good sam

Evolution

Celebrating 50 years of Good Sam Parks

Everything evolves and RVing and camping are no exception. Camping looks a lot different today than it did 50 years ago when we launched the Good Sam Park Network.

Back then you reserved your campsite over the phone with a park ranger or showed up at a campground you knew nothing about and hoped for the best. You didn't research ratings, reviews or amenities, and you certainly couldn't book your reservation online.

You owned your RV (that may or may not have been pulled by a large station wagon), or possibly borrowed one from a family member but you didn't rent it from a stranger.

Even with all the changes, there are some things that have remained constant, like the importance of a good campground. You can have the most elaborate RV on the market and all the high-tech camping gear money can buy but it's the campground that can make or break your experience. This is exactly why we have a team of dedicated and enthusiastic professionals who personally inspect and rate each of thousands of RV parks and campgrounds to bring you this valuable and easy-to-use guide.

It's also why we've included Coast to Coast resorts in this edition for the first time – we want to ensure that you have all campground and resort options at your fingertips.

Good Sam Parks' commitment to making your RVing adventures that much better provides you with a network of more than 2,000 top-quality parks and campgrounds across North America. We want to be part of an exciting and positive camping experience for all. Within our vast network we believe there's something for everyone — the weekend warrior, solo traveler, adventure-seeker, full-timer, family camper — and even more for the 2 million Good Sam members who save 10% on nightly camping fees.

Above all, the most important constant are the reasons we love RVing — spending quality time with loved ones, exploring new places, meeting new people and the flexibility to go where we want. Now get out there and plan your next adventure at one of these amazing parks!

Marcus Lemonis
Chairman and CEO of Camping World Holdings
@ MarcusLemonis

PACK LIKE THE PROS

Three Good Sam bloggers share some of their favorite items to bring on the road.

Rene Agredano

- full-time RV traveler and entrepreneur

Tire Pressure Monitoring System (TPMS). Even the best RV tires can fail, but a good TPMS can prevent tire failure from turning into catastrophe.

Pour-Over Coffee Filter. Use boiling water from a kettle to make coffee — it beats space-hogging coffee makers.

Oxygenics Handheld Shower Head. Install an Oxygenics RV model. This delivers high-pressure shower streams while conserving water, too.

Coty Perry

- angler, camper and rock climber

Large Reusable Water Bottles. You have to stay hydrated, whether you're road-tripping up the coast or beelining to the mountains.

Small Board Games. I like bringing portable board games like chess and Othello on long road trips. It's a great way to keep the young ones entertained as well.

My Comfy Shorts/Sweatpants. We all have that one pair of shorts or pants, right? Nope? Just me? After a long hike or day on the water, I love throwing on my favorite pair of sweatpants and lounging out under the stars.

Peter Mercer

- snowbird and decades-long RVer

Some Spare Automotive Fluids. These should include automatic transmission fluid, engine oil, glycol coolant, etc. Fluids might not be available in all service or repair centers.

A Flashlight and Spare Batteries. Even if you don't travel after dark, a flashlight may be needed when looking in a lower outside locker or poorly lit engine compartment areas during the day.

Find it at CampingWorld.com or GanderRV.com. Get more RV advice at Blog.Goodsam.com.

Contents

DIRECTORY LISTING SECTION

★ NEW ★ COAST TO COAST RV RESORTS AND CAMPGROUNDS!

Starting after page 1216

▶ **MORE MONEY SAVING COUPONS!** PGS. 1219-1237

Published by Good Sam Enterprises, LLC
2750 Park View Court, Suite 240
Oxnard, CA 93036
(800) 765-7070
www.GoodSam.com

Printed in the U.S.A.
Printed on Recyclable Paper
Book Trade Distribution by
National Book Network
(800) 462-6420

ISBN: 978-1-73415-862-5 (Bookstore) • 978-1-937321-58-1 (Other Circulation)

Front Cover Photography: Sean Pierce, Shasta Lake, California

NASCAR TRACKS
AND NEARBY GOOD SAM PARKS

good sam | NASCAR
Official Campground Directory

NEW HAMPSHIRE MOTOR SPEEDWAY | LOUDON, NH

Sandy Beach RV Resort
Contoocook, NH

Twin Tamarack Family Camping & RV Resort
Meredith, NH

POCONO RACEWAY | LONG PONG, PA

Four Seasons Campgrounds
Scotrun, PA

Mountain Vista Campground
Stroudsburg, PA

Timothy Lake North RV Park
East Stroudsburg, PA

Timothy Lake South RV Park
East Stroudsburg, PA

RICHMOND RACEWAY | RICHMOND, VA

Americamps RV Resort
Ashland, VA

Chesapeake Bay RV Resort
Gloucester, VA

Cozy Acres Campground/RV Park
Powhatan, VA

Picture Lake Campground
Petersburg, VA

R & D Family Campground
Milford, VA

South Forty RV Campground
Petersburg, VA

ATLANTA MOTOR SPEEDWAY | HAMPTON, GA

Atlanta South RV Resort
McDonough, GA

BRISTOL MOTOR SPEEDWAY | BRISTOL, TN

Lazy Llama Campground
Greeneville, TN

Shadrack Campground
Bristol, TN

CHARLOTTE MOTOR SPEEDWAY | CONCORD, NC

Camping World Racing Resort
Charlotte, NC

CHICAGOLAND SPEEDWAY | JOLIET, IL

RV Park At Hollywood Casino Joliet
Joliet, IL

DAYTONA INTERNATIONAL SPEEDWAY | DAYTONA BEACH, FL

Beverly Beach Camptown RV Resort & Campers Village
Flagler Beach, FL

Bulow RV Resort
Flagler Beach, FL

Coral Sands Oceanfront RV Resort
Ormond Beach, FL

Highbanks Marina & Campresort
Debary, FL

Miami Everglades Resort
Miami, FL

Nova Family Campground
Daytona Beach, FL

Rose Bay Travel Park
Port Orange, FL

Sugar Mill Ruins Travel Park
New Smyrna Beach, FL

DOVER INTERNATIONAL SPEEDWAY | DOVER, DE

Holly Lake Campsites
Millsboro, DE

Massey's Landing
Millsboro, DE

HOMESTEAD-MIAMI SPEEDWAY | HOMESTEAD, FL

Boardwalk RV Resort
Homestead, FL

INDIANAPOLIS MOTOR SPEEDWAY | INDIANAPOLIS, IN

Indy Lakes RV Campground
Indianapolis, IN

Lake Haven Retreat
Indianapolis, IN

IOWA SPEEDWAY | NEWTON, IA

Kellogg RV Park
Kellogg, IA

ISM RACEWAY | AVONDALE, AZ

Cotton Lane RV Resort
Goodyear, AZ

Desert Shadows RV Resort
Phoenix, AZ

Horspitality RV Resort
Wickenburg, AZ

Phoenix Metro RV Park
Phoenix, AZ

Pueblo El Mirage RV & Golf Resort
El Mirage, AZ

Sunflower RV Resort
Surprise, AZ

KANSAS SPEEDWAY | KANSAS CITY, KS

Beacon RV Park
St. Joseph, MO

Owl Creek Market & RV Park
Odessa, MO

Walnut Grove RV Park
Merriam, KS

KENTUCKY SPEEDWAY | SPARTA, KY

Follow the River RV Resort
Florence, IN

Northern KY RV Park
Dry Ridge, KY

KERN COUNTY RACEWAY PARK | BAKERSFIELD, CA

A Country RV Park
Bakersfield, CA

Bakersfield River Run RV Park
Bakersfield, CA

Bakersfield RV Resort
Bakersfield, CA

LAS VEGAS MOTOR SPEEDWAY | LAS VEGAS, NV

Arizona Charlie's Boulder RV Park
Las Vegas, NV

Duck Creek RV Park
Las Vegas, NV

Hitchin' Post RV Park
Las Vegas, NV

Las Vegas RV Resort
Las Vegas, NV

Riviera RV Park
Las Vegas, NV

LEE USA SPEEDWAY | LEE, NH

Pine Acres Resort
Raymond, NH

MICHIGAN INTERNATIONAL SPEEDWAY | BROOKLYN, MI

Apple Creek Campground & RV Park
Grass Lake, MI

Indian Creek Camp & Conference Center
Tecumseh, MI

ROAD AMERICA | ELKHART LAKE, WI

Plymouth Rock Camping Resort
Plymouth, WI

STAFFORD MOTOR SPEEDWAY | STAFFORD SPRINGS, CT

Oak Haven Family Campground
Wales, MA

TALLADEGA SUPER SPEEDWAY | TALLADEGA, AL

Talladega Pit Stop RV Park & Campground
Talladega, AL

TEXAS MOTOR SPEEDWAY | FORT WORTH, TX

Northlake Village RV Park
Roanoke, TX

The Vineyards Campground & Cabins
Grapevine, TX

THOMPSON SPEEDWAY MOTORSPORTS PARK | THOMPSON, CT

Stateline Campresort & Cabins
East Killingly, CT

WATKINS GLEN INTERNATIONAL | WATKINS GLEN, NY

Camp Bell Campground
Corning, NY

MAJOR LEAGUE BASEBALL STADIUMS
AND NEARBY GOOD SAM PARKS

good sam | Official Partner of Major League Baseball

ARIZONA DIAMONDBACKS
CHASE FIELD | PHOENIX, AZ

Royal Palm RV Resort
Phoenix, AZ
Holiday Village
Mesa, AZ
Desert Shadows RV Resort
Phoenix, AZ
Palm Gardens MHC & RV Park
Mesa, AZ
Phoenix Metro RV Park
Phoenix, AZ
Mesa Spirit RV Resort
Mesa, AZ
Pueblo El Mirage RV & Golf Resort
El Mirage, AZ
Good Life RV Resort
Mesa, AZ
Val Vista Village RV Resort
Mesa, AZ
Paradise RV Resort
Sun City, AZ

ATLANTA BRAVES
TRUIST PARK | CUMBERLAND, GA

Atlanta-Marietta RV Resort
Marietta, GA
Sweetwater Creek RV Reserve
Austell, GA
Stone Mountain Park Campground
Stone Mountain, GA
Allatoona Landing Marine Resort
Cartersville, GA
Atlanta South RV Resort
McDonough, GA
Harvest Moon RV Park
Adairsville, GA
Forest Glen Mobile Home & RV Park
Jackson, GA
Iron Mountain Resort
Dahlonega, GA
Calhoun AOK Campground
Calhoun, GA

BALTIMORE ORIOLES
ORIOLE PARK | BALTIMORE, MD

Ramblin' Pines Family Campground & RV Park
Woodbine, MD
Cherry Hill Park
College Park, MD
Tucquan Park Family Campground
Holtwood, PA
Round Top Campground
Gettysburg, PA
Drummer Boy Camping Resort
Gettysburg, PA
Oma's Family Campground
Kirkwood, PA
Gettysburg Farm RV Campground
Dover, PA

BOSTON RED SOX
FENWAY PARK | BOSTON, MA

Circle CG Farm Campground
Bellingham, MA
Tuxbury Pond RV Resort
South Hampton, NH
Field & Stream RV Park
Brookline, NH
Gateway To Cape Cod RV Campground
Rochester, MA
Pine Acres Resort
Raymond, NH
Pine Acres Family Camping Resort
Oakham, MA
Stateline Campresort & Cabins
East Killingly, CT

CHICAGO WHITE SOX
GUARANTEED RATE FIELD | CHICAGO, IL

RV Park at Hollywood Casino Joliet
Joliet, IL
Leisure Lake Resort
Joliet, IL
Lehman's Lakeside RV Resort
Marengo, IL

CHICAGO CUBS
WRIGLEY FIELD | CHICAGO, IL

RV Park at Hollywood Casino Joliet
Joliet, IL
Leisure Lake Resort
Joliet, IL
Lehman's Lakeside RV Resort
Marengo, IL

CINCINNATI REDS
GREAT AMERICAN BALL PARK | CINCINNATI, OH

Little Farm On the River RV Park Camping Resort
Rising Sun, IN
Rising Star Casino Resort & RV Park
Rising Sun, IN
Kings Island Camp Cedar
Mason, OH
Northern KY RV Park
Dry Ridge, KY
Olive Branch Campground
Lebanon, OH
Follow the River RV Resort
Florence, IN
Indian Lakes RV Campground
Batesville, IN
Thousand Trails Wilmington
Wilmington, OH
Three Springs Campground
Corinth, KY

CLEVELAND GUARDIANS
PROGRESSIVE FIELD | CLEVELAND, OH

American Wilderness Campground
Grafton, OH
Woodside Lake Park
Streetsboro, OH
Roundup Lake Campground
Aurora, OH
Maple Lakes Recreational Park
Seville, OH
Cherokee Park Campground
Akron, OH
Countryside Campground
Akron, OH
Kenisee Lake
Jefferson, OH

COLORADO ROCKIES
COORS FIELD | DENVER, CO

Dakota Ridge RV Resort
Golden, CO
Loveland RV Resort
Loveland, CO
Riverview RV Park & Campground
Loveland, CO
Greeley RV Park
Greeley, CO
Manor RV Park
Estes Park, CO
Spruce Lake RV Resort
Estes Park, CO

DETROIT TIGERS
COMERICA PARK | DETROIT, MI

Wildwood Golf & RV Resort
Essex, ON
Wayne County Fairgrounds RV Park
Belleville, MI
Northpointe Shores RV Resort
Fair Haven, MI
Camp Lord Willing RV Park & Campground
Monroe, MI
Campers Cove Campground
Wheatley, ON
Saint Clair (Thousand Trails)
St Clair, MI
Indian Creek Camp & Conference Center
Tecumseh, MI

HOUSTON ASTROS
MINUTE MAID PARK | HOUSTON, TX

Advanced RV Resort
Houston, TX
Houston Central RV Park
Houston, TX
Sheldon Lake RV Resort
Houston, TX
Cullen RV Resort
Pearland, TX
Traders Village RV Park
Houston, TX
San Jacinto Riverfront RV Park
Highlands, TX
Katy Lake RV Resort
Katy, TX
Safari Mobile Home & RV Community
League City, TX
Rayford Crossing RV Resort
The Woodlands, TX

KANSAS CITY ROYALS
KAUFFMAN STADIUM | KANSAS CITY, MO

Walnut Grove RV Park
Merriam, KS
Owl Creek Market & RV Park
Odessa, MO
Beacon RV Park
St Joseph, MO

LOS ANGELES ANGELS
ANGEL STADIUM | ANAHEIM, CA

Orangeland RV Park
Orange, CA
Waterfront RV Park
Huntington Beach, CA
Newport Dunes Waterfront Resort & Marina
Newport Beach, CA
Arbor Mobile Village
Long Beach, CA
Bonelli Bluffs RV Resort & Campground
San Dimas, CA
Fairplex RV Park
Pomona, CA
Wilderness Lakes RV Resort
Menifee, CA
Soledad Canyon RV & Camping Resort
Acton, CA
Walnut RV Park
Northridge, CA

LOS ANGELES DODGERS
DODGER STADIUM | LOS ANGELES, CA

Arbor Mobile Village
Long Beach, CA
Walnut RV Park
Northridge, CA
Los Angeles RV Resort (formerly KOA)
Acton, CA
Soledad Canyon RV & Camping Resort
Acton, CA
Bonelli Bluffs RV Resort & Campground
San Dimas, CA
Fairplex RV Park
Pomona, CA
Orangeland RV Park
Orange, CA
The Californian RV Resort
Acton, CA
Valencia Travel Village
Valencia, CA

MIAMI MARLINS
MARLINS PARK | MIAMI, FL

Miami Everglades Resort
Miami, FL
Boardwalk RV Resort
Homestead, FL
Sunshine Holiday Ft. Lauderdale
Fort Lauderdale, FL
Paradise Island RV Resort
Fort Lauderdale, FL
Breezy Hill RV Resort
Pompano Beach, FL
Highland Woods RV Resort
Pompano Beach, FL

MILWAUKEE BREWERS

AMERICAN FAMILY FIELD | MILWAUKEE, WI

Lakeland Camping Resort
Milton, WI

Blackhawk Camping Resort
Milton, WI

Plymouth Rock Camping Resort
Plymouth, WI

MINNESOTA TWINS

TARGET FIELD | MINNEAPOLIS, MN

Wildwood Campground
Shafer, MN

St Cloud/Clearwater RV Park
Clearwater, MN

St Cloud Campground & RV Park
St. Cloud, MN

NEW YORK YANKEES

YANKEE STADIUM | BRONX, NY

Fla-Net Park
Flanders, NJ

Black Bear Campground
Florida, NY

Tip Tam Camping Resort
Jackson, NJ

NEW YORK METS

CITI FIELD | QUEENS, NY

Fla-Net Park
Flanders, NJ

Black Bear Campground
Florida, NY

Tip Tam Camping Resort
Jackson, NJ

OAKLAND ATHLETICS

RING CENTRAL COLISEUM | OAKLAND, CA

San Francisco RV Resort
Pacifica, CA

Marin RV Park
Greenbrae, CA

Tradewinds RV Park Of Vallejo
Vallejo, CA

Novato RV Park
Novato, CA

Olema Campground
Olema, CA

Duck Island RV Park & Fishing Resort
Rio Vista, CA

Coyote Valley RV Resort
San Jose, CA

Midway RV Park
Vacaville, CA

Vineyard RV Park
Vacaville, CA

PHILADELPHIA PHILLIES

CITIZENS BANK PARK | PHILADELPHIA, PA

Country Oaks Campground
Dorothy, NJ

Mays Landing Campground
Mays Landing, NJ

Holly Acres Campground
Egg Harbor City, NJ

Timberland Lake Campground
Jackson, NJ

Indian Rock RV Park
Jackson, NJ

Chestnut Lake RV Campground
Port Republic, NJ

Atlantic Shore Pines Campground
Tuckerton, NJ

Spring Gulch Resort Campground
New Holland, PA

Oma's Family Campground
Kirkwood, PA

PITTSBURGH PIRATES

PNC PARK | PITTSBURGH, PA

Pine Cove Beach Club & Resort
Washington, PA

Bear Run Campground
Portersville, PA

Austin Lake RV Park & Cabins
Toronto, OH

Mountain Pines Campground
Champion, PA

SAN DIEGO PADRES

PETCO PARK | SAN DIEGO, CA

Mission Bay RV Resort
San Diego, CA

Campland On the Bay
San Diego, CA

Santee Lakes Recreation Preserve
Santee, CA

Rancho Los Coches RV Park
Lakeside, CA

Pio Pico RV Resort & Campground
Jamul, CA

Olive Avenue RV Resort
Vista, CA

Oceanside RV Resort
Oceanside, CA

Oakzanita Springs RV Campground
Descanso, CA

Champagne Lakes RV Resort
Escondido, CA

Pala Casino RV Resort
Pala, CA

SAN FRANCISCO GIANTS

ORACLE PARK | SAN FRANCISCO, CA

San Francisco RV Resort
Pacifica, CA

Marin RV Park
Greenbrae, CA

Tradewinds RV Park Of Vallejo
Vallejo, CA

Novato RV Park
Novato, CA

Olema Campground
Olema, CA

Duck Island RV Park & Fishing Resort
Rio Vista, CA

Sonoma County RV Park-At the Fairgrounds
Santa Rosa, CA

Midway RV Park
Vacaville, CA

Vineyard RV Park
Vacaville, CA

SEATTLE MARINERS

T-MOBILE PARK | SEATTLE, WA

Eagle Tree RV Park
Poulsbo, WA

Cedar Glen RV Park
Poulsbo, WA

Issaquah Village RV Park
Issaquah, WA

Tall Chief RV & Camping Resort
Fall City, WA

Maple Grove RV Resort
Everett, WA

Majestic RV Park
Puyallup, WA

Thunderbird Resort
Monroe, WA

Cedar Grove Shores RV Park
Stanwood, WA

Glen Ayr Resort
Hoodsport, WA

The Waterfront At Potlatch Resort & RV Park
Hoodsport, WA

ST. LOUIS CARDINALS

BUSCH STADIUM | ST. LOUIS, MO

DraftKings at Casino Queen RV Park
East St. Louis, IL

Cahokia RV Parque
Cahokia, IL

Sundermeier RV Park
St. Charles, MO

Stone Park Resort & Amphitheatre
Bonne Terre, MO

TAMPA BAY RAYS

TROPICANA FIELD | ST. PETERSBURG, FL

Vacation Village RV Resort
Largo, FL

Yankee Traveler RV Park
Largo, FL

Hawaiian Isles
Ruskin, FL

Avalon RV Resort
Clearwater, FL

River Vista RV Village
Ruskin, FL

Terra Ceia RV Resort
Palmetto, FL

Fiesta Grove RV Resort
Palmetto, FL

The Tides RV Resort
Palmetto, FL

Fisherman's Cove RV Resort
Palmetto, FL

TEXAS RANGERS

GLOBE LIFE FIELD | ARLINGTON, TX

Traders Village RV Park
Grand Prairie, TX

Loyd Park Camping Cabins & Lodge
Grand Prairie, TX

Lakeview RV & MH Community
Fort Worth, TX

The Vineyards Campground & Cabins
Grapevine, TX

Texan RV Ranch
Mansfield, TX

Mockingbird Hill Mobile Home & RV Park
Burleson, TX

Northlake Village RV Park
Roanoke, TX

Texas Ranch RV Resort
Alvarado, TX

Cowtown RV Park
Fort Worth, TX

TORONTO BLUE JAYS

ROGERS CENTRE | TORONTO, ON

N.E.T. Camping Resort
Vineland, ON

Scott's Family RV-Park Campground
Niagara Falls, ON

Campark Resorts Family Camping & RV Resort
Niagara Falls, ON

Bissell's Hideaway Resort
Pelham, ON

Emerald Lake Trailer Resort & Waterpark
Puslinch, ON

Nicolston Dam Campground & Travellers Park
Alliston, ON

Yogi Bear's Jellystone Park Camp-Resort
Niagara Falls, ON

AA Royal Motel & Campground
Niagara Falls, NY

Niagara County Camping Resort
Lockport, NY

WASHINGTON NATIONALS

NATIONALS PARK | WASHINGTON D.C.

Cherry Hill Park
College Park, MD

Prince William Forest RV Campground
Dumfries, VA

Greenville Farm Family Campground
Haymarket, VA

Ramblin' Pines Family Campground & RV Park
Woodbine, MD

Monroe Bay Campground
Colonial Beach, VA

Harbor View RV Park
Colonial Beach, VA

Get the Most out of Your Travel Guide

This Guide is organized alphabetically, first by U.S. state, then by Canadian province. Within each state and province, the listing information is alphabetized by town. Each town name is followed by map-grid coordinates and the appropriate county name. The map grid coordinate (a letter and a number, such as A1) refers to coordinates on the maps found at the beginning of each state or province. Each campground is listed alphabetically by town.

Welcome Sections, Spotlights & Road Trips

Each state and province includes valuable travel information. The Welcome Section contains road/highway information, travel and tourism contact information, time zone and more. Spotlights are a collection of areas that feature local points of interest as well as fun things to see and do. You'll also find a Road Trip adventure, taking you along some of each state and province's most scenic routes.

How To Read Our Campground Information

Included is basic information for thousands of campgrounds. You will find expanded listings which have more detail, and are outlined below.

1. TOWN NAME: This indicates the campground's location. If the campground isn't located in a municipality, we list the nearest town.

2. MAP COORDINATES: The letter and number next to a town correspond to the coordinates on the state/provincial map noted.

3. COUNTY NAME: Shows the county in which that town is located.

4. DIRECTIONAL ARROW: Indicates the facility's location relative to the town.

5. FACILITY NAME: The name of the facility.

good sam parks

6. GOOD SAM PARK LOGO: Indicates parks that offer the 10% discount to Good Sam members on an overnight stay for two people in one recreational vehicle. You must present a valid Good Sam membership card at the time of registration.

7. TRIPLE DIGIT RATING: We rate Good Sam Parks and other private parks in three categories: Development of Facilities, Cleanliness & Construction of Restrooms and Showers, and Visual Appearance & Environmental Quality. See page 8 for more information on our exclusive triple-digit rating system. Note: Due to special circumstances not all private parks were rated and inspected in 2021 and reflect the prior year's rating.

8. TYPE OF FACILITY: Classifies parks into several unique categories to help envision the park setting before arrival.

RV Resort: Designs and caters to larger RVs and has highly developed grounds.

RV Park: Includes formal site and grounds development and is primarily designed for RVs.

Campground: Usually located in a rural or natural setting, with less formal grounds and site development; accepts tents as well as RVs.

RV Spaces: A handful of RV spaces reserved for overnight travelers, and often has few, if any, additional facilities or amenities.

Membership Park: Primary business is selling memberships.

RV Area in Mobile Home Park: A designated area for RVs within a mobile home park.

Condo Park: A condo park sells its sites to individuals then reserves the right to rent out the sites when not in use by owner.

Public Campground: Campgrounds with camping sites open to the public that are owned and operated by a government agency, includes state, national, city parks, etc.

9. DIRECTIONS: Beginning with the nearest highway exit or major intersection, you may locate the facility by following the directions and mileage. Note: (L), (R) and (E) denote whether the facility entrance is to the left, right or end of the road respectively.

10. SPECIAL INFORMATION: Unique information that is high-lighted in yellow and gives you a little extra nugget of information not found in our standardized listing information.

11. INTERIOR ROADS: Unless "poor" is noted, the condition and surface of the interior roads is fair to good. Note: When the primary interior roads are paved, yet those leading to the sites are gravel, we label them as paved/gravel. When interior roads are a mixture of gravel and dirt, we label them as gravel/dirt.

12. DESCRIPTION OF SITES: Site description includes total number of RV spaces, surface preparation at most sites (paved, all weather, gravel, grass or dirt), hookup information, width and length of pull-thru sites and back-ins, etc.

Big Rig: We also indicate here if sites accept Big Rigs. A Big Rig designation is only offered to parks which have 25% or more of sites that meet this criteria: minimum of 14-ft.

ABBREVIATION KEY

Alt	alternate
Bus	business
Corps	Corps of Engineers-managed
COE	Corps of Engineers-managed
CR	county road
Elev	elevation
Expwy	expressway
FAC	facilities & sites available at location
FM Rd	farm-to-market road
FR	forest road
Frntg	frontage
hkups	hookups
km	kilometer
LP	liquid propane
MHP	mobile home park
mi	mile
MP	mile post
no cc	does not accept credit cards
NP	National Park
NRA	National Recreation Area
pk	park
PR	provincial road
QEW	Queen Elizabeth Way
REC	recreation available at location
RR	rural route
SF	State Forest
SP	State Park
SR	state route
SRA	State Recreation Area
Tpk	turnpike
TCH	Trans-Canada Highway
Twp	township
UI	uninspected
yd	yard
yr	year

overhead clearance, 12-ft. wide roads (1-way), 50-amp full hookup sites, sites that are a minimum of 24 ft. by 60 ft., and adequate site access. Parks without a Big Rig designation may still have a few such sites.

Side-by-Side Hookups: Indicates that the configuration of some hookups may create space limitations for slide outs, as you could be close to your neighbor.

Full Hookups: Indicates sites that have all three: water, electric and sewer. If the hookups are not full, we indicate how many sites have at least water (W), electric (E), and sewer (S). We also note the minimum and maximum type of electrical receptacles that will be found at sites (15, 20, 30 or 50 amps). We only list the availability of 50-amp receptacles when at least 25% of the sites have them. The type of receptacle doesn't guarantee exact amperage or voltage.

13. INTERNET ACCESS: WiFi @ Sites indicates that Internet can be accessed wirelessly for overnight RVers at their sites. WiFi indicates that Internet can be accessed wirelessly at the park in a location such as a rec hall. $ indicates an extra charge not included in the nightly rate.

14. BASIC FACILITIES: This includes restaurant, laundry, etc. A $ after the facilities (e.g., showers $) indicates an extra charge not included in the overnight rate listed.

15. RECREATION (REC): Notes the types of recreational facilities the campground offers.

16. PET INFORMATION: Pet Restrictions are noted when they apply, such as breed (B), quantity (Q) or size (S). If pets are not allowed at all, No Pets will appear. Pet $ indicates the park charges extra for pets. Note: Call ahead to ask for the park's specific pet policy and limitations.

17. PARTIAL HANDICAP ACCESS: Indicates the park has been adapted in one or more ways to accommodate RVers/campers with disabilities. This listing may include showers with benches and handrails, wheelchair-accessible sinks and toilets, wide doorways with no curbs or steps, wheelchair ramps, signs on buildings and/or hiking trails printed in Braille, TDD equipment, etc. If you or a family member has special needs, please call ahead to determine the type of services/facilities available. This indication does not necessarily mean the park is ADA compliant.

18. AGE RESTRICTIONS: Parks with this designation usually cater to 55+ guests. Children are usually restricted. Call the park for details.

19. RV AGE RESTRICTIONS: Parks with this designation may have an RV Age restriction. Call the park for details.

ANATOMY OF OUR LISTING

1. TOWN NAME
2. MAP COORDINATES
3. COUNTY NAME
4. DIRECTIONAL ARROW
5. FACILITY NAME
6. GOOD SAM PARK LOGO
7. RATINGS
8. TYPE OF FACILITY & MANAGEMENT
9. DIRECTIONS

10. SPECIAL INFORMATION

11. INTERIOR ROADS
12. DESCRIPTION OF SITES
13. INTERNET ACCESS
14. BASIC FACILITIES
15. RECREATION
16. PET INFORMATION
17. PARTIAL HANDICAP ACCESS
18. AGE RESTRICTIONS
19. RV AGE RESTRICTIONS
20. RV RESTRICTIONS
21. 2021 RATES
22. SEASON (OPEN/CLOSE)

23. CONTACT INFORMATION
24. ADVERTISER REFERENCE

TITUSVILLE – A3 *Pinelas*

↗ RIVERSIDE RV PARK

good sam park **Ratings: 9/9.5★/9.5** (Campground) From jct I-10 and I-5: Go 5 N on I-5 to Exit 23, Go 1/2 W on Green Valley Road (R).

ENJOY THE SPACE COAST'S BEST!
Enjoy activities galore in the beautiful setting of the Cocoa Beach Area! Visit Kennedy Space Center. Enjoy the Atlantic Ocean Beaches or just relax at one of our beautiful sites. Our RV Resort is near all area attractions.

FAC: paved/gravel rds. (200 spaces). 100 Avail: 50 paved, 50 gravel, patios, 20 pull-thrus (30 x 60), back-ins (30 x 60), mostly side by side hkups, 90 full hkups, 10 W, 10 E (30/50 amps), seasonal sites, cable, WiFi @ sites, tent sites. Rentals. Dump, mobile sewer, laundry, groc, LP gas, fire rings, firewood, restaurant, controlled access. **REC:** Atlantic Ocean: fishing, marina, boating nearby, golf, shuffleboard, playground, hunting nearby, rec open to public. Pets OK, partial handicap access. Age restrict may apply. Big rig sites, RV age restrict, No Class B, 28 day max stay, eco-friendly. 2021 rates: $25 - $50. Military discount. Nov 1 to May 30. No reservations.

(888) 123-4567 Lat : 12.34567, Lon: -89.87654
123 Main Street, Titusville, FL 12345
www.riversidervp.com
See ad page 65.

➔ ADVERTISERS WANT YOUR BUSINESS

The basic listings in this Guide are provided at no charge to the business owner. Any campground that meets our minimum requirements receives a listing. Many campground owners want to tell you more about their campground than the listing includes and have purchased advertising for that purpose.

20. RV RESTRICTIONS: Parks with this designation may have restrictions on Class A, B or C motorhomes. Call the park for details.

21. RATES, CREDIT CARDS & DISCOUNTS: Rates are listed as minimum to maximum, for two adults in one RV, based on information gathered in 2021. Rates include any additional fees that may typically be found at the site such as air conditioning, TV service and heating. Rates and discounts are shown as a guideline only. They can change without notice. Call for the most current information. This information is deemed accurate but is not guaranteed. Unless "no cc" is noted; credit cards are accepted. Call park for credit card policies.

22. SEASON: Indicates opening and closing dates. Otherwise, facilities are open year-round.

23. CONTACT INFO: Easy, at-a-glance information gives you everything you need to contact and reserve a site at the park.

24. ADVERTISER REFERENCE: This line will refer you to the specific page for the listed facilities advertisement(s).

Special Notes & Misc. Info

Cancellations: Policies regarding canceling reservations vary with each campground. Remember to ask what that policy is when making a reservation.

Toilets & Showers: Unless otherwise noted, all campgrounds have flush toilets and hot showers. If only pit toilets are available, the listing will note pit toilet. If the restroom and showers are coin operated, the listing will indicate it with a $ in the listing. If the Restroom Rating is NA, this indicates that restrooms are not available at the facility. If the Restroom Rating is UI, this means that the restrooms could not be inspected by our consultants during the time of the visit.

Rates And Discounts: All information about rates and discounts are based on information gathered in 2021. These are not guaranteed. Please call ahead for detailed, up-to-date rates.

✓ **The Preferred Location Logo:** Indicates locations that meet certain criteria and invest in providing more information about their business; earning them a check mark next to their listing.

COMMENTS? To give us feedback about our listings, email us at: Parks@GoodSam.com

Good Sam Ratings 101

Our Good Sam Triple Rating System can be a great help when looking for the perfect RV park or campground for your next trip. Each year our highly trained Good Sam Review Teams personally inspect and rate private RV parks and campgrounds, assigning ratings to Facilities, Restroom & Showers, and Visual Appearance.

A small percentage of campgrounds receive the coveted 10/10★/10 rating, meaning top marks in every category. In order to qualify as a Good Sam Park, campgrounds must receive a minimum 5/7/5 rating and meet specific requirements within each category.

The below gives a quick look at what gets evaluated in each of our ratings categories.

good sam park
Rated 10/10★/10

Our Triple Rating System is comprehensive and covers every aspect of what RVers look for when choosing a campground. If you're curious about how we determine our ratings, try it for yourself at the next RV park you visit. You'll find our official Rating Guidelines Form – the one used by our review teams – at Goodsam.com/RatingGuidelines.

RATING CATEGORIES

☑ Facilities

The first rating in our rating system takes a look at the facilities at each park, evaluating the level of development of the following items. Each area is assigned 0, ½ or 1 point. A maximum of 10 points can be earned:

1. Interior Roads
2. Registration
3. Sites ➔
4. Hookups
5. Recreation
6. Swimming
7. Security
8. Laundry
9. On-site services
10. Internet access

Facilities Rating Tips:

- To get 1 point in the Hookup category, a minimum of 75% of sites must have full hookups with the remaining sites having water & electric hookups
- For 1 point in the Sites category, 100% of sites must have 14-foot overhead clearance
- For 1 point in the Internet category, a park must provide online access to at least 50% of overnight sites

0	½	1
Sites not level, no prepared surface	More than 50% of Sites are level with a prepared surface	100% have paved or all-weather surface. Minimal leveling is required

☑ Restrooms & Showers

The second rating evaluates the restrooms and showers, and also takes into consideration the number of showers and toilets available for guests. Each area is assigned 0, ½ or 1 point. A maximum of 10 points can be earned:

1. Toilets
2. Showers ➔
3. Floors
4. Walls
5. Sinks/Counters/Mirrors
6. Interior construction
7. Supplies/Odor
8. Number of facilities
9. Exterior Appearance
10. Interior Appearance

The coveted ★ next to the restroom rating indicates exceptionally clean restrooms!

Bathroom/Shower Rating Tips:

- To get 1 point in Interior Appearance, the bathhouse must be superior – no hard water deposits, pitting, rusting, chipping or cracking of sinks, toilets, dividers, tiling or hardware. No graffiti. Well lighted throughout the restroom and shower stalls

0	½	1
Unacceptable amount of dirt, litter and mildew	Some dirt, litter and mildew	Clean and free of dirt, litter and mildew

☑ Environment/Visual Appearance

The third rating appraises the park's overall look and is based on the following. Each area is assigned 0, ½ or 1 point. A maximum of 10 points can be earned:

1. Function of Park Entrance/Signage
2. Appearance of Entrance Area
3. Appearance of Park Grounds
4. Appearance of Sites
5. Litter & Debris throughout the Park
6. Overall Exterior Building Maintenance
7. Trash Disposal ➔
8. Noise
9. Park Setting
10. Site Layout

Appearance Rating Tips:

- For 1 point in the Noise category, a park must be adequately distant from airports, railroads, interstates, etc.
- For 1 point in the Site Layout category, a park must not have side-by-side hookups

0	½	1
No trash receptacles or receptacles overflowing	Trash receptacles of ample capacity. Well maintained, regularly empties	Trash pickup at site daily

Rules of the Road

An at-a-glance guide to state and provincial laws pertaining to RVs and automobiles

	SIZE LIMITS				TOWING		RIDING			MISC.	EQUIPMENT REQUIRED						CELL PHONE	
	WIDTH	TRAILER LENGTH	MOTORHOME LENGTH	HEIGHT	TWO-VEHICLE COMBINED LENGTH	TRIPLE TOWING	IN-PICKUP CAMPER	IN FIFTH-WHEEL TRAILER	IN TRAVEL TRAILER	OVERNIGHT PARKING IN STATE REST AREAS	WEIGHT OF TRAILER REQUIRING BRAKES	BREAKAWAY SWITCH	SAFETY CHAIN	FLARES / REFLECTIVE SIGNS	FIRE EXTINGUISHER IN RV	LIGHTS REQUIRED ON (DISTANCE OF VISIBILITY)	VOICE CALLING	TEXT MESSAGING
AK	8½'	40'	45'	14'	75'	•	•			•	5000	•[3]	•	•	•	1000[12]	•	
AL	8½'	40'	45'	13½'	65'		•			P	3000[7]	•[2]	•	•	•	500[12]	•[1,24]	
AR	8½'	43½'	45'	13½'	65'	•				•	3000	•[2]	•	•	•	500[11,12]	•[1,24]	
AZ	8½'	40'	45'	13½'[1]	65'	•[1]	•	•	•	•	3000	•[2]	NS	NS	•	[12]	•[25]	
CA	8½'	40'	45'	14'	65'	•[1]	•[20]	•[20]		•[16]	1500	•	•	•	•	1000[11,12]	•[25]	
CO	8½'	45'	45'	14½'[1]	70'	•	•			P	3000	•[2]	•	•	•	1000,[12]	•[24]	
CT	8½'	45'	45'	13½'	65'	•	•			•	3000	NS	•	•	•	1000	•[25]	
DC	8'	40'	40'	13½'	55'	•	•				3000[7]	•[2]	•	•	•	500[11,12]	•[25]	
DE	8½'	40'	45'	13½'	65'		•			P	4000	NS	•	NS	•	1000[11,12]	•[25]	
FL	8½'	40'	45'	13½'	65'		•			•[16]	3000[7]	•[2]	•	•	•	[12]	•[24]	
GA	8½'	NS	45'	13½'	60'		•[21]			•	3000	NS	•	•	•	[11,12]	•[25]	
HI	9'	48'	45'	14'	65'	•	•[19]				3000[7]	NS	•	NS	•	500[11,12]	•[25]	
IA	8½'	40'	45'	13½'	65'[1]	•	•	•	•	•[16]	3000	NS	•	•	•	500[12]	•[24]	
ID	8½'	48'	45'	14'	75'	•	•			•	1500	•	NS	NS	•	500[12]	•[25]	
IL	8½'	42'	45'	13½'	60'		•				3000	•[3]	•	•	•	[11,12]	•[25]	
IN	8½'	45'	45'	13½'	65'	•	•	•	•	P	3000	•[2]	•	•	•	500[12]	•[25]	
KS	8½'	NS	45'	14'	65'		•[19]	•[19]	•[19]	•	[1,8]	NS	•	•	•	1000[11,12]	•[24]	
KY	8½'	45'	45'	13½'[1]	65'	•	•			•[16]	4000[8]	NS	•	•	•	[12]	•[1,24]	
LA	8½'	45'	45'	13½'[1]	65'[1]	•	•			•	3000	•[2]	•	•	•	500[11,12]	•[1,24]	
MA	8½'	40'	45'	13½'	65'		•			P	10000	NS	•	NS	•	500[11,12]	•[25]	
MD	8½'	40'	45'	13½'	55'		•	•	•		3000[7]	•	•	•	•	1000[11]	•[25]	
ME	8½'	45'	45'	13½'[1]	65'					•	3000	NS	•	NS	•	1000[11,12]	•[25]	
MI	8½'	40'	45'	13½'	65'[1]		•	•	•	•	3000[7]	NS	•	NS	•	500[11,12]	•[1,24]	
MN	8½'	45'	45'	13½'	70'[1]	•	•	•	•	P	3000	•[3]	•	•	•	500[11,12]	•[25]	
MO	8½'	45'	45'	13½'[1]	65'[1]	•	•	•	•	•	NS	NS	•	NS	•	[11,12]	•	•[1,24]
MS	8½'	40'	45'	13½'	53'					•	2000	•	•	•	•	500[12]	•	
MT	8½'	NS	55'	14'	65'[1]	•	•	•		•	3000[7]	•	•	•	•	500[12]	•	•
NC	8½'	45'	45'	13½'	60'	•	•	•	•		1000	NS	•	NS	•	400[11,12]	•[1,24]	
ND	8½'	50'	50'	14'	75'	•	•	•		•	3000	•	•	•	•	1000[11,12]	•[24]	
NE	8½'	40'	45'	14½'	65'	•	•	•	•	•[16]	3000	•[2]	•	•	•	500[12]	•[1]	
NH	8½'	45'	45'	13½'	53'					•	1500	•[2]	•	NS	•	1000[11,12]	•[25]	
NJ	8½'	40'	40'	13½'	62'		•	•		P	3000[7]	•[2]	•	•	•	500[11,12]	•[25]	
NM	8½'	40'	45'	14'	65'	•	•			P	3000	NS	•	•	•	500[12]	•[1,25]	
NV	8½'	NS	45'	14'	70'		•			•[16]	1500	•[2]	•	NS	•	1000[12]	•[25]	
NY	8½'	45'	45'	13½'	65'		•			•[16]	3000	NS	•	NS	•	1000[11,12]	•[25]	
OH	8½'	45'	45'	13½'	65'	•	•			•	2000	•	•	NS	•	1000[11,12]	•[24]	
OK	8½'	40'	45'	13½'	65'[1]		•			•	3000	•[2]	•	•	•	1000[11,12]	•[1,24]	
OR	8½'	45'	45'	14'	65'		•	•[17,20]		•[16]	NS	NS	•	NS	•	1000[12]	•[25]	
PA	8½'	NS	45'	13½'	60'	•		•[17,20]		•[16]	3000[7]	•[2]	•	•	•	1000[11,12]	•	

	SIZE LIMITS				TOWING		RIDING			MISC.	EQUIPMENT REQUIRED						CELL PHONE	
	WIDTH	TRAILER LENGTH	MOTORHOME LENGTH	HEIGHT	TWO-VEHICLE COMBINED LENGTH	TRIPLE TOWING	IN-PICKUP CAMPER	IN FIFTH-WHEEL TRAILER	IN TRAVEL TRAILER	OVERNIGHT PARKING IN STATE REST AREAS	WEIGHT OF TRAILER REQUIRING BRAKES	BREAKAWAY SWITCH	SAFETY CHAIN	FLARES / REFLECTIVE SIGNS	FIRE EXTINGUISHER IN RV	LIGHTS REQUIRED ON (DISTANCE OF VISIBILITY)	VOICE CALLING	TEXT MESSAGING
RI	8 ½'	45'	45'	13 ½'	60'		•			•	4000	•	NS	•	•	500 [11, 12]	• [25]	
SC	8 ½'	48'	45'	13 ½'	53'	•	•			P	3000 [7]	• [2]	•	•	•	500 [11, 12]	•	
SD	8 ½'	45'	45'	14'	75'	•	•	• [17, 20]		P	3000 [7]	• [2]	•	•	•	200 [12]	•	
TN	8 ½'	40'	45'	13 ½'	65'	•	•			• [16]	3000	• [2]	•	•	•	200 [11, 12]	• [25]	
TX	8 ½'	45'	45'	14'	65'	•	•			• [16]	4500	• [2]	•	•	•	1000 [12]	• [1, 24]	
UT	8 ½'	45'	45'	14'	65'	•	•			•	3000	NS	•	•	•	1000 [12]	• [1, 25]	
VA	8 ½'	45'	45'	13 ½'	65'		•			P	3000	• [2]	•	NS	•	500 [11, 12]	• [25]	
VT	8 ½'	46'	46'	13 ½'	65'	•	•			•	3000 [7]	• [2]	•	•	•	500 [12]	• [25]	
WA	8 ½'	40'	46'	14'	60'		•			• [16]	3000 [7]	• [2]	•	•	•	[12]	• [25]	
WI	8 ½'	45'	45'	13 ½'	65'		•	• [20]		•	3000	NS	•	NS	•	500 [12]	• [1]	
WV	8 ½'	40'	45'	13 ½'	65'		•	•		•	3000	• [2]	•	•	•	500 [11, 12]	• [25]	
WY	8 ½'	60'	60'	14'	85'	•	•			•	[8]	NS	•	NS	•	1000 [12]	•	

CANADA

	WIDTH	TRAILER LENGTH	MOTORHOME LENGTH	HEIGHT	TWO-VEHICLE COMBINED LENGTH	TRIPLE TOWING	IN-PICKUP CAMPER	IN FIFTH-WHEEL TRAILER	IN TRAVEL TRAILER	OVERNIGHT PARKING IN STATE REST AREAS	WEIGHT OF TRAILER REQUIRING BRAKES	BREAKAWAY SWITCH	SAFETY CHAIN	FLARES / REFLECTIVE SIGNS	FIRE EXTINGUISHER IN RV	LIGHTS REQUIRED ON (DISTANCE OF VISIBILITY)	VOICE CALLING	TEXT MESSAGING
AB	2.6m	12.5m	14m	4.15m	20m	• [1]	•			P	909kg [6]	•	•	•	•	150m	• [25]	
BC	2.6m	12.5m	14m	4.15m	20m		•			P	1400kg [6]	• [2]	•	•	•	150m [12]	• [24, 25]	
MB	2.6m	12.5m	14m	4.15m	21.5m	• [1]	•			P	910kg	•	•	•	•	60m [12]	• [25]	
NB	2.6m	12.5m	14m	4.15m	23m					P	1500kg	NS	• [9]	•	•	• [13]	• [25]	
NL	2.6m	12.5m [1]	12.5m [1]	4.15m	23m		•			P	4500kg	NS	•	•	•	•	• [25]	
NS	2.6m	12.5m	14m	4.15m	23m					P	1800kg	• [2]	• [9]	•	•	• [13]	• [25]	
NT	2.6m	12.5m	14m	4.2m	20m		NS			P	1360kg [6]	NS	NS	•	•	• [13]	• [25]	
ON	2.6m	12.5m	14m	4.15m	23m	• [1]	•			P	1360kg	NS	•	•	•	150m [12]	• [25]	
PE	2.6m	12.5m	14m	4.15m	23m					P	1500kg	NS	• [9]	•	•	150m [12]	• [25]	
QC	2.6m	12.5m	14m	4.15m	23m [1]	• [1]	•			P	1300kg	• [2]	•	•	•	•	• [25]	
SK	2.6m	12.5m	14m	4.15m	23m	• [1]	•			P	1360kg	•	• [9]	•	•	• [12]	• [24, 25]	
YT	2.6m	12.5m	14m	4.2m	25m	• [1]	NS			P	910kg [6]	NS	• [9]	•	•	• [13]	• [24, 25]	

Gross Weight: Maximum operating weight of vehicle as specified by Mfg. | **Weight:** Weight of vehicle as manufacture at factory

NOTE: The regulations in the table above may have changed since the publication date. Please call state or provincial motor vehicle agencies for up-to-date rules and complete details. State/provincial department of transportation numbers and websites are found on each Welcome page in the Listings section.

- • Indicates "yes" item is permitted or required
- NS Indicates "not specified"
- P Indicates "as posted"
- 1 Some exceptions
- 2 Required if weight is more than 3000 lbs
- 3 Required if weight is more than 6000 lbs
- 4 Required if gross weight is more than 3000 lbs
- 5 Required if gross weight is more than 6000 lbs
- 6 Required if the gross weight of the trailer is more than half the tow vehicle weight
- 7 Required if the trailer weight exceeds 40% of the tow vehicle weight
- 8 Must be able to stop within 40 feet at 20 mph
- 9 Two safety chains or breakaway switch required on trailers
- 10 Laden weight noted (gross weight of the trailer plus the cargo)
- 11 Required when wipers are in continuous use
- 12 Required 30 min. after sunset and 30 min. before sunrise
- 13 Headlights or running lights required at all times
- 14 Required when speeds exceed 45 mph on designated highways
- 15 Prohibited where posted
- 16 12-hour limit; CA: 8-hour limit; FL: 3-hour limit; IA: 24-hour limit; NV: 18-hour limit; TN: 2-hour limit; TX: 24-hour limit; WA: 8-hour limit; WI: 24-hour limit
- 17 Safety glass in windows required
- 18 With approved safety belt
- 19 Must be 13 years of age or older; WI: 12+ years
- 20 If passenger can communicate with driver and exits can be opened from both exterior and interior
- 21 Must have free access to drive compartment
- 22 Only if required by CSA at time of manufacturer
- 23 Suggested but not required
- 24 Restrictions apply for minor drivers and/or newer drivers, or under certain conditions such as school zones, etc.
- 25 Permitted only if "hands-free"

NOTE: Child safety restraints are required in ALL states and provinces. For more details, contact the motor vehicle agency of the state or province you plan to visit.

NHRA MEMBER TRACKS

VISIT GOODSAM.COM TO FIND GOOD SAM PARKS NEARBY

CAMPING WORLD | CHAMPIONSHIP NHRA DRAG RACING

The Official RV & Outdoor Company

ALABAMA

Atmore Dragway
Atmore

Huntsville Dragway
Harvest

Capital City Motorsports Park
Montgomery

ALASKA

Alaska Raceway Park
Palmer

ARIZONA

Tucson Dragway
Tucson

Wild Horse Pass Motorsports Park
Chandler

CALIFORNIA

Auto Club Dragway at Auto Club Speedway
Fontana

Famoso Dragstrip
McFarland

Barona 1/8-Mile Drag Strip
Lakeside

Irwindale Dragstrip
Irwindale

Redding Drag Strip
Redding

Sacramento Raceway
Sacramento

Samoa Dragstrip
Samoa

Sonoma Raceway
Sonoma

COLORADO

Bandimere Speedway
Morrison

Julesburg Dragstrip
Julesburg

Pueblo Motorsports Park
Pueblo

Western Colorado Dragway
Grand Junction

FLORIDA

Bradenton Motorsports Park
Bradenton

Emerald Coast Dragway
Holt

Gainesville Raceway
Gainesville

Orlando Speed World Dragway
Orlando

Sebring International Raceway
Sebring

GEORGIA

Atlanta Dragway
Commerce

Silver Dollar Raceway
Reynolds

South Georgia Motorsports Park
Cecil

U.S. 19 Dragway
Albany

ILLINOIS

Byron Dragway
Byron

Coles County Dragway USA, LLC
Charleston

Route 66 Raceway
Joliet

World Wide Technology Raceway
Madison

IDAHO

Firebird Raceway
Eagle

INDIANA

Crossroads Dragway
Terre Haute

Lucas Oil Raceway
Indianapolis

Wagler Motorsports Park
Lyons

IOWA

Cedar Falls Motorsports Park
Cedar Falls

I29 Dragway
Pacific Junction

Tri-State Raceway
Earlville

KANSAS

Heartland Motorsports Park
Topeka

Kansas International Dragway
Maize

Mid America Dragway
Arkansas City

SRCA Dragstrip
Great Bend

KENTUCKY

Beech Bend Raceway Park
Bowling Green

Kentucky Dragway
Clay City

Ohio Valley Raceway
West Point

LOUISIANA

No Problem Raceway Park
Belle Rose

MARYLAND

Cecil County Dragway
Rising Sun

Mason-Dixon Dragway
Boonsboro

MICHIGAN

Milan Dragway
Milan

MINNESOTA

Brainerd International Raceway
Brainerd

Grove Creek Raceway
Grove City

Interstate Raceway
Glyndon

MONTANA

Lewistown Raceway
Lewistown

Lost Creek Raceway
Anaconda

Yellowstone Drag Strip
Acton

NEBRASKA

Kearney Raceway Park
Kearney

NEVADA

The Strip at Las Vegas Motor Speedway
Las Vegas

Top Gun Dragstrip
Fallon

NEW HAMPSHIRE

New England Dragway
Epping

NEW JERSEY

Atco Dragway
Atco

NEW MEXICO

Albuquerque Dragway
Albuquerque

Roswell Dragway
Roswell

Hobbs Motorsports Park
Hobbs

NEW YORK

Esta Safety Park
Cicero

Island Dragway
Great Meadows

Lebanon Valley Dragway
West Lebanon

NORTH CAROLINA

Galot Motorsports Park
Benson

Mooresville Dragway
Mooresville

Piedmont Dragway
Julian

Rockingham Dragway
Rockingham

ZMax Dragway
Concord

OHIO

Edgewater Sports Park
Cleves

Kil-Kare Raceway
Xenia

National Trail Raceway
Hebron

Pacemakers Dragway Park
Mount Vernon

Summit Motorsports Park
Norwalk

OKLAHOMA

Ardmore Dragway
Ardmore

Osage Casino Tulsa Raceway Park
Tulsa

Thunder Valley Raceway Park
Lexington

OREGON

Coos Bay Speedway
Coos Bay

Madras Dragstrip
Madras

Medford Dragstrip
White City

Portland International Raceway
Portland

Woodburn Dragstrip
Woodburn

PENNSYLVANIA

Maple Grove Raceway
Mohnton

Numida Dragway
Numida

South Mountain Raceway
Boiling Springs

SOUTH CAROLINA

Carolina Dragway
Aikens

SOUTH DAKOTA

Oahe Speedway
Pierre

Sturgis Dragway
Sturgis

TENNESSEE

Bristol Dragway
Bristol

Music City Raceway
Goodlettsville

TEXAS

Alamo City Motorplex
San Antonio

Big Country Race Way
Abilene

Houston Motorsports Park
Houston

Houston Raceway Park Powered by Pennzoil
Baytown

Paris Drag Strip
Paris

Texas Motorplex
Ennis

VIRGINIA

Virginia Motorsports Park
Petersburg

WASHINGTON

Bremerton Raceway
Bremerton

Pacific Raceways
Kent

Renegade Raceway
Yakima

Walla Walla Drag Strip
Walla Walla

WISCONSIN

Rock Falls Raceway
Eau Claire

CANADA

ALBERTA

Castrol Raceway
Edmonton Int'l Airport

M.H.D.R.A. Raceway
Medicine Hat

BRITISH COLUMBIA

Mission Raceway
Mission

NEW BRUNSWICK

Miramichi Dragway Park
Miramichi

ONTARIO

Toronto Motorsports Park
Cayuga Canada

QUEBEC

Luskville Dragway
Luskville

Napierville Dragway
Napierville

good sam member exclusive offers!

JANUARY MEMBERS EXCLUSIVE

TUESDAY-THURSDAY ONLY

$10 OFF

Any Purchase

Valid for Good Sam Members at Camping World and Gander RV retail locations only. Offer redeemable on merchandise only excluding generators, electronics and RV covers. Offer is not retroactive and cannot be used in combination with any other offer. Must present coupon at time of purchase. Limit one coupon per customer. Any unused portion of this dollar amount cannot be exchanged for cash or used on a later transaction. Offer valid Tuesdays thru Thursdays 1/1/22-1/31/22 only.

CC2700

JANUARY MEMBERS EXCLUSIVE

$20 OFF

Any Two Chairs

Valid for Good Sam Members at Camping World and Gander RV retail locations only. Offer is not retroactive and cannot be used in combination with any other offer. Must present coupon at time of purchase. Limit one coupon per customer. Offer valid 1/1/22-1/31/22 only.

CC2701

JANUARY MEMBERS EXCLUSIVE

$20 OFF

Coleman Grills

Valid for Good Sam Members at Camping World and Gander RV retail locations only. Offer is not retroactive and cannot be used in combination with any other offer. Must present coupon at time of purchase. Limit one coupon per customer. Offer valid 1/1/22-1/31/22 only.

CC2702

JANUARY MEMBERS EXCLUSIVE

TUESDAY-THURSDAY ONLY

$5 OFF

Any Purchase

Valid for Good Sam Members at Camping World and Gander RV retail locations only. Offer redeemable on merchandise only excluding generators, electronics and RV covers. Offer is not retroactive and cannot be used in combination with any other offer. Must present coupon at time of purchase. Limit one coupon per customer. Any unused portion of this dollar amount cannot be exchanged for cash or used on a later transaction. Offer valid Tuesdays thru Thursdays 1/1/22-1/31/22 only.

CC2703

JANUARY MEMBERS EXCLUSIVE

ONLINE ONLY

15% OFF

Purchase of $99 or More

Must use promo code TRAVELGUIDE15 at online checkout

Valid for Good Sam Members at CampingWorld.com. Offer redeemable on merchandise only excluding generators, electronics and RV covers. Offer is not retroactive and cannot be used in combination with any other offer. Limit one coupon per customer. Offer valid 1/1/22-1/31/22 only.

JANUARY MEMBERS EXCLUSIVE

$1,000 OFF

New Motorhome Purchase

Discount can be applied to new units only. Discount taken off Special Online Price. Must present this coupon at time of purchase. Prior sales excluded. Not applicable on wholesale units. Cannot be combined with any other promotion or used as a down payment. Valid only at Camping World RV Sales, Gander RV Sales or Freedom Roads RV Sales location. Offer valid 1/1/22-1/31/22.

coast to coast

a good sam company

Visit CoastResorts.com/FreeCamping to learn about this special offer!

FREE

3 Day & 2 Night RV Getaway

($100 value) at one of the participating RV resorts in 18 states across the U.S. where Coast to Coast memberships are accepted.*

$100 Value!

*Free 3-day, 2-night RV stay requires a 90-minute tour of the resort. The offer is available to U.S. residents only. Offer valid for new guests only, one free stay per household, not valid for current Coast to Coast members. Offer valid at a participating RV resort in the following states: Alabama, Arizona, Arkansas, California, Georgia, Louisiana, Michigan, Minnesota, Mississippi, Missouri, New York, North Carolina, Ohio, Oregon, Pennsylvania, South Dakota, Texas, and Washington. States subject to change. Some restrictions apply. Advance reservations required. RV resorts are independently owned and operated. Offer valid until 12/31/22.

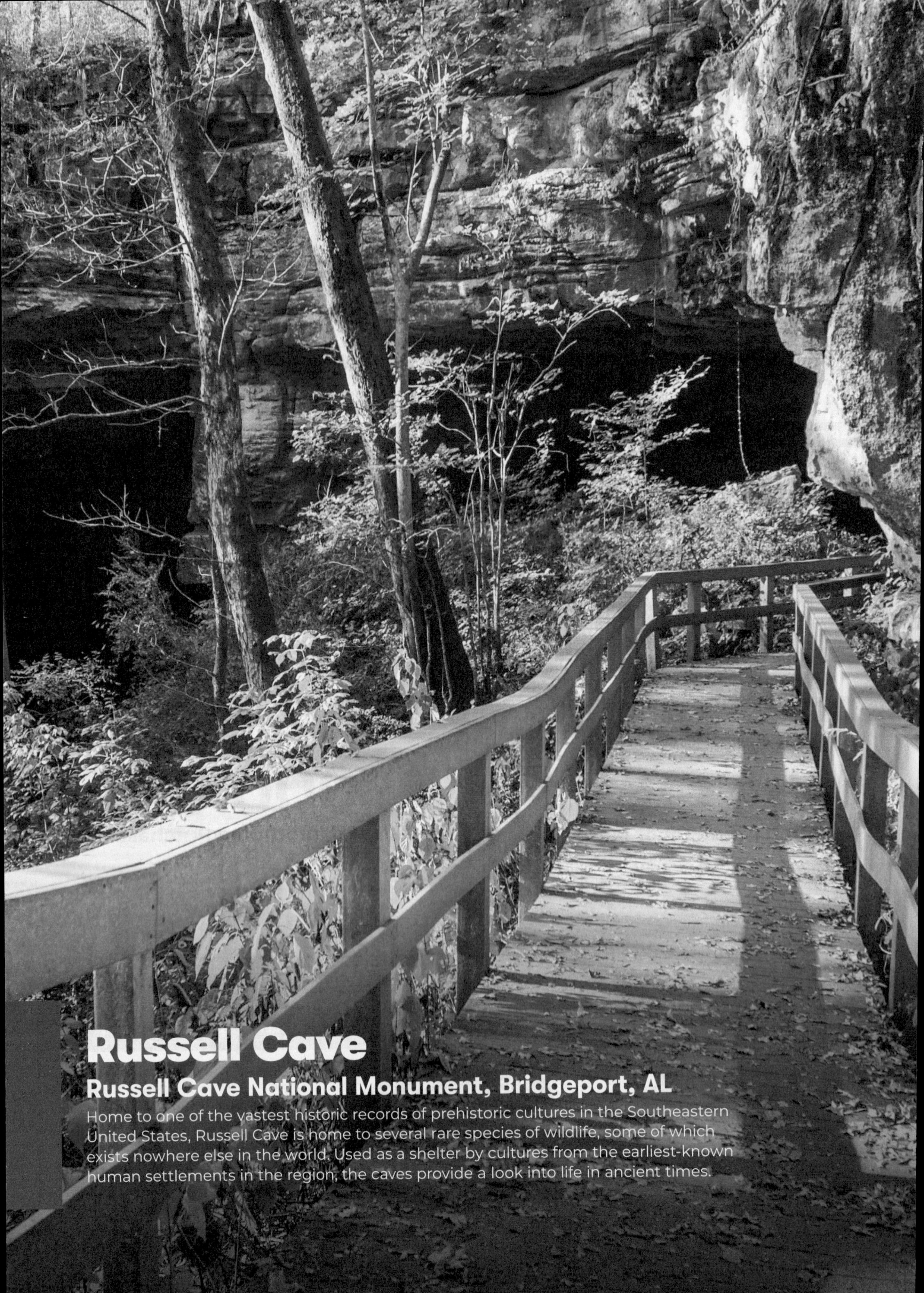

Russell Cave

Russell Cave National Monument, Bridgeport, AL

Home to one of the vastest historic records of prehistoric cultures in the Southeastern United States, Russell Cave is home to several rare species of wildlife, some of which exists nowhere else in the world. Used as a shelter by cultures from the earliest-known human settlements in the region, the caves provide a look into life in ancient times.

Getty Images

YOU ARE HERE

Alabama

DID YOU KNOW?

Clocking in at 212.8 mph, the Talladega Superspeedway holds the record for the fastest qualifying lap speed in NASCAR history.

With a rich history that covers both the Civil War and Space Age, Alabama tantalizes visitors. Explore giant space rockets at the U.S. Space & Rocket Center or watch epic sunsets from the shores of Dauphin Island.

Water Fun

Fishing is stellar in 'Bama. To make your dream catch, motor over to Guntersville Lake in the state's northeast corner. These waters are also great for boating and water sports. Experienced paddlers will want to head to northeast Alabama's Little River Canyon National Preserve for some scenic views and whitewater rapids. For a more relaxed paddling experience, check out the Sipsey Fork of the Black Warrior River, a National Wild and Scenic River. Lewis Smith Lake in the Bankhead National Forest is another favorite for fishing, paddling and boating.

Super Shores

Alabama's Gulf Coast is only 60 miles, but the state packs plenty of diversion along this strip of shoreline. Here, visitors will encounter sugary white sands and endless emerald waters. From beachside towns like Orange Beach and Gulf Shores to the beauty of Bon Secour National Wildlife Refuge, Alabama's Gulf Coast is a delight. Northeastern Alabama is home to recreation on the Tennessee River and in the Appalachian Mountains.

Spectacular Southern Cities

Birmingham honors it storied past with an array of monuments. On the top of nearby Red Mountain, a massive statue of Vulcan, the Roman god of fire, overlooks the city in a nod to the town's vibrant steel industry. Take a trip up the tower that forms the pedestal to check out the views. Less than 100 miles to the south, Montgomery, the state's capital, celebrates the arts with a vibrant cultural scene. On the southern coast, Mobile is an action-packed hot spot.

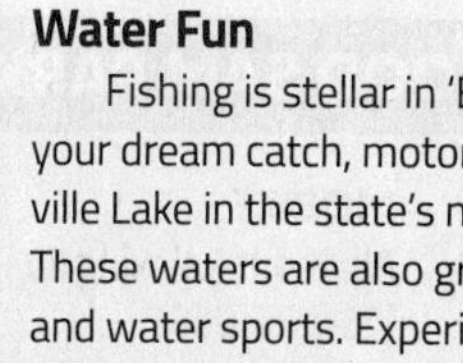

Alabama White Sauce

Unique to the state, Alabama white sauce is a mayonnaise-based dressing consisting of vinegar, horseradish, cayenne pepper and other flavor-packed ingredients. Decatur's Big Bob Gibson Bar-B-Q first concocted the condiment in 1925 and has been making the dangerously addictive stuff ever since. Drizzle the sauce over smoked chicken or use it as a secret ingredient in homemade coleslaw.

VISITOR CENTER

TIME ZONE
Central Standard

ROAD & HIGHWAY INFORMATION
334-242-6356
dot.state.al.us

FISHING & HUNTING LICENSES
334-242-3465
outdooralabama.com/license-information

BOATING INFORMATION
334-272-7930
outdooralabama.com/boating

NATIONAL PARKS
nps.gov/al

STATE PARKS
alapark.com/parks

TOURISM INFORMATION
Alabama Tourism Department
800-ALABAMA
alabama.travel

TOP TOURISM ATTRACTIONS
1) US Space and Rocket Center
2) Talladega Superspeedway
3) Cheaha State Park

MAJOR CITIES
Birmingham, Montgomery (capital), Mobile, Huntsville, Tuscaloosa

good sam park

Featured Good Sam Parks

ALABAMA

When you stay with Good Sam, you can expect the highest degree of cleanliness and friendliness, and better yet, you get **10% off** overnight campground fees.

If you're not already a Good Sam member you can purchase your membership at one of these locations:

ANDALUSIA
The Oaks Family Campground

ARLEY
Hidden Cove Outdoor Resort

ATMORE
Wind Creek Atmore Casino RV Park

ATTALLA
Big Wills Creek Campground & Tubing

AUBURN
Eagle's Landing RV Park

BIRMINGHAM
Carson Village Mobile Home & RV Park

COTTONDALE
Bama RV Station

CULLMAN
Cullman Campground

DOTHAN
Dothan RV Park

ELBERTA
Lake Osprey RV Resort

EUFAULA
Lake Eufaula Campground

FAIRHOPE
Wales West RV Resort & Light Railway

FOLEY
Ahoy RV Resort
Alabama Coast Campground

FORT PAYNE
Wills Creek RV Park

GADSDEN
Noccalula Falls Campground
The Cove Lakeside RV Resort and Campground

GULF SHORES
RV Hideaway Campground

HARTSELLE
Quail Creek RV Resort

JASPER
Sleepy Holler Campground

MOBILE
All About Relaxing RV Park
I-10 Kampground
I-65 RV Campground
Shady Acres Campground

MONTGOMERY
Capital City RV Park
Montgomery South RV Park & Cabins

OPELIKA
Lakeside RV Park

PRATTVILLE
Kountry Air RV Park

TALLADEGA
Talladega Pit Stop RV Park & Campground

TANNER
Swan Creek Community (MHP)

WOODVILLE
Parnell Creek RV Park

10/10★/10 GOOD SAM PARKS

FOLEY
Ahoy RV Resort
(251)233-7250

MOBILE
All About Relaxing RV Park
(251)375-0661

What's This?

An RV park with a 10/10★/10 rating has scored perfect grades in amenities, cleanliness and appearance ("See Understanding the Campground Rating System" on pages 8 and 9 for an explanation of the trusted Good Sam Rating System). Stay in a 10/10★/10 park on your next trip for a nearly flawless camping experience.

Getty Images/iStockphoto

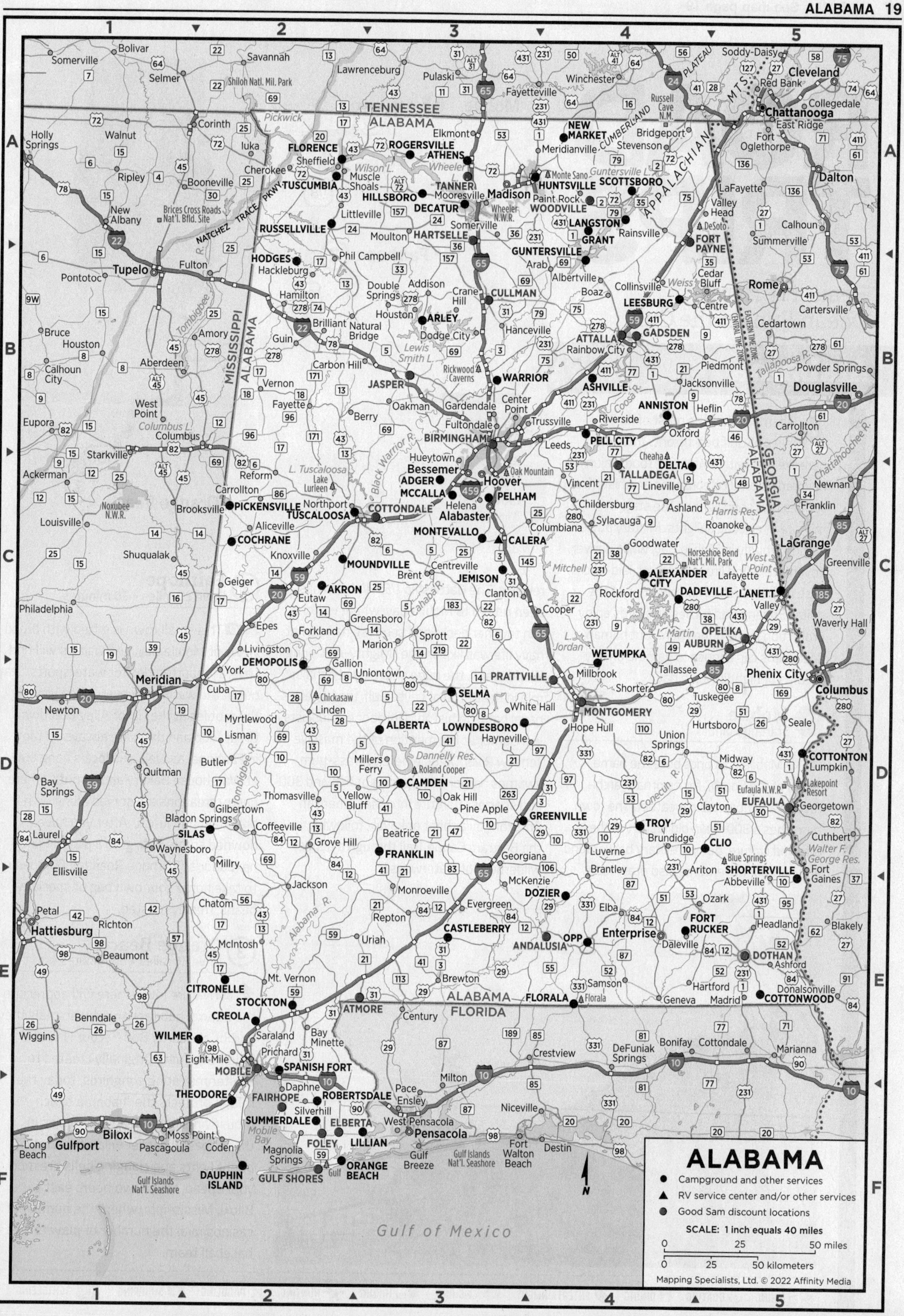
ALABAMA
Campground and other services
RV service center and/or other services
Good Sam discount locations
SCALE: 1 inch equals 40 miles
0 25 50 miles
0 25 50 kilometers
Mapping Specialists, Ltd. © 2022 Affinity Media
Gulf of Mexico
TENNESSEE
ALABAMA
MISSISSIPPI
GEORGIA
FLORIDA
CENTRAL TIME ZONE
EASTERN TIME ZONE
NATCHEZ TRACE PKWY.
CUMBERLAND PLATEAU
APPALACHIAN MTS.
FLORENCE
ROGERSVILLE
ATHENS
TUSCUMBIA
TANNER
HILLSBORO
DECATUR
Madison
HUNTSVILLE
SCOTTSBORO
WOODVILLE
NEW MARKET
LANGSTON
GRANT
RUSSELLVILLE
HARTSELLE
GUNTERSVILLE
FORT PAYNE
HODGES
CULLMAN
ARLEY
LEESBURG
ATTALLA
GADSDEN
JASPER
WARRIOR
ASHVILLE
ANNISTON
BIRMINGHAM
PELL CITY
Bessemer
ADGER
MCCALLA
Hoover
PELHAM
TALLADEGA
DELTA
PICKENSVILLE
TUSCALOOSA
COTTONDALE
Alabaster
MONTEVALLO
CALERA
COCHRANE
MOUNDVILLE
AKRON
JEMISON
ALEXANDER CITY
DADEVILLE
LANETT
OPELIKA
AUBURN
WETUMPKA
DEMOPOLIS
PRATTVILLE
SELMA
MONTGOMERY
Phenix City
Columbus
ALBERTA
LOWNDESBORO
CAMDEN
COTTONTON
EUFAULA
GREENVILLE
TROY
CLIO
SILAS
FRANKLIN
SHORTERVILLE
DOZIER
CASTLEBERRY
FORT RUCKER
Enterprise
ANDALUSIA
OPP
DOTHAN
CITRONELLE
STOCKTON
CREOLA
ATMORE
FLORALA
COTTONWOOD
WILMER
MOBILE
SPANISH FORT
THEODORE
FAIRHOPE
ROBERTSDALE
SUMMERDALE
ELBERTA
FOLEY
LILLIAN
Pensacola
DAUPHIN ISLAND
GULF SHORES
ORANGE BEACH
Meridian
Tupelo
Hattiesburg
Gulfport
Biloxi
Chattanooga
Cleveland
Dalton
Rome
Douglasville
LaGrange
Gulf Islands Nat'l. Seashore
Lake Lurleen
Dannelly Res.
Roland Cooper
L. Martin
West Point L.
Walter F. George Res.
Lakepoint Resort
Mobile Bay
Fort Walton Beach
Destin
Niceville
Crestview
DeFuniak Springs
Marianna
Bonifay
Cottondale

ROAD TRIPS

Beautiful 'Bama: Ocean Fun on the Gulf

Alabama

Alabama makes the most of its 32 miles of Gulf beachfront. Travelers here are met with tantalizing food, Cajun-flavored cultural celebrations and historical venues that shed light on the state's mixture of eclectic delights. Military power stands proudly in Mobile Bay, while upriver adventurers find life at a slower, laid-back pace in the marshes and swamps of the delta. Endangered turtles and birds enjoy protection in the dunes here, but human specimens can choose to gamble on day-dreams or nightlife each day.

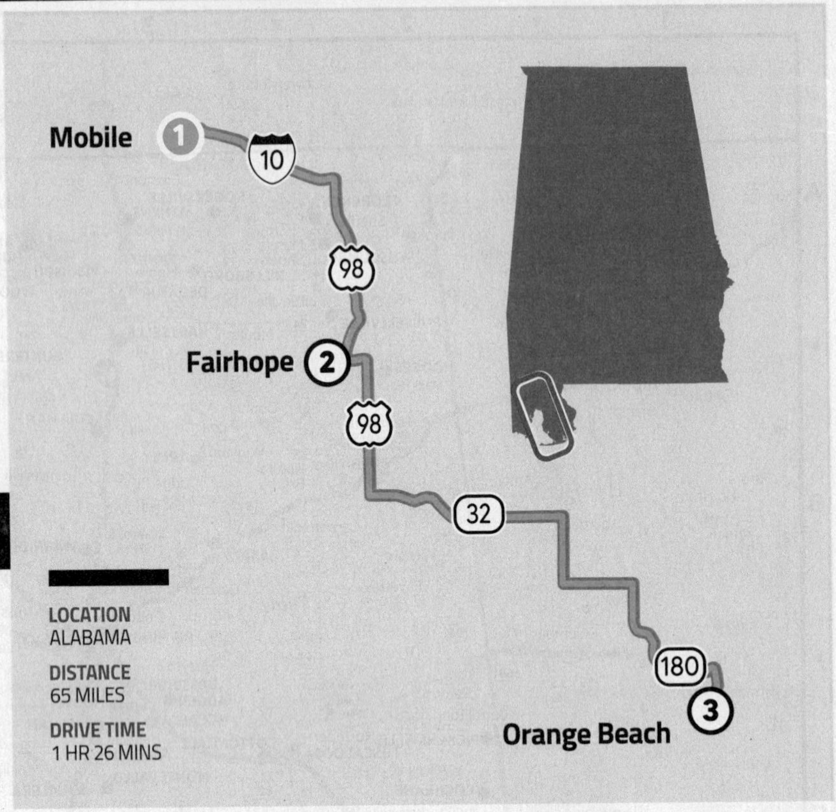

LOCATION
ALABAMA

DISTANCE
65 MILES

DRIVE TIME
1 HR 26 MINS

1 Mobile
Starting Point

Mobile was once bore the name, "Paris of the South," for its ornate architecture and hospitable weather. The town burnishes a 300-year-old history in the arts and culture, but its military background and outdoor adventures also draw rave reviews. The Battleship *USS Alabama* has been retired to Mobile Bay, where visitors can tour her decks and see first-hand what navy life was like on the "Mighty-A." During World War II, the huge ship played a major role in the Battle of Leyte Gulf, the largest naval battle in history. Outdoor enthusiasts will clamor at the mention of the massive Tensaw River Delta, where cypress-gum swamps harbor 120 species of fish and 300 bird species. Venture into the "American Amazon" by airboat or kayak, following the Bartram Canoe Trail through a dense wilderness of waterways.

2 Fairhope
Drive 29 miles • 30 minutes

This small town is gifted with broad views of Mobile Bay, and visitors will find several opportunities for watersports. Stay out of the water, however, when viewing the reptiles at the Gator Alley Boardwalk. Great food and drink are always on tap in Fairhope, as well, and locals hang out at Warehouse Bakery and Donuts, where pastry creations are served along with breakfast and lunch. After you have downed some grub, grab a place in line next door at Fairhope Roasting Company to take home your own bag of specialty beans, freshly roasted.

3 Orange Beach
Drive 36 miles • 56 minutes

Nature lovers here will appreciate the natural habitats and the animals they harbor at nearby Bon Secour National Wildlife Refuge. Originally created to shelter migrating songbirds, today the refuge protects the Alabama beach mouse and loggerhead sea turtles in these coastal barrier wildlands. But if bright lights and clanging bells are more your speed, travel two hours east to Biloxi, Mississippi, where the number of casinos rival the number of players on a baseball team.

BIKING BOATING DINING ENTERTAINMENT FISHING HIKING HUNTING PADDLING SHOPPING SIGHTSEEING

Alabama SPOTLIGHTS

Race to Dixie for Thrills and Football

The Yellowhammer State is home to championship college football, thrilling NASCAR racing and a welcoming attitude that can't be beat. Take time exploring its unspoiled coastline or venture into the rich forests that sprawl across the heart of the state. You won't see Dixie the same way again.

SAMFORD HALL'S CLOCK TOWER PLAYS THE "WAR EAGLE" FIGHT SONG.

The elegant Samford Hall clock tower in Auburn University in Auburn.

Getty Images/iStockphoto

Auburn-Opelika

The largest city in Eastern Alabama, Auburn — and its nearby sister city of Opelika — are known for their historic homes, thriving fine and performing arts scenes, and easy access to beautiful parklands and world-class golf. Much of the area's activities are centered on Auburn University, which dates to its 1856 charter and was the first four-year college in the state to admit women.

Toomer's Corner

At the intersection of Magnolia Avenue and College Street in the heart of town sits Toomer's Corner, named for Toomer's Drugs, a landmark dating back to 1896. This busy spot is the place to be when Auburn University celebrates a major sports win; as per tradition, students and fans alike descend on the area armed with toilet paper in order to "roll Toomer's Corner." Don't be surprised if you pass by to find the corner's trees and structures covered with long strands of sanitary paper. If you're inspired, feel free to join in the fun — celebratory TPing in Auburn is not only legal, but encouraged.

Chewacla State Park

Just a 10-minute drive from Auburn will take you to Chewacla State Park, a 696-acre expanse and home to Lake Chewacla. The lake is the biggest draw here for many, with ample room for swimming, fishing (Alabama fishing license required), and nonmotorized boating, with canoes, kayaks and paddleboards available for rent. Other popular activities include geocaching, mountain biking, hiking and birding. Don't miss the chance to stroll along the Creek View Trail, which passes along the cascading Natural Falls.

Jule Collins Smith Museum of Fine Art

Situated on the Auburn University campus, this American Alliance of Museums-accredited institution features six galleries full of art along with seven additional acres of sprawling gardens and forest. Here you'll find a solid collection of artwork, with a strong focus on American and European art from the 19th and 20th centuries. Highlights include works by the likes of Jacob Lawrence and Georgia O'Keeffe, along with a collection of European art boasting works by Picasso, Renoir, Matisse, Chagall and Dali. Fans of nature won't want to miss the Louise Hauss and David Brent Miller Audubon Collection, which features prints by John James Audubon himself. And when you visit the museum, remember to look up! You'll be rewarded with a view of Amber Luster, a gold-hued glass chandelier by famed American artist Dale Chihuly.

Jay and Susie Gogue Performing Arts Center

Also on the Auburn University campus, this sprawling arts complex is home to a 1,200-seat theater and a 3,500-capacity outdoor amphitheater. Shows here run the gamut from student performances to touring Broadway musicals.

Grand National Golf Course

Part of the Robert Trent Jones Golf Trail, a system of golf courses across Alabama, this golf course sits on the 600-acre Lake Saugahatchee just outside of Opelika. There are three 18-hole courses, along with a practice

LOCAL FAVORITE

Iron Bowl Dip

This dip is named after the annual football game between two 'Bama college powerhouses: the University of Alabama Crimson Tide and the Auburn Tigers.

INGREDIENTS

- ☐ 1 8 oz pkg. cream cheese
- ☐ 1 can condensed cheddar cheese soup
- ☐ 1 cup chunky salsa (you choose the level of spice)
- ☐ Tortilla chips

DIRECTIONS

Spread cream cheese in a 9-inch microwavable pie plate. Top with soup and salsa. Microwave on high for 2 to 3 minutes, or until hot. Stir until creamy. Serve with your favorite tortilla chips.

range, putting greens, a shop, and on-site dining and accommodations.

Opelika Northside Historic District

If you like Victorian architecture, you won't want to miss the chance to see some of the region's finest examples at the Opelika Northside Historic District. The area is easy to explore independently, encompassing 8th and 9th streets, Avenue A and Railroad Avenue. Tours are also an option. Although the district is a year-round attraction, it's at its prime in the holiday season, when residence deck their front porches and facades with all sorts of holiday decorations. The area is closed to vehicular traffic on Saturday nights, when pedestrians and carolers garbed in Victorian dress descend upon the area for some holiday cheer!

Pioneer Park

In nearby Loachapoka sits Pioneer Park, which offers visitors a glimpse into what life was like in the area's early days. The park is home to a number of structures — some original, others reproductions — including an old frontier log cabin and a local history museum housed in the circa 1845 Old Trade Center. There are also four on-site gardens featuring crops that were grown in the area in the 19th century, medicinal herbs, and foods cultivated by the indigenous Creek People such as corn and squash.

Gulf Shores/Orange

Something incredible happens when you arrive at the white sandy beaches and cozy waterfront towns of Alabama's southern Gulf Coast: The outside world melts away, and only a landscape of sun-soaked relaxation and adventure remains. More than 50 miles from the nearest big city in the state (Mobile), and essentially surrounded by water on three sides, this is a prime vacation destination.

Sparkling Getaway

Once a little-known hidden gem, this sparkling beachfront region is now a go-to getaway destination for families from far and wide. It's no surprise why — 32 miles of soft sandy beaches rim the region's coastal edges, offering an inexhaustible supply world-class fishing, scuba diving, boating, swimming, kayaking, hiking and guided wildlife tours for outdoors enthusiasts.

Decatur

Throughout its history, the small city of Decatur in northern Alabama has been anything but forgettable. Founded in 1820 as a scrappy backcountry ferry crossing, it was soon transformed — almost overnight — with the arrival of the railroad and major industry. The burgeoning settlement expanded and the population boomed. The first glimmers of a city on the rise began to emerge.

Point Mallard

When it's time to jump back into the present day and unwind with a bit of family fun, head for Point Mallard Park. There's a water park, 18-hole golf course and driving range. It's a great place for families to relax.

FOR MORE INFORMATION

Alabama Travel, 800-ALABAMA, www.alabama.travel

Auburn and Opelika Tourism Bureau, 866-880-8747, www.aotourism.com

Alabama Gulf Coast, 800-745-SAND, www.gulfshores.com

Visit Mobile, 800-5-MOBILE, www.mobile.org

Decatur Morgan County Tourism, 256-350-2028, decaturcvb.org

Alabama

ADGER — C3 *Jefferson*

BLACK WARRIOR-TOMBIGBEE - COE/ BURCHFIELD BRANCH (Public Corps) From I-20 (exit 86), N 24.5 mi on CR-59 to Lock 17 Rd/CR-54, W 6.3 mi on Lock 17 Rd/CR-54 to Bankhead Rd, W 2 mi on Bankhead Rd (E). **FAC:** paved rds. Avail: 36 paved, 2 pull-thrus, (14x60), back-ins (14x60), 36 W, 36 E (50 amps), tent sites, dump, laundry, groc. **REC:** Holt Lake: swim, fishing, boating nearby, playground. Pets OK. Partial handicap access. 2021 rates: $20 to $40. no cc.
(205)497-9828 Lat: 33.440037, Lon: -87.372142
15036 Bankhead Rd, Adger, AL 35006
www.recreation.gov

AKRON — C2 *Hale*

BLACK WARRIOR-TOMBIGBEE - COE/JENNINGS FERRY (Public Corps) From town, E 5.3 mi on SR-14, follow signs (E). 52 Avail: 52 W, 52 E (50 amps). 2021 rates: $24 to $26. (205)372-1217

ALBERTA — D3 *Wilcox*

DANNELLY LAKE - COE/CHILATCHEE CREEK (Public Corps) From town, SE 9 mi on CR-29 to access rd, E 2 mi, follow signs (E). 53 Avail: 46 W, 46 E (30/50 amps). 2021 rates: $14 to $24. Mar 01 to Oct 11. (334)573-2562

ALEXANDER CITY — C4 *Tallapoosa*

WIND CREEK (Public State Park) From Jct of US-280 & Hwy 63, S 4.3 mi on Hwy 63 to Hwy 128, E 1.5 mi (R). 586 Avail: 268 full hkups, 318 W, 318 E (30/50 amps). 2021 rates: $22.50 to $56. (256)329-0845

ANDALUSIA — E4 *Covington*

POINT A PARK (Public) From Jct US Hwy 84 & US 29: Go 6 mi N on US 29, then 2-1/2 mi W on CR 59 (Point A Rd), then 1/4 mi S on Conecuh Cove Rd, then (R) on Sailboat Rd (E). Avail: 28 full hkups (30/50 amps). 2021 rates: $40. (334)388-0342

THE OAKS FAMILY CAMPGROUND
good sam park **Ratings: 9.5/10★/9.5** (Campground) Avail: 26 full hkups (30/50 amps). 2021 rates: $35 to $45. (334)804-2267, 13421 Brooklyn Rd, Andalusia, AL 36421

ANNISTON — B4 *Calhoun*

GANDER RV-CAMPGROUND OF OXFORD **Ratings: 6.5/6.5/6.5** (RV Park) Avail: 39 full hkups (30/50 amps). 2021 rates: $31.95 to $48. (256)241-2295, 20 Garrett Circle, Anniston, AL 36207

SCENIC DRIVE RV PARK & CAMPGROUND
Ratings: 6.5/8.5/7.5 (Campground) From jct I-20 (exit 191) & 431 S: Go 1/4 mi S on 431 (R). **FAC:** gravel rds. (38 spaces). Avail: 34 gravel, 9 pull-thrus, (30x80), back-ins (35x65), 34 full hkups (30/50 amps), seasonal sites, WiFi @ sites, tent sites, dump, laundry, fire rings, firewood. **REC:** boating nearby. Pets OK. 2021 rates: $38, Military discount.
(256)201-8012 Lat: 33.613140, Lon: -85.723934
24 Cheaha State Park Dr, Anniston, AL 36207
www.scenicdrivervpark.com
See ad this page

Travel Services

GANDER RV OF ANNISTON/OXFORD Your new hometown outfitter offering the best regional gear for all your outdoor needs. Your adventure awaits. **SERVICES:** RV, tire, RV appliance, MH mechanical, sells outdoor gear, sells firearms, restrooms. RV Sales. RV supplies, LP gas, RV accessible. Hours: 9am to 7pm. ATM.
(888)473-0038 Lat: 33.61435, Lon: -85.77309
2772 US Hwy 78 E, Suite 1, Anniston, AL 36207
rv.ganderoutdoors.com

Save 10% at Good Sam Parks & Campgrounds. Stay at any of the Good Sam RV Parks & Campgrounds in the U.S. and Canada and save 10% on the regular nightly RV site rate! No Blackout dates! Good Sam RV Parks are inspected and rated annually-look for the exclusive Triple Rating System. Visit GoodSam.com for more details.

ARLEY — B3 *Winston*

HIDDEN COVE OUTDOOR RESORT
good sam park **Ratings: 8/7.5/9** (Membership Park) 17 Avail: 16 full hkups, 1 W, 1 E (30/50 amps). 2021 rates: $48. (888)563-7040, 687 CR 3919, Arley, AL 35541

ASHVILLE — B4 *St Clair*

GREENSPORT RV PARK & CAMPGROUND **Ratings: 8.5/9/9.5** (RV Park) Avail: 47 full hkups (30/50 amps). 2021 rates: $40. (205)505-0027, 130 Greensport, Ashville, AL 35953

ATHENS — A3 *Limestone*

NORTHGATE RV-TRAVEL PARK **Ratings: 3.5/NA/6.5** (RV Park) 24 Avail: 20 full hkups, 4 W, 4 E (30/50 amps). 2021 rates: $30. (256)232-8800, 1757 Hwy 31 N, Athens, AL 35613

ATMORE — E3 *Escambia*

LITTLE RIVER/ CLAUDE D. KELLEY REC AREA (Public State Park) From jct I-65 & Hwy 21: Go 12 mi N on Hwy 21. 28 Avail: 6 full hkups, 22 W, 22 E (30/50 amps). 2021 rates: $20 to $22. (251)862-2022

MAGNOLIA BRANCH WILDLIFE RESERVE **Ratings: 4.5/7/6.5** (RV Park) 73 Avail: 44 full hkups, 29 W, 29 E (30/50 amps). 2021 rates: $25 to $30. (251)446-3423, 24 Big Creek Road, Atmore, AL 36502

WIND CREEK ATMORE CASINO RV PARK
good sam park **Ratings: 10/9★/10** (RV Park) From jct Curtis Rd & SR 21: Go 1 mi N on SR 21, then ¼ mi W on Poarch Rd, then 1/4 mi on Madison Circle (R); From jct I-65 & SR 21: Go 1 mi SW on SR 21, then ¼ mi W on Poarch Rd, then 1/4 mi on Madison Circle (R). **FAC:** paved rds. Avail: 28 paved, patios, 28 pull-thrus, (25x75), 28 full hkups (30/50 amps), WiFi @ sites, dump, laundry, restaurant. **REC:** pool, hot tub, playground, rec open to public. Pets OK. Partial handicap access. No tents. Big rig sites, eco-friendly. 2021 rates: $38. ATM.
(866)946-3360 Lat: 31.101059, Lon: -87.484983
303 Poarch Rd, Atmore, AL 36502
windcreekatmore.com
See ad this page

Things to See and Do

WIND CREEK ATMORE CASINO Casino Partial handicap access. RV accessible. Restrooms. Food. Hours: open 24 hours. ATM.
(866)946-3360 Lat: 31.101059, Lon: -87.484983
303 Poarch Street, Atmore, AL 36502
windcreekcasino.com
See ad this page

ATTALLA — B4 *Etowah*

BIG WILLS CREEK CAMPGROUND & TUBING
good sam park **Ratings: 8.5/8.5★/8** (Campground) Avail: 37 full hkups (30/50 amps). 2021 rates: $32.50 to $39.50. (256)344-2473, 2075 Hwy 77, Attalla, AL 35954

AUBURN — C5 *Lee*

A SPOTLIGHT Introducing Auburn-Opelika's colorful attractions appearing at the front of this state section.

AUBURN RV PARK AT LEISURE TIME CAMPGROUND **Ratings: 7/9★/8** (Campground) Avail: 80 full hkups (30/50 amps). 2021 rates: $39.25 to $117. (334)821-2267, 2670 S College St, Auburn, AL 36832

CHEWACLA (Public State Park) From Jct of I-85 & US-29 (exit 51), S 0.2 mi on US-29 to Shell Toomer Pkwy, E 1.7 mi (E). Avail: 36 full hkups (30/50 amps). 2021 rates: $38.69 to $44.22. (334)887-5621

EAGLE'S LANDING RV PARK
good sam park **Ratings: 8/9.5★/9** (RV Park) Avail: 45 full hkups (30/50 amps). 2021 rates: $35 to $85. (334)821-8805, 1900 Wire Road, Auburn, AL 36832

Things to See and Do

AUBURN-OPELIKA TOURISM BUREAU Home of Auburn University & Robert Trent Jones Golf Trail. The area has restaurants, shopping, nightlife, arts and culture, recreation, sports facilities, parks, mountain biking trails and Agritourism. Hours Monday thru Friday. RV accessible. Restrooms. Hours: 8am to 5pm. No CC.
(866)880-8747 Lat: 32.60845, Lon: -85.46747
714 East Glenn Avenue, Auburn, AL 36830
www.aotourism.com
See ad opposite page

BIRMINGHAM — B3 *Jefferson*

BIRMINGHAM See also Pelham.

CARSON VILLAGE MOBILE HOME & RV PARK
good sam park **Ratings: 8/NA/8** (RV Area in MH Park) Avail: 10 full hkups (30/50 amps). 2021 rates: $31.50. (205)854-0059, 400 North Carson Rd, Birmingham, AL 35215

HOOVER RV PARK (Public) From jct of I-459 (exit 10) & Hwy 150/John Hawkins Pkwy: Go 1/2 mi E on Hwy 150, then 1-1/2 mi S on Stadium Trace Pkwy, then ¼ mi SE on Mineral Trace, then ¼ mi SE then NE on Feldspar Way (E) *Follow RV Parking Signs. Avail: 170 full hkups (30/50 amps). 2021 rates: $35 to $45. (205)739-7364

Alabama Privately Owned Campground Information Updated by our Good Sam Representatives

Ed & Susan DeWitt

Susan and I will be married for 48 years as this Good Sam edition goes to print. It has been a pleasure to be with Good Sam since 2014, helping parks along the way. Our goal has always been to assist our customers to be successful.

CALERA — C3 *Shelby*

Travel Services

CAMPING WORLD OF CALERA As the nation's largest retailer of RV supplies, accessories, services and new and used RVs, Camping World is committed to making your total RV experience better. **SERVICES:** RV, RV appliance, MH mechanical, staffed RV wash, restrooms. RV Sales. RV supplies, LP gas, dump, RV accessible. Hours: 9am to 7pm.
(888)875-2097 Lat: 33.09549, Lon: -86.46331
730 George Roy Parkway, Calera, AL 35040
www.campingworld.com

CAMDEN — D3 *Wilcox*

DANNELLY LAKE - COE/MILLER'S FERRY (Public Corps) From Camden, W 11 mi on Hwy 28 to corps access rd, follow signs (E). 52 Avail: 52 W, 52 E (30/50 amps). 2021 rates: $22 to $24. (334)682-4191

ROLAND COOPER (Public State Park) From Jct of SR-10 & CR-43, NE 5 mi on CR-43, follow signs (L). Avail: 47 full hkups (30 amps). 2021 rates: $27.88. (334)682-4838

CASTLEBERRY — E3 *Conecuh*

COUNTRY SUNSHINE CAMPGROUND **Ratings: 3/7.5/6.5** (Campground) Avail: 15 full hkups (30/50 amps). 2021 rates: $30. (251)966-5540, 3876 W. Cleveland Ave, Castleberry, AL 36432

CITRONELLE — E2 *Mobile*

CITRONELLE LAKEVIEW RV PARK (CITY PARK) (Public) From jct US 45 & Hwy 96: Go 5 mi W on Hwy 96 to Citronelle Lakeside Park entrance, then 3 mi S. 24 Avail: 7 full hkups, 17 W, 17 E (30/50 amps), Pit toilets. 2021 rates: $20 to $22. (251)866-9647

CLIO — D5 *Barbour*

BLUE SPRINGS (Public State Park) From Jct of SR-10 & SR-51, E 7 mi on SR-10 (R). 47 Avail: 7 full hkups, 40 W, 40 E (30/50 amps). 2021 rates: $21.50 to $28.50. (334)397-4875

COCHRANE — C2 *Pickens*

TENNESSEE-TOMBIGBEE - COE/COCHRANE (Public Corps) From Aliceville, S 10 mi on Hwy-17, W on Perry Long Rd (E). 60 Avail: 60 W, 60 E (30 amps). 2021 rates: $16 to $18. (205)373-8806

COTTONDALE — C3 *Tuscaloosa*

BAMA RV STATION
Ratings: 5.5/NA/7 (RV Park) 76 Avail: 67 full hkups, 9 W, 9 E (30/50 amps). 2021 rates: $40. (205)722-7005, 5461 Skyland Blvd East, Cottondale, AL 35453

Park owners and staff are rightly proud of their business. Let them know how much you enjoyed your stay.

COTTONTON — D5 *Russell*

WALTER F GEORGE - COE/BLUFF CREEK (Public Corps) From Jct of US-431 & SR-165, W 25 mi on SR-165 (E). 87 Avail: 87 W, 87 E (50 amps). 2021 rates: $26 to $48. Feb 28 to Sep 12. (334)855-2746

COTTONWOOD — E5 *Houston*

HIDDEN HOLLOW RV PARK AT THE CROSSING **Ratings: 6.5/8.5★/8.5** (RV Park) Avail: 78 full hkups (30/50 amps). 2021 rates: $40. (334)316-9300, 11295 South Highway 231, Cottonwood, AL 36320

CREOLA — E2 *Mobile*

MOBILE RIVER DELTA (MOBILE COUNTY PARK) (Public) From Jct of I-65 & Sailor Rd (exit 22), N 200 ft on Exit Rd to Dead Lake Rd, E 4.1 mi on Dead Lake Rd, follow signs (L). Avail: 60 full hkups (30/50 amps). 2021 rates: $19.80. (251)574-2266

CULLMAN — B3 *Cullman*

CULLMAN CAMPGROUND
Ratings: 8/9.5★/9 (Campground) From Jct of I-65 (exit 310) & Hwy 157: Go 1-1/2 mi W on Hwy 157, then 1/2 mi S on CR 1184 (L) *follow signs. **FAC:** paved/gravel rds. (90 spaces). Avail: 31 all weather, 30 pull-thrus, (25x80), back-ins (25x80), 31 full hkups (30/50 amps), seasonal sites, WiFi @ sites, dump, laundry, LP gas. **REC:** pond, playground. Pet restrict (B). Partial handicap access. No tents. Big rig sites, eco-friendly. 2021 rates: $36, Military discount.
(256)734-5853 Lat: 34.21444, Lon: -86.90426
220 County Road 1185, Cullman, AL 35057
cullman-campground.business.site
See ad this page

DADEVILLE — C4 *Tallapoosa*

MILITARY PARK LAKE MARTIN REC AREA (MAXWELL AFB) (Public) From jct I-85 & Exit 32/AL-49: go N on AL-49 to CR-34 (Stillwater Rd), W 2.5 mi, follow signs. 76 Avail: 66 full hkups, 10 W, 10 E (30/50 amps). 2021 rates: $20 to $25. Apr 01 to Sep 30. (334)953-3509

DAUPHIN ISLAND — F2 *Mobile*

DAUPHIN ISLAND CAMPGROUND (Public) From Jct of I-10 (Exit 17A) & Hwy 193: Go 27 1/2 mi S on Hwy 193 to Bienville Ave, then 2 mi E (R). 125 Avail: 90 full hkups, 35 W, 35 E (30/50 amps). 2021 rates: $36 to $43. (251)861-2742

DECATUR — A3 *Morgan*

POINT MALLARD CAMPGROUND (Public) From Jct of I-65 (exit 340) & Hwy 20/US-ALT 72: Go 3-1/4 mi W on Hwy 20/US-ALT 72 (across Tennessee River Bridge), then 1-3/4 mi S on US-31/Hwy 20/US-ALT 72, then 3-1/2 mi SE on Church St (2nd light past TN River Bridge) (E) *Move to left lane as you approach bridge. Avail: 119 full hkups (30/50 amps). 2021 rates: $33. (256)341-4826

DELTA — C4 *Clay*

CHEAHA (Public State Park) From Lineville, N 17 mi on SR-49 to SR-281, W 3 mi (R); or From Jct of I-20 & US-431 (exit 191), S 3.6 mi on US-431 to SR-281, SW 13.3 mi on SR-281S (R). Avail: 77 full hkups (20/50 amps). 2021 rates: $27.50 to $29.70. (205)488-5111

DEMOPOLIS — D2 *Greene*

BLACK WARRIOR-TOMBIGBEE - COE/FORKLAND (Public Corps) From town, N 9 mi on Hwy 43, W 1 mi on gravel rd (E). 42 Avail: 42 W, 42 E (30/50 amps). 2021 rates: $20 to $26. (334)289-5530

Camping World RV & Outdoors ProCare, service you can trust from the RV experts.

BLACK WARRIOR-TOMBIGBEE - COE/FOSCUE CREEK (Public Corps) From Jct of US-80W & Maria Ave exit, N 2 mi on Maria Ave (R). 54 Avail: 49 full hkups, 5 W, 5 E (50 amps). 2021 rates: $25 to $28. (334)289-5535

DOTHAN — E5 *Houston*

DOTHAN RV PARK
Ratings: 9.5/9.5★/9 (RV Park) From Jct Hwy 210 (Ross Clark Cir) & US 231S: Go 1-1/2 mi S on US 231S (R) south of town. **FAC:** paved rds. (102 spaces). Avail: 47 paved, 32 pull-thrus, (30x70), back-ins (36x65), 47 full hkups (30/50 amps), seasonal sites, cable, WiFi @ sites, laundry. **REC:** pool, playground, hunting nearby. Pets OK. Partial handicap access. No tents. Big rig sites, eco-friendly. 2021 rates: $56, Military discount.
(334)792-3313 Lat: 31.16722, Lon: -85.40249
4100 S Oates (Hwy 231 S), Dothan, AL 36301
www.cherryblossomrv.com
See ad this page

Travel Services

GANDER RV & OUTDOORS OF DOTHAN Your new hometown outfitter offering the best regional gear for all your outdoor needs. Your adventure awaits. **SERVICES:** RV, tire, RV appliance, MH mechanical, sells outdoor gear, sells firearms, staffed RV wash, restrooms. RV Sales. RV supplies, LP gas, dump, emergency parking, RV accessible. Hours: 9am - 7pm.
(866)504-3880 Lat: 31.218961, Lon: -85.431892
2691 Ross Clark Circle SW, Suite 2, Dothan, AL 36301
rv.ganderoutdoors.com

DOZIER — E4 *Crenshaw*

CYPRESS LANDING RV PARK **Ratings: 7.5/8.5/7.5** (Campground) Avail: 56 full hkups (30/50 amps). 2021 rates: $45. (334)388-1008, 32249 US Hwy 29, Dozier, AL 36028

ELBERTA — F2 *Baldwin*

JELLYSTONE PARK **Ratings: 8.5/8.5/7** (RV Park) Avail: 20 full hkups (30/50 amps). 2021 rates: $50 to $56. (251)986-3566, 12160 Wortel Rd, Elberta, AL 36530

LAKE OSPREY RV RESORT
Ratings: 10/9.5★/10 (RV Resort) Avail: 48 full hkups (30/50 amps). 2021 rates: $70 to $85. (251)986-3800, 12054 Gateway Drive, Elberta, AL 36530

EUFAULA — D5 *Barbour*

LAKE EUFAULA CAMPGROUND
Ratings: 9/9.5★/8.5 (RV Park) From Jct US 82 & US 431: Go 1-1/4 mi N on US 431, then 1/2 mi W on Chewalla Creek Dr (L). **FAC:** gravel rds. (50 spaces). Avail: 38 grass, 32 pull-thrus, (25x45), back-ins (25x35), 38 full hkups (30/50 amps), seasonal sites, cable, WiFi @ sites, tent sites, rentals, laundry, fire rings, firewood. **REC:** pool, Lake Eufaula: fishing, boating nearby, hunting nearby. Pet restrict (B). eco-friendly. 2021 rates: $27 to $30, Military discount.
(334)687-4425 Lat: 31.911643, Lon: -85.154457
151 West Chewalla Creek Drive, Eufaula, AL 36027
lakeeufaulacampground.com
See ad previous page

LAKEPOINT (Public State Park) From Jct of US-82W & US-431, N 6 mi on US-431 (R). 192 Avail: 80 full hkups, 112 W, 112 E (30/50 amps). 2021 rates: $20.90 to $30.50. (334)687-6710

WALTER F GEORGE - COE/WHITE OAK CREEK (Public Corps) From town, S 8 mi on US-431 to Hwy 95, SE 4 mi (L). 129 Avail: 129 W, 129 E (30/50 amps). 2021 rates: $26 to $52. (334)687-3101

FAIRHOPE — F2 *Baldwin*

COASTAL HAVEN RV PARK **Ratings: 8/10★/9** (RV Park) Avail: 55 full hkups (30/50 amps). 2021 rates: $42. (251)929-4298, 10151 CR 32, Fairhope, AL 36532

DRIFTWOOD RV PARK **Ratings: 7.5/8/7.5** (RV Park) Avail: 20 full hkups (30/50 amps). 2021 rates: $25. (251)597-9825, 9318 US Hwy 98, Fairhope, AL 36532

WALES WEST RV RESORT & LIGHT RAILWAY
Ratings: 9/10★/9.5 (RV Park) From Jct I-10 (exit 44) & Hwy 59: Go 13-3/4 mi S on Hwy 59, then 5-1/4 mi W on CR 32, then 2-1/4 mi N on CR 9 (R). **FAC:** paved/gravel rds. (100 spaces). 60 Avail: 55 gravel, 5 grass, 34 pull-thrus, (30x70), back-ins (22x27), 60 full hkups (30

50 amps), seasonal sites, WiFi @ sites, tent sites, laundry, LP gas, restaurant. **REC:** heated pool, hot tub, Lake Victoria: swim, fishing, boating nearby, playground, rec open to public. Pet restrict (B/Q). Partial handicap access. Big rig sites, eco-friendly. 2021 rates: $40 to $60, Military discount.
(251)232-2322 Lat: 30.503509, Lon: -87.790440
13670 Smiley Street, Silverhill, AL 36576
www.waleswest.com
See ad page 26

Things to See and Do

→ **WALES WEST LIGHT RAILWAY** Full size train that has special events throughout the year for visitors. RV accessible. Restrooms. Food. Hours: call. Adult fee: $8.00.
(888)569-5337 Lat: 30.50351, Lon: -87.79057
13670 Smiley St, Silverhill, AL 36576
See ad next page

FLORALA — E4 *Covington*

LAKE JACKSON RV PARK AT FLORALA (Public State Park) From Jct of US-331 & SR-54 (East edge of town), S 0.2 mi on US-331 to 3rd Ave, W 0.5 mi on 3rd Ave, follow signs (L). Avail: 38 full hkups (30/50 amps). 2021 rates: $30.16 to $34.80. (334)858-6425

FLORENCE — A2 *Colbert*

FLORENCE See also Tuscumbia.

MCFARLAND PARK (Public) From Jct of US-43/US-72 & Hwy 20, W 0.1 mi on Hwy 20 (L). Avail: 60 full hkups (30/50 amps). 2021 rates: $25. Apr 01 to Nov 30. (205)760-6416

FOLEY — F2 *Baldwin*

→ **AHOY RV RESORT**
good sam park **Ratings: 10/10★/10** (RV Resort) From jct 1-10 (exit 49) & Baldwin Beach Express: Go 13 mi S on Baldwin Beach Express, then 4 mi E on Foley Beach Express, then 500 ft W on US 98, then 1/4 mi N on Springsteen Ln (L).

****GREAT LOCATION...MORE AMENITIES****
NEW RV RESORT - Ideally located off US 98 & Foley Beach Express. Ahoy is dedicated to providing prompt, personable service in clean & comfortable resort atmosphere. So many great amenities. Come as guests...leave as family.
FAC: paved rds. (82 spaces). Avail: 62 all weather, patios, 15 pull-thrus, (30x95), back-ins (30x70), 62 full hkups (30/50 amps), seasonal sites, cable, WiFi @ sites, laundry, groc, LP gas, fire rings, firewood. **REC:** pool, wading pool, Lake Rougaroux: swim, fishing, kayaking/canoeing, boating nearby, shuffleboard, hunting nearby. Pet restrict (B). Partial handicap access. No tents. Big rig sites, eco-friendly. 2021 rates: $55 to $65, Military discount.
(251)233-7250 Lat: 30.414138, Lon: -87.650231
13000 Springsteen Ln, Foley, AL 36535
www.ahoyrvresort.com
See ad this page

→ **ALABAMA COAST CAMPGROUND**
good sam park **Ratings: 6/NA/9** (Campground) Avail: 43 full hkups (30/50 amps). 2021 rates: $36 to $39. (251)752-0474, 11959 Barin Field Rd, Foley, AL 36535

→ ANCHORS AWEIGH RV RESORT **Ratings: 10/8.5/9.5** (RV Park) Avail: 14 full hkups (30/50 amps). 2021 rates: $50 to $55. (251)971-6644, 19814 County Road 20 S, Foley, AL 36535

→ BEACH EXPRESS RV PARK **Ratings: 7/9★/6.5** (RV Park) Avail: 46 full hkups (30/50 amps). 2021 rates: $40. (251)970-7277, 22225 US Hwy 98, Foley, AL 36535

→ BLUEGRASS RV PARK **Ratings: 5.5/8/7** (RV Park) Avail: 10 full hkups (30/50 amps). 2021 rates: $50. (251)971-1874, 21403 Hwy 98, Foley, AL 36535

JOHNNY'S LAKESIDE RV RESORT **Ratings: 9/8/9.5** (RV Park) Avail: 48 full hkups (30/50 amps). 2021 rates: $55 to $70. (251)260-0582, 15810 State Hwy 59 North, Foley, AL 36535

MAGNOLIA FARMS RV PARK **Ratings: 7/10★/9** (RV Park) Avail: 48 full hkups (30/50 amps). 2021 rates: $40. (251)928-7335, 13381 Lipscomb Road, Foley, AL 36535

FORT PAYNE — A4 *DeKalb*

DESOTO (Public State Park) From Jct of I-59 & CR-35 (exit 218), E 4.5 mi on CR-35 (passing thru town) to CR-89, N 5 mi (L). Avail: 94 full hkups (30/50 amps). 2021 rates: $34.65. (254)845-5380

→ LITTLE RIVER RV PARK & CAMPGROUND **Ratings: 5/7.5/8.5** (RV Park) Avail: 19 full hkups (30/50 amps). 2021 rates: $25 to $37. (256)619-2267, 1357 Co. Rd. 261, Fort Payne, AL 35967

WILLS CREEK RV PARK
good sam park **Ratings: 8/9.5★/10** (RV Park) Avail: 34 full hkups (30/50 amps). 2021 rates: $28 to $30. (256)845-6703, 1310 Airport Rd W, Fort Payne, AL 35968

FORT RUCKER — E4 *Dale*

FORT RUCKER See also Dothan & Troy.

MILITARY PARK LAKE THOLOCCO RV PARK & CAMPGROUND (FORT RUCKER) (Public) From Jct of US -231 & Andrew Ave (L) on Andrew to Ozark gate, right on Whitaker, right on Christian Rd, right on Johnston Rd, follow Johnston 2.2 miles. 48 Avail: 48 W, 48 E (15/50 amps). 2021 rates: $16 to $25. (334)255-4234

FRANKLIN — D3 *Monroe*

CLAIBORNE LAKE - COE/ISAAC CREEK (Public Corps) From Monroeville, N 8 mi on SR-41 to CR-17, W 10 mi, follow signs (E). 60 Avail: 60 W, 60 E (50 amps). 2021 rates: $22 to $24. (251)282-4254

GADSDEN — B4 *Etowah*

NOCCALULA FALLS CAMPGROUND
good sam park **Ratings: 8.5/9.5★/9** (Public) From Jct of I-59 (exit 188) & Hwy 211: Go 2 mi E on Noccalula Rd (R). **FAC:** paved/gravel rds. Avail: 127 paved, 6 pull-thrus, (25x70), back-ins (24x40), 77 full hkups, 50 W, 50 E (30/50 amps), cable, WiFi @ sites, tent sites, rentals, dump, laundry, fire rings, firewood. **REC:** pool, Noccalula Falls: fishing, boating nearby, playground. Pet restrict (B). Partial handicap access. Big rig sites, 28 day max stay, eco-friendly. 2021 rates: $25, Military discount. no cc.
(256)549-4663 Lat: 34.04219, Lon: -86.02062
1600 Noccalula Rd, Gadsden, AL 35904
noccalulafallspark.com
See ad this page

RIVER ROCKS LANDING **Ratings: 9/9★/8.5** (RV Park) Avail: 119 full hkups (30/50 amps). 2021 rates: $40 to $61. (256)543-7111, 1 River Road, Gadsden, AL 35901

→ **THE COVE LAKESIDE RV RESORT AND CAMPGROUND**
good sam park **Ratings: 9/10★/8.5** (RV Park) From Jct I-759 & I-59: Go 1-1/4 mi SW on I-59 (to exit 181), then 1/2 mi E on Hwy 77/ Gilbert Ferry Road, then 1/2 mi NE on Old Pump Station Rd (E). **FAC:** gravel rds. (60 spaces). Avail: 40 gravel, 20 pull-thrus, (30x70), back-ins (30x55), 40 full hkups (30/50 amps), seasonal sites, cable, WiFi @ sites, dump, laundry, firewood, controlled access. **REC:** pool, wading pool, The Cove Lake: fishing, boating nearby, playground, hunting nearby. Pet restrict (B/Q). Partial handicap access. No tents. Big rig sites, eco-friendly. 2021 rates: $34 to $42, Military discount.
(256)467-3158 Lat: 34.002827, Lon: -86.080697
4122 Old Pump Station Rd, Gadsden, AL 35904
www.thecoverv.com
See ad this page

Things to See and Do

NOCCALULA FALLS PARK Tourist attraction, garden, daily train rides, petting zoo. Legend of Noccalula. Partial handicap access. RV accessible. Restrooms. Food. Hours: 9am to 5pm. Adult fee: $6 .
(256)549-4663 Lat: 34.04219, Lon: -86.02062
1600 Noccalula Rd, Gadsden, AL 35904
noccalulafallspark.com
See ad this page

GRANT — A4 *Marshall*

HONEYCOMB CAMPGROUND **Ratings: 7.5/7/8** (Campground) 61 Avail: 61 W, 61 E (30/50 amps). 2021 rates: $31 to $37. Jan 01 to Dec 15. (256)582-9884, 188 Campground Road, Grant, AL 35747

GREENVILLE — D3 *Butler*

SHERLING LAKE PARK & CAMPGROUND (Public) From Jct of I-65 (Exit 130) & Hwy 185: Go 2-1/4 mi N on Hwy 185, then 1-1/2 mi N on Hwy 263 (L) *note: Do not follow GPS coordinates last two miles on Braggs Rd, follow these directions and signs. 40 Avail: 30 full hkups, 10 W, 10 E (30/50 amps). 2021 rates: $25 to $28. (334)382-3638

GULF SHORES — F2 *Baldwin*

GULF SHORES See also Elberta, Fairhope, Foley, Lillian, Mobile, Orange Beach, Robertsdale & Summerdale, AL; Pensacola & Perdido Key, FL.

→ **AHOY RV RESORT**
good sam park **Ratings: 10/10★/10** (RV Resort) From jct West Beach Blvd & AL 59 (Gulf Shores Pkwy): Go 8-1/2 mi N on AL 59, then 2 mi E on US 98, then ¼ mi N on Springsteen Ln (L). **FAC:** paved rds. (82 spaces). Avail: 62 all weather, patios, 15 pull-thrus, (30x95), back-ins (30x70), 62 full hkups (30/50 amps), seasonal sites, cable, WiFi @ sites, laundry, groc, LP gas, fire rings, firewood. **REC:** pool, wading pool, Lake Rougaroux: swim, fishing, kayaking/canoeing, boating nearby, shuffleboard, hunting nearby. Pet restrict (B). No tents, eco-friendly. 2021 rates: $55 to $65, Military discount.
(251)233-7250 Lat: 30.414138, Lon: -87.650231
1300 Springsteen Ln, Foley, AL 36535
www.ahoyrvresort.com
See primary listing at Foley and ad this page

GULF SHORES (CONT)

➡ BELLA TERRA OF GULF SHORES **Ratings: 10/9.5★/10** (Condo Park) Avail: 100 full hkups (30/50 amps). 2021 rates: $52 to $105. (866)417-2416, 101 Via Bella Terra, Foley, AL 36535

➡ GULF (Public State Park) From Jct of SR-59 & SR-182, E 2.1 mi on SR-182 to CR-2, N 0.5 mi (R). Avail: 496 full hkups (30/50 amps). 2021 rates: $37 to $52. (251)948-7275

⬆ GULF BREEZE RV RESORT **Ratings: 10/8.5/9** (RV Park) Avail: 42 full hkups (30/50 amps). 2021 rates: $45. (251)968-8462, 19800 Oak Rd W, Gulf Shores, AL 36542

⬅ ISLAND RETREAT RV PARK **Ratings: 9.5/8.5★/9** (RV Park) Avail: 30 full hkups (30/50 amps). 2021 rates: $50 to $90. (251)967-1666, 18201 State Hwy 180 (FT Morgan Rd), Gulf Shores, AL 36542

⬅ LAZY LAKE RV PARK **Ratings: 4/6/5.5** (Campground) Avail: 15 full hkups (30/50 amps). 2021 rates: $36. (251)968-7875, 18950 Old Plash Isl Rd, Gulf Shores, AL 36547

We rate what RVers consider important.

↗ RV HIDEAWAY CAMPGROUND

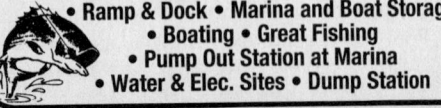

good sam park **Ratings: 8/9.5★/10** (RV Park) From Jct Hwy 59 & US 98 (in Foley): Go 5-1/4 mi W on US 98, then 2 mi S on CR 49 (R). **FAC:** paved/gravel rds. (128 spaces). Avail: 106 paved, patios, 10 pull-thrus, (35x75), back-ins (35x62), 106 full hkups (30/50 amps), seasonal sites, WiFi @ sites, dump, laundry. **REC:** boating nearby, shuffleboard, playground, hunting nearby. Pet restrict (B/Q). Partial handicap access. No tents, Age restrict may apply. Big rig sites, eco-friendly. 2021 rates: $36.
(251)965-6777 Lat: 30.381, Lon: -87.76806
10723 Magnolia Springs Hwy, Foley, AL 36535
rvhideawaycampground.com
See ad previous page

⬅ SUN-RUNNERS RV PARK **Ratings: 4.5/5/5.5** (RV Park) 30 Avail: 24 full hkups, 6 W, 6 E (30/50 amps). 2021 rates: $35. (251)955-5257, 19480 Co. Rd 8, Gulf Shores, AL 36542

GUNTERSVILLE — B4 *Marshall*

⬆ LAKE GUNTERSVILLE (Public State Park) From Jct of US-431 & SR-227, NE 7 mi on SR-227 to park access rd, N 1 mi (L). Avail: 295 full hkups (30 amps). 2021 rates: $23 to $25. (256)571-5455

⬅ RIVERVIEW CAMPGROUND **Ratings: 6.5/8.5★/8** (Campground) 21 Avail: 2 full hkups, 13 W, 13 E (30/50 amps). 2021 rates: $25. Mar 01 to Oct 31. (256)582-3014, 1450 Cha-La-Kee Rd, Guntersville, AL 35976

⬆ SEIBOLD CAMPGROUND

Ratings: 7/7/7.5 (Campground) From Jct of US 431 & Hwy 79: Go 1 mi N on Hwy 79. **FAC:** paved rds. (136 spaces). Avail: 11 paved, back-ins (40x60), 11 W, 11 E (30/50 amps), seasonal sites, dump, mobile sewer, controlled access. **REC:** pool, Lake Guntersville: fishing, marina, kayaking/canoeing, boating nearby, playground. Pets OK. No tents. 2021 rates: $22 to $27. Mar 01 to Oct 31.
(256)582-0040 Lat: 34.43553, Lon: -86.24843
54 Seibold Creek Rd, Guntersville, AL 35976
See ad this page

HARTSELLE — A3 *Morgan*

↘ QUAIL CREEK RV RESORT

good sam park **Ratings: 9.5/9.5★/8** (RV Resort) From Jct of I-65 (exit 322) & CR 55: Go 3/4 mi E on CR 55, then 1-3/4 mi N on CR 27 (Mount Zion Rd), then 1 mi E on Nat Key Rd, then 1/4 mi S on Quail Creek Dr (R). **FAC:** all weather rds. (35 spaces). Avail: 28 all weather, patios, 23 pull-thrus, (34x95), back-ins (30x95), 28 full hkups (30/50 amps), seasonal sites, WiFi @ sites, tent sites, rentals, laundry, fire rings, firewood. **REC:** pool, pond, fishing, boating nearby, golf, playground, hunting nearby, rec open to public. Pet restrict (B/Q). Big rig sites, eco-friendly. 2021 rates: $35, Military discount.
(256)784-5033 Lat: 34.391668, Lon: -86.863554
233 Quail Creek Drive, Hartselle, AL 35640
qcresort.com
See ad this page

HILLSBORO — A3 *Lawrence*

⬅ DECATUR / WHEELER LAKE KOA **Ratings: 8.5/8/8.5** (Campground) 52 Avail: 5 full hkups, 47 W, 47 E (30/50 amps). 2021 rates: $37 to $52. Mar 01 to Nov 30. (256)280-4390, 44 County Road 443, Hillsboro, AL 35643

HODGES — B2 *Franklin*

⬅ HORSESHOE BEND (Public) From town, W 14 mi on Hwy 24 to CR-88, S 2 mi to CR-16, E 4 mi to Horseshoe Bend Rd, W 2 mi (R). 28 Avail: 26 W, 26 E (30/50 amps). 2021 rates: $20. Apr 01 to Oct 30. (256)331-5681

HOPE HULL — D4 *Montgomery*

HOPE HULL See also Montgomery & Prattville.

HUNTSVILLE — A3 *Madison*

⬇ DITTO LANDING (Public) From Jct of US-431 & US-231, S 7 mi on US-231 to Hobbs Island Rd, N 2 mi (R). 32 Avail: 32 W, 32 E (30/50 amps). 2021 rates: $19 to $22. (256)882-1057

↗ MILITARY PARK REDSTONE ARSENAL MWR RV PARK (REDSTONE ARSENAL) (Public) From Jct of I-65 & I-565, E 15 mi on I-565 to Jordan Ln (Patton Rd) S 2 mi to Gate 10; Gate is open 5am to 12am. Avail: 70 full hkups (20/50 amps). 2021 rates: $25. (256)876-4868

➡ MONTE SANO (Public State Park) From Jct of US-231 & US-431/Governors Dr, E 3.6 mi on US-431S/Governors Dr to Monte Sano Blvd, N 2.5 mi to Nolen Dr, E 1 mi (L) Caution: Some steep & switchback entry roads. 89 Avail: 15 full hkups, 59 W, 59 E (30 amps). 2021 rates: $27 to $29. (256)534-6589

↗ U.S. SPACE & ROCKET CENTER CAMPGROUND **Ratings: 5/7.5/7** (Campground) Avail: 27 full hkups (30 amps). 2021 rates: $28 to $32. (256)830-4987, 1 Tranquility Base , Huntsville, AL 35805

JASPER — B3 *Walker*

➡ SLEEPY HOLLER CAMPGROUND

good sam park **Ratings: 5.5/NA/6.5** (Campground) From Jct Hwy 78 (exit 65) & Industrial Pky: Go 3-1/2 mi N on Industrial Pky, then 3-1/4 mi E on Hwy 5, then 3/4 mi S on Buttermilk Rd (L) *Do not use GPS). **FAC:** gravel rds. (130 spaces). 75 Avail: 40 gravel, 35 grass, 60 pull-thrus, (18x60), back-ins (20x60), 75 full hkups (30/50 amps), seasonal sites, dump, laundry. **REC:** Campground Lake: fishing, hunting nearby. Pets OK. Partial handicap access. No tents, eco-friendly. 2021 rates: $35 to $40, Military discount. no cc.
(205)332-0017 Lat: 33.807503, Lon: -87.181029
174 Sleepy Holler Circle, Cordova, AL 35550
See ad this page

JEMISON — C3 *Chilton*

MINOOKA PARK (CHILTON COUNTY PARK) (Public) From Jct of I-65 & CR-42 (Exit 219), W 3.8 mi on CR-42 to Jct of CR-42 & Hwy 31, N 3.9 mi on Hwy 31 to CR-146, E 1.8 mi on CR-146 (L). 18 Avail: 10 full hkups, 8 W, 8 E (30/50 amps). 2021 rates: $25 to $30. (205)312-1376

➡ PEACH QUEEN CAMPGROUND **Ratings: 7.5/6.5/6.5** (Campground) Avail: 12 full hkups (30/50 amps). 2021 rates: $40. (205)688-2573, 12986 County Road 42, Jemison, AL 35085

LANETT — C5 *Chambers*

⬆ WEST POINT LAKE - COE/AMITY (Public Corps) From town, N 7 mi on CR-212 to CR-393, E 0.5 mi (E). 72 Avail: 67 W, 72 E (30/50 amps). 2021 rates: $16 to $28. Apr 02 to Sep 06. (334)499-2404

LANGSTON — A4 *Jackson*

⬇ NORTHSHORE CAMPGROUND AT THE BIG ROCK

Ratings: 5.5/NA/8.5 (Campground) From Jct US 431 & Hwy 227: Go 11-3/4 mi NE on Hwy 227, then continue 7 mi NE on S Sauty Rd (CR 67) (R). **FAC:** paved rds. (81 spaces). Avail: 40 gravel, back-ins (40x60), 40 full hkups (30/50 amps), seasonal sites, fire rings, restaurant, controlled access. **REC:** pool, Lake Guntersville: swim, fishing, kayaking/canoeing, boating nearby. Pet restrict (B). No tents. Big rig sites. 2021 rates: $28. Mar 01 to Oct 31. no cc.
(256)582-6157 Lat: 34.51506, Lon: -86.11020
6845 S Sauty Rd, Langston, AL 35755
www.southsautyresort.com
See ad this page

RV MYTH #2: ""Class A and fifth-wheel trailers require special drivers' license endorsements and training.'' In most states and provinces, there are no extra license requirements for these popular RV types. You should, however, verify the local regulations in your home area.

SOUTH SAUTY CREEK RESORT **Ratings: 5.5/7/6.5** (Campground) From Jct US 431 & Hwy 227: Go 11-3/4 mi NE on Hwy 227, then continue 7 mi NE on South Sauty Rd (CR 67) (L). **FAC:** paved/gravel rds. (86 spaces). Avail: 36 gravel, back-ins (24x60), 36 W, 36 E (30/50 amps), seasonal sites, WiFi, rentals, dump, mobile sewer, groc, fire rings, restaurant. **REC:** pool, Lake Gunterville: swim, fishing, marina, kayaking/canoeing, boating nearby. Pet restrict (B). No tents. 2021 rates: $22. no cc.
(256)582-6157 Lat: 34.51506, Lon: -86.11020
122 Murphy Hill Dr, Langston, AL 35755
www.southsautyresort.com
See ad opposite page

WINDEMERE COVE RV RESORT **Ratings: 10/9.5★/10** (Condo Park) Avail: 106 full hkups (30/50 amps). 2021 rates: $38.50 to $49.50. (256)228-3010, 10174 County Rd 67, Langston, AL 35755

LEESBURG — B4 *Cherokee*

CHESNUT BAY RV RESORT **Ratings: 9.5/10★/10** (RV Resort) Avail: 38 full hkups (30/50 amps). 2021 rates: $50. (256)526-7778, 4507 CR 147 , Leesburg, AL 35983

LILLIAN — F3 *Baldwin*

LOST BAY KOA **Ratings: 8/7/7.5** (Campground) 110 Avail: 103 full hkups, 7 W, 7 E (30/50 amps). 2021 rates: $42.99 to $68. (251)961-1717, 11650 CR 99, Lillian, AL 36549

LOWNDESBORO — D3 *Lowndes*

WOODRUFF LAKE - COE/PRAIRIE CREEK (Public Corps) From Jct of US-80 & CR-23 (milepost 108.6), N 3 mi on CR-23 to CR-40, W 3.5 mi (R). 55 Avail: 55 W, 55 E (50 amps). 2021 rates: $22 to $24. (334)418-4919

MCCALLA — C3 *Tuscaloosa*

TANNEHILL IRONWORKS HISTORICAL (Public) From Jct of I-59 & Bucksville (exit 100), SE 2.5 mi on Tannehill Parkway to Eastern Valley Rd, W 200 ft (L); or From Jct of I-459 & Eastern Valley Rd (exit 1), W 7.2 mi on Eastern Valley Rd (L). 195 Avail: 195 W, 195 E (30/50 amps). 2021 rates: $25 to $30. (205)477-5711

MOBILE — E2 *Baldwin*

MOBILE See also Fairhope, Robertsdale, Summerdale & Theodore.

ALL ABOUT RELAXING RV PARK **Ratings: 10/10★/10** (RV Park) From Jct 1-10 (exit 10) & CR 39 (McDonald Rd): Go 3-1/4 mi N on McDonald Rd, then ¾ mi W (through roundabout) on Three Notch Rd (R). **FAC:** all weather rds. (41 spaces). Avail: 27 all weather, patios, 16 pull-thrus, (28x74), back-ins (27x74), accepts full hkup units only, 27 full hkups (30/50 amps), seasonal sites, WiFi @ sites, laundry, LP gas, controlled access. **REC:** pool, boating nearby. Pets OK. Partial handicap access. No tents. Big rig sites, eco-friendly. 2021 rates: $38 to $60, Military discount.
(251)375-0661 Lat: 30.589167, Lon: -88.252814
8950 Three Notch Road, Theodore, AL 36582
www.allaboutrelaxingrv.com
See ad this page

BAY PALMS RV RESORT **Ratings: 8/6/7** (RV Park) Avail: 31 full hkups (30/50 amps). 2021 rates: $45 to $55. (251)873-4700, 15440 Dauphin Island Parkway, Coden, AL 36523

CHICKASABOGUE PARK (MOBILE COUNTY PARK) (Public) From Jct of I-65 & Hwy 158 (exit 13), Hwy 158 W 0.1 to Hwy 213, S 2.2 mi to Whistler, E 0.7 mi to Aldock Rd, N 1 mi, follow signs (E). 53 Avail: 53 W, 25 S, 53 E (30/50 amps). 2021 rates: $15.60 to $18.72. (251)574-2267

EAGLE'S LANDING RV PARK **Ratings: 6.5/8/8** (RV Park) Avail: 66 full hkups (30/50 amps). 2021 rates: $30. (251)653-1034, 7970 Bellingrath Rd, Theodore, AL 36582

I-10 KAMPGROUND **Ratings: 9/8.5★/8** (Campground) From Jct of I-10 & Theodore Dawes Rd (Exit 13), S 0.5 mi on Theodore Dawes Rd (L). **FAC:** all weather rds. (146 spaces). 15 Avail: 6 paved, 9 gravel, 15 pull-thrus, (20x60), 15 full hkups (30/50 amps), seasonal sites, WiFi @ sites, laundry. **REC:** pool, boating nearby, hunting nearby. Pets OK. Partial handicap access. No tents. Big rig sites, eco-friendly. 2021 rates: $45, Military discount.
(251)653-9816 Lat: 30.55831, Lon: -88.19182
6430 Theodore Dawes Rd, Theodore, AL 36582
i10kamp.com
See ad this page

I-65 RV CAMPGROUND **Ratings: 7.5/8/7.5** (RV Park) From Jct I-65 & Hwy 43 (exit 19): Go 1/4 mi N on Hwy 43, then 1 mi W on Jackson Rd (L) Follow signs. **FAC:** paved/gravel rds. (87 spaces). Avail: 11 gravel, patios, 11 pull-thrus, (30x90), 11 full hkups (30/50 amps), seasonal sites, WiFi @ sites, tent sites, dump, laundry, LP gas. **REC:** boating nearby. Pet restrict (S/B). Partial handicap access. Big rig sites. 2021 rates: $37, Military discount.
(251)675-6347 Lat: 30.87320, Lon: -88.05476
730 Jackson Rd, Creola, AL 36525
www.i65rvcampground.com
See ad this page

SHADY ACRES CAMPGROUND **Ratings: 7.5/8.5/8.5** (Campground) From Jct of I-10 (W-Bnd, exit 22B), (E-bnd, exit 22) & SR 163 S: Go 1/2 mi S on SR 163, then 1/3 mi W on Old Military Rd (R) Caution W-bnd: After tunnel, exit 22B from Left Lane. **FAC:** paved rds. (92 spaces). Avail: 25 all weather, 9 pull-thrus, (25x85), back-ins (25x75), 25 full hkups (30/50 amps), seasonal sites, cable, WiFi @ sites, laundry. **REC:** Dog River: fishing, boating nearby. Pet restrict (B). Partial handicap access. No tents. Big rig sites, eco-friendly. 2021 rates: $37, Military discount.
(251)478-0013 Lat: 30.62771, Lon: -88.09512
2500 Old Military Road, Mobile, AL 36605
shadyacresmobile.com
See ad this page

MONTEVALLO — C3 *Bibb*

BRIERFIELD IRONWORKS HISTORICAL PARK (Public) From Jct of SR-25 & SR-119 (downtown Montevallo), S 7 mi on SR-25 to CR-62, S 0.4 mi (L). 42 Avail: 42 W, 42 E (20/50 amps). 2021 rates: $16 to $24. (205)665-1856

MONTGOMERY — D4 *Montgomery*

CAPITAL CITY RV PARK **Ratings: 9/10★/10** (RV Park) Avail: 40 full hkups (30/50 amps). 2021 rates: $44 to $50. (334)271-8063, 4655 Old Wetumpka Hwy, Montgomery, AL 36110

MILITARY PARK MAXWELL/GUNTER AFB FAMCAMP (MAXWELL AFB) (Public) From jct I-85 S & I-65 N: take Herron exit off I-65 N to Bell St (E). Avail: 71 full hkups (30/50 amps). 2021 rates: $18 to $26. (334)953-5161

Had a great stay? Let us know by emailing us Parks@goodsam.com

MONTGOMERY SOUTH RV PARK & CABINS **Ratings: 7.5/9.5★/9** (RV Park) Avail: 33 full hkups (30/50 amps). 2021 rates: $51. (334)284-7006, 731 Venable Rd, Hope Hull, AL 36043

THE WOODS RV PARK & CAMPGROUND **Ratings: 6.5/9★/8.5** (RV Park) Avail: 65 full hkups (30/50 amps). 2021 rates: $65. (334)356-1887, 4350 Sassafras Circle, Montgomery, AL 36105

WOODRUFF LAKE - COE/GUNTER HILL (Public Corps) From Jct of I-65 & exit 167 (Hwy 80), W 9 mi on Hwy 80 to CR-7, N, follow signs (L). 140 Avail: 140 W, 140 E (30/50 amps). 2021 rates: $18 to $26. Mar 01 to Oct 31. (334)269-1053

MOUNDVILLE — C2 *Hale*

MOUNDVILLE ARCHAEOLOGICAL PARK (Public) From Jct of US-82 & Hwy 69, S 15 mi on Hwy 69 (R). 34 Avail: 5 full hkups, 24 W, 24 E (30 amps). 2021 rates: $10 to $20. (205)371-2234

Be prepared! Bridge, Tunnel & Ferry Regulations and Rules of the Road can be found in the front of the Guide.

NEW MARKET — A4 *Madison*

SHARON JOHNSTON PARK (MADISON COUNTY PARK) (Public) North on Memorial Parkway, right on Winchester, left on Coleman Rd. 50 Avail: 19 full hkups, 14 W, 14 E (50 amps). 2021 rates: $20 to $30. (256)379-2868

OPELIKA — C5 *Lee*

A SPOTLIGHT Introducing Auburn-Opelika's colorful attractions appearing at the front of this state section.

LAKESIDE RV PARK

Ratings: 7.5/7/7.5 (Campground) Avail: 30 full hkups (30/50 amps). 2021 rates: $50. (334)705-0701, 5664 US Hwy 280E, Opelika, AL 36804

SPRING VILLA CAMPGROUND (Public) From Jct of I-85 & SR-169, SE 4 mi on SR-169 to CR-148, E 1 mi (R). Avail: 30 full hkups (30/50 amps). 2021 rates: $35. (334)705-5552

OPP — E4 *Covington*

FRANK JACKSON (Public State Park) From Jct of US-331/US 84/Hwy 12, N 0.7 mi on US 331, W 1.0 mi on Opine Rd, N 0.2 mi on Jerry Adams Dr. (L) Entrance fee required. Avail: 32 full hkups (30/50 amps). 2021 rates: $30.69 to $37.52. (334)493-6988

ORANGE BEACH — F2 *Baldwin*

AHOY RV RESORT

Ratings: 10/10★/10 (RV Resort) From jct AL 182/Orange Beach Blvd & AL 161/ Alabama Coastal Connection: Go 1-3/4 mi N on AL 161, then 3 mi W on AL 180/ Alabama Coastal Connection/Canal Rd, then 9 mi N on Foley Beach Blvd, then 500 ft W on US 98, then 1/4 mi N on Springsteen Ln (L). **FAC:** paved rds. (82 spaces). Avail: 62 all weather, patios, 15 pull-thrus, (30x95), back-ins (30x70), 62 full hkups (30/50 amps), seasonal sites, cable, WiFi @ sites, laundry, groc, LP gas, fire rings, firewood. **REC:** pool, wading pool, Lake Rougaroux: swim, fishing, kayaking/canoeing, boating nearby, shuffleboard, hunting nearby. Pet restrict (B). No tents. Big rig sites, eco-friendly. 2021 rates: $55 to $65, Military discount.
(251)233-7250 Lat: 30.414138, Lon: -87.650231
1300 Springsteen Ln, Foley, AL 36535
www.ahoyrvresort.com
See primary listing at Foley and ad page 25

BUENA VISTA COASTAL RV RESORT **Ratings: 9.5/9.5★/9.5** (Condo Park) Avail: 30 full hkups (30/50 amps). 2021 rates: $95 to $420. (251)980-1855, 23601 Perdido Beach Blvd., Orange Beach, AL 36561

HERITAGE MOTORCOACH RESORT & MARINA **Ratings: 10/9.5★/10** (Condo Park) Avail: 29 full hkups (30/50 amps). 2021 rates: $80 to $195. (800)730-7032, 28888 Canal Road, Orange Beach, AL 36561

PANDION RIDGE LUXURY RV RESORT **Ratings: 9.5/9.5★/9.5** (RV Resort) Avail: 100 full hkups (30/50 amps). 2021 rates: $59 to $109. (888)978-2080, 22800 Canal Rd, Orange Beach, AL 36561

PELHAM — C3 *Shelby*

BIRMINGHAM SOUTH RV PARK **Ratings: 9.5/9★/9.5** (Campground) Avail: 71 full hkups (30/50 amps). 2021 rates: $50. (205)664-8832, 222 Hwy 33, Pelham, AL 35124

OAK MOUNTAIN (Public State Park) From Jct of I-65 & SR-119 (exit 246), W 300 ft on SR-119 to state park rd, S 2 mi to entrance, NE 6 mi (E). 145 Avail: 57 full hkups, 27 W, 27 E (30 amps). 2021 rates: $17.60 to $33. (205)620-2527

PELL CITY — B4 *St Clair*

LAKESIDE LANDING MARINA & RV RESORT **Ratings: 8/7.5/8** (RV Park) Avail: 68 full hkups (30/50 amps). 2021 rates: $35 to $65. (205)525-5701, 4600 Martin St South, Cropwell, AL 35054

PICKENSVILLE — C2 *Pickens*

TENNESSEE-TOMBIGBEE - COE/PICKENSVILLE (Public Corps) From Jct Hwy 388 & W Lock and Dam Rd, W 0.6 mi on W Lock and Dam Rd, L 0.1 mi on Camp Rd (E). 174 Avail: 27 full hkups, 147 W, 147 E (50 amps). 2021 rates: $20 to $24. (205)373-6328

PRATTVILLE — D4 *Autagua*

AUTAUGA CREEK LANDING RV CAMPGROUND **Ratings: 3.5/NA/4.5** (Campground) Avail: 20 full hkups (30/50 amps). 2021 rates: $25 to $35. (334)361-3999, 951 Langford Ct, Prattville, AL 36067

KOUNTRY AIR RV PARK

Ratings: 9/9★/9.5 (Campground) From Jct I-65 (exit 179) & Cobb Ford Rd: Go 1 mi W on Cobb Ford Rd, then 14 mi W on US 82/W (L). **FAC:** all weather rds. (43 spaces). Avail: 10 gravel, 10 pull-thrus, (30x75), 10 full hkups (30/50 amps), seasonal sites, WiFi @ sites, rentals, laundry, LP gas, fire rings, firewood. **REC:** pool, boating nearby, playground, hunting nearby. Pet restrict (B). Partial handicap access. No tents. Big rig sites, eco-friendly. 2021 rates: $40 to $45, Military discount.
(334)365-6861 Lat: 32.51504, Lon: -86.592695
2133 Hwy 82 West, Prattville, AL 36067
www.kountryairrv.com
See ad this page

ROBERTSDALE — F2 *Baldwin*

AZALEA ACRES RV PARK **Ratings: 8/10★/10** (RV Park) Avail: 35 full hkups (30/50 amps). 2021 rates: $35 to $40. (251)947-9530, 27450 Glass Rd, Robertsdale, AL 36567

HILLTOP RV PARK **Ratings: 7/8.5★/7.5** (RV Park) Avail: 40 full hkups (30/50 amps). 2021 rates: $40 to $45. (251)229-5880, 23420 CR-64, Robertsdale, AL 36567

RIVERSIDE RV RESORT **Ratings: 8.5/9★/8** (RV Park) Avail: 33 full hkups (30/50 amps). 2021 rates: $35 to $45. (251)945-1110, 25625 Water Rapids Rd, Robertsdale, AL 36567

WILDERNESS RV PARK

Ratings: 8/9★/8.5 (RV Park) From I-10 (exit 53) & CR 64: Go S 1/4 mi on CR 64, then turn left on Patterson Rd for 1.3 mi. (Ignore GPS). **FAC:** gravel rds. (81 spaces). Avail: 30 grass, 30 pull-thrus, (25x65), 30 full hkups (30/50 amps), seasonal sites, WiFi @ sites, laundry, LP gas. **REC:** pool, pond, fishing, boating nearby, hunting nearby. Pet restrict (B/Q). Partial handicap access. No tents. Big rig sites, eco-friendly. 2021 rates: $40 to $45.
(251)960-1195 Lat: 30.61870, Lon: -87.61132
24280 Patterson Rd, Robertsdale, AL 36567
wildernessrvpark.com
See ad this page

Travel Services

CAMPING WORLD OF ROBERTSDALE As the nation's largest retailer of RV supplies, accessories, services and new and used RVs, Camping World is committed to making your total RV experience better. **SERVICES:** RV, tire, RV appliance, MH mechanical, staffed RV wash, restrooms. RV Sales. RV supplies, LP gas, dump, emergency parking, RV accessible. Hours: 9am to 7pm.
(866)906-6968 Lat: 30.534835, Lon: -87.70835
21282 Hwy 59 South, Robertsdale, AL 36567
www.campingworld.com

ROGERSVILLE — A3 *Lauderdale*

JOE WHEELER (Public State Park) From Jct of US-72 & SR-207, W 1.5 mi on US-72 to park rd, S 3 mi (L). 116 Avail: 110 full hkups, 6 W, 6 E (30/50 amps). 2021 rates: $25 to $29. (256)247-1184

RUSSELLVILLE — A2 *Franklin*

PINEY POINT (Public) From town, W 18 mi on Hwy 24 to CR-16, S 8 mi to CR-4, S 1.2 mi to CR-37, S 3 mi, cross dam (L). 19 Avail: 19 W, 19 E (30 amps). 2021 rates: $20. Mar 15 to Oct 15. (256)436-3018

SLICKROCK (Public) From town, W 13 mi on Hwy 24 to CR-33, N 2.3 mi (L). 53 Avail: 53 W, 53 E (30 amps). 2021 rates: $20. Mar 15 to Nov 15. (256)332-4392

SCOTTSBORO — A4 *Jackson*

GOOSEPOND COLONY RESORT (Public) From jct US 72 & AL 79: Go 1-3/4 mi SE on AL 79, then 1 mi SW on AL 79 (Broad St), then 1-1/2 mi E on Ed Hembree Dr (R). 133 Avail: 109 full hkups, 24 W, 24 E (30/50 amps). 2021 rates: $32 to $49. (800)268-2884

JACKSON COUNTY PARK (Public) From jct AL 279 & US 72 (John T Reed Pky): Go 1/4 mi E on US 72, then 1 mi SE on County Park Rd (L). Avail: 16 full hkups (30/50 amps). 2021 rates: $29 to $41. (256)574-4719

SELMA — D3 *Dallas*

DANNELLY LAKE - COE/SIX MILE CREEK (Public Corps) From town, S 9 mi on Hwy 41 to CR-139, W 1 mi (L). 31 Avail: 31 W, 31 E (30/50 amps). 2021 rates: $22. Apr 01 to Sep 07. (334)872-9554

PAUL GRIST (Public State Park) From town: Go 15 mi N on Hwy 22. Avail: 11 full hkups (30/50 amps). 2021 rates: $22 to $25. (334)872-5846

SHORTERVILLE — E5 *Henry*

WALTER F GEORGE - COE/HARDRIDGE CREEK (Public Corps) From Jct Hwy 10 & CR-97, N 6 mi on CR-97 (E). 74 Avail: 18 full hkups, 55 W, 56 E (30/50 amps). 2021 rates: $26 to $52. Feb 28 to Sep 12. (334)585-5945

SILAS — D2 *Choctaw*

BLACK WARRIOR-TOMBIGBEE - COE/SERVICE (Public Corps) From town, W 4 mi on Hwy 84 (R). 30 Avail: 30 W, 30 E (50 amps). 2021 rates: $24 to $26. Mar 15 to Dec 15. (251)753-6935

SPANISH FORT — E2 *Baldwin*

BLAKELEY (Public State Park) From jct I-10 & US 98: Go N 1 mi on Hwy 98 to Hwy 31, then N 4/5 mi to Hwy 225, follow signs. 31 Avail. 2021 rates: $30. (251)626-0798

MEAHER (Public State Park) From jct US 90 and I-10: Go 3 mi E on US 90 (Battleship Pkwy) (R). Avail: 61 full hkups (20/50 amps). 2021 rates: $37. (251)626-5529

STOCKTON — E2 *Baldwin*

LIVE OAK LANDING (Public) From jct I-65 (exit 31) & Hwy 225: Go 3/4 mi N on Hwy 225, then 1 mi W on Live Oak Rd (R). Avail: 18 full hkups (30/50 amps). 2021 rates: $40. (251)800-7464

SUMMERDALE — F2 *Baldwin*

EMMAUS MOTORCOACH & RV RESORT **Ratings: 6.5/7.5/8** (RV Park) Avail: 17 full hkups (30/50 amps). 2021 rates: $30 to $50. (251)989-9888, 23051 Cty Rd 38, Summerdale, AL 36580

ESCAPEES RAINBOW PLANTATION **Ratings: 8/7.5/7** (RV Park) Avail: 61 full hkups (30/50 amps). 2021 rates: $27.50. (251)988-8132, 14301 County Rd 28, Summerdale, AL 36580

TALLADEGA — C4 *Talladega*

TALLADEGA See also Anniston & Pell City.

TALLADEGA CREEKSIDE RESORT **Ratings: 3/UI/7** (Campground) Avail: 15 full hkups (30/50 amps). 2021 rates: $25 to $60. (256)362-9053, 760 Lake Whitland Dr, Talladega, AL 35160

TALLADEGA PIT STOP RV PARK & CAMPGROUND

Ratings: 6/10★/8 (RV Park) Avail: 83 full hkups (30/50 amps). 2021 rates: $40. (256)581-5955, 4889 Speedway Blvd, Lincoln, AL 35096

SNOWBIRD TIP: Imagine your perfect destination. RV parks reflect our personalities, lifestyles and budgets. Eastern RV parks offer a more urban experience and conveniences, while parks out west typically have more elbow room. Research before reserving to find your ideal spot.

TANNER — A3 *Lime Stone*

SWAN CREEK COMMUNITY (MHP)
good sam park **Ratings: 6/UI/7.5** (RV Area in MH Park) Avail: 30 full hkups (30/50 amps). 2021 rates: $40. (256)355-5392, 10420 US Hwy 31 Lot 67, Tanner, AL 35671

THEODORE — F2 *Mobile*

PECAN GROVE MOTORHOME RV PARK **Ratings: 5/NA/7** (Campground) Avail: 18 full hkups (30/50 amps). 2021 rates: $30.60. (251)973-1013, 10420 Dauphin Island Pkwy, Theodore, AL 36582

TROY — D4 *Pike*

ALABAMA MUD PARK **Ratings: 6/7.5/6.5** (Campground) 65 Avail: 20 full hkups, 45 W, 45 E (30 amps). 2021 rates: $30. (334)770-0589, 4162 County Road 7708 (Needmore Rd), Troy, AL 36081

DEER RUN RV PARK **Ratings: 9/9★/8.5** (Campground) Avail: 82 full hkups (30/50 amps). 2021 rates: $38. (334)566-6517, 25629 US Hwy 231, Troy, AL 36081

RV parks in remote locations are sometimes unable to provide all amenities, like 30/50-amp service. Don't let that stop you - the tradeoff is a once-in-a-lifetime trip to some of the most beautiful wilderness areas on the planet!

TUSCALOOSA — C2 *Tuscaloosa*

BLACK WARRIOR-TOMBIGBEE - COE/DEERLICK CREEK (Public Corps) From Jct of I-59/I-20 & US-82, W 4 mi on US-82 to Rice Mine Rd (CR-30), NE 3 mi to CR-87, NE 3 mi to CR-42, E 3 mi to CR-89, S 3 mi (E). 46 Avail: 3 full hkups, 42 W, 42 E (15/50 amps). 2021 rates: $25 to $30. Mar 01 to Nov 28. (205)759-1591

LAKE LURLEEN (Public State Park) From Jct of I-59/I-20 & US-82W (exit 73), NW 12.1 mi on US-82W to CR-21, N 2.5 mi to Lk Lurleen Rd, N 2 mi (E); or From Jct of I-59/I-20 & SR-69 (exit 71B), N 5 mi on SR-69 to US-82W, W 5.3 mi to CR -21, N 2.5 mi to Lk Lurleen Rd, N 2 mi (E). 91 Avail: 35 full hkups, 56 W, 56 E (30 amps). 2021 rates: $27. (205)339-1558

TUSCUMBIA — A2 *Colbert*

HERITAGE ACRES RV PARK **Ratings: 8/10★/9.5** (Campground) Avail: 20 full hkups (30/50 amps). 2021 rates: $39 to $59. (256)383-7368, 1770 Neil Morris Rd, Tuscumbia, AL 35674

WARRIOR — B3 *Blount*

RICKWOOD CAVERNS (Public State Park) From Jct of I-65 & SR-160 (exit 284), W 0.2 mi on SR-160 to CR-8, N 2.5 mi to Rickwood Caverns Rd, E 1.3 mi (R); or From Jct of I-65 & CR-5 (exit 289), W 0.6 mi on CR-5 to Rickwood Caverns Rd/CR 4, S 2.3 (L). 13 Avail: 13 W, 13 E (30/50 amps). 2021 rates: $15 to $28. (205)647-9692

WETUMPKA — C4 *Elmore*

FORT TOULOUSE - JACKSON PARK (Public) From Jct of I-65 & Hwy 231, N 10 mi on Hwy 231 to Ft Toulouse Rd, W 2.5 mi (E). 39 Avail: 39 W, 39 E (20/50 amps). 2021 rates: $20. (334)567-3002

WILMER — E2 *Mobile*

ESCATAWPA HOLLOW PARK AND CAMPGROUND (MOBILE COUNTY PARK) (Public) From US 98 (in town of Wilmer): Go 4-1/4 mi W on US-98 to AL/MS state line (L). 22 Avail: 6 full hkups, 16 W, 16 E (30 amps). 2021 rates: $25. (251)547-2267

WOODVILLE — A4 *Jackson*

CATHEDRAL CAVERNS (Public State Park) From Huntsville: Take Hwy 72 E to Hwy 63, then right until you see the Cathedral Caverns rock sign, turn left & follow signs. 11 Avail: 11 W, 11 E (30 amps), Pit toilets. 2021 rates: $20. (256)728-8193

PARNELL CREEK RV PARK
good sam park **Ratings: 9/8.5★/9** (RV Park) 36 Avail: 28 full hkups, 8 W, 8 E (30/50 amps). 2021 rates: $27 to $32. (256)508-7308, 115 Parnell Circle, Woodville, AL 35776

Check out a campground's ad. In it you might find a locator map, photos, and a lot more information about the park to help you find just the right place to stay.

Getty Images/iStockphoto

YOU ARE HERE

Alaska

DID YOU KNOW?

Larger than Yellowstone and Yosemite combined, Wrangell-St. Elias National Park and Preserve is the largest national park in the country.

Alaska has no shortage of dramatic landscapes. Monstrous mountains, vast wilderness areas and rollicking rivers set the stage for adventure. Watch for whales, wrestle a trophy fish or paddle a kayak at the foot of a towering glacier.

A Wild Town

Come to Anchorage to experience a town that blends big-city amenities and untamed wilderness. While the skyscrapers might be the biggest in the state, the surrounding mountain peaks make them appear tiny.

Fun Frontier

Although Anchorage serves a major business and tourism nexus, it makes visitors feel at home with its many locally owned and operated restaurants, shops, outfitters and tour companies. Far south of the Arctic Circle, protected by the Chugach Mountains and warmed by Pacific Rim ocean currents, the climate is mild and the city is generally spared from extreme cold. Nevertheless, dress in layers and arrive prepared, as weather conditions can shift quickly. Of course, outdoor action is the name of the game here, and Anchorage has it all. Ice climbing, white-water rafting, paragliding, mountain biking, kayaking, ziplining, skiing, snowboarding and heli-skiing options abound for the more adrenaline-prone adventure seekers.

Larger-Than-Life Spectacle

Seeking nearly endless expanses of wilderness? You can't go wrong with a visit to Alaska. You'll find sprawling landscapes at Wrangell-St. Elias National Park and Preserve, the nation's biggest national park. Located in southeast Alaska, the park consists of 13.2 million acres of untamed mountains and forests. For something more accessible to major travel routes, check out Kenai Fjords National Park, home to nearly 40 glaciers that bring visitors close to nature.

Alaska Chinook

Chinook, also known as king salmon, is the largest type of Pacific salmon and the official state fish. Boasting a melt-in-your-mouth consistency, this hefty catch can be transformed into delicious steaks or fillets. Locals prefer cooking them over charcoal or open flame. Get your fill at seafood restaurants or purchase some smoked salmon and layer it with cream cheese on a morning bagel.

VISITOR CENTER

TIME ZONE
Alaska Standard

ROAD & HIGHWAY INFORMATION
907-465-8952
511.alaska.gov

FISHING & HUNTING INFORMATION
907-465-2376
adfg.alaska.gov

BOATING INFORMATION
907-269-8700
dnr.alaska.gov/parks/boating/

NATIONAL PARKS
nps.gov/ak

STATE PARKS
dnr.alaska.gov/parks/

TOURISM INFORMATION
Alaska Travel Industry Association
907-929-2842
travelalaska.com

TOP TOURISM ATTRACTIONS
1) Denali National Park and Preserve
2) Glacier Bay National Park and Preserve
3) Alaska Native Heritage Center

MAJOR CITIES
Anchorage, Fairbanks, Juneau (capital), Badger, Knik, Fairview

VALDEZ, ALASKA
VALDEZ SPIRIT
THE LOCAL EXPERTS
AT HOME IN VALDEZ
SINCE 1971
MEARES GLACIER
COLUMBIA GLACIER
VALDEZ
Visit us in scenic Valdez, Alaska
Stan Stephens
GLACIER & WILDLIFE CRUISES
VALDEZ, ALASKA
stephenscruises.com
Valdez: 907.835.4731 | 866.867.1297
See listing Valdez, AK

ALASKA

A mother brown bear with her cubs in Alaska wilderness. Brown bears can weight up to 1,700 pounds and reach nine feet in height when standing on their back legs.

Located south of Anchorage, this park gives visitors a chance to hike an icefield, kayak the fjords or see gargantuan glaciers.

Go for the Gold in Fairbanks

When it became one of the launching pads for the Klondike Gold Rush in the late 1800s, Fairbanks earned the nickname, "Golden Heart of Alaska." Indeed, Fairbanks is a prime spot for exploring Alaska's interior. This is the Land of the Midnight Sun, where the sun doesn't set for 70 days between May and July. The rest of the year, the night skies often put on a show, as Fairbanks is one of the best locations to see the aurora borealis.

Dazzling Denali

You can access the magnificent, six-million-acre Denali National Park and Preserve via a single road. Take a bus tour to reach the interior, which offers views of Denali, rising over 20,310 feet above sea level, making it North America's highest mountain. Keep your binoculars handy and watch for bears, moose and caribou along the route. Located in Alaska's famed Inside Passage, Glacier Bay National Park and Preserve offers visitors a dizzying array of landscapes to explore, from verdant rainforests to sapphire glaciers to rugged coasts.

Epic Waterways

Alaska's nearly 7,000 miles of coastline pack adventures that you won't find anywhere else. That doesn't even include the endless rivers and lakes found inland. Anglers can snag trophy-sized halibut, salmon and trout across the state, with the Kenai River, Brooks Range and Bristol Bay being top picks.

Launch in Alaska

Hit the Alaska water in a kayak or canoe to get up close to its rich waterways. The lakes glimmer with clear, cold glacial waters, often reflecting mountain peaks, and the pristine rivers run untamed for hundreds of miles. The Kenai Lake is popular for water sports, while Wonder Lake has awe-inspiring views of Denali. Kayak to Mendenhall Glacier, outside of Juneau, for a quintessential Alaskan adventure.

Native Peoples

More than 200 federally recognized indigenous tribes comprising 100,000 Alaska Natives call the Frontier State their home. Celebrate this rich cultural heritage with a visit to one of the small Native villages where traditional customs and crafts are proudly preserved. Learn more with a visit to the Alaska Native Heritage Center in Anchorage, the Alaska State Museum in Juneau or the amazing Totem Bight State Historical Park in Ketchikan.

Gold Among the Glaciers

The glint of gold inspired waves of prospectors to invade the Alaska Territory during the Klondike Gold Rush in 1896-1899. Step back in time with a tour of the Klondike Gold Rush National Historical Park. Stroll through the colorful boomtown of Skagway's Historic District and explore the Chilkoot Trail and White Pass Trail.

Sound Travel

Stunning snow-capped mountain peaks loom over spectacular Prince William Sound. The small coastal town of Valdez in southern Alaska is renowned for its state parks, glaciers and alpine atmosphere. Plundering eclectic antique shops and exploring the history of this one-time Gold Rush outpost.

Riches on the Richardson Highway

You can reach Valdez from Anchorage by taking a drive that can be made in about six hours via the Richardson Highway. At the turn of the century, scrappy prospectors traveling north to the Alaskan gold fields arrived by way of the town's waterfront, and even more than one hundred years later the small harbor still finds itself as the undisputed heart of Valdez. It's from here that the town center expands backward, with a handful of streets offering local food, shopping and adventure-activity outfitters.

Sights on the Water

Take a day cruise to Columbia Glacier, which sits 25 miles east of Valdez. Columbia is the second-largest tidewater glacier in the world and sports a front face that's as tall as a football field is long — it's a must-visit.

good sam park Featured ALASKA Good Sam Parks

When you stay with Good Sam, you can expect the highest degree of cleanliness and friendliness, and better yet, you get **10% off** overnight campground fees.

If you're not already a Good Sam member you can purchase your membership at one of these locations:

ANCHORAGE
Anchorage Ship Creek RV Park

FAIRBANKS
River's Edge RV Park & Campground

FAIRBANKS
Tanana Valley Campground

GLENNALLEN
Northern Nights Campground & RV Park

HAINES
Haines Hitch-Up RV Park

HOMER
Ocean Shores RV Park & Resort

JUNEAU
Glacier Nalu Campground Resort

NINILCHIK
Alaskan Angler RV Resort & Cabins

PALMER
Mountain View RV Park

TOK
Tok RV Village & Cabins

TRAPPER CREEK
Trapper Creek Inn & RV Park

VALDEZ
Eagle's Rest RV Park & Cabins

Getty Images/iStockphoto

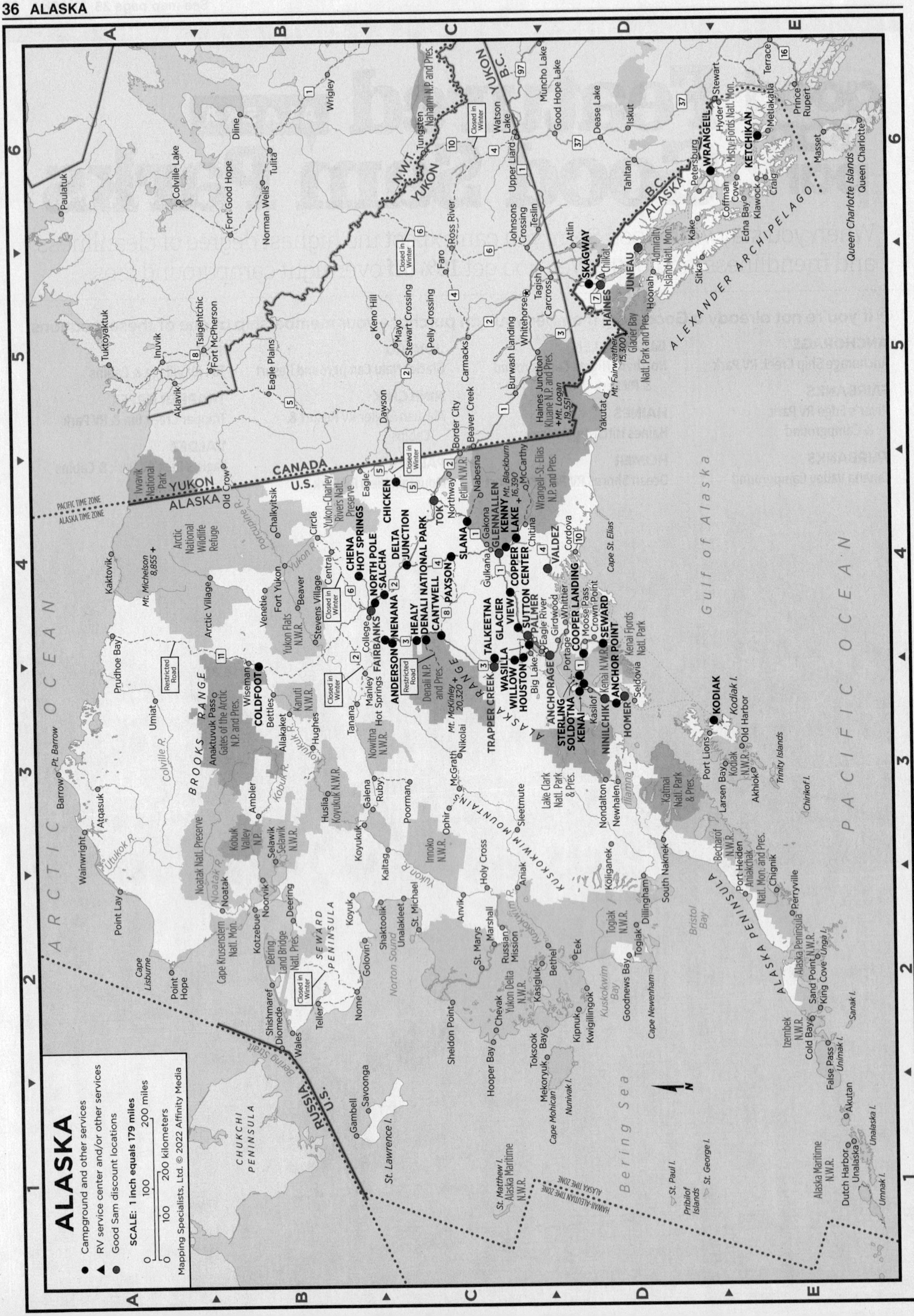
ALASKA
Campground and other services
RV service center and/or other services
Good Sam discount locations
SCALE: 1 inch equals 179 miles
0 100 200 miles
0 100 200 kilometers
Mapping Specialists, Ltd. © 2022 Affinity Media
ARCTIC OCEAN
PACIFIC OCEAN
Gulf of Alaska
Bering Sea
Bristol Bay
Norton Sound
ALEXANDER ARCHIPELAGO
BROOKS RANGE
ALASKA RANGE
KUSKOKWIM MOUNTAINS
SEWARD PENINSULA
ALASKA PENINSULA
CHUKCHI PENINSULA
PACIFIC TIME ZONE
ALASKA TIME ZONE
HAWAII-ALEUTIAN TIME ZONE
YUKON
ALASKA
CANADA
U.S.
RUSSIA
N.W.T.
B.C.
Closed in Winter
Restricted Road
ANCHORAGE
FAIRBANKS
JUNEAU
KETCHIKAN
WRANGELL
SKAGWAY
HAINES
KODIAK
HOMER
ANCHOR POINT
NINILCHIK
KENAI
SOLDOTNA
STERLING
SEWARD
COOPER LANDING
PALMER
SUTTON
GLACIER VIEW
WASILLA
WILLOW
HOUSTON
TALKEETNA
TRAPPER CREEK
CANTWELL
DENALI NATIONAL PARK
HEALY
ANDERSON
NENANA
NORTH POLE
SALCHA
CHENA HOT SPRINGS
DELTA JUNCTION
PAXSON
GLENNALLEN
COPPER CENTER
KENNY LAKE
SLANA
TOK
CHICKEN
VALDEZ
COLDFOOT
Mt. McKinley 20,320
Mt. Logan 19,551
Mt. Fairweather 15,300
Mt. Blackburn 16,390
Mt. Michelson 8,855
Denali N.P. and Pres.
Wrangell-St. Elias N.P. and Pres.
Kluane N.P. and Pres.
Glacier Bay Natl. Park and Pres.
Gates of the Arctic N.P. and Pres.
Arctic National Wildlife Refuge
Katmai Natl. Park & Pres.
Kenai Fjords Natl. Park
Lake Clark Natl. Park & Pres.
Misty Fjords Natl. Mon.
Admiralty Island Natl. Mon.
Whitehorse
Dawson
Watson Lake
Prince Rupert
Inuvik
Barrow
Nome
Bethel
Dillingham
Kotzebue
Prudhoe Bay
Sitka
Cordova
Whittier
Yakutat

ROAD TRIPS

Greet the Glaciers on an Epic Frontier Trip

Alaska

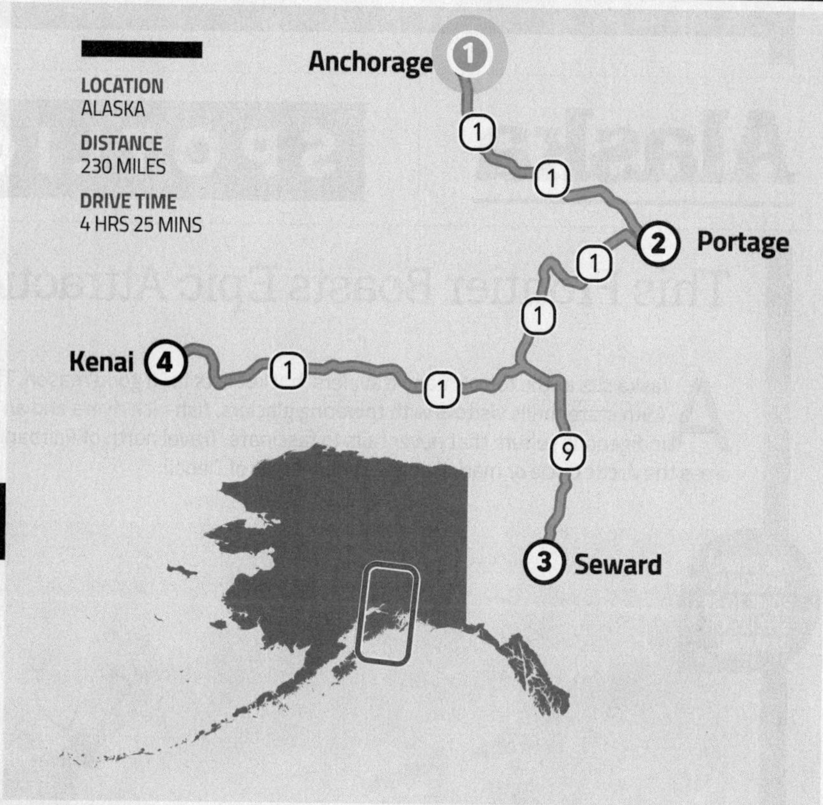

Carpeted with ancient glaciers, dramatic fjords and national parks larger than many countries, the Last Frontier is one of the last places on Earth where the wild remains untamed. Hit the road and prepare for epic adventures at every stop. From exploring blue ice tunnels and sailing alongside orca pods to trekking snow-capped mountains under the midnight sun, this Alaskan road trip offers experiences you'll never come across in the continental United States.

1 Anchorage
Starting Point

Anchorage is where adventurous souls and culture seekers come to play. Unravel Alaska's past through art and history galleries at the Anchorage Museum and discover indigenous traditions at the Alaska Native Heritage Center. When it's time for a breath of fresh air, trek the popular Tony Knowles Coastal Trail or reel in king salmon from Ship Creek. You can also encounter moose, arctic ground squirrels and the willow ptarmigan (Alaska's state bird) in the nearby Chugach Mountains.

2 Portage
Drive 48 Miles ▪ 58 Minutes

Nestled at the end of a lake, Portage Glacier is 10 stories high and miles long. Get up close to this blue wonder by taking a sightseeing cruise. Aboard the boat, hear rangers tell the story of Portage Valley's unique geology and history as a connection point between Prince William Sound and Turnagain Arm. You'll find more glaciers waiting to be explored back on land. Follow the five-mile Trail of Blue Ice, which connects glaciers to campgrounds or the Byron Glacier Trail for a short hike to blue ice.

3 Seward
Drive 78 Miles ▪ 1 Hour, 24 Minutes

Seward is a charming town lined with restaurants, shops and a waterfront park. It's also the gateway to Kenai Fjords National Park. Board a cruise and sail out to these majestic waters teeming with orcas, humpback whales and sea otters. For a different perspective, take a flightseeing tour to admire the park's glaciers and fjords from a bird's-eye view. Round out your visit with a trip to Exit Glacier, located just a 10-minute drive from town.

4 Kenai
Drive 104 Miles ▪ 2 Hours, 3 Minutes

Bust out your tackle box and get ready for world-class salmon fishing in Kenai. The lower Kenai River is home to a variety of salmon species including king salmon, sockeye and coho. These waters produced the world-record-holding king salmon at over 97 pounds, so it's not uncommon to reel in big fish weighing between 50 to 80 pounds. After your angling adventures, spot whales from Beluga Whale Lookout and stop by the Kenai Visitor and Cultural Center to learn about the city's Russian heritage.

Getty Images/iStockphoto

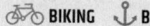

BIKING BOATING DINING ENTERTAINMENT FISHING HIKING HUNTING PADDLING SHOPPING SIGHTSEEING

Alaska SPOTLIGHTS

This Frontier Boasts Epic Attractions

Alaska sits at the top of many travelers' bucket lists for a good reason. The 49th state thrills visitors with towering glaciers, fish-rich rivers and an indigenous culture that never fails to fascinate. Travel north of Fairbanks to cross the Arctic Circle or marvel at the sheer height of Denali.

THE DENALI REGION IS HOME TO 39 SPECIES OF MAMMAL.

Caribou on a slope near Denali, the highest mountain in North America.

Getty Images/iStockphoto

Fairbanks

Founded at the turn of the 20th century, the little city of Fairbanks attracts visitors throughout the year. In the fall, winter and spring people brave subfreezing temperatures with hopes of catching a glimpse of the northern lights, while summertime travelers often use the city as a base for exploring nearby natural attractions, notably Denali National Park.

Denali National Park and Preserve

One of the biggest draws in the Fairbanks area, if not all of Alaska, is the expansive Denali National Park and Preserve. Designated to protect Alaska's native wildlife, this park is home to over 150 types of birds and more than three dozen species of mammals, including bears, moose and caribou. Note that in order to protect Denali's fragile ecosystem, visitors are not allowed to drive past mile marker 15. Instead, visitors will need to take a bus tour (narrated tours and transit buses are available). Free park-operated buses also operate along the first 15 miles of the road.

Museum of the North

Situated on the University of Alaska Fairbanks campus, the Museum of the North is an excellent spot to familiarize yourself with the natural and cultural history of Alaska. Visitors are greeted by an 8-foot taxidermic bear standing on his hind legs. Permanent exhibits cover everything from the ecosystems of Alaska to indigenous art and culture, and there's an outdoor sculpture area complete with a 20-foot Ketchikan totem pole.

Aurora Ice Museum

On the Chena Hot Springs property, the Aurora Ice Museum bills itself as the largest year-round ice environment on earth. Comprising upward of 1,000 tons of ice and snow, the space is filled with expertly crafted ice sculptures illuminated with multicolored lights that evoke the aurora borealis. The highlight for many, however, is the chance to mosey on up to the ice bar to drink an appletini out of an ice glass.

Trans-Alaska Pipeline Viewpoint

Fans of engineering won't want to miss the chance to see part of the Trans-Alaska Pipeline, which carries crude oil through 800 miles of the state. Much of it is elevated, including this section just a few minutes' drive outside of Fairbanks. The site also has a number of informational panels.

Wedgewood Wildlife Sanctuary

If you're looking for a quiet place to stroll, while maybe getting the chance to spot local birds and mammals, Wedgewood Wildlife Sanctuary is a great option. Here you'll find plenty of well-maintained trails dotted with informational panels and benches. For a good sense of the place, you can walk around the perimeter of Wander Lake via the 2-mile Wander Lake Trail.

LOCAL FAVORITE

E-Z Salmon

Alaska's waterways teem with hefty salmon. After the big catch, whip up a recipe that delivers hearty Frontier State flavor. *Recipe adapted from Best Ever RV Recipes.*

INGREDIENTS

- ☐ 2 medium-size fresh salmon fillets
- ☐ ½ cup soy sauce
- ☐ ½ cup water
- ☐ 1 Tbsp freshly grated ginger
- ☐ 1 Tbsp dark brown sugar
- ☐ 4 cloves fresh garlic, minced
- ☐ Extra-virgin olive oil

DIRECTIONS

Wash salmon and pat dry. Place in a large resealable plastic bag. Mix soy, water, ginger, brown sugar and garlic in a bowl with a whisk and add a bag. Close the bag, let set for about 15 minutes and turn it over for another 15 minutes.

Oil fish and place over medium heat (direct) grill and cook on each side for approximately 6-8 minutes or until fish flakes.

North Pole

Do visions of sugarplums dance in your head? Do you crave candy canes all year round, even during the warm summer months? It's possible you're in need of a little Christmas, and the best place to find that is North Pole. Only 15 minutes north of Fairbanks, North Pole is a year-round Christmas destination and the perfect place for any RV family.

The Alaska town of North Pole celebrates the holidays year-round, but things really heat up in December.

Santa's Workshop

North Pole was incorporated in 1952 by investors who thought toy makers from the lower 48 would want to be able to say their toys were made at the North Pole. Unfortunately, the prospects of high shipping costs kept the Santa's Workshop idea from taking off and no toy maker has yet to build here.

Santa's Mail

The name, however, stuck, along with the Christmas theme. The North Pole Post Office becomes one of the busiest in the nation beginning shortly after Thanksgiving, when mountains of letters to Santa start pouring in. Obviously, Santa is a little busy at that time of the year, so he asks students from the local high school to help him answer the hundreds of thousands of letters that come in annually.

Downtown North Pole

Travel along the streets named Santa Claus Lane, St. Nicholas Drive and Snowman Drive, where Candy Canes light the way. You may be able to catch a glimpse of Santa himself as he makes his way to the Santa Claus House where he hears Christmas wishes all year round.

Miller's Magic

The Santa Claus House was the first Christmas-themed business in North Pole. A young entrepreneur named Con Miller would dress up as Santa and visit children in the Fairbanks area around the Christmas season. He quickly gained fame, and in 1952, Con and his wife Nellie decided to open a trading post near the newly formed "North Pole" but couldn't come up with a name for his business. While working on the building, one of the village children came past and noticed "Santa" and said, "Hello Santa, are you building a new house?" The idea inspired Miller and the Santa Claus House was born. Visitors can find the Santa Claus House by its 42-foot tall Santa statue, which sits in front of the building. It's said to be the largest plastic Santa in the world.

Winterfest and Summerfest

Since everyday is a holiday at North Pole, it seems fitting that locals and visitors should celebrate winter. Every December, the town rolls out its annual Winterfest Celebration. Winterfest has lots to offer visitors including the "Christmas in Ice" ice carving contest. This contest attracts carvers from all across Alaska and few from as far away as China and Russia. During the Fourth of July, North Pole holds its annual Summerfest celebration. Summerfest brings lots of people to town because of the Cruis'n with Santa Classic Car Cruise. In addition to the vintage wheels, visitors can also enjoy old-fashioned drive-in movies, a street dance and live entertainment. Browse vendors at the event's street fair and enjoy some rock 'n' roll tunes.

FOR MORE INFORMATION

Alaska Travel Industry Association, 907-929-2842, www.travelalaska.com
Fairbanks Convention & Visitors Bureau, 800-327-5774, www.explorefairbanks.com
City of North Pole, 907-488-2281, www.northpolealaska.com

Alaska

ANCHOR POINT — D3 *Kenai Peninsula*

➔ KYLLONEN RV PARK **Ratings: 6.5/8.5★/9** (RV Park) Avail: 23 full hkups (30 amps). 2021 rates: $45.32 to $50.47. May 15 to Sep 15. (907)235-7762, 74160 Anchor Point Rd, Anchor point, AK 99556

Alaska Privately Owned Campground Information Updated by our Good Sam Representatives

Tony & Nanette Martin

In 2014, Tony and I decided to sell everything we owned, buy a motorhome and travel for a year with our two dogs. That year turned into five, traveling from Mexico to Alaska. Along the way we met some Good Sam rep teams, and we thought, "what a perfect job." And so it all began; we have been lucky to live the lifestyle.

↑ WHISKEY POINT CABINS AND RV PARK **Ratings: 7/9.5★/9** (RV Park) Avail: 29 full hkups (30 amps). 2021 rates: $50. May 01 to Sep 30. (907)235-1961, 30475 Sterling Hwy, Anchor Point, AK 99556

ANCHORAGE — D4 *Anchorage*

ANCHORAGE See also Wasilla.

➚ ANCHORAGE SHIP CREEK RV PARK

good sam park **Ratings: 7/9.5★/8** (RV Park) From Jct Glenn Hwy & Ingra St: Go 1/4 mi N on Ingra St to 1st Ave, then go 500 feet W (L).

MAKE THE MOST OF YOUR ALASKAN TOUR
Anchorage Ship Creek RV Park puts a variety of activities & amusements at your doorstep. Located just a few blocks from downtown Anchorage, it offers easy access to Alaska's largest city & local attractions.
FAC: gravel rds. Avail: 130 gravel, 4 pull-thrus, (18x60), back-ins (15x45), 130 full hkups (30 amps), WiFi @ sites, tent sites, dump, laundry. **REC:** boating nearby, hunting nearby, rec open to public. Pets OK. Partial handicap access, eco-friendly. 2021 rates: $29 to $59. May 01 to Sep 30.
(907)277-0877 Lat: 61.22169, Lon: -149.86906
150 N Ingra St, Anchorage, AK 99501
www.alaskatraveladventures.com
See ad this page

↑ CENTENNIAL CAMPGROUND
(Public) From jct Seward Hwy 1 & Glenn Hwy 1 (Downtown Anchorage): Go 4-1/2 mi E on Glenn Hwy 1, then 1/4 mi S on Muldoon Rd, then 1 block E on Boundry Ave, then 3/4 mi N on Frontage Rd. **FAC:** Avail: 82 gravel, 6 pull-thrus, 21 E tent sites, shower$, dump, fire rings, firewood. **REC:** playground. Pets OK. Partial handicap access, 14 day max stay. 2021 rates: $25 to $35. May 28 to Sep 06.
(907)343-6986 Lat: 61.22853, Lon: -149.72245
8400 Starview Dr, Anchorage, AK 99504
www.muni.org/parks

➘ CREEKWOOD INN MOTEL & RV PARK **Ratings: 6.5/9.5★/6.5** (RV Park) Avail: 50 full hkups (30/50 amps). 2021 rates: $45 to $58. May 01 to Oct 01. (907)258-6006, 2150 Seward Highway, Anchorage, AK 99503

➔ GOLDEN NUGGET RV PARK **Ratings: 8/10★/9.5** (RV Park) Avail: 190 full hkups (30/50 amps). 2021 rates: $39 to $50. (907)333-2012, 4100 Debarr Rd, Anchorage, AK 99508

➚ MILITARY PARK BLACK SPRUCE RV PARK (FORT RICHARDSON) (Public) From AK1/Glenn Hwy & main gate entrance (NE Anchorage) N to main gate, follow D St, E 100 yds on Otter Loop Rd (L). 45 Avail: 40 full hkups, 5 W, 5 E (30 amps). 2021 rates: $33. May 01 to Oct 31. (907)552-2023

↑ MILITARY PARK JOINT BASE ELMENDORF/RICHARDSON FAMCAMP (ELMENDORF AFB) (Public) N of Anchorage, take Boniface Pkwy off AK-1 (Glenn Hwy) to base gate. 68 Avail: 60 W, 60 E (30/50 amps). 2021 rates: $30. (907)552-2023

Things to See and Do

↑ ALASKA CAMPGROUND OWNER'S ASSOCIATION ACOA represents privately owned Campgrounds throughout Alaska that provide outdoor hospitality services to campers visiting the State. .
Hours: .
(866)339-9082
PO Box 111005, Anchorage, AK 99511
www.alaskacampgrounds.net

ANDERSON — C4 *Denali*

← RIVERSIDE PARK (ANDERSON CITY PARK) (Public) From jct Parks Hwy 3 & Anderson Rd: Go 6 mi W on Clear/Anderson Rd. Avail: 18 E. 2021 rates: $20. (907)582-2500

CANTWELL — C4 *Denali*

← CANTWELL RV PARK **Ratings: 7.5/10★/9.5** (RV Park) 70 Avail: 41 W, 70 E (30 amps). 2021 rates: $40.50 to $45.50. May 20 to Sep 10. (907)888-6850, .3 MI Cantwell Station Rd, Cantwell, AK 99729

CHENA HOT SPRINGS — B4 *Fairbanks North Star Borough*

➔ CHENA RIVER SRA/TORS TRAIL (Public State Park) On Chena Hot Springs Rd at MP-39. 24 Avail. 2021 rates: $15. May 21 to Sep 15. (907)451-2695

County names help you follow the local weather report.

CHICKEN — C4 *Southeast Fairbanks*

→ CHICKEN CREEK RV PARK **Ratings: 5/9.5★/7.5** (Campground) Avail: 29 E (20/30 amps). 2021 rates: $24 to $44. May 15 to Sep 15. (907)505-0231, MP 66.8 Taylor Highway, Chicken, AK 99732

← CHICKEN GOLD CAMP & OUTPOST **Ratings: 6/NA/9** (Campground) Avail: 39 E (20/30 amps), Pit toilets. 2021 rates: $20 to $40. May 15 to Sep 20. (907)782-4427, 1/4 Mile Airport Road, Chicken, AK 99732

↓ WEST FORK CAMPGROUND (BLM) (Public Corps) From town: Go 19 mi S on the Taylor Hwy 5. 25 Avail: Pit toilets. 2021 rates: $10. (907)474-2200

COLDFOOT — B3 *Yukon Koyukuk*

↑ MARION CREEK (BLM) (Public Corps) From town: Go 5 mi N on Dalton Hwy. 28 Avail: Pit toilets. 2021 rates: $8. (907)474-2200

COOPER LANDING — D4 *Kenai Peninsula*

↘ KENAI PRINCESS RV PARK **Ratings: 8/8.5★/9** (RV Park) Avail: 22 full hkups (30 amps). 2021 rates: $45. May 20 to Sep 15. (907)595-1425, 17225 Frontier Circle, Cooper Landing, AK 99572

← KENAI RIVERSIDE CAMPGROUND & RV PARK/ B & B **Ratings: 5/9★/7.5** (Campground) 23 Avail: 18 W, 18 E (20/30 amps). 2021 rates: $27 to $35. May 30 to Sep 01. (888)536-2478, 16918 Sterling Hwy, Cooper Landing, AK 99572

COPPER CENTER — C4 *Valdez Cordova*

← KING FOR A DAY CAMPGROUND **Ratings: 6/6.5/7** (RV Park) 63 Avail: 8 full hkups, 8 W, 8 E (20/30 amps). 2021 rates: $25 to $45. May 25 to Aug 31. (907)822-3092, 100.5 Richardson Hwy, Copper Center, AK 99573

↑ SQUIRREL CREEK (Public State Park) On Richardson Hwy, at milepost 79.5. 25 Avail: Pit toilets. 2021 rates: $25. Jun 15 to Sep 15. (907)822-5932

DELTA JUNCTION — C4 *Southeast Fairbanks*

↑ BIG DELTA STATE HISTORICAL PARK (Public State Park) From town: Go 14 mi N on Richardson Hwy 26 to Milepost 274.5, then NE on Rika's Rd. 25 Avail. 2021 rates: $20. Jun 15 to Sep 15. (907)451-2695

↓ CLEARWATER SRA (Public State Park) On AK Hwy at MP-1415. Avail: 17 W. 2021 rates: $15. Jun 01 to Sep 30. (907)451-2695

↑ DELTA SRA (Public State Park) On Richardson Hwy at MP-267. Avail: 25 W. 2021 rates: $15. Jun 01 to Sep 30. (907)451-2695

↓ DONNELLY CREEK (Public State Park) 32 miles south of Delta Junction on Richardson Hwy at MP-238. 12 Avail. 2021 rates: $15. (907)269-8400

↖ FIELDING LAKE (Public State Park) From Jct of SR-2 & Richardson Hwy, SW 200.5 mi on Richardson Hwy/SR-4, follow signs. 17 Avail. 2021 rates: $5 to $10. Jun 15 to Sep 15. (907)451-2695

↑ QUARTZ LAKE (Public State Park) On Richardson Hwy at MP-277.8 to Quartz Lake Rd, N 2.5 mi (E). 103 Avail. 2021 rates: $15. Jun 15 to Sep 15. (907)451-2695

DENALI NATIONAL PARK — C4 *Denali*

↑ DENALI GRIZZLY BEAR RESORT **Ratings: 7/9.5★/9** (Campground) 21 Avail: 21 W, 21 E (30 amps). 2021 rates: $45. May 20 to Sep 15. (866)583-2696, 231.1 Parks Hwy, Denali National Park, AK 99755

↑ DENALI RAINBOW VILLAGE RV PARK, MOTEL & COUNTRY MALL **Ratings: 7/8.5★/7.5** (RV Park) 52 Avail: 21 full hkups, 31 W, 31 E (30/50 amps). 2021 rates: $53 to $63. May 15 to Sep 20. (907)683-7777, Mile 238.6 Parks Hwy, Denali National Park, AK 99755

↑ DENALI RV PARK & MOTEL **Ratings: 7/10★/9.5** (RV Park) 80 Avail: 73 full hkups, 7 W, 7 E (30 amps). 2021 rates: $58 to $68. May 20 to Sep 10. (907)683-1500, Mile 245.1 Parks Hwy, Denali National Park, AK 99755

↘ DENALI/RILEY CREEK (Public National Park) From Healy, 5.12 mi on AK Hwy 3 (R) Entrance fee required. RV or Trailer Max 40'. 142 Avail. 2021 rates: $24 to $30. (907)683-9532

← DENALI/SAVAGE RIVER (Public National Park) From Hwy 3: Go 12 mi W on Park Rd from entrance: Register first at Visitor Center (1/2 mi on Park Rd). 32 Avail. 2021 rates: $24 to $30. (907)683-9532

← DENALI/TEKLANIKA RIVER (Public National Park) From Hwy 3: Go 29 mi W on Park Rd from entrance. Register first at Visitor Center (1/2 mi on Park Rd) Note: Minimum 3 night stay for RVs. 53 Avail. 2021 rates: $25. (907)683-9532

FAIRBANKS — B4 *Burrough*

FAIRBANKS See also Nenana, North Pole & Salcha.

→ CHENA RIVER SRA/ROSEHIP (Public State Park) On Chena Hot Springs Rd at MP-27. 37 Avail. 2021 rates: $15. (907)451-2695

↙ CHENA RIVER SRA/WAYSIDE (Public State Park) From Jct of Richardson Hwy (Hwy 2) & Lawrence Rd, E 2.6 mi to entrance (L). 60 Avail: 16 W, 16 E (20/30 amps). 2021 rates: $20 to $30. May 15 to Sep 15. (907)455-8881

↑ LOWER CHATANIKA/OLNES POND (Public State Park) On Elliott Hwy at MP-10.5. Note: Park not maintained or managed. 15 Avail: Pit toilets. 2021 rates: $15. Jun 15 to Sep 15. (907)451-2695

↑ LOWER CHATANIKA/WHITEFISH (Public State Park) On Elliott Hwy at MP-11. Note: Park not maintained or managed. 25 Avail: Pit toilets. 2021 rates: $15. Jun 15 to Sep 15. (907)451-2705

↓ MILITARY PARK BIRCH LAKE RECREATION AREA (EIELSON AFB) (Public) From base, S 38 mi on AK-2 (Richardson Hwy) at milepost 305. Avail: 29 E (30 amps). 2021 rates: $21. May 31 to Sep 07. (907)377-1232

→ MILITARY PARK EIELSON AFB BEAR LAKE FAMCAMP (EIELSON AFB) (Public) On base, from Fairbanks, NW 26 mi on Richardson Hwy. 41 Avail: 41 W, 41 E (20/50 amps). 2021 rates: $22. May 15 to Sep 15. (907)377-1317

↙ **RIVER'S EDGE RV PARK & CAMPGROUND**
Ratings: 7/10★/8.5 (RV Park) E-bnd: From Jct of AK Hwy 3 & Fairbanks exit (East Airport Way), E 0.5 mi on Airport Way to Sportsman Way, N 50 ft to Boat St, W 0.3 mi (R); or W-bnd: From Jct of AK Hwy 3 & University Ave, N 0.8 mi on University Ave to Airport Way, W 0.25 mi to Sportsman Way, N 50 ft to Boat St, W 0.3 mi (R). **FAC:** gravel rds. Avail: 167 gravel, 82 pull-thrus, (25x60), back-ins (25x35), 135 full hkups, 32 W, 32 E (30/50 amps), WiFi @ sites, tent sites, rentals, dump, laundry, restaurant. **REC:** Chena River: fishing, kayaking/canoeing, boating nearby. Pets OK. Partial handicap access. Big rig sites. 2021 rates: $55 to $65, Military discount. May 25 to Sep 12. ATM.
(907)474-0286 Lat: 64.83944, Lon: -147.83411
4140 Boat Street, Fairbanks, AK 99709
www.riversedge.net
See ad this page

↘ RIVERVIEW RV PARK **Ratings: 8/10★/9.5** (RV Park) 155 Avail: 153 full hkups, 2 W, 2 E (30/50 amps). 2021 rates: $49.95 to $57.95. May 15 to Sep 15. (907)488-6392, 1316 Badger Rd, North Pole, AK 99705

↘ **TANANA VALLEY CAMPGROUND**
Ratings: 5/8.5/7 (Campground) From Jct of A2 Steese Hwy & College Rd (E of town), N 2.2 mi on College Rd (R); or From Jct of A3 Mitchell Expressway & Giest Rd (W of town), E 1.5 mi on Geist Rd to University Ave, N 0.5 mi to College Rd, E 1.7 mi (L). **FAC:** gravel rds. Avail: 29 gravel, back-ins (25x40), 17 E (20/30 amps), WiFi @ sites, tent sites, dump, laundry, fire rings, firewood. **REC:** boating nearby, rec open to public. Pets OK. 2021 rates: $20 to $35. May 15 to Sep 15.
(907)456-7956 Lat: 64.51846, Lon: -147.45533
1800 College Road, Fairbanks, AK 99709
www.tananavalleycampgroundandrv.com
See ad this page

↑ UPPER CHATANIKA RIVER REC SITE (Public State Park) On Steese Hwy at MP-39. 24 Avail: Pit toilets. 2021 rates: $15. Jun 15 to Sep 15. (907)456-1104

Travel Services

↙ **GABE'S TRUCK & AUTO REPAIR** Napa Truck Care Center. Auto, truck and RV service. General automotive repair for RVs, trucks and cars. Towing services (not for Class A motorhomes). **SERVICES:** MH mechanical, engine/chassis repair, emergency rd svc, restrooms. **TOW:** RV, auto, emergency parking, RV accessible, waiting room. Hours: 7:30am to 6pm.
(907)456-6156 Lat: 64.810210, Lon: -147.766425
2015 Frank Ave, Fairbanks, AK 99707
gabesauto.com
See ad this page

Things to See and Do

↑ **GOLD DAUGHTERS** Gold panning, largest mining relic collection in Alaska and great collection of ice age fossils, gift shop and gold jewelry May 30 to Sep 04. Partial handicap access. RV accessible. Restrooms.. Hours: 10am to 6pm. Adult fee: $20. (907)347-4749 Lat: 64.929528, Lon: -147.633455 1671 Steese Hwy , Fairbanks, AK 99712 golddaughters.com

GLACIER VIEW — C4 *Matanuska Susitna*

↖ GRAND VIEW CAFE & RV CAMPGROUND **Ratings: 7.5/10★/8.5** (RV Park) 25 Avail: 10 full hkups, 15 W, 15 E (30/50 amps). 2021 rates: $38 to $43. May 25 to Sep 15. (907)746-4480, MP 109.7 Glenn Hwy, Glacier View, AK 99674

GLENNALLEN — C4 *Valdez Cordova*

↑ DRY CREEK (Public State Park) 4 miles north of Glennallen on Richardson Hwy, at milepost 117.5. 50 Avail. 2021 rates: $20. Jun 15 to Sep 15. (907)205-0766

↓ LAKE LOUISE (Public State Park) Mile 158 Glenn Highway to Lake Louise Road. Drive 0.4 miles to "T"; turn left for Lake Louise Campground. 67 Avail. 2021 rates: $20. Jun 15 to Sep 15. (907)441-7575

Laundry & dishwasher detergent liquids contain up to 80 percent water. It costs energy and packaging to bring this water to the consumer. When there is a choice - choose dry powders.

GLENNALLEN (CONT)

→ **NORTHERN NIGHTS CAMPGROUND & RV PARK**
Ratings: 7/9.5★/9.5 (Campground) From Jct Glenn Hwy & Richardson Hwy: Go W 600 yds on Glenn Hwy (R). **FAC:** gravel rds. Avail: 25 gravel, 16 pull-thrus, (30x70), back-ins (25x55), 5 full hkups, 19 W, 19 E (30 amps), WiFi @ sites, tent sites, rentals, shower$, dump, laundry, fire rings, firewood. **REC:** boating nearby, hunting nearby. Pets OK. eco-friendly. 2021 rates: $44.25, Military discount. May 15 to Sep 15. no cc.
(907)822-3199 Lat: 62.107943, Lon: -145.486399
Mile Post 188.7 Glenn Hwy, Glennallen, AK 99588
northernnightscampground.com
See ad previous page

← RANCH HOUSE LODGE & RV CAMPING **Ratings: 8/10★/9** (RV Park) Avail: 21 full hkups (30/50 amps). 2021 rates: $40 to $55. May 15 to Sep 15. (907)822-5634, Mile 173 Glenn Hwy, Glennallen, AK 99588

← SLIDE MOUNTAIN CABINS & RV PARK **Ratings: 6.5/9★/9.5** (Campground) 15 Avail: 5 full hkups, 10 W, 10 E (30/50 amps). 2021 rates: $35 to $40. (907)822-3883, Mile 135 Glenn Highway, Glennallen, AK 99588

↑ SOURDOUGH CREEK CAMPGROUND (BLM) (Public Corps) From town: Go 32 mi N on Richardson Hwy 4 to MP 147.5 (R). 42 Avail. 2021 rates: $12. (907)822-3217

← TOLSONA WILDERNESS CAMPGROUND **Ratings: 7.5/6/8.5** (Campground) 80 Avail: 50 W, 50 E (30/50 amps). 2021 rates: $37 to $47. Apr 01 to Oct 31. (907)822-3900, Mile 173 Glenn Hwy, Glennallen, AK 99588

HAINES — D5 *Haines*

↖ CHILKAT (Public State Park) From town, S 7 mi on Mud Bay Rd (E). 35 Avail: Pit toilets. 2021 rates: $20. May 15 to Sep 15. (907)766-2292

↖ CHILKOOT LAKE REC SITE (Public State Park) On Lutak Rd at MP-10 (E) Note: 35' RV Size Limit. 32 Avail: Pit toilets. 2021 rates: $20. May 15 to Oct 15. (907)465-4563

← **HAINES HITCH-UP RV PARK**
Ratings: 7.5/10★/10 (RV Park) Avail: 92 full hkups (30/50 amps). 2021 rates: $42 to $57. May 15 to Sep 15. (907)766-2882, 851 Main St, Haines, AK 99827

→ OCEANSIDE RV PARK (RV Park) (Rebuilding) Avail: 22 full hkups (30 amps). 2021 rates: $25 to $45. (907)766-3730, 14 Front St, Haines, AK 99827

HEALY — C4 *Denali*

← TATLANIKA TRADING COMPANY & RV PARK **Ratings: 6/9★/9.5** (Campground) 22 Avail: 2 W, 22 E (20/30 amps). 2021 rates: $25 to $30. May 01 to Sep 15. (907)582-2341, Mile 276 Parks Hwy, Healy, AK 99743

HOMER — D3 *Kenai Peninsula*

↓ DEEP CREEK SRA (Public State Park) From town: Go 1/2 mi S on Sterling Hwy (R) Note: 35' RV size limit. 100 Avail. 2021 rates: $20. May 01 to Sep 30. (907)262-5581

← DRIFTWOOD INN & RV PARK **Ratings: 6.5/9.5★/7.5** (RV Park) Avail: 14 full hkups (30 amps). 2021 rates: $39 to $79. (907)235-8019, 135 W Bunnell Ave, Homer, AK 99603

↖ **HERITAGE RV PARK Ratings: 8/9.5★/8** (RV Park) Avail: 107 full hkups (30/50 amps). 2021 rates: $68. May 15 to Sep 15. (907)226-4500, 3550 Homer Spit Rd, Homer, AK 99603

↖ HOMER BAYCREST KOA **Ratings: 8/9.5★/9** (RV Park) Avail: 45 full hkups (30/50 amps). 2021 rates: $55.89 to $63.89. May 15 to Oct 01. (907)435-7995, 3425 Sterling Hwy, MP 169, Homer, AK 99603

↖ HOMER SPIT CAMPGROUND **Ratings: 5.5/7/4.5** (Campground) 124 Avail: 9 full hkups, 90 E (20/30 amps). 2021 rates: $30 to $50. May 15 to Sep 15. (907)235-8206, 4535 Homer Spit Rd, Homer, AK 99603

↓ NINILCHIK (Public State Park) Located at milepost 135 of the Sterling Hwy. 62 Avail: Pit toilets. 2021 rates: $20. May 01 to Oct 30. (907)262-5581

↖ **OCEAN SHORES RV PARK & RESORT**
Ratings: 6.5/9.5★/8 (RV Park) From Jct of Sterling Hwy and Ohlson Ln: Go N .1 mi on Sterling Hwy (L). **FAC:** gravel rds. Avail: 78 gravel, 17 pull-thrus, (21x40), back-ins (21x38), 65 full hkups, 8 W, 8 E (30/50 amps), cable, WiFi @ sites, tent sites, rentals, dump, laundry, fire rings, firewood, restaurant. **REC:** Kachemak Bay of the Gulf of Alaska: fishing, kayaking/canoeing, boating nearby, rec open to public. Pets OK. Partial handicap access. 2021 rates: $25 to $65, Military discount. May 01 to Oct 01.
(907)435-0800 Lat: 59.641138, Lon: -151.553599
455 Sterling Highway, Homer, AK 99603
homeralaskarvpark.com
See ad this page

↑ STARISKI (Public State Park) On Sterling Hwy at milepost 151. 13 Avail. 2021 rates: $20. May 15 to Oct 15. (907)522-8368

HOUSTON — C4 *Matanuska Susitna*

LITTLE SUSITNA RIVER (CITY PARK) (Public) On George Parks Hwy 3 at MP 57.5. 80 Avail: Pit toilets. 2021 rates: $15. May 25 to Sep 07. (907)892-6869

← RIVERSIDE CAMPER PARK **Ratings: 6.5/9★/7.5** (RV Park) Avail: 56 full hkups (30 amps). 2021 rates: $40. May 15 to Sep 30. (907)892-9020, Mile 57.7 Parks Hwy, Houston, AK 99694

JUNEAU — D5 *Juneau*

↖ **GLACIER NALU CAMPGROUND RESORT**
Ratings: 7.5/10★/10 (Campground) Avail: 64 full hkups (30 amps). 2021 rates: $44.10 to $46.20. (907)789-1990, 10200 Mendenhall Loop Rd, Juneau, AK 99801

Things to See and Do

↑ **ADVENTURE BOUND ALASKA** Cruise by waterfalls & through ice floes en route to Sawyer glaciers. Whales, bears, mountain goats & eagles are common sights. May 01 to Sep 25. Restrooms. Food.. Hours: 7am to 6pm. Adult fee: $165.00.
(907)463-2509 Lat: 58.299396, Lon: -134.409672
76 Egan Dr , Juneau, AK 99801
www.adventureboundalaska.com

KENAI — D3 *Kenai Peninsula*

↑ CAPTAIN COOK/DISCOVERY CAMPGROUND (Public State Park) On Kenai Spur at MP-39 (E). 53 Avail. 2021 rates: $20. May 15 to Oct 15. (907)522-8368

↖ DIAMOND M RANCH RESORT **Ratings: 8.5/10★/10** (RV Park) Avail: 77 full hkups (30/50 amps). 2021 rates: $48 to $98. (907)283-9424, 48500 Diamond M Ranch Rd, Kenai, AK 99611

KENNY LAKE — C4 *Valdez Cordova*

← KENNY LAKE MERCANTILE & RV PARK **Ratings: 7/8.5/8.5** (Campground) Avail: 10 E (30 amps). 2021 rates: $15 to $45. May 01 to Sep 30. (907)822-3313, Mile 7.2 Edgerton Hwy, Kenny Lake, AK 99573

KETCHIKAN — E6 *Ketchikan Gateway*

↑ CLOVER PASS RESORT **Ratings: 7/9.5★/6** (Campground) Avail: 29 full hkups (30/50 amps). 2021 rates: $43 to $50. May 01 to Sep 30. (907)247-2234, 708 N. Point Higgins Rd, Ketchikan, AK 99901

↖ SETTLERS COVE (Public State Park) Ferry to Ketchikan, on Tongass Rd at MP-18N (E) Note: 35' RV size limit. 13 Avail. 2021 rates: $15. May 15 to Sep 15. (907)465-4563

Things to See and Do

↑ **ALASKA MARINE HIGHWAY SYSTEM** Alaska Marine Highway is part of the state highway system, connecting those parts of Alaska not reached by traditional roads with the rest of the state and the lower 48. Cars, RVs, cabins, dining, movies, lounges. One-way or round trip. Partial handicap access. RV accessible. Restrooms. Food. Hours: 9am to 5pm.
(800)642-0066 Lat: 55.3543, Lon: -131.6933
7559 N Tongass Hwy, Ketchikan, AK 99901
www.ferryalaska.com
See ad page 34

KODIAK — D3 *Kokiak Island*

↓ BUSKIN RIVER SRA (Public State Park) South of town, on W Rezanof at mile 4.5. 15 Avail. 2021 rates: $15. May 15 to Sep 15. (907)486-6339

NENANA — C4 *Denali*

← NENANA RV PARK & CAMPGROUND **Ratings: 7/9.5★/9** (Campground) 36 Avail: 15 W, 29 E (30 amps). 2021 rates: $20 to $37.50. May 15 to Sep 30. (907)750-4008, 210 E. 4th St, Nenana, AK 99760

NINILCHIK — D3 *Kenai Peninsula*

↑ **ALASKAN ANGLER RV RESORT & CABINS**
Ratings: 8/9.5★/9 (RV Park) S-bnd: From Jct of Sterling Hwy & Kingsley Rd (MP-135.4), E 100 yds on Kingsley Rd (L). **FAC:** gravel rds. Avail: 58 gravel, back-ins (24x60), 48 full hkups, 10 W, 10 E (50 amps), WiFi @ sites, tent sites, rentals, shower$, dump, laundry, LP gas, firewood. **REC:** Kenai River: fishing, boating nearby, hunting nearby, rec open to public. Pets OK. Big rig sites. 2021 rates: $39 to $58, Military discount. May 01 to Sep 15.
(800)347-4114 Lat: 60.04494, Lon: -151.66662
15640 Kingsley Rd, Ninilchik, AK 99639
alaskabestrvpark.com
See ad this page

→ ALL SEASONS CAMPGROUND **Ratings: 6.5/7.5/8** (Campground) Avail: 52 full hkups (30 amps). 2021 rates: $36 to $42. May 01 to Sep 01. (907)567-3396, 63960 Oil Well Rd, Ninilchik, AK 99639

→ REEL 'EM INN & COOK INLET CHARTERS **Ratings: 7/9★/8.5** (Campground) Avail: 11 full hkups (30 amps). 2021 rates: $39. May 15 to Sep 01. (907)567-7335, 65910 Oil Well Dr, Ninilchik, AK 99639

↓ SCENIC VIEW RV PARK (RV Park) (Rebuilding) 22 Avail: 10 full hkups, 12 W, 12 E (30 amps). 2021 rates: $45. May 01 to Sep 30. (907)567-3909, 74360 Sterling Hwy, Ninilchik, AK 99639

Things to See and Do

↗ **AFISHUNT CHARTERS** Chartering fishing expeditions for Halibut and Salmon spanning the entire Kenai Peninsula. May 01 to Sep 15. RV accessible. Hours: 6am-6pm. Adult fee: $255 to $375. ATM.
(800)347-4114 Lat: 60.04494, Lon: -151.66662
15640 Kingsley Road, Ninilchik, AK 99639
afishunt.com
See ad this page

NORTH POLE — C4 *Fairbanks North Star*

A SPOTLIGHT Introducing North Pole's colorful attractions appearing at the front of this state section.

↓ CHENA LAKE RECREATION AREA (Public) From Jct of Richardson Hwy (Hwy 2) & Laurance Rd, E 2.6 mi to entrance (L). 80 Avail. 2021 rates: $20. (907)488-1655

Things to See and Do

→ **ANTLER ACADEMY** Training Academy & petting zoo that gives visitors a chance to interact with Santa's reindeer. Partial handicap access. RV accessible. Restrooms. Food. Hours: 8am to 8pm Summer. No CC.
(800)588-4078 Lat: 64.75513, Lon: -147.34359
101 St. Nicholas Dr, North Pole, AK 99705
www.santaclaushouse.com
See ad page 39

↓ **SANTA CLAUS HOUSE** Christmas ornaments, Alaskan gifts, apparel, toys & collectibles, espresso & homemade fudge. Mail cards & letters for North Pole postmark. Santa & Mrs. Claus available for photos. Extended summer hours.

SANTA - A HOLIDAY TRADITION FOR ALL
Santa Claus House is one of the top attractions in Interior Alaska, and has welcomed millions of visitors from all over the world. For over sixty years we've put smiles on the faces of millions of children all over the world!
Partial handicap access. RV accessible. Restrooms. Food. Hours: 9am to 8pm summer.
(800)588-4078 Lat: 64.75513, Lon: -147.34359
101 St Nicholas Dr, North Pole, AK 99705
www.santaclaushouse.com
See ad page 39

PALMER — C4 *Matanuska Susitna*

→ CHUGACH/EKLUTNA LAKE (Public State Park) From town, 13 mi NE. 50 Avail. 2021 rates: $20. May 15 to Sep 15. (907)345-5014

↖ FINGER LAKE (Public State Park) From town, W 4 mi on Palmer-Wasilla Hwy to Trunk Rd, N 1 mi to Bogart Rd, W 1 mi (L). 24 Avail: Pit toilets. 2021 rates: $25 to $35. May 15 to Sep 15. (907)745-8950

↙ FOX RUN CAMPGROUND & RV PARK **Ratings: 5.5/7/7** (Campground) 40 Avail: 22 full hkups, 7 W, 18 E (30/50 amps). 2021 rates: $45. (907)745-6120, 4466 S. Glenn Hwy, Palmer, AK 99645

→ KING MOUNTAIN (Public State Park) Take the Glenn Hwy. eastbound to Mile 78.6, Chickaloon. 22 Avail. 2021 rates: $25 to $30. May 15 to Sep 15. (907)240-9797

↓ **MOUNTAIN VIEW RV PARK**
Ratings: 7.5/10★/9.5 (RV Park) Avail: 80 full hkups (30 amps). 2021 rates: $45. (907)745-5747, 1405 N Smith Rd, Palmer, AK 99645

PAXSON — C4 *Valdez Cordova*

PAXSON LAKE (BLM) (Public Corps) On Richardson Hwy 4 at milepost 175. 50 Avail. 2021 rates: $12. (907)822-3217

← TANGLE LAKES (BLM) (Public Corps) From town: Go 21.7 mi W on Denali Hwy 8. 45 Avail. 2021 rates: $12. (907)822-3217

SALCHA — C4 *Fairbarnks-North Star*

↓ "C" LAZY MOOSE **Ratings: 5/6/7** (Campground) 28 Avail: 18 full hkups, 10 W, 10 E (30/50 amps). 2021 rates: $40 to $45. May 01 to Sep 30. (907)488-8141, Milepost 315 Richardson Hwy, Salcha, AK 99714

↑ HARDING LAKE (Public State Park) On Richardson Hwy at MP-321.4. 83 Avail. 2021 rates: $15. Jun 15 to Sep 15. (907)451-2695

SEWARD — D4 *Kenai Peninsula*

↑ MILITARY PARK SEWARD RESORT (FORT WAINWRIGHT) (Public) Take Seward Hwy (AK1) S to AK9, continue S to Seward City Limit sign, right on Hemlock, left on Dimond. 40 Avail: 40 W, 40 E (30/50 amps). 2021 rates: $26 to $30. May 15 to Sep 07. (907)224-5559

↑ STONEY CREEK RV PARK **Ratings: 7/10★/8.5** (RV Park) 81 Avail: 68 full hkups, 13 W, 13 E (30/50 amps). 2021 rates: $45 to $49.50. May 21 to Sep 10. (877)437-6366, 13760 Leslie Place, Seward, AK 99664

→ WATERFRONT PARK (Public) In town, at Jct of 4th Ave & Ballaine Ave. 441 Avail: 99 W, 99 E (30/50 amps). 2021 rates: $10 to $40. (907)224-4055

SKAGWAY — D5 *Haines*

↑ GARDEN CITY RV PARK **Ratings: 4.5/9.5★/8** (RV Park) Avail: 81 full hkups (30 amps). 2021 rates: $45 to $55. Apr 15 to Oct 15. (907)983-3884, 15th & E State St, Skagway, AK 99840

SLANA — C4 *Valdez Cordova*

→ HART D RANCH DOUBLETREE RV PARK **Ratings: 5.5/9.5★/9** (Campground) 43 Avail: 14 full hkups, 20 W, 6 E (30 amps). 2021 rates: $30 to $40. (907)822-3973, 1/2 mi Nabesna Rd, Slana, AK 99586

↓ PORCUPINE CREEK (Public State Park) From jct Hwy 1 & Hwy 2: Go 14 mi S on Hwy 1 to MP 64 (R). 12 Avail. 2021 rates: $25. Jun 15 to Sep 15. (907)822-3973

SOLDOTNA — D3 *Kenai Peninsula*

← ANCHOR RIVER SRA (Public State Park) In town, W 0.5 mi on Sterling Hwy at MP 157 (R). Avail: 186 W, Pit toilets. 2021 rates: $20. May 01 to Sep 30. (907)522-8368

↓ CENTENNIAL PARK (Public) From jct Kenai Spur Rd & Hwy 1 (Sterling Hwy Mile Post 94.2): Go 2 mi S on Hwy 1, then 500 feet W on Kalifornsky, then 1/4 mi N on Centennial Park Rd. 176 Avail: Pit toilets. 2021 rates: $21 to $26. (907)262-3151

↓ CLAM GULCH SRA (Public State Park) From town, S 25 mi on Sterling Hwy, follow signs. MP-117. 120 Avail. 2021 rates: $20. May 01 to Oct 31. (907)262-5581

↓ CROOKED CREEK SRA (Public State Park) From town: Go 14 mi S on Sterling Hwy, then 2 mi No Coho Loop Rd (R) Note: 35' RV size limit. 79 Avail. 2021 rates: $20. May 15 to Oct 15. (907)262-5581

↓ EDGEWATER RV PARK **Ratings: 6.5/8/7** (RV Park) 55 Avail: 44 full hkups, 11 W, 11 E (30 amps). 2021 rates: $45 to $55. May 15 to Aug 31. (907)262-7733, 48798 Funny River Rd, Soldotna, AK 99669

↓ JOHNSON LAKE (Public State Park) On Sterling Hwy at MP-110 to Johnson Lake Loop Road. Note: 35' RV size limit. 51 Avail. 2021 rates: $20. (907)269-8400

→ KENAI NATIONAL WILDLIFE REFUGE/HIDDEN LAKE (Public National Park) From town: Go 22 mi E on Sterling Hwy to milepost 72.5, then 14-1/2 mi S on Skilak Rd. 44 Avail. 2021 rates: $10. (907)262-7021

→ KENAI NATIONAL WILDLIFE REFUGE/UPPER SKILAK LAKE (Public National Park) From town: Go 22 mi E on Sterling Hwy to milepost 72.5, then 8 mi S on Skilak Rd. 25 Avail. 2021 rates: $5 to $10. (907)262-7021

← KING SALMON MOTEL & RV PARK **Ratings: 6/9.5★/6.5** (RV Park) Avail: 39 full hkups (30/50 amps). 2021 rates: $35. May 15 to Sep 15. (907)262-5857, 35546-A Kenai Spur Hwy, Soldotna, AK 99669

↓ **KLONDIKE RV PARK & COTTAGES**
Ratings: 8/9.5★/10 (RV Park) From jct of Sterling Hwy & Funny River Rd: Go 1/4 mi E on Funny River Rd (R). **FAC:** all weather rds. Avail: 35 all weather, 4 pull-thrus, (30x60), back-ins (30x50), 35 full hkups (30/50 amps), WiFi @ sites, rentals, laundry. **REC:** Kenai River: boating nearby, hunting nearby. Pets OK. No tents. Big rig sites. 2021 rates: $42 to $58. May 01 to Sep 10.
(907)262-6035 Lat: 60.28452, Lon: -151.04623
48665 Funny River Rd, Soldotna, AK 99669
klondikervpark.com
See ad this page

← MORGAN'S LANDING SRA (Public State Park) On Sterling Hwy at MP-85 Note: 35' RV size limit. 51 Avail. 2021 rates: $20. May 15 to Oct 15. (907)269-8400

→ SWIFTWATER PARK (SOLDOTNA CITY PARK) (Public) From jct Kenai Spur Rd & Hwy 1 (Sterling Hwy Mile Post 94.2): Go 500 feet on Hwy 1, then 1/2 mi E on E Redoubt Ave, then 1/4 mi S on Swiftwater Park Rd. 40 Avail. 2021 rates: $21 to $26. (907)262-1337

STERLING — D3 *Kenai Peninsula*

← ALASKA CANOE & CAMPGROUND **Ratings: 6/7/6.5** (Campground) Avail: 30 full hkups (30/50 amps). 2021 rates: $35. May 01 to Sep 30. (907)262-2331, 35292 Sterling Hwy, Sterling, AK 99672

↑ BING'S LANDING (Public State Park) On Sterling Hwy at MP-79. 36 Avail. 2021 rates: $20. May 15 to Oct 15. (907)262-5581

↙ IZAAK WALTON (Public State Park) From town, S 1 mi on Hwy 1 (Sterling Hwy) to Izaak Walton State Park Rd (MP-81), W 0.25 mi (E). 31 Avail. 2021 rates: $20. May 15 to Oct 30. (907)262-5581

← MOOSE RIVER RV PARK **Ratings: 4.5/9★/6** (Campground) Avail: 30 full hkups (30/50 amps). 2021 rates: $35. May 01 to Sep 01. (907)260-7829, 33219 Sterling Hwy, Sterling, AK 99672

SUTTON — C4 *Matanuska Susitna*

→ PINNACLE MOUNTAIN RV PARK & CAFE **Ratings: 6/7/5.5** (Campground) 36 Avail: 22 full hkups, 14 E (30 amps). 2021 rates: $20 to $35. (907)746-6531, Mile 70 Glenn Hwy, Sutton, AK 99674

TALKEETNA — C4 *Matanuska Susitna*

↑ DENALI/LOWER TROUBLESOME (Public State Park) From Talkeentna cutoff, N 40 mi on Parks Hwy(L). 20 Avail. 2021 rates: $15. (907)745-3975

← TALKEETNA CAMPER PARK **Ratings: 6/9.5★/8** (RV Park) 35 Avail: 5 full hkups, 30 W, 30 E (30/50 amps). 2021 rates: $43 to $48. May 01 to Sep 30. (907)733-2693, 22763 S. Talkeetna Spur Rd, Talkeetna, AK 99676

TOK — C4 *Southeast Fairbanks*

↙ EAGLE TRAIL (Public State Park) On Tok Cutoff at MP-109.5. 35 Avail. 2021 rates: $20. (907)505-0319

↖ MOON LAKE REC SITE (Public State Park) On AK Hwy at MP-1332. 15 Avail. 2021 rates: $20. Jun 01 to Sep 15. (907)505-0319

← SOURDOUGH CAMPGROUND & CAFE **Ratings: 7/9★/8.5** (Campground) 60 Avail: 32 full hkups, 28 W, 28 E (20/30 amps). 2021 rates: $25 to $55. (907)883-5543, 1 Prospector Way, Tok, AK 99780

↖ TOK RIVER (Public State Park) On AK Hwy at MP-1309. Note: 60' RV site limit. 27 Avail: Pit toilets. 2021 rates: $20. Jun 15 to Sep 15. (907)505-0319

→ **TOK RV VILLAGE & CABINS**
Ratings: 8/10★/10 (RV Park) 145 Avail: 100 full hkups, 44 W, 44 E (30/50 amps). 2021 rates: $53.45 to $63.78. May 15 to Sep 30. (907)883-5877, 1313.4 Mile Alaska Hwy, Tok, AK 99780

↑ TUNDRA RV PARK AND BAR **Ratings: 5.5/8.5/8** (RV Park) 54 Avail: 30 full hkups, 24 W, 24 E (30/50 amps). 2021 rates: $45 to $50. May 15 to Sep 15. (907)883-7875, MP 1315 Alaska Hwy, Tok, AK 99780

TRAPPER CREEK — C3 *Matanuska Susitna*

↑ DENALI/BYERS LAKE (Public State Park) On Parks Hwy, at MP 147. As of Spring 2019 park currently closed until further notice. Call for updates. 73 Avail. 2021 rates: $20. May 15 to Sep 15. (907)745-3975

↑ DENALI/DENALI VIEWPOINT NORTH (Public State Park) On Parks Hwy, at MP 162.7. 20 Avail. 2021 rates: $15. (907)745-3975

↓ **TRAPPER CREEK INN & RV PARK**
Ratings: 7/10★/8.5 (Campground) 34 Avail: 19 full hkups, 1 E (30/50 amps). 2021 rates: $20 to $40. May 15 to Sep 15. (907)733-1444, 23471 S Parks Highwy, Trapper Creek, AK 99683

VALDEZ — D4 *Nia*

↖ ALLISON POINT (Public State Park) From town, E 6 mi on Richardson Hwy to Dayville Rd, W 5 mi (R) Dry camp site with overnight & day use parking. 51 Avail. 2021 rates: $20. May 15 to Sep 15. (907)835-2282

Directional arrows indicate the campground's position in relation to the nearest town.

VALDEZ (CONT)

BAYSIDE RV PARK **Ratings: 7/9.5★/8.5** (RV Park) 110 Avail: 69 full hkups, 21 W, 21 E (30/50 amps). 2021 rates: $40 to $52. May 01 to Sep 08. (907)255-4425, 230 E. Egan Dr, Valdez, AK 99686

BEAR PAW ADULT PARK
Ratings: 8/10★/9.5 (RV Park) From jct Richardson Hwy & Meals Ave: Go 1/4 mi S on Meals Ave, then 300 feet E on Wyatt Way (L). **FAC:** gravel rds. Avail: 28 gravel, back-ins (20x60), 28 full hkups (50 amps), WiFi @ sites, tent sites, dump, laundry, fire rings, firewood. **REC:** Prince William Sound: boating nearby, hunting nearby. Pets OK. Age restrict may apply. Big rig sites, eco-friendly. 2021 rates: $55. May 20 to Sep 15.
(907)835-2530 Lat: 61.07500, Lon: -146.21537
300 Wyatt Way, Valdez, AK 99686
www.bearpawrvpark.com
See ad previous page

BEAR PAW CAMPER PARK
Ratings: 7.5/9.5★/8.5 (RV Park) From jct Richardson Hwy & Meals Ave: Go 500 feet S on Meals Ave to N Harbor Dr, then 150 feet E on North Harbor Dr (L). **FAC:** gravel rds. Avail: 61 gravel, 19 pull-thrus, (20x60), back-ins (20x40), 51 full hkups, 10 W, 10 E (30 amps), WiFi @ sites, dump, laundry, firewood. **REC:** Prince William Sound: marina, boating nearby, playground, hunting nearby. Pets OK. Partial handicap access. No tents, eco-friendly. 2021 rates: $45. May 01 to Sep 25.
(907)835-2530 Lat: 61.12748, Lon: -146.349800
101 North Harbor Drive, Valdez, AK 99686
www.bearpawrvpark.com
See ad previous page

EAGLE'S REST RV PARK & CABINS
good sam park
Ratings: 8/10★/9.5 (RV Park) Avail: 197 full hkups (30/50 amps). 2021 rates: $40 to $59. May 15 to Sep 15. (800)553-7275, 139 E Pioneer, Valdez, AK 99686

VALDEZ GLACIER CAMPGROUND (CITY PARK) (Public) From jct Richardson Hwy (Milepost O) & Airport Rd: Go 1-1/2 mi N on Airport Rd. Avail: 14 E. 2021 rates: $20 to $40. (907)835-2282

VALDEZ KOA **Ratings: 6.5/9★/8** (RV Park) 90 Avail: 3 full hkups, 71 W, 71 E (30/50 amps). 2021 rates: $34.89 to $49.89. May 25 to Sep 12. (907)835-2723, 3181 Richardson Hwy, Valdez, AK 99686

Things to See and Do

STAN STEPHENS GLACIER & WILDLIFE CRUISES Discover the Glaciers & Wildlife of Prince William Sound from Valdez. Tours feature Columbia or Meares Glaciers. Daily departures. May 15 to Sep 15. Partial handicap access. RV accessible. Restrooms. Food. Hours: 8am to 7pm. Adult fee: $135 to $170.
(907)835-4731 Lat: 61.12647, Lon: -146.35007
112 North Harbor Drive, Valdez, AK 99686
www.stephenscruises.com
See ad page 32

WASILLA — C4 *Matanuska Susitna*

BIG BEAR RV PARK **Ratings: 7.5/10★/10** (RV Park) 47 Avail: 24 full hkups, 9 W, 14 E (30/50 amps). 2021 rates: $40 to $55. (907)745-7445, 2010 S Church St, Palmer, AK 99645

BIG LAKE NORTH REC SITE (Public State Park) From town, W 15 mi on Parks Hwy to Big Lake Rd, S 3 mi (E). 80 Avail. 2021 rates: $20 to $25. May 15 to Sep 15. (907)746-4644

BIG LAKE SOUTH REC SITE (Public State Park) From town, W 15 mi on Parks Hwy to Big Lake Rd, S 5 mi (E). 23 Avail. 2021 rates: $20 to $25. May 15 to Sep 15. (907)240-9797

ROCKY LAKE (Public State Park) From town, W 15 mi on Parks Hwy to Big Lake Rd to Beaver Lake Rd, N 1 mi (L). 10 Avail. 2021 rates: $20 to $25. May 15 to Sep 15. (907)240-9797

CLEAN RESTROOMS GET A STAR

Campgrounds that receive the maximum 5 points for restroom cleanliness (toilets, showers, floors, walls and sinks/counters/mirrors) achieve a star beside their total restroom rating.

Rated 10/10★/10

WILLOW — C4 *Matanuska Susitna*

MAT-SU RV PARK & CAMPGROUND (RV Park) (Rebuilding) 46 Avail: 44 full hkups, 2 E (30/50 amps). 2021 rates: $20 to $45. May 01 to Sep 30. (907)495-6300, 47442 S Yancey, Willow, AK 99688

MONTANA CREEK CAMPGROUND **Ratings: 6.5/NA/8** (Campground) Avail: 18 E (30/50 amps), Pit toilets. 2021 rates: $25 to $55. May 15 to Sep 01. (907)733-5268, Mile 96.5 Parks Hwy, Willow, AK 99688

NANCY LAKE/SOUTH ROLLY LAKE (Public State Park) At MP 67.3 of the Parks Highway, travel on the Nancy Lake Parkway for 6.5 miles southwest to South Rolly Lake. 98 Avail. 2021 rates: $20 to $25. May 15 to Sep 15. (907)745-3975

SUSITNA LANDING AND CAMPGROUND **Ratings: 4.5/NA/9** (RV Park) Avail: 19 E (30/50 amps). 2021 rates: $15 to $25. (907)495-7700, 14400 E Susitna Landing Rd, Willow, AK 99688

WILLOW CREEK CAMPGROUND (Public State Park) From town, N on Parks Hwy to MP 70.8 (L). 140 Avail: Pit toilets. 2021 rates: $15. May 15 to Sep 15. (907)745-3975

WRANGELL — D6 *Wrangell*

SHOEMAKER RV PARK AND TENT CAMPGROUND (Public) From ferry dock: Go 4-9/10 mi E on Zimouia Hwy. Avail: 16 E Pit toilets. 2021 rates: $20 to $30. (907)874-2444

RV Tech Tips - Front Curtains for Privacy: Let the sun shine in but keep the gawkers from looking through the large front windshield of your Class A motorhome with the installation of mid-height cafe curtains. If your coach has a split-front windshield, buy two spring-tension curtain rods. If yours is a one-piece window, buy one that will span side-to-side. They simply spring into place and can easily be adjusted for height. You can now enjoy the sunlight and sights without feeling like you are on display.

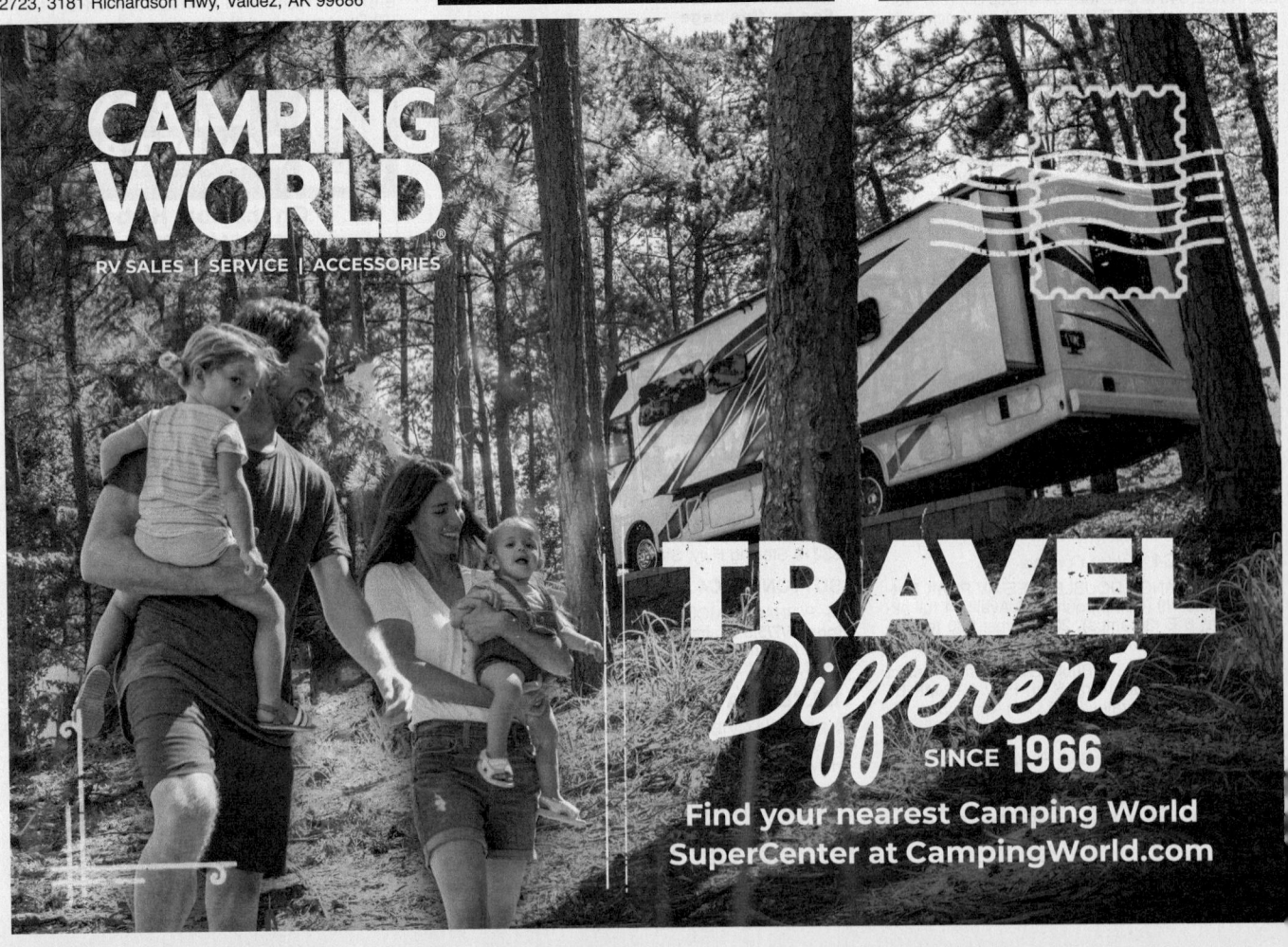

AZ

YOU ARE HERE

Arizona

DID YOU KNOW?

There are no dinosaur fossils in the Grand Canyon because the rocks there are older than the oldest known species.

Arizona is synonymous with America's desert Southwest, and there's a good reason for this distinction. The state is home to spectacles like the Grand Canyon and Meteor Crater, as well as cities like Tucson and Phoenix.

The Grandest National Park

It's a safe bet that the Grand Canyon occupies a high place in many travelers' bucket lists. Whether you prefer to peer down into the mile-deep canyon depths from the rim or take a journey down the Colorado River on the canyon floor, Grand Canyon National Park offers a memorable glimpse into a world-famous geological marvel.

A Tale of Two Cities: Flagstaff and Sedona

The town of Flagstaff showcases Arizona's alpine side. Sitting at an elevation of 7,000 feet about 140 miles north of Phoenix, the town entices visitors to lush forested, mountain landscapes. Green pine trees are a departure from the cacti found elsewhere in Arizona. Just south of Flagstaff, Sedona sits amid red rock formations that boggle the mind. Spend the day riding a bike around these geological marvels, then relax the night away at a five-star restaurant.

Jewel of the Desert

In the heart of Arizona, Phoenix entertains visitors with its big city attractions, scores of top-rated golf courses and surrounding mountains and hills. In the state's southeast corner, Tucson is a vibrant hub in the midst of the Sonoran Desert, offering both outdoor adventures and big-city experiences.

Indigenous Imprint

Long before European explorers reached the Southwest, Native American tribes flourished in throughout Arizona, growing crops and creating irrigation systems of impressive complexity. This

Arizona Sonoran Dog

Originating from the 1940s, the Sonoran hot dog is a twist on an American classic – sausage is wrapped in crispy bacon and piled high with pinto beans, onions, tomatoes, mayo and jalapeño sauce. A split-top roll called a bolillo is also used instead of a normal bun. You can sample this culinary treasure in El Guero Canelo and BK Carne Asada and Hot Dogs in Tucson.

VISITOR CENTER

TIME ZONE
Mountain Standard

ROAD & HIGHWAY INFORMATION
888-411-7623
az511.com

FISHING & HUNTING INFORMATION
azgfd.com/license
602-942-3000

BOATING INFORMATION
azgfd.com/boating

NATIONAL PARKS
nps.gov/az

STATE PARKS
azstateparks.com

TOURISM INFORMATION
Arizona Office of Tourism
866-275-5816
visitarizona.com

TOP TOURISM ATTRACTIONS
1) The Grand Canyon
2) Saguaro National Park
3) Navajo Nation

MAJOR CITIES
Phoenix (capital), Tucson, Mesa, Chandler, Gilbert

INDULGE YOUR PASSION FOR SUN AND FUN AT
CAL AM RESORTS
good sam park

rich history can be explored at places like Montezuma Castle National Monument, Wupatki National Monument and Homolovi State Park. While not as notorious at Tombstone, mining towns like Oatman, Bisbee and Jerome offer glimpses into Arizona's frontier history.

Plan to Visit Lake Powell

Arizona's most popular water playground, Lake Powell entices recreation seekers to enjoy water sports amid rugged desert shores. Whether you are boating, fishing or paddling, Lake Powell will challenge you with seemingly endless inlets and bays. In central Arizona, the Salt River hypnotically snakes its way through the Tonto National Forest wilderness.

Spires, Mesas and More

In Monument Valley on Arizona's northern border, iconic sandstone towers and buttes formed the backdrops of so many American Westerns. Dozens of classic films were filmed on this expanse, and visitors will certainly recognize the otherworldly rock formations. This border is also home to Horseshoe Bend and the Wave rock formation, two of the state's most photographed sights.

Haul It to Havasu

Lake Havasu is home to Arizona's cool and quirky side. Here, you'll find a legendary European bridge, kitschy English village and 20 lighthouses. Indeed, this city has twists and surprises at every turn. Pair that with a magnificent human-made lake and 300 days of sunshine and you've got a recipe for a getaway that's truly one of a kind.

"I've Got a Bridge to Sell You..."

A bridge too far? A publicity scheme concocted by city founder Robert McCulloch eventually turned into a beloved local landmark. McCulloch purchased the old London Bridge in 1968 and had it shipped — stone by stone — more than 5,400 miles to the Arizona desert. Over half a century later, the world's largest antique ever sold is still standing over the Colorado River. Take a stroll across the bridge for stellar views of the Bridgewater Channel and be sure to admire the decorative lampposts made from the cannons of Napoleon's army. For the full English experience, go to the London Bridge Resort for afternoon tea. Wafer cookies, cheesecakes and scones with clotted cream and jam are just some of the sophisticated delights you can enjoy. Your host will also tell how the London Bridge arrived in Havasu.

Built by the Singua people around 1400 A.D., Montezuma's castle in Verde sits 90 feet up a limestone cliff.

Rev Your Outboard

Lake Havasu with a vast expanse of water and a spirit of fun, Lake Havasu has cemented its status as a top water recreation hotspot. Spend your days jet skiing on 60 continuous miles of waterways, taking your family on relaxing pontoon rides through the Brightwater Channel or exploring hidden beaches by paddleboard. If you're an angler, haul up everything from bass to crappie from several public fishing docks and piers.

Tucson, Arizona's Second City

Second only to Phoenix in population, Tucson blends cosmopolitan charms with raw desert wilderness. With a multicultural vibe, eclectic food scene and to-die-for desert landscape, Tucson is an outdoor mecca with a modern edge.

Where Saguaros Tower Overhead

The iconic saguaro cactus grows in profusion just outside of Tucson. Split between two sections that lie on either side of Tucson, Saguaro National Park is the first stop on almost every visitor's itinerary and one of the few places left in the country to get up close and personal with its namesake flora. Learn more at the Arizona-Sonora Desert Museum or the Tucson Botanical Gardens. For a different kind of exploration, head about an hour southwest and try Kitt Peak National Observatory, where stellar discoveries await. Or head north where Biosphere 2 preserves diverse ecosystems in controlled indoor landscapes.

Drop a Line in the Desert

South of Tucson, a refreshing watery sanctuary glitters in the desert. Patagonia Lake State Park is the perfect place to cool off after a day in the desert. Join local fishermen casting for bass, bluegill and catfish, or enjoy a day on the water in canoes, paddleboats and pontoons available for rent at the marina.

Cycle Among the Saguaro

Hiking and biking trails provide endless exploration in Tucson. Start easy with a stroll along the Rillito River Park Trail that cuts 12 miles through downtown Tucson before heading to one of the five mountain ranges that surround the city. Colossal Cave Mountain Park southeast of town plays host to archaeological sites and incredible underground geological formations. More intrepid hikers should try the 8.2-mile round-trip route to Seven Falls in Sabino Canyon. Rated the No. 1 trail in the area, it's home to waterfalls, wildlife and lush mountain landscapes.

good sam park

Featured Good Sam Parks

ARIZONA

When you stay with Good Sam, you can expect the highest degree of cleanliness and friendliness, and better yet, you get **10% off** overnight campground fees.

If you're not already a Good Sam member you can purchase your membership at one of these locations:

10/10★/10 GOOD SAM PARKS

AMADO
De Anza RV Resort
(520)398-8628

APACHE JUNCTION
Sundance West RV Resort
(480)982-5856

Sunrise RV Resort
(480)983-2500

Superstition Sunrise RV Resort
(800)624-7027

Weaver's Needle RV Resort
(480)982-3683

BLACK CANYON CITY
Black Canyon Ranch RV Resort
(623)374-9800

BULLHEAD CITY
Vista Del Sol RV Resort
(928)754-0182

CAMP VERDE
Verde Ranch RV Resort
(928)567-7126

CASA GRANDE
Sundance 1 RV Resort
(520)426-9662

EL MIRAGE
Pueblo El Mirage RV & Golf Resort
(623)583-0464

FORT MCDOWELL
Eagle View RV Resort Asah Gweh Oou-o At Fort McDowell
(480)789-5310

GOLD CANYON
Arizonian RV Resort
(520)463-2978

Canyon Vistas RV Resort
(480)288-8844

Gold Canyon RV & Golf Resort
(480)982-5800

MESA
Apache Wells RV Resort
(480)832-4324

Good Life RV Resort
(480)832-4990

Mesa Regal RV Resort
(480)830-2821

Sun Life RV Resort
(480)981-9500

Towerpoint Resort
(480)832-4996

Valle Del Oro RV Resort
(480)984-1146

PHOENIX
Desert Shadows RV Resort
(800)595-7290

TUCSON
Far Horizons RV Resort
(520)296-1234

Mission View RV Resort
(800)444-8439

Rincon Country East RV Resort
(520)448-4449

Rincon Country West RV Resort
(520)294-5608

YUMA
Bonita Mesa RV Resort
(928)342-2999

Del Pueblo RV Resort
(928)341-2100

Villa Alameda RV Resort
(928)344-8081

Westwind RV & Golf Resort
(928)342-2992

What's This?

An RV park with a 10/10★/10 rating has scored perfect grades in amenities, cleanliness and appearance ("See Understanding the Campground Rating System" on pages 8 and 9 for an explanation of the trusted Good Sam Rating System). Stay in a 10/10★/10 park on your next trip for a nearly flawless camping experience.

AMADO
De Anza RV Resort

APACHE JUNCTION
Campground USA RV Resort
Countryside RV Resort
Golden Sun RV Resort
Meridian RV Resort
Sundance West RV Resort
Sunrise RV Resort
Superstition Sunrise RV Resort
VIP RV Resort & Storage
Weaver's Needle RV Resort

ASH FORK
Interstate 40 Grand Canyon RV Park

BEAVER DAM
Beaver Dam Lodge RV Resort

BENSON
Butterfield RV Resort & Observatory
CT RV Resort
Pato Blanco Lakes RV Resort
San Pedro Resort Community
Valley Vista RV Resort

BLACK CANYON CITY
Black Canyon Ranch RV Resort

BOUSE
Desert Pueblo RV Resort

BRENDA
3 Dreamers RV Park
Black Rock RV Village
Desert Gold RV Resort
Wagon West RV Park

Getty Images/iStockphoto

BULLHEAD CITY
Colorado River Oasis Resort
Vista Del Sol RV Resort

CAMP VERDE
Verde Ranch RV Resort
Verde River RV Resort & Cottages

CASA GRANDE
Casa Grande RV Resort & Cottages
Casita Verde RV Resort
Fiesta Grande RV Resort
Foothills West RV Resort
Sundance 1 RV Resort

CLARKDALE
Rain Spirit RV Resort

COOLIDGE
Ho Ho Kam RV Park

COTTONWOOD
Verde Valley RV & Camping Resort

DUNCAN
Valley View RV Park & MH Community

EHRENBERG
Riversands RV Resort

EL MIRAGE
Pueblo El Mirage RV & Golf Resort

ELOY
Las Colinas RV Resort

FLAGSTAFF
Black Barts RV Park
Greer's Pine Shadows RV Park
J & H RV Park

FORT MCDOWELL
Eagle View RV Resort Asah Gweh Oou-o At Fort McDowell

FREDONIA
Kaibab Paiute Tribal RV Park

GOLD CANYON
Arizonian RV Resort
Canyon Vistas RV Resort
Gold Canyon RV & Golf Resort

GOLDEN VALLEY
Adobe RV Park
Tradewinds RV Park

GOODYEAR
Cotton Lane RV Resort

HOLBROOK
OK RV Park

HUACHUCA CITY
Mountain View RV Park

KINGMAN
Blake Ranch RV Park
Zuni Village RV Park

LAKE HAVASU CITY
Campbell Cove RV Resort

MARANA
Valley Of the Sun RV Resort

MEADVIEW
Meadview RV Park & Cozy Cabins

MESA
Apache Wells RV Resort
Good Life RV Resort
Holiday Village
Mesa Regal RV Resort
Mesa Spirit RV Resort
Mesa Sunset RV Resort
Monte Vista Village RV Resort
Palm Gardens MHC & RV Park
Sun Life RV Resort
Towerpoint Resort
Val Vista Village RV Resort
Valle Del Oro RV Resort
Viewpoint RV & Golf Resort
Western Acres

MOHAVE VALLEY
Crossroads RV Park

OVERGAARD
Heber RV Resort

PAGE
Antelope Point Marina RV Park
Page Lake Powell Campground

PHOENIX
Desert Shadows RV Resort
Phoenix Metro RV Park
Pioneer RV Resort
Royal Palm RV Resort

PICACHO
Picacho Peak RV Resort

PRESCOTT VALLEY
Fairgrounds RV Park

QUARTZSITE
88 Shades RV Park
Holiday Palms Resort
Quail Run RV Park
The Scenic Road RV Park

SAN MANUEL
Rancho San Manuel Mobile Home & RV Park

SCENIC
Scenic Orchard RV Park

SEDONA
Rancho Sedona RV Park

SHOW LOW
Venture In RV Resort

SPRINGERVILLE
OM Place RV Park

ST JOHNS
St Johns RV Resort

SUN CITY
Paradise RV Resort

SURPRISE
Sunflower RV Resort

TACNA
Copper Mountain RV Park

TOMBSTONE
Tombstone RV Park
Tombstone Territories RV Resort

TOPOCK
Route 66 Golden Shores RV Park

TUCSON
Crazy Horse RV Campgrounds
Crescent Manor MH Village
El Frontier
Far Horizons RV Resort
Mesa Ridge
Mission View RV Resort
Palo Verde Estates
Prince Of Tucson RV Park
Rincon Country East RV Resort
Rincon Country West RV Resort
South Forty RV Ranch
The RV Park at the Pima County Fairgrounds
Voyager RV Resort & Hotel

WELLTON
Sun Country RV Park

WICKENBURG
Horspitality RV Resort

WILLIAMS
Canyon Gateway Grand Canyon RV Park & Glamping
Grand Canyon Railway RV Park

WILLOW BEACH
Willow Beach Marina & Campground

YUMA
Araby Acres RV Resort
Blue Sky RV Resort
Bonita Mesa RV Resort
Cactus Gardens RV Resort
Capri RV Resort
Caravan Oasis RV Resort
Del Pueblo RV Resort
Desert Paradise RV Resort
Foothill Village RV Resort
Fortuna de Oro RV Resort
Garden Oasis RV Resort
Goldwater Mobile Home & RV Park
Mesa Verde RV Resort
Shady Acres MH & RV Park
Southern Mesa RV Park
Sundance RV Resort
Suni Sands RV Resort
Villa Alameda RV Resort
Westwind RV & Golf Resort

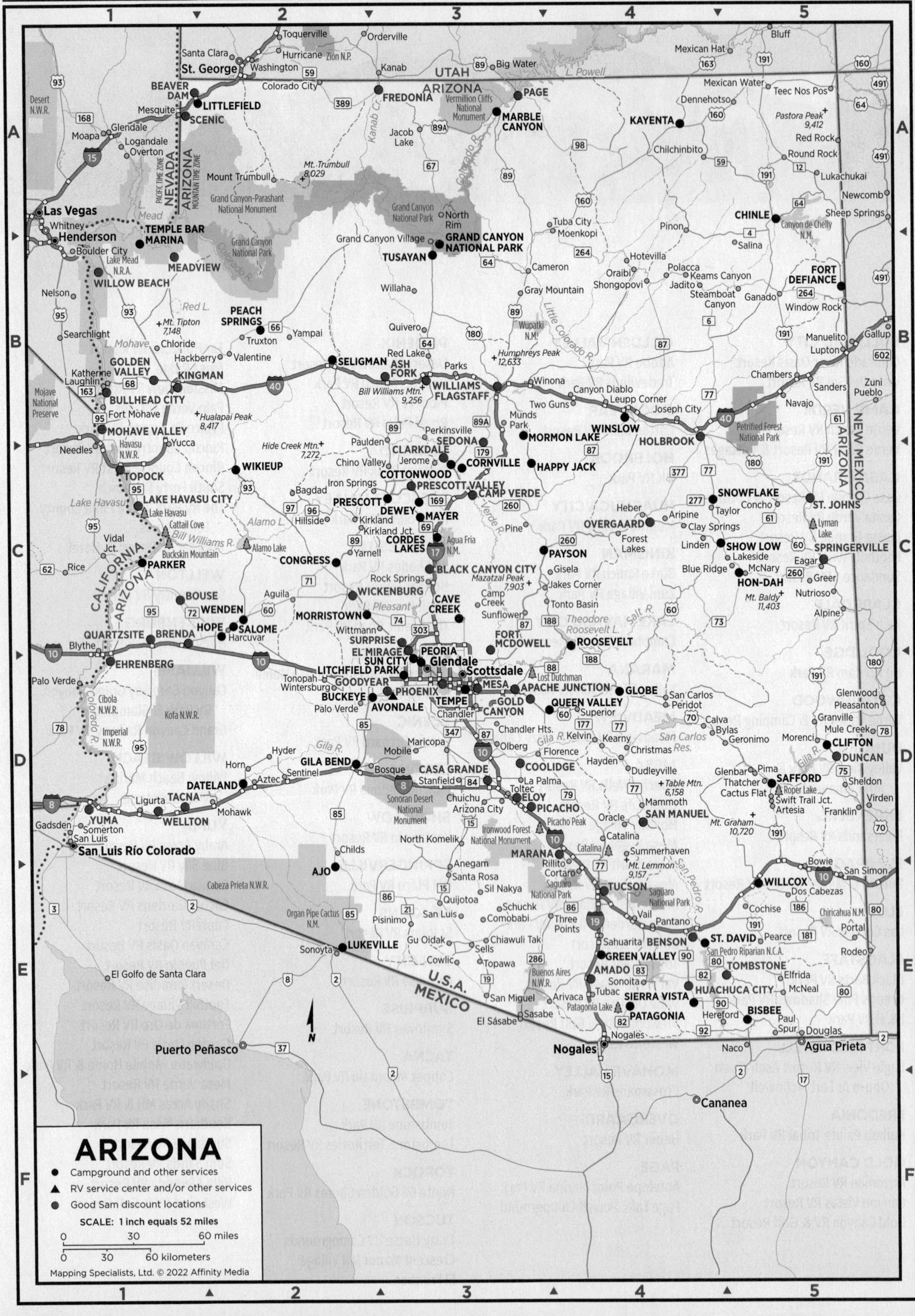
ARIZONA
Campground and other services
RV service center and/or other services
Good Sam discount locations
SCALE: 1 inch equals 52 miles
0 30 60 miles
0 30 60 kilometers
Mapping Specialists, Ltd. © 2022 Affinity Media
UTAH
NEVADA
ARIZONA
CALIFORNIA
NEW MEXICO
U.S.A.
MEXICO
PACIFIC TIME ZONE
MOUNTAIN TIME ZONE
Toquerville
Orderville
Santa Clara
Hurricane
Zion N.P.
St. George
Washington
Kanab
Big Water
L. Powell
Bluff
Mexican Hat
Colorado City
BEAVER DAM
LITTLEFIELD
Mesquite
SCENIC
FREDONIA
Vermillion Cliffs National Monument
PAGE
MARBLE CANYON
Desert N.W.R.
Glendale
Moapa
Logandale
Overton
Jacob Lake
Mount Trumbull
Mt. Trumbull 8,029
Grand Canyon-Parashant National Monument
Grand Canyon National Park
North Rim
Las Vegas
Whitney
Henderson
Boulder City
TEMPLE BAR MARINA
Lake Mead N.R.A.
MEADVIEW
Mead
WILLOW BEACH
Nelson
Grand Canyon Village
GRAND CANYON NATIONAL PARK
TUSAYAN
Willaha
Red L.
Mt. Tipton 7,148
PEACH SPRINGS
Searchlight
L. Mohave
Chloride
Truxton
Yampai
Quivero
Hackberry
Valentine
Katherine
Laughlin
GOLDEN VALLEY
KINGMAN
SELIGMAN
ASH FORK
Red Lake
Parks
WILLIAMS
FLAGSTAFF
Bill Williams Mtn. 9,256
Mojave National Preserve
BULLHEAD CITY
Fort Mohave
Hualapai Peak 8,417
MOHAVE VALLEY
Havasu N.W.R.
Yucca
Needles
TOPOCK
WIKIEUP
Hide Creek Mtn. 7,272
Paulden
Perkinsville
SEDONA
CLARKDALE
Jerome
Chino Valley
CORNVILLE
COTTONWOOD
Iron Springs
PRESCOTT VALLEY
CAMP VERDE
Bagdad
PRESCOTT
DEWEY
MAYER
Hillside
Kirkland
Kirkland Jct.
CORDES LAKES
Agua Fria N.M.
Yarnell
CONGRESS
Lake Havasu
LAKE HAVASU CITY
Cattail Cove
Bill Williams R.
Alamo L.
Alamo Lake
Buckskin Mountain
Vidal Jct.
PARKER
Rice
BOUSE
WENDEN
HOPE
SALOME
Harcuvar
Aguila
WICKENBURG
Rock Springs
BLACK CANYON CITY
Mazatzal Peak 7,903
Camp Creek
CAVE CREEK
L. Pleasant
MORRISTOWN
Wittmann
SURPRISE
EL MIRAGE
PEORIA
SUN CITY
Glendale
LITCHFIELD PARK
GOODYEAR
Scottsdale
Tonopah
Wintersburg
BUCKEYE
PHOENIX
AVONDALE
Palo Verde
MESA
TEMPE
Chandler
GOLD CANYON
APACHE JUNCTION
Lost Dutchman
QUARTZSITE
BRENDA
Blythe
EHRENBERG
Palo Verde
Cibola N.W.R.
Kofa N.W.R.
Imperial N.W.R.
Colorado R.
Gila R.
Hyder
Horn
GILA BEND
Sentinel
Aztec
DATELAND
Ligurta
TACNA
Mohawk
WELLTON
YUMA
Somerton
Gadsden
San Luis
San Luis Río Colorado
Maricopa
Mobile
Bosque
CASA GRANDE
Stanfield
Chuichu
Arizona City
Sonoran Desert National Monument
Chandler Hts.
Olberg
Florence
COOLIDGE
La Palma
Toltec
ELOY
PICACHO
Picacho Peak
Ironwood Forest National Monument
North Komelik
MARANA
Rillito
Cortaro
Saguaro National Park
TUCSON
Childs
AJO
Cabeza Prieta N.W.R.
Organ Pipe Cactus N.M.
Anegam
Santa Rosa
Sil Nakya
Quijotoa
Schuchk
Comobabi
San Luis
Pisinimo
Three Points
Gu Oidak
Chiawuli Tak
Sells
Cowlic
Topawa
LUKEVILLE
Sonoyta
Buenos Aires N.W.R.
San Miguel
Arivaca
Sasabe
El Sásabe
El Golfo de Santa Clara
Puerto Peñasco
Nogales
Tubac
Sonoita
Patagonia Lake
PATAGONIA
AMADO
GREEN VALLEY
Sahuarita
SIERRA VISTA
HUACHUCA CITY
Hereford
BISBEE
Naco
Paul Spur
Douglas
Agua Prieta
Cananea
BENSON
ST. DAVID
San Pedro Riparian N.C.A.
TOMBSTONE
Elfrida
McNeal
Pearce
Portal
Rodeo
Chiricahua N.M.
Cochise
Dos Cabezas
WILLCOX
Bowie
San Simon
Pantano
Vail
Summerhaven
Mt. Lemmon 9,157
Catalina
Oracle
SAN MANUEL
Mammoth
Dudleyville
Table Mtn. 6,158
Hayden
Kearny
Kelvin
Christmas
Superior
QUEEN VALLEY
GLOBE
San Carlos
Peridot
San Carlos Res.
Calva
Bylas
Geronimo
Glenbar
Pima
Thatcher
SAFFORD
Cactus Flat
Roper Lake
Swift Trail Jct.
Artesia
Mt. Graham 10,720
Franklin
Virden
Sheldon
DUNCAN
CLIFTON
Morenci
Mule Creek
Granville
Glenwood
Pleasanton
Alpine
Nutrioso
Mt. Baldy 11,403
HON-DAH
McNary
Greer
Eagar
SPRINGERVILLE
Lyman Lake
ST. JOHNS
Concho
SHOW LOW
Lakeside
Linden
Pinetop
Blue Ridge
Clay Springs
Aripine
Taylor
SNOWFLAKE
Heber
OVERGAARD
Forest Lakes
PAYSON
Gisela
Jakes Corner
Tonto Basin
Sunflower
FORT MCDOWELL
Theodore Roosevelt L.
ROOSEVELT
Salt R.
Pine
Verde R.
Munds Park
MORMON LAKE
HAPPY JACK
Two Guns
Winona
Canyon Diablo
Leupp Corner
WINSLOW
Joseph City
HOLBROOK
Petrified Forest National Park
Navajo
Sanders
Chambers
Zuni Pueblo
Manuelito
Gallup
Lupton
Window Rock
Ganado
FORT DEFIANCE
Keams Canyon
Steamboat Canyon
Polacca
Jadito
Hotevilla
Oraibi
Shongopovi
Cameron
Gray Mountain
Wupatki N.M.
Humphreys Peak 12,633
Little Colorado R.
Tuba City
Moenkopi
Pinon
CHINLE
Canyon de Chelly N.M.
Salina
Sheep Springs
Newcomb
Lukachukai
Round Rock
Red Rock
Pastora Peak 9,412
Teec Nos Pos
Mexican Water
Dennehotso
KAYENTA
Chilchinbito
Kanab Cr.
Colorado R.

AZ

ROAD TRIPS

Grand Adventures and Compelling Treasures

Arizona North

LOCATION
ARIZONA NORTH

DISTANCE
225 MILES

DRIVE TIME
4 HRS 13 MINS

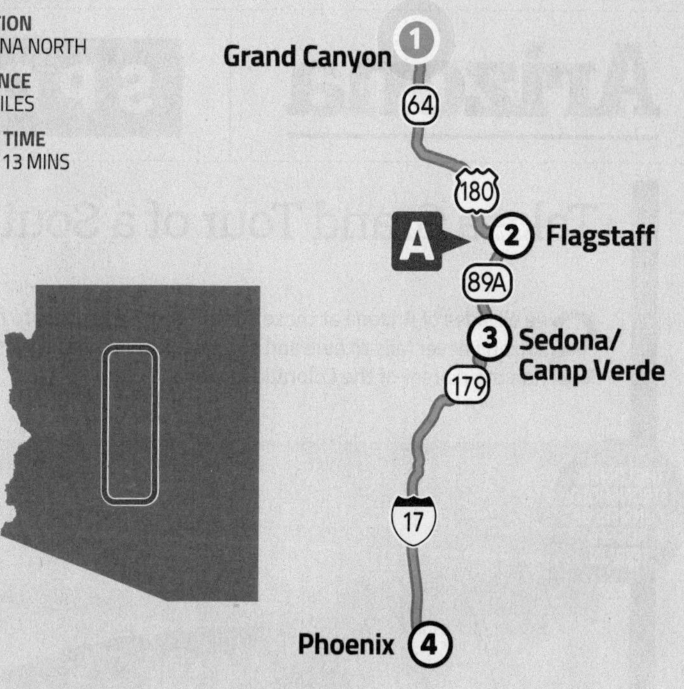

In Northern Arizona, the journey is just as thrilling as the destinations. Scenic drives weave through mysterious archaeological sites, hip college towns and spiritual communities before unveiling natural wonders like the Grand Canyon and Cathedral Rock. Get out of the car often if you don't want to miss a thing — from wine tastings in Camp Verde to art walks in Phoenix, this part of the Grand Canyon State doesn't skimp on unforgettable pit stops.

1 Grand Canyon
Starting Point

The Grand Canyon is one of the seven natural wonders of the world and easily Arizona's most iconic landmark. Start your adventure at the South Rim, where lookouts like Mather Point and Yavapai Point offer sweeping views of rippling rock faces that seem to go on for eternity. If you're an avid hiker, tackle popular routes such as Bright Angel Trail or the South Kaibab Trail. You can also take a helicopter tour to see the multicolored landscape from a bird's-eye view or walk along the Skywalk, a glass-bottomed platform suspended over 4,000 feet above the canyon floor.

2 Flagstaff
Drive 79 Miles ▪ 1 Hour, 28 Minutes

Home to Northern Arizona University, this college town is a hub of activity and the perfect pit stop after exploring the Grand Canyon. Refuel at over 200 restaurants and microbreweries — locals rave about the generous portions at MartAnne's Burrito Palace and the English muffin burgers at Diablo Burger. Afterward, head to the Lowell Observatory (where Pluto was discovered) for guided stargazing sessions and constellation tours. Other popular attractions in town include the Museum of Northern Arizona, Arizona Snowbowl and Flagstaff Extreme Adventure Course.

RECOMMENDED STOPOVER
A GRAND CANYON RAILWAY RV PARK
WILLIAMS, AZ (800) 843-8724

3 Sedona/Camp Verde
Drive 29 Miles ▪ 48 Minutes

Stretch your legs in Sedona's spectacular red rock mesas. Hiking trails like Cathedral Rock, Bell Rock Pathway and Devil's Bridge lead to panoramic vistas, while trout-filled streams in deep canyon gorges offer fly-fishing destinations. Sedona is also believed to be a vortex that radiates spiritual energy. Take a tour to discover these hot spots and then see more of the city's spiritual side at crystal shops and yoga classes. Just a 40-minute drive away is Camp Verde. Meet local winemakers and enjoy wine tastings at Clear Creek Vineyard & Winery, Salt Mine Wine or Alcantara Vineyards.

4 Phoenix
Drive 117 Miles ▪ 1 Hour, 57 Minutes

America's fifth-largest city has captivating desert scenery and every urban luxury imaginable, making it easy to forge your own path in the Valley of the Sun. Work up a sweat summiting Camelback Mountain and walk among towering saguaros in the Desert Botanical Garden. If you're into art, view masterpieces from around the globe at the Phoenix Art Museum and then wander past vibrant murals in Roosevelt Row and Old Town Scottsdale. Round out your visit by sampling delicious Southwest dishes like the Sonoran hot dog, cheese crisp and chimichanga.

Getty Images/iStockphoto

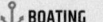

BIKING BOATING DINING ENTERTAINMENT FISHING HIKING HUNTING PADDLING SHOPPING SIGHTSEEING

Arizona SPOTLIGHTS

Take a Grand Tour of a Southwestern Gem

See all sides of Arizona at these spots. From wide rivers to mile-deep canyons, Arizona never fails to awe and surprise. Relive the Old West in Tombstone or ride the current of the Colorado in Yuma.

THE COCHISE STRONGHOLD CONSISTS OF RUGGED TERRAIN.

Towering buttes loom over Kartchner Caverns State Park.

Getty Images/iStockphoto

Benson

Benson was founded in the heyday of the mining boom and hasn't changed much since then. Step inside the railway town and prepare to be whirled back to the Old West with lively festivals, artifact-filled museums and historic downtown streets. Benson also acts as the gateway to Cochise County, opening the doors to lush river valleys and still-living caverns. With so much to do inside and out, you'll find this charming community is anything but sleepy.

Caving Adventures

Benson's top attraction is Kartchner Caverns State Park. Discovered in 1974, this sprawling limestone cave has the world's longest stalactite formation. Water still seeps from the surface, causing the formation to grow constantly. Tour through the living cave and learn more about the ecosystem from a guide. Next, visit the Discovery Center for interactive exhibits showing how the cave was formed and displays covering the local bat population. Round out your visit by stretching your legs above ground. The 1.7-mile Ocotillo Trail unveils diverse desert flora, while the 2.5-mile Foothills Loop Trail leads to the scenic Mountain Viewpoint.

Abundant Desert Lakes

You're never too far from a fishing lake. Drop a line in Cochise County's Willow Lake to catch largemouth bass, rainbow trout and bluegill. Roper Lake State Park near Stafford is another population destination with tons of largemouth bass, sunfish and channel catfish. The park also has lakeside cabins so consider turning your fishing excursion into an overnight trip. About an hour south of Benson, Patagonia Lake State Park is stocked with rainbow trout from November through March and boasts healthy populations of crappie, sunfish and bass. Whether you're angling from shore or boat, you're sure to reel in some impressive catches that will tip the scale in a big way.

A Birdwatcher's Paradise

Flowing north out of Mexico, the San Pedro River attracts a diverse array of animals. See them up close in the San Pedro Riparian National Conservation Area. Spanning 50,000 acres, this refuge is home to more than 350 bird species, 80 mammal species and 40 types of amphibians and reptiles. As you search for wildlife, keep an eye out for historical and archaeological remains like the Murray Springs Clovis Site, one of North America's most important early human sites, and the San Pedro House, a 1930s ranch now turned bookstore and visitor center. For more wildlife sightings, head to Benson's Waterfowl Viewing Pond, Ash Canyon or Miller Canyon. Be sure to stop by Whitewater Draw to see thousands of sandhill cranes if you're visiting between October and February.

Wild West Calling

Harken back to the Old West at Gammons Gulch Movie Set. Just a stone's throw away from downtown Benson, the recreated town

LOCAL FAVORITE

Desert Hominy Dessert

The prickly pear cactus doesn't just pepper the Arizona landscape, it's also a regional specialty. Enjoy a savory and tart stew. *Recipe by Ray Miller.*

INGREDIENTS

- ☐ 1 jar prickly pear cactus, use pickling juice to reach the level of tartness you like
- ☐ 1 jar medium banana peppers sliced
- ☐ 1 smoked sausage sliced or diced
- ☐ 1 medium jar of red or green salsa or 2 cups of homemade red or green salsa
- ☐ 1 small can of diced green chilis
- ☐ 1 can of white or yellow hominy
- ☐ ¼ onion diced

DIRECTIONS

Brown sausage and onion in a Dutch oven over open fire. Then add cactus, banana peppers, salsa and hominy. Stir well. Add pickling juice from cactus jar or pepper jar to season for tartness. Add a pinch of salt. Cover and cook for 30 to 45 minutes over open fire. You may need to add a bit of cactus juice or water if it becomes too thick.

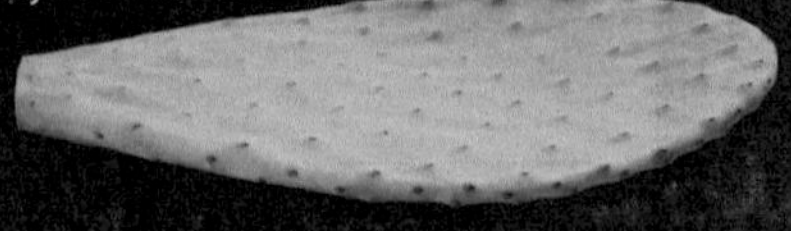

AZ

Trails lead hikers along the South Rim of the Grand Canyon, treating sightseers to remarkable scenery.

has been featured in over 64 films such as Day of Redemption and The Gundown. Over 15 functional buildings bring the past to life, including a saloon, jail and mining camp. The venue isn't open to the general public, however you can call ahead and organize a private tour. In town, swing by the Benson Historical Museum to see art and exhibits covering local cultures. Next, go for a stroll and look for 14 historic murals peppered throughout the streets. The murals were painted by artist Doug Quarles and depict the town's rich railroading heritage. Finish your stay at the Singing Wing Book Shop. Set on a working cattle ranch, this shop is stocked with a great selection of Southwest and Western America titles.

Illuminating Events

Benson goes all out for the Fourth of July. Come for the morning parade and stay for water fights, live music and fireworks. If you're visiting on September 11, honor the heroes of 9/11 at the annual Lantern Festival. Watch the sky light up with the warm glow of hundreds of lanterns and enjoy music, dancing and food vendors. In October, the Butterfield Stagecoach Days invites you to experience the town's Native American and Western heritage through Aztec dancing, folk music and historical re-enactments.

Spiritual Delights

Located near St. David, the Holy Trinity Monastery welcomes visitors of all faiths to its tranquil grounds. Admire the beautiful chapel and then wander through the pecan orchard and bird sanctuary trail. The 92-acre site also has a museum containing artifacts from around the globe. Before you go, make sure to pick up a loaf of fresh-baked bread at the bookstore.

Grand Canyon

Easily the most iconic natural wonder in the American West, the Grand Canyon is a 277-mile-long canyon and up to a mile deep that was carved out by the Colorado River over millions of years. Here you can go on hikes and mule rides or learn about geology from rangers.

Yavapai Museum of Geology

Looking out over the Grand Canyon at Yavapai Point, this small museum features large windows that afford visitors panoramic views out over the canyon. There's also an interpretive section with three-dimensional models of the North and South rims as well as old photos and informational panels that detail the geologic history of the area.

Go Back in History on the Trail of Time

If you want to learn about the geologic history of the Grand Canyon, head to the Trail of Time, a paved walkway featuring interpretive signage and rock displays designed to give visitors an idea of how long the canyon took to form. For perspective, the trail spans 2.83 miles (4.56 k) and each meter represents a million years of history. You can either walk west from the Yavapai Geology Museum to explore the canyon's history backwards or start at the beginning of the trail at Grand Canyon Village.

Kolb Studio

Situated inside a structure dating back to 1905, the Kolb Studio got its start as a photography shack used as a studio by a pair of photographer

See listing Williams, AZ

SPOTLIGHTS

AZ

The Grand Canyon Railway in Williams takes tourists to the South Rim of Grand Canyon National Park.

brothers to photograph mule riders. The shack was later expanded into a home and tollgate and today serves as an art gallery and book-store, complete with old-time ephemera, art, photography, and film screenings.

Test your Nerves on the Grand Canyon Skywalk

If you're not afraid of heights (or if you are and want to face your fears, full-on), the Grand Canyon Skywalk is a must-do experience. Jutting out around 70 feet over the rim of the Grand Canyon, this glass viewing platform allows daring visitors to walk right out over the canyon and gaze down 2,000 feet below. It's part of the Grand Canyon West attraction run by the Hualapai Indian Nation, which also features tours and a zipline.

Explore the Canyon by Mule

Visitors have been exploring the Grand Canyon by mule for generations, and one of the most popular ways of getting down into the depths of the canyon--and back up again-- is by riding one of these sturdy beasts. Two-hour rides are available for those short on time, though for the quintessential experience, take an overnight trip down to the Phantom Ranch. Note that due to their popularity, ranch stays are only available through a lottery system, 14 months in advance.

Take a Hike

The Grand Canyon's South Rim offers no shortage of opportunities for day hikes, from the easy-to-manage Rim Trail, which connects the South Rim Village to Hermits Rest, to steeper jaunts such as the Bright Angel Trail and the Grandview Trail.

Northern Trails

The North Rim area offers plenty hikes of all lengths, from the easy Cape Royal Trail which offers great views over the Canyon to the more challenging North Kaibab Trail, the only trail that descends deep into the canyon from the North Rim.

Hop Aboard the Grand Canyon Railway

If you want to experience the Grand Canyon the way early visitors did, leave your car or RV behind for a few hours and hop aboard the Grand Canyon Railway. This tourist train departs from Williams, Arizona every morning and makes the 2.25-hour trip to the South Rim's Grand Canyon Depot, which dates back to 1910. The train features six different classes of carriage, from the budget-friendly Pullman Class, which offers bench seating, clear up to the plus Luxury Dome and Luxury Parlor, both of which have private bars. While the views of the Arizona landscapes are enough to merit a ride on the train, there are plenty of little added bonuses, including onboard musical performances and even make-believe train robberies by costumed outlaws.

Discover the Park through a Ranger Program

One of the best ways to learn about the Grand Canyon is from those who know it best—the local park rangers. Most of the ranger programs take place at one of three centers: North Rim, the South Rim Village's McKee Amphitheater, and at the Desert View Watchtower. Programs include lectures on everything from geology to cultural history to bats, along with cultural presentations and special activities for children.

Heritage Week

If you happen to visit in August, don't miss a chance to attend the North Rim Heritage Week, which features a variety of educational programs and performances led by rangers and members of local tribes.

Mesa/Apache Junction

Not far from Phoenix in the immense Arizona Desert sit the paired towns of Mesa and Apache Junction. Here you'll find great museums, beautiful desert landscapes, and plenty of chances to learn about—and celebrate—the history and culture of the Wild West. Mesa and Apache Junction are also ideal for art lovers, with over 200 outdoor sculptures scattered across public areas.

Treasure Loop Trail leads hikers into into Lost Dutchman State Park in the Superstition Mountains near Mesa.

SPOTLIGHTS

The Arizona Museum of Natural History

This Mesa museum is a must-visit for anyone interested in paleontology, and features the largest dinosaur exhibit west of the Mississippi. Highlights include an animatronic exhibit — Dinosaur Mountain — complete with a three-story indoor waterfall and moving replicas of creatures that lived throughout the various periods of the Mesozoic Era. There's also a hands-on Paleo Dig Pit for kids who want to play fossil hunter for the day, as well as real jail cells that date to Arizona's early days as a U.S. territory. If you're interested in indigenous culture, the Southwest Gallery is definitely worth checking out, and features a solid collection of indigenous art and artifacts from the region as well as replica dwellings of the Hohokam people, who lived in the area thousands of years ago.

Mesa Arts Center

Fans of the performing arts may end up finding themselves at the Mesa Arts Center, a gargantuan complex that's home to four theaters, 14 classrooms, and the Mesa Contemporary Arts Museum (MCA). The MCA is divided into four galleries: one hosting paintings, sculptures, and decorative objects from the permanent collection, a second exhibiting the works of Arizona artists, and two others that are used for everything from instillations to curated exhibitions.

Mesa Historical Museum

If you're interested in history or just want to get a better sense of the area, head to the Mesa Historical Museum, which features both temporary and permanent exhibits. Permanent exhibits focus on the history of Mesa and its early settlers as well as topics such as local baseball and the feline-inspired creations of 20th-century Arizona artist Karen Kuykendall. There's also a replica adobe schoolhouse built to resemble a 19th-century school, complete with antique desks.

Goldfield Ghost Town

One of Apache Junction's quirkiest attractions, the Goldfield Ghost Town offers a realistic window into life in the Wild West, with all sorts of family-friendly attractions that harken back to the days of yore. There's a zipline, a narrow-gauge railroad complete with guided narration, and even an old gold mine. If you want to try your hand at prospecting yourself, be sure to pay a visit to Prospector's Palace, where you can pan for gold or sluice for gemstones using traditional tools and techniques. Other popular attractions at the town include the Mystery Shack, a vortex-style attraction in which objects don't quite act as they should and the Eagle Eye Shooting Gallery, where make-believe target shooting takes center stage. If you'd like to learn more about local history, don't miss Goldfield's Historic Museum, which traces the history of mining in the area, or pay a visit to Lu Lu's Bordello, which tells the story of women settlers in 19th-century Arizona.

Lost Dutchman State Park

If you love the great outdoors, you won't want to miss the chance to visit Lost Dutchman State Park, which gets its name from the mysterious Lost Dutchman Goldmine, a legendary Superstition Mountain mine that may or may not actually exist. While there are plenty of people who spend their time in this region searching for the old mine, you don't need to be on the hunt for gold to warrant a visit here. The park features plenty of great trails, many of which are short enough to do on a quick visit — both Prospector's View Trail and Jacob's Crosscut Trail are less than a mile long. There's also a mountain biking trail that spans about

SPOTLIGHTS

four miles. Lost Dutchman and the surrounding Superstition Mountains are also ideal for wildlife spotting, with desert mule deer, bobcats, coyotes, roadrunners, and even Gila monsters calling the region home.

Park of the Canals

The area now known as Mesa has been inhabited for millennia, and a great way to learn a bit about some of the area's prehistoric people is by visiting the Park of the Canals. Spread over 30 acres, this park is home to a system of ancient canals constructed by the Hohokam people as early as 700 BC. There's also a desert botanical garden with 25 types of prickly pear as well as a playground and picnic areas.

Getty Images/iStockphoto

A trail snakes through the hills overlooking Phoenix. There are more than 200 trails in the greater metro area.

Valley of the Sun

Nicknamed the Valley of the Sun, Greater Phoenix is the fifth largest metro area in America. It encompasses over 20 unique communities, including Scottsdale, Mesa, Chandler, Tempe and Glendale. Every district shows off a different side of the Southwest, making it easy to pursue whatever your passions are. From summiting canyons and sipping wine in desert vineyards to viewing contemporary art in renowned galleries and searching for fabled gold, the memories you make in the Valley of the Sun are ones you'll remember for a lifetime.

Revel in Resort Life

The Valley of the Sun takes R&R to a whole other level with destination spas set in the heart of the Sonoran Desert. Feel the tension melt away with spa treatments infused with local botanicals at Alvadora Spa. You can also relax poolside at the swanky Sanctuary Resort or Omni Scottsdale Resort and Spa at Montelucia. When you're all rested, taste your way through Phoenix's wineries. Swirl reds while basking in the red rock canyons of the Verde Valley or sample vintages close to the city at Peoria's Winery 101. Consider teeing off at nearly 200 golf courses too.

Watersports Galore

Six Greater Phoenix lakes offer the perfect escape on hot days. Go boating, windsurfing or jet skiing on Lake Pleasant, located just 45 minutes from downtown Phoenix. You can also fish for bass, carp and bluegill in Tonto National Forest's Saguaro Lake, Apache Lake and Canyon Lake. The Bartlett Reservoir is another popular angling spot, with smallmouth bass, carp and catfish ready for the taking.

Desert Adventures

Hundreds of hiking and biking trails mean there's an adventure for every kind of traveler. Enjoy leisurely jaunts around the red rock buttes of Papago Park and take your time discovering over 50,000 desert plants in the Desert Botanical Garden. If you want to kick it up a notch, climb the Echo Canyon Trail for sweeping vista views on top of Camelback Mountain. Some paths even lead to petroglyphs. Follow the Holbert Trail in South Mountain Park or the Waterfall Trail in White Tank Mountain Regional Park to see intricate rock carvings left behind by ancient native civilizations.

Southwest Soul

Whether you're seeking art, history or a bit of bit, you'll find eclectic neighborhoods packed with all sorts of cultural attractions. Architecture enthusiasts can marvel at Taliesin West in Scottsdale, the desert masterpiece designed by Frank Lloyd Wright. Art lovers won't want to miss the Phoenix Art Museum's collection of 17,000 modern works from around the world. More contemporary art can be found in Roosevelt Row, a thriving arts hub. If you prefer to peer into the past, go to the acclaimed Heard Museum to view an impressive collection of Native American artifacts. You can also discover an archaeological site once home to a Hohokam tribe at the Pueblo Grande Museum and Cultural Park.

FIND YOURSELF
IN ALL-NEW EVERYTHING
Arizona's newest casino destination invites you to an experience like nowhere else in the Southwest. Indulge in a world of endless gaming action, incredible dining, live entertainment, two award-winning golf courses, AAA Four-Diamond luxury, and the outdoor escapes you'll find with Fort McDowell Adventures: off-roading, horseback riding, Segway tours, and more.
For RV enthusiasts, the Eagle View RV Resort provides a scenic, comfortable, and convenient setting for your next excursion.
See listing Fort McDowell, AZ

PHOENIX MAGAZINE
2021 Best of the Valley
READERS' PICK
good sam park
2022 Top Rated 10/10★/10
We-Ko-Pa CASINO RESORT
FORT McDOWELL YAVAPAI NATION ARIZONA
Eagle View RV Resort
Asah gweh oou-o at Fort McDowell
FIND YOURSELF HERE
10438 WEKOPA WAY • FORT MCDOWELL, AZ
1-855-WKP-WINS (1-855-957-9467) • WEKOPACASINORESORT.COM
9605 N. FORT MCDOWELL RD • FORT MCDOWELL, AZ
480-789-5310 • EAGLEVIEWRVRESORT.COM
AN ENTERPRISE OF THE FORT MCDOWELL YAVAPAI NATION

Clear, clean desert air. Minutes from Desert Hiking Trails, surrounded by undeveloped state land.

good sam park

ARIZONIAN RV RESORT

NEAR MEDICAL, SHOPPING, BANKS, ENTERTAINMENT, SPORTS, RESTAURANTS AND TRAILS.

2022 Top Rated 10/10★/10

(520) 463-2978

15976 E. Highway 60
Apache Junction (Gold Canyon), AZ 85118

Wi-Fi Available Limited

www.ArizonianResort.com
arizonianresort@yahoo.com

COUNTRY LIVING WITH GREAT AMENITIES!

- SWIMMING POOL • SPA
- SHUFFLEBOARDS • PICKLEBALL
- ATV TRAIL ACCESS DIRECTLY FROM RESORT
- PUTTING GREEN
- BILLIARDS
- FITNESS CENTER
- LARGE CLUBHOUSE
- LIVE ENTERTAINMENT
- LARGE QUILTING ROOM

See listing Gold Canyon, AZ

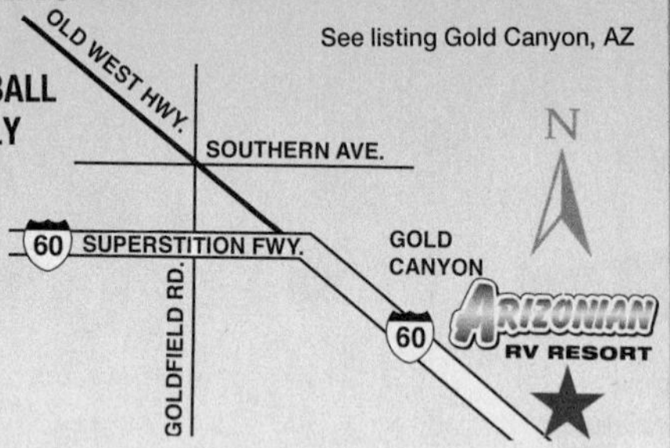

WEAVER'S NEEDLE RV RESORT

55+ SENIOR PARK

good sam park

A NEW MODERN RESORT IN THE SUN

250 S. Tomahawk Road • Apache Junction, AZ 85119

(480) 982-3683

2022 Top Rated 10/10★/10

www.weaversneedle.com
weaversneedle@yahoo.com

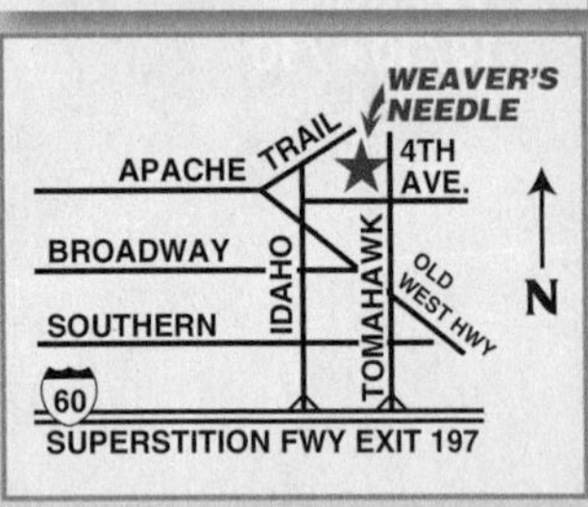

- CLASSES • CRAFTS • CERAMICS • DANCES
- WIFI • HEATED POOLS • SHUFFLEBOARD
- PICKLEBALL • PUTTING GREEN • BILLIARDS
- LARGE QUILTING ROOM • WOODSHOP • LIBRARY
- CLOSE TO HORSE BOARDING FACILITIES

Wi-Fi Available Limited

See listing Apache Junction, AZ

WESTERN ACRES

Best for Less in the West

- LONG PULL-THRU LOTS *(Call for Availability)*
- SHUFFLEBOARD • LARGE CLUBHOUSE
- NEAR SHOPPING & MEDICAL
- REASONABLE RATES • HORSESHOE PIT

Fun in the Sun

Friendliest MH/RV Park in Arizona!

Wi-Fi Available Limited

(480) 986-1158
9913 East Apache Trail
Mesa, Arizona 85207
www.western-acres.com
westernacres@yahoo.com

good sam park

Rated 8.5/9.5★/8.5

See listing Mesa, AZ

SPOTLIGHTS

A four-wheel-drive vehicle explores the backroads in Red Rock Country outside of Sedona.

Festivals of Fun

It doesn't matter what season you come, there's always something fun happening in the Valley of the Sun. Every spring, the Phoenix Raceway hosts the thrilling FanShield 500 Speed Fest. Cactus League Spring Training also occurs during this time, allowing you to watch 15 major league teams play over 200 games in a span of a month. During the holidays, Glendale Glitters covers over 16 blocks of downtown Glendale in 1.6 million twinkling lights, while Las Noches de Las Luminarias illuminates the Desert Botanical Garden with over 8,000 hand-lit luminaria bags. Other popular winter events include the Barrett-Jackson Collector Car Auction, World Championship Hoop Dance Contest and the Scottsdale Arabian Horse Show.

From Boom to Bust

Remnants of the Old West can be found in every corner of Greater Phoenix. In the Superstition Mountains, go back to the gold rush at Goldfield Ghost Town. The recreated boomtown makes the past come alive with mock gunfights, train rides and gold panning activities. Afterward, head to the Arizona Museum of Natural History in Mesa to learn about the Southwest's rich natural and cultural history. Engaging exhibits share the legend of the Lost Dutchman's Mine and even allow you to star in your own western movie. Finish the day by hunting for antiques in downtown Mesa. From Western art to vintage décor, you never know what treasures you'll unearth.

Verde Valley/Sedona

Humans have inhabited the Verde Valley for over 10,000 years, but that doesn't mean a visit here is all about the past. New Age spirituality, forward-looking design and a burgeoning wine scene are all a part of a reinvention that has made Sedona and the surrounding communities among the most exciting destinations in the country. Whether you're a history buff, an outdoor lover, or a bit of both, you'll find lots to enjoy among the stunning rock formations, verdant forests and cultural scene of a locale once voted the "Most Beautiful Place in America."

Sedona Chapel of the Holy Cross

One of the most unique sites in the red rocks is the iconic Chapel of the Holy Cross, a Roman Catholic chapel built directly into the buttes that surround it. Featuring a 90-foot iron cross and a steel and concrete frame, the landmark is an unmistakable part of Sedona's landscape and one of the city's most visited sites by people of all faiths. Designed by sculptor Marguerite Brunswig Staude, a student of Frank Lloyd Wright, and constructed in 1956, the religious site boasts expansive desert views, but most visitors say the incredible calm they feel touring the wonder is the reason they return.

Local Wineries in Verde Valley

A day trip on the Verde Valley Wine Trail is the perfect way to see how local vintners are putting Arizona on the wine-making map.

Featuring over 20 wineries and tasting rooms in nearby towns like Jerome, Cottonwood and Page Springs, you can try everything from award-winning blends to sustainably grown local varietals while taking in a diverse array of northern Arizona landscapes. Adventurous wine lovers can even pair an outing with a trip on the endlessly scenic Verde River. Tours include kayaking your way through easy-going rapids while enjoying the sight of bald eagles and other local wildlife, before ending your day with a quick hike to a riverside winery for a tasting led by professional sommeliers.

Sedona Rock Formations, Hiking and Biking Opportunities

Surrounded by a national forest, four wilderness areas and two state parks, Sedona is a veritable paradise for outdoor adventurers. There are endless opportunities for paddling, hiking, biking and climbing, but most visitors come simply for a glimpse of the famed red rocks. These otherworldly sandstone formations glow a brilliant red and orange in the dawn and dusk light. There are hundreds of trails that offer stunning views of the singular landscape, but the 1.2-mile Doe Mountain Trail and the steep, one-mile hike to the top of Cathedral Rock are among the most popular. Mountain bikers should head to the Long Canyon Trail or Mescal Trail for beginner and intermediate routes, respectively.

Montezuma's Castle

When it comes to wondrous structures, Montezuma's Castle National Monument in nearby Camp Verde is one of the most spectacularly preserved cave dwellings in the world. The five-story, apartment-like structure consists of more than 40 rooms carved out of an almost sheer cliff face. The amazing will and determination of the Sinagua people, who made a home for themselves in the unforgiving desert, is something to behold. In fact, Teddy Roosevelt was so struck by the site that in 1906 he declared it one of the nation's first National Monuments. These days, you can join a formal park ranger program to learn more details about the structure and the people who built it, or simply enjoy the scenic and history as you picnic in a sycamore grove at the cliff's base.

The Yuma Territorial Prison was named "Best Haunted Destination" by USA Today. It's easy to see why.

Yuma

Sitting on the banks of the Colorado River, Yuma entices travelers seeking recreation on the current and adventure in rugged landscapes. Surrounding the city, lush, green fields stretch out to the city limits. Yuma has managed to make the most of its location, providing cooling activities in and out of the water, and bundling historic destinations with newfound experiences. From working the blackjack table to dropping a line in a favorite fishing hole, the Gateway of the Great Southwest is a good bet on a great getaway.

Imprisoned History

One of the city's top attractions is a grim reminder of the fate of outlaws during the 1800s. Built in 1875, the Yuma Territorial Prison housed inmates for over 30 years, but today the abandoned cell blocks constitute one of the most popular state parks in Arizona. Equally compelling is the Arizona Historical Society Sanguinetti House Museum & Garden, which showcases the residence of E.F. Sanguinetti, a luminary from the early 1900s who was nicknamed the "Merchant Prince of Yuma." Another popular destination is the Saint Thomas Yuma Indian Mission just across the state line in Winterhaven, California.

Yuma Knows How to Party

Yuma packs its event calendar with exciting festivals and riveting historical events. January brings Civil War Days to the desert with battle reenactments on the grounds of the Colorado River State Historic Park. Occurring mid-November, the Colorado River Crossing Balloon Festival will take visitors up, up and away with daily liftoffs. Yuma certainly rises to the occasion with tethered rides, entertainment and a balloon glow at Desert Sun Stadium.

Getting Tubular

For many visitors, floating down the current on an inner tube scratches the itch for fun. Visitors can hit the water via boating or paddling canoes and kayaks on the slow current. Several outfitters in town provide the watercraft of your choice. You can also take a speed boat tour of the waterway. If swimming is more desirable, head to Centennial Beach or go fishing upstream along the river.

Taking Wing

Military and civilian aircraft that helped make aviation history are on display during the Yuma Air Show. Usually held in March, the desert skies fill with plane demonstrations, while back on solid ground, attendees will find modern airplanes, helicopters and jet displays, along with entertainment. See the Marine Corps Mounted Color Guard and see the Fireworks Finale.

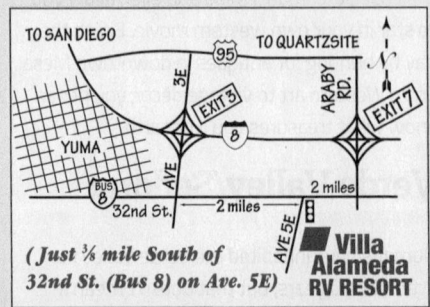

Agriculture Hotspot

The region's warm climate and proximity to the river make it ideal for agriculture. Yuma County is a thriving farming community that produces over $3 billion a year in winter vegetables and other agricultural products. In fact, a third of Arizona's agricultural produce comes from the Yuma County area, making it a prime winter snowbird spot for Field to Feast farm tours with gourmet farm-to-table lunches, farmer's wife dinners, progressive dinners and other special events.

Snowbirds Soar Here

Yuma has shed its roustabout past and now welcomes RVing snowbirds with open arms. With warm winters (and even warmer summers), the region has become a haven for snowbirds looking for balmy winter retreats. The town's population easily doubles in size, as it offers a warm welcome to more than 85,000 temporary residents. Snowbirds come from as far as Canada to enjoy Colorado River views and the warm desert sun.

Views From Above

The surrounding landscape of Yuma is a vibrant mixture of desert terrain, riparian habitat and rugged mountains. Castle Dome Peak is a distinctive, blocky summit with hidden gullies and solid rock footing that allow experienced hikers a reasonably safe trek up to the top. If you'd prefer not to make the hike, you can enjoy spectacular views of the summit from afar. Bighorn sheep make their home among the peaks and valleys of the Castle Dome Mountains. For a moderate hike, head out to Telegraph Pass Trail, a 2.2-mile round-trip trail east of the city with scenic views.

Wild in Yuma

Yuma's diverse species invite licensed sportsmen to bag big game such as bighorn sheep and mule deer, as well as dove, quail and waterfowl. Cast a line at Fortuna Pond for largemouth bass, channel catfish, bluegill, mullet and carp—seasonally, the pond is also stocked with rainbow trout. Away from waterlogged recreation, Yuma's untamed terrain beckons daredevils. Imperial Sand Dunes National Recreation Area is open to riders of all-terrain vehicles, campers and hikers. The stark backdrop has served as a setting for "Star Wars," "Jarhead" and "The Scorpion King."

The Rush to Riches

Mining success in the 1860s led to the birth of the town of Castle Dome Landing, about one hour north of Yuma along the Colorado River. During its heyday, the population of Castle Dome exceeded the population of Yuma, but when the mines ran dry, the town was abandoned. Today, the ghost town stands as the Castle Dome Mines Museum, and visitors can tour buildings dating back to the 1800s, including a stamp mill, five saloons, a stone cabin and dozens of preserved artifacts from the town's heyday. Fortuna Mine was another quick boom-and-bust town near Yuma that today is marked by an interpretive trail.

▸ FOR MORE INFORMATION

Arizona Office of Tourism, 866-275-5816, www.visitarizona.com

Benson Visitor Center, 520-586-4293, www.bensonvisitorcenter.com

Grand Canyon National Park, 928-638-7888, www.nps.gov/grca

Visit Mesa, 800-283-6372, www.visitmesa.com

Greater Phoenix Convention and Visitors Bureau (Valley of the Sun), 877-225-5749, www.visitphoenix.com

Sedona Verde Valley Tourism Council, 877-847-4829, www.sedona-verdevalley.com

Visit Yuma, 800-293-0071, www.visityuma.com

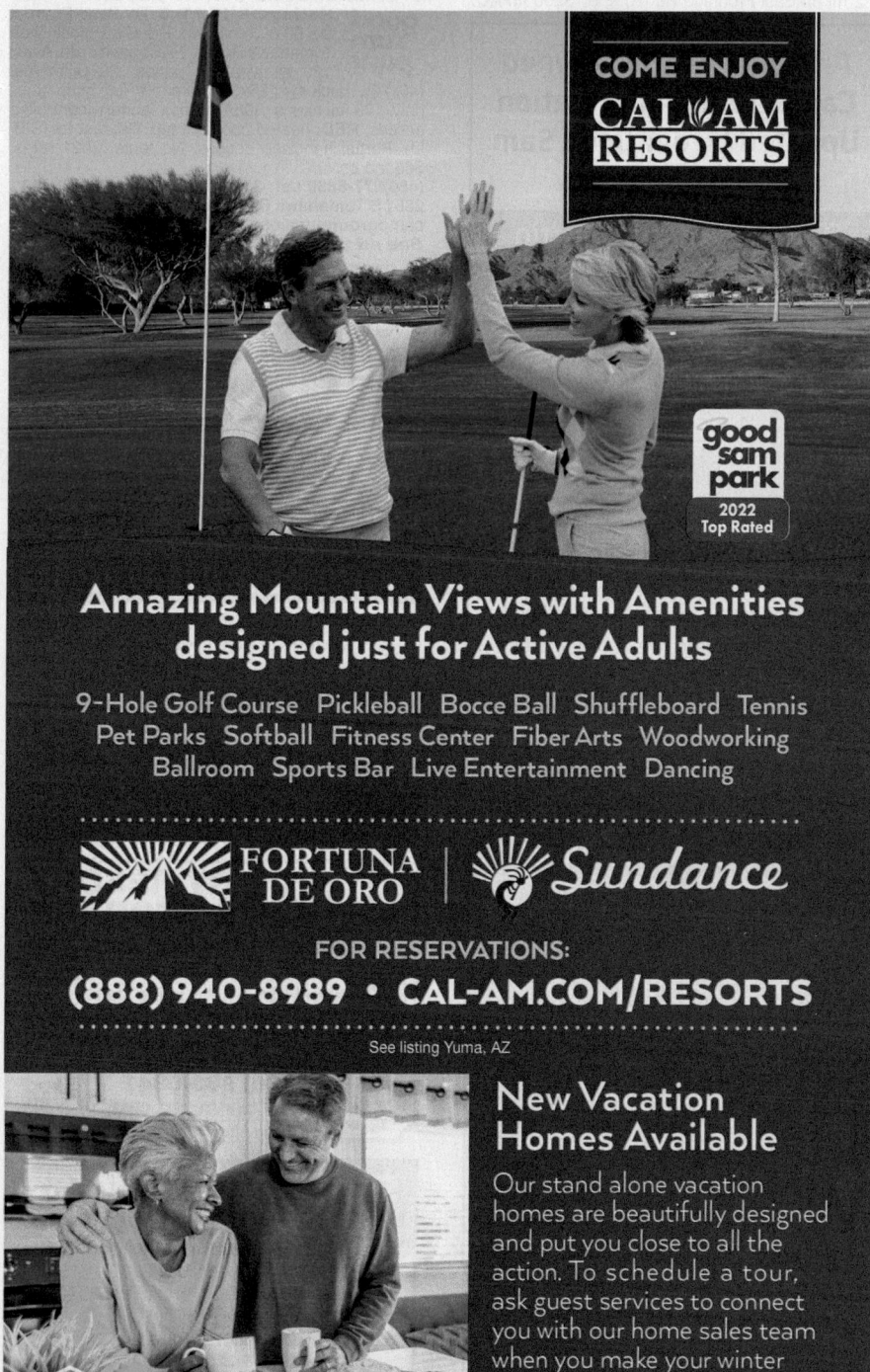

Arizona

AJO — E2 *Pima*

AJO HEIGHTS RV PARK **Ratings: 8.5/9★/9.5** (RV Park) Avail: 40 full hkups (30/50 amps). 2021 rates: $38. Oct 01 to May 01. (520)387-6796, 2000 N Ajo Gila Bend Hwy, Ajo, AZ 85321

SHADOW RIDGE RV RESORT **Ratings: 8/9★/8.5** (RV Park) Avail: 105 full hkups (30/50 amps). 2021 rates: $41.70. (520)387-5055, 431 N 2nd Ave (Hwy 85), Ajo, AZ 85321

AMADO — E4 *Santa Cruz*

DE ANZA RV RESORT
good sam park
Ratings: 10/10★/10 (RV Park) S-bnd: From Jct of I-19 & Arivaca Rd (Exit 48), S 1.5 mi on East Frontage Rd (L); N-bnd: From Jct of I-19 & Agualinda Rd (Exit 42), N 2 mi on East Frontage Rd (R). Elev 3200 ft.**FAC:**

Arizona Privately Owned Campground Information Updated by our Good Sam Representatives

Tony & Nanette Martin

In 2014, Tony and I decided to sell everything we owned, buy a motorhome and hit the road for a year with our two dogs. That year turned into five, traveling from Mexico to Alaska as well as Canada. Along the way we ran into a couple of Good Sam rep teams, and we thought, "what a perfect job." And so it all began; we have been lucky enough to live the lifestyle we love.

Randy & Debbie Block

We come from different places: Randy is from Missouri Valley, Iowa, home of the World Championship Goose Calling contest; Debbie is from Greenwood, South Carolina, home to the World's Widest Main Street. We met in St Louis and married within one month in 1978. Now we are living the greatest lifestyle ever invented.

paved rds. (130 spaces). Avail: 90 all weather, patios, 16 pull-thrus, (30x70), back-ins (35x55), accepts full hkup units only, 90 full hkups (30/50 amps), seasonal sites, WiFi @ sites, rentals, laundry, restaurant, controlled access. **REC:** heated pool, hot tub. Pet restrict (Q) $. Partial handicap access. No tents. Big rig sites, eco-friendly. 2021 rates: $38 to $55. ATM.
(520)398-8628 Lat: 31.70562, Lon: -111.06379
2869 E Frontage Rd, Amado, AZ 85645
deanzarvresort.com
See ad page 69

APACHE JUNCTION — D3 *Maricopa*

A SPOTLIGHT Introducing Valley of the Sun's colorful attractions appearing at the front of this state section.

APACHE JUNCTION See also Fort McDowell, Gold Canyon, Mesa & Queen Valley.

BLUE STAR RV RESORT **Ratings: 9/10★/8** (RV Resort) Avail: 150 full hkups (30/50 amps). 2021 rates: $41 to $55. (480)984-5570, 11050 E Apache Trail, Apache Junction, AZ 85120

CAMPGROUND USA RV RESORT
good sam park
Ratings: 9/10★/9.5 (RV Park) From jct US 60 & Tomahawk Rd: Go 1 block N on Tomahawk Rd (R). **FAC:** paved rds. Avail: 129 all weather, patios, 20 pull-thrus, (40x70), back-ins (30x50), accepts full hkup units only, 129 full hkups (30/50 amps), laundry, controlled access. **REC:** heated pool, hot tub. Pet restrict (S/B/Q). Partial handicap access. No tents. 2021 rates: $65. no cc.
(480)877-8880 Lat: 33.389483, Lon: -111.528700
2851 S Tomahawk Rd, Apache Junction, AZ 85119
campgroundusa.org
See ad this page

CAREFREE MANOR RV RESORT **Ratings: 8.5/10★/9** (RV Park) Avail: 44 full hkups (30/50 amps). 2021 rates: $40. (480)982-4008, 1615 N Delaware Dr, Space 57, Apache Junction, AZ 85120

COUNTRYSIDE RV RESORT
good sam park
Ratings: 8.5/9.5★/8 (Membership Park) Avail: 270 full hkups (30/50 amps). 2021 rates: $49. (888)563-7040, 2701 S Idaho Rd, Apache Junction, AZ 85119

GOLDEN SUN RV RESORT
good sam park
Ratings: 9/9.5★/9.5 (RV Park) Avail: 135 full hkups (30/50 amps). 2021 rates: $49. (888)563-7040, 999 W Broadway Ave, Apache Junction, AZ 85120

LOST DUTCHMAN
(Public State Park) From Jct of US 60 & S Idaho Rd (AZ-88), N 1.9 mi on S Idaho to N Apache Trail, NE 5 mi (R). **FAC:** paved rds. Avail: 138 paved, 42 pull-thrus, (25x80), back-ins (25x50), 68 W, 68 E (30/50 amps), tent sites, dump, fire rings. **REC:** rec open to public. Pets OK. Partial handicap access, 14 day max stay. 2021 rates: $20 to $35, Military discount.
(480)982-4485 Lat: 33.460735, Lon: -111.486156
6109 N Apache Trail, Apache Junction, AZ 85119
azstateparks.com

MERIDIAN RV RESORT
good sam park
Ratings: 9.5/9.5★/9.5 (RV Resort) Avail: 154 full hkups (30/50 amps). 2021 rates: $50. (888)563-7040, 1901 S Meridian, Apache Junction, AZ 85120

MESA APACHE JUNCTION KOA **Ratings: 9/9.5★/9.5** (Campground) 107 Avail: 94 full hkups, 13 W, 13 E (30/50 amps). 2021 rates: $45 to $65. (480)982-4015, 1540 S Tomahawk Rd, Apache Junction, AZ 85119

SIERRA DEL SAGUARO/MHP **Ratings: 8/7/8** (RV Park) Avail: 20 full hkups (30/50 amps). 2021 rates: $48. (480)982-2444, 1855 W Southern, Apache Junction, AZ 85120

SUNDANCE WEST RV RESORT
good sam park
Ratings: 10/10★/10 (RV Park) From Jct of Hwy 60 & Tomahawk Rd (exit 197), N 1 mi on Tomahawk Rd to Old West Highway, E 0.6 mi to Cortez Rd, S 0.1 mi (R). **FAC:** paved rds. (176 spaces). Avail: 100 all weather, patios, 16 pull-thrus, (30x60), back-ins (30x45), 100 full hkups (30/50 amps), seasonal sites, WiFi @ sites, laundry. **REC:** heated pool, hot tub. Pet restrict (S/B/Q). No tents, Age restrict may apply. 2021 rates: $65.
(480)982-5856 Lat: 33.39697, Lon: -111.52046
2024 S Cortez Rd, Apache Junction, AZ 85119
sundancewestrv.com
See ad this page

SUNRISE RV RESORT
good sam park
Ratings: 10/10★/10 (RV Resort) Avail: 138 full hkups (30/50 amps). 2021 rates: $50 to $55. (480)983-2500, 1403 W Broadway Ave, Apache Junction, AZ 85120

SUPERSTITION SUNRISE RV RESORT
good sam park
Ratings: 10/10★/10 (RV Resort) Avail: 250 full hkups (30/50 amps). 2021 rates: $50. (800)624-7027, 702 S Meridian Rd, Apache Junction, AZ 85120

VIP RV RESORT & STORAGE
good sam park
Ratings: 9/10★/9.5 (RV Park) From Jct of US Hwy 60 & Ironwood Dr (Exit 195), N 1.8 mi on Ironwood Dr (R). **FAC:** paved rds. (128 spaces). Avail: 41 all weather, patios, back-ins (30x45), 41 full hkups (30/50 amps), seasonal sites, WiFi @ sites, rentals, laundry. **REC:** hot tub, shuffleboard. Pet restrict (S/B/Q). Partial handicap access. No tents, Age restrict may apply, eco-friendly. 2021 rates: $45.
(480)983-0847 Lat: 33.41203, Lon: -111.56219
401 S Ironwood Drive, Apache Junction, AZ 85120
www.viprvresort.com
See ad this page

WEAVER'S NEEDLE RV RESORT
good sam park
Ratings: 10/10★/10 (RV Park) From Jct of US Hwy 60 & Tomahawk Rd (exit 197), N 1.7 mi on Tomahawk Rd (L).

A FUN RESORT IN VALLEY OF THE SUN
Park yourself with us and enjoy all the amenities. Swim in our heated pools-6 hole golf course, ceramics, crafts, lapidary, wood shop and hiking club. Fun people enjoying other fun people. Make your reservation now!

FAC: paved rds. (400 spaces). Avail: 200 all weather, patios, back-ins (30x40), 200 full hkups (30/50 amps), seasonal sites, WiFi @ sites, laundry. **REC:** heated pool, hot tub, shuffleboard. Pet restrict (B/Q). Partial handicap access. No tents, Age restrict may apply, eco-friendly. 2021 rates: $48.
(480)982-3683 Lat: 33.41214, Lon: -111.52808
250 S Tomahawk Rd, Apache Junction, AZ 85119
www.weaversneedle.com
See ad page 60

ASH FORK — B3 *Yavapai*

INTERSTATE 40 GRAND CANYON RV PARK
good sam park
Ratings: 8/7.5/7 (RV Park) From Jct of I-40 & Exit 144, N 0.5 mi on Old Rt 66 to 8th St, E 0.2 Mi on 8th St. (L). Elev 5100 ft.**FAC:** gravel rds. Avail: 39 gravel, patios, 25 pull-thrus, (30x50), back-ins (20x40), 31 full hkups, 8 W,

8 E (30/50 amps), WiFi @ sites, tent sites, rentals, shower$, dump, laundry, LP gas, fire rings, firewood. **REC:** pool, hunting nearby. Pets OK. eco-friendly. 2021 rates: $47.86 to $58.49, Military discount.
(928)637-9897 Lat: 35.22211, Lon: -112.49184
783 S Old Route 66, Ash Fork, AZ 86320
See ad this page

AVONDALE — D3 *Maricopa*

Travel Services

➡ **CAMPING WORLD OF AVONDALE** As the nation's largest retailer of RV supplies, accessories, services and new and used RVs, Camping World is committed to making your total RV experience better. **SERVICES:** tire, RV appliance, MH mechanical, staffed RV wash, restrooms. RV Sales. RV supplies, emergency parking, RV accessible. Hours: 9am to 7pm.
(888)457-4931 Lat: 33.45988, Lon: -112.28304
10255 W. Papago Freeway, Avondale, AZ 85323
www.campingworld.com

BEAVER DAM — A1 *Mohave*

BEAVER DAM LODGE RV RESORT
good sam park
Ratings: 7.5/9.5★/8.5 (RV Park) From jct I-15 & Hwy 91: Go 2 mi E on Hwy 91 (L). **FAC:** all weather rds. Avail: 35 all weather, 10 pull-thrus, (36x60), back-ins (36x50), 35 full hkups (30/50 amps), WiFi @ sites, rentals, dump, fire rings, restaurant. **REC:** golf, hunting nearby. Pet restrict (Q). No tents. Big rig sites. 2021 rates: $35 to $40.
(928)347-2222 Lat: 36.898892, Lon: -113.933049
452 Old Highway 91 North, Beaver Dam, AZ 86432
www.historicalbeaverdamlodge.com
See ad page 589

BENSON — E4 *Cochise*

A SPOTLIGHT Introducing Benson's colorful attractions appearing at the front of this state section.

BENSON I-10 RV PARK **Ratings: 6.5/9★/6** (RV Park) Avail: 88 full hkups (30/50 amps). 2021 rates: $50. (520)586-4252, 840 N Ocotilllo Rd , Benson, AZ 85602

BENSON KOA Ratings: 7.5/9★/7.5 (Campground) 97 Avail: 81 full hkups, 16 W, 16 E (30/50 amps). 2021 rates: $45. (520)586-3977, 180 W Four Feathers, Benson, AZ 85602

BUTTERFIELD RV RESORT & OBSERVATORY
good sam park
Ratings: 10/10★/9.5 (RV Park) From Jct of I-10 & Ocotillo Ave (exit 304), go S 0.6 mi on Ocotillo Ave/past Safeway shopping center to 3rd entrance on (L). Elev 3580 ft.**FAC:** paved rds. (173 spaces). 163 Avail: 27 paved, 136 all weather, 24 pull-thrus, (30x55), back-ins (30x50), 163 full hkups (30/50 amps), seasonal sites, WiFi @ sites, rentals, laundry, LP gas. **REC:** heated pool, hot tub. Pet restrict (B). Partial handicap access. No tents, eco-friendly. 2021 rates: $45, Military discount.
(520)586-4400 Lat: 31.96720, Lon: -110.30677
251 S Ocotillo Ave , Benson, AZ 85602
www.rv-resort.com
See ad page 53

CT RV RESORT
good sam park
Ratings: 10/10★/9.5 (RV Park) From Jct of I-10 & Hwy 90 (exit 302), S 0.9 mi on Hwy 90 (R).

HIGH DESERT BEAUTY AWAITS
Enjoy spectacular views and luxury living at your premier RV resort in Southern AZ. Visit area wineries, Kartchner Caverns, Tucson, Bisbee, go hiking or enjoy the many amenities here where your comfort is our goal

FAC: paved rds. (302 spaces). 70 Avail: 14 paved, 56 all weather, 14 pull-thrus, (25x60), back-ins (40x50), 70 full hkups (30/50 amps), seasonal sites, cable, WiFi @ sites, laundry, LP gas. **REC:** pool, hot tub. Pet restrict (S/B/Q). Partial handicap access. No tents. Big rig sites, eco-friendly. 2021 rates: $42 to $49, Military discount.
(520)720-0911 Lat: 31.95256, Lon: -110.34481
1030 S Barrel Cactus Ridge , Benson, AZ 85602
www.ctrvresort.com
See ad this page

KARTCHNER CAVERNS (Public State Park) From Jct of I-10 & Hwy 90 (exit 302) S 9 mi on Hwy 90 (R). 62 Avail: 62 W, 62 E (30/50 amps). 2021 rates: $30. (520)586-2283

PATO BLANCO LAKES RV RESORT
good sam park
Ratings: 9.5/9.5★/9 (RV Park) From Jct of I-10 & Pomerene Rd (Exit 306) S 0.1 mi on Pomerene Rd to 4th St, W 0.7 mi to County Rd, N 0.3 mi to Pearl St, W 500 ft (R). Elev 3580 ft.**FAC:** all weather rds. Avail: 105 all weather, patios, 10 pull-thrus, (35x80), back-ins (35x55), 105 full hkups (30/50 amps), cable, WiFi @ sites, rentals, dump, laundry, LP gas, controlled access. **REC:** heated pool, hot tub, pond, fishing. Pets OK. Partial handicap access. No tents, Age restrict may apply. Big rig sites, eco-friendly. 2021 rates: $59.54, Military discount.
(520)586-8966 Lat: 31.97142, Lon: -110.28841
635 E Pearl St, Benson, AZ 85602
www.patoblancolakes.com
See ad this page

RED BARN CAMPGROUND **Ratings: 2.5/7/5** (Campground) Avail: 10 full hkups (30/50 amps). 2021 rates: $49. (520)586-2035, 711 N Madison, Benson, AZ 85602

SAN PEDRO RESORT COMMUNITY
good sam park
Ratings: 10/8.5★/9.5 (RV Park) From Jct of I-10 & Ocotillo St (exit 304), S 0.5 mi on Ocotillo St to Bus 10, E 0.9 mi to SR-80, S 1.3 mi (R). Elev 3600 ft.**FAC:** paved rds. (270 spaces). Avail: 50 all weather, patios, 27 pull-thrus, (30x55), back-ins (30x40), accepts full hkup units only, 50 full hkups (30/50 amps), seasonal sites, cable, WiFi @ sites, $, laundry. **REC:** heated pool, hot tub. Pet restrict (B/Q). No tents, Age restrict may apply, eco-friendly. 2021 rates: $42.
(520)586-9546 Lat: 31.94832, Lon: -110.28600
1110 South Hwy 80 , Benson, AZ 85602
www.sanpedrorvresortaz.com
See ad this page

VALLEY VISTA RV RESORT
good sam park
Ratings: 8/9★/8 (Membership Park) Avail: 123 full hkups (30/50 amps). 2021 rates: $43.50. (888)563-7040, 1060 South Hwy 80, Benson, AZ 85602

Things to See and Do

BUTTERFIELD OBSERVATORY University grade Observatory open year-round. Free nightly showings of the heavens and beyond. Elev 3600 ft. RV accessible. Restrooms. Hours: . No CC.
(800)863-8160 Lat: 31.96732, Lon: -110.30699
251 S Ocotillo Ave, Benson, AZ 85602
See ad page 53

BISBEE — E5 *Cochise*

BISBEE RV PARK AT TURQUOISE VALLEY **Ratings: 5/8/8** (RV Park) Avail: 85 full hkups (30/50 amps). 2021 rates: $25. (520)505-1642, 1791 W Newell St , Naco, AZ 85620

➡ DESERT OASIS CAMPGROUND **Ratings: 7.5/8.5★/9** (Campground) Avail: 20 full hkups (50 amps). 2021 rates: $30 to $40. (520)979-6650, 5311 W Double Adobe Rd, McNeal, AZ 85617

BLACK CANYON CITY — C3 *Yavapai*

BLACK CANYON CAMPGROUND **Ratings: 8.5/8.5★/7.5** (Campground) Avail: 23 full hkups (30/50 amps). 2021 rates: $40 to $50. (844)562-5314, 19600 E St Joseph Rd, Black Canyon City, AZ 85324

BLACK CANYON RANCH RV RESORT
good sam park
Ratings: 10/10★/10 (RV Park) N-bnd: From Jct of I-17 & Exit 242 (W over Fwy to Old Black Canyon Hwy), N 1.3 mi (L); or S-bnd: From Jct of I-17 & Exit 244, S 1 mi on S Old Black Canyon Hwy (R). **FAC:** paved rds. (107 spaces). Avail: 43 all weather, patios, 11 pull-thrus, (30x50), back-ins (30x50), accepts full hkup units only, 43 full hkups (30/50 amps), seasonal sites, cable, WiFi @ sites, laundry, restaurant. **REC:** heated pool, hot tub. Pet restrict (Q). No tents, eco-friendly. 2021 rates: $60 to $75, Military discount.
(623)374-9800 Lat: 34.07164, Lon: -112.15262
33900 S Old Black Canyon Hwy, Black Canyon City, AZ 85324
www.blackcanyonranchrv.com
See ad this page

BOUSE — C1 *La Paz*

BOUSE RV PARK **Ratings: 7.5/8★/7** (RV Park) Avail: 38 full hkups (30/50 amps). 2021 rates: $30. (928)851-2508, 44255 Winters St, Bouse, AZ 85325

DESERT PUEBLO RV RESORT
good sam park
Ratings: 8.5/10★/10 (RV Park) Avail: 60 full hkups (30/50 amps). 2021 rates: $30. Oct 01 to Apr 15. (928)851-2206, 28726 Highway 72, Bouse, AZ 85325

LA MESA VERDE RV PARK **Ratings: 6.5/8.5★/7** (RV Park) 50 Avail: 45 full hkups, 5 W, 5 E (30/50 amps). 2021 rates: $15 to $30. Oct 01 to Apr 01. (928)851-2456, 43254 AZ 72, Bouse, AZ 85325

BRENDA — C1 *La Paz*

3 DREAMERS RV PARK
Ratings: 7/8★/8 (RV Park) Avail: 25 full hkups (30/50 amps). 2021 rates: $32. (928)859-4145, 54000 Hwy 60, Salome, AZ 85348

BLACK ROCK RV VILLAGE
Ratings: 9/10★/10 (RV Park) From Jct of I-10 & Hwy 60 (exit 31), NE 4 mi on Hwy 60 (L). **FAC:** gravel rds. (408 spaces). Avail: 178 all weather, 26 pull-thrus, (30x100), back-ins (40x55), 178 full hkups (30/50 amps), seasonal sites, WiFi, rentals, laundry, LP gas, firewood, restaurant. **REC:** heated pool, hot tub, shuffleboard. Pet restrict (B/Q). No tents. Big rig sites, eco-friendly. 2021 rates: $37 to $44. ATM.
(928)927-4206 Lat: 33.68009, Lon: -113.94547
46751 E Hwy 60, Salome, AZ 85348
www.blackrockrv.com
See ad this page

BRENDA RV RESORT **Ratings: 8.5/9★/8** (RV Park) Avail: 20 full hkups (30/50 amps). 2021 rates: $27 to $32. (877)927-5249, 46251 E Hwy 60, Salome, AZ 85348

DESERT GOLD RV RESORT
Ratings: 10/9★/10 (RV Park) From Jct of I-10 & Hwy 60 E (exit 31), NE 4 mi on Hwy 60 E (R); or W-bnd: From Jct of I-10 & Exit 45 (Vicksburg Rd), N 7 mi on Vicksburg Rd to Hwy 60, SW 10 mi (L). **FAC:** paved rds. (550 spaces). Avail: 125 all weather, patios, 25 pull-thrus, (30x70), back-ins (35x50), 125 full hkups (30/50 amps), seasonal sites, WiFi @ sites, rentals, laundry, LP gas. **REC:** heated pool, hot tub, hunting nearby. Pet restrict (B/Q). Partial handicap access. No tents. Big rig sites, eco-friendly. 2021 rates: $39 to $45, Military discount.
(800)927-2101 Lat: 33.67869, Lon: -113.94677
46628 E Hwy 60, Salome, AZ 85348
www.g7rvresorts.com
See ad page 74

GATEWAY RANCH RV RESORT **Ratings: 6.5/7.5/7** (RV Park) Avail: 60 full hkups (30/50 amps). 2021 rates: $25. (928)927-7770, 44660 S Ave 42 E, Salome, AZ 85348

WAGON WEST RV PARK
Ratings: 6/8.5★/7 (RV Park) From jct of I-10 & Hwy 60 (exit 31): Go 8 mi NE on Hwy 60/MP 39 (R). **FAC:** gravel rds. (215 spaces). Avail: 30 gravel, 11 pull-thrus, (25x45), back-ins (30x50), 30 full hkups (30/50 amps), seasonal sites, WiFi, shower$, laundry, LP gas. **REC:** golf, shuffleboard. Pet restrict (B/Q). No tents, Age restrict may apply, eco-friendly. 2021 rates: $35 to $39. Oct 15 to Apr 15.
(928)927-7077 Lat: 33.69361, Lon: -113.88491
50126 E Hwy 60, Salome, AZ 85348
wagonwestrvpark.com
See ad this page

BUCKEYE — D2 *Maricopa*

LEAF VERDE RV RESORT **Ratings: 9.5/10★/9** (RV Resort) Avail: 100 full hkups (30/50 amps). 2021 rates: $39 to $49. (623)386-3132, 1500 S Apache Rd, Buckeye, AZ 85326

BULLHEAD CITY — B1 *Mohave*

COLORADO RIVER OASIS RESORT
Ratings: 10/10★/9.5 (RV Park) From Jct of Hwy 95 & Bullhead City Pkwy (Laughlin Bridge), S 3.4 mi on Hwy 95 (R). **FAC:** all weather rds. Avail: 27 all weather, patios, back-ins (30x45), 27 full hkups (30/50 amps), cable, WiFi @ sites, rentals, dump, laundry. **REC:** pool, hot tub, Colorado River: swim, fishing, boating nearby. Pet restrict (B/Q). No tents, eco-friendly. 2021 rates: $40 to $60, Military discount.
(928)763-4385 Lat: 35.12665, Lon: -114.57882
1641 Highway 95, Bullhead City, AZ 86442
coloradoriveroasis.com
See ad this page

DAVIS CAMP (MOHAVE COUNTY PARK) (Public) From jct Bullhead Pkwy (Casino Bridge) & Hwy 68: Go 1/2 mi N on Hwy 68 to milepost 250. 185 Avail: 155 full hkups, 30 W, 30 E (50 amps). 2021 rates: $20 to $35. (877)757-0915

FIESTA RV RESORT **Ratings: 9/8.5/8.5** (RV Resort) Avail: 112 full hkups (30/50 amps). 2021 rates: $25 to $30. (800)982-1750, 3190 Hwy 95, Bullhead City, AZ 86442

LAKE MEAD NRA/KATHERINE LANDING CAMPGROUND (Public National Park) From Jct of SR-95 & SR-68, N 1 mi on SR-68 to Katherine Rd, W 3.1 mi (E). Avail: 173 full hkups. 2021 rates: $20. (928)754-3245

RIVER CITY RV PARK **Ratings: 8.5/9/8.5** (RV Park) Avail: 35 full hkups (30/50 amps). 2021 rates: $36 to $40. (928)754-2121, 2225 Merrill Ave, Bullhead City, AZ 86442

RIVERSIDE ADVENTURE TRAILS **Ratings: 7.5/6.5/5.5** (Membership Park) Avail: 314 full hkups (30/50 amps). 2021 rates: $25. (928)763-8800, 4750 Hwy 95, Bullhead City, AZ 86426

SILVER CREEK RV PARK **Ratings: 9/9.5★/7.5** (RV Park) Avail: 30 full hkups (30/50 amps). 2021 rates: $27. (928)763-2444, 1515 Gold Rush Rd, Bullhead City, AZ 86442

SILVER VIEW RV RESORT **Ratings: 10/9.5★/10** (RV Resort) Avail: 267 full hkups (30/50 amps). 2021 rates: $40 to $55. (928)763-5500, 1501 Gold Rush Rd, Bullhead City, AZ 86442

VISTA DEL SOL RV RESORT
Ratings: 10/10★/10 (RV Resort) Avail: 89 full hkups (30/50 amps). 2021 rates: $33 to $47. (928)754-0182, 3249 Felipe Dr, Bullhead City, AZ 86442

CAMP VERDE — C3 *Yavapai*

A SPOTLIGHT Introducing Verde Valley/Sedona's colorful attractions appearing at the front of this state section.

DISTANT DRUMS RV RESORT **Ratings: 10/10★/10** (RV Resort) Avail: 157 full hkups (30/50 amps). 2021 rates: $38 to $46. (928)554-8000, 583 W Middle Verde Rd, Camp Verde, AZ 86322

KRAZY K RV PARK **Ratings: 7/8.5/7.5** (RV Park) Avail: 10 full hkups (30/50 amps). 2021 rates: $30 to $60. (928)567-0565, 2075 N Arena del Loma, Camp Verde, AZ 86322

RANCHO VERDE RV PARK **Ratings: 7.5/9★/9.5** (RV Park) Avail: 10 full hkups (30/50 amps). 2021 rates: $42 to $49. (928)567-7037, 1488 W Horseshoe Bend Dr, Camp Verde, AZ 86322

VERDE RANCH RV RESORT
Ratings: 10/10★/10 (RV Resort) Avail: 302 full hkups (30/50 amps). 2021 rates: $36 to $81. (928)567-7126, 1105 N Dreamcatcher Dr, Camp Verde, AZ 86322

VERDE RIVER RV RESORT & COTTAGES
Ratings: 9/10★/9.5 (RV Resort) From Jct Hwy 260 & Horseshoe Bend Dr: Go 1 1/2 mi N on Horseshoe Bend Dr (R). Elev 3300 ft.

SEDONA/NORTHERN AZ LOCATION
Easy I-17 access, exit #287, 160 HUGE, level RV sites, 50+ cottages, 1400 ft Verde River front, pool, spa, fitness center, new private bath suites, free LD phone, WiFi and Cable TV. 3000 ft elev for year-round family fun.

FAC: paved/gravel rds. (160 spaces). Avail: 135 all weather, 17 pull-thrus, (30x110), back-ins (30x70), accepts full hkup units only, 135 full hkups (30/50 amps), seasonal sites, cable, WiFi @ sites, rentals, laundry, groc, controlled access. **REC:** heated pool, hot tub, Verde River: fishing, kayaking/canoeing, playground. Pets OK $. Partial handicap access. No tents. Big rig sites, eco-friendly. 2021 rates: $35 to $69, Military discount.
(928)202-3409 Lat: 34.59953, Lon: -111.88461
1472 W Horseshoe Bend Dr, Camp Verde, AZ 86322
verderiverrvresort.com
See ad page 62

ZANE GREY RV VILLAGE
Ratings: 8/9★/9.5 (RV Park) Avail: 63 full hkups (30/50 amps). 2021 rates: $42 to $44. (928)567-4320, 4500 E State Route 260, Camp Verde, AZ 86322

CASA GRANDE — D3 *Pinal*

A SPOTLIGHT Introducing Valley of the Sun's colorful attractions appearing at the front of this state section.

CASA GRANDE See also Coolidge, Eloy & Picacho.

CASA GRANDE RV RESORT & COTTAGES
Ratings: 10/10★/9.5 (RV Park) From Jct of I-10 and Pinal Rd (Exit 185) S 5 mi on Pinal Rd to Rodeo Rd, E 300ft (R).

BEST RV RESORT VALUE IN CENTRAL AZ
Easy I-10 access: AZ #185 Hwy 387/Pinal Rd. Excellent long term rates! Fitness center, 2 pools, 4 pickleball, 8 stunning pro billiard tables, free waffle breakfast M-F, dinners 3/nts week, free WiFi, Great Group facilities.

FAC: paved rds. (340 spaces). Avail: 15 all weather, patios, 15 pull-thrus, (20x60), accepts full hkup units only, 15 full hkups (30/50 amps), seasonal sites, WiFi @ sites, rentals, laundry. **REC:** heated pool, hot tub, shuffleboard, playground. Pets OK. No tents, Age restrict may apply. Big rig sites, eco-friendly. 2021 rates: $46 to $54, Military discount.
(520)421-0401 Lat: 32.92311, Lon: -111.7546
195 W Rodeo Rd, Casa Grande, AZ 85122
casagrandervresort.com
See ad page 61

CASITA VERDE RV RESORT
good sam park
Ratings: 9/9★/9 (RV Park) Avail: 90 full hkups (30/50 amps). 2021 rates: $49 to $56. (888)563-7040, 2200 N Trekell Rd, Casa Grande, AZ 85122

FIESTA GRANDE RV RESORT
good sam park
Ratings: 9/9★/10 (RV Park) Avail: 20 full hkups (30/50 amps). 2021 rates: $47 to $56. (888)563-7040, 1511 E Florence Blvd, Casa Grande, AZ 85122

FOOTHILLS WEST RV RESORT
good sam park
Ratings: 8.5/8.5★/9.5 (RV Park) Avail: 65 full hkups (30/50 amps). 2021 rates: $57.91. (888)563-7040, 10167 N Encore Dr, Casa Grande, AZ 85122

LEISURE VALLEY RV RESORT **Ratings: 8/8.5★/7.5** (RV Park) Avail: 13 full hkups (30/50 amps). 2021 rates: $45.02. (520)836-9449, 9985 N Pinal Ave, Casa Grande, AZ 85122

PALM CREEK GOLF & RV RESORT **Ratings: 10/10★/10** (RV Resort) Avail: 954 full hkups (30/50 amps). 2021 rates: $45 to $79. (800)421-7004, 1110 N Henness Rd, Casa Grande, AZ 85122

SUNDANCE 1 RV RESORT
good sam park
Ratings: 10/10★/10 (RV Resort) From Jct of I-10 & Pinal Ave (exit 185), S 7.3 mi on Pinal Ave to Cottonwood, W 1 mi to Thornton Rd, N 0.2 mi (L); or From Jct of I-8 & Thornton Rd (Exit 172), N 5 mi on Thornton Rd (L). **FAC:** paved rds. (707 spaces). Avail: 186 all weather, patios, 13 pull-thrus, (39x55), back-ins (40x50), accepts full hkup units only, 186 full hkups (30/50 amps), seasonal sites, cable, WiFi @ sites, $, rentals, laundry, controlled access. **REC:** heated pool, hot tub, shuffleboard. Pet restrict (B/Q). Partial handicap access. No tents, Age restrict may apply, eco-friendly. 2021 rates: $42 to $58.
(520)426-9662 Lat: 32.8977, Lon: -111.77521
1703 N Thornton Rd, Casa Grande, AZ 85122
sundance1rv.com
See ad this page

CAVE CREEK — C3 *Maricopa*

CAVE CREEK (MARICOPA COUNTY PARK) (Public) From jct I-17 (exit 223) & Carefree Hwy: Go 5 mi E on Carefree Hwy, then 1-1/2 mi N on 32nd St. 44 Avail: 44 W, 44 E (30/50 amps). 2021 rates: $15 to $40. (602)506-2930

CHINLE — A5 *Apache*

CANYON DE CHELLY/COTTONWOOD (Public National Park) From Jct of Hwy 191 & Rte 7 (in Chinle), E 2.5 mi on Rte 7 to visitor center, follow signs (E). 90 Avail. 2021 rates: $14. (928)674-2106

CLARKDALE — C3 *Yavapai*

RAIN SPIRIT RV RESORT
good sam park
Ratings: 10/10★/9.5 (RV Park) From jct Hwy 89A & S Main St: Go 3-1/2 mi NW on S Main/S Broadway St (R). Elev 3545 ft.**FAC:** paved rds. Avail: 63 all weather, patios, 5 pull-thrus, (30x62), back-ins (26x50), 63 full hkups (30/50 amps), WiFi @ sites, laundry. **REC:** pool, hot tub, Verde River: swim, fishing, kayaking/canoeing, hunting nearby. Pet restrict (S/B) $. No tents. Big rig sites, eco-friendly. 2021 rates: $46 to $52, Military discount.
(928)202-3230 Lat: 34.76376, Lon: -112.042298
551 S Broadway, Clarkdale, AZ 86324
rainspiritrvresort.com
See ad page 61

It's the law! Rules of the Road and Towing Laws are updated each year. Be sure to consult this chart to find the laws for every state on your traveling route.

CLIFTON — D5 *Greenlee*

NORTH CLIFTON RV PARK (Public) From Historic Railroad Station: Go 300 ft N on US 191, then turn E on Zorilla St, then go 100 ft to Frisco Ave, then 1/2 mi N on Frisco Ave. 59 Avail: 55 full hkups, 4 S, 4 E (30/50 amps). 2021 rates: $19. (928)865-9064

CONGRESS — C2 *Yavapai*

NORTH RANCH RV ESCAPEES **Ratings: 7/8/8.5** (Membership Park) Avail: 40 full hkups (30 amps). 2021 rates: $28.18. (928)427-3657, 30625 Hwy 89 MP 264, Congress, AZ 85332

COOLIDGE — D3 *Pinal*

HO HO KAM RV PARK
good sam park
Ratings: 10/8.5★/8.5 (RV Area in MH Park) From N Jct of Hwys 87 & 287, S 2.9 mi on Hwys 87/287 (L). **FAC:** paved rds. (202 spaces). Avail: 93 all weather, patios, back-ins (25x45), accepts full hkup units only, 93 full hkups (30/50 amps), seasonal sites, WiFi @ sites, laundry. **REC:** heated pool, hot tub, shuffleboard. Pet restrict (S/B/Q). Partial handicap access. No tents, Age restrict may apply, eco-friendly. 2021 rates: $35 to $40.
(520)723-3697 Lat: 32.96107, Lon: -111.52390
1925 S Arizona Blvd, Coolidge, AZ 85128
westcoastmobilehomeparks.com
See ad opposite page

CORDES LAKES — C3 *Yavapai*

CORDES JCT MOTEL, RV PARK, 50'S DINER & BACKSEAT BAR **Ratings: 7/8★/8** (RV Park) Avail: 17 full hkups (30/50 amps). 2021 rates: $44. (928)632-5186, 19780 E Hitching Post Way, Cordes Lakes, AZ 86333

CORNVILLE — C3 *Yavapai*

SUNRISE RESORTS AT PAGE SPRINGS **Ratings: 5/7/5.5** (Membership Park) 56 Avail: 24 full hkups, 32 W, 32 E (30 amps). 2021 rates: $42 to $54. (928)634-4309, 1951 N Page Springs Rd, Cornville, AZ 86325

COTTONWOOD — C3 *Yavapai*

DEAD HORSE RANCH (Public State Park) From Jct of US-89A & SR-260, NW 0.6 mi on US-89A to (Historic 89A) Main St, NW 1.4 mi to N 10th St, NE 0.8 mi (R). 106 Avail: 106 W, 106 E (30/50 amps). 2021 rates: $30 to $35. (928)634-5283

RIO VERDE RV PARK **Ratings: 7/8★/9** (RV Park) Avail: 63 full hkups (30/50 amps). 2021 rates: $55 to $75. (928)634-5990, 3420 E SR 89A, Cottonwood, AZ 86326

VERDE VALLEY RV & CAMPING RESORT
good sam park
Ratings: 7.5/8.5/8.5 (Membership Park) 371 Avail: 327 full hkups, 44 W, 44 E (30/50 amps). 2021 rates: $48 to $69. (888)563-7040, 6400 E Thousand Trails Rd, Cottonwood, AZ 86326

DATELAND — D2 *Yuma*

DATELAND PALMS VILLAGE **Ratings: 2.5/7/7** (RV Park) Avail: 46 full hkups (30/50 amps). 2021 rates: $20. (928)454-2772, 1737 S Ave 64 E, Dateland, AZ 85333

DEWEY — C3 *Yavapai*

ORCHARD RANCH RV RESORT **Ratings: 9.5/9★/10** (RV Park) Avail: 25 full hkups (30/50 amps). 2021 rates: $55. (928)772-8266, 11250 E State Rt 69, Dewey, AZ 86327

We give campgrounds one rating for development, a second for restrooms and a third for visual appearance and environmental quality. That's the Triple Rating System.

DUNCAN — D5 *Greenlee*

VALLEY VIEW RV PARK & MH COMMUNITY
good sam park
Ratings: 6/7/7.5 (RV Park) From jct US 191 & State Hwy 75 (N of Duncan and York from 3 Way): Go 2-1/4 mi S on Hwy 75 (R). **FAC:** paved rds. (145 spaces). Avail: 120 gravel, back-ins (40x65), accepts full hkup units only, 120 full hkups (30/50 amps), WiFi @ sites, laundry. Pet restrict (S/B/Q). No tents. Big rig sites. 2021 rates: $30. no cc.
(928)687-1541 Lat: 32.92401, Lon: -109.202359
441 Corral Rd, Duncan, AZ 85534
www.valleyviewaz.com
See ad this page

EHRENBERG — D1 *La Paz*

ARIZONA OASIS RV RESORT **Ratings: 8.5/9/9** (RV Park) Avail: 130 full hkups (30/50 amps). 2021 rates: $50 to $70. (928)923-8230, 50238 Ehrenberg/Parker Hwy, Ehrenberg, AZ 85334

OXBOW (BLM) (Public Corps) From town, S 3 mi on Hwy 78, E on gravel rd btwn mileposts 77 & 78, 0.75 mi to Colorado River (E). 75 Avail: Pit toilets. 2021 rates: $15. (928)317-3200

RIVERSANDS RV RESORT
good sam park
(RV Resort) (Not Visited) Avail: 375 full hkups (30/50 amps). 2021 rates: $50 to $109. (800)714-7249, 49960 Ehrenberg Rd, Ehrenberg, AZ 85334

EL MIRAGE — C3 *Maricopa*

PUEBLO EL MIRAGE RV & GOLF RESORT
good sam park
Ratings: 10/10★/10 (RV Resort) Avail: 475 full hkups (30/50 amps). 2021 rates: $54 to $84. (623)583-0464, 11201 N El Mirage Rd, El Mirage, AZ 85335

RV DRIVING TIPS: Adjust your vehicle's environment so that it helps you to stay alert. Keep the temperature cool, with open windows or air conditioning in the summer and minimal amounts of heat in the winter. Avoid listening to soft, sleep-inducing music and switch radio stations frequently.

ELOY — D3 *Pinal*

LAS COLINAS RV RESORT
good sam park **Ratings: 10/9★/10** (RV Park) From Jct of I-10 & Exit 200 (Sunland Gin Rd): Go N on Sunland Gin Rd for .5 mi to Redd Rd (First St), turn W on Redd Rd, go 300 ft (L). **FAC:** paved rds. (150 spaces). Avail: 100 all weather, patios, 6 pull-thrus, (32x70), back-ins (30x45), accepts full hkup units only, 100 full hkups (30/50 amps), seasonal sites, WiFi @ sites, laundry. **REC:** heated pool, hot tub, shuffleboard. Pet restrict (B/Q). Partial handicap access. No tents, Age restrict may apply. Big rig sites, eco-friendly. 2021 rates: $42, Military discount. no cc.
(520)836-5050 Lat: 32.81531, Lon: -111.67354
7136 Sunland Gin Rd , Eloy, AZ 85131
www.lascolinasrvresort.com
See ad this page

SILVERADO RV RESORT **Ratings: 9.5/9.5★/8.5** (RV Park) Avail: 300 full hkups (30/50 amps). 2021 rates: $40. (520)466-4500, 4555 W Tonto Rd , Eloy, AZ 85131

FLAGSTAFF — B3 *Coconino*

FLAGSTAFF See also Mormon Lake & Sedona.

BLACK BARTS RV PARK
good sam park **Ratings: 6.5/10★/7.5** (RV Park) From Jct of I-40 & exit 198 (Butler), go SE 0.25 mi on Butler (L). Elev 6838 ft.**FAC:** paved/gravel rds. (174 spaces). Avail: 94 gravel, patios, 42 pull-thrus, (25x50), back-ins (20x37), 94 full hkups (30/50 amps), seasonal sites, tent sites, laundry, restaurant. **REC:** rec open to public. Pets OK. 21 day max stay, eco-friendly. 2021 rates: $60, Military discount.
(928)774-1912 Lat: 35.19304, Lon: -111.61728
2760 E Butler, Flagstaff, AZ 86004
blackbartsrvpark.com
See ad this page

FLAGSTAFF KOA HOLIDAY **Ratings: 6.5/8/7.5** (Campground) 174 Avail: 45 full hkups, 129 W, 129 E (30/50 amps). 2021 rates: $39 to $83. (928)526-9926, 5803 N Hwy 89, Flagstaff, AZ 86004

FORT TUTHILL (COCONINO COUNTY PARK) (Public) From Jct of I-17 & Exit 337, W 200 yards, follow signs to park (E). 96 Avail: 8 W, 8 S. 2021 rates: $23 to $28. May 01 to Oct 01. (928)679-8000

GREER'S PINE SHADOWS RV PARK
good sam park **Ratings: 8/NA/8** (RV Park) From Jct of I-40 & Exit 201, NW 0.4 mi on Country Club Dr to US-89N, NE 1.7 mi on US-89N (L) Note: Follow signage to Page, AZ. Elev 6965 ft.**FAC:** paved/gravel rds. (76 spaces). Avail: 18 gravel, 13 pull-thrus, (20x70), back-ins (20x70), 18 full hkups (30/50 amps), seasonal sites, WiFi @ sites, laundry. **REC:** hunting nearby. Pet restrict (S/Q). No tents, eco-friendly. 2021 rates: $37 to $56, Military discount.
(928)526-4977 Lat: 35.24121, Lon: -111.56984
7101 N Hwy 89N, Flagstaff, AZ 86004
www.greerspineshadowsrvpark.com
See ad this page

J & H RV PARK
good sam park **Ratings: 9/10★/10** (RV Park) Avail: 51 full hkups (30/50 amps). 2021 rates: $65.49. May 01 to Oct 15. (928)526-1829, 7901 North US Highway 89, Flagstaff, AZ 86004

MILITARY PARK FORT TUTHILL RECREATION AREA (LUKE AFB) (Public) From Jct of I-17 & Flagstaff Airport Rd/Exit 337, W on Flagstaff Airport Rd thru intersection of US-89A & Fort Tuthill Rd, straight to rec area. 27 Avail: 27 W, 27 E (20/30 amps). 2021 rates: $19. May 01 to Oct 15. (928)774-8893

Things to See and Do

BLACK BARTS STEAKHOUSE Steakhouse, Saloon and Musical Revue featuring local entertainment. Elev 6838 ft. RV accessible. Restrooms. Food. Hours: 5pm to 9pm.
(928)779-3142 Lat: 35.19304, Lon: -111.61728
2760 E Butler Ave, Flagstaff, AZ 86004
blackbartssteakhouse.com
See ad this page

FORT DEFIANCE — B5 *Apache*

WHEATFIELDS LAKE (Public) From town, N 43 mi on Rte 12 (E) Navajo fishing & boat permits required. You will cross AZ/NE border several times. 25 Avail: Pit toilets. 2021 rates: $15 to $25. (928)871-6647

FORT MCDOWELL — D3 *Maricopa*

A SPOTLIGHT Introducing Valley of the Sun's colorful attractions appearing at the front of this state section.

FORT MCDOWELL See also Apache Junction, Gold Canyon, Mesa, Phoenix & Tempe.

EAGLE VIEW RV RESORT ASAH GWEH OOU-O AT FORT MCDOWELL
good sam park **Ratings: 10/10★/10** (RV Resort) From Jct of SR-87 (Beeline Hwy) & N Fort McDowell Rd, S 0.4 mi on N Fort McDowell Rd (E).

THE RESORT DESTINATION FOR ALL AGES
Serenity & solitude nestled along the Verde River with majestic mountain views, yet only minutes from We-Ko-Pa Golf Club, We-Ko-Pa Casino, art festivals and auto auctions. Enjoy boating & fishing at nearby lakes.
FAC: paved rds. (150 spaces). Avail: 140 paved, back-ins (30x69), accepts full hkup units only, 140 full hkups (30/50 amps), seasonal sites, cable, WiFi @ sites, rentals, laundry, restaurant, controlled access. **REC:** heated pool, hot tub, Verde River: boating nearby, golf, rec open to public. Pet restrict (B/Q) $. No tents. Big rig sites, eco-friendly. 2021 rates: $38 to $64, Military discount.
(480)789-5310 Lat: 33.57389, Lon: -111.67469
9605 N Fort McDowell Rd, Fort McDowell, AZ 85264
www.eagleviewrvresort.com
See ad page 58

MCDOWELL MOUNTAIN REGIONAL PARK (Public) From jct Scottsdale Rd & Shea Blvd: Go 12 mi E on Shea Blvd, then 4 mi N on Saguaro Blvd, then 4 mi E on McDowell Mtn. Rd. 76 Avail: 76 W, 76 E. 2021 rates: $15 to $32. (480)471-0173

Things to See and Do

WE-KO-PA CASINO RESORT Just minutes away from Scottsdale and Mesa Fort McDowell Resort and destination offers a variety of gaming options, fine dining, golf and world class entertainment. New casino building in 2020. Partial handicap access. RV accessible. Restrooms. Food. Hours: 24 hours. ATM.
(855)957-9467 Lat: 33.58246, Lon: -111.67877
10438 Wekopa Way, Fort McDowell, AZ 85264
wekopacasinoresort.com
See ad page 58

WE-KO-PA GOLF CLUB Honored as one of the the Best Resort Courses by Golfweek magazine, We-Ko-Pa is designed by golf course veterans Bill Coore, Ben Crenshaw and Scott Miller. A daily fee golf facility with two 18-hole courses. Restrooms. Food. Hours: .
(480)836-9000 Lat: 33.57857, Lon: -111.68576
18200 E Toh Vee Circle, Fort McDowell, AZ 85264
wekopa.com
See ad page 58

FREDONIA — A3 *Coconino*

KAIBAB CAMPER VILLAGE **Ratings: 5/NA/7.5** (Campground) 51 Avail: 40 full hkups, 11 W, 11 E (30 amps). 2021 rates: $40 to $45. May 14 to Oct 15. (928)643-7804, 770 Forest Service Rd 461, Fredonia, AZ 86022

KAIBAB PAIUTE TRIBAL RV PARK
good sam park **Ratings: 7.5/10★/8** (RV Park) Avail: 58 full hkups (30/50 amps). 2021 rates: $25. (928)643-6601, 406 N Pipe Spring Rd, Fredonia, AZ 86022

WHEEL INN RV PARK **Ratings: 5/NA/7** (RV Park) Avail: 32 full hkups (30/50 amps). 2021 rates: $25. (435)689-1908, 295 W Pratt St, Fredonia, AZ 86022

GILA BEND — D2 *Maricopa*

MILITARY PARK GILA BEND FAMCAMP (GILA BEND AFAF) (Public) From Jct of I-10 & AZ-85/Exit 112, S 45 mi on AZ-85 to Gila Bend AFAF/Ajo sign, W 4.5 mi (L). Avail: 37 full hkups (15/50 amps). 2021 rates: $12. (623)856-5211

SONORAN DESERT RV PARK
Ratings: 9.5/10★/9.5 (RV Park) From Jct of I-8 & Butterfield Trail (exit 119), N 1 mi on Butterfield Trail (Bus 8) (R); or From Jct of SR-85 & Bus 8, SE 1 mi on Bus 8 (L). **FAC:** all weather rds. Avail: 130 gravel, 34 pull-thrus, (55x100), back-ins (55x80), 130 full hkups (30/50 amps), WiFi @

EXCLUSIVE! Every listing includes a special "arrow" symbol. This valuable tool shows you where the facility is located (N, S, E, W, NE, NW, SE, SW) in relation to the town.

sites, tent sites, laundry, LP bottles. **REC:** heated pool, playground. Pet restrict (B/Q). Big rig sites, eco-friendly. 2021 rates: $37.25 to $68.90.
(928)683-2850 Lat: 32.93798, Lon: -112.68084
800 Butterfield Trail, Gila Bend, AZ 85337
www.sonorandesertrvpark.com
See ad this page

GLOBE — D4 *Gila*

APACHE GOLD RV PARK **Ratings: 8.5/8.5/7.5** (RV Park) Avail: 60 full hkups (30/50 amps). 2021 rates: $45. (928)475-7608, 777 Geronimo Springs Blvd, San Carlos, AZ 85550

GOLD CANYON — D3 *Pinal*

GOLD CANYON See also Apache Junction, Fort McDowell, Mesa & Queen Valley.

ARIZONIAN RV RESORT
good sam park **Ratings: 10/10★/10** (RV Resort) From Jct of US Hwy 60 & Goldfield Rd (Exit 198), E 9.2 mi on Hwy 60 (L).

ENJOY THIS SONORAN DESERT RESORT!
Hundreds of miles of ATV and hiking trails right out our back gate. Big rig friendly. Live entertainment, pickle ball, fitness center, pool and spa await you. Near shopping, restaurants, medical facilities & attractions.

FAC: paved rds. (354 spaces). Avail: 248 all weather, patios, back-ins (40x50), 248 full hkups (30/50 amps), seasonal sites, WiFi @ sites, laundry. **REC:** heated pool, hot tub, golf, shuffleboard. Pet restrict (S/B/Q). Partial handicap access. No tents, Age restrict may apply, eco-friendly. 2021 rates: $50.
(520)463-2978 Lat: 33.30003, Lon: -111.39457
15976 East US Hwy 60, Apache Junction, AZ 85118
www.arizonianresort.com
See ad page 60

CANYON VISTAS RV RESORT
good sam park **Ratings: 10/10★/10** (RV Resort) From Jct Hwy 88 & US 60: Go E 4.9 mi on US 60 for 4.9 mi.

NOW TAKING RESERVATIONS
Nestled at base of Superstition Mts. for quiet morning walks or bike rides. Keep in shape in our fitness center. Meet friends for a round at our Pitch & Putt Golf Course. Enjoy a desert breeze & cool drink under the veranda!

FAC: paved rds. (634 spaces). Avail: 60 all weather, patios, back-ins (40x50), accepts full hkup units only, 60 full hkups (30/50 amps), seasonal sites, WiFi @ sites, laundry. **REC:** heated pool, hot tub, shuffleboard. Pet restrict (B/Q). Partial handicap access. No tents, Age restrict may apply, eco-friendly. 2021 rates: $80. ATM, no cc.
(480)288-8844 Lat: 33.36141, Lon: -111.47491
6601 E US Hwy 60, Gold Canyon, AZ 85118
www.cal-am.com/resorts/canyon-vistas
See ad pages 46, 56

GOLD CANYON RV & GOLF RESORT
good sam park **Ratings: 10/10★/10** (RV Resort) Avail: 200 full hkups (30/50 amps). 2021 rates: $72 to $83. (480)982-5800, 7151 E US Hwy 60, Gold Canyon, AZ 85118

GOLDEN VALLEY — B1 *Mohave*

ADOBE RV PARK
good sam park **Ratings: 7.5/9.5★/9.5** (RV Park) From Jct of I-40 & US 93 (Exit 48), W 3.5 mi on US 93 to AZ-68, W 4.4 mi on AZ-68 (toward Laughlin, NV) to Adobe Rd (Maverick Country Store), N 600 ft to West Apache Way, E 0.1 mi (R). Elev 2800 ft.**FAC:** paved rds. (75 spaces). Avail: 25 gravel, 4 pull-thrus, (32x58), back-ins (32x58), 25 full hkups (30/50 amps), seasonal sites, WiFi @ sites, $, dump, laundry. Pet restrict (S/B/Q). Partial handicap access. No tents, Age restrict may apply. Big rig sites, eco-friendly. 2021 rates: $27. no cc.
(928)565-3010 Lat: 35.22343, Lon: -114.19763
4950 West Apache Way, Golden Valley, AZ 86413
adobervpark.com
See ad this page

SETTLIN' IN RV PARK **Ratings: 6/9★/6.5** (RV Park) Avail: 220 full hkups (30/50 amps). 2021 rates: $33. (928)565-3005, 7930 W Hwy 68, Golden Valley, AZ 86413

TRADEWINDS RV PARK
good sam park **Ratings: 8/9★/9** (RV Park) Avail: 13 full hkups (30/50 amps). 2021 rates: $40. (928)565-5115, 152 S Emery Park Rd, Golden Valley, AZ 86413

GOODYEAR — D3 *Maricopa*

A SPOTLIGHT Introducing Valley of the Sun's colorful attractions appearing at the front of this state section.

COTTON LANE RV RESORT
good sam park **Ratings: 9.5/10★/9** (RV Resort) Avail: 238 full hkups (30/50 amps). 2021 rates: $49 to $54. (888)907-7223, 17506 W Van Buren, Goodyear, AZ 85338

DESTINY RV RESORT **Ratings: 10/9.5★/10** (RV Park) Avail: 34 full hkups (30/50 amps). 2021 rates: $50 to $52. (623)853-0537, 416 N Citrus Rd, Goodyear, AZ 85338

GRAND CANYON NATIONAL PARK — B3 *Coconino*

A SPOTLIGHT Introducing Grand Canyon's colorful attractions appearing at the front of this state section.

GRAND CANYON NATIONAL PARK See also Ash Fork & Williams.

GRAND CANYON TRAILER VILLAGE RV PARK **Ratings: 8/8★/8** (RV Resort) Avail: 123 full hkups (30/50 amps). 2021 rates: $59. (877)404-4611, 100 Trailer Village Rd, Grand Canyon National Park, AZ 86023

GRAND CANYON/DESERT VIEW (Public National Park) From Jct of US-89 & AZ Rte 64 (at Cameron), NW 33 mi on AZ Rte 64 (R). Entrance fee required. 50 Avail. 2021 rates: $12. May 15 to Oct 15. (928)638-7888

GRAND CANYON/MATHER (Public National Park) From Jct of I-180 & SR-64, N 30 mi on SR-64 to entrance station, continue N 3 mi to Mather Camp Rd, E 0.2 mi, follow signs. 327 Avail. 2021 rates: $6 to $50. (928)638-7888

GRAND CANYON/NORTH RIM (Public National Park) From Jct of US-89 Alt. & Hwy 67 (N entrance), S 43 mi on Hwy 67 (E). 90 Avail. 2021 rates: $18 to $25. May 15 to Oct 31. (928)638-7888

Things to See and Do

GRAND CANYON VISITOR CENTER & IMAX Discover 4,000 years of Grand Canyon history in this IMAX film presentation. Outdoor gear & Souvenirs, Pizza Hut Express, deli & Canyon Creamery. Sales of Grand Canyon Nat'l Park Pass, Pink Jeep Tours, free maps & tourist information. Elev 7000 ft. Partial handicap access. RV accessible. Restrooms. Food.. Hours: 8am to 10pm. Adult fee: $13.59. ATM.
(928)638-2468 Lat: 35.97454, Lon: -112.12683
450 State Route 64, Grand Canyon Village, AZ 86023
explorethecanyon.com

GREEN VALLEY — E4 *Pima*

GREEN VALLEY RV RESORT **Ratings: 8.5/9★/8.5** (RV Park) Avail: 84 full hkups (30/50 amps). 2021 rates: $50. (520)625-3900, 19001 S Richfield Ave, Green Valley, AZ 85614

HAPPY JACK — C3 *Coconino*

CLINT'S WELL RESORT- SUNRISE RESORTS **Ratings: 5/7/6** (Membership Park) Avail: 40 full hkups (30 amps). 2021 rates: $42. May 01 to Oct 15. (928)477-2299, 291 Forest Hwy 3, Happy Jack, AZ 86024

HAPPY JACK LODGE & RV RESORT **Ratings: 6/7/7.5** (RV Park) Avail: 74 full hkups (30/50 amps). 2021 rates: $42. (928)477-2805, 57383 Lake Mary Rd, Happy Jack, AZ 86024

HOLBROOK — B4 *Navajo*

HOLBROOK/PETRIFIED FOREST KOA JOURNEY **Ratings: 8/7/7** (Campground) 90 Avail: 75 full hkups, 15 W, 15 E (30/50 amps). 2021 rates: $38 to $60. (800)562-3389, 102 Hermosa Ave, Holbrook, AZ 86025

OK RV PARK
good sam park **Ratings: 7/10★/8.5** (RV Park) From jct I-40 & Navajo Blvd (exit 286): Go 1/2 mi NE on Bus I-40/Navajo Blvd, then 1/2 mi NW on Buzzard Blvd, then 800 feet NE on Roadrunner Rd (R). Elev 5000 ft.**FAC:** paved/gravel rds. Avail: 89 gravel, patios, 89 pull-thrus, (18x108), mostly side by side hkups, 89 full hkups (30/50 amps), cable, WiFi @ sites, tent sites, laundry. **REC:** hunting nearby. Pet restrict (B/Q). Partial handicap access, eco-friendly. 2021 rates: $40 to $45, Military discount.
(928)524-3226 Lat: 34.91921, Lon: -110.15411
1576 Roadrunner Rd, Holbrook, AZ 86025
www.okrvholbrook.com
See ad this page

HON-DAH — C5 *Navajo*

HON-DAH RV PARK **Ratings: 7/7/7.5** (RV Park) Avail: 30 full hkups (30/50 amps). 2021 rates: $34.77. (928)369-7400, 1 Hwy 73, Pinetop, AZ 85935

HOPE — C2 *La Paz*

RAMBLIN' ROADS RV RESORT **Ratings: 7/8★/7.5** (RV Park) Avail: 27 full hkups (30/50 amps). 2021 rates: $35. (928)859-3187, 60655 E US Hwy 60, Salome, AZ 85348

HUACHUCA CITY — E4 *Cochise*

MOUNTAIN VIEW RV PARK
good sam park **Ratings: 9/10★/8.5** (RV Park) From jct of Hwy 90 (Huachuca Blvd) & 82: Go S 0.5 mi on Hwy 90 (R). Elev 4700 ft.**FAC:** paved rds. (81 spaces). Avail: 61 all weather, patios, 57 pull-thrus, (25x60), back-ins (21x40), 61 full hkups (30/50 amps), seasonal sites, WiFi @ sites, tent sites, laundry. Pet restrict (B). Big rig sites, eco-friendly. 2021 rates: $27.50 to $40.
(520)456-2860 Lat: 31.68252, Lon: -110.35307
99 W Vista Ln , Huachuca City, AZ 85616
www.mountainviewrvpark.com
See ad next page

QUAIL RIDGE RV RESORT **Ratings: 6.5/8.5★/9** (RV Park) Avail: 153 full hkups (30/50 amps). 2021 rates: $13.81. (520)456-9301, 2207 N Yucca Dr , Huachuca City, AZ 85616

Canada -- know the rules, regulations and tips before crossing the border. This is listed at the beginning of the country.

KAYENTA — A4 *Navajo*

KAYENTA See also Monument Valley, UT.

NAVAJO NATIONAL MONUMENT/SUNSET VIEW (Public National Park) From town, SW 19 mi on Hwy 160 to Hwy 564, N 10 mi (E). 31 Avail. (928)672-2700

KINGMAN — B1 *Mohave*

BLAKE RANCH RV PARK

good sam park **Ratings: 8/9.5★/9.5** (RV Park) From jct of I-40 & Blake Ranch Rd (exit 66): Go 0.2 mi N on Blake Ranch Rd (E). Elev 4300 ft.**FAC:** paved rds. (55 spaces). Avail: 24 all weather, 24 pull-thrus, (30x65), 24 full hkups (30/50 amps), seasonal sites, WiFi @ sites, rentals, dump, laundry, LP gas. **REC:** hunting nearby. Pets OK. Partial handicap access. No tents. Big rig sites, eco-friendly. 2021 rates: $32.49 to $44.69, Military discount.
(928)757-3336 Lat: 35.17951, Lon: -113.78903
9315 E Blake Ranch Road, Kingman, AZ 86401
blakeranchrv.com
See ad this page

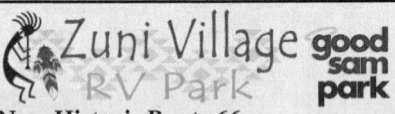

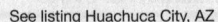

FORT BEALE RV PARK **Ratings: 8/9.5★/8** (RV Park) Avail: 12 full hkups (30/50 amps). 2021 rates: $37. (928)753-3355, 300 Metcalfe Road, Kingman, AZ 86401

HUALAPAI MOUNTAIN (MOHAVE COUNTY PARK) (Public) From Jct of I-40 & Exit 51 (Stockton Hill Rd becomes Hualapai Mountain Rd), S 15 mi on Hualapai Mnt Rd (R). Avail: 47 full hkups (50 amps). 2021 rates: $30. (928)681-5700

KINGMAN KOA JOURNEY **Ratings: 8/8.5★/8.5** (Campground) 84 Avail: 69 full hkups, 15 W, 15 E (30/50 amps). 2021 rates: $43.88 to $47.88. (800)562-3991, 3820 N Roosevelt, Kingman, AZ 86409

SUNRISE RV PARK **Ratings: 7/9★/7** (RV Park) Avail: 15 full hkups (30/50 amps). 2021 rates: $40. (928)753-2277, 3131 Macdonald Ave, Kingman, AZ 86401

ZUNI VILLAGE RV PARK

good sam park **Ratings: 8/9/8** (RV Park) From Jct of I-40 & US 66 (Andy Devine Ave/Exit 53), NE 0.6 mi on US 66 to Airway Ave, W 0.6 mi (L). Elev 3200 ft.**FAC:** paved rds. (130 spaces). Avail: 18 gravel, 18 pull-thrus, (30x60), accepts full hkup units only, 18 full hkups (30/50 amps), seasonal sites, WiFi @ sites, dump, laundry, LP gas. **REC:** pool. Pet restrict (B/Q). Partial handicap access. No tents. Big rig sites. 2021 rates: $43.65 to $48.50, Military discount.
(866)887-9864 Lat: 35.22506, Lon: -114.01380
2840 Airway Ave, Kingman, AZ 86409
See ad this page

LAKE HAVASU CITY — C1 *Mohave*

CAMPBELL COVE RV RESORT

good sam park **Ratings: 9/9.5★/8** (RV Park) Avail: 100 full hkups (30/50 amps). 2021 rates: $41 to $49. (928)854-7200, 1523 Industrial Blvd, Lake Havasu City, AZ 86403

CATTAIL COVE (Public State Park) From Jct of Hwy 95 & London Bridge Rd, S 14.5 mi on Hwy 95 (between MP-167 & 168) to Cat Tail Cove Rd, SW 0.5 mi (E). 61 Avail: 61 W, 61 E (30/50 amps). 2021 rates: $30 to $40. (928)855-1223

CRAZY HORSE CAMPGROUNDS **Ratings: 7.5/4.5/5.5** (Campground) 497 Avail: 275 full hkups, 222 W, 222 E (30/50 amps). 2021 rates: $45 to $70. (928)855-4033, 1534 Beachcomber Blvd, Lake Havasu City, AZ 86403

Park policies vary. Ask about the cancellation policy when making a reservation.

DJ'S RV PARK **Ratings: 9/9★/8** (RV Park) Avail: 40 full hkups (30/50 amps). 2021 rates: $40 to $50. (928)764-3964, 3501 Hwy 95N, Lake Havasu City, AZ 86404

HAVASU FALLS RV RESORT **Ratings: 10/9/8** (RV Park) Avail: 59 full hkups (30/50 amps). 2021 rates: $45 to $55. (928)764-0050, 3493 Hwy 95 N, Lake Havasu City, AZ 86404

ISLANDER RESORT **Ratings: 9.5/10★/9** (RV Park) Avail: 80 full hkups (30/50 amps). 2021 rates: $59 to $95. (928)680-2000, 751 Beachcomber Blvd, Lake Havasu City, AZ 86403

LAKE HAVASU/WINDSOR BEACH (Public State Park) From Jct of I-40 & Hwy 95, S 20 mi on Hwy 95 to Industrial Blvd, follow signs (R). Entrance fee required. 47 Avail: 47 W, 47 E (30/50 amps). 2021 rates: $35 to $40. (928)855-2784

PROSPECTORS RV RESORT **Ratings: 7/8/7.5** (RV Park) Avail: 108 full hkups (30/50 amps). 2021 rates: $39. (928)764-2000, 4750 N London Bridge Road, Lake Havasu City, AZ 86404

SAM'S BEACHCOMBER RV RESORT **Ratings: 8.5/10★/8.5** (RV Resort) Avail: 100 full hkups (30/50 amps). 2021 rates: $55 to $65. (928)453-1550, 555 Beachcomber Blvd, Lake Havasu City, AZ 86403

LAKE POWELL — A3 *Coconino*

LAKE POWELL See also Page.

LITCHFIELD PARK — D3 *Maricopa*

WHITE TANK MOUNTAIN (MARICOPA COUNTY PARK) (Public) From Jct of I-17 & Dunlap Ave, W 20 mi on Dunlap Ave/Olive; or From Jct of I-10 & Cotton Ln, N 7 mi on Cotton Ln to Olive, W 4 mi (E). Entrance fee required. 40 Avail. 2021 rates: $15 to $40. (602)506-2930

LITTLEFIELD — A2 *Mohave*

VIRGIN RIVER GORGE (BLM) (Public Corps) From St George, UT, SW 20 mi on I-15 to Cedar Pockets exit, follow signs (L). 77 Avail. 2021 rates: $8. (435)688-3200

LUKEVILLE — E2 *Pima*

ORGAN PIPE CACTUS/TWIN PEAKS CAMPGROUND (Public National Park) From Lukeville: Go 5 mi N on AZ-85 N, then 350 yds W on Puerto Blanco Dr, then 1-1/4 mi S (L). 174 Avail. 2021 rates: $20. (520)387-6849

MARANA — D4 *Pima*

VALLEY OF THE SUN RV RESORT

good sam park **Ratings: 10/10★/9.5** (RV Park) From Jct of I-10 & Marana Rd (exit 236), S 0.7 mi on Sandario Rd (R). **FAC:** all weather rds. (121 spaces). Avail: 71 all weather, patios, 15 pull-thrus, (23x70), back-ins (35x70), accepts full hkup units only, 71 full hkups (30/50 amps), seasonal sites, WiFi @ sites, $, laundry, LP gas. **REC:** heated pool, hot tub. Pet restrict (S/B). No tents. Big rig sites, eco-friendly. 2021 rates: $39.98 to $50.11, Military discount.
(520)682-3434 Lat: 32.45086, Lon: -111.21729
13377 N Sandario Rd, Marana, AZ 85653
www.valleyofthesunrv.com
See ad page 77

MARBLE CANYON — A3 *Coconino*

GLEN CANYON/LEES FERRY (Public National Park) From Jct of US-89 & US-89A, NE 16 mi on US-89A to park access rd, N 5 mi (L). 51 Avail. 2021 rates: $20. (928)608-6200

MAYER — C3 *Yavapai*

QUAIL RIDGE RV PARK **Ratings: 8/8.5★/9.5** (Campground) Avail: 10 full hkups (30/50 amps). 2021 rates: $52. (928)227-1919, 18825 E Copper Star Road, Mayer, AZ 86333

MEADVIEW — B1 *Mohave*

MEADVIEW RV PARK & COZY CABINS

good sam park **Ratings: 7/7.5★/8.5** (Campground) Avail: 32 full hkups (30/50 amps). 2021 rates: $30 to $33. (928)564-2662, 28100 N Pierce Ferry Rd, Meadview, AZ 86444

MESA — D3 *Maricopa*

A SPOTLIGHT Introducing Valley of the Sun's colorful attractions appearing at the front of this state section.

MESA See also Apache Junction, Fort McDowell, Gold Canyon, Peoria, Phoenix & Tempe.

Always do a Pre-Drive Safety Check!

➔ AGAVE VILLAGE RV RESORT **Ratings: 9/9★/9.5** (RV Park) Avail: 74 full hkups (30/50 amps). 2021 rates: $55. (480)986-5451, 7807 E Main St, Mesa, AZ 85207

APACHE WELLS RV RESORT

Ratings: 10/10★/10 (RV Resort) From Jct of Loop 202 & Higley Rd, S 1 mi on Higley Rd to Mc Dowell Rd, E 0.5 mi to N 56th St, S 200 ft (R).

NOW TAKING RESERVATIONS
Enjoy with friends an invigorating game of tennis on lighted courts, shuffleboard or a fun game of bridge. Don't forget our pool & spa. High speed internet in the computer room to keep in touch with family and friends.

FAC: paved rds. (320 spaces). Avail: 88 all weather, patios, back-ins (32x45), 88 full hkups (30/50 amps), seasonal sites, WiFi @ sites, laundry. **REC:** heated pool, hot tub, shuffleboard. Pet restrict (B/Q). No tents, Age restrict may apply, eco-friendly. 2021 rates: $49.
(480)832-4324 Lat: 33.46424, Lon: -111.71028
2656 N 56th St, Mesa, AZ 85215
www.cal-am.com/resorts/apache-wells
See ad pages 46, 56

➔ DESERT VISTA RV RESORT **Ratings: 9.5/NA/9.5** (RV Park) Avail: 46 full hkups (50 amps). 2021 rates: $53.89. (480)663-3383, 124 S. 54th St, Mesa, AZ 85206

➔ **GOOD LIFE RV RESORT**

Ratings: 10/10★/10 (RV Resort) From Jct of US Hwy 60 & Val Vista Rd (exit 184), N 2 mi on Val Vista Rd to Main St, W 0.2 mi (L).

NOW TAKING RESERVATIONS
Guests enjoy a wide range of activities, fun dancing events, great pool, games under lighted tennis/shuffleboard courts, shopping, restaurants and a short distance to fabulous golf courses. A new dog park for your pet!

FAC: paved rds. (1156 spaces). Avail: 400 all weather, patios, back-ins (30x42), accepts full hkup units only, 400 full hkups (30/50 amps), seasonal sites, WiFi @ sites, laundry, restaurant, controlled access. **REC:** heated pool, hot tub, shuffleboard. Pet restrict (B/Q). Partial handicap access. No tents, Age restrict may apply. Big rig sites, eco-friendly. 2021 rates: $56, Military discount. ATM.
(480)832-4990 Lat: 33.41476, Lon: -111.75791
3403 E Main St, Mesa, AZ 85213
www.cal-am.com/resorts/good-life
See ad pages 46, 56

➔ **HOLIDAY VILLAGE**

Ratings: 8.5/8.5★/8.5 (RV Area in MH Park) Avail: 78 full hkups (50 amps). 2021 rates: $38. (480)962-1694, 701 S. Dobson Rd, Mesa, AZ 85202

➔ M & M MOBILE VILLA **Ratings: 6/NA/8** (RV Area in MH Park) Avail: 100 full hkups (30/50 amps). 2021 rates: $45.71. (480)461-6000, 320 E McKellips Rd, Mesa, AZ 85201

➔ **MESA REGAL RV RESORT**

Ratings: 10/10★/10 (RV Resort) From Jct of US Hwy 60 (Superstition Fwy) & Greenfield Rd (exit 185), N 2 mi on Greenfield Rd to Main St, E 0.4 mi (L).

NOW TAKING RESERVATIONS
Enjoy 4 outdoor pools & spa, computer, fitness centers plus in-house beauty/barber shops, massage therapy, travel agency, 5 lighted tennis courts, batting/driving cages, water volleyball, bocce ball, pickle ball & much more!

FAC: paved rds. (2005 spaces). Avail: 800 all weather, patios, back-ins (35x45), accepts full hkup units only, 800 full hkups (30/50 amps), seasonal sites, WiFi @ sites, laundry, restaurant. **REC:** heated pool, wading pool, hot tub, shuffleboard. Pet restrict (B/Q). No tents, Age restrict may apply, eco-friendly. 2021 rates: $74. ATM.
(480)830-2821 Lat: 33.41571, Lon: -111.72971
4700 E Main, Mesa, AZ 85205
www.cal-am.com/resorts/mesa-regal
See ad pages 46, 56

➔ **MESA SPIRIT RV RESORT**

Ratings: 9.5/9.5★/9.5 (RV Resort) Avail: 1000 full hkups (30/50 amps). 2021 rates: $63 to $86. (888)563-7040, 3020 E Main St, Mesa, AZ 85213

➔ **MESA SUNSET RV RESORT**

Ratings: 9.5/8.5/9.5 (RV Park) Avail: 178 full hkups (30/50 amps). 2021 rates: $59.99. (480)984-6731, 9252 E Broadway Rd, Mesa, AZ 85208

MONTE VISTA VILLAGE RV RESORT

Ratings: 8.5/9/9.5 (RV Resort) Avail: 384 full hkups (30/50 amps). 2021 rates: $60 to $89. (888)563-7040, 8865 E Baseline Rd, Mesa, AZ 85209

➔ **PALM GARDENS MHC & RV PARK**

Ratings: 9/9.5★/9 (RV Area in MH Park) From Jct of US-60 & Gibbert St (Exit 132): Go N on Gilbert St for 2 mi, turn E onto E. Main for 1.1 mi to Park on right.

FAC: paved rds. (439 spaces). Avail: 324 gravel, patios, back-ins (30x50), accepts full hkup units only, 324 full hkups (30/50 amps), seasonal sites, WiFi, dump, laundry, controlled access. **REC:** pool, hot tub, shuffleboard. Pet restrict (S/B/Q). Partial handicap access. No tents, Age restrict may apply, eco-friendly. 2021 rates: $45. no cc.
(480)832-0290 Lat: 33.41471, Lon: -111.76896
2929 E. Main St, Mesa, AZ 85213
palmgardensonline.com
See ad opposite page

➔ **SUN LIFE RV RESORT**

Ratings: 10/10★/10 (RV Resort) From Jct of Hwy 60 & Higley Rd (exit 186), N 2.5 mi on Higley Rd to University Dr, W 0.2 mi (L).

NOW TAKING RESERVATIONS
Best location to see & do it all...casinos-golfing-bowling-museums-sports stadiums-shopping-restaurants-local hiking. Social director has a full schedule of activities/events like ever popular dancing in the Grand Ballroom!

FAC: paved rds. (761 spaces). Avail: 235 all weather, patios, back-ins (32x45), accepts full hkup units only, 235 full hkups (30/50 amps), seasonal sites, WiFi @ sites, laundry, restaurant, controlled access. **REC:** heated pool, hot tub, shuffleboard. Pet restrict (S/B/Q). Partial handicap access. No tents, Age restrict may apply. Big rig sites, eco-friendly. 2021 rates: $67. ATM.
(480)981-9500 Lat: 33.42001, Lon: -111.72228
5055 E University Dr, Mesa, AZ 85205
www.cal-am.com/resorts/sun-life
See ad pages 46, 56

➔ **TOWERPOINT RESORT**

Ratings: 10/10★/10 (RV Resort) From Jct of US Hwy 60 & Higley Rd (exit 186), N 2 mi on Higley Rd to Main St, W 0.4 mi (R).

NOW TAKING RESERVATIONS
Endless activities-silversmithing-woodworking-cards-games-sewing-concerts-chapel services-Bible studies-tennis/shuffleboard courts-swimming-dancing (square & round) all winter long. Relax in our 2 large therapy pools & more.

FAC: paved rds. (1112 spaces). Avail: 287 all weather, patios, back-ins (30x50), accepts full hkup units only, 287 full hkups (30/50 amps), seasonal sites, WiFi @ sites, laundry, restaurant. **REC:** heated pool, hot tub, shuffleboard. Pet restrict (S/B/Q). Partial handicap access. No tents, Age restrict may apply. Big rig sites, eco-friendly. 2021 rates: $62. ATM.
(480)832-4996 Lat: 33.41905, Lon: -111.72572
4860 E Main St, Mesa, AZ 85205
www.cal-am.com/resorts/towerpoint
See ad pages 46, 56

USERY MOUNTAIN (MARICOPA COUNTY PARK) (Public) From Jct of US-60 & Ellsworth/Usery Pass Rd (exit 191), N 7.5 mi (R). Entrance fee required. Avail: 73 full hkups (30/50 amps). 2021 rates: $15 to $40. (602)506-2930

VAL VISTA VILLAGE RV RESORT

Ratings: 9/10★/9.5 (RV Resort) From Jct of US Hwy 60 & Val Vista Dr (exit 184), N 2.3 mi on Val Vista Dr (R). Note: No Pickup campers.

NOW TAKING RESERVATIONS
Stay with us in our RV resort or a new beautiful manufactured home (for sale or rent) deluxe RV super sites w/gas BBQs and privacy fence or invite family/friends to enjoy a vacation home (fully furnished) to rent or purchase.

FAC: paved rds. (1498 spaces). Avail: 498 gravel, patios, 61 pull-thrus, (32x82), back-ins (30x40), accepts full hkup units only, 498 full hkups (30/50 amps), seasonal sites, WiFi, laundry, controlled access. **REC:** heated pool, hot tub, shuffleboard. Pet restrict (S/B/Q). No tents, Age restrict may apply. Big rig sites, eco-friendly. 2021 rates: $59. ATM.
(480)832-2547 Lat: 33.41940, Lon: -111.75340
233 N Val Vista Dr, Mesa, AZ 85213
www.cal-am.com/resorts/val-vista-villages
See ad pages 46, 56

Say you saw it in our Guide!

➔ **VALLE DEL ORO RV RESORT**

Ratings: 10/10★/10 (RV Resort) From Jct of US Hwy 60 & Ellsworth Rd (exit 191), N 0.1 mi on Ellsworth Rd (L).

NOW TAKING RESERVATIONS
Enjoy our 2 pools & 2 spas-premier fitness center-fantastic wood shop-tennis courts-bocce ball-softball field & dancing. Join a hiking/biking club-ceramics-stained glass-computer class or enjoy discount at local golf courses

FAC: paved rds. (1761 spaces). Avail: 487 all weather, patios, back-ins (35x50), accepts full hkup units only, 487 full hkups (30/50 amps), seasonal sites, WiFi @ sites, laundry, controlled access. **REC:** heated pool, hot tub, shuffleboard. Pet restrict (B/Q). Partial handicap access. No tents, Age restrict may apply. Big rig sites, eco-friendly. 2021 rates: $73. ATM.
(480)984-1146 Lat: 33.38885, Lon: -111.63307
1452 S Ellsworth Rd, Mesa, AZ 85209
www.cal-am.com/resorts/valle-del-oro
See ad pages 46, 56

➔ **VIEWPOINT RV & GOLF RESORT**

Ratings: 9.5/9★/10 (RV Park) Avail: 355 full hkups (30/50 amps). 2021 rates: $73 to $85. (888)563-7040, 8700 E University Dr, Mesa, AZ 85207

➔ **WESTERN ACRES**

Ratings: 8.5/9.5★/8.5 (RV Area in MH Park) From Jct of US Hwy 60 & Crismon Rd (Exit 192), N 2 mi on Crismon Rd to E Apache Trail, W 0.2 mi, E 0.1 mi (R).

GREAT QUALITY AT AFFORDABLE PRICES!
Friendliest park in the West! Convenient to shopping malls, hospitals & medical facilities, groceries & major freeways with easy access to the Phoenix area, lakes and Superstition recreational area. We hope you visit soon.

FAC: paved rds. (180 spaces). Avail: 33 all weather, patios, 12 pull-thrus, (25x35), back-ins (25x35), accepts full hkup units only, 33 full hkups (30/50 amps), seasonal sites, WiFi @ sites, laundry. **REC:** shuffleboard. Pet restrict (B/Q). Partial handicap access. No tents, eco-friendly. 2021 rates: $47.20. no cc.
(480)986-1158 Lat: 33.41485, Lon: -111.61742
9913 East Apache Trail, Mesa, AZ 85207
www.western-acres.com
See ad page 60

Travel Services

➔ **CAMPING WORLD OF MESA** As the nation's largest retailer of RV supplies, accessories, services and new and used RVs, Camping World is committed to making your total RV experience better. **SERVICES:** RV, RV appliance, MH mechanical, sells outdoor gear, sells firearms, staffed RV wash, restrooms. RV Sales. RV supplies, LP gas, dump, RV accessible. Hours: 9am to 7pm.
(877)882-9815 Lat: 33.41553, Lon: -111.78377
2222 E. Main Street, Mesa, AZ 85213
www.campingworld.com

MOHAVE VALLEY — B1 *Mohave*

CROSSROADS RV PARK

Ratings: 8/9★/9 (RV Park) Avail: 136 full hkups (30/50 amps). 2021 rates: $35 to $45. (928)768-3303, 3299 Boundary Cone Rd, Mohave Valley, AZ 86440

HAPPY TOGETHER RV RESORT **Ratings: 8/9★/8** (RV Park) Avail: 87 full hkups (30/50 amps). 2021 rates: $45. (917)848-5288, 8545 S Highway 95, Mohave Valley, AZ 86440

MOON RIVER RV RESORT **Ratings: 9/9★/9** (RV Park) Avail: 50 full hkups (30/50 amps). 2021 rates: $36 to $39. (928)788-6666, 1325 E Boundary Cone Rd, Mohave Valley, AZ 86440

MORMON LAKE — B3 *Coconino*

MORMON LAKE LODGE & RV PARK & CAMPGROUND **Ratings: 5/7.5/6.5** (Campground) Avail: 24 full hkups (30/50 amps). 2021 rates: $44. (928)354-2227, 1991 Mormon Lake Rd, Mormon Lake, AZ 86038

MORRISTOWN — C2 *Maricopa*

LAKE PLEASANT (Public) From Jct of I-17 & SR-74 (Carefree Hwy), W 15 mi on SR-74 (R). Avail: 97 full hkups (30 amps). 2021 rates: $15 to $45. (928)501-1710

Find it fast! Use our alphabetized index of campgrounds and parks.

OVERGAARD — C4 *Navajo*

ELK PINES RV RESORT **Ratings: 8.5/9★/9** (RV Park) Avail: 68 full hkups (30/50 amps). 2021 rates: $53. Apr 15 to Oct 31. (928)535-3833, 2256 Hwy 260, Overgaard, AZ 85933

HEBER RV RESORT

good sam park **Ratings: 9/9.5★/9** (RV Park) From Jct of 260 & 277: Go NE 1.3 mi on 277 (R). Elev 6563 ft.**FAC:** all weather rds. Avail: 71 all weather, patios, 11 pull-thrus, (24x45), back-ins (24x50), 71 full hkups (30/50 amps), WiFi @ sites, dump, laundry, controlled access. **REC:** hunting nearby. Pet restrict (B/Q). No tents, eco-friendly. 2021 rates: $48.
(928)535-4004 Lat: 34.42704, Lon: -110.55564
3065 Hwy 277, Overgaard, AZ 85933
heberrvresort.com
See ad page 589

WHITE MOUNTAIN RESORT- SUNRISE RESORT **Ratings: 5/6/6.5** (Membership Park) 61 Avail: 31 full hkups, 30 W, 30 E (30 amps). 2021 rates: $33 to $40. May 01 to Sep 30. (928)535-5978, 2162 Camperland Rd, Overgaard, AZ 85933

PAGE — A3 *Coconino*

ANTELOPE POINT MARINA RV PARK

good sam park (RV Park) (Too New to Rate) Avail: 104 full hkups (30/50 amps). 2021 rates: $70 to $80. (928)645-5900, 537 Marina Pkwy, Page, AZ 86040

PAGE LAKE POWELL CAMPGROUND

good sam park **Ratings: 8.5/9★/9** (RV Park) From Jct of Hwy 89 & AZ 98 E, go E 2.6 mi on AZ 98 E to Coppermine Rd/N 20, then N 0.7 mi on Coppermine Rd (R). Elev 4300 ft.- **FAC:** paved/gravel rds. (120 spaces). Avail: 70 gravel, 29 pull-thrus, (28x50), back-ins (30x50), 60 full hkups, 10 W, 10 E (30/50 amps), seasonal sites, cable, WiFi @ sites, tent sites, rentals, dump, laundry, groc, LP gas. **REC:** heated pool, hot tub, boating nearby, playground. Pet restrict (Q). Partial handicap access. Big rig sites, 21 day max stay, eco-friendly. 2021 rates: $51.37 to $59.36, Military discount.
(928)645-3374 Lat: 36.90156, Lon: -111.45299
849 S Coppermine Rd, Page, AZ 86040
www.pagecampground.com
See ad page 47

WAHWEAP RV PARK & CAMPGROUND **Ratings: 8.5/8.5/9** (RV Park) Avail: 139 full hkups (30/50 amps). 2021 rates: $68.18. (800)528-6154, 100 Lake Shore Dr, Page, AZ 86040

PARKER — C1 *La Paz*

BLUE WATER RV PARK **Ratings: 8/7.5/6.5** (RV Park) Avail: 135 full hkups (30/50 amps). 2021 rates: $40 to $61. (928)669-2433, 1001 Bluewater Dr, Parker, AZ 85344

BUCKSKIN MOUNTAIN (Public State Park) From Jct of Hwys 62 & 95, N 10.5 mi on Hwy 95, at N Jct of Bus 95 & Hwy 95 (L). 64 Avail: 13 full hkups, 51 W, 51 E (30/50 amps). 2021 rates: $35 to $43. (928)667-3231

CASTLE ROCK SHORES RESORT **Ratings: 6.5/4.5/6.5** (RV Park) Avail: 100 full hkups (30/50 amps). 2021 rates: $30 to $50. (928)667-2344, 5220 Hwy 95, Parker, AZ 85344

LA PAZ COUNTY PARK (Public) From North city limits: Go 7 mi N on Hwy 95, then W onto Golf Course Dr, then 1/2 mi N on Riverside Dr (R). 114 Avail: 114 W, 114 E (30 amps). 2021 rates: $18 to $24. (928)667-2069

RIVER ISLAND (Public State Park) From Jct of Hwys 62 & 95, N 12 mi on Hwy 95 (L). 37 Avail: 3 full hkups, 34 W, 34 E (30/50 amps). 2021 rates: $30 to $33. (928)667-3386

PATAGONIA — E4 *Santa Cruz*

PATAGONIA LAKE (Public State Park) From Jct of I-19 & Hwy 82, NE 12 mi on Hwy 82 to Patagonia Rd, W 4 mi (E). 105 Avail: 105 W, 105 E (30/50 amps). 2021 rates: $27 to $30. (520)287-6965

PAYSON — C3 *Gila*

OXBOW RV PARK **Ratings: 6/6.5/7** (RV Park) Avail: 26 full hkups (30/50 amps). 2021 rates: $40. (928)474-2042, 962 W Oxbow Trail, Payson, AZ 85541

PAYSON CAMPGROUND AND RV RESORT **Ratings: 9/10★/9.5** (RV Park) Avail: 56 full hkups (30/50 amps). 2021 rates: $42 to $52. (928)472-2267, 808 E Hwy 260, Payson, AZ 85541

PEACH SPRINGS — B2 *Mohave*

GRAND CANYON CAVERNS RV PARK & CAMPGROUND **Ratings: 7/7/8** (Campground) 48 Avail: 48 W, 48 E (30/50 amps). 2021 rates: $40 to $44.95. (928)422-4565, Mile Marker 115 Route 66, Peach Springs, AZ 86434

PEORIA — D3 *Maricopa*

A SPOTLIGHT Introducing Valley of the Sun's colorful attractions appearing at the front of this state section.

PLEASANT HARBOR MARINA & RV RESORT **Ratings: 9.5/9.5★/9.5** (RV Park) Avail: 125 full hkups (30/50 amps). 2021 rates: $45 to $59. (623)235-6140, 8708 W Harbor Blvd, Peoria, AZ 85383

SUNDIAL BUDGET RV PARK **Ratings: 3.5/NA/4** (RV Park) Avail: 60 full hkups (30/50 amps). 2021 rates: $46. (623)979-1921, 9250 N 75th Ave, Peoria, AZ 85345

VALLEY OF THE SUN RV PARK **Ratings: 6.5/6.5/5.5** (RV Park) Avail: 50 full hkups (30/50 amps). 2021 rates: $45.92 to $52.82. (623)334-1977, 8955 NW Grand Ave, Peoria, AZ 85345

PHOENIX — D3 *Maricopa*

A SPOTLIGHT Introducing Valley of the Sun's colorful attractions appearing at the front of this state section.

PHOENIX See also Apache Junction, Black Canyon City, Buckeye, El Mirage, Fort McDowell, Gold Canyon, Goodyear, Mesa, Peoria, Sun City, Surprise & Tempe.

DEER VALLEY RV PARK **Ratings: 6.5/NA/5.5** (RV Park) Avail: 10 full hkups (30/50 amps). 2021 rates: $50. (623)581-3969, 2550 W Louise Drive, Phoenix, AZ 85027

DESERT SHADOWS RV RESORT

good sam park **Ratings: 10/10★/10** (RV Park) N-bnd: From Jct of I-17 & Union Hills Dr (Exit 214 A & B), W 0.4 mi on Union Hills Dr to 29th Ave, N 0.4 mi (R); or S-bnd: From Jct of I-17 & Union Hills Dr/Yorkshire (Exit 214 A & B), S 0.6 mi on N Black Canyon Hwy/Frontage Rt to Union Hills Dr, W 0.4 mi to 29th Ave, N 0.4 mi (R).

FEEL AT HOME WITH US!
A beautiful resort in North Phoenix. A friendly, tranquil place with all the amenities you can imagine. Close to golf, restaurants, shopping & sporting events. Visit soon - short or long term - and experience all we have.
FAC: paved rds. (638 spaces). Avail: 38 all weather, patios, 28 pull-thrus, (30x75), back-ins (30x45), accepts full hkup units only, 38 full hkups (30/50 amps), seasonal sites, WiFi @ sites, $, laundry. **REC:** heated pool, hot tub, shuffleboard. Pet restrict (B/Q). Partial handicap access. No tents. Big rig sites, eco-friendly. 2021 rates: $52 to $64.
(800)595-7290 Lat: 33.66037, Lon: -112.1216
19203 N 29th Ave, Phoenix, AZ 85027
www.phoenixrvresorts.com
See ad opposite page

DESERT'S EDGE RV PARK **Ratings: 9.5/9.5★/10** (RV Park) Avail: 14 full hkups (30/50 amps). 2021 rates: $54 to $65. (623)587-0940, 2398 W Williams Dr, Phoenix, AZ 85027

PHOENIX METRO RV PARK
good sam park **Ratings: 9.5/10★/9.5** (RV Park) Avail: 100 full hkups (30/50 amps). 2021 rates: $50. (623)582-0390, 22701 N Black Canyon Hwy, Phoenix, AZ 85027

PIONEER RV RESORT
good sam park **Ratings: 9.5/10★/9** (RV Resort) From Jct of I-17 & Pioneer Rd exit (225), NW 0.3 mi on Pioneer Rd (L). **FAC:** paved rds. (583 spaces). Avail: 48 gravel, 48 pull-thrus, (28x98), accepts full hkup units only, 48 full hkups (30/50 amps), seasonal sites, WiFi @ sites, $, laundry. **REC:** heated pool, hot tub. Pet restrict (B/Q). Partial handicap access. No tents, Age restrict may apply. Big rig sites, eco-friendly. 2021 rates: $39.27.
(800)658-5895 Lat: 33.82114, Lon: -112.14690
36408 N Black Canyon Hwy, Phoenix, AZ 85086
www.arizonarvresorts.com
See ad page 57

ROYAL PALM RV RESORT
good sam park **Ratings: 9.5/9★/9.5** (RV Area in MH Park) From jct of I-10 & I-17: Go 6.5 mi N on I-17 (Exit 207), then .8 mi E on Dunlap Ave (L). **FAC:** paved rds. (425 spaces). Avail: 103 gravel, patios, 4 pull-thrus, (32x75), back-ins (32x40), accepts full hkup units only, 103 full hkups (30/50 amps), seasonal sites, WiFi @ sites, laundry, controlled access. **REC:** heated pool, hot tub. Pet restrict (B/Q). No tents, Age restrict may apply, eco-friendly. 2021 rates: $70.
(602)943-5833 Lat: 33.56957, Lon: -112.10299
2050 West Dunlap Ave, Phoenix, AZ 85021
continentalcommunities.com
See ad this page

PICACHO — D3 *Pinal*

PICACHO PEAK (Public State Park) From Jct of I-10 & Exit 219, W 0.7 mi on E Picacho Peak Rd, S 1 mi on State Park Rd (E). Avail: 85 E (30/50 amps). 2021 rates: $30. Sep 12 to May 24. (520)466-3183

PICACHO PEAK RV RESORT
good sam park **Ratings: 10/10★/9.5** (RV Park) From Jct of I-10 & exit 219, exit to S Frontage Rd, SE 0.5 mi (R). **FAC:** paved rds. (305 spaces). Avail: 137 all weather, patios, 63 pull-thrus, (31x65), back-ins (40x50), 137 full hkups (30/50 amps), seasonal sites, WiFi @ sites, $, rentals, laundry, LP gas. **REC:** heated pool, hot tub. Pet restrict (B/Q). Partial handicap access. No tents, Age restrict may apply. Big rig sites, eco-friendly. 2021 rates: $40 to $45, Military discount.
(520)466-7841 Lat: 32.64093, Lon: -111.38468
17065 E Peak Lane, Picacho, AZ 85141
www.picachopeakrvpark.com
See ad page 67

PICACHO/TUCSON NORTHWEST KOA **Ratings: 7/9★/7.5** (Campground) Avail: 58 full hkups (30/50 amps). 2021 rates: $44 to $59. (520)466-2966, 18428 S Picacho Hwy, Picacho, AZ 85141

PRESCOTT — C3 *Yavapai*

POINT OF ROCKS RV CAMPGROUND **Ratings: 6.5/8/8** (Campground) Avail: 74 full hkups (30/50 amps). 2021 rates: $43 to $47. (928)445-9018, 3025 N State Route 89, Prescott, AZ 86301

WATSON LAKE (PRESCOTT CITY PARK) (Public) From town, N 3.7 mi on Hwy 89, follow signs (R). Campground closed Tuesday, Wednesday, and Thursday nights. 34 Avail. 2021 rates: $20. Apr 01 to Sep 30. (928)777-1100

WILLOW LAKE RV & CAMPING PARK **Ratings: 6/6.5/6.5** (Campground) Avail: 20 full hkups (30/50 amps). 2021 rates: $39. (928)445-6311, 1617 Heritage Park Road, Prescott, AZ 86301

PRESCOTT VALLEY — C3 *Yavapai*

FAIRGROUNDS RV PARK
good sam park **Ratings: 8.5/NA/10** (RV Park) From Jct of SR-89A & Roberts Rd, E 2.1 mi on 89A to Yavapai County Fairgrounds, S 0.2 mi (L). Elev 5040 ft.**FAC:** paved rds. (230 spaces). Avail: 110 all weather, patios, 63 pull-thrus, (45x70), back-ins (35x60), accepts full hkup units only, 110 full hkups (30/50 amps), seasonal sites, cable, WiFi @ sites, laundry, LP gas. Pet restrict (B/Q). Partial handicap access. No tents. Big rig sites, eco-friendly. 2021 rates: $49.
(928)227-3310 Lat: 34.64778, Lon: -112.28305
10443 Hwy 89A, Prescott Valley, AZ 86315
fairgroundsrvpark.com
See ad this page

QUARTZSITE — C1 *La Paz*

QUARTZSITE See also Bouse, Brenda & Ehrenberg, AZ; Blythe, CA.

88 SHADES RV PARK
good sam park **Ratings: 8.5/8★/7.5** (RV Park) Avail: 32 full hkups (30/50 amps). 2021 rates: $35. (928)927-6336, 575 W Main St, Quartzsite, AZ 85346

AMERICAN TRAILS RV PARK **Ratings: 8/9★/6.5** (RV Park) Avail: 55 full hkups (30/50 amps). 2021 rates: $25 to $50. (928)927-5733, 310 N Central Blvd, Quartzsite, AZ 85346

SAVE! Camping World coupons can be found at the front and back of this Guide!

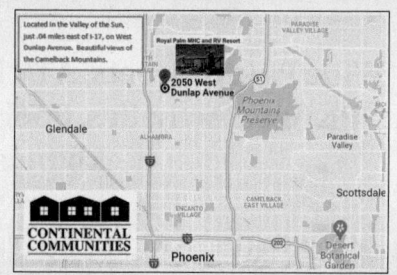

QUARTZSITE (CONT)

ARIZONA SUN RV RESORT **Ratings: 7/9★/7.5** (RV Park) Avail: 84 full hkups (30/50 amps). 2021 rates: $25 to $45. Oct 01 to Apr 01. (928)927-5057, 715 E Quail Trail / 425 N Las Palomas Ave, Quartzsite, AZ 85346

DESERT GARDENS INTERNATIONAL RV & MHP **Ratings: 5.5/6.5/5.5** (RV Park) 110 Avail: 90 full hkups, 20 W, 20 S (30 amps). 2021 rates: $40. (928)927-6361, 1240 Acacia Blvd, Quartzsite, AZ 85346

HASSLER'S RV PARK **Ratings: 6.5/7.5★/7.5** (RV Park) Avail: 25 full hkups (30/50 amps). 2021 rates: $27.75. (928)927-6950, 400 W Main St, Quartzsite, AZ 85346

HOLIDAY PALMS RESORT

good sam park **Ratings: 9.5/10★/8.5** (RV Park) From Jct of I-10 & Bus Loop 10 (exit 19), W 1.4 mi on Bus Loop 10 (L). **FAC:** paved rds. (243 spaces). Avail: 93 all weather, 14 pull-thrus, (27x75), back-ins (30x50), 93 full hkups (30/50 amps), seasonal sites, WiFi @ sites, laundry, LP gas, firewood. **REC:** heated pool, hot tub. Pet restrict (B/Q). Partial handicap access. No tents. Big rig sites, eco-friendly. 2021 rates: $32 to $37, Military discount.
(928)927-5666 Lat: 33.66587, Lon: -114.22256
355 W Main, Quartzsite, AZ 85346
holidaypalmsrv.com
See ad this page

Rancho San Manuel
MOBILE HOME & RV PARK
FHU 30/50 AMPS · Escort To Site
Playground · Snack Shop · Pet Friendly
good sam park
402 S. San Carlos St. • San Manuel, AZ
See listing San Manuel, AZ
520-385-4007 | ranchosanmanuel.com

KOFA MOUNTAIN RV PARK **Ratings: 7/8★/7.5** (RV Park) Avail: 30 full hkups (30/50 amps). 2021 rates: $22 to $44. (928)927-6778, 170 N Central Blvd, Quartzsite, AZ 85346

LA PAZ VALLEY RV PARK **Ratings: 5/NA/5.5** (RV Park) Avail: 44 full hkups (30/50 amps). 2021 rates: $30 to $35. Oct 15 to May 01. (928)927-9754, 52301 Century Dr, Quartzsite, AZ 85346

PARK PLACE RV PARK **Ratings: 6.5/7/6.5** (RV Park) Avail: 44 full hkups (30/50 amps). 2021 rates: $29 to $47. (928)927-6699, 250 N Riggles Ave, Quartzsite, AZ 85346

QUAIL RUN RV PARK

good sam park **Ratings: 9/10★/9** (RV Park) From Jct of I-10 & Quartzsite Blvd (Exit 17), N 0.2 mi on Quartzsite Blvd to Bus Loop 10, E 1.4 mi on Bus Loop 10 to Central Blvd, N 0.9 mi (L).

BRING YOUR BIG RIGS & OFF ROAD TOYS
We can handle any rig of any size with a tow car or trailer. We neighbor the Arizona Peace Trail, an off-roaders dream, full of exciting and fun terrain with picturesque landscapes, historical sites, and incredible wildlife.

FAC: paved rds. Avail: 168 all weather, patios, 88 pull-thrus, (30x90), back-ins (40x60), 168 full hkups (30/50 amps), WiFi @ sites, shower$, laundry. Pet restrict (S/B/Q). Partial handicap access. No tents. Big rig sites, eco-friendly. 2021 rates: $25 to $38.
(928)927-8810 Lat: 33.67998, Lon: -114.21742
918 N Central Blvd, Quartzsite, AZ 85346
www.quailrv.com
See ad previous page

RIGGLES RV COMMUNITY & EVENT CENTER **Ratings: 6/NA/7** (RV Park) Avail: 19 full hkups (30/50 amps). 2021 rates: $25 to $40. (928)927-2091, 240 N Riggles Ave, Quartzsite, AZ 85346

SHADY LANE RV PARK **Ratings: 6/9★/7.5** (RV Park) 93 Avail: 90 full hkups, 3 W, 3 E (30/50 amps). 2021 rates: $17.90 to $37. Oct 01 to Apr 01. (928)927-6844, 185 N Central Blvd, Quartzsite, AZ 85346

SPLIT RAIL RV PARK **Ratings: 6/7.5/6** (RV Park) Avail: 30 full hkups (30/50 amps). 2021 rates: $20 to $30. Oct 01 to May 01. (928)927-5296, 1258 N Central Blvd/N Hwy 95, Quartzsite, AZ 85346

THE SCENIC ROAD RV PARK

good sam park **Ratings: 7.5/8.5★/8** (RV Park) From Jct of Bus. I-10 & AZ 95/N. Central Blvd, N 0.3 mi on AZ 95/N. Central Blvd (L). **FAC:** gravel rds. Avail: 97 gravel, patios, 38 pull-thrus, (30x60), back-ins (30x40), 97 full hkups (30/50 amps), WiFi @ sites, rentals, laundry. Pets OK. No tents. Big rig sites, eco-friendly. 2021 rates: $34 to $44. Oct 01 to Apr 30.
(928)927-6443 Lat: 33.67459, Lon: -114.21806
480 N Central Blvd, Quartzsite, AZ 85346
www.thescenicroad.com
See ad previous page

QUEEN VALLEY — D3 *Pinal*

QUEEN VALLEY RV RESORT **Ratings: 9.5/9.5★/9.5** (RV Park) Avail: 39 full hkups (30/50 amps). 2021 rates: $70.78. (520)463-2300, 50 West Oro Viejo Dr, Queen Valley, AZ 85118

ROOSEVELT — C4 *Gila*

ROOSEVELT LAKE MARINA AND RV PARK **Ratings: 5.5/NA/7** (Campground) 50 Avail: 35 full hkups, 15 W, 15 E (30/50 amps). 2021 rates: $48. (602)977-7170, 28085 AZ Hwy 188, Roosevelt, AZ 85545

SAFFORD — D5 *Graham*

LEXINGTON PINES RESORT **Ratings: 9/9.5★/9.5** (RV Park) Avail: 24 full hkups (30/50 amps). 2021 rates: $40. (928)428-7570, 1535 Thatcher Blvd, Safford, AZ 85546

ROPER LAKE (Public State Park) From Jct of US 70 & US 191, S 5.3 mi to Roper Lake Rd, E 1 mi (E). 50 Avail: 45 W, 45 E (30/50 amps). 2021 rates: $28. (928)428-6760

SALOME — C2 *La Paz*

DESERT PALMS RV RESORT **Ratings: 10/9★/9.5** (RV Park) Avail: 170 full hkups (30/50 amps). 2021 rates: $32. (928)859-2000, 39258 Harquahala Rd, Salome, AZ 85348

DESERT VISTA KOA CAMPGROUND **Ratings: 8/8.5★/7.5** (RV Park) Avail: 125 full hkups (30/50 amps). 2021 rates: $38.50 to $44. (888)563-7040, 64812 Harcuvar Dr, Salome, AZ 85348

SAN MANUEL — D4 *Pinal*

RANCHO SAN MANUEL MOBILE HOME & RV PARK

good sam park (RV Spaces) From jct AZ-77 & AZ-76 (Reddington Rd): Go 6 mi E on Reddington Rd, then 1/4 mi SE on Main St, then 1 Block N on South San Carlos St (E). Elev 3345 ft.**FAC:** paved rds. (386 spaces). Avail: 30 grass, back-ins (45x65), accepts full hkup units only, 30 full hkups (30/50 amps), seasonal sites, cable, . **REC:** playground, hunting nearby. Pet restrict (S/B). No tents. 2021 rates: $52.72.
(520)385-4007 Lat: 32.605611, Lon: -110.626127
402 S San Carlos St, San Manuel, AZ 85631
www.ranchosanmanuel.com
See ad this page

HOLIDAY PALMS RESORT
good sam park
2022 Top Rated 9.5/10★/8.5
· 2 NEW PICKLEBALL COURTS · POOL & HOT TUB
· BIG RIG FRIENDLY (PAVED STREETS, FHU, 30/50 AMP)
· WI-FI & CABLE · ATV TRAIL ENTRY FROM PARK
See listing Quartzsite, AZ
355 W. Main
Quartzsite, AZ 85346
www.holidaypalmsrv.com
928-927-5666

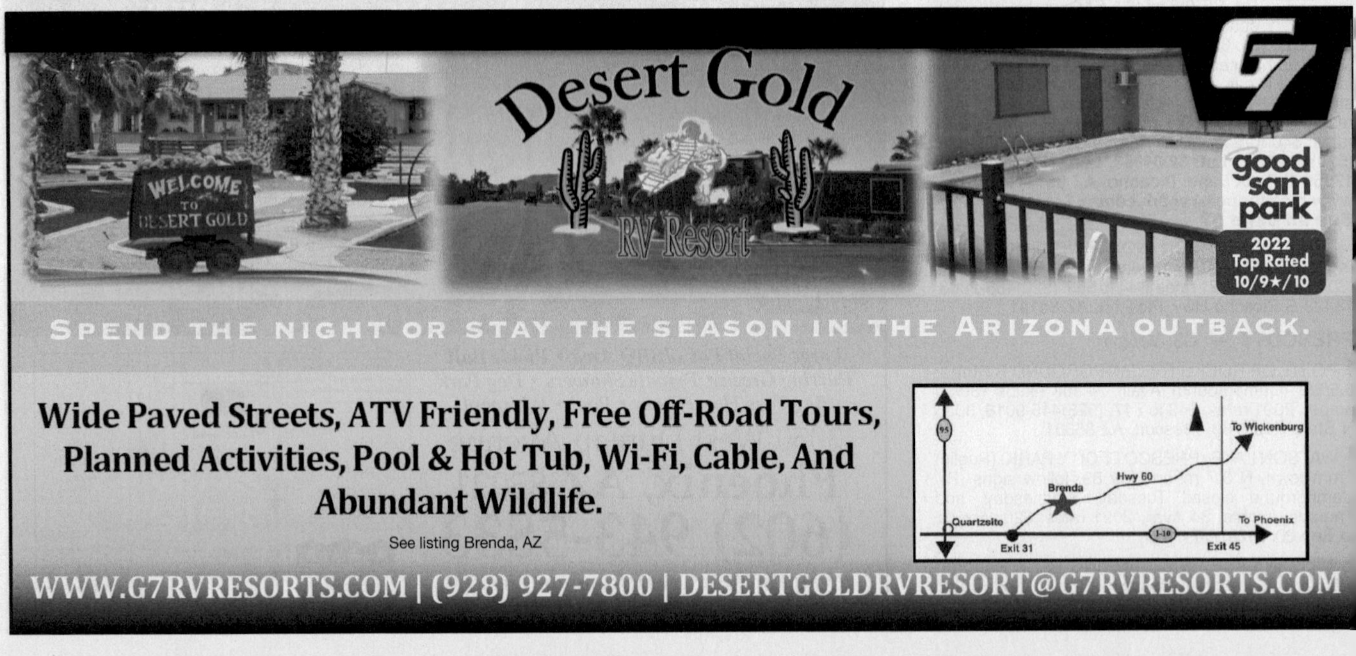
G7
Desert Gold
RV Resort
WELCOME TO DESERT GOLD
good sam park
2022 Top Rated 10/9★/10
SPEND THE NIGHT OR STAY THE SEASON IN THE ARIZONA OUTBACK.
Wide Paved Streets, ATV Friendly, Free Off-Road Tours, Planned Activities, Pool & Hot Tub, Wi-Fi, Cable, And Abundant Wildlife.
See listing Brenda, AZ
95
To Wickenburg
Hwy 60
Brenda
Quartzsite
To Phoenix
I-10
Exit 31
Exit 45
WWW.G7RVRESORTS.COM | (928) 927-7800 | DESERTGOLDRVRESORT@G7RVRESORTS.COM

SCENIC — A1 *Mohave*

SCENIC ORCHARD RV PARK

good sam park (RV Park) (Under Construction) From jct Spring Rain Dr & Scenic Blvd: Go 1/2 mi E on Spring Rain Dr, then 1-1/4 mi S on Scenic Blvd (L). **FAC:** paved rds. Avail: 75 paved, 75 pull-thrus, (30x80), 75 full hkups (30/50 amps), . Pets OK. No tents. 2021 rates: $32 to $45
Lat: 36.785678, Lon: -113.994358
3594 Scenic Blvd, Littlefield, AZ 86432
See ad page 589

SEDONA — C3 *Coconino*

A SPOTLIGHT Introducing Verde Valley/Sedona's colorful attractions appearing at the front of this state section.

SEDONA See also Camp Verde, Clarkdale, Cornville, Cottonwood, Flagstaff & Mormon Lake.

LO LO MAI SPRINGS RESORT **Ratings: 7.5/7/7.5** (Campground) 55 Avail: 44 full hkups, 11 W, 11 E (30 amps). 2021 rates: $59 to $85. (928)634-4700, 11505 E Lolomai Rd, Cornville, AZ 86325

RANCHO SEDONA RV PARK

good sam park **Ratings: 8.5/10★/10** (RV Park) From jct I-17 & SR-179 (Exit 298): Go 14 mi N on SR-179, then 1/4 mi NE on Schnebly Hill Rd, then 500 feet W on Bear Wallow Ln (L). Elev 4300 ft.**FAC:** all weather rds. Avail: 84 all weather, patios, 2 pull-thrus, (30x32), back-ins (30x45), accepts full hkup units only, 84 full hkups (30/50 amps), cable, WiFi @ sites, laundry. **REC:** Sedona Stream: fishing. Pets OK $. No tents. Big rig sites, eco-friendly. 2021 rates: $42 to $84, Military discount.
(888)641-4261 Lat: 34.86530, Lon: -111.75897
135 Bear Wallow Lane, Sedona, AZ 86336
ranchosedona.com
See ad this page

SELIGMAN — B2 *Yavapai*

SELIGMAN ROUTE 66 KOA JOURNEY **Ratings: 7/8/7.5** (Campground) 56 Avail: 29 full hkups, 27 W, 27 E (30/50 amps). 2021 rates: $41 to $50. (800)562-4017, 801 E Hwy 66, Seligman, AZ 86337

SHOW LOW — C4 *Navajo*

FOOL HOLLOW LAKE RECREATION AREA (Public State Park) From Jct US 60 & Hwy 260: Go 2 mi W on Hwy 260, then .6 mi E on Old Linden Rd (L). 123 Avail: 92 W, 63 S, 92 E (30/50 amps). 2021 rates: $20 to $35. (928)537-3680

SHOW LOW LAKE CAMPGROUND (Public) From Jct of SR-77 & US-60, W 0.8 mi on US-60 to SR-260, S 5 mi to Show Low Lake Rd, E 1 mi, follow signs (L). 75 Avail: 10 W, 10 E (30 amps). 2021 rates: $18 to $30. (888)537-7762

VENTURE IN RV RESORT

good sam park **Ratings: 8.5/9★/9.5** (RV Park) Avail: 100 full hkups (30/50 amps). 2021 rates: $55 to $59.46. Apr 01 to Nov 30. (888)563-7040, 270 N Clark Rd / Hwy 260 W, Show Low, AZ 85901

WOODFIELD RV PARK **Ratings: 7.5/NA/9** (RV Park) Avail: 20 full hkups (30/50 amps). 2021 rates: $50. May 01 to Oct 31. (928)242-9049, 3851 S Vacation Village Dr, Show Low, AZ 85901

SIERRA VISTA — E4 *Cochise*

SIERRA VISTA See also Benson, Huachuca City, St David & Tombstone.

MILITARY PARK APACHE FLATS RV RESORT (FORT HUACHUCA) (Public) From I-10 take exit 302, S 35 mi on Hwy-90 to Ft Huachuca (Use the East Gate), go through gate on Hatfield Rd, R on Smith Rd, R on unnamed road (after passing Johnson Rd) which becomes Clarkson. Avail: 56 full hkups (30/50 amps). 2021 rates: $30 to $33. (520)533-1335

MOUNTAIN VISTA MOBILE HOME & RV PARK **Ratings: 3.5/6/4.5** (RV Park) Avail: 49 full hkups (30/50 amps). 2021 rates: $24.54. (520)452-0500, 700 S Carmichael Ave , Sierra Vista, AZ 85635

SIERRA VISTA RV PARK **Ratings: 9.5/8.5★/9.5** (RV Resort) Avail: 39 full hkups (30/50 amps). 2021 rates: $30 to $40. (520)459-1690, 733 S Deer Creek Lane, Sierra Vista, AZ 85635

SNOWFLAKE — C4 *Navajo*

PUTTER'S PARADISE RV PARK **Ratings: 7/8.5★/7.5** (RV Park) Avail: 35 full hkups (30/50 amps). 2021 rates: $45. (928)536-2127, 2085 W Snowflake Blvd , Snowflake, AZ 85937

We appreciate your business!

SPRINGERVILLE — C5 *Apache*

CASA MALPAIS RV PARK **Ratings: 7.5/9★/8.5** (RV Park) Avail: 58 full hkups (30/50 amps). 2021 rates: $33. (928)333-4632, 272 W Main St, Springerville, AZ 85938

LYMAN LAKE (Public State Park) From Jct of US 180 & US 191, go S 11.4 mi on US 180/191, then E 1.6 mi (R). 56 Avail: 13 full hkups, 25 W, 25 S (30/50 amps). 2021 rates: $28 to $33. May 15 to Oct 15. (928)337-4441

OM PLACE RV PARK

good sam park **Ratings: 5/NA/5.5** (RV Park) Avail: 12 full hkups (30/50 amps). 2021 rates: $22 to $25. (928)221-9325, 741 E Main St, Springerville, AZ 85938

SPRINGERVILLE RV PARK **Ratings: 5.5/NA/6.5** (RV Park) Avail: 44 full hkups (30/50 amps). 2021 rates: $25 to $40. (505)215-0712, 1630 E Main Street, Springerville, AZ 85938

ST DAVID — E4 *Cochise*

APACHE MOBILE HOME AND RV PARK **Ratings: 7.5/8.5★/8** (RV Park) Avail: 60 full hkups (30/50 amps). 2021 rates: $25 to $35. (520)720-4634, 79 N Apache Trail, St David, AZ 85630

ST JOHNS — C5 *Apache*

ST JOHNS RV RESORT

good sam park **Ratings: 7.5/9★/8** (RV Park) From jct US-180 & US-191: Go 1 mi S on US-191/White Mtn Dr, then 1-1/2 mi W on 7th St S (R). Elev 5815 ft.**FAC:** paved rds. (140 spaces). Avail: 70 gravel, patios, 3 pull-thrus, (40x90), back-ins (40x90), 70 full hkups (30/50 amps), seasonal sites, WiFi @ sites, tent sites, rentals, laundry, firewood. **REC:** boating nearby, playground, hunting nearby. Pets OK. Big rig sites. 2021 rates: $20. no cc.
(928)337-3726 Lat: 34.49781, Lon: -109.39678
2135 West 7th South, St Johns, AZ 85936
www.stjohnrv.com
See ad this page

SUN CITY — D3 *Maricopa*

SUN CITY See also Buckeye, El Mirage, Goodyear, Peoria, Phoenix, Surprise & Tempe.

PARADISE RV RESORT

good sam park **Ratings: 8.5/9★/8.5** (Membership Park) Avail: 250 full hkups (30/50 amps). 2021 rates: $32 to $48. (888)563-7040, 10950 W Union Hills Dr, Sun City, AZ 85373

SURPRISE — C3 *Maricopa*

A SPOTLIGHT Introducing Valley of the Sun's colorful attractions appearing at the front of this state section.

SUNFLOWER RV RESORT

good sam park **Ratings: 9.5/9★/10** (RV Resort) N-bnd: From Jct of I-10 & 101 Loop (Exit 133), N 12.5 mi on the 101 Loop to Bell Rd (Exit 14), W 5.6 mi on Bell Rd to N El Mirage Rd, S 0.3 mi (L); or S-bnd: From Jct of I-17 & 101 Loop (Exit 285), W 8 mi on 101 Loop to Bell Rd (Exit 14), W 5.6 mi on to El Mirage Rd, S 0.3 mi (L). Min. length 22 ft.

NOW TAKING RESERVATIONS
Sunflower offers endless activities and outstanding amenities amid intimate surroundings. Choose from hundreds of activities, classes and clubs to find the event just for you. Close to great shopping-restaurants-local events.

FAC: paved rds. (1139 spaces). Avail: 30 gravel, patios, 30 pull-thrus, (30x60), accepts full hkup units only, 30 full hkups (30/50 amps), seasonal sites, WiFi @ sites, dump, laundry, restaurant, controlled access. **REC:** heated pool, hot tub, shuffleboard. Pet restrict (B/Q). Partial handicap access. No tents, Age restrict may apply. Big rig sites, eco-friendly. 2021 rates: $35 to $69. ATM.
(623)583-0100 Lat: 33.63380, Lon: -112.32376
16501 N El Mirage Rd, Surprise, AZ 85378
www.cal-am.com/resorts/sunflower
See ad page 46

TACNA — D1 *Yuma*

COPPER MOUNTAIN RV PARK

good sam park **Ratings: 9/9.5★/9.5** (RV Park) From Jct of I-8 & Ave 40E (Exit 42), S 0.5 mi on Ave 40 E (R). **FAC:** paved/gravel rds. (204 spaces). Avail: 100 gravel, patios, back-ins (45x50), 100 full hkups (30/50 amps), seasonal sites, WiFi @ sites, laundry. **REC:** pool, shuffleboard. Pets OK. Partial handicap access. No tents. 2021 rates: $38, Military discount. no cc.
(928)750-6652 Lat: 32.68637, Lon: -113.95420
39886 E. County 9 1/2 St, Tacna, AZ 85352
coppermountainrvpark.com
See ad page 78

Find Good Sam member specials at GanderOutdoors.com

TEMPE — D3 *Maricopa*

APACHE PALMS RV PARK **Ratings: 9/9.5★/8** (RV Park) Avail: 80 full hkups (30/50 amps). 2021 rates: $50 to $65. (480)966-7399, 1836 E Apache Blvd, Tempe, AZ 85281

TEMPLE BAR MARINA — B1 *Mohave*

LAKE MEAD NRA/TEMPLE BAR (Public National Park) From Jct of US-93 & Temple Bar Rd, NE 26 mi on Temple Bar Rd CR-148, follow signs (R). 153 Avail. 2021 rates: $10 to $20. (702)293-8990

TOMBSTONE — E4 *Cochise*

TOMBSTONE RV PARK

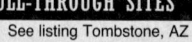

good sam park **Ratings: 9/9.5★/10** (RV Park) From Jct of Hwy 82 & SR-80, S 1.7 mi on SR-80 (R). Elev 4350 ft.**FAC:** gravel rds. (83 spaces). Avail: 63 gravel, 38 pull-thrus, (30x45), back-ins (35x50), 63 full hkups (30/50 amps), seasonal sites, WiFi @ sites, rentals, laundry, LP gas, firewood. **REC:** heated pool, playground. Pet restrict (Q) $. No tents, eco-friendly. 2021 rates: $45, Military discount.
(520)457-3829 Lat: 31.73036, Lon: -110.07935
1475 N Hwy 80, Tombstone, AZ 85638
www.tombstonervparkandcampground.com
See ad this page

Keep one Guide at home, and one in your RV! To purchase additional copies, call 877-209-6655.

So you're the one with ""pooch'' duty? Please make a clean sweep of it! Your fellow RVers will appreciate it!

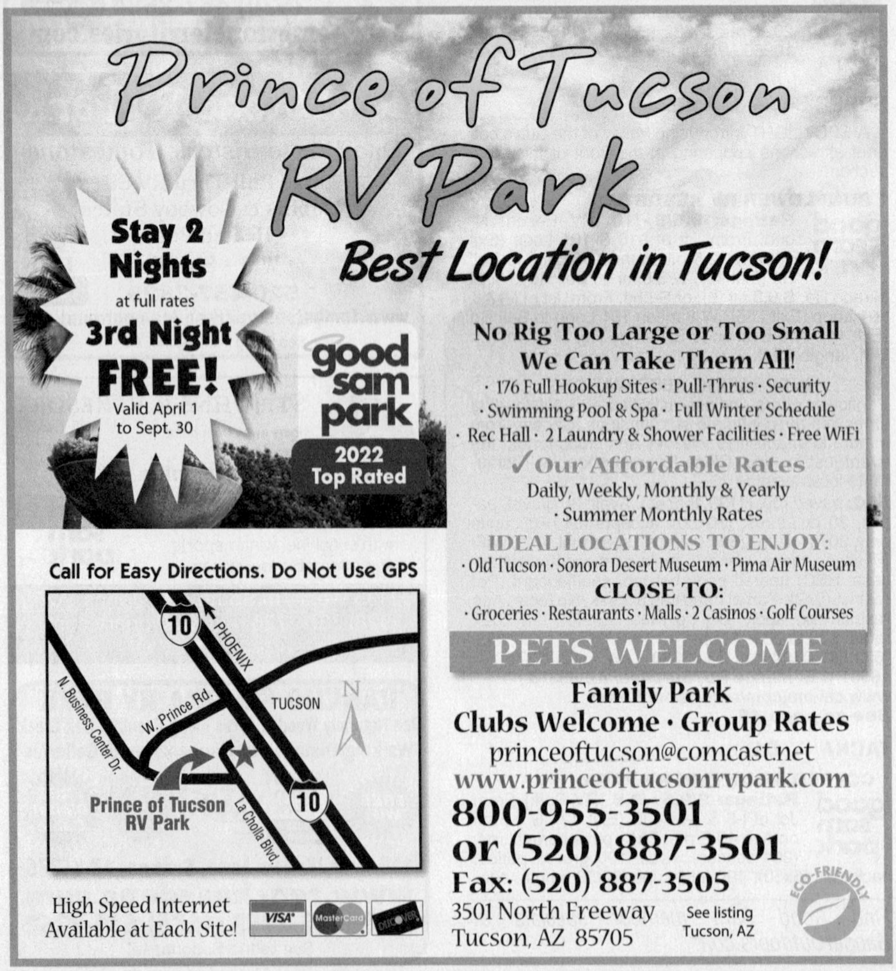

TOMBSTONE (CONT)

TOMBSTONE TERRITORIES RV RESORT

good sam park **Ratings: 10/9.5★/10** (RV Park) From Jct of I-10 & AZ Hwy 90 (Exit 302), go S on AZ-90 for 19 mi to AZ-82, turn E on to AZ-82, go 7.8 mi (L). Elev 4000 ft.**FAC:** paved rds. (102 spaces). Avail: 90 all weather, patios, 90 pull-thrus, (40x80), 90 full hkups (30/50 amps), seasonal sites, cable, WiFi @ sites, laundry, LP gas. **REC:** heated pool, hot tub, shuffleboard. Pet restrict (B/Q) $. Partial handicap access. No tents. Big rig sites, eco-friendly. 2021 rates: $33 to $38, Military discount.
(520)457-2584 Lat: 31.72107, Lon: -110.22435
2111 E Hwy 82, Tombstone, AZ 85616
www.tombstoneterritories.com
See ad previous page

TOPOCK — C1 *Mohave*

ROUTE 66 GOLDEN SHORES RV PARK

good sam park **Ratings: 7/8.5★/7.5** (RV Park) Avail: 33 full hkups (30/50 amps). 2021 rates: $32 to $38. (928)788-1001, 13021 Water-reed Way, Topock, AZ 86436

TUCSON — E4 *Pima*

TUCSON See also Green Valley & Marana.

CACTUS COUNTRY RV RESORT **Ratings: 9/9★/9** (RV Resort) Avail: 199 full hkups (30/50 amps). 2021 rates: $37 to $53. (520)574-3000, 10195 S Houghton Rd, Tucson, AZ 85747

CASINO DEL SOL RV PARK **Ratings: 7/9★/9.5** (RV Resort) Avail: 73 full hkups (30/50 amps). 2021 rates: $55. (520)324-9070, 5655 W Valencia Rd, Tucson, AZ 85757

CATALINA (Public State Park) From Jct of I-10 & W Tangerine Rd, E 13.5 mi on W Tangerine Rd to N Oracle Rd, S 0.4 mi on N Oracle Rd. (L). 120 Avail: 95 W, 95 E (30/50 amps). 2021 rates: $20 to $30. (520)628-5798

CRAZY HORSE RV CAMPGROUNDS

good sam park **Ratings: 9.5/9★/9** (RV Park) From Jct of I-10 & Craycroft Rd (Exit 268) take Frontage Rd to Craycroft Rd, N 1/4 mi on Craycroft Rd (L).

FUN CAMPING IN TUCSON!

Minutes from Gem Shows, downtown & many attractions. Come relax in the recreation hall with your friends & neighbors. Pet friendly. Low monthly rates. Call for a complete list of our amenities and discounts.

FAC: all weather rds. (176 spaces). Avail: 108 gravel, patios, 80 pull-thrus, (20x55), back-ins (20x50), 108 full hkups (30/50 amps), seasonal sites, WiFi @ sites, dump, laundry, LP gas. **REC:** heated pool. Pet restrict (S/B/Q). No tents, eco-friendly. 2021 rates: $39 to $46, Military discount.
(800)279-6279 Lat: 32.13072, Lon: -110.87533
6660 S Craycroft Rd, Tucson, AZ 85756
crazyhorserv.com
See ad this page

CRESCENT MANOR MH VILLAGE

good sam park **Ratings: 7.5/NA/8.5** (RV Area in MH Park) Avail: 23 full hkups (30 amps). 2021 rates: $42. (520)887-4452, 1150 W Prince Road, Tucson, AZ 85705

DESERT TRAILS RV PARK **Ratings: 9/9★/8.5** (RV Park) Avail: 244 full hkups (30/50 amps). 2021 rates: $32.50 to $39. (520)883-8340, 3551 S San Joaquin Rd, Tucson, AZ 85735

EL FRONTIER

good sam park **Ratings: 7/NA/6.5** (RV Area in MH Park) Avail: 10 full hkups (30/50 amps). 2021 rates: $45. (520)887-6369, 4233 N. Flowing Wells Rd. #193, Tucson, AZ 85705

FAR HORIZONS RV RESORT

good sam park **Ratings: 10/10★/10** (RV Resort) From jct I-10 & Kolb Rd (Exit 270): Go 9 mi N on Kolb Rd to Speedway, then 1 mi E to Pantano Rd, then 0.5 mi S (R).

NOW TAKING RESERVATIONS

Celebrate historic Tucson at our beautiful RV Resort with breathtaking mountain views, fun & relaxing amenities and activities that help you build long-lasting friendships. Stop by and see why so many RVers love Far Horizons.

FAC: paved rds. (514 spaces). Avail: 40 paved, patios, back-ins (36x47), accepts full hkup units only, 40 full hkups (30/50 amps), seasonal sites, WiFi @ sites, laundry, controlled access. **REC:** heated pool,

Are you using a friend's Guide? Want one of your own? Call 877-209-6655.

hot tub. Pet restrict (Q). No tents, Age restrict may apply. Big rig sites, eco-friendly. 2021 rates: $40 to $57.
(520)296-1234 Lat: 32.22802, Lon: -110.82414
555 N Pantano Rd, Tucson, AZ 85710
www.cal-am.com/resorts/far-horizons
See ad page 46

GILBERT RAY (PIMA COUNTY PARK) (Public) From jct Hwy 86 & Kinney Rd: Go 5 mi N on Kinney Rd, then 1/2 mi W on McCain Loop Rd (L). Avail: 130 E (30 amps). 2021 rates: $20. (520)883-4200

JUSTINS DIAMOND J RV PARK **Ratings: 7/NA/9** (RV Park) Avail: 100 full hkups (30/50 amps). 2021 rates: $37 to $40. (520)883-6706, 3451 S San Joaquin Rd, Tucson, AZ 85735

MESA RIDGE
Ratings: 7/NA/8 (RV Area in MH Park) Avail: 10 full hkups (30/50 amps). 2021 rates: $45. (520)294-2617, 1402 W. Ajo Way, Tucson, AZ 85713

MILITARY PARK FAMCAMP (DAVIS-MONTHAN AFB) (Public) W-bnd: From Jct of I-10 & Kolb Rd exit 270, N 6.6 mi to Golf Links, W to Craycroft Ave, L into main gate, L on Quijota Blvd, 1.1 mi to FampCamp (R). E-bnd: From Jct of I-10 & Alvernon Way exit 265, L on Alvernon Way (becomes Golf Links Rd) for 4.5 mi, R on Craycroft Ave to main gate. Avail: 197 full hkups (20/50 amps). 2021 rates: $24 to $29. (520)747-9144

MISSION VIEW RV RESORT
Ratings: 10/10★/10 (RV Park) From Jct of I-10 & I-19 (Exit 260), S 8.5 mi on I-19 to San Xavier Loop Rd (Exit 92), E 1.4 mi on San Xavier Loop Rd (L). **FAC:** paved rds. (342 spaces). Avail: 160 all weather, patios, back-ins (36x50), 160 full hkups (30/50 amps), seasonal sites, WiFi @ sites, rentals, laundry. **REC:** heated pool, hot tub, shuffleboard. Pet restrict (B/Q). No tents, Age restrict may apply, eco-friendly. 2021 rates: $36 to $46. no cc.
(800)444-8439 Lat: 32.11721, Lon: -110.97208
31 West Los Reales, Tucson, AZ 85756
www.missionviewrv.com
See ad opposite page

PALO VERDE ESTATES
Ratings: 5.5/NA/7.5 (RV Area in MH Park) From jct I-10 & S Palo Verde Rd (Exit 264A): Go 1 mi S on Palo Verde Rd (L). **FAC:** paved rds. (162 spaces). Avail: 45 gravel, back-ins (40x70), 45 full hkups (30/50 amps), seasonal sites, laundry. **REC:** pool. Pets OK. No tents. 2021 rates: $35. no cc.
(520)889-9674 Lat: 32.143519, Lon: -110.91634
6001 S Palo Verde Rd, Tucson, AZ 85706
www.paloverdemhp.com
See ad this page

PRINCE OF TUCSON RV PARK
Ratings: 9.5/9.5★/9.5 (RV Park) From Jct of I-10 & Prince Rd (Exit 254), Go W 0.2 mi on Prince Rd to stop sign, (do not turn onto frontage Rd) then S 0.1 mi on Business Center Dr, (L). **FAC:** all weather rds. Avail: 176 all weather, patios, 42 pull-thrus, (24x70), back-ins (25x45), accepts full hkup units only, 176 full hkups (30/50 amps), WiFi, dump, laundry. **REC:** heated pool, hot tub, shuffleboard. Pet restrict (B/Q). No tents. Big rig sites, eco-friendly. 2021 rates: $46.50.
(520)887-3501 Lat: 32.27146, Lon: -111.01092
3501 N Freeway, Tucson, AZ 85705
www.princeoftucsonrvpark.com
See ad opposite page

RINCON COUNTRY EAST RV RESORT
Ratings: 10/10★/10 (RV Park) From Jct of I-10 & Kolb Rd (exit 270), N 5 mi on Kolb Rd to Escalante Rd, E 2.5 mi (L).

VOTED ARIZONA'S BEST
Located near many attractions Tucson has to offer; Kartchner Caverns, Saguaro National Park, Arizona Desert Museum. Come enjoy our sunshine, hospitality & experience the resort you bought the RV for in the first place.

FAC: paved rds. (456 spaces). Avail: 55 paved, patios, back-ins (30x45), 55 full hkups (30/50 amps), seasonal sites, cable, WiFi @ sites, rentals, laundry, controlled access. **REC:** heated pool, hot tub, shuffleboard. Pet restrict (Q). Partial handicap access. No tents, Age restrict may apply, eco-friendly. 2021 rates: $55 to $61.
(520)448-4449 Lat: 32.17878, Lon: -110.80155
8989 E Escalante Rd, Tucson, AZ 85730
rinconcountry.com
See ad this page

Get the GOOD SAM CAMPING APP

RINCON COUNTRY WEST RV RESORT
Ratings: 10/10★/10 (RV Resort) From Jct of I-10 & I-19 (exit 260), S 1.5 mi on I-19 to Ajo Way (exit 99), W 1 mi to Mission Rd, S 0.5 mi (L). **FAC:** paved rds. (1112 spaces). 382 Avail: 24 paved, 358 all weather, patios, 24 pull-thrus, (22x57), back-ins (35x50), accepts full hkup units only, 382 full hkups (30/50 amps), seasonal sites, cable, WiFi @ sites, rentals, laundry, controlled access. **REC:** heated pool, hot tub, shuffleboard. Pet restrict (B/Q). Partial handicap access. No tents, Age restrict may apply, eco-friendly. 2021 rates: $57 to $63.
(520)294-5608 Lat: 32.16873, Lon: -111.00249
4555 S Mission Rd, Tucson, AZ 85746
rinconcountry.com
See ad this page

SENTINEL PEAK RV PARK **Ratings: 9.5/NA/9.5** (RV Park) Avail: 23 full hkups (30/50 amps). 2021 rates: $42 to $52. (520)495-0175, 450 N Grande Ave, Tucson, AZ 85745

SOUTH FORTY RV RANCH
Ratings: 9.5/10★/9.5 (RV Park) From jct of I-10 & Orange Grove Rd (exit 250): Go 1/2 mi E on Orange Grove Rd (L). **FAC:** paved rds. (230 spaces). Avail: 103 all weather, patios, 90 pull-thrus, (30x50), back-ins (35x45), 103 full hkups (30/50 amps), seasonal sites, WiFi, rentals, laundry. **REC:** heated pool, hot tub. Pet restrict (S/B/Q). No tents. 2021 rates: $45.02 to $53, Military discount.
(520)297-2503 Lat: 32.323961, Lon: -111.041473
3600 W Orange Grove, Tucson, AZ 85741
southfortyrvranch.com
See ad this page

THE RV PARK AT THE PIMA COUNTY FAIRGROUNDS
Ratings: 8/9★/8 (RV Park) From jct I-10 & Houghton Rd (Exit 275): Go 1 mi S on Houghton Rd to Brekke, then 0.2 mi N (L). **FAC:** paved/gravel rds. 350 Avail: 45 paved, 305 gravel, 26 pull-thrus, (20x45), back-ins (25x45), 310 full hkups, 40 W, 40 E (30/50 amps), WiFi @ sites, dump, laundry, LP gas, restaurant, controlled access. **REC:** rec open to public. Pets OK. Partial handicap access. No tents. Big rig sites, eco-friendly. 2021 rates: $30.
(520)762-8579 Lat: 32.04851, Lon: -110.77380
11300 S Houghton Rd, Tucson, AZ 85747
www.pimacountyfair.com
See ad this page

TUCSON LAZYDAYS KOA **Ratings: 9.5/9.5★/10** (RV Resort) Avail: 360 full hkups (30/50 amps). 2021 rates: $31.95 to $56.95. (520)799-3701, 5151 S Country Club Rd, Tucson, AZ 85706

VOYAGER RV RESORT & HOTEL
Ratings: 9.5/9.5★/8.5 (RV Park) Avail: 976 full hkups (30/50 amps). 2021 rates: $42 to $54. (888)563-7040, 8701 S Kolb Rd, Tucson, AZ 85756

Travel Services

CAMPING WORLD OF TUCSON As the nation's largest retailer of RV supplies, accessories, services and new and used RVs, Camping World is committed to making your total RV experience better. **SERVICES:** tire, RV appliance, staffed RV wash, restrooms. RV Sales. RV supplies, LP gas, emergency parking, RV accessible. Hours: 9am to 7pm.
(888)544-8470 Lat: 32.176007, Lon: -110.917790
4700 S. Palo Verde Road, Tucson, AZ 85714
www.campingworld.com

TUSAYAN — B3 *Coconino*

GRAND CANYON CAMPER VILLAGE **Ratings: 3.5/5/5** (Campground) 96 Avail: 50 full hkups, 46 W, 46 E (30/50 amps). 2021 rates: $52 to $66. (928)638-2887, 549 Camper Village Lane, Tusayan, AZ 86023

WELLTON — D1 *Yuma*

ARROWHEAD RV PARK **Ratings: 8.5/8.5★/7.5** (RV Park) 79 Avail: 74 full hkups, 5 W, 5 E (30/50 amps). 2021 rates: $27. (928)785-3971, 30115 Wellton-Mohawk Dr, Wellton, AZ 85356

RANCHO EL MIRAGE MFH AND RV RESORT **Ratings: 9/10★/9** (RV Park) Avail: 60 full hkups (30/50 amps). 2021 rates: $45. (928)785-4960, 26532 Red Rock Rd, Wellton, AZ 85356

SUN COUNTRY RV PARK
Ratings: 5/7.5★/5 (RV Park) Avail: 40 full hkups (30 amps). 2021 rates: $27. (928)785-4072, 10321 Fresno St, Wellton, AZ 85356

TIER DROP RV PARK **Ratings: 8/7.5/8** (RV Park) Avail: 60 full hkups (30/50 amps). 2021 rates: $27. (928)785-9295, 28320 E Co 11th St, Wellton, AZ 85356

WENDEN — C2 *La Paz*

ALAMO LAKE (Public State Park) From the city of Wenden, go north 38 miles on Alamo Dam Road to reach Alamo Lake State Park. 194 Avail: 18 full hkups, 45 W, 176 E (30/50 amps). 2021 rates: $22 to $28. (928)669-2088

Things change ... last year's rates serve as a guideline only.

WICKENBURG — C2 *Maricopa*

COUNTRY CLUB PARK **Ratings: 7.5/7.5/8.5** (RV Area in MH Park) Avail: 21 full hkups (30/50 amps). 2021 rates: $60. (928)684-2110, 1855 W Wickenburg Way, Wickenburg, AZ 85390

DESERT CYPRESS RV & MH PARK **Ratings: 8.5/8.5★/9** (RV Area in MH Park) Avail: 60 full hkups (30/50 amps). 2021 rates: $45. (928)684-2153, 610 Jack Burden Rd Space 33, Wickenburg, AZ 85390

HORSPITALITY RV RESORT
good sam park **Ratings: 9/9.5★/10** (RV Park) From Jct of US-60/89 & SR-93, SE 2 mi on Hwys 60/89/93, between MP-112 & 113 (R). **FAC:** paved rds. (100 spaces). Avail: 50 all weather, patios, 7 pull-thrus, (30x100), back-ins (30x65), 50 full hkups (30/50 amps), seasonal sites, WiFi @ sites, dump, laundry, LP gas, firewood. Pet restrict (B). No tents, Age restrict may apply, eco-friendly. 2021 rates: $35 to $59, Military discount.
(928)684-2519 Lat: 33.95275, Lon: -112.70964
51802 US Hwy 60-89, Wickenburg, AZ 85390
horspitality.com
See ad this page

WIKIEUP — C2 *Mohave*

BURRO CREEK (BLM) (Public Corps) From town: Go 60 mi N on Hwy 93, then 1.5 mi W on Burro Creek Rd (R). 23 Avail. 2021 rates: $14. (928)718-3700

HIDDEN OASIS RV PARK **Ratings: 7/8★/7.5** (RV Park) Avail: 43 full hkups (30/50 amps). 2021 rates: $30. (928)765-2439, 17653 S Hwy 93, Wikieup, AZ 85360

WILLCOX — E5 *Cochise*

CHIRICAHUA NATIONAL MONUMENT/BONITA CANYON (Public National Park) From town, SE 34 mi on Hwy 186 to Hwy 181, E 3 mi (L). Avail: 1 E. 2021 rates: $12. (520)824-3560

GRANDE VISTA RV PARK **Ratings: 9/9★/8.5** (RV Park) Avail: 36 full hkups (30/50 amps). 2021 rates: $36 to $38. (520)384-4002, 711 North Prescott Ave, Willcox, AZ 85643

LIFESTYLE RV RESORT **Ratings: 8/8★/8** (RV Park) Avail: 52 full hkups (30/50 amps). 2021 rates: $39. (520)384-3303, 622 N Haskell Ave, Willcox, AZ 85643

WILLCOX-COCHISE KOA **Ratings: 10/10★/8** (RV Park) Avail: 57 full hkups (30/50 amps). 2021 rates: $39.89 to $62.89. (520)384-3212, 700 N Virginia Ave, Willcox, AZ 85643

WILLIAMS — B3 *Coconino*

CANYON GATEWAY GRAND CANYON RV PARK & GLAMPING
good sam park **Ratings: 8/10★/8** (RV Park) Avail: 40 full hkups (30/50 amps). 2021 rates: $46.73. (928)635-2718, 1060 N Grand Canyon Blvd, Williams, AZ 86046

CANYON MOTEL & RV PARK **Ratings: 9/9★/9** (RV Park) Avail: 47 full hkups (30/50 amps). 2021 rates: $46.99 to $56.99. (928)635-9371, 1900 E Rodeo Rd/Route 66, Williams, AZ 86046

GRAND CANYON KOA JOURNEY **Ratings: 7/8/7** (Campground) 54 Avail: 16 full hkups, 38 W, 38 E (30/50 amps). 2021 rates: $29 to $75. (800)562-5771, 5333 N Hwy 64, Williams, AZ 86046

GRAND CANYON RAILWAY RV PARK
good sam park **Ratings: 9.5/10★/9** (RV Resort) From Jct of I-40 & Grand Canyon Blvd (exit 163), S 0.3 mi on Grand Canyon Blvd to Franklin Ave, SW 0.2 mi (L). Elev 6800 ft.

We've listened to thousands of RVers like you, so we know exactly how to rate campgrounds. Got feedback? Call us! 877-209-6655.

ALL ABOARD GRAND CANYON NATL PARK
Take the historic train into Grand Canyon National Park without having to worry about navigating through the busy local roadways. Park your RV in the clean mountain air in Williams, just two blocks away from Route 66.
FAC: paved rds. Avail: 124 paved, 73 pull-thrus, (30x65), back-ins (30x55), 124 full hkups (30/50 amps), WiFi @ sites, tent sites, rentals, laundry, restaurant. **REC:** heated pool, hot tub, playground, hunting nearby. Pets OK. Partial handicap access. Big rig sites, 28 day max stay, eco-friendly. 2021 rates: $46.20 to $51.25, Military discount. ATM.
(800)843-8724 Lat: 35.25157, Lon: -112.19410
601 W Franklin Ave, Williams, AZ 86046
www.thetrain.com
See ad page 54

RAILSIDE RV RANCH & CABIN RESORT **Ratings: 7/9★/8** (RV Park) Avail: 96 full hkups (30/50 amps). 2021 rates: $45 to $51. Mar 01 to Dec 21. (928)635-4077, 877 E Rodeo Rd, Williams, AZ 86046

RAPTOR RANCH RV PARK & CAMPGROUND (Campground) (Rebuilding) 24 Avail: 8 full hkups, 16 W, 16 E (30/50 amps). 2021 rates: $50 to $75. (928)635-3072, 332 State Route 64, Williams, AZ 86046

WILLIAMS/CIRCLE PINES KOA HOLIDAY **Ratings: 8/8.5/7.5** (Campground) 125 Avail: 84 full hkups, 41 W, 41 E (30/50 amps). 2021 rates: $50 to $105.84. Mar 15 to Oct 31. (800)562-9379, 1000 Circle Pines Rd, Williams, AZ 86046

Things to See and Do

GRAND CANYON RAILWAY Grand Canyon Railway offers train trips from Williams to the Grand Canyon on trains that made their first journey in 1901. Elev 6800 ft. Partial handicap access. RV accessible. Restrooms. Food. Hours: . Adult fee: $65.00 to $219.00. ATM.
(800)843-8724 Lat: 35.25157, Lon: -112.1941
235 N Grand Canyon Blvd, Williams, AZ 86046
www.thetrain.com
See ad page 54

GRAND CANYON RAILWAY PET RESORT Pet Resort has 28 spacious rooms for dogs & 16 comfortable condos for cats. Elev 7000 ft. Partial handicap access. RV accessible. Restrooms. Food. Hours: 8am to 8pm.
(800)843-8724 Lat: 35.25157, Lon: -112.1941
601 W Franklin, Williams, AZ 86046
www.thetrain.com
See ad page 54

WILLOW BEACH — B1 *Mohave*

WILLOW BEACH MARINA & CAMPGROUND
good sam park **Ratings: 9/9.5/9** (Campground) Avail: 27 full hkups (30/50 amps). 2021 rates: $60. (928)767-4747, 25804 N Willow Beach Rd, Willow Beach, AZ 86445

WINSLOW — B4 *Navajo*

HOMOLOVI (Public State Park) From Jct of I-40 & AZ 87, go N 1.9 mi on AZ 87, then SE 0.9 mi on State Park Rd (E). 53 Avail: 53 W, 45 E (30/50 amps). 2021 rates: $25 to $30. (928)289-4106

MCHOOD PARK (Public) From town, S 1.5 mi on SR-87 to SR-99, E 5 mi (L). 22 Avail. (928)289-5714

METEOR CRATER RV PARK **Ratings: 8.5/10★/10** (RV Park) 57 Avail: 26 full hkups, 31 W, 31 E (30/50 amps). 2021 rates: $37 to $42. (800)478-4002, I-40 Exit 233, Winslow, AZ 86047

YUMA — D1 *Yuma*

A SPOTLIGHT Introducing Yuma's colorful attractions appearing at the front of this state section.

ARABY ACRES RV RESORT
good sam park **Ratings: 9/9.5★/9.5** (RV Park) Avail: 39 full hkups (30/50 amps). 2021 rates: $68. (888)563-7040, 6649 E 32nd St, Yuma, AZ 85365

BLUE SKY RV RESORT
good sam park **Ratings: 9.5/10★/9.5** (RV Resort) Avail: 32 full hkups (30/50 amps). 2021 rates: $42 to $52.50. (877)367-5220, 10247 S Frontage Rd, Yuma, AZ 85365

BONITA MESA RV RESORT
good sam park **Ratings: 10/10★/10** (RV Park) From Jct of I-8 & exit 12 (Fortuna Rd), N on Fortuna Rd to Frntg rd, W 1.5 mi (R). **FAC:** paved rds. (470 spaces). Avail: 200 all weather, patios, back-ins (30x50), 200 full hkups (30/50 amps), seasonal sites, WiFi @ sites, rentals, laundry. **REC:** heated pool, hot tub, kayaking/canoe-

ing, shuffleboard. Pet restrict (B/Q). Partial handicap access. No tents, eco-friendly. 2021 rates: $46, Military discount.
(928)342-2999 Lat: 32.67159, Lon: -114.47103
9400 N Frontage Rd, Yuma, AZ 85365
bonitamesa.com
See ad this page

→ **CACTUS GARDENS RV RESORT**
good sam park **Ratings: 9/8.5★/8.5** (RV Park) Avail: 240 full hkups (30/50 amps). 2021 rates: $43 to $50. (888)563-7040, 10657 S Ave 9E, Yuma, AZ 85365

↓ **CAPRI RV RESORT**
good sam park **Ratings: 7.5/9★/7** (RV Park) Avail: 40 full hkups (30 amps). 2021 rates: $43 to $45. (888)563-7040, 3380 S 4th Ave, Yuma, AZ 85365

→ **CARAVAN OASIS RV RESORT**
good sam park **Ratings: 9.5/9★/9** (RV Park) Avail: 200 full hkups (30/50 amps). 2021 rates: $50. (928)342-1480, 10500 N Frontage Rd, Yuma, AZ 85365

← COCOPAH BEND RV & GOLF RESORT **Ratings: 9.5/9★/9.5** (RV Park) Avail: 375 full hkups (30/50 amps). 2021 rates: $50. (800)537-7901, 6800 S Strand Ave, Yuma, AZ 85364

↓ **DEL PUEBLO RV RESORT**
good sam park **Ratings: 10/10★/10** (RV Park) Jct of I-8 & Ave 3E (exit 3), S 5.2 mi on Ave 3E (R).

COUNTRY CLUB STYLE RV RESORT
Stay a night, month or year in our top rated, 55+ family owned RV resort. Guests appreciate our angled pull through sites that easily accommodate rigs to 70 feet long. Come enjoy our beautiful, friendly and active resort.

FAC: paved rds. (478 spaces). Avail: 398 all weather, patios, 30 pull-thrus, (40x90), back-ins (40x55), 398 full hkups (30/50 amps), seasonal sites, cable, WiFi @ sites, rentals, laundry, restaurant. **REC:** heated pool, hot tub, shuffleboard. Pet restrict (Q). Partial handicap access. No tents, Age restrict may apply. Big rig sites, eco-friendly. 2021 rates: $52 to $56. Oct 01 to May 01.
(928)341-2100 Lat: 32.61330, Lon: -114.58139
14794 S. Ave 3E, Yuma, AZ 85365
www.delpueblorv.com
See ad this page

→ **DESERT PARADISE RV RESORT**
good sam park **Ratings: 9/8.5★/8.5** (RV Park) Avail: 187 full hkups (30/50 amps). 2021 rates: $53.56 to $58.69. (888)563-7040, 10537 S Ave 9E, Yuma, AZ 85365

→ **FOOTHILL VILLAGE RV RESORT**
good sam park **Ratings: 8/8.5★/8.5** (RV Park) Avail: 78 full hkups (30 amps). 2021 rates: $51. (888)563-7040, 12705 E S Frontage Rd, Yuma, AZ 85367

→ **FORTUNA DE ORO RV RESORT**
good sam park **Ratings: 9.5/10★/9** (RV Resort) From Jct of I-8 & Foothills Blvd (exit 14), N 50 ft on Foothills Blvd to N frntg rd, E 0.6 mi (L).

NOW TAKING RESERVATIONS
Fill your days with fun! With over 1200 sites, a 9-hole golf course and on-site restaurant, you won't have to go anywhere to enjoy this 5-star resort. Located in the foothills of Yuma, AZ with lakes and casinos nearby.

FAC: paved rds. (1294 spaces). Avail: 794 gravel, patios, 34 pull-thrus, (30x50), back-ins (34x50), 794 full hkups (30/50 amps), seasonal sites, WiFi @ sites, laundry, LP bottles. **REC:** heated pool, hot tub, golf, shuffleboard. Pet restrict (B/Q). Partial handicap access. No tents, Age restrict may apply, eco-friendly. 2021 rates: $55 to $65. ATM.
(928)342-5051 Lat: 32.66831, Lon: -114.39853
13650 N Frontage Rd, Yuma, AZ 85367
www.cal-am.com/resorts/fortuna-de-oro
See ad pages 46, 63

↑ **GARDEN OASIS RV RESORT**
good sam park **Ratings: 8/9★/8.5** (RV Area in MH Park) From jct I-8 & US 95 S (exit 2): Go 2-1/2 mi W on US 95 S, then 1 mi N on S Avenue B, then 1/4 mi W on 8th St, then 1/4 mi N on S Clifford Way (R). **FAC:** paved rds. (78 spaces). Avail: 10 gravel, patios, back-ins (30x60), 10 full hkups (30/50 amps), seasonal sites, WiFi @ sites, laundry. **REC:** heated pool. Pets OK. No tents, Age restrict may apply. 2021 rates: $36.
(928)782-7747 Lat: 32.716038, Lon: -114.653283
669 S Clifford Way, Yuma, AZ 85364
gardenoasisrv.com
See ad opposite page

→ GILA MOUNTAIN RV PARK **Ratings: 8/8.5★/8.5** (RV Park) Avail: 59 full hkups (30/50 amps). 2021 rates: $35. (928)342-1310, 12325 S Frontage Rd, Yuma, AZ 85367

↑ **GOLDWATER MOBILE HOME & RV PARK**
good sam park **Ratings: 7.5/9★/8.5** (RV Park) From jct I-8 & Winterhaven Dr (exit 172 CA): Go 1/2 mi S on Winterhaven Dr, then 2 mi W on W 1st St (L). **FAC:** paved rds. (99 spaces). Avail: 35 gravel, back-ins (30x60), 35 full hkups (30/50 amps), seasonal sites, WiFi @ sites, laundry. Pets OK. No tents. 2021 rates: $30.
(928)783-8063 Lat: 32.724091, Lon: -114.655875
2837 W 1st St, Yuma, AZ 85364
goldwaterrv.com
See ad opposite page

↓ **MESA VERDE RV RESORT**
good sam park **Ratings: 9/8.5★/8** (RV Park) Avail: 30 full hkups (30/50 amps). 2021 rates: $54.10. (888)563-7040, 3649 S 4th Ave, Yuma, AZ 85365

↑ MILITARY PARK DESERT BREEZE TRAVEL CAMP (YUMA ARMY PROVING GROUND) (Public) On base, from Jct I-8 & S Fortuna Ave, N 2 mi to US-98, R on US-98 10.5 mi, L on Imperial Dam Rd, W 5.5 mi, R into gate, L at A Street. Avail: 113 full hkups (20/50 amps). 2021 rates: $35. (928)328-3989

↑ MILITARY PARK LAKE MARTINEZ RECREATION FACILITY (MCAS YUMA) (Public) From town, NE 32 mi to Martinez Lake Rd, L on Martinez Lake Rd for 10.5 mi, R on Red Cloud Mine Rd for 2.5 mi, L on Egret Rd. 20 Avail: 20 W, 20 E (20/50 amps). 2021 rates: $29 to $32. (928)783-3422

↖ RIVER FRONT RV PARK **Ratings: 7/7/7** (RV Park) Avail: 170 full hkups (30/50 amps). 2021 rates: $30 to $40. Oct 01 to Jun 01. (928)783-5868, 2300 Water St, Yuma, AZ 85364

← ROLLE'S LYNDA VISTA RV PARK **Ratings: 7/8.5★/6.5** (RV Park) Avail: 40 full hkups (30 amps). 2021 rates: $39. (928)782-9009, 2900 W 5th St, Yuma, AZ 85364

↑ **SHADY ACRES MH & RV PARK**
good sam park **Ratings: 8.5/9★/8** (RV Park) From Jct of I-8 & 4th Ave (Exit 172 in CA), S 0.7 mi on 4th Ave to W 3rd St, W .7 mi (R). **FAC:** paved rds. (155 spaces). 69 Avail: 50 gravel, 19 grass, back-ins (20x50), 69 full hkups (30/50 amps), seasonal sites, cable, WiFi @ sites, laundry. **REC:** heated pool, hot tub. Pets OK. No tents, Age restrict may apply, eco-friendly. 2021 rates: $45.
(928)783-9431 Lat: 32.72367, Lon: -114.63605
1340 W. 3rd Street, Yuma, AZ 85364
shadyacresyuma.com
See ad opposite page

→ SHANGRI-LA RV RESORT **Ratings: 10/10★/10** (RV Park) Avail: 18 full hkups (30/50 amps). 2021 rates: $46.88 to $59.23. (928)342-9123, 10498 N Frontage Rd, Yuma, AZ 85365

Save 10% at Good Sam Parks 365 days a year with no blackout dates!!

YUMA (CONT)

SOUTHERN MESA RV PARK

good sam park **Ratings: 8.5/8.5★/8.5** (RV Park) From Jct of I-8 & Ave 3E (Exit 3), S 8.9 mi on Ave 3E (R). **FAC:** gravel rds. (164 spaces). Avail: 100 dirt, patios, back-ins (35x40), 100 full hkups (30/50 amps), seasonal sites, WiFi @ sites, laundry. **REC:** heated pool. Pets OK. No tents, eco-friendly. 2021 rates: $35.
(928)726-5167 Lat: 32.55919, Lon: -114.58078
18540 S Ave 3E, Yuma, AZ 85365
southernmesarvpark.com
See ad page 78

SUNDANCE RV RESORT

good sam park **Ratings: 9.5/10★/9** (RV Park) From Jct of I-8 & Foothills Blvd (exit 14), N 50 ft on Foothills Blvd to N Frontage Rd, E 0.3 mi (L).

NOW TAKING RESERVATIONS
Resort is located in the scenic Foothills area of Yuma, Arizona where the beauty of the desert can be enjoyed while still close to shopping, medical facilities and a brief drive to old Mexico.
FAC: paved rds. (460 spaces). Avail: 160 gravel, patios, back-ins (30x40), 160 full hkups (30/50 amps), seasonal sites, WiFi @ sites, laundry. **REC:** heated pool, hot tub, shuffleboard. Pet restrict (Q). Partial handicap access. No tents, Age restrict may apply, eco-friendly. 2021 rates: $47.
(928)342-9333 Lat: 32.66895, Lon: -114.40320
13502 N Frontage Rd, Yuma, AZ 85367
www.cal-am.com/resorts/sundance
See ad pages 46, 63

SUNI SANDS RV RESORT

good sam park **Ratings: 8.5/8.5★/7.5** (RV Park) Avail: 100 full hkups (30 amps). 2021 rates: $51. (888)563-7040, 1960 E 32nd St, Yuma, AZ 85365

VILLA ALAMEDA RV RESORT

good sam park **Ratings: 10/10★/10** (RV Park) From Jct of I-8 & Ave 3E (exit 3), Go 1-1/4 mi S on Ave 3E, then 2 mi E on 32nd St (Bus 8), then 1/2 mi S on Ave 5E (L); or From Jct of I-8 & Araby Rd (Exit 7), Go 1/2 mi S on Araby Rd, then 1-1/2 mi W on 32nd St (Bus 8), then 1/2 mi S on Ave 5E (L).

A FUN PLACE-NOT JUST ANOTHER SPACE
Villa Alameda RV Resort is luxurious RV living in a grove! Whether you're looking for a daily, weekly or monthly site, we have sites just for you! You will find a friendly, active community and a great place to call home!
FAC: paved rds. (302 spaces). Avail: 20 all weather, patios, back-ins (33x52), 20 full hkups (30/50 amps), seasonal sites, cable, WiFi @ sites, laundry. **REC:** heated pool, hot tub, shuffleboard. Pet restrict (S/B/Q). Partial handicap access. No tents, Age restrict may apply, eco-friendly. 2021 rates: $40. no cc.
(928)344-8081 Lat: 32.66280, Lon: -114.54618
3547 S Ave 5E, Yuma, AZ 85365
villaalamedarvresort.com
See ad page 62

WESTWIND RV & GOLF RESORT

good sam park **Ratings: 10/10★/10** (RV Resort) From Jct of I-8 & Fortuna Rd (exit 12), S 50 ft on Fortuna Rd to S Frontage Rd, W 1 mi (L). **FAC:** paved rds. (1075 spaces). Avail: 475 all weather, patios, 3 pull-thrus, (32x84), back-ins (30x45), 475 full hkups (30/50 amps), seasonal sites, WiFi @ sites, $, rentals, laundry, restaurant, controlled access. **REC:** heated pool, hot tub, golf, shuffleboard. Pet restrict (S/B/Q). No tents, Age restrict may apply, eco-friendly. 2021 rates: $30 to $60. ATM.
(928)342-2992 Lat: 32.66957, Lon: -114.46294
9797 South Frontage Road, Yuma, AZ 85365
www.westwindrvgolfresort.com
See ad previous page

Driving a big rig? Average site width and length measurements tell you which campgrounds can accommodate your Big Rig.

Read RV topics at blog.GoodSam.com

Check out those views! From awe-inspiring redwood giants to the soaring towers of the Golden Gate Bridge, we've put the Spotlight on North America's most popular travel destinations. Turn to the Spotlight articles in our State and Province sections to learn more.

Getty Images/iStockphoto

Arkansas

DID YOU KNOW?

On average, two diamonds a day are found by visitors to Crater of Diamonds State Park in Murfreesboro. Treasure finders get to keep them.

AR

Arkansas stays true to its roots as a welcoming region that basks in its southern influences. Fiddlers play their tunes at community gatherings and time-honored, homespun recipes grace the tables of cozy restaurants.

Vibrant Towns

Little Rock, the capital of Arkansas, serves up a unique brand of food and fun that has put Arkansas on the map. A revitalized area along the Arkansas River connects several historic sites, family-friendly attractions, green spaces and recreational trails, including the nation's longest pedestrian bridge. Another wonderful place to explore is the town of Hot Springs, an hour southwest of Little Rock. Hot Springs National Park preserves the history of the grand Bathhouse Row, which sprang up along the town's namesake mineral water springs in the 1800s. In the northwest, the town of Bentonville is home to the Walmart Museum.

Diamonds and Delights

Arkansas is home to 52 state parks that preserve remarkable environments. You'll hit the trifecta with a visit to Mount Magazine, Mount Nebo and Petit Jean State Parks. Each offers unforgettable views from some of Arkansas' highest points. In Central Arkansas, Crater of Diamonds State Park is the only spot in the world where visitors can dig for diamonds. Unearth gems in the 37 acres of exposed surface.

Ozarks All Day Long

Northwest Arkansas is home to some of the state's best hiking trails. Hawksbill Crag, a large rock formation, provides a natural platform with views of the rolling Ozark hills receding into the distance. Those with a fear of heights will find friendlier trails nearby. Bicyclists can also find their paradise in Northwest Arkansas. The 36-mile Razorback Regional Greenway connects several small towns.

Arkansas Cheese Dip

Arkansas likes to call itself the birthplace of cheese dip. Locals love it so much that they've even created a cheese dip trail that runs through the entire state. Start your cheesy adventure in Little Rock, where Casa Manana Rock offers a white dip with queso añejo and queso Chihuahua. It's a great appetizer.

VISITOR CENTER

TIME ZONE
Central Standard

ROAD & HIGHWAY INFORMATION
501-569-2374
idrivearkansas.com

FISHING & HUNTING INFORMATION
800-364-4263
agfc.com/en

BOATING INFORMATION
www.agfc.com/en/fishing/boating-information

NATIONAL PARKS
nps.gov/ar

STATE PARKS
arkansasstateparks.com

TOURISM INFORMATION
Arkansas Department of Parks and Tourism
501-682-7777
arkansas.com

TOP TOURISM ATTRACTIONS
1) Hot Springs National Park
2) Boyhood Home of Johnny Cash
3) Clinton Presidential Center

MAJOR CITIES
Little Rock (capital), Fort Smith, Fayetteville, Springdale, Jonesboro

 See map page 83

good sam park Featured Good Sam Parks

ARKANSAS

When you stay with Good Sam, you can expect the highest degree of cleanliness and friendliness, and better yet, you get **10% off** overnight campground fees.

If you're not already a Good Sam member you can purchase your membership at one of these locations:

ALMA
Fort Smith-Alma RV Park

ARKADELPHIA
Caddo Valley RV Park

BELLA VISTA
Blowing Springs RV Park

CAVE SPRINGS
The Creeks Golf & RV Resort

CONWAY
Forest Lake Estates MH and RV Community

COTTER
Denton Ferry RV Park & Cabin Rental

EUREKA SPRINGS
Kettle Campground
Wanderlust RV Park

HORSESHOE BEND
Crown Lake RV Resort

HOT SPRINGS NATIONAL PARK
Cloud Nine RV Park
J & J RV Park
Treasure Isle RV Park

JUDSONIA
Red River RV Park

LAKE VILLAGE
Pecan Grove RV Park

MAGNOLIA
Magnolia RV Park

MOUNTAIN VIEW
Ozark RV Park

NORTH LITTLE ROCK
Downtown Riverside RV Park

RUSSELLVILLE
Ivys Cove RV Retreat
Outdoor Living Center RV Park

TEXARKANA
Sunrise RV Park

VAN BUREN
Overland RV Park
Park Ridge RV Campground

WEST MEMPHIS
Tom Sawyer's RV Park

Getty Images/iStockphoto

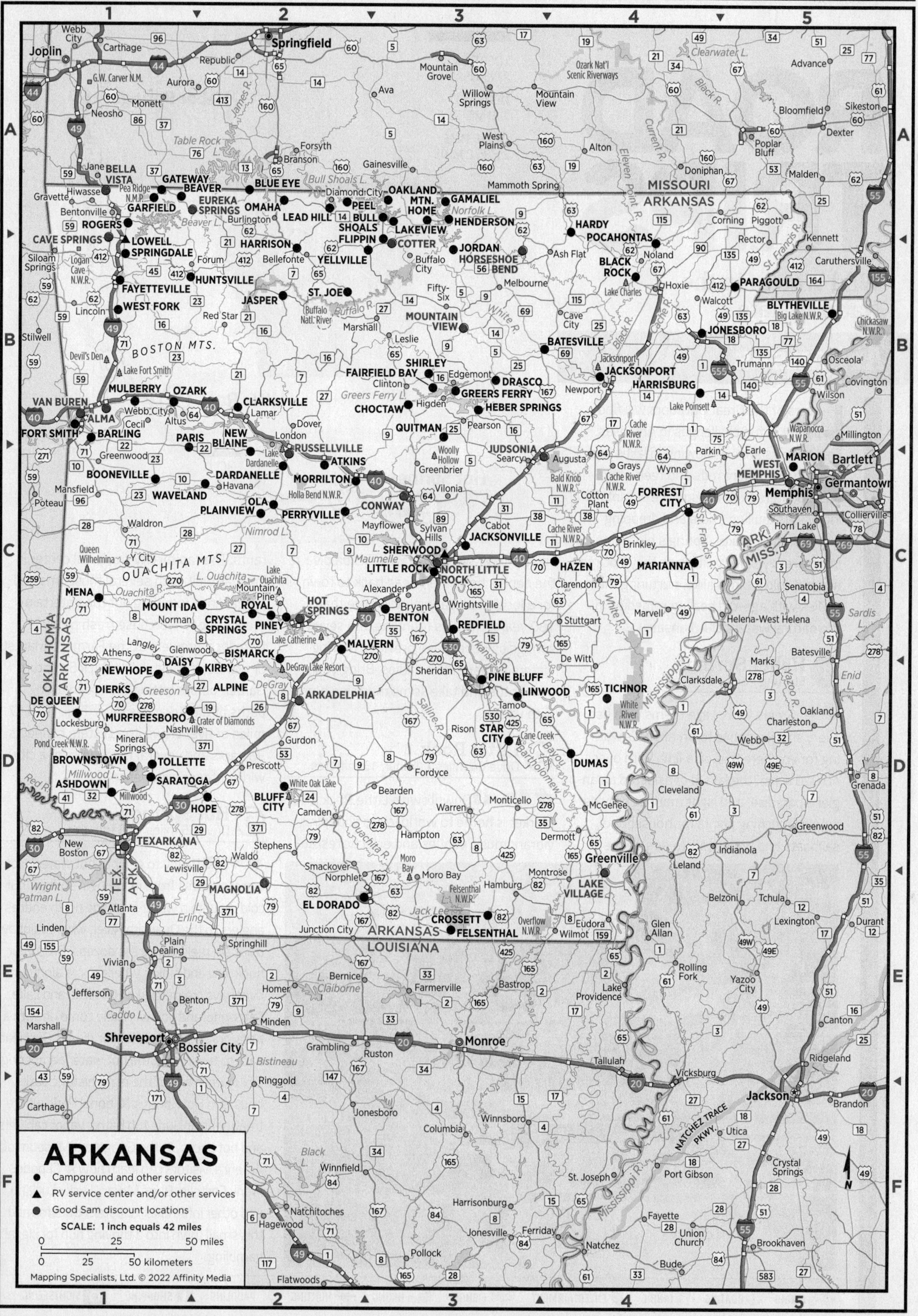
ARKANSAS
Campground and other services
RV service center and/or other services
Good Sam discount locations
SCALE: 1 inch equals 42 miles
0 25 50 miles
0 25 50 kilometers
Mapping Specialists, Ltd. © 2022 Affinity Media
MISSOURI
ARKANSAS
LOUISIANA
OKLAHOMA
TEX.
ARK.
ARK.
MISS.
BOSTON MTS.
OUACHITA MTS.
Springfield
Joplin
BELLA VISTA
GATEWAY
BEAVER
BLUE EYE
EUREKA SPRINGS
GARFIELD
OMAHA
LEAD HILL
OAKLAND
PEEL
MTN. HOME
GAMALIEL
BULL SHOALS
LAKEVIEW
HENDERSON
FLIPPIN
COTTER
YELLVILLE
HARRISON
ROGERS
CAVE SPRINGS
LOWELL
SPRINGDALE
HUNTSVILLE
FAYETTEVILLE
WEST FORK
JASPER
ST. JOE
JORDAN
HORSESHOE BEND
HARDY
POCAHONTAS
BLACK ROCK
PARAGOULD
BLYTHEVILLE
JONESBORO
MOUNTAIN VIEW
BATESVILLE
JACKSONPORT
HARRISBURG
SHIRLEY
FAIRFIELD BAY
DRASCO
GREERS FERRY
HEBER SPRINGS
CHOCTAW
QUITMAN
VAN BUREN
MULBERRY
OZARK
ALMA
FORT SMITH
BARLING
CLARKSVILLE
PARIS
NEW BLAINE
RUSSELLVILLE
ATKINS
DARDANELLE
MORRILTON
BOONEVILLE
WAVELAND
JUDSONIA
OLA
PLAINVIEW
PERRYVILLE
CONWAY
WEST MEMPHIS
MARION
Memphis
FORREST CITY
SHERWOOD
JACKSONVILLE
LITTLE ROCK
NORTH LITTLE ROCK
HAZEN
MARIANNA
MENA
MOUNT IDA
ROYAL
HOT SPRINGS
CRYSTAL SPRINGS
PINEY
BENTON
REDFIELD
BISMARCK
MALVERN
NEWHOPE
DAISY
KIRBY
ALPINE
DIERKS
DE QUEEN
ARKADELPHIA
PINE BLUFF
LINWOOD
TICHNOR
MURFREESBORO
STAR CITY
DUMAS
BROWNSTOWN
TOLLETTE
SARATOGA
ASHDOWN
HOPE
BLUFF CITY
TEXARKANA
MAGNOLIA
EL DORADO
CROSSETT
FELSENTHAL
LAKE VILLAGE
Greenville
Shreveport
Bossier City
Monroe
Vicksburg
Jackson
NATCHEZ TRACE PKWY.

ROAD TRIPS

Wild Waters in the Natural State

Arkansas

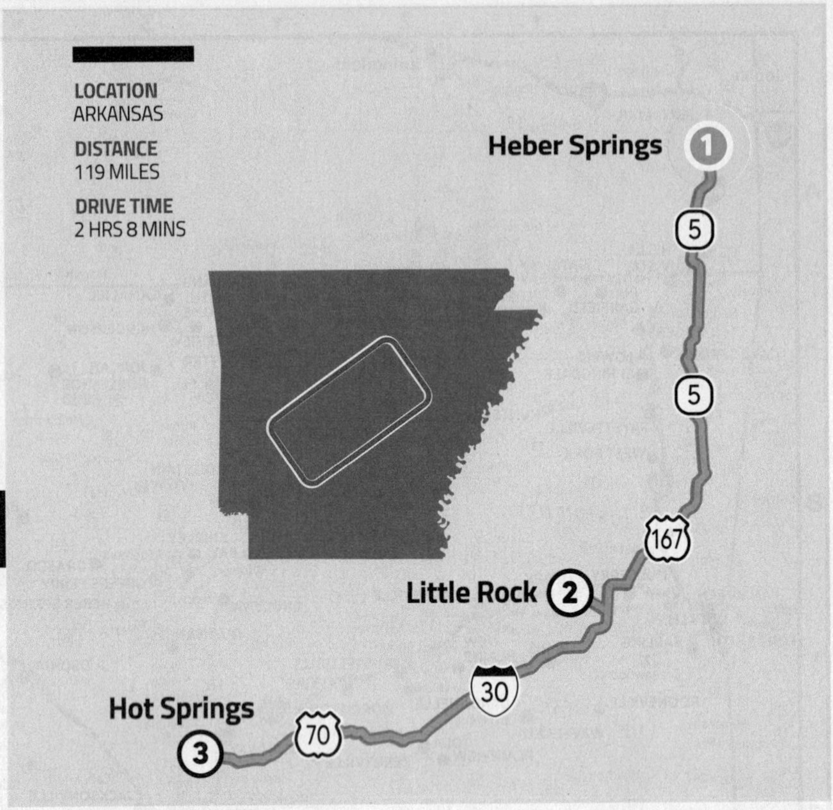

Lovers of the Great Outdoors will find plenty of fun challenges in Arkansas. Fish baskets are overflowing in lakes and along rivers, where rods and reels stay busy. Boaters skim the surface of tantalizing waters, pulling skiers and dropping divers in their wakes. Spring's blossoms inspire renewal for visitors as they flock to hot and cold springs alike, nurturing their bodies with age-old healing remedies in the natural waters of Arkansas.

1 Heber Springs
Starting Point

Greers Ferry Lake teems with fish: every species native to Arkansas is waiting for you here to drop a line. With over 40,000 acres, the lake is considered an angler's paradise, and eight marinas provide ample launching points for houseboats, sailboats and watercraft to peruse the crystal-clear waters, as well. Scuba dive the depths here, then head back to town for a local ritual dating back more than 180 years. Since its founding, the seven springs of Heber have provided healing waters for various maladies. Bring your own bottle and take some medicine home with you.

2 Little Rock
Drive 64 miles • 1 hour, 13 minutes

Downtown's Little Rock River Market is home to world-class shopping, vibrant music venues and eclectic restaurants. The capital city's cultural center is here, as well, with several museums and art galleries rounding out the entertainment options. Purchase fresh produce from local growers at the Farmer's Market, or wander through Little Rock Sculpture Garden before hitting the urban hiking paths of the Arkansas River Trail. With 17 miles of river views, the system connects 38 parks and several museums for a city-wide outdoor experience.

3 Hot Springs
Drive 55 miles • 55 minutes

Ready to get into hot water? Hot water streams from its renown springs, but cold mountain water from the north entices anglers to the Ouachita River, where rainbow trout are reeled in by the dozens. Drop your hook, line and sinker where dams along the river have created Lake Hamilton and Lake Catherine, and you will likely come up with a bass, crappie and catfish for dinner. But head back to town for some hot water pampering. Luxuriate in any of the eight historic bathhouses in Hot Springs National Park, where treatments include tub baths, vapor cabinets and hot packs. At the Gangsters Museum of America, visitors can learn how Al Capone, Frank Costello, Bugs Moran, Lucky Luciano and other infamous mobsters transformed this small town into a thriving hub for illegal gambling.

Getty Images/iStockphoto

BIKING · BOATING · DINING · ENTERTAINMENT · FISHING · HIKING · HUNTING · PADDLING · SHOPPING · SIGHTSEEING

Arkansas SPOTLIGHTS

Make Your Natural State Getaway

Shop at the very first Walmart and soak in hot springs that are renowned for their medicinal properties. Arkansas caters to everything a traveler could want, some with great fishing and hiking thrown in.

ARKANSAS BOASTS MORE THAN 400 MILES OF BIKING TRAILS.

Biking one of the many family-friendly mountain trails in Arkansas. Getty Images/iStockphoto

Bella Vista

Developed in the early 20th century as a summer resort town, Bella Vista is a cozy community that attracts visitors from across the South and beyond. Here you'll find world-class golf courses, seven area lakes, an interesting medley of museums, diverse dining opportunities, and extensive networks of public walking and mountain biking trails, all within a short drive of central Bella Vista. Nearby, you can visit priceless works of art at an iconic museum and visit the small store that spawned a retail empire.

The Trails of Bella Vista

Bella Vista is a major mountain biking destination, with many popular trails for cyclists of all strokes. The Back 40 Loop is among the most popular, featuring 40 miles of single-track trails. Other major trail systems include the Little Sugar Trail, around 35 miles of trails, including the Tunnel Vision Loop, which spans 25 miles. For slightly more experienced riders, the moderately rated Blowing Springs Loop takes visitors through a cave and past a waterfall. Note that the trails here are multi-use, so mountain bikers and hikers should be aware that they may encounter one another on the trails, some of which can be quite narrow.

Museums in and Around Town

Bella Vista and the surrounding area offer more than just outdoor recreation. There are several museums both within city limits and just a short drive from town. If you want to learn about local history, the Bella Vista Museum tells the story of the resort town's evolution since its establishment over a century ago. Bentonville's Museum of Native American History is worth a visit, with over 10,000 Native artifacts, many from the private collection of the museum's founder, a member of the Cherokee Nation.

Beautiful Bridges

Also in Bentonville, the Crystal Bridges Museum of American Art boasts a solid collection of priceless treasures, much of it contemporary American works, as well as 120 acres of grounds featuring sculptures and walking trails. For an off-beat museum experience, Bentonville's Walmart Museum traces the history and vision of the gargantuan American chain. It's located in the original "Walton's Five and Dime" store, the retail chain's humble predecessor. Browse the items on sale for a souvenir. For families, the Scott Family Amazeum offers all sorts of hands-on, interactive exhibits, with a heavy focus on science and industry.

Golf Country

Bella Vista has long been celebrated as a golf destination—in fact, its first golf course

LOCAL FAVORITE

Fiesta Fish

In Arkansas, catfish graces restaurant menus and can be caught in Natural State rivers, lakes and streams. *Recipe by Mike Robinson.*

INGREDIENTS

- ☐ 4 meaty fish fillets (cat fish, cod, snapper, any firm meaty fillet will work)
- ☐ 1 green bell pepper sliced
- ☐ 1 tomato sliced
- ☐ 1 onion sliced
- ☐ 1 lemon sliced
- ☐ 8 oz shredded cheddar cheese
- ☐ 4 Tbsp butter or margarine
- ☐ Salt and pepper to taste

DIRECTIONS

Tear 4 aluminum foil sheets long enough to make a tent around each fish fillet. Place a filet in the center of the foil sheet. Salt and pepper each filet to taste. Then add a layer of each vegetable (pepper, onion, and tomato) on top of the fish. Place about ¼ cup of the grated cheese on top of the veggies. Place 3 slices of the lemon on top of the pile. Put a dollop of the butter or margarine on the top then seal the packets closed. Sealing them tightly ensures the juices stay in and steam cook everything.

The dish can be cooked on a grill or in the oven. If cooking inside, preheat the oven to 350°F. Place your packets of fish on a cookie sheet and bake for 30 minutes.

If cooking on a grill, place the packets over direct heat and grill for 30 minutes. Serve with your favorite crusty bread to soak up juices. and a good rice dish. Serves 4.

opened in the 1920s. These days the area is home to a nine-hole executive golf course and six regulation 18-hole golf courses, from the beginner-friendly course at Bella Vista Country Club to the more challenging Scottsdale Golf Course. If you're just looking to warm up or perfect your form, the Tanyard Creek Practice Center offers 36 hard-surface stations, some of which are heated and covered for the cooler winter months.

Local Architecture

While you won't see any old antebellum houses in this 20th-century community, there are a couple of architectural features that are worth checking out. Perhaps the most impressive is the Mildred B. Cooper Memorial Chapel, a one-of-a-kind steel-and-glass chapel tucked away on a forested hilltop. The church incorporates elements from Gothic architecture, with 15 main arches and three or four intertwining additional arches that reach some 50 feet in the air. Dating to 2004, the Veterans Wall of Honor is dedicated to all veterans, with thousands of names of former service people etched onto its edifice.

On the Water

Bella Vista's seven lakes are a big part of its charm, though you will need to be the guest of a local resident to get out on the water. However, if you do want to get out on the water and don't know any locals, you can head out to the nearby Beaver Lake reservoir, about an hour's drive away, which offers 12 recreational areas and ample opportunities for swimming, boating, waterskiing, and bass fishing and is open to the general public.

Thorncrown Chapel in the Ozark Mountains near Eureka Springs serves as a religious retreat.

Bella Vista Dining

Bella Vista is home to all sorts of restaurants, from classic fast-food favorites to standalone restaurants unique to the city. Lakepoint Restaurant and Event Center is among the most popular spots in town, with classic American food and views over the waters of Loch Lomond, plus semi-frequent live music performances. If you're in the mood for something a bit spicier, Las Fajitas Mexican Restaurant and El Pueblito Mexican Restaurant both get rave reviews. If you want a taste of authentic barbecue, Alabama style, Bubba's BBQ serves up ribs, smoked meats, sandwiches, and hearty sides in a no-frills atmosphere. For something a bit lighter, the Veggie Table offers healthy, veggie-heavy meals, with options for meat lovers and herbivores alike.

Eureka Springs

Combine a laid-back Ozark Mountain vibe with elegant Victorian architecture and a rich spirit of fun and eccentricity. Eureka Springs stands at the crossroads of hipster and yesteryear, with a well-preserved downtown from the 1800s. These elegant structures are full of eclectic shops and bistros, all brimming with today's trinkets, cosmopolitan dining experiences and fine arts. Throw in a resident ghost or two, and this little Ozark gem will charm its way into everyone's trip itinerary.

Launch Your Watercraft

West of town, Beaver Lake satisfies boaters' hunger for adventure. Rent a kayak, paddle-

Steam rises from a mossy pool in Hot Springs. Local bathhouses tap the thermal springs for customers.

board or canoe to skim across the lake's surface or explore its depths at several swim beaches. Beaver Lake is located in northwest Arkansas, the birthplace of the White River, and offers great water for paddling and bass fishing. And don't miss reeling in enormous trout on the White River or canoeing down the country's first national waterway, Buffalo National River.

The Ozarks Via Two Wheels

There are abundant opportunities for mountain biking along the Oz Trails of Northwest Arkansas. And hiking and biking in Hobbs State Park are just two activities available there. Check out the Blue Springs Heritage Center, which preserves a unique body of water.

Religious Roots

Hidden deep in the woodlands is Thorncrown Chapel. Boasting 425 windows comprising 6,000 square feet of glass, this stunning 48-foot-tall structure is considered by many to be the most beautiful chapel in the world. Step inside to experience its exquisite open-air design and be captivated by the contrasting wood and glass architecture. If you prefer historical churches, check out St. Elizabeth's Catholic Church. Listed on the National Register of Historic Places and in Ripley's Believe It or Not, the 1904 structure is the only house of worship in which congregants enter through the bell tower. The structure is also unique in that it blends Byzantine, Romanesque and Gothic architectural styles.

Hot Springs

Hot Springs, Arkansas, attracts visitors for a soothing dip in therapeutic waters. Flowing out of the ground at an average temperature of 143 degrees Fahrenheit, the hot springs produce almost one million gallons of water each day.

Valued Vapors

Native Americans called this area "the Valley of the Vapors," and it was said to have been a neutral territory where all tribes could enjoy its healing waters in peace. Spanish and French settlers claimed the area in the mid-1500s. In fact, famous explorer Hernando de Soto was the first European to visit Hot Springs in 1541. The hot springs were such a coveted natural wonder that in 1832, President Andrew Jackson designed Hot Springs as the first federal reservation. Hot Springs Reservation was essentially America's first national park, predating Yellowstone National Park by 40 years. In just a decade, the area changed from a rough frontier town to an elegant spa city centered on a row of attractive Victorian-style bathhouses, the last ones completed in 1888. When Congress established the National Park Service, Hot Springs Reservation became Hot Springs National Park in 1921.

Soothing Soaks

Find warm bliss in the thermal waters on historic Bathhouse Row. The hot springs are also pumped into several downtown hotels and spas. The water is even available at public fountains. The beautifully restored Fordyce Bathhouse now serves as a visitor center. You'll find lots of activities and attractions in Hot Springs. Bring the whole gang to the National Park Aquarium, which houses the state's largest fish and reptile exhibit. Or, get up close and personal with reptiles and animals at the Arkansas Alligator Farm & Petting Zoo.

Great Garvan Gardens

The beauty of nature is on display at Garvan Woodland Gardens, located on a 210-acre peninsula on Lake Hamilton. Soar 1,200 feet above the city at Hot Springs Mountain Tower overlooking 140 miles of Ouachita Mountain scenery. Experience excitement at every twist and turn at Magic Springs Water and Theme Park, featuring roller coasters, water slides and family rides.

▸ **FOR MORE INFORMATION**

Arkansas Dept. of Parks & Tourism, 501-682-7777, www.arkansas.com
Eureka Springs Arkansas, www.eurekasprings.com
Greater Bentonville Area Chamber of Commerce, 479-273-2841
www.greaterbentonville.com
Hot Springs Convention & Visitors Bureau, 800-SPA-CITY
www.hotsprings.org

See listing Eureka Springs, AR

Arkansas

ALMA — B1 *Crawford*

CLEAR CREEK - COE/CLEAR CREEK CAMPGROUND (Public Corps) From town, S 5.2 mi on Hwy 162 to Clear Creek Rd., E 3.6 mi (E). Avail: 25 E (30 amps). 2021 rates: $10 to $18. (479)632-4882

CRABTREE RV PARK **Ratings: 7/8★/6** (RV Park) Avail: 11 full hkups (30/50 amps). 2021 rates: $27.77 to $29.99. (479)632-0909, 405 Heather Ln, Alma, AR 72921

FORT SMITH-ALMA RV PARK
Ratings: 9.5/9.5★/8 (Campground) From jct of I-40 (exit 13) & US-71: Go 2-1/4 mi N on US-71 (L). **FAC:** paved rds. (58 spaces). 52 Avail: 5 paved, 47 gravel, patios, 39 pull-thrus, (18x70), back-ins (18x40), mostly side by side hkups, 39 full hkups, 13 W, 13 E (30/50 amps), seasonal sites, WiFi @ sites, tent sites, rentals, dump, laundry, groc, LP gas. **REC:** pool, pond, fishing, boating nearby, playground, hunting nearby, rec open to public. Pets OK. eco-friendly. 2021 rates: $45.64 to $50.71, Military discount.
(479)632-2704 Lat: 35.5221, Lon: -94.2218
3539 N US-71, Alma, AR 72921
fortsmithalmarvpark.com
See ad page 90

Refer to the Table of Contents in front of the Guide to locate everything you need.

Arkansas Privately Owned Campground Information Updated by our Good Sam Representatives

Don & Peggy Holloway

After being high school sweethearts (the football player and the cheerleader) and married for 52 years, we've owned several businesses, allowing us to travel. Joining Good Sam in 2017, we follow two passions: seeing the U.S. and meeting new people.

ALPINE — D2 *Clark*

DEGRAY LAKE - COE/ALPINE RIDGE
(Public Corps) From Jct of I-30 & Exit 73/Hwy 8, W 19 mi on Hwy 8 to Fendley Rd (in Alpine), N 9 mi (E). **FAC:** paved rds. Avail: 49 paved, back-ins (15x65), 49 E (30/50 amps), tent sites, dump, fire rings. **REC:** DeGray Lake: swim, fishing, kayaking/canoeing, boating nearby, playground. Pets OK. 14 day max stay. 2021 rates: $20.
(870)246-5501 Lat: 34.26149, Lon: -93.22891
757 Alpine Ridge Landing Rd, Amity, AR 71921
www.recreation.gov

ARKADELPHIA — D2 *Clark*

CADDO VALLEY RV PARK
Ratings: 9/9.5★/8.5 (Campground) From Jct of I-30 & SR-7 (exit 78), N 0.3 mi on SR-7 to Service rd/ Frost Rd, NE 1 mi on Frost Rd (L). **FAC:** gravel rds. (46 spaces). Avail: 26 gravel, 14 pull-thrus, (30x100), back-ins (30x60), 26 full hkups (30/50 amps), seasonal sites, WiFi @ sites, dump, laundry. **REC:** pool, boating nearby, hunting nearby. Pet restrict (B). Partial handicap access. No tents. Big rig sites. 2021 rates: $45, Military discount.
(870)246-4922 Lat: 34.19637, Lon: -93.05746
221 Frost Road, Arkadelphia, AR 71923
www.caddovalleyRVpark.com
See ad this page

DE GRAY LAKE RESORT (Public State Park) From Jct of I-30 & SR-7 (exit 78), N 5 mi on SR-7 to park entrance rd, NW 1 mi (L). 113 Avail: 113 W, 113 E (30 amps). 2021 rates: $22 to $34. (501)865-5850

DEGRAY LAKE - COE/EDGEWOOD (Public Corps) From Jct of I-30 & Exit 78/Hwy 7, N 6 mi on Hwy 7 to Edgewood Rd, W 2 mi (E). Avail: 49 E (30/50 amps). 2021 rates: $20 to $40. May 01 to Sep 03. (870)246-5501

DEGRAY LAKE - COE/IRON MOUNTAIN CAMPGROUND (Public Corps) From Jct of I-30 & Exit 78/Hwy 7, N 2.5 mi on Hwy 7 to Skyline Dr, W 2.5 mi to Iron Mountain Rd, N to park (E). Avail: 69 E (50 amps). 2021 rates: $16. May 01 to Sep 03. (870)246-5501

GOLDENS RIVERSIDE RV PARK **Ratings: 5/NA/8** (RV Park) Avail: 26 full hkups (30/50 amps). 2021 rates: $40. (870)397-3553, 116 Valley St., Arkadelphia, AR 71923

ASHDOWN — D1 *Little River*

MILLWOOD (Public State Park) From Jct of US-71 & SR-32, E 9 mi on SR-32 (L). 42 Avail: 42 W, 42 E (30/50 amps). 2021 rates: $22 to $34. (870)898-2800

MILLWOOD LAKE - COE/BEARD'S BLUFF (Public Corps) From town, E 12.5 mi on AR-32 to CR-196, N 1 mi (E). 28 Avail: 27 W, 2 S, 27 E (30/50 amps). 2021 rates: $12 to $21. (870)388-9556

OCP - MILLWOOD LANDING RESORT **Ratings: 9/8.5★/9** (Membership Park) Avail: 37 full hkups (30/50 amps). 2021 rates: $50.10. (866)888-1655, 596 Hwy 317, Ashdown, AR 71822

ATKINS — C2 *Pope*

ARKANSAS RIVER - COE/SWEEDEN ISLAND PARK (Public Corps) From town, S 15 mi on Hwy 105 (L). 28 Avail: 22 W, 22 E (30 amps), Pit toilets. 2021 rates: $10 to $16. (479)968-5008

Don't miss a thing! Check out the Table of Contents for everything the Guide has to offer.

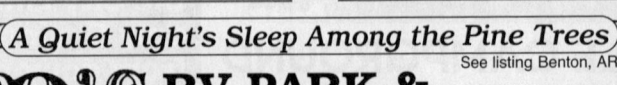

BARLING — B1 *Sebastian*

JOHN PAUL HAMMERSCHMIDT LAKE - COE/SPRINGHILL (Public Corps) From town, N 1.6 mi on Hwy 59 (R). Avail: 44 E (30/50 amps). 2021 rates: $18 to $20. (479)452-4598

BATESVILLE — B4 *Independence*

BRECKS RV PARK & COUNTRY STORE **Ratings: 8/10★/8** (RV Park) Avail: 44 full hkups (30/50 amps). 2021 rates: $32.95 to $54.95. (870)569-8031, 897 Batesville Blvd, Batesville, AR 72501

BEAVER — A1 *Lawrence*

BEAVER RV PARK (BEAVER CITY PARK) (Public) From Jct of Hwy 62 W & Hwy 187 E (10 mi W. of Eureka Springs), E 4.3 mi on Hwy 187 E to Golden Gate Road (in town) N 500'. Avail: 31 full hkups (20/30 amps). 2021 rates: $25 to $35. Apr 01 to Oct 31. (479)253-5469

BELLA VISTA — A1 *Benton*

A SPOTLIGHT Introducing Bella Vista's colorful attractions appearing at the front of this state section.

BLOWING SPRINGS RV PARK
Ratings: 8/9.5★/8.5 (RV Park) From jct Hwy US-71 & Mercy Way: Go 1/4 mi E on Mercy Way, then 1/4 mi E on Blowing Springs Rd (L). **FAC:** paved rds. (64 spaces). Avail: 60 paved, patios, back-ins (25x50), 60 full hkups (30/50 amps), seasonal sites, WiFi @ sites, tent sites, dump, laundry, firewood, controlled access. **REC:** Blowing Springs: boating nearby. Pets OK. Partial handicap access, 14 day max stay, eco-friendly. 2021 rates: $35.
(479)855-8075 Lat: 36.44115, Lon: -94.22869
700 Blowing Spring Rd, Bella Vista, AR 72715
bellavistapoa.com
See ad page 86

BENTON — C3 *Saline*

JB'S RV PARK & CAMPGROUND
Ratings: 6/8★/7.5 (Campground) From jct of I-30 & (exit 106) & US 67: Go 1/4 mi NE on US 67, then 500 feet SE on J.B. Baxley Rd (R). **FAC:** gravel rds. (50 spaces). Avail: 36 gravel, 26 pull-thrus, (30x150), back-ins (30x50), 36 full hkups (30/50 amps), seasonal sites, dump, laundry. **REC:** pond, fishing, boating nearby, hunting nearby. Pet restrict (B). No tents. Big rig sites. 2021 rates: $33 to $35. no cc.
(501)778-6050 Lat: 34.48095, Lon: -92.72022
8601 J.B. Baxley Rd., Benton, AR 72015
www.jbsrvpark.com
See ad this page

BENTONVILLE — A1 *Benton*

BENTONVILLE See also Bella Vista, Cave Springs, Fayetteville, Rogers & Springdale, AR; Noel, MO.

BISMARCK — D2 *Hot Spring*

DEGRAY LAKE - COE/ARLIE MOORE (Public Corps) From town, S 2.3 mi on Hwy 7 to Arlie Moore Rd (CR-254), W 2 mi (E). Avail: 68 E (30/50 amps). 2021 rates: $16. (870)246-5501

BLACK ROCK — B4 *Lawrence*

LAKE CHARLES (Public State Park) From town, NW 8 mi on US-63 to Hwy 25, S 6 mi (R). 60 Avail: 60 W, 60 E (30/50 amps). 2021 rates: $22 to $34. (870)878-6595

BLUE EYE — A2 *Carroll*

OZARKS RV RESORT ON TABLE ROCK LAKE **Ratings: 10/10★/10** (Condo Park) Avail: 64 full hkups (30/50 amps). 2021 rates: $75 to $95. (888)749-7396, 1229 CR-663, Oak Grove, AR 72660

BLUFF CITY — D2 *Nevada*

WHITE OAK LAKE (Public State Park) From Jct of SR-24 & SR-299 (in Bluff City), S 100 yds on SR-299 to SR-387, SE 2 mi (L). 41 Avail: 41 W, 41 E (20/30 amps). 2021 rates: $22 to $27. (870)685-2748

BLYTHEVILLE — B5 *Mississippi*

SHEARIN'S RV PARK **Ratings: 6/NA/8** (RV Park) Avail: 10 full hkups (30/50 amps). 2021 rates: $35. (870)763-4858, 2953 N US Hwy 61, Blytheville, AR 72315

BOONEVILLE — C1 *Logan*

BOONEVILLE MUNICIPAL PARK (Public) From Jct of AR-23 & AR-10, E 4.5 blks on AR-10 (L). Avail: 5 full hkups (30 amps). 2021 rates: $15 to $17.50 (479)675-3811

BROWNSTOWN — D1 *Sevier*

MILLWOOD LAKE - COE/PARALOMA LANDING (Public Corps) From town, E 3 mi on Hwy 234 to Jackson Rd, S 2 mi (E). 34 Avail: 34 W, 34 E (30/50 amps), Pit toilets. 2021 rates: $13. (870)898-3343

MILLWOOD LAKE - COE/WHITE CLIFFS (Public Corps) From town, S 4 mi on Rte 317 (E). Avail: 25 E Pit toilets. 2021 rates: $15 to $21. (870)898-3343

BULL SHOALS — A3 *Marion*

BULL SHOALS-WHITE RIVER (Public State Park) From Mountain Home, N 6 mi on SR-5 to SR-178, W 8 mi (L). Avail: 93 full hkups (30/50 amps). 2021 rates: $19 to $30. (870)445-3629

DAM SITE PARK (Public) From town, SE 1 mi on Hwy 178 (L). Avail: 33 E (30/50 amps). 2021 rates: $20 to $75. Apr 01 to Sep 30. (870)445-4424

CAVE SPRINGS — B1 *Benton*

THE CREEKS GOLF & RV RESORT

good sam park

Ratings: 8.5/9.5★/10 (RV Park) From jct of I-49 (exit 77) & St Hwy 612: Go 3-1/2 mi W on St Hwy 612, then 1-1/2 mi N on St Hwy 112 (L). **FAC:** paved rds. (113 spaces). Avail: 103 paved, patios, 30 pull-thrus, (30x77), back-ins (30x74), 103 full hkups (30/50 amps), seasonal sites, cable, WiFi @ sites, dump, laundry, LP gas, restaurant. **REC:** Osage Creek: fishing, boating nearby, golf, rec open to public. Pets OK. Partial handicap access. No tents, Age restrict may apply. Big rig sites. 2021 rates: $50. ATM.
(479)248-1000 Lat: 36.24545, Lon: -94.23905
1499 S Main Street, Cave Springs, AR 72718
nwarvresort.com
See ad this page

Things to See and Do

THE CREEKS GOLF & RV RESORT The Creeks Golf Course and RV Resort is a public golf course with an on site RV park located just on the outskirts of Cave Springs. RV accessible. Restrooms. Food. Hours: 7am to 8pm. Adult fee: $42 to $48.
(479)248-1000 Lat: 36.24545, Lon: -94.23905
1499 S. Main Street, Cave Springs, AR 72718
nwarvresort.com
See ad this page

CHOCTAW — B3 *Van Buren*

GREERS FERRY LAKE - COE/CHOCTAW (Public Corps) From Clinton, S 5 mi on US-65 to Hwy 330, E 3.5 mi (R). Avail: 91 E (30/50 amps). 2021 rates: $16 to $20. May 16 to Sep 05. (501)745-8320

CLARKSVILLE — B2 *Johnson*

DARDANELLE LAKE - COE/SPADRA (Public Corps) From Jct of I-40 & Hwy 103, S 2 mi on Hwy 103 (E). 23 Avail: 23 W, 23 E (30 amps). 2021 rates: $12 to $18. (479)968-5008

CONWAY — C3 *Faulkner*

CONWAY See also Morrilton, North Little Rock & Perryville.

FOREST LAKE ESTATES MH AND RV COMMUNITY

good sam park

Ratings: 5.5/NA/6 (Campground) Avail: 20 full hkups (30/50 amps). 2021 rates: $40. (501)329-2240, 1001 McNutt Rd. #1000, Conway, AR 72034

WOOLLY HOLLOW (Public State Park) From Jct of US-65 & SR-285, E 6 mi on SR-285 (L). 30 Avail: 30 W, 30 E (30/50 amps). 2021 rates: $34. (501)679-2098

COTTER — B3 *Baxter*

DENTON FERRY RV PARK & CABIN RENTAL

good sam park

Ratings: 9/9.5★/9.5 (RV Park) From jct of Hwy 62/412 & Denton Ferry Rd: Go 1/2 mi N on Denton Ferry Rd (L). **FAC:** all weather rds. (44 spaces). Avail: 40 all weather, 27 pull-thrus, (30x65), back-ins (30x65), 40 full hkups (30/50 amps), seasonal sites, WiFi @ sites, rentals, laundry, LP gas, fire rings, firewood. **REC:** White River: fishing, kayaking/canoeing, boating nearby, hunting nearby. Pets OK. Partial handicap access. No tents. Big rig sites, eco-friendly. 2021 rates: $40 to $55, Military discount.
(870)435-7275 Lat: 36.29259, Lon: -92.52139
740 Denton Ferry Rd., Cotter, AR 72626
dentonrv.com
See ad this page

Do you know how to read each part of a listing? Check the How to Use This Guide in the front.

CROSSETT — E3 *Ashley*

CROSSETT HARBOR RV PARK (Public) From town: Go 8 mi W on US 82. 119 Avail: 119 W, 119 E (30/50 amps). 2021 rates: $16. (870)364-6136

CRYSTAL SPRINGS — C2 *Garland*

OUACHITA LAKE - COE/CRYSTAL SPRINGS (Public Corps) From Jct of US-7 & US-270, W 15 mi on US-270 to park access rd, N 3 mi, follow signs (E). 68 Avail: 63 W, 63 E (30/50 amps). 2021 rates: $20 to $30. (501)991-3390

DAISY — D1 *Pike*

DAISY (Public State Park) From Jct SR-84 & US-70 (in Kirby), W 6 mi on US-70 (L). 82 Avail: 82 W, 82 E (30/50 amps). 2021 rates: $19 to $32. (870)398-4487

GREESON LAKE - COE/SELF CREEK (Public Corps) From town, W 1.5 mi on US-70 (L). 72 Avail: 1 full hkups, 40 E (20/30 amps). 2021 rates: $10 to $18. (870)285-2151

DARDANELLE — C2 *Yell*

ARKANSAS RIVER - COE/RIVERVIEW (Public Corps) From town, NW 0.75 mi on Second St, adjacent to Dardanelle Power House (E). 18 Avail: 8 W, 8 E (20/30 amps), Pit toilets. 2021 rates: $10 to $18. Mar 01 to Oct 31. (479)968-5008

MOUNT NEBO (Public State Park) From jct Hwy 22 & Hwy 155: Go 7 mi W on Hwy 155 (E). 24 Avail: 24 W, 24 E (30 amps). 2021 rates: $11 to $30. (479)229-3655

DE QUEEN — D1 *Sevier*

DEQUEEN LAKE - COE/BELLAH MINE (Public Corps) From town, N 7 mi on US-71 to Bellah Mine Rd, W 5 mi, follow signs (E). Avail: 24 E (30/50 amps). 2021 rates: $14 to $25. Mar 01 to Oct 31. (870)386-7511

DEQUEEN LAKE - COE/PINE RIDGE (Public Corps) From town: Go 3 mi N on US-71, then 5-1/2 mi W on DeQueen Lake Rd (R). 45 Avail: 17 W, 17 E (30 amps). 2021 rates: $14 to $18. (870)584-4161

DIERKS — D1 *Howard*

DIERKS LAKE - COE/BLUE RIDGE (Public Corps) From town, E 3 mi on Hwy 70 to Hwy 278, N 4 mi, W on Blue Ridge Rd. follow signs (E). 22 Avail: 22 W, 22 E (30 amps). 2021 rates: $8 to $14. (870)286-2346

DRASCO — B3 *Cleburne*

GREERS FERRY LAKE - COE/CHEROKEE REC AREA (Public Corps) From town, W 7.5 mi on Hwy 92 to Brownsville, S 4.5 mi (E). Avail: 17 E (20/30 amps), Pit toilets. 2021 rates: $16 to $18. May 15 to Sep 15. (501)745-8320

GREERS FERRY LAKE - COE/HILL CREEK (Public Corps) From town, W 12 mi on Hwy 92 to Hwy 225, NW 3 mi to paved access rd, S 2 mi (E). Avail: 30 E (30 amps). 2021 rates: $16 to $18. May 15 to Sep 15. (870)948-2419

DUMAS — D4 *Arkansas*

ARKANSAS RIVER - COE/PENDLETON BEND PARK (Public Corps) From town, NE 10.5 mi on US-165 to AR-212, E 2 mi (E). 31 Avail: 31 W, 31 E (30/50 amps). 2021 rates: $16 to $19. (870)548-2291

ARKANSAS RIVER - COE/WILBUR D MILLS PARK (Public Corps) From town, N 10.5 mi on US-165 to AR-212, E 5 mi (E). 21 Avail: 21 W, 21 E (20/30 amps). 2021 rates: $16. Feb 27 to Nov 01. (870)548-2291

EL DORADO — E2 *Union*

MORO BAY (Public State Park) From Warren, SW 29 mi on US-63 (L). 23 Avail: 23 W, 23 E (30/50 amps). 2021 rates: $34. (870)463-8555

EUREKA SPRINGS — A2 *Carroll*

A SPOTLIGHT Introducing Eureka Springs' colorful attractions appearing at the front of this state section.

EUREKA SPRINGS See also Bella Vista, Rogers & Springdale, AR; Branson, Cassville & Kimberling City, MO.

BEAVER LAKE - COE/DAM SITE LAKE CAMPGROUND (Public Corps) From town, W 4.8 mi on US-62 to Hwy 187, S 2.5 mi (L). Avail: 48 E (30/50 amps). 2021 rates: $20 to $25. Apr 01 to Oct 30. (479)253-5828

BEAVER LAKE - COE/DAM SITE RIVER (Public Corps) From town, W 9 mi on US-62 to Hwy 187, S 2.5 mi (E). Avail: 58 E (30/50 amps). 2021 rates: $20 to $25. Apr 01 to Oct 31. (479)253-9865

BEAVER LAKE - COE/STARKEY (Public Corps) From town, W 2.5 mi on US-62 to Hwy 187, SW 4.2 mi to CR-2176 (Mundel Rd), W 4.3 mi (E). Avail: 23 E (30 amps). 2021 rates: $20 to $24. May 01 to Sep 08. (479)253-5866

KETTLE CAMPGROUND

good sam park

Ratings: 8/9.5★/8.5 (Campground) From jct US-62 & SR-23S: Go 3 mi E on US-62 (L).

RELAXING IN THE OZARK MOUNTAINS

Nestled in heart of the Ozarks, enjoy our pool, 4-person swing, or catch the downtown trolley that stops at our park. Stay in one of our cabins or enjoy an RV site set under tall pine trees that whisper in the gentle breeze.

FAC: gravel rds. (57 spaces). Avail: 47 gravel, 10 pull-thrus, (26x70), back-ins (26x40), 31 full hkups, 16 W, 16 E (30/50 amps), seasonal sites, WiFi @ sites, tent sites, rentals, dump, laundry, LP gas, fire rings, firewood. **REC:** pool, boating nearby, playground. Pets OK. Big rig sites, eco-friendly. 2021 rates: $36 to $44, Military discount.
(479)253-9100 Lat: 36.39627, Lon: -93.70579
4119 E Van Buren, Eureka Springs, AR 72632
www.KettleCampground.net
See ad page 87

LAKE LEATHERWOOD CITY PARK (Public) From north Jct Hwy 23 & US 62: Go 3-1/4 mi NW on US 62, then 1-1/2 mi N on entry road. (Not suitable for Big Rigs). 4 Avail. 2021 rates: $14.50 to $19.50. Mar 01 to Nov 30. (479)253-7921

EUREKA SPRINGS (CONT)

WANDERLUST RV PARK
good sam park **Ratings: 9.5/9.5★/9.5** (RV Park) Avail: 83 full hkups (30/50 amps). 2021 rates: $37 to $60. (479)253-7385, 468 Passion Play Road, Eureka Springs, AR 72632

FAIRFIELD BAY — B3 *Van Buren*

FAIRFIELD BAY RV CAMPGROUND & MARINA (Public) From Jct of US-65 & SR-16, E 1.8 mi on SR-16 to Burnt Ridge Rd, E 7.7 mi to SR-330, S 1.4 mi (R). 49 Avail: 33 W, 49 E (30/50 amps). 2021 rates: $12 to $17. (501)253-8408

FAYETTEVILLE — B1 *Washington*

SOUTHGATE RV PARK OF FAYETTEVILLE **Ratings: 5.5/7.5/8** (RV Park) Avail: 42 full hkups (30/50 amps). 2021 rates: $38. (479)442-2021, 2331 S. School Ave., Fayetteville, AR 72701

FELSENTHAL — E3 *Union*

GRAND MARAIS (UNION COUNTY PARK) (Public State Park) From jct Hwy 129 & Hwy 129B: Go 1 mi NE on Hwy 129B, then 3-1/2 mi W on CR 30. 50 Avail: 50 W, 50 E (30 amps). 2021 rates: $21 to $30. (870)943-2930

FLIPPIN — B3 *Marion*

BLUE HERON RV CAMPGROUND & RESORT **Ratings: 6/8.5★/8.5** (RV Park) 33 Avail: 14 full hkups, 19 W, 19 E (30/50 amps). 2021 rates: $30 to $36. (870)453-4678, 150 Blue Heron Lane, Flippin, AR 72634

WHITE RIVER CAMPGROUND & CABINS **Ratings: 7.5/8/8.5** (Campground) Avail: 40 full hkups (30/50 amps). 2021 rates: $41.50 to $50. (870)453-2299, 258 White River Trail, Flippin, AR 72634

FORREST CITY — C4 *St Francis*

VILLAGE CREEK (Public State Park) From Jct of I-40 & Hwy 284 (exit 242), N 13 mi on Hwy 284 (R). 96 Avail: 24 full hkups, 72 W, 72 E (30/50 amps). 2021 rates: $22 to $34. (870)238-9406

FORT SMITH — B1 *Crawford*

FORT SMITH See also Alma & Van Buren, AR; Sallisaw, OK.

MILITARY PARK FORT CHAFFEE RV PARK (FORT CHAFFEE) (Public) From Jct of I-40 & I-540, S 2 mi on I-540 to AR-22/Rogers Ave, E through Barling to base. Avail: 39 full hkups (20/50 amps). 2021 rates: $10 to $12.40. (479)484-2252

GAMALIEL — A3 *Baxter*

NORFORK LAKE - COE/GAMALIEL (Public Corps) From Mountain Home, E 9 mi on Hwy 62/412 to Hwy 101, N 5 mi to CR-42, SE 3 mi (E). 64 Avail: 64 W, 64 E (30/50 amps). 2021 rates: $20 to $21. Apr 01 to Oct 31. (870)467-5680

GARFIELD — A1 *Benton*

BEAVER LAKE - COE/LOST BRIDGE NORTH (Public Corps) From Jct of US-62 & SR-127, SE 6.1 mi on SR-127 (follow 127 spur) to Marina Rd, E into park (E). Avail: 48 E (30/50 amps). 2021 rates: $17 to $25. Apr 01 to Sep 29. (479)359-3312

BEAVER LAKE - COE/LOST BRIDGE SOUTH (Public Corps) From town, SE 5 mi on SR-127 (E). Avail: 36 E (50 amps). 2021 rates: $21 to $23. May 01 to Sep 29. (479)359-3755

GATEWAY — A1 *Benton*

BEAVER LAKE - COE/INDIAN CREEK (Public Corps) From town, E 3 mi on Hwy 62 to Indian Creek Rd (E). Avail: 33 E (20/30 amps). 2021 rates: $20 to $38. May 01 to Sep 29. (479)253-5866

GREERS FERRY — B3 *Cleburne*

GREERS FERRY LAKE - COE/DEVILS FORK (Public Corps) From Jct of AR-16 & AR-92, N 0.5 mi on AR-16 (L). Avail: 55 E (30/50 amps). 2021 rates: $18 to $24. Mar 15 to Oct 30. (501)825-8618

GREERS FERRY LAKE - COE/MILL CREEK (Public Corps) From town, SW 2 mi on AR-16 to AR-92, W 0.5 mi to Mill Creek Rd, N 3 mi (E). 39 Avail: Pit toilets. 2021 rates: $16. May 15 to Sep 15. (501)362-2416

GREERS FERRY LAKE - COE/NARROWS CAMPGROUND (Public Corps) From town, W 2 mi on Hwy 16/92 (R). Avail: 59 E (30 amps). 2021 rates: $18 to $24. May 15 to Sep 15. (501)825-7602

GREERS FERRY LAKE - COE/SHILOH (Public Corps) From town, SE 3 mi on AR-110 (E). Avail: 60 E (20/30 amps). 2021 rates: $16 to $18. May 15 to Sep 15. (501)825-8619

GREERS FERRY LAKE - COE/SUGAR LOAF (Public Corps) From town, SW 2 mi on Hwy 16 to Hwy 92, W 1 mi to SR-337, W 1 mi (E). Avail: 57 E (30/50 amps). 2021 rates: $16 to $18. May 15 to Sep 15. (501)654-2267

HARDY — A4 *Sharp*

HARDY RV PARK (Public) From west jct US 62 & US 63: Go 1/4 mi E on US 62/63, then 2 blocks S on Spring St. 76 Avail: 76 W, 76 E (30 amps). 2021 rates: $25. Mar 01 to Oct 31. (870)856-2356

HARRISBURG — B4 *Poinsett*

LAKE POINSETT (Public State Park) From Jct of SR-14 & SR-163 (E of Harrisburg), S 3 mi on SR-163 (L). 26 Avail: 26 W, 26 E (30/50 amps). 2021 rates: $12 to $32. (870)578-2064

HARRISON — B2 *Boone*

HARRISON See also Blue Eye, Jasper & Omaha.

HARRISON KOA **Ratings: 9/9.5★/10** (RV Park) Avail: 36 full hkups (30/50 amps). 2021 rates: $39.87 to $59.87. (870)743-2267, 3629 Hwy 65 N, Harrison, AR 72601

Show Your Good Sam Membership Card!

HARRISON VILLAGE CAMPGROUND & RV PARK **Ratings: 8.5/10★/9** (Campground) 72 Avail: 55 full hkups, 17 W, 17 E (30/50 amps). 2021 rates: $36.50 to $41.50. (870)743-3388, 2364 Hwy 65 S, Harrison, AR 72601

HAZEN — C4 *Prairie*

LOWER WHITE RIVER RV PARK **Ratings: 5/NA/8** (RV Park) Avail: 22 full hkups (30/50 amps). 2021 rates: $35. (501)388-0998, 4100 Hwy 11 N, Hazen, AR 72064

HEBER SPRINGS — B3 *Cleburne*

GREERS FERRY LAKE - COE/DAM SITE (Public Corps) From town, N 3 mi on SR-25 (L). 252 Avail: 148 W, 148 E (30/50 amps). 2021 rates: $16 to $24. Mar 15 to Oct 30. (501)362-5233

GREERS FERRY LAKE - COE/HEBER SPRINGS (Public Corps) From town, W 2 mi on Hwy 110 to park access rd, N 0.5 mi (E). Avail: 101 E (30/50 amps). 2021 rates: $16 to $20. Mar 15 to Oct 30. (501)250-0485

GREERS FERRY LAKE - COE/JOHN F KENNEDY (Public Corps) From town, NE 4 mi on Hwy 25 to access rd, E 1 mi, follow signs (E). 73 Avail: 13 W, 73 E (30/50 amps). 2021 rates: $18 to $24. Apr 15 to Sep 05. (501)250-0481

GREERS FERRY LAKE - COE/OLD HWY 25 (Public Corps) From town, NE 7 mi on Hwy 25 to Hwy 25S, W 3 mi (E). Avail: 84 E (20/30 amps). 2021 rates: $16 to $20. May 15 to Sep 15. (501)250-0483

HENDERSON — A3 *Baxter*

NORFORK LAKE - COE/HENDERSON PARK (Public Corps) From jct Hwy-101 & US-62: Go 1/4 mi S off US-62. Avail: 36 E (30 amps). 2021 rates: $20. May 01 to Sep 30. (870)488-5282

HOPE — D2 *Hempstead*

FAIR PARK RV PARK (Public) From jct I-30 & Rte 278 (exit 30): Go 1/4 mi SE on Rte 278, then 1 mi SE on Rte 278B, then 1/4 mi W on Rte 67, the 1/4 mi S on Rte 174, then 1/4 mi W on Park Dr (E). 200 Avail: 20 full hkups, 180 W, 180 E (30 amps). 2021 rates: $25. (870)777-7500

HORSESHOE BEND — B3 *Fulton*

CROWN LAKE RV RESORT
good sam park **Ratings: 9.5/10★/9.5** (RV Resort) From jct Hwy 56 & Main St: Go 3/4 mi NE on Hwy 56, then 2-1/4 mi NE on Hwy 289, then 1/4 mi SE on E Tri Lakes Dr, then 1/2 mi N on Ivory Ln (L); or From jct US Hwy 412 & Hwy 289: Go 7-3/4 mi S on Hwy 289, then 1/2 mi E on Tri Lakes Dr, then 1/2 mi N Ivory Ln (L).

BEAUTIFUL OZARK MOUNTAIN RETREAT!!
Relaxing resort with fantastic views! A fun time in the Arkansas Ozarks! Enjoy fishing, a white sandy beach, mini golf, shuffleboard, fitness center, a restaurant, cable, 2 pools & Wi-Fi. Bring your ATVs and Ride the Trails!

FAC: gravel rds. Avail: 73 paved, patios, 60 pull-thrus, (40x65), back-ins (40x65), 73 full hkups (30/50 amps), WiFi @ sites, tent sites, rentals, dump, laundry, groc, LP bottles, fire rings, firewood, restaurant. **REC:** heated pool, hot tub, Crown Lake: swim, fishing, kayaking/canoeing, boating nearby, playground. Pet restrict (Q). Partial handicap access. Big rig sites, eco-friendly. 2021 rates: $39 to $99. ATM.
(870)291-5171 Lat: 36.2088, Lon: -91.7476
1601 Ivory Ln, Horseshoe Bend, AR 72512
www.crownlakervresort.com
See ad this page

HOT SPRINGS NATIONAL PARK — C2 *Garland*

CATHERINE'S LANDING AT HOT SPRINGS **Ratings: 10/10★/10** (Campground) Avail: 181 full hkups (30/50 amps). 2021 rates: $55 to $110. (501)262-2550, 1700 Shady Grove Rd., Hot Springs, AR 71901

CLOUD NINE RV PARK
good sam park **Ratings: 8.5/9.5★/10** (RV Park) Avail: 30 full hkups (30/50 amps). 2021 rates: $45 to $50. (501)262-1996, 136 Cloud Nine Drive, Hot Springs National Park, AR 71901

HOT SPRINGS NATIONAL PARK KOA **Ratings: 9.5/9.5★/8.5** (Campground) Avail: 75 full hkups (30/50 amps). 2021 rates: $46.96 to $91.60. (501)624-5912, 838 Mc Clendon Road, Hot Springs National Park, AR 71901

Check out 10/10/10 Good Sam Parks on the Good Sam Park page.*

→ HOT SPRINGS/GULPHA GORGE CAMPGROUND (Public National Park) From Jct of Hwy 70 & 70B (E of town), N 0.25 mi on 70B, follow signs (L). Avail: 40 full hkups (30/50 amps). 2021 rates: $15 to $30. (501)620-6743

→ **J & J RV PARK**
Ratings: 8/9★/7.5 (RV Park) From jct of US-270B/70B & SR-7: Go 4 mi E on US-70B, then 1/4 mi E onto East Grand Ave (exit 4) (R). **FAC:** paved rds. Avail: 46 gravel, 17 pull-thrus, (30x70), back-ins (26x40), 46 full hkups (30/50 amps), cable, WiFi @ sites, laundry, fire rings. **REC:** Gulpha Creek: boating nearby, playground. Pet restrict (B). Partial handicap access. No tents. Big rig sites. 2021 rates: $41, Military discount.
(501)321-9852 Lat: 34.50833, Lon: -93.01000
2000 E Grand Ave, Hot Springs, AR 71901
www.jjrvpark.com
See ad this page

↑ LAKE OUACHITA (Public State Park) From jct US-270 & SR-227: Go 12 mi N on SR-227 (E). 81 Avail: 58 full hkups, 23 W, 23 E (30/50 amps). 2021 rates: $34. (501)767-9366

← **TREASURE ISLE RV PARK**
Ratings: 8.5/9.5★/8.5 (Campground) From jct of US-70/US-270 & SR-7: Go 9-1/4 mi W on US-270, then 1/4 mi N on Treasure Isle Rd. (L). **FAC:** paved/gravel rds. 65 Avail: 8 paved, 57 gravel, 20 pull-thrus, (24x55), back-ins (24x55), 65 full hkups (30/50 amps), cable, WiFi @ sites, rentals, laundry, fire rings, firewood. **REC:** pool, Lake Hamilton: swim, fishing, kayaking/canoeing, boating nearby, playground, hunting nearby. Pet restrict (B). No tents, eco-friendly. 2021 rates: $35 to $50, Military discount.
(501)767-6852 Lat: 34.51147, Lon: -93.18088
205 Treasure Isle Rd , Hot Springs, AR 71913
www.treasureislerv.com
See ad this page

HUNTSVILLE — B2 *Madison*

↑ WITHROW SPRINGS (Public State Park) From Jct of SR-412 & SR-23, N 5 mi on SR-23 (L). Avail: 30 full hkups (30/50 amps). 2021 rates: $34. (479)559-2593

JACKSONPORT — B4 *Jackson*

↖ JACKSONPORT (Public State Park) In town, NW 0.25 mi on AR-69S (L). 20 Avail: 20 W, 20 E (50 amps). 2021 rates: $27. (870)523-2143

JACKSONVILLE — C3 *Pulaski*

↖ MILITARY PARK LITTLE ROCK AFB FAMCAMP (LITTLE ROCK AFB) (Public) At Jct of US-67 N from Little Rock to Jacksonville, exit at AFB (Exit 11) and follow signs through gate. Avail: 24 full hkups (20/50 amps). 2021 rates: $20. (501)987-3365

JASPER — B2 *Newton*

↑ DOGWOOD SPRINGS CAMPGROUND/RESORT **Ratings: 6/7.5★/7** (Campground) Avail: 28 full hkups (30/50 amps). 2021 rates: $32 to $36. (870)446-2163, 621 East Court Street, Jasper, AR 72641

JONESBORO — B4 *Craighead*

↑ CRAIGHEAD FOREST PARK (Public) From jct US 63 (exit 44) & Hwy 1B: Go 1 block S on Hwy 1B, then 1 mi W on Parker Rd, then 2 mi S on Culberhouse St (Hwy 141) to Forest Park Dr. (R). 26 Avail: 26 W, 26 E (50 amps). 2021 rates: $25. (870)933-4604

↓ PERKINS RV PARK **Ratings: 4.5/NA/6** (RV Park) Avail: 35 full hkups (30/50 amps). 2021 rates: $30 to $35. (870)897-5700, 1821 E Parker Rd, Jonesboro, AR 72404

JORDAN — B3 *Izard*

↖ NORFORK LAKE - COE/JORDAN CAMPGROUND (Public Corps) From town, SE 12 mi on Hwy 5 to Hwy 177, E 5 mi to CR-64, N 3 mi (E). Avail: 33 E (20 amps). 2021 rates: $25. (870)499-7223

JUDSONIA — B4 *White*

← **RED RIVER RV PARK**
Ratings: 7/NA/9 (RV Park) From Jct. US 167 and CW Road (exit 48) Go E 1/4 mi. on CW Road (R). **FAC:** gravel rds. (71 spaces). Avail: 43 gravel, patios, 8 pull-thrus, (25x60), back-ins (25x50), 43 full hkups (30/50 amps), seasonal sites, WiFi @ sites, laundry. **REC:** Little Red River: fishing, kayaking/canoeing, boating nearby, playground, hunting nearby. Pets OK. No tents. Big rig sites. 2021 rates: $30, Military discount.
(501)729-0937 Lat: 35.2672, Lon: -91.6715
416 CW Road, Judsonia, AR 72081
rrrpark.com
See ad this page

KIRBY — D2 *Pike*

← GREESON LAKE - COE/KIRBY LANDING (Public Corps) From town, W 2.5 mi on US-70 to park access rd, SW 1.5 mi (E). 105 Avail: 105 W, 105 E (50 amps). 2021 rates: $20 to $36. (870)285-2151

LAKE VILLAGE — E4 *Chicot*

→ CHICOT COUNTY RV PARK (CHICOT COUNTY PARK) (Public) From Jct of Hwy 65 & Hwy 82 E 5.2 mi on Hwy 82 to CR 403 Levee Rd (just before Mississippi River Bridge) N 1.3 mi to Lake Hall Rd SW 3 mi (L). Avail: 98 E (30 amps). 2021 rates: $20 to $30. (870)265-3500

↗ LAKE CHICOT (Public State Park) From jct US-82 & US-65: Go 4 mi N on US-65, then 4 mi E on SR-257, then 4 mi NE on SR-144 (R). 122 Avail: 55 full hkups, 67 W, 67 E (30/50 amps). 2021 rates: $17 to $34. (870)265-5480

↓ **PECAN GROVE RV PARK**
Ratings: 8/9★/9 (RV Park) S-bnd: From Jct of US 65 & US 82 (in Lake Village), S 2.7 mi on US 65 & US 82 (R); or N-bnd: From Jct US 65 & US 82, 1.7 mi on US 65 & US 82 (L). **FAC:** gravel rds. (104 spaces). 39 Avail: 4 paved, 35 gravel, 39 pull-thrus, (35x90), 39 full hkups (30/50 amps), seasonal sites, WiFi @ sites, tent sites, rentals, dump, laundry, fire rings, firewood. **REC:** Lake Chicot: fishing, kayaking/canoeing, boating nearby, playground, hunting nearby. Pets OK. Big rig sites, eco-friendly. 2021 rates: $25 to $40, Military discount.
(870)265-3005 Lat: 33.29610, Lon: -91.27530
3768 Highway 82 & 65 South, Lake Village, AR 71653
www.pecangrove.net
See ad this page

LAKEVIEW — A3 *Baxter*

↑ BULL SHOALS LAKE - COE/LAKEVIEW PARK (Public Corps) From town, N 1 mi on Hwy 178 to Boat Dock Rd, N 1.5 mi (E). Avail: 78 E (30/50 amps). 2021 rates: $20 to $54. (870)431-8116

LEAD HILL — A2 *Boone*

↑ BULL SHOALS LAKE - COE/LEAD HILL (Public Corps) From town, N 4 mi on Hwy 7 (E). Avail: 75 E (30 amps). 2021 rates: $20 to $54. Apr 01 to Oct 31. (870)422-7555

↖ BULL SHOALS LAKE - COE/TUCKER HOLLOW (Public Corps) From town, NW 7.5 mi on Hwy 14 to Hwy 281, N 3 mi (E). Avail: 28 E (30/50 amps). 2021 rates: $22. May 01 to Sep 30. (870)422-7555

LINWOOD — D3 *Jefferson*

↑ ARKANSAS RIVER - COE/RISING STAR (Public Corps) From Pine Bluff, S 7.8 mi on US-65 to Blankinship Rd (in Linwood), N 3.5 mi (E). 25 Avail: 25 W, 25 E (20/30 amps). 2021 rates: $19. Mar 01 to Oct 31. (870)479-3292

LITTLE ROCK — C3 *Pulaski*

LITTLE ROCK See also Conway & North Little Rock.

↖ ARKANSAS RIVER - COE/MAUMELLE PARK (Public Corps) From Jct of I-430 & Hwy 10 (exit 9), W 2.6 mi on Hwy 10 to Pinnacle Valley Rd, N 2.1 mi (E). Avail: 128 E (30/50 amps). 2021 rates: $22 to $26. (501)868-9477

LOWELL — B1 *Benton*

Travel Services

→ **GANDER RV OF LOWELL** Your new hometown outfitter offering the best regional gear for all your outdoor needs. Your adventure awaits. **SERVICES:** restrooms. RV Sales. RV supplies, LP gas, RV accessible. Hours: 9am - 7pm.
(888)540-8764 Lat: 36.256023, Lon: -94.148316
317 North 6th Place, Lowell, AR 72745
rv.ganderoutdoors.com

MAGNOLIA — E2 *Columbia*

↑ **MAGNOLIA RV PARK**
Ratings: 8/10★/10 (RV Park) Avail: 32 full hkups (30/50 amps). 2021 rates: $40. (870)562-2908, 1399 W University, Magnolia, AR 71753

MALVERN — C2 *Hot Spring*

↖ LAKE CATHERINE (Public State Park) From jct I-30 & SR-171 (exit 97): Go 12 mi N on SR-171 (E). 70 Avail: 70 W, 44 S, 70 E (30/50 amps). 2021 rates: $22 to $34. (501)844-4176

MARIANNA — C4 *Lee*

↖ STORM CREEK LAKE (Public State Park) From town: Go 2-1/2 mi SE on Hwy 44 (L). 14 Avail: Pit toilets. 2021 rates: $13 to $30. Apr 01 to Sep 05. (870)295-5278

MARION — C5 *Crittenden*

← MEMPHIS KOA **Ratings: 9/9★/8** (RV Park) 53 Avail: 40 full hkups, 13 W, 13 E (30/50 amps). 2021 rates: $35 to $76. (870)739-4801, 7037 I-55, Marion, AR 72364

MENA — C1 *Polk*

↓ IRON MOUNTAIN **Ratings: 6.5/8.5/9** (Campground) Avail: 80 full hkups (30/50 amps). 2021 rates: $30. (870)389-6560, 106 Iron Mountain Lane, Mena, AR 71953

← QUEEN WILHELMINA (Public State Park) From Jct of SR-88 & US 71/59, W 13 mi on SR-88 (L). 35 Avail: 35 W, 35 E (20/30 amps). 2021 rates: $17 to $27. (479)394-2863

↓ SHADOW MOUNTAIN RV PARK **Ratings: 8/8.5★/7.5** (Campground) 64 Avail: 45 full hkups, 19 W, 19 E (30/50 amps). 2021 rates: $30 to $45. (479)394-6099, 3708 Hwy 71 South, Mena, AR 71953

MORRILTON — C2 *Conway*

ARKANSAS RIVER - COE/TOAD SUCK CHEROKEE PARK (Public Corps) From Jct of I-40 & Hwy 95, S to Hwy 64, follow signs (E). 48 Avail: 33 W, 33 E (30/50 amps). 2021 rates: $18 to $20. Mar 01 to Oct 31. (501)329-2986

MORRILTON I40/107 RV PARK **Ratings: 7/9★/7.5** (Campground) Avail: 30 full hkups (30/50 amps). 2021 rates: $35. (501)354-8262, 30 Kamper Lane, Morrilton, AR 72110

PETIT JEAN (Public State Park) From Jct of I-40 & SR-9 (exit 108), S 9 mi on SR-9 to SR-154, W 12 mi (R). 125 Avail: 35 full hkups, 90 W, 90 E (30/50 amps). 2021 rates: $15 to $34. (501)727-5441

MOUNT IDA — C2 *Montgomery*

OUACHITA LAKE - COE/BIG FIR (Public Corps) From town, N 6 mi on Hwy 27 to Hwy 188, E 8 mi (E). 50 Avail: Pit toilets. (501)767-2101

OUACHITA LAKE - COE/DENBY POINT (Public Corps) From town, E 9 mi on US-270 to Ouachita Shores Pkwy, N 1 mi, follow signs (E). 58 Avail: 58 W, 58 E (50 amps). 2021 rates: $18 to $30. May 01 to Sep 25. (870)867-4475

OUACHITA LAKE - COE/JOPLIN CAMPGROUND (Public Corps) From town, E 11 mi on US-270 to Mountain Harbor Rd, N 3 mi (E). Avail: 59 E (30 amps). 2021 rates: $16 to $24. May 01 to Sep 25. (501)767-2108

OUACHITA LAKE - COE/LITTLE FIR (Public Corps) From town, NE 7 mi on SR-27 to Hwy 188, E 9 mi (E). 29 Avail: 29 W, 29 E (50 amps). 2021 rates: $12 to $18. (501)767-2101

OUACHITA LAKE - COE/TOMPKINS BEND (Public Corps) From town, E 10.7 mi on US-270 to Shangri La Dr., N 2.4 mi (E). 77 Avail: 39 W, 63 E (30/50 amps). 2021 rates: $22 to $30. (501)767-2108

MOUNTAIN HOME — A3 *Baxter*

NORFORK LAKE - COE/BIDWELL POINT (Public Corps) From town, E 9 mi on US-62/412 to AR-101, N 2 mi, over bridge, E on access rd (R). 48 Avail: 48 W, 48 E (30/50 amps). 2021 rates: $20 to $22. May 01 to Sep 30. (870)467-5375

NORFORK LAKE - COE/CRANFIELD PARK (Public Corps) From town NE 5 mi on Hwy 62 to Cranfield Rd, N 2 mi (L). Avail: 66 E (30/50 amps). 2021 rates: $20 to $22. Apr 01 to Oct 31. (870)492-4191

NORFORK LAKE - COE/DAM-QUARRY CAMPGROUND (Public Corps) From jct US 62 & Hwy 5: Go 11 mi SE on Hwy 5 to Salesville, then 2 mi E on Hwy 177 to Norfork Dam. Avail: 68 E (50 amps). 2021 rates: $20 to $22. (870)499-7216

NORFORK LAKE - COE/PANTHER BAY PARK (Public Corps) From town, E 9 mi on US-412/Hwy 62 to Hwy 101, N 1 mi (R). Avail: 15 E (30 amps), Pit toilets. 2021 rates: $20 to $21. May 01 to Sep 30. (870)425-2700

Go to GoodSam.com/Trip-Planner for Trip Routing.

NORFORK LAKE - COE/ROBINSON POINT (Public Corps) From town, E 9 mi on US-421/Hwy 62 to Robinson Point Rd (CR-279), S 3 mi (E). Avail: 102 E (30/50 amps). 2021 rates: $20 to $40. Apr 01 to Oct 31. (870)492-6853

MOUNTAIN VIEW — B3 *Stone*

ANGLERS HOLIDAY MOUNTAIN RESORT **Ratings: 7/6.5/7.5** (Membership Park) Avail: 113 full hkups (30/50 amps). 2021 rates: $35 to $40. Apr 01 to Nov 15. (870)585-2231, 473 Swinging Bridge Rd, Mountain View, AR 72560

OZARK RV PARK

good sam park **Ratings: 8/9.5★/9.5** (Campground) N-bnd: Jct of SR-5/9/14, N 0.5 mi on SR14 to E Webb, W 0.7 mi to Park Ave, N 0.4 mi (L); S-bnd: Jct of SR-5/9/14, N of town, S 5 mi on SR9 to SR382, W 0.2 mi to Roper, SW 0.5 mi to Park Ave, N 0.1 mi (L); E-bnd: Jct of 65/66, E 27 mi on 66 to Peabody, N 500' to Webb, E 150' to Park Ave, N 0.4 mi (L). **FAC:** gravel rds. (76 spaces). Avail: 56 gravel, 21 pull-thrus, (24x60), back-ins (24x45), 56 full hkups (30/50 amps), seasonal sites, cable, WiFi @ sites, tent sites, rentals, dump, laundry, fire rings, firewood. **REC:** boating nearby, hunting nearby. Pet restrict (B). Big rig sites, eco-friendly. 2021 rates: $28 to $34.
(870)269-2542 Lat: 35.87908, Lon: -92.11608
1022 Park Ave., Mountain View, AR 72560
ozarkrvpark.com
See ad this page

SYLAMORE CREEK CAMP **Ratings: 6/5.5/7** (Campground) 36 Avail: 12 full hkups, 24 W, 24 E (20/30 amps). 2021 rates: $30 to $35. (870)585-2326, 214 Sylamore Creek Rd., Mountain View, AR 72560

WHITEWATER BLUEGRASS RV PARK **Ratings: 6/8/7.5** (Campground) Avail: 60 full hkups (30/50 amps). 2021 rates: $28 to $32. (870)269-8047, 108 East Webb St., Mountain View, AR 72560

MULBERRY — B1 *Crawford*

ARKANSAS RIVER - COE/VINE PRAIRIE (Public Corps) From town, S 1.7 mi on Hwy 917 to access rd (E). Avail: 13 full hkups (30 amps). 2021 rates: $10 to $20. (479)667-2129

MURFREESBORO — D1 *Pike*

CRATER OF DIAMONDS (Public State Park) From town, SE 2 mi on Hwy 301, follow signs (R). Avail: 47 full hkups (30/50 amps). 2021 rates: $34. (870)285-3113

GREESON LAKE - COE/COWHIDE COVE (Public Corps) From town, N 9 mi on Hwy 27 to Laurel Creek Rd., W 1.4 mi, S 1.8 mi CR-77 (E). Avail: 48 E (30 amps). 2021 rates: $18 to $20. Mar 01 to Nov 30. (870)285-2151

GREESON LAKE - COE/LAUREL CREEK (Public Corps) From town, N 10 mi on SR-27 to access rd, W 5 mi (E). 24 Avail: Pit toilets. 2021 rates: $5. Mar 01 to Oct 31. (877)444-6777

GREESON LAKE - COE/NARROWS DAM REC AREA (Public Corps) From town, N 6 mi on Hwy 19 to access rd, NW 0.5 mi (E). 24 Avail: 2 full hkups, 16 E (20/30 amps). 2021 rates: $13 to $14. (870)285-2151

GREESON LAKE - COE/PARKER CREEK (Public Corps) From town, N 6 mi on Hwy 19, NW (across dam) 3 mi on Beacon Hill/Parker Creek Rd. Avail: 49 E (20/30 amps). 2021 rates: $14 to $20. Mar 01 to Dec 15. (870)285-2151

NEW BLAINE — C2 *Logan*

DARDANELLE LAKE - COE/SHOAL BAY PARK (Public Corps) From town, N 2 mi on Hwy 197 to access rd (E). 82 Avail: 62 W, 82 E (30 amps). 2021 rates: $16 to $20. Mar 01 to Oct 31. (479)938-7335

NEWHOPE — D1 *Pike*

GREESON LAKE - COE/STAR OF THE WEST (Public Corps) From town, E 2.8 mi on US-70, at bridge (R). 21 Avail: Pit toilets. 2021 rates: $5. Mar 01 to Oct 31. (870)285-2151

NORTH LITTLE ROCK — C3 *Pulaski*

ARKANSAS RIVER - COE/WILLOW BEACH (Public Corps) From town, SE 2.5 mi on US-165 to Col. Maynard Rd, S 3 mi to Blue Heron, W 1 mi, follow signs (R). 23 Avail: 23 W, 23 E (50 amps). 2021 rates: $19. (501)961-1332

"Full hookups" in a campground listing means there are water, electric and sewer hookups at the sites.

BURNS PARK CAMPGROUND (Public) W-bnd I-40 (Exit 150): .3 mi on ramp to SR-176 (Military Dr), L .3 mi on SR-176 to Burns Park Dr, R .6 mi on Burns Park Dr (R) E-bnd I-40 (Exit 150): .2 mi on ramp to SR-176 (Military Dr), R .1 mi on SR-176 to Burns Park Dr, R .6 mi on Burns Park Dr (R). 38 Avail: 38 W, 38 E (30/50 amps). 2021 rates: $25 to $35. (501)771-0702

DOWNTOWN RIVERSIDE RV PARK

good sam park **Ratings: 7.5/8★/7** (Public) W-bnd: From jct I-30 (exit 141B) & Cypress St: Go 1/2 mi S on Cypress St, then 600 feet E on Riverfront Dr (R). E-bnd: From jct I-30 (Exit 141B) & US 70: Go 1/4 mi E on US 70, then 1/2 mi S on Riverfront Dr (L). **FAC:** paved rds. 61 Avail: 42 paved, 19 gravel, 14 pull-thrus, (40x100), back-ins (20x50), mostly side by side hkups, 61 full hkups (50 amps), WiFi @ sites, dump, laundry, controlled access. **REC:** Arkansas River: boating nearby. Pet restrict (B). No tents. Big rig sites, eco-friendly. 2021 rates: $25 to $33, Military discount.
(501)340-5312 Lat: 34.75233, Lon: -92.26153
250 South Locust St, North Little Rock, AR 72114
downtownriversidervpark.com
See ad this page

KOA LITTLE ROCK NORTH **Ratings: 9/9★/7.5** (Campground) 77 Avail: 70 full hkups, 7 W, 7 E (30/50 amps). 2021 rates: $57.50 to $63.26. (501)758-4598, 7820 Kampground Way, North Little Rock, AR 72118

TRAILS END RV PARK **Ratings: 6.5/UI/6.5** (RV Park) Avail: 30 full hkups (30/50 amps). 2021 rates: $40. (501)851-4594, 14223 Stricklin Cove, North Little Rock, AR 72118

Travel Services

CAMPING WORLD OF NORTH LITTLE ROCK

CAMPING WORLD As the nation's largest retailer of RV supplies, accessories, services and new and used RVs, Camping World is committed to making your total RV experience better. **SERVICES:** RV, tire, RV appliance, MH mechanical, restrooms. RV Sales. RV supplies, LP gas, RV accessible. Hours: 9am - 7pm.
(888)409-7366 Lat: 34.784026, Lon: -92.139666
9801 Diamond Drive, North Little Rock, AR 72117
www.campingworld.com

OAKLAND — A3 *Marion*

BULL SHOALS LAKE - COE/OAKLAND PUBLIC USE AREA (Public Corps) From town, SW 8 mi on Hwy 202 (E). Avail: 32 E (30/50 amps). 2021 rates: $19 to $38. May 01 to Sep 30. (870)425-2700

OLA — C2 *Yell*

NIMROD LAKE - COE/QUARRY COVE (Public Corps) From town, E 7 mi on Hwy 60 to access rd (E). Avail: 31 E (30 amps). 2021 rates: $18 to $36. (479)272-4233

OMAHA — A2 *Boone*

OZARK VIEW RV PARK **Ratings: 8/8.5★/9** (Campground) Avail: 28 full hkups (30/50 amps). 2021 rates: $32. (870)715-0131, 18412 Old Hwy 65, Omaha, AR 72662

TABLE ROCK LAKE - COE/CRICKET CREEK (Public Corps) From town, N 4 mi on Hwy 65 to Hwy 14, W 5.9 mi (E). Avail: 37 E (30/50 amps). 2021 rates: $21 to $23. Apr 01 to Sep 15. (870)426-3331

Set your clocks. Time zones are indicated in the front of each state and province.

Get the Facts!

Essential tips, travel and outdoor recreation info can be found in the Welcome Section at the beginning of each State/Province.

You may just discover something new to see and do at your destination!

OZARK — B1 *Franklin*

➡ OZARK LAKE - COE/AUX ARC (Public Corps) From Ozark, S 1.5 mi on Hwy 23 to Hwy 309, E 1 mi (L). Avail: 60 E (30/50 amps). 2021 rates: $10 to $20. (479)667-1100

PARAGOULD — B5 *Greene*

➚ CROWLEY'S RIDGE (Public State Park) From Jct of SR-141 & SR-168 (in town), E 0.25 mi on SR-168 (R). 18 Avail: 18 W, 18 E (30 amps). 2021 rates: $22. (870)573-6751

PARIS — C1 *Logan*

⬇ MT MAGAZINE/CAMERON BLUFF CAMPGROUND (Public State Park) From town, S 17 mi on Hwy 309 (E). Avail: 18 full hkups (30/50 amps). 2021 rates: $30 to $34. (479)963-8502

PEEL — A2 *Marion*

⬆ BULL SHOALS LAKE - COE/HIGHWAY 125 (Public Corps) From town, NW 14 mi on Hwy 14 to Hwy 125, N 13 mi (R). Avail: 39 E (30/50 amps). 2021 rates: $22. Apr 01 to Oct 31. (870)436-5711

PERRYVILLE — C2 *Perry*

➘ HARRIS BRAKE LAKE RESORT **Ratings: 8/8.5★/8.5** (RV Resort) Avail: 15 full hkups (30/50 amps). 2021 rates: $29.50. (501)889-2745, 18 Coffee Creek Landing, Perryville, AR 72126

PINE BLUFF — D3 *Jefferson*

⬆ PINE BLUFF REGIONAL PARK (Public) From Jct of US-79 & US-65 (in town), E 1.25 mi on US-65B (avoid Loop 530) to Convention Center Dr, N 2 mi (beyond golf course) (E); or From Jct of US-65 & US-65B (E of town), N 3.4 mi on US-65B to Convention Center Dr, N 2 mi (beyond golf course) (E). 52 Avail: 52 W, 52 E (30 amps). 2021 rates: $20. (870)634-2121

PINEY — C2 *Garland*

⬆ DARDANELLE LAKE - COE/PINEY BAY (Public Corps) From town, W 3.7 mi on US-64 to SR-359, N 3.5 mi (L). 91 Avail: 70 W, 85 E (30/50 amps). 2021 rates: $10 to $20. Mar 01 to Oct 31. (479)885-3029

PLAINVIEW — C2 *Yell*

➡ NIMROD LAKE - COE/CARTER COVE (Public Corps) From town, SE 3 mi on Hwy 60 to access rd, S 1 mi (E). 34 Avail: 34 W, 34 E (30 amps). 2021 rates: $18 to $36. (479)272-4983

➡ NIMROD LAKE - COE/RIVER ROAD (Public Corps) From town, E 6 mi on Hwy 60 to access rd (E). 21 Avail: 21 W, 21 E (30/50 amps). 2021 rates: $17 to $40. Mar 01 to Oct 31. (479)272-4835

➡ NIMROD LAKE - COE/SUNLIGHT BAY (Public Corps) From town, W 0.25 mi on Hwy 28 to Sunlight access rd, S 2 mi (R). 29 Avail: 29 W, 29 E (30 amps). 2021 rates: $18 to $40. (479)272-4234

POCAHONTAS — B4 *Randolph*

⬇ DAVIDSONVILLE (Public State Park) From Jct of US-62 & SR-166, S 9 mi on SR-166 (E); or From Jct of US-63 & SR-361, N 6 mi on SR-361 (R). 20 Avail: 20 W, 20 E (30/50 amps). 2021 rates: $27 to $34. (870)892-4708

QUITMAN — B3 *Cleburne*

⬉ GREERS FERRY LAKE - COE/COVE CREEK (Public Corps) From town, NW 3 mi on Hwy 16 to access rd, right (E). Avail: 31 E (30/50 amps). 2021 rates: $16 to $24. May 15 to Sep 15. (501)589-3568

REDFIELD — C3 *Jefferson*

➡ ARKANSAS RIVER - COE/TAR CAMP (Public Corps) From town, E 6 mi on River Rd, follow signs (E). 48 Avail: 45 W, 45 E (50 amps). 2021 rates: $19. Mar 01 to Oct 31. (501)397-5101

ROGERS — A1 *Benton*

ROGERS See also Bella Vista, Cave Springs, Eureka Springs, Fayetteville & Springdale, AR; Cassville, MO.

➡ BEAVER LAKE - COE/HORSESHOE BEND (Public Corps) From Jct of US-62/I-546 & SR-94, E 7.5 mi on SR-94/New Hope Rd.(E). Avail: 184 E (30 amps). 2021 rates: $20 to $50. Apr 01 to Oct 30. (479)925-2561

➡ BEAVER LAKE - COE/PRAIRIE CREEK (Public Corps) From Jct of US-62 & SR-12, E 4 mi on SR-12 to North Park Rd, N into park (E). Avail: 112 E (30 amps). 2021 rates: $20 to $38. Apr 01 to Oct 31. (479)925-3957

⬆ BEAVER LAKE - COE/ROCKY BRANCH (Public Corps) From town, E 11 mi on Hwy 12 to SR-303, NE 4.5 mi to paved access road (E). Avail: 44 E (30/50 amps). 2021 rates: $20 to $25. May 01 to Oct 30. (479)925-2526

⬆ MONTE NE FAMILY CAMPGROUND RV PARK & CABINS **Ratings: 5.5/7/7** (RV Park) Avail: 30 full hkups (30/50 amps). 2021 rates: $30. (479)925-1265, 15039 E Highway 94, Rogers, AR 72758

ROYAL — C2 *Garland*

⬅ OUACHITA LAKE - COE/BRADY MOUNTAIN (Public Corps) From town, W 2 mi on US-270 to SH 926, N 6 mi (E). Avail: 74 E (30/50 amps). 2021 rates: $16 to $30. Mar 01 to Oct 01. (501)760-1146

RUSSELLVILLE — C2 *Pope*

⬇ DARDANELLE LAKE - COE/OLD POST ROAD (Public Corps) From Jct of I-40 & Hwy 7, S 6 mi on Hwy 7 to Old Post Rd, W 2 mi (E). 37 Avail: 37 W, 37 E (30 amps). 2021 rates: $20. Mar 01 to Oct 31. (501)968-7962

➡ **IVYS COVE RV RETREAT**

Ratings: 9/9.5★/10 (RV Park) Avail: 46 full hkups (30/50 amps). 2021 rates: $43.45 to $45. (479)280-1662, 321 Bradley Cove Rd., Russellville, AR 72802

➚ LAKE DARDANELLE (Public State Park) From Jct of I-40 & SR-7 (exit 81) to Aspen Rd, W (left) 0.1 mi on Aspen Rd to Rte 7, S 0.1 mi to SR 326, W 5.5 mi (R). 75 Avail. 2021 rates: $20 to $34. (479)967-5516

⬆ **OUTDOOR LIVING CENTER RV PARK**

Ratings: 7.5/9★/9 (RV Park) Avail: 26 full hkups (30/50 amps). 2021 rates: $37 to $40. (800)828-4307, 10 Outdoor Ct., Russellville, AR 72811

SARATOGA — D1 *Hempstead*

⬇ MILLWOOD LAKE - COE/SARATOGA PARK (Public Corps) From town, S 1 mi on Hwy 32 to Hwy 234, W 1 mi (E). 17 Avail: 17 W, 17 E. 2021 rates: $13. Mar 01 to Oct 31. (870)898-3343

SHERWOOD — C3 *Pulaski*

Travel Services

⬆ **GANDER RV OF SHERWOOD/NORTH LITTLE ROCK** Your new hometown outfitter offering the best regional gear for all your outdoor needs. Your adventure awaits.
SERVICES: RV appliance, MH mechanical, restrooms. RV Sales. RV supplies, RV accessible. Hours: 9am - 7pm.
(866)789-0643 Lat: 34.820342, Lon: -92.199191
6721 Warden Rd, Sherwood, AR 72120
rv.ganderoutdoors.com

SHIRLEY — B3 *Van Buren*

➡ GOLDEN POND RV PARK **Ratings: 8.5/8.5★/9** (RV Park) 39 Avail: 37 full hkups, 2 W, 2 E (30/50 amps). 2021 rates: $45. (501)723-8212, 241 Hwy 330 S., Shirley, AR 72153

SPRINGDALE — B1 *Benton*

SPRINGDALE See also Bella Vista, Cave Springs, Fayetteville & Rogers.

➡ BEAVER LAKE - COE/HICKORY CREEK (Public Corps) From Jct of US-71 & SR-264, E 4.5 mi on SR-264 to Cow Face Rd, S 1 mi to Hickory Creek Rd, E 1 mi (R). Avail: 61 E (30/50 amps). 2021 rates: $21 to $25. Apr 01 to Oct 30. (479)750-2943

⬉ BEAVER LAKE - COE/WAR EAGLE (Public Corps) From town, E 14 mi on SR-412 to Knob Hill Loop (CR-389), N 2.1 mi, follow signs (L). Avail: 26 E (30 amps). 2021 rates: $17 to $20. May 01 to Sep 14. (479)636-1210

➡ NWA HIDEAWAY **Ratings: 6/8★/7.5** (RV Park) Avail: 33 full hkups (30/50 amps). 2021 rates: $35. (479)789-7152, 21225 Hickory Flatt Road, Springdale, AR 72764

ST JOE — B2 *Searcy*

➚ BUFFALO NATIONAL RIVER/TYLER BEND (Public) From town: Go 3 mi S on US 65, then 3 mi W on access road. 28 Avail. 2021 rates: $20. (877)444-6777

STAR CITY — D3 *Lincoln*

➡ CANE CREEK (Public State Park) From Jct of US-425 & SR-293 (in town), E 5 mi on SR-293 (L). 29 Avail: 29 W, 29 E (30/50 amps). 2021 rates: $22 to $27. (870)628-4714

RV Park ratings you can rely on!

TEXARKANA — D1 *Miller*

➚ **SUNRISE RV PARK**

Ratings: 8.5/9.5★/9 (RV Park) Avail: 70 full hkups (30/50 amps). 2021 rates: $38.22. (870)772-0751, 8225 Camper Lane, Texarkana, AR 71854

TICHNOR — D4 *Desha*

⬇ ARKANSAS POST RIVER - COE/NOTREBES BEND (Public Corps) From town: Go 10 mi S on County Road, then follow signs 6-1/2 mi SW & SE on paved access road. Avail: 30 E (30 amps). 2021 rates: $19. Mar 01 to Oct 27. (870)548-2291

⬇ ARKANSAS RIVER - COE/MERRISACH LAKE (Public Corps) From town, S 10 mi on Tichnor Balcktop Rd to Merrisach Lake Ln, W 1 mi (E). Avail: 62 E (30/50 amps). 2021 rates: $11 to $19. (870)548-2291

TOLLETTE — D1 *Howard*

⬅ MILLWOOD LAKE - COE/COTTONSHED LANDING (Public Corps) From town, W 4 mi on CR-332 to access rd (E). 43 Avail: 43 W, 43 E (30/50 amps). 2021 rates: $15. (870)287-7118

VAN BUREN — B1 *Crawford*

⬆ **OVERLAND RV PARK**

Ratings: 6.5/8.5★/5.5 (RV Park) From jct of I-40 (exit 5) & SR-59: Go 1/4 mi S on SR-59, then 500 feet E on unnamed Access Rd (past shell station) (E). **FAC:** gravel rds. Avail: 50 gravel, 30 pull-thrus, (20x55), back-ins (20x30), 50 full hkups (30/50 amps), cable, WiFi @ sites, laundry. Pets OK. No tents. 2021 rates: $35 to $40, Military discount. no cc.
(479)471-5474 Lat: 35.46071, Lon: -94.35335
1716 1/2 Fayetteville Hwy, Van Buren, AR 72956
See ad this page

⬅ **PARK RIDGE RV CAMPGROUND**

Ratings: 8/10★/9.5 (Campground) From jct of I-40 (exit 3) & Lee Creek Rd: Go 1/4 mi N on Lee Creek Rd, then 1/4 mi E on Rena Rd (L).

STAY ON LEE CREEK NEAR FORT SMITH

Enjoy shady sites near I-40 on beautiful Lee Creek. Our new bath house and showers, as well as laundry are now open. Only minutes to restaurants, shopping and sightseeing in downtown Van Buren and historic Fort Smith.

FAC: gravel rds. (56 spaces). Avail: 40 gravel, 31 pull-thrus, (25x65), back-ins (28x45), 40 full hkups (30/50 amps), seasonal sites, cable, WiFi @ sites, tent sites, dump, laundry, firewood. **REC:** Lee Creek: fishing, boating nearby, playground, hunting nearby. Pets OK. Big rig sites, eco-friendly. 2021 rates: $42 to $45, Military discount.
(479)410-4678 Lat: 35.46693, Lon: -94.38724
1616 Rena Rd., Van Buren, AR 72956
parkridgerv.com
See ad this page

Keeping pets quiet and on a leash is common courtesy. ""Pet Restrictions'' which you'll find in some listings refers to limits on size, breed or quantity of pets allowed.

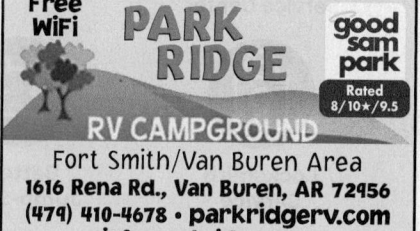

WAVELAND — C2 *Yell*

BLUE MOUNTAIN LAKE - COE/OUTLET AREA (Public Corps) From town: Go 1 mi S on Hwy 309, then 1 mi W on Blue Mountain Dam, follow signs (E). 36 Avail: 36 W, 36 E (30 amps). 2021 rates: $18 to $40. Mar 15 to Oct 26. (479)947-2101

BLUE MOUNTAIN LAKE - COE/WAVELAND PARK (Public Corps) From town, S 1 mi on Hwy 309 to paved cnty rd, W 1 mi, follow signs. 51 Avail: 51 W, 51 E (30/50 amps). 2021 rates: $18 to $20. Mar 01 to Oct 30. (479)947-2102

WEST FORK — B1 *Washington*

DEVIL'S DEN (Public State Park) From jct US-71 & SR-170: Go 18 mi SW on SR-170 (R). 127 Avail: 44 full hkups, 25 W, 25 E (30/50 amps). 2021 rates: $18 to $34. (479)761-3325

RV MAINTENANCE CHECKLIST: Check for fluid leaks and that they are all at their desired levels. Change the engine oil and filter or put it on your checklist to have it done before your first Spring trip. Check battery connections for corrosion and clean terminals. Spray with anti-corrosive. Test batteries in all smoke detectors and CO detectors. Verify that your fire extinguisher's pressure gauge is still in the green zone. If not, have it serviced.

WEST MEMPHIS — C5 *Crittenden*

WEST MEMPHIS See also Marion, AR; Horn Lake & South Haven, MS; Memphis, TN.

TOM SAWYER'S RV PARK

good sam park **Ratings: 7.5/9★/8** (RV Park) From Jct of I-40 (exit 280) & ML King Dr: Go 2-1/2 mi S on ML King Dr (becomes South Loop Dr), then 1/4 mi S on 8th St (over Levy) (L). **FAC:** paved/gravel rds. (121 spaces). 110 Avail: 47 paved, 63 all weather, 103 pull-thrus, (30x130), back-ins (30x60), 110 full hkups (30/50 amps), seasonal sites, WiFi @ sites, tent sites, laundry, firewood, controlled access. **REC:** Mississippi River: fishing, kayaking/canoeing, boating nearby. Pet restrict (B). Big rig sites. 2021 rates: $40 to $55.
(870)735-9770 Lat: 35.12999, Lon: -90.16714
1286 S 8th St, West Memphis, AR 72301
tomsawyersrvpark.com
See ad page 856

Good Sam Roadside Assistance has unlimited distance towing to the nearest service center and help from people who have RV specific expertise and equipment. Plus, for less than one tank of gas, you're covered even when you're not RVing - cars, trucks, SUVs, motorcycles, even boat trailers are included. Visit GoodSamRoadside.com

YELLVILLE — B2 *Marion*

BUFFALO NATIONAL RIVER/BUFFALO POINT (Public National Park) From town: Go 14 mi S on AR-14, then 3 mi E on AR-268 (E). 83 Avail: 83 W, 83 E (50 amps). 2021 rates: $30. Mar 13 to Nov 15. (877)444-6777

Like Us on Facebook.

CLEAN RESTROOMS GET A STAR

Campgrounds that receive the maximum 5 points for restroom cleanliness (toilets, showers, floors, walls and sinks/counters/mirrors) achieve a star beside their total restroom rating.

Rated 10/10★/10

YOU ARE HERE
DID YOU KNOW?
Soaring to a height of 380 feet, the world's tallest-known living tree - nicknamed Hyperion - stands in Redwood National Park.
Getty Images/iStockphoto

California

The Golden State caters to every traveler, from hikers seeking backwoods adventure to epicures seeking prime restaurants and wineries. Meet Mickey and Minnie in Disneyland or motor the coastline of Big Sur.

Two Vibrant Valleys and Legendary City

Northern California's owns much of its fame to two iconic valleys. You can tour proving grounds of the latest high-tech gadgets in Silicon Valley and then sip world-class vintages in Napa Valley. Nothing beats San Francisco, where you can dig into fresh seafood along Fisherman's Wharf, admire the iconic Golden Gate Bridge and ride a cable car to the stars on steep, scenic streets. You can also take a ferry to Alcatraz Island to see the infamous prison that once housed America's most notorious felons.

Terrific Tahoe

Located on Northern California's eastern border with Nevada, Lake Tahoe shimmers with topaz waters that will make you want to bust out the canoes and sailboats. If you're new to water sports, enroll at the High Sierra Waterski School to learn the ins and outs of its namesake pastime along with jet skiing, kayaking or paddleboarding. The lake also supports large populations of mackinaw, kokanee salmon and brown and rainbow trout. You can reel in these prized catches from the Truckee River on the west shore, Boca and Stampede reservoirs in the north or Taylor Creek in the south.

Happiest Place on Earth

Ready to escape? Located in Anaheim, Disneyland immerses visitors deep in the fantasy worlds of some of the most creative minds in the entertainment business. The Happiest Place on Earth is located in Anaheim and promises a magical day filled with rides, shows and character experiences. Planning a

California Burrito

You can't leave San Diego without trying the California Burrito. Head to Mike's Taco Club or Nico's Mexican Food to sample this hefty roll loaded with carne asada, cheese, guacamole, sour cream, salsa and French fries. Foodies say the fries put the burrito over the top by giving it an extra satisfying crunch. Judge for yourself on your next trip to San Diego.

VISITOR CENTER

TIME ZONE
Pacific Standard

ROAD & HIGHWAY INFORMATION
800-427-7623
dot.ca.gov

FISHING & HUNTING INFORMATION
888-326-2822
wildlife.ca.gov/licensing

BOATING INFORMATION
dbw.ca.gov

NATIONAL PARKS
nps.gov/ca

STATE PARKS
parks.ca.gov

TOURISM INFORMATION
California Travel and Tourism Commission
877-225-4367
visitcalifornia.com

TOP TOURISM ATTRACTIONS
1) Disneyland Park
2) Golden Gate Bridge
3) The Hollywood Sign

MAJOR CITIES
Los Angeles, San Diego, San Jose, San Francisco, Fresno, Sacramento (capital)

romantic getaway? Whisk your partner to Sonoma or Napa Valley and spend your time touring scenic vineyards.

I Love LA

Old Hollywood landmarks, glitzy neighborhoods and scenic ocean shorelines coalesce in Los Angeles. Visit iconic attractions like the TCL Chinese Theatre, Walk of Fame and Grammy Museum. When you're done being star-struck, head to Santa Monica pier for old-fashioned amusements or Venice Beach to watch the region's most eccentric characters stroll the boardwalk.

Islands Out of Time

Off the shores of Ventura County a chain of islands harbor unique wildlife. Channel Islands National Park is located just off the coast of Ventura County and is home to wildlife found nowhere else in the world, resulting in the nickname, "Galapagos of North America." This environment is filled with rare plants and an abundance of wildlife. Paddle around the five islands and you've got a good chance of seeing whales, seals and dolphins.

Walk Among Giants

Northern California's nutritious soil and damp climate create conditions that are perfect for some of the largest living organisms in the world. Witness these treasures at Redwood National and State Parks. Encompassing 139,000 acres, this contiguous ecosystem stretches northward along the Pacific Coast, almost all the way to Oregon, hosting the tallest trees on the planet. Hike the Trillium Falls Trail or Prairie Creek Trail to gawk at ancient redwoods or drive down the Newton B. Drury Scenic Parkway to enjoy the peaceful landscape.

Wind forms ripples in the the dunes of Death Valley National Park. The park has six dune environments.

Death Valley Days

Badlands, mountainous sand dunes and endless salt flats enthrall visitors to Death Valley National Park. Located along California's eastern border with Nevada, this arid expanse preserves desert terrain that ranges from creamy dunes to jagged peaks. These otherworldly landscapes have been used as backdrops for countless movies including "Star Wars" and "Blade." Visit in spring to see "super blooms" of colorful desert flowers.

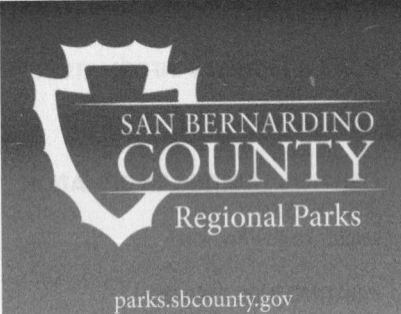

Featured Good Sam Parks

CALIFORNIA

CA

When you stay with Good Sam, you can expect the highest degree of cleanliness and friendliness, and better yet, you get **10% off** campground fees.

If you're not already a Good Sam member you can purchase your membership at one of these locations:

10/10★/10 GOOD SAM PARKS

BAKERSFIELD
Bakersfield RV Resort
(661)833-9998

BORREGO SPRINGS
The Springs At Borrego RV Resort & Golf Course
(760)767-0004

CORNING
The RV Park At Rolling Hills Casino and Resort
(530)528-3500

GREENFIELD
Yanks RV Resort
(831)740-8007

INDIO
Indian Waters RV Resort & Cottages
(760)342-8100

JACKSON
Jackson Rancheria RV Park
(800)822-WINN

OROVILLE
Berry Creek Rancheria RV Park
(866)991-5061

PALA
Pala Casino RV Resort
(844)472-5278

REDDING
JGW RV Park
(530)365-7965

Redding Premier RV Resort
(530)246-0101

SAN JOSE
Coyote Valley RV Resort
(866)376-5500

TEMECULA
Pechanga RV Resort
(877)997-8386

VACAVILLE
Vineyard RV Park
(866)447-8797

What's This?

An RV park with a 10/10★/10 rating has scored perfect grades in amenities, cleanliness and appearance ("See Understanding the Campground Rating System" on pages 8 and 9 for an explanation of the trusted Good Sam Rating System). Stay in a 10/10★/10 park on your next trip for a nearly flawless camping experience.

ACTON
Los Angeles RV Resort (formerly KOA)
Soledad Canyon RV & Camping Resort
The Californian RV Resort

ANGELS CAMP
Angels Camp RV Resort

BAKERSFIELD
A Country RV Park
Bakersfield River Run RV Park
Bakersfield RV Resort
Orange Grove RV Park

BARSTOW
Shady Lane RV Camp

BISHOP
Highlands RV Park

BLYTHE
Destiny RV Resorts-McIntyre

BORON
Arabian RV Oasis

Getty Images/iStockphoto

BORREGO SPRINGS
Leapin Lizard RV Ranch
Palm Canyon Hotel and RV Resort
The Springs At Borrego RV Resort & Golf Course

BUELLTON
Flying Flags RV Resort & Campground

CATHEDRAL CITY
Palm Springs Oasis RV Resort

CHICO
Almond Tree RV Park

CHOWCHILLA
The Lakes RV & Golf Resort

CLOVERDALE
Russian River RV Campground

COACHELLA
Coachella Lakes RV Resort

COLUMBIA
49er RV Ranch

CORNING
The RV Park At Rolling Hills Casino and Resort

CRESCENT CITY
Village Camper Inn RV Park

DESCANSO
Oakzanita Springs RV Campground

DESERT HOT SPRINGS
Sam's Family Spa

EL CENTRO
Rio Bend RV & Golf Resort

EMIGRANT GAP
Snowflower RV Resort

ESCONDIDO
Champagne Lakes RV Resort

FORESTVILLE
River Bend Resort

FORT BRAGG
Pomo RV Park & Campground

FORTUNA
Riverwalk RV Park & Campground

FRESNO
Fresno Mobile Home & RV Park

GREENBRAE
Marin RV Park

GREENFIELD
Yanks RV Resort

GROVELAND
Yosemite Lakes RV Resort
Yosemite Pines RV Resort

HEMET
Casa Del Sol RV Resort

HOLLISTER
Casa de Fruta RV Park

HUNTINGTON BEACH
Waterfront RV Park

IDYLLWILD
Idyllwild RV Resort

INDIO
Indian Waters RV Resort & Cottages
Shadow Hills RV Resort

JACKSON
Jackson Rancheria RV Park

JAMUL
Pio Pico RV Resort & Campground

JOSHUA TREE NATIONAL PARK
TwentyNine Palms Resort RV Park and Cottages

KERNVILLE
Frandy Park Campground

KLAMATH
Kamp Klamath RV Park & Campground
Klamath River RV Park

LAKEPORT
Konocti Vista RV Park

LAKESIDE
Rancho Los Coches RV Park

LEMON COVE
Lemon Cove Village RV Park

LODI
Flag City RV Resort

LONE PINE
Boulder Creek RV Resort

LONG BEACH
Arbor Mobile Village

LOTUS
Ponderosa RV Resort

MANTECA
Turtle Beach

MARINA
Marina Dunes RV Resort

MCARTHUR
Lassen RV Resort

MENIFEE
Wilderness Lakes RV Resort

MORGAN HILL
Morgan Hill RV Resort

MYERS FLAT
Giant Redwoods RV and Cabin Destination

NEEDLES
Pirate Cove Resort & Marina

NEWPORT BEACH
Newport Dunes Waterfront Resort & Marina

NICOLAUS
Lake Minden RV Resort

NILAND
Fountain Of Youth Spa RV Resort

NORTHRIDGE
Walnut RV Park

NOVATO
Novato RV Park

OAKHURST
High Sierra RV Park & Mobile Park

OCEANO
Pacific Dunes Ranch RV Resort

OCEANSIDE
Oceanside RV Resort

OLANCHA
Lake Olancha RV Park

OLD STATION
Hat Creek Resort & RV Park

OLEMA
Olema Campground

ORANGE
Orangeland RV Park

OREGON HOUSE
Lake of the Springs RV Resort

OROVILLE
Berry Creek Rancheria RV Park
River Reflections RV Park & Campground

PACIFICA
San Francisco RV Resort

PAICINES
San Benito RV & Camping Resort

PALA
Pala Casino RV Resort

PALM DESERT
Palm Springs RV Resort

PASO ROBLES
Paso Robles RV Ranch

POMONA
Fairplex RV Park

REDCREST
Ancient Redwoods RV Park

REDDING
JGW RV Park
Redding Premier RV Resort

REDWAY
Dean Creek Resort

RIO VISTA
Duck Island RV Park & Fishing Resort

SAN DIEGO
Campland On the Bay
Mission Bay RV Resort

SAN DIMAS
Bonelli Bluffs RV Resort & Campground

SAN JOSE
Coyote Valley RV Resort

SAN JUAN BAUTISTA
Betabel RV Park

SANTA BARBARA
Rancho Oso RV & Camping Resort

SANTA NELLA
Santa Nella RV Park

SANTA ROSA
Sonoma County RV Park-At the Fairgrounds

SANTEE
Santee Lakes Recreation Preserve

SCOTTS VALLEY
Santa Cruz Ranch RV Resort

SHOSHONE
Shoshone RV Park

SOUTH LAKE TAHOE
Tahoe Valley Campground

STANDISH
Days End RV Park

SUSANVILLE
Eagle Lake RV Park
Susanville RV Park

TEMECULA
Pechanga RV Resort

TRINIDAD
Sounds Of the Sea RV Park & Cabins

TRUCKEE
Coachland RV Park

TULARE
Sun & Fun RV Park

TUOLUMNE
The RV Park at Black Oak Casino Resort

VACAVILLE
Midway RV Park
Vineyard RV Park

VALENCIA
Valencia Travel Village

VALLEJO
Tradewinds RV Park Of Vallejo

VISALIA
Country Manor RV & MH Community

VISTA
Olive Avenue RV Resort

WEED
Hi-Lo RV Park

WEST SACRAMENTO
Sac-West RV Park and Campground

WILLITS
Mendocino Redwoods RV Resort

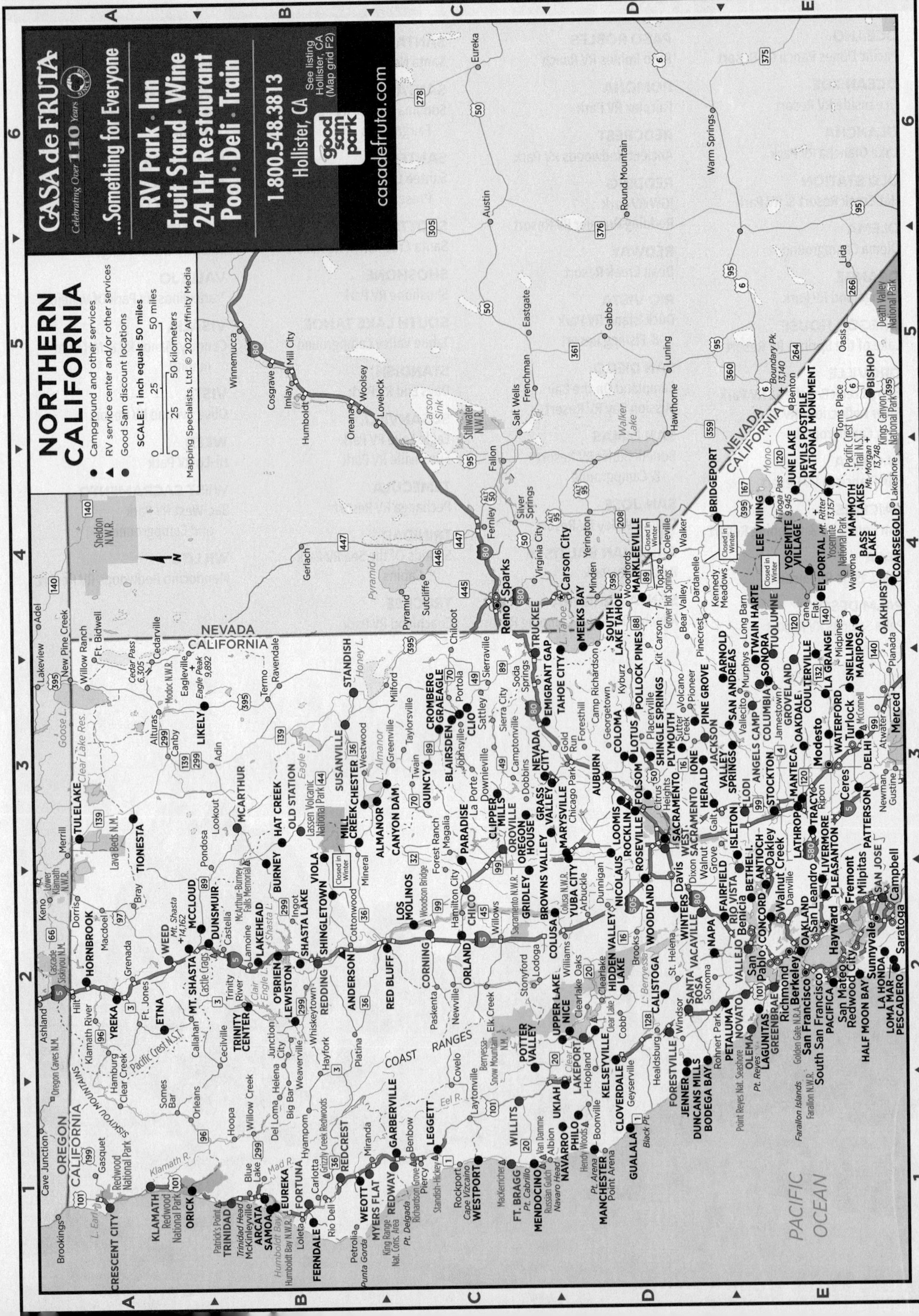
NORTHERN CALIFORNIA
Campground and other services
RV service center and/or other services
Good Sam discount locations
SCALE: 1 inch equals 50 miles
0 25 50 miles
0 25 50 kilometers
Mapping Specialists, Ltd. © 2022 Affinity Media
CASA de FRUTA
Celebrating Over 110 Years
...Something for Everyone
RV Park · Inn
Fruit Stand · Wine
24 Hr Restaurant
Pool · Deli · Train
1.800.548.3813
Hollister, CA
good sam park
See listing Hollister, CA (Map grid F2)
casadefruta.com
OREGON
CALIFORNIA
NEVADA
PACIFIC OCEAN
COAST RANGES
SISKIYOU MOUNTAINS
Reno
Sparks
Carson City
Sacramento
San Francisco
Oakland
San Jose
Redding
Eureka
Chico
Stockton
Modesto
Merced
Lake Tahoe
Winnemucca
Fallon
Bishop
Death Valley National Park

SOUTHERN CALIFORNIA
● Campground and other services
▲ RV service center and/or other services
● Good Sam discount locations
SCALE: 1 inch equals 54 miles
0 25 50 miles
0 25 50 kilometers
Mapping Specialists, Ltd. © 2022 Affinity Media
PACIFIC OCEAN
MOJAVE DESERT
NEVADA
CALIFORNIA
ARIZONA
MEXICO
BAJA CALIFORNIA
SONORA
SEE LOS ANGELES METRO MAP FOR ENLARGEMENT OF BOXED AREA

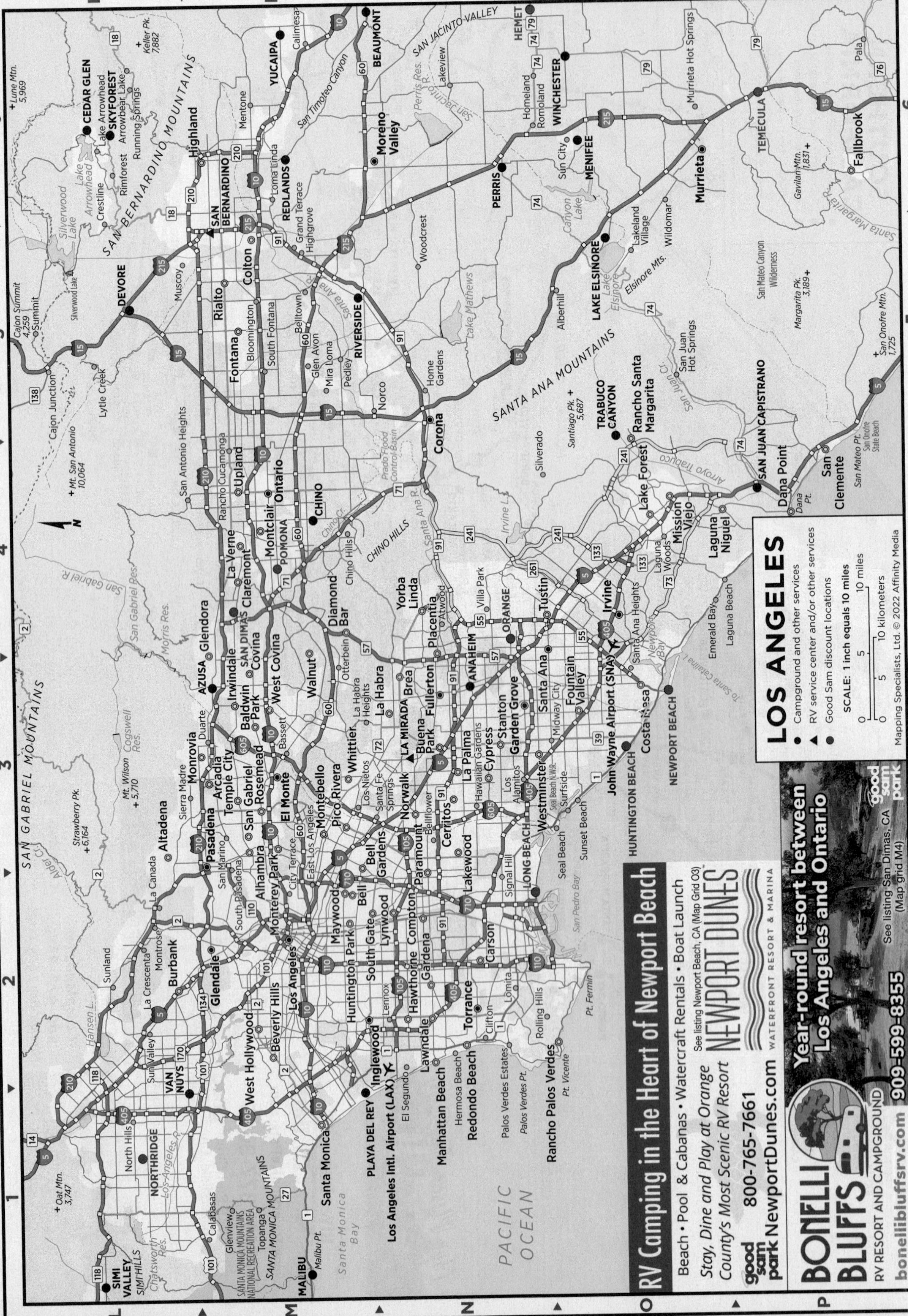
LOS ANGELES
Campground and other services
RV service center and/or other services
Good Sam discount locations
SCALE: 1 inch equals 10 miles
Mapping Specialists, Ltd. © 2022 Affinity Media

ROAD TRIPS

See Where the Golden State Really Shines

California South

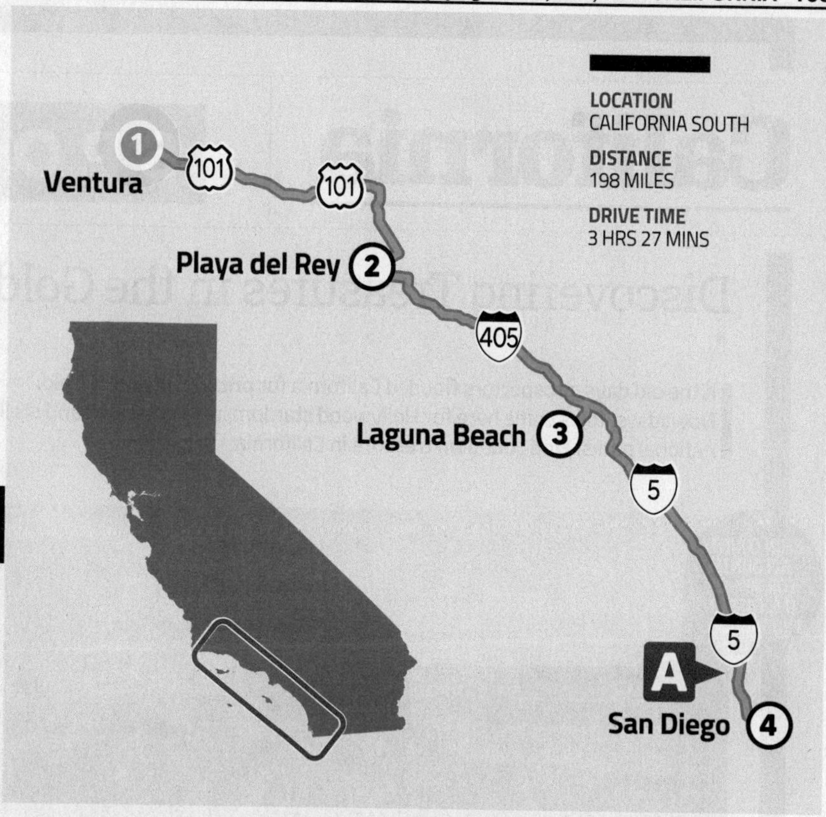

Follow SoCal's coast for adventure. Whether you're a budding surfer, seashell hunter or freewheeling hippy, you'll find a beach that's right up your alley. Inland, you'll uncover artsy enclaves teeming with galleries and a striking blend of architecture ranging from Spanish-inspired missions to futuristic concert halls. The food scene is also out of this world, so make sure you fill up on the region's famous fish tacos before you go.

1 Ventura
Starting point

Get a taste of California history. Traditional homes, antique shops and a wide array of restaurants occupy the palm tree-lined streets of Ventura's historic downtown district. Admire the 18th-century Mission San Buenaventura and consider catching a show at the award-winning Rubicon Theater. You can also pick up produce at the farmer's market. The city also acts as the entry point to Channel Islands National Park. Nicknamed the "Galapagos of North America," these five remote islands are home to 150 species of endemic flora and fauna. Board a boat and go hiking, kayaking or diving. Keep an eye out for the island fox.

2 Playa del Rey
Drive 69 miles ▪ 1 hour, 14 minutes

LA's eclectic offerings all gather on this stretch of coast. Head to the north end of Playa Del Rey Beach to hit the waves on a surfboard and then stroll the Venice Beach Boardwalk to mingle with fortune-tellers, street performers and other eccentric characters. In Marina del Rey, cycle down the 22-mile Marvin Braude Coastal Bike Trail or take a YOGAqua class, an activity that blends yoga with stand-up paddleboarding. Finish your day with a dinner cruise where champagne and seasonal dishes are served alongside sweeping harbor views.

3 Laguna Beach
Drive 56 miles ▪ 59 minutes

Fine California living is on full display in this upscale coastal enclave. View works by local artists at the Laguna Art Museum and pick up a piece for your home at galleries like Kush Fine Art and Virga Gallery. In the summer, watch actors pose for living paintings during the Festival of Arts Pageant of the Masters and admire everything from hand-blown glass to fine photography during the Sawdust Art and Craft Festival. Before you leave, stop by the Pacific Marine Mammal Center to meet rescued sea lions and seals. There is no admission fee, but donations are appreciated.

4 San Diego
Drive 73 miles ▪ 1 hour, 14 minutes

San Diego's temperate climate and outstanding ocean shore makes it a top vacation destination. Bring the family to the La Jolla Shores for a day of paddleboarding and beachcombing or perfect your surfing skills at Mission Beach. There are dozens of beaches to choose from, so you're sure to find the perfect patch of sand for your outdoor pursuits. When the sun goes down, go to the historic Gaslamp Quarter for dinner or head north to guzzle down craft beers in Miramar, a neighborhood that locals call "Beer-a-Mar." Discover new flavors and take some bottles home.

RECOMMENDED STOPOVER
A SANTEE LAKES RECREATION PRESERVE
SANTEE, CA (619) 596-3141

Getty Images/iStockphoto

BIKING BOATING DINING ENTERTAINMENT FISHING HIKING HUNTING PADDLING SHOPPING SIGHTSEEING

California SPOTLIGHTS

Discovering Treasures in the Golden State

In the old days, prospectors flooded California for prized nuggets of gold. Nowadays, folks come here for Hollywood stardom, amazing cities and stellar national parks. Find your own treasure in California.

KERN COUNTY ACCOUNTS FOR 80% OF U.S. CARROT PRODUCTION.

Getty Images/iStockphoto

Bakersfield's fertile soil has made it a top U.S. agricultural center.

Bakersfield

This city in the San Joaquin Valley has long been an agricultural hub growing everything from grain to citrus fruits. The discovery of black gold in 1899 brought migrants from the Great Plains and it was their descendants who gave the region its distinct western flair. Bakersfield has come a long way since its humble beginnings — it's now a hotbed for music and art, yet continues to honor its rich past.

Art and Music Hub

Bakersfield is known as Nashville West because of its country music roots. During the 1950s, legendary artists like Merle Haggard and Buck Owens began popularizing a gritty style of country music called the Bakersfield Sound. This raw rock-meets-country genre continues to play in the city's top music venues. Hear it for yourself at the famed Buck Owens' Crystal Palace, a country venue that has hosted some of the biggest names in country. Browse the exhibits at the onsite museum or order a serving of "Cryin' Time" onion rings at the restaurant. Buy a ticket for one of the top country acts that regularly perform at the Palace.

Creative Capital

The arts flourish here too, especially in the downtown Arts District. Catch a film screening or musical at the Art Deco Fox Theater and check out the many galleries nearby. You can admire abstract and contemporary pieces at Metro Galleries and take weekly art classes at the Art Center Gallery. The Bellmoore Gallery is also worth a visit for its works by up-and-coming artists.

Wild Whitewater

Get ready for a thrilling whitewater experience on the Kern River. Thanks to Class I to Class V rapids, this river offers several rafting trips for paddlers of all skill levels. River's End Rafting provides guided expeditions through the mouth of the Kern Canyon to Lake Ming, a scenic stretch with Class II to III whitewater. The tour company also gives you the chance to pan for gold in Greenhorn Creek, a fun activity before or after your rafting adventure.

Hit the Trail

Wildflowers carpet the landscape every spring and one of the best places to view them is in Wind Wolves Preserve. This 93,000-acre swath of ancient trees and lush grasslands is the West Coast's largest non-profit preserve. Within it, you'll find a multitude of hiking and biking trails along with well-maintained amenities such as picnic areas and campgrounds.

California's Secret

Kern Canyon Trail is another top spot for wildflower viewing. Called "California's best-kept secret" by residents, this 9.4-mile path begins in Sequoia National Park's Keyesville Recreation Site and weaves through scenic hillsides before leading hikers to fantastic overlooks of the Kern River. The Kern River Parkway Trail is also a popular cycling destination, as 21 miles span nature preserves, parks and the Kern River Oil Field.

Basque Cuisine

You're in for a treat if you love trying new foods. Bakersfield has the largest number of Basque restaurants in the entire country and you can find most of them in Old Town Kern, aka the Basque Block. This cuisine came from the northern part of Spain and was imported here by Spanish and French Pyrenees immigrants during the late 1800s. Head to the 125-year-old Noriega Hotel to sample classic dishes such as oxtail stew, roasted lamb and pickled tongue. Wash it all down

CATCH A FILM SCREENING OR MUSICAL AT THE ICONIC ART DECO FOX THEATER IN BAKERSFIELD.

Stretching 1, 620 feet into the Pacific Ocean, the Ventura pier is the eighth-longest pier in California and a magnet for anglers. Seafood restaurants overlook the pier.

with Picon Punch, a cocktail crafted with Basque brandy, grenadine and bitter orange liqueur. Other restaurants in town include the Chalet Basque Restaurant, Wool Growers Restaurant and Pyrenees Café.

Land of Concerts, Rodeos and Food Festivals

Major events occur almost every month, so it's easy to fill your calendar with fun activities. Experience the city's rich musical talent at The Great 48-Hour Bluegrass Jam in January, Jazz Festival in April and Celtic Music Festival in October. If food is your passion, come during April to feast on gastronomic delights at the Macaroni and Cheese Festival and Jewish Food Festival.

Bakersfield's Beginnings

Home to 56 historic buildings, the Kern County Museum acts as a window into the past. Stroll 16 acres of preserved structures to discover significant sites like Merle Haggard's childhood home, an 1860 general store and an antique Southern Pacific engine. Check out the Bakersfield Sound exhibit and displays about Kern County's oil industry.

History in your Hands

If you want to take home a piece of local history, hunt for vintage treasures on Antique Row. From cowboy boots to traditional furnishings, you'll find all sorts of old gems at dozens of consignment shops. Mill Creek Antique Mall, Great American Antiques and Central Park Antique Mall are excellent places to start your search.

Depression Legacy

Walk in the steps of the Okies of the Dust Bowl era with a stop at the Weedpatch Camp, a temporary settlement for migrants described in John Steinbeck's 1939 novel of the Great Depression, "The Grapes of Wrath." Several historic buildings preserve the lives of itinerant farmers who journeyed to the area in ramshackle caravans. Signage tells the story of the thousands of migrants who traveled west in search of a better life.

California's Central Coast

The Central Coast is what California dreams are made of. Home to Santa Barbara's romantic vineyards, hidden beaches in Big Sur and the Galapagos of North America, this 350-mile stretch from Ventura to Santa Clara has been hailed as one of the best road trips in the world. Every wine region, state park and beach town worth visiting is easily accessible via Highway One, so buckle up and get ready to discover America's most enchanting coastline.

Discover Ventura and the Galapagos of North America

Ventura has that classic beach town vibe that casts a spell on visitors. Spend your days riding waves at Surfers Point, fishing off of Ventura Pier and enjoying the view from the Ventura Botanical Gardens. The waterfront community also acts as the gateway to Channel Islands National Park. Located an hour away from the mainland, these five remote islands are coined the "Galapagos of North America" because they support more than 2,000 species of flora and fauna, 150 of which can only be found here. The hiking, kayaking and diving opportunities are infinite, with approximately 175 miles of undeveloped coastline to explore. You can also expect epic sunset views from places like Cavern Point on Santa Cruz Island and Torrey Pines on Santa Rosa Island. Keep an eye out for the Island fox, unique to the islands, and marvel at the flora that flourishes there.

Santa Barbara is the American Riviera

Make your next stop Santa Barbara, a seaside city with a Mediterranean flair. Spanish colonial-style architecture dominates the landscape with standout structures being the Old Mission Santa Barbara and El Cuartel, California's second oldest building in El Presidio Historic Park. State Street breathes new life into the city with upscale restaurants, art galleries and designer boutiques. The Santa Barbara Urban Wine Trail also runs through the street, a route consisting of 33 wineries and tasting rooms. You'll find vineyards all around Santa Barbara too so plan a day trip to Lompoc, Santa Maria and Santa Ynez if you want to sample some more world-class wines.

Founded in 1772 by Father Junipero Serro, Mission San Luis Obispo de Tolosa is the fifth California mission.

Play in Pismo Beach's Natural Wonderland of Sea and Sand

Coastal hills and teal waters make Pismo Beach an ideal place to connect with nature. Saddle up and traverse the dunes in the south part of town by horseback. For a more adrenaline-packed excursion, rent an ATV and whiz through the Oceano Dunes State Vehicular Recreation Area. On the water, take a surf lesson or paddle out to nearby sea caves. If you're in town between late October to February, make sure to visit the Pismo Beach Monarch Butterfly Grove to view over 10,000 migrating butterflies.

Take it SLO in San Luis Obispo

Referred to as "SLO" by the locals, San Luis Obispo invites you to take life at a slower pace. Dine on freshly caught seafood at ocean-to-table restaurants and pick up fresh produce and local souvenirs at the SLO Farmers Market. Love wine? Book a day tour to Paso Robles and San Luis Obispo wine regions to sample over 40 grape varieties. San Luis Obispo County is also home to spectacular mountain and ocean scenery, the perfect backdrop for your outdoor adventures. The Reservoir Canyon Trail and Cerro San Luis Trail are two popular hikes ending with sweeping vistas of the surrounding area. Hike the three major peaks that overlook San Luis Obispo, then celebrate your accomplishment by dining on tri-tip beef afterward.

Wildlife spotting at Morro Bay

Bird-watchers come to this coastal town to spot peregrine falcons nesting on Morro Rock, an ancient volcanic plug jutting out of Morro Beach. The community hosts the Morro Bay Winter Bird Festival every Martin Luther King weekend, a fantastic opportunity to view and photograph over 200 species. For marine wildlife, join a whale-watching cruise or stop by the Estuary Nature Center to meet otters and pelicans. On land, take a stroll down the Embarcadero, an oceanfront street lined with guesthouses, restaurants and the Morro Bay Skateboard Museum.

Motorists crossing Bixby Creek Bridge on Highway 1 along the Big Sur coast 120 miles south of San Francisco.

Artistic Cambria

Creative Cambria charms with its artsy atmosphere. Housed in the old Bank of Cambria building, the Vault Gallery displays works by plein air and contemporary artists. There are also a few galleries in the West Village including Ephraim Pottery which showcases handmade furniture and lamps. Eleven miles up the coast is Hearst Castle, the lavish 1940s estate of publishing magnate William Randolph Hearst. Guided tours give you the chance to explore the mansion's 165 rooms and gardens teeming with elaborate fountains and palm trees.

Unforgettable Road Trips along Big Sur

It's not every day you get to take a scenic drive through a place like Big Sur. Spanning 90 miles from Carmel-by-the-Sea to Hearst Castle, this stretch of coastline will cast a spell on you with its dramatic cliffs, misty shores, and towering redwood forests. Make a stop at the famed Bixby Creek Bridge (you'll want photos for sure) and stay on the lookout for California condors, the largest birds in North America. Continue your journey to Pfeiffer Big Sur State Park which has countless trails for you to explore.

Whale-watching in Monterey

Wildlife encounters are plentiful in Monterey. The picturesque town is one of the best places in the country for whale watching so join a naturalist-led tour and keep your eyes open for orcas, dolphins and more. Other popular attractions in town include the revitalized Cannery Row and historic Old Fisherman's Wharf. If you're a John Steinbeck fan, don't miss the National Steinbeck Museum in nearby Salinas.

Monterey Aquarium

The waterfront aquarium has won accolades as one of the most sophisticated exhibits of sea life.

The keystone attraction is the 28-foot, three-story kelp forest. It remains as one of the stalwart features of the aquarium displaying a real life version of California coastal marine life. The water in its 333,000-gallon tank appears to be rising and falling with the outside bay's incoming waves. Piped in from Monterey Bay, the water sources are actually connected. The live kelp and fish within the saltwater tank behave as if they were in the very ocean itself and the aquarium was the first location to ever grow live kelp in a saltwater tank. The close-up view of the three story tank's inhabitants looking up from the lowest level of the tank or down from the top gives you a feeling of being suspended along with the tank's occupants in their watery environment.

You Otter See It

In the aquarium, the sea otter exhibit attract throngs for good reason. Ever moving, these creatures could delight visitors for hours on end. It is possible to watch them under the water or above the surface as they roll and dive in the water or float upon its surface. There is also a huge "Open Sea" tank with yellow fin tuna, sharks and ocean sunfish.

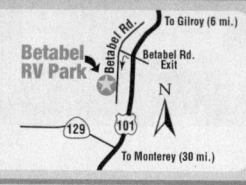

CA

SPOTLIGHTS

Located 45 miles east of Monterey, Hollister sits in California's "hidden wine country" with its own wine trail.

A Major Mission

The Basilica of Mission San Carlos Borromeo Del Rio Carmelo, dating back to 1770, is the crown jewel of this historic town. Mission Ranch, nearby, is also a great example of early Spanish architecture. This, along with downtown Hog's Breath Inn Restaurant and Bar, is owned by the one time-mayor of Carmel and the famous film star Clint Eastwood.

Linking Up

There are many world-class links here, with Pebble Beach Golf Course serving as the home of world-class tournaments. Bring your own bike or rent one, as these offer a great way to tour the coastal communities and picturesque coastline. Hiking also is popular. Using Monterey as your base, you are located well for a host of day trips to additional attractions.

Hollister

Located fewer than 100 miles south of the San Francisco Bay Area, Hollister is a quiet getaway in the western foothills of California's Diablo Range. These peaks rise on the distant horizon, turning into undulating grasslands closer to town. These hills are home to farms and vineyards. Those exploring the California missions on the El Camino Real route may find Hollister an inviting waypoint. Head east to explore the exquisite Pacific Coast and Monterey Bay region.

Relaxation on Tap

The rolling hills of Hollister and the surrounding region make it a prime location for wineries. Let the day slip away while you sip on local chardonnays. The beautiful vineyards form a striking backdrop for your adventures. Head to downtown Hollister to explore the charming shops and cafes. Guided walking tours take you by the architectural gems and murals, which commemorate Hollister as "The Birthplace of the American Biker." Farm-to-table restaurants take advantage of the local bounty, as does Casa de Fruta, a 110-year-old fruit stand. Head to the Mission San Juan Bautista, one of California's oldest missions, dating to 1797.

Making Waves

With three lakes, the San Luis Reservoir State Recreation Area is a watery playland. Though there is a potential for strong winds, these waterways are popular spots for boating and paddling. Anglers will find a variety of species to hook, including largemouth black bass, crappie, bluegill, trout, catfish, and more. Seasonally, waterfowl hunting is allowed. Developed facilities include boat launches, a swim beach, and hiking trails. In spring, the surrounding grasslands pop with colorful wildflower blooms.

Get your Motors Roaring

Hollister Hills State Vehicular Recreation Area offers almost 7000 acres to explore on foot or on wheels. In the Lower Ranch section, you will find trails and hill climbs to traverse on your motorcycle or all-terrain vehicle. Those with four-wheeled vehicles can head to the Upper Ranch, where trails offer specially designed challenging obstacles. The San Andreas Fault crosses the park, and visitors can enjoy diverse habitats on either side. Hiking, biking, and equestrian trails offer a slower, quieter place to soak in the scenery.

Los Angeles

Los Angeles is nothing if not interesting. This sunny SoCal megacity is best known for its film industry, and while Hollywood definitely plays a big role in defining the city, LA is so much more. With its funky beach neighborhoods, world-class museums and surprisingly spacious natural areas, Los Angeles offers plenty to keep travelers entertained.

Completed in 1870 as a water reservoir, Echo Park Lake is an oasis amid the cityscape of Los Angeles.

Welcome to Tinseltown

The first thing that comes to many people's minds when they think about Los Angeles is Hollywood, and it's no surprise why. The film industry's presence can be felt everywhere in LA, and it's not unusual to spot film stars going about their days around town. However, there are a few key spots that film buffs won't want to miss. The most obvious is the Hollywood Walk of Fame, a 15-block stretch of Hollywood Boulevard that showcases thousands of star-shaped tiles bearing the names of some of the world's most celebrated actors and musicians. Other key attractions include the TCL Chinese Theatres (formerly Grauman's Chinese Theatre), which has its own set of stars complete with autographs and cement handprints of their honorees. Other popular activities for the starstruck include bus tours that ferry visitors past the homes of superstars as well as tours of working studios, such as Warner Bros. and Paramount Pictures. And no visit to Hollywood would be complete without a pilgrimage to the iconic Hollywood sign, nestled in the hills of Griffith Park.

Beach Time

Southern California is known for its beaches, and while those seeking sand and sun often end up heading south to Orange County and beyond, there are plenty of great beaches right in LA County. Manhattan Beach is a good option, as it's one of the nicer beaches in town — it's also a popular surf spot. Just up the coast, on the other side of swanky Marina del Rey,

See listing San Dimas, CA

sits Venice Beach, where street performers, roller skaters, skateboarders, eccentric locals, and tourists all rub shoulders. Along with plenty of surf and sand, this area is home to Muscle Beach, a free outdoor gym that's long been a hit with hardcore bodybuilders — it's also a bit of a tourist attraction so if you plan to pump some iron yourself, be prepared for onlookers.

Meander to Santa Monica

Just up the coast, Santa Monica attracts families and couples with its lively commercial area full of shops and restaurants, but the biggest reason to visit is to get the chance to stroll along the Santa Monica Pier. Here you'll find Pacific Park, a seaside amusement park with a smattering of rides and other carnival activities — don't leave without taking a ride on the solar-powered Ferris wheel. Up the coast from Santa Monica, Malibu is also a great option, with about 20 miles of coastline, including scenic El Matador State Beach, known for sea caves, and Zuma Beach, a wide stretch that's popular with surfers.

Museums and Culture

You may be surprised to learn that Los Angeles has a huge number of museums, from UCLA's funky Hammer Museum (which focuses on contemporary art, not tools) to the Petersen Automotive Museum, one of the largest car museums in the world. However, the city's best-known museum is undeniably the Getty Center. Constructed from around 16,000 tons of Italian travertine, with only half the floors above ground due to height restrictions, the museum focuses primarily on pre-20th-century European art, though they also host plenty of special and traveling exhibits across themes, eras and geographies. Best of all, admission is free. While the Getty has some pretty old pieces, if you really want to go back in history, consider a visit to the La Brea Tar Pits. Here you'll see actual tar pits, where many prehistoric fossils have been found, along with an on-site museum full of paleontology-related exhibits.

Getty Images/iStockphoto

Originally built in 1909, the Santa Monica Pier has an amusement park and an aquarium, as well as restaurants.

City of Nature

While it's easy to equate LA with traffic jams, smog and urban sprawl, the City of Angels is actually full of parks and natural areas to get a little respite. If you're into hiking, the 4,310-acre Griffith Park — the city's largest — is worth exploring. Many visitors start at the base of the park and make their way up to the park's star attraction, the Griffith Observatory, via the East or West Observatory Trail. The second-largest, and the oldest park in town, Elysian Park offers plenty of trails and green spaces; it's also the site of Dodger Stadium. Not far from Elysian Park, Echo Park features a large lake surrounded by a jogging trail. The lake is flanked with plenty of benches plus a large grassy area that's popular with picnicking families. There's also an on-site cafe, and you'll often stumble upon local vendors selling popsicles and snacks.

North Coast and the Giant Redwoods

In Redwood National and State Parks, you're free to walk among the tallest trees on the planet. Spread over 130,000 acres of misty forest, these towering redwoods can reach staggering heights of 367 feet and ages of up to 2,000 years old. Admire these giants and then wander through the quaint harbor towns and rugged shoreline on the North Coast.

A walkway leads through a grove of sequioas, which can grow as tall as 300 feet with diamaters of up to 20 feet.

Walk Among Mammoth Trees

California's North Coast is the gateway to the mystifying Redwood National and State Parks. It doesn't matter if it's your first or fiftieth time visiting, the ancient redwood trees here will shock you with their mighty grandeur. View them from the comfort of your car by cruising along the 31-mile Avenue of the Giants or 10-mile Newton B. Drury Redwood Scenic Parkway. Get even closer to the astounding redwoods by hiking the Trillium Falls Trail or Prairie Creek Trail. Jurassic Park 2 was also shot here, in Fern Canyon to be exact, and you can visit the same filming areas by trekking along the James Irvine Trail.

Breath-taking Beaches

Behind every corner are postcard-worthy beaches just waiting to be explored. Fort Bragg's Glass Beach is one of them. The shore is home to one of the world's largest collection of sea glass, giving it a bright, mesmerizing sparkle. If you're in Point Arena during low tide, walk out from Schooner Gulch State Beach to Bowling Ball Beach to see tons of round rock formations which took millions of years to create.

See the Whales

From December to May, approximately 20,000 gray whales pass through the North Coast. High Bluff Beach in Klamath and Mendocino Headlands State Park make excellent vantage points so bring your binoculars and watch this annual migration occur before your eyes.

Wandering Wildlife Encounters

Just like hiking, cycling in Redwood National and State Parks is an incredibly rewarding experience. You can do a guided mountain bike tour with Redwood Adventures to access off-the-beaten-path pockets of the park or venture off on your own. Several bike trails snake through coastline and verdant forest so it's easy to put together your own DIY adventure. Pack animals are also permitted on designated trails, allowing you to enjoy horseback riding through old-growth redwoods.

New England Ambiance

The hamlet of Mendocino will make you feel like you're in New England with its preserved historic homes, seafood restaurants and cute boutiques. Many Victorian homes have been converted into bed and breakfasts too which add to the town's romantic charm. Artists like coming here to capture the dramatic landscape and you can see their works in a handful of galleries. A few hours up the coast is Eureka, an old logging town teeming with gilded mansions that could rival the lavish estates in Newport. Take a gander at the Carson Mansion, an impressive example of Queen Anne-style architecture and then visit the waterfront for scenic views of Humboldt Bay. Just a little further north is Trinidad. Resting on a bluff overlooking Trinidad Bay, this scenic spot is a great place for whale watching. Other popular activities include crabbing off of Trinidad Pier, exploring the Trinidad Memorial Lighthouse and gulping down delicious bowls of chowder at Seascape Restaurant.

Local Arts and Flavors

Live to eat? You're in the right spot – many North Coast festivals center around food so make sure to bring your appetite. Mendocino hosts Feast Mendocino every November, a ten-day event featuring foraged mushrooms and wine tastings. The town also hosts the Crab and Wine Festival in January with all-you-can-eat crab buffets, crab cruises and even a crab cake cook-off. If you're into the weird and wacky, check out the Kinetic Grand Championship. This Memorial Day weekend event has been called the "triathlon of the art world" with bizarre race vehicles made out of all sorts of scrap metal. The three-day race runs from Arcata to Ferndale and ends with a fun, family-friendly shindig on the streets.

All Aboard the Skunk Train

Named after its strong fumes, the historic Skunk Train used to move redwood logs to the coast during the late 19th-century. Today, it transports sightseers from Fort Braff to Willits, chugging past ancient redwood forests and the Noyo River along the way. The Pudding Creek Express and Wolf Tree Turn trips depart year-round. During the journey, you'll get to see some of the first tracks ever installed by the California Western Railroad and may even spot deer, egrets and river otters

With great views of the San Bernardino Mountains, Indian Wells Golf Resort in Palm Springs is one of 124 irrigated links that attracts golfers to the Coachella Valley.

too. The Skunk Train also offers pedal-powered railbike excursions for a different, yet just as amazing, experience. Embark on the rails and enjoy the scenery.

Palm Springs

Situated in Southern California's Coachella Valley, Palm Springs is a chic little city that has attracted well-heeled Angelinos, retirees and more than a few celebrities in its days. This desert town offers a solid selection of museums, great shopping, and quick-and-easy access to a variety of great desert hikes.

Palm Canyon Drive

As Palm Springs' main drag, Palm Canyon Drive is a great place to shop, eat or just sit back and people-watch. Palm Canyon drive also has its own Hollywood-style "Walk of Stars," with hundreds of stars dedicated to celebrities, many of whom once called Palm Springs home. Thursday evenings are particularly lively here, when the stretch of Palm Canyon Drive between Alejo and Ramon Road is shut down to traffic to make way for VillageFest. This weekly event features a couple hundred booths selling everything from vegetables to locally crafted fine art.

The Palm Springs Aerial Tramway

For the best views of the city, hop aboard the Palm Springs Aerial Tramway, the largest rotating aerial tramway in the world, with an 80-passenger capacity. The experience starts at the base of the Coachella Valley and makes the two-and-a-half-mile journey up to the top of Mount San Jacinto (elevation 8,516 feet) in about 10 minutes. At the top, you'll find restaurants, observation decks, and a natural history museum along with around 50 miles of hiking trails.

The Palm Springs Air Museum

Considered one of the foremost aviation museums in the United States, this popular spot boasts an impressive collection of restored aircraft, including one of the largest assemblage of WWII fighter planes on the planet. Visitors can also book a seat or an entire private ride on one of the museum's five vintage Warbirds, including aboard a P-51 Mustang that served in WWII and the Korean War. If you happen to visit during Memorial Day Weekend, you'll have the chance to witness the annual Flower Drop & Air Fair, in which Warbirds scatter flowers over the Coachella Valley.

Palm Springs Art Museum

Established in 1938, this museum hosts a huge permanent collection, with over 12,000 objects plus an additional 50,000 documents and photos in their archive. The museum focuses on modern and contemporary art, architecture and design, photography and art from the western Americas. There are also a few pieces by famous glass artist Dale Chihuly. Other museum highlights include the Palm Springs Art Museum Architecture and Design Center, the Annenberg Theater (a popular performing arts venue) and the modernist Aluminaire House, designed by architect Albert Frey, the father of what's now known as "desert modernism."

Agua Caliente Cultural Museum

This museum focuses on the history and culture of the Indigenous Cahuilla people. It's housed in a new complex that draws its design inspiration from the art and traditions of the Agua Caliente Band of Cahuilla Indians and from the surrounding desert landscape. The museum also sponsors the annual Native FilmFest, held in spring, which showcases films created by Indigenous people around the world.

The Palm Springs Aerial Tramway transports riders two-and-one-half miles along the cliffs of Chino Canyon.

Rancho Mirage

Touted as the "Camp David of the West," Rancho Mirage, is a must-visit for those interested in 20th-century Americana. An impressive list of celebrities have stayed at the estate over the years, including Fred Astaire, Sammy Davis Junior, Dwight Eisenhower and even Queen Elizabeth II. Tours of the house are available for a fee and there's an on-site sculpture garden.

Indian Canyons

Just south of Palm Springs, Indian Canyons offers around 60 miles of hiking trails, with options suitable for all levels. One easy jaunt is the Andreas Trail, which is just over a mile in length. For something a bit more challenging, consider the six-mile Palm Canyon Trail to the Stone Pools or the strenuous Hahn Buena Vista hike, which rewards those willing to climb to an elevation of around 1915 feet with panoramic views out over the area.

Joshua Tree National Park

A short drive from Palm Springs, where the Colorado and Mojave Deserts meet, Joshua Tree National Park awes sightseers. Spread out over 1,235 miles, this park is best known for its namesake yucca brevifolia plants, or Joshua trees, and its massive boulders. It's popular for hiking, camping and rock climbing, and is surrounded by interesting attractions, including the Joshua Tree Retreat Center, designed by Frank Lloyd Wright.

San Diego

California's second-largest city stays on vacation mode with over 60 beaches and the best weather in America. Dig your toes in the sand and then venture beyond the beautiful waterfront to explore epic trails, award-winning craft breweries and renowned museums.

World-famous Attractions

Kick off your vacation at Balboa Park, the largest urban cultural park in America. Here you'll find 17 museums, many of which are

The San Diego skyline stands on the edge of San Diego Bay, shared by both pleasure craft and navy vessels.

located in ornate Spanish Colonial Revival buildings. The park is also home to the famous San Diego Zoo. Step inside the menagerie to meet animals from all over the world and ride the Skyfari Aerial Tram for a bird's-eye view of the zoo. South of the park is the hip and historic Gaslamp Quarter where restaurants, nightclubs and breweries inhabit beautifully restored 19th-century buildings.

San Diego Zoo Safari Park

Rhinos, elephants and giraffes roam free in SoCal's version of wild savannah. Located 30 miles north of downtown, the San Diego Zoo Safari Park occupies 1,800 acres of semi-arid, free-range terrain for animals from Africa, along with creatures from Asia, Europe, North and South America and Australia. Trams take wildlife watchers through the property to see the distinctive animal habitats, and wildlife watchers can attend educational animal shows like the Frequent Flyers Bird Show and Tiger Keeper Talk.

Aquatic Adventures

Much of San Diego's outdoor recreation revolves around the ocean. Guided kayaking tours give you the chance to spot dolphins and seals while paddling to picturesque destinations such as Mission Bay, Coronado Island and Carlsbad Lagoon. Fishing charters can take you out to the deep sea where tuna, marlin and mahi-mahi lurk. There are also seven ocean piers where you can cast a line from and over 20 lakes and reservoirs teeming with everything from trout and carp to catfish and sturgeon. The city's three harbors (Oceanside, Mission Bay and The Big Bay) all have boat rentals, marina facilities and more. Narrated boat tours depart from these locations too and provide views of landmarks and marine animals.

Captivating Landscapes

San Diego County is rich in ecological diversity with over 2,100 plant species and more than 500 types of birds. It's also one of the only places in the world growing Torrey pine trees. You can view this rare species along with panoramic ocean views at Torrey Pines Natural Reserve. Some of California's most famous natural events occur here as well. In spring, Anza-Borrego Desert State Park bursts with vibrant wildflowers, while the Pacific Flyway sees countless migratory birds. Fall foliage is awe-inspiring here too with vivid golds and reds blanketing the landscape every November. Take in the autumn colors by hiking the Sunset Trail in Laguna Mountain Recreation Area and the Observatory Trail within Cleveland National Forest.

Bring Your Appetite

Originating from San Diego and Baja California, Cali-Baja cuisine merges fresh ingredients with bold Baja-Med flavors. You can try this unique style of cooking all over town. Make sure to order the fish tacos at Rubio's and the grilled octopus tostada at Galaxy Taco. If you're feeling adventurous, go to La Fachada for beef tongue tacos. For a meal with a view, dine at Harbor Island's Coasterra which serves fresh Mexican fare in a romantic seaside setting. The craft beer scene here is also out of this world. San Diego has over 85 breweries, including internationally recognized names like Ballast Point and AleSmith. Sip your way through the city with a beer tour or have a meal and pint at popular gastropubs like Stone Brewing's World Bistro and Gardens.

Play Your Way

San Diego events cater to a broad spectrum of hobbies and interests. If you love golf, watch your favorite PGA pros sink birdies at the Farmers Insurance Open at Torrey Pines Golf Course every January. Traveling with kids? Bring them to the County Fair in June and July for a fun-filled day of rides, games and live entertainment. In July, superhero fans can don their masks and capes at Comic-Con, the largest pop culture event in the country. The Del Mar Racetrack is also open from July to September, so put a wager on your favorite horse and watch them speed around the course. America's largest military air show takes place here too. Every September, the Miramar Air Show dazzles with performances by the U.S. Navy Blue Angels.

The Birthplace of California

Juan Rodriguez Cabrillo was the first European explorer to reach America's West Coast and you can learn all about his landing at Cabrillo National Monument. The visitor center hosts presentations and short films, providing an insight into San Diego's beginnings. A stone's throw away is the Old Point Loma Lighthouse, a restored beacon that lets you see what life was like for 19th-century lightkeepers.

Mexican Flavor

California was part of Mexico until 1850 and you can still feel its Latin roots at Old Town San Diego. The living history park takes you back to the 1800s with more than 20 preserved buildings. Many of them still contain working businesses like Racine and Laramie, the oldest smoke shop in the city, and the Rust General Store which sells vintage-style goods. On the outer edge is a Mexican handicraft market selling handcrafted tiles, copperware and more.

A cable car ascends California Street in San Francisco near the Financial District less than a mile from the bay.

San Francisco

This compact city has long attracted tourists with its fabulous museums, hilly streets traversed by iconic cable cars and cityscapes that never fail to charm. Visitors can get an eyeful of sea, rolling hills, long, elegant bridges and a lot of fog. It's a great place to get out and explore, with great parks with ample hiking trails in and around town.

Alcatraz

One of San Francisco's darker attractions, the former penal island of Alcatraz served as a fort, military prison and federal penitentiary. Famous criminals such as Al Capone and George "Machine Gun" Kelly were both locked up here. Today, the island is managed by the National Parks Service and is accessible by boat, with a variety of tours available, from a special night tour to an extra-long behind-the-scenes tour that takes visitors to areas not normally seen by the public.

Angel Island State Park

Sometimes combined with a tour to Alcatraz, Angel Island is the largest natural island in the area, reachable by ferry or private boat (ferries depart from San Francisco, Oakland, Alameda and Tiburon). Here, you'll find a variety of hiking and mountain biking trails along with picnic areas and ample opportunities to fish. The island is also home of the Angel Island Immigration Station, which operated from 1910 to 1940 and used to screen immigrants, primarily coming across the Pacific from Asia. Today it's an educational museum.

Fisherman's Wharf

One of the most popular spots for tourists, Fisherman's Wharf is a charming area and a great place for people-watching. At its heart is Pier 39, where there's almost always a street performer or two along with the occasional basking sea lion. Don't miss the chance to try out some locally made clam chowder served up San Francisco style: in a bread bowl.

Spanning 4,200 feet over bustling San Francisco Bay, the Golden Gate Bridge is one of the longest suspension bridges in the world. The bridge was completed in 1937.

Golden Gate Bridge

San Francisco's most iconic attraction is undoubtedly the Golden Gate Bridge, a mile-long expanse of bridge that connects San Francisco with Marin County up to the north. At the time of its launch in 1937, it was the longest and tallest suspension bridge on earth. While it's fun to drive over (it's part of Highway 101), an even better way to experience its grandeur is by walking across it (or at least across part of it). There's even a Welcome Center as well as an array of exhibits chronicling its past. Free walking tours are also available on Thursdays and Sundays.

Golden Gate Park

Spanning over 1,000 acres, this huge park is a popular spot for strolls and picnics, and home to a variety of museums, gardens and event spaces. Museums here include De Young Museum, which features large collections of American and African art and the California Academy of Sciences, one of the largest natural history museums on earth. Other notable features include the Japanese Tea Garden, the Conservatory of Flowers, and even a paddock housing a herd of American bison. The park is accessible from various points throughout town; if you happen to be visiting the Haight-Ashbury neighborhood, you can access it via Hippie Hill, which still attracts a counterculture crowd to this day. Snag a tie dye shirt or enjoy a street performer. Take a walking tour to admire the well-preserved Victorian homes that line many streets.

Chinatown

The largest Chinatown outside of Asia, San Francisco's Chinatown has long played an important role in the city's cultural life. Although Chinatown is known as a popular tourist attraction, it's really an authentic part of town. It's home to a large number of Chinese immigrants and their children and grandchildren, with plenty of restaurants, clubs and supermarkets catering to the local residents. Visit in September for the Autumn Moon Festival, which features parades and special events.

Palace of Fine Arts

Commissioned for the 1915 Panama-Pacific Exposition, the Palace of Fine Arts is a Beaux Arts-style structure that stretches partway around a humanmade lagoon. Today, this picturesque dome and columns serve as the setting for events. The palace boasts a 961-seat theater and a lobby that can accommodate receptions of 400 people, though most people come here just to take pictures.

Mitchell Ice Cream

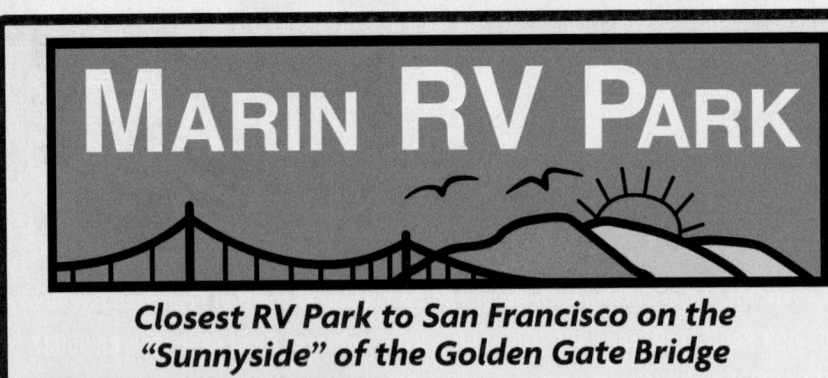

Lines snaking out the door testify to the popularity of Mitchell's Ice Cream, a popular family-run store that has been a local institution in Bernal Heights since 1953. Hand-made daily, with a primo ratio of 16 percent butterfat (for an extra dose of creaminess), the beloved store is famed for its eclectic range of flavors, including avocado, lychee, lucuma (a superfruit imported from Peru), jackfruit and the store's top seller, mango imported from the Philippines. The store's second generation, Brian and Linda,

A golden sunset over the Santa Barbara Channel at the El Capitan State Beach near Santa Barbara.

have taken over the store's reigns and still passionately churn out small batches of the award-winning ice cream.

Twin Peaks

In the heart of San Francisco, the Twin Peaks are an excellent place to go if you want great views of the city (provided it's a clear day, which is really a crapshoot in the foggy city). You can drive up to the top where there's a small but free parking lot and then continue up well-maintained paths with wooden stairs that will lead you all the way to the top of the peaks.

Exploratorium

Learning about science is fun at the Exploratorium on the Embarcadero. Here, you'll find exhibits that focus on everything from human behavior to the life sciences, with plenty of interactive, hands-on play. While it's geared toward kids, adults love it, too. If you want a more grown-up experience, come on a Thursday evening for the special "after dark" program. Only those aged 18 and above area allowed.

Santa Barbara County

Known as "the American Riviera," this charming, quaint, coastal region just 90 miles north of Los Angeles is nestled between the Santa Ynez Mountains and the Pacific Ocean leading to a magical mix of sea breeze and mountain views. Between the perfect weather, beautiful architecture and amazing restaurants, it's no surprise that so many Hollywood A-listers call the county home. For laid-back luxury, this dreamy destination is hard to beat.

Pismo

With some of the best waves, weather and wine anywhere on the coast, Pismo Beach serves up an exciting array of activities sure to appeal to outdoor lovers. You can explore the surf on horseback, conquer towering dunes on ATV and kayak nearby coves along the coast all in the same day. The diverse food and wine options also pair well with the stunning ocean views and spectacular sunsets in this iconic

LOCAL FAVORITE

Grilled Eggy Portobello Mushroom Cups

The Golden State produces nearly half of the country's fruits, nuts and vegetables, including mushrooms. Whip up this protein-packed portobello dish for your next breakfast, lunch or dinner. Recipe by Maria Remington.

INGREDIENTS

- ☐ Portobello mushrooms (1 per serving)
- ☐ 1 egg yolk per mushroom
- ☐ 1 Tbsp Italian dressing per mushroom
- ☐ 1 Tbsp olive oil per mushroom (optional)
- ☐ Salt and pepper to taste (optional)

DIRECTIONS

Preheat your grill to medium heat. Wash the mushrooms and remove the stems. Apply olive oil, salt and pepper to both sides of the mushroom if you like.

Place mushrooms on the grill cup-side down and grill for 2 minutes with the lid closed. Flip over mushrooms and apply 1 tbsp of Italian dressing to each mushroom cup.

Carefully pour one egg yolk into each mushroom and close the lid. Cook for approximately 5 minutes or until desired doneness of eggs and mushrooms.

When serving, cut egg yolks in half and allow the gooey eggy goodness to create a sauce with the Italian dressing.

Enjoy with toast or hash browns for breakfast, in a hamburger bun for lunch or over rice for dinner.

CA

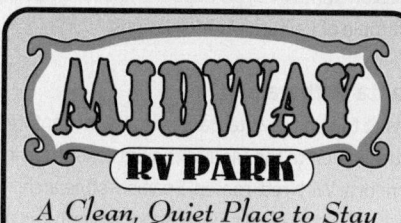

A humpback whale breaches off the coast of Santa Barbara. Humpbacks can grow as long as 50 feet and travel 3,000 miles during migrations in the Pacific Ocean.

beach town. Make sure you don't miss the historic Pismo Beach Pier, perfect for sunset strolls, first-time fishing, or watching the surfers below.

Los Olivos

The world-class wineries dotting the Santa Ynez Mountains are quickly becoming a must-visit for wine lovers around the world and Los Olivos, a quaint, charming town off Highway 154, is the perfect jumping-off point for exploring the best the region has to offer. Spend the afternoon eating fresh, farm-to-table foods and enjoying the decadent tasting rooms and breweries scattered along downtown. With expansive views of the county's vineyards and horse ranches, take the Foxen Canyon Wine Trail.

Solvang

Known as the "Danish Capital of America," the small town of Solvang was founded in 1911 by a group of Danes looking to escape the harsh Midwestern winter. These days, the Danish-style architecture, bakeries, restaurants and boutiques, offer a little taste of Europe in California. Don't miss the chance to travel back in time and ride in an old-fashioned, horse-drawn streetcar while passing by the village's many shops, tasting rooms and traditional windmills. No visit to Solvang would be complete without touring the Mission Santa Ines, perhaps the finest remaining example of California's 21 missions.

Santa Barbara

A visit to sunny Santa Barbara is an enchanting introduction to the Mediterranean coast here in America. With red-roofed, Spanish-style architecture, incredible dining, outdoor adventures and a buzzing art scene, Santa Barbara is brimming with cultural cool. For the nature-lover on the trip, there's no shortage of adventures at Channel Islands National Park, where you can kayak through caves, snorkel in the serene waters and marvel at the harbor seals, sea lions and peregrine falcons that call the park home. For even more fun, several companies offer whale-watching excursions that often include sightings of humpback, blue, gray and killer whales.

Perfect Presidio

The life of early Spanish settlers is re-created at El Presidio de Santa Barbara. This state historic park is nestled downtown and preserves the remains of the last Spanish fortress built in Central California, which dates to 1782. Two adobe buildings still stand.

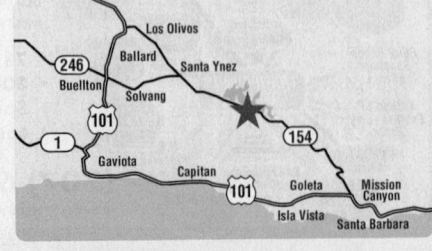

SPOTLIGHTS

CA

Temecula

This sun-soaked valley has no shortage of luxury amenities. Dozens of wineries carpet the lush hillsides and hot air balloons lift off for romantic flights all throughout the year. There are also spa resorts and golf courses ready to soothe your stress away. Take all the time you need to unwind and then visit Old Town Temecula for specialty boutiques, craft breweries and Old West charms.

Wine break: Visitors to a Temecula winery relax and enjoy one of the vintner's products in the fields.

Sip, Sip Hooray

Warm sunshine, cool ocean breezes and crisp nights are what make Temecula's microclimate special. These unique conditions allow grapes to flourish and help producers craft internationally acclaimed wines. From Chardonnay to Syrah, you can taste a wide selection of varietals at more than 40 wineries. Visit a handful of tasting rooms with a wine tour or stay at a winery resort for the ultimate getaway. Locals say the restaurant at Leoness Cellars is divine, with seasonal fare served in a stunning outdoor setting. Miramonte Winery also offers live music every weekend, while Hart Family Winery encourages you to pack a picnic and enjoy it at the vineyard. Many wineries also produce their own artisanal products such as the authentic Argentinian chimichurri at Doffo Wines and fresh marinara sauce at Robert Renzoni Vineyards.

Relaxing Lake Days

Bust out your tackle box and flick your rod into Vail Lake, one of California's top largemouth bass destinations. You can also catch a big one in Diamond Valley Lake. Rent a boat and sail to the lake's west end to nab rainbow trout. Bass, catfish, panfish and striper can also be caught here. Diamond Valley Lake also hosts the annual National Bass West Tournament where anglers reel in hefty hauls. If you get bored with the water, take a hike on the Wildflower Trail, which leads to colorful blooms in spring.

Balloonists blow hot air into their craft before conducting an aerial tour of Temecula and surrounding area.

Valley Views

Temecula Valley has more than 100 miles of cycling trails, so hop on your bike and pedal through picturesque wine country. Santa Rosa Plateau's Ecological Reserve makes for an excellent day trip, thanks to mountain biking terrain, diverse ecosystems and easy trails that end with superb views. Keep your eyes peeled for mule deer and turtles and consider venturing into the nearby Cleveland National Forest to hike to Tenaja Falls. The forest is also home to the Dripping Springs Trail, a challenging 13-mile trek that rewards outdoor enthusiasts with sweeping mountain vistas. If you're into birdwatching, head to the Lake Skinner Recreation Area for your chance to spot herons, owls and hawks.

Experience the Finer Things in Life

There are infinite ways to pamper yourself here. Indulge in a rejuvenating facial and massage at Murrieta Day Spa or sign up for a vino-vinyasa yoga class at South Coast Winery Resort and Spa. For a romantic date, surprise your sweetie with a hot air balloon ride over the valley. Flights operate year-round and promise unbeatable views of rolling hills and vineyards. Wedged in the idyllic landscape are premier golf courses, so don't forget to pack your clubs too. Set a tee time at CrossCreek, a course designed by Arthur Hill himself, or take lessons with a PGA instructor at Temecula Creek. Pechanga, the largest casino out west, also promises Vegas-level excitement with delicious dining options, nightly entertainment and every betting game under the sun.

Wine Country Festivities

Music, great food and even better wine are the cornerstones of almost every festival in the Temecula Valley. At the end of January, attend the Annual Barrel Tasting event to sample unfinished barrel and tank wines along with newly released bottles at up to 30 wineries. In the spring, view hundreds of vintage vehicles at the Temecula Rod Run and listen to legendary musicians during the Annual Jazz Festival. You also won't want to miss the Balloon and Wine Festival which features sunset flights, live entertainment and chef demonstrations. In July and August, Summerfest heats things up with concerts, craft beer tastings and fantastic dining. No matter what time of year you come, pop in the Temecula Stampede for live country music, mechanical bull riding and free dance lessons.

Old Town Temecula

The city's roots are on full display in Old Town Temecula. Most of the frontier-style buildings in this 12-block neighborhood were constructed during the late 19th century. Take a stroll to see historic landmarks like the St. Catherine of Alexandria Church and Hotel Temecula. Local businesses inhabit the rest of the western-era storefronts including the Temecula Olive Oil Company, Serendipity Antiques and 1909, a burger joint that used to be a trading post. The Temecula Valley Museum is also located here and allows you to dive deeper into the region's past. Photographs, documents and original items like ranching equipment and Native American artifacts shed light on the different cultures that helped developed the area.

Visit SLO Cal

Life moves a little slower on California's charming Central Coast, where down-home dining, luxurious wineries and unbeatable views come together to create a once-in-a-lifetime vacation destination. From the dunes of Oceano to the volcanic rocks of Morro Bay, outdoors lovers will relish in the combination of sea, surf and mountains to explore, while food and wine lovers will be right at home among some of the state's top vineyards and farm-to-table restaurants. For that perfect blend of wild and refined, San Luis Obispo County awaits.

Wine Scene

Home to 14 distinct American Viticultural Areas (AVAs), the SLO region is considered one of the finest winemaking regions in the West and a must-visit for connoisseurs across the country. To discover the best of the

A kayaker navigates the cliffs at Shell beach, a stretch of coast along Pismo Beach in San Luis Obispo County.

SPOTLIGHTS

Sea lions bask in the sun on a Morro Bay dock. These mammals can weigh as much as 860 pounds.

bunch, try the Santa Barbara Downtown Urban Wine Trail, which features 11 tasting rooms within easy walking distance. From there, head to the inland hills where hundreds of operations in towns like Paso Robles and the Edna Valley serve up world-class bottles of some 40 different varietals, and equally stunning vineyard views. Since many of the wineries are small, family-owned businesses, you may even find yourself treated to an expert tasting directly from the winemaker. Get the full measure of the region's famous chardonnay, pinot noir and Syrah wines.

Oceano

Stretching for thousands of acres, the windswept dunes of this coastal haven are sure to take your breath away. As the only state park in California where you can drive on the beach, most visitors enjoy the limitless off-roading opportunities or rent ATVs for an even more thrilling excursion, but swimming, clamming and camping are also popular pastimes. Hike on the manicured nature trails that wind between the dunes and the rugged oceanfront. History buffs should stop by the historic Oceano Train Depot, which houses hundreds of artifacts related to the town's railroading past. Try the nearby Rock & Roll Diner, an entire restaurant housed in a 1946 dining car and a 1947 lounge car. Try American, Mexican and Greek food.

SLO By Horse

Whether you prefer coastal views from Oceano or Morro Bay or are looking for hill top peaks in Atascadero or Paso Robles, horseback riding is an activity the crew will love. Trot beside the waves or through vineyards until you're saddle sore, then hitch your pony and enjoy a picnic.

Morro Bay

Speaking of dynamic coastlines, it's hard to find anywhere with a view more ruggedly beautiful than Morro Bay. Highlighted by the stunning Morro Rock in the distance, the bay is home to dolphins, otters, seals and more, all of which meander in between kayakers and paddleboarders exploring the coast either solo or as part of tours guided by local experts. Back on land, the Embarcadero is home to funky boutiques and hip galleries, as well as seafood joints that specialize in the catch of the day. Lucky visitors might even catch one of the town's popular festivals like January's California Bird Festival where over 200 shorebirds are likely to make an appearance. Cyclists can ride from the south end of the Embarcadero along the waterfront and out towards Morro Rock utilizing the Harbor Walk. Take a paddleboard out to the Sandspit, the secluded dune peninsula in the middle of the bay.

Pecho Coast Trail

Limited to 20 hikers on Wednesdays and 40 hikers on Saturdays, docent-led tours of the Pecho Coast Trail are a truly unique experience. The 3.6-mile trek to the Point San Luis Lighthouse features sweeping views of Avila Beach and San Luis Obispo Bay, as well as a diverse landscape of chaparral, oak groves and coastal bluffs. Guides are experts in local geology, history and flora and fauna so the relatively easy route is informative as well as picturesque. At the lighthouse, you can explore the grounds or join another brief tour of the historic Victorian lighthouse tower built in 1890, showing examples of the original Fresnel bulbs of the era.

FOR MORE INFORMATION

California Tourism, 877-225-4367 www.visitcalifornia.com
Bakersfield Convention and Visitor Bureau, 866-425-7353, www.visitbakersfield.com
Central Coast Tourism Council, www.centralcoast-tourism.com
LA Tourism and Convention Board, 888-733-6952, www.discoverlosangeles.com
Humboldt County Convention and Visitors Bureau, 800-346-3482, www.visitredwoods.com
Palm Springs Visitors Center, 800-347-7746, www.visitpalmsprings.com
Visit Sacramento, 800-292-2334, www.visitsacramento.com
San Diego Tourism Authority, 619-232-3101, www.sandiego.org
San Francisco Travel, 415-391-2000, www.sanfrancisco.travel
Visit Santa Barbara, 800-676-1266, www.santabarbaraca.com
Visit Temecula Valley, 888-363-2852, www.visittemeculavalley.com
Visit SLO CAL, 805-541-8000, www.SLOCAL.com

A boardwalk leads to the beach at Oceano, one of the largest dune areas in California.

California

ACTON — H4 *Los Angeles*

LOS ANGELES RV RESORT (FORMERLY KOA)
good sam park **Ratings: 6.5/7.5/5.5** (Campground) From Jct of Hwy 14 and Soledad Canyon Rd (Exit 11): Go 8.5 mi E on Soledad Canyon Rd (L).

ULTIMATE CAMPING & PCT BASE CAMP
Get away to beautiful Soledad Canyon & be just a short drive from the beach or the best adventures of the LA area theme parks, shopping, dining, theaters, museums etc. Glamp in your RV or rent a teepee, woody tent or cabin.
FAC: dirt rds. (79 spaces). Avail: 46 dirt, 9 pull-thrus, (15x60), back-ins (15x34), 46 full hkups (30/50 amps), seasonal sites, WiFi @ sites, tent sites, rentals, laundry, groc, LP gas, fire rings. **REC:** pool, hot tub, Santa Clara River: shuffleboard, playground, rec open to public. Pets OK. Partial handicap access, eco-friendly. 2021 rates: $65 to $110.
(661)268-1214 Lat: 34.43776, Lon: -118.26565
7601 Soledad Canyon Rd, Acton, CA 93510
LArvresort.com
See ad page 110

SOLEDAD CANYON RV & CAMPING RESORT
good sam park **Ratings: 7/7/6.5** (RV Resort) 50 Avail: 45 full hkups, 5 W, 5 E (30/50 amps). 2021 rates: $65 to $72.50. (888)563-7040, 4700 Crown Valley Road, Acton, CA 93510

THE CALIFORNIAN RV RESORT
good sam park **Ratings: 10/9.5★/9** (RV Park) N-bnd: From Jct of Hwy 14 & Soledad Canyon Rd (Exit 27): Go 3/4 mi W on Sierra Hwy (R) or S-bnd: From Jct of Hwy 14 & Soledad Canyon Rd (Exit 27): Go 1/4 mi E on Sierra Hwy (L). Elev 3079 ft.**FAC:** paved rds. (193 spaces). Avail: 51 paved, 51 pull-thrus, (25x60), 51 full hkups (30/50 amps), seasonal sites, WiFi @ sites, laundry, LP gas, controlled access. **REC:** heated pool, hot tub. Pet restrict (B/Q). Partial handicap access. No tents. Big rig sites, eco-friendly. 2021 rates: $65, Military discount.
(888)787-8386 Lat: 34.486545, Lon: -118.143256
1535 Sierra Hwy, Acton, CA 93510
calrv.com
See ad page 140

ADELANTO — H4 *San Bernardino*

ADELANTO RV PARK **Ratings: 8.5/8/8** (RV Park) Avail: 10 full hkups (30/50 amps). 2021 rates: $39. (877)246-5554, 11301 Airbase Rd / Air Expressway, Adelanto, CA 92301

AGUANGA — J5 *Riverside*

RANCHO CALIFORNIA RV RESORT **Ratings: 10/9.5★/10** (Condo Park) Avail: 30 full hkups (30/50 amps). 2021 rates: $70 to $175. (951)383-4222, 45525 Hwy 79 S., Aguanga, CA 92536

Explore America's Top RV Destinations! Turn to the Spotlight articles in our State and Province sections to learn more.

ALMANOR — B3 *Plumas*

PG & E/FEATHER RIVER/COOL SPRINGS
(Public) From Jct of Hwys 147 & 89, NW 5 mi on Hwy 89 to Butt Lake Rd, SW 5 mi (R). Elev 4150 ft.**FAC:** paved rds. Avail: 25 paved, no slide-outs, back-ins (15x20), pit toilets, firewood. **REC:** Butt Valley Reservoir: swim, fishing, kayaking/canoeing, boating nearby. Pets OK. Partial handicap access. No tents, 14 day max stay. 2021 rates: $40.36. no cc, no reservations.
(916)386-5164 Lat: 40.16750, Lon: -121.18500
Butt Valley Road , Canyon Dam, CA 95947
recreation.pge.com

ANAHEIM — N3 *Orange*

ANAHEIM See also Huntington Beach, Long Beach, Newport Beach, Orange, Pomona & San Dimas.

ANAHEIM HARBOR RV PARK **Ratings: 8/8.5/6.5** (RV Park) Avail: 63 full hkups (30/50 amps). 2021 rates: $45 to $70. (888)835-6495, 1009 S Harbor Blvd, Anaheim, CA 92805

CANYON RV PARK **Ratings: 7.5/6/7.5** (RV Park) Avail: 120 full hkups (30/50 amps). 2021 rates: $75. (714)637-0210, 24001 Santa Ana Canyon Rd, Anaheim, CA 92808

ORANGELAND RV PARK
good sam park **Ratings: 10/10★/9** (RV Park) From Jct of I-5 & W.Lincoln Ave (exit 112),Go 2.7 mi S on I-5 to Katella Ave (exit 109A) then go 2 mi E on Katella Ave to W.Struck Ave, then go 150ft SE. (L). **FAC:** paved rds. Avail: 195 paved, patios, 18 pull-thrus, (26x50), back-ins (22x50), 195 full hkups (30/50 amps), cable, WiFi @ sites, laundry, groc. **REC:** heated pool, hot tub, boating nearby, shuffleboard, playground. Pet restrict (B/Q) $. Partial handicap access. No tents, eco-friendly. 2021 rates: $75 to $90, Military discount. ATM.
(714)633-0414 Lat: 33.80545, Lon: -117.86957
1600 W Struck Ave, Orange, CA 92867
www.orangeland.com
See primary listing at Orange and ad this page

Find Good Sam member specials at CampingWorld.com

California Privately Owned Campground Information Updated by our Good Sam Representatives

George Daunis & Diana Fleming

We are proud to represent Good Sam by visiting and evaluating parks. We have been full-timers for seven years now and would not change a thing. We have had the opportunity to visit parts of this beautiful country and meet people that we otherwise would never have met.

Jeff & Peggy Harmann

We have worked with Good Sam from coast to coast, north to south. After a career largely focused around customer support and marketing, we see that the "magic" happens when RVers find the right RV park for them.

ANDERSON — B2 *Shasta*

Travel Services

CAMPING WORLD OF ANDERSON/REDDING

CAMPING WORLD As the nation's largest retailer of RV supplies, accessories, services and new and used RVs, Camping World is committed to making your total RV experience better. **SERVICES:** RV, tire, RV appliance, MH mechanical, restrooms. RV Sales. RV supplies, LP gas, RV accessible. Hours: 9am to 7pm.
(888)450-0282 Lat: 40.767029, Lon: -122.317376
3700 Auto Mall Drive, Anderson, CA 96007
www.campingworld.com

GANDER RV OF ANDERSON/REDDING Your new hometown outfitter offering the best regional gear for all your outdoor needs. Your adventure awaits. **SERVICES:** RV, restrooms. RV Sales. RV supplies, RV accessible. Hours: 9am - 7pm.
(888)892-4765 Lat: 40.466694, Lon: -122.304657
3750 Auto Mall Drive, Anderson, CA 96007
rv.ganderoutdoors.com

ANGELS CAMP — E3 *Calaveras*

ANGELS CAMP RV RESORT

good sam park **Ratings: 10/9.5★/10** (Campground) Avail: 67 full hkups (30/50 amps). 2021 rates: $61 to $77. (209)736-0404, 3069 Hwy 49 South, Angels Camp, CA 95222

FROGTOWN RV PARK (Public) From Jct of Hwy 49 & Hwy 4, S 1.2 mi on Hwy 49 to Gun Club Road, E 0.4 mi (E). Avail: 68 full hkups (20/30 amps). 2021 rates: $35. (209)736-2561

GLORYHOLE REC AREA/BIG OAK (Public) From town, S 3 mi on Hwy 49 (R). 75 Avail. 2021 rates: $18 to $22. (209)536-9094

GLORYHOLE REC AREA/IRONHORSE (Public) From town, S 3 mi on Hwy 49 (R). 69 Avail. 2021 rates: $18 to $22. (209)536-9094

ANTIOCH — E2 *Contra Costa*

CONTRA COSTA COUNTY FAIR RV PARK (Public) From Jct of SR-4 & Exit 26B (Auto Center Dr), N 0.8 mi on Auto Center Dr to W 10th St, E 0.3 mi to fair entrance, S 200 ft on entry rd (L). Avail: 18 full hkups (20/30 amps). 2021 rates: $35. (925)757-4400

ARCATA — B1 *Humboldt*

MAD RIVER RAPIDS RV PARK **Ratings: 10/9.5★/9.5** (RV Park) Avail: 43 full hkups (30/50 amps). 2021 rates: $47 to $59. (800)822-7776, 3501 Janes Rd, Arcata, CA 95521

ARNOLD — D3 *Calaveras*

CALAVERAS BIG TREES (Public State Park) From town, NE 4 mi on Hwy 4 (R). 129 Avail. 2021 rates: $20 to $35. (209)795-2334

We rate what RVers consider important.

GOLDEN PINES RV RESORT & CAMPGROUND **Ratings: 8/9.5★/8.5** (Campground) Avail: 27 full hkups (20/30 amps). 2021 rates: $50 to $60. (209)795-2820, 2869 Golden Torch Drive, Arnold, CA 95223

ARROYO GRANDE — G2 *San Luis Obispo*

LOPEZ LAKE REC AREA (Public) From Jct of US-101 & Grand Ave exit, E 0.9 mi on Grand Ave to Huasna Rd/Lopez Dr, SE 10 mi, follow signs (E). 354 Avail: 143 full hkups, 67 E (20/30 amps). 2021 rates: $23 to $40. (805)788-2381

AUBURN — D3 *Placer*

AUBURN GOLD COUNTRY RV PARK **Ratings: 10/9.5★/9.5** (RV Park) 20 Avail: 15 full hkups, 5 W, 5 E (30/50 amps). 2021 rates: $68 to $78. (530)885-0990, 3550 KOA Way, Auburn, CA 95602

AZUSA — M3 *Los Angeles*

CARAVAN MOBILE HOME PARK

(RV Spaces) From Jct of I 210 & Exit 40 (Azusa Ave exit): Go S 0.3 mi on S Azusa Ave to W Gladstone St, W 0.4mi (L). **FAC:** paved rds. (120 spaces). Avail: 13 paved, no slide-outs, 5 pull-thrus, (12x36), back-ins (14x40), accepts full hkup units only, 13 full hkups (30/50 amps), seasonal sites, laundry. **REC:** pool, boating nearby. Pet restrict (S/B/Q). No tents. 2021 rates: $40. no cc.
(626)334-2306 Lat: 34.11406, Lon: -117.91439
600 W Gladstone St, Azusa, CA 91702
See ad page 142

BAKERSFIELD — G3 *Kern*

A SPOTLIGHT Introducing Bakersfield's colorful attractions appearing at the front of this state section.

BAKERSFIELD See also Lost Hills.

A COUNTRY RV PARK

good sam park **Ratings: 10/10★/9** (RV Park) From Jct of Hwy 99 & Hwy 58: Go 6 mi E on Hwy 58 to Fairfax Rd, then 1/4 mi S on Fairfax Rd (R).

GREAT FOR SNOWBIRDS AND FAMILIES!

The perfect home base for Sequoia National Park, Fort Tejon State Park, and all the outdoor fun of the Kern River. A great stop whether heading north or south. Family built, owned and operated since 1998. Pool, spa, WiFi.

FAC: paved rds. (120 spaces). Avail: 20 paved, patios, 20 pull-thrus, (25x65), 20 full hkups (30/50 amps), seasonal sites, cable, WiFi @ sites, tent sites, laundry, groc, LP gas, controlled access. **REC:** pool, hot tub, boating nearby. Pet restrict (B). Partial handicap access. Big rig sites, eco-friendly. 2021 rates: $48, Military discount.

(866)787-2750 Lat: 35.349673, Lon: -118.932431
622 S Fairfax Rd, Bakersfield, CA 93307
acountryrvpark.com
See ad page 127

BAKERSFIELD RIVER RUN RV PARK

good sam park **Ratings: 10/10★/9** (RV Park) From Jct of Hwy 99 & Hwy 58 W/Rosedale Hwy (Exit 26): Go 1/2 mi W on Hwy 58 to Gibson St, then 1/4 mi S on Gibson St to Burr St, then 1/4 mi E on Burr St (E).

THE PLACE TO STAY IN BAKERSFIELD

Newer park centrally located, walk to many of Bakersfield's finest restaurants, attractions and hotels. Enjoy our sites with lots of grass and large patios. The wide roads and big sites makes it easy for the largest RVs.

FAC: paved rds. (121 spaces). Avail: 71 all weather, patios, 31 pull-thrus, (24x60), back-ins (30x40), 71 full hkups (30/50 amps), seasonal sites, cable, WiFi @ sites, dump, laundry, groc, LP gas. **REC:** pool, hot tub, Kern River (seasonal):. Pet restrict (S/B/Q) $. Partial handicap access. No tents. Big rig sites, 28 day max stay, eco-friendly. 2021 rates: $47 to $88.

(661)377-3616 Lat: 35.378573, Lon: -119.047051
3715 Burr St, Bakersfield, CA 93308
www.riverrunrvpark.com
See ad this page, 101, 105

BAKERSFIELD RV RESORT

good sam park **Ratings: 10/10★/10** (RV Park) From Jct of Hwy 99 & White Lane (exit 21): Go 100 ft W on White Lane to Wible Road, then 1/2 mi S on Wible Rd (R).

ENJOY LUXURY IN CENTRAL CA

Luxury, style, and comfort COMBINE to make us the ideal stop on your travels, with exceptional amenities and superior customer service. Enjoy the pool and our full bar and restaurant, Crest Bar & Grill, during your stay.

FAC: paved rds. Avail: 215 all weather, patios, 88 pull-thrus, (30x65), back-ins (30x50), 215 full hkups (30/50 amps), cable, WiFi @ sites, dump, laundry, groc, LP gas, restaurant, controlled access. **REC:** heated pool, hot tub. Pet restrict (B/Q) $. Partial handicap access. No tents. Big rig sites, eco-friendly. 2021 rates: $55, Military discount.

(661)833-9998 Lat: 35.308642, Lon: -119.039610
5025 Wible Rd, Bakersfield, CA 93313
www.bakersfieldrvresort.com
See ad this page

BEAR MOUNTAIN RV RESORT **Ratings: 4/NA/6.5** (RV Park) Avail: 16 full hkups (30/50 amps). 2021 rates: $34. (661)834-3811, 16501 S Union Ave, Bakersfield, CA 93307

BUENA VISTA AQUATIC REC AREA (Public) From Jct of I-5 & Hwy 119 (Exit 244), W 1.6 mi on Hwy 119 to Hwy 43, S 2.7 mi (E). Entrance fee required. Avail: 82 full hkups (30/50 amps). 2021 rates: $24 to $40. (661)868-7000

KERN RIVER COUNTY PARK (Public) From town, E 8 mi on Hwy 178 to Lake Ming Rd exit, follow signs (R). 50 Avail. 2021 rates: $12 to $24. (661)868-7000

ORANGE GROVE RV PARK

good sam park **Ratings: 9.5/9.5★/10** (RV Park) From Jct of Hwy 99 & Hwy 58E (exit 24): Go 8 mi E on Hwy 58 to S Edison Rd (exit 119), then 1/8 mi S on S Edison Rd (R). **FAC:** paved rds. (185 spaces). Avail: 91 gravel, 83 pull-thrus, (30x90), back-ins (30x65), 83 full hkups, 8 W, 8 E (30/50 amps), seasonal sites, cable, WiFi @ sites, dump, laundry, LP gas. **REC:** pool, boating nearby. Pets OK. Partial handicap access. No tents. Big rig sites, 21 day max stay, eco-friendly. 2021 rates: $43 to $62.50, Military discount.

(661)366-4662 Lat: 35.341833, Lon: -118.879139
1452 - S Edison Rd, Bakersfield, CA 93307
www.orangegrovervpark.com
See ad this page

Travel Services

CAMPING WORLD OF BAKERSFIELD As the nation's largest retailer of RV supplies, accessories, services and new and used RVs, Camping World is committed to making your total RV experience better. **SERVICES:** RV, tire, RV appliance, restrooms. RV Sales. RV supplies, LP gas, emergency parking, RV accessible. Hours: 9am to 7pm.
(888)441-9065 Lat: 35.304481, Lon: -119.038863
5500 Wible Road, Bakersfield, CA 93313
www.campingworld.com

Join in the fun. Like us on FACEBOOK!

See listing Ventura, CA

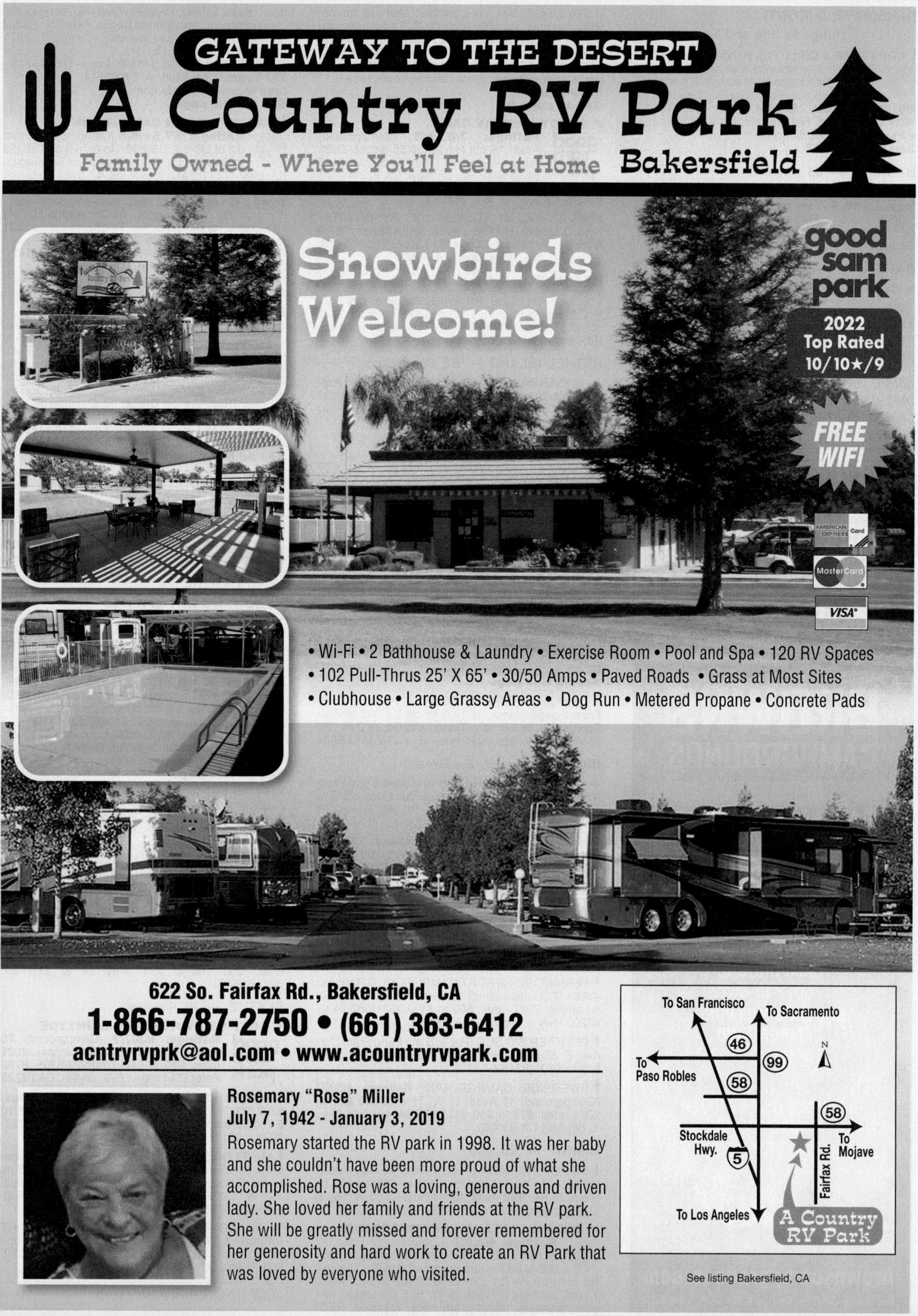
GATEWAY TO THE DESERT
A Country RV Park
Family Owned - Where You'll Feel at Home
Bakersfield
Snowbirds Welcome!
good sam park
2022 Top Rated 10/10★/9
FREE WIFI
AMERICAN EXPRESS Card
MasterCard
VISA
• Wi-Fi • 2 Bathhouse & Laundry • Exercise Room • Pool and Spa • 120 RV Spaces
• 102 Pull-Thrus 25' X 65' • 30/50 Amps • Paved Roads • Grass at Most Sites
• Clubhouse • Large Grassy Areas • Dog Run • Metered Propane • Concrete Pads
622 So. Fairfax Rd., Bakersfield, CA
1-866-787-2750 • (661) 363-6412
acntryrvprk@aol.com • www.acountryrvpark.com
Rosemary "Rose" Miller
July 7, 1942 - January 3, 2019
Rosemary started the RV park in 1998. It was her baby and she couldn't have been more proud of what she accomplished. Rose was a loving, generous and driven lady. She loved her family and friends at the RV park. She will be greatly missed and forever remembered for her generosity and hard work to create an RV Park that was loved by everyone who visited.
To San Francisco
To Sacramento
46
99
To Paso Robles
58
N
58
Stockdale Hwy.
5
Fairfax Rd.
To Mojave
To Los Angeles
A Country RV Park
See listing Bakersfield, CA

BAKERSFIELD (CONT)

Things to See and Do

CREST BAR & GRILL Full service restaurant with bar area serving lunch & dinner. Catering for groups. Partial handicap access. RV accessible. Restrooms. Food. Hours: 11am to 8pm.
(661)833-9998 Lat: 35.308642, Lon: -119.039610
5025 Wible Road, Bakersfield, CA 93313
www.crestbarandgrill.com
See ad page 125

BANNING — J5 *Riverside*

BANNING STAGECOACH KOA JOURNEY **Ratings: 8.5/8/8.5** (Campground) Avail: 60 full hkups (30/50 amps). 2021 rates: $54.89 to $71.89. (951)849-7513, 1455 S San Gorgonio Ave, Banning, CA 92220

BARSTOW — H4 *San Bernardino*

CALICO GHOST TOWN CAMPGROUND
(Public) From Jct of Hwy 58 & I-15: Go 8 mi NE on I-15 to Ghost Town Rd (Exit 191), then 3-1/2 mi N on Ghost Town Rd (L). Elev 2938 ft.**FAC:** paved/gravel rds. Avail: 265 dirt, 23 pull-thrus, (20x50), back-ins (30x40), 64 full hkups, 20 W, 60 E (30/50 amps), tent sites, rentals, shower$, dump. **REC:** rec open to public. Pets OK $. Partial handicap access, 14 day max stay. 2021 rates: $25 to $40.
(800)862-2542 Lat: 34.941538, Lon: -116.866778
36600 Ghost Town Rd, Yermo, CA 92398
parks.sbcounty.gov/park/calico-ghost-town-regional-park
See ad page 96

Before you head north, know the rules and regulations for crossing the border into Canada. Read all about it in our Crossing into Canada section.

SHADY LANE RV CAMP
Ratings: 7/8.5★/8 (Campground) Avail: 18 full hkups (30/50 amps). 2021 rates: $45 to $49. (760)256-5322, 36445 Soap Mine Rd, Barstow, CA 92311

BASS LAKE — E4 *Madera*

BASS LAKE AT YOSEMITE RV RESORT **Ratings: 9.5/8★/9** (RV Park) Avail: 89 full hkups (30/50 amps). 2021 rates: $69.50 to $99.50. (559)608-3418, 39744 Rd 274, Bass Lake, CA 93604

BEAUMONT — N6 *Riverside*

COUNTRY HILLS RV PARK **Ratings: 8.5/7.5/7** (RV Park) Avail: 10 full hkups (30/50 amps). 2021 rates: $53. (951)845-5919, 14711 Manzanita Park Rd, Beaumont, CA 92223

BETHEL ISLAND — E2 *Contra Costa*

SUGAR BARGE RV RESORT AND MARINA **Ratings: 9.5/10★/10** (RV Park) Avail: 70 full hkups (30 amps). 2021 rates: $50 to $60. (800)799-4100, 1440 Sugar Barge Rd, Bethel Island, CA 94511

BIG PINE — F4 *Inyo*

BAKER CREEK CAMPGROUND (Public) From town, N 0.5 mi on US-395 to Baker Creek Rd (at N end of town), W 1 mi (E). 43 Avail: Pit toilets. 2021 rates: $14. (760)878-5577

GLACIER VIEW CAMPGROUND
Ratings: 2.5/5.5/6 (Campground) From Jct of US-395 & SR-168E: Go E on SR-168E at corner of US-395 and SR-168E (R). Elev 4000 ft.**FAC:** gravel rds. Avail: 40 dirt, patios, back-ins (26x36), 9 W, 9 E (30 amps), tent sites, shower$. **REC:** boating nearby, hunting nearby. Pets OK. 14 day max stay, eco-friendly. 2021 rates: $25. no cc, no reservations.
(760)872-6911 Lat: 37.173469, Lon: -118.290204
SE Corner of US-395 & SR-168E, Big Pine, CA 93513
See ad this page

TINNEMAHA CREEK COUNTY PARK (Public) From Independence, N 19.5 mi on US-395 to Fish Springs Rd, W 0.5 mi to Tinnemaha Rd, W 2 mi (R). 35 Avail: Pit toilets. 2021 rates: $14. (760)873-5564

BIG RIVER — H6 *San Bernardino*

BIG RIVER RV PARK **Ratings: 8/8/8.5** (RV Park) Avail: 63 full hkups (30/50 amps). 2021 rates: $47 to $60. (760)665-9359, 1 Marina St, Big River, CA 92242

RIO DEL SOL RV HAVEN **Ratings: 7/6.5/7.5** (Campground) Avail: 10 full hkups (30/50 amps). 2021 rates: $50 to $70. (760)665-2981, 7905 Rio Vista Dr, Big River, CA 92242

BIG SUR — F1 *Monterey*

BIG SUR CAMPGROUND & CABINS **Ratings: 4/8★/8** (Campground) 21 Avail: 21 W, 21 E (30/50 amps). 2021 rates: $80 to $100. (831)667-2322, 47000 Hwy 1, Big Sur, CA 93920

FERNWOOD RESORT CAMPGROUND **Ratings: 4.5/9★/7** (Campground) 16 Avail: 16 W, 16 E (30/50 amps). 2021 rates: $50 to $110. (831)667-2422, 47200 Hwy 1, Big Sur, CA 93920

PFEIFFER BIG SUR (Public State Park) From Carmel, S 26 mi on Hwy 1 (L). 189 Avail. 2021 rates: $35 to $50. (831)667-1112

RIVERSIDE CAMPGROUND **Ratings: 4/5.5/7** (Campground) 11 Avail: 11 W, 11 E (20/30 amps). 2021 rates: $75 to $80. (831)667-2414, 47020 Hwy 1, Big Sur, CA 93920

BISHOP — E5 *Inyo*

BISHOP RV PARK (Public) From jct Hwy 168 & US 395: Go 1 mi N on US 395, then 900 feet W on Sierra St (R). 192 Avail: 42 full hkups, 150 W, 150 E (30/50 amps). 2021 rates: $35. (760)873-3588

BROWN'S MILLPOND CAMPGROUND
Ratings: 4/6.5/7 (Campground) From Jct of Hwy 6 & US-395: Go 4-1/2 mi N on Hwy 395 to Ed Powers Rd, then 1/4 mi S to Sawmill Rd, then 1 mi W (L). Elev 4200 ft.**FAC:** dirt rds. Avail: 72 dirt, back-ins (27x54), 19 W, 19 E (30 amps), tent sites, shower$, laundry, fire rings, firewood. **REC:** pond, swim, fishing, kayaking/canoeing, playground, hunting nearby, rec open to public. Pets OK. Partial handicap access, 14 day max stay, eco-friendly. 2021 rates: $35. Mar 01 to Oct 31.
(760)873-5342 Lat: 37.374309, Lon: -118.493713
230 Sawmill Rd, Bishop, CA 93514
brownscampgrounds.com
See ad this page

BROWN'S TOWN CAMPGROUND
Ratings: 5/7.5★/8.5 (Campground) From Jct of US-6 & US-395: Go 3 mi S on US-395 to Schober Ln, then 1/8 mi W on Schober Ln (L). Elev 4137 ft.**FAC:** gravel rds. 47 Avail: 20 grass, 27 dirt, 10 pull-thrus, (22x40), back-ins (24x36), 47 W, 47 E (30 amps), tent sites, shower$, dump, laundry, groc, fire rings, firewood. **REC:** playground. Pets OK. Partial handicap access, 14 day max stay. 2021 rates: $35. Mar 01 to Nov 30.
(760)873-8522 Lat: 37.346299, Lon: -118.396187
20 Schober Lane, Bishop, CA 93514
brownscampgrounds.com
See ad this page

HIGHLANDS RV PARK
Ratings: 9/9★/9 (RV Park) From Jct of US-6 & US-395: Go 1 mi N on US-395 to N Sierra Hwy (R). Elev 4140 ft.**FAC:** paved rds. Avail: 103 paved, patios, 50 pull-thrus, (20x55), back-ins (20x55), 103 full hkups (30/50 amps), cable, WiFi @ sites, dump, laundry, LP gas. **REC:** Bishop Creek: hunting nearby. Pets OK. No tents, eco-friendly. 2021 rates: $45.
(760)873-7616 Lat: 37.376197, Lon: -118.414922
2275 N Sierra Hwy, Bishop, CA 93514
See ad this page

HORTON CREEK (BLM) (Public Corps) From town: Go 8.5 mi N on US-395, then S on Round Valley Rd, then W 3 mi on Round Valley Rd (L). 49 Avail: Pit toilets. 2021 rates: $8. May 01 to Oct 30. (760)872-5000

J DIAMOND MOBILE RANCH **Ratings: 6/6.5/6** (Campground) Avail: 21 full hkups (30/50 amps). 2021 rates: $45. (760)872-7341, 771 N Main St, Bishop, CA 93514

KEOUGH'S HOT SPRINGS
Ratings: 5.5/6/7 (RV Park) From Jct of US-395 & US-6: Go 8 mi S on US-395 to Keough Hot Springs Rd, then 1 mi W on Keough Hot Springs Rd (E). Elev 4350 ft.**FAC:** gravel/dirt rds. 19 Avail: 10 grass, 9 dirt, 1 pull-thrus, (24x57), back-ins (20x40), 11 W, 11 E (20/30 amps), WiFi @ sites, tent sites, rentals, shower$, fire rings, firewood. **REC:** heated pool $, hot tub, rec open to public. Pet restrict (S/Q). 14 day max stay. 2021 rates: $30 to $35.
(760)872-4670 Lat: 37.253555, Lon: -118.374905
800 Keough's Hot Springs Rd, Bishop, CA 93514
www.keoughshotsprings.com
See ad this page

PLEASANT VALLEY COUNTY PARK (Public) From Jct of US-6 & US-395, NW 7 mi on US-395 to Pleasant Valley Rd, N 1 mi (R). 75 Avail: Pit toilets. 2021 rates: $14. (760)873-5564

BLAIRSDEN — C3 *Plumas*

LITTLE BEAR RV PARK **Ratings: 9/8.5★/9.5** (Campground) 40 Avail: 30 full hkups, 10 W, 10 E (30/50 amps). 2021 rates: $39 to $55. Apr 15 to Oct 28. (530)836-2774, 102 Little Bear Rd, Blairsden, CA 96103

PLUMAS-EUREKA (Public State Park) From Jct of SR-89 & CR-A14, SW 5.5 mi on CR-A14 (L). 60 Avail. 2021 rates: $35. May 24 to Sep 29. (530)836-2380

BLYTHE — J6 *Riverside*

DESTINY RV RESORTS-MCINTYRE
Ratings: 6.5/7/7 (Campground) 10 Avail: 10 W, 10 E (30/50 amps). 2021 rates: $40 to $42. (760)922-8205, 8750 Peter D McIntyre Ave, Blythe, CA 92225

HIDDEN BEACHES RIVER RESORT **Ratings: 6.5/7.5/8** (RV Park) 20 Avail: 10 full hkups, 10 W, 10 E (30/50 amps). 2021 rates: $42 to $49. (760)922-7276, 6951 Sixth Ave, Blythe, CA 92225

MAYFLOWER REGIONAL PARK (Public) From town, N 3.5 mi on State Hwy 95 to 6th Ave, E 3 mi to the Colorado River Rd, N 0.5 mi (E). 179 Avail: 152 W, 152 E (30 amps). 2021 rates: $20 to $30. (760)922-4665

THE COVE COLORADO RIVER RV RESORT **Ratings: 8.5/5.5/7.5** (RV Resort) Avail: 75 full hkups (30/50 amps). 2021 rates: $55 to $77. (760)922-5350, 500 Riviera Drive, Blythe, CA 92225

JOIN GoodSamRoadside.com

BODEGA BAY — D2 *Sonoma*

BODEGA BAY RV PARK
Ratings: 9/10★/9.5 (RV Park) From Jct of SR-1 & Bay Hill Rd (1.2 mi N of town), NW 100 ft on SR-1 (L).

ENJOY THE BEST OF THE NORTH COAST
When you stay with us, you'll have easy access to fine dining, fine wine and shopping. Great fishing, boating, clamming, crabbing and whale watching. Hiking, biking and kayaking. Art galleries, artist studios and local events

FAC: paved rds. Avail: 68 all weather, 26 pull-thrus, (29x62), back-ins (24x40), accepts full hkup units only, 55 full hkups, 13 W, 13 E (30/50 amps), cable, WiFi @ sites, dump, laundry, restaurant. **REC:** Bodega Bay: fishing, boating nearby, hunting nearby. Pets OK. Partial handicap access. No tents. Big rig sites, eco-friendly. 2021 rates: $64 to $66, Military discount.
(707)875-3701 Lat: 38.34068, Lon: -123.04906
2001 Hwy 1, Bodega Bay, CA 94923
www.bodegabayrvpark.com
See ad this page

DORAN REGIONAL PARK (Public) From Jct of Hwy 1 & Doran Pk Rd, S 1 mi on Doran Pk Rd, follow signs (R). 120 Avail. 2021 rates: $32 to $35. (707)875-3540

SONOMA COAST STATE BEACH/BODEGA DUNES (Public State Park) From town, N 0.5 mi on Hwy 1 (L). 98 Avail. 2021 rates: $35. (707)875-3483

SONOMA COAST STATE BEACH/WRIGHTS BEACH (Public State Park) From town, N 6 mi on Hwy 1 (L). 27 Avail. 2021 rates: $35 to $45. (707)875-3483

WESTSIDE REGIONAL PARK (Public) From Jct of Hwy 1 & Eastshore Rd, exit onto Bay Flat Rd, W 2 mi (L). 45 Avail. 2021 rates: $32 to $35. (707)875-3540

BONITA — K5 *San Diego*

SWEETWATER SUMMIT COUNTY PARK (Public) From Jct of I-5 & I-805 (exit 31), S 20 mi on I-805 to Bonita Rd (exit 7C), E 4 mi to San Miguel Rd (do not cross bridge), continue 2 mi to entrance (L). 112 Avail: 63 full hkups, 20 W, 20 E (30 amps). 2021 rates: $29 to $33. (619)472-7572

BORON — H4 *Kern*

ARABIAN RV OASIS
Ratings: 5.5/7/5.5 (RV Park) From Hwy 58 & Boron Ave (Exit 199): Go 1/4 mi S on Boron Ave (R). Elev 2550 ft. **FAC:** paved rds. (52 spaces). Avail: 30 gravel, patios, 12 pull-thrus, (25x80), back-ins (25x40), accepts full hkup units only, 30 full hkups (30/50 amps), seasonal sites, cable, WiFi @ sites, tent sites, dump, laundry. Pets OK $. eco-friendly. 2021 rates: $36.
(760)762-5008 Lat: 35.004831, Lon: -117.65024
12401 Boron Ave, Boron, CA 93516
See ad this page

BORREGO SPRINGS — J5 *San Diego*

ANZA-BORREGO DESERT (Public State Park) From Jct of CR-S3 & CR-S22 (in town), W 2 mi on CR-S22/Palm Canyon Dr (R). Avail: 47 full hkups (30 amps). 2021 rates: $20 to $35. (760)767-4205

BLU IN PARK RV RESORT AND CAFE **Ratings: 7.5/9★/7** (RV Park) Avail: 150 full hkups (30/50 amps). 2021 rates: $60 to $70. Oct 15 to Apr 30. (760)561-1370, 2189 Hwy 78, Borrego Springs, CA 92004

LEAPIN LIZARD RV RANCH
Ratings: 7.5/9.5★/9 (RV Park) Avail: 40 full hkups (30/50 amps). 2021 rates: $40 to $50. Oct 01 to Jun 01. (760)767-4526, 5929 Kunkler Ln, Borrego Springs, CA 92004

PALM CANYON HOTEL AND RV RESORT
Ratings: 8.5/8★/9 (RV Park) Avail: 80 full hkups (30/50 amps). 2021 rates: $48 to $86. Aug 31 to May 31. (760)767-5341, 221 Palm Canyon Drive, Borrego Springs, CA 92004

THE SPRINGS AT BORREGO RV RESORT & GOLF COURSE
Ratings: 10/10★/10 (RV Resort) From Jct of Hwys S-3 & S-22 (in town), E 0.5 mi on Hwy S-22 to Di Giorgio Rd, N 0.6 mi (R). **FAC:** paved rds. Avail: 160 paved, patios, 90 pull-thrus, (35x60), back-ins (40x70), 160 full hkups (30/50 amps), cable, WiFi @ sites, tent sites, rentals, dump, laundry, LP gas, controlled access. **REC:** heated pool, hot tub, Golf Lake: fishing, golf. Pet restrict (Q). Partial handicap access. Big rig sites, eco-friendly. 2021 rates: $45 to $116, Military discount.
(760)767-0004 Lat: 33.26626, Lon: -116.36526
2255 Digiorgio Road, Borrego Springs, CA 92004
www.springsatborrego.com
See ad this page

BOULDER CREEK — F1 *Santa Cruz*

BIG BASIN REDWOODS (Public State Park) From Santa Cruz, N 14 mi on SR-9 to SR-236 (at Boulder Creek), NW 9 mi (R). 142 Avail. 2021 rates: $35. (831)338-8860

BRADLEY — G2 *Monterey*

LAKE SAN ANTONIO REC AREA/NORTH SHORE (Public) N-bnd: From Jct of Hwy 101 & Exit 252, Jolon Rd (G-18), NW 9.3 mi on Jolon Rd (G-18) to New Pleyto Rd, S 1.8 mi (E); or S-bnd: From Jct of Hwy 101 & Jolon Rd exit (G-14), S 22.8 mi on Jolon Rd to Lockwood (G-18/go straight), S 6.3 mi to New Pleyto Rd, S 1.8 mi (E). 90 Avail: 18 full hkups, 72 W, 72 E (30 amps). 2021 rates: $15 to $45. (800)323-3839

LAKE SAN ANTONIO REC AREA/SOUTH SHORE (Public) From Jct of Hwy 101 & Exit 252 (SR-G18), W 0.1 mi on G18 (Jolon Rd) to G19 (Nacimiento Lake Dr), SW 11.7 mi to G14 (Interlake Rd), N 8 mi to San Antonio Rd, NE 2 mi (E). 481 Avail: 140 full hkups, 249 W, 26 E (30 amps). 2021 rates: $15 to $45. (800)323-3839

BRIDGEPORT — D4 *Mono*

BRIDGEPORT RESERVOIR MARINA & CAMPGROUND **Ratings: 5/6.5/7.5** (Campground) 24 Avail: 12 full hkups, 2 W, 2 E (30/50 amps). 2021 rates: $42 to $45. Mar 15 to Nov 15. (760)932-7001, 1845 Hwy 182, Bridgeport, CA 93517

PARADISE SHORES RV PARK **Ratings: 5.5/8.5★/7.5** (RV Park) Avail: 35 full hkups (30 amps). 2021 rates: $42 to $48. Apr 26 to Oct 15. (760)932-7735, 2399 Hwy 182, Bridgeport, CA 93517

TWIN LAKES RESORT **Ratings: 5.5/7/6** (Campground) Avail: 26 full hkups (30/50 amps). 2021 rates: $35 to $50. Apr 15 to Nov 15. (760)932-7751, 10316 Twin Lakes Rd, Bridgeport, CA 93517

WILLOW SPRINGS MOTEL & RV PARK **Ratings: 6/8★/8.5** (RV Park) Avail: 24 full hkups (20/30 amps). 2021 rates: $45 to $65. May 01 to Nov 01. (760)932-7725, 70970 Hwy 395, Bridgeport, CA 93517

BROWNS VALLEY — C3 *Yuba*

COLLINS LAKE RECREATION AREA **Ratings: 7/8★/9** (Campground) 135 Avail: 3 full hkups, 132 W, 132 E (20/30 amps). 2021 rates: $48 to $68. (800)286-0576, 7530 Collins Lake Rd, Browns Valley, CA 95918

BUELLTON — H2 *Santa Barbara*

FLYING FLAGS RV RESORT & CAMPGROUND
Ratings: 9.5/10★/9 (RV Park) Avail: 274 full hkups (30/50 amps). 2021 rates: $68 to $350. (805)688-3716, 180 Avenue of Flags, Buellton, CA 93427

BURNEY — B3 *Plumas*

BURNEY See also Hat Creek, McArthur & Old Station.

MCARTHUR-BURNEY FALLS MEMORIAL (Public State Park) From Jct of SR-299 & SR-89, N 6 mi on SR-89 (L). 84 Avail. 2021 rates: $30 to $35. (530)335-2777

PG & E/PIT RIVER/CASSEL CAMPGROUND (Public) From Jct of Hwys 299 & 89, E 2 mi on Hwy 299 to Cassel Rd, S 3.6 mi (L). 27 Avail: Pit toilets. 2021 rates: $32.72. (916)386-5164

CALISTOGA — D2 *Napa*

BOTHE-NAPA VALLEY (Public State Park) From town, N 5 mi on SR-29 (L). 24 Avail. 2021 rates: $35. (800)942-4575

CALISTOGA RV PARK (Public) From Jct of SR-128 & 29, NE 0.4 mi on SR-29 (Lincoln Ave) to Fairway, NW 0.3 mi to N Oak St, NE 500 ft (L). 69 Avail: 24 full hkups, 45 W, 45 E (30/50 amps). 2021 rates: $37 to $60. (707)942-5221

CANYON DAM — C3 *Plumas*

PG & E/FEATHER RIVER/ROCKY POINT CAMPGROUND (Public) From Jct of Hwys 147 & 89, NW 5 mi on Hwy 89. 131 Avail: Pit toilets. 2021 rates: $45.88 to $91.76. May 23 to Sep 05. (916)386-5164

CAPITOLA — F1 *Santa Cruz*

NEW BRIGHTON STATE BEACH (Public State Park) From Jct of Hwy 1 & Park Ave (exit 456/frntg rd), W 0.5 mi on frntg rd (R). 102 Avail. 2021 rates: $35 to $50. (831)464-6329

CARDIFF BY THE SEA — J4 *San Diego*

SAN ELIJO STATE BEACH (Public State Park) From Jct of I-5 & Encinitas Blvd exit (Exit 41B), W 0.75 mi on Encinitas Blvd to US-101(1st St), S 2 mi (R). 171 Avail. 2021 rates: $35 to $75. (760)753-5091

CARLSBAD — J4 *San Diego*

SOUTH CARLSBAD STATE BEACH (Public State Park) From Jct of I-5 & Palomar Airport Rd (Exit 47), W on Palomar Airport Rd to Carlsbad Blvd, S 3 mi (R). Avail: 13 full hkups. 2021 rates: $35 to $50. (760)438-3143

CARMEL — F1 *Monterey*

CARMEL BY THE RIVER RV PARK **Ratings: 7.5/9.5★/9.5** (RV Park) Avail: 35 full hkups (30/50 amps). 2021 rates: $95 to $210. (831)624-9329, 27680 Schulte Rd, Carmel, CA 93923

SADDLE MOUNTAIN RV & CAMPGROUND **Ratings: 6.5/9★/9** (RV Park) Avail: 20 full hkups (30 amps). 2021 rates: $75 to $130. (831)624-1617, 27625 Schulte Rd, Carmel, CA 93923

CARPINTERIA — H3 *Santa Barbara*

CARPINTERIA STATE BEACH (Public State Park) From Jct of US-101 & Casitas Pass exit (Exit 86A), SW 0.1 mi on exit rd to Carpinteria St, N 0.1mi to Palm, W 0.5 mi (E). 150 Avail: 80 full hkups, 30 W, 30 E (30 amps). 2021 rates: $35 to $65. (805)968-1033

CASTAIC — H3 *Los Angeles*

CASTAIC LAKE (Public) From Jct of I-5 & Lake Hughes Rd exit (exit 176B), E 1.5 mi on Lake Hughes Rd to 2nd park entrance, cross lake bridge, follow signs (L). 66 Avail. 2021 rates: $20. (661)257-4050

CATHEDRAL CITY — J5 *Riverside*

CATHEDRAL PALMS RV RESORT **Ratings: 8/8.5★/7.5** (RV Resort) Avail: 20 full hkups (30/50 amps). 2021 rates: $52. (760)324-8244, 35901 Cathedral Canyon Drive, Cathedral City, CA 92234

OUTDOOR RESORT PALM SPRINGS
Ratings: 10/10★/10 (Condo Park) From Jct of I-10 & Bob Hope Dr (Exit 130), S 0.3 mi on Bob Hope Dr to Ramon Rd, W 2.1 mi (L) (3 night minimum stay). **FAC:** paved rds. (1213 spaces). Avail: 200 paved, patios, back-ins (35x65), accepts full hkup units only, 200 full hkups (30/50 amps), seasonal sites, cable, WiFi @ sites, $, laundry, groc, restaurant, controlled access. **REC:** heated pool, wading pool, hot tub, golf. Pet restrict (Q). Partial handicap access. No tents. Big rig sites, No Class B, eco-friendly. 2021 rates: $60 to $90.
(800)843-3131 Lat: 33.81509, Lon: -116.44833
69411 Ramon Rd, Cathedral City, CA 92234
orps.com
See ad page 112

PALM SPRINGS OASIS RV RESORT
good sam park **Ratings: 9/9★/7.5** (RV Resort) Avail: 140 full hkups (30/50 amps). 2021 rates: $71.58 to $85.12. (888)563-7040, 36100 Date Palm Dr, Cathedral City, CA 92234

CEDAR GLEN — L6 *San Bernardino*

SAN BERNARDINO/NORTH SHORE (Public State Park) From town: Go 1-1/2 mi N on Hwy-173, then 1/4 mi E on Hospital Rd (CR-3N41). 28 Avail. 2021 rates: $26. Apr 24 to Oct 04. (909)382-2790

CHERRY VALLEY — J5 *Riverside*

BOGART PARK (Public) From jct Hwy 60 & I-10: Go 3/4 mi E on I-10, then 2-1/4 mi N on Beaumont Ave, then 3/4 mi E on Brookside Ave, then 1 mi N on Cherry Ave. 29 Avail. 2021 rates: $15 to $23. (951)845-3818

CHESTER — B3 *Plumas*

NORTH SHORE CAMPGROUND **Ratings: 6.5/9★/8** (RV Park) Avail: 101 full hkups (20/30 amps). 2021 rates: $40 to $60. May 01 to Oct 01. (530)258-3376, 541 Catfish Beach Rd., Chester, CA 96020

Thank you for being one of our best customers!

CHICO — C2 *Butte*

ALMOND TREE RV PARK
good sam park **Ratings: 10/10★/9** (RV Park) From Jct of SR-99 & SR-32 (SE of town/Exit 389), N 3.7 mi on SR-99 to Eaton Rd, SW 0.2 mi to Esplanade, SE 0.4 mi (L). **FAC:** paved rds. Avail: 42 all weather, patios, 26 pull-thrus, (25x65), back-ins (25x60), 42 full hkups (30/50 amps), cable, WiFi @ sites, dump, laundry, groc. **REC:** pool, boating nearby, hunting nearby. Pets OK. Partial handicap access. No tents. Big rig sites, eco-friendly. 2021 rates: $55, Military discount.
(530)899-1271 Lat: 39.76880, Lon: -121.87062
3124 Esplanade Ave, Chico, CA 95973
www.almondtreervandstorage.com
See ad this page

CHINO — M4 *San Bernardino*

PRADO REGIONAL PARK
(Public) From Jct of Hwy 91 & Hwy 71 exit, N 3.7 mi on Hwy 71 to Euclid Ave (Hwy 83), NE 1 mi (R). Minimum 2 ngts stay on weekends. **FAC:** paved rds. Avail: 75 paved, patios, 58 pull-thrus, (25x60), back-ins (25x40), 75 full hkups (20/50 amps), tent sites, shower$, dump, laundry, fire rings, firewood, controlled access. **REC:** Prado Lake: fishing, golf, playground, rec open to public. Pet restrict (Q) $. 14 day max stay. 2021 rates: $47.
(909)597-4260 Lat: 33.94618, Lon: -117.65157
16700 S Euclid Ave, Chino, CA 91708
parks.sbcounty.gov/park/prado-regional-park
See ad page 96

CHOWCHILLA — F2 *Madera*

ARENA RV PARK **Ratings: 6/8.5★/7.5** (RV Park) 10 Avail: 6 full hkups, 4 W, 4 E (30/50 amps). 2021 rates: $42 to $48. (559)598-9696, 203 S Chowchilla Blvd, Chowchilla, CA 93610

THE LAKES RV & GOLF RESORT
good sam park **Ratings: 10/10★/9.5** (RV Resort) From Jct of Hwy 99 & E Robertson Blvd (Exit 170): Go 1-1/4 mi E on Robertson Blvd (R).

FREE GOLF FOR TWO WITH YOUR STAY!
Enjoy California's Heartland. Easy access to Hwy 99. Drive to San Francisco, Napa, Yosemite, Tahoe & Monterey. Lake front sites, refreshing pool & spa. Restaurant on site, free golfing for two. Big Rigs welcome. Pet friendly.

FAC: paved rds. (87 spaces). Avail: 77 paved, patios, 18 pull-thrus, (30x77), back-ins (26x54), accepts full hkup units only, 77 full hkups (30/50 amps), seasonal sites, WiFi @ sites, dump, laundry, restaurant, controlled access. **REC:** heated pool, hot tub, pond, boating nearby, golf. Pet restrict (Q). Partial handicap access. No tents. Big rig sites, eco-friendly. 2021 rates: $42 to $60, Military discount.
(866)665-6980 Lat: 37.12714, Lon: -120.22880
5001 E Robertson Blvd, Chowchilla, CA 93610
thelakesrv.com
See ad opposite page

Always do a Pre-Drive Safety Check!

Things to See and Do

PHEASANT RUN GOLF CLUB 18 hole championship golf course Par 72 RV accessible. Restrooms. Food. Hours: 7am to 5pm.
(559)665-3411 Lat: 37.12547, Lon: -120.23061
19 Clubhouse Dr, Chowchilla, CA 93610
www.pheasantrungolfclub.com
See ad opposite page

THE FINAL ROUND BAR & GRILL Breakfast, lunch and dinner served daily. Outdoor, wood fire pizza oven. RV accessible. Restrooms. Food. Hours: 7am to 9pm.
(559)744-7000 Lat: 37.12549, Lon: -120.23061
19 Clubhouse Dr, Chowchilla, CA 93610
thefinalround.net
See ad opposite page

CHULA VISTA — K4 *San Diego*

CHULA VISTA RV RESORT **Ratings: 9.5/9/9.5** (RV Park) Avail: 237 full hkups (30/50 amps). 2021 rates: $79 to $123. (800)759-0148, 460 Sandpiper Way, Chula Vista, CA 91910

SAN DIEGO METROPOLITAN KOA RESORT **Ratings: 9.5/9/8.5** (RV Park) Avail: 150 full hkups (30/50 amps). 2021 rates: $70 to $120. (800)562-9877, 111 North 2nd Ave, Chula Vista, CA 91910

CLEARLAKE — D2 *Lake*

CLEARLAKE See also Cloverdale, Hidden Valley Lake, Lakeport, Nice & Upper Lake.

CLIO — C3 *Plumas*

CLIO'S RIVERS EDGE RV PARK **Ratings: 8/8/8.5** (RV Park) Avail: 165 full hkups (30/50 amps). 2021 rates: $42 to $55. Apr 15 to Oct 15. (530)836-2375, 3754 Hwy 89, Clio, CA 96106

CLIPPER MILLS — C3 *Butte*

QUAIL RIDGE RV PARK **Ratings: 3/4.5/5** (RV Resort) Avail: 66 full hkups (30/50 amps). 2021 rates: $35. (530)675-9313, 12468 LaPorte Rd, Clipper Mills, CA 95930

CLOVERDALE — D2 *Sonoma*

CLOVERDALE CITRUS FAIR
(Public) From Jct of US-101 & Citrus Fair Dr exit (S of town), exit Fwy W to stop light, W 300 ft (straight across intersection) on Citrus Fair Dr (R). After 5pm or on weekends, check phone numbers on Washington Street gate. **FAC:** paved rds. Avail: 40 paved, patios, 6 pull-thrus, (12x35), back-ins (20x60), mostly side by side hkups, 4 full hkups, 36 W, 36 E (20/50 amps), WiFi @ sites, dump. **REC:** hunting nearby. Pets OK. Partial handicap access. No tents, 14 day max stay, eco-friendly. 2021 rates: $25.
(707)894-3992 Lat: 38.27353, Lon: -122.68046
1 Citrus Fair Drive, Cloverdale, CA 95425
www.cloverdalecitrusfair.org
See ad opposite page

New to RVing? Visit Blog.GoodSam.com for tips on everything camping and RVing.

CLOVERDALE/HEALDSBURG KOA CAMPING RESORT **Ratings: 9/8.5★/8.5** (Campground) Avail: 140 full hkups (30/50 amps). 2021 rates: $75 to $89.50. (707)894-3337, 1166 Asti Ridge Rd, Cloverdale, CA 95425

RUSSIAN RIVER RV CAMPGROUND
good sam park **Ratings: 8/8/8.5** (RV Park) 117 Avail: 117 W, 117 E (30 amps). 2021 rates: $57 to $78. (888)563-7040, 33655 Geysers Rd, Cloverdale, CA 95425

COACHELLA — J5 *Riverside*

COACHELLA LAKES RV RESORT
good sam park (RV Resort) (Planned) Avail: 355 full hkups (30/50 amps). (928)554-7710, 44-790 Dillon Rd, Coachella, CA 92236

COALINGA — G2 *Fresno*

ALMOND TREE OASIS RV PARK **Ratings: 9.5/9.5★/8** (RV Park) Avail: 14 full hkups (30/50 amps). 2021 rates: $47.50 to $57.50. (559)935-0711, 41191 S Glenn Ave, Coalinga, CA 93210

COARSEGOLD — E4 *Madera*

YOSEMITE RV RESORT **Ratings: 8/9.5★/8.5** (RV Park) 78 Avail: 72 full hkups, 6 W, 6 E (30/50 amps). 2021 rates: $85.92 to $137.86. (559)683-7855, 34094 Hwy 41, Coarsegold, CA 93614

COLOMA — D3 *El Dorado*

AMERICAN RIVER RESORT **Ratings: 7.5/8.5★/8.5** (Campground) Avail: 17 full hkups (30 amps). 2021 rates: $45 to $50. (530)622-6700, 6019 New River Rd, Coloma, CA 95613

COLOMA RESORT **Ratings: 8/9.5★/9.5** (RV Park) 71 Avail: 43 full hkups, 28 W, 28 E (30/50 amps). 2021 rates: $48 to $65. (800)238-2298, 6921 MT Murphy, Coloma, CA 95613

FOLSOM LAKE SRA/PENINSULA (Public State Park) From Jct of Hwy 49 & Rattlesnake Bar Rd, W 9 mi on Rattlesnake Bar Rd (E). 100 Avail. 2021 rates: $28 to $33. (916)988-0205

We shine ""Spotlights" on interesting cities and areas.

COLUMBIA — E3 *Tuolumne*

49ER RV RANCH
good sam park **Ratings: 8.5/9★/9.5** (RV Park) Avail: 20 full hkups (30/50 amps). 2021 rates: $40 to $49. (209)532-4978, 23223 Italian Bar Rd, Columbia, CA 95310

TUTTLETOWN REC AREA/ACORN (Public) From town, N 8 mi on Hwy 49 to Reynolds Fairy Rd (access rd), W 2 mi (E). 35 Avail. 2021 rates: $18 to $22. (209)536-9094

TUTTLETOWN REC AREA/MANZANITA (Public) From town, N 8 mi on Hwy 49 to Reynolds Fairy Rd (acess rd), W 2 mi (E). 32 Avail. 2021 rates: $18 to $22. (209)536-9094

COLUSA — C2 *Colusa*

COLUSA COUNTY FAIRGROUNDS (Public) W-bnd: From Jct of SR-20 & SR-45 (in town), W 0.7 mi on SR-20 (L); or E-bnd: From Jct of I-5 & SR-20, E 7.9 mi on SR-20 (R). Register at office on side next to SR-20. 147 Avail: 32 full hkups, 50 W, 50 E (20/50 amps). 2021 rates: $20. (530)458-2641

COLUSA SACRAMENTO RIVER SRA (Public State Park) From Jct of I-5 & Hwy 20 (exit 578), E 9 mi on Hwy 20 (becomes 10th St), follow signs (E). 12 Avail. 2021 rates: $15 to $28. (530)329-9198

Say you saw it in our Guide!

CONCORD — E2 *Contra Costa*

SUNNY ACRES MOBILE HOME AND RV PARK
(RV Spaces) From jct Hwy 4 & I-680: Go 3-1/2 mi S on I-680 to Gregory Lane/Pleasant Hill exit, then 2-1/4 mi E on Monument Blvd, then 1 block S on Systron, then 1/4 mi S on San Miguel Road. **FAC:** paved rds. (80 spaces). Avail: 9 paved, 2 pull-thrus, (20x45), back-ins (20x40), 9 full hkups (30/50 amps), seasonal sites, WiFi, laundry. **REC:** heated pool, boating nearby, hunting nearby. Pet restrict (Q). No tents. 2021 rates: $55. no cc.
(925)685-7048 Lat: 37.96245, Lon: -122.02962
1080 San Miguel Road, Concord, CA 94518
See ad this page

CA

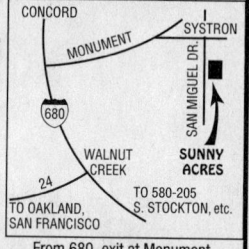

See listing Corning, CA

CORNING — C2 *Tehama*

HERITAGE RV PARK **Ratings: 10/10★/9** (RV Park) Avail: 74 full hkups (30/50 amps). 2021 rates: $46.89 to $53.89. (530)824-6130, 975 Hwy 99W, Corning, CA 96021

THE RV PARK AT ROLLING HILLS CASINO AND RESORT
good sam park
Ratings: 10/10★/10 (Campground) From jct of I-5 & Exit 628 (cross to West side of fwy) W on Liberal Ave, then 1/2 mi S on Everett Freeman Way (R).

YOUR ESCAPE TO N CALIFORNIA'S BEST!
Come experience Northern California's finest Casino Resort! Located just off I-5! Great gaming, two hotels, four restaurants, an RV Park, championship golf, and fun around the clock are just the beginning of 'Your Escape!'

FAC: paved rds. Avail: 96 all weather, 96 pull-thrus, (55x80), accepts full hkup units only, 96 full hkups (30/50 amps), WiFi @ sites, shower$, laundry. **REC:** heated pool, hot tub, boating nearby, golf, hunting nearby. Pets OK. Partial handicap access. No tents. Big rig sites, eco-friendly. 2021 rates: $40. ATM.
(530)528-3500 Lat: 39.8728, Lon: -122.2024
2655 Everett Freeman Way, Corning, CA 96021
www.rollinghillscasino.com
See ad opposite page

WOODSON BRIDGE RV PARK **Ratings: 6.5/8/7** (RV Park) Avail: 14 full hkups (30/50 amps). 2021 rates: $40 to $50. (530)839-2151, 25433 South Ave, Corning, CA 96021

WOODSON BRIDGE SRA (Public State Park) From Jct of I-5 & South Ave (Exit 630), E 6 mi on South Ave (L); or From Jct of E Hwy 99 & South Ave, W 3 mi on South Ave (R). 37 Avail. 2021 rates: $31. (530)839-2112

Things to See and Do

ROLLING HILLS CASINO AND RESORT Gaming Machines & Restaurant RV accessible. Restrooms. Food. Hours: 24 hour.
(888)331-6400 Lat: 39.87406, Lon: -122.20216
2655 Everett Freeman Way, Corning, CA 96021
www.rollinghillscasino.com
See ad opposite page

COULTERVILLE — E3 *Mariposa*

BAGBY RECREATION AREA (Public) From town, N 15 mi on Hwy 49 at Lake McClure (E). 30 Avail: 10 W, 10 E (20/30 amps). 2021 rates: $15 to $31. (855)800-2267

HORSESHOE BEND (Public) From Jct of Hwys 49 & 132, W 3 mi on Hwy 132 (L). 97 Avail: 35 W, 35 E (20/30 amps). 2021 rates: $22 to $34. (209)378-2521

CRESCENT CITY — A1 *Del Norte*

CRESCENT CITY See also Klamath, CA; Brookings, OR.

CRESCENT CITY REDWOODS KOA **Ratings: 8.5/10★/9** (Campground) 41 Avail: 24 full hkups, 17 W, 17 E (30/50 amps). 2021 rates: $52.50 to $67.50. Mar 01 to Nov 15. (800)562-5754, 4241 US Hwy 101 N, Crescent City, CA 95531

DEL NORTE COAST REDWOODS (Public State Park) From city center, S 7 mi on US-101 to park entrance rd, E 2.5 mi, follow signs (R). 107 Avail. 2021 rates: $35. (707)465-7335

JEDEDIAH SMITH REDWOODS (Public State Park) From Jct of US-101 & US-199 (exit 197), E 6 mi on US-199 (R). 106 Avail. 2021 rates: $35. (707)465-7335

RAMBLIN' REDWOODS CAMPGROUND **Ratings: 7.5/8.5★/9** (RV Park) 74 Avail: 61 full hkups, 13 W, 13 E (30/50 amps). 2021 rates: $52 to $70. (707)487-7404, 6701 Highway 101 N, Crescent City, CA 95531

REDWOOD MEADOWS RV RESORT **Ratings: 8.5/9.5★/8.5** (RV Park) Avail: 90 full hkups (30/50 amps). 2021 rates: $45 to $53. (707)458-3321, 2000 US Hwy 199, Crescent City, CA 95531

SHORELINE RV PARK (Public) From Jct US-101 & Front St (S end of downtown), SE 0.1 mi on US-101 to Sunset Circle, SW 500 ft (E). Avail: 196 full hkups (20/30 amps). 2021 rates: $50. (707)464-2473

SUNSET HARBOR RV PARK **Ratings: 7.5/9★/7** (RV Park) Avail: 15 full hkups (30/50 amps). 2021 rates: $35.70 to $37.74. (707)465-1246, 205 King St., Crescent City, CA 95531

We appreciate your business!

VILLAGE CAMPER INN RV PARK
good sam park
Ratings: 9/9★/9 (Campground) Avail: 70 full hkups (30/50 amps). 2021 rates: $55 to $59. (707)464-3544, 1543 Parkway Dr, Crescent City, CA 95531

CROMBERG — C3 *Plumas*

GOLDEN COACH RV PARK **Ratings: 8/8.5★/7** (Campground) Avail: 29 full hkups (30/50 amps). 2021 rates: $38.50. May 01 to Oct 31. (530)836-2426, 59704 Hwy 70, Cromberg, CA 96103

DANA POINT — J4 *Orange*

DOHENY STATE BEACH (Public State Park) From Jct of PCH & Dana Point Harbor Dr, W 0.8 mi on Dana Point Harbor Dr (L). 122 Avail. 2021 rates: $40 to $60. (949)496-6171

DELHI — E3 *Merced*

MERCED RIVER RV RESORT **Ratings: 9.5/9.5★/9.5** (RV Park) Avail: 38 full hkups (30/50 amps). 2021 rates: $50. (209)634-6056, 7765 Campground Rd, Delhi, CA 95315

DESCANSO — K5 *San Diego*

OAKZANITA SPRINGS RV CAMPGROUND
good sam park
Ratings: 8/8/7.5 (Membership Park) 95 Avail: 47 full hkups, 48 W, 48 E (30/50 amps). 2021 rates: $59 to $84. (888)563-7040, 11053 Hwy 79, Descanso, CA 91916

DESERT HOT SPRINGS — J5 *Riverside*

CALIENTE SPRINGS RESORT **Ratings: 8.5/8.5★/9** (RV Resort) Avail: 200 full hkups (30/50 amps). 2021 rates: $55 to $72. (760)329-8400, 70200 Dillon Rd, Desert Hot Springs, CA 92241

CATALINA SPA AND RV RESORT **Ratings: 9.5/9.5★/9** (RV Resort) Avail: 160 full hkups (30/50 amps). 2021 rates: $45 to $60. (760)329-4431, 18800 Corkill Rd, Desert Hot Springs, CA 92241

PALM SPRINGS/JOSHUA TREE KOA **Ratings: 8.5/8.5/9** (RV Resort) Avail: 194 full hkups (30/50 amps). 2021 rates: $45 to $80. (760)251-6555, 70405 Dillon Rd, Desert Hot Springs, CA 92241

SAM'S FAMILY SPA
good sam park
Ratings: 9/8★/9.5 (RV Park) From Jct of I-10 & Palm Dr (exit 123), N 3 mi on Palm Dr to Dillon Rd, E 4.2 mi (R).

PALM SPRINGS MOST RELAXING RESORT
Soak in one of our therapeutic pools or hot mineral spas naturally heated by underground wells. Enjoy a wet or dry sauna after taking in all the fun of the Palm Springs area. Near golf, restaurants, Coachella and Joshua Tree.

FAC: paved rds. (184 spaces). Avail: 178 gravel, patios, back-ins (32x50), 178 full hkups (30/50 amps), seasonal sites, cable, WiFi @ sites, tent sites, rentals, laundry, groc. **REC:** heated pool, wading pool, hot tub, playground, rec open to public. Pets OK. Partial handicap access, eco-friendly. 2021 rates: $60, Military discount.
(760)329-6457 Lat: 33.92488, Lon: -116.42535
70875 Dillon Rd, Desert Hot Springs, CA 92241
samsfamilyspa.com
See ad this page

SKY VALLEY RESORT **Ratings: 9/8.5★/9** (RV Resort) Avail: 100 full hkups (30/50 amps). 2021 rates: $40 to $70. (760)329-8400, 74711 Dillon Rd, Desert Hot Springs, CA 92241

THE SANDS GOLF & RV RESORT **Ratings: 9.5/9★/9.5** (RV Park) Avail: 250 full hkups (30/50 amps). 2021 rates: $28 to $95. (877)426-5882, 16400 Bubbling Wells Road, Desert Hot Springs, CA 92240

Get the GOOD SAM CAMPING APP

Things to See and Do

SAM'S FAMILY SPA RESORT AND MOTEL 13 Motel units, refrigerators in all rooms plus color satellite TV, doubles & queens, some with kitchen. Pool views & sun decks. Hours: . Adult fee: $95 to $185.
(760)329-6457 Lat: 33.92325, Lon: -116.42522
70875 Dillon Rd, Desert Hot Springs, CA 92241
www.samsfamilyspa.com
See ad this page

DEVILS POSTPILE NATIONAL MONUMENT — E4 *Madera*

DEVILS POSTPILE NATIONAL MONUMENT (Public National Park) From Jct of Hwys 395 & 203, W 9 mi on Hwy 203 to Minerate Summit, W 8 mi follow signs (E). CAUTION: Narrow mountain road. 20 Avail. 2021 rates: $20. Jun 29 to Sep 01. (760)934-2289

DEVORE — L5 *San Bernardino*

GLEN HELEN REGIONAL PARK (Public) From Jct of I-15 Glen Helen Parkway, N 0.5 mi on Glen Helen Pkwy to Glen Helen Park Rd, W 0.1 mi (R). **FAC:** paved rds. Avail: 20 paved, 15 pull-thrus, (25x40), back-ins (25x40), 20 full hkups (30/50 amps), tent sites, shower$, dump. **REC:** pool $, Glen Helen Lake: fishing, playground. Pets OK. eco-friendly. 2021 rates: $47.
(909)887-7540 Lat: 34.20869, Lon: -117.40953
2555 Glen Helen Pkwy, San Bernardino, CA 92407
parks.sbcounty.gov/park/glen-helen-regional-park
See ad page 96

DUNCANS MILLS — D2 *Sonoma*

CASINI RANCH FAMILY CAMPGROUND Ratings: 8.5/8.5★/9 (Campground) 220 Avail: 36 full hkups, 137 W, 137 E (30/50 amps). 2021 rates: $63 to $120. (800)451-8400, 22855 Moscow Rd, Duncans Mills, CA 95430

DUNLAP — F3 *Fresno*

SEQUOIA RV PARK **Ratings: 6/NA/6.5** (RV Park) Avail: 29 full hkups (30/50 amps). 2021 rates: $49. (559)338-2350, 35671 E Kings Canyon Rd, Dunlap, CA 93621

DUNSMUIR — B2 *Siskiyou*

CASTLE CRAGS (Public State Park) From Jct of I-5 & Castle Creek Rd, W 0.5 mi on Castle Creek Rd (R). 76 Avail. 2021 rates: $15 to $25. (530)235-2684

EARP — H6 *San Bernardino*

RIVERLAND RESORT **Ratings: 7.5/7.5/7.5** (RV Park) Avail: 10 full hkups (30/50 amps). 2021 rates: $62 to $89. (760)663-3733, 3401 Parker Dam Rd, Earp, CA 92242

WINDMILL RESORT **Ratings: 4.5/NA/6.5** (RV Resort) Avail: 20 full hkups (30 amps). 2021 rates: $49 to $55. (760)663-3717, 1451 Parker Dam Rd, Earp, CA 92242

EL CAJON — K5 *San Diego*

CIRCLE RV RESORT - SUNLAND **Ratings: 10/9★/7.5** (RV Park) Avail: 59 full hkups (30/50 amps). 2021 rates: $70 to $95. (619)373-0905, 1835 E Main St, El Cajon, CA 92021

OAK CREEK RV RESORT - SUNLAND **Ratings: 10/10★/7** (RV Park) Avail: 34 full hkups (30/50 amps). 2021 rates: $60 to $90. (616)219-0661, 15379 Oak Creek Rd, El Cajon, CA 92021

VACATIONER RV PARK - SUNLAND **Ratings: 10/9.5★/7** (RV Park) Avail: 46 full hkups (30/50 amps). 2021 rates: $50 to $80. (616)202-6789, 1581 E Main St, El Cajon, CA 92021

EL CENTRO — K5 *Imperial*

DESERT TRAILS RV PARK & GOLF COURSE **Ratings: 8/8.5/8** (RV Park) 20 Avail: 16 full hkups, 4 W, 4 E (30/50 amps). 2021 rates: $37 to $45. (760)352-7275, 225 Wake Ave, El Centro, CA 92243

MILITARY PARK PALM OASIS RV PARK & RESORT (EL CENTRO NAVAL AIR FACILITY) (Public) From jct I-8 & Forester Rd to Evan Hewen, left to Bennet Rd, 3/4 mi N(R). Avail: 106 full hkups (30/50 amps). 2021 rates: $22 to $35. (760)339-2486

RIO BEND RV & GOLF RESORT
good sam park
Ratings: 10/10★/9.5 (RV Resort) From Jct of I-8 & Hwy 86 (Imperial Ave), W 8 mi on I-8 to Drew Rd (Exit 107), S 0.4 mi (R). **FAC:** paved rds. (458 spaces). Avail: 188 all weather, 23 pull-thrus, (30x50), back-ins (30x50), 188 full hkups (30/50 amps), seasonal sites, WiFi @ sites, rentals, dump, laundry, LP gas, restaurant, controlled access. **REC:** heated pool, hot tub, Rio Bend Lake: fishing, golf, shuffleboard. Pet restrict (B/Q). Partial handicap access. No tents, Age restrict may apply, eco-friendly. 2021 rates: $30 to $60, Military discount. ATM.
(760)352-7061 Lat: 32.76540, Lon: -115.69423
1589 Drew Rd, El Centro, CA 92243
www.riobendrvgolfresort.com
See ad this page

EL PORTAL — E4 *Mariposa*

INDIAN FLAT RV PARK **Ratings: 5.5/7/6.5** (Campground) 28 Avail: 16 full hkups, 12 W, 12 E (30/50 amps). 2021 rates: $42 to $48. (209)379-2339, 10008 Hwy 140, El Portal, CA 95318

EMIGRANT GAP — C3 *Placer*

PG & E/DONNER SUMMIT AREA/LAKE SPAULDING (Public) From Jct of I-80 & Hwy 20 (exit 161), W 2 mi on Hwy 20 (R). 25 Avail: Pit toilets. 2021 rates: $22 to $48. Jun 01 to Sep 30. (916)386-5164

PG & E/DONNER SUMMIT AREA/LODGEPOLE (Public) From Jct of I-80 & Yuba Gap (exit160), S 1.5 mi on access rd/Yuba Gap exit (follow rt fork) (E). 35 Avail: Pit toilets. 2021 rates: $50. (916)386-5164

SNOWFLOWER RV RESORT
good sam park
Ratings: 7.5/7/8 (Membership Park) 14 Avail: 14 W, 14 E (30 amps). 2021 rates: $60. (888)563-7040, 41776 Yuba Gap Dr, Emigrant Gap, CA 95715

ESCONDIDO — J4 *San Diego*

CHAMPAGNE LAKES RV RESORT
good sam park
Ratings: 8.5/8.5★/9 (Campground) Avail: 65 full hkups (30/50 amps). 2021 rates: $50 to $55. (760)749-7572, 8310 Nelson Way, Escondido, CA 92026

ESCONDIDO RV RESORT - SUNLAND **Ratings: 10/10★/8.5** (RV Park) Avail: 95 full hkups (30/50 amps). 2021 rates: $55 to $101. (619)648-8565, 1740 Seven Oakes Road, Escondido, CA 92026

ETNA — A2 *Siskiyou*

MOUNTAIN VILLAGE RV PARK **Ratings: 6.5/9.5★/8.5** (RV Park) Avail: 29 full hkups (30/50 amps). 2021 rates: $35. (530)467-5678, 30 Commercial Way, Etna, CA 96027

EUREKA — B1 *Humboldt*

GIANT REDWOODS RV AND CABIN DESTINATION
good sam park
Ratings: 9/9.5★/9.5 (Campground) From jct Hwy 345 & US 101: Go 37-3/4 mi on S on US 101, then 300 feet NW on Ave of Giants, then ½ mi SW on Myers Ave (R) Caution: Do not use Boy Scout Rd. **FAC:** paved rds. Avail: 64 all weather, 33 pull-thrus, (18x50), back-ins (20x40), 13 full hkups, 51 W, 51 E (30/50 amps), cable, WiFi @ sites, rentals, dump, laundry, groc, fire rings, firewood. **REC:** South Fork Eel River: swim, fishing, playground. Pet restrict (B) $. Partial handicap access. No tents, eco-friendly. 2021 rates: $60 to $80.
(707)943-9999 Lat: 40.26247, Lon: -123.87744
400 Myers Ave, Myers Flat, CA 95554
giantredwoodsrv.com
See primary listing at Myers Flat and ad page 143

REDWOOD ACRES FAIRGROUNDS (Public) N-bnd: From Jct of US-101 & Harris St (S end of town), E 3 mi on Harris St (R); or S-bnd: From Jct of US-101 & V St (N edge of town), S 0.3 mi on V St to Myrtle Ave, SE 0.4 mi to Harrison Ave, S 1.2 mi to Harris St (unmarked), E 0.5 mi (R). Note: Gate closes 10pm, Park only accepts RVs 2005 and newer. Avail: 52 full hkups (30/50 amps). 2021 rates: $35. (707)499-6187

REDWOOD COAST CABINS & RV RESORT **Ratings: 9.5/9.5★/7.5** (Campground) Avail: 50 full hkups (30/50 amps). 2021 rates: $46 to $51. (707)822-4243, 4050 N Hwy 101, Eureka, CA 95503

SHORELINE RV PARK **Ratings: 7.5/10★/8** (RV Park) Avail: 39 full hkups (30/50 amps). 2021 rates: $42 to $56. (707)443-2222, 2600 6th St, Eureka, CA 95501

EXETER — F3 *Tulare*

Travel Services

EXETER RV STORAGE Modern secure storage facility with indoor storage for boats, cars, trailers and RVs, offering short and long term leases. **RV Storage:** indoor, outdoor, secured fencing, electric gate, easy reach keypad, 24/7 access, well-lit facility, well-lit roads, well-lit perimeter, security cameras, on-site staff, level gravel/paved spaces, battery charger, power to charge battery, water, compressed air, office. **SERVICES:** self RV wash, restrooms. Hours: 9am to 5pm.
Special offers available for Good Sam Members
(559)202-0794 Lat: 36.325180, Lon: -119.082410
21945 Ave 296 , Exeter, CA 93221
www.exeterrvstorage.com

FAIRFIELD — D2 *Solano*

MILITARY PARK TRAVIS FAMCAMP (TRAVIS AFB) (Public) From jct I-80 & Fairfield Airbase Pkwy: go 8 mi E on Airbase Pkwy to main gate (R). Avail: 72 full hkups (30/50 amps). 2021 rates: $25. (707)424-3583

FELTON — F1 *Santa Cruz*

COTILLION GARDENS RV PARK **Ratings: 7.5/6.5/8** (RV Park) 65 Avail: 39 full hkups, 26 W, 26 E (20/30 amps). 2021 rates: $60 to $66. (831)335-7669, 300 Old Big Trees Rd, Felton, CA 95018

HENRY COWELL REDWOODS (Public State Park) From Jct of SR-9 & Graham Hill Rd, SE 2.5 mi on Graham Hill Rd (R). 113 Avail. 2021 rates: $35. (831)335-4598

SMITHWOODS RV PARK (MHP) **Ratings: 7/NA/7.5** (Campground) Avail: 80 full hkups (30/50 amps). 2021 rates: $55 to $82. (831)335-4321, 4770 Hwy 9, Felton, CA 95018

FERNDALE — B1 *Humboldt*

HUMBOLDT COUNTY FAIRGROUNDS (Public) From Jct of US-101 & Hwy 1 (Fernbridge, exit 621), SW 5 mi on Hwy 1 to Van Ness St, W 0.25 mi (L). 60 Avail: 60 W, 60 E (30 amps). 2021 rates: $12 to $28. (707)786-9511

FILLMORE — H3 *Ventura*

KENNEY GROVE PARK (Public) From town, W 2 mi on Hwy 126, E 0.25 mi on Old Telegraph Rd, follow signs (L). 33 Avail: 33 W, 33 E (20 amps). 2021 rates: $23 to $37. (805)524-0750

FOLSOM — D3 *Sacramento*

FOLSOM LAKE SRA/BEALS POINT (Public State Park) From Jct of Hwy 80 & Douglas Blvd E (exit 103A), E 5 mi on Douglas Blvd to Auburn-Folsom Rd, S 2 mi (L). Avail: 19 full hkups. 2021 rates: $28 to $58. (916)988-0205

FORESTVILLE — D2 *Sonoma*

A SPOTLIGHT Introducing Northcoast and the Giant Redwoods' colorful attractions appearing at the front of this state section.

RIVER BEND RESORT
good sam park
Ratings: 9/9.5★/9 (Campground) W-bnd: From Jct of US-101/River Rd (Mark West Exit 494), W 11.2 mi on River Rd (L); or E-bnd: From Jct of SR-116/River Rd (at E end of Guerneville SR-116 turns S over Russian River Bridge), E 4.2 mi on River Rd (R).

EXPLORE THE RUSSIAN RIVER VALLEY!
We are centrally located amidst several world famous wineries & the quaint towns of Forestville & Guerneville, offering shopping and dining. Ziplining, hiking, canoeing, swimming, backpacking and fishing are all close by.

FAC: paved rds. (98 spaces). Avail: 55 all weather, 3 pull-thrus, (17x50), back-ins (20x30), 22 full hkups, 33 W, 33 E (30/50 amps), seasonal sites, WiFi @ sites, tent sites, rentals, dump, laundry, groc, LP gas, fire rings, firewood. **REC:** Russian River: swim, fishing, boating nearby, playground, hunting nearby. Pet restrict (B) $. Partial handicap access, eco-friendly. 2021 rates: $95 to $115, Military discount.
(707)887-7662 Lat: 38.50475, Lon: -122.94186
11820 River Road, Forestville, CA 95436
riverbendresort.net
See ad page 111

FORT BRAGG — C1 *Mendocino*

MACKERRICHER (Public State Park) From N end of town, N 3 mi on SR-1 (L). 75 Avail. 2021 rates $40 to $45. (707)964-9112

POMO RV PARK & CAMPGROUND

Ratings: 9/10★/10 (RV Park) From Jct of SR-20 & SR-1, S 1 mi on SR-1 to Tregoning Ln, E 0.1 mi (E).

NICEST PARK ON THE MENDOCINO COAST!

17 wooded acres-secluded large individual sites-paved roads-clean restrooms-RV supplies & convenience items. Group area-meeting room-tent area-fishing-diving-Skunk Train-Botanical Gardens nearby. Quiet.

FAC: paved rds. Avail: 96 all weather, 6 pull-thrus, (30x60), back-ins (30x60), 74 full hkups, 22 W, 22 E (30/50 amps), cable, WiFi @ sites, tent sites, shower$, dump, laundry, LP gas, fire rings, firewood. **REC:** boating nearby, hunting nearby. Pets OK $. Big rig sites, eco-friendly. 2021 rates: $51. no cc.
(707)964-3373 Lat: 39.40455, Lon: -123.80663
17999 Tregoning Lane, Fort Bragg, CA 95437
www.pomorv.com
See ad opposite page, 110

FORTUNA — B1 *Humboldt*

GRIZZLY CREEK REDWOODS (Public State Park) From Jct of Hwy 101 & exit SR-36, E 17 mi on SR-36 (R). 28 Avail. 2021 rates: $35. (707)777-3683

RIVERWALK RV PARK & CAMPGROUND

Ratings: 10/10★/9.5 (Campground) From Jct of US-101 & Kenmar Rd/Riverwalk Dr (Exit 687), W 0.2 mi on Riverwalk Dr (R).

YOUR REDWOOD ADVENTURE STARTS HERE

The North Coast's finest RV Park. Immaculately maintained grounds and facilities add to the beauty and relaxed atmosphere of our park. The friendly staff makes this the perfect base to visit the amazing Redwood Coast.

FAC: paved rds. Avail: 89 paved, 54 pull-thrus, (25x60), back-ins (25x50), 89 full hkups (30/50 amps), cable, WiFi @ sites, tent sites, rentals, dump, laundry, groc, LP gas, firewood. **REC:** heated pool, hot tub, playground, hunting nearby. Pet restrict (B). Partial handicap access. Big rig sites, eco-friendly. 2021 rates: $56 to $60, Military discount.
(707)725-3359 Lat: 40.57625, Lon: -124.15082
2189 Riverwalk Dr, Fortuna, CA 95540
riverwalkrvpark.com
See ad this page

FRESNO — F3 *Fresno*

FRESNO See also Kingsburg & Sanger.

BLACKSTONE NORTH RV PARK **Ratings: 6.5/7/8** (RV Park) Avail: 47 full hkups (30/50 amps). 2021 rates: $43 to $50. (559)785-9020, 6494 N Blackstone Ave, Fresno, CA 93710

FRESNO MOBILE HOME & RV PARK

Ratings: 8/9.5★/9 (RV Park) Avail: 22 full hkups (30/50 amps). 2021 rates: $55. (559)417-3059, 1362 N Hughes Ave, Fresno, CA 93728

PG & E/KINGS RIVER AREA/TRAPPER SPRINGS (Public) From Jct of Hwy 168 & Dinkey Creek Rd (exit 1), E 12.5 mi on Dinkey Creek Rd to McKinley Grove Rd, E 14.1 mi to Courtright Rd, N 7.5 mi (R). 70 Avail: Pit toilets. 2021 rates: $48. (916)386-5164

Travel Services

CAMPING WORLD OF FRESNO As the nation's largest retailer of RV supplies, accessories, services and new and used RVs, Camping World is committed to making your total RV experience better. **SERVICES:** RV appliance, restrooms. RV Sales. RV supplies, LP gas, RV accessible. Hours: 9am - 7pm.
(866)983-0515 Lat: 36.679732, Lon: -119.744867
3672 South Maple Avenue, Fresno, CA 93725
www.campingworld.com

FRIANT — F3 *Fresno*

MILLERTON LAKE SRA (Public State Park) From Fresno, NE 20 mi on Hwy 41 to SR-145, E 7 mi (E). Avail: 27 E. 2021 rates: $30 to $40. (559)822-2332

FURNACE CREEK — F5 *Inyo*

DEATH VALLEY/FURNACE CREEK (Public National Park) From Jct of SR-127 & Hwy 190 (Death Valley Jct), E 30 mi on Hwy 190 (L). 136 Avail. 2021 rates: $22 to $36. (800)365-2267

DEATH VALLEY/MESQUITE SPRING (Public National Park) From Jct of Hwy 190 & Scotty's Castle Rd, NW 28 mi on Scotty's Castle Rd to Mesquite Spring Rd, W 2 mi (E). Entrance fee required. 30 Avail. 2021 rates: $14. (760)786-2331

DEATH VALLEY/SUNSET (Public National Park) From Jct of Hwy 190 & Campground Rd, E 0.25 mi on Campground Rd (L). Entrance fee required. 270 Avail. 2021 rates: $16. Oct 15 to Apr 15. (760)786-2331

DEATH VALLEY/TEXAS SPRINGS (Public National Park) From Jct of Hwy 190 & Campground Rd, E 0.25 mi on Campground Rd (E). Entrance fee required. 92 Avail. 2021 rates: $16. Oct 15 to Apr 15. (760)786-3247

GARBERVILLE — C1 *Humboldt*

BENBOW KOA **Ratings: 9.5/9/9.5** (RV Park) Avail: 103 full hkups (30/50 amps). 2021 rates: $45 to $90. (707)923-2777, 7000 Benbow Dr, Garberville, CA 95542

RICHARDSON GROVE (Public State Park) From town, S 7 mi on US-101 (R). 170 Avail. 2021 rates: $35 to $45. (707)247-3318

GAVIOTA — H2 *Santa Barbara*

GAVIOTA (Public State Park) 1 mi NW on US-101. 41 Avail. 2021 rates: $35 to $45. (805)968-1033

GILROY — F2 *Santa Clara*

GILROY See also Hollister, Marina, Morgan Hill, Moss Landing, Salinas, San Jose, San Juan Bautista, Scotts Valley & Watsonville.

GILROY GARLIC USA RV PARK **Ratings: 9/7.5/8** (RV Park) Avail: 31 full hkups (30/50 amps). 2021 rates: $59.96 to $65.40. (408)848-8081, 650 Holloway Rd, Gilroy, CA 95020

GOLETA — H3 *Santa Barbara*

EL CAPITAN STATE BEACH (Public State Park) From town, N 10 mi on US-101 (L). 128 Avail. 2021 rates: $35 to $45. (805)968-1033

REFUGIO STATE BEACH (Public State Park) From town, N 15 mi on SR-101 to Refugio State Beach exit (Exit 120), W 0.2 mi on state beach service rd (L). 85 Avail. 2021 rates: $35 to $55. (805)968-1033

GRAEAGLE — C3 *Plumas*

GRAEAGLE See also Blairsden, Clio, Cromberg & Quincy.

DREAM CATCHER CAMPGROUND & LODGE **Ratings: 6/8/7.5** (Campground) Avail: 22 full hkups (30/50 amps). 2021 rates: $45. Apr 01 to Oct 31. (530)836-2747, 70099 Hwy 70, Graeagle, CA 96103

MOVIN' WEST RV PARK (MHP) **Ratings: 6/8.5★/8.5** (RV Park) 23 Avail: 15 full hkups, 8 W, 8 E (30 amps). 2021 rates: $51 to $58. May 01 to Oct 21. (530)836-2614, 305 Johnsville, Graeagle, CA 96103

GRASS VALLEY — C3 *Nevada*

NEVADA COUNTY FAIRGROUNDS (Public) From Jct of SR-49 & SR-20, W 500 ft on SR-20 to Mill St exit, S 200 ft on Mill St to McCourtney Rd, W 0.6 mi to Gate 4 (R); or E-bnd: From Jct of SR-20 & McCourtney Rd exit (500 ft prior to Jct of SR-49 & SR-20), SW 0.6 mi on McCourtney Rd to Gate 4 (R). 144 Avail: 44 full hkups, 100 W, 100 E (30/50 amps). 2021 rates: $30 to $50. (530)273-6217

ORCHARD SPRINGS RESORT (Public) From Jct of SR 174 & Orchard Springs Rd, E 0.5 mi on Orchard Springs Rd, S 0.2 mi to entrance gate. Avail: 15 full hkups (20/30 amps). 2021 rates: $56. (530)346-2212

GREENBRAE — E2 *Marin*

MARIN RV PARK

Ratings: 10/10★/8 (RV Park) N-bnd: From Jct of US-101 & Exit 450A (Lucky Dr), N 0.1 mi on frntg rd (R); or S-bnd: From Jct of US-101 & Exit 450A (Lucky Dr), W 300 ft on Fifer Ave to Tamal Vista Blvd, S 0.2 mi to Wornum, E 0.1 mi on Wornum (under Fwy) to Redwood Hwy (Frntg Rd), N 0.3 mi (R).

MAKE US YOUR TOURING HEADQUARTERS

We are the closest RV Park to San Francisco and 10 miles north of the Golden Gate Bridge. A ten-minute walk from the Bus/Ferry to San Francisco. Ride the Trolley Cars, trek to the Muir Woods, Pt Reyes, Napa Valley and more.

FAC: paved rds. (89 spaces). Avail: 84 all weather, back-ins (17x50), accepts full hkup units only, 84 full hkups (30/50 amps), seasonal sites, cable, WiFi @ sites, dump, laundry. **REC:** heated pool, boating nearby. Pet restrict (Q). No tents. Big rig sites, eco-friendly. 2021 rates: $99.
(888)461-5199 Lat: 37.94111, Lon: -122.51518
2140 Redwood Hwy, Greenbrae, CA 94904
www.marinrvpark.com
See ad page 116

GREENFIELD — F2 *Monterey*

YANKS RV RESORT

Ratings: 10/10★/10 (RV Resort) From Jct Hwy 101 & Thorne Rd (Exit 295): Go 1/10 mi E on Livingston Rd (E). **FAC:** paved rds. Avail: 110 paved, patios, 77 pull-thrus, (32x70), back-ins (30x50), 110 full hkups (30/50 amps), cable, WiFi @ sites, dump, laundry, groc, LP gas, controlled access. **REC:** heated pool, hot tub. Pet restrict (B/Q). Partial handicap access. No tents. Big rig sites, eco-friendly. 2021 rates: $51 to $71, Military discount.
(831)740-8007 Lat: 36.342459, Lon: -121.254156
40399 Livingston Rd, Greenfield, CA 93927
www.yanksrvresort.com
See ad page 143

GRIDLEY — C2 *Butte*

GRIDLEY INN & RV PARK **Ratings: 9.5/10★/9.5** (RV Park) Avail: 10 full hkups (30/50 amps). 2021 rates: $45.99. (530)846-4520, 1490 Hwy 99, Gridley, CA 95948

GROVELAND — E3 *Tuolumne*

MOCCASIN POINT REC AREA (Public) From Jct of Hwys 120 & 49 (Chinese Camp), SE 6.2 mi on Hwy 120/49 to Jacksonville Rd exit, N 100 ft (R). Avail: 18 full hkups (20/30 amps). 2021 rates: $28 to $50. (209)852-2396

YOSEMITE LAKES RV RESORT

Ratings: 8/9★/8 (Membership Park) Avail: 35 full hkups (30 amps). 2021 rates: $98. (888)563-7040, 31191 Hardin Flat Rd, Groveland, CA 95321

YOSEMITE PINES RV RESORT

Ratings: 8.5/8/8 (Campground) 158 Avail: 96 full hkups, 62 W, 62 E (30/50 amps). 2021 rates: $40 to $77. (209)962-7690, 20450 Old Hwy 120, Groveland, CA 95321

YOSEMITE RIDGE RESORT (RV Park) (Rebuilding) Avail: 10 full hkups (30/50 amps). 2021 rates: $40 to $60. (800)706-3009, 7589 Hwy 120, Groveland, CA 95321

GROVER BEACH — H2 *San Luis Obispo*

LE SAGE RIVIERA RV PARK
Ratings: 5.5/8.5★/7.5 (RV Park) N-bnd: From Jct of US-101 & Grand Ave exit: Go 2-1/2 mi W on Grand Ave to Hwy-1, then 1/10 mi N on Hwy-1 (L); or S-bnd: From Jct of US-101 & Grand Ave (Arroyo Grande exit): Go 2 mi W on Grand Ave to Hwy-1, then 1/10 mi N on Hwy-1 (L). **FAC:** paved rds. (62 spaces). Avail: 10 gravel, 5 pull-thrus, (20x45), back-ins (20x40), 10 full hkups (30/50 amps), seasonal sites, WiFi @ sites, laundry. **REC:** boating nearby. Pet restrict (B). Partial handicap access. No tents, eco-friendly. 2021 rates: $54.20 to $76.
(805)489-5506 Lat: 35.124038, Lon: -120.630908
319 N Hwy 1, Grover Beach, CA 93433
lesageriviera.com
See ad page 121

GUALALA — D1 *Mendocino*

GUALALA POINT (Public) From town: Go 1 mi S on Hwy-1. 19 Avail. 2021 rates: $32 to $35. (707)565-2041

HALF MOON BAY — E2 *San Mateo*

HALF MOON BAY STATE BEACH (Public State Park) From Hwy 1 in town: Go 1/2 mi W on Kelly Ave. 52 Avail. 2021 rates: $35 to $65. (650)726-8819

PELICAN POINT RV PARK **Ratings: 6/8.5★/7.5** (RV Park) Avail: 15 full hkups (30/50 amps). 2021 rates: $83. (650)726-9100, 1001 Miramontes Point Rd, Half Moon Bay, CA 94019

HAT CREEK — B3 *Shasta*

HAT CREEK HEREFORD RANCH RV PARK & CAMPGROUND **Ratings: 7.5/5.5/9** (Campground) 53 Avail: 42 full hkups, 11 W, 11 E (30 amps). 2021 rates: $45 to $50. Apr 15 to Oct 15. (530)335-7171, 17855 Doty Rd, Hat Creek, CA 96040

RANCHERIA RV PARK **Ratings: 7.5/9.5★/8.5** (RV Park) Avail: 65 full hkups (30/50 amps). 2021 rates: $45 to $55. (530)335-7418, 15565 Black Angus Lane, Hat Creek, CA 96040

HAVASU LAKE — H6 *San Bernardino*

HAVASU LANDING RESORT CAMPGROUND **Ratings: 7.5/8/7.5** (Campground) Avail: 132 full hkups (30/50 amps). 2021 rates: $40 to $260. (760)858-4592, #1 Main St, Havasu Lake, CA 92363

HEMET — N6 *Riverside*

CASA DEL SOL RV RESORT
good sam park
Ratings: 8/9★/7.5 (RV Park) From Jct of Hwys 74 W & 79 S (Florida Ave) W 2.3 mi on Hwy 74W & 79S to Kirby St, S 0.1 mi (R).

PREMIER PARK MODELS & RV SITES
Enjoy our sparkling heated pool, invigorating indoor whirlpool spa, indoor shuffleboard courts, pool tables & huge recreation hall. Practice on our own green, enjoy the relaxing library, join crafts, dances & more!
FAC: paved rds. (358 spaces). Avail: 100 dirt, patios, 10 pull-thrus, (30x80), back-ins (30x40), accepts full hkup units only, 100 full hkups (30/50 amps), seasonal sites, cable, laundry, controlled access. **REC:** heated pool, hot tub, shuffleboard. Pet restrict (S/B/Q). Partial handicap access. No tents, eco-friendly. 2021 rates: $65 to $79.
(951)925-2515 Lat: 33.74508, Lon: -116.99798
2750 W Acacia Ave, Hemet, CA 92545
casadelsolrvpark.com
See ad this page

GOLDEN VILLAGE PALMS RV RESORT - SUNLAND **Ratings: 10/10★/9.5** (RV Resort) Avail: 870 full hkups (30/50 amps). 2021 rates: $65 to $90. (888)474-8519, 3600 W Florida Ave, Hemet, CA 92545

HERALD — D3 *Sacramento*

RANCHO SECO RECREATIONAL AREA **Ratings: 7.5/7/8.5** (Campground) 21 Avail: 20 full hkups, 1 W, 1 E (20/30 amps). 2021 rates: $30 to $40. (209)748-2318, 14440 Twin Cities Rd, Herald, CA 95638

HESPERIA — H4 *San Bernardino*

DESERT WILLOW RV RESORT (RV Park) (Seasonal Stay Only) Avail: 1 full hkups (30/50 amps). (760)949-0377, 12624 Main St, Hesperia, CA 92345

HESPERIA LAKE PARK (Public) From Jct of I-15 & Main St/Arrowhead Lake Rd, E 9.5 mi on Main St/Arrowhead Lake Rd (L). 53 Avail: 30 W, 30 E (20 amps). 2021 rates: $35 to $50. (760)244-5951

MOJAVE RIVER FORKS REGIONAL PARK
(Public) From Jct of I-15 & Phelan/Main St exit: Go 7 mi E on Main St, turns into Arrowhead Lake Rd, then 5-1/2 mi SE on Arrowhead Lake Rd to SR 173, then 1 mi E on SR 173 (R). Elev 3500 ft.**FAC:** paved/gravel rds. Avail: 25 gravel, 8 pull-thrus, (20x40), back-ins (20x40), 25 full hkups (15/30 amps), tent sites, dump, fire rings. **REC:** Silverwood Lake: fishing, kayaking/canoeing, boating nearby, rec open to public. Pets OK $. 14 day max stay. 2021 rates: $47.
(760)389-2322 Lat: 34.3301758, Lon: -117.267795
17891 CA Hwy 173, Hesperia, CA 92345
parks.sbcounty.gov/park/mojave-river-forks-regional-park
See ad page 96

HIDDEN VALLEY LAKE — D2 *Lake*

HIDDEN VALLEY LAKE RV PARK/CAMPGROUND **Ratings: 4.5/6.5/7** (RV Park) Avail: 18 full hkups (30/50 amps). 2021 rates: $44. (707)987-3138, 19234 Hidden Valley Lake Rd, Hidden Valley Lake, CA 95467

HOLLISTER — F2 *Santa Clara*

BOLADO PARK EVENT CENTER & CAMPGROUND (Public) From San Benito St and 4th St: Go 2 mi S to Union Rd, then 1-1/2 mi E to Airline Hwy, then 8 miles SE (R). 38 Avail: 30 full hkups, 8 W, 2 E (30/50 amps). 2021 rates: $35. (831)628-3421

CASA DE FRUTA RV PARK
good sam park
Ratings: 9.5/10★/8.5 (RV Park) From Jct of 4th St & San Benito St (Hwy 156B): Go 5 mi N to Jct of Hwy 156B & Hwy 156, then 3-1/2 mi N on Hwy 156 to Jct of Hwy 156 & Hwy 152 (Pacheco Pass Hwy), then 1-1/2 mi N on Hwy 152 to Casa de Fruta Pkwy Exit, then E to Frontage Rd, then 1/2 mi N on Frontage Rd (R).

CALIFORNIA'S DESTINATION LOCATION
Stay, play, dine, wine taste, swim, relax without leaving the property. Huge Farmer's Market, rides for kids, sweet shop, coffee shop & year round fun for the whole family. Close to Gilroy, Pinnacles, Hollister, and Monterey
FAC: paved rds. (250 spaces). Avail: 126 paved, 100 pull-thrus, (22x45), back-ins (24x46), mostly side by side hkups, 126 full hkups (30/50 amps), seasonal sites, WiFi @ sites, tent sites, rentals, dump, laundry, groc, LP gas, firewood, restaurant. **REC:** pool, wading pool, Pacheco Creek: boating nearby, playground. Pet restrict (Q) $. Partial handicap access, eco-friendly. 2021 rates: $50 to $60. ATM.
(408)842-9316 Lat: 36.99448, Lon: -121.37793
10031 Pacheco Pass Hwy, Hollister, CA 95023
www.casadefruta.com
See ad pages 100, 108

HOLLISTER HILLS SRVA (Public State Park) From town: Go 6 mi S on Cienega Rd. 125 Avail. 2021 rates: $10. (831)637-3874

Things to See and Do

CASA DE FRUTA FRUIT STAND California fresh fruit, dried fruit & nuts, local vegetables, gift packs and mail order. Partial handicap access. RV accessible. Restrooms. Food. Hours: 7am to 9pm.
(408)842-9316 Lat: 36.98862, Lon: -121.38252
10021 Pacheco Pass Hwy, Hollister, CA 95023
www.casadefruta.com/visit/fruitstands.php
See ad pages 100, 108

CASA DE FRUTA PLAZA 24-Hour Chevron Plaza & Casa de Burrito Food Mart Partial handicap access. RV accessible. Restrooms. Food. Hours: Gas 24 Hr/Casa de Burrito 10am-8pm. ATM.
(408)842-9316 Lat: 36.98862, Lon: -121.38252
10021 Pacheco Pass Hwy, Hollister, CA 95023
www.casadefruta.com
See ad page 108

CASA DE FRUTA RESTAURANT & BAKERY Open 24 Hours featuring Kobe burgers, char-broiled steaks and homemade desserts. Partial handicap access. RV accessible. Restrooms. Food. Hours: Open 24 Hrs..
(408)842-9316 Lat: 36.98862, Lon: -121.38252
10021 Pacheco Pass Hwy, Hollister, CA 95023
www.casadefruta.com/visit/restaurant.php
See ad pages 100, 108

CASA DE FRUTA SWEET SHOP & COFFEE BAR Fresh baked pastries, espresso bar, homemade pies, ice cream and gelato with mix-ins, fudge, chocolates and gift items. Partial handicap access. RV accessible. Restrooms. Food. Hours: 7am to 7pm.
(408)842-9316 Lat: 36.99448, Lon: -121.37793
10021 Pacheco Pass Hwy, Hollister, CA 95023
www.casadefruta.com
See ad pages 100, 108

CASA DE FRUTA WINE & DELI Wine tasting room, gourmet sandwiches, award-winning wines, deli trays. Partial handicap access. RV accessible. Restrooms. Food. Hours: 8:30am to 7pm.
(408)842-9316 Lat: 36.98862, Lon: -121.38252
10021 Pacheco Pass Hwy, Hollister, CA 95023
www.casadefruta.com
See ad pages 100, 108

HORNBROOK — A2 *Siskiyou*

KLAMATH RANCH RESORT / BLUE HERON RV PARK **Ratings: 7/9★/9.5** (RV Park) Avail: 27 full hkups (30/50 amps). 2021 rates: $65 to $70. (530)475-3270, 6930 Copco, Hornbrook, CA 96044

HUNTINGTON BEACH — O3 *Orange*

SUNSET VISTA RV PARK (Public) From jct I-405 & Hwy 39: Go 5-1/2 mi S on Hwy 39, then 3/4 mi NE on Pacific Coast Hwy (Hwy 1). 46 Avail: 46 W, 46 E. 2021 rates: $70. Oct 01 to May 31. (714)536-5286

WATERFRONT RV PARK
good sam park
Ratings: 8.5/UI/6 (RV Park) From Jct of Pacific Coast Hwy & Hwy 39/Beach Blvd, S 0.5 mi on Pacific Coast Hwy to Newland St, E 100 ft (L).

BY THE OCEAN - RELAX OR GET ACTIVE!
Day trips to Disneyland, California Adventure, Knott's Berry Farm, day trips to Catalina. Enjoy nearby dining, shopping and entertainment. Stroll down the Huntington Beach Pier then relax on the beach.
FAC: paved rds. (96 spaces). Avail: 76 paved, patios, 29 pull-thrus, (20x50), back-ins (20x50), 76 full hkups (30/50 amps), seasonal sites, cable, WiFi, laundry. **REC:** heated pool, hot tub, boating nearby. Pet restrict (B/Q). Partial handicap access. No tents. 2021 rates: $70 to $135.
(714)536-8316 Lat: 33.64492, Lon: -117.98083
21871 Newland St, Huntington Beach, CA 92646
hometownamerica.com/WaterFront
See ad opposite page

IDYLLWILD — J5 *Riverside*

IDYLLWILD COUNTY PARK (Public) From Jct o SR-243 & Riverside Cnty Playground, W 0.5 mi o Riverside Cnty Playground (E). 88 Avail. 2021 rates $20. (951)659-2656

IDYLLWILD RV RESORT
good sam park
Ratings: 8/8.5/8 (RV Park) 200 Avai 36 full hkups, 164 W, 164 E (30 amps 2021 rates: $59 to $77. (888)563-704C 24400 Canyon Trail , Idyllwild, CA 9254

↑ MOUNT SAN JACINTO/IDYLLWILD (Public State Park) From Jct of I-215 & I-10 (exit 40A), E 21 mi on I-10 to SR-243 (8th St, exit 100), S 28 mi (R). Avail: 3 full hkups (20 amps). 2021 rates: $20 to $45. (951)659-2607

↑ MOUNT SAN JACINTO/STONE CREEK (Public State Park) From town, N 6 mi on State Hwy 243 (R). 50 Avail: Pit toilets. 2021 rates: $15 to $20. (951)659-2607

INDEPENDENCE — F4 *Inyo*

↑ GOODALE CREEK (BLM) (Public Corps) From town, N 16 mi on US-395 to Aberdeen Cut-off Rd, W 2 mi (R). 43 Avail: Pit toilets. 2021 rates: $5. Apr 15 to Nov 30. (760)872-5000

← INDEPENDENCE CREEK (Public) From Jct of US-395 & Market St, W 0.5 mi on Market St to Creek Rd, 2.5 mi (R). 25 Avail: Pit toilets. 2021 rates: $14. (760)878-0272

↑ TABOOSE CREEK COUNTY PARK (Public) From Jct of US-395 & Taboose Creek Rd (14 mi N of Independence), W 2.5 mi on Taboose Creek Rd (L). 35 Avail: Pit toilets. 2021 rates: $14. (760)878-0272

INDIO — J5 *Riverside*

↘ **INDIAN WATERS RV RESORT & COTTAGES**
good sam park
Ratings: 10/10★/10 (RV Resort) From Jct of I-10 & Golf Center Pky (Exit 144): Go SW 0.9 mi on Golf Center Pkwy to Hwy 111, then W 0.3 mi to Jackson St, then S 0.7 mi (L).

PALM SPRINGS AREA BEST RESORT VALUE
Top Rated Resort 10/10/10! Total renovation with cottages, 2nd pool, lighted pickleball courts, new fitness room, billiard room, office area, dining area and lounge/computer center. Stay for a day or a season.
FAC: paved rds. (265 spaces). Avail: 115 paved, 15 pull-thrus, (30x60), back-ins (35x48), accepts full hkup units only, 115 full hkups (30/50 amps), seasonal sites, WiFi @ sites, rentals, dump, laundry, controlled access. **REC:** heated pool, hot tub, pond. Pets OK. Partial handicap access. No tents. Big rig sites, eco-friendly. 2021 rates: $25 to $92, Military discount.
(760)342-8100 Lat: 33.70674, Lon: -116.21637
47202 Jackson St, Indio, CA 92201
indianwatersrvresort.com
See ad page 111

← INDIAN WELLS RV RESORT **Ratings: 10/9★/9** (RV Park) Avail: 179 full hkups (30/50 amps). 2021 rates: $59 to $97. (760)347-0895, 47-340 Jefferson Street, Indio, CA 92201

↓ JOSHUA TREE/COTTONWOOD (Public National Park) From Jct of I-10 & Joshua Tree Park exit, N 7 mi (R). Entrance fee required. 62 Avail. 2021 rates: $20. (760)367-7511

← **MOTORCOACH COUNTRY CLUB**
Ratings: 10/10★/10 (Condo Park) From Jct of I-10 & Jefferson St (Exit 139), S 3 mi on Jefferson St to Ave 48, E 0.5 mi (R) Note: Min.length of Motorhome - 30 ft. **FAC:** paved rds. (400 spaces). Avail: 100 paved, patios, back-ins (35x63), accepts full hkup units only, 100 full hkups (30/50 amps), WiFi @ sites, laundry, restaurant, controlled access. **REC:** heated pool, wading pool, hot tub, Waterway: boating nearby, golf. Pet restrict (Q). Partial handicap access. No tents. Big rig sites, No Class B/C, 30 day max stay, eco-friendly. 2021 rates: $139 to $236.
(888)277-0789 Lat: 33.69980, Lon: -116.26005
80501 Avenue 48, Indio, CA 92201
www.motorcoachcountryclub.com
See ad page 112

← OUTDOOR RESORT INDIO **Ratings: 10/9.5★/10** (Condo Park) Avail: 37 full hkups (50 amps). 2021 rates: $110 to $180. (800)892-2992, 80394 Avenue 48, Indio, CA 92201

↑ **SHADOW HILLS RV RESORT**
good sam park
Ratings: 10/10★/9 (RV Park) From Jct of I-10 & Jefferson St (Exit 139), N 0.25 mi on Jefferson St (L). **FAC:** paved rds. Avail: 100 paved, patios, 1 pull-thrus, (25x96), back-ins (28x45), 100 full hkups (30/50 amps), cable, WiFi @ sites, tent sites, rentals, dump, laundry, LP gas, controlled access. **REC:** heated pool, hot tub, pond, shuffleboard. Pet restrict (B/Q) $. Partial handicap access, eco-friendly. 2021 rates: $45 to $85, Military discount.
(760)360-4040 Lat: 33.75423, Lon: -116.27004
40655 Jefferson Street, Indio, CA 92203
www.shadowhillsrvresort.com
See ad page 112

Show Your Good Sam Membership Card!

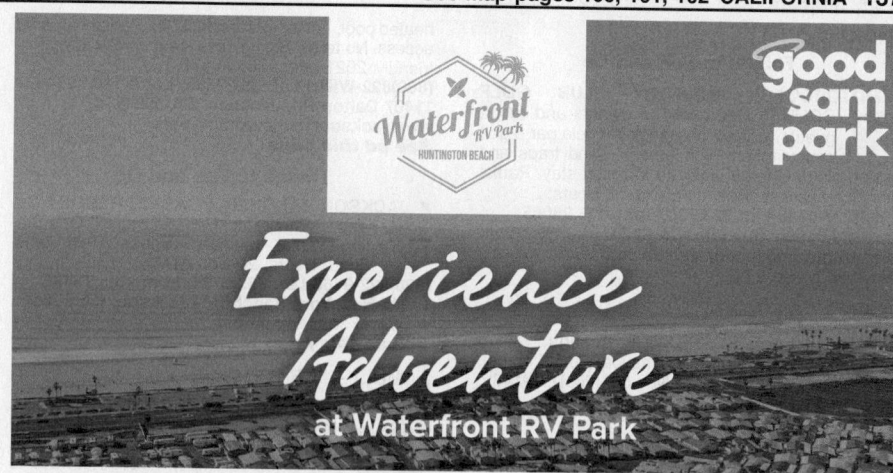

CA

INDIO (CONT)

Things to See and Do

MOTORCOACH COUNTRY CLUB GOLF COURSE Open only to owners and resort guests, private, challenging 9 hole par 3 golf course offers lush greens, sand traps and water. Note: Charge included in resort stay. Partial handicap access. Restrooms. Food. Hours: .
(888)277-0789 Lat: 33.6998, Lon: -116.26005
80501 Avenue 48, Indio, CA 92201
www.motorcoachcountryclub.com
See ad page 112

IONE — D3 *Amador*

PARDEE LAKE RECREATION **Ratings: 7.5/7/8** (Campground) Avail: 12 full hkups (30/50 amps). 2021 rates: $40. Feb 17 to Nov 06. (209)772-1472, 4900 Stony Creek Rd, Ione, CA 95640

ISLETON — D3 *Sacramento*

KO-KET RESORT **Ratings: 7.5/9.5★/8** (RV Resort) Avail: 19 full hkups (30/50 amps). 2021 rates: $56 to $68. (916)776-1488, 14174 Isleton Rd, Isleton, CA 95641

VIEIRA'S RESORT MHP **Ratings: 6.5/8/7.5** (Campground) 47 Avail: 24 full hkups, 23 W, 23 E (30/50 amps). 2021 rates: $52 to $55. (916)777-6661, 15476 State Hwy 160, Isleton, CA 95641

JACKSON — D3 *Amador*

JACKSON RANCHERIA RV PARK
Ratings: 10/10★/10 (RV Resort) From Jct of Hwy 49 & Hwy 88 (in Jackson), E 2.5 mi on Hwy 88 to Dalton Rd, N 0.9 mi (L).

STAY AND PLAY AT JACKSON RANCHERIA
Northern CA's best RV Park. Located in a beautiful forest setting, minutes from the casino as well as the Historic Mother Lode Gold and Wine Country. Enjoy free WI-FI, a clubhouse, pool & spas, pet park, outdoor games & more!

FAC: paved rds. Avail: 100 paved, 30 pull-thrus, (35x60), back-ins (35x45), accepts full hkup units only, 100 full hkups (30/50 amps), cable, WiFi @ sites, dump, laundry, groc, LP gas, restaurant. **REC:** heated pool, hot tub. Pet restrict (Q). Partial handicap access. No tents. Big rig sites, 14 day max stay, eco-friendly. 2021 rates: $65 to $75.
(800)822-WINN Lat: 38.37568, Lon: -120.73648
11407 Dalton Rd, Jackson, CA 95642
www.jacksoncasino.com/rv-park
See ad this page

Things to See and Do

JACKSON RANCHERIA CASINO RESORT Casino, Restaurants, General Store & Gas Station Partial handicap access. Restrooms. Food. Hours: 24 Hrs. ATM.
(800)822-9466 Lat: 38.38734, Lon: -120.73703
12222 New York Ranch Rd, Jackson, CA 95642
www.jacksoncasino.com
See ad this page

JAMUL — K5 *San Diego*

PIO PICO RV RESORT & CAMPGROUND
Ratings: 8/8.5★/7.5 (Membership Park) 476 Avail: 319 full hkups, 157 W, 157 E (30/50 amps). 2021 rates: $62 to $84. (888)563-7040, 14615 Otay Lakes Rd, Jamul, CA 91935

JENNER — D2 *Sonoma*

FORT ROSS STATE HISTORIC PARK (Public State Park) From town: Go 10 mi N on Hwy 1. Dirt road access. 20 Avail. 2021 rates: $25. (707)847-3286

SALT POINT (Public State Park) From town: Go 20 mi N on Hwy-1. 109 Avail. 2021 rates: $35. (707)847-3221

STILLWATER COVE REGIONAL PARK (Public) From town, N 16 mi on Hwy 1 (R). 23 Avail. 2021 rates: $32. (707)847-3245

JOSHUA TREE NATIONAL PARK — J5 *San Bernardino*

JOSHUA TREE/INDIAN COVE (Public National Park) From I-10 to Hwy 62, E 39 mi to Indian Cove Rd (7 mi W of Twentynine Palms), S 3 mi (E). 101 Avail. 2021 rates: $20. (760)362-4367

RV Park ratings you can rely on!

JOSHUA TREE/JUMBO ROCKS (Public National Park) From Jct of I-10 & Hwy 62, E 45 mi on Hwy 62 to Twentynine Palms, S 4 mi on Utah Trail (L). Sharp left, 8 mi uphill. Entrance fee required. 124 Avail: Pit toilets. 2021 rates: $15. (760)367-7511

TWENTYNINE PALMS RESORT RV PARK AND COTTAGES
(RV Park) (Rebuilding) Avail: 139 full hkups (30/50 amps). 2021 rates: $44 to $47. (800)874-4548, 4949 Desert Knoll Ave, Twentynine Palms, CA 92277

JULIAN — J5 *San Diego*

AGUA CALIENTE COUNTY PARK (Public) From Jct of Hwy S-2 & Agua Caliente Springs Rd, SE 0.5 mi on Agua Caliente Springs Rd (E). 140 Avail: 53 full hkups, 53 W, 53 E (20 amps). 2021 rates: $24 to $33. Sep 01 to May 31. (877)565-3600

CUYAMACA RANCHO/GREEN VALLEY (Public State Park) From Jct I-8 & Descanso Rd, NE 1 mi on Descanso Rd to Hwy 79, N 4 mi (L). 81 Avail. 2021 rates: $30. (760)765-0755

CUYAMACA RANCHO/PASO PICACHO (Public State Park) From Jct of I-8 & SR-79 (exit 40), N 15 mi on SR-79 (L). 85 Avail. 2021 rates: $30. (760)765-0755

LAKE CUYAMACA (Public) From Jct of I-8 & Hwy 79 (exit 40), N 12 mi on Hwy 79 (R). 29 Avail: 29 W, 29 E (30 amps). 2021 rates: $25 to $35. (760)765-0515

PINEZANITA RV PARK & CAMPGROUNDS **Ratings: 6.5/8/8.5** (Campground) 48 Avail: 48 W, 48 E (30/50 amps). 2021 rates: $43 to $48. (760)765-0429, 4446 Hwy 79, Julian, CA 92036

STAGECOACH TRAILS RV PARK **Ratings: 8/7.5/8** (RV Park) Avail: 239 full hkups (30/50 amps). 2021 rates: $51 to $69. (760)765-3765, 7878 Great Southern Overland Stage Rte of 1849(S-2), Julian, CA 92036

VALLECITO COUNTY PARK (Public) From Jct of Hwy S-2 & Agua Caliente Springs Rd, N 4.5 mi on S-2 (L). 44 Avail. 2021 rates: $22. Sep 01 to May 31. (877)565-3600

Like Us on Facebook.

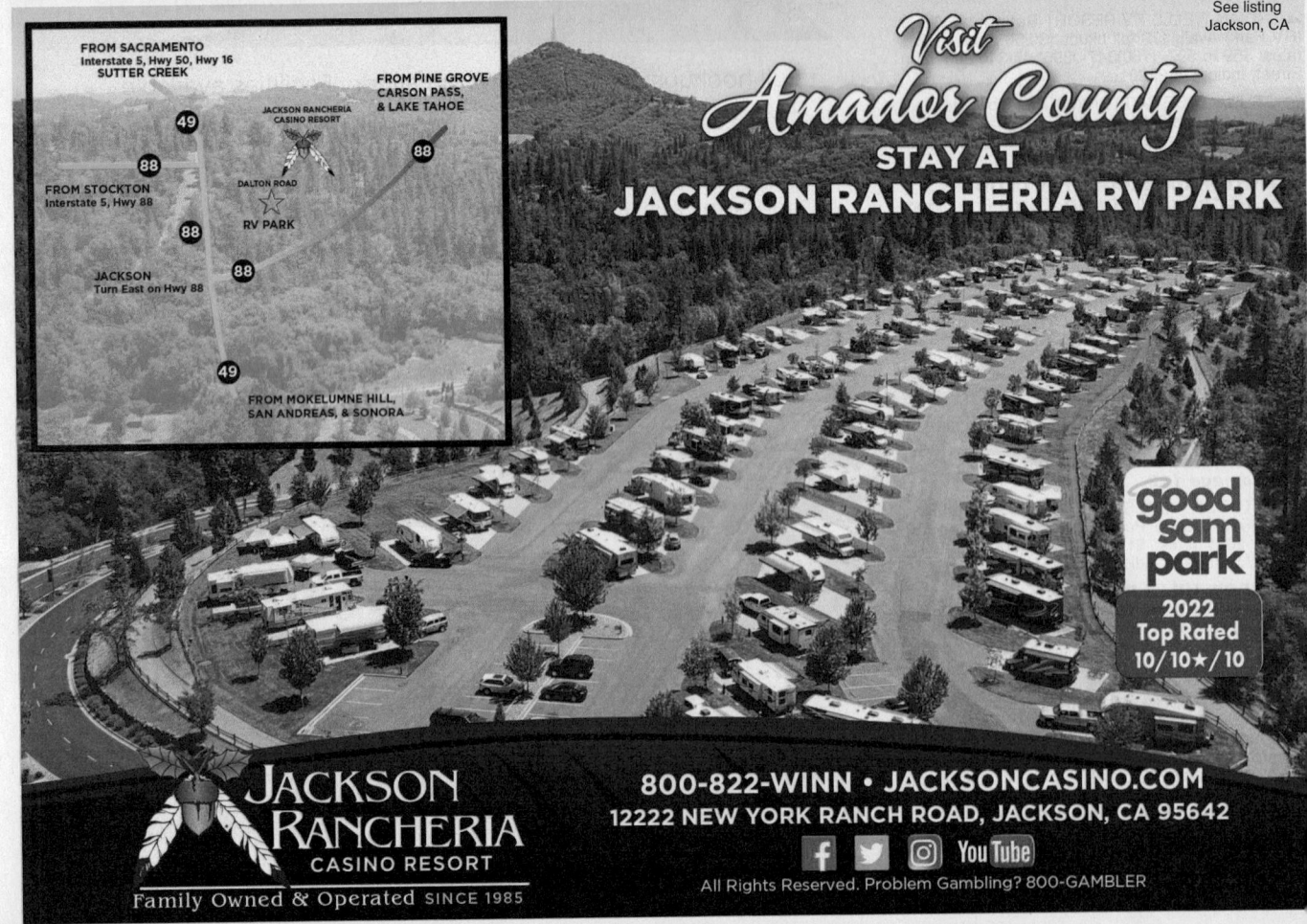

WILLIAM HEISE COUNTY PARK (Public) From Jct of Hwy 79 & Pine Hills Rd (1 mi W of town), S 2 mi on Pine Hills Rd to Frisius Rd, E 2 mi (R). Avail: 21 E (30 amps). 2021 rates: $24 to $29. (760)765-0650

JUNE LAKE — E4 *Mono*

GRANT LAKE RESORT **Ratings: 3.5/7.5/5.5** (Campground) 35 Avail: 35 W, 35 S. 2021 rates: $30. Apr 25 to Oct 15. (760)648-7964, 1 Grant Lake Rd, June Lake, CA 93529

PINE CLIFF RESORT **Ratings: 3/5.5/5.5** (Campground) 122 Avail: 107 full hkups, 15 W, 15 E (30 amps). 2021 rates: $34 to $41. Apr 15 to Oct 31. (760)648-7558, 1 Pine Cliff Rd, June Lake, CA 93529

SILVER LAKE RESORT **Ratings: 4.5/8/7.5** (RV Park) Avail: 78 full hkups (30 amps). 2021 rates: $46. Apr 29 to Oct 17. (760)648-7525, 6957 Hwy 158, June Lake, CA 93529

KELSEYVILLE — D2 *Lake*

CLEAR LAKE (Public State Park) From Jct of US-101 & SR-20 (Exit 555B), E 13 mi on SR-20 to SR-29, S 8 mi to Soda Bay Rd, E 6 mi (L). 147 Avail. 2021 rates: $30 to $45. (707)279-2267

KERNVILLE — G4 *Kern*

CAMP KERNVILLE **Ratings: 6/6.5/7.5** (RV Area in MH Park) 49 Avail: 33 full hkups, 16 W, 16 E (30/50 amps). 2021 rates: $42 to $104. (760)376-1000, 24 Sirretta St, Kernville, CA 93238

FRANDY PARK CAMPGROUND
good sam park **Ratings: 5/9.5★/7.5** (Campground) 92 Avail: 33 W, 33 E (30/50 amps). 2021 rates: $45 to $115. (760)376-6483, 11252 Kernville Rd, Kernville, CA 93238

RIVERNOOK CAMPGROUND **Ratings: 7/8.5★/8.5** (Campground) 76 Avail: 29 full hkups, 45 W, 45 E (30/50 amps). 2021 rates: $55 to $60. (760)376-2705, 14001 Sierra Way, Kernville, CA 93238

KING CITY — F2 *Monterey*

CIUDAD DEL REY RV PARK & MOTEL
Ratings: 7.5/7.5/7 (RV Park) From Jct of US-101 & Wild Horse Rd exit: Go 100 ft W on Wild Horse Rd to Mesa Verde Rd, then 2/10 mi N on Mesa Verde Rd (L). **FAC:** paved rds. (38 spaces). Avail: 18 gravel, 5 pull-thrus, (22x50), back-ins (22x45), 18 full hkups (30/50 amps), seasonal sites, cable, WiFi @ sites, tent sites, rentals, shower$, dump, laundry, groc, LP gas, firewood, restaurant. **REC:** heated pool, playground. Pets OK $. eco-friendly. 2021 rates: $45 to $55, Military discount. ATM.
(831)385-4828 Lat: 36.188693, Lon: -121.075255
50620 Mesa Verde Rd, King City, CA 93930
See ad this page

SAN LORENZO COUNTY PARK (Public) From Jct of US-101 & Broadway exit, W (left at stoplight) 0.2 mi on Broadway (L). 98 Avail: 26 full hkups, 72 W, 71 E (20/30 amps). 2021 rates: $32 to $42. (831)755-4899

Things to See and Do

CIUDAD DEL REY STORE Convenience store with snacks, quick meals, local wines, beer, cookies, pastries, specialty items and memorabilia. Adjacent to RV park. RV accessible. Restrooms. Food. Hours: 6am to 7pm. ATM.
(831)385-4312 Lat: 36.188693, Lon: -121.075255
50640 Mesa Verde Rd, King City, CA 93930
See ad this page

WILDHORSE CAFE Cafe serving breakfast, lunch and dinner. Partial handicap access. RV accessible. Restrooms. Food. Hours: 6:30am to 8pm. ATM.
(831)385-4312 Lat: 36.188693, Lon: -121.075255
50630 Mesa Verde Rd, King City, CA 93930
www.mywildhorsecafe.com/home
See ad this page

KINGS CANYON NATIONAL PARK — F3 *Fresno*

KINGS CANYON/AZALEA (Public National Park) From N end of town, N 0.5 mi on SR-180 (L). 110 Avail. 2021 rates: $18. (559)565-3341

KINGS CANYON/CRYSTAL SPRINGS (Public National Park) From town, N 0.5 mi on Grant Grove Village (R). Big rigs not recommended. 36 Avail. 2021 rates: $18. (559)565-3341

KINGS CANYON/MORAINE (Public National Park) From Cedar Grove Ranger Station, E 1 mi on Hwy 180 (L). 121 Avail. 2021 rates: $18. (559)565-3341

KINGS CANYON/SENTINEL (Public National Park) At Cedar Grove Ranger Station on Hwy 180 (E). 82 Avail. 2021 rates: $22. May 10 to Nov 12. (559)565-3341

KINGS CANYON/SHEEP CREEK (Public National Park) From Cedar Grove Ranger Station, W 0.5 mi on Hwy 180 (R). 111 Avail. 2021 rates: $18. Jul 03 to Sep 04. (559)565-3341

KINGS CANYON/SUNSET (Public National Park) From Grant Grove Village, N 0.2 mi on Grant Grove Village Rd (L). 157 Avail. 2021 rates: $22. Jul 03 to Sep 04. (559)565-3341

KINGSBURG — F3 *Fresno*

KINGS RIVER RV RESORT Ratings: 7.5/8.5★/9 (RV Park) 55 Avail: 35 full hkups, 20 W (30/50 amps). 2021 rates: $59 to $200. (559)897-0351, 39700 Road 28, Kingsburg, CA 93631

RIVERLAND RV RESORT **Ratings: 6.5/5.5/5** (RV Park) 34 Avail: 14 full hkups, 20 W, 20 E (30/50 amps). 2021 rates: $42 to $75. (559)897-5166, 38743 Hwy 99, Kingsburg, CA 93631

KLAMATH — A1 *Del Norte*

CHINOOK RV RESORT **Ratings: 7.5/8/8.5** (RV Park) Avail: 70 full hkups (30/50 amps). 2021 rates: $35. (866)482-3511, 17465 Hwy 101 S, Klamath, CA 95548

GOLDEN BEAR RV PARK **Ratings: 7.5/7/7.5** (Campground) Avail: 54 full hkups (30/50 amps). 2021 rates: $45. (707)482-3333, 17581 Hwy 101 S, Klamath, CA 95548

KAMP KLAMATH RV PARK & CAMPGROUND
good sam park **Ratings: 8/8★/9.5** (Campground) 49 Avail: 40 full hkups, 9 W, 9 E (30/50 amps). 2021 rates: $48 to $55. (866)KLAMATH, 1661 W Klamath Beach Rd, Klamath, CA 95548

KLAMATH CAMPER CORRAL **Ratings: 9/10★/9.5** (Campground) Avail: 124 full hkups (30/50 amps). 2021 rates: $48 to $58. Apr 01 to Nov 01. (800)701-7275, 18151 Hwy 101, Klamath, CA 95548

KLAMATH RIVER RV PARK
good sam park **Ratings: 8.5/9.5★/9** (RV Park) Avail: 75 full hkups (30 amps). 2021 rates: $56.10 to $71.40. Apr 15 to Nov 01. (707)482-2091, 700 W Klamath Beach Rd, Klamath, CA 95548

MYSTIC FOREST RV PARK **Ratings: 8/9.5★/9** (RV Park) Avail: 28 full hkups (20/30 amps). 2021 rates: $38. (707)482-4901, 15875 US Hwy 101, Klamath, CA 95548

RIVERSIDE RV PARK **Ratings: 7/8★/7.5** (Campground) Avail: 45 full hkups (20/30 amps). 2021 rates: $40 to $45. May 01 to Sep 30. (707)482-1111, 17505 Hwy 101, Klamath, CA 95548

LA GRANGE — E3 *Stanislaus*

BARRETT COVE RECREATION AREA (Public) From Jct of Hwy 132 & Merced Falls Rd, S 3 mi on Merced Falls Rd to Ranchito Dr, E 1 mi (E). 249 Avail: 89 W, 89 E (30 amps). 2021 rates: $22 to $34. (209)354-2966

BLUE OAKS REC AREA (Public) From Jct of Hwy 132 & CR-J59 (La Grange Rd), N 8 mi on La Grange Rd to Bonds Flat Rd, S 1 mi (L). 34 Avail: 34 W, 34 E (20/30 amps). 2021 rates: $28 to $50. (209)852-2396

FLEMING MEADOWS REC AREA (Public) From Jct of Hwy 132 & CR-J59 (La Grange Rd), N 8 mi on CR-J59 to Bonds Flat Rd, S 3.2 mi (L). Avail: 96 full hkups (30 amps). 2021 rates: $28 to $50. (209)852-2396

LA HONDA — E2 *San Mateo*

PORTOLA REDWOODS (Public State Park) From Jct of Hwy 35 & Alpine Rd exit, W 3 mi on Alpine Rd to Portola State Park Rd, S 3 mi (E). Steep & winding rds to park. 53 Avail. 2021 rates: $35. (650)948-9098

LA MESA — K5 *San Diego*

SAN DIEGO RV RESORT - SUNLAND **Ratings: 10/9.5★/8** (RV Park) Avail: 72 full hkups (30/50 amps). 2021 rates: $70 to $150. (619)373-0877, 7407 Alvarado Rd, La Mesa, CA 91942

LA MIRADA — N3 *Los Angeles*

Travel Services

CAMPING WORLD OF LA MIRADA As the nation's largest retailer of RV supplies, accessories, services and new and used RVs, Camping World is committed to making your total RV experience better. **SERVICES:** RV, tire, RV appliance, staffed RV wash, restrooms. RV supplies, LP gas, RV accessible. Hours: 9am to 6pm.
(800)854-8422 Lat: 33.87504, Lon: -118.012642
14900 S Firestone Blvd, La Mirada, CA 90638
www.campingworld.com

LA QUINTA — J5 *Riverside*

LAKE CAHUILLA VETERANS REGIONAL PARK (Public) From Jct of I-10 & Monroe Ave (exit 142), S 7.5 mi on Monroe Ave to Ave 58, W 2.5 mi (R). 120 Avail: 55 full hkups, 10 W (20/50 amps). 2021 rates: $15 to $35. (760)564-4712

LAGUNITAS — E2 *Marin*

SAMUEL P TAYLOR (Public State Park) From Jct of US-101 & Sir Francis Drake Blvd exit (Exit 450B), W 16 mi on Sir Francis Drake Blvd (L); or From Jct of US-1 & Sir Francis Drake Blvd at Olema, E 6 mi on Sir Francis Drake Blvd (R). 59 Avail. 2021 rates: $35 to $50. (415)488-9897

LAKE ALMANOR — B3 *Plumas*

LAKE ALMANOR See also Chester, Mill Creek & Quincy.

LAKE ELSINORE — O5 *Riverside*

LAKE ELSINORE MARINA & RV RESORT **Ratings: 6/5/6** (Campground) Avail: 31 full hkups (30/50 amps). 2021 rates: $40 to $48. (800)328-6844, 32700 Riverside Drive, Lake Elsinore, CA 92530

LAUNCH POINTE RECREATION DESTINATION & RV PARK (Public) From Jct of US-91 & US-15 (Exit 96), S 15 mi on US-15 to Central St, S 3 mi (E). Avail: 200 full hkups (30/50 amps). 2021 rates: $60 to $240. (951)471-1212

LAKE ISABELLA — G4 *Kern*

LAKE ISABELLA RV RESORT **Ratings: 7.5/7.5/8** (RV Park) Avail: 24 full hkups (30/50 amps). 2021 rates: $37. (760)379-2046, 11936 Hwy 178, Lake Isabella, CA 93240

LAKE ISABELLA/KERN RIVER KOA **Ratings: 7/7/7.5** (Campground) 44 Avail: 35 full hkups, 9 W, 9 E (30/50 amps). 2021 rates: $42 to $51. (800)562-2085, 15627 Hwy 178, Weldon, CA 93283

LAKE MORENA VILLAGE — K5 *San Diego*

LAKE MORENA COUNTY PARK (Public) From San Diego, E 46 mi on I-8 to Buckman Spgs Rd (exit 51), S 4 mi to Oak Dr, W 3 mi to Lake Morena Dr (R). 86 Avail: 58 W, 58 E (30 amps). 2021 rates: $22 to $33. (877)565-3600

LAKE TAHOE — D3 *El Dorado*

LAKE TAHOE See also Arnold, Coloma, Emigrant Gap, Lotus, South Lake Tahoe & Truckee, CA; Carson City, Dayton, Gardnerville, Minden, Reno, Smith Valley, Sparks, Verdi, Yerington & Zephyr Cove, NV.

LAKEHEAD — B2 *Shasta*

ANTLERS RV PARK & CAMPGROUND **Ratings: 6/5/6.5** (Campground) Avail: 70 full hkups (30/50 amps). 2021 rates: $38.18 to $59.99. (800)642-6849, 20682 Antlers Rd, Lakehead, CA 96051

LAKEHEAD CAMPGROUND & RV PARK **Ratings: 6/5/7** (RV Park) Avail: 24 full hkups (30 amps). 2021 rates: $35. (530)238-8450, 20999 Antlers, Lakehead, CA 96051

LAKESHORE VILLA RV PARK **Ratings: 5.5/4.5/6** (RV Park) 62 Avail: 48 full hkups, 14 W, 14 E (30/50 amps). 2021 rates: $38 to $55. (530)238-8688, 20672 Lakeshore Dr, Lakehead, CA 96051

LAKEHEAD (CONT)

SHASTA LAKE RV RESORT & CAMPGROUND **Ratings: 7/4.5/6.5** (Campground) Avail: 50 full hkups (20/30 amps). 2021 rates: $46. (800)374-2782, 20433 Lakeshore Drive, Lakehead, CA 96051

LAKEPORT — D2 *Lake County*

KONOCTI VISTA RV PARK
good sam park **Ratings: 8.5/7.5★/7** (RV Park) From N Jct of SR-29 & SR-175 (Soda Bay Rd exit), NE 200 ft to S Main St/Soda Bay Rd, SE 1.7 mi on Soda Bay Rd to Mission Rancheria Rd, N 0.4 mi (E). **FAC:** paved rds. Avail: 74 paved, 32 pull-thrus, (15x42), back-ins (15x36), accepts full hkup units only, 74 full hkups (30/50 amps), cable, WiFi @ sites, dump, laundry, groc, restaurant. **REC:** pool, Clear Lake: marina, boating nearby, hunting nearby. Pets OK. No tents. Big rig sites, 28 day max stay, eco-friendly. 2021 rates: $40 to $45. ATM.
(707)262-1900 Lat: 39.01964, Lon: -122.88864
2755 Mission Rancheria Road, Lakeport, CA 95453
konocti-vista-casino.com
See ad this page

Things to See and Do

KONOCTI VISTA CASINO Casino, hotel, restaurant & marina. Partial handicap access. RV accessible. Restrooms. Food. Hours: 24 hours. ATM.
(707)262-1900 Lat: 39.0195, Lon: -122.88736
2755 Mission Rancheria Rd, Lakeport, CA 95453
www.kvcasino.com
See ad this page

LAKESIDE — K5 *San Diego*

LAKE JENNINGS (Public) From Jct of I-8 & Lake Jennings Park Rd, NW 0.3 mi on Lake Jennings Park Rd to Harritt Rd, N 0.4 mi to Bass Dr, E 0.7 mi (E). 52 Avail: 35 full hkups, 17 W, 17 E (20/50 amps). 2021 rates: $30 to $44. (619)390-1623

RANCHO LOS COCHES RV PARK
good sam park **Ratings: 10/10★/9.5** (RV Park) From jct I-8 & Los Coches Rd (Exit 22): Go 1/2 mi N on Los Coches Rd, stay in right lane, then 1/2 mi E on Hwy 8 Bus (L) Do not use GPS. **FAC:** paved rds. (135 spaces). Avail: 49 all weather, patios, 2 pull-thrus, (22x42), back-ins (20x40), 49 full hkups (30/50 amps), seasonal sites, cable, WiFi @ sites, tent sites, dump, laundry. **REC:** heated pool, hot tub, Los Coches Creek: boating nearby. Pet restrict (B/Q). Partial handicap access, eco-friendly. 2021 rates: $63 to $93, Military discount.
(800)630-0448 Lat: 32.83638, Lon: -116.90037
13468 Hwy 8 Business, Lakeside, CA 92040
RanchoLosCochesRV.com
See ad page 114

LANCASTER — H4 *Los Angeles*

ANTELOPE VALLEY FAIRGROUNDS RV PARK
(Public) From Jct of Hwy 14 & Ave H: Go 3/4 mi W on Ave H to 30th St W, then 1/2 mi N to Ave G8, then 1/4 mi E to Gate 5 (R). **FAC:** paved rds. (85 spaces). Avail: 55 paved, 22 pull-thrus, (22x60), back-ins (22x50), 55 full hkups (30/50 amps), seasonal sites, WiFi @ sites, . **REC:** rec open to public. Pets OK. No tents, 21 day max stay. 2021 rates: $40 to $45.
(661)206-0427 Lat: 34.725613, Lon: -118.176721
2551 W Ave G-8 Gate-5, Lancaster, CA 93536
avfair.com
See ad this page

CRESTVIEW MH COMMUNITY (RV Spaces) Avail: 10 full hkups (30/50 amps). 2021 rates: $30. (661)942-3487, 1449 East Ave I, Lancaster, CA 93535

MILITARY PARK EDWARDS FAMCAMP (EDWARDS AFB) (Public) From jct Hwy 14 & Edwards AFB exit/Rosamond Blvd: Go 18 mi E on Rosamond Blvd, follow signs. Avail: 25 full hkups (30/50 amps). 2021 rates: $30. (661)275-2267

SADDLEBACK BUTTE (Public State Park) From the Jct of Hwy 14 & Ave J (Exit 43), E 20 mi on East Ave J (R). 37 Avail. 2021 rates: $20. (661)946-6092

THE CALIFORNIAN RV RESORT
good sam park **Ratings: 10/9.5★/9** (RV Park) N-bnd: From jct Hwy 14 & Soledad Canyon Rd (Exit 27): Go 3/4 mi W on Sierra Hwy (R) or S-bnd: From jct Hwy 14 & Soledad Canyon Rd (Exit 27): Go 1/4 mi E on Sierra Hwy (L). Elev 3079 ft.**FAC:** paved rds. (193 spaces). Avail: 51 paved, 51 pull-thrus, (25x60), 51 full hkups (30/50 amps), seasonal sites, WiFi @ sites, laundry, LP gas, controlled access. **REC:** heated pool, hot tub. Pet restrict (B/Q). Partial handicap access. No tents. Big rig sites, eco-friendly. 2021 rates: $65, Military discount.
(888)787-8386 Lat: 34.486545, Lon: -118.143256
1535 Sierra Hwy, Acton, CA 93510
calrv.com
See primary listing at Acton and ad this page

Things to See and Do

ANTELOPE VALLEY FAIRGROUNDS Antelope Valley Fairgrounds is a multi-purpose, year-round facility and event venue used for education and entertainment including buildings of various sizes, an outdoor pavilion, a waterfall display and BBQ areas. Partial handicap access. RV accessible. Restrooms. Food. Hours: 9am to 5pm. ATM.
(661)948-6060 Lat: 34.725613, Lon: -118.176721
2551 West Ave H Ste 102, Lancaster, CA 93536
www.avfair.com
See ad this page

LATHROP — E3 *San Joaquin*

DOS REIS REGIONAL PARK (Public) From Jct of I-5 & Lathrop Rd, (Exit 463) Lathrop Rd onto Manthey Rd (frntg rd), N 0.3 mi to Dos Reis Rd, W 1.4 mi (R). Avail: 26 full hkups (20/30 amps). 2021 rates: $25. (209)953-8800

LEE VINING — E4 *Mono*

LUNDY CANYON CAMPGROUND (Public) From Jct of US-395 & SR-120, W 3.5 mi on SR-120 (E). Avail: 36 full hkups (30/50 amps). 2021 rates: $16. Apr 15 to Oct 15. (760)932-5231

MONO VISTA RV PARK **Ratings: 6.5/9★/7.5** (RV Park) 54 Avail: 26 full hkups, 28 W, 28 E (30/50 amps). 2021 rates: $35 to $41. Apr 01 to Oct 31. (760)647-6401, 57 Beaver's Ln, Lee Vining, CA 93541

LEGGETT — C1 *Mendocino*

REDWOODS RIVER RESORT & CAMPGROUND **Ratings: 8/7/8.5** (RV Park) 38 Avail: 31 full hkups, 7 W, 7 E (30/50 amps). 2021 rates: $36 to $55. (707)925-6249, 75000 Hwy 101, Leggett, CA 95585

STANDISH-HICKEY SRA (Public State Park) From town, N 1.5 mi on Hwy 101 (L). 162 Avail. 2021 rates: $35. (707)925-6482

LEMON COVE — F3 *Tulare*

KAWEAH LAKE - COE/HORSE CREEK CAMPGROUND (Public Corps) From town, E 6 mi on SR-198 (L). 80 Avail. 2021 rates: $20 to $40. (559)597-2301

LEMON COVE VILLAGE RV PARK
good sam park **Ratings: 9/9.5★/9.5** (RV Park) From US Hwy 99 and CA-198: Go 21 miles E on CA-198 (L). **FAC:** gravel rds. Avail: 32 gravel, 32 pull-thrus, (28x50), 32 full hkups (30/50 amps), WiFi @ sites, tent sites, dump, laundry, groc, fire rings, firewood. **REC:** pool, boating nearby, playground. Pet restrict (B). Partial handicap access, eco-friendly. 2021 rates: $55 to $60.
(559)370-4152 Lat: 36.369458, Lon: -119.032715
32075 Sierra Dr, Lemon Cove, CA 93244
www.lemoncovevillagervpark.com
See ad this page

Had a great stay? Let us know by emailing us Parks@goodsam.com

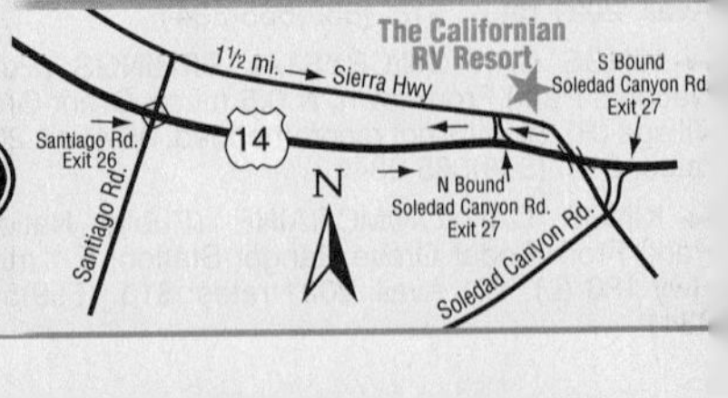

LEMOORE — F3 *Kings*

MILITARY PARK LEMOORE RV PARK AND CAMPGROUND (LEMOORE NAS) (Public) From jct 99 & 198: Go 19 mi E on 198 to main gate, right at traffic light, 1/2 mi to Ranger Ave, left 1/4 mi (E). Avail: 18 full hkups (30/50 amps). 2021 rates: $24. (559)998-0183

LEWISTON — B2 *Trinity*

OLD LEWISTON BRIDGE RV RESORT **Ratings: 7.5/9★/9.5** (Campground) Avail: 27 full hkups (20/30 amps). 2021 rates: $32. (530)778-3894, 8460 Rush Creek Rd, Lewiston, CA 96052

LIKELY — A3 *Lassen*

LIKELY PLACE GOLF COURSE AND RESORT **Ratings: 8.5/9★/8.5** (RV Park) 52 Avail: 42 full hkups, 10 W, 10 E (30/50 amps). 2021 rates: $42. (530)233-4466, 1255 Likely Place, Likely, CA 96116

LIVERMORE — E2 *Alameda*

DEL VALLE FAMILY CAMPGROUND (Public) From Jct of Hwy 580 & N Livermore Ave exit (Exit 52), S 1.5 mi on Livermore Ave through town (becomes Tesla Rd outside of town) to Mines Rd, S 3.5 mi to Del Valle Rd, S 4 mi (E). Avail: 21 full hkups (30/50 amps). 2021 rates: $35 to $50. (888)327-2757

LODI — E3 *San Joaquin*

FLAG CITY RV RESORT

good sam park

Ratings: 10/10★/8.5 (RV Park) From Jct of I-5 & SR 12, E 0.2 mi on SR 12 to Star St, S 500 ft to Banner St, E 0.1 mi (R). **FAC:** paved rds. (180 spaces). Avail: 166 paved, patios, 135 pull-thrus, (28x60), back-ins (20x40), 166 full hkups (30/50 amps), seasonal sites, cable, WiFi @ sites, laundry, groc, LP gas. **REC:** pool, hot tub, boating nearby, hunting nearby. Pet restrict (B/Q) $. Partial handicap access. No tents, Age restrict may apply. Big rig sites, eco-friendly. 2021 rates: $65, Military discount.
(866)371-4855 Lat: 38.11420, Lon: -121.38995
6120 Banner St, Lodi, CA 95242
www.flagcityrvresort.com
See ad page 150

We rate what RVers consider important.

JELLYSTONE PARK CAMP-RESORT AT TOWER PARK **Ratings: 9/10★/10** (Campground) Avail: 210 full hkups (30/50 amps). 2021 rates: $65 to $200. (209)369-1041, 14900 W Hwy 12, Lodi, CA 95242

WESTGATE LANDING REGIONAL PARK (Public) From jct I-5 & Hwy 12 (exit 485): Go 5 mi W on Hwy 12, then 1 mi N. 14 Avail. 2021 rates: $20. (209)953-8800

LOMA MAR — E2 *San Mateo*

SAN MATEO COUNTY MEMORIAL PARK (Public) From Jct of Hwy 1 & Pescadero Rd, E 9.5 mi on Pescadero Rd (R). 158 Avail. 2021 rates: $25 to $4,500. (650)879-0238

LOMPOC — H2 *Santa Barbara*

JALAMA BEACH CAMPGROUND

(Public) From Jct of Hwy 246 & Hwy 1, S 4.2 mi on Hwy 1 to Jalama Rd, SW 14 mi (E). **FAC:** paved rds. 102 Avail: 33 paved, 69 dirt, 9 pull-thrus, (20x45), back-ins (20x45), 29 E (30 amps), tent sites, rentals, shower$, dump, groc, firewood. **REC:** Pacific Ocean: swim, fishing, playground. Pets OK $. Partial handicap access, 14 day max stay. 2021 rates: $30 to $50.
(805)736-6316 Lat: 34.50980, Lon: -120.50073
9999 Jalama Road, Lompoc, CA 93436
www.countyofsb.org/parks/jalama.sbc
See ad page 118

MILITARY PARK VANDENBERG FAMCAMP (VANDENBERG AFB) (Public) From jct US-101 & CA-1: Go W on CA-1 (E). Avail: 49 full hkups (20/50 amps). 2021 rates: $26 to $30. (805)606-8579

RIVER PARK (CITY PARK) (Public) From Jct of Hwys 1 & 246: Go 1/2 mi E on Hwy 246 (L). Avail: 35 full hkups (30 amps). 2021 rates: $30. (805)875-8034

LONE PINE — F4 *Inyo*

BOULDER CREEK RV RESORT

good sam park

Ratings: 9.5/9★/9 (RV Park) From Jct of US-395 & SR-136: Go 2.6 mi S on US-395 (L). Elev 3730 ft.

Join in the fun. Like us on FACEBOOK!

GREAT FOR OUTDOOR ENTHUSIASTS
Fish, Boat, Hike, 4-Wheel, Trail Ride, Star Gaze. Horse Corral, Dog Park & Dog Day Care. Mt Whitney, Ghost Towns, Fish Hatchery, Alabama Hills, Movie Locations, Film Museum, Manzanar. All while staying in a beautiful Park.

FAC: paved rds. (109 spaces). Avail: 78 gravel, 64 pull-thrus, (33x60), back-ins (25x50), 78 full hkups (30/50 amps), seasonal sites, WiFi @ sites, tent sites, rentals, laundry, groc, LP gas, fire rings, firewood. **REC:** heated pool, hot tub, boating nearby, playground, hunting nearby. Pets OK. Partial handicap access. Big rig sites, 28 day max stay, eco-friendly. 2021 rates: $60, Military discount.
(760)876-4243 Lat: 36.54303, Lon: -118.04702
2550 S Hwy 395, Lone Pine, CA 93545
www.bouldercreekrvresort.com
See ad this page

DIAZ LAKE (Public) From Jct of US-395 & SR-136, S 1 mi on US-395 (R). 200 Avail. 2021 rates: $14. (760)873-5577

PORTAGEE JOE COUNTY PARK (Public) From Jct of US-395 & Whitney Portal Rd, W 0.5 mi on Whitney Portal Rd to Tuttle Creek Rd, turn left (R). 20 Avail: Pit toilets. 2021 rates: $14. (760)878-5564

TUTTLE CREEK (BLM) (Public Corps) From Jct of I-395 & Whitney Portal Rd, W 3.5 mi on Whitney Portal Rd to Horseshoe Meadows Rd, S 1.5 mi (E). 83 Avail: Pit toilets. 2021 rates: $8. (760)872-5000

LONG BEACH — N2 *Los Angeles*

LONG BEACH See also Anaheim, Huntington Beach, Newport Beach & Orange.

ARBOR MOBILE VILLAGE

good sam park

Ratings: 6/8/5 (RV Park) Avail: 10 full hkups (30/50 amps). 2021 rates: $45 to $55. (562)422-3666, 300 E Arbor St, Long Beach, CA 90805

LOOMIS — D3 *Placer*

LOOMIS RV PARK **Ratings: 6.5/6.5/6.5** (Campground) Avail: 14 full hkups (30/50 amps). 2021 rates: $59.40. (916)652-6737, 3945 Taylor Rd, Loomis, CA 95650

JOIN GoodSamRoadside.com

LOS ANGELES — M2 *Los Angeles*

A SPOTLIGHT Introducing Los Angeles' colorful attractions appearing at the front of this state section.

LOS ANGELES See also Anaheim, Long Beach, Northridge, Orange & Van Nuys.

CARAVAN MOBILE HOME PARK
(RV Spaces) From Jct of I-5 & I-10: Go E 12.6 mi on I-10 to I-605, N 5.6 mi to I-210, E 3 mi to exit 40 (Azusa Ave exit) S 0.3 mi on S Azusa Ave to W Gladstone St, W 0.4mi (L). **FAC:** paved rds. (120 spaces). Avail: 13 paved, no slide-outs, 5 pull-thrus, (12x36), back-ins (14x40), accepts full hkup units only, 13 full hkups (30/50 amps), seasonal sites, laundry. **REC:** pool, boating nearby. Pet restrict (S/B/Q). No tents. 2021 rates: $40. no cc.
(626)334-2306 Lat: 34.11406, Lon: -117.91439
600 W Gladstone St, Azusa, CA 91702
See primary listing at Azusa and ad this page

LOS BANOS — F2 *Merced*

SAN LUIS RESERVOIR SRA (Public State Park) From Jct of I-5 & Hwy 152 (Exit 403B), W 6 mi on Hwy 152, follow Basalt Area signs (L). 132 Avail: 132 W, 132 E. 2021 rates: $30 to $35. (209)826-1197

LOS MOLINOS — C2 *Tehama*

HUNTERS RESORT **Ratings: 5.5/7.5/7** (Campground) Avail: 10 full hkups (30/50 amps). 2021 rates: $40. (530)527-5293, 10675 Bryne Ave, Los Molinos, CA 96055

LOST HILLS — G3 *Kern*

LOST HILLS RV PARK **Ratings: 7/8/7** (Campground) Avail: 41 full hkups (30/50 amps). 2021 rates: $42.50 to $47.50. (661)797-2719, 14831 Warren Street, Lost Hills, CA 93249

LOTUS — D3 *El Dorado*

PONDEROSA RV RESORT
Ratings: 7.5/8/8 (Membership Park) Avail: 19 full hkups (30/50 amps). 2021 rates: $63 to $76. (888)563-7040, 7291 Hwy 49, Lotus, CA 95651

MALIBU — M1 *Los Angeles*

LEO CARRILLO (Public State Park) From town, N 13 mi on PCH 1 (R) Closed until further notice due to the damages caused by the wildfire. 135 Avail. 2021 rates: $35. (310)457-8143

MAMMOTH LAKES — E4 *Madera*

MAMMOTH LAKES See also June Lake & Lee Vining.

BROWN'S OWENS RIVER CAMPGROUND
Ratings: 3.5/8★/7.5 (Campground) From Jct of US-395 & Hwy 203 (Mammoth Lakes exit): Go 5-1/4 mi S on US-395 to Benton Crossing Rd, then 6-3/4 mi E on Benton Crossing Road (R). Elev 7000 ft.**FAC:** gravel rds. Avail: 92 grass, 11 pull-thrus, (30x50), back-ins (40x50), tent sites, shower$, groc, fire rings, firewood. **REC:** Owens River: fishing, boating nearby. Pets OK. Partial handicap access. 2021 rates: $35. May 01 to Sep 30.
(760)920-0975 Lat: 37.694685, Lon: -118.758601
6766 Benton Crossing Rd, Mammoth Lakes, CA 93546
brownscampgrounds.com
See ad page 128

CAMP HIGH SIERRA (Public) From Jct of SR-203/395 & Lake Mary Rd, N 1 mi on Lake Mary Rd (L). Caution: Winding, dirt road. 39 Avail: 9 W, 9 E (15 amps). 2021 rates: $30 to $40. May 25 to Sep 05. (800)626-6684

CROWLEY LAKE (BLM) (Public Corps) From Jct of US-395 & Crowley Lake Dr, N 5.5 mi (L). 47 Avail: Pit toilets. 2021 rates: $8. Apr 15 to Oct 31. (760)872-4881

MAMMOTH MOUNTAIN RV PARK **Ratings: 7.5/8.5/7** (RV Park) 128 Avail: 49 full hkups, 79 W, 79 E (30/50 amps). 2021 rates: $65 to $70. (760)934-3822, 2667 Main Street, Mammoth Lakes, CA 93546

MCGEE CREEK RV PARK **Ratings: 4/8.5★/8.5** (RV Park) 54 Avail: 35 full hkups, 10 W, 10 E (30/50 amps). 2021 rates: $40 to $49. Apr 23 to Oct 08. (760)935-4233, 110 McGee Creek Rd, Mammoth Lakes, CA 93546

MANCHESTER — D1 *Mendocino*

MANCHESTER (Public State Park) From town, N 1 mi on Hwy 1 to Kinny Rd, W 1 mi (R). 46 Avail: Pit toilets. 2021 rates: $35. (707)882-2463

MANCHESTER BEACH/MENDOCINO COAST KOA **Ratings: 8.5/9.5★/9.5** (Campground) 61 Avail: 28 full hkups, 33 W, 33 E (30/50 amps). 2021 rates: $65 to $80. (800)562-4188, 44300 Kinney Road, Manchester, CA 95459

MANTECA — E3 *San Joaquin*

CASWELL MEMORIAL PARK (Public State Park) From Jct of Hwy 99 & Austin Rd (Exit 240), S 6 mi on Austin Rd (E). 65 Avail. 2021 rates: $30. (209)599-3810

FRENCH CAMP RV PARK RESORT **Ratings: 9.5/9.5★/8.5** (RV Park) Avail: 53 full hkups (30/50 amps). 2021 rates: $49.50 to $59.50. (209)234-1544, 3919 E French Camp Rd, Manteca, CA 95336

TURTLE BEACH
Ratings: 6/8★/7.5 (Membership Park) 14 Avail: 10 full hkups, 4 W, 4 E (30/50 amps). 2021 rates: $58 to $62. (888)563-7040, 703 E Williamson Rd, Manteca, CA 95337

MARINA — F1 *Monterey*

MARINA DUNES RV RESORT
Ratings: 8.5/10★/9 (RV Park) 89 Avail: 85 full hkups, 4 W, 4 E (30/50 amps). 2021 rates: $70 to $89. (888)563-7040, 3330 Dunes Dr, Marina, CA 93933

MARIPOSA — E4 *Mariposa*

MARIPOSA FAIRGROUNDS (Public) From No. Jct of Hwys 140 & 49, S 1.5 mi on Hwy 49 (L). 200 Avail: 17 full hkups, 183 W, 183 E (20/30 amps). 2021 rates: $45. (209)966-2432

MARKLEEVILLE — D4 *Alpine*

GROVER HOT SPRINGS (Public State Park) From Jct of Hwy 89 & Hot Springs Rd, W 4 mi on Hot Springs Rd (R). 48 Avail. 2021 rates: $35. (530)694-2248

INDIAN CREEK (BLM) (Public Corps) From town: Go 4 mi S on Hwy 89, then 4 mi E on Airport Rd (L). 19 Avail. 2021 rates: $20 to $32. (702)885-6000

PG & E/CARSON PASS/LOWER BLUE LAKE (Public) From Jct of Hwys 89 & 88, W 2.5 mi on Hwy 88 to Blue Lakes Rd, S 12 mi (L). 16 Avail: Pit toilets. 2021 rates: $23 to $42. May 31 to Oct 15. (916)386-5164

PG & E/CARSON PASS/UPPER BLUE LAKE (Public) From Jct of Hwys 89 & 88, W 2.5 mi on Hwy 88 to Blue Lakes Rd, S 11 mi (L). 32 Avail: Pit toilets. 2021 rates: $21. May 31 to Oct 01. (916)386-5164

PG & E/CARSON PASS/UPPER BLUE LAKE DAM (Public) From Jct of Hwys 89 & 88, W 2.5 mi on Hwy 88 to Blue Lakes Rd, S 12 mi (R). 25 Avail: Pit toilets. 2021 rates: $21. May 30 to Oct 15. (916)386-5164

MARYSVILLE — D3 *Yuba*

MILITARY PARK BEALE FAMCAMP (BEALE AFB) (Public) From Marysville: Go 1 mi S on US-70 to N Beale Rd exit, then 6 mi E (E). Avail: 44 full hkups (30/50 amps). 2021 rates: $18 to $20. (530)634-3382

MCARTHUR — B3 *Lassen*

INTER-MOUNTAIN FAIR OF SHASTA COUNTY (Public) From Jct of SR-299 & CR-A19, E 0.1 mi on SR-299 to Grove St (L). Avail: 53 full hkups (30/50 amps). 2021 rates: $20 to $30. Apr 01 to Oct 31. (530)336-5694

LASSEN RV RESORT
Ratings: 10/9.5★/9 (RV Park) 44 Avail: 42 full hkups, 2 W, 2 E (30/50 amps). 2021 rates: $40 to $80. Apr 15 to Oct 31. (530)336-5657, 548-335 Old Hwy Rd, McArthur, CA 96056

MCCLOUD — A2 *Siskiyou*

MCCLOUD RV RESORT **Ratings: 6.5/8/9.5** (RV Park) 130 Avail: 106 full hkups, 24 W, 24 E (30/50 amps). 2021 rates: $51.15 to $60.50. (530)964-2252, 106 Squaw Valley, McCloud, CA 96057

MECCA — J5 *Riverside*

SALTON SEA SRA (Public State Park) From Jct of Hwys 195 & 111, S 11 mi on Hwy 111 (R). 149 Avail: (30 amps). 2021 rates: $20 to $30. (760)393-3052

MEEKS BAY — D4 *El Dorado*

D L BLISS (Public State Park) From Jct of SR-28 & SR-89, S 17 mi on SR-89 (L). 265 Avail. 2021 rates: $35 to $45. May 15 to Sep 15. (530)525-7277

EMERALD BAY (Public State Park) From Jct of 50 & SR-89, N 8 mi on SR-89 (R). 69 Avail. 2021 rates: $35. May 31 to Sep 30. (916)541-3030

MENDOCINO — C1 *Mendocino*

CASPAR BEACH RV PARK & CAMPGROUND **Ratings: 8/7.5/8.5** (Campground) 52 Avail: 40 full hkups, 12 W, 12 E (20/30 amps). 2021 rates: $51 to $68. (707)964-3306, 14441 PT Cabrillo Rd, Mendocino, CA 95460

RUSSIAN GULCH (Public State Park) From town, N 2 mi on Hwy 1 (L). 30 Avail. 2021 rates: $35. (707)937-5804

VAN DAMME (Public State Park) From town, S 3 mi on Hwy 1 (L). 74 Avail. 2021 rates: $25 to $45. (707)937-5804

MENIFEE — O6 *Riverside*

WILDERNESS LAKES RV RESORT
Ratings: 9/8.5/7.5 (Membership Park) Avail: 523 full hkups (30/50 amps). 2021 rates: $55. (888)563-7040, 30605 Briggs Rd, Menifee, CA 92584

MILL CREEK — B3 *Tehama*

THE VILLAGE AT CHILDS MEADOW **Ratings: 6/NA/7** (Campground) Avail: 22 full hkups (30/50 amps). 2021 rates: $35. May 01 to Oct 31. (530)595-3383, 41500 Highway 36 E, Mill Creek, CA 96061

MOJAVE — H4 *Kern*

RED ROCK CANYON (Public State Park) From town, NE 25 mi on Hwy 14 (L). 50 Avail: Pit toilets. 2021 rates: $25. (661)946-6092

MONTEREY — F1 *Monterey*

MONTEREY See also Big Sur, Carmel, Marina, Moss Landing, Salinas, San Juan Bautista & Watsonville.

COYOTE VALLEY RV RESORT
Ratings: 10/10★/10 (RV Resort) From Jct Del Monte Rd and Hwy 1: Go 12 miles NE on Hwy 1 to Hwy 156 then 18 miles W on Hwy 156 to Hwy 101 then 41 3/4 miles NE on Hwy 101 to Cochrane Rd (Exit 367) then 3/4 mi W on Cochrane Rd to Monterey Rd, then 4 mi N on Monterey Rd (R). **FAC:** paved rds. Avail: 197 paved, patios, back-ins (30x60), accepts full hkup units only, 197 full hkups (30/50 amps), WiFi @ sites, dump, laundry, groc, LP gas. **REC:** pool, hot tub, boating nearby. Pet restrict (B/Q) $. Partial handicap access. No tents. Big rig sites, eco-friendly. 2021 rates: $70 to $80.
(866)376-5500 Lat: 37.191388, Lon: -121.713097
9750 Monterey Rd, San Jose, CA 95037
www.coyotevalleyresort.com
See primary listing at San Jose and ad pages 106, 115, 154

MILITARY PARK MONTEREY PINES RV CAMPGROUND (NSA MONTEREY) (Public) From jct Hwy 1 & Casa Verde Way: turn left to Fairgrounds Rd, then W to Garden Rd, then S to park (L). 38 Avail: 30 full hkups, 8 S, 8 E (15/30 amps). 2021 rates: $30 to $42. (831)656-7563

MONTEREY COUNTY FAIR & EVENTS CENTER RV PARK (Public) From Jct of Hwy 1 & Casa Verde exit: Go 3/10 mi SE on Casa Verde to Fairground Rd, then 200 ft NE to Gate 6 (R). Avail: 56 full hkups (30/50 amps). 2021 rates: $65. (831)717-7167

VETERANS MEMORIAL PARK (CITY PARK) (Public) In town, from jct Pacific St & Jefferson Dr: Go 1 mi up narrow, winding Jefferson Dr. 40 Avail 2021 rates: $30. (831)646-3865

MORGAN HILL — F2 *Santa Clara*

MAPLE LEAF RV PARK **Ratings: 8.5/8.5/7** (RV Park) Avail: 62 full hkups (30/50 amps). 2021 rates $60. (408)776-1818, 15200 Monterey Rd, Morgan Hill, CA 95037

MORGAN HILL RV RESORT
good sam park **Ratings: 6.5/8.5★/8** (Membership Park) 320 Avail: 320 W, 320 E (30/50 amps). 2021 rates: $69 to $79. (888)563-7040, 12895 Uvas Rd, Morgan Hill, CA 95037

UVAS PINES RV PARK **Ratings: 7/7.5/9** (RV Park) 24 Avail: 20 full hkups, 4 W, 4 E (30/50 amps). 2021 rates: $60. (408)779-3417, 13210 Uvas Rd, Morgan Hill, CA 95037

MORRO BAY — G2 *San Luis Obispo*

BAY PINES TRAVEL TRAILER PARK
Ratings: 8/8.5★/8 (RV Park) From Hwy 1 & South Bay Blvd (Exit 277): Go 1/10 mi S to Quintana Rd, then 100 ft E on Quintana Rd (L). **FAC:** paved rds. (110 spaces). Avail: 10 gravel, back-ins (23x40), 10 full hkups (30 amps), seasonal sites, cable, WiFi @ sites, laundry. **REC:** heated pool, hot tub, boating nearby. Pet restrict (S/B/Q). No tents, eco-friendly. 2021 rates: $48.
(805)772-3223 Lat: 35.362443, Lon: -120.823693
1501 Quintana Rd, Morro Bay, CA 93442
www.baypinesrv.net
See ad page 121

CYPRESS RV & MOBILE HOME PARK
Ratings: 6/8.5★/8.5 (RV Park) N-bnd: From Jct of Hwy 1 & Main St exit: Go 4/10 mi S on Main St (R); or S-bnd: From Jct of Hwy 1 & Hwy 41: Go 4/10 mi S on Hwy 1 to Main St (Exit 279A), then 3/10 mi S On Main St (R). **FAC:** paved rds. (34 spaces). Avail: 23 all weather, patios, back-ins (22x44), 23 full hkups (30 amps), seasonal sites, cable, WiFi @ sites, laundry. **REC:** boating nearby. Pets OK. No tents, eco-friendly. 2021 rates: $55.
(805)772-2515 Lat: 35.369335, Lon: -120.850718
1121 Main St, Morro Bay, CA 93442
www.slocal.com/listing/cypress-rv-mh-park/2197
See ad page 121

HARBORVIEW RV PARK
(RV Park) (Seasonal Stay Only) From jct CA-1 & Morro Bay Blvd: Go 0.7 mi W to Monterey Ave, then 0.2 mi N (R). **FAC:** gravel rds. (10 spaces). Avail: 1 paved, back-ins (20x30), accepts full hkup units only, 1 full hkups (30/50 amps), seasonal sites, WiFi @ sites, rentals, shower$. **REC:** boating nearby. Pet restrict (B/Q). No tents.
(805)470-9929 Lat: 35.368600, Lon: -120.848519
1078 Monterey Ave, Morro Bay, CA 93442
www.harborviewrvpark.com
See ad page 121

MONTANA DE ORO (Public State Park) From Jct Hwy 101 & Los Osos Valley Rd (exit 200), W 9 mi on Los Osos Valley Rd to Pecho Valley Rd, S 3 mi (L). 47 Avail: Pit toilets. 2021 rates: $20 to $50. (805)772-6101

MORRO BAY (Public State Park) From town, S 1 mi on Main St (state park rd) (L). 135 Avail: 27 W, 27 E (20 amps). 2021 rates: $35 to $50. (805)772-6101

MORRO DUNES RV PARK
Ratings: 8.5/8.5★/9 (RV Park) From Jct of Hwy 1 & Rte 41 (Atascadero exit): Go 1/2 mi W on Atascadero Rd (L).

CAMP JUST STEPS AWAY FROM THE BEACH
From golfing to surfing, sunbathing to wine tasting, if you're looking for excitement or relaxation it's here in Morro Bay. We have the only pull thru sites in town. Great views of Morro Rock. A short drive to Hearst Castle.

FAC: paved rds. Avail: 152 gravel, 35 pull-thrus, (20x48), back-ins (30x40), 152 full hkups (30/50 amps), cable, WiFi @ sites, tent sites, dump, laundry, groc, LP bottles, fire rings, firewood. **REC:** Morro Bay: swim, boating nearby. Pet restrict (Q) $. Partial handicap access, 14 day max stay, eco-friendly. 2021 rates: $40 to $50.
(805)772-2722 Lat: 35.378893, Lon: -120.861511
1700 Embarcadero, Morro Bay, CA 93442
morrodunes.com
See ad pages 107, 121

MORRO STRAND RV PARK
Ratings: 6.5/8/7 (RV Park) From Jct of Hwy 1 & Rte 41 (Atascadero exit): Go 2/10 mi W on Atascadero Rd (R). **FAC:** paved rds. Avail: 43 gravel, back-ins (24x70), 43 full hkups (30/50 amps), cable, WiFi @ sites, laundry, firewood. **REC:** boating nearby. Pets OK $. Partial handicap access. No tents. Big rig sites. 2021 rates: $51 to $62.
(800)799-6030 Lat: 35.380433, Lon: -120.858428
221 Atascadero Rd, Morro Bay, CA 93442
morrostrandrvpark.com
See ad page 121

MORRO STRAND STATE BEACH (Public State Park) From Jct SR-41 & SR-1, N 2 mi on SR-1 to Yerba Buena Rd, W 0.3 mi (L). Avail: 5 full hkups. 2021 rates: $35 to $50. (805)772-6101

RANCHO COLINA RV PARK **Ratings: 6/8.5★/6** (RV Park) Avail: 47 full hkups (30/50 amps). 2021 rates: $50. (805)772-8420, 1045 Atascadero Rd, Morro Bay, CA 93442

SILVER CITY RESORT
Ratings: 6/7.5/7 (RV Area in MH Park) From jct of CA-1 & CA-41/Atascadero Rd: Go 0.2 mi W (R). **FAC:** paved rds. Avail: 32 gravel, back-ins (22x40), accepts full hkup units only, 32 full hkups (30/50 amps), cable, WiFi, laundry. **REC:** boating nearby. Pet restrict (B/Q). No tents, Age restrict may apply, eco-friendly. 2021 rates: $50. no cc.
(805)772-7478 Lat: 35.380854, Lon: -120.853090
500 Atascadero Road, Morro Bay, CA 93442
silvercitymorrobay.com
See ad page 121

Travel Services

MORRO DUNES RV REPAIR RV Repairs **SERVICES:** RV, RV appliance, restrooms. **TOW:** RV, RV supplies, dump, RV accessible. Hours: 8:30am to 4:30pm.
(805)772-2722 Lat: 35.378893, Lon: -120.861511
1700 Embarcadero, Morro Bay, CA 93442
See ad page 107

MOSS LANDING — F1 *Monterey*

MOSS LANDING KOA EXPRESS **Ratings: 7.5/8/8.5** (RV Park) Avail: 46 full hkups (30/50 amps). 2021 rates: $77 to $87. (800)562-3390, 7905 Sandholdt Rd, Moss Landing, CA 95039

MOUNT SHASTA — A2 *Siskiyou*

MOUNT SHASTA See also McCloud & Weed.

ABRAMS LAKE RV PARK **Ratings: 7.5/7.5/7.5** (RV Area in MH Park) Avail: 15 full hkups (30/50 amps). 2021 rates: $50. (530)926-2312, 2601 N Old Stage Road, Mount Shasta, CA 96067

MT. SHASTA KOA **Ratings: 8.5/8.5/8** (Campground) Avail: 30 full hkups (30/50 amps). 2021 rates: $55.24. (800)562-3617, 900 N Mt Shasta Blvd, Mount Shasta, CA 96067

MOUNTAIN CENTER — J5 *Riverside*

HURKEY CREEK PARK (Public) From Jct of SR-243 & SR-74, SE 4 mi on SR-74 (L). 130 Avail. 2021 rates: $20. (951)659-2050

LAKE HEMET (Public) From Jct of I-215 & SR-74 (Exit 15), E 36 mi on SR-74 (R). 289 Avail: 82 full hkups, 18 W, 18 E (30 amps). 2021 rates: $30 to $40. (951)659-2680

MCCALL MEMORIAL EQUESTRIAN PARK (Public) From jct Hwy 79 & Hwy 74: Go 17-1/2 mi E on Hwy 74, then N on McCall Park Rd. (E). 30 Avail. 2021 rates: $17. (951)659-2311

MYERS FLAT — B1 *Humboldt*

GIANT REDWOODS RV AND CABIN DESTINATION
good sam park **Ratings: 9/9.5★/9.5** (Campground) N-bnd: From Jct of US-101/Myers Flat (Exit 656), exit to Ave of Giants, N 0.2 mi to Myers Ave, SW 0.4 mi (E); or S-bnd: From Jct of US-101/Myers Flat, exit to Ave of Giants, NW 100 ft to Myers Ave, SW 0.4 mi (E) (Caution: Do not use Boy Scout Rd). **FAC:** paved rds. Avail: 64 all weather, 33 pull-thrus, (18x50), back-ins (20x40), 13 full hkups, 51 W, 51 E (30/50 amps), cable, WiFi @ sites, rentals, dump, laundry, groc, fire rings, firewood. **REC:** South Fork Eel River: swim, fishing, playground. Pet restrict (B) $. Partial handicap access. No tents, eco-friendly. 2021 rates: $60 to $80.
(707)943-9999 Lat: 40.26247, Lon: -123.87744
400 Myers Ave, Myers Flat, CA 95554
giantredwoodsrv.com
See ad this page

NAPA — D2 *Napa*

NAPA VALLEY EXPO RV PARK **Ratings: 9/10★/9.5** (Public) From Jct of SR-12/121 & SR-29, N 1.4 mi on SR-29/121 to SR-121/Imola Ave, E 1.4 mi to Soscol Ave/SR-121, N 0.6 mi to Silverado Trail/SR-121, N 0.5 mi (L). Avail: 28 full hkups (50 amps). 2021 rates: $60. (707)253-4900

SKYLINE WILDERNESS PARK (Public) From jct Hwy 12 & Hwy 29: Go 1-1/2 mi N on Hwy 29, then 2-1/2 mi E on Imola Ave (exit 16). 39 Avail. 2021 rates: $25 to $35. (707)252-0481

NAVARRO — C1 *Mendocino*

NAVARRO RIVER REDWOODS/PAUL M. DEMMICK (Public State Park) From jct Hwy-1 & Hwy-128: Go 8 mi E on Hwy-128. As of Spring 2019 park currently closed until further notice. Call for updates. 23 Avail: Pit toilets. 2021 rates: $25. (707)937-5804

NEEDLES — H6 *San Bernardino*

DESERT VIEW RV RESORT
good sam park **Ratings: 9/9.5★/10** (RV Park) Avail: 14 full hkups (30/50 amps). 2021 rates: $38 to $48. (760)333-0617, 5300 Route 66, Needles, CA 92363

FENDER'S RIVER ROAD RESORT **Ratings: 7.5/7/6** (RV Park) Avail: 55 full hkups (30/50 amps). 2021 rates: $38.50 to $60.50. (760)326-3423, 3408 River Rd, Needles, CA 92363

MOJAVE NATIONAL PRESERVE/HOLE-IN-THE-WALL (Public National Park) From Jct of I-40 & Essex Rd (exit 100), N 10 mi on exit rd to Jct with Black Canyon Rd, N 10 mi on Black Canyon Rd., follow signs (R). 35 Avail: Pit toilets. 2021 rates: $12. (760)252-6100

NEEDLES KOA JOURNEY **Ratings: 7/7.5/7.5** (Campground) 88 Avail: 70 full hkups, 18 W, 18 E (30 amps). 2021 rates: $33.95 to $36.95. (800)562-3407, 5400 Route 66, Needles, CA 92363

NEEDLES MARINA RESORT **Ratings: 9/8.5/7** (RV Park) Avail: 157 full hkups (30/50 amps). 2021 rates: $48 to $55. (760)326-2197, 100 Marina Dr, Needles, CA 92363

PIRATE COVE RESORT & MARINA
good sam park **Ratings: 8.5/9.5★/8.5** (RV Park) 145 Avail: 134 full hkups, 11 W, 11 E (30/50 amps). 2021 rates: $55 to $70. (866)301-3000, 100 Park Moabi Rd, Needles, CA 92363

THE PALMS RIVER RESORT **Ratings: 9/9★/9** (RV Park) Avail: 55 full hkups (30/50 amps). 2021 rates: $50 to $55. (760)326-0333, 4170 Needles Hwy, Needles, CA 92363

NEVADA CITY — C3 *Nevada*

INN TOWN CAMPGROUND **Ratings: 8.5/10★/9** (RV Park) 15 Avail: 11 full hkups, 4 W, 4 E (30/50 amps). 2021 rates: $50 to $68. (530)265-9900, 9 Kidder Ct., Nevada City, CA 95959

Always do a Pre-Drive Safety Check!

MALAKOFF DIGGINS STATE HISTORICAL PARK (Public State Park) From town: Go 6 mi N on Hwy-49, then 7 mi on Tyler-Foote Crossing Rd, then 5 mi on Lake City Rd, then 3 mi on N. Bloomfield Rd. (N. Bloomfield) (Caution: steep, gravel road). 32 Avail. 2021 rates: $35 to $40. (530)265-2740

NEWBERRY SPRINGS — H5 *San Bernardino*

NEWBERRY MOUNTAIN RV PARK **Ratings: 7.5/8.5★/6.5** (RV Park) Avail: 11 full hkups (30/50 amps). 2021 rates: $45. (760)257-0066, 47800 National Trails Hwy, Newberry Springs, CA 92365

NEWHALL — H3 *Los Angeles*

Travel Services

CAMPING WORLD STORE OF NEWHALL/VALENCIA As the nation's largest retailer of RV supplies, accessories, services and new and used RVs, Camping World is committed to making your total RV experience better. **SERVICES:** RV, tire, RV appliance, sells outdoor gear, restrooms. RV Sales. RV supplies, LP gas, emergency parking, RV accessible. Hours: 9am to 7pm.
(888)654-5177 Lat: 34.380663, Lon: -118.569699
24901 W Pico Canyon Rd, Newhall, CA 91381
www.campingworld.com

NEWPORT BEACH — O3 *Orange*

NEWPORT DUNES WATERFRONT RESORT & MARINA
good sam park **Ratings: 9.5/10★/9** (RV Park) From Jct of Pacific Coast Hwy (Hwy 1) & Jamboree Rd exit, N 0.2 mi on Jamboree Rd to Back Bay Dr, W 0.1 mi (L); or From Jct of I-405 & Jamboree Rd exit (in Irvine), S 5 mi on Jamboree Rd to Back Bay Dr, W 0.1 mi (L).

LUXURIOUS WATERFRONT RESORT
Newport Dunes Waterfront Resort surrounds its own beach and lagoon connected to the Pacific Ocean. Featuring our deluxe beachfront cottages. We are close to Disneyland! Come and stay a day, a week, or a few months!

FAC: paved rds. (371 spaces). 281 Avail: 5 paved, 276 dirt, patios, back-ins (24x40), 281 full hkups (30/50 amps), seasonal sites, cable, WiFi @ sites, tent sites, rentals, laundry, groc, LP bottles, firewood, restaurant, controlled access. **REC:** heated pool, wading pool, hot tub, Newport Bay: swim, marina, kayaking/canoeing, boating nearby, playground, rec open to public. Pet restrict (B/Q) $. Partial handicap access, eco-friendly. 2021 rates: $67 to $460, Military discount. ATM.
(800)765-7661 Lat: 33.61480, Lon: -117.89670
1131 Back Bay Dr, Newport Beach, CA 92660
www.newportdunes.com
See ad pages 102, 124

NICE — D2 *Lake*

AURORA RV PARK & MARINA **Ratings: 8/9.5★/8** (RV Park) Avail: 40 full hkups (30/50 amps). 2021 rates: $48 to $66. (707)274-5531, 2985 Lakeshore Blvd, Nice, CA 95464

NICOLAUS — D3 *Sutter*

LAKE MINDEN RV RESORT
good sam park **Ratings: 8/8.5★/9** (Membership Park) 126 Avail: 106 full hkups, 20 W, 20 E (30 amps). 2021 rates: $41. (888)563-7040, 1256 Marcum Rd, Nicolaus, CA 95659

NILAND — J6 *Imperial*

BASHFORD'S HOT MINERAL SPA RV PARK **Ratings: 7.5/6.5/6** (RV Park) Avail: 10 full hkups (30/50 amps). 2021 rates: $40. Oct 15 to May 15. (760)354-1315, 10590 Hot Mineral Spa Rd, Niland, CA 92257

FOUNTAIN OF YOUTH SPA RV RESORT
good sam park **Ratings: 9/9★/8.5** (RV Resort) Avail: 100 full hkups (30/50 amps). 2021 rates: $42 to $110. (888)800-0772, 1500 Spa Rd, Niland, CA 92257

GLAMIS NORTH HOT SPRINGS RESORT **Ratings: 7.5/7/7** (RV Resort) Avail: 167 full hkups (30/50 amps). 2021 rates: $55 to $99. Oct 15 to Apr 15. (760)354-1010, 10595 Hot Mineral Spa Rd, Niland, CA 92257

NORTHRIDGE — L1 *Los Angeles*

WALNUT RV PARK
good sam park **Ratings: 9/9★/7.5** (RV Park) From Jct of I-405 & Nordhoff exit (Exit 69), W 4.5 mi on Nordhoff (L) (Maximum Length 40 ft). **FAC:** paved rds. (114 spaces). Avail: 15 all weather, back-ins (26x42), 15 full hkups (30/50 amps), seasonal sites, WiFi @ sites, laundry. **REC:** heated pool, boating nearby. Pet restrict (S/B/Q). No tents, eco-friendly. 2021 rates: $80, Military discount.
(800)868-2749 Lat: 34.23515, Lon: -118.55082
19130 Nordhoff St, Northridge, CA 91324
www.walnutrvpark.com
See ad this page

NOVATO — E2 *Marin*

NOVATO RV PARK
good sam park **Ratings: 10/10★/9.5** (RV Park) Avail: 10 full hkups (30/50 amps). 2021 rates: $100. (800)733-6787, 1530 Armstrong Ave, Novato, CA 94945

OAKDALE — E3 *Stanislaus*

WOODWARD RESERVOIR (Public) From Jct of SR-120 & CR-J14, N 4 mi on CR-J14 (R). 155 Avail: (30 amps). 2021 rates: $30 to $35. (209)847-3304

OAKHURST — E4 *Madera*

HIGH SIERRA RV PARK & MOBILE PARK
good sam park **Ratings: 7/7/7.5** (RV Park) 29 Avail: 23 full hkups, 6 W, 6 E (30/50 amps). 2021 rates: $30 to $60. (559)683-7662, 40389 Hwy 41, Oakhurst, CA 93644

OAKLAND — E2 *Alameda*

OAKLAND See also Greenbrae, Pacifica, Pleasanton, San Francisco & Vallejo.

ANTHONY CHABOT REGIONAL PARK (Public) E-bnd: From Hwy 13 to Redwood Rd exit (Exit 1), E & S 7.5 mi on Redwood Rd to Marciel Gate (R); or W-bnd: From Hwy 580 to Castro Valley Blvd exit (Exit 37), W 1 mi on Castro Valley Blvd to Redwood Rd, NW 5 mi to Marciel Gate (L). Avail: 12 full hkups (30 amps). 2021 rates: $25 to $45. (888)327-2757

O'BRIEN — B2 *Shasta*

HOLIDAY HARBOR SHASTA LAKE RESORT & MARINA **Ratings: 5.5/8/6** (Campground) Avail: 29 full hkups (30/50 amps). 2021 rates: $40.25 to $51.95. Apr 01 to Nov 01. (800)776-2628, 20061 Shasta Caverns Rd, O'Brien, CA 96070

OCEANO — H2 *San Luis Obispo*

COASTAL DUNES RV PARK & CAMPGROUNE (Public) S-Bnd: From Jct of Hwy 101 & Pismo Beach exit (Dolliver, Hwy 1), S 2.5 mi on Hwy 1 (L); or N-bnd: From Jct of Hwy 101 N & Grand exit, W 2.7 mi on Grand to Hwy 1, S 0.5 mi (L). Avail: 230 full hkups (30/50 amps). 2021 rates: $23 to $40. (805)781-4900

PACIFIC DUNES RANCH RV RESORT
good sam park **Ratings: 7.5/7/5.5** (RV Park) Avail 185 full hkups (30/50 amps). 2021 rates $68 to $84. (888)563-7040, 1205 Silve Spur Pl, Oceano, CA 93445

➔ PISMO SANDS RV PARK **Ratings: 10/9.5★/8.5** (RV Park) Avail: 103 full hkups (30/50 amps). 2021 rates: $70 to $73. (800)404-7004, 2220 Cienaga St, Oceano, CA 93445

PISMO STATE BEACH/OCEANO (Public State Park) From town, S 2 mi on Hwy 1 to Pier Ave, W 2 blks (R). 82 Avail: 39 W, 39 E (20 amps). 2021 rates: $25 to $50. (805)473-7220

OCEANSIDE — J4 *San Diego*

➔ GUAJOME COUNTY PARK (Public) From Jct of I-5 & Mission Ave (exti 53), E 7 mi on Mission Ave (L). 35 Avail: 35 W, 35 E (30 amps). 2021 rates: $29. (877)565-3600

➔ MILITARY PARK DEL MAR BEACH COTTAGES & CAMPSITES (MCB CAMP PENDLETON) (Public) From I-5: Take Camp Pendleton/Oceanside exit, then follow Del Mar sign on Wire Mountain Rd, turn left on 12th St (R). Avail: 106 full hkups (30/50 amps). 2021 rates: $35 to $55. (760)725-2134

MILITARY PARK LAKE O'NEILL REC PARK (MCB CAMP PENDLETON) (Public) From I-5 and exit 54B: Go through gate then 9 mil to left on Santa Margarita Rd (R). 61 Avail: 18 full hkups, 43 W, 43 E (30 amps). 2021 rates: $33 to $44. (760)725-5611

OCEANSIDE RV RESORT

good sam park **Ratings: 9.5/9★/7.5** (RV Park) From Jct of I-5 & Oceanside Blvd (exit 52), W 0.5 mi on Oceanside Blvd to S. Coast Hwy, S 0.1 mi across railway track-4th Entrance (L). **FAC:** paved rds. (178 spaces). Avail: 138 paved, patios, 33 pull-thrus, (20x50), back-ins (22x40), accepts full hkup units only, 138 full hkups (30/50 amps), seasonal sites, cable, WiFi @ sites, tent sites, rentals, dump, laundry, groc. **REC:** heated pool, hot tub, boating nearby. Pet restrict (B/Q). Partial handicap access, eco-friendly. 2021 rates: $105 to $190, Military discount.
(760)722-4404 Lat: 33.18222, Lon: -117.36663
1510 S Coast Hwy, Oceanside, CA 92054
www.traveloceanside.com
See ad page 152

PARADISE BY THE SEA BEACH RV RESORT **Ratings: 10/10★/8** (RV Park) Avail: 91 full hkups (30/50 amps). 2021 rates: $75 to $200. (760)439-1376, 1537 S Coast Hwy, Oceanside, CA 92054

OJAI — H3 *Ventura*

➔ CAMP COMFORT (Public) From Jct of Hwy 33 (Ojai Ave) & Creek Rd, S 2 mi on Creek Rd (L). Avail: 15 full hkups (30/50 amps). 2021 rates: $42. (805)654-3951

OLANCHA — F4 *Inyo*

➔ **LAKE OLANCHA RV PARK**

good sam park (RV Park) (Under Construction) From jct US 395N & CA 190E: Go 1/4 mi S on US 395N (L). Elev 3661 ft.**FAC:** dirt rds. Avail: 33 dirt, back-ins (21x60), accepts full hkup units only, 33 full hkups (30/50 amps), tent sites, rentals, . **REC:** pond. Pets OK. 2021 rates: $35.
(760)792-2034 Lat: 36.281319, Lon: -118.00022
200 S Hwy 395, Olancha, CA 93549
www.lakeolancha.com
See ad this page

OLD STATION — B3 *Lassen*

➔ **HAT CREEK RESORT & RV PARK**

good sam park **Ratings: 6/8.5★/7.5** (RV Park) Avail: 51 full hkups (20/30 amps). 2021 rates: $39 to $80. Apr 15 to Oct 31. (530)335-7121, 12533 Hwy 44/89, Old Station, CA 96071

➔ LASSEN VOLCANIC/BUTTE LAKE (Public National Park) From jct Hwy-89/44 & Hwy-44 (Feather Lake Hwy): Go 10 mi E on Hwy-44, then 5 mi S on Halls Flat Rd. 37 Avail. 2021 rates: $15 to $22. Jun 05 to Oct 26. (530)595-6121

OLEMA — E2 *Marin*

OLEMA CAMPGROUND

good sam park **Ratings: 7.5/9★/8.5** (RV Park) From Jct of SR-1 & Sir Francis Drake Blvd (in town), N 0.2 mi on SR-1 (L).

ESCAPE THE CHAOS OF DAILY LIVING
Located next to the Point Reyes National Seashore and just north of San Francisco. Explore the 65,000 acres of unspoiled wilderness that surrounds us. Spend a day visiting San Francisco or Wine Country. **FAC:** paved/gravel rds. (80 spaces). Avail: 60 gravel, back-ins (20x50), 26 full hkups, 34 W, 34 E (30/50 amps), seasonal sites, WiFi @ sites, tent sites, dump, mobile sewer, laundry, LP gas, fire rings, firewood. **REC:** boating nearby, shuffleboard, playground, hunting nearby. Pet restrict (B/Q). 14 day max stay. 2021 rates: $47 to $65. ATM.
(415)663-8106 Lat: 38.04409, Lon: -122.78994
10155 Hwy 1, Olema, CA 94950
www.olemacampground.net
See ad this page

ORANGE — N4 *Orange*

➔ **ORANGELAND RV PARK**

good sam park **Ratings: 10/10★/9** (RV Park) S-bnd: From Jct of I-5 & Katella Ave (exit 109A), E 2 mi on Katella Ave to W Struck Ave, SE 150 ft (R). **FAC:** paved rds. Avail: 195 paved, patios, 18 pull-thrus, (26x45), back-ins (22x45), 195 full hkups (30/50 amps), cable, WiFi @ sites, laundry, groc. **REC:** heated pool, hot tub, boating nearby, playground. Pet restrict (B/Q) $. Partial handicap access. No tents, eco-friendly. 2021 rates: $75 to $90, Military discount. ATM.
(714)633-0414 Lat: 33.80545, Lon: -117.86957
1600 W Struck Ave, Orange, CA 92867
www.orangeland.com
See ad page 123

OREGON HOUSE — C3 *Yuba*

LAKE OF THE SPRINGS RV RESORT

good sam park **Ratings: 9/8/9** (Membership Park) 310 Avail: 21 full hkups, 289 W, 289 E (30 amps). 2021 rates: $57 to $67. (888)563-7040, 14152 French Town Road, Oregon House, CA 95962

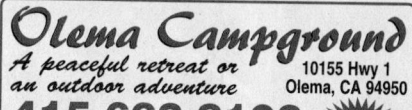

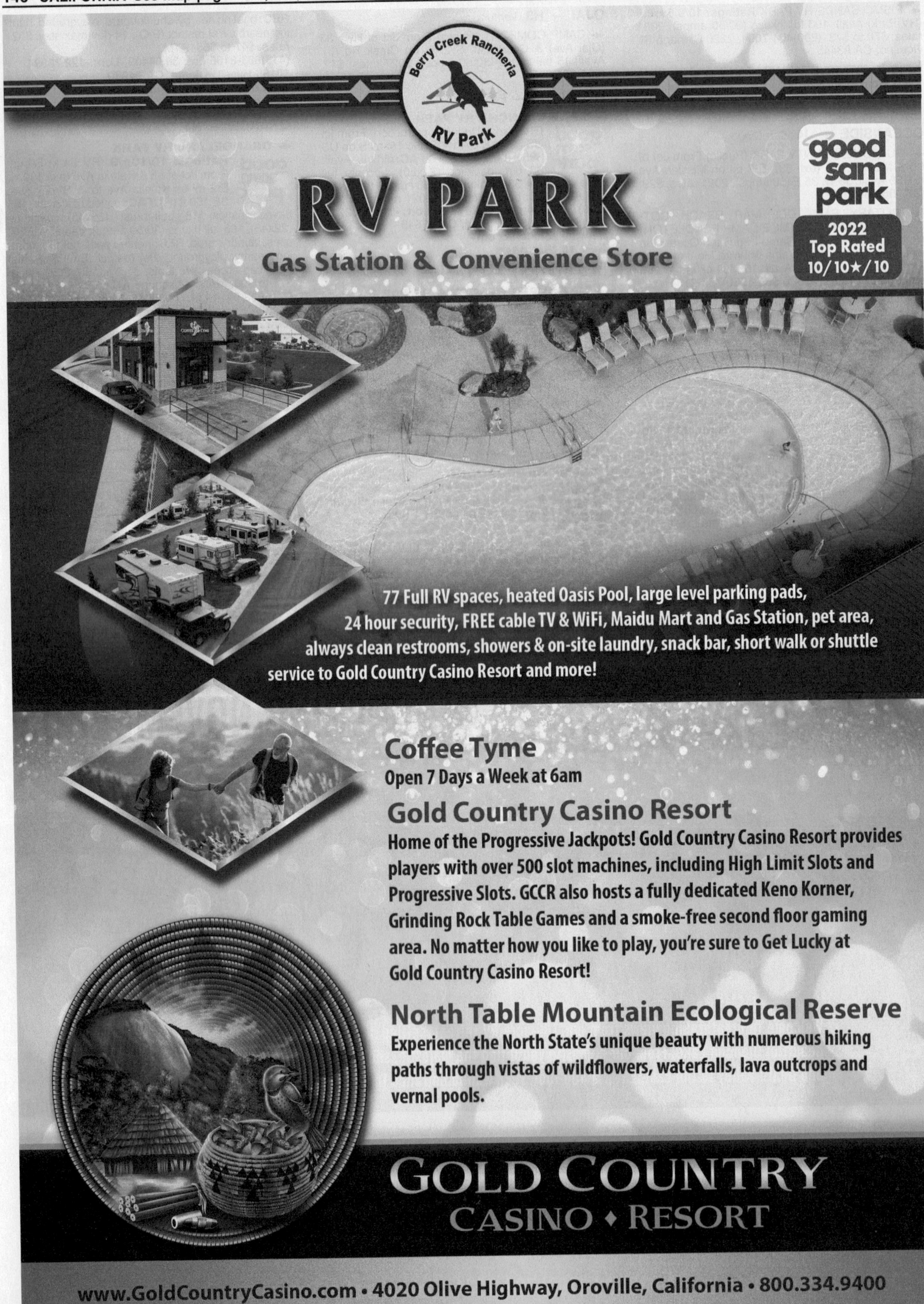

See listing Oroville, CA

ORICK — A1 *Humboldt*

PRAIRIE CREEK REDWOODS/ELK PRAIRIE (Public State Park) From town, N 3 mi on US-101 to Davison Rd, W 4 mi (L). 70 Avail. 2021 rates: $35. (707)488-2039

PRAIRIE CREEK REDWOODS/GOLD BLUFFS BEACH (Public State Park) From town: Go 3 mi N on US-101, then 7 mi W on Davidson Rd/Fern Canyon (caution: graded, dirt road). 25 Avail. 2021 rates: $35. (707)488-2039

ORLAND — C2 *Glenn*

THE PARKWAY RV RESORT & CAMPGROUND **Ratings: 10/10★/9.5** (RV Park) Avail: 34 full hkups (30/50 amps). 2021 rates: $57.55 to $69.55. (530)865-9188, 6330 County Road 200, Orland, CA 95963

OROVILLE — C3 *Butte*

BERRY CREEK RANCHERIA RV PARK
good sam park **Ratings: 10/10★/10** (RV Resort) From jct 70 & SR 162 exit 46 (SR 162 Oroville Dam Blvd): Go 1-1/2 mi E on SR 162 to Olive Hwy (SR 162), then 2-1/4 mi E on Olive Hwy (R). **FAC:** paved rds. Avail: 79 paved, patios, 30 pull-thrus, (30x50), back-ins (30x40), 79 full hkups (30/50 amps), cable, WiFi @ sites, rentals, laundry, groc, LP gas. **REC:** pool, hot tub, boating nearby, playground, hunting nearby. Pets OK. Partial handicap access. No tents. Big rig sites, eco-friendly. 2021 rates: $52 to $68. no cc.
(866)991-5061 Lat: 39.505, Lon: -121.507
3900 Olive Hwy, Oroville, CA 95966
www.goldcountrycasino.com
See ad opposite page

FEATHER FALLS KOA & CASINO **Ratings: 10/9★/10** (RV Park) Avail: 34 full hkups (30/50 amps). 2021 rates: $54.89 to $72.89. (800)562-5079, 3 Alverda Drive, Oroville, CA 95966

LAKE OROVILLE SRA/BIDWELL CANYON (Public State Park) From Jct of SR-70 & SR-162 (exit 46), E 7 mi on SR-162 to Kelly Ridge Rd, N 0.5 mi to Arroyo Dr, follow signs (E). Avail: 75 full hkups (30 amps). 2021 rates: $40. (530)538-2218

LAKE OROVILLE SRA/LOAFER CREEK (Public State Park) From Jct of SR-70 & SR-162 (exit 46), E 8 mi on SR-162 (L). 137 Avail. 2021 rates: $35. Apr 01 to Sep 30. (530)538-2217

RIVER REFLECTIONS RV PARK & CAMPGROUND
good sam park **Ratings: 9/9★/10** (Campground) From Jct of SR-70 & SR-162 (at Oroville), S 1.6 mi on SR-70 to Pacific Heights Rd, NW 0.1 mi (L). **FAC:** paved rds. 91 Avail: 10 paved, 81 grass, 18 pull-thrus, (30x70), back-ins (30x70), 85 full hkups, 6 W, 6 E (30/50 amps), WiFi @ sites, rentals, dump, laundry, fire rings, firewood. **REC:** Feather River: swim, fishing, boating nearby, hunting nearby. Pet restrict (B). No tents. Big rig sites. 2021 rates: $50.
(530)533-1995 Lat: 39.47915, Lon: -121.57757
4360 Pacific Heights Rd, Oroville, CA 95965
www.rvparkresorts.com
See ad this page

SEACLIFF STATE BEACH (Public State Park) From Jct of Hwy 1 & State Park Dr (Seacliff Beach exit), SW 0.4 mi on State Park Dr (E). Avail: 26 full hkups (20/30 amps). 2021 rates: $55 to $65. (831)685-6500

Things to See and Do

COFFEE TYME Drive thru coffee shop located near Berry Creek Rancheria RV Park and Gold Country Casino Resort. No CC.
(800)334-9400 Lat: 39.504214, Lon: -121.507773
3910 Olive Hwy, Oroville, CA 95966
See ad opposite page

GOLD COUNTRY CASINO RESORT Nor-Cal's premier award-winning getaway. Enjoy the Gaming, Rewards Club, Hotel, Dining and Entertainment/Nightlife. Partial handicap access. RV accessible. Restrooms. Food. Hours: 24 hour. No CC.
(800)916-4339 Lat: 39.50380, Lon: -121.50307
4020 Olive Hwy, Oroville, CA 95966
www.goldcountrycasino.com
See ad opposite page

OXNARD — H3 *Ventura*

PT MUGU/BIG SYCAMORE CANYON (Public State Park) From town, S 14 mi on PCH 1 (L). 58 Avail. 2021 rates: $45. (310)457-8143

PT MUGU/THORNHILL BROOME BEACH (Public State Park) From town, S 10 mi on PCH 1 (R). 62 Avail: Pit toilets. 2021 rates: $35. (310)457-9143

PACIFICA — E2 *San Mateo*

SAN FRANCISCO RV RESORT
good sam park **Ratings: 10/9★/7** (RV Park) Avail: 61 full hkups (30/50 amps). 2021 rates: $111 to $136. (888)563-7040, 700 Palmetto Ave, Pacifica, CA 94044

PAICINES — F2 *San Benito*

SAN BENITO RV & CAMPING RESORT
good sam park **Ratings: 6.5/5.5/7** (RV Park) 537 Avail: 417 full hkups, 83 W, 83 E (30/50 amps). 2021 rates: $70. (888)563-7040, 16225 Cienega Road, Paicines, CA 95043

PALA — J5 *San Diego*

PALA CASINO RV RESORT
good sam park **Ratings: 10/10★/10** (RV Resort) From Jct I-15 & CA-76 (exit 46): Go 5.5 mi E on CR-76 (R).

SPOIL YOURSELF AT OUR LUXURY RESORT
Discover the fun and excitement in the shade of the Palomar Mountains at our perfectly rated resort. Take in the views, relax at one of 5 pools, play your favorite table game & slots, or explore nearby San Diego and Temecula.
FAC: paved rds. Avail: 100 paved, patios, 17 pull-thrus, (30x72), back-ins (30x55), accepts full hkup units only, 100 full hkups (30/50 amps), cable, WiFi @ sites, laundry, groc, LP gas, restaurant. **REC:** heated pool, hot tub. Pet restrict (Q) $. Partial handicap access. No tents. Big rig sites, 14 day max stay, eco-friendly. 2021 rates: $113 to $225. ATM.
(844)472-5278 Lat: 33.36413, Lon: -117.09012
11042 Hwy 76, Pala, CA 92059
www.palacasino.com/rv
See ad page 156

Things to See and Do

PALA CASINO SPA & RESORT Pala Casino Spa & Resort features a 507 room hotel a full-service spa & salon, a fitness center, swimming pool & whirlpool. There are 11 restaurants. A 24 hour shuttle service runs between the casino & the 100 site RV Resort. Partial handicap access. Restrooms. Food. Hours: 24 hrs. ATM.
(877)946-7252 Lat: 33.36449, Lon: -117.08638
11154 Hwy 76, Pala, CA 92059
www.palacasino.com
See ad page 156

PALM DESERT — J5 *Riverside*

EMERALD DESERT RV RESORT - SUNLAND **Ratings: 10/9.5★/8.5** (RV Park) Avail: 161 full hkups (30/50 amps). 2021 rates: $56 to $141. (866)290-2487, 76000 Frank Sinatra Dr, Palm Desert, CA 92211

PALM SPRINGS RV RESORT
good sam park **Ratings: 8.5/8.5/7.5** (Membership Park) Avail: 348 full hkups (30/50 amps). 2021 rates: $77. Sep 15 to May 15. (888)563-7040, 77500 Varner Rd, Palm Desert, CA 92211

PALM SPRINGS — J5 *Riverside*

A SPOTLIGHT Introducing Palm Springs' colorful attractions appearing at the front of this state section.

SAM'S FAMILY SPA
good sam park **Ratings: 9/8★/9.5** (RV Park) From jct E Alejo Rd & N Indian Canyon Dr: Go 6-1/2 mi N on N Indian Canyon Dr, then 7 mi E on Dillon Rd (R). **FAC:** paved rds. (184 spaces). Avail: 178 gravel, back-ins (32x50), 178 full hkups (30/50 amps), seasonal sites, cable, WiFi @ sites, tent sites, rentals, laundry, groc. **REC:** heated pool, wading pool, hot tub, playground, rec open to public. Pets OK. Partial handicap access, eco-friendly. 2021 rates: $60, Military discount.
(760)329-6457 Lat: 33.92488, Lon: -116.42535
70875 Dillon Rd, Desert Hot Springs, CA 92241
samsfamilyspa.com
See primary listing at Desert Hot Springs and ad page 133

PALOMAR MOUNTAIN — J5 *San Diego*

PALOMAR MOUNTAIN/DOANE VALLEY (Public State Park) From town, E on State Hwy 76 to CR-S6, N 7 mi to CR-S7, W 3 mi (E). 31 Avail. 2021 rates: $30. (760)742-3462

PARADISE — C3 *Butte*

PG & E/FEATHER RIVER/PHILBROOK (Public) From Jct of Elliot Rd & Skyway, N 27.3 mi on Skyway to Humbug Summit Rd, NE 1.9 mi to Philbrook Rd, E 3.1 mi (R). 20 Avail: Pit toilets. 2021 rates: $41.50. (916)386-5164

PARKER DAM — H6 *San Bernardino*

BIG BEND RESORT **Ratings: 7.5/7.5/7.5** (RV Park) Avail: 52 full hkups (50 amps). 2021 rates: $59 to $75. (760)663-3755, 501 Parker Dam Rd, Parker Dam, CA 92267

BLACK MEADOW LANDING **Ratings: 7.5/7/7** (Campground) Avail: 200 full hkups (30 amps). 2021 rates: $35 to $70. (800)742-8278, 156100 Black Meadow Rd, Parker Dam, CA 92267

ECHO LODGE RESORT **Ratings: 6.5/6.5/7** (RV Park) Avail: 101 full hkups (30 amps). 2021 rates: $59 to $75. (760)663-4931, 451 Parker Dam Rd, Parker Dam, CA 92267

RIO DEL COLORADO RV RESORT **Ratings: 7/7/7.5** (Membership Park) Avail: 16 full hkups (30 amps). 2021 rates: $35. (760)663-3636, 2054 Parker Dam Rd, Parker Dam, CA 92267

RIVER LODGE RESORT **Ratings: 7.5/6.5/6.5** (RV Park) Avail: 100 full hkups (30/50 amps). 2021 rates: $40 to $50. (760)663-4934, 675 N Parker Dam Road, Parker Dam, CA 92267

PASO ROBLES — G2 *San Luis Obispo*

CAVA ROBLES RV RESORT
Ratings: 10/10★/10 (RV Resort) From jct US 101 & CA-46: Go 1-1/2 mi E on CA-46, then 1/2 mi N on Golden Hill Rd (R). **FAC:** paved rds. Avail: 312 all weather, patios, 21 pull-thrus, (35x65), back-ins (30x60), 312 full hkups (30/50 amps), cable, WiFi @ sites, rentals, laundry, groc, LP gas, fire rings, firewood, restaurant. **REC:** heated pool, hot tub, playground. Pet restrict (Q). Partial handicap access. No tents. Big rig sites, 28 day max stay, eco-friendly. 2021 rates: $80 to $128. no cc.
(888)886-2477 Lat: 35.6521544, Lon: -120.6580817
3800 Golden Hill Rd, Paso Robles, CA 93446
www.sunrvresorts.com
See ad page 121

PASO ROBLES (CONT)

LAKE NACIMIENTO RESORT (Public) From Jct of Hwy 101 & 24th St (Hwy 46E exit), W 16.2 mi on 24th St (Becomes Nacimiento Lake Rd)/G14 (L). Avail: 40 full hkups (20/30 amps). 2021 rates: $30 to $45. (805)238-3256

PASO ROBLES RV RANCH
Ratings: 10/9★/9.5 (RV Park) From Jct of US-101 & Hwy 46E: Go 3 mi N on US-101 to Exline Rd Exit (N-bnd left lane exit), then 200 ft S on Stockdale Rd (R) (Note: Entry turn is before Exline Rd). **FAC:** paved rds. (67 spaces). Avail: 46 all weather, 30 pull-thrus, (22x60), back-ins (24x35), 46 full hkups (30/50 amps), seasonal sites, WiFi @ sites, laundry, LP gas, fire rings. **REC:** pool, hunting nearby. Pet restrict (B). Partial handicap access. No tents. Big rig sites, eco-friendly. 2021 rates: $60 to $65, Military discount.
(805)237-8685 Lat: 35.681529, Lon: -120.697893
398 Exline Rd, Paso Robles, CA 93446
See ad previous page

VINES RV RESORT **Ratings: 9.5/9.5★/8** (RV Resort) Avail: 113 full hkups (30/50 amps). 2021 rates: $63 to $99. (888)710-6552, 88 Wellsona Rd, Paso Robles, CA 93446

WINE COUNTRY RV RESORT
Ratings: 10/9.5★/9 (RV Resort) From Jct of Hwy 101 & Hwy 46E: Go 2-1/4 mi E on Hwy 46E to Airport Rd, then 2/10 mi N on Airport Rd (R). **FAC:** paved rds. (180 spaces). 165 Avail: 81 paved, 84 all weather, 44 pull-thrus, (24x80), back-ins (25x54), 165 full hkups (30/50 amps), seasonal sites, cable, WiFi @ sites, rentals, laundry, groc, LP gas. **REC:** heated pool, hot tub, playground. Pet restrict (Q). Partial handicap access. No tents. Big rig sites, eco-friendly. 2021 rates: $63 to $113, Military discount.
(888)713-0819 Lat: 35.648137, Lon: -120.640381
2500 Airport Rd, Paso Robles, CA 93446
www.sunrvresorts.com
See ad page 121

PATTERSON — E3 *Stanislaus*

FRANK RAINES REGIONAL PARK (Public) From jct I-5 & Del Puerto Canyon Rd (exit 434): Go 17 mi W on Del Puerto Canyon Rd. Avail: 34 full hkups (15/20 amps). 2021 rates: $15 to $25. (209)525-6750

KIT FOX RV PARK **Ratings: 8.5/9★/8.5** (RV Park) Avail: 91 full hkups (30/50 amps). 2021 rates: $45 to $50. (209)892-2638, 240 Rogers Rd, Patterson, CA 95363

PERRIS — N6 *Riverside*

LAKE PERRIS SRA/LUISENO (Public State Park) From Jct of I-215 & Ramona Expwy, E 2.5 mi on Ramona Expwy to Lake Perris Dr, N 1 mi (E). 265 Avail: 265 W, 265 E (30 amps). 2021 rates: $25 to $30. (951)940-5600

PESCADERO — E2 *San Mateo*

SANTA CRUZ NORTH COSTANOA KOA **Ratings: 8/8★/8.5** (RV Park) Avail: 87 full hkups (30/50 amps). 2021 rates: $88 to $195. (650)879-7302, 2001 Rossi Rd, Pescadero, CA 94060

PETALUMA — D2 *Sonoma*

SAN FRANCISCO NORTH/PETALUMA KOA **Ratings: 9.5/10★/10** (Campground) 218 Avail: 118 full hkups, 100 W, 100 E (30/50 amps). 2021 rates: $65 to $175. (800)992-2267, 20 Rainsville Rd, Petaluma, CA 94952

PHILO — D1 *Mendocino*

HENDY WOODS (Public State Park) From town, NW 2 mi on Hwy 128 to Philo-Greenwood Rd, SW 0.5 mi (L). 85 Avail. 2021 rates: $40 to $45. (707)895-3141

PIEDRA — F3 *Fresno*

CHOINUMNI PARK (Public) From Jct of SR-180 & Piedra Rd, NE 5 mi on Piedra Rd to Trimmer Springs Rd, E 4 mi to Pine Flat Rd, S 0.25 mi (R). 75 Avail. 2021 rates: $25. (559)600-3004

PINE FLAT LAKE - COE/ISLAND PARK (Public Corps) From town, NE 8 mi on Trimmer Springs Rd (R). Avail: 25 E. 2021 rates: $20 to $30. (559)787-2589

PINE FLAT LAKE - COE/TRIMMER (Public Corps) From Jct of Pine Flat Rd & Trimmer Springs Rd, NE 15 mi on Trimmer Springs Rd (R). 10 Avail. 2021 rates: $20. (559)787-2589

PINE GROVE — D3 *Amador*

INDIAN GRINDING ROCK (Public State Park) From Jackson, E 10 mi on Hwy 88 to Pine-Grove/Volcano Rd, N 2 mi (L). 22 Avail. 2021 rates: $30 to $35. (209)296-7488

PIRU — H3 *Ventura*

LAKE PIRU REC AREA (Public) From Jct of I-5 & Hwy 126, W 12 mi on Hwy 126 to Main St, N 7 mi, follow signs (E). 238 Avail: 5 full hkups, 102 E (20/30 amps). 2021 rates: $22 to $44. (805)521-1500

PISMO BEACH — G2 *San Luis Obispo*

A SPOTLIGHT Introducing Central Coast's colorful attractions appearing in the front of the state section.

PISMO BEACH See also Grover Beach, Morro Bay, Oceano, San Luis Obispo & Santa Margarita.

HOLIDAY RV PARK
Ratings: 8.5/8/6.5 (RV Park) N-bnd: From Jct of Hwy 101 & Price St: Go 75 ft N on Price St to Ocean View, then 1/10 mi W to Dolliver St, then 1/4 mi S on Dolliver St (L); or S-bnd: From Jct of Hwy 101 & Dolliver St (Pismo Beach Exit): Go 3/4 mi S on Dolliver St (L). **FAC:** paved rds. (195 spaces). Avail: 125 all weather, back-ins (20x36), 125 full hkups (30/50 amps), seasonal sites, cable, WiFi @ sites, laundry. **REC:** heated pool, hot tub, boating nearby. Pet restrict (Q) $. Partial handicap access. No tents, eco-friendly. 2021 rates: $55 to $140, Military discount.
(800)272-3672 Lat: 35.136303, Lon: -120.637868
100 S Dolliver St, Pismo Beach, CA 93449
www.holidayrvpark.org
See ad page 121

PISMO COAST VILLAGE RV RESORT
Ratings: 9.5/10★/8.5 (RV Park) N-bnd: From Jct of US-101 & Price St: Go 75 ft N on Price St to Ocean View Rd, then 1/10 mi W to Dolliver St (US-1), then 1/2 mi S (R); or S-bnd: From Jct of US-101 & Dolliver St (Pismo Beach exit): Go 9/10 mi S on Dolliver St (R).

A UNIQUE RV PARADISE ON THE OCEAN
Relax to the sound of the surf, scent of the salt air, and the feel of an ocean breeze. This award winning resort is located within walking distance from downtown Pismo Beach shopping, restaurants, and the famous Pismo Pier.

FAC: paved rds. Avail: 400 gravel, back-ins (26x45), 400 full hkups (30/50 amps), cable, WiFi @ sites, laundry, groc, LP gas, fire rings, firewood, restaurant, controlled access. **REC:** heated pool, wading pool, Pacific Ocean: swim, boating nearby, playground. Pet restrict (B/Q). Partial handicap access. No tents. Big rig sites, 29 day max stay, eco-friendly. 2021 rates: $59 to $76. ATM.
(888)782-3224 Lat: 35.134770, Lon: -120.637282
165 S Dolliver St, Pismo Beach, CA 93449
pismocoastvillage.com
See ad this page, 121

Travel Services

PISMO COAST RV SERVICE Full service RV repair facility. **SERVICES:** RV, RV appliance, mobile RV svc, staffed RV wash, restrooms. RV supplies, LP gas, RV accessible. Hours: 8am to 5pm.
(805)773-3868 Lat: 35.134770, Lon: -120.637282
2096 Nipomo St, Oceano, CA 93445
pismocoastvillage.com
See ad this page

PLAYA DEL REY — M1 *Los Angeles*

DOCKWEILER RV PARK (Public) From Jct of I-405 & I-105, W 2.5 mi on I-105 to end of Fwy-becoming Imperial Hwy, continue W 1.9 mi on Imperial Hwy to Vista del Mar (Entrance to RV park at state beach entrance). Avail: 113 full hkups (30/50 amps). 2021 rates: $65 to $85. Feb 01 to Jan 01. (800)950-7275

PLEASANTON — E2 *Alameda*

THE FAIR PARK RV (Public) From jct I-680 & Exit 26 (Bernal Ave): Go 1/3 mi E on Bernal Ave, then 1/3 mi N on Valley Ave to Gate 12 (R). Avail: 176 full hkups (30/50 amps). 2021 rates: $50 to $65. (925)426-7600

PLYMOUTH — D3 *Amador*

49ER VILLAGE RV RESORT **Ratings: 10/9/9.5** (RV Park) Avail: 290 full hkups (30/50 amps). 2021 rates: $54 to $92. (844)726-5472, 18265 Hwy 49, Plymouth, CA 95669

POLLOCK PINES — D3 *El Dorado*

SLY PARK RECREATION AREA (Public) From Jct of Hwy 50 & Sly Park Rd (exit 60), S 5 mi on Sly Park Rd (L). 191 Avail: Pit toilets. 2021 rates: $35 to $80. (530)295-6810

POMONA — M4 *Los Angeles*

FAIRPLEX RV PARK
Ratings: 10/9.5/7.5 (RV Park) Avail: 60 full hkups (30/50 amps). 2021 rates: $65 to $79. (909)593-8915, 2200 N White Ave, Pomona, CA 91768

PORT HUENEME — H3 *Ventura*

MILITARY PARK FAIRWAYS RV RESORT (PORT HUENEME) (Public) From jct US-101 & Rice Ave: Go 2 mi S on Rice Ave, then right onto Wooley for 3-3/4 mi, then left onto Patterson for 1 mi, then left on to W Channel Islands (R). Avail: 85 full hkups (30/50 amps). 2021 rates: $40 to $45. (805)982-6123

MILITARY PARK POINT MUGU REC FACILITIES (NAS POINT MUGU) (Public) From US-101 & Las Posas Rd: Go 5 mi S on Las Posas to gate (E). Avail: 68 full hkups (30/50 amps). 2021 rates: $40 to $45. (805)989-8407

County names help you follow the local weather report.

PORTERVILLE — G3 *Tulare*

SUCCESS LAKE - COE/TULE (Public Corps) Freeway 99: Take the highway 190 exit east to the park (8 miles east of Porterville). Avail: 29 E. 2021 rates: $20 to $30. Mar 01 to Sep 30. (559)784-0215

POTRERO — K5 *San Diego*

POTRERO COUNTY PARK (Public) From town, E 1 mi on Hwy 94 to Potrero Valley Rd to Potrero Park Rd, E 1 mi (E). 37 Avail: 37 W, 37 E (20/30 amps). 2021 rates: $22 to $27. (619)478-5212

POTTER VALLEY — C2 *Lake*

PG & E/SAN JOAQUIN RIVER/TROUT CREEK (Public) From Jct of Eel River Rd & E Potter Valley Rd, E 6.5 mi on Eel River Rd (R). 17 Avail: Pit toilets. 2021 rates: $32. (916)386-5164

QUINCY — C3 *Plumas*

PG & E/FEATHER RIVER/HASKINS VALLEY (Public) From Jct of Hwy 70 & Bucks Lake Rd, SW 16.5 mi on Bucks Lake Rd (R). 65 Avail: Pit toilets. 2021 rates: $45.88. May 01 to Oct 31. (916)386-5164

PIONEER RV PARK **Ratings: 9/9/9.5** (RV Park) Avail: 28 full hkups (30/50 amps). 2021 rates: $55.50. (530)283-0769, 1326 Pioneer Rd, Quincy, CA 95971

RAMONA — J5 *San Diego*

DOS PICOS COUNTY PARK (Public) From Jct of SR-67 & Mussey Grade Rd, SE 1 mi on Mussey Grade Rd to Dos Picos Rd, E 0.2 mi (E). 57 Avail: 57 W, 57 E (15/20 amps). 2021 rates: $24 to $29. (877)565-3600

RAMONA OAKS RV RESORT **Ratings: 8.5/8/8** (RV Resort) Avail: 10 full hkups (30/50 amps). 2021 rates: $65. (760)788-3085, 24340 Hwy 78, Ramona, CA 92065

RED BLUFF — C2 *Tehama*

RED BLUFF KOA JOURNEY **Ratings: 10/10★/10** (RV Resort) Avail: 174 full hkups (30/50 amps). 2021 rates: $60 to $68. (530)527-5300, 100 Lake Ave, Red Bluff, CA 96080

RED BLUFF RV PARK **Ratings: 9/9★/9** (RV Park) Avail: 10 full hkups (30/50 amps). 2021 rates: $35 to $40. (530)838-4652, 80 Chestnut Ave, Red Bluff, CA 96080

REDCREST — B1 *Humboldt*

ANCIENT REDWOODS RV PARK

good sam park **Ratings: 8.5/10★/9** (RV Park) Avail: 49 full hkups (30/50 amps). 2021 rates: $55. May 01 to Oct 31. (707)722-4396, 28101 Avenue Of The Giants, Redcrest, CA 95569

REDDING — B2 *Shasta*

JGW RV PARK

good sam park **Ratings: 10/10★/10** (RV Park) From Jct of I-5 & Knighton Rd exit 673 (6 mi S of town), exit to W side of I-5 to Riverland Dr (Frntg Rd), S 2 mi (R).

CLOSE TO TOWN IN A NATURAL SETTING

The park has a grassy, natural setting for viewing birds & wildlife or for just strolling along the Sacramento Riverbank. Fish for steelhead, trout & salmon or just enjoy a BBQ and a friendly game of horseshoes or corn hole.

FAC: paved rds. (75 spaces). Avail: 50 paved, 38 pull-thrus, (30x60), back-ins (30x60), accepts full hkup units only, 50 full hkups (30/50 amps), seasonal sites, cable, WiFi @ sites, laundry, LP gas. **REC:** pool, Sacramento River: fishing, boating nearby, hunting nearby. Pets OK. Partial handicap access. No tents. Big rig sites, eco-friendly. 2021 rates: $45 to $65, Military discount.

(530)365-7965 Lat: 40.48062, Lon: -122.32066
6612 Riverland Dr, Redding, CA 96002
jgwrvpark.com
See ad this page

MARINA RV PARK **Ratings: 9/9.5★/8.5** (RV Park) Avail: 36 full hkups (20/30 amps). 2021 rates: $35 to $40. (530)241-4396, 2615 Park Marina Dr, Redding, CA 96001

Drop in at one of our social media stomping grounds on Facebook, Twitter or the Good Sam Blog to mingle with thousands of fellow RVers. Learn about new RV destinations, share some hard-earned RV advice and make new friends - all with a few clicks of the mouse.

MOUNTAIN GATE RV PARK **Ratings: 10/10★/9.5** (RV Park) Avail: 72 full hkups (30/50 amps). 2021 rates: $37 to $43. (800)404-6040, 14161 Holiday Rd, Redding, CA 96003

REDDING PREMIER RV RESORT

good sam park **Ratings: 10/10★/10** (Campground) From Jct of I-5 & Exit 680 (SR-299E/Lake Blvd/Burney-Alturas), W 0.2 mi on Lake Blvd to N Boulder Dr, N 0.1 mi (L). **FAC:** paved rds. (104 spaces). Avail: 54 paved, patios, 50 pull-thrus, (25x70), back-ins (25x65), accepts full hkup units only, 54 full hkups (30/50 amps), seasonal sites, WiFi @ sites, rentals, dump, laundry, LP gas. **REC:** pool, boating nearby, playground, hunting nearby. Pet restrict (B). Partial handicap access. No tents. Big rig sites, eco-friendly. 2021 rates: $56.56 to $77.28.

(530)246-0101 Lat: 40.61314, Lon: -122.37035
280 N Boulder Dr, Redding, CA 96003
www.premierrvresorts.com
See ad this page

REDDING RV PARK **Ratings: 10/9★/9** (RV Park) Avail: 22 full hkups (30/50 amps). 2021 rates: $40 to $43. (530)241-0707, 11075 Campers Ct, Redding, CA 96003

SACRAMENTO RIVER RV PARK **Ratings: 9/9.5★/8** (RV Park) Avail: 25 full hkups (30/50 amps). 2021 rates: $45. (530)365-6402, 6596 Riverland Dr, Redding, CA 96002

WHISKEYTOWN NRA/BRANDY CREEK (Public National Park) From Redding, W 8 mi on Hwy 299 to visitor center, W 5 mi(E). 32 Avail. 2021 rates: $15. (530)242-3400

WHISKEYTOWN NRA/OAK BOTTOM (Public National Park) From W-end of town, W 14 mi on SR-299 (L). 22 Avail. 2021 rates: $14 to $21. (530)242-3400

REDLANDS — M6 *San Bernardino*

MISSION RV PARK **Ratings: 8/9.5★/7.5** (RV Park) Avail: 95 full hkups (30/50 amps). 2021 rates: $43. (909)796-7570, 26397 W Redlands Blvd, Redlands, CA 92373

REDWAY — C1 *Humboldt*

DEAN CREEK RESORT

good sam park **Ratings: 8.5/9★/8.5** (Campground) 52 Avail: 6 full hkups, 46 W, 46 E (20/30 amps). 2021 rates: $35 to $55. (707)923-2555, 4112 Redwood Drive, Redway, CA 95560

RIDGECREST — G4 *Kern*

MILITARY PARK SIERRA VISTA RV PARK (NAWS CHINA LAKE) (Public) From US-395 & SR-178: Go 12 miles W on SR-178 to the NAWS China Lake Main Gate (E). Avail: 60 full hkups (30 amps). 2021 rates: $15 to $28. (877)628-9233

RIO VISTA — D2 *Solano*

BRANNAN ISLAND SRA (Public State Park) From Jct of SR-12 & SR-160, S 3.5 mi on SR-160 (L). Avail: 140 W. 2021 rates: $25 to $40. (916)777-6671

DELTA MARINA YACHT HARBOR (RV RESORT) **Ratings: 7.5/9/8** (Campground) Avail: 19 full hkups (30/50 amps). 2021 rates: $45 to $55. (866)774-2315, 100 Marina Dr, Rio Vista, CA 94571

DUCK ISLAND RV PARK & FISHING RESORT

good sam park **Ratings: 8.5/NA/8.5** (RV Park) Avail: 25 full hkups (30/50 amps). 2021 rates: $55. (916)777-6663, 16814 Hwy 160, Rio Vista, CA 94571

RIO VIENTO RV PARK **Ratings: 5.5/9★/8.5** (RV Park) Avail: 60 full hkups (30/50 amps). 2021 rates: $50. (925)382-4193, 4460 W. Sherman Island Rd, Rio Vista, CA 94571

SANDY BEACH COUNTY PARK AND CAMPGROUND

(Public) From Jct of Hwy 12 & Main St, E 0.4 mi on Main St to 2nd St, S 0.5 mi on 2nd St to Beach Dr, E 0.7 mi (R). **FAC:** paved rds. Avail: 42 paved, 42 pull-thrus, (25x45), 42 W, 42 E (30 amps), tent sites, dump, fire rings, firewood. **REC:** wading pool, Sacramento River: swim, fishing, boating nearby, hunting nearby. Pets OK. Partial handicap access, 14 day max stay, eco-friendly. 2021 rates: $34.

(707)374-2097 Lat: 38.08184, Lon: -121.41273
2333 Beach Drive, Rio Vista, CA 94571
www.solanocounty.com/Parks
See ad this page

We appreciate your business!

RIVERSIDE — M5 *Riverside*

RANCHO JURUPA REGIONAL PARK (Public) From Jct of Hwy 60 & Rubidioux (exit 50), S 0.6 mi on Rubidioux to Mission Blvd, E 0.8 mi to Crestmore, S 1 mi (E). 131 Avail: 70 full hkups, 61 W, 61 E (20/30 amps). 2021 rates: $35 to $40. (951)684-7032

ROCKLIN — D3 *Placer*

Travel Services

CAMPING WORLD OF ROCKLIN As the nation's largest retailer of RV supplies, accessories, services and new and used RVs, Camping World is committed to making your total RV experience better. **SERVICES:** tire, RV appliance, restrooms. RV supplies, emergency parking, RV accessible. Hours: 9am to 6pm.
(800)437-5332 Lat: 38.799142, Lon: -121.213046
4435 Granite Drive, Rocklin, CA 95677
www.campingworld.com

ROSEVILLE — D3 *Placer*

PLACER COUNTY FAIR (Public) From Jct of I-80 & Hwy 65 (Exit 106), N 2 mi on Hwy 65 to Pleasant Grove Blvd, SE 1.4 mi to Washington Blvd, S 1.5 mi to Corporation Yard Rd., W 0.2 mi (Left through Gate J, follow signs) (R). Closed during month of June. 70 Avail: 60 full hkups, 10 W, 10 E (30/50 amps). 2021 rates: $45. Jul 01 to May 31. (916)701-8181

Travel Services

CAMPING WORLD OF ROSEVILLE/SACRAMENTO As the nation's largest retailer of RV supplies, accessories, services and new and used RVs, Camping World is committed to making your total RV experience better. **SERVICES:** RV, restrooms. RV Sales. RV supplies, RV accessible. Hours: 9am to 7pm.
(888)306-5486 Lat: 38.726719, Lon: -121.28668
1039 Orlando Ave, Roseville, CA 95661
www.campingworld.com

We give you what you want. First, we surveyed thousands of RVers just like you. Then, we developed our exclusive Triple Rating System for campgrounds based on the results. That's why our rating system is so good at explaining the quality of facilities and cleanliness of campgrounds.

SACRAMENTO — D3 *Sacramento*

SACRAMENTO See also Isleton, Loomis, Nicolaus & West Sacramento.

➔ CAL EXPO RV PARK (Public) From Jct of Capitol City Fwy (Bus 80) & Cal Expo/Exposition Blvd exit, E 1.3 mi on Exposition Blvd to Ethan Way, S 0.4 mi (past Gate 12) onto service rd (continuing straight), S 0.1 mi (R). Avail: 176 full hkups (30/50 amps). 2021 rates: $45. (916)263-3187

➚ SACRAMENTO SHADE RV PARK **Ratings: 9/7.5★/9.5** (RV Park) Avail: 80 full hkups (30/50 amps). 2021 rates: $62. (916)922-0814, 2150 Auburn Blvd, Sacramento, CA 95821

SALINAS — F2 *Monterey*

➔ LAGUNA SECA RECREATION AREA (Public) From Jct of Hwy 101 & Exit 326B/Monterey Peninsula exit (in Salinas), SW 2.4 mi on S Sanborn Rd (becomes E Blanco Rd) to Hwy 68 (S Main St), S 9.0 mi (R); or From Jct of Hwy 1 & Hwy 68E, E 7 mi on Hwy 68E (L). 16% grade at park. 93 Avail: 93 W, 93 E (30 amps). 2021 rates: $40. (831)242-8200

⬆ SALINAS/MONTEREY KOA **Ratings: 8/7/6** (RV Park) Avail: 57 full hkups (30/50 amps). 2021 rates: $58 to $73. (800)541-0085, 8710 Prunedale North Rd, Salinas, CA 93907

SALTON CITY — J5 *Imperial*

➔ SEA VIEW ESTATES & RV RESORT & SPA **Ratings: 9/9★/7.5** (RV Park) Avail: 125 full hkups (30/50 amps). 2021 rates: $49. (760)394-4333, 336 Seaview Drive, Salton City, CA 92275

➔ WEST SHORES RV PARK **Ratings: 5/7.5/6.5** (RV Park) Avail: 46 full hkups (30/50 amps). 2021 rates: $49. (760)343-9091, 2740 Sea Garden Ave, Salton City, CA 92274

SAMOA — B1 *Humboldt*

⬅ SAMOA BOAT RAMP (Public) From Hwy 101, exit Hwy 255W (exit 713) to Samoa Peninsula, S 5 mi on New Navy Base, follow signs (L). Avail: 13 W. 2021 rates: $25. (707)445-7651

Directional arrows indicate the campground's position in relation to the nearest town.

SAN ANDREAS — D3 *Calaveras*

⬆ GOLD STRIKE VILLAGE **Ratings: 6/8★/8** (RV Area in MH Park) 20 Avail: 1 full hkups, 19 W, 19 E (30/50 amps). 2021 rates: $50. (209)754-3180, 1925 Gold Strike Rd, San Andreas, CA 95249

SAN BERNARDINO — M5 *San Bernardino*

Travel Services

⬇ **CAMPING WORLD OF SAN BERNARDINO** As the nation's largest retailer of RV supplies, accessories, services and new and used RVs, Camping World is committed to making your total RV experience better. **SERVICES:** tire, RV appliance, restrooms. RV supplies, RV accessible. Hours: 9am to 6pm.
(800)423-7569 Lat: 34.06035, Lon: -117.28252
151 E Redlands Blvd, San Bernardino, CA 92408
www.campingworld.com

Things to See and Do

➔ **SAN BERNARDINO COUNTY REGIONAL PARKS** Camp at any of the six scenic parks - from the mountains to the Inland Empire. Reserve your spot online.

THE GREAT OUTDOORS JUST GOT BETTER
Visit any of our scenic parks where you will find lots to do in the great outdoors. We offer a wide variety of programs and events. Reserve online at www.sbcountyparks.com.
Partial handicap access. Hours: 9am to 5pm. No CC.
(909)38-PARKS
777 E Rialto Ave, San Bernardino, CA 92415
www.sbcountyparks.org
See ad page 96

SAN CLEMENTE — J4 *Orange*

⬇ MILITARY PARK SAN ONOFRE REC BEACH (MCB CAMP PENDLETON) (Public) From jct I-5 & Basilone Rd: Go 1-1/2 mi E on Basilone Rd (E). 144 Avail: 46 full hkups, 98 W, 98 E (30/50 amps). 2021 rates: $35 to $45. (760)763-7263

⬇ SAN CLEMENTE STATE BEACH (Public State Park) From town, S 1 mi on I-5 to Avenida Calafia exit (Exit 73), follow signs (L). 160 Avail: (30 amps). 2021 rates: $40 to $65. (949)492-3156

⬇ SAN ONOFRE SB-BLUFFS (Public State Park) From Jct of I-5 & Basilone Rd exit (Exit 71), S 3 mi on Basilone Rd (E). 221 Avail: Pit toilets. 2021 rates: $40. (949)492-4872

⬇ SAN ONOFRE SB-SAN MATEO (Public State Park) From Jct of I-5 & Christianitos Rd (exit 72), E 1 mi on Christianitos Rd (R). 157 Avail: 67 W, 67 E (20 amps). 2021 rates: $40 to $65. (949)492-4872

SAN DIEGO — K4 *San Diego*

A SPOTLIGHT Introducing San Diego's colorful attractions appearing at the front of this state section.

SAN DIEGO See also Chula Vista, El Cajon, Jamul, La Mesa, Lakeside & Santee.

⬉ **CAMPLAND ON THE BAY**
good sam park **Ratings: 9/9.5★/9.5** (RV Park) N-bnd: Jct of I-5 & Grand/Garnet exit 23A (becomes Mission Bay Dr), N 0.2 mi to Grand Ave, W 0.8 mi to Olney, S 0.2 mi to Pacific Beach Dr(R) S-bnd: Jct of I-5 & Balboa/Garnet St (Mission Bay Dr), S 0.5 mi to Mission Bay Dr to Grand Ave, follow N-bnd directions (E).

SANDY BEACH ON MISSION BAY
We have our own fabulous beach overlooking Mission Bay! Enjoy our cantina, spas, heated pools, game room & market. Year-round activities & entertainment for all ages! New skateboard park! Close to SeaWorld & San Diego Zoo.
FAC: paved rds. Avail: 568 paved, 26 pull-thrus, (20x43), back-ins (20x37), 405 full hkups, 145 W, 145 E (30/50 amps), cable, WiFi @ sites, tent sites, dump, laundry, groc, LP gas, fire rings, firewood, restaurant, controlled access. **REC:** heated pool, hot tub, Mission Bay: swim, fishing, kayaking/canoeing, boating nearby, playground. Pet restrict (B/Q) $. Partial handicap access, eco-friendly. 2021 rates: $55 to $164, Military discount. ATM.
(800)422-9386 Lat: 32.79630, Lon: -117.22390
2211 Pacific Beach Drive, San Diego, CA 92109
www.campland.com
See ad opposite page, 101

➚ MILITARY PARK ADMIRAL BAKER RV PARK (NAS SAN DIEGO) (Public) From jct I-8 and Friars Rd, follow Friars Rd to Santo Rd left, then right on Admiral Baker Rd (R). Avail: 48 full hkups (30/50 amps). 2021 rates: $40 to $52. (619)487-0019

⬇ MILITARY PARK FIDDLER'S COVE RV PARK (NAS NORTH ISLAND) (Public) From I-5 & Coronado Bridge: cross the bridge to city of Coronado, then left on Orange Ave for approximately 6 mi (R). Avail: 57 full hkups (30/50 amps). 2021 rates: $40 to $51. (877)628-9233

⬆ **MISSION BAY RV RESORT**
good sam park **Ratings: 9/9★/8.5** (RV Park) From Jct of I-5 & Clairemont Dr (East Mission Bay Dr/Exit 22), N 0.8 mi on East Mission Bay Dr to De Anza Rd, W 0.1 mi (R).

EXPERIENCE SAN DIEGO BAY'S FINEST
Our beautiful spacious resort is big rig, pet & family friendly with breathtaking views. Near Sea World, San Diego Zoo, Old Town, Sunset Cliffs and more, our surrounding fun is endless! Make us your next vacation destination.
FAC: paved rds. Avail: 260 paved, patios, back-ins (24x48), 260 full hkups (30/50 amps), cable, WiFi @ sites, laundry, firewood, controlled access. **REC:** Mission Bay: swim, fishing, kayaking/canoeing, boating nearby. Pet restrict (B/Q) $. Partial handicap access. No tents, eco-friendly. 2021 rates: $75 to $197.
(877)219-6900 Lat: 32.79433, Lon: -117.21898
2727 De Anza Road, San Diego, CA 92109
www.missionbayrvresort.com
See ad opposite page

RV Tech Tips - Get Custom Floor Protection: If your new trailer has wall-to-wall carpeting, and you are forever tracking in dirt and getting the carpet at the entrance dirty, try this handy tip. Make a cardboard template of the entryway area. Then buy a plastic floor mat - the type used over carpet to allow office chairs to move about - from an office-supply store. Using the template of the entrance area, cut the plastic mat to custom-fit the space. Then spray-paint the backside of the mat the approximate color of the carpet. Editor's Note: Be sure to allow the paint to dry fully before placing the mat on your carpet. Evaporating solvent from the paint could damage the carpet if the paint isn't cured first.

good sam park
Family Friendly Fun
Nestled along Mission Bay, Campland on the Bay® offers waterfront RV sites, watercraft rentals, dining, amenities galore and easy access to San Diego's many attractions.
San Diego's Most Beloved RV Resort
Campland on the Bay
Campland.com • 800-422-9386
• 2211 Pacific Beach Dr. • San Diego, CA 92109
Escape to San Diego's Mission Bay
good sam park
Relish waterview RV sites, pool, clubhouse, restrooms, showers, laundry, lounge & game room, 24-hour security, and access to Campland's amenities.
Camp on the Mellow Side of Mission Bay
MissionBayRVResort.com • 877-219-6900
2727 De Anza Road • San Diego, CA
MISSION BAY
RV RESORT

SAN DIEGO (CONT)

RANCHO LOS COCHES RV PARK
good sam park **Ratings: 10/10★/9.5** (RV Park) From jct I-5 & I-8 at San Diego (Exit 22): Go 21 mi E on I-8 (Exit 22), then 1/2 mi N on Los Coches Rd, stay in right lane, then 1/2 mi E on Hwy 8 Bus (L) Do not use GPS. **FAC:** paved rds. (135 spaces). Avail: 49 all weather, patios, 2 pull-thrus, (22x42), back-ins (20x40), 49 full hkups (30/50 amps), seasonal sites, cable, WiFi @ sites, tent sites, dump, laundry. **REC:** heated pool, hot tub, Los Coches Creek: boating nearby. Pet restrict (B/Q). Partial handicap access, eco-friendly. 2021 rates: $63 to $93, Military discount.
(800)630-0448 Lat: 32.83638, Lon: -116.90037
13468 Hwy 8 Business, Lakeside, CA 92040
rancholoscochesrv.com
See primary listing at Lakeside and ad page 114

SANTA FE PARK & RV RESORT Ratings: 9/9★/7.5 (RV Park) Avail: 110 full hkups (30/50 amps). 2021 rates: $125 to $175. (858)272-4051, 5707 Santa Fe St, San Diego, CA 92109

SANTEE LAKES RECREATION PRESERVE
good sam park **Ratings: 9.5/9.5★/9.5** (Public) From Jct of I-5 (Mission Valley Fwy) & I-15 (Escondido Fwy) N 4.4 mi on I-15 (Escondido Fwy) to Hwy 52, E 5. 9mi to Mast Blvd, NE 1.4 mi to Fanita Pkwy, S 0.2 mi (R). **FAC:** paved rds. (300 spaces). 83 Avail: 70 paved, 13 dirt, 60 pull-thrus, (30x62), back-ins (30x60), 83 full hkups (30/50 amps), seasonal sites, cable, WiFi @ sites, tent sites, rentals, dump, laundry, LP gas, firewood, restaurant, controlled access. **REC:** pool, hot tub, Santee Lakes: fishing, kayaking/canoeing, boating nearby, playground, rec open to public. Pet restrict (Q) $. Partial handicap access. Big rig sites, eco-friendly. 2021 rates: $57 to $80.
(619)596-3141 Lat: 32.84594, Lon: -117.00381
9310 Fanita Parkway, Santee, CA 92071
www.santeelakes.com
See primary listing at Santee and ad page 113

SAN DIMAS — M4 *Los Angeles*

BONELLI BLUFFS RV RESORT & CAMPGROUND
good sam park **Ratings: 9.5/8.5★/9** (Campground) From Jct of I-10 & Fairplex Dr (exit 44), N 0.5 mi on Fairplex Dr to Via Verde, W 0.6 mi to Camper View Rd, N 0.3 mi (E).

DISCOVER BREATHTAKING LAKE VIEWS!
Discover breathtaking lake views at Bonelli Bluffs RV Resort & Campground. We offer Spacious Lots, Level Hard Pads, Pull-Thru Sites, Full Hookups, Laundry Facilities, and a Family, Senior & Pet Friendly Atmosphere.

FAC: paved rds. (504 spaces). Avail: 329 paved, patios, 15 pull-thrus, (33x45), back-ins (27x50), 329 full hkups (30/50 amps), seasonal sites, cable, WiFi, tent sites, dump, laundry, groc, LP gas, fire rings, firewood, controlled access. **REC:** pool, Puddingstone Lake: swim, fishing, kayaking/canoeing, boating nearby, golf, playground. Pet restrict (S/B/Q) $. Partial handicap access, 20 day max stay, eco-friendly. 2021 rates: $57 to $77, Military discount. ATM.
(909)599-8355 Lat: 34.08404, Lon: -117.79150
1440 Camper View Rd, San Dimas, CA 91773
www.bonellibluffsrv.com
See ad pages 102, 109

SAN FRANCISCO — E2 *San Francisco*

A SPOTLIGHT Introducing San Francisco's colorful attractions appearing at the front of this state section.

SAN FRANCISCO See also Bethel Island, Greenbrae, Half Moon Bay, Napa, Novato, Olema, Pacifica, Pescadero, Petaluma, Pleasonton, Rio Vista, San Jose, Santa Rosa, Vacaville & Vallejo.

COYOTE VALLEY RV RESORT
good sam park **Ratings: 10/10★/10** (RV Resort) From Jct I-280 and Hwy 101: Go 52 miles S on Hwy 101 to Cochrane Rd (Exit 367), then 3/4 mi W on Cochrane Rd to Monterey Rd, then 4 mi N on Monterey Rd (R). **FAC:** paved rds. Avail: 197 paved, patios, back-ins (30x60), accepts full hkup units only, 197 full hkups (30/50 amps), WiFi @ sites, dump, laundry, groc, LP gas. **REC:** heated pool, hot tub, boating nearby. Pet restrict (B/Q) $. Partial handicap access. No tents. Big rig sites, eco-friendly. 2021 rates: $70 to $80.
(866)376-5500 Lat: 37.191388, Lon: -121.713097
9750 Monterey Rd, San Jose, CA 95037
www.coyotevalleyresort.com
See primary listing at San Jose and ad pages 106, 115, 154

MARIN RV PARK
good sam park **Ratings: 10/10★/8** From jct Veterans Blvd & US 101: Go 10 mi N on US 101, then 460 feet N on Lucky Dr (exit 450A), then 1000 feet N on Redwood Hwy/frntg rd (R). **FAC:** paved rds. (89 spaces). Avail: 84 all weather, back-ins (20x50), accepts full hkup units only, 84 full hkups (30/50 amps), seasonal sites, ca-

Get the GOOD SAM CAMPING APP

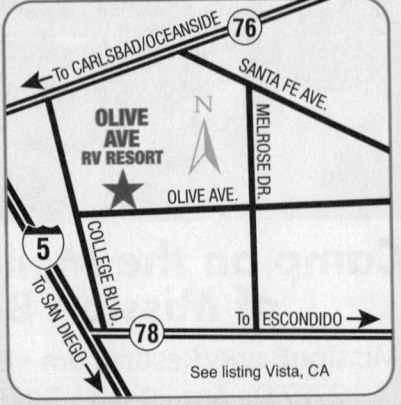

ble, WiFi @ sites, dump, laundry. **REC:** heated pool, boating nearby. Pet restrict (Q). No tents. Big rig sites, eco-friendly. 2021 rates: $99.
(888)461-5199 Lat: 37.94111, Lon: -122.51518
2140 Redwood Hwy, Greenbrae, CA 94904
www.marinrvpark.com
See primary listing at Greenbrae and ad page 116

VINEYARD RV PARK
Ratings: 10/10★/10 (RV Park) From Jct of I-80 & I-580: Go 50 mi N on I-80, then 3 mi W to Midway Rd (R). **FAC:** paved rds. (256 spaces). Avail: 35 paved, patios, 27 pull-thrus, (30x64), back-ins (30x45), 35 full hkups (30/50 amps), seasonal sites, cable, WiFi @ sites, rentals, dump, laundry, LP gas, fire rings, firewood. **REC:** pool, pond, fishing, boating nearby, playground, hunting nearby. Pets OK $. No tents, eco-friendly. 2021 rates: $69 to $79.
(866)447-8797 Lat: 38.41832, Lon: -121.93687
4985 Midway Rd, Vacaville, CA 95688
www.vineyardrvpark.com
See primary listing at Vacaville and ad page 144

SAN JACINTO — J5 *Riverside*

REFLECTION LAKE RV PARK & CAMPGROUND Ratings: 7/6.5/5.5 (Campground) 57 Avail: 57 W, 57 E (30 amps). 2021 rates: $35 to $45. (951)654-7906, 3440 Cottonwood Ave, San Jacinto, CA 92582

SAN JOSE — E2 *Santa Clara*

SAN JOSE See also Morgan Hill, Pleasanton & Scotts Valley.

COYOTE VALLEY RV RESORT
Ratings: 10/10★/10 (RV Resort) From Jct of Hwy 101 & Cochrane Rd (Exit 367): Go 3/4 mi W on Cochrane Rd to Monterey Rd, then 4 mi N on Monterey Rd (R).

NEWLY EXPANDED LUXURY RESORT!
A magnificent valley setting with access to everything in the San Francisco Bay Area. Stay in a Top Rated RV Resort with easy access to the entire Bay Area; including Silicon Valley, Monterey, Carmel & SF.
FAC: paved rds. Avail: 197 paved, patios, back-ins (30x60), accepts full hkup units only, 197 full hkups (30/50 amps), WiFi @ sites, dump, laundry, groc, LP gas. **REC:** heated pool, hot tub, boating nearby. Pet restrict (B/Q) $. Partial handicap access. No tents. Big rig sites, eco-friendly. 2021 rates: $70 to $80.
(866)376-5500 Lat: 37.191388, Lon: -121.713097
9750 Monterey Rd, San Jose, CA 95037
coyotevalleyresort.com
See ad next page, 106, 115

SAN JUAN BAUTISTA — F2 *San Benito*

BETABEL RV PARK
Ratings: 10/9.5★/9.5 (RV Park) From Jct of US-101 & Hwy 156: Go 2 mi N on US-101 to Betabel Rd (exit 349), then W across the overpass to Betabel Rd, then 2/10 mi S on Betabel Rd (R). **FAC:** paved rds. (164 spaces). Avail: 44 paved, patios, 19 pull-thrus, (24x60), back-ins (22x50), 44 full hkups (30/50 amps), seasonal sites, WiFi @ sites, dump, laundry, groc, LP gas, controlled access. **REC:** heated pool, playground. Pet restrict (B/Q). Partial handicap access. No tents. Big rig sites, eco-friendly. 2021 rates: $60.20, Military discount.
(831)623-2202 Lat: 36.90098, Lon: -121.55788
9664 Betabel Rd, San Juan Bautista, CA 95045
www.betabel.com
See ad page 107

FREMONT PEAK (Public State Park) From jct Hwy 156E & CR G1: Go 11 mi S on CR G1 (San Juan Canyon Rd). 25 Avail: Pit toilets. (831)623-4255

SAN JUAN CAPISTRANO — P4 *Orange*

RONALD W. CASPERS WILDERNESS PARK (Public) From jct I-5 (San Diego Fwy) & Hwy 74 (exit 82) (Ortega Hwy): Go 7-1/2 mi E on Hwy 74. 72 Avail. 2021 rates: $15 to $21. (949)923-2210

SAN LUIS OBISPO — G2 *San Luis Obispo*

A SPOTLIGHT Introducing San Luis Obispo County's colorful attractions appearing at the front of the state section.

AVILA PISMO BEACH KOA **Ratings: 9.5/8★/8.5** (Campground) Avail: 82 full hkups (30/50 amps). 2021 rates: $55 to $150. (800)562-1244, 7075 Ontario Rd, San Luis Obispo, CA 93405

EL CHORRO REGIONAL PARK (Public) From town, N 5 mi on Santa Rosa St/Hwy 1 to Dairy Creek Rd., turn right to entrance (L). Avail: 43 full hkups (20/30 amps). 2021 rates: $23 to $40. (805)781-5930

MILITARY PARK CAMP SAN LUIS OBISPO RV PARK (SAN LUIS OBISPO) (Public) From jct US 101 & SR-1: Go 5 mi NW toward Morro Bay (L). Avail: 12 full hkups (30/50 amps). 2021 rates: $25 to $28. (805)594-6500

Things to See and Do

VISIT SLO CAL - SAN LUIS OBISPO COUNTY
Visit SLOCAL: providing area information for travelers.

LIFE'S TOO BEAUTIFUL TO RUSH
Find your perfect spot in SLO CAL! Stay just steps from the beach or minutes from wineries. Our area parks offer different amenities. Heated pools, free Wi-Fi, bike rentals, & cafes, but all have plenty of sunshine year round
Restrooms. Hours: . No CC.
(805)541-8000
1334 Marsh St. , San Luis Obispo, CA 93401
www.slocal.com
See ad page 121

SAN MARCOS — J4 *San Diego*

Travel Services

CAMPING WORLD OF SAN MARCOS As the nation's largest retailer of RV supplies, accessories, services and new and used RVs, Camping World is committed to making your total RV experience better. **SERVICES:** tire, RV appliance, restrooms. RV supplies, LP gas, RV accessible. Hours: 9am to 6pm.
(800)874-4346 Lat: 33.138356, Lon: -117.172309
200 Travelers Way, San Marcos, CA 92069
www.campingworld.com

SAN MARTIN — F2 *Santa Clara*

Travel Services

CAMPING WORLD OF SAN MARTIN As the nation's largest retailer of RV supplies, accessories, services and new and used RVs, Camping World is committed to making your total RV experience better. **SERVICES:** tire, RV appliance, restrooms. RV supplies, emergency parking, RV accessible. Hours: 9am to 6pm.
(800)782-0061 Lat: 37.092073, Lon: -121.599859
13575 Sycamore Avenue, San Martin, CA 95046
www.campingworld.com

SAN SIMEON — G2 *Monterey*

HEARST SAN SIMEON (Public State Park) From town, 5 mi S on Hwy-1. 115 Avail. 2021 rates: $35. (805)772-6101

SANGER — F3 *Fresno*

RIVERBEND RV PARK **Ratings: 6.5/8★/7** (RV Park) Avail: 29 full hkups (30/50 amps). 2021 rates: $50 to $70. (559)787-3627, 17604 E Kings Canyon Rd, Sanger, CA 93657

SANTA BARBARA — H3 *Santa Barbara*

A SPOTLIGHT Introducing Santa Barbara's colorful attractions appearing at the front of the state section.

CACHUMA LAKE CAMPGROUND
(Public) From Jct of Hwy 101 & 154, NW 18 mi on Hwy 154 (R) Note: Reservation required for group area. **FAC:** paved rds. 157 Avail: 120 paved, 37 gravel, 7 pull-thrus, (23x56), back-ins (30x50), 120 full hkups, 37 W, 37 E (30/50 amps), WiFi @ sites, tent sites, rentals, shower$, dump, laundry, groc, LP gas, firewood, restaurant. **REC:** pool, Lake Cachuma: fishing, marina, kayaking/canoeing, boating nearby, playground, hunting nearby, rec open to public. Pets OK $. Partial handicap access, 14 day max stay. 2021 rates: $25 to $50.
(805)568-2460 Lat: 34.57434, Lon: -119.95856
2225 Hwy 154, Santa Barbara, CA 93105
countyofsb.org/parks/cachuma.sbc
See ad page 118

EARL WARREN SHOWGROUNDS RV PARK (Public) From jct US 101 & Las Positas Rd (exit 100): Go 1/4 mi N on Las Positas Rd to Gate A (L). Avail: 44 full hkups (30/50 amps). 2021 rates: $65 to $70. (805)350-4556

OCEAN MESA AT EL CAPITAN **Ratings: 10/8.5/9** (RV Resort) Avail: 80 full hkups (30/50 amps). 2021 rates: $95 to $125. (866)410-5783, 100 El Capitan Terrace Lane, Goleta, CA 93117

RANCHO OSO RV & CAMPING RESORT
Ratings: 7/7.5/7.5 (RV Park) 99 Avail: 74 full hkups, 25 W, 25 E (30 amps). 2021 rates: $60 to $80. (888)563-7040, 3750 Paradise Rd, Santa Barbara, CA 93105

SANTA BARBARA SUNRISE RV PARK **Ratings: 5.5/8★/5.5** (RV Park) Avail: 31 full hkups (30/50 amps). 2021 rates: $60 to $75. (805)966-9954, 516 S Salinas St, Santa Barbara, CA 93103

SANTA CRUZ — F1 *Santa Cruz*

SANTA CRUZ See also Felton, Marina, Morgan Hill, Moss Landing, Pescadero, Salinas, San Jose & Watsonville.

SANTA CRUZ HARBOR RV PARK (Public) S-bnd: From Jct of Hwy 1 & Soquel Ave, W 0.1 mi (right) on Frontage Rd to Soquel Ave (stay in Left lane), W 0.1 mi to 7th Ave; N-bnd: From Jct of Hwy 1 & Soquel Ave exit, W 0.2 mi on Soquel Ave to 7th Ave, S 1 mi to Brommer Ave, W 0.2 mi (L). Avail: 12 full hkups (30/50 amps). 2021 rates: $52. (831)475-3279

SANTA MARGARITA — G2 *San Luis Obispo*

SANTA MARGARITA LAKE (Public) From town: Go 10 mi SE on Pozo Rd, then E on Santa Margarita Lake Rd. 60 Avail: Pit toilets. 2021 rates: $25 to $36. (805)788-2397

SANTA MARGARITA LAKE KOA **Ratings: 8/6/6.5** (Campground) Avail: 18 full hkups (30/50 amps). 2021 rates: $70 to $90. (800)562-5619, 4765 Santa Margarita Lake Rd, Santa Margarita, CA 93453

SANTA NELLA — F2 *Merced*

OASIS WEST RV PARK **Ratings: 7.5/9★/8.5** (Campground) Avail: 35 full hkups (30/50 amps). 2021 rates: $50. (209)370-0603, 28485 Gonzaga Rd, Santa Nella, CA 95322

SAN LUIS RESERVOIR/ SAN LUIS CREEK (Public State Park) From Jct of I-5 & Hwy 152 (Exit 402B), W 7 mi on Hwy 152, follow San Luis Creek signs (E). 53 Avail: 53 W, 53 E (30 amps), Pit toilets. 2021 rates: $40 to $45. (209)826-1197

SANTA NELLA RV PARK
Ratings: 8.5/9.5★/9 (RV Park) From Jct of I-5 & Exit 407 (Santa Nella exit): Go 1/4 mi S on Hwy 33 (R).

EASY ACCESS OFF I-5. BIG RIG SITES!
At nearby San Luis Reservoir you can fish, boat, swim, or just relax on the water or shoreline. Extra wide Big Rig sites with concrete pads. Free WiFi, pet friendly, restaurants nearby. Open year round. High Def Dish Network.
FAC: paved rds. Avail: 57 paved, patios, 55 pull-thrus, (30x65), back-ins (30x38), 57 full hkups (30/50 amps), cable, WiFi @ sites, laundry, LP gas. **REC:** boating nearby, hunting nearby. Pets OK. Partial handicap access. No tents. Big rig sites, eco-friendly. 2021 rates: $44 to $48, Military discount.
(209)826-3105 Lat: 37.100661, Lon: -121.016658
13023 State Hwy 33, Santa Nella, CA 95322
www.santanellarvpark.com
See ad page 155

SANTA PAULA — H3 *Ventura*

VENTURA RANCH KOA HOLIDAY **Ratings: 7/5.5/8** (RV Park) 61 Avail: 15 full hkups, 46 W, 46 E (30/50 amps). 2021 rates: $66 to $115. (877)779-8080, 7400 Pine Grove Rd, Santa Paula, CA 93060

According to the Wall Street Journal, 100 billion plastic shopping bags are consumed in the United States annually. Consider toting your own reusable shopping bags instead of using plastic.

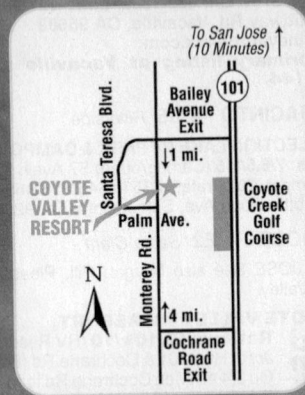

SANTA ROSA — D2 *Sonoma*

SONOMA COUNTY RV PARK-AT THE FAIRGROUNDS
Ratings: 8/8.5★/7 (Public) From Jct of Hwy 101 & CA 12 E, E 0.5 mi on CA 12 E/Bennett Valley, NE 0.6 mi on Bennett Valley to Brookwood, S 0.4 mi to Aston, W 0.1 mi (L) (Note: Closed July 15 to Aug 15 for fair).

MAKE US YOUR TOURING HEADQUARTERS
Conveniently located near Hwy 101 and Hwy 12 in Santa Rosa. This is the perfect home base for travelers seeking to explore. Just minutes from world class wineries, Bodega Bay, Lake Sonoma & the Lush Russian River Region.

FAC: all weather rds. Avail: 164 all weather, 5 pull-thrus, (22x70), back-ins (25x35), accepts full hkup units only, 164 full hkups (30/50 amps), WiFi @ sites, dump, laundry. **REC:** boating nearby, golf, hunting nearby. Pets OK. No tents, Age restrict may apply, 28 day max stay, eco-friendly. 2021 rates: $50 to $55.
(707)293-8410 Lat: 38.42594, Lon: -122.69838
1500 Aston Ave, Santa Rosa, CA 95404
www.sonomacountyfair.com/rv-park.php
See ad this page

SPRING LAKE REGIONAL PARK (Public) From Jct of SR-101 & SR-12 (Exit 488B), E 3 mi on SR-12 to Hoen Ave, N 2 mi to Newanga Ave (E). 31 Avail. 2021 rates: $32. May 01 to Sep 30. (707)539-8092

SUGARLOAF RIDGE (Public State Park) From Jct of Hwys 12 & 101, E 7 mi on Hwy 12 to Adobe Canyon Rd, N 3 mi (E). 50 Avail. 2021 rates: $35. (707)833-5712

SANTEE — K5 *San Diego*

SANTEE LAKES RECREATION PRESERVE
Ratings: 9.5/9.5★/9.5 (Public) From Jct of Hwy 52 & Mast Blvd, NE 1.4 mi on Mast Blvd to Fanita Pkwy, S 0.2 mi (R).

GREAT FACILITIES AND GREAT LOCATION
Over 190 acres of Parkland! Enjoy the quiet tranquility of the country, while being close enough to visit the many attractions of San Diego County. The perfect location to explore the mountains, deserts, beaches, and lakes.

FAC: paved rds. (300 spaces). 83 Avail: 70 paved, 13 dirt, 60 pull-thrus, (30x62), back-ins (30x60), 83 full hkups (30/50 amps), seasonal sites, cable, WiFi @ sites, tent sites, rentals, dump, laundry, LP gas, firewood, restaurant, controlled access. **REC:** heated pool, hot tub, Santee Lakes: fishing, kayaking/canoeing, boating nearby, playground, rec open to public. Pet restrict (Q) $. Partial handicap access. Big rig sites, eco-friendly. 2021 rates: $57 to $80.
(619)596-3141 Lat: 32.84594, Lon: -117.00381
9310 Fanita Parkway, Santee, CA 92071
www.santeelakes.com
See ad page 113

SCOTTS VALLEY — F1 *Santa Cruz*

SANTA CRUZ RANCH RV RESORT
Ratings: 8/9★/7.5 (RV Park) Avail: 25 full hkups (30 amps). 2021 rates: $90 to $98. (888)563-7040, 917 Disc Dr, Scotts Valley, CA 95066

SEQUOIA NATIONAL PARK — F3 *Fresno*

SEQUOIA/DORST CREEK (Public National Park) From town: Go 12 mi N on Generals Hwy. 218 Avail. 2021 rates: $22. Jun 17 to Sep 08. (559)565-3341

SEQUOIA/LODGEPOLE (Public National Park) From town, E 18 mi on CA-198 (Gen Hwy) (R); or From Giant Forest Vlg, N 5 mi on CA-198 (R). 214 Avail. 2021 rates: $22. May 20 to Sep 29. (559)565-3341

SEQUOIA/POTWISHA (Public National Park) From town, NE 9 mi on SR-198 (E). 42 Avail. 2021 rates: $22. (559)565-3341

SHASTA LAKE — B2 *Shasta*

SHASTA LAKE See also Lakehead, Lewiston, O'Brien & Redding.

LAKESHORE INN & RV **Ratings: 7/5/5.5** (Campground) 40 Avail: 13 full hkups, 27 W, 27 E (30/50 amps). 2021 rates: $44 to $45. May 15 to Sep 15. (530)238-2003, 20483 Lakeshore Dr, Lakehead, CA 96051

SHAVER LAKE — F3 *Fresno*

CAMP EDISON (Public) From Jct of Hwys 99 & 180, 3.2 mi on Hwy 180 to Hwy 168, E 46.5 mi (R). 252 Avail: 43 full hkups, 209 E (30 amps). 2021 rates: $32 to $80. (559)841-3134

SHINGLE SPRINGS — D3 *El Dorado*

PLACERVILLE KOA **Ratings: 9.5/9.5★/9.5** (Campground) 59 Avail: 30 full hkups, 29 W, 29 E (30/50 amps). 2021 rates: $82 to $104. (530)676-2267, 4655 Rock Barn Rd, Shingle Springs, CA 95682

SHINGLETOWN — B2 *Shasta*

MT LASSEN/SHINGLETOWN KOA **Ratings: 9/9.5★/9.5** (Campground) 58 Avail: 37 full hkups, 12 W, 12 E (30/50 amps). 2021 rates: $58.89 to $70.89. Apr 01 to Oct 31. (530)474-3133, 7749 KOA Rd, Shingletown, CA 96088

SHOSHONE — G5 *Inyo*

SHOSHONE RV PARK
Ratings: 8/8★/8 (RV Park) Avail: 35 full hkups (30/50 amps). 2021 rates: $45. (760)852-4569, State Hwy 127, Shoshone, CA 92384

SIMI VALLEY — L1 *Ventura*

OAK PARK (Public) From Jct of Fwy 118 & Collins Dr, exit 19B (W-side of town), W 2 mi on Collins Dr, follow signs (R). 59 Avail: 29 W, 29 E (20/30 amps). 2021 rates: $32. (805)654-3951

SKYFOREST — L6 *San Bernardino*

SKYPARK CAMP + RV RESORT **Ratings: 9/9.5★/9.5** (RV Park) Avail: 57 full hkups (30/50 amps). 2021 rates: $100 to $120. (909)774-9927, 29297 Hwy 18, Skyforest, CA 92385

SNELLING — E3 *Mariposa*

LAKE MCSWAIN (Public) From Jct of SR-99 & G St (in Merced), NE 20 mi on G St (Snelling Rd) to Hwy 59, (follow signs). 111 Avail: 65 W, 65 E (30 amps). 2021 rates: $22 to $34. (209)378-2521

MCCLURE POINT RECREATION AREA (Public) From Jct of SR-99 & G St (in Merced), NE 20 mi on G St (Snelling Rd) to Hwy 59, E 13 mi (follow signs) (R). 100 Avail: 52 W, 52 E (30 amps). 2021 rates: $22 to $34. (855)800-2267

SOLVANG — H2 *Santa Barbara*

SOLVANG See also Buellton & Santa Barbara.

SONOMA — D2 *Sonoma*

SONOMA See also Greenbrae, Napa, Novato, Olema, Petaluma, Santa Rosa & Vallejo.

SONORA — E3 *Tuolumne*

SONORA See also Angels Camp, Arnold, Columbia, Groveland, San Andreas, Toulumne & Twain Harte.

MOTHER LODE FAIRGROUNDS - SONORA (Public) From Jct of Hwy 108 (in town) & Hwy 49 (Downtown Sonora Exit), N 1.1 mi on Hwy 49 to Southgate Dr, SE 0.3 mi on Southgate Dr (R). 60 Avail: 50 full hkups, 10 W, 10 E (30/50 amps). 2021 rates: $50. (209)532-7428

SOUTH LAKE TAHOE — D4 *El Dorado*

CAMP RICHARDSON RESORT **Ratings: 6.5/5.5/6** (Campground) 98 Avail: 22 full hkups, 76 W, 76 E (30 amps). 2021 rates: $65 to $77. May 26 to Nov 01. (800)544-1801, 1900 Jameson Beach Rd, South Lake Tahoe, CA 96158

CAMPGROUND BY THE LAKE (Public) From Jct of Hwy 50 & Rufus Allen Blvd (in South Lake Tahoe), S 200 yds on Rufus Allen Blvd (E). 140 Avail. 2021 rates: $30 to $46. Apr 01 to Oct 31. (530)542-6096

TAHOE VALLEY CAMPGROUND
Ratings: 8/7.5/7.5 (Campground) 295 Avail: 275 full hkups, 20 W, 20 E (30/50 amps). 2021 rates: $79 to $150. (888)563-7040, 1175 Melba Dr, South Lake Tahoe, CA 96150

STANDISH — B3 *Lassen*

DAYS END RV PARK
Ratings: 8/10★/9 (RV Park) From Jct of US-395 & CR-A3 (in Standish), W 150 ft on CR-A3 (R). Elev 4100 ft.**FAC:** all weather rds. Avail: 27 all weather, 10 pull-thrus, (23x75), back-ins (27x60), accepts full hkup units only, 27 full hkups (30/50 amps), WiFi @ sites, laundry. **REC:** hunting nearby. Pets OK. Partial handicap access. No tents. Big rig sites. 2021 rates: $38.50, Military discount.
(530)254-1094 Lat: 40.36568, Lon: -120.42320
718-755 Hwy 395, Standish, CA 96128
www.daysendrv.com
See ad this page

STOCKTON — E3 *San Joaquin*

RIVER POINT LANDING MARINA-RESORT **Ratings: 7.5/9★/8.5** (RV Park) 32 Avail: 32 W, 32 E (30/50 amps). 2021 rates: $49 to $59. (209)951-4144, 4950 Buckley Cove Way, Stockton, CA 95219

STOVE PIPE WELLS — F4 *Inyo*

DEATH VALLEY/STOVEPIPE WELLS VILLAGE (Public National Park) From Furnace Creek, NW 25 mi on Hwy 190 (R). Entrance fee required. 190 Avail. 2021 rates: $14. Oct 01 to May 10. (760)786-2331

SUSANVILLE — B3 *Lassen*

EAGLE LAKE RV PARK
Ratings: 9/9★/8.5 (RV Park) Avail: 57 full hkups (30/50 amps). 2021 rates: $40. May 15 to Nov 15. (530)825-3133, 687-125 Palmetto Way, Susanville, CA 96130

NORTH EAGLE LAKE (BLM) (Public Corps) From town, 29 mi on SR-139 to CR-A1, W 1 mi (R). 20 Avail: Pit toilets. 2021 rates: $8 to $11. May 15 to Nov 05. (530)257-0456

Looking for places the ""locals'' frequent? Make friends with park owners and staff to get the inside scoop!

SUSANVILLE (CONT)

➜ SUSANVILLE RV PARK

good sam park **Ratings: 9/9.5★/9.5** (RV Park) E-bnd: From Jct of SR-36 & SR-139, SE 1.1 mi on SR-36 to E Riverside Dr, NE (left turn) 0.1 mi to Johnstonville Rd (1st left turn), NW 0.1 mi (R); or W-bnd: From Jct of SR-36 & US-395, NW 2.9 mi on SR-36 to E Riverside Dr, NE (right turn) 0.1 mi to Johnstonville Rd (1st left turn), NW 0.1 mi (R). Elev 4200 ft.**FAC:** paved rds. (101 spaces). Avail: 48 paved, patios, 25 pull-thrus, (30x60), back-ins (30x60), accepts full hkup units only, 48 full hkups (30/50 amps), seasonal sites, cable, WiFi @ sites, dump, laundry, LP gas. **REC:** hunting nearby. Pet restrict (B). Partial handicap access. No tents. Big rig sites. 2021 rates: $50 to $55, Military discount.
(877)686-7878 Lat: 40.408025, Lon: -120.631723
3075 Johnstonville Rd, Susanville, CA 96130
www.susanvillervpark.com
See ad page 155

TAHOE CITY — D4 *Placer*

➜ ED Z'BERG SUGAR PINE POINT/GENERAL CREEK (Public State Park) From Tahoma, S 1 mi on Hwy 89 (R). 175 Avail. 2021 rates: $35. (530)525-7982

➚ TAHOE SRA (Public State Park) From town, NE 0.25 mi on Hwy 28 (R). 27 Avail. 2021 rates: $35. May 31 to Oct 01. (530)583-3074

TECOPA — G5 *Inyo*

⬆ DELIGHT'S HOT SPRINGS RESORT **Ratings: 6/7/6.5** (RV Park) 38 Avail: 35 full hkups, 3 W, 3 E (30/50 amps). 2021 rates: $70 to $110. (760)852-4343, 368 Tecopa Hot Springs Road, Tecopa, CA 92389

TEHACHAPI — G4 *Kern*

➚ INDIAN HILL RANCH RV PARK **Ratings: 4/NA/5** (RV Park) Avail: 10 full hkups (30/50 amps). 2021 rates: $26 to $40. (661)822-6613, 18061 Arosa Rd, Tehachapi, CA 93561

➚ MOUNTAIN VALLEY RV PARK **Ratings: 5.5/7.5/6.5** (Campground) 27 Avail: 27 W, 27 E (30/50 amps). 2021 rates: $43. (661)822-1213, 16334 Harris Rd, Tehachapi, CA 93581

⬇ TEHACHAPI MOUNTAIN PARK (Public) From town, S 3 mi on Tucker Rd to Highline Rd, SW 1 mi to Water Canyon Rd, S 3 mi (E). 61 Avail. 2021 rates: $18. (661)822-4632

TEMECULA — P6 *Riverside*

A SPOTLIGHT Introducing Temecula's colorful attractions appearing at the front of this state section.

➘ PECHANGA RV RESORT

good sam park **Ratings: 10/10★/10** (RV Resort) From Jct of I-15 & Hwy 79S/Temecula Pkwy), E 0.8 mi on Hwy 79S/Temecula Pkwy) to Pechanga Pkwy, SE 2.1 mi to Pechanga Resort Dr, S 0.25 mi (L).

MINUTES FROM WINE COUNTRY AND GOLF!
Nestled in the picturesque hills of Temecula Wine Country, the award-winning Pechanga RV Resort offers guests endless opportunities for excitement, relaxation and fun! Wine tasting, casino, golf, Historic Old Town and more!
FAC: paved rds. Avail: 210 paved, patios, 66 pull-thrus, (28x55), back-ins (28x55), 210 full hkups (30/50 amps), cable, WiFi @ sites, dump, laundry, groc, LP gas, restaurant. **REC:** heated pool, hot tub, golf, rec open to public. Pet restrict (Q) $. Partial handicap access. No tents, 29 day max stay, eco-friendly. 2021 rates: $60 to $145, Military discount. ATM.
(877)997-8386 Lat: 33.45264, Lon: -117.10373
45000 Pechanga Hwy, Temecula, CA 92592
www.pechanga.com/rvresort
See ad this page, 119

➘ TEMECULA/VAIL LAKE KOA **Ratings: 7/6/8** (Campground) 520 Avail: 250 full hkups, 270 W, 270 S (30/50 amps). 2021 rates: $49 to $85. (951)303-0173, 38000 Hwy 79 S, Temecula, CA 92592

RV DRIVING TIPS: Don't get too comfy. Although today's RV cockpits are designed for maximum driver comfort, you should drive with your head up, your shoulders back and your lower back against the seat back. Legs should not be fully extended, but flexed at about a 45-degree angle. Don't use cruise control; keep your body involved in the driving.

Things to See and Do

➘ **PECHANGA CASINO RESORT** Use Pechanga Resort and Casino as a base from which to explore the area's wineries. Casino with 15 delectable dining options and 1085 luxury suites. Shuttle service from casino to the RV park. Partial handicap access. RV accessible. Restrooms. Food. Hours: 24 hours. ATM.
(888)732-4264 Lat: 33.45264, Lon: -117.10373
45000 Pechanga Pkwy, Temecula, CA 92589
www.pechanga.com
See ad this page, 119

THERMAL — J5 *Riverside*

➜ OASIS PALMS RV RESORT **Ratings: 9/8/7** (RV Park) Avail: 81 full hkups (30/50 amps). 2021 rates: $40. (760)397-1011, 90123 81st Ave, Thermal, CA 92274

THREE RIVERS — F3 *Tulare*

⬇ SEQUOIA CAMPGROUND & LODGE **Ratings: 7/5/7.5** (Campground) Avail: 32 full hkups (30/50 amps). 2021 rates: $54 to $200. (559)561-4424, 40457 Sierra Dr, Three Rivers, CA 93271

⬆ SEQUOIA RV RANCH **Ratings: 8/7.5/8** (RV Park) 47 Avail: 34 full hkups, 13 W, 13 E (30/50 amps). 2021 rates: $34 to $71. (559)561-4333, 43490 North Fork Dr, Three Rivers, CA 93271

➜ THREE RIVERS HIDEAWAY **Ratings: 5/6.5/7** (RV Park) 30 Avail: 16 full hkups, 14 W, 10 S, 4 E (30/50 amps). 2021 rates: $49 to $54. (559)561-4413, 43365 Sierra Dr, Three Rivers, CA 93271

TIONESTA — A3 *Modoc*

➘ HAWKS NEST RV & CABINS **Ratings: 6/7.5/8** (RV Park) Avail: 18 full hkups (30/50 amps). 2021 rates: $45 to $55. (530)664-3187, 200 CR 97A, Tulelake, CA 96134

TRABUCO CANYON — O4 *Orange*

➚ O'NEILL REGIONAL PARK (Public) From jct I-5 & El Toro Rd (exit 91) (CR S18): Go 7 mi NE on El Toro Rd, then 3 mi S on Live Oak Canyon Rd (CR S19). 79 Avail. 2021 rates: $20. (949)923-2260

Read RV topics at blog.GoodSam.com

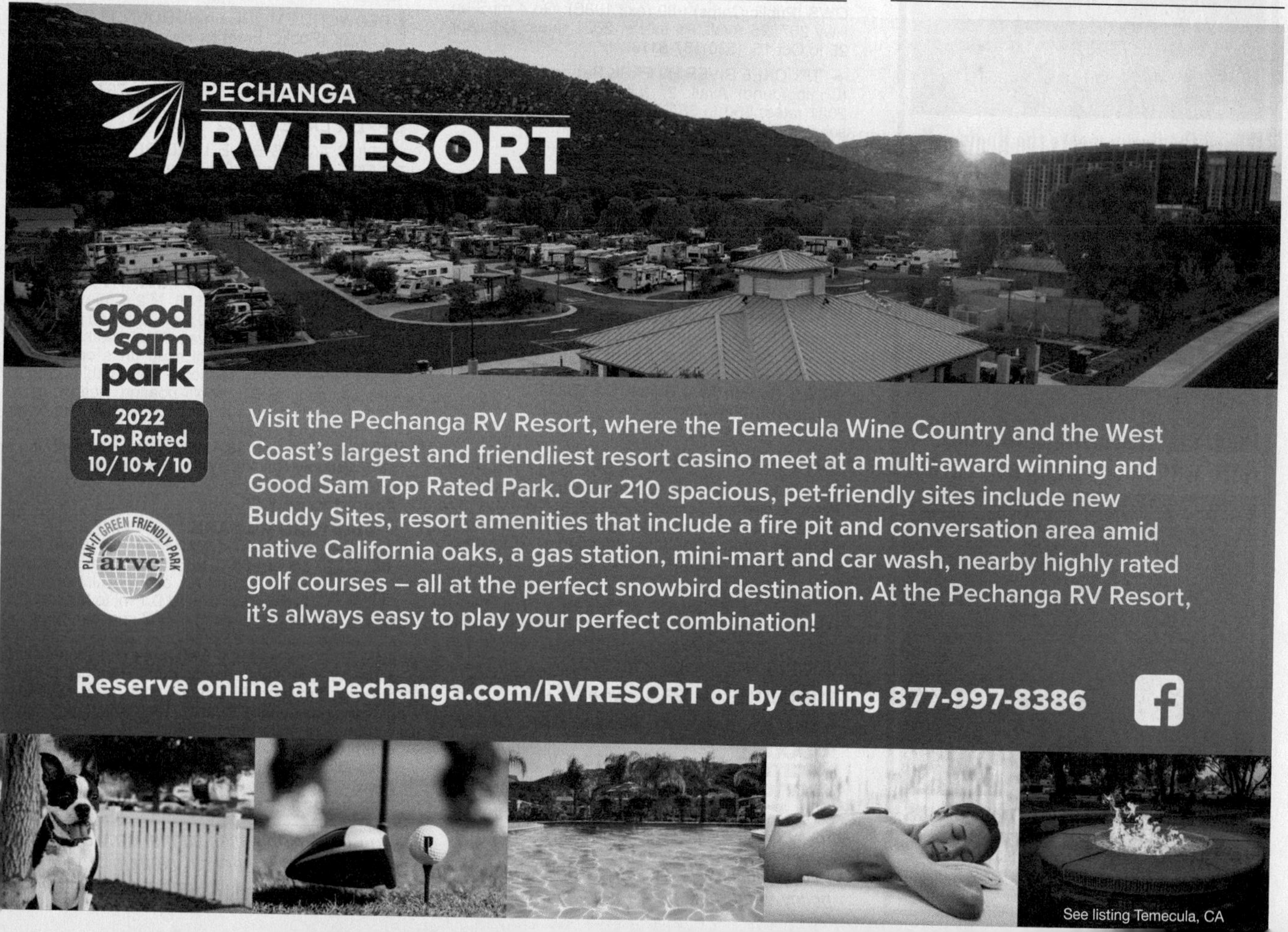

TRACY — E3 *San Joaquin*

CARNEGIE SVRA (Public State Park) From town: Go 10 mi W on Telsa/Corral Hollow Rd. 25 Avail. 2021 rates: $10. (925)447-9027

TRINIDAD — B1 *Humboldt*

EMERALD FOREST CABINS & RV **Ratings: 7/9★/9** (Campground) 52 Avail: 22 full hkups, 30 W, 30 E (20/30 amps). 2021 rates: $38 to $52. (707)677-3554, 753 Patricks Point Dr, Trinidad, CA 95570

PATRICKS POINT (Public State Park) From town, N 5 mi on Hwy 101 (L). 121 Avail. 2021 rates: $35 to $45. (707)677-3570

SOUNDS OF THE SEA RV PARK & CABINS
Ratings: 9/9★/9.5 (RV Park) From Jct of US-101 & Patricks Point State Park Exit/Exit 734, (5 mi N of town), S 1.2 mi on Patricks Point Dr (L). **FAC:** paved/gravel rds. Avail: 52 all weather, 10 pull-thrus, (40x110), back-ins (25x80), 52 full hkups (30/50 amps), cable, WiFi @ sites, tent sites, rentals, laundry, groc, firewood. **REC:** boating nearby, hunting nearby. Pet restrict (B). Big rig sites, eco-friendly. 2021 rates: $40 to $60, Military discount. Mar 01 to Oct 31.
(707)677-3271 Lat: 41.12326, Lon: -124.15578
3443 Patrick's Point Drive, Trinidad, CA 95570
www.soundsofthesea.us
See ad this page

TRINITY CENTER — B2 *Trinity*

PINEWOOD COVE RESORT **Ratings: 9/8.5/8** (Campground) Avail: 34 full hkups (30/50 amps). 2021 rates: $56. Apr 15 to Oct 31. (530)286-2201, 45110 State Hwy 3, Trinity Center, CA 96091

TRINITY LAKE KOA **Ratings: 9/9★/9** (Campground) Avail: 141 full hkups (30/50 amps). 2021 rates: $57.32 to $89.25. May 15 to Sep 30. (800)562-7706, 60260 State Hwy 3, Trinity Center, CA 96091

TRUCKEE — C4 *Nevada*

COACHLAND RV PARK
Ratings: 8.5/9★/8.5 (RV Park) Avail: 63 full hkups (30/50 amps). 2021 rates: $65 to $120. (530)587-3071, 10100 Pioneer Trail #35, Truckee, CA 96161

DONNER MEMORIAL (Public State Park) From Jct of Donner Pass Rd (Exit 184) & Hwy 80, W 0.1 mi on Donner Pass Rd (L) Park is closed until August. 154 Avail. 2021 rates: $35. May 01 to Sep 30. (530)582-7894

MARTIS CREEK LAKE - COE/ALPINE MEADOWS (Public Corps) I-80 (exit 188B): Go 4 mi S on Hwy 267. 25 Avail: Pit toilets. 2021 rates: $20. Apr 25 to Oct 15. (530)587-8113

TRUCKEE RIVER RV PARK **Ratings: 8.5/9★/8.5** (Campground) Avail: 27 full hkups (30/50 amps). 2021 rates: $60 to $65. (530)448-4650, 10068 Hirschdale Rd, Truckee, CA 96161

TULARE — F3 *Tulare*

SUN & FUN RV PARK
Ratings: 9.5/8.5★/7.5 (RV Park) From Jct of Hwy 99 & Ave 200 (Exit 83): Go 1/4 mi W on Ave 200 (R). **FAC:** paved rds. (69 spaces). Avail: 12 paved, patios, 5 pull-thrus, (20x50), back-ins (24x40), 12 full hkups (30/50 amps), seasonal sites, cable, WiFi @ sites, dump, laundry. **REC:** pool, hot tub, playground. Pet restrict (S/B/Q). Partial handicap access. No tents, eco-friendly. 2021 rates: $60.
(559)686-5779 Lat: 36.152991, Lon: -119.334194
1000 E Rankin Ave, Tulare, CA 93274
sunandfuntulare.com
See ad this page

TULELAKE — A3 *Siskiyou*

LAVA BEDS/INDIAN WELL (Public National Park) From Tulelake, S 4 mi on Hwy 139, to CR-111, S 4.5 mi on CR-111 to Lava Beds Rd (park entrance), W 18 mi (E) Entrance fee required. 43 Avail. 2021 rates: $10. (530)667-8113

TULELAKE-BUTTE VALLEY FAIR RV PARK (Public) From Jct of Hwy 139 & Main St (in Tulelake) S 0.5 mi on Main St, W 0.2 mi on G St (L). 100 Avail: 100 W, 100 E (20/30 amps). 2021 rates: $20 to $36. (530)667-5312

TUOLUMNE — E3 *Tuolumne*

THE RV PARK AT BLACK OAK CASINO RESORT
Ratings: 10/9.5/10 (RV Resort) From jct US-49 & CR-108 (Mono Way): Go 6-3/4 mi NE on CR-108 (Mono Way), then 6-1/2 mi E on CR-17 (Tuolumne Road North), then 1/2 mi on Tuolumne Road North (R). Elev 2590 ft.

STAY HERE, PLAY EVERYWHERE
Your base camp for excitement near Yosemite! Enjoy gaming, live entertainment, bowling and a video game arcade, buffets and more. Amenities include 85 full hook-up sites, a club house, pool and spa, satellite TV and WiFi.

FAC: paved rds. Avail: 85 paved, patios, 48 pull-thrus, (30x45), back-ins (30x40), 85 full hkups (30/50 amps), cable, WiFi @ sites, rentals, laundry, groc, LP gas, restaurant. **REC:** pool, hot tub, boating nearby, hunting nearby. Pets OK. Partial handicap access. No tents. Big rig sites, eco-friendly. 2021 rates: $60 to $70. ATM.
(877)747-8777 Lat: 37.97249, Lon: -120.24025
19400 Tuolumne Road N, Tuolumne, CA 95379
www.blackoakcasino.com/stay/rv-park
See ad opposite page

Things to See and Do

BLACK OAK CASINO RESORT Come to where the fun never ends. Enjoy gaming, dining, bowling, entertainment, night life & hotel. Elev 2570 ft. Partial handicap access. RV accessible. Restrooms. Food. Hours: Open 24 hours. ATM.
(877)747-8777 Lat: 37.973, Lon: -120.237
19400 Tuolumne Road North, Tuolumne, CA 95379
www.blackoakcasino.com
See ad opposite page

TWAIN HARTE — E3 *Tuolumne*

SUGAR PINE RV PARK & RESORT **Ratings: 8/9★/6.5** (Campground) Avail: 12 full hkups (30/50 amps). 2021 rates: $50. (209)586-4631, 23699 Hwy 108, Twain Harte, CA 95832

TWENTYNINE PALMS — H5 *San Bernardino*

MILITARY PARK TWILIGHT DUNES (MCAGCC 29 PALMS) (Public) From town: Go 3-1/2 mi N on Adobe Rd, then 1-1/2 mi E on Condor Rd, left on Rainbow Canyon, right onto Sunshine Peak Rd, left onto Cleghorn St (L). Avail: 83 full hkups (30/50 amps). 2021 rates: $25. (760)830-6583

UKIAH — C1 *Mendocino*

LAKE MENDOCINO - COE (Public Corps) From jct Hwy 101 & Hwy 20E (exit 555B): Go 2 mi E on Hwy 20. 314 Avail. 2021 rates: $25 to $40. (707)467-4200

REDWOOD EMPIRE FAIRGROUNDS VACATION RV PARK (Public) From jct Hwy 253 & US 101: Go 4-1/2 mi N on US 101 (N State St Exit), then S on N State St, 0.5 mi. 28 Avail: 18 full hkups, 10 W, 10 E (30 amps). 2021 rates: $35 to $40. (707)462-3884

UPPER LAKE — C2 *Lake*

PINE ACRES BLUE LAKE RESORT **Ratings: 7/6.5/8.5** (Campground) 29 Avail: 4 full hkups, 25 W, 25 E (20/30 amps). 2021 rates: $40 to $60. (707)275-2811, 5328 Blue Lake Road, Upper Lake, CA 95485

VACAVILLE — D2 *Solano*

MIDWAY RV PARK
Ratings: 9.5/9★/9.5 (RV Park) From Jct of I-80 & I-505, N 2.5 mi on I-505 to Midway Rd, E 0.2 mi (L). **FAC:** paved rds. (64 spaces). Avail: 10 all weather, 10 pull-thrus, (32x55), accepts full hkup units only, 10 full hkups (30/50 amps), seasonal sites, cable, WiFi @ sites, laundry. **REC:** pool, boating nearby, playground, hunting nearby. Pet restrict (B). No tents, eco-friendly. 2021 rates: $65.
(707)446-7679 Lat: 38.41900, Lon: -121.93970
4933 Midway Rd, Vacaville, CA 95688
midwayrvpark.com
See ad page 117

VINEYARD RV PARK
Ratings: 10/10★/10 (RV Park) From Jct of I-80 & I-505, N 3.3 mi to Midway Rd, E 0.4 mi (L) or From Jct of I-80 & Midway Rd exit, W 0.1 mi to Midway Rd, W 3 mi (R). **FAC:** paved rds. (307 spaces). Avail: 30 all weather, patios, 27 pull-thrus, (30x64), back-ins (30x45), 30 full hkups (30/50 amps), seasonal sites, cable, WiFi @ sites, rentals, dump, laundry, LP gas, fire rings, firewood. **REC:** pool, pond, boating nearby, playground, hunting nearby. Pets OK $. No tents, eco-friendly. 2021 rates: $69 to $79.
(866)447-8797 Lat: 38.41832, Lon: -121.93687
4985 Midway Rd, Vacaville, CA 95688
www.vineyardrvpark.com
See ad page 144

BLACK OAK
THE RV PARK
good sam park
2022
Top Rated
10/9.5/10
ESCAPE TO Adventure
24 HOUR CASINO EXCITEMENT ON SITE!
With 1100 slots, 22 tables games, 6 restaurants and bars.
1.877.747.8777
PLUS
blackoakcasino.com
Restrooms / Showers / Laundry • Clubhouse / Pool / Spa • Recreational Area
Complimentary Coffee • 30 and 50 amp service • Convenience Store with
Propane and RV Dump • Free Cable with 40 Channels • Dog Park
Courtesy Shuttle to and from Casino • Pull through spots • Trash Pickup
See listing Tuolumne, CA

VACAVILLE (CONT)

Travel Services

CAMPING WORLD OF VACAVILLE As the nation's largest retailer of RV supplies, accessories, services and new and used RVs, Camping World is committed to making your total RV experience better. **SERVICES:** tire, RV appliance, restrooms. RV Sales. RV supplies, LP gas, emergency parking, RV accessible. Hours: 9am to 7pm.
(855)546-1888 Lat: 38.390669, Lon: -121.932118
5065 Quinn Road, Vacaville, CA 95688
www.campingworld.com

VALENCIA — H3 *Los Angeles*

VALENCIA TRAVEL VILLAGE
Ratings: 9.5/9.5★/8.5 (Campground) Avail: 64 full hkups (30/50 amps). 2021 rates: $65 to $85. (661)257-3333, 27946 Henry Mayo Dr (Hwy 126), Castaic, CA 91384

VALLEJO — E2 *Solano*

THE RV PARK AT THE SOLANO COUNTY FAIRGROUNDS (Public) From I-80, go W on 37 to Fairgrounds Dr, turn L at ramp, 2nd light. Or from I-80 go E on 37 (R) at ramp, next light, turn L at main entrance. 34 Avail: 23 full hkups, 11 W, 11 E (30/50 amps). 2021 rates: $40. Apr 01 to Oct 31. (707)551-2007

TRADEWINDS RV PARK OF VALLEJO
Ratings: 8/9.5★/7.5 (RV Park) W-bnd (to San Fran): From Jct of I-780 & I-80, W 0.25 mi on I-80 to Magazine St exit, sharp rt immediately after exit for 600 ft on Lincoln Rd/W service rd (L). **FAC:** paved rds. (78 spaces). Avail: 28 all weather, patios, 13 pull-thrus, (19x52), back-ins (22x35), accepts full hkup units only, 28 full hkups (30/50 amps), seasonal sites, cable, WiFi @ sites, laundry. **REC:** boating nearby, playground. Pet restrict (S/B/Q). Partial handicap access. No tents. 2021 rates: $47 to $55, Military discount.
(707)643-4000 Lat: 38.08628, Lon: -122.23321
239 Lincoln Rd West, Vallejo, CA 94590
tradewindsrvpark.net
See ad page 117

VALLEY CENTER — J5 *San Diego*

WOODS VALLEY KAMPGROUND & RV PARK **Ratings: 7/7/7.5** (Campground) 49 Avail: 5 full hkups, 44 W, 44 E (30 amps). 2021 rates: $45 to $50. (760)749-2905, 15236 Woods Valley Rd, Valley Center, CA 92082

VALLEY SPRINGS — D3 *Calaveras*

LAKE CAMANCHE SOUTH **Ratings: 6.5/NA/8** (RV Park) Avail: 200 full hkups (30/50 amps). 2021 rates: $54. (866)763-5121, 11700 Wade Lane, Valley Springs, CA 95252

NEW HOGAN LAKE - COE/ACORN WEST (Public Corps) From jct Hwy 12 & Hwy 26: Go 1 mi S on Hwy 26, then 2-1/2 mi E on Hogan Dam Rd. 128 Avail. 2021 rates: $20. (209)772-1343

NEW HOGAN LAKE - COE/OAK KNOLL (Public Corps) From jct Hwy 12 & Hwy 26: Go 1 mi S on Hwy 26, then 2-1/2 mi E on Hogan Dam Rd. 30 Avail. 2021 rates: $20. Apr 01 to Sep 30. (209)772-1343

VAN NUYS — L1 *Los Angeles*

HOLLYWOOD RV PARK **Ratings: 8/9★/7** (RV Park) Avail: 20 full hkups (30/50 amps). 2021 rates: $65. (818)785-0949, 7740 Balboa Blvd, Van Nuys, CA 91406

VENTURA — H3 *Ventura*

EMMA WOOD STATE BEACH (Public State Park) From US-101 exit State Beaches (Exit 72), N 0.25 mi on Old US-1/Pacific Coast Hwy (L). 90 Avail. 2021 rates: $30 to $40. (805)968-1033

FARIA BEACH PARK (Public) From Jct of US-101 & State Beaches exit (Exit 72), N 6 mi on Old US-1/Pacific Coast Hwy (L). Avail: 15 full hkups (30/50 amps). 2021 rates: $36 to $53. (805)654-3951

FOSTER PARK (Public) From Jct of Hwy 33 & Casitas Vista Rd, W 0.4 mi on Casitas Vista Rd (R). Avail: 10 full hkups. 2021 rates: $21 to $36. (805)654-3951

HOBSON BEACH PARK (Public) From Jct of US-101 & State Beaches, exit 72 (Pacific Coast Hwy), N 7 mi on Old US-101/Pacific Coast Hwy (L). Avail: 10 full hkups (30/50 amps). 2021 rates: $36 to $48. (805)654-3951

Show Your Good Sam Membership Card!

LAKE CASITAS RECREATION AREA (Public) From jct Hwy 101 & Hwy 33: Go 11 mi N on Hwy 33, then 3 mi W on Hwy 150, then S on Santa Ana Rd. 400 Avail: (30/50 amps). 2021 rates: $30 to $66. (805)649-2233

RINCON PARKWAY (Public) From US-101 & State Beaches (exit 72), N 6.5 mi on Old US-101/Pacific Coast Hwy (R). 127 Avail. 2021 rates: $32 to $35. (805)654-3951

VENTURA BEACH RV RESORT
Ratings: 9.5/8.5★/8 (RV Park) N-bnd: From Jct of Hwy 101 & California St (Exit 70A): Go 100 ft. N on California St to Thompson Blvd, then 1/2 mi W to Ventura Ave, then 1/10 mi N to Main, then 1/2 mi W (L); or S-bnd: From Jct of Hwy 101 & Main St (Ventura exit): Go 1/4 mi E on Main St (R).

ESCAPE TO PARADISE AT VENTURA BEACH
14 acres of lush green grass & palms. We offer tent sites, RV sites, Travel Trailer Rentals, Yurt Rentals & more! Enjoy a 6-minute walk to the ocean or a 15-minute bike ride to the pier. Surf, shop, dine & play under the sun!

FAC: paved rds. (180 spaces). Avail: 140 paved, patios, 89 pull-thrus, (27x60), back-ins (27x36), 125 full hkups, 15 W, 15 E (30/50 amps), seasonal sites, WiFi @ sites, tent sites, rentals, dump, laundry, groc, LP gas, fire rings, firewood. **REC:** heated pool, hot tub, boating nearby, playground, rec open to public. Pet restrict (B/Q) $. Partial handicap access. Big rig sites, eco-friendly. 2021 rates: $79.50 to $175.50. ATM.
(805)643-9137 Lat: 34.28161, Lon: -119.31222
800 W Main St, Ventura, CA 93001
www.vbrvresort.com
See ad page 126

VICTORVILLE — H4 *San Bernardino*

MOJAVE NARROWS COUNTY REGIONAL PARK
(Public) From Jct of I-15 & Bear Valley Rd: Go 4 mi E on Bear Valley Rd to Ridgecrest Rd, then 2-1/2 mi N on Ridgecrest Rd (L). Elev 2850 ft.**FAC:** paved rds. Avail: 38 paved, 7 pull-thrus, (50x55), back-ins (30x50), 38 full hkups (30/50 amps), tent sites, dump, firewood, controlled access. **REC:** Horse Lake: fishing, playground, rec open to public. Pets OK $. Partial handicap access, 14 day max stay. 2021 rates: $47.
(877)387-2757 Lat: 34.50748, Lon: -117.27299
18000 Yates Rd, Victorville, CA 92392
parks.sbcounty.gov/park/mojave-narrows-regional-park
See ad page 96

VIOLA — B3 *Shasta*

LASSEN VOLCANIC/MANZANITA LAKE (Public National Park) From town: Go 6 mi E on Hwy-44, then 3/4 mi E on Lassen Park Rd. 83 Avail. 2021 rates: $15 to $26. May 22 to Nov 30. (530)595-6121

LASSEN VOLCANIC/SUMMIT LAKE (Public National Park) From town: Go 6 mi E on Hwy-44, then 12 mi E/NE/SE on Lassen Park Rd. 94 Avail. 2021 rates: $15 to $22. Jun 27 to Sep 30. (530)595-6121

VISALIA — F3 *Tulare*

COUNTRY MANOR RV & MH COMMUNITY
Ratings: 9/9★/9 (RV Area in MH Park) Avail: 40 full hkups (30/50 amps). 2021 rates: $70. (559)732-8144, 820 S Chinowth St, Visalia, CA 93277

VISALIA SEQUOIA NATIONAL PARK KOA **Ratings: 8/7.5/7** (Campground) 49 Avail: 42 full hkups, 7 W, 7 E (30/50 amps). 2021 rates: $58 to $68. (800)562-0540, 7480 Ave 308, Visalia, CA 93291

Travel Services

BULLDOG RV STORAGE Modern secure storage facility with storage for boats, cars, trailers and RVs, offering short and long term leases. **RV Storage:** outdoor, covered canopy, secured fencing, electric gate, 24/7 access, well-lit facility, well-lit roads, well-lit perimeter, security cameras, on-site staff, level gravel/paved spaces, power to charge battery, water, compressed air, office. **SERVICES:** self RV wash, restrooms. Hours: 8am - 5pm.
Special offers available for Good Sam Members
(559)627-4000 Lat: 36.338490, Lon: -119.281490
1010 E Douglas Ave, Visalia, CA 93292
rvstoragevisalia.com

How can we make a great Travel Guide even better? We ask YOU! Please share your thoughts with us. Drop us a note and let us know if there's anything we haven't thought of.

VISTA — J4 *San Diego*

OLIVE AVENUE RV RESORT
Ratings: 9/9.5★/9 (RV Park) From Jct of N Melrose Dr & Olive Ave, W 450 ft on Olive Ave (R).

MAKE US YOUR 'HOME BASE'
Stay a day or a season with us as you explore Southern CA. Central location with easy access to Vista, Carlsbad, Oceanside and Escondido. Enjoy all that San Diego County has to offer. Family oriented. Groups welcome.

FAC: paved rds. (60 spaces). Avail: 50 paved, 32 pull-thrus, (25x62), back-ins (25x60), accepts full hkup units only, 50 full hkups (30/50 amps), seasonal sites, cable, WiFi @ sites, $, laundry. **REC:** heated pool, hot tub, boating nearby. Pet restrict (B/Q) $. Partial handicap access. No tents, eco-friendly. 2021 rates: $60 to $75, Military discount.
(760)295-9243 Lat: 33.20471, Lon: -117.25660
713 Olive Ave, Vista, CA 92083
oliveavervresort.com
See ad page 152

WATERFORD — E3 *Stanislaus*

MODESTO RESERVOIR REGIONAL PARK (Public) From Jct of SR-99 & SR-132 (exit 226B), E 35 mi on SR-132 to Reservoir Rd, N 0.5 mi (E). Avail: 150 full hkups (30 amps). 2021 rates: $30 to $35. (209)874-9540

TURLOCK LAKE SRA (Public State Park) From Jct of Hwys 99 & 132, E 14 mi on Hwy 132 to Hickman Rd (CR-J9), S 1 mi to Lake Rd, E 10 mi (L). 66 Avail. 2021 rates: $36. (209)874-2056

WATSONVILLE — F1 *Santa Cruz*

PINTO LAKE RV PARK (Public) N-bnd: From Jct of Hwy 1 & Green Valley Rd, NE 2.5 mi on Green Valley Rd (L); or S-bnd: From Jct of Hwy 1 & Watsonville/Gilroy (Hwy 152) exit, take immediate left (N) onto Green Valley Rd, NE 2 mi (L). Avail: 28 full hkups (30 amps). 2021 rates: $45. (831)768-3240

SANTA CRUZ/MONTEREY BAY KOA **Ratings: 9.5/8/9** (Campground) 119 Avail: 99 full hkups, 20 W, 20 E (30/50 amps). 2021 rates: $85 to $170. (831)722-0551, 1186 San Andreas Rd, Watsonville, CA 95076

SUNSET STATE BEACH (Public State Park) From Santa Cruz, S on Hwy 1 to Larkin Valley Rd/San Andreas Rd, W 5 mi on San Andreas Rd to Sunset Beach Rd (R). 73 Avail. 2021 rates: $35. (831)763-7063

Check the air pressure on your tires and inflate any that are lower than the pressure recommended in the owner's manual. Properly inflated tires can increase fuel efficiency by 3.3 percent.

WEED — A2 *Siskiyou*

FRIENDLY RV PARK **Ratings: 8/10★/10** (Campground) Avail: 26 full hkups (30 amps). 2021 rates: $48. (530)938-2805, 1800 Black Butte Drive, Weed, CA 96094

HI-LO RV PARK
good sam park **Ratings: 6/9★/6** (RV Park) Avail: 16 full hkups (15/30 amps). 2021 rates: $41. (530)938-2731, 88 S. Weed Blvd, Weed, CA 96094

TRAILER LANE RV PARK **Ratings: 7/9★/7** (RV Park) Avail: 20 full hkups (30/50 amps). 2021 rates: $40. Apr 01 to Sep 15. (530)938-4554, 27535 Edgewood Rd, Weed, CA 96094

WEOTT — B1 *Humboldt*

HUMBOLDT REDWOODS/ALBEE CREEK (Public State Park) From town, N 2 mi on Hwy 101 to Mattole Rd, W 5 mi (R). 40 Avail. 2021 rates: $35. May 15 to Oct 15. (707)946-2409

HUMBOLDT REDWOODS/BURLINGTON (Public State Park) From Jct of US-101 & Weott exit (Ave of the Giants), S 2 mi on Ave of the Giants (L). 57 Avail. 2021 rates: $35. (707)946-2409

HUMBOLDT REDWOODS/HIDDEN SPRINGS (Public State Park) From town, S 1 mi on Hwy 254 (L). 154 Avail. 2021 rates: $35. May 01 to Sep 07. (707)946-2409

WEST SACRAMENTO — D3 *Yolo*

SAC-WEST RV PARK AND CAMPGROUND
good sam park **Ratings: 9.5/9.5★/9** (Campground) Avail: 50 full hkups (30/50 amps). 2021 rates: $67 to $90. (916)371-6771, 3951 Lake Rd, West Sacramento, CA 95691

WESTPORT — C1 *Mendocino*

WESTPORT BEACH **Ratings: 8.5/8★/8.5** (Campground) Avail: 75 full hkups (30/50 amps). 2021 rates: $65 to $75. (707)964-2964, 37700 North Hwy 1, Westport, CA 95488

WESTPORT-UNION LANDING STATE BEACH (Public State Park) From town: Go 1-1/2 mi N on Hwy 1. 86 Avail: Pit toilets. 2021 rates: $35. (707)937-5804

WILLITS — C1 *Mendocino*

MENDOCINO REDWOODS RV RESORT
good sam park **Ratings: 9.5/10★/9.5** (Campground) From Jct of US-101 & SR-20, W 1.5 mi on SR-20 (R). **FAC:** all weather rds. (109 spaces). Avail: 90 all weather, 17 pull-thrus, (24x65), back-ins (20x40), 13 full hkups, 77 W, 77 E (30/50 amps), seasonal sites, cable, WiFi @ sites, tent sites, rentals, dump, mobile sewer, laundry, groc, LP bottles, fire rings, firewood, controlled access. **REC:** heated pool, wading pool, hot tub, pond, fishing, boating nearby, playground, hunting nearby, rec open to public. Pet restrict (B). Partial handicap access, eco-friendly. 2021 rates: $55 to $77.
(707)459-6179 Lat: 39.40822, Lon: -123.37920
1600 Hwy 20, Willits, CA 95490
www.mendocinoredwoods.com
See ad this page

WINCHESTER — O6 *San Bernardino*

LAKE SKINNER (Public) From Jct of I-15 & Hwy 215 (exit 123), S 3 mi on I-15 to Rancho California Rd (exit 59), E 10 mi (R). 257 Avail: 199 full hkups, 58 W, 18 E (20/50 amps). 2021 rates: $15 to $30. (951)926-1541

WINTERHAVEN — K6 *Imperial*

MCCOY MOBILE HOME & RV PARK **Ratings: 7/7/6** (RV Park) Avail: 10 full hkups (30/50 amps). 2021 rates: $45. (760)572-0744, 640 1st St, Winterhaven, CA 92283

PICACHO SRA (Public State Park) From I-8 in town: Go 25 mi N on unpaved road. 54 Avail. 2021 rates: $25 to $35. (760)996-2963

PILOT KNOB RV RESORT **Ratings: 7.5/8.5/8** (RV Resort) Avail: 70 full hkups (30/50 amps). 2021 rates: $22.50 to $40. Nov 01 to Apr 01. (928)750-3775, 3707 W Hwy 80, Winterhaven, CA 92283

RV SPACE-SAVING TIP: Line your trashcans with multiple bags at once and keep the roll in the bottom of the wastebasket for easy refills. Also, you could even reuse the same bag, if it hasn't gotten too soiled, by simply dumping the trash and leaving the existing bag in it for multiple uses.

RIVERS EDGE RV RESORT **Ratings: 8/8.5★/7.5** (RV Park) Avail: 39 full hkups (30/50 amps). 2021 rates: $55 to $65. (760)572-5105, 2299 Winterhaven Drive, Winterhaven, CA 92283

SANS END RV PARK **Ratings: 7.5/8.5/8** (RV Park) Avail: 75 full hkups (30/50 amps). 2021 rates: $35. (760)572-0797, 2209 Winterhaven Dr, Winterhaven, CA 92283

SENATOR WASH RESERVOIR (BLM) (Public Corps) From Jct of 4th St & I-8 (exit 172), N 0.25 mi on 4th St to Imperial County Hwy S-24, NE 16 mi (through Indian Reservation) to Senator Wash Rd, W 2.5 mi, (across canal) follow signs (E). 350 Avail: Pit toilets. 2021 rates: $15. (928)317-3200

SQUAW LAKE (BLM) (Public Corps) From town, E 20 mi on SR-24 to Senator Wash Rd, N 4 mi (E). 125 Avail. 2021 rates: $15. (928)317-3200

WINTERS — D2 *Solano*

LAKE SOLANO COUNTY PARK AND CAMPGROUND
(Public) From Jct of I-80 & I-505 (Exit 56), N 15 mi on I-505 to Winters exit, W 4 mi to Pleasant Valley Rd, S 0.25 mi (R). **FAC:** paved rds. Avail: 32 paved, 9 pull-thrus, (15x65), back-ins (15x60), 2 full hkups, 30 W, 30 E (30 amps), tent sites, dump, fire rings, firewood, controlled access. **REC:** wading pool, Putah Creek: boating nearby, playground, hunting nearby. Pet restrict (Q) $. Partial handicap access, 14 day max stay. 2021 rates: $30 to $37.
(530)795-2990 Lat: 38.49305, Lon: -122.02833
8685 Pleasant Valley, Winters, CA 95694
www.solanocounty.com/parks
See ad this page

WOFFORD HEIGHTS — G4 *Kern*

GREENHORN MOUNTAIN PARK (Public) From Jct of I-5 & SR-99 (Exit 221), N 20 mi on SR-99 to SR-178 (Exit 26), E 50 mi to SR-155 (thru Woffard Heights & Lake Isabella), W 10 mi (L). Steep, 13% grade. 70 Avail. 2021 rates: $18. (760)376-6780

WOODLAND — D2 *Yolo*

CACHE CREEK CANYON (Public) From Jct of I-505 & SR-16, NW 40 mi on SR-16 (L). 45 Avail. 2021 rates: $25. (530)666-8115

YOLO COUNTY FAIRGROUNDS' RV PARK (Public) From Jct of I-5 & Exit 537 (Main St), W 1 mi on Main St to Thomas St, S 0.6 mi on Gum St, SW 0.2 mi (L). 200 Avail: 40 full hkups, 160 W, 160 E (30/50 amps). 2021 rates: $35. (530)402-2203

YERMO — H5 *San Bernardino*

BARSTOW CALICO KOA JOURNEY **Ratings: 7.5/9★/7.5** (Campground) 54 Avail: 25 full hkups, 29 W, 29 E (30/50 amps). 2021 rates: $55.35 to $57.41. (760)904-3069, 35250 Outer Hwy 15 N, Yermo, CA 92398

Things to See and Do

CALICO GHOST TOWN Authentic Old West mining boom town featuring silver mine, saloon, general store, train ride, shops, gold panning and historical tours. Partial handicap access. RV accessible. Restrooms. Food. Hours: 9am to 5pm. Adult fee: $5 to $8.50. ATM.
(760)254-2122 Lat: 34.94515, Lon: -116.86475
36600 Ghost Town Rd, Yermo, CA 92398
parks.sbcounty.gov/park/calico-ghost-town-regional-park
See ad page 96

YOSEMITE NATIONAL PARK — E4 *Mariposa*

YOSEMITE NATIONAL PARK See also Angels Camp, Bass Lake, Bridgeport, Chowchilla, Coarsegold, Columbia, Delhi, El Portal, Fresno, Groveland, June Lake, Lee Vining, Mammoth Lakes, Oakhurst, Tuolumne & Twain Harte.

YOSEMITE/BRIDALVEIL CREEK (Public National Park) From town, S on Hwy 41 to Chinquapin, E 10 mi to Glacier Point Rd (R). 110 Avail. 2021 rates: $18. Aug 01 to Sep 23. (209)372-0200

YOSEMITE/CRANE FLAT (Public National Park) From Groveland, W 33 mi SR-120 (R). Entrance fee required. 166 Avail. 2021 rates: $26. Jul 12 to Oct 13. (209)372-0200

YOSEMITE/HODGDON MEADOW (Public National Park) From Groveland, E 25 mi on SR-120, follow signs (L). 105 Avail. 2021 rates: $26. (209)372-0200

YOSEMITE/LOWER PINES (Public National Park) In Yosemite Valley, on Yosemite Village loop. 60 Avail. 2021 rates: $26. Apr 06 to Nov 02. (209)372-0200

YOSEMITE/NORTH PINES (Public National Park) In Yosemite Valley, on Yosemite Village loop. 81 Avail. 2021 rates: $26. Mar 30 to Nov 02. (209)372-0200

YOSEMITE/TUOLUMNE MEADOWS (Public National Park) From Jct of SR-120 & Tioga Pass Rd, E 39 mi on Tioga Pass Rd (R). 304 Avail. 2021 rates: $26. Jul 12 to Sep 27. (209)372-0200

YOSEMITE/UPPER PINES (Public National Park) In Yosemite Valley, on Yosemite Village loop. 238 Avail. 2021 rates: $26. (209)372-0200

YOSEMITE/WAWONA (Public National Park) From N end of Wawona, N 1 mi on SR-41 (L). 93 Avail. 2021 rates: $26. (209)372-0200

YOSEMITE/WHITE WOLF (Public National Park) From Jct of SR-120 & Tioga Pass Rd, E 15 mi on Tioga Pass Rd (L). 74 Avail. 2021 rates: $18. Jul 01 to Sep 14. (209)372-0200

YREKA — A2 *Siskiyou*

WAIIAKA RV PARK **Ratings: 9/10★/8.5** (Campground) Avail: 50 full hkups (30/50 amps). 2021 rates: $40 to $42. (530)842-4500, 240 Sharps Road, Yreka, CA 96097

YREKA RV PARK **Ratings: 8.5/8.5/9** (RV Park) Avail: 12 full hkups (30/50 amps). 2021 rates: $39. (530)841-0100, 767 Montague Rd, Yreka, CA 96097

YUBA CITY — D3 *Sutter*

YUBA-SUTTER FAIRGROUNDS RV PARK (Public) From Jct of SR-99 & SR-20, S 1.0 mi on SR-99 to Franklin Ave, E 1.3 mi to Wilbur Ave, S 50 ft, go left into fenced parking lot (L). 100 Avail: 70 W, 100 E (30/50 amps). 2021 rates: $30. (530)674-1280

YUCAIPA — M6 *San Bernardino*

YUCAIPA REGIONAL PARK
(Public) From Jct of I-10 & Oak Glen Rd/Live Oak Cyn. Dr. (exit 85): Go 3-1/2 mi N on Oak Glen Rd (L). Elev 2659 ft.**FAC:** paved rds. Avail: 42 paved, patios, 20 pull-thrus, (33x96), back-ins (30x60), 42 full hkups (30/50 amps), WiFi, tent sites, shower$, dump, firewood, controlled access. **REC:** pool $, pond, swim, fishing, playground, rec open to public. Pets OK $. Partial handicap access. Big rig sites, 14 day max stay. 2021 rates: $40 to $50.
(909)790-3127 Lat: 34.04963, Lon: -117.04791
33900 Oak Glen Rd, Yucaipa, CA 92399
parks.sbcounty.gov/park/yucaipa-regional-park
See ad page 96

YUCCA VALLEY — H5 *San Bernardino*

JOSHUA TREE/BLACK ROCK CANYON (Public National Park) From Jct of I-10 & Hwy 62, E 25 mi on Hwy 62 to Yucca Valley, S 5 mi on Joshua Ln (E). 99 Avail: 51 W, 51 E. 2021 rates: $20. (760)367-3001

Download the FREE GOOD SAM CAMPING APP Today! Search RV parks nearby, by City, State or Province. Filter detailed results by offers, distance and ratings. Tag favorite parks and add your own notes. Available from the App Store and Google Play.

good sam
RV Rentals
Experience more for less.
Coleman
List or Rent, it's 5%.
That's **up to 75% less in fees** than the competition.
LEARN MORE AT RVRENTALS.COM

DID YOU KNOW?
The Trail Ridge Road in Rocky Mountain National Park is the highest continuously paved road in the U.S.
Getty Images/iStockphoto

YOU ARE HERE

Colorado

CO

Reach new travel heights in Colorado. This outdoor playground is home to world-class skiing, stellar mountain biking and glorious fishing. Historic mining towns and big, vibrant cities are equally at home here.

Home of the Rockies

Mountain peaks dominate the horizon in the heart of the state. In Rocky Mountain National Park, northwest of Denver, colorful flowers dot the alpine meadows and mountain peaks reflect in turquoise ponds. In Great Sand Dunes National Park and Preserve, an astonishing sea of sand serves up epic adventures. Wilderness areas offer scenic spots for ATVing, horseback riding, rock climbing and mountain biking. Across the state, hot springs bubble and steam, furnishing comforting spots for relaxation after a day of adventuring.

Friendly Fishing

Centennial State rivers and lakes teem with trout. Eleven rivers and three lakes have earned the distinction of being named Gold Medal Waters by the Colorado Wildlife Commission. Not only do these offer the best chance to snag trout, most are scenic spots. With over 150 miles of rapids, the Arkansas River is one of the top picks in the U.S. for whitewater rafting. With calmer waters for paddling or boating, glacial Grand Lake offers abundant scenery.

Mile High Fun

There are few places where hikers can hit the trail all day and enjoy a gourmet meal during the evening. Denver checks off both boxes. Whether you want to browse a cutting-edge museum or take a day trip into Rocky Mountain National Park, the Mile High City is sure to delight. About 70 miles to the south on Interstate 25, Colorado Springs beckons with the Garden of the Gods, along with Pikes Peak.

Colorado Steak

Steaks taste phenomenal in the Centennial State. That's no surprise, considering Colorado is one of the nation's top cattle-producing states. Order your favorite cut from famous steakhouses that dot the state or try a bison steak if you're feeling adventurous. Hungry carnivores can also sink their teeth in the Denver steak, an incredibly tender cut with plenty of marbling.

VISITOR CENTER

TIME ZONE
Mountain Standard

ROAD & HIGHWAY INFORMATION
303-639-1111
codot.gov

FISHING & HUNTING INFORMATION
303-297-1192
www.cpwshop.com/licensing.page

BOATING INFORMATION
303-297-1192
cpw.state.co.us/placestogo/Pages/Boating.aspx

NATIONAL PARKS
nps.gov/co

STATE PARKS
cpw.state.co.us

TOURISM INFORMATION
Colorado Tourism Office
800-COLORADO
colorado.com

TOP TOURISM ATTRACTIONS
1) Pikes Peak, America's Mountain
2) Red Rocks Park and Amphitheatre
3) Mesa Verde National Park

MAJOR CITIES
Denver (capital), Colorado Springs, Aurora, Fort Collins, Lakewood

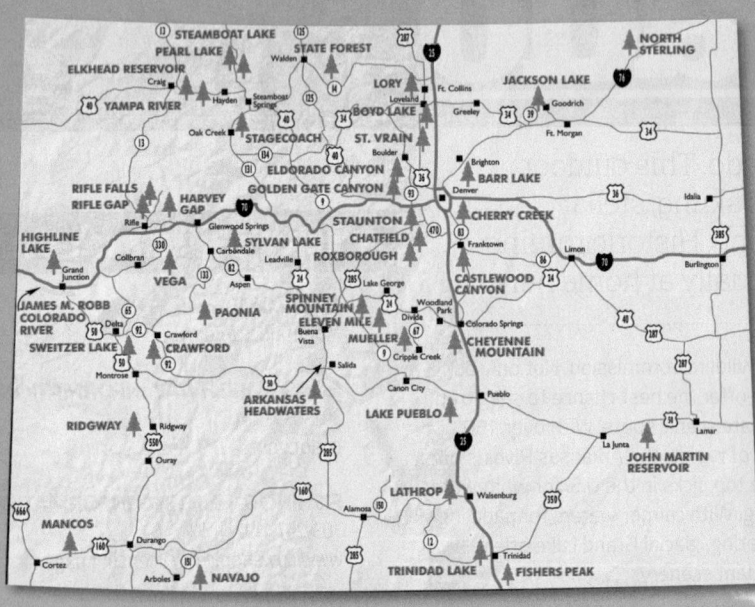

Cañon City-Royal Gorge

Located among the Sangre de Cristo Mountains, Cañon City delivers a dose of Old West culture and rugged scenery that has provided the backdrop for TV series such as "How the West Was Won" and "True Grit." Nearby, one of Colorado's most spectacular natural attractions, the Royal Gorge is a dramatic gash in the earth carved over three million years by the Arkansas River. Known as the "Grand Canyon of the Arkansas River," the 10-mile-long spectacle plummets 1,250 feet at its deepest point. Many visitors start their visit at the Royal Gorge Bridge and Park, built near the 1,260-foot-long namesake suspension bridge.

Built in 1929, Royal Gorge Bridge hangs almost 1,000 feet above the Arkansas River.

Going Deep in the Gorge

One of Colorado's deepest canyons, Royal Gorge is located 125 miles south of Denver and 50 miles southwest of Colorado Springs at the head of the Arkansas River Valley, just off U.S. Route 50. From the mouth of Grape Creek, 2 miles west of Cañon City, the canyon funnels northwest for approximately 10 miles. The best times to visit the Gorge are from March to May and from September to October, when cooler but comfortable temperatures prevail and there are fewer crowds. Averaging 250 sunny days per year, July temperatures nudge 90 degrees, while in January daytime temps can drop to 45 degrees.

Superb Span

One of the world's highest suspension bridges, the Royal Gorge Bridge, built in 1929, is the centerpiece to a diverse medley of attractions and recreational pursuits in the Royal Gorge Bridge and Park. Crossing the bridge in your vehicle is thrilling, but nothing beats standing on the span's walkway as a brisk breeze blows through the canyon. Peer down at the river, a dizzying 950-plus feet below, or ride the trolley that crosses the bridge, allowing you to make it to the other side in a comfortable car. Running parallel to the bridge, bright red gondolas glide along cables, giving passengers views of the nearby Sangre de Cristo Mountains.

Rushing River

With gaping canyons, towering walls up to 1,000 feet, rushing waters and a breathtaking mountainous landscape, the Royal Gorge region delivers superb hiking, rafting, four-wheeling, mountain biking and horseback riding. Rafting the world-class rapids of the Arkansas River is a rite of passage for many rafters, and local outfitters offer trips on Class III, IV and V rapids that allow for moderate to extreme thrills while surrounded by the towering red granite walls. The Royal Gorge region is woven with dozens of trails ranging from novice rambles to steep ascents that require more technical expertise. One of the most accessible (but incredibly scenic) hikes in the area, the Royal Gorge Rim Trail is a mellow 3-mile loop trail with just over 100 feet of elevation gain.

Glenwood Springs

Situated on the confluence of two rivers in a geothermally rich part of Colorado, Glenwood Springs attracts outdoorsy travelers looking to take advantage of the area's abundance of water sports activities, as well as vacationers looking for a little R&R in one of the compact city's hot springs resorts. While summers here are particularly popular thanks to the area's ample hiking, mountain biking, fishing, and even paragliding opportunities, the resort town also attracts plenty of winter travelers, owing largely to its proximity to the popular Sunlight Mountain Resort.

In Hot Water

One of Glenwood Springs' biggest draws is its thermal hot springs. The granddaddy is Glenwood Hot Springs Resort, the first public spring in town to open to visitors — the resort also claims to have the world's largest hot springs pool! The big main pool here is kept slightly cooler than your typical hot spring (around 90 to 93 degrees); the resort's hotter therapy pool is kept at around 104 degrees. There's also an aquatic park — Sopris Splash Zone — with a lazy river feature that's been designed to mimic a whitewater rafting river, plus a kids' slide that's suited to smaller guests. Also worth visiting, particularly if you want something quieter, is Iron Mountain Hot Springs on the banks of the Colorado River. Here, you'll find 16 pools in a designated "quiet zone" plus a family pool.

Getting Out on the River

Rafting is among the most popular summertime activities in Glenwood Springs, with plenty of Class IV and Class V rapids as well as an abundance of highly trained guides who can help less experienced rafters have a safe and exciting experience. Kayaking is also popular, with a mix of smoother areas and spots with more challenging rapids. Canoeing and stand-up paddleboarding are also popular, with plenty of local outfitters offering rentals. Glenwood Springs and its surrounding lakes and rivers are also great for fly-fishing, particularly in the spring and fall; locally found species include cutthroats and rainbow trout.

good sam park Featured Good Sam Parks COLORADO

When you stay with Good Sam, you can expect the highest degree of cleanliness and friendliness, and better yet, you get **10% off** overnight campground fees.

If you're not already a Good Sam member you can purchase your membership at one of these locations:

ALAMOSA
Cool Sunshine RV Park

BATTLEMENT MESA
Saddleback RV

BAYFIELD
Bayfield Riverside RV Park

BUENA VISTA
Arrowhead Point Campground and Cabins

CANON CITY
Royal View RV Park

COLORADO SPRINGS
Fountain Creek RV Park
Goldfield RV Park

CORTEZ
La Mesa RV Park
Sleeping Ute RV Park
Sundance RV Park

DURANGO
Oasis RV Resort & Cottages - Durango

ESTES PARK
Elk Meadow Lodge and RV Resort
Manor RV Park
Spruce Lake RV Resort

FAIRPLAY
Middlefork RV Resort

FORT MORGAN
Emerald RV Park

FRUITA
Monument RV Resort

GOLDEN
Dakota Ridge RV Resort

GRAND JUNCTION
Canyon View RV Resort

GRAND LAKE
Winding River Resort

GREELEY
Greeley RV Park

GYPSUM
Aunt Sara's River Dance RV Resort

IGNACIO
Sky Ute Casino RV Park

LOVELAND
Loveland RV Resort
Riverview RV Park & Campground

MANCOS
Mesa Verde RV Resort

MEEKER
Trail & Hitch RV Park and Tiny Home Hotel

MONTROSE
Cedar Creek RV Park

OLATHE
Uncompahgre River Adult RV Park

PAGOSA SPRINGS
Pagosa Riverside Campground

SILVERTON
Silver Summit RV Park

WESTCLIFFE
Grape Creek RV Park Campground & Cabins

10/10★/10 GOOD SAM PARKS

CANON CITY
Royal View RV Park
(719)275-1900

MANCOS
Mesa Verde RV Resort
(800)776-7421

GRAND JUNCTION
Canyon View RV Resort
(970)730-2600

What's This?

An RV park with a 10/10★/10 rating has scored perfect grades in amenities, cleanliness and appearance ("See Understanding the Campground Rating System" on pages 8 and 9 for an explanation of the trusted Good Sam Rating System). Stay in a 10/10★/10 park on your next trip for a nearly flawless camping experience.

Getty Images/iStockphoto

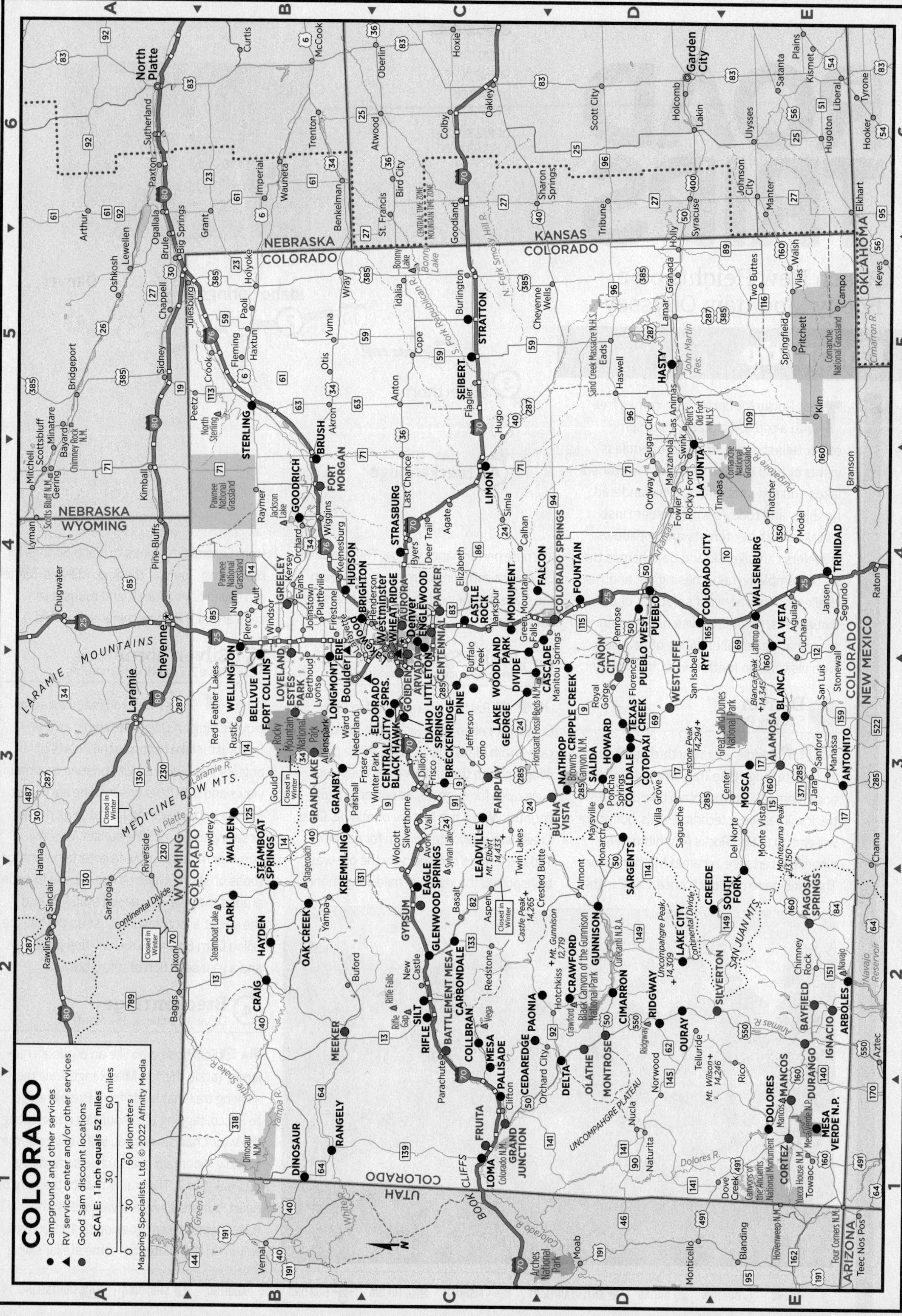
COLORADO
Campground and other services
RV service center and/or other services
Good Sam discount locations
SCALE: 1 inch equals 52 miles
60 miles
60 kilometers
Mapping Specialists, Ltd. © 2022 Affinity Media
NEBRASKA
WYOMING
KANSAS
OKLAHOMA
NEW MEXICO
UTAH
ARIZONA
COLORADO
Denver
Boulder
North Platte
Garden City
Cheyenne
Laramie
LARAMIE MOUNTAINS
MEDICINE BOW MTS.
SAN JUAN MTS.
UNCOMPAHGRE PLATEAU
BOOK CLIFFS
CENTRAL TIME ZONE
MOUNTAIN TIME ZONE
STERLING
BRUSH
FORT MORGAN
GOODRICH
STRASBURG
LIMON
STRATTON
SEIBERT
HASTY
LA JUNTA
COLORADO CITY
WALSENBURG
TRINIDAD
LA VETA
BLANCA
ALAMOSA
ANTONITO
MOSCA
PUEBLO
PUEBLO WEST
COLORADO SPRINGS
FOUNTAIN
FALCON
MONUMENT
CASTLE ROCK
PARKER
AURORA
BRIGHTON
HUDSON
GREELEY
FORT COLLINS
WELLINGTON
LOVELAND
ESTES PARK
LONGMONT
GRAND LAKE
GRANBY
KREMMLING
WALDEN
STEAMBOAT SPRINGS
CLARK
HAYDEN
CRAIG
OAK CREEK
MEEKER
RANGELY
DINOSAUR
RIFLE
SILT
GLENWOOD SPRINGS
CARBONDALE
GYPSUM
EAGLE
LEADVILLE
FAIRPLAY
BRECKENRIDGE
BUENA VISTA
NATHROP
SALIDA
HOWARD
COALDALE
COTOPAXI
CAÑON CITY
CRIPPLE CREEK
WESTCLIFFE
RYE
GUNNISON
SARGENTS
LAKE CITY
CREEDE
SOUTH FORK
PAGOSA SPRINGS
ARBOLES
IGNACIO
BAYFIELD
DURANGO
MANCOS
MESA VERDE N.P.
CORTEZ
DOLORES
SILVERTON
OURAY
RIDGWAY
MONTROSE
OLATHE
DELTA
CEDAREDGE
PAONIA
CRAWFORD
CIMARRON
GRAND JUNCTION
FRUITA
LOMA
PALISADE
MESA
COLLBRAN
BATTLEMENT MESA

ROAD TRIPS

Reach New Heights on a Rocky Mountain Odyssey

Colorado

LOCATION
COLORADO

DISTANCE
82 MILES

DRIVE TIME
1 HR 43 MINS

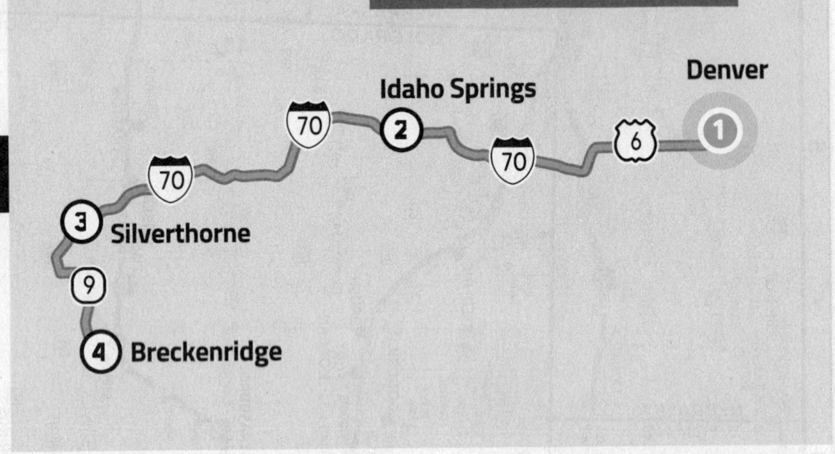

That Rocky Mountain high comes free with a trip to Colorado. Hike some of her tallest peaks to discover endless vistas or hold the line with trout in storied lakes and streams. Dinosaurs wandered her hills, and today's wildlife seem just as taken with her forests and meadows. Travelers can bike, ski and boat across the state's ample terrain, chasing yet another challenge from her vast selection of activities. Yes, Colorado loves nothing more than sharing her abundance of beauty with visitors, no matter what the season.

1 Denver
Starting Point

Peddle your way through time on Dakota Ridge Bike Trail, where dinosaurs once roamed. This mountain bike double track will test your technical skills, but riders will end up at Red Rocks Amphitheater, where concerts are set amid Mother Nature. The sandstone outdoor "concert hall" is the ultimate performance venue. Then head to LoDo for a sampling of micro brews from the state that helped to put craft beers on the map.

2 Idaho Springs
Drive 33 miles ▪ 41 minutes

Rafting spring runoff in Clear Creek is an adrenaline kick, with rapids rated from Class II to Class V. While paddling through the narrow river, keep your eyes open for nuggets, as you are in gold country. With a rich history of mining, Clear Creek was a favorite stream for panning. Today's visitors can see how the ore was transported through a 4-mile-long tunnel from Central City mines to Idaho Springs for processing. Tours of the Argo Mill and Tunnel run seven days a week, and tourists can keep any of the shiny mineral they find.

3 Silverthorne
Drive 35 miles ▪ 37 minutes

Get your rod ready for some trout fishing on Dillon Reservoir, as this freshwater lake captures the hearts of anglers everywhere. With pristine mountain views and 300 days of sunshine each year, it is the perfect setting for catching dinner or sailing away into the sunset. Weekly summer regattas provide entertainment for those offshore, while others choose to cycle around the lake on a paved trail. And end the day at a local favorite just up the hill, the Dillon Dam Brewery. You will find good eats and a vast selection of micro brews.

4 Breckenridge
Drive 14 miles ▪ 25 minutes

For those who like an outdoor challenge, tackle the Ten Mile Range Traverse, a hiking trail that leads from Breckenridge to Frisco, tagging ten mountain peaks along the way. Chances are you will run into some friendly mountain goats while scrambling up Peak 1 or 2. The trail is not for the faint of heart, but the views are well worth the effort, as your ascent goes up to 13,500 feet. Return in the winter for some stellar skiing.

Getty Images/iStockphoto

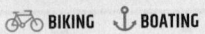

BIKING BOATING DINING ENTERTAINMENT FISHING HIKING HUNTING PADDLING SHOPPING SIGHTSEEING

CO

Colorado SPOTLIGHTS

See Mountains and Cities Reach New Heights

The Centennial State will inspire you with its towering peaks and endless possibilities for recreation. The state that gives birth to the Colorado River is home to world-class river rafting, off-the-charts hiking and biking, and a craft beer scene that will whet any whistle. See where Olympians soar and discover downhill thrills.

SOME COLORADO NATIONAL MONUMENT ROCKS RISE 450 FEET.

Fourteen hiking trails snake through the majestic Colorado National Monument.

Getty Images/iStockphoto

Grand Junction

Get your outdoor recreation fix at Grand Junction on Colorado's Western Slope on the banks of the Colorado River. From digging for dinosaur bones to high-desert hikes to backcountry bike trips and more, visitors to the Centennial State's Western Slope are spoiled for choices when it comes to adventure. But a trip to Grand Junction isn't just full-throttle fun. An award-winning wine and beer scene, coupled with vibrant downtown shopping and galleries, means there's a little something for everyone. There's also plenty of boating and fishing recreation on nearby waterways.

Major Monument

Trek 14 miles west from the city to visit the jaw-dropping towering red rocks of Colorado National Monument. Whether you're exploring the miles of hiking trails or taking in the sights from the 23-mile Rim Rock Drive, it's the area's must-see outdoor escape.

Hiking is Huge Here

Colorado National Monument is a top spot in the region for trail buffs. Many casual hikers start with the Canyon Rim, Coke Ovens or Window Rock trails. Each of these top out at under 2 miles out and back but offer canyon views and the chance to see the deer, bighorn sheep and golden eagles that inhabit the park. Just outside the park, the town of Fruita is a cycling mecca with everything from easily accessible loops to the 140-mile Kokopelli's Trail, a true backcountry gem for lovers of two wheels.

One Flat Top That's Always in Tyle

Ready for record breaking? Grand Mesa is the largest flat-topped mountain in the world and the namesake national forest that surrounds the city boasts expansive views, rugged woods and incredible fall foliage. For an indoor adventure, don't skip the Museum of the West for an immersive and interactive glimpse into the area's 1,000-year history of human habitation. The Dinosaur Journey Museum in Fruita is another popular destination.

Cast a Line in the Current

You'll find a lot of streams perfect for flyfishing in the area. Adventurous anglers should head to the Lake of the Woods trail in Grand Mesa National Forest for backcountry access to Bull Creek, one of the park's best trout pools. For more family-friendly amenities, try Ward, Alexander and Baron lakes, which have become boating and canoeing hot spots. For a new level of excitement, test your mettle against some of the country's finest whitewater with a trip down the Colorado River's Westwater Canyon. Just 30 miles downstream from the city center, the town has plenty of outfitters who can help organize this trip of a lifetime.

Loving the Lake

Slow things down on a sprawling lake. Set out for the James M. Robb-Colorado River

LOCAL FAVORITE

Colorado Cowboy Beans

When the temperature dips in the Rockies, any mountain man can stay warm and satisfied with a pot of these meaty and filling legumes. Add a buttery piece of cornbread and dig-in.

INGREDIENTS

- ☐ 1 lb ground beef
- ☐ 1 pkg bacon cut into small pieces
- ☐ 1 cup chopped onion
- ☐ 2 large cans of pork and beans
- ☐ 1 can of red beans, drained
- ☐ 1 can of kidney beans, drained
- ☐ 1 can of butter beans, drained
- ☐ 1 ¼ cup ketchup
- ☐ ⅓ cup brown sugar
- ☐ 1 Tbsp liquid smoke
- ☐ 4 Tbsp white vinegar
- ☐ Salt and pepper to taste

DIRECTIONS

Brown meats and onion, drain off fat and place in crockpot, slow cooker or large pot. Add the remaining ingredients. Stir well, cover and cook on low 4-6 hours.

State Park, which is situated around Corn Lake near the north bank of the Colorado River. Drop a line for bass or northern pike in this tranquil environment. There's also a one-mile natural-surface trail following the course of the Colorado River, giving hikers a view of the park while taking a pleasant stroll through the area's geology.

High Country Winery

Visitors may be surprised to learn that the Grand Junction area is home to one of Colorado's two viticulture areas: the Grand Valley AVA. There are more than 20 wineries in the area, with tasting rooms open throughout the year, and plenty of local operators offering bicycles and horse-drawn carriages to enhance the experience. Most of the wineries in the area are in and around nearby Palisade, though the city of Grand Junction has vintners of its own.

Rocky Mountain National Park

No visit to the Rocky Mountains are complete without a visit to their namesake national park. Rocky Mountain National Park encompasses 265,000 acres of placid mountain lakes and rugged mountain terrain. Rocky Mountain National Park attracts adventurers from both sides of the continent. The Continental Divide runs through the park, and the headwaters of the Colorado River are found here. With so many superlatives, it is hard to narrow down high points.

A bull moose wades through a lake in Rocky Mountain National Park. An estimated 2,500 moose live in Colorado.

Powerful Peak

Toward the west, one stalwart mountain stands out among the crowd. Longs Peak is one of 58 mountains in the state that rise above 14,000 feet (called 14ers). Its diamond-shaped face is immediately recognizable, but to scale this mountain takes some real grit, as hikers traverse tremendous boulder fields, pass through a granite "keyhole" and scale narrow rock ledges, all to be rewarded with a view for miles.

High Life Hotel

Built six years before Rocky Mountain became a national park, the Stanley Hotel in Estes Park is an ethereal attraction, bringing fans of the paranormal to the region. Built by inventor F.O. Stanley (of Stanley Steamer car fame) as a showcase for wealthy friends visiting from back East, the hotel was outfitted with the latest amenities for the time, including a hydraulic elevator and electric heat. But it never made a profit for Stanley.

Supernatural Stanley

The second half of the 20th century wasn't kind to the hotel, as it fell into disrepair. Then author Steven King and his wife spent a night there, and its fortunes changed. King's nightmare in room 217 became the inspiration for one of his most popular books, "The Shining," and bookings at the hotel soared as guests reported seeing ghostly figures and apparitions. Management has embraced the spooky stories, offering popular evening ghost tours of the property.

Grand Lake Goings On

Take Trail Ridge Road through the park from the east and descend into the charming town of Grand Lake. Once the destination for wealthy

With awesome views, Trail Ridge Road in Rocky Mountain National Park links Estes Park and Grand Lake.

resort guests in the late 1800s, this area is dominated by an enormous mountain lake, where canoes, fishing boats and catamarans glide on smooth waters. Spend a day on the water dropping a line, paddling along the shore or tacking with the wind.

Boots Made for Hiking

Trails lead hikers to endless vistas at Rocky Mountain National Park. Over 350 miles of trails challenge summer visitors, with elevations from 7,500 feet to over 12,000 feet. Winter hiking on the trail is also quite remarkable, but mainly achieved with snowshoes or on cross-country skis.

Telescopes and Top Movies

If you love starry skies, then Rocky Mountain National Park is the place for you. High altitude mixed with no light pollution presents a perfect stage from which to count constellations. Join a ranger-led program. Other events in the park revolve around its five visitor centers. Beaver Meadows offers a gift shop and screenings of a 20-minute film on the park.

Watching the Wildlife

Big mammals roam freely in the park, making it ideal for wildlife buffs. It's not unusual to see elk, mule deer and bighorn sheep grazing along the road or on a backcountry hiking trek. Moose and black bear are a little shy, but can usually be found near forested areas.

Ride the Trail Ridge Road

For a drive of a lifetime, take Trail Ridge Road. It is the only path that connects the east side of the park to the west, but it is also the highest paved road in the country, rising to over 12,000 feet. One can only imagine the amount of snow that falls at that altitude in winter, but snowplow drivers do an amazing job of bulldozing through it, usually around Memorial Day. During clear summer days, the views are awesome.

Rugged Scenery

Native Americans inhabited this rugged wilderness for thousands of years before the Ute and Arapaho tribes hunted here, but it went unnoticed by early European pioneers. So remote was this land that it wasn't explored until the 1820s, and the discovery of gold in Colorado brought miners, who established towns. Within 10 years, the settlements were abandoned.

Preserving Beauty

In the early 20th century, an effort to preserve pristine American lands made serious inroads. In 1915, the region officially became a national park. It wasn't until 1932, however, that transportation could move from one side of the park to the other when Trail Ridge Road was completed, connecting Estes Park and Grand Lake.

SPOTLIGHTS

The Spirit of Southwestern Colorado

Southwest Colorado is a place where canyons, deserts and mesas take center stage, the past comes shrouded in mystery and the legacy of the Old West endures. A haven for nature lovers and history buffs, this rugged slice of the Centennial State has all the makings of an unforgettable vacation. From desolate landscapes rich in outdoor recreation and spellbinding byways, to abandoned mining towns and the largest archaeological preservation site in the country, there's no limit to what you can experience here. Come visit this enthralling part of America's West and see what adventurers have been gushing about.

Rugged range: View of the Gunnison River during sunset along the Tabeguach Trail near Grand Junction.

Black Canyon Adventures

Discover one of the continent's deepest chasms and some of its oldest rock in Black Canyon of the Gunnison. Located 14 miles from Montrose and 63 miles from Gunnison, this national park is named after the plunging cliff walls that are blanketed in black shadow. The most dramatic cliff of them all is the Painted Wall, the highest in Colorado, standing 2,250 feet from the rim to the Gunnison River below.

Hiking Near the Canyon

See the Painted Wall in all its glory by traversing the Cedar Point Nature Trail. This easy 0.6-mile path found in the South Rim of the park weaves through plenty of local flora and ends with two overlooks offering marvelous views of the Painted Wall and river below. Hikers looking for more of a challenge can take on the North Rim's Chasm View Nature Trail, a moderate 0.3-mile journey through pinyon and juniper forest that eventually leads to a lookout with the Painted Wall and Serpent Point as its backdrop. Don't forget to look up during your trek as raptors, swifts and swallows are often spotted. Only the most seasoned hikers should tackle the inner canyon as maintained and marked trails are nonexistent.

River Wild

World-class hiking isn't the only draw here — the Gunnison River has been awarded the title of Gold Medal Water and Wild Trout Water. Drop a line anywhere between Crystal Dam to the river's North Fork to bag some monster trout. On land, a diverse array of wildlife calls Black Canyon home. Bring binoculars and keep your eyes open for yellow-bellied marmots, mule deer, elk, badgers and Rocky Mountain bighorn sheep. If you're lucky, you may even catch a glimpse of the "ghost of the Rockies," also known as the mountain lion. Other popular activities in the park include camping, kayaking, rock climbing and stargazing.

Ride into Black Canyon's Past

Situated just 20 miles east of Montrose is Cimarron, which originally served as a link to transport ore from the San Juan Mountains' mines and later functioned as a livestock shipping hub. Visit the area today and you'll stumble upon an outdoor exhibit featuring original railroad stock cars and loading corrals. The National Park Service also runs a campground and picnic space here.

Durango Delights

Just over 100 miles south of Black Canyon via U.S. Route 550 lies the dynamic town of Durango. The time-honored traditions of the area's native and gold rush occupants are preserved through a host of historic attractions, while the timeless beauty of nature is evident in the stunning mountains that soar into the sky.

High-Altitude Valley

Durango sits tucked into the Animas River Valley at an elevation of 6,512 feet. Early visitors weren't drawn here for the natural beauty of the landscape. Instead they were more interested in what they could find below the

The Durango & Silverton Narrow Gauge Railway chugging through the San Juan Mountains.

surface: silver and gold. Snowcapped mountain peaks, roaring waterways and soaring pine trees make this area a picturesque destination. Head downtown to learn more about the town's history in the Durango & Silverton Narrow Gauge Railroad & Museum or find out about local flora and fauna at the Durango Fish Hatchery & Wildlife Museum. There are a number of camping areas in the San Juan National Forest that lies to the north of town.

Frontier Fun

One of Colorado's top attractions, the Durango & Silverton Narrow Gauge Railroad has been in continuous operation since 1882, when the Denver and Rio Grande Railroad line was extended to Silverton to carry gold, silver and other minerals from the state's high-country mines. A ride on the historic Durango & Silverton Narrow Gauge Railroad takes you through spectacular mountainous scenery, with a layover in the colorful town of Silverton. Don't overlook the heritage left by the predecessors of the cowboys. Relive the sights and sounds of yesteryear on the Cascade Canyon Express where you can take in incredible geological features and jaw-dropping scenery. The journey north to Silverton traces the course of the Río de Las Animas Perdidas (The River of Lost Souls) and climbs 3,000 feet as it traverses the breathtaking canyons and the majestic mountains of beautiful San Juan National Forest.

Cascade Creek

Many more adventurous trails can be found in the hills and valleys surrounding Durango. Pick your desired level of difficulty and head to the hills. Hike up Smelter Mountain for expansive views of the city below. The Cascade Creek Trail takes you through a forest of pine trees to a spectacular view of a tumbling waterfall. After a day of hiking and adventuring, sink into the Pinkerton Hot Springs or Trimble Spa and Natural Hot Springs to relax your cares away in one of Mother Nature's hot tubs.

Explore Durango

Elegant historic buildings rise high above the streets, dwarfed only by the snowcapped mountain peaks in the distance, giving downtown Durango a stunning beauty not found in many other cities. The famous archeological sites of Mesa Verde are only a scenic 45-minute drive west. The Animas River offers a range of water sports, and numerous spots to fish with convenient access from downtown. Experience the adrenaline-pumping excitement of a rafting adventure on this turbulent waterway. Wander Main Street and soak in the sights and enjoy all the unique shops and restaurants Durango has to offer. The Strater Hotel is also in Downtown and has been in operation since the 1887. The well-preserved hotel boasts the largest collection of walnut Victorian furniture on the planet. Hoist a beer at the Diamond Belle Saloon to get the full experience.

Aggie Community

Foodies will love sampling the eclectic menu of restaurants found here. Agriculture is the heart of the community with the "eat local" mantra and an abundance of locally grown and raised meat and vegetables. Agritourism brings visitors in to truly experience some of the best of the region's resources. Savor local farmers markets, farm-to-table meals and wine dinners with San Juan region's best locally grown foods. Durango Mountain Resort even hosts foraging and cooking demonstrations during summer. For a hearty meal, order a burger at Grassburger, which uses only grassfed beef for its food. Eat it with fries cooked in non-GMO sunflower fry oil and chase it with a delicious Vegan Bliss Shake.

Famous Mountains and Super Skiing

With 2 million acres of wild national forest, it makes sense that Durango has been chosen dozens of times as the set for movies and film. And it has hosted a number of famous artists and writers over the years. Find the exact room where Louis L'Amour wrote his famed western novels, the Sackett Series at the Strater Hotel on Main Avenue.

CO

SPOTLIGHTS

Heavenly Resort

Winter abounds with activity and beauty as Purgatory Resort, named in the top 10 on Conde Naste's list of best ski resorts in the U.S. and Canada, according to their readers. It was also named as the "Best Value Ski Resort in North America" by TripAdvisor. Located about 30 minutes north of town, this winter paradise in the heart of the San Juan Mountains resort has all the amenities a skier wants with alpine skiing, a vibrant downtown and private lounge. During the summer and fall, book a mountain biking tour with Durango Bike Tours where they customize a ride that will match the trails and terrain to your skill level. This mountain biker's playground is a place where arid desert terrain meets lush spruce forests. If you're craving a few hours of bike playtime, check out the Horse Gulch trail system.

Get Crafty

Within a short drive of Durango, in all four directions, there's over 30 craft breweries, wineries and distilleries (and a cider house!). Colorado is known for having some of the best craft breweries in the country and Durango is no exception. Visit some of the best microbreweries and pubs and taste award-winning libations that will satisfy even the most discerning craft beer lover. Ska Brewing has been brewing since 1995, boasting flavorful brews like the award-winning Euphoria Pale Ale. Their True Blonde Ale recently received the 2019 Good Food Award. Durango Brewing Company is one of the oldest breweries in Colorado, having brewed their Amber Ale in the fall of 1990. Pick up their Great American Beer Festival Bronze medal winner, the Durango Dark Lager.

Snow-covered mountains outside of Silverton, which is one of the tallest U.S. towns at 9,318 feet.

Spirits on Hand

Honey House Distillery creates hand crafted, small batch honey spirits. All of their spirits contain Honeyville Wildflower Honey, found in the Hermosa Valley. After you return from the slopes, grab something warm and boozy at the Office Spiritorium, where you can sit by the fire and sip hand-crafted drinks.

Beautiful Bayfield

While visiting the area, many visitors take a side trip to scenic Bayfield, a small town just east of Durango. Sitting at an altitude of about 6,900 feet, Bayfield is close to the Four Corners of Colorado, New Mexico, Arizona and Utah. Bayfield is the "Heart of the Pine River Valley," featuring a small historic district with a few shops and restaurants in town. Vallecito Lake is one of southwest Colorado's most cherished and secluded destinations. This secluded mountain valley is less than 20 miles from Durango, offering breathtaking mountain views and clear sparkling waters. Enjoy year-round fishing, great hiking trails and of course boating, kayaking and paddle boarding. The area's waters are filled with kokanee salmon, rainbow trout and small mouth bass. Located 25 minutes from Bayfield and less than 40 minutes from Durango, the Vallecito Marina is the best way to enjoy Vallecito Lake.

The Front Range

Occupying the eastern slope of the Rocky Mountains, Colorado's Front Range is dotted with Alpine vistas, laid-back mountain towns and Wild West heritage sites. Occupying the eastern edge of the Rocky Mountains, this region strikes the perfect balance of outdoor adventure and urban pleasures. Spend your days conquering majestic peaks and then unwind in vibrant cities like Denver, Colorado Springs, Pueblo and Boulder.

Mountain Majesty

Rocky Mountain National Park is one of the Front Range's premier attractions. This natural wonderland contains an endless array of outdoor recreation, with 355 miles of trails, 150 lakes and towering peaks as far as the eye can see. Trek a portion of the Continental Divide

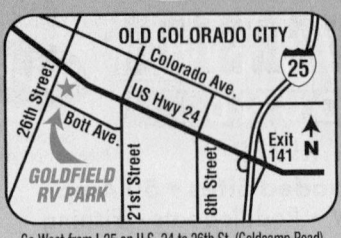

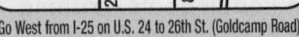

See listing Colorado Springs, CO

Trail to reach meadows and waterfalls and keep an eye out for bighorn sheep, mule deer and elk along the way. Bring your tackle box too, as the streams and lakes support four species of trout. The scenic drives are just as rewarding as the waterways, so cruise along Trail Ridge Road or Old Fall River Road to admire Mother Nature from the comfort of your vehicle.

Reelin' in Rocky Fish

Rivers, lakes and stocked reservoirs have put this region high on anglers' wish lists. The reservoirs and lakes between Fort Collins and Denver are filled with walleye and smallmouth bass. Cast a line from popular spots like Carter Lake, Horsetooth Reservoir and Boyd Lake State Park. If you're in the Denver metro area, try your luck at Cherry Creek State Park, Chatfield State Park and Stanley Lake, or venture into Boulder Creek to catch a bounty of rainbow and brown trout. Watersports are big in this region too, with activities ranging from tame to extreme. Rent a canoe and relax on Lake Estes or get the ultimate adrenaline rush by whitewater rafting on the Arkansas River.

Soaring Summits

Mountain adventure is just a short trip from Colorado Springs. Just minutes from town is Garden of the Gods, a National Landmark consisting of 1,367 acres overflowing with soaring red rock formations. Cross the dramatic landscape by horseback just as the pioneers did over a century ago or cycle down winding roads to get to pull-offs with the best views.

Spectacular Pikes Peak

A short jaunt south of Colorado Springs takes visitors to Pikes Peak, the world's second-most-visited mountain. A popular way to get to the 14,000-foot peak is by hiking Barr Trail. The 26-mile path weaves through rock formations and dense forest before unveiling a 360-degree view at the top. You can also get to the summit by driving or biking along the Pikes Peak Highway or riding the Broadmoor Pikes Peak Cog Railway from Manitou Springs. On a clear day, you can spot Denver's skyscrapers.

A fly-fisherman casts a line on the Taylor River near Gunnison. The waterway is known for some of the largest rainbow trout in the Centennial State.

Merriment in the Mile-High City

Denver ranks as one of the top cities in the U.S., thanks to its professional sports teams, premier museums and endless brewpubs. Let your imagination soar at the Denver Museum of Nature and Science and view one of the largest collections of Native American art at the Denver Art Museum.

Pioneering Spirit

Back in the 1800s, Pueblo's streets were walked by characters like Wild Bill Hickok and Buffalo Bill Cody. Get an idea of what life was like in this rough-and-tumble town at the El Pueblo History Museum.

▸ FOR MORE INFORMATION

Colorado Tourism Office, 800-265-6723, www.colorado.com
Visit Grand Junction, 970-244-1480, www.visitgrandjunction.com
Rocky Mountain National Park, 970-586-1206, www.nps.gov/romo
Colorado Front Range, 800-265-6723, www.colorado.com/front-range

CO

Colorado

ALAMOSA — E3 *Alamosa*

ALAMOSA KOA **Ratings: 8.5/9★/8.5** (Campground) 53 Avail: 49 full hkups, 4 W, 4 E (30/50 amps). 2021 rates: $48 to $87. May 01 to Oct 15. (800)562-9157, 6900 Juniper Ln, Alamosa, CO 81101

BASE CAMP FAMILY CAMPGROUND **Ratings: 5.5/10★/7.5** (Campground) Avail: 13 full hkups (30/50 amps). 2021 rates: $45. (719)589-2938, 7001 Base Camp Road, Alamosa, CO 81101

COOL SUNSHINE RV PARK
Ratings: 9/10★/9.5 (RV Park) Avail: 41 full hkups (30/50 amps). 2021 rates: $47 to $52. (719)992-9105, 1055 7th St, Alamosa, CO 81101

ANTONITO — E3 *Conejos*

CANON BONITO RV PARK & ANGLERS CLUB **Ratings: 6/7/8** (Campground) Avail: 24 full hkups (30/50 amps). 2021 rates: $34. May 01 to Nov 15. (719)376-2274, 6819 CR D5, Antonito, CO 81120

CONEJOS RIVER CAMPGROUND **Ratings: 7.5/9.5★/9** (RV Park) Avail: 33 full hkups (30/50 amps). 2021 rates: $36 to $38. May 01 to Oct 31. (719)376-5943, 26714 Hwy 17, Antonito, CO 81120

MOGOTE MEADOW CABINS AND RV PARK Ratings: 7.5/6.5/6 (Campground) Avail: 37 full hkups (30/50 amps). 2021 rates: $32.50 to $34.75. (719)376-5774, 34127 State Hwy 17, Antonito, CO 81120

TWIN RIVERS CABINS & RV PARK **Ratings: 6.5/8★/8** (RV Park) Avail: 39 full hkups (30/50 amps). 2021 rates: $34.95 to $42.95. Apr 01 to Nov 30. (719)376-5710, 34044 State Hwy 17, Antonito, CO 81120

ARBOLES — E2 *Archuleta*

NAVAJO
(Public State Park) From Jct of US-160 & SR-151, SW 18 mi on SR-151 to CR-982, S 2 mi (E). Entrance fee required. Elev 6100 ft.**FAC:** paved rds. 105 Avail: 9 paved, 96 gravel, 68 pull-thrus, (15x80), back-ins (15x80), 39 full hkups, 41 E (30/50 amps), tent sites, rentals, shower$, dump, laundry, firewood. **REC:** Navajo Reservoir: swim, fishing, marina, boating nearby, hunting nearby, rec open to public. Pets OK. Partial handicap access. Big rig sites, 14 day max stay. 2021 rates: $18 to $41.
(970)883-2208 Lat: 37.00931, Lon: -107.40732
1526 CR-982, Arboles, CO 81121
cpw.state.co.us
See ad page 164

Find it fast! Use our alphabetized index of campgrounds and parks.

Colorado Privately Owned Campground Information Updated by our Good Sam Representatives

Tim & Sheryl Heath

Originally from Indiana, we have been traveling full-time in our motorcoach and working for Good Sam for eight years. We have formed lasting friendships with campground owners. Our puppies, Mork and Mindie, love the adventure.

NAVAJO LAKE RESORT RV PARK & CAMPGROUND **Ratings: 6.5/9.5★/7.5** (RV Park) Avail: 31 full hkups (30/50 amps). 2021 rates: $37. Apr 01 to Nov 30. (970)883-3636, 19 Lazy Lane, Arboles, CO 81121

ARVADA — C3 *Adams*

Travel Services

UNCLE JON'S OUTDOOR STORAGE Secure, fully paved outdoor storage with 24/7 keypad access. Well lighted for nighttime parking of your RV, boat, trailer or toy. Elev 5955 ft.**RV Storage:** outdoor, secured fencing, electric gate, easy reach keypad, 24/7 access, well-lit facility, well-lit roads, well-lit perimeter, security cameras, on-site staff, level gravel/paved spaces, battery charger, office. **SERVICES:**. Hours: 9am to 5pm.
Special offers available for Good Sam Members
(303)420-5252 Lat: 39.51588, Lon: -105.11739
17190 Hwy 72, Arvada, CO 80007
ujstorage.com

UNCLE JON'S OUTDOOR STORAGE WEST Open outdoor storage for RVs, boats, trailers and toys. 500+ secure spaces surrounded by mountain and city views with 24 hour keypad access. Elev 6112 ft.**RV Storage:** outdoor, secured fencing, electric gate, easy reach keypad, 24/7 access, well-lit facility, well-lit roads, well-lit perimeter, security cameras, level gravel/paved spaces. **SERVICES:**. Hours: 8am to 8pm.
Special offers available for Good Sam Members
(303)420-5252 Lat: 39.51744, Lon: -105.12951
18930 Hwy 72, Arvada, CO 80007
ujstorage.com

AURORA — C4 *Adams*

CHERRY CREEK
(Public State Park) From Jct of I-225 & Parker Rd/SR-83 (exit 4), S 1.2 mi on Parker Rd/SR-83 at Lehigh Ave (R). Entrance fee required. Elev 5550 ft.**FAC:** paved rds. Avail: 101 paved, 61 pull-thrus, (30x45), back-ins (30x45), 101 full hkups (30/50 amps), WiFi @ sites, tent sites, shower$, dump, laundry, fire rings, firewood. **REC:** Cherry Creek Reservoir: swim, fishing, marina, kayaking/canoeing, playground, rec open to public. Pets OK. Partial handicap access, 14 day max stay. 2021 rates: $28 to $41.
(303)690-1166 Lat: 39.647341, Lon: -104.829570
4201 S Parker Rd, Aurora, CO 80014
cow.state.co.us
See ad page 164

Travel Services

RV VAULT - AURORA Spacious RV Canopy and Outdoor Storage near Denver International Airport just off the freeway with secure 24/7 gated access and roaming security. Water, electric, dump station and compressed air included. Elev 5689 ft. **RV Storage:** outdoor, covered canopy, secured fencing, electric gate, easy reach keypad, 24/7 access, well-lit facility, well-lit roads, well-lit perimeter, security cameras, level gravel/paved spaces, power to charge battery, water, compressed air. **SERVICES:**. Hours: 8am to 5pm.
Special offers available for Good Sam Members
(720)903-2619 Lat: 39.67722, Lon: -104.72969
2151 S Rome Way, Aurora, CO 80019
rvvault.com

BATTLEMENT MESA — C2 *Garfield*

SADDLEBACK RV
Ratings: 6/9★/7 (RV Park) Avail: 99 full hkups (30/50 amps). 2021 rates: $29. (970)285-5640, 95 Eldora Dr, Parachute, CO 81635

BAYFIELD — E2 *La Plata*

BAYFIELD See also Arboles, Durango, Ignacio & Pagosa Springs.

BAYFIELD RIVERSIDE RV PARK
Ratings: 9.5/10★/9.5 (RV Park) Avail: 100 full hkups (30/50 amps). 2021 rates: $48 to $75. (970)884-2475, 41743 US Hwy 160, Bayfield, CO 81122

BLUE SPRUCE RV PARK & CABINS **Ratings: 8/9.5★/9.5** (RV Park) Avail: 77 full hkups (30/50 amps). 2021 rates: $41 to $49. Apr 15 to Oct 31. (970)884-2641, 1875 CR-500, Bayfield, CO 81122

VALLECITO RESORT **Ratings: 7.5/10★/8.5** (RV Park) Avail: 90 full hkups (30/50 amps). 2021 rates: $45.95. May 01 to Oct 01. (970)884-9458, 13030 County Road 501, Bayfield, CO 81122

BELLVUE — B3 *Larimer*

Things to See and Do

LORY STATE PARK CO State Park. Back country camping only. Entrance fee required. Elev 5134 ft. Partial handicap access. Hours: 5am to 10pm. Adult fee: $18 .
(970)493-1623 Lat: 40.5903, Lon: -105.1841
708 Lodgepole Dr, Bellvue, CO 80512
www.cpw.state.co.us
See ad page 164

BLACK HAWK — C3 *Gilpin*

BASE CAMP @ GOLDEN GATE CANYON **Ratings: 6.5/9.5★/8** (Campground) 21 Avail: 3 full hkups, 18 W, 18 E (30/50 amps). 2021 rates: $60. (303)582-9979, 661 Hwy 46, Black Hawk, CO 80422

BLANCA — E3 *Costilla*

BLANCA RV PARK **Ratings: 5.5/4.5/5.5** (RV Park) Avail: 26 full hkups (30/50 amps). 2021 rates: $33 to $38. (719)379-3201, 521 Main, Blanca, CO 81123

BOULDER — B3 *Boulder*

BOULDER See also Brighton, Central City, Denver, Estes Park, Golden & Loveland.

BRECKENRIDGE — C3 *Summit*

TIGER RUN RESORT **Ratings: 10/10★/10** (RV Resort) Avail: 144 full hkups (30/50 amps). 2021 rates: $60 to $160. (970)453-9690, 85 Revett Dr, Breckenridge, CO 80424

BRIGHTON — B4 *Adams*

BARR LAKE RV PARK **Ratings: 5.5/6.5/6** (RV Park) 85 Avail: 75 full hkups, 10 W, 10 E (30/50 amps). 2021 rates: $45 to $56. (303)659-6180, 17180 E 136th Ave, Brighton, CO 80601

Things to See and Do

BARR LAKE STATE PARK Day use only. No camping. Entrance fee required. Fishing, multi-use trail, boating, bird watching, archery range. Elev 5137 ft. Restrooms. Hours: 5am to 10pm. Adult fee: $9.00. No CC.
(303)659-6005 Lat: 39.944665, Lon: -104.733515
13401 Picadilly Road, Brighton, CO 80603
cpw.state.co.us
See ad page 164

BRUSH — B4 *Morgan*

BRUSH MEMORIAL RV PARK & CAMPGROUND
(Public) From Jct of SR-34 & Cameron St, S .27 mi on Cameron St, right on Ellsworth, left on Jordan Pl (R). Elev 4320 ft.**FAC:** gravel rds. Avail: 18 gravel, back-ins (12x35), 12 W, 12 E (20 amps), tent sites, dump. **REC:** pool, playground. Pets OK. Partial handicap access, 7 day max stay. 2021 rates: $25. Apr 01 to Oct 15. no cc.
(970)842-5001 Lat: 40.24923, Lon: -103.62345
S Clayton Street, Brush, CO 80723
www.brushcolo.com

BUENA VISTA — D3 *Chaffee*

ARKANSAS HEADWATERS RECREATION AREA/RAILROAD BRIDGE CAMPGROUND
(Public State Park) From jct H-24 & Main St: Go 2 blocks E, then 6-1/4 mi N on CR-371 (L). Elev 8039 ft.**FAC:** gravel rds. Avail: 8 gravel, 3 pull-thrus, (30x60), back-ins (20x60), accepts self-contain units only, tent sites, pit toilets, fire rings. **REC:** Arkansas River: fishing, boating nearby, hunting nearby, rec open to public. Pets OK. 14 day max stay. 2021 rates: $28.
(719)539-7289 Lat: 38.9228, Lon: -106.1699
CR 371, Buena Vista, CO 81211
cpw.state.co.us
See ad page 164

ARKANSAS HEADWATERS RECREATION AREA/RUBY MOUNTAIN CAMPGROUND
(Public State Park) From jct US-285 & CR-301: Go 1/2 mi N on CR-301, then 2-1/2 mi E on CR-300 (R). Elev 6689 ft.**FAC:** gravel rds. Avail: 14 gravel, 2 pull-thrus, (30x100), back-ins (30x55), accepts self-contain units only, tent sites, pit toilets, fire rings. **REC:** Arkansas River: fishing, boating nearby, hunting nearby, rec open to public. Pets OK. 14 day max stay. 2021 rates: $28.
(719)539-7289 Lat: 38.7528, Lon: -106.0701
CR 300, Buena Vista, CO 81211
cpw.state.co.us
See ad page 164

ARKANSAS RIVER RIM CAMPGROUND & RV PARK **Ratings: 5.5/6.5/6.5** (Campground) Avail: 38 full hkups (30/50 amps). 2021 rates: $40 to $60. Apr 01 to Oct 31. (719)395-8883, 33198 US Hwy 24N, Buena Vista, CO 81211

ARROWHEAD POINT CAMPGROUND AND CABINS
good sam park
Ratings: 8.5/10★/10 (Campground) 66 Avail: 50 full hkups, 16 W, 16 E (30/50 amps). 2021 rates: $48 to $71. May 01 to Sep 30. (719)395-2323, 33975 U.S. Hwy 24 North, Buena Vista, CO 81211

MT PRINCETON RV PARK & CABINS **Ratings: 8/9.5★/10** (RV Park) Avail: 86 full hkups (30/50 amps). 2021 rates: $47 to $59.50. Apr 01 to Oct 31. (719)395-6206, 30380 County Rd 383, Buena Vista, CO 81211

SNOWY PEAKS RV PARK AND RENTALS **Ratings: 7.5/9★/9.5** (RV Park) 91 Avail: 76 full hkups, 15 W, 15 E (30/50 amps). 2021 rates: $39 to $75. (719)395-8481, 30430 US Hwy 24, Buena Vista, CO 81211

CANON CITY — D3 *Fremont*

CANON CITY See also Colorado Springs, Cripple Creek & Pueblo West.

ARKANSAS HEADWATERS RECREATION AREA/FIVE POINTS CAMPGROUND
(Public State Park) From jct US-50 & Royal Gorge Rd: Go 10 mi W on US-50 (L). Elev 6000 ft.**FAC:** gravel rds. Avail: 20 gravel, 4 pull-thrus, (30x45), back-ins (30x45), accepts self-contain units only, pit toilets, fire rings. **REC:** Arkansas River: fishing, boating nearby, hunting nearby, rec open to public. Pets OK. No tents, 14 day max stay. 2021 rates: $28.
(719)539-7289 Lat: 38.452925, Lon: -105.492827
Highway 50, Canon City, CO 81212
cpw.state.co.us
See ad page 164

FARMHOUSE RV RESORT AT ROYAL GORGE **Ratings: 8/NA/9** (RV Resort) 50 Avail: 44 full hkups, 6 W, 6 E (30/50 amps). 2021 rates: $47 to $77. May 01 to Sep 30. (719)800-6008, 43595 Hwy 50 West, Canon City, CO 81212

MOUNTAIN VIEW RV RESORT **Ratings: 8.5/9★/8.5** (RV Park) Avail: 41 full hkups (30/50 amps). 2021 rates: $55 to $72. Apr 01 to Oct 31. (719)275-0900, 45606 Highway 50W, Canon City, CO 81212

ROYAL GORGE KOA **Ratings: 8.5/9/8** (Campground) Avail: 66 full hkups (30/50 amps). 2021 rates: $47.58 to $80. (800)562-5689, 559 Cr 3A, Canon City, CO 81212

ROYAL VIEW RV PARK
good sam park
Ratings: 10/10★/10 (RV Park) Avail: 56 full hkups (30/50 amps). 2021 rates: $50 to $85. May 15 to Sep 30. (719)275-1900, 43590 US Hwy 50 W, Canon City, CO 81212

CARBONDALE — C2 *Garfield*

CARBONDALE/CRYSTAL RIVER KOA **Ratings: 8.5/9.5★/8.5** (Campground) 24 Avail: 24 W, 24 E (30/50 amps). 2021 rates: $39 to $70. Apr 01 to Nov 01. (970)963-2341, 7202 Hwy 133, Carbondale, CO 81623

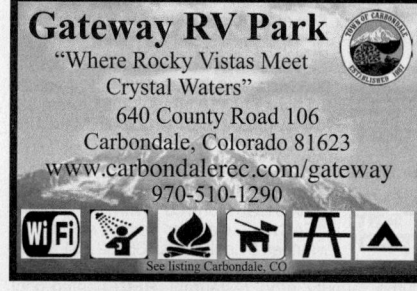

GATEWAY RV PARK
(Public) From Jct of Hwy 133 & Hwy 82: Go W on Hwy 82 1 mi to Satank (CR 106), then go .9 mi (at each Jct, veer left) (L). Elev 6192 ft.**FAC:** gravel rds. Avail: 18 gravel, 5 pull-thrus, (24x45), back-ins (24x35), 11 full hkups, 5 W, 7 E (30/50 amps), WiFi @ sites, dump, fire rings. **REC:** Roaring Fork River: swim, fishing, kayaking/canoeing, boating nearby, hunting nearby. Pets OK. Partial handicap access. No tents, 14 day max stay, eco-friendly. 2021 rates: $25 to $45. May 01 to Oct 01.
(970)510-1290 Lat: 39.41558, Lon: -107.22498
640 CR 106, Carbondale, CO 81623
www.carbondalerec.com/gateway
See ad this page

CASCADE — D4 *El Paso*

LONE DUCK CAMPGROUND **Ratings: 8/9.5★/8** (Campground) 39 Avail: 9 full hkups, 30 W, 30 E (30/50 amps). 2021 rates: $55 to $59. May 01 to Sep 28. (719)684-9907, 8855 W Hwy 24, Cascade, CO 80809

CASTLE ROCK — C4 *Douglas*

YOGI BEARS JELLYSTONE PARK @ LARKSPUR **Ratings: 10/10★/10** (Campground) Avail: 404 full hkups (50 amps). 2021 rates: $109 to $200. (720)325-2393, 650 Sky View Lane, Larkspur, CO 80118

CEDAREDGE — C2 *Delta*

ASPEN TRAILS CAMPGROUND **Ratings: 7/7/7.5** (RV Park) Avail: 23 full hkups (30/50 amps). 2021 rates: $40. (970)856-6321, 19991 Hwy 65, Cedaredge, CO 81413

CENTENNIAL — C4 *Arapahoe*

Travel Services

RV VAULT - CENTENNIAL Deluxe outdoor RV storage spaces from 16x15 to 16x65 with 24/7 secured access. Water, electric, dump station and compressed air included. Elev 5724 ft. **RV Storage:** outdoor, secured fencing, electric gate, easy reach keypad, 24/7 access, well-lit facility, well-lit roads, well-lit perimeter, security cameras, level gravel/paved spaces, power to charge battery, water, compressed air. **SERVICES:**. Hours: 8am to 5pm.
good sam RV Storage
Special offers available for Good Sam Members
(720)903-2619 Lat: 39.58385, Lon: -104.81747
7354 South Eagle Street, Centennial, CO 80012
rvvault.com

CENTRAL CITY — C3 *Gilpin*

DENVER WEST/CENTRAL CITY KOA **Ratings: 8.5/10★/9.5** (RV Park) Avail: 75 full hkups (30/50 amps). 2021 rates: $69 to $89. (800)562-8613, 605 Lake Gulch Road, Central City, CO 80427

CIMARRON — D2 *Gunnison*

BLACK CANYON RV PARK & CAMPGROUND **Ratings: 7.5/9★/8.5** (RV Park) Avail: 26 full hkups (30/50 amps). 2021 rates: $45. Apr 01 to Nov 30. (970)249-1147, 348 Hwy 50, Cimarron, CO 81220

CURECANTI/CIMARRON (Public National Park) On US 50, 20 mi E of Montrose. 21 Avail. 2021 rates: $16. (970)641-2337

CLARK — B2 *Routt*

PEARL LAKE
(Public State Park) From Jct US-40 and CR-129 (2 mi W of Steamboat Springs); Go 23 mi N on CR-129 to CR-209, then 2 mi E on CR-209 to Pearl Lake Campground Loop. Entrance fee required. Elev 8065 ft.**FAC:** gravel rds. Avail: 38 dirt, tent sites, rentals, restrooms only, fire rings. **REC:** Pearl Lake: fishing, boating nearby, rec open to public. Pets OK. 14 day max stay. 2021 rates: $16 to $24.
(970)879-3922 Lat: 40.78632, Lon: -106.88976
61105 CR-129, Clark, CO 80428
cpw.state.co.us
See ad page 164

STEAMBOAT LAKE
(Public State Park) From Jct of US-40 & CR-129, N 26 mi on CR-129 (L). Entrance fee required. Elev 8060 ft.**FAC:** paved rds. Avail: 188 gravel, 99 pull-thrus, (10x50), back-ins (10x35), 74 E (50 amps), tent sites, rentals, shower$, dump, laundry, fire rings. **REC:** Steamboat Lake: swim, fishing, marina, boating nearby, hunting nearby, rec open to public. Pets OK. Partial handicap access, 14 day max stay. 2021 rates: $16 to $32.
(970)879-3922 Lat: 40.798660, Lon: -106.965376
61105 RCR 129, Clark, CO 80428
cpw.state.co.us
See ad page 164

COALDALE — D3 *Fremont*

BIGHORN RV PARK **Ratings: 7.5/8.5★/8.5** (RV Park) 21 Avail: 19 full hkups, 2 W, 2 E (30/50 amps). 2021 rates: $36 to $45. (719)942-4266, 16373 Hwy 50 W, Coaldale, CO 81222

CUTTY'S HAYDEN CREEK RV CAMPING & RESORT **Ratings: 6.5/7.5/8** (Campground) 123 Avail: 63 full hkups, 60 W, 60 E (30/50 amps). 2021 rates: $50 to $82. May 01 to Oct 09. (719)942-4222, 3428 Hayden Creek Rd, Coaldale, CO 81222

COLLBRAN — C2 *Mesa*

VEGA
(Public State Park) From town, E 6 mi on CR-330E to Vega Reservoir Rd, SE 6 mi (E). Entrance fee required. Elev 8000 ft.**FAC:** paved/gravel rds. 99 Avail: 60 paved, 39 gravel, back-ins (12x30), 33 W, 33 E (30/50 amps), tent sites, rentals, shower$, dump, fire rings. **REC:** Vega Reservoir: fishing, boating nearby, hunting nearby, rec open to public. Pets OK. Partial handicap access, 14 day max stay. 2021 rates: $20 to $30.
(970)487-3407 Lat: 39.2156, Lon: -107.8145
15247 North 64 6/10 Road, Collbran, CO 81624
www.cpw.state.co.us
See ad page 164

RV Park ratings you can rely on!

COLORADO CITY — D4 *Pueblo*

PUEBLO SOUTH/COLORADO CITY KOA **Ratings: 10/10★/10** (RV Park) Avail: 100 full hkups (30/50 amps). 2021 rates: $54 to $79. (800)562-8646, 9040 I-25 S @ Exit 74, Pueblo, CO 81004

COLORADO SPRINGS — D4 *El Paso*

A SPOTLIGHT Introducing The Front Range's colorful attractions appearing at the front of this state section.

COLORADO SPRINGS See also Cascade, Castle Rock, Cripple Creek, Falcon, Fountain, Monument & Woodland Park.

CHEYENNE MOUNTAIN
(Public State Park) From I-25 (Exit 135): Go W on S Academy 2 mi to Hwy 115. Go S on Hwy 115 2 mi. Go W on JL Ranch Heights Rd (L) Note: Pets welcome in developed areas only. Entrance fee required. Elev 6010 ft.**FAC:** paved rds. Avail: 51 paved, 12 pull-thrus, (20x40), back-ins (20x40), 51 full hkups (30/50 amps), tent sites, shower$, dump, laundry, fire rings, firewood. **REC:** rec open to public. Pets OK. Partial handicap access, 14 day max stay. 2021 rates: $28 to $41.
(719)576-2016 Lat: 38.738314, Lon: -104.808414
410 JL Ranch Heights, Colorado Springs, CO 80926
cpw.state.co.us
See ad page 164

FOOT OF THE ROCKIES RV RESORT **Ratings: 7/NA/8.5** (RV Park) Avail: 44 full hkups (30/50 amps). 2021 rates: $45 to $55. (719)447-0670, 53 Resort Pointe, Colorado Springs, CO 80905

Wasn't that a beautiful campground you visited ten years ago? But can you remember where it was? Use our ""Find-it-Fast'' index, located in the back of the Guide. It's an alphabetical list, by state, of every private and public park and campground in the Guide.

COLORADO SPRINGS (CONT)

FOUNTAIN CREEK RV PARK

good sam park **Ratings: 8/8.5★/8** (RV Park) From Jct of I-25 & US-24 (exit 141), W 2.7 mi on US-24 to 31st St, N 0.1 mi to Colorado Ave, E 1/4 Blk to Golden Lane Rd, S 300 ft (E). Elev 6077 ft.**FAC:** all weather rds. Avail: 86 all weather, patios, 36 pull-thrus, (30x60), back-ins (18x40), 86 full hkups (30/50 amps), cable, WiFi @ sites, laundry, LP gas. **REC:** Fountain Creek: boating nearby. Pets OK. No tents. Big rig sites. 2021 rates: $58, Military discount.
(719)633-2192 Lat: 38.851494, Lon: -104.871352
3023 W Colorado Avenue, Colorado Springs, CO 80904
See ad previous page

GARDEN OF THE GODS RV RESORT **Ratings: 10/10★/9.5** (RV Park) 147 Avail: 141 full hkups, 6 W, 6 E (30/50 amps). 2021 rates: $69.73 to $139.48. (800)248-9451, 3704 W Colorado Ave, Colorado Springs, CO 80904

GOLDEN EAGLE CAMPGROUND **Ratings: 7/7.5★/7.5** (Campground) 216 Avail: 112 full hkups, 74 W, 74 E (30/50 amps). 2021 rates: $38 to $55. (719)576-0450, 710 Rock Creek Canyon Road, Colorado Springs, CO 80926

GOLDFIELD RV PARK

good sam park **Ratings: 8/10★/8.5** (RV Park) From Jct of I-25 & US-24 (exit 141), W 2.1 mi on US-24 to 26th St, S 100 ft (L). Elev 6096 ft.**FAC:** all weather rds. Avail: 54 all weather, 11 pull-thrus, (20x75), back-ins (20x60), 54 full hkups (30/50 amps), cable, WiFi @ sites, dump, laundry. **REC:** boating nearby, hunting nearby. Pets OK. No tents. Big rig sites. 2021 rates: $39 to $50, Military discount.
(719)471-0495 Lat: 38.84494, Lon: -104.86694
411 S 26th Street, Colorado Springs, CO 80904
goldfieldrvpark.com
See ad page 174

MILITARY PARK PEREGRINE PINES FAMCAMP (USAF ACADEMY) (Public) On base. From Jct of I-25 & North Gate Blvd (exit 156), W 1 mi on North Gate Blvd to Stadium Blvd, NW 1.3 mi on Stadium Blvd to base entrance (L). Avail: 105 full hkups (30/50 amps). 2021 rates: $30 to $35. (719)333-4980

MOUNTAINDALE CABINS & RV RESORT **Ratings: 8/10★/9.5** (RV Park) Avail: 79 full hkups (30/50 amps). 2021 rates: $60. (719)576-0619, 2000 Barrett Road, Colorado Springs, CO 80926

ROCKY TOP MOTEL & CAMPGROUND **Ratings: 7/7.5/7.5** (Campground) Avail: 48 full hkups (30/50 amps). 2021 rates: $48 to $54. (719)684-9044, 10090 W. Hwy 24, Green Mountain Falls, CO 80819

CORTEZ — E1 *Montezuma*

A SPOTLIGHT Introducing the Spirit of Southwestern Colorado's colorful attractions appearing at the front of this state section.

CORTEZ See also Dolores, Mancos & Mesa Verde National Park.

LA MESA RV PARK

good sam park **Ratings: 6/8.5/8.5** (RV Park) Avail: 33 full hkups (30/50 amps). 2021 rates: $30 to $42. (505)215-0712, 2380 E Main, Cortez, CO 81321

SLEEPING UTE RV PARK

good sam park **Ratings: 10/10★/9** (RV Park) From Jct 160/491: Go S on 160 11 mi (R). Elev 5843 ft.**FAC:** all weather rds. Avail: 61 all weather, 61 pull-thrus, (35x62), 61 full hkups (30/50 amps), cable, WiFi @ sites, tent sites, dump, laundry, groc, restaurant. **REC:** heated pool, hunting nearby. Pets OK. Big rig sites, eco-friendly. 2021 rates: $42, Military discount. Apr 01 to Nov 01. ATM.
(970)565-6544 Lat: 37.20642, Lon: -108.68837
3 Weeminuche Drive, Towaoc, CO 81334
www.utemountaincasino.com
See ad this page

SUNDANCE RV PARK

good sam park **Ratings: 9/10★/9.5** (RV Park) E-Bnd: From Jct of US-160 & US-491, E 1 mi on US-160 (R); or W-Bnd: From Jct of US-160 & SR-145, W 1.3 mi on US-160 (L). Elev 6200 ft.**FAC:** paved rds. Avail: 64 all weather, 13 pull-thrus, (30x65), back-ins (30x50), 64 full hkups (30/50 amps), cable, WiFi @ sites, laundry. **REC:** boating nearby. Pets OK. No tents. Big rig sites, eco-friendly. 2021 rates: $48, Military discount.
(970)565-0997 Lat: 37.34847, Lon: -108.57442
815 E Main St, Cortez, CO 81321
sundancervpark.com
See ad page 172

Things to See and Do

UTE MOUNTAIN CASINO Casino, Hotel, RV Park and Travel Center Elev 5670 ft. Partial handicap access. RV accessible. Restrooms. Food. Hours: 24 Hrs. ATM.
(800)258-8007 Lat: 37.204711, Lon: -108.685835
#3 Weeminuche Dr, Towaoc, CO 81321
www.utemountaincasino.com
See ad this page

SAVE! Camping World coupons can be found at the front and back of this Guide!

COTOPAXI — D3 *Fremont*

ARKANSAS HEADWATERS RECREATION AREA/VALLIE BRIDGE CAMPGROUND

(Public State Park) From jct US-50 & CR-6: Go 2 mi W on US-50 (R). Elev 6500 ft.**FAC:** gravel rds. Avail: 1 gravel, back-ins (30x50), tent sites, pit toilets, fire rings. **REC:** Arkansas River: boating nearby, hunting nearby, rec open to public. Pets OK. 14 day max stay. 2021 rates: $28. no cc.
(719)539-7289 Lat: 38.3915, Lon: -105.7731
CR45, Cotopaxi, CO 81223
cpw.state.co.us
See ad page 164

CRAIG — B2 *Moffat*

ELKHEAD RESERVOIR

(Public State Park) From Jct Hwy 40 and Moffat CR-29 (6 mi E of Craig); Go 5 mi N on Moffat CR-29 then .6 mi E on Moffat CR-28. Entrance fee required. Elev 6300 ft.**FAC:** gravel rds. Avail: 16 grass, back-ins (18x60), tent sites, restrooms only, fire rings. **REC:** Elkhead Reservoir: swim, fishing, boating nearby, hunting nearby, rec open to public. Pets OK. Partial handicap access, 14 day max stay. 2021 rates: $22 to $30. no cc.
(970)276-2061 Lat: 40.562678, Lon: -107.388170
135 County Rd 28, Craig, CO 81625
cpw.state.co.us
See ad page 164

CRAWFORD — D2 *Delta*

CRAWFORD

(Public State Park) From Jct of Hwy 133 & Hwy 92 (in Hotchkiss), SE 12.3 mi on Hwy 92 (R) (1 mi S of Crawford) Entrance Fee Required. Elev 6600 ft.**FAC:** gravel rds. 66 Avail: 4 paved, 62 gravel, 33 pull-thrus, (20x70), back-ins (30x60), 45 W, 45 E (30/50 amps), tent sites, shower$, dump, firewood. **REC:** Crawford Reservoir: swim, fishing, boating nearby, playground, hunting nearby, rec open to public. Pets OK. Partial handicap access, 14 day max stay. 2021 rates: $22 to $35.
(970)921-5721 Lat: 38.687178, Lon: -107.594649
40468 Hwy 92, Crawford, CO 81415
cpw.state.co.us
See ad page 164

CREEDE — D2 *Mineral*

ANTLER'S RIO GRANDE LODGE & RV PARK **Ratings: 8.5/9★/9.5** (RV Park) Avail: 24 full hkups (30/50 amps). 2021 rates: $55 to $65. May 15 to Oct 01. (719)658-2423, 26222 Hwy 149, Creede, CO 81130

MOUNTAIN VIEWS AT RIVERS EDGE RV RESORT **Ratings: 9.5/10★/10** (RV Resort) Avail: 98 full hkups (30/50 amps). 2021 rates: $60. May 01 to Oct 01. (719)658-2710, 539 Airport Rd, Creede, CO 81130

CRIPPLE CREEK — D3 *Teller*

CRIPPLE CREEK HOSPITALITY HOUSE & TRAVEL PARK **Ratings: 6/8/7** (RV Park) Avail: 36 full hkups (30/50 amps). 2021 rates: $39 to $50. May 15 to Oct 01. (719)689-2513, 600 N B Street, Cripple Creek, CO 80813

CRIPPLE CREEK KOA **Ratings: 7/10★/9.5** (Campground) 52 Avail: 32 full hkups, 20 W, 20 E (30/50 amps). 2021 rates: $47 to $90. May 22 to Oct 03. (719)689-5647, 2576 CR 81, Cripple Creek, CO 80813

CRIPPLE CREEK RV PARK **Ratings: 5/9★/6** (RV Park) Avail: 47 full hkups (30/50 amps). 2021 rates: $55 to $75. (719)689-2006, 202 E May Ave, Cripple Creek, CO 80813

DELTA — D2 *Delta*

VALLEY SUNSET RV RANCH **Ratings: 8.5/9★/7** (RV Park) Avail: 20 full hkups (30/50 amps). 2021 rates: $30. (970)874-0200, 1675 Hwy 92, Delta, CO 81416

Things to See and Do

SWEITZER LAKE STATE PARK CO State Park. Day use only, no camping. Entrance fee required. Elev 4953 ft. Restrooms. Hours: 8am to 10pm . Adult fee: $9.
(970)874-4258 Lat: 38.716308, Lon: -108.02874
1735 E Rd, Delta, CO 81416
www.cpw.state.co.us
See ad page 164

DENVER — C4 *Jefferson*

DENVER See also Aurora, Black Hawk, Brighton, Castle Rock, Central City, Englewood, Golden, Hudson, Idaho Springs & Strasburg.

PROSPECT PLACE RV PARK & CAMPGROUND **Ratings: 6.5/9.5★/8** (RV Park) 47 Avail: 22 full hkups, 25 W, 25 E (30/50 amps). 2021 rates: $39 to $42. (303)424-4414, 11600 W. 44th Ave, Wheat Ridge, CO 80033

Things to See and Do

CASTLEWOOD CANYON STATE PARK CO State Park. Day use only. No camping. Entrance fee required. Elev 6635 ft. Restrooms. Hours: 5am to 10pm. Adult fee: $10. No CC.
(303)688-5242 Lat: 39.323425, Lon: -104.735029
2989 S State Hwy 83, Franktown, CO 80116
cpw.state.co.us
See ad page 164

COLORADO PARKS & WILDLIFE Colorado's 42 state parks offer some of the highest quality outdoor recreation destinations in the state. See individual park listings for campground information. Elev 5800 ft. Partial handicap access. Restrooms. Hours: 8am to 5pm. No CC.
(303)297-1192
6060 Broadway, Denver, CO 80216
cpw.state.co.us
See ad page 164

DINOSAUR — B1 *Moffat*

DINOSAUR NATL MON/GATES OF LODORE (Public National Park) From town, E 54 mi on US-40 to SR-318, NW 72 mi (L). 19 Avail: Pit toilets. 2021 rates: $6 to $10. (435)781-7700

DIVIDE — C3 *Teller*

MUELLER

(Public State Park) From Jct US 24 & Hwy 67, S 3.5 mi on Hwy 67 (E). Entrance fee required. Elev 9600 ft.**FAC:** paved rds. Avail: 123 paved, 80 pull-thrus, (14x40), back-ins (14x40), 101 E (30 amps), tent sites, rentals, shower$, dump, laundry, fire rings, firewood. **REC:** pond, fishing, playground, hunting nearby, rec open to public. Pets OK. Partial handicap access, 14 day max stay. 2021 rates: $28 to $36.
(719)687-2366 Lat: 38.89254, Lon: -105.15788
21045 Hwy 67 S, Divide, CO 80814
cpw.state.co.us
See ad page 164

DOLORES — E1 *Montezuma*

DOLORES RIVER CAMPGROUND & CABINS **Ratings: 8.5/10★/10** (Campground) 76 Avail: 75 full hkups, 1 W, 1 E (30/50 amps). 2021 rates: $44 to $65. May 01 to Oct 11. (970)882-7761, 18680 Hwy 145, Dolores, CO 81323

THE VIEWS RV PARK & CAMPGROUND **Ratings: 7/9.5★/9** (Campground) Avail: 49 full hkups (30/50 amps). 2021 rates: $40 to $55. Apr 15 to Oct 31. (970)749-6489, 24990 Hwy 184, Dolores, CO 81323

WEST VIEW RV RESORT **Ratings: 9/9.5★/9.5** (RV Resort) Avail: 93 full hkups (50 amps). 2021 rates: $55. (970)565-3388, 12092 Highway 145, Dolores, CO 81323

DURANGO — E2 *La Plata*

DURANGO See also Bayfield & Ignacio.

ALPEN ROSE RV PARK Ratings: 9.5/10★/9.5 (RV Park) Avail: 100 full hkups (30/50 amps). 2021 rates: $55 to $82. (970)247-5540, 27847 Hwy 550 N, Durango, CO 81301

DURANGO NORTH RIVERSIDE **Ratings: 9/8.5/9.5** (RV Park) Avail: 98 full hkups (30/50 amps). 2021 rates: $66 to $150. May 01 to Oct 15. (970)247-4499, 13391 CR-250, Durango, CO 81301

OASIS RV RESORT & COTTAGES - DURANGO

Ratings: 10/9★/9.5 (Campground) From W Jct of US-550 & US-160 (in town), E 7 mi on US-160 (R); or From E Jct of US-160 & US-550, E 2.5 mi on US-160 (R). Elev 6987 ft.

ENDLESS OUTDOOR RECREATION!

Hiking, rafting, boating, fishing--we are close to it all. Experience Durango's Narrow Gauge Train ride, festivals, rodeos, lakes & more for days of wild & mild activities that will satisfy even the most adventurous of souls.

FAC: all weather rds. Avail: 99 all weather, 62 pull-thrus, (30x80), back-ins (28x45), 89 full hkups, 10 W, 10 E (30/50 amps), cable, WiFi @ sites, tent sites, rentals, dump, laundry, groc, LP gas. **REC:** heated pool, boating nearby, playground, hunting nearby. Pets OK. Partial handicap access. Big rig sites, eco-friendly. 2021 rates: $42 to $94, Military discount.
(970)247-0783 Lat: 37.22839, Lon: -107.80282
30090 Hwy 160 E, Durango, CO 81303
myrvoasis.com/durango
See ad page 173

WESTERLY RV PARK Ratings: 7/NA/7.5 (RV Park) Avail: 24 full hkups (30/50 amps). 2021 rates: $52. (970)247-1275, 6440 CR 203, Durango, CO 81301

EAGLE — C2 *Eagle*

SYLVAN LAKE

(Public State Park) From Jct of I-70 & Eagle exit (#147), S 1 mi on Main St to West Brush Creek Rd, S 16 mi (road becomes unpaved - stay right at the fork) (R) Entrance fee required. Elev 8500 ft.**FAC:** gravel rds. Avail: 44 gravel, 16 pull-thrus, (12x36), back-ins (12x40), tent sites, rentals, shower$, dump, laundry. **REC:** Sylvan Lake: fishing, hunting nearby, rec open to public. Pets OK. Partial handicap access, 14 day max stay. 2021 rates: $28.
(970)328-2021 Lat: 39.4810, Lon: -106.7347
10200 Brush Creek Road, Eagle, CO 81631
cpw.state.co.us
See ad page 164

ELDORADO SPRINGS — B3 *Boulder*

Things to See and Do

ELDORADO CANYON STATE PARK Day use only. Hiking. No camping. Visitor Center and picnic sites. Entrance fee required. Elev 6108 ft. Hours: 5am to 10pm. Adult fee: $10. No CC.
(303)543-8882 Lat: 39.929083, Lon: -105.294138
9 Kneale Road, Eldorado Springs, CO 80025
www.cpw.state.co.us
See ad page 164

ENGLEWOOD — C4 *Arapahoe*

SOUTH PARK MOBILE HOME AND RV COMMUNITY **Ratings: 9/9★/8.5** (RV Park) Avail: 18 full hkups (30/50 amps). 2021 rates: $50. (303)761-0121, 3650 S. Federal Blvd #97, Englewood, CO 80110

ERIE — B3 *Boulder*

Things to See and Do

CAMP COLORADO Camp Colorado represents privately owned campgrounds throughout Colorado that provide outdoor hospitality to campers. Elev 5023 ft. Hours: . No CC.
1472 Allen Ave, Erie, CO 80516
campcolorado.com
See ad page 165

ESTES PARK — B3 *Larimer*

A SPOTLIGHT Introducing Rocky Mountain National Park's colorful attractions appearing at the front of this state section.

ELK MEADOW LODGE AND RV RESORT

Ratings: 9/10★/9 (RV Park) From W Jct of Bus US 34 & US 36 (Elkhorn Ave), W 0.3 mi on Elkhorn Ave to Moraine Ave (US 36 W), SW 1.2 mi to Hwy-66, SW 0.2 mi (R) Note: do not follow GPS. Elev 7750 ft.**FAC:** gravel rds. Avail: 169 gravel, 50 pull-thrus, (30x60), back-ins (30x50), 169 full hkups (30/50 amps), cable, WiFi @ sites, tent sites, rentals, laundry, LP gas, firewood. **REC:** heated pool, boating nearby, playground, hunting nearby. Pet restrict (Q). Partial handicap access. Big rig sites, eco-friendly. 2021 rates: $75, Military discount. May 08 to Oct 03.
(970)586-5342 Lat: 40.36203, Lon: -105.55320
1665 CO Hwy 66, Estes Park, CO 80517
elkmeadowrv.com
See ad page 171

ESTES PARK AT EAST PORTAL (Public) From W Jct of Bus US-34 & US-36 (in town), S 1.6 mi on US-36 to SR-66 (Rocky Mountain Natl Park to W on US-36), SW 3.2 mi on SR-66 (E). Small rigs only. 68 Avail: 27 W, 27 E (30/50 amps). 2021 rates: $45 to $80. May 15 to Oct 15. (800)964-7806

ESTES PARK CAMPGROUND AT MARY'S LAKE (Public) From jct US 34 & US 36: Go 1/2 mi SE on US 36, then 1-1/2 mi S on Hwy 7, then 1-1/2 mi W on Peak View Dr. 128 Avail: 39 full hkups, 21 W, 21 E (30/50 amps). 2021 rates: $45 to $65. May 15 to Oct 15. (970)577-1026

MANOR RV PARK

Ratings: 7/9.5★/8.5 (RV Park) From E Jct of US-34 & US-36, W 0.2 mi on Bus US-34/US-36 to Riverside Dr (on left in center of town), 3rd light W-bnd, SW 1.5 mi on Riverside Dr (R) Note: RV length restriction of 38'. Elev 7644 ft.**FAC:** paved/gravel rds. Avail: 117 gravel, patios, 9 pull-thrus, (25x65), back-ins (25x40), 117 full hkups (30/50 amps), WiFi @ sites, rentals, laundry, LP bottles. **REC:** Big Thompson River: fishing, boating nearby, playground, hunting nearby. Pet restrict (Q). No tents, eco-friendly. 2021 rates: $65 to $87, Military discount.
(970)586-3251 Lat: 40.36171, Lon: -105.53824
815 Riverside Dr, Estes Park, CO 80517
www.trouthavenresorts.com
See ad page 171

ROCKY MTN/ASPENGLEN (Public National Park) From Rocky Mountain National Park entrance, S 0.2 mi on US-34 (L). 39 Avail. 2021 rates: $30. May 21 to Sep 27. (970)586-1206

ROCKY MTN/GLACIER BASIN (Public National Park) From town, W 5 mi on Bear Lake Rd (L). 80 Avail. 2021 rates: $30. May 21 to Sep 07. (970)586-1206

ROCKY MTN/MORAINE PARK (Public National Park) From Jct US-34 & US-36, W 5 mi on US-36 (L). 143 Avail: Pit toilets. 2021 rates: $20 to $30. (970)586-1206

SPRUCE LAKE RV RESORT

Ratings: 9/9.5★/9 (RV Park) From W Jct of Bus US 34 & US 36 (Elkhorn Ave), W 0.3 mi on Elkhorn Ave to Moraine Ave (US 36W), SW 0.8 mi to Mary's Lake Rd, S 0.1 mi (L) Note: do not follow GPS. Elev 7622 ft.**FAC:** gravel rds. Avail: 110 gravel, back-ins (40x40), 88 full hkups, 22 W, 22 E (30/50 amps), cable, WiFi @ sites, rentals, dump, laundry, LP gas. **REC:** heated pool, hot tub, Big Thompson River: fishing, boating nearby, playground, hunting nearby. Pet restrict (Q). Partial handicap access. No tents, eco-friendly. 2021 rates: $73 to $79, Military discount. May 08 to Oct 03.
(970)586-2889 Lat: 40.36246, Lon: -105.54265
1050 Marys Lake Rd, Estes Park, CO 80517
sprucelakerv.com
See ad page 171

YOGI BEAR'S JELLYSTONE PARK OF ESTES **Ratings: 9/8.5★/8.5** (Campground) Avail: 99 full hkups (30/50 amps). 2021 rates: $55 to $120. May 10 to Sep 27. (970)586-4230, 5495 US Hwy 36, Estes Park, CO 80517

FAIRPLAY — C3 *Park*

MIDDLEFORK RV RESORT

Ratings: 8/8★/7.5 (RV Park) 46 Avail: 33 full hkups, 13 E (30/50 amps). 2021 rates: $42 to $72. (719)836-4857, 255 US Hwy 285, Fairplay, CO 80440

FALCON — C4 *El Paso*

FALCON MEADOW RV CAMPGROUND

Ratings: 7.5/9★/7.5 (RV Park) From Jct of US-24 & Power Blvd (E Edge of Colorado Springs), NE 7.9 mi on US 24 (L). Elev 6800 ft.**FAC:** gravel rds. Avail: 58 gravel, 51 pull-thrus, (28x60), back-ins (25x60), 46 full hkups, 12 W, 12 E (30/50 amps), WiFi @ sites, tent sites, dump, laundry, groc, LP gas. **REC:** playground. Pets OK. Partial handicap access. Big rig sites. 2021 rates: $36 to $50.
(719)495-2694 Lat: 38.92408, Lon: -104.61981
11150 Hwy 24, Falcon, CO 80831
www.falconmeadowrvcampground.com
See ad page 177

FORT COLLINS — B3 *Larimer*

FORT COLLINS KOA LAKESIDE **Ratings: 9.5/9.5★/9.5** (Campground) Avail: 168 full hkups (30/50 amps). 2021 rates: $50 to $106. (800)562-9168, 1910 Lakeside Resort Ln, Fort Collins, CO 80524

HORSETOOTH RESERVOIR (Public) From jct I-25 (exit 265) & Hwy 68 (Harmony Rd): Go 7 mi W on Hwy 68, then 1 mi N on CR 19 (Taft Hill Rd), then W on CR 38E. Avail: 124 E (30/50 amps), Pit toilets. 2021 rates: $20 to $60. (970)619-4570

FORT MORGAN — B4 *Morgan*

EMERALD RV PARK

Ratings: 6/10★/7 (RV Park) From jct I-76 (exit 75) & US-34: Go 500 feet E on US-34, then 1/4 mi SW on Frontage Rd (L) Note: between Shell station and Baymont hotel. Elev 4402 ft.**FAC:** gravel rds. Avail: 88 gravel, 88 pull-thrus, (35x60), 88 full hkups (30/50 amps), dump, laundry, LP bottles. Pet restrict (B). Partial handicap access. No tents. Big rig sites. 2021 rates: $40, Military discount.
(970)380-5679 Lat: 40.251707, Lon: -103.879767
14390 US Hwy 34, Fort Morgan, CO 80701
www.webreserv.com/emeraldparkco
See ad next page

FOUNTAIN — D4 *El Paso*

COLORADO SPRINGS KOA **Ratings: 9.5/9.5★/10** (RV Park) Avail: 162 full hkups (30/50 amps). 2021 rates: $85 to $125. (719)382-7575, 8100 Bandley Drive, Fountain, CO 80817

Travel Services

CAMPING WORLD OF FOUNTAIN/COLORADO SPRINGS As the nation's largest retailer of RV supplies, accessories, services and new and used RVs, Camping World is committed to making your total RV experience better. Elev 5720 ft. **SERVICES:** RV, RV appliance, restrooms. RV Sales. RV supplies, emergency parking, RV accessible. Hours: 9am to 7pm.
(855)546-1778 Lat: 38.73251, Lon: -104.73804
6830 Bandley Drive, Fountain, CO 80817
www.campingworld.com

FRUITA — C1 *Mesa*

COLORADO NATL MON/SADDLEHORN (Public National Park) From Jct of I-70 & SR-340, S 3 mi on SR-340 to park entrance, S 4.5 mi (L). Entrance fee required. Note: 40' RV length limit. 79 Avail. 2021 rates: $22. (877)444-6777

JAMES M. ROBB - COLORADO RIVER/ FRUITA

(Public State Park) From Jct of I-70 & SR-340 (exit 19), S 0.3 mi (R) Note: Park entrance fee is required. Elev 4495 ft.**FAC:** paved rds. Avail: 44 paved, 34 pull-thrus, (25x60), back-ins (25x60), 22 full hkups, 22 E (30/50 amps), tent sites, shower$, dump, laundry, fire rings, firewood. **REC:** Colorado River: boating nearby, playground, rec open to public. Pets OK. Partial handicap access. Big rig sites, 14 day max stay. 2021 rates: $22 to $41.
(970)858-9188 Lat: 39.149914, Lon: -108.738272
595 Hwy 340, Fruita, CO 81521
cpw.state.co.us
See ad page 164

From fishing along the Cape to boating on the Great Lakes, we've put the Spotlight on North America's most popular travel destinations. Turn to the Spotlight articles in our State and Province sections to learn more.

FRUITA (CONT)

MONUMENT RV RESORT

Ratings: 10/10★/9.5 (RV Park) From Jct of I-70 & SR-340 (exit 19), S 0.3 mi on SR-340 (L). Elev 4466 ft. **FAC:** paved rds. Avail: 88 all weather, 37 pull-thrus, (30x95), back-ins (30x60), 72 full hkups, 16 W, 16 E (30/50 amps), cable, WiFi @ sites, tent sites, rentals, dump, laundry, LP gas. **REC:** pool, hot tub, boating nearby, playground, hunting nearby. Pets OK. Partial handicap access. Big rig sites, eco-friendly. 2021 rates: $35 to $52.
(970)858-4405 Lat: 39.149319, Lon: -108.736335
607 Hwy 340, Fruita, CO 81521
www.monumentrvresort.com
See ad page 170

GLENWOOD SPRINGS — C2 *Garfield*

AMI'S ACRES CAMPING **Ratings: 5/7.5/8** (Campground) Avail: 50 full hkups (30/50 amps). 2021 rates: $44 to $52. Mar 15 to Nov 15. (970)945-5340, 50235 Hwy 6, Glenwood Springs, CO 81601

GLENWOOD CANYON RESORT **Ratings: 9.5/10★/9.5** (RV Park) 64 Avail: 49 full hkups, 15 W, 15 E (30/50 amps). 2021 rates: $75 to $85. (800)958-6737, 1308 CR-129, Glenwood Springs, CO 81601

GOLDEN — C3 *Jefferson*

CHIEF HOSA (Public) From Jct of I-70 & Exit 253, S 100 ft on Exit Rd (R). 24 Avail: 24 W, 24 E (30/50 amps). 2021 rates: $30 to $32.50. May 01 to Sep 30. (303)526-1324

CLEAR CREEK RV PARK (Public) W-bnd: From Jct of I-70 & SR-58 (Exit 265), W 4.5 mi on SR-58 to Washington Ave, S 0.3 mi to 10th St, W 0.5 mi (E)); or E-bnd: From Jct of I-70 & US-40 (Exit 262), SW (left turn) 1 mi on US-40 to US-6, W 3.5 mi to SR-58, NE 0.5 mi to Washington Ave, to 10th St. SE 0.3 (L). 33 Avail: 22 full hkups, 11 W, 11 E (30/50 amps). 2021 rates: $48 to $65. May 01 to Sep 30. (303)278-1437

DAKOTA RIDGE RV RESORT

Ratings: 10/10★/9 (RV Park) E-bnd: From Jct of I-70 & US-40 (exit 259), NE 1.5 mi on US-40/Colfax Ave (R); or W-bnd: From Jct of I-70 & US-40 (exit 262), W 1.7 mi on US-40/Colfax Ave (L). Elev 6049 ft. **FAC:** paved rds. Avail: 141 paved, 84 pull-thrus, (28x70), back-ins (24x50), 141 full hkups (30/50 amps), WiFi @ sites, dump, laundry, LP gas. **REC:** heated pool, hot tub, playground. Pet restrict (Q). Partial handicap access. No tents. Big rig sites. 2021 rates: $61 to $82, Military discount
(303)279-1625 Lat: 39.71952, Lon: -105.20124
17800 W Colfax Ave, Golden, CO 80401
dakotaridgerv.com
See ad page 175

GOLDEN GATE CANYON

(Public State Park) From Golden, go W 27 mi on SR-6 N then SR-119 to Gap Rd, E 1 mi (L). Entrance fee required. Elev 9100 ft. **FAC:** paved rds. Avail: 59 paved, 32 pull-thrus, (20x60), back-ins (20x30), 59 E (30/50 amps), tent sites, rentals, shower$, dump, laundry, firewood. **REC:** pond, fishing, hunting nearby, rec open to public. Pets OK. Partial handicap access, 14 day max stay. 2021 rates: $18 to $36. no cc.
(303)582-3707 Lat: 39.830911, Lon: -105.411648
92 Crawford Gulch Road, Golden, CO 80403
cpw.state.co.us
See ad page 164

Travel Services

CAMPING WORLD OF GOLDEN/DENVER As the nation's largest retailer of RV supplies, accessories, services and new and used RVs, Camping World is committed to making your total RV experience better. Elev 5280 ft. **SERVICES:** RV, restrooms. RV Sales. RV supplies, RV accessible. Hours: 9am to 7pm.
(855)561-2864 Lat: 39.728183, Lon: -105.18035
16000 W Colfax, Golden, CO 80401
www.campingworld.com

GOODRICH — B4 *Morgan*

JACKSON LAKE

(Public State Park) From Jct of I-76 & US-34/CR-39 (exit 66B), N 7.9 mi on CR-39 through Goodrich to RD Y5, W 2.4 mi (E) Entrance Fee Required. Elev 4440 ft. **FAC:** paved/gravel rds. Avail: 260 gravel, 100 pull-thrus, (14x40), back-ins (15x30), 163 E (30/50 amps), tent sites, shower$, dump, laundry, LP bottles, firewood. **REC:** Jackson Lake: swim, fishing, marina, kayaking/canoeing, boating nearby, hunting nearby, rec open to public. Pets OK. Partial handicap access, 14 day max stay. 2021 rates: $28 to $36. ATM.
(970)645-2551 Lat: 40.384682, Lon: -104.091635
26363 County Road 3, Orchard, CO 80649
cpw.state.co.us
See ad page 164

GRANBY — B3 *Grand*

RIVER RUN RESORT **Ratings: 10/10★/10** (RV Resort) Avail: 203 full hkups (30/50 amps). 2021 rates: $50 to $125. (888)303-7027, 1051 Summit Trail, Granby, CO 80446

GRAND JUNCTION — C1 *Mesa*

A SPOTLIGHT Introducing Grand Junction's colorful attractions appearing at the front of this state section.

GRAND JUNCTION See also Fruita, Mesa & Palisade.

CANYON VIEW RV RESORT

Ratings: 10/10★/10 (RV Resort) From jct I-70 & US-6 E/US-50: Go 1/2 mi S on US-6 E, then 1/2 mi E on G Rd, then 1/2 mi N on 23 1/2 Rd (R). Elev 4561 ft. **FAC:** paved rds. (161 spaces). Avail: 77 all weather, patios, 44 pull-thrus, (40x80), back-ins (40x80), 77 full hkups (30/50 amps), WiFi @ sites, tent sites, laundry, groc, LP gas, fire rings, firewood. **REC:** heated pool, hot tub, boating nearby, playground, hunting nearby. Pet restrict (Q). Partial handicap access. Big rig sites, eco-friendly. 2021 rates: $55 to $85, Military discount
(970)730-2600 Lat: 39.113064, Lon: -108.616943
746 23 1/2 Road, Grand Junction, CO 81505
www.canyonviewrvresort.com
See ad page 170

GRAND JUNCTION KOA

Ratings: 10/10★/9.5 (RV Park) E-bnd: From Jct of I-70 & US-50 (exit 26), SE 9 mi on US-50 (R); or W-bnd: From Jct of I-70 & Bus I-70 (exit 37), SW 0.8 mi on Bus I-70 to SR-141 (turn left), S 5.4 mi to US-50, N 3.3 mi (L). Elev 4665 ft. **FAC:** all weather rds. Avail: 66 all weather, patios, 43 pull-thrus, (30x75), back-ins (25x55), 66 full hkups (30/50 amps), cable, WiFi @ sites, tent sites, rentals, dump, laundry, groc, LP gas, fire rings, firewood. **REC:** heated pool, playground. Pets OK. Partial handicap access. Big rig sites, eco-friendly. 2021 rates: $57 to $75, Military discount
(800)562-1510 Lat: 39.03550, Lon: -108.52976
2819 Hwy 50, Grand Junction, CO 81503
www.grandjunctionkoa.com
See ad page 170

JUNCTION WEST RV PARK **Ratings: 8.5/9★/9.5** (RV Park) Avail: 67 full hkups (30/50 amps). 2021 rates: $37 to $52. (970)245-8531, 793 - 22 Rd, Grand Junction, CO 81505

RV RANCH AT GRAND JUNCTION **Ratings: 9.5/9.5/9** (RV Park) 128 Avail: 126 full hkups, 2 W, 2 E (30/50 amps). 2021 rates: $40 to $55. (970)434-6644, 3238 E I-70 Bus Loop, Clifton, CO 81520

GRAND LAKE — B3 *Boulder*

ELK CREEK CAMPGROUND & RV RESORT **Ratings: 7.5/9.5★/8.5** (RV Park) 50 Avail: 16 full hkups, 34 W, 34 E (30/50 amps). 2021 rates: $56 to $62. May 15 to Oct 05. (970)627-8502, 143 CR 48/Golf Course Rd, Grand Lake, CO 80447

ROCKY MTN/TIMBER CREEK (Public National Park) From town, N 11 mi on Hwy 34 (L). 98 Avail. 2021 rates: $30. (970)586-1206

WINDING RIVER RESORT

Ratings: 8/10★/9.5 (Campground) 125 Avail: 50 full hkups, 75 W, 75 E (30/50 amps). 2021 rates: $65 to $90. May 25 to Sep 30. (970)627-3215, 1447 CR 491, Grand Lake, CO 80447

GREELEY — B4 *Weld*

GREELEY RV PARK

Ratings: 6.5/9★/8 (RV Park) Avail: 15 full hkups (30/50 amps). 2021 rates: $40. (970)353-6476, 501 E 27th Street, Greeley, CO 80631

GUNNISON — D2 *Gunnison*

BLUE MESA OUTPOST **Ratings: 7/8★/8** (RV Park) Avail: 12 full hkups (30/50 amps). 2021 rates: $42 to $47. May 01 to Oct 31. (970)641-4044, 940 Cove Rd, Gunnison, CO 81230

BLUE MESA RECREATIONAL RANCH **Ratings: 9/10★/10** (Membership Park) 358 Avail: 325 full hkups, 33 W, 33 E (30/50 amps). 2021 rates: $55. May 01 to Oct 01. (970)642-4150, 27601 W. Hwy 50, Gunnison, CO 81230

CURECANTI/ELK CREEK (Public National Park) From town, W 16 mi on US-50 (L). Avail: 27 E (50 amps). 2021 rates: $16 to $22. (970)641-2337

CURECANTI/LAKE FORK (Public National Park) From town, W 27 mi on US-50 (R). 90 Avail. 2021 rates: $16. Apr 01 to Oct 15. (970)641-2337

CURECANTI/STEVENS CREEK (Public National Park) From town: Go 12 mi W on US 50. 53 Avail: Pit toilets. 2021 rates: $16. (970)641-2337

GUNNISON KOA **Ratings: 7.5/9★/8.5** (Campground) 58 Avail: 42 full hkups, 16 W, 16 E (30/50 amps). 2021 rates: $45 to $75. May 01 to Oct 15. (970)641-1358, 105 CR-50, Gunnison, CO 81230

MESA CAMPGROUND **Ratings: 7.5/9.5★/9** (Campground) Avail: 100 full hkups (30/50 amps). 2021 rates: $44 to $88. Apr 15 to Oct 15. (970)641-3186, 36128 US Hwy 50, Gunnison, CO 81230

OASIS RV RESORT & COTTAGES GUNNISON LAKESIDE **Ratings: 8/9.5★/9.5** (RV Park) Avail: 81 full hkups (30/50 amps). 2021 rates: $49 to $59. Apr 01 to Oct 31. (970)641-0477, 28357 US Hwy 50, Gunnison, CO 81230

TALL TEXAN RV PARK & CABINS **Ratings: 8/9★/8** (RV Park) 93 Avail: 89 full hkups, 4 W, 4 E (30/50 amps). 2021 rates: $49 to $64. May 01 to Oct 01. (970)641-2927, 194 County Rd 11, Gunnison, CO 81230

GYPSUM — C2 *Eagle*

AUNT SARA'S RIVER DANCE RV RESORT

Ratings: 5.5/8.5★/8.5 (RV Park) 34 Avail: 8 full hkups, 26 W, 26 E (30/50 amps). 2021 rates: $47. (720)933-9212, 6700 US Hwy 6, Gypsum, CO 81637

HASTY — D5 *Bent*

JOHN MARTIN RES/LAKE HASTY REC. AREA

(Public State Park) From Jct of US-50 & CR-24, S 3 mi on CR-24 (E). Entrance fee required. Elev 3750 ft. **FAC:** paved/gravel rds. Avail: 213 gravel, 17 pull-thrus, (20x120), back-ins (20x60), 109 E (30/50 amps), tent sites, shower$, dump, laundry. **REC:** Lake Hasty: swim, fishing, kayaking/canoe

ing, boating nearby, playground, rec open to public. Pets OK. Partial handicap access, 14 day max stay. 2021 rates: $17 to $28.
(719)829-1801 Lat: 38.077563, Lon: -102.957241
30703 Rd 24, Hasty, CO 81044
cpw.state.co.us
See ad page 164

HAYDEN — B2 *Routt*

YAMPA RIVER HEADQUARTERS
(Public State Park) From Hayden, W 2 mi on Hwy 40 (follow signs). Entrance fee required. Elev 6300 ft.**FAC:** gravel rds. Avail: 35 gravel, back-ins (25x60), 35 E (30/50 amps), tent sites, rentals, shower$, dump, laundry, fire rings. **REC:** Yampa River: swim, fishing, boating nearby, playground, hunting nearby, rec open to public. Pets OK. Partial handicap access, 14 day max stay. 2021 rates: $24 to $32.
(970)276-2061 Lat: 40.49184, Lon: -107.30457
6185 W US Hwy 40, Hayden, CO 81639
cpw.state.co.us
See ad page 164

HOWARD — D3 *Fremont*

BLACK BEAR MOTEL & RV PARK **Ratings: 5.5/8.5★/8** (RV Park) 19 Avail: 15 full hkups, 4 W, 4 S (30/50 amps). 2021 rates: $42. (719)207-5194, 7528 US Hwy 50, Howard, CO 81233

PLEASANT VALLEY RV PARK **Ratings: 9/UI/9** (RV Park) Avail: 44 full hkups (30/50 amps). 2021 rates: $45 to $65. (719)942-3484, 18 CR 47, Howard, CO 81233

ROCKY TOP RIVER RANCH **Ratings: 6/5.5/7** (RV Park) Avail: 10 full hkups (30/50 amps). 2021 rates: $40. (719)942-3811, 10281 Hwy 50, Howard, CO 81233

SUGARBUSH CAMPGROUND **Ratings: 6/9★/8** (Campground) 19 Avail: 11 full hkups, 8 W, 8 E (30/50 amps). 2021 rates: $35 to $45. (719)942-3363, 9229 Hwy 50, Howard, CO 81233

HUDSON — B4 *Weld*

PEPPER POD CAMPGROUND Ratings: 5.5/8.5★/7 (RV Park) 16 Avail: 6 full hkups, 10 W, 10 E (30/50 amps). 2021 rates: $25 to $35. (303)536-4763, 450 5th Ave, Hudson, CO 80642

IDAHO SPRINGS — C3 *Clear Creek*

COTTONWOOD RV CAMPGROUND
Ratings: 5.5/NA/8.5 (RV Park) From Jct of I-70 & SR-103 (exit 240), SW 1.4 mi on SR-103 (L). Elev 7750 ft.**FAC:** gravel rds. 22 Avail: 18 gravel, 4 grass, back-ins (20x60), accepts full hkup units only, 22 full hkups (30/50 amps), cable, WiFi @ sites, . **REC:** Chicago Creek:. Pet restrict (B). No tents. Big rig sites, eco-friendly. 2021 rates: $50. no cc.
(303)567-2617 Lat: 39.72974, Lon: -105.53986
1485 Hwy 103, Idaho Springs, CO 80452
www.cottonwoodrvcolorado.com
See ad this page

IGNACIO — E2 *La Plata*

SKY UTE CASINO RV PARK
good sam park
Ratings: 10/10★/9.5 (RV Park) Avail: 24 full hkups (30/50 amps). 2021 rates: $50. Apr 01 to Nov 15. (970)563-7777, 14324 Hwy 172N, Ignacio, CO 81137

SKY UTE FAIRGROUNDS & RV PARK
Ratings: 7.5/8.5/8.5 (RV Park) From Jct of Hwy 172 & Hwy 151 (in Ignacio), E 0.1 mi on CR-151 (R). Elev 6500 ft.**FAC:** all weather rds. Avail: 64 all weather, 59 pull-thrus, (32x60), back-ins (32x60), 64 full hkups (30/50 amps), WiFi @ sites, $, tent sites, shower$, dump, laundry. **REC:** Los Pinos River: hunting nearby. Pet restrict (B). Partial handicap access. Big rig sites. 2021 rates: $30.
(970)563-5540 Lat: 37.11378, Lon: -107.63030
200 E Hwy 151, Ignacio, CO 81137
www.skyutefairgrounds.com
See ad this page

KREMMLING — B3 *Grand*

RED MOUNTAIN RV PARK **Ratings: 6.5/8.5★/8** (RV Park) Avail: 45 full hkups (30/50 amps). 2021 rates: $39 to $42. (970)724-9593, 2201 Central Ave, Kremmling, CO 80459

LA JUNTA — D4 *Otero*

LA JUNTA KOA **Ratings: 9/9★/8** (Campground) Avail: 58 full hkups (30/50 amps). 2021 rates: $40 to $72. (800)562-9501, 26680 W. Hwy 50, La Junta, CO 81050

LA VETA — E4 *Huerfano*

A SPOTLIGHT Introducing the Spirit of Southwestern Colorado's colorful attractions appearing at the front of this state section.

LA VETA PINES RV PARK **Ratings: 5/7.5★/6.5** (RV Park) Avail: 27 full hkups (30/50 amps). 2021 rates: $37 to $42. May 01 to Oct 10. (719)742-3252, 226 W Grand, La Veta, CO 81055

LAKE CITY — D2 *Hinsdale*

CASTLE LAKES CAMPGROUND & CABINS **Ratings: 6.5/9★/7.5** (Campground) 45 Avail: 38 full hkups, 7 W, 7 E (30/50 amps). 2021 rates: $39 to $43. May 24 to Oct 01. (970)944-2622, 8201 HC Rd 30, Lake City, CO 81235

ELKHORN RV RESORT **Ratings: 6.5/9.5★/8** (RV Park) Avail: 22 full hkups (30/50 amps). 2021 rates: $42. Apr 15 to Oct 01. (970)944-2920, 713 N Bluff, Lake City, CO 81235

HIGHLANDER RV CAMPGROUND **Ratings: 8/9.5★/8** (RV Park) Avail: 35 full hkups (30/50 amps). 2021 rates: $42. May 15 to Oct 01. (888)580-4636, 1245 Cty Rd 30, Lake City, CO 81235

RIVER FORK RV CAMPGROUND **Ratings: 5.5/8★/7.5** (RV Park) Avail: 26 full hkups (30/50 amps). 2021 rates: $39. Jun 01 to Oct 01. (970)944-9519, 112 Henson St, Lake City, CO 81235

Are you using a friend's Guide? Want one of your own? Call 877-209-6655.

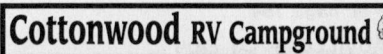

LAKE CITY (CONT)

↓ WOODLAKE PARK **Ratings: 7/8★/8** (RV Park) Avail: 53 full hkups (30/50 amps). 2021 rates: $42. Jun 01 to Sep 30. (800)201-2694, 2690 S. Colorado Hwy 149, Lake City, CO 81235

LAKE GEORGE — C3 *Park*

↗ **ELEVEN MILE**

(Public State Park) From town, W 1 mi on US-24 to CR-90, S 6 mi (stay on pavement) to CR-92, S 5 mi (E). Entrance fee required. Elev 8597 ft.**FAC:** paved/gravel rds. Avail: 348 dirt, 50 pull-thrus, (25x115), back-ins (20x85), 52 E (20/30 amps), tent sites, shower$, dump, laundry, fire rings, firewood. **REC:** Eleven Mile Reservoir: fishing, marina, kayaking/canoeing, boating nearby, playground, hunting nearby, rec open to public. Pets OK. Partial handicap access, 14 day max stay. 2021 rates: $28 to $36.
(719)748-3401 Lat: 38.948475, Lon: -105.526519
4229 CR-92, Lake George, CO 80827
cpw.state.co.us
See ad page 164

Things to See and Do

← **SPINNEY MOUNTAIN STATE PARK** Day use only. Fishing and boating on Reservoir. No Camping. Entrance fee required. Elev 8715 ft. Apr 15 to Nov 15. Restrooms. Hours: 6am to 10pm. Adult fee: $9. No CC.
(719)748-3401 Lat: 38.9821, Lon: -105.6571
4229 CR 92, Lake George, CO 80827
cpw.state.co.us
See ad page 164

LEADVILLE — C3 *Eagle*

↗ LEADVILLE RV CORRAL **Ratings: 5.5/6.5/6** (RV Park) Avail: 10 full hkups (30/50 amps). 2021 rates: $45. (719)486-3111, 135 West 2nd St, Leadville, CO 80461

← SUGAR LOAFIN' RV/CAMPGROUND AND CABINS **Ratings: 6/9★/7** (Campground) 68 Avail: 42 full hkups, 26 W, 26 E (30/50 amps). 2021 rates: $42 to $50. May 12 to Oct 01. (719)486-1031, 2665 CR 4, Leadville, CO 80461

LIMON — C4 *Lincoln*

→ LIMON KOA **Ratings: 9/10★/8** (RV Park) 57 Avail: 50 full hkups, 7 W, 7 E (30/50 amps). 2021 rates: $57 to $70. (800)562-2129, 575 Colorado Ave, Limon, CO 80828

LITTLETON — C4 *Arapahoe*

↓ **CHATFIELD**

(Public State Park) From Jct of SR-470 & Wadsworth Blvd (SR-121), S 1 mi on SR-121 (L); or From Jct of SR-470 & Santa Fe Dr (US-85), S 4.2 mi on US-85 to Titan Rd, W 3.6 mi to Roxborough Park Rd, N 1.5 mi (E) Entrance Fee Required. Elev 5550 ft.**FAC:** paved rds. Avail: 197 paved, 120 pull-thrus, (30x60), back-ins (30x60), 146 full hkups, 51 E (30/50 amps), WiFi @ sites, shower$, dump, laundry, firewood. **REC:** Chatfield Reservoir: swim, fishing, marina, playground, rec open to public. Pets OK. Partial handicap access. No tents, No Class A, 14 day max stay. 2021 rates: $36 to $41.
(303)791-7275 Lat: 39.530507, Lon: -105.054387
11500 N Roxborough Park Rd, Littleton, CO 80125
cpw.state.co.us
See ad page 164

LOMA — C1 *Mesa*

↑ **HIGHLINE LAKE**

(Public State Park) From Jct of I-70 & SR-139, N 6 mi on SR-139 to Rd Q, W 1.2 mi to Rd 11.8, N 1 mi (E). Entrance fee required. Elev 4700 ft.**FAC:** paved rds. Avail: 36 grass, no slide-outs, 22 pull-thrus, (15x45), back-ins (15x45), tent sites, shower$, dump, laundry, fire rings, firewood. **REC:** Highline Lake: swim, fishing, boating nearby, playground, hunting nearby, rec open to public. Pets OK. Partial handicap access, 14 day max stay. 2021 rates: $14 to $28.
(970)858-7208 Lat: 39.270781, Lon: -108.837358
1800 11.8 Rd, Loma, CO 81524
cpw.state.co.us
See ad page 164

LONGMONT — B3 *Boulder*

← **ST VRAIN**

(Public State Park) From Jct of I-25 & SR-119, W 1 mi on SR-119 to CR-7, N until it turns into CR-24 1/2 (R). Entrance fee required. Elev 4830 ft.**FAC:** paved/gravel rds. 87 Avail: 41 paved, 46 gravel, patios, back-ins (15x40), 46 full hkups, 41 E (30/50 amps), tent sites, shower$, dump, fire rings. **REC:** Blue Heron Reservoir: fishing, rec open to public. Pets OK. Partial handicap access, 14 day max stay. 2021 rates: $36 to $41.
(303)678-9402 Lat: 40.16933, Lon: -104.98800
3525 Highway 119, Firestone, CO 80504
cpw.state.co.us
See ad page 164

Travel Services

↗ **CAMPING WORLD OF LONGMONT** As the nation's largest retailer of RV supplies, accessories, services and new and used RVs, Camping World is committed to making your total RV experience better. Elev 4979 ft. **SERVICES:** RV, tire, RV appliance, MH mechanical, staffed RV wash, restrooms. RV Sales. RV supplies, LP gas, emergency parking, RV accessible. Hours: 9am to 7pm.
(855)966-0076 Lat: 40.204551, Lon: -104.97866
14504 E I-25 Frontage Road, Longmont, CO 80504
www.campingworld.com

LOVELAND — B3 *Larimer*

A SPOTLIGHT Introducing The Front Range's colorful attractions appearing at the front of this state section.

→ **BOYD LAKE**

(Public State Park) From Jct of I-25 & US-34 (exit 257B), W 3.4 mi on US-34 to Madison Ave, N 1.5 mi to CR-24E, E 0.7 mi to CR-11C, N 0.3 mi (R). Follow signs. Entrance Fee Required. Elev 5300 ft.**FAC:** paved rds. Avail: 148 paved, 148 pull-thrus, (25x40), 148 E (30/50 amps), shower$, dump, laundry, firewood. **REC:** Boyd Lake: swim, fishing, marina, playground, hunting nearby, rec open to public. Pets OK. Partial handicap access. No tents, 14 day max stay. 2021 rates: $36.
(970)669-1739 Lat: 40.43313, Lon: -105.04440
3720 N CR 11-C, Loveland, CO 80538
cpw.state.co.us
See ad page 164

← CARTER LAKE COUNTY PARK (Public) From jct I-25 & Hwy 56: Go 9 mi W on Hwy 56, then W on CR 8E. Avail: 92 E (50 amps), Pit toilets. 2021 rates: $20 to $60. (970)619-4570

← FLATIRON RESERVOIR (Public) From town: Go 6 mi W on US 34, then 2-1/2 mi S on CR 29E. Avail: 33 E (50 amps), Pit toilets. 2021 rates: $20 to $48. (970)619-4570

→ **LOVELAND RV RESORT**

Ratings: 9.5/9.5★/8.5 (RV Park) From Jct of I-25 & US-34 (Exit 257), W 1 mi on US-34 (R). Elev 5000 ft.

IN THE HEART OF THINGS TO SEE & DO!
Base camp here--the GATEWAY to ADVENTURES! Visit Rocky Mtn Nat'l Park for beauty, wildlife & trails. Stroll Benson's Sculpture Park & nearby quaint towns. Shop, dine or relax & enjoy our heated pool & mini golf. Fun for all!

FAC: paved rds. Avail: 156 gravel, 125 pull-thrus, (25x60), back-ins (25x40), mostly side by side hkups, 156 full hkups (30/50 amps), WiFi @ sites, dump, laundry, groc, LP gas. **REC:** heated pool, boating nearby, playground, hunting nearby. Pet restrict (B/Q). No tents. Big rig sites, eco-friendly. 2021 rates: $58 to $72, Military discount.
(970)667-1204 Lat: 40.40789, Lon: -105.01328
4421 E Hwy 34, Loveland, CO 80537
www.lovelandrvresort.com
See ad page 175

← PINEWOOD LAKE (Public) From jct US 34 & Hwy 29: Go 2 mi S on Hwy 29, then 6-1/2 mi W on CR 18E. Avail: 16 E Pit toilets. 2021 rates: $20 to $26. (970)619-4570

← **RIVERVIEW RV PARK & CAMPGROUND**

Ratings: 7.5/9★/8 (RV Park) 111 Avail: 101 full hkups, 10 W, 10 E (30/50 amps). 2021 rates: $45 to $72. (970)667-9910, 2444 River Rim Rd, Loveland, CO 80537

MANCOS — E1 *Montezuma*

← ANCIENT CEDARS MESA VERDE RV PARK **Ratings: 10/10★/9.5** (RV Park) 63 Avail: 52 full hkups, 11 W, 11 E (30/50 amps). 2021 rates: $38 to $55. Mar 15 to Nov 01. (970)565-3517, 34979 Hwy 160, Mancos, CO 81328

→ ECHO BASIN CABIN AND RV RESORT **Ratings: 9.5/9★/10** (RV Park) Avail: 76 full hkups (30/50 amps). 2021 rates: $45 to $55. (970)533-7000, 43747 Road M , Mancos, CO 81328

↑ **MANCOS**

(Public State Park) From Jct of Hwy 160 & Hwy 184, N 0.5 mi on Hwy 184 to CR-42, E 4 mi to CR-N, W 0.5 mi (L) Entrance fee required. Elev 7800 ft.**FAC:** gravel/dirt rds. Avail: 32 gravel, back-ins (15x50), tent sites, rentals, pit toilets, dump, fire rings, firewood. **REC:** Jackson Gulch Reservoir: fishing, boating nearby, rec open to public. Pets OK. Partial handicap access, 14 day max stay. 2021 rates: $18 to $22.
(970)533-7065 Lat: 37.39999, Lon: -108.2693
42545 County Road N, Mancos, CO 81328
www.cpw.state.co.us
See ad page 164

↗ **MESA VERDE RV RESORT**

Ratings: 10/10★/10 (RV Park) 48 Avail: 36 full hkups, 12 W, 12 E (30/50 amps). 2021 rates: $38.95 to $48.95. Mar 01 to Nov 01. (800)776-7421, 35303 Hwy 160, Mancos, CO 81328

↘ RIVERWOOD RV RESORT **Ratings: 7/9.5★/9** (RV Resort) Avail: 68 full hkups (30/50 amps). 2021 rates: $44. Apr 01 to Nov 30. (970)533-9142, 350 E Grand Ave, Mancos, CO 81328

MEEKER — B2 *Rio Blanco*

→ **TRAIL & HITCH RV PARK AND TINY HOME HOTEL**

Ratings: 9/10★/10 (RV Park) Avail: 28 full hkups (30/50 amps). 2021 rates: $45 to $55. (970)329-1077, 322 County Road 8, Meeker, CO 81641

MESA — C2 *Mesa*

↑ GRAND MESA RV PARK **Ratings: 5.5/9.5★/5.5** (RV Park) Avail: 23 full hkups (30/50 amps). 2021 rates: $49. (970)268-5651, 11674 Hwy 65, Mesa, CO 81643

MESA VERDE NATIONAL PARK — E1 *Montezuma*

↑ MOREFIELD CAMPGROUND **Ratings: 7/9★/7.5** (Campground) Avail: 18 full hkups (30 amps). 2021 rates: $36 to $50. May 18 to Oct 28. (800)449-2288, Mile Marker 4 U.S. 160, Mesa Verde National Park, CO 81330

MONTROSE — D2 *Montrose*

↑ BLACK CANYON OF THE GUNNISON NPS (SOUTH RIM) (Public National Park) From jct US-50 & Hwy-347: Go 6 mi N on Hwy-347. Avail: 23 E (30/50 amps), Pit toilets. 2021 rates: $16 to $22. May 30 to Sep 15. (970)641-2337

→ **CEDAR CREEK RV PARK**

Ratings: 8.5/9★/9 (RV Park) 44 Avail: 37 full hkups, 7 W, 7 E (30/50 amps). 2021 rates: $40.50 to $51.50. (970)249-3884, 126 Rose Ln, Montrose, CO 81401

↓ CENTENNIAL RV PARK & CAMPGROUND **Ratings: 8.5/9.5★/9.5** (RV Park) Avail: 60 full hkups (30/50 amps). 2021 rates: $46 to $52. Apr 01 to Oct 31. (970)240-3832, 23449 Hwy 550, Montrose, CO 81403

↓ MEADOWS OF SAN JUAN RV RESORT **Ratings: 7.5/9.5★/8** (RV Park) Avail: 142 full hkups (30/50 amps). 2021 rates: $40 to $52. (970)249-6382, 22045 S US 550, Montrose, CO 81403

→ MONTROSE/BLACK CANYON KOA **Ratings: 9/10★/9.5** (RV Park) Avail: 50 full hkups (30/50 amps). 2021 rates: $59 to $63. (800)562-9114, 200 N Cedar Ave, Montrose, CO 81401

↓ RIVERBEND RV PARK & CABINS **Ratings: 9.5/10★/9.5** (RV Park) Avail: 59 full hkups (30/50 amps). 2021 rates: $42 to $79. (970)249-8235, 65120 Old Chipeta Trail, Montrose, CO 81403

MONUMENT — C4 *El Paso*

↑ COLORADO HEIGHTS **Ratings: 8/7.5★/8.5** (RV Park) 241 Avail: 187 full hkups, 54 W, 54 E (30/50 amps). 2021 rates: $55 to $65. (719)481-2336, 19575 Monument Hill Rd, Monument, CO 80132

MOSCA — E3 *Alamosa*

→ GREAT SAND DUNES OASIS **Ratings: 4/9.5★/6.5** (RV Park) Avail: 20 full hkups (30/50 amps). 2021 rates: $38. May 01 to Oct 15. (719)378-2222, 7800 Hwy 150 N, Mosca, CO 81146

↗ GREAT SAND DUNES/PINON FLATS (Public National Park) From Jct of US-160 & Hwy 17, E 15 mi on US-160 to SR-150, N 18 mi (E); or From Jct of US-160 & Hwy 17, N 14 mi on US-160 to County Six Mile Lane, E 20 mi (E). 88 Avail. 2021 rates: $20. Apr 01 to Oct 31. (719)378-6395

NATHROP — D3 *Chaffee*

↘ CHALK CREEK CAMPGROUND & RV PARK **Ratings: 7/10★/9** (RV Park) 57 Avail: 29 full hkups, 28 E (30/50 amps). 2021 rates: $45 to $70. Apr 10 to Oct 15. (719)395-8301, 11430 Cty Rd 197, Nathrop, CO 81236

OAK CREEK — B2 *Routt*

STAGECOACH

(Public State Park) From Jct of US-40 & SR-131 (S of Steamboat Springs), S 6.4 mi on SR-131 to CR-14, S 5.3 mi (L); or From Jct of SR-131 & CR-14 (S edge of Oak Creek), N 5 mi on CR-14 (R) Entrance fee required. Elev 7250 ft.**FAC:** gravel rds. Avail: 92 gravel, 9 pull-thrus, (25x45), back-ins (25x35), 64 E (30 amps), tent sites, shower$, dump, fire rings. **REC:** Stagecoach Reservoir: swim, fishing, marina, boating nearby, hunting nearby, rec open to public. Pets OK. Partial handicap access, 14 day max stay. 2021 rates: $28 to $36.
(970)736-2436 Lat: 40.29015, Lon: -106.86341
25500 CR 14, Oak Creek, CO 80467
cpw.state.co.us
See ad page 164

OLATHE — D2 *Montrose*

UNCOMPAHGRE RIVER ADULT RV PARK

Ratings: 9/9.5★/9.5 (RV Park) Avail: 46 full hkups (30/50 amps). 2021 rates: $48. (970)323-8706, 804 S Church Ave, Olathe, CO 81425

OURAY — D2 *Ouray*

4 J + 1 + 1 CAMPGROUND **Ratings: 7/9.5★/8** (RV Park) 55 Avail: 35 full hkups, 20 W, 20 E (30/50 amps). 2021 rates: $44 to $48. May 01 to Oct 31. (970)325-4418, 790 Oak, Ouray, CO 81427

OURAY KOA **Ratings: 7/9★/9** (Campground) 77 Avail: 57 full hkups, 20 W, 20 E (30/50 amps). 2021 rates: $69 to $85. (970)325-4736, 225 CR #23, Ouray, CO 81427

OURAY RIVERSIDE RESORT **Ratings: 9/10★/9.5** (RV Park) Avail: 70 full hkups (30/50 amps). 2021 rates: $50 to $90. (970)325-4523, 1700 N Main, Ouray, CO 81427

PAGOSA SPRINGS — E2 *Archuleta*

BRUCE SPRUCE RANCH **Ratings: 6.5/7.5★/7.5** (Campground) Avail: 33 full hkups (30 amps). 2021 rates: $44. May 25 to Oct 15. (970)264-5374, 231 FS 648, Pagosa Springs, CO 81147

HAPPY CAMPER RV PARK **Ratings: 6/6.5/5** (RV Park) Avail: 45 full hkups (30/50 amps). 2021 rates: $45. (970)731-5822, 9260 West Hwy 160 , Pagosa Springs, CO 81147

MOUNTAIN LANDING SUITES & RV PARK **Ratings: 7/10★/8** (RV Park) 36 Avail: 33 full hkups, 3 W, 3 E (30/50 amps). 2021 rates: $50. May 01 to Oct 31. (970)731-5345, 345 Piedra Road, Pagosa Springs, CO 81147

PAGOSA PINES RV PARK **Ratings: 8.5/9★/9.5** (RV Park) Avail: 23 full hkups (30/50 amps). 2021 rates: $60 to $70. May 01 to Oct 01. (970)264-9130, 1501 W Hwy 160 #3, Pagosa Springs, CO 81147

PAGOSA RIVERSIDE CAMPGROUND

Ratings: 9/10★/9.5 (Campground) From Jct of US-84 & US-160, NE 1.3 mi on US-160 (L). Elev 7200 ft.**FAC:** all weather rds. Avail: 60 gravel, 24 pull-thrus, (35x60), back-ins (20x35), 45 full hkups, 15 W, 15 E (30/50 amps), cable, WiFi @ sites, tent sites, rentals, dump, laundry, groc, fire rings, firewood. **REC:** pool, San Juan River: fishing, kayaking/canoeing, playground, hunting nearby, rec open to public. Pets OK. Big rig sites, eco-friendly. 2021 rates: $53 to $59, Military discount. Apr 15 to Nov 15.
(970)264-5874 Lat: 37.28608, Lon: -106.97950
2270 E Hwy 160, Pagosa Springs, CO 81147
www.pagosariverside.com
See ad page 173

PAGOSA SPRINGS RV PARK **Ratings: 7/10★/9** (RV Park) 45 Avail: 42 full hkups, 3 W, 3 E (30/50 amps). 2021 rates: $52.50 to $67.95. May 15 to Oct 10. (970)264-9264, 10 Leisure Court, Pagosa Springs, CO 81147

WOLF CREEK RUN MOTOR COACH RESORT **Ratings: 8.5/9.5★/10** (RV Resort) Avail: 27 full hkups (30/50 amps). 2021 rates: $89 to $129. May 15 to Oct 15. (970)264-0365, 1742 E Hwy 160, Pagosa Springs, CO 81147

How much will it all cost? Use this as a guide: Rates shown are the minimum and maximum for two adults in one RV at the time of inspection (excluding any additional fees for items not at the site). Remember, these rates serve as guidelines only. It's always best to call ahead for the most current rate information.

PALISADE — C1 *Mesa*

JAMES M. ROBB - COLORADO RIVER/ CONNECTED LAKES SECTION

(Public State Park) From Jct I-70 & Exit 47 (5 mi NE of town), exit N to Frontage Rd, E 0.4 mi (E) Park Entrance Fee Required. Elev 4800 ft.**FAC:** paved rds. Avail: 68 gravel, 45 pull-thrus, (25x50), back-ins (25x50), 40 full hkups, 22 E (30/50 amps), tent sites, shower$, dump, laundry, fire rings, firewood. **REC:** Colorado River: swim, fishing, boating nearby, playground, hunting nearby, rec open to public. Pets OK. Partial handicap access, 14 day max stay. 2021 rates: $22 to $37.
(970)464-0548 Lat: 39.168586, Lon: -108.299741
@ Exit 47/I 70, Palisade, CO 81526
cpw.state.us.co
See ad page 164

PALISADE BASECAMP RV RESORT **Ratings: 9/10★/9** (RV Resort) Avail: 71 full hkups (30/50 amps). 2021 rates: $66 to $106. (970)462-9712, 985 North River Road, Palisade, CO 81526

PAONIA — D2 *Delta*

PAONIA

(Public State Park) From Jct of Hwy 82 & Hwy 133 (Colorado) in Carbondale, S 46 mi; or From Jct of Hwy 92 & Hwy 133 (through Paonia), N 16 mi. Entrance fee required. Elev 6500 ft.-**FAC:** gravel rds. Avail: 13 gravel, back-ins (15x30), tent sites, pit toilets, fire rings. **REC:** North Fork Gunnison River: fishing, boating nearby, hunting nearby, rec open to public. Pets OK. 14 day max stay. 2021 rates: $18. May 01 to Oct 01.
(970)921-5721 Lat: 38.9602, Lon: -107.3457
Hwy 133, Paonia, CO 81428
cpw.state.co.us
See ad page 164

PARKER — C4 *Douglas*

Travel Services

RV VAULT - PARKER State of the Art saw-tooth faced Premier indoor RV storage facility with garages up to 60 feet deep. Lights, power and fire protection in each unit. 24/7 secured access. Water, dump station and compressed air included. Elev 5810 ft. **RV Storage:** indoor, covered canopy, secured fencing, electric gate, easy reach keypad, 24/7 access, well-lit facility, well-lit roads, well-lit perimeter, security cameras, power to charge battery, water, compressed air. **SERVICES:**. Hours: 8am to 5pm.
Special offers available for Good Sam Members
(720)903-2619 Lat: 39.52966, Lon: -104.77382
18525 Apache Drive, Parker, CO 80134
rvvault.com

PINE — B3 *Jefferson*

STAUNTON

(Public State Park) From US Hwy 285 S: Go 1-1/2 mi N on Elk Creek Road (R). Elev 8877 ft.**FAC:** dirt rds. Avail: 25 dirt, tent sites, pit toilets. **REC:** boating nearby, rec open to public. Pets OK. 14 day max stay. 2021 rates: $28.
(303)816-0912 Lat: 39.31050, Lon: -105.23220
12102 S Elk Creek Road, Pine, CO 80470
cpw.state.co.us
See ad page 164

PUEBLO — D4 *Pueblo*

LAKE PUEBLO

(Public State Park) From Jct of I-25 & SR-45/ Pueblo Blvd (exit 94), NW 4.6 mi on Pueblo Blvd to SR-96 (Thatcher Ave), W 3.8 mi (R); or From Jct of US-50 & SR-45 (Pueblo Blvd), S 4 mi on Pueblo Blvd to SR-96(Thatcher Ave), W 3.8 mi (R) Park Entrance Fee Required. Elev 5000 ft.**FAC:** paved rds. Avail: 393 paved, 126 pull-thrus, (35x60), back-ins (35x40), 281 E (20/30 amps), tent sites, shower$, dump, firewood. **REC:** Lake Pueblo: swim, fishing, marina, kayaking/canoeing, boating nearby, playground, hunting nearby, rec open to public. Pets OK. Partial handicap access, 14 day max stay. 2021 rates: $24 to $36. no cc.
(719)561-9320 Lat: 38.254362, Lon: -104.731960
640 Pueblo Reservoir Rd, Pueblo, CO 81005
www.cpw.state.co.us
See ad page 164

PUEBLO KOA **Ratings: 8.5/9.5★/8** (RV Park) Avail: 60 full hkups (30/50 amps). 2021 rates: $48 to $75. (800)562-7453, 4131 I-25 N, Pueblo, CO 81008

PUEBLO WEST — D4 *Pueblo*

HAGGARD'S RV CAMPGROUND **Ratings: 7/7.5/8.5** (Campground) Avail: 40 full hkups (30/50 amps). 2021 rates: $47 to $57. Mar 01 to Oct 31. (719)547-2101, 7910 W Hwy 50, Pueblo West, CO 81007

RANGELY — B1 *Rio Blanco*

BUCK 'N' BULL RV PARK **Ratings: 7.5/10★/8** (RV Park) 17 Avail: 13 full hkups, 4 W, 4 E (30/50 amps). 2021 rates: $45. Apr 01 to Oct 31. (970)675-9335, 2811 East Main Street, Rangely, CO 81648

RIDGWAY — D2 *Ouray*

RIDGWAY/DUTCH CHARLIE

(Public State Park) From Jct Hwy 62 & US-550 (in town), N 4.5 mi on US-550 (L); or From Jct US-50 & US-550 (in Montrose), S 22.7 mi on US-550 (R) Entrance fee required. Elev 6900 ft.**FAC:** paved rds. Avail: 187 paved, 123 pull-thrus, (45x60), back-ins (45x50), 167 W, 167 E (20/30 amps), tent sites, rentals, shower$, dump, laundry, fire rings. **REC:** Ridgway Reservoir: swim, fishing, marina, boating nearby, playground, hunting nearby, rec open to public. Pets OK. Partial handicap access, 14 day max stay. 2021 rates: $26 to $41.
(970)626-5822 Lat: 38.1967, Lon: -107.7417
28555 Hwy 550, Ridgway, CO 81432
cpw.state.co.us
See ad page 164

RIDGWAY/PA CO-CHU PUK

(Public State Park) From Jct of Hwy 62 & US-550 (in town), N 8.1 mi on US-550 (L); or From Jct of US-50 & US-550 (in Montrose), S 19.1 mi on US-550 (R) Entrance fee required. Elev 6800 ft.**FAC:** paved rds. Avail: 95 paved, 80 pull-thrus, (45x60), back-ins (45x50), 88 full hkups (20/30 amps), tent sites, shower$, laundry, fire rings. **REC:** Uncompahgre River: swim, fishing, boating nearby, playground, hunting nearby, rec open to public. Pets OK. Partial handicap access, 14 day max stay. 2021 rates: $26 to $41.
(970)626-5822 Lat: 38.1967, Lon: -107.7417
28555 Hwy 550, Ridgway, CO 81432
cpw.state.co.us
See ad page 164

RIFLE — C2 *Garfield*

RIFLE FALLS

(Public State Park) From town, N 3 mi on SR-13 to SR-325, E 9.8 mi (L). Entrance fee required. Elev 6500 ft.**FAC:** gravel rds. Avail: 20 dirt, 6 pull-thrus, (15x40), back-ins (15x40), 13 E (30 amps), tent sites, restrooms only, fire rings. **REC:** Rifle Gap Reservoir: swim, fishing, rec open to public. Pets OK. Partial handicap access, 14 day max stay. 2021 rates: $22 to $36.
(970)625-1607 Lat: 39.6747, Lon: -107.6998
5775 Hwy 325, Rifle, CO 81650
cpw.state.co.us
See ad page 164

RIFLE GAP

(Public State Park) From Jct I-70 & Hwy 13, N 3 mi on Hwy 13 to Colorado 325, R 9.8 mi on Colorado 325 to County Road 252, stay on County Road 252 2 mi to County Road 219, R 0.1 mi on County Road 219 Entrance fee required. Elev 6000 ft.**FAC:** gravel rds. 89 Avail: 45 paved, 44 gravel, 40 pull-thrus, (15x40), back-ins (15x40), 36 full hkups, 24 E (30/50 amps), tent sites, shower$, dump, fire rings. **REC:** Rifle Gap Reservoir: swim, fishing, boating nearby, hunting nearby, rec open to public. Pets OK. Partial handicap access, 14 day max stay. 2021 rates: $20 to $38.
(970)625-1607 Lat: 39.6154, Lon: -107.6656
5775 Hwy 325, Rifle, CO 81650
www.cpw.state.co.us
See ad page 164

Things to See and Do

HARVEY GAP STATE PARK Day use fishing Elev 6400 ft. Restrooms. Hours: 6am to 10pm. Adult fee: $9.
(970)625-1607 Lat: 39.633560, Lon: -107.745213
5775 Highway 325, Rifle, CO 81650
cpw.state.co.us
See ad page 164

RYE — D4 *Pueblo*

ASPEN ACRES CAMPGROUND **Ratings: 6/9.5★/8.5** (Campground) 49 Avail: 42 full hkups, 7 W, 7 E (30/50 amps). 2021 rates: $31 to $65. May 15 to Nov 02. (719)485-3275, 16561 Hwy 165 , Rye, CO 81069

Exclusive! According to our research, restroom cleanliness is of the utmost importance to RVers. Of course, you knew that already. The cleanest campgrounds have a star in their restroom rating!

SALIDA — D3 *Chaffee*

ARKANSAS HEADWATERS RECREATION AREA/HECLA JUNCTION CAMPGROUND
(Public State Park) From jct US-24 & US-285: Go 10 mi S on US-285, then 2-1/2 mi E on CR-194 (L). Elev 7423 ft.**FAC:** gravel rds. Avail: 23 gravel, 2 pull-thrus, (30x40), back-ins (30x35), accepts self-contain units only, pit toilets, fire rings. **REC:** Arkansas River: fishing, boating nearby, hunting nearby, rec open to public. Pets OK. No tents, 14 day max stay. 2021 rates: $28.
(719)539-7289 Lat: 38.653051, Lon: -106.051603
CR 194, Salida, CO 81201
cpw.state.co.us
See ad page 164

ARKANSAS HEADWATERS RECREATION AREA/RINCON CAMPGROUND
(Public State Park) From US 50 in Howard: Go 2-1/2 mi N on US 50 (R). Elev 6791 ft.**FAC:** paved rds. Avail: 8 gravel, 5 pull-thrus, (30x70), back-ins (30x25), accepts self-contain units only, pit toilets, fire rings. **REC:** Arkansas River: fishing, boating nearby, hunting nearby, rec open to public. Pets OK. No tents, 14 day max stay. 2021 rates: $28.
(719)539-7289 Lat: 38.4707, Lon: -105.8653
Hwy 50, Salida, CO 81201
cpw.state.co.us
See ad page 164

ARKANSAS HEADWATERS RECREATION AREA/SALIDA EAST CAMPGROUND
(Public State Park) From Jct of US-50 & SR-291, E 1.5 mi on US-50 (L). Elev 7500 ft.**FAC:** gravel rds. Avail: 25 gravel, 6 pull-thrus, (20x50), back-ins (20x40), accepts self-contain units only, pit toilets, fire rings. **REC:** Arkansas River: fishing, boating nearby, hunting nearby, rec open to public. Pets OK. No tents, 14 day max stay. 2021 rates: $28.
(719)539-7289 Lat: 38.53780, Lon: -105.99250
Hwy 50 , Salida, CO 81201
cpw.state.co.us
See ad page 164

FOUR SEASONS RV RESORT **Ratings: 7.5/9.5★/8.5** (RV Park) Avail: 65 full hkups (30/50 amps). 2021 rates: $46 to $83. (719)539-3084, 4305 E Hwy 50, Salida, CO 81201

SALIDA/MT SHAVANO KOA **Ratings: 7.5/8.5★/7** (RV Park) Avail: 45 full hkups (30/50 amps). 2021 rates: $57.95 to $80.54. (800)562-7398, 16105 Hwy 50 W, Salida, CO 81201

SARGENTS — D3 *Saguache*

TOMICHI CREEK TRADING POST **Ratings: 6.5/8★/7.5** (RV Park) Avail: 20 full hkups (30/50 amps). 2021 rates: $40 to $45. (970)641-0674, 71420 Highway 50, Sargents, CO 81248

SEIBERT — C5 *Kit Carson*

SHADY GROVE CAMPGROUND **Ratings: 6.5/8.5★/7** (RV Park) Avail: 30 full hkups (30/50 amps). 2021 rates: $34 to $39. (970)664-2218, 306 Colorado Ave, Seibert, CO 80834

SILT — C2 *Garfield*

GLENWOOD SPRINGS WEST/SILT COLORADO RIVER KOA **Ratings: 10/10★/9** (RV Park) Avail: 98 full hkups (30/50 amps). 2021 rates: $38 to $79. Mar 15 to Nov 15. (970)876-4900, 629 River Frontage Road, Silt, CO 81652

SILVERTON — E2 *San Juan*

SILVER SUMMIT RV PARK
good sam park
Ratings: 8/9.5★/8.5 (RV Park) From Jct of US-550 & SR-110, N 0.2 mi on SR-110 to E 7th St, E 0.1 mi (R). Elev 9265 ft.**FAC:** all weather rds. Avail: 39 gravel, 1 pull-thrus, (25x60), back-ins (25x60), 39 full hkups (30/50 amps), WiFi @ sites, dump, laundry. **REC:** hunting nearby. Pets OK. Partial handicap access. No tents. Big rig sites. 2021 rates: $52, Military discount. Jun 01 to Oct 01.
(970)387-0240 Lat: 37.80596, Lon: -107.66697
640 Mineral St, Silverton, CO 81433
www.silversummitrvpark.com
See ad this page

Like Us on Facebook.

SOUTH FORK — E2 *Rio Grande*

ALPINE TRAILS RV PARK **Ratings: 8/9★/9** (RV Park) Avail: 42 full hkups (30/50 amps). 2021 rates: $43 to $55. May 15 to Sep 30. (719)873-0261, 0111 Wharton Rd, South Fork, CO 81154

ASPEN RIDGE RV PARK **Ratings: 8/9★/8.5** (RV Park) Avail: 45 full hkups (30/50 amps). 2021 rates: $42 to $49. May 01 to Oct 01. (719)873-2248, 700 State Hwy 149, South Fork, CO 81154

FUN VALLEY FAMILY RESORT **Ratings: 7.5/8/7.5** (RV Park) Avail: 450 full hkups (30/50 amps). 2021 rates: $47.50 to $65.50. May 21 to Sep 12. (970)661-2220, 36000 Hwy 160 W, South Fork, CO 81154

GRANDVIEW CABINS & RV RESORT **Ratings: 7.5/8.5/7.5** (RV Park) Avail: 81 full hkups (30/50 amps). 2021 rates: $42. May 01 to Oct 31. (719)873-5541, 0613 Hwy 149, South Fork, CO 81154

MOON VALLEY RV RESORT **Ratings: 7/7.5/6.5** (Campground) Avail: 18 full hkups (30 amps). 2021 rates: $30. May 01 to Oct 31. (719)873-5216, 180173 W. Hwy 160, South Fork, CO 81154

PEACOCK MEADOWS RIVERSIDE RV PARK **Ratings: 8.5/9★/9** (RV Park) Avail: 56 full hkups (30/50 amps). 2021 rates: $44 to $54. (719)657-1129, 29059 US-160, South Fork, CO 81154

RIVERBEND RESORT **Ratings: 8/9★/8.5** (RV Park) Avail: 51 full hkups (30/50 amps). 2021 rates: $42 to $44. (800)621-6512, 33846 W. Hwy 160, South Fork, CO 81154

SOUTH FORK CAMPGROUND **Ratings: 8/9.5★/9** (Campground) Avail: 51 full hkups (30/50 amps). 2021 rates: $36 to $46. May 01 to Oct 01. (719)873-5500, 26359 W US-160, South Fork, CO 81154

SOUTH FORK LODGE AND RV PARK **Ratings: 7/7/8** (RV Park) Avail: 29 full hkups (30/50 amps). 2021 rates: $44. May 15 to Oct 01. (719)873-5303, 364 Hwy 149, South Fork, CO 81154

UTE BLUFF LODGE & RV PARK **Ratings: 8/9★/8** (RV Park) Avail: 27 full hkups (30/50 amps). 2021 rates: $45 to $50. Apr 01 to Nov 30. (800)473-0595, 27680 Hwy 160, South Fork, CO 81154

STEAMBOAT SPRINGS — B2 *Routt*

STEAMBOAT SPRINGS KOA **Ratings: 9/10★/8.5** (Campground) 115 Avail: 91 full hkups, 24 W, 24 E (30/50 amps). 2021 rates: $55 to $80. (970)879-0273, 3603 Lincoln Ave, Steamboat Springs, CO 80487

STERLING — B5 *Logan*

NORTH STERLING
(Public State Park) From Jct of I-76 & US-6 (exit 125), W 2.3 mi on Chestnut St (to 3rd Ave, N 0.3 mi to Broadway, W 0.3 mi to 7th Ave/Hwy 37, N 9.3 mi to CR-46, W 2 mi to CR-33, N 0.3 mi, follow signs (L) Entrance fee required. Elev 4000 ft.**FAC:** paved/gravel rds. Avail: 141 gravel, 130 pull-thrus, (20x50), back-ins (20x50), 97 E (30/50 amps), tent sites, shower$, dump, laundry, fire rings, firewood. **REC:** North Sterling Reservoir: swim, fishing, boating nearby, playground, hunting nearby, rec open to public. Pets OK. Partial handicap access, 14 day max stay. 2021 rates: $28 to $36.
(970)522-3657 Lat: 40.78945, Lon: -103.26480
24005 County Road 330, Sterling, CO 80751
www.cpw.state.co.us
See ad page 164

STRASBURG — C4 *Arapahoe*

DENVER EAST/STRASBURG KOA **Ratings: 9/9★/8** (Campground) 81 Avail: 67 full hkups, 14 W, 14 E (30/50 amps). 2021 rates: $56 to $85. (800)562-6538, 1312 Monroe St, Strasburg, CO 80136

STRATTON — C5 *Kit Carson*

PAINTED ROCK PARK **Ratings: 6.5/NA/8** (RV Park) Avail: 28 full hkups (30/50 amps). 2021 rates: $30. (719)349-2183, 13850 CR 31, Stratton, CO 80836

TEXAS CREEK — D3 *Fremont*

SWEETWATER RIVER RANCH **Ratings: 5/6.5/6** (RV Park) Avail: 15 full hkups (30/50 amps). 2021 rates: $55 to $75. (719)276-3842, 24871 US Hwy 50, Texas Creek, CO 81223

TRINIDAD — E4 *Las Animas*

TRINIDAD LAKE
(Public State Park) From Jct of I-25 & Hwy 12(Exit 13b), W 4 mi on Hwy 12 (L). Entrance fee required. Elev 6300 ft.**FAC:** paved rds. 73 Avail: 20 paved, 53 gravel, 11 pull-thrus, (15x45), back-ins (15x35), 7 full hkups, 56 E (50 amps), tent sites, shower$, dump, laundry. **REC:** Trinidad Lake: fishing, boating nearby, playground, hunting nearby, rec open to public. Pets OK. Partial handicap access, 14 day max stay. 2021 rates: $28 to $41.
(719)846-6951 Lat: 37.14554, Lon: -104.57020
32610 Hwy 12, Trinidad, CO 81082
www.cpw.state.co.us
See ad page 164

VALLECITO — E2 *La Plata*

VALLECITO See also Arboles, Bayfield, Durango, Ignacio & Pagosa Springs.

WALDEN — B3 *Jackson*

STATE FOREST/BOCKMAN
(Public State Park) From town, SE 20.25 mi, E 4 mi on CR-41 (R) Entrance fee required. Elev 9500 ft.**FAC:** gravel rds. Avail: 52 gravel, 13 pull-thrus, (30x40), back-ins (15x50), tent sites, pit toilets, dump. **REC:** Michigan River: fishing, boating nearby, hunting nearby, rec open to public. Pets OK. 14 day max stay. 2021 rates: $18 to $28.
(970)723-8366 Lat: 40.5505, Lon: -106.0371
56666 Hwy 14, Walden, CO 80480
cpw.state.co.us
See ad page 164

STATE FOREST/NORTH MICHIGAN
(Public State Park) From town: Go 24-1/4 mi SE on CR 41 (R) Note: Entrance fee required. **FAC:** gravel rds. Avail: 48 gravel, 6 pull-thrus, (20x50), back-ins (15x50), tent sites, rentals, pit toilets, fire rings. **REC:** North Michigan Reservoir: fishing, boating nearby, hunting nearby, rec open to public. Pets OK. 14 day max stay. 2021 rates: $18 to $28.
(970)723-8366 Lat: 40.5553171, Lon: -105.994430
56750 Hwy 14, Walden, CO 80480
cpw.state.co.us
See ad page 164

STATE FOREST/NORTH PARK
(Public State Park) From town, SE 20.25 mi, E 4 mi on CR-41 (R). Entrance fee required. The North Park campground and cabins will be closed through the 2022 season for renovations. Elev 8800 ft.**FAC:** gravel rds. Avail: 29 gravel, 9 pull-thrus, (20x50), back-ins (20x50) (30/50 amps), tent sites, rentals, fire rings. **REC:** boating nearby, hunting nearby, rec open to public. Pets OK. 14 day max stay. 2021 rates: $18 to $36, Military discount.
(970)723-8366 Lat: 40.553379, Lon: -106.037024
53337 Hwy 14, Walden, CO 80480
cpw.state.co.us
See ad page 164

STATE FOREST/RANGER LAKES
(Public State Park) From Jct of Hwy 287 & Hwy 14, N 75 mi on Hwy 14 (L). Entrance fee required. Elev 9200 ft.**FAC:** dirt rds. Avail: 31 gravel, back-ins (12x50), 31 E (30 amps), tent sites, pit toilets, fire rings. **REC:** Ranger Lakes: fishing, hunting nearby, rec open to public. Pets OK. 14 day max stay. 2021 rates: $36.
(970)723-8366 Lat: 40.550356, Lon: -106.036731
59955 Hwy 14, Walden, CO 80480
cpw.state.co.us
See ad page 164

RV Galley Space Savers: Use square or rectangular plastic containers to contain bulk buy dry foods (pasta, rice and other dry snacks). Mount a spice rack on the inside of a cabinet door near the food prep area where spices can all be seen. Store canned food in a shallow drawer, tops up. Identify each can (nothing fancy or laborious, just a letter like P for peas, B for beans, etc.). Small hammocks strung between cup hooks are perfect for fruits and vegetables that don't need to be refrigerated, like bananas, oranges, lemons and tomatoes. Buy liquids in plastic-not glass-bottles to reduce risk of breakage. What glass you do buy, store in empty cardboard wine cartons with dividers. Keep your refrigerator as full as possible, and store most of your vertical and spillable items on the same shelf.

WALSENBURG — E4 *Huerfano*

LATHROP

(Public State Park) From Jct of I-25 & US-160 (Exit 49 or 52), W 4.5 mi on US-160 (R). Entrance fee required. Elev 6400 ft. **FAC:** paved/gravel rds. 103 Avail: 82 paved, 21 gravel, 77 pull-thrus, (15x50), back-ins (15x40), 103 W, 82 E (30/50 amps), tent sites, shower$, dump, firewood. **REC:** Martin Lake: swim, fishing, kayaking/canoeing, boating nearby, golf, playground, hunting nearby, rec open to public. Pets OK. Partial handicap access, 14 day max stay. 2021 rates: $28 to $36.
(719)738-2376 Lat: 37.60245, Lon: -104.833432
70 County Rd 502, Walsenburg, CO 81089
cpw.state.co.us
See ad page 164

RV Tech Tips - Get a Charge Out of This Nifty Battery Water Filler. The placement of batteries in some motorhomes can make them difficult to service. Here's an easy, fool-proof tool that works for any battery, regardless of location. Purchase a one-gallon or smaller garden pump sprayer. Remove the wand attachment, leaving the hose and trigger assembly. Add distilled water to the sprayer's tank, pump a few times to add air pressure and squirt the water into each battery cell with no mess or overfill.

WELLINGTON — B4 *Larimer*

FORT COLLINS NORTH/WELLINGTON KOA **Ratings: 9/10★/9** (Campground) Avail: 74 full hkups (30/50 amps). 2021 rates: $50 to $70. (800)562-8142, 4821 E CR 70, Wellington, CO 80549

WESTCLIFFE — D3 *Custer*

GRAPE CREEK RV PARK CAMPGROUND & CABINS

good sam park

Ratings: 9/10★/10 (RV Park) Avail: 34 full hkups (30/50 amps). 2021 rates: $57.47 to $64.67. May 01 to Oct 30. (719)783-2588, 56491 Hwy 69, Westcliffe, CO 81252

WHEAT RIDGE — C4 *Jefferson*

Travel Services

GANDER RV OF WHEAT RIDGE/DENVER Your new hometown outfitter offering the best regional gear for all your outdoor needs. Your adventure awaits. **SERVICES:** RV appliance, MH mechanical, restrooms. RV Sales. RV supplies, RV accessible. Hours: 9am- 7pm, closed Sun.
(855)507-3474 Lat: 39.783508, Lon: -105.108067
9870 W 48th Ave, Wheat Ridge, CO 80033
rv.ganderoutdoors.com

Making campground reservations? Remember to ask about the cancellation policy when making your reservation.

WOODLAND PARK — C4 *Teller*

BRISTLECONE LODGE **Ratings: 7/8.5★/8** (RV Park) Avail: 40 full hkups (30/50 amps). 2021 rates: $45. (719)687-9518, 510 N State Hwy 67, Woodland Park, CO 80863

DIAMOND CAMPGROUND & RV PARK **Ratings: 8/9.5★/9** (RV Park) 80 Avail: 70 full hkups, 10 W, 10 E (30/50 amps). 2021 rates: $46 to $52. May 10 to Sep 30. (719)687-9684, 900 N Hwy 67, Woodland Park, CO 80863

MILITARY PARK FARISH RECREATION AREA (USAF ACADEMY) (Public) From jct I-25 & US-24: Go 17 mi W on US-24, then 4 mi N on Baldwin/Rampart Range Rd, then 2 mi E on Loy Creek Rd (E) Caution: RVs over 26 ft call for special directions. 15 Avail: 6 W, 6 E. 2021 rates: $25. May 15 to Oct 15. (719)687-9098

CLEANING YOUR RV: Use the proper cleaning products for fiberglass, rubber, windows, and for removing bugs; A long-handled telescoping pole with multiple attachments (brushes, squeegee, soft mitt for waxing, etc.) will make your job easier; This is also the right time to inspect for cracks in caulking around windows and roof mounted vents and TV antenna; Inspect inside for any evidence of water leaks.

CO

Getty Images/iStockphoto

Connecticut

DID YOU KNOW?

The white clam pizza at Pepe's in New Haven was once voted the best pie in the country.

CT

Connecticut's famous universities in historic ports make it a top New England destination. Take a scenic drive during the fall colors, sample a creamy lobster roll or catch a wave on the seashore.

Mystic Pizza Memories

In 1988, a movie titled "Mystic Pizza" made Mystic synonymous with a disc-shaped Italian entree. For a real slice of heaven, head to New Haven where the local style known as "apizza" has made loyalists across the country. The thin, charred crust is chewy and savory, but for a truly unique experience, try the white clam pie at Pepe's.

New England Towns

A state with a history steeped in nautical trade, many of Connecticut's biggest cities lie along the Long Island Sound. On the shore, lighthouses, wind-swept vistas and rugged beaches entice visitors to explore. Step back to 19th-century Connecticut with a stop at the Mystic Seaport, renowned for its historic village, nautical exhibits and dynamic shipyard. Inland, the state capital, Hartford, boasts a thriving cultural scene. Get acquainted with the author of "Huckleberry Finn" and "Tom Sawyer" with a visit to the town's Mark Twain House & Museum. Swing by New Haven and stroll the campus of Yale University.

Off to the Atlantic

The Atlantic Ocean continues to attract adventures seekers to Connecticut. Walk Connecticut's sweeping coastline and catch sight of thriving aquatic habitat. Book a fishing charter to head out to the deep Atlantic or find a pier along the shore for flounder, bluefish and striped bass. Paddlers can explore the inlets and islands along the coast while watching for wildlife. Head inland to the Farmington River for some of the best rapids and scenery in the state.

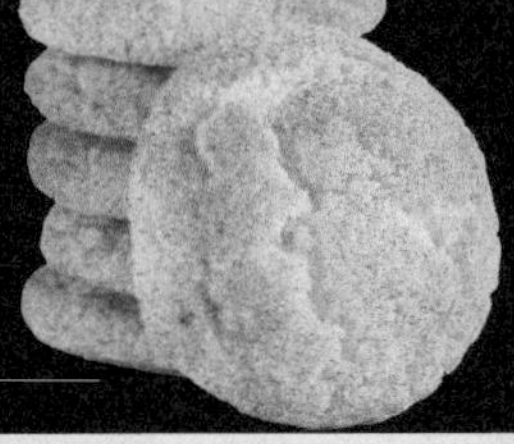

Connecticut Snickerdoodle

Get your sweet tooth fix with the snickerdoodle. Soft, chewy and warm to the bite, this cinnamon- and sugar-coated cookie is believed to have been brought to New England by Dutch and German immigrants in the 1800s. Eat them on their own or with a scoop (or two) of ice cream for a hearty snack.

VISITOR CENTER

TIME ZONE
Eastern Standard

ROAD & HIGHWAY INFORMATION
860-594-2000
ct.gov/dot

FISHING & HUNTING INFORMATION
860-434-8638
portal.ct.gov/DEEP/Fishing

BOATING INFORMATION
ct.gov/deep/boating

NATIONAL PARKS
nps.gov/ct

STATE PARKS
portal.ct.gov/DEEP/State-Parks/Connecticut-State-Parks-and-Forests

TOURISM INFORMATION
Connecticut Office of Tourism
888-CTVISIT
ctvisit.com

TOP TOURISM ATTRACTIONS
1) Mystic Seaport
2) Mystic Aquarium
3) Mark Twain House & Museum

MAJOR CITIES
Bridgeport, New Haven, Stamford, Hartford (capital), Waterbury

Featured Good Sam Parks

good sam park

CONNECTICUT

When you stay with Good Sam, you can expect the highest degree of cleanliness and friendliness, and better yet, you get **10% off** overnight campground fees.

If you're not already a Good Sam member you can purchase your membership at one of these locations:

EAST KILLINGLY
Stateline Campresort & Cabins

JEWETT CITY
Campers World on Hopeville Pond

PLYMOUTH
Gentile's Campground

PRESTON
Hidden Acres Family Campground

SALEM
Salem Farms Campground

THOMASTON
Branch Brook Campground

VOLUNTOWN
Natures Campsites

Getty Images/iStockphoto

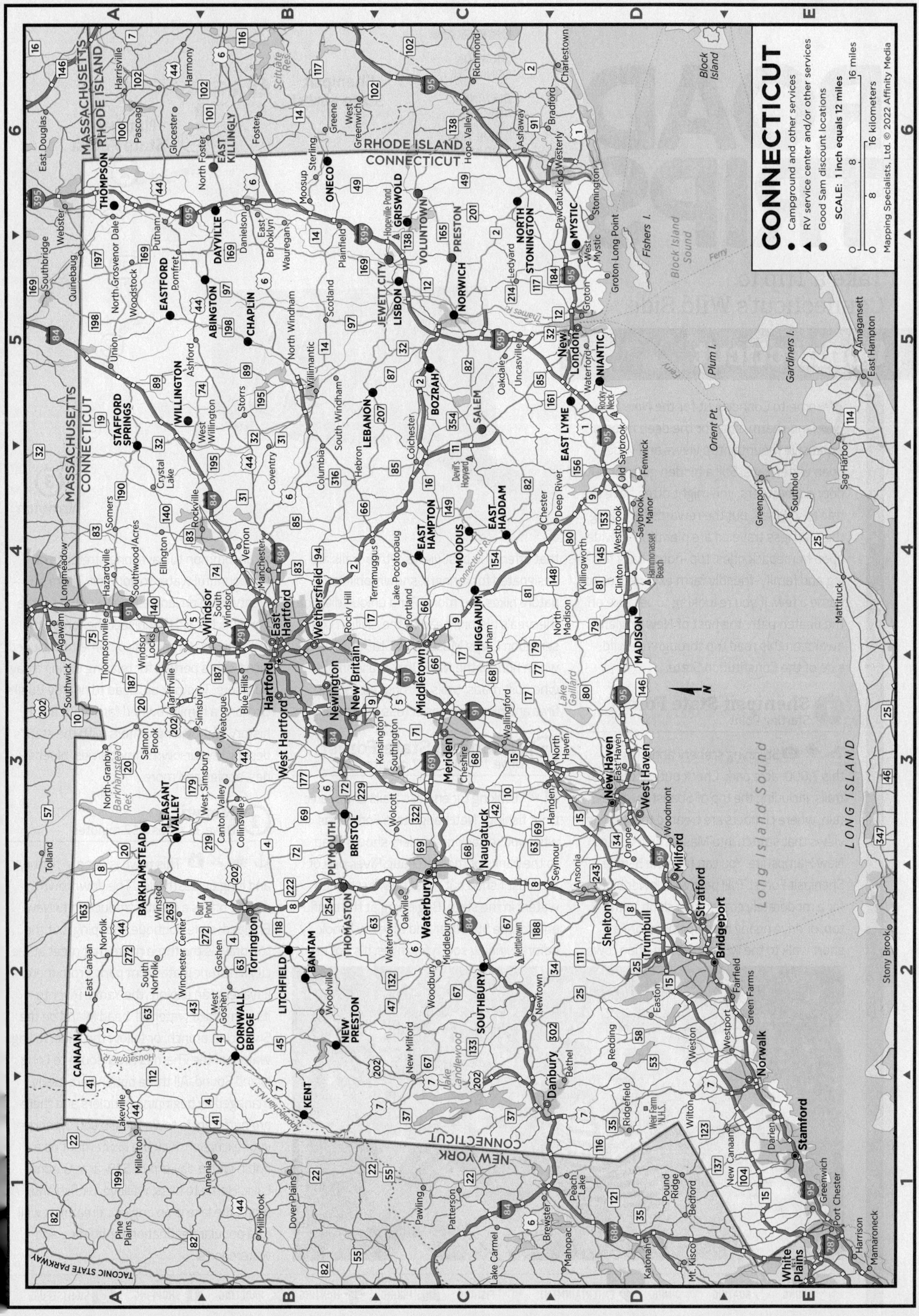
CONNECTICUT
Campground and other services
RV service center and/or other services
Good Sam discount locations
SCALE: 1 inch equals 12 miles
0 8 16 miles
0 8 16 kilometers
Mapping Specialists, Ltd. © 2022 Affinity Media
MASSACHUSETTS
CONNECTICUT
RHODE ISLAND
NEW YORK
Long Island Sound
LONG ISLAND
Block Island Sound
Block Island
Fishers I.
Plum I.
Gardiners I.
Orient Pt.
THOMPSON
EAST KILLINGLY
DAYVILLE
ONECO
GRISWOLD
VOLUNTOWN
PRESTON
NORTH STONINGTON
MYSTIC
JEWETT CITY
LISBON
NORWICH
EASTFORD
ABINGTON
CHAPLIN
WILLINGTON
STAFFORD SPRINGS
LEBANON
BOZRAH
SALEM
NIANTIC
EAST LYME
New London
EAST HAMPTON
MOODUS
EAST HADDAM
HIGGANUM
MADISON
Hartford
East Hartford
Wethersfield
Windsor
West Hartford
Newington
New Britain
Middletown
Meriden
New Haven
West Haven
Milford
Stratford
Bridgeport
Norwalk
Stamford
Danbury
Waterbury
Naugatuck
Shelton
Trumbull
Torrington
BRISTOL
PLYMOUTH
THOMASTON
BANTAM
LITCHFIELD
NEW PRESTON
KENT
CORNWALL BRIDGE
CANAAN
BARKHAMSTEAD
PLEASANT VALLEY
SOUTHBURY
White Plains
TACONIC STATE PARKWAY
Appalachian N.S.T.

ROAD TRIPS

Take a Trip to Connecticut's Wild Side

Connecticut

LOCATION
CONNECTICUT

DISTANCE
48 MILES

DRIVE TIME
1 HR 19 MINS

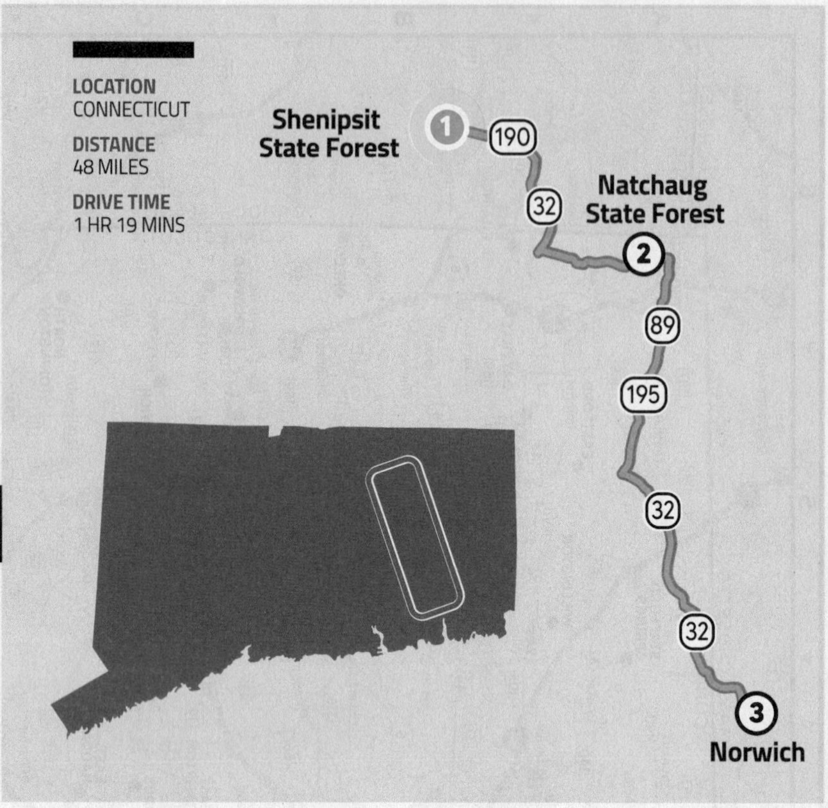

Come to Connecticut for the New England charm, stay for the deep forests, expansive mountaintop views and wide-open waterways. Still a hidden gem for outdoor adventurers, you might often have the trail to yourself, but the rewards for taking the road less traveled are plentiful — wide-open horseback rides, top-notch bass fishing and family-friendly farm experiences to name a few. If you're looking to venture off the beaten path, the best of New England awaits on this road trip through the wild side of the Constitution State.

1 Shenipsit State Forest
Starting Point

Stunning scenery abounds in this 7,000-acre park. Check out picturesque trails, including the top of Soapstone Mountain, where climbers are treated to stunning views that stretch into Massachusetts and New Hampshire. You can take the 5-mile Shenipsit Forest Trail past wildflower blooms for a moderately challenging climb to the top, or drive nearly to the peak before a short walk to the wooden observation tower that offers the best views. Other trails are designated for runners, snowmobilers, nature hikes and more. For a unique dive into the area's history, head to the Civilian Conservation Corps Museum in Stafford Springs, which honors the New Deal-era workers who built roads, trails, campsites, fought fires and planted trees across the state.

2 Natchaug State Forest
Drive 17 miles • 27 minutes

Looking for endless trails and scenic trout fishing? Natchaug State Forest has what you're seeking Anglers should head to the banks of the Natchaug River, one of the least fished but most heavily stocked waters in the state. Beginning at the confluence of the Still River and Bigelow Brook before winding south for miles, it's not at all uncommon to have long stretches of the bountiful water to yourself. There's plenty to do on land as well. Known for the horseback trails that bisect the forest, the expansive network is also home to secluded picnic spots perfect for relaxing during a day outdoors. To stock up, head to nearby Buell's Orchard, a family-owned farm with a long history of providing visitors with the state's best pick-your-own strawberries, blueberries, apples and more.

Getty Images/iStockphoto

3 Norwich
Drive 31 miles • 52 minutes

This town is deep in history and long on aesthetics. The downtown district offers a great introduction to New England-style boutique shopping, but the top draw is the three rivers that meet at the city's historic waterfront park. From there, kayakers can explore the Yantic River to its namesake waterfall, head inland on the Shetucket branch, or follow the wide, rolling waters of the Thames River south to Long Island Sound. All three options are easily managed by beginning paddlers and there are outfitters in town to help you organize your excursion. Kick the excitement up a notch with a day trip to 529-acre Gardner Lake. Home to bass, walleye, catfish and more, the lake is an angler's dream, as well as a popular destination for boating and watersports.

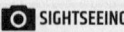

BIKING · BOATING · DINING · ENTERTAINMENT · FISHING · HIKING · HUNTING · PADDLING · SHOPPING · SIGHTSEEING

Connecticut SPOTLIGHTS

Enjoy the Right to Fun in the Constitution State

Connecticut packs a lot of attractions in a small package. Tour legendary towns like the port town of Mystic, or head inland for biking, kayaking and New England villages in some of the Constitution State's beautiful forests and mountains.

MYSTIC-BASED SEA CAPTAINS FOUNDED KEY WEST, FLORIDA.

Getty Images/iStockphoto

Historical ships are preserved in Mystic, Connecticut, a pivotal colonial seaport.

Bristol

This community might not be on the radar for most travelers, but the central Connecticut town sports an impressive menu of attractions. From wine tasting to boating, Bristol can keep you and your family busy for weeks.

Lovely Lake

If you're an amusement park addict, then you need to cross this unique attraction off your bucket list. Lake Compounce is the nation's oldest continually operating amusement park, enticing both the young and old since 1846 with rides and live shows, and today it's home to the state's largest water park, Crocodile Cove. During summer, these venues swell with fun seekers. Catch the autumn breeze on the Boulder Dash, voted the world's Number One roller coaster, and stroll through the park during winter holidays for spectacular displays of lights.

Connecticut Conifers

Connecticut's wild side calls you to explore. Venture into Mattatuck State Forest, west of Bristol, and the adjacent Black Rock State Park. These well-maintained state lands are home to a variety of wildlife and are open to exploration by hikers and mountain bikers. Learn about the Legend of the Leatherman.

Mystic

The nation's dynamic nautical past is preserved in this coastal town. Mystic Seaport is one of America's top maritime museums, featuring several historical vessels and replicas that bring the seafaring olden days to life. Step onboard the *Charles W. Morgan*, the last wooden whaleship on the globe, and three other National Historic Landmark vessels. Duck into Mystic Pizza — made famous by the namesake 1988 movie starring Julia Roberts — for a slice of culinary heaven.

New Haven History

What's the deal with Connecticut and pizza? New Haven serves up its own style of pie that's as delicious as the pizza served in Mystic. But that's not the only draw to this classic New England college town. New Haven offers up historic architecture, world-class museums and easy access to Long Island Sound's tranquil shores, but that's not all. Take a tour through the campus of Yale University and see where Albert Einstein taught during his tenure at the hallowed institution.

FOR MORE INFORMATION

Connecticut Commission, 888-CT VISIT, www.ctvisit.com

Bristol, www.ci.bristol.ct.us

Greater Mystic Chamber of Commerce, 860-572-9578, www.thisismystic.com

Visit New Haven, 203-777-8550, www.visitnewhaven.com

LOCAL FAVORITE

Turkey Burgers

The humble hamburger got its start in Connecticut, with Louis' Lunch of New Haven serving up the first sandwiches way back in 1900. Give this turkey variation a try.

INGREDIENTS

- ☐ 1 lb ground turkey meat
- ☐ 1 tsp paprika
- ☐ 2 Tbsp gourmet burger seasoning
- ☐ ½ tsp pepper
- ☐ Sprinkle of salt
- ☐ 4 slices of bacon
- ☐ 4 slices of white cheddar or Swiss cheese
- ☐ 8 slices of sourdough bread
- ☐ Red onion sliced
- ☐ Tomato sliced
- ☐ Green leaf lettuce

DIRECTIONS

Combine ground turkey, paprika, gourmet burger seasoning, pepper and salt. Mix well and then form into patties.

Heat up a cast iron skillet on the grill. Put bacon in and cook each side until crispy.

While bacon is crisping up, place turkey burgers on the grill. Cook each side for 5 minutes until it has nice grill marks. Place cheese on top of the burgers and heat until melted.

When bacon is crispy, remove the cast iron skillet. Butter sourdough bread and place on the grill.

Once toasted, stack burgers with tomato, red onion and green leaf lettuce. Finish with condiments like mayonnaise, ketchup and mustard. You can also add grilled zucchini, squash and other vegetables.

CT

Connecticut

ABINGTON — B5 *Windham*

MASHAMOQUET BROOK
(Public State Park) From Jct of US-44 & SR-101, W 1.5 mi on US-44(L). **FAC:** paved/gravel rds. Avail: 53 paved, back-ins (25x35), 1 S, 1 E tent sites, dump, firewood. **REC:** pond, swim, fishing. Partial handicap access, 14 day max stay. 2021 rates: $14 to $24. Apr 25 to Sep 03. no cc.
(860)928-6121 Lat: 41.850806, Lon: -71.978972
147 Wolf Den Drive, Pomfret, CT 06259
www.ct.gov

BANTAM — B2 *Litchfield*

COZY HILLS CAMPGROUND **Ratings: 8.5/10★/9.5** (Campground) Avail: 74 full hkups (30/50 amps). 2021 rates: $62 to $72. Apr 15 to Oct 15. (860)567-2119, 1311 Bantam Rd, Bantam, CT 06750

WHITE MEMORIAL FAMILY CAMPGROUND (POINT FOLLY) (Public) From jct Hwy-63 & US-202: Go 2 mi W on Hwy-202, then 1 mi S on Bissell Rd, then .3 mi W on Whitehall Rd. 47 Avail: Pit toilets. 2021 rates: $19. (860)567-0089

BARKHAMSTED — A3 *Litchfield*

WHITE PINES CAMPSITES **Ratings: 7/7/8.5** (Campground) Avail: 113 full hkups (30/50 amps). 2021 rates: $35 to $65. Apr 14 to Oct 15. (860)379-0124, 232 Old North Rd, Barkhamsted, CT 06063

BOZRAH — C5 *New London*

ODETAH CAMPING RESORT **Ratings: 9/9.5★/10** (Campground) 150 Avail: 40 full hkups, 110 W, 110 E (30/50 amps). 2021 rates: $30 to $93. May 01 to Nov 03. (860)889-4144, 38 Bozrah St. Ext, Bozrah, CT 06334

BRISTOL — B3 *Hartford*

LAKE COMPOUNCE CAMPGROUND **Ratings: 9/10★/10** (Campground) 56 Avail: 56 W, 56 E (30/50 amps). 2021 rates: $32 to $62. May 04 to Oct 29. (860)583-3300, 185 Enterprise Drive, Bristol, CT 06010

CANAAN — A2 *Litchfield*

LONE OAK CAMPSITES **Ratings: 8/9.5★/9.5** (RV Park) 183 Avail: 117 full hkups, 66 W, 66 E (30/50 amps). 2021 rates: $72 to $90. Apr 15 to Oct 15. (800)422-2267, 360 Norfolk, East Canaan, CT 06024

CHAPLIN — B5 *Windham*

NICKERSON PARK **Ratings: 7.5/8.5/10** (Campground) 50 Avail: 20 full hkups, 30 W, 30 E (30/50 amps). 2021 rates: $45 to $60. (860)455-0007, 1036 Phoenixville Rd, Chaplin, CT 06235

CORNWALL BRIDGE — B2 *Litchfield*

HOUSATONIC MEADOWS (Public State Park) From jct Rte 4 & Rte 7: Go 2 mi N on Rte 7 (R). 57 Avail. 2021 rates: $17 to $27. May 25 to Oct 08. (860)672-6772

DAYVILLE — B6 *Windham*

HIDE-A-WAY-COVE FAMILY CAMPGROUND **Ratings: 7/6.5/7** (Campground) 90 Avail: 90 W, 90 E (20/30 amps). 2021 rates: $35. May 01 to Oct 08. (860)774-1128, 1060 North Rd, Dayville, CT 06241

EAST HADDAM — C4 *Middlesex*

DEVIL'S HOPYARD (Public State Park) From town: Go 10 mi E on SR-82 (L). 21 Avail: Pit toilets. 2021 rates: $14 to $24. Apr 15 to Sep 30. (860)526-2336

WOLF'S DEN FAMILY CAMPGROUND **Ratings: 8/10★/8.5** (Campground) 59 Avail: 59 W, 59 E (30/50 amps). 2021 rates: $52. May 03 to Oct 27. (860)873-9681, 256 Town St (Rte 82), East Haddam, CT 06423

EAST HAMPTON — C4 *Middlesex*

MARKHAM MEADOWS CAMPGROUND **Ratings: 7/5/8.5** (Campground) 70 Avail: 70 W, 70 E (30/50 amps). 2021 rates: $50. Apr 19 to Oct 14. (860)267-9738, 9 Markham Rd, East Hampton, CT 06424

NELSON'S FAMILY CAMPGROUND **Ratings: 8.5/9★/9** (Campground) 110 Avail: 22 full hkups, 88 W, 88 E (30/50 amps). 2021 rates: $62. Apr 16 to Oct 14. (860)267-5300, 71 Mott Hill Rd, East Hampton, CT 06424

EAST KILLINGLY — B6 *Windham*

STATELINE CAMPRESORT & CABINS
good sam park **Ratings: 8.5/9.5★/9.5** (RV Park) From Jct of I 395 & Rte 101 (Exit 93), E 5 mi on Rte 101 (R).

LOCATED ON THE CT AND RI STATE LINE
Centrally located near Federal Hill, Newport and the Water Fires in Providence, RI. Come explore CT wine trails. Forested, family friendly place with a great pool & planned activities for adults and kids to enjoy.
FAC: paved/gravel rds. (235 spaces). Avail: 50 gravel, back-ins (32x43), 50 full hkups (30/50 amps), seasonal sites, cable, WiFi @ sites, rentals, dump, mobile sewer, laundry, groc, LP gas, fire rings, firewood, controlled access. **REC:** pool, Campground Lake: fishing, boating nearby, playground. Pet restrict (B/Q) $. No tents. 2021 rates: $58 to $83, Military discount. Apr 15 to Oct 15. ATM.
(860)774-3016 Lat: 41.84802, Lon: -71.79518
1639 Hartford Pike, East Killingly, CT 06243
statelinecampresort.com
See ad this page

EAST LYME — D5 *New London*

ACES HIGH RV PARK **Ratings: 10/9.5/10** (RV Park) Avail: 61 full hkups (30/50 amps). 2021 rates: $70 to $82. (860)739-8858, 301 Chesterfield Road, East Lyme, CT 06333

EASTFORD — A5 *Windham*

CHARLIE BROWN CAMPGROUND **Ratings: 8/9★/10** (Campground) 50 Avail: 14 full hkups, 36 W, 36 E (30/50 amps). 2021 rates: $49.50 to $69. Apr 15 to Oct 13. (860)974-0142, 98 Chaplin Rd, Rte 198, Eastford, CT 06242

PEPPERTREE CAMPING **Ratings: 7/7.5/9** (Campground) 40 Avail: 18 full hkups, 22 W, 22 E (30 amps). 2021 rates: $45 to $65. Apr 01 to Oct 13. (860)974-1439, 146 Chaplin Rd, Eastford, CT 06242

GRISWOLD — C6 *New London*

COUNTRYSIDE RV PARK **Ratings: 8.5/8.5★/9.5** (Campground) Avail: 54 full hkups (30/50 amps). 2021 rates: $60. May 01 to Oct 14. (860)376-0029, 75 Cook Hill Rd, Griswold, CT 06351

HARTFORD — B3 *Hartford*

HARTFORD See also Barkhamsted, Bristol, East Hampton, Higganum, Lebanon, Moodus, Plymouth, Stafford Springs, Thomaston & Willington, CT; Granville, MA.

HIGGANUM — C4 *Middlesex*

LITTLE CITY CAMPGROUND **Ratings: 5.5/6/5.5** (RV Park) 25 Avail: 7 full hkups, 18 W, 18 E (30/50 amps). 2021 rates: $38 to $42. May 01 to Oct 01. (860)345-8469, 733 Little City Rd, Higganum, CT 06441

JEWETT CITY — C5 *New London*

CAMPERS WORLD ON HOPEVILLE POND
good sam park **Ratings: 7.5/8/7** (RV Park) From jct I-395 Hwy 201: Go 1/2 mi E on Hopeville Rd, then 1 mi S on Bishop Crossing Rd, then 1 mi SE on Nowakowski Rd (E).
FAC: all weather rds. (90 spaces). Avail: 15 dirt, 3 pull-thrus, (50x50), back-ins (50x50), accepts full hkup units only, 15 full hkups (30/50 amps), seasonal sites, cable, WiFi @ sites, tent sites, shower$, dump, laundry, fire rings, firewood, controlled access. **REC:** pond, swim, kayaking/canoeing, boating nearby, playground, hunting nearby. Pet restrict (Q). Partial handicap access, eco-friendly. 2021 rates: $62.
(860)245-1882 Lat: 41.608559, Lon: -71.938575
28 Nowakowski Rd, Jewett City, CT 06351
campersworldcampground.com
See ad this page

HOPEVILLE POND (Public State Park) From I-395: Take Exit 86, from N, Go (L) From S, Go (R); Follow Hopeville Rd to Y intersection, Proceed to (R). Entrance is 1/2 Mile on (R), Off Rte 201. 80 Avail: (15 amps). 2021 rates: $17 to $27. May 25 to Sep 30. (860)376-0313

KENT — B1 *Litchfield*

MACEDONIA BROOK (Public State Park) From Jct of US-7 & SR-341, NW 2 mi on SR-341 to Macedonia Brook Rd, N 2 mi (R). Note: Alcohol-free campground. 46 Avail: Pit toilets. 2021 rates: $14 to $24. Apr 13 to Sep 03. (860)927-4100

LEBANON — C5 *New London*

WATER'S EDGE **Ratings: 8/7.5/8.5** (Campground) 72 Avail: 72 W, 72 E (20/30 amps). 2021 rates: $49 to $63. Apr 15 to Oct 15. (860)642-7470, 271 Leonard Bridge Rd, Lebanon, CT 06249

RV Tech Tips - You Screen, I Screen, We All Screen: Like the screen door of many coaches, opening your door from the inside requires sliding a plastic panel to access and pull the spring-loaded handle. This can be very inconvenient at times, especially when carrying something. To eliminate the sliding of the panel and make it easier to unlock the handle, attach a nylon cord between the handle and the hinged edge of the door. After drilling a small hole in the handle, wind the cord through the hole and tie it to the handle. The other end of the cord is attached to a screw along the edge of the screen door. The string can be easily pulled down to open the door handle from inside or outside without ever needing to slide the plastic and pull the handle.

LISBON — C5 *New London*

ROSS HILL PARK **Ratings: 6.5/5.5/8.5** (Campground) 108 Avail: 20 full hkups, 88 W, 88 E (30/50 amps). 2021 rates: $50 to $59. Apr 19 to Oct 27. (860)376-9606, 170 Ross Hill Rd, Lisbon, CT 06351

SUNFOX CAMPGROUND **Ratings: 8/9★/10** (Campground) 29 Avail: 4 full hkups, 25 W, 25 E (30 amps). 2021 rates: $39 to $79. Apr 01 to Oct 31. (860)376-1081, 15 Kenyon Rd, Lisbon, CT 06351

LITCHFIELD — B2 *Litchfield*

HEMLOCK HILL CAMP-RESORT COOPERATIVE **Ratings: 7/8/6** (Campground) Avail: 40 full hkups (30/50 amps). 2021 rates: $50 to $56. Apr 25 to Oct 18. (860)361-6888, 118 Hemlock Hill Rd, Litchfield, CT 06759

MADISON — D4 *New Haven*

HAMMONASSET BEACH (Public State Park) From jct I-95 & Hammonasset Connecter (exit 62): Go 1/2 mi S on Hammonasset Connecter (E). 552 Avail. 2021 rates: $20 to $45. May 25 to Oct 08. (203)245-1817

MOODUS — C4 *Middlesex*

GRANDVIEW CAMPING RESORT **Ratings: 7/9.5★/9.5** (Campground) 45 Avail: 23 full hkups, 22 W, 22 E (30/50 amps). 2021 rates: $54 to $64. Apr 15 to Oct 31. (860)873-3332, 89 North Moodus Rd, Moodus, CT 06469

MYSTIC — D5 *New London*

SEAPORT RV RESORT & CAMPGROUND **Ratings: 8.5/10★/9.5** (Campground) 101 Avail: 101 W, 101 E (30/50 amps). 2021 rates: $59 to $110. Apr 15 to Oct 15. (888)472-4189, 45 Camp Ground Road, Old Mystic, CT 06372

NEW PRESTON — B2 *Litchfield*

LAKE WARAMAUG (Public State Park) From town, NW 3 mi on Hwy 45 to North Shore Rd, W 5 mi (R). 70 Avail. 2021 rates: $17 to $27. May 25 to Sep 03. (860)868-0220

Things change ... last year's rates serve as a guideline only.

NIANTIC — D5 *New London*

ROCKY NECK (Public State Park) From Jct of I-95 & Rte 156 (exit 72), S 0.5 mi on Rte 156, E .25 mi (R). 160 Avail. 2021 rates: $20 to $30. May 25 to Sep 30. (860)739-1339

NORTH STONINGTON — C6 *New London*

MYSTIC KOA **Ratings: 8/9.5/10** (Campground) 200 Avail: 69 full hkups, 131 W, 131 E (30/50 amps). 2021 rates: $87 to $115. (800)562-3451, 118 Pendleton Hill Rd, North Stonington, CT 06359

NORWICH — C5 *New London*

ACORN ACRES **Ratings: 8.5/8/8.5** (Campground) 60 Avail: 20 full hkups, 40 W, 40 E (30/50 amps). 2021 rates: $55 to $70. Apr 12 to Oct 14. (860)859-1020, 135 Lake Rd, Bozrah, CT 06334

ONECO — B6 *Windham*

RIVER BEND CAMPGROUND **Ratings: 8/10★/9** (Campground) 125 Avail: 25 full hkups, 100 W, 100 E (30/50 amps). 2021 rates: $41 to $53. Apr 19 to Oct 14. (860)564-3440, 41 Pond St, Oneco, CT 06373

PLEASANT VALLEY — A3 *Litchfield*

AMERICAN LEGION/AUSTIN HAWES CAMPGROUND (Public) From jct Rte 8 & 44: Go 1/2 mi E on Rte 44, then 1 mi E on Rte 318, then 2 mi N on W Center Hill Rd (R). 30 Avail. 2021 rates: $17 to $27. Apr 12 to Oct 13. (860)379-0922

PLYMOUTH — B3 *Litchfield*

GENTILE'S CAMPGROUND

good sam park **Ratings: 8/10★/8.5** (Campground) From jct US 6 & CT Hwy 8: Go 3 mi S on CT Hwy 8 (exit 37), then 1/4 mi E on Echo Lake Road, then 3/4 mi S on Hwy 262, then 2 mi E on Spruce Brook Road (R). **FAC:** all weather rds. (120 spaces). Avail: 105 all weather, 2 pull-thrus, (30x80), back-ins (30x40), 75 full hkups, 30 W, 30 E (30/50 amps), seasonal sites, WiFi @ sites, tent sites, shower$, dump, LP gas, fire rings, controlled access. **REC:** pool, boating nearby, playground, hunting nearby. Pet restrict (B/Q). 2021 rates: $50 to $53, Military discount. ATM, no cc.
(860)283-8437 Lat: 41.6294076, Lon: -73.048408
223 Mount Tobe Rd. (Rt 262), Plymouth, CT 06782
gentilescampground.com
See ad this page

PRESTON — C5 *New London*

HIDDEN ACRES FAMILY CAMPGROUND

good sam park **Ratings: 8.5/10★/10** (Campground) 73 Avail: 28 full hkups, 37 W, 37 E (30/50 amps). 2021 rates: $62 to $72. May 01 to Oct 10. (860)887-9633, 47 River Rd, Preston, CT 06365

STRAWBERRY PARK RV RESORT **Ratings: 7.5/10★/10** (Campground) 300 Avail: 162 full hkups, 138 W, 138 E (30/50 amps). 2021 rates: $47 to $110. May 01 to Oct 23. (860)886-1944, 42 Pierce Rd., Preston, CT 06365

SALEM — C5 *New London*

SALEM FARMS CAMPGROUND

good sam park **Ratings: 9/10★/9.5** (Campground) 59 Avail: 59 W, 59 E (30/50 amps). 2021 rates: $55 to $59. May 01 to Oct 14. (860)859-2320, 39 Alexander Rd, Salem, CT 06420

WITCH MEADOW LAKE FAMILY CAMPGROUND **Ratings: 9/10★/10** (Campground) Avail: 80 full hkups (30/50 amps). 2021 rates: $54 to $64. May 01 to Oct 13. (860)859-1542, 139 Witch Meadow Rd, Salem, CT 06420

SOUTHBURY — C2 *Fairfield*

KETTLETOWN (Public State Park) From Jct of I-84 & SR-67, E 0.1 mi on SR-67 to Kettletown Rd, S 3.5 mi to Georges Hill Rd, W 0.75 mi (L).From Labor Day to Memorial Day, campground is open weekends only. No rigs over 28 ft long. 61 Avail: 1 W, 1 E. 2021 rates: $17 to $27. May 24 to Sep 01. (203)264-5678

STAFFORD SPRINGS — A4 *Tolland*

MINERAL SPRINGS FAMILY CAMPGROUND **Ratings: 7/8.5/7.5** (Campground) 94 Avail: 15 full hkups, 79 W, 79 E (20/30 amps). 2021 rates: $50 to $57. May 01 to Oct 15. (860)684-2993, 135 Leonard Rd, Stafford Springs, CT 06076

Clean Green! Vinegar and baking soda can be used to clean almost anything. Mix in a little warm water with either of these and you've got yourself an all-purpose cleaner.

THOMASTON — B2 *Litchfield*

BLACK ROCK (Public State Park) From jct I-84 & Rte 8N (exit 38): Go 10 mi N on Rte 8N, then 1/2 mi W on Rte 6W (R). 96 Avail. 2021 rates: $17 to $27. Apr 15 to Sep 30. (860)283-8088

BRANCH BROOK CAMPGROUND

good sam park **Ratings: 9.5/9★/9.5** (Campground) S-bnd: From Jct of Rtes 8 & 6W (exit 38 in Thomaston), W 0.8 mi on Rte 6W (L) or N-bnd: From Jct of Rtes 8 & 6W (Exit 38) L (N) 0.4 mi on Waterbury Rd to Watertown Rd (US 6), W 0.8 mi (L). **FAC:** all weather rds. (71 spaces). 58 Avail: 26 gravel, 32 grass, 1 pull-thrus, (28x60), back-ins (28x42), 58 full hkups (30/50 amps), seasonal sites, cable, WiFi @ sites, tent sites, rentals, laundry, LP gas, fire rings, firewood. **REC:** pool, Branch Brook: fishing, boating nearby, hunting nearby. Pets OK. Big rig sites. 2021 rates: $60. Apr 01 to Nov 01. no cc.
(860)283-8144 Lat: 41.65469, Lon: -73.09328
435 Watertown Rd, Thomaston, CT 06787
branchbrookcampgroundct.com
See ad this page

CT

THOMPSON — A6 *Windham*

WEST THOMPSON LAKE - COE/WEST THOMPSON LAKE (Public Corps) From jct I-395 (exit 99) & Hwy 200: Go 1 mi W on Hwy 200 to Thompson Center, then 2 mi S on Hwy 193, straight across Hwy 12 at traffic light, then 1/4 mi W on Reardon Rd to Campground Rd. 22 Avail: 11 W, 11 E. 2021 rates: $15 to $30. May 15 to Sep 12. (860)923-3121

VOLUNTOWN — C6 *New London*

CIRCLE C CAMPGROUND **Ratings: 7.5/7.5/7.5** (Campground) 76 Avail: 70 W, 70 E (30/50 amps). 2021 rates: $43 to $60. Apr 15 to Oct 14. (860)564-4534, 21 Bailey Pond Rd, Voluntown, CT 06384

NATURES CAMPSITES

good sam park **Ratings: 7.5/10★/10** (Campground) 114 Avail: 37 full hkups, 36 W, 36 E (30/50 amps). 2021 rates: $50 to $70. May 01 to Oct 15. (860)376-4203, 96 Ekonk Hill Rd, Voluntown, CT 06384

PACHAUG/GREEN FALLS CAMPGROUND (Public State Park) From town, E 2.5 mi on Rte-138 to Forest Park Rd, S 2.5 mi (R). 18 Avail: Pit toilets. 2021 rates: $17 to $27. Apr 13 to Sep 03. (860)376-4075

PACHAUG/MOUNT MISERY (Public State Park) From town, N 0.6 mi on Rte 49 (L). 22 Avail: Pit toilets. 2021 rates: $17 to $27. Apr 13 to Sep 03. (860)376-4075

WILLINGTON — A5 *Tolland*

MOOSE MEADOW **Ratings: 8/10★/9** (Campground) 94 Avail: 42 full hkups, 52 W, 52 E (30/50 amps). 2021 rates: $40 to $62. Apr 19 to Oct 13. (860)429-7451, 28 Kechkes Rd, W Willington, CT 06279

WILDERNESS LAKE PARK **Ratings: 6.5/8/7.5** (Campground) 30 Avail: 30 W, 30 E (30/50 amps). 2021 rates: $60. Apr 01 to Nov 20. (860)684-6352, 150 Village Hill Rd, Willington, CT 06279

good sam
Extended Service Plan

You make the priceless memories. We'll pay for the pricey repair bills.

We know that time spent traveling with your family is precious. When your RV needs a mechanical repair, let us pick up the bill, so that you can get back on the road and back to spending time with your family.

Program Benefits:

- No waiting for reimbursement, we pay the shop directly.
- Take your vehicle to the repair shop of your choice.
- Choose the deductible and payment schedule that works for you, and lock in your rate for up to 3 years.
- Trip Interruption: If your RV is not usable due to a covered loss, we'll help cover costs for meals and lodging for $100 a day, for up to 5 days per repair visit.
- Rental Car Reimbursement: If you can't drive your vehicle due to a covered loss, we'll help cover costs for a rental car for $60 a day, for up to 5 days per repair visit.

Rental car benefit is not available on 5th wheel and travel trailer coverage.

Visit **GoodSamESP.com/Guide**

Call **866-601-2317**

To qualify, towable RVs must be 15 model years or newer. Cars, trucks, SUVs, and gas Motorhomes must be 15 model years or newer with less than 100,000 miles, and rear engine diesel Motorhomes must be 15 model years or newer with less than 120,000 miles. Coverage is renewable up to 18 model years or 150,000 miles. All program benefits are subject to limitations set forth in the current Terms & Conditions.

The Good Sam Extended Service Plan is not available to residents of New York or Indiana. If you are a resident of New York or Indiana, please call 1-866-524-7842 as other products may be available to you.

The Good Sam Extended Service Plan, which was designed for Good Sam by Affinity Brokerage, LLC, a Colorado surplus lines brokerage (Lic. #185640), is available exclusively for active members of Good Sam. Membership is required for eligibility in this program. Termination of your membership in Good Sam during the policy period may result in termination of The Good Sam Extended Service Plan. The cost of Good Sam Membership is the responsibility of the certificate holder and will be available at the then current rate. The Good Sam Extended Service Plan is available to U.S. residents only.

YOU ARE HERE

Delaware

Getty Images/iStockphoto

DID YOU KNOW?

Reggae legend Bob Marley worked at the Chrysler plant in Wilmington before his music career took off.

DE

Don't let Delaware's diminutive size fool you. With ample coastlines and fun-filled cities, you won't run out of stuff to do. Start by exploring the banks of the Delaware Bay and River, which extends the fun deep into the state.

Summer Fun

The beach beckons in the First State. The coastal resort town of Rehoboth Beach has a classic boardwalk. Colorful carnival rides spin and undulate through the air, as game barkers call out for your chance to win the big prize. All of that contrasts the serenity found in a sunset stroll along the beach. Shopping malls, craft breweries, upscale restaurants and plenty of nature trails ensure you'll stay busy in "The Nation's Summer Capital."

Brandywine Beauty

Head inland to experience Delaware's lush Brandywine Valley. Once a farm owned by the renowned du Pont family, Brandywine Creek State Park offers charm in spades. Stone walls dating to the 1800s give the park an otherworldly European feel. Get lost in the woods of the old-growth Tulip Poplar forest or hit one of the 14 miles of trails. Two creeks snake through the park, providing anglers a chance to catch trout, bass and bluegill.

Bye, Bye City, Hello Beach

Delaware has cemented its cred among summer vacationers seeking to escape East Coast cities, thanks to its many miles of beaches. Try Cape Henlopen State Park, which has been preserved for public use. Today's visitors come to see the historic lighthouse and to enjoy recreation in the water.

Break a Sweat at Breakwater

Bike or hike the Junction Breakwater Trail, which runs for five miles between Rehoboth Beach and Lewes. This pathway passes by marshlands and through woodlands and is worth the effort.

Delaware Peach Pie

Peaches were brought to Delaware in colonial times and have become a key part of the region's agricultural heritage. The sweet fruit is so important that the peach pie was recognized as the official state dessert in 2009. Make your own pie with the last peaches of summer or treat yourself to a slice at Fifer Orchards Farm and Markets in Camden-Wyoming and Dewey Beach.

VISITOR CENTER

TIME ZONE
Eastern Standard

ROAD & HIGHWAY INFORMATION
800-652-5600
deldot.gov

FISHING & HUNTING INFORMATION
302-739-9918
alpha.delaware.gov/guides/recreation

BOATING INFORMATION
302-739-9916
dnrec.alpha.delaware.gov/fw/boating

NATIONAL PARKS
nps.gov/de

STATE PARKS
destateparks.com

TOURISM INFORMATION
Delaware Tourism
866-284-7483
visitdelaware.com

TOP TOURISM ATTRACTIONS
1) Rehoboth Beach
2) Dover International Speedway
3) Cape Henlopen State Park

MAJOR CITIES
Wilmington, Dover (capital), Newark, Middletown, Bear

good sam park Featured Good Sam Parks

DELAWARE

When you stay with Good Sam, you can expect the highest degree of cleanliness and friendliness, and better yet, you get **10% off** overnight campground fees.

If you're not already a Good Sam member you can purchase your membership at one of these locations:

LINCOLN
Yogi Bear's Jellystone Park At Delaware Beach

MILLSBORO
Holly Lake Campsites
Massey's Landing

Getty Images/iStockphoto

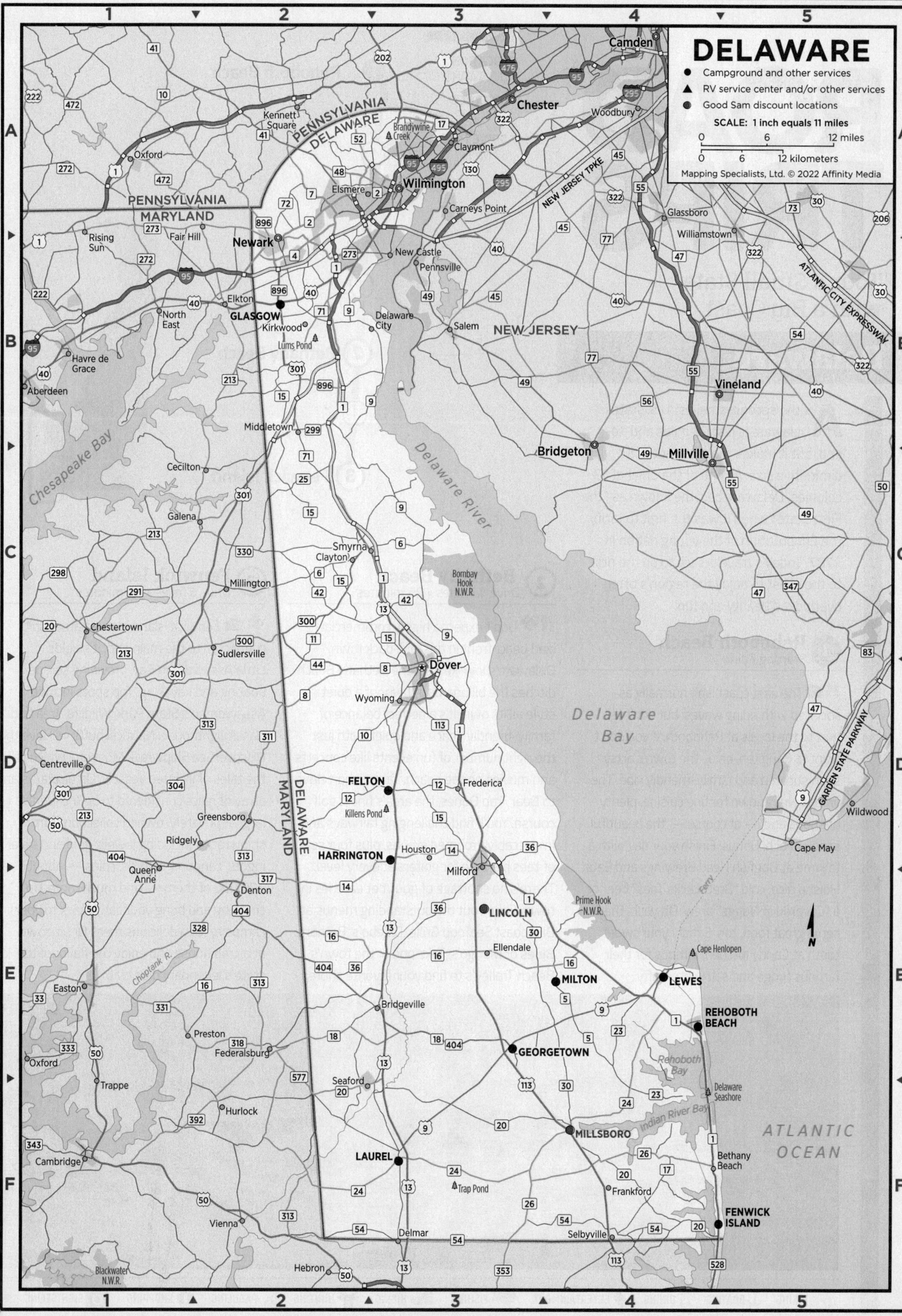
DELAWARE
Campground and other services
RV service center and/or other services
Good Sam discount locations
SCALE: 1 inch equals 11 miles
0 6 12 miles
0 6 12 kilometers
Mapping Specialists, Ltd. © 2022 Affinity Media
PENNSYLVANIA
DELAWARE
MARYLAND
NEW JERSEY
Camden
Chester
Woodbury
Kennett Square
Brandywine Creek
Claymont
Oxford
Wilmington
Elsmere
Carneys Point
NEW JERSEY TPKE
Glassboro
Williamstown
ATLANTIC CITY EXPRESSWAY
Rising Sun
Fair Hill
Newark
New Castle
Pennsville
Elkton
GLASGOW
Kirkwood
Delaware City
Salem
North East
Lums Pond
Havre de Grace
Aberdeen
Vineland
Middletown
Bridgeton
Millville
Chesapeake Bay
Cecilton
Delaware River
Galena
Smyrna
Clayton
Bombay Hook N.W.R.
Millington
Chestertown
Sudlersville
Dover
Wyoming
Delaware Bay
GARDEN STATE PARKWAY
Centreville
FELTON
Frederica
Killens Pond
Wildwood
Greensboro
Ridgely
Houston
HARRINGTON
Cape May
Queen Anne
Milford
Denton
Prime Hook N.W.R.
Ferry
LINCOLN
Ellendale
Cape Henlopen
Choptank R.
MILTON
LEWES
Easton
Bridgeville
REHOBOTH BEACH
Preston
Federalsburg
GEORGETOWN
Rehoboth Bay
Oxford
Trappe
Seaford
Delaware Seashore
Hurlock
Indian River Bay
MILLSBORO
ATLANTIC OCEAN
Cambridge
LAUREL
Bethany Beach
Trap Pond
Frankford
FENWICK ISLAND
Vienna
Delmar
Selbyville
Hebron
Blackwater N.W.R.
N
DE

ROAD TRIPS

Tour a Small State with a Big Coast

Delaware

As the second-smallest U.S. state, Delaware is just 96 miles end-to-end, but it makes the most out of its diminutive size. As one of the original 13 colonies, Delaware became known as "the First State" when it was the first to ratify the Constitution of the young nation in 1787. Today's travelers vie to be the first to the coast to enjoy the region's often-overlooked beauty and fun.

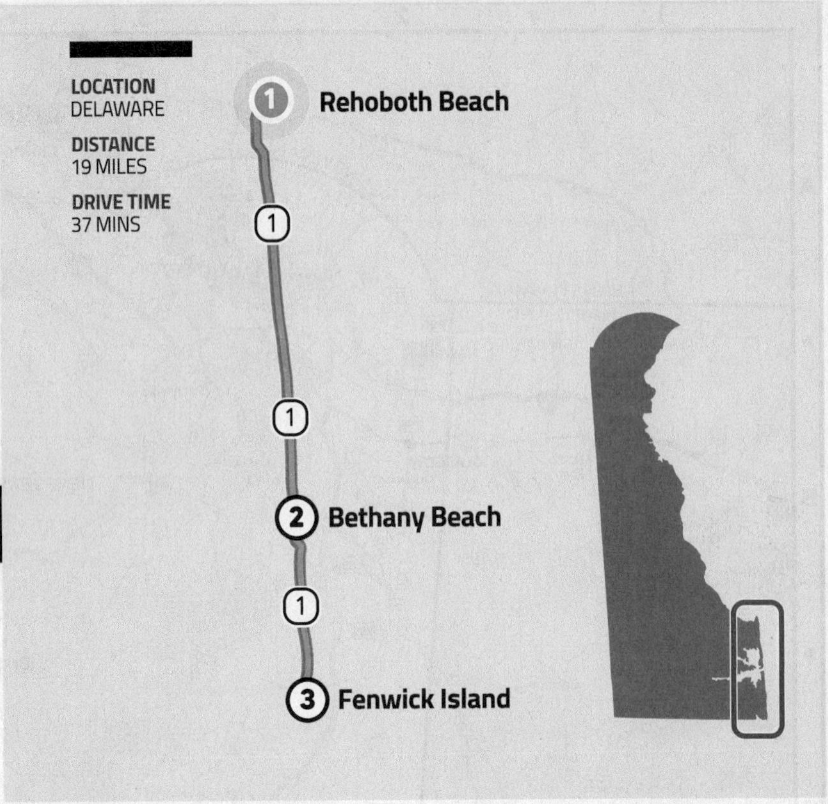

1 Rehoboth Beach
Starting Point

The east coast isn't normally associated with riding waves, but don't tell that to the locals at Rehoboth. If you don't want to hang ten, enjoy the town's artsy, sophisticated and family-friendly vibe. The area is well known for fine cuisine, plenty of shops and — of course — the beautiful sandy beach. Bonus: Finish your day with a tall one at Dogfish Head Brewings and Eats. Hoist a nice, cold "Brett Lacks Toes" beer or a "Covered in Nuggs" brew. Oh yeah, they serve great food, too. Satisfy your sweet tooth at Candy Kitchen, famous for their famous fudge and salt-water taffy.

2 Bethany Beach
Drive 13 miles ▪ 25 minutes

Don't expect a highly commercialized beachfront in this laid-back town. Delaware's low-key, serene Bethany Beach ditches the billboards in favor of a quiet style all its own. It's a perfect balance of family-friendly peace and quiet, with just the right number of fun events like concerts and movies on the beach. Take a short drive to Bear Trap Dunes, the area's finest golf course. You'll find challenging fairways and impeccably groomed greens, plus four sets of tees per hole for golfers at every level. There's no shortage of gourmet eateries in town. Check out the outstanding menus at Bluecoast Seafood Grille, DiFebo's, Bethany Blues or Mango's. Take one of the town's Beach Trolley's to find your favorite shore.

3 Fenwick Island
Drive 6 miles ▪ 12 minutes

Fenwick Island is on a barrier spit connected to the mainland. It shields Little Assawoman Bay, providing serene boating and kayaking. Top spots include Assawoman's State Park, Wildlife Area and classic lighthouse. Nautical buffs will love the DiscoverSea Shipwreck Museum, which tells the tales of ill-fated vessels. On display is an array of relics considered to be the world's largest privately-owned collection from shipwrecks, including jewels, gold and silver ingots, cannons, swords, coins — about 200,000 of them — and much more. Go crabbing and bring your catch back to your campsite for a delicious meal. Or sit down at a crab house and enjoy the flavor of the state's legendary blue crab.

Getty Images/iStockphoto

BIKING BOATING DINING ENTERTAINMENT FISHING HIKING HUNTING PADDLING SHOPPING SIGHTSEEING

Delaware SPOTLIGHTS

Experience Adventure on the Atlantic Shore

Consider Delaware for your next Atlantic getaway. The state has hundreds of miles of Atlantic shoreline, a famous NASCAR track and several natural attractions. Find a spot to catch some waves or dine at a crab shack for delicious Maryland crustaceans.

A BELL FROM A REVOLUTIONARY WARSHIP IS DISPLAYED IN DOVER.

Delaware's First State Heritage Park preserves structures from the 1700s.

Getty Images/iStockphoto

Dover

Dover's tree-lined streets echo with the history that shaped the 330-year-old city. Whether exploring the cultural sites of First State Heritage Park or the wild tidal marshes of Bombay Hook National Wildlife Refuge, it's easy to step back to simpler times with a visit to this capital city. Walk in teh footsteps of Revolutionary War leaders.

First State Icons

Begin your time travel at the First State Heritage Park, with 19 different historic sites within a few blocks. Start with a visit to the Old State House, originally built in 1791, before admiring the stunning collections at the Biggs Museum of American Art and the John Bell House, which offers interactive tours of the city Green. On display is a bell from the *USS Delaware*, a Revolutionary War frigate.

Pond of Plenty

Less than half an hour to the south, Killens Pond State Park is a picturesque retreat perfect for day-tripping families. Home to bass, catfish, crappie and more, the park's 66-acre pond will keep anglers happy.

Rehoboth Beach

Hit the beach in the coastal city of Rehoboth. Better known as Rehoboth Beach, the coastal playground offers year-round attractions and activities for vacationers.

Boardwalk This Way

Rehoboth's mile-long wooden boardwalk leads visitors to quirky shops and laidback crab shacks that serve up steaming crustaceans. Catch the Rehoboth Beach Bandstand Summer Concert Series, a free event that's been held since 1963 and draws more than 50 bands to perform in the open-air concert venue on weekend evenings.

Sussex County

Immerse yourself in sprawling countryside away from the hustle and bustle of the big cities. Stretching from the Atlantic Coast inland to Maryland, Sussex County fills much of southern Delaware. Whether you want to relax with your toes in the sand or actively explore ruggedly beautiful landscapes, Sussex County has a place for you.

DE

FOR MORE INFORMATION

Visit Delaware, 866-284-7483, www.visitdelaware.com

Dover Attractions, www.visitdelaware.com/cities-regions/dover/attractions

Rehoboth Beach, 302-245-0304

Visit Southern Delaware (Sussex) 800-357-1818, visitsoutherndelaware.com

LOCAL FAVORITE

Caribbean Crockpot

Snag some fresh Delaware seafood and throw it into a crockpot for an exotic and flavorful meal. Bring a taste of the tropics to the Mid-Atlantic region. *Recipe by Jay and Robin Fogle.*

INGREDIENTS

- ☐ 1 fresh lime
- ☐ 4 servings of either chicken, pork, beef, fish, or shrimp, clams and scallops
- ☐ 1 bunch fresh parsley
- ☐ 1 each green, yellow, orange, red bell peppers, seeds and stems removed
- ☐ Lemon pepper seasoning, to taste
- ☐ 1 box chicken broth bouillon cubes or 1 box chicken stock
- ☐ 10 oz can tomato paste
- ☐ Salt and pepper, to taste
- ☐ Seasoning salt, to taste
- ☐ 1 clove garlic minced

DIRECTIONS

Drench your protein in lime juice. Place in the crockpot. Chop parsley. Place the bell peppers, garlic, season salt, lemon pepper and black pepper into a food processor and medium chop. Mix tomato paste, processed peppers and parsley. Pour over your choice of protein. Cook on medium in the slow cooker for 2-3 hours until meat is tender.

Delaware

FELTON — D3 *Kent*

KILLENS POND

(Public State Park) From Jct of US-13 & SR-12, S 2.4 mi on US-13 to Paradise Alley Rd, E 1.7 mi (L). **FAC:** paved/gravel rds. Avail: 59 gravel, back-ins (24x38), 59 W, 59 E (30 amps), tent sites, rentals, dump, laundry, groc, fire rings, firewood. **REC:** pool, wading pool, pond, fishing, kayaking/canoeing, shuffleboard, playground. Pets OK. Partial handicap access, 14 day max stay. 2021 rates: $20 to $37. Mar 01 to Nov 30.
(302)284-4526 Lat: 38.986929, Lon: -75.542342
5025 Killens Pond Rd, Felton, DE 19943
www.destateparks.com

FENWICK ISLAND — F4 *Sussex*

TREASURE BEACH RV PARK **Ratings: 8.5/8★/8.5** (RV Park) Avail: 326 full hkups (30/50 amps). 2021 rates: $95 to $150. Apr 15 to Oct 31. (302)436-8001, 37291 Lighthouse Rd, Selbyville, DE 19975

GEORGETOWN — E3 *Sussex*

HOMESTEAD CAMPGROUND **Ratings: 8.5/9★/10** (Campground) Avail: 39 full hkups (30/50 amps). 2021 rates: $75 to $90. May 01 to Sep 30. (302)684-4278, 25165 Prettyman Rd, Georgetown, DE 19947

GLASGOW — B2 *New Castle*

LUMS POND (Public State Park) From Glasgow (I-95 exit 1A): Go 3 mi S on SR-896, then 2 mi N on SR-71 (L). Avail: 64 full hkups (30/50 amps). 2021 rates: $20 to $45. (302)368-6989

Save 10% at Good Sam Parks 365 days a year with no blackout dates!!

Delaware Privately Owned Campground Information Updated by our Good Sam Representatives

James & Mary Margrave

We've been involved in the RV lifestyle for over 20 years, and for the past 5 years or so, we've done it full time. We love being around our fellow RVers, who are great people. And we love seeing the great variety in the parks on our travels.

HARRINGTON — D3 *Kent*

G & R CAMPGROUND **Ratings: 7/7.5/8** (Campground) 240 Avail: 54 full hkups, 186 W, 186 E (30/50 amps). 2021 rates: $45 to $60. (302)398-8108, 4075 Gun & Rod Club Rd, Houston, DE 19954

LAUREL — F3 *Sussex*

TRAP POND (Public State Park) From Jct of US-13 & SR-24, E 4.7 mi on SR-24 to CR-450, S 0.8 mi (L). 137 Avail: 137 W, 137 E (30/50 amps). 2021 rates: $20 to $37. (302)875-2392

LEWES — E4 *Sussex*

CAPE HENLOPEN (Public State Park) From town: Go 1 mi E on US-9, follow signs (E). 120 Avail: 120 W, 120 E (30/50 amps). 2021 rates: $25 to $59. (302)645-8983

TALL PINES CAMPGROUND RESORT **Ratings: 9/9★/9.5** (RV Park) 22 Avail: 22 W, 22 E (50 amps). 2021 rates: $59 to $70. (302)684-0300, 29551 Persimmon Rd, Lewes, DE 19958

LINCOLN — E3 *Sussex*

YOGI BEAR'S JELLYSTONE PARK AT DELAWARE BEACH

good sam park

Ratings: 9/9.5★/9.5 (Campground) Avail: 229 full hkups (30/50 amps). 2021 rates: $55 to $159. Apr 01 to Oct 31. (302)491-6614, 8295 Brick Granary Rd, Lincoln, DE 19960

MILLSBORO — F4 *Sussex*

HOLLY LAKE CAMPSITES

good sam park

Ratings: 8/8.5★/8.5 (Campground) 620 Avail: 420 full hkups, 200 W, 200 E (30/50 amps). 2021 rates: $60 to $70. (800)227-7170, 32087 Holly Lake Road, Millsboro, DE 19966

LIGHTHOUSE BEACH RV RESORT **Ratings: 9.5/10★/9.5** (RV Park) Avail: 9 full hkups (30/50 amps). 2021 rates: $75 to $95. Apr 01 to Oct 31. (302)515-2300, 26162 Bay Blvd, Millsboro, DE 19966

MASSEY'S LANDING

good sam park

Ratings: 9.5/10★/9.5 (RV Resort) From Jct of US 113 and Hwy 24, S on Hwy 113 to Jct of Hwy 113 & Rt 24, N 8.0 mi on Rt 24 to Jct of Rt 24 & Long Neck Rd, E 3.0 mi on Long Neck Rd (L).

LUXURY IS IN SITE
A luxury RV resort in the heart of the DE Seashore. Beachfront RV and tent sites redefine camping as you know it. Pampered with the luxury you have come to expect. The Resort at Massey's Landing...Your choice, our pleasure.

FAC: paved rds. 254 Avail: 53 paved, 201 gravel, patios, 7 pull-thrus, (40x90), back-ins (35x55), 254 full hkups (30/50 amps), cable, WiFi @ sites, tent sites, rentals, laundry, groc, LP bottles, fire rings, firewood, restaurant, controlled access. **REC:** heated pool, Roman Pond: swim, fishing, kayaking/canoeing, boating nearby, playground, hunting nearby. Pets OK. Partial handicap access. Big rig sites, eco-friendly. 2021 rates: $61 to $259, Military discount. Mar 30 to Oct 31. ATM.
(302)947-2600 Lat: 38.625340, Lon: -75.103807
20628 Long Beach Drive, Millsboro, DE 19966
www.masseyslanding.com
See ad this page

OFF SEASON RVING TIP: Find out which campground sections are open. With fewer campers to contend with, many campgrounds limit off-season camping to a smaller area of the campground. You may find your favorite area off-limits or without hookups.

MILTON — E4 *Sussex*

BRUMBLEY'S FAMILY PARK **Ratings: 4/6.5/6** (RV Park) Avail: 10 full hkups (30/50 amps). 2021 rates: $65. (302)684-5189, 25601 Amy's Lane, Milton, DE 19968

REHOBOTH BEACH — E4 *Sussex*

BIG OAKS FAMILY CAMPGROUND Ratings: 9.5/10★/9.5 (Campground) Avail: 45 full hkups (30/50 amps). 2021 rates: $57 to $74. May 01 to Oct 01. (302)645-6838, 35567 Big Oaks Lane, Rehoboth Beach, DE 19971

DELAWARE SEASHORE (Public State Park) From Jct SR-24 and SR-1, S 10.2 mi on SR-1 to Entrance on S side of Indian River Inlet (R). Avail: 239 full hkups (30/50 amps). 2021 rates: $20 to $55. (302)227-2800

SEA AIR VILLAGE MANUFACTURED HOME & RV RESORT **Ratings: 8.5/8.5/9** (RV Area in MH Park) Avail: 7 full hkups (30/50 amps). 2021 rates: $70 to $75. Apr 15 to Nov 15. (888)465-8909, 19837 Sea Air Ave., Rehoboth Beach, DE 19971

Know The Rules Of The Road!

Our Rules of the Road table shows you RV-related laws in every state and province. Also in this section is a roundup of bridge and tunnel restrictions.

Find the Rules in the front of this Guide.

YOU ARE HERE

District of Columbia

Getty Images/iStockphoto

DID YOU KNOW?

There's no J Street in Washington D.C. because the original city planners thought it looked way too much like the letter I.

Washington, D.C., keeps American history alive. Pick a page from time, and you'll find a way to explore it in the U.S. capital. While monuments and museums honor the past, history is still being made in dynamic D.C.

A Major Mall

Connecting many of the city's venerable attractions is the National Mall, a two-mile green space in the heart of the metro area. The iconic 555-foot Washington Monument rises above it all. Pay homage to past heroes at stately memorials, or tour the dozens of free museums, each presenting a different slice of the nation's story. See where history is currently being made with a visit to the White House or one of the many government institutions.

Honest Abe

Start your mall exploration at the west end, where you'll find the iconic Lincoln Memorial. Featuring a colossal marble statue of Abraham Lincoln deep in thought amid 36 Doric columns symbolizing the states of his era, the shrine to the nation's 16th president is a captivating space. Abe's weathered visage gazes eastward at the magnificent Lincoln Memorial Reflecting Pool, which runs 2,000 feet along the axis.

Birth of a 'Dream'

From this vantage point at the top of the monument's stairs, Martin Luther King Jr. gave his famous "I have a dream speech" in 1963. Fittingly, just a short walk to the southeast of the monument lies the stunning Martin Luther King Jr. Memorial, home to an imposing statue of the Civil Rights leader along with some of his memorable quotes etched in stone.

Honoring Veterans

Other nearby memorials include the Vietnam Veterans Memorial and Korean Veterans Memorial. At the east end of

District of Columbia Half Smoke

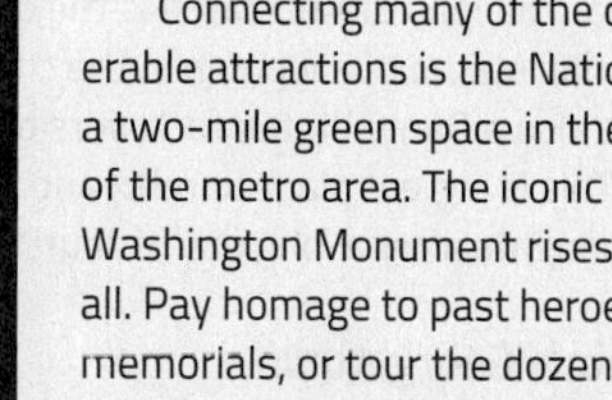

Ahh, the half-smoke. Similar to a hot dog, this delicious combo of coarsely ground pork and beef with a touch of hot pepper on a bun is guaranteed to satisfy the pickiest meat eater's appetite. Some people like to top their half-smoke with onions and spicy mustard, while others prefer chili and cheese.

VISITOR CENTER

TIME ZONE
Eastern Standard

ROAD & HIGHWAY INFORMATION
311 (in-district only)
ddot.dc.gov

FISHING & HUNTING INFORMATION
https://doee.dc.gov/service/fishdc

BOATING INFORMATION
202-nl-9099
mpdc.dc.gov/page/harbor-and-boating-safety-regulations

NATIONAL PARKS
nps.gov/dc

DISTRICT PARKS
dpr.dc.gov

TOURISM INFORMATION
District of Columbia
202-789-7000
washington.org

TOP TOURISM ATTRACTIONS
1) Houses of Government
2) National Monuments
3) Smithsonian Institution

DC

the pool sits the World War II Memorial, with its circle of 56 granite columns representing unity between the U.S. states, territories and District of Columbia.

The First House

Less than a mile north of the Washington Monument stands the White House, the official residence of the president. You can also stop by the White House Visitor Center to explore intriguing exhibits on the famous building and learn about the lives of previous presidential families.

Major Museums

The city also is home many world-class museums, making it so much more than a history lesson. Marvel at dazzling collections of gems and minerals at the National Museum of Natural History. Satisfy your fascination with flight at the National Air and Space Museum. Take in approximately 141,000 works of art dating back to the Middle Ages at the National Gallery of Art. Or gain valuable insight into the life, history and culture of African Americans at the Smithsonian National Museum of African American History and Culture. If you're in town during spring, be sure to meander along Tidal Basin to see cherry blossoms envelop the landscape in endless pink and white tufts.

Green Spaces Between the Stone

Despite its small footprint, D.C. has found plenty of room for sprawling green spaces. The 1700-acre Rock Creek Park offers bountiful recreational opportunities in a tranquil environment that feels far from the surrounding city. This national park offers 32 miles of hiking trails, paved biking trails, guided horseback tours, boat rentals, tennis, golf and so much more. The U.S. National Arboretum is another spot to find respite from the hustle and bustle, with over 400 acres of lush foliage. Stroll along the nine miles of trails to admire eclectic gardens.

Nicknamed the "Marble Palace," the Supreme Court Building was made with marble from across the U.S.

Capital Waters

Both the Potomac River and the lakes and ponds in the city's parks give visitors an alternative perspective of D.C. Boathouses and marinas throughout the district provide access for personal watercraft. From the Washington Sailing Marina, tourists can enjoy beautiful views of the city's skyline from a sailboat, kayak or stand-up paddleboard. Cruise to Daingerfield Island, a great spot for a picnic.

Cool Canal

During his presidency, George Washington touted a vision of opening up new avenues to the west. This dream was partially realized with the establishment of the Chesapeake & Ohio Canal, which originates in Georgetown and extends 185 miles east into Cumberland, Maryland. Ground was broken on the project in 1828, and the long stretch of waterway, which runs parallel to the Potomac River, is now a national park. The canal's tow path is today used by walkers and runners taking advantage of the park's beautiful scenery. Take one of the boat tours of the canal that disembark from Georgetown.

Perfect Park

Once the site of an encampment for Union troops during the Civil War, the 12-acre Meridian Hill Park makes up for its small size with several notable attractions. The park's centerpiece is a 13-basin cascade fountain, the longest of its kind in North America. The Joan of Arc statue is the only equestrian statue of a woman in the city. There's also a Dante statue for lovers of literature. This is a great place to relax and collect your thoughts after a long day of touring.

Gorgeous Georgetown

In Georgetown, visitors will discover 200-year-old mansions in elegant Federal and Victorian styles, along with row houses that once served as homes to celebrated leaders. The town's shopping and restaurant district treats visitors to fine cuisine and opulent retail goods. Visitors can see the elegant Federal-style home occupied by John F. Kennedy and his family during his campaign for president and sit down for a meal at Martin's Tavern, a family-owned establishment where Kennedy reportedly proposed to Jackie. Founded in 1933, the family-run restaurant displays pictures on its walls of the iconic leaders who visited the establishment, from Harry S. Truman to George W. Bush.

Biking to Mount Vernon

From Washington, D.C., cyclists can follow the Mount Vernon Bike Trail, which starts at the foot of the Washington Monument and takes cyclists to the front doors of George Washington's Mount Vernon.

ROAD TRIPS

Take a Walk in Washington D.C.

LOCATION
WASHINGTON, D.C.

DISTANCE
2.3 MILES

WALKING TIME TIME
47 MINS

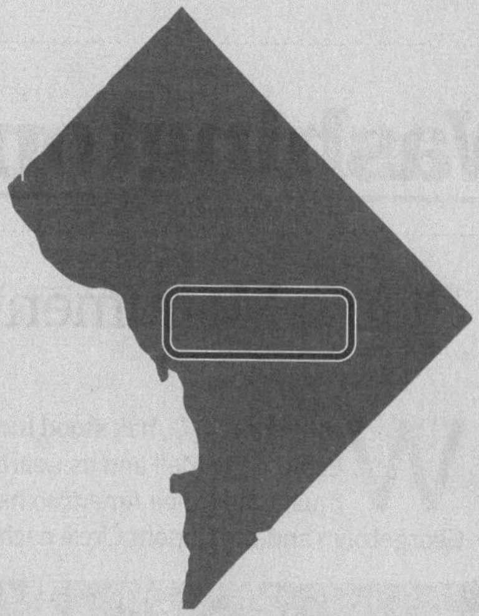

Washington, D.C.

This D.C. route is for walkers. Check out the ample greenbelts and walkways between the Lincoln Memorial Capitol Hill, a two-mile strip that allows walkers to stretch their legs as they take in the sights. If only the nation's legislative process was so easy.

1 Capitol Hill
Starting Point

The U.S. Capitol cuts an imposing figure against the D.C. skyline. While the building is a fascinating look into the legislative branch, it's worthwhile to explore some of the neighboring attractions, including the Library of Congress, the U.S. Supreme Court and U.S. Botanic Garden. If you'd like to see legislation in action, stop by the Visitor Galleries of the chambers of the House of Representatives and the Senate. The Capitol Visitor Center has an Exhibition Hall, two gift shops and a 530-seat restaurant. Emancipation Hall features statues and exhibits dedicated to the enslaved workers who helped build the U.S. Capitol.

2 Smithsonian Castle
Walk 1 mile ▪ 20 minutes

A series of memorials greets folks who hike along the banks of the reflecting pool. See the Martin Luther King, Jr. Memorial, the Korean War Veterans Memorial and the Vietnam Veterans Memorial. At the very east end of the reflecting pool, the World War II Memorial pays homage to the fallen soldiers of the United States as well as U.S. allies. After peering up at the 555-foot-tall Washington Monument, spend some time at the Smithsonian Castle, a majestic neo-gothic structure that serves as the gateway to the other Smithsonian Museums in the district. Along the journey, you'll pass the Smithsonian National Museum of Natural History, the National Gallery of Art and Smithsonian national Air and Space Museum.

3 Lincoln Memorial
Walk 1.3 miles ▪ 27 minutes

This monument was constructed in 1922 in a Doric-temple style and houses a 19-foot-tall statue of America's 16th president sitting and gazing thoughtfully toward the city in the distance. Climb the steps leading to Abe and turn around to see the majestic reflecting pool. The water of this 2,029-foot artificial lake reflects the obelisk-like Washington Monument in the distance. It may be Washington D.C.'s most iconic vista. Inscribed on the monument's south wall is Lincoln's Gettysburg Address.

Getty Images/iStockphoto

Washington, D.C. SPOTLIGHTS

Plan a Monumental Vacation in the District of Columbia

Washington, D.C., has stood for two centuries as a shrine of democracy. Explore the Mall and its nearby monuments or drop into one of the museums to see American history unfold. Compelling neighborhoods like Georgetown and the Dupont Circle each deserve a day of exploration.

IN 1912, JAPAN GAVE CHERRY BLOSSOM TREES TO THE U.S. AS A GIFT.

Cherry blossoms during spring across the Potomac from the Jefferson Memorial.

Getty Images/iStockphoto

Dupont Circle

Upscale stores, world-class restaurants and a cosmopolitan vibe prevails in D.C.'s Dupont Circle neighborhood. Take a stroll and do some shopping in one of the capital's most famed neighborhoods.

Embark on the Potomac

Known for history and governance, Washington doesn't seem like the place to visit for outdoor fun. But visitors are never far from open-air adventure. The Washington Sailing Marina and Belle Haven Marina, both on the western shores of the Potomac River, offer kayaking and sailing opportunities that give you the chance to experience the skyline from a truly unique perspective.

TR's Island

Hikers will relish in a visit to Theodore Roosevelt Island, an 88-acre memorial in honor of the 26th president's love of the great outdoors. Within walking distance of D.C.'s top attractions, the island park is accessed by a footbridge on the western side of the Potomac and has both swampland and wooded trails that recreate the area's environment in its natural state. With no bikes or cars are allowed on the grounds, it's a chance to get away from it all.

Georgetown

John F. Kennedy lived here during his early political career, and basketball great Patrick Ewing made hoops history at the local university. Come here to see D.C.'s fashionable side. A tour of the area, which sits on the banks of the Potomac River on the district's southeast border, bears this out. Visitors will discover 200-year-old mansions in Federal and Victorian styles. Looking for exercise? Jog or walk along the towpath of the historic Chesapeake & Ohio Canal, which originates in Georgetown.

The Smithsonian

Discover some of the greatest treasures in the fields of history, science, art and culture. The Smithsonian Institution invites you to discover the most intriguing parts of our planet at 19 museums, galleries, gardens and a zoo. Admission is free at all their locations, making it a treasure trove for visitors.

National Air and Space Museum

Have you always dreamt of taking flight? Aspiring pilots and astronauts will get to see the famous 1903 Wright Flyer, touch a moon rock brought back from Apollo 17 and gaze at stars in the public observatory.

▸ FOR MORE INFORMATION

Dupont Circle Historic District, washingtonwalks.com/tours/dupont-circle

Georgetown DC, www.georgetowndc.com

Smithsonian Institution, 202-633-1000, www.si.edu

LOCAL FAVORITE

D.C. Comfort Skillet

This dish whips up in as little as 10-15 minutes, giving you lots of time to tour the sights of the U.S. capital. *Recipe by Michelle Horn.*

INGREDIENTS

- ☐ 1 lb small yellow creamer potatoes
- ☐ 3 corncobs worth of kernels (removed)
- ☐ 1 green bell pepper
- ☐ ½ yellow onion
- ☐ Salt & pepper to taste

DIRECTIONS

Use a cooking rack over barbecue coals. Place butter in bottom of an iron skillet, set on rack and melt.

Dice onion and pepper and add to skillet. Add potatoes and corn and let cook until potatoes are soft, stirring occasionally, for 10-15 minutes. Let cool 5 minutes and enjoy.

For a twist, you could add precooked shredded chicken at the end or add seafood and Old Bay seasoning with garlic powder.

District of Columbia

WASHINGTON — C6 *District of Columbia*

WASHINGTON See also Brunswick, College Park, Lothian, Rock Hall & Woodbine, MD; Colonial Beach, Dumfries, Haymarket & Stafford, VA.

← PRINCE WILLIAM FOREST RV CAMPGROUND

good sam park

Ratings: 9/10★/9 (RV Park) From Jct I395 & I95: Go 26 miles S on I95 (exit 152B/Manassas), then 2.5 mi NW on SR-234 (L). **FAC:** paved rds. Avail: 71 paved, 54 pull-thrus, (24x45), back-ins (24x75), 36 full hkups, 35 W, 35 E (30/50 amps), WiFi @ sites, tent sites, dump, laundry, LP gas, fire rings, firewood. **REC:** pool, boating nearby, playground, hunting nearby. Pet restrict (B). Partial handicap access, eco-friendly. 2021 rates: $38 to $65, Military discount.

(888)737-5730 Lat: 38.60398, Lon: -77.35073
16058 Dumfries Rd, Dumfries, VA 22025
www.princewilliamforestrvcampground.com
See primary listing at Dumfries, VA and ad this page

↑ RAMBLIN' PINES FAMILY CAMPGROUND & RV PARK

good sam park

Ratings: 9.5/9.5★/10 From jct US 50 & I-495: Go 6-3/4 mi N on I-495 (exit 25), then 12 mi NE on I-95 (exit 38), then 16-3/4 mi NW on MD 32, then 3-1/2 on W I-70, then 2-3/4 mi on SR97, then 1/2 mi N on Hoods Mill Rd (L). **FAC:** paved rds. (200 spaces). 90 Avail: 3 paved, 87 gravel, 14 pull-thrus, (30x70), back-ins (30x70), 90 full hkups (30/50 amps), seasonal sites, cable, WiFi @ sites, tent sites, rentals, dump, laundry, groc, LP gas, fire rings, firewood. **REC:** heated pool, pond, fishing, shuffleboard, playground. Pet restrict (B). Partial handicap access. Big rig sites. 2021 rates: $70, Military discount. ATM.

(410)795-5161 Lat: 39.36728, Lon: -77.02505
801 Hoods Mill Road, Woodbine, MD 21797
ramblinpinescampground.com
See primary listing at Woodbine, MD and ad pages 202, 461, 466

The Ratings & What They Mean

Turn to "Understanding the Rating System" section at the front of this Guide to get information on how we rate and inspect parks with our handy three number system!

Rated 10/10★/10

The **FIRST NUMBER** represents Development of Facilities

The **SECOND NUMBER** represents Cleanliness and Physical Characteristics of Restrooms and Showers (plus, a Star is awarded to parks who receive maximum points for cleanliness!)

The **THIRD NUMBER** represents Visual Appearance/Environmental Quality

TIPS FOR THE BBQ CHEF - CHARCOAL BRIQUETTES: Fill the top of a chimney starter with briquettes, the bottom with crumpled newspaper and place chimney in center of grill. Light newspaper, which will light the bottom briquettes. After about 10 minutes you will see flames at the top. Dump the coals onto the grill. When all coals are covered with a gray ash (5 to 10 minutes), spread them out and you're ready to cook. GAS GRILLING: Turn on gas supply and ignite grill. When desired temperature is reached you are ready to cook. DIGITAL MEAT THERMOMETERS: Inexpensive and easy to use. Set dial for type of meat you are cooking and insert probe into thickest part of meat to read. Remove food when desired temperature is reached.

Be a Greener RVer: Turn off utilities at home before you hit the road and conserve water as much as possible when in the RV. Work with nature to avoid using the A/C and heater. Try to park in the shade or use your awning in the heat of the day. In the winter, park in the sun and where the wind will be resisted. Use non-toxic tank additives and cleaning supplies. Observe and follow fire rules, which can change with the weather. Don't put anything in a fire pit that will not burn. Keep campfires small to minimize ash and pollution. Recycle when possible, use less plastic cups/plates/utensils. Keep your RV well-tuned to conserve energy/reduce emissions. Always stay in marked campsites so as not to disturb the natural habitat.

DC

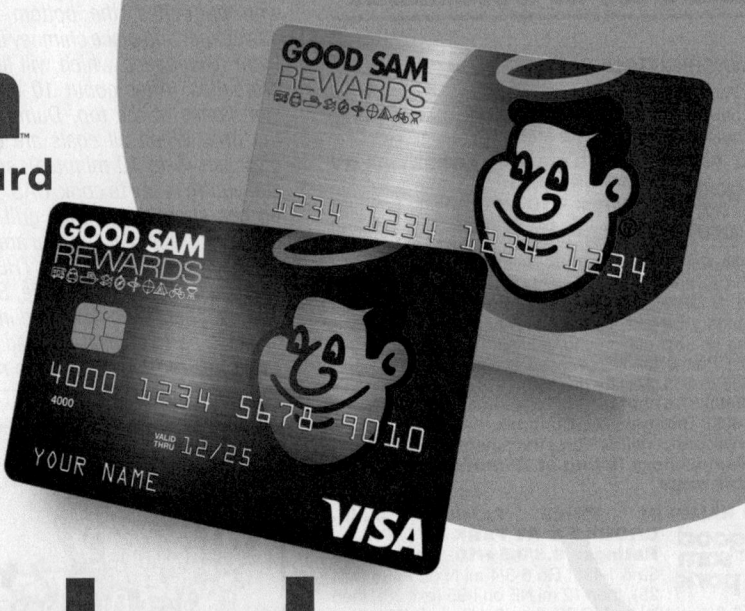

DID YOU KNOW ?
No matter where you go, you're never more than 60 miles from saltwater anywhere in the Sunshine State.
YOU ARE HERE

Getty Images/iStockphoto

Florida

FL

With the Atlantic Ocean to the east and Gulf of Mexico to the west, Florida has the most coastline of all the Lower 48 states. From the northern Emerald Coast to the Florida Keys, the Sunshine State offers beauty and adventure.

Superb Cities

Come to the Gulf Coast for a taste of old Cuba. Tampa Bay packs lots of amusement parks as well as brilliant Ybor City, a Cuban enclave that serves up outstanding food and cigars. Head south to Miami and South Beach for trendy entertainment spots, iconic architecture and beautiful beaches. A bevy of small towns and big cities line Florida's shores. St. Petersburg, Daytona, Destin and Pensacola are just a few of the sublime coastal retreats.

Ocean Waters and Pretty Pinelands

Located on Florida's southwest coast, Everglades National Park protects over 1.5 million acres of Florida's wetlands. Explore the prairies, pinelands, marshes and mangroves by foot, on a bike or in a boat, while watching for abundant wildlife. Take an airboat tour to skim across the water at high speeds, enjoying the sights along the way. Several trails snake through Everglades terrain for unforgettable hikes.

Theme Park Central

In the heart of Florida, Orlando rolls out larger-than-life theme park thrills. Walt Disney World, Legoland, Universal Orlando and SeaWorld offering magical adventures to eager guests. Where else can you swim with real dolphins, play Quidditch with Harry Potter, see mind-blowing Lego creations and have a play date with Mickey Mouse?

Sunshine State Getaways

Even though Florida doesn't have dramatic elevation changes — its highest point, Britton Hill, is 345 feet

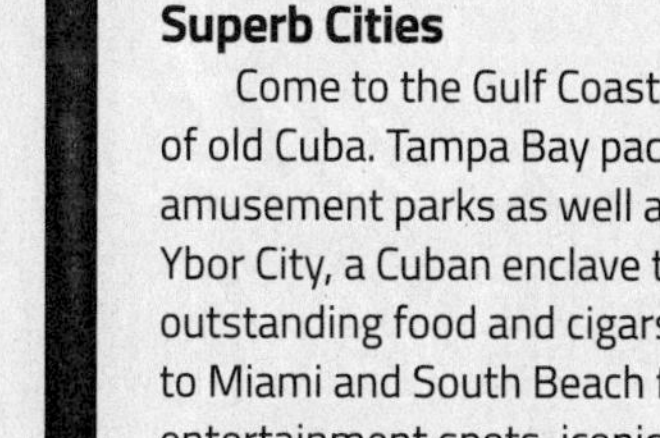

Florida Cuban Sandwich

Florida is home to the world-famous Cuban sandwich. The lunch meal was born in 1915 at Columbia Restaurant, the state's oldest eatery. The simple yet satisfying sandwich consists of two slices of fluffy Cuban bread hugging a mix of meats, swiss cheese, pickles and mustard. You can find Cuban sandwiches everywhere, but locals say the best ones are in Tampa's Ybor City neighborhood.

VISITOR CENTER

TIME ZONE
Eastern Standard

ROAD & HIGHWAY INFORMATION
866-511-3352
fl511.com

FISHING & HUNTING INFORMATION
850-488-4676
myfwc.com/license/recreational

BOATING INFORMATION
850-488-4676
myfwc.com/boating

NATIONAL PARKS
nps.gov/fl

STATE PARKS
floridastateparks.org

TOURISM INFORMATION
Florida Department of Tourism
888-735-2872
visitflorida.com

TOP TOURISM ATTRACTIONS
1) Walt Disney World
2) Kennedy Space Center
3) Everglades National Park

MAJOR CITIES
Jacksonville, Miami, Tampa, Orlando, St Petersburg, Tallahassee (capital)

A manatee in Crystal River. Manatees can grow up to 14 feet long and weigh as much as 3,000 pounds.

above sea level — Florida's trails still lead hikers to some exciting discoveries. Some of the state's best hikes can be found along the Florida National Scenic Trail, which runs 1,300 miles from Florida's panhandle through myriad landscapes all the way to the state's southern tip. For a quintessential Floridian experience, check out the Bulow Woods Trail between Flagler Beach and Ormond Beach, taking hikers under a canopy of massive live oak trees. Cyclists will find an abundance of trails in the Sunshine State. Check out Sebastian Inlet State Park, which boasts a 40-mile multi-use beach trail that's perfect for cycling. The path runs parallel to state road A1A and the Indian River Lagoon on the inland side.

Daytona Days

In mid-February, stock car engines rev as top racers vie for one of the top honors in NASCAR. The 500-mile Daytona 500 at the Daytona International Speedway ranks as one of the top events in motorsports. Feel like dining with Mickey? While any time is an excellent time to visit Walt Disney World, foodies won't want to miss the annual Epcot International Food & Wine Festival, held each fall.

Colonial Past and Rocketing Future

In the 1500s, Spanish settlers established the city of St. Augustine as the capital of colonial Florida. The town honors this legacy with prominent Spanish architecture throughout town and cultural events featuring Spanish food and music. Take a drive along the Old Florida Heritage Highway to experience "Old Florida," where small towns and simpler times beckon visitors. Visit the sleepy antique stores and sample the local cuisine at welcoming eateries. Along the Atlantic coast, Florida has played an essential role in the nation's space exploration, from the launch of early rockets from Cape Canaveral in the 1950s to the human-crewed space shuttles from the Kennedy Space Center.

A Pirate's Life for Me

Raise the Jolly Roger and don an eye patch at the annual Gasparilla Pirate Fest. For over a century, Tampa has hosted this lively event each January. The festivities start with the pirate invasion of Tampa Bay with a flotilla of boats, followed by a spirited parade modeled after Mardi Gras.

Sharks and Shells

Get the blood pumping at the Shark Valley Trail in the Everglades. This 15-mile loop trail goes right through alligator territory. Off the Fort Myers coast, Sanibel Island's network of trails provide a relaxing way to explore this beautiful destination. On Sanibel's beaches, visitors are allowed to bring home some of the ample seashells that litter the shore. For unique hiking, paddling and hunting opportunities, head to Big Cypress National Preserve, with its 700,000 acres of swamplands.

Getty Images/iStockphoto

A panther lurks amid a grove of palmetto trees in Charlotte County on Florida's Gulf Coast.

Franklin County

Named after the Founding Father whose likeness is on the $100 bill, Franklin County is a quaint and cozy coastal county that's as green as the currency. The verdant region sits on the Florida Panhandle and is one of the least populated counties in the state, but its human presence has nonetheless been significant. Archaeologists have discovered traces of human settlements dating back 12,000 years, and Native American tribes thrived in the area for eons, subsisting on fishing off the warm Gulf waters. These days, fishing is still a big industry in Franklin County, and its mellow way of life attracts visitors seeking relaxation, adventure and a chance of catching "the big one."

Guiding Lights

Lighthouse fans will enjoy touring the Cape St. George Light on St. George Island. A museum and interactive archive tell the story of this landmark, which traces its history back to 1848.

Okeechobee County

Known as "Florida's Inland Sea," the sprawling Lake Okeechobee

Fun on the Water

Virtually 90 percent of Franklin County falls under the rubric of protected parkland or nature preserve. The community's mammal inventory includes black bears and the elusive Florida panther, while the region's swamps, beaches and waterways entice passionate bird-watchers. Find fun in the form of canoeing along the 100 miles of the Apalachicola River's swamplands or go hiking across pristine white-sand beaches. With the small-town hospitality of the county's rough diamond towns Franklin is a flashback to sultry "Old Florida."

Fun if By Boat

There's no point going to the coast if you're not going to enjoy the water, and in Franklin County, a number of relaxing and eye-opening boat tours are available. If you prefer dry land, take a trip into the Apalachicola National Forest, Apalachicola Bay National Estuarine Research Reserve or Tate's Hell State Forest.

Historical Franklin County

The Apalachicola Maritime Museum reflects on the things that made this region great, including fishing and trade, while at the John Gorrie State Museum, you can learn about another big part of Franklin County's history, and one that has nothing to do with the coast. John Gorrie lived in Apalachicola during the early 1800s, and is known for his pioneering work in the fields of air conditioning and refrigeration. The museum looks back on his life and work.

is the centerpiece of this fun-loving Florida region. Visitors from all over the world come each year to make the most of its recreational opportunities, while taking some time to enjoy its surroundings.

Built in 1846 west of Key West, Fort Jefferson protected shipping and is part of Dry Tortugas National Park.

Welcome to Florida's Finest

Encompassing more than 700 square miles is Lake Okeechobee, the largest lake in Florida. One of the largest freshwater lakes in the United States, Lake Okeechobee is approximately half the size of Rhode Island and serves as a magnet for anglers from across the United States. Indeed, the lake is home to champion-size catches. Charter fishing excursions are ready to take anglers to the prime fishing spots for largemouth bass, crappie and bluegill. Guided nature and Eco tours are also available.

Bird Business

The lake is home to a variety of plant life and is known as a place to spot bald eagles, brown pelicans and other bird species. If you're a hunter, local outfitters can help you bag boar, turkey and even alligators. If catching a big reptile isn't on your "to-do" list, you may still see them on one of the tour-operated airboats that specialize in finding the variety of wildlife in the region.

Hiking Okeechobee County

For a land tour option, try Lake Okeechobee Scenic Trail. More than 100 miles of paved and unpaved routes circle the lake with plenty of shaded spots for picnics. There is a sweeping view of Lake Okeechobee from Herbert Hoover Dike, which is found along the trail. Keep a lookout for a wood stork or heron, as well as otters.

Florida Main Street

The arts play a big role in the town of Okeechobee located on the north side of the lake. Okeechobee's Main Street is lined with murals presenting the history and popular activities of the Okeechobee region with a Smithsonian Waterway Exhibit stopping at the Historic County Courthouse, December 2016 through January 2017. Events like the Speckled Perch Festival and Car Show keep the town rocking. The town is also home to Quail Creek Plantation and OK Corral, which both offer quail, turkey and pheasant hunting along with clay shooting.

Okeechobee Art

In June, the Okeechobee's Art & Wine Walk kicks off. Each downtown business will feature an artist showcasing their artwork or music, and will offer guests wine tasting, appetizers and promotional offers. In July, Okeechobee celebrates the National Day of the American Cowboy with a cattle drive through town, a livestock market and the Cattlemen's Ranch Rodeo. Also on tap is a barbecue competition and vendors selling western wear and goods. The event salutes Okeechobee's heritage as center for cattle ranching and commerce.

Taking it Easy

To slow things down a bit, take a leisurely visit to Wagon Wheel Horse Farm. Here, you'll find pony rides for the kids, horse riding lessons for grown-ups and farm animals on-site. If you would like to experience the more exotic animals that make their home in the area, visit Arnold's Wildlife Rehabilitation Center. Here, you can get a close look at Florida panthers and other wild cats. There is nothing like a walk through the butterfly garden at Arnold's to finish your day.

Deep Hole Gators

Looking for some animal-related thrills on your Florida trip? Look no further than Deep Hole at Myakka State Park. Deep Hole may possibly be the best place to see American Alligators in their natural habitat. But this isn't a zoo or managed environment. These are real gators. Deep Hole is 4.4-mile round trip easy hike into the backcountry at Myakka State Park's Lower Lake. A permit is required for entrance into this area.

good sam park

Featured Good Sam Parks

FLORIDA

When you stay with Good Sam, you can expect the highest degree of cleanliness and friendliness, and better yet, you get **10% off** campground fees.

If you're not already a Good Sam member you can purchase your membership at one of these locations:

ALACHUA
Travelers Campground

APOPKA
Lost Lake RV Park

ARCADIA
Craig's RV Park
Toby's RV Resort

AUBURNDALE
Fish Haven

BIG PINE KEY
Big Pine Key Resort
Sunshine Key RV Resort & Marina

BONITA SPRINGS
Bonita Lake RV Resort
Bonita Terra
Gulf Coast Camping Resort
Imperial Bonita Estates RV Resort

BOWLING GREEN
Pioneer Creek RV Resort

BRADENTON
Winter Quarters Manatee RV Resort

BRONSON
Black Prong Equestrian Village

BROOKSVILLE
Belle Parc RV Resort
Clover Leaf Forest RV Resort

BUSHNELL
Breezy Oaks RV Park

CALLAHAN
Kelly's Countryside RV Park

CEDAR KEY
Anglers RV Campground

CHATTAHOOCHEE
Flat Creek Family Campground

CHOKOLOSKEE
Chokoloskee Island Resort

CITRA
Orange Lake RV Resort

CLEARWATER
Avalon RV Resort

CLERMONT
Clerbrook Golf & RV Resort
Lake Magic RV Resort
Orlando RV Resort

CLEWISTON
Big Cypress RV Resort

COCOA
JOY RV Resort
Sonrise Palms RV Park

CORTEZ
Buttonwood Inlet RV Resort

CRYSTAL RIVER
Crystal Isles RV Park

DADE CITY
Seven Acres RV Park
Sunburst RV Park
Town and Country RV Resort

10/10★/10 GOOD SAM PARKS

BROOKSVILLE
Belle Parc RV Resort
(352)593-5852

KEYSTONE HEIGHTS
Keystone Heights RV Resort
(352)645-4330

LAKE WALES
Resort at Canopy Oaks
(407)630-7000

PALMETTO
The Tides RV Resort
(941)212-0777

REDDICK
Ocala North RV Resort
(352)591-1723

SUMMERFIELD
Sunkissed Village RV Resort
(352)480-5000

TITUSVILLE
The Great Outdoors RV Nature & Golf Resort
(321)269-5004

WILLISTON
Williston Crossings RV Resort
(877)785-4405

What's This?

An RV park with a 10/10★/10 rating has scored perfect grades in amenities, cleanliness and appearance ("See Understanding the Campground Rating System" on pages 8 and 9 for an explanation of the trusted Good Sam Rating System). Stay in a 10/10★/10 park on your next trip for a nearly flawless camping experience.

Getty Images/iStockphoto

FL

Getty Images/iStockphoto

DAVENPORT
Rainbow Chase RV Resort

DAYTONA BEACH
Nova Family Campground

DEBARY
Highbanks Marina & Campresort

DEFUNIAK SPRINGS
Sunset King Lake RV Resort
Twin Lakes Camp Resort

DESTIN
Camping on the Gulf
Geronimo RV Park

EUSTIS
Southern Palms RV Resort

FIESTA KEY
Fiesta Key RV Resort

FLAGLER BEACH
Beverly Beach Camptown RV Resort & Campers Village
Bulow RV Resort

FORT LAUDERDALE
Paradise Island RV Resort
Sunshine Holiday Ft. Lauderdale

FORT MYERS
Blueway RV Village
Fort Myers Beach RV Resort
Fort Myers RV Resort
Iona Ranch MH/RV Resort
Lazy J RV & Mobile Home Park
Pioneer Village RV Resort
Seminole Campground
Sunseekers RV Park
Tamiami RV Park
Tice Courts & RV Park
Upriver RV Resort

FORT MYERS BEACH
Gulf Air RV Resort
Red Coconut RV Park

FORT PIERCE
Road Runner Travel Resort

FROSTPROOF
Camp Inn RV Resort

GLEN ST MARY
Island Oaks RV Resort

GREEN COVE SPRINGS
Clay Fair RV Park

HIGH SPRINGS
High Springs Campground

HOLIDAY
Holiday Travel Park

HOLT
Rivers Edge RV Campground

HOMESTEAD
Boardwalk RV Resort

HOMOSASSA
Chassahowitzka River Campground
Nature's Resort

HUDSON
Barrington Hills RV Resort
Winter Paradise RV Resort

JACKSONVILLE
Sunny Oaks RV Park

KENANSVILLE
Lake Marian Resort

KEYSTONE HEIGHTS
Keystone Heights RV Resort

KISSIMMEE
Merry D RV Sanctuary
Sherwood Forest RV Resort
Tropical Palms RV Resort

LABELLE
Grandma's Grove RV Park
The Glades RV Resort
Whisper Creek RV Resort

LADY LAKE
Blue Parrot RV Resort
Grand Oaks Resort

LAKE CITY
Lake City Campground
Lake City RV Resort

LAKE PANASOFFKEE
Lake Pan RV Village

LAKE PLACID
Sunshine RV Resort

LAKE WALES
Resort at Canopy Oaks

LAKELAND
Sanlan RV & Golf Resort

LARGO
Vacation Village RV Resort
Yankee Traveler RV Park

LEESBURG
Haines Creek RV Park
Holiday RV Village

LUTZ
Winter Quarters Pasco RV Resort

MADISON
Madison RV & Golf Resort
Ragans Family Campground

MARATHON
Grassy Key RV Park and Resort
Jolly Roger RV Resort

MARIANNA
Alliance Hill RV Resort
Florida Caverns RV Resort at Merritt's Mill Pond
Stay N Go RV

MCINTOSH
Sportsman's Cove Campground

MIAMI
Miami Everglades Resort

MILTON
Avalon Landing RV Park
Splash! RV Resort & Waterpark

MONTICELLO
A Campers World
Tallahassee East Campground

NAPLES
Northtide Naples RV Resort

NAVARRE
Emerald Beach RV Park
Navarre Beach Camping Resort

NEW PORT RICHEY
Orchid Lake RV Resort
Seven Springs Travel Park

NEW SMYRNA BEACH
Sugar Mill Ruins Travel Park

NOKOMIS
Royal Coachman RV Resort

OCALA
Ocala RV Camp Resort
Wandering Oaks RV Resort
Wild Frontier RV Resort

ODESSA
Silver Dollar Golf, Trap Club & RV Resort

OKEECHOBEE
Okeechobee KOA Resort & Golf Course
Zachary Taylor RV Resort

ORMOND BEACH
Coral Sands Oceanfront RV Resort
Sunshine Holiday Daytona RV Resort

PAHOKEE
Pahokee Campground & Marina

PALMETTO
Fiesta Grove RV Resort
Fisherman's Cove RV Resort
Terra Ceia RV Resort
The Tides RV Resort

PANACEA
Panacea RV Park

PANAMA CITY BEACH
Camper's Inn

PENSACOLA
Pensacola Beach RV Resort
Pensacola North RV Resort
Pensacola RV Park

PERDIDO KEY
Perdido Key RV Resort

POLK CITY
LeLynn RV Resort

POMPANO BEACH
Breezy Hill RV Resort
Highland Woods RV Resort

PONCE DE LEON
Vortex Spring Adventures

PORT CHARLOTTE
Harbor Lakes RV Resort
Riverside RV Resort

PORT ORANGE
Rose Bay Travel Park

PORT RICHEY
Ja-Mar North RV Resort
Oak Springs RV Resort
Sundance Lakes RV Resort

PORT ST JOE
Presnell's Bayside Marina
& RV Resort

PORT ST LUCIE
Port St Lucie RV Resort

PUNTA GORDA
Gulf View RV Resort
Sun N Shade RV Resort

REDDICK
Ocala North RV Resort

RIVERVIEW
Rice Creek RV Resort

ROCKLEDGE
Space Coast RV Resort

RUSKIN
Hawaiian Isles
River Vista RV Village
Sun Lake RV Resort

SEBASTIAN
Vero Beach Kamp

SEBRING
Outback RV Resort At Tanglewood
Sebring Gardens RV Community

SILVER SPRINGS
The Springs RV Resort

SPRING HILL
Big Oaks RV Park
& Mobile Home Community
Topics RV Resort

ST AUGUSTINE
North Beach Camp Resort
St Augustine RV Resort
Stagecoach RV Park

ST JAMES CITY
Pine Island KOA

STEINHATCHEE
Steinhatchee River Club

SUMMERFIELD
Sunkissed Village RV Resort

SUMTERVILLE
Shady Brook Golf & RV Resort

TALLAHASSEE
Tallahassee RV Park

TAMPA
Bay Bayou RV Resort
Tampa RV Park

TAVARES
Fisherman's Cove Golf & RV
Resort

THONOTOSASSA
Southern Aire RV Resort

TITUSVILLE
The Great Outdoors RV Nature
& Golf Resort
Whispering Pines

VENICE
Florida Pines Mobile Home Court
Ramblers Rest RV Campground

VERO BEACH
Sunshine Travel RV Resort

WALDO
Dixieland RV Park - Gainesville

WAUCHULA
Peace River RV Resort

WEBSTER
Sunshine Village

WESLEY CHAPEL
Quail Run RV Resort

WILDWOOD
Three Flags RV Campground
Wildwood RV Village

WILLISTON
Williston Crossings RV Resort

WINTER GARDEN
Stage Stop Campground
Winter Garden RV Resort

ZEPHYRHILLS
Ducky's Day Off RV Park
Forest Lake Estates RV Resort
Happy Days RV Park
Palm View Gardens RV Resort

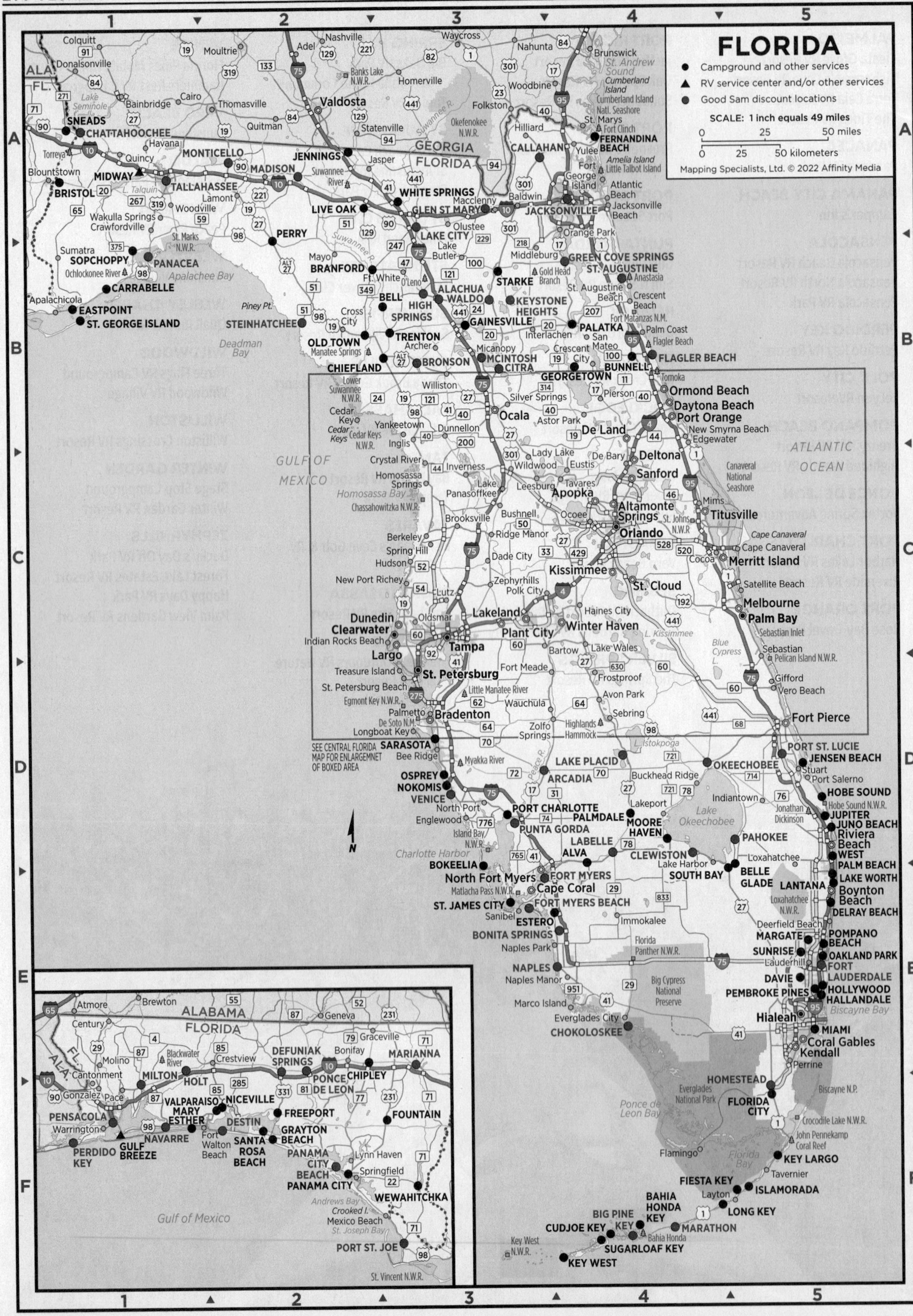
FLORIDA
● Campground and other services
▲ RV service center and/or other services
● Good Sam discount locations
SCALE: 1 inch equals 49 miles
0 25 50 miles
0 25 50 kilometers
Mapping Specialists, Ltd. © 2022 Affinity Media
GEORGIA
FLORIDA
ALA.
FL.
GULF OF MEXICO
ATLANTIC OCEAN
SEE CENTRAL FLORIDA MAP FOR ENLARGEMENT OF BOXED AREA
SNEADS
CHATTAHOOCHEE
MIDWAY
BRISTOL
TALLAHASSEE
MONTICELLO
MADISON
JENNINGS
WHITE SPRINGS
LIVE OAK
GLEN ST MARY
CALLAHAN
FERNANDINA BEACH
JACKSONVILLE
LAKE CITY
PERRY
SOPCHOPPY
PANACEA
CARRABELLE
EASTPOINT
ST. GEORGE ISLAND
STEINHATCHEE
BRANFORD
BELL
HIGH SPRINGS
ALACHUA
WALDO
STARKE
KEYSTONE HEIGHTS
GREEN COVE SPRINGS
ST. AUGUSTINE
GAINESVILLE
PALATKA
TRENTON
OLD TOWN
BRONSON
CHIEFLAND
MCINTOSH
CITRA
GEORGETOWN
BUNNELL
FLAGLER BEACH
Ormond Beach
Daytona Beach
Port Orange
Ocala
De Land
Deltona
Sanford
Apopka
Altamonte Springs
Orlando
Titusville
Merritt Island
Kissimmee
St. Cloud
Melbourne
Palm Bay
Lakeland
Plant City
Winter Haven
Dunedin
Clearwater
Largo
Tampa
St. Petersburg
Bradenton
Fort Pierce
SARASOTA
OSPREY
NOKOMIS
VENICE
LAKE PLACID
ARCADIA
OKEECHOBEE
PORT ST. LUCIE
JENSEN BEACH
HOBE SOUND
JUPITER
JUNO BEACH
Riviera Beach
WEST PALM BEACH
LAKE WORTH
LANTANA
Boynton Beach
DELRAY BEACH
PORT CHARLOTTE
PUNTA GORDA
PALMDALE
MOORE HAVEN
LABELLE
ALVA
CLEWISTON
PAHOKEE
BELLE GLADE
SOUTH BAY
BOKEELIA
North Fort Myers
FORT MYERS
Cape Coral
ST. JAMES CITY
FORT MYERS BEACH
ESTERO
BONITA SPRINGS
NAPLES
MARGATE
SUNRISE
POMPANO BEACH
OAKLAND PARK
FORT LAUDERDALE
DAVIE
PEMBROKE PINES
HOLLYWOOD
HALLANDALE
Hialeah
MIAMI
Coral Gables
Kendall
CHOKOLOSKEE
HOMESTEAD
FLORIDA CITY
KEY LARGO
ISLAMORADA
FIESTA KEY
LONG KEY
MARATHON
BAHIA HONDA KEY
BIG PINE KEY
CUDJOE KEY
SUGARLOAF KEY
KEY WEST
ALABAMA
FLORIDA
MILTON
HOLT
DEFUNIAK SPRINGS
PONCE DE LEON
CHIPLEY
MARIANNA
PENSACOLA
PERDIDO KEY
GULF BREEZE
NAVARRE
MARY ESTHER
VALPARAISO
NICEVILLE
DESTIN
FREEPORT
SANTA ROSA BEACH
GRAYTON BEACH
FOUNTAIN
PANAMA CITY BEACH
PANAMA CITY
WEWAHITCHKA
PORT ST. JOE
Gulf of Mexico

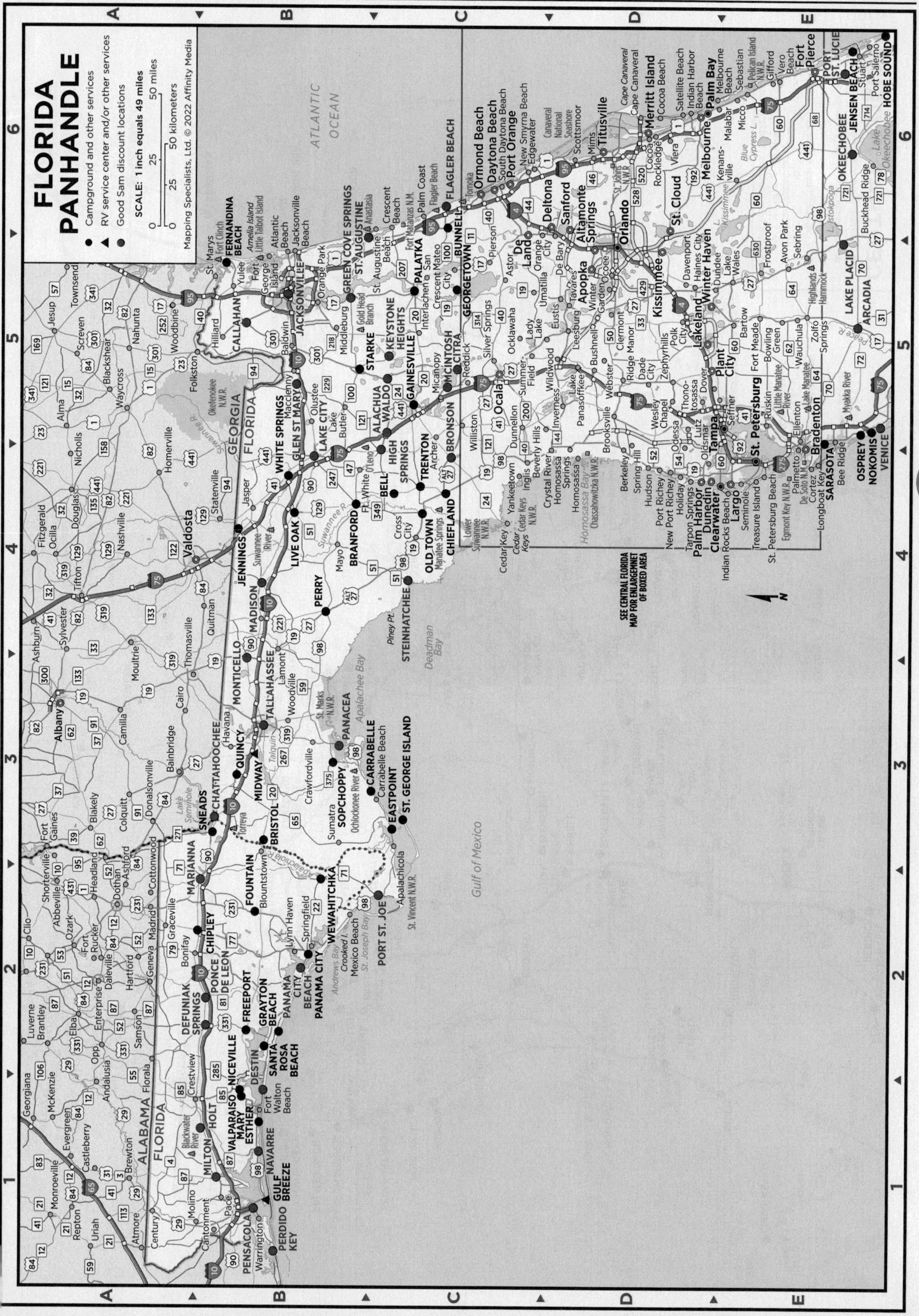
FLORIDA PANHANDLE
Campground and other services
RV service center and/or other services
Good Sam discount locations
SCALE: 1 inch equals 49 miles
0 25 50 miles
0 25 50 kilometers
Mapping Specialists, Ltd. © 2022 Affinity Media
ATLANTIC OCEAN
Gulf of Mexico
Apalachee Bay
Deadman Bay
SEE CENTRAL FLORIDA MAP FOR ENLARGEMENT OF BOXED AREA
ALABAMA
FLORIDA
GEORGIA
PENSACOLA
PERDIDO KEY
GULF BREEZE
NAVARRE
MILTON
HOLT
VALPARAISO
MARY ESTHER
NICEVILLE
DESTIN
SANTA ROSA BEACH
GRAYTON BEACH
FREEPORT
PANAMA CITY BEACH
PANAMA CITY
DEFUNIAK SPRINGS
PONCE DE LEON
CHIPLEY
MARIANNA
FOUNTAIN
WEWAHITCHKA
PORT ST. JOE
SNEADS
CHATTAHOOCHEE
BRISTOL
QUINCY
MIDWAY
TALLAHASSEE
MONTICELLO
SOPCHOPPY
PANACEA
CARRABELLE
EASTPOINT
ST. GEORGE ISLAND
MADISON
JENNINGS
PERRY
STEINHATCHEE
LIVE OAK
WHITE SPRINGS
LAKE CITY
GLEN ST MARY
BRANFORD
BELL
HIGH SPRINGS
TRENTON
OLD TOWN
CHIEFLAND
BRONSON
ALACHUA
WALDO
GAINESVILLE
STARKE
KEYSTONE HEIGHTS
MCINTOSH
CITRA
JACKSONVILLE
CALLAHAN
FERNANDINA BEACH
GREEN COVE SPRINGS
ST. AUGUSTINE
PALATKA
GEORGETOWN
BUNNELL
FLAGLER BEACH
Ormond Beach
Daytona Beach
Port Orange
Ocala
De Land
Deltona
Sanford
Altamonte Springs
Apopka
Orlando
Titusville
Merritt Island
St. Cloud
Kissimmee
Melbourne
Palm Bay
Winter Haven
Lakeland
Plant City
Tampa
St. Petersburg
Clearwater
Dunedin
Palm Harbor
Largo
Bradenton
SARASOTA
OSPREY
NOKOMIS
VENICE
ARCADIA
LAKE PLACID
OKEECHOBEE
JENSEN BEACH
PORT ST. LUCIE
Fort Pierce
HOBE SOUND
Valdosta
Albany
FL

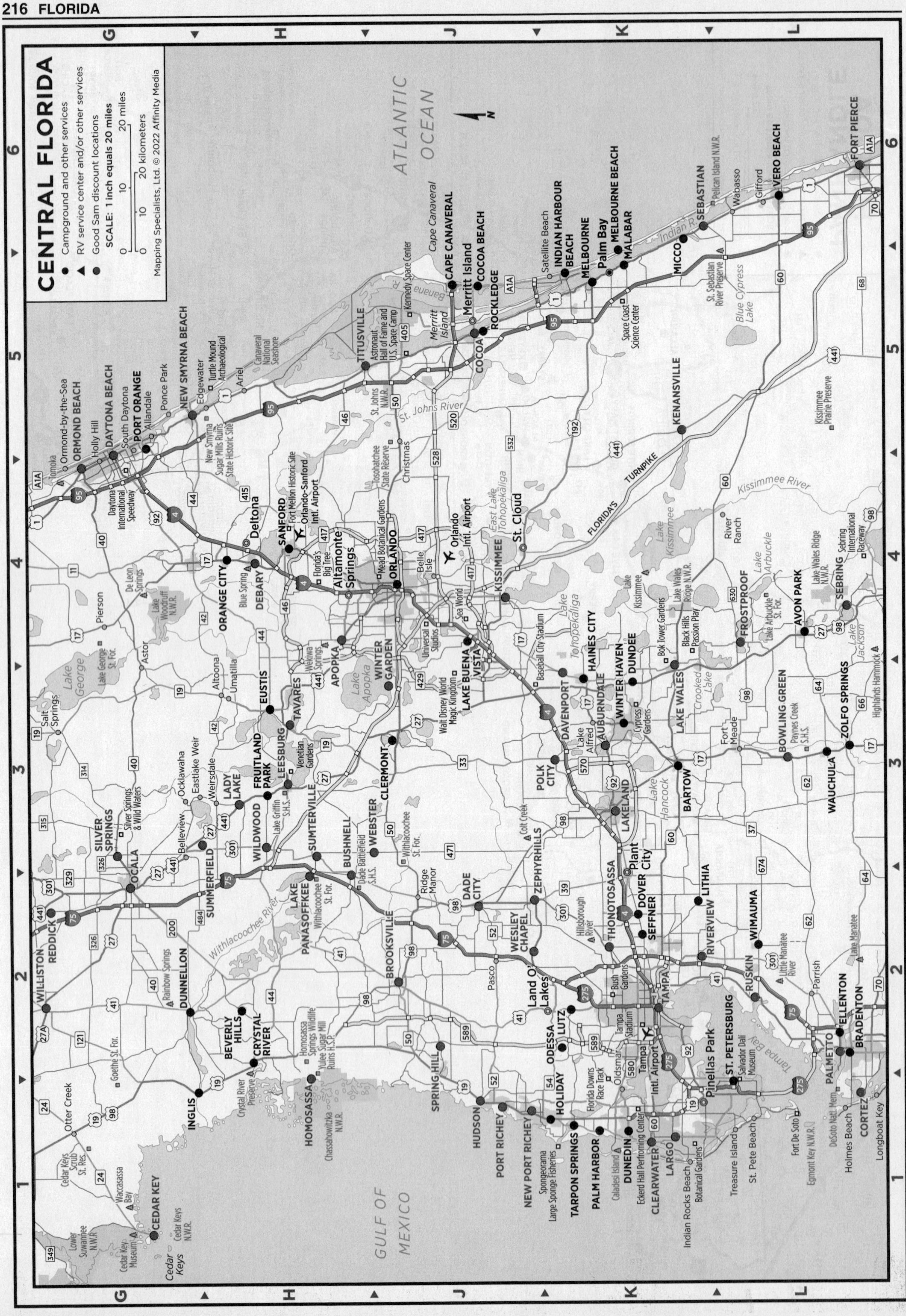
CENTRAL FLORIDA
Campground and other services
RV service center and/or other services
Good Sam discount locations
SCALE: 1 inch equals 20 miles
0 10 20 miles
0 10 20 kilometers
Mapping Specialists, Ltd. © 2022 Affinity Media
ATLANTIC OCEAN
GULF OF MEXICO
Cape Canaveral
DAYTONA BEACH
ORMOND BEACH
PORT ORANGE
NEW SMYRNA BEACH
TITUSVILLE
CAPE CANAVERAL
COCOA BEACH
COCOA
ROCKLEDGE
Merritt Island
INDIAN HARBOUR BEACH
MELBOURNE
MELBOURNE BEACH
Palm Bay
MALABAR
MICCO
SEBASTIAN
VERO BEACH
FORT PIERCE
ORANGE CITY
DEBARY
Deltona
SANFORD
Altamonte Springs
ORLANDO
APOPKA
WINTER GARDEN
KISSIMMEE
St. Cloud
LAKE BUENA VISTA
CLERMONT
EUSTIS
TAVARES
LEESBURG
FRUITLAND PARK
LADY LAKE
WILDWOOD
SUMTERVILLE
BUSHNELL
WEBSTER
OCALA
SILVER SPRINGS
SUMMERFIELD
REDDICK
WILLISTON
DUNNELLON
INGLIS
CRYSTAL RIVER
BEVERLY HILLS
HOMOSASSA
BROOKSVILLE
SPRING HILL
HUDSON
PORT RICHEY
NEW PORT RICHEY
HOLIDAY
TARPON SPRINGS
PALM HARBOR
DUNEDIN
CLEARWATER
LARGO
Pinellas Park
ST. PETERSBURG
TAMPA
LUTZ
ODESSA
Land O' Lakes
WESLEY CHAPEL
ZEPHYRHILLS
DADE CITY
LAKE PANASOFFKEE
THONOTOSASSA
DOVER
SEFFNER
Plant City
LAKELAND
POLK CITY
DAVENPORT
HAINES CITY
AUBURNDALE
WINTER HAVEN
DUNDEE
LAKE WALES
BARTOW
FROSTPROOF
AVON PARK
SEBRING
BOWLING GREEN
WAUCHULA
ZOLFO SPRINGS
LITHIA
RIVERVIEW
WIMAUMA
RUSKIN
ELLENTON
PALMETTO
BRADENTON
CORTEZ
KENANSVILLE
CEDAR KEY
Tampa Bay
Lake George
Lake Apopka
Lake Tohopekaliga
East Lake Tohopekaliga
Lake Kissimmee
Kissimmee River
St. Johns River
Withlacoochee River
Indian R.
FLORIDA'S TURNPIKE

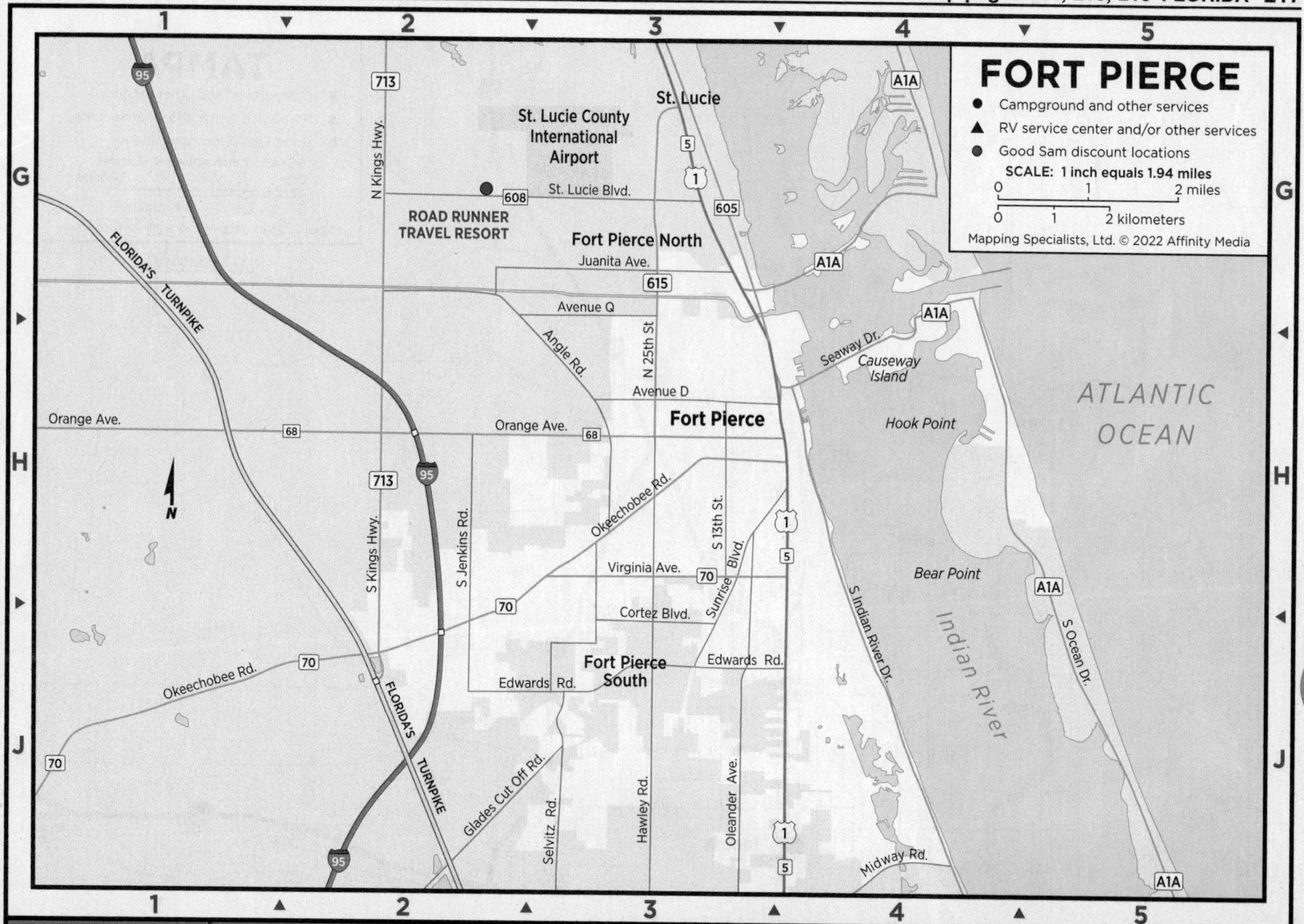

See listing Fort Pierce, FL

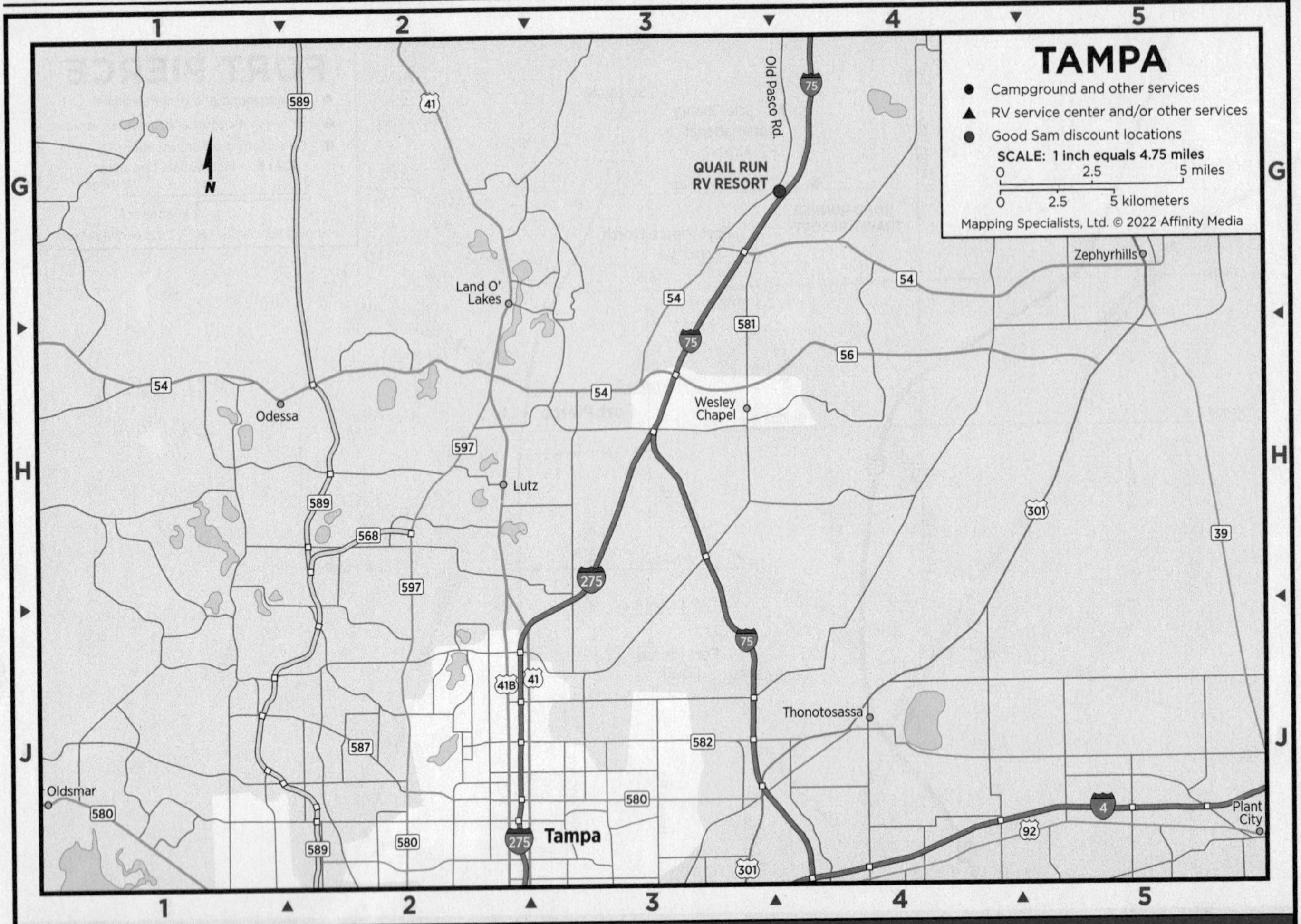
TAMPA
Campground and other services
RV service center and/or other services
Good Sam discount locations
SCALE: 1 inch equals 4.75 miles
0 2.5 5 miles
0 2.5 5 kilometers
Mapping Specialists, Ltd. © 2022 Affinity Media
1 2 3 4 5
G H J
Old Pasco Rd.
QUAIL RUN RV RESORT
Zephyrhills
Land O' Lakes
Odessa
Wesley Chapel
Lutz
Thonotosassa
Oldsmar
Tampa
Plant City
589 41 75 54 581 56 597 568 275 301 39 41B 587 582 580 92 4

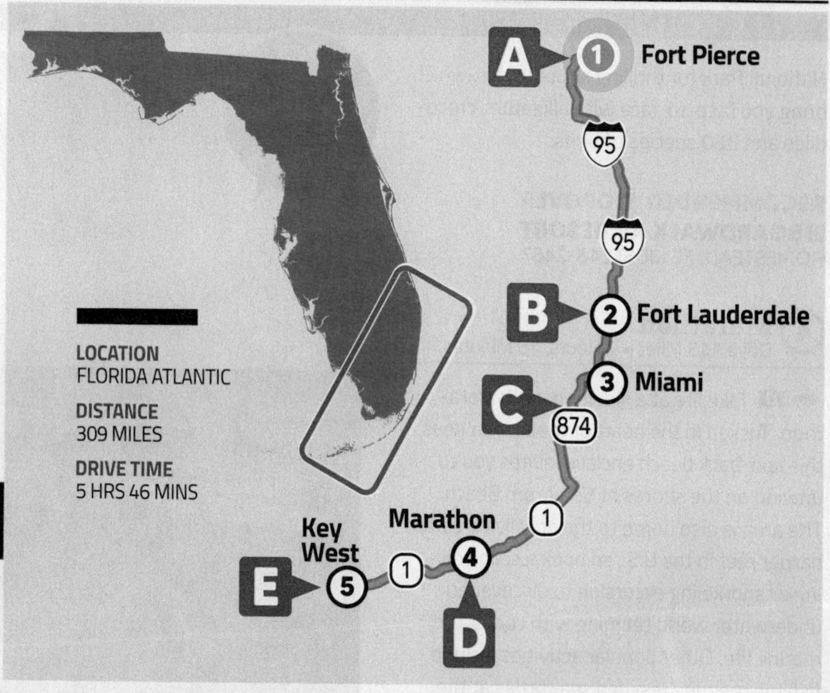

ROAD TRIPS

Follow Trails Blazed by Hemingway

Florida Atlantic

Stretching 285 miles from Fort Pierce to Key West, this road trip along Florida's Atlantic Coast promises unspoiled nature, quirky historical attractions and lavish getaways under the tropical sun. Spend some time lounging on white-sand beaches and then set off in search of authentic Cuban food, wildlife encounters in the Everglades and Ernest Hemingway's favorite hangout spots. Whether you want to take it easy on island time or party in the playgrounds of the rich and famous, you'll get to do it all and more in this slice of the Sunshine State.

1 Fort Pierce
Starting Point

Dubbed Sunrise City, Fort Pierce is one of the oldest communities on Florida's east coast. Stroll through the historic downtown and enjoy period Spanish architecture houses, contemporary shopping, dining and entertainment like Friday Fest and the Jazz Market. Afterward, tee off at Indian Hills Golf Course or come face-to-face with gentle giants at the Manatee Observation and Education Center. It's also no secret Fort Pierce has some of the best angling on the Treasure Coast. Drop a line in the Indian River or head out on the Atlantic to reel in trophy catches.

RECOMMENDED STOPOVER
A ROAD RUNNER TRAVEL RESORT
FORT PIERCE, FL (800) 833-7108

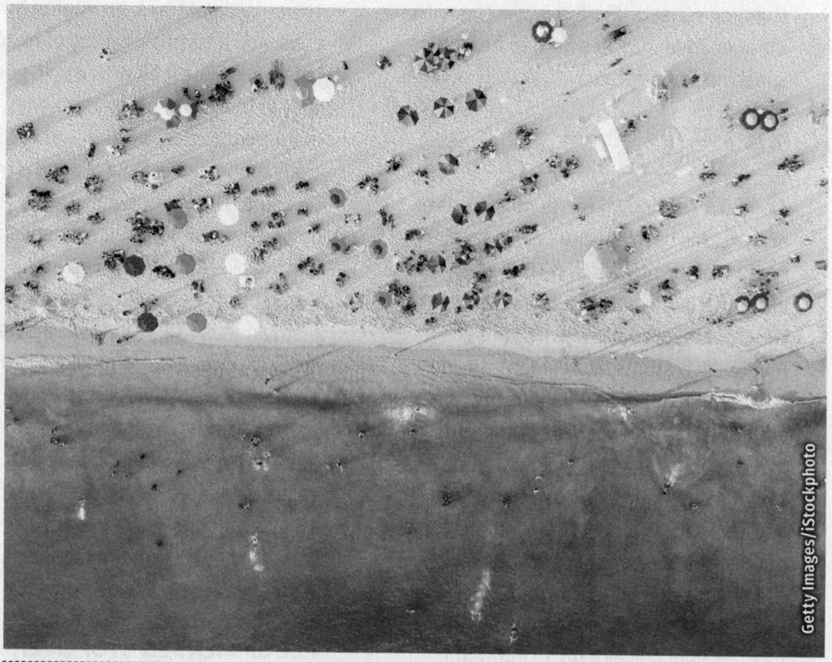

Getty Images/iStockphoto

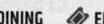

2 Fort Lauderdale
Drive 110 Miles ▪ 1 Hour, 44 Minutes

More than 160 miles of canals run through Fort Lauderdale, hence the city's nickname, the "Venice of America." Kick off your visit with a sightseeing cruise through Millionaire's Row. From mega-yachts to sprawling waterfront mansions, you'll get to see lavish homes owned by Hollywood stars. Next, soak up the sun at Fort Lauderdale Beach or Las Olas Beach and then enjoy dining and nightlife at the Riverwalk Arts & Entertainment District. If you want to get outdoors, head to Hugh Taylor Birch State Park to hike the Coastal Hammock Trail or wet your paddle in coastal dune lakes.

RECOMMENDED STOPOVER
B PARADISE ISLAND RV RESORT
FORT LAUDERDALE, FL (800) 487-7395

3 Miami
Drive 29 Miles ▪ 39 Minutes

Bring your appetite because you're going to need it for all the delicious Cuban cuisine. Locals recommend the Cubanos at Enriqueta's Sandwich Shop, croquettes at Islas Canarias and extra-large portions of Cuban comfort food at Rio Cristal. Walk off all the food by admiring vibrant murals in the Wynwood Arts District or exploring the Vizcaya Museum and Gardens, an extravagant Italian Renaissance-style villa in Coconut Grove. You can also drive 30 miles to Everglades

FL

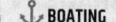

National Park for thrilling airboat rides, which bring you face-to-face with alligators, crocodiles and 360 species of birds.

RECOMMENDED STOPOVER
C BOARDWALK RV RESORT
HOMESTEAD, FL (305) 248-2487

4 Marathon
Drive 115 Miles • 2 Hours, 15 Minutes

Take life at a slower pace in Marathon. Tucked in the heart of the Florida Keys, this laid-back beach enclave invites you to unwind on the shores of Sombrero Beach. The area is also home to the only living coral barrier reef in the U.S., so book a scuba diving or snorkeling excursion to discover an underwater world teeming with corals and marine life. Other popular activities include fishing, meeting rescued sea turtles at the Turtle Hospital and interacting with dolphins at the Dolphin Research Center. The Florida Keys Aquarium in Marathon gives visitors a truly immersive experience with reef fish, invertebrates, stingrays and sharks. The facility's reef exhibit and shark habitat occupies a massive 200,000-gallon interconnected saltwater aquarium.

RECOMMENDED STOPOVER
D JOLLY ROGER RV RESORT
MARATHON, FL (305) 289-0404

5 Key West
Drive 50 Miles • 1 Hour, 8 Minutes

The southernmost point of the contiguous U.S. offers an eclectic mix of history and fun. Fans of Ernest Hemingway can visit his favorite watering hole, Sloppy Joe's, and wander through his old estate at the Ernest Hemingway Home and Museum. In the center of town, the Key West Cemetery gives you a sense of the island's offbeat humor with gravestone inscriptions like "I told you I was sick" and "I'm just resting my eyes." You'll find the best beaches at Fort Zachary Taylor Historic State Park and Dry Tortugas National Park, which is easily accessible by ferry or seaplane charter. On nearby Stock Island, the Key West Tropical Forest and Botanical Garden thrills visitors with its lush native landscapes, two ponds and neotropical migrating birds that stop on the island from as far away as South America. Hundreds of butterfly species thrive here.

RECOMMENDED STOPOVER
E BOYD'S KEY WEST CAMPGROUND
KEY WEST, FL (305) 294-1465

Getty Images/iStockphoto

Florida Gulf

Go Big for Gulf Adventures

Blending rich cultural history with amazing natural wonders, this trip down Florida's Gulf Coast is sure to impress. From Tampa's vibrant downtown neighborhoods to the wild interior of the Everglades, you'll discover firsthand the diverse landscapes and fascinating communities that make this region so unique. The best part? The entire journey comes with a backdrop of pristine beaches and stunning sunsets. For fun in the sun with a hint of adventure, it's hard to beat this Sunshine State getaway.

1 Tampa
Starting Point

Known for its multicultural history, this bayfront city serves up plenty of inspiring attractions. Thrill-seekers will relish in the pulse-pounding rides at Busch Gardens, while the picturesque Riverwalk features hip restaurants and shopping. To learn more about the role Cuban, Italian and Spanish immigrants played in helping grow Tampa's world-famous cigar industry, head to the must-see Ybor City Museum State Park. Once dubbed the "Cigar Capital of the World," the historic neighborhood features classic brick-paved streets and iconic architecture. You can still pick up an authentic, hand-rolled stogie at one of the many family-owned cigar shops that dot 7th Avenue. For a more soulful experience, the protected mangrove-fringed beaches and turquoise waters of Caladesi Island State Park (only accessible by boat) deliver pure Gulf Coast magic without the crowds. A three-mile paddling trail traverses the island's mangroves and affords great wildlife watching.

2 Punta Gorda
Drive 104 Miles • 1 Hour, 32 Minutes

Brimming with Old Florida charm, this small, laid-back city boasts towering palm trees, tin-roofed bungalows, and a surprising array of historic landmarks. See it all with a self-guided tour of the Punta Gorda Pathways, a web of interconnected walking and cycling trails that make getting around a true pleasure. The Harborwalk, Linear Park and Fisherman's Village are especially worthwhile. Eighteen miles east of town, the Babcock Ranch Preserve offers up plenty of recreation and wildlife viewing, including over 5 miles of hiking, biking and buggy trails that wind through cypress swamps, coastal forests and wide-open pasture. You might see herons, eagles and more. Keep an eye out for the 13 different species of endangered wildlife — including the rare Florida panther — that call the preserve home.

RECOMMENDED STOPOVER
A SUN N SHADE RV RESORT
PUNTA GORDA, FL (941) 639-5388

ANGLERS GET READY FOR ACTION AT THE FORT MYERS BEACH FISHING PIER.

Getty Images/iStockphoto

③ Fort Myers
Drive 24 Miles ▪ 35 Minutes

Situated 20 miles inland on the shores of the Caloosahatchee River, the "City of Palms" has been drawing visitors since as far back as 1916 when both Thomas Edison and Henry Ford had established their winter estates here. These days, you can explore the homes, gardens and laboratories of the famous inventors as part of a self-guided tour or alongside expert historians who help bring the immersive experience to life. Twenty miles west, where the river meets the Gulf, the area opens up into miles of soft, white-sand beaches. Home to some of the best seashell collecting on the planet, as well as endless opportunities for charter and surf fishing, the unspoiled shorelines of Sanibel Island, Lovers Key and Estero are truly one-of-a-kind destinations.

④ Bonita Springs
Drive 28 Miles ▪ 34 Minutes

Benefitting from a tropical climate, Bonita Springs is located on both the Gulf of Mexico and Estero Bay. The Imperial River flows through the city's downtown district, emptying into Estero Bay. Bonita Beach Park features a swimming area and boardwalk along with picnic shelters and a gazebo. *Forbes* ranked Barefoot Beach Preserve Park—one of the last undeveloped barrier islands on Florida's southwest coast—the sixth best beach in the nation. Wildlife lovers and sightseers alike will enjoy Lover's Key State Park, a wildlife haven composed of four barrier islands that feature hiking and biking trails and miles of pristine beaches. Just east of Bonita Springs, visitors will discover the Corkscrew Swamp Sanctuary, a bald cypress reserved managed by the National Audubon Society.

⑤ Everglades City
Drive 51 Miles ▪ 1 Hour

Near the state's southwestern tip, this end-of-the-road outpost is the perfect jumping-off point for exploring Everglades National Park, the country's largest subtropical wilderness. Home to manatees, alligators and a dizzying array of shorebirds, the unique landscape is begging to be explored by canoe or kayak. For a truly memorable adventure, head to the rugged Ten Thousand Islands region, where endless miles of mangrove forest await. There are plenty of outfitters available to help you organize a trip. If you'd rather stay on dry land, try Big Cypress National Preserve, where hikers, bikers and birders can enjoy miles of wilderness trails, as well as daily activities led by park rangers.

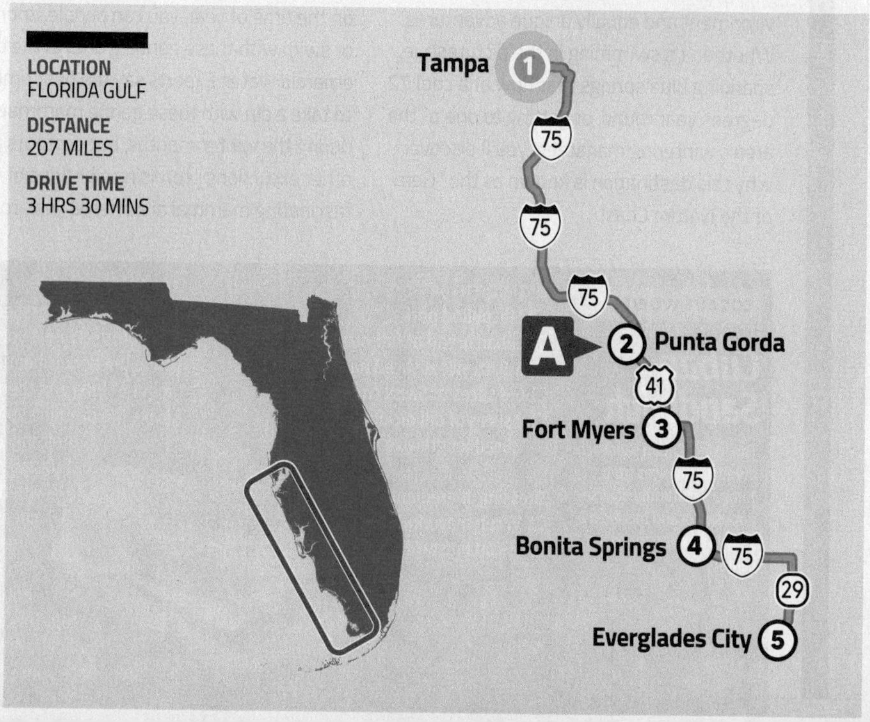

Florida SPOTLIGHTS

Bright Spots in the Sunshine State

Walk the shores of Florida's sugar-sand beaches or relax on the banks of one of its inland rivers. Florida serves up a menu of adventure with as many flavors as a Key West drink menu.

FLORIDA HAS MORE SPRINGS THAN ANY OTHER STATE IN THE U.S.

Kayakers navigate the crystal-clear waters of Three Sister Springs. CityofCrystalRiver

Crystal River

Located just 80 miles north of Tampa, this inland maze of springs, lakes and mangroves make for a one-of-a-kind environment and equally unique adventures. Whether it's swimming in the picturesque, sparkling blue springs that flow at a cool 72 degrees year round, or getting to one of the area's wintering manatees, you'll discover why this destination is known as the "Gem of the Nature Coast."

Three Sisters Springs

If seeing a manatee (or two or three) is on your agenda, don't miss Three Sisters Springs, a natural inlet that hosts hundreds of unique animals each winter. Depending on the time of year, you can paddle, snorkel, or swim with these gentle giants in the clear, emerald water. Experts say the best time to take a dip with these gentle mammals is during the winter months, but ecotours and other excursions promising sightings of this fascinating mammal are offered year-round.

On the Boardwalk

If you chose to stay on land, enjoy the incredible views from the boardwalk that circles the manatee area. Birdwatchers won't want to miss the restored wetlands that surround the springs and are home to dozens of unique bird varieties. Bring your camera to capture this wildlife.

Homosassa Spring Wildlife State Park

Just south of Crystal River, this park boasts some of the most diverse wildlife you'll see anywhere in the state. A section featuring captive animals unable to live in the wild includes alligators, black bears, red wolf, key deer, flamingoes and other species found naturally in the region. That is, except for "Lu," the park's beloved hippopotamus that was given Florida residency status instead of being removed. The paved trails are a great way to see these animals in the wild, especially for birdwatchers looking to check a few unique species off their list. In addition to what you'll see along the trails, the Fish Bowl underwater observatory allows visitors a view of the fish and manatees that inhabit the spring throughout the year.

Crystal River Preserve State Park

Visiting Crystal River Preserve State Park is like taking a trip back in time, as much of the area has been left untouched for centuries. Combining freshwater from spring-fed rivers and saltwater from the Gulf of Mexico,

LOCAL FAVORITE

Cuban Sandwich

The iconic Cuban sandwich blends influences from Tampa's culturally diverse population and has been a Florida favorite for over a century.

INGREDIENTS

- ☐ 1 lb. pulled pork
- ☐ Cuban bread or full-size hoagie rolls
- ☐ 6-8 oz. sweet sliced ham
- ☐ 6-8 slices of Swiss cheese
- ☐ 8 slices of dill pickles, sliced lengthwise

Dressing Ingredients

- ☐ ⅓ cup mayonnaise
- ☐ ⅓ cup mustard

DIRECTIONS

Heat the griddle to medium heat. Add pulled pork and a little pork stock liquid. Beef broth is fine if you don't have pork stock.

While the pork is heating up, start preparing the sandwich. Cut the bread to be about 6" long and then slice it lengthwise.

Make the dressing spread by combining mayonnaise and mustard. Take the dressing and smear it over both sides of the bread. Cover it good and heavy. Add Swiss cheese slices and then the hot pulled pork. Top it with dill pickles and sliced ham. Finish with another layer of Swiss cheese. Place the top half of the bread. Using a brush, apply melted butter to both sides of the bread.

To press the sandwich, place one side of the sandwich on the hot griddle and put a heavy pan such as a cast iron skillet on top. This will gently press the sandwich and allow all the ingredients to mingle. After a couple of minutes, flip the sandwich and do the other side. Slice your sandwich diagonally and enjoy!

FL

See listing Crystal River, FL

Stretching for seven miles along the western shore of Estero Island, Fort Myers Beach faces the Gulf of Mexico.

the park's 27,500 acres are one of Florida's most biologically diverse estuaries, including pinewoods, mangroves, salt marshes and hardwood forests to be explored by bike on the park's seven-mile loop or by boat for a waterfront view. Lucky naturalists should keep an eye out for the resident otter families or a dolphin cruising the water for its next meal.

Town of Homosassa

In Homosassa, water is central to everyday life. The town was one of Florida's original fishing villages and remains a top sport fishing destination as well as a working commercial fishing port on the Gulf of Mexico. It's also world-renowned for the size of its tarpon, so anglers looking to reel in a trophy-size catch should consider booking a local charter to get the inside scoop on the area's hot spots.

Fresh Catches

And after a day on the water, there's nothing better than stopping by one of the fresh fish markets for the catch of the day or visiting one of Florida's most famous hole-in-the-wall seafood joints: the funky and fun Freezer Tiki Bar.

Try Kayaking Along the Crystal River

If you love the idea of adventure, kayaking the Crystal River with a planned route is the way to go. Kayak rentals are easy to find and there are guides to show you the routes, which range anywhere from a 10-minute journey to 10 miles or more. Try exploring Homosassa Springs, Three Sisters Springs or Kings Bay. Kayaking is also a way to get up close and personal with manatees. Try not to scare these gentle giants.

History Unfolding

To step even further back into Florida living, visit the Crystal River Archaeological State Park, where pre-Columbian burial mounds and temple sites rise from the landscape. Interpretive walks and a museum at the visitors center are a great way to learn about Florida's unique Native American history.

Dive Into History

Of particular interest is the 28-foot Native American mound that dates to 500 B.C. Set along extensive marshlands, the pre-Columbia center ranks as one of the longest continuously occupied sites in Florida; thousands of Native Americans visited the site over the course of 1,600 years. The site is also located on a marsh plain so bird-watchers will have a field day.

Perennial Plantation

It's not just nature, though, that draws visitors to this year-round destination. The Plantation on Crystal River is a 232-acre eco-friendly resort that has been serving up locally sourced seafood, surf-and-turf and world-class golf for over 50 years.

Cool Croom

For terrain that is more challenging, the unpaved trails in the Croom area of the forest on the western side of the Withlacoochee River spice things up with hilly inclines and tricky technical areas in three loop trails over 19 miles. The Crystal River Preserve State Park preserves thousands of acres of coastline and is home to over half a dozen marked nature trails that snake through pinewoods, hardwood forests, salt marshes and mangrove islands, including a short boardwalk walking trail and a 7-mile unpaved biking/hiking loop trail.

Fort Myers

On the western shores of Florida's Gulf Coast, about 20 miles from the popular island of Sanibel, Fort Myers offers all of the sea and sun one would expect from a coastal Florida destination, but also great museums, restaurants, family activities, and even sporting events.

Historic Fort Myers

Fort Myers offers plenty for those interested in history. The 21-acre Edison and Ford Winter Estates showcase the winter homes of Thomas Edison and his friend and neighbor Henry Ford, and feature botanical gardens, a research lab, and museum exhibits. There's also the Mound

Point Ybel Light stands 98 feet on Sanibel Island's eastern tip and was one of the region's first nautical beacons.

House, a historic house on a shell mound that houses a museum full of shells that were collected and used by the indigenous Calusa tribes.

Standing up to four feet tall, great white egrets are some of the largest wading birds in Everglades National Park.

Beachfront Fun

Fort Myers' biggest draw is its beach, a 7-mile-long expanse of powdery white sand, dubbed "sugar sand," and its turquoise seas. Popular activities include kayaking and parasailing, and if you want to go fishing, you can rent a rod at the Fort Myers Beach Pier (no licenses required). Popular beaches in the region include North Captiva and Cayo Costa State Park, both of which are only accessible by boat. If you've brought your dog along, don't miss Bonita Beach, with its off-leash dog park. For an unusual treat, head to Bowman's Beach on Sanibel, characterized by its miles of vibrantly hued seashell and abundance of loggerhead sea turtles.

Urban Adventure

Fort Myers offers plenty more than just beaches, with a lively downtown and plenty of great dining and shopping options. In the heart of the city, Times Square and its vicinity is dotted with shops and restaurants, with plenty of terrace seating for summer evenings and regular live music performances. Fort Myers River District is also home to plenty of great restaurants and bars. If you're into architecture, don't miss the neighborhood's star attraction, the historic Georgian Revival Burroughs Home and Gardens.

One With Nature

Just as Fort Myers offers plenty of city fun, it's also a good base for exploring nature. A popular spot for nonmotorized watersports, the Great Calusa Blueway spans 190 miles and is home to a wide variety of birds and mammals, including dolphins, manatees and spoonbills. Another popular spot for wildlife lovers, the 3,500-acre Six Mile Cypress Slough

Covering more than 730 square miles, Lake Okeechobee is the second largest freshwater lake in the U.S.

Preserve is home to alligators, turtles, otters, and—in the winter months—a wide variety of migratory birds. A boardwalk runs through the park and guided tours are available. And if you happen to make your way to Sanibel, the J.N. "Ding" Darling National Wildlife Refuge is not to be missed, with its 6,400 acres of mangrove, nearly half of which is a protected Federal Wilderness Area. Along with a visitors center with educational displays, the refuge offers a tram service and regular guided tours. If you have access to a boat, Lovers Key State Park is also worth considering, with plenty of trails and excellent fishing opportunities (fish found here include tarpon, grouper and Spanish mackerel).

Take Me Out to the Ballgame

Fort Myers has long been popular with ball fans and teams alike, and its great weather attracts both the Boston Red Sox and Minnesota Twins to town for their annual spring training. The Twins play at Hammond Stadium and the Red Sox play at JetBlue Park, and with games almost every day, it's usually easy to grab tickets. The parks also host everything from college games to sports camps when they aren't being used by MLB teams.

Bring the Grandkids

Whether you've got little ones in tow or simply enjoy family-friendly fun yourself, Fort Myers will deliver. Popular area attractions include the IMAG History and Science Center, which offers educational, hands-on exhibits with a heavy focus on science. Highlights include a "touch tank" (essentially an aquatic petting zoo), a history section, and a huge globe that's animated with video mapping to help teach visitors more about the planet we call home. The Calusa Nature Center and Planetarium is also a hit across generations, and offers planetarium shows, guided nature hikes, and animal shows on its 105-acre protected property. Lakes Regional Park offers plenty for visitors of all ages, with a freshwater lake, ample trails, paddleboat rentals, a playground and even a mini train. The Shell Factory and Nature Park is also worth visiting, with plenty of water activities, from paddleboats to water balloon games, along with make-believe gem sifting, a climbing wall, ziplining and a petting zoo.

Hendry County

In Hendry County, sprawling patches of pristine wetlands and bass-filled waterways give you a front-row seat to South Florida's wild side. Whether you choose to take an airboat ride through the Everglades, cast a line in Lake Okeechobee or traverse miles upon miles of forest trails, you'll find an infinite amount of ways to explore this untamed part of the Sunshine State.

Swamp Safari

Located within the Big Cypress Reservation, the Billie Swamp Safari offers a range of activities guaranteed to get your heart pumping. Watch a snake demonstration, whiz across the Everglades by airboat or board the swamp buggy safari to come face-to-face with alligators, hogs and maybe even a Florida panther. Riding on large tractor wheels, swamp buggies can handle almost any terrain, giving you an amazing ride. Be sure to try the tasty Seminole fry bread at the Swamp Water Café too. If you'd like to stay the night, reserve one of the traditional chickees in the park. The rustic thatched-roof dwellings may be simple, but they give you the chance to hear the wetlands come alive after the sun goes down.

Fantastic Freshwater Fishing

Lake Okeechobee is one of the nation's top destinations for largemouth bass. If you're ready to reel in a big one, head to Roland and Mary Ann Martin Marina on the west side of the lake. The resort and marina have everything you need for your angling adventure, including a tackle shop, boat rentals, fishing guides and more. Uncle Joe's Fish Camp at Liberty Point is another great location to launch your boat from. Spend the day catching bass and then stay overnight at a campsite or air-conditioned cabin.

River of Fish

For more angling action, make your way to the Caloosahatchee River. Beginning at Lake Okeechobee and running through LaBelle, this 67-mile-long river is a hotspot for trout, bass, tarpon and catfish. Discover the river's most bountiful spots.

Florida Untamed

Swaths of dense forest remain untouched in this part of the Sunshine State. If you're set on getting away from it all, go to the 32,370-acre Okaloacoochee Slough State Forest where loads of hiking and biking trails await. The Spirit-of-the-Wild Wildlife Management Area is also an excellent place for wildlife viewing with opportunities to see sandhill cranes, white-tailed deer and a variety of wading birds. Hunting can be done in both places, as well as in private estates like Black Boar Ranch, Big "O" Hunts and Gator Glades Hunts.

Sweet Towns

Resting on the southern shores of Lake Okeechobee is Clewiston, the largest city in Hendry County. You can get a sense of the town's Old South roots at the historic Clewiston Inn. Listed on the National Register of Historic Places, this 57-room hotel looks just like it did when it was built in 1926. Don't miss the spectacular wildlife mural wrapping around the inn's Everglades Lounge. More local history is on display at the Clewiston Museum. Step inside to view fossils discovered in Hendry County, original tools used in sugar cane production and Native American artifacts.

LaBelle

Beautiful LaBelle is just a stone's throw away. Nestled along the banks of the Caloosahatchee River, this quaint community has a lovely commercial district lined with restaurants and shops. Pop in the Harold P. Curtis Honey Company for beeswax candles and all sorts of honey products and check out the gallery and gift shop in Barron Park just a few blocks away.

Southern Celebrations

Get to know the community by attending local fairs and festivals throughout the year. The Hendry County Fair and Livestock Show takes place mid-February in Clewiston and draws quite the crowd with its youth livestock shows, carnival rides, beauty pageants and parade. In the same month is LaBelle's Swamp Cabbage Festival. The two-day event promises family fun with a car show, rodeo, fishing tournament and 5K run. Live entertainment in Barron Park rounds out the experience. Got a sweet tooth? Fill up on all kinds of treats at the Clewiston Sugar Festival. Dating back to the 1930s, this March festival originally marked the end of the sugarcane harvest season and has evolved into the largest event in Hendry County.

The Land of the Unconquered

The Big Cypress Reservation is home to the Seminole clan, the only Native American tribe that has never been conquered by the United States government. You can hear their stories at the Smithsonian-affiliated Ah-Tah-Thi-Ki Museum. Exhibits, films and a research center touch on many topics like how the Seminole hunted, traded and traveled. There is also a boardwalk weaving through tranquil woodlands and a small village where you can purchase beautiful crafts from Seminole elders.

Florida Cowboys

Cattle ranching also has deep roots in the region. The area was named after Francis A. Hendry, a cattle rancher who founded the city of LaBelle. He named the town after Hendry's two daughters, Laura and Belle. That ranching legacy is celebrated during the Annual Swamp Cabbage Festival Ranch Rodeo, held in conjunction with the Swamp Cabbage Festival in February in the LaBelle Rodeo Grounds. The event features some of the top ropers and riders in the nation along with Florida cowboys and cowgirls whose horse- and cattle-handling skills have been shared between generations.

Retail Heaven

While you're in Hendry County you'll want to set aside some time to check the many small-town niche stores and restaurants that serve up the unique flavor of the area. Several antique shops in the county sell historical treasures that shed light onto "old Florida." Check out the Country Peddlers Antique Mall for a trip into the Sunshine State's colorful history.

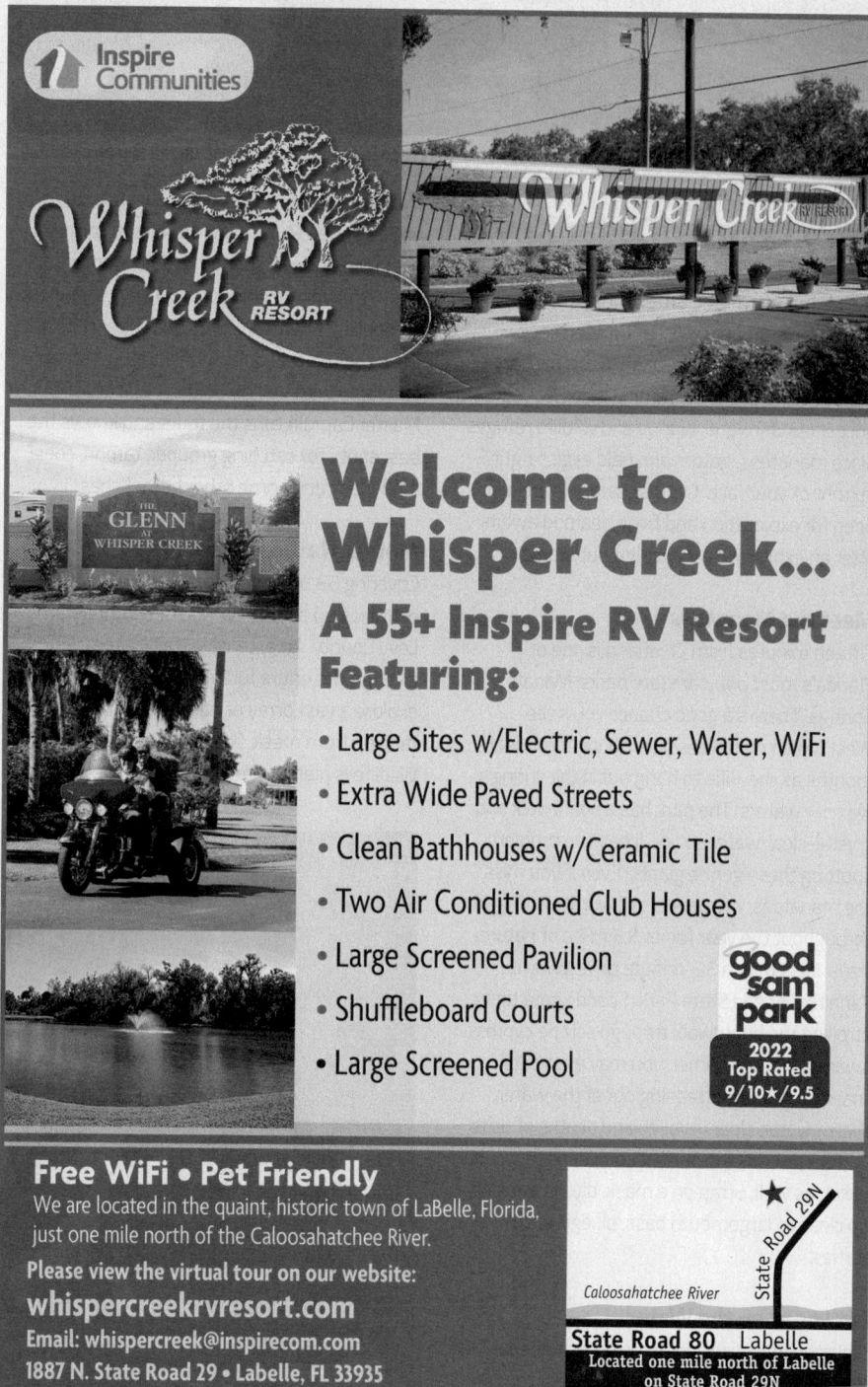

FL

Basking turtles, like this yellow-bellied slider, like to rest on logs or rocks and soak up the sun on clear days.

Levy County/Cedar Key

Leave the man-made attractions behind and prepare to experience Cedar Key and Levy County, aka the Nature Coast. In this part of the Sunshine State, swimming holes let you uncover underwater worlds and wildlife refuges place manatees, gators and bald eagles right in front of your face. Cypress swamps are also open for exploration and fresh seafood awaits after an exhilarating day spent outdoors.

Meet the Manatees

Fifteen minutes from Chiefland is one of Florida's most popular state parks: Manatee Springs. There's a good chance you'll see West Indian manatees here during the colder months as they like to hang out in the spring's warmer waters. The park has a boardwalk and crystal-clear water so you'll have no problem spotting these gentle giants. Even if you miss the manatees, the park is still worth visiting all throughout the year for its 8.5 miles of nature trails. Less than a 30-minute drive away is Fanning Springs State Park. Spend some time strolling the boardwalk through serene cypress swamp. In the summer, you may even catch massive sturgeons leaping out of the water. Warm water, clear visibility and depths of up to 21 feet provide the perfect conditions for scuba diving as well. Strap on a mask, dive in and get up close to largemouth bass, bluegill and musk turtles.

Let Loose on the Water

Sightseeing cruises open the doors to Cedar Key's alluring tidal marsh eco-system. You can book a cruise with Tidewater Tours and choose from three routes: the island, coastal marsh or Suwannee River. Expert guides accompany every trip and will share their knowledge about the unique landscape while pointing out compelling migratory birds and marine life. If you're set on scalloping or fishing, opt for an excursion with Voyles Guide. A U.S. Coast Guard Master Captain runs the tours and knows the best spots for catching grouper, tarpon, cobia, amberjack and some other hefty fishes.

Mother Nature Calls

Covering 53,587 acres, the Goethe State Forest takes up a hefty portion of southeastern Levy County. An extensive trail system winds through the entire forest which allows you to explore a vast array of natural environments ranging from mesic flatwoods to basin swamp. Wildlife is plentiful too so keep an eye out for woodpeckers, gopher tortoises and striped newts. More animals can be seen at two national wildlife refuges: Lower Suwannee and Cedar Keys. The Lower Suwannee is a haven for otters, turtles and alligators. It's also prime hunting grounds for white-tailed deer. Over in Cedar Keys, look out for dolphins, eagle rays and white pelicans. Shore fishing is permitted in most months so feel free to bring your tackle box too.

Happy as a Clam

Cedar Key thrives on commercial clamming and you can see all the action at Southern Cross Sea Farms, one of the largest hard-shell clam producers in the state. Free tours walk you through the entire clam production process from the hatchery to the harvest. Fresh clams and fish are also available for purchase on-site. After the tour, head down the street to Tony's Seafood. The clam chowder here has won the annual Great Clam Chowder Cook-Off in Rhode Island three times so you'll definitely want to order a bowl or two. You can also pick up fresh, frozen or canned chowder if you want to bring some home. Keep in mind Tony's chowder is also served in many restaurants all over Florida.

Community Events

There's no shortage of family-friendly festivals in this section of Florida. Come to the Cedar Key Arts Festival in April to see ceramics, paintings, glasswork and more by over a hundred artists. The two-day event also hosts art demonstrations on both afternoons. In May, check out the Annual Garden Show and Spring Festival at Cedar Lakes Woods and Gardens. Musical performances, food trucks and plant vendors

Florida manatees are called "gentle giants" for good reason: They are friendly and come to people to get pet.

On Florida's Atlantic side, condos line the beach just north of Fort Pierce Inlet State Park on Jack Island.

guarantee a fun day out. If you're an environmentalist, sign up for September's International Coastal Cleanup. The cleanup starts at the Cedar Key City Marina and ends with a hot dog lunch for volunteers. Don't miss the Cedar Key Seafood Festival too. The two-day event in October is sure to satisfy your hunger with hearty bowls of chowder and fried oysters. A parade, live music and craft exhibits round out the experience.

The Heart of Old Florida

Cedar Key's rustic marinas and retro diners keep the spirit of Old Florida alive. Get a feel for its old-timey atmosphere on Second Street, a commercial district lined with weathered buildings from the 1800s. Just a stone's throw away is the Island Hotel and Restaurant, an 1859 establishment listed on the National Register of Historic Places. Stop for a drink inside the Neptune Bar and admire the beautiful murals which were painted in 1948. You can also unravel the town's colorful past at two places.

History, Museums & Monuments

Get an overview of Cedar Key's history as a port city and railroad town with a visit to the Cedar Key Museum State Park. You can also learn about the Native Americans who once lived in the region and the town's role in the Civil War. An expansive seashell collection and a restored farmstead round out the offerings. Housed in a building that dates to 1871, the Cedar Key Historical Society Museum is another pick for exploring the story of the area. Dedicated guides and a variety of artifacts bring the past to life. Those with an interest in military history will want to explore the Fort Fanning Historic Park. Located on the Suwannee River, this fort played a prominent role in the Second Seminole War.

Paynes Prairie Reserve

A 10-minute drive south of Gainesville, Paynes Prairie Preserve State Park ranks as one of Florida's most environmentally sensitive and historic areas. A National Natural Landmark, the 21,000-acre park is hailed for its biodiversity. More than 20 unique biological ecosystems, ranging from wet prairie to pine flat woods, hammocks and ponds, give refuge to a captivating array of wildlife, including alligators, bison and 270 bird species. Eight trails snake through the terrain.

St. Lucie County

St Lucie County is blessed. The area's 21 miles of uncrowded, pristine beaches are lapped by clear waters, and almost half this coastline is protected from development, a rarity in these parts. In addition to its beautiful setting and array of activities on land and sea, St. Lucie County offers a clutch of historic and cultural sites in revitalized Lincoln Park, Fort Pierce and St. Lucie Village.

Riding Free

With the Indian River Lagoon's abundance of biodiversity and pristine beaches and dunes, St Lucie is a land of wild and scenic beauty. St. Lucie is famed among equestrians as one of the few places in Florida where riders can experience Florida's wild beaches on horseback. On Hutchinson Island, Bathtub Beach draws families to its shallow reef, which provides rewarding snorkeling just 100 yards from the beach. On South Hutchinson Island, white sand Waveland Beach has all the requisite beach amenities for a fun and convenient daytrip. It's the starting point for the 13.2-mile bike path that funnels north to Fort Pierce.

All Creatures Great and Small

The Fort Pierce City Marina is the launching pad for myriad on-the-water tours and activities. Wildlife watching tours on the Indian River Lagoon provide close encounters with over 4,000 native plants and animals, including manatees, sea turtles and bottlenose dolphins. This teeming 156-mile estuary is a magnet for anglers with prize-winning catches of

FL

Accessible from Tampa, the Hillsborough River Paddling Trail runs 30 miles to Hillsborough River State Park.

tarpon, snook, red drum and huge sea trout. Novice surfers can take lessons through a local surf shop at Fort Pierce Inlet State Park, St. Lucie's most consistent break.

Fishing for History

One of the oldest towns in eastern Florida, steeped in centuries-old fishing traditions, Fort Pierce remains a haven for seasoned anglers. With healthy waters populated with tuna, sailfish, barracuda, amberjack, cobia, snapper and grouper, records are constantly challenged and broken in these parts, including a colossal 17-pound, 7-ounce sea trout plucked from these waters in 1995.

Diamond Days

Baseball fans know that Florida becomes a hot spot for both fans and scouts during the spring months when major league teams head south for spring training. The New York Mets have called Port St. Lucie their springtime home for years, and there's nothing quite like seeing the team play in the casual preseason atmosphere. You can also explore the historic downtown.

Golf Nirvana

The nearby PGA Village Golf Resort offers the chance to try your luck on the greens with a state-of-the-art training facility, multiple courses and a performance center where experts can help you improve your game. Learn about the rich heritage of golf or take your choice of three challenging 18-hole courses. Learn about famous golfers at the museum.

American Heroes

The area is also home to the world's only museum dedicated to the fearless spirit of the naval warriors who trained in the area's coastal waters. The National Navy UDT-SEAL Museum boasts displays on the exploits of the legendary fighters.

Tampa

Situated on Florida's Tampa Bay, the city of Tampa offers great museums, easy access to white-sand beaches, and more animal-related attractions than most people could fit into one trip. It's also home to historic Ybor City, once at the heart of the Florida cigar trade. While Tampa certainly has a big-city vibe, a number of expansive nature preserves are mere minutes away.

Animal Adventures

If you're interested in getting up close with wildlife, Tampa won't disappoint. The city and its surrounding areas have a huge range of animal-related attractions—so many, in fact, that you could easily devote an entire vacation just to zoos and sanctuaries. The most famous of the lot is Busch Gardens, a mix between a zoo and an amusement park, complete with thrilling roller coasters and all sorts of creatures; there's even a wallaby petting zoo. The park also offers a number of animal encounter programs; sign up for the Serengeti Safari for the chance to hand feed a giraffe! Giraffe feeding is also an option at Giraffe Ranch in Dade City, a large park that houses creatures such as hippos, rhinos and zebras, to name a few. You can visit in a 4WD vehicle, on the back of a camel, or even on a Segway.

Life Below the Surface

Closer to town, The Florida Aquarium focuses on life under the sea, while the 56-acre ZooTampa at Lowry Park is home to over 1,100 animals. Also in town, the nonprofit Big Cat Rescue sanctuary is devoted to protecting exotic and large felines from poaching and the pet trade, while Tampa Electric's Manatee Viewing Center (open November through mid-April) offers travelers the chance to learn about manatees and even see some of the majestic "sea cows" swimming in the wild.

Cigar City

One of Tampa's most popular places for visitors and locals alike is Ybor City, a historic district dating to the Victorian era. The area had a large Cuban population and was originally a hub for cigar manufacture (though the industry began to decline due to the Great Depression). Today, Ybor City is best known for its great dining options and nightlife, though its historic roots have certainly not been forgotten. If you want to learn more about the neighborhood's early days, the Ybor City Museum, housed inside a century-old bakery building, is a great place to start. Walking tours are also popular in the area—themes include foodie exploration, local history, and even ghost hunting. If you're particularly interested in cigars, you can take a factory tour of Tabanero Cigars, where you can learn all about cigar manufacture and watch employees roll up stogies by hand.

Plant Perfections

Tampa has a number of fantastic museums, the most eye-catching of which is the Henry B. Plant Museum. It's housed in part of the Moorish-Revival style Plant Hall at the University of Tampa, an 1891 building with onion-domed turrets and grand latticed arches. While the building is an attraction unto itself, the museum inside reveals all sorts of decorative arts from the Victorian era.

Terrific Tampa Art

Not far from Plant Hall, the Tampa Museum of Art offers works dating from ancient times to the modern era, and regularly hosts special exhibits. If you're interested in history, the Tampa Bay History Center focuses on local history, from pre-European settlement to the 20th century. The Museum of Science & Industry (MOSI) is also worth visiting, especially with kids, and offers science and technology exhibits focusing on topics ranging from environmental conservation to space exploration.

One With Nature

Although Tampa very much has a city vibe, it's still close enough to parks, swamplands, and protected areas for those itching to get out in nature. One of the most popular (and easy to get to) options is Lettuce Lake Park, just outside of town. It's a popular spot for canoeing and kayaking (rentals are available on-site), and getting out on the water is a good way to spot some of the park's many aquatic birds. If you'd rather stay on land, there's also a boardwalk with an observation deck as well as a paved running trail and plenty of picnic areas. Take your time exploring this dynamic terrain.

Protected Wilderness

A little further out, but still within half an hour or so of town, the Lower Hillsborough Wilderness Preserve features over 60 miles of forest trails and plenty of opportunities to paddle through dense swampland. It connects to the 3,000-acre Hillsborough River State Park, with additional trails as well as opportunities to fish for bass, catfish and bream. On the opposite side of Tampa, in St. Petersburg, Weedon Island Preserve spans 3,190 acres and offers a ton of outdoor recreation opportunities, from fishing off a long pier to exploring the preserve's extensive network of trails and boardwalks. There's also a visitors center that's full of exhibits focusing on both local ecology and the traditions of local indigenous people, although the real highlight for history fans is the chance to view an 1,100-year-old dugout canoe that was excavated from the area in 2011.

▸ FOR MORE INFORMATION

Discover Crystal River, 800-587-6667, www.discovercrystalriverfl.com

The Beaches of Fort Myers and Sanibel, 800-237-6444, www.fortmyers-sanibel.com

Hendry County Tourist Development Council, 863-983-7979, www.discoverhendrycounty.com

Levy County Visitors Bureau, 877-387-5673, www.visitnaturecoast.com

Visit Tampa Bay, 800-448-2672, www.visittampabay.com

Florida

ALACHUA — B3 *Alachua*

TRAVELERS CAMPGROUND
good sam park **Ratings: 9.5/9.5★/8.5** (Campground) From Jct of I-75 & US-441 (exit 399), E 100 ft on US-441 to service rd (April Blvd, Waffle House), N 1 mi (R).

RIGHT OFF 1-75 CLOSE TO GAINESVILLE
Your home away from home in the rolling hills of central Florida. Close to the University of Florida and other fun venues. Enjoy our spacious park with Big Rig friendly pull thrus, heated pool, free WiFi, & social activities.
FAC: paved rds. (148 spaces). Avail: 48 all weather, 48 pull-thrus, (30x70), 48 full hkups (30/50 amps), seasonal sites, cable, WiFi @ sites, tent sites, dump, laundry, groc, LP gas. **REC:** pool, playground. Pets OK. Partial handicap access. Big rig sites, eco-friendly. 2021 rates: $69 to $89, Military discount. no cc.
(386)462-2505 Lat: 29.81820, Lon: -82.51371
17701 April Blvd, Alachua, FL 32615
www.travelerscampground.com
See ad page 258

ALVA — D4 *Hendry*

FRANKLIN LOCK & DAM/W.P. FRANKLIN NORTH COE
(Public Corps) From Jct of SR-31 & SR-78, E 3 mi on CR-78 to N Franklin Lock Rd, follow signs (R). **FAC:** paved rds. Avail: 29 paved, 5 pull-thrus, (15x50), back-ins (15x50), 29 W, 29 E (50 amps), tent sites, dump, laundry. **REC:** Caloosahatchee River: swim, fishing, kayaking/canoeing, playground. Pets OK. Partial handicap access, 14 day max stay. 2021 rates: $30 to $35.
(239)694-8770 Lat: 26.727424, Lon: -81.692608
17850 N. Franklin Lock Rd, Alva, FL 33920
www.recreation.gov

APOPKA — H4 *Orange*

LOST LAKE RV PARK
good sam park **Ratings: 7.5/9.5★/7.5** (RV Park) From jct I-4 & FL 414 (Maitland Blvd): Go 6-3/4 mi W on Maitland Blvd, then 1/2 mi W on Keene Rd, then 3/4 mi S on Clarcona Rd (SR435) (R). **FAC:** gravel rds. 81 Avail: 10 paved, 71 gravel, back-ins (25x45), 81 full hkups (30/50 amps), WiFi @ sites, laundry, groc. **REC:** pool. Pet restrict (S/B). No tents. Big rig sites, eco-friendly. 2021 rates: $41 to $50. no cc.
(407)886-1996 Lat: 28.6300, Lon: -81.4986
3400 Clarcona Rd, Apopka, FL 32703
See ad page 288

ORANGE BLOSSOM KOA **Ratings: 8/9★/8** (Campground) Avail: 80 full hkups (30/50 amps). 2021 rates: $55 to $95. (407)886-3260, 3800 W Orange Blossom Trail, Apopka, FL 32712

WEKIWA SPRINGS (Public State Park) From Jct of I-4 & SR-434 (exit 94), W 1 mi on SR-434 to Wekiwa Springs Rd, NW 4.9 mi to Park Entrance Rd, follow signs (R). 53 Avail: 53 W, 53 E (20/30 amps). 2021 rates: $24. (407)884-2008

ARCADIA — D3 *De Soto*

BIG TREE RV RESORT **Ratings: 8.5/8.5★/8.5** (RV Park) Avail: 20 full hkups (30/50 amps). 2021 rates: $46 to $127. (863)494-7247, 2626 NE Hwy 70, Arcadia, FL 34266

CRAIG'S RV PARK
good sam park **Ratings: 8.5/9★/8.5** (RV Park) From Jct of SR-70 & US-17, N 6.7 mi on US-17 to NE Cubitis Ave, W 0.1 mi (R).

ENJOY COUNTRY LIVING AT ITS BEST!
Relax this season at our family owned destination park. Our planned activities can keep you busy inside & out. Enter the park as strangers & leave as family. The experience will keep you coming back, again and again.
FAC: paved rds. (333 spaces). Avail: 172 grass, patios, 25 pull-thrus, (30x45), back-ins (30x45), 172 full hkups (30/50 amps), seasonal sites, cable, WiFi @ sites, $, dump, laundry, LP gas. **REC:** heated pool, boating nearby, shuffleboard. Pet restrict (B/Q). Partial handicap access. No tents. 2021 rates: $35 to $68, Military discount.
(863)494-1820 Lat: 27.30908, Lon: -81.81987
7895 NE Cubitis Ave, Arcadia, FL 34266
www.craigsrvpark.com
See ad opposite page

CROSS CREEK RV RESORT **Ratings: 10/10★/10** (RV Resort) Avail: 75 full hkups (30/50 amps). 2021 rates: $50 to $75. (863)494-7300, 6837 NE Cubitis Ave, Arcadia, FL 34266

LETTUCE LAKE TRAVEL RESORT **Ratings: 8.5/8.5/8.5** (Campground) Avail: 50 full hkups (30/50 amps). 2021 rates: $50. (863)494-6057, 8644 SW Reese St, Arcadia, FL 34269

LITTLE WILLIES RV RESORT **Ratings: 8.5/9/8.5** (RV Park) Avail: 100 full hkups (30/50 amps). 2021 rates: $58. (863)494-2717, 5905 NE Cubitis Ave, Arcadia, FL 34266

OAK HAVEN MH & RV PARK **Ratings: 8/9★/8.5** (RV Park) Avail: 63 full hkups (30/50 amps). 2021 rates: $55 to $70. (863)494-4578, 10307 SW Lettuce Lake Ave, Arcadia, FL 34269

PEACE RIVER CAMPGROUND **Ratings: 8/5.5/7** (Campground) Avail: 127 full hkups (30/50 amps). 2021 rates: $85. (863)494-9693, 2998 NW Hwy 70, Arcadia, FL 34266

TOBY'S RV RESORT
good sam park **Ratings: 8.5/8/8.5** (RV Park) Avail: 150 full hkups (30/50 amps). 2021 rates: $30 to $71. (888)563-7040, 3550 NE Hwy 70, Arcadia, FL 34266

AUBURNDALE — K3 *Polk*

CAMP MARGARITAVILLE **Ratings: 10/10★/10** (RV Park) Avail: 151 full hkups (30/50 amps). 2021 rates: $64 to $85. (863)455-7335, 361 Denton Ave, Auburndale, FL 33823

FISH HAVEN
good sam park (RV Area in MH Park) (Seasonal Stay Only) Avail: 1 full hkups (50 amps). (863)984-1183, 201 Fish Haven Road, Auburndale, FL 33823

AVON PARK — L4 *Highlands*

BONNET LAKE CAMPGROUNDS **Ratings: 8.5/8.5/7** (RV Park) Avail: 25 full hkups (30/50 amps). 2021 rates: $50. (863)385-3700, 2825 SR-17 S, Avon Park, FL 33825

LAKE GLENADA RV RESORT **Ratings: 7.5/9.5★/7** (RV Park) Avail: 119 full hkups (30/50 amps). 2021 rates: $50. (863)453-7007, 2525 US Hwy 27 S, Avon Park, FL 33825

REFLECTIONS ON SILVER LAKE **Ratings: 9/10★/9** (RV Park) Avail: 50 full hkups (30/50 amps). 2021 rates: $67. (863)453-5756, 3522 Bill Sachsenmaier, Avon Park, FL 33825

BAHIA HONDA KEY — F4 *Monroe*

BAHIA HONDA (Public State Park) S-bnd: On US-1 (oceanside), at MP-37 (L). 80 Avail: 72 W, 72 E (30/50 amps). 2021 rates: $36. (305)872-2353

BARTOW — K3 *Polk*

GOOD LIFE RV RESORT **Ratings: 9/9.5★/8.5** (RV Park) Avail: 14 full hkups (30/50 amps). 2021 rates: $40. (863)537-1971, 6815 SR-60E, Bartow, FL 33830

Travel Services

GANDER RV OF BARTOW Your new hometown outfitter offering the best regional gear for all your outdoor needs. Your adventure awaits. **SERVICES:** RV, tire, RV appliance, MH mechanical, sells outdoor gear, sells firearms, staffed RV wash, restrooms. RV Sales. RV supplies, LP gas, RV accessible. Hours: 9am - 7pm. (866)906-9517 Lat: 27.889193, Lon: -81.820519 7400 S.R. 60 East, Bartow, FL 33830 rv.ganderoutdoors.com

County names are provided after the city names. If you're tracking the weather, this is the information you'll need to follow the reports.

BELL — B3 *Gilchrist*

◄ HART SPRINGS PARK (Public) From Jct of US 19 & SR-26 to CR-232 (in Fanning Springs), E 2 mi on SR-26 to CR-232, N 4 mi to CR-344, W 1 mi (R). Avail: 71 full hkups (30/50 amps). 2021 rates: $35. (352)463-3444

BELLE GLADE — D5 *Palm Beach*

▲ TORRY ISLAND CAMPGROUND & MARINA (Public) From jct Hwy 80 & Hwy 715: Go 2-1/4 mi N on Hwy 715, then 2 mi W on Torry Rd. (Turn left immediately after crossing bridge.). 380 Avail: 240 full hkups, 140 W, 140 E (50 amps). 2021 rates: $16.80 to $29.12. (561)996-6322

BEVERLY HILLS — H2 *Citrus*

▲ SANDY OAKS RV RESORT **Ratings: 9.5/9.5★/9** (RV Park) Avail: 85 full hkups (30/50 amps). 2021 rates: $52 to $57. (352)465-7233, 6760 N Lecanto Hwy (CR 491), Beverly Hills, FL 34465

BIG PINE KEY — F4 *Monroe*

↘ BIG PINE KEY RESORT

good sam park **Ratings: 7.5/9★/8** (RV Park) S-bnd: On US-1 (Oceanside) at MP-33 (L). **FAC:** gravel rds. Avail: 169 gravel, back-ins (23x35), 97 full hkups (30/50 amps), cable, WiFi @ sites, tent sites, laundry, groc, LP bottles, controlled access. **REC:** heated pool, Atlantic Ocean: swim, fishing, marina, kayaking/canoeing, boating nearby, shuffleboard. Partial handicap access. 2021 rates: $79 to $86, Military discount.
(786)386-0982 Lat: 24.64778, Lon: -81.33184
33000 Overseas Hwy, Big Pine Key, FL 33043
www.covecommunities.com
See ad this page

↗ SUNSHINE KEY RV RESORT & MARINA

good sam park **Ratings: 9/9★/9** (RV Park) Avail: 200 full hkups (30/50 amps). 2021 rates: $93 to $220. (888)563-7040, 38801 Overseas Hwy, Big Pine Key, FL 33043

BOKEELIA — D3 *Lee*

▼ TROPICAL WATERS RV RESORT **Ratings: 7.5/7.5/7.5** (RV Park) Avail: 50 full hkups (30/50 amps). 2021 rates: $78. (239)283-4456, 15175 Stringfellow Rd, Bokeelia, FL 33922

RV SPACE-SAVING TIPS: Install an over-the-counter trashcan for the bathroom to save space and for easy clean up that isn't going to get knocked over. Keep a handheld vacuum handy (ideally attached to the wall/ceiling in the bathroom or closet) for quick and easy clean-up for after a sandy day at the beach or after the kids or grandkids eat lunch.

Pre-Drive Safety INTERIOR Checklist: Secure all loose items; Ensure stove burners and oven are in off position; Securely latch cabinet and closet doors; Close roof vents and windows; Turn OFF air conditioner/heat pump/furnace; Turn OFF refrigerator and securely latch doors; Turn OFF water pump; Turn OFF interior RV lights; Fully retract slides and secure.

FL

BONITA SPRINGS — E4 *Lee*

BONITA LAKE RV RESORT
good sam park
Ratings: 8.5/8.5★/8.5 (RV Park) From Jct of I-75 & Bonita Beach Rd (Exit 116), W 1.7 mi on Bonita Beach Rd to Old 41 Rd, N 1.7 mi (R). **FAC:** paved rds. (181 spaces). 148 Avail: 51 paved, 97 grass, patios, back-ins (30x45), 148 full hkups (30/50 amps), WiFi @ sites, dump, laundry. **REC:** heated pool, Bonita Lake: fishing, boating nearby, shuffleboard. Pet restrict (B). Partial handicap access. No tents, eco-friendly. 2021 rates: $60 to $85, Military discount.
(239)992-2481 Lat: 26.35594, Lon: -81.78226
26325 Old 41 Rd, Bonita Springs, FL 34135
www.bonitalake.com
See ad this page

BONITA TERRA
good sam park
Ratings: 8/9★/8.5 (RV Park) 160 Avail: 130 full hkups, 30 W, 30 E (30/50 amps). 2021 rates: $45 to $70. (239)992-3030, 25581 Trost Blvd, Bonita Springs, FL 34135

Refer to the Table of Contents in front of the Guide to locate everything you need.

GULF COAST CAMPING RESORT
good sam park
Ratings: 7.5/8.5★/7.5 (RV Park) From jct I-75 (exit 116) & CR-865/Bonita Beach Rd: Go 4-1/4 mi W on Bonita Beach Rd, then 3-1/2 mi N on US-41/Tamiami Trail, then 1/4 mi E on Production Circle (R). **FAC:** paved rds. (260 spaces). 186 Avail: 2 paved, 184 grass, back-ins (40x50), 186 full hkups (30/50 amps), WiFi @ sites, tent sites, dump, laundry. **REC:** pool, pond, fishing, boating nearby, shuffleboard. Pets OK. 2021 rates: $55 to $70. Oct 01 to Jun 01.
(239)992-3808 Lat: 26.38475, Lon: -81.80530
24020 Production Circle, Bonita Springs, FL 34135
www.gulfcoastcampingresort.com
See ad this page

IMPERIAL BONITA ESTATES RV RESORT
good sam park
Ratings: 9/9.5★/9 (RV Park) From Jct of I-75 & CR-865 (exit 116/Bonita Beach Rd), W 0.7 mi on CR-865 (Bonita Beach) to Imperial Pkwy, N 0.2 mi to Dean St, E 0.1 mi (L). **FAC:** paved rds. (307 spaces). Avail: 218 all weather, patios, 30 pull-thrus, (30x60), back-ins (28x50), accepts full hkup units only, 218 full hkups (30/50 amps), WiFi @ sites, dump, laundry. **REC:** heated pool, Imperial River: fishing, kayaking/canoeing, boating nearby, shuffleboard. Pet restrict (Q). Partial handicap access. No tents, Age restrict may apply. Big rig sites, eco-friendly. 2021 rates: $52 to $95, Military discount.
(239)992-0511 Lat: 26.33679, Lon: -81.75849
27700 Bourbonniere Dr, Bonita Springs, FL 34135
www.imperialbonitaestates.com
See ad this page

SANCTUARY RV RESORT **Ratings: 9/8.5/8** (RV Resort) Avail: 185 full hkups (30/50 amps). 2021 rates: $67 to $105. (239)495-9700, 13660 Bonita Beach Rd SE, Bonita Springs, FL 34135

BOWLING GREEN — L3 *Hardee*

ORANGE BLOSSOM ADULT RV PARK
Ratings: 8.5/8/7 (RV Park) From Jct Hwy 62 & US 17: Go N .5 mi on US-17 (L). **FAC:** paved rds. (173 spaces). Avail: 26 grass, patios, back-ins (24x45), 26 full hkups (30/50 amps), WiFi @ sites, $, laundry. **REC:** heated pool, shuffleboard. Pet restrict (S/B/Q). No tents, Age restrict may apply. 2021 rates: $29.15. no cc.
(863)773-2282 Lat: 27.60109, Lon: -81.82386
2829 US Highway 17 N, Bowling Green, FL 33834
www.orangeblossomrvpark.com
See ad this page

PIONEER CREEK RV RESORT
good sam park
Ratings: 8.5/9★/8.5 (RV Area in MH Park) From Jct of SR-62 & US-17: Go N 2.3 mi on US-17, then E 0.1 mi on Broward St (R). **FAC:** paved rds. (375 spaces). Avail: 102 grass, patios, 1 pull-thrus, (30x50), back-ins (30x50), 102 full hkups (30/50 amps), seasonal sites, WiFi @ sites, $, rentals, laundry, LP bottles. **REC:** heated pool, Paynes Creek: boating nearby, shuffleboard. Pet restrict (S). Partial handicap access. No tents, eco-friendly. 2021 rates: $50.
(863)375-4343 Lat: 27.62710, Lon: -81.82360
138 E Broward St, Bowling Green, FL 33834
www.rvresorts.com
See ad this page

We rate what RVers consider important.

TORREY OAKS RV RESORT **Ratings: 8.5/9/9** (Condo Park) Avail: 139 full hkups (30/50 amps). 2021 rates: $40 to $45. (863)773-3157, 2908 Country Club Dr, Bowling Green, FL 33834

BRADENTON — L2 *Manatee*

BRADENTON See also Cortez, Ellenton, Nokomis, Palmetto, Ruskin, Sarasota & Venice.

ARBOR TERRACE RV RESORT **Ratings: 7.5/9.5★/8.5** (RV Park) Avail: 100 full hkups (30/50 amps). 2021 rates: $79 to $98. (888)310-4975, 405 57th Ave W, Bradenton, FL 34207

HORSESHOE COVE RV RESORT **Ratings: 8/9.5★/9** (RV Park) Avail: 161 full hkups (30/50 amps). 2021 rates: $45 to $93. (800)291-3446, 5100 60th St E, Bradenton, FL 34203

LAKE MANATEE (Public State Park) From Jct I-75 (Exit 220) & SR-64, E 9 mi on SR-64 (L). 54 Avail: 54 W, 54 E (30 amps). 2021 rates: $22. (941)741-3028

PLEASANT LAKE RV RESORT **Ratings: 9/9.5★/8.5** (RV Park) Avail: 60 full hkups (30/50 amps). 2021 rates: $54 to $98. (941)756-5076, 6633 53rd Ave E, Bradenton, FL 34203

SARASOTA BAY RV PARK **Ratings: 9/9/8.5** (RV Park) Avail: 60 full hkups (30/50 amps). 2021 rates: $60 to $110. (941)794-1200, 10777 Cortez Rd W, Bradenton, FL 34210

TROPICAL GARDENS RV PARK **Ratings: 8.5/9★/8** (RV Park) Avail: 46 full hkups (30/50 amps). 2021 rates: $50 to $85. (941)756-1135, 1120 53rd Ave East (Hwy 70), Bradenton, FL 34203

VISTA DEL LAGO RV RESORT **Ratings: 6/NA/8** (RV Area in MH Park) Avail: 4 full hkups (30/50 amps). 2021 rates: $40 to $55. (941)755-5680, 801 53rd Ave W, Bradenton, FL 34207

WINTER QUARTERS MANATEE RV RESORT
good sam park
Ratings: 9/9/8 (RV Park) Avail: 100 full hkups (30/50 amps). 2021 rates: $43 to $98. (888)563-7040, 800 Kay Rd NE, Bradenton, FL 34212

BRANFORD — B3 *Bradford*

ELLIE RAY'S RIVER RV RESORT **Ratings: 7/7.5/7.5** (RV Park) Avail: 59 full hkups (30/50 amps). 2021 rates: $52 to $85. (386)935-1099, 3349 NW 110TH St, Branford, FL 32008

BRISTOL — A1 *Liberty*

TORREYA (Public State Park) From Jct of S.R. 12 & CR 1641, NW 7 mi on CR 1641 (E). Entrance fee required. 26 Avail: 26 W, 26 E (30 amps). 2021 rates: $16. (850)643-2674

BRONSON — B3 *Levy*

BLACK PRONG EQUESTRIAN VILLAGE
good sam park
Ratings: 9/9★/9.5 (RV Resort) Avail: 28 full hkups (30/50 amps). 2021 rates: $70 to $100. (352)486-1234, 450 SE CR 337, Bronson, FL 32621

Things to See and Do

LEVY COUNTY VISITORS BUREAU With nearly one fifth of the county set aside for state and national wildlife areas, Levy is blessed with numerous parks, preserves, springs and wildlife refuges where visitors can discover rest and recreation in abundance. Hours: 8am to 5pm. No CC.
(877)387-5673
607 SW 1st Ave, Williston, FL 32696
visitnaturecoast.com
See ad page 229

RV SPACE-SAVING TIPS: Use a hanging fruit basket as a catch-all for keys, sunglasses, etc. Use brackets to attach tools and/or cleaning accessories to the ceiling in your storage compartments for storing longer items, such as mops, brooms, etc. Install a peg board in your kitchen for hanging utensils and other cooking items. Install a shelf system above your kitchen and/or toilet for light items, such as toilet paper etc.

BROOKSVILLE — J2 *Hernando*

BELLE PARC RV RESORT
good sam park **Ratings: 10/10★/10** (RV Resort) From Jct of I-75 (exit 301) & US-98: Go W 9.6 mi on US-98, then N 2.3 mi on US-41 (L).

FABULOUS NEW SITES
Enjoy Brooksville - a location close to everything the Sunshine State has to offer, yet away from it all in the peace and quiet of Central Florida. Belle Parc offers large sites, free WiFi, a heated pool, lake views and more!

FAC: paved rds. Avail: 280 paved, patios, 8 pull-thrus, (35x60), back-ins (35x60), 280 full hkups (50 amps), cable, WiFi @ sites, laundry, controlled access. **REC:** heated pool, hot tub, pond, fishing, boating nearby, shuffleboard. Pet restrict (Q). Partial handicap access. No tents. Big rig sites. 2021 rates: $63 to $95, Military discount.
(352)593-5852 Lat: 28.58613, Lon: -82.37573
11050 Elliots Way, Brooksville, FL 34601
www.belleparcrvresorts.com
See ad next page, 237

CLOVER LEAF FOREST RV RESORT
good sam park **Ratings: 8/8.5★/7.5** (RV Park) Avail: 154 full hkups (30/50 amps). 2021 rates: $63 to $72. (888)563-7040, 910 N Broad St, Brooksville, FL 34601

BUNNELL — B4 *Flagler*

FLAGLER COUNTY BULL CREEK CAMPGROUND (Public) From Jct of US-1 & SR-100, W 7 mi on SR-100 to CR-305, S 4 mi to CR-2006, W 3.8 mi (E). Avail: 25 full hkups (30/50 amps). 2021 rates: $35. (386)313-4020

FL

BUSHNELL — H2 *Sumter*

BLUEBERRY HILL RV RESORT **Ratings: 9.5/9.5★/8** (RV Park) Avail: 100 full hkups (30/50 amps). 2021 rates: $43 to $53. (888)759-4957, 6233 Lowery St, Bushnell, FL 33513

BREEZY OAKS RV PARK
good sam park **Ratings: 9/9★/8.5** (RV Park) From jct I-75 & CR 673 (exit 309): Go 3/4 mi E on CR 673, then 1 mi N on CR 671 (E).

NEAR ORLANDO, OCALA & TAMPA ON I-75
Located close to all the fun cities of Central Florida. Easy access on and off the highway, pet friendly, full hookups, spacious park. Make us your home for a night, a week, or a season. Free WiFi, heated pool. Family owned.

FAC: paved rds. Avail: 161 grass, 56 pull-thrus, (35x75), back-ins (25x50), 161 full hkups (30/50 amps), cable, WiFi @ sites, laundry, LP gas. **REC:** heated pool, shuffleboard. Pets OK. No tents. Big rig sites, eco-friendly. 2021 rates: $54.95, Military discount.
(352)569-0300 Lat: 28.61507, Lon: -82.18794
9683 CR 671, Bushnell, FL 33513
breezyoaksrvpark.com
See ad page 238

PARADISE OAKS RV RESORT **Ratings: 9.5/9.5★/9** (RV Park) Avail: 440 full hkups (30/50 amps). 2021 rates: $45 to $70. (352)793-1823, 4628 CR 475, Bushnell, FL 33513

RED OAKS RV RESORT **Ratings: 8.5/7.5/8** (RV Area in MH Park) Avail: 500 full hkups (30/50 amps). 2021 rates: $42 to $56. (352)793-7117, 5551 SW 18th Terrace, Bushnell, FL 33513

CALLAHAN — A3 *Nassau*

KELLY'S COUNTRYSIDE RV PARK
good sam park **Ratings: 8/9★/9** (Campground) From Jct of US-1 & US-301, N 7 mi on US-1/301 (L). **FAC:** gravel rds. (70 spaces). Avail: 10 grass, 5 pull-thrus, (25x50), back-ins (25x50), 10 full hkups (30/50 amps), seasonal sites, WiFi @ sites, tent sites, dump, laundry, firewood. **REC:** boating nearby. Pet restrict (B). Partial handicap access. Big rig sites. 2021 rates: $38.
(904)845-4252 Lat: 30.64492, Lon: -81.86980
36065 Kelly's Ln, Callahan, FL 32011
kellyscountrysidervpark.com
See ad page 261

CAPE CANAVERAL — J5 *Brevard*

JETTY PARK (CANAVERAL PORT AUTH) (Public) From Jct US-1 & SR-528: Go E 8 mi on SR-528, then take the George J King Blvd/Port Canaveral/B Cruises Terminal exit, go N 1.3 mi on George J King Blvd, then continue on Jetty Park Dr (E). 187 Avail: 95 full hkups, 92 W, 92 E (30/50 amps). 2021 rates: $20 to $49. (321)783-7111

Belle Parc
RV Resort

LUXURY FOR LESS – WEST CENTRAL FLORIDA'S PREMIER RV RESORT

Our friendly staff will escort you to your site, arrange for propane delivery during the season, set up special planned activities such as bike rides and kayak trips and provide other concierge services that you expect at a luxury resort.

good sam park

2022 Top Rated 10/10★/10

11050 Elliots Way • Brooksville, FL 34601

352-593-5852

BelleParcRVResorts.com

See listing Brooksville, FL

FIRST CLASS AMENITIES AND A GREAT LOCATION!

- Spacious 1,000 Sq. Ft. Concrete Sites
- Full Service Hookups
- Free Complimentary Wi-Fi Throughout The Park
- Free Cable • Gated Entry
- High Speed Internet (For Additional Charge)
- Seasonally Heated Pool • Hot Tub
- Paddle Boats • Sitting and Fishing Dock
- Luxury Fire Pit and Free Wood
- State Of The Art Fitness Center
- Beautiful Lakeside Lodge & Clubhouse
- Television Room & Library
- Shuffleboard And Horseshoes
- Seasonally Planned Activities
- Cottage & Park Model Rentals
- Clean, Upscale Restroom, Shower, and Laundry Facilities
- Open Year Round - Adults Only October Through April
- Non-Smoking Park (Smoking Is Allowed On Your Site)
- Large Group Outdoor Grill, with Oven
- Pet Friendly, Fenced Dog Runs, and Designated Pet Areas

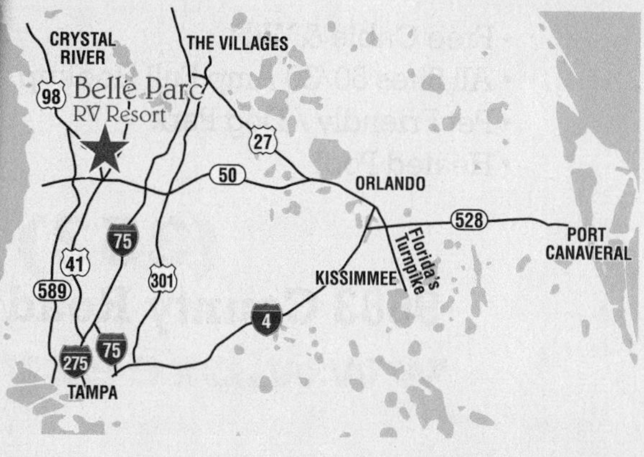

FL

good sam park
Rated 9/9★/8.5

INTERSTATE FLORIDA I-75 CAMP

Breezy Oaks RV PARK

Big Rig Friendly
Large Pull-Thru Sites

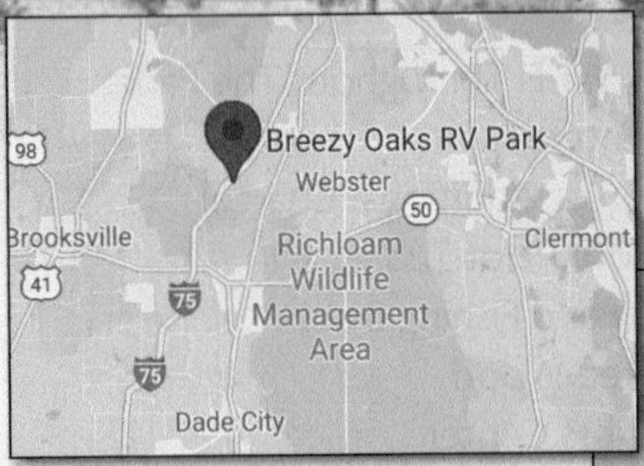

Easy On/Off I-75, Exit 309

Centrally located to Ocala, Tampa & Orlando

- Free Cable & WiFi
- All Sites 50/30 Amp Full Hookup
- Pet Friendly / Dog Park
- Heated Pool
- Clean Showers, Restrooms & Laundry
- Nearby Restaurants and Shopping
- Nice Amenities & Planned Activities
- And Much, Much More!

(352) 569-0300

9683 County Road 671 • Bushnell, FL 33513

www.breezyoaksrvpark.com

See listing Bushnell, FL

CARRABELLE — B1 *Franklin*

CARRABELLE BEACH RV RESORT **Ratings: 10/9.5★/9** (RV Resort) Avail: 68 full hkups (50 amps). 2021 rates: $59.95 to $69.95. (850)697-2638, 1843 Hwy 98 W, Carrabelle, FL 32322

HO HUM RV PARK **Ratings: 7.5/7.5/7** (RV Park) Avail: 60 full hkups (30/50 amps). 2021 rates: $69. (850)697-3926, 2132 Hwy 98 East, Carrabelle, FL 32322

CEDAR KEY — G1 *Levy*

A SPOTLIGHT Introducing Levy County/Cedar Key's colorful attractions appearing at the front of this state section.

ANGLERS RV CAMPGROUND

good sam park **Ratings: 8.5/8/7.5** (Campground) From Jct of Hwy 19/98 & SR 24 (Otter Creek), W 15 mi on Hwy 24 (R). **FAC:** gravel rds. (78 spaces). Avail: 28 grass, patios, 18 pull-thrus, (25x60), back-ins (25x60), accepts full hkup units only, 28 full hkups (30/50 amps), seasonal sites, cable, WiFi @ sites, tent sites, dump, laundry, LP gas, firewood, controlled access. **REC:** pool, boating nearby. Pet restrict (Q). Partial handicap access. 2021 rates: $39 to $42.
(352)543-6268 Lat: 29.21714, Lon: -82.96823
11951 SW Shiloh Rd, Cedar Key, FL 32625
www.anglersrv.com
See ad this page

CEDAR KEY RV RESORT **Ratings: 9/9★/9.5** (RV Park) Avail: 50 full hkups (30/50 amps). 2021 rates: $43 to $60. (352)543-5097, 11980 SW Shiloh Rd, Cedar Key, FL 32625

CHATTAHOOCHEE — A1 *Gadsden*

FLAT CREEK FAMILY CAMPGROUND

good sam park **Ratings: 8.5/9★/8.5** (Campground) From Jct of I-10 & CR-270A (exit 166), S 0.9 mi on CR-269A (L). **FAC:** paved/gravel rds. 56 Avail: 7 paved, 49 gravel, 48 pull-thrus, (25x60), back-ins (30x60), 55 full hkups, 1 W, 1 E (30/50 amps), WiFi, tent sites, rentals, dump, laundry, groc, LP gas, firewood. **REC:** pool, boating nearby, playground. Pets OK. Partial handicap access. Big rig sites. 2021 rates: $44, Military discount.
(850)442-3333 Lat: 30.60922, Lon: -84.80995
2309 Flat Creek Rd, Chattahoochee, FL 32324
fcfcamp.com
See ad page 303

CHIEFLAND — B3 *Levy*

MANATEE SPRINGS (Public State Park) From Jct of US-19/98 & SR-320, W 6 mi on SR-320 (E). 43 Avail: 43 W, 43 E (30/50 amps). 2021 rates: $20. (352)493-6072

SOUTHERN LEISURE RV RESORT **Ratings: 10/10★/10** (RV Park) Avail: 499 full hkups (30/50 amps). 2021 rates: $62 to $72. (352)284-9900, 505 NW 21st Ave , Chiefland, FL 32626

CHIPLEY — E2 *Washington*

FALLING WATERS (Public State Park) From Jct of I-10 & SR-77 (exit 120), S 0.5 mi on SR-77 to SR-77A, E 2 mi (E). 24 Avail: 24 W, 24 E (30/50 amps). 2021 rates: $18. (850)638-6130

CHOKOLOSKEE — E4 *Collier*

CHOKOLOSKEE ISLAND RESORT

good sam park **Ratings: 6/7.5/8** (RV Area in MH Park) From Jct of US-41 & SR-29, S 7.4 mi on SR-29 to Demere Ln, W 0.1 mi to Mamie St, SW 200 ft to Hamilton Ln (E). **FAC:** paved rds. (82 spaces). Avail: 35 grass, 1 pull-thrus, (25x35), back-ins (25x35), 35 full hkups (20/30 amps), seasonal sites, cable, WiFi, tent sites, rentals, dump, laundry, LP bottles. **REC:** Gulf of Mexico: fishing, kayaking/canoeing, boating nearby, hunting nearby, rec open to public. Pet restrict (S/B/Q). eco-friendly. 2021 rates: $59 to $69, Military discount.
(239)296-2925 Lat: 25.81429, Lon: -81.36294
1150 Hamilton Lane, Chokoloskee, FL 34138
www.covecommunities.com
See ad this page

OUTDOOR RESORTS/CHOKOLOSKEE ISLAND **Ratings: 9.5/9.5★/10** (Condo Park) Avail: 50 full hkups (30/50 amps). 2021 rates: $99 to $149. (239)695-3788, 150 Smallwood Dr, Hwy 29 S, Chokoloskee, FL 34138

Replace clogged air filters. A clogged air filter can cut a vehicle's fuel efficiency by 10 percent.

CITRA — B3 *Marion*

GRAND LAKE RV & GOLF RESORT **Ratings: 9.5/9★/9.5** (RV Park) 407 Avail: 337 full hkups, 70 W, 70 E (30/50 amps). 2021 rates: $45 to $79. (888)842-9219, 18545 NW 45th Avenue Road, Citra, FL 32113

ORANGE LAKE RV RESORT

good sam park (RV Resort) (Under Construction) From jct I-75 (exit 368) & Hwy 318: Go 3 mi E on Hwy 318 (cross over Hwy 441), then 1 mi N on NW 45th Avenue Rd (L).

OCALA'S NEWEST RV RESORT IS COMING!
Surrounded by beautiful horse country, close to crystal clear springs, hiking and biking trails, and endless outdoor fun sits a piece of heaven that we are turning into THE premiere RV destination. Come and visit us in 2022!

FAC: all weather rds. Avail: 70 all weather, 10 pull-thrus, (30x65), back-ins (30x65), 70 full hkups (30/50 amps), . No tents. Big rig sites. no cc, no reservations.
(352)878-4855 Lat: 29.41605, Lon: -82.20012
18365 NW 45th Avenue Road, Citra, FL 32113
orangelakervresort.com
See ad pages 282, 283

CLEARWATER — K1 *Pinellas*

CLEARWATER See also Dunedin, Holiday, Largo, Lutz, New Port Richey, Odessa, Palm Harbor, Port Richey, St Petersburg, Tampa & Tarpon Springs.

AVALON RV RESORT

good sam park **Ratings: 7/8/7** (RV Park) From jct of US 19 & SR 60: Go 2-1/4 mi S on US 19, then 1/4 mi S on Whitney Rd (R). **FAC:** paved rds. (258 spaces). Avail: 146 grass, patios, back-ins (30x60), mostly side by side hkups, 146 full hkups (30/50 amps), WiFi, $, dump, laundry, LP gas. **REC:** heated pool, boating nearby, shuffleboard. Pet restrict (B). No tents. Big rig sites. 2021 rates: $46 to $48.
(727)531-6124 Lat: 27.924694, Lon: -82.733141
16860 US Hwy 19 N, Clearwater, FL 33764
www.avalonrvresort.com
See ad page 209

CLEARWATER RV RESORT **Ratings: 9/9★/8.5** (RV Park) Avail: 75 full hkups (30/50 amps). 2021 rates: $53 to $60. (727)791-0550, 2946 Gulf To Bay Blvd, Clearwater, FL 33759

TRAVEL WORLD RV PARK **Ratings: 8/NA/7.5** (RV Park) Avail: 150 full hkups (30/50 amps). 2021 rates: $50 to $55. (727)536-1765, 12400 US 19 N, Clearwater, FL 33764

Don't miss the best part! Look in the front of most state/province sections for articles that focus on areas of special interest to RVers. These ""Spotlights'' tell you about interesting tourist destinations you might otherwise miss.

CLERMONT — J3 *Lake*

BEE'S RV RESORT **Ratings: 8.5/9.5★/7.5** (Membership Park) Avail: 166 full hkups (30/50 amps). 2021 rates: $29 to $39. (352)429-2116, 20260 US Hwy 27, Clermont, FL 34715

CLERBROOK GOLF & RV RESORT

good sam park **Ratings: 8.5/8.5★/8.5** (RV Area in MH Park) Avail: 821 full hkups (30/50 amps). 2021 rates: $37 to $69. (888)563-7040, 20005 Hwy 27, Clermont, FL 34715

ELITE RESORTS AT CITRUS VALLEY **Ratings: 9/9★/9** (Condo Park) Avail: 50 full hkups (30/50 amps). 2021 rates: $55 to $180. (352)432-5934, 16246 Citrus Parkway, Clermont, FL 34714

LAKE MAGIC RV RESORT

good sam park **Ratings: 8.5/7.5/8.5** (RV Park) Avail: 470 full hkups (30/50 amps). 2021 rates: $48 to $88. (888)563-7040, 9600 Hwy 192 W, Clermont, FL 34714

ORLANDO RV RESORT

good sam park **Ratings: 8.5/9★/8.5** (Membership Park) Avail: 185 full hkups (30/50 amps). 2021 rates: $48 to $75. (888)563-7040, 2110 Thousand Trail Blvd, Clermont, FL 34714

Join in the fun. Like us on FACEBOOK!

FL

CLEWISTON — D4 *Hendry*

BIG CYPRESS RV RESORT

good sam park **Ratings: 9/10★/8.5** (RV Park) S-bnd: From Jct of US-27 & SR-80 (W of town), W 2.9 mi on SR-80 to CR-833, S 35.2 mi to Halls Rd, E 0.2 mi (L); or N-bnd: From Jct of I-75 & SR-833 (Exit 49), N 18 mi on SR-833 to Halls Rd, E 0.2 mi (L). **FAC:** paved rds. (110 spaces). Avail: 100 paved, patios, 10 pull-thrus, (25x60), back-ins (25x60), 100 full hkups (30/50 amps), seasonal sites, cable, WiFi @ sites, $, rentals, dump, laundry, LP bottles, firewood. **REC:** heated pool, boating nearby, shuffleboard. Pet restrict (B). Partial handicap access. No tents. Big rig sites. 2021 rates: $55 to $60.
(863)983-1330 Lat: 26.32818, Lon: -80.99539
34950 Halls Rd, Clewiston, FL 33440
www.bigcypressrvresort.com
See ad this page

CROOKED HOOK RV RESORT **Ratings: 7.5/9.5★/9** (Campground) Avail: 60 full hkups (30/50 amps). 2021 rates: $59. (863)983-7112, 51700 E US-27, Clewiston, FL 33440

OKEECHOBEE LANDINGS RV RESORT **Ratings: 7.5/8.5★/7** (RV Park) Avail: 196 full hkups (30/50 amps). 2021 rates: $35 to $48. (863)983-4144, 420 Holiday Blvd, Clewiston, FL 33440

Follow the arrow. The arrow in each listing indicates where the facility is located in relation to the listed town.

COCOA — J5 *Brevard*

JOY RV RESORT

good sam park **Ratings: 9/9.5★/8.5** (RV Park) From jct I-95 & SR-520 (exit 201): Go 1/4 mi W on SR-520, then 1/2 mi S on Tucker Ln, then 150 feet W on Flamingo Connector, then 1/2 mi S on Flamingo Dr (E). **FAC:** paved rds. (75 spaces). Avail: 43 grass, patios, 5 pull-thrus, (26x45), back-ins (26x65), 43 full hkups (30/50 amps), seasonal sites, WiFi @ sites, rentals, laundry. **REC:** heated pool, boating nearby. Pet restrict (S/B/Q). No tents. Big rig sites. 2021 rates: $41 to $51.
(321)631-0305 Lat: 28.35501, Lon: -80.79247
245 Flamingo Drive, Cocoa, FL 32926
joyrvpark.com
See ad this page

SONRISE PALMS RV PARK

good sam park **Ratings: 9/9.5★/9** (RV Park) From Jct of I-95 (Exit 201) & SR-520: Go W 0.1 mi on SR-520, then S 1 mi on Tucker Ln (R). **FAC:** paved rds. Avail: 96 gravel, patios, back-ins (30x60), 83 full hkups, 13 W, 13 E (30/50 amps), cable, WiFi @ sites, rentals, dump, laundry, LP gas. **REC:** heated pool, pond, fishing, boating nearby. Pet restrict (B). Partial handicap access. No tents. Big rig sites. 2021 rates: $59.59 to $63.50, Military discount.
(321)633-4335 Lat: 28.35061, Lon: -80.79176
660 Tucker Ln, Cocoa, FL 32926
www.sonrisepalmsrv.com
See ad opposite page

Travel Services

CAMPING WORLD OF COCOA As the nation's largest retailer of RV supplies, accessories, services and new and used RVs, Camping World is committed to making your total RV experience better. **SERVICES:** RV, RV appliance, MH mechanical, staffed RV wash, restrooms. RV Sales. RV supplies, LP gas, RV accessible. Hours: 9am to 7pm.
(888)409-8104 Lat: 28.360835, Lon: -80.799275
4700 King Street Hwy 520, Cocoa, FL 32926
www.campingworld.com

Don't miss a thing! Check out the Table of Contents for everything the Guide has to offer.

COCOA BEACH — J5 *Brevard*

MILITARY PARK MANATEE COVE CAMPGROUND (PATRICK AFB) (Public) From I-95 S & FL-404: Go 7 mi E on FL-404, then 3 mi N on A1A, then 1-3/4 mi W on Rescue Rd (E). Avail: 165 full hkups (30/50 amps). 2021 rates: $22 to $30. (321)494-4787

CORTEZ — L1 *Manatee*

BUTTONWOOD INLET RV RESORT

good sam park **Ratings: 9/9.5★/9** (RV Park) Avail: 80 full hkups (30/50 amps). 2021 rates: $65 to $110. (941)798-3090, 12316 Cortez Rd W, Cortez, FL 34215

HOLIDAY COVE RV RESORT **Ratings: 9.5/10★/9.5** (Condo Park) Avail: 24 full hkups (30/50 amps). 2021 rates: $100 to $180. (941)251-7809, 11900 Cortez Rd W, Cortez, FL 34215

CRYSTAL RIVER — H2 *Citrus*

A SPOTLIGHT Introducing Crystal River's colorful attractions appearing at the front of this state section.

CRYSTAL ISLES RV PARK

good sam park **Ratings: 9/9★/8.5** (RV Park) Avail: 246 full hkups (30/50 amps). 2021 rates: $54 to $85. (888)563-7040, 11419 W Fort Island Trail, Crystal River, FL 34429

LAKE ROUSSEAU RV & FISHING RESORT **Ratings: 8.5/8.5★/8** (RV Park) Avail: 80 full hkups (30/50 amps). 2021 rates: $56 to $79. (352)795-6336, 10811 N Coveview Terrace, Crystal River, FL 34428

QUAIL ROOST RV CAMPGROUND **Ratings: 8/8.5★/8** (Campground) Avail: 72 full hkups (30/50 amps). 2021 rates: $40 to $56. (352)563-0404, 9835 N Citrus Ave, Crystal River, FL 34428

ROCK CRUSHER CANYON RV RESORT **Ratings: 9.5/9.5★/9.5** (RV Park) Avail: 291 full hkups (30/50 amps). 2021 rates: $50 to $70. (888)886-2477, 237 S Rock Crusher Rd, Crystal River, FL 34429

Average site width and length are indicated in many campground listings to give you an idea of how much room and privacy you can expect.

FL

Away From It All...
CENTRAL FLORIDA...
Close To Everything

- Reasonable Rates
- Open All Year
- Cable TV • New Clubhouse
- 98 Sites • 30/50 Amp
- Heated Pool • Laundry
- Showers • Wi-Fi $
- Fishing • Propane
- Park Models/Cabins
- Fenced Dog Park
- Across from Cocoa Expo Sports Center & Camping World

Find us on Facebook

See listing Cocoa, FL

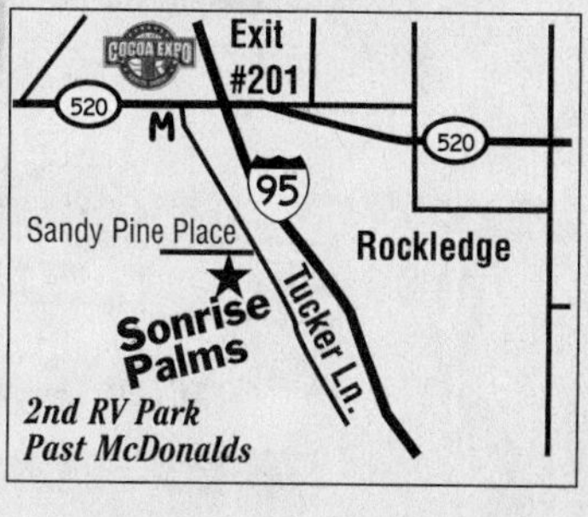

660 Tucker Lane • Cocoa, FL 32926

(321) 633-4335

www.sonrisepalmsrv.com

sonrisepalmsrvpark@aol.com

Come Stay Where the Manatee Play

Nature's Resort

Closest Park to Homosassa Springs

good sam park

Rated 9/9.5★/9

See listing Homosassa, FL

Direct Gulf Access

TIKI BAR w/FOOD & MUSIC

We Welcome Rallies & Groups

Air Conditioned Club House

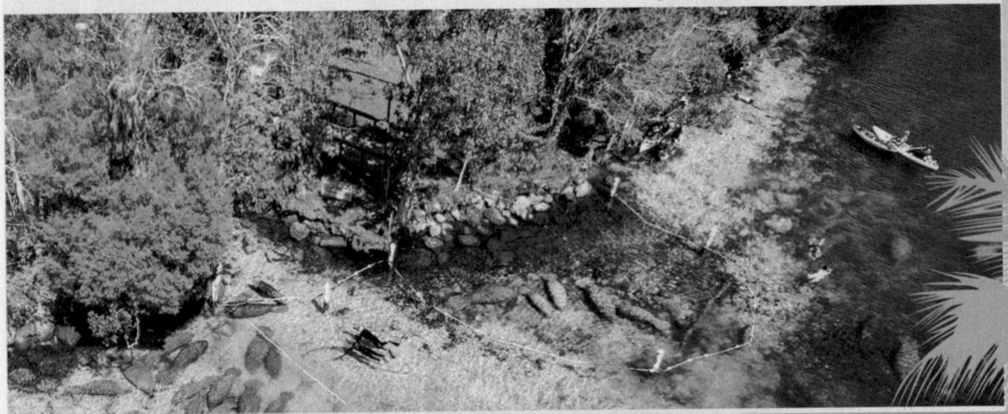

- 400 Sites
- New Pull-Thrus
- 97 Shady Acres
- Full Hookups on River
- 30/50 Amp
- Big Rigs Welcome
- Extra Large Sites
- Concrete Pads
- 2000 ft Riverfront
- Pontoon & Kayak Rentals
- Marina • Cabin Rental
- Large Heated Pool
- Free Wi-Fi & Cable TV
- Salt & Fresh Water Fishing
- 2 New Dog Parks
- Golf Cart Rentals
- Park Model Sales

800-301-7880

naturesresortfla.com

10359 W. Halls River Rd.
Homosassa, FL 34448

CRYSTAL RIVER (CONT)

Things to See and Do

DISCOVER CRYSTAL RIVER Tourism Office & Convention Bureau providing a complete compliment of brochures and information about the area. Hours: 9am to 5pm. No CC.
(800)587-6667
915 N. Suncoast Blvd, Crystal River, FL 34429
www.discovercrystalriverfl.com
See ad page 223

CUDJOE KEY — F4 *Monroe*

VENTURE OUT AT CUDJOE CAY **Ratings: 8.5/8.5★/9.5** (Condo Park) Avail: 250 full hkups (30/50 amps). 2021 rates: $56 to $135. (305)414-8936, 701 Spanish Main Dr, Cudjoe Key, FL 33042

DADE CITY — J2 *Pasco*

BLUE JAY RV RESORT **Ratings: 7.5/8.5★/8** (RV Area in MH Park) Avail: 15 full hkups (30 amps). 2021 rates: $40 to $46. (352)567-9678, 38511 Wilds Rd, Dade City, FL 33525

CITRUS HILL RV RESORT **Ratings: 7/8★/8** (RV Area in MH Park) Avail: 45 full hkups (30/50 amps). 2021 rates: $47. (352)567-6045, 9267 US-98, Dade City, FL 33525

COUNTRY AIRE MANOR **Ratings: 8/7/7** (RV Area in MH Park) Avail: 53 full hkups (50 amps). 2021 rates: $39. (352)523-1228, 10249 Wellington Ave, Dade City, FL 33525

GROVE RIDGE RV RESORT **Ratings: 8/9.5★/8** (RV Area in MH Park) Avail: 96 full hkups (30/50 amps). 2021 rates: $40 to $52. (352)523-2277, 10721 US Hwy 98, Dade City, FL 33525

MANY MANSIONS RV RESORT **Ratings: 8/8.5★/8.5** (RV Park) Avail: 78 full hkups (30/50 amps). 2021 rates: $44. (352)567-8667, 40703 Stewart Rd, Dade City, FL 33525

MORNINGSIDE RV ESTATES **Ratings: 9/9★/8.5** (RV Area in MH Park) Avail: 42 full hkups (50 amps). 2021 rates: $38.95 to $43.95. (352)523-1922, 12645 Morning Drive, Dade City, FL 33525

SEVEN ACRES RV PARK
good sam park **Ratings: 7/NA/7.5** (RV Park) Avail: 25 full hkups (30/50 amps). 2021 rates: $50. (352)567-3510, 16731 US 301, Dade City, FL 33523

SUNBURST RV PARK
good sam park **Ratings: 7/NA/7.5** (RV Park) Avail: 25 full hkups (30/50 amps). 2021 rates: $50. (352)567-3411, 17031 US 301, Dade City, FL 33523

TOWN AND COUNTRY RV RESORT
good sam park **Ratings: 8.5/8.5★/8.5** (RV Area in MH Park) From jct US 98 & US 301: Go 4-1/4 mi N on US 301 (L). **FAC:** paved rds. (200 spaces). Avail: 20 grass, patios, 3 pull-thrus, (40x60), back-ins (40x60), 20 full hkups (30/50 amps), seasonal sites, WiFi @ sites, rentals, dump, laundry. **REC:** heated pool, boating nearby, shuffleboard, playground. Pet restrict (S/B/Q). No tents, Age restrict may apply. Big rig sites, eco-friendly. 2021 rates: $36.99 to $44. no cc.
(352)567-7707 Lat: 28.42010, Lon: -82.19091
18005 US 301 , Dade City, FL 33523
townandcountryrvresortfl.com
See ad page 307

WITHLACOOCHEE RIVER PARK (Public) From Jct US-301/US-98 & River Rd: Go E 2.6 mi on River Rd, then L to stay on River Rd for 1.9 mi, then S 0.2 mi on Auton Rd (L). Avail: 15 full hkups (30/50 amps). 2021 rates: $25. (352)567-0264

DAVENPORT — K3 *Polk*

KISSIMMEE SOUTH RV RESORT **Ratings: 9.5/9.5★/9** (RV Area in MH Park) Avail: 137 full hkups (30/50 amps). 2021 rates: $44 to $97. (863)424-1286, 3700 US Hwy 17-92N, Davenport, FL 33837

MOUSE MOUNTAIN RV RESORT **Ratings: 9/8.5★/8** (RV Park) Avail: 138 full hkups (30/50 amps). 2021 rates: $40 to $50. (888)709-1167, 7500 Osceola Polk Line Rd, Davenport, FL 33896

RV parks in remote locations are sometimes unable to provide all amenities, like 30/50-amp service. Although these inconveniences can lower a park's facility rating, the tradeoff is a once-in-a-lifetime trip to some of the most beautiful wilderness areas on the planet!

ORLANDO SW/FORT SUMMIT KOA **Ratings: 8.5/8.5★/7.5** (RV Park) Avail: 95 full hkups (30/50 amps). 2021 rates: $81 to $99. (863)424-1880, 2525 Frontage Rd, Davenport, FL 33837

RAINBOW CHASE RV RESORT
good sam park **Ratings: 8.5/8.5★/8.5** (RV Park) From Jct of I-4 (exit 58) & CR-532: Go E 1.5 mi on CR-532, then S 0.9 mi on CR-545 (Lake Wilson Rd) (L). **FAC:** paved rds. (162 spaces). 50 Avail: 20 paved, 30 grass, patios, 40 pull-thrus, (30x60), back-ins (40x60), 50 full hkups (30/50 amps), seasonal sites, WiFi @ sites, dump, laundry, LP gas, controlled access. **REC:** boating nearby, shuffleboard. Pet restrict (S/B). Partial handicap access. No tents, Age restrict may apply. Big rig sites, eco-friendly. 2021 rates: $48.
(863)424-2688 Lat: 28.24727, Lon: -81.59031
6300 W Lake Wilson Rd, Davenport, FL 33896
www.rainbowchaserv.com
See ad this page

THEME WORLD RV RESORT **Ratings: 6.5/8.5★/5.5** (RV Park) 62 Avail: 39 full hkups, 23 W, 23 E (30/50 amps). 2021 rates: $38 to $48. (888)691-1320, 2727 Frontage Rd, Davenport, FL 33837

DAVIE — E5 *Broward*

DAVIE/FORT LAUDERDALE KOA **Ratings: 8/9/7.5** (RV Park) Avail: 100 full hkups (30/50 amps). 2021 rates: $55 to $95. (954)473-0231, 3800 SW 142nd Avenue, Davie, FL 33330

DAYTONA BEACH — G5 *Volusia*

DAYTONA BEACH See also Flagler Beach, New Smyrna Beach, Orange City, Ormond Beach & Port Orange.

DAYTONA SPEEDWAY RV **Ratings: 8/8.5★/8.5** (RV Park) Avail: 98 full hkups (30/50 amps). 2021 rates: $55 to $177. (386)257-6137, 3003 W International Speedway Blvd, Daytona Beach, FL 32124

JOIN GoodSamRoadside.com

DAYTONA'S RACETRACK RV **Ratings: 6/8.5★/6.5** (RV Park) 295 Avail: 295 W, 295 E (30/50 amps). 2021 rates: $56.25 to $195. (877)787-2246, 330 Innovation Way, Daytona Beach, FL 32124

INTERNATIONAL RV PARK CAMPGROUND **Ratings: 9.5/9★/8.5** (RV Park) Avail: 300 full hkups (30/50 amps). 2021 rates: $60 to $90. (386)239-0249, 3175 W International Speedway Blvd., Daytona Beach, FL 32124

Save 10% at Good Sam Parks!

Sandy Beach
25 Minutes to Historic St. Augustine
Three Miles North of the Flagler Beach Pier
25 Minutes to World Famous Daytona Beach
2815 N. Oceanshore Blvd. Flagler Beach, Fl.

Beverly Beach
Camptown RV Resort
& Campers Village
good sam park
386.439.3111
See listing Flagler Beach, FL
beverlybeachcamptown.com
SCAN ME

FL

DAYTONA BEACH (CONT)

NOVA FAMILY CAMPGROUND

Ratings: 8/8/8.5 (Campground) From Jct of I-95 (Exit 256-Port Orange) & Taylor/Dunlawton Ave, E 0.7 mi on Dunlawton Ave to Clyde Morris Blvd, N (Left) 0.9 mi to Herbert St, E 0.7 mi on Herbert St (R). **FAC:** paved/gravel rds. (371 spaces). 174 Avail: 124 grass, 50 dirt, 10 pull-thrus, (21x55), back-ins (21x55), 40 full hkups, 134 W, 134 E (30/50 amps), seasonal sites, cable, WiFi @ sites, tent sites, rentals, dump, mobile sewer, laundry, groc, LP gas, firewood. **REC:** heated pool, shuffleboard. Pet restrict (B/Q) $. eco-friendly. 2021 rates: $39 to $93.

(386)767-0095 Lat: 29.13451, Lon: -81.01434
1190 Herbert St, Port Orange, FL 32129
novacamp.com
See ad page 243

DEBARY — H4 *Volusia*

HIGHBANKS MARINA & CAMPRESORT

Ratings: 9.5/9.5★/8.5 (RV Park) From Jct of I-4 & CR-4162/Dirksen Dr (exit 108), W 2 mi on CR-4162 to US-17/92, N 1.8 mi to Highbanks Rd, W 2.8 mi. (E). **FAC:** paved rds. (235 spaces). Avail: 56 gravel, patios, 10 pull-thrus, (30x60), back-ins (25x50), 56 full hkups (30/50 amps), seasonal sites, cable, WiFi @ sites, $, laundry, groc, LP gas, restaurant. **REC:** pool, St John's River: fishing, marina, boating nearby. Pet restrict (S/B/Q). Partial handicap access. No tents. Big rig sites, eco-friendly. 2021 rates: $48 to $75.

(386)668-4491 Lat: 28.89061, Lon: -81.35384
488 West Highbanks Rd, Debary, FL 32713
www.campresort.com
See ad page 289

LAKE MONROE PARK (Public) From town, S 3 mi on US-17/92, follow signs (L). 25 Avail: 25 W, 25 E (30 amps). 2021 rates: $15. (386)668-3825

Things to See and Do

SWAMP HOUSE RIVER FRONT GRILL Located at Highbanks Marina & Campresort. Seating for 150 overlooking the beautiful St John's River. Restrooms. Hours: 11am to 10pm.

(386)668-8891 Lat: 28.89089, Lon: -81.35396
488 W Highbanks Rd, Debary, FL 32713
www.swamphousegrill.com
See ad page 289

DEFUNIAK SPRINGS — E2 *Walton*

SUNSET KING LAKE RV RESORT

Ratings: 9.5/9★/9 (RV Park) From Jct of I-10 & Hwy 331 (exit 85), N 2 mi on Hwy 331 to Hwy 90/331, W 2 mi to Hwy 331 N, N 5.3 mi to Kings Lake Rd, S.W. 0.8 mi to Paradise Island Dr, S.E. 0.3 mi (R). **FAC:** paved rds. (205 spaces). Avail: 155 grass, patios, 90 pull-thrus, (30x60), back-ins (30x60), mostly side by side hkups, 155 full hkups (30/50 amps), seasonal sites, cable, WiFi @ sites, tent sites, rentals, dump, laundry, LP gas, firewood. **REC:** pool, hot tub, King Lake: fishing, kayaking/canoeing, boating nearby, playground. Pets OK. Partial handicap access. Big rig sites, eco-friendly. 2021 rates: $43 to $49, Military discount.

(850)892-7229 Lat: 30.78901, Lon: -86.19703
366 Paradise Island Dr, Defuniak Springs, FL 32433
sunsetking.com
See ad this page

TWIN LAKES CAMP RESORT

Ratings: 9.5/10★/10 (RV Park) From the jct of I10 & US331 (exit 85), Non US331 2 mi. to US331 North, N 3 mi to Holley King Rd, W .5 mi. (E).

MINS FROM I-10, MILES FROM ORDINARY
Pull thru the gates 'unplug' & just relax. We feature 66 new FHU sites, 12 big pull thrus 75X100'. Sits between two lakes, fish, kayak, paddle board or sit back & enjoy the view. Five 2 bedroom suites, 70 channel Cable TV.

FAC: gravel rds. Avail: 66 paved, 16 pull-thrus, (30x60), back-ins (30x60), 66 full hkups (30/50 amps), cable, WiFi @ sites, rentals, dump, laundry, groc, firewood, controlled access. **REC:** heated pool, Holley Lake: boating nearby, playground. Pets OK. No tents. 2021 rates: $52 to $60, Military discount. ATM.

(850)892-5914 Lat: 30.77763, Lon: -86.18099
580 Holley King Rd, Defuniak Springs, FL 32433
www.twinlakescampresort.com
See ad next page, 249

Do you know how to read each part of a listing? Check the How to Use This Guide in the front.

RV SPACE-SAVING TIPS: Hang a fruit and veggie hammock/basket. Use magnetic strips for hanging knives and scissors. Use dish cradles for storing dishes. Install a shelf system above your kitchen and/or toilet. This allows for extra storage space for light items, such as toilet paper, paper towels, bath towels, etc.

TRAVELING WITH YOUR PET: Know the rules. Visit GoodSam.com/campgrounds-rv-parks for pet restrictions at RV parks you're considering for your trip. Always call and ask before visiting. If you are allowed to bring a commonly prohibited breed, like a Pit Bull, Doberman or Rottweiler, go the extra mile to be an exemplary canine citizen.

Twin Lakes
- DeFuniak Springs, Florida
- All Waterfront & Waterview
Twin Lakes Camp Resort
-Google rated
4.8 stars, 475+ reviews
-Good Sam Rated
9.5-10★-10

Camp Resort
- Easy Access From I-10
80' Pull Thrus
(850) 892-5914
-Facebook Ratings
4.9 stars
-Trip Advisor:
Rated #1 Specialty Lodging
4.5 stars
good sam park
2022
Top Rated
See listing
Defuniak Springs, FL

DELRAY BEACH — E5 *Palm Beach*

DEL RATON RV PARK **Ratings: 5.5/8.5★/7** (RV Park) Avail: 59 full hkups (30/50 amps). 2021 rates: $51 to $65. (561)278-4633, 2998 S Federal Hwy (US-1), Delray Beach, FL 33483

DESTIN — F2 *Okaloosa*

CAMPING ON THE GULF

good sam park **Ratings: 10/10★/9.5** (RV Park) Avail: 190 full hkups (30/50 amps). 2021 rates: $75 to $232. (850)502-5282, 10005 W Emerald Coast Pkwy, Destin, FL 32550

GERONIMO RV PARK

good sam park **Ratings: 8/10★/9** (RV Park) E-bnd: From Jct of Hwy 98 & SR-293 (Mid Bay Bridge), E 4 mi on US 98 to Geronimo St, S 0.2 mi to Arnett Ln (R); or W-bnd: From Jct of Hwy 98 & US 331, W 11.1 mi on Hwy 98 to Geronimo St, S 0.2 mi to Arnett Ln (R). **FAC:** paved rds. Avail: 34 paved, patios, 5 pull-thrus, (30x60), back-ins (30x60), 34 full hkups (30/50 amps), cable, WiFi @ sites, laundry. **REC:** boating nearby. Pets OK. Partial handicap access. No tents. Big rig sites. 2021 rates: $80 to $105, Military discount.
(850)424-6801 Lat: 30.37844, Lon: -86.36095
75 Arnett Ln, Destin, FL 32550
www.geronimorvresort.com
See ad opposite page

HENDERSON BEACH (Public State Park) From town, S 305 ft on Benning Dr to US-98 E, 3 mi on US 98 E to Henderson Beach Rd (R). 52 Avail: 52 W, 52 E (30/50 amps). 2021 rates: $30. (850)837-7550

MILITARY PARK DESTIN ARMY INFANTRY CENTER REC AREA (FORT BENNING) (Public) From jct US-98 & Benning Drive: Go N 1 mi on Benning Dr, then left onto Calhoun Ave (R). Avail: 46 full hkups (30/50 amps). 2021 rates: $30 to $55. (850)837-6423

DOVER — K2 *Hillsborough*

CITRUS HILLS RV PARK **Ratings: 6.5/7/7.5** (RV Park) Avail: 155 full hkups (30/50 amps). 2021 rates: $25. (813)737-4770, 5401 Boca Grande Circle, Dover, FL 33527

TAMPA EAST RV RESORT **Ratings: 8.5/9★/9** (RV Park) Avail: 448 full hkups (30/50 amps). 2021 rates: $47 to $70. (877)361-5208, 4630 McIntosh Rd, Dover, FL 33527

Travel Services

CAMPING WORLD OF DOVER/TAMPA As the nation's largest retailer of RV supplies, accessories, services and new and used RVs, Camping World is committed to making your total RV experience better. **SERVICES:** RV, tire, RV appliance, sells outdoor gear, staffed RV wash, restrooms. RV Sales. RV supplies, LP gas, RV accessible. Hours: 9am - 7pm.
(888)451-4197 Lat: 28.024655, Lon: -82.2446
4811 McIntosh Road, Dover, FL 33527
www.campingworld.com

DUNDEE — K3 *Polk*

ROYAL OAKS MOBILE HOME PARK AND TRAVEL RESORT **Ratings: 6.5/7.5/7** (Condo Park) Avail: 37 full hkups (30/50 amps). 2021 rates: $36.75. (863)439-5954, 1012 Dundee Rd, Dundee, FL 33838

DUNEDIN — K1 *Pinellas*

DUNEDIN RV RESORT **Ratings: 9/9/9.5** (RV Park) Avail: 50 full hkups (30/50 amps). 2021 rates: $59 to $104. (727)784-3719, 2920 Alternate 19 N, Dunedin, FL 34698

DUNNELLON — G2 *Levy*

RAINBOW SPRINGS (Public State Park) From jct I-75 (exit 341) and Hwy 484: Go 19 mi W on Hwy 484, then 2-1/4 mi N on SW 180th Ave Rd. Avail: 49 full hkups (30/50 amps). 2021 rates: $30. (352)465-8555

EASTPOINT — B1 *Franklin*

COASTLINE RV RESORT **Ratings: 9/10★/9** (RV Resort) Avail: 72 full hkups (30/50 amps). 2021 rates: $46 to $70. (850)799-1016, 957 Hwy 98, Eastpoint, FL 32328

SNOWBIRD TIP: Get social and active. Winter getaways are a chance to try activities you've been curious about. From line dancing to woodworking, pickle ball to rock hounding, you'll never get bored at snowbird RV parks with jam-packed activity calendars.

ELLENTON — L2 *Manatee*

ELLENTON GARDENS RV RESORT **Ratings: 8.5/9.5★/7.5** (RV Area in MH Park) Avail: 30 full hkups (30/50 amps). 2021 rates: $50 to $62. (941)722-0341, 7310 US Hwy 301 N, Ellenton, FL 34222

ESTERO — E4 *Lee*

KORESHAN (Public State Park) From Jct of I-75 & CR-850/Corkscrew Rd (exit 123/old exit 19), W 2.2 mi on CR-850/Corkscrew Rd (R). 44 Avail: 44 W, 44 E (30 amps). 2021 rates: $26. (239)992-0311

EUSTIS — H3 *Lake*

SOUTHERN PALMS RV RESORT

good sam park **Ratings: 8/8.5★/7** (RV Park) Avail: 500 full hkups (30/50 amps). 2021 rates: $51 to $56. (888)563-7040, 1 Avocado Ln, Eustis, FL 32726

FERNANDINA BEACH — A4 *Nassau*

FORT CLINCH (Public State Park) From Jct of I-95 & SR-A1A (exit 373), E 16 mi on SR-A1A to Atlantic Ave, E 2 mi (L). 63 Avail: 63 W, 63 E (30/50 amps). 2021 rates: $26. (904)277-7274

FIESTA KEY — F4 *Monroe*

FIESTA KEY RV RESORT

good sam park **Ratings: 8/7.5/9** (Campground) Avail: 245 full hkups (30/50 amps). 2021 rates: $121 to $249. (888)563-7040, 70001 Overseas Hwy, Long Key, FL 33001

FLAGLER BEACH — B4 *Flagler*

BEVERLY BEACH CAMPTOWN RV RESORT & CAMPERS VILLAGE

good sam park **Ratings: 9/10★/8.5** (RV Park) From Jct of I-95 & SR-100 exit 284, E 3.25 mi on SR-100 to SR-A1A, N 3 mi (R).

ENJOY 1500 FEET OF BEACHFRONT VIEWS
Come experience our beautiful beachfront resort. Air-conditioned bathhouses and a complete convenience store on site. Close to Daytona and St Augustine. Families and clubs welcome, all sites full hookups. Pet friendly beach.
FAC: paved rds. Avail: 150 gravel, patios, back-ins (30x60), 150 full hkups (30/50 amps), cable, WiFi @ sites, rentals, laundry, groc, firewood. **REC:** Atlantic Ocean: swim, fishing, kayaking/canoeing, boating nearby. Pets OK. Partial handicap access. No tents. Big rig sites, eco-friendly. 2021 rates: $75 to $240, Military discount.
(386)439-3111 Lat: 29.52104, Lon: -81.14767
2815 N Oceanshore Blvd , Flagler Beach, FL 32136
beverlybeachcamptown.com
See ad pages 244, 245

Check out 10/10/10 Good Sam Parks on the Good Sam Park page.*

BULOW RV RESORT

good sam park **Ratings: 8.5/7.5/8.5** (RV Park) 303 Avail: 251 full hkups, 52 W, 52 E (30/50 amps). 2021 rates: $56 to $85. (888)563-7040, 3345 Old Kings Road South, Flagler Beach, FL 32136

GAMBLE ROGERS MEM REC AREA AT FLAGLER BEACH (Public State Park) From Jct of Hwys 100 & A1A, S 3 mi on Hwy A1A (R). 34 Avail: 34 W, 34 E (30/50 amps). 2021 rates: $28 to $30. (386)517-2086

FLORIDA CITY — F5 *Miami-Dade*

FLORIDA CITY CAMPSITE & RV PARK (Public) From Jct of FL Tpke & Exit 1 (Florida City North/336 th St), W 0.5 mi on 336th St/Davis Pkwy to NW 2nd Ave, N 0.1 mi (R); or From Jct of SR-997/Krome Ave & 312th St/Campbell Dr (in center of Homestead), S 1.6 mi on SR-997/Krome Ave to Davis Pkwy (336th St), W 0.1 mi to NW 2nd Ave, N 0.1 mi (R). 30 Avail: 30 W, 30 E (30 amps). 2021 rates: $35. (305)248-7889

FLORIDA KEYS — F4 *Monroe*

FLORIDA KEYS See also Big Pine Key, Fiesta Key & Marathon.

FORT LAUDERDALE — E5 *Broward*

KOZY KAMPERS RV PARK & STORAGE **Ratings: 7/9★/6.5** (RV Park) Avail: 40 full hkups (30/50 amps). 2021 rates: $45 to $75. (954)731-8570, 3631 W Commercial Blvd, Fort Lauderdale, FL 33309

Want to know how we rate? Our campground inspection guidelines are detailed in the front pages of the Guide.

FL

FORT LAUDERDALE (CONT)

PARADISE ISLAND RV RESORT
Ratings: 9/9.5★/8 (RV Park) From Jct of I-95 & W Oakland Park Blvd (exit 31), W 0.7 mi on Oakland Park Blvd to NW 21st Ave, S 0.1 mi to 29th Ct (R).

FUN IN THE SUN YEAR ROUND
Four miles from beautiful beaches, famous shopping, finest dining and entertainment in the world. Newly renovated, well-maintained RV Park with heated pool, recreation rooms, exercise equipment and billiard tables.

FAC: paved rds. Avail: 232 paved, patios, 18 pull-thrus, (30x61), back-ins (26x45), 232 full hkups (30/50 amps), WiFi @ sites, dump, laundry. **REC:** heated pool, boating nearby, shuffleboard. Pet restrict (S/B/Q). Partial handicap access. No tents, eco-friendly. 2021 rates: $50 to $65, Military discount.
(800)487-7395 Lat: 26.16350, Lon: -80.17158
2121 NW 29th Ct, Fort Lauderdale, FL 33311
paradiserv.com
See ad previous page

SUNSHINE HOLIDAY FT. LAUDERDALE
Ratings: 8/7.5/7.5 (RV Park) Avail: 70 full hkups (30/50 amps). 2021 rates: $45 to $74. (888)563-7040, 2802 W Oakland Park Blvd, Oakland Park, FL 33311

YACHT HAVEN PARK & MARINA **Ratings: 9/9★/8** (RV Park) Avail: 200 full hkups (30/50 amps). 2021 rates: $88 to $190. (954)583-2322, 2323 State Road 84, Fort Lauderdale, FL 33312

FORT MYERS — E3 *Lee*

A SPOTLIGHT Introducing Fort Myers' colorful attractions appearing at the front of this state section.

FORT MYERS See also Bokeelia, Bonita Springs, Fort Myers Beach, La Belle, Naples, Punta Gorda & St James City.

BLUEWAY RV VILLAGE
Ratings: 9/8.5★/8 (RV Park) From Jct of I-75 N-bnd & Alico Rd (exit 128), W (left) 3 mi on Alico Rd to US-41, S (left) 3 mi (R); or From Jct of I-75 S-bnd & Alico Rd (Exit 128), W (right) 3 mi on Alico Rd to US-41, S (left) 3 mi (R). **FAC:** paved rds. (325 spaces). 267 Avail: 5 paved, 135 gravel, 127 grass, patios, 4 pull-thrus, (30x50), back-ins (30x50), 267 full hkups (30/50 amps), seasonal sites, WiFi @ sites, laundry. **REC:** heated pool, hot tub, pond, boating nearby, shuffleboard. Pet restrict (B) $. Partial handicap access. No tents, eco-friendly. 2021 rates: $64 to $80.
(239)990-3302 Lat: 26.45757, Lon: -81.83121
19370 S Tamiami Trail, Fort Myers, FL 33908
www.covecommunities.com
See ad this page

CYPRESS TRAIL RV RESORT **Ratings: 10/10★/10** (Condo Park) Avail: 457 full hkups (30/50 amps). 2021 rates: $50 to $150. (239)333-3246, 5400 Tice Street, Fort Myers, FL 33905

FORT MYERS BEACH RV RESORT
Ratings: 7.5/7.5/7.5 (RV Park) Avail: 168 full hkups (30/50 amps). 2021 rates: $49 to $86. (888)563-7040, 16299 San Carlos Blvd, Fort Myers, FL 33908

FORT MYERS RV RESORT
Ratings: 8/8.5★/8 (RV Park) From Jct of I-75 & Alico Rd (Exit 128), W 3.1 mi on Alico Rd to US-41, N 0.3 mi (L). **FAC:** paved rds. (345 spaces). 205 Avail: 15 paved, 10 gravel, 180 grass, patios, 30 pull-thrus, (30x75), back-ins (28x60), accepts full hkup units only, 205 full hkups (30/50 amps), WiFi @ sites, $, dump, laundry, LP gas. **REC:** heated pool, Ten Mile Canal: fishing, boating nearby, shuffleboard. Pet restrict (S/B/Q). Partial handicap access. No tents, Age restrict may apply, eco-friendly. 2021 rates: $60.
(239)267-2141 Lat: 26.49803, Lon: -81.85300
16800 Tamiami Trail, Fort Myers, FL 33908
www.rvresorts.com
See ad this page

GROVES RV RESORT **Ratings: 8.5/10★/8.5** (RV Park) Avail: 13 full hkups (30/50 amps). 2021 rates: $48 to $76. (877)540-1931, 16175 John Morris Rd, Fort Myers, FL 33908

IONA RANCH MH/RV RESORT
Ratings: 8/9★/8.5 (RV Park) Avail: 29 full hkups (30/50 amps). 2021 rates: $60. (239)466-0440, 16295 Davis Rd, Fort Myers, FL 33908

LAZY J RV & MOBILE HOME PARK
Ratings: 5.5/7.5/6 (RV Area in MH Park) From jct Hwy 82 & I-75: Go 1-1/2 mi N on I-75 (exit 139), then 1/4 mi W on Luckett Rd, then 1/2 mi S on Golden Lake Rd (L). **FAC:** paved rds. (127 spaces). Avail: 52 gravel, patios, back-ins (25x42), accepts full hkup units only, 52 full hkups (30/50 amps), seasonal sites, WiFi, dump, laundry. **REC:** pond, fishing, kayaking/canoeing, boating nearby. Pets OK. No tents, eco-friendly. 2021 rates: $35 to $65, Military discount.
(239)694-5038 Lat: 26.65389, Lon: -81.80637
1263 Golden Lake Rd, Fort Myers, FL 33905
www.lazyjpark.com
See ad this page

ORANGE GROVE RV RESORT **Ratings: 8/8.5/8** (RV Area in MH Park) Avail: 79 full hkups (30/50 amps). 2021 rates: $60. (239)694-5534, 647 Nuna Ave, Fort Myers, FL 33905

ORANGE HARBOR CO-OP & RV RESORT **Ratings: 9/8/9.5** (RV Area in MH Park) Avail: 146 full hkups (50 amps). 2021 rates: $40 to $80. (239)694-3707, 5749 Palm Beach Blvd, Fort Myers, FL 33905

PIONEER VILLAGE RV RESORT
Ratings: 8/8/7.5 (RV Park) Avail: 169 full hkups (30/50 amps). 2021 rates: $49 to $89. (888)563-7040, 7974 Samville Rd, North Fort Myers, FL 33917

RAINTREE RV RESORT **Ratings: 9/9.5★/10** (RV Park) Avail: 110 full hkups (30/50 amps). 2021 rates: $65 to $85. (239)731-1441, 19250 N Tamiami Trail, North Fort Myers, FL 33903

SEMINOLE CAMPGROUND

good sam park **Ratings: 8.5/10★/9.5** (RV Park) From Jct Hwy 82 & I-75: Go 5 1/2 mi N on I-75 (exit 143), then 1/4 mi E on Hwy 78 (Bayshore Rd), then 1/4 mi N on Wells Rd, then 1/4 mi W on Triplett Rd (R). **FAC:** gravel rds. Avail: 129 gravel, patios, 7 pull-thrus, (30x70), back-ins (30x70), 129 full hkups (30/50 amps), WiFi @ sites, laundry, LP bottles, fire rings, firewood. **REC:** heated pool, boating nearby, shuffleboard, playground, hunting nearby. Pet restrict (Q). Partial handicap access. No tents. Big rig sites, eco-friendly. 2021 rates: $55 to $70.
(239)543-2919 Lat: 26.71867, Lon: -81.80989
8991 Triplett Rd, N Fort Myers, FL 33917
www.seminolecampground.com
See ad opposite page

SIESTA BAY RV RESORT **Ratings: 9.5/10★/9** (RV Park) Avail: 31 full hkups (30/50 amps). 2021 rates: $48 to $79. (877)326-4261, 19333 Summerlin Rd, Fort Myers, FL 33908

SOUTHWIND VILLAGE MOBILE HOME & RV PARK

(RV Area in MH Park) (Not Visited) From jct Hwy 78 (Bayshore Rd) & Bus US-41: Go 3/4 mi S on US-41, then 1/4 mi S on River Rd (R). **FAC:** paved rds. (79 spaces). 28 Avail: 6 paved, 22 grass, back-ins (30x65), accepts full hkup units only, 28 full hkups (50 amps), seasonal sites, WiFi @ sites, restrooms only, laundry. **REC:** boating nearby, shuffleboard. Pet restrict (S/B). No tents, Age restrict may apply. 2021 rates: $45.
(239)995-8005 Lat: 26.66869, Lon: -81.88327
1269 River Road, North Fort Myers, FL 33903
www.garbercommunities.com/properties/southwind-village
See ad opposite page

SUNSEEKERS RV PARK

good sam park **Ratings: 7.5/9.5★/9** (RV Park) Avail: 190 full hkups (30/50 amps). 2021 rates: $55 to $81. (888)563-7040, 19701 N Tamiami Trail, North Fort Myers, FL 33903

SWAN LAKE VILLAGE & RV RESORT **Ratings: 8/10★/8** (RV Area in MH Park) Avail: 114 full hkups (30/50 amps). 2021 rates: $40 to $75. (239)995-3397, 2400 N Tamiami Tr, North Fort Myers, FL 33903

TAMIAMI RV PARK

good sam park **Ratings: 9/9★/8** (RV Park) From N Jct of US-41 & US-41 Bus, S 0.5 mi on US-41 (R). **FAC:** paved rds. (242 spaces). Avail: 185 grass, patios, back-ins (28x47), 185 full hkups (30/50 amps), seasonal sites, WiFi @ sites, dump, laundry. **REC:** heated pool, boating nearby, shuffleboard. Pet restrict (B/Q). Partial handicap access. No tents, eco-friendly. 2021 rates: $32.50 to $36.50.
(866)573-2041 Lat: 26.70520, Lon: -81.90133
16555-A N Cleveland Ave, North Fort Myers, FL 33903
www.tamiamicommunity.com
See ad page 226

TICE COURTS & RV PARK

good sam park **Ratings: 7/8★/7.5** (RV Area in MH Park) From Jct of I-75 & SR-80 (exit 141), W 1.7 mi on SR-80 to New York Dr, S 300 ft (L). **FAC:** paved rds. (98 spaces). Avail: 36 grass, patios, 3 pull-thrus, (25x50), back-ins (25x35), 36 full hkups (30/50 amps), WiFi, tent sites, dump, laundry. **REC:** heated pool, boating nearby, shuffleboard. Pet restrict (S). Age restrict may apply. 2021 rates: $57, Military discount.
(239)694-3545 Lat: 26.66919, Lon: -81.82218
541 New York Dr, Fort Myers, FL 33905
www.ticemobilehomecourt.com
See ad page 226

UPRIVER RV RESORT

good sam park **Ratings: 9/9.5★/9.5** (RV Park) From Jct of I-75 & SR-78 (exit 143/Bayshore Rd), E 1.6 mi on SR-78 (R).

#1 RV RESORT IN SWFL IS UPRIVER
Upriver offers fun activities for active adults, enjoy our heated pool/spa & newly renovated rec hall/library/billiards rooms. New paved sites for all sized rigs. New boat ramp & the best fishing in FL. Paradise on the water!

FAC: paved rds. (407 spaces). Avail: 282 paved, patios, 123 pull-thrus, (35x100), back-ins (32x60), accepts full hkup units only, 282 full hkups (30/50 amps), cable, WiFi @ sites, rentals, laundry, controlled access. **REC:** heated pool, Caloosahatchee River: fishing, kayaking/canoeing, boating nearby, shuffleboard. Pet restrict (S/B/Q) $. Partial handicap access. No tents. Big rig sites, eco-friendly. 2021 rates: $55 to $110, Military discount.
(239)543-3330 Lat: 26.71156, Lon: -81.78521
17021 Upriver Dr, North Fort Myers, FL 33917
www.upriver.com
See ad page 225

WOODSMOKE CAMPING RESORT **Ratings: 9/9.5★/9** (RV Park) Avail: 102 full hkups (30/50 amps). 2021 rates: $58 to $97. (800)231-5053, 19551 S Tamiami Trail (US 41S), Fort Myers, FL 33908

Travel Services

CAMPING WORLD OF FORT MYERS As the nation's largest retailer of RV supplies, accessories, services and new and used RVs, Camping World is committed to making your total RV experience better. **SERVICES:** RV, tire, sells outdoor gear, staffed RV wash, restrooms. RV Sales. RV supplies, LP gas, emergency parking, RV accessible. Hours: 9am to 7pm.
(888)306-2356 Lat: 26.66383, Lon: -81.80018
4681 Waycross Rd., Fort Myers, FL 33905
www.campingworld.com

RV BOAT STORAGE WORKS Covered storage with 30/15-amp service, 60 degree angled spaces, 27 to 65 foot pull-thru spaces.Open spaces up to 45 ft. 24/7 gate access, smartphone app, security system, monitored surveillance, wash/air station, dump station & free ice. **RV Storage:** outdoor, covered canopy, secured fencing, electric gate, easy reach keypad, 24/7 access, well-lit facility, well-lit roads, well-lit perimeter, security cameras, level gravel/paved spaces, power to charge battery, water, compressed air, office. **SERVICES:** self RV wash, restrooms. Hours: 10am to 4pm M-Sat .
Special offers available for Good Sam Members
(239)333-4444 Lat: 26.62394, Lon: -81.84401
2950 Work Drive, Fort Myers, FL 33916
rvboatstorageworks.com

Things to See and Do

THE BEACHES OF FORT MYERS & SANIBEL Discover The Beaches of Fort Myers & Sanibel through the new free guidebook from Lonely Planet. Explore naturally preserved islands, white sand beaches, and warm Gulf waters. Hours: . No CC.
(800)237-6444
2201 Second St, Suite 600, Fort Myers, FL 33901
www.fortmyers-sanibel.com
See ad page 208

FORT MYERS BEACH — E3 *Lee*

GULF AIR RV RESORT

good sam park **Ratings: 8/10★/7.5** (RV Park) Avail: 82 full hkups (30/50 amps). 2021 rates: $57 to $86. (888)563-7040, 17279 San Carlos Blvd SW, Fort Myers Beach, FL 33931

GULF WATERS RV RESORT **Ratings: 10/10★/10** (Condo Park) Avail: 100 full hkups (30/50 amps). 2021 rates: $55 to $112. (866)437-5888, 11201 Summerlin Sq. Dr, Fort Myers Beach, FL 33931

INDIAN CREEK RV RESORT **Ratings: 9.5/9.5★/9.5** (RV Park) Avail: 50 full hkups (30/50 amps). 2021 rates: $56 to $80. (888)382-8752, 17340 San Carlos Blvd, Fort Myers Beach, FL 33931

RED COCONUT RV PARK

good sam park **Ratings: 7/8.5★/7.5** (RV Park) From Jct of I-75 & Daniels Pkwy (Exit 131), W 5.5 mi on Daniels Pkwy/Cypress Lake Dr to Summerlin Rd, SW 5.6 mi to San Carlos Blvd, S 3 mi to Estero Blvd, SE 1.4 mi (L). **FAC:** paved/gravel rds. (256 spaces). 170 Avail: 15 paved, 77 gravel, 78 grass, patios, 12 pull-thrus, (25x52), back-ins (20x30), 170 full hkups (30/50 amps), seasonal sites, cable, WiFi @ sites, tent sites, rentals, dump, laundry, LP gas, restaurant. **REC:** Gulf of Mexico: swim, fishing, kayaking/canoeing, boating nearby, shuffleboard. Pet restrict (B/Q) $. Partial handicap access, eco-friendly. 2021 rates: $73.59 to $127.11, Military discount.
(888)262-6226 Lat: 26.44540, Lon: -81.93588
3001 Estero Blvd, Fort Myers Beach, FL 33931
www.redcoconut.com
See ad this page

SAN CARLOS RV RESORT AND MARINA **Ratings: 8.5/9★/9** (RV Park) Avail: 139 full hkups (30/50 amps). 2021 rates: $55 to $124. (239)466-3133, 18701 San Carlos Blvd, Fort Myers Beach, FL 33931

FORT PIERCE — L6 *St Lucie*

A SPOTLIGHT Introducing St Lucie County's colorful attractions appearing at the front of this state section.

CAUSEWAY COVE RV PARK **Ratings: 9/9★/9.5** (RV Park) Avail: 10 full hkups (30/50 amps). 2021 rates: $60 to $130. (772)242-3552, 601 Seaway Drive, Fort Pierce, FL 34949

FORT PIERCE WEST KOA **Ratings: 8.5/9★/9.5** (RV Park) Avail: 117 full hkups (30/50 amps). 2021 rates: $42.50 to $115. (772)812-7200, 3180 S Jenkins Rd, Fort Pierce, FL 34981

FORT PIERCE/PORT ST LUCIE KOA **Ratings: 7/9.5/7.5** (RV Park) Avail: 31 full hkups (30/50 amps). 2021 rates: $42.50 to $80. (772)812-7200, 1821 N US Hwy 1, Fort Pierce, FL 34946

ROAD RUNNER TRAVEL RESORT

good sam park **Ratings: 9.5/10★/9** (RV Park) From Jct of FL Tpke & SR-713 (exit 152), N 5 mi on SR-713 to CR-608, E 1.2 mi (L); or From Jct of I-95 & Indrio Rd (exit 138), E 3.2 mi on Indrio Rd to SR-713, S 2.5 mi to CR-608 (St Lucie Blvd), E 1.2 mi (L).

ROAD RUNNER TRAVEL RESORT, FLORIDA
East Coast RV resort nestled in a 38-acre natural Florida Hammock. Full-service resort with immaculate facilities, pool, great recreation, restaurant & 3 hole golf course on site. 5 miles from beach & fantastic FL weather.

FAC: paved rds. (452 spaces). 275 Avail: 20 paved, 185 all weather, 70 grass, patios, 11 pull-thrus, (30x70), back-ins (30x55), 275 full hkups (30/50 amps), seasonal sites, WiFi @ sites, rentals, laundry, groc, LP gas, firewood, restaurant, controlled access. **REC:** heated pool, pond, fishing, boating nearby, golf, shuffleboard. Pet restrict (B/Q). Partial handicap access. No tents. Big rig sites, eco-friendly. 2021 rates: $58 to $68, Military discount. ATM.
(800)833-7108 Lat: 27.48544, Lon: -80.38001
5500 St Lucie Blvd, Fort Pierce, FL 34946
www.roadrunnertravelresort.com
See ad next page, 217

THE SAVANNAS REC AREA (Public) From Jct of US-1 & Hwy 712, E 1.3 mi on Hwy 712 (L). 64 Avail: 54 W, 17 S, 54 E (30 amps). 2021 rates: $22.42 to $26.01. (772)464-7855

TREASURE COAST RV RESORT **Ratings: 10/9/10** (RV Resort) Avail: 165 full hkups (30/50 amps). 2021 rates: $60 to $73. (772)468-2099, 2550 Crossroads Parkway, Fort Pierce, FL 34945

Travel Services

GANDER RV OF FORT PIERCE Your new hometown outfitter offering the best regional gear for all your outdoor needs. Your adventure awaits. **SERVICES:** RV appliance, sells outdoor gear, sells firearms, staffed RV wash, restrooms. RV Sales. RV supplies, LP gas, dump, RV accessible. Hours: 9am - 7pm.
(844)975-2003 Lat: 27.427210, Lon: -80.383109
2123 S Jenkins Rd, Fort Pierce, FL 34947
rv.ganderoutdoors.com

FOUNTAIN — F3 *Bay*

PINE LAKE RV PARK **Ratings: 7/8.5★/6** (RV Park) Avail: 20 full hkups (30/50 amps). 2021 rates: $34.95. (850)722-1401, 21036 Hwy 231, Fountain, FL 32438

FREEPORT — F2 *Walton*

LIVE OAK LANDING **Ratings: 9/9.5★/10** (RV Park) Avail: 66 full hkups (30/50 amps). 2021 rates: $50 to $70. (877)436-5063, 229 Pitts Ave, Freeport, FL 32439

Find 'em fast. Our advertisers often include extra information or provide a detailed map in their ads to help you find their facilities quickly and easily.

FL

Road Runner Travel Resort
TOP RATED RV PARK in South Florida – Fort Pierce.
NO COYOTES
BEST PARKS IN AMERICA
AAA
good sam park
"Nestled in a beautiful 38 acre Florida Hammock"
One of the country's Top Rated R.V. destinations, the Road Runner Travel Resort in Ft. Pierce, Florida, offers 452 full hook-up sites with an unbeatable location! Situated on Florida's Treasure Coast, the Road Runner Travel Resort is just three miles from the pristine shoreline of the Atlantic Ocean. The friendly atmosphere at the Road Runner welcomes you from the moment you arrive. On site is a wide array of amenities, including a heated swimming pool, restaurant & grill, free Wi-Fi porch area, a three-hole golf course, tennis courts, shuffleboard and a general store with everything you need for your pantry and your R.V.
Sites
Cabin Suites
Cabins
The Road Runner Travel Resort also offers over 25 cabin accommodations. Each cabin comes beautifully decorated and furnished, fully equipped with dishes, cookware and bedding. The villas are also a great way to get away from it all when you want to "travel light," yet still experience the benefits of an R.V. vacation.
Fishing on the lake
3 hole golf course
Bike Riding
Pets welcome
Swimming pool
Family Owned & Operated!
Toll Free: 1-800 833-7108
For Reservations & Information
Ph: 772-464-0969
Address: 5500 St. Lucie Blvd., Fort Pierce, FL34946
Website: www.RoadrunnerTravelResort.com
Email: info@RoadrunnerResort.com
You Tube
Florida
See listing Fort Pierce, FL

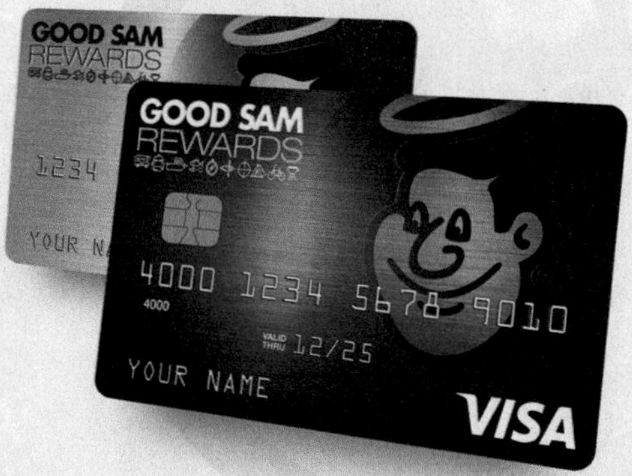

FROSTPROOF — L4 *Polk*

CAMP INN RV RESORT

good sam park **Ratings: 7/8/8.5** (RV Park) From jct of SR 60 & US 27: Go 4-3/4 mi S on US 27 (R). **FAC:** paved rds. (796 spaces). Avail: 179 grass, 20 pull-thrus, (25x50), back-ins (30x60), 155 full hkups, 24 W, 24 E (30/50 amps), tent sites, dump, laundry, LP gas. **REC:** heated pool, hot tub, boating nearby, shuffleboard. Pet restrict (B/Q). Big rig sites. 2021 rates: $36.
(863)635-2500 Lat: 27.77558, Lon: -81.600248
10400 Hwy 27, Frostproof, FL 33843
www.campinnrvresort.com
See ad page 209

RAINBOW RV RESORT **Ratings: 9/10★/9** (RV Park) Avail: 40 full hkups (50 amps). 2021 rates: $38 to $75. (888)650-8189, 700 CR-630A, Frostproof, FL 33843

FRUITLAND PARK — H3 *Lake*

LAKE GRIFFIN (Public State Park) From town, N 0.5 mi on US-27/441 (R). 36 Avail: 36 W, 36 E (30/50 amps). 2021 rates: $18. (352)360-6760

GAINESVILLE — B3 *Alachua*

PAYNES PRAIRIE PRESERVE (Public State Park) From town, N 1 mi on US-441, follow signs (R). 30 Avail: 30 W, 30 E (30/50 amps). 2021 rates: $18. (352)466-3397

GEORGETOWN — B4 *Putnam*

RIVERS EDGE RV PARK **Ratings: 5.5/5.5/6.5** (RV Park) Avail: 10 full hkups (30/50 amps). 2021 rates: $45 to $50. (386)467-7147, 1393 CR 309, Georgetown, FL 32139

GLEN ST MARY — A3 *Baker*

ISLAND OAKS RV RESORT

good sam park (RV Resort) (Under Construction) From jct I-10 & CR 125 (South Glen Ave): Go 500 feet N on CR 125, then 1000 feet W on Nursery Blvd (R). **FAC:** paved rds. Avail: 350 paved, patios, 100 pull-thrus, (30x60), back-ins (30x60), accepts full hkup units only, 350 full hkups (30/50 amps), WiFi @ sites, dump, laundry, LP gas, restaurant. **REC:** heated pool, hot tub, pond, swim, fishing, kayaking/canoeing, boating nearby, shuffleboard. Pets OK. Partial handicap access. No tents. Big rig sites. 2021 rates: $64. ATM.
(904)420-7822 Lat: 30.2638, Lon: -82.1696
9664 Nursery Rd Blvd, Glen St Mary, FL 32040
www.islandoaksrvresort.com
See ad page 260

GRAYTON BEACH — F2 *Walton*

GRAYTON BEACH (Public State Park) From Jct of US-98 & CR-C283, S 1 mi on CR-C283 to SR-30A, E 0.6 mi (R). 59 Avail: 59 W, 59 E (30/50 amps). 2021 rates: $30. (850)267-8300

Williston Crossings RV RESORT

Florida's Premier Camping Resort

- Large Pull-Thru or Back-In Sites Available with High Speed WiFi Service
- 450 Full Hookup, Oversized, Big Rig Friendly, Luxury RV Sites • Gated Community
- Free WiFi and Cable Television
- 9,000+ Sq Ft Clubhouse with Full Service Kitchen
- 2,000+ Sq Ft Activity Center
- Fitness Center, Game Room, Craftroom, Outdoor Bar-B-Q Function Hall, Pavilion
- Large, Heated Swimming Pools
- Two Modern Laundry Facilities
- Full-Time Activity Director with Daily Planned Schedules
- Pet Friendly • Large Fenced In Dog Parks

www.WillistonCrossingRV.com

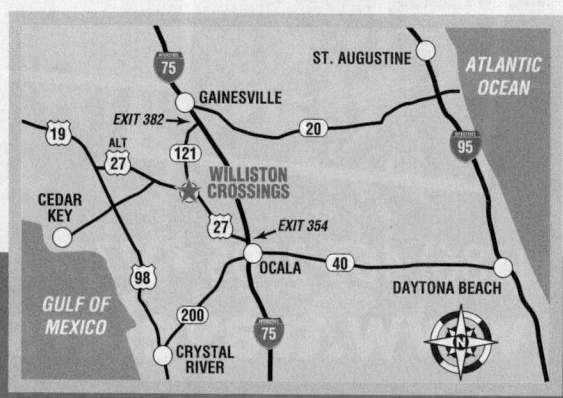

Travelers
Campground
INTERSTATE
FLORIDA
I-75 CAMP
10 Minutes from Gainesville on I-75
I-75 Exit 399 (old 78) (US 441), Left 100' to Waffle House, Left on April Blvd. 1 Mile
good sam park
Rated 9.5/9.5★/8.5
(386) 462-2505 • 17701 April Blvd. • Alachua, FL 32615
www.travelerscampground.com
See listing Alachua, FL

GREEN COVE SPRINGS — B4 *Clay*

CLAY FAIR RV PARK

good sam park **Ratings: 5.5/9★/8.5** (Public) From jct US 17 & SR 16: Go 4 mi W on SR 16 (L). **FAC:** all weather rds. Avail: 68 grass, back-ins (25x45), 68 full hkups (30/50 amps), WiFi @ sites, dump, controlled access. Pets OK. Partial handicap access. No tents. 2021 rates: $35.
(904)284-1615 Lat: 29.980500, Lon: -81.744669
2493 SR 16 West, Green Cove Springs, FL 32043
www.claycountyfair.org
See ad this page

GULF BREEZE — F1 *Santa Rosa*

Travel Services

GANDER RV OF GULF BREEZE Your new hometown outfitter offering the best regional gear for all your outdoor needs. Your adventure awaits. **SERVICES:** RV appliance, MH mechanical, staffed RV wash, restrooms. RV Sales. RV supplies, LP gas, dump, RV accessible. Hours: 9am - 7pm.
(888)219-3441 Lat: 30.403927, Lon: -86.961284
6242 Gulf Breeze Pkwy, Gulf Breeze, FL 32563
rv.ganderoutdoors.com

HAINES CITY — K3 *Polk*

CENTRAL PARK RV RESORT **Ratings: 9/9★/8.5** (RV Park) Avail: 81 full hkups (30/50 amps). 2021 rates: $44 to $74. (863)422-5322, 1501 W Commerce Ave, Haines City, FL 33844

OAK HARBOR LODGING & RV PARK **Ratings: 7.5/8.5★/8.5** (RV Park) Avail: 125 full hkups (30/50 amps). 2021 rates: $40. (863)956-1341, 10000 Lake Lowery Rd, Haines City, FL 33844

PARADISE ISLAND RV PARK **Ratings: 7/7.5/6.5** (RV Park) Avail: 51 full hkups (30/50 amps). 2021 rates: $40. (863)439-1350, 32000 Hwy 27, Haines City, FL 33844

HALLANDALE — E5 *Broward*

HOLIDAY PARK **Ratings: 7/9.5★/7** (RV Area in MH Park) Avail: 65 full hkups (30/50 amps). 2021 rates: $45 to $55. (954)981-4414, 3140 W. Hallandale Beach Blvd, Hallandale, FL 33009

HIGH SPRINGS — B3 *Gilchrist*

HIGH SPRINGS CAMPGROUND

good sam park **Ratings: 8/8.5★/8.5** (Campground) From Jct of I-75 & CR-236 (exit 404), W 0.3 mi on CR-236 to Old Bellamy Rd, N 1000 ft (L). **FAC:** paved/gravel rds. Avail: 45 grass, 17 pull-thrus, (30x75), back-ins (30x45), 45 full hkups (30/50 amps), WiFi @ sites, tent sites, dump, laundry, fire rings, firewood. **REC:** pool, boating nearby, playground. Pets OK. 2021 rates: $39.95, Military discount. no cc.
(386)454-1688 Lat: 29.87520, Lon: -82.54955
24004 NW Old Bellamy Rd, High Springs, FL 32643
www.highspringscampground.com
See ad this page

O'LENO (Public State Park) From Jct of I-75 & US-441/41 (exit 414), S 5 mi on US-441 to park access rd, E 0.4 mi (L). 50 Avail: 50 W, 50 E (20/30 amps). 2021 rates: $18. (386)454-1853

HOBE SOUND — D5 *Martin*

FLORIDAYS RV PARK **Ratings: 6/9.5/7.5** (RV Park) Avail: 62 full hkups (30/50 amps). 2021 rates: $44.60. (772)546-5060, 10705 SE Federal Hwy, Hobe Sound, FL 33455

JONATHAN DICKINSON (Public State Park) N-bnd: From Jct of I-95 & SR-706 (exit 87A), E 4 mi on SR-706 to US-1, N 5.5 mi (L); or S-bnd: From Jct of I-95 & CR-708 (exit 96), E 6.4 mi on SR-708 to US-1, S 3 mi (R). 122 Avail: 122 W, 122 E (30/50 amps). 2021 rates: $26. (772)546-2771

HOLIDAY — K1 *Pasco*

HOLIDAY TRAVEL PARK

good sam park **Ratings: 8/8/8.5** (RV Area in MH Park) Avail: 83 full hkups (30/50 amps). 2021 rates: $44 to $53. (888)563-7040, 1622 Aires Dr., Holiday, FL 34690

Travel Services

CAMPING WORLD OF HOLIDAY/NEW PORT RICHEY As the nation's largest retailer of RV supplies, accessories, services and new and used RVs, Camping World is committed to making your total RV experience better. **SERVICES:** RV, tire, RV appliance, MH mechanical, staffed RV wash, restrooms. RV Sales. RV supplies, LP gas, RV accessible. Hours: 9am to 7pm.
(866)469-0989 Lat: 28.18991, Lon: -82.73965
2112 US Hwy 19 , Holiday, FL 34691
www.campingworld.com

HOLLYWOOD — E5 *Broward*

HOLLYWOOD KOA **Ratings: 6/9.5★/8** (RV Park) Avail: 38 full hkups (30/50 amps). 2021 rates: $60 to $85. (954)983-8225, 5931 Polk St, Hollywood, FL 33021

LAKESIDE PARK ESTATES **Ratings: 7.5/8.5/8.5** (RV Park) Avail: 20 full hkups (30/50 amps). 2021 rates: $35 to $53. (954)962-7400, 3300 Pembroke Rd, Hollywood, FL 33021

TY (TOPEEKEEGEE YUGNEE) (Public) From Jct of I-95 & Sheridan St (Exit 21), W 0.75 mi to North Park Rd, N 0.1 mi (R). Avail: 61 full hkups (50 amps). 2021 rates: $40 to $50. (954)357-8811

HOLT — E1 *Okaloosa*

BLACKWATER RIVER (Public State Park) From town, W 10 mi on US-90 to cnty rd (Deaton Bridge Rd), N 3 mi (E) Entrance fee required. Avail: 30 full hkups (30/50 amps). 2021 rates: $20. (850)983-5363

RIVERS EDGE RV CAMPGROUND

good sam park **Ratings: 7.5/8★/8** (Campground) Avail: 98 full hkups (30/50 amps). 2021 rates: $30. (850)537-2267, 4001 Log Lake Rd, Holt, FL 32564

HOMESTEAD — F5 *Miami-Dade*

HOMESTEAD See also Key Largo & Miami.

BOARDWALK RV RESORT

good sam park **Ratings: 8.5/9★/8.5** (RV Park) From FL Turnpike S (exit 2): Go 1-1/2 mi W on Campbell Dr, then 3/4 mi S on US-1, then 500 feet E on NE 6th Ave (L).

GATEWAY TO EVERGLADES & FL KEYS
Gated RV resort located close to shopping and restaurants. Nearby attractions include Biscayne National Park, Everglades National Park, Pennekamp Coral Reef State Park, Homestead-Miami Speedway, and Coral Castle.
FAC: paved rds. (311 spaces). Avail: 145 grass, patios, back-ins (30x60), 145 full hkups (30/50 amps), WiFi, laundry, controlled access. **REC:** heated pool, boating nearby, shuffleboard, playground. Pet restrict (S/B/Q). Partial handicap access. No tents, eco-friendly. 2021 rates: $69 to $79, Military discount.
(305)248-2487 Lat: 25.47142, Lon: -80.46889
100 NE 6TH Ave, Homestead, FL 33030
boardwalkrv.com
See ad this page

EVERGLADES/FLAMINGO (Public National Park) From jct FL Tpk & US-1: Go 500 feet S on US-1, then 45 mi W on SR-9336 (Palm Dr) (L). Avail: 41 E (30/50 amps). 2021 rates: $25 to $50. (855)708-2207

Set your clocks. Time zones are indicated in the front of each state and province.

FL

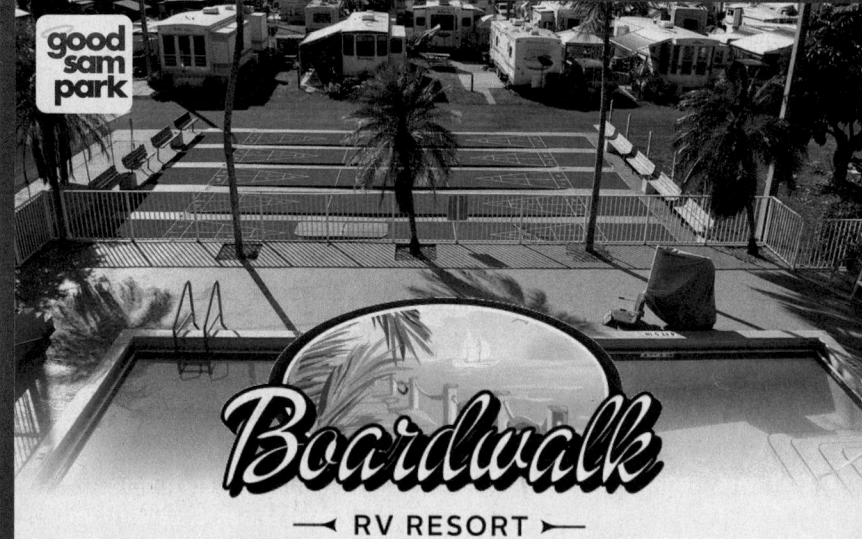

Island Oaks
RV RESORT
It's Happening at Island Oaks!
NORTHEAST FLORIDA'S NEWEST OUTDOOR RESORT
LUSH GREENERY • LARGE WATER FEATURES • RECREATION CENTER
FOREST
EVENT LAWN
SWIMMING LAKE
SANDY BEACH
Island
FISHING LAKE
Pool
EVENT LAWN
good sam park
ABUNDANT RECREATION & DAILY GROUP ACTIVITIES
JOIN IN THE FUN - MAKE NEW FRIENDS!
• 60'+ RV sites, 30/50 amp sites
• Free WiFi
• Cable TV available
• Golf cart, segway & bike rentals
• Convenience store
• Dog park, pet wash
• Spacious bathrooms
• Club house, restaurant & bar, fitness gym, laundry centers
• Kid's arcade, ping pong, air hockey, pool tables
• Badminton, corn hole, horse shoes & card room
• Miniature golf
• Pickle ball, bocce ball & shuffle board courts
• Tiki bar
• Heated swimming pool & hot tub
• Concert lawn
• Recreation area
• Swimming lake beach, blow up slides & bounce platforms
• Two acre fishing lake
• Fishing gear and boat rentals
See listing Glen St. Mary, FL
Visit us online to see our progress and sign up for special offers and news at
www.islandoaksrvresort.com
10
30 miles west of Jacksonville
9664 Nursery Blvd
Glen St. Mary FL 32040
(904) 420-7822
info@islandoaksrv.com

HOMESTEAD (CONT)

EVERGLADES/LONG PINE KEY (Public National Park) From Jct of US-1 & SR-9336, SW 10 mi on SR-9336 to park entrance, W 6 mi (E) Entrance fee required. 79 Avail. 2021 rates: $25. Nov 01 to Apr 30. (855)708-2207

GOLD COASTER RV RESORT AND MANUFACTURED HOME COMMUNITY **Ratings: 8.5/9/8.5** (RV Area in MH Park) Avail: 14 full hkups (30/50 amps). 2021 rates: $62 to $91. (877)466-9758, 34850 SW 187th Ave, Homestead, FL 33034

HOMOSASSA — H2 *Citrus*

CHASSAHOWITZKA RIVER CAMPGROUND
good sam park
Ratings: 8/8.5★/8.5 (Campground) From Jct Hwy 19 & Hwy 98: Go W 2 mi on Miss Magee Dr (E). **FAC:** gravel rds. Avail: 52 grass, 10 pull-thrus, (35x50), back-ins (35x50), 52 full hkups (30/50 amps), WiFi @ sites, tent sites, dump, laundry, groc, fire rings, firewood. **REC:** Chassahowitzka River: swim, fishing, kayaking/canoeing, boating nearby, playground. Pet restrict (Q). Big rig sites. 2021 rates: $55.
(352)382-2200 Lat: 28.71320, Lon: -82.57625
8600 W Miss Maggie Dr, Homosassa, FL 34448
www.campnpaddle.com
See ad page 243

HOMOSASSA RIVER RV RESORT **Ratings: 8.5/8.5★/9** (RV Park) Avail: 122 full hkups (30/50 amps). 2021 rates: $43 to $71. (352)628-2928, 10200 W Fishbowl Dr, Homosassa Springs, FL 34448

NATURE'S RESORT
good sam park
Ratings: 9/9.5★/9 (RV Park) From Jct of US-19 & Hwy 490A (Halls River Rd), W 1.8 mi on Halls River Rd (R). **FAC:** paved rds. (400 spaces). Avail: 250 gravel, patios, 34 pull-thrus, (30x60), back-ins (30x52), 250 full hkups (30/50 amps), seasonal sites, cable, WiFi @ sites, rentals, dump, laundry, groc, LP gas, firewood, restaurant. **REC:** heated pool, Halls River: swim, fishing, marina, kayaking/canoeing, boating nearby, playground. Pets OK. Partial handicap access. No tents. Big rig sites. 2021 rates: $58 to $68.
(800)301-7880 Lat: 28.79806, Lon: -82.60614
10359 W Halls River Rd, Homosassa, FL 34448
naturesresortfla.com
See ad page 242

HUDSON — J1 *Pasco*

7 OAKS RV PARK **Ratings: 7.5/7.5★/7.5** (RV Area in MH Park) Avail: 30 full hkups (30/50 amps). 2021 rates: $40 to $50. (727)862-3016, 9207 Bolton Ave, Hudson, FL 34667

BARRINGTON HILLS RV RESORT
good sam park
Ratings: 8.5/8/8 (RV Area in MH Park) Avail: 100 full hkups (30/50 amps). 2021 rates: $46 to $52. (888)563-7040, 9412 New York Ave, Hudson, FL 34667

THREE LAKES RV RESORT **Ratings: 9/9★/8.5** (RV Park) Avail: 111 full hkups (30/50 amps). 2021 rates: $40 to $54. (888)316-6991, 10354 Smooth Water Drive, Hudson, FL 34667

Don't miss out on great savings - find Camping World coupons at the front and back of this Guide!

WINTER PARADISE RV RESORT
good sam park
Ratings: 7.5/7.5/6.5 (RV Area in MH Park) From jct US 19 & Denton Ave: Go 500 feet N on US 19. (R). **FAC:** paved rds. (290 spaces). Avail: 140 grass, patios, back-ins (25x45), 140 full hkups (30/50 amps), seasonal sites, WiFi, laundry, LP gas. **REC:** heated pool, boating nearby, shuffleboard. Pet restrict (B). No tents. 2021 rates: $33. no cc.
(727)868-2285 Lat: 28.39143, Lon: -82.66713
16108 US Hwy 19, Hudson, FL 34667
www.winterparadiserv.com
See ad page 209

INDIAN HARBOUR BEACH — K5 *Brevard*

LUCKY CLOVER RV & MHP **Ratings: 6.5/NA/7** (RV Area in MH Park) Avail: 47 full hkups (50 amps). 2021 rates: $40. (321)773-3661, 635 E Eau Gallie Blvd (SR-518), Melbourne, FL 32937

INGLIS — G1 *Levy*

GULF COAST RV RESORT **Ratings: 9/8.5★/8.5** (RV Park) Avail: 30 full hkups (30/50 amps). 2021 rates: $35 to $39. (352)447-2900, 10885 N Suncoast Blvd, Inglis, FL 34449

ISLAMORADA — F5 *Monroe*

SAN PEDRO VILLAGE RV RESORT (RV Park) (Rebuilding) Avail: 2 full hkups (30/50 amps). 2021 rates: $75. (305)289-0011, 87401 Old Hwy, Islamorada, FL 33036

JACKSONVILLE — A4 *Duval*

JACKSONVILLE See also Callahan, Glen St Mary & Green Cove Springs.

COUNTRY OAKS RV PARK & CAMPGROUND
good sam park
Ratings: 8.5/9★/9 (RV Park) From North Jct I-295 & I-95: Go 19 mi N on I-95 (GA exit 1), then 1/4 mi W on St. Mary's Rd. (L). **FAC:** paved rds. (43 spaces). Avail: 23 gravel, 18 pull-thrus, (28x60), back-ins (30x40), 23 full hkups (30/50 amps), seasonal sites, WiFi @ sites, laundry, LP gas, fire rings, firewood. **REC:** pond, fishing, boating nearby. Pet restrict (B). Partial handicap access. No tents. Big rig sites. 2021 rates: $38 to $42.
(912)729-6212 Lat: 30.76032, Lon: -81.65920
2456 Scrubby Bluff Road, Kingsland, GA 31548
www.countryoaksrv.com
See primary listing at Kingsland, GA and ad this page

CROSSBOW RV CAMPGROUND
(RV Park) (Seasonal Stay Only) From jct I-295 & New Kings Rd (exit 28B): Go 1/2 mi N on New Kings Rd, then 1/2 mi E on Trout Blvd, then 2-1/2 mi N on Old Kings Rd (L). **FAC:** gravel rds. Avail: 9 gravel, 3 pull-thrus, (40x60), back-ins (40x60), 9 full hkups (30/50 amps), WiFi, controlled access. **REC:** hunting nearby. Pet restrict (B). No tents. 2021 rates: $66.
(904)351-8118 Lat: 30.4502165, Lon: -81.7776537
11950 Old Kings Road, Jacksonville, FL 32219
crossbowrv.com
See ad this page

FLAMINGO LAKE RV RESORT **Ratings: 9/9★/9** (RV Park) Avail: 433 full hkups (30/50 amps). 2021 rates: $56 to $94. (800)782-4323, 3640 Newcomb Rd, Jacksonville, FL 32218

Find Good Sam member specials at CampingWorld.com

FLEETWOOD MHP RV PARK **Ratings: 6.5/9★/7** (RV Area in MH Park) Avail: 84 full hkups (30/50 amps). 2021 rates: $50. (904)737-4733, 5001 Phillips Hwy, Jacksonville, FL 32207

HANNA PARK CAMPGROUND (Public) From Jct of SR-10 (Atlantic Ave) & A1A (Mayport Rd), N 2 mi on A1A (Mayport Rd) until becomes CR-101, N 1 mi to Wonderwood Dr, E 0.1 mi (E). Avail: 252 full hkups (30/50 amps). 2021 rates: $33.84. (904)249-4700

LITTLE TALBOT ISLAND (Public State Park) From Jct of I-95 & SR-A1A exit 373, E 32.4 mi on SR-A1A (L). 20 Avail: 20 W, 20 E (20/30 amps). 2021 rates: $24. (904)251-2320

MILITARY PARK JACKSONVILLE RV PARK (NAS JACKSONVILLE) (Public) From town: Go 11 mi S on US-17 S/Roosevelt Blvd, then 1-1/2 mi E Yorktown/Birminham Ave (R). Avail: 38 full hkups (30/50 amps). 2021 rates: $27 to $29. (904)542-5898

PECAN PARK RV RESORT **Ratings: 10/10★/9** (RV Park) Avail: 183 full hkups (30/50 amps). 2021 rates: $60 to $94. (866)981-9759, 650 Pecan Park Rd, Jacksonville, FL 32218

Always do a Pre-Drive Safety Check!

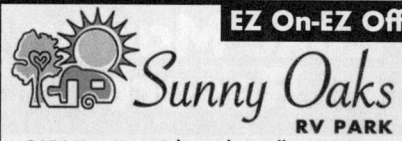

JACKSONVILLE (CONT)

SUNNY OAKS RV PARK

Ratings: 8.5/9★/8.5 (RV Park) From jct I 295 & New Kings Rd (exit 28): Go 1/4 mi S on New Kings Rd (R). **FAC:** paved rds. Avail: 160 gravel, patios, back-ins (30x60), accepts full hkup units only, 160 full hkups (30/50 amps), WiFi @ sites, dump, laundry, LP gas. Pets OK. No tents, eco-friendly. 2021 rates: $50. no cc.
(904)619-6118 Lat: 30.406975, Lon: -81.746301
8654 New Kings Rd, Jacksonville, FL 32219
www.SunnyOaksCommunityRV.com
See ad previous page

Travel Services

CAMPING WORLD OF JACKSONVILLE As the nation's largest retailer of RV supplies, accessories, services and new and used RVs, Camping World is committed to making your total RV experience better. **SERVICES:** RV, tire, RV appliance, MH mechanical, . RV Sales. RV supplies, LP gas, emergency parking. Hours: 9am to 7pm.
(877)261-4327 Lat: 30.421820, Lon: -81.658268
10101 Interstate Center Drive, Jacksonville, FL 32218
www.campingworld.com

Thank you for being one of our best customers!

JENNINGS — A2 *Hamilton*

JENNINGS KOA HOLIDAY **Ratings: 9.5/10★/8.5** (RV Park) Avail: 102 full hkups (30/50 amps). 2021 rates: $52 to $76. (386)938-3321, 2039 Hamilton Ave, Jennings, FL 32053

JENSEN BEACH — D5 *Martin*

OCEAN BREEZE RESORT **Ratings: 10/10★/10** (RV Resort) Avail: 124 full hkups (30/50 amps). 2021 rates: $60 to $85. (772)334-2494, 3000 NE Indian River Drive, Jensen Beach, FL 34957

JUNO BEACH — D5 *Palm Beach*

JUNO OCEAN WALK RV RESORT **Ratings: 9/9.5★/9** (Condo Park) Avail: 70 full hkups (30/50 amps). 2021 rates: $55 to $120. (561)622-7500, 900 Juno Ocean Walk, Juno Beach, FL 33408

JUPITER — D5 *Palm Beach*

PALM BEACH MOTORCOACH RESORT **Ratings: 10/10★/10** (Condo Park) Avail: 50 full hkups (30/50 amps). 2021 rates: $75 to $145. (561)741-1555, 11075 W Indiantown Rd, Jupiter, FL 33478

WEST JUPITER RV RESORT **Ratings: 9/9.5★/8** (Campground) Avail: 91 full hkups (30/50 amps). 2021 rates: $45 to $85. (561)746-6073, 17801 130th Avenue N, Jupiter, FL 33478

KENANSVILLE — K5 *Osceola*

LAKE MARIAN RESORT

Ratings: 7/7.5/8 (RV Park) From Jct US-441 & Hwy 523: Go W 3.25 mi on Hwy 523, then S 0.5 mi on Arnold Rd (E). **FAC:** paved/gravel rds. (126 spaces). 37 Avail: 26 gravel, 11 grass, 11 pull-thrus, (24x40), back-ins (22x41), 37 full hkups (30/50 amps), seasonal sites, WiFi @ sites, rentals, dump, laundry, groc. **REC:** Lake Marian: fishing, marina, kayaking/canoeing, boating nearby, shuffleboard, playground. Pet restrict (B/Q). No tents. 2021 rates: $40 to $85, Military discount.
(407)436-1464 Lat: 27.87023, Lon: -81.04365
901 Arnold Rd Office, Kenansville, FL 34739
www.lakemarianresort.com
See ad this page

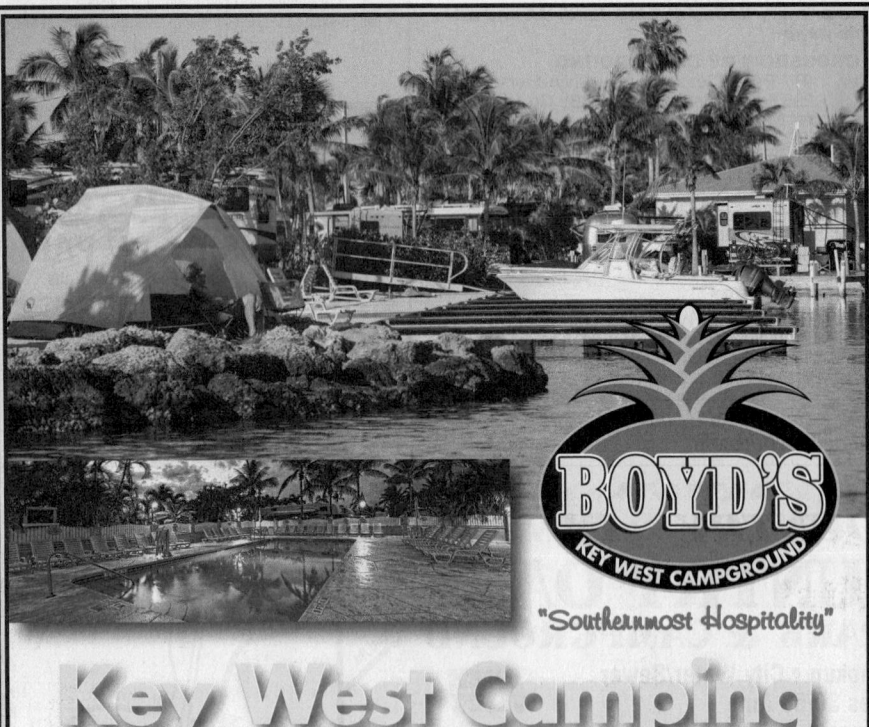

KEY LARGO — F5 *Monroe*

CALUSA CAMPGROUND **Ratings: 9/9.5/8.5** (Condo Park) Avail: 167 full hkups (30/50 amps). 2021 rates: $65 to $85. (305)451-0232, 325 Calusa Street, Key Largo, FL 33037

JOHN PENNEKAMP CORAL REEF (Public State Park) S-bnd: On US-1 at MP-102.5 (L). 42 Avail: 42 W, 42 E (30/50 amps). 2021 rates: $32. (305)451-1202

KEY LARGO KAMPGROUND & MARINA **Ratings: 8/8/8.5** (Condo Park) Avail: 57 full hkups (30/50 amps). 2021 rates: $100 to $115.50. (305)451-1431, 101551 Overseas Hwy, Key Largo, FL 33037

KEYS PALMS RV RESORT **Ratings: 9.5/9/10** (RV Resort) Avail: 30 full hkups (30/50 amps). 2021 rates: $115 to $175. (305)440-2832, 104200 Overseas Hwy, Key Largo, FL 33037

KINGS KAMP, RV, TENT & MARINA **Ratings: 6/9.5★/7** (Campground) Avail: 48 full hkups (30/50 amps). 2021 rates: $65 to $118. (305)451-0010, 103620 Overseas Hwy, Key Largo, FL 33037

RIPTIDE RV RESORT & MARINA **Ratings: 5.5/9★/8** (RV Park) Avail: 8 full hkups (30/50 amps). 2021 rates: $75 to $155. (305)852-8481, 97680 Overseas Hwy, Key Largo, FL 33037

KEY WEST — F4 *Monroe*

KEY WEST See also Cudjoe Key & Sugarloaf Key.

BLUEWATER KEY RV RESORT **Ratings: 9/9.5★/10** (Condo Park) Avail: 75 full hkups (30/50 amps). 2021 rates: $112 to $410. (305)745-2494, 2950 US Hwy 1, Key West, FL 33040

BOYD'S KEY WEST CAMPGROUND

Ratings: 8.5/9★/9 (Campground) From Jct of US-1 & 3rd St at MP-5, S 0.2 mi on 3rd St to MacDonald Ave/Maloney Ave, E 0.3 mi (L).

TROPICAL CAMPING AT ITS BEST!

Tropical waterfront camping at the southernmost campground in the USA. Excellent boating access to both the Atlantic and the Gulf of Mexico. Heated pool, game room, picnic pavilion, boat ramp, and more.
FAC: paved rds. (203 spaces). 163 Avail: 138 gravel, 25 grass, patios, back-ins (24x44), 163 full hkups (30/50 amps), seasonal sites, cable, WiFi @ sites, tent sites, rentals, dump, laundry, groc, firewood, restaurant. **REC:** heated pool, Atlantic Ocean: fishing, kayaking/canoeing, boating nearby. Pet restrict (B). Partial handicap access. 2021 rates: $105 to $205. ATM.
(305)294-1465 Lat: 24.57111, Lon: -81.73372
6401 Maloney Ave, Key West, FL 33040
www.boydscampground.com
See ad this page

MILITARY PARK NASKW CAMPGROUND (KEY WEST NAS) (Public) From town: Go 1 mi NE on Flagler Ave, then 1/2 mi W on Kennedy Dr, continue onto Sigsbee Rd for 1 mi (R). Avail: 90 full hkups (30/50 amps). 2021 rates: $27 to $32. (305)293-4432

KEYSTONE HEIGHTS — B3 *Clay*

KEYSTONE HEIGHTS RV RESORT

Ratings: 10/10★/10 (RV Resort) From jct SR-21 & SR-100: Go 2 mi NW on SR-100, then 500 feet S on SE County Rd 21b, then 500 feet SW on Keystone Ave (R).

LUXURY MADE AFFORDABLE

Come experience for yourself one of Florida's newest parks with every amenity you can imagine. First Class all the way. Centrally located to many of the places you know & love. Many great fishing lakes nearby.
FAC: paved rds. Avail: 413 paved, patios, 33 pull-thrus, (30x80), back-ins (40x70), accepts full hkup units only, 413 full hkups (30/50 amps), cable, WiFi @ sites, $, dump, laundry, LP gas, controlled access. **REC:** heated pool, hot tub, boating nearby. Pets OK. Partial handicap access. No tents. Big rig sites. 2021 rates: $62 to $72, Military discount.
(352)645-4330 Lat: 29.8044, Lon: -82.0630
1177 SE Keystone Ave., Keystone Heights, FL 32656
www.keystoneheightsrv.com
See ad pages 264, 265

MIKE ROESS GOLD HEAD BRANCH (Public State Park) From Jct of SR-100 & SR-21, NE 6 mi on SR-21 (R). 39 Avail: 39 W, 39 E (20/30 amps). 2021 rates: $20. (352)473-4701

Welcome to Paradise...

Keystone Heights RV Resort is an RV Community designed purely for your enjoyment. We cater to our guests who enjoy an active, adult, RV lifestyle. We offer outstanding accommodations for your Big Rig, Class A, B or C motorhome, 5th Wheel or Travel Trailer. We have over 400 spacious RV Sites with concrete pads and exquisite landscaping.

A secure and gated resort

Your home away from home

Beautifully landscaped sites

Stay in a Real Covered Wagon

It's a unique experience complete with electricity, full bathroom and shower, air conditioning and heating. All wagons are covered with the highest quality canvas to protect from the elements and keep our guests comfortable.

2,700sf swimming pool with spa

Dedicated game room

An Experience You'll Never Forget!

See listing Keystone Heights, FL

Ultra clean laundry facility

Glamp in our covered wagons

KISSIMMEE — J4 *Osceola*

KISSIMMEE See also Apopka, Clermont, Davenport, Dundee, Haines City, Lake Buena Vista, Lake Wales, Orlando, Polk City, Winter Garden & Winter Haven.

BOGGY CREEK RESORT & RV PARK **Ratings: 7.5/7.5★/7** (Campground) Avail: 300 full hkups (30/50 amps). 2021 rates: $75 to $105. (407)348-2040, 3705 Big Bass Rd, Kissimmee, FL 34744

GREAT OAK RV RESORT **Ratings: 7/7/7** (RV Area in MH Park) Avail: 10 full hkups (30/50 amps). 2021 rates: $39.50. (407)396-9092, 4440 Yowell Rd, Kissimmee, FL 34746

KISSIMMEE RV PARK **Ratings: 8/7/8** (Campground) Avail: 43 full hkups (30/50 amps). 2021 rates: $45 to $63. (407)396-6655, 2425 Old Vineland Rd, Kissimmee, FL 34746

MERRY D RV SANCTUARY

good sam park **Ratings: 8/8★/8** (Campground) From jct Florida Tpke (exit 249) & Osceola Pkwy: Go W 2.6 mi on Osceola Pkwy, then S 6.2 mi on John Young Pkwy, then S 6.8 mi on Pleasant Hill Rd (L). **FAC:** paved rds. (121 spaces). Avail: 79 all weather, patios, 34 pull-thrus, (50x100), back-ins (50x100), 79 full hkups (30/50 amps), cable, WiFi @ sites, tent sites, dump, laundry, LP gas, controlled access. **REC:** pond, fishing, boating nearby, shuffleboard. Pet restrict (B/Q). Partial handicap access. Big rig sites. 2021 rates: $46.54. **(800)208-3434 Lat: 28.16347, Lon: -81.43984**
4261 Pleasant Hill Rd, Kissimmee, FL 34746
www.merryd.com
See ad page 288

MILL CREEK RV RESORT **Ratings: 8.5/9★/7.5** (RV Area in MH Park) Avail: 30 full hkups (30/50 amps). 2021 rates: $60 to $81. (407)847-6288, 2775 Michigan Ave, Kissimmee, FL 34744

ORLANDO/KISSIMMEE KOA **Ratings: 8.5/10★/9** (RV Park) Avail: 68 full hkups (30/50 amps). 2021 rates: $55 to $94. (407)396-2400, 2644 Happy Camper Place, Kissimmee, FL 34746

SHERWOOD FOREST RV RESORT

good sam park **Ratings: 8/8.5★/7.5** (RV Park) Avail: 398 full hkups (30/50 amps). 2021 rates: $68 to $101. (888)563-7040, 5302 W Irlo Bronson Hwy, Kissimmee, FL 34746

TROPICAL PALMS RV RESORT

good sam park **Ratings: 9/9.5★/9** (RV Resort) 329 Avail: 289 full hkups, 40 W, 40 E (30/50 amps). 2021 rates: $62 to $95. (888)563-7040, 2650 Holiday Trail, Kissimmee, FL 34746

Travel Services

CAMPING WORLD OF KISSISSMMEE/ORLANDO As the nation's largest retailer of RV supplies, accessories, services and new and used RVs, Camping World is committed to making your total RV experience better. **SERVICES:** RV, tire, RV appliance, sells outdoor gear, sells firearms, staffed RV wash, restrooms. RV Sales. RV supplies, LP gas, RV accessible. Hours: 9am to 7pm.
(888)253-3918 Lat: 28.333024, Lon: -81.490498
5175 W. Irlo Bronson Hwy, Kissimmee, FL 34746
www.campingworld.com

LABELLE — D4 *Glades*

A SPOTLIGHT Introducing Hendry County's colorful attractions appearing at the front of this state section.

GRANDMA'S GROVE RV PARK

good sam park **Ratings: 7.5/8.5/8.5** (RV Park) From jct SR-80 & SR-29: Go 3 mi W on SR-80 (R). **FAC:** paved rds. (205 spaces). Avail: 55 gravel, patios, back-ins (35x60), 55 full hkups (30/50 amps), seasonal sites, WiFi, dump, laundry. **REC:** heated pool, pond, fishing, boating nearby, shuffleboard. Pet restrict (S/B/Q). Partial handicap access. No tents, Age restrict may apply. Big rig sites. 2021 rates: $40 to $45. no cc.
(863)675-2567 Lat: 26.73664, Lon: -81.47404
2250 SR 80 W, LaBelle, FL 33935
www.grandmasgrove.com
See ad this page

MOSS LANDING RV RESORT **Ratings: 8.5/9/9** (RV Area in MH Park) Avail: 140 full hkups (30/50 amps). 2021 rates: $47. (863)674-7119, 900 Aqua Isle Blvd, LaBelle, FL 33935

ORTONA LOCK & DAM - COE/ORTONA SOUTH (Public Corps) From town, E 8 mi on SR 80 to Dalton Ln, N 1 mi (E). 49 Avail: 49 W, 49 E (50 amps). 2021 rates: $30. (863)675-8400

RIVERBEND MOTORCOACH RESORT **Ratings: 10/10★/10** (Condo Park) Avail: 60 full hkups (30/50 amps). 2021 rates: $75 to $154. (866)787-4837, 5800 West SR-80, LaBelle, FL 33935

THE GLADES RV RESORT

good sam park **Ratings: 8.5/9★/8.5** (RV Park) From Jct of SR-80 & SR-29, E 13 mi on SR-80 (L). **FAC:** paved rds. (360 spaces). Avail: 100 grass, patios, 6 pull-thrus, (30x70), back-ins (45x70), 100 full hkups (30/50 amps), seasonal sites, WiFi @ sites, $, rentals, dump, laundry, groc, restaurant. **REC:** heated pool, Caloosahatchee River: fishing, marina, kayaking/canoeing, boating nearby, golf, shuffleboard. Pets OK. Partial handicap access. No tents. Big rig sites, eco-friendly. 2021 rates: $49 to $60, Military discount.
(800)803-2750 Lat: 26.77723, Lon: -81.22821
1682 Indian Hills Dr, Moore Haven, FL 33471
www.thegladesresort.com
See ad opposite page

WHISPER CREEK RV RESORT

good sam park **Ratings: 9/10★/9.5** (RV Park) From Jct of SR-80 & SR-29, N 1.8 mi on SR-29 (L).

RELAX AT WHISPER CREEK
Centrally located in South Florida one mile north of quaint LaBelle and the Caloosahatchee River. Enjoy small town living with waterways and natural beauty. Visit famous attractions, or take a quiet walk on a nature trail.

FAC: paved rds. (462 spaces). 142 Avail: 20 paved, 122 grass, patios, 3 pull-thrus, (50x60), back-ins (50x60), accepts full hkup units only, 142 full hkups (30/50 amps), seasonal sites, WiFi @ sites, rentals, laundry, controlled access. **REC:** heated pool, pond, fishing, boating nearby, shuffleboard, hunting nearby. Pet restrict (B/Q). Partial handicap access. No tents, Age restrict may apply. Big rig sites, eco-friendly. 2021 rates: $58 to $68, Military discount.
(863)656-3475 Lat: 26.78713, Lon: -81.43482
1887 North State Rd 29, LaBelle, FL 33935
www.inspirecom.com/communities/whisper-creek
See ad previous page, 227

Things to See and Do

THE GLADES RV & GOLF RESORT Championship length par-36 9-hole golf course with water features, natural landscaping & has a grill. Open to the public. Restrooms. Food. Hours: Call for tee times. Adult fee: $15 to $40.
(863)983-8464 Lat: 26.76863, Lon: -81.22736
1682 Indian Hills Dr, Moore Haven, FL 33471
www.thegladesresort.com
See ad this page

THE GLADES RV RESORT & MARINA Marina sits on the Caloosahatchee River, intercoastal waterway connecting the Atlantic Ocean & Gulf of Mexico. Public boat launch for park guests, accommodates watercraft up to 60 feet. Pump-out station available. $2.00 to $10 per foot. Partial handicap access. Restrooms. Hours: 8am to 6pm.
(863)673-5653 Lat: 26.76863, Lon: -81.22736
1682 Indian Hills Dr, Moore Haven, FL 33471
www.thegladesresort.com
See ad this page

New to RVing? Visit Blog.GoodSam.com for tips on everything camping and RVing.

LADY LAKE — H3 *Lake*

BLUE PARROT RV RESORT
good sam park **Ratings: 8.5/9★/8.5** (RV Park) N-Bnd: From Jct of US-27/US-441 & CR-25, N 1.3 mi on CR-25 (R); or S-Bnd: From Jct of US 27/US 441 & Griffin Rd, E 0.7 mi on Griffin Rd to CR-25, N 0.2 mi (R). **FAC:** paved rds. (448 spaces). Avail: 150 grass, 20 pull-thrus, (30x60), back-ins (30x60), 150 full hkups (30/50 amps), WiFi, dump, laundry, LP gas. **REC:** heated pool, boating nearby, golf, shuffleboard. Pets OK. No tents. Big rig sites. 2021 rates: $50.
(352)753-2026 Lat: 28.94210, Lon: -81.92827
40840 CR-25, Lady Lake, FL 32159
www.rvresorts.com
See ad this page

Thank You to our active and retired military personnel. Look for military parks within the state listings section of your 2022 Guide.

GRAND OAKS RESORT
good sam park **Ratings: 10/10★/9.5** (RV Resort) Avail: 60 full hkups (30/50 amps). 2021 rates: $50 to $75. (352)750-5500, 3525 Griffin Ave, Lady Lake, FL 32159

RECREATION PLANTATION **Ratings: 9/9★/8** (RV Area in MH Park) Avail: 404 full hkups (30/50 amps). 2021 rates: $63. (800)448-5646, 609 Hwy 466, Lady Lake, FL 32159

Find new and exciting itineraries in our ""Road Trip" article at the front of each state and province.

FL

LAKE CITY
Campground
LAKE
CITY
CAMPGROUND
• Long Paved Pull-thrus, some 120 ft.
• Big Rig Friendly
• Cabin & Cottage Rentals
• 30/50 Amp • Propane • Free Cable
• Clean Laundry & Bathrooms
• RV & Boat Storage • Pool
• Playground • Fishing Pond
• Weekly & Monthly Rates
• Luxury Tent Sites
FREE WI-FI
good sam park
Rated
9/9★/8.5
See listing Lake City, FL
TOLL FREE 866-773-CAMP
4743 N. US Hwy 441 • Lake City, FL 32055
Lakecitycampground@aol.com
www.lakecitycampground.com

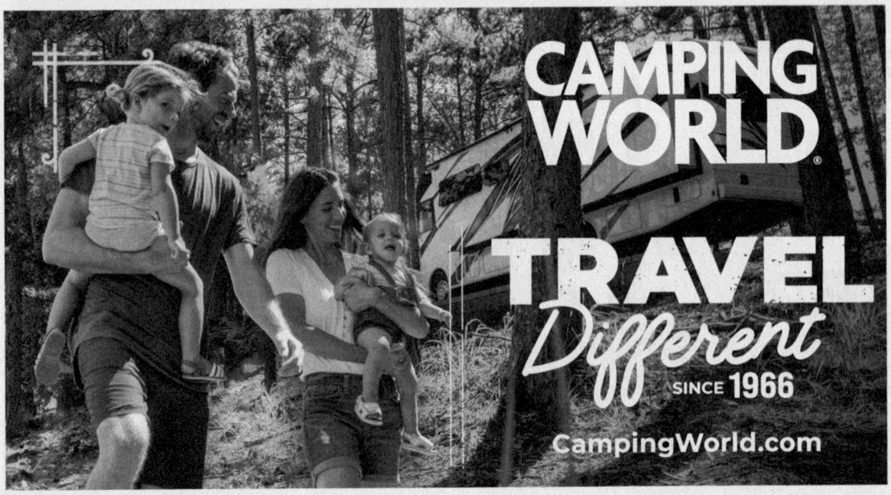

LAKE BUENA VISTA — J4 *Lake*

DISNEY'S FORT WILDERNESS RESORT & CAMPGROUND **Ratings: 10/10★/10** (Campground) 843 Avail: 753 full hkups, 90 W, 90 E (30/50 amps). 2021 rates: $80 to $285. (407)939-7723, 4510 N. Fort Wilderness Trail, Lake Buena Vista, FL 32830

LAKE CITY — A3 *Columbia*

LAKE CITY CAMPGROUND

good sam park **Ratings: 9/9★/8.5** (Campground) From Jct of I-75 & I-10, E 5.5 mi on I-10 to US-441 (exit 303), N 1 mi (R). **FAC:** paved rds. 40 Avail: 25 paved, 15 grass, 40 pull-thrus, (25x70), 40 full hkups (30/50 amps), cable, WiFi @ sites, tent sites, rentals, dump, laundry, groc, LP gas, fire rings, firewood. **REC:** pool, pond, fishing, boating nearby, shuffleboard, playground. Pets OK. Partial handicap access. Big rig sites. 2021 rates: $40 to $42.

(386)752-9131 Lat: 30.25697, Lon: -82.63701
4743 N US 441, Lake City, FL 32055
www.lakecitycampground.com
See ad this page

LAKE CITY RV RESORT

good sam park **Ratings: 8/9★/8.5** (RV Park) Avail: 60 full hkups (30/50 amps). 2021 rates: $50. (386)752-0830, 3864 N US Hwy 441, Lake City, FL 32055

Travel Services

CAMPING WORLD OF LAKE CITY As the nation's largest retailer of RV supplies, accessories, services and new and used RVs, Camping World is committed to making your total RV experience better. **SERVICES:** RV, tire, RV appliance, MH mechanical, staffed RV wash, restrooms. RV Sales. RV supplies, LP gas, emergency parking, RV accessible. Hours: 9am to 7pm.
(888)347-0448 Lat: 30.175074, Lon: -82.686803
530 SW Florida Gateway Dr., Lake City, FL 32024
www.campingworld.com

LAKE OKEECHOBEE — D4 *Okeechobee*

LAKE OKEECHOBEE See also Clewiston, LaBelle, Moore Haven, Okeechobee, Pahokee & Palmdale.

LAKE PANASOFFKEE — H2 *Sumter*

COUNTRYSIDE RV PARK **Ratings: 7.5/8.5★/8.5** (RV Park) 29 Avail: 26 full hkups, 3 W, 3 E (30/50 amps). 2021 rates: $35 to $39. (352)793-8103, 741 CR-489, Lake Panasoffkee, FL 33538

LAKE PAN RV VILLAGE

good sam park **Ratings: 9/9★/9** (Campground) From Jct of I-75 (exit 321) & SR-470: Go W 0.25 mi on SR-470 (R).

A CHARMING NEW WATERFRONT JEWEL
Located right on Lake Pan with a boat ramp and dock. All this and a beautiful pool set in the majestic ancient oaks. All of this with EZ access to I-75 rounds out this centrally located park.

FAC: paved/gravel rds. (130 spaces). Avail: 100 gravel, patios, 45 pull-thrus, (30x60), back-ins (35x60), 100 full hkups (30/50 amps), cable, WiFi @ sites, rentals, laundry, LP gas, firewood. **REC:** heated pool, Lake Panasoffkee: fishing, kayaking/canoeing, boating nearby, shuffleboard. Pets OK. No tents, Age restrict may apply. Big rig sites. 2021 rates: $40 to $68.

(352)793-2051 Lat: 28.75587, Lon: -82.10742
190 NW 4th Dr, Lake Panasoffkee, FL 33538
www.lakepanrvvillage.com
See ad opposite page

RV Tech Tips - Precision Fifth-Wheel Hitching: If, like many fellow fifth-wheel owners, you often have trouble gauging how high to position the front of your trailer for a smooth hitch-up process, try this RV Tech Tip. After unhitching pull the tow vehicle forward a couple of feet and measure the distance between the truck bed and the pin plate with a tape measure. When preparing to hitch up, set the tape to the same height, stand it on the truck bed and raise or lower the front of the trailer until the pin plate is even with the end of the tape. The distance remains the same each time, so there's no guesswork.

LAKE PAN
RV VILLAGE
good sam park
Rated 9/9★/9
Catch Your Dreams
Come Enjoy One Of Our Many Ways To Relax
Just 20 Minutes to "The Villages"
Centrally Located & EZ On/EZ Off I-75

• Long 50 Amp Pull-Thrus • Boat Ramp • Fishing Dock • Heated Pool • Airboat Rides Nearby • RV Rentals • Cable TV Included • Free Wifi • 20 minutes to Brownwood in The Villages • 1 Hour to Disney • Located at Heart of Central Florida I-75/ Turnpike

190 NW 4th Dr • Lake Panasoffkee Florida 33538

352-793-2051 • office@lakepanrvvillage.com

www.lakepanrvvillage.com

See listing Lake Panasoffkee, FL

FL

LAKE PLACID — D4 *Highlands*

CAMP FLORIDA RV RESORT **Ratings: 8.5/8.5/9** (RV Resort) Avail: 24 full hkups (30/50 amps). 2021 rates: $45 to $55. (863)699-1991, 100 Shoreline Dr, Lake Placid, FL 33852

LAKE PLACID CAMPGROUND **Ratings: 7/8/8.5** (RV Park) Avail: 37 full hkups (30/50 amps). 2021 rates: $45. (863)465-2934, 1801 US 27 South, Lake Placid, FL 33852

SUNSHINE RV RESORT

good sam park **Ratings: 8.5/9★/8** (RV Park) From Jct of US-27 & SR-70: Go E 0.25 mi on SR-70 (R). **FAC:** paved rds. (328 spaces). Avail: 110 gravel, patios, 20 pull-thrus, (30x52), back-ins (30x52), 110 full hkups (30/50 amps), seasonal sites, cable, WiFi @ sites, laundry. **REC:** heated pool, Ridge Lake: fishing, boating nearby, shuffleboard, playground. Pet restrict (S/B/Q). Partial handicap access. No tents. 2021 rates: $37 to $49.
(863)465-4815 Lat: 27.20721, Lon: -81.32362
303 SR-70E, Lake Placid, FL 33852
www.sunshinervresort.com
See ad this page

LAKE WALES — K3 *Polk*

CAMP CENTRAL RV PARK **Ratings: 8/8.5★/8** (RV Park) Avail: 52 full hkups (30/50 amps). 2021 rates: $45. (863)638-1015, 15860 Hwy 27, Lake Wales, FL 33859

CAMP MACK, A GUY HARVEY LODGE, MARINA & RV RESORT **Ratings: 8/8/7** (Condo Park) Avail: 250 full hkups (50 amps). 2021 rates: $45 to $55. (863)696-1108, 14900 Camp Mack Rd, Lake Wales, FL 33898

LAKE KISSIMMEE (Public State Park) From Jct of US-27 & SR 60, E 9.5 mi on SR-60 to Boy Scout Rd, N 3.5 mi to Camp Mack Rd, E 5.1 mi (R); or From Jct of Florida's Tnpk and SR-60, NW 40 mi to Boy Scout Rd, N 3.5 mi to Camp Mack Rd, E 5.1 mi (R). 53 Avail: 53 W, 53 E (20/30 amps). 2021 rates: $20. (863)696-1112

LAKE WALES RV & CAMPSITES **Ratings: 9/8.5★/8** (RV Park) Avail: 45 full hkups (30/50 amps). 2021 rates: $40. (863)638-9011, 15898 Hwy 27, Lake Wales, FL 33859

PARAKEET MOBILE HOME & RV PARK (RV Park) (Not Visited) Avail: 27 full hkups (30/50 amps). 2021 rates: $35. (863)676-2812, 2400 Parakeet Park Blvd, Lake Wales, FL 33859

RESORT AT CANOPY OAKS

good sam park **Ratings: 10/10★/10** (RV Resort) From jct Hwy 60 & Hwy 630: Go 1 mi S on Hwy 630 (L). **FAC:** paved rds. Avail: 400 paved, back-ins (45x90), accepts full hkup units only, 400 full hkups (30/50 amps), WiFi @ sites, rentals, laundry, groc, LP gas, fire rings, firewood, restaurant, controlled access. **REC:** heated pool, pond, fishing, kayaking/canoeing, boating nearby, golf, shuffleboard, playground, hunting nearby. Pet restrict (Q) $. Partial handicap access. No tents. Big rig sites, eco-friendly. 2021 rates: $69 to $150, Military discount. ATM.
(407)630-7000 Lat: 27.753545, Lon: -81.564873
16950 County Rd 630, Lake Wales, FL 33898
www.sunlight-resorts.com
See ad opposite page

Traveling with Fido? Many campground listings indicate pet-friendly amenities and pet restrictions.

See listing Lake Wales, FL

FL

Know the name? Then you can use our special ""Find-it-Fast'' index to locate your campground on the map. The index arranges private and public campgrounds alphabetically, by state. Next to the name, you'll quickly find the name of the town the park is in, plus the Listing's page number.

LAKE WORTH — E5 *Palm Beach*

JOHN PRINCE PARK CAMPGROUND (Public) From Jct of I-95 & exit 63 (6th Ave S Lake Worth), W 1.5 mi on 6th Ave S to Congress Ave, S 0.2 mi (L); or From Jct of FL Tpke & Lake Worth Rd exit, E 5 mi on Lake Worth Rd to Congress Ave, S 0.5 mi (L). 300 Avail: 198 full hkups, 102 W, 102 E (30/50 amps). 2021 rates: $24 to $32. (561)582-7992

LAKELAND — K3 *Polk*

LAKELAND See also Auburndale, Bartow, Clermont, Dade City, Davenport, Dover, Dundee, Haines City, Lake Wales, Polk City, Riverview, Seffner, Thonotosassa, Wesley Chapel, Winter Haven & Zephyrhills.

LAKELAND RV RESORT **Ratings: 8.5/10★/8** (RV Park) Avail: 14 full hkups (30/50 amps). 2021 rates: $50 to $83. (863)687-6146, 900 Old Combee Rd, Lakeland, FL 33805

LELYNN RV RESORT

good sam park **Ratings: 9/8.5★/9** (RV Park) From jct of I-4 & State Road-559 (exit 44): Go N 3 mi on State Road-559 (L). **FAC:** paved rds. (370 spaces). Avail: 220 paved, patios, 10 pull-thrus, (33x66), back-ins (34x74), 220 full hkups (30/50 amps), seasonal sites, WiFi @ sites, $, dump, laundry, LP gas. **REC:** pool, Little Lake Agnes: fishing, kayaking/canoeing, boating nearby, shuffleboard. Pet restrict (S/B/Q). Partial handicap access. No tents. Big rig sites. 2021 rates: $50.60, Military discount. no cc.
(800)736-0409 Lat: 28.16321, Lon: -81,80183
1513 State Road-559, Polk City, FL 33868
See primary listing at Polk City and ad this page

SANLAN RV & GOLF RESORT

good sam park **Ratings: 8.5/8.5★/9** (RV Park) From Jct Hwy 570 (exit 10) & US 98: Go S 0.5 mi on US-98 (R).

SCENIC & NATURAL RV RESORT
Convenient to Central Florida's top attractions & Gulf Coast beaches. Close to Disney World, Universal Studios and Detroit Tigers' winter home. Enjoy 8 miles of shaded trails on Banana Lake and 3 distinct 9-hole golf courses.

FAC: paved/dirt rds. (531 spaces). 162 Avail: 103 paved, 59 grass, patios, 52 pull-thrus, (40x60), back-ins (40x60), 162 full hkups (30/50 amps), seasonal sites, cable, WiFi @ sites, dump, laundry, LP gas, controlled access. **REC:** heated pool, wading pool, pond, fishing, boating nearby, golf, shuffleboard, playground. Pet restrict (Q) $. Partial handicap access. No tents. Big rig sites, eco-friendly. 2021 rates: $33 to $75, Military discount.
(863)665-1726 Lat: 27.99387, Lon: -81.90461
3929 US Hwy 98 South, Lakeland, FL 33812
www.sanlan.com
See ad this page

VALENCIA ESTATES **Ratings: 7/8.5★/7.5** (RV Area in MH Park) Avail: 39 full hkups (30/50 amps). 2021 rates: $40. (863)665-1611, 3325 Highway 98 S, Lakeland, FL 33803

WOODALL'S MOBILE HOME VILLAGE & RV PARK **Ratings: 8/NA/8** (RV Area in MH Park) Avail: 50 full hkups (30/50 amps). 2021 rates: $60. (863)686-7462, 2121 New Tampa Hwy, Lakeland, FL 33815

LANTANA — E5 *Palm Beach*

PALM BEACH TRAVELER RV PARK **Ratings: 8.5/8/8** (RV Park) Avail: 96 full hkups (30/50 amps). 2021 rates: $50 to $90. (561)967-3139, 6159 Lawrence Rd, Lake Worth, FL 33462

LARGO — K1 *Pinellas*

INDIAN ROCKS TRAVEL PARK

Ratings: 8/8/8 (RV Park) From Jct of US-19Alt & SR-688 (Ulmerton Rd): Go W 2.9 mi on SR-688, then N 0.2 mi on Vonn Rd (R). **FAC:** paved rds. (175 spaces). Avail: 45 grass, patios, back-ins (30x50), 45 full hkups (30/50 amps), WiFi @ sites, dump, laundry, LP gas. **REC:** heated pool, boating nearby, shuffleboard. No tents. 2021 rates: $42 to $53.
(727)595-2228 Lat: 27.88301, Lon: -82.81884
12121 Vonn Rd, Largo, FL 33774
www.indianrockstravelpark.com
See ad this page

Shop at Camping World and SAVE with coupons. Check the front of the Guide for yours!

RAINBOW VILLAGE OF LARGO RV RESORT **Ratings: 9/9/9** (RV Park) Avail: 108 full hkups (30/50 amps). 2021 rates: $45 to $68. (727)536-3545, 11911 66th St N, Largo, FL 33773

SCOTTISH TRAVELER RV PARK **Ratings: 8/8.5★/8** (RV Park) Avail: 60 full hkups (30/50 amps). 2021 rates: $47. (727)536-2050, 1610 Belcher Rd S, Largo, FL 33771

VACATION VILLAGE RV RESORT
good sam park **Ratings: 8.5/9★/7.5** (RV Resort) Avail: 143 full hkups (30/50 amps). 2021 rates: $51 to $64. (888)563-7040, 6900 Ulmerton Rd, Largo, FL 33771

YANKEE TRAVELER RV PARK
good sam park **Ratings: 9.5/10★/8.5** (RV Park) From Jct US-19 & Hwy 688 (Ulmerton Rd): Go W 2 mi on Ulmerton Rd (L).

BEST RV PARK IN CENTRAL FLORIDA
Centrally located between Clearwater-St Petersburg-Tampa and minutes to the beaches! Beautiful landscaping-heated pool-free WiFi-new private bathrooms & extensive activities. Perfect anytime of the year. Come Stay & Play!

FAC: paved rds. (218 spaces). 35 Avail: 26 gravel, 9 grass, patios, back-ins (25x60), accepts full hkup units only, 35 full hkups (30/50 amps), seasonal sites, WiFi @ sites, laundry, LP gas. **REC:** heated pool, hot tub, pond, boating nearby, shuffleboard. Pet restrict (S/Q). Partial handicap access. No tents, Age restrict may apply. Big rig sites, eco-friendly. 2021 rates: $52 to $70, Military discount.
(727)531-7998 Lat: 27.89361, Lon: -82.75691
8500 Ulmerton Rd, Largo, FL 33771
yankeetraveler.net
See ad this page

We shine ""Spotlights'' on interesting cities and areas.

Camping World RV & Outdoors offers new and used RV sales and so much more! Find a SuperCenter near you at CampingWorld.com

LEESBURG — H3 *Lake*

HAINES CREEK RV PARK
good sam park **Ratings: 8/9★/8.5** (RV Park) From jct CR 473 & CR 44 E: Go 500 feet E on CR 44 E (L). **FAC:** paved rds. Avail: 86 grass, back-ins (30x50), accepts full hkup units only, 86 full hkups (30/50 amps), WiFi @ sites, dump, laundry. **REC:** Haines Creek Canal: fishing, kayaking/canoeing, boating nearby. Pets OK. No tents. 2021 rates: $40 to $55, Military discount. no cc.
(352)728-5939 Lat: 28.872, Lon: -81.7899
10121 CR 44 , Leesburg, FL 34788
hainescreekrvvillage.com
See ad page 276

Stay at any of the Good Sam RV Parks & Campgrounds in the U.S. and Canada and save 10% on the regular nightly RV site rate! No Blackout dates! Good Sam RV Parks are inspected and rated annually-look for the exclusive Triple Rating System.

FL

SPOTLIGHT ON
TOP RV & CAMPING DESTINATIONS

We've put the Spotlight on popular RV & camping travel destinations. Turn to the Spotlight articles in our State and Province sections to learn more.

Welcome!
Come, stay and enjoy at Florida's
favorite Lake Front Resort
3950 N Eichelberger Road
Tavares, FL 32778

Fisherman's Cove
MARINA · RV SITES · LODGE
on beautiful Lake Harris
Call or Book Online Today!
352-343-1233
www.fishermanscoverv.us
good sam park
2022
Top Rated

LEESBURG (CONT)

HOLIDAY RV VILLAGE
Ratings: 9.5/10★/9.5 (RV Park) From Jct of I-75 & SR-44 (Exit 329 Wildwood), E 12 mi on SR-44 to US-27, S 2.8 mi to SR-33, W 0.5 mi (R) or From Jct of FL Tnpk & SR-470 (Exit 296), E 3 mi on SR-470 to SR-33, N 1 mi (L). **FAC:** paved rds. (935 spaces). Avail: 200 gravel, 200 pull-thrus, (35x65), 200 full hkups (30/50 amps), seasonal sites, cable, WiFi @ sites, dump, laundry, LP gas, controlled access. **REC:** heated pool, hot tub, Big Lake Harris: fishing, marina, boating nearby, shuffleboard, playground. Pets OK. Partial handicap access. No tents. Big rig sites. 2021 rates: $64, Military discount.
(866)737-0441 Lat: 28.75658, Lon: -81.88581
28229 CR-33, Leesburg, FL 34748
www.CoveCommunities.com
See ad this page

RIDGECREST RV RESORT **Ratings: 8.5/8★/8** (RV Area in MH Park) Avail: 79 full hkups (30/50 amps). 2021 rates: $40 to $55. (352)787-1504, 26125 US Hwy 27, Leesburg, FL 34748

LITHIA — K2 *Hillsborough*

ALAFIA RIVER (Public State Park) From town, S 0.9 mi on Bryant Rd to Lithia Pinecrest Rd, E 1.5 mi to CR-39, S 5.1 mi on CR-39 (L). 27 Avail: 16 W, 16 E (30/50 amps). 2021 rates: $22. (813)672-5320

LIVE OAK — A2 *Suwannee*

SUWANNEE RIVER (Public State Park) From town, W 13 mi on US-90 to access rd (R). Avail: 24 full hkups (50 amps). 2021 rates: $22. (386)362-2746

LONG KEY — F4 *Monroe*

LONG KEY (Public State Park) S-bnd: On US-1 at MP-67.5 (L) Entrance is on ocean side, look for lrg brown sign & stop at ranger station for directions. 42 Avail: 42 W, 42 E (20/30 amps). 2021 rates: $36. (305)664-4815

We appreciate your business!

LUTZ — K2 *Hillsborough*

WINTER QUARTERS PASCO RV RESORT
Ratings: 7.5/7.5/8.5 (RV Area in MH Park) Avail: 30 full hkups (30/50 amps). 2021 rates: $50 to $78. (888)563-7040, 21632 State Road 54, Lutz, FL 33549

MADISON — A2 *Madison*

MADISON RV & GOLF RESORT
Ratings: 9/9.5★/10 (RV Resort) Avail: 95 full hkups (30/50 amps). 2021 rates: $50 to $70. (850)688-0363, 445 SW Country Club Rd, Madison, FL 32340

RAGANS FAMILY CAMPGROUND
Ratings: 9/9★/9 (Campground) From Jct of I-10 (exit 258) & SR-53, S 0.2 mi on SR-53 to St. Augustine Rd, W 0.5 mi (L). **FAC:** gravel rds. Avail: 175 gravel, 77 pull-thrus, (35x60), back-ins (30x50), 142 full hkups, 33 W, 33 E (30/50 amps), WiFi @ sites, tent sites, rentals, dump, mobile sewer, laundry, groc, LP gas, fire rings, firewood, controlled access. **REC:** pool, Ragans Lake: fishing, playground, rec open to public. Pets OK. Partial handicap access. Big rig sites, eco-friendly. 2021 rates: $59 to $98, Military discount.
(850)973-8269 Lat: 30.39611, Lon: -83.36816
1051 SW Old St Augustine Rd, Madison, FL 32340
ragansfamilycampground.com
See ad opposite page

MALABAR — K5 *Brevard*

ENCHANTED LAKES RV RESORT **Ratings: 7.5/8/8** (RV Park) Avail: 40 full hkups (30/50 amps). 2021 rates: $52.50. (321)723-8847, 750 Malabar Rd, Malabar, FL 32950

MARATHON — F4 *Monroe*

COCONUT CAY RV PARK & MARINA **Ratings: 8/9★/9.5** (RV Park) Avail: 25 full hkups (30/50 amps). 2021 rates: $99 to $375. (305)289-1870, 7200 Aviation Blvd, Marathon, FL 33050

GRASSY KEY RV PARK AND RESORT
Ratings: 10/NA/10 (RV Park) S-bnd: On US-1 at MP 58.7, Gulfside (R). **FAC:** all weather rds. Avail: 38 all weather, 8 pull-thrus, (30x62), back-ins (30x50), accepts full hkup units only, 38 full hkups (30/50 amps), cable, WiFi @ sites, laundry. **REC:** heated pool, Gulf of Mexico: fishing, kayaking/canoeing, boating nearby. Pet restrict (S/B/Q). No tents. Big rig sites. 2021 rates: $71 to $210, Military discount.
(305)289-1606 Lat: 24.76501, Lon: -80.94814
58671 Overseas Hwy (US-1), Marathon, FL 33050
www.grassykeyrvpark.com
See ad page 278

Get ready for your next camping trip at CampingWorld.com

JOLLY ROGER RV RESORT
Ratings: 8/10★/8 (RV Park) S-bnd: On US-1 at MP-59.5 (R).

JOLLY ROGER IN HEART OF FL KEYS
Spacious shady, grassy sites on 11 acres-rare find in the Florida Keys! NEW premier RV sites and heated/chilled pool. Enjoy our high-speed internet, cable TV, Gulf fishing, or snorkel and fish off the dock and seawall.

FAC: paved rds. Avail: 162 grass, patios, 34 pull-thrus, (25x60), back-ins (24x44), 162 full hkups (30/50 amps), cable, WiFi @ sites, tent sites, rentals, laundry. **REC:** heated pool, Gulf of Mexico: swim, fishing, kayaking/canoeing, boating nearby. Pet restrict (Q). Partial handicap access. Big rig sites, eco-friendly. 2021 rates: $77 to $115, Military discount.
(305)289-0404 Lat: 24.76965, Lon: -80.94196
59275 Overseas Hwy, Marathon, FL 33050
www.jrtp.com
See ad page 278

PELICAN RV RESORT & MARINA **Ratings: 7.5/9.5★/8** (RV Park) Avail: 73 full hkups (30/50 amps). 2021 rates: $75 to $155. (305)289-0011, 59151 Overseas Hwy, Marathon, FL 33050

RV Tech Tips - Water Hookups: When hooking up at the campground water faucet, a 25-foot hose is often a bit excessive. Whether it's sunny or not, the coiled-up 25-footer generally acts as a heat sink, making the water too warm before it enters the trailer. To solve this, cut a 25-foot hose into three pieces (two 10 feet and one 5 feet in length). Use two sets of 3/8-inch repair connectors to make three complete hoses. Now, you have five hose lengths to choose from: 5 feet, 10 feet, 15 feet (one 5-footer and one 10-footer), 20 feet (two 10-footers) and 25 feet (using all three). Most of the time the 5- or 10-footers will do. It keeps things clean, and you don't have to drain all the excess water from a longer hose length.

MADISON, FLORIDA
good sam park
WATER FEATURES NOW OPEN
Ragans Family Campground
Cabins • RV Sites • Waterpark
"Family camping at its best"
Come Enjoy Our New Lazy River
Located on I-10 at Exit 258
Near the Center of the State.
Great Destination
Yet on the Way Everywhere!
• 30 & 50 Amp Sites • Long Pull-Thrus
• Large, Spacious Sites • Big Rigs Welcome
• Group Camping • We Cater to Snowbirds!
• Lakeside RV Sites Available
• We Recommend Calling Ahead of Time (They Fill Up Fast!)
WiFi
1051 SW Old St. Augustine Rd.
I10 & Exit 258 • Madison, FL 32340
See listing Madison, FL
1-800-347-0174 • www.ragansfamilycampground.com

MARGATE — E5 *Broward*

AZTEC RV RESORT **Ratings: 10/10★/10** (Condo Park) Avail: 645 full hkups (30/50 amps). 2021 rates: $70 to $129. (888)493-2856, 1 Aztec Blvd, Lot #1, Margate, FL 33068

MARIANNA — E3 *Jackson*

ALLIANCE HILL RV RESORT
good sam park **Ratings: 10/10★/9.5** (RV Park) Avail: 14 full hkups (30/50 amps). 2021 rates: $44. (850)260-8154, 639 Plymouth Loop, Marianna, FL 32448

FLORIDA CAVERNS (Public State Park) From Jct of Hwy 90 & SR-166, N 3 mi on SR-166 (L). 28 Avail: 28 W, 28 E (50 amps). 2021 rates: $20. (850)482-1228

FLORIDA CAVERNS RV RESORT AT MERRITT'S MILL POND
good sam park **Ratings: 9/10★/9** (RV Park) Avail: 105 full hkups (30/50 amps). 2021 rates: $50 to $66. (850)482-5583, 4820 Hwy 90E, Marianna, FL 32446

STAY N GO RV
good sam park **Ratings: 7/NA/8** (RV Park) Avail: 51 full hkups (30/50 amps). 2021 rates: $44. (850)372-4198, 4951 Malloy Plaza East, Marianna, FL 32448

MARY ESTHER — F1 *Okaloosa*

MILITARY PARK HURLBURT FIELD FAMCAMP (HURLBURT AFB) (Public) From town: Go 1/4 mi N on Cristobal Rd to Hollywood Blvd E, then 2 m N on Hill Ave, then right on Down Circle (E). Avail: 40 full hkups (30/50 amps). 2021 rates: $20. (850)797-0103

MCINTOSH — B3 *Marion*

SPORTSMAN'S COVE CAMPGROUND
good sam park **Ratings: 7/8★/7.5** (Campground) From the jct of US441 & Ave F, E on Ave F 1/2 mi (E). **FAC:** gravel rds. Avail: 49 gravel, 3 pull-thrus, (24x50), back-ins (30x60), 49 full hkups (30/50 amps), WiFi @ sites, tent sites, rentals, dump, laundry, fire rings, firewood. **REC:** Orange Lake: fishing, marina, kayaking/canoeing, boating nearby. Pets OK. eco-friendly. 2021 rates: $36 to $40.
(352)591-1435 Lat: 29.449895, Lon: -82.214857
5423 Avenue F Box 107, McIntosh, FL 32664
cove.campground.world
See ad page 255

MELBOURNE — K5 *Brevard*

LAND YACHT HARBOR RV PARK **Ratings: 6/NA/9** (RV Park) Avail: 129 full hkups (30/50 amps). 2021 rates: $40. (321)254-6398, 201 N John Rodes Blvd, Melbourne, FL 32934

WICKHAM PARK (Public) From Jct of I-95 & Exit 191 (Wickham Rd), E 8.4 mi on Wickham Rd to Parkway Dr, E 0.5 mi (R). NOTE: N-bnd follow Exit 72 E to Wickham Rd. Avail: 133 full hkups (30 amps). 2021 rates: $17.80 to $21. (321)255-4307

MELBOURNE BEACH — K5 *Brevard*

MELBOURNE BEACH MOBILE PARK **Ratings: 5/7.5/7** (RV Area in MH Park) Avail: 84 full hkups (30/50 amps). 2021 rates: $54. (321)723-4947, 2670 So. A1A, Melbourne Beach, FL 32951

OUTDOOR RESORTS/MELBOURNE BEACH **Ratings: 8.5/10★/9.5** (Condo Park) Avail: 25 full hkups (30/50 amps). 2021 rates: $50 to $80. (321)724-2600, 214 Horizon Ln, Melbourne Beach, FL 32951

MIAMI — E5 *Miami-Dade*

MIAMI See also Davie, Fort Lauderdale, Hallandale & Hollywood.

LARRY & PENNY THOMPSON CAMPGROUND (Public) From Jct of FL Tpke & SW 184th St (exit 13), W 1.1 mi on 184th St (Eureka) (R). Avail: 240 full hkups (30/50 amps). 2021 rates: $33.90. (305)232-1049

MIAMI EVERGLADES RESORT
good sam park **Ratings: 8.5/9★/9** (Campground) 120 Avail: 108 full hkups, 12 W, 12 E (30/50 amps). 2021 rates: $51 to $78. (888)563-7040, 20675 SW 162 Ave, Miami, FL 33187

MICCO — K5 *Brevard*

BREEZEWAY TRAILER & RV PARK
Ratings: 4.5/NA/6.5 (RV Park) From Jct Hwy 505 & US-1: Go N 3 mi on US-1 (L). **FAC:** gravel rds. (43 spaces). Avail: 15 gravel, patios, 5 pull-thrus, (28x50), back-ins (28x50), accepts full hkup units only, 15 full hkups (30/50 amps), WiFi, laundry. **REC:** Indian River: fishing, boating nearby. Pet restrict (B). No tents, Age restrict may apply. 2021 rates: $40.
(772)664-5073 Lat: 27.866554, Lon: -80.496241
8860 US Hwy 1, Micco, FL 32976
www.breezewaytrailerpark.com
See ad this page

MIDWAY — A1 *Gadsden*

Travel Services

CAMPING WORLD OF MIDWAY/TALLAHASSEE As the nation's largest retailer of RV supplies, accessories, services and new and used RVs, Camping World is committed to making your total RV experience better. **SERVICES:** RV, tire, RV appliance, restrooms. RV Sales. RV supplies, LP gas, dump, emergency parking, RV accessible. Hours: 9am to 7pm.
(888)413-0741 Lat: 30.50063, Lon: -84.45085
31300 Blue Star Hwy, Midway, FL 32343
www.campingworld.com

MILTON — E1 *Santa Rosa*

AVALON LANDING RV PARK
good sam park **Ratings: 10/10★/9** (RV Park) From Jct of IH10 & SR 281 (Avalon Blvd Exit 22), S 0.4 mi on SR 281 (L).

SCENIC, CONVENIENT, WATERFRONT PARK
Waterfront Big Rig sites on Indian Bayou, 1/2 mi South I-10, 5 mi East of Pensacola with white sand beaches, Museum & Historic sites. Kayak/canoe off our private launch. No Lic Req'd Saltwater Bridge Fishing for Reg Guests.

FAC: paved rds. (79 spaces). Avail: 75 all weather, patios, 8 pull-thrus, (30x60), back-ins (30x60), 75 full hkups (30/50 amps), cable, WiFi @ sites, dump, laundry, LP gas. **REC:** pool, Escambia Bay: fishing, kayaking/canoeing, boating nearby. Pet restrict (B/Q). Partial handicap access. No tents. Big rig sites, eco-friendly. 2021 rates: $43 to $59.
(850)995-5898 Lat: 30.52509, Lon: -87.08662
2444 Avalon Blvd, Milton, FL 32583
avalonlandingrvpark.com
See ad page 292

GULF PINES KOA **Ratings: 9.5/9.5★/8.5** (RV Park) Avail: 75 full hkups (30/50 amps). 2021 rates: $72. (877)684-2307, 8700 Gulf Pines Dr, Milton, FL 32583

SPLASH! RV RESORT & WATERPARK
good sam park (RV Resort) (Under Construction) From jct IH 10 & SR 87: Go 1000 feet S on SR 87, then 1/2 mi W on Welcome Church Rd (E).

NEW LUXURY RV RESORT & WATER PARK
A fantastic water park located in Florida's newest luxury RV resort. All of that and just a short 20 minute drive to some of the best white sand beaches on the Gulf. Come experience the fun firsthand!

FAC: paved rds. Avail: 350 paved, 60 pull-thrus, (40x80), back-ins (40x80), accepts full hkup units only, 350 full hkups (30/50 amps), . Pets OK. No tents. Big rig sites. 2021 rates: $75 to $85.
(850)626-8500 Lat: 30.616750, Lon: -86.96776
8500 Welcome Church Rd, Milton, FL 32583
splashrvresort.com
See ad page 294

SUNBURST RV RESORT **Ratings: 9/8★/9** (RV Resort) Avail: 50 full hkups (30/50 amps). 2021 rates: $35 to $45. (850)889-3391, 2375 Horn Road, Milton, FL 32570

MONTICELLO — A2 *Jefferson*

A CAMPERS WORLD
Ratings: 7/8.5★/7.5 (Campground) From Jct of I-10 & Hwy 19 (exit 225), N 0.2 mi on Hwy 19 to campground rd, W 0.25 mi (L). **FAC:** gravel rds. Avail: 29 gravel, 23 pull-thrus, (22x60), back-ins (22x60), 29 full hkups (30/50 amps), WiFi @ sites, laundry. **REC:** pool. Pets OK. No tents. 2021 rates: $31 to $33. no cc, no reservations.
(850)997-3300 Lat: 30.47816, Lon: -83.89466
397 Campground Rd , Lamont, FL 32336
See ad page 303

TALLAHASSEE EAST CAMPGROUND
Ratings: 8/8.5★/8 (Campground) From Jct of I-10 & US-19 (exit 225), S 0.5 mi on US-19 to 158B, W 2 mi to Hwy 259, N 0.5 mi to access rd, E 0.25 mi (E). **FAC:** gravel rds. 66 Avail: 29 gravel, 19 grass, 18 dirt, 66 pull-thrus, (32x60), 58 full hkups, 8 W, 8 E (30/50 amps), WiFi, tent sites, rentals, dump, laundry, groc, LP gas. **REC:** pool, Lake Catherine: fishing, playground. Pets OK. Big rig sites. 2021 rates: $46.
(850)997-3890 Lat: 30.47766, Lon: -83.91598
346 Koa Rd, Monticello, FL 32344
tallahasseeeastcampground.com
See ad page 303

MOORE HAVEN — D4 *Glades*

ARUBA RV RESORT **Ratings: 7.5/8.5★/8.5** (RV Park) Avail: 43 full hkups (30/50 amps). 2021 rates: $35 to $55. (863)946-1324, 1073 Old Lakeport Rd, Moore Haven, FL 33471

MOORE HAVEN KOA **Ratings: 7.5/9/8.5** (RV Park) Avail: 227 full hkups (30/50 amps). 2021 rates: $32 to $80. (863)946-6616, 17192 US Hwy 27, Moore Haven, FL 33471

NORTH LAKE ESTATES RV RESORT **Ratings: 9.5/9/9.5** (RV Park) Avail: 34 full hkups (30/50 amps). 2021 rates: $49 to $58. (877)417-6193, 12044 East State Rd 78, Moore Haven, FL 33471

NAPLES — E4 *Collier*

CLUB NAPLES RV RESORT **Ratings: 9/9.5★/9** (RV Park) Avail: 30 full hkups (30/50 amps). 2021 rates: $51 to $91. (888)898-6463, 3180 Beck Blvd, Naples, FL 34114

COLLIER-SEMINOLE (Public State Park) From Jct of US-41 & SR-84, SE 15 mi on US-41 (R). Avail: 124 E (30/50 amps). 2021 rates: $22. (239)394-3397

CRYSTAL LAKE RV RESORT **Ratings: 10/10★/10** (Condo Park) Avail: 120 full hkups (30/50 amps). 2021 rates: $60 to $110. (239)348-0017, 14960 Collier Blvd, Naples, FL 34119

ENDLESS SUMMER RV PARK **Ratings: 6.5/7.5/6.5** (RV Area in MH Park) Avail: 61 full hkups (30/50 amps). 2021 rates: $55. (239)643-1511, 2 Tina Lane, Naples, FL 34104

LAKE SAN MARINO RV RESORT **Ratings: 9/10★/8.5** (RV Park) Avail: 209 full hkups (50 amps). 2021 rates: $50 to $78. (877)720-1982, 1000 Wiggins Pass Rd, Naples, FL 34110

MARCO-NAPLES RV RESORT **Ratings: 8/10★/7.5** (RV Park) Avail: 108 full hkups (30/50 amps). 2021 rates: $65 to $87. (239)774-1259, 100 Barefoot Williams Rd, Naples, FL 34113

NAPLES MOTORCOACH RESORT & BOAT CLUB - SUNLAND **Ratings: 10/10★/10** (Condo Park) Avail: 184 full hkups (50 amps). 2021 rates: $110 to $204. (888)474-8856, 13300 Tamiami Trail E, Naples, FL 34114

NAPLES RV RESORT **Ratings: 8/9.5★/8.5** (RV Park) Avail: 59 full hkups (30/50 amps). 2021 rates: $62 to $118. (877)361-5197, 8230 Collier Blvd, Naples, FL 34114

NAPLES/MARCO ISLAND KOA **Ratings: 8.5/9★/8** (Campground) 98 Avail: 75 full hkups, 23 W, 23 E (30/50 amps). 2021 rates: $67 to $121. (239)774-5455, 1700 Barefoot Williams Rd, Naples, FL 34113

NEAPOLITAN COVE RV RESORT **Ratings: 9/NA/9** (RV Park) Avail: 65 full hkups (30/50 amps). 2021 rates: $53 to $87. (239)793-0091, 3790 Tamiami TR-E, Naples, FL 34112

NORTHTIDE NAPLES RV RESORT
Ratings: 8/9★/9 (RV Park) Avail: 110 full hkups (30/50 amps). 2021 rates: $60 to $86. (239)643-3100, 3100 North Rd, Naples, FL 34104

PELICAN LAKE MOTORCOACH RESORT **Ratings: 10/10★/10** (Condo Park) Avail: 52 full hkups (50 amps). 2021 rates: $115 to $200. (239)417-1600, 4555 Southern Breeze Dr, Naples, FL 34114

SILVER LAKES RV RESORT & GOLF CLUB **Ratings: 9.5/10★/10** (Condo Park) Avail: 255 full hkups (30/50 amps). 2021 rates: $64 to $120. (239)775-2575, 1001 Silver Lakes Blvd, Naples, FL 34114

NAVARRE — F1 *Santa Rosa*

EMERALD BEACH RV PARK
Ratings: 10/10★/9 (RV Park) E-bnd: From the Jct of US 87 & US 98, E 1 mi on US 98 (R); W-bnd: From entrance to Hurlburt Field (US Army Installation) & US 98, W 9 mi on US 98 (past park entrance) to Navarre Sound Circle, U-turn if possible or S onto Navarre Sound Circle & back to Hwy 98, E 0.1 mi (R). **FAC:** paved rds. Avail: 76 paved, patios, 37 pull-thrus, (37x60), back-ins (25x60), 76 full hkups (30/50 amps), cable, WiFi @ sites, dump, laundry, LP gas. **REC:** heated pool, Santa Rosa Sound: swim, fishing, kayaking/canoeing, boating nearby. Pet restrict (B/Q). No tents. Big rig sites. 2021 rates: $54 to $90.
(850)939-3431 Lat: 30.40477, Lon: -86.85124
8885 Navarre Pkwy, Navarre, FL 32566
www.emeraldbeachrvpark.com
See ad page 251

NAVARRE BEACH CAMPING RESORT
Ratings: 9/10★/9 (Campground) Avail: 116 full hkups (30/50 amps). 2021 rates: $75 to $180. (888)668-0770, 9201 Navarre Parkway, Navarre, FL 32566

SANTA ROSA WATERFRONT RV RESORT **Ratings: 10/10★/9.5** (RV Park) Avail: 88 full hkups (30/50 amps). 2021 rates: $60 to $160. (888)936-4791, 8315 Navarre Pkwy, Navarre, FL 32566

NEW PORT RICHEY — J1 *Pasco*

ORCHID LAKE RV RESORT
Ratings: 9/10★/8.5 (RV Area in MH Park) From Jct of US 19 & SR-54: Go N 4.7 mi on US 19, then E 2.5 mi on Ridge Rd, then S 0.5 mi on Little Rd, then W 0.25 mi on Arevee Dr (E). **FAC:** paved rds. (465 spaces). Avail: 125 all weather, patios, back-ins (30x50), 125 full hkups (30/50 amps), WiFi @ sites, laundry, controlled access. **REC:** heated pool, Orchid Lake: fishing, boating nearby, shuffleboard. Partial handicap access. No tents, Age restrict may apply, eco-friendly. 2021 rates: $57, Military discount.
(727)847-1925 Lat: 28.27408, Lon: -82.67898
8225 Arevee Drive, New Port Richey, FL 34653
orchidlakervresort.com
See ad this page

SEVEN SPRINGS TRAVEL PARK
Ratings: 8.5/8/8.5 (RV Park) From Jct of US-19 & SR-54: Go E 3.3 mi on SR-54, then NE 0.2 mi on Old County Rd 54 (L). **FAC:** paved rds. (220 spaces). Avail: 70 gravel, patios, back-ins (30x65), 70 full hkups (30/50 amps), seasonal sites, WiFi @ sites, $, dump, laundry, LP gas, controlled access. **REC:** heated pool, pond, fishing, boating nearby, shuffleboard. Partial handicap access. No tents, Age restrict may apply. Big rig sites, eco-friendly. 2021 rates: $45.
(727)376-0000 Lat: 28.21758, Lon: -82.68102
8039 Old County Road 54, New Port Richey, FL 34653
sevenspringsrvpark.com
See ad this page

NEW SMYRNA BEACH — G5 *Volusia*

NEW SMYRNA BEACH RV PARK & CAMPGROUND **Ratings: 9/9.5★/9** (RV Park) Avail: 161 full hkups (30/50 amps). 2021 rates: $50 to $57. (386)427-3581, 1300 Old Mission Rd, New Smyrna Beach, FL 32168

Had a great stay? Let us know by emailing us Parks@goodsam.com

SUGAR MILL RUINS TRAVEL PARK
Ratings: 8/8/8.5 (RV Park) Avail: 25 full hkups (30/50 amps). 2021 rates: $36.95 to $45.95. (386)427-2284, 1050 Old Mission Rd, New Smyrna Beach, FL 32168

NICEVILLE — F2 *Okaloosa*

FRED GANNON ROCKY BAYOU (Public State Park) From Jct of I-10 & SR-85, S 14 mi on SR-85 to SR-20 (in Niceville), E 3 mi (L). 38 Avail: 38 W, 38 E (30/50 amps). 2021 rates: $16. (850)833-9144

MILITARY PARK MID BAY SHORES MAXWELL/GUNTER RECREATION AREA (MAXWELL AFB) (Public) From town: Go 5 mi E on FL-20, then 2 mi S on White Point Rd (L). Avail: 26 full hkups (30/50 amps). 2021 rates: $22 to $27. (334)953-3509

NOKOMIS — D3 *Sarasota*

ROYAL COACHMAN RV RESORT
Ratings: 9/9★/9 (RV Resort) Avail: 160 full hkups (30/50 amps). 2021 rates: $62 to $125. (888)563-7040, 1070 Laurel Rd E, Nokomis, FL 34275

OAKLAND PARK — E5 *Broward*

EASTERLIN PARK (Public) From Jct of I-95 & Commercial Blvd, W 0.5 mi on Commercial Blvd to Powerline Rd, S 1.5 mi to NW 38th St, W 1 blk across railroad tracks (L). 55 Avail: 45 full hkups, 6 W, 6 E (30/50 amps). 2021 rates: $35 to $45. (954)357-5190

OCALA — G2 *Marion*

CHAMPIONS RUN LUXURY RV RESORT (RV Resort) (Under Construction) Avail: 482 full hkups (30/50 amps). 2021 rates: $69 to $99. (407)630-7000, 3019 NW 44th Ave, Ocala, FL 34482

CLIFTWOOD MHC & RV PARK **Ratings: 7.5/NA/8** (RV Area in MH Park) Avail: 29 full hkups (30/50 amps). 2021 rates: $40. (352)368-3887, 7101 W Anthony Rd, Ocala, FL 34479

OCALA RV CAMP RESORT
Ratings: 6.5/7.5/6.5 (Campground) From Jct of I-75 & SR-200 (Exit 350), W 300 ft on SR-200 to SW 38th Ave (beside Cracker Barrel), N 0.1 mi to stop, E 0.5 mi on 38th Ave (L). **FAC:** paved/dirt rds. (191 spaces). Avail: 131 dirt, 115 pull-thrus, (25x50), back-ins (25x50), 131 full hkups (30/50 amps), seasonal sites, cable, WiFi, rentals, dump, laundry, LP gas. **REC:** pool, wading pool, pond, boating nearby, shuffleboard. Pets OK. Partial handicap access. No tents. Big rig sites. 2021 rates: $40 to $47.
(866)858-3400 Lat: 29.15648, Lon: -82.18621
3200 SW 38th Ave, Ocala, FL 34474
rvcampocala.com
See ad page 288

OCALA SUN RV RESORT **Ratings: 9/10★/9.5** (RV Resort) Avail: 387 full hkups (50 amps). 2021 rates: $47 to $52. (352)307-1100, 2559 SW Hwy 484, Ocala, FL 34473

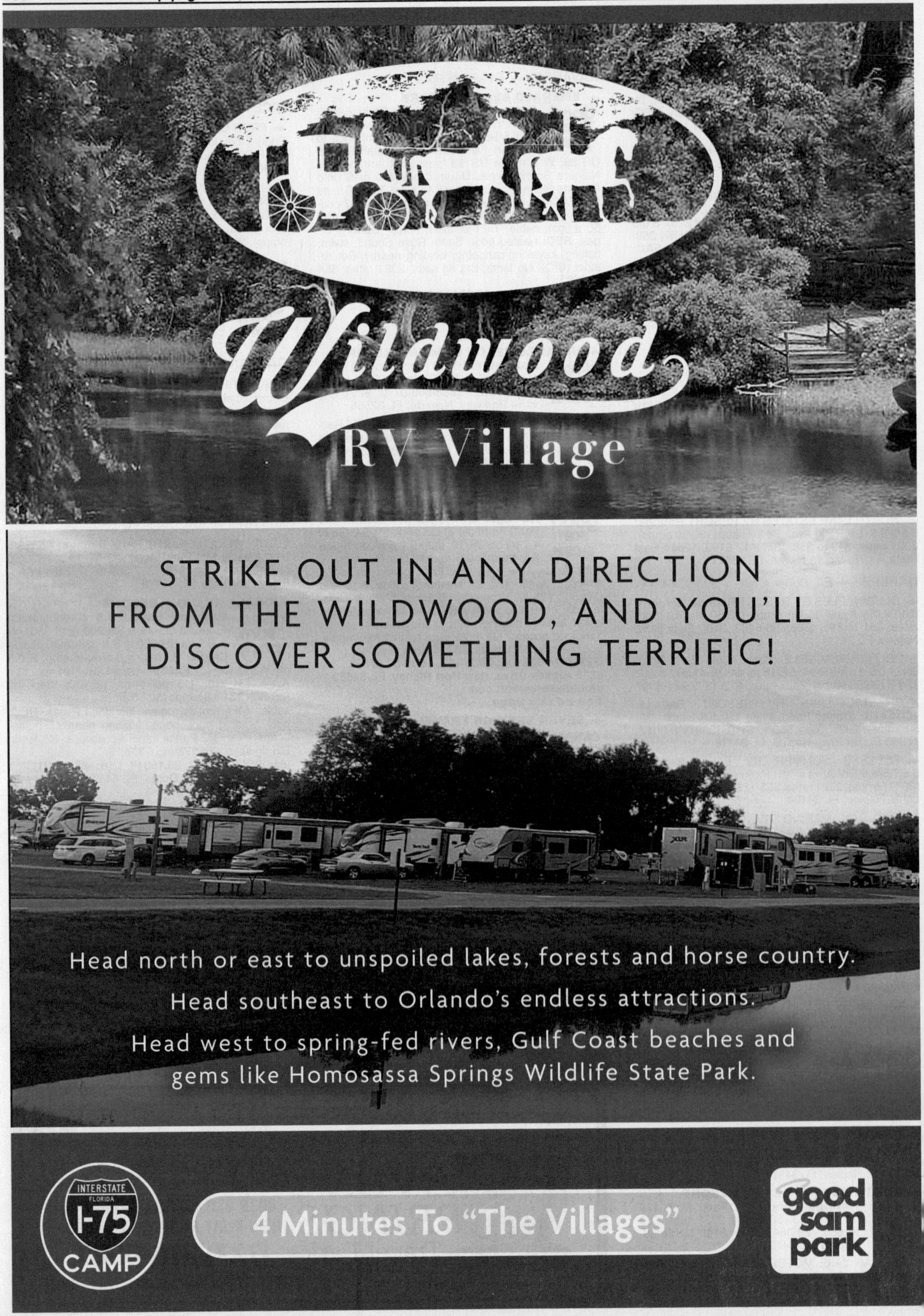
Wildwood
RV Village
STRIKE OUT IN ANY DIRECTION
FROM THE WILDWOOD, AND YOU'LL
DISCOVER SOMETHING TERRIFIC!
Head north or east to unspoiled lakes, forests and horse country.
Head southeast to Orlando's endless attractions.
Head west to spring-fed rivers, Gulf Coast beaches and
gems like Homosassa Springs Wildlife State Park.
INTERSTATE
FLORIDA
I-75
CAMP
4 Minutes To "The Villages"
good sam park

- Easy In & Out • Pet Friendly
- 50 Amp Service • Free Cable TV • WiFi
- Pull-Thru Lots – Big Rig Friendly
- Heated Pool
- Club House, Rec Hall
- Clean Bathrooms, Showers & Laundry
- Brownwood Farmers Market

NEARBY :

- RV Service Center • RV Wash
- Groceries • Restaurants • Shopping
- Canoe & Kayak • Year Round Golf
- Horseback Riding • Bike Trails
- Flea Markets • Amusement Parks

Wildwood RV Village

882 East State Road 44 • Exit 329 • Wildwood, FL 34785
352-748-2774 email: office@wildwoodrvvillage.com
www.wildwoodrvvillage.com

See listing Wildwood, FL

Coming Soon...
Ocala Area's Newest First Class Waterfront RV Resort
• Great Snowbird Location
• 500+ Paved RV Sites
• All First Class Amenities
• Fishing, Swimming, Dog Park...
Follow our progress at www.orangelakervresort.com

Orange Lake
RV RESORT
good sam park
See listing Citra, FL
For Reservations Call 352-878-4855

FL

OCALA NORTH
RV Resort
This is the best kept secret as far as RV resorts go.
Very clean, a friendly staff and Pull-Thrus everywhere!
Ocala North RV Resort
16905 N.W. Hwy 225, Reddick, FL 32686
info@ocalanorthrv.com
352-591-1723 We are available by phone 24 hours everyday
www.ocalanorthrvresort.com
Office Hours: Mon-Fri 9:00am to 5:00pm Sat-Sun 9:00am to 5:00pm

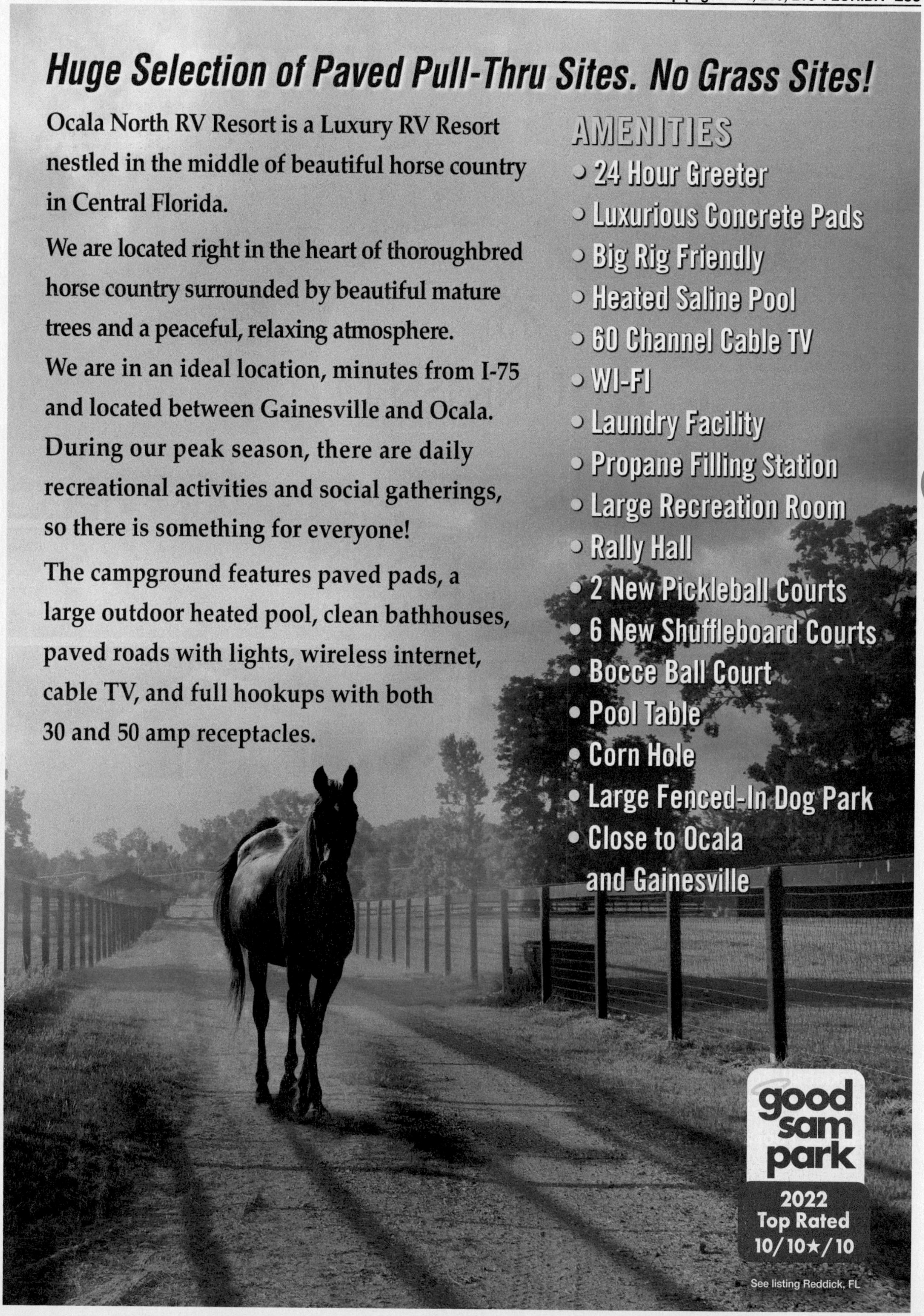
Huge Selection of Paved Pull-Thru Sites. No Grass Sites!
Ocala North RV Resort is a Luxury RV Resort nestled in the middle of beautiful horse country in Central Florida.
We are located right in the heart of thoroughbred horse country surrounded by beautiful mature trees and a peaceful, relaxing atmosphere.
We are in an ideal location, minutes from I-75 and located between Gainesville and Ocala.
During our peak season, there are daily recreational activities and social gatherings, so there is something for everyone!
The campground features paved pads, a large outdoor heated pool, clean bathhouses, paved roads with lights, wireless internet, cable TV, and full hookups with both 30 and 50 amp receptacles.
AMENITIES
• 24 Hour Greeter
• Luxurious Concrete Pads
• Big Rig Friendly
• Heated Saline Pool
• 60 Channel Cable TV
• WI-FI
• Laundry Facility
• Propane Filling Station
• Large Recreation Room
• Rally Hall
• 2 New Pickleball Courts
• 6 New Shuffleboard Courts
• Bocce Ball Court
• Pool Table
• Corn Hole
• Large Fenced-In Dog Park
• Close to Ocala and Gainesville
good sam park
2022 Top Rated 10/10★/10
See listing Reddick, FL

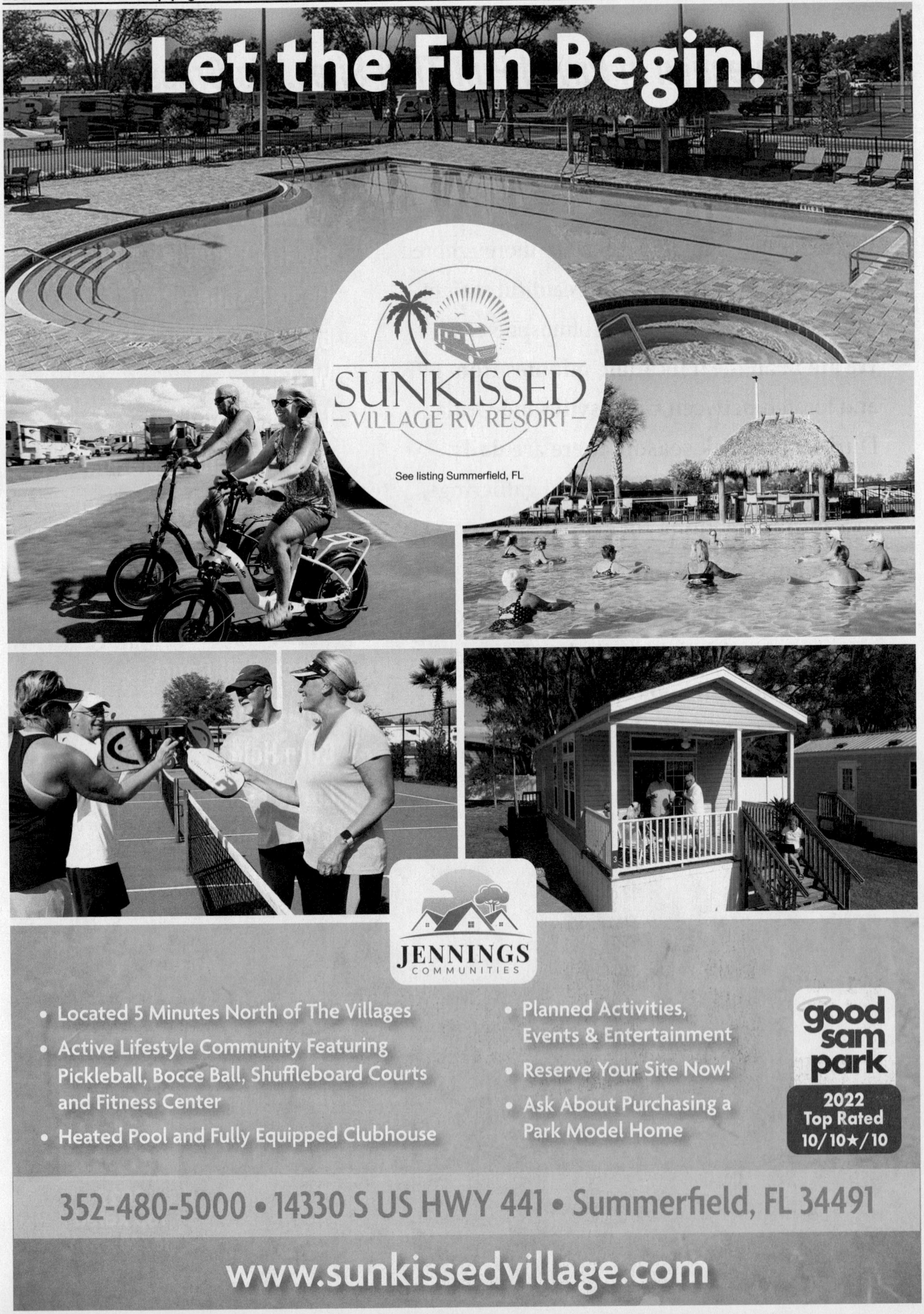
Let the Fun Begin!
SUNKISSED
–VILLAGE RV RESORT–
See listing Summerfield, FL
JENNINGS
COMMUNITIES
• Located 5 Minutes North of The Villages
• Active Lifestyle Community Featuring Pickleball, Bocce Ball, Shuffleboard Courts and Fitness Center
• Heated Pool and Fully Equipped Clubhouse
• Planned Activities, Events & Entertainment
• Reserve Your Site Now!
• Ask About Purchasing a Park Model Home
good sam park
2022 Top Rated 10/10★/10
352-480-5000 • 14330 S US HWY 441 • Summerfield, FL 34491
www.sunkissedvillage.com

WILD FRONTIER RV RESORT

NICE, CLEAN RV PARK. EXPANDED, UPGRADED, REMODELED.

Come See all of the Fantastic Improvements, A Hidden Jewel

- Free WiFi • Digital Cable Television
- 4,200 sq. ft. Rec Center/Clubhouse
- Music and Events
- Full Kitchen and Dining Facility
- Lounge Area, Pool Table, Dart Board, Dining Tables
- Outdoor Pool
- On-Site Laundry Facility
- Clean, Spacious Bathrooms
- Handicap Parking and Accessibility
- Dog Park
- Paved Roads

good sam park

2022 Top Rated 10/9.5★/9.5

See listing Ocala, FL

3101 NW 16th Ave, Ocala FL • (352) 629-3540

www.wildfrontierrvresort.com

29.21799 • -82.14891

OCALA (CONT)

WANDERING OAKS RV RESORT
good sam park **Ratings: 8.5/8.5★/8.5** (RV Park) From Jct of I-75 & SR-326 (Exit 358), E 2.2 mi on SR-326 (R). **FAC:** paved rds. Avail: 85 grass, 40 pull-thrus, (45x100), back-ins (45x100), 85 full hkups (30/50 amps), cable, WiFi @ sites, dump, laundry, LP gas, firewood. **REC:** boating nearby. Pet restrict (S/B). No tents, Age restrict may apply. Big rig sites, eco-friendly. 2021 rates: $40.
(866)380-6700 Lat: 29.25764, Lon: -82.15498
1860 W Hwy 326, Ocala, FL 34475
See ad this page

WILD FRONTIER RV RESORT
good sam park **Ratings: 10/9.5★/9.5** (RV Resort) Sbnd: From jct US 441 & NW 35th St: Go 1/3 mi W on NW 35th St, then 1/4 mi S on 16th Ave (L) Nbnd: From jct I75 & US 27(exit 354): Go 1/3 mi E on US 27, then 3 mi N on NW 35th Ave, then 1-1/2 E on 35th St, then 1/3 mi SE on 16th Ave (L). **FAC:** paved rds. Avail: 333 paved, back-ins (30x60), 333 full hkups (30/50 amps), WiFi @ sites, laundry, LP gas, controlled access. **REC:** heated pool, boating nearby. Pet restrict (B). Partial handicap access. No tents. Big rig sites. 2021 rates: $53 to $65, Military discount.
(352)629-3540 Lat: 29.21799, Lon: -82.14891
3101 NW 16th Ave, Ocala, FL 34475
www.wildfrontierrvresort.com
See ad previous page

WILDWOOD RV VILLAGE
good sam park **Ratings: 9/10★/8** (RV Resort) From jct FL-40 & I-75: Go 22 mi S on I-75, then 300 feet E on SR-44 (L). **FAC:** paved rds. Avail: 233 grass, 86 pull-thrus, (30x60), back-ins (30x40), 233 full hkups (30/50 amps), cable, WiFi @ sites, dump, laundry, LP gas, firewood. **REC:** heated pool, boating nearby, shuffleboard. Pets OK. Partial handicap access. No tents. Big rig sites, eco-friendly. 2021 rates: $50 to $74.
(352)748-2774 Lat: 28.87461, Lon: -82.08931
882 E. State Road 44, Wildwood, FL 34785
wildwoodrvvillage.com
See primary listing at Wildwood and ad pages 280, 281

ODESSA — K2 *Hillsborough*

SILVER DOLLAR GOLF, TRAP CLUB & RV RESORT
good sam park **Ratings: 8/8★/8** (Membership Park) Avail: 27 full hkups (30/50 amps). 2021 rates: $40 to $90. (888)563-7040, 12515 Silver Dollar Drive, Odessa, FL 33556

OKEECHOBEE — D4 *Glades*

BRIGHTON RV RESORT **Ratings: 9.5/9★/8.5** (RV Park) Avail: 54 full hkups (30/50 amps). 2021 rates: $60. (863)467-0474, 14685 Reservation Rd, Okeechobee, FL 34974

LAKE OKEECHOBEE RV PARK (RV Park) (Too New to Rate) Avail: 53 full hkups (50 amps). 2021 rates: $60. (505)382-6068, 6070 Hwy 441 SE, Okeechobee, FL 34974

LAKE SUN LODGE & RV PARK **Ratings: 4.5/6.5/6.5** (RV Park) Avail: 24 full hkups (30/50 amps). 2021 rates: $35 to $55. (863)763-4638, 8680 Hwy 441 S.E., Okeechobee, FL 34974

LAKESIDE NORTH RV RESORT **Ratings: 8.5/7.5/7.5** (RV Park) Avail: 46 full hkups (30/50 amps). 2021 rates: $46. (863)763-6200, 6500 Highway 441 SE, Okeechobee, FL 34974

OKEECHOBEE KOA RESORT & GOLF COURSE
good sam park **Ratings: 9/9.5/8.5** (RV Park) Avail: 425 full hkups (30/50 amps). 2021 rates: $62 to $96. (888)563-7040, 4276 US Hwy 441 S, Okeechobee, FL 34974

SILVER PALMS RV RESORT - SUNLAND **Ratings: 9.5/10★/10** (Condo Park) Avail: 199 full hkups (30/50 amps). 2021 rates: $65 to $128. (888)474-9678, 4143 U.S. Hwy 441 S, Okeechobee, FL 34974

TAYLOR CREEK RV RESORT **Ratings: 6/8★/7.5** (RV Park) Avail: 106 full hkups (50 amps). 2021 rates: $40 to $100. (863)763-4417, 2730 Hwy 441 SE, Okeechobee, FL 34974

WATER'S EDGE RV RESORT **Ratings: 9/NA/10** (RV Park) Avail: 30 full hkups (30/50 amps). 2021 rates: $45 to $90. (863)357-5757, 12766 Hwy 441 SE, Okeechobee, FL 34974

ZACHARY TAYLOR RV RESORT
good sam park **Ratings: 8.5/8.5★/8.5** (Campground) From Jct of SR-70 & US-Hwy 441, S 5.3 mi on US-Hwy 441 to SE 30th Terrace (across bridge), N 0.1 mi (L). **FAC:** paved rds. (204 spaces). 126 Avail: 55 gravel, 71 grass, patios, 30 pull-thrus, (20x46), back-ins (30x50), 126 full hkups (30/50 amps), seasonal sites, WiFi @ sites, rentals, laundry, LP bottles, firewood. **REC:** heated pool, Taylor Creek: fishing, kayaking/canoeing, boating nearby, shuffleboard, hunting nearby. Pet restrict (B). Partial handicap access. No tents, eco-friendly. 2021 rates: $35 to $65, Military discount.
(863)763-3377 Lat: 27.21231, Lon: -80.79830
2995 US Highway 441 SE, Okeechobee, FL 34974
www.flrvresort.com
See ad this page

OLD TOWN — B2 *Dixie*

LUCKY CHARM RV PARK **Ratings: 8.5/8.5★/9** (RV Park) Avail: 75 full hkups (30/50 amps). 2021 rates: $32. (352)542-0033, 4114 NE Hwy 349 , Old Town, FL 32680

SUWANNEE RIVER HIDEAWAY CAMPGROUND **Ratings: 8.5/8★/8.5** (Campground) 59 Avail: 46 full hkups, 13 W, 13 E (30/50 amps). 2021 rates: $40.50 to $43.20. (352)542-7800, 1218 SE 346 Hwy, Old Town, FL 32680

ORANGE CITY — H4 *Volusia*

BLUE SPRING (Public State Park) 2 mi W of Orange City - off US-17-92. 51 Avail: 51 W, 51 E. 2021 rates: $24. (386)775-3663

LUNA SANDS RV RESORT **Ratings: 8/8.5★/7.5** (RV Resort) 145 Avail: 125 full hkups, 20 W, 20 E (30/50 amps). 2021 rates: $42 to $52. (866)953-3358, 1440 E Minnesota Ave, Orange City, FL 32763

ORANGE CITY RV RESORT **Ratings: 9/9★/9** (RV Park) Avail: 200 full hkups (30/50 amps). 2021 rates: $46 to $67. (888)653-1480, 2300 E Graves Ave, Orange City, FL 32763

ORLANDO — J4 *Orange*

ORLANDO See also Apopka, Clermont, Cocoa, Davenport, Debary, Eustis, Kissimmee, Lake Buena Vista, Leesburg, Orange City, Polk City, Sanford, Tavares, Titusville, Webster, Winter Garden & Winter Haven.

BILL FREDERICK PARK AT TURKEY LAKE (Public) From Jct of I-4 (exit 75B) & SR-435/Kirkman Rd-N: Go N 1.5 mi on Kirkman Rd, then W 1.5 mi on Conroy Rd, then N 0.9 mi Hiawassee Rd. (R). 36 Avail: 14 full hkups, 22 W, 22 E (30/50 amps). 2021 rates: $13.33 to $20.44. (407)246-4486

MOSS PARK (Public) From Jct of Hwy 528 & SR-15, S 2.5 mi on SR-15 to Moss Park Rd, N 4.5 mi (E) Note: No alcohol allowed in park. 54 Avail: 54 W, 54 E (20/50 amps). 2021 rates: $15 to $23. (407)254-6840

County names help you follow the local weather report.

St. John's River Retreat
good sam park
Highbanks
Marina & Campresort
Swamp House Grill & Tiki
St. Johns River Eco Tours
NEW SUPER SITES!
SOME 70' LONG, PULL-THRU, 50 AMP, CABLE
• Pontoon Rentals • Overnight Rentals • Cable TV
• Swimming Pool • Billiards • Bingo
• Bait Shop • Country Store • Year Round Activities
• Narrated Wildlife River Tours
• Non-Ethanol & LP Gas
• 30 and 50 Amp Sites Available
• Halfway Between Orlando and Daytona
• Off of I-4
WI-FI Available At Your Site
like us on facebook
www.facebook.com/highbanksmarinacampresort
SWAMP HOUSE RIVER FRONT GRILL
Swamp House Grill
150 SEATING
OVERLOOKING
THE BEAUTIFUL
ST. JOHN'S RIVER
Full Bar
Daily Specials
Steak to Seafood
For Hours,
Call (386) 668-8891
Highbanks Marina
Highbanks Rd.
2.8 MI
Saxon Blvd.
Exit 111B
4
N
17 92
1.5 MI
Exit 108
Dirksen Rd.
1.5 MI
GPS
Lat: 28.89089
Lon: 81.35396
488 West Highbanks Rd. • Debary, FL 32713
(386) 668-4491 • www.campresort.com
See listing Debary, FL

FL

ORMOND BEACH — G4 *Flagler*

CORAL SANDS OCEANFRONT RV RESORT
good sam park **Ratings: 8.5/8.5★/8** (RV Resort) From the Jct of I-95 & US40/Granada Blvd (Exit 268) E 4.1 mi on US40/Granada Blvd to SRA1A, N 2 mi (R). **FAC:** all weather rds. Avail: 33 gravel, 2 pull-thrus, (20x50), back-ins (20x40), 33 full hkups (30/50 amps), WiFi @ sites, tent sites, rentals, laundry. **REC:** heated pool, Atlantic Ocean: swim, fishing, boating nearby. Pets OK. 2021 rates: $65 to $180, Military discount. ATM.
(800)441-1831 Lat: 29.317592, Lon: -81.052521
1047 Ocean Shore Blvd, Ormond Beach, FL 32176
coralsandsinn.com
See ad page 243

SUNSHINE HOLIDAY DAYTONA RV RESORT
good sam park **Ratings: 8/7.5/7.5** (RV Park) 258 Avail: 220 full hkups, 38 W, 38 E (30/50 amps). 2021 rates: $59 to $89. (888)563-7040, 1701 N US-1, Ormond Beach, FL 32174

TOMOKA (Public State Park) From Jct of US-1 & SR-40, E 0.5 mi on SR-40 to Beach St, N 3 mi (R). CAUTION: Max height 11ft, length 34 ft. 88 Avail: 88 W, 88 E (30 amps). 2021 rates: $24. (386)676-4050

OSPREY — D3 *Sarasota*

OSCAR SCHERER (Public State Park) From Jct of US-41 & SR-681, N 1.6 mi on US-41 (R). 97 Avail: 97 W, 97 E (30/50 amps). 2021 rates: $26. (941)483-5956

Directional arrows indicate the campground's position in relation to the nearest town.

PAHOKEE — D5 *Palm Beach*

PAHOKEE CAMPGROUND & MARINA
good sam park **Ratings: 8/9★/8** (Public) From jct S Hwy 715 & N US-441: Go 100 ft N on US-441, then 1 blk W on S Lake Ave (E). **FAC:** paved rds. (118 spaces). 112 Avail: 5 paved, 107 grass, back-ins (30x50), 50 full hkups (30/50 amps), WiFi, tent sites, dump, laundry. **REC:** pool, Lake Okeechobee : fishing, marina, kayaking/canoeing, boating nearby. Pets OK. Partial handicap access. 2021 rates: $34.95 to $37, Military discount.
(561)924-7832 Lat: 26.82502, Lon: -80.66639
190 North Lake Avenue, Pahokee, FL 33476
www.cityofpahokee.com
See ad this page

PALATKA — B4 *Putnam*

RODMAN CAMPGROUND (Public State Park) From jct Hwy 20 & Hwy 19: Go 12 mi S on Hwy 19, then 2 mi W on Rodman Dam Rd. 39 Avail: 39 W, 39 E. 2021 rates: $12 to $22. (386)326-2846

PALM HARBOR — K1 *Pinellas*

BAY AIRE RV PARK **Ratings: 8/7.5/7** (RV Park) Avail: 20 full hkups (30/50 amps). 2021 rates: $50 to $75. (727)784-4082, 2242 Alt US-19, Palm Harbor, FL 34683

CLEARWATER/LAKE TARPON KOA **Ratings: 8/9.5★/8.5** (Campground) Avail: 103 full hkups (30/50 amps). 2021 rates: $59 to $150. (727)937-8412, 37061 US-19N, Palm Harbor, FL 34684

SHERWOOD FOREST RV PARK **Ratings: 7/8/8** (RV Park) Avail: 49 full hkups (30/50 amps). 2021 rates: $55 to $88. (727)784-4582, 175 Alt 19 So, Palm Harbor, FL 34683

PALMDALE — D4 *Glades*

FISHEATING CREEK OUTPOST (Public) From jct Hwy 29 & US 27: Go 1 mi N on US 27. Avail: 48 full hkups (30/50 amps). 2021 rates: $29. (863)675-5999

SABAL PALM RV RESORT **Ratings: 7.5/8.5★/7.5** (RV Park) 97 Avail: 93 full hkups, 4 W, 4 E (30/50 amps). 2021 rates: $35. (863)675-1778, 1947 Main Ave N, Palmdale, FL 33944

PALMETTO — L2 *Manatee*

FIESTA GROVE RV RESORT
good sam park **Ratings: 8.5/9/8.5** (RV Park) 66 Avail: 53 full hkups, 13 W, 13 E (30/50 amps). 2021 rates: $40 to $54. (941)722-7661, 8615 Bayshore Rd, Palmetto, FL 34221

FISHERMAN'S COVE RV RESORT
good sam park **Ratings: 8.5/10★/8** (RV Park) From Jct US-301 & Hwy 41: Go N 2 mi on Hwy 41, then N 1 mi on US-19 (L).

WATERFRONT NEAR ANNA MARIA ISLAND
Secluded Terra Ceia Bay frontage leading to the Gulf of Mexico. Tampa, St Petersburg, Clearwater & Sarasota close by. NEW water view pavered Big Rig sites with majestic Oak trees, swaying palms & breathtaking sunsets.
FAC: paved rds. (82 spaces). Avail: 29 paved, patios, back-ins (24x60), 29 full hkups (30/50 amps), seasonal sites, WiFi, rentals, laundry. **REC:** heated pool, hot tub, Terra Ceia Bay: fishing, kayaking/canoeing, boating nearby. Pet restrict (Q) $. Partial handicap access. No tents, Age restrict may apply. Big rig sites. 2021 rates: $99 to $159.
(941)729-3685 Lat: 27.56682, Lon: -82.56492
100 61st St. E, Palmetto, FL 34221
myfishermanscove.com
See ad this page

TERRA CEIA RV RESORT
good sam park **Ratings: 8/8.5/8** (RV Park) 46 Avail: 44 full hkups, 2 W, 2 E (30/50 amps). 2021 rates: $40 to $81. (888)563-7040, 9303 Bayshore Dr, Palmetto, FL 34221

THE TIDES RV RESORT
good sam park **Ratings: 10/10★/10** (RV Resort) Avail: 389 full hkups (30/50 amps). 2021 rates: $100 to $180. (941)212-0777, 6310 Bayshore Road, Palmetto, FL 34221

WINTERSET RV RESORT **Ratings: 9/9★/8** (RV Park) 50 Avail: 34 full hkups, 16 W, 16 E (30/50 amps). 2021 rates: $34 to $54. (877)946-8376, 8515 US Hwy 41 N #73, Palmetto, FL 34221

Lend a hand. During the busy season park services are stretched to the max! Please do your best to keep your area ""ship-shape".

PANACEA — B1 *Wakulla*

HOLIDAY CAMPGROUND **Ratings: 7.5/8.5★/7.5** (Campground) Avail: 75 full hkups (30/50 amps). 2021 rates: $47 to $52. (850)984-5757, 14 Coastal Hwy, Panacea, FL 32346

PANACEA RV PARK
good sam park **Ratings: 7.5/8.5★/8.5** (RV Park) From jct US 319 & SR 98: Go 6 mi S on SR 98/Coastal Hwy (L). **FAC:** paved/gravel rds. (80 spaces). Avail: 50 gravel, 18 pull-thrus, (30x60), back-ins (30x60), 50 full hkups (30/50 amps), seasonal sites, cable, WiFi @ sites, laundry. **REC:** boating nearby. Pet restrict (B). No tents. Big rig sites. 2021 rates: $37 to $44.
(850)984-5883 Lat: 30.0178, Lon: -84.3920
1089 Coastal Hwy, Panacea, FL 32346
www.panacearvpark.com
See ad this page

PANAMA CITY — F2 *Bay*

MILITARY PARK PANAMA CITY FAMILY CAMPGROUND & MARINA (PANAMA CITY COASTAL SYSTEMS STATION) (Public) From town: Go 2 mi Won Beach Dr, then 3/4 mi N on Frankford Ave, then 4 mi W on US-98, then 1 mi S on Thomas Dr, then 1 mi on Vernon/Solomans Dr (L). 49 Avail: 45 full hkups, 4 W, 4 E (30/50 amps). 2021 rates: $22 to $24. (850)234-4402

MILITARY PARK RAPTOR RANCH (TYNDALL AFB) (Public) From town: Go 5-3/4 mi E on US-98 Bus E, then 2-1/2 mi S on US-98 E/Tyndall Pkwy, then right onto Fam Camp Rd (L). Avail: 100 full hkups (30/50 amps). 2021 rates: $25 to $35. (850)283-2798

Travel Services

CAMPING WORLD OF PANAMA CITY As the nation's largest retailer of RV supplies, accessories, services and new and used RVs, Camping World is committed to making your total RV experience better. **SERVICES:** RV appliance, MH mechanical, staffed RV wash, restrooms. RV Sales. RV supplies, LP gas, RV accessible. Hours: 9am to 7pm.
(877)857-9110 Lat: 30.191104, Lon: -85.713355
4100 W. 23rd Street, Panama City, FL 32405
www.campingworld.com

PANAMA CITY BEACH — F2 *Bay*

CAMPER'S INN
good sam park **Ratings: 9/9★/7.5** (RV Park) W-bnd: From Hathaway Bridge, W 0.25 mi on US-98 to C-3031 (Thomas Dr), S 7 mi (R); or E-bnd: From Jct of US-98 & C-3033, E 0.7 mi on C-3033 to Hwy 392 (Thomas Dr), SE 2 mi (L). **FAC:** paved rds. 105 Avail: 78 paved, 27 grass, patios, 11 pull-thrus, (20x65), back-ins (30x40), 105 full hkups (30/50 amps), cable, WiFi @ sites, dump, laundry, groc, LP gas, controlled access. **REC:** pool, wading pool, Grand Lagoon: boating nearby, shuffleboard, playground. Pets OK. Partial handicap access. No tents. Big rig sites, eco-friendly. 2021 rates: $54.95 to $64.95. ATM.
(866)872-2267 Lat: 30.17072, Lon: -85.79302
8800 Thomas Dr, Panama City Beach, FL 32408
campersinn.net
See ad opposite page

EMERALD COAST RV BEACH RESORT **Ratings: 10/10★/10** (RV Resort) Avail: 242 full hkups (30/50 amps). 2021 rates: $78 to $106. (850)235-0924, 1957 Allison Ave, Panama City Beach, FL 32407

PANAMA CITY BEACH RV RESORT **Ratings: 9.5/9★/8.5** (RV Park) Avail: 69 full hkups (50 amps). 2021 rates: $75 to $94. (850)249-7352, 4702 Thomas Dr, Panama City Beach, FL 32408

PINEGLEN MOTORCOACH & RV PARK **Ratings: 8/9★/8.5** (RV Park) Avail: 60 full hkups (30/50 amps). 2021 rates: $58 to $68. (850)230-8535, 11930 Panama City Beach Parkway, Panama City Beach, FL 32407

RACCOON RIVER RESORT **Ratings: 7.5/8.5★/8** (RV Park) Avail: 138 full hkups (30/50 amps). 2021 rates: $56 to $65. (877)234-0181, 12209 Hutchinson Blvd, Panama City Beach, FL 32407

ST ANDREWS (Public State Park) From Jct of US-98 & Hwy 3031, S 3.5 mi on Hwy 3031 to Thomas Dr, E 0.25 mi (E). 147 Avail: 147 W, 147 E (30/50 amps). 2021 rates: $28. (850)708-6100

Don't take any chances when it comes to cleanliness. We rate campground restrooms and showers for cleanliness and physical characteristics such as supplies and appearance.

CAMPERS INN INC. PANAMA CITY BEACH FL

good sam park

See listing Panama City Beach, FL

Reservations: 866-872-2267 (Toll Free) 850- 234-5731 (local)

FULL HOOK UPS • 30 & 50 AMP
PAVED • PATIO • WIFI & CABLE
PULL THRU'S • GROCERIES/ICE
RESTROOMS & SHOWERS • POOL
LAUNDRY • RV SUPPLIES • ATM
FISHING TACKLE & SUPPLIES

ONLY 300 YARDS TO THE BEACH

CABIN RENTALS

ACCOMMODATES UP TO 4 PEOPLE, OUTDOOR GRILL AIR CONDITIONED

POOL

SEPARATE KIDDIE POOL SHADED AREA

PET FRIENDLY!

NEW DOG RUN AREA & DOG WASHING STATION

LOCATED NEARBY

RESTAURANTS / NIGHTLIFE
FAMILY FRIENDLY ATTRACTIONS
GOLF COURSE / MINI GOLF
FISHING CHARTERS
SHOPPING

ONE STOP SHOPPING

FOR YOUR CAMPING AND OUTDOOR NEEDS.
BEACH SUPPLIES, COOLERS, ICE, BEVERAGES, GROCERY, FISHING TACKLE, APPAREL, & RV/CAMP SUPPLIES

Visit our website for more information or call us to reserve a site!
CAMPERSINN.NET • 8800 THOMAS DR PANAMA CITY BEACH FL 32408

FL

PEMBROKE PINES — E5 *Broward*

CB SMITH PARK (Public) From Jct of I-75 & Pine Blvd, E 1 mi on Pine Blvd to Flamingo Rd, N 0.5 mi (L). Avail: 83 full hkups (30/50 amps). 2021 rates: $35 to $45. (954)357-5170

PENSACOLA — F1 *Escambia*

AHOY RV RESORT

Ratings: 10/10★/10 (RV Resort) From jct I-10 (FL) & US 90/US 98: Go 5-1/2 mi W on US 90, then 7 mi W on FL 298, then 17 mi W on US 98 (AL), then ¼ mi N on Springsteen Ln (L). **FAC:** all weather rds. (82 spaces). Avail: 62 all weather, patios, 15 pull-thrus, (30x95), back-ins (30x70), 62 full hkups (30/50 amps), seasonal sites, cable, WiFi @ sites, laundry, groc, LP gas, fire rings, firewood. **REC:** pool, wading pool, Lake Rougaroux: swim, fishing, kayaking/canoeing, boating nearby, shuffleboard, hunting nearby. Pet restrict (B). No tents. Big rig sites, eco-friendly. 2021 rates: $55 to $65, Military discount.
(251)233-7250 Lat: 30.414138, Lon: -87.650231
1300 Springsteen Ln, Foley, AL 36535
www.ahoyrvresort.com
See primary listing at Foley, AL and ad page 25

AVALON LANDING RV PARK

Ratings: 10/10★/9 (RV Park) From jct I-10 & SR 281 (Avalon Blvd Exit 22): Go S 1/2 mi S on SR 281 (L). **FAC:** paved rds. (79 spaces). Avail: 75 all weather, patios, 8 pull-thrus, (30x60), back-ins (30x60), 75 full hkups (30/50 amps), cable, WiFi @ sites, dump, laundry, LP gas. **REC:** pool, Escambia Bay: fishing, boating nearby. Pet restrict (B/Q). Partial handicap access. No tents. Big rig sites, eco-friendly. 2021 rates: $43 to $59.
(850)995-5898 Lat: 30.52509, Lon: -87.08662
2444 Avalon Blvd, Milton, FL 32583
avalonlandingrvpark.com
See primary listing at Milton and ad this page

BIG LAGOON (Public State Park) From jct Hwy 292 & Hwy 292A: Go 2 mi E on Hwy 292A. 75 Avail: 75 W, 75 E. 2021 rates: $20. (850)492-1595

GULF ISLANDS/FORT PICKENS (Public National Park) From jct US-98 & Hwy-399: Go 15 mi SW on Hwy-399 & Ft. Pickens Rd. 137 Avail: 137 W, 137 E (50 amps). 2021 rates: $20 to $30. (850)934-2622

MILITARY PARK BLUE ANGEL NAVAL REC AREA (CORRY STATION) (Public) From town: Go 2 mi W on US-98 W/W Navy Blvd, then 8 mi W on US-98, then 2 mi N on Bronson Rd (R). Avail: 158 full hkups (30/50 amps). 2021 rates: $16 to $25. (850)390-6133

MILITARY PARK OAK GROVE PARK (PENSACOLA NAS) (Public) From town: Go 10 mi SW on E Garden St/Barrancas Ave/Duncan Rd/Taylor Rd, then 1 mi SW on Shell Rd (R). Avail: 51 full hkups (30/50 amps). 2021 rates: $26 to $32. (850)452-2535

PENSACOLA BEACH RV RESORT

Ratings: 10/10★/9 (RV Resort) From Jct of US 98 & Pensacola Beach Blvd, E 2.2 mi on Pensacola Beach Blvd (becomes Via De Luna Dr at Fort Pickens Rd) (L). **FAC:** paved rds. Avail: 72 paved, patios, 1 pull-thrus, (30x60), back-ins (30x60), accepts full hkup units only, 72 full hkups (30/50 amps), cable, WiFi @ sites, rentals, laundry. **REC:** heated pool, Santa Rosa Sound: swim, boating nearby, shuffleboard, playground. Pets OK. Partial handicap access. No tents. Big rig sites, eco-friendly. 2021 rates: $70 to $130, Military discount.
(850)932-4670 Lat: 30.33473, Lon: -87.13560
17 Via De Luna Dr, Pensacola, FL 32561
pensacolarvresorts.com
See ad opposite page

PENSACOLA NORTH RV RESORT

Ratings: 10/9★/8 (RV Park) From jct I-10 & Pine Forest Rd: Go 1000 feet N on Pine Forest Rd (L). **FAC:** paved rds. Avail: 38 paved, patios, back-ins (22x45), accepts full hkup units only, 38 full hkups (30/50 amps), cable, WiFi @ sites, dump, laundry. **REC:** pool, boating nearby. Pets OK. No tents. 2021 rates: $60.
(850)285-0574 Lat: 30.4907, Lon: -87.3056
7800 Pine Forest Rd, Pensacola, FL 32526
pensacolarvresorts.com
See ad opposite page

PENSACOLA RV PARK

Ratings: 8/9.5★/9 (RV Park) From the Jct of IH 10 & Pine Forest Rd (Exit 7), S 0.1 mi on Pine Forest Rd to Wilde Lake Blvd., W (past the hotels & large church), 0.5 mi (L).

PRETTY & CONVENIENT IN-TOWN PARK
Located in town but still close to the freeway, beaches, shopping and services. Pretty little park with really friendly natives. Clean, quiet & peaceful. Come see our great new spaces. Free High Speed Wi-Fi. Big Rig friendly

FAC: gravel rds. Avail: 87 gravel, patios, 25 pull-thrus, (34x80), back-ins (34x70), 87 full hkups (30/50 amps), cable, WiFi @ sites, laundry, LP gas. **REC:** pond, fishing, boating nearby. Pet restrict (B/Q). Partial handicap access. No tents. Big rig sites, eco-friendly. 2021 rates: $46, Military discount.
(850)944-1734 Lat: 30.51950, Lon: -87.32617
3117 Wilde Lake Blvd, Pensacola, FL 32526
www.pensacolarvpark.net
See ad page 295

PERDIDO KEY — F1 *Escambia*

PERDIDO KEY RV RESORT

Ratings: 9.5/9★/9 (RV Park) Avail: 55 full hkups (30/50 amps). 2021 rates: $85 to $130. (850)492-7304, 13770 River Rd, Pensacola, FL 32507

PERRY — B2 *Jefferson*

PERRY KOA **Ratings: 8.5/8.5★/7** (RV Park) Avail: 115 full hkups (30/50 amps). 2021 rates: $32 to $88. (850)584-3221, 3641 US-19 S, Perry, FL 32348

ROCKY'S CAMPGROUND **Ratings: 7/9★/8** (Campground) Avail: 47 full hkups (30/50 amps). 2021 rates: $32.95. (850)584-6600, 5175 W US 98, Perry, FL 32348

POLK CITY — K3 *Polk*

LELYNN RV RESORT

Ratings: 9/8.5★/9 (RV Park) From Jct of I-4 & State Road-559 (exit 44), N 0.3 mi on State Road-559 (L). **FAC:** paved rds. (370 spaces). Avail: 220 paved, patios, 10 pull-thrus, (33x66), back-ins (34x74), 220 full hkups (30/50 amps), seasonal sites, WiFi @ sites, $, dump, laundry, LP gas. **REC:** pool, Little Lake Agnes: fishing, kayaking/canoeing, boating nearby, shuffleboard. Pet restrict (S/B/Q). Partial handicap access. No tents. Big rig sites. 2021 rates: $50.60, Military discount. no cc.
(800)736-0409 Lat: 28.16321, Lon: -81.80183
1513 State Road-559, Polk City, FL 33868
See ad page 272

POMPANO BEACH — E5 *Broward*

BREEZY HILL RV RESORT

Ratings: 8.5/8.5★/7.5 (RV Park) Avail: 594 full hkups (30/50 amps). 2021 rates: $44 to $84. (888)563-7040, 800 NE 48th St, Pompano Beach, FL 33064

HIGHLAND PINES RV RESORT **Ratings: 7.5/7.5/7.5** (RV Park) Avail: 141 full hkups (30/50 amps). 2021 rates: $50 to $75. (954)421-5372, 875 NE 48th St, Deerfield Beach, FL 33064

HIGHLAND WOODS RV RESORT

Ratings: 7/9.5★/7.5 (RV Park) Avail: 129 full hkups (30/50 amps). 2021 rates: $44 to $81. (888)563-7040, 900 NE 48th St, Pompano Beach, FL 33064

PONCE DE LEON — E2 *Holmes*

VORTEX SPRING ADVENTURES

Ratings: 7.5/NA/8 (Campground) From jct I-10 & SR 81 (exit 96): Go 4-1/4 mi N on US-81, then 250 feet E on Vortex Spring Lane (E). **FAC:** gravel rds. Avail: 88 grass, 26 pull-thrus, (30x60), back-ins (30x60), 2 full hkups, 86 W, 86 E (30/50 amps), WiFi @ sites, tent sites, rentals, dump, fire rings, firewood, restaurant. **REC:** pool, Vortex Spring: swim, kayaking/canoeing, boating nearby, playground. Pets OK. Big rig sites. 2021 rates: $37.
(850)836-4979 Lat: 30.7732, Lon: -85.9554
1517 Vortex Spring Lane, Ponce De Leon, FL 32455
Vortexspring.com
See ad page 290

PORT CHARLOTTE — D3 *De Soto*

HARBOR LAKES RV RESORT

Ratings: 9/9.5/9 (RV Park) Avail: 99 full hkups (30/50 amps). 2021 rates: $49 to $99. (888)563-7040, 3737 El Jobean Rd, Port Charlotte, FL 33953

MYAKKA RIVER MOTORCOACH RESORT **Ratings: 10/10★/10** (RV Resort) Avail: 99 full hkups (50 amps). 2021 rates: $90 to $157. (941)740-2599, 14100 Myakka Ave, Port Charlotte, FL 33953

RIVERSIDE RV RESORT

Ratings: 9/10★/9.5 (RV Park) Avail: 449 full hkups (30/50 amps). 2021 rates: $55 to $79. (888)563-7040, 9770 SW CR-769 , Arcadia, FL 34269

RV SPACE-SAVING TIP: Keep multiple layers of sheets on the bed for easy changes (without having to remake the entire bed). This comes in especially handy if you have a potty-training child sleeping in one of the beds. If they wake up soaking wet in the middle of the night, it's not a big deal, since you strip the sheets down to the waterproof mattress cover. Thus, revealing a clean set of dry sheets, with yet another mattress cover under those.

Get the GOOD SAM CAMPING APP

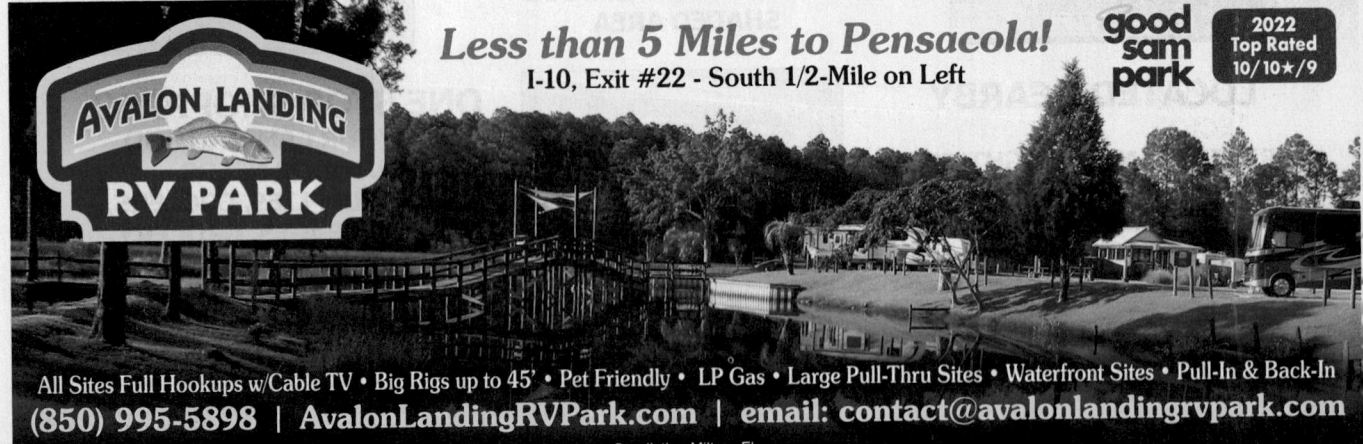

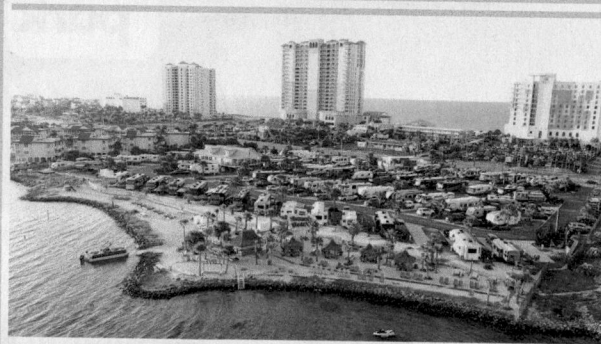

- 60+ Acre Campground and Water Park
- Lazy River • Golf Cart Rentals
- Lake With Paddle Board, Canoe, and Kayak Rentals
- Four Pickleball Courts • One Basketball Court
- One Kids Playground • One Bocce Ball Court
- Adults-Only Pool with Bar • Three Additional Pools
- 40 Cottages and Luxury Conestoga Wagons
- All Concrete RV Pads and Pull-Thru Sites
- Full RV Hookups • Fire Pits • Dog Parks • Amphitheater

In Historic Milton, close to the white sandy beaches of Navarre Beach and Pensacola

Navarre Beach~Milton
Splash! RV RESORT & WATERPARK

8500 Welcome Church Rd
Milton, FL 32583

850-626-8500

See listing Milton, FL

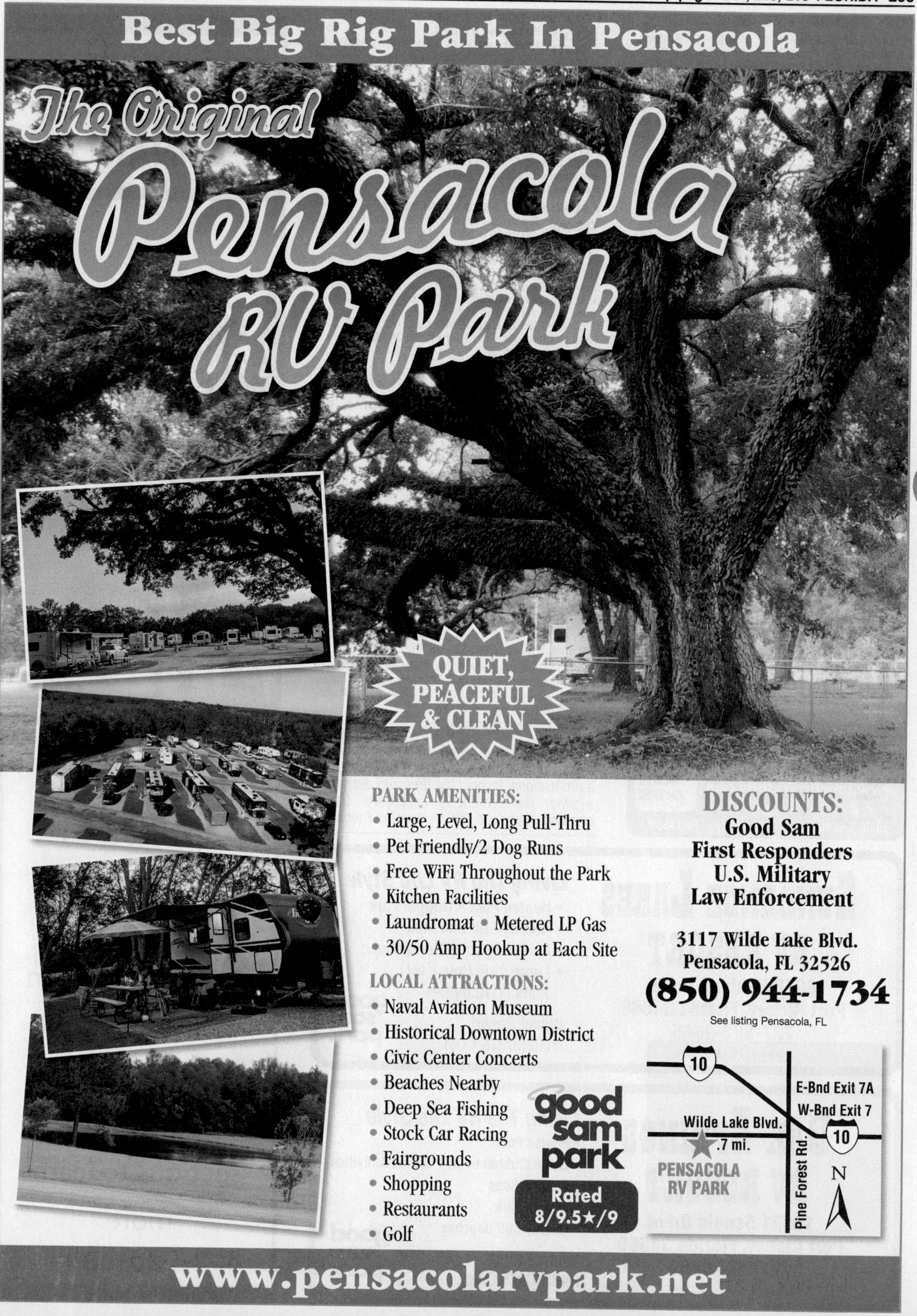
Best Big Rig Park In Pensacola
The Original
Pensacola
RV Park
QUIET, PEACEFUL & CLEAN
PARK AMENITIES:
• Large, Level, Long Pull-Thru
• Pet Friendly/2 Dog Runs
• Free WiFi Throughout the Park
• Kitchen Facilities
• Laundromat • Metered LP Gas
• 30/50 Amp Hookup at Each Site
LOCAL ATTRACTIONS:
• Naval Aviation Museum
• Historical Downtown District
• Civic Center Concerts
• Beaches Nearby
• Deep Sea Fishing
• Stock Car Racing
• Fairgrounds
• Shopping
• Restaurants
• Golf
good sam park
Rated 8/9.5★/9
DISCOUNTS:
Good Sam
First Responders
U.S. Military
Law Enforcement
3117 Wilde Lake Blvd.
Pensacola, FL 32526
(850) 944-1734
See listing Pensacola, FL
10
E-Bnd Exit 7A
W-Bnd Exit 7
Wilde Lake Blvd.
.7 mi.
10
PENSACOLA RV PARK
Pine Forest Rd.
N
www.pensacolarvpark.net

PORT ORANGE — G5 *Volusia*

DAYTONA BEACH RV RESORT **Ratings: 9.5/10★/8.5** (RV Park) Avail: 176 full hkups (30/50 amps). 2021 rates: $52 to $115. (877)618-7544, 4601 S Clyde Morris Blvd, Port Orange, FL 32129

DAYTONA'S ENDLESS SUMMER CAMPGROUND **Ratings: 9/9★/8** (RV Park) 280 Avail: 160 full hkups, 120 W, 120 E (30/50 amps). 2021 rates: $39 to $150. (386)767-9170, 3520 S Nova Rd, Port Orange, FL 32129

ROSE BAY TRAVEL PARK
good sam park **Ratings: 9/8.5/8** (RV Park) Avail: 108 full hkups (30/50 amps). 2021 rates: $41 to $63. (888)563-7040, 5200 S Nova Rd, Port Orange, FL 32127

PORT RICHEY — J1 *Pasco*

JA-MAR NORTH RV RESORT
good sam park **Ratings: 8.5/9.5★/9.5** (RV Park) From Jct of SR-52 & US-19: Go S 0.5 mi on US-19, then W 0.2 mi on San Marco Dr. (E). **FAC:** paved rds. (353 spaces). Avail: 202 grass, patios, back-ins (35x57), 202 full hkups (30/50 amps), seasonal sites, WiFi, rentals, laundry. **REC:** heated pool, pond, fishing, boating nearby, shuffleboard. Pet restrict (B). Partial handicap access. No tents, Age restrict may apply. 2021 rates: $42. no cc.
(727)862-8882 Lat: 28.324078, Lon: -82.701649
6650 San Marco Dr, Port Richey, FL 34668
www.ja-marrvresorts.com
See ad this page

JA-MAR TRAVEL PARK
Ratings: 8/9★/8 (RV Area in MH Park) From Jct of SR-52 & US-19: Go S 0.8 mi on US-19 (R). **FAC:** paved rds. (396 spaces). 245 Avail: 60 paved, 185 grass, patios, back-ins (30x50), 245 full hkups (30/50 amps), seasonal sites, WiFi, laundry. **REC:** heated pool, pond, fishing, boating nearby, shuffleboard. Pet restrict (B). Partial handicap access. No tents, Age restrict may apply. 2021 rates: $58. no cc.
(727)863-2040 Lat: 28.31982, Lon: -82.69937
11203 US-Hwy 19-N, Port Richey, FL 34668
www.ja-marrvresorts.com
See ad this page

OAK SPRINGS RV RESORT
good sam park **Ratings: 7.5/8/8.5** (RV Area in MH Park) From Jct of US-19 & Hwy 52: Go S 2 mi on US-19, then W 0.2 mi on Jasmine Blvd, then S 500 ft on Scenic Dr (R). **FAC:** paved rds. (528 spaces). Avail: 100 paved, back-ins (22x38), 100 full hkups (30/50 amps), seasonal sites, laundry, LP gas. **REC:** heated pool, pond, boating nearby, shuffleboard. Pet restrict (B). Partial handicap access. No tents. 2021 rates: $50 to $55.
(727)863-5888 Lat: 28.31031, Lon: -82.70348
10521 Scenic Dr, Port Richey, FL 34668
www.rvresorts.com
See ad this page

SUNDANCE LAKES RV RESORT
good sam park **Ratings: 8/8.5★/8** (RV Park) From Jct of US-19 & SR-52: Go S 0.25 mi on US-19 (R). **FAC:** paved rds. (523 spaces). Avail: 10 grass, patios, back-ins (30x50), 10 full hkups (30/50 amps), seasonal sites, WiFi, laundry, LP gas. **REC:** heated pool, pond, fishing, boating nearby, shuffleboard. Pet restrict (S/B/Q). No tents. 2021 rates: $50 to $55.
(727)862-3565 Lat: 28.32745, Lon: -82.70045
6848 Hachem Dr, Port Richey, FL 34668
www.rvresorts.com
See ad this page

PORT ST JOE — F3 *Gulf*

PRESNELL'S BAYSIDE MARINA & RV RESORT
good sam park **Ratings: 9/9★/9.5** (RV Resort) From the jct of US98 & SR30A: Go 2-1/3 mi S on CR30A (R). **FAC:** gravel rds. Avail: 71 gravel, 8 pull-thrus, (30x65), back-ins (30x65), 71 full hkups (30/50 amps), cable, WiFi @ sites, laundry, groc, LP gas. **REC:** heated pool, Gulf of Mexico: fishing, marina, kayaking/canoeing, boating nearby. Pet restrict (Q). No tents. Big rig sites, eco-friendly. 2021 rates: $59.50 to $69.50.
(850)229-9229 Lat: 29.7476, Lon: -85.3031
2115 Highway C-30, Port St Joe, FL 32456
presnells.com
See ad opposite page

ST JOSEPH PENINSULA (Public State Park) From town, E 2 mi on US-98 to C-30, S 10 mi to Cape San Blas Rd (C-30E), N 11 mi (E). 88 Avail: 88 W, 88 E (30 amps). 2021 rates: $24. (850)227-1327

WATERS EDGE RV PARK **Ratings: 7/8★/8** (RV Park) Avail: 12 full hkups (30/50 amps). 2021 rates: $49.99. (251)284-1776, 8300 CR 30A, Port St Joe, FL 32456

CLEANING YOUR RV: Clean your wheels and tires. Inspect tire tread depth and look for cracks in tread and sidewalls. If in doubt, have a professional inspect the tires and determine whether replacement is necessary. Use a cleaning agent specific for tires and wheels.

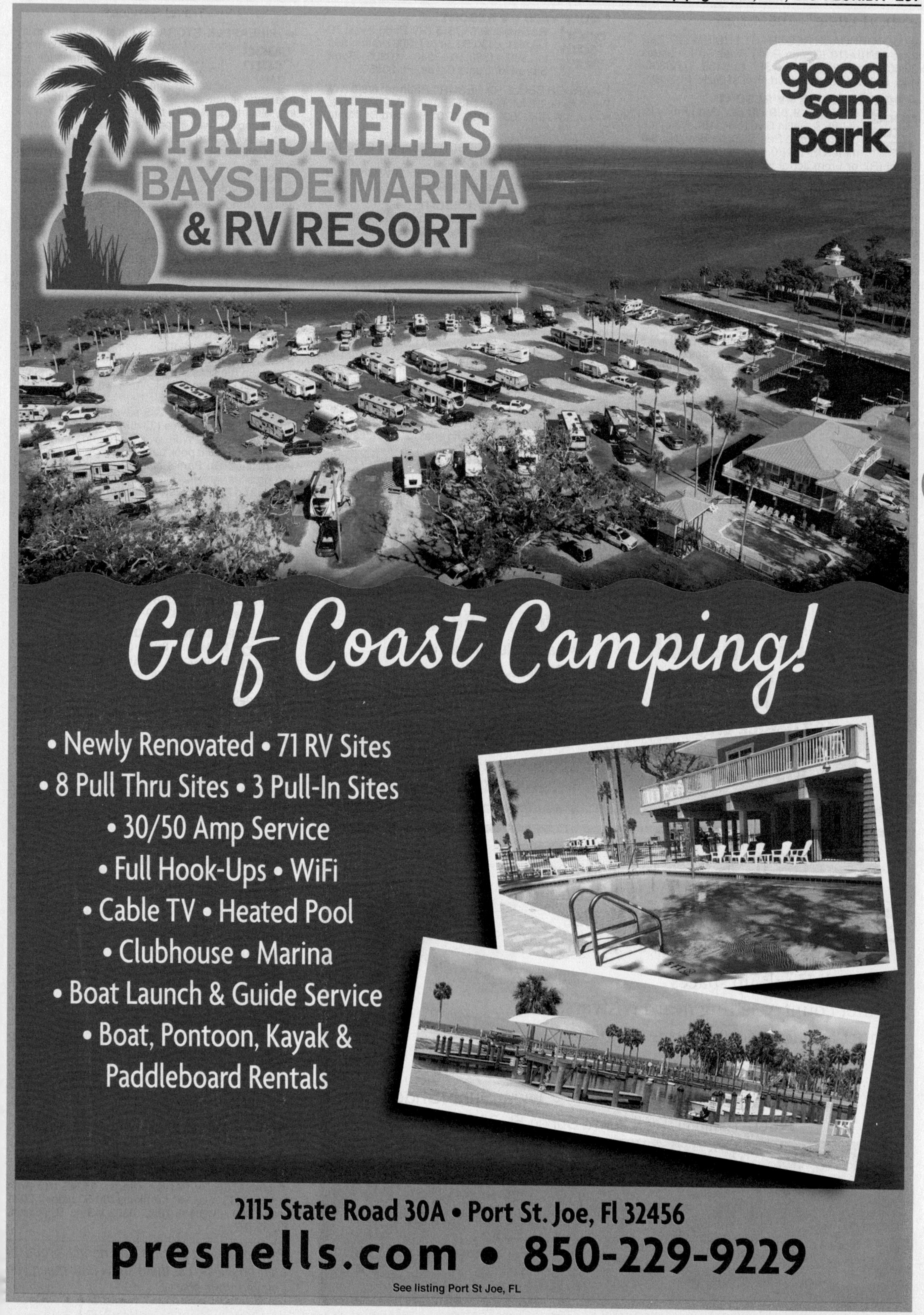
PRESNELL'S
BAYSIDE MARINA
& RV RESORT
good sam park
Gulf Coast Camping!
• Newly Renovated • 71 RV Sites
• 8 Pull Thru Sites • 3 Pull-In Sites
• 30/50 Amp Service
• Full Hook-Ups • WiFi
• Cable TV • Heated Pool
• Clubhouse • Marina
• Boat Launch & Guide Service
• Boat, Pontoon, Kayak &
Paddleboard Rentals
2115 State Road 30A • Port St. Joe, Fl 32456
presnells.com • 850-229-9229
See listing Port St Joe, FL

PORT ST LUCIE — D5 *St Lucie*

MOTORCOACH RESORT ST. LUCIE WEST **Ratings: 10/10★/10** (Condo Park) Avail: 90 full hkups (30/50 amps). 2021 rates: $80 to $135. (772)336-1135, 800 NW Peacock Blvd, Port St Lucie, FL 34986

PORT ST LUCIE RV RESORT
good sam park **Ratings: 9.5/9★/8** (RV Park) From Jct of I-95 & Gatlin Blvd (exit 118), E 3 mi on Gatlin Blvd to Port St Lucie Blvd, NE 5.9 mi to US-1, N 0.5 mi to Jennings Rd, E 0.1 mi (R); or From Jct of FL Tpke & Port St Lucie Blvd (exit 142), E 4 mi on Port St Lucie Blvd to US-1, N 0.5 mi to Jennings Rd, E 0.1 mi (R). **FAC:** paved rds. (117 spaces). Avail: 82 paved, patios, 4 pull-thrus, (24x66), back-ins (24x55), 82 full hkups (30/50 amps), seasonal sites, cable, WiFi @ sites, laundry. **REC:** heated pool, boating nearby. Pet restrict (B/Q). Partial handicap access. No tents. Big rig sites. 2021 rates: $55 to $59.
(772)337-3340 Lat: 27.27584, Lon: -80.28770
3703 SE Jennings Rd, Port St Lucie, FL 34952
portstlucievresort.com
See ad page 230

PSL VILLAGE RV RESORT **Ratings: 8.5/9★/8.5** (RV Park) Avail: 71 full hkups (30/50 amps). 2021 rates: $45 to $60. (772)337-0333, 3600 SE Mariposa Ave, Port St Lucie, FL 34952

PUNTA GORDA — D3 *Charlotte*

ALLIGATOR PARK **Ratings: 9.5/8.5/8.5** (Condo Park) Avail: 68 full hkups (30/50 amps). 2021 rates: $35 to $52. (941)639-7000, 6400 Taylor Rd #112, Punta Gorda, FL 33950

CREEKSIDE RV RESORT **Ratings: 10/10★/10** (RV Resort) Avail: 208 full hkups (30/50 amps). 2021 rates: $75 to $135. (941)833-3334, 27005 Jones Loop Rd., Punta Gorda, FL 33982

GULF VIEW RV RESORT
good sam park **Ratings: 9/9★/8.5** (RV Park) Avail: 78 full hkups (30/50 amps). 2021 rates: $53 to $90. (888)563-7040, 10205 Burnt Store Rd, Punta Gorda, FL 33950

HARBOR BELLE RV RESORT **Ratings: 8/8/8** (RV Park) Avail: 21 full hkups (30/50 amps). 2021 rates: $79 to $84. (941)639-2010, 3701 Baynard Dr, Punta Gorda, FL 33950

SHELL CREEK RV RESORT **Ratings: 8.5/9★/9** (RV Park) Avail: 40 full hkups (30/50 amps). 2021 rates: $43 to $54. (941)639-4234, 35711 Washington Loop Rd, Punta Gorda, FL 33982

SUN N SHADE RV RESORT
good sam park **Ratings: 8/8/8.5** (Campground) From Jct of I-75 & CR-762/Tuckers Grade Rd (Exit 158), W 1 mi on CR-762 to US-41, S 3.4 mi (L) Note: Watch for tall American flag.

SUN-N-SHADE NESTLED IN COUNTRY
Peaceful RV Park between Punta Gorda and Fort Myers, FL - a great place to enjoy all that Florida has to offer. Entertainment, beaches, shopping, nature all nearby. We welcome traveling RVers, 6/6 and yearly residents.

FAC: paved rds. (191 spaces). Avail: 116 grass, patios, back-ins (30x60), 116 full hkups (30/50 amps), seasonal sites, WiFi @ sites, $, dump, laundry. **REC:** heated pool, pond, fishing, boating nearby, shuffleboard, hunting nearby. Pet restrict (B/Q). Partial handicap access. No tents. Big rig sites. 2021 rates: $38 to $50, Military discount.
(941)639-5388 Lat: 26.81390, Lon: -81.95707
14880 Tamiami Trail, Punta Gorda, FL 33955
sunnshade.com
See ad this page

WATER'S EDGE RV RESORT OF PUNTA GORDA **Ratings: 8/8.5/8.5** (Condo Park) 56 Avail: 46 full hkups, 10 W, 10 E (50 amps). 2021 rates: $38 to $55. (800)637-9224, 6800 Golf Course Blvd, Punta Gorda, FL 33982

Travel Services

PINEAPPLE STORAGE Locally owned facility. good sam RV Storage Storage for RVs, boats, trailers and more. Security cameras, pest maintenance and 24/7 access. Open Mon-Fri 9am to 6pm, Sat 9am to 2pm, closed Sunday. **RV Storage:** indoor, outdoor, covered canopy, secured fencing, electric gate, easy reach keypad, 24/7 access, well-lit facility, well-lit perimeter, security cameras, level gravel/paved spaces, power to charge battery, water, office. **SERVICES:** restrooms. Hours: 9am to 6pm.
Special offers available for Good Sam Members
(941)505-0626 Lat: 26.94227, Lon: -82.02520
25477 Marion Ave, Punta Gorda, FL 33950
pineapplestorage.com

REDDICK — G2 *Athens*

OCALA NORTH RV RESORT
good sam park **Ratings: 10/10★/10** (RV Resort) From Jct of I-75 & SR-318 exit 368 W 0.1 mi on SR-318 to CR 225, .9 mi (L).

200 PAVED BIG RIG PULL THRU SITES!
Nestled in the heart of Ocala's horse country within a short drive to great shopping, dining, and entertainment. Big Rig sites in the forest with the convenience of the city. Heated pool, WiFi, and every activity imaginable.

FAC: paved rds. Avail: 385 paved, patios, 279 pull-thrus, (30x80), back-ins (27x55), 385 full hkups (30/50 amps), cable, WiFi @ sites, dump, laundry, LP gas. **REC:** heated pool, boating nearby, shuffleboard. Pet restrict (B). Partial handicap access. No tents. Big rig sites, eco-friendly. 2021 rates: $65 to $75.
(352)591-1723 Lat: 29.39282, Lon: -82.24637
16905 NW Hwy 225, Reddick, FL 32686
ocalanorthrvresort.com
See ad pages 284, 285

RIVERVIEW — K2 *Hillsborough*

HIDDEN RIVER RESORT **Ratings: 8/9.5★/8.5** (RV Park) Avail: 91 full hkups (30/50 amps). 2021 rates: $45 to $66. (813)677-1515, 12500 McMullen Loop, Riverview, FL 33569

RICE CREEK RV RESORT
good sam park **Ratings: 8/8/8** (RV Area in MH Park) From Jct of I-75 (Exit 2500 & Gibsonton Dr: Go E 1 mi on Gibsonton Dr, then, S 0.8 mi on US 301 (L). **FAC:** paved rds. (573 spaces). Avail: 258 grass, patios, back-ins (30x50), 258 full hkups (30/50 amps), WiFi @ sites, $, rentals, dump, laundry, LP gas. **REC:** heated pool, hot tub, pond, fishing, boating nearby, shuffleboard. Pet restrict (S/B/Q). No tents, eco-friendly. 2021 rates: $50, Military discount.
(813)677-6640 Lat: 27.84521, Lon: -82.32573
10719 Rice Creek Dr, Riverview, FL 33578
www.rvresorts.com
See ad this page

ROCKLEDGE — J5 *Brevard*

SPACE COAST RV RESORT
good sam park **Ratings: 9/8.5★/8.5** (Campground) Avail: 118 full hkups (30/50 amps). 2021 rates: $78 to $90. (888)563-7040, 820 Barnes Blvd, Rockledge, FL 32955

RUSKIN — L2 *Hillsborough*

HAWAIIAN ISLES
good sam park **Ratings: 8.5/9.5★/8.5** (RV Area in MH Park) From Jct of I-75 (Exit 240) & SR-674: Go W 2.9 mi on SR-674, S 2.9 mi on US-41, then W 1.5 mi on Cockroach Bay Rd (L). **FAC:** paved rds. (939 spaces). Avail: 211 grass, patios, back-ins (35x60), accepts full hkup units only, 211 full hkups (30/50 amps), WiFi, rentals, dump, laundry, LP gas. **REC:** heated pool, hot tub, Cockroach Bay/Tampa Bay: swim, fishing, kayaking/canoeing, boating nearby, golf, shuffleboard. Pet restrict (B/Q). No tents. Big rig sites. 2021 rates: $58, Military discount.
(813)645-1098 Lat: 27.68615, Lon: -82.49375
4054 Aloha Blvd, Ruskin, FL 33570
www.rvresorts.com
See ad opposite page

MANATEE RV PARK **Ratings: 7.5/6/8** (RV Area in MH Park) Avail: 40 full hkups (30/50 amps). 2021 rates: $60. (813)645-7652, 6302 US-41 S, Ruskin, FL 33570

Park owners and staff are rightly proud of their business. Let them know how much you enjoyed your stay.

↓ **RIVER VISTA RV VILLAGE**
Ratings: 9/8★/9 (RV Park) From Jct of I-75 (exit 240) & SR-674: Go W 2.9 mi on SR-674, then S 2.6 mi on US-41, then E 0.7 mi on Chaney Dr (E). **FAC:** paved rds. (397 spaces). 114 Avail: 88 paved, 26 gravel, patios, 10 pull-thrus, (30x45), back-ins (40x60), 114 full hkups (30/50 amps), seasonal sites, WiFi @ sites, rentals, laundry, LP gas. **REC:** heated pool, Little Manatee River: fishing, kayaking/canoeing, boating nearby, shuffleboard. Pets OK. Partial handicap access. No tents, Age restrict may apply. Big rig sites. 2021 rates: $49 to $69, Military discount.
(813)522-8032 Lat: 27.68973, Lon: -82.45593
2206 Chaney Dr, Ruskin, FL 33570
www.covecommunities.com
See ad this page

→ **SUN LAKE RV RESORT**
Ratings: 9/9★/8 (RV Park) From Jct of I-75 (Exit 240) & SR-674: Go W 1.0 mi on SR-674, then S 0.5 mi on 27th St SE, then E 0.3 mi on 14th Ave SE (L).

WATERFRONT BY TAMPA BAY ATTRACTIONS
Short distance from Tampa Bay next to Sun City Center. 32 acre bass lake for fishing, kayaking & paddle boarding. Conveniently located for day trips to beaches and city amenities. New paver patio sites, roads, and bathrooms.

FAC: paved rds. (49 spaces). Avail: 30 grass, patios, 18 pull-thrus, (25x50), back-ins (40x60), 30 full hkups (30/50 amps), seasonal sites, WiFi @ sites, dump, laundry. **REC:** heated pool, Sun Lake: fishing, boating nearby, shuffleboard. Pet restrict (Q). No tents, Age restrict may apply. Big rig sites. 2021 rates: $59 to $79.
(813)645-7860 Lat: 27.70636, Lon: -82.39371
3006 14th Ave SE, Ruskin, FL 33570
sunlakervresort.com
See ad this page

↓ TAMPA SOUTH RV RESORT **Ratings: 8.5/10★/8** (RV Park) Avail: 53 full hkups (30/50 amps). 2021 rates: $45 to $65. (813)645-1202, 2900 US Hwy 41 South, Ruskin, FL 33570

SANFORD — H4 *Seminole*

← TWELVE OAKS RV RESORT **Ratings: 6.5/9★/8** (RV Park) Avail: 100 full hkups (30/50 amps). 2021 rates: $50. (407)323-0880, 161 Twelve Oaks Pl, Sanford, FL 32771

← WEKIVA FALLS RV RESORT **Ratings: 9/10★/9** (RV Park) Avail: 486 full hkups (30/50 amps). 2021 rates: $60 to $87. (352)383-8055, 30700 Wekiva River Rd, Sorrento, FL 32776

SANTA ROSA BEACH — F2 *Walton*

← TOPSAIL HILL PRESERVE (Public State Park) From Jct of US-331 & US-98, W 5.7 mi on US-98 to CR-30A, SE 0.4 mi on CR-30A (R). Avail: 156 full hkups (30/50 amps). 2021 rates: $42. (850)267-8330

SARASOTA — D3 *Sarasota*

↘ MYAKKA RIVER (Public State Park) From Jct of I-75 & SR-72 (exit 205/old exit 37), E 8.7 mi on SR-72 (L). 80 Avail: 80 W, 80 E (30/50 amps). 2021 rates: $26. (941)361-6511

↓ SARASOTA SUNNY SOUTH RV RESORT **Ratings: 9/10★/9** (RV Park) Avail: 60 full hkups (30/50 amps). 2021 rates: $85 to $100. (941)921-4409, 2100 Doud St Lot 100, Sarasota, FL 34231

→ SUN OUTDOORS SARASOTA **Ratings: 9/9.5★/9.5** (RV Park) Avail: 619 full hkups (30/50 amps). 2021 rates: $69 to $130. (941)371-2505, 7125 Fruitville Rd, Sarasota, FL 34240

← TURTLE BEACH CAMPGROUND (Public) From Jct I-75 (Exit 205) & Clark Rd: Go W 4 mi on Clark Rd, continue W 1.8 mi on Sticking Point Rd, then S 2.5 mi on Midnight Pass Rd (R). Avail: 39 full hkups (30/50 amps). 2021 rates: $42 to $60. (941)861-2267

SEBASTIAN — K6 *Indian River*

↓ LONG POINT REC & CAMPING PARK (Public) From Sebastian Inlet, N 1.5 mi on Hwy A1A (L); or from town, S 14 mi on Hwy A1A (R). 170 Avail: 15 full hkups, 155 W, 155 E (20/30 amps). 2021 rates: $28. (321)952-4532

↓ SEBASTIAN INLET (Public State Park) S-Bnd: From Jct of I-95 & exit 180 (in Melbourne), E 11 mi on Hwy 192 to A1A, S 18 mi to State Rec Area (R); or N-Bnd: From Jct of US-1 & SR-510 (in Wabasso), E 2.6 mi on SR-510 to A1A, N 7 mi (L). 51 Avail: 51 W, 51 E (30 amps). 2021 rates: $28. (321)984-4852

Park policies vary. Ask about the cancellation policy when making a reservation.

↑ **VERO BEACH KAMP**
Ratings: 9/9.5★/9.5 (RV Park) From Jct of I-95 (Exit 156) & CR-512: Go E 2.4 mi on CR-512, then S 5.8 mi on CR-510, then N 0.4 mi on US-1 (R).

SUMMER FUN ALL YEAR LONG
Only 2 mi to ocean beaches and 5 mi to the fishing mecca. The baseball stadium is close, but we are away from the hustle and bustle in this paradise called Vero Beach - WHERE THE TROPICS BEGIN ON FL'S TREASURE COAST

FAC: paved rds. Avail: 130 all weather, patios, back-ins (30x70), 130 full hkups (30/50 amps), cable, WiFi @ sites, tent sites, rentals, dump, laundry, LP gas. **REC:** heated pool, boating nearby, playground. Pet restrict (B). Partial handicap access. Big rig sites, eco-friendly. 2021 rates: $48 to $69, Military discount.
(877)589-5643 Lat: 27.75450, Lon: -80.43652
8850 N US Hwy-1, Sebastian, FL 32958
www.verobeachkamp.com
See ad page 305

↓ WHISPERING PALMS RV RESORT **Ratings: 9/9★/8.5** (RV Park) Avail: 204 full hkups (30/50 amps). 2021 rates: $57 to $76. (800)414-0814, 10305 US Hwy 1, Sebastian, FL 32958

SEBRING — L4 *Highlands*

↓ BUTTONWOOD BAY RV RESORT & MANUFACTURED HOME COMMUNITY **Ratings: 9/9.5★/9** (RV Area in MH Park) Avail: 169 full hkups (30/50 amps). 2021 rates: $68 to $120. (888)469-1733, 10001 US 27 S, Sebring, FL 33876

↓ HIGHLAND OAKS RV RESORT **Ratings: 6/8.5★/7.5** (RV Park) Avail: 50 full hkups (30/50 amps). 2021 rates: $40. (863)655-1685, 7001 Old Plantation Ave, Sebring, FL 33876

← HIGHLANDS HAMMOCK (Public State Park) From Jct of US-27-98 & CR-634, W 4 mi on CR-634 (E). 118 Avail: 118 W, 118 E (30/50 amps). 2021 rates: $18 to $22. (863)386-6094

↓ LAKE JOSEPHINE RV RESORT **Ratings: 7.5/9.5★/8.5** (RV Area in MH Park) Avail: 74 full hkups (30/50 amps). 2021 rates: $49 to $52. (863)655-0925, 10809 US Hwy 27 S, Sebring, FL 33876

↓ LEISURE ACRES **Ratings: 7.5/9★/8** (RV Resort) Avail: 41 full hkups (30/50 amps). 2021 rates: $42. (863)385-8959, 3651 US Hwy 27 South, Sebring, FL 33870

Read RV topics at blog.GoodSam.com

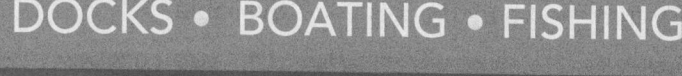

FL

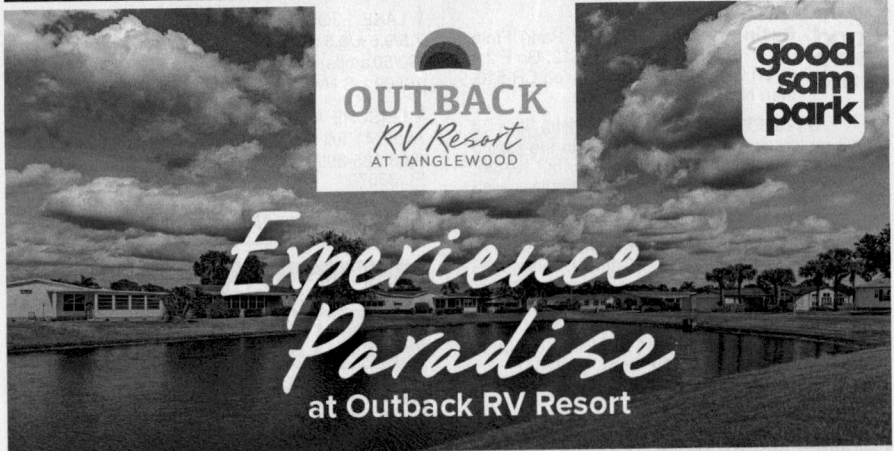

SEBRING (CONT)

OUTBACK RV RESORT AT TANGLEWOOD

good sam park **Ratings: 8.5/9.5★/9** (RV Park) From Jct of US-27 & CR-634A: Go N 0.7 mi on US-27 (L).

CENTRAL FLORIDA PREMIER RV RESORT

Outback RV Resort, for ages 40+, is located within Tanglewood, a 350-acre community in Sebring, FL. It includes 2 clubhouses, fishing, horseshoes, pickleball, shuffleboard, tennis, a swimming pool, a chipping green and more.

FAC: paved rds. (151 spaces). 100 Avail: 31 paved, 69 grass, patios, back-ins (50x85), accepts full hkup units only, 100 full hkups (30/50 amps), seasonal sites, cable, WiFi @ sites, rentals, dump, laundry, controlled access. **REC:** heated pool, pond, fishing, boating nearby, shuffleboard. Pet restrict (B/Q). Partial handicap access. No tents, Age restrict may apply. Big rig sites. 2021 rates: $50 to $99.
(863)837-4100 Lat: 27.51860, Lon: -81.50798
3000 Tanglewood Pkwy, Sebring, FL 33872
www.OutbackRvResort.com
See ad this page

SEBRING GARDENS RV COMMUNITY

good sam park **Ratings: 7/8★/7.5** (RV Park) From Jct of US-27 & Alt CR-634 (Flare Rd): Go W 0.3 mi on Flare Rd, then S 0.1 mi on Brunns Rd S (L).

EZ IN & OUT

Quiet, peaceful park with 5 acres adjacent for walking. Easy access from US-27. Close to stores and restaurants. Small, friendly get-to-know you park.

FAC: paved rds. (62 spaces). Avail: 30 grass, patios, 9 pull-thrus, (25x65), back-ins (25x50), 30 full hkups (30/50 amps), seasonal sites, WiFi @ sites, laundry. **REC:** pond, boating nearby, shuffleboard. Pet restrict (B). No tents. Big rig sites. 2021 rates: $28. no cc.
(863)385-7624 Lat: 27.48296, Lon: -81.48562
1920 Brunns Rd, Sebring, FL 33872
See ad previous page

SEBRING GROVE RV RESORT **Ratings: 7.5/7/7** (RV Park) Avail: 90 full hkups (30/50 amps). 2021 rates: $50. (863)382-1660, 4105 US-27 S, Sebring, FL 33870

SUNNY PINES RV & MHC **Ratings: 6.5/8/6.5** (RV Park) Avail: 50 full hkups (30/50 amps). 2021 rates: $45. (863)385-4144, 1200 US 27 N, Sebring, FL 33870

WHISPERING PINES VILLAGE **Ratings: 8/8.5★/7** (RV Park) Avail: 140 full hkups (30/50 amps). 2021 rates: $30 to $45. (863)385-8806, 2323 Brunns Rd, Sebring, FL 33872

WOODY'S RV RESORT **Ratings: 8.5/8/8.5** (RV Park) Avail: 30 full hkups (30/50 amps). 2021 rates: $39 to $45. (863)385-0500, 2009 Fortune Blvd, Sebring, FL 33870

SEFFNER — K2 *Hillsborough*

BETHESDA RV PARK **Ratings: 6.5/9★/8** (RV Park) Avail: 43 full hkups (30/50 amps). 2021 rates: $40. (813)330-0389, 5482 Roger Duncan Ln, Seffner, FL 33584

LAZYDAYS RV RESORT **Ratings: 10/9.5★/9** (RV Park) Avail: 300 full hkups (30/50 amps). 2021 rates: $39.99 to $65.99. (866)456-7015, 6210 County Rd 579, Seffner, FL 33584

SILVER SPRINGS — G3 *Marion*

LAKE WALDENA RESORT **Ratings: 8/8★/9** (Campground) Avail: 100 full hkups (30/50 amps). 2021 rates: $39 to $45. (352)625-2851, 13582 East Hwy 40, Lot#300, Silver Springs, FL 34488

SILVER SPRINGS RV PARK **Ratings: 8/8.5★/7** (RV Park) Avail: 38 full hkups (30/50 amps). 2021 rates: $39.95 to $51.95. (352)236-3700, 3151 NE 56th Ave, Silver Springs, FL 34488

THE SPRINGS RV RESORT

good sam park **Ratings: 7.5/8/8.5** (RV Park) From Jct of US-27/301/441 & SR-40, E 7 mi on SR-40 to NE 52nd Ct, N 0.1 mi (L). **FAC:** paved rds. (618 spaces). Avail: 280 grass, 256 pull-thrus, (30x60), back-ins (30x60), 280 full hkups (30/50 amps), seasonal sites, WiFi, dump, laundry, LP gas. **REC:** heated pool, boating nearby, shuffleboard. Pet restrict (B/Q). Partial handicap access. No tents. Big rig sites. 2021 rates: $50.
(352)236-5250 Lat: 29.21698, Lon: -82.06218
2950 NE 52nd Ct, Silver Springs, FL 34488
www.rvresorts.com
See ad opposite page

Show Your Good Sam Membership Card!

→ WHISPERING PINES RV PARK **Ratings: 5.5/7.5/7** (RV Park) 25 Avail: 24 full hkups, 1 W, 1 E (30 amps). 2021 rates: $30. (352)625-1295, 1700 NE 115TH Ave, Silver Springs, FL 34488

→ WILDERNESS RV RESORT AT SILVER SPRINGS **Ratings: 9/8.5/9.5** (Condo Park) Avail: 138 full hkups (30/50 amps). 2021 rates: $50. (352)625-1122, 2771 NE 102nd Ave Rd, Silver Springs, FL 34488

SNEADS — A1 *Gadsden*

↑ THREE RIVERS (Public State Park) From town, N 2 mi on SR-271 (R). 27 Avail: 27 W, 27 E (30/50 amps). 2021 rates: $16. (850)482-9006

SOPCHOPPY — B1 *Wakulla*

↓ OCHLOCKONEE RIVER (Public State Park) From Jct of SR-375 & US-319, S 4 mi on US-319 (L). 25 Avail: 25 W, 25 E (30 amps). 2021 rates: $18. (850)962-2771

SOUTH BAY — E4 *Palm Beach*

↖ SOUTH BAY RV CAMPGROUND (Public) From Jct of US-27 & SR-80 in South Bay, N 1.5 mi on US-27 (R). Avail: 72 full hkups (30/50 amps). 2021 rates: $21 to $30. (561)992-9045

SPRING HILL — J2 *Hernando*

↖ **BIG OAKS RV PARK & MOBILE HOME COMMUNITY**
Ratings: 8/8★/7 (RV Area in MH Park) Avail: 15 full hkups (30/50 amps). 2021 rates: $50. (352)799-5533, 16654 US-41, Spring Hill, FL 34610

↓ HOLIDAY SPRINGS RV RESORT **Ratings: 8.5/8.5/8** (RV Park) Avail: 58 full hkups (30/50 amps). 2021 rates: $65. (352)683-0034, 138 Travel Park Dr, Spring Hill, FL 34607

↖ **TOPICS RV RESORT**
Ratings: 7/8★/8 (RV Area in MH Park) Avail: 41 full hkups (30/50 amps). 2021 rates: $52 to $61. (888)563-7040, 13063 County Line Rd, Spring Hill, FL 34609

ST AUGUSTINE — B4 *St Johns*

↖ ANASTASIA (Public State Park) From Jct of US-1 & SR-312, E 2.5 mi on SR-312 to SR-AIA, N 1.5 mi (R). 139 Avail: 139 W, 139 E (20/30 amps). 2021 rates: $28. (904)461-2033

↙ COMPASS RV PARK **Ratings: 9.5/10★/9.5** (RV Park) Avail: 175 full hkups (30/50 amps). 2021 rates: $52 to $97. (877)394-6577, 1505 St Rd. 207, St Augustine, FL 32086

↓ FAVER-DYKES (Public State Park) From town: Go 15 mi S on US-1. 30 Avail: 30 W, 30 E (30 amps). 2021 rates: $18. (904)794-0997

↑ **NORTH BEACH CAMP RESORT**
Ratings: 9/9★/9 (Campground) From Jct of Bus US-1 & SR-A1A, N 4 mi on SR-A1A (L).

OCEAN OUT FRONT & RIVER OUT BACK!
Sunrise on the ocean, sunset on the river, a bit of Olde Florida in between! From spectacular ocean sunrises to river sunset vistas and endless stars at night, here's your ticket to the best camping vacation ever!

FAC: gravel rds. Avail: 150 gravel, 26 pull-thrus, (40x90), back-ins (40x60), 150 full hkups (30/50 amps), cable, WiFi @ sites, tent sites, rentals, dump, laundry, groc, LP bottles, controlled access. **REC:** heated pool, hot tub, Atlantic Ocean: boating nearby, shuffleboard, playground. Pet restrict (S/B/Q). Partial handicap access. Big rig sites. 2021 rates: $80 to $100, Military discount.
(800)542-8316 Lat: 29.95217, Lon: -81.30484
4125 Coastal Hwy (SR A1A), St Augustine, FL 32084
northbeachcamp.com
See ad next page

↖ ST AUGUSTINE BEACH KOA HOLIDAY **Ratings: 8.5/8★/7** (RV Park) 120 Avail: 94 full hkups, 26 W, 26 E (30/50 amps). 2021 rates: $75 to $100. (800)562-4022, 525 West Pope Road, St Augustine, FL 32080

← **ST AUGUSTINE RV RESORT**
Ratings: 6/8/7 (RV Park) Avail: 135 full hkups (30/50 amps). 2021 rates: $57.44 to $59.44. (904)824-9840, 2493 SR-207, ST Augustine, FL 32086

Find it fast! Use our alphabetized index of campgrounds and parks.

Good Sam's Trip Planner features tools and information designed to help you have the best road trip - every time. Visit GoodSam.com/Trip-Planner.

Reducing your speed to 55 mph from 65 mph may increase your fuel efficiency by as much as 15 percent; cut it to 55 from 70, and you could get a 23 percent improvement.

FL

ST AUGUSTINE (CONT)

← **STAGECOACH RV PARK**

good sam park **Ratings: 8/10★/9** (RV Park) From Jct of I-95 & SR-16 (exit 318), W 0.2 mi on SR-16 to Toms Rd, S 0.1 mi to CR 208, W 0.2 mi (L).

CLOSE TO THE FUN, OUT OF THE HASSLE
Ideally located with easy access to I-95, St Augustine's beautiful beaches & many attractions in America's oldest city. Enjoy a day trip to Daytona Beach or Jacksonville. Close to shopping, restaurants & surrounded by nature.

FAC: gravel rds. Avail: 80 grass, patios, 60 pull-thrus, (40x60), back-ins (40x60), 80 full hkups (30/50 amps), cable, WiFi @ sites, laundry, LP gas. **REC:** boating nearby. Pet restrict (S/B). Partial handicap access. No tents. Big rig sites. 2021 rates: $56, Military discount.
(904)824-2319 Lat: 29.91940, Lon: -81.42218
2711 CR 208, St Augustine, FL 32092
www.stagecoachrv.net
See ad previous page

Travel Services

← **GANDER RV & OUTDOORS OF ST AUGUSTINE** Your new hometown outfitter offering the best regional gear for all your outdoor needs. Your adventure awaits. **SERVICES:** tire, RV appliance, MH mechanical, gunsmithing svc, archery svc, sells outdoor gear, sells fishing gear, sells firearms, staffed RV wash, restrooms. RV Sales. RV supplies, LP gas, RV accessible. Hours: 9am to 7pm.
(866)413-8680 Lat: 29.925596, Lon: -81.414229
600 Outlet Mall Blvd, St Augustine, FL 32084
rv.ganderoutdoors.com

ST GEORGE ISLAND — B1 *Franklin*

→ ST GEORGE ISLAND (Public State Park) Cross the bridge to St George Island & go East. 60 Avail: 60 W, 60 E. 2021 rates: $24. (850)927-2111

Be prepared! Bridge, Tunnel & Ferry Regulations and Rules of the Road can be found in the front of the Guide.

ST JAMES CITY — E3 *Lee*

↑ **PINE ISLAND KOA**

good sam park **Ratings: 8.5/10★/8** (RV Park) Avail: 210 full hkups (30/50 amps). 2021 rates: $80 to $115. (888)563-7040, 5120 H Stringfellow Rd, St James City, FL 33956

ST PETERSBURG — L1 *Pinellas*

ST PETERSBURG See also Bradenton, Clearwater, Cortez, Dunedin, Ellenton, Largo, Odessa, Palm Harbor, Palmetto, Riverview, Ruskin & Tampa.

↗ ROBERTS MH & RV RESORT **Ratings: 8/8.5★/8** (RV Area in MH Park) Avail: 300 full hkups (30/50 amps). 2021 rates: $70 to $95. (727)577-6820, 3390 Gandy Blvd, St Petersburg, FL 33702

↖ ST PETERSBURG/MADIERA BEACH KOA **Ratings: 8.5/9.5★/8.5** (Campground) 267 Avail: 263 full hkups, 4 W, 4 E (30/50 amps). 2021 rates: $74 to $140. (727)392-2233, 5400 95th St N, St Petersburg, FL 33708

STARKE — B3 *Bradford*

↓ STARKE/GAINESVILLE NE KOA HOLIDAY **Ratings: 9.5/9★/8** (RV Park) Avail: 114 full hkups (30/50 amps). 2021 rates: $45 to $58. (800)562-8498, 1475 S Walnut St, Starke, FL 32091

STEINHATCHEE — B2 *Levy*

↑ **STEINHATCHEE RIVER CLUB**

good sam park **Ratings: 7/NA/8.5** (RV Park) Avail: 7 full hkups (30/50 amps). 2021 rates: $65. (352)498-3222, 5800 SW Hwy 358, Steinhatchee, FL 32359

SUGARLOAF KEY — F4 *Monroe*

↑ LAZY LAKES RV RESORT **Ratings: 8/7/7.5** (RV Park) Avail: 100 full hkups (30/50 amps). 2021 rates: $47.50 to $125. (305)745-1079, 311 Johnson Rd, Sugarloaf Key, FL 33042

↖ SUGARLOAF KEY/KEY WEST KOA HOLIDAY (Campground) (Rebuilding) Avail: 157 full hkups (30/50 amps). 2021 rates: $145 to $215. (305)745-3549, 251 SR 939, Summerland Key, FL 33042

SUMMERFIELD — H3 *Marion*

→ SOUTHERN OAKS RV RESORT **Ratings: 9/9★/8** (RV Park) Avail: 160 full hkups (30/50 amps). 2021 rates: $45 to $65. (352)347-2550, 14140 SE US Hwy 441, Summerfield, FL 34491

↓ **SUNKISSED VILLAGE RV RESORT**

good sam park **Ratings: 10/10★/10** (RV Resort) From jct US 27/441 & SE 92nd Loop: Go 1-1/3 mi S on US27/441 (R).

A PREMIERE PARK FOR THE VILLAGES!
All the great amenities you expect in a luxury resort with easy access to the extraordinary list of goods and services located around The Villages. Come be a part of a First Class community. The fun begins now and never ends!

FAC: paved rds. (267 spaces). Avail: 199 paved, patios, 33 pull-thrus, (35x70), back-ins (35x60), accepts full hkup units only, 199 full hkups (30/50 amps), seasonal sites, cable, WiFi @ sites, laundry, LP gas. **REC:** heated pool, hot tub, shuffleboard. Pet restrict (B/Q). Partial handicap access. No tents, Age restrict may apply. Big rig sites, eco-friendly. 2021 rates: $60.
(352)480-5000 Lat: 29.0145, Lon: -82.0113
14330 S US 441, Summerfield, FL 34491
sunkissedvillage.com
See ad page 286

Travel Services

↓ **CAMPING WORLD OF SUMMERFIELD/OCALA**

CAMPING WORLD As the nation's largest retailer of RV supplies, accessories, services and new and used RVs, Camping World is committed to making your total RV experience better. **SERVICES:** tire, RV appliance, MH mechanical, sells outdoor gear, sells firearms, staffed RV wash, restrooms. RV Sales. RV supplies, LP gas, RV accessible. Hours: 9am to 7pm.
(877)878-7662 Lat: 29.15153, Lon: -82.12312
14200 South US Hwy 441, Summerfield, FL 34491
www.campingworld.com

Got something to tell us? We welcome your comments and suggestions regarding the ratings for a particular campground, or our rating system in general. Please email them to: Parks@goodsam.com

SUMTERVILLE — H3 *Sumter*

SHADY BROOK GOLF & RV RESORT
good sam park **Ratings: 8/8.5★/9** (RV Park) From Jct of I-75 and CR-470 (exit 321), E 2.5 mi on CR-470 to US-301, N 0.5 mi to entrance (L). **FAC:** paved rds. (172 spaces). Avail: 100 grass, 5 pull-thrus, (45x75), back-ins (40x60), 100 full hkups (50 amps), seasonal sites, WiFi, dump, laundry. **REC:** boating nearby, golf. Pets OK. Partial handicap access. No tents, Age restrict may apply. Big rig sites. 2021 rates: $34 to $44.
(352)568-2244 Lat: 28.75648, Lon: -82.06170
178 N US 301, Sumterville, FL 33585
www.shadybrookrvandgolf.com
See ad page 239

SUNRISE — E5 *Broward*

MARKHAM PARK & RANGE (Public) From Jct of US-441 & SR-84, W 11 mi on SR-84 to entrance across from Weston Rd (R). Avail: 88 full hkups (30/50 amps). 2021 rates: $31 to $70. (954)357-8868

TALLAHASSEE — A1 *Leon*

BAYHEAD RV & MHP **Ratings: 8/8★/8** (RV Area in MH Park) Avail: 11 full hkups (30/50 amps). 2021 rates: $55. (850)580-1197, 356 Bayhead Dr, Tallahassee, FL 32304

BIG OAK RV PARK **Ratings: 8/9.5★/8** (RV Park) Avail: 117 full hkups (30/50 amps). 2021 rates: $57. (850)562-4660, 4024 N Monroe St, Tallahassee, FL 32303

TALLAHASSEE RV PARK
good sam park **Ratings: 9/9★/9** (RV Park) Avail: 66 full hkups (30/50 amps). 2021 rates: $55.60. (850)878-7641, 6504 Mahan Dr, Tallahassee, FL 32308

TAMPA — K2 *Hillsborough*

A SPOTLIGHT Introducing Tampa's colorful attractions appearing at the front of this state section.

TAMPA See also Clearwater, Dover, Dunedin, Holiday, Largo, Lutz, New Port Richey, Odessa, Palm Harbor, Palmetto, Riverview, Ruskin, Seffner, St Petersburg, Tarpon Springs, Thonotosassa, Wesley Chapel & Zephyrhills.

BAY BAYOU RV RESORT
good sam park **Ratings: 9/10★/9.5** (RV Park) From Jct of I-275 (exit 47) & SR-580/Hillsborough Ave: Go W 10.8 mi, then N 0.5 mi on Country Way Blvd, then W 0.75 mi on Memorial Hwy (L).

PREMIER WATERFRONT RESORT IN TAMPA
Natural surroundings on Double Branch Creek just minutes from Tampa and Clearwater's top attractions and Gulf beaches. Bay Bayou offers deluxe facilities and amenities with a friendly staff to assist you.
FAC: paved rds. (300 spaces). 190 Avail: 53 paved, 137 gravel, patios, back-ins (35x60), accepts full hkup units only, 190 full hkups (30/50 amps), seasonal sites, cable, WiFi @ sites, dump, laundry, LP gas, firewood, controlled access. **REC:** heated pool, Double Branch Creek: fishing, kayaking/canoeing, boating nearby, shuffleboard. Pet restrict (B/Q). Partial handicap access. No tents. Big rig sites, eco-friendly. 2021 rates: $50 to $96, Military discount.
(813)855-1000 Lat: 28.02971, Lon: -82.63068
8492 Manatee Bay Dr, Tampa, FL 33635
www.baybayou.com
See ad page 231

MILITARY PARK RACCOON CREEK REC AREA (MACDILL AFB) (Public) From town: Go 5 mi SW on FL-618 Toll/Selmon Expwy, then 2 mi S on FL-573 S, then 1 mi S on Boundary Rd, then 1 mi S on Hangar Loop Dr, then 2 mi S on Marina Bay Dr (E). 389 Avail: 268 full hkups, 21 W, 21 E (30/50 amps). 2021 rates: $17 to $23. (813)840-6919

SAVE! Camping World coupons can be found at the front and back of this Guide!

Time and rates don't stand still. Remember that last year's rates serve as a guideline only. Call ahead for the most current rate information.

Got a different point of view? We want to know. Rate the campgrounds you visit using the rating guidelines located in front of this Guide, then compare your ratings to ours.

TAMPA (CONT)

TAMPA RV PARK

good sam park **Ratings: 6/8★/7** (RV Park) From Jct of I-275 & SR-582 (Exit 51), E 0.2 mi on SR-582 (Fowler Ave) to US-41, S 0.7 mi on US-41 (Nebraska Ave) to E Bougainvillea Ave, W 250 ft (L). **FAC:** paved/gravel rds. Avail: 86 grass, patios, 15 pull-thrus, (20x50), back-ins (20x50), 86 full hkups (30/50 amps), WiFi @ sites, laundry. Pet restrict (S/B/Q). No tents. 2021 rates: $38 to $47, Military discount.
(813)971-3460 Lat: 28.04323, Lon: -82.45219
10314 N Nebraska Ave, Tampa, FL 33612
www.tampa-rv-park-camp-nebraska.com
See ad previous page

TARPON SPRINGS — K1 *Pinellas*

HICKORY POINT RV PARK **Ratings: 7/8★/8** (Campground) Avail: 47 full hkups (30/50 amps). 2021 rates: $77 to $225. (727)937-7357, 1181 Anclote Rd, Tarpon Springs, FL 34689

TAVARES — H3 *Lake*

FISHERMAN'S COVE GOLF & RV RESORT

good sam park **Ratings: 10/10★/9.5** (RV Park) From Jct of US 441 & SR-19, SW 3.4 mi on SR-19 to N. Eichelberger, N 0.1 mi (L).

FLORIDA'S FAVORITE LAKEFRONT RESORT
Friends, fishing and golf are always a winning combination. Live the good life on scenic Lake Harris. Close to shopping, restaurants & attractions. Come see our new luxury upgrades.

FAC: paved rds. Avail: 300 paved, patios, 8 pull-thrus, (30x60), back-ins (30x60), 300 full hkups (30/50 amps), cable, WiFi @ sites, rentals, dump, laundry, controlled access. **REC:** heated pool, hot tub, Harris Chain of Lakes: fishing, marina, kayaking/canoeing, boating nearby, golf, shuffleboard. Pet restrict (B). No tents. Big rig sites, eco-friendly. 2021 rates: $70 to $85.
(352)343-1233 Lat: 28.76515, Lon: -81.75411
3950 N Eichelberger Rd, Tavares, FL 32778
www.fishermanscoverv.us
See ad pages 274, 275

THE VILLAGES — H3 *Sumter*

SUNSHINE VILLAGE

good sam park **Ratings: 9.5/10★/9.5** (RV Park) From jct CR 466 & US 301: Go 13 mi S on US 301, then 10 mi S on SR 471, then 1/2 mi W on W Central Ave (L). **FAC:** paved rds. 85 Avail: 67 paved, 18 gravel, back-ins (30x60), 85 full hkups (30/50 amps), WiFi @ sites, $, rentals, dump, laundry. **REC:** heated pool, boating nearby. Pet restrict (Q). Partial handicap access. No tents. Big rig sites. 2021 rates: $49 to $89, Military discount.
(352)793-8626 Lat: 28.60990, Lon: -82.06724
2236 SE 100 Lane, Webster, FL 33597
sunshinevillageflorida.com
See primary listing at Webster and ad this page

THONOTOSASSA — K2 *Hillsborough*

HAPPY TRAVELER RV RESORT **Ratings: 8/8.5/8.5** (RV Park) Avail: 82 full hkups (30/50 amps). 2021 rates: $50 to $60. (813)986-3094, 9401 E Fowler Ave, Thonotosassa, FL 33592

HILLSBOROUGH RIVER (Public State Park) From Jct of US-301 & SR-54, S 7 mi on US-301 (R). 98 Avail: 98 W, 98 E (30/50 amps). 2021 rates: $24. (813)987-6771

SOUTHERN AIRE RV RESORT

good sam park **Ratings: 7.5/8/8** (RV Area in MH Park) From Jct of I-4 (Exit 10) & CR-579: Go N 3.9 mi on CR-579, then E 200 ft on Florence Ave (R). **FAC:** paved rds. (430 spaces). Avail: 113 grass, 4 pull-thrus, (30x60), back-ins (30x60), 113 full hkups (30/50 amps), seasonal sites, WiFi, rentals, dump, laundry, LP bottles. **REC:** heated pool, hot tub, pond, fishing, shuffleboard. Pet restrict (S/B/Q). No tents. 2021 rates: $50.
(813)986-1596 Lat: 28.06454, Lon: -82.30127
10511 Florence Ave, Thonotosassa, FL 33592
www.rvresorts.com
See ad this page

SPANISH MAIN RV RESORT **Ratings: 8/9.5★/8** (RV Area in MH Park) Avail: 30 full hkups (30/50 amps). 2021 rates: $48 to $60. (813)986-2415, 12110 Spanish Main Resort Trail, Thonotosassa, FL 33592

TITUSVILLE — H5 *Brevard*

CHRISTMAS RV PARK **Ratings: 8/9★/7** (RV Park) Avail: 10 full hkups (30/50 amps). 2021 rates: $52 to $72. (407)568-5207, 25525 E Colonial Dr, Christmas, FL 32709

MANATEE HAMMOCK PARK (Public) From Jct of I-95 & SR-50 (exit 215), E 3.3 mi on SR-50 to US-1, S 3.7 mi (L). 186 Avail: 166 full hkups, 20 W, 20 E (30/50 amps). 2021 rates: $26. (321)264-5083

SEASONS IN THE SUN RV RESORT **Ratings: 8.5/9★/9** (RV Park) Avail: 175 full hkups (30/50 amps). 2021 rates: $55 to $85. (321)385-0440, 2400 Seasons in the Sun Blvd, Mims, FL 32754

THE GREAT OUTDOORS RV NATURE & GOLF RESORT

good sam park **Ratings: 10/10★/10** (Condo Park) From Jct of I-95 (exit 215) & SR-50: Go W 0.5 mi on SR-50 (Cheney Hwy) to entrance rd (L).

STAY A NIGHT OR A LIFETIME!
Near Florida's premier attractions. Kennedy Space Center, Orlando theme parks, Daytona racing, cruise terminals, casinos. Enjoy onsite restaurants, 18-hole golf course, tennis, church, pools, fishing, pickle ball & much more.

FAC: paved rds. (600 spaces). Avail: 50 paved, patios, back-ins (40x80), 50 full hkups (30/50 amps), seasonal sites, WiFi @ sites, $, dump, laundry, LP gas, restaurant, controlled access. **REC:** heated pool, hot tub, Lake Judy: fishing, boating nearby, golf, shuffleboard. Pet restrict (Q). Partial handicap access. No tents. Big rig sites, eco-friendly. 2021 rates: $60 to $75.
(321)269-5004 Lat: 28.55026, Lon: -80.86089
125 Plantation Dr, Titusville, FL 32780
www.tgoresort.com
See ad this page

TITUSVILLE/KENNEDY SPACE CENTER KOA **Ratings: 8/8.5★/6.5** (Campground) Avail: 10 full hkups (30/50 amps). 2021 rates: $45 to $64. (321)267-2417, 4513 W Main St, Mims, FL 32754

WHISPERING PINES

good sam park **Ratings: 8/9★/8.5** (RV Area in MH Park) From Jct I-95 (exit 215) & Hwy 50: Go E 3 mi on Hwy 50 (Cheney Hwy) (R). **FAC:** paved rds. (200 spaces). 63 Avail: 30 gravel, 33 grass, patios, back-ins (26x50), 63 full hkups (30/50 amps), seasonal sites, WiFi, laundry. **REC:** boating nearby, shuffleboard. Pet restrict (S). No tents, Age restrict may apply, eco-friendly. 2021 rates: $50. no cc.
(321)267-2081 Lat: 28.55719, Lon: -80.80255
359 Cheney Hwy, Titusville, FL 32780
mywhisperingpines.com
See ad this page

TRENTON — B3 *Gilchrist*

OTTER SPRINGS PARK & CAMPGROUND (Public) From Jct of US-19 & SR-26 (Fanning Springs): E 2 mi on SR-26 to CR-232, N 1.7 mi to 70th St (Otter Springs Rd), W 1 mi (R). Avail: 100 full hkups (30/50 amps). 2021 rates: $31. (800)883-9107

VALPARAISO — F2 *Okaloosa*

MILITARY PARK EGLIN FAMCAMP (EGLIN AFB) (Public) From town: Go 1/2 mi E on Lincoln Ave, then 1-1/2 mi S on John Sims Pkwy (L). Avail: 82 full hkups (30/50 amps). 2021 rates: $29. (850)883-1243

TRAVELING WITH YOUR PET: Consistency is key. Dogs thrive on routine, try to maintain a consistent schedule of feeding, walking and playtime. If your dog is in good shape, summertime swimming holes are great for extra exercise, but play it safe with a canine flotation jacket for peace of mind in unfamiliar waters. If bad weather keeps you inside the rig, interactive doggy ""brain games" can engage a bored pet.

VENICE — D3 *Sarasota*

FLORIDA PINES MOBILE HOME COURT
Ratings: 8/9.5★/8 (RV Area in MH Park) From Jct of I-75 (exit 193) & Jacaranda Blvd: Go S 4 mi on Jacaranda Blvd, then N 0.5 mi on SR-776(Englewood Rd) (R). **FAC:** paved rds. (130 spaces). Avail: 30 paved, patios, back-ins (45x65), accepts full hkup units only, 30 full hkups (30/50 amps), seasonal sites, cable, WiFi @ sites, laundry. **REC:** pond, fishing, boating nearby, shuffleboard. Pets OK. No tents, Age restrict may apply. Big rig sites, eco-friendly. 2021 rates: $48 to $60. no cc.
(941)493-0019 Lat: 27.04838, Lon: -82.40494
150 Satulah Cir, Venice, FL 34293
www.goodsamcamping.com.s3.amazonaws.-com/gsparks/731000284/index.html
See ad opposite page

RAMBLERS REST RV CAMPGROUND
Ratings: 8.5/9.5★/8.5 (RV Area in MH Park) 325 Avail: 313 full hkups, 12 W, 12 E (30/50 amps). 2021 rates: $42 to $110. (888)563-7040, 1300 N River Rd, Venice, FL 34293

VERO BEACH — L6 *Indian River*

MIDWAY ESTATES/MHP **Ratings: 7.5/NA/8** (RV Area in MH Park) Avail: 50 full hkups (50 amps). 2021 rates: $45. (772)567-2764, 1950 S US Hwy 1, Vero Beach, FL 32962

SUNSHINE TRAVEL RV RESORT
Ratings: 9/9.5/8.5 (RV Park) Avail: 171 full hkups (30/50 amps). 2021 rates: $52 to $77. (888)563-7040, 9455 108th Ave, Vero Beach, FL 32967

WALDO — B3 *Alachua*

DIXIELAND RV PARK - GAINESVILLE
Ratings: 8/9★/9 (RV Park) From the Jct of US 301 & SR 24 (in Waldo) N 1.5 mi on US 301 (L). **FAC:** gravel rds. (150 spaces). Avail: 48 grass, patios, 40 pull-thrus, (30x70), back-ins (30x60), 48 full hkups (30/50 amps), seasonal sites, WiFi @ sites, tent sites, dump, laundry, LP gas, firewood, restaurant, controlled access. **REC:** pond, fishing, boating nearby. Pet restrict (Q). Big rig sites, eco-friendly. 2021 rates: $40 to $100.
(352)468-3988 Lat: 29.81603, Lon: -82.16884
17500 NE US Hwy 301, Waldo, FL 32694
gainesvillervpark.com
See ad page 255

WAUCHULA — L3 *Hardee*

CRYSTAL LAKE VILLAGE **Ratings: 9/9.5/8.5** (RV Park) Avail: 84 full hkups (30/50 amps). 2021 rates: $30 to $40. (800)661-3582, 237 Maxwell Dr, Wauchula, FL 33873

PEACE RIVER RV RESORT
Ratings: 8/8.5/7 (Membership Park) 400 Avail: 200 full hkups, 200 W, 200 E (30/50 amps). 2021 rates: $43 to $57. (888)563-7040, 2555 US Hwy 17 South, Wauchula, FL 33873

WEBSTER — J3 *Sumter*

FLORIDA GRANDE MOTORCOACH RESORT **Ratings: 9.5/10★/9.5** (Condo Park) Avail: 214 full hkups (50 amps). 2021 rates: $70. (352)569-1169, 9675 SE 49th Terrace, Webster, FL 33597

SUNSHINE VILLAGE
Ratings: 9.5/10★/9.5 (RV Park) From jct CR 478 & SR 471: Go S 0.3 mi on SR 471, then W 0.6 mi on W Central Ave (L). **FAC:** paved rds. 85 Avail: 67 paved, 18 grass, back-ins (30x60), 85 full hkups (30/50 amps), WiFi @ sites, $, rentals, dump, laundry. **REC:** heated pool, boating nearby. Pet restrict (Q). Partial handicap access. No tents. Big rig sites. 2021 rates: $49 to $89, Military discount.
(352)793-8626 Lat: 28.60990, Lon: -82.06724
2236 SE 100 Lane, Webster, FL 33597
www.sunshinevillageflorida.com
See ad opposite page

WEBSTER RV RESORT **Ratings: 8.5/8.5★/8.5** (RV Park) Avail: 80 full hkups (30/50 amps). 2021 rates: $40 to $49. (352)793-6765, 2085 County Road 740, Webster, FL 33597

Enjoy the scenery as you travel North America. We exclusively rate campgrounds for their visual appearance and environmental quality, and represent their score, 1 through 10, as the third rating in our Triple Rating System.

WESLEY CHAPEL — J2 *Pasco*

QUAIL RUN RV RESORT
Ratings: 10/9.5★/10 (RV Park) From Jct of I-75 (exit 279) & SR-54: Go W 0.5 mi on SR-54 then N 2 mi on Old Pasco Rd (R).

NO RIG TOO BIG
Nestle into our friendly country setting. Enjoy our rec hall, exercise room, pool & fun activities. Fabulous shopping & restaurants close by. NEW SUPER SIZED BIG RIG SITES with concrete pads & patios. Your Home Away from Home
FAC: paved rds. (292 spaces). 242 Avail: 148 paved, 94 all weather, patios, 39 pull-thrus, (35x70), back-ins (35x55), 242 full hkups (30/50 amps), seasonal sites, cable, WiFi @ sites, dump, laundry, groc, LP gas, controlled access. **REC:** heated pool, pond, fishing, boating nearby, shuffleboard. Pet restrict (S/B/Q). Partial handicap access. No tents, Age restrict may apply. Big rig sites, eco-friendly. 2021 rates: $64 to $90.
(800)582-7084 Lat: 28.25814, Lon: -82.34162
6946 Old Pasco Rd, Wesley Chapel, FL 33544
www.quailrunrv.com
See ad next page, 218

WEST PALM BEACH — D5 *Palm Beach*

LION COUNTRY SAFARI KOA
Ratings: 9.5/9.5★/9 (Campground) From Jct of I-95 & Southern Blvd (exit 68/SR-80), W 15.5 mi on Southern Blvd to Lion Country Safari Rd, N (right) 2 mi (E). **FAC:** paved rds. (211 spaces). Avail: 104 dirt, patios, 52 pull-thrus, (30x50), back-ins (24x45), 104 full hkups (30/50 amps), seasonal sites, WiFi @ sites, tent sites, rentals, laundry, groc, LP gas, controlled access. **REC:** heated pool, shuffleboard, playground. Pet restrict (B/Q). Partial handicap access. Big rig sites. 2021 rates: $99, Military discount. ATM.
(561)793-9797 Lat: 26.71411, Lon: -80.31819
2000 Lion Country Safari Rd, West Palm Beach, FL 33470
www.lioncountrysafari.com
See ad page 210

Find Good Sam member specials at GanderOutdoors.com

VACATION INN RESORT OF THE PALM BEACHES **Ratings: 9.5/10★/10** (Condo Park) Avail: 50 full hkups (30/50 amps). 2021 rates: $56 to $100. (561)848-6170, 6500 N. Military Trl, West Palm Beach, FL 33407

Things to See and Do

LION COUNTRY SAFARI A 245 acre wild animal preserve with over 800 wild animals roaming free within inches of your vehicle. Visit Safari World Amusement Park with giraffe feeding, carousel, animals, gift shop, restaurant & more. Partial handicap access. RV accessible. Restrooms. Food. Hours: 9:30am to 4:30pm. Adult fee: $39.00. ATM.
(561)793-1084 Lat: 26.71339, Lon: -80.32249
2003 Lion Country Safari Rd, Loxahatchee, FL 33470
www.lioncountrysafari.com
See ad page 210

WEWAHITCHKA — F3 *Gulf*

DEAD LAKES SRA (Public State Park) From jct Hwy-71 & Hwy-22: Go 4 mi N on Hwy-71. Avail: 12 E. 2021 rates: $10 to $50. (850)639-2702

WHITE SPRINGS — A3 *Columbia*

STEPHEN FOSTER FOLK CULTURE CENTER (Public State Park) From Jct of I-75 & SR-136 (exit 439), E 3 mi on SR-136 to US-41, N 0.1 mi (L). 39 Avail: 39 W, 39 E (30 amps). 2021 rates: $20. (386)397-4331

WILDWOOD — H3 *Sumter*

RAILS END RV & MHP **Ratings: 8.5/8★/7.5** (RV Area in MH Park) Avail: 54 full hkups (30/50 amps). 2021 rates: $40. (352)748-1224, 7250 E SR 44, Wildwood, FL 34785

THOUSAND PALMS RV RESORT **Ratings: 8/8.5★/8.5** (RV Park) 95 Avail: 77 full hkups, 18 W, 18 E (30/50 amps). 2021 rates: $50 to $55. (352)748-2237, 6545 W State Rd 44, Lake Panasoffkee, FL 33538

THREE FLAGS RV CAMPGROUND
Ratings: 9/8.5★/8 (Membership Park) Avail: 211 full hkups (30/50 amps). 2021 rates: $55 to $65. (888)563-7040, 1755 E SR Rd 44, Wildwood, FL 34785

Quail Run R.V. Resort
"No Rig Too Big!"
6946 Old Pasco Road, Wesley Chapel, FL 33544
Exit 279 West Off I-75 to SR54 • (813) 973-0999
For Reservations Only: 1-800-582-7084
www.quailrunrv.com • info@quailrunrv.com
Close to Attractions, Restaurants, Shopping and Entertainment!
See listing Wesley Chapel, FL
FREE 70+ CHANNEL CABLE
FREE WI-FI
Selected By BIG RIGS Best Bets
www.big-rigs-rv.com
good sam park
2022 Top Rated 10/9.5★/10

WILDWOOD (CONT)

WILDWOOD RV VILLAGE

good sam park **Ratings: 9/10★/8** (RV Park) From jct I-75 & Hwy 44 (exit 329): Go 300 feet E on Hwy 44 (L).

EASY ACCESS TO I-75 & THE VILLAGES
A great place to spend the night or all season. This park is all new. Ownership, attitude and amenities. Conveniently located by The Villages and all it has to offer.

FAC: paved rds. Avail: 233 grass, 86 pull-thrus, (30x60), back-ins (30x40), 233 full hkups (30/50 amps), cable, WiFi @ sites, dump, laundry, LP gas, firewood. **REC:** heated pool, boating nearby, shuffleboard. Pets OK. Partial handicap access. No tents. Big rig sites, eco-friendly. 2021 rates: $50 to $74.
(352)748-2774 Lat: 28.87461, Lon: -82.08931
882 E. State Road 44, Wildwood, FL 34785
wildwoodrvvillage.com
See ad pages 280, 281

WILLISTON — G2 *Marion*

WILLISTON CROSSINGS RV RESORT

good sam park **Ratings: 10/10★/10** (RV Resort) S-bnd: From Jct of I-75 & CR-121/Williston Rd (Exit 382), SW 15 mi on CR-121/Williston Rd to US 27/41, S 0.3 mi to US 27/Alt 27, SE 0.4 mi to NE 5th St, N 0.2 mi (R); or N-bnd: From Jct of I-75 & US 27 (Exit 354) NW 21 mi on US 27 to NE 5th St, N 0.2 mi (R).

NORTHERN FLORIDA'S BEST KEPT SECRET
Our one-week campers wind up staying all year! Williston Crossings offers a pristine 135-acre paradise complete with large, paved sites, a lively social scene, onsite amenities, free WiFi and cable TV, and so much more!

FAC: paved rds. Avail: 455 paved, patios, 35 pull-thrus, (35x100), back-ins (40x70), accepts full hkup units only, 455 full hkups (30/50 amps), cable, WiFi @ sites, laundry, LP gas, controlled access. **REC:** heated pool, Williston Crossing Lake: boating nearby, shuffleboard, playground. Pet restrict (Q). Partial handicap access. No tents. Big rig sites, eco-friendly. 2021 rates: $70 to $80.
(877)785-4405 Lat: 29.40038, Lon: -82.43993
410 NE 5th St, Williston, FL 32696
willistoncrossingrv.com
See ad pages 256, 257

WIMAUMA — L2 *Hillsborough*

LITTLE MANATEE RIVER (Public State Park) From jct Hwy 674 & US 301: Go 5 mi S on US 301, then W on Lightfoot Rd. 27 Avail: 27 W, 27 E (50 amps). 2021 rates: $22. (813)671-5005

WINTER GARDEN — J3 *Orange*

STAGE STOP CAMPGROUND

good sam park **Ratings: 9/9★/8.5** (RV Park) From Jct FL Tpk (exit 267B) & Hwy 50: Go W 2.5 mi on Hwy 50 (L). **FAC:** paved rds. (248 spaces). Avail: 158 grass, patios, back-ins (35x50), 158 full hkups (30/50 amps), WiFi @ sites, dump, laundry, groc. **REC:** pool, boating nearby, shuffleboard. Pet restrict (Q). Partial handicap access. No tents. 2021 rates: $55.
(407)656-8000 Lat: 28.55064, Lon: -81.59929
14400 W Colonial Dr, Winter Garden, FL 34787
stagestoprvcampground.com
See ad this page

WINTER GARDEN RV RESORT

good sam park **Ratings: 8/7.5/7** (RV Area in MH Park) Avail: 175 full hkups (30/50 amps). 2021 rates: $50 to $69. (888)563-7040, 13905 W Colonial Dr, Winter Garden, FL 34787

WINTER HAVEN — K3 *Polk*

CYPRESS CAMPGROUND & RV PARK **Ratings: 8/9★/8.5** (RV Park) Avail: 59 full hkups (30/50 amps). 2021 rates: $46.95 to $59.95. (863)324-7400, 7400 Cypress Gardens Blvd, Winter Haven, FL 33884

EAST HAVEN RV PARK **Ratings: 7.5/8/7.5** (RV Park) Avail: 50 full hkups (30/50 amps). 2021 rates: $45. (863)324-2624, 4320 Dundee Rd, Winter Haven, FL 33884

HAMMONDELL CAMPSITES **Ratings: 7.5/7.5/8** (RV Area in MH Park) Avail: 53 full hkups (30/50 amps). 2021 rates: $55 to $60. (863)324-5775, 5601 Cypress Gardens Rd, Winter Haven, FL 33884

THE OUTPOST RV RESORT **Ratings: 8.5/9★/7.5** (RV Park) Avail: 55 full hkups (30/50 amps). 2021 rates: $53 to $58. (863)289-0104, 2250 US Highway 92, Winter Haven, FL 33881

ZEPHYRHILLS — J2 *Pasco*

BAKER ACRES RV RESORT **Ratings: 9/NA/8** (RV Park) Avail: 60 full hkups (30/50 amps). 2021 rates: $44 to $51. (813)782-3950, 7820 Wire Rd, Zephyrhills, FL 33540

DUCKY'S DAY OFF RV PARK

good sam park **Ratings: 8/9★/7** (RV Park) From S Jct of US-301 & SR-54: Go W 2.5 mi on SR-54 (L). **FAC:** paved rds. (350 spaces). Avail: 40 grass, patios, 15 pull-thrus, (16x45), back-ins (16x40), 40 full hkups (30/50 amps), seasonal sites, WiFi, laundry. **REC:** pool, pond, shuffleboard. Pet restrict (S/B/Q). No tents, Age restrict may apply. 2021 rates: $45. no cc.
(813)782-8223 Lat: 28.21859, Lon: -82.24739
34408 State Rd. 54 West, Zephyrhills, FL 33543
duckysdayoff.com
See ad this page

FOREST LAKE ESTATES RV RESORT

good sam park **Ratings: 9/8★/8.5** (RV Park) Avail: 194 full hkups (30/50 amps). 2021 rates: $42 to $54. (888)563-7040, 41219 Hockey Dr, Zephyrhills, FL 33540

GLEN HAVEN RV RESORT **Ratings: 9/9★/8** (RV Area in MH Park) Avail: 50 full hkups (30/50 amps). 2021 rates: $34 to $46. (813)782-1856, 37251 Chancey Rd, Zephyrhills, FL 33541

HAPPY DAYS RV PARK

good sam park **Ratings: 9/8.5★/8.5** (RV Park) From Jct of US-301 & SR-54: Go W 1.25 mi on SR-54, then S 0.3 mi on Allen Rd (R). **FAC:** paved rds. (292 spaces). Avail: 130 grass, back-ins (30x60), accepts full hkup units only, 130 full hkups (30/50 amps), seasonal sites, WiFi @ sites, $, rentals, dump, laundry. **REC:** heated pool, shuffleboard. Pet restrict (S/B/Q). No tents, Age restrict may apply. Big rig sites. 2021 rates: $34 to $39, Military discount.
(813)788-4858 Lat: 28.22399, Lon: -82.20536
4603 Allen Rd, Zephyrhills, FL 33541
happy-days-rv-park.com
See ad this page

HILLCREST RV RESORT **Ratings: 8/8.5★/8** (RV Park) Avail: 146 full hkups (30/50 amps). 2021 rates: $39. (813)782-1947, 4421 Lane Rd, Zephyrhills, FL 33541

LANDING RESORT **Ratings: 9/9★/8** (RV Park) Avail: 22 full hkups (30/50 amps). 2021 rates: $45. (813)783-1644, 37400 Chancey Rd, Zephyrhills, FL 33541

LEISURE DAYS RV RESORT **Ratings: 8/9.5★/8** (RV Park) Avail: 40 full hkups (50 amps). 2021 rates: $35 to $42. (813)788-2631, 34533 Leisure Days Drive, Zephyrhills, FL 33541

MAJESTIC OAKS RV RESORT **Ratings: 9/8★/8.5** (RV Area in MH Park) Avail: 45 full hkups (30/50 amps). 2021 rates: $51. (813)783-7518, 3751 Laurel Valley Blvd, Zephyrhills, FL 33542

RV Tech Tips - Hose Close: To keep your RV's cabinet doors closed in case the standard door-catches fail while on the road, use a 6-inch length of 1/2-inch inside-diameter clear plastic hose (from the hardware store) and slip the hose between the handles.

FL

ZEPHYRHILLS (CONT)

PALM VIEW GARDENS RV RESORT

good sam park **Ratings: 7.5/8.5★/8** (RV Area in MH Park) From Jct of US-301 & SR-54: Go S 2 mi on US-301 (R). **FAC:** paved rds. (497 spaces). Avail: 47 grass, patios, back-ins (30x60), 47 full hkups (30/50 amps), seasonal sites, WiFi, rentals, laundry, LP gas. **REC:** heated pool, pond, fishing, boating nearby. Pet restrict (S/B/Q). No tents. 2021 rates: $50.
(813)782-8685 Lat: 28.20640, Lon: -82.18755
3331 Gall Blvd, Zephyrhills, FL 33541
www.rvresorts.com
See ad previous page

RAINBOW VILLAGE RV RESORT **Ratings: 9/9★/8.5** (RV Area in MH Park) Avail: 65 full hkups (30/50 amps). 2021 rates: $37 to $46. (813)782-5075, 4150 Lane Rd, Zephyrhills, FL 33541

SETTLER'S REST RV RESORT **Ratings: 7/8.5★/8** (RV Area in MH Park) Avail: 60 full hkups (30/50 amps). 2021 rates: $38 to $44. (813)782-2003, 37549 Chancey Rd, Zephyrhills, FL 33541

SOUTHERN CHARM RV RESORT **Ratings: 8/8/8.5** (RV Area in MH Park) Avail: 47 full hkups (30/50 amps). 2021 rates: $37 to $42. (813)783-3477, 37811 Chancey Rd, Zephyrhills, FL 33541

SWEETWATER RV RESORT **Ratings: 9/9.5★/8.5** (RV Area in MH Park) Avail: 50 full hkups (30/50 amps). 2021 rates: $38 to $44. (813)788-7513, 37647 Chancey Rd, Zephyrhills, FL 33541

WATERS EDGE RV RESORT **Ratings: 8.5/9.5★/8.5** (RV Area in MH Park) Avail: 75 full hkups (30/50 amps). 2021 rates: $35 to $70. (813)783-2708, 39146 Otis Allen Rd, Zephyrhills, FL 33540

ZEPHYR PALMS RV RESORT **Ratings: 8.5/8★/8** (RV Park) Avail: 46 full hkups (30/50 amps). 2021 rates: $50. (813)782-5610, 35120 State Road 54, Zephyrhills, FL 33541

ZOLFO SPRINGS — L3 *Hardee*

THE OASIS AT ZOLFO SPRINGS **Ratings: 7.5/7/6.5** (RV Park) Avail: 60 full hkups (30/50 amps). 2021 rates: $40. (863)735-0030, 937 Sabal Palm Dr, Zolfo Springs, FL 33890

CLEANING YOUR RV: Air out your RV. Open the windows. Dust all surfaces and the dash area. Use lens wipes for the glass gauges. Use the proper product if you have leather seats. For cloth seats, you can vacuum or launder the removable covers. Vacuum the floors and carpeting, your carpeted sidewalls, curtains, and draperies as well. Use a hand vacuum for inside cabinets, lockers, and drawers. Inspect for rodent droppings, mold, and mildew as well. Check for water leaks while you have your head in the cabinets. Wash the inside of windows.

Each privately owned campground has been rated three times. The first rating is for development of facilities. The second one is for cleanliness and physical characteristics of restrooms and showers. The third is for campground visual appearance and environmental quality.

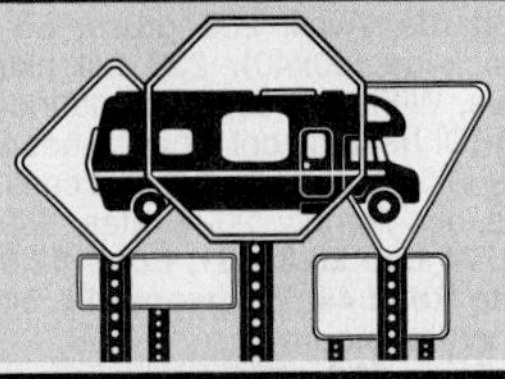

Know The Rules Of The Road!

RV-related laws in every state and province. Also in this section is a roundup of bridge and tunnel restrictions

Find the Rules in the front of this Guide.

YOU ARE HERE

Georgia

DID YOU KNOW?

Home to dozens of famous specters, ghost hunters consider Savannah to be one of the most haunted cities in America.

etty Images/iStockphoto

Georgia never fails to enchant visitors. From the scenic mountain landscapes of the north to the rugged Atlantic coast, there's beauty to be found across the Peach State. Relics of the Old South mingle with modern sensibilities.

Atlanta Achievements

Atlanta has enough tourist attractions to go toe-to-toe with any of the nation's heavy hitters, from Orlando to LA. Sample Coke from around the world at the World of Coca-Cola, tour one of the world's largest exhibits of aquatic creatures at the Georgia Aquarium or walk above the forest canopy at the Atlanta Botanical Garden.

Sweet Savannah

Georgia's Atlantic coast is bejeweled with a glittering city, Savannah. At first glance, it might seem like time has stood still here, as horse-drawn carriages roll along the cobblestone streets, passing by antebellum mansions. Those who dig a little deeper will find that Savannah also has its finger on the pulse of the future, as dining and entertainment abounds.

Georgia's Wild Side

Discover the untamed side of the Peach State off the Atlantic Coast. Cumberland Island National Seashore preserves the state's largest barrier island, offering 17 miles of silky sand, 50 miles of hiking trails and ample sites to explore. One of Georgia's most spectacular habitats can be found in Okefenokee National Wildlife Refuge, home to North America's largest blackwater swamp. Diverse flora and fauna fill the waterways and woodlands.

Civil War Flash Point

During the Civil War, the Confederacy enjoyed their last major victory in Georgia before the tide finally turned. This piece of history is shared at the Chickamauga & Chattanooga National Military Park, commemorating a clash between the

Georgia Grits

Centuries ago, Native Americans prepared the first servings of grits. Today, the simple food, derived from ground corn or hominy, is a Southern staple that graces kitchen tables and restaurant menus all over the state. The dish is usually eaten at breakfast and often served with shrimp, cheese or butter.

VISITOR CENTER

TIME ZONE
Eastern Standard

ROAD & HIGHWAY INFORMATION
404-635-8000
dot.ga.gov

FISHING & HUNTING INFORMATION
404-656-3500
georgiawildlife.com

BOATING INFORMATION
770-918-6408
gadnrle.org/boating-rules-regulations

NATIONAL PARKS
nps.gov/ga

STATE PARKS
gastateparks.org

TOURISM INFORMATION
Georgia Department of Economic Development
800-VISIT GA
exploregeorgia.org

TOP TOURISM ATTRACTIONS
1) Georgia Aquarium
2) World of Coca-Cola
3) Centennial Olympic Park

MAJOR CITIES
Atlanta (capital), Columbus, Augusta, Macon, Savannah

gray and blue in 1863. Just over a year after these battles, the Union's General Sherman would capture the city of Atlanta and go on his March to the Sea, burning entire towns along the way.

Civil Rights Crusaders

Georgia's 100-mile Antebellum Trail in Savannah is a window into an outdated way of life. Nearly a century later, Georgia would also play a pivotal role in the civil rights movement. Martin Luther King Jr. was born in the state and spent his formative years in his father's church before becoming a pastor there himself. Several memorials and museums commemorate his life and tell the story of the movement he inspired.

Hit Georgia Trails

Georgia is the starting point of the famed Appalachian Trail, which runs nearly 2,200 miles north to Maine. Those not up for the full, epic experience can find shorter excursions along the 79 miles of the trail that cut across the mountainous landscape of northern Georgia.

Magical Macon

Located near the geographic center of Georgia, Macon boasts a rich past. Native Americans made the region home more than 17,000 years ago, and the 1600s and 1700s saw waves of settlers putting down roots. Today, living history abounds on the streets of Macon, with 14 designated historic districts and more than 6,000 structures nominated for the National Register of Historic Places.

Musical Legacy

Nothing makes Maconites prouder than their musical heritage. Jazz vocalist Lena Horne began her career with City Hall youth choir performances in the 1930s; the Reverend Pearly Brown, blind from birth and the last of America's great street blues singers, began arriving from his hometown of Americus by bus in the 1940s to play his guitar with a cup attached; native son Richard Wayne Penniman—better known as Little Richard—redefined rock and roll in the 1950s; Otis Redding, "The Mad Man from Macon," became the 1960s' seminal soul artist; and the Allman Brothers honed Southern Rock here in the 1970s. You can still walk in the footsteps of musical Macon giants in places like Grant's Lounge, the Original Home of Southern Rock, and the Big House, a Tudor Revival mansion on Vineville Avenue where the Allman Brothers lived in the early 1970s.

The 145-foot-tall Tybee Island Light was built in 1866. The beacon is still a functional navigation aid.

Making Hay

Seeking more traditional touring? The Hay House on Macon's Georgia Avenue is often called the "Palace of the South" for its 18,000 square feet and stunning Antebellum-era Italian Renaissance architecture. Builder William Butler Johnston, a prosperous merchant, oversaw the Confederate treasury. Macon blends its historical roots with outdoor recreation on the 11-mile Ocmulgee Heritage Trail, Middle Georgia's only riverside trail and park system. A life-size bronze statue of Otis Redding resides trailside.

Ocean Adventures and Civil War

Take the ferry to Cumberland Island National Seashore to explore the natural coastal landscape. Watch the feral horses that run free along the sandy shores and through forests. Tour the historic structures to learn the story of the island's earliest inhabitants and visitors. Fun for the whole family can be found about 17 miles east of Atlanta at Stone Mountain, named for the massive quartz dome that rises over the landscape below. Check out the Confederate Memorial Carving etched into the rock's side. The surrounding woodlands are contrasted by colorful theme park attractions. Fifteen miles of trails wind through the terrain, with the mile-long climb to the top offering expansive views.

Ocean Adventures

Georgia's Atlantic coast is studded with gems. Near Savannah, Tybee Island is a perennial vacation favorite. Also off the coast is a hidden oasis, Jekyll Island. With a history of human habitation stretching back as far as 5000 B.C., the island has been a retreat for English colonial troops, the world's most influential millionaires, and now, family and friends from far and wide.

Beaches

Ten miles of shoreline and five distinct beaches provide a stretch of sand to suit every taste. Home to "nature's jungle gym," Driftwood Beach is a must-see. Great Dunes, with its central location and abundant pavilions, is the go-to for a full family beach day. The wide expanses of sand at Glory Beach make for great lounging. Saint Andrews is perfect for birding and shelling. South Dunes, with its elevated observation deck and picnic area, is the excellent for lovers of wildlife.

Shopping and Dining

For those who want to unplug, but still want modern conveniences, Jekyll's Beach Village and historic Pier Road are home to unique shopping and dining options. From frozen yogurt to flip flops, these shops have all the things you need and none of the things you don't.

Featured Good Sam Parks

good sam park

GEORGIA

When you stay with Good Sam, you can expect the highest degree of cleanliness and friendliness, and better yet, you get **10% off** overnight campground fees.

If you're not already a Good Sam member you can purchase your membership at one of these locations:

ADAIRSVILLE
Harvest Moon RV Park

AUSTELL
Sweetwater Creek RV Reserve

BAINBRIDGE
Flint River RV Park

BRUNSWICK
Coastal Georgia RV Resort
Southern Retreat RV Park

CALHOUN
Calhoun AOK Campground

CARTERSVILLE
Allatoona Landing Marine Resort

CAVE SPRING
Cedar Creek RV & Outdoor Center

CECIL
Cecil Bay RV Park

CLEVELAND
Leisure Acres Campground
Yonah Mountain Campground

COLUMBUS
Lake Pines RV Park & Campground

DAHLONEGA
Iron Mountain Resort

DANVILLE
4County RV Park & Campground

DILLARD
River Vista RV Resort

ELKO
Twin Oaks RV Park

ELLIJAY
Talona Ridge RV Resort

FOLKSTON
Jenny Ridge Venue & RV Park

FORSYTH
L & D RV Park

HIAWASSEE
Bald Mountain Camping Resort
Enota Mountain Retreat

JACKSON
Forest Glen Mobile Home & RV Park

KINGSLAND
Country Oaks RV Park & Campground

LAKE PARK
Eagles Roost RV Resort & Conference Center

MARIETTA
Atlanta-Marietta RV Resort

MCDONOUGH
Atlanta South RV Resort

METTER
Beaver Run RV Park

MILLEDGEVILLE
Scenic Mountain RV Park & Campground

MORGANTON
Waterside at Blue Ridge Tiny Home and RV Community

OCHLOCKNEE
Sugar Mill RV Park

PERRY
Crossroads Travel Park
Fair Harbor RV Park
Perry Ponderosa Park

ROSSVILLE
Hawkins Pointe Park, Store & More

SAVANNAH
Biltmore RV Park
CreekFire RV Resort
Red Gate Campground & RV Park
Savannah Oaks RV Resort

STONE MOUNTAIN
Stone Mountain Park Campground

TIFTON
I75 RV Park

TOWNSEND
Lake Harmony RV Park and Campground

TYBEE ISLAND
River's End Campground

UNADILLA
Southern Trails RV Resort

VALDOSTA
Valdosta Oaks RV Park

10/10★/10 GOOD SAM PARK

BRUNSWICK
Coastal Georgia RV Resort
(912)264-3869

DILLARD
River Vista RV Resort
(706)746-2722

ELLIJAY
Talona Ridge RV Resort
(706)636-2267

MORGANTON
Waterside at Blue Ridge Tiny Home and RV Community
(706)851-8855

What's This?

An RV park with a 10/10★/10 rating has scored perfect grades in amenities, cleanliness and appearance ("See Understanding the Campground Rating System" on pages 8 and 9 for an explanation of the trusted Good Sam Rating System). Stay in a 10/10★/10 park on your next trip for a nearly flawless camping experience.

Getty Images/iStockphoto

GA

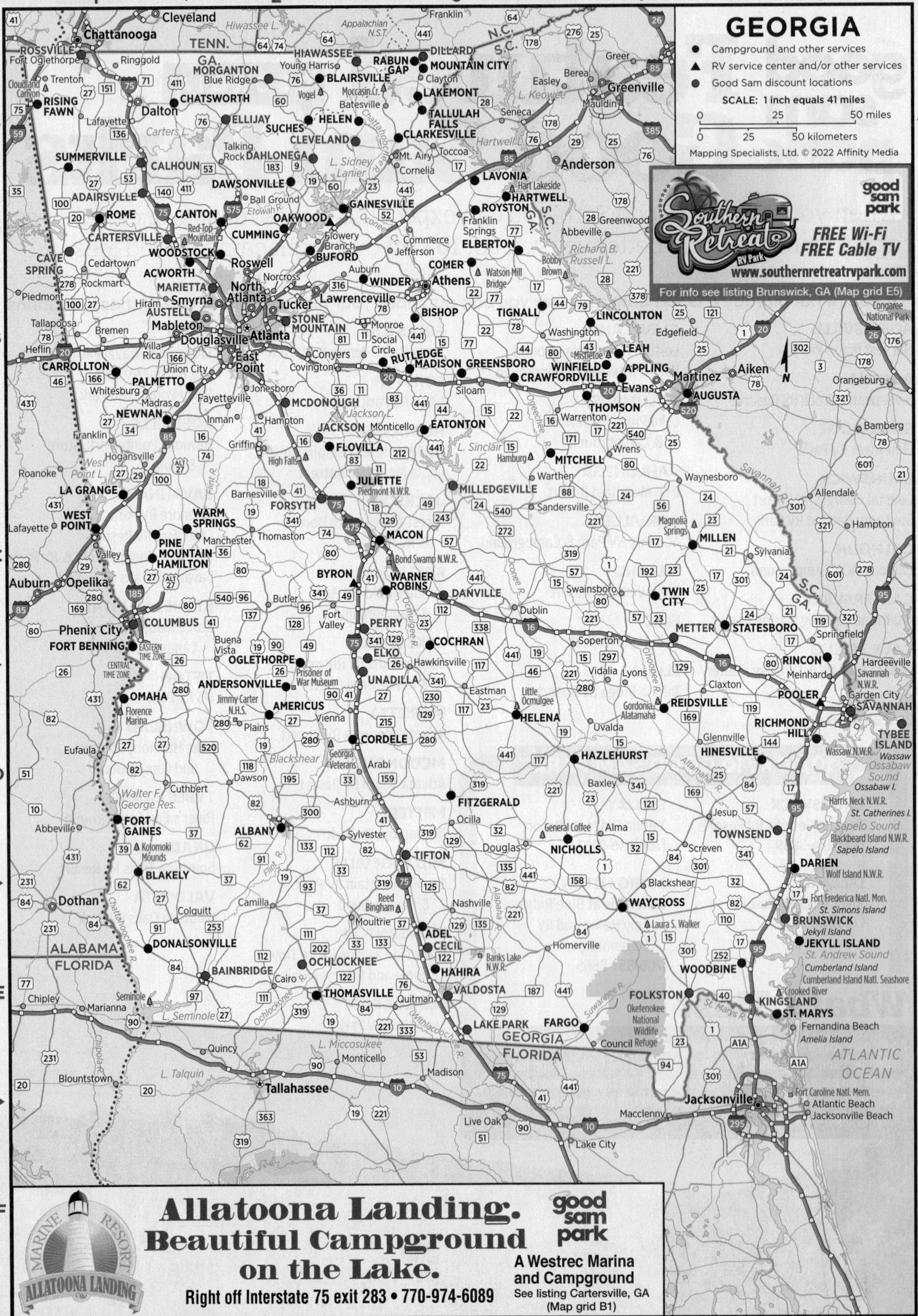
GEORGIA
Campground and other services
RV service center and/or other services
Good Sam discount locations
SCALE: 1 inch equals 41 miles
0 25 50 miles
0 25 50 kilometers
Mapping Specialists, Ltd. © 2022 Affinity Media
1 2 3 4 5
A B C D E F
Chattanooga
Cleveland
ROSSVILLE
Fort Oglethorpe
Ringgold
HIAWASSEE
DILLARD
RABUN GAP
MOUNTAIN CITY
MORGANTON
BLAIRSVILLE
LAKEMONT
RISING FAWN
CHATSWORTH
Dalton
TALLULAH FALLS
ELLIJAY
HELEN
SUCHES
CLEVELAND
CLARKESVILLE
SUMMERVILLE
CALHOUN
DAHLONEGA
LAVONIA
HARTWELL
DAWSONVILLE
ADAIRSVILLE
GAINESVILLE
ROYSTON
ROME
CANTON
OAKWOOD
CARTERSVILLE
CUMMING
ELBERTON
WOODSTOCK
BUFORD
CAVE SPRING
Roswell
COMER
Athens
ACWORTH
WINDER
MARIETTA
North Atlanta
Smyrna
Tucker
Lawrenceville
AUSTELL
Mableton
STONE MOUNTAIN
BISHOP
TIGNALL
LINCOLNTON
Douglasville
Atlanta
East Point
RUTLEDGE
MADISON
GREENSBORO
LEAH
APPLING
CARROLLTON
WINFIELD
CRAWFORDVILLE
Martinez
Aiken
Evans
AUGUSTA
PALMETTO
THOMSON
MCDONOUGH
NEWNAN
JACKSON
EATONTON
FLOVILLA
MITCHELL
JULIETTE
MILLEDGEVILLE
LA GRANGE
FORSYTH
WEST POINT
WARM SPRINGS
PINE MOUNTAIN
HAMILTON
MACON
MILLEN
Auburn
Opelika
BYRON
WARNER ROBINS
DANVILLE
TWIN CITY
COLUMBUS
Phenix City
FORT BENNING
PERRY
METTER
STATESBORO
COCHRAN
OGLETHORPE
ELKO
RINCON
UNADILLA
POOLER
ANDERSONVILLE
SAVANNAH
OMAHA
AMERICUS
REIDSVILLE
HELENA
RICHMOND HILL
TYBEE ISLAND
CORDELE
HINESVILLE
HAZLEHURST
FITZGERALD
FORT GAINES
ALBANY
TOWNSEND
NICHOLLS
TIFTON
DARIEN
BLAKELY
WAYCROSS
Dothan
BRUNSWICK
ADEL
JEKYLL ISLAND
DONALSONVILLE
CECIL
HAHIRA
OCHLOCKNEE
WOODBINE
BAINBRIDGE
THOMASVILLE
VALDOSTA
FOLKSTON
KINGSLAND
ST. MARYS
LAKE PARK
FARGO
GEORGIA
FLORIDA
ALABAMA
Tallahassee
Jacksonville
ATLANTIC OCEAN

ROAD TRIPS

Follow Itineraries That Will Keep Georgia on Your Mind

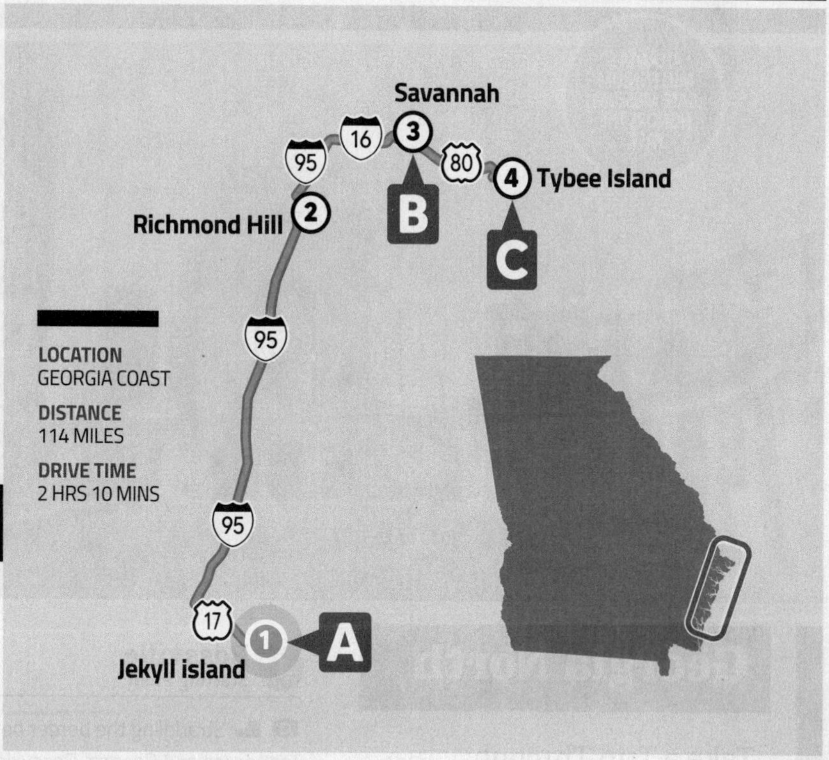

Georgia Coast

Georgia's gorgeous Atlantic Coast blends southern hospitality with nautical adventure. From Gilded Age mansions to ghostly beaches to iconic gardens, the cultural and historical attractions here are sure to delight, but the untouched beauty of the coastline remains the real winner. Whether it's adventure you're after, or just the chance to lay with your feet in the sand, Southern living has never been more enticing.

1 Jekyll Island
Starting Point

Part of the Golden Isles chain, this small barrier island was the one-time retreat of America's richest families, including the Carnegies, Rockefellers and Vanderbilts. These days, you too can enjoy the highlife with a tour of those families' impressive estates. Driftwood Beach, at the island's northern tip, is an eerie must-see destination where salt air and saltier water has preserved gnarled trees up and down the coast. It's not a swim spot, but you'll be hard-pressed to take more magical pictures anywhere else. Finish off your stay with a kayak tour of the Tidelands Nature Center.

RECOMMENDED STOPOVER
A SOUTHERN RETREAT RV PARK
BRUNSWICK, GA (912) 2616-1025

2 Richmond Hill
Drive 29 miles ▪ 30 minutes

Wander Richmond Hill's historic Coastal Bryan Heritage Trail and visit the deep history of this lovely region. See the Guale (WA-lee) Indian village site, where the locals built a defense against a possible Spanish invasion; learn about the Union Army's famous March to the Sea, which passed right through town as it rampaged through the Peach State.

3 Savannah
Drive 36 miles ▪ 56 minutes

Revered as one of the most beautiful cities in the South, it's hard not to fall in love with the hospitality, architecture and landscape of this Georgian gem. First-time visitors should book a bicycle tour of the Historic District, including the 22 park-like squares that give the city its famed Gothic atmosphere. Lined with live oaks drenched in Spanish moss, the photo opportunities alone are worth the ride. Don't skip on a visit to the eerily magical Bonaventure Cemetery.

RECOMMENDED STOPOVER
B SAVANNAH OAKS RV RESORT
SAVANNAH, GA (800) 851-0717

4 Tybee Island
Drive 36 miles ▪ 56 minutes

Families have been flocking to this small barrier island since the 1800's and it's easy to see why. Five miles of beautiful beaches, spectacular views and a rich maritime history combine to make this a near-perfect vacation spot. Try a swim or paddle at Back River Beach, the so-called "secret beach" of the island. Boasting some of the best views and seafood around, you'll wonder why the secret isn't out. No visit to the island would be complete without a tour of the Tybee Island Light Station and Museum, home of the state's oldest and tallest lighthouse. Climb the 178 steps to the top.

RECOMMENDED STOPOVER
C RIVER'S END CAMPGROUND
TYBEE ISLAND, GA (987) 654-3210

Getty Images/iStockphoto

BIKING · BOATING · DINING · ENTERTAINMENT · FISHING · HIKING · HUNTING · PADDLING · SHOPPING · SIGHTSEEING

ATLANTA'S MILLENNIUM GATE MUSEUM HONORS THE PAST.
Getty Images/iStockphoto

Georgia North

Take a Trip Through the Heart of the Peach

Showcasing winding rivers, preserved battlefields and some of the South's most famous museums, this itinerary proves that Georgia has a whole lot more than antebellum homes and sweet peaches. Cruise down the highvway and get ready to discover attractions right up your alley. From pristine forests and ancient archaeological sites to world-class art galleries and hospitable towns rich in musical heritage, you'll find plenty of reasons to pull over and explore.

1 Rossville
Starting Point

Straddling the border between Tennessee and Georgia, Rossville is a charming town that's big on family fun. Park your RV and enjoy more than 40 rides and attractions at Lake Winnepesaukah Amusement Park. The 5-acre Water Park is also housed here, so don't forget to bring your swimsuit on hot days. Just a 10-minute drive away is the Chickamauga and Chattanooga National Military Park, where Union and Confederate forces fought for control over the "Gateway to the Deep South." Take a ranger-led tour through these preserved battlegrounds to hear what happened here during the bloody Civil War.

2 Calhoun
Drive 46 Miles • 50 Minutes

Make Calhoun your base camp for exploring Chattahoochee-Oconee National Forest. Hikers can traverse a section of the Appalachian Trail, while anglers can reel in trout from abundant streams and rivers. Other points of interest within the preserve are the Scull Shoals Historic Site, Track Rock Gap Petroglyph Site and Anna Ruby Falls. After your outdoor excursions, shop for local goods at Calhoun's seasonal farmers markets and visit the Rock Garden to see an impressive collection of miniature castles and cathedrals crafted from tiny pebbles.

RECOMMENDED STOPOVER
A CALHOUN OAK CAMPGROUND
CALHOUN, GA (706) 629-7511

3 Cartersville
Drive 28 miles • 36 minutes

Cartersville provides easy access to Red Top Mountain State Park. Located on Allatoona Lake, this popular park offers every water sport under the sun, including fishing, and even has a sand beach for swimming. There are also over 15 miles of hiking trails, including the 4-mile loop Iron Hill Trail which serves up picturesque views of the lake's shoreline. In town, stop by the Booth Western Art Museum to view the world's largest permanent exhibition space for Western art and explore an archaeological area from A.D. 1000.

RECOMMENDED STOPOVER
B ALLATOONA LANDING MARINE RESORT
CARTERSVILLE, GA (770) 974-6089

4 Atlanta
Drive 43 miles • 44 minutes

World-class attractions, professional sports teams and myriad annual festivals make Atlanta the entertainment center of the South. Kick off your visit by sampling beverages around the globe at the World of Coca-Cola and meet thousands of marine animals at the Georgia Aquarium. You can also look into the past at the Atlanta History Center, National Center for Civil and Human Rights, and the Martin Luther King, Jr. National Historical Park. Art is big here too – check out over 17,000 works at the High Museum of Art and keep an eye out for colorful murals and art installations.

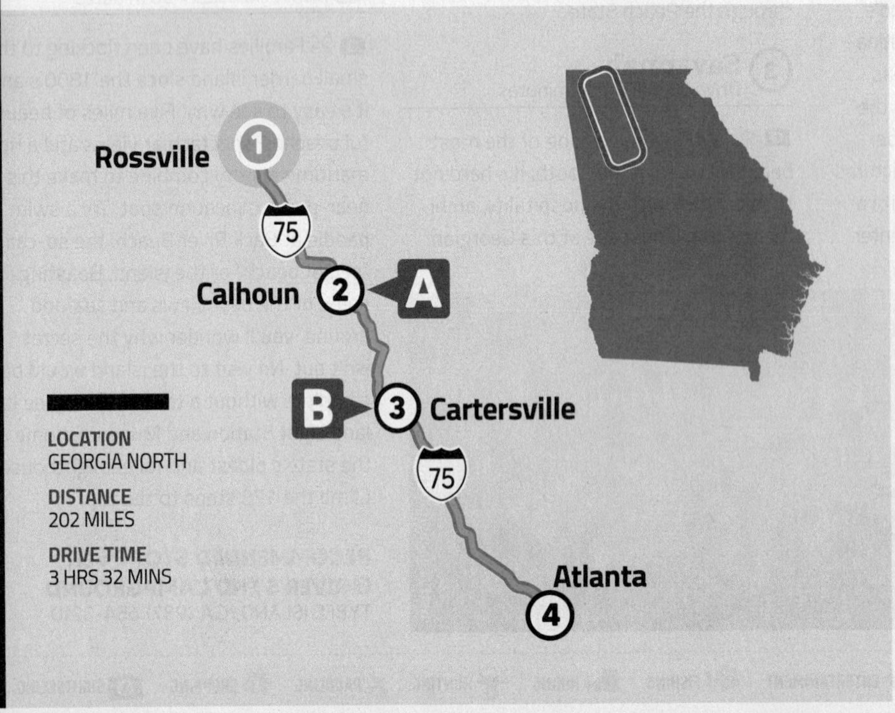

Georgia SPOTLIGHTS

Prepare for Peach State Fun

If Georgia's on your mind, then it belongs on your travel itinerary. The Peach State serves up Southern Culture in every variety. Dine at a five-star restaurant in Atlanta or ride the rapids on the Chattahoochee River in Columbus. Macon preserves music history, while northern Georgia is a hiker's paradise.

MORE THAN 100,000 SHADE TREES HAVE BEEN PLANTED IN ATLANTA.

Piedmont Park's 185 lush acres sprawl on the outskirts of downtown Atlanta.

Getty Images/iStockphoto

Atlanta

The perfect blend of big-city cosmopolitanism and laid-back Southern charm, Atlanta offers a huge range of activities and attractions for visitors of all ages and walks of life. The Georgia capital is an excellent place to deepen your knowledge of U.S. history, particularly when it comes to Martin Luther King Jr. and the civil rights movement. Atlanta also boasts some great museums focused on topics as wide-ranging as puppetry and Coca-Cola.

Georgia Aquarium

Among Atlanta's most popular attractions, the Georgia Aquarium is home to an impressive variety of marine life, with thousands of resident creatures across hundreds of species, from dolphins to penguins to beluga whales. It's the largest aquarium in the U.S. (and one of the largest in the world), with over 10 million gallons of water. While wandering through the aquarium's expansive grounds is a treat unto itself, visitors can pay a little more to get up close and personal with sea creatures; encounter activities range from marine petting zoos to the chance to cage dive with sharks.

The Martin Luther King Jr. National Historical Park

If you're interested in U.S. history, particularly the civil rights movement, you won't want to miss the chance to visit the Martin Luther King Jr. National Historical Park. Managed by the National Park Service, this park encompasses sites such as King's childhood home and the Ebenezer Baptist Church, where the young King was baptized. Other highlights include a visitors center featuring educational exhibits about MLK's life and works and the King Center, established by the late reverend's widow upon his death in 1968, and the site of the leader's grave. The King Center also has a library, exhibits on civil rights movements and nonviolent resistance, and a reflecting pool with an eternal flame symbolizing the continued march toward the goal of equality for all people.

The World of Coca-Cola

Although Georgia has long been known for its delicious peaches, the state's most famous export is undoubtedly Coca-Cola. You can learn all about the world-famous fizzy drink at The World of Coca-Cola, a sprawling museum full of all sorts of artifacts, from old-time Coke ads to an extensive collection of Coke bottles and dispensers. There's also a 4D theater and an imitation bottling plant, and—unsurprisingly—a gargantuan gift shop. You may even get a chance to snap a selfie with a costumed Coca-Cola polar bear.

Sweet Secrets

Don't miss the Vault of the Secret Formula, where the mystery-shrouded recipe is stored. For many, the biggest highlight of a visit is the chance to try all sorts of Coke products from around the world. (Spoiler alert: The carbonation levels and sweeteners can change the taste and feel of the product quite a bit.)

GA

LOCAL FAVORITE

Campfire Peach Cobbler

Use Georgia peaches to create a dessert that will satisfy the most demanding sweet tooth. *Recipe by Diane Ashbury.*

INGREDIENTS

- ☐ 3 jars of the canned peaches that had simple syrup on them
- ☐ 2 white cake mixes
- ☐ ½ stick of butter
- ☐ 1 cup of pecans
- ☐ 6 qt Dutch oven
- ☐ Aluminum foil

DIRECTIONS

Line the Dutch oven with aluminum foil.
Dump the peaches into the Dutch oven and cover the peaches with the two boxes of white cake mix.
Dot the top with butter and sprinkle the pecans over the top.
Cook over the charcoal for about an hour Turing every 15 minutes.

LAKE PINES

RV PARK & CAMPGROUND

SINCE 1967

- ★ GREAT RALLY DESTINATION
- ★ UNIQUE ON-SITE EVENT CENTER FOR FAMILY REUNIONS & CELEBRATIONS.
- ★ CALL FOR GROUP RATES.
- ★ BIG RIG FRIENDLY
- ★ 30/50 AMP SERVICE
- ★ LONG PULL-THRUS
- ★ CONCRETE PATIOS
- ★ SWIMMING POOL
- ★ LAUNDRY
- ★ NATURE TRAILS
- ★ WEEKLY & MONTHLY RATES
- ★ FISHING
- ★ WI-FI HOTSPOT
- ★ NEAR CALLAWAY GARDENS,
- ★ WARMS SPRINGS, ANDERSONVILLE, AND PLAINS.

Family-owned & operated since 1967

Lake Pines is just minutes from Ft. Benning, historic sites, art and history museums, unique dining, antiquing, shopping, whitewater rafting and paddleboarding, golfing, zip-lining, hiking, biking, segwaying, and many more adventures!

706.561.9675
www.lakepines.net

6404 Garrett Road,
Midland (Columbus),
Georgia 31820

SEE LISTING COLUMBUS, GA

good sam park

GPS: 32.53804 84.82728

SPOTLIGHTS

Columbus

Columbus combines history, thrills and great food. For travelers in the know, this town in western Georgia hosts world-class museums, gorgeous antebellum homes and a flourishing arts and culinary scene. Excellent walking, hiking and biking trails allow for close encounters with Georgia's majestic landscapes. The Chattahoochee River forms the boundary between Georgia and Alabama and delivers prime on-the-water opportunities.

Libations and Lounges

Wine and dine like a true Southerner. In Columbus' entertainment district, Old Southern rituals of mint juleps and sultry jazz coexist nicely with the craft beer culture and a buzzing live music scene. The Loft is a perennial local favorite with fine food and an upstairs bar/lounge that hosts top regional musicians on Wednesday, Friday (jazz night) and Saturday nights. Columbus' authentic culinary scene trades the hype and hip factor for down-home classics with deep flavors, served in a welcoming ambiance.

Raging Waters

Columbus expertly puts outdoor recreation in an urban environment. Ranked as the world's longest urban whitewater rafting experience, the Chattahoochee Whitewater Park is a rafting course that has been rated as one of the top 12 human-made adventures in the world by *USA Today*. A dam-controlled release system allows local tour operators to operate tame, family-oriented floats as well as Class IV and V trips on the same 2.5-mile sections of the river. Kayaking and stand-up paddleboarding are also popular on the more placid stretches.

Confederate Vessels

Civil War history is a prominent feature of Columbus. Check out the salvaged wrecks of the ironclad *CSS Jackson* and the gunboat *CSS Chattahoochee* in the National Civil War Naval Museum, which recreates the days when steam-powered vessels fired cannon balls in hotly contested rivers, lakes and coastal areas. Or head to the National Infantry Museum and Soldier Center to immerse yourself in over 240 years of US military history.

The Chattahoochee River in Columbus is a popular rafting spot. Some spots have Class IV rapids.

Columbus Blues

Columbus' long and diverse heritage is on display year-round in some of its lesser-known museums. Try the Ma Rainey House and Blues Museum to learn more about the "Mother of the Blues" and her massive impact on both blues and jazz.

Dixie Relics on Display

For those history buffs seeking out a hidden gem to call their own, try not to get lost at the River Market Antiques & Lunch Box Museum, which offers over 16 acres worth of vintage art, furniture and collectibles. Displays include the iconic metal lunch boxes that have grown to become a vital part of pop culture.

Into Space

The Coca-Cola Space Science Center, located on the waterfront in Columbus' historic district, is an out-of-this-world opportunity to experience a trip to the final frontier. Flight simulators and hands-on mission-learning exhibits thrill visitors.

Cool Canyon

Forty-two miles to the south, the stunning Providence Canyon Recreation Area delights visitors with its red-hued rock walls. Formed by thousands of years of wind and water erosion, this colorful spectacle has been nicknamed "Georgia's Little Grand Canyon" and attracts photographers from all over.

"COCA-COLA SPACE SCIENCE CENTER IS A CHANCE TO EXPERIENCE A TRIP TO THE FINAL FRONTIER."

Milledgeville

With a past that extends as far back as the early 1800s, Milledgeville is one of Georgia's oldest and most celebrated cities. Home to incredible architecture, an award-winning downtown, and a beautifully refined landscape, it's the kind of place that will linger in your memory for years to come. For a taste of Southern hospitality with a side of family-friendly fun, it's hard to beat this gem of the Old South.

Historic Homes

For many visitors, Milledgeville's biggest draw is the endless examples of historic architecture on display throughout the downtown district. Start at the Old Governor's Mansion, a Greek Revival estate that now doubles as a museum. Completed in 1839, the building has played host to some of the state's most iconic speeches and deliberations both before and after the Civil War, including its capture as part of Gen. William T. Sherman's March to the Sea. After an informative tour led by expert guides, board one of the popular Historic Trolley Tours which visit many of the town's other top landmarks. Along the way, you'll have special access to the beautifully crafted St. Stephen's Episcopal Church, the distinctive architectural style of the Rose Hill estate, and the singular elegance of the Brown-Stetson-Sanford House. Finish your outing at the Old Capitol Building, one of the oldest of its kind in the country.

Luxurious Landscapes

As the former home of one of America's most famous authors, Andalusia Farm is a must-see for both history buffs and book lovers alike. For

GA

SPOTLIGHTS

Built in 1858, the elegant fountain at the north end of Savannah's Forsyth Park is a top attraction.

13 years beginning in 1951, Flannery O'Connor lived and wrote on the plantation estate as she recovered from lupus under the care of her mother. These days, the more than 500-acre property is preserved as a museum honoring O'Connor's Southern Gothic style and the pristine landscape that influenced her work. Don't be surprised if you meet a few of the famous peacocks that so often inspired her imagination during your visit.

Literary Arboretum

For even more natural beauty, head to Lockerly Arboretum, on the grounds of the Rose Hill home. Boasting 50 acres of local shrub, tree and rhododendron varieties, there's plenty to see as you wander the property's nature trails. Keep a close eye out for the brilliant collection of camellia flowers that bloom each winter.

Wondrous Waters

For an outdoors excursion with a bit more adventure, head to the shores of Lake Sinclair, a sprawling reservoir home to bass, crappie, and plenty of catfish. Anglers, boaters, and swimmers alike will revel in the seemingly endless coves and inlets that branch off the main waterway, as well as marvel at the more than 500 miles of scenic shoreline. Between the fishing tournaments, personal watercraft rentals, and its reputation as the cleanest lake in the state, it's hard to beat for relaxing family fun. Even closer to downtown, the Oconee River Greenway, a 3-mile boardwalk and nature trail, offers up individual fishing stations, as well as boat ramps and bird-watching. It's also the perfect place for a canoe or kayaking outing, coupled with a picnic lunch. Contact one of the three main outfitters in town rentals.

Savannah

Established by the British in 1733, Savannah, Georgia's former state capital, exudes quintessential Southern charm. This historic city's roots are in the cotton trade, and it was a major port for cotton distribution until the Civil War. Today it's popular for its beautiful antebellum homes and museums. The book (and, later film) "Midnight in the Garden of Good and Evil" was also set in Savannah, and its legacy is a major draw for tourists from around the world.

Historic Landmark District

Savannah's stunning Historic District is easily the city's biggest draw. Here you'll find stately old houses and squares, most of which date back to the 18th and 19th centuries, and a mix of architectural styles, notably neo-Gothic, Beaux Arts, Georgian, and Greek Revival. The district is home to Forsyth Park, the largest park in town, with its iconic cast-iron fountain modeled after a similar fountain in Paris' Place de la Concorde, plus an expansive grove of Southern live oaks covered with drooping Spanish moss.

Iconic Squares

The district is also home to 22 public park squares, many dating to the 18th century (the four oldest ones were constructed in 1733). While the area is small enough to see most of the squares in one day, make sure to at least visit Lafayette Square, site of the gorgeous Cathedral of St. John the Baptist. Pay a visit to Marshall House, the oldest hotel in town (rumor has it that the 1851 building is haunted).

If the majestic 200 year old oak trees could talk, perhaps they would tell us about the Indians & Colonists who have walked this land or the wild animals who once roamed here. The land was used as an encampment for Confederate soldiers, and later occupied by General Sherman after the March to the Sea. Many civil war artifacts have been found on the land.

Mr. Harry E Martin, Jr. purchased the wooded 440 acres in1931, which he and his wife named Red Gate Farms.

The Martins began a dairy farm and cultivated 300 acres for crops as well as for 140 Jersey cows.

Over the years the family has operated several businesses from Red Gate: A Feed Center, Sod & Landscaping Co, The Mackey House Event Venue, The Barn at Red Gate Farms Event Venue and of course, Red Gate Campground & RV Park!

Today they continue the tradition of Southern Hospitality in the development of Savannah's finest RV Campground & Park and The Event Venues.

We think you will agree with many that Red Gate Farms is one of the most beautiful places in Savannah. We love Red Gate Farms and we know you will too.

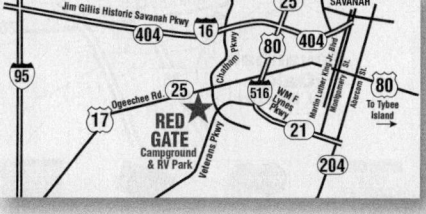

GA

Bonaventure Cemetery

One of Savannah's many "Midnight in the Garden of Good and Evil" attractions, Bonaventure Cemetery was founded in 1846 (as Evergreen Cemetery) and has since grown from 60 acres to nearly 103. In its early days, it was a popular picnic spot, as was the tradition in the Victorian era. Noteworthy gravesites include the grave of American song lyricist Johnny Mercer and the final resting place of "Little Gracie" Watson, who died of pneumonia at the young age of 6. Her gravesite features a life-size sculpture of the young child, and visitors often leave small toys in her honor. Among the more unusual statues in the cemetery is the Bonaventure Jogger, a sculpture of a jogging woman, the late Julie Denise Backus Smith, who was an avid runner until her death. While it can be fun to just wander through the undeniably eerie cemetery independently, the local Bonaventure Historical Society does offer tours.

Tybee Island

About a 25-minute drive from the heart of Savannah, at the easternmost part of Georgia, Tybee Island offers plenty of sand and surf along with a rich history. Plenty of people come here to relax, swim, and kayak, and there are plenty of tour operators offering dolphin-watching excursions and fishing trips (grouper and snapper are commonly caught in these parts). Historic highlights include the Tybee Island Light Station, a lighthouse that was partially built in 1736, and rebuilt several times over the years. Climb the 178 steps to the top for stunning 360-degree views of Tybee Island. There's also the Fort Screven Historic District, with its mix of early 20th-century buildings and ruined fortifications. It was also one of the few places an atom bomb has ever been dropped by the U.S. Air Force (fortunately, the bomb never detonated). The bomb has never been found.

Savannah's Beach

Just 17 miles east of Savannah, Tybee Island is cut off from the mainland by the Savannah River to the north and the Bull River to the west. It is on the northern tip of Georgia's barrier islands and once served as a strategic position for U.S. military forces guarding the entrance to the Port of Savannah. The beautiful beach town offers visitors 3 miles of warm

Where the River Meets the Sea • Walk to the Ocean

RIVER'S END CAMPGROUND

TYBEE ISLAND, GA • SAVANNAH'S BEACH

• New Cabins • Big Rigs Welcome • Picnic Tables
• Fire Rings • Coin Operated Laundry

Close to local attractions and Tybee Lighthouse & Museum

The Perfect Place for Your Beach Side Rally
Close to Charter Fishing & Kayaking

GROUPS WELCOME

OPEN ALL YEAR

Big Rigs Welcome

Club Facilities

Cabin Rentals

A SNOWBIRD OASIS
GROUP MEETING FACILITIES

(912) 786-5518

5 Fort Avenue • Tybee Island, GA 31328
e-mail: riversend@cityoftybee.org
www.riversendcampground.com

RESERVE ONLINE

VISA • MasterCard • DISCOVER

VIRTUAL TOUR

good sam park

2022 Top Rated 9.5/10★/9

LAT: 32.02274
LON: -80.85020

FREE Wi-Fi

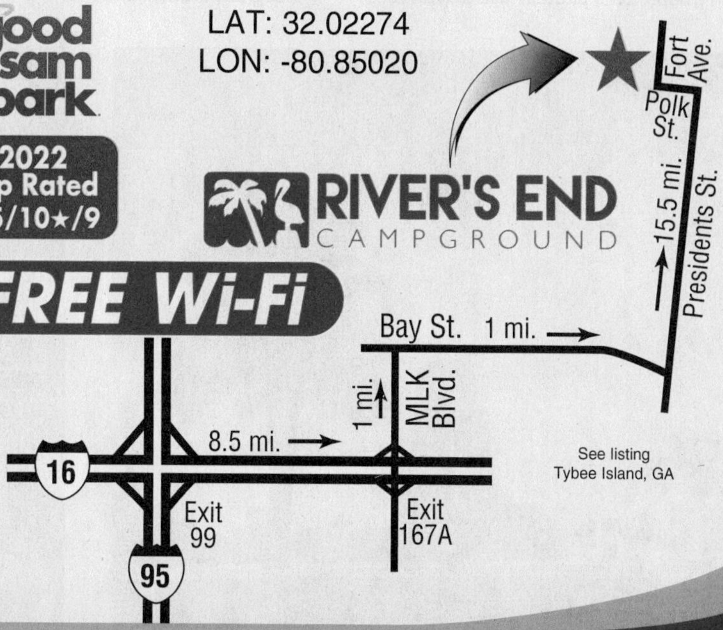

See listing Tybee Island, GA

beaches, year-round beach weather and sunrises over the Atlantic Ocean that will take your breath away.

Play in the Sun

With a scenic trail that circles the island, Tybee Island is ideal for biking or walking. If you brought your kayak, or need to rent one, you can paddle on some of Georgia's most unspoiled waterways. Stand-up paddleboarding is another popular pastime. You can take your personal watercraft out on the Savannah River or just go for a swim. Maybe you want to do some deep-sea fishing or dolphin watching as well.

Tybee Island Marine Science Center

At Tybee's small but well-conceived science center, a series of exhibits present the flora and fauna indigenous to southern Georgia and reveals the fascinating dynamics between barrier islands. In addition to a tidal pool "Touch Tank" of marine invertebrates, and a small aquarium that provides sanctuary to injured fish and turtles, the star of the show is Ike, a loggerhead sea turtle hatchling. Guided "Walks, Talks & Treks" aim to foster close encounters with the inhabitants of the salt marsh and reveal the importance of the intertidal zone and forces behind tides and waves and sand dune formation.

Tides of History

Tybee Island has seen some of the most exciting chapters of American history. Tybee Island, which once served as a hunting ground for Native Americans, has been occupied by the Spanish, French, English, Confederate and Union troops. Even pirates have called Tybee Island home for a time. The area's military past is preserved at Fort Pulaski National Monument, a coastal fortification overlooking the Savannah River that saw action during the Civil War. Today, visitors can explore the still-formidable brick walls of the well-preserved cannon positions.

Island Living

Relish Tybee Island entertainment. Every April, wine connoisseurs can sample some of the region's finest wine and food pairings at the Tybee Wine Festival. Independence Day always brings the area's best fireworks, and you won't want to miss the annual Labor Day Beach Bash. In October, you can practice your best "arrrgh" to get ready for the annual Tybee Island Pirate Fest.

Georgia Lights

Are you a lover of nautical beacons? You've come to the right place. The Tybee Island Light Station and Museum is a majestic black-and-white tower that has guided mariners into the Savannah River for well over a century and still functions as a navigational aid.

Southern Smiles

The Island's laid-back Southern hospitality can best be found at its classic eateries like the Original Crab Shack at Chimney Creek. Serving up kitschy vibes, alligator viewing and one of the area's oldest low country boils, it's a family-friendly gem that keeps guests coming back year after year. The Deck Beach Bar and Kitchen has true seaside dining, while Tybee Island Social Club offers a can't-miss bluegrass brunch. End your trip with a visit to the iconic Tybee Pier and Pavilion, where excellent fishing, stunning ocean views and the best people-watching in town come together in one memorable locale.

Find the Right Spot

Tybee has the right beach for every kind of visitor. Adjacent to Tybee's town kernel, South Beach is the busiest stretch (and the only surfing beach). Mid Beach caters to travelers in search of solitude, while the more enclosed North Beach, located at the mouth of the Savannah River surrounding Fort Screven, is popular with families for its gently shelving sands (great for shelling) and calm waters, where dolphins conspicuously cavort.

Island Waterways

Kayak tours are the perfect way to explore the meandering inlets and channels that surround Tybee Island. Classic paddles include Little Tybee Island, where low country nature remains largely untouched, or along Lazaretto Creek to Dolphin Bay where lucky adventurers can catch a glimpse of the area's dolphins at play. It's also a great place to stop off for food and drinks during sunset.

FOR MORE INFORMATION

Georgia Department of Economic Development, 800-847-4842, www.exploregeorgia.org
Atlanta CVB, 800-285-2682, www.atlanta.net
Columbus Convention & Visitors Bureau, 800-999-1613, www.visitcolumbusga.com
Milledgeville-Baldwin Convention & Visitors Bureau, 800-653-1804, www.visitmilledgeville.org
Visit Savannah, 877-728-2662, www.visitsavannah.com

Standing 144 feet tall, the Tybee Lighthouse has 178 steps to the top.

Tybee Island Pier in Georgia attracts anglers and sightseers

Georgia

ACWORTH — B2 *Bartow*

ALLATOONA LAKE - COE/MCKINNEY (Public Corps) From Jct of I-75 & Exit 278, NE 3 mi on Glade Rd to Kings Camp Rd, W 1 mi, follow signs (E). 150 Avail: 150 W, 150 E (50 amps). 2021 rates: $28 to $32. (678)721-6700

ALLATOONA LAKE - COE/OLD HWY 41 #3 (Public Corps) From Jct of I-75 & exit 278, NW 1 mi to Hwy 92, left 1 mi to Hwy 293, follow signs (E). 44 Avail: 1 full hkups, 43 W, 43 E (30 amps). 2021 rates: $28 to $64. May 15 to Sep 07. (678)721-6700

ALLATOONA LAKE - COE/PAYNE (Public Corps) From Jct of I-75 & Hwy 92 (exit 277), N 2 mi on Hwy 92 to Kellogg Crk Rd, NE 3 mi (R). 60 Avail: 2 full hkups, 48 W, 48 E (30/50 amps). 2021 rates: $20 to $60. Mar 22 to Sep 02. (678)721-6700

LAKE ALLATOONA - COE/CLARK CREEK NORTH (Public Corps) From Jct of I-75 & Exit 278, NW 2 mi on Glade Rd, follow signs (L). 24 Avail: 24 W, 24 E (50 amps). 2021 rates: $28. May 15 to Sep 07. (678)721-6700

ADAIRSVILLE — A1 *Bartow*

HARVEST MOON RV PARK

good sam park

Ratings: 6.5/9★/8 (RV Park) From Jct of I-75 (exit 306) & Hwy 140: Go 1/4 mi W on Hwy 140, then 1/4 mi S on Poplar Springs Rd (R). **FAC:** paved/gravel rds. (77 spaces). Avail: 10 gravel, 10 pull-thrus, (35x90), 10 full hkups (30/50 amps), seasonal sites, cable, WiFi, laundry, LP gas. Pet restrict (B/Q). Partial handicap access. No tents. Big rig sites. 2021 rates: $46.58, Military discount.
(770)773-7320 Lat: 34.37450, Lon: -84.91673
1001 Poplar Springs Rd, Adairsville, GA 30103
harvestmoonrvparkga.com
See ad this page

ADEL — E3 *Colquitt*

REED BINGHAM (Public State Park) From Jct of I-75 & SR-37 (Exit 39), W 5.5 mi on SR-37 to Evergreen Church Rd, N 0.3 mi to Reed Bingham Rd, W 0.9 mi (E). Entrance fee required. 46 Avail: 19 full hkups, 27 W, 27 E (30/50 amps). 2021 rates: $30 to $49. (800)864-PARK

ALBANY — D2 *Dougherty*

THE PARKS AT CHEHAW CAMPGROUND (Public) From Jct of US-19 & SR-91, NE 1.3 mi on SR-91 (L). 44 Avail: 44 W, 44 E (30/50 amps). 2021 rates: $28 to $35. (229)430-5277

AMERICUS — D2 *Sumter*

AMERICUS KOA AT BRICKYARD PLANTATION **Ratings: 7.5/9★/8.5** (RV Park) Avail: 48 full hkups (30/50 amps). 2021 rates: $25 to $45. (229)874-1234, 1619 US Hwy 280 E, Americus, GA 31709

ANDERSONVILLE — D2 *Sumter*

ANDERSONVILLE RV PARK (Public) From jct Hwy 49 & Hwy 228: Go 1/4 mi W on Hwy 228, then 1 block S to Monument, then 1 block W (follow signs). Avail: 25 full hkups (30 amps). 2021 rates: $25. (229)924-2558

APPLING — B4 *Columbia*

MILITARY PARK POINTES WEST ARMY RESORT (FORT GORDON) (Public) From I-20 take Exit 183, L 4.2 mi on 221N Appling GA, straight on Ray Owens Rd for 8.5 mi, L 0.8 mi on Rte 47W, R on Pointes West Resort (follow signs). 85 Avail: 65 full hkups, 20 E (30/50 amps). 2021 rates: $7 to $18. (706)541-1057

MISTLETOE (Public State Park) From Jct of I-20 & SR-150 (Exit 175), N 7.8 mi on Hwy 150 to Mistletoe Rd, W 3 mi (E). Parking fee required. 92 Avail: 92 W, 92 E (30/50 amps). 2021 rates: $32 to $49. (800)864-PARK

WILDWOOD PARK (COLUMBIA COUNTY PARK)
(Public) From Jct of US Hwy 221 & SR-47 (in Pollards Corner), NW 3 mi on SR-47 (R). **FAC:** paved/gravel rds. Avail: 61 dirt, 7 pull-thrus, (24x80), back-ins (22x50), 61 W, 61 E (30/50 amps), tent sites, dump, firewood. **REC:** Clarks Hill Lake: swim, fishing, playground. Pets OK $. Partial handicap access. 2021 rates: $25.
(706)541-0586 Lat: 33.64109, Lon: -82.28673
3780 Dogwood Lane, Appling, GA 30802
www.columbiacountyga.gov

ATLANTA — B2 *Cobb*

ATLANTA See also Austell, Cartersville, Cumming, Forsyth, Jackson, Marietta, McDonough, Palmetto & Stone Mountain.

ALLATOONA LANDING MARINE RESORT

good sam park

Ratings: 9.5/10★/9.5 (Campground) From Jct I-285 & I-75: Go 24 mi N on I-75 (exit 283), then 2 mi E on Allatoona Rd (L). **FAC:** paved rds. Avail: 113 paved, 14 pull-thrus, (30x75), back-ins (30x70), 21 full hkups, 92 W, 92 E (30/50 amps), cable, WiFi @ sites, tent sites, rentals, dump, mobile sewer, laundry, groc, LP gas, fire rings, firewood, controlled access. **REC:** pool, Lake Allatoona: fishing, marina, kayaking/canoeing, boating nearby, playground, rec open to public. Pets OK. 2021 rates: $48 to $59.
(770)974-6089 Lat: 34.10903, Lon: -84.71144
24 Allatoona Landing Rd, Cartersville, GA 30121
www.allatoonalandingmarina.com
See primary listing at Cartersville and ad next page, 312

FOREST GLEN MOBILE HOME & RV PARK

good sam park

Ratings: 9/9★/7.5 (RV Park) From jct I-75 (exit 237A) & Hwy 285/407: Go 32 mi S on I-75 (exit 205), then1/4 mi W on Hwy 16, then 500 ft S on Windy Lane Circle, then 1/2 mi E on Forest Glen Rd, then 500 ft S on Entrance Rd (E). **FAC:** paved rds. (148 spaces). Avail: 44 paved, 42 pull-thrus, (22x50), back-ins (22x50), 44 full hkups (30/50 amps), seasonal sites, WiFi @ sites, laundry. **REC:** pool, boating nearby. Pet restrict (S/B). No tents. 2021 rates: $40 to $45.
(770)228-3399 Lat: 33.25707, Lon: -84.09341
218 Glade Rd, Jackson, GA 30233
See primary listing at Jackson and ad next page, 310

GA

Got a big rig? Look for listings indicating ""big rig sites". These campgrounds are made for you, with 12'-wide roads and 14' overhead clearance. They guarantee that 25% or more of their sites measure 24' wide by 60' long or larger, and have full hookups with 50-amp electricity.

AUGUSTA — B4 *Richmond*

HERITAGE RV PARK **Ratings: 5/NA/7.5** (RV Park) Avail: 90 full hkups (30/50 amps). 2021 rates: $40 to $100. (706)863-3333, 3863 Wrightsboro Road, Augusta, GA 30909

Travel Services

GANDER RV OF AUGUSTA Your new hometown outfitter offering the best regional gear for all your outdoor needs. Your adventure awaits. **SERVICES:** gunsmithing svc, archery svc, sells outdoor gear, sells fishing gear, sells firearms, restrooms. RV Sales. RV supplies, LP gas, RV accessible. Hours: 9am - 8pm.
(844)434-1296 Lat: 33.492361, Lon: -82.105058
145 Mason McKnight Jr Pkwy, Augusta, GA 30907
rv.ganderoutdoors.com

AUSTELL — B2 *Cobb*

SWEETWATER CREEK RV RESERVE
good sam park **Ratings: 6.5/8.5/7** (Campground) From Jct I-20 (exit 44) & Hwy 6 (Thornton Road): Go 1-1/4 mi NW on Hwy 6, then 1/2 mi N on Maxham Rd, then 1/2 mi W on Old Alabama, then 500 ft NW on Love St, then 1/4 mi NE on Wren Circle (R) Note: Do not use Brookforest Rd. **FAC:** paved rds. (85 spaces). Avail: 6 grass, back-ins (30x45), 6 full hkups (30/50 amps), seasonal sites, WiFi, laundry, LP gas. **REC:** boating nearby. Pet restrict (B). No tents. Big rig sites. 2021 rates: $62.50 to $63.25, Military discount.
(770)743-4378 Lat: 33.81260, Lon: -84.63437
2558 Wren Circle, Austell, GA 30168
swcrv.com
See ad previous page

Are you using a friend's Guide? Want one of your own? Call 877-209-6655.

BAINBRIDGE — E2 *Decatur*

FLINT RIVER RV PARK
good sam park **Ratings: 8/8.5★/8** (RV Park) Avail: 55 full hkups (30/50 amps). 2021 rates: $40 to $45. (229)246-5802, 801 W. Shotwell St, Bainbridge, GA 39819

BISHOP — B3 *Oconee*

PINELAKE CAMPGROUND **Ratings: 7.5/9.5★/8** (Campground) Avail: 23 full hkups (30/50 amps). 2021 rates: $45 to $110. (706)769-5486, 5540 High Shoals Rd (Hwy 186), Bishop, GA 30621

BLAIRSVILLE — A2 *Union*

POTEETE CREEK (UNION COUNTY PARK) (Public) From jct US-19/129 & Hwy-325: Go 3-1/2 mi W on Hwy-325, then follow signs 1 mi E on county road. Avail: 59 E. 2021 rates: $18 to $25. Apr 01 to Oct 15. (706)439-6103

TRACKROCK CAMPGROUND & CABINS **Ratings: 8.5/7.5/9** (Campground) Avail: 54 full hkups (30/50 amps). 2021 rates: $40 to $45. (706)745-2420, 141 Trackrock Camp Rd, Blairsville, GA 30512

VOGEL (Public State Park) From Jct of US 76 & US 129, S 11 mi on US 129 (R). Parking fee required. CAUTION: Several tight turn arounds. 85 Avail: 85 W, 85 E (30/50 amps). 2021 rates: $27 to $49. (800)864-PARK

BLAKELY — D1 *Early*

KOLOMOKI MOUNDS (Public State Park) From Jct of 27 Bus & SR-62, N on 27 Bus 1.2 mi to First Kolomoki Rd, N 4.4 mi (R) Entrance fee required. 24 Avail: 24 W, 24 E (30 amps). 2021 rates: $26 to $49. (800)864-PARK

Things change ... last year's rates serve as a guideline only.

BLUE RIDGE — A2 *Fannin*

WATERSIDE AT BLUE RIDGE TINY HOME AND RV COMMUNITY
Ratings: 10/10★/10 (RV Park) From jct GA 5 (Blue Ridge Dr) & US 76/GA 515: Go 6-1/2 mi NE on US 76/GA 515, then 1/4 mi S on Loving Rd (L). **FAC:** paved rds. (100 spaces). 100 Avail: 50 paved, 50 all weather, 15 pull-thrus, (30x60), back-ins (30x60), 100 full hkups (30/50 amps), cable, WiFi @ sites, rentals, laundry, firewood, controlled access. **REC:** heated pool, hot tub, pond, fishing, boating nearby, playground. Pets OK. No tents. Big rig sites. 2021 rates: $60 to $115.
(706)851-8855 Lat: 34.884228, Lon: -84.223977
984 Loving Road, Morganton, GA 30560
www.watersidegeorgia.com
See primary listing at Morganton and ad page 332

BRUNSWICK — E5 *Glynn*

BLYTHE ISLAND REGIONAL PARK CAMPGROUND (Public) From Jct of I-95 (Exit 29) & US 17: Go 1/2 mi W on US 17, then 2-3/4 mi NE on Hwy 303 (R). Avail: 75 full hkups (30/50 amps). 2021 rates: $40 to $45. (912)279-2812

COASTAL GEORGIA RV RESORT
Ratings: 10/10★/10 (RV Park) From the Jct of I-95 (Exit 29) & US 17/US 82: Go 1/2 mi W on US 17/US-82, then 1/4 mi S on US 17 S, then 1/2 mi SE on Martin Palmer Dr (E).

BEAUTIFUL HIGH-END RESORT
Long, Level, Paved Pull-Thru Sites. Check out our NEW Buddy Sites & Rally Center. Walk along our Lake on the beautiful new Wooden Walkway. Open-air & closed pavilion. Sparkling Clean Restrooms & Facilities.

FAC: paved rds. (157 spaces). Avail: 117 paved, patios, 110 pull-thrus, (35x75), back-ins (35x60), 117 full hkups (30/50 amps), seasonal sites, cable, WiFi @ sites, laundry, LP gas, firewood. **REC:** pool, Lake Earl: fishing, boating nearby. Pet restrict (B). Partial handicap access. No tents. Big rig sites. 2021 rates: $50, Military discount.
(912)264-3869 Lat: 31.13385, Lon: -81.58251
287 South Port Parkway, Brunswick, GA 31523
www.coastalgarvresort.com
See ad page 327

SOUTHERN RETREAT RV PARK
Ratings: 9.5/9.5★/9 (Campground) From Jct of I-95 (Exit 29) & US Hwy 82/17: Go 1/2 mi W on US Hwy 82/17, then 1/4 mi N on GA 303 (L).

95 FT. SITES FOR THE BIG RIGS
I-95 (Exit 29) Country Cooking Buffet at Fran's Place. Beautiful beaches, history, water park & cruise ships. Golf, fish & sightsee. Affordable family fun! Relax by our pool or a campfire! Free WIFI & 63 Channel Cable TV.

FAC: paved rds. (162 spaces). Avail: 122 gravel, 96 pull-thrus, (28x80), back-ins (28x45), 122 full hkups (30/50 amps), seasonal sites, cable, WiFi @ sites, tent sites, rentals, dump, laundry, groc, LP gas, firewood, restaurant. **REC:** pool, boating nearby, playground. Pets OK. Partial handicap access. Big rig sites. 2021 rates: $42 to $45, Military discount.
(912)261-1025 Lat: 31.14542, Lon: -81.57653
7445 Blythe Island Hwy, Brunswick, GA 31523
www.southernretreatrvpark.com
See ad next page, 310, 312

Things to See and Do

FRAN'S PLACE RESTAURANT Full service restaurant, serving breakfast & lunch, featuring country cooking & special menu items. RV accessible. Restrooms. Food. Hours: 11am to 2pm Sun - Fri.
(912)262-9663 Lat: 31.14438, Lon: -81.57933
7445 Blythe Island Hwy, Brunswick, GA 31523
www.southernretreatrvpark.com
See ad next page

BUFORD — B2 *Gwinnett*

MARGARITAVILLE WATERFRONT RV RESORT **Ratings: 9/9.5★/10** (RV Resort) Avail: 122 full hkups (30/50 amps). 2021 rates: $60 to $170. (470)323-3486, 7650 Lanier Islands Parkway, Buford, GA 30518

SHOAL CREEK CAMPGROUND **Ratings: 5.5/7/7** (Campground) 63 Avail: 63 W, 63 E (30/50 amps). 2021 rates: $39 to $55. (678)482-0332, 6300 Shadburn Ferry Rd, Buford, GA 30518

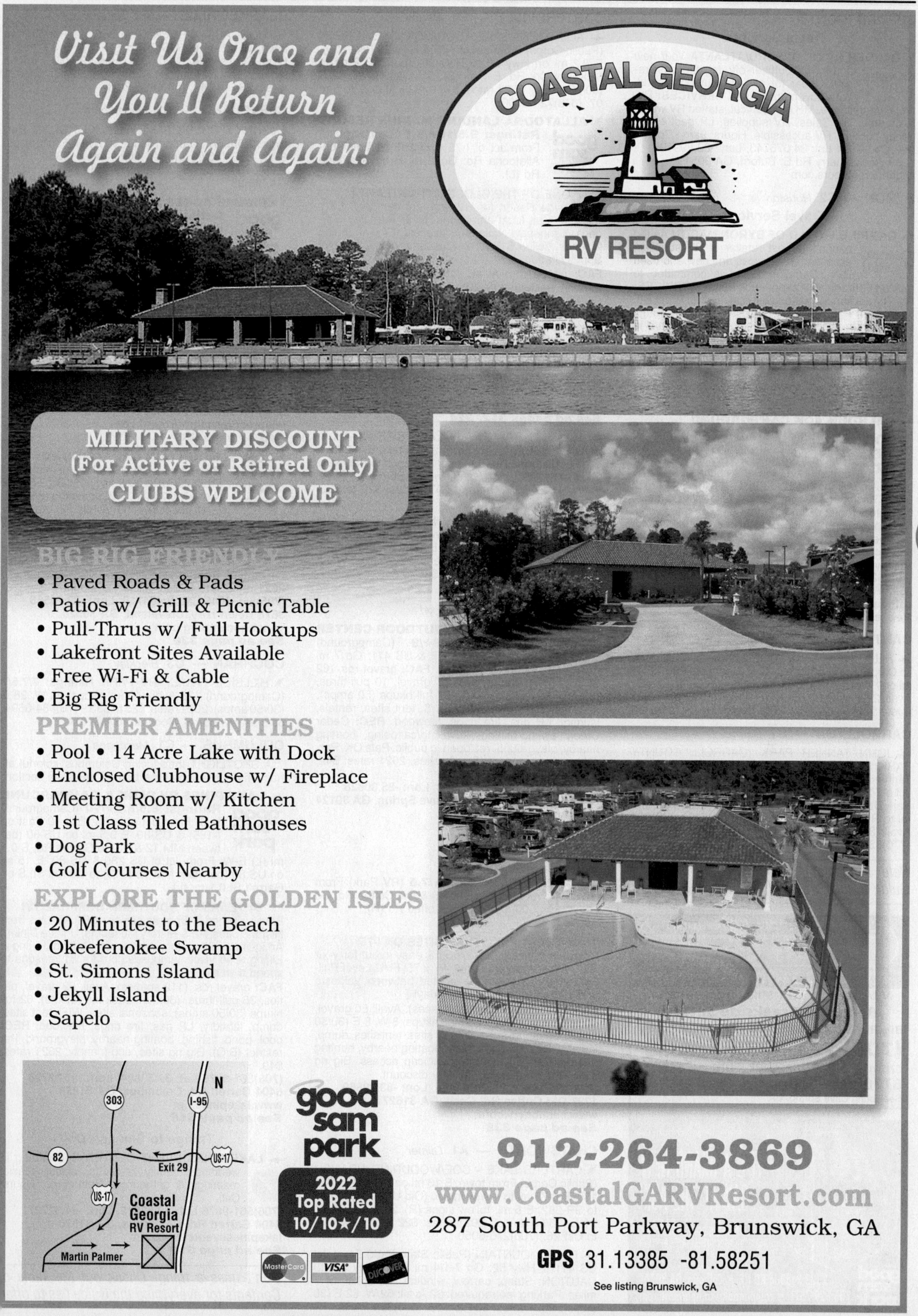
Visit Us Once and You'll Return Again and Again!
COASTAL GEORGIA
RV RESORT
MILITARY DISCOUNT
(For Active or Retired Only)
CLUBS WELCOME
BIG RIG FRIENDLY
• Paved Roads & Pads
• Patios w/ Grill & Picnic Table
• Pull-Thrus w/ Full Hookups
• Lakefront Sites Available
• Free Wi-Fi & Cable
• Big Rig Friendly
PREMIER AMENITIES
• Pool • 14 Acre Lake with Dock
• Enclosed Clubhouse w/ Fireplace
• Meeting Room w/ Kitchen
• 1st Class Tiled Bathhouses
• Dog Park
• Golf Courses Nearby
EXPLORE THE GOLDEN ISLES
• 20 Minutes to the Beach
• Okeefenokee Swamp
• St. Simons Island
• Jekyll Island
• Sapelo
N
303
I-95
82
US-17
Exit 29
US-17
Coastal Georgia RV Resort
Martin Palmer
good sam park
2022 Top Rated 10/10★/10
MasterCard
VISA
DISCOVER
912-264-3869
www.CoastalGARVResort.com
287 South Port Parkway, Brunswick, GA
GPS 31.13385 -81.58251
See listing Brunswick, GA
GA

BUFORD (CONT)

Travel Services

GANDER RV OF BUFORD/ATLANTA Your new hometown outfitter offering the best regional gear for all your outdoor needs. Your adventure awaits. **SERVICES:** RV, tire, RV appliance, MH mechanical, staffed RV wash, restrooms. RV Sales. RV supplies, LP gas, emergency parking, RV accessible. Hours: 9am - 7pm. (844)241-7054 Lat: 34.075743, Lon: -83.899195 2289 Rock Quarry Rd E, Buford, GA 30519 rv.ganderoutdoors.com

BYRON — C2 *Houston*

Travel Services

CAMPING WORLD OF BYRON/MACON As the nation's largest retailer of RV supplies, accessories, services and new and used RVs, Camping World is committed to making your total RV experience better. **SERVICES:** RV, RV appliance, MH mechanical, staffed RV wash, restrooms. RV Sales. RV supplies, LP gas, dump, emergency parking, RV accessible. Hours: 9am to 7pm.
(888)270-8505 Lat: 32.652742, Lon: -83.745104
225 W.E. Green Jr. Parkway, Byron, GA 31008
www.campingworld.com

CALHOUN — A1 *Gordon*

CALHOUN AOK CAMPGROUND
Ratings: 8/8★/8 (Campground) From Jct I-75 (exit 315) & Hwy 156/Red Bud Rd: Go 1-3/4 mi E on Hwy 156 (R). **FAC:** paved/gravel rds. (69 spaces). Avail: 45 gravel, 45 pull-thrus, (25x60), 23 full hkups, 22 W, 22 E (30/50 amps), seasonal sites, cable, WiFi @ sites, tent sites, rentals, dump, laundry, LP gas, firewood. **REC:** pool, pond, fishing, boating nearby, playground, rec open to public. Pet restrict (S/B/Q). Partial handicap access. Big rig sites. 2021 rates: $36 to $55, Military discount.
(706)629-7511 Lat: 34.517853, Lon: -84.890244
2523 Redbud Rd NE, Calhoun, GA 30701
calhounaokrvcampground.com
See ad this page

CANTON — A2 *Cherokee*

ALLATOONA LAKE - COE/SWEETWATER (Public Corps) From Jct of I-75 & Hwy 20 (exit 290), E 11 mi on Hwy 20 to Field's Chapel Rd, S 1.4 mi (E). 151 Avail: 2 full hkups, 118 W, 2 S, 118 E (50 amps). 2021 rates: $22 to $64. Mar 15 to Sep 07. (678)721-6700

CARROLLTON — B1 *Carroll*

JOHN TANNER PARK (CARROLL COUNTY PARK) (Public) From town, W 6 mi on Hwy 16 to Tanner Beach Rd, follow signs S 0.6 mi (E); or From Jct of I-20 (Exit 11) & US 27, S 0.4 mi on John Tanner Park Dr to Bowden Jct Rd, W 3.1 mi to SR-16, S 1.5 mi to Rte 224 (Tanner Beach Rd), W 0.6 mi (E). 31 Avail: 31 W, 31 E (20/30 amps). 2021 rates: $30. (770)830-2222

Refer to the Table of Contents in front of the Guide to locate everything you need.

CARTERSVILLE — B1 *Bartow*

ALLATOONA LAKE - COE/MCKASKEY CREEK (Public Corps) From Jct of I-75 & Hwy 20 (exit 290), E 0.2 mi on Hwy 20 to Hwy 20 Spur, SE 2 mi to McKasky Crk Rd, E 1 mi (E). 51 Avail: 32 W, 32 E (30/50 amps). 2021 rates: $18 to $28. Mar 27 to Sep 07. (678)721-6700

ALLATOONA LANDING MARINE RESORT
Ratings: 9.5/10★/9.5 (Campground) From Jct of I-75 (exit 283) & Emerson-Allatoona Rd: Go 2 mi E on Allatoona Rd (L).

ONE OF THE CLOSEST TO ATLANTA
A Lakeside Resort for RV and tent campers. Fish, relax, or visit local attractions. Near Barnsley Gardens, Kennesaw National Battlefield, Etowah Indian Mounds, Tellus & Boothe Museums plus Lakepoint Sports Station.

FAC: paved rds. Avail: 113 paved, 14 pull-thrus, (30x75), back-ins (30x70), 21 full hkups, 92 W, 92 E (30/50 amps), cable, WiFi @ sites, tent sites, rentals, dump, mobile sewer, laundry, groc, LP gas, fire rings, firewood, controlled access. **REC:** pool, Lake Allatoona: fishing, marina, kayaking/canoeing, boating nearby, playground, rec open to public. Pets OK. 2021 rates: $48 to $59, Military discount.
(770)974-6089 Lat: 34.10903, Lon: -84.71144
24 Allatoona Landing Rd, Cartersville, GA 30121
www.allatoonalandingmarina.com
See ad pages 312, 324

MILITARY PARK NAVY LAKE SITE AT ALLATOONA (NSB) (Public) From I-75 S take Exit 283, L on Old Allatoona Rd, L 4 mi on Lakepointe Parkway/Old 41 Hwy NW, L on Sandtown Rd SE (R). 11 Avail: 11 W, 11 E (30/50 amps). 2021 rates: $20 to $22. (770)974-6309

RED TOP MOUNTAIN (Public State Park) From Jct of I-75 & Red Top Mountain Rd (Exit 285), E 2 mi on Red Top Mountain Rd (E). Entrance fee required. CAUTION: Narrow winding roads. 92 Avail: 92 W, 92 E (30/50 amps). 2021 rates: $35 to $49. (800)864-7275

CAVE SPRING — B1 *Floyd*

CEDAR CREEK RV & OUTDOOR CENTER
Ratings: 8.5/8★/9 (Campground) From Jct of US 27 & US 411: Go 7 mi W on US 411 (R). **FAC:** gravel rds. (62 spaces). Avail: 57 gravel, 10 pull-thrus, (30x65), back-ins (30x45), 57 full hkups (50 amps), seasonal sites, WiFi @ sites, $, tent sites, rentals, laundry, LP gas, fire rings, firewood. **REC:** Cedar Creek: swim, fishing, kayaking/canoeing, boating nearby, playground, rec open to public. Pets OK. Partial handicap access. Big rig sites. 2021 rates: $42, Military discount.
(706)777-3030 Lat: 34.13313, Lon: -85.30828
6770 Cave Spring Rd SW, Cave Spring, GA 30124
www.bigcedarcreek.com
See ad this page

CECIL — E3 *Cook*

CECIL BAY RV PARK
Ratings: 8/8.5★/7.5 (RV Park) From Jct of I-75 (Exit 32) & Old Coffee Rd: Go 500 ft W on Old Coffee Rd (R).

BEST PULL-THRU SITES ON I-75
I-75 (exit 32). An easy off/on & easy in/out for your RIG. We are proud to offer 40' x 75' FHU Level Pull-thru sites. Conveniently located between Valdosta and Tifton. Book Your Site Today!

FAC: all weather rds. (104 spaces). Avail: 50 gravel, 50 pull-thrus, (40x75), 42 full hkups, 8 W, 8 E (30/50 amps), seasonal sites, WiFi @ sites, tent sites, dump, laundry. **REC:** pond, fishing, boating nearby, hunting nearby. Pets OK. Partial handicap access. Big rig sites. 2021 rates: $36, Military discount.
(229)794-1484 Lat: 31.04404, Lon: -83.39869
1787 Old Coffee Rd, Cecil, GA 31627
www.cecilbayrv.com
See ad page 338

CHATSWORTH — A1 *Gilmer*

CARTERS LAKE - COE/WOODRING BRANCH (Public Corps) From town, S 13 mi on US-411 to SR-136, E 0.75 mi to 4-way intsec (Old US-411), N 5 mi to SR-282, E 5 mi, follow signs (R). 31 Avail: 31 W, 31 E (30/50 amps). 2021 rates: $22 to $28. Apr 05 to Oct 26. (706)276-6050

FORT MOUNTAIN (Public State Park) From Jct US 411 & Hwy 52: Go 7-1/4 mi E on Hwy 52 (L) CAUTION: Steep, narrow, winding Rd, uphill for 7 miles. Parking fee required. 62 Avail: 62 W, 62 E (30 amps). 2021 rates: $34 to $49. (800)864-PARK

CLARKESVILLE — A3 *Habersham*

MOCCASIN CREEK (Public State Park) From town, W 12 mi on US 76 to SR-197, S 3.6 mi; or From Clarkesville, N 20 mi on Hwy 197 (R). Parking fee required. 54 Avail: 54 W, 54 E (20/30 amps). 2021 rates: $34 to $49. (800)864-PARK

CLEVELAND — A2 *Habersham*

JENNY'S CREEK FAMILY CAMPGROUND **Ratings: 7.5/8.5/7** (Campground) 13 Avail: 5 full hkups, 8 W, 8 E (30/50 amps). 2021 rates: $36 to $40. (706)865-6955, 4542 Highway 129 N, Cleveland, GA 30528

LEISURE ACRES CAMPGROUND
Ratings: 9/9★/9 (Campground) S-bnd: From Cleveland, From Jct of US 129 & Hwy 115: Go 3-3/4 mi S on US-129, then 1/2 mi W on Westmoreland Rd (L); N-bnd: From Clermont, From Jct of US 129 & Hwy 254: Go 2-3/4 N on US 129 then 1/2 mi W on Westmoreland Rd (L). **FAC:** gravel rds. (134 spaces). Avail: 54 gravel, 29 pull-thrus, (25x60), back-ins (25x45), 54 full hkups (30/50 amps), seasonal sites, WiFi @ sites, dump, laundry, LP gas, fire rings, firewood. **REC:** pool, wading pool, pond, fishing, boating nearby, playground. Pet restrict (B/Q). Partial handicap access. No tents. Big rig sites, eco-friendly. 2021 rates: $50 to $60, Military discount.
(706)865-6466 Lat: 34.53684, Lon: -83.76715
3840 Westmoreland Rd, Cleveland, GA 30528
leisureacrescampground.com
See ad page 330

YONAH MOUNTAIN CAMPGROUND
Ratings: 9/10★/9 (Membership Park) From Jct US 129 & Hwy 75: Go 3-3/4 mi N on Hwy 75 (R). **FAC:** paved/gravel rds. (110 spaces). 100 Avail: 92 gravel, 8 grass, 6 pull-thrus, (35x60), back-ins (30x37), 100 full hkups (30/50 amps), seasonal sites, WiFi @ sites, tent sites, laundry, LP gas, fire rings, firewood. **REC:** pool, pond, shuffleboard, playground. Pet restrict (B/Q). Partial handicap access. Big rig sites, eco-friendly. 2021 rates: $45 to $65, Military discount.
(706)865-6546 Lat: 34.64765, Lon: -83.73565
3678 Helen Hwy, Cleveland, GA 30528
yonahgocamping.com
See ad page 330

COCHRAN — C3 *Bleckley*

HILLSIDE FAMILY RV PARK **Ratings: 7/7.5/7** (Campground) 138 Avail: 40 full hkups, 98 W, 98 E (30/50 amps). 2021 rates: $25 to $33. (478)934-6694, 592 GA Hwy 87 S, Cochran, GA 31014

COLUMBUS — C1 *Muscogee*

A SPOTLIGHT Introducing Columbus' colorful attractions appearing at the front of this state section.

LAKE PINES RV PARK & CAMPGROUND
Ratings: 8.5/8.5★/10 (Campground) N-S: From Jct of I-185 (Exit 10 East on I-185) & US-80, E 9.5 mi on US-80 (between MM 12 & 13) to Garrett Rd, S 0.1 mi (L) E-W: From Jct of US 280 & US 80, E 15 mi on US 80 (between MM 12 & 13) to Garrett St, S on Garrett St 0.1 mi (L).

54 YEARS OF SOUTHERN HOSPITALITY!
Family Owned & Operated since 1967. Minutes from Historic Sites, Art & History Museums, Unique Dining, Antiquing & Shopping, Whitewater Rafting, Hiking & Biking. See visitcolumbusga.com for 51 reasons to spend a week or two!

FAC: gravel rds. (112 spaces). Avail: 62 gravel, patios, 36 pull-thrus, (30x75), back-ins (27x70), 62 full hkups (30/50 amps), seasonal sites, WiFi, tent sites, dump, laundry, LP gas, fire rings, firewood. **REC:** pool, pond, fishing, boating nearby, playground. Pet restrict (B/Q). Big rig sites, eco-friendly. 2021 rates: $49.
(706)561-9675 Lat: 32.53804, Lon: -84.82728
6404 Garrett Rd, Columbus, GA 31820
www.lakepines.net
See ad page 316

Things to See and Do

LAKE PINES EVENT CENTER Specializing in weddings, family reunions, clubs, special meetings & gatherings. Restrooms. Hours: Call.
(706)561-9675 Lat: 32.53812, Lon: -84.82727
6404 Garrett Rd, Columbus, GA 31820
lakepineseventcenter.com
See ad page 316

Don't miss a thing! Check out the Table of Contents for everything the Guide has to offer.

COMER — B3 *Oglethorpe*

WATSON MILL BRIDGE (Public State Park) From town, S 3 mi on Hwy 22 to Watson Mill Rd, E 3.3 mi (E). Caution: Low branches, narrow internal roads, tight turns. Parking fee required. 31 Avail: 31 W, 31 E (30/50 amps). 2021 rates: $30 to $49. (800)864-PARK

CORDELE — D2 *Crisp*

CORDELE KOA KAMPGROUND **Ratings: 6.5/8.5/7** (Campground) 38 Avail: 13 full hkups, 25 W, 25 E (30/50 amps). 2021 rates: $44 to $55. (800)562-0275, 373 Rockhouse Rd E, Cordele, GA 31015

GEORGIA VETERANS (Public State Park) From Jct of I-75 & US 280 (Exit 101): Go 9-1/4 mi W on US 280 (L). 77 Avail: 77 W, 77 E (30 amps). 2021 rates: $35 to $70. (800)864-PARK

CRAWFORDVILLE — B3 *Taliaferro*

A.H. STEPHENS (Public State Park) From jct I-20 & Hwy 22 (exit 148): Go 2 mi N on Hwy 22, then 1 mi E on US 278, then 1/2 mi N on Monument St (Crawfordville), Follow signs (E). 40 Avail: 22 W, 40 E (30/50 amps). 2021 rates: $23 to $50. (800)864-PARK

CUMMING — B2 *Forsyth*

LAKE SIDNEY LANIER - COE/BALD RIDGE CREEK (Public Corps) From town, N 2.5 mi on GA-400 to exit 16 (Pilgrim Mill Rd), S 3 mi on Sinclair Shores Rd to Bald Ridge Rd, E follow signs (E). 82 Avail: 82 W, 82 E (30 amps). 2021 rates: $26 to $36. Apr 02 to Sep 30. (770)889-1591

LAKE SIDNEY LANIER - COE/BOLDING MILL (Public Corps) From town, SW 5 mi on Hwy 53 to Sardis Rd, N 0.5 mi to Chestatee Rd, follow signs (E). 88 Avail: 88 W, 88 E (50 amps). 2021 rates: $26 to $36. (770)534-6960

LAKE SIDNEY LANIER - COE/SAWNEE (Public Corps) From town, E 4 mi on Buford Dam Rd (L). 43 Avail: 43 W, 43 E (30/50 amps). 2021 rates: $24 to $36. Mar 28 to Oct 20. (770)887-0592

SHADY GROVE CAMPGROUND (FORSYTH COUNTY PARK) (Public) From Jct of GA-400 & CSR-306 (exit 17), N 1 mi on CSR-306 to Hwy 369, E 2 mi to Shady Grove Rd, follow signs (E). 107 Avail: 94 W, 94 E (30/50 amps). 2021 rates: $26 to $28. Mar 30 to Nov 08. (770)205-6850

TWIN LAKES RV PARK
Ratings: 7/NA/8.5 (RV Park) From Jct of Hwy 400 (exit 13) & Hwy 141: Go 500 feet W on Hwy 141, then 1 mi SW on Hwy 9, then 1/4 mi W on Lake Rd (E). **FAC:** paved rds. (130 spaces). Avail: 45 gravel, 7 pull-thrus, (25x50), back-ins (25x60), 35 full hkups, 10 W, 10 E (30/50 amps), seasonal sites, WiFi @ sites, dump, LP gas. **REC:** Twin Lakes: fishing, boating nearby. Pets OK. No tents. Big rig sites. 2021 rates: $45 to $55. no cc.
(770)887-4400 Lat: 34.16316, Lon: -84.19444
3300 Shore Drive, Cumming, GA 30040
twinlakes-rvpark.com
See ad page 324

DAHLONEGA — A2 *Lumpkin*

IRON MOUNTAIN RESORT
good sam park **Ratings: 7/10★/7.5** (RV Resort) From jct GA 183 & GA 52 E: Go 9 mi E on GA 52, then S at the Iron Mountain Park Sign, follow signs to the office (E). **FAC:** paved/gravel rds. Avail: 82 gravel, back-ins (40x60), 65 full hkups, 17 E (30/50 amps), WiFi @ sites, tent sites, rentals, dump, laundry, groc, LP gas, fire rings, firewood, controlled access. **REC:** rec open to public. Pet restrict (B). Big rig sites. 2021 rates: $50, Military discount.
(706)216-7275 Lat: 34.5476, Lon: -84.1380
116 Iron Mountain Parkway, Dahlonega, GA 30533
ironmountainresort.com
See ad this page

DANVILLE — C3 *Twiggs*

4COUNTY RV PARK & CAMPGROUND
good sam park **Ratings: 6/NA/7.5** (Campground) Avail: 12 full hkups (30/50 amps). 2021 rates: $40. (478)308-3292, 405 GA Hwy 112, Danville, GA 31017

DARIEN — D5 *McIntosh*

INLAND HARBOR RV PARK **Ratings: 7.5/8.5★/8** (RV Park) Avail: 30 full hkups (30/50 amps). 2021 rates: $40. (912)437-6172, 13566 Georgia Hwy 251, Darien, GA 31305

Do you know how to read each part of a listing? Check the How to Use This Guide in the front.

DAWSONVILLE — A2 *Dawson*

AMICALOLA FALLS (Public State Park) From Jct Hwy 53 & Hwy 9: Go 10 mi NE Hwy 9, then 15 mi W on Hwy 52 (R) Half-way between Elijay & Dahlonega. Parking fee required. CAUTION: 25 degree grade to campsites, not recommended for RVs over 30'. 25 Avail: 25 W, 25 E (30/50 amps). 2021 rates: $25 to $50. (800)864-PARK

WAR HILL PARK (DAWSON COUNTY PARK) (Public) From Jct of Hwy 53 & Hwy 400, SE 1.8 mi SH-53, E 3.75 mi SH 318. 14 Avail. 2021 rates: $16. Mar 20 to Oct 03. (706)344-3646

DILLARD — A3 *Rabun*

RIVER VISTA RV RESORT
good sam park **Ratings: 10/10★/10** (RV Resort) From Jct US 441 & Hwy 246: Go 1 mi E on Hwy 246 (R). **FAC:** paved rds. (124 spaces). Avail: 89 paved, 28 pull-thrus, (35x75), back-ins (35x60), 89 full hkups (30/50 amps), seasonal sites, cable, WiFi @ sites, rentals, laundry, LP gas, firewood. **REC:** heated pool, hot tub, Mud Creek: fishing, boating nearby, playground. Pet restrict (Q). Partial handicap access. No tents. Big rig sites, 180 day max stay, eco-friendly. 2021 rates: $40 to $85, Military discount.
(706)746-2722 Lat: 34.986062, Lon: -83.368359
20 River Vista Dr, Dillard, GA 30537
rvmountainvillage.com
See ad this page

DONALSONVILLE — E1 *Seminole*

SEMINOLE (Public State Park) From Jct of US 84 & SR-39, S 16 mi on SR-39 to SR-253, E 0.3 mi (R). Entrance fee required. 46 Avail: 46 W, 46 E (30 amps). 2021 rates: $32 to $49. (800)864-PARK

EATONTON — B3 *Putnam*

LAWRENCE SHOALS PARK (GEORGIA POWER) **Ratings: //** (Public) From Jct US 129/441 & Hwy 16: Go 15 mi E on Hwy 16, then 150 yds N on Wallace Dam Rd, then 1-1/2 mi W (E). 49 Avail: 49 W, 49 E (30/50 amps). 2021 rates: $25. Feb 25 to Oct 04. (706)485-5494

OCONEE SPRINGS PARK (PUTNAM COUNTY PARK) (Public) From Jct of US-441 & Hwy 16, E 10 mi on Hwy 16 to Oconee Springs Rd, S 1.5 mi to Rockville Rd, SE 3.5 mi (L). 43 Avail: 6 full hkups, 37 W, 37 E (30 amps). 2021 rates: $30 to $40. (706)485-8423

ELBERTON — B3 *Elbert*

BOBBY BROWN (Public State Park) From town, E 11 mi on SR-72 to Bobby Brown State Park Rd, SE 7 mi (E). Parking fee required. 61 Avail: 61 W, 61 E (30 amps). 2021 rates: $25 to $50. Mar 15 to Sep 15. (800)864-PARK

RICHARD B. RUSSELL (Public State Park) From Jct of SR-77 & SR-17, N 1.2 mi on SR-77 to Ruckersville Rd, E 7.8 mi (R) 35' maximum length RV (parking fee required). 28 Avail: 28 W, 28 E (30 amps). 2021 rates: $33 to $49. (800)864-PARK

ELKO — C3 *Houston*

TWIN OAKS RV PARK
good sam park **Ratings: 9/9★/9.5** (RV Park) From Jct of I-75 (exit 127) & GA 26: Go 500 ft E on GA 26 (L). **FAC:** gravel rds. (64 spaces). Avail: 44 gravel, patios, 38 pull-thrus, (30x83), back-ins (30x60), 44 full hkups (30/50 amps), seasonal sites, WiFi @ sites, tent sites, rentals, laundry, LP gas, fire rings, firewood. **REC:** pool, playground. Pet restrict (B). Big rig sites. 2021 rates: $42 to $45.
(478)987-9361 Lat: 32.33598, Lon: -83.76465
305 GA Hwy 26 E, Elko, GA 31025
www.twinoaksrvpark.com
See ad this page

ELLIJAY — A2 *Gilmer*

CARTERS LAKE - COE/DOLL MOUNTAIN (Public Corps) From town, S 9 mi on Hwy 411 to GA-136, E 9.1 mi to Harris Branch Rd., W 1.5 mi CAUTION: Steep entrance road. 39 Avail: 4 full hkups, 35 W, 35 E (30/50 amps). 2021 rates: $24 to $28. Apr 05 to Oct 26. (706)276-4413

ELLIJAY (CONT)

↓ PLUM NELLY CAMPGROUND **Ratings: 7/8.5★/6** (Campground) Avail: 22 full hkups (30/50 amps). 2021 rates: $39.50. (706)698-7586, 15828 Highway 515 S, Ellijay, GA 30536

↑ **TALONA RIDGE RV RESORT**
good sam park **Ratings: 10/10★/10** (RV Resort) From jct GA-52 & GA-515: Go 2-1/4 mi S on GA-515, then 1/2 mi E on Highland Pkwy (L). **FAC:** paved rds. (142 spaces). Avail: 132 paved, patios, 132 full hkups (30/50 amps), seasonal sites, WiFi @ sites, laundry, LP gas, fire rings, firewood, controlled access. **REC:** heated pool, hot tub, boating nearby. Pets OK. No tents. Big rig sites, eco-friendly. 2021 rates: $75 to $120.
(706)636-2267 Lat: 34.655210, Lon: -84.489440
723 Highland Parkway, East Ellijay, GA 30540
www.talonaridgervresort.com
See ad this page

Check out 10/10★/10 Good Sam Parks on the Good Sam Park page.

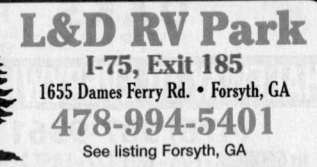

FARGO — E4 *Charlton*

↗ STEPHEN C. FOSTER (Public State Park) From town, S 1 mi on US 441 to Jct of US 441 & SR-177, NE 18 mi on Georgia Hwy 177 (E). Entrance fee required. 64 Avail: 64 W, 64 E (30 amps). 2021 rates: $28 to $49. (800)864-PARK

FITZGERALD — D3 *Ben Hill*

← PAULK PARK RV PARK CAMPGROUND (Public) From Jct of US Hwy 129/90 & Main St (in town), S 0.6 mi on Main St to W Roanoke Dr, W 0.4 mi to Perry House Rd, S 1.2 mi to Paulk Park Rd, W 0.3 mi (L). Avail: 25 full hkups (30/50 amps). 2021 rates: $30. (229)426-5050

FLOVILLA — C2 *Butts*

↑ INDIAN SPRINGS (Public State Park) S-bnd: From Jct of I-75 & SR-16 (Exit 205), E 7.5 mi on SR-16 to Merge with SR 42, continue W on SR 42 6.2 mi (R); or N-bnd: From Jct of I-75 & SR-42 (Exit 188), NE 15 mi on SR-42 (L). Entrance fee required. 60 Avail: 60 W, 60 E (20/30 amps). 2021 rates: $32 to $49. (800)864-PARK

FOLKSTON — E4 *Charlton*

↓ **JENNY RIDGE VENUE & RV PARK**
good sam park **Ratings: 7/8★/7** (RV Park) Avail: 45 full hkups (30/50 amps). 2021 rates: $38.85. (912)496-1172, 2790 Second St. South, Folkston, GA 31537

↑ OKEFENOKEE RV PARK **Ratings: 7/8★/7** (Campground) Avail: 30 full hkups (30/50 amps). 2021 rates: $30 to $32. (912)496-2220, 252 Bowery Ln, Homeland, GA 31537

↓ TRADERS HILL PARK (Public) From town, S 5 mi on Hwy 121, E 1.5 to stop sign (E). Avail: 12 full hkups (30 amps). 2021 rates: $12 to $20. (912)496-3412

FORSYTH — C2 *Monroe*

→ FORSYTH KOA **Ratings: 8.5/7.5/6.5** (Campground) 61 Avail: 50 full hkups, 11 W, 11 E (30/50 amps). 2021 rates: $49 to $52. (478)994-2019, 414 S Frontage Rd, Forsyth, GA 31029

→ **L & D RV PARK**
good sam park **Ratings: 7.5/9★/8.5** (RV Park) From Jct of I-75 (Exit 185) & Hwy 18: Go 2-1/2 mi E on Hwy 18 (R). **FAC:** paved rds. 30 Avail: 21 gravel, 9 grass, 15 pull-thrus, (22x65), back-ins (22x35), 24 full hkups, 6 W, 6 E (30/50 amps), WiFi @ sites, dump, laundry, fire rings, firewood. **REC:** pool, boating nearby, hunting nearby. Pets OK. No tents. 2021 rates: $30 to $35, Military discount.
(478)994-5401 Lat: 33.02757, Lon: -83.86998
1655 Dames Ferry Rd, Forsyth, GA 31029
rvparkforsythga.com
See ad this page

FORT BENNING — C1 *Muscogee*

← MILITARY PARK UCHEE CREEK CAMPGROUND/MARINA (FORT BENNING) (Public) S on I-85 through Columbus to end on Fort Benning, W 1 mi on First Division Rd to Dixie Rd, S 2.8 mi to Uchee Creek Rd, N 1.5 mi (L). Avail: 72 full hkups (15/50 amps). 2021 rates: $27 to $30. (706)545-4053

FORT GAINES — D1 *Clay*

↑ WALTER F GEORGE LAKE - COE/COTTON HILL (Public Corps) From town, N 7 mi on SR-39, follow signs (L). 101 Avail: 91 W, 101 E (50 amps). 2021 rates: $24 to $56. (229)768-3061

GAINESVILLE — A2 *Hall*

↗ DON CARTER (Public State Park) From Clarks Bridge Rd, go S on N. Browning Bridge Rd. At the "Y" take the left fork and go 1/2 mi to park entrance (L). 44 Avail: 44 W, 44 E (30/50 amps). 2021 rates: $25 to $50. (800)864-7275

← LAKE SIDNEY LANIER - COE/DUCKETT MILL (Public Corps) From town, W 5 mi on Hwy 53 to Duckett Mill Rd, S 2 mi (E). 97 Avail: 97 W, 97 E (50 amps). 2021 rates: $26 to $36. Apr 02 to Sep 08. (770)532-9802

↖ LAKE SIDNEY LANIER - COE/OLD FEDERAL (Public Corps) From town, N 7 mi on McEver Rd to Jim Crow Rd, W 3 mi (E). 65 Avail: 65 W, 65 E (50 amps). 2021 rates: $26 to $36. Apr 02 to Sep 30. (770)967-6757

← RIVER FORKS PARK & CAMPGROUND (HALL COUNTY PARK) (Public) SE of town, Jct I-985 & Hwy 53 (Exit 16) NW 2.6 mi on Hwy 53 to McEver Rd, N 1.8 mi on McEver Rd to SR-369, W 0.5 mi on SR-369 (R). 47 Avail: 47 W, 47 E (30/50 amps). 2021 rates: $30. Mar 01 to Dec 31. (770)531-3952

GREENSBORO — B3 *Greene*

← LAKE OCONEE/GREENSBORO KOA **Ratings: 8.5/7.5/8.5** (Campground) Avail: 107 full hkups (30/50 amps). 2021 rates: $45 to $75. (706)453-4505, 2541 Carey Station Rd, Greensboro, GA 30642

← NORTH SHORE LANDING **Ratings: 8.5/7.5/8.5** (RV Park) Avail: 107 full hkups (30/50 amps). 2021 rates: $45 to $70. (706)453-4505, 2541 Carey Station Rd, Greensboro, GA 30642

↓ OLD SALEM PARK (GEORGIA POWER) (Public) From jct I-20 (exit 130) & Hwy 44: Go 7 mi SW on Hwy 44, then 3/4 mi SE on Linger Longer Rd, then 1 mi SW on Old Salem Rd (E). 100 Avail: 100 W, 100 E (30/50 amps). 2021 rates: $25. Mar 01 to Sep 30. (706)467-2850

↓ PARK'S FERRY PARK (GEORGIA POWER) (Public) From Jct I-20 (exit 130) & Hwy 44: Go 5-1/2 mi SW on Hwy 44, then 3-1/2 mi N on Carey Station Rd, then 1 mi W on Parks Mill Rd (R). 53 Avail: 53 W, 53 E (30/50 amps). 2021 rates: $25. Apr 27 to Sep 13. (706)453-4308

HAHIRA — E3 *Lowndes*

↑ CAIN'S CREEKSIDE RV PARK **Ratings: 5.5/8★/8.5** (RV Park) Avail: 12 full hkups (30/50 amps). 2021 rates: $40. (229)794-9416, 6143 US Hwy 41 North, Hahira, GA 31632

HAMILTON — C1 *Harris*

↑ BLANTON CREEK PARK (GEORGIA POWER) (Public) From Jct I-185 (Exit 25) & Hwy 116: Go 1,000 feet W on Hwy 116, then 3-1/2 mi W on Hwy 103, then 3/4 mi S on Lickskillet Rd (R). 43 Avail: 43 W, 43 E (30/50 amps). 2021 rates: $30 to $35. Mar 01 to Sep 02. (706)643-7737

HARTWELL — A3 *Hart*

↑ HARTWELL LAKE - COE/MILLTOWN (Public Corps) From town, N 4 mi on SR-51 to New Prospect Rd, E 4 mi, follow signs to park (R). 25 Avail. 2021 rates: $10. May 01 to Sep 06. (888)893-0678

↑ HARTWELL LAKE - COE/PAYNES CREEK (Public Corps) From town, N 7 mi on Hwy 51 to CR-301, W 5 mi (R). 44 Avail: 44 W, 44 E (30 amps). 2021 rates: $26 to $56. May 01 to Sep 29. (888)893-0678

↘ HARTWELL LAKE - COE/WATSADLER (Public Corps) From town, N 5 mi on US-29, follow signs (L). 51 Avail: 51 W, 51 E (50 amps). 2021 rates: $26 to $52. (888)893-0678

↗ HARTWELL LAKESIDE KOA HOLIDAY **Ratings: 6/7.5★/8** (Campground) 62 Avail: 5 full hkups, 57 W, 57 E (30/50 amps). 2021 rates: $45 to $88. (706)376-1340, 330 Hart Park Rd, Hartwell, GA 30643

HAZLEHURST — D4 *Jeff Davis*

↑ TOWNS BLUFF PARK (Public) S-bnd: From Jct of US 221 & SR 56 (in Uvalda), S 6.1 mi on US 221 to Uvalda Landing Rd, E 0.1 mi to River Rd, E 0.5 mi (R); or N-bnd: From Jct of US 341 & US 221 (in Hazlehurst), N 5.3 mi on US 221 to Uvalda Landing Rd, E 0.1 mi to River Rd, E 0.5 mi (R). 24 Avail: 24 W, 24 E (30/50 amps). 2021 rates: $25. (912)379-9303

HELEN — A2 *Habersham*

HELEN See also Blairsville, Cleveland, Dahlonega, Hiawassee, Lakemont & Suches.

↑ CHEROKEE CAMPGROUND **Ratings: 5.5/7.5★/7** (Campground) Avail: 33 full hkups (30/50 amps). 2021 rates: $27. (888)878-2268, 45 Bethel Rd, Sautee Nacoochee, GA 30571

→ CREEKWOOD RESORT **Ratings: 7.5/9★/10** (RV Park) Avail: 17 full hkups (30/50 amps). 2021 rates: $50 to $100. (706)878-2164, 5730 Hwy 356, Sautee Nacoochee, GA 30571

↗ UNICOI (Public State Park) From Jct of SR-75 & SR-356, E 1.5 mi on SR-356 (L). Parking fee required. 50 Avail: 13 full hkups, 37 W, 37 E (30/50 amps). 2021 rates: $50 to $65. (800)864-PARK

HELENA — D3 *Telfair*

↑ LITTLE OCMULGEE (Public State Park) From Jct of US 280 & US 319/441, N 0.5 mi on US 319/441 (L). Parking fee required. 54 Avail: 54 W, 54 E (30/50 amps). 2021 rates: $35 to $49. (800)864-PARK

RV Park ratings you can rely on!

HIAWASSEE — A2 *Towns*

BALD MOUNTAIN CAMPING RESORT
good sam park **Ratings: 9.5/9★/9.5** (Campground) From E Jct of US 76 & Hwy 288: Go 1/4 mi SW on Hwy 288, the 3-1/2 mi S on Fodder Creek Rd (L). **FAC:** paved rds. (300 spaces). 180 Avail: 7 paved, 173 all weather, 47 pull-thrus, (30x100), back-ins (30x70), 180 full hkups (30/50 amps), seasonal sites, WiFi @ sites, tent sites, rentals, dump, laundry, groc, LP gas, fire rings, firewood. **REC:** pool, Mountain Lake: fishing, boating nearby, shuffleboard, playground. Pet restrict (B). Partial handicap access. Big rig sites. 2021 rates: $45 to $55.
(706)896-8896 Lat: 34.89177, Lon: -83.77051
751 Gander Gap Rd, Hiawassee, GA 30546
www.baldmountainpark.com
See ad this page

ENOTA MOUNTAIN RETREAT
good sam park **Ratings: 8.5/9.5★/9** (Campground) 46 Avail: 35 full hkups, 11 W, 11 E (30/50 amps). 2021 rates: $60 to $70. (706)896-9966, 1000 Highway 180, Hiawassee, GA 30546

GEORGIA MOUNTAIN FAIRGROUNDS (Public) From Jct of US-76 & SR-75 (W side of town), W 1 mi on US-76 (R). 139 Avail: 96 full hkups, 43 W, 43 E (30/50 amps). 2021 rates: $35 to $45. (706)896-4191

HINESVILLE — D5 *Liberty*

MILITARY PARK HOLBROOK POND RECREATION AREA & CAMPGROUND (FORT STEWART) (Public) From Jct I-95 & Exit 15, W 17 mi on Hwy 144 to Brown Holbrook Recreation Area, follow sign (L). 20 Avail: 20 W, 20 E (30/50 amps). 2021 rates: $27 to $30. (912)435-8213

JACKSON — B2 *Butts*

FOREST GLEN MOBILE HOME & RV PARK
good sam park **Ratings: 9/9★/7.5** (RV Park) From Jct of I-75 (exit 205) & Hwy 16: Go 1/4 mi W on Hwy 16, then 500 ft S on Windy Lane Circle, then 1/2 mi E on Forest Glen Rd, then 500 ft S on Entrance Rd (E). **FAC:** paved rds. (148 spaces). Avail: 44 paved, 42 pull-thrus, (22x50), back-ins (22x50), 44 full hkups (30/50 amps), seasonal sites, WiFi, laundry. **REC:** pool, boating nearby. Pet restrict (S/B). No tents, eco-friendly. 2021 rates: $40 to $45.
(770)228-3399 Lat: 33.25707, Lon: -84.09341
218 Glade Rd, Jackson, GA 30233
See ad pages 310, 324

HIGH FALLS (Public State Park) From Jct of I-75 & High Falls Rd (Exit 198), E 1.5 mi on High Falls Rd (L). Entrance fee required. 107 Avail: 107 W, 107 E (30/50 amps). 2021 rates: $35 to $38. (800)864-PARK

JEKYLL ISLAND — E5 *Glynn*

JEKYLL ISLAND CAMPGROUND
(Public) From Jct I-95 (exit 29) & US-17 (Hwy 520): Go 5-1/2 mi N on US-17, then 6-1/2 mi SE on Jekyll Island Causeway to Jekyll Island Entrance Gate, then continue straight to Roundabout, take 3rd exit, then 5 mi NE on N Beach Rd (L) Do Not Use GPS. Admission fee required.

WELCOME TO JEKYLL ISLAND
Discover miles of beach, salt marsh teeming with life, and live oaks draped in moss. You'll find out why the Jekyll Island experience is unlike that of any other. Jekyll Island, a secret we're proud to share.
FAC: gravel rds. (175 spaces). Avail: 150 gravel, 60 pull-thrus, (25x70), back-ins (25x50), 150 full hkups (30/50 amps), seasonal sites, cable, WiFi @ sites, tent sites, laundry, groc, LP gas, fire rings, firewood. **REC:** Atlantic Ocean: swim, fishing, kayaking/canoeing, boating nearby, playground. Pets OK $. Partial handicap access. Big rig sites. 2021 rates: $48 to $67.
(912)635-3021 Lat: 31.10741, Lon: -81.41300
1197 Riverview Dr, Jekyll Island, GA 31527
www.jekyllisland.com/campground
See ad this page

Things to See and Do

JEKYLL ISLAND PARK Park is 7-1/2 mi long & 1-1/3 mi wide. Activities include golf, miles of beaches, bicycle and walking paths, historical sites and a water park. Partial handicap access. RV accessible. Restrooms. Food. Hours: 8am to 5pm. Adult fee: $8.00. ATM. No CC.
(912)635-3636 Lat: 31.05916, Lon: -81.41944
100 James Rd, Jekyll Island, GA 31527
www.jekyllisland.com
See ad this page

Like Us on Facebook.

JULIETTE — C2 *Monroe*

DAMES FERRY PARK (GEORGIA POWER) (Public) From Jct I-75 (Exit 171) & US 23/Hwy 87: Go 9-1/4 mi N on US 23/Hwy 87 (L). 31 Avail: 31 W, 31 E (30/50 amps). 2021 rates: $23 to $50. Mar 01 to Oct 31. (478)994-7945

KINGSLAND — E5 *Camden*

COUNTRY OAKS RV PARK & CAMPGROUND
good sam park **Ratings: 8.5/9★/9** (RV Park) From jct I-95 & St Marys Rd (exit 1): Go 1/4 mi W on St Marys Rd (L). **FAC:** paved rds. (43 spaces). Avail: 23 gravel, 18 pull-thrus, (28x60), back-ins (30x40), 23 full hkups (30/50 amps), seasonal sites, WiFi @ sites, laundry, LP gas, fire rings, firewood. **REC:** pond, fishing, boating nearby. Pet restrict (B). Partial handicap access. No tents. Big rig sites. 2021 rates: $38 to $42.
(912)729-6212 Lat: 30.76032, Lon: -81.65920
2456 Scrubby Bluff Road, Kingsland, GA 31548
www.countryoaksrv.com
See ad page 261

JACKSONVILLE NORTH / ST MARYS KOA **Ratings: 8/7.5/8** (Campground) 82 Avail: 57 full hkups, 25 W, 25 E (30/50 amps). 2021 rates: $53 to $74. (912)729-3232, 2970 Scrubby Bluff Rd, Kingsland, GA 31548

LAGRANGE — C1 *Troup*

STATE LINE PARK (Public) From town, W 11 mi on SR-109 to Chambers CR-288, S 3 mi (E). 122 Avail: 56 W, 56 E (20/30 amps). 2021 rates: $14 to $20. Mar 01 to Sep 30. (706)882-5439

WEST POINT LAKE - COE/HOLIDAY (Public Corps) From town, W 8 mi on SR-109 to Abbottsford Rd, S 2 mi (E). 112 Avail: 71 W, 112 E (30/50 amps). 2021 rates: $16 to $48. Mar 22 to Sep 02. (706)884-6818

WEST POINT LAKE - COE/WHITETAIL RIDGE (Public Corps) From town, W 8 mi on Hwy 109 to Abbottsford Rd exit, S 1.2 mi, SE .5 mi on Freeman Rd. 58 Avail: 58 W, 58 E (30/50 amps). 2021 rates: $24 to $48. Mar 01 to Dec 01. (706)884-8972

LAKE PARK — E3 *Lowndes*

EAGLES ROOST RV RESORT & CONFERENCE CENTER
good sam park **Ratings: 9/9.5★/9** (Campground) From Jct of I-75 (Exit 5) & Hwy 376: Go 200 ft E on Hwy 376, then 1/2 mi S on Mill Store Rd (L). **FAC:** paved/gravel rds. (111 spaces). 101 Avail: 50 paved, 51 grass, 101 pull-thrus, (26x70), 101 full hkups (30/50 amps), seasonal sites, WiFi @ sites, tent sites, rentals, dump, laundry, LP gas. **REC:** pool, boating nearby, shuffleboard, playground. Pets OK. Partial handicap access. Big rig sites, eco-friendly. 2021 rates: $43 to $51, Military discount.
(229)559-5192 Lat: 30.66882, Lon: -83.21207
5465 Mill Store Rd, Lake Park, GA 31636
www.eaglesroostresort.com
See ad page 339

Travel Services

CAMPING WORLD OF LAKE PARK/VALDOSTA As the nation's largest retailer of RV supplies, accessories, services and new and used RVs, Camping World is committed to making your total RV experience better. **SERVICES:** RV, tire, RV appliance, MH mechanical, staffed RV wash, restrooms. RV Sales. RV supplies, LP gas, RV accessible. Hours: 8am to 6pm.
(888)239-4005 Lat: 30.67651, Lon: -83.22102
5244 Jewell Futch Rd, Lake Park, GA 31636
www.campingworld.com

We rate what RVers consider important.

LAKEMONT — A3 *Rabun*

RIVER FALLS AT THE GORGE **Ratings: 6/7/6** (Campground) 111 Avail: 34 full hkups, 77 W, 77 E (30/50 amps). 2021 rates: $49 to $69. (706)754-0292, 32 US 441, Lakemont, GA 30552

LAVONIA — A3 *Franklin*

TUGALOO (Public State Park) From Jct of I-85 & SR-17 (Exit 173), S 1.2 mi on SR-17 to SR-59, E 1.2 mi to SR-328, N 3.9 mi to park rd, SE 1.6 mi (E). CAUTION: Narrow internal roads, sharp curves, low branches. Parking fee required. 113 Avail: 113 W, 113 E (30 amps). 2021 rates: $38 to $49. (800)864-PARK

LEAH — B4 *Columbia*

J. STROM THURMOND LAKE - COE/PETERSBURG (Public Corps) From town, NE 8 mi on US-221 to cnty rd, N 1 mi (E). 94 Avail: 86 W, 86 E (50 amps). 2021 rates: $18 to $28. Feb 27 to Nov 28. (706)541-9464

J. STROM THURMOND LAKE - COE/RIDGE ROAD (Public Corps) From town, S 1 mi on Hwy 47 to Ridge Rd, E 5 mi (E). 69 Avail: 63 W, 63 E (50 amps). 2021 rates: $18 to $54. Mar 29 to Sep 28. (706)541-0282

LINCOLNTON — B4 *Lincoln*

ELIJAH CLARK (Public State Park) From Jct of I-20 & Hwy 78 (Exit 172), NW 2 mi on Hwy 78 to Hwy 43, N 19 mi to Lincolnton (US 378), NE 7 mi (L). Parking fee required. 165 Avail: 165 W, 165 E (30 amps). 2021 rates: $25 to $50. (800)864-PARK

J. STROM THURMOND LAKE - COE/CLAY HILL (Public Corps) From town, S 8 mi on Hwy 43 to Clay Hill rd, E 2 mi (E). 17 Avail: 10 W, 10 E (30 amps). 2021 rates: $15 to $27. Mar 13 to Sep 30. (706)359-7495

J. STROM THURMOND LAKE - COE/HESTERS FERRY (Public Corps) From town, go 12 miles north on Hwy 79. Turn east onto Graball Rd; Continue on Graball Rd for 4.7 miles continue to follow the signs to the park. 26 Avail: 16 W, 16 E (30 amps). 2021 rates: $15 to $27. (706)359-2746

MACON — C3 *Bibb*

LAKE TOBESOFKEE RECREATION AREA-ARROWHEAD (Public) From Jct of I-475 & US 80 (Exit 3) W on US 80 4.9 mi to Columbus Rd, NE on Columbus Rd 0.8 mi to Arrowhead Rd, N on Arrowhead Rd 0.7 mi (E). 52 Avail: 17 full hkups, 35 W, 35 E (30/50 amps). 2021 rates: $27 to $35. (478)474-8770

LAKE TOBESOFKEE RECREATION AREA-CLAYSTONE (Public) From Jct of I-475 & Hwy 74 (Exit 5), W on Hwy 74 0.8 mi to Moseley Dixon Rd, SW on Moseley Dixon Rd 1.8 mi (L). Avail: 37 full hkups (30/50 amps). 2021 rates: $27 to $35. (478)474-8770

Canada -- know the rules, regulations and tips before crossing the border. This is listed at the beginning of the country.

MADISON — B3 *Morgan*

COUNTRY BOY'S RV PARK **Ratings: 6/7/5.5** (Campground) Avail: 12 full hkups (30/50 amps). 2021 rates: $35. (706)342-1799, 2750 Eatonton Rd (Hwy 441), Madison, GA 30650

MARIETTA — B2 *Cobb*

ATLANTA-MARIETTA RV RESORT
good sam park
Ratings: 7/8.5★/8 (RV Park) From Jct I-75 (Exit 261) & Hwy 280 (Delk Rd): Go 1 mi SW on Hwy 280, then 1/4 mi N on Hwy 41, then 500 ft E on Wylie Rd (R). **FAC:** paved rds. (60 spaces). 25 Avail: 23 paved, 2 gravel, patios, back-ins (26x45), 25 full hkups (30/50 amps), seasonal sites, WiFi @ sites, dump, laundry, LP gas. **REC:** boating nearby. Pet restrict (B). Partial handicap access. No tents. 2021 rates: $54, Military discount.
(770)427-6853 Lat: 33.92823, Lon: -84.50684
1031 Wylie Rd SE, Marietta, GA 30067
amrvresort.com
See ad page 324

MCDONOUGH — B2 *Henry*

ATLANTA SOUTH RV RESORT
good sam park
Ratings: 8.5/9★/9 (RV Park) From jct I-675 & I-75: Go 4-1/2 mi S on I-75 (exit 222), then 1/4 mi W on Jodeco Rd, then 3/4 mi S on Mt Olive Rd, then continue 3/4 mi SE on Mt Olive Rd (E). **FAC:** paved/gravel rds. (170 spaces). Avail: 45 gravel, 45 pull-thrus, (20x70), 45 full hkups (30/50 amps), seasonal sites, cable, WiFi @ sites, rentals, dump, laundry, LP gas, fire rings, firewood. **REC:** pool, playground. Pet restrict (B/Q). Partial handicap access. No tents, eco-friendly. 2021 rates: $45 to $55, Military discount.
(770)957-2610 Lat: 33.474510, Lon: -84.216646
281 Mt Olive Rd, McDonough, GA 30253
www.atlantasouthrvresort.com
See ad page 323

METTER — C4 *Candler*

BEAVER RUN RV PARK
good sam park
Ratings: 8.5/9.5★/9.5 (Campground) Avail: 15 full hkups (30/50 amps). 2021 rates: $38. (912)362-4737, 22321 Excelsior Church Rd, Metter, GA 30439

MILLEDGEVILLE — C3 *Baldwin*

A SPOTLIGHT Introducing Milledgeville's colorful attractions appearing at the front of this state section.

SCENIC MOUNTAIN RV PARK & CAMPGROUND
good sam park
Ratings: 9.5/10★/9 (RV Park) From Jct GA 22 & GA 441 By-Pass (GA 29): Go 7 mi S on 441 By-Pass, then ¼ mi N on Bus 441 (GA 243) (R).

HISTORIC HEARTLAND'S HIDDEN GEM
4 mi S of Historic Milledgeville. A Quiet Friendly Park, Six stocked fishing ponds plus Hiking Trails thru our 112 Wooded Acres. Beautiful New Event Center, Sparkling clean Swimming Pool/Whirlpool. Clubhouse with a kitchen.

FAC: paved rds. (83 spaces). Avail: 53 gravel, 10 pull-thrus, (30x90), back-ins (45x45), 53 full hkups (30/50 amps), seasonal sites, cable, WiFi @ sites, tent sites, rentals, laundry, LP bottles, fire rings, firewood. **REC:** pool, hot tub, pond, fishing, boating nearby, playground. Pets OK. Partial handicap access. Big rig sites, eco-friendly. 2021 rates: $48 to $55, Military discount.
(478)454-1013 Lat: 33.02898, Lon: -83.23576
2686 Irwinton Road, Milledgeville, GA 31061
scenicmountainrvresort.com
See ad page 318

MILLEN — C4 *Jenkins*

MAGNOLIA SPRINGS (Public State Park) From Jct of US 25 & Hwy 23 (in town), N 5 mi on US 25 (R). Parking fee required. 26 Avail: 26 W, 26 E (30/50 amps). 2021 rates: $33 to $49. (800)864-PARK

MITCHELL — C4 *Glascock*

HAMBURG (Public State Park) From town, S 2 mi on Hwy 102 to Hamburg/Agricola Rd, NW 4 mi (L) Parking fee required. 30 Avail: 30 W, 30 E (30/50 amps). 2021 rates: $28 to $49. Mar 15 to Nov 30. (800)864-PARK

MORGANTON — A2 *Fannin*

WATERSIDE AT BLUE RIDGE TINY HOME AND RV COMMUNITY
good sam park
Ratings: 10/10★/10 (RV Park) From jct GA 60 & US 76/GA 515: Go 2-1/2 mi E on US 76/GA 515, then 1/4 mi S on Loving Rd (L).

EXPERIENCE BLUE RIDGE IN A NEW WAY
Waterside at Blue Ridge is a tiny home and RV community that has everything you need for a relaxing getaway in Blue Ridge, Georgia.

FAC: paved rds. 100 Avail: 50 paved, 50 all weather, 15 pull-thrus, (30x60), back-ins (30x60), 100 full hkups (30/50 amps), cable, WiFi @ sites, rentals, laundry, firewood, controlled access. **REC:** heated pool, hot tub, pond, fishing, boating nearby, playground. Pets OK. No tents. Big rig sites. 2021 rates: $60 to $115.
(706)851-8855 Lat: 34.884228, Lon: -84.223977
984 Loving Road, Morganton, GA 30560
www.watersidegeorgia.com
See ad this page

WHISPERING PINES CAMPGROUND & RV PARK **Ratings: 8/7.5★/7** (Campground) Avail: 18 full hkups (30/50 amps). 2021 rates: $32 to $42. (706)374-6494, 290 Whispering Pines Rd, Morganton, GA 30560

MOUNTAIN CITY — A3 *Rabun*

BLACK ROCK MOUNTAIN (Public State Park) From Jct of SR-441 & SR-76, N 2.9 mi on SR-441 to Black Rock Mtn Rd, W 3 mi (E). Caution: Last 3 mi are steep and winding, interior roads also winding with sharp curves (max RV length 25'). Parking fee required. 44 Avail: 44 W, 44 E (30 amps). 2021 rates: $27 to $50. Mar 16 to Nov 30. (800)864-PARK

NEWNAN — B1 *Coweta*

CHATTAHOOCHEE BEND (Public State Park) From Newman, Hwy 34-W to Thomas Powers Rd (R). Go 5.5 mi to Flatrock Rd (R), 1 mi to park entrance. 35 Avail: 35 W, 35 E (30/50 amps). 2021 rates: $25 to $49. (800)864-7275

NICHOLLS — D4 *Coffee*

GENERAL COFFEE (Public State Park) From Jct of US 441 & SR-32 (in town), E 6 mi on SR-32 (L). Parking fee required. 40 Avail: 40 W, 40 E (30/50 amps). 2021 rates: $32 to $49. (800)864-7275

OAKWOOD — B2 *Hall*

Travel Services

CAMPING WORLD OF OAKWOOD As the nation's largest retailer of RV supplies, accessories, services and new and used RVs, Camping World is committed to making your total RV experience better. **SERVICES:** RV, tire, RV appliance, MH mechanical, restrooms. RV Sales. RV supplies, LP gas, emergency parking, RV accessible. Hours: 9am to 7pm.
(877)709-5791 Lat: 34.222776, Lon: -83.87131
4696 Smithson Blvd, Oakwood, GA 30566
www.campingworld.com

OCHLOCKNEE — E2 *Thomas*

SUGAR MILL RV PARK
good sam park
Ratings: 7.5/9.5★/8 (RV Park) From Jct of US 19/SR 300 (GA/FL Pkwy) & US 319: Go 6-1/2 mi N on US-19/SR-300, the 500 ft W on McMillan Rd (R). **FAC:** paved/gravel rds. (121 spaces). Avail: 61 grass, 15 pull-thrus, (30x65), back-ins (30x60), 61 full hkups (30/50 amps), seasonal sites, WiFi, tent sites, rentals, laundry, LP gas. **REC:** pond, fishing, boating nearby, shuffleboard, hunting nearby. Pet restrict (B). Big rig sites. 2021 rates: $30 to $33, Military discount.
(229)227-1451 Lat: 30.94970, Lon: -84.02605
4857 McMillan Rd, Ochlocknee, GA 31773
www.sugarmillrvpark.com
See ad this page

OGLETHORPE — D2 *Macon*

WHITEWATER CREEK PARK (MACON COUNTY PARK) (Public) From jct Hwy 26 & Hwy 49/128: Go 6-1/4 mi N on Hwy 128 or Hwy 128 Bypass. 29 Avail: 17 full hkups, 12 W, 12 E (30 amps). 2021 rates: $30 to $35. (478)472-8171

OMAHA — D1 *Stewart*

FLORENCE MARINA (Public State Park) From Jct of Hwy 27 & Rt 1 (in Lumpkin): Go 1/4 mi N on Rt 1, then 15 mi W on Hwy 39C (E). Entrance fee required. Avail: 43 full hkups (30/50 amps). 2021 rates: $32 to $50. (800)864-7275

PALMETTO — B2 *Coweta*

SOUTH OAKS MOBILE HOME & RV COMMUNITY
Ratings: 4.5/NA/4.5 (RV Area in MH Park) From Jct of I-85 (exit 56) & Collinsworth Road: Go 200 ft N on Collinsworth Rd, then 1/4 mi E on Tingle Lane (L). **FAC:** paved rds. (310 spaces). 140 Avail: 135 paved, 5 grass, 4 pull-thrus, (18x60), back-ins (35x60), 140 full hkups (30/50 amps), seasonal sites, dump. **REC:** Justa Stream: playground. Pet restrict (B). No tents. Big rig sites. 2021 rates: $35. no cc.
(770)463-3070 Lat: 33.50457, Lon: -84.63689
240 Tingle Lane, Palmetto, GA 30268
See ad page 323

PERRY — C2 *Houston*

PERRY See also Cochran, Elko & Unadilla.

CROSSROADS TRAVEL PARK
good sam park
Ratings: 8.5/8/8 (RV Park) From Jct of I-75 & US-341 (exit 136), W 0.2 mi on US-341/Sam Nunn Blvd (L). **FAC:** paved rds. (72 spaces). Avail: 49 paved, 33 pull-thrus, (26x60), back-ins (30x40), 49 full hkups (30/50 amps), seasonal sites, cable, WiFi @ sites, dump, laundry, LP gas. **REC:** pool, boating nearby. Pet restrict (B). Partial handicap access. No tents. Big rig sites. 2021 rates: $45, Military discount.
(478)987-3141 Lat: 32.47372, Lon: -83.74663
1513 Sam Nunn Blvd, Perry, GA 31069
www.crossroadstravelpark.com
See ad page 336

FAIR HARBOR RV PARK
good sam park
Ratings: 8.5/10★/9 (RV Park) From Jct of I-75 (exit 135) & GA 127: Go 1/4 mi W on GA 127 (R). **FAC:** paved rds. (280 spaces). Avail: 105 gravel, 90 pull-thrus, (28x75), back-ins (28x60), 105 full hkups (30/50 amps), seasonal sites, cable, WiFi @ sites, rentals, dump, laundry, LP gas, fire rings, firewood. **REC:** pond, fishing, boating nearby, playground. Pets OK. Partial handicap access. No tents. Big rig sites, eco-friendly. 2021 rates: $46 to $49, Military discount.
(478)988-8844 Lat: 32.44752, Lon: -83.75840
515 Marshallville Rd, Perry, GA 31069
www.GaCampground.com
See ad page 336

PERRY PONDEROSA PARK
good sam park
Ratings: 6/9.5★/8 (Campground) From Jct of I-75 (Exit 142) & GA 96: Go 1/4 mi E on GA 96 (L). **FAC:** all weather rds. (60 spaces). 35 Avail: 20 grass, 15 dirt, 35 pull-thrus, (25x55), 35 full hkups (30/50 amps), seasonal sites, WiFi @ sites, laundry, LP gas. **REC:** boating nearby, playground. Pet restrict (S/B). No tents. 2021 rates: $42 to $45. no cc.
(478)825-8030 Lat: 32.54694, Lon: -83.73919
13841 Hwy 96 E, Fort Valley, GA 31030
See ad page 336

PINE MOUNTAIN — C1 *Harris*

FD ROOSEVELT (Public State Park) From Jct of US 27 & SR-190, E 3 mi on SR-190 (R). Entrance fee required. 109 Avail: 109 W, 109 E (30/50 amps). 2021 rates: $25 to $50. (800)864-PARK

PINE MOUNTAIN RV RESORT AN RVC OUTDOOR DESTINATION **Ratings: 8.5/8/9** (RV Park) Avail: 183 full hkups (30/50 amps). 2021 rates: $65 to $90. (706)663-4329, 8804 Hamilton Rd/Hwy 27, Pine Mountain, GA 31822

Go to GoodSam.com/Trip-Planner for Trip Routing.

Southern Trails RV Resort

Welcome to Southern Trails RV Resort - Located in the Heart of Georgia

Southern Trails RV Resort is rated the #1 Value Campground in Georgia. You'll enjoy peace and quiet in a country setting far from the big city while still having access to plenty of fun activities. A favorite among vacationers looking to take a break as they are traveling North or South on Interstate 75. Southern Trails is the perfect place to get away and meet the friendly locals while enjoying the small town feel it has to offer.

Southern Trails RV Resort
2690 Arena Road, Unadilla, GA 31091
info@southerntrailsrvresort.com

good sam park

478-627-3254

www.southerntrailsrvresort.com

Office Hours: Monday - Friday 8:00am to 4:00pm

See listing Unadilla, GA

Amenities

- Free Wi-Fi
- 30/50 Amp available
- Big rig friendly
- Laundry
- Bath house
- Swimming pool
- Propane station
- Clubhouse
- Fire pit

Activities

- Basketball
- Horseshoes
- Swimming
- Fishing
- Recreation room with games and activities
- Pecan gathering
- Miniature golf
- Playground

Location

Southern Trails RV Resort is located in the heart of Georgia in the town of Unadilla just east of Interstate 75 at exit 121 with eazy on/off access

Nearby Attractions

- Aviation Museum
- Sam Shortline Excursion
- Little Grand Canyon
- Plains, Georgia
- Camp Sutter
- Windsor Hotel
- Houston Lake Golf Course
- Andersonville Historic Site
- Museum of Arts and Science

Providence Canyon State Park - Little Grand Canyon

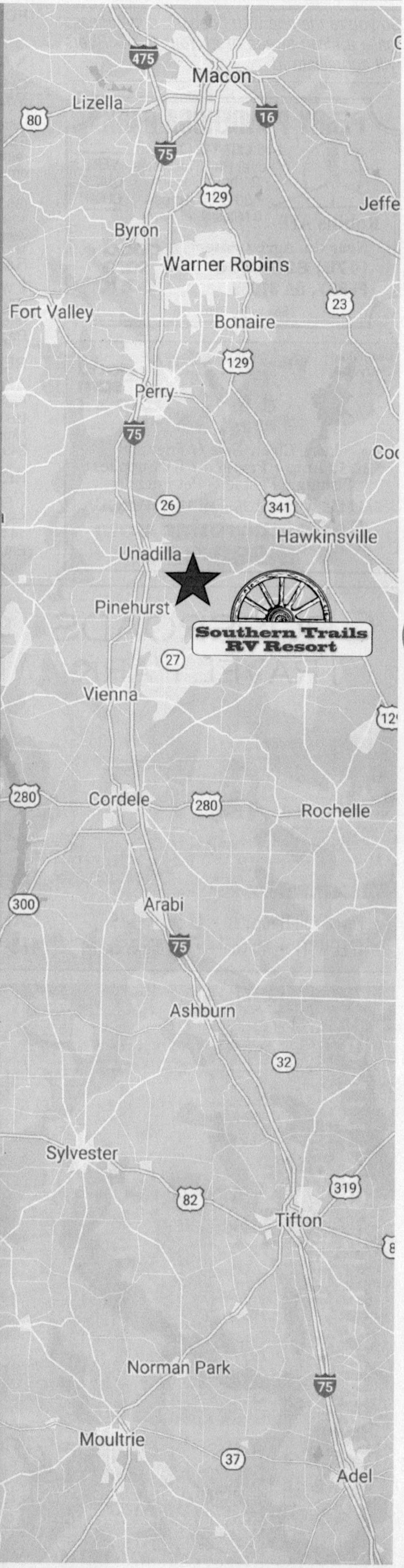

So you're the one with ""pooch'' duty? Please make a clean sweep of it! Your fellow RVers will appreciate it!

POOLER — D5 *Chatham*

Travel Services

CAMPING WORLD OF POOLER/SAVANNAH As the nation's largest retailer of RV supplies, RV accessories, services and new and used RVs, Camping World is committed to making your total RV experience better. **SERVICES:** RV, tire, RV appliance, staffed RV wash, restrooms. RV Sales. RV supplies, LP gas, dump, emergency parking, RV accessible. Hours: 9am to 7pm.
(866)886-7694 Lat: 32.109525, Lon: -81.235305
129 Continental Blvd., Pooler, GA 31322
www.campingworld.com

RABUN GAP — A3 *Rabun*

WILLOW VALLEY RV RESORT **Ratings: 8/10★/8** (RV Park) Avail: 39 full hkups (30/50 amps). 2021 rates: $39 to $70. (706)746-0078, 323 Yorkhouse Rd, Rabun Gap, GA 30568

REIDSVILLE — D4 *Tattnall*

GORDONIA - ALATAMAHA (Public State Park) From Jct of SR-57 & US 280 (in town), W 0.4 mi on US 280 (R). Parking fee required. 29 Avail: 5 full hkups, 24 W, 24 E (30/50 amps). 2021 rates: $32 to $49. (800)864-PARK

RICHMOND HILL — D5 *Bryan*

FORT MCALLISTER (Public State Park) From Jct I-95 & Hwy 144 (Exit 90): Go 6-1/2 mi SE on Hwy 144, then 4 mi E on Spur Rte 144, follow signs (E) Entrance fee required. 65 Avail: 65 W, 65 E (20/30 amps). 2021 rates: $32 to $49. (800)864-PARK

KOA SAVANNAH SOUTH **Ratings: 9/9★/8** (Campground) Avail: 56 full hkups (30/50 amps). 2021 rates: $52.50 to $99. (912)756-3396, 4915 Hwy 17 S, Richmond Hill, GA 31324

RINCON — C5 *Effingham*

WHISPERING PINES RV PARK **Ratings: 8/8.5★/8.5** (RV Park) 24 Avail: 20 full hkups, 4 W, 4 E (30/50 amps). 2021 rates: $30 to $55. (912)728-7562, 1755 Hodgeville Rd, Rincon, GA 31326

RISING FAWN — A1 *Dade*

CLOUDLAND CANYON (Public State Park) From Jct I-59 & SR-136 (exit 11), SE 5.9 mi on SR-136 (L) Note: Parking fee required. 72 Avail: 72 W, 72 E (20/30 amps). 2021 rates: $25 to $49. (800)864-PARK

ROME — A1 *Floyd*

COOSA RIVER CAMPGROUND AT LOCK & DAM PARK (Public) From Jct of US-411 & US-27S, S 3.4 mi on US-27S to Walker Mtn Rd, changes to Blacks Bluff Rd, W 3.2 mi to Lock & Dam Rd, N 0.2 mi (E). 31 Avail: 31 W, 31 E (30/50 amps). 2021 rates: $22 to $24. (706)234-5001

ROSSVILLE — A1 *Walker*

HAWKINS POINTE PARK, STORE & MORE good sam park **Ratings: 6.5/NA/7.5** (RV Park) From jct I-75 (exit 1-TN) & US 41: Go 1/4 mi W on US 41 (Ringgold Rd), then 3/4 mi S on Mack Smith Rd, then 1 block E on Emerson Circle (L).

CHATTANOOGA'S NEWEST PARK
I-75 (exit 1-TN) 70 ft Long, Level 50 AMP FHU Sites. Stay nightly or weekly; enjoy our great City. Luxury A/C Indoor Storage & Covered, Gated Storage with Concierge services. 100 ft Dog Park, washing station, walking trails.

FAC: paved rds. Avail: 50 paved, 32 pull-thrus, (24x75), back-ins (32x55), accepts full hkup units only, 50 full hkups (50 amps), WiFi @ sites, dump. **REC:** boating nearby. Pets OK. Partial handicap access. No tents. Big rig sites. 2021 rates: $45 to $70.
(706)820-6757 Lat: 34.979311, Lon: -85.209864
182 Emerson Circle, Rossville, GA 30741
hawkinspointe.com
See ad page 851

ROYSTON — A3 *Hart*

VICTORIA BRYANT (Public State Park) From Jct of I-85 & SR-51 (Exit 160), S 10 mi on SR-51 to SR-145, S 1.2 mi to US 29, E 1 blk to SR-327, N 1 mi (L). Parking fee required. 27 Avail: 27 W, 27 E (30 amps). 2021 rates: $28 to $49. (800)864-PARK

RUTLEDGE — B3 *Morgan*

HARD LABOR CREEK (Public State Park) From Jct of I-20 & Exit 105, N 4.9 mi thru Rutledge (E) Parking fee required. 46 Avail: 46 W, 46 E (30/50 amps). 2021 rates: $35 to $59. (800)864-PARK

SAVANNAH — D5 *Chatham*

A SPOTLIGHT Introducing Savannah's colorful attractions appearing at the front of this state section.

SAVANNAH See also Richmond Hill, Rincon & Tybee Island, GA; Hardeeville & Hilton Head Island, SC.

BILTMORE RV PARK good sam park **Ratings: 6/NA/8** (RV Park) From Jct I-95 & I-16: Go 5 mi E on I-16 (exit 162), then 1-1/2 mi S on Chatham Pkwy, then 1/2 mi SW on US 17 (Ogeechee Rd) (L) Closed Sunday. **FAC:** paved rds. 38 Avail: 30 gravel, 8 grass, 5 pull-thrus, (30x60), back-ins (30x60), accepts full hkup units only, 38 full hkups (30/50 amps), cable, WiFi, firewood. **REC:** boating nearby. Pet restrict (B/Q). No tents. Big rig sites. 2021 rates: $50 to $55.
(912)236-4065 Lat: 32.04469, Lon: -81.17985
4707 Ogeechee Rd, Savannah, GA 31405
www.biltmorerv.com
See ad opposite page

CREEKFIRE RV RESORT good sam park **Ratings: 9.5/9.5★/10** (RV Park) From jct I-95 (exit 94) & Hwy 204: Go 1/2 mi W on Hwy 204 (L). **FAC:** paved rds. (209 spaces). 109 Avail: 75 paved, 34 gravel, patios, 36 pull-thrus, (30x100), back-ins (30x90), 109 full hkups (30/50 amps), seasonal sites, WiFi @ sites, tent sites, rentals, laundry, LP gas, fire rings, firewood, restaurant, controlled access. **REC:** heated pool, wading pool, hot tub, Creekfire Motor Ranch Lake: fishing, kayaking/canoeing, boating nearby, play-

Join in the fun. Like us on FACEBOOK!

ground, hunting nearby. Pet restrict (B). Big rig sites, eco-friendly. 2021 rates: $50 to $100, Military discount.
(912)244-6985 Lat: 32.011748, Lon: -81.296065
275 Fort Argyle Rd, Savannah, GA 31419
www.covecommunities.com
See ad opposite page

RED GATE CAMPGROUND & RV PARK
good sam park **Ratings: 9/9★/9** (RV Park) From Jct of I-95 & I-16: Go 5 mi E on I-16 (Exit 162), then 2-1/4 mi S on Chatham Pkwy, then 500 ft W on Red Gate Farms Trail (R).

AN OASIS OF SOUTHERN CHARM
Set up your base camp to explore Savannah from the Closest RV Park to The Historic District - ONLY 6 MILES! Big Rig Friendly. Explore Georgia's Gorgeous Scenery on one of our Guided Horseback Trail Rides.
FAC: all weather rds. (31 spaces). 29 Avail: 25 gravel, 4 grass, 6 pull-thrus, (30x75), back-ins (30x60), 24 full hkups, 5 W, 5 E (30/50 amps), seasonal sites, WiFi @ sites, dump, laundry, LP gas, fire rings, firewood. **REC:** pool, pond, fishing, kayaking/canoeing, boating nearby, playground. Pets OK. No tents. Big rig sites. 2021 rates: $42.50 to $77.50, Military discount.
(912)272-8028 Lat: 32.040640, Lon: -81.165750
136 Red Gate Farms Trail, Savannah, GA 31405
redgatecampground.com
See ad page 319

SAVANNAH OAKS RV RESORT
good sam park **Ratings: 9/9.5★/8.5** (Campground) From Jct of I-95 (exit 94) & Hwy 204: Go 2-1/2 mi W on Hwy 204 (L).

TROLLEY STOPS AT OUR CAMPGROUND!
We are a convenient base camp to explore Coastal GA and Historical Savannah. You can relax by the sparkling pool, drop a line in the river or rent a canoe or kayak. Our area of GA has lots to offer for day trips. Y'all come!
FAC: paved/gravel rds. (139 spaces). 99 Avail: 21 paved, 78 gravel, 76 pull-thrus, (24x60), back-ins (24x60), 86 full hkups, 13 W, 13 E (30/50 amps), seasonal sites, cable, WiFi @ sites, rentals, dump, laundry, groc, LP gas, firewood, controlled access. **REC:** pool, Ogeechee River: fishing, kayaking/canoeing, boating nearby, playground. Pets OK. Partial handicap access. No tents. Big rig sites. 2021 rates: $44 to $49, Military discount.
(800)851-0717 Lat: 32.025745, Lon: -81.31976
805 Fort Argyle Rd Hwy 204, Savannah, GA 31419
savannahoaksrvresort.com
See ad page 320

SKIDAWAY ISLAND (Public State Park) From Jct of I-95 & SR-204 (Exit 94), E 10.6 mi on SR-204 to Spur 204, SE 6.8 mi on Spur 204 to park gate (L). Parking fee required. 87 Avail: 17 full hkups, 70 W, 70 E (30/50 amps). 2021 rates: $45 to $53. (800)864-7275

ST MARYS — E5 *Camden*

CROOKED RIVER (Public State Park) N-bnd: From Jct of I-95 & St Marys Rd (Exit 1), E 5.1 mi on St Marys Rd to Charlie Smith Sr Hwy, N 4 mi (R). Entrance fee required. 62 Avail: 62 W, 62 E (30 amps). 2021 rates: $25 to $50. (800)864-PARK

STATESBORO — C4 *Bulloch*

PARKWOOD RV PARK & COTTAGES **Ratings: 9/8.5★/9.5** (RV Park) Avail: 33 full hkups (30/50 amps). 2021 rates: $42 to $47. (912)681-3105, 12188 US Hwy 301 S, Statesboro, GA 30458

STONE MOUNTAIN — B2 *DeKalb*

STONE MOUNTAIN PARK CAMPGROUND
good sam park **Ratings: 8.5/8.5/8.5** (Campground) From Jct of I-285 & Hwy 78 (Stone Mtn Fwy, Exit 39B): Go 7-1/2 mi E on Hwy 78, then follow signs to Exit #8 (E) (entrance fee required).

FAMILY FUN IN THE GREAT OUTDOORS
Georgia's most popular attraction features a wide variety of activities for the whole family. Located on 3,200 acres of natural beauty, you'll discover interactive family adventure, historical sites, and fun annual events.
FAC: paved rds. (385 spaces). Avail: 335 gravel, 20 pull-thrus, (25x50), back-ins (40x55), 206 full hkups, 129 W, 129 E (30/50 amps), seasonal sites, cable, WiFi @ sites, tent sites, rentals, dump, laundry, groc, LP gas, fire rings, firewood, restaurant, controlled access. **REC:** pool, Stone Mountain Lake: fishing, kayaking/canoeing, boating nearby, golf, playground, rec open to public. Pets OK. Partial handicap access. Big rig sites. 2021 rates: $44 to $77. ATM.
(770)498-5710 Lat: 33.819794, Lon: -84.133466
4003 Stonewall Jackson Dr., Stone Mountain, GA 30083
www.stonemountainpark.com
See ad page 323

Set your clocks. Time zones are indicated in the front of each state and province.

Things to See and Do

STONE MOUNTAIN PARK Outdoor entertainment & recreation on 3300 acres of family fun including a riverboat, railroad, summit skyride, crossroads, an 1870 town, treehouse challenge, ride the Duck & see the world's largest laser show spectacular. RV accessible. Restrooms. Food. Hours: 8am to 8pm. Adult fee: $20 to $34.95. ATM.
(800)317-2006 Lat: 33.819794, Lon: -84.133466
1900 Stonewall Jackson Dr, Stone Mountain, GA 30086
www.stonemountainpark.com
See ad page 323

SUCHES — A2 *Union*

WILDCAT LODGE & CAMPGROUND **Ratings: 4.5/7/6** (Campground) Avail: 17 full hkups (30/50 amps). 2021 rates: $40 to $45. (706)973-0321, 7475 Georgia Hwy 60, Suches, GA 30572

SUMMERVILLE — A1 *Chattooga*

JAMES H (SLOPPY) FLOYD (Public State Park) From Jct of US 27 & Sloppy Floyd Lake Rd (4 mi S of town), SW 3 mi on Sloppy Floyd Lake Rd (E). Caution: Steep, narrow roads. 25 Avail: 25 W, 25 E (30/50 amps). 2021 rates: $31 to $33. (800)864-7275

TALLULAH FALLS — A3 *Rabun*

TALLULAH GORGE (Public State Park) From Jct of US 441 & Main St (in town), N 0.6 mi on US 441 to Jane Hurt Yarn Dr, E 0.2 mi (R). Parking fee required. 50 Avail: 50 W, 50 E (30/50 amps). 2021 rates: $40 to $49. (800)864-7275

THOMASVILLE — E2 *Thomas*

THOMASVILLE See also Ochlocknee.

EASTERN PINES RV PARK **Ratings: 6/8/7** (RV Park) Avail: 32 full hkups (30/50 amps). 2021 rates: $40. (833)682-4508, 277 Old Boston Rd, Thomasville, GA 31792

THOMSON — B4 *McDuffee*

J. STROM THURMOND LAKE - COE/BIG HART (Public Corps) From Jct of I-20 & US-78, N 8 mi on US-78 to Russell Landing Rd, E 4 mi (E). 31 Avail: 31 W, 31 E (50 amps). 2021 rates: $26 to $30. Mar 27 to Oct 03. (706)595-8613

RAYSVILLE CAMPGROUND (Public) From town, W 5 mi on Hwy 78 to GA-43, N 6.8 mi (L). 55 Avail: 55 W, 55 E (50 amps). 2021 rates: $26. Mar 01 to Oct 30. (706)595-6759

TIFTON — D3 *Tift*

I75 RV PARK
good sam park **Ratings: 6/9.5★/7.5** (RV Park) From Jct I75 (Exit 61) & Omega Rd: Go 500 ft W on Omega Rd, then 500 ft S on Casseta Rd (L). **FAC:** gravel rds. (13 spaces). Avail: 11 gravel, patios, 11 pull-thrus, (30x60), 11 full hkups (30/50 amps), seasonal sites, cable, WiFi @ sites, laundry. **REC:** boating nearby. Pets OK. Partial handicap access. No tents. Big rig sites. 2021 rates: $30 to $33.
(229)392-0808 Lat: 31.43648, Lon: -83.52700
15 Casseta Rd, Tifton, GA 31793
i75rvpark.com
See ad this page

PINES RV PARK I-75 **Ratings: 7.5/9.5★/8** (RV Park) Avail: 26 full hkups (30/50 amps). 2021 rates: $33. (229)382-3500, 18 Casseta Rd, Tifton, GA 31793

TIFTON KOA **Ratings: 7/7.5/6.5** (RV Park) Avail: 44 full hkups (30/50 amps). 2021 rates: $49.50 to $51.50. (229)386-8441, 4632 Union Rd, Tifton, GA 31794

TIGNALL — B3 *Wilkes*

BROAD RIVER CAMPGROUND (Public State Park) From town, N 19 mi on Hwy 79 (L). 31 Avail: 31 W, 31 E (30 amps). 2021 rates: $25 to $27. (800)405-1033

TOWNSEND — D5 *McIntosh*

LAKE HARMONY RV PARK AND CAMPGROUND
good sam park **Ratings: 9/9.5★/8.5** (Campground) From Jct of I-95 (exit 58) & Hwy 57: Go 1/2 mi W on Hwy 57 (L). **FAC:** paved rds. (54 spaces). Avail: 34 gravel, 31 pull-thrus, (25x60), back-ins (25x50), 34 full hkups (30/50 amps), seasonal sites, cable, WiFi @ sites, laundry, LP gas, fire rings, firewood, controlled access. **REC:** Lake Harmony: swim, fishing, kayaking/canoeing, boating nearby. Pets OK. Partial handicap access. No tents. Big rig sites. 2021 rates: $39, Military discount.
(912)832-4338 Lat: 31.53692, Lon: -81.45537
1088 Lake Harmony Dr. SW, Townsend, GA 31331
www.lakeharmonypark.com
See ad this page

MCINTOSH LAKE RV PARK **Ratings: 6/NA/7.5** (Campground) Avail: 31 full hkups (30/50 amps). 2021 rates: $39. Sep 01 to May 31. (912)832-6215, 1093 McIntosh Lake Ln SW, Townsend, GA 31331

Keep one Guide at home, and one in your RV! To purchase additional copies, call 877-209-6655.

GA

TWIN CITY — C4 *Emanuel*

GEORGE L SMITH (Public State Park) From Jct US 80 & Hwy 23 (in town): Go 3-1/2 mi S on Hwy 23, the 1-3/4 mi E on George L. Smith Park Rd (E) Entrance fee required. 25 Avail: 25 W, 25 E (30/50 amps). 2021 rates: $33 to $49. (800)864-PARK

TYBEE ISLAND — D5 *Chatham*

A SPOTLIGHT Introducing Tybee Island's colorful attractions appearing at the front of this state section.

RIVER'S END CAMPGROUND

good sam park **Ratings: 9.5/10★/9** (Public) From Jct I-95 (Exit 94) & Hwy 204: Go 10 mi E on Hwy 204, then 8 mi N on Harry Truman Parkway, then 15-1/2 mi E on US 80E, then ¼ mi N on Polk St, then 500 ft E on Fort Ave (L).

TYBEE ISLAND, GA * SAVANNAH'S BEACH

A place for all seasons. Sandy beaches, great fishing & history at every turn. Walking distance to the beach. 16 mi to historic Savannah. Enjoy Tybee Time under our live oak canopy. See our website for a detailed rate guide.

FAC: paved rds. (92 spaces). Avail: 80 gravel, 30 pull-thrus, (20x45), back-ins (20x40), 73 full hkups, 7 W, 7 E (30/50 amps), seasonal sites, cable, WiFi @ sites, tent sites, rentals, dump, laundry, LP gas, fire rings, firewood. **REC:** pool, boating nearby. Pet restrict (Q). Partial handicap access, eco-friendly. 2021 rates: $49 to $99, Military discount. ATM.

(912)786-5518 Lat: 32.02274, Lon: -80.85020
5 Fort Ave, Tybee Island, GA 31328
www.riversendcampground.com
See ad page 321

UNADILLA — D2 *Dooly*

SOUTHERN TRAILS RV RESORT

good sam park **Ratings: 7/9★/6** (Membership Park) From Jct I-75 (Exit 121) & Hwy 41: Go 1/4 mi E on Hwy 41, then 1/4 mi S on Speeg Rd, then 1/2 mi SW on E Railroad St (Arena Rd) (L).

ENJOY PEACE & QUIET IN THE COUNTRY!

Come and see our newly renovated resort located in the heart of Georgia off I-75. Surrounded by museums, history, and fun as well as endless on-site amenities we are the perfect place to stop whether traveling north or south.

FAC: gravel rds. (191 spaces). 161 Avail: 141 gravel, 20 grass, 114 pull-thrus, (20x50), back-ins (20x45), 103 full hkups, 58 W, 58 E (30/50 amps), seasonal sites, WiFi, dump, laundry, LP gas. **REC:** pool, pond, fishing, playground. Pets OK. No tents. 2021 rates: $30. no cc.

(478)627-3254 Lat: 32.24037, Lon: -83.73928
2690 Arena Rd, Unadilla, GA 31091
southerntrailsresort.com
See ad pages 334, 335

VALDOSTA — E3 *Lowndes*

VALDOSTA See also Cecil, Hahira & Lake Park, GA; Jennings and Madison, FL.

MILITARY PARK GRASSY POND RECREATION AREA (MOODY AFB) (Public) From Jct I-75 & GA-376 (exit 5), W on GA-376 to Loch Laurel Rd, turn L and follow signs to gate, N 1.8 mi. Avail: 39 full hkups (30/50 amps). 2021 rates: $30 to $40. (229)559-5840

RIVER PARK RV PARK **Ratings: 7.5/9★/8.5** (Campground) Avail: 57 full hkups (30/50 amps). 2021 rates: $44. (229)560-6352, 1407 St Augustine Rd, Valdosta, GA 31602

VALDOSTA OAKS RV PARK

good sam park **Ratings: 7/8★/7** (RV Park) From Jct I-75 (Exit 22) & Hwy 41: N-Bnd, Go 1/4 mi W on Hwy 41 to Citgo, then 1/4 mi N on N Valdosta Rd (E); S-Bnd (Exit 22) continue straight 1/4 mi N on Valdosta Rd (E). **FAC:** all weather rds. (76 spaces). Avail: 55 gravel, 55 pull-thrus, (35x65), accepts full hkup units only, 55 full hkups (30/50 amps), seasonal sites, cable, WiFi @ sites, tent sites, laundry. Pet restrict (Q). Big rig sites. 2021 rates: $36, Military discount.

(229)247-0494 Lat: 30.897239, Lon: -83.358980
4630 N Valdosta Rd, Valdosta, GA 31602
www.valdostaoaksrv.com
See ad opposite page

WARM SPRINGS — C2 *Meriwether*

RAMSEY RV PARK **Ratings: 3/5/5.5** (Campground) Avail: 12 full hkups (30/50 amps). 2021 rates: $26 to $36.75. (706)655-2480, 5153 White House Pkwy (Hwy 85 Alt N), Warm Springs, GA 31830

Find Good Sam member specials at CampingWorld.com

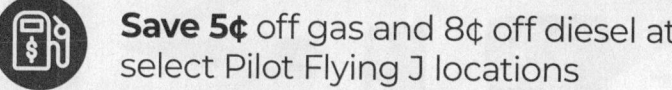

WARNER ROBINS — C3 *Houston*

→ MILITARY PARK ROBINS AFB FAMCAMP (ROBINS AFB) (Public) From Jct I-129 & GA-247 (at Warner-Robins), E 7 mi on GA-247. Avail: 31 full hkups (20/50 amps). 2021 rates: $15 to $25. (478)926-4500

WAYCROSS — E4 *Ware*

↖ LAURA S WALKER (Public State Park) From Jct of US 82 & SR-177, S 2 mi on SR-177 (R). Parking fee required. 44 Avail: 44 W, 44 E (30 amps). 2021 rates: $32 to $49. (800)864-PARK

WEST POINT — C1 *Troup*

↑ WEST POINT LAKE - COE/R SHAEFER HEARD PARK (Public Corps) From town, N 4 mi on US-29, follow signs (L). 117 Avail: 117 W, 117 E (30/50 amps). 2021 rates: $24 to $56. (706)645-2404

WINDER — B2 *Barrow*

↓ FORT YARGO (Public State Park) From Jct I-85 & Hwy 53 (Exit 129): Go 11 mi S on Hwy 53, then 3/4 mi S on Hwy 81 (in town), follow signs (L) Parking fee required. 40 Avail: 40 W, 40 E (20/30 amps). 2021 rates: $34 to $49. (800)864-PARK

WINFIELD — B4 *Columbia*

↗ J. STROM THURMOND LAKE - COE/WINFIELD (Public Corps) From Jct of I-20 & Hwy 150, NE 8 mi on Hwy 150 to Winfield Rd, N 3.5 mi (Left at intersection). 80 Avail: 80 W, 80 E (50 amps). 2021 rates: $28. Mar 29 to Sep 28. (706)541-0147

WOODBINE — E5 *Camden*

↓ WALKABOUT CAMP & RV PARK **Ratings: 8.5/8.5★/8.5** (RV Park) Avail: 60 full hkups (30/50 amps). 2021 rates: $39 to $42. (912)729-4110, 742 Old Still Rd, Woodbine, GA 31569

WOODSTOCK — B2 *Cherokee*

↓ ALLATOONA LAKE - COE/VICTORIA (Public Corps) From Jct of I-575 & Old Alabama Rd (exit 7), W 3 mi on Old Alabama Rd to Bells Ferry Rd, N 4 mi to Victoria Landing Dr, W 3 mi (R). 74 Avail: 2 full hkups, 72 W, 72 E (30/50 amps). 2021 rates: $22 to $32. Mar 22 to Oct 26. (678)721-6700

Travel Services

↓ **CAMPING WORLD OF WOODSTOCK** As the nation's largest retailer of RV supplies, accessories, services and new and used RVs, Camping World is committed to making your total RV experience better. **SERVICES:** RV, RV appliance, MH mechanical, staffed RV wash, restrooms. RV Sales. RV supplies, LP gas, RV accessible. Hours: 9am to 7pm.
(888)380-0095 Lat: 34.088942, Lon: -84.531262
505 Parkway 575, Woodstock, GA 30188
www.campingworld.com

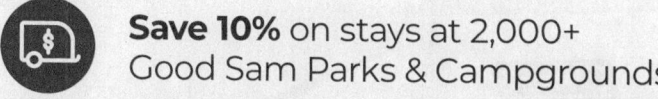

Thank you for using our 2022 Guide. Now you have all the latest information about RV parks, campgrounds and RV resorts across North America!

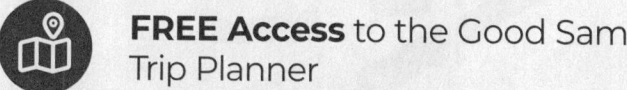

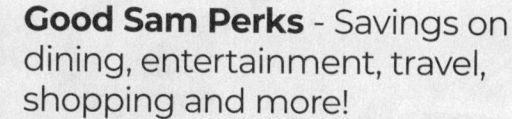

Getty Images/iStockphoto

YOU ARE HERE

Idaho

DID YOU KNOW?

Spanning 3.1 miles, the world's longest gondola ride stretches across the Silver Mountain ski resort in the town of Kellogg.

You don't have to look far to find outdoor recreation in Idaho. Larger-than-life Idaho will keep you busy. Raft the roaring rapids, ski down endless slopes, catch a bounty of fish from the waterways or hit the trail.

Boise is the Best

In Boise, Idaho's biggest city, visitors can enjoy big city amenities just minutes from outdoor thrills. Tour the many museums and art galleries, dine in chic restaurants, partake in the microbrewery culture or enjoy the scenery along the Boise River Greenbelt. To the east, small cities like Pocatello and Idaho Falls provide welcoming base camps for adventures in the nearby mountains and rivers. In North Idaho, the city of Coeur d'Alene is bejeweled by more than 55 glacial lakes.

Yellowstone's Idaho Allotment

Did you know that one percent of Yellowstone National Park lies within Idaho's eastern border (the rest of the park is in Wyoming and Montana)? The Gem State serves as a welcoming gateway to this legendary park. Within the state, Shoshone Falls is an epic natural wonder, known as the "Niagara Falls of the West." These roaring waters tumble 212 feet. After taking in the views, enjoy the surrounding park. An otherworldly landscape greets visitors at the Craters of the Moon National Monument & Preserve, where visitors can explore a 600-square-mile lava field.

Riding the Snake

The Snake River slithers along Idaho's western border and across its southern half, giving anglers lots of spots to catch the fish that make the waterway home. For epic views, hike the 10-mile trail that runs along the south bank. Spanning the river in a graceful arc, the Perrine Bridge in Twin Falls is a site to behold.

Idaho Ice Cream Potato

You'll love the ice cream potato if you like sweet, whimsical creations. Vanilla ice cream is shaped into an oval, covered in cocoa and capped with a generous dollop of whipped cream. The finished creation looks exactly like a baked potato. Get your hands on this offbeat dessert at fairs and festivals throughout the summer.

ID

VISITOR CENTER

TIME ZONE
Mountain Standard

ROAD & HIGHWAY INFORMATION
888-432-7623
511.idaho.gov

FISHING & HUNTING INFORMATION
208-334-3700
idfg.idaho.gov/licenses

BOATING INFORMATION
208-334-4199
parksandrecreation.idaho.gov/activities/boating

NATIONAL PARKS
nps.gov/id

STATE PARKS
parksandrecreation.idaho.gov

TOURISM INFORMATION
Idaho Division of Tourism Development
800-VISIT ID
visitidaho.org

TOP TOURISM ATTRACTIONS
1) Craters of the Moon National Monument
2) Mesa Falls
3) Hells Canyon National Recreation Area

MAJOR CITIES
Boise (capital), Nampa, Meridian, Idaho Falls, Pocatello

good sam park

Featured Good Sam Parks

IDAHO

When you stay with Good Sam, you can expect the highest degree of cleanliness and friendliness, and better yet, you get **10% off** overnight campground fees.

If you're not already a Good Sam member you can purchase your membership at one of these locations:

AMERICAN FALLS
Indian Springs Resort & RV
Willow Bay Campground

ARCO
Mountain View RV Park

BOISE
Hi Valley RV Park
Mountain View RV Park

CALDWELL
Ambassador RV Resort
Country Corners RV Park and Campground

CHALLIS
Challis Golf Course RV Park
Round Valley Park

COEUR D'ALENE
Wolf Lodge Campground

DECLO
Village Of Trees RV Resort

FORT HALL
Buffalo Meadows RV Park

FRUITLAND
Neat Retreat RV Park

GLENNS FERRY
Y Knot Winery & RV Park

GRANGEVILLE
Bear Den RV Park

HAGERMAN
Hagerman RV Village

HEYBURN
Heyburn Riverside RV Park

IDAHO FALLS
Snake River RV Park and Campground

KAMIAH
Long Camp RV Park

MCCALL
McCall RV Resort

MOUNTAIN HOME
Gem State RV Park
Mountain Home RV Resort

MOYIE SPRINGS
The Hemlocks RV and Lodging

NORTH FORK
Wagonhammer RV Park & Campground

POCATELLO
Cowboy RV Park
The Flamingo

POST FALLS
Coeur d'Alene RV Resort

REXBURG
Wakeside Lake RV Park

TWIN FALLS
Anderson Camp

Getty Images/iStockphoto

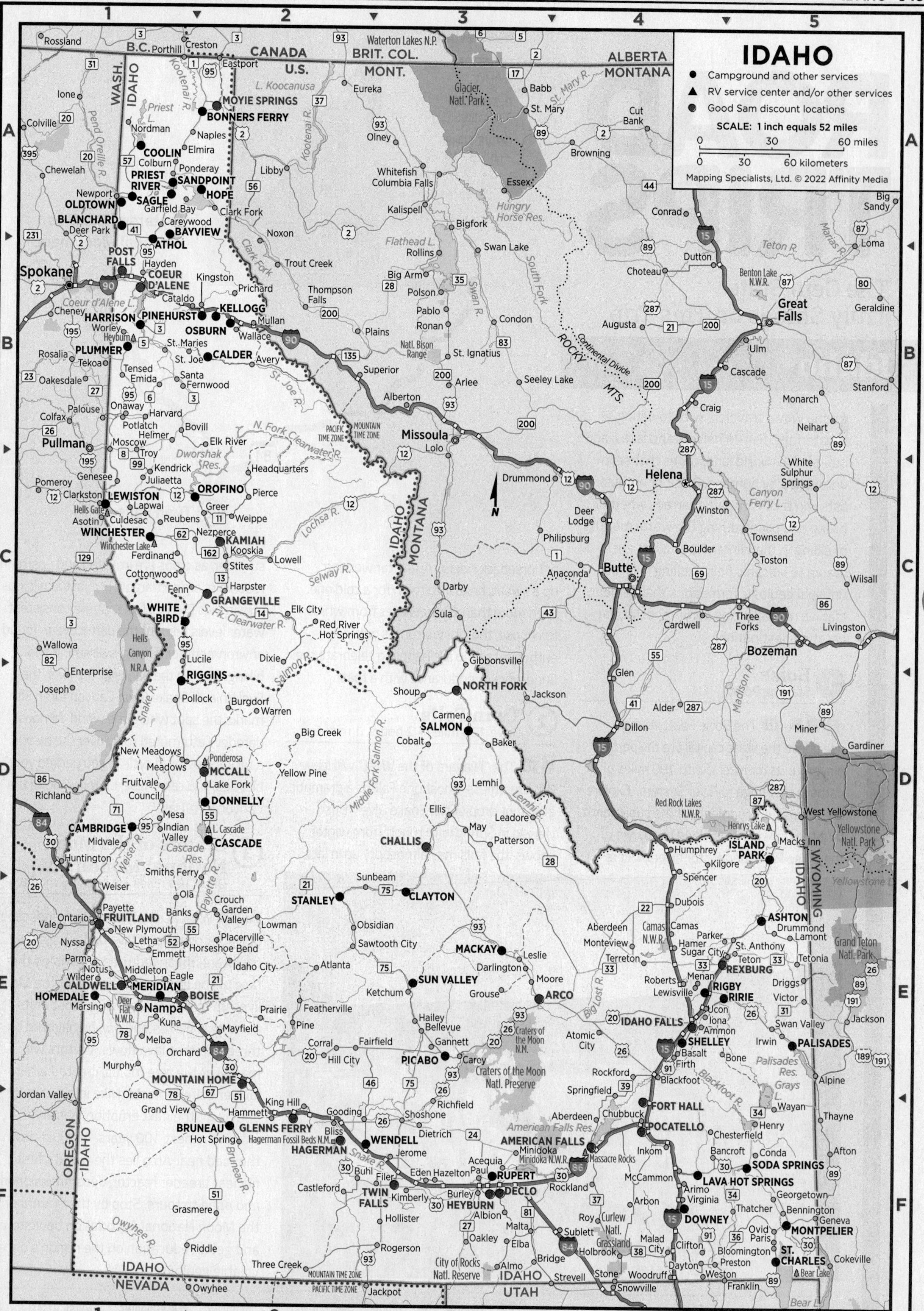
IDAHO
Campground and other services
RV service center and/or other services
Good Sam discount locations
SCALE: 1 inch equals 52 miles
0 30 60 miles
0 30 60 kilometers
Mapping Specialists, Ltd. © 2022 Affinity Media
1 2 3 4 5
A B C D E F
CANADA
U.S.
B.C.
BRIT. COL.
MONT.
ALBERTA
MONTANA
WASH.
IDAHO
OREGON
NEVADA
UTAH
WYOMING
Spokane
Pullman
Missoula
Helena
Butte
Great Falls
Bozeman
Livingston
Dillon
West Yellowstone
BONNERS FERRY
MOYIE SPRINGS
COOLIN
PRIEST RIVER
SANDPOINT
HOPE
SAGLE
OLDTOWN
BLANCHARD
BAYVIEW
ATHOL
POST FALLS
COEUR D'ALENE
HARRISON
PINEHURST
KELLOGG
OSBURN
PLUMMER
CALDER
LEWISTON
OROFINO
WINCHESTER
KAMIAH
GRANGEVILLE
WHITE BIRD
RIGGINS
MCCALL
DONNELLY
CAMBRIDGE
CASCADE
FRUITLAND
CALDWELL
MERIDIAN
BOISE
HOMEDALE
Nampa
MOUNTAIN HOME
BRUNEAU
GLENNS FERRY
HAGERMAN
WENDELL
TWIN FALLS
HEYBURN
RUPERT
DECLO
AMERICAN FALLS
POCATELLO
FORT HALL
LAVA HOT SPRINGS
SODA SPRINGS
DOWNEY
MONTPELIER
ST. CHARLES
IDAHO FALLS
SHELLEY
RIGBY
RIRIE
REXBURG
ASHTON
ISLAND PARK
PALISADES
ARCO
MACKAY
SUN VALLEY
PICABO
STANLEY
CLAYTON
CHALLIS
SALMON
NORTH FORK
Glacier Natl. Park
Hells Canyon N.R.A.
Craters of the Moon Natl. Preserve
Yellowstone Natl. Park
Grand Teton Natl. Park
City of Rocks Natl. Reserve
Hagerman Fossil Beds N.M.
Red Rock Lakes N.W.R.
PACIFIC TIME ZONE
MOUNTAIN TIME ZONE
Continental Divide
ROCKY MTS.

ID

ROAD TRIPS

The Gem State Truly Shines on This Trip

Idaho

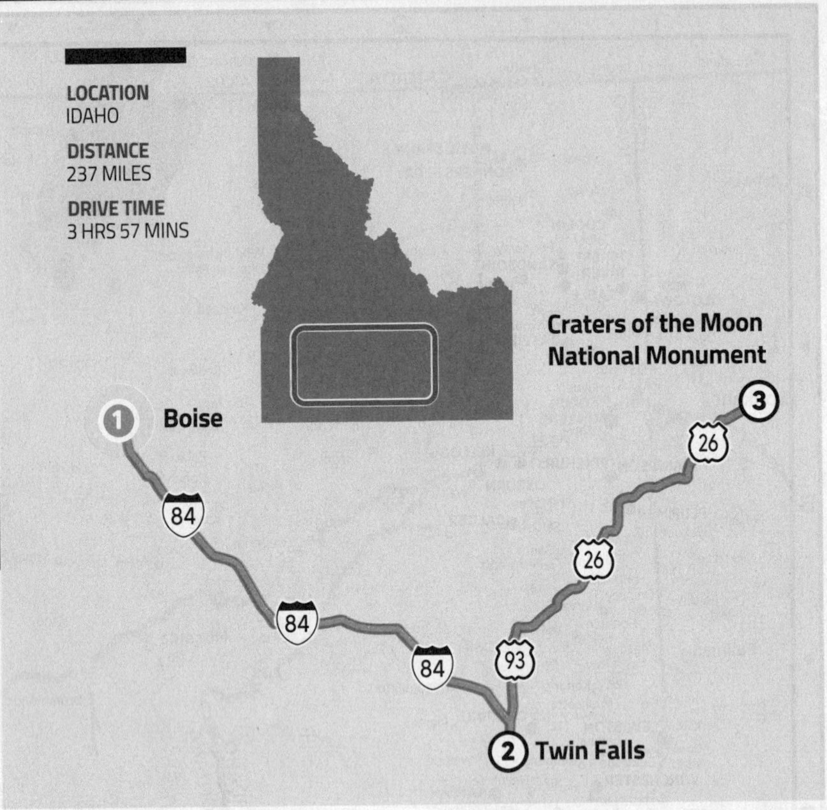

Idaho wows travelers with towering waterfalls, fish-rich rivers and lakes, and out-of-this-world landscapes that seem untouched by humans. Outdoor enthusiasts can tackle inspiring terrain, whether hiking and biking during the warm months or skiing in the winter. Naturalists are drawn to volcanic fields, rolling hills and unusual geologic formations that cement Idaho's reputation as a truly spectacular vacation destination.

1 Boise
Starting Point

The Boise Foothills that rise above the state capital are the perfect playgrounds for hikers, with 190 miles of paths in the Ridge to River System. Explore the natural environments of the public lands that the trails connect along the banks of the Boise River, perfect for hikers, bikers or horseback riders. And after working up a sweat, head into town for a cold one. With more than 20 breweries from which to choose, the city welcomes outdoor enthusiasts who are happy to celebrate their endeavors of endurance with a toast.

2 Twin Falls
Drive 128 miles ▪ 2 hours, 1 minute

The "Niagara of the West" will leave you breathless. Shoshone Falls is a dramatic, 200-foot drop of the Snake River. Best viewed in Spring with runoff from winter snows, the falls may almost dry up in late summer, as crops are irrigated and upstream reservoirs are recharged. But just a mile upstream lies Dierkes Lake, where consistent water levels present the perfect year-round environment for fishing, swimming and hiking. Also on the banks of the river, the Evel Knievel Snake River Canyon Jump Site marks the spot where the world-famous daredevil attempted to fly over the river in a rocket-powered cycle. If you packed your bicycles, you can cruise 1.8 miles along the Canyon Rim Trail.

Getty Images/iStockphoto

3 Craters of the Moon National Monument
Drive 109 miles ▪ 1 hour, 56 minutes

Walk across tormented landscape of cinder cones and lava beds. To early explorers, these features resembled the face of the moon, and Craters of the Moon lives up to its namesake, as most of its acreage is barren and dry, highlighted by three different lava flows. Visitors will marvel at the tree molds, created when lava engulfed forests. Hike in a lava tube and await the next eruption, possibly within the next 100 years. And just down the road near Arco lies the world's first nuclear breeder reactor, decommissioned and open to tours. Stop by the Craters of the Moon National Association bookstore and get an education on the region's once-volatile geology.

BIKING BOATING DINING ENTERTAINMENT FISHING HIKING HUNTING PADDLING SHOPPING SIGHTSEEING

Idaho SPOTLIGHTS

Find New Facets in the Gem State

Idaho has natural attractions found nowhere else on the planet. Explore otherworldly landscapes in Craters of the Moon National Park or take a trip deep into Hells Canyon. Hop on a Boise brew bus in Boise to cap your adventure.

CRIBS: BALD EAGLE NESTS ARE UP TO 4 FEET DEEP AND 5 FEET WIDE.

A bald eagle gracefully alights on a branch in Idaho outside of Boise.

Getty Images/iStockphoto

Boise

Nestled in Treasure Valley in the high desert of the southwestern region of the state, Boise is the cultural center of Idaho. This "City of Trees" is safe, walkable and bikeable. The Rocky Mountain foothills provide a stunning backdrop for recreational activities or imbibing in local brews from the area's emerging craft beer industry.

A Wooded Paradise

Boise, named one of North America's coolest downtowns by major travel companies, has the Boise River Greenbelt running through the heart of the city. Tree-lined paths meander along the river for more than 25 miles, providing a wonderful spot to experience nature. Birders might spot a belted kingfisher, blue heron or an elusive bald eagle while river anglers cast for steelhead, mountain whitefish and chinook salmon.

Fun in the Foothills

Outside Magazine put Boise on its "Best Towns Ever" list. Home to the Rocky Mountain foothills that provide the perfect backdrop for 190 miles of interconnected trails making up the Ridge to Rivers trail system, these routes for walking, running and hiking accommodate families, visitors with pets and other wayfarers.

Post Falls

Sitting on the banks of the Spokane River, Post Falls is an under-the-radar gem that attracts nature lovers and adventure seekers. Post Falls slowly grew from a solitary lumber mill constructed by a German immigrant in 1871. These days, because of its abundance of natural beauty, Post Falls is a popular getaway.

Twin Falls

Legendary daredevil Evel Knievel made history 1974 when he attempted to launch himself over the Snake River on a rocket-powered motorcycle. His failed attempt is still memorialized at the site of the jump.

Double Your Fun

Located near Idaho's southern border, Twin Falls is named for a matching pair of waterfalls on the Snake River. The town was once a stopping point on the Oregon Trail in the late 1800s. Though the original twins of the falls are now a single stream due to a dam built upriver, many impressive waterfalls are found here. At 213 feet high, the striking Shoshone Falls are taller than Niagara Falls.

FOR MORE INFORMATION

Idaho Division of Tourism Development, 800-VISITID, visitidaho.org

Boise, 800-635-5240, www.boise.org

Post Falls Chamber of Commerce, 800-292-2553, www.visitpostfalls.org

Visit South Idaho (Twin Falls), 208-732-5569, visitsouthidaho.com

ID

LOCAL FAVORITE

Easy Cottage Potatoes

Idaho is legendary for its robust potatoes. This one-pot recipe brings out the rich Gem State spud flavor. *Recipe by Pat Pullum.*

INGREDIENTS

- ☐ 2 medium potatoes, cut into quarters
- ☐ 1 lb ground beef
- ☐ 1 medium onion, diced
- ☐ 8 oz frozen mixed vegetables
- ☐ ½ cup stock or gravy mix
- ☐ Shredded cheese (optional)
- ☐ Seasonings to taste

DIRECTIONS

Boil the potatoes in a large pan until soft.
Drain and mash and place in another bowl.
Rinse pan, dry and add ground beef and onions. Cook until slightly browned. Drain off the excess fat. Add the stock, mixed vegetables and any seasonings you like. Cook for about 10 minutes.
Pour meat mixture into a microwave bowl and spread the mashed potatoes on the top. Add the cheese if desired. Place bowl in microwave for about 2 minutes until potatoes are reheated and the cheese is melted. Serve on its own or with a side salad.

Idaho

AMERICAN FALLS — F4 *Power*

INDIAN SPRINGS RESORT & RV
good sam park **Ratings: 6.5/8/7.5** (RV Park) From Jct I-86 and Hwy 37 (exit 36): Go 1.5 mi S on Rockland Hwy to Indian Springs Road, then .1 mi SE on Indian Springs Rd (E). Elev 4499 ft.**FAC:** gravel rds. (138 spaces). Avail: 131 grass, 30 pull-thrus, (20x42), back-ins (20x42), 76 full hkups, 55 W, 55 E (30/50 amps), seasonal sites, WiFi, tent sites, shower$, dump, fire rings, firewood. **REC:** heated pool $, wading pool, pond, boating nearby, playground, hunting nearby, rec open to public. Pets OK. Partial handicap access, eco-friendly. 2021 rates: $19 to $38, Military discount. Apr 01 to Oct 31.
(208)226-7700 Lat: 42.7248, Lon: -112.8741
3249 Indian Springs Rd, American Falls, ID 83211
indianspringsresortandrv.com
See ad this page

Thank you for being one of our best customers!

Idaho Privately Owned Campground Information Updated by our Good Sam Representatives

Jim & Julie Golden

We reside in Tucson, Arizona. We enjoy escaping to Montana and Idaho to avoid the hot desert summers. We love the great outdoors and the freedom that RVing offers. We have been consultants with Good Sam for seven years.

MASSACRE ROCKS (Public State Park) From Jct I-86 & Exit 28 N 0.1 mi (E). 42 Avail: 42 W, 42 E (30 amps). 2021 rates: $12 to $29. (208)548-2672

WILLOW BAY CAMPGROUND
good sam park **Ratings: 9/9★/8** (RV Park) Avail: 32 full hkups (30/50 amps). 2021 rates: $20 to $45. (208)226-2688, 2700 Marina Rd, American Falls, ID 83211

ARCO — E3 *Butte*

CRATERS OF THE MOON/LAVA FLOW
(Public National Park) From Jct of US-26 & US-20, SW 18 mi on US-20 (L). Entrance fee required. Elev 5900 ft.**FAC:** paved rds. Avail: 42 gravel, 6 pull-thrus, (50x100), back-ins (40x80), tent sites, restrooms only. Pets OK. Partial handicap access, 14 day max stay. 2021 rates: $8 to $15. Apr 15 to Nov 15. no cc.
(208)527-3257 Lat: 43.461861, Lon: -113.562889
NULL, Arco, ID 83213
www.nps.gov/crmo

MOUNTAIN VIEW RV PARK
good sam park **Ratings: 8/9.5★/9.5** (RV Park) Avail: 35 full hkups (30/50 amps). 2021 rates: $44.50 to $48.50. (208)527-3707, 705 W Grand Ave, Arco, ID 83213

ASHTON — E5 *Fremont*

YELLOWSTONE GOLF RESORT @ ASPEN ACRES **Ratings: 6/7/6.5** (Campground) Avail: 31 full hkups (30/50 amps). 2021 rates: $30 to $70. May 01 to Sep 30. (208)652-3524, 4179 E 1100 N, Ashton, ID 83420

ATHOL — B1 *Kootenai*

FARRAGUT (Public State Park) From Jct of US-95 & SR-54, E 4 mi on SR-54 (E). 265 Avail: 48 full hkups, 156 W, 156 E (30/50 amps). 2021 rates: $12 to $5,500. (208)683-2425

RAVENWOOD RV RESORT **Ratings: 7/NA/8.5** (RV Resort) 113 Avail: 33 full hkups, 77 W, 77 E (30/50 amps). 2021 rates: $35 to $55. May 01 to Sep 30. (208)683-0891, 25700 N Pope Rd, Athol, ID 83801

SILVERWOOD RV PARK **Ratings: 7/9/8.5** (Campground) Avail: 126 full hkups (30/50 amps). 2021 rates: $52.92 to $69.12. May 02 to Nov 02. (208)683-3400, 27843 N Hwy 95, Athol, ID 83801

BAYVIEW — A1 *Kootenai*

LAKELAND RV PARK **Ratings: 6/6.5/6.5** (Campground) Avail: 25 full hkups (30/50 amps). 2021 rates: $50. May 01 to Oct 01. (208)683-4108, 20139 E Perimeter Rd, Bayview, ID 83803

BLANCHARD — A1 *Bonner*

STONERIDGE GOLF AND MOTOR COACH VILLAGE **Ratings: 10/10★/10** (RV Resort) Avail: 20 full hkups (30/50 amps). 2021 rates: $75 to $125. Apr 01 to Oct 15. (800)952-2948, 364 Stoneridge Rd, Blanchard, ID 83804

BOISE — E1 *Ada*

BOISE See also Caldwell & Meridian.

BOISE RIVERSIDE RV PARK **Ratings: 8/9★/9.5** (Campground) 80 Avail: 31 full hkups, 49 W, 49 E (30/50 amps). 2021 rates: $44.10 to $54. (208)375-7432, 6000 N Glenwood St, Garden City, ID 83714

JOIN GoodSamRoadside.com

HI VALLEY RV PARK
good sam park **Ratings: 9.5/9.5★/9** (RV Park) From Jct I-84 & Hwy 55 / Eagle Rd (exit 46) : Go 6 mi N on Hwy 55 / Eagle Rd, then 2 mi E on West State St (Hwy 44), then 1 mi N on Horseshoe Bend Rd (L). **FAC:** paved rds. (194 spaces). Avail: 45 gravel, patios, 45 pull-thrus, (24x70), 45 full hkups (30/50 amps), seasonal sites, cable, WiFi @ sites, rentals, dump, laundry, LP gas. **REC:** heated pool, hot tub, boating nearby, playground, hunting nearby. Pet restrict (B/Q). Partial handicap access. No tents. Big rig sites, eco-friendly. 2021 rates: $50, Military discount. ATM.
(888)457-5959 Lat: 43.69797, Lon: -116.31573
10555 Horseshoe Bend Rd, Garden City, ID 83714
www.g7rvresorts.com
See ad this page

MOUNTAIN VIEW RV PARK
good sam park **Ratings: 8/10★/8** (RV Park) From Jct I-84 & US 20/26 / Broadway Ave (exit 54): Go 1/8 mi S on Broadway Ave, then 1/2 mi W on Commerce Ave, then 1/4 mi N on S Development Ave, then 1/8 mi E on W Airport Way (L). Elev 2883 ft.

ONLY RV PARK IN BOISE CITY LIMITS
60 full hookup pull thrus. Within 4 miles of Bronco Stadium & State Capitol. Close to downtown Boise & amazing restaurants & entertainment venues. Beautiful rivers, mountains & lush landscaping surround our city. Come enjoy!

FAC: paved rds. (60 spaces). Avail: 45 paved, 45 pull-thrus, (20x65), 45 full hkups (30/50 amps), seasonal sites, WiFi @ sites, dump, laundry. **REC:** boating nearby, hunting nearby. Pets OK. Partial handicap access. No tents, eco-friendly. 2021 rates: $51.84, Military discount.
(877)610-4141 Lat: 43.56793, Lon: -116.20437
2040 W Airport Way, Boise, ID 83705
www.boiservpark.com
See ad opposite page

Travel Services

NELSON'S RVS Fully equipped state of the art service dept, newly expanded parts dept, full truck hitch & accessory shop, experienced and certified service tech & parts personnel, professional sales staff with in-depth product knowledge. **SERVICES:** RV appliance, MH mechanical, restrooms. RV Sales. RV supplies, RV accessible. Hours: 9am - 6pm, 11am - 5pm Sun.
(888)503-1026 Lat: 43.640571, Lon: -116.265224
4911 W Chinden Blvd, Boise, ID 83714
www.nelsonsrvs.com

BONNERS FERRY — A2 *Boundary*

BLUE LAKE RV RESORT Ratings: 8/8.5★/7 (Campground) 42 Avail: 19 full hkups, 19 W, 23 E (30/50 amps). 2021 rates: $34.99 to $50.99. (208)946-3361, 242 Blue Lake Rd, Bonners Ferry, ID 83847

BRUNEAU — F2 *Elmore*

BRUNEAU DUNES (Public State Park) From Jct of I-84 & So. State Hwy 51, S 17 mi on So State Hwy 51 to Jct State Hwy 78, E 2 mi on State Hwy 78 (R). 117 Avail: 82 W, 82 E (30/50 amps). 2021 rates: $12 to $29. (208)366-7919

COVE (BLM) (Public Corps) From Jct of SR-51 & SR-78, W 7 mi on SR-78, NE 1.1 mi on Cottonwood Rd. 28 Avail: Pit toilets. 2021 rates: $12. (208)384-3300

BURLEY — F3 *Cassia*

BURLEY See also Declo, Heyburn & Twin Falls.

CALDER — B2 *Shoshone*

HUCKLEBERRY FLAT (BLM) (Public Corps) From town, Jct of NF-50 and Elk Prairie Rd. East on NF-50 for 5.3 mi. 30 Avail: 30 W, 30 E (50 amps), Pit toilets. 2021 rates: $23. May 15 to Oct 15. (208)769-5000

CALDWELL — E1 *Canyon*

ABUNDANT LIFE RV PARK **Ratings: 8.5/9.5★/8** (RV Park) Avail: 20 full hkups (30/50 amps). 2021 rates: $45 to $55. (208)714-0667, 4924 Laster Lane, Caldwell, ID 83607

AMBASSADOR RV RESORT
good sam park **Ratings: 10/10★/9.5** (RV Park) From Jct I-84 & US 20/26 (exit 29): Go 3/4 mi E on US 20/26, then 1/8 mi N on Smeed Pkwy (R). **FAC:** paved rds. (187 spaces). Avail: 85 all weather, patios, 85 pull-thrus, (33x80), 85 full hkups (30/50 amps), seasonal sites, cable, WiFi @ sites, rentals, dump, laundry, LP gas. **REC:** heated pool, wading pool, hot tub, boating nearby.

playground, hunting nearby. Pet restrict (B/Q). Partial handicap access. No tents. Big rig sites, eco-friendly. 2021 rates: $50, Military discount. ATM.
(888)877-8307 Lat: 43.66439, Lon: -116.64215
615 Smeed Pkwy, Caldwell, ID 83605
www.g7rvresorts.com
See ad page 348

CALDWELL CAMPGROUND & RV PARK
Ratings: 8/9★/8 (Campground) From Jct I-84 & Hwy 20/26 (exit 26): Go 1/8 mi E on US 20/26 to Old Hwy 30, then 1/8 mi S on Old Hwy 30 to Town Circle, then 1/4 mi SW on Town Circle (L). **FAC:** paved/gravel rds. (133 spaces). Avail: 73 gravel, 55 pull-thrus, (27x65), back-ins (30x45), 73 full hkups (30/50 amps), seasonal sites, cable, WiFi @ sites, tent sites, dump, laundry, LP gas, fire rings, firewood. **REC:** Bass Lake: fishing, boating nearby, hunting nearby, rec open to public. Pet restrict (B). Big rig sites, eco-friendly. 2021 rates: $35.
(208)454-0279 Lat: 43.68556, Lon: -116.68686
21830 Town Circle #34, Caldwell, ID 83607
www.caldwellcampgroundandrvparkllc.com
See ad next page

COUNTRY CORNERS RV PARK AND CAMPGROUND
good sam park
Ratings: 8/9.5★/9.5 (Campground) From Jct I-84 & Oasis Rd (exit 17): Go 1/4 mi E Oasis on Rd (R). **FAC:** gravel rds. (62 spaces). Avail: 17 gravel, 17 pull-thrus, (30x66), 17 full hkups (30/50 amps), seasonal sites, WiFi @ sites, tent sites, laundry, groc, LP gas, fire rings, firewood. **REC:** pond, fishing, boating nearby, hunting nearby. Pet restrict (B/Q). Partial handicap access. Big rig sites, eco-friendly. 2021 rates: $40.74 to $45.37, Military discount.
(208)453-8791 Lat: 43.80690, Lon: -116.74588
17671 Oasis Rd, Caldwell, ID 83607
www.countrycornersrvpark.com
See ad this page

We make finding the perfect campground easier. Just use the ""Find-it-Fast'' index in the back of the Guide. It's a complete, state-by-state, alphabetical listing of our private and public park listings.

CALDWELL (CONT)

Travel Services

GANDER RV OF CALDWELL Your new hometown outfitter offering the best regional gear for all your outdoor needs. Your adventure awaits. **SERVICES:** staffed RV wash, restrooms. RV Sales. RV supplies, RV accessible. Hours: 9am- 7pm; closed Sunday.
(888)325-7181 Lat: 43.630834, Lon: -116.640562
5500 Cleveland Blvd, Caldwell, ID 83607
rv.ganderoutdoors.com

New to RVing? Visit Blog.GoodSam.com for tips on everything camping and RVing.

CAMBRIDGE — D1 *Washington*

MCCORMICK PARK (Public) From town, N 28 mi on Hwy 71 to Snake River, follow signs (R) Note: 45' RV length maximum. 28 Avail: 28 W, 28 E (30 amps). 2021 rates: $16. (208)257-3332

WOODHEAD PARK (Public) From town, S 0.1 mi on SR-82 to SR-350, E 7.5 mi to FR 39, SE 25 mi follow signs (E). 118 Avail: 118 W, 118 E (50 amps). 2021 rates: $16. (208)388-2231

CASCADE — D2 *Valley*

ARROWHEAD RV PARK ON THE RIVER **Ratings: 7.5/8.5/8.5** (Campground) Avail: 16 full hkups (30/50 amps). 2021 rates: $40. May 01 to Oct 01. (208)382-4534, 955 S Main St, Cascade, ID 83611

LAKE CASCADE/BUTTERCUP (Public State Park) From town, N 11 mi on US-55 to W Roseberry Rd (in Donnelly), W 1.6 mi, S 1 mi Rainbow Pt. Rd., W 1.7 to W. Mountain Rd., S 2.25 mi. Avail: 1 full hkups, Pit toilets. 2021 rates: $12 to $45. May 24 to Dec 31. (208)382-6544

LAKE CASCADE/HUCKLEBERRY (Public) From town, N 11 mi on US-55 to Tamarack Rd (in Donnelly), W 5 mi to Tamarack Falls Store, W to West Mountain Rd, W 3 mi (L). Avail: 1 full hkups. 2021 rates: $12 to $45. (208)382-6544

LAKE CASCADE/SUGARLOAF (Public State Park) From town, N 7 mi on US-55 (L). Avail: 1 full hkups (30 amps). 2021 rates: $12 to $45. (208)382-6544

LAKE CASCADE/VAN WYCK (Public State Park) From Jct of SR-55 & Old State Hwy, W 2 mi on Old State Hwy (E) Note: 32' RV length max. 30 Avail: Pit toilets. 2021 rates: $12 to $45. May 01 to Oct 20. (208)382-6544

LAKE CASCADE/WEST MOUNTAIN (Public State Park) From town, N 11 mi on US-55, W 1.5 mi W Roseberry Rd., SW 2.6 mi Rainbow Point Rd., S W. Mountain Rd. 2.5 mi. Avail: 1 E (30 amps). 2021 rates: $12 to $45. May 24 to Dec 31. (208)382-6544

CHALLIS — D3 *Custer*

CHALLIS GOLF COURSE RV PARK
Ratings: 6/9.5★/7.5 (RV Park) From Jct US 93 & Hwy 75: Go 2-1/4 mi N on US 93, then 1-1/4 mi W on Main (becomes Garden Creek Rd), then 1/8 mi S on Emily Ln (R). Elev 5355 ft.**FAC:** gravel rds. Avail: 30 gravel, 24 pull-thrus, (25x60), back-ins (40x40), 30 full hkups (30/50 amps), WiFi @ sites, laundry. **REC:** pond, fishing, boating nearby, golf, hunting nearby, rec open to public. Pets OK. Partial handicap access. No tents. Big rig sites. 2021 rates: $35 to $41. Apr 15 to Oct 15.
(208)879-5500 Lat: 44.50391, Lon: -114.24709
210 Golf Club Lane , Challis, ID 83226
www.golfcourserv.com
See ad this page

Save 10% at Good Sam Parks!

CHALLIS HOT SPRINGS & RV PARK **Ratings: 7/7.5/7** (Campground) 37 Avail: 37 W, 37 E (30/50 amps). 2021 rates: $40 to $43. Mar 15 to Oct 31. (208)879-4442, 5025 Hot Springs Rd, Challis, ID 83226

PIONEER MOTEL & RV PARK **Ratings: 5.5/UI/6** (Campground) Avail: 12 full hkups (30/50 amps). 2021 rates: $34 to $38. (208)879-6791, 220 Hwy 93 S, Challis, ID 83226

ROUND VALLEY PARK
Ratings: 7/9★/9 (RV Park) Avail: 67 full hkups (30/50 amps). 2021 rates: $39. Apr 15 to Nov 30. (208)879-2393, 211 Ramshorn Dr, Challis, ID 83226

CLAYTON — E3 *Custer*

THE SAWMILL STATION **Ratings: 8/7.5/8.5** (RV Park) Avail: 49 full hkups (30/50 amps). 2021 rates: $30 to $40. May 01 to Nov 08. (208)838-2400, 21855 Highway 75, Clayton, ID 83227

COEUR D'ALENE — B1 *Kootenai*

COEUR D'ALENE See also Athol, Bayview, Plummer & Post Falls, ID; Liberty Lake & Spokane Valley, WA.

BLACKWELL ISLAND RV RESORT **Ratings: 8.5/9.5★/8** (RV Park) Avail: 182 full hkups (30/50 amps). 2021 rates: $45 to $80. Apr 01 to Oct 15. (888)571-2900, 800 S Marina Dr, Coeur d'Alene, ID 83814

CAMP COEUR D'ALENE **Ratings: 7/9★/6.5** (Campground) 38 Avail: 30 full hkups, 8 W, 8 E (30/50 amps). 2021 rates: $40 to $60. May 01 to Oct 15. (208)664-4471, 10588 E Wolf Lodge Bay Rd, Coeur d'Alene, ID 83814

WOLF LODGE CAMPGROUND
Ratings: 8/8.5★/9 (Campground) From Jct I-90 & Hwy 97 (exit 22): Go 1/8 mi N on Hwy 97, then 1-1/2 mi E on Frontage Rd (L). **FAC:** gravel rds. (65 spaces). 63 Avail: 10 paved, 16 gravel, 37 grass, 23 pull-thrus, (23x70), back-ins (30x40), 27 full hkups, 36 W, 36 E (30/50 amps), seasonal sites, WiFi @ sites, tent sites, rentals, dump, laundry, groc, firewood. **REC:** Wolf Lodge Creek: swim, fishing, kayaking/canoeing, boating nearby, shuffleboard, playground. Pets OK. eco-friendly. 2021 rates: $50 to $60, Military discount. May 01 to Sep 30.
(208)664-2812 Lat: 47.63113, Lon: -116.61620
12329 E Frontage Rd, Coeur D'Alene, ID 83814
www.wolflodgecampground.com
See ad this page

COOLIN — A1 *Bonner*

PRIEST LAKE/INDIAN CREEK UNIT (Public State Park) From Jct of SR-57 & Coolin Rd, NE 5.4 mi on Coolin Rd to East Shore Rd, N 11.5 mi (E). 151 Avail: 11 full hkups, 63 W, 63 E (20/50 amps), Pit toilets. 2021 rates: $12 to $31. (208)443-2200

PRIEST LAKE/LIONHEAD UNIT (Public State Park) From jct US 2 & Hwy 57: Go 22-1/2 mi N on Hwy 57, then 5 mi NE on Dickensheet Rd to Coolin, then 23 mi N on East Shore Rd. 47 Avail: Pit toilets. 2021 rates: $12 to $21. (208)443-2200

TIPS FOR THE BBQ CHEF: BURGERS - Use fresh meat and mix in ingredients-onions, garlic, chopped jalapeno or bell peppers, oregano, BBQ or hot sauce-sprinkle salt and pepper just before going on the grill. Cook 3 to 5 mins per side to 140-degree internal temp. Tip: Don't press down on the patties during cooking or you'll squeeze out the delicious juices. BEEF BRISKET - Marinate a 3 to 4 lb brisket for 24 hrs. or more in Worcestershire or teriyaki sauce with garlic and black pepper. Cook for 3 to 5 mins per side on direct high heat, then indirect heat for 15-20 mins to 130-degree internal temp (medium-rare). FISH FILLETS OR STEAKS (such as salmon, striped bass, and mahi-mahi) - Cook 5 to 8 mins per side (depending on heat) or to 130 to 135-degree internal temp. BONELESS CHICKEN BREASTS - Marinate for 30 mins or more or rub both sides with a spice mix. Cook over high heat (375-400 degrees) for 4 to 5 mins per side, then indirect heat for 8 to 12 mins to 160-165 internal temp.

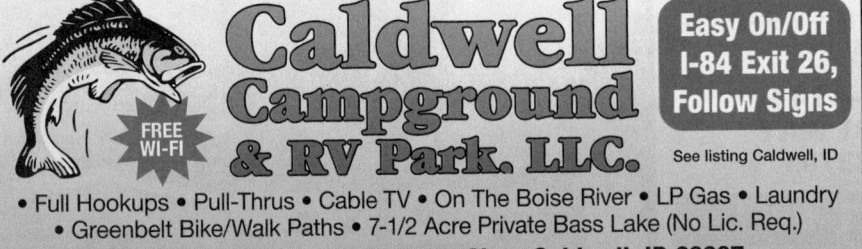

DECLO — F3 *Cassia*

VILLAGE OF TREES RV RESORT

good sam park **Ratings: 8/9★/8.5** (Campground) From Jct I-84 & Rupert-Declo Rd (exit 216): Go 1/4 mi N on Rupert-Declo Rd (L). Elev 4200 ft.**FAC:** gravel rds. (84 spaces). Avail: 54 gravel, 54 pull-thrus, (30x70), 54 full hkups (30/50 amps), seasonal sites, cable, WiFi @ sites, tent sites, rentals, dump, laundry, groc, LP gas, fire rings, firewood, restaurant. **REC:** heated pool, Snake River: fishing, boating nearby, playground. Pets OK. Partial handicap access. Big rig sites, eco-friendly. 2021 rates: $32, Military discount. ATM.
(208)654-2133 Lat: 42.57195, Lon: -113.62503
274 Highway 25, Declo, ID 83323
www.villageoftreesrvresort.com
See ad this page

Travel Services

TRAVEL STOP 216 C-STORE & RESTAURANT The Village of Trees RV Resort Travel Stop 216 offers 24 hour Phillips 66 gas & diesel, propane, convenience store, groceries, gift shop, RV supplies and full service grill. Elev 4200 ft. **SERVICES:** restaurant, restrooms. RV supplies, LP gas, dump, emergency parking, RV accessible. Hours: 6am to 9pm. ATM.
(208)654-2133 Lat: 42.57195, Lon: -113.62503
274 Hwy 25, Declo, ID 83323
www.villageoftreesrvresort.com
See ad this page

DONNELLY — D2 *Valley*

CHALET FAMILY CAMPGROUND **Ratings: 8/9.5★/8.5** (Campground) Avail: 41 full hkups (30/50 amps). 2021 rates: $45 to $50. May 01 to Nov 01. (208)325-8223, 418 S Hwy 55 (Main St), Donnelly, ID 83615

DOWNEY — F4 *Bannock*

DOWNATA HOT SPRINGS CAMPGROUND **Ratings: 6.5/8/7.5** (Campground) 81 Avail: 39 W, 76 E (30/50 amps). 2021 rates: $25 to $39. (208)897-5736, 25900 S Downata Rd, Downey, ID 83234

Get a FREE Quote at GoodSamESP.com

FORT HALL — F4 *Bingham*

BUFFALO MEADOWS RV PARK

good sam park **Ratings: 8.5/9★/7.5** (RV Park) From Jct I-15 & Simplot Rd (exit 80): Go 1/4 mi W on Simplot Rd (R) (Behind casino). Elev 4525 ft.

ON THE WAY TO YELLOWSTONE!
Perfect stop on your way to Yellowstone & conveniently open year-round! Casino & hotel onsite has lots of menu favorites in our restaurant, plus concerts by well-known entertainers. Come stay & play a few days!

FAC: paved rds. Avail: 37 paved, 37 pull-thrus, (23x60), 37 full hkups (30/50 amps), WiFi @ sites, tent sites, laundry, restaurant. **REC:** boating nearby, hunting nearby, rec open to public. Pets OK. Partial handicap access. 2021 rates: $37. ATM.
(208)238-4800 Lat: 43.02524, Lon: -112.41444
777 Bannock Trl, Fort Hall, ID 83203
www.shobangaming.com
See ad this page

Things to See and Do

SHOSHONE-BANNOCK CASINO HOTEL Multi-Denominational Gaming Machines, Bingo, Live Entertainment, Monthly Promotions Elev 4525 ft. Partial handicap access. RV accessible. Restrooms. Food. Hours: 24 Hrs. ATM.
(208)238-4800 Lat: 43.02242, Lon: -112.41285
777 Bannock Trail, Fort Hall, ID 83203
www.shobangaming.com
See ad this page

FRUITLAND — E1 *Payette*

NEAT RETREAT RV PARK

good sam park **Ratings: 7.5/9.5★/8.5** (RV Park) Avail: 13 full hkups (30/50 amps). 2021 rates: $40 to $44.50. (208)452-4324, 2701 N Alder Dr #0, Fruitland, ID 83619

GLENNS FERRY — F2 *Elmore*

THREE ISLAND CROSSING (Public State Park) From Jct of I-84 & Exit 121 (W-bnd) or Exit 120 (E-bnd), exit rd to Commercial (in center of town), S 0.75 mi to Madison Ave, W 1.0 mi (L). 82 Avail: 1 full hkups, 81 W, 81 E (30 amps). 2021 rates: $22 to $45. (208)366-2394

Y KNOT WINERY & RV PARK

good sam park **Ratings: 6/NA/7.5** (RV Park) Avail: 16 full hkups (30/50 amps). 2021 rates: $35 to $40. (208)366-2313, 1294 W Madison Ave, Glenns Ferry, ID 83623

GRANGEVILLE — C2 *Idaho*

BEAR DEN RV PARK

good sam park **Ratings: 8/9.5★/9** (Campground) Avail: 45 full hkups (30/50 amps). 2021 rates: $40 to $43. (208)983-0140, 20 Fish Hatchery Rd, Grangeville, ID 83530

HAGERMAN — F2 *Gooding*

HAGERMAN RV VILLAGE

good sam park **Ratings: 8/10★/9** (RV Park) From Jct I-84 & US 26 (exit 141) : Go 1/4 mi W on US 26, then 8 mi S on US 30 (R). Elev 2975 ft.**FAC:** gravel rds. (72 spaces). Avail: 57 gravel, 57 pull-thrus, (30x75), 57 full hkups (30/50 amps), seasonal sites, WiFi @ sites, rentals, laundry, LP gas. **REC:** boating nearby, playground, hunting nearby. Pet restrict (S/B/Q). Partial handicap access. No tents. Big rig sites, eco-friendly. 2021 rates: $40.
(208)837-4906 Lat: 42.82347, Lon: -114.89572
18049 Hwy 30, Hagerman, ID 83332
www.hagermanrvvillage.com
See ad next page

We shine ""Spotlights'' on interesting cities and areas.

HARRISON — B1 *Kootenai*

CITY OF HARRISON CAMPGROUND (Public) In town, S on US-97, follow signs (R). 20 Avail: 20 W, 20 E (30 amps). 2021 rates: $36.75 to $44.10. May 15 to Sep 15. (208)689-3212

HEYBURN — F3 *Minidoka*

HEYBURN RIVERSIDE RV PARK
Ratings: 5/9★/9 (Public) From Jct I-84 & Hwy 30 (exit 211): Go 2 mi S on Hwy 30, then 1/4 mi E on 7th St (R). Elev 4150 ft.**FAC:** paved/gravel rds. (29 spaces). 24 Avail: 2 paved, 22 gravel, patios, 11 pull-thrus, (51x64), back-ins (51x45), 24 full hkups (30/50 amps), seasonal sites, WiFi @ sites, . **REC:** Snake River: fishing, boating nearby, playground, hunting nearby, rec open to public. Pets OK. Partial handicap access. No tents. Big rig sites, eco-friendly. 2021 rates: $31 to $38, Military discount. Mar 01 to Nov 30.
(208)431-2977 Lat: 42.54665, Lon: -113.75904
1175 7th St, Heyburn, ID 83336
heyburn.id.gov
See ad this page

Always do a Pre-Drive Safety Check!

KASOTA RV RESORT **Ratings: 7/NA/9** (RV Park) Avail: 43 full hkups (30/50 amps). 2021 rates: $35 to $50. (208)438-5500, 1325 W Hwy 25, Heyburn, ID 83336

HOMEDALE — E1 *Owyhee*

SNAKE RIVER RV RESORT **Ratings: 6.5/9★/8.5** (Campground) Avail: 36 full hkups (30/50 amps). 2021 rates: $40 to $45. (208)337-3744, 4030 River Resort Dr, Homedale, ID 83628

HOPE — A2 *Bonner*

BEYOND HOPE RESORT **Ratings: 5.5/7.5/6.5** (Campground) 70 Avail: 70 W, 70 E (30/50 amps). 2021 rates: $60. May 15 to Sep 30. (208)264-5251, 1267 Peninsula Rd, Hope, ID 83836

ISLAND VIEW RV PARK **Ratings: 5.5/NA/6** (Campground) Avail: 55 full hkups (30/50 amps). 2021 rates: $45 to $50. May 01 to Sep 30. (208)264-5509, 1767 Peninsula Rd, Hope, ID 83836

IDAHO FALLS — E4 *Bonneville*

KELLY ISLAND (BLM) (Public Corps) From town, NE 23 mi on Hwy 26 (L) Note: 40' RV length maximum. 14 Avail: Pit toilets. 2021 rates: $10 to $20. May 15 to Sep 15. (208)524-7500

SNAKE RIVER RV PARK AND CAMPGROUND
Ratings: 9/9★/9 (Campground) From Jct I-15 (Exit 119) & US 20 (Grandview Dr): Go 1/8 mi E on US 20 (Grandview Dr) to Lindsay Blvd exit, then 1/2 mi N on Lindsay Blvd (R). Elev 4710 ft.**FAC:** paved/gravel rds. Avail: 158 gravel, 58 pull-thrus, (24x72), back-ins (20x38), 134 full hkups, 24 W, 24 E (30/50 amps), WiFi @ sites, tent sites, rentals, dump, laundry, groc, LP gas, fire rings, firewood. **REC:** heated pool, hot tub, boating nearby, playground, hunting nearby. Pets OK $. Big rig sites, eco-friendly. 2021 rates: $37 to $57, Military discount.
(208)523-3362 Lat: 43.50878, Lon: -112.05312
1440 Lindsay Blvd, Idaho Falls, ID 83402
www.snakeriverrvpark.com
See ad this page

SUNNYSIDE ACRES PARK & MHP **Ratings: 6.5/8.5/7** (RV Area in MH Park) Avail: 24 full hkups (30/50 amps). 2021 rates: $55. (208)523-8403, 905 W Sunnyside Rd, Idaho Falls, ID 83402

Travel Services

CAMPING WORLD OF IDAHO FALLS As the nation's largest retailer of RV supplies, accessories, services and new and used RVs, Camping World is committed to making your total RV experience better. **SERVICES:** tire, RV appliance, MH mechanical, staffed RV wash, restrooms. RV Sales. RV supplies, LP gas, dump, emergency parking, RV accessible. Hours: 9am to 7pm.
(855)691-4253 Lat: 43.48774, Lon: -112.060158
1355 Tara St, Idaho Falls, ID 83402
www.campingworld.com

ISLAND PARK — D5 *Fremont*

BUFFALO RUN RV PARK & CABINS **Ratings: 6/UI/8** (Campground) 20 Avail: 20 W, 20 E (30/50 amps). 2021 rates: $50. May 15 to Oct 15. (208)558-7112, 3402 N Hwy 20, Island Park, ID 83429

HENRYS LAKE (Public State Park) From Jct of US-20 & SR-87, S 1.2 mi on US-20 to Henry Lake Rd (MP 401), W 2 mi (E). 83 Avail: 25 W, 83 E (30 amps). 2021 rates: $20 to $31. May 23 to Oct 13. (888)922-6743

REDROCK RV AND CAMPING PARK **Ratings: 8.5/10★/10** (RV Park) Avail: 90 full hkups (30/50 amps). 2021 rates: $78. May 10 to Sep 25. (800)473-3762, 3707 Red Rock Rd, Island Park, ID 83429

VALLEY VIEW RV PARK **Ratings: 7.5/UI/7.5** (RV Park) Avail: 57 full hkups (30/50 amps). 2021 rates: $72 to $76. May 15 to Oct 01. (208)558-7443, 5152 North Highway 20, Island Park, ID 83429

YELLOWSTONE RV PARK AT MACK'S INN **Ratings: 8/9.5★/10** (RV Park) Avail: 70 full hkups (30/50 amps). 2021 rates: $65 to $75. May 21 to Sep 30. (208)716-5959, 4270 Old Highway 191, Island Park, ID 83429

KAMIAH — C2 *Idaho*

KAMIAH/CLEARWATER VALLEY KOA **Ratings: 7.5/UI/5.5** (Campground) 125 Avail: 75 full hkups, 50 W, 50 E (30/50 amps). 2021 rates: $35.59 to $42.89. (208)935-2556, 4243 Hwy 12, Kamiah, ID 83536

LONG CAMP RV PARK
Ratings: 7/8.5★/9 (Campground) Avail: 22 full hkups (30/50 amps). 2021 rates: $35 to $40. (208)935-7922, 4192 Hwy 12, Kamiah, ID 83536

KELLOGG — B2 *Shoshone*

CRYSTAL GOLD MINE & RV PARK **Ratings: 6/NA/7.5** (Campground) Avail: 15 full hkups (30/50 amps). 2021 rates: $39. (208)783-4653, 51931 Silver Valley Rd., Kellogg, ID 83837

LAVA HOT SPRINGS — F4 *Bannock*

LAVA HOT SPRINGS KOA **Ratings: 6/9.5★/8** (Campground) Avail: 106 full hkups (30/50 amps). 2021 rates: $49.95 to $125. (208)776-5295, 100 Bristol Park Lane, Lava Hot Springs, ID 83246

MARY'S PLACE RV CAMPGROUND **Ratings: 6.5/UI/7** (Campground) 69 Avail: 67 full hkups, 2 W, 2 E (30/50 amps). 2021 rates: $50 to $85. May 15 to Sep 03. (208)776-5026, 300 Bristol Park Lane, Lava Hot Springs, ID 83246

LEWISTON — C1 *Nez Perce*

LEWISTON See also Clarkston, WA.

CLEARWATER RIVER CASINO & RV PARK **Ratings: 5.5/9/6** (Campground) Avail: 21 full hkups (30/50 amps). 2021 rates: $25. (208)298-1400, 17500 Nez Perce Rd, Lewiston, ID 83501

HELLS GATE (Public State Park) From Jct of US-12 & Snake River Ave, S 3.7 mi on Snake River Ave. 89 Avail: 9 full hkups, 51 W, 51 E (50 amps). 2021 rates: $12 to $31. (208)799-5015

Say you saw it in our Guide!

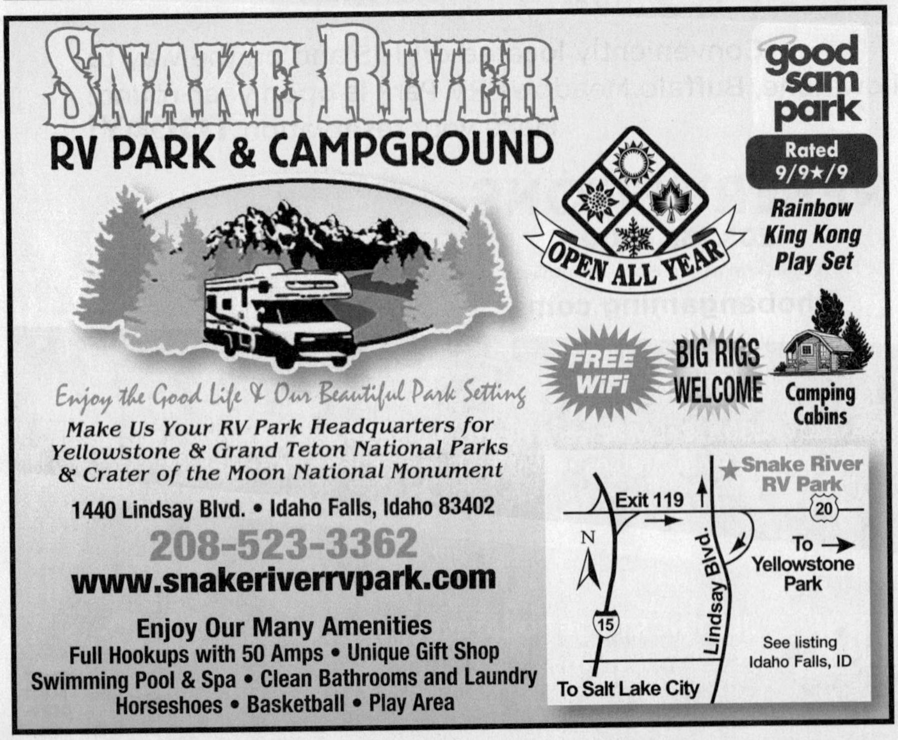

MACKAY — E3 *Custer*

JOSEPH T. FALLINI CAMPGROUND (BLM) (Public Corps) From town, N 6 mi on US-93 (L). 22 Avail: 22 W, 22 E Pit toilets. 2021 rates: $14 to $20. (208)879-6200

MOOSE CROSSING RV PARK **Ratings: 6/8★/6** (RV Park) Avail: 27 full hkups (30/50 amps). 2021 rates: $35 to $40. May 01 to Sep 30. (208)588-2994, 3794 N US Highway 93, Mackay, ID 83251

MCCALL — D2 *Valley*

BLACK BEAR RV PARK **Ratings: 7/9★/9** (Campground) 42 Avail: 42 W, 42 E (30/50 amps). 2021 rates: $48. May 01 to Nov 01. (208)634-5165, 190 Krahn Ln, McCall, ID 83638

MCCALL RV RESORT

good sam park **Ratings: 9.5/10★/10** (RV Resort) From Jct of Hwy 55 (East Lake St) & Hwy 55 (3rd St): Go 1-1/2 mi S on Hwy 55 to Deinhard Ln, then 1/2 mi NW on Deinhard Ln to Mission St, then 1/4 mi S on Mission St to Scott St, then 1/8 mi W on Scott St (E). Elev 5067 ft.**FAC:** paved rds. (157 spaces). 107 Avail: 41 paved, 66 gravel, patios, 56 pull-thrus, (45x75), back-ins (30x70), 107 full hkups (30/50 amps), seasonal sites, cable, WiFi @ sites, rentals, dump, laundry, LP gas. **REC:** heated pool, hot tub, North Fork of Payette River: fishing, kayaking/canoeing, boating nearby, playground, hunting nearby, rec open to public. Pets OK. Partial handicap access. No tents. Big rig sites, eco-friendly. 2021 rates: $65, Military discount. ATM.
(855)634-5646 Lat: 44.89600, Lon: -116.10629
200 Scott St, McCall, ID 83638
www.g7rvresorts.com
See ad this page

PONDEROSA (Public State Park) From Jct of SR-55 & 3rd/Railroad St, follow signs (E). 185 Avail: 163 W, 163 E (30/50 amps). 2021 rates: $12 to $31. Apr 15 to Oct 01. (208)634-2164

MERIDIAN — E1 *Ada*

BOISE MERIDIAN KOA RV RESORT **Ratings: 9.5/10★/9** (Campground) Avail: 62 full hkups (30/50 amps). 2021 rates: $57.78 to $62.64. (866)988-7003, 184 W Pennwood, Meridian, ID 83642

Travel Services

CAMPING WORLD OF MERIDIAN As the nation's largest retailer of RV supplies, accessories, services and new and used RVs, Camping World is committed to making your total RV experience better. **SERVICES:** RV, tire, RV appliance, sells outdoor gear, sells firearms, restrooms. RV Sales. RV supplies, LP gas, RV accessible. Hours: 9am to 7pm.
(877)847-5681 Lat: 43.590126, Lon: -116.412428
1580 W Overland Road, Meridian, ID 83642
www.campingworld.com

MONTPELIER — F5 *Bear Lake*

MONTPELIER CREEK KOA **Ratings: 8/UI/8.5** (Campground) 36 Avail: 18 full hkups, 18 W, 18 E (30/50 amps). 2021 rates: $49 to $58.85. Apr 15 to Oct 31. (800)562-7576, 28501 US Hwy 89 N, Montpelier, ID 83254

MOUNTAIN HOME — E2 *Elmore*

FORT RUNNING BEAR RV RESORT **Ratings: 7/UI/6.5** (Membership Park) 72 Avail: 44 full hkups, 28 W, 28 E (30/50 amps). 2021 rates: $39.33 to $43.70. May 01 to Sep 30. (208)653-2494, CTC Deluxe #784/25094 Little Camas Reservoir Rd, Mountain Home, ID 83647

GEM STATE RV PARK

good sam park **Ratings: 7/9★/7** (Campground) From jct I-84 & Hwy 51 (Exit 95): Go 1-3/4 mi S on Hwy 51 to 2nd St, then 3/4 mi N on 2nd St to E 10th St N, then 1/4 mi E on E 10th St N (L). Elev 3150 ft.**FAC:** paved rds. (61 spaces). Avail: 46 grass, 40 pull-thrus, (34x87), back-ins (34x42), 46 full hkups (30/50 amps), seasonal sites, cable, WiFi @ sites, tent sites, rentals, laundry. **REC:** playground, hunting nearby. Pets OK. Partial handicap access. Big rig sites, eco-friendly. 2021 rates: $35, Military discount.
(208)587-5111 Lat: 43.14156, Lon: -115.69900
220 E 10th North , Mountain Home, ID 83647
www.gemstatervpark.com
See ad this page

MILITARY PARK MOUNTAIN HOME AFB FAMCAMP (MTN HOME AFB) (Public) From Jct I-84 & ID-67, SW 12 mi on ID-67. Avail: 22 full hkups (20/50 amps). 2021 rates: $15. (208)828-6333

We appreciate your business!

MOUNTAIN HOME RV RESORT

good sam park **Ratings: 10/10★/9.5** (RV Park) From Jct I-84 & Hwy 51/American Legion Blvd (Exit 95): Go 1/2 mi S on Hwy 51/American Legion Blvd (L). Elev 3200 ft.**FAC:** paved rds. (212 spaces). Avail: 80 paved, patios, 80 pull-thrus, (32x90), 80 full hkups (30/50 amps), seasonal sites, cable, WiFi @ sites, rentals, dump, laundry, LP gas. **REC:** heated pool, hot tub, boating nearby, playground, hunting nearby. Pet restrict (B). Partial handicap access. No tents. Big rig sites, eco-friendly. 2021 rates: $50, Military discount. ATM.
(208)580-1211 Lat: 43.13105, Lon: -115.67274
2295 American Legion Blvd, Mountain Home, ID 83647
www.g7rvresorts.com
See ad this page

MOYIE SPRINGS — A2 *Boundary*

THE HEMLOCKS RV AND LODGING

good sam park **Ratings: 7/8.5★/8** (Campground) From Jct US Hwy 95 & US Hwy 2: Go 9.2 mi E on US Hwy 2 (R). Elev 2600 ft.**FAC:** gravel/dirt rds. Avail: 37 gravel, 21 pull-thrus, (35x76), back-ins (28x50), 31 full hkups, 6 W, 6 E (30/50 amps), WiFi @ sites, tent sites, rentals, dump, laundry, LP gas, fire rings, firewood, restaurant. **REC:** boating nearby, hunting nearby. Pets OK. eco-friendly. 2021 rates: $59 to $69, Military discount. Apr 01 to Oct 31.
(208)267-4363 Lat: 48.709374, Lon: -116.127666
73400 US-2, Moyie Springs, ID 83845
hemlockslodging.com
See ad page 347

NORTH FORK — D3 *Lemhi*

THE VILLAGE AT NORTH FORK **Ratings: 7/UI/8** (Campground) 20 Avail: 17 full hkups, 3 E (30/50 amps). 2021 rates: $37. Mar 01 to Nov 30. (208)865-7001, 2046 Hwy 93 N, North Fork, ID 83466

WAGONHAMMER RV PARK & CAMPGROUND

good sam park **Ratings: 8/10★/10** (RV Park) S-bnd: From US 93 (in North Fork): Go 2 mi S on Hwy 93 (R) (MP 324) or N-bnd: From US 93 & Hwy 28 (in Salmon): Go 18 mi N on Hwy 93 (L) (MP 324). Elev 3650 ft.**FAC:** gravel rds. 52 Avail: 25 gravel, 27 grass, 15 pull-thrus, (25x80), back-ins (35x80), 12 full hkups, 40 W, 40 E (30/50 amps), WiFi @ sites, tent sites, rentals, dump, laundry, fire rings, firewood. **REC:** Salmon River: swim, fishing, kayaking/canoeing, boating nearby, hunting nearby. Pets OK. Partial handicap access. Big rig sites, eco-friendly. 2021 rates: $37.80 to $42, Military discount. Apr 25 to Nov 10.
(208)865-2477 Lat: 45.38465, Lon: -113.96165
1826 Hwy 93 N, North Fork, ID 83466
wagonhammercampground.com
See ad this page

Get the GOOD SAM CAMPING APP

WATERS EDGE RV PARK & PIZZERIA **Ratings: 6/8/9** (Campground) 11 Avail: 9 full hkups, 2 E (30/50 amps). 2021 rates: $35. Apr 15 to Nov 08. (208)865-2476, 2570 Hwy 93 N, North Fork, ID 83466

OLDTOWN — A1 *Bonner*

LAKE PEND OREILLE - COE/ALBENI COVE (Public Corps) From town, E 3 mi on 4th St (E). 10 Avail. 2021 rates: $22. May 14 to Sep 10. (208)437-3133

OROFINO — C2 *Clearwater*

CLEARWATER CROSSING RV PARK **Ratings: 8/9.5★/8** (Campground) Avail: 49 full hkups (30/50 amps). 2021 rates: $29 to $40. (208)476-4800, 500 Riverfront Rd, Orofino, ID 83544

DWORSHAK RESERVOIR - COE/DENT ACRES (Public Corps) From jct US-12 & Hwy-7: Go 1 block N (across bridge) & 1 block W on Hwy-7, then 17 mi N on paved & gravel county road, then 2 mi W on access road. Avail: 43 full hkups (50 amps). 2021 rates: $20. Apr 11 to Dec 14. (208)476-1255

OROFINO (CONT)

DWORSHAK/FREEMAN CREEK (Public State Park) From town: Go 14 mi NW on Hwy 7 to Cavendish, then 10 mi E on county road. Follow signs. 105 Avail: 1 full hkups, 45 W, 56 E (50 amps). 2021 rates: $12 to $29. (208)476-3132

OSBURN — B2 *Shoshone*

BLUE ANCHOR RV PARK **Ratings: 8.5/9★/8.5** (Campground) Avail: 25 full hkups (30/50 amps). 2021 rates: $47. (208)752-3443, 300 W Mullan Ave, Osburn, ID 83849

PALISADES — E5 *Bonneville*

PALISADES CABINS & RV **Ratings: 4.5/UI/7** (Campground) 16 Avail: 15 full hkups, 1 W, 1 E (30 amps). 2021 rates: $44 to $52. May 01 to Oct 01. (208)351-0511, 3804 Swan Valley Hwy, Irwin, ID 83428

PICABO — E3 *Blaine*

PICABO ANGLER SILVER CREEK RV PARK **Ratings: 5/8/8** (Campground) 17 Avail: 17 W, 17 E (30/50 amps). 2021 rates: $40 to $50. Apr 01 to Nov 01. (208)788-3536, 18915 Hwy 20, Picabo, ID 83348

PINEHURST — B2 *Shoshone*

BY THE WAY CAMPGROUND **Ratings: 7/7/6.5** (Campground) 10 Avail: 10 W, 10 E (30/50 amps). 2021 rates: $32.40. (208)682-3311, 907 N Division St, Pinehurst, ID 83850

PLUMMER — B1 *Benewah*

HEYBURN (Public State Park) From Jct of US-95 & SR-5, E 6 mi on SR-5 (L). Avail: 57 E (20/30 amps). 2021 rates: $12 to $29. (208)686-1308

SOARING HAWK RV RESORT **Ratings: 7.5/NA/7.5** (RV Park) 50 Avail: 50 W, 50 E (30/50 amps). 2021 rates: $55. May 01 to Oct 18. (208)582-3980, 3201 Highway 5, Plummer, ID 83851

POCATELLO — F4 *Bannock*

POCATELLO See also American Falls & Fort Hall.

BANNOCK COUNTY EVENT CENTER (Public) From jct I-15 & Bus 15 / Pocatello Creek Rd (exit 71): Go 1/4 mi E on Pocatello Creek Rd, then 1-1/2 mi N on Olympus Dr, then 1/2 mi W on E. Chubbuck Rd, then 1/2 mi S on Fairgrounds Dr (E). 187 Avail: 69 full hkups, 118 W, 118 E (30/50 amps). 2021 rates: $35 to $45. Apr 01 to Oct 15. (208)237-1340

COWBOY RV PARK
good sam park **Ratings: 7.5/9.5★/9** (RV Park) From Jct I-15 & 5th Ave (Exit 67): Go 3/4 mi N on 5th Ave, then 1/4 mi N on Barton Rd (R). Elev 4500 ft.**FAC:** paved rds. (77 spaces). Avail: 41 paved, patios, 10 pull-thrus, (25x60), back-ins (25x40), 41 full hkups (30/50 amps), seasonal sites, WiFi @ sites, dump, laundry. **REC:** playground, hunting nearby, rec open to public. Pets OK. Partial handicap access. No tents. Big rig sites, eco-friendly. 2021 rates: $46.60 to $51, Military discount.
(208)232-4587 Lat: 42.84971, Lon: -112.42031
845 Barton Rd, Pocatello, ID 83204
www.cowboyrvpocatello.com/cowboy-rv-park
See ad this page

THE FLAMINGO
good sam park **Ratings: 6.5/8.5★/8.5** (RV Area in MH Park) Avail: 10 full hkups (30/50 amps). 2021 rates: $35. (208)232-1325, 1002 Samuel St #145, Pocatello, ID 83204

Travel Services

GANDER RV OF POCATELLO Your new hometown outfitter offering the best regional gear for all your outdoor needs. Your adventure awaits. **SERVICES:** sells outdoor gear, restrooms. RV accessible. Hours: 9am - 6pm. (844)641-1390 Lat: 42.89383, Lon: -112.47670 3385 Hawthorne Rd, Pocatello, ID 83201 rv.ganderoutdoors.com

POST FALLS — B1 *Kootenai*

COEUR D'ALENE RV RESORT
good sam park **Ratings: 9.5/9★/9.5** (RV Park) Avail: 100 full hkups (30/50 amps). 2021 rates: $50 to $54. (208)773-3527, 2652 E Mullan Ave, Post Falls, ID 83854

PRIEST RIVER — A1 *Bonner*

PRIEST RIVER See also Athol, Bayview, Blanchard & Sandpoint, ID; Cusick & Newport, WA.

LAKE PEND OREILLE - COE/PRIEST RIVER (Public Corps) From town, E 0.5 mi on US-2 (R). 20 Avail. 2021 rates: $22. May 09 to Sep 12. (208)437-3133

LAKE PEND OREILLE - COE/RILEY CREEK (Public Corps) From town, W 0.1 mi on US-2 to Riley Creek Rd, S 1.5 mi (E). 67 Avail: 67 W, 67 E (50 amps). 2021 rates: $30. May 09 to Sep 26. (208)437-3133

REXBURG — E4 *Madison*

WAKESIDE LAKE RV PARK
good sam park **Ratings: 6.5/8.5★/8.5** (Campground) 37 Avail: 30 full hkups, 7 W, 7 E (30/50 amps). 2021 rates: $35 to $48. (208)356-3681, 2245 South 2000 West, Rexburg, ID 83440

WIND WILLOWS RV PARK **Ratings: 6.5/UI/6.5** (Campground) Avail: 21 full hkups (30/50 amps). 2021 rates: $40. (208)701-9941, 4816 S Yellowstone Hwy, Rexburg, ID 83440

RIGBY — E4 *Jefferson*

YELLOWSTONE LAKESIDE RV PARK **Ratings: 7.5/9.5/7.5** (RV Park) Avail: 97 full hkups (30/50 amps). 2021 rates: $32 to $45. (208)745-5115, 731 N Rigby Lake Dr, Rigby, ID 83442

RIGGINS — D1 *Idaho*

RIGGINS See also White Bird.

CANYON PINES RV RESORT **Ratings: 7.5/9.5★/10** (Campground) 42 Avail: 42 W, 42 E (30/50 amps). 2021 rates: $39 to $42. (208)628-4006, 159 Barn Rd, Pollock, ID 83547

RIRIE — E5 *Jefferson*

7 N RANCH **Ratings: 4.5/8/8** (Campground) 46 Avail: 26 full hkups, 20 W, 20 E (30/50 amps). 2021 rates: $38. Apr 15 to Oct 15. (208)538-5097, 5109 7N Ranch Rd, Ririe, ID 83443

HEISE HOT SPRINGS RV CAMP **Ratings: 7/6/8** (Campground) 60 Avail: 23 full hkups, 37 E (30/50 amps). 2021 rates: $32 to $39. Apr 15 to Oct 15. (208)538-7312, 5130 E Heise Rd, Ririe, ID 83443

MOUNTAIN RIVER RANCH **Ratings: 6.5/9★/8** (Campground) 64 Avail: 64 W, 64 E (30/50 amps). 2021 rates: $39. May 01 to Oct 15. (208)538-7337, 98 N 5050 E, Ririe, ID 83443

RUPERT — F3 *Minidoka*

LAKE WALCOTT (Public State Park) From town: Go 11 mi NE on Hwy 24. 37 Avail: 23 W, 23 E. 2021 rates: $10 to $29. (208)436-1258

SAGLE — A1 *Bonner*

GARFIELD BAY CAMPGROUND (Public) From town, E 9 mi on cnty rd, follow signs (L). 29 Avail: Pit toilets. 2021 rates: $15. May 01 to Oct 01. (208)255-5681

SALMON — D3 *Lemhi*

SALMON See also North Fork.

BUDDY'S RV PARK **Ratings: 5.5/7/5.5** (RV Park) Avail: 12 full hkups (30/50 amps). 2021 rates: $38. (208)756-3630, 609 River Front Dr, Salmon, ID 83467

CENTURY 2 CAMPGROUND & RV PARK **Ratings: 5/UI/7** (Campground) Avail: 19 full hkups (30/50 amps). 2021 rates: $33 to $44. May 15 to Nov 01. (208)756-2063, 603 Riverfront Dr, Salmon, ID 83467

SANDPOINT — A1 *Bonner*

SANDPOINT See also Bayview, Bonners Ferry, Hope, ID; Newport, WA.

BONNER COUNTY FAIRGROUNDS CAMPGROUND **Ratings: 5.5/7/7** (Campground) 32 Avail: 1 full hkups, 31 W, 31 E (30/50 amps). 2021 rates: $30. (208)263-8414, 4203 N Boyer Rd, Sandpoint, ID 83864

EDGEWATER RESORT-BEST WESTERN **Ratings: 6.5/9★/5** (Campground) Avail: 21 full hkups (30/50 amps). 2021 rates: $35 to $75. (208)263-3194, 56 Bridge St, Sandpoint, ID 83864

LAKE PEND OREILLE - COE/SPRINGY POINT (Public Corps) From town, S 2 mi on US-95 to Lakeshore Dr, W 3 mi (R). 37 Avail. 2021 rates: $22. May 11 to Sep 28. (208)437-3133

ROUND LAKE (Public State Park) From Jct of US-2 & US-95 (in Sandpoint), S 10 mi on US-95 to Dufort Rd, W 2 mi (L). 51 Avail: 16 W, 16 E (30 amps). 2021 rates: $12 to $29. (208)263-3489

TRAVEL AMERICA RV PARK
Ratings: 5.5/8.5★/8 (Campground) From Jct US 2 & US 95: Go 5 1/2 mi S on US 95 (MP 468.5) (R). **FAC:** gravel/dirt rds. (76 spaces). Avail: 58 grass, 58 pull-thrus, (30x60), 38 full hkups, 20 W, 20 E (30/50 amps), seasonal sites, WiFi @ sites, tent sites, dump, laundry, groc, LP gas, firewood. **REC:** boating nearby, hunting nearby. Pet restrict (B). Partial handicap access. Big rig sites, eco-friendly. 2021 rates: $35. ATM.
(208)263-6522 Lat: 48.20363, Lon: -116.56641
468800 Hwy 95, Sagle, ID 83860
See ad this page

SHELLEY — E4 *Bingham*

NORTH BINGHAM PARK (BINGHAM COUNTY PARK) (Public) From Jct I-15 & Exit 108, E on Fir 1.3 mi (R). 12 Avail: 12 W, 12 E (30/50 amps). 2021 rates: $25. May 01 to Sep 30. (208)357-1895

SODA SPRINGS — F5 *Caribou*

CARIBOU COUNTY PARK (Public) From town, N 12 mi on SR-34 to Blackfoot River Rd, E 0.5 mi (L). 20 Avail. (208)547-4324

ST CHARLES — F5 *Bear Lake*

BEAR LAKE (Public State Park) From town, S 6 mi on Hwy 89 to N Beach Rd, E 11 mi, follow signs (R). Avail: 47 E (30/50 amps). 2021 rates: $12 to $23. (208)945-2565

BEAR LAKE NORTH RV PARK & CAMPGROUND **Ratings: 6/7/6.5** (Campground) Avail: 30 full hkups (30/50 amps). 2021 rates: $42 to $70. May 01 to Oct 31. (208)945-2941, 220 N Main St, St Charles, ID 83272

STANLEY — E2 *Custer*

SMILEY CREEK LODGE **Ratings: 6.5/UI/6** (Campground) Avail: 23 full hkups (30 amps). 2021 rates: $45 to $65. Jun 01 to Sep 30. (208)774-3547, 16546 N Highway 75, Sawtooth City, ID 83278

TORREY'S BURNT CREEK INN & RV PARK **Ratings: 5.5/7.5/6.5** (Campground) Avail: 10 full hkups (30/50 amps). 2021 rates: $45. Apr 01 to Nov 01. (208)838-2313, 21021 State Hwy 75, Stanley, ID 83278

SUN VALLEY — E3 *Custer*

THE MEADOWS RV PARK **Ratings: 6.5/8.5★/6.5** (Campground) Avail: 43 full hkups (30/50 amps). 2021 rates: $51 to $54. (208)726-5445, 13 Broadway Run, Ketchum, ID 83340

TWIN FALLS — F3 *Jerome*

TWIN FALLS See also Hagerman & Wendell.

ANDERSON CAMP
good sam park **Ratings: 8.5/9★/8.5** (Campground) From Jct I-84 & Hwy 50 (Exit 182): Go 1/8 mi N on Hwy 50, then 1/2 mi E on Tipperary Rd (L). Elev 3747 ft.**FAC:** gravel rds. (93 spaces). Avail: 62 gravel, 62 pull-thrus, (30x60), 62 full hkups (30/50 amps), seasonal sites, WiFi @ sites, $, tent sites, rentals, dump, laundry, groc, LP gas, firewood, restaurant. **REC:** heated pool, boating nearby, playground, hunting nearby, rec open to public. Pets OK. Partial handicap access. Big rig sites, eco-friendly. 2021 rates: $39 to $45, Military discount. ATM.
(208)825-9800 Lat: 42.57735, Lon: -114.28989
1188 East 990 South, Eden, ID 83325
andersoncamp.com
See ad this page

Dealing with Extreme Weather Conditions: When flooding conditions are encountered, seek higher ground. If a section of roadway is flooded, do not drive through it. If you must cross it, observe other vehicles to determine depth of water. Be sure there are no downed electrical lines in the water. Depending on type of RV you are traveling in, a safe still water maximum depth must be established. That figure should not exceed much more than about half the height of your wheel/tire radius. E.g., a 22.5'' wheel with an 80-series tire, would be about 14'' or so. A 15'' wheel with a 70-series tire may be about 10''. Drive slowly and do not stop. In addition to water depth, the roadway below may be eroded or starting to collapse. If the water is moving at any speed across the roadway the vehicle could easily lose control. Items in the water can pose an additional hazard. Do not camp in low elevation locations. Avoid areas near any mountain washes. If a flood watch is upgraded to a warning, hold up in the highest ground you can find. Early warning is one of the best defenses when facing severe weather events. Monitor your local weather broadcasts. Consider getting an automatic ""First Alert'' or ""NOAA Radio'' to keep you safe and informed.

NAT-SOO-PAH HOT SPRINGS & CAMPGROUND **Ratings: 6.5/UI/7.5** (Campground) 75 Avail: 29 full hkups, 46 W, 46 E (20/30 amps). 2021 rates: $20 to $30. May 01 to Sep 06. (208)655-4337, 2738 E 2400 N, Twin Falls, ID 83301

OREGON TRAIL CAMPGROUND **Ratings: 7.5/8/8.5** (Campground) Avail: 30 full hkups (30/50 amps). 2021 rates: $38 to $39.50. (208)733-0853, 2733 Kimberly Rd, Twin Falls, ID 83301

TWIN FALLS / JEROME KOA **Ratings: 8/8/7** (Campground) 70 Avail: 47 full hkups, 23 W, 23 E (30/50 amps). 2021 rates: $45 to $90. Mar 01 to Oct 31. (800)562-4169, 441 S Liberty Lane, Jerome, ID 83338

TWIN FALLS 93 RV PARK **Ratings: 6.5/8.5★/9** (RV Park) 72 Avail: 47 full hkups, 25 W, 25 E (30/50 amps). 2021 rates: $40 to $50. (208)326-5092, 2404 E 3830 N, Filer, ID 83328

Travel Services

ANDERSON CAMP FULL SERVICE STOP Located at Jct I-84 and Hwy 50 (Exit 182). Full service: gasoline, diesel & propane for vehicles of any size, convenience store and restaurant. Elev 4150 ft. **SERVICES:** restrooms. emergency parking, RV accessible. Hours: 8am to 6pm. ATM.
(208)825-9800 Lat: 42.57735, Lon: -114.28989
1188 East 990 South, Eden, ID 83325
andersoncamp.com
See ad this page

WALLACE — B2 *Shoshone*

WALLACE See also Kellogg, Osburn & Pinehurst.

WEISER — E1 *Washington*

WEISER See also Fruitland, ID; Vale & Huntington, OR.

WENDELL — F3 *Gooding*

WILSON'S RV & PARK **Ratings: 6.5/8★/8.5** (Campground) 23 Avail: 23 W, 23 E (20/30 amps). 2021 rates: $36. Mar 01 to Nov 15. (208)536-2301, 1894 N Frontage Rd , Wendell, ID 83355

WHITE BIRD — C1 *Idaho*

SALMON RIVER RESORT **Ratings: 5.5/8/7.5** (Campground) Avail: 14 full hkups (30/50 amps). 2021 rates: $45. (208)839-9990, 3252 Waterfront Dr, White Bird, ID 83554

SWIFTWATER RV PARK **Ratings: 7/8.5★/9.5** (Campground) 21 Avail: 1 full hkups, 20 W, 20 E (30/50 amps). 2021 rates: $37. (208)839-2700, 3154 Salmon River Ct, White Bird, ID 83554

WINCHESTER — C1 *Lewis*

WINCHESTER LAKE (Public State Park) From Jct of US-95 & US-95 ALT, SW 1 mi on US-95 Alt to Camas St, W 0.25 mi (L). 68 Avail: 46 W, 46 E (20/30 amps). 2021 rates: $12 to $49. (208)924-7563

Our rating system is fair and thorough. We know the kinds of things that are important to you - like clean restrooms and showers, attractive, secure, well-tended grounds, and extras like swimming pools. We give the first rating for development of facilities, the second for cleanliness and physical characteristics of restrooms and showers, and the third for visual appearance.

Illinois

Getty Images/iStockphoto

DID YOU KNOW?

The "Windy City" moniker was originally used in reference to Chicago's long-winded politicians, not the weather.

Few Midwestern states can boast the verve and dynamism of the Land of Lincoln. This Heartland state is home to the city of Chicago, with its iconic skyline rising above the waters of Lake Michigan.

Lush Illinois

Between Illinois's bustling towns, vast forests proliferate with enticing trails and overlooks. Covering 280,000 acres, the Shawnee National Forest invites adventurers to explore its trails. Hiking, biking, paddling, horseback riding and more can all be enjoyed in the diverse landscapes, ranging from prairies to woodlands. Unique rock formations seem to rise from nowhere in an area known as the Garden of the Gods. Look out at expansive views of the rolling Shawnee Hills and follow the interpretive signs explaining the area's geology.

Beyond the Big Blocks

About 100 miles southwest of Chicago, visitors will discover rugged wilderness. At Starved Rock State Park in Oglesby, the Illinois River has carved canyons of sandstone bluffs. At LaSalle Canyon, waterfalls tumble down smooth cliffs. Hike the narrow French Canyon, with sheer walls rising on each side.

City of the Big Shoulders

Few cities cut such a dramatic silhouette against the horizon. But the contours of skyscrapers rising in the distance are no mirage. The nation's third largest city is the cultural capital of the Midwest, boasting world-class theater and music, major museums and high-end shopping along the Magnificent Mile. Aside from its urban appeal, Chicago is known for the natural beauty of Lake Michigan, a popular spot for city dwellers seeking cool breezes. Don't forget to take a photo of the reflective Cloud Gate, the smooth, gleaming sculpture affectionately known as "The Bean."

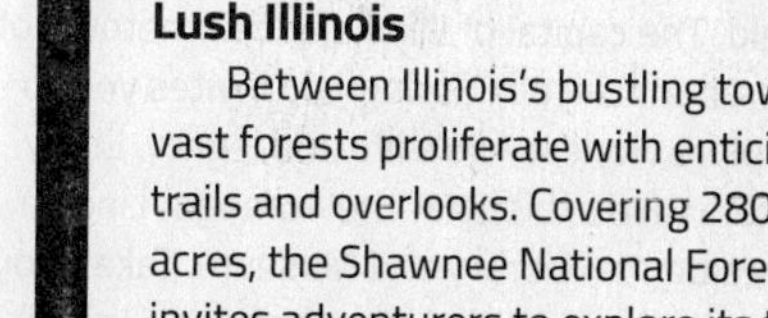

Illinois Popcorn

Residents of the Land of Lincoln love popcorn so much they named it the official state snack food in 2003. Remember to stock up on Chicago mix popcorn when you're in the Windy City. Half cheddar cheese and half caramel, this popcorn offers the perfect blend of sweet and salty to make your tastebuds sing.

VISITOR CENTER

IL

TIME ZONE
Central Standard

ROAD & HIGHWAY INFORMATION
800-452-4368
idot.illinois.gov

FISHING & HUNTING INFORMATION
217-785-3423
www.dnr.illinois.gov

BOATING INFORMATION
217-782-6302
www.dnr.illinois.gov/boating

NATIONAL PARKS
nps.gov/il

STATE PARKS
www.dnr.illinois.gov/parks

TOURISM INFORMATION
Illinois Office of Tourism
800-2-Connect
enjoyillinois.com

TOP TOURISM ATTRACTIONS
1) Millennium Park
2) Skydeck Chicago – Willis Tower
3) Wrigley Field

MAJOR CITIES
Chicago, Aurora, Rockford, Joliet, Naperville, Springfield (capital)

Sky-High Attractions

A perfect blend of high society and casual cool, America's third-largest city has been making its case as a bucket-list destination for years. Architecture lovers can gawk at some of the world's tallest buildings, while artists, sports fans and foodies will be busy soaking in their own world-class attractions. With a little something for everyone, the Windy City is a remarkable and sprawling urban getaway that somehow hasn't lost its small town feel.

Magic Mile

Considered one of the world's great thoroughfares, the famed Magnificent Mile is the perfect introduction to the Midwest's largest city. From high-end boutiques, to sights like the Historic Water Tower (now a gallery) and Pumping Station, a stroll down the flower-lined boulevard offers the chance to bask in Chicago's low-key but cosmopolitan vibe. Head to the observation deck at the top of the John Hancock Center — dubbed 360 Chicago — for panoramic views of the cityscape and lakefront. Throughout the city, world-class cuisine awaits foodies. Enjoy the city's legendary deep-dish pizza or dig into the offerings from restaurants serving food from across the globe.

Local son: An Abraham Lincoln statue in front of the Illinois State Capital Building in Springfield.

Loving the Lake

Head east from Millennium Park and you'll quickly find yourself on the shores of Lake Michigan, where nature loving visitors can really let loose. Kayak Chicago offers paddleboard and kayak rentals that allow you to see the skyline from a whole new perspective, whether you're in the open lake waters or cruising between the downtown high-rises on the Chicago River. Sunset and firework tours are available. Sport fishing is also on the menu as the many charters lining Lake Shore Drive are available for top-notch salmon and trout excursions. Of course, if you would rather stay on dry land, urban anglers can head to local hotspots along the Chicago River for plentiful bass, carp, crappie and bluegill without leaving the city limits.

Hiking and Biking the City

Winding along the shores of Lake Michigan for 18-miles, the Lakefront Trail is heaven for hikers and bikers who want to stretch their legs while still taking in some of Chicago's must-see sights. Spanning the relatively quiet scenery of Foster Beach in the north, to the country club feel of South Shore, the route passes by Grant Park, the Art Institute of Chicago, Lincoln Park Zoo and plenty of sandy stretches giving you ample opportunity to enjoy the ride at your own pace. The South Shore Nature Sanctuary and farther afield destinations like the Indiana Dunes National Lakeshore and the Fox River Trail in Aurora make for excellent, nature-friendly day trips.

Big Catches

Incredible salmon fishing awaits in the north on Lake Michigan, while Lake Shelbyville to the south gives anglers a chance to reel in catfish and 20-pound bigmouth buffalo. The best time to catch largemouth bass is in April in areas like Fox Chain O Lakes, Sand Pond, Newton Lake and Lake Springfield. Boaters can also launch their watercraft from hundreds of ramps in Lake County, which is home to more than 170 lakes and rivers.

Capital Fun

On Route 66 and you'll wind up in Springfield. The capital of Illinois and hometown of Abraham Lincoln, Springfield invites you to explore Honest Abe's life and legacy. Enjoy interactive exhibits at the Abraham Lincoln Presidential Library and Museum. Take a tour through the Lincoln Home National Historic Site or stop by the Old State Capitol to see where the 16th president gave his historic "House Divided" speech.

Super Sanctuary

One of the cooler attractions in Springfield is Adams' Wildlife Sanctuary. Miss Margery Adams donated this beautiful parcel of land to the Illinois Audubon Society in 1983. The society, which is the state's oldest non-profit independent conservation organization, has turned Miss Adams' property into an urban nature center and trails system that is open to the public and free of charge.

Pontiac

About 100 miles northwest of Springfield, the town of Pontiac honors the iconic route with historic murals on the buildings that line the road. The murals honor farming, industry and other local achievements that helped put Pontiac on the map. The Roszell's Soda Shop Mural celebrates a day when ice cream, hot dogs and tall glasses of fizzy beverages were served in local hangouts.

good sam park

Featured Good Sam Parks

ILLINOIS

When you stay with Good Sam, you can expect the highest degree of cleanliness and friendliness, and better yet, you get **10% off** overnight campground fees.

If you're not already a Good Sam member you can purchase your membership at one of these locations:

AMBOY
O'Connell's Yogi Bear Park

ANNAPOLIS
Hickory Holler Campground

BELVIDERE
Pine Country RV & Camping Resort

CAHOKIA
Cahokia RV Parque

CARLOCK
Kamp Komfort RV Park & Campground

EAST PEORIA
Millpoint RV Park

EAST ST LOUIS
DraftKings at Casino Queen RV Park

EFFINGHAM
Camp Lakewood Campground & RV Park

GALESBURG
Galesburg East Campground

JOLIET
Leisure Lake Resort
RV Park At Hollywood Casino Joliet

MARENGO
Lehman's Lakeside RV Resort

MARSEILLES
Glenwood RV Resort

MOUNT VERNON
Archway RV Park

PANA
Oak Terrace RV Resort

SPRING BAY
Sankoty Lakes

SPRINGFIELD
Double J Campground

10/10★/10 GOOD SAM PARK

SPRINGFIELD
Double J Campground
(217)483-9998

What's This?

An RV park with a 10/10★/10 rating has scored perfect grades in amenities, cleanliness and appearance ("See Understanding the Campground Rating System" on pages 8 and 9 for an explanation of the trusted Good Sam Rating System). Stay in a 10/10★/10 park on your next trip for a nearly flawless camping experience.

Getty Images/iStockphoto

IL

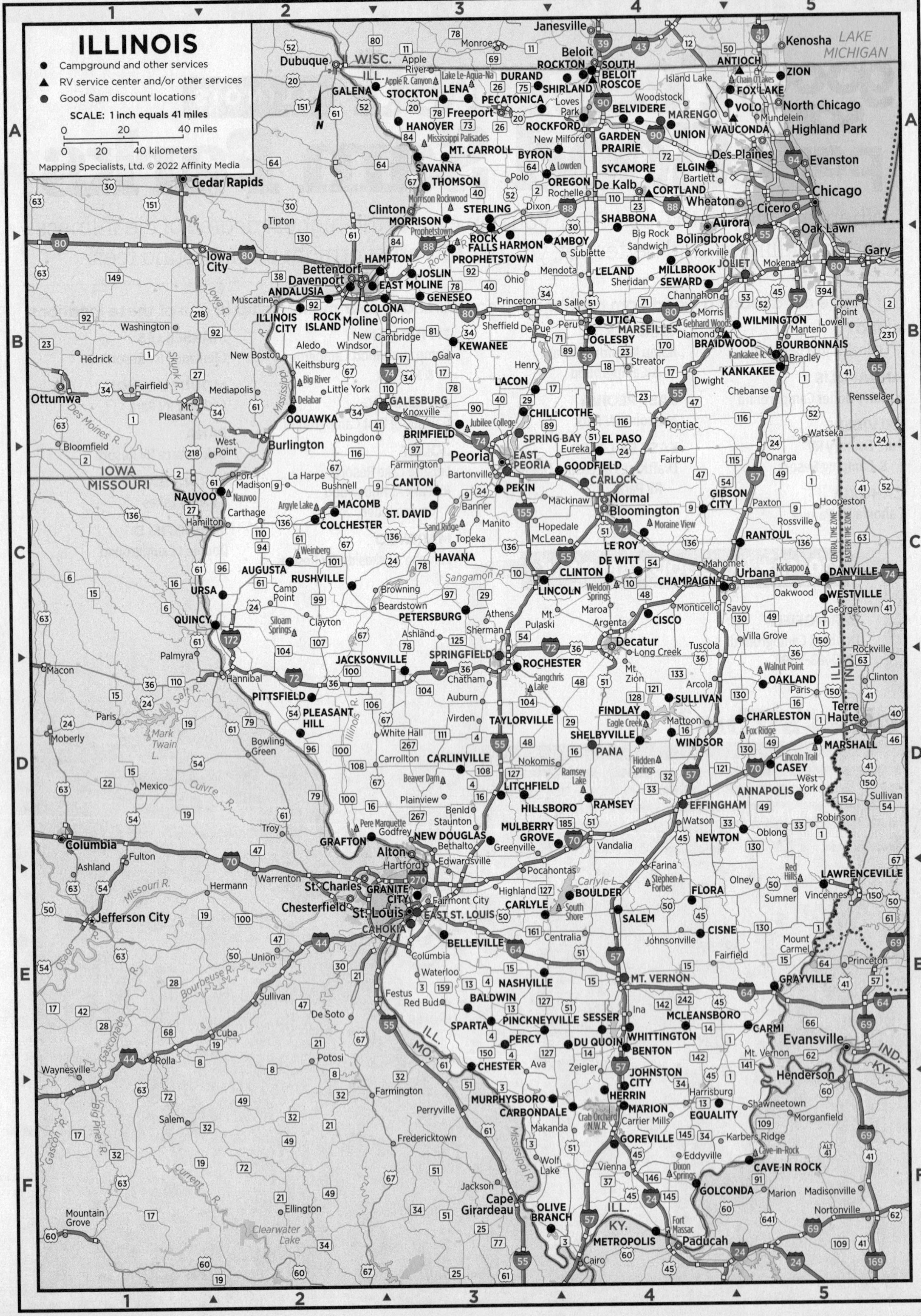

ILLINOIS
Campground and other services
RV service center and/or other services
Good Sam discount locations
SCALE: 1 inch equals 41 miles
0 20 40 miles
0 20 40 kilometers
Mapping Specialists, Ltd. © 2022 Affinity Media
1 2 3 4 5
A B C D E F
Janesville
Beloit
ROCKTON
SOUTH BELOIT
ROSCOE
Kenosha
LAKE MICHIGAN
ANTIOCH
ZION
Island Lake
FOX LAKE
VOLO
North Chicago
Mundelein
WAUCONDA
Highland Park
Woodstock
MARENGO
UNION
BELVIDERE
Dubuque
WISC.
ILL.
Apple River
Apple R. Canyon
Lake Le-Aqua-Na
Monroe
DURAND
SHIRLAND
LENA
STOCKTON
GALENA
PECATONICA
Freeport
Loves Park
ROCKFORD
HANOVER
Mississippi Palisades
MT. CARROLL
New Milford
GARDEN PRAIRIE
BYRON
Lowden
Des Plaines
ELGIN
Evanston
SAVANNA
THOMSON
Polo
OREGON
SYCAMORE
De Kalb
CORTLAND
Bartlett
Wheaton
Chicago
Cicero
Cedar Rapids
Morrison Rockwood
Rochelle
Dixon
Clinton
STERLING
MORRISON
Prophetstown
ROCK FALLS
HARMON
AMBOY
SHABBONA
Aurora
Oak Lawn
Tipton
Big Rock
Sandwich
Bolingbrook
Yorkville
Gary
Iowa City
HAMPTON
Bettendorf
Davenport
JOSLIN
EAST MOLINE
PROPHETSTOWN
Sublette
LELAND
MILLBROOK
SEWARD
JOLIET
Mokena
Mendota
Sheridan
Ohio
Muscatine
ANDALUSIA
GENESEO
COLONA
Princeton
La Salle
Channahon
Crown Point
ILLINOIS CITY
ROCK ISLAND
Moline
Orion
Sheffield
De Pue
Peru
UTICA
MARSEILLES
Gebhard Woods
Morris
Diamond
WILMINGTON
Manteno
Lowell
Washington
New Cambridge
Windsor
KEWANEE
OGLESBY
BRAIDWOOD
BOURBONNAIS
Hedrick
New Boston
Aledo
Keithsburg
Galva
Streator
Kankakee R.
Bradley
KANKAKEE
Big River
Henry
Dwight
Fairfield
Mediapolis
Little York
LACON
Chebanse
Ottumwa
Mt. Pleasant
Delabar
GALESBURG
Knoxville
CHILLICOTHE
Rensselaer
OQUAWKA
Jubilee College
Pontiac
Des Moines R.
West Point
Burlington
Abingdon
BRIMFIELD
SPRING BAY
EL PASO
Watseka
Bloomfield
Peoria
EAST PEORIA
Eureka
Fairbury
Onarga
IOWA
MISSOURI
Farmington
Bartonville
GOODFIELD
Fort Madison
La Harpe
Bushnell
CANTON
PEKIN
CARLOCK
GIBSON CITY
NAUVOO
Nauvoo
Argyle Lake
MACOMB
Banner
Mackinaw
Normal
Bloomington
Paxton
Hoopeston
Hamilton
Carthage
COLCHESTER
ST. DAVID
Manito
Hopedale
Moraine View
Rossville
Sand Ridge
Topeka
McLean
RANTOUL
CENTRAL TIME ZONE
EASTERN TIME ZONE
Weinberg
HAVANA
LE ROY
AUGUSTA
RUSHVILLE
DE WITT
Mahomet
CLINTON
Kickapoo
DANVILLE
Sangamon R.
Browning
Urbana
URSA
Camp Point
LINCOLN
Weldon Springs
CHAMPAIGN
Oakwood
WESTVILLE
Beardstown
Monticello
Savoy
Georgetown
QUINCY
Siloam Springs
Clayton
PETERSBURG
Athens
Mt. Pulaski
Maroa
Argenta
CISCO
Villa Grove
Palmyra
Ashland
Sherman
Decatur
Tuscola
Long Creek
Macon
JACKSONVILLE
SPRINGFIELD
ROCHESTER
Rockville
Walnut Point
Hannibal
Chatham
Mt. Zion
OAKLAND
Clinton
Sangchris Lake
Arcola
Paris
PITTSFIELD
Auburn
SULLIVAN
Terre Haute
PLEASANT HILL
Virden
TAYLORVILLE
FINDLAY
Eagle Creek
Mattoon
CHARLESTON
Moberly
Mark Twain L.
Bowling Green
White Hall
SHELBYVILLE
WINDSOR
Fox Ridge
MARSHALL
PANA
Illinois R.
Carrollton
CARLINVILLE
Nokomis
Hidden Springs
Lincoln Trail
CASEY
Mexico
Cuivre R.
Beaver Dam
Ramsey Lake
West York
LITCHFIELD
ANNAPOLIS
Plainview
Benld
HILLSBORO
RAMSEY
EFFINGHAM
Sullivan
Pere Marquette
Staunton
Watson
Robinson
Troy
Godfrey
MULBERRY GROVE
NEWTON
Oblong
Columbia
GRAFTON
NEW DOUGLAS
Bethalto
Alton
Hartford
Edwardsville
Greenville
Vandalia
Fulton
Ashland
Warrenton
Pocahontas
Farina
Red Hills
LAWRENCEVILLE
Missouri R.
St. Charles
GRANITE CITY
Highland
Carlyle L.
Stephen A. Forbes
Olney
Sumner
Vincennes
Hermann
Chesterfield
St. Louis
Fairmont City
CARLYLE
BOULDER
FLORA
Jefferson City
EAST ST. LOUIS
CAHOKIA
South Shore
SALEM
CISNE
BELLEVILLE
Centralia
Johnsonville
Mount Carmel
Union
Columbia
Fairfield
Princeton
Osage R.
Bourbeuse R.
Waterloo
NASHVILLE
MT. VERNON
GRAYVILLE
Sullivan
De Soto
Festus
Red Bud
BALDWIN
Ina
MCLEANSBORO
Cuba
SPARTA
PINCKNEYVILLE
SESSER
WHITTINGTON
CARMI
Gasconade R.
Rolla
Potosi
ILL.
MO.
PERCY
DU QUOIN
BENTON
Evansville
IND.
KY.
Waynesville
CHESTER
Ava
Zeigler
Mt. Vernon
JOHNSTON CITY
Henderson
Farmington
MURPHYSBORO
HERRIN
Harrisburg
Shawneetown
Big Piney R.
Perryville
CARBONDALE
MARION
EQUALITY
Crab Orchard N.W.R.
Morganfield
Salem
Carrier Mills
Gasconade R.
Fredericktown
Makanda
GOREVILLE
Karbers Ridge
Mississippi R.
Cave-in-Rock
Wolf Lake
Eddyville
Current R.
Vienna
CAVE IN ROCK
Dixon Springs
Jackson
GOLCONDA
Madisonville
Marion
Cape Girardeau
OLIVE BRANCH
Ellington
Mountain Grove
Clearwater Lake
Fort Massac
Nortonville
METROPOLIS
Paducah
Cairo

ROAD TRIPS

Exploring the Land of Lincoln

Illinois

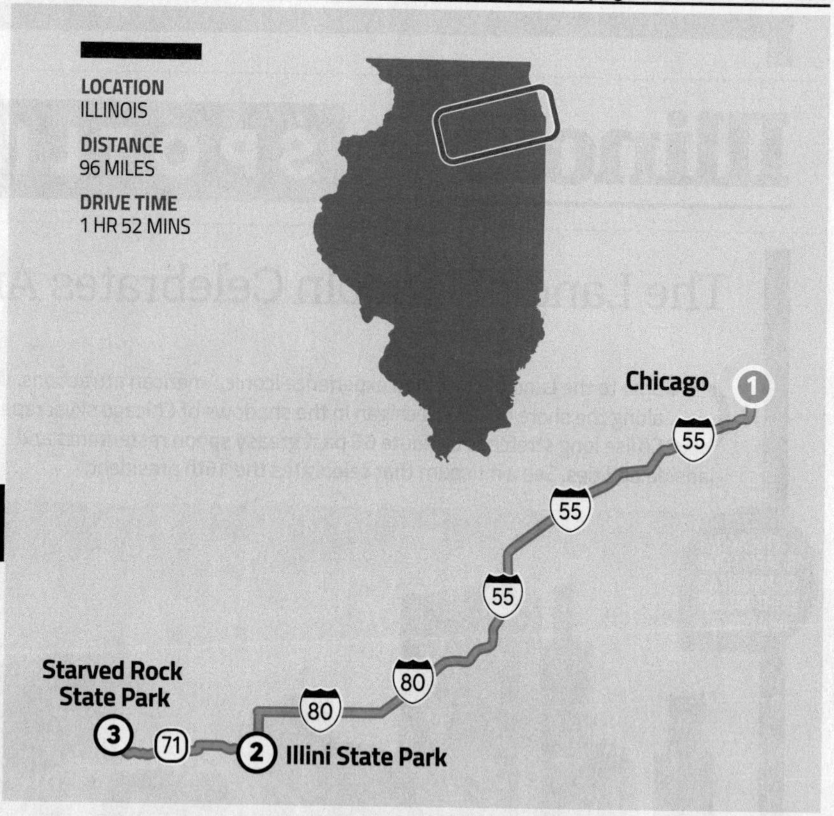

From the skyscrapers of Chicago to the sweeping prairie in the state's heartland, Illinois stands tall as a vacation destination. Enjoy a deep-dish Chicago pizza one day then motor down to Starved Rock State Park the next. Illinois' most popular sights and its best-kept secrets await on this journey through the Land of Lincoln.

1 Chicago
Starting Point

You'll be hard-pressed to enjoy everything Chicago has to offer, but put your best foot forward with a bike trip along the Lakefront Trail. The 18-mile paved pathway connects many of the most popular sights, including Lincoln Park, Soldier Field, the South Shore Cultural Center and Navy Pier. Of course, with sparkling Lake Michigan on one side and downtown skyscrapers on the other, the trail is a destination in its own right. For a one-of-a-kind excursion, head to the Museum Campus to visit the city's world-renowned institutions, including the Field Museum, Adler Planetarium and the unrivaled Shedd Aquarium.

2 Illini State Park
Drive 78 miles ▪ 1 hour, 24 minutes

Illini State Park, on the banks of the Illinois River, is an under-the-radar gem for lovers of the outdoors in search of natural beauty. Dedicated in 1935, the park is next door to the historic Illinois-Michigan Canal and the Marseilles Locks, as well as home to a number of well-maintained Civilian Conservation Corp camps. Anglers are in luck, too, as the water brims with bass, catfish, crappie and bluegill, while hikers can walk along the picturesque rapids that stretch for nearly two miles along the park's shoreline. For an inland excursion, try the scenic Illini-Wek Trail, which offers a glimpse of the park's famed wildflower blooms, including endlessly photogenic Virginia bluebells.

Getty Images/iStockphoto

3 Starved Rock State Park
Drive 18 miles ▪ 28 minutes

Starved Rock State Park stands out as a true natural wonder. Boasting rugged canyons, sweeping vistas and seasonal waterfalls, the park is a favorite among both day-trippers and locals in search of a landscape rich with beauty and history. Hike to the St. Louis, Wildcat, Ottawa and Kaskaskia canyons for some of the best waterfall views, or head straight up the short but steep Lover's Leap Overlook Trail for panoramic views of the Illinois River and beyond. Kick things up a notch with a fun-filled afternoon running the 10-mile stretch of rapids on the nearby Vermillion River from Lowell to Oglesby. Geared towards beginning paddlers, the thrilling whitewater is safe enough you can rent a raft in town and make the trip without an experienced guide.

BIKING BOATING DINING ENTERTAINMENT FISHING HIKING HUNTING PADDLING SHOPPING SIGHTSEEING

IL

 See map page 358

Illinois SPOTLIGHTS

The Land of Lincoln Celebrates American Icons

Come to the Land of Lincoln to experience iconic American attractions. Walk along the shore of Lake Michigan in the shadows of Chicago skyscrapers. Cruise long stretches of Route 66 past greasy spoon restaurants and roadside oddities. See a museum that celebrates the 16th president.

CHICAGO BOASTS FOUR OF AMERICA'S EIGHT TALLEST BUILDINGS.

The Buckingham Fountain in Chicago's Grant Park holds 1.5 million gallons of water.

Getty Images/iStockphoto

Chicago

The United States' third-largest city stands tall with towering skyscrapers, unforgettable dining and outstanding cultural attractions. Nestled against the turquoise waters of Lake Michigan and sporting dazzling skyline, the city of Chicago makes its mark before visitors even begin exploring this megalopolis.

Super City

Since the 1800s, Chicago has burnished its reputation as a major hub of the Midwest. After the Great Chicago Fire destroyed many of the downtown buildings in 1871, the town was rebuilt. Out of the ashes grew the world's first skyscraper. Chicago continued to build skyward throughout the next decade, ultimately gaining the achievement of having one of the tallest skyscrapers in the world with the Sears Tower (now known as the Willis Tower) in 1973. Today's visitors enjoy heading to the Skydeck to get a bird's-eye view of the massive city below and several states in the distance.

Green Goliath

Despite its urban cityscapes, Chicago is dotted with several verdant parks, giving credence to the town's motto, "City in a Garden." As early as the 1860s, city leaders recognized the importance of green spaces as a way to encourage public health and they set aside land to develop them. Lincoln Park offers a popular spot to stroll, along with a free zoo. Grant Park's Buckingham Fountain is an iconic attraction with graceful, arching waters.

Champaign County

Explore the green side of Illinois. With five forest preserves, seemingly endless miles of hiking trails and handfuls of gorgeous gardens and parks, this county teems with outdoor recreation opportunities. In fact, *Time Magazine* named it one of the best places to walk or bike in 2015. Urbana's Market on the Square serves up fresh regional food in a festive setting. Taste succulent sauce at the Word N' Hog Barbecue in Champaign.

Springfield

See where Honest Abe cut his teeth as a fledgling politician. The Old State Capitol Historic Site offers a glimpse into Springfield's early days as the state's political center. The building was the fifth statehouse and the first located in Springfield. Lincoln's final resting place, the Lincoln Tomb at Oak Ridge Cemetery, and the public receiving vault used for his funeral services, are also accessible to visitors.

FOR MORE INFORMATION:

Illinois Office of Tourism, 800-2-Connect, enjoyillinois.com

Choose Chicago, www.choosechicago.com

Visit Champaign County, 800-369-6151 www.visitchampaigncounty.org

Visit Springfield, 800-545-7300 visitspringfieldillinois.com

LOCAL FAVORITE

Dutch Oven Kielbasa and Kraut

If you have never cooked a true Dutch oven campfire meal, it's time to expand your camp-cooking horizons. This dish is packed with German-influenced Midwestern flavors. *Recipe by Linda Henderson.*

INGREDIENTS

- ☐ 1 jar or pouch (2 lb) sauerkraut, drained
- ☐ 2 apples peeled and chopped
- ☐ ½ cup water
- ☐ ½ cup brown sugar
- ☐ 1 lb kielbasa sausage sliced
- ☐ 2 cans sliced potatoes, drained
- ☐ 1 tsp caraway seed
- ☐ 1 can French or flat-cut green beans (optional)
- ☐ Salt and pepper to taste

DIRECTIONS

Layer all ingredients in a cast-iron Dutch oven in order listed. Place hot coals, 8 on the bottom and 15 on top, and allow to bake for 15 minutes. Then remove the bottom coals and continue with the coals on top another 15 to 20 minutes. In a pinch you may also roast in a foil covered pan in the oven at 425 degrees.

Illinois

AMBOY — B3 *Lee*

GREEN RIVER OAKS CAMPING RESORT **Ratings: 7.5/6.5/8.5** (Campground) 100 Avail: 40 full hkups, 60 W, 60 E (30/50 amps). 2021 rates: $55 to $60. Apr 15 to Oct 15. (815)857-2815, 1442 Sleepy Hollow Rd, Amboy, IL 61310

MENDOTA HILLS CAMPGROUND **Ratings: 8/9.5★/9** (Campground) 41 Avail: 6 full hkups, 35 W, 35 E (30/50 amps). 2021 rates: $44 to $50. Apr 15 to Oct 15. (815)849-5930, 642 US Rt 52, Amboy, IL 61310

O'CONNELL'S YOGI BEAR PARK
Ratings: 8.5/10★/8.5 (Campground) 310 Avail: 179 full hkups, 131 W, 131 E (30/50 amps). 2021 rates: $54 to $85. Apr 21 to Oct 15. (888)563-7040, 970 Green Wing Rd, Amboy, IL 61310

PINE VIEW CAMPGROUND **Ratings: 5/7.5★/7** (Campground) 33 Avail: 15 full hkups, 18 W, 18 E (20/30 amps). 2021 rates: $36. Apr 15 to Oct 15. (815)857-3964, 1273 Sleepy Hollow Rd, Amboy, IL 61310

ANDALUSIA — B2 *Rock Island*

MISSISSIPPI RIVER REC AREAS-MUSCATINE AREA - COE/ANDALUSIA SLOUGH (Public Corps) From town: Go 4 mi W on Hwy 92 (follow signs). 25 Avail: Pit toilets. 2021 rates: $10. May 15 to Oct 15. (563)263-7913

ANNAPOLIS — D5 *Crawford*

HICKORY HOLLER CAMPGROUND
Ratings: 6.5/8.5★/8.5 (Campground) From Jct of I-70 & Exit 147 (SR-1), S 19 mi on SR-1 to E 2000th Ave (CR-2), W 4.2 mi (R). **FAC:** gravel rds. (89 spaces). Avail: 72 gravel, 35 pull-thrus, (25x60), back-ins (25x45), 62 full hkups, 10 W, 10 E (30/50 amps), seasonal sites, tent sites, dump, mobile sewer, laundry, LP bottles, fire rings, firewood. **REC:** Lake Guyer: fishing, playground, hunting nearby. Pets OK. Big rig sites, eco-friendly. 2021 rates: $25 to $37.
(618)563-4779 Lat: 39.13984, Lon: -87.76245
9876 E 2000th Ave, West York, IL 62478
www.hickoryholler.com
See ad page 379

ANTIOCH — A5 *Lake*

Travel Services

GANDER RV SERVICE OF ANTIOCH Your new hometown outfitter offering the best regional gear for all your outdoor needs. Your adventure awaits. **SERVICES:** RV appliance, MH mechanical, restrooms. RV supplies, RV accessible. Hours: 9am - 7pm; closed Sun.
(888)893-5121 Lat: 42.467192, Lon: -88.016319
41517 US Hwy 45, Antioch, IL 60002
www.ganderoutdoors.com

AUGUSTA — C2 *Schuyler*

WEINBERG-KING STATE FISH & WILDLIFE AREA (Public State Park) From town, E 3 mi on SR-101 (L). Avail: 48 E Pit toilets. 2021 rates: $10 to $18. (217)392-2345

BALDWIN — E3 *Randolph*

K-RIVER MOTEL & CAMPGROUND **Ratings: 5/NA/8** (Campground) Avail: 32 full hkups (30/50 amps). 2021 rates: $25 to $30. (618)785-2564, 7797 Route 154, Baldwin, IL 62217

RV Tech Tips - Battery Cable Connections: Some vehicles require the negative battery cable to be disconnected when being towed to prevent the dash lights from draining the battery. There are electronic devices and switches available to prevent this problem, but they can be costly and have their own potential problems. One solution is to replace the battery cable bolt with a quick-release seat binder bolt from a bicycle shop. These bolts generally come in two lengths; the shorter one will work the best. With the seat binder bolt installed, the disconnect and reconnect that used to take minutes, has been reduced to seconds.

BELLEVILLE — E3 *St Clair*

MILITARY PARK SCOTT AFB FAMCAMP (SCOTT AFB) (Public) From Jct I-64 & SR-158, S 1 mi on SR-158 to base (L). 22 Avail: 22 W, 22 E (30/50 amps). 2021 rates: $20. (618)256-2067

BELVIDERE — A4 *Boone*

PINE COUNTRY RV & CAMPING RESORT
Ratings: 8.5/9★/9 (RV Park) Avail: 56 full hkups (30/50 amps). 2021 rates: $52 to $84. Apr 19 to Oct 18. (888)563-7040, 5710 Shattuck Rd, Belvidere, IL 61008

BENTON — E4 *Franklin*

BENTON KOA **Ratings: 8/UI/8** (Campground) 75 Avail: 42 full hkups, 33 W, 33 E (30/50 amps). 2021 rates: $36 to $54. (618)439-4860, 1500 N DuQuoin St, Benton, IL 62812

REND LAKE - COE/GUN CREEK (Public Corps) From town, N 6 mi on I-57 to Rte 154, W 0.25 mi to park access rd, S 0.5 mi to Gun Creek Trail, L on Gun Creek Trail/Larry Foster Pkwy, R on Golf Course Rd, .5 mi to park entrance. 100 Avail: 26 full hkups, 74 E (50 amps). 2021 rates: $16 to $25. Mar 15 to Nov 24. (618)724-2493

REND LAKE - COE/NORTH SANDUSKY (Public Corps) From Jct of Rte 57 & Rte 154, W 4 mi on Rte 154 to Rend City Rd, S 1 mi (E). 118 Avail: 15 full hkups, 103 E (50 amps). 2021 rates: $16 to $24. Mar 29 to Oct 27. (618)724-2493

REND LAKE - COE/SOUTH MARCUM (Public Corps) From Jct of Rte 37N & Petroff Rd, W 0.5 mi on Petroff Rd to Duquoin St, N 2 mi to Rend City Rd, N 0.5 mi (E). Avail: 146 E (50 amps). 2021 rates: $16 to $40. Mar 29 to Oct 27. (618)724-2493

REND LAKE - COE/SOUTH SANDUSKY (Public Corps) From Jct of I-57 & SR-14, W 2.5 mi on SR-14 to Rend City Rd, N 4 mi (R). 129 Avail: 18 full hkups, 103 E (30/50 amps). 2021 rates: $12 to $24. Mar 27 to Nov 01. (618)724-2493

BOULDER — E4 *Clinton*

CARLYLE LAKE - COE/BOULDER REC AREA (Public Corps) From town, E 7 mi on Rte 50 to Boulder Rd, N 6 mi (L). 83 Avail: 8 full hkups, 75 W, 75 E (30/50 amps). 2021 rates: $16 to $32. Apr 15 to Oct 14. (618)226-3586

CARLYLE LAKE - COE/COLES CREEK REC AREA (Public Corps) From town, E 7 mi on Rte 50 to Boulder-Ferrin Rd, N 4 mi, follow signs (L). Avail: 119 E (50 amps). 2021 rates: $16 to $32. May 01 to Sep 29. (618)226-3211

BOURBONNAIS — B5 *Kankakee*

KANKAKEE RIVER
(Public State Park) From town, NW 8 mi on SR-102, follow signs (L). **FAC:** paved rds. Avail: 208 gravel, back-ins (15x35), 110 E tent sites, dump, firewood. **REC:** Kankakee River: fishing, kayaking/canoeing, playground, hunting nearby. Pets OK. Partial handicap access, 14 day max stay. 2021 rates: $25 to $35.
(815)933-1383 Lat: 41.208452, Lon: -88.012938
5314 W Route 102, Bourbonnais, IL 60914
www.dnr.illinois.gov

BRAIDWOOD — B5 *Will*

Travel Services

CAMPING WORLD OF BRAIDWOOD As the nation's largest retailer of RV supplies, accessories, services and new and used RVs, Camping World is committed to making your total RV experience better. **SERVICES:** restrooms. RV Sales. RV supplies, RV accessible. Hours: 9am - 6pm, closed Sun.
(844)977-3577 Lat: 41.28392, Lon: -88.23382
800 EZ St, Braidwood, IL 60408
rv.campingworld.com

BRIMFIELD — B3 *Peoria*

JUBILEE COLLEGE (Public State Park) From town, E 4 mi on US-150, follow signs (L). Avail: 107 E (30 amps). 2021 rates: $10 to $35. Apr 15 to Nov 01. (309)446-3758

BYRON — A4 *Ogle*

LAKE LOUISE CAMPGROUND **Ratings: 7/5.5/6.5** (Campground) 62 Avail: 15 full hkups, 47 W, 47 E (30/50 amps). 2021 rates: $70 to $90. Apr 01 to Oct 31. (815)234-8483, 8840 N IL Route 2, Byron, IL 61010

Camping World RV & Outdoors ProCare, service you can trust from the RV experts.

CAHOKIA — E3 *St Clair*

CAHOKIA RV PARQUE
Ratings: 9/9.5★/7.5 (RV Park) From Jct of I-255 & SR-157 (exit 13), W 2 mi on SR-157 to SR-3, N 500 ft (L).

RELAX BY OUR POOL OR DAYTRIP TO STL
Enjoy the sun by our sparkling pool, or day-trips to the Arch or to the fabulous & free St Louis Zoo! End your day with GREAT BBQ right in our own park at Sawmill BBQ. Friendly staff and clean restrooms always.

FAC: paved/gravel rds. (119 spaces). Avail: 52 gravel, patios, 14 pull-thrus, (25x55), back-ins (25x55), 40 full hkups, 12 W, 12 E (30/50 amps), seasonal sites, WiFi @ sites, tent sites, rentals, dump, laundry, LP gas, fire rings, firewood. **REC:** pool, playground. Pets OK. Partial handicap access. Big rig sites, eco-friendly. 2021 rates: $45 to $50, Military discount.
(618)332-7700 Lat: 38.573721, Lon: -90.187979
4060 Mississippi Ave, Cahokia, IL 62206
www.cahokiarvparque.com
See ad page 544

Things to See and Do

SAWMILL BBQ Located next to Cahokia RV Parque. Serving hickory smoked barbeque. Partial handicap access. RV accessible. Restrooms. Food. Hours: 11am to 8pm Mon - Sat.
(618)332-3000 Lat: 38.573233, Lon: -90.187025
4060 Mississippi Ave (Rt 3), Cahokia, IL 62206
www.sawmillbbq.com
See ad page 544

CANTON — C3 *Fulton*

RICE LAKE STATE FISH & WILDLIFE AREA (Public State Park) From Jct of US-9 & US-24, S 2.5 mi on US-24 (L). Avail: 32 E (30/50 amps), Pit toilets. 2021 rates: $10 to $35. (309)647-9184

CARBONDALE — F4 *Williamson*

CRAB ORCHARD LAKE (Public) From Jct of I-57 & SR-13, E 9 mi on SR-13 (R). Avail: 128 E (30 amps). 2021 rates: $10 to $25. Apr 01 to Oct 31. (618)985-4983

GIANT CITY (Public State Park) From Jct of US-51 & Makanda Rd, E 2.5 mi on Makanda Rd, follow signs (E). 85 Avail: 85 W, 85 E (30 amps). 2021 rates: $20 to $30. (618)457-4836

LITTLE GRASSY LAKE CAMPGROUND & MARINA **Ratings: 5/5.5/5** (Campground) 66 Avail: 14 full hkups, 52 W, 52 E (30/50 amps). 2021 rates: $25 to $35. Mar 15 to Nov 25. (618)457-6655, 788 Hidden Bay Lane, Makanda, IL 62958

CARLINVILLE — D3 *Macoupin*

BEAVER DAM (Public State Park) From Jct of Rte 108 & Carlinville-Shipman Rd (in town), S 8 mi on Carlinville-Shipman Rd, follow signs (R). Avail: 40 E (50 amps). 2021 rates: $20 to $35. (217)854-8020

IL

CARLOCK — C4 *McLean*

KAMP KOMFORT RV PARK & CAMPGROUND
good sam park **Ratings: 9.5/10★/9.5** (RV Park) From jct I-74 & 2050 N (Exit 120): Go 3/4 mi W on 2050, then 1 mi N on 600 East Rd (L).
FAC: all weather rds. Avail: 68 all weather, 68 pull-thrus, (35x70), 68 full hkups (30/50 amps), WiFi @ sites, dump, laundry, fire rings, firewood. **REC:** pool, playground. Pets OK. Partial handicap access. No tents. Big rig sites, eco-friendly. 2021 rates: $40 to $45, Military discount. Apr 01 to Oct 31.
(309)376-4411 Lat: 40.595458, Lon: -89.156468
21408 N 600 East Rd, Carlock, IL 61725
kampkomfortcampground.com
See ad this page

CARLYLE — E3 *Clinton*

CARLYLE LAKE - COE/DAM WEST REC AREA (Public Corps) From town, N 0.5 mi on SR 127 to William Rd, E 0.5 mi (L). 109 Avail: 24 full hkups, 85 E (50 amps). 2021 rates: $18 to $52. Apr 01 to Oct 31. (618)594-4410

ELDON HAZLET SRA (Public State Park) From N Jct of US-50 & SR-127, N 2.9 mi on SR-127 to Hazlet Park Rd, E 0.9 mi to CR-1860E, E 1.4 mi (E). Avail: 328 E (30/50 amps). 2021 rates: $18 to $35. (618)594-3015

LAKE CARLYLE - COE/MCNAIR CAMPGROUND (Public Corps) From jct Hwy-127 & US-50: Go 1 mi E on US-50. 47 Avail: 32 W, 32 E (50 amps). 2021 rates: $16 to $32. (618)594-2484

CARMI — E5 *White*

BURRELL PARK CAMPGROUND (Public) From Jct of I-64 & SR-1 (exit 130), S 13 mi on SR-1 to SR-14, W 0.2 mi to 6th St, N 0.3 mi to Stewart St, W 2 mi (L). Avail: 25 full hkups (30/50 amps). 2021 rates: $20. (618)382-2693

CASEY — D5 *Clark*

CASEY KOA CAMPGROUND **Ratings: 8/8.5/8** (Campground) 63 Avail: 21 full hkups, 42 W, 42 E (30/50 amps). 2021 rates: $45.95 to $54.95. Apr 01 to Nov 01. (217)932-5319, 1248 E 1250 Rd, Casey, IL 62420

CAVE IN ROCK — F5 *Hardin*

CAVE-IN-ROCK (Public State Park) From Jct of Hwys 146 & 1, S 2 mi on Hwy 1 (L). Avail: 34 E (30 amps). 2021 rates: $20 to $30. (618)289-4325

CHAMPAIGN — C4 *Champaign*

CHAMPAIGN See also Gibson City & Rantoul.

D & W LAKE RV PARK Ratings: 7/9.5★/9 (Campground) 37 Avail: 33 full hkups, 4 W, 4 E (30/50 amps). 2021 rates: $35. (217)356-3732, 411 W Hensley Rd, Champaign, IL 61822

CHARLESTON — D5 *Coles*

FOX RIDGE (Public State Park) From Jct of SR-16 & SR-130, S 7 mi on SR-130 (R). Avail: 42 E (30 amps). 2021 rates: $20 to $30. (217)345-6416

CHESTER — E3 *Randolph*

RANDOLPH COUNTY SRA (Public State Park) From Jct of SR-3 & 150, E 3 mi on SR-150, follow signs (L). Avail: 51 E (50 amps). 2021 rates: $10 to $35. (618)826-2706

CHICAGO — A5 *Cook*

CHICAGO See also Joliet, Marengo, Millbrook, Union & Volo, IL; Cedar Lake, Chesterton, Michigan City & Portage, IN.

SANKOTY LAKES
good sam park **Ratings: 8/10★/10** (RV Resort) From jct I-57 S & I-80 W: Go 73 mi W on I-80, then 18 mi S on I-39 S/US-51, then 14 mi W on IL-18, then 24 mi S on IL-26 (R).
FAC: all weather rds. Avail: 21 paved, patios, 21 pull-thrus, (35x45), 21 full hkups (30/50 amps), WiFi @ sites, rentals, groc, fire rings, firewood, restaurant, controlled access. **REC:** Lake Canada: swim, fishing, kayaking/canoeing, boating nearby. Pets OK. Partial handicap access. No tents, Age restrict may apply. Big rig sites, eco-friendly. 2021 rates: $95, Military discount.
(309)570-1111 Lat: 40.8180306, Lon: -89.5221788
1583 Spring Bay Rd, Spring Bay, IL 61611
www.sankotylakes.com
See primary listing at Spring Bay and ad page 356

CHILLICOTHE — B3 *Peoria*

CHILLICOTHE RV & RECREATION AREA **Ratings: 7.5/10★/9.5** (RV Park) 22 Avail: 11 full hkups, 11 W, 11 E (30/50 amps). 2021 rates: $35 to $50. Apr 15 to Oct 15. (309)274-2000, 20205 State Route 29 N, Chillicothe, IL 61523

CISCO — C4 *Platt*

FRIENDS CREEK CONSERVATION AREA (Public) From Jct of I-72 & exit 156, S 0.2 mi on exit Rd to CR-18, W 2 mi to 2300N, N 1.2 mi (R). Avail: 26 E (30 amps). 2021 rates: $10 to $20. May 01 to Nov 01. (217)423-7708

CISNE — E4 *Wayne*

SAM DALE LAKE STATE FISH & WILDLIFE AREA (Public State Park) From Jct of US-45 & CR-161 (in Cisne), W 8 mi on CR-161 to CR-700, N 1 mi, follow signs (L). Avail: 68 E (30/50 amps), Pit toilets. 2021 rates: $18 to $35. (618)835-2292

CLINTON — C4 *DeWitt*

WELDON SPRINGS (Public State Park) From town, E 1 mi on SR-10 to cnty park access rd, S 1 mi, follow signs (R). Avail: 79 E (30/50 amps). 2021 rates: $10 to $35. (217)935-2644

COLCHESTER — C2 *McDonough*

ARGYLE LAKE (Public State Park) From Jct of SR-67 & SR-136, W 7 mi on SR-136 to Argyle Lake Rd, N 2 mi (R). Avail: 110 E (30 amps). 2021 rates: $18 to $30. (309)776-3422

COLONA — B3 *Henry*

COLONA'S SCOTT FAMILY PARK (Public) From Jct I-80 & Hwy 6 (exit 9): Go E 1 mi on Hwy 6, then N 1 mi on Green River Rd, then W 100 yds on Poppy Garden Rd. 180 Avail: 180 W, 180 E (30 amps). 2021 rates: $40 to $50. (309)949-2128

CORTLAND — A4 *DeKalb*

Travel Services

GANDER RV OF CORTLAND/DEKALB Your new hometown outfitter offering the best regional gear for all your outdoor needs. Your adventure awaits. **SERVICES:** . RV Sales. RV supplies. Hours: 9am - 7pm, closed Sun. (888)892-3560 Lat: 41.918642, Lon: -88.701538 350 W Lincoln Hwy, Cortland, IL 60112 rv.ganderoutdoors.com

DANVILLE — C5 *Vermilion*

KICKAPOO (Public State Park) From I-74 (exit 206), N 2.1 mi on New Town Rd, follow signs (R). Avail: 101 E (30/50 amps). 2021 rates: $20 to $30. (217)442-4915

DE WITT — C4 *DeWitt*

CLINTON LAKE SRA (Public State Park) From jct Hwy-54 & CR-14: Go 2 mi S on CR-14. Avail: 91 E (30/50 amps). 2021 rates: $20 to $35. (217)935-8722

DU QUOIN — E4 *Perry*

DU QUOIN STATE FAIR CAMPGROUND (Public) From jct Hwy-152 & US-51: Go 2-1/4 mi S on US-51. During fair, enter through Gate 3 off US-51; Off-season, enter through Main Gate. 1000 Avail: 1000 W, 1000 E (30 amps). 2021 rates: $15 to $25. (618)542-9373

DURAND — A3 *Winnebego*

SUGAR SHORES RV RESORT **Ratings: 8/9.5★/9** (Membership Park) Avail: 27 full hkups (30/50 amps). 2021 rates: $45. Apr 15 to Oct 15. (815)629-2568, 9938 W Winslow, Durand, IL 61024

EAST MOLINE — B3 *Rock Island*

LUNDEEN'S LANDING (Campground) (Rebuilding) 32 Avail: 1 full hkups, 31 W, 31 E (30/50 amps). 2021 rates: $25 to $30. Apr 01 to Oct 31. (309)496-9956, 21119 Barstow Rd, East Moline, IL 61244

EAST PEORIA — C3 *Tazewell*

↖ CARL SPINDLER CAMPGROUND & MARINA (Public) From Jct of I-74 & SR-116 (exit 95B), N 4 mi on Hwy 150 to access rd 7, W 500 ft (R). 81 Avail: 55 W, 81 E (50 amps). 2021 rates: $21 to $30. Mar 01 to Oct 31. (309)699-3549

→ **MILLPOINT RV PARK**
good sam park **Ratings: 6.5/9.5★/8.5** (Campground) From Jct I-74 & Hwy 116 (Exit 95): Go 5 mi E on Hwy 116, then 3-1/2 mi N on Hwy 26, then 3/4 mi W on Millpoint Rd. (R). **FAC:** gravel rds. Avail: 85 gravel, 30 pull-thrus, (60x100), back-ins (60x75), 85 full hkups (30/50 amps), WiFi @ sites, tent sites, rentals, fire rings, firewood. **REC:** Illinois River: fishing, kayaking/canoeing, boating nearby. Pets OK. Big rig sites, eco-friendly. 2021 rates: $44, Military discount.
(309)231-6497 Lat: 40.780932, Lon: -89.536416
310 Ash Lane, East Peoria, IL 61611
millpointrvpark.com
See ad this page

EAST ST LOUIS — E3 *St Clair*

EAST ST LOUIS See also Cahokia & Granite City, IL; Fenton & St Charles, MO.

← **DRAFTKINGS AT CASINO QUEEN RV PARK**
good sam park **Ratings: 9/8.5/9.5** (RV Park) Avail: 140 full hkups (30/50 amps). 2021 rates: $55 to $60. (800)777-0777, 200 South Front St, East St Louis, IL 62201

EFFINGHAM — D4 *Effingham*

↑ **CAMP LAKEWOOD CAMPGROUND & RV PARK**
good sam park **Ratings: 8.5/9.5★/9.5** (Campground) Avail: 50 full hkups (30/50 amps). 2021 rates: $50 to $88. (217)342-6233, 1217 W Rickelman Ave, Effingham, IL 62401

EL PASO — C4 *Mason*

← HICKORY HILL CAMPGROUND **Ratings: 7/6/7.5** (Campground) 38 Avail: 18 full hkups, 20 W, 20 E (30/50 amps). 2021 rates: $34 to $36. Apr 01 to Nov 01. (309)744-2407, 973 County Road 2250 E, Secor, IL 61771

ELGIN — A4 *Kane*

↖ BURNIDGE FOREST PRESERVE/PAUL WOLFF (Public) From Jct I-90, take the Randall Rd. exit. Go S to Big Timber Rd., approximately 1 mi. Turn right (west) onto Big Timber Rd. until you reach entrance for park, approximately 1.2 mi. Avail: 89 E (50 amps), Pit toilets. 2021 rates: $20 to $35. May 01 to Oct 31. (630)232-5980

EQUALITY — F4 *Saline*

↓ SALINE COUNTY STATE FISH & WILDLIFE AREA (Public State Park) From Jct of SR-13 & SR-142, SE 1 mi on SR-142 to cnty rd, S 5 mi, follow signs (R). Avail: 13 W, Pit toilets. 2021 rates: $10 to $35. (618)276-4405

FINDLAY — D4 *Shelby*

↖ EAGLE CREEK (Public State Park) From Jct of Hwy 16 & Rte 128, N 10 mi on Rte 128 to Findlay Rd, E 4 mi to park access rd, S 2 mi (E). Avail: 103 E (30 amps). 2021 rates: $20 to $30. (217)756-8260

↓ LAKE SHELBYVILLE - COE/LONE POINT (Public Corps) From town, S 2.8 mi on Findlay Concrete Hwy to unmarked rd, E 0.5 mi to unmarked rd, S 0.8 mi to unmarked rd, E 0.5 mi to unmarked rd, S 0.5 mi (E). 82 Avail: 28 full hkups, 54 E (30/50 amps). 2021 rates: $16 to $32. May 16 to Sep 02. (217)774-3951

FLORA — E4 *Clay*

← CHARLEY BROWN PARK (Public) From Jct of Hwy 50 & Rte 45, W 1 mi on Hwy 50 to cnty rd, S 0.75 mi to 2nd cnty rd, W 1 mi (L). 85 Avail: 85 W, 85 E (30 amps). 2021 rates: $18. May 15 to Nov 15. (618)662-8313

FOX LAKE — A5 *Lake*

→ CHAIN O'LAKES (Public State Park) From Jct of US-12 & Wilmot Rd, N 2 mi on Wilmot Rd (R). Avail: 189 E (50 amps). 2021 rates: $12 to $35. (847)587-5512

GALENA — A3 *Jo Daviess*

← PALACE CAMPGROUND **Ratings: 8/6/8** (Campground) 107 Avail: 22 full hkups, 49 W, 85 E (30/50 amps). 2021 rates: $38 to $42. Apr 01 to Nov 01. (815)777-2466, 11357 Rte 20 W, Galena, IL 61036

GALESBURG — B3 *Knox*

→ **GALESBURG EAST CAMPGROUND**
good sam park **Ratings: 9/9.5★/10** (Campground) From Jct I-74 & US-150 (Exit 54): Go E 1/2 mi on US-150 (L). Note: Do not use GPS, follow blue camping signs. **FAC:** gravel rds. (73 spaces). Avail: 62 gravel, 56 pull-thrus, (30x60), back-ins (30x50), 62 full hkups (30/50 amps), seasonal sites, WiFi @ sites, tent sites, rentals, dump, laundry, LP gas, fire rings, firewood. **REC:** heated pool, pond, fishing, boating nearby, playground. Pets OK. Partial handicap access. Big rig sites, eco-friendly. 2021 rates: $34 to $38, Military discount. Apr 01 to Oct 31.
(309)289-2267 Lat: 40.9084, Lon: -90.2358
1081 US Hwy 150 E, Knoxville, IL 61448
www.galesburgeastcampground.com
See ad this page

GARDEN PRAIRIE — A4 *Boone*

↑ NORTHWOODS RV RESORT **Ratings: 7/8.5/8.5** (RV Park) 104 Avail: 12 full hkups, 92 W, 92 E (30/50 amps). 2021 rates: $75 to $99. Apr 10 to Oct 31. (815)317-3775, 7081 Garden Prairie Rd, Garden Prairie, IL 61038

GENESEO — B3 *Henry*

↑ GENESEO CAMPGROUND **Ratings: 7.5/9.5★/9** (Campground) 62 Avail: 40 full hkups, 22 W, 22 E (30/50 amps). 2021 rates: $28 to $35. Apr 01 to Oct 31. (309)944-6465, 22978 IL Hwy 82, Geneseo, IL 61254

GIBSON CITY — C4 *Ford*

SOUTH PARK MUNICIPAL CAMPGROUND (Public) From jct IL47/54/9: Go E one block. 9 Avail: 9 W, 9 E (30 amps). 2021 rates: $10. Apr 01 to Oct 31. (217)784-5872

GOLCONDA — F4 *Pope*

← DIXON SPRINGS (Public State Park) From Jct of I-24 & SR-146 (exit 16), E 12 mi on SR-146 (L). Avail: 13 E (30/50 amps). 2021 rates: $18. (618)949-3394

GOODFIELD — C4 *Woodford*

↗ TIMBERLINE CAMPGROUND **Ratings: 8/5/6.5** (Campground) Avail: 120 full hkups (30/50 amps). 2021 rates: $35 to $38. Apr 01 to Oct 31. (309)965-2224, 1467 Timberline Road, Goodfield, IL 61742

GOREVILLE — F4 *Johnson*

↓ FERNE CLYFFE (Public State Park) From town, S 1 mi on SR-37 (R). Avail: 56 E (30 amps). 2021 rates: $20 to $30. Apr 01 to Dec 31. (618)995-2411

GRAFTON — D2 *Jersey*

← PERE MARQUETTE (Public State Park) From Jct of SR-3 & SR-100, W 5 mi on SR-100, follow signs (R). Avail: 80 E (30/50 amps). 2021 rates: $10 to $35. (618)786-3323

GRANITE CITY — E3 *Madison*

↑ GRANITE CITY KOA JOURNEY **Ratings: 9/9.5★/8** (Campground) Avail: 56 full hkups (30/50 amps). 2021 rates: $46.80 to $55. Apr 01 to Nov 01. (618)931-5160, 3157 W Chain of Rocks Rd, Granite City, IL 62040

↓ HORSESHOE LAKE (Public State Park) From jct I-270 & Hwy 111: Go 4 mi S on Hwy 111. Avail: 48 E Pit toilets. 2021 rates: $8. May 01 to Sep 30. (618)931-0270

GRAYVILLE — E5 *White*

↖ HILLTOP CAMPGROUND (Public) From Jct of I-64 & Hwy 1 (exit 130), N 1.5 mi on Hwy 1 to North St, E 4 blks to Water St, S 0.25 mi to Walnut St, E 1 blk to Oxford St, S 0.25 mi, follow signs (E). Avail: 34 full hkups (30/50 amps). 2021 rates: $10. (618)375-3671

Driving a big rig? Average site width and length measurements tell you which campgrounds can accommodate your Big Rig.

HAMPTON — B3 *Carroll*

↓ MISSISSIPPI RIVER POOLS 11-22 - COE/FISHERMAN'S CORNER (Public Corps) From Jct of I-80 & SR-84, SW 1 mi on SR-84 (R). Avail: 46 E (30/50 amps). 2021 rates: $20. May 01 to Oct 28. (815)259-3628

HANOVER — A3 *Jo Daviess*

← MISSISSIPPI RIVER - POOLS 11-22 - COE/BLANDING LANDING (Public Corps) From Hwy-84 in town: Go 7 mi W on Blanding Rd, follow signs. Avail: 30 E (20/50 amps). 2021 rates: $14 to $25. May 01 to Oct 27. (563)582-0881

HARMON — B3 *Lee*

↖ GREEN RIVER STATE WILDLIFE AREA (Public State Park) From town: Go 6 mi N on hwy 26, then follow signs W on blacktop road. 50 Avail. 2021 rates: $8. (815)379-2324

HAVANA — C3 *Fulton*

↖ ANDERSON LAKE CONSERVATION AREA (Public State Park) From town, NE 11 mi on SR-100 (L). 100 Avail: Pit toilets. 2021 rates: $8. (309)759-4484

HERRIN — F4 *Williamson*

↑ FOUR SEASONS CAMPGROUND **Ratings: 7.5/8.5★/7** (Campground) Avail: 37 full hkups (30/50 amps). 2021 rates: $30. (618)942-2069, 720 E Carroll St, Herrin, IL 62948

HILLSBORO — D3 *Montgomery*

↗ SHERWOOD FOREST CAMPGROUND (Public) From Jct of SR-16 & SR-127 (in town), N 0.4 mi on SR-16/SR-127 to Seward St, E 100 ft to Main St, S around square to N Main, N 1.6 mi to CR-1275N, E 1.4 mi (E). Avail: 200 E (20/30 amps). 2021 rates: $25 to $35. Apr 01 to Oct 31. (217)532-5211

ILLINOIS CITY — B2 *Rock Island*

← MISSISSIPPI RIVER REC AREAS-MUSCATINE AREA - COE/BLANCHARD ISLAND (Public Corps) From town: Go 6 mi W on Hwy 92/New Boston Rd, follow signs. 34 Avail: Pit toilets. 2021 rates: $12. (563)263-7913

JACKSONVILLE — D3 *Morgan*

↗ CRAZY HORSE CAMPGROUND **Ratings: 8.5/9.5★/9** (Campground) Avail: 33 full hkups (30/50 amps). 2021 rates: $49. Apr 01 to Oct 31. (217)886-2089, 2113 Crazy Horse Rd, Ashland, IL 62612

JOHNSTON CITY — F4 *Williamson*

→ ARROWHEAD LAKE CAMPGROUND (Public) From Jct of I-57 & Exit 59(Broadway), E 2 mi on Broadway (thru town) to entrance rd (L). 66 Avail: 66 W, 66 E (30/50 amps). 2021 rates: $18 to $23. (618)983-3535

We've listened to thousands of RVers like you, so we know exactly how to rate campgrounds. Got feedback? Call us! 877-209-6655.

IL

JOLIET — B5 *Will*

LEISURE LAKE RESORT

good sam park **Ratings: 10/10★/9** (Membership Park) S-bnd: From Jct I-55 & IL-59 (Exit 251): Go W 0.1 mi on Seil Rd, then S 2 mi on Frontage Rd (R) or N-bnd: From Jct I-55 & US 52 (Exit 253): Go W 0.5 mi on US 52 (Jefferson St), then S 1 mi on IL-59 (Cottage St), then W 0.1 mi on Seil Rd,then S 2 mi on Frontage Rd (R).

ONLY 40 MILES TO DOWNTOWN CHICAGO!
Near Chicago Land's Route 66 Speedway & Metra Train Station. Offering Planned Activities, Dances, Entertainment, a stocked fishing lake, sand bottom swimming lake, pool, pickle ball & much more. Come experience our resort!

FAC: all weather rds. (265 spaces). 175 Avail: 75 paved, 100 all weather, 18 pull-thrus, (30x70), back-ins (30x60), 155 full hkups, 20 W, 20 E (30/50 amps), seasonal sites, WiFi @ sites, dump, mobile sewer, laundry, LP gas, fire rings, firewood, controlled access. **REC:** pool, Leisure Lake: swim, fishing, playground. Pets OK. Partial handicap access. No tents. Big rig sites, eco-friendly. 2021 rates: $53.50. Mar 01 to Nov 30.
(815)741-9405 Lat: 41.485113, Lon: -88.201225
21900 SW Frontage Rd, Joliet, IL 60404
leisurelakeresort.com
See ad page 362

RV PARK AT HOLLYWOOD CASINO JOLIET

good sam park **Ratings: 7.5/8.5★/9** (RV Park) 80 Avail: 80 W, 80 E (30/50 amps). 2021 rates: $40 to $69. (815)744-9400, 777 Hollywood Blvd, Joliet, IL 60436

JOSLIN — B3 *Rock Island*

SUNSET LAKES RESORT **Ratings: 9/10★/9** (RV Park) 190 Avail: 58 full hkups, 132 W, 132 E (30/50 amps). 2021 rates: $46 to $74. Apr 11 to Oct 19. (888)460-1197, 3333 290th St North, Hillsdale, IL 61257

KANKAKEE — B5 *Kankakee*

KANKAKEE SOUTH KOA **Ratings: 9/9★/8.5** (Campground) 74 Avail: 60 full hkups, 14 W, 14 E (30/50 amps). 2021 rates: $40 to $80. Apr 01 to Oct 31. (815)939-4603, 425 E 6000 S Rd, Chebanse, IL 60922

KEWANEE — B3 *Henry*

FRANCIS PARK (Public) From town, E 4 mi on US 34, follow signs (L). Avail: 60 E (20/30 amps). 2021 rates: $13. May 01 to Sep 30. (309)852-0511

JOHNSON/SAUK TRAIL (Public State Park) From town, N 5 mi on SR-78 to park access rd; or From Jct of I-80 (exit 33) & SR-78, S 5 mi on SR-78 (L). Avail: 70 E (30/50 amps). 2021 rates: $18 to $55. (309)853-5589

Show Your Good Sam Membership Card!

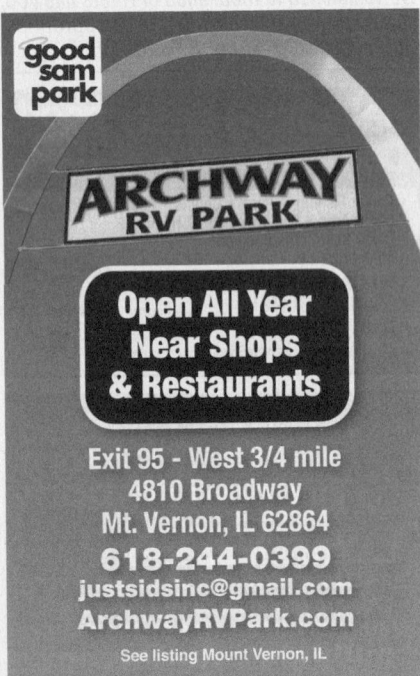

LA SALLE — B4 *La Salle*

LA SALLE See also Amboy, Leland, Marseilles, Oglesby & Utica.

LACON — B3 *Marshall*

MARSHALL STATE FISH & WILDLIFE AREA (Public State Park) From Jct of Hwys 17 & 26, S 5 mi on Hwy 26, follow signs (R). Avail: 15 E (30 amps). 2021 rates: $10 to $35. (309)246-8351

LAWRENCEVILLE — E5 *Lawrence*

RED HILLS (Public State Park) From Jct of SR-1 & US-50, W 8 mi on US-50, follow signs (L). Avail: 104 E (30/50 amps). 2021 rates: $10 to $35. Apr 01 to Nov 30. (618)936-2469

LE ROY — C4 *McLean*

MORAINE VIEW (Public State Park) From Jct of I-74 & Rte. 21, N 5.6 mi to CR-36, E 2 mi, follow signs (R). Avail: 102 E (30 amps). 2021 rates: $10 to $35. (309)724-8032

LELAND — B4 *La Salle*

HI-TIDE BEACH & CAMPGROUND **Ratings: 8/9.5★/9.5** (Campground) 99 Avail: 20 full hkups, 79 W, 79 E (30/50 amps). 2021 rates: $52. Apr 15 to Oct 15. (815)495-9032, 4611 E 22nd Rd, Leland, IL 60531

LENA — A3 *Stephenson*

LAKE LE-AQUA-NA (Public State Park) From Jct of Hwy 73 & US-20, N 5.75 mi on Hwy 73 to Lake Rd, W 2.1 mi on Lake Rd (L). 138 Avail: (30/50 amps). 2021 rates: $20 to $35. (815)369-4282

LENA KOA **Ratings: 9/9.5★/9.5** (Campground) 67 Avail: 55 full hkups, 12 W, 12 E (30/50 amps). 2021 rates: $55.95 to $79.95. Apr 15 to Nov 01. (815)369-2612, 10982 W Hwy 20, Lena, IL 61048

LINCOLN — C3 *Logan*

CAMP A WHILE **Ratings: 1.5/UI/7** (Campground) 10 Avail: 5 full hkups, 2 W, 5 E (30/50 amps). 2021 rates: $30 to $40. Apr 01 to Oct 31. (217)732-8840, 1779-1250th Avenue, Lincoln, IL 62656

LITCHFIELD — D3 *Montgomery*

COUNTRY BEND CAMPGROUND **Ratings: 7.5/10★/9** (Campground) 100 Avail: 54 full hkups, 46 W, 46 E (30/50 amps). 2021 rates: $33 to $43. Apr 01 to Nov 01. (217)324-2363, 3279 Honey Bend Ave, Litchfield, IL 62056

KAMPER KOMPANION RV PARK **Ratings: 6/9.5★/7.5** (RV Park) Avail: 23 full hkups (30/50 amps). 2021 rates: $44. (217)324-4747, 18388 E Frontage Rd, Litchfield, IL 62056

MACOMB — C2 *McDonough*

SPRING LAKE PARK CAMPGROUND (CITY PARK) (Public) From west jct US 136 & US 67: Go 4 mi N on US 67, then 2 mi W on CR N1500. (Spring Lake Park Rd). 120 Avail. 2021 rates: $20 to $40. (309)833-2052

MARENGO — A4 *McHenry*

LEHMAN'S LAKESIDE RV RESORT

good sam park **Ratings: 8.5/10★/8.5** (RV Park) 152 Avail: 114 full hkups, 38 W, 38 E (30/50 amps). 2021 rates: $45 to $60. (815)923-4533, 19609 Harmony Rd, Marengo, IL 60152

MARION — F4 *Williamson*

MARION CAMPGROUND & RV PARK **Ratings: 7/9★/8.5** (RV Park) Avail: 58 full hkups (30/50 amps). 2021 rates: $39.95. (618)997-3484, 119 N 7th St, Marion, IL 62959

Travel Services

GANDER RV OF MARION Your new hometown outfitter offering the best regional gear for all your outdoor needs. Your adventure awaits. **SERVICES:** sells outdoor gear, sells firearms, restrooms. RV Sales. RV supplies, LP gas, dump, emergency parking, RV accessible. Hours: 9am - 8pm.
(855)214-4531 Lat: 37.749538, Lon: -88.957517
2480 Blue Heron Drive, Marion, IL 62959
rv.ganderoutdoors.com

Slow down. For most vehicles, fuel efficiency begins to drop rapidly at 60 mph. Driving within the speed limit can improve fuel efficiency by up to 23 percent.

MARSEILLES — B4 *La Salle*

GLENWOOD RV RESORT

good sam park **Ratings: 6.5/7.5★/7.5** (Campground) 400 Avail: 36 full hkups, 364 W, 364 E (30/50 amps). 2021 rates: $36 to $45. (815)795-6000, 551 Wilson St, Marseilles, IL 61341

ILLINI (Public State Park) From Jct of I-80 & Marseilles exit/CR-15, S 4 mi on CR-15 (L). Avail: 45 E (30/50 amps). 2021 rates: $10 to $55. (815)795-2448

MARSHALL — D5 *Clark*

LINCOLN TRAIL (Public State Park) From Jct of I-70 & SR-1 (exit 147), S 5 mi on SR-1, follow signs (R). Avail: 177 E (30 amps). 2021 rates: $10 to $35. (217)826-2222

MILL CREEK PARK CAMPGROUND (CLARK COUNTY PARK) (Public) From jct I-70 (exit 147) & Hwy 1: Go 1 mi S on Hwy 1, then 3/4 mi W on US 40, then 7 mi NW on Lincoln Heritage Tr. Avail: 139 E. 2021 rates: $22 to $30. (217)889-3901

MCLEANSBORO — E4 *Hamilton*

HAMILTON COUNTY CONSERVATION AREA (Public State Park) From town, E 8 mi on Rte 14 to park access rd, S 1 mi, follow signs (E). Avail: 60 E (30 amps). 2021 rates: $20 to $35. (618)773-4340

METROPOLIS — F4 *Massac*

FORT MASSAC (Public State Park) From Jct of I-24 & US-45 (exit 37), W 2.5 mi on US-45 (L). Avail: 50 E (30/50 amps). 2021 rates: $10 to $30. (618)524-4712

MILLBROOK — B4 *Cook*

YOGI BEAR'S JELLYSTONE PARK CAMP RESORT **Ratings: 8.5/10★/9** (RV Park) 184 Avail: 57 full hkups, 127 W, 127 E (30/50 amps). 2021 rates: $75 to $95. (800)438-9644, 8574 Millbrook Rd, Millbrook, IL 60536

MORRISON — A3 *Whiteside*

MORRISON-ROCKWOOD (Public State Park) From Jct of US-30 & SR-78, N 1 mi on SR-78 to Damen Rd, E 1.5 mi to Crosby Rd, N 0.5 mi (E). Avail: 92 E (30/50 amps). 2021 rates: $10 to $35. (815)772-4708

MOUNT CARROLL — A3 *Carroll*

TIMBER LAKE RESORT **Ratings: 9/9★/9.5** (Campground) 46 Avail: 38 full hkups, 8 W, 8 E (30/50 amps). 2021 rates: $52 to $80. Apr 15 to Nov 01. (800)485-0145, 8216 Black Oak Rd, Mount Carroll, IL 61053

MOUNT VERNON — E4 *Jefferson*

ARCHWAY RV PARK

good sam park **Ratings: 8/10★/8** (RV Park) Jct I-57 & IL Hwy-15 (Exit 95): Go 3/4 mi W on IL Hwy-15/Broadway St (R). **FAC:** all weather rds. Avail: 49 all weather, 42 pull-thrus, (25x65), back-ins (30x60), mostly side by side hkups, 49 full hkups (30/50 amps), WiFi @ sites, tent sites, rentals, dump, laundry, LP bottles. **REC:** pond, fishing, playground. Pets OK. Partial handicap access. Big rig sites, eco-friendly. 2021 rates: $45, Military discount.
(618)244-0399 Lat: 38.312921, Lon: -88.965569
4810 Broadway, Mount Vernon, IL 62864
archwayrvpark.com
See ad this page

MULBERRY GROVE — D3 *Bond*

CEDARBROOK RV PARK & CAMPGROUND **Ratings: 7.5/6.5/8.5** (Campground) 15 Avail: 10 full hkups, 5 W, 5 E (30/50 amps). 2021 rates: $40. Apr 01 to Oct 31. (618)326-8865, 1109 Mulberry Grove Rd, Mulberry Grove, IL 62262

TIMBER TRAILS CAMPGROUND **Ratings: 4.5/7/7.5** (Campground) 18 Avail: 5 full hkups, 13 W, 13 E (30/50 amps). 2021 rates: $46 to $52. Apr 01 to Nov 01. (618)326-8264, 1276 Matts Lane, Mulberry Grove, IL 62262

MURPHYSBORO — F3 *Jackson*

LAKE MURPHYSBORO (Public State Park) From Jct of SR-149 & SR-127, W 3.5 mi on SR-149 (R). Avail: 54 E (30/50 amps). 2021 rates: $10 to $35. (618)684-2867

NASHVILLE — E3 *Washington*

WASHINGTON COUNTY SRA (Public State Park) From Jct of I-64 & SR-127 (exit 50), S 8 mi on SR-127, follow signs (L). Avail: 37 E (30 amps). 2021 rates: $10 to $35. (618)327-3137

NAUVOO — C2 *Hancock*

NAUVOO (Public State Park) From Jct of Hwy 96 & US-136, N 11 mi on Hwy 96, follow signs (R). Avail: 35 E (30 amps). 2021 rates: $10 to $35. (217)453-2512

NEW DOUGLAS — D3 *Madison*

RUSTIC ACRES CAMPGROUND **Ratings: 8/9.5★/9** (Campground) 80 Avail: 72 full hkups, 8 W, 8 E (30/50 amps). 2021 rates: $35 to $50. Apr 01 to Oct 31. (217)456-1122, 12246 Binney Rd, New Douglas, IL 62074

NEWTON — D5 *Jasper*

SAM PARR STATE FISH & WILDLIFE AREA (Public State Park) From town, NE 3 mi on SR-33 (L). Avail: 10 E (50 amps), Pit toilets. 2021 rates: $10 to $35. (618)783-2661

OAKLAND — D5 *Coles*

WALNUT POINT (Public State Park) From town, N 1 mi on Hwy 3 (becomes Hwy 7), N 2 mi, follow signs (L). Avail: 34 E (30/50 amps). 2021 rates: $10 to $35. (217)346-3336

OGLESBY — B4 *LaSalle*

PLEASANT CREEK CAMPGROUND **Ratings: 5.5/8.5★/7.5** (Campground) 92 Avail: 92 W, 92 E (30/50 amps). 2021 rates: $38 to $44. May 01 to Oct 31. (815)431-0936, 926 N. 2150th Rd, Oglesby, IL 61348

OLIVE BRANCH — F3 *Alexander*

HORSESHOE LAKE STATE FISH & WILDLIFE AREA (Public State Park) From S end of town, SE 2 mi on SR-3, follow signs (R). Avail: 78 E (30 amps). 2021 rates: $8 to $35. May 01 to Oct 31. (618)776-5689

OQUAWKA — B2 *Henderson*

DELABAR (Public State Park) From town, N 1 mi on cnty rd (L) Note: Must obtain permit from park staff upon arrival. Avail: 56 E (30 amps). 2021 rates: $20 to $25. (309)374-2496

HENDERSON COUNTY STATE CONSERVATION AREA (Public State Park) From town: Go 4 mi S on Hwy 164. Turn Right on Hwy 34 and then Right again on Gladstone Lake Rd. 35 Avail: Pit toilets. 2021 rates: $8. (309)374-2496

OREGON — A3 *Ogle*

HANSEN'S HIDEAWAY RANCH & FAMILY CAMPGROUND Ratings: 5.5/9★/8 (Campground) 10 Avail: 1 full hkups, 9 W, 9 E (30 amps). 2021 rates: $32 to $37. Apr 15 to Oct 20. (815)732-6489, 2916 South Harmony Rd, Oregon, IL 61061

LAKE LADONNA FAMILY CAMPGROUND **Ratings: 6/7.5/8** (Campground) 73 Avail: 73 W, 73 E (30/50 amps). 2021 rates: $45. Apr 15 to Oct 15. (815)732-6804, 1302 S Harmony Rd, Oregon, IL 61061

LOWDEN (Public State Park) From Jct of Hwy 64 & River Rd, N 2 mi on River Rd (L). Avail: 80 E (20 amps). 2021 rates: $10 to $35. (815)732-6828

WHITE PINES FOREST (Public State Park) From town, W 8 mi on W Pines Rd, follow signs (R). Avail: 3 E (30 amps). 2021 rates: $10. (815)946-3717

PANA — D4 *Christian*

OAK TERRACE RV RESORT

good sam park **Ratings: 8.5/9.5★/10** (RV Park) Avail: 20 full hkups (30/50 amps). 2021 rates: $40 to $60. Apr 15 to Oct 15. (217)539-4477, 100 Beyers Lake Rd, Pana, IL 62557

PECATONICA — A3 *Winnebego*

PECATONICA RIVER FOREST PRESERVE (Public) From Jct of US-20 & SR-70, NW 12 mi on SR-70 to Judd Rd, S 1.5 mi, follow signs (R). Avail: 68 E (30/50 amps), Pit toilets. 2021 rates: $8 to $23. (815)877-6100

PEKIN — C3 *Tazewell*

SPRING LAKE FISH & WILDLIFE AREA (Public State Park) From town, N 2 mi on CR-16 to CR-21, W 3 mi (E). 60 Avail: Pit toilets. 2021 rates: $8. (309)968-7135

PERCY — E3 *Perry*

LAKE CAMP-A-LOT **Ratings: 4/4.5/5.5** (Campground) 21 Avail: 21 W, 21 E (30/50 amps). 2021 rates: $18. (618)497-2942, 13520 Community Lake Rd, Percy, IL 62272

RV Park ratings you can rely on!

PETERSBURG — C3 *Menard*

LINCOLN'S NEW SALEM STATE HISTORIC SITE (Public State Park) From Jct of SR-125 & SR-97, N 13.2 mi on SR-97 (L). Avail: 100 E (30/50 amps). 2021 rates: $5 to $30. (217)632-4000

PINCKNEYVILLE — E3 *Perry*

PYRAMID (Public State Park) From Jct of SR-154 & SR-13, S 6 mi on SR-13 to Pyatt Cutler Rd., W 2.75 mi, follow signs (R). 54 Avail: Pit toilets. 2021 rates: $8 to $10. (618)357-2574

PITTSFIELD — D2 *Pike*

YOGI BEAR'S JELLYSTONE PARK AT PINE LAKES **Ratings: 8.5/10★/9** (Campground) 101 Avail: 87 full hkups, 14 W, 14 E (30/50 amps). 2021 rates: $66 to $86. Apr 15 to Oct 18. (217)285-6719, 1405 Lakeview Heights, Pittsfield, IL 62363

PLEASANT HILL — D2 *Pike*

GREAT RIVER ROAD CAMPGROUND (Public) From Hwy 96 & S Main St: Go 1/2 mi S on S Main St. to Campground Rd. 59 Avail: 59 W, 59 E (30 amps). 2021 rates: $10 to $16. Apr 01 to Oct 31. (217)285-7000

PROPHETSTOWN — B3 *Whiteside*

PROPHETSTOWN (Public State Park) From Jct of Hwys 78 & 172, E 0.25 mi on Hwy 172 (L). Avail: 43 E (30 amps). 2021 rates: $10 to $35. May 01 to Oct 31. (815)537-2926

QUINCY — C2 *Adams*

SILOAM SPRINGS (Public State Park) From Jct of SR-24 & CR-2950E, S 10 mi on CR-2950E; or From Jct SR-104 & CR-2873E, N 6 mi on CR-2873E, follow signs (R). Avail: 98 E (30/50 amps). 2021 rates: $10 to $35. (217)894-6205

RAMSEY — D4 *Fayette*

RAMSEY LAKE (Public State Park) From Jct of I-70 & US-51 (exit 63), N 12 mi on US-51, follow signs (L). Avail: 90 E (30/50 amps). 2021 rates: $10 to $35. (618)423-2215

RANTOUL — C5 *Champaign*

PRAIRIE PINES CAMPGROUND (Public) From Jct of I-57 & US-136 (exit 250), E 1.6 mi on US-136 to US-45, S 2 mi to Chandler Rd, E 1 mi on Chandler/S Perimeter Rds (L); or From Jct of I-74 & US-45 (exit 184), N 10.4 mi on US-45 to Chandler Rd, E 1 mi (L). Avail: 95 full hkups (30/50 amps). 2021 rates: $26.50. (217)893-0438

ROCHESTER — D3 *Christian*

SANGCHRIS LAKE (Public State Park) From Jct of I-55 & Hwy 29 (exit 96A), S 5 mi on Hwy 29 to Walnut, S 5 mi to New City, E 3 mi (E); or N-bnd: From Jct of I-55 & Rte 104 (exit 82), W 5 mi on Rte 104, follow signs. Avail: 135 E (30/50 amps). 2021 rates: $10 to $20. Apr 01 to Jan 16. (217)498-9208

ROCK FALLS — B3 *Whiteside*

CRYSTAL LAKE RV PARK **Ratings: 7/10★/7.5** (RV Park) Avail: 42 full hkups (30/50 amps). 2021 rates: $50 to $55. Apr 15 to Nov 01. (815)499-0520, 600 E 17th St, Rock Falls, IL 61071

LEISURE LAKE CAMPGROUND **Ratings: 5.5/UI/7.5** (Campground) Avail: 65 full hkups (30/50 amps). 2021 rates: $30 to $32. Apr 01 to Oct 15. (815)626-0005, 2304 French St, Rock Falls, IL 61071

ROCK ISLAND — B2 *Rock Island*

ROCK ISLAND/QUAD CITIES KOA **Ratings: 9/10★/8.5** (Campground) Avail: 58 full hkups (30/50 amps). 2021 rates: $55 to $75. (888)562-4502, 2311 78th Ave W, Rock Island, IL 61201

ROCKFORD — A4 *Winnebago*

BLACKHAWK VALLEY CAMPGROUND **Ratings: 7/8.5★/8.5** (Campground) 40 Avail: 17 full hkups, 23 W, 23 E (30/50 amps). 2021 rates: $40 to $50. Apr 15 to Oct 15. (815)874-9767, 6540 Valley Trail Rd, Rockford, IL 61109

ROCK CUT (Public State Park) From Jct of I-90 & Riverside Blvd exit, W 3 mi on Riverside Blvd to Forest Hills Rd, N 3.3 mi to SR-173, E 1 mi, follow signs (L). Avail: 270 E (30/50 amps). 2021 rates: $10 to $35. (815)885-3311

Dispose of old paint, chemicals, and oil properly. Don't put batteries, antifreeze, paint, motor oil, or chemicals in the trash. Use proper toxics disposal sites.

ROCKTON — A4 *Winnebago*

HONONEGAH FOREST PRESERVE (Public) From Jct of SR-251 & Hononegah Rd, W 2 mi on Hononegah Rd (L). 57 Avail: (30/50 amps), Pit toilets. 2021 rates: $13 to $23. Apr 16 to Nov 19. (815)877-6100

ROSCOE — A4 *Winnebago*

Travel Services

RUSHVILLE — C2 *Schuyler*

SCHUY-RUSH PARK (Public) Jct of Hwy 24 & Hwy 67: Go 2 mi S on Hwy 67, turn W on CR 190 E. 77 Avail: (30/50 amps). 2021 rates: $10 to $35. (217)322-6628

SALEM — E4 *Marion*

STEPHEN A FORBES (Public State Park) From Jct of I-57 & US-50 (Salem exit), E 17 mi on US-50 to Omega luka Rd, N 7 mi, follow signs (R). 115 Avail: 115 W, 115 E (30/50 amps). 2021 rates: $10 to $35. (618)547-3381

SAVANNA — A3 *Carroll*

MISSISSIPPI PALISADES (Public State Park) From Jct US-52 & SR-84, N 2 mi on SR-84, follow signs (R). Avail: 110 E (30 amps). 2021 rates: $10 to $35. May 01 to Oct 31. (815)273-2731

SESSER — E4 *Franklin*

WAYNE FITZGERRELL SRA (Public State Park) From Jct of I-57 & Rte 154 (exit 77), W 1 mi on Rte 154 (R). 243 Avail: 243 S, 243 E (30/50 amps). 2021 rates: $20 to $30. (618)629-2320

SEWARD — B4 *Winnebago*

SEWARD BLUFFS FOREST PRESERVE (Public) From Jct of US-20 & SR-70, W 13 mi on US-20 to Pecatonica Rd, S 1 mi to Comly Rd, W 0.5 mi, follow signs (R). Avail: 36 E (30/50 amps), Pit toilets. 2021 rates: $11 to $31. Apr 16 to Nov 19. (815)877-6100

SHABBONA — B4 *DeKalb*

SHABBONA SRA (Public State Park) From town, S 0.75 mi on Shabbona Rd, follow signs (R). Avail: 150 E (30/50 amps). 2021 rates: $10 to $35. (815)824-2106

SHELBYVILLE — D4 *Shelby*

LAKE SHELBYVILLE - COE/COON CREEK (Public Corps) From town: Go 4-1/2 mi N on SR 128, then 1 mi E on CR 1750 N, then ¼ mi N on CR 1900 E, then 1-3/4 mi E on CR 1785 N, then 1-3/4 mi S on CR 2075 E (E). 181 Avail: 23 full hkups, 158 E (30/50 amps). 2021 rates: $18 to $48. May 07 to Oct 11. (217)774-3951

LAKE SHELBYVILLE - COE/LITHIA SPRINGS (Public Corps) From town, E 3.2 mi on SR-16 to cnty rd, N 2.1 mi to unmarked rd, W 1.4 mi (E). Avail: 113 E (30/50 amps). 2021 rates: $18 to $36. Apr 18 to Oct 26. (217)774-3951

LAKE SHELBYVILLE - COE/OPOSSUM CREEK (Public Corps) From town, N 3.4 mi on SR-128 to CR-1650, E 0.9 mi to unmarked rd, S 0.5 mi to unmarked rd, E 1.2 mi (E). 80 Avail: 17 full hkups, 2 W, 55 E (20/50 amps). 2021 rates: $16 to $32. May 16 to Sep 02. (217)774-3951

ROBIN HOOD WOODS CAMPGROUND & RESORT **Ratings: 8.5/9★/9** (Campground) 100 Avail: 60 full hkups, 40 W, 40 E (30/50 amps). 2021 rates: $35 to $43. Apr 01 to Oct 31. (217)774-4222, 2151 State Hwy 16, Shelbyville, IL 62565

SHIRLAND — A4 *Winnebago*

SUGAR RIVER FOREST PRESERVE (Public) From Jct of SR-70 & SR-75, E 8 mi on SR-75 to Harrison Rd, N 1.2 mi to Shirland Rd, E 0.5 mi to Boswell Rd, N 1 mi to Forest Preserve Rd, W 2 mi, follow signs (L). Avail: 63 E (30/50 amps). 2021 rates: $11 to $33. Apr 16 to Nov 19. (815)877-6100

Like Us on Facebook.

SOUTH BELOIT — A4 *Winnebago*

PEARL LAKE **Ratings: 6.5/10★/8** (Campground) 90 Avail: 70 full hkups, 20 W, 20 E (30/50 amps). 2021 rates: $50 to $60. Apr 20 to Oct 15. (815)389-1479, 1220 Dearborn Ave, South Beloit, IL 61080

SPARTA — E3 *Randolph*

WORLD SHOOTING & RECREATIONAL COMPLEX (Public State Park) From jct Hwy 154 & Hwy 4: Go 4-1/2 mi N on Hwy 4, then 3 mi W on CR 18. 1001 Avail: 341 full hkups, 350 W, 660 E (50 amps). 2021 rates: $10 to $35. (618)295-2700

SPRING BAY — B3 *Woodford*

SANKOTY LAKES

good sam park **Ratings: 8/10★/10** (RV Resort) From jct IL-116 & IL-26: Go 6 mi NE on IL-26/ Spring Bay Rd (L).

LUXURY FISHING AND RV RESORT

Relax under pristine sunsets from your spacious lakeside big rig pull-through site. Premier amenities, full hookups, spring-fed lakes and a trout stream await you with relaxed farm-to-table dining and an expansive patio.

FAC: all weather rds. Avail: 21 paved, patios, 21 pull-thrus, (35x45), 21 full hkups (30/50 amps), WiFi @ sites, rentals, groc, fire rings, firewood, restaurant, controlled access. **REC:** Lake Canada : swim, fishing, kayaking/canoeing, boating nearby. Pets OK. Partial handicap access. No tents, Age restrict may apply. Big rig sites, eco-friendly. 2021 rates: $95, Military discount.

(309)570-1111 Lat: 40.8180306, Lon: -89.5221788
1583 Spring Bay Rd, Spring Bay, IL 61611
www.sankotylakes.com

See ad page 356

SPRINGFIELD — D3 *Sangamon*

DOUBLE J CAMPGROUND

good sam park **Ratings: 10/10★/10** (RV Park) Avail: 103 full hkups (30/50 amps). 2021 rates: $50. (217)483-9998, 9683 Palm Rd, Chatham, IL 62629

ILLINOIS STATE FAIRGROUNDS (Public State Park) From jct I-55 & I-72: Go 2 mi W on SR 97, then 1 mi N on 5th St, then 1/4 mi E on Taintor Rd, then 1/8 mi N on Natural Resources Way (Rates change during Fair). 300 Avail: 300 W, 300 E (30/50 amps). 2021 rates: $15 to $35. (217)524-9894

RIVERSIDE CAMPGROUND (Public) From Jct I-55 & S Sherman Blvd, S 3 mi. 87 Avail: 8 full hkups, 67 W, 67 E (30/50 amps). 2021 rates: $25 to $30. May 01 to Oct 31. (217)753-0630

SPRINGFIELD KOA **Ratings: 7.5/10★/8** (Campground) 90 Avail: 75 full hkups, 15 W, 15 E (30/50 amps). 2021 rates: $40 to $59. Apr 01 to Nov 01. (217)498-7002, 4320 KOA Rd, Rochester, IL 62563

Travel Services

GANDER RV OF SPRINGFIELD Your new hometown outfitter offering the best regional gear for all your outdoor needs. Your adventure awaits. **SERVICES:** tire, RV appliance, MH mechanical, staffed RV wash, restrooms. RV Sales. RV supplies, LP gas, dump, emergency parking, RV accessible. Hours: 9am - 7pm.
(888)886-0396 Lat: 39.742217, Lon: -89.697814
2371 Chuckwagon Drive, Springfield, IL 62711
rv.ganderoutdoors.com

ST DAVID — C3 *Fulton*

FULTON COUNTY CAMPING & REC AREA (Public) From town, SW 1.5 mi on SR-100 (L) Entrance fee required. Avail: 40 E (20/30 amps). 2021 rates: $30. (309)668-2931

STERLING — A3 *Whiteside*

CROW VALLEY CAMPGROUND **Ratings: 7/5.5/7** (Campground) 35 Avail: 35 W, 35 E (30/50 amps). 2021 rates: $30 to $40. Apr 15 to Oct 15. (815)626-5376, 23807 Moline Rd, Sterling, IL 61081

STOCKTON — A3 *Jo Daviess*

APPLE RIVER CANYON (Public State Park) From Jct of US-20 & Hwy 78, N 6 mi on Hwy 78 to E Canyon Rd, W 4 mi (L). 49 Avail: Pit toilets. 2021 rates: $20 to $30. May 01 to Nov 01. (815)745-3302

SULLIVAN — D4 *Moultrie*

LAKE SHELBYVILLE - COE/FORREST W BO WOOD (Public Corps) From Jct of SR-32 & SR-121, S 2.6 mi on SR-32 to access rd, W 0.5 mi (E). 137 Avail: 58 full hkups, 7 W, 79 E (20/30 amps). 2021 rates: $18 to $48. Apr 16 to Oct 24. (217)774-3951

SYCAMORE — A4 *DeKalb*

SYCAMORE RV RESORT **Ratings: 7.5/9.5★/8** (Campground) 31 Avail: 29 full hkups, 2 W, 2 E (30/50 amps). 2021 rates: $40 to $44. (815)895-5590, 375 E North Ave, Sycamore, IL 60178

TAYLORVILLE — D3 *Christian*

LAKE TAYLORVILLE (Public) From Jct of SR-48 & SR-29, SE 2 mi on SR-29 to Lake Dr, SW 50 yds to Lake Shore Dr, NW 0.5 mi, follow signs (L). 12 Avail: 12 W, 12 E (30/50 amps). 2021 rates: $20. Apr 01 to Oct 31. (217)824-5606

THOMSON — A3 *Carroll*

MISSISSIPPI RIVER - POOLS 11-22 - COE/ THOMSON CAUSEWAY (Public Corps) From town, E 0.5 mi on Main St to Lewis Ave, S 0.25 mi (E). Avail: 120 E (30/50 amps). 2021 rates: $20 to $25. May 01 to Oct 24. (815)259-2353

UNION — A4 *McHenry*

CHICAGO NORTHWEST KOA KAMPGROUND **Ratings: 8/9.5★/9** (Campground) 73 Avail: 40 full hkups, 33 W, 33 E (30/50 amps). 2021 rates: $43 to $100. Apr 16 to Oct 10. (815)923-4206, 8404 S Union Rd, Union, IL 60180

URSA — C2 *Adams*

MISSISSIPPI RIVER - COE LOCK & DAM 21/ BEAR CREEK (Public Corps) From jct Hwy 96 & CR 2150: Go 3 mi W on CR 2150, then 2-1/2 mi N on CR 500E, then 2-1/2 mi W on CR 2400N, then 1 mi W over levee on gravel road. 30 Avail: Pit toilets. 2021 rates: $4. (563)263-7913

RV Myth #3: ""Maintenance on a motorhome is very costly.'' Not necessarily so. One oil change per year with filters similar to that of your car. Diesel maintenance is higher due to a larger quantity of oil and additional larger filters. However, the oil change interval on diesel pushers is fifteen to twenty thousand miles.

UTICA — B4 *La Salle*

LA SALLE-PERU KOA **Ratings: 7.5/10★/8** (Campground) 46 Avail: 16 full hkups, 30 W, 30 E (30/50 amps). 2021 rates: $38 to $52. Apr 15 to Oct 15. (815)667-4988, 756 N 3150th Road, Utica, IL 61373

STARVED ROCK (Public State Park) From Jct of I-80 & Rte 178, S 4 mi on Rte 178 to Rte 71, E 2 mi, follow signs (R). Avail: 129 E (30/50 amps). 2021 rates: $10 to $35. (815)667-4726

VOLO — A5 *Lake*

FISH LAKE BEACH CAMPING RESORT **Ratings: 7/7.5/9** (Campground) 58 Avail: 40 full hkups, 18 W, 18 E (30/50 amps). 2021 rates: $35 to $55. May 01 to Oct 15. (847)546-2228, 32223 North US Hwy 12, Volo, IL 60073

WAUCONDA — A5 *Lake*

Travel Services

CAMPING WORLD OF WAUCONDA/CHICAGO

CAMPING WORLD As the nation's largest retailer of RV supplies, accessories, services and new and used RVs, Camping World is committed to making your total RV experience better. **SERVICES:** RV, tire, RV appliance, staffed RV wash, restrooms. RV Sales. RV supplies, LP gas, dump, emergency parking, RV accessible. Hours: 9am to 7pm.
(866)885-7621 Lat: 42.276968, Lon: -88.194371
27794 N. Darrell Road, Wauconda, IL 60084
www.campingworld.com

WESTVILLE — C5 *Vermilion*

FOREST GLEN PRESERVE (VERMILION COUNTY PARK) (Public) From jct I-74 & Hwy 1: Go 5 mi S on Hwy 1, then 7 mi E on CR 5. Avail: 34 E (50 amps). 2021 rates: $17 to $22. (217)662-2142

WHITTINGTON — E4 *Franklin*

WHITTINGTON WOODS CAMPGROUND **Ratings: 9.5/9.5★/10** (Campground) 100 Avail: 97 full hkups, 3 W, 3 E (30/50 amps). 2021 rates: $36 to $42. (618)435-3401, 14297 State Highway 37, Whittington, IL 62897

WILMINGTON — B5 *Will*

DES PLAINES STATE FISH & WILDLIFE AREA (Public State Park) From I-55 (exit 241): Go 1 mi W. Avail: 22 W, Pit toilets. 2021 rates: $8. Apr 15 to Oct 15. (815)423-5326

WINDSOR — D4 *Shelby*

WOLF CREEK (Public State Park) From town, N 6 mi on Rte 32 to CH-4, W 3.8 mi to park access rd, S 2.2 mi. Avail: 304 E (30/50 amps). 2021 rates: $10 to $55. (217)459-2831

ZION — A5 *Lake*

ILLINOIS BEACH (Public State Park) Hwy 173 to Rte 41, R to Wadsworth Rd (E). Avail: 241 E (30/50 amps). 2021 rates: $20 to $35. (847)662-4811

Don't forget to show your Good Sam Membership card when you check in. Stay at any of the Good Sam RV Parks & Campgrounds in the U.S. and Canada and save 10% on the regular nightly RV site rate! No Blackout Dates! Visit GoodSam.com for more details.

Getty Images/iStockphoto

Indiana

DID YOU KNOW?

Picturesque Parke County is home to more covered bridges than anywhere else in the world.

Indiana sits in the center of it all. Some of the nation's pivotal events occurred here, and it celebrates this legacy with well-preserved towns and traditions. Travelers crossing the Midwest should linger in the Hoosier State.

Parks Aplenty

The urban planners in Indianapolis embraced a vision of an urban metropolis with big parks and lush landscapes. Today, its sprawling open spaces preserve natural attractions. Check out White River State Park, right in the heart of town. Take a gondola ride down the tranquil river for epic views of the skyscrapers, then hop off to explore the museums, green spaces and art pieces connected by this urban park. Sports fanatics and families will find much to do in this vibrant city.

Doorway to the Great Lakes

Visitors enjoy spectacular access to a Great Lake. Ascend to Mount Tom in northwest Indiana, where visitors can look out over the blue waters of Lake Michigan, with the Chicago skyline rising above the horizon. Mount Tom isn't a traditional mountain; instead, it is the tallest of the sand dunes found at the Indiana Dunes National Park, rising upward of 190 feet above the water. Considered one of Indiana's greatest natural wonders, the massive dunes running along Lake Michigan extend into the adjacent Indiana Dunes State Park.

Make Waves on Monroe

Lake Michigan isn't the only game in town. Boating, paddling and fishing are popular activities on the coast. Indiana's largest reservoir, Lake Monroe, just south of Indianapolis, is another great choice for boating and reeling in the big one. The crystal-clear waters are perfect for watersports, with many no-wake zones providing calm coves for quiet pursuits. In the town of Corydon, Caverns take explorers into a deep cave system.

Indiana Hoosier Sandwich

Bring your appetite to the Heartland because you're going to need it for the Hoosier sandwich. Inside the toasted bun is a thinly pounded, breaded and deep-fried pork tenderloin. Restaurants, diners and country fairs have perfected the art of the Hoosier so you can expect meat that's juicy and well-seasoned every time.

VISITOR CENTER

TIME ZONE
Eastern/Central Standard

ROAD & HIGHWAY INFORMATION
800-261-7623
in.gov/dot

FISHING & HUNTING INFORMATION
317-232-4200
in.gov/dnr/fishwild

BOATING INFORMATION
812-837-9536
in.gov/dnr/lawenfor

NATIONAL PARKS
nps.gov/in

STATE PARKS
in.gov/dnr/parklake

TOURISM INFORMATION
Indiana Office of Tourism Development
in.gov/visitindiana

TOP TOURISM ATTRACTIONS
1) Indianapolis Motor Speedway
2) Holiday World & Splashin' Safari
3) White River State Park

MAJOR CITIES
Indianapolis (capital), Fort Wayne, Evansville, South Bend, Carmel

IN

good sam park

Featured Good Sam Parks

INDIANA

When you stay with Good Sam, you can expect the highest degree of cleanliness and friendliness, and better yet, you get **10% off** overnight campground fees.

If you're not already a Good Sam member you can purchase your membership at one of these locations:

BATESVILLE
Indian Lakes RV Campground

CLARKSVILLE
Louisville North Campground
Silver Lakes

CLINTON
Horseshoe Lakes RV Campground

COLUMBUS
Ceraland Park & Campground
Columbus Woods-N-Waters Kampground

ELKHART
Elkhart Campground

FLORENCE
Follow the River RV Resort

GREENFIELD
Heartland Resort

HOWE
Twin Mills RV Resort

INDIANAPOLIS
Indy Lakes RV Campground
Lake Haven Retreat

NEW CARLISLE
Lakeside RV Resort

OAKTOWN
New Vision RV Park

REMINGTON
Caboose Lake Campground

RICHMOND
Deer Ridge Camping Resort

RISING SUN
Little Farm On the River RV Park Camping Resort
Rising Star Casino Resort & RV Park

ST PAUL
Hidden Paradise Campground

TERRE HAUTE
Terre Haute Campground

VINCENNES
Vincennes RV Park

Getty Images/iStockphoto

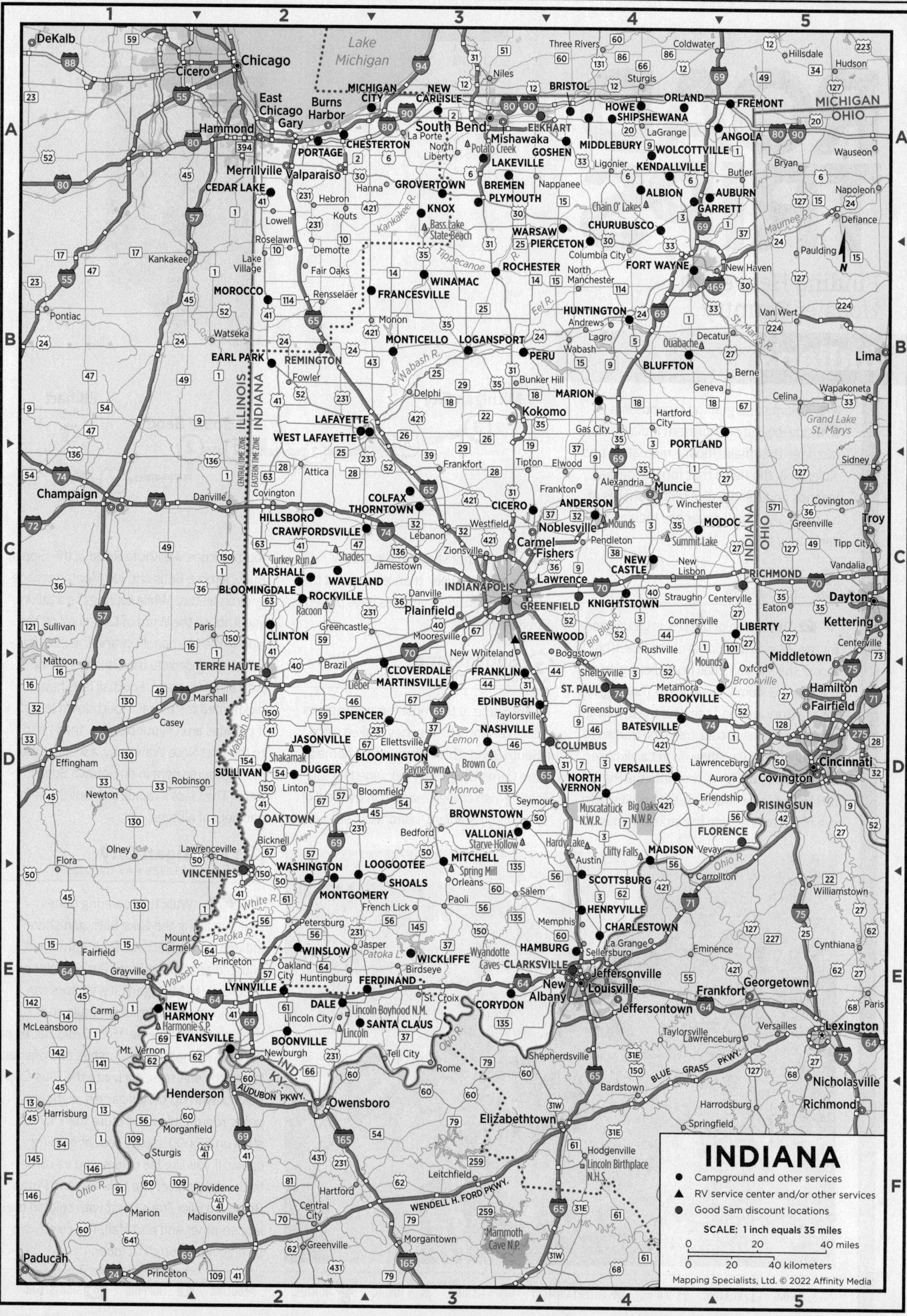
INDIANA
Campground and other services
RV service center and/or other services
Good Sam discount locations
SCALE: 1 inch equals 35 miles
0 20 40 miles
0 20 40 kilometers
Mapping Specialists, Ltd. © 2022 Affinity Media
Lake Michigan
DeKalb
Chicago
Cicero
East Chicago
Burns Harbor
Gary
Hammond
MICHIGAN CITY
NEW CARLISLE
South Bend
Mishawaka
ELKHART
BRISTOL
HOWE
SHIPSHEWANA
ORLAND
FREMONT
ANGOLA
MICHIGAN
OHIO
Three Rivers
Coldwater
Hillsdale
Hudson
Niles
Sturgis
LaGrange
La Porte
CHESTERTON
PORTAGE
Merrillville
Valparaiso
CEDAR LAKE
North Liberty
Potato Creek
LAKEVILLE
GOSHEN
MIDDLEBURY
WOLCOTTVILLE
Ligonier
KENDALLVILLE
Butler
Bryan
Wauseon
Napoleon
Defiance
Hanna
GROVERTOWN
BREMEN
PLYMOUTH
Nappanee
ALBION
AUBURN
GARRETT
Hebron
Kouts
Lowell
KNOX
Bass Lake State Beach
Kankakee R.
Chain O' Lakes
CHURUBUSCO
WARSAW
PIERCETON
Columbia City
Roselawn
Demotte
Lake Village
Kankakee
Fair Oaks
Tippecanoe
ROCHESTER
North Manchester
FORT WAYNE
New Haven
Paulding
Maumee R.
WINAMAC
MOROCCO
Rensselaer
FRANCESVILLE
Pontiac
Watseka
Monon
HUNTINGTON
Andrews
Eel R.
Van Wert
St. Marys R.
MONTICELLO
LOGANSPORT
PERU
Wabash
Lagro
Decatur
Ouabache
EARL PARK
REMINGTON
Wabash R.
BLUFFTON
Berne
Lima
Fowler
Bunker Hill
MARION
Geneva
Celina
Wapakoneta
ILLINOIS
INDIANA
CENTRAL TIME ZONE
EASTERN TIME ZONE
Delphi
Kokomo
Hartford City
Grand Lake St. Marys
LAFAYETTE
WEST LAFAYETTE
Gas City
PORTLAND
Sidney
Frankfort
Tipton
Elwood
Attica
Covington
Alexandria
Muncie
Champaign
Danville
COLFAX
THORNTOWN
Frankton
CICERO
ANDERSON
Winchester
HILLSBORO
CRAWFORDSVILLE
Lebanon
Westfield
Noblesville
Mounds
MODOC
Greenville
Troy
Carmel
Fishers
Pendleton
Summit Lake
Tipp City
Turkey Run
Shades
Zionsville
Jamestown
NEW CASTLE
New Lisbon
Vandalia
MARSHALL
WAVELAND
Lawrence
INDIANAPOLIS
RICHMOND
BLOOMINGDALE
ROCKVILLE
Danville
GREENFIELD
KNIGHTSTOWN
Straughn
Centerville
Dayton
Eaton
Racoon
Plainfield
Kettering
Sullivan
Paris
CLINTON
Greencastle
Mooresville
GREENWOOD
Connersville
LIBERTY
Centerville
New Whiteland
Boggstown
Rushville
Big Blue R.
Middletown
Mattoon
TERRE HAUTE
Brazil
CLOVERDALE
MARTINSVILLE
FRANKLIN
Shelbyville
Mounds
Oxford
Marshall
Lieber
EDINBURGH
ST. PAUL
Metamora
BROOKVILLE
Brookville L.
Hamilton
Fairfield
Casey
SPENCER
Taylorsville
Greensburg
BATESVILLE
Ellettsville
NASHVILLE
Lemon
COLUMBUS
JASONVILLE
BLOOMINGTON
Shakamak
DUGGER
Brown Co.
Effingham
SULLIVAN
Paynetown
VERSAILLES
Lawrenceburg
Cincinnati
Covington
Aurora
Robinson
Linton
Bloomfield
Monroe L.
NORTH VERNON
Newton
Seymour
Muscatatuck N.W.R.
Big Oaks N.W.R.
Friendship
RISING SUN
OAKTOWN
BROWNSTOWN
Bedford
VALLONIA
Starve Hollow
Hardy Lake
FLORENCE
Bicknell
Olney
Lawrenceville
MITCHELL
Spring Mill
Orleans
Clifty Falls
MADISON
Vevay
Ohio R.
Flora
VINCENNES
WASHINGTON
LOOGOOTEE
SHOALS
Austin
Carrollton
MONTGOMERY
Paoli
SCOTTSBURG
Salem
Williamstown
White R.
French Lick
HENRYVILLE
Petersburg
Memphis
CHARLESTOWN
Mount Carmel
Patoka R.
Jasper
Fairfield
WINSLOW
Patoka L.
WICKLIFFE
Wyandotte Caves
HAMBURG
La Grange
Sellersburg
Eminence
Cynthiana
Princeton
Oakland City
Birdseye
CLARKSVILLE
Grayville
Huntingburg
FERDINAND
Jeffersonville
New Albany
Louisville
Georgetown
Frankfort
LYNNVILLE
St. Croix
DALE
CORYDON
Jeffersontown
Carmi
NEW HARMONY
Harmonie S.P.
Lincoln Boyhood N.M.
Lincoln City
SANTA CLAUS
Lincoln
Versailles
Lexington
Paris
McLeansboro
EVANSVILLE
BOONVILLE
Taylorsville
Lawrenceburg
Mt. Vernon
Newburgh
Tell City
Shepherdsville
IND. KY.
Rome
Henderson
AUDUBON PKWY.
Owensboro
Bardstown
BLUE GRASS PKWY.
Nicholasville
Richmond
Harrisburg
Morganfield
Elizabethtown
Harrodsburg
Springfield
Sturgis
Hodgenville
Lincoln Birthplace N.H.S.
Leitchfield
Providence
Hartford
WENDELL H. FORD PKWY.
Marion
Madisonville
Central City
Morgantown
Mammoth Cave N.P.
Greenville
Paducah
Princeton
IN
1 2 3 4 5
A B C D E F

ROAD TRIPS

Finding Heaven in Hoosier Country

Indiana

LOCATION
INDIANA

DISTANCE
55 MILES

DRIVE TIME
1 HR 18 MINS

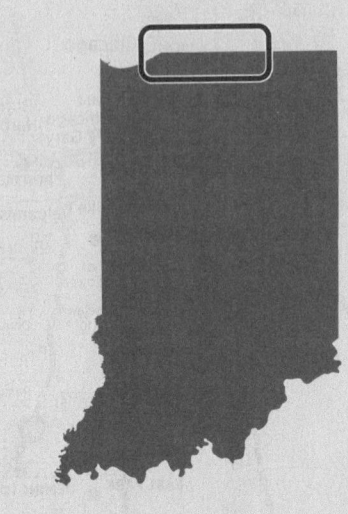

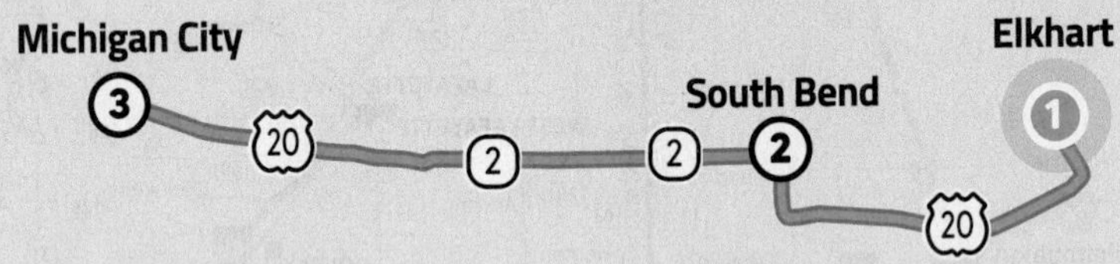

RV giants and gridiron legends live side-by-side in northern Indiana. Tour factories that make mobile recreation possible, walk the fields that forged football legends and roll the dice on the shores of a Great Lake. You'll never see Indiana the same way again.

1 Elkhart
Starting Point

This region of the U.S. is ground zero for the RV industry. Some of the heavy hitters of the RV world hail from this region of the country, from Coachmen to Thor. Sign up for a factory tour and see how these rolling condos are constructed, from the frames to furniture to paint coating. To get a glimpse of the history of RVing, drop into the RV/MH Hall of Fame Museum, with multimedia exhibits that celebrate the industry's past. Tour exhibits that showcase iconic RV models of yesteryear, then learn about the role that recreational vehicles have played in American culture.

2 South Bend
Drive 21 miles ▪ 31 minutes

Some of the most famous exploits in college sports history have taken place in South Bend. This community is home to Notre Dame University, renowned for its Fighting Irish college teams. On the field of Notre Dame Stadium, visitors can see where football icons like Knute Rockne, the Gipper, Rudy, Jerome Betis and Joe Montana made gridiron history. While touring the stadium, you'll notice the Word of Life mural on the side of the Memorial Library. The 200-foot-tall painting depicts the Christian savior with arms upraised. Football fans have nicknamed the mural, "Touchdown Jesus." If pigskins aren't your passion, then head to the East Race Waterway, a whitewater rafting course right in downtown South Bend. The Class II rapids dish out thrills for paddlers of all ages.

Getty Images/iStockphoto

3 Michigan City
Drive 34 miles ▪ 47 minutes

Walk the towering dunes that rise along the Lake Michigan shore. Indiana Dunes National Park, combined with Indiana Dunes State Park, stretches from Gary to Michigan City. Visitors can embark on several miles of trails and through wildly diverse 15,000-plus acres of dunes, swamps, bogs marshes and prairies. When the sun sets, duck into the Blue Chip Casino, with 40 tables games, eight live poker room tables and more than 1,700 slots on 65,000 square feet of gaming space. If you like fall colors, you've come to the right place: The Calumet and Porter Brickyard Bike Trails burst with color in the late summer and early fall. The colors can be enjoyed through October.

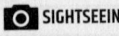

BIKING BOATING DINING ENTERTAINMENT FISHING HIKING HUNTING PADDLING SHOPPING SIGHTSEEING

Indiana SPOTLIGHTS

Get Your Heart Racing in the Heartland

The Hoosier State thunders with the Indy 500 and whispers with quiet country lanes. Explore a Great Lake, discover Midwest wineries and try your luck at fun-filled games. Climb towering dunes on Lake Michigan and sample fine wines at your own pace.

NATIVE AMERICAN TRIBES OWN THREE INDIANA CASINOS.

Casinos operate in 13 locations in Indiana, and sports betting is allowed.

Getty Images

Casino Country

Tucked away in the state's southeast corner, this riverside region might just be Indiana's best-kept secret. Boasting top-notch golf courses, unique outdoor adventures and small towns brimming with old-fashioned American charm, it's easy to see why visitors keep coming back year after year. Of course, it might also have something to do with the one-of-a-kind riverboat resorts that dot the Ohio River.

Rocking the Boat

In 2011, the legendary steamboat Grand Victoria II was renamed the Rising Sun Casino Resort after the small town where it was moored. These days, visitors from across the Midwest flock to the sprawling ship to enjoy over 40,000 square feet of gaming, from slots to table games and more. With a busy calendar of concerts, sporting events and musical revues, there's a little something for everyone.

Spas and Spades

About 20 miles south, the Belterra Casino Resort and Spa is a popular spot for riverboat gamblers, with special treats like thoroughbred racing and a full-service spa. Hollywood Casino in Lawrenceburg is another destination with easy access to big cities. Just twenty minutes west of Cincinnati, the resort prides itself on luxury attractions and easy-going attitude.

Betting on Fishing

Well-known for its catfish tournaments, the Ohio River is the perfect getaway for anglers looking to take a break from the blackjack table. The area around Rising Sun offers up some of the region's best fishing holes, while the Markland Dam near Florence is a hotspot for sauger, gar and freshwater drum. Both Kentucky and Indiana recognize each other's fishing licenses, so anglers in the know will try both banks, especially at popular stretches where Kentucky is known to stock the river with striped bass.

Canoes and Cardinals

Head to the quiet town of Patriot to canoe serene stretches of the river or head into one of the small streams that meander away from the main waterway. Bird-watchers especially will delight in the large variety of species that call the region home.

Golfing and Gaming

The rolling hills of the Ohio River Valley

INDIANA DUNES NATIONAL PARK HAS 15,000 ACRES OF PRIMITIVE LANDS WITH 50 MILES OF TRAILS.

IN

LOCAL FAVORITE

Tom's Apple Orchard Bean Bake

You have Johnny Appleseed to thank for Indiana's apples. Beginning in 1792, the American legend spent 50 years planting apple seeds throughout the Midwest. *Recipe by Kathy and Tom Heffron.*

INGREDIENTS

- ☐ 1 lb pork breakfast sausage
- ☐ ½ can tomato soup
- ☐ 1 tall can and 1 small can of baked beans with molasses
- ☐ ⅛ tsp pepper
- ☐ 1 sliced medium cored apple (not peeled)
- ☐ ¼ cup brown sugar

DIRECTIONS

Brown the sausage and add pepper, tomato soup and beans until bubbly. Pour the mixture into a 1.5-quart baking casserole dish. Arrange apple slices on top. Sprinkle brown sugar on top of the casserole. Bake for 25 minutes uncovered at 450°F. Cover and let stand for 5 minutes before serving. Serves 4.

Fond of shallow-water habitats, herons are frequently seen wading in Indiana waters in search of food.

make the perfect backdrop for world-class golf courses and it seems like each one brings something new to the table. The Links at the Rising Sun Casino have a Scottish-style design that feature panoramic views of the riverside landscape. Not to be outdone, Belterra's links were once ranked among the top 30 courses in the country.

Where the Wolves Are

For a distinctly different outdoors experience, try a visit to the Red Wolf Sanctuary, a non-profit organization rehabilitating and preserving American wildlife. Tours of the grounds need to be scheduled in advance, but lucky visitors can see wolves, coyotes, bears, foxes and more in their natural habitats.

NW Hoosier Country

Welcome to the Lake Michigan coast of Northwest Hoosier Country, a land composed of rugged shores, pristine beaches, sandy dunes, forests, farmland and prairies. With 15 miles of shoreline and more than 70 miles of trails, the Indiana Dunes offers up adventures for families seeking fun under the sun.

Dynamic Dunes

The Indiana Dunes is a wind-swept land comprising bogs, marshes, rivers and forests. Indiana Dunes National Park has 15,000 acres of primitive lands with 50 miles of trails providing the chance to ramble through an ever-changing landscape. Take a ranger-guided tour to the top of Mount Baldy, a sand dune that rises 126 feet.

Taking Wing

Birding opportunities are excellent, with more than 350 species establishing habitats in the area. Visit Heron Rookery for a close look at the great blue heron, a wading bird known for its azure feathers. Explore Bailly Homestead, a National Historic Landmark that housed one of the earliest settlers of northern Indiana, and Chellberg Farm, a preserved homestead occupied by a Swedish family that is managed by the National Park Service.

State Park Supreme

Three miles of spectacular beaches, undulating dunes and lush forests are accessible by more than 16 miles of trails in Indiana Dunes State Park. Camp at Indiana Dunes and listen to tales about the local legend of Diana of the Dunes — a free spirit whose ghost purportedly haunts the beach — told 'round a flickering campfire.

Water, Water Everywhere

No matter the season, Lake Michigan offers the ultimate in water adventures. Angle for trout, perch and salmon onboard a charter fishing excursion. Looking to get physical? Paddlers can get down in the water at a no-wake lake or explore a South Shore waterway like Deep River Water Trail, with 1.6 miles of estuaries along rugged shores with picturesque scenery. Kayak or canoe the longest continuous looping water route in the world on the Lake Michigan Water Trail.

Fair Oaks Farm

Some 45 miles south of Gary, Fair Oaks Farms offers a rich, back-to-country experience. In the heart of Indiana's bucolic farm country, acres of flourishing pastures and undulating hills provide the backdrop for outdoor play married with a fascinating insight into the workings of a modern farm. With a strong environmental ethos (the facility generates power from cow and pig manure alone) and a commitment to educational programs and resources, the farm's attractions incorporate child-friendly lessons in sustainability, nutrition and animal safety.

SPOTLIGHTS

Located within the racing complex, the Indianapolis Motor Speedway Museum tells the story of racing history.

Dairy Nice

The two-hour Dairy Experience includes a tour of the barns to observe cows being milked, free play in "Mooville" (think rides, inflatables, ropes and swings with a farmyard theme), a visit to the birthing center and a series of engaging exhibits on modern farm practices. In the Pig Experience, you can play with piglets, explore a towering treehouse, try out a virtual sonogram and even pick up some excellent pork recipes. Another great garden spot is the Chellberg Farm, which hosts festivals all year.

Washington Park Zoo

With its 100-year anniversary approaching, Michigan City's Washington Park Zoo is a classic summer's day trip that continues to pull in families with young children. On the southern shore of Lake Michigan, the zoo is home to around 90 species housed in exhibits spread across 15 acres of rolling dunes (it's quite a workout) and botanical gardens. Crowd-pleasing creatures include Bengal tigers, American alligators, a grizzly bear and eagles.

Making Discoveries

About 27 miles to the west along the coat, Bellaboo's Play and Discovery Center features several educational activities to keep little ones entertained.

Blue Chip Adventures

Not many boating excursions include an evening of high-stakes enjoyment, but the Blue Chip Casino riverboat offers exactly that. The three-story vessel can host more than 6,000 guests and crew members from its spot on the edge of Lake Michigan, and is the largest casino boat by hull size in the U.S.

Breweries and Wineries

Over recent years, craft beer culture has grown exponentially in northwest Indiana. In Munster, the irreverent but top-notch 3 Floyds, which first opened its doors in 1996, has become an internationally recognized brew pub famed for its award-winning regional, seasonal and collaborative brews. Take one of the brewery's Saturday tours to learn the process of creating distinctive flavors.

Switzerland County

As the name suggests, Switzerland County is a community with roots stretching back to immigrants from the central European nation. Situated on the Ohio River, Switzerland County is a destination that presents ample opportunities for relaxation, adventure and cultural endeavors.

Swiss Wine

The area is known for its wine grape production and is considered the birthplace of the nation's first successful commercial winery. Visitors can sample a taste of this legacy by visiting a winery along the Ohio River and a wine cellar in downtown Vevay, where Hoosier wines are featured. Late summer means another run of the historic Swiss Wine Festival in Vevay, which draws thousands to the streets for tastings, treats and more.

Foodie Fun

Weekends are all about the food of Florence. The Farmers and Artisans Market, a Saturday staple, is a tasty trip for foodies who want locally sourced culinary creations, as well as fresh-from-the-farm produce.

The Sun Also Rises

Satisfy the need for an adrenaline rush with a trip down a zipline at Dagasz Acres, north of Vevay. One- and two-hour tours are available for adventurers of all skill levels. Wind down from a day in the canopy with an easy boat ride down the river. Several boat ramps and marinas are located along the river in the towns of Florence, Patriot and Vevay.

Indianapolis

To add big city fun to your travels, check out Indianapolis. You'll find all the perks of big-city living — major league sports, cultural attractions and a dynamic downtown area — along with outdoorsy pursuits.

Racing Cars

The Indianapolis Motor Speedway, also known as the Brickyard, annually hosts the Indy 500, the world's largest single-day spectator sporting event. Held every Labor Day Weekend, this open-wheeled racing event attracts top drivers from around the world and is considered by many to be the greatest spectacle of racing. Visit the Indianapolis Motor Speedway Hall of Fame Museum, housing priceless memorabilia, including more than 75 racing cars. Want to play a round of golf with a racing twist? Try booking a tee time at Brickyard Crossing, an 18-hole course with four of its holes located in the infield of the speedway.

White River

The sprawling White River State Park is a significant link to the culture and history of Indianapolis. Visitors can walk along the gentle waters on paved walkways for a pleasurable blend of city and nature. Or sit back and relax while a Gondolier transports travelers into the romance of old Italy. Within its 250 acres, the park boasts several museums, the Indianapolis Zoo, an IMAX Theater, Indiana State Museum, a concert venue and the White River Gardens.

FOR MORE INFORMATION

Indiana Office of Tourism Development, 800-677-9800, www.visitindiana.com

Casino Country — Indiana Gaming Commission, www.in.gov/igc

NW Hoosier Country/ South Shore Convention and Visitors Authority, 219-989-7770 www.southshorecva.com

Switzerland County Tourism, 800-435-5688, www.switzcotourism.com

Visit Indianapolis, 800-323-4639, www.visitindy.com

Indiana

ALBION — A4 *Noble*

CHAIN O'LAKES (Public State Park) From town, S 5 mi on SR-9 (L). Avail: 331 E (20 amps). 2021 rates: $7.63 to $90. (260)636-2654

ANDERSON — C4 *Madison*

ANDERSON/MUNCIE KOA **Ratings: 8.5/9.5★/9.5** (RV Park) Avail: 62 full hkups (30/50 amps). 2021 rates: $43 to $71. (765)378-5909, 3230 E CR-75 N, Anderson, IN 46017

MOUNDS (Public State Park) From town, E 2.5 mi on Hwy 232 (L). Avail: 75 E (30 amps). 2021 rates: $12 to $29. (765)642-6627

ANGOLA — A4 *Steuben*

ANGOLA/ HOGBACK LAKE KOA **Ratings: 9/8.5★/9** (RV Park) 140 Avail: 105 full hkups, 35 W, 35 E (30/50 amps). 2021 rates: $56 to $84. (260)665-5353, 5251 US Hwy 20 W, Angola, IN 46703

BUCK LAKE RANCH ENTERTAINMENT CENTER **Ratings: 5/6.5/7.5** (Campground) 45 Avail: 29 full hkups, 16 W, 16 E (30 amps). 2021 rates: $40. Apr 15 to Oct 15. (260)665-6699, 2705 W Buck Lake Rd, Angola, IN 46703

CAMP SACK-IN **Ratings: 4/7/5.5** (Campground) 73 Avail: 73 W, 73 E (20/30 amps). 2021 rates: $35 to $40. Apr 15 to Oct 15. (260)665-5166, 8740 E 40 S, Angola, IN 46703

MILLER'S HAPPY ACRES **Ratings: 6.5/5/6** (Campground) 34 Avail: 12 full hkups, 22 W, 22 E (30/50 amps). 2021 rates: $35 to $50. Apr 15 to Oct 31. (260)665-9843, 1940 S 300 W, Angola, IN 46703

POKAGON (Public State Park) From Jct of I-69 & exit 154, W on exit 154, follow signs (E) Entrance fee required. 273 Avail: 166 W, 200 E (30/50 amps). 2021 rates: $10 to $40. (260)833-2012

AUBURN — A4 *DeKalb*

FIRESIDE RESORT **Ratings: 3/8.5★/6.5** (RV Park) 55 Avail: 49 full hkups, 6 W, 6 E (30/50 amps). 2021 rates: $36 to $38. (260)925-6747, 5612 CR 11A, Auburn, IN 46706

BATESVILLE — D4 *Ripley*

INDIAN LAKES RV CAMPGROUND

Ratings: 8/9★/9.5 (RV Park) 550 Avail: 450 full hkups, 100 W, 100 E (30/50 amps). 2021 rates: $45 to $65. Apr 01 to Nov 01. (888)563-7040, 7234 E State Rd 46, Batesville, IN 47006

BLOOMINGDALE — C2 *Parke*

PEACEFUL WATERS CAMPGROUND AND CABINS **Ratings: 6/9★/9** (Campground) 63 Avail: 15 full hkups, 48 W, 48 E (30/50 amps). 2021 rates: $30 to $45. Apr 16 to Nov 01. (765)592-6458, 3325 N Hwy 41, Bloomingdale, IN 47832

TIPS FOR THE BBQ CHEF: BURGERS - Use fresh meat and mix in ingredients-onions, garlic, chopped jalapeno or bell peppers, oregano, BBQ or hot sauce-sprinkle salt and pepper just before going on the grill. Cook 3 to 5 mins per side to 140-degree internal temp. Tip: Don't press down on the patties during cooking or you'll squeeze out the delicious juices. BEEF BRISKET - Marinate a 3 to 4 lb brisket for 24 hrs. or more in Worcestershire or teriyaki sauce with garlic and black pepper. Cook for 3 to 5 mins per side on direct high heat, then indirect heat for 15-20 mins to 130-degree internal temp (medium-rare). FISH FILLETS OR STEAKS (such as salmon, striped bass, and mahi-mahi) - Cook 5 to 8 mins per side (depending on heat) or to 130 to 135-degree internal temp. BONELESS CHICKEN BREASTS - Marinate for 30 mins or more or rub both sides with a spice mix. Cook over high heat (375-400 degrees) for 4 to 5 mins per side, then indirect heat for 8 to 12 mins to 160-165 internal temp.

BLOOMINGTON — D3 *Monroe*

LAKE MONROE VILLAGE **Ratings: 9/10★/9.5** (Campground) Avail: 52 full hkups (30/50 amps). 2021 rates: $65 to $80. (812)824-2267, 8107 S Fairfax Rd, Bloomington, IN 47401

MONROE LAKE (Public State Park) From Jct of SR-46 & SR-446, S 7 mi on SR-446 (R). Entrance fee required. Avail: 226 E (20/30 amps). 2021 rates: $12 to $40. (812)837-9546

BLUFFTON — B4 *Wells*

CREEKSIDE RV CAMPGROUND AND MOBILE HOME PARK **Ratings: 3/NA/7** (RV Area in MH Park) Avail: 14 full hkups (30/50 amps). 2021 rates: $35. (260)824-5365, 3427 E State Rd 124, Bluffton, IN 46714

OUABACHE (Public State Park) From town, E 2 mi on Hwy 124 to Hwy 201, S .75 mi to SH-316, SE .5 mi. Avail: 124 E (30/50 amps). 2021 rates: $12 to $55. (260)824-0926

BOONVILLE — E2 *Warrick*

SCALES LAKE PARK (WARRICK COUNTY PARK) (Public) From Jct of I-64 & Hwy 61 (exit 39), S 10 mi on Hwy 61 to Hwy 62, E 0.5 mi to Walnut St, E 0.2 mi to Park Lane Dr, N 0.5 mi (L). 128 Avail: 42 full hkups, 47 E (30/50 amps). 2021 rates: $13 to $28. (812)897-6200

BREMEN — A3 *Marshall*

PLA-MOR CAMPGROUND **Ratings: 8/7.5★/8** (Campground) 410 Avail: 91 full hkups, 319 W, 319 E (30/50 amps). 2021 rates: $45 to $50. Apr 15 to Oct 15. (574)546-3665, 2162 US 6 East, Bremen, IN 46506

BRISTOL — A4 *Elkhart*

EBY'S PINES RV PARK & CAMPGROUND **Ratings: 8.5/9.5★/9.5** (RV Park) 160 Avail: 24 full hkups, 136 W, 136 E (30/50 amps). 2021 rates: $45 to $70. Apr 01 to Nov 01. (574)848-4583, 14583 SR 120, Bristol, IN 46507

BROOKVILLE — D4 *Franklin*

BROOKVILLE LAKE

(Public State Park) From town, N 7 mi on Hwy 101 (L). **FAC:** paved rds. Avail: 450 paved, back-ins (20x45), 62 full hkups, 388 E (20 amps), tent sites, dump, fire rings, firewood, restaurant. **REC:** Brookville Lake: swim, fishing, marina, playground. Partial handicap access, 14 day max stay. 2021 rates: $30 to $90. no cc.
(765)647-2657 Lat: 39.504320, Lon: -84.948352
14108 SR 101, Brookville, IN 47012
www.in.gov

BROWNSTOWN — D3 *Jackson*

JACKSON-WASHINGTON STATE FOREST (Public State Park) From Business Center: Go 2.5 mi SE of Brownstown. 56 Avail: Pit toilets. 2021 rates: $13. (812)358-2160

CEDAR LAKE — A2 *Lake*

CEDAR LAKE MINISTRIES RV PARK **Ratings: 5.5/8.5/8.5** (RV Park) 30 Avail: 23 full hkups, 7 W, 7 E (30/50 amps). 2021 rates: $38. (219)374-5941, 8816 W 137th Ave, Cedar Lake, IN 46303

CHARLESTOWN — E4 *Clark*

CHARLESTOWN (Public State Park) 7 miles East on Hwy 62, straight through stoplight, one more milegate is on the right. 192 Avail: 60 full hkups, 132 E (30/50 amps). 2021 rates: $12 to $55. (812)256-5600

CHESTERTON — A2 *Porter*

INDIANA DUNES (Public State Park) From Jct of I-94 & SR-49, N 2 mi on SR-49 (E). Avail: 140 E (50 amps). 2021 rates: $16 to $65. (219)926-1952

SAND CREEK CAMPGROUND **Ratings: 6.5/9★/7.5** (Campground) 74 Avail: 31 full hkups, 43 W, 43 E (30/50 amps). 2021 rates: $48.15 to $53.50. Apr 15 to Oct 15. (219)926-7482, 1000 N 350 E, Chesterton, IN 46304

CHURUBUSCO — A4 *Whitley*

BLUE LAKE RESORT CAMPGROUND **Ratings: 7.5/7/8.5** (Campground) 44 Avail: 34 full hkups, 10 W, 10 E (30/50 amps). 2021 rates: $35 to $45. Apr 15 to Oct 15. (260)693-2265, 5453 N Blue Lake Rd, Churubusco, IN 46723

""Full hookups'' in a campground listing means there are water, electric and sewer hookups at the sites.

CICERO — C3 *Hamilton*

WHITE RIVER CAMPGROUND (HAMILTON COUNTY PARK) (Public) From Jct of SR-37 & SR-32 (in Noblesville), N 6.3 mi on SR-37 to Strawtown Rd, W 1.2 mi (L). 106 Avail: 53 full hkups, 42 W, 42 E (30/50 amps). 2021 rates: $20 to $30. Apr 15 to Oct 31. (317)770-4430

CLARKSVILLE — E4 *Clark*

ADD-MORE CAMPGROUND **Ratings: 6.5/8.5★/8.5** (RV Park) Avail: 75 full hkups (30/50 amps). 2021 rates: $40 to $45. (812)283-4321, 2411 Addmore Lane, Clarksville, IN 47129

LOUISVILLE NORTH CAMPGROUND

Ratings: 8.5/10★/7.5 (RV Park) From Jct of I-65 & Stansifer Ave (exit 1), W 50 ft on Stansifer Ave to Marriott Dr, S 0.3 mi (L). N-bnd: Stay on exit ramp until you reach Stansifer Ave. **FAC:** paved rds. (108 spaces). Avail: 78 paved, 26 pull-thrus, (18x60), back-ins (18x35), 78 full hkups (30/50 amps), seasonal sites, WiFi @ sites, tent sites, rentals, dump, laundry, groc, LP gas. **REC:** boating nearby, playground. Pets OK. Partial handicap access. 2021 rates: $50, Military discount. ATM.
(812)282-4474 Lat: 38.27924, Lon: -85.75462
900 Marriott Dr, Clarksville, IN 47129
louisvillenorthcampground.com
See ad page 424

SILVER LAKES

(RV Area in MH Park) (Seasonal Stay Only) Avail: 1 full hkups (50 amps). (812)282-6667, 5935 US 31 E, Clarksville, IN 47129

CLINTON — C2 *Vermillion*

HORSESHOE LAKES RV CAMPGROUND

Ratings: 8/9★/10 (Membership Park) 28 Avail: 19 full hkups, 9 E (30/50 amps). 2021 rates: $48 to $68. May 02 to Oct 20. (888)563-7040, 12962 S CR 225 W, Clinton, IN 47842

CLOVERDALE — D3 *Putnam*

CAGLES MILL LAKE/LIEBER SRA (Public State Park) From town, SW 5 mi on Hwy 42 to Hwy 243, N 1 mi (E). Avail: 115 E (20/30 amps). 2021 rates: $10 to $75. (765)795-4576

CLOVERDALE RV PARK **Ratings: 6/8/9** (Campground) 60 Avail: 27 full hkups, 33 W, 33 E (20/30 amps). 2021 rates: $35 to $40. (765)795-3294, 2789 E CR-800 S, Cloverdale, IN 46120

COLFAX — C3 *Clinton*

BROADVIEW ACRES CAMPGROUND **Ratings: 8/7.5/8** (Campground) 20 Avail: 20 W, 20 E (30/50 amps). 2021 rates: $35. Apr 15 to Oct 15. (765)324-2622, 4850 South Broadview Rd, Colfax, IN 46035

We rate what RVers consider important.

Indiana Privately Owned Campground Information Updated by our Good Sam Representatives

James & Mary Margrave

We've been involved in the RV lifestyle for over 20 years, and for the past 5 years or so, we've done it full time. We love being around our fellow RVers, who are great people. And we love seeing the great variety in the parks on our travels.

COLUMBUS — D4 *Bartholomew*

CERALAND PARK & CAMPGROUND
good sam park **Ratings: 8.5/9.5★/9.5** (RV Park) Jct I-65 & Walesboro Rd (Exit 64), E 6.4 mi on 450S to US 31, N 2.0 mi on US 31 to State Rd 46, E 1.5 mi on State Rd 46 to CR525 E, S .07 mi on CR525 E (L).

IT'S ALL HERE - CERALAND PARK!
It's all here...in one place - Ceraland! 345 acres, 308 sites, 6 cabins, 18-hole mini golf, aquatic center, sports center, driving range & more! Live music every Fri/Sat at The Landing, our waterfront bar.

FAC: paved/gravel rds. Avail: 308 gravel, 12 pull-thrus, (25x70), back-ins (25x60), 234 full hkups, 74 W, 74 E (30/50 amps), WiFi @ sites, tent sites, rentals, dump, laundry, groc, fire rings, firewood, restaurant, controlled access. **REC:** pool, wading pool, pond, fishing, kayaking/canoeing, playground, rec open to public. Pets OK. Partial handicap access. Big rig sites, eco-friendly. 2021 rates: $49 to $59. Apr 01 to Nov 15. ATM.
(812)377-5849 Lat: 39.16237, Lon: -85.81384
3989 South 525 East, Columbus, IN 47203
www.ceraland.org
See ad this page

COLUMBUS WOODS-N-WATERS KAMPGROUND
good sam park **Ratings: 8/10★/9** (Campground) 100 Avail: 26 full hkups, 74 W, 74 E (30/50 amps). 2021 rates: $38 to $40. (812)342-1619, 8855 S 300 W, Columbus, IN 47201

CORYDON — E3 *Harrison*

O'BANNON WOODS (Public State Park) From jct Hwy-135 & Hwy-62: Go 7 mi W on Hwy-62, then 1 mi S on Hwy-462. Avail: 281 E. 2021 rates: $10.49 to $32. (812)738-8232

CRAWFORDSVILLE — C2 *Montgomery*

CRAWFORDSVILLE KOA KAMPGROUND **Ratings: 8/9.5★/8.5** (Campground) 50 Avail: 30 full hkups, 20 W, 20 E (30/50 amps). 2021 rates: $48. (765)230-0965, 1600 Lafayette Rd, Crawfordsville, IN 47933

SUGAR CREEK CAMPGROUND & CANOE RENTALS **Ratings: 6.5/9.5★/8** (Campground) Avail: 47 full hkups (30/50 amps). 2021 rates: $39 to $44. (765)362-5528, 841 W 83 North, Crawfordsville, IN 47933

DALE — E2 *Spencer*

LINCOLN (Public State Park) From Jct of I-64 & US-231 (exit 57), S 8 mi on US-231 to SR-162, E 2 mi (R). Entrance fee required. 269 Avail: 150 W, 150 E (30 amps). 2021 rates: $6.12 to $38.76. (812)937-4710

DUGGER — D2 *Sullivan*

GREENE-SULLIVAN STATE FOREST (Public State Park) From town: Go 2 mi S on Hwy-159. 100 Avail: Pit toilets. (812)648-2810

EARL PARK — B2 *Benton*

EARL PARK COMMUNITY PARK (Public) From jct US-41/52 & Seventh St (550N): Go 1/2 mi W on Seventh St. 30 Avail: 20 W, 20 E (20/30 amps). 2021 rates: $8 to $15. (219)474-6108

EDINBURGH — D3 *Bartholomew*

MILITARY PARK WHITAKER PLACE CAMPGROUND (CAMP ATTERBURY) (Public) From Jct I-65 & 31, Exit 76B N to Hwy 31 (Hospital Rd/252) approx. 3 mi to main camp entrance, E one block. Avail: 33 full hkups (30/50 amps). 2021 rates: $30. (812)526-1128

ELKHART — A3 *Elkhart*

ELKHART CAMPGROUND
good sam park **Ratings: 9.5/10★/9.5** (Campground) From Jct of Toll Rd 80/90 & SR-19 (exit 92), N 0.25 mi on SR-19 to CR-4E, E 0.75 mi (R). **FAC:** paved rds. (364 spaces). 314 Avail: 303 paved, 11 grass, 314 pull-thrus, (30x70), 239 full hkups, 75 W, 75 E (30/50 amps), seasonal sites, cable, WiFi @ sites, rentals, dump, laundry, groc, LP gas, fire rings, firewood. **REC:** heated pool, boating nearby, playground. Pets OK. Partial handicap access. No tents. Big rig sites, eco-friendly. 2021 rates: $30 to $60, Military discount. Mar 15 to Nov 25.
(574)264-2914 Lat: 41.73844, Lon: -85.95911
25608 CR 4 E, Elkhart, IN 46514
elkhartcampground.com
See ad this page

EVANSVILLE — E2 *Vanderburgh*

BURDETTE PARK (Public) From Jct of Hwy 62/Lloyd Expressway & Red Bank Rd, S 3.2 mi on Red Bank Rd (becomes Nurrenburn) (R). 27 Avail: 18 full hkups, 6 W, 6 E (30/50 amps). 2021 rates: $20 to $30. (812)435-5602

VANDERBURGH 4-H CENTER **Ratings: 6/8.5★/8** (Campground) Avail: 41 full hkups (30/50 amps). 2021 rates: $40. (812)867-6217, 201 E. Boonville-New Harmony Rd, Evansville, IN 47725

FERDINAND — E3 *Dubois*

FERDINAND STATE FOREST (Public State Park) From jct Hwy-162 & Hwy-264: Go 5 mi NE on Hwy-264. 57 Avail. (812)827-2857

FLORENCE — D5 *Switzerland*

FOLLOW THE RIVER RV RESORT
good sam park **Ratings: 9/10★/10** (RV Park) From Jct of I-71 & (Kentucky SR 1039) Exit 55, N 6 mi on SR 1039, W 1 mi on (Indiana SR 156) (R). **FAC:** paved/gravel rds. Avail: 130 paved, patios, 31 pull-thrus, (40x85), back-ins (40x75), 130 full hkups (30/50 amps), WiFi @ sites, laundry, groc, LP gas, fire rings, firewood. **REC:** heated pool, pond, fishing, boating nearby, playground. Pets OK. Partial handicap access. No tents. Big rig sites, eco-friendly. 2021 rates: $43 to $53.
(812)427-3330 Lat: 38.78279, Lon: -84.98149
12273 Markland Town Rd, Florence, IN 47020
www.followtheriverrvresort.com
See ad page 372

FORT WAYNE — B4 *Allen*

JOHNNY APPLESEED CAMPGROUND (Public) From Jct I-69 & Coldwater Rd, S 1.4 mi on Coldwater Rd to Harry Baals Dr, E 0.5 mi on Harry Baals Dr to Parnell Ave, S 0.25 mi (L). Avail: 45 E (30/50 amps). 2021 rates: $22. Apr 15 to Oct 31. (260)427-6720

FRANCESVILLE — B3 *Pulaski*

ACORN OAKS CAMPGROUND **Ratings: 5/8.5★/7.5** (Campground) 68 Avail: 32 full hkups, 36 W, 36 E (30/50 amps). 2021 rates: $28. (219)567-2524, 16614 W SR 114, Francesville, IN 47946

FRANKLIN — D3 *Johnson*

JOHNSON COUNTY PARK (Public) From jct Hwy 144/Hwy 44 & US 31: Go 3 mi S on US 31, then 3-1/2 mi W on Hwy 252, then 2-1/2 mi S on Schoolhouse Rd (CR 550S), follow signs. Avail: 54 E (30/50 amps). 2021 rates: $25. (812)526-6809

FREMONT — A5 *Steuben*

YOGI BEAR'S JELLYSTONE PARK-BARTON LAKE **Ratings: 8.5/9.5★/9** (Campground) 325 Avail: 175 full hkups, 150 W, 150 E (30/50 amps). 2021 rates: $58 to $83. Apr 22 to Oct 16. (260)833-1114, 140 Lane 201 Barton Lake, Fremont, IN 46737

GARRETT — A4 *DeKalb*

INDIAN SPRINGS CAMPGROUND **Ratings: 7.5/6.5/6.5** (Campground) Avail: 230 full hkups (30/50 amps). 2021 rates: $40 to $50. Apr 15 to Oct 15. (260)357-5572, 0981 CR 64, Garrett, IN 46738

GOSHEN — A4 *Elkhart*

GOSHEN See also Bremen, Bristol, Elkhart, Howe, Lakeville, Middlebury, Pierceton, Shipshewana, Warsaw, Wolcotville, IN; Jones & Niles, MI.

ELKHART COUNTY FAIRGROUNDS (Public) From S Jct of SR 15 & US 33, E 0.6 mi on US 33 to Monroe St (left turn) 0.8 mi (R). 347 Avail: 275 full hkups, 72 W, 72 E (30/50 amps). 2021 rates: $25 to $33. (574)533-3247

GREENFIELD — C4 *Hancock*

HEARTLAND RESORT
good sam park **Ratings: 7.5/8/9** (Campground) W-bnd: From jct of I-70 & Hwy 9 (exit 104): Go 1/2 mi N on Hwy 9, then 4 mi W on CR 300 N (L); or E-bnd: From jct of I-70 & Mt Comfort Rd (exit 96): Go 1/2 mi N on Mt Comfort Rd, then 4-1/4 mi E on CR 300 N (R). **FAC:** paved/gravel rds. (290 spaces). Avail: 110 gravel, 60 pull-thrus, (25x60), back-ins (25x40), 55 full hkups, 55 W, 55 E (30/50 amps), seasonal sites, WiFi @ sites, tent sites, dump, laundry, groc, LP bottles, fire rings, firewood. **REC:** pond, swim, fishing, golf, playground, hunting nearby, rec open to public. Pets OK. Partial handicap access. Big rig sites. 2021 rates: $45, Military discount.
(317)326-3181 Lat: 39.82740, Lon: -85.83297
1613 W 300 N, Greenfield, IN 46140
www.heartlandresort.com
See ad this page

INDIANAPOLIS KOA **Ratings: 8.5/10★/8.5** (Campground) 127 Avail: 101 full hkups, 26 W, 26 E (30/50 amps). 2021 rates: $52 to $96. Mar 15 to Nov 15. (317)894-1397, 5896 W 200N, Greenfield, IN 46140

Check out a campground's ad. In it you might find a locator map, photos, and a lot more information about the park to help you find just the right place to stay.

GREENWOOD — C3 *Johnson*

Travel Services

CAMPING WORLD OF GREENWOOD/INDIANAPOLIS As the nation's largest retailer of RV supplies, accessories, services and new and used RVs, Camping World is committed to making your total RV experience better. **SERVICES:** RV, tire, RV appliance, MH mechanical, restrooms. RV Sales. RV supplies, LP gas, emergency parking, RV accessible. Hours: 9am to 7pm. (866)395-7711 Lat: 39.610376, Lon: -86.076163 303 Sheek Road, Greenwood, IN 46143 www.campingworld.com

GROVERTOWN — A3 *Starke*

EZ KAMP **Ratings: 8.5/8.5★/7.5** (RV Park) Avail: 87 full hkups (30/50 amps). 2021 rates: $45 to $50. Apr 15 to Nov 01. (574)867-5267, 9415 E 500 N Rd, Grovertown, IN 46531

HAMBURG — E4 *Clark*

DEAM LAKE SRA (Public State Park) From town, E 6 mi on Hwy 60, follow signs (L); or From Hamburg, NW 8 mi on Hwy 60, follow signs (R). Entrance fee required. Avail: 174 E (20/30 amps). 2021 rates: $12 to $46. (812)246-5421

HENRYVILLE — E4 *Clark*

CLARK STATE FOREST (Public State Park) From town: Go 1 mi N on US-31. 38 Avail: Pit toilets. 2021 rates: $12. (812)294-4306

HILLSBORO — C2 *Fountain*

CHARLAROSE LAKE & CAMPGROUND **Ratings: 6/9★/8** (Campground) 38 Avail: 8 full hkups, 30 W, 30 E (30/50 amps). 2021 rates: $35. Apr 01 to Nov 01. (765)234-7286, 3204 E 300S, Hillsboro, IN 47949

HOWE — A4 *LaGrange*

GRAND VIEW BEND **Ratings: 5.5/9★/8.5** (Membership Park) 40 Avail: 40 W, 40 E (30/50 amps). 2021 rates: $30 to $40. Apr 15 to Oct 15. (574)575-5927, 4630 N 100 E, Howe, IN 46746

TWIN MILLS RV RESORT
Ratings: 8.5/8.5★/9 (RV Park) 151 Avail: 40 full hkups, 111 W, 111 E (30/50 amps). 2021 rates: $55 to $71. Apr 15 to Nov 01. (888)563-7040, 1675 W SR 120 (West State Road), Howe, IN 46746

HUNTINGTON — B4 *Huntington*

CAMP TIMBER LAKE **Ratings: 6/8★/8** (Campground) 44 Avail: 30 full hkups, 14 E (30/50 amps). 2021 rates: $36 to $45. (260)672-3251, 1740 E 675 N, Huntington, IN 46750

J.E. ROUSH LAKE (Public State Park) From town: Go 1-1/2 mi S on Hwy 5. Avail: 41 E (30 amps), Pit toilets. (260)468-2165

SALAMONIE LAKE (Public State Park) From town, S 9 mi on SR-105 (cross the Salamonie Reservoir), W 0.1 mi on park access rd/Lost Bridge West Rd (R). Avail: 245 E (30/50 amps). 2021 rates: $10 to $29. (260)468-2125

INDIANAPOLIS — C3 *Indianapolis*

INDIANAPOLIS See also Greenfield.

INDIANA STATE FAIRGROUNDS (Public) From Jct of I-465N & SR-31 (Meridian St), S 7.2 mi on SR-31 to 38th St, E 2 mi (L); or From Jct of I-70 & Keystone (exit 85B), N 2 mi on Keystone to 38th St, W 0.9 mi (R). 170 Avail: 80 full hkups, 90 W, 90 E (30/50 amps). 2021 rates: $40. (317)927-7503

INDY LAKES RV CAMPGROUND
Ratings: 6.5/9★/8.5 (Campground) Avail: 51 full hkups (30/50 amps). 2021 rates: $39.95. (317)888-6006, 4001 W Southport Rd, Indianapolis, IN 46217

LAKE HAVEN RETREAT
Ratings: 8/8.5★/8.5 (Campground) From jct of I-465 & Hwy 37 (Exit 4): Go 1-1/2 mi S on Hwy 37, then 1/4 mi E on W Edgewood Ave (R). **FAC:** paved/gravel rds. (100 spaces). Avail: 30 gravel, 30 pull-thrus, (28x65), mostly side by side hkups, 30 full hkups (30/50 amps), seasonal sites, cable, WiFi @ sites, dump, laundry, fire rings, firewood, controlled access. **REC:** Fishing Lake: fishing, playground. Pets OK. Partial handicap access. No tents. Big rig sites, eco-friendly. 2021 rates: $40, Military discount.
(317)783-5267 Lat: 39.67817, Lon: -86.19492
1739 W Edgewood Ave, Indianapolis, IN 46217
www.lakehavenretreat.com
See ad this page

JASONVILLE — D2 *Clay*

SHAKAMAK (Public State Park) From Jct of SR-59 & SR-48, W 4 mi on SR-48 (L). 174 Avail: 8 full hkups, 114 E (30/50 amps). 2021 rates: $7.63 to $29. (812)665-2158

KENDALLVILLE — A4 *LaGrange*

BIXLER LAKE CAMPGROUND (Public) From Jct of US-6 & SR-3, E 1.3 mi on US-6 to Fair St, S 0.3 mi to Wayne St, E 500 ft to Park Ave, S 0.3 mi to Lake Park Dr, E 0.2 mi (L) Follow signs. 103 Avail: 78 W, 78 E (20/30 amps). 2021 rates: $25 to $30. Apr 27 to Oct 15. (260)242-6898

KNIGHTSTOWN — C4 *Henry*

YOGI BEAR'S JELLYSTONE PARK CAMP-RESORT **Ratings: 8/8.5★/9** (Campground) 50 Avail: 10 full hkups, 40 W, 40 E (30/50 amps). 2021 rates: $52 to $69. Apr 01 to Oct 31. (765)737-6585, 5964 South SR-109, Knightstown, IN 46148

KNOX — A3 *Starke*

BASS LAKE STATE BEACH AND CAMPGROUND (Public) From town, S 5 mi on US-35 to IN-10, E 3.4 mi (R). Avail: 60 E (20 amps). 2021 rates: $30 to $40. May 15 to Oct 31. (574)405-5322

LAFAYETTE — B3 *Tippecanoe*

WOLFE'S LEISURE TIME CAMPGROUND **Ratings: 7.5/8.5★/7** (Campground) 53 Avail: 13 full hkups, 17 W, 23 E (30/50 amps). 2021 rates: $33 to $38. (765)589-8089, 7414 Old SR 25 North, Lafayette, IN 47905

LAKEVILLE — A3 *St Joseph*

MAPLE RIDGE CAMPGROUND **Ratings: 8/9.5★/8** (Campground) 68 Avail: 7 full hkups, 61 W, 61 E (30/50 amps). 2021 rates: $32 to $40. Apr 15 to Oct 15. (574)784-8532, 65777 Maple Rd, Lakeville, IN 46536

POTATO CREEK (Public State Park) From Jct of SR-23 & SR-4, E 4 mi on SR-4 (L). Avail: 287 E (30/50 amps). 2021 rates: $12 to $32. (574)656-8186

LIBERTY — C5 *Union*

WHITEWATER MEMORIAL (Public State Park) From Jct of US-27 & SR-101, S 1.5 mi on SR-101 (R). Entrance fee required. Avail: 236 E (30 amps). 2021 rates: $10 to $29. (765)458-5565

LOGANSPORT — B3 *Cass*

FRANCE PARK (Public) From town, W 4 mi on US-24 (L). 200 Avail: 130 W, 130 E (30 amps). 2021 rates: $18 to $25. (574)753-2928

LOOGOOTEE — E2 *Daviess*

WEST BOGGS PARK (DAVIESS-MARTIN COUNTY) (Public) From Jct of US-50 & US-231, N 4.1 mi on US-231 (L). 250 Avail: 241 W, 241 E (30/50 amps). 2021 rates: $26 to $42. (812)295-3421

LYNNVILLE — E2 *Warrick*

LYNNVILLE RV PARK (Public) From Jct of I-64 & SR-61 (exit 39), N 0.1 mi on SR-61 to SR-68, W 1.5 mi (R). 39 Avail: 25 full hkups, 14 W, 14 E (30/50 amps). 2021 rates: $25 to $30. Apr 01 to Nov 30. (812)922-5144

MADISON — D4 *Jefferson*

CITY OF MADISON CAMPGROUND (Public) From Jct of Hwys 421 & 56 (Jefferson St), S 0.2 mi on Jefferson St to Vaughn Dr, E 0.2 mi (R). 34 Avail: 34 W, 34 E (30/50 amps). 2021 rates: $30 to $40. Apr 01 to Oct 31. (812)265-8333

CLIFTY FALLS (Public State Park) From town, W 1 mi on SR-56/62 (R). Avail: 106 E (20/30 amps). 2021 rates: $7.63 to $50. (812)273-8885

MARION — B4 *Grant*

SPORTS LAKE CAMPING RESORT **Ratings: 6.5/8.5★/7.5** (Campground) 50 Avail: 10 full hkups, 40 W, 40 E (30/50 amps). 2021 rates: $35. May 01 to Oct 01. (765)998-2558, 7230 East 400 S, Marion, IN 46953

WHITE OAKS **Ratings: 5/NA/8.5** (RV Park) Avail: 16 full hkups (30/50 amps). 2021 rates: $30. (765)674-6166, 7145 S. Meridian Street, Marion, IN 46953

Explore America's Top RV Destinations! Turn to the Spotlight articles in our State and Province sections to learn more.

MARSHALL — C2 *Parke*

TURKEY RUN (Public State Park) From Jct of US-41 & SR-47, E 1.8 mi on SR-47 (L). Entrance fee required. Avail: 213 E (20/50 amps). 2021 rates: $12 to $29. (765)597-2635

MARTINSVILLE — D3 *Monroe*

MORGAN-MONROE STATE FOREST (Public State Park) From Jct of Hwy 37 & Old 37 access rd, S 3 mi on Old 37 access rd to forest entrance, E 4.5 mi (L). 29 Avail: Pit toilets. 2021 rates: $6 to $16. (765)342-4026

MICHIGAN CITY — A3 *La Porte*

MICHIGAN CITY CAMPGROUND **Ratings: 9/9★/8.5** (Campground) 95 Avail: 85 full hkups, 10 W, 10 E (30/50 amps). 2021 rates: $48 to $59. (219)872-7600, 1601 N US 421, Michigan City, IN 46360

MIDDLEBURY — A4 *Elkhart*

ELKHART COUNTY MIDDLEBURY KOA **Ratings: 8/9★/8.5** (RV Park) 95 Avail: 60 full hkups, 35 W, 35 E (30/50 amps). 2021 rates: $49.78 to $96. Apr 01 to Oct 31. (800)562-5892, 52867 SR 13, Middlebury, IN 46540

MITCHELL — D3 *Lawrence*

SPRING MILL (Public State Park) From Jct of SR-37 & SR-60, E 3 mi on SR-60 (L). Avail: 187 E (30 amps). 2021 rates: $10 to $29. (812)849-3534

MODOC — C4 *Randolph*

ADVENTURE BOUND KAMP MODOC **Ratings: 6/10★/8** (Campground) Avail: 86 full hkups (30/50 amps). 2021 rates: $50 to $100. Apr 15 to Oct 15. (765)853-5290, 9773 S 800 W, Modoc, IN 47358

MONTGOMERY — E2 *Daviess*

MONTGOMERY REC PARK (Public) From Jct of Hwy 50/150 & First St, N 0.3 mi on First St to Park St (cross RR tracks), E 0.4 mi (L). 150 Avail: 50 full hkups, 100 W, 100 E (30/50 amps). 2021 rates: $20 to $24. Apr 15 to Oct 15. (812)486-3255

MONTICELLO — B3 *White*

INDIANA BEACH CAMPGROUND **Ratings: 8/7.5/8** (Campground) 733 Avail: 204 full hkups, 466 W, 466 E (30/50 amps). 2021 rates: $46 to $52. May 01 to Oct 31. (574)583-4141, 2732 NW Schafer Drive, Monticello, IN 47960

INDIANA BEACH MONTICELLO KOA **Ratings: 8/8.5★/8.5** (RV Park) 135 Avail: 71 full hkups, 64 W, 64 E (30/50 amps). 2021 rates: $63.24 to $70.68. May 01 to Oct 31. (574)583-8646, 2882 North West Shafer Dr, Monticello, IN 47960

LOST ACRES RV PARK (RV Park) (Rebuilding) 70 Avail: 4 full hkups, 66 W, 66 E (20/30 amps). 2021 rates: $65.10 to $70.10. May 01 to Oct 23. (574)870-9436, 3148 N 400 E, Monticello, IN 47960

MOROCCO — B2 *Newton*

WILLOW SLOUGH STATE FISH & WILDLIFE AREA (Public State Park) From jct US-41 & CR-275S: Go 2 mi W on CR-275S. Avail: 50 E. (219)285-2704

NASHVILLE — D3 *Brown*

BILL MONROE MEMORIAL MUSIC PARK & CAMPGROUND **Ratings: 6/9.5★/8.5** (Campground) 260 Avail: 260 W, 260 E (30/50 amps). 2021 rates: $32 to $38. (812)988-6422, 5163 SR 135 N, Morgantown, IN 46160

BROWN COUNTY (Public State Park) From Jct of SR-135N & SR-46W, SW 2.2 mi on SR-46W (L). RVs use west gate. Entrance fee required. Avail: 519 E (30 amps). 2021 rates: $6.12 to $38.76. (812)988-6406

BROWN COUNTY KOA Ratings: 8/10★/9.5 (Campground) Avail: 41 full hkups (30/50 amps). 2021 rates: $50 to $90. Apr 01 to Nov 01. (812)988-4675, 2248 SR-46 East, Nashville, IN 47448

IN

NASHVILLE (CONT)

FRIENDS O'MINE CAMPGROUND & CABINS **Ratings: 7.5/9★/8** (RV Park) Avail: 80 full hkups (30/50 amps). 2021 rates: $38 to $45. Apr 01 to Nov 01. (812)988-0008, 4557 E SR-46, Nashville, IN 47448

YELLOWWOOD STATE FOREST (Public) From business center: Go 7 mi W on Hwy-46. 80 Avail: Pit toilets. 2021 rates: $10 to $40. (812)988-7945

NEW CARLISLE — A3 *St Joseph*

LAKESIDE RV RESORT
(RV Resort) (Seasonal Stay Only) Avail: 1 full hkups (30/50 amps). 2021 rates: $46. Apr 01 to Nov 01. (888)563-7040, 7089 N Chicago Rd, New Carlisle, IN 46552

MINI MOUNTAIN CAMPGROUND **Ratings: 7/5/7.5** (Campground) 140 Avail: 120 full hkups, 20 W, 20 E (30/50 amps). 2021 rates: $45. (574)340-9923, 32351 State Rd 2, New Carlisle, IN 46552

NEW CASTLE — C4 *Henry*

CORNERSTONE RETREAT AND FAMILY CAMPGROUND **Ratings: 7.5/9★/9** (Campground) 91 Avail: 18 full hkups, 73 W, 73 E (30/50 amps). 2021 rates: $45 to $55. Apr 01 to Nov 01. (765)987-8700, 75 W County Road 500 S, New Castle, IN 47362

SUMMIT LAKE (Public State Park) From Jct of SR-3N & US-36, E 4 mi on US-36 to Messick Rd, N 1 mi (E). Avail: 125 E (20/30 amps). 2021 rates: $12 to $29. (765)766-5873

WESTWOOD PARK & CAMPGROUND (Public) From Jct of SR-38 & SR-3, W 2.75 mi on SR-38 to RD 275W, S 2 mi to park access rd, follow signs (L). 38 Avail: 38 W, 38 E (30/50 amps), Pit toilets. 2021 rates: $29. (765)987-1232

NEW HARMONY — E1 *Posey*

HARMONIE (Public State Park) From town, S 4 mi on Hwy 69 to SR-269, W 1 mi (E). Avail: 200 E (30/50 amps). 2021 rates: $12 to $95. (812)682-4821

NORTH VERNON — D4 *Jennings*

MUSCATATUCK PARK (JENNINGS COUNTY PARK) (Public) From Jct of US-50 & Hwy 7/3, S 1.3 mi on Hwy 7/3 (R). 50 Avail: 8 full hkups, 42 W, 42 E (20/30 amps). 2021 rates: $23 to $30. (812)346-2953

OAKTOWN — D2 *Knox*

NEW VISION RV PARK
Ratings: 7.5/8.5★/9.5 (RV Park) Avail: 39 full hkups (30/50 amps). 2021 rates: $30 to $32. (812)745-2125, 13552 N US Hwy 41, Oaktown, IN 47561

ORLAND — A4 *Steuben*

MANAPOGO PARK Ratings: 7.5/9★/7 (Campground) 70 Avail: 3 full hkups, 67 W, 67 E (30/50 amps). 2021 rates: $40 to $45. Apr 21 to Oct 08. (260)833-3902, 5495 W 760 N, Orland, IN 46776

Had a great stay? Let us know by emailing us Parks@goodsam.com

PERU — B3 *Miami*

HONEY BEAR HOLLOW FAMILY CAMPGROUND
Ratings: 7.5/10★/8 (Campground) From Jct of US-24 & US-31, N 1.3 mi on US-31 to CR-200N, W 1.2 mi (R). **FAC:** gravel rds. (98 spaces). 61 Avail: 51 gravel, 10 grass, 22 pull-thrus, (30x50), back-ins (30x50), 5 full hkups, 56 W, 56 E (30/50 amps), seasonal sites, WiFi, tent sites, rentals, dump, mobile sewer, laundry, groc, LP gas, fire rings, firewood. **REC:** pool, pond, fishing, boating nearby, playground. Pets OK. eco-friendly. 2021 rates: $30, Military discount. Mar 15 to Oct 31.
(765)473-4342 Lat: 40.79516, Lon: -86.15291
4252 W 200 N, Peru, IN 46970
See ad this page

MISSISSINEWA LAKE (Public State Park) From Jct of Main/Bus SR-24 & Broadway/SR-19 (in town), S 6 mi on SR-19 to SR-500S, E 2.9 mi (L). Entrance fee required. 431 Avail: 39 full hkups, 335 E (30/50 amps). 2021 rates: $12 to $29. (765)473-6528

PIERCETON — B4 *Kosciusko*

YOGI BEAR'S JELLYSTONE PARK CAMP-RESORT **Ratings: 8.5/9★/8.5** (Campground) 65 Avail: 58 full hkups, 7 W, 7 E (30 amps). 2021 rates: $44.95 to $64.95. May 13 to Sep 15. (574)594-2124, 1916 N 850 E, Pierceton, IN 46562

PLYMOUTH — A3 *Marshall*

HIDDEN LAKE PARADISE CAMPGROUND **Ratings: 6.5/8★/8** (Campground) 15 Avail: 15 W, 15 E (30/50 amps). 2021 rates: $34 to $38. (574)936-2900, 12589 Rose Rd, Plymouth, IN 46563

YOGI BEAR'S JELLYSTONE PARK PLYMOUTH **Ratings: 8.5/9★/8** (RV Park) Avail: 85 full hkups (30/50 amps). 2021 rates: $45 to $55. May 02 to Sep 30. (574)936-7851, 7719 Redwood Rd, Plymouth, IN 46563

PORTAGE — A2 *Porter*

LAKESHORE CAMP RESORT **Ratings: 7.5/8.5★/8** (Campground) Avail: 100 full hkups (30 amps). 2021 rates: $37 to $64. May 15 to Sep 30. (219)762-7757, 5300 Old Porter Rd, Portage, IN 46368

WOODLAND VILLAGE RV PARK **Ratings: 5.5/NA/7** (RV Area in MH Park) Avail: 10 full hkups (30/50 amps). 2021 rates: $40. (219)762-6578, 5757 Melton Road, Portage, IN 46368

PORTLAND — B5 *Jay*

FOX LAKE CAMPGROUND **Ratings: 5/5/7.5** (Campground) 83 Avail: 63 full hkups, 20 W, 20 E (30/50 amps). 2021 rates: $45 to $50. Apr 15 to Oct 15. (260)335-2639, 7424 South 300 E, Portland, IN 47371

REMINGTON — B2 *Jasper*

A SPOTLIGHT Introducing NW Hoosier Country's colorful attractions appearing at the front of this state section.

CABOOSE LAKE CAMPGROUND
Ratings: 8.5/9.5★/9 (RV Park) From jct I-65 & US-24 (exit 201): Go 528 ft E on US-24 (R).

AN AFFORDABLE PLACE TO ENJOY
Beautiful RV sites on a 20-acre spring fed stocked lake. FREE Streaming WIFI. Perfect 75' overnight pull-thrus. Located off I-65 & convenient to Chicago. Stay longer & enjoy our SUMMER BEACH FAMILY FUN ZONE!

FAC: gravel rds. (125 spaces). Avail: 105 gravel, 43 pull-thrus, (30x75), back-ins (35x60), 105 full hkups (30/50 amps), seasonal sites, WiFi @ sites, tent sites, rentals, dump, laundry, groc, LP gas, fire rings, firewood, controlled access. **REC:** Caboose Lake: swim, fishing, playground, rec open to public. Pet restrict (B). Partial handicap access. Big rig sites. 2021 rates: $55, Military discount.
(219)261-3828 Lat: 40.76555, Lon: -87.11518
3657 West US Hwy 24 , Remington, IN 47977
www.cabooselake.com
See ad page 373

Things to See and Do

SUMMER BEACH FAMILY FUN ZONE 35' Hippo Slide, Bumper Boats, Inflatable Slides, Water Wars, Jumpshot, Water Inflatables, and Dunk Tank. A day-cation located at Caboose Lake Campground. Jun 01 to Aug 30. Partial handicap access. RV accessible. Restrooms. Food. Hours: 11am to 5pm Sun-Th,11am to 7pm Fri-Sat. Adult fee: $10 to $30 daily.
(219)261-3828 Lat: 40.76555, Lon: -87.11518
3657 West US Hwy 24, Remington, IN 47977
www.cabooselake.com
See ad page 373

Join in the fun. Like us on FACEBOOK!

RICHMOND — C5 *Wayne*

ARROWHEAD CAMPGROUND
Ratings: 10/10★/10 (RV Park) From Jct of I-70 & US 40 (Indiana exit 156) go E 1 mi on US 40, go N 1.5 mi on OH 320 onto OH 121 N for 8.5 mi to Thomas Rd, go W on Thomas 1 mi (L). **FAC:** all weather rds. (131 spaces). Avail: 26 all weather, patios, 10 pull-thrus, (35x70), back-ins (30x40), 26 full hkups (30/50 amps), seasonal sites, WiFi @ sites, tent sites, rentals, dump, laundry, LP gas, fire rings, firewood. **REC:** pool, pond, fishing, playground. Pet restrict (B). Big rig sites, eco-friendly. 2021 rates: $44 to $56, Military discount. Apr 15 to Oct 27.
(937)996-6203 Lat: 39.94380, Lon: -84.74400
1361 Thomas Rd, New Paris, OH 45347
arrowhead-campground.com
See primary listing at New Paris, OH and ad this page

DEER RIDGE CAMPING RESORT
Ratings: 8.5/9★/8.5 (Campground) Avail: 30 full hkups (30/50 amps). 2021 rates: $40 to $50. May 01 to Oct 31. (765)939-0888, 3696 Smyrna Rd, Richmond, IN 47374

GRANDPA'S FARM **Ratings: 8.5/9★/10** (Campground) 70 Avail: 25 full hkups, 45 W, 45 E (30/50 amps). 2021 rates: $40 to $50. Apr 01 to Nov 01. (765)962-7907, 4244 State Road 227 N, Richmond, IN 47374

RICHMOND KOA KAMPGROUND **Ratings: 8.5/10★/9** (Campground) 56 Avail: 22 full hkups, 34 W, 34 E (30/50 amps). 2021 rates: $52.75 to $61.50. Mar 15 to Nov 01. (765)962-1219, 3101 Cart Rd, Richmond, IN 47374

Travel Services

CAMPING WORLD OF RICHMOND As the nation's largest retailer of RV supplies, accessories, services and new and used RVs, Camping World is committed to making your total RV experience better. **SERVICES:** RV, RV appliance, MH mechanical, sells outdoor gear, restrooms. RV Sales. RV supplies, LP gas, dump, RV accessible. Hours: 9am to 7pm.
(888)708-2569 Lat: 39.85905, Lon: -84.91678
2250 Williamsburg Pike, Richmond, IN 47374
www.campingworld.com

RISING SUN — D5 *Ohio*

A SPOTLIGHT Introducing Casino Country's colorful attractions appearing at the front of this state section.

LITTLE FARM ON THE RIVER RV PARK CAMPING RESORT
Ratings: 9/9★/8 (RV Park) From Jct of I 275 & US 50, W 7.9 mi on US 50 to SR 56, S 8 mi to E Bellview Lane, E 0.2 mi (R). **FAC:** gravel rds. (192 spaces). Avail: 152 gravel, 54 pull-thrus, (35x90), back-ins (26x75), 152 full hkups (30/50 amps), seasonal sites, WiFi @ sites, tent sites, rentals, dump, laundry, groc, LP gas, fire rings, firewood. **REC:** pool, pond, fishing, boating nearby, shuffleboard, playground. Pets OK. Partial handicap access. Big rig sites. 2021 rates: $43 to $50, Military discount.
(812)438-4500 Lat: 38.97387, Lon: -84.84468
1343 E Bellview Lane, Rising Sun, IN 47040
www.littlefarmresort.com
See ad page 372

RISING STAR CASINO RESORT & RV PARK
Ratings: 10/10★/9.5 (RV Resort) From jct Hwy 262 (Main St) & Hwy 56 (N High St): Go 1/4 mi N on Hwy 56 (N High St), then 150 yards E on 6th St, then 200 yards N on Rising Star Dr (L). **FAC:** paved rds. Avail: 56 paved, 6 pull-thrus, (30x50), back-ins (30x40), 56 full hkups (30/50 amps), cable, WiFi @ sites, laundry, restaurant, controlled access. **REC:** pool, Ohio River: golf, shuffleboard, rec open to public. Pets OK. Partial handicap access. No tents. Big rig sites, 10 day max stay, eco-friendly. 2021 rates: $39.99, Military discount. ATM.
(800)472-6311 Lat: 38.952906, Lon: -84.846794
777 Rising Star Drive, Rising Sun, IN 47040
risingstarcasino.com
See ad page 372

Things to See and Do

RISING STAR CASINO RESORT Casino with slot machines, game tables, hotel rooms, spa, pool, sauna, health club, golf course, dining options, and RV Park. Partial handicap access. RV accessible. Restrooms. Food. Hours: Open 24 hours a day. ATM.
(812)438-1234 Lat: 38.95725, Lon: -84.847399
777 Rising Star Dr, Rising Sun, IN 47040
risingstarcasino.com
See ad page 372

ROCHESTER — B3 *Fulton*

LAKEVIEW CAMPGROUND **Ratings: 7/6/8.5** (Campground) 45 Avail: 2 full hkups, 43 W, 43 E (30/50 amps). 2021 rates: $33. Apr 15 to Oct 15. (574)353-8114, 7781 E 300 N, Rochester, IN 46975

ROCKVILLE — C2 *Parke*

CECIL M HARDEN LAKE/RACCOON SRA (Public State Park) From Jct of US-36 & US-41, E 9 mi on US-36 (R). Avail: 240 E (20 amps). 2021 rates: $10 to $40. (765)344-1412

ROCKVILLE LAKE PARK (PARK COUNTY PARK) (Public) From Jct of US 41 & US 36, E 0.5 mi on US 36 to Erie St., N 0.4 mi to Stark St, E 0.2 mi to Marshall Rd., NE 1.2 mi (L). 152 Avail: 12 full hkups, 12 S, 31 E (30/50 amps). 2021 rates: $21.05 to $42.45. Mar 26 to Oct 31. (765)569-6541

SANTA CLAUS — E2 *Spencer*

LAKE RUDOLPH CAMPGROUND & RV RESORT **Ratings: 9.5/10★/9.5** (RV Park) Avail: 205 full hkups (30/50 amps). 2021 rates: $49 to $83. May 01 to Oct 31. (888)349-9733, 78 N Holiday Blvd, Santa Claus, IN 47579

SCOTTSBURG — E4 *Scott*

CAMP RAINTREE LAKE **Ratings: 8.5/9.5★/9.5** (Campground) 40 Avail: 12 full hkups, 25 W, 25 E (30/50 amps). 2021 rates: $43 to $65. Mar 01 to Dec 01. (812)752-4062, 4577 W State Road 56, Scottsburg, IN 47170

HARDY LAKE (Public State Park) From Jct of I-65 & Hwy 256, E 7 mi on Hwy 256 to N Sunnyside Rd., N 4 mi (E). Avail: 149 E (30/50 amps). 2021 rates: $10 to $45. (812)794-3800

SHIPSHEWANA — A4 *LaGrange*

SHIPSHEWANA CAMPGROUND NORTH PARK & AMISH LOG CABIN LODGING Ratings: 7/9★/9 (RV Park) 55 Avail: 30 full hkups, 25 W, 25 E (30/50 amps). 2021 rates: $36 to $44. Apr 01 to Oct 24. (260)768-7770, 5970 North State Road 5, Shipshewana, IN 46565

SHIPSHEWANA CAMPGROUND SOUTH PARK Ratings: 8.5/9.5★/9 (RV Park) Avail: 151 full hkups (30/50 amps). 2021 rates: $43 to $46. Apr 15 to Oct 15. (260)768-4669, 1105 S Van Buren St, Shipshewana, IN 46565

SHOALS — E3 *Martin*

MARTIN STATE FOREST (Public State Park) From business center: Go 4 mi E on US-50. 26 Avail: Pit toilets. (812)247-3491

SPENCER — D3 *Owen*

MCCORMICK'S CREEK (Public State Park) From town, E 2 mi on Hwy 46, follow signs (L). Avail: 189 E (20/30 amps). 2021 rates: $6.12 to $38.76. (812)829-2235

OWEN-PUTNAM STATE FOREST (Public State Park) From town: Go 5 miles W on Hwy 46, then 1 mile N on Fish Creek Rd. Avail: 14 W, Pit toilets. 2021 rates: $10 to $40. (812)829-2462

ST PAUL — D4 *Decatur*

HIDDEN PARADISE CAMPGROUND

good sam park **Ratings: 8/10★/8.5** (Campground) From Jct I-74 (Exit 123) & N CR-800E: Go 2 mi S on N CR-800E, then 1/2 mi E on Jefferson St (L). **FAC:** gravel rds. (183 spaces). 113 Avail: 77 gravel, 36 grass, 53 pull-thrus, (50x40), back-ins (50x70), mostly side by side hkups, 56 full hkups, 57 W, 57 E (50 amps), seasonal sites, WiFi @ sites, tent sites, rentals, dump, mobile sewer, laundry, groc, LP bottles, fire rings, firewood. **REC:** Dream Lake: swim, fishing, playground. Pets OK. Partial handicap access, eco-friendly. 2021 rates: $42 to $48, Military discount.
(765)525-6582 Lat: 39.42318, Lon: -85.62453
802 East Jefferson St, St Paul, IN 47272
www.hiddenparadise.info
See ad this page

SULLIVAN — D2 *Sullivan*

SULLIVAN COUNTY PARK & LAKE (Public) From Jct of US-41 & W Washington St, E 1.8 on W Washington St to Foley St, N 0.25 mi (E) Entrance fee required. 451 Avail: 451 W, 451 E (50 amps). 2021 rates: $15 to $30. Mar 01 to Oct 31. (812)268-5537

TERRE HAUTE — D2 *Vigo*

FOWLER PARK (VIGO COUNTY PARK) (Public) From jct I-70 & US 41: Go 7 mi S on US 41. Avail: 53 E. 2021 rates: $18. May 01 to Oct 15. (812)462-3413

HAWTHORN PARK (VIGO COUNTY PARK) (Public) From jct I-70 W & Hwy 46: Go 3 mi N on Hwy 46, then 1 mi E on US 40, then 1/2 mi N on Hunt Rd, then 1/2 mi W. Avail: 75 E. 2021 rates: $12 to $20. May 01 to Oct 15. (812)462-3225

PRAIRIE CREEK PARK (VIGO COUNTY PARK) (Public) From jct I-70 & US 41: Go 11 mi S on US 41, then W on W French Dr. Avail: 42 E (20/30 amps). 2021 rates: $20. (812)462-3392

TERRE HAUTE CAMPGROUND

good sam park **Ratings: 8.5/10★/9** (Campground) 78 Avail: 31 full hkups, 47 W, 47 E (30/50 amps). 2021 rates: $55 to $85. (812)917-5671, 5995 E Sony Dr, Terre Haute, IN 47802

THORNTOWN — C3 *Boone*

OLD MILL RUN PARK **Ratings: 8.5/8.5★/9** (Campground) Avail: 45 full hkups (30/50 amps). 2021 rates: $37 to $40. Apr 01 to Oct 15. (765)436-7190, 8544 W 690 N, Thorntown, IN 46071

VALLONIA — D3 *Jackson*

STARVE-HOLLOW SRA (Public State Park) From Jct of US-50 & Hwy 135, S 3 mi on Hwy 135 to CR-310, E 2.5 mi (L). 150 Avail: 53 full hkups, 87 E (30/50 amps). 2021 rates: $10 to $40. (812)358-3464

VERSAILLES — D4 *Ripley*

VERSAILLES (Public State Park) From Jct of US-421 & US-50, E 1 mi on US-50 (L). Avail: 226 E (50 amps). 2021 rates: $12 to $29. (812)689-6424

VINCENNES — E2 *Knox*

OUABACHE TRAILS PARK (Public) S-bnd: From Jct of US-41 & US-50, S 0.1 mi on US-41(turns into 6th St) to Executive Blvd, W 0.5 mi to Oliphaunt Rd, S 0.25 mi to Old Fort Knox Rd, W 0.5 mi (E). 35 Avail: 35 W, 35 E (30 amps). 2021 rates: $18. Apr 15 to Oct 15. (812)882-4316

VINCENNES RV PARK

good sam park (RV Park) (Rebuilding) Avail: 50 full hkups (30/50 amps). 2021 rates: $35. (812)891-0007, 500 E Robinson Ln, Vincennes, IN 47591

Looking for places the ""locals'' frequent? Make friends with park owners and staff to get the inside scoop!

WARSAW — A4 *Kosciusko*

JTS LAKESIDE CAMPGROUND **Ratings: 5.5/NA/6** (Campground) 35 Avail: 35 W, 35 E (30 amps), Pit toilets. 2021 rates: $40. Apr 15 to Oct 15. (574)594-2635, 6402 E McKenna Rd, Warsaw, IN 46582

PIKE LAKE CAMPGROUND (Public) From business center: Go 1/2 mi N on Hwy-15, then 1/2 mi E on Arthur St. Avail: 47 full hkups (30/50 amps). 2021 rates: $32. Apr 15 to Oct 01. (574)269-1439

WASHINGTON — E2 *Daviess*

GLENDALE FISH & WILDLIFE AREA (Public) From Jct of US-50E & CR-550/Sportsman's Rd, S 7.5 mi on Sportsman's Rd (E). Avail: 67 E (20/30 amps). 2021 rates: $7 to $11. Apr 01 to Oct 31. (812)644-7711

WAVELAND — C2 *Montgomery*

LAKE WAVELAND PARK (Public) From Jct of SR-59 & SR-47, W 1 mi on SR-47 (R). 54 Avail: 54 W, 54 E (30/50 amps). 2021 rates: $16 to $28. Mar 15 to Oct 15. (765)435-2073

SHADES (Public State Park) From town, N 3 mi on CR-750W to SR-234, W 1 mi (L). 105 Avail. 2021 rates: $7.63 to $20. Apr 01 to Sep 30. (765)435-2810

WEST LAFAYETTE — B2 *Tippecanoe*

PROPHETSTOWN (Public State Park) From I-65, take exit 178 (St Rd 43), south on State Road 43 to Burnett Road, (1/4 mi), left on Burnett Rd to 9th St Road (3/4 mi), right on 9th St Road to Swisher Road (3/4 mi), left on Swisher Road to park entrance (1-1/2 mi). 110 Avail: 55 full hkups, 55 E (30/50 amps). 2021 rates: $12 to $40. (765)567-4919

WICKLIFFE — E3 *Crawford*

PATOKA LAKE SRA (Public State Park) From Jct of SR-145 & SR-164, W 1 mi on SR-164, turn right on Dillard Rd, continue to Patoka Station (L). Avail: 455 E (30/50 amps). 2021 rates: $16.21 to $29. (812)685-2464

WINAMAC — B3 *Pulaski*

TIPPECANOE RIVER (Public State Park) From town, N 4 mi on US-35 (R). Avail: 112 E (30/50 amps). 2021 rates: $10 to $29. (574)946-3213

WINSLOW — E2 *Pike*

PIKE STATE FOREST (Public State Park) From jct Hwy-61 & Hwy-364: Go 3 mi E on Hwy-364. 36 Avail: Pit toilets. 2021 rates: $10 to $40. (812)827-2851

WOLCOTTVILLE — A4 *LaGrange*

ATWOOD LAKE CAMPGROUND **Ratings: 5.5/7/7** (Campground) 114 Avail: 114 W, 114 E (30 amps). 2021 rates: $35. Apr 15 to Oct 15. (260)854-3079, 655 E 800 S, Wolcottville, IN 46795

GORDONS CAMPGROUND **Ratings: 6.5/5.5/6.5** (Campground) 191 Avail: 191 W, 191 E (30/50 amps). 2021 rates: $40. Apr 15 to Oct 15. (260)351-3383, 9500 E 600 S, Wolcottville, IN 46795

IN

good sam

Extended Service Plan

You make the priceless memories. We'll pay for the pricey repair bills.

We know that time spent traveling with your family is precious. When your RV needs a mechanical repair, let us pick up the bill, so that you can get back on the road and back to spending time with your family.

Program Benefits:

- No waiting for reimbursement, we pay the shop directly.
- Take your vehicle to the repair shop of your choice.
- Choose the deductible and payment schedule that works for you, and lock in your rate for up to 3 years.
- Trip Interruption: If your RV is not usable due to a covered loss, we'll help cover costs for meals and lodging for $100 a day, for up to 5 days per repair visit.
- Rental Car Reimbursement: If you can't drive your vehicle due to a covered loss, we'll help cover costs for a rental car for $60 a day, for up to 5 days per repair visit.

Rental car benefit is not available on 5th wheel and travel trailer coverage.

Visit **GoodSamESP.com/Guide**

Call **866-601-2317**

To qualify, towable RVs must be 15 model years or newer. Cars, trucks, SUVs, and gas Motorhomes must be 15 model years or newer with less than 100,000 miles, and rear engine diesel Motorhomes must be 15 model years or newer with less than 120,000 miles. Coverage is renewable up to 18 model years or 150,000 miles. All program benefits are subject to limitations set forth in the current Terms & Conditions.

The Good Sam Extended Service Plan is not available to residents of New York or Indiana. If you are a resident of New York or Indiana, please call 1-866-524-7842 as other products may be available to you.

The Good Sam Extended Service Plan, which was designed for Good Sam by Affinity Brokerage, LLC, a Colorado surplus lines brokerage (Lic. #185640), is available exclusively for active members of Good Sam. Membership is required for eligibility in this program. Termination of your membership in Good Sam during the policy period may result in termination of The Good Sam Extended Service Plan. The cost of Good Sam Membership is the responsibility of the certificate holder and will be available at the then current rate. The Good Sam Extended Service Plan is available to U.S. residents only.

YOU ARE HERE
DID YOU KNOW?
Edible sweet corn only makes up 1 percent of Iowa's yield. The rest is used for livestock feed and manufacturing.
Getty Images/iStockphoto

Iowa

Endless fields of corn, an epic state fair and a presidential caucus all have a home in the Hawkeye State. But there's so much more to this Midwestern gem than what meets the eye. Take some time to explore Iowa.

Splendid Cities

Des Moines hosts the annual Iowa State Fair, but there's more to this town than corn dogs and livestock competition. Des Moines is a city rich with history, natural beauty and cultural impact. Visit the grand Capitol, with its golden dome, then interact with the quirky artworks of Pappajohn Sculpture Park. For wholesome food, gather homegrown produce at the weekly farmers market, or seek out trendy restaurants downtown. Located on the Mississippi River, Dubuque is a big getaway in eastern Iowa. Learn more about this national waterway's history, flora and fauna with a visit to the National Mississippi River Museum & Aquarium.

Outdoor Treasures

Despite its location on the Great Plains, you'll find lots of landscapes that undulate. Take the Loess Hills in western Iowa. Here, the flatlands and farmlands give way to rippling hills. Take a drive along the Loess Hills National Scenic Byway, hike Loess Hills State Forest, or enjoy a variety of outdoor activities at Stone State Park. Head underground at Maquoketa Caves State Park.

Lakes to Live For

Paddlers will find lots of space to explore on the Upper Iowa River, known for its limestone bluffs, or the Maquoketa River Water Trail. Those chasing thrills can find them at the whitewater parks sprinkled across the state. Northeast Iowa is the place for trout streams. Boaters and anglers should fish the Iowa Great Lakes, a chain of natural glacial lakes renowned for their exceptionally clear, blue, fish-rich waters.

Iowa Maid-Rite Sandwich

Featuring the perfect blend of spices and ground meat, the Maid-Rite sandwich first came about in 1926 when a customer told Fred Angell his sandwich was "made right." The edible icon continues to be an Iowa tradition served at Maid-Raid restaurant locations in Des Moines, Cedar Rapids and beyond.

VISITOR CENTER

TIME ZONE
Central Standard

ROAD & HIGHWAY INFORMATION
800-288-1047
www.511ia.org

FISHING & HUNTING INFORMATION
515-725-8200
iowadnr.gov

BOATING INFORMATION
515-725-8200
iowadnr.gov/Things-to-Do/Boating

NATIONAL PARKS
nps.gov/ia

STATE PARKS
www.iowadnr.gov/Places-to-Go/State-Parks

TOURISM INFORMATION
Iowa Tourism Office
800-345-IOWA
www.traveliowa.com

TOP TOURISM ATTRACTIONS
1) Amana Colonies
2) Greater Des Moines Botanical Center
3) Field of Dreams

MAJOR CITIES
Des Moines (capital), Cedar Rapids, Davenport, Sioux City, Iowa City

Featured Good Sam Parks

IOWA

When you stay with Good Sam, you can expect the highest degree of cleanliness and friendliness, and better yet, you get **10% off** overnight campground fees.

If you're not already a Good Sam member you can purchase your membership at one of these locations:

AMANA
Amana RV Park & Event Center

CHARLES CITY
R Campground

DAVENPORT
Interstate RV Park

DECATUR
Ted's RV Park

EARLHAM
Shady Brook Camping & RV Adventures

KELLOGG
Kellogg RV Park

MOUNT PLEASANT
Crossroads RV Park

OELWEIN
Lakeshore RV Resort & Campground

ONAWA
On-Ur-Wa RV Park

OXFORD
Beyonder Getaway at Sleepy Hollow

TIPTON
Cedar River Campground (formerly Hunt's)

URBANA
Lazy Acres RV Park

WAUKEE
Timberline Campground

Getty Images/iStockphoto

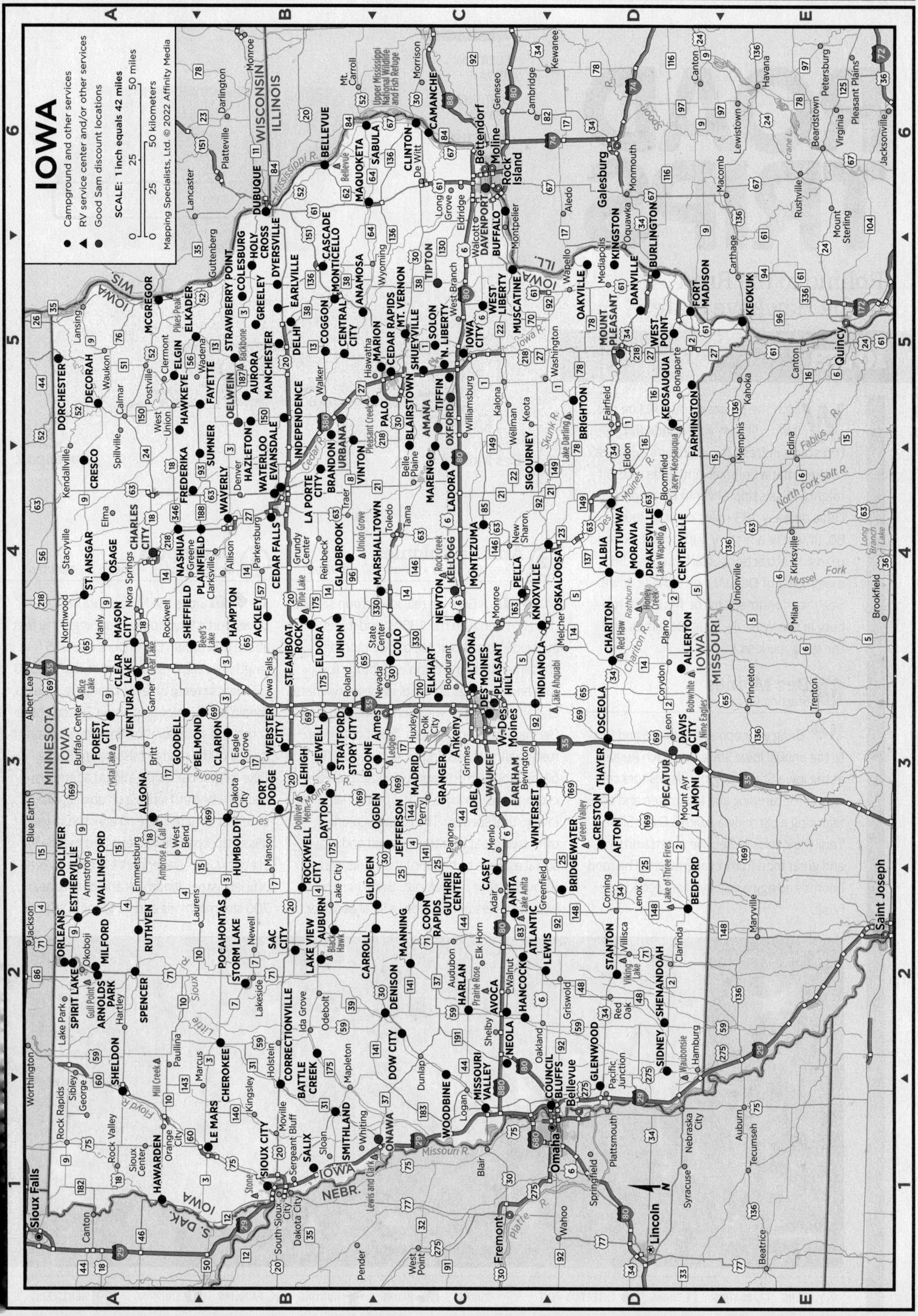
IOWA
Campground and other services
RV service center and/or other services
Good Sam discount locations
SCALE: 1 inch equals 42 miles
0 25 50 miles
0 25 50 kilometers
Mapping Specialists, Ltd. © 2022 Affinity Media

ROAD TRIPS

Rolling to the River in the Hawkeye State

Iowa

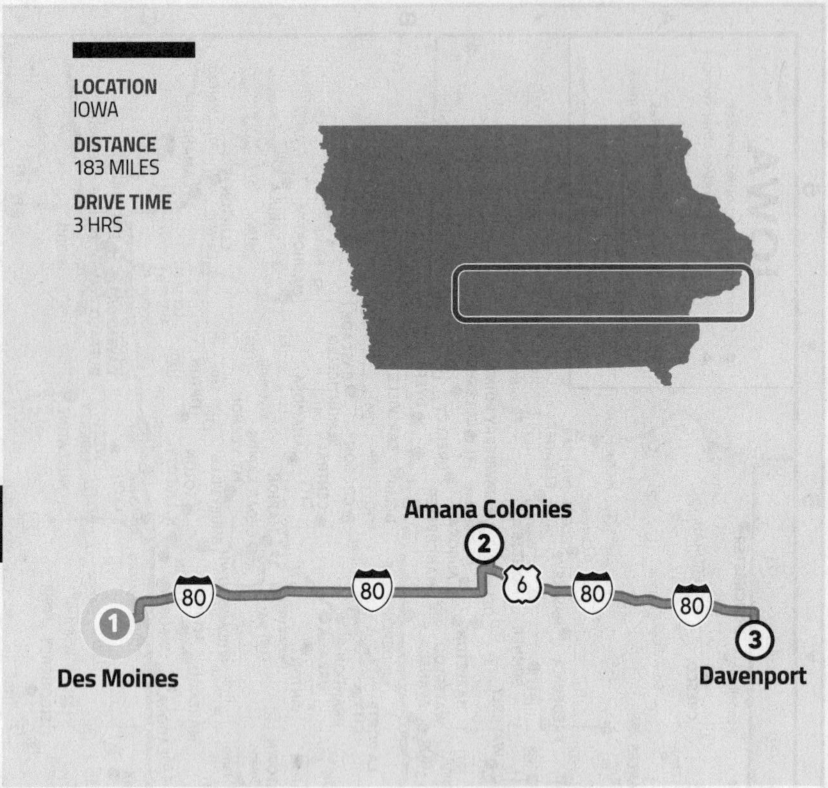

Watch the pastoral countryside of Iowa roll past your window. This trip starts in Des Moines, heads due east to the Amana Colonies and ends at the mighty Mississippi River in Davenport. Drive an easy 183 miles on U.S. Route 80. (If you're a history buff or just like odd roadside attractions, start your trip 55 miles west of Des Moines in Adair, Iowa. See the monument to the first train robbery in the West — by Jesse James and the gang, no less.)

1 Des Moines
Starting Point

Bring your appetite for food and fun to the annual Iowa State Fair. Each August at the Iowa State Fairgrounds, visitors can expect RV camping and lots to see and do, featuring a big midway with a Giant Slide, Thrill Park, tons of free live entertainment and great food from local growers. The food booths and aggie displays are second to none.

2 Amana Colonies
Drive 104 miles ▪ 1 hour, 37 minutes

A German religious group settled this community in the 1800s, and it has evolved into a showcase of outstanding craftsmanship. The colonies' historic furniture and buildings are on display everywhere and are celebrated with numerous authentic German-themed festivals. Traditional inns, restaurants, shops and foods abound. Go biking around the beautiful landscape. Bicycling's easy in Iowa — it's pretty flat with lovely rural scenery. The Amana Colonies offer two great bike trails: paved and gravel surfaces. Spin by historic landmarks and through native hardwoods. Bring your own two-wheelers or rent from a local outfitter.

3 Davenport
Drive 79 miles ▪ 1 hour, 23 minutes

Cross the Mississippi in style. Davenport's Skybridge is dazzling. Fifty feet above downtown Davenport, and 575 feet in length, the cable-stayed footbridge's 8,000 LED lights create an ever-changing, kaleidoscopic, multi-color light show. Pause at the south end's observation deck for a panoramic view of the mighty Mississippi. Bonus: Take a riverboat cruise aboard a famous paddle wheeler. Here's a unique chance to take a romantic ride on a Victorian-era Mississippi paddle wheeler and maybe win big bucks, too. Davenport's President is an official historic landmark and boasts nearly 700 slot machines and 32 gaming tables.

Getty Images/iStockphoto

BIKING BOATING DINING ENTERTAINMENT FISHING HIKING HUNTING PADDLING SHOPPING SIGHTSEEING

Iowa SPOTLIGHTS

Come Home to Midwest Bounty

The Hawkeye State brims with Midwestern treasures. The annual state fair in Des Moines showcases the region's agricultural bounty, while the community of Amana Colonies is a treasure-trove of handcrafted goods. Don't leave without taking a paddleboat ride on the Mississippi River.

THE AMANA COLONIES ARE COMPOSED OF SEVEN VILLAGES.

Fall decorations adorn a house in the historic Amana Colonies in eastern Iowa.

Smallbones

Amana Colonies

Willkommen to the Amana Colonies, one of the oldest communal religious societies in America. Originally called the "Community of True Inspiration," the Colonies are made up of seven distinct villages and designated as a National Historic Landmark in 1965. Take a cell-phone driving tour that highlights history, culture and the special ambience of each community or enjoy an app-guided walking tour of Amana, the largest town in the Colonies. The Village Voyage Driving Tour provides well-versed guides at four historical sites.

Handcrafted Goods

"Handcrafted" is the watchword in this community, whether it's wooden furniture, woolen blankets or delightful German foods. Famous "Sampling Tours" allow visitors to partake in authentic family-style lunches served in Amana's only remaining communal kitchen.

Super Store

History whispers down brick and stone streets as centuries-old clapboard homes grace one of Iowa's top historical attractions. Step into the past at the High Amana General Store, still boasting its original tin ceiling, wooden floor and glass-topped display cases from 1857. This authentic shop is stocked with quaint items, and games that will bring the past to life.

House of Worship

Breathe in the tranquil atmosphere of Amana Homestead Church. Built in 1865, worshippers sit on simple wooden benches in a sanctuary infused with tranquility. The Amana religion is a combination of simplicity, spirited worship and time spent in silent reflection, and visitors are invited to attend services.

Hiking the Heartland

Three hiking and biking trails snake across the pastoral prairie into timbered forests and along the scenic Iowa River Valley. Traverse from Amana to Middle Amana by the Kolonieweg Recreational Trail, ambling along the Millrace Canal. Prehistoric Native American mounds vie for attention along the Amana Colonies Nature Trail near Homestead. The bluff overlook showcases breathtaking views of the valley below. Take a spin along Amana Colonies Gravel Bike Route and roll from the leafy shade of hardwood forests into bucolic open fields.

A Slice of Germany

The Amana Colonies are known for authentic German food served in the comfortable ambiance of the last communal dining room in the region. These one-of-a-kind dining feasts are served in the "Rüdy Küche" (Ruedy Kitchen) located in the Communal Kitchen and Cooper Shop, preserved as it was the day it closed in 1932. The Communal Kitchen Museum supplies historical context by explaining how "kitchen bosses" organized the feeding of 40 people in 50 communal kitchens scattered throughout the villages five times each day.

More Shopping

Throughout the area, there's everything from clock shops, broom and basket stores, and German furniture makers to tempt you.

IA

LOCAL FAVORITE

Campfire Corn Dogs

Ask an Iowan what their favorite summer food is and they'll say it's sweet corn. Enjoy it on the cob or go for its tasty cousin, the corn dog. *Recipe by Jennifer Maitland.*

INGREDIENTS

- ☐ 1 pack Pillsbury corn bread swirls
- ☐ 6 hot dogs
- ☐ Honey mustard sauce
- ☐ Campfire cooking sticks

DIRECTIONS

Place your hot dog on a cooking stick and wrap a corn bread swirl around it. Cook over a low flame until your corn bread is puffy and slightly browned. Dip in honey mustard or your favorite dipping sauce. Serves 6.

SPOTLIGHTS

Snuggle up with an Amana woolen blanket or comfy cotton throw from the Amana Woolen Mill, Iowa's only operating woolen mill, and the oldest business in the Colonies. Learn how baskets are made at the Philip Dickel Basket Museum or mosey over to the Mini-Americana Barn Museum with the largest known collection of 1/12 scale miniatures. Looking for a rollicking selfie? Take a seat in the World's Largest Indoor Rocking Chair, standing 11 feet tall.

Oktober Surprise

Oktoberfest is the largest Deutsch celebration in the Amana Colonies. Experience Bavarian-style hospitality as you pull on lederhosen or a dirndl, and sing along with the German folk songs or dance a lively polka. Tuck into steaming brats with all the trimmings while quaffing excellent German beers. There's even an official keg tapping ceremony on Friday evening.

Des Moines

You'll find a host of family-friendly attractions in the state capital. As you drive across town, you might catch a glimpse of a golden dome glittering in the sun from Iowa's gold-capped capitol. Downtown's Pappajohn Sculpture Park is an interesting place to explore, with its massive artworks displayed against a backdrop of the city's skyline. Hit the Downtown Farmers Market to sample some amazing cuisine and take home locally grown produce.

The Iowa Woman of Achievement Bridge crosses the Des Moines River with the capital skyline in the distance.

History Comes Alive

A trip through Iowa wouldn't be complete without visiting Living History Farms just outside of Des Moines. This 500-acre estate is an interactive museum with working Indian and pioneer farms and re-enactments of prairie life. Head back into Des Moines for a visit to the eye-catching capitol, the epicenter of state politics and first stop on many presidential campaigns. The guided tours are excellent and, if you're brave enough, you'll have the chance to climb the narrow, winding steps to the top of the building's dome.

Okoboji

In the northwest of Iowa, a chain of beautiful, glacier-carved lakes constitutes the Okoboji region. Known as the Iowa Great Lakes, these waterways offer 12,000 acres of natural fun. Find a quiet cove and toss in a line. You'll likely snag some walleye, bass or crappie. A number of state parks can be found in the region, offering beaches, boating, hiking trails and an abundance of recreational opportunities.

Walking Around Okoboji

Lace-up those hiking boots and set out on a trail. The Iowa Great Lakes Trail network winds its way around the stunning blue waterways and through grassy prairies, allowing you to experience Iowa's great outdoors on foot or on wheels. Several resort communities dot the region, hearkening back to earlier days of small mom-and-pop stores and friendly diners serving Midwestern blue-plate specials.

▸ FOR MORE INFORMATION

Iowa Tourism Office, 800-345-4692, www.traveliowa.com

Amana Colonies Visitors Center, 319-622-7622, www.amanacolonies.com

Catch Des Moines, 800-451-2625, www.catchdesmoines.com

Vacation Okoboji, 800-270-2574, www.vacationokoboji.com

Iowa

ACKLEY — B4 *Franklin*

PRAIRIE BRIDGES PARK (Public) From Jct of St Hwy 20 & SR-S-56, N 0.2 mi on SR-S-56 (L). 120 Avail: 30 W, 120 E (30/50 amps). 2021 rates: $10 to $15. Apr 01 to Nov 01. (641)485-1623

ADEL — C3 *Dallas*

DALLAS COUNTY FAIR CAMPGROUNDS (Public) From jct I-80 (exit 110) & US 169: Go 5 mi N on US 169. 80 Avail: 30 full hkups, 50 W, 50 E (20/50 amps). 2021 rates: $15 to $20. Apr 01 to Nov 01. (515)993-3728

DES MOINES WEST KOA **Ratings: 9/10★/9.5** (RV Park) Avail: 77 full hkups (30/50 amps). 2021 rates: $60.89 to $97.64. Apr 01 to Oct 31. (515)834-2729, 34308 L Ave, Adel, IA 50003

AFTON — D3 *Union*

THREE MILE REC AREA (UNION COUNTY PARK) (Public) From town, N 3 mi on Creamery Rd to 150th St, W 0.5 mi (L). Avail: 80 E (30/50 amps). 2021 rates: $10 to $17. (641)347-5100

ALBIA — D4 *Monroe*

LAKE MIAMI PARK (MONROE COUNTY PARK) (Public) From town, N 2 mi on Hwy 5 to cnty rd, E 0.25 mi, follow signs (R). 43 Avail: 16 full hkups, 27 E (30/50 amps). 2021 rates: $11 to $16. Apr 01 to Nov 01. (641)946-8112

ALGONA — A3 *Kossuth*

AMBROSE A CALL (Public State Park) From Jct of US-169 & Call Park Dr, W 2 mi on Call Park Dr (L). Avail: 13 E (30 amps), Pit toilets. 2021 rates: $9 to $16. Apr 01 to Nov 01. (641)581-4835

SMITH LAKE PARK (KOSSUTH COUNTY PARK) (Public) From Jct of US-18 & US-169, N 3 mi on US-169 (L). 65 Avail: 16 full hkups, 49 E (20/50 amps). 2021 rates: $15 to $18. Apr 15 to Oct 31. (515)295-2138

ALLERTON — D3 *Wayne*

BOBWHITE
(Public State Park) From Jct Hwy 40 & Main St (CR J46): Go 1-1/2 mi W on CR J46. **FAC:** paved rds. Avail: 30 dirt, 30 E tent sites, **REC:** Bobwhite Lake: swim, fishing, kayaking/canoeing. Pets OK. 2021 rates: $10. Apr 01 to Dec 01. no cc.
(641)873-4670 Lat: 40.710194, Lon: -93.394306
2303 Bobwhite Rd, Allerton, IA 50008
www.mycountyparks.com

ALTOONA — C3 *Polk*

ADVENTURELAND CAMPGROUND **Ratings: 9/8★/9** (RV Park) Avail: 25 full hkups (15/30 amps). 2021 rates: $35 to $45. Apr 01 to Oct 31. (800)532-1286, 2600 Adventureland Dr , Altoona, IA 50009

GRIFF'S VALLEY VIEW RV PARK
Ratings: 7.5/10★/9.5 (RV Park) From jct I-35 (exit 89) & Corporate Woods: Go 2-3/4 mi E on Corporate Woods Dr, then 1/4 mi N on NE 46th St. (Office located off property at 5200 NE 62nd Ave.) (L). **FAC:** paved rds. Avail: 142 paved, 21 pull-thrus, (40x70), back-ins (40x60), accepts full hkup units only, 142 full hkups (30/50 amps), laundry, LP gas. **REC:** pond, fishing, playground. Pets OK. Partial handicap access. No tents. Big rig sites. 2021 rates: $30.
(515)967-5474 Lat: 41.67717, Lon: -93.52214
6429 NE 46th St, Altoona, IA 50009
www.griffsrv.com
See ad this page

AMANA — C5 *Iowa*

A SPOTLIGHT Introducing the Amana Colonies' colorful attractions appearing at the front of this state section.

AMANA RV PARK & EVENT CENTER
good sam park
Ratings: 7.5/9★/8.5 (Public) From jct of I-80 & US 151 (Exit 225), N 9.9 mi on US 151 to C St, W 0.5 mi (L). **FAC:** gravel rds. (450 spaces). 425 Avail: 230 gravel, 195 grass, 100 pull-thrus, (30x75), back-ins (24x75), 230 full hkups, 195 W, 195 E (30/50 amps), seasonal sites, WiFi @ sites, tent sites, dump, laundry, LP gas, fire rings, firewood. **REC:** playground. Pets OK. Partial handicap access. Big rig sites. 2021 rates: $36 to $39. Apr 01 to Oct 31.
(319)622-7616 Lat: 41.81396, Lon: -91.87819
3850 C St, Amana, IA 52203
amanarvpark.com
See ad opposite page

You have high expectations, so we point out campgrounds, service centers and tourist attractions with elevations over 2,500 feet.

Things to See and Do

AMANA COLONIES CONVENTION & VISITORS BUREAU Located in a restored corn crib, the visitor center provides information about the Amana Colonies; Visitors Guides, maps and brochures for area businesses, including menus for local restaurants. RV accessible. Restrooms. Hours: 9am to 5pm. No CC.
(800)579-2294 Lat: 41.79990, Lon: -91.86796
622 46th Ave, Amana, IA 52203
amanacolonies.com
See ad opposite page

ANAMOSA — B5 *Jones*

WAPSIPINICON (Public State Park) From town, S 0.5 mi Elm St. Avail: 13 E (20/30 amps). 2021 rates: $6 to $16. (319)462-2761

ANITA — C2 *Cass*

LAKE ANITA (Public State Park) From Jct of I-80 & SR-148 (exit 70), S 4.5 mi on SR-148 (R). 161 Avail: 40 full hkups, 52 E (20 amps). 2021 rates: $6 to $19. (712)762-3564

ARNOLDS PARK — A2 *Dickinson*

ARNOLDS PARK CITY CAMPGROUND (Public) From Jct of US-71 & Broadway, E on Broadway, to Rohr St (R). 15 Avail: 3 W, 15 E (30 amps). 2021 rates: $25 to $50. May 15 to Sep 01. (712)332-2341

ATLANTIC — C2 *Cass*

CASS COUNTY FAIRGROUNDS CAMPGROUND (Public) From I 80 & US 71/US 6 (Exit 60): Go 6-1/4 mi S on US 71/US 6, then 5 mi W on US 6. Avail: 26 E (30 amps). 2021 rates: $20. Apr 01 to Nov 01. (712)254-3203

AUBURN — B2 *Sac*

GRANT PARK (SAC COUNTY PARK) (Public) From jct US-71 & Hwy-175: Go W on US-71/Hwy-175, then 1/2 mi N on CR-D54, then 1/4 mi W. 20 Avail: 9 full hkups, 11 W, 11 E (30/50 amps). 2021 rates: $12 to $17. May 01 to Oct 15. (712)662-4530

AURORA — B5 *Buchanan*

JAKWAY AREA (BUCHANAN COUNTY PARK) (Public) From town: Go 1-1/2 mi S on CR W45. Avail: 40 E (30 amps). 2021 rates: $10 to $15. Apr 15 to Oct 01. (319)636-3378

AVOCA — C2 *Pottawattamie*

POTTAWATTAMIE COUNTY FAIR CAMPGROUND (Public) From jct I-80 (exit 40) & US 59: Go 1-3/4 mi S on US 59, then 200 yds W on West Lincoln. 334 Avail: 34 full hkups, 300 E (30/50 amps). 2021 rates: $20. (712)307-0509

BATTLE CREEK — B2 *Ida*

CRAWFORD CREEK REC AREA (IDA COUNTY PARKS) (Public) From Jct of Hwy 175 & CR-L51, S 3.3 mi on CR-L51 (R). Avail: 37 E (30/50 amps). 2021 rates: $12 to $18. Apr 01 to Oct 31. (712)364-3300

BEDFORD — D2 *Taylor*

LAKE OF THREE FIRES (Public State Park) From Jct of Hwy 2 & Hwy 49, NE 4 mi on Hwy 49 (L). Avail: 30 E (50 amps). 2021 rates: $6 to $16. (712)523-2700

County names help you follow the local weather report.

BELLEVUE — B6 *Dubuque*

BELLEVUE (Public State Park) From Jct of US-52 & Hwy 62, S 2.5 mi on US-52 (R). Avail: 31 E (30 amps). 2021 rates: $6 to $19. Apr 01 to Oct 31. (563)872-4019

MISSISSIPPI RIVER - COE/PLEASANT CREEK (Public Corps) From town, S 3 mi on US-52, follow signs (L). 55 Avail: Pit toilets. 2021 rates: $12. May 15 to Oct 15. (563)872-5782

OFFSHORE RV PARK **Ratings: 7.5/8.5★/8** (RV Park) Avail: 15 full hkups (30/50 amps). 2021 rates: $69 to $79. Apr 01 to Oct 31. (563)872-5000, 4115 North Riverview St, Bellevue, IA 52031

SPRUCE CREEK PARK (JACKSON COUNTY PARK) (Public) From town, N 2.5 mi on US-52 to 395th Ave, E 0.75 mi (R). Avail: 86 E (30/50 amps). 2021 rates: $17 to $20. Apr 01 to Oct 31. (563)652-3783

BELMOND — B3 *Wright*

IOWA RIVER RV PARK (Public) From Jct of US-69 & Main St, S 3 blks on Main St (R). 16 Avail: 8 full hkups, 8 W, 8 E (30 amps). 2021 rates: $10 to $12. Apr 15 to Oct 15. (641)444-3498

BLAIRSTOWN — C4 *Benton*

HANNEN PARK (BENTON COUNTY PARK) (Public) From town: Go 1 mi S on CR-V56, then 3 mi SE on blacktop road. Avail: 83 E (30 amps). 2021 rates: $10 to $16. (319)560-9804

BOONE — C3 *Boone*

LEDGES (Public State Park) From Jct of SR-30 & SR-17, S 2.8 mi on SR-17 to 250th St, W 3.1 mi (R). Avail: 40 E (30 amps). 2021 rates: $6 to $11. (515)432-1852

BRANDON — B5 *Buchanan*

LIME CREEK AREA (BUCHANAN COUNTY PARK) (Public) From jct Hwy 150 & Hwy 283: Go 5 mi W on Hwy 283, then 1-1/2 mi NE on CR W17. Avail: 20 E (20 amps), Pit toilets. 2021 rates: $8 to $14. Apr 15 to Oct 01. (319)636-2617

Iowa Privately Owned Campground Information Updated by our Good Sam Representatives

Randy & Debbie Block

We come from different places: Randy is from Missouri Valley, Iowa, home of the World Championship Goose Calling contest; Debbie is from Greenwood, SC, home to the World's Widest Main Street. We are living the greatest lifestyle ever.

IA

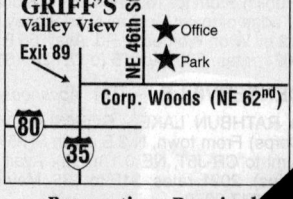

BRIDGEWATER — D2 *Adair*

MORMON TRAIL PARK (ADAIR COUNTY PARK) (Public) From jct CR N51 & Hwy 92: Go 1 mi E on Hwy 92, then 1-1/2 mi S on gravel road. Avail: 15 E Pit toilets. 2021 rates: $6 to $9. (641)743-6450

BRIGHTON — D5 *Washington*

LAKE DARLING (Public State Park) From W-end of town, W 3 mi on SR-78/1 (R). 80 Avail: 15 full hkups, 51 E (30 amps). 2021 rates: $6 to $19. (319)694-2323

BUFFALO — C6 *Scott*

BUFFALO SHORES CAMPGROUND (Public) From Davenport, W 4 mi on Hwy 22 (L). 65 Avail: 65 W, 65 E (50 amps). 2021 rates: $20 to $23. (563)328-3280

BURLINGTON — D5 *Des Moines*

BURLINGTON See also Mount Pleasant.

WELTER RECREATION AREA (DES MOINES COUNTY PARK) (Public) 7 mi S of Burlington on Hwy 61, turn west/northwest onto Skunk River Rd. Avail: 12 E Pit toilets. 2021 rates: $8 to $15. (319)753-8260

CAMANCHE — C6 *Clinton*

ROCK CREEK MARINA & CAMPGROUND (CLINTON COUNTY PARK) (Public) From jct I-80 (exit 306) & US 67: Go 14 mi N on US 67, then 1 mi E on 291st St (gravel road). 77 Avail. 2021 rates: $14 to $25. (563)259-1876

CARROLL — C2 *Carroll*

SWAN LAKE (Public State Park) From Jct of US-30 & US-71, S 2.7 mi on US-71 to 220th St., E 1.4 mi. 175 Avail: 46 full hkups, 100 W, 125 E (30 amps). 2021 rates: $16 to $19. Apr 15 to Oct 31. (712)792-4614

CASCADE — B5 *Dubuque*

FILLMORE REC AREA (DUBUQUE COUNTY PARK) (Public) From town: Go 5 mi E on Hwy 151. Avail: 4 E (30 amps). 2021 rates: $12 to $18. (563)852-7105

CASEY — C2 *Guthrie*

CASEY CITY PARK (Public) From jct Hwy-25 & I-80: Go 2 mi W on I-80. Avail: 25 E (20 amps). 2021 rates: $10. May 01 to Oct 01. (641)746-3315

CEDAR FALLS — B4 *Black Hawk*

BLACK HAWK PARK (BLACK HAWK COUNTY PARK) (Public) From Jct of US-218 & SR-58, N 1.3 mi on US-218 to E Lone Tree Rd, W 2.3 mi (E). 197 Avail: 21 full hkups, 176 E (30/50 amps). 2021 rates: $13 to $30. (319)433-7275

GEORGE WYTH MEMORIAL (Public State Park) From Jct of Hwys 20 & 218, N 9.8 mi on Hwy 218 to George Wyth Park exit (L). Avail: 46 E (30/50 amps). 2021 rates: $6 to $16. Apr 15 to Oct 15. (319)232-5505

Travel Services

CAMPING WORLD OF CEDAR FALLS As the nation's largest retailer of RV supplies, accessories, services and new and used RVs, Camping World is committed to making your total RV experience better. **SERVICES:** RV appliance, MH mechanical, staffed RV wash, restrooms. RV Sales. RV supplies, LP gas, dump, RV accessible. Hours: 9am - 7pm.
(888)833-3901 Lat: 42.467568, Lon: -92.44390
7805 Ace Place, Cedar Falls, IA 50613
www.campingworld.com

CEDAR RAPIDS — C5 *Linn*

CEDAR RAPIDS See also Amana, Marengo, Oxford & Urbana.

MORGAN CREEK PARK (LINN COUNTY PARK) (Public) From jct 16th Ave SW & Stoney Point Rd at W edge of town: Go 2 mi N on Stoney Point Rd, then 1/2 mi W on Worcester Rd. Avail: 36 E (30/50 amps). 2021 rates: $20. Apr 15 to Oct 25. (319)892-6450

— **D4** *Appanoose*

E - COE/ISLAND VIEW (Public ... N 2.5 mi on SR-5 to CR-29, NW ... 0.1 mi (L). Avail: 187 E (30/50 ... $18 to $36. May 01 to Sep 30.

- COE/ROLLING COVE (Public ... V on Hwy 2 to CR-T14, N 6 mi ... to 150 Ave, N 2.5 mi to 435 St, ... E). 45 Avail. May 19 to Sep 02.

CENTRAL CITY — B5 *Linn*

PINICON RIDGE PARK (LINN COUNTY PARK) (Public) From town: Go 1 mi N on Hwy 13, then 1/4 mi W on county road. 119 Avail: 75 W, 95 E (30/50 amps). 2021 rates: $19. Apr 15 to Oct 15. (319)892-6450

CHARITON — D3 *Lucas*

RED HAW LAKE (Public State Park) From Jct of SR-14 & US-34, E 1 mi on US-34 (R). Avail: 62 E (30/50 amps). 2021 rates: $6 to $16. (641)774-5632

CHARLES CITY — A4 *Floyd*

R CAMPGROUND
Ratings: 7/8.5★/7 (Campground) 62 Avail: 54 full hkups, 8 W, 8 E (30/50 amps). 2021 rates: $26 to $32. (641)257-0549, 1910 Clark St, Charles City, IA 50616

CHEROKEE — B2 *Cherokee*

KOSER SPRING LAKE PARK (Public) From Jct of Hwy 59 & Hwy 3, S 3 mi on Hwy 59 to campground, 0.05 mi S of Little Sioux River Bridge (L). Avail: 48 full hkups (30/50 amps). 2021 rates: $15. Apr 15 to Nov 15. (712)225-2715

CLARION — B3 *Wright*

LAKE CORNELIA (Public) From town, E 1 mi on Hwy 3 to CR-R45, N 5 mi (R). 70 Avail: 13 full hkups, 57 E (20/50 amps). 2021 rates: $17 to $22. Apr 15 to Oct 15. (515)532-3185

CLEAR LAKE — A3 *Cerro Gordo*

CLEAR LAKE (Public State Park) From Jct of I-35 & Hwy 106 (exit 193), W 1 mi on Hwy 106 to S 8th St, S 1.4 mi to 27th Ave, W 0.5 mi to B35, S 100 ft (R). 177 Avail: 8 full hkups, 161 E (50 amps). 2021 rates: $6 to $19. (641)357-4212

OAKWOOD RV PARK **Ratings: 7/7.5/7** (RV Park) Avail: 68 full hkups (30/50 amps). 2021 rates: $35. Apr 15 to Oct 15. (641)357-4019, 5419 240th St, Clear Lake, IA 50428

CLINTON — C6 *Clinton*

MISSISSIPPI RIVER - COE/BULGER'S HOLLOW REC AREA (Public Corps) From town, N 3 mi on Hwy 67 (R). 17 Avail: Pit toilets. 2021 rates: $12. May 15 to Oct 15. (815)259-3628

COGGON — B5 *Linn*

BUFFALO CREEK PARK-WALNUT GROVE CAMPGROUND (LINN COUNTY PARK) (Public) From town: Go 1/2 mi W on CR-D62. 13 Avail: 13 W, 13 E (50 amps), Pit toilets. 2021 rates: $17. Apr 15 to Oct 15. (319)892-6450

COLESBURG — B5 *Delaware*

TWIN BRIDGES (DELAWARE COUNTY PARK) (Public) From town: Go 5 mi W on Hwy 3. 15 Avail: 10 W, 15 E Pit toilets. 2021 rates: $15 to $17. May 01 to Nov 01. (563)927-3410

COLO — C3 *Story*

HICKORY GROVE PARK (STORY COUNTY PARK) (Public) From town, W 2 mi on US-30 to 680th Ave, S 1 mi on county rd, continues W 0.5 mi (L). Avail: 43 E (30/50 amps). 2021 rates: $17. Apr 01 to Oct 31. (515)232-2516

COON RAPIDS — C2 *Carroll*

RIVERSIDE PARK (CARROLL COUNTY PARK) (Public) From jct SR 141 & 330th St: Go 1 mi E on 330th, then 1/2 mi N on Walnut St. 20 Avail: 20 W, 20 E. 2021 rates: $14. Apr 15 to Oct 15. (712)792-4614

CORRECTIONVILLE — B2 *Woodbury*

LITTLE SIOUX PARK (WOODBURY COUNTY PARK) (Public) From Jct of US-20 & SR-31, S 2 mi on SR-31 (L). 194 Avail: 53 W, 148 E (30 amps). 2021 rates: $15 to $18. May 01 to Oct 31. (712)372-4984

COUNCIL BLUFFS — D1 *Douglas*

BLUFFS RUN RV PARK **Ratings: 5.5/9★/3.5** (RV Park) 44 Avail: 44 W, 44 E (30/50 amps). 2021 rates: $40 to $50. May 01 to Oct 31. (712)396-3715, 2701 23rd Ave, Council Bluffs, IA 51501

LAKE MANAWA (Public State Park) From Jct of I-80 & exit 3, S 1 mi on S Expwy to Hwy 275 & 92, W 1 mi to S 11th St; or From Jct of I-29 & exit 47 to W Hwy 92/275, W 1.5 mi to S 11th St, S 2 blks, follow signs (E). Avail: 37 E (30 amps). 2021 rates: $6 to $16. (712)366-0220

JOIN GoodSamRoadside.com

Travel Services

CAMPING WORLD OF COUNCIL BLUFFS/ OMAHA As the nation's largest retailer of RV supplies, accessories, services and new and used RVs, Camping World is committed to making your total RV experience better. **SERVICES:** tire, RV appliance, MH mechanical, restrooms. RV Sales. RV supplies, LP gas, RV accessible. Hours: 9am to 7pm.
(888)896-9850 Lat: 41.233661, Lon: -95.87493
2802 South 21st Street, Council Bluffs, IA 51501
www.campingworld.com

CRESCO — A4 *Winneshiek*

HARVEST FARM CAMPGROUND **Ratings: 7/9.5★/9.5** (Campground) 60 Avail: 32 W, 60 E (30 amps). 2021 rates: $38. Apr 01 to Oct 31. (563)883-8562, 3690 318th Ave, Cresco, IA 52136

CRESTON — D3 *Adair*

GREEN VALLEY (Public State Park) From Jct. of SH25 & Howard St., N .7 mi to W Townline Dr., W .7 mi to Cottonwood Rd. (L). 100 Avail: 18 full hkups, 82 E (30 amps). 2021 rates: $11 to $19. Apr 15 to Nov 01. (641)782-5131

MCKINLEY PARK (Public) From jct SH-25 & W Adams St., W .5 mi (L). 38 Avail: 38 W, 38 E (30 amps). 2021 rates: $12 to $14. May 15 to Oct 15. (641)782-8220

DANVILLE — D5 *Henry*

GEODE (Public State Park) From town: Go 2-1/2 mi S on Main St, then 3 mi W on SR-79 (E). Avail: 87 E (30 amps). 2021 rates: $6 to $16. (319)392-4601

DAVENPORT — C6 *Scott*

DAVENPORT See also Geneseo, Joslin & Rock Island, IL.

INTERSTATE RV PARK
Ratings: 10/9.5★/9 (Campground) From Jct of I-80 & SR-130 (Exit 292), NW 0.6 mi on SR-130 to Fairmount St, W 0.1 mi (R).

INTERSTATE RV PARK IN DAVENPORT, IA
Visit all the excitement of the Quad City Area! 3 Casinos, 25 Golf Courses, Excursion/Dinner Riverboat Cruises, John Deere Commons Pavilion, Historic Shopping, many museums and theaters.
FAC: all weather rds. (100 spaces). Avail: 56 all weather, patios, 49 pull-thrus, (24x75), back-ins (22x50), 49 full hkups, 7 W, 7 E (30/50 amps), seasonal sites, WiFi @ sites, dump, laundry, groc, fire rings. **REC:** pool, playground. Pet restrict (B). No tents. Big rig sites. 2021 rates: $47 to $52, Military discount.
(563)386-7292 Lat: 41.60589, Lon: -90.63126
8448 N. Fairmount St, Davenport, IA 52806
iowarvpark.com
See ad opposite page

MISSISSIPPI RIVER - POOLS 11-22 - COE/ CLARKS FERRY (Public Corps) From Davenport, W on Hwy 22 15 mi to Clark's Ferry sign (in Montpelier). Avail: 44 E (50 amps). 2021 rates: $20. May 01 to Oct 27. (563)419-7594

SCOTT COUNTY PARK (Public) From Davenport, N 9 mi on Hwy 61, to Exit 129 (R). 398 Avail: 48 W, 85 E (30 amps). 2021 rates: $13 to $21. Apr 15 to Oct 15. (563)328-3282

WEST LAKE PARK (Public) From Jct of I-280 & US-61, W 0.8 mi on US-61 to CR Y-48, N 1 mi (R). 127 Avail: 74 full hkups, 53 W, 53 E (30 amps). 2021 rates: $13 to $21. Apr 15 to Oct 15. (563)328-3280

Travel Services

CAMPING WORLD OF DAVENPORT As the nation's largest retailer of RV supplies, accessories, services and new and used RVs, Camping World is committed to making your total RV experience better. **SERVICES:** RV appliance, MH mechanical, sells outdoor gear, restrooms. RV Sales. RV supplies, LP gas, emergency parking, RV accessible. Hours: 9am to 7pm.
(888)445-6159 Lat: 41.509973, Lon: -90.690125
14040 110th Ave, Davenport, IA 52804
www.campingworld.com

DAVIS CITY — D3 *Decatur*

NINE EAGLES (Public State Park) From Jct of US-69 & CR-J66, SE 6 mi on CR-J66 (L). Avail: 27 E (50 amps). 2021 rates: $6 to $16. (641)442-2855

Making campground reservations? Remember to ask about the cancellation policy when making your reservation.

DAYTON — B3 *Hamilton*

OAK PARK (Public) From town, S 0.4 mi of town center on Hwy 175 (R). 44 Avail: 20 W, 40 E (20 amps). 2021 rates: $12. Apr 01 to Sep 30. (515)547-2711

DECATUR — D3 *Decatur*

TED'S RV PARK

good sam park **Ratings: 7/10★/9** (RV Park) Avail: 26 full hkups (30/50 amps). 2021 rates: $30. (641)446-3080, 308 SE Vine Street, Decatur, IA 50067

DECORAH — A5 *Winneshiek*

PULPIT ROCK CAMPGROUND (Public) From Jct of US-52 & SR-9, N 1 mi on US-52 to Pulpit Rock Rd, E 0.25 mi (R). Avail: 75 E (30/50 amps). 2021 rates: $22 to $42. Mar 29 to Nov 03. (563)382-9551

DELHI — B5 *Delaware*

TURTLE CREEK PARK (DELAWARE COUNTY PARK) (Public) From jct US-20 & CR-D-5X: Go 4 mi SE on CR-D-5X, then 4 mi S on CR-X21, then 3 mi E. 28 Avail: 15 W, 24 E. 2021 rates: $10 to $17. (563)927-3410

DENISON — C2 *Crawford*

YELLOW SMOKE PARK (Public) From town, E 1 mi on US-30 to Yellow Smoke Rd, N 0.5 mi (L). 61 Avail: 15 W, 15 E (30 amps). 2021 rates: $16. Apr 15 to Oct 15. (712)263-2748

DES MOINES — C3 *Boone*

DES MOINES See also Adel, Altoona, Earlham, Kellogg, Newton, Osceola, Story City & Waukee.

IOWA STATE FAIR CAMPGROUNDS (Public) From jct I-35/80 & I-235: Go 3-1/2 mi S on I-235, then 1-1/2 mi E on Hwy 163 (University Ave.), then 1/4 mi S on E 30th St (Hwy 46). 3034 Avail: 734 full hkups, 1566 W, 1566 E. 2021 rates: $28 to $30. Jun 01 to Oct 15. (515)262-3111

SAYLORVILLE LAKE - COE/ACORN VALLEY (Public Corps) From town, N 4 mi on Merle Hay Rd to NW Beaver Dr, W 3.7 mi to NW Coryden Dr (at Natl Weather Service bldg), N 0.5 mi (R). 29 Avail: 2 W, 29 E (30/50 amps). 2021 rates: $22. May 01 to Oct 19. (515)276-0429

SAYLORVILLE LAKE - COE/BOB SHETLER REC AREA (Public Corps) From Jct. of I-80 & Hwy 401,N 3.5 mi on Hwy 401, N 2 mi to Beaver Dr, NW 0.5 mi to 78th Ave, E 0.75 mi (E). Avail: 67 E (30/50 amps). 2021 rates: $20 to $22. May 01 to Sep 29. (515)276-0873

SAYLORVILLE LAKE - COE/CHERRY GLEN (Public Corps) From Jct of I-35 & Hwy 160 (exit 90), W 3 mi on Hwy 160 to Hwy 415, NW 5.5 mi to 94th Ave, W 0.9 mi (E). 125 Avail: 2 S, 123 E (50 amps). 2021 rates: $22 to $26. Apr 15 to Oct 09. (515)964-8792

SAYLORVILLE LAKE - COE/PRAIRIE FLOWER REC AREA (Public Corps) From town, SE 2.5 mi on Hwy 415 (R). Avail: 153 E (30/50 amps). 2021 rates: $18 to $24. May 01 to Oct 21. (515)984-6925

THOMAS MITCHELL PARK (POLK COUNTY PARK) (Public) From Jct of I-35 & I-80, E 5 mi on I-80 to exit 143 to 1st Ave., S 1 mi to 8th St, E 4 mi (R). Avail: 24 E (30/50 amps). 2021 rates: $18 to $23. Apr 01 to Nov 30. (515)967-4889

WALNUT WOODS (Public State Park) From Jct I-35 & 64th Ave, E 0.8 mi to 105th Ave, N 0.7 mi. 22 Avail: 8 full hkups, 13 E (30 amps). 2021 rates: $11 to $17. (515)285-4502

DOLLIVER — A2 *Emmet*

TUTTLE LAKE (Public) From town, N 1.5 mi on N52 to Hwy A13, E 0.4 mi (L). 60 Avail: 60 W, 60 E (30 amps). 2021 rates: $10 to $20. Apr 15 to Nov 15. (712)260-6697

DORCHESTER — A5 *Allamakee*

UPPER IOWA RESORT & RENTAL **Ratings: 6.5/7.5/8** (Campground) 38 Avail: 32 W, 38 E (30/50 amps). 2021 rates: $38. Apr 15 to Oct 15. (563)568-3263, 578 Lonnings Drive, Dorchester, IA 52140

DOW CITY — C2 *Crawford*

NELSON PARK (CRAWFORD COUNTY PARK) (Public) From Jct US-59 & US-30, W 11 mi on US-30 to Nelson Park Rd, NW 4 mi (E). Avail: 60 E (30 amps). 2021 rates: $15 to $18. (712)643-5426

Directional arrows indicate the campground's position in relation to the nearest town.

DRAKESVILLE — D4 *Appanoose*

LAKE WAPELLO (Public State Park) From Jct of US-63 & Hwy 273, W 8 mi on Hwy 273, NW 2.2 mi on Eagle Blvd (L). Avail: 42 E (30 amps). 2021 rates: $6 to $16. (641)722-3371

DUBUQUE — B6 *Dubuque*

FINLEY'S LANDING (DUBUQUE COUNTY PARK) (Public) From town, NW 5.3 mi on Hwy 3, NW 6 mi. Sherrill Rd., N 3.2 mi Finley's Landing Rd. 42 Avail: 24 W, 24 E (20/30 amps). 2021 rates: $12 to $18. Apr 15 to Nov 01. (563)556-6745

MASSEY PARK (DUBUQUE COUNTY PARK) (Public) From town: Go 4 mi SE on US 52, then 7 mi E on Massey Station Rd. 60 Avail: 42 W, 46 E (30 amps). 2021 rates: $23. (563)556-3416

MUD LAKE PARK (DUBUQUE COUNTY PARK) (Public) From Jct of US-3 & Hwy 52, NW 5 mi on Hwy 52 to Mud Lake access rd, E 3 mi (R). 58 Avail: 18 W, 26 E (20/30 amps). 2021 rates: $10 to $16. (563)552-2746

SWISS VALLEY PARK (DUBUQUE COUNTY PARK) (Public) From town, W 6 mi on US-20 to Swiss Valley Rd, S 3 mi to Whitetop Rd, N 0.25 mi (L). 86 Avail: 26 W, 60 E (20/30 amps). 2021 rates: $10 to $16. Apr 15 to Oct 15. (563)556-6745

DYERSVILLE — B5 *Dubuque*

NEW WINE PARK (DUBUQUE COUNTY PARK) (Public) From town, N 4 mi on Hwy 136, W at sign on Vaske Rd, then 1 mi to New Wine Rd (E). 36 Avail: 21 W, 26 E (20/30 amps). 2021 rates: $10 to $16. Apr 01 to Nov 30. (563)921-3475

EARLHAM — C3 *Madison*

SHADY BROOK CAMPING & RV ADVENTURES

good sam park **Ratings: 7/8.5★/10** (Campground) 13 Avail: 13 W, 13 E (30/50 amps). 2021 rates: $40 to $45. Apr 01 to Oct 31. (515)238-1998, 36026 Jewel Court, Earlham, IA 50072

The best things happen outdoors. Start your adventure today at GanderOutdoors.com

EARLVILLE — B5 *Delaware*

TRI STATE RACEWAY & RV PARK **Ratings: 5/6/4.5** (Campground) Avail: 86 full hkups (30/50 amps). 2021 rates: $35. Apr 15 to Oct 31. (563)923-2267, 2217 270th Ave, Earlville, IA 52041

ELDORA — B4 *Hardin*

PINE LAKE (Public State Park) From Jct of SR-175 & CR-S56, NE 1 mi on CR-S56 (E). 120 Avail: 2 full hkups, 94 E (50 amps). 2021 rates: $6 to $16. (641)858-5832

ELGIN — A5 *Fayette*

GILBERTSON CONSERVATION EDUCATION AREA (Public) From Jct of US-18 & CR-B64, E 9 mi on CR-B64 (R). Avail: 28 E (30 amps). 2021 rates: $10 to $15. Apr 15 to Nov 15. (563)426-5740

ELKADER — B5 *Clayton*

DEER RUN RESORT **Ratings: 8.5/9.5★/10** (RV Park) Avail: 34 full hkups (30/50 amps). 2021 rates: $49 to $54. Apr 15 to Oct 15. (563)245-3337, 501 High St SE, Elkader, IA 52043

ELKHART — C3 *Polk*

CHICHAQUA BOTTOMS GREENBELT (POLK COUNTY PARK) (Public) From Jct of I-35N & Elkhart exit, E 7.8 mi on 142nd Ave. to NE 72nd, N 1.5 mi (R). Avail: 10 E (30/50 amps). 2021 rates: $18 to $23. Apr 01 to Nov 30. (515)967-2596

ESTHERVILLE — A2 *Emmet*

FORT DEFIANCE (Public State Park) From Jct of Hwys 4 & 9, W 2 mi on Hwy 9 to county rd, S 1 mi (L). Avail: 8 E (20 amps), Pit toilets. 2021 rates: $6 to $14. (712)337-3211

EVANSDALE — B4 *Black Hawk*

DEERWOOD CAMPGROUND & PARK (Public) From jct I-380 (exit 70) & River Forest Rd: Go 1 block N on River Forest Rd, then 1/4 mi W on campground road. Avail: 94 E (30 amps). 2021 rates: $12 to $19. (319)493-0655

Park policies vary. Ask about the cancellation policy when making a reservation.

IA

FARMINGTON — D5 *Van Buren*

INDIAN LAKE PARK (Public) From Jct of Hwys 218 & 2, W 11 mi on Hwy 2 to Hwy 81, S 0.4 mi (L). 30 Avail: 10 full hkups, 20 E (30 amps). 2021 rates: $13 to $18. (319)878-3706

FAYETTE — B5 *Fayette*

VOLGA RIVER SRA (Public State Park) From town: Go 4 mi N on Hwy-150, then 2 mi E on gravel road. 48 Avail: 33 full hkups, 10 E. 2021 rates: $6 to $19. (563)425-4161

FOREST CITY — A3 *Hancock*

PILOT KNOB (Public State Park) From town, E 3.4 mi on Hwy 9 to 205th Ave, S 1 mi (L). 61 Avail: 1 full hkups, 48 E (30 amps). 2021 rates: $6 to $16. (641)581-4835

FORT DODGE — B3 *Webster*

KENNEDY MEMORIAL PARK (WEBSTER COUNTY PARK) (Public) From Jct of Hwys 7 & 169, N 2 mi on Hwy 169 to CR-D14, E 2 mi to CR-P56, N 3 mi (L). 100 Avail: 29 full hkups, 49 E (30/50 amps). 2021 rates: $12 to $20. May 01 to Sep 30. (515)576-4258

FORT MADISON — D5 *Lee*

WILSON LAKE (LEE COUNTY PARK) (Public) From town, E 3.5 mi on Hwy 2 (L). Avail: 15 E (30 amps). 2021 rates: $15 to $20. (319)463-7673

FREDERIKA — A4 *Bremer*

ALCOCK PARK (BREMER COUNTY PARK) (Public) From Jct of US-63 & CR-C16, E 1 mi on CR-C16 to gravel rd, N 0.2 mi (R). Avail: 50 E (20/30 amps). 2021 rates: $9 to $12. May 01 to Oct 31. (319)882-4742

GLADBROOK — B4 *Tama*

UNION GROVE (Public State Park) From Jct of SR-96 & CR-T47, S 4 mi on CR-T47 to 220th St., W 1 mi (R). Avail: 9 full hkups (30/50 amps). 2021 rates: $14. (641)473-2556

GLENWOOD — D1 *Mills*

GLENWOOD LAKE PARK (Public) E edge of town on Hwy 34 (L). 20 Avail: 12 full hkups, 8 W, 8 E (30/50 amps). 2021 rates: $17 to $25. Apr 01 to Oct 24. (712)520-7275

GLIDDEN — C2 *Carroll*

DICKSON TIMBER (CARROLL COUNTY PARK) (Public) From town, E 2 mi on US 30 to Velvet Rd., N 5.2 mi on Velvet Rd. to park access rd, N 1 mi (R). Avail: 20 E (20 amps), Pit toilets. 2021 rates: $10 to $14. Apr 15 to Oct 15. (712)792-4614

RICHEY ACCESS (Public) From jct SR 30 & CR N58: Go 3 mi N on CR N58. Note: maximum RV width is 20'. 13 Avail: 8 W, 8 E (30 amps), Pit toilets. 2021 rates: $10 to $12. Apr 15 to Oct 15. (712)792-4614

GOODELL — A3 *Hancock*

ELDRED SHERWOOD PARK (HANCOCK COUNTY PARK) (Public) From town, E 3 mi on CR-B63 to CR-68, N 2.7 mi (L). Avail: 40 E (30 amps). 2021 rates: $10 to $15. Apr 15 to Oct 15. (641)923-2720

GRANGER — C3 *Polk*

JESTER PARK (POLK COUNTY PARK) (Public) From jct I-80/35 (exit 127) & Hwy 141: Go 7-1/2 mi W on Hwy 141, then 3 mi N on NW 121st St, then 1/2 mi E on NW 118th Ave, then 1/2 mi on NW 128th St. Avail: 80 E. 2021 rates: $15 to $20. Apr 01 to Nov 30. (515)323-5366

GREELEY — B5 *Delaware*

FOUNTAIN SPRINGS (DELAWARE COUNTY PARK) (Public) From town: Go 3 mi NE on gravel county roads, follow signs. 25 Avail: Pit toilets. 2021 rates: $15. Apr 15 to Oct 15. (563)927-3410

GUTHRIE CENTER — C3 *Des Moines*

SPRINGBROOK (Public State Park) From Jct of SR-44 & SR-25, N 7.5 mi on SR-25 to 160 Rd., E 1 mi (L). Avail: 73 E (30/50 amps). 2021 rates: $6 to $16. (641)747-3591

HAMPTON — B4 *Franklin*

BEEDS LAKE (Public State Park) From Jct of SR-3 & CR-S42, N 1.5 mi on Beeds Lake Rd. Avail: 99 E (30/50 amps). 2021 rates: $11 to $19. Apr 01 to Oct 31. (641)456-2047

HANCOCK — C2 *Pottawattamie*

BOTNA BEND PARK (POTTAWATTAMIE COUNTY PARK) (Public) From Jct of I-80 & Hwy 59, S 8 mi on Hwy 59 to Jct Hwy 59 & G-30, W 1.5 mi on G-30 (R). Avail: 57 E (30 amps). 2021 rates: $15. (712)741-5465

HARLAN — C2 *Cass*

PRAIRIE ROSE (Public State Park) From town, E 6 mi on SR-44 to M-47, S 3 mi (R). 88 Avail: 8 full hkups, 69 E (50 amps). 2021 rates: $6 to $16. (712)773-2701

HAWARDEN — A1 *Sioux*

OAK GROVE PARK (SIOUX COUNTY PARK) (Public) From Jct of Hwy 10 & CR-K18, NE 6 mi on CR-K18 (L). Avail: 57 E (30 amps). 2021 rates: $18. May 15 to Oct 15. (712)552-1047

HAWKEYE — A5 *Fayette*

GOULDSBURG PARK (FAYETTE COUNTY PARK) (Public) From town, N 5 mi on W-14 to Sunset Rd, W 0.5 mi (E). Avail: 29 E (20 amps). 2021 rates: $10 to $15. (563)425-3613

HAZLETON — B5 *Buchanan*

FONTANA PARK (BUCHANAN COUNTY PARK) (Public) From jct CR C-57 & Hwy 150: Go 1-1/2 mi SW on Hwy 150. Avail: 54 E. 2021 rates: $12 to $18. Apr 15 to Nov 01. (319)636-2617

MORWOOD CAMPGROUND & RESORT **Ratings: 8.5/8/9** (Campground) 40 Avail: 24 full hkups, 16 W, 16 E (30/50 amps). 2021 rates: $29 to $37. Apr 15 to Oct 15. (319)636-2422, 1865 150th St, Hazleton, IA 50641

HOLY CROSS — B5 *Dubuque*

BANKSTON PARK (DUBUQUE COUNTY PARK) (Public) From town: Go 2 mi E on US 52, then 1-1/2 mi S on Bankston Park Rd. 50 Avail: Pit toilets. 2021 rates: $12 to $18. Apr 01 to Nov 01. (563)556-6745

HUMBOLDT — B3 *Humboldt*

FRANK A GOTCH (Public State Park) From Jct of I-169 & I-3, S 5 mi on I-169 to CR-49, E 1 mi, N 1 mi on CR-49 to Gotch Park Rd (R). 32 Avail: 32 W, 32 E (30/50 amps). 2021 rates: $10 to $15. Apr 01 to Oct 31. (515)332-9017

JOE SHELDON PARK (HUMBOLDT COUNTY PARK) (Public) From Jct of US-169 & Hwy 3, W 2 mi on Hwy 3, follow signs (L). Avail: 43 full hkups (30/50 amps). 2021 rates: $10 to $15. Apr 01 to Oct 31. (515)332-4087

Visit Camping World RV & Outdoors and stock up on accessories and supplies while on the road. Find your nearest location at CampingWorld.com

INDEPENDENCE — B5 *Buchanan*

INDEPENDENCE See also Hazleton, Oelwein, Urbana & Waterloo.

INDEPENDENCE RV PARK & CAMPGROUND (Public) From Jct of US 20 & SR 150 (exit 254), N 0.9 mi to 8th St (across bridge), E 500 ft (R). Avail: 42 full hkups (30/50 amps). 2021 rates: $20.50 to $23. May 01 to Oct 01. (319)440-0472

INDIANOLA — C3 *Warren*

LAKE AHQUABI (Public State Park) From Jct of Hwys 69 & 349, W 1 mi on Hwy 349 to 118th Ave, N 1 mi (L). Avail: 85 E (30 amps). 2021 rates: $6 to $16. May 24 to Sep 02. (515)961-7101

IOWA CITY — C5 *Johnson*

IOWA CITY See also Amana, Oxford, Tipton & West Liberty.

CORALVILLE LAKE - COE/LINDER POINT (Public Corps) From Jct of I-80 & exit 244 (Dubuque St), N 2 mi on Dubuque St to West Overlook Rd, E 1 mi (E). 18 Avail: 8 full hkups, 6 E (30/50 amps). 2021 rates: $16 to $26. May 01 to Oct 30. (319)338-3685

CORALVILLE LAKE - COE/TAILWATER WEST (Public Corps) From I-80 (exit 244): Go 3 mi N, then follow signs 1-1/2 mi E. 20 Avail: 8 full hkups, 12 W, 12 E (50 amps). 2021 rates: $24 to $26. May 01 to Oct 30. (319)338-3543

CORALVILLE LAKE - COE/WEST OVERLOOK (Public Corps) From Jct of I-80 & exit 244, N 2 mi on exit rd to cnty rd, E 1 mi (L). Avail: 89 E (30 amps). 2021 rates: $20. May 01 to Oct 30. (319)338-3685

JEFFERSON — C3 *Boone*

SPRING LAKE PARK (GREENE COUNTY PARK) (Public) From town, E 7 mi on US-30 to S Ave, N 2.5 mi to 195th St, W 0.5 mi (L). Avail: 121 E (30/50 amps). 2021 rates: $10 to $17. (515)386-5674

JEWELL — B3 *Hamilton*

LITTLE WALL LAKE (HAMILTON COUNTY PARK) (Public) From Jct of I-35 & SR-175, W 4 mi on SR-175 to US-69, S 1.5 mi (l). 106 Avail: 53 full hkups, 53 W, 53 E (30/50 amps). 2021 rates: $22 to $25. (515)832-9570

KELLOGG — C4 *Jasper*

KELLOGG RV PARK

good sam park **Ratings: 7.5/9.5★/8** (Campground) From Jct of I-80 & SR-224 (Exit 173), N 0.1 mi on SR-224 (R). Register at Phillips 66 station. **FAC:** all weather rds. Avail: 38 all weather, 38 pull-thrus, (27x85), 38 full hkups (30/50 amps), WiFi @ sites, tent sites, dump, laundry, groc, fire rings, firewood, restaurant. Pets OK. Big rig sites. 2021 rates: $35. ATM.

(641)526-8535 Lat: 41.68493, Lon: -92.90029
1570 Hwy 224 S, Kellogg, IA 50135
kelloggrv.com
See ad this page

ROCK CREEK (Public State Park) From Jct of I-80 & SR-224, N 6 mi on SR-224 to CR-F27, E 3 mi (R). Avail: 98 E (30/50 amps). 2021 rates: $6 to $16. (641)236-3722

Things to See and Do

IOWA'S BEST BURGER CAFE Sit down restaurant serving burgers, BBQ, chicken and sandwiches. RV accessible. Restrooms. Food. Hours: 11am to 9pm. ATM.

(641)526-8535 Lat: 41.68486, Lon: -92.90275
1570 Hwy 224 S, Kellogg, IA 50135
iowasbestburgercafe.com
See ad this page

KEOKUK — E5 *Lee*

CHATFIELD PARK (Public) From town, N 1.5 mi on SR-61/218 to CR-W62 (Argyle Rd), W 1 mi, follow signs (L). Avail: 15 E (30 amps), Pit toilets. 2021 rates: $10 to $15. Apr 01 to Nov 30. (319)463-7673

HICKORY HAVEN CAMPGROUND **Ratings: 9/9★/9.5** (Campground) Avail: 29 full hkups (30/50 amps). 2021 rates: $35. (319)795-4822, 2413 353rd St, Keokuk, IA 52632

VICTORY PARK & HUBINGER LANDING CAMPING (CITY PARKS) (Public) From jct US 136 & S 2nd St (Iowa end of Miss. River bridge): Go 1 block W on S 2nd St, then 2 blocks S on Johnson St, then 1/2 block E on Water St, then 100 feet S across RR tracks (under bridge), then 1 block W on frontage road (pass museum). 21 Avail: 21 W, 21 E (30/50 amps). 2021 rates: $14 to $16. (319)524-7122

KEOSAUQUA — D5 *Van Buren*

LACEY-KEOSAUQUA (Public State Park) From town, S 1 mi on Hwy 1 (R). Avail: 45 E (30/50 amps). 2021 rates: $9 to $16. Apr 10 to Nov 01. (319)293-3502

KINGSTON — D5 *Des Moines*

4TH PUMPING PLANT RECREATION PARK (DES MOINES COUNTY PARK) (Public) From town: Go 6 mi N on Hwy 99, then 5 mi E on Pumping Station Rd. Avail: 22 E (30/50 amps), Pit toilets. 2021 rates: $10 to $15. (319)753-8260

KNOXVILLE — C4 *Marion*

ELK ROCK (Public State Park) From Hwy 92 in Knoxville, 6 mi N on Hwy 14. From I-80 at Newton, 20 mi S on Hwy 14. Avail: 22 E (20/30 amps). 2021 rates: $6 to $16. (641)842-6008

LAKE RED ROCK - COE/WHITEBREAST CAMP (Public Corps) From town, W 2 mi on CR-G28 to CR-T15, S 6.8 mi to Hwy S-71, N 2.5 mi (E). Avail: 132 E (30/50 amps). 2021 rates: $20. Apr 27 to Sep 24. (641)828-7522

MARION COUNTY PARK (Public) From Jct of Hwy 14 & McKimber St., W 0.5 mi on McKimber St. to Willets Dr, S 0.25 mi (R). 100 Avail: 52 full hkups, 28 W, 28 E (50 amps). 2021 rates: $20 to $25. Apr 03 to Oct 25. (641)828-2214

LA PORTE CITY — B4 *Black Hawk*

HICKORY HILLS PARK (BLACK HAWK COUNTY PARK) (Public) From Jct of US-218 & CR-D56 (50th St), W 5.1 mi on 50th St to CR-V37 (Dystart Rd), S 1.1 mi (R). 80 Avail: 27 full hkups, 16 E (30/50 amps). 2021 rates: $13 to $25. (319)433-7276

MCFARLANE PARK (BLACK HAWK COUNTY PARK) (Public) From Jct US-218 & Fourth St, 0.6 mi on Fourth St to Bishop Rd, E 2 mi on Bishop Rd to King Rd, N 0.5 (E). Avail: 64 E (30/50 amps). 2021 rates: $13 to $30. (319)342-3844

LADORA — C4 *Iowa*

LAKE IOWA PARK (IOWA COUNTY PARK) (Public) From Jct I-80 & H Ave (exit 211), S 1 mi on H Ave to 230th St, W 1.5 mi to 'G' Ave, follow signs (L). Avail: 120 E (30 amps). 2021 rates: $9 to $12. (319)655-8465

LAKE VIEW — B2 *Sac*

BLACK HAWK LAKE (Public State Park) From town, E 2 mi on Hwy 175, follow signs (R). Avail: 92 E (20/30 amps). 2021 rates: $6 to $25. May 01 to Sep 30. (712)657-8712

CAMP CRESCENT (Public) From Jct of Hwy 196 & US 71, W 4.3 mi on US 71 to 3rd St., SW 0.3 mi, follow signs (L). 167 Avail: 74 full hkups, 93 W, 93 E (20/50 amps). 2021 rates: $18 to $22. Apr 15 to Oct 01. (712)657-2189

LAMONI — D3 *Decatur*

SLIP BLUFF PARK (Public) From I-35 & Hwy 69 intchg (exit 4), W 0.3 mi on Hwy 69, N 1 mi on Spruce Rd., E 2 mi on CR-J52, N 1 mi on cnty rd, follow signs (E). Avail: 16 E (20 amps). 2021 rates: $10 to $15. (641)446-7307

LE MARS — B1 *Plymouth*

WILLOW CREEK CAMPGROUND (Public) From Jct of Hwy 3 & US-75, E 0.8 mi on Hwy 3 to 4th Ave NE, N 0.6 mi (R) (Dump station offsite 0.5 mi). 30 Avail: 30 W, 30 E (20/30 amps). 2021 rates: $18. Apr 15 to Oct 15. (712)546-8360

LEHIGH — B3 *Webster*

BRUSHY CREEK SRA (Public State Park) From Jct US-169 & Hwy-50: Go 7 mi E on Hwy-50, then 5 mi NE on CR-D46. 256 Avail: 8 full hkups, 112 E (50 amps). 2021 rates: $11 to $22. (515)543-8298

DOLLIVER MEMORIAL (Public State Park) From town: Go 1-1/4 mi W on Hwy 50, then 1 mi N on CR D33. Avail: 19 E (50 amps). 2021 rates: $6 to $16. (515)359-2539

LEWIS — C2 *Cass*

COLD SPRINGS PARK (CASS COUNTY PARK) (Public) From Jct of US-6 & CR-M56, S 1.75 mi on CR-M56 (R). Avail: 26 E (20/30 amps). 2021 rates: $10 to $15. Apr 01 to Oct 31. (712)769-2372

MADRID — C3 *Boone*

SWEDE POINT PARK (Public) From town, W 1 mi on Hwy 210 to QM Ave., N .8 mi, W .5 mi on 322nd Ln. Shelterhouse available by reservation only. Avail: 24 E (30 amps). 2021 rates: $11 to $18. Apr 15 to Oct 15. (515)353-4237

MANCHESTER — B5 *Delaware*

BAILEYS FORD PARK (DELAWARE COUNTY PARK) (Public) From jct US-20 & CR-D-5X: Go 3 mi SE on CR-D-5X. 71 Avail: 33 W, 65 E Pit toilets. 2021 rates: $14 to $16. (563)927-3410

COFFINS GROVE PARK (DELAWARE COUNTY PARK) (Public) From jct Hwy 13 & CR D-22: Go 2-1/2 mi W on CR D-22, then 1/2 mi W on gravel CR W-69. 20 Avail: 20 W, 20 E (30 amps), Pit toilets. 2021 rates: $12 to $20. Apr 15 to Oct 15. (563)927-3410

MANNING — C2 *Carroll*

GREAT WESTERN PARK (CARROLL COUNTY PARK) (Public) From jct SR 141 & CR M66: Go 1/4 mi S on M66. 8 Avail: 8 W, 8 E (20 amps). 2021 rates: $10 to $12. Apr 15 to Oct 15. (712)792-4614

MAQUOKETA — B6 *Jackson*

MAQUOKETA CAVES (Public State Park) From Town, N 1 mi on US 61, W 6 mi on Caves Rd (E). Avail: 17 E (30 amps). 2021 rates: $6 to $16. (563)652-5833

MARENGO — C4 *Iowa*

SUDBURY COURT MOTEL & RV PARK **Ratings: 6.5/8★/5.5** (RV Park) Avail: 18 full hkups (30/50 amps). 2021 rates: $29.75 to $35. (319)642-5411, 2211 Highway 6 Trial, Marengo, IA 52301

MARION — C5 *Linn*

SQUAW CREEK PARK (LINN COUNTY PARK) (Public) From Jct of US-151 & SR-13, S 1 mi on SR-13 to park access rd (just past Hwy 100), W 0.5 mi (L). 69 Avail: 24 full hkups, 45 W, 45 E (50 amps). 2021 rates: $19 to $30. Apr 15 to Oct 15. (319)892-6450

MARSHALLTOWN — C4 *Marshall*

RIVERVIEW PARK (Public) From Jct of SR-14 & Woodland Ave (in town), E 0.1 mi on Woodland Ave (L). 60 Avail: 10 full hkups, 8 S, 30 E (30/50 amps). 2021 rates: $15 to $20. Apr 15 to Oct 31. (641)754-5715

MASON CITY — A4 *Mitchell*

MASON CITY See also Clear Lake.

MARGARET MACNIDER PARK (Public) From Jct of US-65 & 4th St., E 0.7 mi on 4th St. to N Kentucky Ave, N 0.7 mi to Birch Dr, W 0.5 mi (L). 75 Avail: 20 full hkups, 55 W, 55 E (30/50 amps). 2021 rates: $16 to $25. Apr 15 to Oct 15. (641)421-3679

MCGREGOR — A5 *Clayton*

PIKES PEAK (Public State Park) From town, SE 3 mi on Hwy 340 to park access rd, S 1 mi (E). 68 Avail: 1 full hkups, 52 E (30/50 amps). 2021 rates: $6 to $14. Apr 15 to Oct 15. (563)873-2341

SPOOK CAVE CAMPGROUND **Ratings: 7.5/7.5/8** (Campground) 47 Avail: 23 full hkups, 24 W, 24 E (30/50 amps). 2021 rates: $33 to $58. May 01 to Oct 31. (563)539-4114, 13299 Spook Cave Rd, Mc Gregor, IA 52157

MILFORD — A2 *Dickinson*

EMERSON BAY SRA (Public State Park) From town: Go 2-1/2 mi N on Hwy 86. 82 Avail: 23 full hkups, 59 E (50 amps). 2021 rates: $11 to $19. (712)337-3211

GULL POINT (Public State Park) From Jct of US-71 & Hwy 86, N 3 mi on Hwy 86 (R). Avail: 60 E (30 amps). 2021 rates: $6 to $16. (712)337-3211

MISSOURI VALLEY — C1 *Harrison*

WILSON ISLAND SRA (Public State Park) From jct of I-29 & Hwy 30, W 4 mi on US-30, S 4.6 mi on Desoto Ln, W .9 mi. 125 Avail: 1 full hkups, 78 E (30 amps). 2021 rates: $11 to $19. (712)642-2069

MONTEZUMA — C4 *Marion*

DIAMOND LAKE PARK (POWESHIEK COUNTY PARK) (Public) From Jct of US-63 & SR-85, N 1 mi on US-63 (L). Avail: 50 E (30 amps). 2021 rates: $10 to $20. (641)623-3191

MONTICELLO — B5 *Jones*

MONTICELLO JELLYSTONE RV PARK **Ratings: 8/7/7.5** (Campground) 185 Avail: 69 full hkups, 86 W, 116 E (30/50 amps). 2021 rates: $46 to $71. Apr 15 to Oct 15. (319)465-4665, 22128 Hwy 38 N, Monticello, IA 52310

MORAVIA — D4 *Appanoose*

HONEY CREEK (Public State Park) From jct IA-5 & IA-142: Go 8-1/4 mi W on IA-142, then 3-1/2 mi SE on 160th (L). 148 Avail: 28 full hkups, 76 E (30/50 amps). 2021 rates: $11 to $19. (641)724-3739

HONEY CREEK RESORT (Public) From Jct of Hwy 5 & SR-142 (in Moravia), W 5.5 mi on SR-142 to Resort Dr (185th Ave) (L). Avail: 20 full hkups (30/50 amps). 2021 rates: $49. Apr 15 to Oct 15. (877)677-3344

RATHBUN LAKE - COE/BRIDGEVIEW (Public Corps) From town, W 8 mi on Hwy 2 to Hwy 142, N 11 mi (R). Avail: 94 E (30/50 amps). 2021 rates: $14 to $36. May 01 to Sep 30. (641)724-3062

RATHBUN LAKE - COE/BUCK CREEK (Public Corps) From town, N 5 mi on US-5 to CR-J29, NW 4 mi to CR-J5T, NE 2 mi (L). Avail: 42 E (30/50 amps). 2021 rates: $18 to $20. May 08 to Sep 30. (641)724-3206

RATHBUN LAKE - COE/PRAIRIE RIDGE (Public Corps) From town, N 11 mi on SR-5 to SR-142, W 4 mi to cnty rd, S 3 mi, follow signs (E). Avail: 54 E (50 amps). 2021 rates: $18. May 15 to Sep 15. (641)724-3103

MOUNT PLEASANT — D5 *Henry*

CROSSROADS RV PARK

good sam park

Ratings: 9/9.5★/9.5 (RV Park) From Jct of US 27/218 & US 34 (Exit 42/42B), W 0.4 mi to S Iris St, S 0.2 mi (L); or W-bnd From Jct of US 34 & US 27/218, W 0.4 mi on Bus Hwy 34 (towards town) to S Iris St, S 0.2 mi (L).

BIG TO SMALL, WE WELCOME ALL

Located at the crossroads of SE Iowa. Long, wide, full hookups sites with free wifi and cable TV. Enjoy a fabulous clubhouse with full kitchen. Rallies are welcome. Pristine restroom and laundry facilities.

FAC: all weather rds. Avail: 34 all weather, 34 pull-thrus, (34x90), 34 full hkups (30/50 amps), cable, WiFi @ sites, dump, laundry, LP gas, fire rings. **REC:** playground. Pet restrict (B/Q). Partial handicap access. No tents. Big rig sites. 2021 rates: $40.66, Military discount.

(319)385-9737 Lat: 40.95789, Lon: -91.52507
708 S Iris St., Mount Pleasant, IA 52641
www.xrdsrv.com
See ad this page

MOUNT VERNON — C5 *Linn*

PALISADES-KEPLER (Public State Park) From Jct of SR-1 & US-30, W 3.5 mi on US-30 (L). Avail: 31 E (20/50 amps). 2021 rates: $6 to $16. (319)895-6039

MUSCATINE — C5 *Muscatine*

FAIRPORT SRA (Public State Park) From town, E 5 mi on SR-22 (R). Avail: 43 E (30 amps). 2021 rates: $11 to $16. (563)263-4337

MISSISSIPPI RIVER - COE/SHADY CREEK (Public Corps) From town, E 10 mi on US-22 (R). Avail: 53 E (50 amps). 2021 rates: $20. May 01 to Oct 21. (800)645-0248

WILDCAT DEN (Public State Park) From jct US-61 & Hwy-22: Go 11 mi NE on Hwy-22. 28 Avail: Pit toilets. 2021 rates: $6 to $9. (563)263-4337

NASHUA — A4 *Chickasaw*

CEDAR VIEW PARK (Public) From Jct of SR-346 & Charles City Rd, N 0.2 mi on Charles City Rd (R). 43 Avail: 43 W, 43 E (30 amps). 2021 rates: $12 to $15. May 15 to Oct 20. (641)435-4156

NEOLA — C2 *Pottawattamie*

ARROWHEAD PARK (Public) From Jct of I-80 & L-55 (exit 23), SE 1 mi on L-55, follow signs (L). Avail: 48 E (30/50 amps). 2021 rates: $15. (712)485-2295

NEWTON — C4 *Jasper*

NEWTON/DES MOINES EAST KOA **Ratings: 9/9.5★/8.5** (RV Park) 77 Avail: 62 full hkups, 15 W, 15 E (30/50 amps). 2021 rates: $33.95 to $65. Apr 01 to Oct 31. (641)792-2428, 1601 E 36th St. S, Newton, IA 50208

IA

NORTH LIBERTY — C5 *Johnson*

CORALVILLE LAKE - COE/SUGAR BOTTOM (Public Corps) From town, NE 4 mi on CR-F28 to access rd (E). 204 Avail: 13 full hkups, 25 W, 191 E (30/50 amps). 2021 rates: $14 to $26. May 01 to Sep 30. (319)338-3543

OAKVILLE — D5 *Louisa*

MISSISSIPPI RIVER - COE/FERRY LANDING (Public Corps) From town, NE 6 mi on CR-X71 (E). 22 Avail: Pit toilets. May 01 to Oct 01. (563)263-7913

OELWEIN — B5 *Fayette*

LAKESHORE RV RESORT & CAMPGROUND

good sam park **Ratings: 8.5/9★/9.5** (RV Resort) Avail: 30 full hkups (30/50 amps). 2021 rates: $40. May 01 to Oct 15. (319)800-9968, 1418 Q Ave, Oelwein, IA 50662

OELWEIN CITY PARK (Public) From Jct of Hwys 150 & 281, W 0.3 mi on Hwy 281 (R). 40 Avail: 40 W, 40 E (20/30 amps). 2021 rates: $8 to $12. (319)283-5440

OGDEN — C3 *Boone*

DON WILLIAMS REC AREA (BOONE COUNTY PARK) (Public) From Jct of Hwy 30 & CR-P70, N 6.3 mi on CR-P70 (R). Avail: 148 E (30/50 amps). 2021 rates: $11 to $18. Apr 01 to Oct 31. (515)353-4237

OKOBOJI — A2 *Dickinson*

OKOBOJI See also Spirit Lake, IA; Jackson, MN.

ONAWA — C1 *Monona*

LEWIS AND CLARK (Public State Park) From Jct of I-29 & Hwy 175, W 1.5 mi on Hwy 175 to Hwy 324, N 1 mi (E). 112 Avail: 12 full hkups, 100 E (20/30 amps). 2021 rates: $11 to $19. (712)423-2829

ON-UR-WA RV PARK

good sam park **Ratings: 9/10★/10** (RV Park) Avail: 44 full hkups (30/50 amps). 2021 rates: $38 to $41. Apr 15 to Oct 15. (712)423-1387, 1111 28th St, Onawa, IA 51040

ORLEANS — A2 *Dickinson*

MARBLE BEACH STATE REC AREA (Public State Park) From town, N 4 mi on Lake Shore Dr. (R). Avail: 102 E (30 amps). 2021 rates: $6 to $16. (712)337-3211

OSAGE — A4 *Mitchell*

SPRING PARK (Public) From town, W 2 mi on Hwy 9 to Spring Park Rd, S .5 mi (E). 12 Avail. 2021 rates: $5. (641)732-3709

OSCEOLA — D3 *Clarke*

LAKESIDE HOTEL-CASINO RV PARK **Ratings: 7.5/NA/7.5** (RV Park) Avail: 65 full hkups (30/50 amps). 2021 rates: $25. (877)477-5253, 777 Casino Dr., Osceola, IA 50213

OSKALOOSA — D4 *Appanoose*

LAKE KEOMAH (Public State Park) From Jct. of SR-92 & SR-63, E 6.3 mi on SR-92, S 1.1 mi on Royal Ln. Avail: 41 E (30/50 amps). 2021 rates: $6 to $16. (641)673-6975

OTTUMWA — D4 *Wapello*

OTTUMWA PARK (Public) From Jct of US-63 & 34W, S 0.5 mi on Wapello St (R). 200 Avail: 150 W, 150 E (30/50 amps). 2021 rates: $17. Apr 01 to Oct 31. (641)682-1307

VALLEY VILLAGE MH COMMUNITY **Ratings: 5/NA/7.5** (RV Area in MH Park) Avail: 60 full hkups (30/50 amps). 2021 rates: $25. (641)682-8481, 11620 Rabbit Run Rd. Lot 162, Ottumwa, IA 52501

OXFORD — C5 *Johnson*

BEYONDER GETAWAY AT SLEEPY HOLLOW

good sam park **Ratings: 8/9★/9** (Campground) 60 Avail: 40 full hkups, 20 W, 20 E (30/50 amps). 2021 rates: $28 to $45. (319)628-6900, 3340 Black Hawk Ave NW, Oxford, IA 52322

PALO — B5 *Linn*

PLEASANT CREEK SRA (Public State Park) From town: Go 4 mi N on CR-W36. 70 Avail: 2 full hkups, 55 E. 2021 rates: $6 to $19. (319)436-7716

Replace clogged air filters. A clogged air filter can cut a vehicle's fuel efficiency by 10 percent.

PELLA — C4 *Marion*

LAKE RED ROCK - COE/HOWELL STATION (Public Corps) From Jct of SR-163 & CR-T15, SW 2.8 mi on CR-T15, follow signs (L). Avail: 143 E (50 amps). 2021 rates: $22. Apr 12 to Oct 28. (641)828-7522

LAKE RED ROCK - COE/NORTH OVERLOOK (Public Corps) From town, W 2 mi on CR-G28 to CR-T15, S 2 mi, follow signs (R). Avail: 46 E (50 amps). 2021 rates: $20. Apr 27 to Sep 24. (641)828-7522

LAKE RED ROCK - COE/WALLASHUCK (Public Corps) From town, W 4 mi on Hwy-G28, then 0.8 mi S on 190th Ave. Avail: 83 E (30/50 amps). 2021 rates: $18. Apr 27 to Sep 24. (641)828-7522

ROBERTS CREEK PARK (MARION COUNTY PARK) (Public) From town, W 7 mi on CR-G28 (R). 129 Avail: 40 full hkups, 89 E (30/50 amps). 2021 rates: $12 to $25. Apr 03 to Oct 25. (641)627-5507

PLAINFIELD — B4 *Bremer*

NORTH CEDAR PARK (BREMER COUNTY PARK) (Public) From town, E 1 mi on Hwy 188 (L). Avail: 48 E (20/30 amps). 2021 rates: $9 to $12. May 01 to Oct 31. (319)882-4742

PLEASANT HILL — C3 *Polk*

YELLOW BANKS PARK (POLK COUNTY PARK) (Public) From jct US 65 & Vandalia Rd: Go 3 mi E on Vandalia Rd, then turn S on SE 68th St. Follow signs. Avail: 48 E (50 amps). 2021 rates: $13. Apr 01 to Nov 30. (515)266-1563

POCAHONTAS — B2 *Pocahontas*

ELBERT PARK (Public) From Jct of Hwy 3 & Main St, N 0.3 mi on Main St (R). 26 Avail: 26 W, 26 E (30 amps). 2021 rates: $7 to $15. Apr 15 to Oct 15. (712)335-4841

ROCKWELL CITY — B2 *Calhoun*

FEATHERSTONE MEMORIAL PARK (CALHOUN COUNTY PARK) (Public) From Jct of Hwy 20 & CR-N57, N 5.2 mi on CR-N57 (L). 49 Avail: 49 W, 49 E (30 amps). 2021 rates: $15. Apr 01 to Oct 31. (712)297-7131

RUTHVEN — A2 *Palo Alto*

LOST ISLAND - HUSTON PARK (PALO ALTO COUNTY PARK) (Public) From Jct US-18 & 350th Ave, N 2 mi on 350th Ave to 340th St, E 0.5 mi to 355th Ave, N 2 mi to 320th St, W 0.5 mi (L). Avail: 38 E (20/30 amps). 2021 rates: $10 to $15. Apr 15 to Oct 15. (712)837-4866

SABULA — B6 *Jackson*

SOUTH SABULA LAKE PARK (JACKSON COUNTY PARK) (Public) Take Hwy 52/64 into Sabula. Go S on Broad St (turns into South Ave). Follow South Ave into park. 39 Avail: 25 W, 39 E (30/50 amps). 2021 rates: $17 to $20. Apr 01 to Oct 31. (563)652-3783

SAC CITY — B2 *Sac*

HAGGE PARK (SAC COUNTY PARK) (Public) From town, S 2 mi on CR-M54 to CR-D42, E 0.25 mi (R). Avail: 15 full hkups (30 amps). 2021 rates: $10 to $15. Apr 01 to Oct 31. (712)662-4530

SALIX — B1 *Woodbury*

BROWN'S LAKE BIGELOW PARK (WOODBURY COUNTY PARK) (Public) From I-29 (Salix exit): Go 2 mi W on county road. Avail: 40 E (30/50 amps). 2021 rates: $15 to $20. May 01 to Oct 31. (712)946-7114

SNYDER BEND PARK (WOODBURY COUNTY PARK) (Public) From Jct of I-29 & CR-K25 (Salix exit), W 2 mi on CR-K25 to park access rd, S 1.5 mi (L). Avail: 28 E (30 amps). 2021 rates: $15 to $20. May 01 to Oct 31. (712)946-5622

SHEFFIELD — A4 *Mitchell*

GALVIN MEMORIAL PARK (Public) From Jct US-65 & CR-13, W 1 mi on CR-13, follow signs (L). Avail: 12 E (20/30 amps). 2021 rates: $5 to $10. May 01 to Sep 30. (641)892-4718

SHELDON — A1 *Lyon*

HILLS PARK (Public) From town, N 0.25 mi on SR-60 (L). 26 Avail: 26 W, 26 E (20/30 amps). 2021 rates: $15. (712)324-4651

SHENANDOAH — D2 *Page*

PIERCE CREEK REC AREA (Public) From town, N 4 mi on Hwy 59 to 150th St, E 1 mi (L). Avail: 12 E (50 amps), Pit toilets. 2021 rates: $6 to $15. (712)542-3864

SHUEYVILLE — C5 *Johnson*

CORALVILLE LAKE - COE/SANDY BEACH (Public Corps) From jct I-380 (Swisher/Shueyville exit) & CR F12: Go 1 mi E on CR F12, then follow signs 4 mi. 50 Avail: 2 full hkups, 48 E (30 amps). 2021 rates: $20 to $24. May 01 to Sep 29. (319)338-3543

SIDNEY — D2 *Fremont*

VICTORIAN ACRES RV PARK

good sam park **Ratings: 8.5/9.5★/9.5** (RV Park) From jct Hwy 275 & Clay St: Go 3 mi S on Hwy 275, then 13 mi W on Hwy 2 (R). **FAC:** all weather rds. Avail: 88 all weather, 69 pull-thrus, (30x75), back-ins (28x35), 69 full hkups, 19 W, 19 E (30/50 amps), WiFi @ sites, dump, laundry, LP gas, fire rings, firewood. **REC:** boating nearby, playground. Pets OK. Partial handicap access. No tents. Big rig sites, eco-friendly. 2021 rates: $36 to $39, Military discount. Mar 01 to Nov 30.
(402)873-6866 Lat: 40.659382, Lon: -95.841545
6591 Hwy 2, Nebraska City, NE 68410
www.victorianacresrvpark.com
See primary listing at Nebraska City, NE and ad page 570

WAUBONSIE (Public State Park) From Jct of US-275 & Hwy 2, W 2 mi on Hwy 2 to CH L48, S 0.5 mi (E). Avail: 25 E (50 amps). 2021 rates: $6 to $11. (712)382-2786

SIGOURNEY — C4 *Marion*

LAKE BELVA DEER PARK (KEOKUK COUNTY) (Public) From town, NE 1.3 mi on Hwy 92, N 4.2 mi on Hwy 149, E 1.8 mi on 180th St. 66 Avail: 56 W, 56 E (30 amps). 2021 rates: $10 to $18. (641)622-3757

SIOUX CITY — B1 *Plymouth*

SIOUX CITY See also North Sioux City, SD.

STONE (Public State Park) From Jct of I-29 & Riverside Blvd, N 5 mi on SR-12 (R). Avail: 10 E (30/50 amps). 2021 rates: $6 to $16. (712)255-4698

SMITHLAND — B1 *Woodbury*

SOUTHWOOD CONSERVATION AREA (WOODBURY COUNTY PARK) (Public) From jct Hwy 31 & US 141: Go 1-1/2 mi W on US 141, then 3/4 mi S & E on gravel road. Avail: 19 E. 2021 rates: $15 to $20. May 01 to Oct 31. (712)889-2215

SOLON — C5 *Johnson*

LAKE MACBRIDE (Public State Park) From town, W 5 mi on SR-382 to N campground; or W 4 mi on 5th St to S campground (L). 98 Avail: 10 full hkups, 38 E (50 amps). 2021 rates: $6 to $16. (319)624-2200

SPENCER — A2 *Clay*

EAST LEACH PARK (Public) From S Jct of US-18 & US-71 (S of town), N on US-18/71 to 4th St SE, E 0.2 mi (L); or from N Jct of US-18 & US-71 (N of town), S on US-18/71, over bridge to 4th St SE, E 0.2 mi (L). 120 Avail: 100 W, 100 E (30 amps). 2021 rates: $12 to $15. Apr 15 to Oct 15. (712)264-7265

SPIRIT LAKE — A2 *Dickinson*

CENLA RV PARK **Ratings: 8/9.5★/8.5** (RV Park) 42 Avail: 35 full hkups, 7 W, 7 E (30/50 amps). 2021 rates: $32.50 to $38.50. Apr 15 to Oct 15. (712)336-2925, 3200 US Hwy 71, Spirit Lake, IA 51360

ST ANSGAR — A4 *Mitchell*

HALVORSON PARK (MITCHELL COUNTY PARK) (Public) From Jct of US-218 & Hwy 9, W 10 mi on Hwy 9 to Foothill Ave (St Ansgar sign), N 5 mi (R). Avail: 50 E (20/30 amps). 2021 rates: $10 to $18. May 15 to Oct 15. (641)732-5204

STANTON — D2 *Montgomery*

VIKING LAKE (Public State Park) From Jct of US-71 & 34, W 4 mi on US-34 to Q Ave, S 0.5 mi to 230th St., E 0.8 mi. 120 Avail: 22 full hkups, 94 E (20/30 amps). 2021 rates: $6 to $16. (712)829-2235

STEAMBOAT ROCK — B4 *Hardin*

PINE RIDGE PARK (HARDIN COUNTY PARK) (Public) From Jct of Hwy 556 & D 35, S .3 mi on Hwy S56, (R). Avail: 30 E (30 amps). 2021 rates: $10 to $15. Apr 15 to Nov 01. (641)648-4361

STORM LAKE — B2 *Buena Vista*

SUNRISE PARK (Public) From Jct US Hwy 71 & Hwy 7/Bus 71: Go 1 1/2 mi W on Hwy 7/Bus 71 (at Lighthouse), then 1/4 mi S on Sunrise Rd (L). 104 Avail: 101 full hkups, 3 E (30/50 amps). 2021 rates: $16 to $25. Apr 01 to Oct 01. (712)732-8023

STORY CITY — B3 *Story*

WHISPERING OAKS RV PARK **Ratings: 4.5/7.5★/6.5** (Campground) Avail: 16 full hkups (30/50 amps). 2021 rates: $27 to $32. (515)733-4663, 1011 Timberland Dr, Story City, IA 50248

STRATFORD — B3 *Hamilton*

BELLS MILL PARK (HAMILTON COUNTY PARK) (Public) From town, N 3 mi on CR-R21 to CR-D56, E 1.5 mi to park access rd, N 2.5 mi, follow signs (R). Avail: 45 E (30/50 amps). 2021 rates: $12 to $20. Apr 01 to Nov 30. (515)832-9570

RV Generator Care Tips: Don't forget to clean out the spark arrestor (every 50 hours for gas or propane -150 hours for diesel). Don't forget to exercise your generator regularly. Long dormancy of any motor-driven machine can lead to problems. Even if you don't need it, run it with a load from time to time. Don't shut down the generator while it's still under a heavy load. Always turn off the loads and allow it to run for 3 minutes or so to even out the heat and start to cool down. Don't start your generator with a load already present. Allow the genset to stabilize and add the loads one at a time. Air conditioners tend to do this for you as they are equipped with delayed starting sequence modules. If your unit is AGS (Automatic Generator Start) equipped, don't set the low battery start setting too high. Generally, this setting will be at around 11.8 volts to equal a rested state battery level of 50% discharged of 12.2 VDC or specific gravity of 1.190. Don't operate your generator while driving on a gravel road or parking lot if you can avoid it. The cooling fan air flow often causes an abundance of dust that gets ingested into the air intake filter. If you care for and look after your generator, it will be there when you need it for years to come.

STRAWBERRY POINT — B5 *Clayton*

BACKBONE (Public State Park) From town, N 1 mi on CR-W-69 (L). 125 Avail: 1 full hkups, 49 E (30 amps). 2021 rates: $6 to $19. (563)924-2527

SUMNER — B4 *Bremer*

NORTH WOODS PARK (BREMER COUNTY PARK) (Public) From town, N 1.5 mi on CR-V62 (R). Avail: 30 E (20/30 amps). 2021 rates: $10 to $15. May 01 to Oct 31. (319)882-4742

THAYER — D3 *Union*

THAYER LAKE PARK (UNION COUNTY PARK) (Public) From Jct of 34 & cnty rd, S 0.05 mi on cnty rd to 2nd cnty rd, W 0.7 mi (R). 16 Avail: Pit toilets. 2021 rates: $8. (641)782-7111

TIFFIN — C5 *Johnson*

F.W. KENT PARK (JOHNSON COUNTY PARK) (Public) From I-80 (exit 237): Go 1 mi N, then 3-1/2 mi W on US-6. Avail: 86 E (30/50 amps). 2021 rates: $20. (319)645-2315

TIPTON — C5 *Cedar*

CEDAR RIVER CAMPGROUND (FORMERLY HUNT'S)
good sam park **Ratings: 8/8.5★/8** (Campground) From Jct of I-80 & SR-38 (exit 267), N 0.2 mi on SR-38 to Frntg Rd, W 0.7 mi (E). **FAC:** gravel rds. (152 spaces). Avail: 65 grass, 32 pull-thrus, (25x60), back-ins (25x50), 45 full hkups, 20 W, 20 E (30/50 amps), seasonal sites, WiFi @ sites, dump, laundry, LP gas, fire rings, firewood. **REC:** pool, Cedar River: fishing, kayaking/canoeing, playground. Pet restrict (B). No tents. Big rig sites. 2021 rates: $32 to $40. Apr 15 to Oct 15.
(563)946-2431 Lat: 41.64600, Lon: -91.12746
1231 306th St, Tipton, IA 52772
huntscedarrivercampground.com
See ad this page

UNION — B4 *Hardin*

DAISY LONG MEMORIAL PARK (HARDIN COUNTY PARK) (Public) From Jct of Hwys 175 & 215, S on Hwy 215 to Union, E 1 mi to SR-D65, N 0.125 mi (L). Avail: 30 E (30 amps). 2021 rates: $10 to $15. Apr 15 to Nov 01. (641)648-4361

URBANA — B5 *Benton*

LAZY ACRES RV PARK
good sam park **Ratings: 9/10★/10** (RV Park) 76 Avail: 67 full hkups, 9 W, 9 E (30/50 amps). 2021 rates: $35 to $40. Apr 01 to Oct 31. (319)443-4000, 5486 32nd Ave, Center Point, IA 52213

WILDCAT BLUFF PARK (BENTON COUNTY PARK) (Public) From jct Hwy 150 & Hwy 363: Go 1 mi E on Hwy 363 into Urbana, then S on CR W28. Avail: 30 E. 2021 rates: $13. (319)472-3318

VENTURA — A3 *Cerro Gordo*

MCINTOSH WOODS (Public State Park) From town: Go 3/4 mi E on US 18, then 1/2 mi S on McIntosh Rd. Avail: 45 E. 2021 rates: $6 to $16. (641)829-3847

VINTON — B5 *Benton*

BENTON CITY-FRY CAMPGROUND (BENTON COUNTY PARK) (Public) From Hwy 150 & 13th St: Go 4-1/2 mi E on 13th St, then follow signs. Avail: 16 E Pit toilets. 2021 rates: $10 to $15. Mar 20 to Dec 21. (319)472-3318

MINNE ESTEMA PARK (BENTON COUNTY PARK) (Public) From jct US 218 & Hwy 150: Go 3-1/2 mi N on Hwy 150, then follow signs. Avail: 10 E Pit toilets. (563)472-3318

RODGERS PARK (BENTON COUNTY PARK) (Public) From town: Go 3 mi W on US-218, then 1 mi N on CR-V61, then 1/4 mi E. Avail: 52 E. 2021 rates: $15. (319)472-4942

WALLINGFORD — A2 *Emmet*

WOLDEN REC AREA & CAMPGROUND (Public) From town, E 3 mi on A-34 (R). 90 Avail: 90 W, 90 E (30/50 amps). 2021 rates: $18 to $20. Apr 15 to Oct 31. (712)867-4422

WATERLOO — B4 *Black Hawk*

WATERLOO See also Hazleton & Oelwein.

BAMBOO RIDGE KOA **Ratings: 9.5/9.5★/9** (RV Park) Avail: 148 full hkups (30/50 amps). 2021 rates: $41 to $69. (319)233-3485, 4550 Hess Rd, Waterloo, IA 50701

WAUKEE — C3 *Dallas*

TIMBERLINE CAMPGROUND
good sam park **Ratings: 9.5/10★/9.5** (Campground) From Jct of I-35 & I-80 (West Jct), W 5 mi on I-80 to CR-R22 (Exit 117), N 0.9 mi to CR-F64 (Ashworth Rd), E 0.4 mi (L). **FAC:** all weather rds. Avail: 153 all weather, patios, 105 pull-thrus, (35x100), back-ins (25x55), 115 full hkups, 38 W, 38 E (30/50 amps), WiFi @ sites, tent sites, rentals, dump, laundry, groc, LP gas, fire rings, firewood. **REC:** pool, playground. Pet restrict (B). Big rig sites, eco-friendly. 2021 rates: $44 to $49.
(515)987-1714 Lat: 41.57954, Lon: -93.87400
31635 Ashworth Rd, Waukee, IA 50263
www.timberlineiowa.com
See ad this page

WAVERLY — B4 *Bremer*

CEDAR BEND PARK (BREMER COUNTY PARK) (Public) From Jct of Hwy 3 & 12th St NW (in Waverly), N 2.6 mi on 12th NW (R). Avail: 60 E (20/30 amps). 2021 rates: $12 to $20. May 01 to Oct 31. (319)882-4742

WEBSTER CITY — B3 *Hamilton*

BRIGGS WOODS PARK & GOLF COURSE (HAMILTON COUNTY PARK) (Public) From Jct of Hwys 520 & 17, S 2 mi on Hwy 17 (L). 79 Avail: 30 full hkups, 49 W, 49 E (30/50 amps). 2021 rates: $20 to $25. (515)832-9570

WEST LIBERTY — C5 *Cedar*

LITTLE BEAR CAMPGROUND **Ratings: 7/8.5★/7.5** (Campground) Avail: 45 full hkups (30/50 amps). 2021 rates: $33. Apr 15 to Nov 01. (319)627-2676, 1961 Garfield Ave, West Liberty, IA 52776

WEST POINT — D5 *Lee*

POLLMILLER PARK (LEE COUNTY PARK) (Public) From town, E 0.5 mi on Hwy 103 (R). Avail: 20 E (50 amps). 2021 rates: $10 to $15. (319)463-7673

WINTERSET — C3 *Madison*

WINTERSET CITY PARK CAMPGROUND (Public) From Jct of Hwys 169 & 92, E 0.5 mi on Hwy 92 to 10th St, S 0.5 mi (E). Avail: 34 full hkups (30/50 amps). 2021 rates: $20. Apr 01 to Nov 01. (515)462-3258

WOODBINE — C2 *Harrison*

WILLOW LAKE REC AREA (HARRISON COUNTY PARK) (Public) From jct US 30 & CR F20L (Easton Trail): Go 6 mi W on CR F20L (Easton Trail). Avail: 41 E (20/50 amps). 2021 rates: $20. Apr 01 to Oct 31. (712)647-2785

SNOWBIRD TIP: Imagine your perfect destination. RV parks reflect our personalities, lifestyles and budgets. Eastern RV parks offer a more urban experience and conveniences, while parks out west typically have more elbow room. Research before reserving to find your ideal spot.

Getty Images/iStockphoto

DID YOU KNOW?

With an average wind speed of 14 miles per hour, Dodge City is the windiest city in America.

YOU ARE HERE

Kansas

Wide-open prairies, wholesome small towns and more than a few jaw-dropping wonders constitute the Sunflower State. Kansas is a quintessential slice of America's heartland, connecting Midwest to true West.

Cattle Heritage

Wichita has deep roots in the cattle business stretching back to the mid-1800s. Over the decades, it has grown to become the state's largest city. Wichita's first visitors stopped at this trading post as they drove cattle along the Chisholm Trail. Today's visitors will find the town packed with historical museums, family-friendly attractions and a thriving recreation area along the riverbanks. Head about 170 miles west and transport back to Kansas' Old West days at Dodge City. Once a stop on the Santa Fe Trail, this town retains its Western charm.

Big Catches and Cool Rivers

You'll find lots of fish on the Great Plains. Scott State Fishing Lake will challenge your angling skills with robust catches. Located in the wooded canyons of the western prairie, this lake offers cold, spring-fed waters, teeming with bluegill and saugeye. Paddlers will want to hit the waters of the Kansas River Trail, which connects several spots along this 173-mile waterway.

On the Prairie

Long before cities and highways, the region that is now Kansas was once sprawling prairie. But as settlers began to work the soil, much of the prairies were turned into farmland, and towns and roads took over in between. But not all of it was occupied by humans. In Kansas, you can tour the remaining 11,000 acres of untouched grasslands at Tallgrass Prairie National Preserve. Guided bus tours help visitors learn about this habitat. While there, hop on the Flint Hills Scenic Byway to tour beautiful landscapes.

Kansas Barbecue Ribs

The barbecue ribs in the Sunflower State are smoked slow and smothered in a sweet and tangy sauce. The result? Tender slabs of meat that practically fall off the bone. Prepare to get your fingers sticky and don't forget to pair your baby backs with a side of smoked mac and cheese or herbed potato salad.

VISITOR CENTER

TIME ZONE
Central Standard

ROAD & HIGHWAY INFORMATION
800-585-7623
ksdot.org

FISHING & HUNTING INFORMATION
ksoutdoors.com/license-permits

BOATING INFORMATION
620-672-5911
ksoutdoors.com/boating

NATIONAL PARKS
nps.gov/ks

STATE PARKS
ksoutdoors.com/State-Parks

TOURISM INFORMATION
Kansas Office of Tourism and Travel
785-296-2009
travelks.com

TOP TOURISM ATTRACTIONS
1) Dodge City
2) Oz Museum
3) Tallgrass Prairie National Preserve

MAJOR CITIES
Wichita, Overland Park, Kansas City, Olathe, Topeka (capital)

good sam park

Featured Good Sam Parks

KANSAS

When you stay with Good Sam, you can expect the highest degree of cleanliness and friendliness, and better yet, you get **10% off** overnight campground fees.

If you're not already a Good Sam member you can purchase your membership at one of these locations:

ABILENE
Covered Wagon RV Resort
Flatland RV Park

EL DORADO
Deer Grove RV Park

HALSTEAD
Spring Lake RV Resort

LIBERAL
Seven Winds RV Park

LYNDON
Crossroads RV Park

MCPHERSON
McPherson RV Ranch

MERRIAM
Walnut Grove RV Park

OAKLEY
High Plains Camping

PITTSBURG
Parkview MH & RV Community

RUSSELL
Triple 'J' RV Park

SENECA
Bailey's RV Resort

SOUTH HUTCHINSON
Lighthouse Landing RV Park & Cabins

TOPEKA
Deer Creek Valley RV Park

VALLEY CENTER
North Star RV Park

WELLINGTON
Wellington KOA

WICHITA
Air Capital RV Park
All Seasons RV Park
Camp The Range
K & R RV Park

Getty Images/iStockphoto

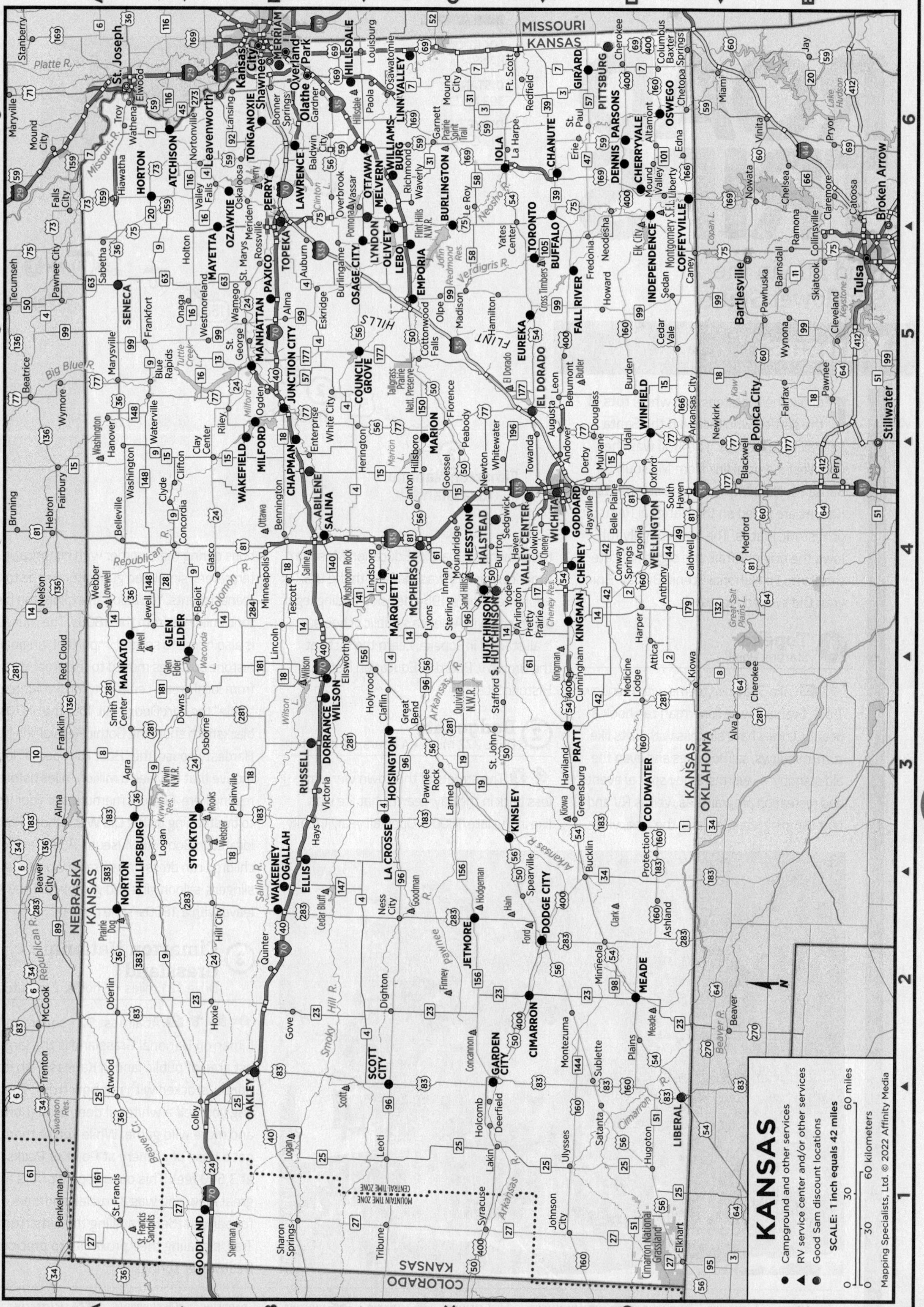
KANSAS
Campground and other services
RV service center and/or other services
Good Sam discount locations
SCALE: 1 inch equals 42 miles
0 30 60 miles
0 30 60 kilometers
Mapping Specialists, Ltd. © 2022 Affinity Media
NEBRASKA
MISSOURI
OKLAHOMA
COLORADO
MOUNTAIN TIME ZONE
CENTRAL TIME ZONE
TOPEKA
WICHITA
DODGE CITY
GARDEN CITY
SALINA
LAWRENCE
MANHATTAN
HUTCHINSON
EMPORIA
GOODLAND
LIBERAL

 See map page 397

ROAD TRIPS

Find Fun in the Sunflower State

Kansas

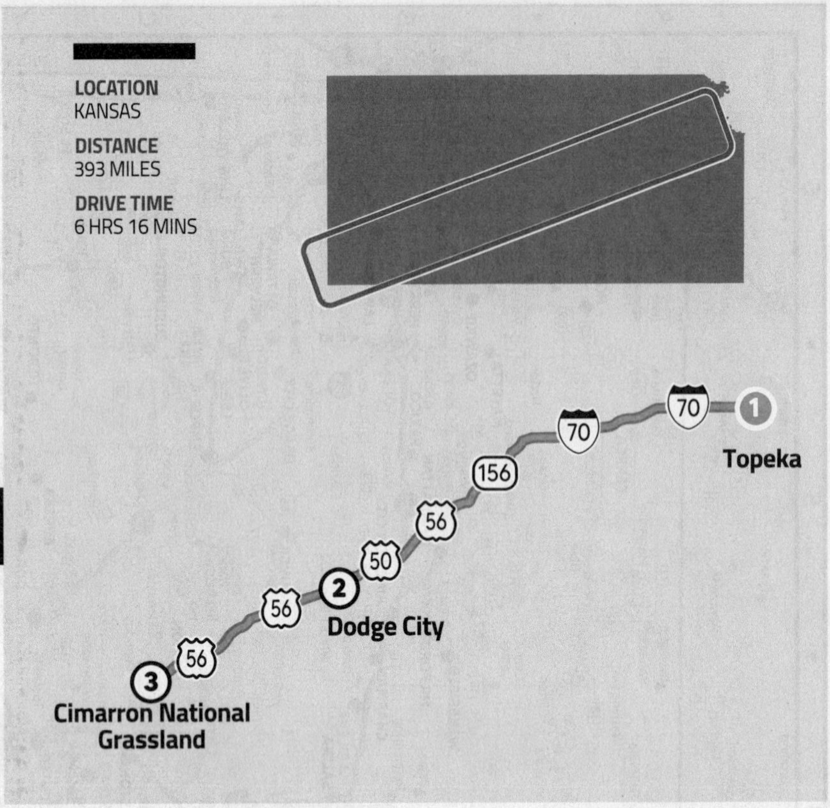

Follow the footsteps and wheel ruts of the settles who followed the Santa Fe Trail in the 1800s. The Trail was the Old West's crucial link from Missouri to Santa Fe, New Mexico; some segments in Kansas are listed on the National Register of Historic Places. The road roughly follows the original Trail, and signs indicate the Santa Fe National Scenic Byway. Enjoy your Old West adventure!

1 Topeka
Starting Point

Lake Shawnee teems with Rainbow Trout. Even a novice fisherman can hook a beauty. Locals have success with baits like corn, minnows, salmon eggs and even the old standby — worms. Enjoy special events and recreation programs as well as RV and tent camping sites. While in the area, visit the Brown vs. Board of Education Museum. American history was made with the U.S. Supreme Court's 1954 decision ending legal segregation in America's public schools. It all started in Topeka. Learn the facts at the Brown v. Board of Education National Historic Site.

2 Dodge City
Drive 272 miles • 4 hours, 14 minutes

The streets of this town were lawless back in the day. Learn what life was like in the late 1800's. Open all year, it really hops during the summer with historical interpreters, simulated gunfights and historic reenactments. You also can explore the historic buildings from the 1800s. The museum is also home to several important, original, historic buildings moved to the property from local areas. Learn why local volunteers "stole" the Fort Dodge Jail. Tour the 1870s blacksmith shop, the Gothic Revival, kit-built Hardesty house, the "Boot Hill Special" locomotive that traveled a million miles before resting here. Capture memories of your visit to by stopping by the Old West Photo Parlor located in Boot Hill Museum. Adults and children can dress up as prairie women, gunslingers, saloon girls and gamblers. They'll leave with a 1800s-style portrait.

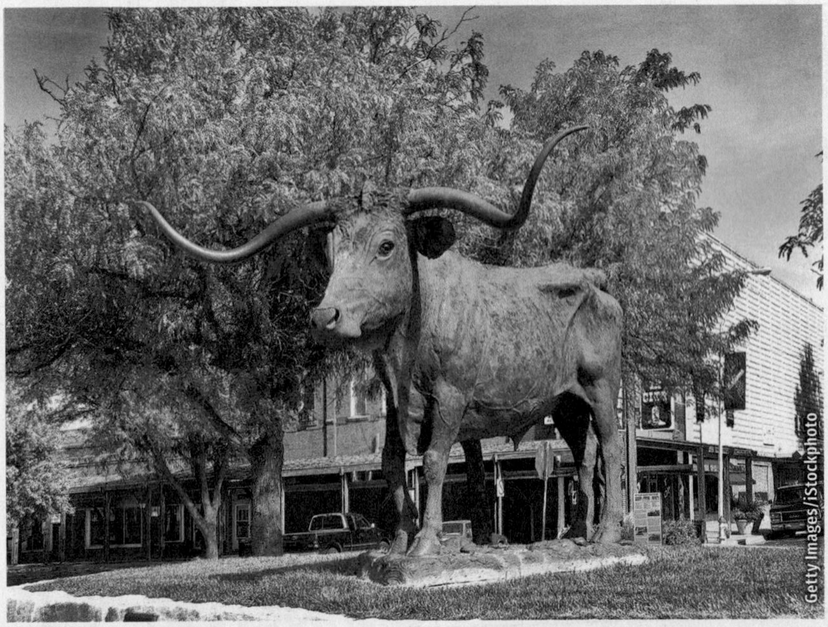
Getty Images/iStockphoto

3 Cimarron National Grassland
Drive 121 miles • 2 hours, 2 minutes

At almost 521 square miles, Cimarron National Grassland is the largest area of public land in Kansas. Fish its ponds, stocked with rainbow trout. Then bag yourself a whitetail deer, pronghorn and more wild game. While you're there, get a dose of scenery at Point of Rocks at 3,540 feet. This outcropping offers a great view and was a crucial landmark for early settlers traveling the Cimarron Trail, signaling their proximity to precious freshwater springs.

BIKING BOATING DINING ENTERTAINMENT FISHING HIKING HUNTING PADDLING SHOPPING SIGHTSEEING

Kansas SPOTLIGHTS

Discover Wide-Open Adventure in the Sunflower State

You won't find the Land of Oz in the Sunflower State, but you will discover outlaws, cattle drivers and iconic pilots. Visitors can explore sprawling grasslands and stand in the spots where gunslingers exchanged fire.

WYATT EARP BECAME THE MARSHAL OF DODGE CITY FOR $250 PER MONTH.

The Boot Hill Museum in Dodge City recreates Old West stores and sidewalks. Lithistman

Dodge City

Dodge City's compelling frontier history comes to life in an evocative medley of museums, landmarks and living history re-enactments. It was here that Wyatt Earp gained notoriety as an assistant city Marshal in 1876 before he made his move to Tombstone, Arizona, scene of the infamous Gunfight at the OK Corral. Dodge City's historic Front Street recalls the Wild West days with a smattering of evocative artifacts and historical re-enactments at the Boot Hill Museum and the Boot Hill Cemetery.

Trolley to the Past

A fun and illuminating way to get under the skin of Dodge is to hop on the Dodge City Trolley, which takes in the original locations of the Long Branch Saloon (where Frank Loving killed Levi Richardson in the notorious 1879 gunfight), Gospel Hill and the "deadline." Follow the path of the Santa Fe Trail, where Fort Dodge was established in 1859 to protect wagon trains from raids. Tourists can peruse the historic structures of Gospel Hill, including the First Presbyterian Church and the Spanish Mission-style Sacred Heart Cathedral.

Historic Front Street

The city's legendary Front Street gained notoriety in 1872 when the Atchison, Topeka and Santa Fe Railway transformed Dodge City into a lawless boomtown and breeding ground for every conceivable sin. Front Street became its main thoroughfare, and today, the city's Wild West stories and legends are interpreted through historic Front Street's audiovisual programs and exhibits. There's even a reconstruction of Dodge City as it looked in 1867 along with living history demonstrations. Exhibits recall the days when Front Street was bisected by the railroad tracks; an ordinance stated that guns could not be worn north of the "deadline" demarcated by the tracks. More than 60,000 artifacts are displayed in the Boot Hill Museum, including photographs, documents and an extensive Old West gun collection.

History Comes Alive

Visitors can take a self-guided tour of the historic structures that have been moved onto the property, including Fort Dodge Jail, the First Union Church, a blacksmith shop, school house and the 1878 Hardesty House (a restoration of a Victorian-era cattleman's home), the working Rath's General Store, Long Branch Saloon and a 19th-century ice cream parlor. During the summer, the immensely popular Long Branch Variety Show (the longest-running show in the nation) still draws the crowds from across the nation with its themed shows and can-can dancers. The saloon was the scene of innumerable

KS

LOCAL FAVORITE

Monkey Bread

The Sunflower State is home to sprawling vistas of wheat. If this makes you hungry for bread, try this warm and gooey Midwestern treat. *Recipe by Barbara Tysak.*

INGREDIENTS

- ☐ ½ cup granulated sugar
- ☐ 1 Tbsp cinnamon
- ☐ 2 cans refrigerated biscuits
- ☐ ½ cup chopped walnuts
- ☐ ½ cup raisins
- ☐ ¾ cup firmly packed brown sugar
- ☐ ¾ cup butter, melted

DIRECTIONS

Heat oven to 350°F. Generously grease 12-cup fluted tube pan with shortening or cooking spray. In large, 1-gallon plastic food storage bag or a bowl, mix granulated sugar and cinnamon. Separate dough into 16 biscuits; cut each into quarters. Coat pieces well in the sugar mixture.

Arrange in the pan, adding walnuts and raisins among the biscuit pieces. Sprinkle any remaining sugar over the dough. In small bowl, mix brown sugar and butter; pour over biscuit pieces. Bake 30 to 40 minutes or until golden brown and no longer doughy in center. Loosen edges of pan with a knife. Cool 5 minutes. Turn upside down onto serving plate. Serve warm and simply pull apart and enjoy.

Wild West gunfights and standoffs, making this one of the most dangerous places on the continent.

Bullets and Blackboards

The Gunfighters Wax Museum hones in on the city's notorious past by immortalizing the town's storied outlaws, hustlers and gunslingers in wax. With more than a whiff of early tourism eccentricity, the museum has its origins in 1957 when it formed the showpiece of a traveling carnival with a handful of Wild West wax dummies. While the colorful exhibits are rather short on subtlety, there's sufficient historical information (via an audio application) to accompany the life-size wax figures to keep it interesting.

Topeka

Situated near the geographic center of the lower 48, Topeka has long been at the crossroads of American history. Between its abolitionist past, and its storied place in the civil rights movement, visitors here can expect plenty of eye-opening experiences, not to mention an exciting array of cultural attractions. Toss in a heavy dose of heartland hospitality and it's easy to see why this capital city is quickly becoming one of the Sunflower State's must-see destinations.

Rich History

Built in the late 19th century, the Kansas State Capitol offers the perfect introduction to Topeka's outsized influence on historic events. You can visit many of the legislative chambers on your own, but for a truly educational experience it's worth joining one of the free guided tours. Highlights include the governor's ceremonial office, as well as the brilliant murals that decorate each floor of the rotunda. The nearby Historic Ritchie House, one of the oldest homes in the city, is another must-see, though it's best to make an appointment before arriving. Built by abolitionists in 1856, the house was a key stop along the Underground Railroad.

Sprawling Green Spaces

Outdoors lovers will rejoice in an afternoon spent exploring the 160-acre Gage Park, one of the city's star attractions. Boasting a children's discovery center, an outdoor theater, and a rose garden, as well as walking trails and plenty of room to picnic, it's no wonder locals have been flocking here for over a hundred years. Families should make sure to save time for a ride on the park's famous vintage 1908 carousel or the miniature train, which follows a mile-long course through the most scenic part of the park. The area's most famous feature, however, is the renowned Topeka Zoo, which after an overhaul in 2003 has steadily earned a reputation as an innovative and enthralling conservation center.

Motorsports Galore

Just south of town, Heartland Motorsports Park is a must-do for anyone who loves the sound of roaring engines and the smell of burnt rubber. From drag racing, to motocross, to musical performances, the track is buzzing with events many weekends throughout the year, but to witness the best drivers in action you'll have to time your visit for late summer. That's when Heartland plays host to one of the most thrilling, pulse-pounding events in racing — the NHRA Nationals. One of the state's largest events, the weekend-long gathering features record-setting drag races, meet-and-greets with top drivers and plenty of entertainment.

Wichita

Wichita has a vast Western history stretching from Native American culture to pioneers who settled at the end of the Chisholm Trail. Today, art and culture play a central role with more than 50 art galleries and museums in Old Town, to the Douglas Design District, home to amazing street murals. With more than one air museum in town, you can virtually experience "slipping the surly bonds of earth." If you're more grounded in terra firma, walking and biking trails are plentiful throughout the city and the waterfront. Sports fans can cheer for everything from a professional Double A baseball team to minor league hockey to a flat track roller derby league.

Come Fly with Me

Discover how Wichita, "Air Capital of the World," helped end World War II. This was where nearly 1,650 Boeing Superfortress bombers were built — the most B-29s manufactured during WWII. A restored B-29 can be seen at the Doc Hangar, Education and Visitors Center at Eisenhower National Airport. "Doc" is one of only two B-29s still airworthy and visitors can pay for the ride of a lifetime in this rare warbird. Once you've touched down, soar into the Kansas Aviation Museum with three floors of aerial displays and learn why Kansas manufactured 67% of all general aviation aircraft in the world.

Overlooking the Arkansas River, the Keeper of the Plains statue in Wichita stands over 70 feet tall.

Rolling on the Plains

Railroad enthusiasts can hop aboard for a trip to the Great Plains Transportation Museum, one of the best railroad museums in the country, featuring six locomotives including steam, diesel and electric.

Slip, Slide or Glide

Glide along the Arkansas River through the center of town for scenic views. Rent watercraft like kayaks, canoes and paddleboats or take a lazy float down the river. Several city lakes are stocked with fish on a regular basis so look to reel in bass, trout, catfish, carp, bluegill and gizzard shad. Thirty miles west of town water lovers can take the plunge at Cheney State Park's 9,500-acre lake — one of the premier sailing lakes in the country. Anglers cast for channel cats, crappie, striped bass, walleye and white bass. Take the kids to Rock River Rapids, the largest waterpark in the area complete with waterslides, a lazy river, lap pool and zero depth pool.

Get Up Close to the Natural West

Should you take South Lake Loop for an easy stroll with your best four-legged friend? Or maybe the Pawnee Prairie Park Trail, a moderate route accessible year-round. Chisholm Creek Park, one of the largest parks in the city, offers 240 acres of wetlands, prairies and woodlands dotted with Great Plains wildlife.

Wild in Kansas

Visit the Kansas Wildlife Exhibit with more than 25 native species of animals, birds and reptiles. Tanganyika Wildlife Park, home to more than 400 animals and 40 exhibits, is one of only a handful of wildlife parks in the country to receive the Humane Certified seal of approval. Spin along the 10-mile Arkansas River Path for beautiful scenery and access to city museums and attractions.

Art, Civil Rights and Sports

Known for his horizontal prairie style, legendary architect Frank Lloyd Wright designed the Allen House in 1918 with a living room architectural writers have deemed "one of the great rooms of the 20th century." *USA Today* lists it as one of its top-10 Frank Lloyd Wright tours in the country. In July 1958, Dockum Drug Store was the site of the first student-led sit-in to end segregation. Today a life-size bronze sculpture of a lunch counter is located at the Chester I. Lewis Reflection Square Park.

Batter Up

This is a sports lover's town! Batter up for great baseball with the Wichita Wind Surge. The Wichita Wizards are considered the "mecca of basketball west of the Mississippi." Wichita Force is a member of the Champions Indoor Football League. Watch ice fly from the Wichita Thunder hockey team, and don't miss the rough-and-tumble ICT Roller Girls.

Get Ready for Riverfest

Riverfest is the largest and longest-running festival in the state. For nine days, Wichita is filled with music and entertainment as dozens of performers and bands take to the stages. Don't miss the Sundown Parade, a River Run, Paddle Board 5K and fireworks during the most anticipated festival in the area.

Step Back in Time

Wichita began as a stopover for cattle drives headed to Abilene, but thanks to the railroad, it became a major cattle-shipping destination. The city proudly embraces its bovine history at the Old Cowtown Museum providing a glimpse of life during the 1860s and '70s when cowboys herded longhorn steer through the streets, and Wichita marked the end of the Chisholm Trail.

Native American Past

Explore the history of the Plains Indians at the Mid-America All-Indian Museum with outdoor exhibits including a full-size tipi and grass houses. Traditional artifacts and contemporary exhibits represent the 73 tribes in the Wichita area. An annual powwow takes place each summer. Keeper of the Plains, a 44-foot-tall, 5-ton Native American statue, stands as a tribute to regional tribes and is illuminated nightly.

FOR MORE INFORMATION

Kansas Office of Tourism & Travel, 785-296-2009, www.travelks.com

Dodge City CVB, 800-766-3777, www.visitdodgecity.org

Greater Topeka Partnership, 800-235-1030, visit.topekapartnership.com

Wichita Convention & Visitors Bureau, 800-288-9424, www.visitwichita.com

KS

Kansas

ABILENE — B4 *Dickinson*

COVERED WAGON RV RESORT
good sam park
Ratings: 8.5/10★/7.5 (Campground) From jct I-70 (exit 275) & Buckeye St: Go S 2-1/4 mi on Buckeye St. (R). **FAC:** gravel rds. (60 spaces). Avail: 45 gravel, 43 pull-thrus, (25x70), back-ins (25x40), 45 full hkups (30/50 amps), seasonal sites, cable, WiFi @ sites, tent sites, dump, laundry, LP bottles. **REC:** pool, playground, hunting nearby. Pets OK. Big rig sites. 2021 rates: $38, Military discount.
(785)263-2343 Lat: 38.90743, Lon: -97.214058
803 S Buckeye, Abilene, KS 67410
coveredwagonrvks.com
See ad this page

FLATLAND RV PARK
good sam park
Ratings: 8/9.5★/7.5 (RV Park) Avail: 21 full hkups (30/50 amps). 2021 rates: $40. (785)263-1684, 2200 N Buckeye Ave, Abilene, KS 67410

ATCHISON — A6 *Atchison*

WARNOCK (Public) From town, W 1 mi on US-59 to Phillips Rd, S .5 mi on Phillips Rd to 274th Rd, E 0.5 mi (R). Avail: 16 E (30 amps), Pit toilets. 2021 rates: $10. (913)367-5561

BUFFALO — D6 *Wilson*

WILSON STATE FISHING LAKE (Public) From Jct of US-75 & SR-39, E .8 mi on Hwy 75/SH-39 (L). 20 Avail: Pit toilets. 2021 rates: $7.50 to $8.50. (620)637-2748

BURLINGTON — C5 *Coffey*

JOHN REDMOND RESERVOIR - COE/DAM SITE (Public Corps) From town, N 3.5 mi on US-75 to 16th St, W 0.3 mi to Embankment Rd, W 1.2 mi, follow signs (E). 26 Avail: 22 W, 9 E (30 amps). 2021 rates: $10 to $15. Apr 01 to Oct 31. (620)364-8613

JOHN REDMOND RESERVOIR - COE/RIVERSIDE EAST (Public Corps) From Jct of I-35 & US-75, S 11 mi on US-75 to Embankment Rd, W 1.5 mi, follow signs (E). Avail: 53 E (30 amps). 2021 rates: $15. May 01 to Sep 30. (620)364-8613

JOHN REDMOND RESERVOIR - COE/RIVERSIDE WEST (Public Corps) From town, N 3.5 mi on US-75 to Embankment Rd, W 2.5 mi (across dam) follow signs (R). Avail: 32 E (15/50 amps). 2021 rates: $14 to $15. May 01 to Sep 30. (620)364-8613

CHANUTE — D6 *Neosho*

SANTA FE PARK
(Public) From town, S 2 mi on Santa Fe Ave (R). **FAC:** paved rds. Avail: 28 paved, back-ins (20x50), 28 W, 28 E (50 amps), tent sites, dump. **REC:** Santa Fe Lake: fishing, golf, playground. Pets OK. 10 day max stay. 2021 rates: $10. no cc, no reservations.
(620)431-5250 Lat: 37.656000, Lon: -95.452928
Chanute, KS 66720
www.chanute.org

CHAPMAN — B4 *Dickinson*

CHAPMAN CREEK RV PARK **Ratings: 7.5/9.5★/8.5** (RV Park) Avail: 23 full hkups (30/50 amps). 2021 rates: $28 to $38. (785)922-2267, 2701 N Marshall Dr, Chapman, KS 67431

CHENEY — D4 *Kingman*

CHENEY (EAST SHORE) (Public State Park) From Jct US-54 & SR-251: Go 5-1/2 mi N on SR-251 (L). 223 Avail: 223 W, 223 E (30/50 amps). 2021 rates: $5 to $35. (316)542-3664

CHENEY (WEST SHORE) (Public State Park) From Jct US-54 & SR-251: Go 3-1/2 mi N on SR-251, then 2-1/4 mi W on 21st St (R). 245 Avail: 245 W, 245 E (30/50 amps). 2021 rates: $10 to $24. (316)542-3664

CHERRYVALE — D6 *Labette*

BIG HILL LAKE - COE/CHERRYVALE (Public Corps) From Jct of Hwy 169 & Main St, E 2 mi on Main St to Olive St, S 0.25 mi to Montgomery CR-5000, E 4.5 mi to Big Hill Lake, W 0.75 mi (E). Avail: 22 E (50 amps). 2021 rates: $17 to $22. Mar 30 to Nov 01. (620)336-2741

BIG HILL LAKE - COE/TIMBER HILL (Public Corps) From Parsons: Go 6 mi W on Hwy 400 (E). 20 Avail: Pit toilets. 2021 rates: $8. Mar 29 to Nov 03. (620)336-2741

CIMARRON — C2 *Gray*

CIMARRON RV PARK **Ratings: 6.5/9.5★/6** (RV Park) Avail: 32 full hkups (30/50 amps). 2021 rates: $25. (620)855-2017, 809 E. Ave A, Cimarron, KS 67835

COFFEYVILLE — D6 *Montgomery*

WALTER JOHNSON PARK CAMPGROUND (Public) From west jct US 166 & US 169: Go 1-1/4 mi E on US 166/169 (to Old Locomotive/Fairgrounds). 117 Avail: 117 W, 117 E (30/50 amps). 2021 rates: $8 to $15. (620)252-6100

COLDWATER — D3 *Comanche*

LAKE COLDWATER (Public) From Jct of US-160 & US-183 (N of town), S 1.5 mi on US-183 to Lake Coldwater Rd, W 1 mi (R). 100 Avail: 21 full hkups, 79 W, 79 E (30 amps). 2021 rates: $12.50 to $22. (620)582-2702

COUNCIL GROVE — B5 *Morris*

COUNCIL GROVE LAKE - COE/CANNING CREEK COVE (Public Corps) From town: Go 3/4 mi N on SR-177, then 3 mi NW on City Lake Rd (R). 40 Avail: 32 W, 37 E (30/50 amps). 2021 rates: $12 to $22. Apr 01 to Oct 31. (620)767-5195

COUNCIL GROVE LAKE - COE/RICHEY COVE (Public Corps) From town: Go 3 mi N on SR-177 (L). Avail: 39 E (30/50 amps). 2021 rates: $17 to $25. Apr 01 to Oct 31. (620)767-5195

COUNCIL GROVE LAKE - COE/SANTA FE TRAIL (Public Corps) From west jct Hwy 177 & US 56: Go 1 block W on US 56, then 2-1/2 mi NW on Mission St (R). Avail: 31 E (30/50 amps). 2021 rates: $14 to $25. Apr 15 to Oct 31. (620)767-7125

DENNIS — D6 *Labette*

BIG HILL LAKE - COE/MOUND VALLEY (Public Corps) From Parsons, W 6 mi on Hwy 400 to Dennis-Mound Valley Rd, S 5 mi to Labette CR-19000, W 4 mi (R). Avail: 74 E (30 amps). 2021 rates: $12 to $20. Mar 27 to Nov 01. (620)336-2741

DODGE CITY — C2 *Ford*

DODGE CITY KOA **Ratings: 7/9.5★/8** (RV Resort) 98 Avail: 30 full hkups, 68 W, 68 E (30/50 amps). 2021 rates: $30 to $57. (620)371-7177, 701 Park St., Dodge City, KS 67801

GUNSMOKE RV PARK **Ratings: 9/10★/9.5** (RV Park) Avail: 74 full hkups (30/50 amps). 2021 rates: $49.50. (620)227-8247, 11070 108 Rd, Dodge City, KS 67801

RIVERSIDE RV PARK **Ratings: 6.5/8.5★/5.5** (RV Park) 116 Avail: 104 full hkups, 12 W, 12 E (30/50 amps). 2021 rates: $24. (620)225-8044, 500 Cherry St., Dodge City, KS 67801

DORRANCE — B3 *Russell*

WILSON LAKE - COE/MINOOKA PARK (Public Corps) From Jct I-70 & Dorrance exit 199 (Hwy 231): Go 6 mi N on Hwy 231 (E). 159 Avail: 117 W, 117 E (30/50 amps). 2021 rates: $18 to $24. (785)658-2551

EL DORADO — C5 *Butler*

DEER GROVE RV PARK
good sam park
Ratings: 8/9★/9.5 (RV Park) N-bnd: From Jct I-35 (KS Turnpike) & Exit 71: Go 5.6 mi E on Hwy 254 (Hwy 254 turns into Hwy 54), follow blue camper signs to park (R). S-bnd: From Jct I-35 & Hwy 177 (Exit 92): Go 18 mi S on Hwy 177 to US 54, then W 3 mi (L). **FAC:** all weather rds. Avail: 50 gravel, 19 pull-thrus, (25x65), back-ins (20x45), 50 full hkups (30/50 amps), cable, WiFi @ sites, tent sites, laundry, fire rings, firewood. **REC:** boating nearby, hunting nearby. Pet restrict (B). eco-friendly. 2021 rates: $37 to $40, Military discount.
(316)321-6272 Lat: 37.81010, Lon: -96.79176
2873 S.E. US Hwy 54, El Dorado, KS 67042
www.deergrovervpark.com
See ad previous page

EL DORADO/BLUESTEM POINT (Public State Park) From jct US-54 & US-77: Go 4-3/3 mi E on US-54, then 4 mi N on SR-177 (L). 500 Avail: 70 full hkups, 197 W, 197 E (30/50 amps). 2021 rates: $10 to $35. (316)321-7180

EL DORADO/BOULDER BLUFF (Public State Park) From Jct I-35 & US-77: Go 528 ft S on US-77, then 2 mi E on Meyers Rd, then 700 ft S on Boulder Bluff Rd (L). 148 Avail: 24 W, 24 E. 2021 rates: $15 to $25. (316)321-7180

EL DORADO/SHADY CREEK (Public State Park) From town, E 3 mi on US-54 to Bluestem Dr, N 2 mi to access rd, E 0.2 mi (L). Entrance fee required. 71 Avail. 2021 rates: $10 to $35. (316)321-7180

EL DORADO/WALNUT RIVER (Public State Park) From jct US-54 & US-77: Go 3 mi E on US-54, then 1-1/2 mi N on Bluestem Rd, then 1-3/4 mi W on Cross Creek (R). 166 Avail: 95 full hkups, 63 W, 63 E (20/30 amps). 2021 rates: $10 to $35. (316)321-7180

ELLIS — B3 *Ellis*

ELLIS LAKESIDE CAMPGROUND (Public) From Jct of I-70 & Washington St (exit 145), S 7 blks on Washington St to 8th St, E 2 blks (E). 17 Avail: 17 W, 17 E (30/50 amps). 2021 rates: $15 to $20. (785)726-4812

EMPORIA — C5 *Lyon*

EMPORIA RV PARK **Ratings: 7/9★/5.5** (RV Park) Avail: 36 full hkups (30/50 amps). 2021 rates: $36. (620)343-3422, 4601 W Hwy 50, Emporia, KS 66801

EUREKA — C5 *Greenwood*

DUNHAM'S RV PARK **Ratings: 4.5/NA/7.5** (RV Park) Avail: 12 full hkups (30/50 amps). 2021 rates: $30 to $35. (620)583-6616, 309 S Jefferson, Eureka, KS 67045

FALL RIVER — D5 *Greenwood*

FALL RIVER LAKE - COE/DAMSITE (Public Corps) From town: Go 3-1/2 mi W on Hwy 96, then 1-1/2 mi N on Cummings Rd. Follow signs. Avail: 27 E (30/50 amps). 2021 rates: $10 to $21. Mar 29 to Oct 30. (620)658-4445

FALL RIVER LAKE - COE/ROCK RIDGE COVE NORTH (Public Corps) From town: Go 3-1/2 mi W on Hwy 96, then 1-1/2 mi N on Cummings Rd. Follow signs. 44 Avail: 2 W, 23 E (30 amps), Pit toilets. 2021 rates: $10 to $16. Apr 01 to Oct 31. (620)658-4445

FALL RIVER LAKE - COE/WHITEHALL BAY AREA (Public Corps) From town, N on US-400, immediate right turn at Fall River exit, follow signs (E). 26 Avail: 11 W, 26 E (30/50 amps). 2021 rates: $16 to $21. Apr 01 to Oct 30. (620)658-4445

FALL RIVER LAKE/QUARRY BAY AREA (Public State Park) From town, W 4 mi on Hwy 400 to Country Rd, N 3 mi (R). 17 Avail. 2021 rates: $10 to $35. Apr 15 to Oct 15. (620)637-2213

FALL RIVER/FREDONIA BAY AREA (Public State Park) From Jct of US-54 & SR-99, S 12 mi on SR-99 to US-400, E 7.7 mi to park access rd (Cummings Rd), N 2.4 mi (E). Entrance fee required. 34 Avail: 1 full hkups, 29 W, 29 E (30/50 amps), Pit toilets. 2021 rates: $10 to $35. (620)637-2213

GARDEN CITY — C2 *Finney*

RJ'S RV PARK **Ratings: 5.5/4.5/4.5** (RV Park) Avail: 15 full hkups (30/50 amps). 2021 rates: $29. (620)276-8741, 4100 E Hwy 50, Garden City, KS 67846

GIRARD — D6 *Crawford*

LAKE CRAWFORD (Public State Park) From Jct of SR-47 & SR-7 (in town), N 9.3 mi on SR-7 to SR-277, E 0.8 mi (E) Caution: Rapid water crossing at dam during heavy rainfall. 112 Avail: 45 W, 83 E (30/50 amps). 2021 rates: $10 to $35. (620)362-3671

GLEN ELDER — B4 *Mitchell*

GLEN ELDER (Public State Park) From Jct of US-24 & SR-128, E 1.1 mi on US-24 (R). Entrance fee required. 355 Avail: 77 W, 82 E (30/50 amps). 2021 rates: $10 to $35. (785)545-3345

GODDARD — D4 *Sedgwick*

LAKE AFTON PARK (SEDGWICK COUNTY PARK) (Public) From town, S 3 mi on 199th Rd to 39th St S, W 3 mi (L). 190 Avail: 16 W, 154 E (30 amps). 2021 rates: $7 to $12. (316)794-2774

GOODLAND — B1 *Sherman*

GOODLAND KOA KAMPGROUND **Ratings: 7/9.5★/8.5** (Campground) 36 Avail: 18 full hkups, 18 W, 18 E (30/50 amps). 2021 rates: $33 to $49. Apr 15 to Oct 31. (785)890-5701, 1114 E Hwy 24, Goodland, KS 67735

MID AMERICA CAMP INN

Ratings: 6.5/6/6 (RV Park) From Jct I-70 & Hwy 27 (West Goodland exit 17): Go 1/4 mi S on Hwy 27 (R). Elev 3700 ft.**FAC:** paved rds. Avail: 91 paved, 91 pull-thrus, (35x60), 91 full hkups (30/50 amps), WiFi @ sites, tent sites, dump, laundry. **REC:** playground, hunting nearby. Pets OK. Big rig sites. 2021 rates: $40 to $45.
(785)899-5431 Lat: 39.32393, Lon: -101.72813
2802 Commerce Rd, Goodland, KS 67735
See ad this page

HALSTEAD — C4 *Harvey*

SPRING LAKE RV RESORT

Ratings: 8.5/9★/9 (Membership Park) 149 Avail: 81 full hkups, 68 W, 68 E (30/50 amps). 2021 rates: $30 to $32. (316)835-3443, 1308 South Spring Lake Rd., Halstead, KS 67056

HESSTON — C4 *Harvey*

COTTONWOOD GROVE CAMPGROUND **Ratings: 4.5/7.5/6** (Campground) Avail: 22 full hkups (30/50 amps). 2021 rates: $35. (620)327-4173, 1001 E Lincoln Blvd, Hesston, KS 67062

HILLSDALE — B6 *Miami*

HILLSDALE (Public State Park) S-bnd: From Jct of US-169 & 255 St, W 5 mi on 255 St (R); or N-bnd: From Jct of US-169 & SR-68, W 5.5 mi on SR-68 to Osawatomie Rd, N 2.5 mi (L). Entrance fee required. 248 Avail: 180 W, 180 E (30 amps). 2021 rates: $10 to $35. (913)783-4507

HOISINGTON — C3 *Barton*

HOISINGTON RV PARK (Public) From E jct US 281 & K-4: Go 2 blks E on K-4, then 1 blk N on Susank Rd (E). 12 Avail: 12 W, 12 E (20/50 amps). 2021 rates: $15. (620)653-4050

HORTON — A6 *Brown*

HORTON MISSION LAKE CAMPGROUND (Public) From Jct of Hwys 159 & 73, E 3 blks on Hwy 73 to Wilson Dr, N 0.25 mi (E). Avail: 100 E (30 amps). 2021 rates: $17. Apr 01 to Oct 31. (785)486-2324

HUTCHINSON — C4 *Reno*

KANSAS STATE FAIR RV PARK (Public State Park) From jct KS-61 & E 30th Ave: Go W 2-3/4 mi on 30th Ave, then S 3/4 mi on N Main St, then E 330 yds on 20th Ave. (L). Avail: 211 full hkups (30/50 amps). 2021 rates: $30. (620)669-3630

INDEPENDENCE — D6 *Montgomery*

ELK CITY (Public State Park) W-bnd: From Jct of US-75 & US-160 (in town), W 1.8 mi on US-160 to Peter Pan rd., N 1 mi to CR-4600, W 2.2 mi to County Park Rd, ; or N-bnd: From Jct of US-75 (from Okla) & US-160, E 0.2 mi on US-160 to Peter Pan Rd., follow above directions. 240 Avail: 120 full hkups, 63 W, 63 E (30/50 amps). 2021 rates: $10 to $35. Apr 15 to Oct 31. (620)331-6295

IOLA — C6 *Allen*

STORAGE & RV OF IOLA **Ratings: 5.5/10★/7** (RV Park) Avail: 26 full hkups (30/50 amps). 2021 rates: $28. (620)365-2200, 1327 US-54 Hwy, Iola, KS 66749

JETMORE — C2 *Hodgeman*

JETMORE See also Dodge City.

HORSETHIEF RESERVOIR (Public) From jct US-283/Main St & Hwy 156: Go 9-1/2 mi W on Hwy 156 (L) Note: Do not rely on GPS. 32 Avail: 32 W, 32 E (30/50 amps). 2021 rates: $10 to $18. (620)253-8464

JUNCTION CITY — B5 *Geary*

MILFORD LAKE - COE/CURTIS CREEK (Public Corps) From jct I-70 & US-77: Go 5 mi N on US-77, then 4 mi W on SR-244, then 6 mi N on CR-837 (R). Avail: 48 E (30 amps). 2021 rates: $14 to $20. Apr 15 to Sep 30. (785)238-5714

MILFORD LAKE - COE/WEST ROLLING HILLS (Public Corps) From Jct of I-70 & US-77, N 5 mi on US-77 to SR-244, W 3 mi (R). 44 Avail: 38 W, 38 E (30/50 amps). 2021 rates: $14 to $21. Apr 15 to Sep 30. (785)784-4447

KANSAS CITY — B6 *Wyandotte*

KANSAS CITY See also Lawrence, Linn Valley & Merriam, KS; Grain Valley, Higginsville, Independence, Kansas City, Maysville, Oak Grove, Odessa, Peculiar, Platte City & St Joseph, MO.

KINGMAN — D4 *Kingman*

KINGMAN STATE FISHING LAKE (Public State Park) From Jct of US-54 & SR-14, W 7.8 mi on US-54 to Kingman Lake Rd, N 0.5 mi (L). 50 Avail: Pit toilets. 2021 rates: $5. (620)532-3242

KINSLEY — C3 *Edwards*

FOUR ACES RV PARK **Ratings: 7/9★/9** (Campground) 35 Avail: 34 full hkups, 1 W, 1 E (30/50 amps). 2021 rates: $38. (620)659-2321, 1004 Massachusetts, Kinsley, KS 67547

LA CROSSE — C3 *Rush*

LA CROSSE CITY PARK (Public) In town on US-183, E side, between 2nd & 4th St. Avail: 4 E. (785)222-2511

LAWRENCE — B6 *Douglas*

CLINTON (Public State Park) From Jct of I-70 & 10 Hwy (exit 197), E 3.6 mi on East 10 Hwy to Clinton Pkwy, W 100 ft to E-900 Rd, N 0.2 mi (2nd left to entrance). 383 Avail: 214 W, 214 E (30/50 amps). 2021 rates: $10 to $35. (785)842-8562

LAWRENCE / KANSAS CITY WEST KOA **Ratings: 9/10★/9.5** (Campground) Avail: 70 full hkups (30/50 amps). 2021 rates: $55 to $85. (785)842-3877, 1473 N. 1800 Rd/Hwy 24/40, Lawrence, KS 66044

LEBO — C5 *Osage*

MELVERN LAKE - COE/SUN DANCE PARK (Public Corps) From town, N 3 mi on cnty rd, follow signs (R). 25 Avail: Pit toilets. 2021 rates: $10. (785)549-3318

LIBERAL — D1 *Seward*

ARKALON RV PARK (Public) From US 54 & US 83: Go 10 mi E on US 54. Avail: 36 E (15/30 amps). 2021 rates: $5 to $15. Apr 01 to Oct 31. (620)626-0531

SEVEN WINDS RV PARK

Ratings: 6.5/8★/6 (RV Park) Avail: 33 full hkups (30/50 amps). 2021 rates: $32. (620)624-5581, 5924 W. Old Hwy 54, Liberal, KS 67901

WESTERN STAR RV RANCH Ratings: 8/8.5★/8 (RV Park) Avail: 38 full hkups (30/50 amps). 2021 rates: $35. (620)391-0628, 13916 Road 7, Liberal, KS 67901

Follow the arrow. The arrow in each listing indicates where the facility is located in relation to the listed town.

LINN VALLEY — B6 *Linn*

LINN VALLEY LAKES **Ratings: 8.5/7/8** (Membership Park) Avail: 47 full hkups (30/50 amps). 2021 rates: $15. (913)757-4591, 9 Linn Valley Ave., Linn Valley, KS 66040

LYNDON — C6 *Osage*

LYNDON See also Topeka & Williamsburg.

CROSSROADS RV PARK

Ratings: 7.5/8.5/9.5 (RV Park) Avail: 45 full hkups (30/50 amps). 2021 rates: $35. (785)221-5482, 23313 S. US Hwy 75, Lyndon, KS 66451

EISENHOWER (Public State Park) From jct US-75 & SR-278: Go 3 mi W on SR-278 (L). 186 Avail: 37 full hkups, 81 W, 68 E (30/50 amps). 2021 rates: $10 to $35. (785)528-4102

POMONA LAKE - COE/CARBOLYN PARK (Public Corps) From Jct of US-75 & SR-268, N 2 mi on US-75 (R). 32 Avail: 29 W, 29 E (30/50 amps). 2021 rates: $18. May 01 to Sep 30. (785)453-2201

MANHATTAN — B5 *Pottawatomie*

TUTTLE CREEK LAKE - COE/STOCKDALE CAMPGROUND (Public Corps) From town, N 12 mi on US-24 to CR-895, N 1.5 mi to CR-396, E 2.5 mi (L). 12 Avail: 12 W, 12 E (50 amps). 2021 rates: $20. Apr 15 to Oct 31. (785)539-8511

TUTTLE CREEK LAKE - COE/TUTTLE CREEK COVE (Public Corps) From town, N 5 mi on US-24 to KS-13, N 0.2 mi to CR-897S, NW 4 mi (E). 56 Avail: 39 W, 39 E (50 amps). 2021 rates: $14 to $20. Apr 15 to Oct 31. (785)539-6523

TUTTLE CREEK/FANCY CREEK (Public State Park) From town: Go 20 mi N on Hwy 24 (R). Avail: 24 E (30/50 amps). 2021 rates: $10 to $35. (785)539-7941

TUTTLE CREEK/RIVER POND (Public State Park) From town, N 5 mi on Hwy 24 to park (R). 715 Avail: 8 full hkups, 167 W, 167 E (30/50 amps). 2021 rates: $10 to $35. (785)539-7941

MANKATO — A4 *Jewell*

LOVEWELL (Public State Park) From Jct of US-36 & K-14, N 8.8 mi on K-14 to unmarked cnty rd (pk access rd), E 4 mi to park access rd, S 0.4 mi (E). 482 Avail: 19 full hkups, 32 W, 82 E (30 amps). 2021 rates: $10 to $35. (785)753-4971

MARION — C4 *Marion*

MARION COUNTY PARK & LAKE (MARION COUNTY PARK) (Public) From town, E 2 mi on US-256 to Upland Rd, S 2 mi on Upland Rd to Lakeshore Dr, W 0.5 mi on Lakeshore Dr (E). 90 Avail: 40 W, 44 E (30 amps). 2021 rates: $6 to $12. (620)382-3240

KS

MARQUETTE — C4 *Ellsworth*

KANOPOLIS LAKE - COE/RIVERSIDE AREA (Public Corps) From town, W 9 mi on Hwy 4 to Hwy 141, N 3 mi (R). Avail: 16 E (30 amps). 2021 rates: $14 to $26. (785)546-2294

KANOPOLIS LAKE - COE/VENANGO AREA (Public Corps) From town, NW 8 mi on Hwy 4 to Hwy 141, N 4 mi (L). 126 Avail: 30 W, 81 E (30/50 amps). 2021 rates: $14 to $26. May 01 to Dec 31. (785)546-2294

KANOPOLIS LAKE/HORSETHIEF CANYON (Public State Park) From town, W 9 mi on K-4 to K-141, N 5 mi to Venango Rd, W 0.25 to park access rd, NW 0.25 (L). 45 Avail: 13 W, 45 E (30 amps). 2021 rates: $10 to $35. (785)546-2565

KANOPOLIS LAKE/LANGLEY POINT (Public State Park) From town, W 9 mi on K-4 to K-141, N 4 mi (L). 193 Avail: 16 full hkups, 31 W, 72 E (30 amps). 2021 rates: $10 to $35. (785)546-2565

Find it fast! Use our alphabetized index of campgrounds and parks.

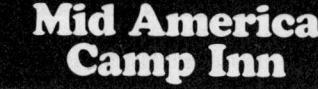

MAYETTA — B5 *Jackson*

PRAIRIE BAND CASINO RESORT RV PARK **Ratings: 9/9.5★/10** (RV Park) Avail: 67 full hkups (30/50 amps). 2021 rates: $31.50. (785)966-7778, 12305 150th Rd, Mayetta, KS 66509

MCPHERSON — C4 *McPherson*

MCPHERSON See also Halstead & Hesston.

MCPHERSON RV RANCH

good sam park **Ratings: 7/9.5★/8.5** (RV Park) From Jct I-135 (exit 63) & Mohawk Road: Go 1/2 mi W on Mohawk Road, then 1 mi S on 16th Ave., then 1/4 mi E on Northview Road (L). **FAC:** gravel rds. Avail: 40 gravel, 30 pull-thrus, (30x80), back-ins (30x60), 40 full hkups (30/50 amps), WiFi @ sites, laundry, fire rings, firewood. **REC:** pond, fishing, hunting nearby. Pets OK. No tents. Big rig sites, eco-friendly. 2021 rates: $37, Military discount.

(620)241-5621 Lat: 38.39394, Lon: -97.62487
2201 E Northview Ave, McPherson, KS 67460
mcphersonrvranchks.com
See ad this page

MEADE — D2 *Meade*

MEADE (Public State Park) From Jct of US-54 & K-23, SW 13 mi on K-23 (R). 96 Avail: 42 W, 42 E (30/50 amps). 2021 rates: $10 to $35. (620)873-2572

MELVERN — C6 *Osage*

MELVERN LAKE - COE/COEUR D'ALENE (Public Corps) From Jct of US-75 & SH-31 exit, S 1.5 mi on SH-31 to Coeur D'Alene Pkwy, NW 1 mi (E). Avail: 34 E (30/50 amps). 2021 rates: $14 to $22. May 01 to Sep 30. (785)549-3318

MELVERN LAKE - COE/OUTLET PARK (Public Corps) From Jct of US-75 & SH-31 exit, W 0.25 mi on SH-31 to cut-off rd, NW 0.25 mi to River Pond Pkwy, N 0.5 mi (E). 140 Avail: 140 W, 140 E (30/50 amps). 2021 rates: $20 to $24. Apr 01 to Oct 31. (785)549-3318

MERRIAM — B6 *Johnson*

WALNUT GROVE RV PARK

good sam park **Ratings: 8.5/9★/9** (RV Park) From jct I-35 (exit 229) & Johnson Dr: Go 3/4 mi W on Johnson Dr (R) or from jct I-435 (exit 6C) & Johnson Dr: Go E 3 mi on Johnson Dr (L). **FAC:** paved rds. (50 spaces). Avail: 31 all weather, 6 pull-thrus, (24x65), back-ins (24x45), 31 full hkups (30/50 amps), seasonal sites, WiFi @ sites, dump, laundry, groc, LP bottles, fire rings, firewood. **REC:** hunting nearby. Pets OK. Partial handicap access. No tents. Big rig sites. 2021 rates: $50 to $100, Military discount.

(913)262-3023 Lat: 39.0228, Lon: -94.70520
10218 Johnson Dr, Merriam, KS 66203
walnutgroverv.com
See ad page 540

MILFORD — B5 *Geary*

MILFORD (Public State Park) From Jct of I-70 & US-77 (exit 295), N 4.5 mi on US-77 to SR-57, W 4.1 mi (L). 244 Avail: 51 full hkups, 90 W, 90 E (30/50 amps). 2021 rates: $10 to $35. (785)238-3014

MILFORD LAKE - COE/FARNUM CREEK (Public Corps) From town, S 2 mi on US-77 (R). Avail: 36 E (30/50 amps). 2021 rates: $14 to $21. Apr 15 to Sep 30. (785)463-5791

NORTON — A2 *Norton*

PRAIRIE DOG (Public State Park) W-bnd: From Jct of US-283 & US-36, W 4 mi on US-36 to SR-261, S 1 mi (E); or E-bnd: From Jct of US-36 & SR-383, E 2 mi on US-36 to SR-261, S 1 mi (E). Entrance fee required. 229 Avail: 10 full hkups, 77 W, 89 E (30/50 amps). 2021 rates: $10 to $35. Apr 15 to Oct 15. (785)877-2953

OAKLEY — B2 *Logan*

HIGH PLAINS CAMPING

good sam park **Ratings: 8/9★/7.5** (RV Park) Avail: 68 full hkups (30/50 amps). 2021 rates: $44. (785)672-3538, 462 US 83, Oakley, KS 67748

OGALLAH — B2 *Trego*

CEDAR BLUFF (BLUFFTON AREA) (Public State Park) From jct I-70 (exit 135) & Hwy 147: Go 13 mi S on Hwy 147. 254 Avail: 11 full hkups, 102 W, 122 E (30 amps). 2021 rates: $10 to $12. (785)726-3212

CEDAR BLUFF (PAGE CREEK AREA) (Public State Park) From jct I-70 & Hwy-147: Go 19 mi S on Hwy-147, then 4 mi W on countyroad. 36 Avail: Pit toilets. 2021 rates: $10 to $22. (785)726-3212

OLIVET — C5 *Osage*

MELVERN LAKE - COE/ARROW ROCK (Public Corps) From Jct of US-75 & Olivet exit (CR-276), W 1 mi on CR-276 to S Fairlawn Rd, N 1 mi to Arrow Rock Pkwy, W 1 mi (E). 43 Avail: 19 W, 19 E (30 amps). 2021 rates: $14 to $20. May 01 to Sep 30. (785)549-3318

OSAGE CITY — B5 *Osage*

MELVERN LAKE - COE/TURKEY POINT (Public Corps) From town, S 8 mi on K-170 to 301st St, E 2 mi to Indian Hills Rd, S 1 mi to Turkey Point Pkwy, S 0.5 mi (E). 46 Avail: 34 W, 34 E (30/50 amps). 2021 rates: $14 to $21. May 01 to Sep 30. (785)549-3318

OSWEGO — D6 *Labette*

HILLSIDE RV PARK **Ratings: 6/NA/8** (RV Area in MH Park) Avail: 24 full hkups (30/50 amps). 2021 rates: $30. (620)795-2471, 1108 S Commercial, Oswego, KS 67356

KAMP SIESTA (Public) From Jct of K-96 & Kansas St, N 1 mi on Kansas St to North St, W 1 mi, follow signs (E). 42 Avail: 42 W, 42 E (30/50 amps). 2021 rates: $15. (620)795-4433

OTTAWA — C6 *Franklin*

POMONA (Public State Park) From Jct of US-75 & SR-268, E 4.4 mi on SR-268 to SR-368, N 1 mi (E). 444 Avail: 41 full hkups, 93 W, 93 E (30/50 amps). 2021 rates: $10 to $35. (785)828-4933

POMONA LAKE - COE/ADAMS GROVE (Public Corps) From town: Go 15 mi W on Hwy 68, then 3 mi W on Hwy 268, then 2 mi N on Lake Rd 1, then 3/4 mi N of dam on lake roads. 30 Avail: Pit toilets. 2021 rates: $6. (785)453-2201

POMONA LAKE - COE/MICHIGAN VALLEY (Public Corps) From town, E 6.4 mi on SR-268 to Pomona Dam Rd, N 3 mi to Wolf Creek Rd, W 0.1 mi (E). 89 Avail: 51 W, 51 E (30/50 amps). 2021 rates: $14 to $22. May 01 to Sep 30. (785)453-2201

POMONA LAKE - COE/OUTLET PARK (Public Corps) From Jct of US-75 & Rte 268, E 7 mi on Rte 268 to Pomona Dam Rd, N 0.5 mi to 229th St, E 0.25 mi (E). 34 Avail: 34 W, 34 E (30 amps). 2021 rates: $20. (785)453-2201

POMONA LAKE - COE/WOLF CREEK (Public Corps) From town, N 2 mi on US-75 to Hwy 268, E 6 mi to Pomona Dam Rd, N 2.5 mi to Wolf Creek Pkwy, W 2 mi (E). 78 Avail: 45 W, 45 E (30/50 amps). 2021 rates: $14 to $20. May 01 to Sep 15. (785)453-2201

OZAWKIE — B6 *Jefferson*

PERRY LAKE - COE/OLD TOWN PARK (Public Corps) From town, E 1.5 mi on SR-92 (R). Avail: 33 E (30 amps). 2021 rates: $14 to $19. May 01 to Sep 30. (785)876-3146

PARSONS — D6 *Labette*

LAKE PARSONS (Public) From Jct of Main St & 32nd St to Z6000 Rd, W 3 mi to Kiowa Rd, N 2 mi, follow signs (R). 50 Avail. 2021 rates: $8 to $15. Apr 01 to Nov 01. (620)421-7031

MARVEL PARK (Public) From Jct of US-59 & US-160, E 0.5 mi on US-160 (R). 24 Avail: 24 W, 24 E (30/50 amps). 2021 rates: $10. (620)421-7032

PAXICO — B5 *Wabaunsee*

MILL CREEK CAMPGROUND & RV PARK **Ratings: 7/8.5/7.5** (Campground) Avail: 10 full hkups (30/50 amps). 2021 rates: $30 to $38. (785)636-5321, 22470 Campground Rd, Paxico, KS 66526

PERRY — B6 *Jefferson*

PERRY (Public State Park) From jct US 24 & Hwy 237: Go 4 mi N on Hwy 237. 110 Avail: 110 W, 110 E (30/50 amps). 2021 rates: $10 to $35. (785)246-3449

PERRY CREEK - COE/SLOUGH CREEK PARK (Public Corps) From town, N 7 mi on Ferguson Rd to Slough Creek Rd, SW 1.5 mi (E). Avail: 127 E (30/50 amps). 2021 rates: $14 to $20. Apr 15 to Oct 15. (785)597-5144

PERRY LAKE - COE/LONGVIEW CAMPGROUND (Public Corps) From town: Go 1-1/2 mi E on Hwy 92, then 2 mi S on Ferguson Rd, then 23 mi W on 86th St (E). Avail: 26 E (30 amps). 2021 rates: $12 to $16. May 01 to Sep 30. (785)597-5144

PERRY LAKE - COE/ROCK CREEK (Public Corps) From town, N 3 mi on Ferguson Rd to 39th St, W 5 mi to Perry Park Dr, N 5 mi to Dam Rd, W 1.5 mi to park entrance. 99 Avail: 51 W, 51 E (30/50 amps). 2021 rates: $14 to $20. May 01 to Sep 30. (785)597-5144

PHILLIPSBURG — A3 *Phillips*

PHILLIPSBURG CAMPGROUND (Public) From Jct of US-36 & Hwy 183, W .5 mi on US-36 (L). 10 Avail: 10 W, 10 E (30 amps). 2021 rates: $10. Apr 01 to Oct 31. (785)543-5234

PITTSBURG — D6 *Crawford*

PARKVIEW MH & RV COMMUNITY

good sam park **Ratings: 6.5/8★/8.5** (RV Area in MH Park) Avail: 45 full hkups (30/50 amps). 2021 rates: $30. (620)232-1030, 520 W 20th St, Pittsburg, KS 66762

PRATT — D3 *Pratt*

EVERGREEN INN MOTEL & RV PARK **Ratings: 7.5/7.5★/7.5** (RV Park) Avail: 25 full hkups (30/50 amps). 2021 rates: $30 to $35. (800)456-6424, 20001 W US-54/400, Pratt, KS 67124

RUSSELL — B3 *Russell*

TRIPLE 'J' RV PARK

good sam park **Ratings: 7.5/10★/8.5** (RV Park) From Jct I-70 (exit 184) & US-281: Go 500 ft N on US-281 (at Cenex Gas), then 500 ft W on E Edwards Ave. (E). **FAC:** gravel rds. (68 spaces). Avail: 48 gravel, 48 pull-thrus, (24x70), 48 full hkups (30/50 amps), seasonal sites, cable, WiFi @ sites, tent sites, rentals, laundry, fire rings, firewood. **REC:** playground, hunting nearby. Pets OK. Big rig sites, eco-friendly. 2021 rates: $42, Military discount.

(785)483-4826 Lat: 38.86635, Lon: -98.85729
187 E. Edwards, Russell, KS 67665
www.triplejrvpark.com
See ad this page

SALINA — B4 *Saline*

SALINA KOA HOLIDAY **Ratings: 9/10★/8.5** (Campground) 63 Avail: 56 full hkups, 7 W, 7 E (30/50 amps). 2021 rates: $36.70 to $62.50. (785)827-3182, 1109 W Diamond Dr, Salina, KS 67401

SCOTT CITY — C2 *Scott*

LAKE SCOTT (Public State Park) From Jct of SR-96 & US-83, N 9.7 mi on US-83 to SR-95, NW 3 mi (L). Entrance fee required. 119 Avail: 40 W, 40 E (30/50 amps). 2021 rates: $10 to $35. Apr 10 to Oct 30. (620)872-2061

SENECA — A5 *Nemaha*

BAILEY'S RV RESORT

good sam park **Ratings: 7/9.5★/9** (RV Park) From Jct Hwy 63 & US-36 (in town): Go 1 mi W on US-36 (North Street) (R) Note: Behind Altenofen Inn Hotel & Dollar General.
FAC: gravel rds. 32 Avail: 20 paved, 12 all weather, patios, 20 pull-thrus, (24x60), back-ins (22x45), 32 full hkups (30/50 amps), WiFi @ sites, $, tent sites, dump, laundry. **REC:** pond, fishing, boating nearby, playground, hunting nearby. Pets OK. Partial handicap access. Big rig sites, eco-friendly. 2021 rates: $40, Military discount. no cc.
(785)294-1208 Lat: 39.84171, Lon: -96.07854
1701 North St, Seneca, KS 66538
baileysrvresort.com
See ad this page

SOUTH HUTCHINSON — C4 *Reno*

LIGHTHOUSE LANDING RV PARK & CABINS

good sam park **Ratings: 8/9.5★/8.5** (RV Park) From jct Hwy 61 & Hwy 96: Go 1/4 mi S on Hwy 96 (Main St), then go 1/8 mi W on Heartland Dr (R). **FAC:** all weather rds. Avail: 46 all weather, 37 pull-thrus, (35x70), back-ins (30x60), 46 full hkups (30/50 amps), WiFi @ sites, rentals, dump, laundry, LP gas, fire rings. **REC:** pond, fishing, boating nearby, playground, hunting nearby. Pets OK. No tents. Big rig sites, eco-friendly. 2021 rates: $40, Military discount.
(800)921-1236 Lat: 38.007702, Lon: -97.945474
9 Heartland Dr, South Hutchinson, KS 67505
lighthouselandingrvpark.com
See ad page 401

The Ratings & What They Mean

Turn to "Understanding the Rating System" section at the front of this Guide to get information on how we rate and inspect parks with our handy three number system!

Rated 10/10★/10

The **FIRST NUMBER** represents Development of Facilities

The **SECOND NUMBER** represents Cleanliness and Physical Characteristics of Restrooms and Showers (plus, a Star is awarded to parks who receive maximum points for cleanliness!)

The **THIRD NUMBER** represents Visual Appearance/Environmental Quality

STOCKTON — B3 *Rooks*

ROOKS COUNTY FAIRGROUNDS (CITY PARK) (Public) From jct US 24 & US 183: Go 8-1/2 blocks S on US 183. Avail: 30 E (30 amps). 2021 rates: $20. (785)425-6703

WEBSTER (Public State Park) From Jct of Hwy 183 & Hwy 24, W 8.9 mi on Hwy 24 (L). 93 Avail: 1 full hkups, 82 W, 92 E (30/50 amps). 2021 rates: $10 to $35. Apr 15 to Oct 15. (785)425-6775

TONGANOXIE — B6 *Leavenworth*

LEAVENWORTH STATE FISHING LAKE (Public State Park) From Jct of SR-24 & SR-16, N 3 mi on SR-16 to Hwy 90, W 2 mi (W). 20 Avail: Pit toilets. 2021 rates: $5 to $35. (913)845-2665

TOPEKA — B5 *Shawnee*

TOPEKA See also Lawrence & Mayetta.

CAPITAL CITY KOA **Ratings: 9/9.5★/8.5** (Campground) Avail: 57 full hkups (30/50 amps). 2021 rates: $48.78 to $58.78. (800)562-4793, 1949 SW 49th St, Topeka, KS 66609

DEER CREEK VALLEY RV PARK

good sam park **Ratings: 10/9.5★/10** (RV Park) From jct I-70 (exit 364B) & Carnahan: Go S 1/4 mi on Carnahan, then E 1/4 mi on 21st St. (L).

TOPEKA'S ONLY LUXURY RV PARK!
Experience luxury tonight! Enjoy our level pull-thru concrete pads with patios just off I-70. Amenities include free cable, WiFi and a security access gate. We pamper pets with a fenced Dog Park. Reservations recommended.

FAC: paved rds. Avail: 59 paved, patios, 54 pull-thrus, (35x95), back-ins (35x50), 59 full hkups (30/50 amps), cable, WiFi @ sites, dump, laundry, LP gas, controlled access. **REC:** heated pool, boating nearby, playground. Pet restrict (B). Partial handicap access. No tents. Big rig sites, eco-friendly. 2021 rates: $45, Military discount.
(785)357-8555 Lat: 39.03068, Lon: -95.63377
3140 SE 21st Street, Topeka, KS 66607
www.deercreekvalleyrvpark.com
See ad next page

LAKE SHAWNEE CAMPGROUND (SHAWNEE COUNTY) (Public) From I-70 (East Topeka Tnpk exit): Go 1/2 mi SE on 21st St, then 1-1/2 mi S on Croco Rd, then 1/2 mi W on East Edge Rd. Avail: 121 full hkups (30/50 amps). 2021 rates: $17 to $20. (785)251-6834

TORONTO — C5 *Woodson*

CROSS TIMBERS/DAM SITE & HOLIDAY HILL AREA (Public State Park) From jct US-54 & Hwy 105: Go 9 mi S on Hwy 105 (L). 77 Avail: 50 W, 58 E (50 amps). 2021 rates: $10 to $35. (620)637-2213

CROSS TIMBERS/MANN'S COVE AREA (Public State Park) From jct US-54 & Hwy 105: Go 3-3/4 mi S on Hwy 105, then 2-3/4 mi SE on Hwy 361 (L). 20 Avail: 20 W, 20 E (20/30 amps). 2021 rates: $10 to $35. (620)637-2213

CROSS TIMBERS/TORONTO POINT (Public State Park) From jct US-54 & SR-105: Go 3 mi S on SR-105, then 1 mi S on Point Rd (E). 46 Avail: 15 full hkups, 25 W, 25 E (30 amps). 2021 rates: $10 to $35. (620)637-2213

RV MYTH #1: ""Recreational vehicles are expensive.'' This is not necessarily true. Oh, yes, you can pay a million or more dollars for one, but that is far from normal and represents an extremely small market. RVs are available in many sizes, configurations and affordable prices. Additionally, the running capital cost of a unit is only the difference between the purchase price and the current value.

KS

TOPEKA'S FINEST
DEER CREEK VALLEY
RV PARK
DEER CREEK VALLEY
RV PARK
GATED FOR SECURITY • RESERVATIONS STRONGLY RECOMMENDED
• All Concrete Roads
• All Sites are 35 x 95 Feet
• All Concrete Sites with 10 x 20 Concrete Patio
• Storm Shelter/Laundry Facility
• Large Enclosed Dog Park
• Heated Swimming Pool
• 30 & 50 Amp
• Playground
• Group Meeting Room (10 or more campers)
• 54 Pull-Thru Sites
• 5 Back-Ins
• Free WiFi & Cable TV
good sam park
2022 Top Rated 10/9.5★/10
3140 SE 21st St. • Topeka, KS • Telephone (785) 357-8555
www.deercreekvalleyrvpark.com
VISA/MASTERCARD/DISCOVER
See listing Topeka, KS

VALLEY CENTER — C4 *Sedgwick*

NORTH STAR RV PARK
good sam park **Ratings: 6.5/9★/8** (RV Park) From jct I-135 (exit 19) & 101st St: Go 1 mi W on 101st St. (R).

QUIET COUNTRY SETTING RV PARK
Come enjoy the country setting in our quiet RV park close enough to Wichita for the convenience of shopping and dining, but far enough out to enjoy the peaceful country atmosphere!

FAC: gravel rds. (30 spaces). Avail: 22 gravel, 15 pull-thrus, (35x70), back-ins (35x70), 18 full hkups, 4 W, 4 E (30/50 amps), seasonal sites, WiFi @ sites, dump, laundry. **REC:** playground. Pet restrict (B/Q). No tents. Big rig sites. 2021 rates: $38.
(316)755-0592 Lat: 37.86852, Lon: -97.34452
650 W 101st St North, Valley Center, KS 67147
See ad this page

WAKEENEY — B2 *Trego*

WAKEENEY KOA **Ratings: 8.5/9.5★/8.5** (Campground) Avail: 57 full hkups (30/50 amps). 2021 rates: $41.50. Mar 15 to Oct 31. (800)562-2761, 25027 S. Interstate, Wakeeney, KS 67672

WAKEFIELD — B4 *Clay*

CLAY COUNTY PARK (Public) From Jct of SR-82 & Dogwood St: Go 3 blks S on Dogwood St (L). 292 Avail: 292 W, 292 E (30 amps). 2021 rates: $20 to $35. Apr 15 to Oct 15. (785)447-1547

MILFORD LAKE - COE/SCHOOL CREEK (Public Corps) From town: Go 1-1/2 mi W on SR-82, then 7 mi S on CR-837, then ½ mi E on 2nd Rd (E). 44 Avail: Pit toilets. 2021 rates: $8. (785)238-5714

MILFORD LAKE - COE/TIMBER CREEK (Public Corps) From town, E 1.9 mi on SR-82 (E). 79 Avail: Pit toilets. 2021 rates: $10. (785)238-5714

WELLINGTON — D4 *Sumner*

WELLINGTON KOA
good sam park **Ratings: 8.5/9.5★/9** (Campground) Avail: 40 full hkups (30/50 amps). 2021 rates: $39 to $67.87. (620)326-8300, 100 South KOA Dr., Wellington, KS 67152

WICHITA — D4 *Sedgwick*

A SPOTLIGHT Introducing Wichita Area's colorful attractions appearing at the front of this state section.

WICHITA See also Halstead, Hesston & Valley Center.

AIR CAPITAL RV PARK
good sam park **Ratings: 9/10★/9.5** (RV Park) Avail: 90 full hkups (30/50 amps). 2021 rates: $49 to $59. (316)201-1250, 609 E 47th St South, Wichita, KS 67216

ALL SEASONS RV PARK
good sam park **Ratings: 8/10★/9** (RV Park) West bnd: From jct I-235 & Hwy 54: Go 4-1/2 mi W on Hwy 54 to 119th St, then 1 mi N on 119th St, then 2-1/4 W on Maple St (R) East bnd: From jct Hwy 54 & 167th St: Go 1 mi N on 167th St, then 3/4 mi E on Maple St (L). **FAC:** gravel rds. (48 spaces). Avail: 30 gravel, 30 pull-thrus, (24x65), mostly side by side hkups, 30 full hkups (30/50 amps), seasonal sites, cable, WiFi @ sites, tent sites, dump, laundry, groc, LP gas. **REC:** boating nearby, playground, hunting nearby. Pet restrict (B). Big rig sites, eco-friendly. 2021 rates: $38 to $45, Military discount.
(316)722-1154 Lat: 37.67903, Lon: -97.52080
15520 W Maple Street, Goddard, KS 67052
www.allseasonsrvcampground.com
See ad page 400

CAMP THE RANGE
good sam park **Ratings: 9/10★/8.5** (RV Park) N-bnd: From Jct I-135 (exit 10-A) & K-96 bypass: Go 1mi E on K-96 bypass, then 300 ft N on Hillside, then .1 mi W on N 33rd St. Or S Bnd: From Jct I-135 (Exit 10) & K-96 bypass: Go 1 mi E on K-96 bypass, then 300 ft N on Hillside, then .1 mi W on N 33rd St (R). **FAC:** all weather rds. (75 spaces). Avail: 42 all weather, 42 pull-thrus, (24x60), 42 full hkups (30/50 amps), seasonal sites, WiFi @ sites, dump, laundry, LP gas. **REC:** boating nearby, playground, hunting nearby. Pet restrict (Q). No tents. Big rig sites, eco-friendly. 2021 rates: $40 to $53, Military discount.
(316)838-8699 Lat: 37.74530, Lon: -97.30212
2920 E 33rd St N, Wichita, KS 67219
camptherangervpark.com
See ad this page

Save 10% at Good Sam Parks!

K & R RV PARK
good sam park **Ratings: 6.5/NA/5.5** (RV Park) Avail: 25 full hkups (30/50 amps). 2021 rates: $35 to $45. (316)684-1531, 3200 S Southeast Blvd, Wichita, KS 67216

Travel Services

GANDER RV OF WICHITA Your new hometown outfitter offering the best regional gear for all your outdoor needs. Your adventure awaits. **SERVICES:** RV appliance, MH mechanical, sells outdoor gear, sells firearms, staffed RV wash, restrooms. RV Sales. RV supplies, LP gas, RV accessible. Hours: 9am - 8pm.
(844)981-1380 Lat: 37.624739, Lon: -97.346114
3928 S Oak St, Wichita, KS 67217
rv.ganderoutdoors.com

WILLIAMSBURG — C6 *Franklin*

HOMEWOOD RV PARK **Ratings: 7/8.5★/8.5** (RV Park) Avail: 25 full hkups (30/50 amps). 2021 rates: $35 to $38. (785)242-5601, 2135 Idaho Rd, Williamsburg, KS 66095

WILSON — B3 *Russell*

WILSON (HELL CREEK CAMPGROUND) (Public State Park) Jct I-70 & Hwy 232: Go 8 miles N on Hwy 232. 128 Avail: 4 full hkups, 49 W, 85 E (30/50 amps). 2021 rates: $10 to $35. (785)658-2465

WILSON (OTOE CAMPGROUND) (Public State Park) Jct I-70 & Hwy 232: Go 8 miles N on Hwy 232. 80 Avail: 37 W, 37 E (30/50 amps). 2021 rates: $10 to $35. (785)658-2465

WILSON LAKE - COE/LUCAS PARK (Public Corps) From jct I-70 & SR-232 (exit 206): Go 9 mi N on SR-232, then 2 mi W on access rd (E). 95 Avail: 18 W, 70 E (30/50 amps). 2021 rates: $14 to $28. (785)658-2551

WILSON LAKE - COE/SYLVAN PARK (Public Corps) From jct I-70 & SR-232 (exit 206): Go 10 mi N on SR-232, then 1/4 mi E on Hwy 181 to access road (E). 25 Avail: 24 W, 24 E (30/50 amps). 2021 rates: $14 to $20. (785)658-2551

WINFIELD — D5 *Cowley*

WINFIELD FAIRGROUNDS (Public) From Jct of US-77 & SR-160, W 1 mi on SR-160 (L). 1000 Avail: 50 W, 850 E (30/50 amps). 2021 rates: $3 to $12. (620)221-5525

RV DRIVING TIPS: Take breaks. To be assured of safe driving, you should stop at a travel plaza, restaurant or rest stop every two hours. Get out of the car and walk around, or even jog or stretch. In addition to exercise breaks, stop for light meals and snacks.

KS

DID YOU KNOW?
Kentucky boasts more than 1,100 miles of lakes and rivers - more than any other state outside of Alaska.
YOU ARE HERE
Getty Images/iStockphoto

Kentucky

What do you get when you combine bourbon, bluegrass music and thoroughbred racing? Kentucky blends all three of those elements with verve. Bask in Southern culture mixed with a big Midwestern welcome.

Lay Down Bets in Louisville

Kentucky's largest and most dynamic city is Louisville, a town known for the Churchill Downs racetrack, the Louisville Slugger Museum & Factory, the Muhammad Ali Center along with fine dining and culture. Head downtown to explore a hip foodie scene that's coming into its own. Lexington, meanwhile, just might be Kentucky's signature city. Known as the "Horse Capital of the World," Lexington has over 400 horse farms nestled in its scenic bluegrass hills. Beyond the big towns, hop on the Bourbon Trail to taste test Kentucky's many distilleries.

Wilderness Untamed

The natural break in the Appalachian Mountains known as the Cumberland Gap gave passage to the pioneers who settled in the region. Sitting on the border of Tennessee, Kentucky and Virginia, the Cumberland Gap National Historical Park preserves the beauty of this gateway to the west. Over 80 miles of trails take hikers through woodlands and to scenic vistas. Nearby, the Cumberland Falls State Resort Park plays host to the occasional "moonbow," a nighttime phenomenon that appears over the waters of the "Niagara of the South."

Reel 'em In

Anglers and boaters flock to The Land Between the Lakes National Recreation Area. The two lakes straddling this peninsula in western Kentucky allow recreation lovers to zip across a massive lake or to paddle a tiny creek. Catfish, bass and bluegill can be caught in the large lakes and small ponds. Hike the 500 miles of trails in the surrounding country.

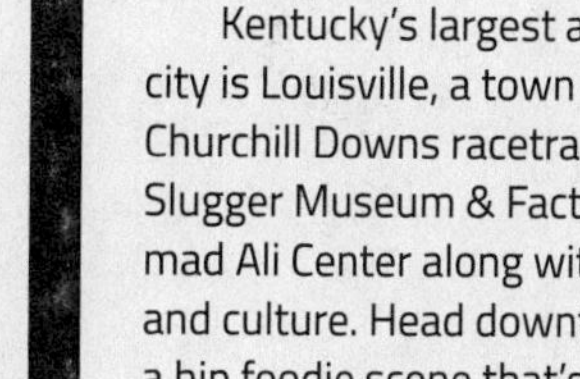

Kentucky Burgoo

Burgoo dates to the Civil War and is still served at large gatherings today. The hearty stew is a popular empty-your-fridge recipe made with various meats (usually chicken, beef or pork) and vegetables like cabbage, potatoes, corn and okra. Burgoo tastes better with age, so prepare a huge pot and enjoy it throughout the week.

VISITOR CENTER

TIME ZONE
Eastern/Central Standard

ROAD & HIGHWAY INFORMATION
866-737-3767
goky.ky.gov

FISHING & HUNTING INFORMATION
800-858-1549
fw.ky.gov/licenses

BOATING INFORMATION
800-858-1549
fw.ky.gov/boat

NATIONAL PARKS
nps.gov/ky

STATE PARKS
parks.ky.gov

TOURISM INFORMATION
Kentucky Department of Travel
800-225-8747
www.kentuckytourism.com

TOP TOURISM ATTRACTIONS
1) Mammoth Cave National Park
2) Churchill Downs
3) Kentucky Horse Park

MAJOR CITIES
Louisville, Lexington-Fayette, Bowling Green, Owensboro, Covington, Frankfort (capital)

good sam park

Featured Good Sam Parks

KENTUCKY

When you stay with Good Sam, you can expect the highest degree of cleanliness and friendliness, and better yet, you get **10% off** overnight campground fees.

If you're not already a Good Sam member you can purchase your membership at one of these locations:

BARDSTOWN
White Acres Campground

CAVE CITY
Cave Country RV Campground
Singing Hills RV Park

CORBIN
Laurel Lake Camping Resort

CORINTH
Three Springs Campground

DRY RIDGE
Northern KY RV Park

EDDYVILLE
Outback RV Resort

ELIZABETHTOWN
Elizabethtown Crossroads Campground

FRANKFORT
Elkhorn Campground

FRANKLIN
Dad's Bluegrass Campground

GEORGETOWN
Whispering Hills RV Park

LONDON
Westgate RV Campground

MOUNT VERNON
Renfro Valley RV Park

PADUCAH
Duck Creek RV Park
Fern Lake Campground & RV Park

PARK CITY
Diamond Caverns RV Resort & Golf Club

RUSSELL SPRINGS
Kumberland Campground

SALT LICK
Outpost RV Park & Campground

SLADE
4 Guys RV Park

SMITHLAND
Birdsville Riverside RV Park

SOMERSET
Happy Camper RV Park

Getty Images/iStockphoto

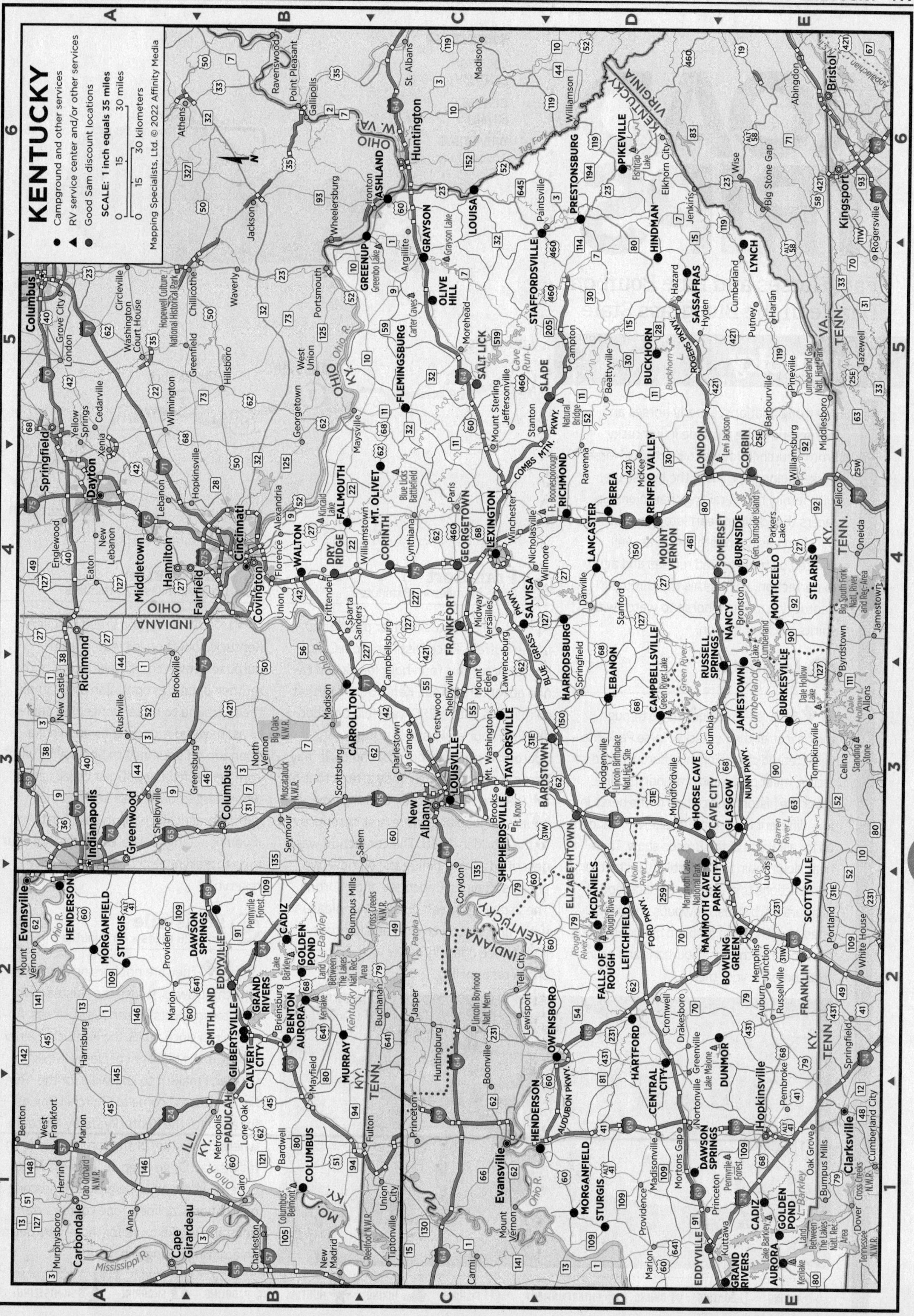
KENTUCKY
Campground and other services
RV service center and/or other services
Good Sam discount locations
SCALE: 1 inch equals 35 miles
Mapping Specialists, Ltd. © 2022 Affinity Media
INDIANA
OHIO
W. VA.
VIRGINIA
TENN.
ILL.
MO.
KY
Columbus
Springfield
Dayton
Middletown
Hamilton
Fairfield
Cincinnati
Covington
Indianapolis
Greenwood
Columbus
Richmond
Evansville
Henderson
Owensboro
Louisville
New Albany
Frankfort
Lexington
Georgetown
Ashland
Huntington
Grayson
Greenup
Louisa
Olive Hill
Salt Lick
Slade
Flemingsburg
Mt. Olivet
Falmouth
Walton
Dry Ridge
Corinth
Carrollton
Shepherdsville
Taylorsville
Bardstown
Harrodsburg
Salvisa
Lancaster
Richmond
Berea
Renfro Valley
Mount Vernon
London
Corbin
Somerset
Burnside
Nancy
Monticello
Stearns
Jamestown
Russell Springs
Burkesville
Campbellsville
Lebanon
Elizabethtown
McDaniels
Falls of Rough
Leitchfield
Horse Cave
Cave City
Glasgow
Mammoth Cave
Park City
Bowling Green
Scottsville
Franklin
Hartford
Central City
Dunmor
Hopkinsville
Dawson Springs
Clarksville
Cadiz
Golden Pond
Aurora
Grand Rivers
Eddyville
Morganfield
Sturgis
Prestonsburg
Pikeville
Staffordsville
Hindman
Sassafras
Buckhorn
Lynch
Kingsport
Bristol
Paducah
Calvert City
Gilbertsville
Benton
Murray
Columbus
Smithland
Cape Girardeau
Carbondale

ROAD TRIPS

Fast Horses and Fine Bourbon Dazzle in the Bluegrass State

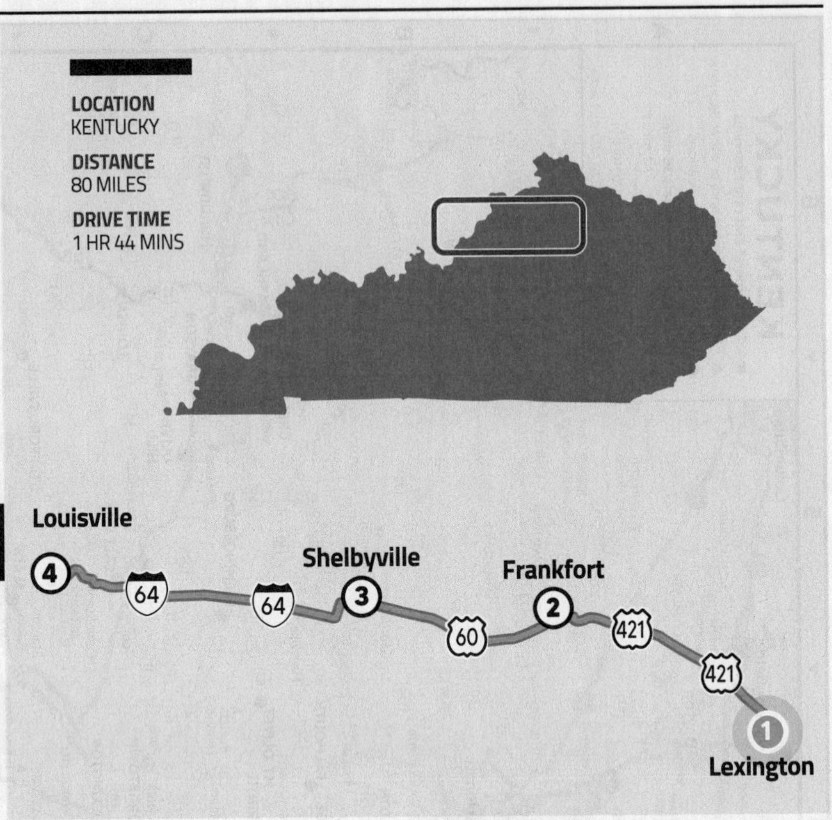

Kentucky

Strong libations, speedy horses and serene living all abide in Kentucky. From Churchill Downs to Kentucky Horse Park, equines dominate the landscape, with family farms raising championship racers that deliver heart-stopping finishes. Bourbon has a smooth finish, as well, created by time-tested recipes and aged to perfection. Follow this trip through Kentucky and find a horse to watch with spirits to cheer him on.

1 Lexington
Starting Point

See well-bred equines go through their paces at the Kentucky Horse Park. Marvel at retired championship thoroughbred racers; meet police and draft horses; discover the history and culture of the horse in four different museums on-site; and saddle up for a Parade of the Breeds show. Then head downtown to the Distillery District for introductions to an entire neighborhood of restaurants, bistros, brewpubs and distilleries. You'll have no problem quenching your thirst here, with prime bourbons and beers to accompany your meal.

2 Frankfort
Drive 32 miles ▪ 38 minutes

Take a Kentucky River paddle trip to the Buffalo Trace Distillery. Join Canoe Kentucky for this four-hour kayak and canoe adventure on the Kentucky River that culminates with a 200-year-old bourbon distillery tour and barbecue lunch. And if bourbon is not your drink of choice, it may become your favorite candy after a tour of the Rebecca-Ruth Candy Factory, where bourbon chocolates were first introduced to the world in 1938. The confection was described as combining the world's two greatest flavors: Chocolate and bourbon. These days, you can double your pleasure with rum, scotch, cognac and Kentucky Irish coffee chocolates, as well. Enjoy, but snack responsibly.

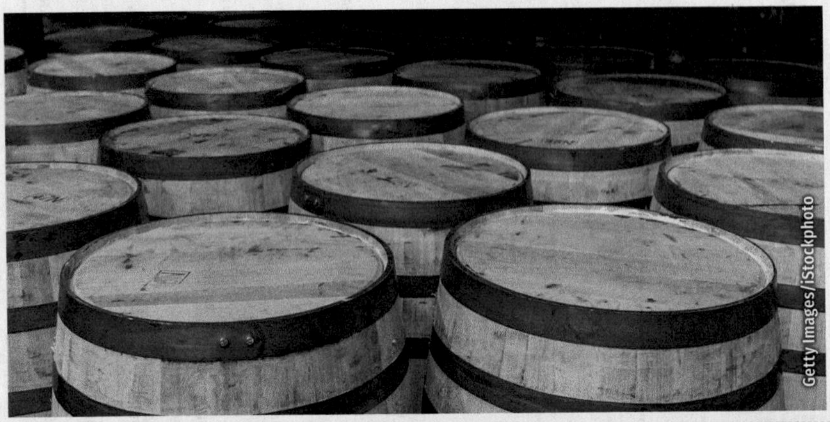
Getty Images/iStockphoto

3 Shelbyville
Drive 22 miles ▪ 23 minutes

At the Jeptha Creed Distillery Kentucky, bourbon is created from purpose-grown crops. Take a tour of this mother-daughter operation and sample their "ground to glass" concept in bourbons, flavored moonshines and vodka. Then top off your visit to Shelbyville with some great fishing at Guist Creek Lake, where largemouth bass and channel catfish practically jump in your boat. And if you're itching for more exercise, tie your rope to a ski boat in this multipurpose reservoir.

4 Louisville
Drive 26 miles ▪ 43 minutes

They are not horsing around at Churchill Downs, where the "fastest two minutes in sports" is serious business. Annually run since 1875, the Kentucky Derby in May is the highlight of Derby Week. If you can't make it to Louisville for the "Run For the Roses," come to Churchill Downs for a visit to the Kentucky Derby Museum, where the history of the competition is on full display. Or go deep at Louisville Mega Cavern, where an underground limestone quarry hosts ziplines, rope courses, tram rides and e-bike tours for those who desire an amazing caving experience.

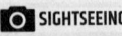

BIKING · BOATING · DINING · ENTERTAINMENT · FISHING · HIKING · HUNTING · PADDLING · SHOPPING · SIGHTSEEING

Kentucky SPOTLIGHTS

Historic Treasures Call Visitors to Explore

Tour the rolling green hills that gave us tasty bourbon and horse-racing thrills. Walk in the footsteps of Daniel Boone, explore a subterranean underworld and see the world's most amazing collection of Corvettes.

MAMMOTH CAVE IS THE LONGEST CAVE SYSTEM IN THE WORLD.

Underground entrance in Mammoth Cave National Park, which covers 52,835 acres.

Getty Images/iStockphoto

Cave Country

Located in the south-central region of Kentucky, Cave Country is home to Mammoth Cave National Park, one of the longest cave systems on the globe. This underground wilderness stretches for more than 360 miles under Kentucky's southern mountains. It is also one of the oldest tourist attractions in the U.S., offering cave tours since 1816. Tours are only available in the spring and summer months.

Out of the Shadows

Although caves take top billing, the area's above-ground activities could keep you busy for days. Take a hike or horse ride along the 70 miles of backcountry trails or explore 31 miles of shoreline along the Green and Nolin rivers. With 52,800 surface acres, the park offers plenty of other interesting things to see and do aside from exploring the caves.

Big Lizards

Come to the Dinosaur World amusement park to see replicas of the fearsome reptiles that once dominated North America. The park showcases over 150 life-size dinosaurs to terrify and amaze the kids. It also includes a fossil dig and a boneyard. The young ones can become paleontologists for the day and make discoveries of their own, some of which they can take home. For kids with a little more adventure in their hearts and for parents who are not too squeamish about accompanying them, there is Mammoth Cave Adventures, a rip-roaring, adrenaline-fueled adventure that will keep all the family happy. At this adventure playground, you can let the professional and well-trained workers take you on a tour of the grounds, flying high and fast on ziplines and walking shakily over sky bridges.

Cool Corvettes

Nearby Bowling Green is the hub of Corvette manufacturing, so it only makes sense that the Bluegrass State pays homage to this sleek set of wheels. The National Corvette Museum in Cave City showcases the history of this proud and powerful American sports car. Also in town, the Historic Railpark Museum will keep rail enthusiasts and history buffs happy, as visitors are invited to step back in time and step inside some fine historic locomotives.

Frankfort

Nestled among the rolling Bluegrass hills, Frankfort is home to horses, history and America's Native Spirit. The equine set can visit up-close with thoroughbreds on area tours. This region was the stomping grounds of statesman Henry Clay, Frankfort founder Gen. James Wilkinson and frontiersman Daniel Boone, adding to the rough-and-tumble early history of the region. Civil War battlefields dot the landscape throughout the commonwealth, and Frankfort is home to several sites and museums along with a stunning war monument. Legendary Kentucky bourbon can be swirled and sipped at several distilleries around the Frankfort area.

KY

LOCAL FAVORITE

Bud's Chicken and Dumplings

Kentucky is known for its succulent chicken. Mix up your poultry routine with some dumplings that taste like they come directly from the Bluegrass State. *Recipe adapted from Best Ever RV Recipes.*

INGREDIENTS

- ☐ 1 6-oz can chicken
- ☐ 2 10¾-oz cans chicken vegetable soup
- ☐ 1 tube large biscuits (from grocery refrigerated section)

DIRECTIONS

Dump the can of chicken and the soup into a fairly large pan with lid. Cover and bring to a low boil. Place the biscuits on the top of the mixture and cook for 10 minutes with the lid off. Then replace the lid and cook for another 10 minutes. Don't let it boil too hard or the dumplings will tear apart.

Wrap up the leftover biscuits and then cook in a small frying pan on the stovetop at low heat until lightly browned.

• FAMILY OWNED & OPERATED FOR OVER 30 YEARS •

good sam park

2022 Top Rated 9.5/10★/9

See listing Frankfort, KY

FREE WI-FI & CABLE

- Full Hookups • 30/50 Amps
- Clean Restrooms/Laundry
- LP Gas • Paved Roads & Sites
- Big Rig Friendly • Sparkling Pool
- Mini Golf • Fishing in Elkhorn Creek
- Hand Dipped Ice Cream
- Limited Winter Facilities

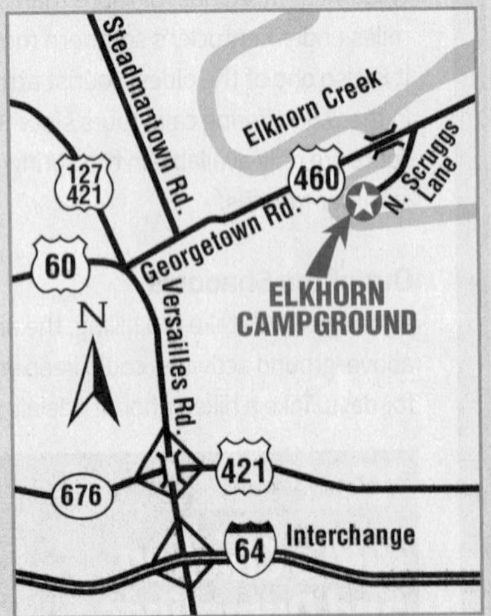

ONLY 10 MI. OR LESS TO:
• Kentucky's Capitol Bldg.
• Major Shopping • Fuel
• Restaurants • Antiques

165 N. Scruggs Ln. (Off US-460, Exit 58) • Frankfort, KY 40601

(502) 695-9154

www.elkhorncampground.com

SPOTLIGHTS

Big Bourbon

Ninety-five percent of all the bourbon in the world is crafted in the Bluegrass State and three of those renowned distilleries are located here. Buffalo Trace Distillery is the most award-winning distillery in Kentucky, crafting their bourbon in the same manner for more than 200 years. In 1887, Old Taylor Distillery was built to resemble a medieval fortress. When Prohibition forced its closing, the castle stood forgotten for nearly a century. Today, Castle & Key Distillery takes the best of the barrels and blends them into iconic spirits using local ingredients.

River or Creek, It's Water You Seek

Rent a canoe, kayak or paddleboard for a fun-filled trip on the Kentucky River filled with beautiful views and a chance to spot wildlife. Elkhorn Creek provides a bit more excitement with whitewater and slower-moving rapids, old-fashioned swimming holes and plenty of fishing.

Graced by an ideal climate for distilling spirits, Kentucky produces 95 percent of the world's supply of bourbon.

Whitley County/ Cumberland Falls

Pioneer Daniel Boone ventured into the Appalachians and across the scenic Cumberland Gap in the latter half of the 18th century. He returned with accounts of a landscape full of thick, dense and incredibly diverse forests. Towering oaks, cedars, pines and sycamores thrived side by side, choking out the sun with canopies as lush as an Amazonian rainforest.

Wild Terrain

This region sprawls across the Cumberland Mountains and houses a large swath of Daniel Boone National Forest, where the last remnants of Kentucky's prehistoric and incredibly diverse forests still proudly stand. Because of its mostly wild and all-natural terrain, the county is a popular spot for adventure-seekers, backcountry campers and wildlife photographers.

High Cliffs

The Pottsville Escarpment — a craggy line of sandstone cliffs and valleys that form the region's transition from rocky mountains to rolling foothills — carves its way through the county, producing a landscape that's positively packed with dramatic natural features like tumbling waterfalls and massive stone arches. An endless supply of well-marked and well-maintained hiking trails snake their way through the forest, and myriad streams and rivers make it easy to explore the forest's 2 million acres by kayak or canoe.

Cumberland Falls forms a stunning curtain of water that plummets 68 feet in the Cumberland River.

Falling for the Cumberland Falls

Cumberland Falls dazzles visitors who see it for the first time. Set within Daniel Boone National Forest itself, Cumberland Falls State Resort Park is home to what locals affectionately refer to as "Niagara of the South." With a wide rock shelf more than 250 million years old, the Cumberland River tumbles over a horseshoe-shaped drop and plummets 65 feet into a large open river basin. At its seasonal peak (when the river is in "flood" status), the width of the falls stretch to upward of 300 feet. At the lowest point, the falls span a 125-foot half-circle.

Walking Cumberland

Finished checking out the state's most scenic natural attractions? The park offers lots of opportunities for hiking, camping and fishing. More than 17 miles of marked trails wind their way around the falls area, and more than 50 campsites with full electrical hookups are available for use, while anglers can cast their lures into the Cumberland River, hoping to snag some hefty bass, catfish, panfish and roughfish.

FOR MORE INFORMATION

Kentucky Department of Tourism, 800-225-8747, www.kentuckytourism.com
Cave Country, 370-782-0800, www.caveslakescorvettes.com
Frankfort/Franklin County Tourist and Convention Commission, 800-960-7200, www.visitfrankfort.com
Whitley County Tourism, 606-549-0530, www.whitleycountytourism.com

KY

Kentucky

ASHLAND — C6 *Boyd*

ASHLAND See also Ashland & Louisa, KY; Huntington & Milton, WV.

ASHLAND/HUNTINGTON WEST KOA **Ratings: 8.5/9.5★/9** (Campground) Avail: 72 full hkups (30/50 amps). 2021 rates: $45 to $79. (606)929-5504, 80 KOA Ln., Argillite, KY 41121

AURORA — B2 *Marshall*

KENLAKE STATE RESORT PARK (Public State Park) From Jct of US-68/SR-80 (west end of Tennessee River bridge), N 1200 ft on US-68 (R). **FAC:** paved rds. Avail: 90 paved, 1 pull-thrus, (40x70), back-ins (30x30), 88 W, 86 E (30/50 amps), tent sites, dump, laundry, groc, firewood, restaurant. **REC:** pool, Kentucky Lake: swim, fishing, marina, boating nearby, golf, playground, hunting nearby. Pets OK. 14 day max stay. 2021 rates: $19 to $30. Apr 01 to Nov 15.
(270)474-2211 Lat: 36.77242, Lon: -88.13712
542 Kenlake Rd, Hardin, KY 42048
parks.ky.gov

LAKESIDE CAMPGROUND & MARINA **Ratings: 8/5.5/8** (Campground) 43 Avail: 7 full hkups, 36 W, 36 E (30 amps). 2021 rates: $30 to $35. Mar 17 to Oct 31. (270)354-8157, 12363 US Hwy 68 East, Benton, KY 42025

It's the law! Rules of the Road and Towing Laws are updated each year. Be sure to consult this chart to find the laws for every state on your traveling route.

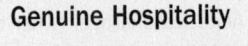

Kentucky Privately Owned Campground Information Updated by our Good Sam Representatives

Carey & Julia Bryant

Texas is home to us, our children and grands. Being with family and friends is our favorite, and dancing, hunting, biking, golfing and the ocean are things we want more time for! Grateful to God for new roads, new opportunities and new memories.

BARDSTOWN — D3 *Nelson*

MY OLD KENTUCKY HOME (Public State Park) From Jct of US-31E & US-150, E 0.5 mi on US-150 to Hwy 49, SE 0.7 mi (R). 39 Avail: 39 W, 39 E (30 amps). 2021 rates: $24 to $37. Mar 15 to Nov 15. (800)323-7803

WHITE ACRES CAMPGROUND **Ratings: 7/7★/8** (Campground) Avail: 49 full hkups (50 amps). 2021 rates: $50. (502)348-9677, 3022 Boston Rd, Bardstown, KY 40004

BENTON — B2 *Marshall*

BIRMINGHAM POINT CAMPGROUND **Ratings: 5/6/8** (Campground) 10 Avail: 10 W, 10 E (30/50 amps). 2021 rates: $30. Mar 15 to Nov 15. (270)354-8482, 5295 Barge Island Rd, Benton, KY 42025

STAGECOACH STATION CAMPGROUND **Ratings: 6.5/9.5★/9** (RV Park) 32 Avail: 32 W, 32 E (30/50 amps). 2021 rates: $30. (270)410-2267, 230 Easy St, Benton, KY 42025

BEREA — D4 *Madison*

OH! KENTUCKY CAMPGROUND **Ratings: 8/10★/7.5** (Campground) 71 Avail: 57 full hkups, 14 W, 14 E (30/50 amps). 2021 rates: $31 to $34. (859)986-1150, 562 Paint Lick Rd, Berea, KY 40403

BOWLING GREEN — E2 *Warren*

BOWLING GREEN See also Cave City, Franklin & Park City.

BOWLING GREEN KOA **Ratings: 8/9.5★/8.5** (Campground) 100 Avail: 76 full hkups, 24 W, 24 E (30/50 amps). 2021 rates: $58 to $64. (270)843-1919, 1960 Three Springs Rd, Bowling Green, KY 42104

Travel Services

CAMPING WORLD/GANDER OUTDOORS OF BOWLING GREEN As the nation's largest retailer of RV supplies, accessories, services and new and used RVs, Camping World is committed to making your total RV experience better. **SERVICES:** RV, RV appliance, MH mechanical, sells outdoor gear, sells firearms, staffed RV wash, restrooms. RV Sales. RV supplies, LP gas, dump, RV accessible. Hours: 9am to 7pm.
(855)666-4472 Lat: 36.92316, Lon: -86.42271
725 Bluegrass Farms Rd. Ste. 2, Bowling Green, KY 42104
www.campingworld.com

BUCKHORN — D5 *Perry*

BUCKHORN LAKE - COE/BUCKHORN CAMPGROUND (Public Corps) From town, S 200 yds, follow signs (L). Avail: 24 E (50 amps). 2021 rates: $20 to $30. May 01 to Sep 29. (606)398-7220

BUCKHORN LAKE - COE/TRACE BRANCH CAMPGROUND (Public Corps) From town, N 8 mi on KY-257 to Grassy Branch Rd, N 6 mi (L). 18 Avail: 14 W, 18 E (20/30 amps). 2021 rates: $24. May 01 to Sep 29. (606)672-3670

BURKESVILLE — E3 *Cumberland*

DALE HOLLOW LAKE STATE RESORT PARK (Public State Park) From jct Hwy 90 & 449: Go 4-1/2 mi S on Hwy 449, then 5 mi S on Hwy 1206 (L). 145 Avail: 145 W, 145 E (20/30 amps). 2021 rates: $25 to $45. Apr 01 to Oct 31. (270)433-7431

SULPHUR CREEK RESORT **Ratings: 8/8.5★/8** (Campground) 32 Avail: 13 full hkups, 19 W, 19 E (30/50 amps). 2021 rates: $40 to $45. Apr 01 to Nov 15. (270)433-7272, 3622 Sulphur Creek Rd, Burkesville, KY 42717

BURNSIDE — E4 *Pulaski*

GENERAL BURNSIDE ISLAND (Public State Park) From Jct of US-27 & SR-90, S 1.7 mi on US-27 (R). 94 Avail: 94 W, 94 E (30/50 amps). 2021 rates: $24 to $30. Apr 01 to Oct 31. (606)561-4104

Take us on the road with the FREE GOOD SAM CAMPING APP. Search thousands of campgrounds & RV parks, plus attractions and service centers. Includes Camping World SuperCenters! Sort and filter results to suit your needs. Download the latest version of the Good Sam Camping app and get essential information, directions and discounts for campgrounds, RV parks, attractions and service centers across the U.S. and Canada. Available from the App Store and Google Play.

SPOTLIGHT ON TOP RV & CAMPING DESTINATIONS

We've put the Spotlight on popular RV & camping travel destinations. Turn to the Spotlight articles in our State and Province sections to learn more.

CADIZ — B2 *Trigg*

⬇ BARKLEY LAKE - COE/HURRICANE CREEK CAMPGROUND (Public Corps) From town, SE 6 mi on Hwy 93 to Hwy 274, S 6 mi (R). 51 Avail: 51 W, 51 E (30/50 amps). 2021 rates: $24 to $30. Apr 25 to Oct 20. (270)522-8821

⬅ LAKE BARKLEY STATE RESORT PARK (Public State Park) From Jct of US 68/SR 80 & SR-1489, NW 3 mi on SR-1489, N 1.1 mi on Park Road (R). NOTE: Rolling wooded hills. Avail: 74 E (20/30 amps). 2021 rates: $14 to $26. Apr 01 to Oct 31. (270)924-1131

⬆ PRIZER POINT/KENTUCKY LAKES KOA **Ratings: 8/9.5★/8.5** (RV Park) 163 Avail: 128 full hkups, 35 W, 35 E (30/50 amps). 2021 rates: $60 to $150. Mar 15 to Nov 15. (270)522-3762, 1777 Prizer Point Rd, Cadiz, KY 42211

CALVERT CITY — B2 *Marshall*

➡ CYPRESS LAKES RV PARK **Ratings: 8/8.5/8** (RV Park) Avail: 47 full hkups (30/50 amps). 2021 rates: $29. (270)395-4267, 30 Cypress Pines Lane, Calvert City, KY 42029

⬇ KY LAKE / I-24 / PADUCAH KOA **Ratings: 7.5/9★/8.5** (Campground) 65 Avail: 20 full hkups, 45 W, 45 E (30/50 amps). 2021 rates: $47 to $55. Mar 01 to Dec 01. (800)562-8540, 4793 US Hwy 62, Calvert City, KY 42029

TRAVELING WITH YOUR PET: Enjoy dog days at the park. Many RV parks have dog parks. For the most freedom to roam, visit during off-peak hours. Bring your own water bowls to avoid contagious diseases like the canine flu, which are spread through common drinking areas. Observe common courtesy at the dog park; clean up after your pet and have your pet play nicely with other dogs. Back at the RV, cleanups are easy when you keep dry dog shampoos and moist towelettes. Many RV parks have dog wash stations just for furry guests.

CAMPBELLSVILLE — D3 *Taylor*

⬇ GREEN RIVER LAKE (Public State Park) From Jct of US-68/SR-70 & SR-55, S 3.5 mi on SR-55 to CR-1061S, S 2 mi (L). 156 Avail: 156 W, 156 E (20/30 amps). 2021 rates: $26 to $36. Apr 01 to Dec 31. (270)465-8255

⬆ GREEN RIVER LAKE - COE/HOLMES BEND (Public Corps) From town center, N 2 mi on Hwy 55 (Campbellsville Rd) to Hwy 551, N 1 mi to Holmes Bend Rd, N 5 mi, follow signs (L). 125 Avail: 52 W, 102 E (50 amps). 2021 rates: $17 to $25. Apr 20 to Sep 22. (270)384-4623

↗ GREEN RIVER LAKE - COE/PIKES RIDGE (Public Corps) From town, E 4 mi on KY-70 to KY-76, SE 4.8 mi to Pikes Ridge Rd, W 2.5 mi, follow signs (R). 60 Avail: 20 W, 20 E (50 amps), Pit toilets. 2021 rates: $15 to $21. May 10 to Sep 22. (270)465-6488

↘ GREEN RIVER LAKE - COE/SMITH RIDGE (Public Corps) From town, E 1 mi on Hwy 70 to Hwy 372, S 3 mi to County Park Rd, follow signs (R). 80 Avail: 50 W, 80 E (50 amps). 2021 rates: $17 to $25. May 11 to Sep 22. (270)789-2743

↗ HEARTLAND CAMPGROUND **Ratings: 6.5/8.5/8** (Campground) Avail: 111 full hkups (50 amps). 2021 rates: $35. (270)789-6886, 278 Heartland Drive, Campbellsville, KY 42718

CARROLLTON — B3 *Carroll*

⬅ 2 RIVERS CAMPGROUND (Public) From Jct I-71 & Exit 44 (SR-227), N 3.6 mi on SR-227 to US-42, W 1.2 mi to 2nd St, N 0.1 mi (L). Avail: 33 full hkups (50 amps). 2021 rates: $35 to $40. (502)732-4665

⬇ GENERAL BUTLER STATE RESORT PARK (Public State Park) From Jct of I-71 & SR-227 (exit 44), N 1.6 mi on SR-227 (L). 111 Avail: 111 W, 111 E (30/50 amps). 2021 rates: $32 to $47. (502)732-4384

CAVE CITY — D3 *Barren*

⬇ **CAVE COUNTRY RV CAMPGROUND**
good sam park **Ratings: 10/10★/9.5** (RV Park) From Jct of I-65 & Hwy 90 (Exit 53), E 0.25 mi on Hwy 90 to Sanders Dr, N 0.25 mi on Sanders Dr to Gaunce Dr, E 0.2 mi (R). **FAC:** all weather rds. Avail: 51 all weather, 51 pull-thrus, (40x65), 51 full hkups (30/50 amps), cable, WiFi @ sites, dump, laundry, LP gas, fire rings, firewood. **REC:** heated pool. Pet restrict (Q). Partial handicap access. No tents. Big rig sites, eco-friendly. 2021 rates: $42 to $45, Military discount.
(270)773-4678 Lat: 37.13496, Lon: -85.96861
216 Gaunce Dr, Cave City, KY 42127
www.cavecountryrv.com
See ad this page

⬅ MOUNTAIN TOP RETREAT CABINS & CAMPGROUND **Ratings: 6.5/NA/8** (Campground) Avail: 18 full hkups (30/50 amps). 2021 rates: $50 to $65. (270)773-2995, 3056 Mammoth Cave Road, Cave City, KY 42127

⬅ **SINGING HILLS RV PARK**
good sam park **Ratings: 6.5/8.5★/9** (Campground) From Jct I-65 & SR-70 (Exit 53), W 2.5 mi on SR-70 (R). **FAC:** gravel rds. Avail: 29 gravel, 20 pull-thrus, (20x70), back-ins (20x40), 17 full hkups, 12 W, 12 E (30/50 amps), WiFi @ sites, tent sites, dump, LP gas, fire rings, firewood. **REC:** pond, fishing. Pets OK. eco-friendly. 2021 rates: $38 to $46, Military discount.
(270)773-3789 Lat: 37.13306, Lon: -86.02213
4110 Mammoth Cave Rd., Cave City, KY 42127
www.singinghillsrvpark.com
See ad opposite page

⬅ YOGI BEAR'S JELLYSTONE PARK CAMP RESORT **Ratings: 9/9★/9** (Campground) 227 Avail: 194 full hkups, 33 W, 33 E (30/50 amps). 2021 rates: $47 to $131. (270)773-3840, 950 Mammoth Cave Rd, Cave City, KY 42127

CENTRAL CITY — B3 *Muhlenberg*

⬇ WESTERN KENTUCKY RV PARK **Ratings: 5.5/9.5★/9** (Campground) Avail: 25 full hkups (30/50 amps). 2021 rates: $35. (270)757-0345, 700 Youngstown Rd, Central City, KY 42330

COLUMBUS — B1 *Hickman*

⬆ COLUMBUS-BELMONT (Public State Park) From SR-80 in town, N 0.25 mi on Cheatham St, follow signs (L). 38 Avail: 10 full hkups, 28 W, 28 E (20/50 amps). 2021 rates: $20 to $22. (270)677-2327

Want to know how we rate? Our campground inspection guidelines are detailed in the front pages of the Guide.

KY

LAUREL LAKE
CAMPING RESORT

Family-Oriented Camping that Brings People Back!

We are looking forward to hosting you and making your stay with us a memorable one.

CAMPGROUND FEATURES

- **CAMP STORE & CAFE**
  Snacks, drinks, souvenirs, gifts, supplies, ice. Deli inside Country Store. Let us make you lunch! Free delivery to campsite upon request.
- **WEEEKLY AMENITIES**
  Join us for days of singing, cooking out on the campfire, games, unique arts and crafts and so much more!
- **RESTROOMS & SHOWERS**
  Placed in central locations around the campgrounds for your convenience.
- **FREE WIRELESS INTERNET**
  We have many access points in the area to cover the campsite and allow you to remain connected via our network.
- **GOLF CART RENTAL**
  Take it easy around the campgrounds in one of our golf-cart rentals.
- **SITES & CABINS**
  We have multiple sites for all to enjoy. Bring a camper or RV to enjoy, or stay in one of our on-site cabins for a cozy camping experience.

CAMPING ACTIVITIES

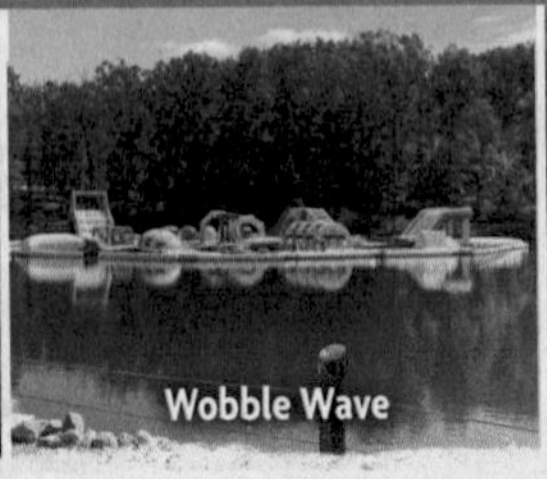

Relax in this Beautiful & Friendly Environment!

Camp out surrounded by an exceptional mountain range, rolling green hills and woodlands!

80 Robert A. Blair Memorial Hwy. in Corbin, KY

Located near the highways & byways of I-75 in southeastern Kentucky

(606) 526-7876 | laurellakecamping@gmail.com

See listing Corbin, KY

CORBIN — E4 *Laurel*

CORBIN KOA **Ratings: 8.5/8.5★/8** (Campground) 42 Avail: 32 full hkups, 10 W, 10 E (30/50 amps). 2021 rates: $38 to $52. (606)528-1534, 171 East City Dam Rd, Corbin, KY 40701

CUMBERLAND FALLS STATE RESORT PARK (Public State Park) S-bnd: From jct I-75 & US-25 (exit 25): Go 7-1/4 mi SW on US-25, then 7-1/4 mi W on Hwy 90 (L); or N-bnd: From jct I-75 & US-25 (exit 15): Go 5-3/4 mi NW on US-25, then 7-1/4 mi W on Hwy 90 (L). 50 Avail: 50 W, 50 E (30/50 amps). 2021 rates: $25 to $34. Mar 16 to Nov 14. (606)528-4121

LAUREL LAKE CAMPING RESORT

good sam park **Ratings: 8.5/9.5★/9.5** (RV Park) From the jct of I 75 & US 25W, SW 4.6 mi on US 25W to SR 1193, W 4.6 mi (R).

BEAUTIFUL RESORT WITH FUN FOR ALL

Enjoy our renovated Resort with RV sites, rental cabins, & hiking trails. Fun activity pond with a wobble wheel, kayak, paddle boats, and sandy beach as well as a large fishing pond. Golf & pedal carts available.

FAC: gravel rds. Avail: 80 gravel, 16 pull-thrus, (30x80), back-ins (30x70), 80 full hkups (30/50 amps), cable, WiFi @ sites, tent sites, rentals, laundry, groc, LP bottles, fire rings, firewood, restaurant, controlled access. **REC:** pond, swim, fishing, kayaking/canoeing, boating nearby, playground, hunting nearby. Pets OK. Partial handicap access. Big rig sites, eco-friendly. 2021 rates: $47 to $57, Military discount. Apr 01 to Nov 01. ATM.

(606)526-7876 Lat: 36.92074, Lon: -84.25977
80 Robert A Blair Memorial Hwy, Corbin, KY 40701
www.laurellakecampingresort.com
See ad opposite page

CORINTH — C4 *Grant*

THREE SPRINGS CAMPGROUND

good sam park **Ratings: 7.5/9.5/8.5** (Campground) 30 Avail: 30 W, 30 E (30/50 amps). 2021 rates: $36 to $42. (859)823-0258, 595 Campground Rd, Corinth, KY 41010

DAWSON SPRINGS — B2 *Christian*

PENNYRILE FOREST STATE RESORT PARK (Public State Park) From Jct of Western Ky Pkwy & Hwy 109 (exit 24), S 9.3 mi on SR-109 to Hwy 398, W 2 mi (R). 44 Avail: 44 W, 44 E (30/50 amps). 2021 rates: $20 to $45. Apr 01 to Oct 31. (270)797-3421

DRY RIDGE — B4 *Grant*

NORTHERN KY RV PARK

good sam park **Ratings: 8.5/9.5★/8.5** (RV Park) From Jct of I-75 & SR-491 (exit 166), E 0.2 mi on SR-491 to US-25, S 2.6 mi (R).

BEAUTIFUL PARK BY GREAT ATTRACTIONS

While enjoying the many attractions only minutes away, such as the Ark Encounter, the Creation Museum, sporting events, and entertainment, come stay in our re-landscaped sites and grounds with New Owners and New Management.

FAC: paved/gravel rds. (80 spaces). Avail: 70 gravel, 59 pull-thrus, (30x65), back-ins (28x40), 70 full hkups (30/50 amps), seasonal sites, WiFi @ sites, dump, laundry, LP gas. **REC:** pond, fishing, boating nearby, playground, hunting nearby. Pets OK. No tents. Big rig sites, eco-friendly. 2021 rates: $45. Mar 15 to Nov 15.

(859)428-2000 Lat: 38.74925, Lon: -84.60307
3315 Dixie Highway , Dry Ridge, KY 41035
www.northernkyrv.com
See ad next page

DUNMOR — B3 *Muhlenberg*

LAKE MALONE (Public State Park) From Jct of Western Kentucky Pkwy & US-431 (Exit 58), S 16.7 mi on US-431 to SR-973, W 3.1 mi on SR-973 to Conservation Rd (Park Access Rd) (L). 25 Avail: 25 W, 25 E (15/30 amps). 2021 rates: $22 to $27. Mar 15 to Dec 15. (270)657-2858

EDDYVILLE — B2 *Lyon*

HOLIDAY HILLS RESORT **Ratings: 7.5/9★/8.5** (RV Park) 12 Avail: 4 full hkups, 8 W, 8 E (30/50 amps). 2021 rates: $41.95. Apr 01 to Oct 30. (270)388-5253, 5631 State Route 93 South, Eddyville, KY 42038

INDIAN POINT RV PARK **Ratings: 8.5/8.5★/8.5** (Campground) Avail: 10 full hkups (30 amps). 2021 rates: $34 to $42. Apr 01 to Nov 01. (270)388-2730, 1136 Indian Hills Trail, Eddyville, KY 42038

KY

See listing Dry Ridge, KY

EDDYVILLE (CONT)

OUTBACK RV RESORT
good sam park **Ratings: 9.5/9.5★/9** (RV Park) Avail: 14 full hkups (30/50 amps). 2021 rates: $42.50. Apr 01 to Nov 01. (270)388-4752, 4481 State Route 93 South, Eddyville, KY 42038

ELIZABETHTOWN — D3 *Hardin*

ELIZABETHTOWN CROSSROADS CAMPGROUND
good sam park **Ratings: 8.5/9.5★/9** (Campground) From US-62 and I-65 (exit 94): Go 8/10 mi E on US-62 then 1/5 mi N on Tunnel Hill Rd. (L). **FAC:** gravel rds. Avail: 48 gravel, 22 pull-thrus, (25x70), back-ins (25x40), 33 full hkups, 15 W, 15 E (30/50 amps), cable, WiFi @ sites, tent sites, rentals, dump, laundry, groc, LP gas, fire rings, firewood. **REC:** pool, pond, fishing, boating nearby, playground, rec open to public. Pet restrict (B). Partial handicap access. Big rig sites, eco-friendly. 2021 rates: $34 to $47, Military discount.
(800)975-6521 Lat: 37.72372, Lon: -85.81611
209 Tunnell Hill Rd, Elizabethtown, KY 42701
www.elizabethtowncrossroadscampgroundky.com
See ad this page

GLENDALE CAMPGROUND **Ratings: 7.5/8.5★/8** (Campground) 55 Avail: 11 full hkups, 44 W, 44 E (30/50 amps). 2021 rates: $33 to $45. (270)369-7755, 4566 Sportsman Lake Rd, Elizabethtown, KY 42701

FALLS OF ROUGH — D2 *Grayson*

ROUGH RIVER DAM (Public State Park) From Jct of Western Kentucky Pkwy & Hwy 79 (Exit 94), N 16.5 mi on Hwy 79 (L). 64 Avail: 33 W, 64 E (30/50 amps). 2021 rates: $12 to $24. Apr 01 to Oct 31. (270)257-2311

ROUGH RIVER LAKE - COE/CAVE CREEK (Public Corps) From town, S 2 mi on Hwy 79 to Hwy 736, E 2 mi, follow signs (R). Avail: 36 E (50 amps), Pit toilets. 2021 rates: $22 to $40. May 15 to Sep 15. (270)879-4304

FALMOUTH — B4 *Pendleton*

KINCAID LAKE (Public State Park) From Jct of SR-22 & SR-159, N 5 mi on SR-159 (R). 84 Avail: 84 W, 84 E (30/50 amps). 2021 rates: $22 to $30. Apr 01 to Nov 12. (859)654-3531

FLEMINGSBURG — C5 *Fleming*

FOX VALLEY REC AREA (FLEMING COUNTY PARK) (Public) S-bnd: From town at Jct of SR-32 & SR-11, SE 5.6 mi on SR-32 to James Rd, E 2 mi (L); or N-bnd: From Jct of I-64 & SR-32 (Exit 137), N 17 mi on SR-32 to James Rd, E 2 mi (L). 85 Avail: 85 W, 85 E (20/30 amps). 2021 rates: $6 to $15. Mar 15 to Oct 31. (606)845-0833

FRANKFORT — C4 *Franklin*

A SPOTLIGHT Introducing Frankfort's colorful attractions appearing at the front of this state section.

ELKHORN CAMPGROUND
good sam park **Ratings: 9.5/10★/9** (RV Park) From jct of I-64 (exit 58) & US 60: Go 2-3/4 mi N on US 60, then 2-1/4 mi E on US 460, then 1/4 mi S on N Scruggs Ln, then 1/4 mi S on McConnel Rd (E). **FAC:** paved rds. (125 spaces). 92 Avail: 82 paved, 10 all weather, patios, 26 pull-thrus, (25x80), back-ins (25x70), 26 full hkups, 66 W, 66 E (30/50 amps), seasonal sites, cable, WiFi @ sites, tent sites, dump, laundry, groc, LP gas, fire rings, firewood. **REC:** pool, Elkhorn Creek: fishing, boating nearby, playground. Pet restrict (B). Partial handicap access. Big rig sites, eco-friendly. 2021 rates: $40 to $44, Military discount.
(502)695-9154 Lat: 38.2100, Lon: -84.8005
165 N Scruggs Ln, Frankfort, KY 40601
www.elkhorncampground.com
See ad page 414

FRANKLIN — E2 *Simpson*

DAD'S BLUEGRASS CAMPGROUND
good sam park **Ratings: 9/9.5★/9.5** (Campground) From jct I-65 (exit 6) & Hwy 100: Go 1/4 mi W on Hwy 100, then 1/4 mi S on KOA Lane (R). **FAC:** paved/gravel rds. (98 spaces). Avail: 88 gravel, 70 pull-thrus, (30x70), back-ins (30x70), 88 full hkups (30/50 amps), seasonal sites, WiFi @ sites, $, tent sites, rentals, dump, laundry, groc, LP gas, fire rings, firewood. **REC:** pool, pond, fishing, boating nearby, playground. Pets OK. Partial handicap access. Big rig sites, eco-friendly. 2021 rates: $54 to $56, Military discount.
(270)253-5191 Lat: 36.7167, Lon: -86.5264
2889 Scottsville Rd, Franklin, KY 42134
dadsbluegrasscampground.com
See ad page 857

Don't miss out on great savings - find Camping World coupons at the front and back of this Guide!

GEORGETOWN — C4 *Scott*

WHISPERING HILLS RV PARK
good sam park **Ratings: 9.5/9.5★/9.5** (RV Park) From Jct of I-75 & Cherry Blossom way (exit 129), W on Cherry Blossom Way 0.5 mi to US-25, N 1.7 mi to Rogers Gap Rd, E 0.6 mi (R). **FAC:** all weather rds. Avail: 212 gravel, 43 pull-thrus, (30x90), back-ins (30x50), 212 full hkups (30/50 amps), WiFi @ sites, laundry, LP gas, fire rings, firewood. **REC:** pool, pond, fishing, playground, hunting nearby. Pets OK. Partial handicap access. No tents. Big rig sites, eco-friendly. 2021 rates: $40 to $55, Military discount.
(502)863-2552 Lat: 38.30173, Lon: -84.55041
257 Rogers Gap Rd, Georgetown, KY 40324
www.whisperinghillsrv.com
See ad page 423

Thank You to our active and retired military personnel. Look for military parks within the state listings section of your 2022 Guide.

Travel Services

CAMPING WORLD OF GEORGETOWN CAMPING WORLD As the nation's largest retailer of RV supplies, accessories, services and new and used RVs, Camping World is committed to making your total RV experience better. **SERVICES:** RV, tire, restrooms. RV Sales. RV supplies, LP gas, dump, RV accessible. Hours: 9am - 7pm.
(877)870-0342 Lat: 38.214450, Lon: -84.536268
151 Wahland Hall Path, Georgetown, KY 40324
www.campingworld.com

Find new and exciting itineraries in our ""Road Trip'' article at the front of each state and province.

KY

GILBERTSVILLE — B2 *Marshall*

KENTUCKY DAM VILLAGE STATE RESORT PARK (Public State Park) From Jct of I 24 & US-62/US-641 (exit 27), S 2.2 mi on US-62/US-641 to SR-282, N 0.5 mi (R). 219 Avail: 219 W, 219 E (30/50 amps). 2021 rates: $22 to $29. Apr 01 to Oct 31. (270)362-4271

KENTUCKY LAKE RESORT AND RV PARK **Ratings: 4.5/5.5/6** (RV Park) 24 Avail: 16 full hkups, 8 W, 8 E (30/50 amps). 2021 rates: $30 to $35. (270)362-8652, 59 Kentucky Lake Resort Rd, Gilbertsville, KY 42044

GLASGOW — E3 *Barren*

BARREN RIVER LAKE - COE/THE NARROWS (Public Corps) From Glasgow, S 10 mi on Old 31E to Narrows Boat Rd, W 2 mi, follow signs (R). 92 Avail: 92 W, 92 E (50 amps). 2021 rates: $23. May 15 to Sep 19. (270)646-3094

BARREN RIVER LAKE STATE RESORT PARK (Public State Park) From Jct of Cumberland Pkwy & US-31E (exit 11), S 11.3 mi on US-31E (R). 98 Avail: 98 W, 98 E (30 amps). 2021 rates: $20 to $40. Apr 30 to Nov 19. (270)646-2151

GOLDEN POND — B2 *Stewart*

LBL NATIONAL RECREATION AREA/ENERGY LAKE (Public National Park) From town, W 2.5 mi on US-68, N 8 mi on the Trace to Mulberry Flat Rd, SE 7 mi. Avail: 35 E (50 amps). 2021 rates: $12 to $24. Mar 01 to Nov 30. (270)924-2270

LBL NATIONAL RECREATION AREA/FENTON (Public National Park) From town, W 4.5 mi on US-68/80, follow signs (L). Avail: 12 E (20/30 amps), Pit toilets. 2021 rates: $18. (270)924-2000

LBL NATIONAL RECREATION AREA/RUSHING CREEK (Public National Park) From town, E 2.5 mi on US-68, S 8 mi on The Trace (Hwy 453) to Rushing Creek Rd., W 2 mi follow signs, (E). 40 Avail. 2021 rates: $9. (270)924-2000

LBL NATIONAL RECREATION AREA/TURKEY BAY OHV AREA (Public National Park) From Jct of US-68/80 & The Trace, S 2 mi on The Trace to CR-167, W 0.5 mi (E). 18 Avail: Pit toilets. 2021 rates: $8. (270)924-2000

LBL NATIONAL RECREATION AREA/WRANGLERS CAMPGROUND (Public) From jct Hwy 94/80/68: Go 5 mi E on Hwy 80/68, then 1 mi S on The Trace Rd, then 5 mi W on Rd 168. 220 Avail: 18 full hkups, 125 W, 127 E (30 amps). 2021 rates: $12 to $34. (270)924-2201

GRAND RIVERS — B2 *Barkley*

BARKLEY LAKE - COE/CANAL CAMPGROUND (Public Corps) From town, S 1 mi on Hwy 453, E .7 mi on Canal Campground Rd. 110 Avail: 17 full hkups, 91 W, 91 E (30/50 amps). 2021 rates: $26 to $34. Mar 29 to Oct 28. (270)362-4840

HILLMAN FERRY (LBL) NATIONAL RECREATION AREA (Public) From jct I-24 & The Trace (Hwy-453): Go 5 mi S on The Trace, then 1 mi W on Hillman Ferry Rd. 374 Avail. 2021 rates: $12 to $40. Mar 01 to Nov 30. (270)924-2181

LBL NATIONAL RECREATION AREA/BIRMINGHAM FERRY (Public National Park) From town, S 9 mi on The Trace (Hwy 453) to Old Ferry Rd/SH-58, W 2.5 mi (E). 16 Avail: Pit toilets. 2021 rates: $7. (270)924-2000

LBL NATIONAL RECREATION AREA/CRAVENS BAY (Public National Park) From town, S 7 mi on The Trace (Hwy 453) to Old Ferry Rd, E 1 mi to CR-118, E 4 mi, follow signs (E). 27 Avail: Pit toilets. 2021 rates: $9. (270)924-2000

TWEEN THE LAKES RV PARK **Ratings: 4.5/NA/7** (Campground) Avail: 28 full hkups (30/50 amps). 2021 rates: $31. (270)252-6520, 831 Vulcan Rd., Grand Rivers, KY 42045

GRAYSON — C5 *Carter*

GRAYSON LAKE (Public State Park) From Jct of I-64 & SR-7 (exit 172), S 11.2 mi on SR-7 (R). 71 Avail: 71 W, 71 E (20/30 amps). 2021 rates: $25 to $32. Apr 01 to Nov 12. (606)474-9727

GREENUP — B5 *Greenup*

GREENBO LAKE STATE RESORT PARK (Public State Park) From Jct of US-23 & SR-1, S 8 mi on SR-1 to park entrance rd, W 2.9 mi (L) or From Jct of I-64 & SR-1 (exit 172), N 15 mi on SR-1 to park entrance rd, W 2.9 mi (L). 94 Avail: 58 W, 58 E (20/30 amps). 2021 rates: $18 to $43. Apr 01 to Oct 31. (606)473-7324

HARRODSBURG — D4 *Mercer*

CHIMNEY ROCK RV PARK **Ratings: 9.5/9★/8** (RV Park) Avail: 20 full hkups (30/50 amps). 2021 rates: $50. Apr 01 to Oct 31. (859)748-5252, 220 Chimney Rock Road, Harrodsburg, KY 40330

HARTFORD — D2 *Ohio*

OHIO COUNTY PARK & CAMPGROUND (Public) From Jct of Western Kentucky Pkwy and William Natcher Pkwy (Exit 77B), N 6.7 mi on William Natcher Pkwy to Hwy 69 (Exit 48), NE 0.8 mi (R). 125 Avail: 125 W, 27 S, 125 E (30 amps). 2021 rates: $19 to $24. (270)298-4466

HENDERSON — A2 *Henderson*

JOHN JAMES AUDUBON (Public State Park) From Jct of US-60 & US-41, N 2 mi on US-41 (R). 73 Avail: 73 W, 73 E (30 amps). 2021 rates: $22 to $26. Apr 01 to Nov 30. (270)826-2247

HINDMAN — D5 *Knott*

CARR CREEK LAKE - COE/LITTCARR CAMPGROUND (Public Corps) From town, S 10 mi on Hwy 160, follow signs (L). 45 Avail: 45 W, 45 E (30 amps). 2021 rates: $24 to $30. Apr 01 to Oct 11. (606)642-3052

HORSE CAVE — D3 *Hart*

HORSE CAVE KOA **Ratings: 9/9.5★/8.5** (Campground) 48 Avail: 21 full hkups, 27 W, 27 E (20/30 amps). 2021 rates: $42 to $55. (800)562-2809, 489 Flint Ridge Rd, Horse Cave, KY 42749

JAMESTOWN — E3 *Russell*

LAKE CUMBERLAND - COE/KENDALL CAMPGROUND (Public Corps) From town, S 10 mi on US-127 to Powerhouse Rd, NW 1 mi (R). 115 Avail: 115 W, 115 E (20/50 amps). 2021 rates: $28. Apr 01 to Nov 01. (270)343-4660

LAKE CUMBERLAND STATE RESORT PARK (Public State Park) From Jct of Cumberland Pkwy & US-127 (exit 62), S 13 mi on US-127 (L) NOTE: Campground 4.5 mi into park. CAUTION roads are hilly with sharp curves. 129 Avail: 129 W, 129 E (30/50 amps). 2021 rates: $20 to $28. Mar 14 to Nov 29. (270)343-3111

LANCASTER — D4 *Garrard*

CAMP NELSON RV PARK **Ratings: 7/6/6.5** (Campground) 46 Avail: 36 full hkups, 10 W, 10 E (30/50 amps). 2021 rates: $33. (859)548-2113, 1470 Old Lexington Rd E, Lancaster, KY 40444

LEBANON — D1 *Marion*

MARION COUNTY FAIR RV PARK (Public) From jct Hwy 49 & US 68; Go 1/2 mi NE on US 68, then 3/4 mi SE on S Woodlawn Ave/Fairgrounds Rd (L). Avail: 20 full hkups (30/50 amps). 2021 rates: $30. (270)402-4036

LEITCHFIELD — D2 *Beckinridge*

NOLIN LAKE (Public State Park) From jct US 62 & Hwy 259: Go 17 mi S on Hwy 259, then E and follow signs. 59 Avail: 32 W, 32 E (30 amps). 2021 rates: $22 to $32. Mar 15 to Nov 15. (270)286-4240

NOLIN RIVER LAKE - COE/DOG CREEK CAMPGROUND (Public Corps) From town: Go 20 mi W on Hwy 88, then 1 mi S on SR-1015 (R). 70 Avail: 50 W, 50 E (30 amps). 2021 rates: $15 to $25. May 15 to Sep 06. (270)524-5454

NOLIN RIVER LAKE - COE/MOUTARDIER (Public Corps) From town, S 12 mi on Hwy 259 to Hwy 2067, E 1.5 mi, follow signs (R). 167 Avail: 81 W, 81 E (20 amps). 2021 rates: $15 to $25. May 01 to Oct 17. (270)286-4230

NOLIN RIVER LAKE - COE/WAX CAMPGROUND (Public Corps) From town, S 7 mi on Hwy 259 to Hwy 226, E 1 mi to KY-88, S 9 mi, follow signs (R). 110 Avail: 56 W, 56 E (30 amps). 2021 rates: $15 to $24. May 15 to Sep 06. (270)242-7578

LEXINGTON — C4 *Fayette*

LEXINGTON See also Frankfort, Georgetown, Harrodsburg, Lancaster & Salvisa.

KENTUCKY HORSE PARK CAMPGROUND (Public) From Jct of I-75 & SR-1973 (exit 120), E 0.7 mi on SR-1973 (L). 260 Avail: 260 W, 260 E (30/50 amps). 2021 rates: $30 to $45. (859)259-4257

We give campgrounds one rating for development, a second for restrooms and a third for visual appearance and environmental quality. That's the Triple Rating System.

KY

See listing Georgetown, KY

LONDON — D4 *Laurel*

LEVI JACKSON WILDERNESS ROAD (Public State Park) From Jct of I-75 & Hwy 192 (exit 38), E 1.8 mi on Hwy 192 to US-25, S 1.4 mi to SR-1006, E 1 mi (L). 136 Avail: 136 W, 136 E (30/50 amps). 2021 rates: $26 to $40. (606)330-2130

WESTGATE RV CAMPGROUND

Ratings: 6.5/9★/6.5 (RV Park) From Jct of I-75 & SR-80 (exit 41), W 0.3 mi on SR-80 (R). **FAC:** gravel rds. Avail: 14 gravel, 2 pull-thrus, (25x45), back-ins (25x45), 14 full hkups (30/50 amps), WiFi @ sites, tent sites, rentals, groc, restaurant. **REC:** heated pool, boating nearby, playground, hunting nearby. Pets OK. Partial handicap access, eco-friendly. 2021 rates: $35.45 to $44.80, Military discount. ATM.
(606)878-7330 Lat: 37.1490, Lon: -84.1158
254 Russell Dyche Memorial Hwy, London, KY 40741
westgatecampground.com
See ad this page

LOUISA — C6 *Lawrence*

THE FALLS CAMPGROUND **Ratings: 7.5/8.5★/8.5** (Campground) 79 Avail: 16 full hkups, 63 W, 63 E (30/50 amps). 2021 rates: $33.50 to $38.50. (606)826-0212, 6072 N Hwy 3, Louisa, KY 41230

YATESVILLE LAKE (Public State Park) From Jct of US-23 & SR-32, SW 4.7 mi on SR-32 to SR-3215, NW 2.7 mi (R). Avail: 27 full hkups (30/50 amps). 2021 rates: $24 to $30. Apr 01 to Oct 31. (606)673-1490

LOUISVILLE — C3 *Fayette*

LOUISVILLE See also Bardstown, Elizabethtown & Shepherdsville, KY; Clarksville & Scottsburg, IN.

MILITARY PARK CAMP CARLSON RECREATION AREA (FORT KNOX) (Public) From Jct I-65 & I-264, W 9.5 mi I-264 to US-31W, S 20 mi to US-60, W 2.5 mi (R). Avail: 62 full hkups (30/50 amps). 2021 rates: $25 to $35. (502)624-4836

LYNCH — E5 *Harlan*

PORTAL #31 RV PARK (Public) From Jct of I-75 & US-25E (exit 27), SE 34.5 mi to US 119, E 51 mi to Hwy 160, S 3.8 mi (R). Avail: 12 full hkups (30 amps). 2021 rates: $16.95. (606)848-3131

MAMMOTH CAVE — D3 *Edmonson*

DOUBLE J RIDING STABLES & HORSEMAN'S CAMPGROUND **Ratings: 6.5/7.5★/8.5** (Campground) 17 Avail: 17 W, 17 E (30 amps). 2021 rates: $25. (270)286-8167, 542 Lincoln School Road, Mammoth Cave, KY 42259

MCDANIELS — D2 *Breckinridge*

ROUGH RIVER LAKE - COE/AXTEL (Public Corps) From town: Go 4-1/2 mi N on KY-79 (L). Avail: 111 E (50 amps). 2021 rates: $17 to $40. Apr 17 to Nov 01. (270)257-2584

ROUGH RIVER LAKE - COE/LAUREL BRANCH (Public Corps) From town, N 2 mi on Hwy 259 to Hwy 110, W 1 mi (L). 71 Avail: 25 W, 48 E (50 amps). 2021 rates: $18 to $40. May 02 to Oct 30. (270)257-8839

ROUGH RIVER LAKE - COE/NORTH FORK (Public Corps) From Jct of KY-79 & KY-259, N 1 mi on KY-259, follow signs (R). 81 Avail: 50 W, 50 E (50 amps). 2021 rates: $17 to $24. May 01 to Sep 15. (270)257-8139

MONTICELLO — E4 *Wayne*

CONLEY BOTTOM RESORT CAMPGROUND **Ratings: 6.5/5.5/7.5** (Campground) 145 Avail: 20 full hkups, 125 W, 125 E (30/50 amps). 2021 rates: $37 to $47. (606)348-6351, 270 Conley Bottom Rd, Monticello, KY 42633

LAKE CUMBERLAND - COE/FALL CREEK CAMPGROUND (Public) From jct SR 90 & SR 1275: Go 5 mi N on SR 1275 (Follow signs). Avail: 10 E. 2021 rates: $20 to $35. May 01 to Sep 12. (606)348-6042

MORGANFIELD — A2 *Union*

MOFFITT REC AREA (Public) From town, SE 6.4 mi on SR-56, S 2 mi on SR-141 to SH-2153, S 3 mi (R). 100 Avail: 100 W, 100 E (30 amps). 2021 rates: $9 to $12. Apr 01 to Oct 31. (270)333-4845

MOUNT OLIVET — C4 *Robertson*

BLUE LICKS BATTLEFIELD (Public State Park) From jct US-68 & SR-165: Go 1/2 mi S on US-68 (R). 51 Avail: 51 W, 51 E (20/30 amps). 2021 rates: $20 to $35. Apr 01 to Oct 31. (859)289-5507

MOUNT VERNON — D4 *Rockcastle*

RENFRO VALLEY RV PARK

Ratings: 6/9/8 (Campground) From Jct of I-75 & US-25 (exit 62), N 0.7 mi on US-25 (R). **FAC:** gravel rds. Avail: 149 gravel, 57 pull-thrus, (28x110), back-ins (26x44), 132 full hkups, 17 W, 17 E (30/50 amps), WiFi @ sites, dump. **REC:** Renfro Creek: boating nearby, rec open to public. Pets OK. No tents. Big rig sites. 2021 rates: $27 to $37. ATM.
(606)256-0101 Lat: 37.3860, Lon: -84.3315
2380 Richmond St, Mount Vernon, KY 40456
www.renfrovalley.com
See ad this page

Things to See and Do

RENFRO VALLEY ENTERTAINMENT CENTER
Tourist attraction; venue for music events. RV accessible. Restrooms. Food. Hours: 9am to 5pm. ATM.
(800)765-7464 Lat: 37.38835, Lon: -84.32986
2380 Richmond St, Mount Vernon, KY 40456
www.renfrovalley.com
See ad this page

MURRAY — B2 *Callaway*

WILDCAT CREEK REC AREA (Public) From jct Hwy 94 & Hwy 280 E of town: Go 5-1/4 mi E on Hwy 280, then 2.1 mi NE on Hwy 614E. Follow signs. 56 Avail: 56 W, 56 E (30 amps). 2021 rates: $40. (270)436-5628

NANCY — E4 *Pulaski*

PULASKI COUNTY PARK (Public) From Jct of US-27 & SR-80, SW 7 mi on SR-80 to local rte 1248, SE 0.1 mi (E). 36 Avail: 36 W, 36 E (50 amps). 2021 rates: $20 to $33. Apr 01 to Oct 31. (606)636-6450

OLIVE HILL — C5 *Carter*

CARTER CAVES STATE RESORT PARK (Public State Park) From jct I-64 & US-60 (exit 161): Go 1-1/2 mi N on US-60E, then 3 mi N on KY-182 (L). 120 Avail: 120 W, 120 E (30/50 amps). 2021 rates: $22 to $32. Apr 01 to Nov 15. (606)286-4411

OWENSBORO — D2 *Daviess*

OWENSBORO See also Santa Claus, IN.

DIAMOND LAKE RESORT **Ratings: 9.5/6.5/8** (RV Park) 180 Avail: 149 full hkups, 31 W, 31 E (30/50 amps). 2021 rates: $36 to $38. (270)229-4900, 7301 Hobbs Rd, Owensboro, KY 42301

WINDY HOLLOW CAMPGROUND & RECREATION AREA **Ratings: 6/8/8.5** (Campground) 110 Avail: 60 full hkups, 50 W, 50 E (30/50 amps). 2021 rates: $45 to $50. Apr 01 to Oct 31. (270)785-4150, 5141 Windy Hollow Rd, Owensboro, KY 42301

PADUCAH — B1 *McCracken*

PADUCAH See also Benton, Calvert City, Gilbertsville, Grand Rivers & Smithland.

DUCK CREEK RV PARK

Ratings: 9.5/10★/7.5 (RV Park) From Jct I 24 & SR 1954/Bus Loop 24 (exit 11), N 0.5 mi on SR 1954 (R).

BIG RIG FRIENDLY-EZ IN/OUT!
1/2 mi N of I-24; LONG pull-thru sites, 30/50 amp, upgraded Wi-Fi, cable, pool & dog park and dog wash station. Fish/boat on KY Lake & Lake Barkley, golfing nearby. Visit Historic Downtown Paducah and The Nat'l Quilt Museum!

FAC: all weather rds. (96 spaces). Avail: 93 gravel, 30 pull-thrus, (30x80), back-ins (30x40), 93 full hkups (30/50 amps), WiFi @ sites, dump, laundry, groc, LP gas, firewood. **REC:** pool, Bee Branch Creek: fishing, hunting nearby. Pets OK. Partial handicap access. No tents. Big rig sites, eco-friendly. 2021 rates: $38 to $40, Military discount.
(800)728-5109 Lat: 37.02137, Lon: -88.58667
2540 John L Puryear Dr, Paducah, KY 42003
duckcreekrv.com
See ad opposite page

FERN LAKE CAMPGROUND & RV PARK

Ratings: 8/9.5★/8.5 (RV Park) From Jct of I-24 & SR-305 (exit 3), SW 1/4 mi on SR-305 (R). **FAC:** paved/gravel rds. Avail: 60 gravel, 41 pull-thrus, (22x60), back-ins (25x50), 45 full hkups, 15 W, 15 E (30/50 amps), WiFi @ sites, tent sites, dump, laundry, fire rings, firewood. **REC:** Fern Lake: fishing, kayaking/canoeing, shuffleboard, playground, hunting nearby. Pet restrict (Q). Partial handicap access, eco-friendly. 2021 rates: $30 to $40, Military discount.
(270)444-7939 Lat: 37.09643, Lon: -88.69545
5535 Cairo Rd, Paducah, KY 42001
www.fernlakecampground.net
See ad page 426

PADUCAH RV PARK & CAMPGROUND **Ratings: 7/8.5★/9.5** (RV Park) Avail: 35 full hkups (30/50 amps). 2021 rates: $27. (888)806-2267, 4300 Shemwell Lane, Paducah, KY 42003

PARK CITY — E3 *Edmonson*

DIAMOND CAVERNS RV RESORT & GOLF CLUB

Ratings: 8.5/7.5/7.5 (Membership Park) 75 Avail: 69 full hkups, 6 W, 6 E (30/50 amps). 2021 rates: $57.20. (888)563-7040, 1878 Mammoth Cave Pkwy, Park City, KY 42160

PIKEVILLE — D6 *Pike*

FISHTRAP LAKE - COE/GRAPEVINE CAMPGROUND (Public Corps) From jct Hwy 80 & US 119: Go 9-1/2 mi E on US 119 to Meta, then 16 mi S on Hwy 194. 28 Avail. 2021 rates: $12 to $20. May 25 to Sep 04. (606)437-7496

PRESTONSBURG — D6 *Floyd*

GERMAN BRIDGE CAMPGROUND **Ratings: 5/9★/8.5** (Campground) 65 Avail: 31 W, 31 E (30/50 amps). 2021 rates: $25. May 01 to Oct 15. (606)874-1150, 7533 Kentucky Hwy 194, Prestonsburg, KY 41653

JENNY WILEY STATE RESORT PARK (Public State Park) From jct US-23 & Hwy 3: Go 2-1/4 mi E on Hwy 3, then 1-1/2 mi E on Hwy 3051 (R). 121 Avail: 121 W, 121 E (30/50 amps). 2021 rates: $23 to $37. Apr 01 to Oct 31. (606)889-1790

RV DRIVING TIPS: Adjust your vehicle's environment so that it helps you to stay alert. Keep the temperature cool, with open windows or air conditioning in the summer and minimal amounts of heat in the winter. Avoid listening to soft, sleep-inducing music and switch radio stations frequently.

Paducah, Kentucky

DUCK CREEK RV PARK

good sam park
Rated 9.5/10★/7.5

- Cable • Pool • Big Rig Friendly
- Long Pull-Thrus • 50 Amp Full Hookups
- EZ In/Out • Propane
- Rallies Welcome • Convenience Store
- Outdoor Games • Free Fitness Center Pass
- New Club Room • 24 Hr. Laundry
- Large Dog Park/Wash Station
- Fire Rings Available

FREE UPGRADED WiFi

Directions: Take I-24 Exit 11, go 1/2 mile North, turn right.

2540 John L. Puryear Drive • Paducah, KY 42003

1-800-728-5109

www.duckcreekrv.com

SPECIAL MILITARY DISCOUNT

VISA MasterCard DISCOVER

See listing Paducah, KY

KY

RENFRO VALLEY — D4 *Rockcastle*

RENFRO VALLEY See also Berea, London & Mount Vernon.

RENFRO VALLEY KOA
Ratings: 9/9.5★/8.5 (Campground) From Jct of I-75 & US-25 (exit 62), N 1.3 mi on US-25 (R). **FAC:** paved/gravel rds. (98 spaces). 92 Avail: 48 paved, 44 gravel, patios, 76 pull-thrus, (24x60), back-ins (22x50), 82 full hkups, 10 W, 10 E (30/50 amps), cable, WiFi @ sites, tent sites, rentals, dump, laundry, groc, LP gas, fire rings, firewood. **REC:** pool, boating nearby, shuffleboard, playground. Pets OK. Partial handicap access, eco-friendly. 2021 rates: $65.95 to $89.95.
(800)562-2475 Lat: 37.39549, Lon: -84.33357
184 KOA Kampground Rd, Mount Vernon, KY 40456
koa.com
See ad this page

RICHMOND — D4 *Madison*

FORT BOONESBOROUGH (Public State Park) From Jct of I-75 & SR-627 (exit 95), N 5.5 mi on SR-627 to SR-388, E 0.2 mi (L) Note: Fort has separate entrance. 167 Avail: 18 full hkups, 149 W, 149 E (30/50 amps). 2021 rates: $31 to $40. (859)527-3454

RUSSELL SPRINGS — E3 *Russell*

KUMBERLAND CAMPGROUND
(Campground) (Too New to Rate) Avail: 90 full hkups (30/50 amps). 2021 rates: $45. (800)521-7316, 240 E L McGowan Road, Russell Springs, KY 42642

Always do a Pre-Drive Safety Check!

RUSSELL SPRINGS KOA **Ratings: 8.5/9★/7.5** (Campground) 27 Avail: 19 full hkups, 8 W, 8 E (30/50 amps). 2021 rates: $43 to $58. Apr 01 to Oct 31. (270)866-5616, 1440 Hwy 1383, Russell Springs, KY 42642

SALT LICK — C5 *Bath*

OUTPOST RV PARK & CAMPGROUND
Ratings: 8.5/9.5★/10 (RV Park) Avail: 82 full hkups (30/50 amps). 2021 rates: $40 to $75. (606)683-2311, 340 Cave Run Lake Road, Salt Lick, KY 40371

SALVISA — C4 *Mercer*

CUMMINS FERRY RESORT CAMPGROUND & MARINA **Ratings: 9.5/9★/9** (RV Park) Avail: 30 full hkups (30/50 amps). 2021 rates: $50 to $60. (859)865-2003, 2558 Cummins Ferry Rd, Salvisa, KY 40372

SASSAFRAS — D5 *Knott*

CARR CREEK (Public State Park) From jct Daniel Boone Pkwy/SR-80 & SR-15 (exit 59): Go 18-1/2 mi S on SR-15 (L). 39 Avail: 39 W, 39 E (30/50 amps). 2021 rates: $22 to $27. Apr 01 to Oct 31. (606)642-4050

SCOTTSVILLE — E2 *Allen*

BARREN RIVER LAKE - COE/BAILEYS POINT (Public Corps) From town, N 7 mi on 31E to Hwy 252, N 1.1 mi to Hwy 517, E 2 mi, follow signs (L). Avail: 151 E (50 amps), Pit toilets. 2021 rates: $17 to $23. Apr 17 to Oct 24. (270)622-6959

BARREN RIVER LAKE - COE/TAILWATER (Public Corps) From Glasgow, N 4 mi on 31E to KY-252, N 4.2 mi, follow signs (L). 48 Avail: 48 W, 48 E. 2021 rates: $18. (270)622-7732

WALNUT CREEK MARINA (Public) From town, NE 6.4 mi Hwy 31E, S 0.7 mi on Hwy 252 to CR-1855, E 2 mi (L). 30 Avail: 30 W, 30 E (20 amps), Pit toilets. 2021 rates: $8 to $10. Apr 15 to Oct 15. (270)622-5858

SHEPHERDSVILLE — C3 *Bullitt*

GRANDMA'S RV CAMPING **Ratings: 7.5/9.5★/7.5** (RV Park) Avail: 60 full hkups (30/50 amps). 2021 rates: $35 to $40. (502)543-7023, 159 Dawson Dr, Shepherdsville, KY 40165

LOUISVILLE SOUTH KOA **Ratings: 9/10★/8.5** (RV Park) 151 Avail: 116 full hkups, 35 W, 35 E (30/50 amps). 2021 rates: $40 to $90. (800)562-1880, 2433 Hwy 44E, Shepherdsville, KY 40165

SLADE — D5 *Powell*

4 GUYS RV PARK
Ratings: 9/10★/8.5 (RV Park) From jct Bert T Combs Mountain Pkwy (exit 33) & SR 11: Go 500 ft E on SR 11, then 2 mi N on SR 15 (L). **FAC:** gravel rds. Avail: 60 gravel, patios, 5 pull-thrus, (30x70), back-ins (35x60), 60 full hkups (30/50 amps), WiFi @ sites, rentals, laundry, groc, LP gas, fire rings, firewood. **REC:** pool, pond, fishing, boating nearby, playground, hunting nearby. Pet restrict (B/Q). No tents. Big rig sites, eco-friendly. 2021 rates: $39 to $44, Military discount.
(859)314-2465 Lat: 37.8205, Lon: -83.7258
10137 Campton Rd, Slade, KY 40376
4guysrvpark.com
See ad this page

NATURAL BRIDGE STATE RESORT PARK (Public State Park) From Jct of Mt Pkwy & SR-11 (exit 33), S 2.5 mi on SR-11 (L). 87 Avail: 87 W, 87 E (20/50 amps). 2021 rates: $26 to $37. Mar 16 to Nov 15. (606)663-2214

SMITHLAND — B2 *Livingston*

BIRDSVILLE RIVERSIDE RV PARK
Ratings: 7/9.5★/9 (Campground) Avail: 34 full hkups (30/50 amps). 2021 rates: $45. Apr 01 to Dec 17. (270)928-2772, 972 River Rd, Smithland, KY 42081

SOMERSET — D4 *Dewayne*

HAPPY CAMPER RV PARK
Ratings: 6.5/NA/8.5 (RV Park) Avail: 12 full hkups (30/50 amps). 2021 rates: $40. (606)872-8640, 332 Falls Dr, Somerset, KY 42503

LAKE CUMBERLAND - COE/CUMBERLAND POINT REC AREA (Public Corps) From town, W 10 mi on Hwy 80 to Hwy 235, S 1 mi to Hwy 761, W 9 mi (E). 30 Avail: 30 W, 30 E (30 amps). 2021 rates: $22. May 15 to Sep 12. (606)871-7886

LAKE CUMBERLAND - COE/FISHING CREEK CAMPGROUND (Public Corps) From town, W 5 mi on Hwy 80 to Hwy 1248, NE 2 mi (L). 26 Avail: 26 W, 26 E (30/50 amps). 2021 rates: $25 to $32. May 01 to Sep 26. (606)679-5174

LAKE CUMBERLAND - COE/WAITSBORO CAMPGROUND (Public Corps) From town, S 5 mi on US-27, follow signs (R). 17 Avail: 17 W, 17 E (30 amps). 2021 rates: $20 to $25. May 01 to Sep 29. (606)561-5513

STAFFORDSVILLE — C6 *Johnson*

PAINTSVILLE LAKE (Public State Park) From Jct of US-23 & SR 40, W 2 mi on SR 40 to Ky 2275, N 1.4 mi (N). Avail: 32 full hkups (30/50 amps). 2021 rates: $30 to $34. (606)297-8486

STEARNS — E4 *McCreary*

BIG SOUTH FORK/BLUE HERON CAMPGROUND (Public National Park) From jct US 27 & Hwy 92: Go 1 mi W on Hwy 92, then 1 mi S on Hwy 1651, then 9 mi S on Hwy 741. 45 Avail: 45 W, 45 E (30/50 amps). 2021 rates: $20. Apr 01 to Oct 31. (423)569-9778

STURGIS — D1 *Union*

UNION COUNTY FAIR & EXPO CENTER (Public) From jct SR-109 & US-60: Go 1 mi E on US-60. 45 Avail. 2021 rates: $33 to $75. (270)333-4107

TAYLORSVILLE — C3 *Spencer*

TAYLORSVILLE LAKE (Public State Park) E-Bnd From Jct of I-64 & KY 55 (exit 32), S 14 mi on KY 55 to KY 44, E 5.2 mi to KY 248, SE 1.9 mi (R) or W-Bnd From Jct of I 64 & KY 53 (exit 35) S 6.2 mi on KY-53 to KY-44 SW 6.2 mi to KY-248, SE 1.9 mi (R). 45 Avail: 45 W, 45 E (30/50 amps). 2021 rates: $26 to $35. Apr 01 to Dec 15. (502)477-8713

WALTON — B4 *Boone*

BIG BONE LICK (Public State Park) From jct US-42 & SR-338: Go 3 mi NW on SR-338 (L). 62 Avail: 62 W, 62 E (30 amps). 2021 rates: $25 to $35. (859)384-3522

OAK CREEK CAMPGROUND **Ratings: 9/9★/9** (Campground) 50 Avail: 50 W, 50 E (30/50 amps). 2021 rates: $35 to $39. (859)485-9131, 13329 Oak Creek Rd, Walton, KY 41094

CLEANING YOUR RV: When you're finished with the exterior cleaning, it's time for waxing. There are products that claim to wax and wash at the same time, while on the other end of the product list are paste waxes that require an electric buffing tool and lots of grunt work. Bottom line - the easier it is the least amount of time the coating will last. Put in the work and you will have a shiny vehicle much longer.

Louisiana

Getty Images/iStockphoto

DID YOU KNOW?

New Orleans' first official Mardi Gras parade kicked off in 1856, though some historians believe similar parties date back as far as 1699.

Louisiana is a hearty mix of world-class cuisine, endless wetlands and a culture like no other on the planet. Towns pulse with rollicking rhythms and the signatures of its French, Spanish, Creole and Cajun settlers.

Chefs in the Crescent City

New Orleans's epic menu of spicy food and rollicking music will put you under its spell. A visit to the so-called Big Easy is not complete without taking in the tunes at a storied jazz bar or sampling the spicy jambalaya. The Big Easy's raucous atmosphere thrives in the French Quarter and on Bourbon Street, while the nearby Jean Lafitte National Historical Park and Preserve serves up a tranquil atmosphere for exploration of the region's landscapes and history. Centrally located, the capital city of Baton Rouge offers up a saucy mix of cultures, as well, with Creole and Cajun influences found in the food and entertainment.

Flyways and Fun on the Mississippi

Before emptying in the Gulf of Mexico, the Mississippi River rolls through southeast Louisiana, bringing migratory birds streaming along the Mississippi Flyway. Grab your binoculars and head to one of the 30 areas along the Mississippi River Birding Trail. The Mississippi Flyway is not only a top spot for birding, it's also a waterfowl-hunting haven. The Pass-a-Loutre Wildlife Management Area promises thrilling hunting action at the mouth of the Mississippi River.

Wetland Wonderland

Louisiana gives watersports enthusiasts access to the Mississippi River, Gulf of Mexico and Atchafalaya Swamp — great places to drop a line or launch watercraft. Rich swamplands, marshes and bayous create distinct habitats to explore on zippy airboat tours or meandering kayaking trips. Watch alligators emerge from coffee-colored waters. The

Louisiana Beignets

You'll find the world's most famous beignets at Café du Monde. Nestled in New Orleans' French Quarter, this iconic coffee shop dishes out these pillowy fried pastries 24 hours a day. Bite into the powdered sugar puffs and then try dunking them in a chicory coffee. Don't leave without picking up a big box of beignet mix to bring home.

VISITOR CENTER

TIME ZONE
Central Standard

ROAD & HIGHWAY INFORMATION
877-452-3683
511la.org

FISHING & HUNTING INFORMATION
800-256-2749
wlf.louisiana.gov/licenses-and-permits

BOATING INFORMATION
800-256-2749
wlf.louisiana.gov

NATIONAL PARKS
nps.gov/la

STATE PARKS
crt.state.la.us/louisiana-state-parks

TOURISM INFORMATION
Louisiana Office of Tourism
800-677-4082
louisianatravel.com

TOP TOURISM ATTRACTIONS
1) French Quarter
2) Avery Island
3) Mardi Gras World

MAJOR CITIES
New Orleans, Baton Rouge (capital), Shreveport, Metairie, Lafayette

LA

There is no limit on joy in Louisiana.
©2021 Louisiana Department of Culture, Recreation & Tourism

LOUISIANA
Feed Your Soul.
LouisianaTravel.com

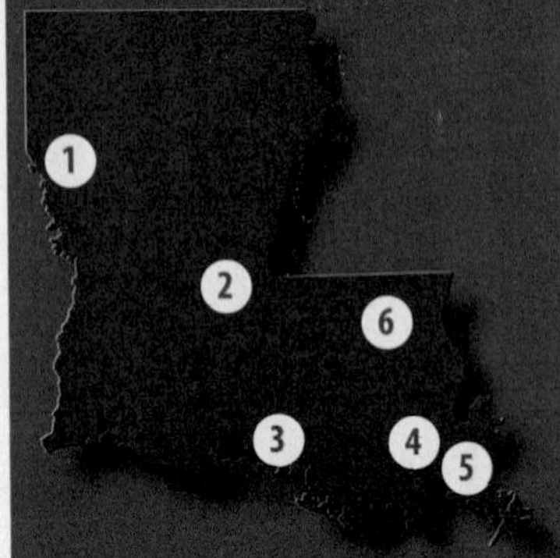

1

TOLEDO BEND Lake Country
SABINE PARISH, LOUISIANA

Come get lost at Louisiana's most popular lake destination! Relax by the campfire as you watch bald eagles soar into the most beautiful sunsets Toledo Bend has to offer.

ToledoBendLakeCountry.com/rv-campgrounds

2

act
Avoyelles Commission of Tourism

Drive to Central Louisiana and RV in Avoyelles Parish off I-49. Select from Gator Grounds RV and Waterpark Resort (118 sites), gatorgrounds.org, indoor/outdoor pools, zip line, and more. Paragon Casino Resort (200 sites), paragoncasinoresort.com, rated 10-10-10 by Good Sam. Both parks adjacent to golf courses and additional amenities, visit websites.

800-833-4195 · travelavoyelles.com

3

IBERIA PARISH
Convention & Visitors Bureau
iberiatravel.com

Ditch the beignets for the hot sauce in New Iberia! Camp at Isle of Iberia RV Resort or KOC Kampground. Visit Avery Island, home of Tabasco®, or Jefferson Island Rip Van Winkle Gardens. Tour the Nationally Registered Main Street, Shadows-on-the-Teche, Bayou Teche Museum, Conrad Rice Mill and Jeanerette Museum. Welcome Center OPEN Mon-Fri 8 am-4 pm.

888-942-3742 · IberiaTravel.com

4

VISIT JEFFERSON PARISH

What better way to explore the outdoors than camping! Bring the whole family in the RV or pitch a tent on the beach at Grand Isle State Park. "Glamp" in one of the floating cabins on Bayou Segnette or experience a cabin or houseboat along the Barataria in Jefferson Parish.

877-572-7474 · visitjeffersonparish.com/outdoors

5

St. Bernard
NEW ORLEANS' MOST HISTORIC NEIGHBOR

From a breath-taking State Park to marinas and other waterside spots, you can bring the comforts of your RV home to enjoy St. Bernard Parish!

504-278-4242 · visitstbernard.com

6

TANGIPAHOA Tourism
Tangipahoa Parish Convention & Visitors Bureau

Tangipahoa Parish, a Camper's Paradise. Our nine unique campgrounds and RV parks are the best place to relax and unwind. Close to nature with amenities that make vacations easier and more fun. Ideal access to exits on Interstate 12 and 55. With great restaurants and annual festivals, we are a Camper's Paradise.

800-617-4503 · tangitourism.com

Barataria Preserve and Palmetto Island State Park are just two of the many places to experience Louisiana's unique landscapes. For a beach retreat, head to Grand Isle State Park, located on a barrier island off the southern coast. Watch pelicans and seagulls skirt the surf, and relax to the sound of waves hitting the shore.

Canoeing, Kayaking and Casting

Get up-close to the bayous in a kayak or canoe. The Bayou Bartholomew and Lake Martin both feature massive, moss-filled cypress trees rising from the inky waters, making them popular spots. For a unique fishing excursion in similar landscapes, head to Caddo Lake, located on the Louisiana-Texas border. Toledo Bend Reservoir, also on the Louisiana-Texas border, consistently offers up quality bass fishing, having been named the best bass lake in the nation two years in a row. The Red River in the northeast is a favorite of anglers, known for its big catfish and bass, while the coastal waters in the south are the places to go for redfish and snapper, staples in Louisianan cuisine. The huge Atchafalaya Basin, west of Baton Rouge, is a paradise for adventurous anglers and paddlers.

Dusk falls as Bourbon Street prepares for a night of revelry in the heart of New Orleans' French Quarter.

Party Time

New Orleans may be the king of Mardi Gras, but several towns in the state give the Big Easy a run for its money. Lafayette, Baton Rouge and Lake Charles are just a few of the towns that go all out for this blowout. New Orleans is the granddaddy of them all, of course. Expect to find rollicking parades, colorful costumes and sweet king cakes making up an epic party. Louisiana is known for the rich mix of cultures that bring spice to the state, and Lafayette celebrates these cultures and more with the Festival International de Louisiane. Held each April, this five-day event is the nation's largest international music and arts festival.

Mounds of Mystery

More than 3,400 years ago, Louisiana's early indigenous people left valuable traces of the past with majestic earthworks. The mound at Poverty Point World Heritage Site is a mystery left by some of Louisiana's earliest peoples. Take a tour and visit the museum to imagine what life was like then. Centuries later, Louisiana would see its first European settlers with the first permanent settlement in what is now the town of Natchitoches. Established in 1714, this historic town is a centerpiece of the Cane River National Heritage Area, which tells the story of the French, Spanish and Creole cultures that shaped Louisiana. Exiled Canadian Acadians added to the cultural mix when they arrived in 1755 and settled along the southern coast. Later known as the Cajuns, these settlers brought a joie de vivre to the music and cuisine of the Gulf Coast.

Flavor Explosion: A homemade Southern crawfish boil with potatoes, sausage, onions and corn.

Tantalizing Tangipahoa

Tangipahoa Parish has been named "Crossroads of the South" for its location on Lake Pontchartrain directly opposite of New Orleans. The word Tangipahoa translates to "ear of corn" or "those who gather corn," describing an agricultural way of life that has endured through the centuries. Located at the intersection of Interstate 55 and Interstate 12, about 45 miles east of Baton Rouge, Hammond, the parish's biggest city, is home to pleasant summer months. Winters reflect a mild, cool subtropical climate. With a vibrant downtown, a tradition of maintaining historical structures and an appreciation for its own unique culture, Hammond is a truly charming Southern town.

Civil War Legacies

During the conflict between the states, Tangipahoa Parish maintained thriving industries. One entrepreneur, Charles Emery Cate, established a shoemaking factory for Confederate soldiers during the war and built Grace Memorial Episcopal Church. The factory was destroyed in the conflict, and the property has been transformed into the Cate Square, a city park. The church, however, remains standing to this day, with a majestic steeple and white, wooden exterior.

good sam park
2022 Top Rated
ALLEGRO
OPEN ROAD
The RV Park Is Just The Start
Pull into a traveler's paradise at Paragon RV Resort in Marksville, Louisiana. We've just scored another 10/10*/10 rating from Good Sam RV Travel & Savings Guide for our cleanliness, environment and facilities. More importantly, we are part of Paragon Casino Resort and only steps away from the casino itself. So you can easily enjoy Louisiana's favorite gaming floor, our restaurants, luxurious spa, award-winning golf, swimming pool with splash pad and so much more. Book your stay now and be sure to ask about Good Sam discounts!
THIS IS HOW WE PLAY
Paragon CASINO | RESORT
PARAGONCASINORESORT.COM
MARKSVILLE, LA

good sam park Featured Good Sam Parks

LOUISIANA

When you stay with Good Sam, you can expect the highest degree of cleanliness and friendliness, and better yet, you get **10% off** overnight campground fees.

If you're not already a Good Sam member you can purchase your membership at one of these locations:

BROUSSARD
Maxie's Campground
Parkside RV Park

COVINGTON
Land-O-Pines Family Campground

DUSON
Frog City RV Park

GREENWOOD
Southern Living RV Park
TravelCenters of America RV Park

IOWA
Blue Heron RV Park

KINDER
Coushatta Luxury RV Resort at Red Shoes Park

LAKE CHARLES
Twelve Oaks RV Park

LIVINGSTON
Lakeside RV Park

MARKSVILLE
Paragon Casino RV Resort

MERRYVILLE
Country Meadow Estates

MINDEN
Cinnamon Creek RV Park

NATCHITOCHES
Grand Ecore RV Park
Nakatosh Campground

NEW IBERIA
KOC Kampground

NEW ORLEANS
Jude Travel Park of New Orleans

OAK GROVE
7 Oaks RV Campground

SLIDELL
Pine Crest RV Park of New Orleans

SULPHUR
A+ Motel & RV Park

VIDALIA
River View RV Park and Resort

10/10★/10 GOOD SAM PARK

MARKSVILLE
Paragon Casino RV Resort
(800)946-1946

What's This?

An RV park with a 10/10★/10 rating has scored perfect grades in amenities, cleanliness and appearance ("See Understanding the Campground Rating System" on pages 8 and 9 for an explanation of the trusted Good Sam Rating System). Stay in a 10/10★/10 park on your next trip for a nearly flawless camping experience.

Getty Images/iStockphoto

LA

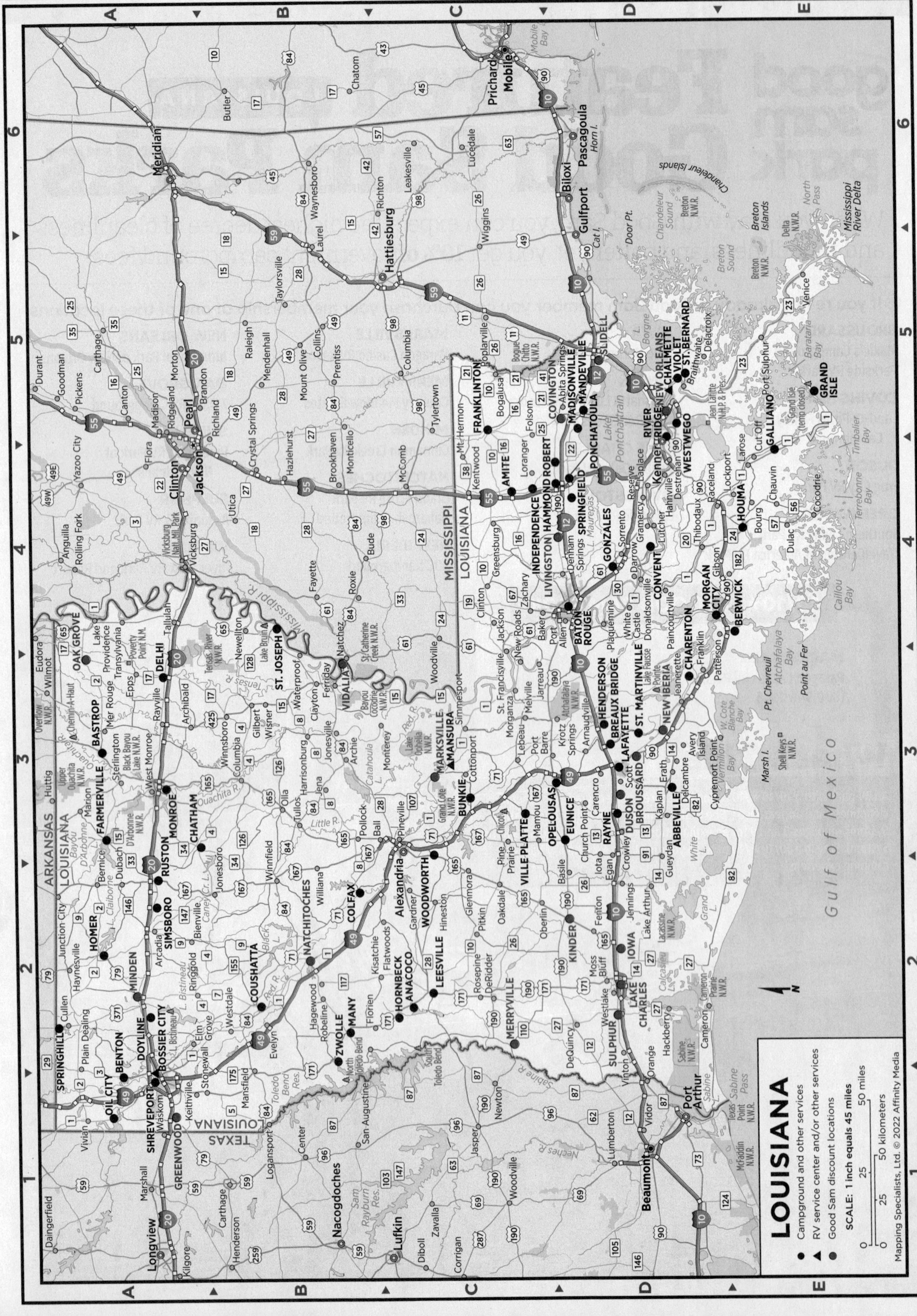

LOUISIANA
Campground and other services
RV service center and/or other services
Good Sam discount locations
SCALE: 1 inch equals 45 miles
0 25 50 miles
0 25 50 kilometers
Mapping Specialists, Ltd. © 2022 Affinity Media
Gulf of Mexico

ROAD TRIPS

Discover New Flavors in the Pelican State

Louisiana

LOCATION
LOUISIANA

DISTANCE
154 MILES

DRIVE TIME
2 HR 45 MINS

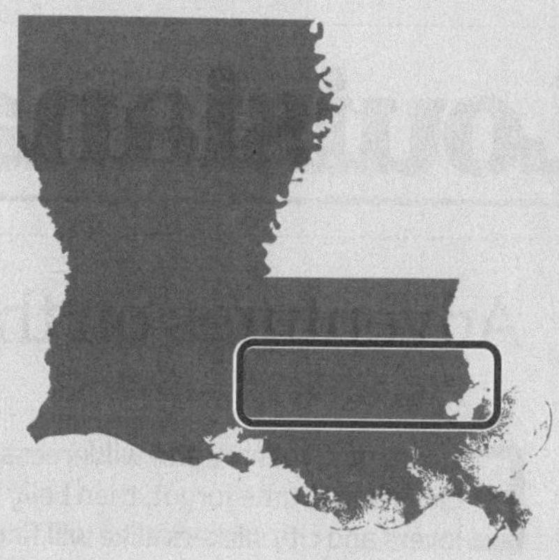

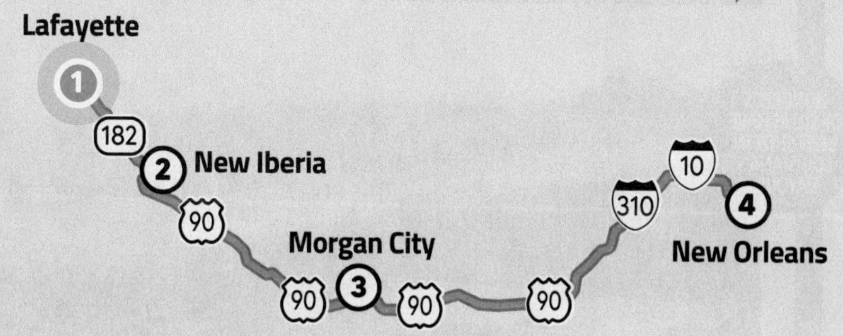

The Cajuns settled in southern Louisiana in the 1700s, bringing their French roots with them. Today, the region offers a distinct kind of food and fun you won't find anywhere else. With delicious Cajun cuisine gracing restaurant menus, soulful zydeco music spilling out from bars, and endless swamps to play in, this stretch from Lafayette to New Orleans makes for an unforgettable journey in the Deep South.

1 Lafayette
Starting Point

The heart of Louisiana's Cajun Country, Lafayette will feed your soul and belly with its unique culinary and cultural identity. Join a food tour to sample local delicacies like gumbo, boudin, etouffee, cracklin' and more. Afterward, visit LARC's Acadian Village, a living history museum showing what Acadian life was like during the 19th century. You can also view native birds and kayak through a swampy ecosystem at nearby Cypress Island Preserve. When night falls, bust a move to the sounds of Cajun and zydeco music at restaurants and dance halls.

2 New Iberia
Drive 21 Miles ▪ 31 Minutes

Rich history, tranquil scenery and warm hospitality make New Iberia one of Louisiana's most interesting places to visit. Start your day by strolling past historic buildings on Main Street and spotting alligators resting in cypress-tupelo swamps from the Bayou Teche Boardwalk. In nearby Vermilion Bay, Cypremort Point State Park has an artificial beach that's great for swimming, fishing and boating. In Jungle Gardens, marvel at alligators, bears, bobcats, deer and other wildlife as you walk or drive along man made lagoons that trail Bayou Petit Anse. Conclude your stay at the Tabasco Factory. See how the famous hot sauce is made from pepper plants and then stock up on spicy souvenirs at the country store. Purchase some Tabasco swag and get some new flavors. Cayenne Garlic Sauce, anyone?

3 Morgan City
Drive 48 Miles ▪ 50 Minutes

Morgan City is best known for hosting the Louisiana Shrimp and Petroleum Festival, but visitors can see how important the seafood and oil business is here year-round. From Main Street, climb the flood barrier to see shrimp boats and industrial ships out on the Atchafalaya River before feasting on fresh shellfish at a local restaurant. If you prefer to catch your meal, drop a line in the freshwater marshes of the Atchafalaya Delta Wildlife Management Area to reel in catfish, bass, bluegill and more.

4 New Orleans
Drive 85 Miles ▪ 1 Hour, 24 Minutes

Mardi Gras may be NOLA's claim to fame, but there's much more than parties and parades here. Wander through the French Quarter, where galleries, shops and music clubs line the street. Make sure to fill up on beignets at Café du Monde and look out for famous landmarks like the St. Louis Cathedral and Jackson Square. You can also cruise the Mississippi River on the iconic Steamboat Natchez and view works by Edgar Degas at the New Orleans Museum of Art. For the best jazz clubs, head to Preservation Hall or the many music clubs on Frenchmen Street. Don't forget to ride one of the town's iconic streetcars.

Getty Images/iStockphoto

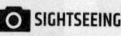

BIKING · BOATING · DINING · ENTERTAINMENT · FISHING · HIKING · HUNTING · PADDLING · SHOPPING · SIGHTSEEING

LA

Louisiana SPOTLIGHTS

Adventures on the Table and on the Bayou

Explore new culinary and wilderness frontiers in the Pelican State. Explore bayous that time forgot, then belly up to a steaming bowl of gumbo. Nature lovers and city slickers alike will find something exciting in Louisiana.

HUNDREDS OF FILMS HAVE BEEN SHOT IN LOUISIANA'S BAYOUS.

A pair of boats ready to go on a bayou near Allen Parish in Southern Louisiana.

Allen Parish-Kinder

Known as the "Gateway to Southwest Louisiana," Allen Parish is home to a deep Cajun culture. The town of Kinder, on the edge of the Cajun Prairie, boasts the largest casino in the state with 100,000 square feet of gaming fun, and the best slots around. A luxury hotel and tasteful RV park along with an award-winning golf course are located at this crossroads of culture where five incredible waterways can be explored. Sports enthusiasts will thrill to two hunting reserves, and there's plenty of history and mystery.

Lady Luck Awaits

Looking for wide-open spaces and a good game? Coushatta Casino Resort, Louisiana's largest gaming palace, features Vegas-style table games, high-stakes salons and off-track betting with 100,000 square feet of gaming floors holding thousands of slots and 70 table games. You'll enjoy bingo, live poker and a chance to bet on horse races around the state. Seven dining experiences serve up everything from sports bar grub, Asian cuisine, juicy burgers, grilled entrees, delicious sandwiches, and custom steaks served just the way you like them. Take a break from the games and enjoy live entertainment at the Pavilion and Dream Pool.

Five Waterways for Fun

Allen Parish is home to the Calcasieu River, Ouiska Chitto Creek, Six Mile Creek, Ten Mile Creek and Bundick Creek — five waterways providing anglers with ample opportunity to reel in channel cats, striped bass, spotted bass and crappie. Float fishing makes the day even more pleasurable. Canoeists and kayakers can paddle some of the most scenic waterways in Louisiana. Beach your boat on the sandy waterfront and set off to explore the Kisatchie National Forest with its aromatic pine and hardwood trees.

Native American Powwow

Step back to an earlier time in our country's history at the Coushatta Indian Powwow, one of the largest Native American celebrations in North America. The event includes the Grand Entry with Native Americans from across the U.S. and Canada performing on the dancing ground in full regalia to the beat of tribal drums and native singers. During the weekend visitors can learn about tribal customs and Native American traditions. This awe-inspiring commemoration honors the culture and heritage of each tribe's ancestors.

A Native Region

Louisiana was bankrupt after the Civil War but that didn't stop Union soldier James A. Kinder from locating in Allen Parish, opening a general store and building a town. But

LOCAL FAVORITE

One Pot Cajun Gumbo

Add a Pelican State twist to this juicy crustacean. *Recipe by Peter Mercer.*

INGREDIENTS

- ☐ 3 Tbsp prepared roux (or make your own with ⅓ cup butter and ⅓ cup flour)
- ☐ 2 Tbsp olive oil
- ☐ 1 red bell pepper, diced
- ☐ 1 green bell pepper, diced
- ☐ 1 onion, diced
- ☐ 1 cup celery, chopped
- ☐ 3 cloves garlic, minced
- ☐ 3 cups chicken stock
- ☐ 14 oz andouille sausage cut into rounds
- ☐ 1 lb chicken, cubed
- ☐ 2 tsp Cajun and/or Creole seasoning
- ☐ 4 oz canned green chiles
- ☐ 2 14.5-oz cans of fire roasted diced tomatoes
- ☐ 1 tsp each salt and pepper (or to taste)
- ☐ Hot sauce to taste

DIRECTIONS

Sauté the celery, onion and peppers in the olive oil until they begin to soften. Add the sausage rounds and brown. Stir in the prepared roux (or make your own roux by melting 1/3 cup butter in a pan and add 1/3 cup flour; simmer and stir constantly until a nice dark brown, but not burned, color develops).

When well combined add the stock, tomatoes, green chiles, garlic, and seasoning to taste. Stir in the cooked chicken. Simmer, stirring often, for 1-3 hours (the longer you simmer, the richer the flavor will be). This recipe may also be finished in a slow cooker (after browning the sausage), or you may follow the appropriate stew instructions for your Instant Pot.

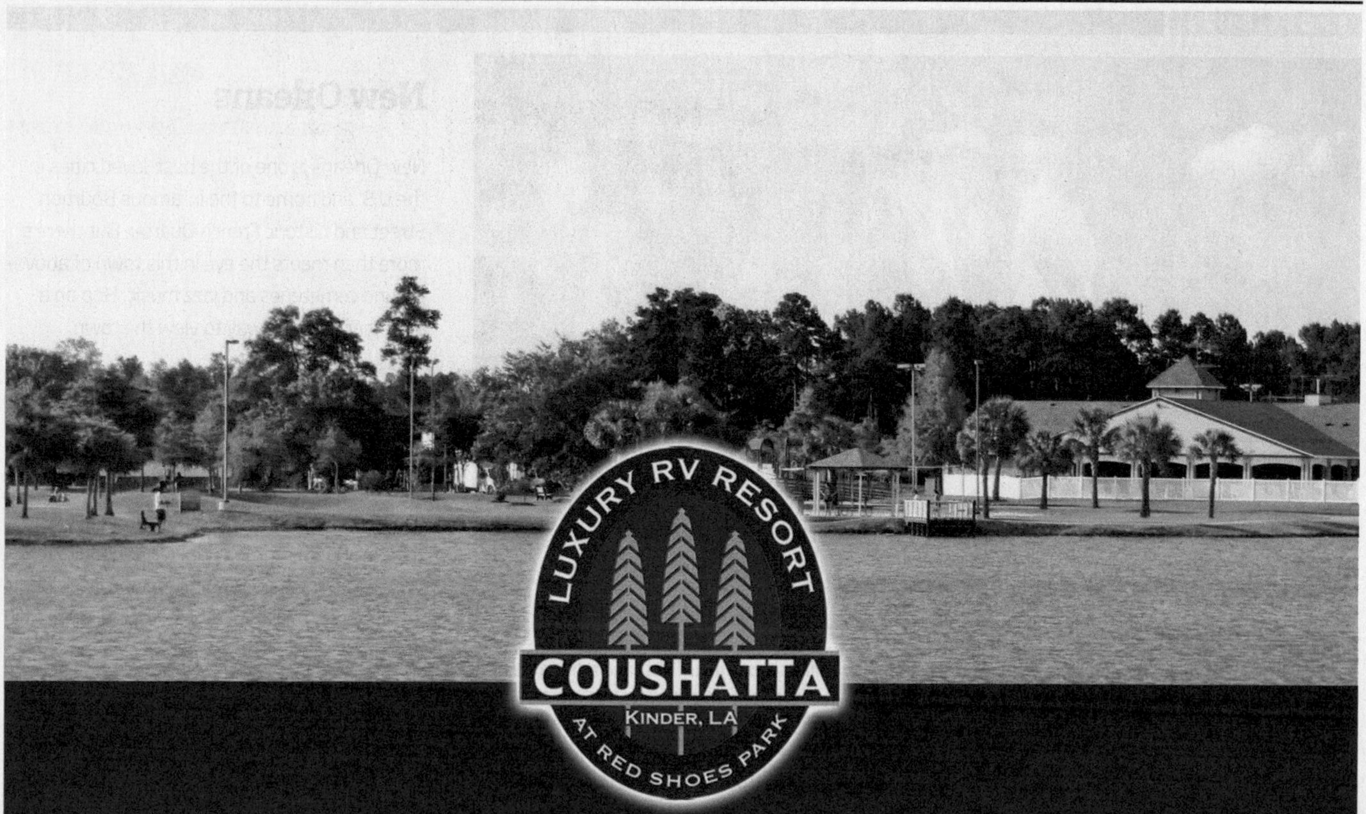

See listing Kinder, LA

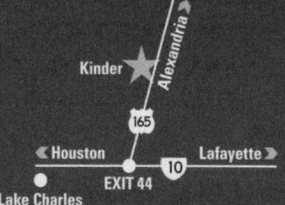

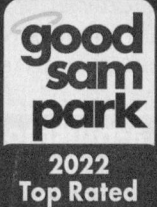

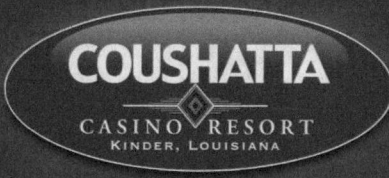

Frequently seen around Louisiana docks, the brown pelican has a wing span of up to 7 feet and is the state bird.

the region's roots run deep — very deep — right back to the Coushatta Tribe that lived along these waterways in the 1700s, and today own the Coushatta Casino Resort, the second-largest private employer in Louisiana. Leatherwood Museum has served as a railroad company house, boarding house, hospital and family home before becoming a museum. The building features furniture from the late 1800s and early 1900s along with medical artifacts, a native wildlife exhibit and the largest arrowhead and point collection in the region.

Lake Charles

A short drive north of the Gulf of Mexico sits historic Lake Charles, known for its strong Cajun influences and myriad annual festivals. The mid-sized city also makes a great base for exploring nearby natural areas, and the surrounding region offers ample opportunities for fishing, boating and birdwatching.

Casinos of Lake Charles

Plenty of people come to Lake Charles primarily to gamble, and there's no shortage of casinos in and around town. Popular spots include Golden Nuggets and L'Auberge Casino Resort. The Isle of Capri Casino & Hotel, Coushatta Casino Resort, and Delta Downs Racetrack Casino and Hotel are all located in nearby towns.

Charpentier Historic District

Fans of history and architecture are likely to enjoy the Charpentier Historic District of Lake Charles, which features 20-odd blocks of historic buildings dating primarily to the late 19th and early 20th centuries. Most of the structures here are private residences, but visitors who want to take a look inside can head to the 1911 Historic City Hall Arts & Cultural Center. This free attraction hosts a variety of art galleries, including the Black Heritage Gallery and Gallery by the Lake.

Creole Nature Trail

If you like exploring nature, you won't want to miss the chance to explore the Creole Nature Trail, which covers a 180-mile expanse in and around the Lake Charles region. The area is particularly popular with boaters and birdwatchers, with ample marshlands that provide a home to over 400 avian species, including egrets, herons, pelicans and warblers. Just be aware that this is also alligator country. Trail features include a 26-mile stretch along the Gulf of Mexico that's ideal for crabbing and collecting shells, a wide variety of walking trails and plenty of spots for fishing. Not into fishing? There are plenty of seafood restaurants in the area serving up gumbo, shrimp and crabs.

New Orleans

New Orleans is one of the best-loved cities in the U.S. and home to the infamous Bourbon Street and historic French Quarter. But there's more than meets the eye in this town of above-ground cemeteries and jazz music. Hop on a streetcar for a fun way to view the town.

The Crown Jewel of New Orleans

When you enter Bourbon Street, you've stepped into 13 blocks of pure New Orleans culture. Grab a bite of authentic Cajun food at a local restaurant or check out a Big Easy bar; they're known for their drinks and hospitality. With an abundance of shopping and interesting architecture, there's plenty to do until night falls and the streets come alive.

Cool French Quarter

The French Quarter is home to Bourbon Street but it's also the oldest neighborhood in NOLA, with late 18th-century architecture and historic homes. Step back to the days of swashbucklers and pirates when you meander Pirates Alley filled with 600 feet of quirky shops and heart-pumping legends. Royal Street is another must-see with its French vibe.

FOR MORE INFORMATION

Louisiana Office of Tourism, 800-677-4082, www.louisianatravel.com
Allen Parish Tourist Commission, 888-639-4868, www.allenparish.com
Cajun Coast Visitors & Convention Bureau, 800-256-2931, www.cajuncoast.com
Lake Charles/Southwest Louisiana CVB, 337-436-9588, www.visitlakecharles.org
New Orleans & Company, 800-672-6124, www.neworleans.com
Toledo Bend Lake Country, 800-358-7802, www.toledobendlakecountry.com

Louisiana

ABBEVILLE — D3 *Vermilion*

ABBEVILLE RV PARK (Public) E-bnd: From jct of I-10 & exit 82: Go S 1 mi on LA-1111/LA-13 Truck Rte, then S 15 mi on LA-13, then E 10 mi on LA-14, then S 1/2 mi on Bus 14 (Port St) (R); or W-bnd: From jct of I-10 & exit 100: Go S 2 mi on LA-3184, then SW 4 mi on LA-3073, then S 15-1/2 mi on US-167, then N 1/2 mi on Port St (L). 45 Avail: 39 full hkups, 6 W, 6 E (30/50 amps). 2021 rates: $24. (337)898-4042

PALMETTO ISLAND (Public State Park) From Jct of US 167 & LA 14 BYP: Go E 0.4 mi on LA 14 BYP to LA 82 (N State St), then S 3.6 mi to Jct of LA 82 & LA 330, then W 4.6 mi on LA 82 to LA 690, then E 0.9 mi to Pleasant Rd, then S 1.8 mi (L). 96 Avail: 96 W, 96 E (20/30 amps). 2021 rates: $20 to $28. (337)893-3930

ALEXANDRIA — C3 *Rapides*

ALEXANDRIA See also Natchitoches.

Things to See and Do

PARAGON CASINO RESORT Full service casino, hotel and RV park. Live entertainment, restaurants, 18 hole golf course, indoor aquatic center, and 3 screen theatre. Partial handicap access. RV accessible. Restrooms. Food. Hours: 24 hrs. ATM.
(800)946-1946 Lat: 31.10674, Lon: -92.05903
711 Paragon Place, Marksville, LA 71351
www.paragoncasinoresort.com
See primary listing at Marksville and ad page 430

AMITE — C4 *St Helena*

NATALBANY CREEK CAMPGROUND & RV PARK **Ratings: 10/9★/9.5** (RV Park) Avail: 100 full hkups (30/50 amps). 2021 rates: $39 to $60. (985)748-4311, 30218 Hwy 16 West, Amite, LA 70422

ANACOCO — C2 *Vernon*

SOUTH TOLEDO BEND (Public State Park) From jct US 171 & Hwy 111/392: Go 10-1/2 mi W on Hwy 111/392, then 1 mi N on Hwy 191, then 1/2 mi W on Bald Eagle Rd. 55 Avail: 55 W, 55 E (20/30 amps). 2021 rates: $20 to $33. (337)286-9075

BASTROP — A3 *Morehouse*

CHEMIN-A-HAUT
(Public State Park) From jct of US-165 & US-425: Go N 9-3/4 mi on US-425, then E 1/4 mi on Loop Park Rd. (L). **FAC:** paved rds. Avail: 26 paved, back-ins (24x60), 26 W, 26 E (30 amps), WiFi @ sites, tent sites, dump, laundry, fire rings, firewood, controlled access. **REC:** pool, wading pool, Bayou Bartholomew: fishing, boating nearby, playground, rec open to public. Pets OK. Partial handicap access, 14 day max stay. 2021 rates: $20 to $28.
(888)677-2436 Lat: 32.907361, Lon: -91.8484978
14656 State Park Rd, Bastrop, LA 71220
www.crt.state.la.us

BATON ROUGE — D4 *East Baton Rouge*

BATON ROUGE See also Livingston.

BATON ROUGE KOA **Ratings: 8.5/9.5★/8.5** (RV Park) Avail: 54 full hkups (30/50 amps). 2021 rates: $58 to $73. (800)562-5673, 7628 Vincent Rd, Denham Springs, LA 70726

FARR PARK EQUESTRIAN CENTER & RV CAMPGROUND (Public) E-bnd: From Jct of I-10 & Exit 155A (right lane on bridge), exit to 2nd left on exit ramp to Nicholson Dr, S 1.7 mi to Skip Bertman Dr, W 0.5 mi to River Rd, S 1.9 mi (L) or W-bnd: From Jct of I-10 & College Dr (exit 158), S 5.3 mi (College becomes Lee Dr then Brighton Ln) to River Rd, S 0.5 mi (L). 108 Avail: 108 W, 108 E (50 amps). 2021 rates: $35. (225)769-7805

LAKESIDE RV PARK
Ratings: 10/10★/9.5 (RV Park) From Baton Rouge; Go east on I-12 to exit 22 (LA63/Frost Rd), South 1 mi on Frost Rd (L). **FAC:** paved rds. (139 spaces). Avail: 139 paved, patios, 13 pull-thrus, (28x95), back-ins (30x55), 139 full hkups (30/50 amps), WiFi @ sites, rentals, laundry, groc, LP gas, fire rings, firewood. **REC:** pool, Campground Lake: fishing, kayaking/canoeing, playground, hunting nearby. Pet restrict (B). Partial handicap access. No tents. Big rig sites, eco-friendly. 2021 rates: $41 to $49, Military discount.
(225)686-7676 Lat: 30.45488, Lon: -90.74368
28370 South Frost Rd, Livingston, LA 70754
lakeside-rvpark.com
See primary listing at Livingston and ad this page

Things to See and Do

LOUISIANA TRAVEL PROMOTION ASSOCIATION The Louisiana Travel Private Association is a non-profit, private sector trade association representing the State's travel and hospitality industry. Hours: 8am to 5pm. No CC.
(225)346-1857
14141 Airline Hwy, Ste 1Q, Baton Rouge, LA 70817
www.louisianatravel.com
See ad page 428

BENTON — A2 *Bossier*

CYPRESS-BLACK BAYOU REC AREA (Public) From Jct of I-220 & Airline Dr (exit 12), N 5.4 mi on Airline Dr to Linton Rd, NE 4.2 mi, follow signs (R). 73 Avail: 28 full hkups, 45 W, 45 E (30/50 amps). 2021 rates: $25 to $30. (318)965-0007

BERWICK — E4 *St Mary*

CYPRESS LAKE RV RESORT **Ratings: 9/9★/8** (Campground) Avail: 36 full hkups (30/50 amps). 2021 rates: $40 to $45. (985)399-5981, 100 Cypress Dr, Berwick, LA 70342

BOSSIER CITY — A2 *Bossier*

SHREVEPORT/BOSSIER KOA JOURNEY
Ratings: 9/9.5★/9 (RV Park) From jct I-20 (exit 10) & Pines Road: Go S 1 mi on Pines Rd, then W 1 mi on W 70th St. (R); or from jct I-49 & LA-3132 (exit 2010: Go W 6-1/4 mi on LA-3132 (exit 1D), then W 2 mi on 70th St. (R). **FAC:** paved/gravel rds. (100 spaces). 85 Avail: 16 paved, 69 gravel, patios, 70 pull-thrus, (35x90), back-ins (25x50), 85 full hkups (30/50 amps), cable, WiFi @ sites, tent sites, rentals, laundry, groc, LP gas. **REC:** pool, pond, fishing, boating nearby, playground, hunting nearby. Pets OK. Partial handicap access. Big rig sites, eco-friendly. 2021 rates: $47.95, Military discount.
(318)687-1010 Lat: 32.44376, Lon: -93.87823
6510 W 70th Street, Shreveport, LA 71129
koa.com/campgrounds/shreveport
See primary listing at Shreveport and ad page 443

Travel Services

CAMPING WORLD OF BOSSIER CITY/SHREVEPORT As the nation's largest retailer of RV supplies, accessories, services and new and used RVs, Camping World is committed to making your total RV experience better. **SERVICES:** RV appliance, MH mechanical, restrooms. RV Sales. RV supplies, LP gas, emergency parking, RV accessible. Hours: 9am - 7pm.
(888)629-6623 Lat: 32.527178, Lon: -93.677505
3625 Industrial Drive, Bossier City, LA 71112
www.campingworld.com

BREAUX BRIDGE — D3 *St Martin*

POCHE'S RV PARK AND FISH-N-CAMP **Ratings: 8.5/8.5★/8.5** (Campground) Avail: 83 full hkups (30/50 amps). 2021 rates: $30 to $55. (337)332-0326, 1080 Sawmill Hwy, Breaux Bridge, LA 70517

Traveling with Fido? Many campground listings indicate pet-friendly amenities and pet restrictions.

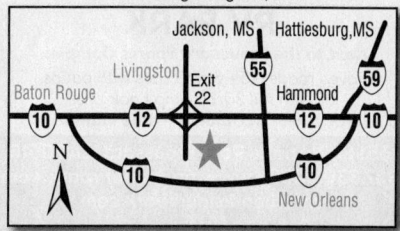

BREAUX BRIDGE (CONT)

Travel Services

CAMPING WORLD OF BREAUX BRIDGE As the nation's largest retailer of RV supplies, accessories, services and new and used RVs, Camping World is committed to making your total RV experience better. **SERVICES:** tire, RV appliance, sells outdoor gear, sells firearms, staffed RV wash, restrooms. RV Sales. RV supplies, LP gas, RV accessible. Hours: 9am - 6pm.
(866)897-4921 Lat: 30.29729, Lon: -91.91261
2310 N Frontage Rd, Breaux Bridge, LA 70517
rv.campingworld.com

BROUSSARD — D3 *Lafayette*

MAXIE'S CAMPGROUND
Ratings: 7/8.5★/7 (Campground) Avail: 57 full hkups (30/50 amps). 2021 rates: $32 to $36. (337)837-6200, 4350 Hwy 90E, Broussard, LA 70518

PARKSIDE RV PARK
Ratings: 8/9.5★/10 (RV Park) From jct US-90 & St Naziaire Rd: Go 3/4 mi E on St Naziaire Rd (L). **FAC:** paved rds. Avail: 54 paved, no slide-outs, back-ins (30x60), 54 full hkups (30/50 amps), WiFi @ sites, laundry. **REC:** boating nearby, hunting nearby. Pets OK. Partial handicap access. No tents. Big rig sites, eco-friendly. 2021 rates: $45, Military discount.
(337)330-2288 Lat: 30.140370, Lon: -91.932291
651 St Naziaire Rd, Broussard, LA 70518
www.parksidervpark.com
See ad this page

BUNKIE — C3 *Avoyelles*

GATOR GROUNDS RV RESORT **Ratings: 9/9/9** (RV Park) Avail: 122 full hkups (30/50 amps). 2021 rates: $45 to $75. (318)295-4030, 200 Golf Course Rd, Bunkie, LA 71322

CHALMETTE — D5 *St Bernard*

Things to See and Do

ST BERNARD PARISH TOURIST COMMISSION St. Bernard Parish is just 5 miles from downtown New Orleans, home to the Battle of New Orleans, outdoor activity paradise, and beautiful waterways. Restrooms. Hours: 8:30am to 4:30pm. No CC.
(504)278-4242 Lat: 29.95106, Lon: -90.00574
409 Aycock St, Arabi, LA 70032
www.visitstbernard.com
See ad page 428

CHARENTON — D3 *St Mary*

CYPRESS BAYOU CASINO RV PARK **Ratings: 6.5/NA/9.5** (RV Park) Avail: 30 full hkups (30/50 amps). 2021 rates: $15 to $22. (800)284-4386, 832 Martin Luther King Road, Charenton, LA 70523

CHATHAM — A3 *Jackson*

JIMMIE DAVIS (Public State Park) From jct of US-167 & LA-4 (in Jonesboro): Go E 12-3/4 mi on LA-4 to Lakeshore Dr, then SE 1-1/2 mi on Lakeshore Dr, then S 1-1/2 mi on State Park Rd. (E). 73 Avail: 73 W, 73 E (20/30 amps). 2021 rates: $20 to $33. (318)249-2595

COLFAX — B2 *Grant*

COLFAX RV PARK (Public) From Jct of I-49 & Hwy 8 (exit 99), N 11 mi on Hwy 8E to Main St, E 0.4 mi to Hwy 158, NW 0.9 mi to Lock & Dam sign, W 0.3 mi (R). Avail: 25 full hkups (30/50 amps). 2021 rates: $32. (318)627-2640

CONVENT — D4 *St James*

POCHE PLANTATION RV RESORT **Ratings: 9/9★/9** (RV Park) Avail: 115 full hkups (30/50 amps). 2021 rates: $40 to $45. (225)715-9510, 6554 Louisiana Hwy 44, Convent, LA 70723

SUGAR HILL RV PARK **Ratings: 7.5/8.5/7.5** (RV Park) Avail: 40 full hkups (30/50 amps). 2021 rates: $30 to $35. (225)715-9510, 9450 Highway 44, Convent, LA 70723

COUSHATTA — B2 *Red River*

GRAND BAYOU RESORT (Public) From Jct of I-49 & LA-177 (exit 162), NE 6 mi on LA-177 to US-84, SE 2.8 mi to US-84E, E 5.2 mi to LA-784, E 1.3 mi (R). 46 Avail: 11 full hkups, 35 W, 35 E (30/50 amps). 2021 rates: $20 to $27. (318)932-0066

COVINGTON — D5 *St Tammany*

LAND-O-PINES FAMILY CAMPGROUND
Ratings: 8.5/8.5★/7.5 (Campground) 92 Avail: 74 full hkups, 18 W, 18 E (30/50 amps). 2021 rates: $42 to $72. (800)443-3697, 17145 Million Dollar Rd, Covington, LA 70435

DELHI — A3 *Richland*

POVERTY POINT RESERVOIR (Public State Park) From jct of I-20 (exit 153) & LA-17: Go N 2-1/2 mi on LA-17. (R). 54 Avail: 45 full hkups, 9 W, 9 E (20/30 amps). 2021 rates: $20 to $33. (318)878-7536

DOYLINE — A2 *Webster*

LAKE BISTINEAU (Public State Park) W-bnd: From Jct of I-20 & LA-371 (exit 47), S 3.4 mi on LA-371 to LA-164, W 6.5 mi to LA-163, S 6.9 mi (L); or E-bnd: From Jct of I-20 & LA-157 (exit 33), S 600 ft on LA-157 to LA-3227, E 2 mi to LA-164, E 4.4 mi to LA-163, S 6.9 mi (L). 61 Avail: 61 W, 61 E (20/30 amps). 2021 rates: $20 to $33. (318)745-3503

DUSON — D3 *Acadia*

FROG CITY RV PARK
Ratings: 9.5/10★/8.5 (RV Park) From Jct of I-10 (exit 92) & LA-95, S 0.4 mi on LA-95 to Service Rd (Daulat Dr), W 1000 ft (E) or From Jct of US 90 & LA 95, N 0.5 mi on LA 95 to Service Rd, W 1000 ft (E). **FAC:** paved rds. (62 spaces). Avail: 32 gravel, 32 pull-thrus, (30x70), 32 full hkups (30/50 amps), seasonal sites, cable, WiFi @ sites, tent sites, dump, laundry, LP gas, restaurant. **REC:** heated pool, playground, hunting nearby. Pet restrict (B/Q). Partial handicap access. Big rig sites, eco-friendly. 2021 rates: $38, Military discount. ATM.
(337)873-9085 Lat: 30.24533, Lon: -92.19544
3003 Daulaut Dr, Duson, LA 70529
www.lafayettervpark.com
See ad opposite page

Travel Services

ROADY'S TRUCK STOP & CASINO Truck Stop with restaurant or fast food. ATM & Frog City RV park next door. Convenience store and casino. **SERVICES:** tire, MH mechanical, mobile RV svc, restaurant, restrooms. emergency parking, RV accessible. Hours: Open 24 hrs. ATM.
(337)873-5400 Lat: 30.24582, Lon: -92.19385
3002 Daulat Dr, Duson, LA 70529
www.lucky2s.com
See ad opposite page

EUNICE — D3 *Evangeline*

LAKEVIEW PARK & BEACH **Ratings: 7.5/7.5/8** (Campground) Avail: 95 full hkups (30/50 amps). 2021 rates: $30 to $80. (337)457-2881, 1717 Veteran Memorial Hwy, Eunice, LA 70535

FARMERVILLE — A3 *Union*

LAKE D'ARBONNE (Public State Park) From Jct of SR-15 & SR-2 (in town), W 5 mi on SR-2 to Evergreen Rd, S 0.3 mi (L). 58 Avail: 58 W, 58 E (20/30 amps). 2021 rates: $20 to $33. (318)368-2086

FRANKLINTON — C5 *Washington*

BOGUE CHITTO (Public State Park) From jct LA-10 & LA-25/LA-16: Go 5-1/2 mi S on LA-25, then 1-1/4 mi E on State Park Blvd. (L). 135 Avail: 46 full hkups, 81 W, 81 E (30/50 amps). 2021 rates: $25 to $33. (886)677-7312

GALLIANO — E4 *Lafourche*

GALLIANO RV PARK **Ratings: 7.5/9.5★/7.5** (RV Park) Avail: 12 full hkups (30/50 amps). 2021 rates: $40. (985)325-4445, 16816 Hwy 3235 , Cut Off, LA 70345

GONZALES — D4 *Ascension*

LAMAR-DIXON EXPO CENTER RV PARK (Public) From Jct of I-10 & LA 30 (Exit 177), W 0.4 mi on LA 30 to St Landry Avenue, S 0.9 mi (R). Avail: 200 full hkups (30/50 amps). 2021 rates: $35 to $45. (225)450-1009

GRAND ISLE — E5 *Jefferson*

GRAND ISLE (Public State Park) From jct of I-10 & US-90: Go S 108 mi, then go SE 68 mi on LA-308/LA-3235/LA-1, then NE 1/4 mi on Admiral Craik Dr. (R). 49 Avail: 49 W, 49 E (30/50 amps). 2021 rates: $25 to $33. (985)787-2559

GREENWOOD — A1 *Caddo*

SOUTHERN LIVING RV PARK
Ratings: 7.5/9★/7.5 (RV Park) From jct of I-20 (exit 5) & Greenwood Road: Go W 1/2 mi on US 79/US 80/Greenwood Road (R). **FAC:** paved rds. (90 spaces). 80 Avail: 12 paved, 68 gravel, 12 pull-thrus, (37x90), back-ins (30x50), 80 full hkups (30/50 amps), WiFi @ sites, laundry. **REC:** pool, boating nearby. Pet restrict (B). Partial handicap access. No tents. Big rig sites. 2021 rates: $35.
(318)938-1808 Lat: 32.44312, Lon: -93.96193
9010 Greenwood Rd, Greenwood, LA 71033
www.southernlivingrvpark.net
See ad page 443

TRAVELCENTERS OF AMERICA RV PARK
Ratings: 8.5/9★/8.5 (RV Park) From Jct of I-20 (exit 5) & Greenwood Rd: Go W 1/4 mi on N service Rd (R).

2 MIN OFF EXIT 5 AT I-20 GREENWOOD
Long level pull-thrus with Wi-Fi, laundry, bath house & cable tv. Next to Travel Center with 2 restaurants, fuel, shopping & casino. Blue Beacon RV Wash nearby. Great for stop over or a place to base while visiting the area.

FAC: paved rds. (60 spaces). Avail: 14 paved, patios, 10 pull-thrus, (24x65), back-ins (24x60), 14 full hkups (30/50 amps), cable, WiFi @ sites, $, dump, laundry, groc, restaurant. **REC:** boating nearby. Pet restrict (B). No tents. Big rig sites, eco-friendly. 2021 rates: $37. ATM.
(318)938-6360 Lat: 32.44591, Lon: -93.95191
8590 Greenwood Rd, Greenwood, LA 71033
www.ta-petro.com
See ad page 443

Things to See and Do

TRAVELCENTERS OF AMERICA - GREENWOOD RV friendly travel plaza, family restaurant (home-style cooking buffet or a la carte), convenience store, Lucky Jack's Casino and space for RV parking. Partial handicap access. RV accessible. Restrooms. Food. Hours: 24 hours. ATM.
(318)938-6360 Lat: 32.44535, Lon: -93.94857
8560 Greenwood Rd, Greenwood, LA 71033
www.tatravelcenters.com
See ad page 443

HAMMOND — D4 *Tangipahoa*

HAMMOND See also Amite, Covington, Independence, Livingston, Ponchatoula & Robert.

PUNKIN PARK CAMPGROUND **Ratings: 6.5/8/6** (Campground) Avail: 10 full hkups (30/50 amps). 2021 rates: $45. (225)567-3418, 43037 North Billville Rd, Hammond, LA 70403

Travel Services

CAMPING WORLD OF HAMMOND As the nation's largest retailer of RV supplies, accessories, services and new and used RVs, Camping World is committed to making your total RV experience better. **SERVICES:** tire, RV appliance, restrooms. RV supplies, emergency parking, RV accessible. Hours: 9am to 6pm.
(866)810-7323 Lat: 30.48239, Lon: -90.542378
43135 Pumpkin Center Road, Hammond, LA 70403
www.campingworld.com

Things to See and Do

TANGIPAHOA PARISH CONVENTION & VISITORS BUREAU Visitors center with brochures & information on accommodations, restaurants & attractions in the area. Open 7 days a week. Sat & Sun hrs 9am to 3pm. Class A parking with tow. Partial handicap access. RV accessible. Restrooms. Hours: 8am to 4pm. No CC.
(800)617-4503 Lat: 30.51956, Lon: -90.50766
13143 Wardline Rd, Hammond, LA 70401
tangitourism.com
See ad page 428

HENDERSON — D3 *St Martin*

CAJUN HERITAGE RV PARK **Ratings: 8.5/9★/9** (Campground) Avail: 140 full hkups (30/50 amps). 2021 rates: $39.99. (337)228-2616, 2026 Atchafalaya River Hwy, Breaux Bridge, LA 70517

CAJUN PALMS RV RESORT **Ratings: 10/10★/10** (RV Park) Avail: 403 full hkups (30/50 amps). 2021 rates: $50 to $109. (337)667-7772, 1055 N Barn Rd, Breaux Bridge, LA 70517

HOMER — A2 *Claiborne*

LAKE CLAIBORNE (Public State Park) E-bnd: From Jct of I-20 & SR-154 (exit 61), N 7.1 mi on SR-154 to SR-518, NE 8.5 mi to SR-146, S 1 mi (L); or W-bnd: From Jct of I-20 & SR-9 (exit 67), N 7.5 mi on SR-9 to SR-518, NE 8 mi to SR-146, S 1 mi (L). 89 Avail: 87 W, 87 E (20/30 amps). 2021 rates: $20 to $33. (318)927-2976

HORNBECK — C2 *Sabine*

SABINE RIVER AUTHORITY/PLEASURE POINT (Public) From Jct of SR-392 & SR-191, N 3.4 mi on SR-191 to park access rd, W 1.1 mi (E). 126 Avail: 50 full hkups, 76 W, 76 E (30 amps). 2021 rates: $20. (318)565-4810

HOUMA — E4 *Terrebonne*

HOUMA See also Galliano.

CAPRI COURT CAMPGROUND **Ratings: 6.5/8.5★/7.5** (Campground) Avail: 10 full hkups (30/50 amps). 2021 rates: $29.80 to $33.40. (800)428-8026, 105 Capri Court, Houma, LA 70364

INDEPENDENCE — C4 *Tangipahoa*

INDIAN CREEK CAMPGROUND & RV PARK **Ratings: 7.5/7.5/7** (Campground) 50 Avail: 50 W, 50 E (30/50 amps). 2021 rates: $34 to $49. (985)878-6567, 53013 West Fontana Rd., Independence, LA 70443

IOWA — D2 *Calcasieu*

BLUE HERON RV PARK

good sam park

Ratings: 7.5/9★/8 (RV Park) Avail: 40 full hkups (30/50 amps). 2021 rates: $55. (337)508-0600, 601 W US 90, Iowa, LA 70647

LACASSINE RV PARK (RV Park) (Rebuilding) Avail: 10 full hkups (30/50 amps). 2021 rates: $35. (337)326-5357, 20500 North Frontage Road, Iowa, LA 70647

LAKE CHARLES EAST / IOWA KOA **Ratings: 7.5/9.5★/8** (RV Park) Avail: 100 full hkups (30/50 amps). 2021 rates: $50. (337)496-7033, 21125 Louisiana Cotton Dr., Iowa, LA 70647

KINDER — D2 *Allen*

A SPOTLIGHT Introducing Allen Parish/Kinder's colorful attractions appearing at the front of this state section.

COUSHATTA LUXURY RV RESORT AT RED SHOES PARK

good sam park

Ratings: 10/9.5★/10 (RV Resort) From jct of I-10 & US-165 (exit 44): Go N 22-1/2 mi on US-165 (L); or from jct of I-49 & US-165 (exit 86): Go S 55 mi on US-165 (R).

LOUISIANA'S LARGEST CASINO RESORT

Louisiana's Best Bet! Enjoy thousands of slots, 70 tables, ten restaurants, an RV resort with furnished chalets, two music venues, supervised childcare, an award-winning golf course, bingo, off-track betting & the Dream Pool!

FAC: paved rds. Avail: 107 paved, patios, 105 pull-thrus, (35x70), back-ins (35x70), 107 full hkups (30/50 amps), cable, WiFi @ sites, rentals, dump, laundry, restaurant. **REC:** heated pool, pond, fishing, golf, playground, hunting nearby. Pets OK. Partial handicap access. No tents. Big rig sites, 14 day max stay, eco-friendly. 2021 rates: $25 to $65. ATM.
(800)584-7263 Lat: 30.54197, Lon: -92.81937
711 Pow Wow Parkway, Kinder, LA 70648
www.ccrla.com
See ad page 435

Things to See and Do

COUSHATTA CASINO RESORT Casino, Hotel, RV Park with Chalets, Golf Course and Restaurants. Partial handicap access. RV accessible. Restrooms. Food. Hours: Open 24 hrs. ATM.
(800)584-7263 Lat: 30.54197, Lon: -92.81937
777 Coushatta Drive, Kinder, LA 70648
www.coushattacasinoresort.com
See ad page 435

KOASATI PINES AT COUSHATTA CASINO RESORT 18 hole, par 72 championship golf course, pro shop, driving range, putting green, bar and grill. Partial handicap access. Restrooms. Food. Hours: 7am to 7pm. Adult fee: $40 to $85.
(800)584-7263 Lat: 30.55450, Lon: -92.80516
300 Koasati Drive, Kinder, LA 70648
www.coushattacasinoresort.com
See ad page 435

PARAGON CASINO RESORT Full service casino with slots, all table games, kid's quest & marketplace buffet. Live entertainment, 7 restaurants, 18 hole golf course, 500 room hotel, indoor aquatic center, spa, 3 screen theatre & over 185 spacious RV sites. Partial handicap access. RV accessible. Restrooms. Food. Hours: 24 hrs. ATM.
(800)946-1946 Lat: 31.10674, Lon: -92.05903
711 Paragon Place, Marksville, LA 71351
www.paragoncasinoresort.com
See primary listing at Marksville and ad page 430

LAFAYETTE — D3 *Lafayette*

LAFAYETTE See also Breaux Bridge, Broussard, Duson, Henderson, New Iberia & St Martinville.

ACADIANA PARK CAMPGROUND (Public) From Jct of I-10 & SR-167, S 1 mi on SR-167 to Willow St, E 0.8 mi to LA Ave, N 0.7 mi to E Alexander St, E 0.5 mi (L). 75 Avail: 75 W, 75 E (30/50 amps). 2021 rates: $25. (337)291-8388

BAYOU WILDERNESS RV CAMPGROUND **Ratings: 9/9★/9** (Campground) Avail: 80 full hkups (30/50 amps). 2021 rates: $39 to $46. (337)896-0598, 600 North Wilderness Trail, Carencro, LA 70520

KOA KAMPGROUND OF LAFAYETTE **Ratings: 9/9.5★/8** (RV Park) 105 Avail: 96 full hkups, 9 W, 9 E (30/50 amps). 2021 rates: $45 to $79. (337)235-2739, 1825 Saint Mary Street, Scott, LA 70583

LAKE CHARLES — D2 *Calcasieu*

A SPOTLIGHT Introducing Lake Charles' colorful attractions appearing at the front of this state section.

LAKE CHARLES See also Iowa & Sulphur.

A+ MOTEL & RV PARK

good sam park

Ratings: 10/9.5★/10 (RV Park) From jct I-210 & I-10: Go 5 mi W on I-10, then 2 mi S on LA-27 (L). **FAC:** paved rds. (134 spaces). Avail: 20 paved, patios, 19 pull-thrus, (30x70), back-ins (30x65), 20 full hkups (30/50 amps), seasonal sites, cable, WiFi @ sites, laundry, LP gas. **REC:** pool, wading pool, hot tub, pond, fishing, boating nearby, playground, hunting nearby. Pet restrict (B). Partial handicap access. No tents. Big rig sites, eco-friendly. 2021 rates: $45 to $50, Military discount. ATM.
(337)583-2631 Lat: 30.1813, Lon: -93.37601
4631 Hwy 27 South, Sulphur, LA 70665
a-plusmotel.com
See primary listing at Sulphur and ad page 436

LITTLE LAKE CHARLES RV RESORT **Ratings: 6.5/7/7.5** (Campground) Avail: 12 full hkups (30/50 amps). 2021 rates: $50 to $75. (337)433-1114, 4200 Luke Powers Rd, Lake Charles, LA 70615

SAM HOUSTON JONES (Public State Park) W-bnd: From Jct of I-10 & US-171 (exit 33), N 3.7 mi on US-171 to SR-378, W 2.8 mi to SR-378 Spur, W 1 mi to Sutherland Rd, S 0.4 mi (R); or From Jct of I-10 & SR-378 (exit 27 in Westlake), N 5 mi on SR-378 to SR-378 Spur, E/N/W 2.4 mi to Sutherland Rd, S 0.4 mi (R). 35 Avail: 35 W, 35 E (30/50 amps). 2021 rates: $20 to $33. (337)855-2665

SAVE! Camping World coupons can be found at the front and back of this Guide!

TWELVE OAKS RV PARK

good sam park

Ratings: 9/9★/8 (RV Park) Avail: 21 full hkups (30/50 amps). 2021 rates: $50 to $60. (337)439-2916, 2736 Conoco St, Lake Charles, LA 70601

LEESVILLE — C2 *Vernon*

MILITARY PARK TOLEDO BEND RECREATION SITE (FORT POLK) (Public) From Leesville, N on US-171 to LA-111. W 15 mi (bear right onto LA-392) to LA-191, N 5 mi to Army Travel Camp sign, W on Army Rec Rd. 28 Avail: 28 W, 28 E (30/50 amps). 2021 rates: $20 to $25. (888)718-9088

LIVINGSTON — D4 *Livingston*

LAKESIDE RV PARK

good sam park

Ratings: 10/10★/9.5 (RV Park) From Jct of I-12 (exit 22) & LA 63/Frost Rd, S 1 mi on Frost Rd (L).

KICK BACK IN OUR COUNTRY SETTING!

Convenient to Baton Rouge & New Orleans. A quick on and off of I-12 Exit 22. Enjoy large concrete roads & sites, dog-friendly walking trail around the lake where you can fish & relax. Come for a night & you'll want to stay!

FAC: paved rds. Avail: 139 paved, patios, 13 pull-thrus, (28x95), back-ins (30x55), 139 full hkups (30/50 amps), WiFi @ sites, rentals, laundry, groc, LP gas, fire rings, firewood. **REC:** pool, Campground Lake: fishing, kayaking/canoeing, playground, hunting nearby. Pet restrict (B). Partial handicap access. No tents. Big rig sites, eco-friendly. 2021 rates: $41 to $49, Military discount.
(225)686-7676 Lat: 30.45488, Lon: -90.74368
28370 S Frost Rd, Livingston, LA 70754
lakeside-rvpark.com
See ad page 437

MADISONVILLE — D5 *St Tammany*

FAIRVIEW-RIVERSIDE (Public State Park) From Jct of I-12 (exit 57) & LA-1077: Go S 7 mi on LA-1077 to Madisonville, then E 2 mi on LA-22. (L). 81 Avail: 81 W, 81 E (30/50 amps). 2021 rates: $20 to $28. (985)845-3318

MANDEVILLE — D5 *St Tammany*

FONTAINEBLEAU (Public State Park) From jct of I-12 (exit 65) & LA-59: Go S 3-1/2 mi on LA-59, then SE 2-1/2 mi on US-190. (L). 163 Avail: 23 full hkups, 103 W, 103 E (30/50 amps). 2021 rates: $20 to $33. (985)624-4443

MANSURA — C3 *Avoyelles*

Things to See and Do

AVOYELLES COMMISSION OF TOURISM Tourist information for the Avoyelles Parish area. Partial handicap access. RV accessible. Restrooms. Hours: . No CC.
(800)833-4195 Lat: 31.06520, Lon: -92.04413
8592 Hwy 1, Mansura, LA 71350
travelavoyelles.com
See ad page 428

MANY — B2 *Sabine*

SABINE RIVER AUTHORITY/CYPRESS BEND PARK (Public) From Jct of SR-6 & SR-191, S 3 mi on SR-191 to Cypress Bend Rd, SW 3 mi (1.5 mi past golf resort entrance) (R). Avail: 68 full hkups (30/50 amps). 2021 rates: $25 to $35. (318)256-4114

TOLEDO BEND RV RESORT AND CABINS **Ratings: 7.5/9.5★/8** (RV Park) Avail: 38 full hkups (30/50 amps). 2021 rates: $30 to $58. (318)256-0002, 114 Shamrock Lane, Many, LA 71449

Find Good Sam member specials at GanderOutdoors.com

LA

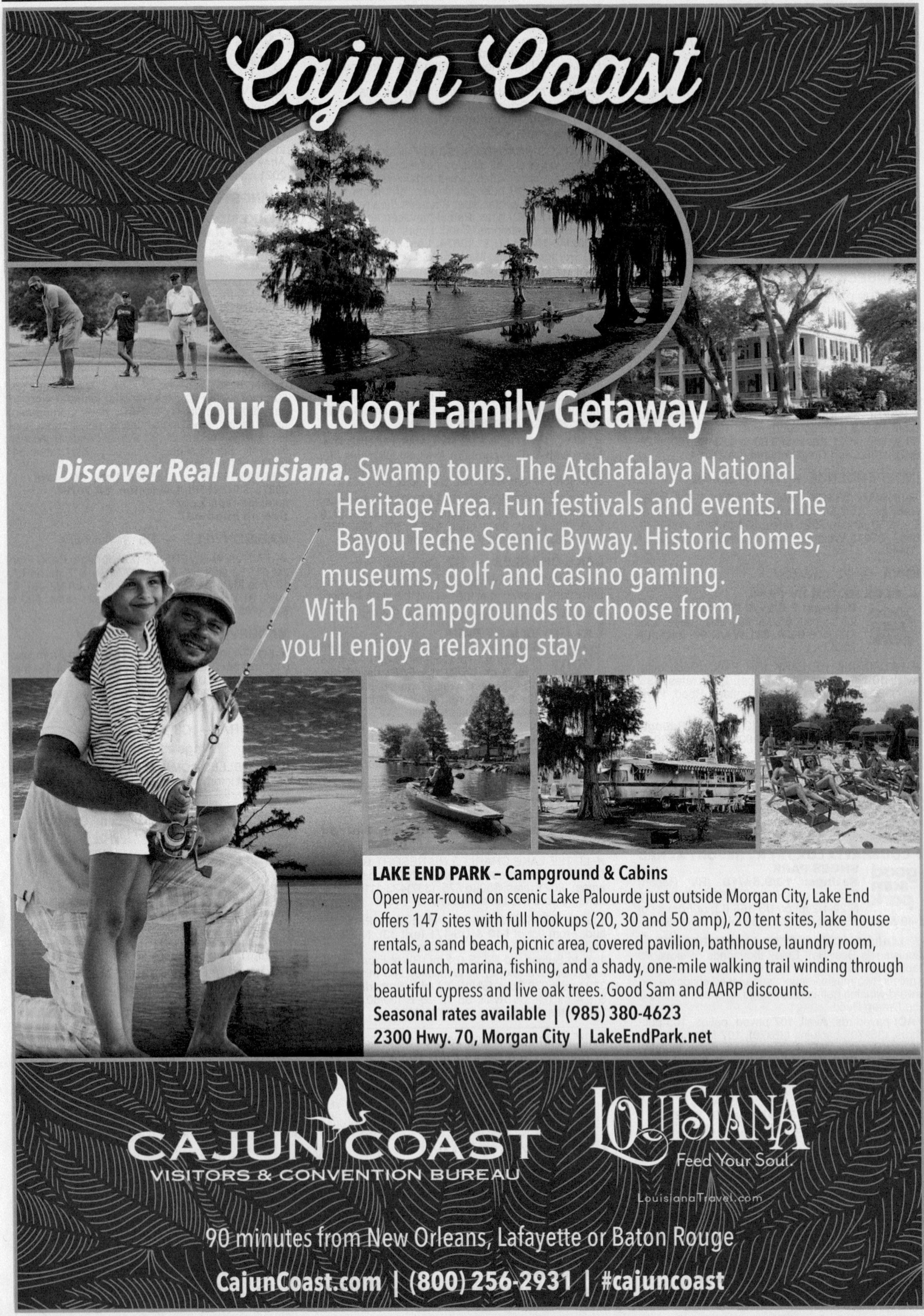
Cajun Coast
Your Outdoor Family Getaway
Discover Real Louisiana. Swamp tours. The Atchafalaya National Heritage Area. Fun festivals and events. The Bayou Teche Scenic Byway. Historic homes, museums, golf, and casino gaming. With 15 campgrounds to choose from, you'll enjoy a relaxing stay.
LAKE END PARK – Campground & Cabins
Open year-round on scenic Lake Palourde just outside Morgan City, Lake End offers 147 sites with full hookups (20, 30 and 50 amp), 20 tent sites, lake house rentals, a sand beach, picnic area, covered pavilion, bathhouse, laundry room, boat launch, marina, fishing, and a shady, one-mile walking trail winding through beautiful cypress and live oak trees. Good Sam and AARP discounts.
Seasonal rates available | (985) 380-4623
2300 Hwy. 70, Morgan City | LakeEndPark.net
CAJUN COAST
VISITORS & CONVENTION BUREAU
LOUISIANA
Feed Your Soul.
LouisianaTravel.com
90 minutes from New Orleans, Lafayette or Baton Rouge
CajunCoast.com | (800) 256-2931 | #cajuncoast

MANY (CONT)

Things to See and Do

TOLEDO BEND LAKE COUNTRY TOURISM Tourism information for the Toledo Bend Lake Country area Partial handicap access. RV accessible. Restrooms. Hours: 9am to 5pm. No CC.
(800)358-7802 Lat: 31.55051, Lon: -93.50732
1601 Texas Hwy, Many, LA 71449
toledobendlakecountry.com/rv-campgrounds
See ad page 428

MARKSVILLE — C3 *Avoyelles*

PARAGON CASINO RV RESORT
good sam park **Ratings: 10/10★/10** (RV Park) From jct of LA-1 & LA-115/107 (in Marksville): Go S 1-1/2 mi on LA-1 (L).

LOUISIANA'S PREMIER RV RESORT
A world-class gaming resort destination, full-service spa & salon, shops, Kids Quest Hourly Childcare and Cyber Quest Arcade, a 3-screen cinema, a variety of dining choices, a championship golf course and live entertainment!

FAC: paved rds. Avail: 205 paved, patios, 166 pull-thrus, (35x80), back-ins (35x60), 205 full hkups (30/50 amps), cable, WiFi @ sites, rentals, dump, laundry, restaurant. **REC:** pool, hot tub, golf, playground, rec open to public. Pets OK. Partial handicap access. No tents. Big rig sites, 14 day max stay, eco-friendly. 2021 rates: $25 to $35, Military discount. ATM.
(800)946-1946 Lat: 31.10556, Lon: -92.05825
124 Earl J Barbry Sr Blvd., Marksville, LA 71351
paragoncasinoresort.com
See ad page 430

Things to See and Do

PARAGON CASINO RESORT Full service casino, hotel and RV park. Live entertainment, restaurants, 18 hole golf course, indoor aquatic center, and 3 screen theatre. Partial handicap access. RV accessible. Restrooms. Food. Hours: 24 hrs. ATM.
(800)946-1946 Lat: 31.10674, Lon: -92.05903
711 Paragon Place, Marksville, LA 71351
www.paragoncasinoresort.com
See ad page 430

PARAGON CASINO'S TAMAHKA TRAILS GOLF CLUB Tamaka Trails is an 18-hole championship golf course associated with Paragon Casino and part of the Audubon Golf Trail. Partial handicap access. RV accessible. Restrooms. Food. Hours: 7:30am to 6:45pm. Adult fee: $42 to $69.
(800)946-1946 Lat: 31.10502, Lon: -92.05721
222 Slim Lemoine Road, Marksville, LA 71351
www.tamahkatrails.com
See ad page 430

Dealing with Extreme Weather Conditions: When flooding conditions are encountered, seek higher ground. If a section of roadway is flooded, do not drive through it. If you must cross it, observe other vehicles to determine depth of water. Be sure there are no downed electrical lines in the water. Depending on type of RV you are traveling in, a safe still water maximum depth must be established. That figure should not exceed much more than about half the height of your wheel/tire radius. E.g., a 22.5'' wheel with an 80-series tire, would be about 14'' or so. A 15'' wheel with a 70-series tire may be about 10''. Drive slowly and do not stop. In addition to water depth, the roadway below may be eroded or starting to collapse. If the water is moving at any speed across the roadway the vehicle could easily lose control. Items in the water can pose an additional hazard. Do not camp in low elevation locations. Avoid areas near any mountain washes. If a flood watch is upgraded to a warning, hold up in the highest ground you can find. Early warning is one of the best defenses when facing severe weather events. Monitor your local weather broadcasts. Consider getting an automatic ""First Alert'' or ""NOAA Radio'' to keep you safe and informed.

MERRYVILLE — C2 *Beauregard Parish*

COUNTRY MEADOW ESTATES
good sam park **Ratings: 5.5/NA/8.5** (RV Park) Avail: 18 full hkups (30/50 amps). 2021 rates: $35 to $55. (315)868-0416, 137 Farris Loop, Merryville, LA 70653

MINDEN — A2 *Webster*

MINDEN See also Simsboro.

CINNAMON CREEK RV PARK
good sam park **Ratings: 7/9.5★/8** (RV Park) From jct of I-20 (exit 44) & LA-371: Go N 1/4 mi on LA-371 (L). **FAC:** gravel rds. (81 spaces). Avail: 61 gravel, 11 pull-thrus, (24x65), back-ins (24x48), 61 full hkups (30/50 amps), cable, WiFi @ sites, tent sites, laundry. **REC:** boating nearby, hunting nearby. Pets OK. Partial handicap access. Big rig sites, eco-friendly. 2021 rates: $37 to $39, Military discount.
(318)371-5111 Lat: 32.59511, Lon: -93.33955
12996 Hwy 371, Minden, LA 71055
www.cinnamoncreekrvpark.com
See ad page 443

MONROE — A3 *Ouachita*

MONROE See also Oak Grove & Simsboro.

OUACHITA RV PARK **Ratings: 5.5/8/7** (Campground) Avail: 20 full hkups (30/50 amps). 2021 rates: $32. (318)343-8672, 7300 Frontage Rd, Monroe, LA 71202

MORGAN CITY — D4 *St Mary*

A SPOTLIGHT Introducing the Cajun Coast/St Mary Parish's colorful attractions appearing at the front of this state section.

MORGAN CITY See also Berwick, Charenton & Houma.

KEMPER WILLIAMS PARK (Public) From Jct of US-90 & W end of Atchafalaya River Bridge, W 3.7 mi on US-90 to Cotton Rd, S 0.3 mi (R) or W-bnd: From Jct of US-90 & Berwick exit, W 4.5 mi on US-90 to Cotton Rd, S 0.3 mi (R) CAUTION: RR crossing. 189 Avail: 26 full hkups, 163 W, 163 E (30/50 amps). 2021 rates: $35. (985)395-2298

LAKE END PARK CAMPGROUND & CABINS
(Public) W-bnd: From Jct of US-90 & SR-70 (Brashear Ave), N 1.5 mi on SR-70 (R); or E-bnd: From Jct of US-90 & SR-182/70 (Morgan City exit), N 1.5 mi on SR-70 (R). **FAC:** paved/gravel rds. (154 spaces). 144 Avail: 129 gravel, 15 grass, 9 pull-thrus, (26x60), back-ins (30x50), 144 full hkups (30/50 amps), seasonal sites, WiFi @ sites, $, tent sites, rentals, dump, laundry, fire rings, firewood. **REC:** Lake Palourde: fishing, marina, playground, hunting nearby, rec open to public. Pet restrict (B). Partial handicap access. Big rig sites, eco-friendly. 2021 rates: $20 to $40, Military discount.
(985)380-4623 Lat: 29.720397, Lon: -91.189610
2300 Hwy 70, Morgan City, LA 70380
lakeendpark.net
See ad opposite page

Things to See and Do

CAJUN COAST VISITORS & CONVENTION BUREAU Exhibits and swamp view. Our new visitors center is your gateway to the Cajun Coast, with brochures, information & assistance on accommodations, restaurants & attractions in the area. Partial handicap access. RV accessible. Restrooms. Hours: 9am to 5pm Mon to Fri. No CC.
(800)256-2931 Lat: 29.69728, Lon: -91.18237
900 Dr. Martin Luther King Blvd., Morgan City, LA 70380
www.cajuncoast.com
See ad opposite page

NATCHITOCHES — B2 *Natchitoches*

NATCHITOCHES See also Many.

GRAND ECORE RV PARK
good sam park **Ratings: 8/9.5★/9** (RV Park) Avail: 59 full hkups (30/50 amps). 2021 rates: $40. (318)238-7446, 1071 Tauzin Island Rd, Natchitoches, LA 71457

JONES RIVERSIDE MARINA **Ratings: 6/NA/7** (Campground) Avail: 30 full hkups (30/50 amps). 2021 rates: $30 to $35. (318)646-0097, 3185 LA 477, Natchitoches, LA 71457

NAKATOSH CAMPGROUND
good sam park **Ratings: 6/7/6.5** (Campground) From Jct of I-49 & SR-6 (exit 138), W 0.2 mi on SR-6. Entrance is at west end of Chevron truck stop (R). **FAC:** gravel rds. (44 spaces). Avail: 25 gravel, 25 pull-thrus, (25x55), 25 full hkups (30/50 amps), WiFi @ sites, tent sites, laundry. **REC:** boating nearby, hunting nearby, rec open to public. Pet restrict (B). Partial handicap access. 2021 rates: $33.14.
(318)352-0911 Lat: 31.72595, Lon: -93.16362
5428 Hwy 6, Natchitoches, LA 71457
nakatoshcampgrounds.com
See ad this page

NEW IBERIA — D3 *Iberia*

ISLE OF IBERIA RV RESORT **Ratings: 9/8/8.5** (RV Resort) Avail: 160 full hkups (30/50 amps). 2021 rates: $45 to $55. (337)256-8681, 911 NW Bypass (Hwy 3212), New Iberia, LA 70560

KOC KAMPGROUND
good sam park **Ratings: 8/9.5★/9** (Campground) From Jct of US-90 & Lewis St (Exit 129), S 0.1 mi on Lewis St to Frontage Rd, W 0.8 mi (L). **FAC:** paved/gravel rds. (200 spaces). 75 Avail: 70 gravel, 5 grass, patios, 5 pull-thrus, (30x50), back-ins (30x50), 75 full hkups (30/50 amps), seasonal sites, cable, WiFi @ sites, tent sites, rentals, laundry, groc. **REC:** pool, pond, fishing, playground, hunting nearby. Pet restrict (B). Partial handicap access, eco-friendly. 2021 rates: $30 to $32.50, Military discount.
(337)364-6666 Lat: 29.97348, Lon: -91.84486
3104 Curtis Ln, New Iberia, LA 70560
www.kockampground.com
See ad this page

WEEKS ISLAND RV **Ratings: 4.5/5.5/6.5** (RV Park) Avail: 15 full hkups (30 amps). 2021 rates: $28 to $30. (337)365-9865, 3004 Weeks Island Rd, New Iberia, LA 70560

Things to See and Do

IBERIA PARISH CONVENTION & VISITORS BUREAU Visitor center with brochures & assistance on attractions, accommodations, RV parks & restaurants. Open Monday thru Saturday. Partial handicap access. RV accessible. Restrooms. Hours: 9am to 5pm. No CC.
(888)942-3742 Lat: 29.98559, Lon: -91.85158
2513 Hwy 14, New Iberia, LA 70560
iberiatravel.com
See ad page 428

NEW ORLEANS — D5 *Jefferson*

NEW ORLEANS See also Convent, Covington, Galliano, Hammond, Houma, Ponchatoula, River Ridge, Robert, Slidell & St Bernard, LA; Bay St Louis & Picayune, MS.

FRENCH QUARTER RV RESORT (FQRV) **Ratings: 10/9.5★/8** (RV Park) Avail: 52 full hkups (30/50 amps). 2021 rates: $105 to $120. (504)586-3000, 500 N. Clairborne Ave., New Orleans, LA 70112

JUDE TRAVEL PARK OF NEW ORLEANS
good sam park **Ratings: 8.5/10★/7.5** (RV Park) Avail: 41 full hkups (30/50 amps). 2021 rates: $35 to $65. (504)241-0632, 7400 Chef Menteur Hwy, New Orleans, LA 70126

PARC D'ORLEANS **Ratings: 3.5/5.5/5** (Campground) Avail: 40 full hkups (30/50 amps). 2021 rates: $29 to $62. (504)243-3052, 7676 Chef Menteur Hwy, New Orleans, LA 70126

LA

TRAVELING WITH YOUR PET: Choose the right chow. Feeding time can be tricky on the road, especially if your pet eats an uncommon food. Consider transitioning to a more common one at least three weeks before leaving. Dehydrated pet food is helpful too; it's made on the spot with hot water, takes up less space and weighs less than cans.

Find it fast! To locate a town on a map, follow these easy instructions: Look for the map grid code after the town heading in the listing section and match it to the letters and numbers on the map borders. Draw a line horizontally from the letter and vertically from the number. You'll find the town near the intersection of the two lines.

NEW ORLEANS (CONT)

PINE CREST RV PARK OF NEW ORLEANS
good sam park
Ratings: 9/9★/9.5 (RV Park) From jct I-610 & I-10: Go NE 25 mi on I-10 (exit 263), then SE 1/4 mi on LA-433. (R). **FAC:** paved rds. (202 spaces). Avail: 30 paved, patios, 30 pull-thrus, (30x65), 30 full hkups (30/50 amps), WiFi @ sites, dump, laundry, LP gas. **REC:** pond, fishing, boating nearby, shuffleboard, playground, hunting nearby. Pet restrict (B). Partial handicap access. No tents, eco-friendly. 2021 rates: $39 to $44.
(800)879-5936 Lat: 30.24194, Lon: -89.75796
2601 Old Spanish Trail, Slidell, LA 70461
www.pinecrestrv.com
See primary listing at Slidell and ad this page

PONTCHARTRAIN LANDING **Ratings: 9/9.5★/9** (RV Park) Avail: 85 full hkups (30/50 amps). 2021 rates: $62 to $250. (877)376-7850, 6001 France Rd, New Orleans, LA 70126

RIVERBOAT TRAVEL PARK **Ratings: 7.5/7/6** (Campground) Avail: 46 full hkups (30/50 amps). 2021 rates: $40. (800)726-0985, 6232 Chef Menteur Hwy, New Orleans, LA 70126

Things to See and Do

JEFFERSON CONVENTION AND VISITORS BUREAU Tourist information for the New Orleans area. Restrooms. Hours: 8:30am to 5pm. No CC.
(877)572-7474 Lat: 29.95733, Lon: -90.18729
1221 Elmwood Park Boulevard Ste. 411, New Orleans, LA 70123
www.visitjeffersonparish.com/outdoors
See ad page 428

OAK GROVE — A3 *West Carroll*

7 OAKS RV CAMPGROUND
good sam park
Ratings: 6/8/7 (RV Park) Avail: 142 full hkups (30/50 amps). 2021 rates: $30 to $35. (318)428-5282, 10284 Hwy 17 South, Oak Grove, LA 71263

Are you using a friend's Guide? Want one of your own? Call 877-209-6655.

OIL CITY — A1 *Caddo*

EARL WILLIAMSON PARK (CADDO PARISH PARK) (Public) From jct Hwy 220 & Hwy 1 (N Market): Go 18 mi N on Hwy 1. 10 Avail: 10 W, 10 E. 2021 rates: $6 to $12. (318)347-5569

OPELOUSAS — D3 *St Landry*

OPELOUSAS See also Breaux Bridge, Duson, Eunice, Henderson & Lafayette.

OPELOUSAS SOUTH CITY PARK (Public) From Jct of I-49 & US-190 (exit 19B), W 1 mi on US-190 to Market St, S 0.8 mi (E). 61 Avail: 61 W, 61 E (20/30 amps). 2021 rates: $11. (337)948-2560

PONCHATOULA — D4 *Tangipahoa*

FIRESIDE RV RESORT **Ratings: 9.5/9.5★/10** (RV Park) Avail: 165 full hkups (30/50 amps). 2021 rates: $55 to $75. (985)277-1059, 42053 Hwy 445, Ponchatoula, LA 70454

REUNION LAKE RV RESORT Ratings: 10/10★/10 (RV Park) Avail: 230 full hkups (30/50 amps). 2021 rates: $55 to $68. (985)520-6600, 43234 Hwy 445, Ponchatoula, LA 70454

RAYNE — D3 *Acadia*

CITY OF RAYNE RV PARK (Public) From jct I-10 (exit 87) & Hwy 98/35: Go 1/4 mi S on Hwy 98/35, then 200 yards W on Oak St, then NW on Gossen Memorial Dr to Frog Festival Blvd. (R) Note: Register at City Hall or Police Station after hours. 737 Avail: 737 W, 737 E (30/50 amps). 2021 rates: $30. (337)334-3121

RIVER RIDGE — D5 *Jefferson*

NEW ORLEANS WEST KOA **Ratings: 9/9★/8** (Campground) Avail: 97 full hkups (30/50 amps). 2021 rates: $40.95 to $80. (504)467-1792, 11129 Jefferson Hwy, River Ridge, LA 70123

ROBERT — D4 *Tangipahoa*

PASSPORT TO LEISURE **Ratings: 9/9★/8** (Membership Park) 80 Avail: 60 full hkups, 20 W, 20 E (30/50 amps). 2021 rates: $10. (985)542-1507, 46049 Hwy 445 N, Robert, LA 70455

YOGI BEAR'S JELLYSTONE PARK **Ratings: 9/9★/8** (RV Park) 247 Avail: 193 full hkups, 54 W, 54 E (30/50 amps). 2021 rates: $45 to $75. (985)542-1507, 46049 Hwy 445N, Robert, LA 70455

RUSTON — A2 *Lincoln*

LINCOLN PARISH PARK (LINCOLN COUNTY PARK) (Public) From Jct of I-20 & SR-33 (exit 86), N 3.5 mi on SR-33 (L). Avail: 33 full hkups (30/50 amps). 2021 rates: $25. (318)251-5156

SHREVEPORT — A1 *Caddo*

SHREVEPORT See also Greenwood & Minden.

CINNAMON CREEK RV PARK

good sam park

Ratings: 7/9.5★/8 (RV Park) From Shreveport: Go E on I-20 to exit 44 / LA-371, then N 1/4 mi on LA-371 (L). **FAC:** gravel rds. (81 spaces). Avail: 61 gravel, 11 pull-thrus, (24x65), back-ins (24x48), 61 full hkups (30/50 amps), cable, WiFi @ sites, tent sites, laundry. **REC:** boating nearby, hunting nearby. Pets OK. Partial handicap access. Big rig sites, eco-friendly. 2021 rates: $37, Military discount.

(318)371-5111 Lat: 32.59511, Lon: -93.33955
12996 Hwy 371, Minden, LA 71055
www.cinnamoncreekrvpark.com
See primary listing at Minden and ad this page

MILITARY PARK BARKSDALE FAMCAMP (BARKSDALE AFB) (Public) From Jct I-20 and US-71, S on US-71 to base entrance. Avail: 62 full hkups (20/50 amps). 2021 rates: $20. (318)456-2679

PARAGON CASINO RV RESORT

good sam park

Ratings: 10/10★/10 (RV Resort) From Shreveport: Go SE 125 on I-49 to exit 80/US-71/US-167, then S 4.5 miles to LA-3170, E 5.5 mi to LA-1, SE 20 mi (L). **FAC:** paved rds. Avail: 205 paved, patios, 166 pull-thrus, (35x80), back-ins (35x60), 205 full hkups (30/50 amps), cable, WiFi @ sites, rentals, dump, laundry, restaurant. **REC:** pool, hot tub, golf, playground, rec open to public. Pets OK. Partial handicap access. No tents. Big rig sites, 14 day max stay, eco-friendly. 2021 rates: $25 to $35, Military discount. ATM.

(800)946-1946 Lat: 31.10556, Lon: -92.05825
124 Earl J Barbry Sr. Blvd., Marksville, LA 71351
paragoncasinoresort.com
See primary listing at Marksville and ad page 430

SHREVEPORT/BOSSIER KOA JOURNEY

Ratings: 9/9.5★/9 (RV Park) From jct I-20 (exit 10) & Pines Rd: Go S 0.6 mi on Pines Rd, then W 1 mi on W 70th St. (R); or From jct I-49 & LA-3132 (exit 201): Go W 6-1/4 mi on LA-3132 (exit 1D), then W 2 mi on 70th St. (R). **FAC:** paved/gravel rds. (100 spaces). 85 Avail: 16 paved, 69 gravel, patios, 70 pull-thrus, (35x90), back-ins (25x50), 85 full hkups (30/50 amps), cable, WiFi @ sites, tent sites, rentals, laundry, groc, LP gas. **REC:** pool, pond, fishing, boating nearby, playground, hunting nearby. Pets OK. Partial handicap access. Big rig sites, eco-friendly. 2021 rates: $47.95, Military discount.

(318)687-1010 Lat: 32.44376, Lon: -93.87823
6510 W 70th Street, Shreveport, LA 71129
koa.com/campgrounds/shreveport
See ad this page

SOUTHERN LIVING RV PARK

good sam park

Ratings: 7.5/9★/7.5 (RV Park) From jct of I-20 (exit 5) & Greenwood Road: Go W 1/2 mi on US 79/US 80/Greenwood Road. (R). **FAC:** paved rds. (90 spaces). 80 Avail: 12 paved, 68 gravel, 12 pull-thrus, (37x90), back-ins (30x50), 80 full hkups (30/50 amps), WiFi @ sites, laundry. **REC:** pool, boating nearby. Pet restrict (B). Partial handicap access. No tents. Big rig sites. 2021 rates: $35.

(318)938-1808 Lat: 32.44312, Lon: -93.96193
9010 Greenwood Rd, Greenwood, LA 71033
www.southernlivingrvpark.net
See primary listing at Greenwood and ad this page

TRAVELCENTERS OF AMERICA RV PARK

good sam park

Ratings: 8.5/9★/8.5 (RV Park) From jct of I-20 & exit 5/Greenwood Rd: Go W 1/4 mi on N Service Rd (R). **FAC:** paved rds. (60 spaces). Avail: 14 paved, patios, 10 pull-thrus, (24x55), back-ins (24x60), 14 full hkups (30/50 amps), cable, WiFi @ sites, $, dump, laundry, groc, restaurant. **REC:** boating nearby. Pet restrict (B). No tents. Big rig sites, eco-friendly. 2021 rates: $37. ATM.

(318)938-6360 Lat: 32.44591, Lon: -93.95191
8590 Greenwood Rd, Greenwood, LA 71033
www.ta-petro.com
See primary listing at Greenwood and ad this page

SIMSBORO — A2 *Lincoln*

ANTIQUE VILLAGE RV PARK **Ratings: 5.5/8.5/8** (RV Park) Avail: 20 full hkups (30/50 amps). 2021 rates: $35. (318)247-1744, 3027 Martha St., Simsboro, LA 71275

Shop at Camping World and SAVE with coupons. Check the front of the Guide for yours!

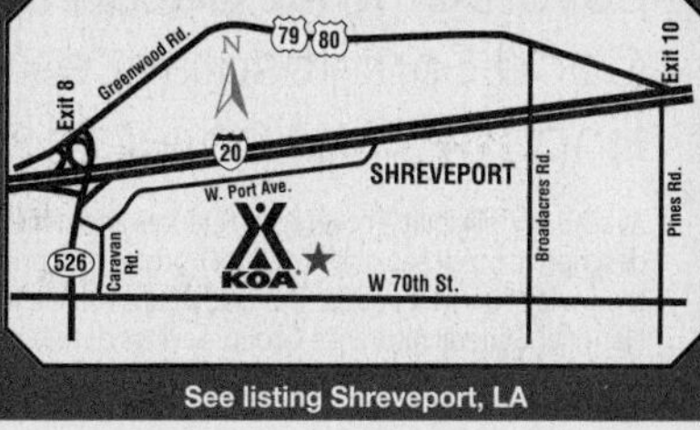

LA

SLIDELL — D5 *St Tammany*

SLIDELL See also New Orleans, LA; Bay St Louis & Picayune, MS.

PINE CREST RV PARK OF NEW ORLEANS
Ratings: 9/9★/9.5 (RV Park) From Jct of I-10 (exit 263) & LA-433, SE 0.2 mi on LA-433 (R). **FAC:** paved rds. (202 spaces). Avail: 30 paved, patios, 30 pull-thrus, (30x65), 30 full hkups (30/50 amps), WiFi @ sites, dump, laundry, LP gas. **REC:** pond, fishing, boating nearby, shuffleboard, playground, hunting nearby. Pet restrict (B). Partial handicap access. No tents, eco-friendly. 2021 rates: $39 to $44.
(800)879-5936 Lat: 30.24194, Lon: -89.75796
2601 Old Spanish Trail, Slidell, LA 70461
www.pinecrestrv.com
See ad page 442

SPRINGFIELD — D4 *Livingston*

TICKFAW (Public State Park) From jct I-55 & LA-22 (exit 26): Go 5-1/2 mi W on LA-22, then 6-1/4 mi SW on LA-1037 to Patterson Rd, follow signs (E); or From jct I-12 & LA-43 (exit 32): Go 2-3/4 mi S on LA-43, then 528 feet E on LA-22, then 6-1/4 mi S on LA-1037 to Patterson Rd, follow signs (E). 50 Avail: 50 W, 30 E (30/50 amps). 2021 rates: $18 to $28. (225)294-5020

SPRINGHILL — A2 *Webster*

FRANK ANTHONY RV PARK (Public) From jct Hwy 157 & US 371: Go 1 block S on US 371, then 2 blocks E on West Church St. Avail: 30 full hkups (30/50 amps). (318)539-5681

ST BERNARD — D5 *St Bernard*

FANZ RV PARK **Ratings: 5/6.5/6** (RV Area in MH Park) Avail: 20 full hkups (30/50 amps). 2021 rates: $35. (504)682-4900, 2100 West Fanz Rd, St Bernard, LA 70085

ST JOSEPH — B4 *Tensas*

LAKE BRUIN (Public State Park) From jct US-65 & LA-607: Go E 1 blk on LA-607, then N 1/2 mi on LA-605, then E 6-1/2 mi on LA-604, then SW 1/4 mi on Lake Bruin Rd. (L). 48 Avail: 48 W, 48 E (20/30 amps). 2021 rates: $20 to $33. (318)766-3530

ST MARTINVILLE — D3 *St Martin*

CATFISH HEAVEN RV PARK **Ratings: 8.5/8.5★/7.5** (Campground) Avail: 34 full hkups (30/50 amps). 2021 rates: $39 to $42. (337)394-9087, 1554 Cypress Island Hwy, Saint Martinville, LA 70582

LAKE FAUSSE POINTE (Public State Park) From jct LA-31 & LA-96 (in town): Go 2-1/4 mi NE on LA-96 to LA-679, then 4 mi E on LA-3083, then 4 mi E (cross bridge), then 7-1/2 mi S on Levee Rd (R). 46 Avail: 46 W, 46 E (20/30 amps). 2021 rates: $20 to $33. (337)229-4764

Camping World RV & Outdoors offers new and used RV sales and so much more! Find a SuperCenter near you at CampingWorld.com

SULPHUR — D2 *Calcasieu*

A+ MOTEL & RV PARK
Ratings: 10/9.5★/10 (RV Park) From Jct of I-10 & LA 27 (exit 20): Go S 2.1 mi on LA 27 (L). **FAC:** paved rds. (134 spaces). Avail: 20 paved, patios, 19 pull-thrus, (30x70), back-ins (30x65), 20 full hkups (30/50 amps), seasonal sites, cable, WiFi @ sites, laundry, LP gas. **REC:** pool, wading pool, hot tub, pond, fishing, boating nearby, playground, hunting nearby. Pet restrict (B). Partial handicap access. No tents. Big rig sites, eco-friendly. 2021 rates: $45 to $50, Military discount. ATM.
(337)583-2631 Lat: 30.1813, Lon: -93.37601
4631 Hwy 27 South, Sulphur, LA 70665
a-plusmotel.com
See ad page 436

VIDALIA — B3 *Concordia*

RIVER VIEW RV PARK AND RESORT
Ratings: 9/9★/9.5 (RV Park) From Jct of US-65/US-84 & LA-131 (on the West side of Mississippi River Bridge), S 0.8 mi on LA-131 (also Martin Luther King Ave) (L). **FAC:** paved/gravel rds. (145 spaces). 135 Avail: 84 paved, 51 grass, 84 pull-thrus, (30x60), back-ins (30x50), 135 full hkups (30/50 amps), seasonal sites, WiFi @ sites, tent sites, rentals, dump, laundry, LP gas, firewood. **REC:** pool, hot tub, Mississippi River: fishing, boating nearby, playground, hunting nearby. Pet restrict (B). Partial handicap access. Big rig sites, eco-friendly. 2021 rates: $32.95 to $44.95, Military discount.
(318)336-1400 Lat: 31.55576, Lon: -91.43441
800 Martin Luther King Ave, Vidalia, LA 71373
www.riverviewrvpark.com
See ad page 526

VILLE PLATTE — C3 *Evangeline*

CHICOT (Public State Park) From Jct of I-49 (exit 23) & US-167: Go NW 16-1/2 mi on US-167, then N 7 mi on LA-3042. (R). 198 Avail: 198 W, 198 E (30 amps). 2021 rates: $20 to $28. (337)363-2403

CROOKED CREEK REC AREA (Public) From Jct of SR-13/SR-106 & SR-3187 (1 mi N of Pine Prairie), W 4.6 mi on SR-3187 to entrance rd, N 0.5 mi (E) or From Jct of US-167 & SR-106 (Bayou Chicot), W 4.5 mi on SR 106 to Jct of SR-134 3187, W 4.6 mi on SR 3187 to entrance rd, N 0.5 mi (E). 148 Avail: 148 W, 148 E (30/50 amps). 2021 rates: $20 to $27. (337)599-2661

RV Tech Tips - A Handy Solution to Open a Gas Cap: Often the simple act of opening the gas cap on your tow vehicle can be bothersome. Cut a notch to fit the raised area on the gas cap on one end of a 6-inch long piece of PVC pipe, drill a hole at the top of the pipe and slide a wooden dowel in the hole to act as a handle. Now, opening the cap is a cinch.

VIOLET — D5 *St Bernard*

ST BERNARD (Public State Park) From Jct of I-10 & I-510/SR-47 (exit 246A), S 9.2 mi on I-510/SR-47 to SR-46 (St Bernard Hwy), E 7.5 mi to SR-39, SW 0.7 mi (L). 51 Avail: 51 W, 51 E (20/30 amps). 2021 rates: $20 to $28. (504)682-2101

WESTWEGO — D5 *Jefferson*

BAYOU SEGNETTE (Public State Park) From jct of Westbank Expwy/Business US-90 & Lapalco Ave: Go SE 2 mi on Lapalco Ave (E). 98 Avail: 98 W, 98 E (30/50 amps). 2021 rates: $25 to $33. (888)677-2296

WOODWORTH — C3 *Rapides*

INDIAN CREEK REC AREA (Public State Park) From Jct of US-165 & Robinson Bridge Rd (at sign in town), E 0.4 mi on Robinson Bridge Rd to Indian Creek Rd, follow signs SE 2.5 mi (E); or From Jct of I-49 & Parish Rd 22 (Exit 73), W 2.2 mi on Parish Rd 22 (Robinson Bridge Rd) to Indian Creek Rd, SE 2.5 mi (E). Avail: 109 full hkups (30/50 amps). 2021 rates: $18 to $54. (318)487-5058

ZWOLLE — B2 *Sabine*

NORTH TOLEDO BEND (Public State Park) From Jct of SR-171 & SR-475 (in town), S 100 ft on SR-475 to SR-482, W 2.3 mi to SR-3229, W 4 mi to N Toledo Park Rd, follow signs 2.4 mi (E). 63 Avail: 63 W, 63 E (20/30 amps). 2021 rates: $20 to $33. (318)645-4715

SABINE RIVER AUTHORITY/SAN MIGUEL (Public) From Jct of SR-475 & SR-191, S 3 mi on SR-191 to Carters Ferry Rd, follow signs, SW 2.5 mi (R). Avail: 39 full hkups (30/50 amps). 2021 rates: $25. (318)645-6748

Flat Towing Versus Tow Dolly - what's the right choice for your dinghy vehicle? Let's look at the pros and cons of each scenario: FLAT TOWING (Towing 4-wheels down) - PRO: Equipment needed usually less costly than a tow dolly. Quick, one-person hook-up and disconnect. No additional storage needed at your destination. CON: Won't work on all vehicles due to drivetrain limitations. Can cause ""Feathering'' of tow vehicle's front tires over time. Most flat-towed dinghies can't be backed more than a few feet. TOW DOLLY (Attaching the dinghy's front two wheels to a dolly trailer) - PRO: No baseplate needed on automobile. Can transport most front-wheel-drive vehicles. Can be backed like other trailers. CON: Capital costs usually more than flat tow. Storage needed both at home and at destination. Additional registration and insurance may be required, depending on location. Generally takes a little longer for loading and unloading.

Getty Images/iStockphoto

YOU ARE HERE

Maine

DID YOU KNOW?

Accounting for all the inlets and bays, Maine's coast is longer than California's. That's not including over 3,000 offshore islands.

Located in the farthest northeast corner of the United States, Maine is known for its beautiful western mountain ranges and the scenic, craggy shores. Visit charming seaside villages and rugged industrial towns.

Sublime Shores

Maine entices lovers of water recreation with a tidal shoreline that stretches for almost 3,500 miles and myriad rivers crossing the state. Relax in the sands along one of Maine's beautiful beaches, or board a boat to hit the seas. Running 375 miles along the Atlantic coast, the Maine Island Trail beckons to paddlers with over 200 wild islands and mainland sites to explore. Anglers can pluck a catch from the depths of the ocean or from babbling mountain creeks.

Superb Cities

Maine's wild landscapes are dotted with several exciting cities. Bar Harbor is a great place to start. The quintessentially New England town is situated on Mount Desert Island, off the Atlantic coast just outside the entrance to Acadia National Park. The town just drips with charm, from the colorful village atmosphere of Main Street to the ships sailing in the harbor. Bar Harbor offers all the human comforts visitors will need after their adventures in the outdoors. Southeast along the coast, Maine's largest city, Portland, maintains a small-town feeling and offers all the natural beauty of the Pine Tree State.

Come to Acadia

Discover unrivaled vistas of the great Atlantic Ocean at Acadia National Park. Wind-swept waves crash into rocky shores, and forests carpet the hills. Peer into tide pools to look for multitudes of marine life, or set your eyes on the endless seas while watching for whales. Experience the remarkable roar of the Atlantic at Thunder Hole.

Maine Lobster Rolls

Lobster rolls are the street food of choice along Maine's rocky coast. The classic New England dish consists of a mayonnaise-based lobster salad packed in a warm buttery bun. Order one from popular seafood shacks like Red's Eats in Wiscasset, Bagaduce Lunch in Penobscot and Five Islands Lobster Company in Georgetown.

VISITOR CENTER

TIME ZONE
Eastern Standard

ROAD & HIGHWAY INFORMATION
207-624-3000
maine.gov/mdot/newengland511

FISHING & HUNTING INFORMATION
207-621-2600
informe.org/moses

BOATING INFORMATION
207-287-8000
maine.gov/ifw/fishing-boating

NATIONAL PARKS
nps.gov/me

STATE PARKS
maine.gov/dad/parks

TOURISM INFORMATION
Maine Office of Tourism
888-624-6345
visitmaine.com

TOP TOURISM ATTRACTIONS
1) Acadia National Park
2) Maine Lighthouses
3) Casco Bay

MAJOR CITIES
Portland, Lewiston, Bangor, South Portland, Auburn, Augusta (capital)

good sam park

Featured Good Sam Parks

MAINE

When you stay with Good Sam, you can expect the highest degree of cleanliness and friendliness, and better yet, you get **10% off** overnight campground fees.

If you're not already a Good Sam member you can purchase your membership at one of these locations:

BANGOR
Paul Bunyan Campground
Pumpkin Patch RV Resort

BAR HARBOR
Mt. Desert Narrows Camping Resort
Narrows Too Camping Resort

BATH
Meadowbrook Camping Area

BOOTHBAY
Shore Hills Campground & RV Park

CASCO
Point Sebago Resort

DAMARISCOTTA
Lake Pemaquid Campground

EASTPORT
Seaview Campground & Cottages

ELLSWORTH
Patten Pond Camping Resort

GOULDSBORO
West Bay Acadia RV Campground

MEDWAY
Katahdin Shadows Campground & Cabins

MOODY
Moody Beach RV Campground

OLD ORCHARD BEACH
Old Orchard Beach Campground
Pinehirst RV Resort

OXFORD
Two Lakes Camping Area

RAYMOND
Kokatosi Campground

SANFORD
Apache Campground

SCARBOROUGH
Wassamki Springs Campground

SKOWHEGAN
Two Rivers Campground

TRENTON
Timberland Acres RV Park

WINTHROP
Augusta-West Lakeside Kampground

Getty Images/iStockphoto

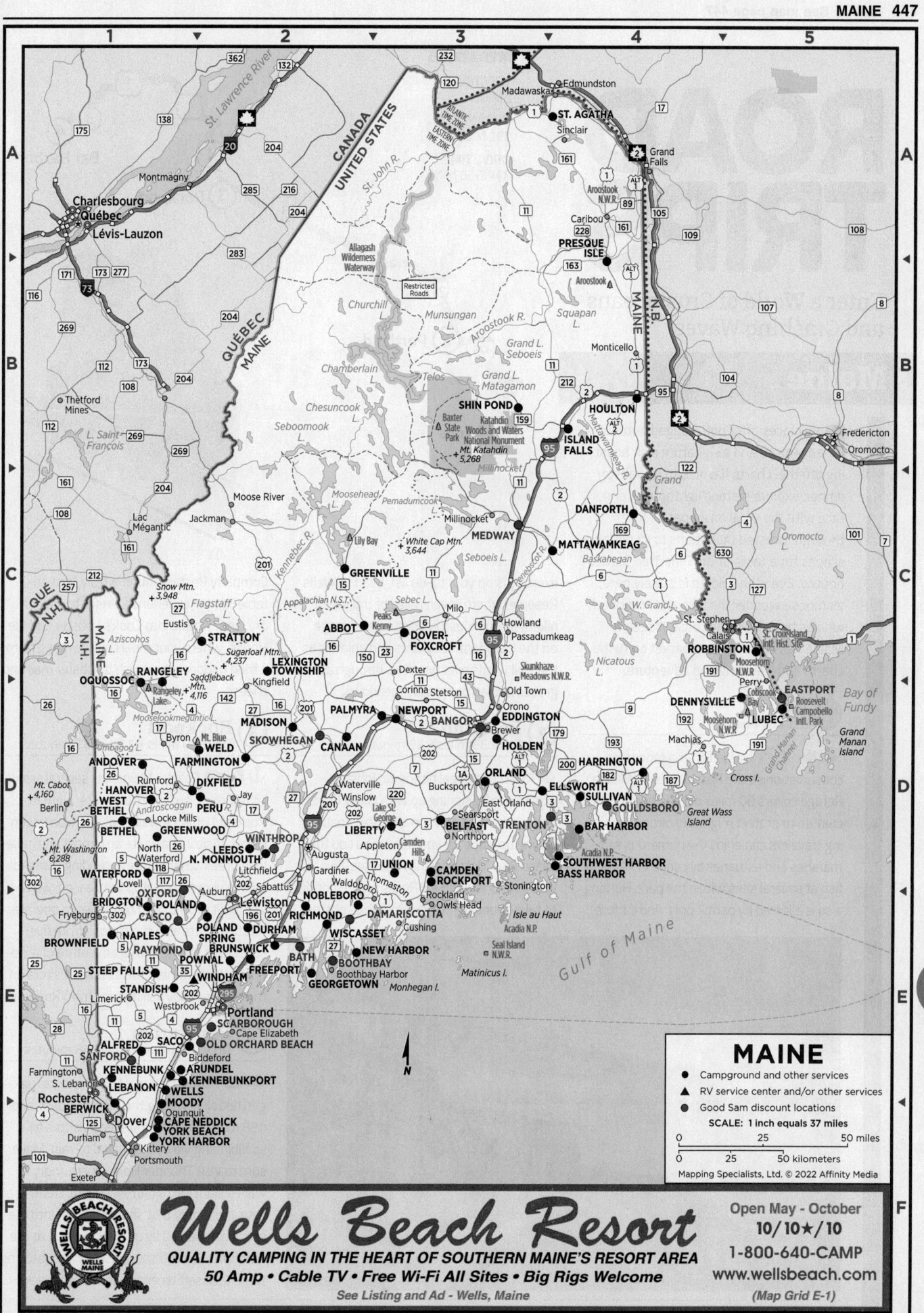

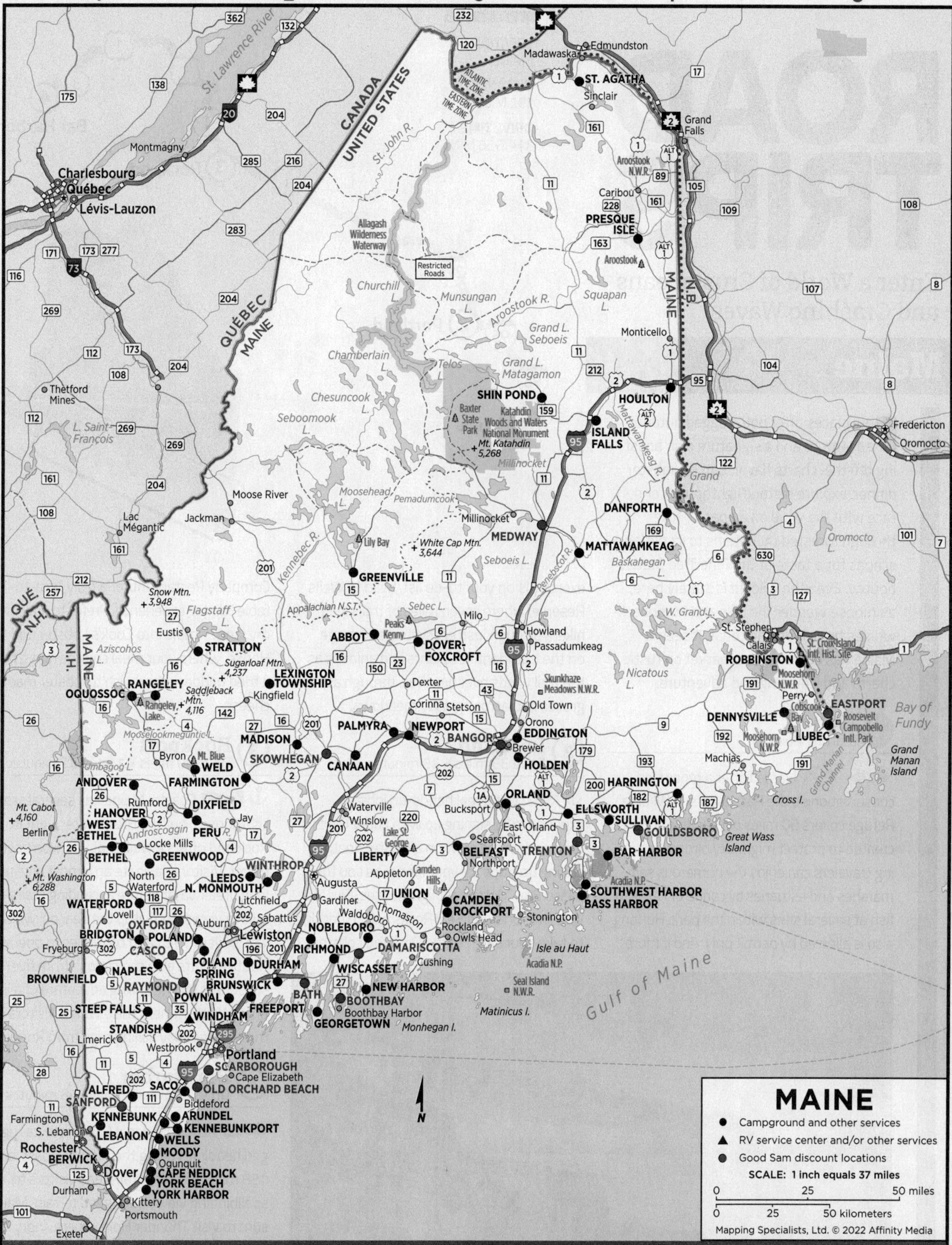
MAINE
Campground and other services
RV service center and/or other services
Good Sam discount locations
SCALE: 1 inch equals 37 miles
0 25 50 miles
0 25 50 kilometers
Mapping Specialists, Ltd. © 2022 Affinity Media
CANADA
UNITED STATES
QUÉBEC
MAINE
N.H.
N.B.
Gulf of Maine
Bay of Fundy
ST. AGATHA
PRESQUE ISLE
SHIN POND
HOULTON
ISLAND FALLS
DANFORTH
MEDWAY
MATTAWAMKEAG
GREENVILLE
STRATTON
ABBOT
DOVER-FOXCROFT
LEXINGTON TOWNSHIP
RANGELEY
OQUOSSOC
MADISON
SKOWHEGAN
CANAAN
PALMYRA
NEWPORT
BANGOR
EDDINGTON
HOLDEN
ORLAND
ROBBINSTON
EASTPORT
DENNYSVILLE
LUBEC
HARRINGTON
ELLSWORTH
SULLIVAN
GOULDSBORO
BAR HARBOR
TRENTON
SOUTHWEST HARBOR
BASS HARBOR
BELFAST
LIBERTY
UNION
CAMDEN
ROCKPORT
WELD
FARMINGTON
ANDOVER
DIXFIELD
HANOVER
WEST BETHEL
BETHEL
PERU
GREENWOOD
WINTHROP
LEEDS
N. MONMOUTH
WATERFORD
OXFORD
POLAND
BRIDGTON
CASCO
NAPLES
BROWNFIELD
RAYMOND
POLAND SPRING
DURHAM
BRUNSWICK
RICHMOND
NOBLEBORO
DAMARISCOTTA
WISCASSET
NEW HARBOR
BOOTHBAY
BATH
GEORGETOWN
FREEPORT
POWNAL
STEEP FALLS
WINDHAM
STANDISH
SCARBOROUGH
OLD ORCHARD BEACH
SACO
ALFRED
SANFORD
ARUNDEL
KENNEBUNK
KENNEBUNKPORT
LEBANON
WELLS
MOODY
BERWICK
CAPE NEDDICK
YORK BEACH
YORK HARBOR
Portland
Augusta
Lewiston
Québec
Lévis-Lauzon
Charlesbourg
Fredericton
Portsmouth
Dover
Rochester

ROAD TRIPS

Enter a World of Crustaceans and Crashing Waves

Maine

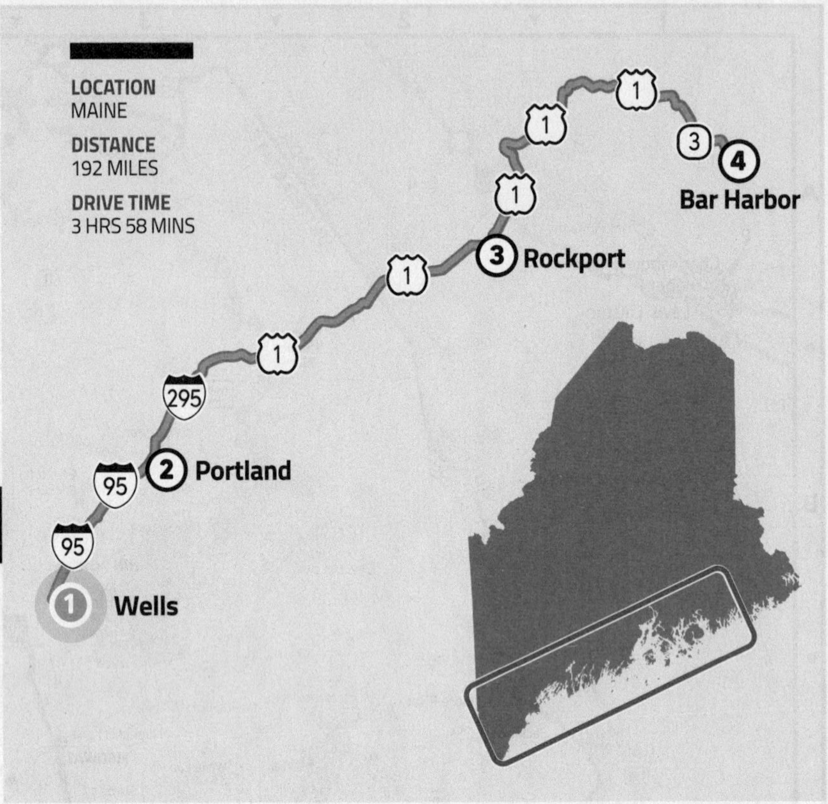

Few places offer both rugged outdoor adventure and a signature dish boasting off-the-charts flavor. Catch a lobster dinner, explore historic lighthouses and race with the wind on a boat, or hike through forested mountains to iconic landscapes for a taste of the Pine Tree State's bounty. Even the wildlife is stately here, as moose wander the hills and humpback whales breach off the coast. It seems Maine has cornered the market on rustic charm and New England adventure.

1 Wells
Starting Point

Named after a renowned conservationist, the Rachel Carson Wildlife Refuge covers 50 miles of coastline and was created to protect migratory birds. Migrating travelers can enjoy the numerous salt marshes and estuaries by canoe or kayak, or fish at several sites within the park. Hunting also is allowed by permit only. And if more exercise is on your to-do list, head to Wells Reserve, where seven miles of trails lead hikers through lush ecosystems. Signage on the trail identifies plants and animals as the trail winds over beaches, through aspen groves and across grassy meadows.

2 Portland
Drive 33 miles ▪ 35 minutes

Get a real hands-on lobster experience by signing up with Lucky Catch Cruises. Join the crew on a lobster boat, pulling up traps for your dinner as you tour Casco Bay. Motor past lighthouses, Civil War-era forts and Seal Rocks before docking to take your catch to the Portland Lobster Company Restaurant for a truly "sea-to-table" dining experience. Prefer to stay on dry land? Amble into Cook's Lobster and Ale House, where your meal choices range from a fried haddock sandwich to lobster mac and cheese.

Getty Images/iStockphoto

3 Rockport
Drive 80 miles ▪ 1 hour, 35 minutes

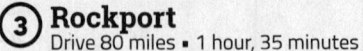

Coastal Maine has several scenic lighthouses, but the Breakwater Light in Rockland offers a walk that you won't soon forget. Visitors navigate an almost one-mile-long breakwater before ascending stairs to take in views from atop the beacon, which was built in 1921 and continues to operate. Nautical buffs also can choose from five schooners for the sailing adventure of a lifetime. Windjammer Cruises takes visitors on three- to six-day sailing trips from Rockland.

4 Bar Harbor
Drive 79 miles ▪ 1 hour, 48 minutes

Acadia National Park protects rugged headlines along the Atlantic Coast, and 158 miles of hiking trails lead visitors to spellbinding views on rugged terrain. Make sure to visit Thunder Hole, where angry waves slam into a narrow chasm, creating a geyser of spray that shoots 40 feet into the sky accompanied by an explosive jolt to the eardrums. Just off the coast, whale watching tours take sightseers close to humpbacks.

BIKING BOATING DINING ENTERTAINMENT FISHING HIKING HUNTING PADDLING SHOPPING SIGHTSEEING

Maine SPOTLIGHTS

Don't Pass Up the Pine Tree State

Behind the Pine Tree State's rugged image lies a warm hospitality that makes this place special. You'll feel at home as you explore the rugged coastlines and deep inland forests of a majestic northeast state.

ACADIA WAS THE 1ST NATIONAL PARK EAST OF THE MISSISSIPPI RIVER.

Getty Images/iStockphoto

Rugged cliffs constitute much of the 64 miles of coastline in Acadia National Park.

Bar Harbor and Acadia National Park

This coastal resort town is nestled among the rugged cliffs of Maine. Bar Harbor has been a resort destination for almost 200 years. Painters and writers came in the 1850s to soak up the ambience of sea and sky. "Rusticators" was the term to describe summer visitors and residents who built quaint cottages here.

A Crown Jewel

Acadia National Park is the "Crown Jewel of the North Atlantic Coast." With more than 48,000 acres and close to 3 million visitors each year, this is one of the top 10 most visited parks in the country. Cadillac Mountain is one of the highest points on the East Coast, with spectacular views of the sunset over Bar Harbor and Frenchman's Bay. Anglers can cast for 30 types of fish, including lake trout, land-locked salmon and white perch in nearly 30 lakes.

Desert Island

Explore the barren beauty of Mount Desert Island along Ocean Trail with massive spruce trees perched upon two granite cliffs and Sand Beach wedged between. The craggy pink face of Otter Cliff accents beautiful views of the coastline. The heart-jolting roar of Thunder Hole is just one of the natural gems tucked along Park Loop Road.

Bangor

Standing over 30 feet tall, the imposing figure of Paul Bunyan rises above the streets of Bangor, massive ax swung over his shoulder. Erected in 1959, the fiberglass-over-metal-frame statue honors the city's lumber industry.

Port of Plenty

Located near the North Maine Woods and the Penobscot River on Interstate 95, Bangor was a major port for shipping Maine's hardwoods out to the world through the late 1800s. Grand mansions from this era can be found tucked in cozy neighborhoods.

Portland

Perched on the edge of Casco Bay is the city of Portland, built by a sturdy community that developed its economy on the sea.

By the Bay

Casco Bay is a year-round port for cruise ships, thanks to its deep water. Nature trails on Long Island beckon hikers and birdwatchers, and Great Diamond Island is home to the parade grounds of old Fort McKinley.

FOR MORE INFORMATION

Maine Office of Tourism, 888-624-6345, www.visitmaine.com

Bar Harbor & Acadia National Park, 207-288-5103, www.visitbarharbor.com

Greater Bangor CVB, 800-91-MOOSE, www.visitbangormaine.com

Visit Portland, 207-772-4994, www.visitportland.com

ME

LOCAL FAVORITE

Cedar Plank Salmon

Maine is known for its robust salmon populations in its rivers, lakes and off the Atlantic coast. Cook up this recipe and enjoy great Pine Tree State flavor. *Recipe by Mike Lloyd.*

INGREDIENTS

- ☐ 1 center cut salmon (Atlantic), skin on
- ☐ 1 large lime or lime juice
- ☐ Sea salt
- ☐ Ground black pepper
- ☐ Olive oil (try red pepper spiced oil)
- ☐ Chef Paul Prudhomme Magic Season Blends (Blackened Redfish Magic)
- ☐ Cedar plank

DIRECTIONS

Place cedar plank in water, let soak 30 minutes. Place Salmon on tinfoil, squeeze juice from ½ lime over fish. slice the other half and set aside. Let fish stand for 5-10 minutes. Coat fish with olive oil. Season lightly with salt and pepper. Season fish with blackened spice.
Set your grill to 600 F°. Place fish on plank skin side down with sliced lime on top of fish. Place on grill, cook for 8½ minutes. (Have a spray bottle of water handy in case your plank catches on fire.)
After the 8½ minutes are complete, turn off grill. DO NOT OPEN. Let grill cool down for another 8 ½ minutes or until fish is flakey.

Maine

ABBOT — C2 *Piscataquis*

BALSAM WOODS CAMPGROUND **Ratings: 8.5/9/9** (Campground) 53 Avail: 50 full hkups, 3 W, 3 E (30/50 amps). 2021 rates: $41 to $52. May 26 to Oct 09. (207)876-2731, 112 Pond Rd, Abbot, ME 04406

ACADIA NATIONAL PARK — D4 *Hancock*

ACADIA NATIONAL PARK See also Bar Harbor, Bass Harbor, Ellsworth, Gouldsboro, Orland, Southwest Harbor & Trenton.

ALFRED — E1 *York*

WALNUT GROVE CAMPGROUND **Ratings: 8.5/8/8** (Campground) 17 Avail: 10 full hkups, 7 W (30/50 amps). 2021 rates: $45.78 to $69.76. May 08 to Oct 15. (207)324-1207, 599 Gore Rd., Alfred, ME 04002

ANDOVER — D1 *Oxford*

SOUTH ARM CAMPGROUND **Ratings: 6.5/8★/8.5** (Campground) 64 Avail: 7 full hkups, 57 W, 57 E (30/50 amps). 2021 rates: $30 to $39. May 15 to Sep 30. (207)364-5155, 62 Kennett Dr, Andover, ME 04216

ARUNDEL — E1 *York*

BENTLEY'S SALOON, MOTEL & CAMPGROUND **Ratings: 6/9★/8.5** (Campground) Avail: 75 full hkups (30/50 amps). 2021 rates: $40 to $60. Apr 15 to Oct 15. (207)985-8966, 1601 Portland Rd., Arundel, ME 04046

AUBURN — E2 *Androscoggin*

AUBURN See also Bridgton, Brunswick, Casco, Durham, Freeport, Leeds, Naples, North Monmouth, Oxford, Poland, Poland Spring, Raymond, Richmond, Waterford & Winthrop.

AUGUSTA — D2 *Kennebec*

AUGUSTA See also Damariscotta, Leeds, Nobleboro, North Monmouth, Richmond & Winthrop.

BANGOR — D3 *Penobscot*

PAUL BUNYAN CAMPGROUND
good sam park
Ratings: 8.5/8.5★/9 (Campground) 30 Avail: 13 full hkups, 17 W, 17 E (30/50 amps). 2021 rates: $36 to $48. May 01 to Oct 15. (207)941-1177, 1858 Union St, Bangor, ME 04401

PLEASANT HILL CAMPGROUND **Ratings: 8.5/9★/9** (Campground) 72 Avail: 20 full hkups, 52 W, 52 E (30/50 amps). 2021 rates: $40 to $50. May 01 to Oct 13. (207)848-5127, 45 Mansell Rd., Hermon, ME 04401

PUMPKIN PATCH RV RESORT
good sam park
Ratings: 9/9.5★/10 (RV Park) 65 Avail: 57 full hkups, 8 W, 8 E (30/50 amps). 2021 rates: $40 to $44. May 01 to Oct 15. (207)848-2231, 149 Billings Rd., Hermon, ME 04401

BAR HARBOR — D4 *Hancock*

ACADIA/BLACKWOODS
(Public National Park) From jct SR-3 & SR-233 (in Bar Harbor): Go 5 mi S on SR-3 (L). **FAC:** paved rds. Avail: 61 gravel, no slide-outs, 25 pull-thrus, back-ins (20x35), tent sites, restrooms only, dump, fire rings. **REC:** Atlantic Ocean:. Pets OK. Partial handicap access, 14 day max stay. 2021 rates: $30. May 01 to Oct 31.
(207)288-3274 Lat: 44.309684, Lon: -68.203501
State Route 3, Bar Harbor, ME 04660
www.nps.gov/acad

BAR HARBOR CAMPGROUND **Ratings: 8.5/9★/8** (Campground) 175 Avail: 70 full hkups, 105 W, 105 E (30/50 amps). 2021 rates: $42 to $48. May 28 to Oct 13. (207)288-5185, 409 State Hwy 3, Bar Harbor, ME 04609

BAR HARBOR OCEANSIDE KOA **Ratings: 7.5/9★/8** (Campground) 168 Avail: 45 full hkups, 123 W, 123 E (30/50 amps). 2021 rates: $81 to $140. May 09 to Oct 07. (888)562-5605, 136 County Rd, Bar Harbor, ME 04609

HADLEY'S POINT CAMPGROUND **Ratings: 8.5/8.5★/9** (Campground) 130 Avail: 16 full hkups, 114 W, 114 E (30/50 amps). 2021 rates: $40 to $52. May 15 to Oct 15. (207)288-4808, 33 Hadley Point Rd., Bar Harbor, ME 04609

MT. DESERT NARROWS CAMPING RESORT
good sam park
Ratings: 7.5/7/8.5 (Campground) 123 Avail: 62 full hkups, 61 W, 61 E (30/50 amps). 2021 rates: $50 to $130. May 15 to Oct 10. (888)563-7040, 1219 State Hwy 3, Bar Harbor, ME 04609

NARROWS TOO CAMPING RESORT
good sam park
Ratings: 9/8.5/9 (RV Park) Avail: 162 full hkups (30/50 amps). 2021 rates: $57 to $161. May 01 to Oct 21. (888)563-7040, 1150 Bar Harbor Rd., Trenton, ME 04605

BASS HARBOR — D4 *Hancock*

BASS HARBOR CAMPGROUND **Ratings: 8/8★/7** (Campground) 51 Avail: 28 full hkups, 23 W, 23 E (30/50 amps). 2021 rates: $44 to $64. May 15 to Oct 15. (207)244-5857, 342 Harbor Dr, Bass Harbor, ME 04653

BATH — E2 *Sagadahoc*

MEADOWBROOK CAMPING AREA
good sam park
Ratings: 8.5/8★/8.5 (Campground) 85 Avail: 42 full hkups, 43 W, 43 E (30/50 amps). 2021 rates: $42.51 to $54.50. May 01 to Oct 01. (207)443-4967, 33 Meadowbrook Rd., Phippsburg, ME 04562

BELFAST — D3 *Waldo*

MOORINGS OCEANFRONT RV RESORT **Ratings: 8/9★/9.5** (Campground) Avail: 31 full hkups (30/50 amps). 2021 rates: $60 to $119. May 11 to Oct 26. (207)338-6860, 191 Searsport Ave., Belfast, ME 04915

Things change ... last year's rates serve as a guideline only.

BERWICK — E1 *York*

➔ BEAVER DAM CAMPGROUND **Ratings: 7.5/9★/9** (Campground) 48 Avail: 15 full hkups, 33 W, 33 E (30/50 amps). 2021 rates: $43 to $66. May 15 to Sep 30. (207)698-2267, 551 School St., Berwick, ME 03901

BETHEL — D1 *Oxford*

⬆ BETHEL OUTDOOR ADVENTURE AND CAMPGROUND **Ratings: 7.5/7/7.5** (Campground) 28 Avail: 22 full hkups, 6 W, 6 E (30/50 amps). 2021 rates: $38.50 to $42.50. May 15 to Oct 15. (207)824-4224, 121 Mayville Rd-US Rte 2, Bethel, ME 04217

BOOTHBAY — E2 *Lincoln*

↖ SHORE HILLS CAMPGROUND & RV PARK

good sam park **Ratings: 8.5/9★/9.5** (Campground) From Jct of US-1 & SR-27, S 7.5 mi on SR-27 (R). **FAC:** paved/gravel rds. (136 spaces). Avail: 102 gravel, 15 pull-thrus, (30x84), back-ins (30x62), 82 full hkups, 20 W, 20 E (30/50 amps), seasonal sites, cable, WiFi @ sites, tent sites, rentals, shower$, dump, laundry, groc, LP gas, fire rings, firewood, controlled access. **REC:** Cross River: swim, fishing, boating nearby, playground. Pet restrict (B). Big rig sites, eco-friendly. 2021 rates: $56 to $60, Military discount. May 15 to Oct 14. ATM, no cc.

(207)633-4782 Lat: 43.90510, Lon: -69.61994
553 Wiscasset Rd., Boothbay, ME 04537
www.shorehills.com
See ad this page

BRIDGTON — E1 *Cumberland*

⬆ LAKESIDE PINES CAMPGROUND **Ratings: 6/6.5/7** (Campground) 43 Avail: 6 full hkups, 37 W, 37 E (30/50 amps). 2021 rates: $50. May 12 to Sep 09. (207)647-3935, 54 Lakeside Pines Rd (Hwy 117), Bridgton, ME 04009

BROWNFIELD — E1 *Oxford*

➔ ON THE SACO FAMILY CAMPGROUND **Ratings: 8/7.5/9** (Campground) Avail: 13 full hkups (30/50 amps). 2021 rates: $40 to $42. May 15 to Oct 15. (207)452-2274, 379 Denmark Road, Brownfield, ME 04010

➔ RIVER RUN CANOE & CAMPGROUND **Ratings: 5.5/9.5★/8** (Campground) 27 Avail. 2021 rates: $20. May 26 to Sep 01. (207)452-2500, 191 Denmark Rd, Brownfield, ME 04010

↗ WOODLAND ACRES CAMPGROUND **Ratings: 8/8.5/9** (Campground) 73 Avail: 39 full hkups, 34 W, 34 E (30/50 amps). 2021 rates: $48 to $56. May 15 to Oct 15. (207)935-2529, 33 Woodland Acres Dr., Brownfield, ME 04010

BRUNSWICK — E2 *Cumberland*

➔ THOMAS POINT BEACH PARK AND CAMPGROUND **Ratings: 7.5/5.5/8.5** (Campground) Avail: 26 E (20/30 amps). 2021 rates: $30 to $35. Apr 01 to Oct 15. (207)725-6009, 29 Meadow Rd, Brunswick, ME 04011

BUCKSPORT — D3 *Hancock*

BUCKSPORT See also Bangor, Bar Harbor, Belfast, Eddington, Ellsworth, Holden, Orland & Trenton.

CAMDEN — D3 *Knox*

⬆ CAMDEN HILLS (Public State Park) From town, N 2 mi on US-1 (L). 107 Avail: 50 W, 50 E (30/50 amps). 2021 rates: $25 to $45. May 18 to Sep 13. (207)236-3109

CANAAN — D2 *Somerset*

➔ SKOWHEGAN/KENNEBEC VALLEY KOA **Ratings: 9/9★/8** (Campground) Avail: 64 full hkups (30/50 amps). 2021 rates: $51.89 to $62.89. May 12 to Oct 09. (207)474-2858, 18 Cabin Rd., Canaan, ME 04924

CAPE NEDDICK — F1 *York*

⬆ DIXON'S COASTAL MAINE CAMPGROUND **Ratings: 6.5/9★/8.5** (Campground) 93 Avail: 93 W, 93 E (30/50 amps). 2021 rates: $38 to $52. May 06 to Sep 23. (207)363-3626, 1740 US Route 1, Cape Neddick, ME 03902

Your neighbor just told you about a great little campground in Kentucky -- what was the name of it again? The ""Find-it-Fast'' index in the back of the Guide can help. It's an alphabetical listing, by state, of every private and public park in the Guide.

CASCO — E1 *Cumberland*

⬇ POINT SEBAGO RESORT

good sam park **Ratings: 8/9★/9.5** (Campground) From jct Hwy-85 & US-302: Go 5 mi N on US-302, then 1 mi W at Casco Alliance Church (Pt. Sebago Rd) (R). **FAC:** paved/gravel rds. (223 spaces). Avail: 88 gravel, 5 pull-thrus, (30x60), back-ins (30x50), 88 full hkups (30/50 amps), seasonal sites, cable, WiFi @ sites, tent sites, rentals, dump, laundry, groc, LP bottles, fire rings, firewood, restaurant, controlled access. **REC:** Sebago Lake: swim, fishing, marina, kayaking/canoeing, boating nearby, golf, shuffleboard, playground, hunting nearby. Pet restrict (Q). Partial handicap access. Big rig sites, eco-friendly. 2021 rates: $97 to $130, Military discount. May 01 to Oct 31. ATM.

(207)506-0165 Lat: 43.91928, Lon: -70.55020
261 Point Sebago Rd., Casco, ME 04015
www.pointsebago.com
See ad this page

ME

DAMARISCOTTA — E2 *Lincoln*

→ **LAKE PEMAQUID CAMPGROUND**

Ratings: 8.5/9★/8.5 (Campground) From Jct Hwy 130 & Bus US-1: Go 1 mi NE on Bus US-1, then 2 mi S on Biscay Rd, then 1/4 mi E on Egypt Rd, then E on Twin Cove Ln (E).

FAMILY FUN LOCATED ON LAKE PEMAQUID
Seven mile Lake Pemaquid in Mid-Coast Maine offers some of the best boating and Fishing. Regularly Scheduled Events and Entertainment for all ages. Join us for Family Fun and Relaxation in the Beautiful State of Maine!

FAC: paved/gravel rds. (263 spaces). 233 Avail: 11 paved, 52 gravel, 170 dirt, 12 pull-thrus, (24x70), back-ins (24x46), 167 full hkups, 66 W, 66 E (30/50 amps), seasonal sites, WiFi @ sites, tent sites, rentals, shower$, dump, laundry, groc, LP bottles, fire rings, firewood, restaurant, controlled access. **REC:** heated pool, hot tub, Pemaquid Lake: swim, fishing, marina, kayaking/canoeing, boating nearby, playground. Pets OK. Partial handicap access. Big rig sites, eco-friendly. 2021 rates: $30 to $57. May 24 to Sep 30. ATM.
(207)563-5202 Lat: 44.03130, Lon: -69.46107
100 Twin Cove Lane, Damariscotta, ME 04543
lakepemaquid.com
See ad this page

DANFORTH — C4 *Washington*

→ GREENLAND COVE CAMPGROUND **Ratings: 8.5/7.5/7** (Campground) 42 Avail: 42 W, 42 E (30/50 amps). 2021 rates: $36. May 15 to Oct 01. (207)448-2863, 70 Brown Rd., Danforth, ME 04424

DENNYSVILLE — D5 *Washington*

↓ COBSCOOK BAY (Public State Park) From jct SR-86 & US-1: Go 4 mi S on US-1, the 1/2 mi E on unnamed cnty rd (L). 106 Avail. 2021 rates: $20 to $30. May 15 to Oct 15. (207)726-4412

DIXFIELD — D2 *Oxford*

↑ MOUNTAIN VIEW CAMPGROUND **Ratings: 8/7/7.5** (Campground) 27 Avail: 21 full hkups, 6 W, 6 E (30/50 amps). 2021 rates: $34 to $36. May 01 to Oct 31. (207)562-8285, 200 Mountainview Dr., Dixfield, ME 04224

DOVER-FOXCROFT — C3 *Piscataquis*

↑ PEAKS-KENNY (Public State Park) From jct SR-150 & SR-153: Go 4-1/2 mi N on SR-153, then 2 mi W on campground rd (E). 56 Avail. 2021 rates: $20 to $40. May 15 to Oct 01. (207)564-2003

DURHAM — E2 *Androscoggin*

↓ FREEPORT DURHAM KOA **Ratings: 8.5/8.5/8** (Campground) 76 Avail: 40 full hkups, 36 W, 36 E (30/50 amps). 2021 rates: $41.50 to $69. Apr 22 to Nov 03. (207)688-4288, 82 Big Skye Ln., Durham, ME 04222

EASTPORT — D5 *Washington*

↑ **SEAVIEW CAMPGROUND & COTTAGES**

Ratings: 8/9.5★/9 (Campground) Avail: 66 full hkups (30/50 amps). 2021 rates: $45 to $66. May 15 to Oct 13. (207)853-4471, 16 Norwood Rd., Eastport, ME 04631

EDDINGTON — D3 *Penobscot*

↑ COLD RIVER CAMPGROUND **Ratings: 9/10★/8.5** (Campground) 39 Avail: 36 full hkups, 3 W, 3 E (30/50 amps). 2021 rates: $47.75 to $55.20. May 15 to Oct 15. (207)922-2551, 211 Riverside Dr., Eddington, ME 04428

ELLSWORTH — D3 *Hancock*

↖ BRANCH LAKE CAMPING AREA **Ratings: 6.5/7.5★/7.5** (Campground) 20 Avail: 7 full hkups, 13 W, 13 E (30/50 amps). 2021 rates: $40 to $45. May 15 to Oct 01. (207)667-5174, 180 Hansons Landing Rd, Ellsworth, ME 04605

← FOREST RIDGE CAMPGROUND AND RV PARK **Ratings: 8/9.5★/8.5** (Campground) Avail: 35 full hkups (30/50 amps). 2021 rates: $50 to $75. May 01 to Oct 15. (207)664-7070, 40 Flockamoosen Way, Ellsworth, ME 04605

↘ LAMOINE (Public State Park) From jct US-1 & Hwy-184: Go 10 mi SE on Hwy-184 (E). 62 Avail. 2021 rates: $20 to $30. May 15 to Oct 15. (207)667-4778

Save 10% at Good Sam Parks 365 days a year with no blackout dates!!

← **PATTEN POND CAMPING RESORT**

Ratings: 8.5/8/8.5 (RV Park) 105 Avail: 79 full hkups, 26 W, 26 E (30/50 amps). 2021 rates: $46 to $84. May 15 to Oct 14. (888)563-7040, 1470 Bucksport Rd., Ellsworth, ME 04605

FARMINGTON — D2 *Franklin*

← TROLL VALLEY CAMPGROUND **Ratings: 2/5/4** (Campground) 11 Avail: 2 full hkups, 9 W, 9 E (30/50 amps). 2021 rates: $37 to $46. May 16 to Oct 18. (207)778-3656, 283 Red Schoolhouse Rd., Farmington, ME 04938

FREEPORT — E2 *Cumberland*

↑ CEDAR HAVEN FAMILY CAMPGROUND **Ratings: 9/9★/10** (Campground) 73 Avail: 45 full hkups, 28 W, 28 E (30/50 amps). 2021 rates: $50.36 to $70.80. May 01 to Oct 31. (207)869-5026, 39 Baker Rd., Freeport, ME 04032

← DESERT OF MAINE CAMPGROUND **Ratings: 6/8.5★/7.5** (Campground) 23 Avail: 23 W, 23 E (15/30 amps). 2021 rates: $45 to $65. May 07 to Oct 12. (207)850-3025, 95 Desert Rd., Freeport, ME 04032

↓ WINSLOW MEMORIAL PARK (Public) From Jct of US-1 & S Freeport Rd, E 0.9 mi on S Freeport Rd to Staples Point Rd, SE 2 mi (R). 100 Avail. 2021 rates: $15 to $35. May 04 to Oct 04. (207)865-4198

→ WOLFES NECK OCEANFRONT CAMPING **Ratings: 6/7.5/7.5** (Campground) 55 Avail: 25 W, 25 E (30/50 amps). 2021 rates: $50 to $73. May 01 to Oct 31. (207)865-9307, 134 Burnett Rd, Freeport, ME 04032

GEORGETOWN — E2 *Sagadahoc*

↓ SAGADAHOC BAY CAMPGROUND **Ratings: 5/7/6.5** (Campground) 31 Avail: 8 full hkups, 23 W, 23 E (20/30 amps). 2021 rates: $52 to $63. May 01 to Nov 01. (207)371-2014, 9 Molly Point Lane, Georgetown, ME 04548

EXCLUSIVE! Every listing includes a special "arrow" symbol. This valuable tool shows you where the facility is located (N, S, E, W, NE, NW, SE, SW) in relation to the town.

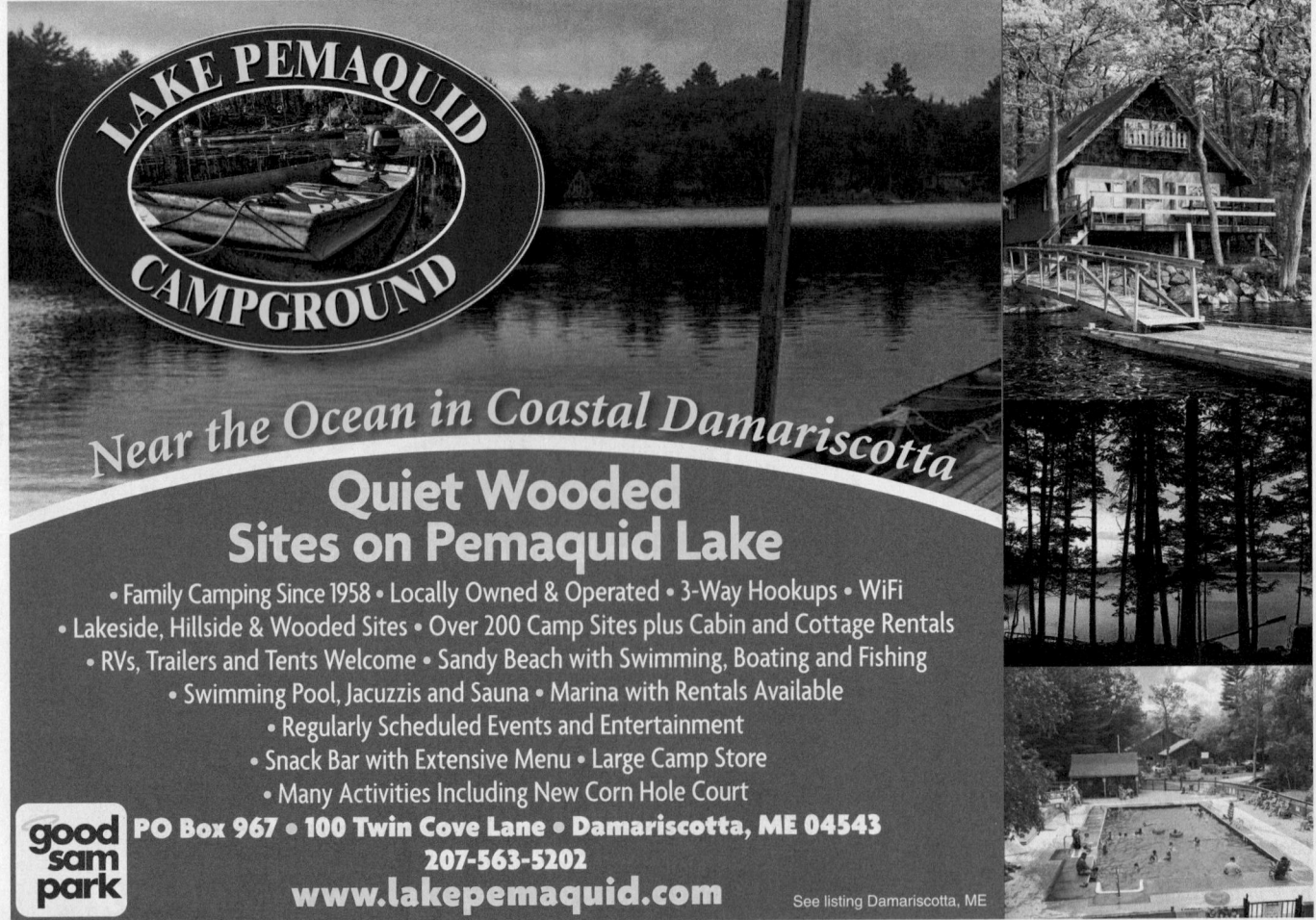

GOULDSBORO — D4 *Hancock*

WEST BAY ACADIA RV CAMPGROUND
good sam park **Ratings: 6.5/NA/10** (RV Park) Avail: 13 full hkups (30/50 amps). 2021 rates: $100 to $165. May 15 to Oct 15. (207)963-9160, 33 Rainbows End, Gouldsboro, ME 04607

GREENVILLE — C2 *Piscataquis*

LILY BAY (Public State Park) From jct Hwy 6/15 & Kokadjo Rd: Go 9 mi N on Kokadjo Rd (L). 90 Avail. 2021 rates: $20 to $30. May 19 to Sep 07. (207)695-2700

MOOSEHEAD FAMILY CAMPGROUND **Ratings: 5.5/NA/7.5** (Campground) 21 Avail: 21 W, 21 E (30/50 amps), Pit toilets. 2021 rates: $37 to $54. May 01 to Oct 15. (207)695-2210, 312 Moosehead Lake Rd. (Route 15), Greenville, ME 04441

GREENWOOD — D1 *Oxford*

LITTLEFIELD BEACHES CAMPGROUND **Ratings: 8/8★/8** (Campground) 50 Avail: 10 full hkups, 40 W, 40 E (20/30 amps). 2021 rates: $41 to $49. May 15 to Sep 25. (207)875-3290, 13 Littlefield Lane, Greenwood, ME 04255

HANOVER — D1 *Oxford*

STONY BROOK RECREATION & CAMPING **Ratings: 8.5/7/8** (Campground) 34 Avail: 14 full hkups, 20 W, 20 E (30/50 amps). 2021 rates: $40 to $45. (207)824-2836, 3036 Main St., Hanover, ME 04237

HARRINGTON — D4 *Washington*

SUNSET POINT CAMPGROUND AT HARRINGTON **Ratings: 6.5/8★/9.5** (Campground) 21 Avail: 13 full hkups, 8 W, 8 E (30/50 amps). 2021 rates: $35 to $39. May 15 to Oct 15. (207)483-4412, 24 Sunset Point Rd., Harrington, ME 04643

HOLDEN — D3 *Penobscot*

BANGOR/HOLDEN KOA **Ratings: 8.5/7.5/9** (Campground) 72 Avail: 37 full hkups, 35 W, 35 E (30/50 amps). 2021 rates: $50.55 to $76.01. May 01 to Oct 15. (207)843-6011, 602 Main Rd., Holden, ME 04429

HOLDEN FAMILY CAMPGROUND **Ratings: 9/9★/8.5** (Campground) Avail: 24 full hkups (30/50 amps). 2021 rates: $45 to $50. May 01 to Oct 15. (207)989-0529, 108 Main Rd., Holden, ME 04429

HOULTON — B4 *Aroostook*

HOULTON/CANADIAN BORDER KOA **Ratings: 9/9.5★/9.5** (Campground) Avail: 50 full hkups (30/50 amps). 2021 rates: $46.05 to $52.59. May 10 to Oct 15. (207)532-6739, 659 North St., Houlton, ME 04730

ISLAND FALLS — B4 *Aroostook*

BIRCH POINT LODGE CAMPGROUND & COTTAGE RESORT **Ratings: 6.5/7.5★/6.5** (Campground) 26 Avail: 3 full hkups, 23 W, 23 E (30 amps). 2021 rates: $35 to $45. May 14 to Oct 31. (207)463-2515, 33 Birch Point Ln, Island Falls, ME 04747

KENNEBUNK — E1 *York*

YANKEELAND CAMPGROUND **Ratings: 7.5/7/8** (Campground) 26 Avail: 10 full hkups, 16 W, 16 E (30/50 amps). 2021 rates: $76.30 to $87.20. May 01 to Oct 08. (207)985-7576, 1 Robinson Way, Kennebunk, ME 04043

KENNEBUNKPORT — E1 *York*

HEMLOCK GROVE CAMPGROUND **Ratings: 9/9.5★/9.5** (Campground) 56 Avail: 46 full hkups, 10 W, 10 E (30/50 amps). 2021 rates: $62. May 01 to Oct 15. (207)985-0398, 1299 Portland Rd, US Route 1, Kennebunkport, ME 04046

RED APPLE CAMPGROUND
Ratings: 10/10★/10 (RV Park) From Jct of ME Tpke & Rte 35 (exit 25), SE 1.8 mi on Rte 35 to US-1, N 1.5 mi to Old Post Rd, E (right) 0.7 mi to Sinnott Rd, E (continue straight) 1.5 mi (L). **FAC:** paved rds. (131 spaces). Avail: 51 paved, 9 pull-thrus, (35x68), back-ins (38x45), 51 full hkups (30/50 amps), seasonal sites, cable, WiFi @ sites, tent sites, rentals, dump, laundry, LP bottles, fire rings, firewood. **REC:** heated pool, boating nearby, shuffleboard, playground. Pets OK. Partial handicap access. Big rig sites, eco-friendly. 2021 rates: $66.04 to $70.64. May 11 to Oct 08.
(207)967-4927 Lat: 43.39128, Lon: -70.49303
111 Sinnott Rd., Kennebunkport, ME 04046
www.redapplecampground.com
See ad this page

SANDY PINES CAMPGROUND **Ratings: 9/10★/10** (Campground) Avail: 61 full hkups (30/50 amps). 2021 rates: $65 to $109. May 11 to Oct 14. (207)967-2483, 277 Mill Rd., Kennebunkport, ME 04046

LEBANON — E1 *York*

LAZY FROG CAMPGROUND **Ratings: 9/8.5★/10** (Campground) Avail: 15 full hkups (30/50 amps). 2021 rates: $52. May 18 to Oct 08. (207)457-1260, 75 Cemetery Road, Lebanon, ME 04027

LEBANON KOA ON SALMON FALLS RIVER Ratings: 7.5/9★/8 (Campground) 133 Avail: 64 full hkups, 69 W, 69 E (30/50 amps). 2021 rates: $59 to $140. May 05 to Oct 14. (207)339-9465, 21 Flat Rock Bridge Rd., Lebanon, ME 04027

POTTER'S PLACE ADULT CAMPING AREA **Ratings: 6.5/7.5/8** (Campground) 25 Avail: 25 W, 25 E (30/50 amps). 2021 rates: $40. May 01 to Oct 15. (207)457-1341, 115 Bakers Grant Rd., Lebanon, ME 04027

SALMON FALLS RIVER CAMPING RESORT **Ratings: 9/8.5★/7.5** (Campground) Avail: 36 full hkups (30/50 amps). 2021 rates: $70 to $75. May 15 to Oct 15. (207)339-8888, 44 Natural High Rd., Lebanon, ME 04027

LEEDS — D2 *Androscoggin*

RIVERBEND CAMPGROUND **Ratings: 8/8★/7** (Campground) 19 Avail: 19 W, 19 E (30/50 amps). 2021 rates: $30 to $35. May 05 to Oct 09. (207)524-5711, 1540 Route 106, Leeds, ME 04263

LEXINGTON TOWNSHIP — C2 *Somerset*

HAPPY HORSESHOE CAMPGROUND **Ratings: 7.5/9.5★/8.5** (Campground) 48 Avail: 48 W, 48 E (30/50 amps). 2021 rates: $45. May 25 to Sep 08. (207)628-3471, 1100 Long Falls Dam Rd., Lexington Township, ME 04961

LIBERTY — D3 *Waldo*

LAKE ST GEORGE (Public State Park) From town: Go 25 mi E on Rte 3 (R). 38 Avail. 2021 rates: $20 to $30. May 18 to Sep 13. (207)589-4255

Get the GOOD SAM CAMPING APP

LUBEC — D5 *Washington*

SUNSET POINT RV PARK **Ratings: 7/9★/8** (Campground) 30 Avail: 30 W, 30 E (30/50 amps). 2021 rates: $40. May 20 to Oct 15. (207)733-2272, 37 Sunset Rd., Lubec, ME 04652

MADISON — D2 *Somerset*

YOGI BEAR'S JELLYSTONE PARK **Ratings: 8.5/9★/9** (Campground) 65 Avail: 59 full hkups, 6 W, 6 E (30/50 amps). 2021 rates: $40 to $72. May 15 to Oct 12. (207)474-7353, 221 Lakewood Rd., Madison, ME 04950

MATTAWAMKEAG — C4 *Penobscot*

MATTAWAMKEAG WILDERNESS PARK CAMPGROUND (Public) From Jct of SR-157 & US-2, S 0.1 mi on US-2 to park access rd, E 9 mi (L). 50 Avail: 6 full hkups, 8 W, 8 E (30/50 amps). 2021 rates: $22 to $35. May 25 to Sep 30. (207)290-0205

MEDWAY — C3 *Penobscot*

KATAHDIN SHADOWS CAMPGROUND & CABINS

good sam park

Ratings: 8.5/9.5★/8.5 (Campground) 65 Avail: 37 full hkups, 28 W, 28 E (30/50 amps). 2021 rates: $38 to $40. May 01 to Nov 01. (207)746-9349, 118 Katahdin Shadows Dr., Medway, ME 04460

PINE GROVE CAMPGROUND & COTTAGES **Ratings: 8/8★/8** (Campground) 27 Avail: 2 full hkups, 25 W, 25 E (20/30 amps). 2021 rates: $37 to $40. May 15 to Oct 31. (207)746-5172, 822 Grindstone Rd, Medway, ME 04460

MOODY — E1 *York*

MOODY BEACH RV CAMPGROUND

good sam park

Ratings: 9/8.5/8 (Membership Park) Avail: 5 full hkups (30/50 amps). 2021 rates: $84 to $85. Apr 15 to Oct 15. (888)563-7040, 266 Post Rd, Wells, ME 04090

NAPLES — E1 *Cumberland*

COLONIAL MAST CAMPGROUND **Ratings: 7.5/8.5★/7** (Campground) 27 Avail: 7 full hkups, 20 W, 20 E (30/50 amps). 2021 rates: $56 to $59. (207)693-6652, 23 Colonial Mast Rd, Naples, ME 04055

FOUR SEASONS CAMPING AREA **Ratings: 7/6.5/6.5** (Campground) 40 Avail: 40 W, 40 E (20/30 amps). 2021 rates: $53 to $71. May 11 to Oct 09. (207)693-6797, 1741 Roosevelt Trail, Naples, ME 04055

LOON'S HAVEN FAMILY CAMPGROUND **Ratings: 7.5/7/8.5** (Campground) 24 Avail: 4 full hkups, 20 W, 20 E (30/50 amps). 2021 rates: $78 to $99.60. May 15 to Oct 15. (207)693-6881, 41 Loon's Haven Dr., Naples, ME 04055

NAPLES KOA CAMPGROUND **Ratings: 8.5/9.5★/10** (Campground) Avail: 68 full hkups (30/50 amps). 2021 rates: $85 to $130. May 01 to Oct 15. (207)693-5267, 295 Sebago Rd. (Route 114/11), Naples, ME 04055

SEBAGO LAKE (Public State Park) From jct Hwy 302 & Hwy 11/114: Go 2 mi S on Hwy 11/114, then 1 mi W on State Park Rd (L). 250 Avail: 92 W, 92 E (30/50 amps). 2021 rates: $25 to $45. (207)693-6613

NEW HARBOR — E2 *Lincoln*

SHERWOOD FOREST CAMPSITE **Ratings: 6.5/7/7** (Campground) 20 Avail: 20 W, 20 E (30/50 amps). 2021 rates: $41. May 15 to Oct 15. (207)677-3642, 32 Pemaquid Trail, New Harbor, ME 04554

NEWPORT — D3 *Penobscot*

CHRISTIES CAMPGROUND & COTTAGES **Ratings: 7.5/8.5★/8.5** (Campground) 18 Avail: 6 full hkups, 12 W, 12 E (30 amps). 2021 rates: $33 to $36. May 15 to Nov 27. (800)688-5141, 83 Christies Campground Rd, Newport, ME 04953

MOOSEHEAD TRAIL CAMPGROUND **Ratings: 8/8/8.5** (Campground) 50 Avail: 48 full hkups, 2 W, 2 E (30/50 amps). 2021 rates: $45. May 15 to Oct 15. (207)974-6241, 781 Moosehead Tr, Newport, ME 04953

SEBASTICOOK LAKE CAMPGROUND **Ratings: 8/9★/8.5** (Campground) 23 Avail: 5 full hkups, 18 W, 18 E (20/30 amps). 2021 rates: $38 to $50. May 11 to Oct 07. (207)368-5047, 52 Tent Village Rd., Newport, ME 04953

Refer to the Table of Contents in front of the Guide to locate everything you need.

NOBLEBORO — E2 *Lincoln*

DUCK PUDDLE CAMPGROUND **Ratings: 7/7.5/7.5** (Campground) 70 Avail: 40 full hkups, 30 W, 30 E (30/50 amps). 2021 rates: $41 to $68. May 01 to Oct 13. (207)563-5608, 60 Campground Rd., Nobleboro, ME 04555

NORTH MONMOUTH — D2 *Kennebec*

BEAVER BROOK CAMPGROUND **Ratings: 7/7/8** (Campground) 155 Avail: 18 full hkups, 137 W, 137 E (30/50 amps). 2021 rates: $31 to $62. May 13 to Oct 10. (207)933-2108, 1 Wilson Pond Rd., North Monmouth, ME 04265

OLD ORCHARD BEACH — E2 *York*

HID'N PINES FAMILY CAMPGROUND **Ratings: 8.5/9.5★/9.5** (Campground) 232 Avail: 179 full hkups, 53 W, 53 E (30/50 amps). 2021 rates: $60 to $90. May 10 to Sep 22. (888)303-7012, 8 Cascade Rd., Old Orchard Beach, ME 04064

OLD ORCHARD BEACH CAMPGROUND

good sam park

Ratings: 10/9.5★/10 (Campground) From Jct I-95 (exit 36) & I-195: Go 2 mi E on I-195, then Rt 5 joins I-195, immediate R.

WHERE FAMILIES LOVE TO CAMP

Beautiful campground one mile from beach. Take the trolley to nearby Amusement Park, restaurants, shopping. Shaded Deluxe RV sites, big rig friendly. New full-service cabins with screened porch. Sport courts, arcades & more!

FAC: paved rds. (276 spaces). Avail: 156 all weather, 37 pull-thrus, (40x80), back-ins (40x60), 156 full hkups (30/50 amps), seasonal sites, cable, WiFi @ sites, tent sites, rentals, dump, laundry, groc, fire rings, firewood, controlled access. **REC:** pool, wading pool, hot tub, boating nearby, playground. Pets OK. Partial handicap access. Big rig sites, eco-friendly. 2021 rates: $55 to $115, Military discount. May 01 to Oct 31.

(207)934-4477 Lat: 43.509397, Lon: -70.429062
27 Ocean Park Rd., Old Orchard Beach, ME 04064
www.gocamping.com
See ad this page

Read RV topics at blog.GoodSam.com

PARADISE PARK RESORT CAMPGROUND **Ratings: 9/10★/9** (Campground) 180 Avail: 150 full hkups, 30 W, 30 E (30/50 amps). 2021 rates: $45 to $79. May 11 to Oct 08. (207)934-4633, 50 Adelaide Rd., Old Orchard Beach, ME 04064

PINEHIRST RV RESORT
good sam park **Ratings: 7.5/6.5/6** (RV Park) Avail: 21 full hkups (30/50 amps). 2021 rates: $87.30 to $107. May 01 to Oct 31. (888)563-7040, 7 Oregon Ave., Old Orchard Beach, ME 04064

POWDER HORN FAMILY CAMPING RESORT **Ratings: 8.5/10★/9.5** (Campground) 261 Avail: 160 full hkups, 101 W, 101 E (30/50 amps). 2021 rates: $67 to $109. May 12 to Oct 14. (207)934-4733, 48 Cascade Rd., Old Orchard Beach, ME 04064

WAGON WHEEL RV RESORT & CAMPGROUND **Ratings: 8.5/8.5★/9** (Campground) Avail: 33 full hkups (30/50 amps). 2021 rates: $67 to $111.60. May 01 to Oct 15. (888)543-0516, 3 Old Orchard Rd, Old Orchard Beach, ME 04064

WILD ACRES RV RESORT & CAMPGROUND **Ratings: 8.5/8.5★/9** (Campground) 285 Avail: 204 full hkups, 81 W, 81 E (30/50 amps). 2021 rates: $83 to $142.60. Apr 30 to Oct 13. (888)451-3586, 179 Saco Ave, Old Orchard Beach, ME 04064

OQUOSSOC — D1 *Franklin*

BLACK BROOK COVE CAMPGROUND **Ratings: 5/5/7** (Campground) 28 Avail: 28 W, 28 E (15 amps). 2021 rates: $32. May 01 to Oct 31. (207)486-3828, 3 Balsam Rd, Lincoln Plantation, ME 04216

CUPSUPTIC LAKE PARK AND CAMPGROUND **Ratings: 7/8.5/9.5** (Campground) 39 Avail: 20 full hkups, 19 W, 19 E (30/50 amps). 2021 rates: $39 to $50. May 01 to Oct 13. (207)864-5249, Route16 West (960 Wilson Mills Rd. or 7 Cupsuptic Campground Rd.), Adamstown Township, ME 04964

ORLAND — D3 *Hancock*

BALSAM COVE CAMPGROUND **Ratings: 8/7/7** (Campground) Avail: 62 full hkups (30/50 amps). 2021 rates: $39 to $62. May 15 to Sep 25. (207)469-7771, 286 Back Ridge Rd., Orland, ME 04472

BUCKSPORT/FORT KNOX KOA **Ratings: 9/9★/9.5** (Campground) Avail: 39 full hkups (30/50 amps). 2021 rates: $51.50 to $86. May 01 to Oct 10. (207)469-7739, 32 Leaches Point, Orland, ME 04472

OXFORD — D1 *Oxford*

TWO LAKES CAMPING AREA
good sam park **Ratings: 7.5/9.5★/8** (Campground) 60 Avail: 12 full hkups, 48 W, 48 E (30/50 amps). 2021 rates: $38 to $60. May 01 to Oct 14. (207)539-4851, 215 Campground Lane, Oxford, ME 04270

PALMYRA — D3 *Somerset*

PALMYRA GOLF & CAMPING **Ratings: 8.5/9.5★/8** (Campground) 65 Avail: 44 full hkups, 21 W, 21 E (30/50 amps). 2021 rates: $41 to $45. May 15 to Oct 15. (207)938-5677, 147 Lang Hill Rd., Palmyra, ME 04965

PERU — D2 *Oxford*

HONEY RUN BEACH & CAMPGROUND **Ratings: 7/7/8** (Campground) Avail: 35 full hkups (30/50 amps). 2021 rates: $45. May 25 to Sep 05. (207)562-4913, 456 East Shore Rd., Peru, ME 04290

POLAND — E2 *Androscoggin*

RANGE POND CAMPGROUND **Ratings: 8/8.5★/8** (Campground) 44 Avail: 30 full hkups, 14 W, 14 E (30/50 amps). 2021 rates: $43 to $50. Apr 15 to Oct 15. (207)998-2624, 94 Plains Rd., Poland, ME 04274

POLAND SPRING — E2 *Androscoggin*

POLAND SPRING CAMPGROUND **Ratings: 8/9★/8.5** (Campground) 68 Avail: 27 full hkups, 41 W, 41 E (30/50 amps). 2021 rates: $41 to $61. May 01 to Oct 09. (207)998-2151, 128 Connor Lane, Poland Spring, ME 04274

PORTLAND — E2 *Cumberland*

PORTLAND See also Arundel, Bath, Brunswick, Casco, Durham, Freeport, Kennebunkport, Old Orchard Beach, Raymond, Saco, Scarborough, Standish & Steep Falls.

WASSAMKI SPRINGS CAMPGROUND
good sam park **Ratings: 8.5/9★/9.5** (Campground) From jct I295 & Forest Ave, Go 0.9 mi S on I295, then 1.9 mi S on Congress St, then 3.9 mi S on CR 22, then 0.3 mi W on Saco St (L). **FAC:** paved/gravel rds. (265 spaces). 165 Avail: 45 grass, 120 dirt, 22 pull-thrus, (30x60), back-ins (30x45), 135 full hkups, 30 W, 30 E (30/50 amps), seasonal sites, cable, WiFi @ sites, tent sites, dump, mobile sewer, laundry, groc, LP gas, fire rings, firewood, controlled access. **REC:** Wassamki Springs Lake: swim, fishing, boating nearby, playground, rec open to public. Pet restrict (B). Partial handicap access. Big rig sites, eco-friendly. 2021 rates: $45 to $78, Military discount. May 01 to Oct 15. ATM.
(207)839-4276 Lat: 43.64687, Lon: -70.39875
56 Saco St, Scarborough, ME 04074
wassamkisprings.com
See primary listing at Scarborough and ad this page

POWNAL — E2 *Cumberland*

BRADBURY MOUNTAIN (Public State Park) From town center: Go 1 mi E on Hwy-9. 35 Avail. 2021 rates: $15 to $25. (207)688-4712

PRESQUE ISLE — B4 *Aroostook*

ARNDT'S AROOSTOOK RIVER LODGE & CAMPGROUND **Ratings: 7.5/8.5★/9.5** (Campground) 55 Avail: 26 full hkups, 29 W, 29 E (30/50 amps). 2021 rates: $33 to $40. May 15 to Oct 15. (207)764-8677, 95 Parkhurst Siding Rd, Presque Isle, ME 04769

AROOSTOOK (Public State Park) From Jct of I-95 & Rte 1, N 38 mi on Rte 1 to Spraqueville Rd, W 1 mi to State Park Rd, S 1 mi (E). 30 Avail. 2021 rates: $15 to $25. (207)768-8341

RANGELEY — D1 *Franklin*

RANGELEY LAKE (Public State Park) From jct SR-16 & SR-4: Go 4 mi S on SR-4, then 6 mi W on S Shore Dr (R). Note: 35' RV length maximum. 50 Avail. 2021 rates: $20 to $30. May 01 to Oct 01. (800)332-1501

RAYMOND — E1 *Cumberland*

KOKATOSI CAMPGROUND
good sam park **Ratings: 8/8★/8.5** (Campground) 71 Avail: 61 full hkups, 10 W, 10 E (30/50 amps). 2021 rates: $54 to $69. May 15 to Oct 09. (207)627-4642, 635 Webbs Mills Rd, Raymond, ME 04071

RICHMOND — E2 *Sagadahoc*

AUGUSTA-GARDINER KOA **Ratings: 8.5/8.5★/8** (Campground) 50 Avail: 25 full hkups, 25 W, 25 E (30/50 amps). 2021 rates: $52 to $62. Apr 01 to Nov 30. (207)582-5086, 30 Mallard Dr, Richmond, ME 04357

ROBBINSTON — C5 *Washington*

HILLTOP CAMPGROUND **Ratings: 8/8.5★/5** (Campground) Avail: 10 full hkups (30/50 amps). 2021 rates: $38. May 15 to Oct 15. (207)454-3985, 317 Ridge Rd., Robbinston, ME 04671

ROCKLAND — E3 *Knox*

ROCKLAND See also Belfast, Damariscotta, New Harbor, Nobleboro, Rockport & Union.

ROCKPORT — D3 *Knox*

CAMDEN HILLS COMMUNITY CAMPGROUND **Ratings: 7.5/7/7.5** (Campground) Avail: 33 full hkups (30/50 amps). 2021 rates: $44 to $77. May 15 to Oct 15. (207)236-2498, 30 Applewood Rd (Route 90), Rockport, ME 04856

MEGUNTICOOK CAMPGROUND BY THE SEA **Ratings: 8.5/8/8** (Campground) 82 Avail: 42 full hkups, 21 W, 21 E (30/50 amps). 2021 rates: $44 to $77. May 15 to Oct 15. (207)594-2428, 620 Commercial St, Rockport, ME 04856

SACO — E1 *York*

HOMESTEAD BY THE RIVER FAMILY CAMPGROUND **Ratings: 7/7/8.5** (Campground) 22 Avail: 10 full hkups, 12 W, 12 E (30/50 amps). 2021 rates: $45 to $50. May 15 to Oct 14. (207)282-6445, 235 New County Rd. (Route 5), Biddeford, ME 04005

SACO/OLD ORCHARD BEACH KOA **Ratings: 9/10★/9.5** (Campground) 148 Avail: 131 full hkups, 17 W, 17 E (30/50 amps). 2021 rates: $62.13 to $149.33. May 01 to Oct 15. (207)282-0502, 814 Portland Rd., Saco, ME 04072

SANFORD — E1 *York*

APACHE CAMPGROUND
good sam park **Ratings: 8.5/9★/9** (Campground) Avail: 20 full hkups (30/50 amps). 2021 rates: $45 to $50. May 01 to Sep 30. (207)324-5652, 165 Bernier Rd, Sanford, ME 04073

SCARBOROUGH — E2 *Cumberland*

BAYLEY'S CAMPING RESORT **Ratings: 8.5/9.5★/9.5** (Campground) 537 Avail: 512 full hkups, 25 W, 25 E (30/50 amps). 2021 rates: $40 to $106. Apr 27 to Oct 14. (207)883-6043, 275 Pine Point Rd., Scarborough, ME 04074

WASSAMKI SPRINGS CAMPGROUND
good sam park **Ratings: 8.5/9★/9.5** (Campground) From Jct I-95 (Exit 46) & Hwy 22: Go 3 mi W on Hwy 22, then 1/4 mi N on Saco St (L). **FAC:** paved/gravel rds. (265 spaces). 165 Avail: 45 grass, 120 dirt, 22 pull-thrus, (30x60), back-ins (30x45), 135 full hkups, 30 W, 30 E (30/50 amps), seasonal sites, cable, WiFi @ sites, tent sites, dump, mobile sewer, laundry, groc, LP gas, fire rings, firewood, controlled access. **REC:** Wassamki Springs Lake: swim, fishing, boating nearby, playground, rec open to public. Pet restrict (B). Partial handicap access. Big rig sites, eco-friendly. 2021 rates: $45 to $78, Military discount. May 01 to Oct 15. ATM.
(207)839-4276 Lat: 43.64687, Lon: -70.39875
56 Saco St., Scarborough, ME 04074
wassamkisprings.com
See ad this page

WILD DUCK ADULT CAMPGROUND & RV PARK **Ratings: 7.5/9.5★/8.5** (Campground) Avail: 35 full hkups (30/50 amps). 2021 rates: $35 to $75. Apr 26 to Oct 21. (207)883-4432, 39 Dunstan Landing Rd., Scarborough, ME 04074

SHIN POND — B3 *Penobscot*

SHIN POND VILLAGE CAMPGROUND & COTTAGES **Ratings: 6.5/7.5★/8** (Campground) 19 Avail: 19 W, 19 E (30/50 amps). 2021 rates: $34.99. May 01 to Oct 31. (207)528-2900, 1489 Shin Pond Rd, Mount Chase, ME 04765

SKOWHEGAN — D2 *Somerset*

TWO RIVERS CAMPGROUND
good sam park **Ratings: 9/9★/9.5** (Campground) 47 Avail: 37 full hkups, 10 W, 10 E (30/50 amps). 2021 rates: $49 to $52. May 15 to Oct 15. (207)474-6482, 327 Canaan Rd., Skowhegan, ME 04976

SOUTHWEST HARBOR — D4 *Hancock*

ACADIA/SEAWALL (Public National Park) From jct SR-102 & SR-102A: Go 5 mi S on SR-102A (R). 60 Avail. 2021 rates: $30. May 20 to Sep 30. (207)244-3600

SMUGGLER'S DEN CAMPGROUND **Ratings: 8/8★/9** (Campground) 82 Avail: 47 full hkups, 10 W, 10 E (30/50 amps). 2021 rates: $55 to $85. May 25 to Oct 26. (207)244-3944, 20 Main St., Southwest Harbor, ME 04679

ST AGATHA — A4 *Aroostook*

LAKEVIEW CAMPING RESORT **Ratings: 7/8.5★/9** (Campground) 29 Avail: 26 full hkups, 3 W, 3 E (30/50 amps). 2021 rates: $29.95 to $36.95. May 20 to Oct 15. (207)543-6331, 9 Lakeview Dr, Saint Agatha, ME 04772

STANDISH — E1 *Cumberland*

FAMILY & FRIENDS CAMPGROUND **Ratings: 7.5/7/7.5** (Campground) 32 Avail: 21 full hkups, 11 W, 11 E (30/50 amps). 2021 rates: $39 to $60. Apr 25 to Oct 12. (207)642-2200, 140 Richville Rd., Standish, ME 04084

ME

Don't miss a thing! Check out the Table of Contents for everything the Guide has to offer.

STEEP FALLS — E1 *Cumberland*

ACRES OF WILDLIFE CAMPGROUND **Ratings: 7/8★/7.5** (Campground) 190 Avail: 40 full hkups, 150 W, 150 E (30/50 amps). 2021 rates: $60 to $81. May 01 to Oct 19. (207)675-2267, 60 Acres Of Wildlife Rd., Steep Falls, ME 04085

STRATTON — C2 *Franklin*

CATHEDRAL PINES CAMPGROUND **Ratings: 6.5/9★/9** (Campground) 73 Avail: 73 W, 73 E (30/50 amps). 2021 rates: $35 to $40. May 15 to Oct 01. (207)246-3491, 945 Arnold Trail Hwy (Rte 27), Eustis, ME 04936

SULLIVAN — D4 *Hancock*

ACADIA SEASHORE CAMPING & CABINS **Ratings: 6.5/8★/9** (Campground) 43 Avail: 7 full hkups, 36 W, 36 E (30/50 amps). 2021 rates: $48 to $55. May 15 to Oct 15. (207)233-0099, 2695 US Hwy 1, Sullivan, ME 04664

TRENTON — D3 *Hancock*

TIMBERLAND ACRES RV PARK

good sam park

Ratings: 10/9.5★/10 (Campground) From Jct of US-1 & SR-3 (in Ellsworth), E 2 mi on SR-3 (R). **FAC:** paved rds. (240 spaces). Avail: 100 all weather, 69 pull-thrus, (30x100), back-ins (30x50), 90 full hkups, 10 W, 10 E (30/50 amps), seasonal sites, WiFi @ sites, tent sites, dump, laundry, LP gas, fire rings, firewood. **REC:** pool, boating nearby, shuffleboard, playground. Pets OK. Partial handicap access. Big rig sites, eco-friendly. 2021 rates: $41 to $55, Military discount. May 11 to Oct 21.
(207)667-3600 Lat: 44.50719, Lon: -68.38911
57 Bar Harbor Rd., Trenton, ME 04605
www.timberlandacresrvpark.com
See ad page 450

UNION — D3 *Knox*

MIC MAC COVE CAMPGROUND **Ratings: 5.5/6/5.5** (Campground) 70 Avail: 70 W, 70 E (30/50 amps). 2021 rates: $35 to $40. May 01 to Oct 12. (207)785-4100, 210 Mic Mac Lane, Union, ME 04862

Do you know how to read each part of a listing? Check the How to Use This Guide in the front.

WATERFORD — D1 *Oxford*

PAPOOSE POND FAMILY CAMPGROUND AND CABINS **Ratings: 7.5/9★/8.5** (Campground) 175 Avail: 109 full hkups, 66 W, 66 E (20/30 amps). 2021 rates: $46 to $115. May 19 to Oct 14. (207)583-4470, 700 Norway Rd., Waterford, ME 04088

WELD — D2 *Franklin*

MT BLUE (Public State Park) From town: Go 3 mi NW on SR-142, then 3-1/2 mi S on West Rd (L). 136 Avail. 2021 rates: $20 to $30. May 15 to Oct 01. (207)585-2347

WELLS — E1 *York*

BEACH ACRES Ratings: 7/8.5★/7.5 (RV Park) 45 Avail: 5 full hkups, 40 W, 40 E (30/50 amps). 2021 rates: $49.05 to $58.86. May 25 to Sep 15. (207)646-5612, 76 Eldridge Rd., Wells, ME 04090

GREGOIRE'S CAMPGROUND **Ratings: 5.5/7.5/8** (Campground) 68 Avail: 40 full hkups, 28 W, 28 E (30/50 amps). 2021 rates: $42 to $50. May 15 to Sep 15. (207)646-3711, 697 Sanford Rd., Wells, ME 04090

OCEAN VIEW COTTAGES & CAMPGROUND **Ratings: 8.5/8.5★/7.5** (Campground) 48 Avail: 22 full hkups, 26 W, 26 E (30/50 amps). 2021 rates: $59 to $79. May 01 to Oct 10. (207)646-3308, 84 Harbor Rd., Wells, ME 04090

RIVERSIDE PARK CAMPGROUND **Ratings: 7/6/7.5** (Campground) Avail: 27 full hkups (30/50 amps). 2021 rates: $45 to $57. May 10 to Oct 15. (207)646-3145, 2295 Post Rd. (US-1), Wells, ME 04090

SEA-VU CAMPGROUND

Ratings: 9.5/10★/9.5 (Campground) From Jct of ME Tpke & Rte 109 (exit 19 Wells-Sanford), E 1.5 mi on Rte 109 to US-1, N 0.4 mi (R). **FAC:** paved rds. (229 spaces). 64 Avail: 54 gravel, 10 grass, back-ins (40x60), 64 full hkups (30/50 amps), seasonal sites, cable, WiFi @ sites, tent sites, dump, laundry, groc, LP gas, fire rings, firewood, controlled access. **REC:** heated pool, wading pool, boating nearby, playground, rec open to public. Pet restrict (Q). Partial handicap access. Big rig sites, eco-friendly. 2021 rates: $65 to $90. May 10 to Oct 14.
(207)646-7732 Lat: 43.32695, Lon: -70.57598
1733 Post Rd., Wells, ME 04090
sea-vucampground.com
See ad this page

SEA-VU WEST **Ratings: 9.5/9.5★/9.5** (Campground) Avail: 45 full hkups (30/50 amps). 2021 rates: $53 to $84. May 06 to Oct 12. (207)646-0785, 23 College Dr., Wells, ME 04090

STADIG CAMPGROUND **Ratings: 5.5/7/7.5** (Campground) 85 Avail: 7 full hkups, 26 W, 18 E (20/30 amps). 2021 rates: $33 to $45. May 24 to Oct 15. (207)646-2298, 146 Bypass Rd, Wells, ME 04090

WELLS BEACH RESORT

Ratings: 10/10★/10 (RV Park) From Jct of ME Tpke (I-95) & Rte 109 (exit 19, Wells-Sanford), E 1.5 mi on Rte 109 to US-1, S 1.4 mi (R). **FAC:** paved rds. (231 spaces). Avail: 200 all weather, 100 pull-thrus, (30x65), back-ins (30x65), 200 full hkups (30/50 amps), seasonal sites, cable, WiFi @ sites, tent sites, dump, laundry, groc, fire rings, controlled access. **REC:** heated pool, boating nearby, playground. Pet restrict (Q). Partial handicap access. Big rig sites, eco-friendly. 2021 rates: $63 to $99. May 15 to Oct 15.
(207)646-7570 Lat: 43.30372, Lon: -70.58595
1000 Post Rd. - US Route 1, Wells, ME 04090
wellsbeach.com
See ad opposite page, 447

WEST BETHEL — D1 *Oxford*

PLEASANT RIVER CAMPGROUND **Ratings: 7.5/8★/8.5** (Campground) 65 Avail: 20 full hkups, 45 W, 45 E (30/50 amps). 2021 rates: $42 to $48. May 01 to Oct 31. (207)836-2000, 800 West Bethel Rd., West Bethel, ME 04286

Check out 10/10/10 Good Sam Parks on the Good Sam Park page.*

RV SPACE-SAVING TIP: Use a hook-and-loop fastener to keep remote controls and cell phones corralled in one location. These fasteners can also be utilized when hanging hoses or other long, burdensome items that take up a lot of storage space.

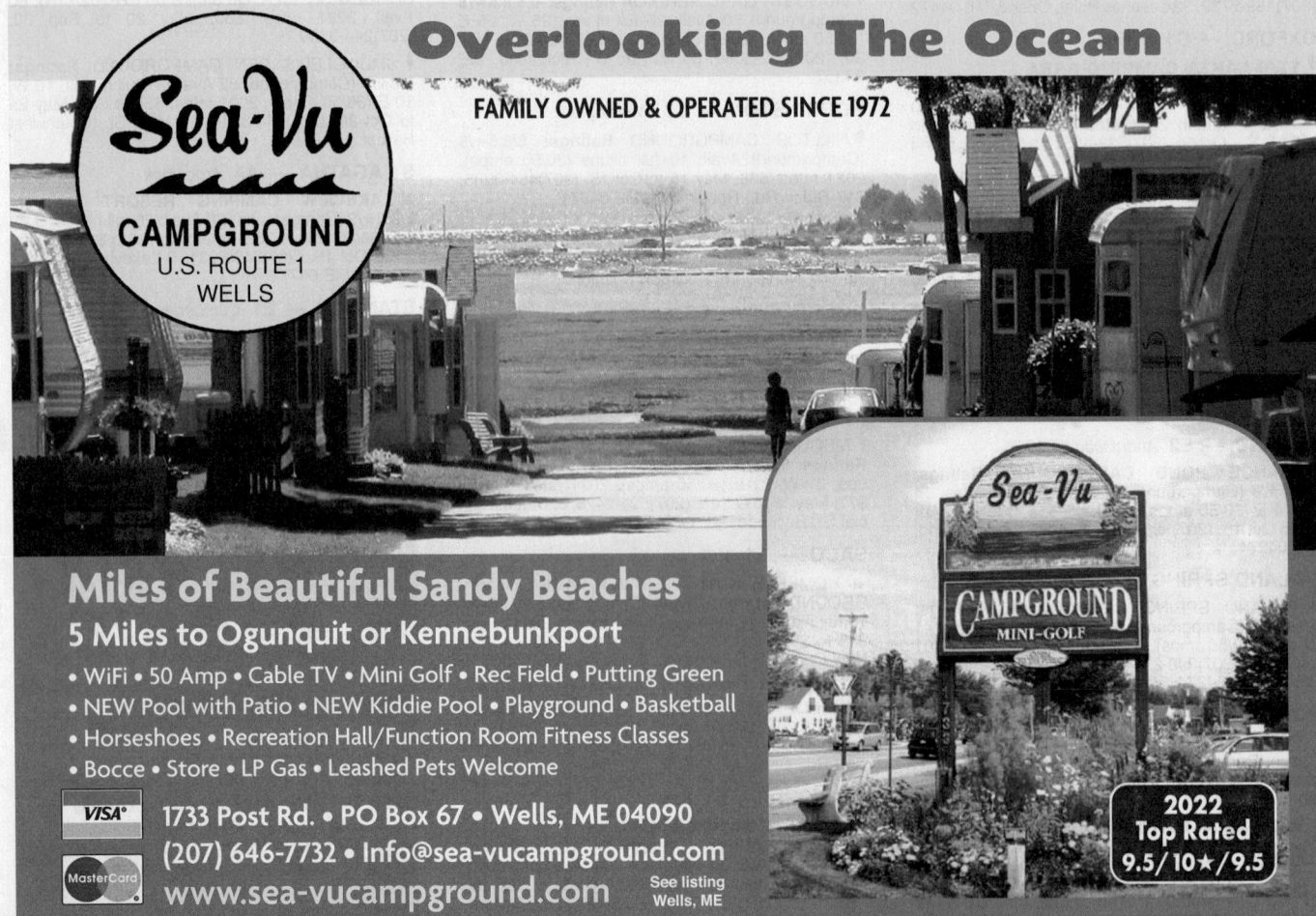

WINDHAM — E2 *Cumberland*

Travel Services

CAMPING WORLD OF WINDHAM As the nation's largest retailer of RV supplies, accessories, services and new and used RVs, Camping World is committed to making your total RV experience better. **SERVICES:** restrooms. RV Sales. RV supplies, RV accessible. Hours: 9am - 6pm.
(844)684-0849 Lat: 43.80869, Lon: -70.41682
480 Roosevelt Trail, Windham, ME 04062
rv.campingworld.com

WINTHROP — D2 *Kennebec*

AUGUSTA-WEST LAKESIDE KAMPGROUND
Ratings: 8/9.5★/8.5 (Campground) 42 Avail: 7 full hkups, 35 W, 35 E (30/50 amps). 2021 rates: $39 to $47.50. May 15 to Oct 15. (207)377-9993, 183 Holmes Brook Ln, Winthrop, ME 04364

MORE TO LIFE CAMPGROUND **Ratings: 7/8.5★/7** (Campground) 23 Avail: 23 W, 23 E (20/30 amps). 2021 rates: $40. May 15 to Oct 15. (207)395-4908, 48 Lady Slipper Ln., Winthrop, ME 04364

WISCASSET — E2 *Lincoln*

CHEWONKI CAMPGROUND **Ratings: 6.5/8.5★/8** (Campground) 41 Avail: 14 full hkups, 12 W, 12 E (30/50 amps). 2021 rates: $58 to $92. May 15 to Oct 15. (207)882-7426, 235 Chewonki Neck Rd, Wiscasset, ME 04578

YORK BEACH — F1 *York*

YORK BEACH CAMPER PARK Ratings: 7/8★/7.5 (Campground) 39 Avail: 34 full hkups, 5 W, 5 E (30/50 amps). 2021 rates: $49. May 22 to Oct 15. (207)363-1343, 11 Cappy's Ln., York Beach, ME 03910

YORK HARBOR — F1 *York*

LIBBY'S OCEANSIDE CAMP
Ratings: 8/10★/8 (RV Park) From Jct of I-95 & The York's Exit 7, E 0.3 mi on connector rd to US-1, S 0.3 mi to Rte 1A, N 3 mi (R).
FAC: paved rds. (85 spaces). 43 Avail: 2 paved, 41 grass, 12 pull-thrus, (20x65), back-ins (20x50), 43 full hkups (30/50 amps), seasonal sites, cable, WiFi @ sites, laundry, fire rings, firewood. **REC:** Atlantic Ocean: swim, fishing, boating nearby. Pets OK. Partial handicap access. No tents, eco-friendly. 2021 rates: $65 to $118. May 15 to Oct 15.
(207)363-4171 Lat: 43.14707, Lon: -70.62620
725 York St., York, ME 03909
libbysoceancamping.com
See ad this page

RV Generator Care Tips: Don't forget to clean out the spark arrestor (every 50 hours for gas or propane -150 hours for diesel). Don't forget to exercise your generator regularly. Long dormancy of any motor-driven machine can lead to problems. Even if you don't need it, run it with a load from time to time. Don't shut down the generator while it's still under a heavy load. Always turn off the loads and allow it to run for 3 minutes or so to even out the heat and start to cool down. Don't start your generator with a load already present. Allow the genset to stabilize and add the loads one at a time. Air conditioners tend to do this for you as they are equipped with delayed starting sequence modules. If your unit is AGS (Automatic Generator Start) equipped, don't set the low battery start setting too high. Generally, this setting will be at around 11.8 volts to equal a rested state battery level of 50% discharged of 12.2 VDC or specific gravity of 1.190. Don't operate your generator while driving on a gravel road or parking lot if you can avoid it. The cooling fan air flow often causes an abundance of dust that gets ingested into the air intake filter. If you care for and look after your generator, it will be there when you need it for years to come.

The Good Sam Extended Service Plan is mechanical breakdown insurance that goes above and beyond a manufacturer's RV warranty to protect RVers from the high costs associated with a mechanical breakdown. Get a FREE Quote at GoodSamESP.com

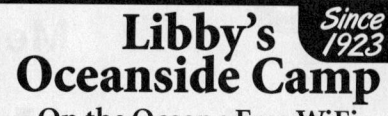

ME

Getty Images/iStockphoto

YOU ARE HERE

Maryland

DID YOU KNOW?

With two of the nation's oldest train stations in Mount Clare and Ellicott City, Baltimore is considered the cradle of U.S. railroading.

You may be surprised when you find out about all the fun you can have in the Old Line State. Maryland prides itself as being "America in Miniature," boasting a diverse slate of landscapes from tall mountains to beautiful coasts.

Baltimore Brims With Fun

Renowned as the place where the "Star Spangled Banner" was penned in 1814, Baltimore preserves history on the Chesapeake Bay. The Baltimore Harbor is the epicenter, with stores and restaurants set against a maritime backdrop. Nearby, Fells Point has a more historic feel, complete with cobblestone streets and colorful buildings. Down the Patapsco River, Fort McHenry showcases the region's birthplace of the national anthem. Dining on crab legs or crab soup is a must while in Maryland.

Wild Horses Roam Here

Come to Assateague Island National Seashore if you want to see herds of wild equines. A band of feral horses, possibly survivors from a long-ago shipwreck, are the top attraction, but there's so much more to explore. Hit the bike trails for seaside views, as you watch for ponies at play. Canoe or kayak along the coast, or try your hand at crabbing, clamming or surf fishing for a fresh taste of Maryland.

Abundant Beaches

Maryland has a beach for you. Ocean City is the place to go to combine your time at the shore with a side of fun. Grab a stick of cotton candy or take a ride to the top of the Ferris wheel for a bird's eye view of the sapphire waters.

Cascades on Display

Take a jaunt to the northwest corner of Maryland to see the spectacular Swallow Falls State Park. Here, the Youghiogheny River plunges over a 53-foot drop, making it one of the state's most breathtaking sites.

Maryland Crab Cakes

Unlike other crab cakes, the Maryland variety doesn't contain a lot of filler. Instead, it's loaded with Old Bay seasoning and thick chunks of blue crab meat. From sauteed to broiled, boardwalk eateries and gourmet restaurants cook these tasty morsels in many ways, but the result is always the same: edges crisped to perfection with tender, meaty filling.

VISITOR CENTER

TIME ZONE
Eastern Standard

ROAD & HIGHWAY INFORMATION
410-582-5605
chart.state.md.us

FISHING & HUNTING INFORMATION
877-620-8DNR
dnr.maryland.gov

BOATING INFORMATION
877-620-8DNR
dnr.maryland.gov/Boating

NATIONAL PARKS
nps.gov/md

STATE PARKS
dnr.maryland.gov/publiclands

TOURISM INFORMATION
Maryland Office of Tourism
800-543-1036
visitmaryland.org

TOP TOURISM ATTRACTIONS
1) Baltimore Inner Harbor
2) Ocean City Boardwalk
3) Assateague Island National Seashore

MAJOR CITIES
Baltimore, Columbia, Germantown, Silver Spring, Waldorf, Annapolis (capital)

good sam park Featured Good Sam Parks

MARYLAND

When you stay with Good Sam, you can expect the highest degree of cleanliness and friendliness, and better yet, you get **10% off** overnight campground fees.

If you're not already a Good Sam member you can purchase your membership at one of these locations:

COLLEGE PARK
Cherry Hill Park

NANTICOKE
Roaring Point Waterfront Campground

WOODBINE
Ramblin' Pines Family Campground & RV Park

Getty Images/iStockphoto

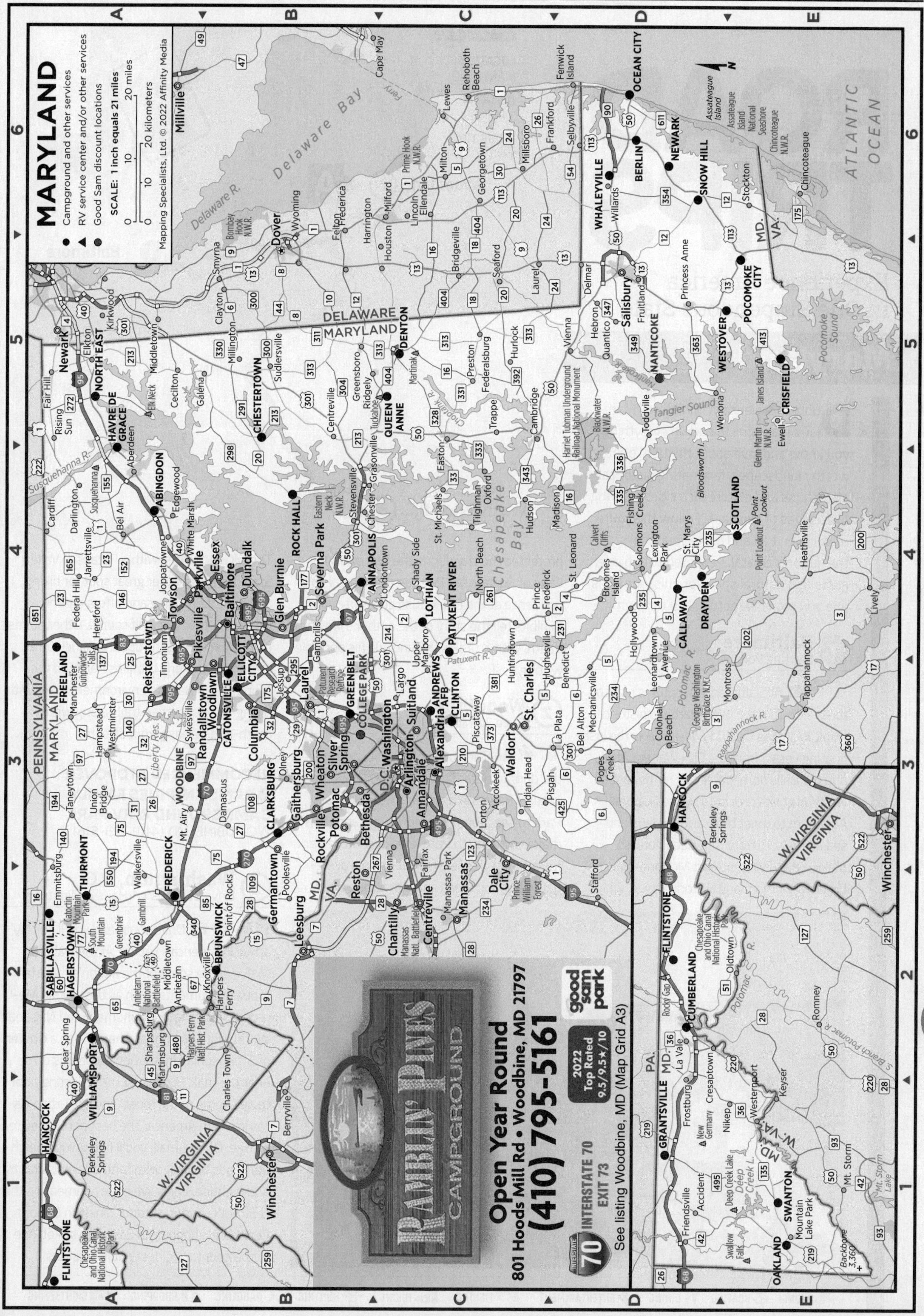
MARYLAND
Campground and other services
RV service center and/or other services
Good Sam discount locations
SCALE: 1 inch equals 21 miles
0 10 20 miles
0 10 20 kilometers
Mapping Specialists, Ltd. © 2022 Affinity Media
Ramblin' Pines Campground
Open Year Round
801 Hoods Mill Rd • Woodbine, MD 21797
(410) 795-5161
2022 Top Rated 9.5/9.5★/10
good sam park
Interstate 70 Exit 73
See listing Woodbine, MD (Map Grid A3)
MD

ROAD TRIPS

Experience America in One Stupendous State

Maryland

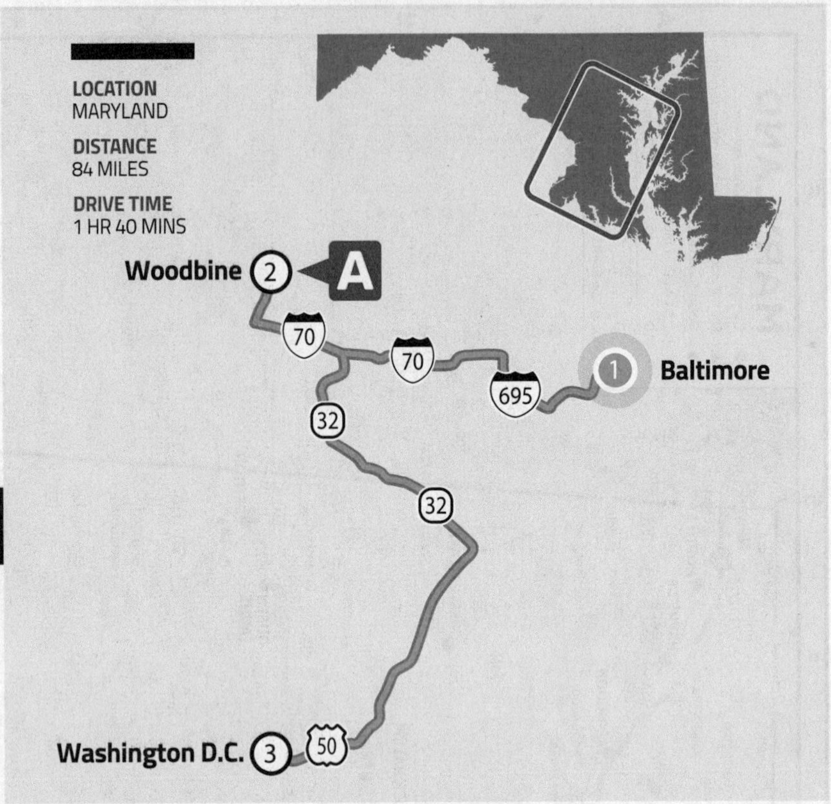

Dubbed "America in Miniature," Maryland manages to pack in everything you know and love about the USA: photo-worthy landscapes, fascinating historical attractions and culture-rich cities catering to all types of travelers. Follow this route to uncover it all and make your final stop the nation's capital. Peppered with hidden gems and natural splendor, this journey is one you won't want to speed through.

1 Baltimore
Starting Point

All Baltimore adventures start by the water. Tour the Inner Harbor's historic ships, including the *USS Constellation*, the last floating vessel from the Civil War era. Next, ride the Baltimore Water Taxi for fantastic waterfront views or stop by the National Aquarium to meet thousands of land and sea animals. History runs deep here, so make sure to visit the Fort McHenry National Monument and Historic Shrine, which protected the city during the War of 1812. Fans of Edgar Allan Poe can also visit his old residence at the Poe House and Museum. Exhibits tell the story of the author's life and death, with artifacts that include his portable writing desk.

2 Woodbine
Drive 32 Miles • 36 Minutes

This rural community opens the door to rustic landscapes and abundant nature. Traverse the loop trail in Gillis Falls Park to see blooming wildflowers and then make your way to Patuxent River State Park for catch-and-release trout fishing, designated hunting areas and equestrian trails. The McKeldin Area within Patapsco Valley State Park is another great spot for hiking and mountain biking and offers amenities like an 18-hole disc golf course. Other points of interest nearby include the Agricultural History Farm Park, Watkins Park and the Morgan Run Natural Environment Area, with hiking and equestrian trails along with a catch-and-release trout stream.

RECOMMENDED STOPOVER
A RAMBLIN' PINES FAMILY CAMPGROUND & RV PARK
WOODBINE, MD (410) 795-5161

3 Washington, D.C.
Drive 52 Miles • 1 Hour, 4 Minutes

Drive south and you'll quickly arrive in America's capital. At the National Mall, admire some of the nation's most famous monuments, such as the Lincoln Memorial, Washington Monument and National World War II Memorial. There's also a cluster of Smithsonian Institution museums on or near the mall. Hike along the reflecting pool to see some of the most amazing urban vistas in North America. The best part? They're all free. Off the mall, you'll find unique neighborhoods buzzing with fantastic restaurants and nightlife. Enjoy live entertainment on the U Street Corridor, outdoor dining in Dupont Circle, and shopping in Eastern Market, one of the country's oldest public markets.

Getty Images/iStockphoto

BIKING · BOATING · DINING · ENTERTAINMENT · FISHING · HIKING · HUNTING · PADDLING · SHOPPING · SIGHTSEEING

Maryland SPOTLIGHTS

Taking the Ultimate Americana Vacation

Find lots of adventure on the banks of the Chesapeake and in lush western forests. Watch cadets transform into officers at the U.S. Naval Academy in Annapolis and get a front-row seat to D.C. happenings at College Park.

BOATS SHOW OFF AT THE CITY DOCK TURNING BASIN, CALLED "EGO ALLEY."

Located in the heart of Historic Annapolis, City Dock is a popular spot for boaters.

Getty Images/iStockphoto

Annapolis

Known as the home of the U.S. Naval Academy, Annapolis has its roots in a Puritanical settlement in the 1600s. Over the centuries, the city has evolved into a cutting-edge center of maritime excellence and home to trendy neighborhoods.

Where River Meets Bay

Annapolis was founded in an ideal location: The point where the Severn River empties out into the Chesapeake Bay. With colorful buildings overlooking the waterfront, the historic downtown district is a picture-perfect place to stroll. The Annapolis City Dock offers restaurants and shops.

Cadets and Currents

America's early leaders realized the importance of a strong navy, and Annapolis, because of its location on the water, was chosen as the site for U.S. Naval Academy. This institution dates to 1845 and visitors will find sites from a time when the grounds served as a fort, as well as several buildings utilized by today's cadets.

Baltimore

Known as Charm City, Baltimore is home to bustling communities, historic ships, exciting museums and the Inner Harbor — the focal point of the city. Explore this Jewel of the Chesapeake with a visit to the art museum with a huge selection of Impressionist paintings while harbor ships provide history lessons that span the centuries.

'O Say Can You See'

Fort McHenry National Monument and Historic Shrine is where Francis Scott Key sat during a battle in the War of 1812 and penned the Star Spangled Banner "by the rocket's red glare." Stroll the historical grounds, visit the casements and brush up on American history. Four miles to the west, the Baltimore and Ohio (B&O) Railroad Museum houses the oldest and most complete railroad collection in America.

College Park

Just a short distance from Washington, D.C., the town of College Park is an ideal base of operation for visitors planning day trips into the nation's capital.

Aviation Heritage

College Park has deep roots in the development of American aviation. The Wright Brothers established an airfield here in 1909 to conduct flight tests and later to train army pilots. Today, the College Park Aviation Museum sits on the grounds of the airfield, the world's oldest continually operating airport.

▸ **FOR MORE INFORMATION**

Maryland Tourism, 800-543-1036, www.visitmaryland.org

Visit Annapolis, 888-302-2852, www.visitannapolis.org

College Park, www.collegeparkmd.gov

Visit Baltimore, 877-225-8466, www.baltimore.org

LOCAL FAVORITE

Crab Salad

Maryland is famous for the big, juicy crabs pulled out of the Chesapeake Bay. This salad can be served alongside your favorite fresh catch, with crackers, or on a bed of salad greens.
Recipe by Rachel Woodard.

INGREDIENTS

- ☐ 1 16-oz bag coleslaw
- ☐ 8 oz fresh lump crab meat, picked and shell bits removed
- ☐ 6 slices bacon, cooked crisp and crumbled
- ☐ 6 mozzarella cheese sticks, sliced into ½-inch pieces
- ☐ 1 cup fresh shelled peas, or 1 can peas, drained
- ☐ 1 English cucumber, diced
- ☐ 1 pint cherry or grape tomatoes, halved
- ☐ 1 cup mayonnaise, not salad dressing
- ☐ 3 green onions, chopped
- ☐ 2 tsp seafood seasoning (such as Chesapeake or Old Bay)
- ☐ Salt and pepper to taste

DIRECTIONS

Mix all the ingredients together in a large bowl and serve immediately, or chill for several hours to allow the flavors to blend.

MD

Maryland

ABINGDON — A4 *Harford*

BAR HARBOR RV PARK & MARINA Ratings: 9/9★/10 (RV Park) Avail: 73 full hkups (30/50 amps). 2021 rates: $70 to $78. (410)679-0880, 4228 Birch Ave, Abingdon, MD 21009

ANDREWS AFB — C3 *Prince Georges*

MILITARY PARK JOINT BASE ANDREWS FAMCAMP (ANDREWS AFB) (Public) From Jct I-95 & Exit 11A S 0.25 mi on exit rd, SE 0.5 mi on PA Ave, R on Suitland Pkwy 400 yds (R). Avail: 18 full hkups (30/50 amps). 2021 rates: $30. (301)981-3279

ANNAPOLIS — B4 *Anne Arundel*

ANNAPOLIS See also College Park, Lothian & Rock Hall.

MILITARY PARK ANNAPOLIS FAMCAMP (US NAVAL ACADEMY/ANNAPOLIS NAVAL STATION) (Public) From Hwys 450 & 648N, N 0.5 mi on 648N to Kinkald Rd (E). 14 Avail: 14 W, 14 E (30 amps). 2021 rates: $22. (410)293-9200

BALTIMORE — B4 *Baltimore*

BALTIMORE See also Abingdon, College Park, Rock Hall & Woodbine.

BERLIN — D6 *Worcester*

ASSATEAGUE NATL SEASHORE/ BAYSIDE
(Public National Park) From jct US-50 & SR-611: Go 9 mi SE on SR-611 (R). **FAC:** paved rds. Avail: 49 paved, back-ins (15x30), tent sites, pit toilets, dump, fire rings. **REC:** Atlantic Ocean: swim, boating nearby, rec open to public. Pets OK. Partial handicap access, 14 day max stay. 2021 rates: $30.
(410)641-3030 Lat: 38.20509, Lon: -75.15401
7206 National Seashore Ln PO Box 38, Berlin, MD 21811
www.nps.gov

ASSATEAGUE NATL SEASHORE/OCEANSIDE (Public National Park) From jct US-50 & SR-611: Go 9 mi SE on SR-611 (R). 104 Avail: Pit toilets. 2021 rates: $30. May 15 to Oct 01. (410)641-3030

BRUNSWICK — B2 *Frederick*

BRUNSWICK FAMILY CAMPGROUND **Ratings: 6.5/7.5★/9** (Campground) 48 Avail: 3 full hkups, 45 W, 45 E (30/50 amps). 2021 rates: $49.50 to $65. Mar 25 to Nov 01. (301)834-9952, 40 Canal Towpath Road, Brunswick, MD 21716

CALLAWAY — D4 *St Mary's*

TAKE-IT-EASY CAMPGROUND **Ratings: 7.5/8★/7.5** (Campground) 160 Avail: 114 full hkups, 46 W, 46 E (30/50 amps). 2021 rates: $55 to $65. (301)994-0494, 45285 Take-It-Easy Ranch Rd, Callaway, MD 20620

CATONSVILLE — B3 *Baltimore*

PATAPSCO VALLEY/HILTON AREA (Public State Park) From jct I-695 (exit 13) & Hwy 144 (Frederick Rd): Go 3/4 mi W on Hwy 144, then 2 mi S on Hilton Ave. 12 Avail. 2021 rates: $20 to $25. (410)461-5005

CHESTERTOWN — B5 *Kent*

DUCKNECK CAMPGROUND **Ratings: 6/8★/6.5** (Campground) Avail: 37 full hkups (30/50 amps). 2021 rates: $65 to $80. Apr 15 to Nov 20. (410)343-9072, 500 Double Creek Point Rd, Chestertown, MD 21620

CLARKSBURG — B3 *Montgomery*

LITTLE BENNETT CAMPGROUND (Public) From Jct of I-270 & SR-121 (exit 18) (Clarksburg), NE 0.6 mi on SR-121 (Stringtown Rd) to SR-355 (Fredrick Rd), N 0.9 mi (R). Avail: 22 full hkups (30/50 amps). 2021 rates: $55 to $66. Mar 29 to Oct 31. (301)528-3430

CLINTON — C3 *Prince Georges*

L F COSCA REGIONAL PARK (PRINCE GEORGE'S COUNTY PARK) (Public) From Jct of I-95 & SR-5 (exit 7A), S 4 mi on SR-5 to SR-223, W 0.7 mi to Brandywine Rd, S 0.9 mi to Thrift Rd, W 1.1 mi (E). 25 Avail: 25 W, 25 E (20 amps). 2021 rates: $12 to $23. (301)868-1397

COLLEGE PARK — B3 *Prince Georges*

CHERRY HILL PARK
good sam park
Ratings: 10/10★/9.5 (RV Park) Avail: 350 full hkups (30/50 amps). 2021 rates: $77 to $119. (301)937-7116, 9800 Cherry Hill Rd, College Park, MD 20740

CRISFIELD — E5 *Somerset*

JANES ISLAND (Public State Park) From town, NE 2 mi on SR-358 (L). Avail: 49 E (30 amps). 2021 rates: $21.49 to $30. Mar 27 to Nov 29. (410)968-1565

CUMBERLAND — D2 *Allegany*

GREEN RIDGE STATE FOREST (Public State Park) From town, E 20 mi on I-68 to Exit 64 (R). Primitive camping only. 100 Avail: Pit toilets. 2021 rates: $10. (301)478-3124

DENTON — C5 *Caroline*

MARTINAK (Public State Park) From town, E 2 mi on SR-404 to Deep Shore Rd, S 1 mi (L). Avail: 30 E (20/30 amps). 2021 rates: $18.49 to $26.49. Mar 27 to Nov 29. (410)820-1668

DRAYDEN — D4 *St Mary's*

DENNIS POINT MARINA & CAMPGROUND **Ratings: 6/8.5★/7** (Campground) 19 Avail: 19 W, 19 E (30/50 amps). 2021 rates: $50 to $60. Mar 15 to Nov 15. (301)994-2288, 46555 Dennis Point Way, Drayden, MD 20630

ELLICOTT CITY — B3 *Howard*

PATAPSCO VALLEY/HOLLOFIELD AREA (Public State Park) From Jct of I-695 & Rte 40, W 3 mi on Rte 40 (R). Avail: 30 E (20 amps). 2021 rates: $20 to $25. (410)461-5005

FLINTSTONE — A1 *Allegany*

ROCKY GAP (Public State Park) From Jct of I-68 (Exit 50) N 0.7 mi to Pleasant Valley Rd (rt turn), NE 1.7 mi to Campers Hill Rd (L). Avail: 30 E (30 amps). 2021 rates: $25 to $30. May 01 to Dec 13. (301)722-1480

FREDERICK — A2 *Frederick*

GAMBRILL (Public State Park) From town, NW 6 mi on US-40 to Gambrill Pk Rd, N 0.5 mi to park entrance. Avail: 8 E. 2021 rates: $20 to $25. Apr 02 to Nov 23. (301)271-7574

FREELAND — A4 *Baltimore*

MERRY MEADOWS RECREATION FARM **Ratings: 9.5/9.5★/9.5** (Campground) 120 Avail: 110 full hkups, 5 W, 5 E (30/50 amps). 2021 rates: $58 to $70. (410)357-4088, 1523 Freeland Rd, Freeland, MD 21053

GRANTSVILLE — D1 *Garrett*

NEW GERMANY (Public State Park) From Jct of I-68 & Chestnut Ridge Rd (exit 22), S 3.5 mi on Chestnut Ridge Rd to New Germany Rd, S 2 mi, park (L). 35 Avail. 2021 rates: $16.75 to $116.75. Apr 03 to Nov 30. (301)895-5453

GREENBELT — B3 *Prince George*

GREENBELT/GREENBELT PARK CAMPGROUND (Public National Park) From I-95/495 (Capital Beltway), take exit 23 Kemilworth Ave S (Rte 201) to Greenbelt Rd E (Rte 193), E 0.25 mi (R). 174 Avail. 2021 rates: $20. (301)344-3944

HAGERSTOWN — A2 *Washington*

FORT FREDERICK (Public State Park) From town: Go 18 mi W on I-70 to exit 12, then 1 mi S on Hwy 56. 29 Avail: Pit toilets. (301)842-2155

GREENBRIER (Public State Park) From Jct of I-70 & (US-40) Exit 42, W 3 mi on US-40 (L). Steep entrance. Avail: 40 E (20 amps). 2021 rates: $21.49 to $30. Apr 01 to Oct 30. (301)791-4767

HANCOCK — A1 *Washington*

HAPPY HILLS CAMPGROUND **Ratings: 6.5/8.5★/7** (Campground) 33 Avail: 27 full hkups, 6 W, 6 E (30/50 amps). 2021 rates: $39 to $44. (301)678-7760, 12617 Seavolt Rd, Hancock, MD 21750

HAVRE DE GRACE — A4 *Harford*

SUSQUEHANNA (Public State Park) From Jct of I-95 & Rte 155 (exit 89), N 2.8 mi on Rte 155, N 1.5 mi. SH 161, E .8 mi. Avail: 6 E (20 amps). 2021 rates: $21.49 to $29.49. Apr 01 to Oct 30. (410)557-7994

LOTHIAN — C4 *Anne Arundel*

ADVENTURE BOUND WASHINGTON DC **Ratings: 8/8.5★/7.5** (Campground) 10 Avail: 10 W, 10 E (30/50 amps). 2021 rates: $45 to $73. (443)607-8609, 5381 Sands Rd, Lothian, MD 20711

NANTICOKE — D5 *Wicomico*

ROARING POINT WATERFRONT CAMPGROUND
good sam park
Ratings: 7.5/8★/8 (Campground) From Jct of US 50 Bus & Hwy 349 (in Salisbury): Go 20 mi SW on Hwy 349, then 1/4 mi W on Nanticoke Wharf Rd (L). **FAC:** gravel rds. (110 spaces). Avail: 30 grass, back-ins (50x50), 14 full hkups, 16 W, 16 E (30/50 amps), seasonal sites, WiFi @ sites, $, tent sites, dump, mobile sewer, laundry, groc, LP gas, fire rings, firewood, controlled access. **REC:** Nanticoke River/Tangier Sound: swim, fishing, kayaking/canoeing, boating nearby, playground. Pets OK. eco-friendly. 2021 rates: $40 to $75. Apr 01 to Nov 15.
(410)873-2553 Lat: 38.26168, Lon: -75.91141
2360 Nanticoke Wharf Rd, Nanticoke, MD 21840
roaringpoint.com
See ad this page

NEWARK — D6 *Worcester*

ISLAND RESORT PARK **Ratings: 8.5/8/9.5** (Campground) Avail: 126 full hkups (30/50 amps). 2021 rates: $70 to $80. Apr 01 to Dec 15. (888)641-9838, 9537 Cropper Island Rd, Newark, MD 21841

NORTH EAST — A5 *Cecil*

ELK NECK (Public State Park) From Jct of US-40 & SR-272, S 10.2 mi on SR-272 (E). Avail: 250 full hkups (30/50 amps). 2021 rates: $27.49 to $38.49. Apr 03 to Oct 26. (410)287-5333

OAKLAND — E1 *Garrett*

DEEP CREEK LAKE (Public State Park) From Jct of US-219 & Glendale Rd, NE 2 mi on Glendale Rd to State Park Rd, NW 1 mi (L). Avail: 26 E (30 amps). 2021 rates: $27.49 to $38.49. Apr 15 to Dec 15. (301)387-5563

SWALLOW FALLS (Public State Park) From town, NW 8 mi on Herrington Manor Rd (L). 65 Avail: 3 full hkups, 3 W, 3 E (30 amps). 2021 rates: $11.75 to $35. May 22 to Sep 07. (301)387-6938

OCEAN CITY — D6 *Worcester*

ASSATEAGUE (Public State Park) From jct Rte 50 & 611: Go 9 mi S on Rte 611 (R). Avail: 39 E (30 amps). 2021 rates: $27.49 to $38.49. Apr 24 to Oct 28. (410)641-2918

CASTAWAYS RV RESORT & CAMPGROUND **Ratings: 9.5/9.5★/9.5** (RV Park) Avail: 335 full hkups (30/50 amps). 2021 rates: $65 to $157. Mar 27 to Nov 01. (410)213-0097, 12550 Eagles Nest Rd, Berlin, MD 21811

FRONTIER TOWN RV RESORT & CAMPGROUND **Ratings: 9.5/10★/9.5** (Campground) 611 Avail: 524 full hkups, 87 W, 87 E (30/50 amps). 2021 rates: $60 to $200. Apr 12 to Dec 01. (800)228-5590, 8428 Stephen Decatur Hwy, Berlin, MD 21811

PATUXENT RIVER — C3 *Prince Georges*

MILITARY PARK GOOSE CREEK CAMPGROUND (PATUXENT RIVER NAVAL AIR STATION) (Public) From Jct I-95 & Exit 7A, SE on exit rd to Branch Ave S (MD-5), S 25 mi (MD-5 turns onto MD-235), SE 24 mi to NAS (L). 14 Avail: 14 W, 14 E (30 amps). 2021 rates: $15.75 to $21. Feb 01 to Oct 31. (301)342-3573

POCOMOKE CITY — E5 *Worcester*

POCOMOKE RIVER/MILBURN LANDING AREA (Public State Park) From Jct of SR-12 & SR-354, SW 7 mi on SR-354 (L). Avail: 10 E (20 amps), Pit toilets. 2021 rates: $11.75 to $24.49. (410)632-2566

QUEEN ANNE — C5 *Queen Anne*

TUCKAHOE (Public State Park) From jct Hwy 404 & Hwy 480: Go 1/10 mi N, then 5 mi N on Eveland Rd. Avail: 33 E. 2021 rates: $21.49 to $30. Mar 27 to Nov 27. (410)820-1668

ROCK HALL — B4 *Kent*

BAY SHORE CAMPGROUND **Ratings: 7.5/UI/10** (Campground) 56 Avail: 56 W, 56 E (30/50 amps). 2021 rates: $61 to $84. (410)639-7485, 4228 Eastern Neck Rd, Rock Hall, MD 21661

SABILLASVILLE — A2 *Frederick*

CATOCTIN MOUNTAIN/OWENS CREEK CAMPGROUND (Public National Park) From Jct of US-15 & MD-77, W 3 mi on MD-77 to Park Central Rd, N 4 mi to park access rd, E 1 mi (E). (Max trailer length 22ft.). 49 Avail. 2021 rates: $30. May 01 to Nov 01. (301)663-9388

SCOTLAND — E4 *St Mary's*

POINT LOOKOUT (Public State Park) From Jct of SR-235 & SR-5, S 4.7 mi on SR-5 (E). 143 Avail: 26 full hkups, 33 E (20/30 amps). 2021 rates: $25 to $35. Mar 29 to Oct 28. (301)872-5688

SNOW HILL — D6 *Worcester*

POCOMOKE RIVER/SHAD LANDING AREA (Public State Park) From town, S 4 mi on US-113 (R). Avail: 59 E (30 amps). 2021 rates: $11.75 to $27.49. (410)632-2566

SOLOMONS — D4 *Calvert*

MILITARY PARK SOLOMONS ISLAND NAVY RECREATION AREA (NRC SOLOMONS) (Public) From Beltway (295) & Exit 11A, S to 4S, S 65 mi to base (E). 298 Avail: 142 full hkups, 156 W, 156 E (20/50 amps). 2021 rates: $22 to $40. (410)326-2840

SWANTON — E1 *Garrett*

BIG RUN (Public State Park) From I-68 (exit 22): Go S on Chestnut Ridge Rd to New Germany Rd to Big Run Rd. 29 Avail: Pit toilets. (301)895-5453

THURMONT — A2 *Frederick*

CUNNINGHAM FALLS/MANOR AREA (Public State Park) From town: Go 3 mi S on US 15. Avail: 10 E. 2021 rates: $25 to $30. (301)271-7574

CUNNINGHAM FALLS/WILLIAM HOUCK (Public State Park) From town: Go 3 mi W on MD-77, then 1/2 mi S on Catoctin Hollow Rd (R). Avail: 33 E (30 amps). 2021 rates: $21.49 to $61.75. Apr 01 to Oct 30. (301)271-7574

WESTOVER — D5 *Somerset*

LAKE SOMERSET CAMPGROUND **Ratings: 8/8.5★/9.5** (Campground) Avail: 22 full hkups (30/50 amps). 2021 rates: $45. May 01 to Sep 30. (410)957-1866, 8658 Lake Somerset Ln, Westover, MD 21871

WHALEYVILLE — D6 *Worcester*

FORT WHALEY RV RESORT & CAMPGROUND **Ratings: 9.5/9.5★/9.5** (RV Park) Avail: 170 full hkups (30/50 amps). 2021 rates: $47 to $120. Mar 15 to Oct 31. (888)322-7717, 11224 Dale Road, Whaleyville, MD 21872

WILLIAMSPORT — A2 *Washington*

HAGERSTOWN/ANTIETAM BATTLEFIELD KOA **Ratings: 8.5/8.5★/7.5** (Campground) 65 Avail: 25 full hkups, 40 W, 40 E (30/50 amps). 2021 rates: $39.25 to $83.50. Mar 25 to Nov 30. (800)562-7607, 11759 Snug Harbor Lane, Williamsport, MD 21795

YOGI BEAR'S JELLYSTONE PARK CAMP-RESORT/WILLIAMSPORT **Ratings: 9/10★/9.5** (Campground) 155 Avail: 137 full hkups, 18 W, 18 E (30/50 amps). 2021 rates: $55 to $163. Apr 12 to Dec 01. (301)223-7117, 9550 Jellystone Park Way, Williamsport, MD 21795

WOODBINE — A3 *Carroll*

RAMBLIN' PINES FAMILY CAMPGROUND & RV PARK

good sam park

Ratings: 9.5/9.5★/10 (Campground) E-bnd: From Jct of I-70 & Hwy 94 (exit 73): Go 3-1/2 mi N on Hwy 94, then 2-1/4 mi E on Hoods Mill Rd (R); W-bnd: From Jct of I-70 & Hwy 97 (exit 76): Go 2-3/4 mi N on Hwy 97, (left turn) onto Hoods Mill Rd, W 1/2 mi (L).

ENJOY THE SERENITY OF PINE FOREST!

Ramblin' Pines is a family campground nestled in a quiet, peaceful wooded setting and located in the center of the Washington-Frederick-Baltimore vacation attractions. Take the metro and be in DC in 20 minutes. Open all year

FAC: paved rds. (200 spaces). 90 Avail: 3 paved, 87 gravel, 14 pull-thrus, (30x70), back-ins (30x70), 90 full hkups (30/50 amps), seasonal sites, cable, WiFi @ sites, tent sites, rentals, dump, laundry, groc, LP gas, fire rings, firewood, controlled access. **REC:** heated pool, pond, fishing, shuffleboard, playground. Pet restrict (B). Partial handicap access. Big rig sites. 2021 rates: $70, Military discount. ATM.
(410)795-5161 Lat: 39.36728, Lon: -77.02505
801 Hoods Mill Rd, Woodbine, MD 21797
ramblinpinescampground.com
See ad next page, 202, 461

Keeping pets quiet and on a leash is common courtesy. ""Pet Restrictions'' which you'll find in some listings refers to limits on size, breed or quantity of pets allowed.

MD

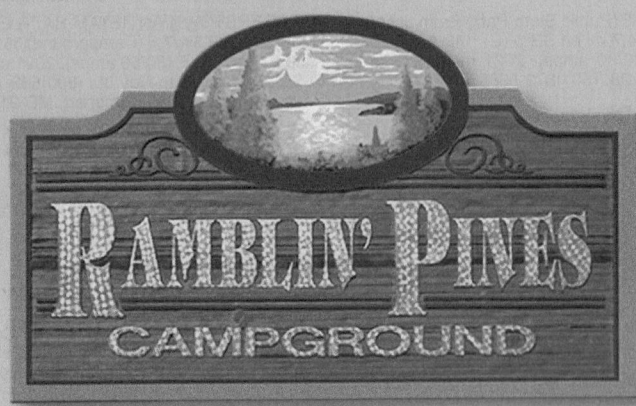

See listing Woodbine, MD

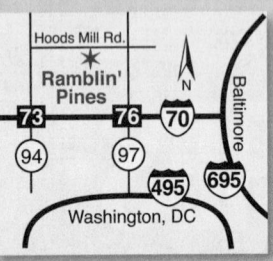

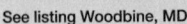

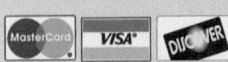

DID YOU KNOW?
Despite what we learned in school, Paul Revere never actually shouted "the British are coming!" during his famous midnight ride.
YOU ARE HERE
Getty Images/iStockphoto

Massachusetts

Once the epicenter of the American Revolution, Massachusetts is a dynamic destination that celebrates past and future. Explore a state that enshrines American history and revels in innovation in places like Boston.

Liberty Lives Here

Rocked by the upheaval of revolution and war, Boston shaped the nation from its earliest days. The 2.5-mile Freedom Trail takes visitors to historic sites hidden amid the city's rising skyscrapers, telling the story of this city's grand past while showcasing its prospering present. Grabbing a meal in the Little Italy neighborhood is not to be missed, with upscale open-air restaurants lining the streets.

Cool Cape Cod

Jutting out into the Atlantic Ocean like a hook, Cape Cod gives visitors endless possibilities for play and exploration on the sea. The slender cape is lined with ceaseless beaches and rolling sand dunes, providing epic backdrops for all forms of recreation. For a magical Cape Cod experience, hit the waters for a whale watching cruise or make an order at a lobster shack for fresh crustacean.

Wonderful Waterways

While Massachusetts' Atlantic shore draws countless visitors to the state, intrepid travelers will find equally compelling bodies of water inland in places like Berkshire hills. Anglers can enjoy trout fishing in cool mountain creeks of bass fishing in the large ponds that dot the state.

Bay State Rambling

Did you know that 90 miles of the epic Appalachian Trail bisect the Bay State? Part of the trail passes through Mount Greylock State Reservation in the state's northwest corner. This scenic expanse is home to Massachusetts's highest peak and over 50 miles of trails.

Massachusetts Boston Cream Pie

Dig into a slice of Boston cream pie. Despite the name, the official state dessert actually is a two-layer cake filled with pastry cream and topped with rich chocolate icing. Make sure to try a Boston cream donut, too — foodies will point you in the direction of Donut King in Weymouth, and Union Square Donuts and Blackbird Doughnuts in Boston.

VISITOR CENTER

TIME ZONE
Eastern Standard

ROAD & HIGHWAY INFORMATION
877-623-6846
mass.gov/orgs/massachusetts-department-of-transportation

FISHING & HUNTING INFORMATION
www.mass.gov/topics/fishing-hunting

BOATING INFORMATION
508-389-7810
www.mass.gov/topics/boats-recreational-vehicles

NATIONAL PARKS
nps.gov/ma

STATE PARKS
mass.gov/visit-massachusetts-state-parks

TOURISM INFORMATION
Massachusetts Office of Travel and Tourism
800-227-MASS
massvacation.com

TOP TOURISM ATTRACTIONS
1) Boston's Freedom Trail
2) Cape Cod Beaches
3) Plymouth Rock and Plimoth Plantation

MAJOR CITIES
Boston (capital), Worcester, Springfield, Lowell, Cambridge

good sam park Featured Good Sam Parks

MASSACHUSETTS

When you stay with Good Sam, you can expect the highest degree of cleanliness and friendliness, and better yet, you get **10% off** overnight campground fees.

If you're not already a Good Sam member you can purchase your membership at one of these locations:

BELLINGHAM
Circle CG Farm Campground

BREWSTER
Shady Knoll Campground

EASTHAM
Atlantic Oaks

OAKHAM
Pine Acres Family Camping Resort

PITTSFIELD
Bonnie Brae Cabins & Campsites

ROCHESTER
Gateway To Cape Cod RV Campground

SOUTH DENNIS
Old Chatham Road RV Campground

STURBRIDGE
Pine Lake RV Resort & Cottages
Sturbridge RV Resort

VINEYARD HAVEN
Martha's Vineyard Family Campground

WALES
Oak Haven Family Campground

10/10★/10 GOOD SAM PARKS

OAKHAM
Pine Acres Family Camping Resort
(508)882-9509

STURBRIDGE
Pine Lake RV Resort & Cottages
(508)347-9570

What's This?

An RV park with a 10/10★/10 rating has scored perfect grades in amenities, cleanliness and appearance ("See Understanding the Campground Rating System" on pages 8 and 9 for an explanation of the trusted Good Sam Rating System). Stay in a 10/10★/10 park on your next trip for a nearly flawless camping experience.

Getty Images/iStockphoto

ROAD TRIPS

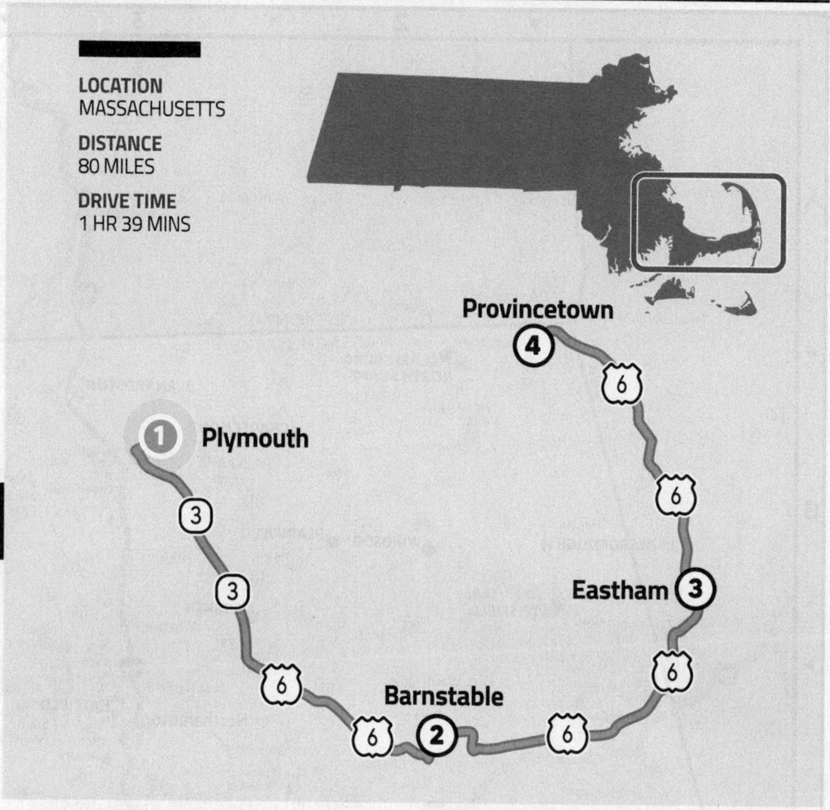

Make Your Cape Cod Escape

Massachusetts

Escape to a place settled by pilgrims and inhabited by Kennedys. Cape Cod is a 65-mile long, sandy peninsula off eastern Massachusetts. Ranging from 1- to 20-miles wide, it boasts over 400 miles of ocean shoreline. This is a prized travel and vacation spot for campers from across the country who love its charming small towns, salt air, extensive beaches, historic pilgrim settlements, art galleries and simple walks on the shore.

1 Plymouth
Starting Point

Pilgrims settled here and made history. Hike or bike many miles of trails, some even for horse riding. Enjoy lots of quiet forest lands plus excellent swimming and fishing. While there, time-travel to the 17th century at Plimouth Plantation and see what life was like for the Pilgrims. Stroll a reconstructed English village and a Wampanoag home site; see the Plimouth Grist Mill and the *Mayflower II.*

2 Barnstable
Drive 32 miles ▪ 37 minutes

Grab a paddle and explore the world of kayaking. The crew at Great Marsh Kayak Tours gets you up to speed quickly on safety and paddling skills. Choose from several interesting tours — beginners love the three-hour Tidal Tour. Chill out in this serene, natural habitat for birds like great blue herons, terns, snowy egrets, and mammals like deer, coyote and fox. While in the area, visit the John F. Kennedy Memorial in nearby Hyannis. The world changed when President Kennedy was assassinated in 1963; take the time to pay your respects to one of America's most-respected leaders.

3 Eastham
Drive 25 miles ▪ 30 minutes

Explore 40 remarkable miles that constitute the Cape Cod National Seashore. Beachcomb endlessly, go hiking, paddling, lighthouse spotting, cranberry-bog exploring or touring with a Park Ranger. Hunt, fish and — surprisingly — you can drive on the beach (restrictions apply). Brought your bike? Traverse the Cape Cod Rail Trail. Developers turned these 25 miles of old railroad right-of-way into a beautifully paved, easy-to-pedal bike touring trail.

4 Provincetown
Drive 23 miles ▪ 32 minutes

The pilgrims landed in this area briefly before landing in Plymouth. While in town, check out the Pilgrim Monument and Provincetown Museum. Construction began in 1907 with President Teddy Roosevelt laying the cornerstone. Today, millions have climbed the 252-foot monument. Learn much more history at the renowned Provincetown Museum.

Getty Images/iStockphoto

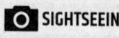

BIKING BOATING DINING ENTERTAINMENT FISHING HIKING HUNTING PADDLING SHOPPING SIGHTSEEING

MA

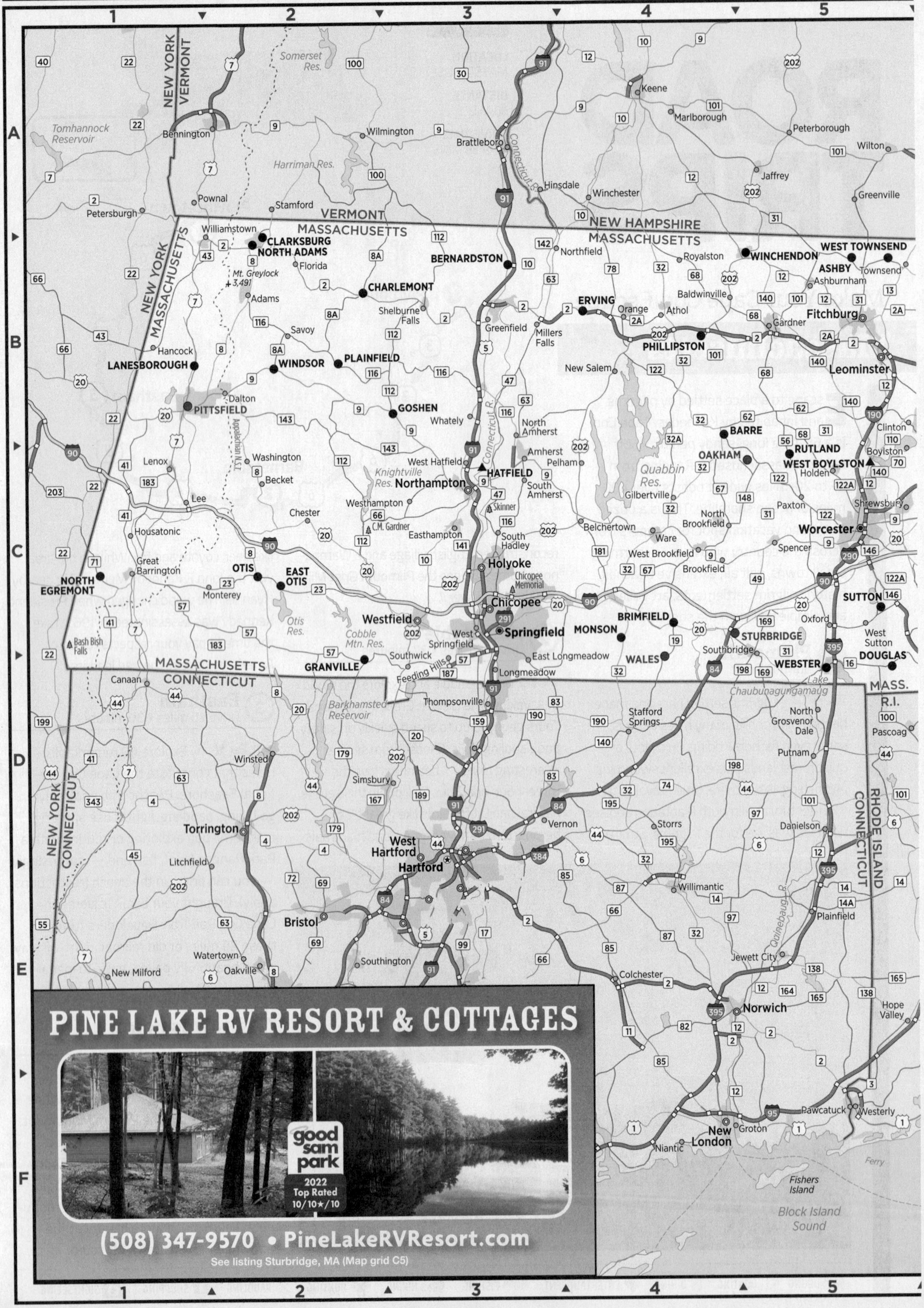
NEW YORK
VERMONT
MASSACHUSETTS
NEW HAMPSHIRE
CONNECTICUT
RHODE ISLAND
R.I.
MASS.
Somerset Res.
Tomhannock Reservoir
Harriman Res.
Bennington
Wilmington
Brattleboro
Keene
Marlborough
Peterborough
Wilton
Jaffrey
Greenville
Hinsdale
Winchester
Pownal
Stamford
Petersburgh
Williamstown
CLARKSBURG
NORTH ADAMS
Mt. Greylock 3,491
Florida
Adams
CHARLEMONT
Shelburne Falls
Savoy
BERNARDSTON
Northfield
Greenfield
Millers Falls
ERVING
Orange
Athol
Royalston
WINCHENDON
WEST TOWNSEND
ASHBY
Townsend
Ashburnham
Baldwinville
Fitchburg
Gardner
PHILLIPSTON
Leominster
New Salem
Hancock
LANESBOROUGH
WINDSOR
PLAINFIELD
Dalton
PITTSFIELD
GOSHEN
Whately
North Amherst
Amherst
Pelham
BARRE
RUTLAND
OAKHAM
WEST BOYLSTON
Clinton
Boylston
Holden
Quabbin Res.
Gilbertville
Lenox
Washington
Becket
Lee
West Hatfield
HATFIELD
Knightville Res.
Northampton
Westhampton
Chester
C.M. Gardner
Easthampton
Skinner
South Amherst
South Hadley
Belchertown
Ware
North Brookfield
Paxton
Shrewsbury
Worcester
Spencer
West Brookfield
Brookfield
Housatonic
Great Barrington
NORTH EGREMONT
OTIS
EAST OTIS
Monterey
Otis Res.
Holyoke
Chicopee Memorial
Chicopee
Westfield
West Springfield
Springfield
MONSON
BRIMFIELD
WALES
STURBRIDGE
Southbridge
Oxford
SUTTON
West Sutton
WEBSTER
DOUGLAS
Lake Chaubunagungamaug
Bash Bish Falls
Cobble Mtn. Res.
GRANVILLE
Southwick
Feeding Hills
East Longmeadow
Longmeadow
Canaan
Barkhamsted Reservoir
Thompsonville
Stafford Springs
North Grosvenor Dale
Putnam
Pascoag
Winsted
Simsbury
Torrington
Litchfield
West Hartford
Hartford
Vernon
Storrs
Danielson
Willimantic
Plainfield
Bristol
Southington
Watertown
Oakville
New Milford
Quinebaug R.
Jewett City
Colchester
Norwich
Hope Valley
Pawcatuck
Westerly
Groton
New London
Niantic
Ferry
Fishers Island
Block Island Sound
Connecticut R.
Appalachian N.S.T.

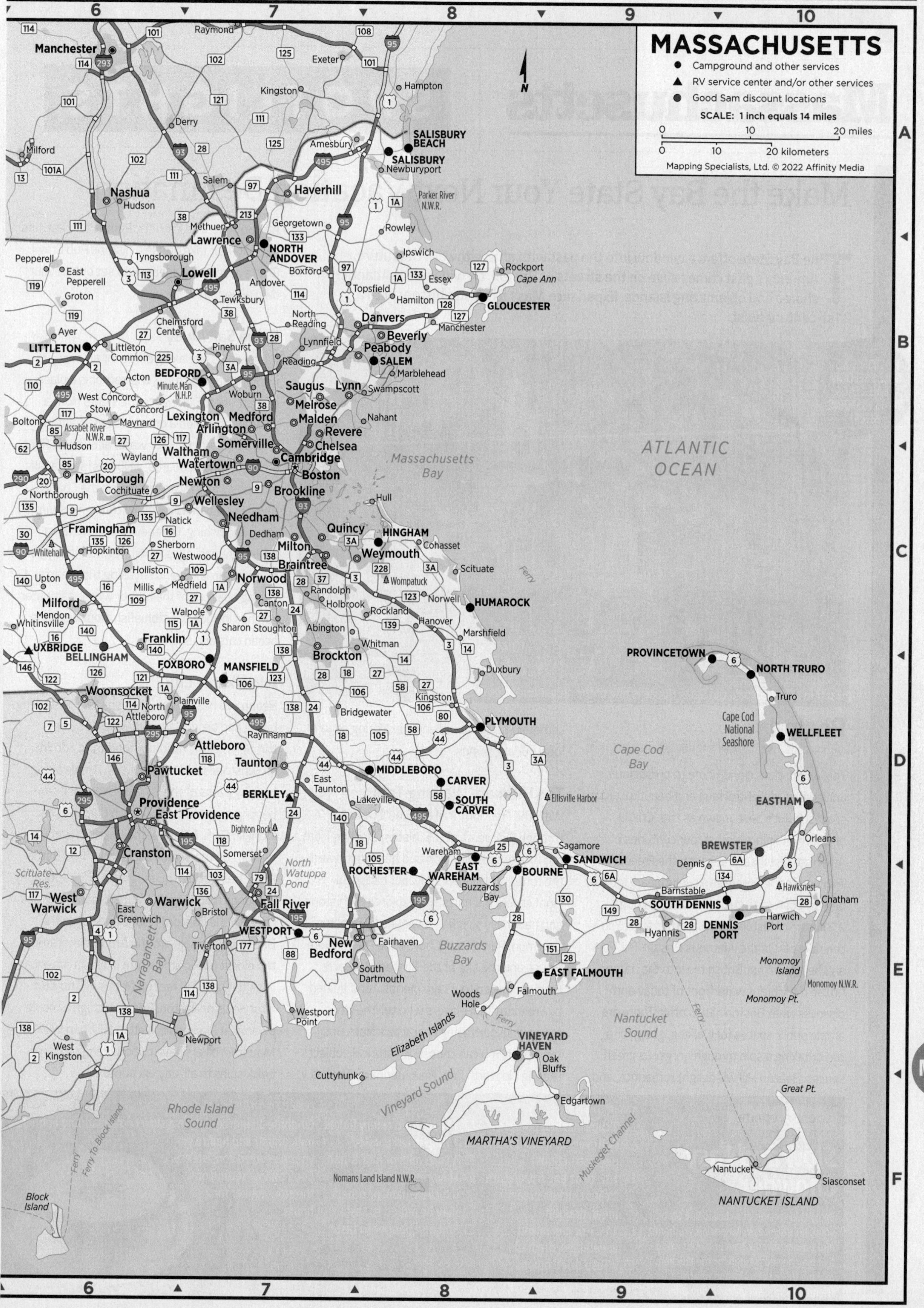
MASSACHUSETTS
Campground and other services
RV service center and/or other services
Good Sam discount locations
SCALE: 1 inch equals 14 miles
0 10 20 miles
0 10 20 kilometers
Mapping Specialists, Ltd. © 2022 Affinity Media
N
ATLANTIC OCEAN
Massachusetts Bay
Cape Cod Bay
Buzzards Bay
Nantucket Sound
Vineyard Sound
Rhode Island Sound
Narragansett Bay
Muskeget Channel
Elizabeth Islands
MARTHA'S VINEYARD
NANTUCKET ISLAND
Block Island
Ferry
Ferry To Block Island
Manchester
Raymond
Exeter
Hampton
Kingston
Derry
Milford
Nashua
Hudson
Salem
Haverhill
Amesbury
SALISBURY BEACH
SALISBURY
Newburyport
Parker River N.W.R.
Rowley
Georgetown
Methuen
Lawrence
NORTH ANDOVER
Ipswich
Pepperell
East Pepperell
Tyngsborough
Lowell
Boxford
Andover
Essex
Rockport
Cape Ann
Groton
Tewksbury
Topsfield
Hamilton
GLOUCESTER
Ayer
Chelmsford Center
North Reading
Danvers
Manchester
LITTLETON
Littleton Common
Pinehurst
Lynnfield
Beverly
Peabody
SALEM
Reading
Marblehead
BEDFORD
Acton
Minute Man N.H.P.
Saugus
Lynn
Swampscott
West Concord
Woburn
Stow
Concord
Melrose
Bolton
Maynard
Lexington
Medford
Malden
Revere
Nahant
Assabet River N.W.R.
Arlington
Hudson
Somerville
Chelsea
Wayland
Waltham
Cambridge
Watertown
Boston
Marlborough
Northborough
Cochituate
Newton
Brookline
Hull
Wellesley
Natick
Needham
Framingham
Quincy
HINGHAM
Cohasset
Sherborn
Dedham
Whitehall
Hopkinton
Westwood
Milton
Weymouth
Holliston
Braintree
Scituate
Upton
Medfield
Norwood
Wompatuck
Millis
Randolph
Norwell
HUMAROCK
Milford
Canton
Holbrook
Rockland
Mendon
Walpole
Whitinsville
Sharon
Stoughton
Abington
Hanover
Marshfield
Franklin
Whitman
UXBRIDGE
BELLINGHAM
Brockton
FOXBORO
MANSFIELD
Duxbury
Woonsocket
Kingston
North Attleboro
Plainville
Bridgewater
PLYMOUTH
Raynham
Attleboro
Taunton
Pawtucket
MIDDLEBORO
CARVER
East Taunton
BERKLEY
Lakeville
SOUTH CARVER
Providence
East Providence
Ellisville Harbor
Dighton Rock
Cranston
Somerset
Wareham
EAST WAREHAM
Sagamore
SANDWICH
ROCHESTER
BOURNE
North Watuppa Pond
Scituate Res.
West Warwick
Warwick
Bristol
Fall River
East Greenwich
WESTPORT
New Bedford
Fairhaven
Tiverton
South Dartmouth
EAST FALMOUTH
Falmouth
Woods Hole
Westport Point
Newport
West Kingston
Cuttyhunk
VINEYARD HAVEN
Oak Bluffs
Edgartown
Nomans Land Island N.W.R.
PROVINCETOWN
NORTH TRURO
Truro
Cape Cod National Seashore
WELLFLEET
EASTHAM
Orleans
BREWSTER
Dennis
Hawksnest
Barnstable
SOUTH DENNIS
Chatham
Hyannis
DENNIS PORT
Harwich Port
Monomoy Island
Monomoy N.W.R.
Monomoy Pt.
Great Pt.
Nantucket
Siasconset
MA
6
7
8
9
10
A
B
C
D
E
F

Massachusetts SPOTLIGHTS

Make the Bay State Your Next Vacation Destination

The Bay State offers a window into the past with an eye toward the future. America's past comes alive on the streets of Boston, on windswept Atlantic shores and on amazing islands. Experience Massachusetts history with a 21st-century twist.

BOSTON'S 2.5-MILE FREEDOM TRAIL LEADS TO 16 HISTORIC SITES.

Built in 1713, Boston's Old State House is one of the oldest buildings in the U.S.

Getty Images/iStockphoto

Boston

This world-class city is home to prestigious universities, delightful food and beautiful urban spaces, but it's best known as the "Cradle of Liberty." Explore almost four centuries of American history starting with the Freedom Trail where the American Revolutionary journey begins. Costumed guides lead you through 250 years of history as it all comes alive. You can take part in the infamous Boston Tea Party and help toss that British tea into the harbor. Cruise the vibrant waterfront of today and discover what Boston has to offer. There are ample public spaces for walking, going for a run or taking a spin through gorgeous green spaces. Beacon Hill will delight romantics, and cemetery buffs should enjoy exploring several local burial grounds.

The Ultimate Walking Trail

Walk the Freedom Trail and you'll traverse through 250 years of U.S. history starting from the American Revolution and heading toward the future. This indoor-outdoor historical jaunt covers 2.5 miles and explores 16 historic and nationally significant venues like Boston Common, Park Street Church, the Paul Revere House and the site of the Boston Massacre. Foundation-led tours are plentiful and guided by Freedom Trail Players who tell the city's story while portraying characters from Boston's past. You can choose a historical subject like the old North End, Revolutionary Women, African American Patriots, Pirates and Patriots to explore or take part in a historic Pub Crawl. Grab a map and guidebook to set out on your own adventure.

Come Sail Away

Whether it's a relaxing dinner or an awe-inspiring sunset cruise, the harbor is a place of memories. Experience the sights from a speedboat, gondola or swan boat. Want to take a different tack for water activities? Rent stand-up paddleboards, sailboats, sea kayaks or windsurfers for adventure on the Charles River. Local park lakes allow canoeing, swimming and fishing. Daredevils will love aqua adventure packages for whitewater rafting or a combo zip lining and kayaking trip. Charter a fishing boat out of the harbor where saltwater catches include bass, bluefish, flounder, tuna, ocean cats and sharks.

A Walkable City

Beantown has myriad open spaces for strolling, hiking and biking. Jaunt up winding streets through historic neighborhoods and admire brownstones and townhouses. Amble along walking paths of the Emerald Necklace connecting six parks from Boston Common to Franklin Park. Meander the Charles River waterfront on the 3-mile Esplanade. Trod Battle Road Trail through quiet forests and captivating wetlands following the route minutemen took to reach the Concord Bridge and battle the British. Take a spin around Arnold Arboretum, the oldest public arboretum in North America; walk the last 200 feet up Peters Hill for stunning views of Boston. Roam through a maple swamp at Roslindale Wetlands Urban Wild. Mountain bikers have options ranging from quick spins to all-day encounters.

LOCAL FAVORITE

Slow and Easy Chowder

Enjoy this version of a classic Bay State soup. It utilizes easy-to-pack ingredients, and turkey, shrimp, ham or a mild white fish may be substituted for the chicken, making this a versatile and pantry-friendly recipe. *Recipe by Peggy Oiler.*

INGREDIENTS

- ☐ 2 cups mashed potatoes (leftovers or instant made per instructions)
- ☐ 1 12-16 oz bag frozen corn
- ☐ 2 cans chicken breast meat, drained
- ☐ 1 14.5-oz can mixed vegetables, drained
- ☐ 2 Tbsp dried onions
- ☐ 1 Tbsp dried celery flakes
- ☐ 1 Tbsp dried parsley
- ☐ 4 cups milk or half & half
- ☐ Flavoring bouillon (chicken, ham, or other) may be added to taste
- ☐ Salt and pepper to taste

DIRECTIONS

Combine all ingredients in a slow cooker, adding enough milk or half and half to get your preferred consistency. Cook on low setting of the slow cooker for 2 hours.

History and Sports

Once Boston's town meeting hall where Revolutionary protests and debates occurred, today Faneuil Hall Marketplace is a cornucopia of entertainment from world-class street performers to more than 100 intriguing shops and push carts filled with locally sourced goods. Fenway Park has been home to the Boston Red Sox for more than a century. The oldest ballpark in Major League Baseball is a mecca for baseball fans. Tours provide history about the legends that played on this hallowed ground. At the Boston Tea Party Ships & Museum enjoy a multisensory experience where you can storm a ship and help dump British tea into the harbor. Griffin's Wharf offers an up-close look of life in port. And you can end your adventure with a spot of tea at Abigail's Tea Room.

Getty Images/iStockphoto

From the Boston Harborwalk, pedestrians can get unmatched views of the water and the city's skyline.

Amped-Up Festival

Boston Calling is a music fest for those who love music — not just certain genres. This multiday event hosts the biggest and best of New England's independent musical performers along with stand-up comedy and visual artists performing on several outdoor stages at Harvard University's sports complex.

Chill Out With Chowder

For the best regional food fest there's Boston Chowderfest, or as locals say it, "chowdahfest." This free event lets you taste some of the best chowder in the city with samples provided by local restaurants. And yes, this is real New England chowder — the hearty white gumbo crafted with heavy cream, a few potatoes and tons of clams. Vote for your favorites and the winner is announced at the end of the day.

History is at Home Here

Boston is filled with Revolutionary history but there are other historic sites to see. Stroll along the narrow cobblestone streets of Beacon Hill where Federal-style homes line the walkways and gaslights cast romantic shadows in the evenings. Step into the African Meeting House, the oldest African American church edifice still standing in the United States and the heart of the abolitionist movement. The Granary Burying Ground, the third-oldest cemetery in Boston, provides a moody stroll among the headstones of famous residents like John Hancock, Paul Revere and Ben Franklin's family. Update your library with tomes from the Old Corner Bookstore highlighting New England history and travel.

Cape Cod

The Cape Cod National Seashore is home to pristine sandy beaches, rugged natural landscapes and charming seafaring villages. This is where a quiet stroll can lead past Gilded Age mansions, expansive dunes and sun-dappled forests. Check out the charming Cape towns for tranquil walks among coastal pine forests, craggy bluffs, salty marshes and sandy beaches. Visit the historic lighthouses, tour the wild cranberry bogs, or walk in the footsteps of our 35th president. Sample succulent lobster and get crackin' with the best oysters in New England. Learn the history of the U.S. Coast Guard and explore where Mayflower residents began a new life. This New England coast is steeped in history, legends and romance.

Paradise Awaits

Cape Cod National Seashore, on the tip of Cape Cod, is a 40-mile natural paradise filled with marshlands, freshwater ponds, wild cranberry bogs and beautiful pristine beaches. Wildlife and sea critters are plentiful along with picturesque lighthouses guiding ships at sea to safe harbor. There's even an ocean graveyard between Chatham and Provincetown where more than 1,000 shipwrecks are buried. Outdoor adventurers can hunt for wild turkeys, ruffed grouse, quail and pheasant along with rabbit, coyote, squirrel and woodchuck. Anglers can land black sea bass, striped bass, trout, bluefin tuna,

MA

false albacore and shark. Take a charter sightseeing cruise to look for whales, porpoises and sea turtles, or head out for a nature hike along the rugged New England coastline.

Nature Calls

Coast through six charming towns along the 22-mile Cape Cod Rail Trail from Dennis to Wellfleet. Ramble past sandy beaches, wooded glades, freshwater ponds and saltwater marshes as you soak up the tranquility of this scenic outdoors. The asphalt trail is open to bikers, inline skaters, hikers and is wheelchair-accessible. Shining Sea Bikeway is 10 miles of paved and off-road routes that embody the spirit of the Cape.

A President, Mansions and Whales

The John F. Kennedy Hyannis Museum provides a fascinating look at our 35th president's deep connection to Cape Cod. Kennedy was a senator when he introduced legislation to make Cape Cod a national seashore, and signed the bill into law in 1961 as president. Take the 1.6-mile Kennedy Legacy Trail with 10 historic stops ending at the JFK Memorial. Newport's Ten Mile Drive showcases stunning views of rocky coastline and Gilded Age mansions. Several yacht clubs are housed in former manses and some turn-of-the-century estates, including The Elms, The Breakers and Marble House, can be toured. Once the Whaling Capital of the World, Nantucket Island is home to 300 years of sea legends and history housed in the Whaling Museum. With nine galleries and more than 1,000 artifacts, visitors will enjoy intimate tours and a chance to see

Nobska Point Light stands at the "elbow" of Cape Cod across from Martha's Vineyard and Nonamesset Island.

the town from the widow's walk. See the places written about in the novel "Moby Dick."

Goodness on the Half Shell

Aw, shucks! Here's a chance to slurp up the tastiness of the Cape at its signature event — the annual Wellfleet OysterFest. This two-day festival features educational programs about shellfish, sharks and seals along with the history of shell fishing in the region.

Pilgrims and Coast Guards

Pilgrim Monument in Provincetown marks the first landing of the Mayflower pilgrims in 1620. Towering at 252 feet, it's the tallest all-granite structure in the U.S. Follow the Pilgrim Landing Trail through 55 miles of Outer and Lower Cape Cod, tracing the lives of these settlers.

Plymouth

Located about 60 miles south of Boston lies one of the most important landing sites in America. From the most famous stepping stone in American history to the first Thanksgiving, the town of Plymouth needs little introduction when it comes to the realm of legend and lore. It was here, in 1620, that the Pilgrims established their first colony.

On the Water

Stop by Plimouth Plantation (don't be confused by the different spelling) and meet costumed interpreters who demonstrate how the early settlers subsisted. Elsewhere, as in those early days, the modern-day city of Plymouth starts at the water's edge. Pay a visit to Pilgrim Memorial State Park, which hugs the shores of Plymouth Bay.

FOR MORE INFORMATION

Massachusetts Office of Travel & Tourism, 800-227-6277, www.massvacation.com
Greater Boston CVB, 888-733-2678
Cape Cod Convention and Visitors Bureau, 888-332-2732, www.capecodchamber.org
Destination Plymouth County, 508-747-7533, www.seeplymouth.com

Massachusetts

ASHBY — B5 *Middlesex*

THE PINES CAMPGROUND **Ratings: 7/6.5/7.5** (Campground) 28 Avail: 16 full hkups, 12 W, 12 E (30/50 amps). 2021 rates: $45 to $50. (978)386-7702, 39 Davis Rd, Ashby, MA 01431

BARRE — B4 *Worcester*

CAMP COLDBROOK GOLF & RV RESORT **Ratings: 8/6.5/7.5** (Campground) 88 Avail: 44 full hkups, 44 W, 44 E (30 amps). 2021 rates: $50.50 to $75. Apr 15 to Oct 15. (978)355-2090, 864 Old Coldbrook Rd, Barre, MA 01005

BEDFORD — B7 *Middlesex*

MILITARY PARK HANSCOM FAMCAMP (HANSCOM AFB) (Public) From jct I-95 & Exit 31B (Bedford St): Go 0.6 mi NW on Bedford St (SR-4/225), 0.5 mi SW on Hartwell Dr, then right on Maguire Rd (E). 72 Avail: 55 full hkups, 13 W, 17 E (30/50 amps). 2021 rates: $26 to $28. May 01 to Oct 30. (781)225-3953

BELLINGHAM — C6 *Norfolk*

CIRCLE CG FARM CAMPGROUND

good sam park

Ratings: 9.5/9.5★/10 (RV Park) From Jct of MA Pike & I-495, S 12 mi on I-495 to Hwy 126 (exit 18), S 1 mi (L); or From Jct of I-95 & I-495, N 13 mi on I-495 to Hwy 126 (exit 18), S 1 mi (L).

PUT FAMILY BACK IN FAMILY CAMPING!
You will need more than a weekend to see all of the attractions in the area. We are located near Boston, Cape Cod and Providence. A quiet, full-service RV Park with a country western theme awaits you and your family.

FAC: paved rds. (150 spaces). 90 Avail: 63 gravel, 27 grass, 20 pull-thrus, (27x63), back-ins (25x51), 73 full hkups, 17 W, 17 E (30/50 amps), seasonal sites, cable, WiFi @ sites, tent sites, dump, laundry, groc, LP gas, fire rings, firewood, controlled access. **REC:** pool, pond, fishing, boating nearby, hunting nearby. Pet restrict (Q). Big rig sites, eco-friendly. 2021 rates: $54 to $60, Military discount.
(508)966-1136 Lat: 42.10128, Lon: -71.47256
131 N Main St, Bellingham, MA 02019
circlecgfarm.com
See ad page 473

BERKLEY — D7 *Bristol*

Travel Services

CAMPING WORLD OF BERKLEY As the nation's largest retailer of RV supplies, accessories, services and new and used RVs, Camping World is committed to making your total RV experience better. **SERVICES:** tire, RV appliance, MH mechanical, . RV Sales. RV supplies, LP gas, emergency parking. Hours: 9am - 7pm.
(888)578-1274 Lat: 41.839492, Lon: -71.012277
137 Myricks Street, Berkley, MA 02779
www.campingworld.com

BERNARDSTON — B3 *Franklin*

TRAVELER'S WOODS OF NEW ENGLAND **Ratings: 7.5/9★/9** (Campground) 69 Avail: 8 full hkups, 61 W, 61 E (30/50 amps). 2021 rates: $30 to $35. May 01 to Oct 15. (413)648-9105, 152 River Street, Bernardston, MA 01337

BOSTON — C7 *Suffolk*

A SPOTLIGHT Introducing Boston's colorful attractions appearing at the front of this state section.

BOSTON See also Foxboro & Mansfield.

CIRCLE CG FARM CAMPGROUND

good sam park

Ratings: 9.5/9.5★/10 (RV Park) From Jct I-93 & I-90: Go 28 mi W on I-90W, then 13-3/4 mi S on I-495S (exit 11A), then 1/4 mi S on Hwy 126S (exit 18), then 1/2 mi S on Main St (Hwy 126S) (L). **FAC:** paved rds. (150 spaces). 90 Avail: 63 gravel, 27 grass, 20 pull-thrus, (27x63), back-ins (25x51), 73 full hkups, 17 W, 17 E (30/50 amps), seasonal sites, cable, WiFi @ sites, tent sites, dump, laundry, groc, LP gas, fire rings, firewood, controlled access. **REC:** pool, pond, fishing, boating nearby, hunting nearby. Pet restrict (Q). Big rig sites, eco-friendly. 2021 rates: $54 to $60, Military discount.
(508)966-1136 Lat: 42.10128, Lon: -71.47256
131 N Main St, Bellingham, MA 02019
circlecgfarm.com
See primary listing at Bellingham and ad page 473

NORMANDY FARMS FAMILY CAMPING RESORT
Ratings: 10/10★/10 (Campground) From Jct of I-95 & Rte 1 (exit 9), S 6.7 mi on Rte 1 to Thurston St, E 1.3 mi (R); or From Jct of I-495 & Rte 1 (exit 14A), N 1 mi on Rte 1 to Thurston St (2nd traffic light), E 1.3 mi (R). **FAC:** all weather rds. (365 spaces). Avail: 345 all weather, patios, 300 pull-thrus, (40x60), back-ins (33x48), 275 full hkups, 70 W, 70 E (30/50 amps), seasonal sites, cable, WiFi @ sites, tent sites, rentals, dump, laundry, groc, LP gas, fire rings, firewood, controlled access. **REC:** heated pool, hot tub, pond, fishing, boating nearby, shuffleboard, playground. Pets OK. Partial handicap access. Big rig sites, eco-friendly. 2021 rates: $56 to $132, Military discount. Apr 01 to Nov 30. ATM.
(866)673-2767 Lat: 42.04033, Lon: -71.28069
72 West St, Foxboro, MA 02035
www.normandyfarms.com
See primary listing at Foxboro and ad opposite page

BOURNE — E8 *Barnstable*

BAY VIEW CAMPGROUND **Ratings: 9/10★/10** (Campground) 130 Avail: 90 full hkups, 40 W, 40 E (30/50 amps). 2021 rates: $55 to $77. May 01 to Oct 15. (508)759-7610, 260 MacArthur Blvd, Bourne, MA 02532

BOURNE SCENIC PARK (Public) From Jct I-495 & US-6, go around Rotary, staying on US-6, N 300 ft on (R) (Beneath north end of Bourne Bridge). 194 Avail: 194 W, 194 E (30/50 amps). 2021 rates: $56 to $64. Apr 01 to Oct 30. (508)759-7873

BREWSTER — D10 *Barnstable*

NICKERSON
(Public State Park) From Jct of Hwy 6A & Hwy 6, W 1.5 mi on Hwy 6A (L). Note: No outside firewood permitted. **FAC:** paved rds. Avail: 190 dirt, back-ins (20x30), tent sites, dump, firewood. **REC:** pond, swim, fishing, kayaking/canoeing, boating nearby, playground, rec open to public. Pets OK. Partial handicap access, 14 day max stay. 2021 rates: $22 to $35. Apr 17 to Nov 01. no cc.
(508)896-3491 Lat: 41.775296, Lon: -70.030592
3488 Main Street, Brewster, MA 02631
www.mass.gov

SHADY KNOLL CAMPGROUND

good sam park

Ratings: 7.5/10★/10 (Campground) 75 Avail: 44 full hkups, 31 W, 31 E (30/50 amps). 2021 rates: $56 to $77. May 15 to Oct 15. (508)896-3002, 1709 Main St, Brewster, MA 02631

SWEETWATER FOREST CAMPING RESORT Ratings: 6/9.5★/9.5 (Campground) 170 Avail: 19 full hkups, 76 W, 76 E (30/50 amps). 2021 rates: $45 to $69. Apr 01 to Nov 01. (508)896-3773, 676 Harwich Rd, Brewster, MA 02631

BRIMFIELD — C4 *Hampden*

QUINEBAUG COVE RESORT **Ratings: 8/9/9** (Campground) 64 Avail: 46 full hkups, 18 W, 18 E (15/30 amps). 2021 rates: $60. Apr 15 to Oct 15. (413)245-9525, 49 E. Brimfield Holland Rd, Brimfield, MA 01010

VILLAGE GREEN FAMILY CAMPGROUND **Ratings: 7.5/8.5★/7.5** (Campground) 33 Avail: 33 W, 33 E (30/50 amps). 2021 rates: $40. May 01 to Nov 01. (413)245-3504, 228 Sturbridge Rd, Brimfield, MA 01010

CAPE COD — D10 *Barnstable*

CAPE COD See also East Falmouth & Dennisport.

CARVER — D8 *Plymouth*

CRANBERRY ACRES JELLYSTONE PARK **Ratings: 9/9★/8** (Campground) 50 Avail: 41 full hkups, 9 W, 9 E (30/50 amps). 2021 rates: $55 to $85. Apr 15 to Oct 15. (508)866-4040, 20 Shoestring Rd, Carver, MA 02330

CHARLEMONT — B2 *Franklin*

COUNTRY AIRE CAMPGROUND **Ratings: 8.5/9★/9** (Campground) 75 Avail: 29 full hkups, 46 W, 46 E (30/50 amps). 2021 rates: $40 to $50. May 01 to Oct 31. (413)625-2996, 1753 Mohawk Trail, Shelburne Falls, MA 01370

MOHAWK TRAIL STATE FOREST (Public State Park) From town: Go 4 mi W on Hwy 2.Note: No outside firewood permitted. 43 Avail. 2021 rates: $17 to $27. Apr 16 to Oct 11. (413)339-5504

CLARKSBURG — B2 *Berkshire*

CLARKSBURG (Public State Park) From town: Go N on Hwy 8, then follow signs on Middle Rd. Note: No outside firewood permitted. 45 Avail. 2021 rates: $17 to $27. May 21 to Oct 11. (413)664-8345

DENNISPORT — E10 *Barnstable*

CAMPERS HAVEN RV RESORT **Ratings: 8/8★/9** (RV Park) Avail: 30 full hkups (30/50 amps). 2021 rates: $85 to $125. May 01 to Oct 31. (508)398-2811, 184 Old Wharf Rd, Dennisport, MA 02639

DOUGLAS — D5 *Worcester*

LAKE MANCHAUG CAMPING **Ratings: 6.5/7/7.5** (Campground) Avail: 20 full hkups (30/50 amps). 2021 rates: $60 to $100. May 01 to Oct 01. (508)476-2471, 76 Oak Street, Douglas, MA 01516

EAST FALMOUTH — E8 *Barnstable*

CAPE COD RV RESORT **Ratings: 10/10★/10** (Campground) Avail: 207 full hkups (30/50 amps). 2021 rates: $69 to $125. May 01 to Oct 15. (508)548-1458, 110 Thomas B Landers Rd, East Falmouth, MA 02536

EAST OTIS — C2 *Berkshire*

LAUREL RIDGE CAMPING AREA **Ratings: 6.5/7/9** (Campground) 15 Avail: 15 W, 15 E (30/50 amps). 2021 rates: $42. May 01 to Oct 11. (413)269-4804, 40 Otis Tolland Rd, Blandford, MA 01008

EAST WAREHAM — D8 *Plymouth*

CAPE COD'S MAPLE PARK CAMPGROUND & RV PARK
Ratings: 7.5/9★/9 (Campground) From Jct of Rte 25 & SR-6 (exit 2), E 0.6 mi on SR-6 to Glen Charlie Rd, N 2 mi (L). **FAC:** paved/gravel rds. (464 spaces). Avail: 220 dirt, 7 pull-thrus, (30x70), back-ins (23x40), 151 full hkups, 69 W, 69 E (30/50 amps), seasonal sites, WiFi, tent sites, rentals, shower$, dump, laundry, groc, LP bottles, fire rings, firewood, controlled access. **REC:** pond, swim, fishing, kayaking/canoeing, boating nearby, playground. Pets OK. Partial handicap access. 2021 rates: $47 to $92.75. May 01 to Oct 15.
(508)295-4945 Lat: 41.78107, Lon: -70.65061
290 Glen Charlie Rd, East Wareham, MA 02538
capecodmaplepark.com
See ad this page

Go to GoodSam.com/Trip-Planner for Trip Routing.

MA

EASTHAM — D10 *Barnstable*

ATLANTIC OAKS

good sam park

Ratings: 8.5/10★/9.5 (Campground) Avail: 72 full hkups (30/50 amps). 2021 rates: $59 to $85. May 01 to Nov 01. (508)255-1437, 3700 State Hwy, Eastham, MA 02642

ERVING — B4 *Franklin*

ERVING STATE FOREST (Public State Park) From town: Go E on Hwy 2, then turn at fire station & follow signs. Note: No outside firewood permitted. 27 Avail. 2021 rates: $17 to $27. May 21 to Sep 06. (978)544-3939

FOXBORO — D7 *Norfolk*

NORMANDY FARMS FAMILY CAMPING RESORT

Ratings: 10/10★/10 (RV Resort) From Jct of I-95 & Rte 1 (exit 9), S 6.7 mi on Rte 1 to Thurston St, E 1.3 mi (R); or From Jct of I-495 & Rte 1 (exit 14A), N 1 mi on Rte 1 to Thurston St (2nd traffic light), E 1.3 mi (R). **FAC:** all weather rds. (387 spaces). Avail: 367 all weather, patios, 212 pull-thrus, (40x60), back-ins (33x48), 310 full hkups, 57 W, 57 E (30/50 amps), seasonal sites, cable, WiFi @ sites, tent sites, rentals, dump, laundry, groc, LP gas, fire rings, firewood, controlled access. **REC:** heated pool, hot tub, pond, fishing, boating nearby, shuffleboard, playground. Pets OK. Partial handicap access. Big rig sites, eco-friendly. 2021 rates: $56 to $132, Military discount. Apr 01 to Nov 15. ATM.
(866)673-2767 Lat: 42.04033, Lon: -71.28069
72 West St, Foxboro, MA 02035
www.normandyfarms.com
See ad page 474

GLOUCESTER — B8 *Essex*

CAPE ANN CAMP SITE

Ratings: 4.5/7.5/8 (Campground) From jct Hwy 128 & Concord St (exit 13): Go 3/4 mi N on Concord St, then 1/2 mi E on Atlantic St (L). **FAC:** paved/gravel rds. (230 spaces). 190 Avail: 110 grass, 80 dirt, back-ins (22x45), 45 full hkups, 145 W, 145 E (30/50 amps), seasonal sites, WiFi, tent sites, shower$, dump, groc, fire rings, firewood. **REC:** boating nearby. Pets OK. Big rig sites. 2021 rates: $50 to $70. May 15 to Oct 15.
(978)283-8683 Lat: 42.63966, Lon: -70.70058
80 Atlantic St, Gloucester, MA 01930
capeanncampsite.com
See ad page 474

GOSHEN — B3 *Hampshire*

DAUGHERS OF THE AMERICAN REVOLUTION (DAR) STATE FOREST (Public State Park) From town, NW 0.25 mi on Rte 9 to Rte 112, N 0.75 mi, E 0.75 mi (L) Note: No outside firewood permitted. 51 Avail. 2021 rates: $17 to $27. May 16 to Oct 13. (413)268-7098

GRANVILLE — D2 *Hampden*

PROSPECT MOUNTAIN CAMPGROUND/RV PARK **Ratings: 8.5/9★/9** (Campground) 101 Avail: 9 full hkups, 92 W, 92 E (30/50 amps). 2021 rates: $37 to $60. May 01 to Oct 15. (888)550-4762, 1349 Main Rd (RT 57), Granville, MA 01034

HATFIELD — C3 *Hampshire*

Travel Services

GANDER RV OF WEST HATFIELD Your new hometown outfitter offering the best regional gear for all your outdoor needs. Your adventure awaits. **SERVICES:** RV, restrooms. RV Sales. RV accessible. Hours: 9am-7pm.
(855)212-0936 Lat: 42.391442, Lon: -72.632516
188 West Street, Route 5, West Hatfield, MA 01088
rv.ganderoutdoors.com

HINGHAM — C8 *Norfolk*

WOMPATUCK (Public State Park) In town, S 1.75 mi on Central St/SR-228 to Free St, E 1 mi to Union St, S 1.5 mi (R) Note: No outside firewood permitted. Avail: 125 E (20 amps). 2021 rates: $17 to $27. May 01 to Oct 11. (617)895-8245

HUMAROCK — C8 *Plymouth*

MILITARY PARK FOURTH CLIFF REC AREA (HANSCOM AFB) (Public) From Jct of I-93 & Rte 3, S 11 mi on Rte 3 to Rte 139 (exit 12), E 1.5 mi to Marshfield, S 1.5 mi to Furnace St, E 2 mi to Ferry St, S 3.5 mi to Sea St, E 100 yds (over bridge) to Central Ave (L). Avail: 11 full hkups (30/50 amps). 2021 rates: $40. May 15 to Jan 15. (800)468-9547

LANESBOROUGH — B2 *Berkshire*

MT. GREYLOCK CAMPSITE PARK

Ratings: 8.5/10★/10 (Campground) From Jct of US 7 & N Main St, N 0.8 mi on N Main St to Scott Rd, N 0.2 mi (L). Caution: Steep Grade Interior Roads. **FAC:** all weather rds. (110 spaces). 70 Avail: 40 gravel, 30 grass, 10 pull-thrus, (40x50), back-ins (40x64), 70 W, 70 E (30/50 amps), seasonal sites, WiFi @ sites, $, tent sites, dump, mobile sewer, laundry, LP gas, fire rings, firewood, controlled access. **REC:** heated pool, pond, fishing, boating nearby, playground. Pet restrict (Q). eco-friendly. 2021 rates: $40 to $55. Apr 15 to Nov 15.
(413)447-9419 Lat: 42.55112, Lon: -73.22956
15 Scott Rd, Lanesborough, MA 01237
www.mtgreylockcampsitepark.com
See ad this page

LITTLETON — B6 *Middlesex*

BOSTON MINUTEMAN CAMPGROUND **Ratings: 9.5/10★/10** (Campground) 93 Avail: 53 full hkups, 39 W, 39 E (30/50 amps). 2021 rates: $54 to $68. May 04 to Oct 19. (978)772-0042, 264 Ayer Road, Littleton, MA 01460

MANSFIELD — D7 *Norfolk*

CANOE RIVER CAMPGROUND **Ratings: 8.5/6.5/8.5** (Campground) Avail: 164 full hkups (30/50 amps). 2021 rates: $49 to $57. Apr 15 to Oct 15. (508)339-6462, 137 Mill St, Mansfield, MA 02048

MIDDLEBORO — D8 *Plymouth*

BOSTON/CAPE COD KOA KAMPGROUND **Ratings: 9/9★/8.5** (Campground) 232 Avail: 199 full hkups, 33 W, 33 E (30/50 amps). 2021 rates: $67 to $120. Apr 01 to Nov 15. (508)947-6435, 438 Plymouth Street, Middleboro, MA 02346

MONSON — C4 *Hampden*

PARTRIDGE HOLLOW CAMPING AREA **Ratings: 8.5/8.5★/9.5** (Campground) 115 Avail: 18 full hkups, 97 W, 97 E (30/50 amps). 2021 rates: $40 to $44. Apr 20 to Oct 15. (413)267-5122, 72 Sutcliffe Rd, Monson, MA 01057

SUNSETVIEW FARM CAMPING AREA

Ratings: 8/10★/10 (Campground) E-bnd: From Jct of Int 90 & Rte 32 (exit 8), S 3.5 mi on Rte 32 to Bethany Rd, S 1.0 mi to Brimfield Rd, E 1.0 mi on Brimfield to Town Farm Rd, 0.5 on Town Farm Rd (R); From CT: From Jct of I-84 & Rte 32 (exit 70), N 17 mi on Rte 32 to Brimfield Rd (in town), E 2 mi to Town Farm Rd, N 0.5 mi (R). **FAC:** gravel rds. (200 spaces). 70 Avail: 40 grass, 30 dirt, 26 pull-thrus, (30x60), back-ins (33x43), 55 full hkups, 15 W, 15 E (30/50 amps), seasonal sites, WiFi, tent sites, dump, laundry, groc, fire rings, firewood, controlled access. **REC:** pool, pond, swim, fishing, boating nearby, shuffleboard, playground. Pet restrict (Q). Partial handicap access, eco-friendly. 2021 rates: $47 to $68. Apr 15 to Oct 15.
(413)267-9269 Lat: 42.12160, Lon: -72.29462
57 Town Farm Rd, Monson, MA 01057
sunsetview.com
See ad this page

NORTH ADAMS — B2 *Berkshire*

HISTORIC VALLEY CAMPGROUND (Public) From Jct of SR-2 & E Main St, W 0.25 mi on E Main St to Kemp Ave, S 1 mi (E). 100 Avail: 100 W, 100 E (20/30 amps). 2021 rates: $30 to $40. May 15 to Oct 15. (413)662-3198

NORTH ANDOVER — B7 *Essex*

HAROLD PARKER (Public State Park) From Jct of I-93 & Hwy 125, N 2.5 mi on Hwy 125 (R) Note: No outside firewood permitted. 25 Avail. 2021 rates: $17 to $27. May 21 to Oct 11. (978)686-3391

NORTH EGREMONT — C1 *Berkshire*

PROSPECT LAKE PARK **Ratings: 7/8★/9** (Campground) 35 Avail: 19 full hkups, 16 W, 16 E (20/30 amps). 2021 rates: $44. May 01 to Oct 15. (413)528-4158, 50 Prospect Lake Rd, North Egremont, MA 01230

NORTH TRURO — D10 *Barnstable*

ADVENTURE BOUND CAMPING RESORTS-NORTH TRURO **Ratings: 6.5/9.5★/9** (Campground) 216 Avail: 18 full hkups, 38 W, 38 E (30 amps). 2021 rates: $119 to $149.99. Apr 12 to Nov 10. (508)487-1847, 46 Highland Rd, North Truro, MA 02652

HORTON'S CAMPING RESORT - NORTH TRURO **Ratings: 4/8.5★/9** (Campground) 155 Avail: 17 full hkups, 37 W, 37 E (20/30 amps). 2021 rates: $119 to $150. Apr 01 to Oct 30. (508)487-1847, 71 South Highland Rd, North Truro, MA 02652

NORTH OF HIGHLAND **Ratings: 5.5/8.5★/7** (Campground) 10 Avail: 10 W, 10 E (30 amps). 2021 rates: $48. May 24 to Sep 09. (508)487-1191, 52 Head of Meadow Dr, North Truro, MA 02652

OAKHAM — C5 *Worcester*

PINE ACRES FAMILY CAMPING RESORT

good sam park

Ratings: 10/10★/10 (Campground) 270 Avail: 250 full hkups, 20 W, 20 E (30/50 amps). 2021 rates: $65 to $105. (508)882-9509, 203 Bechan Rd, Oakham, MA 01068

OTIS — C2 *Berkshire*

TOLLAND STATE FOREST (Public State Park) From Jct of MA Pike (I-90) & Rte 20 (exit 2), E 8 mi on Rte 20 to Rte 8S, S 5 mi to Rte 23, E 4 mi to Reservoir Rd, S follow signs (L) Note: No outside firewood permitted. 45 Avail. 2021 rates: $17 to $27. May 21 to Oct 25. (413)269-6002

PHILLIPSTON — B4 *Worcester*

LAMB CITY CAMPGROUND **Ratings: 9.5/9.5★/10** (Campground) 70 Avail: 58 full hkups, 12 W, 12 E (30/50 amps). 2021 rates: $49 to $67. (800)292-5262, 85 Royalston Rd, Phillipston, MA 01331

PITTSFIELD — B1 *Berkshire*

BONNIE BRAE CABINS & CAMPSITES

good sam park

Ratings: 8/8.5★/9 (Campground) From Jct of Rte 20 & US-7 (in town), N 3.5 mi on US-7 to Broadway, E 0.5 mi (R). **FAC:** all weather rds. (42 spaces). Avail: 28 all weather, patios, back-ins (20x40), 28 full hkups (20/30 amps), seasonal sites, WiFi @ sites, tent sites, rentals, dump, laundry, groc, fire rings, firewood. **REC:** pool, boating nearby, playground. Pets OK. eco-friendly. 2021 rates: $49, Military discount. May 01 to Oct 14.
(413)442-3754 Lat: 42.48910, Lon: -73.23767
108 Broadway, Pittsfield, MA 01201
bonniebraecampground.com
See ad this page

PLAINFIELD — B2 *Hampshire*

➡ PEPPERMINT PARK CAMPING RESORT **Ratings: 8/8★/8.5** (Campground) Avail: 50 full hkups (30/50 amps). 2021 rates: $44 to $50. May 15 to Oct 15. (413)634-5385, 169 Grant St, Plainfield, MA 01070

PLYMOUTH — D8 *Plymouth*

ELLIS HAVEN CAMPING RESORT **Ratings: 8/7.5/8** (Campground) 200 Avail: 65 full hkups, 105 W, 105 E (30/50 amps). 2021 rates: $58 to $75. May 01 to Oct 12. (508)746-0803, 531 Federal Furnace Rd, Plymouth, MA 02360

INDIANHEAD RESORT **Ratings: 4.5/4.5/6** (Campground) 140 Avail: 10 full hkups, 130 W, 130 E (20/50 amps). 2021 rates: $50 to $57. Apr 13 to Oct 10. (508)888-3688, 1929 State Rd, Plymouth, MA 02360

PINEWOOD LODGE CAMPGROUND **Ratings: 8/8.5/9** (Campground) 163 Avail: 68 full hkups, 95 W, 95 E (30/50 amps). 2021 rates: $65 to $95. May 01 to Oct 30. (508)746-3548, 190 Pinewood Rd, Plymouth, MA 02360

SANDY POND CAMPGROUND **Ratings: 7.5/8/8.5** (Campground) 160 Avail: 81 full hkups, 79 W, 79 E (30/50 amps). 2021 rates: $61 to $72. Apr 15 to Oct 15. (508)759-9336, 834 Bourne Rd, Plymouth, MA 02360

PROVINCETOWN — D9 *Barnstable*

COASTAL ACRES CAMPGROUND **Ratings: 5.5/9.5★/9.5** (Campground) Avail: 151 full hkups (30/50 amps). 2021 rates: $80 to $90. Apr 15 to Nov 01. (508)487-1700, 76 R Bayberry Ave, Provincetown, MA 02657

ROCHESTER — E8 *Plymouth*

GATEWAY TO CAPE COD RV CAMPGROUND

good sam park **Ratings: 9/8.5★/9** (Membership Park) Avail: 120 full hkups (30/50 amps). 2021 rates: $55 to $74. Apr 12 to Oct 21. (888)563-7040, 90 Stevens Rd, Rochester, MA 02770

RUTLAND — C5 *Worcester*

POUT & TROUT FAMILY CAMPGROUND **Ratings: 6/5/5.5** (Campground) 38 Avail: 3 full hkups, 35 W, 35 E (30 amps). 2021 rates: $39. Apr 14 to Oct 18. (508)886-6677, 94 River Rd, Rutland, MA 01543

SALEM — B8 *Essex*

WINTER ISLAND PARK (Public) From jct Derby St & Fort Ave in town: Go 3/4 mi NE on Fort Ave, then 1/2 mi E on Winter Island Rd. 28 Avail: 28 W, 28 E (30/50 amps). 2021 rates: $42 to $50. May 01 to Nov 01. (978)745-9430

SALISBURY — A8 *Essex*

BLACK BEAR CAMPGROUND

Ratings: 9/10★/10 (Campground) From jct I-495 & I-95 (exit 90): Go 1/2 mi N on Rabbit Rd, then 1/3 mi E on Main St (L). **FAC:** all weather rds. (262 spaces). Avail: 192 gravel, 20 pull-thrus, (32x65), back-ins (30x50), 192 full hkups (30/50 amps), seasonal sites, cable, WiFi @ sites, tent sites, shower$, dump, laundry, fire rings, firewood, controlled access. **REC:** pool, boating nearby, playground. Pet restrict (S). Partial handicap access. Big rig sites. 2021 rates: $55 to $60. May 15 to Sep 30.
(978)462-3183 Lat: 42.87089, Lon: -70.88153
54 Main St, Salisbury, MA 01952
blackbearcamping.com
See ad this page

SALISBURY BEACH STATE RESERVATION (Public State Park) From Jct I-95 & SR-110, E 3.5 mi on SR-110 to Rte 1A, E 2 mi (R). Avail: 362 E (50 amps). 2021 rates: $22 to $35. Apr 16 to Nov 28. (877)422-6762

➡ THE PINES CAMPING AREA **Ratings: 7.5/8/7.5** (Campground) 40 Avail: 4 full hkups, 36 W, 36 E (30/50 amps). 2021 rates: $50. Apr 15 to Oct 10. (978)465-0013, 28 CCC Rd, Salisbury, MA 01952

SALISBURY BEACH — A8 *Essex*

➡ BEACH ROSE RV PARK **Ratings: 9/8.5★/9.5** (RV Park) Avail: 25 full hkups (30/50 amps). 2021 rates: $55 to $75. Apr 01 to Nov 15. (800)382-2230, 147 Beach Rd, Salisbury, MA 01952

SANDWICH — D9 *Barnstable*

DUNROAMIN' TRAILER PARK & COTTAGES

Ratings: 7/NA/8 (RV Park) From Jct US-6 & Hwy 130, S 3 mi on Hwy 130 to Quaker Meeting House Rd, E 3/4 mi on Quaker Meeting House Rd to Cotuit Rd, S 1 mi on Cotuit to John Ewer Rd, W 500 ft on John Ewer (R). **FAC:** gravel rds. (66 spaces). Avail: 10 gravel, 10 pull-thrus, (40x70), 10 full hkups (30/50 amps), seasonal sites, WiFi, rentals, laundry. **REC:** pond, swim, fishing, kayaking/canoeing, boating nearby, playground, hunting nearby. Pet restrict (B). No tents. 2021 rates: $50 to $75. Apr 13 to Oct 09.
(508)477-0541 Lat: 41.6851370, Lon: -70.4785248
13 John Ewer Rd, Sandwich, MA 02563
www.dunroamintrailerpark.com
See ad this page

PETERS POND RV RESORT **Ratings: 9/8★/10** (Campground) 42 Avail: 33 full hkups, 9 W, 9 E (30/50 amps). 2021 rates: $70 to $300. Apr 15 to Oct 15. (888)434-4381, 185 Cotuit Rd, Sandwich, MA 02563

SCUSSET BEACH STATE RESERVATION (Public State Park) From jct US-6 & SR-3: Go 1-1/4 mi E on Scusset Beach Rd (R). 98 Avail: 98 W, 98 E (30 amps). 2021 rates: $22 to $35. (508)888-0859

➡ SHAWME-CROWELL (Public State Park) From Jct of US-6 & SR-6A, E 2 mi on SR-6A to SR-130, S 0.5 mi (R). Note: No outside firewood permitted. 67 Avail. 2021 rates: $17 to $27. (508)888-0351

SOUTH CARVER — D8 *Plymouth*

➡ MYLES STANDISH (Public State Park) From town, E 3 mi on Cranberry Rd (L). Note: No outside firewood permitted. 220 Avail. 2021 rates: $17 to $27. May 15 to Oct 11. (508)866-2526

SOUTH DENNIS — E10 *Yarmouth*

OLD CHATHAM ROAD RV CAMPGROUND

good sam park **Ratings: 8/6.5/7** (Campground) Avail: 31 full hkups (30/50 amps). 2021 rates: $68 to $149. May 01 to Oct 31. (888)563-7040, 310 Old Chatham Rd, South Dennis, MA 02660

SPRINGFIELD — C3 *Hampden*

SPRINGFIELD See also Brimfield, Charlemont, East Otis, Granville, Monson & Wales, MA; Barkhamsted, Stafford Springs & Willington, CT.

STURBRIDGE — C5 *Worcester*

PINE LAKE RV RESORT & COTTAGES

good sam park **Ratings: 10/10★/10** (Campground) From Jct of MA Pike & I-84 (Exit 9), S 2 mi on I-84 to Exit 2, E over I-84 to River Rd, SE 0.4 mi (R).

BOSTON'S BEST RV AND COTTAGE RESORT
Newly Renovated amenity-rich Resort and Event Center with nearby Old Sturbridge Village, antiques, fine restaurants, and 71 hiking trails with 583 gentle, meandering miles. Enjoy New England's best new get away!

FAC: all weather rds. (209 spaces). Avail: 169 all weather, 45 pull-thrus, (30x65), back-ins (30x45), 169 full hkups (30/50 amps), seasonal sites, cable, WiFi @ sites, rentals, dump, laundry, groc, fire rings, firewood, controlled access. **REC:** pool, hot tub, Pine Lake: swim, fishing, kayaking/canoeing, boating nearby, playground. Pet restrict (Q). Partial handicap access. No tents. Big rig sites, eco-friendly. 2021 rates: $51 to $115, Military discount. Apr 01 to Nov 30.
(508)347-9570 Lat: 42.08978, Lon: -72.08311
30 River Rd, Sturbridge, MA 01566
pinelakervresort.com
See ad this page, 470

STURBRIDGE RV RESORT

good sam park **Ratings: 8.5/9★/8.5** (Membership Park) 71 Avail: 36 full hkups, 35 W, 35 E (30/50 amps). 2021 rates: $57 to $76. Apr 15 to Oct 31. (888)563-7040, 19 Mashapaug Rd, Sturbridge, MA 01566

Show Your Good Sam Membership Card!

➡ WELLS (Public State Park) From town, E 2 mi on Rte 20 to Rte 49, N 1 mi to park access rd (L). Note: No outside firewood permitted. 47 Avail. 2021 rates: $17 to $27. May 08 to Oct 11. (508)347-9257

SUTTON — C5 *Worcester*

SUTTON FALLS CAMPING AREA **Ratings: 8/10★/9** (Campground) 51 Avail: 26 full hkups, 25 W, 25 E (30/50 amps). 2021 rates: $55 to $65. Apr 15 to Oct 01. (508)865-3898, 90 Manchaug Road, Sutton, MA 01590

We give you what you want. First, we surveyed thousands of RVers just like you. Then, we developed our exclusive Triple Rating System for campgrounds based on the results. That's why our rating system is so good at explaining the quality of facilities and cleanliness of campgrounds.

MA

UXBRIDGE — D6 *Worcester*

Travel Services

CAMPING WORLD OF UXBRIDGE As the nation's largest retailer of RV supplies, accessories, services and new and used RVs, Camping World is committed to making your total RV experience better. **SERVICES:** restrooms. RV Sales. RV supplies, RV accessible. Hours: 9am - 6pm.
(833)580-1622 Lat: 42.02542, Lon: -71.60958
865 Quaker Hwy, Uxbridge, MA 01569
rv.campingworld.com

VINEYARD HAVEN — E8 *Dukes*

MARTHA'S VINEYARD FAMILY CAMPGROUND Ratings: 8/10★/9.5 (Campground) From Vineyard Haven Ferry: Go 1/4 mi S on Water St, then 1/4 mi SW on Beach St, then 1 mi S on Edgartown Rd (R). **FAC:** gravel rds. (48 spaces). Avail: 19 dirt, 1 pull-thrus, (45x60), back-ins (30x38), 19 full hkups (30/50 amps), seasonal sites, WiFi @ sites, tent sites, rentals, dump, laundry, groc, fire rings, firewood. **REC:** Atlantic Ocean: boating nearby, playground, hunting nearby. Pet restrict (Q) $. eco-friendly. 2021 rates: $70 to $90, Military discount. May 16 to Oct 16. ATM.
(508)693-3772 Lat: 41.43530, Lon: -70.61029
569 Edgartown Rd, Vineyard Haven, MA 02568
campmv.com
See ad this page

WALES — D4 *Hampden*

OAK HAVEN FAMILY CAMPGROUND Ratings: 8.5/9.5★/9.5 (Campground) From Jct of I-84 & SR-32 (Exit 70 in Connecticut), N 5 mi on SR-32 to Rte 190, E 0.3 mi to SR-19, N 1 mi to MA State Line, Continue N on MA Rte 19, N 2.7 mi (R). **FAC:** gravel rds. (140 spaces). 55 Avail: 14 gravel, 41 grass, 18 pull-thrus, (36x60), back-ins (30x50), 17 full hkups, 38 W, 38 E (30 amps), seasonal sites, WiFi @ sites, tent sites, shower$, dump, laundry, groc, LP gas, fire rings, firewood, controlled access. **REC:** pool, boating nearby, playground. Pet restrict (Q). Partial handicap access, eco-friendly. 2021 rates: $45 to $52, Military discount. May 01 to Oct 15.
(413)245-7148 Lat: 42.06793, Lon: -72.22202
22 Main St., Wales, MA 01081
oakhavencampground.com
See ad this page

WEBSTER — D5 *Worcester*

INDIAN RANCH Ratings: 8.5/8.5★/8.5 (RV Park) Avail: 12 full hkups (30/50 amps). 2021 rates: $65 to $100. May 01 to Oct 15. (508)943-3871, 200 Gore Rd, Webster, MA 01570

WELLFLEET — D10 *Barnstable*

MAURICE'S CAMPGROUND Ratings: 6/7/6.5 (Campground) 80 Avail: 20 full hkups, 60 W, 60 E (20/30 amps). 2021 rates: $75. May 24 to Oct 13. (508)349-2029, 80 Rte 6, Wellfleet, MA 02667

WEST BOYLSTON — C5 *Worcester*

Travel Services

CAMPING WORLD OF WEST BOYLSTON As the nation's largest retailer of RV supplies, accessories, services and new and used RVs, Camping World is committed to making your total RV experience better. **SERVICES:** restrooms. RV Sales. RV supplies, RV accessible. Hours: 9am - 6pm.
(774)450-7033 Lat: 42.35894, Lon: -71.78429
66 W Boylston St, West Boylston, MA 01583
rv.campingworld.com

WEST TOWNSEND — B5 *Middlesex*

PEARL HILL (Public State Park) From Jct of SR-119 & New Fitchburg Rd, S .9 mi on New Fitchburg Rd to Bayberry Hill Rd, W 2.2 mi. Note: No outside firewood permitted. 34 Avail. 2021 rates: $17 to $27. May 21 to Oct 11. (978)597-8802

WESTPORT — E7 *Bristol*

HORSENECK BEACH STATE RESERVATION (Public State Park) From Jct of I-195 & SR-88, S 13 mi on SR-88 (E). Note: No outside firewood permitted. 96 Avail. 2021 rates: $22 to $35. May 15 to Oct 15. (508)636-8817

OFF SEASON RVING TIP: Prepare for limited access to shower houses and restrooms. Some campgrounds close all or some of their shower houses and restrooms during the off-season. If you generally use these, you'll need to know whether or not they will be available. Beware: Some are open but are not heated, which means you may be shivering in the shower.

WINCHENDON — B5 *Worcester*

LAKE DENNISON RECREATION AREA (Public State Park) From Jct of US-202 & SR-68 in Baldwinville, N 3 mi on US-202 (L). Note: No outside firewood permitted. 137 Avail. 2021 rates: $17 to $27. May 21 to Sep 06. (978)939-8962

OTTER RIVER (Public State Park) From N end of town, N 1 mi on US-202 (L). Note: No outside firewood permitted. 10 Avail. 2021 rates: $17 to $27. May 21 to Oct 11. (978)939-8962

WINDSOR — B2 *Berkshire*

WINDSOR STATE FOREST (Public State Park) From town: Go E on Hwy 9, then N on River Rd. Note: No outside firewood permitted. 15 Avail: Pit toilets. (413)684-0948

Before you head north, know the rules and regulations for crossing the border into Canada. Read all about it in our Crossing into Canada section.

DID YOU KNOW?

The Headlands Park in Mackinaw City is considered one of the best places on Earth to observe the night sky.

YOU ARE HERE

Michigan

Part of America's so-called "Third Coast," Michigan has more coastline than any state in the Lower 48. Prefer dry land? Several amazing cities and towns dot the state, along with endless forests and dunes for hunting and off roading.

Great Lakes Galore

Visitors to Michigan will find seemingly endless water recreation possibilities. Surrounded by lakes Michigan, Superior, Huron and Erie, visitors will find no shortage of fun. Paddle along the coast for epic views of cliffs or take a long-range fishing excursion.

Sleeping Splendor

On the shores of Lake Michigan, Sleeping Bear Dunes National Lakeshore is a top pick for families, with a variety of accessible adventures to be found amid the massive sand dunes. One of the dunes has been measured at more than 400 feet tall. Considered one of most scenic spots in North America, Sleeping Bear Dunes features a gorgeous, sandy shoreline and stunning views over expansive Lake Michigan. There's a ton to do here, from hiking up to the viewpoints at Pyramid Point to learning about arts and culture at the area's many museums. The Interlochen Center for the Arts hosts performances throughout the year, and Leelanau Sands Casino offers slots, card games and even bingo.

Inland Adventures

There's more to Michigan than Great Lakes. Head inland and discover an array of smaller bodies of water that will amaze you. While Lake St. Clair and Hubbard Lake are top picks for freshwater fishing and boating, the state has 11,000 other lakes to choose from. Pick up a paddle or a rod and head to the Au Sable River, notable as a National Wild and Scenic River. Running through the Huron-Manistee National Forests, this waterway has exceptional trout fishing.

Michigan Coney Dog

Contrary to popular belief, the coney dog didn't originate from New York's Coney Island. Its birthplace is Michigan, where it was invented by Greek immigrants in the early 20th century. The savory staple consists of a beef hot dog blanketed with chili sauce, chopped raw onions and yellow mustard.

VISITOR CENTER

TIME ZONE
Eastern Standard

ROAD & HIGHWAY INFORMATION
517-373-2090
michigan.gov/mdot

FISHING & HUNTING INFORMATION
517-284-6057
michigan.gov/dnr

BOATING INFORMATION
517-284-6056
michigan.gov/boating

NATIONAL PARKS
nps.gov/mi

STATE PARKS
michigan.gov/dnr

TOURISM INFORMATION
Michigan Economic Development Corporation
888-784-7328
michigan.org

TOP TOURISM ATTRACTIONS
1) Mackinac Island
2) Henry Ford Museum
3) Sleeping Bear Dunes National Lakeshore

MAJOR CITIES
Detroit, Grand Rapids, Warren, Sterling Heights, Ann Arbor, Lansing (capital)

MI

Picture Perfect

Pictured Rocks National Lakeshore is a visual feast that leaves visitors spellbound. Striking standstone cliff faces and gushing waterfalls make this a top photo op along the coast of Lake Superior on the north shore of the Upper Peninsula. Even further north, near the shores of Ontario's Thunder Bay, Isle Royale National Park preserves the tranquil isolation on a forested island. Find a quiet spot for tranquil kayaking, backpacking and scuba diving.

Michigan Metro

From its rise as capital of the U.S. automobile industry to its role in shaping the Motown sound, Detroit has helped define American industry and culture. Michigan's largest city has seen its ups and downs, but visitors will find much to explore in the Motor City. A thriving arts and theater scene finds expression in multiple venues, including the renowned Detroit Institute of Arts and the Fox Theatre. Belle Isle Park, located in the Detroit River, is a refuge for city dwellers, a short distance away from Canada. Just outside of town in neighboring Dearborn, visitors will find the Henry Ford, an indoor and outdoor museum complex dedicated to the auto titan's story.

More than 50-feet wide, Arch Rock on the east side of Mackinac Island beautifully frames Lake Huron.

Grand Rapids Gets in the Groove

For a big city that makes you feel at home, Grand Rapids fits the bill. This town rises above a great waterway, the Grand River, and although it's the second-largest town in the state, it retains a small-town friendliness.

Wooden Shoes in the Wolverine State

In southwestern Michigan on the coast, a small community preserves the customs of old Europe. Holland borrows plenty of elements from its Netherlands namesake. Dutch-inspired attractions include a tulip farm, a windmill and Neil's Dutch Village, a reproduction of a 19th-century Netherlands village, complete with a giant wooden slide in the shape of a shoe. It's also the location of one of the most visited state parks in Michigan, Holland State Park, with scenic beaches on Lake Michigan. Check out the Big Red Lighthouse overlooking the lake.

Souped Up Silver Lake

Also on the west coast, the town of Silver Lake offers a healthy dose of adrenaline. Head over to the Silver Lake Sand Dunes, known for its 2,000-acres of undulating, sandy terrain. Hit the gas in the off-roading northern section (with rentals available), go sandboarding in the middle section or let an experienced guide do the driving in the southern section. While in town, don't miss the Little Sable Point Lighthouse in the nearby town of Mears. Visitors can even ascend the 130 steps to the top in summer months.

Manistee's Magic

Manistee's rich history is rivaled only by opportunities for hiking in lush surrounding trails. The downtown area's 27 historic sites can occupy your whole day. Be sure to stop off at the Manistee County Historical Museum, where elegant Victorian antiques sit on display. The city's historic trolley tours feature guides dressed in period garb.

Take Some Island Time

Cars are prohibited on the quaint Mackinac Island, located on Lake Huron and accessible via a 16-minute ferry ride. Horse-drawn carriages and colorful cruiser bicycles are the best ways to glide down the village streets. Treat your sweet tooth to a piece of candy heaven at Murdick's Fudge, which has been serving its confections since 1887.

Good to Grand

Built in 1880, the majestic Grand Hotel serves as the island's centerpiece, with its front porch considered the largest in the world. Relax in one of the scores of rocking chairs as you take in the views of sprawling Lake Huron. The elegant structure has 385 suites and rooms, and is surrounded by lush landscaping, with more than 5,000 geraniums flourishing in rich soil.

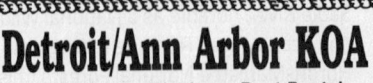

good sam park Featured Good Sam Parks

MICHIGAN

When you stay with Good Sam, you can expect the highest degree of cleanliness and friendliness, and better yet, you get **10% off** overnight campground fees.

If you're not already a Good Sam member you can purchase your membership at one of these locations:

BELLAIRE
Chain O'Lakes Campground

BELLEVILLE
Wayne County Fairgrounds RV Park

BUCHANAN
Bear Cave Resort

COLDWATER
Waffle Farm Campgrounds

DORR
Hungry Horse Family Campground

FAIR HAVEN
Northpointe Shores RV Resort

FRANKENMUTH
Frankenmuth Yogi Bear's Jellystone Park Camp-Resort

GERMFASK
Big Cedar Campground & Canoe Livery

GRASS LAKE
Apple Creek Campground & RV Park

HARRISON
Hidden Hill Family Campground

HOUGHTON LAKE
Houghton Lake Travel Park Campground

IRON MOUNTAIN
Summer Breeze Campground & RV Park

KALKASKA
Kalkaska RV Park & Campground

MARSHALL
Camp Turkeyville RV Resort

MONROE
Camp Lord Willing RV Park & Campground

MOUNT PLEASANT
Soaring Eagle Hideaway RV Park

SOMERSET CENTER
Somerset Beach Campground & Retreat Center

ST CLAIR
Saint Clair (Thousand Trails)

TECUMSEH
Indian Creek Camp & Conference Center

TRAVERSE CITY
Holiday Park Campground
Traverse Bay RV Resort

VASSAR
Ber Wa Ga Na Campground

10/10★/10 GOOD SAM PARKS

MOUNT PLEASANT
Soaring Eagle Hideaway RV Park
(989)817-4803

TRAVERSE CITY
Traverse Bay RV Resort
(231)938-5800

What's This?

An RV park with a 10/10★/10 rating has scored perfect grades in amenities, cleanliness and appearance ("See Understanding the Campground Rating System" on pages 8 and 9 for an explanation of the trusted Good Sam Rating System). Stay in a 10/10★/10 park on your next trip for a nearly flawless camping experience.

Getty Images/iStockphoto

MI

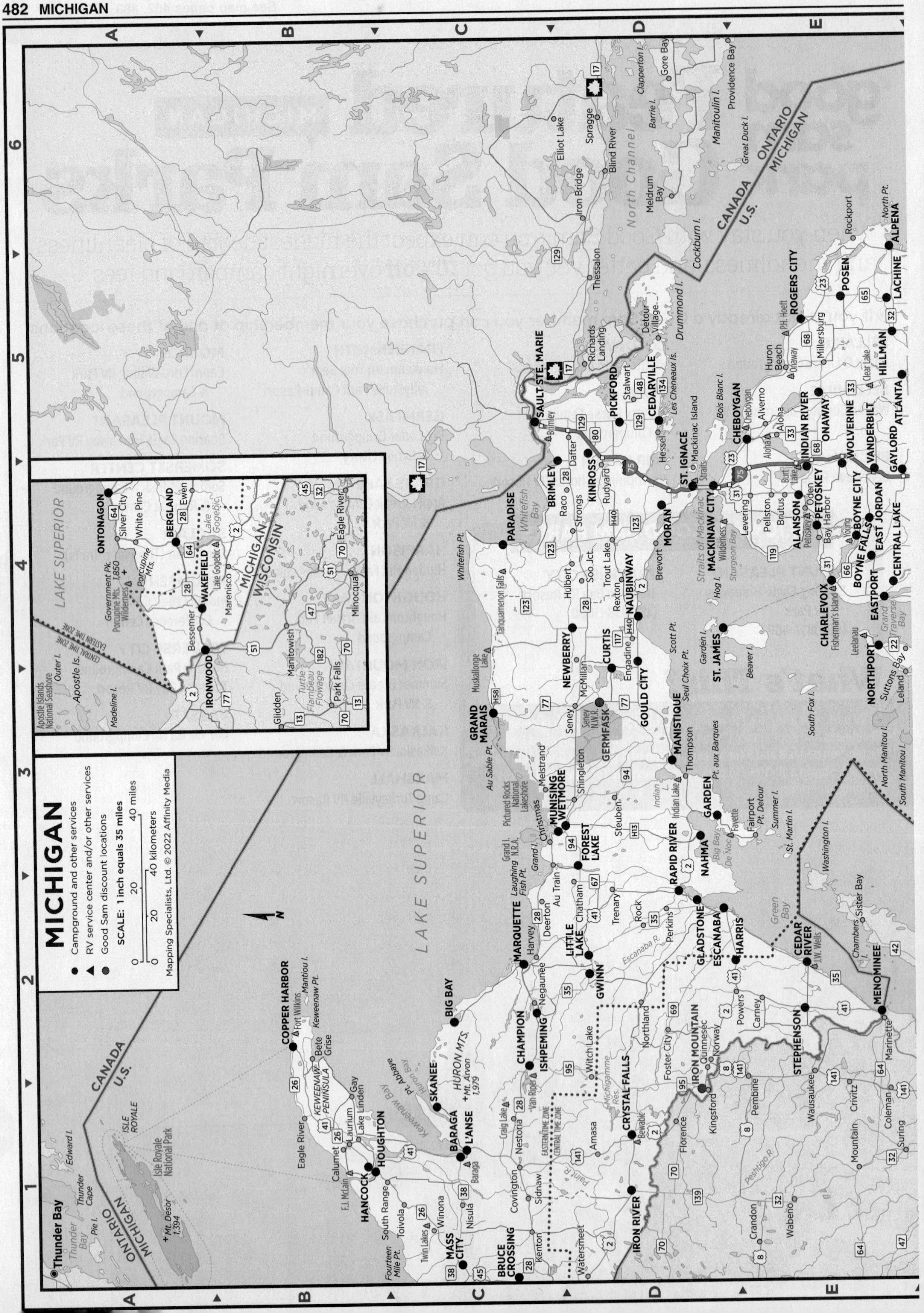
MICHIGAN
Campground and other services
RV service center and/or other services
Good Sam discount locations
SCALE: 1 inch equals 35 miles
0 20 40 miles
0 20 40 kilometers
Mapping Specialists, Ltd. © 2022 Affinity Media
LAKE SUPERIOR
CANADA
U.S.
ONTARIO
MICHIGAN
WISCONSIN
Thunder Bay
Isle Royale National Park
KEWEENAW PENINSULA
HURON MTS.
Mt. Arvon 1,979
Mt. Desor 1,394
Government Pk. 1,850
Porcupine Mts. Wilderness
Apostle Islands National Seashore
Pictured Rocks National Lakeshore
Seney N.W.R.
North Channel
Straits of Mackinac
Whitefish Bay
Green Bay
Grand Traverse Bay
EASTERN TIME ZONE
CENTRAL TIME ZONE
COPPER HARBOR
HOUGHTON
HANCOCK
MASS CITY
BRUCE CROSSING
BARAGA
L'ANSE
SKANEE
BIG BAY
CHAMPION
ISHPEMING
MARQUETTE
GWINN
LITTLE LAKE
CRYSTAL FALLS
IRON RIVER
IRON MOUNTAIN
STEPHENSON
CEDAR RIVER
MENOMINEE
ESCANABA
GLADSTONE
HARRIS
RAPID RIVER
NAHMA
GARDEN
FOREST LAKE
MUNISING
WETMORE
GRAND MARAIS
GERMFASK
MANISTIQUE
GOULD CITY
CURTIS
NEWBERRY
NAUBINWAY
PARADISE
BRIMLEY
KINROSS
SAULT STE. MARIE
PICKFORD
CEDARVILLE
MORAN
ST. IGNACE
MACKINAW CITY
CHEBOYGAN
INDIAN RIVER
ONAWAY
ROGERS CITY
POSEN
ALPENA
LACHINE
HILLMAN
ATLANTA
WOLVERINE
VANDERBILT
GAYLORD
PETOSKEY
ALANSON
BOYNE CITY
BOYNE FALLS
EAST JORDAN
CENTRAL LAKE
EASTPORT
CHARLEVOIX
ST. JAMES
NORTHPORT
IRONWOOD
WAKEFIELD
BERGLAND
ONTONAGON

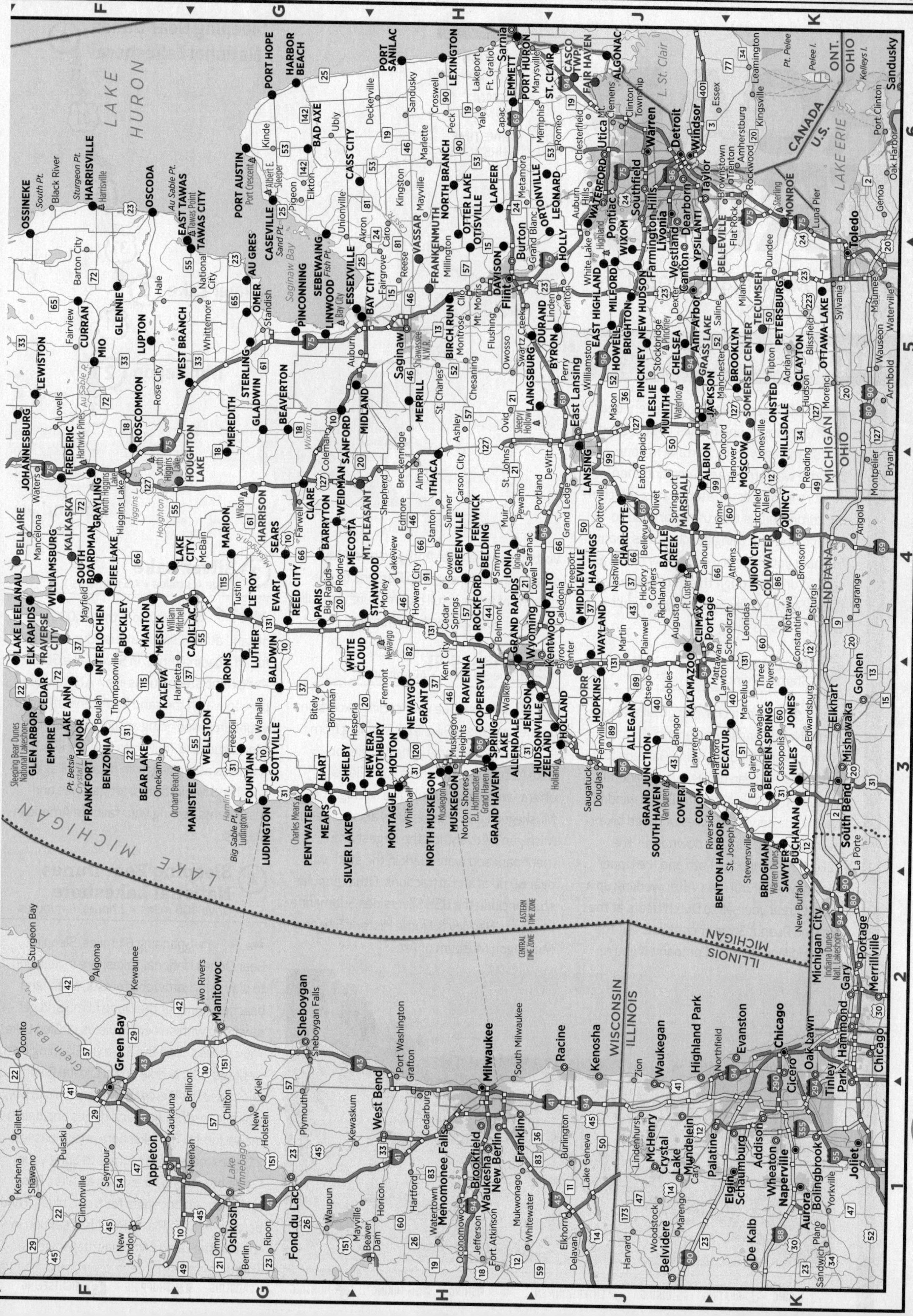
LAKE HURON
LAKE MICHIGAN
LAKE ERIE
L. St. Clair
Saginaw Bay
Green Bay
Lake Winnebago
CANADA
U.S.
ONT.
OHIO
MICHIGAN
INDIANA
ILLINOIS
WISCONSIN
CENTRAL TIME ZONE
EASTERN TIME ZONE
Sleeping Bear Dunes National Lakeshore
Indiana Dunes Natl. Lakeshore
Detroit
Windsor
Lansing
East Lansing
Grand Rapids
Flint
Saginaw
Kalamazoo
Ann Arbor
Toledo
Sarnia
PORT HURON
TRAVERSE CITY
CADILLAC
MIDLAND
BAY CITY
JACKSON
BATTLE CREEK
MUSKEGON
HOLLAND
SOUTH HAVEN
BENTON HARBOR
South Bend
Elkhart
Milwaukee
Chicago
Green Bay
Appleton
Oshkosh
Fond du Lac
Sheboygan
Manitowoc
Racine
Kenosha
Waukegan
Gary
Joliet
Sandusky

ROAD TRIPS

Follow Michigan's Coast with the Most

Michigan West

LOCATION
MICHIGAN WEST

DISTANCE
185 MILES

DRIVE TIME
3 HRS 35 MINS

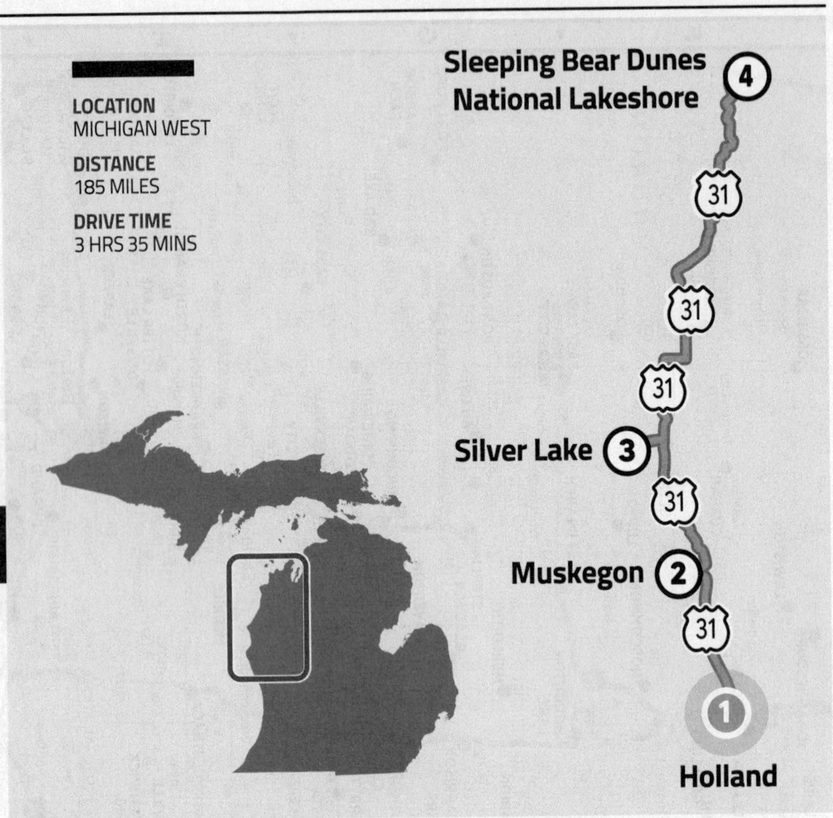

On Michigan's west coast, every beach is the right one thanks to soft sand and sparkling waters. Partake in your favorite waterfront activities and then venture into forested state parks, welcoming communities that transport you to Europe and charming beach towns ready to show you their laid-back way of life. Be sure to drive through this part of the Great Lakes State slowly because you won't want to miss a thing.

1 Holland
Starting Point

You don't have to go all the way to the Netherlands to experience Dutch culture. Go to Windmill Island Gardens to view the 260-year-old DeZwaan windmill, the country's only authentic Dutch windmill. Next, cycle down 155 miles of paved bike paths weaving through downtown, the Lakeshore Connector Path and the Upper Macatawa Natural Area. After working up a sweat, treat yourself to Dutch treats at the Holland Peanut Store or craft beers at the New Holland Brewing Company. If you're visiting between late April and mid-May, stop by the Veldheer Tulip Gardens to see millions of tulips in full bloom. Purchase tulip seeds for your garden back home.

2 Muskegon
Drive 36 miles ▪ 46 minutes

Continue your cycling excursions on the Lakeshore Bike Trail. Running from Pere Marquette Park to the Muskegon Lake Nature Preserve, this 12-mile path offers fantastic views of Lake Michigan and Muskegon Lake. Muskegon is also home to Michigan's Adventure, the largest amusement park and water park in the state with over 60 rides and attractions. Other popular stops include the USS Silversides Submarine Museum, Hackley & Hume Historic Site and Muskegon Museum of Art.

3 Silver Lake
Drive 43 miles ▪ 45 minutes

With more than 2,000 acres of sand dunes, Silver Lake is your destination for off-roading thrills. In Silver Lake State Park, climb steep dunes in an ATV and prepare to watch the sand fly. Afterward, keep your adrenaline going at the 22-mile Hart-Montague Bike Trail State Park, or kick back and relax at the beach. In nearby villages, you'll find family farms, art galleries and restaurants serving your favorite American staples.

4 Sleeping Bear Dunes National Lakeshore
Drive 106 miles ▪ 2 hours, 4 minutes

Spanning 64 miles, Sleeping Bear Dunes National Lakeshore invites you to play in its hardwood forests, bluffs and beaches. Conquer the Dune Climb and get rewarded with sweeping views of Glen Lake. You can also cycle the 22-mile Sleeping Bear Heritage Trail, paddle down Crystal River and cruise the Pierce Stocking Scenic Drive, which loops through sand dunes and beech-maple forest. The lakeshore encompasses 21 lakes too, so don't forget to bring your tackle box. Inland lakes such as Glen, Bass and Otter are hot spots for trout, bluegill and perch, while the Platte River has salmon in the fall. The Dune Climb has stellar views.

BIKING · BOATING · DINING · ENTERTAINMENT · FISHING · HIKING · HUNTING · PADDLING · SHOPPING · SIGHTSEEING

Michigan SPOTLIGHTS

Wander the Wolverine State for Treasure

Expect the unexpected in Michigan. Shop a store that sells only Christmas goods, sample the sweetest cherries on the planet and stroll the streets of an island that outlaws cars. Escape from the big cities and spend time in small towns surrounded by nature.

BRONNER'S CHRISTMAS WONDERLAND STOCKS 3,000 ONLINE ITEMS.

A giant toy soldier guards Frankenmuth, home of Bronner's Christmas Wonderland.

Getty Images/iStockphoto

Frankenmuth

Get a taste of Germany in America's Midwest. Located in the heart of the Wolverine State, Frankenmuth celebrates its ties to the old country in a big way; in fact, the town's nickname is Michigan's Little Bavaria. Looking for great Oktoberfest celebrations? You've come to the right place, but don't limit yourself to the fall Teutonic celebration. Every season gives you a reason to visit Frankenmuth.

Cruising the Cass

Launch a kayak or canoe for a trip down the Cass River. You might even be able to paddle under the Holz Brucke (German for "wooden bridge") Covered Bridge, the longest covered bridge in Michigan and a prime example of Bavarian craftsmanship and design. For a mellower ride, step aboard the *Bavarian Belle Riverboat*. The authentic stern-driven paddlewheel operates historical tours.

St. Nick and Nature

If you prefer shopping, head to Bronner's Christmas Wonderland, the world's largest Christmas store. What began as a mission by beloved founder Wally Bronner has expanded to become a Christmas emporium the size of six football fields. Feeling wild? Head south to the town of Davison and book a tour with Johnny Panther Quests Adventure Trips. Exciting boat tours take riders through Shiawassee National Wildlife Refuge and State Game Area, considered the Everglades of Michigan and the state's largest wildlife and bald eagle habitat.

Mackinaw City

Travel back in time to a town that faithfully preserves the past. Mackinaw City is home to Michilimackinac, a replica of an 18th-century fort and fur trading village, reconstructed based on historic maps and more than 60 years of archaeological excavations.

Launching Point

From Mackinaw City, cross the Mackinac Straits for popular Mackinac Island, where cars are prohibited and visitors can ride in horse-drawn carriages. Mackinaw City sits at the northern tip of Michigan's Lower Peninsula and is linked to the Upper Peninsula by Mackinac Bridge.

Traverse City

Traverse City's modern-day claim to fame dates all the way back to its infancy when, in 1852, a missionary named Peter Dougherty threw agricultural caution to the wind and planted a cherry orchard. More than 160 years and 3.8 million cherry trees later, Traverse City is the undisputed (and self-appointed) "Cherry Capital of the World." More than 70 percent of world's tart cherries are now grown in Michigan, with most of that supply coming from the Traverse Bay area.

FOR MORE INFORMATION

Travel Michigan, 888-784-7328, www.michigan.org

Frankenmuth, 800-386-8696, www.frankenmuth.org

Mackinaw City, 800-666-0160, www.mackinawcity.com

Traverse City Convention & Visitors Bureau, 800-872-8377, www.traversecity.com

MI

LOCAL FAVORITE

Hobo Stew

This easy-to-prepare recipe is ideal for travelers who are tramping around the Wolverine State.

INGREDIENTS

- ☐ 1 lb hamburger
- ☐ 2 cans vegetables
- ☐ 1 can of diced tomatoes
- ☐ Frozen mixed vegetables
- ☐ 3 cups uncooked elbow macaroni (optional)

DIRECTIONS

Cook and drain hamburger.
Place in slow cooker.
Place all vegetables, soup and diced tomatoes in slow cooker.
Cook on low for 6-8 hrs.
Stir and serve.

Michigan

ALANSON — E4 *Emmet*

MACKINAW/MAPLE BAY (Public State Park) From Jct US-31 & Brutus Rd, E 3.5 mi on Brutus Rd to Maple Bay Rd, S 0.5 mi, follow signs. 35 Avail: Pit toilets. 2021 rates: $15. (231)238-9392

ALBION — J4 *Calhoun*

ROCKEY'S CAMPGROUND **Ratings: 6/9★/7.5** (Campground) 35 Avail: 35 W, 35 E (30 amps). 2021 rates: $40. May 15 to Oct 01. (517)857-2200, 19880 27 1/2 Mile Rd, Albion, MI 49224

ALGONAC — J6 *St Clair*

ALGONAC (Public State Park) From town: Go 4 mi N on M-29, follow signs (L). Avail: 296 E (30/50 amps). 2021 rates: $22 to $32. (810)765-5605

ALLEGAN — J3 *Allegan*

ALLEGAN STATE GAME AREA (Public State Park) From town: Go 6 mi W on Monroe Road, then 1 mi S on 48th St, then 1 mi W on 116th Ave. 113 Avail: Pit toilets. 2021 rates: $12. (269)673-2430

DUMONT LAKE CAMPGROUND **Ratings: 7/9.5★/7.5** (Campground) 20 Avail: 7 full hkups, 13 W, 13 E (30/50 amps). 2021 rates: $35 to $40. May 01 to Oct 15. (269)673-6065, 3106 125th Ave, Allegan, MI 49010

TRI PONDS FAMILY CAMP RESORT **Ratings: 9/9★/8.5** (Campground) 102 Avail: 48 full hkups, 54 W, 54 E (30/50 amps). 2021 rates: $45 to $50. May 01 to Oct 31. (269)673-4740, 3687 Dumont Rd, Allegan, MI 49010

ALLENDALE — H3 *Ottawa*

ALLENDALE/WEST GRAND RAPIDS KOA **Ratings: 7.5/8.5★/8.5** (Campground) 105 Avail: 94 full hkups, 11 W, 11 E (30/50 amps). 2021 rates: $45.49 to $67.49. (616)895-6601, 8275 Warner Street, Allendale, MI 49401

ALPENA — E5 *Alpena*

CAMPERS COVE RV PARK & CANOE LIVERY **Ratings: 8.5/8.5★/7.5** (Campground) 59 Avail: 12 full hkups, 47 W, 47 E (30/50 amps). 2021 rates: $33 to $40. May 01 to Oct 15. (989)356-3708, 5005 Long Rapids Rd, Alpena, MI 49707

LONG LAKE PARK (ALPENA COUNTY PARK) (Public) From town, N 10 mi on US-23 to Long Lake Park Rd, W 0.5 mi, follow signs (L). 80 Avail: 80 W, 80 E (20/30 amps). 2021 rates: $25 to $35. May 15 to Oct 15. (989)595-2401

THUNDER BAY CAMPGROUND **Ratings: 2/8.5★/6.5** (Campground) 56 Avail: 56 W, 56 E (30/50 amps). 2021 rates: $30. Apr 01 to Nov 30. (989)354-2528, 4250 US Highway 23 S, Alpena, MI 49707

ALTO — H4 *Kent*

TYLER CREEK GOLF CLUB & CAMPGROUND **Ratings: 7.5/8.5★/7** (Campground) 60 Avail: 60 W, 60 E (30 amps). 2021 rates: $40 to $55. Apr 15 to Oct 15. (616)868-6751, 13495 92nd St, Alto, MI 49302

ANN ARBOR — J5 *Washtenaw*

ANN ARBOR See also Belleville, Grass Lake, Howell, Jackson, Munith, New Hudson, Pinckney, Tecumseh & Ypsilanti.

ATLANTA — E5 *Alpena*

CLEAR LAKE

(Public State Park) From Jct of M-32 & M-33, N 9.6 mi on M-33 (L). **FAC:** paved rds. Avail: 178 grass, back-ins (30x50), 178 E (30/50 amps), tent sites, dump, firewood. **REC:** Clear Lake: swim, fishing, playground, hunting nearby. Pets OK. Partial handicap access, 15 day max stay. 2021 rates: $20 to $29. no cc.
(989)785-4388 Lat: 45.13404, Lon: -84.17715
20500 M-33N, Atlanta, MI 49709
www.michigandnr.com/parksandtrails

MACKINAW/AVERY LAKE (Public State Park) From Jct SR-32 & CR-487: Go 6 mi S on CR-487, then 3 mi W on Avery Lake Rd (R). 13 Avail: Pit toilets. 2021 rates: $15. Apr 15 to Nov 30. (989)785-4388

MACKINAW/BIG OAKS EQUESTRIAN AND TRAIL CAMP (Public State Park) From Jct SR-32 & CR-487: Go 10 mi SW on Cr-487 to Avery Lake Rd (E). 24 Avail: Pit toilets. 2021 rates: $15. (989)785-4388

MACKINAW/ESS LAKE (Public State Park) From town, N 8 mi on SR-33 to CR-624, E 10 mi to park access rd, N 1.5 mi, follow signs (L). 27 Avail: Pit toilets. 2021 rates: $15. Apr 01 to Nov 01. (989)785-4388

MACKINAW/JACKSON LAKE (Public State Park) From Jct of SR-32 & SR-33, N 6 mi to entrance (E). 18 Avail: Pit toilets. 2021 rates: $15. (989)785-4388

MACKINAW/TOMAHAWK CREEK FLOODING (Public State Park) From town: Go 13 mi N on Hwy 33, then 1 mi E on Tomahawk Lake Rd. 47 Avail: Pit toilets. 2021 rates: $15. (989)733-8279

AU GRES — G5 *Arenac*

AU GRES CITY PARK & CAMPGROUND (Public) From Jct of US-23 & Main St, N 0.1 mi on Main St (L). 79 Avail: 30 full hkups, 49 W, 49 E (30 amps). 2021 rates: $32 to $36. Apr 15 to Oct 15. (989)876-8310

BAD AXE — G6 *Huron*

CAMPER'S HAVEN FAMILY CAMPGROUND **Ratings: 7.5/9★/8.5** (Campground) 60 Avail: 60 W, 60 E (30 amps). 2021 rates: $39.95 to $49.95. May 01 to Oct 31. (989)269-7989, 2326 S Van Dyke, Bad Axe, MI 48413

BALDWIN — G3 *Lake*

WHISPERING OAKS CAMPGROUND & CABINS **Ratings: 5.5/8.5★/7** (Campground) 23 Avail: 23 W, 23 E (30 amps). 2021 rates: $32. Apr 01 to Oct 31. (231)745-7152, 8586 M-37 South, Baldwin, MI 49304

BARAGA — C1 *Baraga*

BARAGA (Public State Park) From jct M-38 & US-41: Go 1 mi S on US-41 (R). Avail: 113 E (20/30 amps). 2021 rates: $18 to $20. Apr 15 to Nov 15. (906)353-6558

BARRYTON — G4 *Missaukee*

MERRILL-GORREL PARK (MECOSTA COUNTY PARK) (Public) From the jct of US-10 & M-66/30th Ave: S 3.0 mi on M-66 to 3 mi Rd, W 6.7 mi to Evergreen Rd S 0.1 mi (R). 146 Avail: 122 W, 122 E (30 amps). 2021 rates: $15 to $30. Apr 01 to Oct 27. (231)832-3246

BATTLE CREEK — J4 *Calhoun*

FORT CUSTER REC AREA (Public State Park) From jct I-94 & 35th St (exit 85): Go 1 mi N on 35th St, then 6-1/4 mi E on M-96, follow signs (R). Avail: 219 E (30 amps). 2021 rates: $20 to $25. (269)731-4200

BAY CITY — G5 *Bay*

BAY CITY (Public State Park) From jct I-75 & Beaver Rd (exit 168): Go 5 mi E on Beaver Rd, follow signs (E). Avail: 193 E (30/50 amps). 2021 rates: $25 to $29. May 01 to Oct 31. (989)684-3020

Set your clocks. Time zones are indicated in the front of each state and province.

BEAR LAKE — F3 *Manistee*

HOPKINS PARK RV AND CAMPGROUND (Public) In town, off US-31, follow signs (R). Avail: 30 E (30 amps). 2021 rates: $22 to $27. Apr 15 to Oct 15. (231)383-2402

KAMPVILLA RV PARK **Ratings: 8/10★/9** (Campground) 57 Avail: 34 full hkups, 23 E (30/50 amps). 2021 rates: $42 to $50. Apr 15 to Oct 15. (231)864-3757, 16632 US-31 (Pleasanton Highway), Bear Lake, MI 49614

BEAVERTON — G5 *Gladwin*

CALHOUN CAMPGROUND (BEAVERTON CITY PARK) (Public) From town: Go 1/2 mi S on Hwy 18, then 2 mi W on Brown, then 200 yards S on Roehrs Rd. 58 Avail: 24 full hkups, 22 E (30/50 amps). 2021 rates: $15 to $30. May 15 to Sep 30. (989)312-4401

BELDING — H4 *Ionia*

DOUBLE R RANCH **Ratings: 5.5/5/6** (Campground) 110 Avail: 44 full hkups, 66 W, 66 E (30/50 amps). 2021 rates: $44 to $56. May 01 to Oct 15. (877)794-0520, 4424 N Whites Bridge Rd, Belding, MI 48809

BELLAIRE — F4 *Antrim*

CHAIN O'LAKES CAMPGROUND

Ratings: 7.5/8.5★/8 (Campground) Avail: 37 full hkups (30/50 amps). 2021 rates: $42. (231)533-8432, 7231 S M 88, Bellaire, MI 49615

BELLEVILLE — J5 *Wayne*

WAYNE COUNTY FAIRGROUNDS RV PARK

Ratings: 7/8.5★/8.5 (Public) From Jct of I-94 & Belleville Rd (exit 190), W 0.3 mi on North Service Rd to Quirk Rd, N 0.2 mi to fairgrounds (R). **FAC:** gravel rds. Avail: 107 grass, 55 pull-thrus, (30x60), back-ins (30x68), 43 full hkups, 64 W, 64 E (30/50 amps), WiFi @ sites, dump, mobile sewer, laundry, LP gas, fire rings, firewood. **REC:** boating nearby, hunting nearby, rec open to public. Pet restrict (Q). Partial handicap access. No tents. Big rig sites, eco-friendly. 2021 rates: $39 to $44, Military discount. Apr 01 to Oct 31.
(734)697-7002 Lat: 42.22324, Lon: -83.49414
10871 Quirk Rd, Belleville, MI 48111
www.waynecountyfairgrounds.net
See ad page 480

Travel Services

CAMPING WORLD OF BELLEVILLE/DETROIT

As the nation's largest retailer of RV supplies, accessories, services and new and used RVs, Camping World is committed to making your total RV experience better. **SERVICES:** RV, tire, RV appliance, staffed RV wash, restrooms. RV Sales. RV supplies, LP gas, RV accessible, waiting room. Hours: 9am to 6pm.
(800)446-8929 Lat: 42.220417, Lon: -83.470653
43646 I-94 Service Drive North, Belleville, MI 48111
www.campingworld.com

BENTON HARBOR — J3 *Berrien*

EDEN SPRINGS PARK **Ratings: 7/8.5★/7.5** (Campground) Avail: 36 full hkups (30/50 amps). 2021 rates: $40 to $45. (269)927-3302, 793 M-139, Benton Harbor, MI 49022

BENZONIA — F3 *Benzie*

TIMBERLINE CAMPGROUND **Ratings: 7.5/8.5★/8** (Campground) 95 Avail: 48 full hkups, 47 W, 47 E (30/50 amps). 2021 rates: $39 to $75. Mar 15 to Nov 01. (231)882-9548, 2788 Benzie Hwy, Benzonia, MI 49616

VACATION TRAILER PARK & CANOE LIVERY **Ratings: 8.5/8.5★/8** (Campground) 76 Avail: 17 full hkups, 59 W, 59 E (20/30 amps). 2021 rates: $36.50 to $42. (231)882-5101, 2080 Benzie Hwy, Benzonia, MI 49616

BERGLAND — A4 *Ontonagon*

LAKE GOGEBIC (Public State Park) From Jct US-2 & M-64: Go 10 mi W on M-64 (R). Avail: 105 E (20/30 amps). 2021 rates: $17 to $28. Apr 15 to Nov 15. (906)842-3341

ONTONAGON COUNTY PARK (Public) From Jct of Hwy 64 & M-28, W 5 mi on M-28 to M-64, S 2 mi (L). 56 Avail: 35 W, 40 E (20/30 amps), Pit toilets. 2021 rates: $7 to $9. May 01 to Sep 30. (906)884-2930

BERRIEN SPRINGS — K3 *Berrien*

SHAMROCK PARK (Public) N-bnd: From Jct I 94 (Exit 30) & US 31, S 10 mi on US 31 to Exit 15 (MI 139/Old US 31), SE 3.3 mi (name changes to Old US 31, then to N Cass St) to Ferry St, NE 0.3 mi on Ferry St (Name changes to Old US 31) to Genoa Rd, N 65 yds (L). 124 Avail: 73 W, 40 S, 73 E (30/50 amps). 2021 rates: $25 to $35. (269)473-5691

BIG BAY — C2 *Marquette*

PERKINS PARK (MARQUETTE COUNTY PARK) (Public) In Marquette, from Jct of US-41 & Wright St, N 4 mi on Wright St to CR-550, N 26 mi, follow signs (R). 73 Avail: 29 full hkups, 22 E (50 amps). 2021 rates: $17 to $33. May 15 to Sep 15. (906)345-9353

BIRCH RUN — H5 *Saginaw*

PINE RIDGE RV CAMPGROUND **Ratings: 5/UI/8.5** (Campground) Avail: 195 full hkups (20/50 amps). 2021 rates: $40. May 01 to Oct 31. (989)624-9029, 11700 Gera Rd, Birch Run, MI 48415

BOYNE CITY — E4 *Charlevoix*

YOUNG (Public State Park) From jct SR-75 & CR-56 (Boyne City Rd): Go 2 mi NW on CR-56, follow signs (L). Avail: 240 E (50 amps). 2021 rates: $25 to $37. Apr 01 to Dec 01. (231)582-7523

BOYNE FALLS — E4 *Charlevox*

CHANDLER HILL CAMPGROUND **Ratings: 7/8.5★/8** (Campground) Avail: 66 full hkups (30/50 amps). 2021 rates: $35 to $40. May 01 to Nov 01. (231)549-7878, 2930 Magee Rd N, Boyne Falls, MI 49713

BRIDGMAN — K3 *Berrien*

WEKO BEACH CAMPGROUND (Public) From Jct of I-94 & Red Arrow Hwy (exit 16), N 1 mi on Red Arrow Hwy to Lake St, W 1 mi, follow signs (R). 70 Avail: 18 W, 70 E (30 amps). 2021 rates: $25 to $30. May 01 to Oct 15. (269)465-3406

BRIGHTON — J5 *Livingston*

BRIGHTON BISHOP LAKE SRA (Public State Park) From Jct of I-96 & exit 147 (Spencer Rd), SW 5 mi on Spencer Rd (Main St) (Brighton Rd), to Chilson Rd, S 1.5 mi to Bishop Lake, E 0.75 mi (R). Entrance fee required. Avail: 144 E (30 amps). 2021 rates: $25. Apr 15 to Nov 03. (810)229-6566

BRIMLEY — D4 *Chippewa*

BAY MILLS CASINO RV PARK **Ratings: 7/9.5★/8** (Campground) 120 Avail: 73 full hkups, 47 W, 47 E (30/50 amps). 2021 rates: $20 to $29. (888)422-9645, 11386 West Lakeshore Dr, Brimley, MI 49715

BRIMLEY (Public State Park) From jct I75 & MI 28: Go 7-3/4 mi W on MI 28, then 2-1/2 mi N on MI 221, then 3/4 mi E on 6 Mile Road (L). Avail: 237 E (30/50 amps). 2021 rates: $25 to $29. (906)248-3422

BROOKLYN — J5 *Jackson*

JUNIPER HILLS CAMPGROUND **Ratings: 6/5/5.5** (Campground) 313 Avail: 210 W, 303 E (30/50 amps). 2021 rates: $30 to $41. May 01 to Oct 31. (888)396-8300, 13500 US Hwy 12, Brooklyn, MI 49230

BRUCE CROSSING — C1 *Ontonagon*

STANNARD TOWNSHIP PARK (Public) From jct M28 in Bruce Crossing & US 45: Go 528 feet N on US 45 (R). 12 Avail: 12 W, 12 E (30 amps). 2021 rates: $15. May 15 to Oct 31. (906)827-3778

BUCHANAN — K3 *Berrien*

BEAR CAVE RESORT

good sam park

Ratings: 8/5.5/6.5 (RV Resort) 87 Avail: 5 full hkups, 82 W, 82 E (20/30 amps). 2021 rates: $65. May 01 to Oct 31. (888)563-7040, 4085 Bear Cave Rd, Buchanan, MI 49107

FULLER'S RESORT & CAMPGROUND ON CLEAR LAKE

Ratings: 8/9★/9.5 (Campground) S-bnd: Jct of I-94 & US-12 (Exit 4A), E 17 mi on US-12 to Bakertown Rd, N 1.6 mi to Elm Valley Rd, W 0.7 mi to E Clear Lake Rd, N 1 mi (E). **FAC:** gravel rds. (155 spaces). 75 Avail: 33 gravel, 42 grass, 6 pull-thrus, (30x60), back-ins (33x40), 12 full hkups, 63 W, 63 E (30/50 amps), seasonal sites, WiFi @ sites, tent sites, rentals, dump, mobile sewer, laundry, groc, LP gas, fire rings, firewood, restaurant. **REC:** Clear Lake: swim, fishing, kayaking/canoeing, boating nearby, playground, rec open to public. Pet restrict (B). eco-friendly. 2021 rates: $40 to $60. Apr 15 to Nov 01.
(269)695-3785 Lat: 41.83436, Lon: -86.41836
1622 E Clear Lake Rd, Buchanan, MI 49107
www.fullersresort.com
See ad this page

Thank you for being one of our best customers!

BUCKLEY — F3 *Grand Traverse*

TRAVERSE CITY KOA **Ratings: 9/9.5★/9.5** (Campground) 92 Avail: 80 full hkups, 12 W, 12 E (30/50 amps). 2021 rates: $48 to $72. May 01 to Oct 25. (800)249-3203, 9700 S M 37, Buckley, MI 49620

BYRON — H5 *Genesee*

MYERS LAKE CAMPING & CABINS (Campground) (Rebuilding) Avail: 107 full hkups (30/50 amps). 2021 rates: $45 to $60. May 01 to Oct 31. (810)370-1232, 10575 W Silver Lake Rd, Byron, MI 48418

CADILLAC — G4 *Missaukee*

CAMP CADILLAC **Ratings: 7.5/9.5★/8.5** (Campground) 97 Avail: 51 full hkups, 41 W, 46 E (30/50 amps). 2021 rates: $35 to $65. Apr 15 to Oct 22. (231)775-9724, 10621 E 34 Rd, Cadillac, MI 49601

MITCHELL (Public State Park) From Jct of M-115 & M-55, NW 0.25 mi on M-115 (R). Entrance fee required. Avail: 221 E (30/50 amps). 2021 rates: $33 to $37. (231)775-7911

CASCO TOWNSHIP — J6 *St Clair*

Travel Services

NORTHPOINTE STORAGE Modern storage features secure facility with video surveillance, standard units and climate-controlled units. Outdoor storage (boats and RVs) **RV Storage:** indoor, outdoor, secured fencing, electric gate, easy reach keypad, 24/7 access, well-lit facility, well-lit roads, well-lit perimeter, security cameras, level gravel/paved spaces, compressed air, office. **SERVICES:**. Hours: 6am to 10pm. Special offers available for Good Sam Members (586)725-8871 Lat: 42.722755, Lon: -82.707512 9926 Marine City Highway (26 Mile Road), Casco Township, MI 48064
www.northpointestorage.com

good sam RV Storage

CASEVILLE — G6 *Huron*

ALBERT E SLEEPER (Public State Park) From town: Go 5 mi NE on Hwy M 25 (R). Avail: 226 E (30/50 amps). 2021 rates: $28 to $32. Apr 17 to Oct 18. (800)447-2757

CASEVILLE PARK (HURON COUNTY PARK) (Public) From the Jct of Port Austin Rd (M-25) & Oak St in Downtown Caseville: N 0.3 mi. on Port Austin Rd, cont. on Main St (L). 230 Avail: 172 full hkups, 58 W, 58 E (30/50 amps). 2021 rates: $31 to $57. Apr 15 to Oct 31. (989)856-2080

CASS CITY — G6 *Tuscola*

EVERGREEN PARK (SANILAC COUNTY PARK) (Public) From jct Hwy 46 & Hwy 53: Go 9 mi N on Hwy 53. 147 Avail: 63 full hkups, 84 W, 84 E (30/50 amps). 2021 rates: $20 to $30. (989)872-6600

CEDAR — F3 *Leelanau*

LEELANAU PINES CAMPGROUNDS **Ratings: 8/8.5★/8** (Campground) 48 Avail: 15 full hkups, 26 W, 33 E (30/50 amps). 2021 rates: $46 to $68. May 01 to Oct 15. (231)228-5742, 6500 E Leelanau Pines Dr, Cedar, MI 49621

CEDAR RIVER — E2 *Menominee*

KLEINKE PARK (MENOMINEE COUNTY PARK) (Public) From jct CR G-12 & Hwy 35: Go 6 mi S on Hwy 35. Avail: 31 E (50 amps). 2021 rates: $15 to $21. (906)753-4582

WELLS (Public State Park) From town: Go 1 mi S on M-35 (L). Avail: 150 E (30/50 amps). 2021 rates: $17 to $26. (906)863-9747

CEDARVILLE — D5 *Mackinac*

CEDARVILLE RV PARK **Ratings: 8.5/9.5★/8.5** (Condo Park) Avail: 20 full hkups (30/50 amps). 2021 rates: $55 to $75. May 01 to Oct 01. (906)484-3351, 634 E. Grove St, Cedarville, MI 49719

CENTRAL LAKE — E4 *Cheboygan*

THURSTON PARK CAMPGROUND (Public) From Jct of M-88 & State St, E 2 blks on State St to Lake St, S 1 blk (E). 38 Avail: 12 full hkups, 26 E (20/30 amps). 2021 rates: $20 to $25. Apr 27 to Oct 19. (231)544-6483

CHAMPION — C2 *Marquette*

MICHIGAMME SHORES CAMPGROUND RESORT **Ratings: 7.5/7/8.5** (Campground) 80 Avail: 63 full hkups, 17 W, 17 E (30/50 amps). 2021 rates: $47. May 01 to Oct 15. (906)339-2116, 64 Purple Rd, Michigamme, MI 49861

VAN RIPER (Public State Park) From jct Hwy 95 & US-41: Go 3-3/4 mi W on US-41, follow signs (L). Avail: 147 E (30/50 amps). 2021 rates: $20 to $29. May 01 to Nov 01. (906)339-4461

CHARLEVOIX — E4 *Charlevoix*

FISHERMAN'S ISLAND (Public State Park) From town: Go 5 mi S on US 31, turn right on Bell Bay Rd, then go 2-1/2 mi on Bell Bay Rd to posted entrance. 81 Avail: Pit toilets. 2021 rates: $17. (231)547-6641

CHARLOTTE — J4 *Eaton*

EATON COUNTY FAIRGROUNDS (Public) From jct I-69 & M-50 (exit 60): Go 3/4 mi W on M-50, then 1/4 mi S on Cochran Ave (L). 340 Avail: 340 W, 340 E (30 amps). 2021 rates: $20. Apr 15 to Oct 15. (517)649-8580

CHEBOYGAN — E5 *Cheboygan*

ALOHA (Public State Park) From town: Go 9 mi S on M-33, then 1 mi W on M-212 (E). Avail: 285 E (30/50 amps). 2021 rates: $30 to $34. May 01 to Oct 11. (231)625-2522

CHEBOYGAN (Public State Park) From jct SR-27 & US-23: Go 5 mi E on US-23, follow signs (L). Avail: 6 E (20 amps). 2021 rates: $20 to $25. (231)627-2811

WATERWAYS CAMPGROUND **Ratings: 6.5/8★/8.5** (Campground) 31 Avail: 24 full hkups, 7 W, 7 E (30/50 amps). 2021 rates: $38 to $44. May 01 to Oct 15. (888)882-7066, 9575 M 33 Hwy, Cheboygan, MI 49721

CHELSEA — J5 *Jackson*

WATERLOO SRA/PORTAGE LAKE (Public State Park) From jct I-94 & Mt Hope Rd (exit 150): Go 2-1/2 mi N on Mt Hope Rd, then 1-3/4 mi W on Seymour Rd, follow signs (R). Avail: 136 E (30/50 amps). 2021 rates: $20 to $32. (734)475-8307

WATERLOO SRA/SUGARLOAF (Public State Park) From jct I-94 & Exit 153 (Clear Lake Rd): Go 4 mi N on Clear Lake Rd, then 1 mi E on Loveland Rd (L). Avail: 164 E (20/50 amps). 2021 rates: $28 to $32. May 15 to Sep 13. (734)475-8307

CLARE — G4 *Isabella*

HERRICK REC AREA (ISABELLA COUNTY PARK) (Public) From Jct of US/Bus-10 & Bus-27, E 2.25 mi on US/Bus-10 to Summerton Rd, S 0.75 mi to Herrick Rd, E 0.25 mi (R). Avail: 73 E (20/30 amps). 2021 rates: $20 to $25. May 01 to Oct 15. (989)386-2010

CLAYTON — K5 *Lenawee*

LAKE HUDSON SRA (Public State Park) From jct US 127 & Hwy 34: Go 6-1/2 mi E on Hwy 34, then 1-1/2 mi S on Hwy 156. 50 Avail: Pit toilets. 2021 rates: $20. (517)445-2265

CLIMAX — J4 *Kalamazoo*

COLD BROOK COUNTY PARK (Public) From Jct of I 94 & Mercury Dr (Exit 92), S 0.3 mi on Mercury Dr to MN Ave E, West 1.5 mi (R). 29 Avail: 29 W, 29 E (30/50 amps). 2021 rates: $24. Apr 15 to Oct 31. (269)746-4270

SNOWBIRD TIP: Fire up the barbecue. Even during the holidays, it can get too warm to cook a traditional meal in your RV kitchen. This is your chance to explore great holiday camping recipes so plan on outside festivities with grilled entrees and cold beverages.

MI

COLDWATER — K4 *Branch*

ANGEL COVE PARK (Public) From Jct of I-69 & US-12, W 3.5 mi on US-12 to River Rd, N 4 mi, follow signs (L). 130 Avail: 110 W, 110 E (20/30 amps). 2021 rates: $25. Apr 15 to Oct 15. (517)278-8541

HARBOR COVE RV RESORT **Ratings: 7/6/9.5** (RV Resort) Avail: 156 full hkups (30/50 amps). 2021 rates: $45. May 01 to Oct 31. (517)279-2683, 632 Race St, Coldwater, MI 49036

MEMORIAL PARK (BRANCH COUNTY PARK) (Public) From jct I-69 & US-12: Go 3 mi W on US-12, then 1/2 mi S on Behnke Rd. Avail: 20 E (30/50 amps). 2021 rates: $20 to $25. May 01 to Oct 15. (517)279-2254

WAFFLE FARM CAMPGROUNDS

good sam park **Ratings: 7/10★/9.5** (Campground) From Jct of I-69 & Jonesville Rd (exit 16), W 2.5 mi on Jonesville Rd to Union City Rd, N 0.75 mi (L). **FAC:** gravel rds. (355 spaces). Avail: 110 grass, 24 pull-thrus, (25x75), back-ins (28x75), 18 full hkups, 92 W, 92 E (30/50 amps), seasonal sites, cable, WiFi @ sites, tent sites, rentals, dump, groc, LP gas, firewood. **REC:** Craig-Morrison Chain of 7 Lakes: swim, fishing, kayaking/canoeing, boating nearby, playground. Pet restrict (B). Partial handicap access, eco-friendly. 2021 rates: $35 to $60. Apr 15 to Oct 15.
(517)278-4315 Lat: 41.99736, Lon: -85.02510
790 N Union City Rd, Coldwater, MI 49036
wafflefarm.com
See ad this page

Travel Services

GANDER RV OF COLDWATER Your new hometown outfitter offering the best regional gear for all your outdoor needs. Your adventure awaits. **SERVICES:** RV appliance, MH mechanical, sells outdoor gear, sells firearms, restrooms. RV Sales. RV supplies, LP gas, dump, emergency parking, RV accessible. Hours: 9am to 8pm.
(844)967-0742 Lat: 41.939660, Lon: -84.968415
373 N Willowbrook Rd Ste Y, Coldwater, MI 49036
rv.ganderoutdoors.com

COLOMA — J3 *Van Buren*

COLOMA/ST JOSEPH KOA **Ratings: 9/9.5★/9.5** (Campground) 113 Avail: 40 full hkups, 73 W, 73 E (30/50 amps). 2021 rates: $55.36 to $88.95. May 01 to Oct 15. (269)849-3333, 3527 Coloma Rd, Benton Harbor, MI 49022

DUNE LAKE CAMPGROUND **Ratings: 5.5/7.5★/7.5** (Campground) 70 Avail: 70 W, 40 E (20/30 amps). 2021 rates: $35. May 01 to Oct 01. (269)764-8941, 80855 CR-376, Coloma, MI 49038

New to RVing? Visit Blog.GoodSam.com for tips on everything camping and RVing.

COOPERSVILLE — H3 *Ottawa*

CONESTOGA GRAND RIVER CAMPGROUND **Ratings: 7/8.5★/8.5** (Campground) 51 Avail: 23 full hkups, 28 W, 28 E (30/50 amps). 2021 rates: $50 to $65. May 01 to Oct 31. (616)837-6323, 9720 Oriole Dr, Coopersville, MI 49404

COPPER HARBOR — B2 *Keweenaw*

FORT WILKINS (Public State Park) From jct US-41 & Hwy 26: Go 1 mi E on US-41, then 1-1/2 mi E on park access road (R). Avail: 159 E (30/50 amps). 2021 rates: $20 to $29. Apr 15 to Nov 15. (906)289-4215

COVERT — J3 *Van Buren*

COVERT PARK BEACH & CAMPGROUND (Public) From I-196 exit 13 (Covert): Go W 1 mile to park. 62 Avail: 52 W, 52 E (20/30 amps). 2021 rates: $34. May 15 to Oct 15. (269)764-1421

COVERT/SOUTH HAVEN KOA **Ratings: 8.5/9.5★/9.5** (Campground) 138 Avail: 102 full hkups, 36 W, 36 E (30/50 amps). 2021 rates: $42.99 to $89.99. Apr 15 to Oct 15. (269)764-0818, 39397 M-140 Highway, Covert, MI 49043

CRYSTAL FALLS — D1 *Iron*

BEWABIC (Public State Park) From jct US-141 & US-2: Go 3 mi W on US-2, follow signs (L). Avail: 122 E (20/50 amps). 2021 rates: $17 to $24. (906)875-3324

COPPER COUNTRY (GLIDDEN LAKE CAMPGROUND) (Public State Park) From town, E 4.5 mi on M-69 to Lake Mary Rd, S 1.5 mi to NE-side of lake (R). 23 Avail: Pit toilets. 2021 rates: $15. May 01 to Nov 01. (906)875-3324

PAINT RIVER HILLS CAMPGROUND **Ratings: 4/8.5★/7** (Campground) 23 Avail: 4 full hkups, 19 W, 19 E (30/50 amps). 2021 rates: $25 to $30. May 15 to Nov 30. (906)875-4977, 220 Railway Street , Crystal Falls, MI 49920

PENTOGA PARK (IRON COUNTY PARK) (Public) From Iron Mountain, NE 23.6 mi on US-2 to CR-424, S & W 9 mi on CR 424, follow signs (R). Entrance fee required. 100 Avail: 100 W, 100 E (30/50 amps). 2021 rates: $22 to $23. May 15 to Sep 30. (906)265-3979

RUNKLE LAKE MUNICIPAL PARK (Public) From Jct of US 2 & M69, in Crystal Falls, E 0.75 mi on M69 to Runkle Lake Rd (park sign), N 0.2 mi on Runkle Lake Rd (L). 32 Avail: 16 full hkups, 16 W, 16 E (30/50 amps). 2021 rates: $20 to $25. May 24 to Sep 07. (906)214-4729

CURRAN — F5 *Oscoda*

AU SABLE/MCCOLLUM LAKE (Public State Park) From town, NW 8.5 mi on M-72 to Mc Collum Lake Rd, follow signs (R). 17 Avail: Pit toilets. 2021 rates: $15. (989)848-8545

CURTIS — D3 *Mackinac*

LOG CABIN RESORT & CAMPGROUND **Ratings: 7.5/8★/7.5** (Campground) 30 Avail: 23 full hkups, 7 W, 7 E (30/50 amps). 2021 rates: $40 to $45. May 01 to Oct 01. (906)586-9732, 18024 H42, Curtis, MI 49820

SOUTH MANISTIQUE LAKE (Public State Park) From town: Go 3 mi W on S Curtis Rd, then 2 mi S on Long Point Rd, then 1/2 mi SE, on West side of lake. 29 Avail: Pit toilets. 2021 rates: $15. (906)492-3415

DAVISON — H5 *Genesee*

WOLVERINE CAMPGROUND (GENESEE COUNTY PARK) (Public) From Jct of I-75 & Mt Morris Rd exit, E 14.5 mi on Mt Morris Rd to Baxter Rd, S 0.25 mi (R); or From Jct of M-15 & Mt Morris Rd, E 2.6 mi to Baxter Rd, S 0.25 mi (R). Avail: 151 E (20/50 amps). 2021 rates: $20 to $31. May 22 to Sep 03. (800)648-7275

DECATUR — J3 *Van Buren*

OAK SHORES CAMPGROUND **Ratings: 8.5/6.5/7.5** (Campground) 116 Avail: 90 full hkups, 26 W, 26 E (30/50 amps). 2021 rates: $39 to $52. Apr 15 to Oct 15. (269)423-7370, 86232 CR-215, Decatur, MI 49045

TIMBER TRAILS RV PARK **Ratings: 8/8.5★/9** (Campground) Avail: 32 full hkups (30/50 amps). 2021 rates: $40. May 01 to Sep 30. (269)423-7311, 84981-47 1/2 St, Decatur, MI 49045

DETROIT — J6 *Wayne*

DETROIT See also Belleville, Fair Haven, Holly, Howell, Monroe, New Hudson, Petersburg, Pinckney, St Clair, Tecumseh & Ypsilanti, MI; Amherstburg, Belle River, Essex, Leamington, Wheatley & Windsor, ON.

DORR — J3 *Allegan*

HUNGRY HORSE FAMILY CAMPGROUND

good sam park **Ratings: 8.5/9.5★/10** (Campground) 71 Avail: 40 full hkups, 31 W, 31 E (30/50 amps). 2021 rates: $42 to $55. May 01 to Oct 15. (616)681-9836, 2016 142nd Avenue, Dorr, MI 49323

DURAND — H5 *Shiawassee*

HOLIDAY SHORES RV PARK **Ratings: 8/NA/9.5** (RV Park) Avail: 50 full hkups (30/50 amps). 2021 rates: $40. May 01 to Oct 31. (989)288-4444, 10915 Goodall Rd, Durand, MI 48429

EAST HIGHLAND — J5 *Oakland*

HIGHLAND REC AREA (Public State Park) From jct US-23 & US-59: Go 10 mi E on US-59; or From jct I-75 & US-59: Go 16 mi W on US-59, follow signs (L). 25 Avail: Pit toilets. 2021 rates: $20. (248)889-3750

EAST JORDAN — E4 *Charlevoix*

EAST JORDAN TOURIST PARK (Public) From Jct of M-32 & M-66, N 0.1 mi on M-66 (R). 90 Avail: 75 full hkups, 15 W, 15 E (30/50 amps). 2021 rates: $26 to $36. (231)536-2561

WOODEN SHOE PARK (Public) From jct Hwy-66 & East Jordan-Ellsworth Rd: Go 7 mi W on East Jordan-Ellsworth Rd, follow signs. 45 Avail: 45 W, 45 E. 2021 rates: $30. May 15 to Sep 15. (231)588-6382

EAST TAWAS — F5 *Iosco*

EAST TAWAS CITY PARK (Public) At Jct of US-23 & Newman St. Avail: 178 full hkups (30 amps). 2021 rates: $20 to $40. (989)362-5562

TAWAS POINT (Public State Park) From jct US-23 & Tawas Beach Rd exit: Go 2-1/2 mi SE on Tawas Beach Rd, follow signs (E). Avail: 193 E (30 amps). 2021 rates: $33. Apr 15 to Oct 30. (989)362-5041

EASTPORT — E4 *Antrim*

BARNES PARK CAMPGROUND (ANTRIM COUNTY PARK) (Public) From Jct of US-31 & SR-88, W .25 mi on SR-88/becomes Barnes Park Rd (E). Avail: 76 E (20/30 amps). 2021 rates: $26 to $30. May 12 to Oct 20. (231)599-2712

ELK RAPIDS — F4 *Antrim*

HONCHO REST CAMPGROUND **Ratings: 7.5/8.5★/8.5** (Campground) Avail: 25 full hkups (30/50 amps). 2021 rates: $55 to $75. May 01 to Oct 01. (231)264-8548, 8988 Cairn Highway, Elk Rapids, MI 49629

RV Park ratings you can rely on!

EMMETT — H6 *St Clair*

EMMETT KOA **Ratings: 8/10★/9** (Campground) 90 Avail: 42 full hkups, 48 W, 48 E (30/50 amps). 2021 rates: $46 to $89. May 01 to Oct 25. (888)562-5612, 3864 Breen Rd, Emmett, MI 48022

EMPIRE — F3 *Leelanau*

INDIGO BLUFFS RV PARK Ratings: 9/9.5★/9 (Campground) 187 Avail: 183 full hkups, 4 W, 4 E (30/50 amps). 2021 rates: $37 to $72. May 15 to Oct 15. (231)326-5050, 6760 W Empire Hwy M-72, Empire, MI 49630

INDIGO BLUFFS RV RESORT **Ratings: 10/9.5★/10** (Condo Park) Avail: 43 full hkups (50 amps). 2021 rates: $52 to $86. May 15 to Oct 15. (231)326-5050, 6760 W Empire Hwy M-72, Empire, MI 49630

ESCANABA — D2 *Delta*

FULLER CAMPGROUND (DELTA COUNTY PARK) (Public) From town, S 15 mi on M-35 (L). 44 Avail: 44 W, 44 E (20/50 amps). 2021 rates: $13 to $28. May 07 to Oct 14. (906)786-1020

PIONEER TRAIL PARK (DELTA COUNTY PARK) (Public) N-bnd: On US-2/41 at N-end of town/Escanaba River Bridge (R). 98 Avail: 78 W, 78 E (20/50 amps). 2021 rates: $13 to $28. May 01 to Oct 15. (906)786-1020

ESSEXVILLE — G5 *Bay*

FINN ROAD PARK RV CAMPGROUND & BOAT LAUNCH (Public) From jct Hwy 15 & Hwy 25: Go 5 mi E on Hwy 25, then 2 mi N on Finn Rd. Avail: 56 full hkups (30/50 amps). 2021 rates: $24. May 01 to Oct 31. (989)992-2920

EVART — G4 *Osceola*

RIVERSIDE PARK (Public) From Jct of US-131 & US-10, E 14 mi on US-10 to Main St, S 0.1 mi to 9th St, E 0.25 mi, follow signs (L). Avail: 15 E (30 amps). 2021 rates: $15 to $25. May 01 to Sep 30. (231)734-5901

FAIR HAVEN — J6 *St Clair*

NORTHPOINTE SHORES RV RESORT
good sam park
Ratings: 9.5/10★/10 (RV Resort) Avail: 36 full hkups (30/50 amps). 2021 rates: $66 to $70. Apr 01 to Oct 31. (586)250-2800, 10413 Dixie Highway, Ira Township, MI 48023

FENWICK — H4 *Montcalm*

SNOW LAKE KAMPGROUND **Ratings: 9/8.5★/8** (Campground) 129 Avail: 104 full hkups, 25 W, 25 E (30/50 amps). 2021 rates: $38 to $42. May 01 to Oct 01. (989)248-3224, 644 E Snows Lake Rd, Fenwick, MI 48834

FIFE LAKE — F4 *Grand Traverse*

PERE MARQUETTE/SPRING LAKE (Public State Park) From Jct of US-131 & Hwy 186, SW 1.5 mi on US-131 to park access rd, S 0.5 mi, follow signs (R). 30 Avail: Pit toilets. 2021 rates: $15. (231)775-7911

FOREST LAKE — D3 *Alger*

FOREST LAKE STATE FOREST CAMPGROUND (Public State Park) From town: Go 1/4 mi W on Hwy 94, then 2 mi S on Campground Rd. 23 Avail: Pit toilets. 2021 rates: $15. (906)341-2355

FOUNTAIN — G3 *Mason*

TIMBER SURF RESORT **Ratings: 6/8★/7** (Campground) 32 Avail: 6 full hkups, 19 W, 19 E (30/50 amps). 2021 rates: $32. Apr 01 to Nov 30. (231)462-3468, 6575 Dewey Rd, Fountain, MI 49410

FRANKENMUTH — H5 *Saginaw*

FRANKENMUTH YOGI BEAR'S JELLYSTONE PARK CAMP-RESORT
good sam park
Ratings: 9/10★/9.5 (RV Park) N-bnd: From Jct of I-75 & M-83 (Exit 136), E 2 mi on M-83 (Birch Run Rd) to M-83 (Gera Rd), N 5 mi to Weiss St, NE .01 mi (R). **FAC:** paved/gravel rds. 196 Avail: 64 paved, 103 gravel, 29 grass, 48 pull-thrus, (25x65), back-ins (25x60), 169 full hkups, 27 W, 27 E (30/50 amps), WiFi @ sites, tent sites, rentals, dump, laundry, groc, LP gas, firewood, controlled access. **REC:** heated pool, hot tub, playground. Pets OK. Partial handicap access. Big rig sites, eco-friendly. 2021 rates: $58 to $83, Military discount. Mar 01 to Dec 31. ATM.
(989)652-6668 Lat: 43.31699, Lon: -83.73384
1339 Weiss St, Frankenmuth, MI 48734
www.frankenmuthjellystone.com
See ad this page

FRANKFORT — F3 *Benzie*

BETSIE RIVER CAMPSITE **Ratings: 5.5/8/8.5** (Campground) 84 Avail: 70 W, 84 E (20 amps). 2021 rates: $36 to $39. Apr 01 to Oct 31. (231)352-9535, 1923 River Rd, Frankfort, MI 49635

FREDERIC — F4 *Crawford*

AU SABLE/JONES LAKE (Public State Park) From town, E 9 mi on CR-612, follow signs (R). 42 Avail: Pit toilets. 2021 rates: $15. (989)348-7068

AU SABLE/UPPER MANISTEE RIVER (Public State Park) From town: Go 6-1/2 mi W on CR 612, then S on Manistee Rd. 30 Avail: Pit toilets. 2021 rates: $15. (989)348-7068

GARDEN — D3 *Delta*

FAYETTE HISTORIC PARK (Public State Park) From jct US-2 & M-183: Go 17 mi SW on M-183 (R). Avail: 61 E (20/50 amps), Pit toilets. 2021 rates: $20 to $29. (906)644-2603

PORTAGE BAY STATE FOREST CAMPGROUND (Public State Park) From town, W 2.6 mi on 16th Rd., S 3.25 mi on LL Rd., SE 2 mi 100 Rd. 23 Avail: Pit toilets. 2021 rates: $15. (906)644-2603

GAYLORD — E4 *Otsego*

BENJAMIN'S BEAVER CREEK RESORT **Ratings: 9/9★/9** (Membership Park) 63 Avail: 34 full hkups, 29 W, 29 E (30/50 amps). 2021 rates: $10. (888)249-1995, 5004 West Otsego Lake Dr, Gaylord, MI 49735

GAYLORD KOA **Ratings: 9/9.5★/9** (Campground) 97 Avail: 75 full hkups, 22 W, 22 E (30/50 amps). 2021 rates: $43.81 to $85.81. May 01 to Oct 15. (800)562-4146, 5101 Campfires Parkway, Gaylord, MI 49735

OTSEGO LAKE (Public State Park) From Jct of I-75 & Old US-27, S 6 mi on Old US-27, follow signs (R). Entrance fee required. Avail: 155 E (20/30 amps). 2021 rates: $22 to $30. Apr 06 to Nov 01. (989)732-5485

GERMFASK — D3 *Schoolcraft*

BIG CEDAR CAMPGROUND & CANOE LIVERY
good sam park
Ratings: 7.5/9.5★/9 (Campground) 50 Avail: 9 full hkups, 41 W, 41 E (15/30 amps). 2021 rates: $30 to $35. May 01 to Oct 20. (906)586-6684, 7936 St. Highway M-77, Germfask, MI 49836

NORTHLAND OUTFITTERS **Ratings: 6/6.5/8.5** (Campground) 10 Avail: 5 W, 10 E (20/30 amps). 2021 rates: $35. May 01 to Oct 15. (906)586-9801, 8174 Hwy M-77, Germfask, MI 49836

GLADSTONE — D2 *Delta*

GLADSTONE BAY CAMPGROUND (Public) From N jct Hwy 35 & US 2/41: Go 1/2 mi S on US 2/41, then 1 mi E on Delta Ave. 45 Avail: 28 full hkups, 17 E (30/50 amps). 2021 rates: $25 to $30. May 07 to Oct 07. (906)428-1211

GLADWIN — G5 *Clare*

AU SABLE/TROUT LAKE (Public State Park) From town: Go 3 mi N on Meredith Grade Rd. 35 Avail: Pit toilets. 2021 rates: $15. (989)386-4067

GLADWIN CITY PARK & CAMPGROUND (Public) From Jct of SR-61 & Antler St, S 0.5 mi on Antler St (R). 59 Avail: 59 W, 59 E (20 amps). 2021 rates: $27. May 01 to Nov 30. (989)426-8126

RIVER VALLEY RV PARK **Ratings: 7.5/8.5★/8.5** (Campground) 62 Avail: 62 W, 62 E (30 amps). 2021 rates: $37. May 01 to Oct 15. (989)386-7844, 2165 S Bailey Lake Ave, Gladwin, MI 48624

GLEN ARBOR — F3 *Leelanau*

SLEEPING BEAR DUNES/D H DAY (Public National Park) From town, W 1.5 mi on SR-109, follow signs (R). 88 Avail: Pit toilets. 2021 rates: $20. Apr 04 to Nov 29. (231)326-4700

GLENNIE — F5 *Alcona*

ALCONA PARK (Public) From Jct of M-72 & M-65, S 7 mi on M-65 to Bamfield Rd, W 4.5 mi, follow signs (R). 502 Avail: 48 full hkups, 104 W, 104 E (30/50 amps). 2021 rates: $25 to $30. Apr 15 to Dec 01. (989)735-3881

How can we make a great Travel Guide even better? We ask YOU! Please share your thoughts with us. Drop us a note and let us know if there's anything we haven't thought of.

GOULD CITY — D3 *Mackinac*

MICHIHISTRIGAN BAR CAMPGROUND & CABINS **Ratings: 4/6/6.5** (Campground) 34 Avail: 12 full hkups, 22 W, 22 E (30 amps). 2021 rates: $24 to $28. May 01 to Nov 30. (906)477-6983, W17838 Hwy US 2, Gould City, MI 49838

GRAND HAVEN — H3 *Ottawa*

CAMPERS PARADISE **Ratings: 5.5/8★/5.5** (Campground) 83 Avail: 83 W, 83 E (20/30 amps). 2021 rates: $30 to $40. May 15 to Oct 15. (616)846-1460, 800 Robbins Rd, Grand Haven, MI 49417

EASTPOINTE RV RESORT **Ratings: 10/9.5★/10** (RV Resort) Avail: 30 full hkups (30/50 amps). 2021 rates: $58 to $78. May 01 to Oct 01. (616)414-8137, 200 N Beechtree St, Grand Haven, MI 49417

GRAND HAVEN (Public State Park) From jct US-31 & Washington Ave: Go 3/4 mi N on Washington Ave, then 3/4 mi W on Harbor Ave (R). Avail: 174 E (30/50 amps). 2021 rates: $33 to $37. Mar 26 to Oct 30. (616)847-1309

GRAND JUNCTION — J3 *Van Buren*

WARNER CAMP RV PARK **Ratings: 5.5/7/7.5** (Campground) 62 Avail: 62 W, 62 E (30/50 amps). 2021 rates: $32. May 01 to Oct 01. (269)434-6844, 60 55th St, Grand Junction, MI 49056

GRAND MARAIS — C3 *Alger*

BLIND SUCKER NO. 2 (Public State Park) From town: Go 16 mi E on Grand Marais Truck Trail. 32 Avail: Pit toilets. 2021 rates: $15. (906)658-3338

PICTURED ROCKS NATL LAKESHORE/HURRICANE RIVER (Public National Park) From Grand Marais, W 12 mi on CR-H58, follow signs (R). 21 Avail: Pit toilets. 2021 rates: $20. May 15 to Oct 31. (906)387-3700

PICTURED ROCKS NATL LAKESHORE/TWELVEMILE BEACH (Public National Park) From Grand Marais, W 16 mi on CR-H58, follow signs (R). 36 Avail: Pit toilets. 2021 rates: $20. May 15 to Oct 31. (906)387-3700

WOODLAND PARK CAMPGROUND (Public) From NW end of town, W 0.5 mi on M-77, follow signs (R). 125 Avail: 110 W, 110 E (30/50 amps). 2021 rates: $22 to $34. Apr 20 to Oct 15. (906)494-2613

GRAND RAPIDS — H3 *Kent*

WOODCHIP CAMPGROUND **Ratings: 8.5/9.5★/8.5** (Campground) 69 Avail: 41 full hkups, 28 W, 28 E (30/50 amps). 2021 rates: $50 to $75. (616)878-9050, 7501 Burlingame SW, Byron Center, MI 49315

Travel Services

CAMPING WORLD OF GRAND RAPIDS As the nation's largest retailer of RV supplies, accessories, services and new and used RVs, Camping World is committed to making your total RV experience better. **SERVICES:** RV, tire, RV appliance, MH mechanical, sells outdoor gear, restrooms. RV Sales. RV supplies, emergency parking, RV accessible. Hours: 9am to 7pm. (844)746-5682 Lat: 42.826239, Lon: -85.669525 201 76th Street SW, Grand Rapids, MI 49548 www.campingworld.com

GRANT — H3 *Newaygo*

CHINOOK CAMPING **Ratings: 6.5/7.5/8** (Campground) 101 Avail: 37 W, 37 E (30 amps). 2021 rates: $32 to $36. Apr 15 to Oct 15. (231)834-7505, 5471 W 112th St, Grant, MI 49327

GRASS LAKE — J5 *Jackson*

APPLE CREEK CAMPGROUND & RV PARK good sam park **Ratings: 7.5/9★/9.5** (Campground) 95 Avail: 95 W, 95 E (30 amps). 2021 rates: $35 to $43. Apr 15 to Nov 30. (517)522-3467, 11185 Orban Rd, Grass Lake, MI 49240

HOLIDAY RV CAMPGROUND **Ratings: 8.5/8.5★/8** (Campground) 63 Avail: 12 full hkups, 51 W, 51 E (30/50 amps). 2021 rates: $44.99 to $54.99. Apr 15 to Oct 31. (517)522-5846, 9625 Knight Rd, Grass Lake, MI 49240

GRAYLING — F4 *Crawford*

AU SABLE/CANOE HARBOR (Public State Park) From town: Go 14 mi SE on Hwy 72. 54 Avail: Pit toilets. 2021 rates: $15. (989)275-5151

AU SABLE/LAKE MARGRETHE (Public State Park) From jct Hwy 93 & Hwy 72: Go 5 mi W on Hwy 72, then 1/4 mi S on McIntyres Landing Rd, then 2 mi W on gravel road. 30 Avail: Pit toilets. 2021 rates: $15. (989)348-7068

AU SABLE/MANISTEE RIVER BRIDGE (Public State Park) From town: Go 8 mi W on Hwy 72. 23 Avail: Pit toilets. 2021 rates: $15. (989)348-7068

AU SABLE/SHUPAC LAKE (Public State Park) From Jct of Hwy 612 & Twin Bridge Rd, N 2 mi on Twin Bridge Rd to gravel rd, E 0.5 mi, follow signs (E). 30 Avail: Pit toilets. 2021 rates: $15. (989)348-7068

HARTWICK PINES (Public State Park) From jct I-75 & Harwick Pines Rd (exit 259): Go 2 mi NE on Harwick Pines Rd (L). 100 Avail: 36 full hkups, 64 E (20/30 amps). 2021 rates: $30 to $38. Apr 01 to Nov 30. (989)348-7068

MILITARY PARK CAMP GRAYLING RV PARK (CAMP GRAYLING) (Public) From jct I-75 & 4 Mile Rd (exit 251): Go 4 mi W on 4 Mile Rd, N on Military Rd, then left on M-93, then through the gate right on Lake Rd. Avail: 65 full hkups (30/50 amps). 2021 rates: $17 to $20. May 09 to Sep 20. (989)344-6604

YOGI BEAR'S JELLYSTONE PARK CAMP-RESORT **Ratings: 7.5/10★/9** (Campground) 149 Avail: 35 full hkups, 114 W, 114 E (30/50 amps). 2021 rates: $55 to $75. May 01 to Oct 15. (989)348-2157, 370 W 4 Mile Rd, Grayling, MI 49738

GREENVILLE — H4 *Montcalm*

THREE SEASONS FAMILY CAMPGROUND **Ratings: 8/7.5/8** (Campground) 56 Avail: 2 full hkups, 29 W, 54 E (30/50 amps). 2021 rates: $35 to $38. Apr 21 to Oct 15. (616)754-5717, 6956 W Fuller Rd, Greenville, MI 48838

GWINN — D2 *Marquette*

ESCANABA RIVER/BASS LAKE (Public State Park) From town: Go 1-1/4 mi SE on Rice Lake Dr (L). 18 Avail: Pit toilets. 2021 rates: $15. (906)492-3415

FARQUAR-METSA TOURIST PARK & CAMPGROUND (Public) From Jct of M-35 & Iron St, E 0.35 mi on Iron St (L). Avail: 20 full hkups (30/50 amps). 2021 rates: $26. May 29 to Sep 30. (906)250-1081

HANCOCK — B1 *Houghton*

HANCOCK CAMPGROUND (Public) From Jct of US 41 & CR 203 (Quincy St-in Hancock), W 1.3 mi on CR 203 /Quincy St (changes to Jasberg St) (L). 58 Avail: 13 W, 58 E (30/50 amps). 2021 rates: $22 to $25. May 15 to Oct 15. (906)482-7413

MCLAIN (Public State Park) From town, N 10 mi on M-203, follow signs (L). Entrance fee required. Avail: 98 E (20/30 amps). 2021 rates: $22 to $30. (906)482-0278

HARBOR BEACH — G6 *Huron*

NORTH PARK CAMPGROUND (Public) From Jct of M-142 & M-25 (Huron St, in Harbor Beach), N 0.8 mi on M-25 (L). Avail: 184 full hkups (30/50 amps). 2021 rates: $24 to $25. May 01 to Oct 31. (989)479-9554

WAGENER PARK (HURON COUNTY PARK) (Public) From the Jct of State St & S. Lakeshore Rd (M-25): S 5.3 mi on S. Lakeshore Rd. (L). 75 Avail: 11 full hkups, 64 W, 64 E (30 amps). 2021 rates: $19 to $36. May 01 to Oct 15. (989)479-9131

HARRIS — D2 *Delta*

ISLAND RESORT & CASINO RV PARK **Ratings: 8/9★/7.5** (Campground) 42 Avail: 42 W, 42 E (30/50 amps). 2021 rates: $23. May 01 to Nov 30. (800)682-6040, W399 US 2 & US 41, Harris, MI 49845

Like Us on Facebook.

HARRISON — G4 *Clare*

COUNTRYSIDE CAMPGROUND **Ratings: 8.5/10★/8.5** (Campground) 42 Avail: 29 full hkups, 13 W, 13 E (30/50 amps). 2021 rates: $42 to $48. May 01 to Oct 15. (989)539-5468, 805 Byfield Dr, Harrison, MI 48625

HARRISON RV FAMILY CAMPGROUND **Ratings: 4/9★/7.5** (Campground) 73 Avail: 53 full hkups, 20 W, 20 E (30/50 amps). 2021 rates: $30 to $40. Apr 15 to Oct 08. (989)539-3128, 1820 Hampton Rd, Harrison, MI 48625

HIDDEN HILL FAMILY CAMPGROUND good sam park **Ratings: 9/10★/9.5** (Campground) Avail: 21 full hkups (30/50 amps). 2021 rates: $45 to $65. Apr 15 to Oct 31. (989)539-9372, 300 N Clare Ave, Harrison, MI 48625

WILSON (Public State Park) From jct SR-61 & Old US-127: Go 1/2 mi N on Old US-127, follow signs (R). Avail: 158 E (30 amps). 2021 rates: $22. Apr 01 to Dec 01. (989)539-3021

HARRISVILLE — F6 *Alcona*

HARRISVILLE (Public State Park) From town: Go 1/2 mi S on US-23, then 525 ft E on park access rd, follow signs (L). Avail: 195 E (20/50 amps). 2021 rates: $28 to $32. May 09 to Oct 26. (989)724-5126

HART — G3 *Oceana*

JOHN GURNEY MUNICIPAL PARK (Public) From Jct of US-31 & Exit 149 (Polk Rd), E. 1.9 mi on Polk Rd to S Griswold St, N 0.8 mi (R). 81 Avail: 40 full hkups, 32 W, 32 E (50 amps). 2021 rates: $30 to $40. Apr 15 to Oct 15. (231)873-4959

HASTINGS — J4 *Barry*

CAMP MICHAWANA CHRISTIAN RV CAMP **Ratings: 7.5/8★/7.5** (Campground) 56 Avail: 12 full hkups, 44 W, 44 E (30/50 amps). 2021 rates: $35 to $40. May 01 to Oct 03. (269)623-3035, 5800 Head Lake Rd, Hastings, MI 49058

WELCOME WOODS CAMPGROUND & RV PARK **Ratings: 5/9★/6.5** (Campground) 27 Avail: 27 W, 27 E (30/50 amps). 2021 rates: $40 to $50. May 01 to Oct 15. (269)908-2097, 522 Welcome Road, Hastings, MI 49058

HILLMAN — E5 *Montmorency*

EMERICK PARK (Public) From jct Hwy 65 & Hwy 32: Go 3/4 mi W on Hwy 32, then 5 mi N on State St (R). 36 Avail: 12 full hkups, 22 W, 22 E (30/50 amps). 2021 rates: $16 to $20. May 01 to Oct 31. (989)733-0613

THUNDER BAY RESORT **Ratings: 7.5/NA/9.5** (RV Resort) Avail: 23 full hkups (30/50 amps). 2021 rates: $35 to $55. Apr 15 to Nov 20. (989)742-4502, 27800 M-32, Hillman, MI 49746

HILLSDALE — K4 *Hillsdale*

6 LAKES CAMPGROUND **Ratings: 4.5/8/8** (Campground) 30 Avail: 2 full hkups, 28 W, 28 E (30 amps). 2021 rates: $30 to $38. May 01 to Nov 30. (517)439-5660, 2155 Hudson Rd, Hillsdale, MI 49242

GATEWAY PARK CAMPGROUND **Ratings: 9/9★/10** (Campground) Avail: 27 full hkups (30/50 amps). 2021 rates: $47 to $64. Apr 15 to Oct 15. (517)437-7005, 4111 W Hallett Rd, Hillsdale, MI 49242

HOLLAND — J3 *Ottawa*

HOLLAND (Public State Park) From jct US-31 & Lakewood Blvd: Go 1-1/4 mi W on Lakewood Blvd, then 5-3/4 mi SW on Douglas Ave/Ottawa Beach Rd (R). 309 Avail: 31 full hkups, 278 E (30/50 amps). 2021 rates: $33 to $45. Apr 01 to Oct 31. (616)399-9390

OAK GROVE RESORT **Ratings: 10/10★/10** (Campground) Avail: 62 full hkups (30/50 amps). 2021 rates: $55 to $80. Apr 23 to Oct 04. (616)399-9230, 2011 Ottawa Beach Rd, Holland, MI 49424

HOLLY — J5 *Oakland*

GROVELAND OAKS COUNTY PARK (Public) From Jct of I-75 & Exit 101 (Grange Hall Rd), E 1 mi on Grange Hall Rd to Dixie Hwy, N .3 mi (L). 267 Avail: 60 full hkups, 207 W, 207 E (30/50 amps). 2021 rates: $40 to $55. Apr 27 to Oct 08. (248)634-9811

HOLLY KOA FUN PARK **Ratings: 8/8/8** (Campground) 129 Avail: 6 full hkups, 123 W, 123 E (30/50 amps). 2021 rates: $45 to $130. Apr 15 to Nov 01. (248)634-0803, 7072 Grange Hall Rd, Holly, MI 48442

HOLLY SRA (Public State Park) From jct I-75 & Grange Hall Rd (exit 101): Go 1-1/2 mi E on Grange Hall Rd (R). Avail: 144 E (30/50 amps). 2021 rates: $20 to $29. Apr 01 to Nov 01. (248)634-8811

SEVEN LAKES (Public State Park) From Jct of I-75 & Grange Hall Rd (exit 110), W 5 mi on Grange Rd to Fish Lake Rd, N 0.75 mi (L). Avail: 70 E (20/30 amps). 2021 rates: $25. Apr 01 to Nov 01. (248)634-7271

HOLTON — H3 *Muskegon*

BLUE LAKE PARK (MUSKEGON COUNTY PARK) (Public) From jct Hwy 120 & US 31 (Russell Rd exit): Go 10-1/4 mi N on Russell Rd (CR B23), then 1 mi E on Owassippi Rd, then 1/4 mi N on Nichols Rd. 25 Avail: 25 W, 25 E. 2021 rates: $30. May 15 to Sep 15. (231)894-5574

OAK KNOLL FAMILY CAMPGROUND **Ratings: 6/8★/7.5** (Campground) 12 Avail: 1 full hkups, 11 W, 11 E (30/50 amps). 2021 rates: $43 to $50. May 15 to Sep 30. (231)894-6063, 1522 E. Fruitvale Rd, Holton, MI 49425

HONOR — F3 *Benzie*

PERE MARQUETTE/PLATTE RIVER (Public State Park) From town, E 2.5 mi on US-31 to Goose Rd, SE 1.5 mi, follow signs (L). 26 Avail: Pit toilets. 2021 rates: $15. (231)276-9511

PERE MARQUETTE/VETERAN'S MEMORIAL (Public State Park) From town: Go 3-1/2 mi E on US 31. 24 Avail: Pit toilets. 2021 rates: $15. (231)276-9511

SLEEPING BEAR DUNES/PLATTE RIVER (Public National Park) From Jct of US-31 & CR-708, NW 5 mi on CR-708 to M-22, S 0.25 mi to Lake Michigan Rd, W 0.25 mi (R). 149 Avail: 96 W, 96 E (30 amps). 2021 rates: $26 to $31. (231)326-4700

HOPKINS — J3 *Allegan*

HIDDEN RIDGE RV RESORT **Ratings: 10/9.5★/9.5** (RV Park) Avail: 235 full hkups (30/50 amps). 2021 rates: $52 to $85. Apr 01 to Oct 30. (888)451-2180, 2306 12th St, Hopkins, MI 49328

MILLER LAKE CAMPGROUND **Ratings: 6.5/6/7** (Campground) 41 Avail: 41 W, 41 E (30/50 amps). 2021 rates: $45 to $50. May 01 to Oct 01. (269)672-7139, 2130 Miller Lake Dr, Hopkins, MI 49328

HOUGHTON — B1 *Houghton*

CITY OF HOUGHTON RV PARK (Public) From jct US 41 & Lakeshore Dr (north side of Houghton): Go 1 mi NW on Lakeshore Dr (R). Avail: 25 full hkups (30/50 amps). 2021 rates: $43. May 15 to Oct 30. (906)482-8745

HOUGHTON LAKE — F4 *Roscommon*

AU SABLE/HOUGHTON LAKE (Public State Park) From Jct of Old US-27 & Hwy 55, N 5 mi on Old US-27 to CR-300, E 1 mi (R). 50 Avail. 2021 rates: $19. Apr 15 to Sep 15. (989)821-6125

AU SABLE/REEDSBURG DAM (Public State Park) From jct Hwy 127 & CR-300: Go 2-1/4 mi NW on CR-300 (L). 47 Avail: Pit toilets. 2021 rates: $15. (989)821-6125

HOUGHTON LAKE TRAVEL PARK CAMPGROUND good sam park **Ratings: 8.5/9.5★/9.5** (Campground) 38 Avail: 17 full hkups, 21 W, 21 E (30/50 amps). 2021 rates: $39 to $49. Apr 15 to Oct 15. (989)422-3931, 370 Cloverleaf Ln, Houghton Lake, MI 48629

WEST HOUGHTON LAKE CAMPGROUND **Ratings: 6/5.5/7** (Campground) 57 Avail: 28 W, 57 E (30 amps). 2021 rates: $35. (989)422-5130, 9371 W. Houghton Lake Dr, Houghton Lake, MI 48629

WOODED ACRES FAMILY CAMPGROUND **Ratings: 7.5/9.5★/8.5** (Campground) 58 Avail: 6 full hkups, 22 W, 46 E (30/50 amps). 2021 rates: $36 to $44. Apr 01 to Nov 30. (989)422-3413, 997 Federal Ave, Houghton Lake, MI 48629

Travel Services

HOWELL — J5 *Livingston*

LAKE CHEMUNG OUTDOOR RESORT **Ratings: 9/9.5★/9.5** (RV Park) Avail: 25 full hkups (50 amps). 2021 rates: $55 to $65. (517)546-6361, 320 S Hughes Rd, Howell, MI 48843

TAYLOR'S BEACH CAMPGROUND **Ratings: 7/7.5/7.5** (Campground) 50 Avail: 4 full hkups, 46 W, 46 E (30/50 amps). 2021 rates: $48 to $58. Apr 01 to Oct 31. (517)546-2679, 6197 N Burkhart Rd, Howell, MI 48856

HUDSONVILLE — H3 *Ottawa*

BAZAN BALDWIN OAKS CAMPGROUND **Ratings: 8.5/8/6.5** (Campground) 74 Avail: 74 W, 74 E (30/50 amps). 2021 rates: $40 to $49. Apr 01 to Oct 31. (616)669-1600, 4700 Baldwin St, Hudsonville, MI 49426

INDIAN RIVER — E4 *Cheboygan*

BURT LAKE (Public State Park) From jct I-75 & SR-68 (exit 310): Go 1/4 mi W on SR-68, then 1500 ft on US-27 (R). Avail: 306 E (30/50 amps). 2021 rates: $30 to $34. (231)238-9392

INDIAN RIVER RV RESORT & CAMPGROUND **Ratings: 9.5/10★/9** (Campground) 114 Avail: 104 full hkups, 10 W, 10 E (30/50 amps). 2021 rates: $50 to $79. May 01 to Oct 01. (231)238-0035, 561 N Straits Hwy, Indian River, MI 49749

TWIN BEARS WOODED CAMPGROUND **Ratings: 7.5/8.5★/8.5** (Campground) 134 Avail: 31 full hkups, 55 W, 48 E (30/50 amps). 2021 rates: $36 to $52. May 01 to Oct 15. (231)238-8259, 2201 E. M-68, Indian River, MI 49749

INTERLOCHEN — F3 *Manistee*

INTERLOCHEN (Public State Park) From jct US-31 & M-137: Go 2 mi S on M-137 (L). Avail: 392 E (30/50 amps). 2021 rates: $17 to $29. Apr 15 to Nov 01. (231)276-9511

IONIA — H4 *Ionia*

ALICE SPRINGS RV PARK & CAMPGROUND **Ratings: 8.5/9★/9** (RV Park) Avail: 63 full hkups (30/50 amps). 2021 rates: $45. Apr 15 to Oct 15. (616)527-1608, 5087 Alice Court, Ionia, MI 48846

IONIA SRA (Public State Park) From Jct I-96 & Jordan Lake Rd (Exit 64): Go 3-1/2 mi N on Jordan Lake Rd (E). Avail: 100 E (20/30 amps). 2021 rates: $20 to $22. Mar 31 to Nov 30. (616)527-3750

IRON MOUNTAIN — D1 *Dickinson*

LAKE ANTOINE PARK (DICKINSON COUNTY PARK) (Public) From Jct of US-2 & Lake Antoine Rd, N 1.5 mi on Lake Antoine Rd, follow signs (L). Avail: 80 E (30 amps). 2021 rates: $20 to $24. May 27 to Sep 02. (906)774-8875

RIVERS BEND RV RESORT & CAMPGROUND **Ratings: 7.5/9.5★/8.5** (Campground) 81 Avail: 35 full hkups, 46 W, 46 E (30/50 amps). 2021 rates: $55 to $75. May 15 to Oct 15. (906)779-1171, N 3909 Pine Mountain Rd, Iron Mountain, MI 49801

SUMMER BREEZE CAMPGROUND & RV PARK

good sam park

Ratings: 8.5/9★/8.5 (Campground) 65 Avail: 23 full hkups, 42 W, 42 E (30/50 amps). 2021 rates: $32 to $35. May 01 to Oct 15. (906)774-7701, W8576 Twin Falls Rd, Iron Mountain, MI 49801

IRON RIVER — D1 *Iron*

KLINT SAFFORD MEMORIAL RV PARK (Public) From the Jct of US 2 & M-189 (center of town), E 0.2 mi on US 2 to River St, S 0.1mi to Genesee St, E 250 feet (R). 32 Avail: 17 full hkups, 15 W, 15 E (30 amps). 2021 rates: $35 to $39. (906)265-3822

IRONS — G3 *Lake*

IRONS RV PARK AND CAMPGROUND **Ratings: 8.5/9.5★/8.5** (Campground) 68 Avail: 46 full hkups, 22 W, 22 E (30/50 amps). 2021 rates: $37 to $40. Apr 15 to Oct 15. (231)266-2070, 4623 West 10 1/2 Mile Road, Irons, MI 49644

IRONWOOD — B4 *Gogebic*

CURRY PARK & RV CAMPGROUND (IRONWOOD CITY PARK) (Public) From Jct of US 2 & Superior St, W 0.1 mi on US 2 (R). 56 Avail: 9 full hkups, 37 E (30/50 amps). 2021 rates: $10 to $25. May 15 to Oct 15. (906)932-5050

LITTLE GIRL'S POINT COUNTY PARK (Public) From Jct of US-2 & CR-505, NW 18 mi on CR-505, follow signs (R); or From Jct of US-2 & Saxon, E 11 mi on Saxon to CR-505 (R). Avail: 29 E (30/50 amps). 2021 rates: $20. May 09 to Sep 30. (906)663-4428

ISHPEMING — C2 *Marquette*

COUNTRY VILLAGE RV PARK **Ratings: 9/8.5★/8** (RV Park) 93 Avail: 61 full hkups, 32 W, 32 E (30/50 amps). 2021 rates: $45 to $49. May 15 to Oct 15. (906)486-0300, 1200 Country Lane, Ishpeming, MI 49849

ITHACA — H4 *Gratiot*

JUST-IN-TIME CAMPGROUND **Ratings: 6.5/6.5/6.5** (Campground) 26 Avail: 26 W, 26 E (30/50 amps). 2021 rates: $40. May 01 to Oct 15. (989)875-2865, 8421 E Pierce Rd, Ithaca, MI 48847

JACKSON — J5 *Jackson*

GREENWOOD ACRES FAMILY CAMPGROUND **Ratings: 9/8.5/9** (Campground) 200 Avail: 104 full hkups, 96 W, 96 E (30/50 amps). 2021 rates: $40 to $50. Apr 01 to Oct 31. (517)522-8600, 2401 Hilton Rd, Jackson, MI 49201

JENISON — H3 *Ottawa*

STEAMBOAT PARK CAMPGROUND **Ratings: 8.5/10★/7.5** (Campground) Avail: 62 full hkups (30/50 amps). 2021 rates: $46 to $61. Apr 01 to Jan 15. (616)457-4837, 825 Taylor St., Jenison, MI 49428

JOHANNESBURG — F5 *Otsego*

MACKINAW/BIG BEAR LAKE (Public State Park) From Jct of Hwy 32 & I-75, E 18 mi on Hwy 32 to Meridian Line Rd, S 1.2 mi to Little Bear Lake Rd, SW 0.5 mi to 2nd entrance 0.7 mi (L). 31 Avail: Pit toilets. 2021 rates: $15. Mar 31 to Oct 31. (989)732-5485

JONES — K3 *Cass*

CAMELOT CAMPGROUND **Ratings: 7/5.5/7** (Campground) 29 Avail: 29 W, 29 E (30/50 amps). 2021 rates: $25 to $31. Apr 15 to Oct 31. (269)476-2473, 14630 M-60, Jones, MI 49061

KALAMAZOO — J4 *Kalamazoo*

MARKIN GLEN COUNTY PARK (Public) From Jct of I-94 & US-131 (Exit 44), N 7.5 mi on US-131 to 'D' Ave, E 3.5 mi to N Westnedge Ave, S 2.75 mi (R). Avail: 38 full hkups (30/50 amps). 2021 rates: $30. Apr 29 to Oct 30. (269)383-8778

KALEVA — F3 *Wexford*

KALEVA ROADSIDE VILLAGE PARK (Public) In town, at Jct of N. Highbridge Rd. & 9 Mile Rd. Avail: 6 E (30 amps), Pit toilets. 2021 rates: $15 to $20. (616)362-3366

KALKASKA — F4 *Kalkaska*

KALKASKA RV PARK & CAMPGROUND

good sam park

Ratings: 8.5/9.5★/8.5 (Campground) 96 Avail: 15 full hkups, 81 W, 81 E (30/50 amps). 2021 rates: $37 to $45. (231)258-9863, 580 M-72 SE, Kalkaska, MI 49646

PERE MARQUETTE/CCC BRIDGE (Public State Park) From town: Go 10 mi SE on Hwy 72 & Sunset Trail Rd. 31 Avail: Pit toilets. 2021 rates: $15. (231)922-5270

PERE MARQUETTE/GUERNSEY LAKE (Public State Park) From town, W 7.7 mi on Island Lake Rd to Campground Rd, S 1 mi, follow signs (R). 27 Avail: Pit toilets. 2021 rates: $15. (231)922-5270

KINROSS — D4 *Chippewa*

KINROSS RV PARK EAST (Public) From jct I-75 (exit 378) & Hwy 80: Go 2-3/4 mi E on Hwy 80, then 1 blk N on Riley St. Avail: 64 full hkups (20/30 amps). 2021 rates: $15 to $20. (906)440-4018

KINROSS RV PARK WEST (Public) From I-75 (exit 378): Go 1/2 mi E on Tone Rd, then 1/2 mi N on Fair Rd. 52 Avail: 52 W, 52 E (30 amps). 2021 rates: $15 to $20. (906)259-3318

LACHINE — E5 *Alpena*

BEAVER LAKE CAMPGROUND (ALPENA COUNTY PARK) (Public) From Jct of M-32 & M-65, S 10 mi on M-65 to Beaver Lake Park Rd, W 1.5 mi, follow signs (E). 54 Avail: 54 W, 54 E (30/50 amps). 2021 rates: $20 to $30. May 15 to Oct 15. (989)379-4462

LAINGSBURG — H5 *Shiawassee*

SLEEPY HOLLOW (Public State Park) From Lansing, N 14 mi on US-127, follow signs (L); or From Jct of US-127 & Price Rd, E 5 mi on Price Rd (L). Entrance fee required. Avail: 181 E (20/30 amps). 2021 rates: $25. Apr 26 to Nov 04. (517)651-6217

We rate what RVers consider important.

LAKE ANN — F3 *Benzie*

PERE MARQUETTE/LAKE ANN (Public State Park) From Jct of US-31 & Reynolds Rd, N 4 mi on Reynolds Rd, follow signs (R). 30 Avail: Pit toilets. 2021 rates: $15. (231)276-9511

LAKE CITY — F4 *Houghton*

CROOKED LAKE PARK (MISSAUKEE COUNTY PARK) (Public) From jct Hwy 66 & Jennings Rd: Go 4 mi W on Jennings Rd, then 1 mi N on LaChonce Rd. Avail: 35 E (30 amps). 2021 rates: $25 to $30. (231)839-4945

MAPLE GROVE CAMPGROUND (Public) From Jct of Hwy 55 & E Union St, E 0.4 mi on Union St, follow signs (R). Avail: 33 full hkups (20 amps). 2021 rates: $10. May 01 to Nov 30. (231)839-4429

MISSAUKEE LAKE PARK (MISSAUKEE COUNTY PARK) (Public) From Jct of M-55 & M-66, N 0.1 mi on M-66 to Fisher St, W 0.2 mi (L). 117 Avail: 96 full hkups, 21 E (30 amps). 2021 rates: $30 to $35. May 15 to Oct 01. (231)839-4945

PERE MARQUETTE/GOOSE LAKE (Public State Park) From Jct of M-66 & Goose Lake Rd, NW 2.5 mi on Goose Lake Rd, follow signs (E). 30 Avail: Pit toilets. 2021 rates: $15. (231)775-7911

PERE MARQUETTE/LONG LAKE (Public State Park) From town: Go 3-1/2 mi NW on Hwy 66 & Goose Lake Rd. 11 Avail: Pit toilets. 2021 rates: $15. (231)775-7911

LAKE LEELANAU — F3 *Leelanau*

LAKE LEELANAU RV PARK **Ratings: 9.5/10★/9.5** (Campground) Avail: 72 full hkups (30/50 amps). 2021 rates: $49 to $109. May 01 to Oct 31. (231)256-7236, 3101 Lake Shore Dr, Lake Leelanau, MI 49653

L'ANSE — C1 *Houghton*

L'ANSE TOWNSHIP PARK & CAMPGROUND (Public) From Jct of US 41 & Broad St (sign for downtown L'Anse), N 0.8 mi on Broad St to Main St, 2 mi NE on Main (name changes to Skanee Rd) to Crebassa Dr, L on Crebassa Dr (L). Caution: steep hill. Avail: 30 E (30/50 amps). 2021 rates: $20. May 01 to Oct 15. (906)524-6985

L'ANSE TOWNSHIP PARK AND CAMPGROUND (Public) From Jct of US-41 & Broad St, NE 1 mi on Broad St to Skanee Rd, NE 1.5 mi (L). Avail: 30 E (30/50 amps). 2021 rates: $20. May 15 to Oct 15. (906)524-6985

LANSING — J4 *Ingham*

LANSING COTTONWOOD CAMPGROUND Ratings: 8.5/10★/8.5 (Campground) 100 Avail: 11 full hkups, 89 W, 89 E (30/50 amps). 2021 rates: $37 to $41. Apr 15 to Oct 29. (517)393-3200, 5339 Aurelius Rd, Lansing, MI 48911

LAPEER — H6 *Lapeer*

METAMORA-HADLEY SRA (Public State Park) From Jct of I-75 & SR-24, N 15 mi on SR-24 to Pratt Rd, W 2.3 mi to Herd Rd, S 0.66 mi (L) or From Jct of I-69 & SR-24 (exit 155), S 4.8 mi on SR-24 to Pratt Rd, W 2.3 mi to Herd Rd, S 0.7 mi (L). Entrance fee required. Avail: 214 E (30 amps). 2021 rates: $20 to $25. Apr 01 to Oct 30. (810)797-4439

WATER TOWER RV PARK (Public) From Jct of I-69 & M-24 (exit 155), N 2.8 mi on M-24 (R). Avail: 24 full hkups (30 amps). 2021 rates: $28. May 01 to Oct 31. (810)664-4296

LE ROY — G4 *Osceola*

ROSE LAKE PARK (OSCEOLA COUNTY PARK) (Public) From town: Go 2 mi N on Old US 131, then 4 mi E on 18 Mile Rd. 160 Avail: 160 W, 160 E. 2021 rates: $18 to $26. May 11 to Sep 30. (231)768-4923

LEONARD — H6 *Oakland*

ADDISON OAKS COUNTY PARK CAMPGROUND (Public) From the Jct of I-75 Bus & Route 59 (Huron St) Pontiac MI: W 1.3 mi on Huron St to N. Telegraph Rd, N. 1.7 mi to County Center Dr, S 0.4 mi to Pontiac Rd., W 0.2 mi to Watkins Lake Rd to Buick St NW to 0.1 mi (L). 174 Avail: 174 W, 174 E (30/50 amps). 2021 rates: $30 to $40. May 01 to Oct 17. (248)858-1400

Relax on white sandy beaches under palm fronds or get dancing at Mardi Gras; we've put the Spotlight on North America's most popular destinations. Turn to the Spotlight articles in our State and Province sections to learn more.

LESLIE — J5 *Ingham*

WHEEL INN CAMPGROUND & WHITETAIL ACRES ARCHERY
Ratings: 6.5/7.5★/8 (Campground) From Jct of US 127 & Exit 61 (Barnes Rd), E 3 mi on Barnes Rd to Meridian Rd, S 3 mi to Fogg Rd, E 0.4 mi (R). **FAC:** gravel rds. (150 spaces). Avail: 98 grass, 60 pull-thrus, (30x80), back-ins (30x60), 25 full hkups, 73 W, 73 E (20/30 amps), WiFi @ sites, tent sites, dump, mobile sewer, fire rings, firewood. **REC:** pond, fishing, boating nearby, playground, hunting nearby, rec open to public. Pet restrict (B). Partial handicap access. 2021 rates: $30.
(517)589-8097 Lat: 42.47149, Lon: -84.343799
240 Fogg Rd, Leslie, MI 49251
michigan.org/property/wheel-inn-campground
See ad this page

LEWISTON — F5 *Montmorency*

MACKINAW/LITTLE WOLF LAKE (Public State Park) From town, SE 3 mi on CR-489 to W Wolf Lake Rd, E 2 mi (L). 24 Avail: Pit toilets. 2021 rates: $15. (989)732-5485

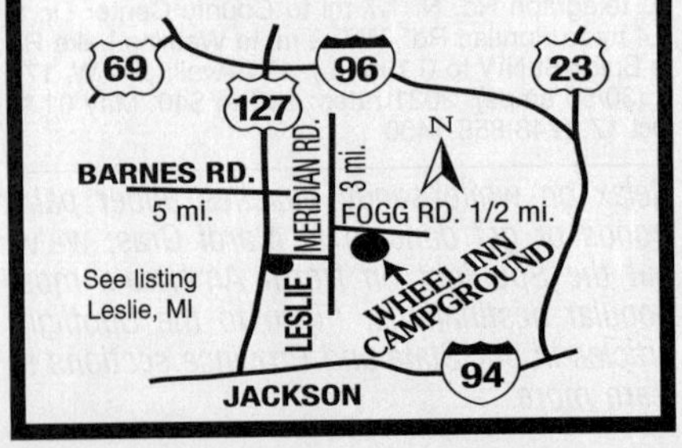

LEXINGTON — H6 *Sanilac*

LEXINGTON PARK (Public) From jct Hwy 90 & Hwy 25: Go 3 mi N on Hwy 25. 41 Avail: 21 full hkups, 6 W, 6 E (30 amps). 2021 rates: $30 to $35. May 01 to Oct 31. (810)359-7473

LINWOOD — G5 *Bay*

LINWOOD BEACH MARINA & CAMPGROUND **Ratings: 6/8.5★/6.5** (Campground) 16 Avail: 5 full hkups, 11 W, 11 E (30/50 amps). 2021 rates: $42. May 01 to Nov 01. (989)697-4415, 135 S Linwood Beach Rd, Linwood, MI 48634

LITTLE LAKE — D2 *Marquette*

ESCANABA RIVER/LITTLE LAKE (Public State Park) From Jct of US-41 & M-35, NW 36 mi on M-35 at E end of lake (R). 16 Avail: Pit toilets. 2021 rates: $15. (906)786-2351

LUDINGTON — G3 *Mason*

CARTIER PARK CAMPGROUND (Public) From W Jct of US-31 & US-10, W 3.1 mi on US-10 to M-116 (Lakeshore Dr), N 1.7 mi (R). 80 Avail: 64 W, 64 S, 80 E (30/50 amps). 2021 rates: $24 to $32. May 01 to Oct 15. (231)845-1522

KIBBY CREEK TRAVEL PARK **Ratings: 8/10★/8** (Campground) 122 Avail: 49 full hkups, 73 W, 73 E (30 amps). 2021 rates: $45 to $57. Apr 15 to Oct 15. (800)574-3995, 4900 W Deren Rd, Ludington, MI 49431

LUDINGTON (Public State Park) From Jct M-116 & US-10: Go 6 mi N on M-116 (E). Avail: 352 E (30/50 amps). 2021 rates: $33 to $37. Apr 15 to Nov 01. (231)843-2423

MASON COUNTY CAMPGROUND (COUNTY PARK) (Public) From jct US 10/31 & US 31: Go 4 mi S on US 31, then 1/2 mi S on Old US 31, then 1-1/2 mi W on Chauvez Rd. 56 Avail: 29 full hkups, 27 E (30/50 amps). 2021 rates: $23 to $27. (231)845-7609

PONCHO'S POND
Ratings: 9.5/10★/10 (RV Park) From W Jct of US-31 & US-10, W 1.5 mi on US-10 to Pere Marquette Rd, S 0.1 mi (L). **FAC:** paved rds. (265 spaces). 182 Avail: 118 paved, 64 gravel, patios, 88 pull-thrus, (30x80), back-ins (30x60), 182 full hkups (30/50 amps), seasonal sites, cable, WiFi @ sites, rentals, laundry, LP gas, fire rings, firewood. **REC:** heated pool, hot tub, pond, fishing, boating nearby, shuffleboard, playground. Pet restrict (Q). Partial handicap access. No tents. Big rig sites, eco-friendly. 2021 rates: $45 to $66, Military discount. Apr 01 to Oct 31.
(888)308-6602 Lat: 43.95357, Lon: -86.41292
5335 W Wallace Lane, Ludington, MI 49431
www.poncho.com
See ad this page

VACATION STATION RV RESORT Ratings: 10/10★/10 (RV Park) Avail: 96 full hkups (30/50 amps). 2021 rates: $40 to $75. Apr 01 to Oct 31. (800)499-1060, 4895 W US-10, Ludington, MI 49431

LUPTON — F5 *Alcona*

RIFLE RIVER GROUSEHAVEN REC AREA (Public State Park) From Jct of I-75 & Exit 202, N 20 mi on SR-33, E 5 mi on CR-28 (Rose City Rd) to park (R). Entrance fee required. Avail: 75 E (20/30 amps). 2021 rates: $28. (989)473-2258

LUTHER — G3 *Lake*

PERE MARQUETTE/SILVER CREEK (Public State Park) From Jct of M-37 & Old 63, E 8 mi on Old 63 to State Rd, N 6 mi, follow signs (L) Entrance fee required. 26 Avail: Pit toilets. 2021 rates: $15. (231)745-9465

MACKINAW CITY — D4 *Cheboygan*

MACKINAW CITY/MACKINAC ISLAND KOA **Ratings: 8/9.5★/8** (Campground) 101 Avail: 33 full hkups, 68 W, 68 E (30/50 amps). 2021 rates: $41.72 to $71.72. May 01 to Oct 24. (800)562-1738, 566 Trail's End Rd, Mackinaw City, MI 49701

TEE PEE CAMPGROUND **Ratings: 7/8.5★/9** (Campground) 95 Avail: 95 W, 95 E (30/50 amps). 2021 rates: $48 to $52. May 05 to Oct 15. (231)436-5391, 11262 W US-23, Mackinaw City, MI 49701

WILDERNESS (Public State Park) From jct I-75 & Wilderness Park Dr: Go 10 mi W on Trails End Rd, follow signs (R). Avail: 250 E (20/30 amps). 2021 rates: $22 to $45. Apr 01 to Dec 31. (231)436-5381

Lend a hand. During the busy season park services are stretched to the max! Please do your best to keep your area ""ship-shape".

MANISTEE — G3 *Mason*

INSTA LAUNCH CAMPGROUND & MARINA **Ratings: 8/9★/8** (Campground) 100 Avail: 16 full hkups, 19 W, 67 E (30/50 amps). 2021 rates: $40 to $45. Apr 01 to Dec 01. (231)723-3901, 20 Park Ave, Manistee, MI 49660

LITTLE RIVER CASINO RESORT RV PARK
Ratings: 9.5/10★/10 (RV Park) 95 Avail: 45 full hkups, 50 W, 50 E (30/50 amps). 2021 rates: $35 to $50. Apr 01 to Oct 31. (888)568-2244, 2700 Orchard Hwy, Manistee, MI 49660

MATSON'S BIG MANISTEE RIVER CAMPGROUND Ratings: 7/8.5★/8 (Campground) 50 Avail: 6 full hkups, 44 W, 44 E (30 amps). 2021 rates: $34. Apr 01 to Dec 01. (888)556-2424, 2680 Bialik Rd, Manistee, MI 49660

ORCHARD BEACH (Public State Park) From Jct of US-31 & SR-110, N 1.4 mi on SR-110, follow signs (L). Entrance fee required. 166 Avail: 166 W, 166 E (20/50 amps). 2021 rates: $30 to $42. Apr 01 to Dec 01. (231)723-7422

THE BLUFFS ON MANISTEE LAKE **Ratings: 9.5/10★/10** (RV Park) Avail: 16 full hkups (30/50 amps). 2021 rates: $52 to $60. Apr 01 to Nov 15. (231)887-4512, 956 Tennessee Ave, Manistee, MI 49660

MANISTIQUE — D3 *Schoolcraft*

INDIAN LAKE (SOUTH SHORE) (Public State Park) From jct US-2 & CR-149: Go 3-1/2 mi N on CR-149, then 1/2 mi E on CR-442 (L). Avail: 145 E (30/50 amps). 2021 rates: $20 to $29. Apr 15 to Nov 01. (906)341-2355

INDIAN LAKE (WEST SHORE) (Public State Park) From town: Go 5-3/4 mi SW on US-2, then 3 mi N on M-149, then 1/2 mi W on CR-442 (R). Avail: 72 E (50 amps), Pit toilets. 2021 rates: $17 to $18. Apr 15 to Nov 01. (906)341-2355

MANISTIQUE LAKESHORE CAMPGROUND
(Public) From jct US 2 & Hwy M 94: Go 1/2 mi W on US 2, then 1/4 mi S on Traders Point Rd (R). **FAC:** paved rds. Avail: 50 paved, 4 pull-thrus, (60x60), back-ins (60x60), 50 full hkups (30/50 amps), cable, WiFi @ sites, tent sites, dump, laundry, fire rings, firewood. **REC:** Lake Michigan: swim, fishing, marina, kayaking/canoeing, boating nearby, playground. Pets OK. Partial handicap access. Big rig sites. 2021 rates: $55 to $75. May 01 to Oct 31. no cc.
(906)286-1696 Lat: 45.95054, Lon: -86.25174
320 Traders Point, Manistique, MI 49854
manistiquelakeshorecampground.org
See ad this page

MANTON — F4 *Wexford*

LAKE BILLINGS RV PARK (Public) From Jct of US 131 & exit 191 (SR 42-Manton), W 1 mi on SR 42 to Bus 131N (Michigan Ave), 0.4 mi to E Main St, E 0.2 mi to Park Dr, N 0.1 mi (Straight ahead). 85 Avail: 37 full hkups, 48 W, 48 E (30 amps). 2021 rates: $24 to $26. May 15 to Oct 15. (231)824-6454

PERE MARQUETTE/BAXTER BRIDGE (Public State Park) From town: Go 6 mi W on Hwy 42, then 6 mi N on Rd 31. 25 Avail: Pit toilets. 2021 rates: $15. (231)775-7911

PERE MARQUETTE/OLD US 131 (Public State Park) From town: Go 6 mi N on US 131 & Old US 131. 20 Avail: Pit toilets. 2021 rates: $15. (231)775-7911

MARION — G4 *Osceola*

VETERANS MEMORIAL PARK (VILLAGE PARK) (Public) From jct Hwy 115 & Hwy 66: Go 5 mi N on Hwy 66. 38 Avail: 12 full hkups, 26 W, 26 E (30/50 amps). 2021 rates: $14 to $20. Apr 15 to Dec 01. (231)667-0100

MARQUETTE — C2 *Marquette*

GITCHE GUMEE RV PARK & CAMPGROUND **Ratings: 4.5/5.5/7** (Campground) 65 Avail: 30 full hkups, 35 W, 35 E (30/50 amps). 2021 rates: $20 to $39. (906)249-9102, 2048 SH 28 East, Marquette, MI 49855

MARQUETTE TOURIST PARK (Public) From Jct of US 41 & Front St (in Marquette, go straight when US 41 turns W), N 1.7 mi on Front St to Fair Ave, W 0.2 mi to Presque Isle Ave, N 0.5 mi to Wright St, W 0.4 mi to Sugarloaf, N 0.4 mi (L). 100 Avail: 38 full hkups, 62 E (30/50 amps). 2021 rates: $30 to $35. May 17 to Oct 15. (906)228-0465

Join in the fun. Like us on FACEBOOK!

MARSHALL — J4 *Calhoun*

CAMP TURKEYVILLE RV RESORT
good sam park **Ratings: 9/9.5★/10** (RV Park) From Jct of I-69 & Exit 42 (N Dr & Turkeyville Rd), W 0.9 mi on Turkeyville Rd (L) Note: Go through blinking light at intersection. Pull into Turkeyville main lot on N Drive. Park drive is on the west side of the main lot. **FAC:** gravel rds. (127 spaces). Avail: 102 gravel, patios, 23 pull-thrus, (40x70), back-ins (40x60), 102 full hkups (30/50 amps), seasonal sites, WiFi @ sites, rentals, dump, laundry, groc, fire rings, firewood, restaurant. **REC:** heated pool, pond, fishing, playground. Pet restrict (B/Q). Partial handicap access. No tents. Big rig sites. 2021 rates: $55. Apr 01 to Oct 31. ATM.
(269)781-4293 Lat: 42.347296, Lon: -84.995507
18935 15 1/2 Mile Rd, Marshall, MI 49068
www.campturkeyville.com
See ad this page

TRI-LAKE TRAILS CAMPGROUND **Ratings: 6/5/6** (Campground) 124 Avail: 124 W, 124 E (20/30 amps). 2021 rates: $38. May 01 to Oct 01. (269)781-2297, 219 Lyon Lake Rd, Marshall, MI 49068

MASS CITY — C1 *Ontonagon*

TWIN LAKES (Public State Park) From Mass City: Go 15 mi NE on M-26, follow signs (E). Avail: 62 E (20 amps). 2021 rates: $20 to $29. Apr 15 to Oct 15. (906)288-3321

MEARS — G3 *Oceana*

HIDEAWAY CAMPGROUND **Ratings: 7.5/8/7** (Campground) 120 Avail: 120 W, 120 E (30 amps). 2021 rates: $40 to $60. May 01 to Oct 01. (231)873-4428, 9671 W Silver Lake Rd, Silver Lake, MI 49436

SANDY SHORES CAMPGROUND **Ratings: 8.5/10★/8.5** (Campground) 70 Avail: 14 full hkups, 56 W, 56 E (30/50 amps). 2021 rates: $46 to $64. May 01 to Sep 19. (231)873-3003, 8595 W Silver Lake Rd, Silver Lake, MI 49436

SILVER CREEK RV RESORT **Ratings: 10/9.5★/10** (RV Park) Avail: 119 full hkups (30/50 amps). 2021 rates: $39 to $100. Apr 01 to Oct 31. (866)401-4592, 1441 N. 34th Ave, Silver Lake, MI 49436

SILVER HILLS CAMPGROUND **Ratings: 7/10★/8** (Campground) 95 Avail: 64 W, 64 E (30/50 amps). 2021 rates: $45 to $85. Apr 15 to Oct 15. (231)873-3976, 7594 W Hazel Rd, Silver Lake, MI 49436

SILVER LAKE RESORT AND CAMPGROUND **Ratings: 8.5/9.5★/9.5** (Campground) 104 Avail: 53 full hkups, 51 W, 51 E (30/50 amps). 2021 rates: $55 to $80. May 01 to Sep 26. (231)873-7199, 1786 N 34th Ave, Silver Lake, MI 49436

MECOSTA — G4 *Mecosta*

BLUEGILL LAKE FAMILY CAMPING RESORT **Ratings: 6.5/8★/7** (Campground) 85 Avail: 85 W, 85 E (30/50 amps). 2021 rates: $32.50 to $45.50. Apr 15 to Oct 15. (231)972-4455, 15854 Pretty Lake Drive, Mecosta, MI 49332

SCHOOL SECTION LAKE PARK (MECOSTA COUNTY PARK) (Public) From Jct of 46 & 127 (Exit 127), S 1 mi on Bus 127 to M-20 W, 22 mi to 9 mile Rd, S 2 mi to 90th Ave (R). 162 Avail: 70 full hkups, 92 W, 92 E (30/50 amps). 2021 rates: $25 to $45. May 07 to Oct 05. (231)832-3246

MENOMINEE — E2 *Menominee*

RIVER PARK CAMPGROUND (Public) From Jct of US-41 & 10th Ave, S 0.25 mi on 10th Ave, behind Kmart (R). 58 Avail: 54 full hkups, 4 E (20/30 amps). 2021 rates: $25 to $35. May 15 to Oct 15. (906)863-5101

MEREDITH — G4 *Clare*

AU SABLE/HOUSE LAKE (Public State Park) From town: Go 2-1/2 mi NE on Meredith Grade Rd. 41 Avail: Pit toilets. 2021 rates: $15. (989)386-4067

MERRILL — H5 *Saginaw*

LAKE OF DREAMS CAMPGROUND Ratings: 7/9★/9 (Campground) 96 Avail: 96 W, 96 E (30/50 amps). 2021 rates: $33. Apr 15 to Oct 15. (989)643-0403, 1000 S Fenmore, Merrill, MI 48637

MESICK — F3 *Manistee*

NORTHERN EXPOSURE CAMPGROUND (Public) From town, W 1 mi on M-115 to cnty rd (Hodenpyle Dam Rd), SW 4.4 mi to N shore of Hodenpyle Dam Impoundment of Manistee River, follow signs (E). 220 Avail: 220 W, 220 E (30/50 amps). 2021 rates: $30 to $45. Apr 26 to Oct 15. (231)885-1199

MIDDLEVILLE — J4 *Barry*

INDIAN VALLEY CAMPGROUND & CANOE LIVERY **Ratings: 8/8.5★/8.5** (Campground) 90 Avail: 21 full hkups, 69 W, 69 E (30/50 amps). 2021 rates: $34 to $46. Apr 15 to Nov 01. (616)891-8579, 8200 108th St SE, Middleville, MI 49333

YANKEE SPRINGS SRA/DEEP LAKE RUSTIC CAMPGROUND (Public State Park) From jct US-131 & M-179 (exit 61): Go 10 mi E on M-179, then 1-1/2 mi S on Yankee Springs Rd (R). 78 Avail: Pit toilets. 2021 rates: $17. Apr 01 to Dec 01. (269)795-9081

YANKEE SPRINGS SRA/GUN LAKE CAMPGROUND (Public State Park) From jct US-131 & M-179 (exit 61): Go 7 mi E on M-179, then 1/2 mi S on Briggs Rd, follow signs (R). Avail: 200 E (20/30 amps). 2021 rates: $20 to $28. Apr 01 to Nov 30. (269)795-9081

MIDLAND — G5 *Bay*

RIVER RIDGE FAMILY CAMPGROUND **Ratings: 8.5/9★/9.5** (Campground) 100 Avail: 31 full hkups, 69 W, 69 E (30/50 amps). 2021 rates: $43 to $47. May 01 to Oct 15. (989)842-5184, 1989 W Pine River Rd, Breckenridge, MI 48615

MILFORD — J5 *Oakland*

CAMP DEARBORN (Public) From Jct of I-96 & Milford Rd (exit 155), N 4.5 mi on Milford Rd to General Motors Rd, W 0.9 mi (R). 191 Avail: 96 full hkups, 95 E (20/50 amps). 2021 rates: $26 to $38. (248)684-6000

MIO — F5 *Oscoda*

AU SABLE/MIO POND (Public State Park) From town: Go 3 mi N on Hwy 72 & W on Popps Rd. 24 Avail: Pit toilets. 2021 rates: $15. (989)473-2258

OSCODA COUNTY PARK (OSCODA COUNTY PARK) (Public) From town, N 1 mi on SR-72 to S side of Mio Dam Impoundment of Au Sable River (R). 153 Avail: 65 W, 65 E (30/50 amps). 2021 rates: $20 to $27. Apr 15 to Dec 01. (989)826-5114

MONROE — K6 *Monroe*

CAMP LORD WILLING RV PARK & CAMPGROUND
good sam park **Ratings: 8.5/9.5★/9.5** (Campground) Avail: 100 full hkups (30/50 amps). 2021 rates: $50. (877)210-8700, 1600 Stumpmier Rd, Monroe, MI 48162

HARBORTOWN RV RESORT **Ratings: 10/10★/10** (RV Park) 173 Avail: 130 full hkups, 43 W, 43 E (30/50 amps). 2021 rates: $53 to $63. (734)384-4700, 14931 Laplaisance Rd, Monroe, MI 48161

WILLIAM C STERLING (Public State Park) From jct I-75 & Dixie Hwy (Exit 15): Go 3/4 mi E on Dixie Hwy (R). 256 Avail: 76 full hkups, 180 E (30/50 amps). 2021 rates: $28 to $40. (734)289-2715

MONTAGUE — H3 *Muskegon*

LUCKY LAKE CAMPGROUND & OUTDOOR CENTER **Ratings: 3/NA/6** (Campground) 95 Avail: 15 W, 55 E (30/50 amps), Pit toilets. 2021 rates: $40 to $45. May 01 to Nov 01. (231)894-3500, 3280 Winston Road, Rothbury, MI 49437

MEINERT PARK (MUSKEGON COUNTY PARK) (Public) From Jct of US-31 & Fruitvale Rd, W 0.5 mi on Fruitvale Rd to Old Bus 31, N 0.9 mi to Meinert Rd, W 4.6 mi (R) Vehicle use fee required. Avail: 67 full hkups (30/50 amps). 2021 rates: $32. May 01 to Sep 27. (231)894-4881

TRAILWAY CAMPGROUND (Public) From jct US-31 (Montague/Whitehall exit) & Bus Hwy 31: Go 2-1/4 mi W Bus Hwy 31 (R). 53 Avail: 53 W, 53 E (30/50 amps). 2021 rates: $45. May 01 to Oct 15. (231)894-4903

WHITE RIVER RV PARK & CAMPGROUND **Ratings: 8.5/9.5★/8.5** (Campground) 142 Avail: 76 full hkups, 66 W, 66 E (30/50 amps). 2021 rates: $50 to $61. May 01 to Oct 15. (231)894-4708, 945 Fruitvale Rd, Montague, MI 49437

MORAN — D4 *Mackinac*

LITTLE BREVORT LAKE-NORTH (Public State Park) From US 2 in town: Go 2 mi NE on Carp River Rd & Worth Rd. 20 Avail: Pit toilets. 2021 rates: $15. (906)643-8620

MOSCOW — K5 *Hillsdale*

MOSCOW MAPLES RV PARK **Ratings: 7.5/8★/7** (Campground) 185 Avail: 100 full hkups, 85 W, 85 E (20/30 amps). 2021 rates: $35 to $47. May 01 to Oct 15. (517)688-9853, 8291 E. Chicago Rd, Moscow, MI 49257

MOUNT PLEASANT — G4 *Isabella*

DEERFIELD NATURE PARK (ISABELLA COUNTY PARK) (Public) From jct US 10 & US 127: Go 13 mi South on US 127 (to Lansing), then .7 mi to US 127 Bus exit toward Mt. Pleasant, then 1.4 mi on N Mission St/US 127 BR, then 6.4 mi on E High St/ M-20 to park. 10 Avail: Pit toilets. 2021 rates: $20. (989)772-2879

SOARING EAGLE HIDEAWAY RV PARK
good sam park **Ratings: 10/10★/10** (RV Park) Avail: 49 full hkups (30/50 amps). 2021 rates: $35 to $94. Apr 01 to Oct 31. (989)817-4803, 5514 E Airport Rd, Mount Pleasant, MI 48858

THE HILL CAMPGROUND **Ratings: 4/9.5★/7.5** (Campground) 35 Avail: 35 W, 35 E (30/50 amps). 2021 rates: $22. (989)775-5899, 7525 E Tomah Rd, Mount Pleasant, MI 48858

MUNISING — D3 *Alger*

MUNISING TOURIST PARK (Public) From M-28 in downtown Munising, W 3 mi on M-28 (R). 104 Avail: 26 full hkups, 78 W, 78 E (30/50 amps). 2021 rates: $25 to $41. May 15 to Oct 28. (906)387-3145

OTTER LAKE CAMPGROUND **Ratings: 5.5/7.5★/7** (Campground) 52 Avail: 5 W, 52 E (20/30 amps). 2021 rates: $25 to $50. May 25 to Oct 01. (906)387-4648, E 7609 Otter Lake Rd, Munising, MI 49862

MUNITH — J5 *Jackson*

THE OAKS CAMPGROUND **Ratings: 7/6/7.5** (Campground) 65 Avail: 65 W, 65 E (20/30 amps). 2021 rates: $35 to $50. (517)596-2747, 7800 Cutler Rd, Munith, MI 49259

MUSKEGON — H3 *Muskegon*

DUCK CREEK RV RESORT **Ratings: 10/10★/10** (RV Park) Avail: 119 full hkups (50 amps). 2021 rates: $55 to $80. Apr 23 to Oct 17. (231)766-3646, 1155 W Riley Thompson Rd, Muskegon, MI 49445

HOFFMASTER (Public State Park) From Jct of US-31 & Pontaluna Rd, W 3 mi on Pontaluna Rd, follow signs (L). Entrance fee required. Avail: 293 E (20/30 amps). 2021 rates: $33 to $37. Apr 09 to Oct 25. (231)798-3711

LAKE SCH-NEPP-A-HO FAMILY CAMPGROUND **Ratings: 8/9.5★/9** (Campground) 73 Avail: 59 W, 73 E (30/50 amps). 2021 rates: $40 to $65. May 01 to Sep 30. (231)766-2209, 390 East Tyler Rd , Muskegon, MI 49445

MUSKEGON KOA **Ratings: 7.5/7/7** (Campground) 69 Avail: 22 full hkups, 47 W, 47 E (30/50 amps). 2021 rates: $40 to $55. May 01 to Oct 11. (800)562-3902, 3500 N Strand Rd, Muskegon, MI 49445

PIONEER PARK (MUSKEGON COUNTY PARK) (Public) From Jct of US-31 & SR-120, SW 1 mi on SR-120 to Giles Rd, W 6 mi to Scenic Drive, N 0.2 mi (L). Entrance fee required. 235 Avail: 235 W, 235 E (30/50 amps). 2021 rates: $30. May 03 to Sep 28. (231)744-3580

NAHMA — D3 *Delta*

NAHMA RESORT **Ratings: 3/NA/6** (Campground) 50 Avail: 50 W, 50 E (30 amps), Pit toilets. 2021 rates: $35. May 25 to Nov 01. (906)644-2728, 13723 Main St, Nahma, MI 49864

We shine ""Spotlights'' on interesting cities and areas.

MI

NAUBINWAY — D4 *Macinac*

BIG KNOB (Public State Park) From town: Go 14 mi SW on US 2 & Big Knob Rd. 23 Avail: Pit toilets. 2021 rates: $15. (906)492-3415

HOG ISLAND POINT (Public State Park) From jct Hwy 117 & US 2: Go 13 mi E on US 2. 50 Avail: Pit toilets. 2021 rates: $15. (906)643-8620

MILAKOKIA LAKE (Public State Park) From jct Hwy 117 & US 2: Go 11-1/2 mi W on US 2, then 1-1/2 mi S on Pike Lake Grade. 35 Avail: Pit toilets. 2021 rates: $15. (906)492-3415

NEW ERA — G3 *Oceana*

HOLIDAY CAMPING RESORT **Ratings: 8.5/9★/8** (Campground) 50 Avail: 27 full hkups, 23 W, 23 E (30/50 amps). 2021 rates: $38 to $45. May 01 to Oct 01. (231)861-5220, 5483 W Stony Lake Rd, New Era, MI 49446

STONY HAVEN CAMPGROUND & CABINS **Ratings: 6/8.5★/7.5** (Campground) 40 Avail: 23 full hkups, 17 W, 17 E (20/30 amps). 2021 rates: $35 to $50. May 01 to Oct 30. (231)861-5201, 8079 W Stony Lake Rd, New Era, MI 49446

NEW HUDSON — J5 *Oakland*

HAAS LAKE PARK RV CAMPGROUND **Ratings: 8.5/9.5★/9.5** (Campground) 160 Avail: 124 full hkups, 36 W, 36 E (30/50 amps). 2021 rates: $39 to $65. Apr 26 to Nov 30. (248)437-0900, 25800 Haas Rd, New Hudson, MI 48165

NEWAYGO — H3 *Newaygo*

CROTON TOWNSHIP PARK (Public) From jct Hwy 37 & Hwy 82: Go 8 mi E on CR to the E side of Muskegon River at Croton Dam. Avail: 150 E. 2021 rates: $18 to $27. (231)652-4642

ED HENNING CAMPGROUND (NEWAYGO COUNTY PARK) (Public) From Jct of M 37 & Croton Rd, E 0.3 mi on Croton Rd (R). Avail: 60 E (30/50 amps). 2021 rates: $16 to $35. Apr 24 to Oct 18. (231)652-1202

NEWAYGO (Public State Park) Take US-131 to exit 125, then go 5 mi W to Beech St, then N on Beech St to park entrance. 99 Avail: Pit toilets. 2021 rates: $17. (231)856-4452

NEWBERRY — D4 *Luce*

KRITTER'S NORTHCOUNTRY CAMPGROUND & CABINS **Ratings: 7.5/8.5★/9** (Campground) 40 Avail: 22 full hkups, 18 W, 18 E (30/50 amps). 2021 rates: $35 to $44. May 12 to Oct 10. (906)293-8562, 13209 State Hwy M 123, Newberry, MI 49868

MOUTH OF TWO HEARTED RIVER (Public State Park) From jct Hwy-28 & Hwy-123: Go 7-1/2 mi N on Hwy-123, then 15 mi NW on CR-407, then 10 mi NE on CR-412, then 3 mi NW on CR-423. 39 Avail: Pit toilets. 2021 rates: $15. (906)492-3415

MUSKALLONGE LAKE (Public State Park) From Jct of M-123 & M-28, N 7 mi on M-123 to H-37, NW 26 mi, follow signs (L). Entrance fee required. Avail: 159 E (20/50 amps). 2021 rates: $20 to $29. May 03 to Oct 30. (906)658-3338

NEWBERRY CAMPGROUND **Ratings: 8.5/9.5★/8.5** (Campground) 77 Avail: 8 full hkups, 69 W, 69 E (30/50 amps). 2021 rates: $47.50 to $58. May 01 to Oct 04. (906)293-5762, 13724 State Hwy M-28, Newberry, MI 49868

PERCH LAKE (Public State Park) From jct Hwy-28 & Hwy-123: Go 7-1/2 mi N on Hwy-123, then 19 mi NW on CR-407. 35 Avail: Pit toilets. 2021 rates: $15. (906)658-3338

NILES — K3 *Cass*

SPAULDING LAKE CAMPGROUND **Ratings: 8.5/10★/9.5** (Campground) From Jct of I-80/90 (IN Toll Rd) & IN 933, Exit 77, (Changes to M 51 in Michigan), N 6 mi on IN 933/MI 51 to Bell Rd, E 1 mi to 17th St, S 1 block to Bell Rd, E 1 mi (L). **FAC:** gravel rds. Avail: 120 gravel, 44 pull-thrus, (30x60), back-ins (30x40), 120 full hkups (30/50 amps), WiFi @ sites, tent sites, laundry, fire rings, firewood. **REC:** Spaulding Lake: swim, fishing, playground, rec open to public. Pets OK. Big rig sites, eco-friendly. 2021 rates: $41 to $45. Apr 01 to Oct 31.
(269)684-1393 Lat: 41.79405, Lon: -86.21507
33524 Bell St, Niles, MI 49120
spauldinglake.com
See ad this page

NORTH BRANCH — H6 *Lapeer*

SUTTER'S RECREATION AREA **Ratings: 7.5/9★/8.5** (Campground) 20 Avail: 3 full hkups, 17 W, 17 E (30 amps). 2021 rates: $35 to $40. Apr 15 to Nov 01. (810)688-3761, 1601 Tozer Rd, North Branch, MI 48461

WASHAKIE GOLF & RV RESORT **Ratings: 7.5/8★/8.5** (Campground) 20 Avail: 20 W, 20 E (30 amps). 2021 rates: $37. May 01 to Oct 31. (810)688-3235, 3461 Burnside Rd, North Branch, MI 48461

NORTH MUSKEGON — H3 *Muskegon*

MUSKEGON (Public State Park) From Jct of US-31 & SR-120, W 2.8 mi on SR-120 to Ruddiman St, W 5 mi, follow signs (E). Entrance fee required. Avail: 244 E (30/50 amps). 2021 rates: $25 to $37. (231)744-3480

NORTHPORT — E4 *Grand Traverse*

LEELANAU (Public State Park) From Jct SR-22 & SR-201: Go 8 mi N on SR-201 (E). 52 Avail: Pit toilets. 2021 rates: $13. May 03 to Nov 03. (231)386-5422

OMER — G5 *Arenac*

BIG BEND FAMILY CAMPGROUND **Ratings: 8/8.5★/8** (Campground) 57 Avail: 57 W, 57 E (30/50 amps). 2021 rates: $33 to $37. Apr 01 to Oct 30. (989)653-2267, 513 Conrad Rd, Standish, MI 48658

ONAWAY — E5 *Presque Isle*

MACKINAW/BLACK LAKE (Public State Park) From Jct of US-23 & Black River Rd, SE 11 mi on Black River Rd. to Twin Lakes Rd, E 3mi to Doriva Beach rd., S 1.4 mi. 52 Avail: Pit toilets. 2021 rates: $15. (989)785-2811

MACKINAW/SHOEPAC LAKE (Public State Park) From jct Hwy-68 & Hwy-33: Go 10-1/2 mi S on Hwy-33, then 2 mi E on Tomahawk Lake Hwy, then 1 mi N on access road. 28 Avail: Pit toilets. 2021 rates: $15. (231)625-2522

ONAWAY (Public State Park) From town, N 6 mi on M-211 (E). Entrance fee required. Avail: 82 E (30 amps). 2021 rates: $20 to $22. Apr 11 to Nov 02. (989)733-8279

ONSTED — K5 *Lenawee*

HAYES (Public State Park) From jct US-127 and US-12 in Cement City: Go 12-1/2 mi E on US-12 (L); or from jct US-23 & US-12 in Ypsilanti: Go 25-3/4 mi W on US-12 (R). 185 Avail: 10 W, 185 E (20/30 amps). 2021 rates: $28 to $32. Apr 09 to Oct 25. (517)467-7401

ONTONAGON — A4 *Ontonagon*

ONTONAGON TOWNSHIP PARK (Public) From Jct of US-45 & Houghton St, NE 1 mi on Houghton St (L). 79 Avail: 79 W, 79 E (30/50 amps). 2021 rates: $19 to $30. May 01 to Oct 18. (906)884-2930

PORCUPINE MOUNTAINS WILDERNESS/ UNION BAY (Public State Park) From Ontonagon, W 13 mi on M-64 to M-107, W 3 mi(R); or From town, W 3 mi on M-107, follow signs (R). Entrance fee required. Avail: 100 E. 2021 rates: $17 to $28. Apr 05 to Nov 03. (906)885-5275

ORTONVILLE — H5 *Brandon*

CLEARWATER CAMPGROUND **Ratings: 8/8.5★/7** (Campground) Avail: 140 full hkups (30/50 amps). 2021 rates: $40 to $55. Apr 15 to Oct 15. (248)627-3820, 1140 M-15 (S Ortonville Rd), Ortonville, MI 48462

OSCODA — F6 *Alcona*

AU SABLE/VAN ETTEN LAKE (Public State Park) From Jct of US-23 & F-41, NW 3 mi on F-41 to park access rd, N 0.1 mi, follow signs (R). 49 Avail: Pit toilets. 2021 rates: $15. (989)362-5041

OLD ORCHARD CAMPGROUND (Public) From Jct of US-23 & River Rd, W 8 mi on River Rd, follow signs (R). 473 Avail: 473 W, 473 E (30 amps). 2021 rates: $23 to $35. Mar 01 to Nov 30. (989)739-7814

OSCODA/TAWAS KOA KAMPGROUND **Ratings: 9/10★/7** (Campground) 117 Avail: 112 full hkups, 5 W, 5 E (30/50 amps). 2021 rates: $54 to $78. Apr 28 to Oct 08. (800)562-9667, 3591 Forest Rd, Oscoda, MI 48750

OSSINEKE — F5 *Alcona*

MACKINAW/OSSINEKE (Public State Park) From Jct of US-23 & Old Ossineke Rd, NE 2 mi on Old Ossineke Rd, follow signs (R). Entrance fee required. 42 Avail: Pit toilets. 2021 rates: $15. (989)734-2543

OTISVILLE — H5 *Genesee*

COVENANT HILLS CAMP & RETREAT **Ratings: 7.5/9.5★/9** (Campground) Avail: 301 full hkups (30/50 amps). 2021 rates: $40. Apr 01 to Nov 01. (810)631-4531, 10359 E. Farrand Rd, Otisville, MI 48463

OTTAWA LAKE — K5 *Monroe*

COVERED WAGON CAMP RESORT Ratings: 7.5/8★/6.5 (Campground) 60 Avail: 30 full hkups, 30 W, 30 E (30/50 amps). 2021 rates: $35 to $45. Apr 15 to Nov 01. (734)856-3058, 5639 M-151, Ottawa Lake, MI 49267

OTTER LAKE — H5 *Genesee*

GENESEE OTTER LAKE CAMPGROUND **Ratings: 6.5/8★/7.5** (Campground) 69 Avail: 69 W, 69 E (30 amps). 2021 rates: $30 to $35. May 01 to Oct 01. (810)793-2725, 12260 Ferrand Rd, Otter Lake, MI 48464

OTTER LAKE VILLAGE PARK (Public) From Jct of SR-24 & Otter Lake Rd, W 7 mi on Otter Lake Rd to 11th St, NE 0.2 mi to Genesee Rd, W 0.2 mi, follow signs (R). Avail: 34 full hkups (30/50 amps). 2021 rates: $33 to $38. Apr 15 to Oct 15. (810)793-4258

PARADISE — C4 *Chippewa*

ANDRUS LAKE STATE FOREST CAMPGROUND (Public State Park) From Jct of Hwys 28 & 123, N 23 mi on Hwy 123 to Wire Rd, N 5 mi to Vermillion Rd, W 2 mi, follow signs (L). 25 Avail: Pit toilets. 2021 rates: $15. (906)293-3293

BODI LAKE (Public State Park) From town: Go 17 mi W on Hwy 123, then N on CR 500 & CR 437. 20 Avail: Pit toilets. 2021 rates: $15. (906)492-3415

CULHANE LAKE (Public State Park) From town: Go 17 mi W on Hwy 123, then N on CR 500 (Northwestern Rd N). 22 Avail: Pit toilets. 2021 rates: $15. (906)492-3415

PIKE LAKE (Public State Park) From town: Go 17 mi W on Hwy 123, then N on CR 500, then W on CR 414. 23 Avail: Pit toilets. 2021 rates: $15. (906)492-3415

TAHQUAMENON FALLS (Public State Park) From town: Go 12 mi SW on M-123 (L). Avail: 260 E (50 amps). 2021 rates: $17 to $32. (906)492-3415

PARIS — G4 *Mecosta*

PARIS PARK (MECOSTA COUNTY PARK) (Public) From Jct of US-131 & 19 Mi Rd, E 1.5 mi on 19 Mi Rd to Northland Dr, N 4 mi (R). 66 Avail: 20 full hkups, 46 W, 46 E (20/30 amps). 2021 rates: $20 to $35. May 04 to Oct 04. (231)796-3420

PENTWATER — G3 *Mason*

CHARLES MEARS (Public State Park) From jct Bus US-31 & Lowell St: Go 1/2 mi W on Lowell St, follow signs (R). Avail: 175 E (30 amps). 2021 rates: $33. Apr 01 to Oct 01. (231)869-2051

HILL & HOLLOW CAMPGROUND **Ratings: 8/9.5★/8.5** (Campground) 110 Avail: 85 full hkups, 25 W, 25 E (30/50 amps). 2021 rates: $47 to $52. May 01 to Oct 15. (231)869-5811, 8915 N Bus US-31, Pentwater, MI 49449

WHISPERING SURF CAMPGROUND AT BASS LAKE **Ratings: 6.5/9★/8.5** (Campground) 47 Avail: 42 full hkups, 4 W, 1 E (30/50 amps). 2021 rates: $43 to $47. May 01 to Oct 15. (231)869-5050, 7070 S Lakeshore Dr, Pentwater, MI 49449

PETERSBURG — K5 *Monroe*

MONROE COUNTY KOA **Ratings: 7/7.5/8** (Campground) 248 Avail: 44 full hkups, 182 W, 204 E (30/50 amps). 2021 rates: $44 to $82. Apr 10 to Oct 30. (734)856-4972, 15600 Tunnicliffe Rd, Petersburg, MI 49270

PETOSKEY — E4 *Emmet*

HEARTHSIDE GROVE MOTORCOACH RESORT **Ratings: 10/NA/9.5** (Condo Park) Avail: 165 full hkups (30/50 amps). 2021 rates: $80 to $170. (888)476-8388, 2400 US 31 North, Petoskey, MI 49770

MAGNUS PARK (Public) From Jct of US-31 & Lake St, W 0.7 mi on Lake St (L). 78 Avail: 36 full hkups, 42 W, 42 E (20/30 amps). 2021 rates: $32. Apr 27 to Oct 21. (231)347-1027

PETOSKEY (Public State Park) From town, N 3 mi on SR-31 to Rte 119, W 1.5 mi, follow signs (L). Entrance fee required. Avail: 180 E (30/50 amps). 2021 rates: $31 to $37. May 15 to Nov 01. (231)347-2311

PETOSKEY KOA **Ratings: 10/10★/10** (Campground) 120 Avail: 94 full hkups, 26 W, 26 E (30/50 amps). 2021 rates: $52 to $98. May 01 to Oct 12. (800)562-0253, 1800 US-31 North, Petoskey, MI 49770

PETOSKEY RV RESORT **Ratings: 10/9.5★/10** (RV Park) Avail: 135 full hkups (50 amps). 2021 rates: $62 to $120. May 01 to Oct 31. (888)517-2340, 5505 Charlevoix Ave, Petoskey, MI 49770

PICKFORD — D5 *Chippewa*

MUNUSCONG RIVER (Public State Park) From jct Hwy 48 & Hwy 129: Go 8 mi E & N on Sterlingville Rd. 26 Avail: Pit toilets. 2021 rates: $15. (906)248-3422

PINCKNEY — J5 *Livingston*

HELL CREEK CAMPGROUND **Ratings: 7.5/9.5★/8** (Campground) 40 Avail: 40 W, 40 E (30 amps). 2021 rates: $30 to $35. Apr 01 to Oct 31. (734)878-3632, 10866 Cedar Lake Rd, Pinckney, MI 48169

PINCKNEY SRA (Public State Park) From US-23 & N Territorial Rd (exit 49), W 14 mi on N Territorial Rd to Hadley Rd, N (right) 4.2 mi to Kaiser Rd, E 0.8 mi, follow signs (R). Entrance fee required. Avail: 161 E (30/50 amps). 2021 rates: $17 to $32. Apr 15 to Dec 01. (734)426-4913

PINCONNING — G5 *Bay*

PINCONNING PARK (BAY COUNTY PARK) (Public) From Jct of I-75 & Pinconning Rd (Exit 181), E 4.6 mi on Pinconning Rd (L). Entrance fee required. 62 Avail: 42 W, 62 E (30/50 amps). 2021 rates: $25. (989)879-5050

PORT AUSTIN — G6 *Huron*

OAK BEACH PARK (HURON COUNTY PARK) (Public) From the Jct of M-25 & M-53 in Downtown Port Austin: SW 8.6 mi on M-25 E (L). Avail: 18 full hkups (30/50 amps). 2021 rates: $27 to $37. May 01 to Oct 15. (989)856-2344

PORT CRESCENT (Public State Park) From Jct of Hwys 53 & 25, SW 5 mi on Hwy 25, follow signs (R). Avail: 142 E (30 amps). 2021 rates: $33 to $45. Apr 01 to Dec 01. (989)738-8663

PORT HOPE — G6 *Huron*

LIGHTHOUSE PARK (HURON COUNTY PARK) (Public) From of Jct of Sand Beach Rd (M-142) & Main St (M-25) in Downtown Harbor Beach: N 13.6 mi on Main St to Lighthouse Rd, E 1.1 mi (L). 108 Avail: 74 full hkups, 29 W, 29 E (30/50 amps). 2021 rates: $19 to $37. May 01 to Oct 15. (989)428-4749

STAFFORD PARK (HURON COUNTY PARK) (Public) From Jct of M 25 & State St in Port Hope: E 0.5 mi on State St to Huron St, N 0.2 mi (L). 73 Avail: 46 full hkups, 27 W, 27 E (30/50 amps). 2021 rates: $19 to $37. May 01 to Oct 15. (989)428-4213

PORT HURON — H6 *Garland*

LAKEPORT (Public State Park) From Jct of I-94 & M-25, N 15 mi on M-25 (R). Avail: 250 E (30/50 amps). 2021 rates: $30 to $34. Apr 11 to Nov 03. (810)327-6224

PORT HURON KOA **Ratings: 8.5/9.5★/9.5** (Campground) 269 Avail: 181 full hkups, 88 W, 88 E (30/50 amps). 2021 rates: $62 to $145. May 01 to Oct 27. (800)562-0833, 5111 Lapeer Rd, Kimball, MI 48074

PORT SANILAC — H6 *Lapeer*

FORESTER PARK (SANILAC COUNTY PARK) (Public) From jct Hwy 46 & Hwy 25: Go 6 1/2 mi N on Hwy 25. 190 Avail: 124 full hkups, 66 W, 66 E (30 amps). 2021 rates: $25 to $30. May 01 to Oct 31. (810)622-8715

NORTH PORT HURON JELLYSTONE PARK **Ratings: 8.5/9.5★/9** (Campground) 272 Avail: 187 full hkups, 85 W, 85 E (30/50 amps). 2021 rates: $55 to $87. Apr 23 to Oct 17. (810)622-0110, 2353 N. Lakeshore Rd, Carsonville, MI 48419

POSEN — E5 *Alpena*

SUNKEN LAKE PARK (ALPENA COUNTY PARK) (Public) From Jct of M-32 & M-65, N 5 mi on M-65 to Long Rapids, N 0.1 mi to Leer Rd, N 5 mi, follow signs (E). 57 Avail: 52 W, 52 E (15 amps). 2021 rates: $23 to $33. May 01 to Oct 15. (989)379-3055

QUINCY — K4 *Branch*

QUINCY MARBLE LAKE PARK (BRANCH COUNTY PARK) (Public) From jct I-69 & US-12: Go 5 mi E on US-12, then 1/4 S on Lake Blvd. 100 Avail: 100 W, 100 E. (517)639-4414

RAPID RIVER — D2 *Delta*

VAGABOND RESORT **Ratings: 7/7/7** (Campground) 36 Avail: 11 full hkups, 25 W, 9 E (30/50 amps). 2021 rates: $30 to $35. May 01 to Nov 01. (906)474-6122, 8935 County 513T Rd, Rapid River, MI 49878

WHITEFISH HILL RV PARK **Ratings: 6.5/UI/7** (RV Park) Avail: 12 full hkups (30/50 amps). 2021 rates: $35. Apr 30 to Oct 31. (906)241-3933, 8455 US 2, Rapid River, MI 49878

RAVENNA — H3 *Muskegon*

CROCKERY CREEK RV PARK **Ratings: 8.5/9★/8.5** (Campground) Avail: 89 full hkups (30/50 amps). 2021 rates: $40 to $45. May 01 to Oct 15. (231)853-0220, 13812 Apple Ave, Ravenna, MI 49451

REED CITY — G4 *Mecosta*

RAMBADT MEMORIAL PARK (Public) From Jct of US-131 & US-10, E 0.1 mi on US-10 to Patterson, S 0.5 mi to Park St, E 0.5 mi, follow signs (L). 13 Avail: 13 W, 13 E (30 amps). 2021 rates: $14. May 15 to Oct 31. (231)832-2245

ROCKFORD — H4 *Kent*

WABASIS LAKE CAMPGROUND (KENT COUNTY PARK) (Public) From Jct of US-131 & SR-57, E 10 mi on SR-57 to Wabasis Ave, S 3 mi (L). 75 Avail: 15 full hkups, 45 W, 45 E (20/30 amps). 2021 rates: $24 to $40. Apr 24 to Nov 01. (616)691-8056

ROGERS CITY — E5 *Presque Isle*

HOEFT (Public State Park) From Jct of Hwy 68 & US-23, NW 4.3 mi on US-23, follow signs (R). Entrance fee required. Avail: 144 E (20/30 amps). 2021 rates: $25 to $33. Apr 01 to Dec 01. (989)734-2543

ROSCOMMON — F4 *Crawford*

NORTH HIGGINS LAKE (Public State Park) From Jct of I-75 & West Higgins (exit 244), W 5 mi on West Higgins (L). Entrance fee required. Avail: 174 E (20/50 amps). 2021 rates: $18 to $31. Apr 01 to Dec 01. (989)821-6125

NORTHERN NIGHTS FAMILY CAMPGROUND **Ratings: 5.5/9★/7.5** (Campground) 29 Avail: 1 full hkups, 28 W, 28 E (20/30 amps). 2021 rates: $45 to $55. May 05 to Oct 08. (989)821-6891, 10058 North Cut Road, Roscommon, MI 48653

SOUTH HIGGINS LAKE (Public State Park) From jct I-75 & SR-18 (exit 239): Go 528 feet S on SR-18, then 3 mi W on CR-100 (R). Avail: 400 E (20/50 amps). 2021 rates: $33 to $45. Apr 15 to Nov 30. (989)821-6374

ROTHBURY — H3 *Oceana*

BACK FORTY RV PARK **Ratings: 6.5/7/6.5** (Campground) 58 Avail: 21 full hkups, 16 W, 21 E (30/50 amps). 2021 rates: $55. Apr 01 to Oct 30. (231)894-4444, 5900 Water Road, Rothbury, MI 49452

SANFORD — G5 *Midland*

AU SABLE/BLACK CREEK (Public State Park) From town: Go 3 mi NW on Saginaw Rd & W River Rd. 23 Avail: Pit toilets. 2021 rates: $15. May 15 to Sep 25. (989)386-4067

SAULT STE MARIE — C5 *Chippewa*

AUNE-OSBORN RV PARK (Public) From jct I-75 & Bus 75/Ashmun (Exit 392): Go 3-1/2 mi NE on Bus 75/Ashman, then 2 mi E on Portage/Riverside (L). 100 Avail: 100 W, 100 E (20/30 amps). 2021 rates: $30 to $32. May 15 to Oct 15. (906)632-5768

KEWADIN CASINO PARK **Ratings: 5.5/8/7** (Campground) Avail: 64 E (30 amps). 2021 rates: $25. May 01 to Oct 31. (906)635-4926, 2186 Shunk Rd, Sault Ste Marie, MI 49783

SOO LOCKS CAMPGROUND **Ratings: 7.5/8.5★/7** (Campground) 100 Avail: 100 W, 100 E (30 amps). 2021 rates: $35 to $45. May 01 to Oct 20. (906)632-3191, 1001 E Portage Ave, Sault Ste Marie, MI 49783

SAWYER — K3 *Berrien*

WARREN DUNES (Public State Park) From jct I-94 & Bridgeman Red Arrow Hwy (exit 16): Go 3 mi SW on Red Arrow Hwy (R). 218 Avail: 1 W, 1 S, 182 E (30/50 amps). 2021 rates: $25 to $45. Apr 01 to Oct 31. (269)426-4013

SCOTTVILLE — G3 *Mason*

CRYSTAL LAKE CAMPGROUND **Ratings: 7.5/7/7** (Campground) 108 Avail: 36 full hkups, 72 W, 72 E (20/30 amps). 2021 rates: $45 to $50. May 01 to Oct 15. (231)757-4510, 1884 W Hansen Rd, Scottville, MI 49454

SCOTTVILLE RIVERSIDE PARK (Public) From Jct of US-31 & US-10/31, E 8 mi on US-10/31 (Ludington) to S Main St, S 0.5 mi, follow signs (L). 52 Avail: 52 W, 52 E (30 amps). 2021 rates: $33. May 01 to Oct 31. (231)757-2429

SEARS — G4 *Osceola*

CRITTENDEN PARK (OSCEOLA COUNTY PARK) (Public) From jct US 131 & US 10: Go 13 mi E on US 10, then 5 mi SE on Big Lake. 58 Avail: 12 full hkups, 36 W, 36 E. 2021 rates: $18 to $26. May 08 to Sep 27. (231)734-2588

SEBEWAING — G5 *Huron*

SEBEWAING PARK (HURON COUNTY PARK) (Public) From Jct of M-25 & Pine St in Downtown Sebewaing: W 0.5 mi on Pine St to Miller St., S 0.3 mi to Union St., NW 0.1 mi (E). Avail: 54 full hkups (30/50 amps). 2021 rates: $19 to $37. May 01 to Oct 15. (989)883-2033

SHELBY — G3 *Oceana*

SILVER LAKE (Public State Park) From town: Go 4 mi SW on CR-B15 (R). Avail: 196 E (20/30 amps). 2021 rates: $25 to $33. Apr 20 to Oct 31. (231)873-3083

SILVER LAKE — G3 *Oceana*

DUNES HARBOR FAMILY CAMP **Ratings: 8/9.5★/10** (Campground) 152 Avail: 128 full hkups, 24 W, 24 E (30/50 amps). 2021 rates: $48 to $79. May 15 to Oct 15. (231)873-3662, 2100 North Ridge Road, Silver Lake, MI 49436

SKANEE — C1 *Baraga*

COPPER COUNTRY (BIG ERIC'S BRIDGE) (Public State Park) From town: Go 6 mi E on Skanee-Big Bay Rd. 20 Avail: Pit toilets. 2021 rates: $15. Apr 01 to Nov 30. (906)353-6558

SOMERSET CENTER — K5 *Hillsdale*

SOMERSET BEACH CAMPGROUND & RETREAT CENTER

good sam park

Ratings: 6/9★/9.5 (Campground) From Jct of US-127 & US-12, W 3.7 mi on US-12 to Fairway Dr, S 0.5 mi to Brooklawn Dr, W 0.4 mi (R). **FAC:** gravel rds. (251 spaces). Avail: 206 grass, back-ins (30x45), 206 E (30 amps), seasonal sites, WiFi @ sites, tent sites, rentals, dump, mobile sewer, LP bottles, fire rings, firewood. **REC:** Mission Lake: swim, fishing, kayaking/canoeing, playground, rec open to public. Pets OK. Partial handicap access, eco-friendly. 2021 rates: $20 to $32.

(517)688-3783 Lat: 42.04195, Lon: -84.43036
9822 Brooklawn Ct, Somerset Center, MI 49282
somersetbeach.org
See ad this page

SOUTH BOARDMAN — F4 *Kalkaska*

VISTA GREEN RV RESORT **Ratings: 10/9.5★/10** (RV Park) Avail: 66 full hkups (30/50 amps). 2021 rates: $59 to $75. May 01 to Oct 31. (231)369-3400, 6100 Larson Road SW, South Boardman, MI 49680

SOUTH HAVEN — J3 *Allegan*

COUSINS CAMPGROUND **Ratings: 5/8.5★/8.5** (Campground) Avail: 20 full hkups (30/50 amps). 2021 rates: $60. May 15 to Oct 15. (269)767-2348, 7317 North Shore Drive, South Haven, MI 49090

SOUTH HAVEN SUNNY BROOK RV RESORT **Ratings: 10/10★/10** (Condo Park) Avail: 86 full hkups (30/50 amps). 2021 rates: $64 to $82. Apr 15 to Oct 31. (888)499-5253, 68300 CR 388 Phoenix Rd, South Haven, MI 49090

VAN BUREN (Public State Park) From Jct of I-196 & Covert Rd exit (Blue Star Hwy): Go 3 mi N on Blue Star Hwy, then 1 mi E on Ruggles Rd (E). Avail: 220 E (30/50 amps). 2021 rates: $20 to $32. Apr 01 to Dec 01. (269)637-2788

YOGI BEAR'S JELLYSTONE PARK CAMP-RESORT **Ratings: 8.5/9.5★/10** (Campground) 99 Avail: 73 full hkups, 26 W, 26 E (30/50 amps). 2021 rates: $43 to $100. Apr 15 to Oct 30. (269)637-6153, 03403 64th Street, South Haven, MI 49090

SPRING LAKE — H3 *Ottawa*

TANGLEFOOT RV PARK (Public) From Jct of US-31 & SR-104, E 0.3 mi on SR-104 to Jackson St, S 0.1 mi to Exchange St, W 0.1 mi, follow signs (L). Avail: 30 full hkups (30/50 amps). 2021 rates: $50. Apr 15 to Oct 15. (616)843-5019

ST CLAIR — H6 *St Clair*

SAINT CLAIR (THOUSAND TRAILS)

good sam park **Ratings: 7.5/8.5★/6.5** (Membership Park) 101 Avail: 50 full hkups, 51 W, 51 E (30/50 amps). 2021 rates: $48 to $58. May 01 to Oct 31. (888)563-7040, 1299 Wadhams Rd, Saint Clair, MI 48079

ST IGNACE — D4 *Mackinac*

CASTLE ROCK LAKEFRONT MACKINAC TRAIL CAMP PARK **Ratings: 8/9★/8.5** (Campground) 88 Avail: 17 full hkups, 71 W, 71 E (30/50 amps). 2021 rates: $38 to $60. May 15 to Oct 15. (906)643-9222, 2811 Mackinac Trail, St Ignace, MI 49781

LAKESHORE RV PARK **Ratings: 8.5/9★/8.5** (Campground) Avail: 53 full hkups (30/50 amps). 2021 rates: $46. May 01 to Oct 15. (906)643-9522, W 1234 Point LaBarbe Rd, St Ignace, MI 49781

ST IGNACE-MACKINAC ISLAND KOA **Ratings: 8/8.5★/8** (Campground) 145 Avail: 85 full hkups, 60 W, 60 E (30/50 amps). 2021 rates: $40 to $80. May 01 to Oct 30. (906)643-9303, W1118 US 2, St Ignace, MI 49781

STRAITS (Public State Park) From jct I-75 & US-2 (exit 344A): Go 1/4 mi E on US-2, then 1000 feet S on Church St (R). Avail: 255 E (30/50 amps). 2021 rates: $22 to $42. Apr 05 to Nov 30. (906)643-8620

TIKI RV PARK & CAMPGROUND **Ratings: 6.5/9★/7** (Campground) 81 Avail: 31 full hkups, 50 W, 50 E (30/50 amps). 2021 rates: $42. May 01 to Oct 31. (906)643-7808, 200 S Airport Rd, St Ignace, MI 49781

ST JAMES — D4 *Charlevoix*

MACKINAW SF/BEAVER ISLAND (Public State Park) From Charlevois: Take ferry to St. James on Beaver Island, then go 7 mi S on East Side Dr. 22 Avail: Pit toilets. 2021 rates: $10. (989)732-3541

STANWOOD — G4 *Mecosta*

BROWER COUNTY PARK (Public) From jct US-131 & Eight Mile Rd: Go 1 mi W on Eight Mile Rd, then 2 mi SW on Old State Rd, then 1 mi W on Polk Rd (E). 230 Avail: 230 W, 230 E (30 amps). 2021 rates: $25 to $40. Apr 01 to Oct 27. (231)823-2561

RIVER RIDGE RV RESORT & MARINA **Ratings: 10/10★/10** (RV Park) Avail: 31 full hkups (30/50 amps). 2021 rates: $60 to $79. Apr 15 to Oct 31. (231)823-8338, 22265 8 Mile Road, Stanwood, MI 49346

STEPHENSON — E2 *Menominee*

COYOTE RV PARK & CAMPGROUND **Ratings: 3/8★/5.5** (Campground) 40 Avail: 5 full hkups, 35 W, 35 E (30/50 amps). 2021 rates: $25 to $30. May 01 to Nov 30. (906)753-4946, W6182 Cty Rd G12, Stephenson, MI 49887

SHAKEY LAKES PARK (MENOMINEE COUNTY PARK) (Public) From Jct of US-41 & CR G-12, W 12 mi on CR-G-12 (R). Entrance fee required. Avail: 74 E (30/50 amps). 2021 rates: $15 to $25. May 23 to Sep 08. (906)753-4582

STERLING — G5 *Arenac*

RIVER VIEW CAMPGROUND & CANOE LIVERY **Ratings: 7/8.5★/8.5** (Campground) 210 Avail: 88 full hkups, 122 W, 122 E (30/50 amps). 2021 rates: $20 to $22. May 01 to Oct 15. (989)654-2447, 5755 Townline Rd, Sterling, MI 48659

TAWAS CITY — F5 *Arenac*

NORTHERN BEAR PAW RV PARK **Ratings: 7.5/10★/10** (RV Park) 29 Avail: 22 full hkups, 7 W, 7 E (30/50 amps). 2021 rates: $35. May 01 to Oct 30. (989)362-8000, 4793 M55, Tawas City, MI 48763

TAWAS RIVER RV PARK **Ratings: 3/5/6** (Campground) 44 Avail: 19 full hkups, 25 W, 25 E (30/50 amps). 2021 rates: $40. May 01 to Oct 15. (989)362-4988, 560 E M-55, Tawas City, MI 48763

TAWAS RV PARK **Ratings: 7/9★/8.5** (Campground) 12 Avail: 7 full hkups, 5 W, 5 E (30/50 amps). 2021 rates: $32 to $37. May 01 to Oct 31. (989)362-0005, 1453 Townline Rd, Tawas City, MI 48763

TECUMSEH — K5 *Lenawee*

INDIAN CREEK CAMP & CONFERENCE CENTER

good sam park **Ratings: 8.5/9.5★/9** (Campground) 39 Avail: 34 full hkups, 5 W, 5 E (30/50 amps). 2021 rates: $46 to $70. Apr 15 to Oct 15. (517)423-5659, 9415 Tangent Hwy, Tecumseh, MI 49286

TRAVERSE CITY — F4 *Grand Traverse*

HOLIDAY PARK CAMPGROUND

good sam park **Ratings: 9/9★/10** (Campground) From SW Jct of M-37 & US-31, SW 1 mi on US-31 (R). Note: No Motorcycles. **FAC:** paved rds. (217 spaces). Avail: 137 all weather, 62 pull-thrus, (40x65), back-ins (40x65), 137 full hkups (30/50 amps), seasonal sites, cable, WiFi @ sites, dump, laundry, groc, LP gas, fire rings, firewood. **REC:** Silver Lake: swim, fishing, kayaking/canoeing, boating nearby, playground. Pets OK. Partial handicap access. No tents. Big rig sites, eco-friendly. 2021 rates: $50 to $95. Apr 25 to Oct 25.
(231)943-4410 Lat: 44.67111, Lon: -85.67390
4860 US-31S, Traverse City, MI 49685
www.holidayparktc.com
See ad this page

NORTHWESTERN MICHIGAN FAIR ASSOCIATION CAMPGROUND **Ratings: 3/9.5★/6.5** (Campground) 133 Avail: 100 W, 133 E (30/50 amps). 2021 rates: $30. May 15 to Oct 15. (231)943-4150, 3606 Blair Townhall Rd, Traverse City, MI 49685

PERE MARQUETTE/ARBUTUS LAKE (Public State Park) From Jct of Hwys 37 & 113, E 6 mi on Hwy 113 into Kingsley, N 10 mi on W side of lake, follow signs (R). 25 Avail: Pit toilets. 2021 rates: $15. (231)922-5270

Save 10% at Good Sam Parks!

PERE MARQUETTE/SCHECK'S PLACE (Public State Park) From town, N 1.4 mi on CR-611 to River Rd, E 4 mi, follow signs (L). 30 Avail: Pit toilets. 2021 rates: $15. May 01 to Oct 15. (231)922-5270

TIMBER RIDGE RV & RECREATION RESORT **Ratings: 7/7.5/7.5** (Campground) 165 Avail: 102 full hkups, 63 W, 63 E (30/50 amps). 2021 rates: $40 to $100. (231)947-2770, 4050 Hammond Rd, Traverse City, MI 49696

TRAVERSE BAY RV RESORT

good sam park **Ratings: 10/10★/10** (Condo Park) From N Jct of US 31N & Hwy 72, E 1.5 mi on Hwy 72 (L). Note: RVs restricted to Class "A" & "C" Motorhomes & Fifth Wheels 10 years or approval and minimum 28'.

NORTHERN MICHIGAN'S PRIME RV RESORT
Traverse Bay offers beautiful scenery & world-class amenities. Shopping, dining, and beaches close by. Adult-oriented RV resort. Come join the lifestyle at Traverse Bay!

FAC: paved rds. Avail: 217 paved, patios, back-ins (48x100), 217 full hkups (30/50 amps), cable, WiFi @ sites, laundry. **REC:** heated pool, hot tub, pond, boating nearby. Pet restrict (Q). Partial handicap access. No tents. Big rig sites, No Class B/C, eco-friendly. 2021 rates: $69 to $95. May 01 to Oct 31.
(231)938-5800 Lat: 44.77329, Lon: -85.46457
5555 M-72 East, Williamsburg, MI 49690
traversebayrv.com
See ad this page

TRAVERSE CITY (Public State Park) From town: Go 2 mi E on US-31, follow signs (R). Avail: 343 E (20/30 amps). 2021 rates: $33. (231)922-5270

UNION CITY — K4 *Branch*

POTAWATOMIE RECREATION AREA **Ratings: 8/8.5/8.5** (Campground) 43 Avail: 14 full hkups, 29 W, 29 E (30/50 amps). 2021 rates: $35. Apr 15 to Oct 15. (517)278-4289, 1117 Bell Rd, Union City, MI 49094

VANDERBILT — E4 *Otsego*

MACKINAW/PICKEREL LAKE OTSEGO (Public State Park) From town, E 10 mi on Sturgeon Valley Rd to Pickerel Lake Rd, N 0.5 mi, follow signs (L). 39 Avail: Pit toilets. 2021 rates: $15. (989)732-5485

VASSAR — H5 *Tuscola*

BER WA GA NA CAMPGROUND

good sam park **Ratings: 7.5/8★/7** (Campground) 82 Avail: 26 full hkups, 52 W, 56 E (20/30 amps). 2021 rates: $38. May 01 to Nov 01. (989)673-7125, 2601 W Sanilac Rd (M-46), Vassar, MI 48768

KRYSTAL LAKE CAMPGROUND **Ratings: 6.5/7.5/7.5** (Campground) 150 Avail: 16 full hkups, 134 W, 134 E (30/50 amps). 2021 rates: $34 to $40. Apr 15 to Oct 15. (989)843-0591, 5475 Washburn Road, Vassar, MI 48768

WESLEYAN WOODS CAMPGROUND (Public) From Jct of Hwy I-75 & M-46 (Exit 149A), E 19 mi to Ringle Rd, S 1 mi to Caine Rd, E 0.5 mi (R). 196 Avail: 50 full hkups, 146 W, 146 E (30/50 amps). 2021 rates: $34 to $39. May 01 to Oct 15. (989)823-8840

TIPS FOR THE BBQ CHEF: BURGERS - Use fresh meat and mix in ingredients-onions, garlic, chopped jalapeno or bell peppers, oregano, BBQ or hot sauce-sprinkle salt and pepper just before going on the grill. Cook 3 to 5 mins per side to 140-degree internal temp. Tip: Don't press down on the patties during cooking or you'll squeeze out the delicious juices. BEEF BRISKET - Marinate a 3 to 4 lb brisket for 24 hrs. or more in Worcestershire or teriyaki sauce with garlic and black pepper. Cook for 3 to 5 mins per side on direct high heat, then indirect heat for 15-20 mins to 130-degree internal temp (medium-rare). FISH FILLETS OR STEAKS (such as salmon, striped bass, and mahi-mahi) - Cook 5 to 8 mins per side (depending on heat) or to 130 to 135-degree internal temp. BONELESS CHICKEN BREASTS - Marinate for 30 mins or more or rub both sides with a spice mix. Cook over high heat (375-400 degrees) for 4 to 5 mins per side, then indirect heat for 8 to 12 mins to 160-165 internal temp.

WAKEFIELD — B4 *Gogebic*

SUNDAY LAKE EDDY PARK & CAMPGROUND (Public) From jct Hwy 28 & US-2: Go 1 mi W on US-2, then 1/2 mi N on Lakeshore Dr, then continue to Eddy Park Rd (R). Avail: 18 full hkups (30/50 amps). 2021 rates: $25 to $40. May 24 to Oct 15. (906)224-4481

WATERFORD — J5 *Oakland*

PONTIAC LAKE RECREATION AREA (Public State Park) From Jct of I-75 & M-59, W 12 mi on M-59 to Teggerdine Rd, N 2.5 mi (R). Entrance fee required. Avail: 176 E (20/30 amps). 2021 rates: $22. May 01 to Oct 31. (248)666-1020

WAYLAND — J4 *Allegan*

DAISY PARK CAMPGROUND **Ratings: 5.5/8.5★/7.5** (Campground) 19 Avail: 19 W, 19 E (30/50 amps). 2021 rates: $33 to $39. May 01 to Oct 15. (269)792-2081, 189 126th Ave, Wayland, MI 49348

WEIDMAN — G4 *Isabella*

COLDWATER LAKE FAMILY PARK (ISABELLA COUNTY PARK) (Public) From Jct of Bus-27 (Mission St) & M-20 (High St), W 7 mi on M-20 to Winn Rd, N 5 mi to Beal City Rd, W 2 mi to Littlefield Rd, S 0.25 mi (R). 95 Avail: 95 W, 95 E (20/30 amps). 2021 rates: $20 to $25. May 01 to Oct 15. (989)317-4083

WELLSTON — G3 *Manistee*

TWIN OAKS CAMPGROUND **Ratings: 6/9.5★/8** (Campground) 58 Avail: 9 full hkups, 4 W, 45 E (20/30 amps). 2021 rates: $36 to $41. Apr 01 to Nov 23. (877)442-3102, 233 Moss Rd, Wellston, MI 49689

WEST BRANCH — F5 *Ogemaw*

AU SABLE/AMBROSE LAKE (Public State Park) From town: Go 11 mi N on CR 15 & CR 20. 19 Avail: Pit toilets. 2021 rates: $15. (989)275-4622

BEAVER TRAIL CAMPGROUND **Ratings: 5/9★/6.5** (Campground) 19 Avail: 19 W, 19 E (30 amps). 2021 rates: $28 to $32. (989)345-7745, 4408 Grass Lake Rd, West Branch, MI 48661

LORANGER PINES RV PARK **Ratings: 5.5/9★/8** (Campground) 24 Avail: 16 full hkups, 8 W, 8 E (30/50 amps). 2021 rates: $35. May 01 to Nov 01. (989)343-0261, 1700 Crawford Lane, West Branch, MI 48661

WEST BRANCH RV PARK (Public) From Jct of I-75 & Exit 212, N 1.5 mi on exit rd (L). 53 Avail: 53 W, 53 E (30 amps). 2021 rates: $20 to $25. Apr 01 to Oct 15. (989)345-3295

WETMORE — D3 *Alger*

MUNISING/PICTURED ROCKS KOA **Ratings: 8/9★/8** (Campground) 87 Avail: 26 full hkups, 61 W, 61 E (30/50 amps). 2021 rates: $39.95 to $69.95. May 15 to Oct 15. (906)387-3315, E10102 Hwy M-28 East, Wetmore, MI 49895

WHITE CLOUD — G3 *Oceana*

BIG BEND PARK (NEWAYGO COUNTY PARK) (Public) From town, E 9 mi on Baseline Rd to S Beech Ave, S 2 mi (E). 230 Avail: 227 W, 227 E (20 amps). 2021 rates: $25 to $26. (231)689-6325

OXBOW TOWNSHIP PARK (Public) From Jct of US-131 & Jefferson Rd, W 9 mi on Jefferson Rd to Chestnut, N 2.5 mi, follow signs (E). Avail: 187 E (30 amps). 2021 rates: $25 to $26. (231)856-4279

SANDY BEACH PARK (NEWAYGO COUNTY PARK) (Public) From Jct of SR-37 & CR-Baseline, E 6 mi on CR-Baseline to Elm Ave, S 4 mi to 30th St, E 0.6 mi (L). 126 Avail: 26 full hkups, 72 W, 100 E (20 amps). 2021 rates: $19 to $39. (231)689-1229

WHITE CLOUD PARK (NEWAYGO COUNTY PARK) (Public) From the Jct. of US-131 & M-20 (Exit 131): W 15.9 mi on M-20 cont. on E. Wilcox Ave 0.8 mi (L). 90 Avail: 90 W, 90 E (30/50 amps). 2021 rates: $19 to $25. May 05 to Sep 29. (231)689-2201

WILLIAMSBURG — F4 *Grand Traverse*

WHITEWATER TOWNSHIP PARK (Public) From town, E 6 mi on Hwy 31/72 to Hwy 72, E 4 mi to Elk Lake Rd (near Turtle Creek Casino), N 3 mi to Park Rd, E 1 mi (E). Avail: 55 E (30/50 amps). 2021 rates: $25 to $30. May 10 to Sep 30. (231)267-5141

WIXOM — J5 *Oakland*

PROUD LAKE SRA (Public State Park) From Jct of I-96 & Wixom Rd (exit 159), N 4.4 mi on Wixom Rd to Glengary Rd, E 0.5 mi (L). Entrance fee required. Avail: 130 E (20/50 amps). 2021 rates: $25 to $29. May 01 to Oct 30. (248)685-2433

WOLVERINE — E4 *Cheboygan*

STURGEON VALLEY CAMPGROUND **Ratings: 6/6.5/7** (Campground) 45 Avail: 45 W, 45 E (20/30 amps). 2021 rates: $33. (231)525-8301, 15247 Trowbridge Rd, Wolverine, MI 49755

YPSILANTI — J5 *Washtenaw*

DETROIT / ANN ARBOR KOA

Ratings: 8/9.5★/9 (Campground) From Jct of I-94 & Rawsonville Rd (exit 187), S 1 mi on Rawsonville Rd to Textile Rd, W 1 mi to Bunton Rd, S 0.7 mi (R). **FAC:** gravel rds. 196 Avail: 176 gravel, 20 grass, 120 pull-thrus, (30x60), back-ins (30x40), 142 full hkups, 54 W, 54 E (30/50 amps), WiFi @ sites, tent sites, rentals, dump, laundry, groc, LP gas, fire rings, firewood. **REC:** Greenfield Lake: swim, fishing, kayaking/canoeing, boating nearby, playground, rec open to public. Pet restrict (B). Partial handicap access. Big rig sites, eco-friendly. 2021 rates: $45 to $75, Military discount. Apr 01 to Oct 31.
(734)482-7722 Lat: 42.19270, Lon: -83.56292
6680 Bunton Rd, Ypsilanti, MI 48197
www.detroitgreenfield.com
See ad page 480

ZEELAND — J3 *Ottawa*

DUTCH TREAT CAMPING & RECREATION **Ratings: 9/8.5★/8** (Campground) 100 Avail: 93 full hkups, 7 W, 7 E (30/50 amps). 2021 rates: $44 to $48. Apr 01 to Nov 01. (616)772-4303, 10300 Gordon Ave, Zeeland, MI 49464

Getty Images/iStockphoto

YOU ARE HERE

Minnesota

DID YOU KNOW?

Minnesota is home to more than a dozen well-known roadside attractions, including a world famous nine-ton ball of twine.

Alaska is America's northernmost state, but did you know that Minnesota takes second place? The notch of Minnesota territory known as the Northwest Angle sticks out above the 49th parallel and deep into Canada.

Terrific Twins

Why settle for one city when you can have two right next to each other? The Twin Cities of Minneapolis and St. Paul offer everything from boundless brews and big buildings to cool culture and cuisine. Whether you prefer to tour an art museum or take in a sporting event, you can do it in the Twin Cities. The nearby Mall of America beckons to shoppers with more than 500 stores. Even Mother Nature is spectacularly grand, with scenic Minnehaha Falls Regional Park perched in the middle of the two towns.

Superb Parks

Minnesota's public lands will delight hunters, boaters and swimmers. Head north toward the Canadian border to paddle the "water highways" of Voyageurs National Park or take a hike to enjoy the verdant scenery. Located along the rocky shores of Lake Superior, Gooseberry Falls State Park is a Minnesota treasure. Named for the spectacular waterfalls along the Gooseberry River, this North Shore park offers 20 miles of scenic trails along the waters and through the woodlands.

Lotsa Lakes

We've all heard the state nickname, "Land of 10,000 Lakes." You might not be able to visit them all, but you won't have a hard time finding cool, clear waters, sandy shores and plenty of summertime sunshine. Isn't that all you need for a beach retreat? Paddlers won't want to miss the Boundary Waters Canoe Area Wilderness, which offers 1,200 miles of water trails set amid a million acres of serene woodlands.

Minnesota Juicy Lucy

You haven't seen a burger like the Juicy Lucy before. Instead of placing a cheese slice on top, the yellow stuff is packed inside the meat patty, creating an oozing molten core when grilled. The burger has origins in south Minneapolis, so head there to tuck into this Minnesotan favorite.

VISITOR CENTER

TIME ZONE
Central Standard

ROAD & HIGHWAY INFORMATION
800-542-0220
511mn.org

FISHING & HUNTING INFORMATION
888-MINNDNR
dnr.state.mn.us

BOATING INFORMATION
888-MINNDNR
dnr.state.mn.us/regulations/boatwater

NATIONAL PARKS
nps.gov/mn

STATE PARKS
dnr.state.mn.us/state_parks

TOURISM INFORMATION
Minnesota Tourism
888-VISITMN
exploreminnesota.com

TOP TOURISM ATTRACTIONS
1) Mall of America
2) Voyageurs National Park
3) Spam Museum

MAJOR CITIES
Minneapolis, St. Paul (capital), Rochester, Duluth, Bloomington

good sam park Featured Good Sam Parks MINNESOTA

When you stay with Good Sam, you can expect the highest degree of cleanliness and friendliness, and better yet, you get **10% off** overnight campground fees.

If you're not already a Good Sam member you can purchase your membership at one of these locations:

BEMIDJI
Royal Oaks RV Park

CASS LAKE
Stony Point Resort RV Park & Campground

CLEARWATER
St Cloud/Clearwater RV Park

GARFIELD
Oak Park Kampground

GILBERT
Sherwood Forest Campground

HINCKLEY
Grand Hinckley RV Resort

HOUSTON
Money Creek Haven

KABETOGAMA
Pines Of Kabetogama Resort

OWATONNA
Hope Oak Knoll Campground
River View Campground

PRESTON
Old Barn Resort

SHAFER
Wildwood Campground

ST CLOUD
St Cloud Campground & RV Park

WABASHA
Big River Resort

10/10★/10 GOOD SAM PARKS

CASS LAKE
Stony Point Resort RV Park & Campground
(218)335-6311

HINCKLEY
Grand Hinckley RV Resort
(800)472-6321

What's This?

An RV park with a 10/10★/10 rating has scored perfect grades in amenities, cleanliness and appearance ("See Understanding the Campground Rating System" on pages 8 and 9 for an explanation of the trusted Good Sam Rating System). Stay in a 10/10★/10 park on your next trip for a nearly flawless camping experience.

Getty Images/iStockphoto

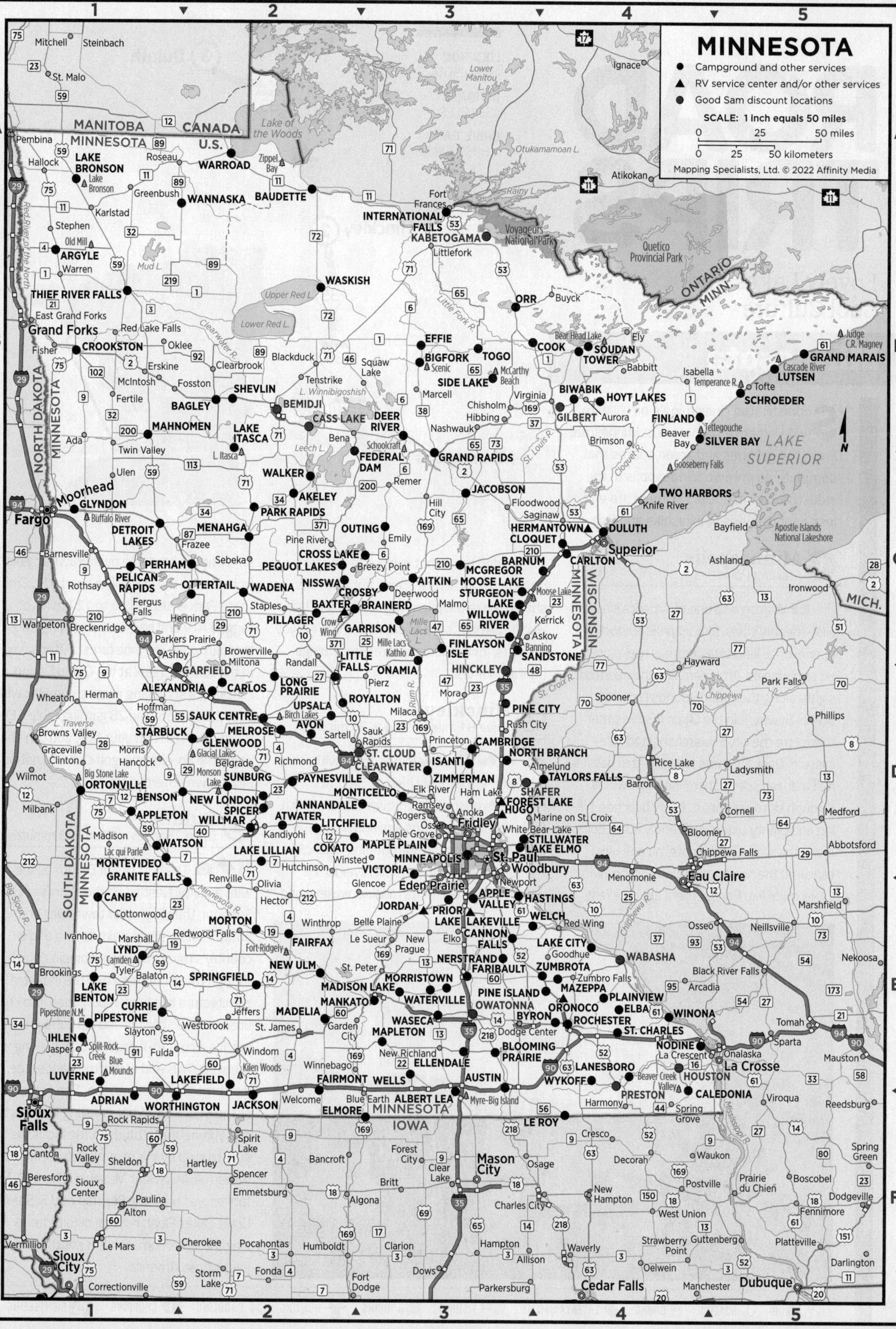
MINNESOTA
Campground and other services
RV service center and/or other services
Good Sam discount locations
SCALE: 1 inch equals 50 miles
0 25 50 miles
0 25 50 kilometers
Mapping Specialists, Ltd. © 2022 Affinity Media
MANITOBA
CANADA
MINNESOTA
U.S.
NORTH DAKOTA
SOUTH DAKOTA
IOWA
WISCONSIN
ONTARIO
MINN.
MICH.
LAKE SUPERIOR
Lake of the Woods
Quetico Provincial Park
Voyageurs National Park
Apostle Islands National Lakeshore
Upper Red L.
Lower Red L.
L. Winnibigoshish
Leech L.
Mille Lacs L.
Rainy L.
Lower Manitou L.
Otukamamoan L.
LAKE BRONSON
WARROAD
WANNASKA
BAUDETTE
INTERNATIONAL FALLS
KABETOGAMA
ARGYLE
THIEF RIVER FALLS
WASKISH
Grand Forks
CROOKSTON
EFFIE
BIGFORK
TOGO
COOK
SOUDAN
TOWER
GRAND MARAIS
LUTSEN
SCHROEDER
SIDE LAKE
SHEVLIN
BAGLEY
BEMIDJI
CASS LAKE
DEER RIVER
BIWABIK
HOYT LAKES
GILBERT
FINLAND
SILVER BAY
MAHNOMEN
LAKE ITASCA
FEDERAL DAM
GRAND RAPIDS
WALKER
AKELEY
JACOBSON
TWO HARBORS
Moorhead
Fargo
GLYNDON
PARK RAPIDS
DETROIT LAKES
MENAHGA
OUTING
HERMANTOWN
CLOQUET
DULUTH
Superior
CROSS LAKE
PEQUOT LAKES
PERHAM
PELICAN RAPIDS
OTTERTAIL
WADENA
NISSWA
CROSBY
AITKIN
BARNUM
CARLTON
MCGREGOR
MOOSE LAKE
STURGEON LAKE
WILLOW RIVER
BAXTER
BRAINERD
PILLAGER
GARRISON
FINLAYSON
ISLE
SANDSTONE
HINCKLEY
LITTLE FALLS
ONAMIA
GARFIELD
ALEXANDRIA
CARLOS
LONG PRAIRIE
UPSALA
ROYALTON
PINE CITY
SAUK CENTRE
AVON
STARBUCK
MELROSE
GLENWOOD
ST. CLOUD
CLEARWATER
CAMBRIDGE
NORTH BRANCH
ISANTI
ZIMMERMAN
TAYLORS FALLS
ORTONVILLE
SUNBURG
PAYNESVILLE
MONTICELLO
SHAFER
FOREST LAKE
HUGO
BENSON
NEW LONDON
SPICER
ANNANDALE
APPLETON
WILLMAR
ATWATER
LITCHFIELD
Fridley
STILLWATER
LAKE ELMO
WATSON
MONTEVIDEO
LAKE LILLIAN
COKATO
MAPLE PLAIN
MINNEAPOLIS
St. Paul
Woodbury
GRANITE FALLS
VICTORIA
Eden Prairie
CANBY
APPLE VALLEY
HASTINGS
JORDAN
PRIOR LAKE
LAKEVILLE
WELCH
MORTON
FAIRFAX
CANNON FALLS
LAKE CITY
WABASHA
LYND
NEW ULM
NERSTRAND
FARIBAULT
ZUMBROTA
LAKE BENTON
SPRINGFIELD
MORRISTOWN
MADISON LAKE
WATERVILLE
PINE ISLAND
MAZEPPA
PLAINVIEW
CURRIE
PIPESTONE
MADELIA
MANKATO
OWATONNA
ORONOCO
ELBA
WINONA
BYRON
ROCHESTER
IHLEN
WASECA
MAPLETON
ST. CHARLES
BLOOMING PRAIRIE
NODINE
La Crosse
ELLENDALE
LANESBORO
HOUSTON
LUVERNE
LAKEFIELD
FAIRMONT
WELLS
AUSTIN
WYKOFF
PRESTON
CALEDONIA
ADRIAN
WORTHINGTON
JACKSON
ALBERT LEA
ELMORE
LE ROY
Sioux Falls
Mason City
Sioux City
Cedar Falls
Dubuque
Eau Claire

MN

 See map page 501

ROAD TRIPS

Lovely Lakes and Cool Culture

Minnesota

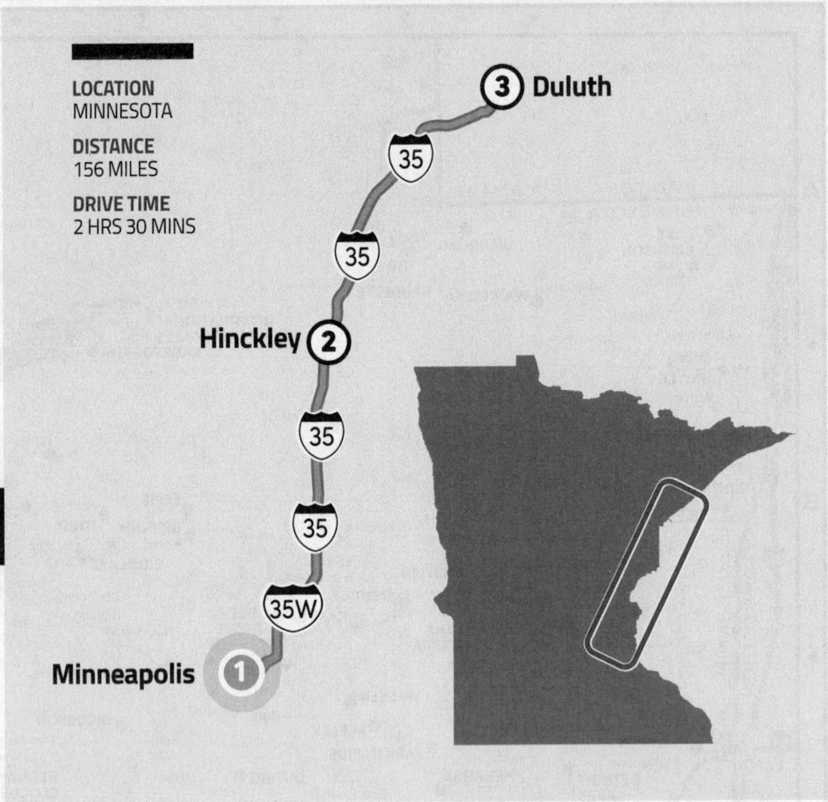

Sophisticated cities mingle nicely with wide expanses of nature in Minnesota. From the galleries and green spaces that dominate downtown Minneapolis to the industrial charm of Duluth, there are endless opportunities to bike, hike and fish.

1 Minneapolis
Starting Point

Welcome to one of America's most bike-friendly cities. Minneapolis is chock full of one-of-a-kind treasures easily explored on two wheels. After perusing the riverfront sights along the Grand Rounds National Scenic Byway, join the Chain of Lakes trail to explore the city's interconnected lake system. Over 15-miles long, the trail passes half a dozen scenic shorelines as it winds through Uptown's heart. Enjoy beaches, hiking and plenty of family-friendly attractions along the way. On that note, no one has captured the hearts and minds of the Twin Cities quite like Prince. There are excellent self-guided tours that explore the singer's roots in the local rock scene, but true fans should make the pilgrimage to Paisley Park, His Purpleness's mansion, where you'll enjoy artifacts, instruments and rare recordings during your visit.

2 Hinckley
Drive 81 miles ▪ 1 hour, 20 minutes

Slow things down with a small town with big history. Start at Hinckley's historic downtown district, which features antique shops and boutiques, before exploring the surrounding landscape including the scenic St. Croix River to the west. Renowned for its muskie, walleye and smallmouth bass, the river draws anglers from across the state. The nearby St. Croix State Park is also home to 127 miles of rugged ATV and backcountry hiking trails through virgin red pine forest. After a day in the country, relax at the Grand Casino Hinckley, a sprawling gaming complex with over 2,000 slots and 28 gaming tables. Even if Lady Luck isn't on your side, you can still enjoy the on-site spa, golf club and nationally known entertainers.

3 Duluth
Drive 75 miles ▪ 1 hour, 10 minutes

The port city of Duluth bustles with activity. Nestled on the shores of Lake Superior, the blue-collar town lives and breathes its historic claim as one of the country's most important shipping hubs, though these days much of the industrial architecture has been repurposed into craft breweries, distilleries and hip coffee roasters. It's a cool, lo-fi aesthetic that, along with the steep hills and waterfront landscape, has led some to dub Duluth the "San Francisco of the Midwest." While enjoying the hearty, entrepreneurial attitude of the locals, be sure to stop by the recently refurbished S.S. William A. Irvin Boat Museum. The 610-foot tanker was once the flagship of U.S. Steel's Great Lakes Fleet, hosting dignitaries in elegant staterooms while it shuttled iron ore east across America.

Getty Images/iStockphoto

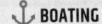

BIKING · BOATING · DINING · ENTERTAINMENT · FISHING · HIKING · HUNTING · PADDLING · SHOPPING · SIGHTSEEING

Minnesota SPOTLIGHTS

Launch a Vacation Voyage in the Gopher State

The Land of 10,000 Lakes has an appeal that goes far beyond boating and fishing. Discover sophisticated cities, charming small towns and lush forests rich with game. Walk the trails blazed by fur traders and Native Americans.

HUMANS LIVED IN THE ST. CROIX RIVER VALLEY AS FAR BACK AS 4,000 YEARS AGO.

A paddleboat and a canoe navigate the St. Croix River by Taylors Falls.

Getty Images/iStockphoto

Hinckley

Hinckley is a town with history; from the Fire Museum and abandoned sandstone quarry to a reconstructed 18th-century trading post, there's so much to see. Water lovers have two rivers to "shoot the rapids" on; for hikers, there are miles of trails to explore or you can cast out a line and fish.

A Wall of Fire

It started with a spark more than 125 years ago, and the town of Hinckley, along with a quarter of a million acres, burned to the ground. Today the community remembers the hundreds who died in 1894 and honors those who fought a wall of fire four miles across. The Fire Museum houses artifacts and exhibits paying tribute to one of the largest wildfires in history. The Hinckley Fire Monument marks the graves of those who perished.

Shoot the Rapids

The St. Croix River, a National Scenic Riverway, is a great place to paddle among lush forestlands while fishing for smallmouth bass, muskies and trout, or shoot step rapids along a rocky shelf. Grindstone Lake is an angler's paradise stocked with lake trout, bullhead, bass, crappie and perch. Kettle River, designated a State Wild and Scenic River, and located at Banning State Park, is one of the most outstanding whitewater rafting rivers in the Midwest. Raft through Mother's Delight, Blueberry Slide and the Dragon's Tooth. Feeling invincible? Tackle the infamous Hell's Gate Canyon, boulder-bed rapids where you'll come out feeling like you've been through...well, you know. The otherworldly rocks on the banks are perfect for photo opportunities.

Explore Nature

Banning State Park is a natural paradise. Hit the trails and discover the Log Creek Arches, rock shelters, gorges and ruins of an abandoned sandstone quarry that still stand as a testament to the late 1890s. A winter trip to Robinson Quarry Ice Cave provides a chance to scale up ice-covered quarry walls. Lace up those hiking boots and head out for a 70-mile trek on Willard Munger State Trail, the fifth-longest continually paved trail in the country.

Step Back in Time

Get an in-depth look at 18th-century life at the Snake River Fur Post, where settlers traded hides for axes, kettles, blankets and tools. Costumed guides escort you to the Ojibwe encampment where birch bark wigwams and canoes reside. Wander 1.5 miles of nature trails through woodlands, wetlands and prairies.

Minneapolis

Minneapolis began life as a humble fur-trading center on the banks of the Mississippi River in the 17th century.

LOCAL FAVORITE

Grilled Spam with Pineapple and Onion

Minnesotans love Spam so much, they have an entire museum devoted to the canned meat in Austin. Hormel Foods, the company behind Spam, was founded in the same city in 1891. *Recipe by Phillip Bryant.*

INGREDIENTS
- ☐ 1 can Spam
- ☐ 1 can pineapple chunks
- ☐ 1 onion
- ☐ Barbecue sauce

DIRECTIONS
Soak wooden sticks in water to prevent them from burning on the grill. Cut Spam and onion into 1" squares. Put 4 to 5 pieces of Spam, onion and pineapple on each skewer and then cook on the grill. Apply BBQ sauce on the skewers before taking them off the grill.

MN

Fast-forward to the 21st century, and the downtown's gleaming skyscrapers show just how far the city has come. Fortunately, locals have gone to great lengths to preserve the past while keeping an eye on the future of this Midwest metropolis.

Water, Water Everywhere

Although Minnesota is known as the Land of 10,000 Lakes, residents of Minneapolis are content with the handful of lakes located in town. Lake Harriet is a great place to go sailing, kayaking or fishing just a few short miles from downtown. The band shell on the north shore of the lake hosts numerous live music events during the summer. Lake Calhoun, the city's largest lake, offers a fishing pier and a boat dock as well as sandy beaches for soaking up the sun and cooling off in the water. Lake of the Isles lets small, four-legged visitors run free at an off-leash dog park.

Fireworks Over the Lake

If you're visiting on July 4, unfold a picnic blanket in the Riverfront area on the Mississippi and watch one of the largest fireworks displays in the country. An even bigger pyrotechnics show erupts over the river during Minneapolis Aquatennial each summer.

Walker Art Center

The Walker Art Center is a 17-acre campus and encompasses 20th-century masterpieces by Edward Hopper, Yves Klein, Chuck Close and more. The Walker's crown jewel, the renowned Minneapolis Sculpture Garden — the largest urban outdoor sculpture garden in the nation — displays more than 40 sculptures, including Claes Oldenburg's "Spoonbridge and Cherry." This is a 29-foot-high sculpture of a cherry perched on the tip of a gargantuan spoon that arches over a pond.

Lake Superior Shores

Several state parks celebrate the stunning beauty of Minnesota's North Shore along Lake Superior. Visit the state park at Gooseberry Falls to stand in awe of the cascading waterfalls and rivers, or head to Split Rock Lighthouse for the iconic site of the grand beacon perched on a rocky bluff overlooking this inland sea. Built in 1910, this beacon is one of Minnesota's most photographed sites.

Cool Cascades

You'll find even more high waterfalls as you traverse the shore. The 120-foot High Falls at Grand Portage State Park are located on the Pigeon River, part of the international boundary with Canada. The highest falls entirely within Minnesota are the 70-foot High Falls of the Baptism River, part of Tettegouche State Park. The falls can be accessed via a 3-mile trail departing from the visitor center.

Raging Rivers

Along the southwest half of the North Shore, rivers churn with whitewater during spring runoff and heavy rains. They can carry up to four times as much water as those with headwaters. From the Manitou River northeast, the rivers have lakes feeding into them, providing a more stable flow. You'll find great rafting here.

FOR MORE INFORMATION

Explore Minnesota Tourism, 888-868-7476, www.exploreminnesota.com
Hinckley Convention and Visitors Bureau, 800-952-4282, www.hinckleymn.com
Meet Minneapolis, 888-676-6757, www.minneapolis.org
Minnesota North Shore Visitor, www.northshorevisitor.com

Minnesota

ADRIAN — F1 *Nobles*

ADRIAN MUNICIPAL CAMPGROUND (Public) From Jct of I-90 & SR-91 (exit 26), S 0.3 mi on SR-91 to Franklin St, W 0.3 mi (E). 104 Avail: 50 full hkups, 54 W, 54 E (30/50 amps). 2021 rates: $26 to $30. Apr 15 to Oct 15. (507)483-2820

AITKIN — C3 *Aitkin*

PETE'S RETREAT FAMILY CAMPGROUND & RV PARK **Ratings: 7.5/9★/9.5** (Campground) Avail: 20 full hkups (30/50 amps). 2021 rates: $54 to $71. May 01 to Oct 01. (320)684-2020, 22337 State Hwy 47, Aitkin, MN 56431

AKELEY — C2 *Hubbard*

AKELEY CITY PARK (Public) From Jct of Hwys 64 & 34, W 0.3 mi on Hwy 34, follow signs (E). 28 Avail: 28 W, 28 E (30/50 amps). 2021 rates: $20 to $30. May 15 to Sep 15. (218)252-4570

ALBERT LEA — E3 *Freeborn*

ALBERT LEA/AUSTIN KOA KAMPGROUND **Ratings: 7.5/9★/8.5** (Campground) 48 Avail: 18 full hkups, 30 W, 30 E (30/50 amps). 2021 rates: $44 to $59. Apr 15 to Oct 15. (507)373-5170, 84259 County Road 46, Hayward, MN 56043

HICKORY HILLS CAMPGROUND **Ratings: 7.5/8★/7.5** (Campground) Avail: 11 full hkups (30/50 amps). 2021 rates: $38 to $50. Apr 15 to Oct 15. (507)852-4555, 15694 717 Ave, Albert Lea, MN 56007

MYRE-BIG ISLAND (Public State Park) From Jct of I-35 & Exit 11/CR-46, E 1 mi on CR-46 to CR-38, S 2 mi (R). Reservation fee & vehicle permit required. Avail: 32 E (20/30 amps). 2021 rates: $17 to $29. (507)668-7060

ALEXANDRIA — D2 *Douglas*

CRUISE INN RV PARKS & LODGING **Ratings: 7/NA/7.5** (RV Park) Avail: 39 full hkups (30/50 amps), Pit toilets. 2021 rates: $38. Apr 15 to Oct 15. (320)763-5121, 910 34th Ave W, Alexandria, MN 56308

ANNANDALE — D2 *Wright*

SCHROEDER (WRIGHT COUNTY PARK) (Public) From Jct of Hwys 55 & 24, N 4.5 mi on Hwy 24 to CR-E 39, E 0.5 mi to Ireland Rd, S 0.25 mi (R). Avail: 50 E (30 amps). 2021 rates: $27.50 to $30. Apr 30 to Sep 30. (320)274-8870

APPLE VALLEY — E3 *Dakota*

LEBANON HILLS CAMPGROUND
(Public) From Jct of I-35 E & Cliff Rd (Exit 93), E 0.6 mi to Johnny Cake Ridge Rd, S 1 mi (L). **FAC:** paved/gravel rds. 93 Avail: 58 gravel, 35 grass, 3 pull-thrus, (30x50), back-ins (30x50), 58 full hkups, 24 E (30/50 amps), WiFi @ sites, tent sites, dump, laundry, fire rings, firewood. **REC:** pond, boating nearby, playground, rec open to public. Pets OK. Partial handicap access, 14 day max stay, eco-friendly. 2021 rates: $30 to $41. May 03 to Oct 17.
(651)480-7773 Lat: 44.77421, Lon: -93.18652
12100 Johnny Cake Ridge Road, Apple Valley, MN 55124
www.dakotacounty.us/parks
See ad this page

APPLETON — D1 *Swift*

APPLETON (CITY PARK) (Public) From Jct of SR-7/US-59 (N of town) & SR-119, S 0.4 mi (L) on SR-7/US-59 (L). Avail: 12 full hkups (30/50 amps). 2021 rates: $25. May 01 to Oct 30. (320)289-1363

ARGYLE — B1 *Marshall*

OLD MILL (Public State Park) From Jct of US-75 & SR-4, E 11 mi on SR-4 to CR-4, N 1 mi to CR-39, N 0.5 mi (L); or From Jct of US-59 & SR-4, W 11 mi on SR-4 to CR-4, N 1 mi (L). Reservation fee. 26 Avail: 10 W, 10 E (20/30 amps). 2021 rates: $15 to $23. May 30 to Oct 31. (218)437-8174

ATWATER — D2 *Kandiyohi*

DIAMOND LAKE (KANDIYOHI COUNTY PARK) (Public) From Atwater, W 3 mi on US-12 to cnty rd, N 4 mi to Diamond Lake, follow signs (L). Avail: 80 full hkups (20/30 amps). 2021 rates: $29.80. (320)974-8520

AUSTIN — E3 *Mower*

ADVENTURE BOUND BEAVER TRAILS **Ratings: 8.5/10★/9.5** (Campground) 189 Avail: 114 full hkups, 75 W, 75 E (30/50 amps). 2021 rates: $53 to $95. May 01 to Oct 15. (507)607-0620, 21943 630th Ave, Austin, MN 55912

AVON — D2 *Stearns*

EL RANCHO MANANA CAMPGROUND & RIDING STABLE **Ratings: 7/8.5★/9** (Campground) 120 Avail: 70 full hkups, 50 W, 50 E (30/50 amps). 2021 rates: $36 to $68. May 01 to Sep 30. (320)597-2740, 27302 Ranch Road, Richmond, MN 56368

BAGLEY — B2 *Clearwater*

BAGLEY CITY PARK (Public) From Jct of US-2 & SR-92, N 0.4 mi on SR-92 (L). 30 Avail: 17 W, 30 E (30 amps). 2021 rates: $25. May 15 to Oct 01. (218)694-2865

BARNUM — C4 *Carlton*

BENT TROUT LAKE CAMPGROUND **Ratings: 6/8★/8.5** (Campground) 11 Avail: 11 W, 11 E (30/50 amps). 2021 rates: $40. May 15 to Oct 01. (218)389-6322, 2928 Bent Trout Lake Road, Barnum, MN 55707

BAUDETTE — A2 *Lake of the Woods*

TIMBER MILL PARK (Public) From Jct Hwy 72 & Hwy 11 (on East side of Baudette), W 0.8 mi on Hwy 11 to Tourist Park Ave NE, N 300 ft (R). 20 Avail. 2021 rates: $35. May 15 to Oct 01. (218)634-1850

ZIPPEL BAY
(Public State Park) From jct Hwy 11 & Hwy 172: Go 12 mi N on Hwy 172, then 6 mi W on CR 8, then 1 mi N on CR 34. **FAC:** Avail: 57 grass, back-ins (20x50), tent sites, pit toilets, dump, firewood. **REC:** Lake of the Woods: swim, fishing, kayaking/canoeing, boating nearby, playground, rec open to public. Pets OK. Partial handicap access. 2021 rates: $15 to $27. no cc.
(218)783-6252 Lat: 48.847889, Lon: -94.849833
Baudette, MN 56623
www.dnr.state.mn.us

BAXTER — C2 *Crow Wing*

Travel Services

GANDER RV OF BAXTER Your new hometown outfitter offering the best regional gear for all your outdoor needs. Your adventure awaits. **SERVICES:** RV appliance, gunsmithing svc, archery svc, sells outdoor gear, sells fishing gear, sells firearms, restrooms. RV Sales. RV supplies, RV accessible. Hours: 9am - 8pm.
(877)873-2188 Lat: 46.357485, Lon: -94.247769
14275 Edgewood Drive North #100, Baxter, MN 56425
rv.ganderoutdoors.com

BEMIDJI — B2 *Beltrami*

BEMIDJI See also Cass Lake.

FOX LAKE CAMPGROUND OF BEMIDJI **Ratings: 8.5/9★/10** (Campground) Avail: 30 full hkups (30/50 amps). 2021 rates: $59. May 03 to Sep 15. (218)586-2231, 2556 Island View Dr NE, Bemidji, MN 56601

KOA BEMIDJI **Ratings: 8.5/9.5★/8.5** (Campground) 54 Avail: 32 full hkups, 22 W, 22 E (30/50 amps). 2021 rates: $49 to $63. May 10 to Sep 10. (218)444-7562, 510 Brightstar Rd NW, Bemidji, MN 56601

LAKE BEMIDJI (Public State Park) From Jct of Hwy 2 & US-71, N 4 mi to Glidden Rd, SE on Glidden, follow signs (L). Entrance fee & reservation fee required. Note: 50' RV length limit. Avail: 43 E (30 amps). 2021 rates: $17 to $31. (218)308-2300

ROYAL OAKS RV PARK
good sam park
Ratings: 7.5/9★/10 (RV Park) W-bnd: From Jct of US-2 & SR71S, R .02 mi to Peaceful Meadows Ln, R .01 mi to Fenske Farm Ln, R .01 mi E-bnd: Stay right on US-2 bypass (3rd exit) from Jct of US-2 & SR-71, S between mile post 116 & 117 (exit 71 S), L .02 mi on 197 to Peaceful Meadows Ln, R .01 mi to Fenske Farm Ln, R .01 mi.

HEADWATERS OF THE MISSISSIPPI RIVER
Experience the headwaters of the Mississippi River at Lake Itasca less than 1 hour away. Bike trails and hiking nearby. Enjoy fishing, swimming and boating any of the many close lakes. Spacious sites including big rig sites.
FAC: gravel rds. (55 spaces). Avail: 49 gravel, 6 pull-thrus, (30x80), back-ins (30x80), 49 full hkups (30/50 amps), seasonal sites, cable, WiFi @ sites, laundry, fire rings, firewood. **REC:** boating nearby, playground, hunting nearby. Pets OK. No tents. Big rig sites, eco-friendly. 2021 rates: $42 to $47. Apr 15 to Oct 15.
(218)751-8357 Lat: 47.43380, Lon: -94.86197
2874 Fenske Farm Lane SE, Bemidji, MN 56601
royaloaksrvpark.com
See ad this page

BENSON — D2 *Swift*

AMBUSH PARK (Public) From Jct of Hwys 29 & 9, W 1 mi on Hwy 9, follow signs (R). Avail: 14 full hkups (30 amps). 2021 rates: $27.47. May 01 to Oct 01. (320)843-4775

BIGFORK — B3 *Itasca*

GEORGE WASHINGTON/OWEN LAKE (Public) From town, SE 10 mi on CR-7 to CR-340, E 7 mi to CR-52, N 1.5 mi to Forestry Rd, W 1 mi, follow signs (E). 18 Avail: Pit toilets. 2021 rates: $14. May 15 to Nov 01. (218)328-8984

SCENIC (Public State Park) From town, SE 7 mi on CR-7 to Scenic State Park Rd, N 1 mi (R). Reservation fee. Avail: 21 E (30 amps). 2021 rates: $15 to $29. Apr 01 to Nov 23. (218)743-3362

MN

BIWABIK — B4 *St Louis*

VERMILION TRAIL CAMPGROUND (Public) From Jct of SR-135 & CR 4 (East of town), E 0.3 mi on SR-135 (R). 40 Avail: 2 full hkups, 9 E (30 amps). 2021 rates: $19 to $22. May 01 to Sep 30. (218)865-6705

BLOOMING PRAIRIE — E3 *Mower*

BROOKSIDE CAMPGROUND **Ratings: 9/10★/9** (Campground) 42 Avail: 32 full hkups, 10 W, 10 E (30/50 amps). 2021 rates: $32 to $45. May 01 to Sep 30. (507)583-2979, 52482-320th St, Blooming Prairie, MN 55917

BRAINERD — C2 *Cass*

CROW WING (Public State Park) From Jct of SR-210 & SR-371, SW 9 mi on SR-371 to CR-27, W 1 mi (E). Entrance fee & reservation fee required. Note: 45' RV length maximum. Avail: 12 E (20/30 amps). 2021 rates: $17 to $29. (218)825-3075

CROW WING LAKE CAMPGROUND **Ratings: 8/8.5★/10** (Campground) 60 Avail: 40 full hkups, 11 W, 11 E (30/50 amps). 2021 rates: $52 to $74. May 01 to Oct 01. (218)829-6468, 2393 Crow Wing Camp Road, Brainerd, MN 56401

LUM PARK (BRAINERD COUNTY PARK) (Public) From Jct of SH-371 & SH-210, E 4 mi on SH-210 to Lum Park Rd, N 0.2 mi (R). 18 Avail: 18 W, 18 E (30/50 amps). 2021 rates: $25 to $35. May 01 to Oct 15. (218)828-2320

MISSISSIPPI RIVER - COE/GULL LAKE (Public Corps) From town, NW 7 mi on Hwy 371 to CR-125 (Gull Lake Dam Rd), W 3 mi (E). Avail: 39 E (30 amps). 2021 rates: $28. May 01 to Oct 31. (651)290-5772

BYRON — E4 *Olmsted*

OXBOW (OLMSTEAD COUNTY PARK) (Public) From Jct of US-14 & CR-5, N 3 mi on CR-5 to CR-105, N 1 mi follow signs (L). Avail: 10 E. 2021 rates: $15. May 01 to Oct 04. (507)328-7340

CALEDONIA — E4 *Houston*

BEAVER CREEK VALLEY (Public State Park) From Jct SR-44 & SR-76, W 1 mi on SR-76 to CR-1, W 4 mi, follow signs (E). Reservation fee. Avail: 16 E (20/30 amps). 2021 rates: $15 to $27. Apr 15 to Oct 01. (507)724-2107

CAMBRIDGE — D3 *Isanti*

FAIRGROUNDS (ISANTI COUNTY PARK) (Public) From jct Hwy 65 & Hwy 95: Go 1/2 mi E on Hwy 95. 78 Avail. 2021 rates: $20 to $25. May 01 to Oct 01. (763)689-2555

CANBY — E1 *Yellow Medicine*

STONE HILL (Public) From Jct of US-75 & SR-68 (in town), W 0.1 mi on SR-68, follow signs 2 mi (L). 54 Avail: 6 full hkups, 48 W, 48 E (30 amps). 2021 rates: $20 to $25. May 01 to Oct 01. (507)223-7586

Had a great stay? Let us know by emailing us Parks@goodsam.com

CANNON FALLS — E3 *Dakota*

CANNON FALLS CAMPGROUND **Ratings: 9/9★/10** (Campground) 111 Avail: 37 full hkups, 69 W, 69 E (30/50 amps). 2021 rates: $42 to $62. Apr 15 to Oct 31. (507)263-3145, 30365 Oak Lane, Cannon Falls, MN 55009

LAKE BYLLESBY CAMPGROUND
(Public) From Jct of US-52 & CR-86, W 30 ft on CR-86 to Harry Ave, S 2.2 mi (L). **FAC:** paved rds. Avail: 83 paved, patios, 15 pull-thrus, (30x60), back-ins (30x60), 46 W, 83 E (30/50 amps), WiFi @ sites, tent sites, dump, groc, fire rings, firewood. **REC:** Lake Byllesby: swim, fishing, playground, rec open to public. Pets OK. Partial handicap access, 14 day max stay, eco-friendly. 2021 rates: $28 to $33. May 03 to Oct 17.
(651)480-7770 Lat: 44.51391, Lon: -92.94715
7650 Echo Point Rd, Cannon Falls, MN 55009
www.dakotacounty.us/parks
See ad previous page

CARLOS — D2 *Douglas*

LAKE CARLOS (Public State Park) From Jct of US-29 & CR-38, W 1.5 mi on CR-38 (L). Reservation fee. Note: 50' RV length limit. Avail: 81 E (30 amps). 2021 rates: $17 to $31. (320)852-7200

CARLTON — C4 *Carlton*

JAY COOKE (Public State Park) From town, E 2 mi on Hwy 210 (R). Avail: 21 E (30 amps). 2021 rates: $17 to $31. (218)673-7000

CASS LAKE — B2 *Beltrami*

STONY POINT RESORT RV PARK & CAMPGROUND
Ratings: 10/10★/10 (Campground) From Jct of US 2 & SR-371, E 1.8 mi on US 2 - between MP 131 & 132 (L). **FAC:** paved rds. (175 spaces). Avail: 60 all weather, patios, 28 pull-thrus, (30x85), back-ins (30x50), 46 full hkups, 14 W, 14 E (30/50 amps), seasonal sites, WiFi @ sites, $, tent sites, rentals, dump, mobile sewer, laundry, groc, LP gas, fire rings, firewood, restaurant. **REC:** heated pool, wading pool, hot tub, Cass Lake: swim, fishing, marina, boating nearby, playground, hunting nearby. Pets OK $. Partial handicap access. Big rig sites, eco-friendly. 2021 rates: $42 to $47, Military discount. May 01 to Oct 15. ATM.
(218)335-6311 Lat: 47.37891, Lon: -94.57393
5510 US 2 NW, Cass Lake, MN 56633
www.stonyptresortcasslake.com
See ad this page

Things to See and Do

CANAL HOUSE RESTAURANT & BAR Restaurant and lounge located at Stony Point Resort. May 01 to Oct 15. Partial handicap access. RV accessible. Restrooms. Food. Hours: 8am to 9pm. ATM.
(218)335-2136 Lat: 47.378670, Lon: -94.57497
5510 US 2 NW, Cass Lake, MN 56633
www.stonyptresortcasslake.com
See ad this page

CLEARWATER — D3 *Stearns*

A-J ACRES Ratings: 7/8★/6.5 (Campground) 75 Avail: 12 full hkups, 63 W, 63 E (30/50 amps). 2021 rates: $43. May 01 to Oct 01. (320)558-2847, 1300 195th Street E, Clearwater, MN 55320

ST CLOUD/CLEARWATER RV PARK
Ratings: 8.5/10★/9.5 (Campground) From Jct of I-94 & SR-24 (exit 178), N 0.5 mi on SR-24 to CR-75, W 1 mi to CR-143, SW 0.3 mi (R); From Jct of US-10 & SR 24 (Clearlake), S 3.5 mi on SR-24 to CR-75, W 1 mi to CR-143, SW 0.3 mi (R). **FAC:** gravel rds. (100 spaces). Avail: 60 gravel, 45 pull-thrus, (30x70), back-ins (30x55), 28 full hkups, 32 W, 32 E (30/50 amps), seasonal sites, WiFi @ sites, tent sites, rentals, dump, laundry, groc, LP bottles, fire rings, firewood. **REC:** heated pool, boating nearby, playground. Pets OK. Partial handicap access. Big rig sites, eco-friendly. 2021 rates: $46 to $55, Military discount. May 01 to Oct 15.
(320)558-2876 Lat: 45.42377, Lon: -94.06521
2454 CR-143, Clearwater, MN 55320
www.time2camp.com
See ad this page

CLOQUET — C4 *Carlton*

CLOQUET/DULUTH KOA **Ratings: 8.5/10★/8.5** (Campground) 45 Avail: 10 full hkups, 35 W, 35 E (30/50 amps). 2021 rates: $47 to $67. May 01 to Oct 04. (218)879-5726, 1381 Kampground Road, Cloquet, MN 55720

SPAFFORD (CLOQUET CITY PARK) (Public) From Jct of Hwys 45 & 33, W 1 blk on Hwy 45 to Broadway, N 1 mi (L). 22 Avail: 22 W, 22 E (15 amps). 2021 rates: $25. May 18 to Oct 06. (218)390-4519

COKATO — D2 *Wright*

COLLINWOOD (WRIGHT COUNTY PARK) (Public) From town, W 2.5 mi on US-12 to Rhodes Ave, S 2 mi (E). Reservation fee. Avail: 40 E (30 amps). 2021 rates: $18.50 to $27.50. Apr 30 to Sep 15. (320)286-2801

COOK — B3 *Itasca*

KABETOGAMA/WAKEMUP BAY (Public State Park) From town: Go 2-1/2 mi N on CR 24, then 3 mi E on CR 78, then 1 mi N. 22 Avail: Pit toilets. 2021 rates: $14. (218)753-2245

CROOKSTON — B1 *Polk*

CENTRAL PARK (CROOKSTON CITY PARK) (Public) From Jct US-75 & US-2 (Robert St E), E 2 blks on Robert St E to Ash St, N 1/2 blk (R). 16 Avail: 16 W, 16 E (15 amps). 2021 rates: $20. May 15 to Sep 30. (218)281-1242

CROSBY — C3 *Crow Wing*

CROSBY MEMORIAL PARK (Public) From Jct of SR-6 & SR-210, S 0.1 mi on SR-210 to 2nd St, SE 0.05 mi (L). Avail: 20 E (20/50 amps). 2021 rates: $25. May 10 to Oct 01. (218)546-5021

CROW WING/GREER LAKE (Public State Park) From town, N 12 mi on SR-6 to CR-36, W 3 mi to CR-14, S 1.5 mi to access rd, W 2 mi, follow signs (R). 31 Avail. 2021 rates: $14. May 01 to Oct 31. (218)546-5926

CROSS LAKE — C3 *Crow Wing*

MISSISSIPPI RIVER - COE/RONALD LOUIS COULTIER (Public Corps) At Jct of Cnty Rds 66 & 3 (E). Avail: 97 E (30 amps). 2021 rates: $20 to $36. May 01 to Sep 30. (218)692-2025

CURRIE — E1 *Murray*

LAKE SHETEK (Public State Park) From Jct of Hwy 30 & CR-38, N 2 mi on CR-38 to CR-37, W 2 mi (R). Reservation fee. 70 Avail: 32 full hkups, 32 E (20/30 amps). 2021 rates: $15 to $27. (507)763-3256

SCHREIER'S ON SHETEK CAMPGROUND **Ratings: 8/9★/10** (Campground) 10 Avail: 10 W, 10 E (30/50 amps). 2021 rates: $33 to $39. May 01 to Oct 15. (507)763-3817, 35 Resort Road, Currie, MN 56123

DEER RIVER — B3 *Cass*

MISSISSIPPI RIVER - COE/WINNIE DAM (Public Corps) From town, W 1 mi on US-2 to Hwy 46, N 11 mi to Hwy 9, W 2 mi (E). Avail: 22 E (30/50 amps), Pit toilets. 2021 rates: $24. May 01 to Sep 15. (218)326-6128

SCHOOLCRAFT (Public State Park) From Jct of US-2 & MN-6, S 8.5 mi on MN-6 to Itasca 28, W 2.5 mi to Cass 74, N 1.5 mi, follow signs (R). Vehicle permit & reservation fee required. Note: 40' RV length limit. 28 Avail: Pit toilets. 2021 rates: $15. (218)328-8982

DETROIT LAKES — C1 *Becker*

DETROIT LAKES See also Perham.

COUNTRY CAMPGROUND **Ratings: 8/10★/10** (Campground) Avail: 30 full hkups (30/50 amps). 2021 rates: $38. May 01 to Oct 01. (218)847-9621, 13639 260th Ave, Detroit Lakes, MN 56501

DETROIT LAKES AMERICAN LEGION (Public) From Jct of Hwy 10 & Washington Ave, S 0.9 mi on Washington Ave to W Lake Dr, W 0.5 mi to Jct of Legion Rd (R) Note: 45' RV length maximum. 33 Avail: 10 full hkups, 23 W, 23 E (30 amps). 2021 rates: $33 to $39. May 15 to Oct 15. (218)847-3759

FOREST HILLS RV & GOLF RESORT **Ratings: 9/9.5★/9** (RV Park) Avail: 11 full hkups (30/50 amps). 2021 rates: $10. May 01 to Sep 30. (800)482-3441, 22931 185th Street, Detroit Lakes, MN 56501

DULUTH — C4 *Carlton*

DULUTH See also Barnum & Cloquet, MN; Superior, WI.

BUFFALO VALLEY RV CAMPING **Ratings: 6.5/10★/8** (Campground) 130 Avail: 38 full hkups, 92 W, 92 E (30/50 amps). 2021 rates: $48 to $54. May 01 to Nov 01. (218)590-8774, 2590 Guss Road, Duluth, MN 55810

Say you saw it in our Guide!

DULUTH INDIAN POINT CAMPGROUND **Ratings: 6/8.5★/8** (RV Park) 82 Avail: 7 full hkups, 22 W, 42 E (30/50 amps). 2021 rates: $39 to $61. May 01 to Oct 18. (855)777-0652, 7000 Pulaski St , Duluth, MN 55807

FOND DU LAC CAMPGROUND AND BOAT LANDING **Ratings: 5.5/7.5/8.5** (Campground) 55 Avail: 5 full hkups, 35 W, 35 E (30/50 amps). 2021 rates: $40 to $50. May 01 to Oct 15. (218)780-2319, 13404 Hwy 23, Duluth, MN 55808

LAKEHEAD BOAT BASIN & RV PARKING Ratings: 7.5/10★/6 (RV Park) 30 Avail: 12 full hkups, 18 W, 18 E (30/50 amps). 2021 rates: $40 to $45. May 15 to Sep 15. (218)722-1757, 1000 Minnesota Ave , Duluth, MN 55802

RED PINE CAMPGROUND **Ratings: 8/9★/9** (RV Park) Avail: 40 full hkups (30/50 amps). 2021 rates: $42. May 01 to Oct 01. (218)481-9210, 5020 Red Pine Dr , Saginaw, MN 55779

SPIRIT LAKE MARINA & RV PARK **Ratings: 6.5/9.5★/7** (RV Park) 25 Avail: 25 W, 25 E (30/50 amps). 2021 rates: $44 to $59. Apr 01 to Oct 30. (218)628-3578, 121 Spring Street, Duluth, MN 55807

SPIRIT MOUNTAIN (Public) At I-35 (exit 249) & Spirit Mountain Place. 73 Avail: 40 W, 73 E. 2021 rates: $40 to $45. May 15 to Oct 10. (218)628-2891

EFFIE — B3 *Itasca*

BASS LAKE (ITASCA COUNTY PARK) (Public) From Jct of SR-38 & SR-1, E 11 mi on SR-1 to Bass Lake Rd, S 2 mi, follow signs (L). 29 Avail: Pit toilets. 2021 rates: $10. May 15 to Nov 15. (218)327-2850

ELBA — E4 *Winona*

WHITEWATER (Public State Park) From Jct of Hwys 14 & 74, N 9 mi on Hwy 74 (L). Entrance fee and reservation fee required. Avail: 47 E (50 amps). 2021 rates: $17 to $31. (507)312-2300

ELLENDALE — E3 *Steele*

CRYSTAL SPRINGS RV RESORT Ratings: 9/9.5★/9.5 (RV Park) Avail: 19 full hkups (30/50 amps). 2021 rates: $40. May 01 to Oct 31. (507)398-3297, 15649 35th Ave SW, Ellendale, MN 56026

ELMORE — F3 *Faribault*

WOODS LAKE (FARIBAULT COUNTY PARK) (Public) From Jct of I-90 & US-169 (exit 119), S 9 mi on US-169 to CR-2, W 1.2 mi, N 0.5 mi, follow signs (L). Avail: 20 E (20/30 amps). 2021 rates: $18 to $20. May 01 to Oct 15. (507)525-7707

FAIRFAX — E2 *Nicollet*

FORT RIDGELY (Public State Park) From Jct of Hwys 19 & 4, S 7 mi on Hwy 4 (R). Reservation fee. Avail: 15 E (30 amps). 2021 rates: $15 to $27. (507)426-7840

FAIRMONT — E2 *Martin*

FLYING GOOSE CAMPGROUND & RESORT **Ratings: 8/9★/10** (Campground) 40 Avail: 21 full hkups, 19 W, 19 E (30/50 amps). 2021 rates: $40 to $45. May 01 to Oct 31. (507)235-3458, 2521 115th St, Fairmont, MN 56031

FARIBAULT — E3 *Rice*

CAMP FARIBO **Ratings: 9/10★/8.5** (Campground) Avail: 41 full hkups (30/50 amps). 2021 rates: $40 to $45. Apr 15 to Oct 15. (507)332-8453, 21851 Bagley Avenue , Faribault, MN 55021

FEDERAL DAM — C2 *Cass*

MISSISSIPPI RIVER - COE/LEECH LAKE (Public Corps) In town, W of CR-8, adjacent to town, follow signs (L). Avail: 73 E (30/50 amps). 2021 rates: $26 to $50. May 01 to Oct 31. (218)654-3145

FINLAND — B4 *Lake*

FINLAND (Public State Park) From town, E 0.5 mi on CR-6 (R). Avail: 39 E (30 amps), Pit toilets. 2021 rates: $14. May 15 to Sep 30. (218)353-8800

FINLAND/ECKBECK (Public State Park) From town, S 3 mi on SR-1 (L). 31 Avail: Pit toilets. 2021 rates: $14. May 15 to Sep 02. (218)353-8800

FINLAYSON — C3 *Pine*

BANNING RV PARK AND CAMPGROUND **Ratings: 6.5/7/7** (Campground) 80 Avail: 55 full hkups, 25 W, 15 E (30/50 amps). 2021 rates: $30 to $60. May 01 to Oct 31. (612)390-0415, 60545 State Hwy 23, Finlayson, MN 55735

FOREST LAKE — D3 *Washington*

Travel Services

GANDER RV OF FOREST LAKE Your new hometown outfitter offering the best regional gear for all your outdoor needs. Your adventure awaits. **SERVICES:** RV appliance, gunsmithing svc, archery svc, sells outdoor gear, sells fishing gear, sells firearms, restrooms. RV Sales. RV supplies, LP gas, RV accessible. Hours: 9am to 8pm.
(833)435-6976 Lat: 45.235247, Lon: -93.031363
14640 West Freeway Dr, Forest Lake, MN 55025
rv.ganderoutdoors.com

GARFIELD — D2 *Douglas*

OAK PARK KAMPGROUND
Ratings: 7.5/9★/8.5 (Campground) 44 Avail: 26 full hkups, 18 W, 18 E (30/50 amps). 2021 rates: $39.58 to $42.84. Apr 15 to Oct 01. (320)834-2345, 9561 CR 8 NW, Garfield, MN 56332

GARRISON — C3 *Crow Wing*

CAMP HOLIDAY RESORT & CAMPGROUND **Ratings: 7.5/8.5★/9** (Campground) 22 Avail: 4 full hkups, 18 W, 18 E (30/50 amps). 2021 rates: $33 to $66. May 01 to Sep 30. (218)678-2495, 27406 Round Lake Road, Deerwood, MN 56444

GILBERT — B4 *St Louis*

SHERWOOD FOREST CAMPGROUND
Ratings: 7.5/9★/9.5 (Public) From Jct of US 53 & SR-37E, E 2.6 mi on SR-37E to Sherwood Forest Drive, N 0.6 mi on Sherwood Forest Drive (R). **FAC:** paved rds. (52 spaces). 41 Avail: 12 paved, 29 gravel, 11 pull-thrus, (24x100), back-ins (30x60), 27 full hkups, 9 W, 9 E (30/50 amps), seasonal sites, WiFi @ sites, tent sites, dump, fire rings, firewood. **REC:** Lake Ore-Be-Gone: swim, fishing, kayaking/canoeing, boating nearby, playground, rec open to public. Pets OK. Partial handicap access. Big rig sites, eco-friendly. 2021 rates: $26.64 to $33.51. May 01 to Oct 01.
(218)748-2221 Lat: 47.48543, Lon: -92.46304
301 Ore-Be-Gone Dr, Gilbert, MN 55741
www.gilbertmn.org
See ad this page

WEST FORTY RV PARK **Ratings: 6.5/7/8.5** (RV Park) 33 Avail: 28 full hkups, 5 W, 5 E (30/50 amps). 2021 rates: $26 to $33. May 01 to Oct 31. (218)248-7362, 245 Highway 37, Gilbert, MN 55741

GLENWOOD — D2 *Pope*

BARNESS PARK (GLENWOOD CITY PARK) (Public) From town, S 0.5 mi on Franklin St (L). Avail: 33 full hkups (30/50 amps). 2021 rates: $42 to $47. May 01 to Oct 01. (320)634-5433

GLYNDON — C1 *Clay*

BUFFALO RIVER (Public State Park) From Jct of Hwys 10 & 9, E 1.5 mi on Hwy 10 (R). Vehicle permit & reservation fee required. Avail: 35 E (30/50 amps). 2021 rates: $17 to $31. (218)498-2124

GRAND MARAIS — B5 *Cook*

GRAND MARAIS RV PARK (CITY PARK) (Public) From Jct of Hwy 61 & 8th Ave W (SW end of town), S 100 ft on 8th Ave W (R). Reservation fee required. 300 Avail: 161 full hkups, 82 W, 82 E (30/50 amps). 2021 rates: $38 to $56. (800)998-0959

JUDGE C R MAGNEY (Public State Park) From town, NE 14 mi on MN-61 (L). Reservation fee. Note: 45' length maximum. 27 Avail. 2021 rates: $17 to $31. (218)387-6300

GRAND RAPIDS — C3 *Itasca*

PRAIRIE LAKE CAMPGROUND **Ratings: 6.5/7/8** (Campground) 15 Avail: 3 full hkups, 12 W, 12 E (30 amps). 2021 rates: $36.95 to $42.95. May 01 to Oct 01. (218)326-8486, 30730 Wabana Rd, Grand Rapids, MN 55744

GRANITE FALLS — E2 *Yellow Medicine*

PRAIRIE VIEW RV PARK & CAMPGROUND Ratings: 10/10★/10 (RV Park) Avail: 42 full hkups (30/50 amps). 2021 rates: $25 to $50. Apr 15 to Oct 31. (866)293-2121, 5590 Prairies Edge Lane, Granite Falls, MN 56241

UPPER SIOUX AGENCY (Public State Park) From jct Hwy 23 & Hwy 67 south of town: Go 8 mi E on Hwy 67. Avail: 14 E (30/50 amps). 2021 rates: $15 to $27. (320)564-4777

HASTINGS — E3 *Washington*

SAINT CROIX BLUFFS (Public) From town, N 1 mi on Hwy 61 to SR-95, N 2 mi to US-10, E 2.6 mi to CR-21, N 0.5 mi (R). Entrance fee required. 62 Avail: 21 W, 62 E (50 amps). 2021 rates: $15 to $22. (651)430-8240

HERMANTOWN — C4 *St Louis*

Travel Services

CAMPING WORLD OF HERMANTOWN As the nation's largest retailer of RV supplies, accessories, services and new and used RVs, Camping World is committed to making your total RV experience better. **SERVICES:** sells outdoor gear, sells fishing gear, sells firearms, restrooms. RV Sales. RV supplies, LP gas, dump, RV accessible. Hours: 9am to 8pm.
(855)852-7586 Lat: 46.8198, Lon: -92.1767
4275 Haines Rd, Hermantown, MN 55811
www.campingworld.com

OFF SEASON RVING TIP: Off season power: Plan for limited utility hookups. If you are planning to camp in an area that generally receives freezing weather during the winter, the RV park may turn off water spigots. Some provide water access at specified frost-free faucets, while others may provide no water at all. Research these details online or by calling the campground, and take the supplies you'll need to replace utilities not offered.

HINCKLEY — D3 *Pine*

A SPOTLIGHT Introducing Hinckley's colorful attractions appearing at the front of this state section.

GRAND HINCKLEY RV RESORT

good sam park **Ratings: 10/10★/10** (RV Park) From Jct of I-35 & SR-48 (Exit 183), E 1 mi on SR-48 (R).

ONE OF THE TOP RATED PARKS IN MN

Enjoy sitting around a campfire with the kids, get your game on at the basketball & volleyball courts, or head over to Grand Casino Hinckley & play your favorite slots. Free shuttle service to the casino and heated pool.

FAC: paved rds. (271 spaces). Avail: 191 paved, patios, back-ins (35x65), 191 full hkups (30/50 amps), seasonal sites, cable, WiFi @ sites, rentals, laundry, groc, fire rings, firewood, restaurant, controlled access. **REC:** heated pool, boating nearby, golf, shuffleboard, playground. Pets OK. Partial handicap access. No tents. Big rig sites. 2021 rates: $32 to $99, Military discount. ATM.

(800)472-6321 Lat: 46.00981, Lon: -92.91177
1326 Fire Monument Rd, Hinckley, MN 55037
grandcasinomn.com
See ad this page, 504

PATHFINDER VILLAGE ST CROIX **Ratings: 8/9★/9.5** (Membership Park) 36 Avail: 36 W, 36 E (30/50 amps). 2021 rates: $35 to $45. Apr 15 to Sep 30. (320)384-7985, 49200 State Hwy 48 #1, Hinckley, MN 55037

ST CROIX (Public State Park) From Jct of I-35 & Hwy 48, E 15 mi on Hwy 48 to CR-22, S 5 mi (E). Reservation fee. Avail: 81 E (30 amps). 2021 rates: $17 to $31. (320)384-6591

Things to See and Do

GRAND CASINO HINCKLEY Casino, Restaurant Partial handicap access. RV accessible. Restrooms. Food. Hours: 24 hours. ATM.
(800)472-6321 Lat: 46.01073, Lon: -92.90183
777 Lady Luck Drive, Hinckley, MN 55037
grandcasinomn.com
See ad this page, 504

HOUSTON — E4 *Houston*

MONEY CREEK HAVEN

good sam park **Ratings: 8.5/8.5★/10** (Campground) 59 Avail: 14 full hkups, 38 W, 38 E (30/50 amps). 2021 rates: $35 to $50. Apr 15 to Oct 15. (507)896-3544, 18502 County Road 26, Houston, MN 55943

HOYT LAKES — B4 *St Louis*

FISHERMAN'S POINT (Public) From Jct of I-53 & Hwy 135 (Gilbert cutoff), E 22 mi on Hwy 135 to Hwy 110, E 4 mi to Hoyt Lakes Rd, S 1 mi (R). Avail: 93 E (30/50 amps). 2021 rates: $12.50 to $25. May 01 to Sep 15. (218)225-3337

HUGO — D3 *Washington*

Travel Services

CAMPING WORLD OF HUGO As the nation's largest retailer of RV supplies, accessories, services and new and used RVs, Camping World is committed to making your total RV experience better. **SERVICES:** restrooms. RV Sales. RV supplies, RV accessible. Hours: 9am - 7pm, closed Sun.
(855)696-5496 Lat: 45.224826, Lon: -93.030543
14025 West Freeway Drive, Hugo, MN 55038
www.campingworld.com

IHLEN — E1 *Pipestone*

SPLIT ROCK CREEK (Public State Park) From Jct of Hwys 30 & 23, S 6 mi on Hwy 23 to CR-2, E 3 blks to CR-20, S 0.75 mi (L). Entrance fee & reservation fee required. Avail: 21 E (30/50 amps). 2021 rates: $17 to $29. (507)348-7908

INTERNATIONAL FALLS — A3 *Koochiching*

RAINY LAKE RV **Ratings: 6.5/NA/9** (RV Park) Avail: 18 full hkups (30/50 amps). 2021 rates: $45. May 01 to Oct 01. (218)288-1130, 2967 Hwy 11 E, International Falls, MN 56649

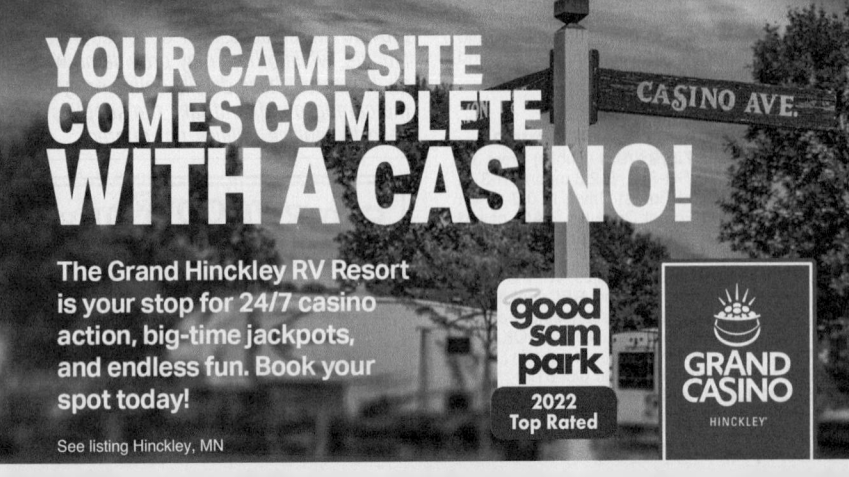

ISANTI — D3 *Isanti*

COUNTRY CAMPING TENT & RV PARK **Ratings: 8.5/9★/9.5** (Campground) 73 Avail: 11 full hkups, 47 W, 47 E (30/50 amps). 2021 rates: $45 to $60. May 01 to Oct 01. (763)444-9626, 27437 Palm Street NW, Isanti, MN 55040

ISLE — C3 *Cook*

FATHER HENNEPIN (Public State Park) From Jct of Hwys 47 & 27, W 1 mi on Hwy 27 (R). Entrance fee required. Reservation fee. Avail: 51 E (20/30 amps). 2021 rates: $17 to $31. (320)676-8763

SOUTH ISLE FAMILY CAMPGROUND **Ratings: 7.5/8/9.5** (Campground) Avail: 45 full hkups (30/50 amps). 2021 rates: $43 to $61. Apr 25 to Oct 15. (320)676-8538, 39002 Highway 47, Isle, MN 56342

JACKSON — F2 *Jackson*

ANDERSON (JACKSON COUNTY PARK) (Public) From town, S 6 mi on Hwy 71 to CR-4, W 5 mi (R). 77 Avail: 77 W, 77 E (30 amps). 2021 rates: $13 to $22. May 15 to Oct 01. (507)847-2525

JACKSON KOA KAMPGROUND **Ratings: 8.5/9.5★/8.5** (Campground) 59 Avail: 34 full hkups, 25 W, 25 E (30/50 amps). 2021 rates: $45 to $52. Apr 15 to Oct 15. (800)KOA-5670, 2035 Hwy 71 N, Jackson, MN 56143

JACOBSON — C3 *Aitkin*

SAVANNA/HAY LAKE (Public State Park) From town: Go 2-1/2 mi S on Hwy 65,then 3 mi E, then 1 mi S. 20 Avail: Pit toilets. 2021 rates: $14. (218)426-3271

JORDAN — E3 *Scott*

Travel Services

CAMPING WORLD OF JORDAN/MINNEAPOLIS As the nation's largest retailer of RV supplies, accessories, services and new and used RVs, Camping World is committed to making your total RV experience better. **SERVICES:** restrooms. RV Sales. RV supplies, RV accessible. Hours: 9am - 6pm, closed Sun.
(952)466-6427 Lat: 44.70791, Lon: -93.59448
16701 Greystone Lane, Jordan, MN 55352
rv.campingworld.com

KABETOGAMA — B3 *St Louis*

KABETOGAMA/WOODENFROG (Public State Park) From Orr, N 30 mi on US-53 to CR-122 (Gamma Rd), N 6 mi follow signs (R). 59 Avail: Pit toilets. 2021 rates: $14. May 01 to Nov 30. (218)753-2245

PINES OF KABETOGAMA RESORT

good sam park **Ratings: 9.5/10★/10** (RV Resort) From Hwy 53 South: Go 1.3 mi N on Gamma Rd, then 1.6 mi E on Gappa Rd, then .02 mi N on Burma Rd (R). **FAC:** all weather rds. 30 Avail: 16 paved, 14 all weather, 3 pull-thrus, (35x65), back-ins (35x65), 30 full hkups (30/50 amps), WiFi @ sites, tent sites, rentals, laundry, groc, fire rings, firewood. **REC:** Lake Kabetogama: swim, fishing, marina, kayaking/canoeing, boating nearby, playground. Pets OK. Big rig sites, eco-friendly. 2021 rates: $75 to $175. May 01 to Oct 15.
(218)875-2000 Lat: 48.438714, Lon: -93.019634
12443 Burma Rd, Kabetogama, MN 56669
thepineskab.com
See ad this page

LAKE BENTON — E1 *Lincoln*

HOLE-IN-THE-MOUNTAIN (LINCOLN COUNTY PARK) (Public) From Jct of US-75 & Hwy 14, W 0.5 mi on Hwy 14 (L). 33 Avail: 33 W, 33 E (30 amps). 2021 rates: $20 to $25. May 15 to Oct 01. (507)368-9350

LAKE BRONSON — A1 *Kittson*

LAKE BRONSON (Public State Park) From Jct of US-59 & CR-28, E 2 mi on CR-28 (E). Reservation fee. Note: 50' RV length limit. Avail: 67 E (20/30 amps). 2021 rates: $15 to $27. (218)754-2200

LAKE CITY — E4 *Wabasha*

FRONTENAC (Public State Park) From town, NW 7 mi on US-61 to CR-2, NE 1 mi, follow signs (L). Entrance fee required. Reservation fee. Note: 53' RV length maximum. Avail: 19 E (30 amps). 2021 rates: $17 to $31. (651)345-3401

LAKE PEPIN CAMPGROUND

Ratings: 5.5/7.5★/8 (Campground) From Jct US-63 & U-61 S, NW 1.4 mi on US-61/63 (R). **FAC:** gravel rds. (120 spaces). Avail: 37 grass, 7 pull-thrus, (30x45), back-ins (28x40), 25 full hkups, 12 W, 12 E (30/50 amps), seasonal sites,

WiFi @ sites, dump, fire rings, firewood. **REC:** boating nearby, playground. Pets OK. No tents, eco-friendly. 2021 rates: $25 to $42. Apr 15 to Oct 15. no cc. **(651)345-2909 Lat: 44.46281, Lon: -92.28629**
1818 North High St, Lake City, MN 55041
See ad opposite page

LAKE ELMO — D3 *Washington*

LAKE ELMO PARK RESERVE (Public) From Jct of I-94 & Kelvin Ave. (exit 251), N 1 mi on CR-19 (E). Entrance fee required. Avail: 80 E (20/30 amps). 2021 rates: $15 to $55. (651)430-8370

LAKE ITASCA — C2 *Clearwater*

ITASCA/BEAR PAW (Public State Park) From Park Rapids, N 20 mi on US-71, follow signs (L). Avail: 35 E (20/30 amps). 2021 rates: $17 to $31. (218)699-7251

ITASCA/PINE RIDGE (Public State Park) From Park Rapids, N 20 mi on US-71 (L). Avail: 64 E (20/30 amps). 2021 rates: $17 to $31. (218)699-7251

LAKE LILLIAN — D2 *Kandiyohi*

BIG KANDIYOHI LAKE EAST (KANDIYOHI COUNTY PARK) (Public) From jct Hwy-7 & CR-8: Go 4 mi N on CR-8, then 1-3/4 mi NW on CR-132. Avail: 80 full hkups. 2021 rates: $28.50. (320)664-4707

BIG KANDIYOHI LAKE WEST (KANDIYOHI COUNTY PARK) (Public) From Jct of US-71 & SR-7, E 3 mi on SR-7 to SR-44/45th St., N 3 mi (R). 94 Avail: 94 W, 94 E (30 amps). 2021 rates: $28.50. (320)995-6599

LAKEFIELD — E2 *Jackson*

KILEN WOODS (Public State Park) From Jct of Hwy 86 & I-90, N 6 mi on Hwy 86 to CR-24, E 5 mi, follow signs (R). Avail: 11 E (30 amps), Pit toilets. 2021 rates: $15 to $27. (507)832-6034

LAKEVILLE — E3 *Dakota*

Travel Services

CAMPING WORLD OF LAKEVILLE As the nation's largest retailer of RV supplies, accessories, services and new and used RVs, Camping World is committed to making your total RV experience better. **SERVICES:** gunsmithing svc, archery svc, sells outdoor gear, sells fishing gear, sells firearms. RV Sales. RV supplies. Hours: 9am to 8pm.
(952)435-3805 Lat: 44.703711, Lon: -93.287445
16861 Kenyon Ave, Lakeville, MN 55044
www.campingworld.com

LANESBORO — E4 *Fillmore*

EAGLE CLIFF CAMPGROUND & LODGING Ratings: 7.5/9.5★/9.5 (Campground) 146 Avail: 40 full hkups, 106 W, 106 E (30/50 amps). 2021 rates: $34 to $41. Apr 15 to Oct 19. (507)467-2598, 35455 State Hwy 16, Lanesboro, MN 55949

SYLVAN PARK (Public) From Jct of US-16 & Parkway Ave (in Lanesboro), N 0.2 mi on Parkway Ave (R). 43 Avail: 43 W, 43 E (15/30 amps). 2021 rates: $30. May 01 to Oct 01. (507)467-3722

LE ROY — F4 *Mower*

LAKE LOUISE (Public State Park) From Jct of Hwy 56 & CR-14, N 1.5 mi on CR-30 (L). Reservation fee. Note: 45' RV length limit. Avail: 11 E (30 amps), Pit toilets. 2021 rates: $15 to $27. (507)352-5111

LITCHFIELD — D2 *Meeker*

LAKE RIPLEY (LITCHFIELD CITY PARK) (Public) From Jct of US-12 & SR-22, S 1.5 mi on SR-22 (R). 32 Avail: 12 full hkups, 20 W, 20 E (30 amps). 2021 rates: $20 to $25. May 02 to Oct 15. (320)693-7201

LITTLE FALLS — D2 *Harrison*

CHARLES A. LINDBERGH (Public State Park) From Jct of N Hwy 10 & Hwy 27 exit, W 2 mi on Hwy 27 to Lindbergh Dr, S 1 mi (R). Reservation fee. Note: 50' RV length limit. Avail: 15 E (30 amps). 2021 rates: $17 to $29. (320)616-2525

LONG PRAIRIE — D2 *Todd*

CAMP S'MORE CAMPGROUND **Ratings: 6.5/9★/9** (Campground) 22 Avail: 14 full hkups, 5 W, 5 E (30/50 amps). 2021 rates: $34. May 01 to Oct 15. (320)732-2517, 24797 US 71, Long Prairie, MN 56347

Clean Green! Vinegar and baking soda can be used to clean almost anything. Mix in a little warm water with either of these and you've got yourself an all-purpose cleaner.

LUTSEN — B5 *Cook*

CASCADE RIVER (Public State Park) From town, SW 9 mi on US-61 (R); Or from Duluth, NE 100 mi on US-61 (Northshore Dr) to Park Entrance Rd, MP 101 N 0.7 mi (E). Reservation fee. Note: 35' length maximum. 40 Avail. 2021 rates: $17 to $31. (218)387-6000

LUVERNE — E1 *Rock*

BLUE MOUNDS (Public State Park) From Jct of US-75 & I-90, N 5 mi on US-75 to CR-20, E 1 mi (E). Reservation fee. Note: 50' RV length limit. Avail: 40 E (30 amps). 2021 rates: $17 to $29. (507)283-6050

LYND — E1 *Lyon*

CAMDEN (Public State Park) From Lynd, SW 3 mi on Hwy 23 (R). Reservation fee. Avail: 29 E (30 amps). 2021 rates: $17 to $29. (507)865-4530

MADELIA — E2 *Watonwan*

MADELIA CAMPGROUND (Public) From Hwy 60 & Main St, W 0.2 mi on Main St to Old Hwy 60, SW 1 mi (R). 49 Avail: 24 full hkups, 4 W, 24 E (30/50 amps). 2021 rates: $15 to $25. Apr 15 to Oct 01. (507)380-9440

Travel Services

CAMPING WORLD OF MADELIA/MANKATO As the nation's largest retailer of RV supplies, accessories, services and new and used RVs, Camping World is committed to making your total RV experience better. **SERVICES:** restrooms. RV Sales. RV supplies, RV accessible. Hours: 9am - 6pm, closed Sun.
(507)550-1130 Lat: 44.06319, Lon: -94.39042
84601 Olson Dr, Madelia, MN 56062
rv.campingworld.com

MADISON LAKE — E3 *Blue Earth*

BRAY PARK (BLUE EARTH COUNTY PARK) (Public) From jct US-14 & Hwy-60: Go 4 mi N on Hwy-60, then 1-1/2 mi E on Hwy-60, then 2 mi S on CR-48. 53 Avail: 17 W, 33 E (30/50 amps). 2021 rates: $25. May 01 to Oct 31. (507)243-3885

MAHNOMEN — B1 *Mahnomen*

SHOOTING STAR CASINO & RV PARK **Ratings: 9.5/9★/8.5** (RV Park) Avail: 47 full hkups (30/50 amps). 2021 rates: $20. May 01 to Oct 30. (800)453-STAR, 777 Casino Drive, Mahnomen, MN 56557

MANKATO — E3 *Blue Earth*

MANKATO See also Waterville.

MINNEOPA (Public State Park) From Jct of Hwys 60 & 68, W 1 mi on Hwy 68, follow signs (R). Reservation fee. Avail: 6 E (30 amps). 2021 rates: $17 to $29. (507)386-3910

MAPLE PLAIN — D3 *Hennepin*

BAKER PARK RESERVE (Public) From Jct of Hwy 12 & CR-19, N 1.5 mi on CR-19, located on Lake Independence, follow signs (L). 203 Avail: 98 W, 98 E (15 amps). 2021 rates: $21 to $29. Apr 30 to Oct 20. (763)694-7860

MAPLETON — E3 *Blue Earth*

DALY PARK (BLUE EARTH COUNTY PARK) (Public) From town: Go 3 mi S on CR-7, then 2 mi W on CR-191. 79 Avail: 18 W, 58 E (50 amps). 2021 rates: $25. May 01 to Oct 31. (507)524-3000

MAZEPPA — E4 *Wabasha*

PONDEROSA CAMPGROUND (Public) From Jct of US-52 & CR-12 (MP66), E 2 mi on CR-12 to CR-27, N 3.5 mi, follow signs (L). 98 Avail: 98 W, 98 E (50 amps). 2021 rates: $28 to $35. Apr 14 to Oct 14. (507)843-3611

MCGREGOR — C3 *Aitkin*

MISSISSIPPI RIVER - COE/SANDY LAKE (Public Corps) From town, N 13 mi on Hwy 65 (R). Avail: 49 E (30 amps). 2021 rates: $26 to $52. May 01 to Sep 30. (218)426-3482

SAVANNA PORTAGE (Public State Park) From town, N 7 mi on Hwy 65 to CR-14, NE 10 mi (R). Reservation fee. Avail: 18 E (30 amps). 2021 rates: $17 to $29. (218)426-3271

MELROSE — D2 *Stearns*

BIRCH LAKES (Public) From Jct of CR-13 & CR-17, E 1.5 mi on CR-17 to Birch Lake Rd, N 2 mi to forest rd (E). Reservation fee. 29 Avail: Pit toilets. 2021 rates: $14. (218)365-4966

We appreciate your business!

MENAHGA — C2 *Wadena*

HUNTERSVILLE/HUNTERSVILLE LANDING (Public State Park) From jct CR 17 & CR 23: Go 1 mi N on CR 23, then 3 mi E on CR 18, then 1 mi S, then 2 mi E. 24 Avail: Pit toilets. 2021 rates: $14. (218)266-2100

MINNEAPOLIS — D3 *Anoka*

MINNEAPOLIS See also Apple Valley, Cannon Falls, Clearwater, Faribault, Isanti, Monticello, Prior Lake, Taylors Falls & Welch, MN; Somerset, WI.

MINNEAPOLIS NW KOA CAMPGROUND Ratings: 8.5/9.5★/9 (Campground) From Jct of I-94 & CR-30 (exit 213), left 0.2 mi on Maple Grove Pkwy (get in rt lane, CR-30 turns R at McDonalds), W 1.7 mi on CR-30 to CR-101, turn R 1 mi (R). **FAC:** gravel rds. 150 Avail: 100 gravel, 50 grass, 50 pull-thrus, (30x75), back-ins (30x55), 61 full hkups, 89 W, 89 E (30/50 amps), WiFi @ sites, tent sites, rentals, dump, laundry, groc, LP gas, fire rings, firewood. **REC:** pool, boating nearby, shuffleboard, playground. Pet restrict (B). Big rig sites, eco-friendly. 2021 rates: $41 to $54, Military discount. Apr 01 to Oct 15.
(763)420-2255 Lat: 45.14474, Lon: -93.52097
10410 Brockton Lane N, Minneapolis, MN 55311
www.mplsnwkoa.com
See ad this page

MINNEAPOLIS SW KOA **Ratings: 8.5/9★/9** (Campground) 83 Avail: 30 full hkups, 53 W, 53 E (30/50 amps). 2021 rates: $41.90 to $66.20. Apr 26 to Oct 05. (952)492-6440, 3315 W 166th Street, Jordan, MN 55352

MONTEVIDEO — D1 *Chippewa*

LAGOON PARK (Public) From Jct of Hwys 7 & 29, N .3 mi on Hwy 29, W .5 mi on Ashmore Ave. 10 Avail: 8 W, 8 E (50 amps). 2021 rates: $20. May 01 to Nov 01. (320)269-6575

MONTICELLO — D3 *Wright*

RIVER TERRACE PARK **Ratings: 8/UI/10** (Campground) Avail: 80 full hkups (30/50 amps). 2021 rates: $38 to $45. Apr 01 to Oct 31. (763)295-2264, 1335 River St W, Monticello, MN 55362

Travel Services

CAMPING WORLD OF MONTICELLO/MINNEAPOLIS As the nation's largest retailer of RV supplies, accessories, services and new and used RVs, Camping World is committed to making your total RV experience better. **SERVICES:** RV, RV appliance, MH mechanical, staffed RV wash, restrooms. RV Sales. RV supplies, LP gas, RV accessible. Hours: 9am - 7pm.
(888)698-3193 Lat: 45.298963, Lon: -93.811708
3801 Chelsea Rd W, Monticello, MN 55362
www.campingworld.com

MOOSE LAKE — C3 *Carlton*

MOOSE LAKE (Public State Park) From Jct of I-35 & Hwy 43 (Willow River exit), W 0.5 mi on Hwy 43 to Hwy 61, N 0.2 mi to park access rd, E 0.75 mi, follow signs (L). Reservation fee. Avail: 20 E (30 amps). 2021 rates: $17 to $31. (218)460-7001

MOOSE LAKE (CITY PARK) (Public) From Jct of I-35 & SR-73, W 1.5 mi on SR-73 to 2nd St, E 0.3 mi to Birch St, N 0.1 mi to 4th St, E 0.1 mi (E). 65 Avail: 43 W, 22 S, 43 E (30/50 amps). 2021 rates: $27 to $30. May 08 to Sep 27. (218)485-4761

MORRISTOWN — E3 *Rice*

CAMP MAIDEN ROCK WEST **Ratings: 7/8★/9** (Campground) 26 Avail: 2 full hkups, 24 W, 24 E (30/50 amps). 2021 rates: $39 to $48. May 15 to Sep 15. (507)685-2280, 24505 Jackson Ave, Morristown, MN 55052

County names help you follow the local weather report.

MORTON — E2 *Redwood*

JACKPOT JUNCTION CASINO HOTEL CAMPGROUND **Ratings: 9/NA/8.5** (RV Park) Avail: 30 full hkups (30/50 amps). 2021 rates: $30 to $40. (800)946-0077, 39375 County Hwy 24, Morton, MN 56270

NERSTRAND — E3 *Rice*

NERSTRAND BIG WOODS (Public State Park) From Jct of SR-246/Main St (in town) & Cherry St, W 0.5 mi on SR-246 to CR-40, W 1.2 mi (R). 51 Avail: 27 W, 27 E (20/30 amps). 2021 rates: $17 to $31. (507)384-6140

NEW LONDON — D2 *Kandiyohi*

GAMES LAKE (KANDIYOHI COUNTY PARK) (Public) From jct US 71 & CR 40: Go 4 mi W on CR 40, then 2 mi N on CR 5. 56 Avail: 56 W, 56 E. 2021 rates: $29.50. (320)354-4453

NEW ULM — E2 *Brown*

FLANDRAU (Public State Park) From Jct US-14 & SR-15, S 1.5 mi on SR-15 to 10th South St, W 1 mi, to Summit Ave, S 0.1 mi, follow signs (R). Reservation fee. Avail: 34 E (30 amps). 2021 rates: $15 to $31. (507)233-9800

NISSWA — C2 *Crow Wing*

BIRCH BAY RV RESORT **Ratings: 8.5/9.5★/8.5** (RV Resort) Avail: 25 full hkups (30/50 amps). 2021 rates: $48 to $58. May 01 to Oct 01. (218)963-4488, 1497 Sandy Point Road SW, Nisswa, MN 56468

FRITZ'S RESORT & CAMPGROUND **Ratings: 8.5/9★/9** (Campground) Avail: 14 full hkups (30/50 amps). 2021 rates: $45. May 01 to Oct 01. (218)568-8988, 26483 Hwy 371, Nisswa, MN 56468

NODINE — E4 *Winona*

GREAT RIVER BLUFFS (Public State Park) From jct I-90 (exit 266) & CR 12: Go N to end of CR 12, then 1 mi E on CR 3 (Scenic Apple Blossom Dr), then right 1 mi on gravel access road. 31 Avail. 2021 rates: $15 to $27. (507)643-6849

NORTH BRANCH — D3 *Chisago*

WILD RIVER (Public State Park) From Jct of I-35 & SR-95, E 10 mi on SR-95 to CR-12, NE 3.5 mi (E). Entrance fee required. Reservation fee. Avail: 34 E (20/30 amps). 2021 rates: $17 to $31. (651)583-2125

ONAMIA — C3 *Mille Lacs*

MILLE LACS KATHIO (Public State Park) From town, N 8 mi on US-169 to CR-26, S 1 mi (R). Reservation fee. Avail: 22 E (20/30 amps). 2021 rates: $15 to $31. (320)532-3523

ORONOCO — E4 *Pine Island*

Travel Services

CAMPING WORLD OF ORONOCO/ROCHESTER As the nation's largest retailer of RV supplies, accessories, services and new and used RVs, Camping World is committed to making your total RV experience better. **SERVICES:** restrooms. RV Sales. RV supplies, RV accessible. Hours: 9am - 6pm, closed Sun.
(507)216-0783 Lat: 44.14731, Lon: -92.53278
1260 Lake Shady Ave S, Oronoco, MN 55960
rv.campingworld.com

ORR — B3 *St Louis*

ASH RIVIERA RV PARK **Ratings: 7/8.5★/9** (RV Park) Avail: 18 full hkups (30/50 amps). 2021 rates: $45. Apr 15 to Oct 15. (218)374-3411, 10351 Ash River Trail, Orr, MN 55771

ORTONVILLE — D1 *Swift*

BIG STONE LAKE (Public State Park) From Jct of Hwy 7 & US-12, NW 8 mi on Hwy 7, follow signs (L). Reservation fee. Avail: 10 E (20 amps). 2021 rates: $15 to $27. May 25 to Sep 07. (320)839-3663

OTTERTAIL — C2 *Otter Tail*

THUMPER POND RV PARK **Ratings: 8/NA/8.5** (RV Park) Avail: 25 full hkups (30/50 amps). 2021 rates: $34.95 to $44.95. May 15 to Oct 01. (218)367-2000, 300 Thumper Lodge Road, Ottertail, MN 56571

OUTING — C3 *Cass*

LAND O' LAKES/CLINT CONVERSE (Public State Park) From town, N 2 mi on Hwy 6 to CR-48 (Lake Washburn Rd), W 2 mi (R). 31 Avail: Pit toilets. 2021 rates: $14. (218)203-4447

Get the GOOD SAM CAMPING APP

OWATONNA — E3 *Steele*

HOPE OAK KNOLL CAMPGROUND
Ratings: 8/9★/9 (Campground) 17 Avail: 15 full hkups, 2 W, 2 E (30/50 amps). 2021 rates: $36. Apr 15 to Oct 15. (507)451-2998, 9545 CR-3, Owatonna, MN 55060

RICE LAKE (Public State Park) From Jct I-35 & Exit 42A/Hoffman Dr, E 0.6 mi on Hoffman Dr to East Rose (CR-19), E 7 mi to park entrance rd (R). Reservation fee. Avail: 18 E (20/30 amps). 2021 rates: $17 to $29. (507)414-6190

RIVER VIEW CAMPGROUND
Ratings: 8.5/10★/10 (Campground) 60 Avail: 10 full hkups, 37 W, 37 E (30/50 amps). 2021 rates: $35 to $55. Apr 15 to Oct 15. (507)451-8050, 2554 SW 28th St, Owatonna, MN 55060

Travel Services

CAMPING WORLD OF OWATONNA As the nation's largest retailer of RV supplies, accessories, services and new and used RVs, Camping World is committed to making your total RV experience better. **SERVICES:** restrooms. RV Sales. RV supplies, RV accessible. Hours: 9am - 6pm, closed Sun.
(507)573-5292 Lat: 44.12481, Lon: -93.24497
3627 N County Rd 45, Owatonna, MN 55060
rv.campingworld.com

PARK RAPIDS — C2 *Clearwater*

BIG PINES RV PARK **Ratings: 8.5/10★/9.5** (Campground) Avail: 15 full hkups (30/50 amps). 2021 rates: $49 to $59. May 01 to Oct 15. (218)237-8815, 501 Central Avenue South, Park Rapids, MN 56470

PAUL BUNYAN/MANTRAP LAKE (Public State Park) From Jct of SR-34 & CR-4, N 12 mi on CR-4 to CR-24, E 1.5 mi to CR-104, N 0.75 mi, follow signs (R). 36 Avail: Pit toilets. 2021 rates: $14. (218)266-2100

VAGABOND VILLAGE CAMPGROUND **Ratings: 9/9.5★/8.5** (Campground) Avail: 55 full hkups (30/50 amps). 2021 rates: $52 to $56. May 15 to Oct 01. (218)732-5234, 23801 Green Pines Road, Park Rapids, MN 56470

PAYNESVILLE — D2 *Meeker*

LAKE KORONIS (MEEKER COUNTY PARK) (Public) From town, SE 5 mi on Hwy 55, S 0.25 mi on US-4 to CSAH-20, W 4 mi (L); or From Jct of US-23 & CSAH-20, S 1.9 mi on CSAH-20, (continue on) E 1.5 mi, follow signs (R). Reservation fee. Avail: 27 E (30 amps). 2021 rates: $16 to $30. May 01 to Sep 30. (320)276-8843

PELICAN RAPIDS — C1 *Otter Tail*

MAPLEWOOD (Public State Park) From Jct of Hwy 108 & US-59, E 7 mi on Hwy 108 (R). Reservation fee. Avail: 32 E (30/50 amps). 2021 rates: $17 to $31. (218)863-8383

SHERIN MEMORIAL (PELICAN RAPIDS CITY PARK) (Public) In town on Hwy-108. 10 Avail. 2021 rates: $15 to $20. May 15 to Sep 15. (218)863-7076

PEQUOT LAKES — C2 *Crow Wing*

RV RESORT VILLAGE AT THE PRESERVE **Ratings: 10/9.5★/10** (Condo Park) Avail: 30 full hkups (30/50 amps). 2021 rates: $49 to $55. Apr 20 to Oct 15. (218)568-8009, 28668 Hurtig Road, Pequot Lakes, MN 56472

PERHAM — C2 *Otter Tail*

GOLDEN EAGLE RV VILLAGE **Ratings: 7.5/8★/9** (Membership Park) Avail: 15 full hkups (30/50 amps). 2021 rates: $50. May 15 to Sep 15. (218)346-4386, 42488 480th Ave, Perham, MN 56573

PILLAGER — C2 *Cass*

PILLSBURY/ROCK LAKE (Public State Park) From town, W 0.5 mi on Hwy 210 to CR-1, N 6 mi, turn left. Note: 30' RV length limit. 48 Avail: Pit toilets. 2021 rates: $14. (218)825-3075

PINE CITY — D3 *Pine*

POKEGAMA LAKE RV PARK & GOLF COURSE **Ratings: 7.5/8.5/8.5** (Campground) Avail: 41 full hkups (30/50 amps). 2021 rates: $50 to $60. May 01 to Oct 01. (320)629-6552, 19193 Island Resort Road, Pine City, MN 55063

SNAKE RIVER (Public State Park) From town, E 6 mi on CR-8 to CR-118, E 3 mi, follow signs (L). Reservation fee. 26 Avail: Pit toilets. 2021 rates: $14. May 05 to Nov 05. (651)583-2125

PINE ISLAND — E4 *Goodhue*

HIDDEN MEADOWS RV PARK **Ratings: 7/8.5★/9** (Campground) 63 Avail: 60 full hkups, 3 W, 3 E (30/50 amps). 2021 rates: $50 to $53. Apr 08 to Nov 01. (507)356-8594, 6450 120th Street NW, Pine Island, MN 55963

PIPESTONE — E1 *Pipestone*

PIPESTONE RV CAMPGROUND **Ratings: 8/8.5★/8.5** (Campground) 27 Avail: 2 full hkups, 25 W, 25 E (30/50 amps). 2021 rates: $35 to $44. May 01 to Oct 15. (507)825-2455, 919 N Hiawatha Ave, Pipestone, MN 56164

PLAINVIEW — E4 *Wabasha*

CARLEY (Public State Park) From town: Go 4 mi S on CR 10. Note: 30' RV length maximum. 20 Avail: Pit toilets. 2021 rates: $15 to $23. (507)312-2300

PRESTON — E4 *Fillmore*

OLD BARN RESORT
Ratings: 8/9★/9.5 (Campground) 125 Avail: 74 full hkups, 19 W, 19 E (30/50 amps). 2021 rates: $37 to $50. Apr 01 to Oct 31. (507)467-2512, 24461 Heron Road, Preston, MN 55965

PRIOR LAKE — E3 *Scott*

DAKOTAH MEADOWS RV PARK **Ratings: 10/9.5★/9** (Campground) Avail: 122 full hkups (30/50 amps). 2021 rates: $40 to $50. (800)653-CAMP, 2341 Park Place NW, Prior Lake, MN 55372

ROCHESTER — E4 *Olmsted*

ROCHESTER See also Pine Island, St Charles & Zumbrota.

AUTUMN WOODS RV PARK **Ratings: 7.5/10★/9.5** (RV Park) Avail: 93 full hkups (30/50 amps). 2021 rates: $38 to $48. Mar 15 to Nov 15. (507)990-2983, 1067 Autumnwoods Circle SW, Rochester, MN 55902

KOA ROCHESTER/MARION **Ratings: 9/8.5★/8** (Campground) Avail: 53 full hkups (30/50 amps). 2021 rates: $44 to $47. Mar 15 to Oct 31. (507)288-0785, 5232 65th Ave SE, Rochester, MN 55904

ROYALTON — D2 *Benton*

TWO RIVERS CAMPGROUND **Ratings: 8.5/9.5★/10** (Campground) 141 Avail: 56 full hkups, 79 W, 79 E (30/50 amps). 2021 rates: $59 to $76. May 01 to Oct 01. (320)584-5125, 5116 145th St N.W., Royalton, MN 56373

SANDSTONE — C3 *Pine*

BANNING (Public State Park) From Jct of I-35 & Hwy 23 (exit 195), E 1.9 mi on Hwy 23, follow signs (R). Avail: 11 E (30 amps). 2021 rates: $14. Apr 01 to Oct 31. (320)245-2668

SAUK CENTRE — D2 *Stearns*

SINCLAIR LEWIS (Public) From Jct of I-94 & US-71, N 1 mi on US-71 to Park Lane, W 0.2 mi, follow signs (R). Reservation fee. 50 Avail: 20 full hkups, 30 W, 30 E (30 amps). 2021 rates: $30. May 01 to Oct 15. (320)352-2203

SCHROEDER — B5 *Cook*

TEMPERANCE RIVER (Public State Park) From town, NE 1 mi on SR-61, follow signs (R). Entrance fee & reservation fee required. Avail: 18 E (30 amps). 2021 rates: $17 to $31. (218)663-3100

SHAFER — D3 *Chisago*

WILDWOOD CAMPGROUND
Ratings: 7.5/9★/8.5 (Campground) 135 Avail: 38 full hkups, 51 W, 51 E (30/50 amps). 2021 rates: $52 to $60. May 01 to Oct 18. (651)465-7162, 20078 Lake Blvd, Shafer, MN 55074

SHEVLIN — B2 *Clearwater*

LONG LAKE (CLEARWATER COUNTY PARK) (Public) From Jct of SR-2 & SR-92, S 20 mi on SR-92 to Clearwater County Campground Rd (R). 91 Avail: 28 W, 49 E (30/50 amps). 2021 rates: $30 to $36. May 08 to Sep 20. (218)657-2275

SIDE LAKE — B3 *St Louis*

MCCARTHY BEACH (Public State Park) From Jct of Hwy 65 & Hwy 1, W 4 mi on Hwy 1 to CR-542, W 1 mi to fork in road, bear right (CR-542), N 3 mi (R). Note: 40' RV length limit. Avail: 21 E (30 amps). 2021 rates: $15 to $31. (218)274-7200

SILVER BAY — B4 *Lake*

TETTEGOUCHE (Public State Park) From town: Go 4-1/2 mi NE on Hwy 61. Avail: 22 E. 2021 rates: $17 to $31. (218)353-8800

SOUDAN — B4 *St Louis*

MCKINLEY PARK (Public) From Jct of US-169 & Main St exit, exit Main St, N 1.2 mi, follow signs (E). 39 Avail: 30 W, 30 E (30 amps). 2021 rates: $26.50 to $39.50. May 01 to Sep 30. (218)753-5921

SPICER — D2 *Kandiyohi*

GREEN LAKE (KANDIYOHI COUNTY PARK) (Public) From town, N 2.5 mi on SR-23 to CR-30, E 4 mi, follow signs (R). Avail: 61 full hkups (20 amps). 2021 rates: $32.20. (320)796-5564

SPRINGFIELD — E2 *Brown*

ROTHENBURG CAMPGROUND (Public) From jct US-14 & Cass Ave (in Springfield): Go 1/4 mi S on Cass Ave (L). 40 Avail: 32 full hkups, 8 W, 8 E (30/50 amps). 2021 rates: $30 to $35. May 01 to Oct 01. (507)723-3517

ST CHARLES — E4 *Winona*

LAZY D CAMPGROUND & TRAIL RIDES **Ratings: 7.5/8/9** (Campground) 82 Avail: 82 W, 82 E (20/30 amps). 2021 rates: $29 to $51. Apr 15 to Nov 30. (507)932-3098, 18748 County Rd 39 , Altura, MN 55910

ST CLOUD — D3 *Benton*

ST CLOUD See also Avon, Clearwater, Monticello & Royalton.

ST CLOUD CAMPGROUND & RV PARK
good sam park **Ratings: 8.5/9.5★/10** (RV Park) 77 Avail: 65 full hkups, 12 W, 12 E (30/50 amps). 2021 rates: $45 to $49. May 01 to Oct 12. (320)251-4463, 2491 2nd St SE, St Cloud, MN 56304

ST PAUL — D3 *Dakota*

ST PAUL See also Apple Valley, Cannon Falls, Clearwater, Faribault, Isanti, Minneapolis, Monticello, Prior Lake & Welch, MN; Somerset, WI.

STARBUCK — D2 *Pope*

GLACIAL LAKES (Public State Park) From town, S 3 mi on SR-29 to CR-41, S 2 mi (L). Reservation fee. Note: 45' RV length maximum. Avail: 14 E (30 amps). 2021 rates: $17 to $29. (320)239-2860

HOBO PARK (Public) From Jct of US-29 & US-28, S 0.5 mi on US-29 (L). 102 Avail: 34 full hkups, 11 W, 11 S (30 amps). 2021 rates: $32 to $42. May 01 to Sep 30. (320)239-2336

STILLWATER — D3 *Washington*

WILLIAM O'BRIEN (Public State Park) From Jct of I-94 & Hwy 95, N 20 mi on Hwy 95 (L). Entrance fee required. Reservation fee. Avail: 70 E (20/30 amps). 2021 rates: $17 to $31. (651)539-4980

STURGEON LAKE — C3 *Pine*

TIMBERLINE RV RESORT **Ratings: 8.5/8.5★/8** (Campground) Avail: 18 full hkups (30/50 amps). 2021 rates: $65 to $75. May 01 to Sep 30. (218)372-3272, 9152 Timberline Road, Sturgeon Lake, MN 55783

SUNBURG — D2 *Kandiyohi*

MONSON LAKE (Public State Park) From town: Go 1-1/2 mi W on Hwy 9, then 2-1/2 mi S on CR 95. Avail: 5 E. 2021 rates: $15 to $27. (320)366-3797

TAYLORS FALLS — D4 *Chisago*

INTERSTATE (Public State Park) From town, S 1 mi on Hwy 8 (L). Reservation fee. Note: 45' RV length maximum. Avail: 22 E (20 amps). 2021 rates: $17 to $31. (651)465-5711

THIEF RIVER FALLS — B1 *Pennington*

THIEF RIVER FALLS TOURIST PARK (Public) From Jct of Hwy 32 & Oakland Park Rd, S 0.25 mi on Oakland Park Rd (L). 72 Avail: 16 full hkups, 56 E (30/50 amps). 2021 rates: $20 to $30. May 05 to Oct 15. (218)681-2519

TOGO — B3 *Itasca*

GEORGE WASHINGTON/THISTLEDEW LAKE (Public State Park) From town: Go 4-1/2 mi W on Hwy 1, then 2 mi S on access road. 21 Avail: Pit toilets. 2021 rates: $14. (218)328-8984

TOWER — B4 *St Louis*

BEAR HEAD LAKE (Public State Park) From town, SW 12 mi on Hwy 169 to CR-128 (Bear Head State Park Rd), S 7 mi, follow signs (R). Reservation fee. Avail: 26 E (20 amps). 2021 rates: $17 to $31. May 15 to Sep 01. (218)235-2520

FORTUNE BAY RESORT RV PARK **Ratings: 7.5/8.5★/8.5** (RV Park) 36 Avail: 36 W, 36 E (30/50 amps). 2021 rates: $40. (800)992-7529, 1430 Bois Forte Road, Tower, MN 55790

HOODOO POINT (Public) From Jct of US-169 & SR-135, N 100 yds on US-169 to Hoodoo Point Rd, N 1.2 mi (L). 85 Avail: 26 W, 26 E (20/50 amps). 2021 rates: $25 to $40. May 01 to Oct 01. (218)753-6868

TWO HARBORS — C4 *Lake*

BURLINGTON BAY (CITY PARK) (Public) From the Jct of Hwy 61 & Park Rd (North end of town), S 100 ft (L). 136 Avail: 70 full hkups, 66 W, 66 E (30 amps). 2021 rates: $20 to $48. May 15 to Oct 15. (218)834-2021

CLOQUET VALLEY/INDIAN LAKE (Public State Park) From town: Go 13 mi N on CR 2, then 12 mi W on CR 14, then 1 mi N. 25 Avail: Pit toilets. 2021 rates: $14. Apr 29 to Oct 30. (218)226-6377

GOOSEBERRY FALLS (Public State Park) From town, NE 14 mi on US-61 (R). 69 Avail. 2021 rates: $17 to $31. (218)595-7100

UPSALA — D2 *Morrison*

CEDAR LAKE MEMORIAL PARK (Public) From Jct of SR-238 & Abaca Rd. (in town), W 3 mi on CR-19 (R). 65 Avail: 65 W, 65 E (30 amps). 2021 rates: $32 to $44. (320)573-2983

VICTORIA — D3 *Carver*

CARVER PARK RESERVE/LAKE AUBURN (CARVER COUNTY PARK) (Public) From Jct of SR-7 & Carver CR-11, S 2 mi on Carver CR-11, follow signs (R). 55 Avail: Pit toilets. 2021 rates: $15.44 to $18.71. Apr 24 to Oct 24. (763)694-1112

WABASHA — E4 *Wabasha*

BIG RIVER RESORT
good sam park **Ratings: 8.5/10★/9.5** (RV Park) Avail: 10 full hkups (30/50 amps). 2021 rates: $56 to $61. Apr 15 to Oct 15. (651)565-9932, 1110 Hiawatha Drive East , Wabasha, MN 55981

WADENA — C2 *Wadena*

SUNNYBROOK PARK (Public) From Jct of US-71 & US-10, E 0.9 mi on US-10 to Harry Rich Dr, N 0.1 mi (R). Avail: 29 full hkups (50 amps). 2021 rates: $15 to $30. May 01 to Oct 01. (218)631-7711

WALKER — C2 *Cass*

TRAILS RV PARK **Ratings: 8.5/9.5★/10** (RV Park) Avail: 19 full hkups (30/50 amps). 2021 rates: $49 to $55. May 01 to Oct 06. (218)547-1138, 9424 State 371 NW, Walker, MN 56484

WANNASKA — A2 *Roseau*

HAYES LAKE (Public State Park) From town, S 15 mi on Hwy 89 to CR-4, E 9 mi, follow signs (E). Reservation fee. Note: 40' RV length maximum. Avail: 18 E (30 amps). 2021 rates: $15 to $23. (218)425-7504

WARROAD — A2 *Roseau*

WARROAD (Public) From Jct of SR-11 & Lake St, E 1 mi on Lake St (L). 172 Avail: 80 full hkups, 32 W, 70 E (50 amps). 2021 rates: $25 to $35. May 03 to Oct 12. (218)386-1004

WASECA — E3 *Waseca*

KIESLER'S CAMPGROUND AND RV RESORT **Ratings: 8.5/10★/9.5** (Campground) 120 Avail: 62 full hkups, 58 W, 58 E (30/50 amps). 2021 rates: $75 to $90. Apr 19 to Oct 06. (507)835-3179, 14360 Old Hwy 14 , Waseca, MN 56093

WASKISH — B2 *Beltrami*

BIG BOG (Public State Park) From Jct of CR-40 & Hwy 72, S 0.1 mi on Hwy 72 (L). Avail: 26 E. 2021 rates: $17 to $31. (218)647-8592

WATERVILLE — E3 *Le Sueur*

KAMP DELS **Ratings: 9/9.5★/10** (Campground) 120 Avail: 105 full hkups, 15 W, 15 E (30/50 amps). 2021 rates: $67 to $92. May 01 to Oct 01. (507)362-8616, 14842 Sakatah Lake Rd, Waterville, MN 56096

SAKATAH LAKE (Public State Park) From Jct of SR-13 & SR-60, E 1 mi on SR-60, follow signs (L). Vehicle permit & reservation fee required. Avail: 14 E (20/30 amps). 2021 rates: $17 to $31. (507)698-7850

WATSON — D1 *Chippewa*

LAC QUI PARLE (Public State Park) From Jct of US-59 & CR-13, W 4 mi on CR-13 (R). Reservation fee. 67 Avail: 9 full hkups, 37 E (30 amps). 2021 rates: $15 to $27. (320)734-4450

WELCH — E3 *Goodhue*

TREASURE ISLAND RV PARK **Ratings: 9.5/9.5★/7.5** (RV Park) Avail: 80 full hkups (30/50 amps). 2021 rates: $35 to $65. Apr 01 to Oct 31. (651)267-3060, 5630 Sturgeon Lake Road , Welch, MN 55089

WELLS — E3 *Faribault*

PIHL'S PARK (FARIBAULT COUNTY PARK) (Public) From Jct of I-90 & Hwy 22 (exit 138), S 1 mi on Hwy 22 (R). Avail: 30 E (20/30 amps). 2021 rates: $18 to $20. May 01 to Oct 15. (507)525-7707

WILLMAR — D2 *Kandiyohi*

SIBLEY (Public State Park) From town, W 5 mi on Hwy 9 to US-71, S 1 mi (R). Entrance fee & reservation fee required. Avail: 53 E (20/30 amps). 2021 rates: $17 to $31. (320)354-2055

WILLOW RIVER — C3 *Pine*

GENERAL C.C. ANDREWS/WILLOW RIVER (Public State Park) E on North St to Int-35 service road. 36 Avail: Pit toilets. 2021 rates: $14. (320)245-2668

WINONA — E4 *Winona*

PRAIRIE ISLAND (Public) From Jct of US-61 & Pelzer St, NE 1.5 mi on Pelzer St to Prairie Island Rd, E 1 mi (R). 201 Avail: 111 W, 111 E (20/30 amps). 2021 rates: $22 to $27. May 01 to Oct 01. (507)452-4501

WORTHINGTON — F2 *Nobles*

OLSON PARK (CITY PARK) (Public) From Jct of I-90 & Hwy 60, W 4.9 mi on Hwy 60 to CR-10, N 1 mi, follow signs (L). Avail: 63 E (50 amps). 2021 rates: $20.50 to $31. Apr 01 to Oct 31. (507)329-0760

WYKOFF — E4 *Fillmore*

FORESTVILLE-MYSTERY CAVE (Public State Park) From Jct of MN-16 & CR-5, S 4 mi on CR-5 to CR-118, E 2 mi, follow signs (R). Entrance fee & reservation fee required. Note: 50' RV length maximum. Avail: 23 E (30 amps). 2021 rates: $17 to $31. (507)352-5111

ZIMMERMAN — D3 *Sherburne*

SAND DUNES/ANN LAKE (Public State Park) From Jct of US-169 & CR-4, W 6 mi on CR-4 to 168 St, S 1.5 mi, follow signs (L). 28 Avail: Pit toilets. 2021 rates: $14 to $16. (763)878-2325

ZUMBROTA — E4 *Goodhue*

COVERED BRIDGE (ZUMBROTA CITY PARK) (Public) From Jct of Hwys 52 & 58, N 1 mi on Hwy 58 (L). 50 Avail: 24 W, 24 E (30 amps). 2021 rates: $20. May 15 to Nov 01. (507)732-7318

SHADES OF SHERWOOD CAMPGROUND **Ratings: 7.5/8.5★/7.5** (Campground) 180 Avail: 180 W, 180 E (30/50 amps). 2021 rates: $52 to $54. Apr 26 to Oct 06. (507)732-5100, 14334 Sherwood Trail, Zumbrota, MN 55992

How can you tell whether you're traveling in the right direction? The arrow in each listing denotes the compass direction of the facility in relation to the listed town. For example, an arrow pointing straight up indicates that the facility is located due north from town. An arrow pointing down and to the right indicates that the facility is southeast of town.

MN

Getty Images/iStockphoto

DID YOU KNOW?

Keeping the flame for more than 60 years in total, female lightkeepers are a mainstay of the Biloxi Lighthouse.

YOU ARE HERE

Mississippi

Life moves slowly in Mississippi, giving you more time to smell the magnolia. Explore the region's natural attractions and visit the historic sites to glimpse the past. Mississippi also has modern cities standing tall for today's traveler.

Cities with Character

Natchez oozes with Mississippi history. Time seems to have stopped in this town, located high on a bluff overlooking the Mississippi River. Hundreds of well-preserved antebellum mansions line the streets, many offering tours. If you're looking for a more energetic pace, head to Jackson. Known as the "Birthplace of American Music," Jackson is where great blues and soul music began.

Sand and Sea

Get away from the mainland. Gulf Islands National Seashore protects the barrier islands along Mississippi's coast. Whispery white sands and grass-spotted dunes are contrasted by endless blue skies and seas. Explore a historic fort, watch for the 300 species of birds that visit, or take a boating tour of several scenic spots. On land, you can enjoy biking and hiking, while the sea offers swimming, snorkeling and diving.

Wonders on the Water

Several major casinos dot the Mississippi shore, but you don't have to lay down bets to feel like a winner. Walk one of the state's many beaches found along the small stretch of the Gulf Coast. Biloxi Beach and Gulf Port take the prize for family. Anglers can also find many ways to get lucky in the state, with crappie waters found in Granada Lake, Enid Lake and Lake Washington.

Turn Back Time

Drive into the past along the Natchez Trace Parkway. Once a Native American footpath, this 444-mile scenic drive starts in Natchez.

Mississippi Okra

Okra can be prepared in a dozen ways, but it's most often sliced into rounds, dunked in cornmeal and deep-fried into crunchy bites. Not sure what to pair with fried okra? Southerners say you can't go wrong with classic soul food — fried chicken, biscuits and gravy, collard greens and catfish all make excellent accompaniments.

VISITOR CENTER

TIME ZONE
Central Standard

ROAD & HIGHWAY INFORMATION
601-987-1211
mdottraffic.com

FISHING & HUNTING INFORMATION
601-432-2400
ms.gov/mdwfp/hunting_fishing

BOATING INFORMATION
601-432-2400
mdwfp.com/law-enforcement/boating-rules-regs

NATIONAL PARKS
nps.gov/ms

STATE PARKS
mdwfp.com/parks-destinations/state-parks

TOURISM INFORMATION
Mississippi Tourism
866-SEE-MISS
visitmississippi.org

TOP TOURISM ATTRACTIONS
1) Natchez Trace Parkway
2) Vicksburg National Military Park
3) Gulf Coast Beaches

MAJOR CITIES
Jackson (capital), Gulfport, Southaven, Hattiesburg, Biloxi

MS

Featured Good Sam Parks

MISSISSIPPI

When you stay with Good Sam, you can expect the highest degree of cleanliness and friendliness, and better yet, you get **10% off** overnight campground fees.

If you're not already a Good Sam member you can purchase your membership at one of these locations:

BAY ST LOUIS
Bay Hide Away RV Park & Campground
Hollywood Casino RV Park- Gulf Coast

BILOXI
Biloxi Bay RV Resort and Marina
Boomtown Casino RV Park
Cajun RV Park
Majestic Oaks RV Resort
Martin Lake Resort
Mazalea Travel Park

CANTON
Movietown RV Park
Springridge RV Park/Mobile Home Estates

COLDWATER
Memphis-South RV Park & Campground

FLORENCE
Wendy Oaks RV Resort

GAUTIER
Indian Point RV Resort

GREENWOOD
Delta Mobile Home & RV Park

GULFPORT
Baywood RV Park & Campground
Campgrounds of the South
Country Side RV Park

MERIDIAN
Benchmark Coach and RV Park
Hill Country RV and MH Community

MORTON
Green Tree RV Park & Campground

PICAYUNE
Sun Roamers RV Resort

SOUTHAVEN
EZ Daze RV Park
Southaven RV Park

STARKVILLE
The Pines MH and RV Community

TUNICA
Hollywood Casino Hotel & RV Park

TUPELO
Campground at Barnes Crossing
Natchez Trace RV Park

TYLERTOWN
Hidden Springs RV Resort

VICKSBURG
Ameristar Casino & RV Park
Magnolia RV Park Resort

10/10★/10 GOOD SAM PARK

BILOXI
Biloxi Bay RV Resort and Marina
(228)529-7866

What's This?

An RV park with a 10/10★/10 rating has scored perfect grades in amenities, cleanliness and appearance ("See Understanding the Campground Rating System" on pages 8 and 9 for an explanation of the trusted Good Sam Rating System). Stay in a 10/10★/10 park on your next trip for a nearly flawless camping experience.

Getty Images/iStockphoto

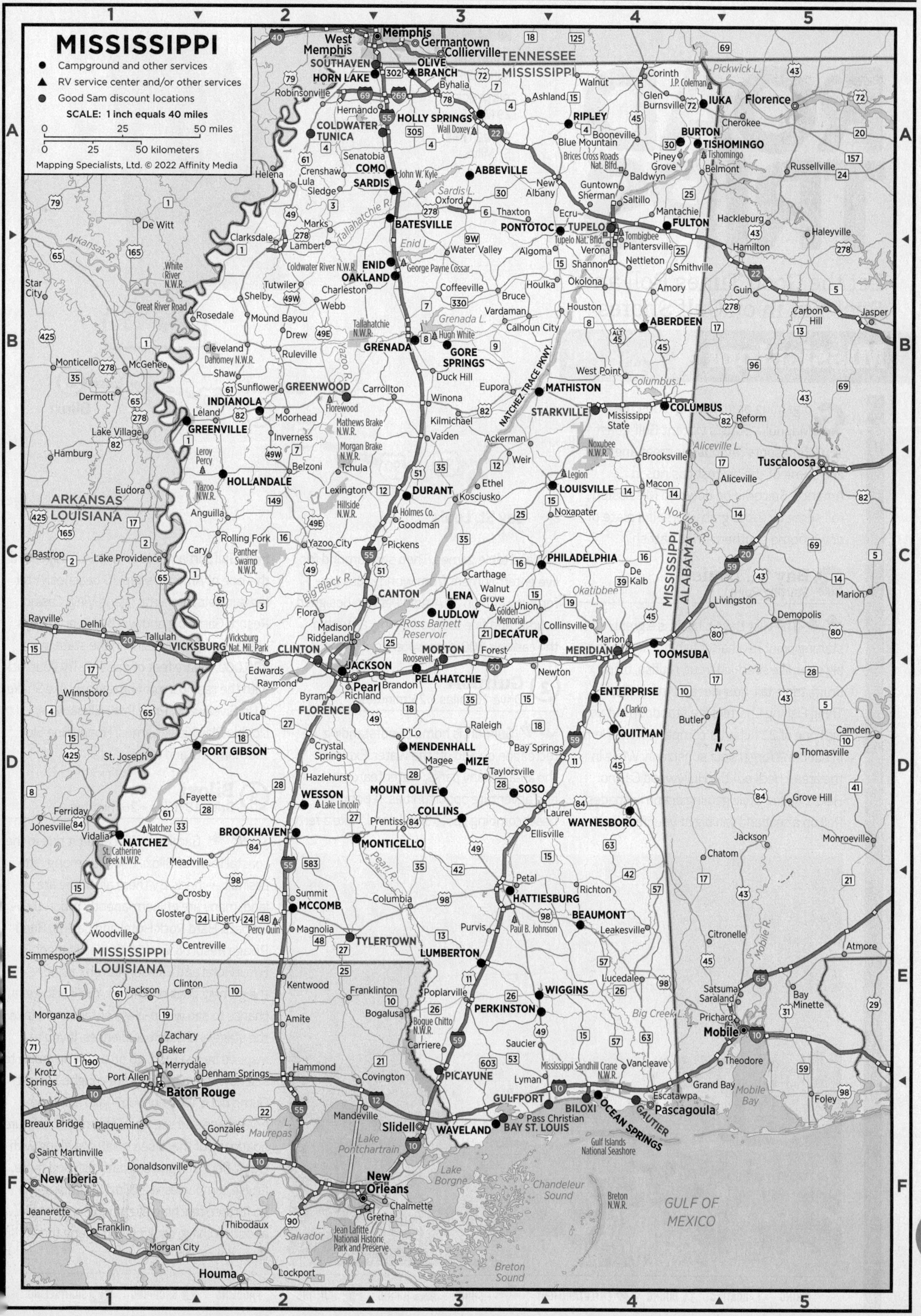
MISSISSIPPI
Campground and other services
RV service center and/or other services
Good Sam discount locations
SCALE: 1 inch equals 40 miles
0 25 50 miles
0 25 50 kilometers
Mapping Specialists, Ltd. © 2022 Affinity Media
1
2
3
4
5
A
B
C
D
E
F
TENNESSEE
MISSISSIPPI
ARKANSAS
LOUISIANA
ALABAMA
West Memphis
Memphis
Germantown
Collierville
SOUTHAVEN
HORN LAKE
OLIVE BRANCH
Byhalia
Robinsonville
Hernando
COLDWATER
TUNICA
HOLLY SPRINGS
Wall Doxey
Walnut
Corinth
J.P. Coleman
Pickwick L.
Glen
Burnsville
IUKA
Florence
Ashland
RIPLEY
Booneville
Blue Mountain
BURTON
TISHOMINGO
Tishomingo
Cherokee
Brices Cross Roads Nat. Bfld.
Piney Grove
Baldwyn
Belmont
Russellville
Senatobia
COMO
John W. Kyle
SARDIS
Sardis L.
Oxford
ABBEVILLE
New Albany
Guntown
Sherman
Saltillo
Helena
Crenshaw
Lula
Sledge
Marks
Thaxton
Ecru
Mantachie
PONTOTOC
TUPELO
Tupelo Nat. Bfld.
Tombigbee
FULTON
Hackleburg
Haleyville
De Witt
Clarksdale
Lambert
BATESVILLE
Tallahatchie R.
Enid L.
Water Valley
Algoma
Verona
Plantersville
Hamilton
Arkansas R.
White River N.W.R.
Coldwater River N.W.R.
ENID
OAKLAND
George Payne Cossar
Shannon
Nettleton
Smithville
Star City
Tutwiler
Charleston
Coffeeville
Houlka
Okolona
Amory
Guin
Shelby
Great River Road
Rosedale
Webb
Bruce
Grenada L.
Vardaman
Houston
Carbon Hill
Jasper
Mound Bayou
Drew
Tallahatchie N.W.R.
Hugh White
GRENADA
Calhoun City
ABERDEEN
Cleveland
Dahomey N.W.R.
Ruleville
GORE SPRINGS
Duck Hill
NATCHEZ TRACE PKWY.
Monticello
McGehee
Shaw
Sunflower
GREENWOOD
Carrollton
Eupora
West Point
Columbus L.
INDIANOLA
Florewood
Winona
MATHISTON
Dermott
Leland
Moorhead
Mathews Brake N.W.R.
Kilmichael
STARKVILLE
Mississippi State
COLUMBUS
Reform
GREENVILLE
Inverness
Vaiden
Ackerman
Lake Village
Morgan Brake N.W.R.
Noxubee N.W.R.
Aliceville L.
Hamburg
Leroy Percy
Tchula
Weir
Brooksville
Belzoni
Legion
Tuscaloosa
HOLLANDALE
Ethel
Macon
Aliceville
Yazoo N.W.R.
Lexington
DURANT
LOUISVILLE
Eudora
Hillside N.W.R.
Kosciusko
Holmes Co.
Noxapater
Goodman
Anguilla
Rolling Fork
Yazoo City
Pickens
Noxubee R.
Bastrop
Lake Providence
Cary
Panther Swamp N.W.R.
PHILADELPHIA
Carthage
De Kalb
Big Black R.
CANTON
Walnut Grove
LENA
Okatibbee L.
Livingston
Marion
Flora
LUDLOW
Golden Memorial
Union
Demopolis
Rayville
Delhi
Madison
Ross Barnett Reservoir
Collinsville
Tallulah
Ridgeland
DECATUR
Marion
VICKSBURG
Vicksburg Nat. Mil. Park
CLINTON
MORTON
Forest
MERIDIAN
TOOMSUBA
Edwards
JACKSON
Roosevelt
Newton
Raymond
PELAHATCHIE
Winnsboro
Byram
Pearl
Brandon
Richland
ENTERPRISE
FLORENCE
Clarkco
Utica
Raleigh
Butler
QUITMAN
Camden
Crystal Springs
D'Lo
MENDENHALL
Bay Springs
Thomasville
St. Joseph
PORT GIBSON
Magee
MIZE
Hazlehurst
Taylorsville
WESSON
Lake Lincoln
MOUNT OLIVE
SOSO
Fayette
Grove Hill
Ferriday
COLLINS
Laurel
WAYNESBORO
Jonesville
Natchez
Prentiss
Vidalia
NATCHEZ
BROOKHAVEN
MONTICELLO
Ellisville
Jackson
Monroeville
St. Catherine Creek N.W.R.
Meadville
Pearl R.
Chatom
Petal
Richton
Crosby
HATTIESBURG
Summit
Columbia
MCCOMB
Gloster
Liberty
Percy Quin
Magnolia
Purvis
Paul B. Johnson
BEAUMONT
Leakesville
Citronelle
Woodville
Centreville
TYLERTOWN
Mobile R.
Atmore
Simmesport
LUMBERTON
Clinton
Kentwood
Franklinton
Lucedale
Jackson
Poplarville
WIGGINS
Satsuma
Saraland
Bay Minette
Morganza
Bogalusa
PERKINSTON
Big Creek L.
Prichard
Amite
Bogue Chitto N.W.R.
Mobile
Zachary
Baker
Carriere
Saucier
Merrydale
Hammond
Mississippi Sandhill Crane N.W.R.
Vancleave
Theodore
Krotz Springs
Port Allen
Denham Springs
Covington
PICAYUNE
Lyman
Grand Bay
Baton Rouge
GULFPORT
BILOXI
OCEAN SPRINGS
GAUTIER
Escatawpa
Pascagoula
Mobile Bay
Foley
Breaux Bridge
Plaquemine
Gonzales
L. Maurepas
Mandeville
Slidell
WAVELAND
BAY ST. LOUIS
Pass Christian
Lake Pontchartrain
Gulf Islands National Seashore
Saint Martinville
Donaldsonville
New Iberia
New Orleans
Lake Borgne
Chandeleur Sound
Breton N.W.R.
GULF OF MEXICO
Jeanerette
Chalmette
Gretna
Franklin
Thibodaux
L. Salvador
Jean Lafitte National Historic Park and Preserve
Morgan City
Houma
Lockport
Breton Sound

MS

ROAD TRIPS

Let the Good Times Roll and Reel 'Em in on Gulf Shores

Mississippi

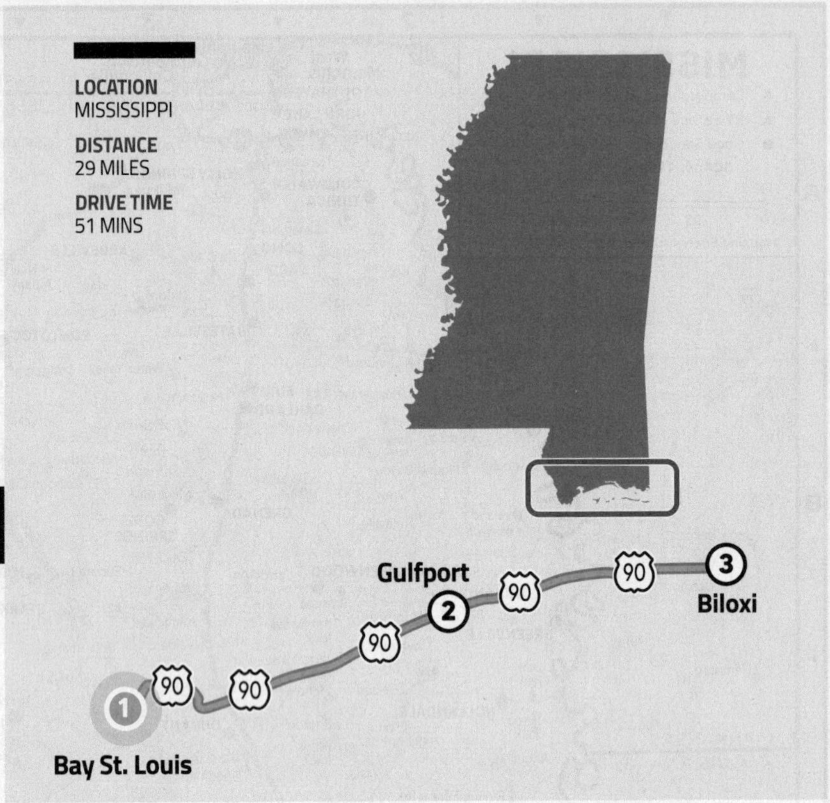

Go gaming or go fishing along the Magnolia State's vibrant Gulf Coast. You'll find spots famous for great angling and some of the hottest casinos in America. So come on down to Mississippi, roll some dice and grab yourself a plate of down home southern-fried catfish.

1 Bay St. Louis
Starting Point

The vast Bay St. Louis is a great starting point for charter fishing. Reel in the big ones like speckled trout, redfish, black drum, triple tail, flounder and more. Shore Thing Fishing Charters is a standout, but you pick one of 231 charter companies. Reel 'em in but don't forget your sunscreen. While in the area, check out the Hollywood Casino. Here's Vegas-style gaming action in spades. Pull up a seat and win big at your favorite slot and table games. Then stick around for live entertainment from world-class performers; golf on an Arnold Palmer-designed course; and fine seafood dining, all within the casino's 600-acre waterfront grounds.

2 Gulfport
Drive 16 miles • 25 minutes

Gulfport is home to outstanding recreation on and off the water. Explore the area's many parks, water features and adventure opportunities. A popular beachcombing spot? Ship Island. Take a ferry from Gulfport and see why *USA Today* called this one of America's top 10 beaches. After the sun sets, drop into Island View Casino Resort. Game big and win big. Everything's big at the biggest casino in the state, with 126,000 square feet of gaming. Try your luck with the casino's rotating specials like Shake It Up Giveaways, Prize Pack Giveaways, Double Play Kiosk Games, Honey Bee Slot Tournaments and more.

3 Biloxi
Drive 13 miles • 26 minutes

Gaming buffs can let it ride in the coastal town of Biloxi. Choose among nine casinos — heck, try them all. Some are on land; many are on permanently moored riverboats. Hard Rock Hotel and Casino, Beau Rivage Resort & Casino, Golden Nugget Biloxi Hotel and Casino, Harrah Casino — the gaming goes on and on. You'll also get a chance to see world-class entertainers take the stage and dazzle audiences. If you're inspired by sea food, go on a shrimp cruise to see how these morsels are caught. Forrest Gump did it, why not you? Take a shrimp boat cruise and see how "shrimpers" capture boatloads of these sea creatures along with crabs, flounder, squid, oyster fish and more. Cruise companies like Biloxi Shrimping Trip go further, teaching everything imaginable about catching, cooking and eating these tasty delicacies.

Getty Images/iStockphoto

BIKING · BOATING · DINING · ENTERTAINMENT · FISHING · HIKING · HUNTING · PADDLING · SHOPPING · SIGHTSEEING

Mississippi SPOTLIGHTS

Make Magnolia State Memories

What does a rock 'n' roll icon, Native American history and tasty seafood have in common? They're all found in Mississippi, where visitors are treated to great food and legendary places.

THE MISSISSIPPI GULF COAST ACCOUNTS FOR 60 MILES OF BEACH.

A Civil War-era cannon on West Ship Island, 11 miles off the coast of Biloxi.

Getty Images/iStockphoto

Gulf Coast

Mississippi's Gulf Coast can be compared to a rich gumbo. Beginning with the French, who arrived at Biloxi Bay in 1698, the area has changed hands many times over its history, and each culture has contributed its own essence and heart to the coastal landscape. Today, in coastal communities like Bay St. Louis, Gulfport and Biloxi, visitors can savor each of the region's flavors.

Casinos, Cabanas and Cuisine

When King Louis XIV of France sent explorers to establish a French colony on what is now Mississippi's Gulf Coast, he could never have imagined the palatial casino resorts holding court there today. About a dozen Gulf Coast gaming establishments in varying size offer blackjack, poker, slot machines and 24 hours of nonstop gaming. Thousands of visitors come each year, earning the region a spot among the top 10 gaming destinations. In addition to thrilling at the prospect of a big jackpot, visitors can enjoy star-studded entertainment and innumerable restaurant choices, serving everything from basic fare to fine dining.

Arts, Culture and Natural Wonders

Like the waves that roll ashore, the historic sights and sounds of Mississippi's Gulf Coast are endless. Explore the region's past to get a sense of the forces that shaped Mississippi into the state it is today. Start with a tour of Beauvoir, a National Historic Landmark and the retirement estate of Confederate President Jefferson Davis, situated on 52 acres overlooking the Gulf of Mexico. Tour the historic landmark to learn about the leader who attempted to lead the Confederate rebellion against the Union and died a political pariah in the South.

Historic Island

For more Civil War history, take a ferry ride into the Gulf for a visit to Fort Massachusetts on West Ship Island. Part of the property features park ranger-led tours of one of the last coastal forts of its kind built in the United States.

Nature

Gautier is where you'll find Shepherd State Park, in the heart of what is called Pascagoula River Country. Also known as Singing River, it's a natural estuary and home to nearly two dozen threatened and endangered species. Migratory birds use the river and its lush marshes as a resting point and breeding ground.

Buccaneer Bounces Back

Buccaneer State Park underwent a total renovation after being destroyed by Hurricane Katrina in 2005. The park, located in Waveland, features a 4.5-acre water park, an 18-hole disc golf course and more. In Gulfport, the Center for Marine Education & Research — also known as The Institute for Marine Mammal Studies — provides a learning experience about marine life in the area. The Maritime & Seafood Industry Museum is the place to learn more.

LOCAL FAVORITE

Bacon-Wrapped Jalapeño Sweet Shrimp

Take a top Mississippi export (shrimp) and give it a spicy and savory kick. *Recipe by Richard Stone.*

INGREDIENTS

- ☐ ¼ cup KC Masterpiece BBQ sauce
- ☐ ⅓ cup brown sugar
- ☐ ¼ tsp pepper
- ☐ ¼ tsp salt
- ☐ 1 tsp chopped garlic
- ☐ 2 Tbsp olive oil
- ☐ 1 tsp apple cider vinegar
- ☐ 20 jalapeño slices
- ☐ 1 lb bacon
- ☐ 1 lb shrimp

DIRECTIONS

Mix ingredients in a bowl with a fork.
Devein shrimp and pull tails off. Place in sauce. Cut bacon strips in half and put each strip in sauce. Marinate overnight (optional). Wrap shrimp in bacon and use toothpick to secure. Place bacon-wrapped shrimp onto a skewer. Place jalapeño slices next to each shrimp.
Cook on low heat until bacon is rendered out, browned and caramelized.

MS

Stay and Play
on the beach!
Located just across Highway 90
from the white sand beach of
the Mississippi Gulf Coast.
good sam park
2022
Top Rated
9.5/10★/9
CAJUN
RV PARK
1860 Beach Blvd.
Biloxi, MS 39531
228/388.5590
www.cajunrvpark.com
From I-10, take exit 46B to Hwy 90 West, park is 3 miles on right.
See listing Biloxi, MS

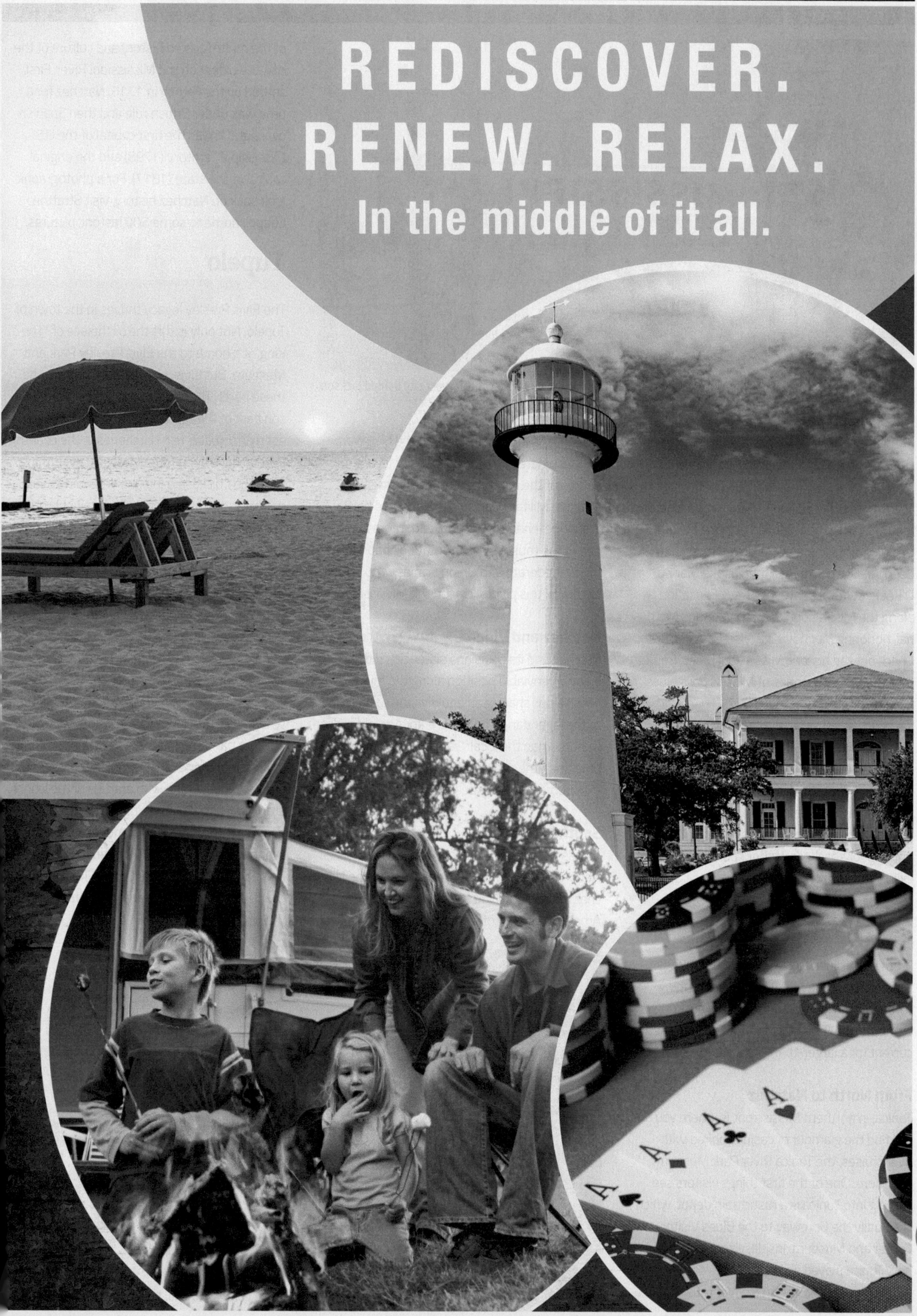
REDISCOVER.
RENEW. RELAX.
In the middle of it all.

See map page 515

SPOTLIGHTS

Once known as Mississippi City, the coastal town of Gulfport is the state's second-largest city behind Jackson.

Mississippi Magic

Mississippi's Gulf Coast has a thriving arts and culture scene. Gulfport venues include Gulfport Little Theatre and Gulf Coast Symphony Orchestra. The Bay St. Louis Mardi Gras Museum features more than a dozen elaborate Mardi Gras costumes housed inside a former train depot. In Ocean Springs, there is the Mary C. O'Keefe Cultural Center of Arts & Education along the Mississippi Vietnam Veterans Memorial, honoring Magnolia State service members. Check out the historic Mississippi Blues Trail in Biloxi, where the stories of Mississippi's blues legends unfold.

Hit the Beach or the Links

Family time on the Mississippi Gulf Coast is like no other. A day at the beach means choosing a spot along 62 miles of scenic shoreline — plenty of room for swimming, sunbathing or hunting for seashells. Water sports like jet skiing and kayaking are available.

River Destinations

From Delta blues to Civil War battlegrounds, this stretch of the Mississippi River running through the Magnolia State boasts amazing stories of the American South. Ride with the current for a larger-than-life adventure.

From North to Natchez

Tunica, in northern Mississippi, is where you will find the glamour of casinos paired with river cruises, the Tunica River Park Museum and more. One of the first things visitors see coming into Tunica is a rustic train depot, which is actually the Gateway to the Blues Visitor Center and Museum. Inside, visitors can learn how Tunica played an important role in the birth of this uniquely American form of music.

Vicksburg Past

Vicksburg is inextricably tied to the Civil War, and it's where one of the most significant battles of the conflict occurred. At Vicksburg National Military Park, visitors can see battleground re-enactments and learn more about one of the toughest confrontations between the Confederate and Union armies, who fought to control this pivotal city on the Mississippi.

Natchez and Vidalia

Natchez and its Louisiana sister city, Vidalia, enjoy an enviable position along the mighty Mississippi, sharing an equally storied past tied to the legendary Jim Bowie, a knife-wielding frontiersman the locals say defended himself time and time again with an infamous weapon — a curved knife — bearing his name.

Southern History

Across the river in Natchez, the Natchez National Historic Park, Grand Village of the Natchez Indians and Natchez Museum of African American History offer distinctive perspectives of the multi-faceted history and culture of the city, the oldest on the Mississippi River. First settled by the French in 1716, Natchez for a time was under British rule and then Spanish oversight. It was the first capital of the U.S. Mississippi Territory (1798) and the original capital of the state (1817). For a photographic look back on Natchez history, visit Stratton Chapel, home to some 500 historic pictures.

Tupelo

The Elvis Presley legacy thrives in the town of Tupelo. Not only is this the birthplace of "The King," it's home to the Elvis Presley Park and Museum. But Elvis isn't the only king around these parts. There's also the largest herd of bison east of the Mississippi and one of the oldest warm-water fish hatcheries in the country. Battles have been fought here — everything from the Chickasaw Indians defending their native land to brother fighting against brother in the Civil War. Tupelo is listed in the annals of the fight for civil rights and is the starting point to an epic road trip through American history on the Natchez Trace Parkway.

Birthplace of the King

People travel from around the world to see where it all began for the star known as the Tupelo Tornado. The two-room shotgun house where Elvis Presley was born is now part of a 15-acre park that includes his childhood church, a memorial chapel, a museum, a theater and an events center, along with statues of the icon. A story wall narrates the singer's life from birth to age 13, when his family moved to Memphis. Wander the Elvis Guitar Trail and explore 12 additional sites on the Elvis Driving Tour, including the Tupelo Hardware Store, where his mother, Gladys, purchased that first guitar.

Elvis Presley was born in 1935 in this two-bedroom house in Tupelo. The structure is open to tours.

One Little Fishy

The Private John Allen National Fish Hatchery is one of the oldest facilities of its kind in the country, founded in 1901. Operated by the U.S. Fish and Wildlife Service, this warm-water hatchery is used to spawn fish for public lakes, rivers, streams and reservoirs in Mississippi and the Gulf Coast. Fish hatched here are used to re-establish the species in their native environments and to sustain existing supplies. Hatchery-raised fish include striped bass, bluegill, paddlefish, lake sturgeon, piebald madtoms, alligator and Gulf Coast walleye. Fun-filled and family-friendly events are held throughout the year including a veterans and children's fish rodeo.

The First Interstate

The Natchez Trace Parkway was a "natural interstate" more than 8,000 years ago. This 444-mile course follows the "Old Natchez Trace," a historical byway trod by Native Americans, pioneers, soldiers, slaves and future presidents, all searching for a better life. Regions traversed by the trace include swamps, lakes and rivers; forests, woods and bottomlands, along with prairies and fields. The region is teeming with wildlife.

For the Love of Elvis

In June, Tupelo honors its native son with the Elvis Presley Festival. The festival is held in Fairpark, the place where Elvis competed in his first talent show at age 10.

Battle Between the States

The Tupelo National Battlefield memorial site commemorates a landmark 1864 battle that saw Union soldiers, including a regiment of African American troops, converge in Tupelo to push back Confederate forces heading north toward Tennessee. Located on Main Street, the 1-acre memorial preserves part of a battleground contested by 20,000 soldiers.

FOR MORE INFORMATION

Mississippi Development Authority, 866-733-6477, www.visitmississippi.org

Mississippi Gulf Coast Regional Convention & Visitors Bureau, 228-896-6699, www.gulfcoast.org

Visit Natchez, 800-647-6724, www.visitnatchez.org

Tupelo Convention & Visitors Bureau, 800-533-0611, www.tupelo.net

Mississippi Privately Owned Campground Information Updated by our Good Sam Representatives

Don & Peggy Holloway

After being high school sweethearts (the football player and the cheerleader) and married for 52 years, we've owned several businesses, allowing us to travel. Joining Good Sam in 2017, we follow two passions: seeing the U.S. and meeting new people.

Mississippi

ABBEVILLE — A3 *Lafayette*

SARDIS LAKE - COE/HURRICANE LANDING (Public Corps) 7 mi W off State Rte 7, on park access rd (E). 19 Avail: (30/50 amps). 2021 rates: $18. (662)563-4531

ABERDEEN — B4 *Monroe*

ABERDEEN LAKE - COE/BLUE BLUFF REC AREA (Public Corps) From Jct of Hwy 45 & Meridian St (in town), N 2 mi on Meridian St (R). 92 Avail: 92 W, 92 E (50 amps). 2021 rates: $20 to $22. (662)369-2832

MORGAN'S LANDING PARK (Public) From jct MS 8 & MS 25 & US 45: Go 1-1/2 mi E on US 45 then 1/2 mi S on Darracot Access Rd, then 1 mi E on Sharpley Bottom Rd. 14 Avail: 13 W, 13 E (30 amps). (662)369-7805

BATESVILLE — A3 *Panola*

BATESVILLE CIVIC CENTER RV PARK
(Public) From jct I-55 (exit 243) & US 278/Hwy 6: Go 1/2 mi E on US 278/Hwy 6, then 1/4 mi S on Medical Center Dr (L). **FAC:** paved/gravel rds. Avail: 20 paved, patios, back-ins (25x55), 20 full hkups (30/50 amps), WiFi @ sites, . **REC:** boating nearby, hunting nearby, rec open to public. Pets OK. No tents. 2021 rates: $30.
(662)563-1392 Lat: 34.3048, Lon: -89.9086
290 Civic Center Drive, Batesville, MS 38606
batesvillecivicenter-ms.com
See ad this page

BAY ST LOUIS — F3 *Hancock*

A SPOTLIGHT Introducing Gulf Coast's colorful attractions appearing at the front of this state section.

BAY ST LOUIS See also Biloxi, Gulfport & Picayune, MS; Slidell, LA.

BAY HIDE AWAY RV PARK & CAMPGROUND
Ratings: 9/9.5★/10 (Campground) Avail: 40 full hkups (30/50 amps). 2021 rates: $46 to $70. (228)466-0959, 8360 Lakeshore Rd, Bay St Louis, MS 39520

HOLLYWOOD CASINO RV PARK- GULF COAST
Ratings: 10/10★/9.5 (RV Park) Avail: 100 full hkups (30/50 amps). 2021 rates: $35 to $99. (866)758-2591, 711 Hollywood Blvd., Bay St Louis, MS 39520

MCLEOD WATER PARK (Public) From town: Go 10 mi N on Hwy 603, then turn W on Texas Flatt Rd. 70 Avail: 70 W, 70 E (30/50 amps). (228)467-1894

Park owners and staff are rightly proud of their business. Let them know how much you enjoyed your stay.

BEAUMONT — E4 *Perry*

LAKE PERRY
(Public State Park) From town, S 3 mi on FS-314/Lake Perry Rd, E 0.8 mi (R). **FAC:** paved rds. 20 Avail: 13 paved, 7 gravel, 2 pull-thrus, (25x40), back-ins (22x40), 20 W, 20 E (30 amps), tent sites, dump. **REC:** Lake Perry: fishing. Pets OK. Partial handicap access, 14 day max stay. 2021 rates: $18, Military discount. no cc, no reservations.
(601)928-3720 Lat: 31.133504, Lon: -88.905536
18 Lake Perry Road, Beaumont, MS 39423
www.mdwfp.com

BILOXI — F4 *Harrison*

A SPOTLIGHT Introducing Gulf Coast's colorful attractions appearing at the front of this state section.

BILOXI See also Gautier & Gulfport.

BILOXI BAY RV RESORT AND MARINA
Ratings: 10/10★/10 (RV Resort) From jct I-10 & Hwy 609 (exit 50): Go 3/4 mi S on Hwy 609, then 3/4 mi W on Lonoyne Blvd, then 1/2 mi S on Riveria Dr (R).

BILOXI BAY RV RESORT AND MARINA
The newest RV hotspot with easy access to everything! Welcome to Biloxi Bay RV Resort - a brand new, 62-acre luxury RV destination and marina in the heart of one of the most celebrated entertainment meccas in the world!

FAC: paved rds. (155 spaces). Avail: 125 paved, patios, 52 pull-thrus, (44x60), back-ins (44x60), 125 full hkups (30/50 amps), seasonal sites, cable, WiFi @ sites, laundry, firewood, restaurant, controlled access. **REC:** pool, Biloxi Bay: boating nearby, playground, hunting nearby. Pets OK. No tents. Big rig sites. 2021 rates: $79 to $129, Military discount.
(228)529-7866 Lat: 30.435716, Lon: -88.854217
6505 Riviera Drive, Biloxi, MS 39532
www.biloxibayrvresort.com
See ad opposite page

BOOMTOWN CASINO RV PARK
Ratings: 7/NA/7.5 (RV Park) Avail: 50 full hkups (30/50 amps). 2021 rates: $39 to $99. (800)627-0777, 676 Bayview Ave., Biloxi, MS 39530

RV Tech Tips - Stable Cables for Towed Vehicles: The various cables from your motorhome to your towed vehicle can get frayed while traveling and when exiting or entering a service station that was a bit higher than the highway. The angle can cause the cables to end up crushed between the dropped receiver and the driveway. A permanent fix for this is to install two pieces of angle iron 1/4-inch higher than the bottom of the receiver, secure with the same huge bolt that secures the receiver to your tow bar. This pair of ""shelves'' keeps the cables out of harm's way. Wire ties, of course, complete the installation.

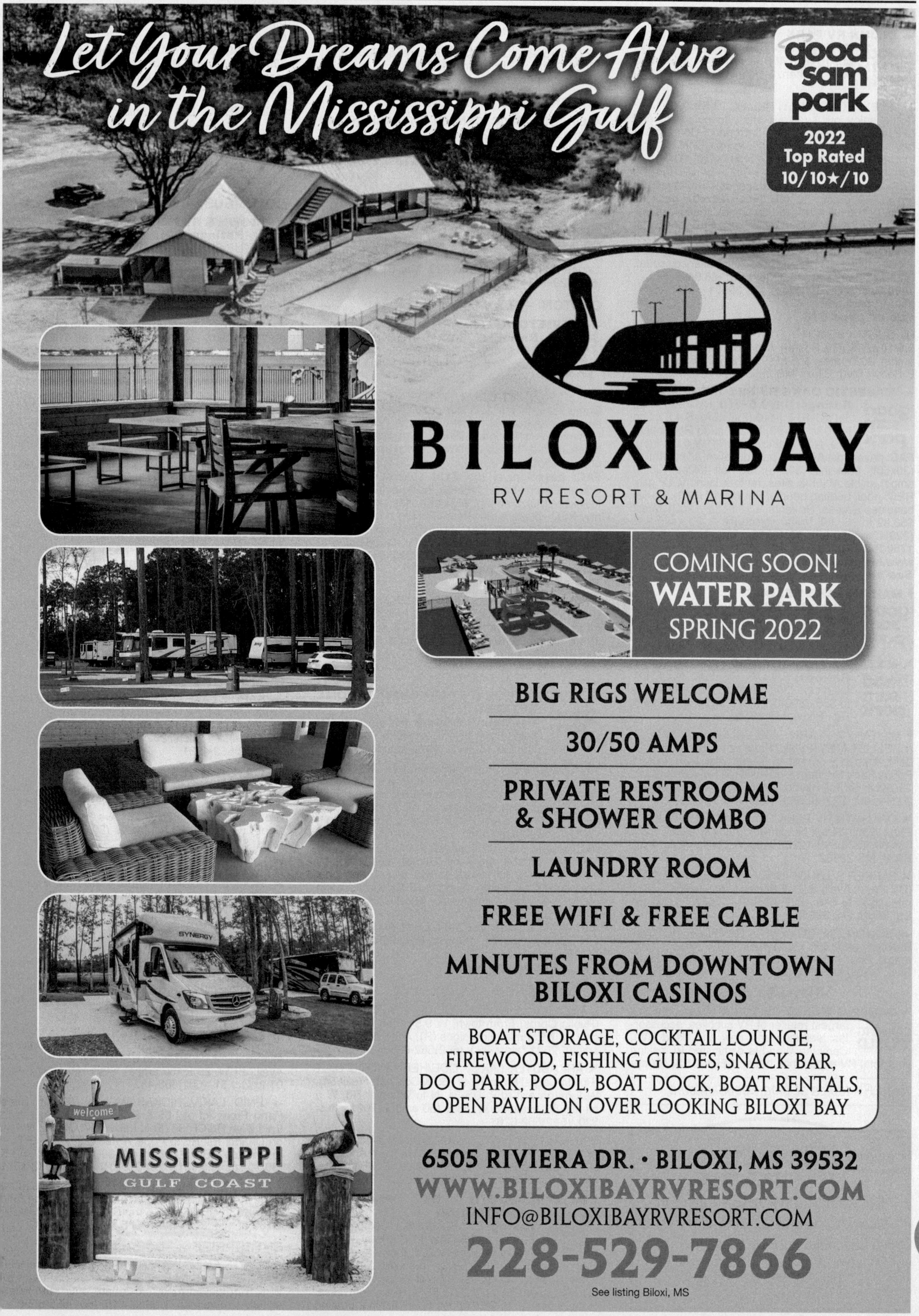

Let Your Dreams Come Alive in the Mississippi Gulf
good sam park
2022 Top Rated 10/10★/10
BILOXI BAY
RV RESORT & MARINA
COMING SOON!
WATER PARK
SPRING 2022
BIG RIGS WELCOME
30/50 AMPS
PRIVATE RESTROOMS & SHOWER COMBO
LAUNDRY ROOM
FREE WIFI & FREE CABLE
MINUTES FROM DOWNTOWN BILOXI CASINOS
BOAT STORAGE, COCKTAIL LOUNGE, FIREWOOD, FISHING GUIDES, SNACK BAR, DOG PARK, POOL, BOAT DOCK, BOAT RENTALS, OPEN PAVILION OVER LOOKING BILOXI BAY
6505 RIVIERA DR. • BILOXI, MS 39532
WWW.BILOXIBAYRVRESORT.COM
INFO@BILOXIBAYRVRESORT.COM
228-529-7866
welcome
MISSISSIPPI
GULF COAST
SYNERGY
See listing Biloxi, MS

MS

BILOXI (CONT)

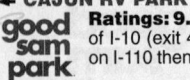

CAJUN RV PARK
Ratings: 9.5/10★/9 (RV Park) From jct of I-10 (exit 46B) & I-110: Go 5-1/2 mi S on I-110 then, 3-1/4 mi W on Hwy 90 (R).

EXPLORE. PLAY. RELAX. IN BILOXI
Come enjoy our spacious sites, friendly staff and beautiful park. Across from the beach. Complimentary casino shuttle, great WiFi access. Only minutes to outstanding restaurants, shopping, jet ski rentals and much more.

FAC: all weather rds. (130 spaces). 100 Avail: 60 gravel, 40 grass, 50 pull-thrus, (24x60), back-ins (36x60), 100 full hkups (30/50 amps), seasonal sites, cable, WiFi @ sites, laundry, LP gas. **REC:** pool, Gulf of Mexico: boating nearby, playground. Pet restrict (S/B/Q). No tents, Age restrict may apply. Big rig sites, eco-friendly. 2021 rates: $44 to $89, Military discount.
(877)225-8699 Lat: 30.3938, Lon: -88.9491
1860 Beach Blvd., Biloxi, MS 39531
cajunrvpark.com
See ad page 518

GULF BEACH RV RESORT **Ratings: 9.5/10★/7.5** (RV Resort) Avail: 65 full hkups (30/50 amps). 2021 rates: $55 to $95. (228)385-5555, 2428-B Beach Blvd, Biloxi, MS 39531

MAJESTIC OAKS RV RESORT
Ratings: 9.5/9.5★/10 (RV Park) From Jct of I-10 & I-110 (Exit 46A), S 4.2 mi on I-110 to US-90, W 3.1 mi to Rodenberg Ave, N 0.6 mi to Pass Rd, W 0.2 mi (R).
FAC: paved rds. Avail: 95 paved, patios, 11 pull-thrus, (30x50), back-ins (30x45), 95 full hkups (30/50 amps), cable, WiFi @ sites, rentals, laundry, LP gas. **REC:** pool, boating nearby. Pet restrict (B/Q). Partial handicap access. No tents, eco-friendly. 2021 rates: $58.99 to $68.99, Military discount.
(228)436-4200 Lat: 30.40360, Lon: -88.94212
1750 Pass Rd, Biloxi, MS 39531
www.majesticoaksrv.com
See ad page 522

MARTIN LAKE RESORT
Ratings: 9/8/7 (Membership Park) Avail: 10 full hkups (30/50 amps). 2021 rates: $34.20 to $38. (228)875-9157, 14605 Parker Rd, Biloxi, MS 39532

MAZALEA TRAVEL PARK
Ratings: 8/9★/8 (RV Park) Avail: 101 full hkups (30/50 amps). 2021 rates: $30 to $35. (800)877-8575, 8220 W Oaklawn Rd., Biloxi, MS 39532

MILITARY PARK KEESLER FAMCAMP (KEESLER AFB) (Public) From jct I-10 & Exit 44 Cedar Lake: Go S on exit 44 Cedar Lake, then right on Popps Ferry Rd, then E on Atkinson Rd, follow signs. 79 Avail: 52 full hkups, 27 W, 27 E (30/50 amps). 2021 rates: $22. (228)377-9050

OAKLAWN RV PARK **Ratings: 7.5/9.5★/7.5** (RV Park) Avail: 34 full hkups (30/50 amps). 2021 rates: $34.50. (228)392-1233, 8400 W Oaklawn Rd #37, Biloxi, MS 39532

PARKER'S LANDING RV PARK **Ratings: 9/8/9** (RV Park) Avail: 81 full hkups (30/50 amps). 2021 rates: $36 to $46. (228)392-7717, 7577 E Oaklawn Rd, Biloxi, MS 39532

SOUTHERN COMFORT CAMPING RESORT **Ratings: 9/8/7** (RV Park) Avail: 46 full hkups (30/50 amps). 2021 rates: $50. (228)432-1700, 1766 Beach Blvd, Biloxi, MS 39531

Travel Services

CAMPING WORLD OF BILOXI As the nation's largest retailer of RV supplies, accessories, services and new and used RVs, Camping World is committed to making your total RV experience better. **SERVICES:** RV appliance, MH mechanical, restrooms. RV Sales. RV supplies, LP gas, dump, RV accessible. Hours: 9am-7pm.
(877)701-5820 Lat: 30.459387, Lon: -88.968487
12020 Shriners Blvd, Biloxi, MS 39532
www.campingworld.com

Read RV topics at blog.GoodSam.com

BROOKHAVEN — D2 *Lincoln*

LINCOLN CIVIC CENTER RV PARK (Public) From jct I-55 (exit 42): Go 1/2 mi SE on Union St Extended NE, then 3-1/4 mi E on W Industrial Park Rd NE. Avail: 39 full hkups (30/50 amps). 2021 rates: $25. (601)823-9064

BURTON — A4 *Prentiss*

BAY SPRINGS LAKE - COE/PINEY GROVE (Public Corps) From Jct of Hwy 4 & Hwy 30 E (in town), E 11 mi on Hwy 30 E to CR-3501 (in Burton), S 3 mi, follow signs. 141 Avail: 141 W, 141 E (30/50 amps). 2021 rates: $18 to $20. Mar 01 to Nov 15. (662)728-1134

CANTON — C3 *Madison*

MOVIETOWN RV PARK
Ratings: 7/8.5★/8 (RV Park) From jct I-55 (exit 119) & Hwy 22: Go 1/2 mi W on Hwy 22, then 1/2 mi N on Virlilia Rd (R).

QUIET COUNTRY SETTING
Come relax in our 120 site park with full hookups and nice restrooms, we are near the Ross Barnett Reservoir so enjoy great fishing, then visit our movie museum in historic downtown Canton and do a little antique shopping.

FAC: paved/gravel rds. (114 spaces). Avail: 67 gravel, 50 pull-thrus, (45x65), back-ins (35x40), 67 full hkups (30/50 amps), WiFi, tent sites, rentals, laundry. **REC:** playground. Pets OK. Big rig sites, eco-friendly. 2021 rates: $30, Military discount.
(601)859-7990 Lat: 32.60736, Lon: -90.08420
109 Movietown Dr., Canton, MS 39046
www.movietownrvpark.com
See ad opposite page

RV PARK AT THE MULTIPURPOSE COMPLEX (Public) From Jct of I 55 & SR 22 (exit 119), W 0.5 mi on SR 22 to Watford Pkwy, S 0.6 mi (L). Avail: 39 full hkups (30/50 amps). 2021 rates: $20 to $25. (601)859-4830

CLINTON — C2 *Hinds*

SPRINGRIDGE RV PARK/MOBILE HOME ESTATES
Ratings: 8.5/10★/8 (RV Area in MH Park) From jct I-20 (exit 36) & Springridge Rd: Go 1/2 mi S on Springridge Rd (L).

EZ ON/OFF I-20, MINUTES TO JACKSON
Paved roads & sites, extremely clean restrooms/showers & laundry. Swim in our pool, use our playground, near restaurants and service stations. Stay and enjoy the nearby Clinton Natchez Trace Visitors Center/museum/gift shop.

FAC: paved rds. (92 spaces). Avail: 42 paved, 30 pull-thrus, (20x55), back-ins (20x33), mostly side by side hkups, 42 full hkups (30/50 amps), seasonal sites, tent sites, dump, laundry. **REC:** pool, boating nearby, playground. Pet restrict (B). 2021 rates: $33, Military discount.
(601)924-0947 Lat: 32.32169, Lon: -90.32380
499 Springridge Rd., Clinton, MS 39056
springridgemhp.com
See ad opposite page

COLDWATER — A3 *Tate*

ARKABUTLA LAKE - COE/DUB PATTON AREA (Public Corps) From town, W 9.5 mi on Rte 304 to cnty rd, NE 4 mi, follow signs (R). Avail: 59 E (30/50 amps). 2021 rates: $20. (662)562-6261

ARKABUTLA LAKE - COE/HERNANDO POINT (Public Corps) From Jct of I-55 & Coldwater (exit 54), W 2 mi on exit rd to US-51, N to Wheeler Rd, W 6 mi (L). 83 Avail: 83 W, 83 E (50 amps). 2021 rates: $20. (662)562-6261

ARKABUTLA LAKE - COE/SOUTH ABUTMENT (Public Corps) From town: Go 10 mi W on Arkabutla Rd. Follow signs N to the dam. Avail: 80 E Pit toilets. 2021 rates: $18 to $20. (662)562-6261

MEMPHIS-SOUTH RV PARK & CAMPGROUND
Ratings: 7.5/8.5★/6 (Campground) From jct of I-55 (exit 271) & Hwy 306: Go 1/4 mi W on Hwy 306, then 1/4 mi S on Campground Dr (E). **FAC:** gravel/dirt rds. (82 spaces). Avail: 47 gravel, 47 pull-thrus, (40x60), 47 full hkups (30/50 amps), WiFi @ sites, tent sites, laundry, firewood. **REC:** pool, pond, fishing, boating nearby, playground, hunting nearby. Pet restrict (B). Big rig sites, eco-friendly. 2021 rates: $32.45 to $47, Military discount.
(662)622-0056 Lat: 34.69600, Lon: -89.96660
256 Campground Dr, Coldwater, MS 38618
memphissouthrvpark.com
See ad page 854

COLLINS — D3 *Covington*

LAKE MIKE CONNER (Public) From Jct of US-49 & US-84, W 3 mi on US-84 to Lake Mike Conner Rd, S 6 mi, NW 0.5 mi on Blackjack New Chapel Rd. 15 Avail: 15 W, 15 E (30 amps). 2021 rates: $18. (601)765-4024

COLUMBUS — B4 *Clay*

BROWN'S RV PARK
Ratings: 6/NA/7 (Campground) From jct US-82 & Military Rd: Go 1/4 mi SW on Military Rd, then 500 ft on Bluecutt Rd (R). **FAC:** gravel rds. Avail: 23 gravel, 3 pull-thrus, (18x45), back-ins (25x45), accepts self-contain units only, 22 full hkups, 1 W, 1 E (30/50 amps), WiFi @ sites, dump, laundry. **REC:** boating nearby, hunting nearby. Pets OK. No tents. 2021 rates: $20. no cc.
(662)328-1976 Lat: 33.5177, Lon: -88.4166
2002 Bluecutt Rd, Columbus, MS 39705
See ad this page

LAKE LOWNDES (Public State Park) From Jct of US 82 & Stokes Rd (Stokes/New Hope exit) (East of Town), S 0.4 mi on Stokes Rd to SR 182, W 2 mi to New Hope Rd, S 3.9 mi, E 1 mi (follow signs) (E). Avail: 50 full hkups (30/50 amps). 2021 rates: $20 to $24. (662)328-2110

PARKWOOD RV PARK **Ratings: 5.5/NA/6.5** (Campground) Avail: 56 full hkups (30/50 amps). 2021 rates: $30. (662)386-3047, 319 E. Plymouth Rd, Columbus, MS 39705

TENNESSEE-TOMBIGBEE WATERWAY - COE/DEWAYNE HAYES (Public Corps) From town, W 4 mi on US-45 to Hwy 373, W 1.5 mi to Stenson Creek Rd, NW 2 mi to Barton's Ferry Rd, W 0.5 mi (L). 100 Avail: 100 W, 100 E (30/50 amps). 2021 rates: $20 to $24. (662)434-6939

TENNESSEE-TOMBIGBEE WATERWAY - COE/TOWN CREEK (Public Corps) From Jct of US-45 & US-50, W 6 mi on US-50 to Witherspoon Rd, N 0.25 mi (E). 100 Avail: 100 W, 100 E (30/50 amps). 2021 rates: $20 to $22. (662)494-4885

COMO — A3 *Lafayette*

SARDIS LAKE - COE/TECKVILLE (Public Corps) From I-55 exit 62 (SR-310), E 16 mi on SR-310 to park access rd, SE 2.1 mi (E). Avail: 16 full hkups (20 amps), Pit toilets. 2021 rates: $15. Mar 01 to Dec 31. (662)563-4531

DECATUR — C3 *Newton*

TURKEY CREEK WATER PARK (Public) From Jct of I-20 & SR-15 (exit 109), N 7 mi on SR-15 to Broad St, W 0.4 mi to S 7th Ave, S 3.8 mi (follow signs) (R). Avail: 20 full hkups (30/50 amps). 2021 rates: $22. (601)635-3314

DURANT — C3 *Holmes*

HOLMES COUNTY (Public State Park) From Jct of I-55 & exit 150, E 0.8 mi on State Park Rd (E). 28 Avail: 28 W, 28 E (30/50 amps). 2021 rates: $18. (662)653-3351

ENID — B3 *Yalobusha*

ENID LAKE - COE/PERSIMMON HILL (Public Corps) From Jct of I-55 & Enid Dam Rd (exit 233), E 1 mi on Enid Dam Rd, S 2 mi across dam (L). 72 Avail: 72 W, 72 E (50 amps). 2021 rates: $10 to $18. Mar 01 to Oct 31. (662)563-4571

ENID LAKE - COE/WATER VALLEY LANDING (Public Corps) From Jct of I-55 & SR-32 (Oakland exit), E 17 mi on SR-32 to CR-53, NW 2.7 mi (R). 29 Avail: 29 W, 29 E (50 amps). 2021 rates: $14. Mar 01 to Oct 31. (601)563-4571

ENID LAKE/CHICKASAW HILL (Public State Park) From Jct of I-55 & Exit 233, follow exit rd to Enid Dam Rd/CR-36 (Enid Lake Field Office), N 3 mi on Chapel Hill Rd to Pope Water Valley Rd, E 7 mi to Chicksaw Rd, S 1.5 mi (L). 53 Avail: 53 W, 53 E (30/50 amps). 2021 rates: $10 to $14. (662)563-4571

ENID LAKE/WALLACE CREEK (Public State Park) From Jct of I-55 & Enid Dam exit 233, E 1 mi on Enid Dam Rd to CR-36, N 3.5 mi (R). 99 Avail: 99 W, 99 E (50 amps). 2021 rates: $20. (662)563-4571

ENTERPRISE — D4 *Clarke*

DUNN'S FALLS WATER PARK (Public) From jct I-20 & I-59: Go 6 mi S on I-59 (exit 142), then 4 mi W & S on paved road (cross back over I-59, follow signs). 15 Avail. 2021 rates: $15. (601)655-8550

FLORENCE — D2 *Rankin*

WENDY OAKS RV RESORT
Ratings: 7.5/8.5★/9 (RV Park) Avail: 10 full hkups (30/50 amps). 2021 rates: $37 to $50. (601)845-CAMP, 4160 Hwy 49 S, Florence, MS 39073

FULTON — A4 *Itawamba*

TENNESSEE-TOMBIGBEE WATERWAY - COE/WHITTEN PARK (Public Corps) From Jct of US-78 & Hwy 25, N 200 yds on Hwy 25 to access rd, N 4.5 mi, follow signs (L). 60 Avail: 60 W, 60 E (15/50 amps). 2021 rates: $22 to $24. (662)862-7070

GAUTIER — F4 *Jackson*

A SPOTLIGHT Introducing Gulf Coast's colorful attractions appearing at the front of this state section.

INDIAN POINT RV RESORT
Ratings: 9/9.5★/9.5 (Campground) From Jct of I-10 & exit 61 (Gautier Vancleave Rd), S 1.8 mi on Gautier Vancleave Rd to Indian Point Parkway, E 1.4 mi (E).

RELAX OR PLAY IN OUR SCENIC RESORT!
Located between Mobile & New Orleans - just minutes from Biloxi. Enjoy our top-rated resort on Sioux Bayou. Swimming, fresh & saltwater fishing, bird watching. Near casinos, golf courses, shopping & the beach.

FAC: paved rds. (175 spaces). 100 Avail: 90 paved, 10 gravel, 17 pull-thrus, (35x75), back-ins (20x60), 100 full hkups (30/50 amps), seasonal sites, cable, WiFi @ sites, rentals, dump, laundry, LP gas, restaurant. **REC:** pool, Sioux Bayou: fishing, kayaking/canoeing, boating nearby, playground. Pet restrict (S/B/Q). No tents. Big rig sites, eco-friendly. 2021 rates: $35.
(228)497-1011 Lat: 30.40631, Lon: -88.63450
1600 Indian Point Parkway, Gautier, MS 39553
indianpt.weebly.com
See ad page 522

SANTA MARIA RV PARK **Ratings: 8/9★/7.5** (Campground) Avail: 20 full hkups (30/50 amps). 2021 rates: $28 to $40. (228)522-3009, 5800 Martin Bluff Rd, Gautier, MS 39553

SHEPARD (Public State Park) From Jct of US-90 & Ladnier Rd, S 1.4 mi on Ladnier Rd to Graveline Rd, E 1.3 mi (L). 28 Avail: 28 W, 28 E (30/50 amps). 2021 rates: $13 to $18. (228)497-2244

GORE SPRINGS — B3 *Grenada*

GRENADA LAKE - COE/NORTH GRAYSPORT (Public Corps) From Jct of I-55 & Hwy 8, E 4 mi to 333 Scenic Drive, follow signs to Dam area (R). 50 Avail: 50 W, 50 E (50 amps). 2021 rates: $10 to $14. (662)226-1679

GREENVILLE — B1 *Washington*

WARFIELD POINT PARK (Public) From Jct of US-82 & SR-1, W 6 mi on US-82 to park access rd, N 2 mi (R). Avail: 52 full hkups (20/30 amps). 2021 rates: $25. (662)335-7275

GREENWOOD — B2 *Leflore*

DELTA MOBILE HOME & RV PARK
Ratings: 6.5/NA/8.5 (RV Area in MH Park) Avail: 21 full hkups (30/50 amps). 2021 rates: $25. (662)374-0002, 32800 CR 512, Greenwood, MS 38930

GRENADA — B3 *Grenada*

FROG HOLLOW CAMPGROUND/RV PARK **Ratings: 8/8.5★/7.5** (Campground) Avail: 10 full hkups (30/50 amps). 2021 rates: $37.45. (662)226-9042, 601 Hwy 7 N, Grenada, MS 38901

HUGH WHITE (Public State Park) From Jct of I-55 & SR-8 (exit 206), E 4.3 mi on SR-8 to Scenic Loop 333, N 2.5 mi, follow signs (bear left before dam) (L). 163 Avail: 163 W, 163 E (30/50 amps). 2021 rates: $18. (662)226-4934

GULFPORT — F3 *Harrison*

A SPOTLIGHT Introducing Gulf Coast's colorful attractions appearing at the front of this state section.

GULFPORT See also Bay St Louis, Biloxi & Perkinston.

BAYWOOD RV PARK & CAMPGROUND
Ratings: 9/9★/8 (Campground) Avail: 44 full hkups (30/50 amps). 2021 rates: $32 to $34. (228)896-4840, 1100 Cowan Rd, Gulfport, MS 39507

Directional arrows indicate the campground's position in relation to the nearest town.

CAMPGROUNDS OF THE SOUTH
Ratings: 7.5/9★/8.5 (RV Park) From Jct of I-10 & US-49 (Exit 34B), N 0.3 mi on US-49 to Landon Rd, E 0.8 mi to Three Rivers Rd, N 0.2 mi (R). **FAC:** paved rds. (140 spaces). 50 Avail: 40 paved, 10 grass, 16 pull-thrus, (25x70), back-ins (25x50), 50 full hkups (30/50 amps), cable, WiFi @ sites, dump, laundry. **REC:** boating nearby. Pet restrict (B). Partial handicap access. No tents. Big rig sites. 2021 rates: $35, Military discount. no cc.
(228)539-2922 Lat: 30.43745, Lon: -89.08292
10406 Three Rivers Rd, Gulfport, MS 39503
www.campgroundsofthesouth.com
See ad this page

COUNTRY SIDE RV PARK
Ratings: 8.5/8.5★/8 (Campground) Avail: 16 full hkups (30/50 amps). 2021 rates: $30 to $33. (228)539-0807, 20278 Hwy 49, Saucier, MS 39574

GULF HAVEN RV RESORT **Ratings: 8.5/9/8** (Campground) Avail: 77 full hkups (30/50 amps). 2021 rates: $45.50 to $55.50. (228)863-9096, 500 Broad Ave, Gulfport, MS 39501

HARRISON COUNTY FAIRGROUNDS (Public) From jct I-10 (exit 28) & County Farm Rd: Go 7-1/2 mi N on County Farm Rd. 46 Avail: 46 W, 46 E. 2021 rates: $20. (228)832-0080

HATTIESBURG — E3 *Covington*

HATTIESBURG See also Lumberton.

HATTIESBURG/OKATOMA HOLIDAY KOA Ratings: 9/8.5★/8.5 (Campground) Avail: 50 full hkups (30/50 amps). 2021 rates: $38 to $53. (601)520-6631, 221 Okatoma River Rd, Hattiesburg, MS 39401

MILITARY PARK LAKE WALKER FAMILY CAMPGROUND (CAMP SHELBY) (Public) From town, S 11 mi on Hwy 49 to Gulf Coast Hwy, S 4 mi to Camp Shelby South Gate exit (L). Avail: 32 full hkups (30/50 amps). 2021 rates: $15. (601)558-2540

PAUL B JOHNSON (Public State Park) From S Jct of US 98 & US 49, S 8.2 mi on US 49 (R). Avail: 125 full hkups (30/50 amps). 2021 rates: $22 to $24. (601)582-7721

HOLLANDALE — C2 *Washington*

LEROY PERCY (Public State Park) W-bnd: From Jct of US 61 & SR 12, W 5.5 mi on SR 12 (R) or; E-bnd: From Jct of Hwy 1 & SR 12, E 7.5 mi on SR 12 (L). 16 Avail: 2 full hkups, 14 W, 14 E (30/50 amps). 2021 rates: $18 to $20. (662)827-5436

HOLLY SPRINGS — A3 *Marshall*

WALL DOXEY (Public State Park) From Jct of US-78 & SR-7 (S. of Holly Springs), S 5.8 mi on SR-7 (R). 64 Avail: 64 W, 64 E (30/50 amps). 2021 rates: $22 to $24. (662)252-4231

HORN LAKE — A3 *DeSoto*

MEMPHIS JELLYSTONE CAMP RESORT **Ratings: 10/9.5★/9** (RV Park) Avail: 10 full hkups (30/50 amps). 2021 rates: $62 to $81. (662)280-8282, 1400 Audubon Point Drive, Horn Lake, MS 38637

INDIANOLA — B2 *Sunflower*

WILLIE'S LAST RESORT **Ratings: 3.5/NA/5** (RV Park) Avail: 14 full hkups (30/50 amps). 2021 rates: $25. (662)887-4551, 508 2nd St, Indianola, MS 38751

IUKA — A4 *Tishomingo*

GOAT ISLAND CAMPGROUND (Campground) (Rebuilding) Avail: 12 full hkups (30/50 amps). 2021 rates: $30. Mar 15 to Nov 15. (662)423-1104, 109 CR 346, Iuka, MS 38852

J P COLEMAN (Public State Park) From Jct of US-72 & SR-25, N 4.5 mi on SR-25 to State Park Rd (CR-989), NE 6.2 mi to CR-321, SE 1.2 mi (E). Avail: 69 full hkups (30/50 amps). 2021 rates: $20 to $24. (662)423-6515

JACKSON — D2 *Hinds*

JACKSON See also Canton, Clinton, Florence & Pelahatchie.

LE FLEUR'S BLUFF (Public State Park) From Jct of I 55 & Lakeland Dr (exit 98B), E 0.7 mi on Lakeland Dr to Lakeland Ter, S 0.2 mi (R). 28 Avail: 28 W, 28 E (30/50 amps). 2021 rates: $18. (601)987-3923

MOVIETOWN RV PARK
Ratings: 7/8.5★/8 (RV Park) From jct I-20 & I-55: Go 25 mi N on I-55 (exit 119), then 1/2 mi W on Hwy 22, then 1/2 mi N on Virillia Rd (R). **FAC:** paved/gravel rds. (114 spaces). Avail: 67 gravel, 50 pull-thrus, (45x65), back-ins (35x40), 67 full hkups (30/50 amps), WiFi, tent sites, rentals, laundry. **REC:** playground. Pets OK. Big rig sites, eco-friendly. 2021 rates: $30, Military discount.
(601)859-7990 Lat: 32.60736, Lon: -90.08420
109 Movietown Dr., Canton, MS 39046
www.movietownrvpark.com
See primary listing at Canton and ad this page

ROSS BARNETT/GOSHEN SPRINGS (Public) From Jct of I-55 & Lakeland Dr/SR-25 (exit 98B), NE 22 mi on Lakeland Dr to SR-43, W 2.9 mi (R). Avail: 75 full hkups (30/50 amps). 2021 rates: $24 to $28. (601)829-2751

ROSS BARNETT/TIMBERLAKE (Public) From I-55 to Lakeland Dr/SR-25 (exit 98B), NE 6 mi on Lakeland Dr/SR-25 to Old Fannin Rd (becomes Northshore Parkway), N 3.7 mi (L). Avail: 108 full hkups (30/50 amps). 2021 rates: $25 to $30. (601)992-9100

SPRINGRIDGE RV PARK/MOBILE HOME ESTATES
Ratings: 8.5/10★/8 (RV Area in MH Park) From jct I-20 and I-55: Go 10 mi W on I-20, then 1/2 mi S on Spring Ridge Rd (L). **FAC:** paved rds. (92 spaces). Avail: 42 paved, 30 pull-thrus, (20x55), back-ins (20x33), mostly side by side hkups, 42 full hkups (30/50 amps), seasonal sites, tent sites, dump, laundry. **REC:** pool, boating nearby, playground. Pet restrict (B). 2021 rates: $33, Military discount.
(601)924-0947 Lat: 32.32169, Lon: -90.32380
499 Springridge Rd, Clinton, MS 39056
springridgemhp.com
See primary listing at Clinton and ad this page

Travel Services

CAMPING WORLD OF JACKSON As the nation's largest retailer of RV supplies, accessories, services and new and used RVs, Camping World is committed to making your total RV experience better. **SERVICES:** tire, MH mechanical, restrooms. RV Sales. RV supplies, LP gas, dump, RV accessible. Hours: 9am to 7pm.
(888)627-2952 Lat: 32.223876, Lon: -90.224904
4601 I-55 South Frontage Rd., Jackson, MS 39212
www.campingworld.com

Be prepared! Bridge, Tunnel & Ferry Regulations and Rules of the Road can be found in the front of the Guide.

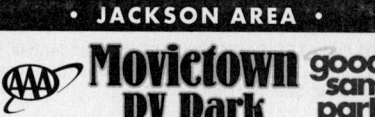

MS

LENA — C3 *Leake*

LEAKE COUNTY WATER PARK (Public) From Jct of SR-43 & SR-25 (E of reservoir), N 11.5 mi on SR-25 to Utah Rd, N 2 mi to Park Rd (Left 10ft, immediate Right, follow signs), N 1.2 mi (E). Avail: 42 full hkups (30/50 amps). 2021 rates: $20 to $22. (601)654-9359

LOW HEAD DAM (LEAKE COUNTY PARK) (Public) From jct Natchez Trace Parkway & Hwy 43: Go 7 mi E on Hwy 43, then 10 mi N on Hwy 25, then 3 mi NW on Utah Rd, then 5 mi W on Lowhead Dam Rd. 42 Avail: 42 W, 42 E (30 amps). (601)654-9359

LOUISVILLE — C4 *Winston*

LEGION (Public State Park) From Northern Jct of SR-15 & SR-25, N 5.5 mi on SR-25 to N Columbus Rd, SW 3.5 mi (R). Caution: Narrow Roads. Avail: 15 full hkups (30/50 amps). 2021 rates: $20. (662)773-8323

LUDLOW — C3 *Scott*

ROSS BARNETT/COAL BLUFF (Public) From Jct of SR-43 & SR-25 (E of reservoir), N 10.3 mi on SR-25 to Riverbend Rd, W 1.9 mi to Coal Bluff Rd, N 1.3 mi (E). 63 Avail: 63 W, 63 E (30/50 amps). 2021 rates: $20 to $22. (601)654-7726

LUMBERTON — E3 *Lamar*

LITTLE BLACK CREEK CAMPGROUND & PARK **Ratings: 7.5/8.5/9.5** (Campground) 124 Avail: 101 full hkups, 23 W, 23 E (30/50 amps). 2021 rates: $30 to $33. (601)794-2957, 2159 Little Black Creek Rd., Lumberton, MS 39455

MATHISTON — B3 *Choctaw*

NATCHEZ TRACE PKWY/JEFF BUSBY (Public National Park) From US-82 (in town) to milepost 204, S 9 mi on Natchez Trace Pkwy, at MP-193.1, follow signs. 18 Avail. (800)305-7417

MCCOMB — E2 *Pike*

BOGUE CHITTO WATER PARK CAMPGROUND (Public) From jct I-55 & Hwy 98 east (exit 15A): Go 12 mi E on Hwy 98, then at Brown Bogue Chitto Water Park sign, go 1 mi S on Dogwood Trail. 81 Avail: 15 full hkups, 66 W, 66 E (30/50 amps). 2021 rates: $10 to $20. (601)684-9568

PERCY QUIN (Public State Park) From Jct of I 55 & Fernwood Rd (exit 13), W 0.7 mi on Fernwood Rd to SR 48, N 0.1 mi (L). Avail: 100 full hkups (30/50 amps). 2021 rates: $22 to $24. (601)684-3938

MENDENHALL — D3 *Simpson*

D'LO WATER PARK (Public) From Mendenhall, W 2 mi on SH-149 (R). Avail: 24 full hkups (30 amps). 2021 rates: $20. (601)847-4310

MERIDIAN — C4 *Lauderdale*

MERIDIAN See also Toomsuba.

BENCHMARK COACH AND RV PARK
good sam park **Ratings: 7.5/9★/8.5** (RV Park) Avail: 27 full hkups (30/50 amps). 2021 rates: $31 to $35. (601)483-7999, 6420 Dale Dr., Meridian, MS 39342

BONITA LAKES RV PARK **Ratings: 9/9★/7.5** (RV Park) Avail: 104 full hkups (30/50 amps). 2021 rates: $27. (601)483-4330, 694 Mitchum Rd, Meridian, MS 39301

HILL COUNTRY RV AND MH COMMUNITY
good sam park **Ratings: 6/NA/7.5** (RV Area in MH Park) Avail: 10 full hkups (30/50 amps). 2021 rates: $40. (601)679-7300, 383 Briarwood Rd, Meridian, MS 39305

OKATIBBEE LAKE - COE/TWILTLEY BRANCH (Public Corps) From Jct of I-20 & Hwy 19 exit, N 12 mi on Hwy 19 to Okatibbee Dam Rd, follow Okatibbee Lake signs (E). 65 Avail: 65 W, 65 E (30/50 amps). 2021 rates: $12 to $20. (601)626-8068

OKATIBBEE WATER PARK (Public) From jct I-20/59 (exit 150) & Hwy 19: Go 5 mi N on Hwy 19, then 8 mi N on Pine Spring Rd. Follow signs. 105 Avail: 75 full hkups, 30 W, 30 E (30/50 amps). 2021 rates: $22 to $24. (601)737-2370

MIZE — D3 *Smith*

PRENTISS WALKER LAKE (Public) From Jct of Mize & SR-35, S 2.4 mi on SR-35, W 1.9 mi on cnty rd, S 0.5 mi (R). 21 Avail: 21 W, 21 E (30 amps). 2021 rates: $18. (601)733-2611

MONTICELLO — D2 *Lawrence*

ATWOOD WATER PARK (Public) From town: Go 1 mi E on Hwy-84. 125 Avail. (601)587-2711

MORTON — C3 *Scott*

GREEN TREE RV PARK & CAMPGROUND
good sam park **Ratings: 7/NA/8** (RV Park) Avail: 19 full hkups (30/50 amps). 2021 rates: $35 to $40. (601)278-4823, 2169 Hwy 80, Morton, MS 39117

ROOSEVELT (Public National Park) From Jct of I 20 & SR 13 (exit 77), N 0.6 mi on SR 13 (L). 109 Avail: 82 full hkups, 27 W, 27 E (30/50 amps). 2021 rates: $18 to $24. (601)732-6316

MOUNT OLIVE — D3 *Covington*

DRY CREEK WATER PARK (Public) From jct US 49 & park road: Go 4-1/2 mi W on park road. Follow signs. Avail: 28 E (30/50 amps). 2021 rates: $18.19. (601)797-4619

NATCHEZ — D1 *Adams*

NATCHEZ (Public State Park) From N Jct of US-61 (NE of Natchez) & US-84, N 5.1 mi on US-61 to State Park Rd, E 0.3 mi to Wickcliff, N 0.3 mi (R). 50 Avail: 6 full hkups, 44 W, 44 E (30/50 amps). 2021 rates: $18 to $20. (601)442-2658

PLANTATION RV PARK **Ratings: 8/8★/9** (Campground) Avail: 34 full hkups (30/50 amps). 2021 rates: $39.95. (601)442-5222, 1 Fredrick Rd., Natchez, MS 39120

RIVER VIEW RV PARK AND RESORT
good sam park **Ratings: 9/9★/9.5** (RV Park) From Jct of US 61 & US 84, NW 3.5 mi on US 84 to LA 131/ Martin Luther King Ave. (First left after bridge) SE 0.8 mi (L). **FAC:** paved/gravel rds. (145 spaces). 135 Avail: 84 paved, 51 grass, 84 pull-thrus, (30x60), back-ins (30x50), 135 full hkups (30/50 amps), seasonal sites, WiFi @ sites, tent sites, rentals, dump, laundry, LP gas, firewood. **REC:** pool, hot tub, Mississippi River: fishing, boating nearby, playground, hunting nearby. Pet restrict (B). Partial handicap access. Big rig sites, eco-friendly. 2021 rates: $32.95 to $44.95, Military discount.
(318)336-1400 Lat: 31.555576, Lon: -91.43441
800 Martin Luther King Ave, Vidalia, LA 71373
riverviewrvpark.com
See primary listing at Vidalia, LA and ad this page

OAKLAND — B3 *Yalobusha*

GEORGE P COSSAR (Public State Park) From Jct of I-55 & SR-32 (exit 227), E 2.5 mi on SR-32 to park rd, N 1.7 mi (E). Avail: 76 full hkups (30/50 amps). 2021 rates: $20. (662)623-7356

OCEAN SPRINGS — F4 *Jackson*

GULF ISLANDS NATIONAL SEASHORE/DAVIS BAYOU CAMPGROUND (Public National Park) From Jct of I-10 & CR-609 (exit 50), S 3 mi on CR-609 to US-90, E 2.6 mi to Park Rd, S 2 mi (R). 52 Avail: 52 W, 52 E (30/50 amps). 2021 rates: $22. (228)875-3962

OLIVE BRANCH — A3 *DeSoto*

Travel Services

CAMPING WORLD OF OLIVE BRANCH/MEMPHIS As the nation's largest retailer of RV supplies, accessories, services and new and used RVs, Camping World is committed to making your total RV experience better. **SERVICES:** restrooms. RV Sales. RV supplies, LP gas, dump, emergency parking, RV accessible. Hours: 9am - 7pm.
(888)671-8595 Lat: 34.978836, Lon: -89.862500
8150 New Craft Road, Olive Branch, MS 38654
www.campingworld.com

PELAHATCHIE — D3 *Rankin*

YOGI ON THE LAKE **Ratings: 9/10★/10** (RV Park) Avail: 164 full hkups (30/50 amps). 2021 rates: $53 to $87. (601)854-6859, 143 Campground Rd, Pelahatchie, MS 39145

PERKINSTON — E3 *Stone*

DIAMOND LAKE RV PARK **Ratings: 7.5/9.5★/8.5** (Campground) Avail: 77 full hkups (30/50 amps). 2021 rates: $40. (228)234-5253, 997 Hwy 49, Perkinston, MS 39573

PHILADELPHIA — C3 *Neshoba*

BURNSIDE LAKE PARK (Public) From town, NE 5 mi on Hwy 15 (L). 22 Avail: 22 W, 22 E (30/50 amps). 2021 rates: $10. (601)656-4101

PICAYUNE — E3 *Hancock*

PICAYUNE See also Bay St Louis, MS; Slidell, LA.

SUN ROAMERS RV RESORT
good sam park **Ratings: 10/10★/9.5** (RV Park) From Jct of I-59 & SR 43 S (exit 4), E 1.4 mi on SR 43S to Stafford Rd, S 0.6 mi to Mississippi Pines Blvd, W 500 ft (E).

NEAR NEW ORLEANS AND MS GULF COAST
Beautiful park among tall pines, Olympic size pool, large fishing pond, miniature golf, rental cabins, great family destination! Rallies welcome (free use of large clubhouse with commercial kitchen for Rallies). Near casinos.

FAC: paved rds. (154 spaces). 118 Avail: 12 paved, 106 all weather, 11 pull-thrus, (25x60), back-ins (28x60), 118 full hkups (30/50 amps), seasonal sites WiFi @ sites, tent sites, rentals, dump, laundry, LP gas, fire rings. **REC:** pool, pond, fishing, boating nearby, playground, hunting nearby, rec open to public. Pet restrict (Q). Partial handicap access. Big rig sites, eco-friendly. 2021 rates: $40 to $43, Military discount.
(601)798-5818 Lat: 30.509977, Lon: -89.649839
41 Mississippi Pines Blvd, Picayune, MS 39466
www.sunroamers.com
See ad page 442

PONTOTOC — A4 *Pontotoc*

HOWARD STAFFORD PARK & LAKE (Public) From Jct of Hwy 6 & 9, W 0.5 mi on Hwy 9S to Lake Dr, S (E). Avail: 13 full hkups (20 amps). 2021 rates: $13. (662)489-1882

PORT GIBSON — D2 *Claiborne*

GRAND GULF MILITARY PARK & CAMPGROUND (Public) From Jct of US 61 & SR 462, W 7 mi on SR 462, follow signs (R); or From Jct of Natchez Trace Pkwy & US 61, N 6.5 mi on US 61 to SR 462, W 7 mi, follow signs (R). Avail: 42 full hkups (30/50 amps). 2021 rates: $25. (601)437-5911

NATCHEZ TRACE PKWY/ROCKY SPRINGS (Public National Park) From Jct of US-61 & SR 18, N 2 mi on SR-18, at MP-54.8, follow signs. 22 Avail. (800)305-7417

QUITMAN — D4 *Clarke*

ARCHUSA CREEK WATER PARK (Public) From Jct of US 45 & SR 18, W 2.1 mi on SR 18 to SR 511, SE 0.3 mi to Shiloh Rd, S 0.4 mi (R). 69 Avail: 69 W, 56 S, 69 E (30/50 amps). 2021 rates: $15 to $22. (601)776-6956

CLARKCO PARK (Public State Park) From Jct of US 45 & SR 145 (N of Quitman), NE 0.3 mi on SR 145 (R). Avail: 43 full hkups (30/50 amps). 2021 rates: $20 to $24. (601)776-6651

RIPLEY — A4 *Tippah*

TIPPAH COUNTY LAKE (Public) From Jct SR-4 & SR-15, N 5 mi on SR-15 to CR-410/Tippah Lake Rd, W 2.5 mi (E). 22 Avail: 22 W, 22 E (30 amps). 2021 rates: $18. (662)837-9850

ROBINSONVILLE — A2 *Tunica*

ROBINSONVILLE See also Coldwater, Horn Lake, Southaven & Tunica, MS; West Memphis, AR; Memphis, TN.

SARDIS — A3 *Lafayette*

JOHN W KYLE (Public State Park) S-bnd: From Jct of I-55 & SR-315 (exit 252), E 6.8 mi on SR-315 (R); or N-bnd: From Jct of I-55 & SR-35 (exit 246), N 7 mi on SR-35 to SR-315, N 2 mi (L). Avail: 200 E (30/50 amps). 2021 rates: $18 to $24. (662)487-1345

SARDIS LAKE - COE/CLEAR CREEK (Public Corps) From Jct of I-55 & Hwy 6, E appx 20 mi on Hwy 6 to SR-314 (in Oxford), N 8 mi, follow signs (E). 52 Avail: 52 W, 52 E (30 amps). 2021 rates: $18. Apr 01 to Sep 30. (662)563-4531

SARDIS LAKE - COE/OAK GROVE (Public Corps) From Jct of I-55 & SR-315 (exit 252), E 8 mi on SR-315, below dam on lower lake (R). 82 Avail: 82 W, 82 E (30/50 amps). 2021 rates: $18. Apr 01 to Sep 30. (662)563-4531

SOSO — D3 *Jones*

BIG CREEK WATER PARK 10 (Public) From Jct of I-59 & US-84W (exit 95B), W 11.9 mi on US-84W to Cooley Park Rd, S 0.6 mi (R). Avail: 30 full hkups (30/50 amps). 2021 rates: $15 to $22. (601)763-8555

SOUTHAVEN — A3 *DeSoto*

EZ DAZE RV PARK

good sam park **Ratings: 10/10★/9** (Campground) From jct of I-55 (exit 287) & Church Rd: Go 1/4 mi W on Church Rd, then 1/2 mi N on Pepper Chase Dr., then 1/4 mi W on W.E. Ross Pkwy (R).

NORTH MISSISSIPPI'S PREMIER RV PARK

We go the extra mile with a reinforced storm room. Let our massage therapist relax those tired muscles. We're a first-class RV park with paved sites, patios & showcase bathrooms located near Memphis & Tunica.

FAC: paved rds. (136 spaces). Avail: 50 paved, patios, 47 pull-thrus, (25x75), back-ins (25x60), 50 full hkups (30/50 amps), seasonal sites, cable, WiFi @ sites, laundry, LP gas. **REC:** pool, boating nearby, playground. Pet restrict (B). Partial handicap access. No tents. Big rig sites, eco-friendly. 2021 rates: $57 to $72, Military discount.

(662)342-7720 Lat: 34.94186, Lon: -89.99883
536 W.E. Ross Pkwy, Southaven, MS 38671
www.ezdazervpark.com
See ad next page, 855

County names are provided after the city names. If you're tracking the weather, this is the information you'll need to follow the reports.

SPOTLIGHT ON
TOP RV & CAMPING DESTINATIONS

We've put the Spotlight on popular RV & camping travel destinations. Turn to the Spotlight articles in our State and Province sections to learn more.

SOUTHAVEN (CONT)

SOUTHAVEN RV PARK
good sam park **Ratings: 7.5/9.5★/8** (RV Park) From jct of I-55 (exit 291) & Stateline Rd: Go 1/2 mi E on Stateline Rd (L).

MEMPHIS ATTRACTIONS MINUTES AWAY
Only minutes from Graceland, downtown Memphis & the historic Beale Street. The park is a safe place to stay will visiting all the area attractions. Enjoy paved roads, 30/50 amp sites, cable tv, a laundry & friendly service!

FAC: paved rds. (44 spaces). Avail: 10 paved, patios, 10 pull-thrus, (20x65), 10 full hkups (30/50 amps), cable, WiFi @ sites, laundry. **REC:** boating nearby. Pet restrict (B). No tents. 2021 rates: $45, Military discount.
(662)393-8585 Lat: 34.9925, Lon: -89.9945
270 Stateline Rd, Southaven, MS 38671
www.southavenrvpark.com
See ad page 854

STARKVILLE — B4 *Oktibbeha*

JOHN W STARR MEMORIAL RVP (Public) From Starkville, S 7.6 mi to St Mark Rd, E 100 yds (R). Avail: 13 full hkups (30/50 amps). 2021 rates: $20. (662)325-4720

THE PINES MH AND RV COMMUNITY
good sam park **Ratings: 7.5/NA/8.5** (RV Area in MH Park) Avail: 65 full hkups (30/50 amps). 2021 rates: $40. (662)323-6423, 1000 Louisville St, Starkville, MS 39759

TISHOMINGO — A4 *Tishomingo*

TISHOMINGO (Public State Park) From Jct of Natchez Trace Pkwy & park entrance road (MP 304), NE 0.5 mi on park entrance rd to CR 90 (park rd), E 0.5 mi, follow signs (E). 62 Avail: 62 W, 62 E (30/50 amps). 2021 rates: $22 to $24. (662)438-6914

TOOMSUBA — C4 *Lauderdale*

LAKE TOM BAILEY (Public) From town, W 1.25 mi on US-80, N 1.3 mi. 22 Avail: 22 W, 22 E (20 amps). 2021 rates: $18. (601)632-4679

MERIDIAN EAST/TOOMSUBA KOA **Ratings: 8/9★/8.5** (Campground) 49 Avail: 29 full hkups, 20 W, 20 E (30/50 amps). 2021 rates: $42 to $52. (800)562-4202, 3953 KOA Campgroun Rd, Toomsuba, MS 39364

TUNICA — A2 *Tunica*

A SPOTLIGHT Introducing Gulf Coast's colorful attractions appearing at the front of this state section.

HOLLYWOOD CASINO HOTEL & RV PARK
good sam park **Ratings: 9.5/9★/8.5** (RV Park) Avail: 123 full hkups (30/50 amps). 2021 rates: $24.60. (800)871-0711, 1150 Casino Strip Blvd, Robinsonville, MS 38664

SAM'S TOWN GAMBLING HALL RV PARK **Ratings: 8/9★/8.5** (RV Park) Avail: 50 full hkups (30/50 amps). 2021 rates: $26.74. (800)456-0711, 1477 Casino Strip Resorts Blvd, Robinsonville, MS 38664

TUPELO — A4 *Lee*

A SPOTLIGHT Introducing Tupelo's colorful attractions appearing at the front of this state section.

CAMPGROUND AT BARNES CROSSING
good sam park **Ratings: 8/10★/10** (Campground) E-bnd: From jct I-22 (exit 82) & Barnes Crossing Rd: Go 2-1/2 mi E on Barnes Crossing Rd, then 1/4 mi N on Hwy 145/Gloster to Campground Rd (R) W-bnd: From jct I-22 (exit 86 B) & US 45: Go 1 mi N on US 45, then 1/2 mi W on Barnes Crossing Rd, then 1/4 mi N on 145/Gloster to Campground Rd (R). **FAC:** paved rds. (55 spaces). Avail: 38 gravel, 25 pull-thrus, (30x68), back-ins (30x35), 38 full hkups (30/50 amps), seasonal sites, cable, WiFi @ sites, laundry. **REC:** boating nearby, hunting nearby. Pets OK. No tents. Big rig sites, eco-friendly. 2021 rates: $45 to $50. no cc.
(662)844-6063 Lat: 34.32301, Lon: -88.70340
125 Campground Rd, Tupelo, MS 38804
www.cgbarnescrossing.com
See ad page 521

ELVIS PRESLEY LAKE CAMPGROUND (Public) From Jct of US 78 & N Veterans Blvd (NE of downtown Tupelo), NE 0.2 mi on Veterans Blvd to CR-1460, E 1.7 mi to CR-995, N 0.6 mi (E). Follow signs, marked well. 16 Avail: 16 W, 16 E (30/50 amps). 2021 rates: $18. (662)620-6314

The best things happen outdoors. Start your adventure today at GanderOutdoors.com

NATCHEZ TRACE RV PARK
good sam park **Ratings: 8/9.5★/9** (Campground) From jct Natchez Trace Pkwy & US-78: Go 12-1/2 mi SW on Natchez Trace Pkwy, then 400 feet E on CR-506 (R). **FAC:** gravel rds. Avail: 25 gravel, 20 pull-thrus, (25x65), back-ins (30x40), 20 full hkups, 5 W, 5 E (30/50 amps), tent sites, dump, laundry, LP gas, firewood. **REC:** pool, pond, fishing, hunting nearby. Pets OK. Big rig sites, eco-friendly. 2021 rates: $30 to $32, Military discount. no cc.
(662)767-8609 Lat: 34.14589, Lon: -88.81812
189 CR-506, Shannon, MS 38868
www.natcheztracervpark.com
See ad this page

TOMBIGBEE (Public State Park) From Jct of US-78 & Veterans Blvd, S 2 mi on Veterans Blvd to SR-6, SE 3.3 mi to park access rd (State Park Rd), E 2.8 mi, follow signs (R). 20 Avail: 18 full hkups, 2 W, 2 E (30/50 amps). 2021 rates: $22 to $24. (662)842-7669

TRACE (Public State Park) E-bnd: From Jct of SR-41 & SR-6/Pontotoc exit (W of Tupelo), E 7.2 mi on SR-6 to Faulkner Rd (CR-65), N 2.1 mi (L); or W-bnd: From Jct of Natchez Trace Pkwy & SR-6 (W of Tupelo), W 7.8 mi on SR-6 to Faulkner Rd (CR-65), N 2.1 mi (L). Avail: 76 full hkups (30/50 amps). 2021 rates: $22 to $24. (662)489-2958

TYLERTOWN — E2 *Walthall*

HIDDEN SPRINGS RV RESORT
good sam park **Ratings: 7.5/9★/8** (Campground) 37 Avail: 20 full hkups, 17 W, 17 E (30/50 amps). 2021 rates: $25 to $45. (601)876-4151, 16 Clyde Rhodus Rd, Tylertown, MS 39667

VICKSBURG — C2 *Warren*

VICKSBURG See also Clinton.

AMERISTAR CASINO & RV PARK
good sam park **Ratings: 9.5/9.5★/9** (RV Park) Avail: 67 full hkups (30/50 amps). 2021 rates: $35 to $45. (800)700-7770, 725 Lucy Bryson St, Vicksburg, MS 39180

MAGNOLIA RV PARK RESORT
good sam park **Ratings: 8/8.5★/7.5** (RV Park) Avail: 66 full hkups (30/50 amps). 2021 rates: $28 to $35. (601)631-0388, 211 Miller St, Vicksburg, MS 39180

WAVELAND — F3 *Hancock*

BUCCANEER (Public State Park) From jct of US-90 & Nicholsan Ave/SR-603, S 1.2 mi on Nicholsan Ave to Central Ave, W 0.7 mi to Coleman, S 0.4 to Beach Blvd, W 2.7 mi, follow signs (R). Avail: 206 full hkups (30/50 amps). 2021 rates: $13 to $35. (228)467-3822

WAYNESBORO — D4 *Wayne*

MAYNOR CREEK WATER PARK (Public) From Jct of US 45 & US 84, W 4.1 mi on US 84 to Reservoir Rd, S 3 mi (L). 69 Avail: 69 W, 36 S, 69 E (30/50 amps). 2021 rates: $22 to $24. (601)735-4365

WESSON — D2 *Copiah*

LAKE LINCOLN (Public State Park) From Jct of I 55 & Sylvarena Rd (exit 51), E 3.8 mi on Sylvarena Rd to US 51, S 0.1 mi to Main St, NE 0.3 mi to E Railroad St, NE 0.7 mi to Timberlane Rd, E 2.3 mi, where road becomes Sunset Rd, SE 1.3 mi (L). 71 Avail: 45 full hkups, 26 W, 26 E (30/50 amps). 2021 rates: $20 to $24. (601)643-9044

WIGGINS — E3 *Stone*

FLINT CREEK WATER PARK (Public) From Jct SR-26 & SR-29, N 2 mi on SR-29, follow signs (L). 152 Avail: 152 W, 77 S, 152 E (30/50 amps). 2021 rates: $28 to $30. (601)928-3051

Show Your Good Sam Membership Card!

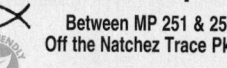

MS

DID YOU KNOW?

Known for their love of grilling, St. Louis residents consume more barbecue sauce per capita than any other American town.

YOU ARE HERE

Missouri

Folks often argue over whether Missouri is part of the Midwest or part of the South. Forget the fuss and enjoy a state that encompasses the Ozarks, rocking nightlife, slow-cooked barbecue and Route 66.

Follow the Arch

Dominating the skyline over St. Louis is the magnificent Gateway Arch National Park, America's tallest national monument. Ride the tram to the top of this 630-foot structure to take in sensational views of the Mississippi River. Afterward, immerse yourself in the world of blues with live performances, interactive galleries and intriguing artifacts at the National Blues Museum.

The Branson Beat

Come to Branson in southern Missouri to enjoy wholesome entertainment. Humming with the sweet sounds of country, rock and pop, the "Live Music Show Capital of the World" will wow you with its electrifying concerts and Broadway-style entertainment. If you're a jazz fan, make your way to Kansas City for the American Jazz Museum and the 18th and Vine Historic Jazz District.

Going Deep

More than 6,400 caves are found under the earth of the Show Me State, and 20 of these subterranean marvels welcome explorers. Wander down twisting passageways inside Onondaga Cave, journey more than 500 feet below the surface at Marvel Cave or gawk at strange-looking limestone formations in the Meramec Caverns.

Two Wheels or Two Legs

Grab your bike or lace up your boots. The scenic Ozark Mountains are accessible with beautiful hiking trails. See them in all their grandeur at the Top of the Rock Ozarks Heritage Preserve. Drink at the Bat Bar in the Lost Canyon Cave.

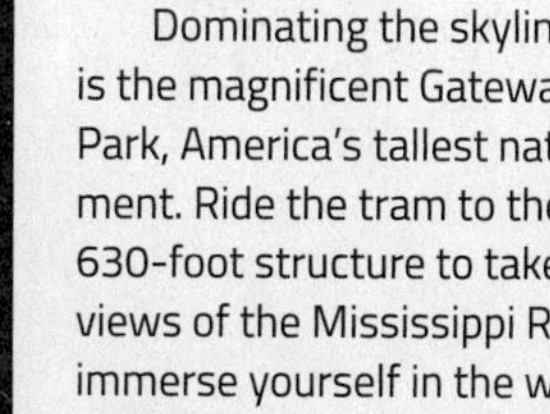

Missouri Toasted Ravioli

A twist on an Italian classic, toasted ravioli is breaded, deep-fried and served with marinara sauce. The indulgent appetizer is said to have come from St. Louis in the 1940s when chefs at Charlie Gitto's and Mama's on the Hill accidentally dropped ravioli in hot oil instead of water. The rest is local culinary history.

VISITOR CENTER

TIME ZONE
Central Standard

ROAD & HIGHWAY INFORMATION
888-275-6636
modot.mo.gov

FISHING & HUNTING INFORMATION
800-392-4115
huntfish.mdc.mo.gov/permits

BOATING INFORMATION
573-751-5071
mo.gov/outdoors/boating

NATIONAL PARKS
nps.gov/mo

STATE PARKS
mostateparks.com

TOURISM INFORMATION
Missouri Division of Tourism
800-519-2100
visitmo.com

TOP TOURISM ATTRACTIONS
1) Gateway Arch National Park
2) Branson/Silver Dollar City
3) Anheuser-Busch Brewery

MAJOR CITIES
Kansas City, Saint Louis, Springfield, Independence, Columbia, Jefferson City (capital)

good sam park Featured Good Sam Parks MISSOURI

When you stay with Good Sam, you can expect the highest degree of cleanliness and friendliness, and better yet, you get **10% off** overnight campground fees.

If you're not already a Good Sam member you can purchase your membership at one of these locations:

BONNE TERRE
Stone Park Resort & Amphitheatre

BOWLING GREEN
Cozy C RV Campground

BRANSON
America's Best Campground
Blue Mountain Campground
Branson Lakeside RV Park
Branson Stagecoach RV Park
Branson Treehouse Adventures
Cooper Creek Resort & Campground
Musicland Kampground

CAPE GIRARDEAU
Cape Camping & RV Park

CAPE GIRARDEAU
The Landing Point RV Park

CARTHAGE
Big Red Barn RV Park

CARUTHERSVILLE
Century Casino & RV Park

COLUMBIA
Cedar Creek Resort & RV Park
Cottonwoods RV Park

DANVILLE
Lazy Day Campground

DIXON
BSC Outdoors Camping & Float Trips

LAKE OZARK
Riverview RV Park

MARSHFIELD
RV Express 66

MOUNTAIN GROVE
Missouri RV Park

ODESSA
Owl Creek Market + RV Park

OSAGE BEACH
Osage Beach RV Park

PORTAGEVILLE
Bootheel RV Park & Event Center

SIKESTON
Cypress Creek RV Park

SPRINGFIELD
Ozark Highlands MHC/RV Park

ST CHARLES
Sundermeier RV Park

ST JOSEPH
AOK Campground & RV Park
Beacon RV Park

ST ROBERT
Motel 6 & RV Park

STRAFFORD
Rustic Meadows RV Park

10/10★/10 GOOD SAM PARKS

COLUMBIA
Cottonwoods RV Park
(573)474-2747

DANVILLE
Lazy Day Campground
(573)564-2949

LAKE OZARK
Riverview RV Park
(573)365-1122

OSAGE BEACH
Osage Beach RV Park
(573)348-3445

What's This?

An RV park with a 10/10★/10 rating has scored perfect grades in amenities, cleanliness and appearance ("See Understanding the Campground Rating System" on pages 8 and 9 for an explanation of the trusted Good Sam Rating System). Stay in a 10/10★/10 park on your next trip for a nearly flawless camping experience.

Getty Images/iStockphoto

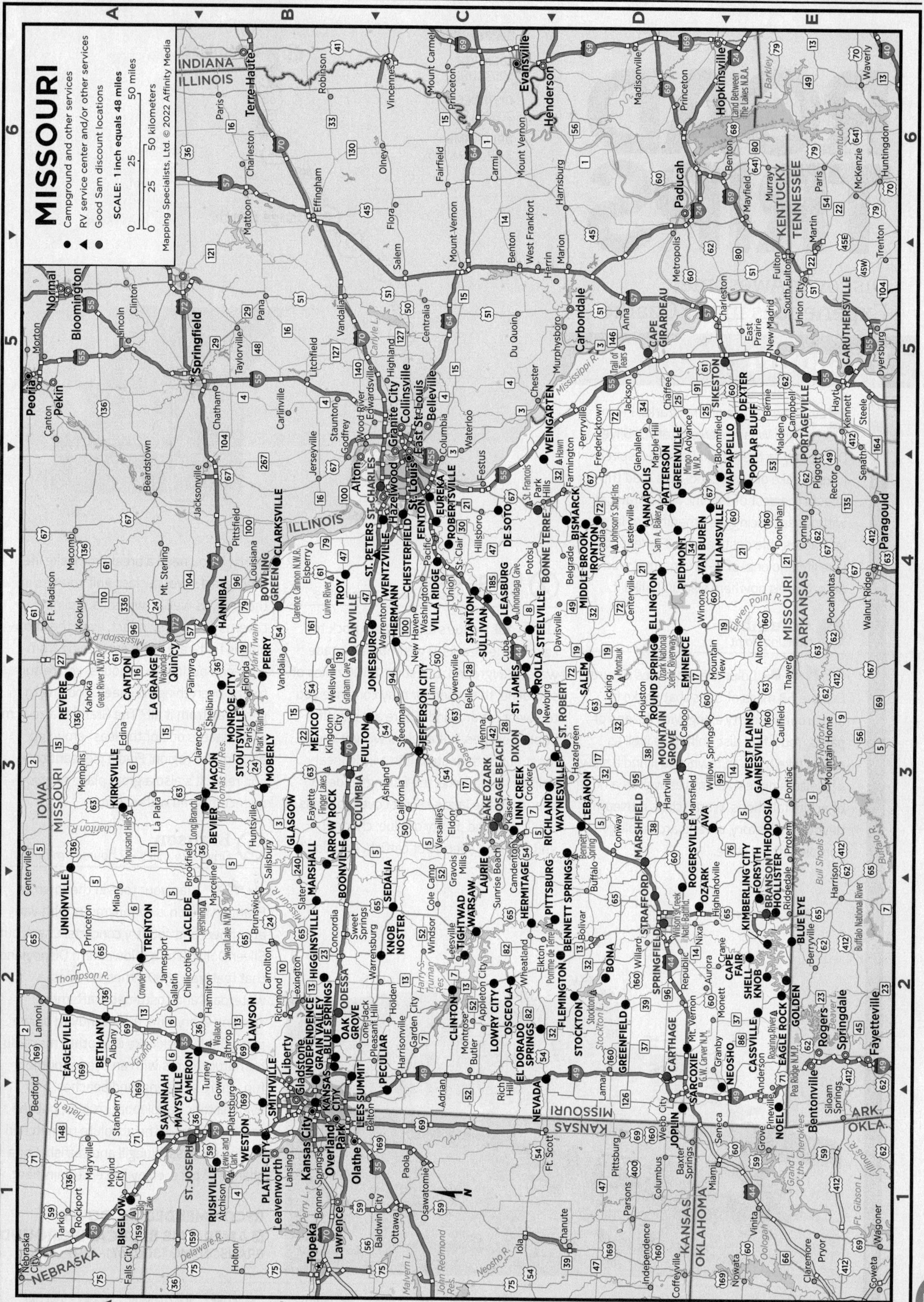
MISSOURI
Campground and other services
RV service center and/or other services
Good Sam discount locations
SCALE: 1 inch equals 48 miles
0 25 50 miles
0 25 50 kilometers
Mapping Specialists, Ltd. © 2022 Affinity Media

ROAD TRIPS

Discover Awesome Experiences in the Ozarks

Missouri

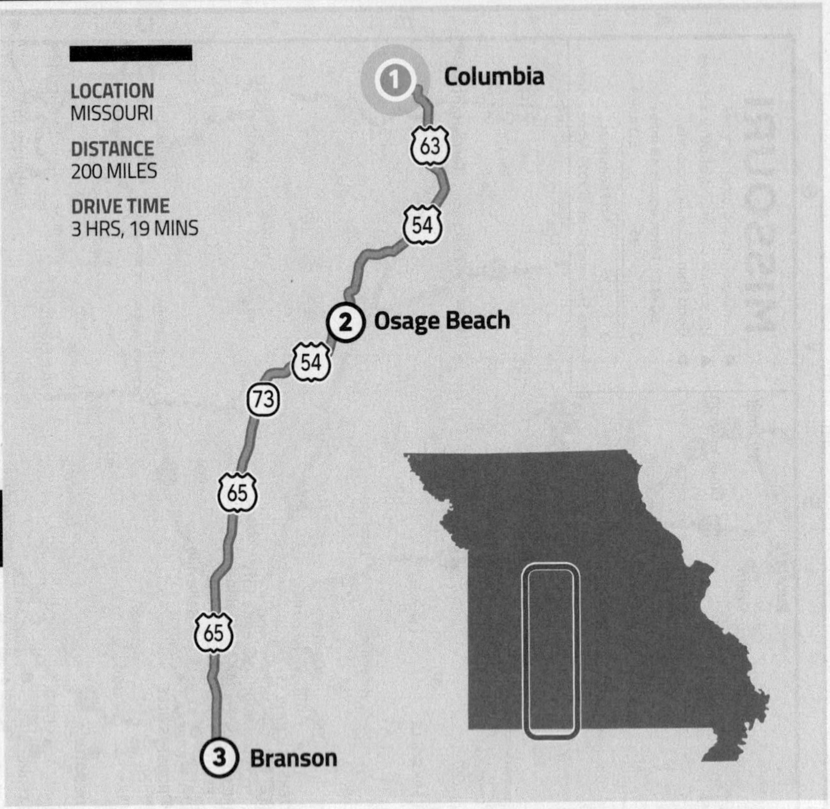

Feel the embrace of the Ozarks. From the Wild West rollercoasters of Silver Dollar City to the Arnold Palmer-inspired links in Lake of the Ozarks, this road trip boasts the best of the Show Me State, all without sacrificing the amenities of larger, less accessible destinations. For legendary lake life and one-of-a-kind natural wonders, there's nowhere else quite like it.

1 Columbia
Starting Point

Columbia embraces nature. Explore 63 miles of trails that snake in and around the city along with dozens of parks. You'll find disc golfing as well as ample bike trails. In town, you'll find a slew of welcoming restaurants as well as a host of art installations. World-class museums devoted to history, art and archaeology complete the picture.

2 Osage Beach
Drive 76 miles • 1 hour, 12 minutes

Boaters and anglers flock to Lake of the Ozarks, a vast human-made water playground. Boasting 1,100 miles of shoreline, this reservoir may convince you to swear off dry land. There are plentiful public beaches, but anglers will get the most out of their stay with a little local help by hiring a charter-fishing guide to show you the lake's secret coves for bass. You'll also find plenty of blue, channel and flathead species of catfish. And don't worry, if you need a break from lake life, there are 13 world-class golf courses in the area, as well as wineries, ziplining, caverns and more. In fact, even the shopping is first-rate. With everything from high-end outlets to antiques, you're sure to find everything you need. Looking to get away from it all? The Grand Glaize Arm of the lake is one of the least crowded parts of the region. Find a pleasant cove and relax. It's also a great place to enjoy unencumbered water skiing.

3 Branson
Drive 124 miles • 2 hours, 7 minutes

Tap your toes in the town of Branson, which is synonymous with variety shows and country concerts. Check out Silver Dollar City, a Midwestern Disneyland that features 1880s-themed rides, a waterpark and costumed craftsmen creating everything from candy to blown glass. Table Rock Lake is another must-do for nature lovers with an eye for outdoor fun. There's boating, and beaches, and even historic paddleboat cruises, but the real draw here is the absolute unmatched fishing for bass, bluegill and catfish. For a change of pace, enjoy live entertainment.

Getty Images/iStockphoto

RECOMMENDED STOPOVER
A AMERICA'S BEST CAMPGROUND
BRANSON, MO (800) 671-4399

BIKING · BOATING · DINING · ENTERTAINMENT · FISHING · HIKING · HUNTING · PADDLING · SHOPPING · SIGHTSEEING

Missouri SPOTLIGHTS

Rolling Out the BBQ and Outdoor Adventure

The Show Me state blends Midwestern hominess with Southern charm. Visitors can get a sense of both regions when they visit Missouri's cities and towns. Savor barbecue, old-fashioned entertainment and rugged landscapes as you explore. Ride to the top of an amazing arch for views of the Mississippi River.

IN 1942, A FIRE GUTTED THE CASTLE IN HA HA TONKA STATE PARK.

Getty Images/iStockphoto

Famous for its castle, Ha Ha Tonka State Park overlooks Lake of the Ozarks.

Kansas City

Kansas City, known as the city of fountains, gushes with exciting entertainment and activities. Catch a summer ballgame at Kauffman Stadium to watch the Royals, or hop in the driver's seat for a NASCAR thrill at the Richard Petty Driving Experience. No matter your interest, Kansas City aims to please.

KC's Roots

Pioneer life comes alive at Shoal Creek Living History Museum, home to authentic, relocated log cabins and other buildings that date from the early- to late-19th century. Walk in the footsteps of a local activist and advocate for social equality at the Bruce R. Watkins Cultural Heritage Center. Here, exhibits and stage performances illustrate the contributions made to the city by its African American community.

Put it in 'Park'

Ready to slow things down? Explore a big patch of nature in the middle of a thriving metropolis at Lakeside Nature Center. The center offers wildlife education programs and is home to a hiking trail and native wildlife exhibit. Wander through stalls of fresh produce at the farmers' market in historic River Market, easily the largest of its kind in the region. The site is also home to the Arabia Steamboat Museum and the world's largest collection of pre-Civil War artifacts.

Lake of the Ozarks

From the air, Lake of the Ozarks resembles a dragon twisting through a rugged landscape. On the ground, this body of water entices visitors to play along 80 miles of shoreline. That means room for zooming in a speedboat or gliding across the surface on water skis. For a slower pace, enjoy fishing, biking, hiking and wildlife spotting on the lake's lush banks. In Ha Ha Tonka State Park, visitors can see the ruins of a castle built in the early 1900s by the Snyder family.

St. Louis

The largest city on the Great Plains stakes its reputation on great barbecue and wholesome American experiences. Just follow the arch overlooking the Mississippi to find out.

Ride the Arch

Originally founded as a fur-trading post on the banks of the Mississippi River, St. Louis's long history as the jumping-off point for pioneers heading west is honored in truly spectacular fashion at the iconic Gateway Arch. Opened to the public in 1965, the arch stands 630 feet high.

FOR MORE INFORMATION

Missouri Division of Tourism, 573-751-4133, www.visitmo.com

Lake of the Ozarks, 800-386-5253, www.funlake.com

Visit Kansas City, 800-767-7700, www.visitkc.com

Explore St. Louis, 800-916-8938, www.explorestlouis.com

LOCAL FAVORITE

Waffle Cone S'mores

The world's first ice cream cone was introduced at the St. Louis World's Fair in 1904.
Recipe by Mary Rumor.

INGREDIENTS

- ☐ 4 waffle cones
- ☐ Miniature chocolate chips
- ☐ Miniature marshmallows
- ☐ Miniature butterscotch chips (optional)
- ☐ Chocolate and/or caramel topping (optional)
- ☐ Whipped cream (optional)
- ☐ Rainbow sprinkles (optional)

DIRECTIONS

Break aluminum foil into square sheets large enough to wrap each waffle cone.
Place 10 miniature chocolate chips at bottom of the cones, followed by mini marshmallows and butterscotch chips. Continue to layer until the waffle cones are full.
Place cones on aluminum square and wrap them entirely. Place on fire pit, grill or propane stove. Rotate with tongs for 15 to 20 minutes or until marshmallows and chips are melted thoroughly. Serves 4.

Missouri

ANNAPOLIS — D4 *Iron*

BIG CREEK RV PARK **Ratings: 10/10★/10** (RV Park) Avail: 65 full hkups (30/50 amps). 2021 rates: $40 to $48. (573)598-1064, 47247 Hwy 49, Annapolis, MO 63620

CLEARWATER LAKE - COE/HIGHWAY K PARK (Public Corps) From Jct of Hwy K & RR 49, W 5 mi on Hwy K (L). 83 Avail: 24 W, 58 E (30/50 amps). 2021 rates: $14 to $20. May 15 to Sep 15. (573)751-4133

ARROW ROCK — B3 *Saline*

ARROW ROCK STATE HISTORIC SITE (Public State Park) From Jct of I-70 & SR-41, N 13 mi on SR-41 (R). 47 Avail: 1 full hkups, 34 E (50 amps). 2021 rates: $12 to $28. (660)837-3330

AVA — D3 *Douglas*

MFTHBA SHOW GROUNDS AND CAMPGROUND (MO FOX TROTTER HORSE BREED ASSOC.) **Ratings: 4.5/7.5/7.5** (Campground) Avail: 216 full hkups (30/50 amps). 2021 rates: $25. Apr 01 to Oct 31. (417)683-2468, Rt 6 Box 65608, Ava, MO 65608

BENNETT SPRINGS — D3 *Dallas*

BENNETT SPRING (Public State Park) From Jct of I-44 & SR-64, W 12 mi on SR-64 to SR-64A, S 0.8 mi (R). Avail: 123 E (30/50 amps). 2021 rates: $12 to $28. (417)532-4338

BETHANY — A2 *Harrison*

QUAIL RIDGE RV PARK Ratings: 3/NA/5 (Campground) Avail: 10 full hkups (30/50 amps). 2021 rates: $30. (660)373-0835, 4130 Miller St, Bethany, MO 64424

BEVIER — B3 *Macon*

SHOEMAKER'S RV PARK **Ratings: 8/7/8.5** (Campground) Avail: 84 full hkups (30/50 amps). 2021 rates: $28. (660)773-5313, 955 N Macon St, Bevier, MO 63532

BIGELOW — A1 *Holt*

BIG LAKE
(Public State Park) From Jct of I-29 & Hwy 159, SW 9 mi on Hwy 159 to Hwy 111, N 3 mi (L). **FAC:** paved rds. Avail: 76 gravel, back-ins (20x50), 58 E (20/30 amps), tent sites, rentals, dump, laundry, groc, firewood. **REC:** pool, Big Lake: swim, fishing, kayaking/canoeing, playground. Pets OK. Partial handicap access, 15 day max stay. 2021 rates: $12 to $23.
(660)442-3770 Lat: 40.086510, Lon: -95.343904
204 Lake Shore Dr, Craig, MO 64437
mostateparks.com

BISMARCK — D4 *St Francois*

ST JOE (Public State Park) From town, W 0.5 mi on Rte W to Bray Rd, N 0.1 mi to Harrington Rd, NW 4.7 mi (R). Avail: 40 E (30/50 amps). 2021 rates: $12 to $26. (573)431-1069

BLUE EYE — E2 *Taney*

TABLE ROCK LAKE - COE/BAXTER (Public Corps) From town, W 5 mi on Hwy H (E). 54 Avail: 49 W, 49 E (30 amps). 2021 rates: $16 to $21. May 01 to Sep 14. (417)779-5370

TABLE ROCK LAKE - COE/COW CREEK PARK (Public Corps) From town: Go 2 mi S on Hwy-86, then 2 mi N on access road. 23 Avail: Pit toilets. 2021 rates: $25. (417)779-5377

TABLE ROCK LAKE - COE/MILL CREEK (Public Corps) From town, N 4 mi on Hwy 13 to Hwy A W 1 mi (E). 67 Avail: 67 W, 67 E (50 amps). 2021 rates: $21 to $38. Apr 01 to Oct 30. (417)779-5378

TABLE ROCK LAKE - COE/OLD HIGHWAY 86 (Public Corps) From town, E 5.5 mi on Hwy 86 to Hwy UU, N 1.5 mi (E). 77 Avail: 77 W, 77 E (30/50 amps). 2021 rates: $21. Apr 01 to Oct 30. (417)779-5376

BLUE SPRINGS — B2 *Jackson*

BLUE SPRINGS LAKE CAMPGROUND (JACKSON COUNTY PARK) (Public) From jct I-70 & I-470: Go 2 mi S on I-470 to exit 14, then 2/10 mi E on Bowlin Rd to park entrance, then N to campground entrance. 82 Avail: 30 full hkups, 13 W, 52 E (30/50 amps). 2021 rates: $25 to $42. Apr 01 to Oct 31. (816)503-4805

BONA — D2 *Dade*

STOCKTON LAKE - COE/CEDAR RIDGE (Public Corps) From town, E 8 mi on Hwy 32 to Hwy 245, S 5 mi to SR-RA, N 1 mi (E). Avail: 30 E (30/50 amps). 2021 rates: $14 to $24. Apr 16 to Sep 30. (417)995-2045

BONNE TERRE — D4 *St Francois*

ST FRANCOIS (Public State Park) From town, N 4 mi on Hwy 67 (R). Avail: 63 E (30 amps). 2021 rates: $12 to $21. (573)358-2173

STONE PARK RESORT & AMPHITHEATRE
good sam park
Ratings: 5/8.5★/7.5 (RV Park) From jct I-55 & US 67 S: Go 25 mi S on US 67, then 1 mi W on Hwy K, then 3/4 mi N on Berry Rd (R). **FAC:** paved rds. Avail: 31 gravel, 31 pull-thrus, (30x65), 31 full hkups (30/50 amps), tent sites, laundry, fire rings, firewood. **REC:** pond, fishing, hunting nearby, rec open to public. Pets OK. Partial handicap access. Big rig sites, eco-friendly. 2021 rates: $44.
(314)769-2283 Lat: 37.96885, Lon: -90.54308
8614 Berry Road, Bonne Terre, MO 63628
stoneparkmo.com
See ad this page

Park policies vary. Ask about the cancellation policy when making a reservation.

BOONVILLE — B3 *Cooper*

BLACK OAKS MH AND RV COMMUNITY **Ratings: 5/NA/8.5** (RV Area in MH Park) Avail: 10 full hkups (30/50 amps). 2021 rates: $30 to $35. (660)882-6420, 1338 W Ashley Rd, Lot 2, Boonville, MO 65233

BOWLING GREEN — B4 *Pike*

COZY C RV CAMPGROUND
good sam park
Ratings: 9/10★/9 (RV Park) From Jct of US-61 & US-54: Go E 2.5 mi on US-54 (R) Do Not rely on GPS. **FAC:** all weather rds. Avail: 45 all weather, 15 pull-thrus, (25x60), back-ins (25x60), 45 full hkups (30/50 amps), WiFi @ sites, tent sites, dump, laundry, LP gas, firewood. **REC:** boating nearby, hunting nearby, rec open to public. Pet restrict (B). Partial handicap access. Big rig sites, eco-friendly. 2021 rates: $35.
(573)324-3055 Lat: 39.37291, Lon: -91.16341
16733 US-54, Bowling Green, MO 63334
cozyccampground.com
See ad this page

BRANSON — E2 *Stone*

BRANSON See also Blue Eye, Forsyth, Kimberling City & Ozark, MO; Harrison & Omaha, AR.

AMERICA'S BEST CAMPGROUND
good sam park
Ratings: 9.5/10★/9.5 (RV Park) From Jct of US 65 & SR-248, W 1.7 mi on SR-248 (move to right turning lane), continue N 1.3 mi on SR-248 to Buena Vista Rd, W 0.3 mi (L) Note: Use these directions, do not use GPS.

'EXPERIENCE THE DIFFERENCE' AT ABC
America's Best Campground's convenient location is city close & country quiet. FREE WiFi, rallies & groups welcome. Come see why Good Sam members voted us their exclusive Welcome Mat Award Winner 9 consecutive years!

FAC: paved rds. (160 spaces). Avail: 154 gravel, patios, 136 pull-thrus, (28x70), back-ins (28x50), 154 full hkups (30/50 amps), seasonal sites, cable, WiFi @ sites, tent sites, rentals, dump, laundry, groc, LP gas. **REC:** pool, hot tub, boating nearby, playground, hunting nearby. Pets OK. Partial handicap access. Big rig sites, eco-friendly. 2021 rates: $60.62, Military discount.
(800)671-4399 Lat: 36.68314, Lon: -93.25802
499 Buena Vista Rd, Branson, MO 65616
www.abc-branson.com
See ad opposite page

BAR M RESORT & CAMPGROUND **Ratings: 8.5/9★/8.5** (Campground) Avail: 12 full hkups (30/50 amps). 2021 rates: $42.50 to $60. Apr 01 to Nov 01. (417)338-2593, 207 Bar M Lane, Branson West, MO 65737

BLUE MOUNTAIN CAMPGROUND
good sam park
Ratings: 8.5/9★/9.5 (Campground) Avail: 50 full hkups (30/50 amps). 2021 rates: $30 to $33. (417)338-2114, 8766 State Hwy 76, Branson, MO 65737

BRANSON KOA & CONVENTION CENTER **Ratings: 9.5/10★/9** (Campground) Avail: 143 full hkups (30/50 amps). 2021 rates: $50 to $90. (800)562-4177, 397 Animal Safari Rd, Branson, MO 65616

BRANSON LAKESIDE RV PARK
good sam park
Ratings: 8.5/10★/9.5 (Public) Jct of Hwy 65 & Hwy 248 (Branson Landing Exit): Go .2 mi E on Branson Landing Blvd to traffic circle, take 3rd exit, then continue 0.6 mi E thru 3 traffic lights (stay in L lane as R lane ends) then 0.1 mi E straight into park. Note: Do not cross bridge & do not use GPS. Avail: 135 full hkups (30/50 amps). 2021 rates: $39 to $60. (417)334-2915

BRANSON SHENANIGANS RV PARK **Ratings: 7/UI/9.5** (RV Park) Avail: 29 full hkups (30/50 amps). 2021 rates: $50 to $55. Mar 01 to Jan 07. (417)334-1920, 3675 Keeter St, Branson, MO 65616

BRANSON STAGECOACH RV PARK
good sam park
Ratings: 8.5/9★/8 (Campground) Avail: 35 full hkups (30/50 amps). 2021 rates: $45 to $50. (417)335-8185, 5751 State Hwy 165, Branson, MO 65616

RV MYTH #2: ""Class A and fifth-wheel trailers require special drivers' license endorsements and training.'' In most states and provinces, there are no extra license requirements for these popular RV types. You should, however, verify the local regulations in your home area

BRANSON • MISSOURI

We Have Cabins!

Beautiful Campsites

Your Hosts Jim And Sue Alkire

Campfires, hotdogs and s'mores

Great Family Fun!

- Free Wi-Fi
- Convenience/Gift Shop
- Concrete Patios BBQ Grills & Picnic Tables
- FREEDOM RING Firepit and Pavilion
- 136 Pull-Thrus
- 30/50/100 Amp Service
- Cable TV • Pool & Spa
- Air Conditioned Camping Cabins/Deluxe Cabins
- 300 Seat Meeting Hall
- RV Wash
- BIG RIG PARADISE!!

good sam park

2022 Top Rated 9.5/10★/9.5

Good Sam Members and Veterans Receive 10% DISCOUNT

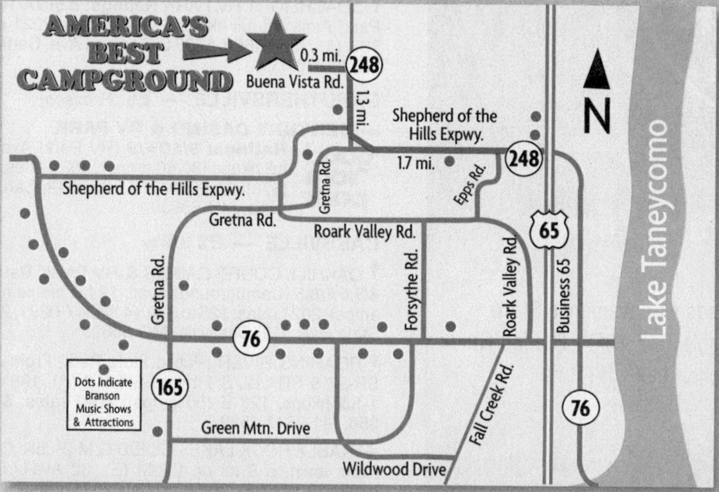

INFO: (417) 336-4399
RESERVATIONS: (800) 671-4399
E-mail: americasbestcampground@gmail.com
499 Buena Vista Road, Branson, MO 65616
Check Our Website for Current Rates & Specials

www.abc-branson.com

See listing Branson, MO

BRANSON (CONT)

BRANSON TREEHOUSE ADVENTURES
good sam park **Ratings: 9/9★/9.5** (Campground) From Jct of US-65 & State Hwy 465/ Ozark Mountain Highroad (North of Branson): Go W 7 mi on State Hwy 465 to Hwy 76, W 2.5 mi (L). **FAC:** gravel rds. (63 spaces). Avail: 56 gravel, 27 pull-thrus, (34x60), back-ins (32x70), 56 full hkups (30/50 amps), seasonal sites, WiFi @ sites, tent sites, rentals, dump, laundry, LP gas, fire rings, firewood. **REC:** pool, boating nearby, playground, hunting nearby. Pets OK. Partial handicap access. Big rig sites, eco-friendly. 2021 rates: $42 to $61.25, Military discount.
(800)338-2504 Lat: 36.67536, Lon: -93.34683
159 Acorn Acres Lane, Branson West, MO 65737
BransonTreeHouseAdventures.com
See ad this page

BRANSON VIEW CAMPGROUND **Ratings: 9/9.5★/8.5** (Campground) Avail: 26 full hkups (30/50 amps). 2021 rates: $50. (417)338-1038, 2362 State Highway 265, Branson, MO 65616

BRANSON VIEW ESTATES MOBILE HOME & RV PARK **Ratings: 4/NA/7.5** (RV Area in MH Park) Avail: 10 full hkups (30/50 amps). 2021 rates: $25. (417)561-2255, 2543 State Hwy F, Branson, MO 65616

COMPTON RIDGE CAMPGROUND & LODGE **Ratings: 7.5/8★/6** (RV Park) Avail: 45 full hkups (30/50 amps). 2021 rates: $47.50. (800)233-8648, 5322 State Hwy 265, Branson, MO 65616

COOPER CREEK RESORT & CAMPGROUND
good sam park **Ratings: 9.5/9.5★/9.5** (Campground) From Jct of US-65 & Hwy 76: Go 1.2 mi W on Hwy 76 to Fall Creek Rd (Yellow Route S), then 1.6 mi S on Fall Creek Rd, then .01 mi E (L) on River Valley Rd, then .1 mi N (L) on Cooper Creek Rd. Follow signs to office. **FAC:** paved rds. Avail: 74 gravel, 28 pull-thrus, (28x70), back-ins (30x50), 74 full hkups (30/50 amps), cable, WiFi @ sites, rentals, laundry, groc, LP bottles, fire rings, firewood. **REC:** pool, Lake Taneycomo: fishing, marina, kayaking/canoeing, boating nearby, playground, hunting nearby. Pets OK. No tents. Big rig sites, eco-friendly. 2021 rates: $41 to $51, Military discount. Mar 01 to Dec 15.
(417)334-4871 Lat: 36.618319, Lon: -93.247985
471 Cooper Creek Road, Branson, MO 65616
coopercreekresort.com
See ad this page

INDIAN POINT PARK (Public State Park) From Jct of Hwys 76 & 76/60, S 2.8 mi on Hwy 76/60 (E). Avail: 74 E (30/50 amps). 2021 rates: $16 to $50. Apr 01 to Oct 30. (417)338-2121

MUSICLAND KAMPGROUND
good sam park **Ratings: 9.5/10★/9.5** (Campground) 101 Avail: 89 full hkups, 12 W, 12 E (30/50 amps). 2021 rates: $42.95 to $53.95. Mar 01 to Dec 30. (417)334-0848, 116 Gretna Rd, Branson, MO 65616

OZARK COUNTRY CAMPGROUND **Ratings: 8.5/9★/9** (Campground) Avail: 20 full hkups (30/50 amps). 2021 rates: $50. (417)334-4681, 679 Quebec Dr, Branson, MO 65616

PEA PATCH RV PARK **Ratings: 7/8.5★/5.5** (RV Park) Avail: 33 full hkups (30/50 amps). 2021 rates: $40 to $48. (417)335-3958, 3330 West Harvey Lane, Branson, MO 65616

SILVER DOLLAR CITY'S CAMPGROUND, CABINS & RVS **Ratings: 9/10★/8** (Campground) Avail: 89 full hkups (30/50 amps). 2021 rates: $37 to $56. Mar 12 to Jan 02. (800)477-5164, 5125 State Hwy 265, Branson, MO 65616

TABLE ROCK (Public State Park) From Jct of US-65 & SR-165, W 5.4 mi on SR-165 (L). Avail: 73 E (50 amps). 2021 rates: $12 to $46. (417)334-4704

TALL PINES CAMPGROUND **Ratings: 7.5/5.5/8.5** (RV Park) 71 Avail: 68 full hkups, 3 W, 3 E (30/50 amps). 2021 rates: $47 to $52. (800)425-2300, 5558 Hwy 265, Branson, MO 65616

TANEYCOMO LAKEFRONT RESORT & RV PARK **Ratings: 7/7.5/7** (RV Park) Avail: 10 full hkups (30/50 amps). 2021 rates: $32. (800)949-9975, 365 Valencia Rd, Branson, MO 65616

TREASURE LAKE RESORT **Ratings: 9/9★/9** (Membership Park) Avail: 573 full hkups (30/50 amps). 2021 rates: $25. (800)455-2961, 1 Treasure Lake Dr, Branson, MO 65616

TURKEY CREEK RV VILLAGE **Ratings: 5.5/9★/7.5** (RV Park) Avail: 15 full hkups (30/50 amps). 2021 rates: $27 to $30. (417)335-8004, 1376 US 65 Business, Hollister, MO 65673

CAMERON — B2 *Clay*

WALLACE (Public State Park) From Jct of I-35 & Wallace State Park exit (Hwy 69), S 0.5 mi on Hwy 69 to Hwy 121, E 2 mi (E). Avail: 42 E (30 amps). 2021 rates: $12 to $23. (816)632-3745

CANTON — A4 *Lewis*

CITY OF CANTON MISSISSIPPI PARK
(Public) From Jct of US 61 & SR-16, E 1.1 mi on SR-16 to 4th St, N 0.1 mi to Henderson St, E 0.2 mi (E). **FAC:** paved rds. Avail: 23 paved, back-ins (16x35), 14 full hkups, 9 W, 9 E (30/50 amps), tent sites, pit toilets, dump, fire rings. **REC:** Mississippi River: fishing, playground, rec open to public. Pets OK. Partial handicap access. Big rig sites, eco-friendly. 2021 rates: $20.
(660)216-5101 Lat: 40.138463, Lon: -91.515728
700 N Front St, Canton, MO 63435
showmecanton.com
See ad this page

CAPE FAIR — E2 *Taney*

TABLE ROCK LAKE - COE/CAPE FAIR (Public Corps) From town, S 1 mi on Hwy 76-82/Lake Rd (E). 81 Avail: 46 W, 68 E (30/50 amps). 2021 rates: $16 to $21. Apr 01 to Oct 30. (417)538-2220

CAPE GIRARDEAU — D5 *Cape Girardeau*

CAPE CAMPING & RV PARK
good sam park **Ratings: 9.5/8.5/8.5** (RV Park) Avail: 40 full hkups (30/50 amps). 2021 rates: $45. (573)332-8888, 1900 N Kings Hwy, Cape Girardeau, MO 63701

THE LANDING POINT RV PARK
good sam park **Ratings: 9/9.5★/9.5** (RV Park) Avail: 48 full hkups (30/50 amps). 2021 rates: $45. (573)334-7878, 3020 Boutin Drive, Cape Girardeau, MO 63701

TRAIL OF TEARS (Public State Park) From Jct of I-55 & US-61 (exit 105, N of town), N 1 mi on US-61 to SR-177, E 10 mi (L). 52 Avail: 7 full hkups, 10 E (20/30 amps). 2021 rates: $12 to $26. (573)290-5268

CARTHAGE — D2 *Jasper*

BALLARD'S CAMPGROUND **Ratings: 5.5/8★/7.5** (Campground) 12 Avail: 6 full hkups, 6 W, 6 E (30/50 amps). 2021 rates: $21 to $30. (417)359-0359, 13965 Ballard Loop, Carthage, MO 64836

BIG RED BARN RV PARK
good sam park **Ratings: 9/10★/10** (RV Park) 55 Avail: 52 full hkups, 3 W, 3 E (30/50 amps). 2021 rates: $45 to $65. (417)358-2432, 5089 County Lane 138, Carthage, MO 64836

CAMP MI CASA ON THE ROUTE RV PARK **Ratings: 8/9★/9** (RV Park) Avail: 35 full hkups (30/50 amps). 2021 rates: $25 to $40. (417)358-7829, 17601 Old 66 Blvd, Carthage, MO 64836

COACHLIGHT RV PARK **Ratings: 8.5/NA/10** (RV Park) Avail: 45 full hkups (30/50 amps). 2021 rates: $35. (417)358-3666, 5305 S Garrison Ave, Carthage, MO 64836

CARUTHERSVILLE — E5 *Pemiscot*

CENTURY CASINO & RV PARK
good sam park **Ratings: 9/10★/9** (RV Park) Avail: 27 full hkups (30/50 amps). 2021 rates: $40. (573)333-6000, 777 E Third St, Caruthersville, MO 63830

CASSVILLE — E2 *Barry*

OAKHILL COURT CABINS & RV PARK **Ratings: 8/8.5★/8.5** (Campground) Avail: 12 full hkups (30/5[illegible] amps). 2021 rates: $25 to $30. (417)847-0291, 2177[illegible] State Hwy 112, Cassville, MO 65625

ROARING RIVER (Public State Park) From Jct o[illegible] SR-37 & SR-112, S 7 mi on SR-112 (R). 168 Avail 1 full hkups, 126 E (50 amps). 2021 rates: $12 t[illegible] $56. (417)847-2539

TABLE ROCK LAKE - COE/BIG M (Public Corps From town, E 8 mi on CR-M (E). 62 Avail: 14 fu[illegible] hkups, 9 W, 9 E (30/50 amps). 2021 rates: $16 t[illegible] $23. May 01 to Sep 14. (417)271-3190

CHESTERFIELD — C4 *St Louis*

DR EDMUND A BABLER MEMORIAL (Public State Park) From Jct of Hwys 44 & 100, E 11 mi on Hwy 100 to Hwy 109, W 0.5 mi on Jct C, N 4 mi, follow signs (L). Two-night minimum stay on weekends. Avail: 43 E (50 amps). 2021 rates: $12 to $23. (636)458-3813

CLARKSVILLE — B4 *Pike*

TIEVOLI HILLS RESORT **Ratings: 8/6/8.5** (Membership Park) Avail: 55 full hkups (30/50 amps). 2021 rates: $38. (573)242-3577, 25795 Hwy N, Clarksville, MO 63336

CLINTON — C2 *Henry*

COZY CORNER RV PARK **Ratings: 8.5/8.5★/8.5** (RV Park) Avail: 110 full hkups (30/50 amps). 2021 rates: $35. (660)885-8824, 460 SE 91 Rd, Clinton, MO 64735

HARRY S. TRUMAN LAKE - COE/SPARROWFOOT PARK (Public Corps) From town, S 4 mi on Hwy 13 to park access rd, E 1 mi (E). Avail: 93 E (30 amps). 2021 rates: $20. (660)885-7546

COLUMBIA — B3 *Boone*

CEDAR CREEK RESORT & RV PARK

good sam park

Ratings: 9.5/9.5★/9.5 (RV Park) From jct I-70 E & MO-J/City Rd 269 (Exit 137): Go 1/4 mi S on MO-J, then 1/2 mi W on County Rd 256/Lloyd Ln, then 1-1/4 mi N on Lloyd Ln (R). **FAC:** all weather rds. Avail: 62 all weather, patios, 18 pull-thrus, (27x80), back-ins (27x40), 62 full hkups (30/50 amps), WiFi @ sites, tent sites, rentals, laundry, fire rings, firewood, controlled access. **REC:** Newman Lake: swim, fishing, kayaking/canoeing, playground, hunting nearby. Pets OK. Partial handicap access. Big rig sites, eco-friendly. 2021 rates: $50.75, Military discount.
(573)239-8340 Lat: 38.945504, Lon: -92.145414
3251 Pinetree Dr. , Columbia, MO 65201
cedarcreekresort.org
See ad this page

COTTONWOODS RV PARK

good sam park

Ratings: 10/10★/10 (RV Park) From Jct of I-70 & US-63 (exit 128A), Go 3 mi N on US-63 to North Oakland Gravel Rd (paved), then 0.25 mi E, then .25 mi N (R); or S-bnd: From Jct of US-63 & Prathersville Rd, Go 0.2 mi E to North Oakland Gravel Rd (paved), then S 0.25 mi (L). **FAC:** paved rds. Avail: 83 all weather, patios, 60 pull-thrus, (30x60), back-ins (30x50), 83 full hkups (30/50 amps), WiFi @ sites, tent sites, dump, laundry, groc, LP gas, fire rings, firewood. **REC:** pool, pond, fishing, playground, hunting nearby. Pets OK. Partial handicap access. Big rig sites, 21 day max stay, eco-friendly. 2021 rates: $48.50, Military discount.
(573)474-2747 Lat: 39.00736, Lon: -92.30191
5170 N. Oakland Gravel Rd, Columbia, MO 65202
cottonwoodsrvpark.com
See ad this page

FINGER LAKES (Public State Park) From town, N 10 mi on US-63 (E). Avail: 16 E (50 amps). 2021 rates: $12 to $23. (573)443-5315

PINE GROVE MHC & RV COMMUNITY **Ratings: 7.5/NA/9** (RV Area in MH Park) Avail: 72 full hkups (30/50 amps). 2021 rates: $45. (573)474-4412, 3900 Clark Ln, Columbia, MO 65202

Travel Services

GANDER RV OF COLUMBIA Your new hometown outfitter offering the best regional gear for all your outdoor needs. Your adventure awaits. **SERVICES:** RV appliance, MH mechanical, staffed RV wash, restrooms. RV Sales. RV supplies, LP gas, dump, emergency parking, RV accessible. Hours: 9am - 7pm.
(866)405-0786 Lat: 38.960157, Lon: -92.202078
8877 Interstate 70 Dr NE, Columbia, MO 65202
rv.ganderoutdoors.com

DANVILLE — B4 *Montgomery*

GRAHAM CAVE (Public State Park) From Jct of I-70 & CR-TT, W 2 mi on CR-TT (E). Avail: 18 E (30 amps). 2021 rates: $12 to $21. (573)564-3476

LAZY DAY CAMPGROUND

good sam park

Ratings: 10/10★/10 (Campground) 54 Avail: 44 full hkups, 8 W, 8 E (30/50 amps). 2021 rates: $41.50. (573)564-2949, 214 Hwy J, Danville, MO 63361

DE SOTO — C4 *Washington*

WASHINGTON (Public State Park) From Jct of SR-110 & SR-21, S 9 mi on SR-21 (R). Avail: 24 E (30 amps). 2021 rates: $8 to $36. (636)586-5768

DEXTER — E5 *Stoddard*

WILDWOOD RV PARK **Ratings: 4.5/NA/5** (RV Park) Avail: 10 full hkups (30/50 amps). 2021 rates: $30. (573)820-0853, 2106 N Outer Rd, Dexter, MO 63841

DIXON — C3 *Pulaski*

BSC OUTDOORS CAMPING & FLOAT TRIPS

good sam park

Ratings: 8/8★/8.5 (RV Park) 40 Avail: 20 full hkups, 15 W, 15 E (30/50 amps). 2021 rates: $40. May 15 to Oct 15. (573)759-7294, 18700 Cliff Road, Dixon, MO 65459

EAGLE ROCK — E2 *Barry*

TABLE ROCK LAKE - COE/EAGLE ROCK (Public Corps) From town, S 3 mi on Hwy 86 (R). 51 Avail: 1 W, 25 E (30/50 amps). 2021 rates: $16 to $21. May 01 to Sep 14. (417)271-3215

EAGLEVILLE — A2 *Harrison*

EAGLE RIDGE RV PARK **Ratings: 7.5/7/8** (Campground) Avail: 23 full hkups (30/50 amps). 2021 rates: $35 to $40. Mar 01 to Nov 30. (660)867-5518, 22708 W 182nd St, Eagleville, MO 64442

EL DORADO SPRINGS — C2 *Cedar*

ARROWHEAD POINT RV PARK & CAMPGROUND **Ratings: 7.5/8/8.5** (Campground) Avail: 43 full hkups (30/50 amps). 2021 rates: $35. (417)876-3016, 755 SW Hwy 54, Osceola, MO 64776

ELLINGTON — D4 *Wayne*

CLEARWATER LAKE - COE/WEBB CREEK (Public Corps) From town, S 2 mi on Hwy 21 to Hwy H, E 10 mi (E). Avail: 26 E (30/50 amps). 2021 rates: $14 to $20. May 15 to Sep 14. (573)223-7777

EMINENCE — D4 *Carter*

OZARK SCENIC RIVERWAY/ALLEY SPRING (Public National Park) From town, W 6 mi on Hwy 106 (L). 161 Avail: 26 W, 26 E (50 amps). 2021 rates: $16 to $38. (573)323-4236

EUREKA — C4 *Jefferson*

ST LOUIS WEST/HISTORIC ROUTE 66 KOA **Ratings: 8.5/10★/8.5** (Campground) 61 Avail: 38 full hkups, 23 W, 23 E (30/50 amps). 2021 rates: $65 to $100. (636)257-3018, 18475 Old Us Hwy 66, Eureka, MO 63025

YOGI BEAR'S JELLYSTONE PARK RESORT AT SIX FLAGS **Ratings: 8.5/8/8.5** (Campground) 47 Avail: 25 full hkups, 22 W, 22 E (30/50 amps). 2021 rates: $31 to $75. Apr 01 to Oct 10. (636)938-5925, 5300 Fox Creek Rd, Pacific, MO 63069

FENTON — C4 *St Louis*

BELLEVILLE RV ESTATES **Ratings: 5/NA/6.5** (RV Area in MH Park) Avail: 10 full hkups (30/50 amps). 2021 rates: $45. (636)343-9182, #1 Heritage Court, Fenton, MO 63026

FLEMINGTON — D2 *Polk*

POMME DE TERRE LAKE - COE/LIGHTFOOT LANDING (Public Corps) From town, S 10 mi on Hwy 83 to CR-RB, E 3 mi (L). 35 Avail: 29 W, 29 E (50 amps). 2021 rates: $16 to $22. Apr 16 to Sep 30. (417)282-6890

FORSYTH — E2 *Taney*

BULL SHOALS LAKE - COE/BEAVER CREEK (Public Corps) From town, E 4 mi on Hwy 160 to Hwy O, S 2.5 mi (R). Avail: 33 E (30/50 amps). 2021 rates: $21 to $22. Apr 01 to Oct 31. (417)546-3708

BULL SHOALS LAKE - COE/RIVER RUN (Public Corps) From Jct of US-160 & 76, S 0.5 mi on US-76 (R) As of Spring 2019 park currently closed until further notice. Call for updates. 32 Avail: 10 W, 32 E (30/50 amps). 2021 rates: $19 to $20. May 01 to Sep 30. (870)425-2700

JELLYSTONE PARK - CAMP RESORT **Ratings: 10/10★/10** (RV Park) Avail: 52 full hkups (30/50 amps). 2021 rates: $45 to $85. Mar 15 to Nov 01. (417)546-3000, 210 Shoals Bend Blvd, Forsyth, MO 65653

SHADOWROCK PARK & CAMPGROUND (Public) N-bnd on US-160 at Jct of SR-76 (R). 110 Avail: 8 full hkups, 102 W, 102 E (30/50 amps). 2021 rates: $7 to $18. Mar 01 to Oct 31. (417)546-2876

FULTON — B3 *Callaway*

RED MAPLES MH AND RV COMMUNITY **Ratings: 6/NA/9** (RV Area in MH Park) Avail: 12 full hkups (30/50 amps). 2021 rates: $35. (573)642-4282, 5315 Red Maples Ln, Fulton, MO 65251

GAINESVILLE — E3 *Ozark*

PONTIAC PARK **Ratings: 5/8★/8** (Campground) 38 Avail: 1 full hkups, 4 W, 18 E (30 amps). 2021 rates: $38. (417)679-3676, 563 Pontiac Cove Road, Pontiac, MO 65729

GLASGOW — B3 *Howard*

STUMP ISLAND RV & CAMPGROUND PARK (Public) From Jct of Hwy 240 & Old Hwy 87, S 0.5 mi on Old Hwy 87 (R). 28 Avail: 6 full hkups, 12 W, 12 E (20 amps). 2021 rates: $20. Apr 01 to Nov 30. (660)338-2377

GOLDEN — E2 *Stone*

VINEY CREEK (Public State Park) From town, NW 4 mi on US-J (E). 45 Avail: 23 W, 23 E (30/50 amps). 2021 rates: $10 to $40. May 01 to Oct 31. (417)271-1001

GRAIN VALLEY — B2 *Jackson*

TRAILSIDE RV PARK & STORE **Ratings: 7.5/UI/6** (Campground) 69 Avail: 40 full hkups, 29 W, 29 E (30/50 amps). 2021 rates: $40 to $42. (800)748-7729, 1000 R.D. Mize Rd, Grain Valley, MO 64029

Travel Services

CAMPING WORLD OF GRAIN VALLEY/KANSAS CITY As the nation's largest retailer of RV supplies, accessories, services and new and used RVs, Camping World is committed to making your total RV experience better. **SERVICES:** tire, RV appliance, MH mechanical, staffed RV wash, restrooms. RV Sales. RV supplies, LP gas, RV accessible. Hours: 9am - 7pm.
(888)504-5167 Lat: 39.025210, Lon: -94.224800
3001 NE Jefferson Rd, Grain Valley, MO 64029
www.campingworld.com

GREENFIELD — D2 *Dade*

MUTTON CREEK MARINA & CAMPGROUND (Public) From town: Go 9 mi N on CR-H, then 1-1/4 mi E on State Hwy Y, then N on Mutton Creek Loop (R). 108 Avail: 53 full hkups, 55 W. 2021 rates: $20 to $25. (417)995-3355

GREENVILLE — D4 *Wayne*

WAPPAPELLO LAKE - COE/GREENVILLE REC AREA (Public Corps) From town, S 2 mi on US-67 (R). 98 Avail: 4 full hkups, 44 W, 94 E (30/50 amps). 2021 rates: $18 to $36. Apr 01 to Nov 18. (573)224-3884

HANNIBAL — B4 *Marion*

HANNIBAL See also Bowling Green, MO; Quincy, IL.

MARK TWAIN CAVE & CAMPGROUND **Ratings: 6.5/8.5/8** (Campground) 77 Avail: 61 full hkups, 9 W, 7 E (30/50 amps). 2021 rates: $33 to $38. (800)527-0304, 300 Cave Hollow Road, Hannibal, MO 63401

HERMANN — C4 *Gasconade*

HERMANN CITY PARK (Public) In town, Hwy 100 to Gasconade St, N 0.5 mi (R). 51 Avail: 43 full hkups, 8 E (30/50 amps). 2021 rates: $20 to $30. Mar 24 to Oct 31. (573)486-5400

HERMITAGE — C2 *Hickory*

POMME DE TERRE LAKE - COE/DAMSITE (Public Corps) From town, S 3 mi on Hwy 254, W 0.5 mi (L). 95 Avail: 1 full hkups, 79 W, 79 E (30/50 amps). 2021 rates: $14 to $22. Apr 16 to Sep 30. (417)745-2244

POMME DE TERRE LAKE - COE/NEMO LANDING (Public Corps) From Jct of Hwys 254 & 64, S 4 mi on Hwy 64 (L). 112 Avail: 29 W, 54 E (30/50 amps). 2021 rates: $14 to $22. Apr 16 to Sep 30. (417)993-5529

POMME DE TERRE LAKE - COE/OUTLET PARK (Public Corps) From town, S 4 mi on Hwy 254 (R). 21 Avail: 15 W, 15 E (15/50 amps). 2021 rates: $14 to $22. Apr 16 to Sep 30. (417)745-2290

POMME DE TERRE LAKE - COE/WHEATLAND (Public Corps) From town, S 4 mi on Hwy 83 to Hwy 254, S 3 mi to Hwy 254/25, S 2 mi (E). 73 Avail: 41 W, 67 E (30/50 amps). 2021 rates: $14 to $22. Apr 16 to Sep 30. (417)745-6411

HIGGINSVILLE — B2 *Clay*

FAIRGROUND PARK (Public) From Jct of I-70 & Hwy 13, N 4 mi on Hwy 13 (R). Avail: 52 E (20/30 amps). 2021 rates: $10. (660)584-7313

GREAT ESCAPE RV & CAMP RESORT **Ratings: 8.5/7.5/8** (RV Park) Avail: 66 full hkups (30/50 amps). 2021 rates: $45. (660)584-2649, 19912 Old Hwy 40, Higginsville, MO 64037

HOLLISTER — E2 *Taney*

HIDDEN VALLEY MOBILE HOME & RV PARK **Ratings: 5/NA/6.5** (RV Area in MH Park) Avail: 11 full hkups (30/50 amps). 2021 rates: $25. (417)335-2322, 110 Creek Drive, Hollister, MO 65672

INDEPENDENCE — B2 *Jackson*

THE CAMPUS RV PARK **Ratings: 8/UI/9** (Campground) Avail: 30 full hkups (30/50 amps). 2021 rates: $35. (816)254-1815, 500 W Pacific, Independence, MO 64050

IRONTON — D4 *Iron*

TAUM SAUK (Public State Park) From jct Hwy 21 and Hwy CC: Go 4 mi W on Hwy CC. 12 Avail: Pit toilets. 2021 rates: $12 to $13. (573)546-2450

JEFFERSON CITY — C3 *Cole*

BINDER CAMPGROUND (Public) From Jct of Hwy 50 & Bus 50 (St Martins Apache Flats Exit), W 1.2 mi on Bus 50 to Binder Rd, N 0.3 mi to Rainbow Dr, W 0.1 mi (R). Avail: 17 full hkups (30/50 amps). 2021 rates: $22. (573)634-6482

MARI OSA DELTA CAMPGROUND **Ratings: 7/8★/7** (Campground) 10 Avail: 6 full hkups, 4 W, 4 E (30/50 amps). 2021 rates: $37. (573)455-2452, 285 Mari Osa Delta Lane, Jefferson City, MO 65101

MILITARY PARK LAKE OF THE OZARKS REC AREA (FORT LEONARD WOOD) (Public) From Jct of I-70 & Hwy 63, S 21 mi on Hwy 63 to US-54, SW 40 mi to SR-A, E 6 mi to McCubbins Dr, N 5 mi, follow signs. Avail: 17 full hkups (30/50 amps). 2021 rates: $25 to $30. (573)346-5640

OSAGE CAMPGROUND RETREAT **Ratings: 5.5/9★/8** (Campground) 38 Avail: 24 full hkups, 14 W, 14 E (30/50 amps). 2021 rates: $38. (573)395-4066, 10407 Marina Rd, Jefferson City, MO 65101

JONESBURG — C4 *Montgomery*

JONESBURG GARDENS CAMPGROUND **Ratings: 7/7/4.5** (Campground) Avail: 45 full hkups (30/50 amps). 2021 rates: $38. (636)488-5630, 15 Hwy E, Jonesburg, MO 63351

Find it fast! Use our alphabetized index of campgrounds and parks.

JOPLIN — D1 *Newton*

JOPLIN See also Carthage, Neosho & Sarcoxi, MO; Pittsburg, KS; Miami & Wyandotte, OK.

BIG SHOAL RV COUNTRY **Ratings: 8/5/7** (Campground) Avail: 32 full hkups (30/50 amps). 2021 rates: $50. (417)438-3003, 6821 Gateway Dr #1, Joplin, MO 64804

DOWNSTREAM Q STORE RV PARK **Ratings: 7/NA/8.5** (RV Park) 36 Avail: 36 W, 36 E (30/50 amps). 2021 rates: $30. (417)626-6750, 4777 Downstream Blvd, Joplin, MO 64804

KANSAS CITY — B1 *Clay*

KANSAS CITY See also Grain Valley, Higginsville, Independence, Kansas City, Maysville, Oak Grove, Odessa, Peculiar, Platte City & St Joseph, MO; Lawrence, Linn Valley & Merriam, KS.

LONGVIEW LAKE (JACKSON COUNTY PARK) (Public) From Jct of US-71 & I-470, E 4.2 mi on I-470 to View High Dr (exit 5), S 2.9 mi to Longview Dr. W 0.4 on Longview Dr (follow signs to campground on no name rd), 2 mi (E). 76 Avail: 17 full hkups, 59 E (30/50 amps). 2021 rates: $20 to $30. Apr 01 to Sep 30. (816)503-4800

WORLDS OF FUN VILLAGE **Ratings: 9.5/9.5★/8.5** (RV Park) Avail: 82 full hkups (30/50 amps). 2021 rates: $29 to $59. Mar 01 to Oct 30. (816)454-4545, 8000 NE Parvin Rd., Kansas City, MO 64161

KIMBERLING CITY — E2 *Stone*

PORT OF KIMBERLING MARINA & RESORT **Ratings: 7.5/9★/9** (Campground) 38 Avail: 30 full hkups, 8 W, 8 E (30/50 amps). 2021 rates: $40 to $70. (417)739-3883, 201 Marina Way, Kimberling City, MO 65686

TABLE ROCK LAKE - COE/AUNTS CREEK PARK (Public Corps) From town: Go 4 mi S on Hwy 13, then 3 mi W on Hwy 00 (E). 55 Avail: 21 W, 53 E (30/50 amps). 2021 rates: $16 to $36. May 01 to Sep 14. (417)739-2792

KIRKSVILLE — A3 *Adair*

LAKEROAD VILLAGE RV PARK **Ratings: 4.5/7.5★/7.5** (RV Park) Avail: 15 full hkups (30/50 amps). 2021 rates: $30. (660)665-2228, 23067 Potter Trail, No 1, Kirksville, MO 63501

THOUSAND HILLS (Public State Park) From town, W 2 mi on Hwy 6 to Hwy 157, S 2 mi (L). Avail: 38 E (30 amps). 2021 rates: $12 to $42. (660)665-6995

KNOB NOSTER — C2 *Benton*

KNOB NOSTER (Public State Park) From town, W 1 mi on US-50 to Hwy 23, S 2 mi (R). Avail: 37 E (30 amps). 2021 rates: $12 to $36. (660)563-2463

LA GRANGE — A4 *Lewis*

WAKONDA (Public State Park) From town, S 3 mi on US-61 to Rte B exit, follow signs (L). 81 Avail: 4 full hkups, 65 E (50 amps). 2021 rates: $12 to $28. (573)655-2280

LACLEDE — B2 *Clay*

PERSHING (Public State Park) From town, W 3 mi on US-36 to SR-130, S 2 mi (R). Avail: 26 E (30 amps). 2021 rates: $13 to $21. (660)963-2299

LAKE OF THE OZARKS — C3 *Miller*

LAKE OF THE OZARKS See also Lake Ozark, Laurie, Linn Creek & Osage Beach.

LAKE OZARK — C3 *Miller*

MAJESTIC OAKS PARK **Ratings: 9/7/8** (Campground) 42 Avail: 33 full hkups, 9 W, 9 E (30/50 amps). 2021 rates: $35 to $39. May 25 to Oct 31. (573)365-1890, 8 Majestic Oaks Rd, Eldon, MO 65026

RIVERVIEW RV PARK
good sam park **Ratings: 10/10★/10** (Campground) Avail: 75 full hkups (30/50 amps). 2021 rates: $45. (573)365-1122, 398 Woodriver Road, Lake Ozark, MO 65049

LAURIE — C3 *Morgan*

LAURIE RV PARK **Ratings: 5/5/6.5** (Campground) Avail: 21 full hkups (30/50 amps). 2021 rates: $37. (573)374-8469, 515 Hwy O, Laurie, MO 65037

LAWSON — B2 *Clay*

WATKINS MILL (Public State Park) From Jct of US-69 & Hwy 92, W 1.5 mi on Hwy 92. Avail: 74 E (50 amps). 2021 rates: $12 to $40. (816)580-3387

LEASBURG — C4 *Crawford*

ONONDAGA CAVE (Public State Park) From Jct of I-44 & Hwy H (Leasburg exit), S 6 mi on Hwy H (R). 64 Avail: 45 W, 45 E (50 amps). 2021 rates: $12 to $50. (573)245-6576

OZARK OUTDOORS/RIVERFRONT RESORT **Ratings: 8/9★/9.5** (Campground) Avail: 210 full hkups (30/50 amps). 2021 rates: $27 to $32.50. (800)888-0023, 200 Ozark Outdoors Lane, Leasburg, MO 65535

LEBANON — D3 *Laclede*

HIDDEN VALLEY FAMILY OUTFITTERS **Ratings: 8.5/9★/10** (RV Park) 88 Avail: 52 full hkups, 26 W, 26 E (30/50 amps). 2021 rates: $34 to $38.50. Mar 01 to Oct 31. (417)533-5628, 27101 Marigold Dr, Lebanon, MO 65536

RUSTIC TRAILS RV PARK **Ratings: 8/9.5★/7** (Campground) 30 Avail: 17 full hkups, 13 W, 13 E (30/50 amps). 2021 rates: $39.95. (417)532-3422, 18376 Campground Rd, Phillipsburg, MO 65722

LEES SUMMIT — B2 *Jackson*

FLEMING PARK/BLUE SPRINGS CAMPGROUND (Public) From Jct of I-70 & I-470 (Exit 14): Go S 2.5 mi on I-470 to Bowlin Rd, then E 0.4 mi on Bowlin Rd to NE Campground Rd, then N 0.4 (E). 82 Avail: 30 full hkups, 13 W, 52 E (30/50 amps). 2021 rates: $23 to $30. May 16 to Sep 03. (816)503-4800

JACOMO CAMPGROUND (Public) W'bound from I-470 (exit 10A): Go 1-3/4 mi E on Colbern Rd to park entrance, then 1/2 mi N to campground entrance. E'bound from I-470 (exit 9) & Douglas St: Go 1/4 mi N, then 2-1/2 mi E on Colbern Rd to park entrance, then 1/2 mi N to campground entrance. 57 Avail: 19 full hkups, 21 E (30/50 amps). 2021 rates: $20 to $30. Apr 01 to Oct 31. (816)503-4805

LINN CREEK — C3 *Camden*

LAKE OF THE OZARKS/LINN CREEK KOA **Ratings: 8.5/10★/9.5** (Campground) 85 Avail: 75 full hkups, 10 W, 10 E (30/50 amps). 2021 rates: $44 to $55. (573)346-5490, 4171 US 54, Linn Creek, MO 65052

LOWRY CITY — C2 *St Clair*

HARRY S. TRUMAN LAKE - COE/TALLEY BEND (Public Corps) From Jct of Hwys 13 & C, E 6 mi on Hwy C/becomes Hwy C (R). Avail: 45 E (30 amps). 2021 rates: $8 to $20. (417)644-2024

MACON — B3 *Monroe*

LONG BRANCH (Public State Park) From Jct of Hwys 63 & 36, W 3 mi on Hwy 36 to park access rd, follow signs (E). Avail: 56 E (50 amps). 2021 rates: $12 to $42. (660)773-5229

MARSHALL — B2 *Saline*

VAN METER (Public State Park) From town, NW 12 mi on Hwy 122 (R). Avail: 12 E (30 amps). 2021 rates: $12 to $23. (660)886-7537

MARSHFIELD — D3 *Webster*

RV EXPRESS 66
good sam park **Ratings: 9/10★/9** (RV Park) From Jct of I-44 & Hwy 38 (Spur Rd) Exit 100: Go S 300 ft on Hwy 38/Spur Rd, take immediate L to enter park. **FAC:** paved rds. Avail: 16 paved, patios, 7 pull-thrus, (30x70), back-ins (30x65), 16 full hkups (30/50 amps), cable, WiFi @ sites, laundry. **REC:** pool, hunting nearby. Pets OK. Partial handicap access. No tents. Big rig sites, eco-friendly. 2021 rates: $34 to $38, Military discount.
(417)859-7837 Lat: 37.34329, Lon: -92.92887
1469 Spur Drive, Marshfield, MO 65706
www.rvexpress66.com
See ad opposite page

MAYSVILLE — A2 *DeKalb*

PONY EXPRESS RV PARK & CAMPGROUND **Ratings: 7.5/9★/9.5** (RV Park) Avail: 40 full hkups (30/50 amps). 2021 rates: $35. (816)449-2039, 4469 S Hwy 33, Maysville, MO 64469

MEXICO — B3 *Saline*

LAKEVIEW PARK (Public) From Jct of I-70 & US-54, N 17 mi on US-54 to Lakeview St, W 0.1 mi, S on Fairground (E). Avail: 16 E (20 amps), Pit toilets. 2021 rates: $8 to $10. Apr 01 to Oct 31. (573)581-2100

MIDDLE BROOK — D4 *Iron/St Francois*

JOHNSON'S SHUT-INS (Public State Park) From Jct of Hwy 49/72 & CR-N, N 6 mi on CR-N (R). 55 Avail: 20 full hkups, 21 E (50 amps). 2021 rates: $12 to $30. (573)546-2450

MOBERLY — B3 *Randolph*

THOMPSON CAMPGROUND (Public) From jct US 63 & US 24: Go 3 mi W on US 24, then 1/4 mi S on Rothwell Park Rd. Avail: 24 full hkups (30 amps). 2021 rates: $30. (660)998-0143

MONROE CITY — B3 *Ralls*

MARK TWAIN LAKE - COE/INDIAN CREEK REC AREA (Public Corps) From Jct of Hwy 24 & Hwy HH, S 1.5 mi on Hwy HH to park access rd, E 3 mi (E). Avail: 190 full hkups (30/50 amps). 2021 rates: $8 to $24. Mar 29 to Nov 17. (573)735-4097

MOUNTAIN GROVE — D3 *Wright*

MISSOURI RV PARK

good sam park **Ratings: 5/9/7.5** (Campground) Avail: 40 full hkups (30/50 amps). 2021 rates: $34. (417)926-4104, 2325 Missouri Park Dr, Mountain Grove, MO 65711

NEOSHO — D2 *Newton*

STAGE STOP CAMPGROUND **Ratings: 8.5/9★/9.5** (Campground) Avail: 10 full hkups (30/50 amps). 2021 rates: $30 to $35. (417)455-1221, 12201 Hammer Rd, Neosho, MO 64850

NEVADA — C2 *Vernon*

OSAGE PRAIRIE RV PARK **Ratings: 9.5/9.5★/8** (RV Park) Avail: 45 full hkups (30/50 amps). 2021 rates: $38 to $44. (417)667-2267, 1501 N Osage Blvd, Nevada, MO 64772

NOEL — E1 *McDonald*

RIVER RANCH RESORT **Ratings: 5.5/5/7.5** (Campground) 31 Avail: 13 full hkups, 18 W, 18 S (20/50 amps). 2021 rates: $40 to $120. May 15 to Sep 15. (800)951-6121, 101 River Road, Noel, MO 64854

OAK GROVE — B2 *Jackson*

KANSAS CITY EAST/OAK GROVE KOA HOLIDAY **Ratings: 9.5/9★/8** (Campground) Avail: 79 full hkups (30/50 amps). 2021 rates: $40 to $75. (816)690-6660, 303 NE 3rd St, Oak Grove, MO 64075

ODESSA — B2 *Lafayette*

OWL CREEK MARKET + RV PARK

good sam park **Ratings: 7.5/10★/9** (RV Park) Avail: 45 full hkups (30/50 amps). 2021 rates: $39 to $55.98. (816)633-8720, 7089 Outer Rd, Odessa, MO 64076

OSAGE BEACH — C3 *Miller*

LAKE OF THE OZARKS (Public State Park) From Jct of US-54 & Hwy 42, E 4 mi on Hwy 42 to Hwy 134, S 5 mi (L). Avail: 124 E (50 amps). 2021 rates: $12 to $40. (573)348-2694

OSAGE BEACH RV PARK

good sam park **Ratings: 10/10★/10** (Campground) From Jct US 54 Expressway & SR-42/ Osage Beach Parkway North Exit: Go N 1/2 mi on SR-42,then E 1/4 mi on (watch for sign on right) to Access Road (watch for sign on R), then S 1/10 mi to office (R). **FAC:** all weather rds. (92 spaces). Avail: 45 all weather, patios, 24 pull-thrus, (26x70), back-ins (34x54), 45 full hkups (30/50 amps), seasonal sites, cable, WiFi @ sites, dump, laundry, LP gas, firewood, controlled access. **REC:** pool, wading pool, boating nearby, shuffleboard, playground, hunting nearby. Pet restrict (B/Q). No tents. Big rig sites, eco-friendly. 2021 rates: $50 to $54, Military discount. Apr 01 to Oct 31.
(573)348-3445 Lat: 38.152729, Lon: -92.602989
3949 Campground Lane, Osage Beach, MO 65065
osagebeachrvpark.net
See ad this page

OSCEOLA — C2 *St Clair*

OSCEOLA RV PARK (Public) S-bnd: Jct SR-13 & Bus 13/Truman Rd (N of town at Hospital H sign), W 0.5 mi on Bus 13/Truman to Parkview Dr, N 300 ft (L); or N-bnd: Jct SR-13 & Bus 13/SR-82 (S of town), W 0.1 on Bus 13/SR-82 to Bus 13, W 1 mi to Lakeshore Dr, N 0.3 mi to Parkview Dr, N 300 ft (L). 52 Avail: 44 full hkups, 8 W, 8 E (30/50 amps). 2021 rates: $17 to $18. Mar 15 to Nov 30. (417)646-8675

OZARK — D2 *Christian*

LAMBERTS CAFE RV PARK **Ratings: 4/NA/5** (RV Park) Avail: 34 full hkups (30/50 amps). 2021 rates: $30. (417)844-6058, 1751 W Boat St, Ozark, MO 65721

SAVE! Camping World coupons can be found at the front and back of this Guide!

PATTERSON — D4 *Wayne*

SAM A BAKER (Public State Park) From Jct of SR-34 & SR-67, W 5 mi to SR-143, N to park entrance (R). Avail: 131 E (30 amps). 2021 rates: $12 to $46. (573)856-4411

PECULIAR — C2 *Cass*

PECULIAR PARK PLACE **Ratings: 9/10★/10** (RV Park) Avail: 95 full hkups (30/50 amps). 2021 rates: $43 to $50. (816)779-6300, 22901 SE Outer Rd, Peculiar, MO 64078

PERRY — B3 *Ralls*

MARK TWAIN LAKE - COE/FRANK RUSSELL (Public Corps) From Jct of Hwy 36 & CR-J, S 12 mi on CR-J (R). Avail: 65 E (30/50 amps). 2021 rates: $18. Mar 29 to Oct 03. (573)735-4097

MARK TWAIN LAKE - COE/RAY BEHRENS (Public Corps) From Jct of Hwys 154 & J, N 7 mi on Hwy J (L). 165 Avail: 43 W, 165 E (50 amps). 2021 rates: $18 to $24. Mar 29 to Nov 17. (573)735-4097

PIEDMONT — D4 *Wayne*

CLEARWATER LAKE - COE/BLUFF VIEW (Public Corps) From town, NW 1 mi on SR-49 to Rte AA, W 6 mi (E). 61 Avail: 35 W, 54 E (30/50 amps). 2021 rates: $14 to $20. May 15 to Sep 15. (573)223-7777

CLEARWATER LAKE - COE/PIEDMONT PARK (Public Corps) From town, SW 7 mi on Rte-HH to Lake Rd 3, N 0.5 mi (L). 92 Avail: 26 W, 84 E (30/50 amps). 2021 rates: $14 to $20. Apr 01 to Sep 30. (573)223-7777

CLEARWATER LAKE - COE/RIVER ROAD PARK (Public Corps) From town, SW 6 mi on Hwy HH (L). 111 Avail: 29 W, 111 E (30/50 amps). 2021 rates: $14 to $40. (573)223-7777

PITTSBURG — D2 *Hickory*

POMME DE TERRE (Public State Park) From town, N 1.7 mi on SR-64, NW 2 mi on SR-64B (E). 256 Avail: 20 W, 201 E (50 amps). 2021 rates: $10 to $40. (417)852-4291

POMME DE TERRE LAKE - COE/PITTSBURG LANDING (Public Corps) From town, S 1 mi on Hwy 64 to SR-RA, E 4 mi (E). 65 Avail. (417)852-4291

PLATTE CITY — B1 *Platte*

BASSWOOD RESORT **Ratings: 9.5/9/9.5** (RV Park) Avail: 63 full hkups (30/50 amps). 2021 rates: $54 to $74. (816)858-5556, 15880 Interurban Rd, Platte City, MO 64079

POPLAR BLUFF — E4 *Butler*

CAMELOT RV CAMPGROUND **Ratings: 8/UI/9** (RV Park) Avail: 66 full hkups (30/50 amps). 2021 rates: $38. (573)785-1016, 100 Camelot Drive, Poplar Bluff, MO 63901

PORTAGEVILLE — E5 *New Madrid*

BOOTHEEL RV PARK & EVENT CENTER

good sam park **Ratings: 8/9.5★/9** (Campground) 38 Avail: 26 full hkups, 12 W, 12 E (30/50 amps). 2021 rates: $35. (573)359-1580, 2824 E Outer Rd., Portageville, MO 63873

REVERE — A3 *Clark*

BATTLE OF ATHENS SHS (Public State Park) From Jct of US-81 & Hwy CC, E 1 mi on Hwy CC, follow signs (L). Avail: 15 E (30 amps). 2021 rates: $12 to $28. Apr 01 to Nov 30. (660)877-3871

Canada -- know the rules, regulations and tips before crossing the border. This is listed at the beginning of the country.

RICHLAND — D3 *Pulaski*

GASCONADE HILLS RESORT **Ratings: 7.5/8.5★/7.5** (Campground) Avail: 18 full hkups (30/50 amps). 2021 rates: $35. Apr 15 to Oct 31. (573)765-3044, 28425 Spring Rd, Richland, MO 65556

ROBERTSVILLE — C4 *Franklin*

ROBERTSVILLE (Public State Park) From Jct of I-44 & Hwy O, S 5 mi on Hwy O (R). Avail: 13 E (30 amps). 2021 rates: $12 to $36. (636)257-3788

ROGERSVILLE — D2 *Greene*

SILVER BELL RV PARK/MHP

Ratings: 5.5/NA/6.5 (RV Area in MH Park) W-bnd: From Jct of US-60 & SR-125, W 0.5 mi on US-60 (R) E-bnd: From Jct of US-65 & US-60, go 7 mi on US-60 to traffic light @ Farm Rd 125, make U-turn to US-60 W 1.2 mi (R). **FAC:** paved rds. (59 spaces). Avail: 26 paved, 26 pull-thrus, (24x75), mostly side by side hkups, accepts full hkup units only, 26 full hkups (30/50 amps), seasonal sites, laundry. **REC:** hunting nearby. Pets OK. No tents. Big rig sites. 2021 rates: $35.
(417)753-2636 Lat: 37.11820, Lon: -93.13007
7711 E. Hwy 60, Rogersville, MO 65742
www.silverbellmhp.com
See ad next page

ROLLA — C3 *Phelps*

THREE SPRINGS RV PARK & CAMPGROUND **Ratings: 6/9★/7** (Campground) Avail: 16 full hkups (30/50 amps). 2021 rates: $32 to $35. (573)458-9185, 24125 CR 6050, South Hwy 63, Rolla, MO 65401

ROUND SPRING — D4 *Shannon*

OZARK SCENIC RIVERWAY/PULLTITE (Public National Park) From town, N 17 mi on Hwy 19 to Rte EE, W 4 mi (E). Avail: 1 W. 2021 rates: $19. (573)323-4236

OZARK SCENIC RIVERWAY/ROUND SPRING (Public National Park) From Jct of US-60 & SR-19, N 25 mi on SR-19 (R). 46 Avail: 7 W, 8 E (15/50 amps). 2021 rates: $19 to $22. (573)858-3297

RUSHVILLE — B1 *Buchanan*

LEWIS & CLARK (Public State Park) From town, SW 20 mi on Hwy 59 to Hwy 45, SE 1 mi (R). Avail: 62 E (50 amps). 2021 rates: $12 to $23. (816)579-5564

SALEM — D4 *Dent*

HAPPY PAPPY'S MONTAUK RV PARK & STORE **Ratings: 4.5/NA/7.5** (RV Park) Avail: 15 full hkups (30/50 amps). 2021 rates: $30. (573)548-7777, 8787 Hwy 119, Salem, MO 65560

MONTAUK (Public State Park) From town, SE 2 mi on SH 137, E 10.3 mi on SH-W. Avail: 116 E (50 amps). 2021 rates: $12 to $46. (573)548-2201

OZARK SCENIC RIVERWAY/TWO RIVERS (Public National Park) From town, W 5.5 mi on SR-106, N 3 mi on SR-V (E). 19 Avail. 2021 rates: $19. (573)323-4236

SARCOXIE — D2 *Jasper*

BEAGLE BAY RV HAVEN & CAMPGROUND (Campground) (Rebuilding) Avail: 36 full hkups (30/50 amps). 2021 rates: $30. (417)548-0000, 2041 Cimarron Road, Sarcoxie, MO 64862

SAVANNAH — A1 *Andrew*

BACK 40 CAMPGROUND AT BARNES ACRES **Ratings: 4.5/4/5** (Campground) Avail: 10 full hkups (30/50 amps). 2021 rates: $33. (816)288-7261, 15609 County Rd 344, Savannah, MO 64485

SEDALIA — C2 *Pettis*

COUNTRYSIDE ADULT RV PARK **Ratings: 6/8.5★/7.5** (RV Park) Avail: 20 full hkups (30/50 amps). 2021 rates: $25. (817)564-3036, 5464 South Limit Avenue (S 65 Hwy), Sedalia, MO 65301

MISSOURI STATE FAIRGROUNDS
(Public) From Jct of US-50 & US-65, S 0.5 mi on US-65 to 16th St, W 0.5 mi to Clarendon, S 1 blk (L). **FAC:** paved/gravel rds. Avail: 1300 grass, 500 pull-thrus, (15x45), back-ins (15x45), mostly side by side hkups, 1300 full hkups (30/50 amps), tent sites, dump, controlled access. **REC:** boating nearby, hunting nearby, rec open to public. Pets OK. Partial handicap access. Big rig sites. 2021 rates: $25. no reservations.
(660)530-5604 Lat: 38.698496, Lon: -93.255040
2503 W 16th St, Sedalia, MO 65301
mostatefairgrounds.com
See ad this page

SHELL KNOB — E2 *Stone*

TABLE ROCK LAKE - COE/CAMPBELL POINT (Public Corps) From town, SE 6 mi on Rte YY (L). 74 Avail: 1 full hkups, 40 W, 64 E (30/50 amps). 2021 rates: $16 to $28. Apr 01 to Oct 30. (417)858-3903

TABLE ROCK LAKE - COE/VIOLA (Public Corps) From town, SW 5 mi on Hwy 39 to Laker Rd 39-48, W 1 mi (E). Avail: 37 E (30/50 amps). 2021 rates: $16 to $28. May 01 to Sep 14. (417)858-3904

SIKESTON — D5 *Scott New Madrid*

CYPRESS CREEK RV PARK
Ratings: 6/NA/8 (RV Park) From Jct of I-55 & US-62 (exit 67), E 1.5 mi on US-62 (R); or From Jct of US-57 & exit 4 (Bertrand), N 0.1 mi to SR-62, W 2 mi (L). **FAC:** paved rds. Avail: 15 gravel, patios, 15 pull-thrus, (30x60), accepts full hkup units only, 15 full hkups (30/50 amps), WiFi @ sites, laundry. **REC:** hunting nearby. Pet restrict (S/B/Q). No tents. Big rig sites. 2021 rates: $40, Military discount.
(573)472-1339 Lat: 36.87286, Lon: -89.53308
1254 U.S. Hwy 62 East, Sikeston, MO 63801
www.cypresscreekrv.com
See ad this page

HINTON RV PARK **Ratings: 8/8.5★/7.5** (RV Park) Avail: 89 full hkups (30/50 amps). 2021 rates: $45. (800)327-1457, 2863 E. Malone Ave, Sikeston, MO 63801

SMITHVILLE — B1 *Clay*

CAMP BRANCH CAMPGROUND (CLAY COUNTY PARK) (Public) From town, N 4 mi on Hwy 169 to Hwy W, E 3 mi to Collins Rd, S 1 mi (R). Avail: 170 E (30/50 amps). 2021 rates: $20 to $25. (816)407-3400

CROWS CREEK (CLAY COUNTY PARK) (Public) From jct I-35 & Hwy 92: Go 4-1/2 mi W on Hwy 92, then 3-1/2 mi N on CR E. 415 Avail: 91 W, 283 E (30/50 amps). 2021 rates: $20 to $50. (816)532-0803

SMITH'S FORK RV PARK (Public) From Jct of I-435 & US 169 (Exit 41B), N 5 mi on US 169 to CR-DD, E 1.9 mi to Litton Way, N 200 ft to Smith Fork Dr, W 0.4 mi (L). Avail: 79 full hkups (30/50 amps). 2021 rates: $30. Apr 01 to Oct 27. (816)532-1028

SPRINGFIELD — D2 *Greene*

SPRINGFIELD See also Marshfield, Ozark & Strafford.

OZARK HIGHLANDS MHC/RV PARK
Ratings: 8/7/7.5 (RV Area in MH Park) Avail: 24 full hkups (30/50 amps). 2021 rates: $40. (417)881-0066, 3731 S Glenstone Ave, Springfield, MO 65804

SPRINGFIELD/RT 66 KOA **Ratings: 7/10★/9.5** (Campground) 72 Avail: 49 full hkups, 23 W, 23 E (30/50 amps). 2021 rates: $45 to $75. (417)831-3645, 5775 W Farm Road 140, Springfield, MO 65802

ST CHARLES — C4 *St Charles*

SUNDERMEIER RV PARK
Ratings: 9/10★/9.5 (RV Park) E-bnd: From Jct I-70 & SR-370 (exit 224): Go E 7-1/2 mi on SR-370, then W 4/10 mi on SR-94/N 3rd St (Exit 7), then E 1/10 mi on Transit St (L) OR W-bnd: From Jct I-270 & SR-370 (Exit 22B): Go W 5-1/2 mi on SR-370, then W 4/10 mi on SR-94/N 3rd St (Exit 7), then E 1/10 mi on Transit St (L).

'AWARD WINNING' FIVE STAR RV PARK
Relive the Early American Spirit in Historic St Charles, convenient to St Louis and St Peters! This charming community, located on the banks of the Missouri River, was Missouri's First State Capitol.

FAC: paved rds. Avail: 114 paved, patios, 39 pull-thrus, (28x80), back-ins (28x55), 114 full hkups (30/50 amps), WiFi @ sites, laundry, LP gas. **REC:** boating nearby, hunting nearby. Pet restrict (B). Partial handicap access. No tents. Big rig sites, eco-friendly. 2021 rates: $56.50 to $60.50, Military discount.
(800)929-0832 Lat: 38.79822, Lon: -90.47381
111 Transit St, St Charles, MO 63301
sundermeierrvpark.com
See ad opposite page

ST JAMES — C3 *Crawford*

MERAMEC SPRINGS COUNTRY STORE & RV PARK **Ratings: 7/UI/8.5** (Campground) Avail: 30 full hkups (30/50 amps). 2021 rates: $32 to $34. (573)265-3796, 20458 Highway 8, St James, MO 65559

PHEASANT ACRES RV PARK **Ratings: 6/UI/8.5** (RV Park) Avail: 10 full hkups (30/50 amps). 2021 rates: $28 to $30. (573)265-5149, 20279 Highway 8 East, St James, MO 65559

ST JOSEPH — B1 *Andrew*

AOK CAMPGROUND & RV PARK
Ratings: 9/10★/8.5 (RV Park) From Jct of I-29 & Bus 71 (exit 53); Go 0.5 N mi on Bus 71 to CR 360, then 0.5 mi W (L) Note: GPS, unless updated, may lead you astray, please follow written directions. **FAC:** gravel rds. (53 spaces). Avail: 35 gravel, 32 pull-thrus, (24x75), back-ins (24x60), mostly side by side hkups, 35 full hkups (30/50 amps), seasonal sites, WiFi @ sites, tent sites, laundry, fire rings, firewood. **REC:** pool, pond, fishing, kayaking/canoeing, playground, hunting nearby. Pets OK. Partial handicap access. Big rig sites, eco-friendly. 2021 rates: $30 to $33.50, Military discount.
(816)324-4263 Lat: 39.864712, Lon: -94.816732
12430 County Rd 360, St Joseph, MO 64505
aokcamping.com
See ad opposite page

BEACON RV PARK
Ratings: 6.5/7/6.5 (RV Park) From Jct of I-29 (exit 46B) & US-36, W 0.2 mi on US-36 to US-169, N 0.8 mi (L). **FAC:** paved rds. (57 spaces). Avail: 37 paved, 8 pull-thrus, (30x60), back-ins (25x60), 37 full hkups (30/50 amps), seasonal sites, WiFi @ sites, laundry, LP gas. **REC:** boating nearby, hunting nearby. Pets OK. No tents. Big rig sites, eco-friendly. 2021 rates: $34.65, Military discount.
(816)279-5417 Lat: 39.759011, Lon: -94.804979
822 S. Belt Hwy, St Joseph, MO 64507
See ad opposite page

SHARP RV PARK Ratings: 6.5/7.5★/8 (Campground) Avail: 10 full hkups (30/50 amps). 2021 rates: $30. (816)262-5799, 18890 Hwy 59, St Joseph, MO 64505

Things to See and Do

GLORE PSYCHIATRIC MUSEUM Recognized as "one of the 500 most unusual Museums in the country". Full sized replicas, interactive displays, audio-visuals, artifacts, documents & photos illustrate how mental illness has been portrayed & treated for the past 7500 years Partial handicap access. Restrooms. Hours: 10am to 5pm. Adult fee: $6. No CC.
(816)232-8471 Lat: 39.77713, Lon: -94.81573
3406 Frederick Ave, St Joseph, MO 64506
www.stjosephmuseum.org
See ad opposite page

PATEE HOUSE MUSEUM NATIONAL HISTORIC LANDMARK This National landmark was a pioneer 140rm luxury hotel, head-quarters for the Pony Express (1860) & where Jesse James died. Visit the Streets of Old St Jo', enjoy western art, antique toys, trains and cars & carousels. Sun 12pm to 4pm Partial handicap access. Restrooms. Hours: 9am to 4pm. Adult fee: $7.
(816)232-8206 Lat: 39.75638, Lon: -94.84494
1202 Penn St, ST Joseph, MO 64502
www.ponyexpressjessejames.com
See ad opposite page

PONY EXPRESS MUSEUM The famous Overland Mail service by horseback began here on April 3, 1860. The state-of-the-art exhibits illustrate the need, creation, operation & termination of the Pony Express. Call for additional hours and rates. Partial handicap access. Restrooms. Hours: 9am to 5pm. Adult fee: $7.00.
(816)279-5059 Lat: 39.75623, Lon: -94.84857
914 Penn, St Joseph, MO 64503
ponyexpress.org
See ad opposite page

ROBIDOUX ROW MUSEUM A series of connected houses built in the late 1840's by city founder Joseph Robidoux. Includes restoration of Robidoux's personal quarters, furnished with some of his own belongings. Hours are Wed - Sat. Restrooms. Hours: 1pm-4pm . Adult fee: $4.00. No CC.
(816)232-5861 Lat: 39.77463, Lon: -94.85722
219 E. Poulin St, St Joseph, MO 64501
www.robidouxrowmuseum.org
See ad opposite page

SOCIETY OF MEMORIES DOLL MUSEUM More than 1,500 dolls & toys ranging from 1840's covered wagon doll, French Jumeau & German antiques, now incorporated into 1879 gothic mansion. Interactive exhibits explore dolls & toys across gender, culture & generations. Apr 05 to Oct 26. Restrooms. Hours: 10am to 5pm. Adult fee: $6.00. No CC.
(816)232-8471 Lat: 39.76510, Lon: -94.84630
3406 Frederick Ave, St Joseph, MO 64506
www.stjosephmuseum.org
See ad opposite page

ST JO FRONTIER CASINO Gambling Showboat on Missouri River. Full Casino and video poker. Sit down restaurant service. Partial handicap access. RV accessible. Restrooms. Food. Hours: 10am to 2am. ATM.
(800)888-2946 Lat: 39.78272, Lon: -94.87487
777 Winners Circle, St Joseph, MO 64505
www.stjofrontiercasino.com
See ad opposite page

ST JOSEPH VISITORS BUREAU Information on St Joseph & all area attractions, hours are Mon - Fri. Partial handicap access. RV accessible. Restrooms. Hours: 9am to 5pm. No CC.
(816)233-6688 Lat: 39.76665, Lon: -94.85537
911 Fredrick, St Joseph, MO 64501
stjomo.com
See ad this page

THE BLACK ARCHIVES MUSEUM OF ST JOSEPH Exhibits include Integration as well as Education; music impact on Blues/Jazz, Underground Railroad and aspects of African-American history in St. Joseph. Includes St Joes African-American Hall of Fame. Open all year, closed holidays. Partial handicap access. Restrooms. Hours: 10am to 5pm Sunday-Friday 10am-4pm Sat.. Adult fee: $6.
(816)232-8471 Lat: 39.77632, Lon: -94.91000
3406 Frederick Ave, St Joseph, MO 64506
www.stjosephmuseum.org
See ad this page

Find Good Sam member specials at GanderOutdoors.com

THE ST JOSEPH MUSEUM Dedicated to the history of St Joseph from prehistoric times to today. Extensive Native American collection. Late soap-opera actress, Ruth Warrick memorabilia. Closed on holidays. Partial handicap access. Restrooms. Hours: 10am to 5pm. Adult fee: $6.
(816)232-8471 Lat: 39.77632, Lon: -94.91000
3406 Frederick Ave, St Joseph, MO 64506
www.stjosephmuseum.org
See ad this page

WYETH-TOOTLE MANSION 1879 Gothic Mansion which illustrates the cultural and economic history of 19th century St Joseph. Open by appointment for groups. Hours are for Friday and Saturday. Apr 05 to Oct 26. Partial handicap access. Restrooms. Hours: 10am to 4pm Thursday & Friday. Adult fee: $7.00. No CC.
(800)530-8866 Lat: 39.76510, Lon: -94.84630
1100 Charles St, St Joseph, MO 64501
www.stjosephmuseum.org
See ad this page

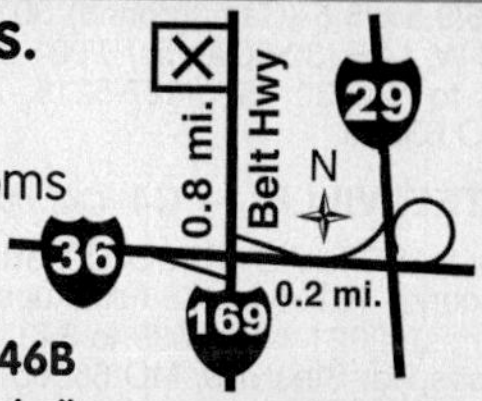

ST LOUIS — C4 *St Louis*

ST LOUIS See also Bonne Terre, Eureka, Fenton, St Charles & Villa Ridge, MO; Baldwin, Cahokia, East St Louis, Granite City & Litchfield, IL.

ST PETERS — C4 *St Charles*

370 LAKESIDE PARK RV CAMPGROUND (Public) From Jct I-70 & Hwy 370 (Exit 224): Go E 2 mi on Hwy 370, then N 1 mi on Truman Rd/Lakeside Park Dr (Exit 2), enter on Lakeside Park Dr (L). Avail: 75 full hkups (30/50 amps). 2021 rates: $45. (636)387-5253

ST ROBERT — D3 *Pulaski*

MOTEL 6 & RV PARK
good sam park **Ratings: 5.5/NA/6** (Campground) Avail: 12 full hkups (30/50 amps). 2021 rates: $35. (573)336-3036, 14175 Hwy Z, St Robert, MO 65584

STANTON — C4 *Franklin*

STANTON/MERAMEC KOA JOURNEY **Ratings: 8.5/9.5★/8.5** (Campground) 30 Avail: 16 full hkups, 14 W, 14 E (30/50 amps). 2021 rates: $42 to $50. Mar 01 to Nov 30. (573)927-5215, 74 Hwy W, Stanton, MO 63080

STEELVILLE — C4 *Crawford*

BASS RIVER RESORT **Ratings: 7/7.5/8** (Campground) 161 Avail: 78 full hkups, 75 W, 83 E (30/50 amps). 2021 rates: $39 to $43. (800)392-3700, 204 Butts Rd, Steelville, MO 65565

CANDY CANE RV PARK **Ratings: 6.5/8/7.5** (Campground) 19 Avail: 5 full hkups, 14 W, 14 E (50 amps). 2021 rates: $34. (573)775-2889, 11 Hwy M, Steelville, MO 65565

HUZZAH VALLEY RESORT **Ratings: 6/8/8.5** (Campground) 135 Avail: 58 full hkups, 77 W, 77 E (30/50 amps). 2021 rates: $25 to $59. (800)367-4516, 970 E Hwy 8, Steelville, MO 65565

STOCKTON — D2 *Cedar*

STOCKTON (Public State Park) From Jct of SR-32 & SR-39, S 4 mi on SR-39 to SR-215, SE 5 m (across bridge). Avail: 53 E (50 amps). 2021 rates: $6 to $40. (417)276-4259

STOCKTON LAKE - COE/CRABTREE COVE (Public Corps) From town, E 2 mi on Hwy 32 (R). Avail: 32 E (30 amps). 2021 rates: $14 to $20. Apr 16 to Sep 30. (417)276-6799

STOCKTON LAKE - COE/HAWKER POINT (Public Corps) From town, S 6 mi on Hwy 39 to Rte H, E 5.2 mi (E). Avail: 30 E (30 amps). 2021 rates: $14 to $20. Apr 16 to Sep 30. (417)276-7266

STOCKTON LAKE - COE/ORLEANS TRAIL (Public Corps) From town, S 0.75 mi on Hwy 39 to SR-RB, E 0.5 mi (E). Avail: 19 E (50 amps). 2021 rates: $14 to $24. Apr 16 to Sep 29. (417)276-6948

STOCKTON LAKE - COE/RUARK BLUFF EAST (Public Corps) From town, S 12 mi on Hwy 39 to Rte Y, E 4.5 mi to Rte H, S 1 mi (E). Avail: 29 E (30 amps). 2021 rates: $14 to $20. Apr 16 to Sep 30. (417)637-5303

STOCKTON MOBILE HOME & RV PARK **Ratings: 4.5/NA/8** (RV Park) Avail: 15 full hkups (30/50 amps). 2021 rates: $25. Apr 15 to Nov 03. (417)276-8212, 416 North 4th St, Stockton, MO 65785

STOUTSVILLE — B3 *Monroe*

MARK TWAIN (Public State Park) From Jct of US-24 & SR-107, S 6 mi on SR-107 (R). Avail: 71 E (50 amps). 2021 rates: $12 to $40. (573)565-3440

STRAFFORD — D2 *Greene*

RUSTIC MEADOWS RV PARK
good sam park **Ratings: 10/9.5★/9** (Campground) W-bnd: From Jct I-44 (Exit 96) & Evergreen Rd: Go 2 1/4 mi W on N service rd (R). E-bnd: From Jct I-44 (Exit 88): Go 0.1 mi N returning over I- 44, then 4.5 Mi E on Evergreen Rd (L). **FAC:** all weather rds. (32 spaces). Avail: 10 all weather, patios, 10 pull-thrus, (24x80), 10 full hkups (30/50 amps), seasonal sites, WiFi @ sites, laundry, LP gas. **REC:** pool, playground, hunting nearby. Pets OK. No tents. Big rig sites, eco-friendly. 2021 rates: $39.35, Military discount.
(417)468-3644 Lat: 37.285548, Lon: -93.039360
2449 Evergreen Rd, Strafford, MO 65757
RusticMeadowsRVPark.com
See ad this page

RV PARK STRAFFORD
Ratings: 6/4.5/5.5 (RV Park) From Jct of I-44 & SR-125 (exit 88), S 0.1 mi on SR-125 to SR-00, E 200 ft (L). **FAC:** gravel rds. (45 spaces). Avail: 10 gravel, 10 pull-thrus, (25x75), 10 full hkups (30/50 amps), seasonal sites, WiFi @ sites, dump, laundry, LP gas. **REC:** hunting nearby. Pets OK. No tents. Big rig sites. 2021 rates: $30. no cc.
(417)736-3382 Lat: 37.27112, Lon: -93.10089
313 E Old Rte 66, Strafford, MO 65757
See ad this page

Travel Services

CAMPING WORLD OF STRAFFORD/SPRINGFIELD As the nation's largest retailer of RV supplies, accessories, services and new and used RVs, Camping World is committed to making your total RV experience better. **SERVICES:** RV, tire, RV appliance, MH mechanical, restrooms. RV Sales. RV supplies, LP gas, dump, emergency parking, RV accessible. Hours: 9am - 7pm.
(888)395-1603 Lat: 37.272125, Lon: -93.123826
373 E Evergreen Rd., Strafford, MO 65757
www.campingworld.com

SULLIVAN — C4 *Crawford*

MERAMEC (Public State Park) From Jct of I-44 & Hwy 185 (exit 226), S 4 mi on Hwy 185 (R). 209 Avail: 21 full hkups, 14 W, 138 E (50 amps). 2021 rates: $12 to $28. May 01 to Oct 01. (573)468-6072

THEODOSIA — E3 *Ozark*

BULL SHOALS LAKE - COE/BUCK CREEK (Public Corps) From town, S 6 mi on Hwy 125 to Buck Creek Park access rd, follow signs (R). 35 Avail: 35 W, 35 E (15/50 amps). 2021 rates: $14 to $22. (417)785-4313

BULL SHOALS LAKE - COE/THEODOSIA PARK (Public Corps) From town, E 1 mi on US-160, follow signs (R). 27 Avail: 19 W, 26 E (30/50 amps). 2021 rates: $16 to $54. May 01 to Sep 30. (417)273-4626

TIGHTWAD — C2 *Henry*

HARRY S. TRUMAN LAKE - COE/BUCKSAW (Public Corps) From Jct MO Hwy 7 to County Hwy U, S 3 mi on CR U to 803 Rd, SE 1.3 mi (R). 167 Avail: 17 full hkups, 75 W, 121 E (30/50 amps). 2021 rates: $10 to $24. (660)477-3402

TRENTON — A2 *Grundy*

CROWDER (Public State Park) From Jct of Hwy 6 & SR-146, N 1 mi on SR-146 (R). Avail: 29 E (50 amps). 2021 rates: $12 to $36. Mar 01 to Nov 30. (660)359-6473

TROY — B4 *Lincoln*

CUIVRE RIVER (Public State Park) From Jct of US-61 & SR-47, E 3 mi on SR-47 to SR-147, N 2 mi, follow signs (E). 100 Avail: 31 full hkups, 19 E (30/50 amps). 2021 rates: $12 to $36. (636)528-7247

Are you using a friend's Guide? Want one of your own? Call 877-209-6655.

UNIONVILLE — A3 *Putnam*

UNIONVILLE CITY PARK (Public) From Jct of US-136 & SR-5, N 3 blks on SR-5 (L). Avail: 45 E (30/50 amps). 2021 rates: $17 to $20. Apr 01 to Oct 31. (660)947-2438

VAN BUREN — D4 *Carter*

BIG SPRING RV CAMP **Ratings: 7/NA/10** (Campground) Avail: 46 full hkups (30/50 amps). 2021 rates: $35. (573)323-8328, 501 Chicopee Road, Van Buren, MO 63965

OZARK SCENIC RIVERWAY/BIG SPRING (Public National Park) From town, S 4 mi on Hwy 103 (R). 119 Avail: 2 W, 31 E (15/50 amps). 2021 rates: $19 to $22. (573)323-4236

THE FAMILY CAMPGROUND ON THE CURRENT RIVER **Ratings: 6/4.5/5.5** (Campground) 68 Avail: 8 full hkups, 60 W, 60 E (30/50 amps). 2021 rates: $35 to $54. Apr 15 to Oct 15. (573)323-4447, County Road M 127/Deer Run #1, Van Buren, MO 63965

VILLA RIDGE — C4 *Franklin*

PIN OAK CREEK RV PARK **Ratings: 8/8/9.5** (RV Park) Avail: 45 full hkups (30/50 amps). 2021 rates: $42 to $80. (636)451-5656, 1302 Highway "AT", Villa Ridge, MO 63089

WAPPAPELLO — D4 *Butler*

WAPPAPELLO LAKE - COE/PEOPLES CREEK (Public Corps) From town, N 2 mi on Hwy D (L). 57 Avail: 19 full hkups, 38 W, 38 E (50 amps). 2021 rates: $20 to $40. (573)222-8234

WAPPAPELLO LAKE - COE/REDMAN CREEK REC AREA (Public Corps) From town, S 2 mi on Hwy T (L). Avail: 105 full hkups (30/50 amps). 2021 rates: $24 to $48. Mar 15 to Oct 31. (573)222-8233

RV SPACE-SAVING TIP: Line your trashcans with multiple bags at once and keep the roll in the bottom of the wastebasket for easy refills. Also, you could even reuse the same bag, if it hasn't gotten too soiled, by simply dumping the trash and leaving the existing bag in it for multiple uses.

WARSAW — C2 *Benton*

HARRY S TRUMAN (Public State Park) From Jct of US-65 & SR-7, W 8 mi on SR-7 to Hwy UU, N 2.5 mi (E). Avail: 117 E (30/50 amps). 2021 rates: $10 to $42. (660)438-7711

HARRY S. TRUMAN LAKE - COE/BERRY BEND (Public Corps) From town, SW 5 mi on Hwy 7 to Hwy Z, S 1.8 mi (L). 119 Avail: 8 full hkups, 110 E (30/50 amps). 2021 rates: $14 to $24. (660)438-3872

HARRY S. TRUMAN LAKE - COE/LONGSHOAL (Public Corps) From town, W 8 mi on Hwy 7 (E). 100 Avail: 2 full hkups, 86 E (30 amps). 2021 rates: $14 to $22. (660)438-2342

HARRY S. TRUMAN LAKE - COE/OSAGE BLUFF (Public Corps) From town, S 2 mi on Hwy 65 to White Branch exit (Old Hwy 65), S 1 mi to Hwy 83, S 5 mi (R). Avail: 41 E (30 amps). 2021 rates: $10 to $20. Apr 15 to Oct 16. (660)438-3873

HARRY S. TRUMAN LAKE - COE/THIBAUT POINT (Public Corps) From town, N 8 mi on Hwy 65 to Hwy T, W 3 mi to Rd 218, S 1 mi (L). 45 Avail: 14 W, 40 E (30/50 amps). 2021 rates: $10 to $22. (660)438-2470

WAYNESVILLE — D3 *Pulaski*

ROUBIDOUX SPRING CAMPGROUND & RV PARK (Public State Park) From jct I-44 (exit 156) & Hwy H & Business I-44: Go 1-3/4 mi NE on Business I-44. Avail: 24 full hkups (30/50 amps). 2021 rates: $20. (573)774-6171

RV Tech Tips - Cat Scratching Solution: RVers like to bring along their cat whenever they travel. But, as cat owners know, kitties have a way of ruining the furniture without a proper outlet for their scratching urges - which makes a scratching post a necessity. To save space - and the furniture - wrap a length of rope around the dinette's table leg for your cat to scratch. It works like a charm, and it lasts for years! Now, you don't have to lug along a bulky scratching post.

WEINGARTEN — C4 *Ste Genevieve*

HAWN (Public State Park) From Jct of I-55 & Hwy 32, W 11 mi on Hwy 32 to Hwy 144, S 4 mi (E). Avail: 25 E (20/30 amps). 2021 rates: $12 to $23. (573)883-3603

WENTZVILLE — C4 *St Charles*

Travel Services

CAMPING WORLD OF WENTZVILLE/ST LOUIS

CAMPING WORLD As the nation's largest retailer of RV supplies, accessories, services and new and used RVs, Camping World is committed to making your total RV experience better. **SERVICES:** RV, MH mechanical, staffed RV wash, restrooms. RV Sales. RV supplies, LP gas, dump, emergency parking, RV accessible. Hours: 9am - 7pm. (888)892-2439 Lat: 38.807780, Lon: -90.803780 2200 E Pitman Ave, Wentzville, MO 63385 www.campingworld.com

WEST PLAINS — E3 *Howell*

ROAD RUNNER RV PARK **Ratings: 8.5/9.5★/8.5** (RV Park) Avail: 10 full hkups (30/50 amps). 2021 rates: $35. (417)257-5658, 4598 County Rd 4620, West Plains, MO 65775

WESTON — B1 *Platte*

WESTON BEND (Public State Park) From town, S 1 mi on Hwy 45 (L). Avail: 32 E (50 amps). 2021 rates: $12 to $46. (816)640-5443

WILLIAMSVILLE — D4 *Wayne*

LAKE WAPPAPELLO (Public State Park) From town,S 15 mi on Hwy 67 to SR-172, E 8 mi (E). Avail: 68 E (50 amps). 2021 rates: $10 to $24. (573)297-3232

How much will it all cost? Use this as a guide: Rates shown are the minimum and maximum for two adults in one RV at the time of inspection (excluding any additional fees for items not at the site). Remember, these rates serve as guidelines only. It's always best to call ahead for the most current rate information.

YOU ARE HERE

Montana

DID YOU KNOW?

Former Montana state capitals Virginia City and Bannack are now two of the best-preserved ghost towns in the country.

What do you get when a "Big Sky" meets big mountains, rivers and lakes? Montana is a place where fat trout leap out of waterways and snowcapped mountains loom above. You won't run out of adventure in Montana.

Good to Great

Billings is Montana's largest town, but many visitors come to know the state through the "Gateway Cities" that welcome guests to Glacier and Yellowstone National Parks. Be spellbound by a stay in Kalispell, gateway to Glacier National Park, where the mountains rise and the rivers run. Refuel for all of your outdoor adventures. Bordered by mountains and public lands, Bozeman is a gorgeous retreat and one of the largest towns near Yellowstone, while smaller towns like West Yellowstone and Gardiner are literally at the doorstep of this enthralling park.

Giant Glacier

While a portion of Yellowstone National Park lies in Montana, Glacier National Park truly is the state's pride and joy. A mesmerizing mixture of mountains and surreal-colored lakes would be enough to make this park beautiful, but what truly sets it apart is the glaciers. These ice behemoths are accessible here. Take a trail or boat and prepare to be amazed. Going-to-the-Sun Road snakes through the park, with picturesque views around each curve. Truly experience the scenery by hiking, biking, fishing or paddling through it.

Nirvana for Fly-fishing

Legions of anglers put Montana at the top of their fishing bucket lists. As one of the nation's legendary fly-fishing regions, Montana's cold, clean rivers are teeming with trout. Places like the Missouri, Madison and Gallatin Rivers not only offer epic fishing, the scenery is absolutely captivating. Boaters and

Montana Huckleberry Pie

Dubbed Montana's purple gems, huckleberries are native to the state and grow at elevations over 3,500 feet. The tart berries taste fantastic in baked goods, especially pies. Locals say you can find the best huckleberry pie at bakeries like Glacier Highland (West Glacier) and Huckleberry Patch (Hungry Horse).

VISITOR CENTER

TIME ZONE
Mountain Standard

ROAD & HIGHWAY INFORMATION
800-226-7623
mdt.mt.gov/travinfo

FISHING & HUNTING INFORMATION
406-444-2535
fwp.mt.gov/aboutfwp/contact-us

BOATING INFORMATION
406-444-2535
fwp.mt.gov/activities/boating/rules-regulations

NATIONAL PARKS
nps.gov/mt

STATE PARKS
stateparks.mt.gov

TOURISM INFORMATION
Montana Office of Tourism
800-847-4868
visitmt.com

TOP TOURISM ATTRACTIONS
1) Glacier National Park
2) Yellowstone National Park
3) Lewis and Clark Trail

MAJOR CITIES
Billings, Missoula, Great Falls, Bozeman, Butte, Helena (capital)

anglers alike will enjoy Flathead Lake, the largest natural lake west of the Mississippi. Just brace yourself if you jump in since these cold waters are literally breathtaking.

A Forest Find

A rain forest in Montana? Don't look surprised. Kootenai National Forest is a unique experience. Walk amid ancient Western Red Cedars in the Ross Creek Scenic Area. These towering beasts reach 175 feet tall and have massive trunks topping eight feet in diameter.

Going Deep in Big Sky Country

Experience a completely different side of the state in Clark Caverns State Park. Explore intricate limestone caverns to gawk at staggering stalactites, stalagmites and other mineral formations. Above ground, take advantage of 10 miles of hiking trails and a variety of camping facilities.

Montana History

Billings is the largest city in the state and a great place to uncover Montana's rich history. Take a step back in time at the historic Moss Mansion, or check out the more than16,000 artifacts at the Western Heritage Center. Just outside of town is Little Bighorn Battlefield National Monument, the site where the 7th Cavalry Regiment, led by General George Custer, met defeat at the hands of the Sioux and Cheyenne in 1876. The historic site features the Custer National Cemetery, Indian Memorial, 7th Cavalry Memorial, Reno-Benteen Battlefield, a visitor center and a museum.

Wildflowers flourish with Glacier National Park in the background. Glacier has 700 miles of hiking trails.

Beautiful Butte

History buffs will make more discoveries in the town of Butte, a mining center that was home to a vibrant Irish and Polish immigrant population. Those in the know can try and time their stay with one of the town's fun-filled annual festivals like Evel Knievel Days, honoring the daredevil every July.

good sam park

Featured Good Sam Parks

MONTANA

When you stay with Good Sam, you can expect the highest degree of cleanliness and friendliness, and better yet, you get **10% off** overnight campground fees.

If you're not already a Good Sam member you can purchase your membership at one of these locations:

ALDER
Ruby Valley Campground & RV Park

ANACONDA
Copper Court RV Park

BIG TIMBER
Spring Creek Campground & Trout Ranch

BILLINGS
Billings Village RV Park
Yellowstone River RV Park & Campground

BOZEMAN
Bozeman Trail Campground

BROWNING
Sleeping Wolf Campground & RV Park

CHOTEAU
Choteau Mountain View RV Campground

COLUMBIA FALLS
Glacier Peaks RV Park
Mountain View RV Park

COLUMBUS
Mountain Range RV Park

CUT BANK
Glacier Mist RV Park

DEER LODGE
Indian Creek RV Park & Campground

DILLON
Beaverhead River RV Park & Campground
Countryside RV Park
Southside RV Park

EAST GLACIER PARK
Red Eagle Campground

EMIGRANT
Yellowstone's Edge RV Park

ENNIS
Ennis RV Village

ESSEX
Glacier Meadow RV Park

GARDINER
Yellowstone RV Park

GARRISON
Riverfront RV Park

GARRYOWEN
7th Ranch RV Camp

GLASGOW
Shady Rest RV Park

GREAT FALLS
Dick's RV Park

HARDIN
Grandview Camp & RV Park

HAVRE
Hansen Family Campground & Storage

HUNGRY HORSE
Mountain Meadow RV Park & Cabins

KALISPELL
Rocky Mountain 'Hi' RV Park and Campground
Spruce Park On the River

LIVINGSTON
Osen's RV Park

MELROSE
The Sportsman Lodge, Cabins & RV

MISSOULA
Jim & Mary's RV Park

POLSON
Big Arm Resort & Marina

PROCTOR
The Lodge & Resort at Lake Mary Ronan

REED POINT
Old West RV Park

ROLLINS
Rollins RV Park & Restaurant

SHELBY
Shelby RV Park and Resort
Trails West RV Park

ST MARY
Chewing Black Bones Campground

ST REGIS
Campground St Regis
Nugget RV Park

WEST GLACIER
West Glacier RV Park & Cabins

WEST YELLOWSTONE
Buffalo Crossing RV Park
Yellowstone Grizzly RV Park
Yellowstone Holiday RV Campground & Marina

10/10★/10 GOOD SAM PARK

ST REGIS
Nugget RV Park
(406)649-2122

What's This?

An RV park with a 10/10★/10 rating has scored perfect grades in amenities, cleanliness and appearance ("See Understanding the Campground Rating System" on pages 8 and 9 for an explanation of the trusted Good Sam Rating System). Stay in a 10/10★/10 park on your next trip for a nearly flawless camping experience.

Getty Images/iStockphoto

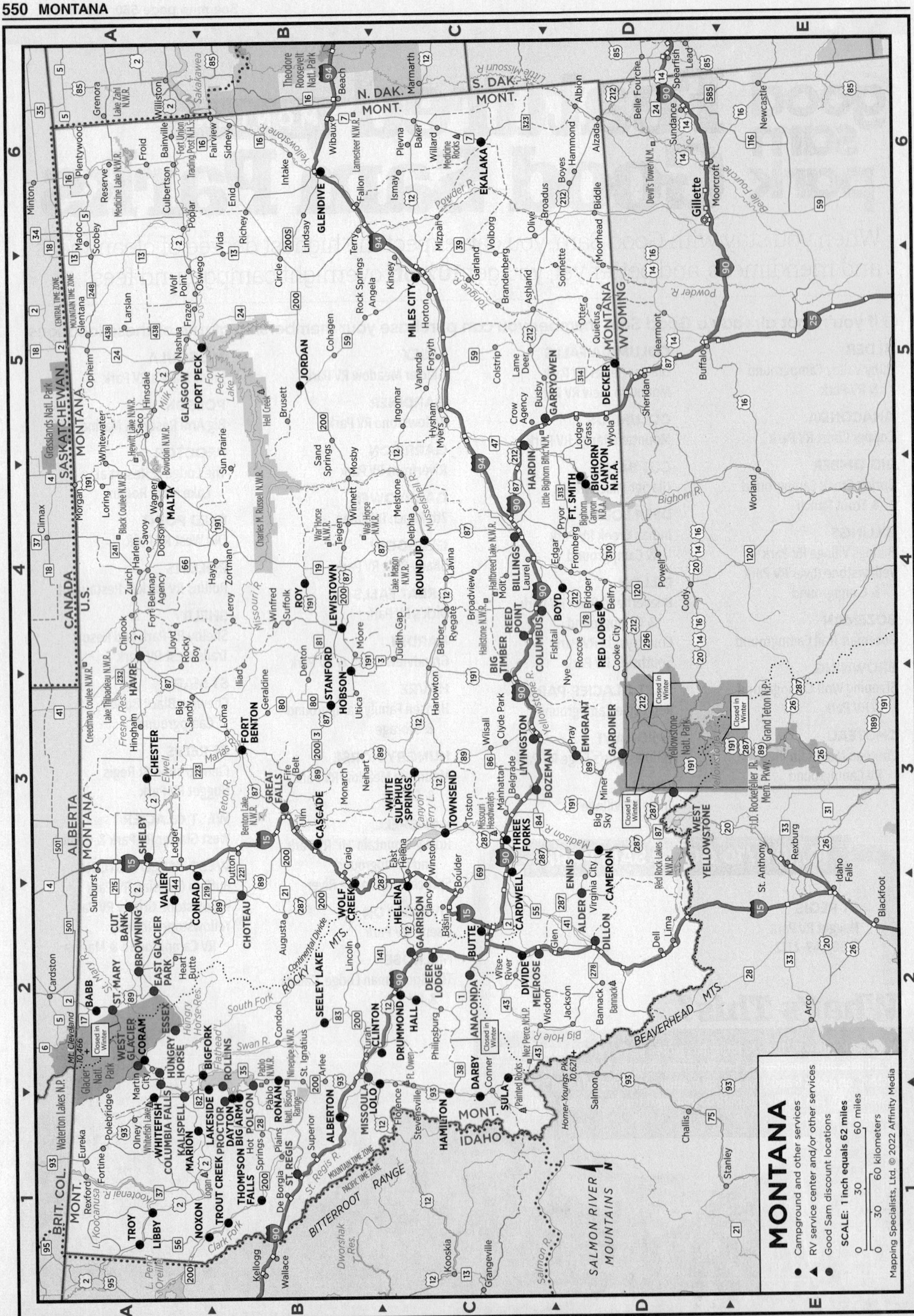
MONTANA
Campground and other services
RV service center and/or other services
Good Sam discount locations
SCALE: 1 inch equals 62 miles
0 30 60 miles
0 30 60 kilometers
Mapping Specialists, Ltd. © 2022 Affinity Media
CANADA
U.S.
ALBERTA
SASKATCHEWAN
BRIT. COL.
N. DAK.
S. DAK.
WYOMING
IDAHO
MONT.
MONTANA
Glacier Natl. Park
Yellowstone Natl. Park
Grand Teton N.P.
Theodore Roosevelt Natl. Park
Charles M. Russell N.W.R.
Fort Peck Lake
BITTERROOT RANGE
BEAVERHEAD MTS.
SALMON RIVER MOUNTAINS
ROCKY MTS.
Continental Divide
MOUNTAIN TIME ZONE
PACIFIC TIME ZONE
CENTRAL TIME ZONE
Yellowstone R.
Missouri R.
Powder R.
Bighorn R.
Closed in Winter
TROY
LIBBY
NOXON
TROUT CREEK
THOMPSON FALLS
ST. REGIS
ALBERTON
MISSOULA
LOLO
HAMILTON
DARBY
SULA
WHITEFISH
COLUMBIA FALLS
KALISPELL
MARION
LAKESIDE
PROCTOR
DAYTON
BIG ARM
POLSON
RONAN
ROLLINS
BIGFORK
HUNGRY HORSE
WEST GLACIER
CORAM
ESSEX
ST. MARY
BABB
EAST GLACIER PARK
BROWNING
CUT BANK
SHELBY
CHESTER
VALIER
CONRAD
CHOTEAU
GREAT FALLS
FORT BENTON
HAVRE
MALTA
GLASGOW
FORT PECK
JORDAN
GLENDIVE
EKALAKA
MILES CITY
ROUNDUP
LEWISTOWN
ROY
STANFORD
HOBSON
CASCADE
WOLF CREEK
HELENA
GARRISON
DEER LODGE
ANACONDA
BUTTE
CLINTON
DRUMMOND
HALL
SEELEY LAKE
WHITE SULPHUR SPRINGS
TOWNSEND
THREE FORKS
CARDWELL
BOZEMAN
LIVINGSTON
BIG TIMBER
REED POINT
COLUMBUS
BILLINGS
BOYD
RED LODGE
HARDIN
FT. SMITH
BIGHORN CANYON N.R.A.
GARRYOWEN
DECKER
GARDINER
EMIGRANT
ENNIS
CAMERON
ALDER
DILLON
DIVIDE
MELROSE
WEST YELLOWSTONE
Gillette

ROAD TRIPS

Witness Beauty Under the Big Sky

Montana

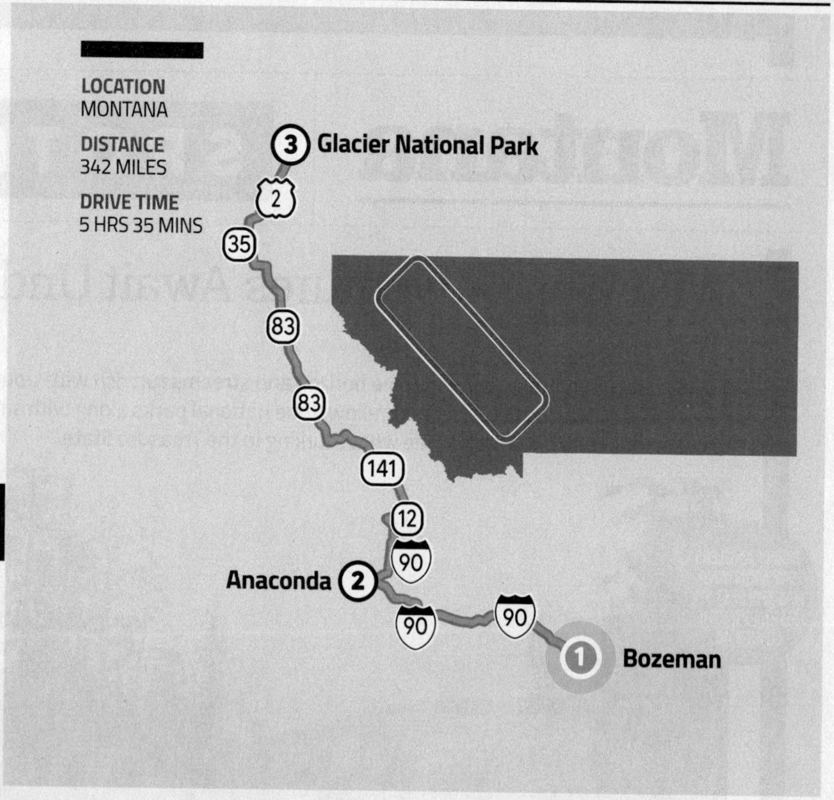

Home to snowcapped peaks, thunderous rivers and a rugged frontier mentality that has come to define the American West, few places on earth stir the senses quite like Big Sky Country. You can enjoy it all on this route through the state's western half, where you'll experience top-notch fly-fishing in Bozeman, rich history in Anaconda and the spectacular vistas of Glacier National Park. If it's outdoors adventure you're after, look no further than this stunning ride through a region aptly known as "The Last Best Place."

1 Bozeman
Starting Point

Surrounded by several iconic mountain ranges, this hip college town has earned a reputation as a haven for artists and outdoors lovers alike. Start your visit with a trip downtown, where quirky galleries and innovative breweries draw in tourists from across the state. From there, the nearby Gallatin, Madison, and Yellowstone rivers offer up some of the best trout fishing opportunities in the country, while the Bridger Range to the north and the Spanish Peaks to the south are home to popular hiking and mountain biking trails. To learn more about the area's singular geologic history, don't miss the renowned Museum of the Rockies, a Smithsonian-affiliated institution that houses some of the finest dinosaur fossil specimens in the world.

2 Anaconda
Drive 109 Miles ▪ 1 Hour, 45 Minutes

Founded in the late 1800s to store copper ore on behalf of the Anaconda Copper Mining Company, this small town is now a hidden gem for history buffs. Learn more about the region's fascinating past at Smoke Stack State Park, the now-closed center of mining operations, and the Copper Village Museum and Art Center, which features heritage-based exhibits on Montanan art and culture. Nestled in a high valley, the town also offers easy access to plenty of hiking and biking, including the ruggedly beautiful Anaconda-Pintler Wilderness. At nearly 250 square miles, the mountainous area is home to an extensive trail system, excellent trout fishing, and a collection of pristine alpine lakes.

3 Glacier National Park
Drive 233 Miles ▪ 3 Hours, 50 Minutes

One of America's great natural wonders, this stunning landscape of sky-high peaks, towering waterfalls and turquoise lakes has to be seen to be believed. The spectacular Going-to-the-Sun Road is considered among the country's most beautiful drives, but to experience the best the park has to offer, nothing beats the over 740 miles of backcountry trails. The popular Highline Trail and Hidden Lake Overlook, which leave from the Logan Pass Visitors Center, are easily accessible day hikes, while the trails to Iceberg Lake, Fishercap Lake and St. Mary Falls offer up family-friendly excursions and incredible vistas. Stop by the adjacent towns of West Glacier and St. Mary for a post-hike drink and a slice of the region's famed huckleberry pie.

Getty Images/iStockphoto

BIKING BOATING DINING ENTERTAINMENT FISHING HIKING HUNTING PADDLING SHOPPING SIGHTSEEING

Montana SPOTLIGHTS

Wild West Adventures Await Under the Big Sky

In Montana, mountains dominate the horizon and streams run rich with trout. You'll find gateways to Glacier and Yellowstone national parks along with small towns that welcome visitors. See what's lurking in the Treasure State.

MANY ANGLERS SAY MONTANA HAS THE BEST FLY FISHING IN THE LOWER 48.

Anglers cast lines for trout in the Gallatin River, which runs near Bozemen.

Getty Images

Anaconda

Located around 100 miles from the larger towns of Missoula, Bozeman and Helena, this mile-high city has great views of the surrounding Anaconda Mountains. Anaconda is a charming and historic city near some of the state's finest outdoor recreational areas. This town began as a copper mining center in the 1880s, but now it's a haven for lovers of the outdoors.

Jaunting Around Anaconda

Anaconda is the kind of town where you can take your time appreciating the little things. Learn about the town's copper ore smelting history with a stop at the Anaconda Smelter Stack State Park and the Copper Village Museum. Take your pick from nearby mountain streams and alpine lakes.

Bozeman

This Montana town is growing so fast that people have given it the nickname "Boz Angeles." But you can rest assured that this town will never lose its wild edge. Hot spring resorts' close proximity to Yellowstone National Park and world-class fishing puts it high on the list for lovers of the outdoors.

Fly-fishing Waters

Winding near town, the gorgeous Gallatin River is a renowned fly-fishing destination, thanks to its spectacular scenery and healthy stocks of mountain whitefish, brown trout and rainbow trout. You'll find many campsites and local lodges that cater to anglers along the river. Another popular spot is the Yellowstone River. This area is usually fished from a drift boat, but you can cast a line from shore at Mallard's Rest fishing access site. Ready for backcountry? Yellowstone National Park is 90 miles from town.

Glacier National Park

With its sky-high peaks, wildflower-filled valleys and ice blue mountaintop lakes, Glacier National Park inspires unequaled wonder. Nestled against the Canadian border in northwestern Montana, the park the "Crown of the Continent."

Going-to-the-Sun

Winding for 50 miles between the east and west entrances to the park, the famed Going-to-the-Sun Road offers almost every visitor their first glimpse of Glacier. Arguably the most beautiful drive in America, its full of narrow twists and hairpin turns as it climbs the steep mountainsides of the Rockies. At Logan Pass, the road's highest point, you'll find one of the park's main visitor centers.

FOR MORE INFORMATION

Travel Montana, 800-847-4868, www.visitmt.com

Bozeman CVB, 406-526-5421, www.bozemancvb.com

Anaconda, 406-563-2400, www.discoveranaconda.com

Glacier National Park, 406-888-7800, www.nps.gov/mt

LOCAL FAVORITE

Grilled Venison Kabobs

Game meat is big in Big Sky Country. Flip through restaurant menus and you'll often find elk in steaks, burgers sausages and stews. *Recipe by Ashley Weems.*

INGREDIENTS

- ☐ 2 lbs cubed venison
- ☐ 2 white onions, quartered
- ☐ 2 bell peppers, quartered
- ☐ 1 cup whole mushrooms
- ☐ 2 tomatoes, quartered

Sauce

- ☐ 1 2/3 cup red wine vinegar
- ☐ 1 1/4 cup ketchup
- ☐ 3/4 cup olive oil
- ☐ 3/4 cup soy sauce
- ☐ 1/2 cup Worcestershire sauce
- ☐ 2 tsp prepared mustard
- ☐ 1 tsp garlic powder
- ☐ 1 tsp salt
- ☐ 1 tsp pepper

DIRECTIONS

Mix sauce ingredients, marinate venison, onions, peppers overnight. Add mushrooms to marinade 6 hours before cooking. Skewer ingredients and grill on low.

Montana

ALBERTON — B1 *Mineral*

→ RIVER EDGE RESORT **Ratings: 5.5/UI/8** (Campground) 16 Avail: 9 full hkups, 7 W, 7 E (30/50 amps). 2021 rates: $35 to $38. (406)722-3375, 168 S Frontage Rd E, Alberton, MT 59820

ALDER — D2 *Madison*

→ **RUBY VALLEY CAMPGROUND & RV PARK**
good sam park
Ratings: 7/8.5★/8 (RV Park) Avail: 37 full hkups (30/50 amps). 2021 rates: $38 to $53. (406)842-5677, 2280 MT Hwy 287, Alder, MT 59710

ANACONDA — C2 *Silver Bow*

↑ BIG SKY RV PARK & CAMPGROUND **Ratings: 5.5/7/7** (Campground) Avail: 20 full hkups (30/50 amps). 2021 rates: $39. (406)563-2967, 350 Copper Sands Rd, Anaconda, MT 59711

← **COPPER COURT RV PARK**
good sam park
(RV Park) (Under Construction) Avail: 103 full hkups (30/50 amps). 2021 rates: $66. Apr 01 to Nov 25. (406)417-1050, 300 North Polk Street, Anaconda, MT 59711

↖ **FAIRMONT RV RESORT**
Ratings: 8/9.5★/9.5 (RV Park) From jct I-90 & Hwy 441/Fairmont Rd (Exit 211): Go 2-1/2 mi W on Fairmont Rd (L). Elev 5150 ft.**FAC:** gravel rds. (113 spaces). Avail: 93 gravel, 53 pull-thrus, (31x75), back-ins (30x48), 93 full hkups (30/50 amps), seasonal sites, WiFi @ sites, dump, laundry, groc. **REC:** boating nearby, playground, hunting nearby. Pets OK $. No tents. Big rig sites. 2021 rates: $50 to $58.
(406)797-3505 Lat: 46.04197, Lon: -112.80511
1700 Fairmont Rd, Anaconda, MT 59711
www.fairmontrvresort.com
See ad this page

RV Tech Tips - Awning Rod Storage: Tired of having to hunt for the awning rod buried under other items in the outside storage compartment? This RV tech tip can help. Cut two short pieces (about 6 inches long) of PVC pipe, drill two holes in each (enlarge the holes on one side for the screwdriver shaft) and attach them to the ceiling of the compartment. Measure the rod and place the pieces of pipe so that the rod tip (bent 90 degrees) will just hang out the end. That way, there is no room for the rod to slide back and forth. Now when you need your awning rod, you know right where it is; you don't have to hunt for it.

BABB — A2 *Glacier*

← **GLACIER/MANY GLACIER**
(Public National Park) From town, W 13 mi on Many Glacier Valley Rd (L). Elev 4500 ft.**FAC:** paved rds. Avail: 109 dirt, 13 pull-thrus, (12x35), back-ins (12x35), tent sites, restrooms only, dump, laundry, groc, firewood, restaurant. **REC:** Swiftcurrent Lake: swim, fishing. Pets OK. Partial handicap access, 7 day max stay. 2021 rates: $23. May 19 to Sep 25. no cc, no reservations.
(406)888-7800 Lat: 48.797300, Lon: -113.674326
West Glacier, MT 59411
home.nps.gov

BIG ARM — B1 *Lake*

↑ FLATHEAD LAKE/BIG ARM (Public State Park) From town, N 14 mi on US-93 (R). Avail: 1 E. 2021 rates: $18 to $34. Mar 01 to Nov 30. (406)752-5501

BIG TIMBER — C3 *Sweet Grass*

→ BIG TIMBER / GREYCLIFF KOA **Ratings: 8/9★/8.5** (Campground) 56 Avail: 33 full hkups, 23 W, 23 E (30/50 amps). 2021 rates: $54.45 to $63.01. Apr 20 to Nov 30. (406)932-6569, 693 Hwy 10E, Big Timber, MT 59011

↓ **SPRING CREEK CAMPGROUND & TROUT RANCH**
good sam park
Ratings: 7/9★/9 (Campground) From I-90 & I-90 Bus (exit 370): Go 2-1/4 mi W on Bus Loop I-90, then 2-1/2 mi S on Hwy 298 (L). Elev 4315 ft.**FAC:** gravel rds. 57 Avail: 9 gravel, 48 grass, 16 pull-thrus, (40x70), back-ins (32x60), 13 full hkups, 44 W, 44 E (30/50 amps), WiFi @ sites, tent sites, rentals, dump, mobile sewer, laundry, groc, LP bottles, fire rings, firewood. **REC:** Boulder River: fishing, playground, hunting nearby, rec open to public. Pets OK. Big rig sites. 2021 rates: $42 to $56, Military discount. Apr 01 to Sep 30.
(406)932-4387 Lat: 45.80212, Lon: -109.96097
257 Main Boulder Rd. Hwy 298 S, Big Timber, MT 59011
www.springcreekcampground.com
See ad this page

BIGFORK — A2 *Flathead*

↓ FLATHEAD LAKE/WAYFARERS (Public State Park) From town, S 0.5 mi on Hwy 35 (R). 40 Avail: (30 amps). 2021 rates: $18 to $34. Apr 01 to Oct 31. (406)752-5501

↓ OUTBACK MONTANA RV PARK & CAMPGROUND **Ratings: 7/8★/8** (Campground) 44 Avail: 34 full hkups, 10 W, 10 E (30/50 amps). 2021 rates: $40 to $45. (406)837-6973, 13772 Outback Lane, Bigfork, MT 59911

BIGHORN CANYON NATIONAL REC — D4 *Big Horn*

↗ BIGHORN CANYON/BARRY'S LANDING (Public National Park) From Lovell, W 3 mi on Hwy 14A, N 25 mi on SR-37 (through Hillsboro). 10 Avail: Pit toilets. 2021 rates: $5. (406)666-2412

RV Park ratings you can rely on!

E2. C5. F1. It's not a cipher; it's our easy-to-use map grid. Draw a line horizontally from the letter, vertically from the number, in the map border. ""X" will mark a spot near your destination.

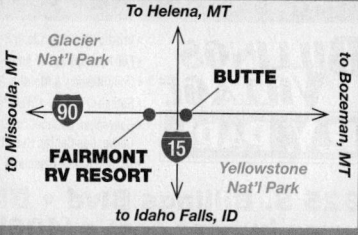

BILLINGS — C4 *Yellowstone*

BILLINGS KOA HOLIDAY **Ratings: 8/9.5★/9.5** (Campground) 118 Avail: 45 full hkups, 73 W, 73 E (30/50 amps). 2021 rates: $54 to $112. Apr 01 to Oct 31. (406)252-3104, 547 Garden Ave, Billings, MT 59101

BILLINGS VILLAGE RV PARK
good sam park **Ratings: 8.5/9.5★/9** (RV Park) From Jct I-90 & S Billings Blvd (exit 447): Go 1/2 mi N on S Billings Blvd (R). Elev 3100 ft.

RV PARK IN THE HEART OF BILLINGS
Stay with us & visit all the sights of Billings. Museums, Moss Mansion, Pompeys Pillar, the Yellowstone River & Custer Battlefield. Award winning golf courses nearby. Enjoy free Wi-Fi & cable TV for your daily or weekly stays

FAC: paved rds. (81 spaces). Avail: 76 paved, back-ins (30x60), 76 full hkups (30/50 amps), seasonal sites, cable, WiFi @ sites, laundry. **REC:** playground. Pet restrict (S). No tents. Big rig sites, eco-friendly. 2021 rates: $56 to $62, Military discount.
(406)248-8685 Lat: 45.76357, Lon: -108.53542
325 S Billings Blvd, Billings, MT 59101
bvrvmt.com
See ad this page

EASTWOOD ESTATES/MHP & RV PARK **Ratings: 3.5/6.5/6** (RV Park) Avail: 14 full hkups (30/50 amps). 2021 rates: $40. (406)245-7733, 1803 Hwy 87 E, Billings, MT 59101

YELLOWSTONE RIVER RV PARK & CAMPGROUND
good sam park **Ratings: 9.5/9.5★/9.5** (Campground) 125 Avail: 97 full hkups, 28 W, 28 E (30/50 amps). 2021 rates: $39 to $97. (406)259-0878, 309 Garden Ave, Billings, MT 59101

Things change ... last year's rates serve as a guideline only.

BOYD — D4 *Carbon*

COONEY (Public State Park) From Jct of I-90 & US-212 (Laurel exit), SW 22 mi on US-212 to Boyd, W 5 mi on cnty rd (E). Avail: 19 E (50 amps). 2021 rates: $15 to $28. (406)445-2326

BOZEMAN — C3 *Gallatin*

BEAR CANYON CAMPGROUND **Ratings: 8.5/8.5★/8** (Campground) 68 Avail: 35 full hkups, 33 W, 33 E (30/50 amps). 2021 rates: $35 to $75. May 01 to Oct 01. (406)587-1575, 4000 Bozeman Trail Road, Bozeman, MT 59715

BOZEMAN HOT SPRINGS CAMPGROUND & RV PARK **Ratings: 8/8/7.5** (Campground) 56 Avail: 46 full hkups, 10 W, 10 E (30/50 amps). 2021 rates: $74.95 to $89.95. (406)587-3030, 81123 Gallatin Rd (US-191), Bozeman, MT 59718

BOZEMAN TRAIL CAMPGROUND
good sam park **Ratings: 8/8.5★/8** (Campground) From Jct of I-90 & E Main / Bus 90 (exit 309): Go 1/2 mi E on frntg rd (R). Elev 4600 ft.**FAC:** paved/gravel rds. Avail: 46 gravel, 26 pull-thrus, (21x64), back-ins (18x50), 44 full hkups, 2 W, 2 E (30/50 amps), WiFi @ sites, tent sites, dump, laundry, LP gas. **REC:** hunting nearby. Pets OK. eco-friendly. 2021 rates: $45 to $65, Military discount. Apr 01 to Oct 31.
(406)587-4797 Lat: 45.67352, Lon: -111.00343
31842 Frontage Rd, Bozeman, MT 59715
bozemantrailcampground.com
See ad page 548

RED MOUNTAIN CAMPGROUND (BLM) (Public Corps) From town, SW 29 mi on SR-84 (R). 17 Avail: Pit toilets. 2021 rates: $8. Apr 01 to Dec 01. (406)683-2337

BROWNING — A2 *Glacier*

SLEEPING WOLF CAMPGROUND & RV PARK
good sam park **Ratings: 7/8★/7.5** (Campground) From Jct US 2 & US 89: Go 1/4 mi W on US 89, then go N on Cemetery Rd 1/4 mi to campground (R). Elev 4377 ft.**FAC:** gravel rds. Avail: 17 grass, 17 pull-thrus, (27x82), 10 W, 10 E (30/50 amps), WiFi @ sites, tent sites, dump, laundry, fire rings, firewood. **REC:** Willow Creek: fishing, boating nearby, hunting nearby. Pets OK. Partial handicap access. 2021 rates: $30 to $35, Military discount. May 15 to Sep 07.
(406)338-5622 Lat: 48.561988, Lon: -113.027274
56 Sleeping Wolf Lane, Browning, MT 59417
www.sleepingwolfcampgrounds.com
See ad this page

BUTTE — C2 *Silver Bow*

BUTTE See also Anaconda & Divide.

2 BAR LAZY H RV PARK **Ratings: 5.5/7/6** (Campground) 36 Avail: 24 full hkups, 12 W, 12 E (30/50 amps). 2021 rates: $37 to $41. (406)782-5464, 122015 W Browns Gulch Rd, Butte, MT 59701

BUTTE MONTANA KOA **Ratings: 8/9★/8** (Campground) 75 Avail: 60 full hkups, 15 W, 15 E (30/50 amps). 2021 rates: $50 to $90. Apr 15 to Oct 15. (406)782-8080, 1601 Kaw Ave, Butte, MT 59701

CAMERON — D3 *Madison*

DRIFTWATERS RESORT **Ratings: 7/UI/7.5** (RV Park) Avail: 10 full hkups (30/50 amps). 2021 rates: $40. May 01 to Dec 01. (406)682-3088, 31 Sagebrush Way, Cameron, MT 59720

CARDWELL — C3 *Jefferson*

CARDWELL RV PARK **Ratings: 5/UI/6.5** (Campground) 35 Avail: 10 full hkups, 25 W, 25 E (30/50 amps). 2021 rates: $54. (406)581-1526, 770 Hwy 2E, Cardwell, MT 59721

CASCADE — B3 *Cascade*

PREWETT CREEK RV PARK & CAMPGROUND **Ratings: 4/UI/7** (RV Park) Avail: 19 full hkups (30/50 amps). 2021 rates: $43.20 to $45.36. (406)788-5360, 2474 Old US Hwy 91, Cascade, MT 59421

CHESTER — A3 *Liberty*

SANFORD PARK CAMPGROUND (Public) From Jct of US-2 & SR-223, S 14 mi on SR-223 to SR-366, W 8 mi. 32 Avail. (406)759-5077

CHOTEAU — B2 *Teton*

CHOTEAU MOUNTAIN VIEW RV CAMPGROUND
good sam park **Ratings: 7/9★/7.5** (RV Park) 44 Avail: 20 full hkups, 24 W, 24 E (30/50 amps). 2021 rates: $40 to $54. May 15 to Oct 01. (406)466-2615, 85 MT-221 , Choteau, MT 59422

CLINTON — C2 *Granite*

BEARMOUTH CHALET RV PARK **Ratings: 7.5/8.5★/9** (Campground) 45 Avail: 45 W, 45 E (30/50 amps). 2021 rates: $37 to $47. May 01 to Oct 31. (406)825-9950, 1611 W Drummond Frontage Rd, Clinton, MT 59825

BEAVERTAIL HILL (Public State Park) From I-90 (milepost 130/Beavertail Hill exit): Go 1/4 mi S on county road. Avail: 28 E. 2021 rates: $12 to $24. May 01 to Oct 31. (406)542-5500

EKSTROM'S STAGE STATION **Ratings: 5/7/7.5** (Campground) 33 Avail: 17 full hkups, 16 W, 16 E (30/50 amps). 2021 rates: $45 to $55. May 01 to Sep 30. (406)825-3183, 81 Rock Creek Rd, Clinton, MT 59825

TURAH RV PARK Ratings: 6.5/8.5/8.5 (RV Park) Avail: 26 full hkups (30/50 amps). 2021 rates: $35 to $45. (406)258-9773, 13555 Turah Rd, Clinton, MT 59825

COLUMBIA FALLS — A2 *Flathead*

COLUMBIA FALLS RV PARK **Ratings: 8.5/9.5★/9** (RV Park) Avail: 62 full hkups (30/50 amps). 2021 rates: $69 to $80. Apr 01 to Oct 31. (888)401-7268, 103 Hwy 2 E, Columbia Falls, MT 59912

GLACIER PEAKS RV PARK
good sam park **Ratings: 7/8.5★/8.5** (Campground) From Jct US 2 & Hwy 40: Go 1/4 mi W on Hwy 40 (R). Elev 3000 ft.**FAC:** paved/gravel rds. (59 spaces). Avail: 41 gravel, 35 pull-thrus, (25x70), back-ins (25x70), 32 full hkups, 9 W, 9 E (30/50 amps), seasonal sites, WiFi @ sites, tent sites, rentals, shower$, laundry. **REC:** boating nearby, hunting nearby, rec open to public. Pets OK. Partial handicap access. Big rig sites, eco-friendly. 2021 rates: $59 to $65, Military discount. Mar 01 to Oct 01.
(406)892-2133 Lat: 48.37107, Lon: -114.24574
3185 MT Hwy 40 W, Columbia Falls, MT 59912
www.glacierpeaksrvpark.com
See ad page 548

LA SALLE RV PARK **Ratings: 7/9★/7.5** (Campground) 16 Avail: 6 full hkups, 10 E (30/50 amps). 2021 rates: $63.18 to $70.20. (406)892-4668, 5618 US Hwy 2 W, Columbia Falls, MT 59912

MOUNTAIN VIEW RV PARK
good sam park **Ratings: 8.5/8.5★/8** (Campground) From Jct of US 93 & Hwy 40 : Go 3-1/4 mi E on Hwy 40 (L). Elev 3063 ft.**FAC:** paved rds. Avail: 45 gravel, 28 pull-thrus, (32x62), back-ins (40x45), 45 full hkups (30/50 amps), WiFi @ sites, laundry, LP gas. **REC:** boating nearby, hunting nearby. Pets OK. No tents. Big rig sites, eco-friendly. 2021 rates: $65, Military discount.
(406)212-7811 Lat: 48.37127, Lon: -114.26937
3621 Hwy 40 W, Columbia Falls, MT 59912
rvparkmontana.com
See ad page 548

COLUMBUS — C4 *Stillwater*

ITCH-KEP-PE PARK (Public) At South edge of town on Hwy-78 at bridge. 30 Avail. Apr 01 to Oct 31. (406)322-5313

MOUNTAIN RANGE RV PARK
good sam park **Ratings: 6.5/8★/7** (RV Park) From Jct I-90 & Hwy 78 (exit 408): Go 1/4 mi N on Hwy 78, then 1/8 mi E on Mountain Range Rd (E). Elev 3650 ft.**FAC:** gravel rds. Avail: 42 gravel, 31 pull-thrus, (27x74), back-ins

(27x66), 31 full hkups, 11 E (30/50 amps), WiFi @ sites, tent sites, dump, laundry. **REC:** hunting nearby, rec open to public. Pets OK. eco-friendly. 2021 rates: $25 to $50, Military discount.
(406)322-1140 Lat: 45.64758, Lon: -109.24483
19 Mountain Range Rd, Columbus, MT 59019
See ad opposite page

CONRAD — A3 *Pondera*

PONDERA RV PARK **Ratings: 5/8★/6** (RV Park) Avail: 13 full hkups (30/50 amps). 2021 rates: $43.20. (406)271-2263, 713 S Maryland St, Conrad, MT 59425

CORAM — A2 *Flathead*

SUNDANCE RV PARK & CAMPGROUND **Ratings: 7/8/7** (Campground) 25 Avail: 25 W, 25 E (30/50 amps). 2021 rates: $52. May 01 to Oct 15. (866)782-2677, 10545 US Hwy 2E MP 147, Coram, MT 59913

CUT BANK — A2 *Glacier*

GLACIER MIST RV PARK
good sam park
Ratings: 6/8.5★/6.5 (RV Park) Avail: 15 full hkups (30/50 amps). 2021 rates: $35. Apr 01 to Dec 01. (406)548-2266, 1 McMisty Loop, Cut Bank, MT 59427

SUNSET RV PARK **Ratings: 8/8.5★/8** (Campground) 28 Avail: 28 W, 28 E (30/50 amps). 2021 rates: $35. May 01 to Sep 30. (406)873-0733, 401 4th Ave SW, Cut Bank, MT 59427

DARBY — C1 *Ravalli*

PAINTED ROCKS (Public State Park) From Hamilton: Go S 17 mi on US 93, then SW 23 mi on Route 473. 25 Avail: Pit toilets. 2021 rates: $18 to $24. (406)542-5500

DAYTON — B1 *Lake*

LAKE MARY RONAN (Public State Park) From US 93 in town: Go 7 mi W on access road. Avail: 22 E Pit toilets. 2021 rates: $18 to $24. May 17 to Sep 15. (406)849-5082

DECKER — D5 *Big Horn*

TONGUE RIVER RESERVOIR (Public State Park) From town: Go 6 mi N on Hwy 314, then 1 mi E on county road. Avail: 40 E Pit toilets. 2021 rates: $15 to $25. (406)234-0900

DEER LODGE — C2 *Powell*

DEER LODGE See also Anaconda, Garrison & Hall.

DEER LODGE A-OK CAMPGROUND **Ratings: 7/8.5★/6** (Campground) 37 Avail: 20 full hkups, 17 W, 17 E (30/50 amps). 2021 rates: $42 to $49. Apr 01 to Oct 20. (406)846-1629, 329 Park St, Deer Lodge, MT 59722

INDIAN CREEK RV PARK & CAMPGROUND
good sam park
Ratings: 7.5/10★/8 (RV Park) From Jct I-90 & Bus I-90 (exit 184): Go 1/8 mi W on Bus I-90 (L). Elev 4200 ft.

CAMP, DINE, FUEL UP AND EXPLORE!
Our top rated facility offers friendly service & savings on gas, diesel & meals. Halfway between Glacier & Yellowstone Natl Parks. We're surrounded by mountain views & near attractions, museums & numerous outdoor events.

FAC: gravel rds. (72 spaces). Avail: 42 gravel, 40 pull-thrus, (25x75), back-ins (25x50), 42 full hkups (30/50 amps), seasonal sites, cable, WiFi @ sites, tent sites, dump, laundry, groc, LP gas, firewood, restaurant. **REC:** hunting nearby. Pets OK. Partial handicap access. Big rig sites, eco-friendly. 2021 rates: $38 to $48, Military discount. ATM.
(800)294-0726 Lat: 46.40931, Lon: -112.72398
745 Maverick Lane, Deer Lodge, MT 59722
indiancreekcampground.net
See ad this page

DILLON — D2 *Beaverhead*

BANNACK (Public State Park) From jct Hwy 278 & county road: Go 4 mi S on county road. 28 Avail. 2021 rates: $12 to $24. (406)834-3413

BEAVERHEAD RIVER RV PARK & CAMPGROUND
good sam park
Ratings: 8/9★/8.5 (Campground) From Jct I-15 & Atlantic St / Bus 15 (exit 62): Go 1-1/4 mi N on Atlantic St / Bus 15, then 1 mi W on Reeder St (R). Elev 5050 ft. **FAC:** gravel rds. 57 Avail: 53 gravel, 4 grass, 29 pull-thrus, (25x72), back-ins (28x54), mostly side by side hkups, 25 full hkups, 32 W, 32 E (30 amps), WiFi @ sites, tent sites, rentals, dump, laundry, groc, LP gas, fire rings, firewood. **REC:** heated pool, Beaverhead River: fishing, kayaking/canoeing, boating nearby, playground, hunting nearby. Pets OK $. Partial handicap access, eco-friendly. 2021 rates: $46.54 to $61.82, Military discount.
(855)683-2749 Lat: 45.21954, Lon: -112.65019
735 W Park St, Dillon, MT 59725
www.beaverheadriverrvpark.com
See ad this page

COUNTRYSIDE RV PARK
good sam park
Ratings: 8/9.5★/9 (RV Park) From Jct I-15 & Hwy 278 (exit 59): Go 1/2 mi W on Hwy 278 (L). Elev 5200 ft. **FAC:** paved/gravel rds. (44 spaces). 34 Avail: 2 paved, 32 gravel, 19 pull-thrus, (32x70), back-ins (32x65), 34 full hkups (30/50 amps), seasonal sites, WiFi @ sites, tent sites, laundry, fire rings, firewood. **REC:** Monty's Pond: fishing, boating nearby, hunting nearby. Pets OK. Partial handicap access. Big rig sites, eco-friendly. 2021 rates: $25 to $55, Military discount.
(406)683-9860 Lat: 45.18039, Lon: -112.70324
30 Sawmill Rd, Dillon, MT 59725
csrvmt.com
See ad this page

SOUTHSIDE RV PARK
good sam park
Ratings: 8/9★/9 (RV Park) Avail: 40 full hkups (30/50 amps). 2021 rates: $45 to $50. Mar 01 to Dec 01. (406)683-2244, 104 E Poindexter, Dillon, MT 59725

DIVIDE — C2 *Silver Bow*

DIVIDE BRIDGE (BLM) (Public Corps) From town: Go 2-1/2 mi W on Hwy 43. 21 Avail: Pit toilets. 2021 rates: $6. May 15 to Sep 15. (406)533-7600

HYDE RV PARK **Ratings: 6/NA/7.5** (RV Park) 11 Avail: 11 W, 11 E (30/50 amps). 2021 rates: $30 to $32. May 01 to Oct 31. (406)832-3107, 70616 MT Highway 43, Divide, MT 59727

DRUMMOND — C2 *Granite*

DRUMMOND CITY PARK (Public) From Jct of I-90 & Old Hwy 10 (Exit 153), S 0.5 mi on Old Hwy 10 (L). 10 Avail: 3 W, 3 E. 2021 rates: $10 to $15. May 15 to Oct 01. (406)288-3231

EAST GLACIER PARK — A2 *Glacier*

GLACIER/TWO MEDICINE (Public National Park) From Jct of US-2 & SR-49, NW 5 mi on SR-49 to Two Medicine CG Rd, W 7 mi (R). 100 Avail. 2021 rates: $20. May 24 to Sep 25. (406)888-7800

Want to see what our inspectors see? The exact reproductions of the rating guidelines our inspectors used for this edition of the Guide are printed in the front of the book. Try using them on your next trip to perform your own inspection. Since our rating system is based on objective criteria, we're confident that your ratings will be similar to ours.

EAST GLACIER PARK (CONT)

RED EAGLE CAMPGROUND
Ratings: 5.5/NA/6.5 (Campground) From jct US Hwy 2 W & MT-49 N: Go 4 mi N on MT-49 N, then go 3/4 W mi on Two Medicine Area Roads (L). Elev 4000 ft.**FAC:** gravel rds. Avail: 26 dirt, 6 pull-thrus, (25x60), back-ins (25x50), accepts self-contain units only, 6 E (30 amps), WiFi, tent sites, rentals, dump, groc, fire rings, firewood. **REC:** Two Medicine River: fishing, boating nearby. Pets OK. 2021 rates: $28.50 to $48.50. Jun 01 to Sep 30.
(406)270-7527 Lat: 48.48741, Lon: -113.26333
30 Two Medicine Area Rd, East Glacier Park, MT 59434
See ad previous page

EKALAKA — C6 *Carter*

MEDICINE ROCKS (Public State Park) From Baker: Go S 25 mi on MT 7 to mile post 10, then W on CR 1 mi. 12 Avail: Pit toilets. 2021 rates: $18 to $24. (406)234-0926

EMIGRANT — D3 *Park*

YELLOWSTONE'S EDGE RV PARK
Ratings: 8/10★/10 (RV Park) From Jct I-90 & US 89 S (exit 333): Go 18 mi S on US 89 (L). Elev 4875 ft.**FAC:** gravel rds. (81 spaces). 64 Avail: 2 paved, 62 gravel, 48 pull-thrus, (30x60), back-ins (30x65), 64 full hkups (30/50 amps), seasonal sites, WiFi @ sites, rentals, laundry, groc, LP gas. **REC:** Yellowstone River: fishing, kayaking/canoeing, boating nearby, hunting nearby. Pets OK. Partial handicap access. No tents. Big rig sites, eco-friendly. 2021 rates: $68 to $78. May 01 to Oct 10.
(406)333-4036 Lat: 45.41712, Lon: -110.68227
3502 US Hwy 89 S, Livingston, MT 59047
yellowstonesedgervpark.com
See ad page 558

ENNIS — D3 *Madison*

ENNIS RV VILLAGE
Ratings: 7.5/10★/9.5 (RV Park) From Jct US 287 & MT Hwy 287: Go 1 mi N on US 287 (R). Elev 5000 ft.

YOUR BASE TO THE YELLOWSTONE AREA!
Float or wade on the river with your fly rod. Hike up streams to fish or just enjoy the fresh air, exercise & remarkable views. Historic towns & fine dining nearby. Stay for a day, a week, a month. An hour to Bozeman.

FAC: gravel rds. (112 spaces). Avail: 97 gravel, 55 pull-thrus, (32x78), back-ins (30x70), 97 full hkups (30/50 amps), seasonal sites, WiFi @ sites, tent sites, dump, laundry. **REC:** boating nearby, hunting nearby. Pets OK. Partial handicap access. Big rig sites, eco-friendly. 2021 rates: $32 to $45. Apr 01 to Nov 01.
(866)682-5272 Lat: 45.36608, Lon: -111.72832
15 Geyser St, Ennis, MT 59729
ennisrv.com
See ad this page, 560

MADISON VALLEY CAMPGROUND **Ratings: 6/UI/7** (Campground) Avail: 18 full hkups (30/50 amps). 2021 rates: $40 to $50. (406)682-4430, 300 W Main St, Ennis, MT 59729

ESSEX — A2 *Flathead*

GLACIER HAVEN RESORT & INN **Ratings: 6.5/8.5★/9** (Campground) Avail: 19 full hkups (30/50 amps). 2021 rates: $60 to $80. Mar 01 to Oct 01. (406)888-9987, 14297 US Hwy 2 East, Essex, MT 59916

GLACIER MEADOW RV PARK
Ratings: 7.5/9★/8 (Campground) From Jct US 2 & Hwy 49 (East Glacier): Go W 17 mi on US 2 (L) (MP 191.5) or From Jct US 2 & Hwy To The Sun (West Glacier): Go 37 mi E on US 2 (R). Elev 4430 ft.**FAC:** all weather rds. (44 spaces). Avail: 40 gravel, 26 pull-thrus, (25x65), back-ins (30x50), 25 W, 40 E (30/50 amps), seasonal sites, WiFi, tent sites, dump, mobile sewer, laundry, LP gas, fire rings, firewood. **REC:** shuffleboard, playground. Pets OK. 2021 rates: $45 to $60, Military discount. May 15 to Sep 30.
(406)226-4479 Lat: 48.26699, Lon: -113.44082
15735 US-2 East, Essex, MT 59916
glaciermeadowrvpark.com
See ad previous page

FORT BENTON — B3 *Chouteau*

BENTON RV PARK & CAMPGROUND **Ratings: 6/7.5/6.5** (RV Park) Avail: 32 full hkups (30/50 amps). 2021 rates: $35 to $40. (406)622-5015, 2410 Chouteau St, Fort Benton, MT 59442

FORT PECK — B5 *Valley*

FORT PECK DAM - COE/DOWNSTREAM (Public Corps) From town, SE 2 mi on Yellowstone Dr (L). Avail: 70 E (15/20 amps). 2021 rates: $18 to $25. May 01 to Oct 30. (406)526-3411

FORT PECK DAM - COE/FORT PECK WEST (Public Corps) From town, W 1.5 mi on Hwy 117, W 0.5 mi on Hwy 24, S 0.5 mi on Duck Creek Rd (L). 12 Avail. 2021 rates: $18. May 15 to Sep 01. (406)526-3411

FORT SMITH — D4 *Big Horn*

BIGHORN CANYON/AFTERBAY (Public National Park) From Hardin, Jct of I-90 & CR-313, S 44 mi on CR-313 (R). 28 Avail: Pit toilets. 2021 rates: $10. (406)666-2412

GARDINER — D3 *Park*

GARDINER See also Emigrant.

ROCKY MOUNTAIN RV PARK AND LODGING **Ratings: 6.5/10★/9.5** (RV Park) Avail: 65 full hkups (30/50 amps). 2021 rates: $79 to $89. May 01 to Sep 30. (406)848-7251, 14 Jardine Rd, Gardiner, MT 59030

YELLOWSTONE RV PARK
Ratings: 6.5/9★/8.5 (Campground) Avail: 30 full hkups (30/50 amps). 2021 rates: $48 to $88. May 01 to Oct 30. (406)848-7496, 121 Hwy 89 S, Gardiner, MT 59030

GARRISON — C2 *Powell*

RIVERFRONT RV PARK
Ratings: 8.5/8.5★/8 (RV Park) W-Bnd: From Jct I-90 & exit 175: Go 1/2 mi N on Frontage Rd (L), E-Bnd: From Jct I-90 & exit 175: Go 1/2 mi W on Frontage Rd to stop sign, Go 1/2 mi N on Frontage Rd (L). Elev 4360 ft.

We rate what RVers consider important.

TIRED OF ORDINARY RV PARKS? We deliver VIP service. Our park hosts personally take you to your long, wide pull-thru full hookup site. Overnight sites are 100' long & 40' wide. Enjoy our shade, lawns & river, plus our mountain views. Special weekly rates

FAC: paved rds. (50 spaces). Avail: 38 gravel, 31 pull-thrus, (26x110), back-ins (32x70), 38 full hkups (30/50 amps), seasonal sites, WiFi @ sites, tent sites, rentals, shower$, dump, laundry, LP gas, fire rings, firewood. **REC:** Little Blackfoot River: fishing, playground, hunting nearby. Pets OK. Partial handicap access. Big rig sites, eco-friendly. 2021 rates: $33 to $35, Military discount.
(406)560-0248 Lat: 46.51918, Lon: -112.79559
115 Riverfront Ln, Garrison, MT 59731
www.riverfrontrvparkmt.com
See ad opposite page

GARRYOWEN — C5 *Big Horn*

7TH RANCH RV CAMP
Ratings: 8/10★/10 (Campground) 60 Avail: 45 full hkups, 15 W, 15 E (30/50 amps). 2021 rates: $42 to $52. Apr 15 to Oct 15. (406)638-2438, 7th Ranch 662 Reno Creek Rd, Garryowen, MT 59031

GLACIER NATIONAL PARK — A2 *Glacier*

GLACIER NATIONAL PARK See also Bigfork, Browning, Columbia Falls, Coram, Cut Bank, East Glacier Park, Essex, Hungry Horse, Kalispell, Lakeside, St Mary, West Glacier & Whitefish.

GLASGOW — A5 *Valley*

COTTONWOOD INN & SUITES & RV PARK **Ratings: 8/9★/9** (RV Park) Avail: 15 full hkups (30/50 amps). 2021 rates: $39 to $45. Apr 01 to Oct 31. (800)321-8213, 54250 US Highway 2 East, Glasgow, MT 59230

SHADY REST RV PARK
Ratings: 6/8.5★/9 (RV Park) From jct US 2 & Hwy 24 (Glasgow): Go 1-1/2 mi W on US 2, then 1/8 mi N on Lasar Dr (E). **FAC:** gravel rds. Avail: 40 gravel, 8 pull-thrus, (22x86), back-ins (27x60), 40 full hkups (30/50 amps), WiFi @ sites, laundry. **REC:** boating nearby, hunting nearby, rec open to public. Pets OK. No tents, eco-friendly. 2021 rates: $40 to $45, Military discount.
(406)228-2769 Lat: 48.19673, Lon: -106.62061
8 Lasar Dr, #15, Glasgow, MT 59230
www.shadyrestrvparkmt.com
See ad this page

GLENDIVE — B6 *Dawson*

MAKOSHIKA (Public State Park) In town on Snyder Ave. 28 Avail. 2021 rates: $18 to $24. (406)377-6256

GREAT FALLS — B3 *Cascade*

DICK'S RV PARK
Ratings: 7.5/9★/8.5 (RV Park) Avail: 114 full hkups (30/50 amps). 2021 rates: $45 to $50. (406)452-0333, 1403 11th St SW, Great Falls, MT 59404

GREAT FALLS KOA **Ratings: 7/9.5★/8** (Campground) 170 Avail: 101 full hkups, 69 W, 69 E (30/50 amps). 2021 rates: $70.62 to $107. (406)727-3191, 1500 51st St S, Great Falls, MT 59405

MILITARY PARK GATEWAY FAMCAMP (MALMSTROM AFB) (Public) From Jct of I-15 & 10th Ave & S exit, E 6 mi on 10th Ave to bypass, follow signs. Avail: 55 full hkups (30/50 amps). 2021 rates: $20 to $25. Apr 15 to Oct 15. (406)731-3263

RV Tech Tips - LP Gas Measuring: Keeping track of the remaining LP gas in your trailer's cylinder is often a challenging task. Many trailer owners apply magnetic strips to the LP gas cylinders that change color at the liquid line when hot water is poured on the cylinder. The problem is remembering how full the cylinder was the last time it was checked without applying hot water again. A magic marker to note the level will certainly work, but that means a streaky mess the next time you pour water on the cylinder. In addition to the magnetic strip, use a refrigerator magnet as a visual aid on the cylinder. Each time you apply hot water, move the magnet to reflect the liquid level.

HALL — C2 *Granite*

BOULDER CREEK LODGE AND RV PARK **Ratings: 6.5/8.5/8.5** (Campground) 10 Avail: 7 full hkups, 3 W, 3 E (30/50 amps). 2021 rates: $43. May 01 to Oct 15. (406)859-3190, 4 Boulder Creek Rd, Hall, MT 59837

HAMILTON — C1 *Ravalli*

ANGLERS ROOST ON THE BITTERROOT RIVER **Ratings: 6/8★/7** (Campground) 39 Avail: 20 full hkups, 19 W, 19 E (30/50 amps). 2021 rates: $29.50 to $42.50. (406)363-1268, 815 Hwy 93 S, Hamilton, MT 59840

BLACK RABBIT RV PARK **Ratings: 7.5/9.5★/7.5** (RV Park) Avail: 39 full hkups (30/50 amps). 2021 rates: $41.85 to $48.60. (406)363-3744, 2101 N 1st St, Hamilton, MT 59840

HARDIN — C5 *Big Horn*

GRANDVIEW CAMP & RV PARK
Ratings: 7/8.5★/8.5 (Campground) Avail: 47 full hkups (30/50 amps). 2021 rates: $28 to $45. (406)665-2489, 1002 N Mitchell Ave, Hardin, MT 59034

HARDIN KOA **Ratings: 8/7/6.5** (Campground) 62 Avail: 27 full hkups, 35 W, 35 E (30/50 amps). 2021 rates: $46. Apr 01 to Oct 15. (406)665-1635, 2205 Hwy 47 N, Hardin, MT 59034

HAVRE — A4 *Blaine*

EVERGREEN CAMPGROUND **Ratings: 7.5/8.5★/8** (Campground) 25 Avail: 19 full hkups, 6 W, 6 E (30/50 amps). 2021 rates: $42. Apr 01 to Nov 15. (406)265-8228, 4850 72nd Ave West, Havre, MT 59501

GREAT NORTHERN FAIR & CAMPGROUNDS (Public) From town, W 1 mi on US-2 (L). 40 Avail: 23 W, 23 E (30 amps). 2021 rates: $20. Apr 15 to Nov 15. (406)265-7121

HANSEN FAMILY CAMPGROUND & STORAGE
Ratings: 7/NA/8.5 (RV Park) Avail: 22 full hkups (30/50 amps). 2021 rates: $36 to $40. (406)945-6629, 39180 US Highway 2 E, Havre, MT 59501

HAVRE RV PARK **Ratings: 8/9.5★/7** (RV Park) Avail: 44 full hkups (30/50 amps). 2021 rates: $48.60 to $54. (800)278-8861, 1415 First St, Havre, MT 59501

HELENA — C2 *Broadwater*

CANYON FERRY/CHINAMANS GULCH (Public) From town, E 9 mi on US-287 to Hwy 284, NE 10 mi (R). 45 Avail. 2021 rates: $8. (406)475-3310

CANYON FERRY/COURT SHERIFF (Public) From town, E 11 mi on US-12 to MP 55 (secondary 284), NE 9 mi (R). 48 Avail. 2021 rates: $15 to $30. (406)475-3921

CANYON FERRY/HELLGATE (Public) From town, E 9 mi on US-287 to SR-284 (MP 55), NE 18 mi (R). 69 Avail. 2021 rates: $10 to $20. (406)475-3310

CANYON FERRY/RIVERSIDE (Public) From town, E 9 mi on US-287 to Hwy 284, NE 9 mi to Eagle Bay Dr., NW 1 mi (R). 27 Avail. 2021 rates: $15. May 26 to Sep 01. (406)475-3921

HAUSER LAKE/BLACK SANDY (Public State Park) From town: Go 7 mi N on I-15 to Lincoln Rd exit/SR-453, then 4 mi E to county rd, 3 mi N, follow signs (R). Avail: 29 E. 2021 rates: $18 to $24. (406)458-3221

HELENA NORTH KOA **Ratings: 7.5/UI/8.5** (RV Park) Avail: 44 full hkups (30/50 amps). 2021 rates: $45 to $85. (406)458-3725, 850 Lincoln Road West, Helena, MT 59602

HOBSON — B4 *Judith Basin*

ACKLEY LAKE (Public State Park) From jct US 87 & Hwy 400: Go 5 mi S on Hwy 400, then 2 mi SW on county road. 15 Avail: Pit toilets. 2021 rates: $12 to $24. (406)727-1212

HUNGRY HORSE — A2 *Flathead*

BEARGRASS LODGING & RV RESORT **Ratings: 7.5/8★/8.5** (Campground) Avail: 26 full hkups (30/50 amps). 2021 rates: $60. Apr 15 to Nov 15. (406)387-5531, 8688 Hwy 2 E, Hungry Horse, MT 59919

Average site width and length are indicated in many campground listings to give you an idea of how much room and privacy you can expect.

MOUNTAIN MEADOW RV PARK & CABINS
Ratings: 7.5/10★/9.5 (Campground) 54 Avail: 31 full hkups, 23 W, 23 E (30/50 amps). 2021 rates: $58 to $63. May 01 to Oct 01. (406)387-9125, 9125 US Hwy 2E, Hungry Horse, MT 59919

JORDAN — B5 *Garfield*

HELL CREEK (Public State Park) From Jct of Hwy 200 & Cnty Rd (at milepost 213), N 26 mi on cnty rd (R). Avail: 45 E (50 amps). 2021 rates: $18 to $24. May 17 to Sep 15. (406)557-2362

KALISPELL — A1 *Flathead*

KALISPELL See also Bigfork, Coram, Columbia Falls, Hungry Horse, Lakeside, Proctor, Rollins, West Glacier & Whitefish.

LIONS BITTERROOT REC YOUTH CAMP (Public) From Jct of US-93 & US-2, W 20 mi on US-2 to Pleasant Valley Rd., NW 5 mi to Bitterroot Rd., (L). 22 Avail: Pit toilets. 2021 rates: $8. May 15 to Oct 01. (406)854-2744

MONTANA BASECAMP **Ratings: 6.5/8/8** (RV Resort) Avail: 62 full hkups (30/50 amps). 2021 rates: $80 to $149. Apr 15 to Oct 15. (406)756-9999, 1000 Basecamp Dr, Kalispell, MT 59901

ROCKY MOUNTAIN 'HI' RV PARK AND CAMPGROUND
Ratings: 9/9★/8.5 (Campground) Avail: 78 full hkups (30/50 amps). 2021 rates: $49 to $54. (800)968-5637, 825 Helena Flats Rd, Kalispell, MT 59901

SPRUCE PARK ON THE RIVER
Ratings: 9/8.5★/8 (Campground) 84 Avail: 68 full hkups, 16 W, 16 E (30/50 amps). 2021 rates: $45 to $75. Apr 01 to Nov 15. (406)752-6321, 1985 MT Hwy 35 , Kalispell, MT 59901

LAKESIDE — B2 *Powell*

EDGEWATER RV RESORT & MOTEL **Ratings: 9/9.5★/8** (RV Park) Avail: 35 full hkups (30/50 amps). 2021 rates: $59. (406)844-3644, 7140 Hwy US 93 S, Lakeside, MT 59922

LEWISTOWN — B4 *Fergus*

MOUNTAIN ACRES RV PARK **Ratings: 7/8.5★/6.5** (RV Park) Avail: 35 full hkups (30/50 amps). 2021 rates: $40.66 to $49.22. (406)538-7591, 103 Rocklyn Ave, Lewistown, MT 59457

LIBBY — A1 *Lincoln*

TWO BIT OUTFIT RV PARK **Ratings: 5/UI/7** (Campground) Avail: 25 full hkups (30/50 amps). 2021 rates: $45 to $50. Apr 01 to Nov 01. (406)293-8323, 17 Two Bit Circle, Libby, MT 59923

WOODLAND RV PARK **Ratings: 7/8★/8.5** (Campground) Avail: 44 full hkups (30/50 amps). 2021 rates: $40 to $55. Apr 15 to Oct 01. (406)293-8395, 31480 US Highway 2, Libby, MT 59923

Save 10% at Good Sam Parks & Campgrounds. Stay at any of the Good Sam RV Parks & Campgrounds in the U.S. and Canada and save 10% on the regular nightly RV site rate! No Blackout dates! Good Sam RV Parks are inspected and rated annually-look for the exclusive Triple Rating System. Visit GoodSam.com for more details.

LIVINGSTON — C3 *Park*

LIVINGSTON See also Bozeman & Emigrant.

LIVINGSTON PARADISE VALLEY KOA **Ratings: 8/8/8.5** (Campground) 55 Avail: 44 full hkups, 11 W, 11 E (30/50 amps). 2021 rates: $54.67 to $116.66. May 01 to Oct 15. (406)222-0992, 163 Pine Cr Rd, Livingston, MT 59047

OSEN'S RV PARK
Ratings: 8/10★/9 (RV Park) From Jct I-90 & US 89 (exit 333) : Go 1/2 mi S on US 89, then 1/8 mi W on Merrill Ln (R). Elev 4500 ft.**FAC:** gravel rds. Avail: 45 all weather, 17 pull-thrus, (30x75), back-ins (25x65), 24 full hkups, 21 W, 21 E (30/50 amps), cable, WiFi @ sites, dump, laundry. **REC:** boating nearby, hunting nearby. Pets OK. No tents. Big rig sites, eco-friendly. 2021 rates: $46 to $59, Military discount. Apr 15 to Oct 10.
(406)222-0591 Lat: 45.63677, Lon: -110.58023
20 Merrill Ln, Livingston, MT 59047
www.osensrvpark.com
See ad page 548

LOLO — C2 *Missoula*

THE SQUARE DANCE CENTER & CAMPGROUND
Ratings: 6.5/7.5★/8.5 (Campground) From Jct US 93 & US 12 (Lolo): Go 2-3/4 mi W on US 12 (L). Elev 3300 ft.**FAC:** paved/gravel rds. Avail: 54 gravel, 7 pull-thrus, (35x75), back-ins (30x60), 23 full hkups, 31 W, 31 E (30/50 amps), WiFi @ sites, tent sites, dump, mobile sewer, firewood. **REC:** Lolo Creek: fishing. Pet restrict (B). eco-friendly. 2021 rates: $35 to $45. May 01 to Sep 30.
(406)273-0141 Lat: 46.74831, Lon: -114.13528
9955 US Hwy 12 W, Lolo, MT 59847
www.lolocampndance.com
See ad this page

MALTA — A4 *Phillips*

EDGEWATER INN & RV PARK **Ratings: 7.5/7.5/4.5** (RV Park) Avail: 21 full hkups (30/50 amps). 2021 rates: $42.50 to $45. (406)654-1302, 47176 US Hwy 2, Malta, MT 59538

TRAFTON (Public) From Jct of US-191 & Hwy 2 (Trafton Park Rd), N 0.1 mi on Trafton Park Rd (E). 22 Avail. 2021 rates: $3. May 15 to Nov 01. (406)654-1251

MARION — A1 *Flathead*

LOGAN (Public State Park) From town, W 60 mi on US-2 to milepost 77 (L). 37 Avail. 2021 rates: $18 to $24. (406)752-5501

MCGREGOR LAKES RV **Ratings: 7/9/8.5** (Campground) Avail: 41 full hkups (30/50 amps). 2021 rates: $43 to $46. Apr 01 to Nov 30. (406)858-2261, 12255 Hwy 2 W, Marion, MT 59925

MELROSE — C2 *Beaverhead*

THE SPORTSMAN LODGE, CABINS & RV
Ratings: 7.5/8.5★/9 (Campground) Avail: 17 full hkups (30/50 amps). 2021 rates: $40 to $45. Mar 01 to Nov 15. (406)835-2141, 540 Main St, Melrose, MT 59743

MILES CITY — C5 *Custer*

BIG SKY CAMP & RV PARK **Ratings: 9/9★/8.5** (Campground) Avail: 25 full hkups (30/50 amps). 2021 rates: $45. (406)234-1511, 1294 US Hwy 12, Miles City, MT 59301

MILES CITY KOA KAMPGROUND **Ratings: 7.5/8.5★/8** (Campground) 53 Avail: 50 full hkups, 3 W, 3 E (30/50 amps). 2021 rates: $49.56 to $75. Apr 15 to Oct 15. (406)232-3991, 1 Palmer St, Miles City, MT 59301

MISSOULA — B2 *Missoula*

MISSOULA See also Alberton, Clinton & Lolo.

GRANITE PEAK RV RESORT **Ratings: 9/9.5★/9.5** (RV Park) 110 Avail: 81 full hkups, 29 W, 29 E (30/50 amps). 2021 rates: $47 to $90. (406)543-9400, 9900 Jellystone Dr, Missoula, MT 59808

JIM & MARY'S RV PARK
Ratings: 8.5/10★/9 (RV Park) Avail: 69 full hkups (30/50 amps). 2021 rates: $49.81 to $53.80. (406)549-4416, 9800 Hwy 93 N, Missoula, MT 59808

MISSOULA KOA **Ratings: 8.5/9.5★/8.5** (RV Park) 130 Avail: 115 full hkups, 15 W, 15 E (30/50 amps). 2021 rates: $41.01 to $74.57. (800)562-5366, 3450 Tina Ave, Missoula, MT 59808

NOXON — B1 *Lincoln*

TWO RIVERS RV PARK **Ratings: 6/UI/6** (Campground) Avail: 25 full hkups (30/50 amps). 2021 rates: $23.54. Apr 15 to Oct 15. (406)847-2291, 33 Blue Jay Lane, Noxon, MT 59853

POLSON — B2 *Lake*

BIG ARM RESORT & MARINA
Ratings: 8.5/9★/9 (RV Resort) From jct MT Hwy 35 & US 93 N: Go 14 mi N on US 93 N (R). **FAC:** paved rds. Avail: 30 paved, patios, back-ins (35x40), 30 full hkups (30/50 amps), WiFi @ sites, rentals, laundry, restaurant. **REC:** Flathead Lake: swim, fishing, marina, kayaking/canoeing, boating nearby, hunting nearby. Pets OK. No tents, eco-friendly. 2021 rates: $45 to $95, Military discount. May 01 to Oct 15. ATM.
(406)883-8363 Lat: 47.799297, Lon: -114.292766
44297 A Street, Big Arm, MT 59910
bigarmresort.com
See ad this page

EAGLE NEST RV RESORT **Ratings: 9.5/10★/9.5** (RV Park) Avail: 43 full hkups (30/50 amps). 2021 rates: $44 to $83. May 01 to Oct 15. (406)883-5904, 35800 Eagle Nest Dr (MT 35), Polson, MT 59860

FLATHEAD LAKE/FINLEY POINT (Public State Park) From Jct of US-93 & SR-35, N 6 mi on SR-35 to Finley Point Rd, W 4 mi (R). Avail: 18 E (30 amps). 2021 rates: $18 to $34. May 01 to Nov 15. (406)752-5501

FLATHEAD RIVER RESORT **Ratings: 7.5/UI/7.5** (Condo Park) Avail: 36 full hkups (30/50 amps). 2021 rates: $55 to $65. (406)883-6400, 9 Regatta Rd, Polson, MT 59860

POLSON MOTORCOACH RESORT **Ratings: 10/10★/10** (Condo Park) Avail: 41 full hkups (50 amps). 2021 rates: $100 to $250. Apr 15 to Oct 15. (406)883-2333, 200 Irvine Flats Rd, Polson, MT 59860

POLSON/FLATHEAD LAKE KOA **Ratings: 9/10★/10** (RV Park) 41 Avail: 33 full hkups, 8 W, 8 E (30/50 amps). 2021 rates: $45 to $89. Apr 15 to Oct 15. (406)883-2151, 200 Irvine Flats Rd, Polson, MT 59860

PROCTOR — B1 *Lake*

THE LODGE & RESORT AT LAKE MARY RONAN
Ratings: 7.5/NA/10 (RV Resort) Avail: 9 full hkups (30/50 amps). 2021 rates: $65 to $100. May 01 to Sep 30. (406)849-6279, 52012 Lake Mary Ronan Rd, Proctor, MT 59929

RED LODGE — D4 *Carbon*

PERRY'S RV & CAMPGROUND **Ratings: 5/9★/7.5** (Campground) 62 Avail: 62 W, 62 E (30/50 amps). 2021 rates: $45. May 15 to Oct 01. (406)446-2722, 6664 US Hwy 212, Red Lodge, MT 59068

RED LODGE KOA **Ratings: 7/9★/7.5** (Campground) 42 Avail: 18 full hkups, 24 W, 24 E (30/50 amps). 2021 rates: $50 to $85. May 01 to Oct 01. (800)562-7540, 7464 US Hwy 212, Red Lodge, MT 59068

REED POINT — C4 *Stillwater*

OLD WEST RV PARK
Ratings: 6.5/8.5★/8 (Campground) Avail: 15 full hkups (30/50 amps). 2021 rates: $43 to $54. May 01 to Oct 31. (406)326-2394, 5 South Division St., Reed Point, MT 59069

ROLLINS — B2 *Lake*

FLATHEAD LAKE/WEST SHORE (Public State Park) From town: Go 5 mi N on US 93. Avail: 19 E Pit toilets. 2021 rates: $18 to $34. May 01 to Nov 30. (406)844-3066

ROLLINS RV PARK & RESTAURANT
Ratings: 8.5/10★/8.5 (RV Park) Avail: 35 full hkups (30/50 amps). 2021 rates: $59. Apr 01 to Sep 30. (406)844-0572, 23711 Hwy 93, Rollins, MT 59931

RONAN — B2 *Lake*

DIAMOND "S" RV PARK **Ratings: 6.5/8.5/8** (Campground) Avail: 38 full hkups (30/50 amps). 2021 rates: $55. May 01 to Sep 30. (406)676-2267, 46711 Old Highway 93, Ronan, MT 59864

ROUNDUP — C4 *Musselshell*

COWBELLES CORRAL (Public) From Jct of Main St & E Second, E 0.5 mi on E Second/at Fairground (L). 35 Avail. 2021 rates: $11. (406)323-1966

ROY — B4 *Fergus*

JAMES KIPP RECREATION AREA (BLM) (Public Corps) From town: Go 30 mi N on US 191 to the Missouri River. 34 Avail: Pit toilets. 2021 rates: $12. Apr 01 to Dec 01. (406)538-1900

SEELEY LAKE — B2 *Missoula*

PLACID LAKE (Public State Park) From town: Go 3 mi S on Hwy 83, then 3 mi W on county road. Avail: 18 E Pit toilets. 2021 rates: $18 to $24. May 17 to Sep 15. (406)677-6804

SALMON LAKE (Public State Park) From town: Go 5 mi S on Hwy 83. Avail: 16 E Pit toilets. 2021 rates: $18 to $25. (406)677-6804

SHELBY — A3 *Toole*

↑ LAKE SHEL-OOLE CAMPGROUND (Public) From town, N 0.75 mi on I-15 Bus Loop to exit 364, S 0.5 mi (L). 46 Avail: 46 W, 46 E (30 amps). 2021 rates: $25. May 15 to Sep 15. (406)434-5222

↑ LEWIS & CLARK RV PARK **Ratings: 7.5/9★/8.5** (RV Park) 54 Avail: 37 full hkups, 17 W, 17 E (30/50 amps). 2021 rates: $32 to $39. (406)434-2710, 1535 Oilfield Ave I-15 North Exit 364, Shelby, MT 59474

↖ **SHELBY RV PARK AND RESORT**
good sam park **Ratings: 8.5/9.5★/8.5** (RV Park) From jct I-15 & US 2 (exit 363): Go 1/4 mi E on US 2, then 1/8 mi S on Wilson Ave, then 1/16 mi W on Joe Irvin Dr, then turn S on McKinley (R). Elev 3350 ft.**FAC:** gravel rds. Avail: 27 gravel, 8 pull-thrus, (42x80), back-ins (42x50), 27 full hkups (30/50 amps), WiFi @ sites, tent sites, rentals, laundry. **REC:** heated pool, hot tub, hunting nearby, rec open to public. Pets OK. Partial handicap access. 2021 rates: $40 to $50, Military discount. ATM.
(406)434-2233 Lat: 48.51212, Lon: -111.87481
455 McKinley Ave, Shelby, MT 59474
www.shelbymtrvpark.com
See ad this page

↖ **TRAILS WEST RV PARK**
good sam park **Ratings: 7/9★/7.5** (RV Park) Avail: 27 full hkups (30/50 amps). 2021 rates: $35 to $40. (406)424-8436, 770 Adams Ave, Shelby, MT 59474

↓ WILLIAMSON RIVER (Public) From Jct of US-2 & I-15 frntg rd (in town), S 7 mi on I-15 frntg rd (L). 25 Avail. 2021 rates: $8 to $15. May 15 to Sep 15. (406)434-5222

Save 10% at Good Sam Parks 365 days a year with no blackout dates!!

ST MARY — A2 *Glacier*

↓ **CHEWING BLACK BONES CAMPGROUND**
good sam park **Ratings: 6.5/8★/7** (Campground) From jct Hwy 464 & US 89 S: Go 1-1/4 mi S on US 89 S (R). Elev 4500 ft.**FAC:** gravel rds. Avail: 71 grass, 37 pull-thrus, (30x60), back-ins (20x45), 14 full hkups, 10 W, 10 S, 47 E (30 amps), WiFi, tent sites, rentals, dump, laundry, groc, fire rings, firewood. **REC:** Lower St Mary's Lake: swim, fishing, kayaking/canoeing, boating nearby, playground. Pets OK. 2021 rates: $25 to $55. Jun 01 to Sep 30.
(406)732-4046 Lat: 48.82618, Lon: -113.41963
3719 Highway 89, Babb, MT 59411
See ad this page

← GLACIER/RISING SUN (Public National Park) From town, W 6 mi on Going-To-The-Sun Rd (R). 84 Avail. 2021 rates: $20. Jun 02 to Sep 11. (406)888-7800

← GLACIER/ST MARY (Public National Park) From Babb, S 10 mi on US-89 (R). 148 Avail. 2021 rates: $10 to $23. (406)888-7800

↑ JOHNSON'S OF ST MARY CAMPGROUND & RV PARK **Ratings: 6.5/8.5★/8** (Campground) 88 Avail: 47 full hkups, 41 W, 41 E (20/30 amps). 2021 rates: $40 to $60. May 15 to Sep 20. (406)732-4207, 21 Red Eagle Rd, St Mary, MT 59417

↑ ST MARY-GLACIER PARK KOA **Ratings: 8/9★/8** (Campground) 98 Avail: 60 full hkups, 26 W, 38 E (30/50 amps). 2021 rates: $62 to $125. May 15 to Sep 30. (800)562-1504, 106 West Shore, St Mary, MT 59417

ST REGIS — B1 *Mineral*

← **CAMPGROUND ST REGIS**
good sam park **Ratings: 8.5/9.5★/9.5** (Campground) 65 Avail: 14 full hkups, 51 W, 51 E (30/50 amps). 2021 rates: $34.20 to $49.49. Apr 15 to Oct 01. (406)649-2470, 660 Frontage Rd West, St Regis, MT 59866

→ **NUGGET RV PARK**
good sam park **Ratings: 10/10★/10** (RV Park) Avail: 86 full hkups (30/50 amps). 2021 rates: $48 to $55. May 01 to Nov 01. (406)649-2122, 1037 Old Highway 10 East, St Regis, MT 59866

STANFORD — B3 *Judith Basin*

LEWIS & CLARK/DRY WOLF (Public State Park) From town: Go 17-1/2 mi SW on gravel CR 251, then 5-1/2 mi SW on FR 251. 25 Avail: Pit toilets. 2021 rates: $5. May 26 to Sep 01. (406)566-2292

SULA — C2 *Ravalli*

↑ CAMP SULA **Ratings: 6/7.5/7** (Campground) 19 Avail: 7 full hkups, 12 W, 12 E (30 amps). 2021 rates: $35 to $40. (406)821-3364, 7060 Hwy 93 S, Sula, MT 59871

THOMPSON FALLS — B1 *Sanders*

↖ BIRDLAND BAY RV RESORT **Ratings: 6.5/7.5/7.5** (Campground) 17 Avail: 16 full hkups, 1 W, 1 E (30/50 amps). 2021 rates: $45. Mar 01 to Oct 31. (406)827-4757, 2148 Blue Slide Rd, Thompson Falls, MT 59873

THOMPSON FALLS (Public State Park) From Thompson Falls: Go NW 1 mi on MT 200. 18 Avail: Pit toilets. 2021 rates: $14 to $24. May 17 to Sep 15. (406)751-4590

THREE FORKS — C3 *Broadwater*

↓ DAILEY LAKE (Public State Park) From Jct I-90 & US-89, S 21 mi on US-89 to Murphy Lane, E 1 mi to SR-540, S 10.6 mi to Dailey Lake Rd., E 3.3. 35 Avail. 2021 rates: $7 to $12. (406)994-4042

→ LEWIS AND CLARK CAVERNS (Public State Park) From Jct of I-90 & US-287, SW 15 mi on US-287 to Hwy 2, W 5 mi (R). Avail: 9 E (50 amps). 2021 rates: $18 to $24. May 17 to Sep 15. (406)287-3541

← THREE FORKS KOA **Ratings: 6/9★/8.5** (Campground) 62 Avail: 18 full hkups, 44 W, 34 E (30/50 amps). 2021 rates: $65 to $75. May 01 to Sep 30. (406)285-3611, 15 KOA Rd, Three Forks, MT 59752

TOWNSEND — C3 *Broadwater*

↑ CANYON FERRY/WHITE EARTH (Public) From Jct of US-287 & West Shore CR, E 5 mi on West Shore CR (E). 34 Avail. 2021 rates: $10 to $20. (406)475-3921

← TOWNSEND/CANYON FERRY LAKE KOA JOURNEY **Ratings: 6.5/9★/9.5** (RV Park) 61 Avail: 41 full hkups, 20 W, 20 E (30/50 amps). 2021 rates: $55 to $80. (406)266-3100, 81 Silos Rd, Townsend, MT 59644

TROUT CREEK — B1 *Sanders*

↑ TROUT CREEK MOTEL & RV PARK **Ratings: 7/UI/8** (Campground) Avail: 16 full hkups (30/50 amps). 2021 rates: $33 to $40. (406)827-3268, 2972 Hwy 200, Trout Creek, MT 59874

TROY — A1 *Lincoln*

← KOOTENAI RIVER CAMPGROUND **Ratings: 7.5/8.5/7** (Campground) 24 Avail: 13 full hkups, 7 W, 7 E (30/50 amps). 2021 rates: $40 to $55. Apr 01 to Nov 30. (406)295-4090, 11251 US Hwy 2, Troy, MT 59935

VALIER — A2 *Pondera*

↖ LAKE FRANCES CAMPGROUND (Public) From Jct of SR-44 & Teton Rd, W 0.4 mi on Teton Rd (R). Avail: 50 E (30 amps). 2021 rates: $10 to $35. May 01 to Sep 30. (406)279-3361

WEST GLACIER — A2 *Glacier*

↗ GLACIER CAMPGROUND **Ratings: 6/8.5★/8** (Campground) 75 Avail: 75 W, 75 E (20/30 amps). 2021 rates: $40 to $50. May 15 to Sep 30. (888)387-5689, 12070 Hwy 2 E, West Glacier, MT 59936

↑ GLACIER/AVALANCHE (Public National Park) From Jct of US-2 & Going-To-The-Sun Rd, NE 13 mi on Going-To-The-Sun Rd (R). Note: 26' RV length limit. 87 Avail. 2021 rates: $20. Jun 16 to Sep 17. (406)888-7800

↖ GLACIER/FISH CREEK (Public National Park) From Jct US-2 & Going-To-The-Sun Rd, N 2 mi on Going-To-The-Sun Rd to Camas Rd, NW 4 mi to Fish Creek Rd, N 1 mi (E). 178 Avail. 2021 rates: $23. Jun 01 to Sep 08. (406)888-7800

↗ MOOSE CREEK RESORT **Ratings: 6/7.5/7.5** (Campground) 55 Avail: 24 full hkups, 31 W, 31 E (30/50 amps). 2021 rates: $50 to $75. May 15 to Sep 30. (406)387-5280, 11505 Hwy 2 E, West Glacier, MT 59936

→ NORTH AMERICAN RV PARK & YURT VILLAGE **Ratings: 7.5/9.5★/8.5** (Campground) Avail: 108 full hkups (30/50 amps). 2021 rates: $70 to $80. May 01 to Oct 15. (406)387-5800, 10640 US Hwy 2 East, Coram, MT 59913

↗ WEST GLACIER KOA RESORT **Ratings: 8/9.5★/9.5** (Campground) 154 Avail: 132 full hkups, 22 W, 22 E (30/50 amps). 2021 rates: $80 to $160. May 01 to Oct 18. (406)387-5341, 355 Halfmoon Flats Rd, West Glacier, MT 59936

← **WEST GLACIER RV PARK & CABINS**
good sam park **Ratings: 8.5/9.5★/9.5** (RV Resort) Avail: 102 full hkups (30/50 amps). 2021 rates: $90 to $130. May 15 to Oct 01. (844)868-7474, 350 River Bend Drive, West Glacier, MT 59936

WEST YELLOWSTONE — D3 *Gallatin*

WEST YELLOWSTONE See also Cameron, MT; Island Park, ID.

BUFFALO CROSSING RV PARK
good sam park **Ratings: 7.5/9★/9** (RV Park) From Jct US 20/Firehole Ave & US 191/Canyon St: Go 1/8 mi S on US 191/Canyon St (L). Elev 6700 ft.**FAC:** gravel rds. Avail: 25 gravel, patios, 15 pull-thrus, (30x70), back-ins (25x45), 25 full hkups (30/50 amps), WiFi @ sites, laundry. **REC:** boating nearby, hunting nearby, rec open to public. Pets OK. Partial handicap access. No tents. Big rig sites, eco-friendly. 2021 rates: $50 to $85, Military discount. May 01 to Oct 23.
(406)646-4300 Lat: 44.65804, Lon: -111.09965
101 B South Canyon St, West Yellowstone, MT 59758
www.buffalocrossingrvpark.com
See ad this page

PONY EXPRESS RV PARK Ratings: 6/8/7 (RV Park) Avail: 16 full hkups (30/50 amps). 2021 rates: $54 to $69. (800)217-4613, 201 Canyon St. , West Yellowstone, MT 59758

YELLOWSTONE GRIZZLY RV PARK
good sam park **Ratings: 8.5/9.5★/10** (RV Park) Avail: 227 full hkups (30/50 amps). 2021 rates: $55.95 to $106.35. May 01 to Oct 15. (406)646-4466, 210 S Electric St., West Yellowstone, MT 59758

YELLOWSTONE HOLIDAY RV CAMPGROUND & MARINA
good sam park **Ratings: 8.5/9★/9** (Campground) From Jct of US 191 & US 287: Go 5-1/2 mi W on US 287 (L). Elev 6600 ft.**FAC:** gravel rds. Avail: 36 gravel, patios, 11 pull-thrus, (40x72), back-ins (36x68), 36 full hkups (30/50 amps), WiFi @ sites, rentals, laundry, groc, LP gas, fire rings, firewood. **REC:** Hebgen Lake: swim, fishing, marina, kayaking/canoeing, boating nearby, hunting nearby, rec open to public. Pets OK. Partial handicap access. No tents. Big rig sites, eco-friendly. 2021 rates: $70 to $85. May 15 to Sep 30.
(406)646-4242 Lat: 44.80320, Lon: -111.21670
16990 Hebgen Lake Rd, West Yellowstone, MT 59758
www.yellowstoneholiday.com
See ad this page

So you're the one with ""pooch'' duty? Please make a clean sweep of it! Your fellow RVers will appreciate it!

YELLOWSTONE PARK / WEST GATE KOA Ratings: 8.5/UI/8.5 (Campground) 244 Avail: 175 full hkups, 69 W, 69 E (30/50 amps). 2021 rates: $76 to $108. May 22 to Oct 01. (800)562-7591, 3305 Targhee Pass/US 20, West Yellowstone, MT 59758

YELLOWSTONE/ MOUNTAINSIDE KOA JOURNEY **Ratings: 7/UI/8** (Campground) 100 Avail: 90 full hkups, 10 W, 10 E (30/50 amps). 2021 rates: $59 to $102. May 20 to Oct 01. (800)562-5640, 1545 Targhee Pass Hwy, West Yellowstone, MT 59758

WHITE SULPHUR SPRINGS — C3 *Meagher*

CONESTOGA CAMPGROUND **Ratings: 6.5/8.5/8** (Membership Park) 47 Avail: 33 full hkups, 14 W, 14 E (30/50 amps). 2021 rates: $35 to $45. Apr 01 to Nov 30. (406)547-3890, 815 8th Ave SW, White Sulphur Springs, MT 59645

WHITEFISH — A1 *Flathead*

WHITEFISH LAKE (Public State Park) From Whitefish, W 3 mi on US-93 (R). Avail: 1 E. 2021 rates: $18 to $34. (406)751-4590

WHITEFISH RV PARK **Ratings: 7/8/7** (Campground) 39 Avail: 33 full hkups, 6 W, 6 E (30/50 amps). 2021 rates: $60 to $65. (406)862-7275, 6404 Hwy 93 S, Whitefish, MT 59937

WHITEFISH/KALISPELL NORTH KOA **Ratings: 8/8.5/8** (Campground) 90 Avail: 85 full hkups, 5 W, 5 E (30/50 amps). 2021 rates: $77 to $100. May 15 to Sep 15. (800)562-8734, 5121 US-93 S, Whitefish, MT 59937

WOLF CREEK — B2 *Lewis & Clark*

HOLTER LAKE (BLM) (Public Corps) From I-15 (exit 226): Go 3 mi SE along Missouri River. 50 Avail: Pit toilets. 2021 rates: $10 to $15. Mar 15 to Oct 15. (406)235-4314

LOG GULCH (BLM) (Public Corps) From I-25 (exit 226): Go 3 mi E on paved road, then 8 mi on gravel road. 72 Avail: Pit toilets. 2021 rates: $15. (406)235-4480

Know the name? Then you can use our special ""Find-it-Fast'' index to locate your campground on the map. The index arranges private and public campgrounds alphabetically, by state. Next to the name, you'll quickly find the name of the town the park is in, plus the Listing's page number.

NE

Getty Images/iStockphoto

YOU ARE HERE

Nebraska

DID YOU KNOW?

On game days, the University of Nebraska football stadium becomes the third most populated place in the state behind Lincoln and Omaha.

Nebraska defies the stereotype of being a "fly-over" state. Everyone who scratches the surface of Cornhusker Country can discover ample fun-filled diversions. Find everything from major sports to gracious cities.

Omaha Magic

As Nebraska's biggest metropolis, Omaha blends big-city energy with distinctly Midwestern diversions. Omaha is located on the banks of the Missouri River in eastern Nebraska. Walk on the wild side with a visit to the Henry Doorly Zoo and Aquarium, considered one of the best in the nation. Feel the heat of the desert, listen to birds calling in the rainforest and walk among the lemurs. With a farmers market, shops, galleries and restaurants, Omaha's Old Market is a favorite spot to relax. Tons of outdoor spaces and family-friendly attractions round out the offerings.

Walk Among Giants

Walk among (bronze) giants at Spirit of Nebraska's Wilderness and Pioneer Courage Park. More than 100 sculptures that weigh anywhere between 400 pounds and six tons are scattered over six blocks of downtown Omaha, telling the story of the pioneer journey out west.

American Royalty

Explore a symbol of American "royalty" on a visit to Joslyn Castle, which is now part of the Nebraska Statewide Arboretum. The Omaha landmark was built by one of the state's wealthiest families in the early 20th century. The Scottish baronial home is four stories tall and has 35 rooms, including a music room, a ballroom and a gold drawing room.

Fantastic Fountain

Scheduled to reopen soon, Heartland of America Park and Fountain will give visitors another reason to explore Omaha. High points will include a 320-foot

Nebraska Chili and Cinnamon Roll

Chili and a cinnamon roll may seem like a strange combination, but don't knock it until you try it. Served between September and April, this sweet and savory pairing is guaranteed to warm you up on a cold winter day. Get your hands on this local specialty at Runza, a chain restaurant found throughout the state.

VISITOR CENTER

TIME ZONE
Mountain/Central Standard

ROAD & HIGHWAY INFORMATION
800-906-9069
511.nebraska.gov

FISHING & HUNTING INFORMATION
402-471-0641
outdoornebraska.gov

BOATING INFORMATION
402-471-0641
mdwfp.com/law-enforcement/boating-rules-regs

NATIONAL PARKS
nps.gov/ne

STATE PARKS
outdoornebraska.gov/stateparks

TOURISM INFORMATION
Nebraska Tourism Commission
877-NEBRASKA
visitnebraska.com

TOP TOURISM ATTRACTIONS
1) Chimney Rock National Historic Site
2) Lake McConaughy
3) Henry Doorly Zoo

MAJOR CITIES
Omaha, Lincoln (capital), Bellevue, Grand Island, Kearney

water jet and light show. There also will be Lewis & Clark Interpretive exhibits, WWII and Airborne Memorial Sculptures and a pedestrian bridge connecting to the Lewis & Clark Landing.

Prairies, Sandhills and Wagons

As pioneers crossed the prairies heading to Oregon and California in covered wagons, they noted the many distinctive landmarks that guided their way. With not much else on the horizon, the dramatic sight of Scotts Bluff rising 800 feet over the river below made it an important landmark. Today, history and natural beauty can be explored at this national monument. Roam the unique landscape of the Sandhills with a drive along the Sandhills Journey Scenic Byway in central Nebraska.

Rad River

Follow Nebraska's Niobrara River through prairies and forests, past waterfalls and dramatic bluffs. Over 70 miles of this waterway has been designated as a National Scenic River, making it one of the state's most popular spots for paddling. White-sand beaches are an unexpected find in the Midwest, but that's what you'll find along the shores of Nebraska's massive Lake McConaughy. Boating, fishing and paddling are popular ways to enjoy this gorgeous lake. North America's longest river, the Missouri, flows for 400 miles along Nebraska's eastern border, providing prime fishing.

Adventure in the Husker State

Where can you view more than 80 percent of the world's sandhill crane population at once? Right here in the heart of Buffalo County. Tucked away in the Platte River Valley, easygoing Kearney hosts one of nature's most awe-inspiring wonders every spring. Come watch the crane migration and stay a little longer for the cultural museums, historical sites and family-friendly activities.

Fast-moving water in Norden Chute on the Niobrara River in northern Nebraska.

Lazy Lake Days

Fort Kearny State Recreation Area invites you to take life at a slower pace. Flick your rod from its wheelchair-accessible fishing pier and dip your paddle in sandpit lakes. Less than 20 miles away is War Axe State Recreation Area. The park is home to a 16-acre lake making it a good destination for boating and fishing. More lakes await in nearby Windmill State Recreation Area. Get on the water and spot the restored windmills that used to pump water for steam locomotives.

Amazing Museums and Sites

Kearney's rich heritage can be discovered in its museums and historical sites. Learn about the Western settlers who traversed this area at the Archway Museum, which spans Interstate 80 in a stunning feat of engineering. Inside, explore a reconstructed blacksmith shop at Fort Kearny State Historical Park, the first fort dedicated to protecting Oregon Trail pioneers. Round out your experience by tracing the evolution of the automobile at the Classic Car Collection and viewing works by regional artists at the Museum of Nebraska Art.

Window to the Past

In Grand Island in the southeast, the Stuhr Museum is 200-acres of living history featuring over 100 structures that tell the story of the pioneers who settled the first communities in Nebraska. Through interpretation, artifacts and more, visitors to the Stuhr Museum will understand the challenges, triumphs and circumstances of those who called Nebraska home in the late 1800s.

Relics of the Frontier

You have to see the Stuhr exhibits to believe them. Railroad Town is a full pioneer town featuring over 50 structures, including historic homes, businesses, a rail depot, blacksmith shop and more. The Stuhr Building, designed by world-renowned architect Edward Durell Stone, features rotating art exhibits and historic artifacts. The Fonner Rotunda houses Native American and cowboy artifacts, and the Antique Farm Machinery building featuring autos and tractors spanning more than a century. The beautiful Hornady Family Arbor and Fonda Rose Garden cultivates lush plants that thrive on the Great Plains.

Rugged Rocks

While much of Nebraska is covered in gently rolling plains, outdoor adventure in the Cornhusker State also involves exquisite and geologically unique landscapes. There's Indian Cave State Park, tucked in the southeastern corner of the state, just south of Omaha. The park sprawls across 3,052 acres astride the mighty Missouri River, and is home to a massive sandstone cavern from which it gets its name.

Toadstools of Stone

In northwestern Nebraska, a visit to Toadstool Geologic Park puts you in the middle of moonlike badlands. You can hike the park's interpretive trail and point your camera at some of the most uniquely spectacular geography in the country.

good sam park

Featured Good Sam Parks

NEBRASKA

When you stay with Good Sam, you can expect the highest degree of cleanliness and friendliness, and better yet, you get **10% off** overnight campground fees.

If you're not already a Good Sam member you can purchase your membership at one of these locations:

ASHLAND
Ashland RV Campground

GERING
Robidoux RV Park

GREENWOOD
Pine Grove RV Park

KEARNEY
Kearney RV Park & Campground

KIMBALL
High Point RV Park

LINCOLN
Camp A Way RV Park

NEBRASKA CITY
Victorian Acres RV Park

NORTH PLATTE
Holiday RV Park & Campground
I-80 Lakeside Campground

OGALLALA
Country View Campground

VALENTINE
Fishberry Campground

YORK
York Kampground

Getty Images/iStockphoto

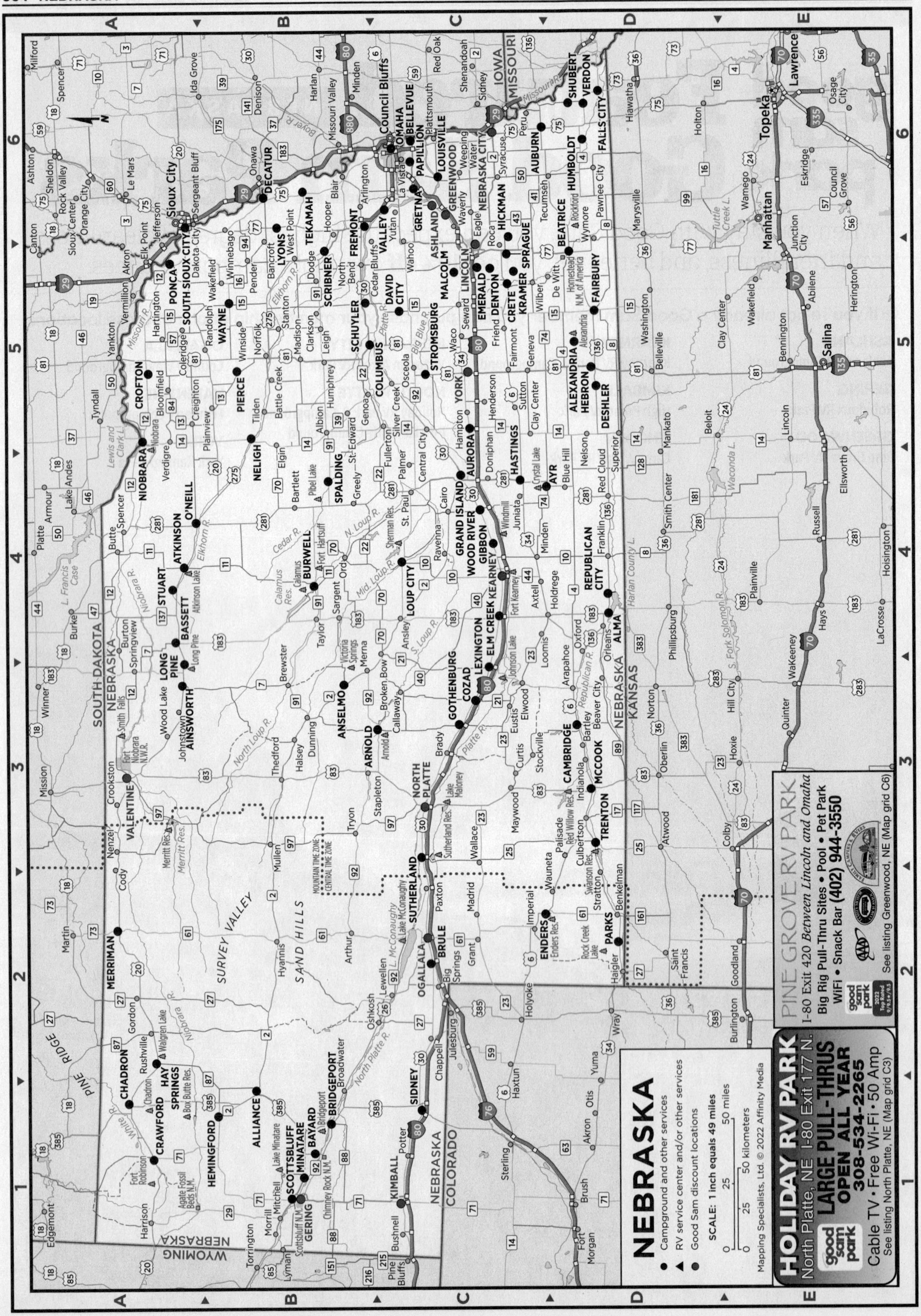
NEBRASKA
● Campground and other services
▲ RV service center and/or other services
● Good Sam discount locations
SCALE: 1 inch equals 49 miles
0 25 50 miles
0 25 50 kilometers
Mapping Specialists, Ltd. © 2022 Affinity Media
HOLIDAY RV PARK
North Platte, NE I-80 Exit 177 N.
LARGE PULL-THRUS
OPEN ALL YEAR
308-534-2265
Cable TV • Free Wi-Fi • 50 Amp
See listing North Platte, NE (Map grid C3)
PINE GROVE RV PARK
I-80 Exit 420 Between Lincoln and Omaha
Big Rig Pull-Thru Sites • Pool • Pet Park
WiFi • Snack Bar (402) 944-3550
See listing Greenwood, NE (Map grid C6)
SOUTH DAKOTA
NEBRASKA
WYOMING
COLORADO
KANSAS
IOWA
MISSOURI
SAND HILLS
SURVEY VALLEY
PINE RIDGE
MOUNTAIN TIME ZONE
CENTRAL TIME ZONE
Omaha
Lincoln
Council Bluffs
Sioux City
North Platte
Grand Island
Kearney
Scottsbluff
Valentine
Topeka
Manhattan
Salina

NE

ROAD TRIPS

Discover a Trove of Heartland Treasures

Nebraska

LOCATION
NEBRASKA

DISTANCE
335 MILES

DRIVE TIME
4 HR 55 MINS

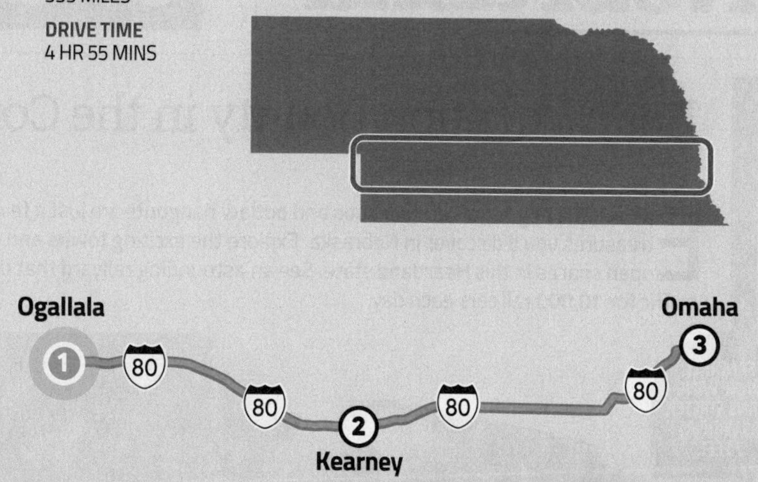

This tour along Interstate 80 will give you a glimpse of some of Nebraska's most awe-inspiring sights, including a lake that teems with hefty rainbow trout and walleye; a museum that dramatically arches over the interstate; and an astonishing zoo with indoor animal habitats built around ecosystems from across the globe. There's nothing plain about this stretch of the Cornhusker State.

1 Ogallala
Starting Point

At 22 miles long and 4 miles across, Lake McConaughy holds endless possibilities for boaters and anglers. The cool, clear, deep waters make it the perfect place to cast a line for rainbow trout and catfish. Walleye also thrive in these waters, and the state record of 16 pounds, 2 ounces came from "Lake Mac," as the locals call it.

In nearby Ogallala, the Mansion on the Hill preserves the area's homesteading past. Tour the structure and marvel at its 10-foot-tall ceilings, solid brass hardware and ornate, curved staircase.

2 Kearney
Drive 149 miles ▪ 2 hours, 12 minutes

The Great Platte River Road Archway Monument can't be missed from Interstate 80; in fact, a large portion of the museum's complex crosses the highway like a bridge, an audacious architectural accomplishment that has made it one of Nebraska's top landmarks. The contents of the museum are no less amazing. On display are exhibits that chronicle the hardships and accomplishments of pioneers who traveled through the region along the same route taken by the interstate. See artifacts from the Pony Express, the Transcontinental Telegraph and the Transcontinental Railroad. On the Archway Campus, visitors can get lost in the Trailblaze Maze and embark on hiking and biking trails. At the onsite Nebraska Visitor Center, travelers can plan even more cornhusker adventures.

Getty Images/iStockphoto

3 Omaha
Drive 186 miles ▪ 2 hours, 43 minutes

When you arrive in Omaha, you can rest assured that there's lots of fun to be had. Omaha is a cosmopolitan city with a small-town feel that boasts unique attractions, great food and ample opportunity for good old-fashioned family fun. Ready to see some exotic animals? Even the cold Nebraska winters can't chill the habitats at Omaha's Henry Doorly Zoo and Aquarium. The geodesic dome is home to the largest indoor desert in the world and supports plants and animals from three distinct environments. In the nocturnal exhibit, visitors can see animals that thrive at night. Stroll from Nebraska to Iowa on the Bob Kerry Pedestrian Bridge, a 3,000-foot walkway that crosses the Missouri River.

BIKING · BOATING · DINING · ENTERTAINMENT · FISHING · HIKING · HUNTING · PADDLING · SHOPPING · SIGHTSEEING

 See map page 564

Nebraska SPOTLIGHTS

Reap Vacation Bounty in the Cornhusker State

Epic animal migrations, indoor zoos and outlaw hangouts are just a few of the treasures you'll discover in Nebraska. Explore the exciting towns and wide-open spaces in this Heartland state. See an astounding railyard that directs traffic for 10,000 rail cars each day.

SANDHILL CRANE WINGSPANS STRETCH AS WIDE AS 7 FEET.

Getty Images/iStockphoto

Sandhill cranes take wing over the Platte River Valley, a major crane migration stop.

Kearny

Where can you witness a gathering of more than 80 percent of the world's sandhill crane population at once? Right in the heart of the Cornhusker State. Tucked away in the Platte River Valley, easygoing Kearney hosts one of nature's most awe-inspiring wonders every spring. Come watch the crane migration and stay a little longer for the museums, historical sites and family-friendly activities.

Witness Sandhill Crane Migration

One of nature's most dazzling spectacles takes place along the Platte River Valley. From late February to early April, more than 600,000 sandhill cranes gather here before continuing their northward migration. You can see these majestic birds at Rowe Sanctuary. Grab a seat in the indoor viewing area or reserve a blind for an up-close viewing experience. Guided tours are available, too, if you want to learn more about sandhill cranes and their spring migration.

Lazy Lake Days

Fort Kearny State Recreation Area is a great place for watersports. Flick your rod from its wheelchair-accessible fishing pier and dip your paddle in sandpit lakes. Less than 20 miles away is War Axe State Recreation Area. The park is home to a 16-acre lake, a great destination for boating and fishing.

North Platte

The sprawling Union Pacific Bailey Yard ranks as the largest railroad classification yard on Earth, spanning 2,850 acres (equivalent to 2,800 football fields). This yard manages more than 150 trains and 10,000 rail cars every day. About 3,000 rail cars are sorted in "hump yards" and depart to different destinations. See all of this taking place from the eight-story Golden Spike Tower.

Ogallala

Get a taste of the Wild West. Ogallala proudly celebrates its roots as a vital frontier community. See where many early Ogallala gunslingers found their final resting places at Boot Hill (not to be confused with the cemetery of the same name in Deadwood, South Dakota). Although the "residents" have since been relocated, historical markers tell the tale of many an outlaw drawn to Ogallala by the booming cattle trade of the late 1900s.

FOR MORE INFORMATION

Nebraska Tourism Commission, 877-NEBRASKA, visitnebraska.com

North Platte/Lincoln County Visitor's Bureau, 800-955-4528, www.visitnorthplatte.com

Visit Ogallala, 800-658-4390, www.explorekeithcounty.com

Visit Omaha, 866-937-662, www.visitomaha.com

LOCAL FAVORITE

A Twist on Chex Party Mix

This wholesome treat is perfect for long drives across Cornhusker country. It's also a great way to dispense of snack-food leftovers. *Recipe by Randy Harwick.*

INGREDIENTS

- ☐ 1 box Corn Chex cereal
- ☐ 1 box Rice Chex cereal
- ☐ 1 box Wheat Chex cereal
- ☐ 1 bag of Bugles (medium size)
- ☐ 1 box Cheese Nips (Cheez-Its work just as well)
- ☐ 1 large can of nuts (I use cashews, but use whatever nuts you like)
- ☐ 2 aluminum turkey roaster pans
- ☐ 5 sticks and 2 Tbsp butter
- ☐ 1 ⅔ Tbsp garlic powder (not garlic salt)
- ☐ 14 Tbsp of Worcestershire sauce. (¼ cup equals 14 tablespoons and close counts)
- ☐ 3 ⅓ Tbsp seasoned salt
- ☐ 1 Tbsp onion powder (not onion salt)

DIRECTIONS

Combine cereal, Bugles, Cheese Nips and nuts and divide between the 2 pans.

Melt the butter in a saucepan and mix in the other ingredients until dissolved (close counts for measuring); pour the mixture over the 2 pans and mix thoroughly.

Bake at 250° for 1 hour, stirring every 15 minutes

Dry on paper towel and allow to cool.

Store in gallon Ziplock bags and it will still be fresh in a month.

Nebraska

AINSWORTH — A3 *Brown*

KELLER PARK SRA (Public State Park) From Jct of Hwys 20 & 183, N 9 mi on Hwy 183 (L).Entrance fee required. Avail: 25 E (20/30 amps), Pit toilets. 2021 rates: $8 to $17. (402)684-2921

ALEXANDRIA — D5 *Jefferson*

ALEXANDRIA STATE REC AREA (Public State Park) From Jct of US-77 & US-136 (in Beatrice), W 37 mi on US-136 to SR-53 (in town), N 6 mi to park access, E 3 mi (R). Entrance fee required. Avail: 25 E (30 amps), Pit toilets. 2021 rates: $7 to $13. Apr 01 to Oct 31. (402)729-5777

ALLIANCE — B1 *Box Butte*

J & C RV PARK **Ratings: 4/NA/7.5** (Campground) Avail: 13 full hkups (30/50 amps). 2021 rates: $45. (308)762-3860, 2491 S Hwy 385, Alliance, NE 69301

JESKE'S OVER THE HILL CAMPGROUND (RV Spaces) 15 Avail: 4 full hkups, 11 W (30/50 amps), Pit toilets. 2021 rates: $27 to $35. (308)762-3763, 2131 CR 59, Alliance, NE 69301

ALMA — D4 *Harlan*

ALMA RV PARK (CITY PARK) (Public) From Jct of US-183 & South St, E 0.6 mi on South St (R). Avail: 36 full hkups (30/50 amps). 2021 rates: $25. Apr 15 to Oct 15. (308)928-2242

HARLAN COUNTY LAKE - COE/METHODIST COVE (Public Corps) From Jct of Hwy 183 & South St (RD-B), E 2 mi on South St (R). Avail: 49 E (50 amps). 2021 rates: $18 to $28. May 01 to Sep 30. (308)799-2105

ANSELMO — B3 *Custer*

VICTORIA SPRINGS SRA (Public State Park) From town, E 6 mi on Spur 21A (R). Entrance fee required. Avail: 21 E (30/50 amps). 2021 rates: $11 to $17. May 01 to Nov 30. (308)749-2235

ARNOLD — C3 *Custer*

ARNOLD SRA (Public State Park) From Jct of US-83 & SR-92, E 16 mi on SR-92 to SR-40, S 1 mi (R). Entrance fee required. 80 Avail: 20 W, 20 E (20/30 amps), Pit toilets. 2021 rates: $6 to $15. (308)848-2228

ASHLAND — C6 *Cass*

ASHLAND RV CAMPGROUND

good sam park **Ratings: 5.5/10★/9.5** (RV Park) From jct US-6 & Hwy 66: Go 1/2 mi NW on Hwy 66, then 161 feet on Ash St (R). **FAC:** paved rds. Avail: 30 paved, patios, 2 pull-thrus, (30x90), back-ins (30x80), 30 W, 30 E (30/50 amps), WiFi @ sites, tent sites, dump, laundry, fire rings, firewood. **REC:** boating nearby, playground, hunting nearby. Pets OK. Partial handicap access. 2021 rates: $38 to $43. Apr 01 to Oct 31.
(402)401-4231 Lat: 41.04569, Lon: -96.36242
1301 Ash Street, Ashland, NE 68003
www.ashlandrvcampground.com
See ad this page

EUGENE T MAHONEY (Public State Park) From Jct of I-80 & SR-66 (exit 426), W 0.5 mi on SR-66 (R). Avail: 74 E (20/30 amps). 2021 rates: $10 to $35. (402)944-2523

MEMPHIS SRA (Public State Park) From town: Go 8 mi N on Hwy 63, then 1 mi W on CR D. 100 Avail: Pit toilets. 2021 rates: $8. (402)471-5497

ATKINSON — A4 *Holt*

OREGON TRAIL RV PARK & CAMPGROUND **Ratings: 5/8★/6** (Campground) Avail: 19 full hkups (30/50 amps). 2021 rates: $28. (402)925-5117, 702 N. Carburry, Atkinson, NE 68713

AUBURN — C6 *Nemaha*

LONGSCREEK RV PARK **Ratings: 6/UI/6** (Campground) Avail: 32 full hkups (30/50 amps). 2021 rates: $30. (402)274-3143, 517 J St., Auburn, NE 68305

AURORA — C5 *Hamilton*

STREETER PARK (Public) From Jct of I-80 & SR-14 (exit 332), N 3 mi on SR-14 to Hwy 34, W 0.25 mi (R). 18 Avail: 8 W, 18 E (30 amps). Apr 01 to Oct 31. (402)694-6992

AYR — C4 *Adams*

CRYSTAL LAKE (Public) From Jct of SR-74 & cnty rd (unnamed-gravel rd in town), N 1.5 mi on cnty rd, follow signs (E). Avail: 12 E (20/30 amps), Pit toilets. 2021 rates: $7 to $13. (402)364-2145

BASSETT — A4 *Rock*

BASSETT CITY PARK (Public) In town, W 1 blk on US-20 (L). Avail: 17 E (30 amps). (402)684-3338

BAYARD — B1 *Morrill*

BAYARD See also Bridgeport, Gering & Scottsbluff.

CHIMNEY ROCK PIONEER CROSSING **Ratings: 5/9★/6.5** (Campground) Avail: 16 full hkups (30/50 amps). 2021 rates: $32 to $36. (308)631-4700, 10012 Road 75, Bayard, NE 69334

BEATRICE — D5 *Gage*

CHAUTAUQUA PARK (Public) From Jct of US-136 & US-77, S 1 mi on US-77 to Grable Ave., E 0.3 mi (L). 20 Avail: (30/50 amps). 2021 rates: $18. (402)228-0315

ROCKFORD SRA (Public State Park) From Jct of US-136 & SR-4, E 7 mi on SR-4 to Rockford Lake Cnty Rd, S 2 mi (L). Entrance fee required. Avail: 32 E (30/50 amps), Pit toilets. 2021 rates: $8 to $17. (402)729-5777

BELLEVUE — C6 *Sarpy*

HAWORTH PARK (CITY PARK) (Public) At the east edge of town at jct Hwy 370 & Payne Dr at the Missouri River. 129 Avail: 109 W, 109 E (30/50 amps). 2021 rates: $20 to $25. Apr 01 to Oct 01. (402)293-3122

MILITARY PARK OFFUTT BASE LAKE FAMCAMP (OFFUTT AFB) (Public) From Jct of I-80W & Hwy 75S, go on Hwy 75S to Hwy 34E, go 2 mi to Harlan-Lewis Rd, N 2.5 mi, follow signs. Avail: 40 full hkups (30/50 amps). 2021 rates: $20 to $25. (402)294-2108

BRIDGEPORT — B1 *Morrill*

BRIDGEPORT SRA (Public State Park) 1/10 mi W of town off US 26. 130 Avail: Pit toilets. 2021 rates: $8. (308)436-3777

MEADOW PARK RV AND MOTEL **Ratings: 7/8/7** (Campground) Avail: 16 full hkups (30/50 amps). 2021 rates: $35. (308)279-1176, 9868 Highway 385, Bridgeport, NE 69336

BRULE — C2 *Keith*

EAGLE CANYON HIDEAWAY **Ratings: 7/8.5★/7.5** (Campground) Avail: 30 full hkups (30/50 amps). 2021 rates: $37 to $41. Mar 15 to Nov 30. (308)287-2673, 1086 Lakeview West Rd, Brule, NE 69127

BURWELL — B4 *Garfield*

CALAMUS RESERVOIR (Public State Park) From town, N 2 mi on Windy Hill Rd., W 3.25 mi. on Pebble Creek Rd., NW 2.25 mi on Dam Rd. Avail: 57 E (30/50 amps). 2021 rates: $15 to $19. (308)346-5666

CAMBRIDGE — D3 *Frontier*

MEDICINE CREEK SRA (TRAIL 4) (Public State Park) From town, W 2 mi on US-6/34 to Medicine Creek Dam Rd, N 8.3 mi to Trail 4, W 1 mi (E). Entrance fee required. Avail: 72 E (20/30 amps). 2021 rates: $8 to $35. (308)697-4667

CHADRON — A1 *Dawes*

CHADRON

(Public State Park) From Jct of US-385 & US-20, S 8.4 mi on US-385 (R). Entrance fee required. Elev 3879 ft.**FAC:** paved rds. Avail: 88 paved, patios, back-ins (30x50), 70 E (30 amps), tent sites, rentals, dump, laundry, firewood. **REC:** heated pool, pond, fishing, playground. Pets OK. Partial handicap access, 14 day max stay. 2021 rates: $10 to $35.
(308)432-6167 Lat: 42.70914, Lon: -103.01974
15951 Hwy 385, Chadron, NE 69337
outdoornebraska.gov

COLUMBUS — C5 *Platte*

LOUP PARK (Public) From Jct of US-30 & 18th Ave, N 4 mi on 18th Ave to 83rd St, W 1 mi (L). Avail: 28 E (20/30 amps). May 01 to Nov 01. (402)562-5709

COZAD — C3 *Dawson*

JOHNSON LAKE SRA/INLET AREA (Public State Park) From Jct of I-80 & US 283 (Exit 237), S 7.4 mi to Johnson Lake Rd, W 0.1 mi on Johnson Lake Rd (L) Entrance fee required. Avail: 30 E (30/50 amps). 2021 rates: $12 to $18. May 01 to Oct 31. (308)785-2685

CRAWFORD — A1 *Dawes*

FORT ROBINSON (Public State Park) From Jct of SR-20 & 1st St (downtown), W 3 mi on SR-20 (R). Entrance fee required. Avail: 100 E (30/50 amps). 2021 rates: $18 to $24. (308)665-2900

CRETE — C5 *Saline*

TUXEDO PARK (Public) From Jct of US-33 & W 13th St, W 1.9 mi on W 13th St to CR-2100, N 2 mi (E). Avail: 20 E (30 amps). 2021 rates: $10. Apr 01 to Oct 15. (402)826-4315

CROFTON — A5 *Knox*

LEWIS & CLARK LAKE - COE/COTTONWOOD (Public Corps) From Yankton, SD, W 4 mi on SD-52, S 1 mi on Dam Toe Rd (L). Avail: 77 E (50 amps). 2021 rates: $16 to $18. Apr 21 to Oct 16. (402)667-2546

LEWIS AND CLARK SRA/BLOOMFIELD AREA (Public State Park) From town, N 7 mi on SR-121 to CR-R54E, W 7 mi (R). Entrance fee required. Avail: 12 E (30/50 amps). 2021 rates: $15. (402)388-4169

DAVID CITY — C5 *Butler*

DAVID (CITY PARK) (Public) From Jct of S Hwy 15 & Kansas St exit, E 0.3 mi on Kansas St (L). Avail: 12 E (20 amps). 2021 rates: $10. Apr 01 to Oct 31. (402)367-3135

DECATUR — B6 *Burt*

BECK MEMORIAL PARK (Public) From Jct of 7th St & Broadway, S 0.4 mi on Broadway to 13th St, E 0.05 mi to 3rd Ave, N 0.05 mi to 11th St, E 0.05 mi (L). 24 Avail: 14 W, 24 E (30/50 amps). 2021 rates: $12 to $20. Apr 01 to Oct 31. (402)349-5360

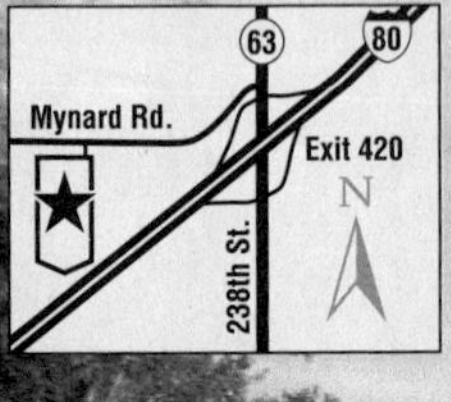

DENTON — C5 *Lancaster*

CONESTOGA SRA (Public State Park) From Denton, N 2 mi on SR-55A to cnty rd, W 0.5 mi (L). Avail: 25 E (30/50 amps), Pit toilets. 2021 rates: $8 to $19. (402)796-2362

DESHLER — D5 *Thayer*

DESHLER (CITY PARK) (Public) From Jct of Hwy 136 & 1st St, S .3 mi on 1st St to Hebron Ave, E 0.2 mi to 4th St, S 0.6 mi (L). Avail: 12 full hkups (20 amps). (402)365-4260

ELM CREEK — C4 *Johnson*

SANDY CHANNEL SRA (Public State Park) From town: Go 3-1/2 mi S on US 183. 30 Avail: Pit toilets. 2021 rates: $8. Sep 15 to May 01. (308)865-5305

THE 4 SEASONS RV PARK **Ratings: 4/4.5/5.5** (RV Park) 43 Avail: 38 full hkups, 5 W, 5 E (30/50 amps). 2021 rates: $40. (308)962-4168, 2005 US Hwy 183, Elm Creek, NE 68836

EMERALD — C5 *Lancaster*

PAWNEE SRA (Public State Park) From Jct of SR-79 & US-34, W 4.1 mi on US-34 to 112th St, S 1.4 mi (R). Avail: 68 E (30/50 amps). 2021 rates: $7 to $18. (402)796-2362

ENDERS — C2 *Chase*

ENDERS RESERVOIR SRA (Public State Park) From town, S 2 mi on US-6/61 (R). Entrance fee required. Avail: 42 E (30/50 amps). 2021 rates: $9 to $19. (308)394-5118

FAIRBURY — D5 *Jefferson*

ROCK CREEK STATION STATE HISTORICAL PARK (Public State Park) From Jct of US-136 & Hwy 15, S 1 mi on Hwy 15 to PWS Rd, E 5.5 mi to 573 Ave, S 1 mi to 710 Ave, E 1.5 mi (E). Entrance fee required. Avail: 13 E (30/50 amps). 2021 rates: $15 to $25. (402)729-5777

FALLS CITY — D6 *Richardson*

STANTON LAKE PARK (Public) From Jct of Hwy 73 & 25th St, W 1 mi on 25th St (E). Avail: 10 full hkups (30 amps). 2021 rates: $20. (402)245-2851

FREMONT — B6 *Dodge*

FREMONT LAKES SRA/PATHFINDER CAMPGROUND (Public State Park) From jct US-77 & US-30: Go 3-1/2 mi SW on US-30, then 1 mi S on CR 20, then 5 mi W on W Military Ave, then 1 mi S on CR 19 (L). Avail: 97 E (30/50 amps). 2021 rates: $16 to $20. (402)727-2922

FREMONT LAKES SRA/VICTORY LAKE CAMPGROUND (Public State Park) From jct of US-77 & US-30: Go 3-1/2 mi SW on US-30, then 1 mi S on CR 20, then 3/4 mi E on W Military Ave, then 500 feet S on Ridge Rd, then 3/4 mi W on State Lakes Rd (L). Avail: 69 E (20/30 amps). 2021 rates: $16 to $20. (402)727-2922

GERING — B1 *Scotts Bluff*

ROBIDOUX RV PARK

good sam park **Ratings: 8.5/8.5★/9.5** (Public) N-bnd: On NE 71 take Gering exit right, then 1-1/2 mi N on Five Rocks Rd (L); S-Bnd: From Jct of NE 71 & NE 92: keep S 4-3/4 mi on Ave I (becomes Five Rocks Rd) (R). Elev 4100 ft.**FAC:** paved rds. Avail: 42 paved, patios, 27 pull-thrus, (35x65), back-ins (35x40), 37 full hkups, 5 W, 5 E (30/50 amps), WiFi @ sites, tent sites, dump, laundry. **REC:** playground. Pets OK. Partial handicap access. Big rig sites. 2021 rates: $34 to $39.50, Military discount.
(308)436-2046 Lat: 41.81134, Lon: -103.67503
585 Five Rocks Rd, Gering, NE 69341
www.gering.org/robidoux-rv-park
See ad this page

GIBBON — C4 *Buffalo*

WINDMILL SRA (Public State Park) From Jct of I-80 & Gibbon (exit 285), N 0.5 mi on Gibbon (R). Entrance fee required. Avail: 69 E (30/50 amps). 2021 rates: $12 to $18. (308)468-5700

GOTHENBURG — C3 *Dawson*

GOTHENBURG BLUE HERON CAMPGROUND (Campground) (Rebuilding) 44 Avail: 14 full hkups, 30 W, 30 E (30/50 amps). 2021 rates: $39 to $42. Apr 01 to Oct 30. (308)537-7387, 1102 South Lake Ave, Gothenburg, NE 69138

LAFAYETTE PARK (Public) From Jct of US-30 & US-47, N 1 mi on US-47 (L). 30 Avail: 30 W, 30 E (30 amps). 2021 rates: $10 to $15. Apr 01 to Nov 01. (308)537-2299

GRAND ISLAND — C4 *Hall*

GRAND ISLAND KOA **Ratings: 9/9.5★/9** (Campground) 84 Avail: 77 full hkups, 7 W, 7 E (30/50 amps). 2021 rates: $45 to $80. Apr 01 to Oct 16. (800)562-0850, 904 South B Rd, Doniphan, NE 68832

MORMON ISLAND SRA (Public State Park) From Jct of I-80 & US-281 (exit 312), N 0.2 mi on US-281 (R). Entrance fee required. Avail: 35 E (30/50 amps). 2021 rates: $12 to $18. (308)385-6211

Things to See and Do

STUHR MUSEUM OF THE PRAIRIE PIONEER
One of America's largest living history museums and greatest treasures. 200 acres & more than 100 structures (including Henry Fonda's birthplace). Antique farm machinery & auto collection, 1890's railroad town, arboretum & mu-

Refer to the Table of Contents in front of the Guide to locate everything you need.

seum shop. Partial handicap access. RV accessible. Restrooms. Food. Hours: 9am to 5pm; Sun 12pm to 5pm. Adult fee: $6 to $10.
(308)385-5316 Lat: 40.88286, Lon: -98.37450
3133 West Hwy 34, Grand Island, NE 68801
stuhrmuseum.org
See ad page 562

GREENWOOD — C6 *Cass*

PINE GROVE RV PARK
good sam park **Ratings: 9/9.5★/9.5** (Campground) W Bnd: From Jct I-80 & NE 63 (exit 420): Go 100 ft N on NE 63; then 1/2 mi W on Mynard Rd (L) or; E Bnd: From Jct I-80 & NE 63 (exit 420): On NE 63 go N over I-80; continue past ramps another 100'; then 1/2 mi W on Mynard Rd (L).

STAY HERE! OMAHA & LINCOLN NEARBY!
A countryside setting with many fun things to do. Relax in our cocktail lounge after city visits. OPEN ALL YEAR! Only 30 minutes from the famous Henry Doorly Zoo, the College World Series Stadium & Cornhuskers Stadium.

FAC: gravel rds. Avail: 100 gravel, 77 pull-thrus, (44x80), back-ins (44x35), 100 full hkups (30/50 amps), WiFi @ sites, tent sites, rentals, dump, laundry, groc, firewood. **REC:** pool, wading pool, playground. Pets OK. Big rig sites, eco-friendly. 2021 rates: $32 to $63, Military discount.
(402)944-3550 Lat: 40.97150, Lon: -96.39558
23403 Mynard Rd, Greenwood, NE 68366
pinegrovervpark.com
See ad opposite page, 564

GRETNA — C6 *Sarpy*

WEST OMAHA KOA **Ratings: 8.5/7.5/7.5** (Campground) 72 Avail: 61 full hkups, 11 W, 11 E (30/50 amps). 2021 rates: $57 to $86. Apr 01 to Oct 31. (402)332-3010, 14601 Hwy 6, Gretna, NE 68028

HASTINGS — C4 *Adams*

ADAMS COUNTY FAIRGROUNDS (Public) From W Jct of US-281, US-6/US-34 & S Baltimore Ave, N 0.2 mi on S Baltimore Ave (R). 396 Avail: 20 full hkups, 86 W, 376 E (20/50 amps). 2021 rates: $14 to $25. (402)462-3247

HAY SPRINGS — A2 *Sheridan*

WALGREN LAKE SRA (Public State Park) From Jct of US-20 & SR-87 (in town), E 3 mi on US-20 to park access cnty rd, S 3 mi to park entrance, E 0.6 mi (R). 40 Avail: Pit toilets. 2021 rates: $8. (308)432-6167

HEBRON — D5 *Thayer*

RIVERSIDE PARK (Public) From Jct of Hwy 81 & Jefferson Ave., W .8 mi. to 7th st., S 1 block. Avail: 16 E (30 amps). 2021 rates: $15. May 01 to Nov 30. (402)768-6322

HEMINGFORD — B1 *Dawes*

BOX BUTTE RESERVOIR SRA (Public State Park) From Jct of SR-87 & Mainstreet (cnty rd), N 10 mi on cnty rd to park access rd, W 1 mi (E). Avail: 14 E (30/50 amps), Pit toilets. 2021 rates: $10 to $35. (308)665-2903

HICKMAN — C6 *Lancaster*

STAGECOACH SRA (Public State Park) From Jct of US-77 & SR-33, S 4 mi on US-77 to Panama rd, E 3.5 mi (L). Entrance fee required. Avail: 22 E (30/50 amps), Pit toilets. 2021 rates: $8 to $17. (402)796-2362

WAGON TRAIN SRA (Public State Park) From Jct of SR-33 & US-77, S 2 mi on US-77 to CR-S55G, E 6 mi (E). Entrance fee required. Avail: 28 E (30/50 amps), Pit toilets. 2021 rates: $8 to $17. (402)796-2362

HUMBOLDT — D6 *Richardson*

HUMBOLDT LAKE PARK (Public) From Jct of SR-105 & SR-4, S 1 mi (N side of lake) on SR-105 (R). Avail: 12 E (20 amps). 2021 rates: $10. Apr 01 to Sep 30. (402)862-2171

KEARNEY — C4 *Buffalo*

FORT KEARNY SRA (Public State Park) From Jct of I-80 & SR-10, S 3 mi on SR-10 (Minden exit #279) to L-50A, W 2 mi then N 1 mi (E). Entrance fee required. Avail: 94 E (30 amps). 2021 rates: $8 to $35. Mar 01 to Oct 31. (308)865-5305

KEARNEY RV PARK & CAMPGROUND
good sam park **Ratings: 8.5/9.5★/9** (RV Park) From Jct I-80 (Exit 272) & Hwy 44 (2nd Ave): Go 1/4 mi N on Hwy 44, then 1/4 mi E on Talmadge, then 1/4 mi S on Central Ave, then 3/4 mi E on 1st St (Archway Pkwy) (L). **FAC:** gravel rds. 96 Avail: 37 paved, 59 gravel, patios, 96 pull-thrus, (30x100), 96 full hkups (30/50 amps), WiFi @ sites, tent sites, dump, laundry, LP gas. **REC:** Getaway Bay: swim, fishing, playground, hunting nearby. Pets OK. Partial handicap access. Big rig sites, eco-friendly. 2021 rates: $45, Military discount.
(308)237-7275 Lat: 40.67049, Lon: -99.06927
1140 E 1st Street, Kearney, NE 68847
kearneyrv.com
See ad this page

KIMBALL — C1 *Kimball*

HIGH POINT RV PARK
good sam park **Ratings: 7/9.5★/9** (Campground) From jct Hwy 32 & S Hwy 71: Go 1/4 mi N on S Hwy 71 (L). **FAC:** gravel rds. Avail: 16 gravel, 16 pull-thrus, (34x65), 16 full hkups (30/50 amps), WiFi @ sites, tent sites, dump, laundry, groc, LP bottles, firewood, restaurant. **REC:** boating nearby, hunting nearby. Pets OK. Big rig sites. 2021 rates: $43. ATM.
(308)230-2003 Lat: 41.221061, Lon: -103.664497
1508 S Hwy 71, Kimball, NE 69145
www.highpointrvpark.net
See ad this page

OLIVER LAKE SRA (Public State Park) From jct Hwy 71 & US 30: Go 8 mi W on US 30. 175 Avail: Pit toilets. 2021 rates: $7. (308)254-2377

KRAMER — C5 *Saline*

OLIVE CREEK SRA (Public State Park) From town: Go 2-3/4 mi SE. 50 Avail: Pit toilets. 2021 rates: $8. (402)796-2362

LEXINGTON — C3 *Dawson*

JOHNSON LAKE SRA/MAIN AREA (Public State Park) From Jct of I-80 & US-283, S 7 mi on US-283 to park access rd, N 0.6 mi (L). Entrance fee required. Avail: 82 E (30/50 amps). 2021 rates: $12 to $18. (308)785-2685

LINCOLN — C5 *Lancaster*

CAMP A WAY RV PARK
good sam park **Ratings: 9/9.5★/10** (Campground) From Jct of I-80 (Downtown Exit) (exit 401/401A) & I-80/Hwy 34 E: Go 1/4 mi S on Hwy 34 E, then 1/4 mi W on Superior St (exit 1), then 1/4 mi N on Campers Circle (E). **FAC:** paved/gravel rds. Avail: 92 gravel, patios, 48 pull-thrus, (35x70), back-ins (40x45), 92 full hkups (30/50 amps), cable, WiFi @ sites, tent sites, rentals, dump, laundry, groc, fire rings, firewood. **REC:** heated pool, hot tub, boating nearby, playground, hunting nearby. Pets OK. Big rig sites, eco-friendly. 2021 rates: $45 to $99, Military discount.
(402)476-2282 Lat: 40.85753, Lon: -96.71765
200 Campers Circle, Lincoln, NE 68521
campaway.com
See ad this page

LONG PINE — A3 *Brown*

LONG PINE SRA (Public State Park) From Jct of US-183 & US-20, E 2.5 mi on US-20 (R). Entrance fee required. Avail: 8 E Pit toilets. 2021 rates: $8 to $10. (402)684-2921

Find 'em fast. Our advertisers often include extra information or provide a detailed map in their ads to help you find their facilities quickly and easily.

LOUISVILLE — C6 *Cass*

LOUISVILLE SRA (Public State Park) W-bnd: From Jct of I-80 & SR-50, S 11 mi on SR-50 (R); or E-bnd: From Jct of I-80 & SR-66 (Exit 426), S 8.5 mi on SR-66 to SR-50, N 1.8 mi (L). Avail: 223 E (30/50 amps). 2021 rates: $8 to $35. (402)234-6855

LOUP CITY — C4 *Sherman*

SHERMAN RESERVOIR SRA (Public State Park) From jct Hwy 92 & Hwy 10: Go 3-1/3 mi E on Hwy 92, then 1 mi N on 477th Ave, then 1 mi E on 790th Rd/ Sherman Lake Recreation Rd. (L). 360 Avail. 2021 rates: $8. May 01 to Nov 30. (308)745-0230

LYONS — B6 *Burt*

ISLAND PARK (LYON CITY PARK) (Public) From Jct of Hwy 77 & Main St, W 1 mi on Main St (L). 16 Avail: 16 W, 16 E (15/30 amps). 2021 rates: $13. Apr 15 to Oct 15. (402)687-2485

MALCOLM — C5 *Lancaster*

BRANCHED OAK SRA (Public State Park) From Jct of SR-79 & W Raymond Rd, W 3.1 mi on Raymond Rd (R). 338 Avail: 11 full hkups, 183 E (30/50 amps). 2021 rates: $8 to $26. (402)783-3400

MCCOOK — D3 *Frontier*

RED WILLOW SRA (Public State Park) From Jct of US-6/34 & US-83, N 10 mi on US-83 to park access Cnty Rd, W 1 mi to park entrance, N 0.25 mi (L). Entrance fee required. Avail: 48 E (30/50 amps). 2021 rates: $8 to $18. (308)345-5899

MERRIMAN — A2 *Cherry*

COTTONWOOD LAKE SRA (Public State Park) From Jct of SR-61 & US-20 (in town), E 0.5 mi on US-20 to park rd, S 0.25 mi (E). 30 Avail: Pit toilets. 2021 rates: $8. (308)684-3428

Get a FREE Quote at GoodSamESP.com

MINATARE — B1 *Scotts Bluff*

LAKE MINATARE SRA (Public State Park) From town, N 9 mi on US-26/Stonegate Rd (R). Entrance fee required. Avail: 101 E (20/30 amps). 2021 rates: $8 to $35. Jan 15 to Oct 15. (308)783-2911

MINDEN — C4 *Kearney*

MINDEN See also Kearney & Wood River.

NEBRASKA CITY — C6 *Otoe*

RIVERVIEW MARINA SRA (Public State Park) From Jct of US-75 & SR-2, E 3 mi on SR-2 to 6th St, N 2 mi to Marina (L). Entrance fee required. Avail: 24 E (20/30 amps). 2021 rates: $12 to $19. (402)873-1035

VICTORIAN ACRES RV PARK
good sam park **Ratings: 8.5/9.5★/9.5** (Campground) E-bnd: From Jct of Hwy 75 & Hwy 2: Go 1-1/4 mi E on Hwy 2 (L); or W-bnd: From Jct of I-29 (in Iowa) & Hwy 2 (exit 10): Go 4 mi W on Hwy 2 (R). **FAC:** all weather rds. Avail: 88 all weather, 69 pull-thrus, (30x75), back-ins (28x35), 69 full hkups, 19 W, 19 E (30/50 amps), WiFi @ sites, dump, laundry, LP gas, fire rings, firewood. **REC:** boating nearby, playground. Pets OK. Partial handicap access. No tents. Big rig sites. 2021 rates: $36 to $39, Military discount. Mar 01 to Nov 30.
(402)873-6866 Lat: 40.659382, Lon: -95.841545
6591 Hwy 2, Nebraska City, NE 68410
www.victorianacresrvpark.com
See ad this page

NELIGH — B5 *Antelope*

RIVERSIDE PARK (Public) In town, S-bnd on US-275 at southern Jct of L St (L). 26 Avail: 26 W, 26 E (30 amps). 2021 rates: $13. Apr 01 to Oct 01. (402)887-4066

NIOBRARA — A5 *Knox*

NIOBRARA (Public State Park) From Jct of SR-12 & SR-14, W 1.2 mi on SR-12 (R). Avail: 76 E (30/50 amps). 2021 rates: $10 to $35. (402)857-3373

NORTH PLATTE — C3 *Lincoln*

BUFFALO BILL SRA (Public State Park) From Jct of I-80 & US-83 (Exit 177 N), N 2.3 mi on US-83 to Rodeo Dr (US-30), W 1.6 mi to Buffalo Bill Ave, N 0.9 mi to dirt road, NE 0.3 mi (E). Entrance fee required. Avail: 23 E (30/50 amps). 2021 rates: $15 to $19. (308)535-8035

HOLIDAY RV PARK & CAMPGROUND
good sam park **Ratings: 9/9.5★/9.5** (Campground) From Jct of I-80 & US 83 (Exit 177 North): Go 1000 ft N on US 83, then 1/2 mi E & S on E Halligan Dr (frontage rd) (L). Elev 2800 ft.**FAC:** gravel rds. Avail: 92 gravel, 72 pull-thrus, (30x70), back-ins (30x55), 80 full hkups, 12 W, 12 E (30/50 amps), cable, WiFi @ sites, tent sites, dump, laundry, groc. **REC:** pool, boating nearby, playground, hunting nearby. Pet restrict (B). Big rig sites, eco-friendly. 2021 rates: $40 to $43, Military discount.
(308)534-2265 Lat: 41.11124, Lon: -100.75597
601 E. Halligan Dr, North Platte, NE 69101
www.holidayparkne.com
See ad this page, 564

I-80 LAKESIDE CAMPGROUND
good sam park **Ratings: 6/8★/6** (Campground) 87 Avail: 58 full hkups, 29 W, 29 E (30/50 amps). 2021 rates: $35 to $38. (877)648-2267, 3800 Hadley Drive, North Platte, NE 69101

LAKE MALONEY SRA (Public State Park) From Jct of I-80 & SR-83, S 4 mi on SR-83 to park access rd, W 0.6 mi (E). Entrance fee required. Avail: 56 E (30 amps), Pit toilets. 2021 rates: $8 to $17. (308)535-8025

OGALLALA — C2 *Keith*

OGALLALA See also Brule.

COUNTRY VIEW CAMPGROUND
good sam park **Ratings: 9/10★/9.5** (Campground) From Jct of I-80 & NE 61 (exit 126): Go 1/2 mi S on NE 61, Then 1/4 mi E on CR East 80 (R). Elev 2950 ft.**FAC:** gravel rds. Avail: 51 gravel, 46 pull-thrus, (24x100), back-ins (25x40), 51 full hkups (30/50 amps), cable, WiFi @ sites, tent sites, dump, laundry, fire rings, firewood. **REC:** heated pool, boating nearby, playground, hunting nearby. Pets OK. Big rig sites. 2021 rates: $39, Military discount. Apr 01 to Nov 01.
(308)284-2415 Lat: 41.10519, Lon: -101.71488
120 Road East 80, Ogallala, NE 69153
www.cvcampground.com
See ad this page

LAKE MCCONAUGHY SRA/CEDAR VIEW CAMPGROUND (Public State Park) From town, NE 12 mi on SR-61 to SR-92, W 12 mi to Public Rd 13 (L). Entrance fee required. Avail: 84 E (30/50 amps). 2021 rates: $8 to $24. (308)284-8800

LAKE MCCONAUGHY SRA/LITTLE THUNDER CAMPGROUND (Public State Park) From jct US-30 & SR-61: Go 10 mi N on SR-61, then 2 mi W on Martin Bay Recreation Rd (L). 42 Avail: 8 full hkups, 34 E (50 amps). 2021 rates: $10 to $35. (308)284-8800

LAKE MCCONAUGHY SRA/LONE EAGLE CAMPGROUND (Public State Park) From Jct of US-30 & SR-61, NE 12 mi on SR-61 to SR-92, W 4.6 mi to Public Rd 4, S .5 mi (L). Entrance fee required. Avail: 84 E (30/50 amps). 2021 rates: $10 to $35. (308)284-8800

LAKE OGALLALA SRA (Public State Park) From Jct of I-80 & SR-61, N 14.6 mi on Hwy 61 N (over dam) to Keystone Lake Rd, E 1.6 mi (R). Entrance fee required. Avail: 82 E (20/30 amps). 2021 rates: $8 to $35. (308)284-8800

OGALLALA LAKE MCCONAUGHY KOA **Ratings: 9/10★/7.5** (Campground) 37 Avail: 29 full hkups, 8 W, 8 E (30/50 amps). 2021 rates: $38. (308)284-1300, 221 Road East 85, Ogallala, NE 69153

OMAHA — C6 *Douglas*

OMAHA See also Ashland & Gretna, NE; Council Bluffs, IA.

GLENN CUNNINGHAM LAKE (CITY PARK) (Public) From jct I-680 & 72nd St exit: Go 1/2 mi N on 72nd St, then 4/5 mi W on Rainwood Rd. Avail: 46 E. 2021 rates: $15. Apr 12 to Oct 14. (402)444-5940

N P DODGE MEMORIAL PARK (Public) From Jct of I-680 & US-75: Go 1 mi E on I-680, then 3/4 mi N on John J Pershing Dr. (R). Avail: 46 E (30 amps). 2021 rates: $15. May 24 to Oct 15. (402)444-5940

PINE GROVE RV PARK
good sam park **Ratings: 9/9.5★/9.5** (Campground) From Jct I-480 & I-80 (in Omaha): Go 33 mi W on I-80; at I-80 (Exit 420) & NE 63; Go 100 ft N on NE 63; then 1/2 mi W on Mynard Rd (L). **FAC:** gravel rds. Avail: 100 gravel, 77 pull-thrus, (44x80), back-ins (44x35), 100 full hkups (30/50 amps), WiFi @ sites, tent sites, rentals, dump, laundry, groc, firewood. **REC:** pool, wading pool, playground. Pets OK. Big rig sites, eco-friendly. 2021 rates: $32 to $63, Military discount.
(402)944-3550 Lat: 40.97150, Lon: -96.3958
23403 Mynard Rd, Greenwood, NE 68366
pinegrovervpark.com
See primary listing at Greenwood and ad pages 564, 568

O'NEILL — A4 *Holt*

CARNEY PARK (Public) From Jct of US-20 & US-281, S 0.4 mi on US-281 (L). 18 Avail: 18 W, 18 E (15 amps). 2021 rates: $10. (402)336-3640

PAPILLION — C6 *Sarpy*

WALNUT CREEK LAKE & REC AREA (Public) From Jct of I-80 & Hwy 370 (Exit 439), E 4.8 mi on Hwy 370 to 96th St, S 0.8 mi to Schram Rd, W 0.6 mi (R). Avail: 44 E (30/50 amps), Pit toilets. 2021 rates: $16. Mar 01 to Dec 01. (402)679-9889

PARKS — D2 *Dundy*

ROCK CREEK LAKE SRA (Public State Park) From Jct of US-61 & US-34, W 12 mi on US-34 to Parks, NW 5.5 mi to Rock Creek Lake (R). 43 Avail: Pit toilets. 2021 rates: $8. (308)394-5118

PIERCE — B5 *Pierce*

WILLOW CREEK SRA (Public State Park) From town, SW 1.5 mi (L). Entrance fee required. Avail: 101 E (20/30 amps). 2021 rates: $12 to $18. (402)329-4053

PONCA — A5 *Dixon*

PONCA (Public State Park) From Jct of SR-20 & SR-12, N 9 mi on SR-12 to 26 E, 3 mi (E). Avail: 92 E (30/50 amps). 2021 rates: $10 to $35. Apr 15 to Oct 31. (402)755-2284

Always do a Pre-Drive Safety Check!

REPUBLICAN CITY — D4 *Harlan*

HARLAN COUNTY LAKE - COE/GREMLIN COVE (Public Corps) From town, S 1.5 mi on Reservoir Rd (R). 70 Avail. 2021 rates: $8 to $10. May 01 to Sep 30. (308)799-2105

HARLAN COUNTY LAKE - COE/HUNTER COVE (Public Corps) From town, S 1.5 mi on Reservoir Rd to Rd-B, W 1 mi (L). Avail: 84 E (15/50 amps). 2021 rates: $14 to $20. Apr 01 to Nov 29. (308)799-2105

HARLAN COUNTY LAKE - COE/SOUTH OUTLET (Public Corps) From jct US 136 & Layne Rd: Go 1/3 mi S on Layne Rd, then 3-1/3 mi S on Corp Rd A, then ½ mi E on 706 Rd, then 1 mi N on Corp Rd 1. (E). 60 Avail: Pit toilets. 2021 rates: $10. (877)444-6777

SCHUYLER — B5 *Colfax*

SCHUYLER PARK (Public) From Jct US-30 & SR-15, S 1.5 mi on SR-15 (L). Avail: 35 full hkups (30/50 amps). 2021 rates: $15 to $20. Apr 01 to Oct 31. (402)352-3101

SCOTTSBLUFF — B1 *Scotts Bluff*

SCOTTSBLUFF See also Bayard & Gering.

CAPTAIN CRITTERS COUNTRY CAMPGROUND (RV Park) (Rebuilding) 35 Avail: 24 full hkups, 11 W, 11 E (30/50 amps). 2021 rates: $28. (308)765-4260, 180454 Highway 26, Scottsbluff, NE 69361

RIVERSIDE (Public) From jct US 26 & S Beltline Hwy: Go 3-3/4 mi W on S Beltline Hwy (Truck Route). 43 Avail: 43 W, 43 E (30/50 amps). 2021 rates: $10 to $25. May 01 to Sep 30. (308)630-6235

SCRIBNER — B5 *Dodge*

DEAD TIMBER SRA (Public State Park) From town, N 5 mi on Hwy 275 to cnty rd, follow signs E 1.5 mi & S 0.5 mi (R). Entrance fee required. Avail: 17 E (20/30 amps), Pit toilets. 2021 rates: $8 to $19. (402)727-2922

SHUBERT — D6 *Nemaha*

INDIAN CAVE (Public State Park) From Jct of I-29 & SR-136 (exit 110), W 8 mi on SR-136 to SR-67, S 9.1 mi to Spur 64 E, E 4.9 mi (E). Avail: 134 E (30/50 amps). 2021 rates: $10 to $35. May 01 to Oct 31. (402)883-2575

SIDNEY — C1 *Cheyenne*

CABELA'S RV PARK **Ratings: 7/9★/8.5** (RV Park) 59 Avail: 31 full hkups, 28 E (30/50 amps). 2021 rates: $30. (308)254-7889, 1 Angler Drive, Sidney, NE 69162

SOUTH SIOUX CITY — A6 *Dakota*

SCENIC PARK (Public) From I-29, go to exit 148 (Wesley Parkway); Go across Veterans Memorial bridge to Riverview Dr, turn left and go 8 blocks on Riverview; or From Hwy 20, go to 77 North/Cornhusker Dr to Dakota Ave, go across Dakota Ave on to 9th St, at 9th & G St, turn left, go 3 blocks and turn right on to Riverview. 125 Avail: 93 full hkups, 32 W, 32 E (30/50 amps). 2021 rates: $25 to $34. (402)494-7531

SPALDING — B4 *Greeley*

PIBEL LAKE REC AREA (Public State Park) From town, S 7 mi on US-281 to cnty rd, E 1 mi (L). 30 Avail: Pit toilets. 2021 rates: $7. (402)471-7670

SPRAGUE — C5 *Lancaster*

BLUESTEM SRA (Public State Park) From town: Go 3 mi W. Avail: 19 E Pit toilets. 2021 rates: $10 to $35. (402)796-2362

STROMSBURG — C5 *Polk*

BUCKLEY PARK (Public) From Jct of US-81 & SR-92, S 5 mi on US-81 (R). Avail: 12 W (30/50 amps). (402)764-8228

STUART — A4 *Holt*

STUART MUNICIPAL PARK (Public) From Jct of US-20 & Main St, N 1 mi on Main St (R). 20 Avail: 10 W, 10 E (30 amps). 2021 rates: $11. Mar 01 to Nov 30. (402)924-3647

SUTHERLAND — C3 *Lincoln*

SUTHERLAND SRA (Public State Park) From Jct of I-80 & SR-25, S 2 mi on SR-25 to blacktop rd, SW 0.4 mi (L). 85 Avail: Pit toilets. 2021 rates: $8 to $25. (308)535-8025

TEKAMAH — B6 *Burt*

PELICAN POINT SRA (Public State Park) From Jct of US-75 & cnty rd, E 8 mi on cnty rd, follow signs (E). Entrance fee required. 6 Avail: Pit toilets. 2021 rates: $10. (402)468-5611

SUMMIT LAKE SRA (Public State Park) From Jct of Hwy 75 & cnty rd, W 5 mi on cnty rd, follow signs (R). Entrance fee required. Avail: 30 E (50 amps), Pit toilets. 2021 rates: $8 to $17. (402)374-1727

TRENTON — D3 *Hitchcock*

SWANSON RESERVOIR SRA (Public State Park) From town, W 5 mi on US-34 (L). Avail: 64 E (20/30 amps). 2021 rates: $8 to $18. May 01 to Sep 30. (308)334-5493

VALENTINE — A3 *Cherry*

FISHBERRY CAMPGROUND

good sam park

Ratings: 7.5/9.5★/9 (Campground) From Jct of US 20 & US 83: Go 5 mi N on US 83 (R). Elev 2728 ft.**FAC:** gravel rds. Avail: 22 gravel, 22 pull-thrus, (25x100), mostly side by side hkups, 22 full hkups (30/50 amps), WiFi @ sites, tent sites, laundry, fire rings, firewood. **REC:** pond, fishing, boating nearby, hunting nearby. Pets OK. Partial handicap access, eco-friendly. 2021 rates: $38, Military discount.
(402)376-1662 Lat: 42.93285, Lon: -100.57162
90440 US Hwy 83, Valentine, NE 69201
www.fishberrycamp.com
See ad this page

MERRITT RESERVOIR SRA (Public State Park) From town: Go 25 mi SW on CR-166. Avail: 89 E (20/30 amps). 2021 rates: $8 to $20. (402)376-3320

VALLEY — C6 *Douglas*

TWO RIVERS SRA (Public State Park) From Jct of US-92 & 264th St, S 1 mi on 264th St to F St, W 1 mi (E). Entrance fee required. 208 Avail: 12 W, 144 E (30/50 amps). 2021 rates: $12 to $21. May 01 to Sep 30. (402)359-5165

VERDON — D6 *Richardson*

VERDON SRA (Public State Park) From Jct of US-75 & US-73, E 6 mi on US-73 (L). Entrance fee required. 20 Avail: Pit toilets. 2021 rates: $8. (402)883-2575

WAYNE — B5 *Wayne*

LIONS RV PARK (Public) From Jct of Hwys 15 & 35, E 1.5 mi on Hwy 35 (L). 6 Avail: 6 W, 6 E (20/50 amps). Apr 01 to Oct 01. (402)375-4803

VICTOR PARK (Public) From Jct of Hwys 35 & 15, S 0.8 mi on Hwy 15 (R). Avail: 12 E (30 amps). 2021 rates: $7. (402)375-1300

WOOD RIVER — C4 *Hall*

FIREFLY MEADOWS RV PARK AND CAMPGROUND **Ratings: 6/9.5★/6** (Campground) 40 Avail: 33 full hkups, 7 W, 7 E (30/50 amps). 2021 rates: $35 to $45. Mar 15 to Nov 15. (308)380-7495, 11774 State Highway 11, Wood River, NE 68883

YORK — C5 *York*

YORK See also Henderson.

DOUBLE NICKEL CAMPGROUND **Ratings: 9/8.5★/9.5** (Campground) Avail: 43 full hkups (30/50 amps). 2021 rates: $45 to $65. Apr 01 to Oct 27. (402)728-5558, 907 Road S, Waco, NE 68460

YORK KAMPGROUND

good sam park

Ratings: 5.5/9★/7 (RV Park) From jct I-80 and US 81 north (exit 353): Go 1/4 mi N to Naomi. Right on Naomi to RV Park. **FAC:** all weather rds. Avail: 139 all weather, 139 pull-thrus, (30x65), 68 full hkups, 71 W, 71 E (30/50 amps), WiFi @ sites, tent sites, dump, laundry. Pet restrict (Q). Partial handicap access. Big rig sites. 2021 rates: $26 to $37, Military discount.
(402)362-0091 Lat: 40.824463, Lon: -97.59430
214 Naomi Rd, York, NE 68467
www.yorkkampground.com
See ad this page

Reducing your speed to 55 mph from 65 mph may increase your fuel efficiency by as much as 15 percent; cut it to 55 from 70, and you could get a 23 percent improvement.

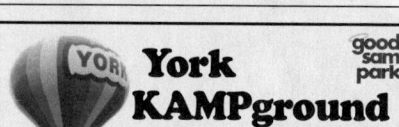

Getty Images/iStockphoto

YOU ARE HERE

Nevada

DID YOU KNOW?

Now a popular tourist attraction, the Nevada stretch of U.S. Route 50 was once called the "Loneliest Road in America."

Nevada is home to the world's gambling capital, but beyond the borders of Vegas, the odds are in your favor for adventure. The surrounding deserts, waterways and mountains promise a great time.

Supercharged Cities

Viva Las Vegas! The world's gambling capital is home to thrills and chills for grownups and kids alike. The simple casinos of decades past have been replaced by extravagant pleasure palaces, with dancing waters, gondola rides and roller coasters. A wealth of live entertainment options, shopping and restaurants mean that even non-gamblers will be pleased. In northern Nevada, Reno offers similar thrills, with the Sierra Nevada nearby.

Big Basin

Great Basin National Park, in the eastern part of the state, is far from the major population centers, making it a popular getaway. Throughout the park, guests can see gnarly bristlecone pines and one of the southernmost glaciers in North America. The alpine hills are home to superb recreational activities, including hiking and biking. A couple hours to the south, Cathedral Gorge State Park is an otherworldly landscape, with deep slot canyons and eye-popping spires.

Big Lakes, Tall Dam

The completion of the Hoover Dam in 1935 resulted in the formation of Lake Mead, 247 square miles of water that's perfect for boating, fishing and paddling. The state's red desert landscape gives way to green pines and turquoise waters at Lake Tahoe, one of the most stunning spots in the nation. North America's largest alpine lake offers boating and fishing, with ample populations of trout and kokanee salmon. Running between Lake Tahoe and Pyramid Lake, the Truckee River entices paddlers and anglers, with amazing mountain views on the horizon.

Nevada Shrimp Cocktail

The shrimp cocktail was born in Las Vegas in 1959 and has been a casino staple ever since. Locals and tourists can't get enough of this simple appetizer, featuring chilled juicy shrimp, cocktail sauce and a lemon wedge. Eat to your heart's content at buffets across the strip or at popular joints like the Oyster Bar at Palace Station.

VISITOR CENTER

TIME ZONE
Pacific Standard

ROAD & HIGHWAY INFORMATION
877-687-6237
nvroads.com

FISHING & HUNTING INFORMATION
775-688-1500
ndow.org

BOATING INFORMATION
775-688-1500
www.ndow.org/Boat

NATIONAL PARKS
nps.gov/nv

STATE PARKS
parks.nv.gov

TOURISM INFORMATION
Nevada Department of Tourism
800-NEVADA8
travelnevada.com

TOP TOURISM ATTRACTIONS
1) Las Vegas Strip
2) Hoover Dam
3) Lake Tahoe

MAJOR CITIES
Las Vegas, Henderson, Reno, North Las Vegas, Paradise, Carson City (capital)

Featured Good Sam Parks

NEVADA

When you stay with Good Sam, you can expect the highest degree of cleanliness and friendliness, and better yet, you get **10% off** overnight campground fees.

If you're not already a Good Sam member you can purchase your membership at one of these locations:

BOULDER CITY
Canyon Trail RV Park
Lake Mead RV Village at Boulder Beach

CARSON CITY
Camp-N-Town RV Park
Comstock Country RV Resort
Gold Dust West Casino & RV Park

COTTONWOOD COVE
Cottonwood Cove Nevada RV Park & Marina

DAYTON
Dayton RV Park

ELKO
Elko RV Park
Iron Horse RV Resort

ELY
Valley View RV Park

FALLON
Fallon RV Park

FERNLEY
Desert Rose RV Park

GARDNERVILLE
Topaz Lodge RV Park & Casino

HAWTHORNE
Whiskey Flats RV Park

HENDERSON
Desert Sands RV Park

JACKPOT
Cactus Petes RV Park

LAS VEGAS
Arizona Charlie's Boulder RV Park
Duck Creek RV Park
Hitchin' Post RV Park
Las Vegas RV Resort
Riviera RV Park
Thousand Trails Las Vegas RV Resort

MESQUITE
Desert Skies RV Resort
Sun Resorts RV Park

MINDEN
Carson Valley RV Resort & Casino

OVERTON
Lake Mead RV Village At Echo Bay

PAHRUMP
Lakeside Casino & RV Park
Nevada Treasure RV Resort
Preferred RV Resort
Wine Ridge RV Resort & Cottages

RENO
Bordertown Casino & RV Resort
Grand Sierra Resort and Casino RV Park
Keystone RV Park
Shamrock RV Park
Silver Sage RV Park

SPARKS
Sparks Marina RV Park
Victorian RV Park

WINNEMUCCA
New Frontier RV Park

10/10★/10 GOOD SAM PARKS

LAS VEGAS
Las Vegas RV Resort
(866)846-5432

PAHRUMP
Lakeside Casino & RV Park
(888)558-5253

Nevada Treasure RV Resort
(800)429-6665

Wine Ridge RV Resort & Cottages
(775)751-7805

SPARKS
Sparks Marina RV Park
(775)851-8888

What's This?

An RV park with a 10/10★/10 rating has scored perfect grades in amenities, cleanliness and appearance ("See Understanding the Campground Rating System" on pages 8 and 9 for an explanation of the trusted Good Sam Rating System). Stay in a 10/10★/10 park on your next trip for a nearly flawless camping experience.

Getty Images/iStockphoto

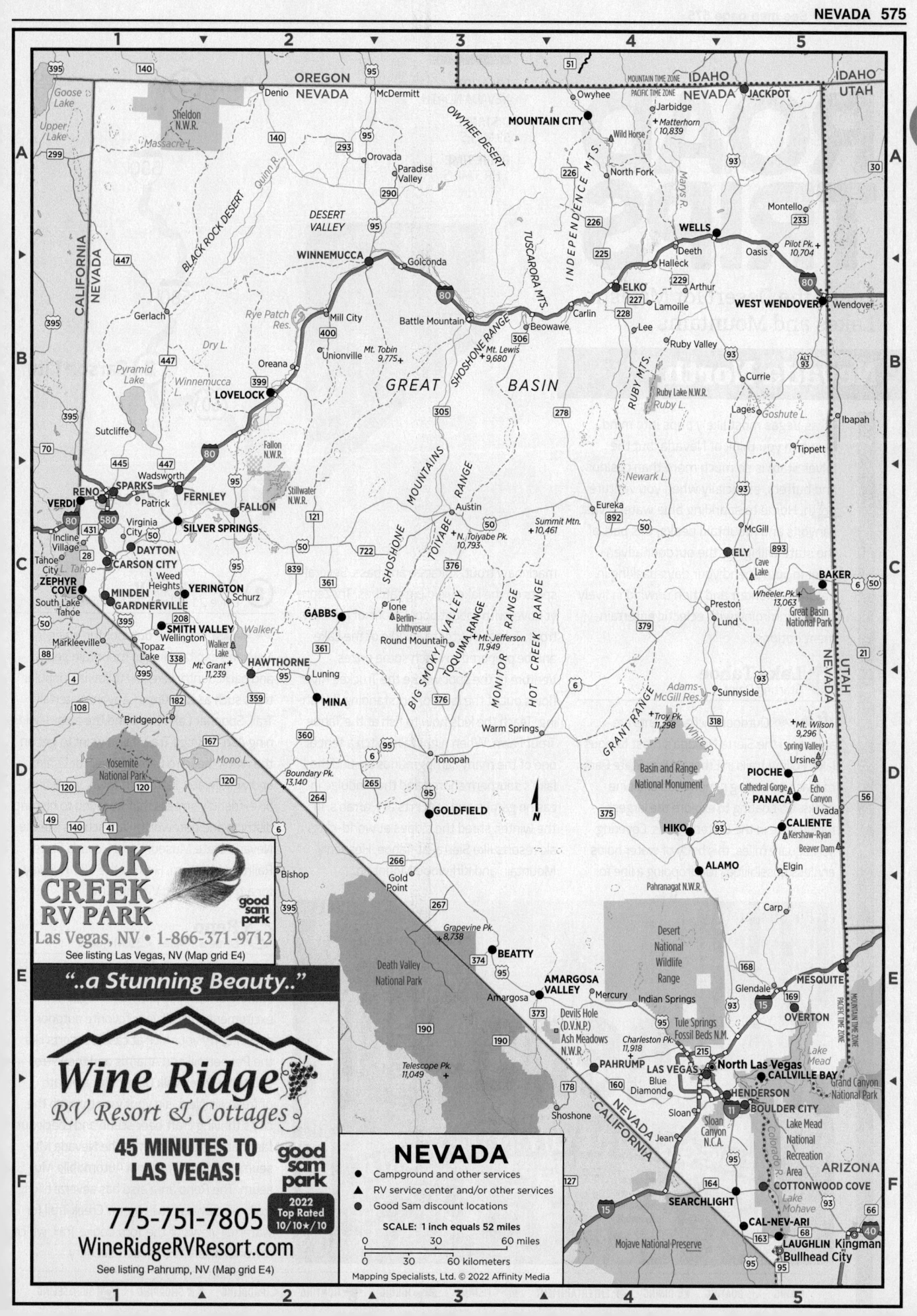

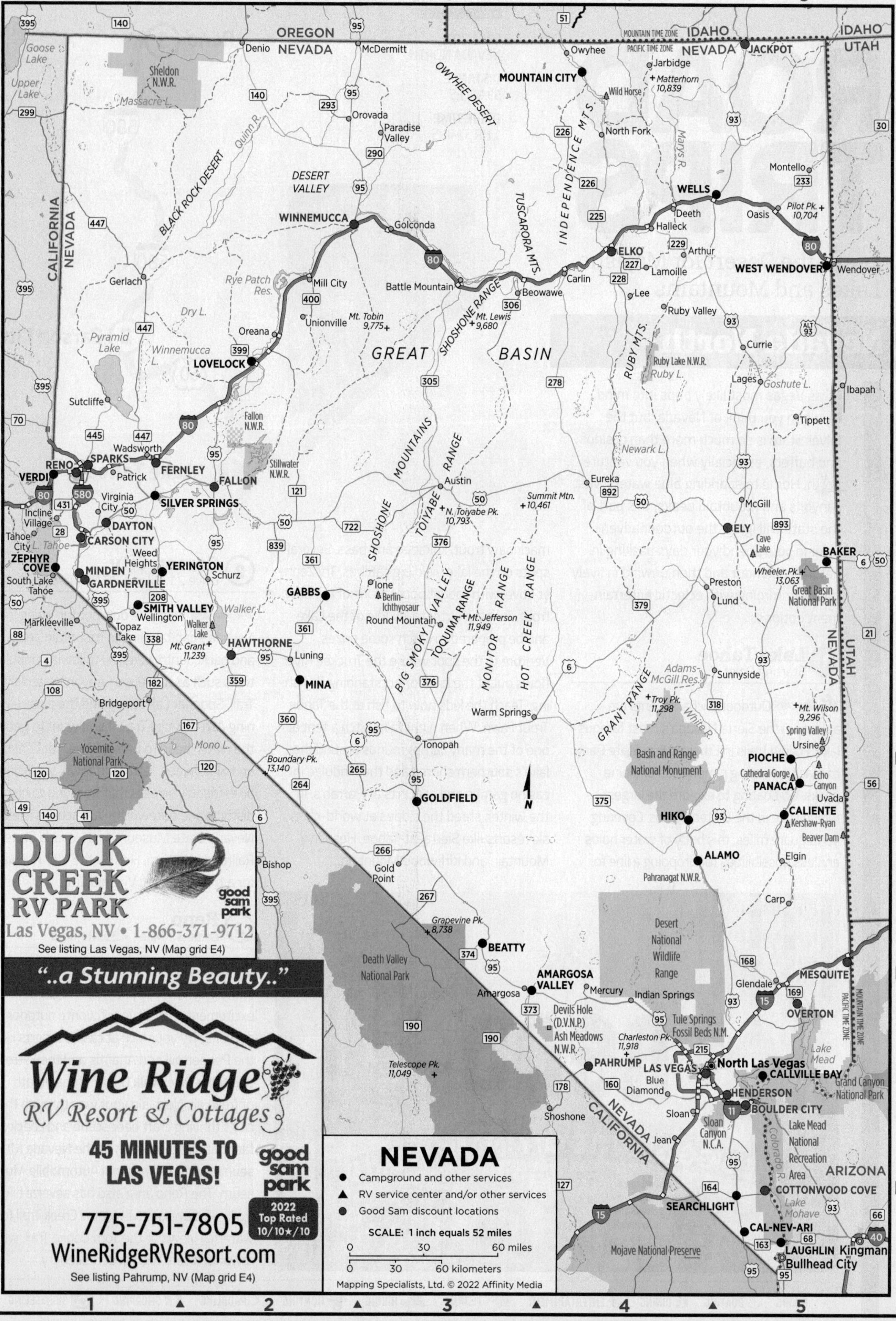
1
2
3
4
5
A
B
C
D
E
F
OREGON
NEVADA
IDAHO
NEVADA
IDAHO
UTAH
CALIFORNIA
NEVADA
UTAH
NEVADA
ARIZONA
NEVADA
CALIFORNIA
MOUNTAIN TIME ZONE
PACIFIC TIME ZONE
NV
Goose Lake
Upper Lake
Sheldon N.W.R.
Massacre L.
Denio
McDermitt
Orovada
Paradise Valley
OWYHEE DESERT
Owyhee
MOUNTAIN CITY
Wild Horse
Jarbidge
Matterhorn 10,839
JACKPOT
North Fork
Marys R.
INDEPENDENCE MTS.
Montello
BLACK ROCK DESERT
Quinn R.
DESERT VALLEY
WINNEMUCCA
Golconda
TUSCARORA MTS.
WELLS
Deeth
Halleck
Arthur
Oasis
Pilot Pk. 10,704
WEST WENDOVER
Wendover
ELKO
Lamoille
Carlin
Beowawe
Battle Mountain
Mill City
Rye Patch Res.
Gerlach
Dry L.
Unionville
Mt. Tobin 9,775
SHOSHONE RANGE
Mt. Lewis 9,680
Lee
Ruby Valley
RUBY MTS.
Ruby Lake N.W.R.
Ruby L.
Currie
Lages
Goshute L.
Ibapah
Tippett
Pyramid Lake
Winnemucca L.
Oreana
LOVELOCK
GREAT BASIN
Sutcliffe
Fallon N.W.R.
Stillwater N.W.R.
Wadsworth
RENO
SPARKS
VERDI
Patrick
FERNLEY
FALLON
Virginia City
SILVER SPRINGS
Incline Village
DAYTON
Tahoe City
L. Tahoe
CARSON CITY
ZEPHYR COVE
South Lake Tahoe
MINDEN
GARDNERVILLE
Weed Heights
YERINGTON
Schurz
SMITH VALLEY
Wellington
Walker L.
Walker Lake
Markleeville
Topaz Lake
Mt. Grant 11,239
HAWTHORNE
Luning
MINA
GABBS
Ione
Berlin-Ichthyosaur
Round Mountain
SHOSHONE MOUNTAINS
TOIYABE RANGE
Austin
N. Toiyabe Pk. 10,793
Summit Mtn. 10,461
Eureka
Newark L.
McGill
ELY
Cave Lake
BAKER
Wheeler Pk. 13,063
Great Basin National Park
Preston
Lund
BIG SMOKY VALLEY
TOQUIMA RANGE
Mt. Jefferson 11,949
MONITOR RANGE
HOT CREEK RANGE
GRANT RANGE
Adams-McGill Res.
Sunnyside
Troy Pk. 11,298
White R.
Mt. Wilson 9,296
Spring Valley
Ursine
PIOCHE
Cathedral Gorge
PANACA
Echo Canyon
Uvada
Basin and Range National Monument
Warm Springs
Bridgeport
Mono L.
Yosemite National Park
Boundary Pk. 13,140
Tonopah
GOLDFIELD
HIKO
CALIENTE
Kershaw-Ryan
Beaver Dam
ALAMO
Elgin
Pahranagat N.W.R.
Carp
Bishop
Gold Point
Grapevine Pk. 8,738
BEATTY
Death Valley National Park
Desert National Wildlife Range
Glendale
MESQUITE
OVERTON
AMARGOSA VALLEY
Amargosa
Mercury
Indian Springs
Devils Hole (D.V.N.P.)
Ash Meadows N.W.R.
Tule Springs Fossil Beds N.M.
Charleston Pk. 11,918
Lake Mead
Telescope Pk. 11,049
PAHRUMP
LAS VEGAS
North Las Vegas
CALLVILLE BAY
Grand Canyon National Park
Blue Diamond
HENDERSON
BOULDER CITY
Sloan
Sloan Canyon N.C.A.
Lake Mead National Recreation Area
Colorado R.
Shoshone
Jean
SEARCHLIGHT
COTTONWOOD COVE
Lake Mohave
CAL-NEV-ARI
Mojave National Preserve
LAUGHLIN
Bullhead City
Kingman
N
NEVADA
Campground and other services
RV service center and/or other services
Good Sam discount locations
SCALE: 1 inch equals 52 miles
0 30 60 miles
0 30 60 kilometers
Mapping Specialists, Ltd. © 2022 Affinity Media

ROAD TRIPS

Leave the Desert for Majestic Lakes and Mountains

Nevada North

LOCATION
NEVADA NORTH

DISTANCE
53 MILES

DRIVE TIME
1 HR 3 MINS

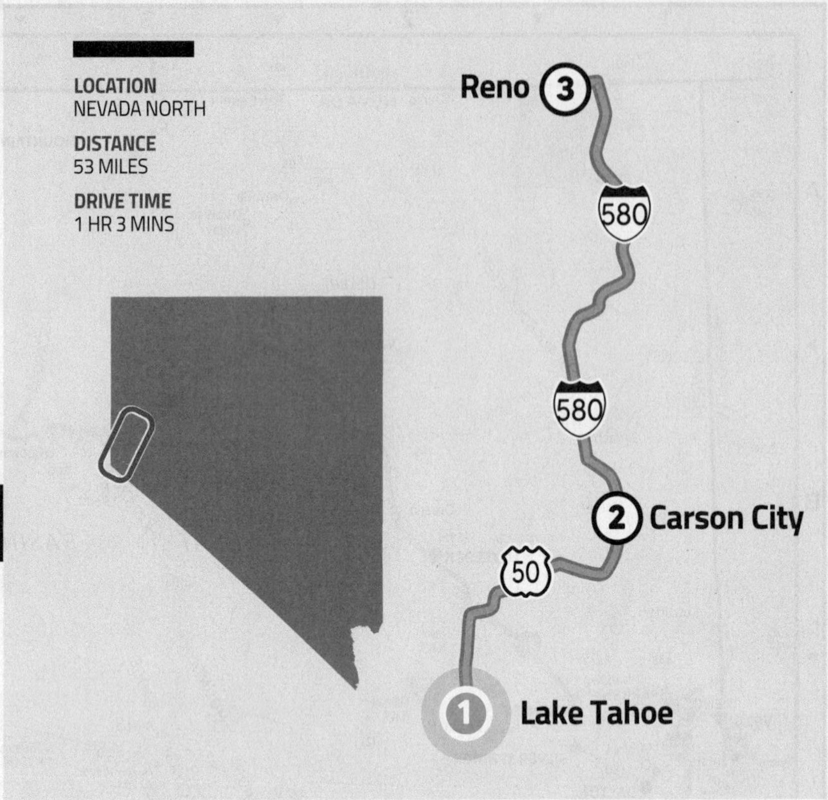

Las Vegas most likely pops into mind when you think of Nevada, but the Silver State is so much more than casinos and buffets, especially when you venture north. Home to sparkling blue waters, vast canyons and mountain peaks, this part of the state will ignite the outdoor adventurer in you. Spend your days basking in nature's splendor and then unwind in lively towns brimming with eclectic entertainment options.

1 Lake Tahoe
Starting Point

Outdoor enchantments are aplenty in the Sierra Nevada's most famous lake. Follow trails in Emerald Bay State Park to reach sweeping panoramas of alpine peaks. Go boating to explore the largest Alpine Lake in the United States. Covering 191 square miles, this body of water holds endless possibilities for dropping a line for mackinaw trout, kokanee and bass. Several spots on the lake yield big catches. Try Zephyr Cove, with robust populations of rainbow trout. Take a charter to Middle of the Lake and be prepared to catch some prizes. Venture to the spot where the Truckee River flows out of the lake for outstanding fly fishing. Teach the kids how to fish at the Tahoe Trout Farm. When night falls, pitch a tent at one of the many campgrounds around the lake's southern shores and then indulge in casino games and concerts at Harrah's. In the winter, shred the slopes at world-class ski resorts like Sierra-at-Tahoe, Heavenly Mountain and Kirkwood Mountain.

2 Carson City
Drive 21 Miles ▪ 28 Minutes

Keep the outdoor fun going in Nevada's capital. Hike to mountain peaks and backcountry lakes by following popular trails such as the Kings Canyon Waterfall Trail, Spooner Lake Loop and the award-winning Ash to Kings Trail. If you want to get on the water, head to Carson River for fishing and whitewater rafting. In town, you'll find bike-friendly streets that take you to historic districts and noteworthy attractions like the Nevada State Museum and Nevada State Railroad Museum. Hop on the V&T Railway for a trip to historic Virginia City.

3 Reno
Drive 32 Miles ▪ 35 Minutes

Dubbed the "Biggest Little City in the World," Reno promises Vegas-level excitement with all your favorite outdoor pursuits. Try your luck at casino resorts like the Peppermill and Atlantis and then stroll down the Riverwalk District for a breath of fresh air. Next, sip your way through the city's thriving craft beer scene and check out fascinating stops, such as the Nevada Museum of Art and National Automobile Museum. The Reno area also has several hiking trails — traverse the Hunter Creek Trail for waterfall views or the Tom Cooke Trail, which rewards hikers with desert scenery.

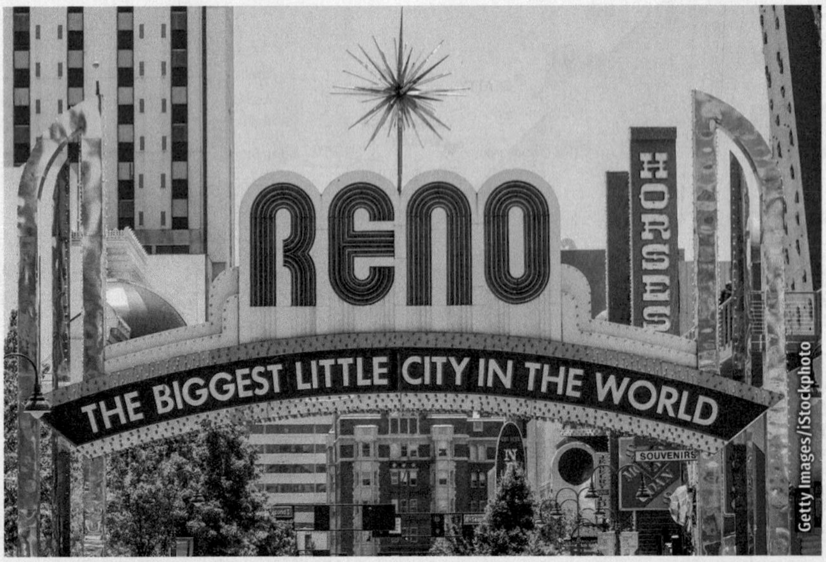

Getty Images/iStockphoto

BIKING · BOATING · DINING · ENTERTAINMENT · FISHING · HIKING · HUNTING · PADDLING · SHOPPING · SIGHTSEEING

NV

Nevada SPOTLIGHTS

Win the Vacation Jackpot in the Silver State

Let it roll in a state known for its glittering cities, sprawling deserts and big waterways. Whether you plan to play it all in Lake Powell or bet the farm in Las Vegas, you're bound to have a wild time in the Silver State.

THERE ARE AN ESTIMATED 200,000 SLOT MACHINES IN LAS VEGAS.

Historically, roulette is the most popular non-blackjack table game in Las Vegas.

Getty Images/iStockphoto

Las Vegas

An oasis of color and lights in the middle of the desert, Las Vegas has been a party hotspot for generations. While Sin City is known as a gambling destination, Vegas offers plenty more to see and do, from unusual dining experiences to family-friendly fun.

Casinos Galore

Vegas is synonymous with casinos, and even if gambling isn't your thing, it can be fun to check out the outrageous architecture and interior décor of these popular spots. Landmark casinos include the Luxor Hotel and Casino, which harkens Ancient Egypt with its own giant Sphinx, as well as The Venetian, which pays tribute to its namesake with gondolas and canals. New York, New York has its own Statue of Liberty, while Treasure Island features costumed pirates who entertain guests with stunts and pyrotechnics. The choreographed musical fountain displays at Bellagio's are also a big hit.

Vegas Museums

While museums aren't necessarily the first things that come to a lot of people's minds when they think of Las Vegas, there are plenty worth visiting. One of the most notable is the Mob Museum, which focuses on the history of organized crime, including how it shaped Las Vegas. Museum highlights include a firearm training simulator, a speakeasy-style distillery, and the electric chair used to execute mobster Albert Anastasia. If you like the bedazzling signs that light up the Las Vegas Strip, be sure to pay your respects at the Neon Museum, where old fluorescent signs are displayed, boneyard style. Not far from town, the Clark County Museum showcases restored old buildings from the turn of the 20th century.

Dining Experiences

You won't go hungry in Vegas — after all, what would Sin City be without a hefty dose of gluttony? All-you-can-eat buffets are part of the quintessential Vegas experience, from the seafood-heavy options at The Wyn to the fancy Bacchanal Buffet at Caesars Palace. If you want a great selection, the Carnival World Buffet and the Bellagio Buffet both offer excellent selections of cuisine from around the world. While buffets are the start of the show in Vegas, the city offers plenty of other unusual dining experiences. If you like your food laden with cholesterol, head over to the Heart Attack Grill, where you can order butterfat milkshakes and four-patty "Quadruple Bypass Burgers" from servers dressed as doctors and nurses. For a healthier, less gimmicky alternative, head to BLACKOUT Dining in the Dark, where you'll be served a seven-course, plant-based dinner in complete darkness.

Fun for the Family

While Vegas is often touted as an adults' playground, the city offers plenty of more wholesome activities suited towards families, too. There are plenty of amusement

LOCAL FAVORITE

Trashed Wings

From the world's gambling mecca comes a recipe for wings that requires you take a chance on your selection of rub and sauce. Get creative, spin the culinary wheel and see if you hit the jackpot with your own creation. *Recipe by Bill Vague.*

INGREDIENTS

- ☐ 12 lb sectioned chicken wings
- ☐ 1 cup olive oil
- ☐ ½ cup of dry rub seasoning, dealer's choice
- ☐ 3 cups BBQ or other wet sauce, dealer's choice

DIRECTIONS

Rub wings with oil and coat with the dry rub. Place wings in a pellet smoker or on grill at 225. Smoke/grill for 1 hr. Remove wings from smoker, brush with chosen BBQ sauce. Place in air fryer or pan fry for 5 to 10 minutes. Brush with sauce one more time then serve.

See listing Las Vegas, NV

SPOTLIGHTS

NV

park-style attractions, from the Stratosphere Hotel's roller coaster and drop tower to the Adventuredome theme park located inside the family-favorite Circus Circus Hotel & Casino. For great views over the city, from 550 feet in the air, head out to the High Roller Observation Wheel, the largest observation wheel in the United States.

Interactive Market

One of the newest attractions in Vegas is Omega Mart, an interactive installation that puts a surreal spin on supermarket shopping. Created by Santa Fe artistic collective Meow Wolf, this family-friendly experience takes visitors through an oddly whimsical faux grocery store full of secret passageways and psychedelic corridors filled with sound, light, and plenty of quirkiness. As such, it can get a little intense, and families with toddlers may prefer something calmer, such as the DISCOVERY Children's Museum, which offers interactive and educational experiences geared toward the youngest of guests.

Getty Images/iStockphoto

Valley of Fire State Park consists of bright red Aztec sandstone outcrops nestled in gray and tan limestone.

Get Outta Town

Although Vegas is very much a city lover's destination, it also makes an excellent base for getting out and exploring some of the epic wilderness of the American Southwest. Nearby outdoorsy attractions include the Valley of Fire State Park, a 40,000-acre expanse of the Mojave Desert and the Red Rock Canyon National Conservation Area, a great spot for hiking and checking out petroglyphs. Red Rock Canyon is also home to Cottonwood Valley, boasting 125-odd miles of track for mountain biking and trail running.

Oasis in the Desert

If you'd like to escape the dryness of the desert, the Clark County Wetlands Park is a great place for checking out wildlife, while the Lake Mead National Recreation Area attracts boating and

SPOTLIGHTS

Gambling oasis: In Laughlin, casinos line the west bank of the Colorado River at the southern tip of Nevada.

kayaking enthusiasts galore. It's also a great fishing spot, particularly for rainbow trout and striped bass. Attractions further afield include the Grand Canyon, which takes about four or five hours to reach by car (helicopter tours are also available). Death Valley National Park in California takes about two and a half hours to reach by car.

Laughlin

Nestled into the west bank of the Colorado River at the southern tip of the Silver State, Laughlin is a friendly, family-oriented. Visitors can choose between entertainment and gaming at a riverside casino or recreation in the surrounding countryside and on the river.

Bank on These Casinos

Eight casinos stretch along the river, and the Tropicana sits just across Casino Drive. That means visitors can walk from casino to casino for gaming fun. Each of the casinos offers many restaurants offering different cuisines. Even though all seven casinos have hotels attached, they all allow dry-camping in their parking lots. You can stay in Laughlin for a week and eat breakfast in a different casino each morning. Take a few chances with Lady Luck before heading out for outdoor adventure.

Full-Throttle Fun on Land and Water

Fans of speed can choose between ATV riding in the Mojave Desert or Jet Skiing on the river. You can bring your own or rent your choice of toys from a huge selection in Laughlin or across the river in Bullhead City, Arizona. Or simply settle back into your seat on a jet boat tour through the beautiful Topock Gorge to Lake Havasu City, Arizona. The jet boat departs from Edgewater and Harrahs' docks.

Colorado Catches

Slow things down a bit with a fishing expedition on the river. Boats can also be rented to enjoy on the river or on Lake Mohave, just upstream from Laughlin. If you happen to notice the difference in the spelling of Mojave/Mohave, an explanation is in order here. The U.S. Post Office decided early on that to avoid confusion between Mojave, California, and Mohave, Arizona, a slight change in spelling was indicated. Therefore, the lake was named with the Arizona spelling, because it was the state border between Nevada and Arizona. For fishing, you'll require a license, which is available at the rental agencies.

Wild Wilderness

You don't have to go far to get away from the bright lights of this gambling mecca. Drive just a few miles north of Laughlin on a well-graded dirt road to find Telephone Cove on the Nevada side of Lake Mohave. It's a quite large, flat beach, where you can park your RV and anchor boat with equal ease. Be advised, on holiday weekends, it can get very crowded. But once you've found your spot, it's a great place to sit back and enjoy the sounds of birds, the gentle waves hitting the beach and the soothing breezes that rustle the leaves on the cottonwood trees. It's a true oasis in the desert.

Laughlin's Legacy: More Than a Desert Mirage

Laughlin has come a long way in the past few decades. Old-timers will harken back to the wild days of the 1970s, when the small community supported only three casinos and two motels. There were no hotels, no RV parks and just a few cafes. At the time, to visit the larger Bullhead City across the river, visitors had to drive over Davis Dam (which has been closed to traffic since 9/11) or ride one of the many shuttle boats plying the river (which are still in use). Then, in 1987, developer Don Laughlin funded and built the Laughlin Bridge at a cost of $3.5 million. He then donated the bridge to the states of Nevada and Arizona. Today, the bridge carries at least 2,000 vehicles daily.

Pahrump

Travel to Pahrump if you have a thirst for scenic trails, high-speed driving and wine tasting. From race cars to rugged hikes to relaxing with a wine glass at one of the state's popular wineries, there's a little something for everyone in the heart of the desert.

High-Speed Thrills

If you have an appetite for adrenaline, Pahrump has you covered. The Spring Mountain Motorsports Ranch is a one-of-a-kind driving school where visitors can learn to handle tight corners and banked turns in Corvettes, Cadillacs and other high-performance vehicles. At nearby Lake Spring Mountain, guests can go paddleboarding, swimming and even take hydro flights strapped to a jet pack. Who needs Vegas thrills when you can truly soar?

Tackling Tough Terrain

Get beyond the pavement with an off-road adventure in the hills around Pahrump. Whether you arrange a rental with an outfitter or travel

LET ADVENTURE TAKE ITS COURSE.
Located 60 miles west of Las Vegas, Pahrump, Nevada is your base camp for adventure. With award-winning wineries, top-rated RV resorts, and adrenaline-boosting attractions, Pahrump has everything you need to make the most of your journey.
Top-Rated Good Sam Resorts
• Nevada Treasure RV Resort
• Wine Ridge RV Resort & Cottages
• Lakeside Casino & RV Park
• Preferred RV Resort
VisitPahrump.com
TRAVEL NEVADA
travelnevada.com
PAHRUMP true NEVADA
60 miles west of Las Vegas. 180 degrees different.
See listing Pahrump, NV

SPOTLIGHTS

No Limits: Tire tracks attest to the popularity of offroading in the Mohave Desert in southern Nevada.

with your own ATV, the many nearby trails, such as Carpenter Canyon Road and Wheeler Wash, deliver visitors to stunning vistas.

Lake in the Desert

Less than two hours east, Lake Mead is a mecca for outdoor lovers. Anglers should head to the lake's hot spots of Boxcar Cove and the Hemingway area to land top-notch stripers and catfish, while families looking to water ski, tube, paddle and swim can find everything they need at the marina. Further south, Lake Mohave is home to black, largemouth and smallmouth bass, as well as endless opportunities for recreation. It's all connected by the Colorado River.

Hiking Boots or Bikes

Hiker and mountain bikes can take advantage of the trails that snake through rugged mountains. Just east of town, the Spring Mountain National Recreation Area boasts over 60 miles of trails, including a challenging hike to the 12,000-foot summit of Mount Charleston. Breaking a sweat on the route to this peak is worth the stellar view at the top. Try the Desert Overlook, Mahogany Grove and Pack Rat routes for easier approaches.

Sliver State Untamed

At the Ash Meadows National Wildlife Refuge, travelers can explore the wild side of the Silver State. The refuge is home to 26 species of flora and fauna found nowhere else in the world. Even closer to downtown, try the Elk Meadows Trail network or Wallace Canyon trail. Red Rock Canyon National Conservation Area and Death Valley National Park are also quick drives from downtown.

Nevada Vintages

Basking in a warm, dry climate, the Pahrump Valley Winery has been producing award-winning vintages for years. The winery's lush, palm tree-covered grounds are worth a visit, whether you're a wine lover or teetotaler. Relax with a visit to the tasting rooms, a tour of the vineyards with desert mountain views in the distance. Discover the unique flavors found only in this desert environment.

Stagecoach Commuting

Nevada's homesteading pioneers are honored during the Wild West Extravaganza and Bluegrass Festival in May. The event celebrates Nevada's settlers with bluegrass music, rodeos and trail rides. The free event has activities for the whole family. Plan on going sky high if you visit during February's Pahrump Balloon Festival.

Delightful Death Valley Days

Get the full measure of the desert with a trip across state lines. Just 48 miles west, Death Valley National Park in California thrills visitors with smooth sand dunes and spectacularly stark vistas.

Reno/Sparks

Situated on the Truckee River, just east of the Sierra Nevada Mountains and about a 15-minute drive from California, sit the neighboring cities of Reno and Sparks. Once a popular stop along the California Goldrush trail, Reno was officially founded in the late 19th century, when the Transcontinental Railroad was established in the area. These days, the area is best

NV

known for its casinos, and while nightlife reigns supreme here, the area also offers plenty more, from art museums to outdoor adventure.

Casinos of Reno

While Reno offers much more than just gambling, casinos play an important role in driving the city's economy. Often touted as a mini–Las Vegas, Reno offers 20-odd casinos in and around town. Three casinos are situated in a strip of downtown known as The Row: Silver Legacy, the family-friendly Circus Circus, and the gargantuan Eldorado. The Peppermill Reno draws its inspiration from Tuscany, Italy.

The Wilbur D. May Center

Situated inside the Rancho San Rafael Regional Park, the Wilbur D. May Center features a museum, an arboretum and a botanical garden. The museum features items from the private collection of Reno philanthropist Wilbur May. It offers a vast collection of objects from around the world, from Chinese pottery to Polynesian carvings, along with ancient Egyptian art, taxidermy, and antique firearms.

Connected the Reno Riverwalk, a pedestrian bridge arches over the Truckee River as it rolls through town.

The National Automobile Museum

Whether you love cars or just appreciate quality design, you'll likely find that the National Automobile Museum is well worth your time. This 100,000-square-foot expanse houses over 200 cars along with automobile-related artifacts and an on-site theater. The museum also hosts plenty of special events, including "Science Saturdays," which feature space-related activities geared toward 8- to 12-year-olds as well as history lectures geared toward adults held on the second Thursday of each month.

The Nevada Museum of Art

Housed in a modern building inspired by the nearby Black Rock Desert, the Nevada Museum of Art is the state's foremost art museum. This 70,000-square-foot expanse features an extensive permanent collection that can be divided into four thematic areas: Altered Landscape Photography, Art of the Greater West, Contemporary Art, and the Work Ethic. There's also a research library, an extensive collection of archives and a "museum school" offering art classes for guests of all ages, as well as a regular rotation of temporary and touring exhibits.

Terry Lee Wells Nevada Discovery Museum

If you're visiting Reno and Sparks with little ones, you'll find the Discovery Museum worth checking out. This 67,000-square-foot spot offers a mix of permanent and changing science-focused educational exhibits offering hands-on fun for the entire family. Here, guests can learn about mining, engineering, anatomy, and astronomy through interactive play.

Animal Ark

A short drive north of town, Animal Ark Wildlife Sanctuary and Nature Center provides a safe sanctuary for animals that, because of injury or other issues, cannot be released back into the wild. This 38-acre property is home to a wide variety of species, including bears, wolves, coyotes, raccoons, cougars, and even cheetahs and tigers. Come early to increase your

SPOTLIGHTS

A trail winds through an alpine forest near Reno during spring. All told, there are 75 trails in the Reno area.

chances of seeing animals at their most active — you might even get to witness a feeding — or sign up for one of the special Ark at Dark evening tours.

Reno Outdoors

With warm, dry, sunny weather throughout the year, the Reno-Sparks area is a great place to go hiking. Good spots include the Tom Cooke Trail, which runs along the Truckee River, and the Huffaker Hills Trail, a 1.8-mile easy loop. For something slightly more challenging, check out the Hunter Creek Trail, which spans 5.7 miles in total and leads to a waterfall. If you're fond of fishing, you'll find plenty of opportunities right on the Truckee River (which is also an excellent spot for whitewater rafting and kayaking), while the 77-acre Sparks Marina Park is good for fishing, swimming, and even scuba diving. A bit further from town, Pyramid Lake is a great place to fish for Lohanton cutthroat, trout, and cui-cu. Getting to Lake Tahoe only takes about 45 minutes, where you'll find more opportunities for hiking, water activities, and gambling.

Carson City

The capital of Nevada, Carson City, sits in the Eagle Valley in the western part of the state, about nine miles east of Lake Tahoe. Its location on the Carson River made it a trading post during the California Gold Rush, when it was still part of the Utah Territory. In 1859, the Comstock Lode — an enormous strike of silver ore (and the first major metal vein to be discovered in the United States) — was found in the nearby Virginia Range. This discovery led to a significant influx of settlers, and by 1864, under Abraham Lincoln, Nevada earned its statehood.

Divine Nine and More

While outdoor sports and activities reign supreme in this region, it's also well known for its excellent golf courses (known collectively as the Divine Nine) and its abundance of antique shops. The immediate Carson City area alone has seven casinos, most of which have amenities for children, and serious gamblers can head over to Reno or Lake Tahoe.

Outdoor Adventureland

Hiking is hugely popular here, and Carson City's position smack in the middle of the Eastern Sierras makes it a good spot to get out into the rugged countryside. Even those who just want a leisurely stroll can find easy, short trails at the 109-acre Riverview Park. Hikers can follow scenic pathways that run along the Carson River. It's also an off-leash space for dogs (though they are not allowed in wetland areas).

Biking the Peak

Carson City is also popular among mountain biking enthusiasts, with lots of single-track trails for experienced bikers in both Ash Canyon and Kings Canyon. Other trails include the 13-mile Scott-McClellan Peak climb, which rises 7,000 feet at its highest point. The Carson River Trail is even longer, at 15 miles in length, but with an elevation gain of around 1,300 feet.

Nevada Paddling

Paddle sports are also a major activity in the summertime, and the city's 12.6-mile Carson River Aquatic Trail is a fantastic stretch for kayakers with a bit of experience. Those just getting started with paddle sports can head to Carson River Park for a 3.3-mile float along cottonwood-lined shores at the Upper River Class I-II stretch.

▸ FOR MORE INFORMATION

Travel Nevada, 775-687-4322, www.travelnevada.com

Visit Las Vegas, 877-847-4858, VisitLasVegas.com

Visit Laughlin, 800-522-4700, www.visitlaughlin.com

Town of Pahrump, 775-727-5107, www.pahrumpnv.org

Visit Reno Tahoe, 800-367-7366, www.visitrenotahoe.com

Visit Carson City, 775-687-7410, www.visitcarsoncity.com

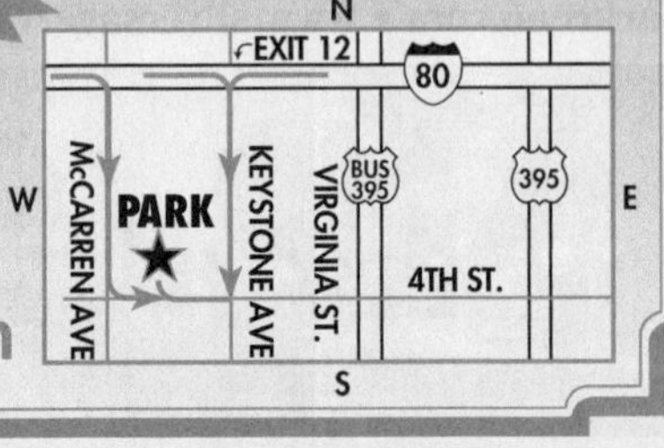

Nevada

ALAMO — D4 *Lincoln*

PICKETTS RV PARK **Ratings: 6/9★/7** (RV Park) Avail: 30 full hkups (30/50 amps). 2021 rates: $35.32 to $39.86. (775)725-3300, 115 Broadway St, Alamo, NV 89001

AMARGOSA VALLEY — E3 *Nye*

LONGSTREET RV RESORT & CASINO **Ratings: 9/10★/7** (RV Park) Avail: 46 full hkups (30/50 amps). 2021 rates: $25 to $30. (775)372-1777, 4400 S Highway 373, Amargosa Valley, NV 89020

BAKER — C5 *White Pine*

BORDER INN & RV PARK **Ratings: 6/7/6.5** (Campground) Avail: 16 full hkups (30/50 amps). 2021 rates: $28. (775)234-7300, Hwy 50 & Hwy 6, Baker, NV 89311

GREAT BASIN/BAKER CREEK CAMPGROUND (Public National Park) From town, W 5 mi on Hwy 488 to Nfd-590, S 3 mi (L). 38 Avail: Pit toilets. 2021 rates: $15. May 01 to Oct 15. (775)234-7331

GREAT BASIN/UPPER LEHMAN CREEK CAMPGROUND (Public National Park) From town, W 5 mi on Hwy 488 to Nfd-446, N 3 mi (L). 22 Avail: Pit toilets. 2021 rates: $15. Apr 15 to Oct 30. (775)234-7331

GREAT BASIN/WHEELER PEAK CAMPGROUND (Public National Park) From town, W 5 mi on Hwy 488 to Nfd 446, N 8.5mi (E). CAUTION: Steep, winding roads. RVs over 24 ft not permitted. 37 Avail: Pit toilets. 2021 rates: $15. Jun 01 to Oct 31. (775)234-7331

WHISPERING ELMS MOTEL/RV PARK & TENT CAMPING **Ratings: 6/7.5/6** (Campground) Avail: 13 full hkups (30/50 amps). 2021 rates: $30 to $35. (775)234-9900, 120 Baker Ave, Baker, NV 89311

BEATTY — E3 *Nye*

BEATTY RV PARK **Ratings: 6/8.5★/5.5** (Campground) Avail: 28 full hkups (30/50 amps). 2021 rates: $25. (775)553-2732, Mile Marker 63 Hwy 95 N, Beatty, NV 89003

DEATH VALLEY INN & RV PARK **Ratings: 6/8.5/7.5** (Campground) Avail: 38 full hkups (30/50 amps). 2021 rates: $35. (775)553-9702, 300 South Highway 95, Beatty, NV 89003

BOULDER CITY — F5 *Clark*

CANYON TRAIL RV PARK
Ratings: 9.5/10★/9.5 (RV Park) Avail: 106 full hkups (30/50 amps). 2021 rates: $52.80 to $63.80. (702)293-1200, 1200 Industrial Rd, Boulder City, NV 89005

LAKE MEAD NRA/BOULDER BEACH (Public National Park) From Jct of US-93 & Lakeshore Rd, N 2 mi on Lakeshore Rd (R). 148 Avail. 2021 rates: $20. (702)293-8990

LAKE MEAD NRA/LAS VEGAS BAY CAMPGROUND (Public National Park) From Jct of US-93 & Lakeshore Rd exit, N 9 mi on Lakeshore Rd (R). 84 Avail. 2021 rates: $20. (702)293-8990

LAKE MEAD RV VILLAGE AT BOULDER BEACH
Ratings: 9/9★/9.5 (RV Park) Avail: 97 full hkups (30/50 amps). 2021 rates: $34 to $50. (702)293-2540, 268 Lakeshore Drive, Boulder City, NV 89005

CALIENTE — D5 *Lincoln*

BEAVER DAM
(Public State Park) From town, N 6 mi on US-93, E 28 mi on gravel road (L). Steep and winding access road. Vehicles over 25 ft not recommended. Entrance fee. Elev 5000 ft.**FAC:** gravel rds. Avail: 33 gravel, no slide-outs, back-ins (18x20), tent sites, pit toilets, fire rings, firewood. **REC:** Beaver Dam Wash: swim, fishing. Pets OK. Partial handicap access, 14 day max stay. 2021 rates: $15. Apr 01 to Nov 15. no cc, no reservations.
(775)728-4460 Lat: 37.723648, Lon: -114.45504
Caliente, NV 89008
www.parks.nv.gov

YOUNG'S RV PARK **Ratings: 6/8★/7** (RV Park) Avail: 37 full hkups (30/50 amps). 2021 rates: $25 to $30. (775)726-3418, 1352 South Front St, Caliente, NV 89008

Say you saw it in our Guide!

CALLVILLE BAY — E5 *Clark*

LAKE MEAD NRA/CALLVILLE BAY (Public National Park) From Jct of US-93 & Northshore Rd, NE 26 mi on Northshore Rd (R). 52 Avail: (30/50 amps). 2021 rates: $20. (702)293-8990

CAL-NEV-ARI — F5 *Clark*

CAL-NEV-ARI MARKET & RV PARK **Ratings: 5/8★/5.5** (RV Park) Avail: 43 full hkups (30/50 amps). 2021 rates: $22.10. (702)297-1115, #2 Spirit Mountain Lane, Cal-Nev-Ari, NV 89039

CARSON CITY — C1 *Carson*

CARSON CITY See also Dayton, Minden, Reno & Zephyr Cove, NV; South Lake Tahoe & Truckee, CA.

CAMP-N-TOWN RV PARK
Ratings: 7.5/9.5★/8 (RV Park) Avail: 32 full hkups (30/50 amps). 2021 rates: $50 to $57. (775)883-1123, 2438 N Carson St, Carson City, NV 89706

COMSTOCK COUNTRY RV RESORT
Ratings: 9.5/9★/9.5 (RV Park) From Jct of US 395 (Carson St) & US 50 W: Go 1600 ft S on NV 395, then 750 ft W on Old Clear Creek Rd (R). Elev 4780 ft.**FAC:** paved rds. Avail: 150 gravel, patios, 120 pull-thrus, (28x60), back-ins (28x60), 150 full hkups (30/50 amps), cable, WiFi @ sites, dump, laundry, groc, LP gas. **REC:** heated pool, hot tub. Pet restrict (B). Partial handicap access. No tents, eco-friendly. 2021 rates: $48 to $55, Military discount.
(775)882-2445 Lat: 39.117858, Lon: -119.774108
5400 S Carson St, Carson City, NV 89701
comstockcountryrvresort.com
See ad this page

DAVIS CREEK CAMPGROUND (Public) From town, N 11 mi on US-395 to Old US-395, W 0.5 mi (L). 62 Avail. 2021 rates: $20. (775)849-0684

Don't miss a thing! Check out the Table of Contents for everything the Guide has to offer.

Good Sam's Trip Planner features tools and information designed to help you have the best road trip - every time. Visit GoodSam.com/Trip-Planner.

NV

Nevada Privately Owned Campground Information Updated by our Good Sam Representatives

Jeff & Peggy Harmann

We have worked with Good Sam from coast to coast, north to south. After a career largely focused around customer support and marketing, we see that the "magic" happens when RVers find the right RV park for them.

Tony & Nanette Martin

In 2014, Tony and I decided to sell everything we owned, buy a motorhome and hit the road for a year with our two dogs. That year turned into five, traveling from Mexico to Alaska as well as Canada. Along the way we ran into a couple of Good Sam rep teams, and we thought, "what a perfect job." And so it all began; we have been lucky enough to live the lifestyle we love.

CARSON CITY (CONT)

GOLD DUST WEST CASINO & RV PARK
Ratings: 10/9.5★/9 (RV Park) From jct I-580 (US 395) & US 50: Go 1/4 mi SW on US 50, then 1/4 mi S on Gold Dust Way (R). Elev 4600 ft.**FAC:** paved rds. Avail: 47 paved, 20 pull-thrus, (21x40), back-ins (21x40), 47 full hkups (30/50 amps), cable, WiFi @ sites, rentals, dump, laundry, restaurant. **REC:** pool, hot tub, boating nearby. Pet restrict (B/Q). Partial handicap access. No tents. 2021 rates: $45 to $60. ATM.
(775)885-9000 Lat: 39.1725, Lon: -119.74416
2171 E William St, Carson City, NV 89701
www.gdwcasino.com
See ad previous page

WASHOE LAKE (Public State Park) From Jct of US-395 & Hwy 50, N 13 mi to Lake Blvd, N 3 mi (L) Entrance fee. Max RV size 45'. 49 Avail. 2021 rates: $15. (775)687-4319

Things to See and Do

GOLD DUST WEST CASINO 24 hour Casino & The Grille Restaurant, 36-lane bowling center. Gold Dust Casino Carson City your one-stop shop. Also Ole Ole Restaurant. Elev 4600 ft. Partial handicap access. RV accessible. Restrooms. Food. Hours: 24 hours. ATM.
(775)885-9000 Lat: 39.1725, Lon: -119.74416
2171 E William St, Carson City, NV 89701
www.gdwcasino.com
See ad previous page

COTTONWOOD COVE — E5 *Clark*

COTTONWOOD COVE NEVADA RV PARK & MARINA
Ratings: 7.5/8.5★/7 (RV Park) Avail: 52 full hkups (30/50 amps). 2021 rates: $35 to $50. (702)297-1464, 10000 Cottonwood Cove Rd, Searchlight, NV 89046

DAYTON — C1 *Lyon*

DAYTON RV PARK
Ratings: 8.5/9.5★/9 (RV Park) Avail: 30 full hkups (30/50 amps). 2021 rates: $50 to $52. (775)246-9300, 75 Pike St, Dayton, NV 89403

ELKO — B4 *Elko*

DOUBLE DICE RV PARK **Ratings: 8/9.5★/7.5** (RV Park) Avail: 64 full hkups (30/50 amps). 2021 rates: $35 to $47. (775)738-5642, 3730 E Idaho St, Elko, NV 89801

ELKO RV PARK
Ratings: 7/7.5/6.5 (RV Park) Avail: 100 full hkups (30/50 amps). 2021 rates: $32 to $40. (775)738-3448, 507 Scott Road, Elko, NV 89801

IRON HORSE RV RESORT
Ratings: 9/10★/9.5 (RV Park) From Jct of I-80 & Exit 303 (Jennings Way): Go 500 ft S on Jennings Way (not marked), then 1/4 mi E on East Idaho St (R). Elev 5100 ft.**FAC:** paved rds. (92 spaces). Avail: 45 gravel, patios, 20 pull-thrus, (28x75), back-ins (28x58), 45 full hkups (30/50 amps), seasonal sites, WiFi @ sites, rentals, dump, laundry. **REC:** heated pool, hot tub, playground, hunting nearby. Pets OK. Partial handicap access. No tents. Big rig sites, eco-friendly. 2021 rates: $35 to $50, Military discount.
(800)782-3556 Lat: 40.8562062, Lon: -115.7400041
3400 East Idaho St, Elko, NV 89801
ironhorservresort.com
See ad this page

SOUTH FORK SRA (Public State Park) From Jct I-80 (exit 301) & Hwy 227, SE 7 mi on Hwy 227, S 6 mi on Hwy 228 (E). Entrance fee required. 25 Avail. 2021 rates: $15. May 01 to Oct 15. (775)744-4346

Things to See and Do

SHUTTERS HOTEL - ELKO AND THE RUBY RESTAURANT Stay in a craftsman inspired hotel with accommodations offering all of the comforts of home and dine at The Ruby Restaurant & Bar featuring elevated comfort food. Elev 5100 ft. Restrooms. Food. Hours: 24 hrs.
(775)777-1200 Lat: 40.86356, Lon: -115.73715
3650 E Idaho St, Elko, NV 89801
www.shuttershotelelko.com
See ad this page

ELY — C5 *White Pine*

CAVE LAKE (Public State Park) From town, N 17.6 mi to SR-486, E 7 mi on SR-486 (R). 35 Avail. 2021 rates: $17. May 01 to Oct 15. (775)728-4467

ELY KOA JOURNEY **Ratings: 7.5/8.5★/9** (Campground) 100 Avail: 83 full hkups, 17 W, 17 E (30/50 amps). 2021 rates: $41.99 to $52.99. (775)289-3413, 15936 Pioche Hwy, Ely, NV 89301

VALLEY VIEW RV PARK
Ratings: 7/9★/8 (RV Park) Avail: 26 full hkups (30/50 amps). 2021 rates: $34. (775)289-3303, 40 US-93 N, Ely, NV 89301

WARD CHARCOAL OVENS (Public State Park) From Jct I-93 & US-50, SW 11 mi to Cave Valley Rd (R) Entrance fee. 14 Avail: Pit toilets. 2021 rates: $14 to $30. (775)289-1693

FALLON — C2 *Churchill*

COLD SPRINGS STATION RESORT **Ratings: 7/8.5★/7** (RV Park) Avail: 24 full hkups (30/50 amps). 2021 rates: $30 to $40. (775)423-1233, 52300 Austin Hwy, Fallon, NV 89406

Do you know how to read each part of a listing? Check the How to Use This Guide in the front.

FALLON RV PARK
Ratings: 7/8/7 (RV Park) From Jct of US-95 & US-50: Go 5 mi W on US-50 (L). Elev 4000 ft.**FAC:** paved rds. (64 spaces). Avail: 47 paved, 28 pull-thrus, (30x70), back-ins (30x60), 47 full hkups (30/50 amps), seasonal sites, cable, WiFi @ sites, tent sites, dump, laundry, groc, LP gas, firewood. Pets OK $. Big rig sites, eco-friendly. 2021 rates: $48 to $51, Military discount. ATM.
(775)867-2332 Lat: 39.485724, Lon: -118.872345
5787 Reno Hwy 50, Fallon, NV 89406
www.fallonrvpark.com
See ad this page

MILITARY PARK FALLON RV PARK (FALLON NAS) (Public) From Jct of US-95 & NV-199 (Berney Rd), go E on NV-199 Berney Rd) to South Gate, then turn left to Carson Rd, turn left to Churchill, turn right to Lanhontan Rd. Avail: 32 full hkups (30/50 amps). 2021 rates: $30. (775)909-4902

Things to See and Do

FALLON RV PARK COUNTRY STORE & GIFT SHOP Country store and gift store. Sells licensed beverages, liquor, groceries and fuel. Elev 4000 ft. Partial handicap access. RV accessible. Restrooms. Food. Hours: 5am to 12am. ATM.
(775)867-2332 Lat: 39.485724, Lon: -118.872345
5787 Reno Hwy 50, Fallon, NV 89406
www.fallonrvpark.com
See ad this page

FERNLEY — C1 *Lyon*

DESERT ROSE RV PARK
Ratings: 8/9.5★/8.5 (RV Park) From Jct of I-80 & exit 48 (Alt US-95 S/Alt US-50 E): Go 1 mi S on Alt US 95, then 4 mi E on US 50 (R). Elev 4200 ft.**FAC:** all weather rds. (115 spaces). Avail: 56 paved, patios, 51 pull-thrus, (35x65), back-ins (30x23), 56 full hkups (30/50 amps), seasonal sites, cable, WiFi @ sites, dump, laundry, LP gas. **REC:** hunting nearby. Pet restrict (B/Q) $. Partial handicap access. No tents. Big rig sites, eco-friendly. 2021 rates: $38 to $45, Military discount.
(775)575-9399 Lat: 39.592391, Lon: -119.156128
3285 Alt US Highway 50 E, Fernley, NV 89408
desertroserv.com
See ad this page

GABBS — C2 *Nye*

BERLIN-ICHTHYOSAUR (Public State Park) From Jct Hwy 361 & Hwy 844, E 22 mi on Hwy 844. 14 Avail: Pit toilets. 2021 rates: $15. (775)964-2440

GARDNERVILLE — C1 *Douglas*

TOPAZ LODGE RV PARK & CASINO
Ratings: 7/7/7.5 (Campground) 59 Avail: 53 full hkups, 6 W, 6 E (30/50 amps). 2021 rates: $30 to $35. (800)962-0732, 1979 US Hwy 395 South, Gardnerville, NV 89410

GOLDFIELD — D3 *Esmeralda*

CLARKS CUSTOM CAMP **Ratings: 5/8★/5** (RV Park) Avail: 10 full hkups (30/50 amps). 2021 rates: $35. (775)485-3460, 560 North 5th Street, Goldfield, NV 89013

HAWTHORNE — D2 *Mineral*

WHISKEY FLATS RV PARK
Ratings: 8/9.5★/8.5 (RV Park) From the Jct of NV 359 & US 95: Go 1 mi N on US 95 (L). Elev 4200 ft.**FAC:** gravel rds. (60 spaces). Avail: 40 paved, 40 pull-thrus, (28x60), 40 full hkups (30/50 amps), seasonal sites, cable, WiFi @ sites, tent sites, dump, laundry, LP gas. **REC:** boating nearby, hunting nearby. Pet restrict (Q). Partial handicap access. Big rig sites, eco-friendly. 2021 rates: $34.54.
(775)945-1800 Lat: 38.5374469, Lon: -118.6332231
3045 US Hwy 95, Hawthorne, NV 89415
www.whiskeyflats.net
See ad opposite page

HENDERSON — F5 *Clark*

DESERT SANDS RV PARK
Ratings: 9/10★/8.5 (RV Park) Avail: 237 full hkups (30/50 amps). 2021 rates: $39. (702)565-1945, 1940 N Boulder Hwy, Henderson, NV 89011

Keep one Guide at home, and one in your RV! To purchase additional copies, call 877-209-6655.

Travel Services

CAMPING WORLD OF HENDERSON As the nation's largest retailer of RV supplies, accessories, services and new and used RVs, Camping World is committed to making your total RV experience better. **SERVICES:** tire, RV appliance, restrooms. RV supplies, emergency parking, RV accessible. Hours: 9am - 6pm. (800)646-4093 Lat: 35.99945, Lon: -114.93896 1600 S Boulder Hwy, Henderson, NV 89015 www.campingworld.com

HIKO — D4 *Lincoln*

GREEN VALLEY GROCERY & RV PARK (Campground) (Rebuilding) Avail: 35 full hkups (30/50 amps). 2021 rates: $22. (775)725-3545, 6799 S Hwy 93, Hiko, NV 89017

JACKPOT — A5 *Elko*

CACTUS PETES RV PARK
Ratings: 8/8/7.5 (RV Park) 84 Avail: 84 W, 84 E (30 amps). 2021 rates: $20 to $26. (775)755-2321, 1385 Highway 93, Jackpot, NV 89825

LAKE TAHOE — C1 *Douglas*

LAKE TAHOE See also Carson City, Dayton, Gardnerville, Minden, Reno, Smith Valley, Sparks, Verdi, Yerington & Zephyr Cove, NV; Arnold, Coloma, Emigrant Gap, Lotus, South Lake Tahoe & Truckee, CA.

LAS VEGAS — E4 *Clark*

A SPOTLIGHT Introducing Las Vegas' colorful attractions appearing at the front of this state section.

LAS VEGAS See also Boulder City & Henderson, NV; Willow Beach, AZ.

ARIZONA CHARLIE'S BOULDER RV PARK
Ratings: 10/10★/8.5 (RV Park) From Jct of I-515 (US 93/95 Expwy) & Boulder Hwy (exit 70): Go 2 mi S on Boulder Hwy (L). **FAC:** paved rds. (221 spaces). Avail: 201 paved, 92 pull-thrus, (20x70), back-ins (20x40), 201 full hkups (30/50 amps), seasonal sites, cable, WiFi @ sites, laundry, LP gas, restaurant. **REC:** heated pool, hot tub. Pet restrict (B/Q). Partial handicap access. No tents. Big rig sites. 2021 rates: $34 to $36, Military discount.
(800)970-7280 Lat: 36.12466, Lon: -115.07733
4445 Boulder Hwy, Las Vegas, NV 89121
www.arizonacharliesboulder.com
See ad next page, 578

CIRCUS CIRCUS RV PARK **Ratings: 7/7.5/4** (RV Park) 60 Avail: 56 full hkups, 4 W, 4 E (30/50 amps). 2021 rates: $41 to $51. (702)691-5988, 500 Circus Circus Drive, Las Vegas, NV 89109

CLARK COUNTY SHOOTING COMPLEX'S RV PARK (Public) From jct of US 95 & Hwy 215 (Bruce Woodbury Beltway): Go 3-1/4 mi E on Hwy 215, then 4-1/4 mi N on N. Decatur Blvd (E). Avail: 59 full hkups (30/50 amps). 2021 rates: $30. (702)455-2000

DUCK CREEK RV PARK
Ratings: 10/10★/9 (RV Park) From Jct of I-515 & Sunset Rd (Exit 64): Go 1 mi E on Sunset Rd, then 1-1/4 mi N on N Boulder Hwy (R).

SPREAD YOUR WINGS AT DUCK CREEK
Come spread your wings and enjoy our friendly staff and the excitement of Las Vegas. Short drive to the Las Vegas strip. Free WIFI, heated pool & Jacuzzi, showers, laundry room & recreation room, cookouts and movie nights.

FAC: paved rds. (207 spaces). Avail: 50 paved, 22 pull-thrus, (20x73), back-ins (20x35), 50 full hkups (30/50 amps), seasonal sites, WiFi @ sites, dump, laundry, groc, LP gas. **REC:** heated pool, hot tub, boating nearby, playground. Pet restrict (S/B/Q). Partial handicap access. No tents, eco-friendly. 2021 rates: $38 to $55, Military discount.
(866)371-9712 Lat: 36.08047, Lon: -115.02583
6635 Boulder Highway, Las Vegas, NV 89122
www.duckcreekrvparklv.com
See ad this page, 575

Each privately owned campground has been rated three times. The first rating is for development of facilities. The second one is for cleanliness and physical characteristics of restrooms and showers. The third is for campground visual appearance and environmental quality.

Time and rates don't stand still. Remember that last year's rates serve as a guideline only. Call ahead for the most current rate information.

Got a different point of view? We want to know. Rate the campgrounds you visit using the rating guidelines located in front of this Guide, then compare your ratings to ours.

LAS VEGAS (CONT)

HITCHIN' POST RV PARK

good sam park **Ratings: 9.5/9.5★/9.5** (RV Park) S-bnd: From Jct of I-15 & Exit 50 (Lamb): Go 2 mi S on Lamb, then 500 ft S on Las Vegas Blvd (L) or N-bnd: From Jct of I-15 & Craig Rd (exit 48): Go 1-1/4 mi E on Craig Rd, then 1 mi SE on Lamb Blvd, then 500 ft on Las Vegas Blvd (L).

FRIENDLIEST RV PARK IN LAS VEGAS!
Highly rated, affordable & gated. Try your luck on our slots, relax in our heated pool, enjoy our Saloon open 24/7, dine in our restaurant & Beer Garden on property. Stop-Stay-Enjoy! Free WiFi, Cable TV & HBO. We have it all.

FAC: paved rds. (196 spaces). Avail: 98 gravel, 98 pull-thrus, (25x70), 98 full hkups (30/50 amps), seasonal sites, cable, WiFi @ sites, rentals, dump, laundry, restaurant, controlled access. **REC:** heated pool, boating nearby. Pet restrict (S/Q). Partial handicap access. No tents. Big rig sites, eco-friendly. 2021 rates: $48.59 to $71.19. ATM.
(888)433-8402 Lat: 36.222656, Lon: -115.084472
3640 Las Vegas Blvd North, Las Vegas, NV 89115
www.hprvp.com
See ad page 579

KINGS ROW RV & MHP **Ratings: 6/9.5★/6** (RV Area in MH Park) Avail: 105 full hkups (30/50 amps). 2021 rates: $25. (702)457-3606, 3660 Boulder Hwy, Las Vegas, NV 89121

LAS VEGAS KOA AT SAM'S TOWN **Ratings: 9.5/9/7** (RV Park) Avail: 487 full hkups (30/50 amps). 2021 rates: $35 to $75. (800)562-7270, 5225 Boulder Highway, Las Vegas, NV 89122

LAS VEGAS RV RESORT

good sam park **Ratings: 10/10★/10** (RV Park) From Jct of Boulder Hwy & Nellis Blvd: Go 1/4 mi N on Nellis Blvd (R). **FAC:** paved rds. (384 spaces). Avail: 150 paved, 129 pull-thrus, (30x60), back-ins (30x50), 150 full hkups (30/50 amps), seasonal sites, WiFi @ sites, rentals, dump, laundry, LP gas, controlled access. **REC:** heated pool, hot tub. Pet restrict (B/Q). Partial handicap access. No tents, Age restrict may apply. Big rig sites, eco-friendly. 2021 rates: $29 to $55.
(866)846-5432 Lat: 36.119078, Lon: -115.063360
3890 S Nellis Blvd, Las Vegas, NV 89121
www.lasvegasrvresort.com
See ad this page

LVM RESORT **Ratings: 10/10★/10** (Condo Park) Avail: 110 full hkups (30/50 amps). 2021 rates: $70 to $120. (866)897-9300, 8175 Arville St, Las Vegas, NV 89139

MAIN STREET STATION RV PARK **Ratings: 6.5/9★/5.5** (RV Park) Avail: 87 full hkups (30/50 amps). 2021 rates: $21. (800)634-6255, 200 North Main, Las Vegas, NV 89101

MILITARY PARK DESERT EAGLE RV PARK (NELLIS AFB) (Public) S-bnd: From jct I-15 & Craig Rd (exit 48): Go 2.5 mi E on Craig Rd, then left on Las Vegas Blvd North (Hwy 604) pass Nellis Main Gate, then W on Range Rd, then left on Stafford Dr, follow signs. 226 Avail: 222 full hkups, 4 W, 4 E (30/50 amps). 2021 rates: $22 to $26. (702)643-3060

OASIS LAS VEGAS RV RESORT **Ratings: 10/10★/9** (RV Resort) Avail: 550 full hkups (30/50 amps). 2021 rates: $54.95 to $81.95. (800)566-4707, 2711 W Windmill Lane, Las Vegas, NV 89123

RIVIERA RV PARK

good sam park **Ratings: 9.5/10★/9** (RV Park) Avail: 14 full hkups (30/50 amps). 2021 rates: $39.03. (702)457-8700, 2200 Palm Street, Las Vegas, NV 89104

ROADRUNNER RV PARK **Ratings: 8/9/8** (RV Park) Avail: 100 full hkups (30/50 amps). 2021 rates: $26 to $30. (702)456-4711, 4711 Boulder Highway, Las Vegas, NV 89121

THOUSAND TRAILS LAS VEGAS RV RESORT

good sam park **Ratings: 8.5/9.5★/7.5** (Membership Park) Avail: 203 full hkups (30/50 amps). 2021 rates: $45 to $55. (888)563-7040, 4295 Boulder Highway, Las Vegas, NV 89121

Travel Services

CAMPING WORLD OF LAS VEGAS As the nation's largest retailer of RV supplies, accessories, services and new and used RVs, Camping World is committed to making your total RV experience better. **SERVICES:** RV, RV appliance, MH mechanical, restrooms. RV Sales. RV supplies, LP gas, RV accessible. Hours: 9am - 7pm.
(877)440-9485 Lat: 35.92804, Lon: -115.19440
13175 South Las Vegas Blvd., Las Vegas, NV 89044
www.campingworld.com

Things to See and Do

ARIZONA CHARLIE'S BOULDER HOTEL, CASINO, RV PARK Casino with 24-hr games, entertainment, restaurant & buffet. Partial handicap access. RV accessible. Restrooms. Food. Hours: 24 hrs. ATM.
(877)951-0002 Lat: 36.12407, Lon: -115.07643
4575 Boulder Highway, Las Vegas, NV 89121
www.arizonacharlies.com
See ad this page, 578

HITCHIN' POST SALOON & CASINO On park property, full-service bar, restaurant, poker machines, outdoor beer garden, horseshoe pits, pool tables, dart boards. Open all year, 24 hours. Partial handicap access. RV accessible. Restrooms. Food. Hours: 24 hrs. ATM.
(888)433-8402 Lat: 36.24390, Lon: -115.05432
3650 Las Vegas Blvd N, Las Vegas, NV 89115
www.hpsslv.com
See ad page 579

LAUGHLIN — F5 *Clark*

LAUGHLIN/AVI CASINO KOA **Ratings: 8.5/9★/7** (RV Park) Avail: 60 full hkups (30/50 amps). 2021 rates: $25 to $50. (800)562-4142, 10000 Aha Macav Parkway, Laughlin, NV 89029

RIVERSIDE RESORT RV PARK **Ratings: 9/9.5★/8** (RV Park) Avail: 640 full hkups (30/50 amps). 2021 rates: $27.53 to $47.69. (800)227-3849, 1650 S Casino Dr, Laughlin, NV 89029

LOVELOCK — B2 *Pershing*

RYE PATCH SRA (Public State Park) From town, N 22 mi on I-80 to exit 129, W 1 mi (L) Entrance fee required. 47 Avail. 2021 rates: $15. (775)538-7321

MESQUITE — E5 *Clark*

CASABLANCA RV PARK RESORT **Ratings: 7/8.5★/6** (RV Park) Avail: 45 full hkups (30/50 amps). 2021 rates: $20. (877)438-2929, 950 W Mesquite Boulevard, Mesquite, NV 89027

DESERT SKIES RV RESORT

good sam park **Ratings: 10/10★/9.5** (RV Park) From Jct of I-15 & Sandhill Blvd (Exit 122): Go 200 ft S on Sandhill Blvd, then 1-1/2 mi E on Hillside Dr (Hwy 91) (R). **FAC:** paved rds. (321 spaces). Avail: 161 all weather, 13 pull-thrus, (32x65), back-ins (33x46), 161 full hkups (30/50 amps), seasonal sites, cable, WiFi @ sites, laundry, LP gas. **REC:** heated pool, hot tub. Pets OK. Partial handicap access. No tents, Age restrict may apply. Big rig sites, eco-friendly. 2021 rates: $35 to $49.
(928)347-6000 Lat: 36.81907, Lon: -114.04140
350 E Hwy 91, Mesquite, NV 89027
desertskiesresorts.com
See ad this page

OASIS RV PARK RESORT **Ratings: 5.5/8.5/6** (RV Park) Avail: 80 full hkups (30/50 amps). 2021 rates: $20 to $30. (800)896-4567, 897 West Mesquite Boulevard, Mesquite, NV 89027

SOLSTICE MOTORCOACH RESORT **Ratings: 8/8.5★/8** (RV Park) Avail: 18 full hkups (30/50 amps). 2021 rates: $45 to $56. (702)346-8522, 345 Mystic Drive, Mesquite, NV 89034

SUN RESORTS RV PARK
good sam park **Ratings: 9/9.5★/9** (RV Park) From I-15 and Mesquite (exit 122): Go 1/4 mi S on Sandhill Blvd, then 1/4 mi E on Hillside (R). **FAC:** paved rds. (71 spaces). Avail: 41 all weather, 24 pull-thrus, (33x87), back-ins (30x54), 41 full hkups (30/50 amps), seasonal sites, cable, WiFi @ sites, laundry. Pet restrict (Q). No tents. Big rig sites, eco-friendly. 2021 rates: $32 to $45.
(702)346-6666 Lat: 36.80971, Lon: -114.06168
400 Hillside Dr, Mesquite, NV 89027
sunresortsrv.com
See ad this page

VIRGIN VALLEY FOOD MART & RV/ TRUCK PARKING
(RV Spaces) From Jct I-15 & N Sandhill Blvd (Exit 122): Go N 1 block on N Sandhill Blvd (R). **FAC:** paved rds. Avail: 110 paved, WiFi @ sites, $, dump, groc, LP gas. Pets OK. No tents. 2021 rates: $3 to $18. ATM, no reservations.
(702)346-8881 Lat: 36.814854, Lon: -114.064223
200 Mesa Blvd, Mesquite, NV 89027
virginvalleyfoodmart.com
See ad this page

MINA — D2 *Mineral*

SUNRISE VALLEY RV PARK **Ratings: 4/6.5/6** (Campground) 24 Avail: 22 full hkups, 2 W, 2 E (30/50 amps). 2021 rates: $38. Mar 02 to Nov 01. (775)573-2214, US Hwy 95, Mina, NV 89422

MINDEN — C1 *Douglas*

CARSON VALLEY RV RESORT & CASINO
good sam park **Ratings: 10/10★/9** (RV Park) From Jct of NV 88 & US 395: Go 1/2 mi SE on US 395 (L). Elev 4750 ft. **FAC:** paved rds. Avail: 59 paved, 25 pull-thrus, (25x54), back-ins (25x35), 59 full hkups (30/50 amps), cable, WiFi @ sites, rentals, dump, laundry, groc, restaurant. **REC:** heated pool, hot tub. Pets OK. Partial handicap access. No tents. Big rig sites, 28 day max stay, eco-friendly. 2021 rates: $39 to $69. ATM.
(800)321-6983 Lat: 38.95660, Lon: -119.76958
1627 Hwy 395 N, Minden, NV 89423
carsonvalleyinn.com
See ad this page

SILVER CITY RV RESORT Ratings: 9/8.5★/8.5 (RV Park) Avail: 40 full hkups (30/50 amps). 2021 rates: $49.95 to $69.95. (800)997-6393, 3165 Hwy 395, Minden, NV 89423

Things to See and Do

CARSON VALLEY INN HOTEL & CASINO Casino with slots, videos, blackjack, craps, keno, race/sports bk, poker room, 3 dining fac., 2 lounges, free nightly live cabaret entertainment. Various lodging options. Indoor pool, 2 spas & fitness center. No resort or parking fees. Elev 4750 ft. Partial handicap access. RV accessible. Restrooms. Food. Hours: 24 hours. ATM.
(775)782-9711 Lat: 38.95660, Lon: -119.76958
1627 US Hwy 395 N, Minden, NV 89423
carsonvalleyinn.com
See ad this page

MOUNTAIN CITY — A4 *Elko*

WILD HORSE SRA (Public State Park) From town: Go 19 mi SE on Hwy-225. Max RV size 45'. 34 Avail. 2021 rates: $15. (775)385-5939

OVERTON — E5 *Clark*

LAKE MEAD NRA/ECHO BAY (Public National Park) From Jct of US-93 & Lakeshore Rd, N 11 mi on Lakeshore Rd to Northshore, NE 37 mi (R). Avail: 166 full hkups (30/50 amps). 2021 rates: $10. (702)394-4000

LAKE MEAD RV VILLAGE AT ECHO BAY
good sam park **Ratings: 8/8.5/7.5** (RV Park) Avail: 34 full hkups (30/50 amps). 2021 rates: $28 to $30. (702)394-4000, 600 Echo Bay Rd, Overton, NV 89040

VALLEY OF FIRE (Public State Park) From Jct of I-15 & SR-169, SW 18 mi on SR-169 (L). Entrance fee required. 72 Avail: 5 W, 5 E. 2021 rates: $20 to $30. (702)397-2088

PAHRUMP — E4 *Nye*

A SPOTLIGHT Introducing Pahrump's colorful attractions appearing at the front of this state section.

PAHRUMP See also Shoshone, CA.

LAKESIDE CASINO & RV PARK
good sam park **Ratings: 10/10★/10** (RV Resort) From Jct of Hwy 160 & Homestead Rd (S end of town): Go S 3-3/4 mi on Homestead Rd, then W 100 ft on Thousandaire Rd (R). Elev 2700 ft.

ESCAPE TO THE OASIS IN THE DESERT
Relax at Lakeside - enjoy our hot tub, swimming pool, sandy beach, cabanas, fire pits, pedal boats & fish in our 7-acre lake. A short walk to the casino for 24-hour action, cafe, buffet and bar. Come relax at Lakeside!

FAC: paved rds. (159 spaces). Avail: 129 paved, patios, 15 pull-thrus, (30x70), back-ins (30x58), 129 full hkups (30/50 amps), seasonal sites, WiFi @ sites, laundry, groc, LP gas, firewood, restaurant. **REC:** pool, hot tub, Lakeside Lake: fishing, kayaking/canoeing, playground. Pet restrict (B/Q). Partial handicap access. No tents. Big rig sites, eco-friendly. 2021 rates: $34.99 to $69.99, Military discount. ATM.
(888)558-5253 Lat: 36.131999, Lon: -115.958804
5870 S Homestead Road, Pahrump, NV 89048
lakesidecasinopahrump.com
See ad this page, 581, 582

Check out 10/10/10 Good Sam Parks on the Good Sam Park page.*

EXTEND YOUR STAY WITH
LAKESIDE CASINO & RV PARK
PAHRUMP, NEVADA
good sam park 2022 Top Rated
ALL THE COMFORTS OF HOME:
CAFE • BINGO ROOM • 24HR CASINO & BAR
THREE COMFORT STATIONS: INCLUDING LAUNDRY AND A 24HR CONVENIENCE STORE
LAKESIDE CASINO & RV PARK
BOOK TODAY 1.888.558.5253
See listing Pahrump, NV

See listing Pahrump, NV
Nevada Treasure RV RESORT
A Jewel in the Desert
NIGHTLY, WEEKLY & LOW MONTHLY RATES
RALLY DISCOUNTS
800.429.6665
775.751.1174
Visit Our Sister Park HEBER RV RESORT
good sam park 2022 Top Rated 10/10★/10
301 West Leslie St • Pahrump, NV 89060
www.nevadatreasurervresort.com

VIRGIN VALLEY FOOD MART & RV PARKING
Exit 122
76
FREE WiFi
PARKING – $1/HOUR
www.virginvalleyfoodmart.com
See listing Mesquite, NV

EZ ON/OFF EXIT 122
SUN RESORTS
R.V. Park–Mesquite, Nevada
702-346-6666
• Large Pull-Thrus • Laundry
• Showers • Putting Green • BBQ
• Next to Smith's Food King
See listing Mesquite, NV
good sam park
702-346-6666 • 400 Hillside Dr.
sunresortsrv.com
See our Sister Parks, Beaver Dam Lodge RV Resort & Our brand new resort Scenic Orchard RV Park

CARSON VALLEY RV RESORT
Only 20 Minutes from Lake Tahoe
★ Full Hookups
★ 30/50 Amp Sites
★ Convenience Store, Gas & Diesel
★ Free Wi-Fi
★ New Showers & Laundry
★ 24-Hour Casino, 590* Slots, Live Poker
★ Table Games, Sports Book & Bar
★ Nightly Live Entertainment
★ Indoor Pool & Spas
★ CV Steak & Katie's Nightly Dinner Specials
*AS OF 2021
good sam park 2022 Top Rated 10/10★/9
Reno/Sparks
Dayton
28
Carson City
Lake Tahoe
395
50
Minden/Gardnerville
See listing Minden, NV
CARSON VALLEY INN ★CASINO★
1627 Hwy 395 N
Minden, Nevada
800-321-6983 • cvinn.com

NV

PAHRUMP (CONT)

NEVADA TREASURE RV RESORT

good sam park **Ratings: 10/10★/10** (RV Resort) From Jct of SR-372 & SR-160: Go N 7-1/2 mi on SR-160, then go 500 ft on Leslie St (L). Elev 2699 ft.**FAC:** paved rds. (202 spaces). Avail: 167 paved, patios, back-ins (36x50), 167 full hkups (30/50 amps), seasonal sites, WiFi @ sites, laundry, LP gas, restaurant, controlled access. **REC:** heated pool, hot tub, rec open to public. Pet restrict (B/Q). Partial handicap access. No tents. Big rig sites, eco-friendly. 2021 rates: $44 to $66. ATM.
(800)429-6665 Lat: 36.310947, Lon: -116.017892
301 West Leslie St, Pahrump, NV 89060
nevadatreasurervresort.com
See ad previous page, 581

PREFERRED RV RESORT

good sam park **Ratings: 9/10★/9.5** (Membership Park) From Jct of SR-160 & Crawford Way: Go NE 1/4 mi on Crawford Way (R). Elev 2700 ft.**FAC:** gravel rds. (270 spaces). Avail: 50 gravel, patios, 25 pull-thrus, (20x60), back-ins (35x45), 50 full hkups (30/50 amps), seasonal sites, WiFi @ sites, rentals, dump, laundry, LP gas, controlled access. **REC:** heated pool, hot tub, shuffleboard, playground. Pets OK. Partial handicap access. No tents, eco-friendly. 2021 rates: $40.
(775)727-4414 Lat: 36.21096, Lon: -115.98184
1801 E Crawford Way, Pahrump, NV 89048
preferredrv.com
See ad page 581

SADDLE WEST RV PARK **Ratings: 8.5/8.5/7** (RV Park) Avail: 20 full hkups (30/50 amps). 2021 rates: $25. (800)433-3987, 1220 S Hwy 160, Pahrump, NV 89048

WINE RIDGE RV RESORT & COTTAGES

good sam park **Ratings: 10/10★/10** (RV Park) From Jct of SR-160 & Winery Rd: Go 3/4 mi on Winery Rd (L). Elev 2850 ft.

MODERN AMENITIES, MOUNTAIN VIEWS
Top Resort: 10/10/10. HWY 160 & Winery Rd. 42 Cottages; new 2-bed Casitas; large, 42 one bed cottages, 129 perfect FHU 50-amp level RV sites. Private bath suites, 2 pools w/spa, free LD phone, free waffle breakfast M-F.

FAC: paved rds. (129 spaces). Avail: 84 all weather, patios, 19 pull-thrus, (33x60), back-ins (33x60), 84 full hkups (30/50 amps), seasonal sites, WiFi @ sites, rentals, laundry, restaurant, controlled access. **REC:** heated pool, hot tub. Pets OK. No tents. Big rig sites, eco-friendly. 2021 rates: $34 to $50, Military discount.
(775)751-7805 Lat: 36.19531, Lon: -115.94223
3800 Winery Road, Pahrump, NV 89048
wineridgervresort.com
See ad pages 575, 580, 581

Things to See and Do

LAKESIDE CASINO Casino with games, entertainment, 24-hr restaurant & buffet. Elev 2700 ft. Partial handicap access. Restrooms. Food. Hours: 24 Hrs. ATM.
(775)751-7770 Lat: 36.13294, Lon: -115.95801
5870 S Homestead Rd, Pahrump, NV 89048
www.lakesidecasinopahrump.com
See ad previous page, 582

PAHRUMP NEVADA Tourist Information for the town of Pahrump, located between Las Vegas and Death Valley. Enjoy the peaceful surroundings of picturesque mountain ranges, wide open spaces and the lush rolling hills of one of Southern Nevada's treasures. Elev 2600 ft. Restrooms. Hours: 9am to 5pm. No CC.
(775)751-6853 Lat: 36.21058, Lon: -115.99591
400 N Hwy 160, Pahrump, NV 89060
visitpahrump.com
See ad page 581

PANACA — D5 *Lincoln*

CATHEDRAL GORGE (Public State Park) From Jct of US-93 & SR-319, N 1 mi on US-93 to park access rd (W side of US-93), W 1.5 mi (L). Entrance fee required. Avail: 22 E. 2021 rates: $15. (775)728-4460

PIOCHE — D5 *Lincoln*

EAGLE VALLEY RESORT **Ratings: 5/7/6.5** (Campground) Avail: 43 full hkups (30/50 amps). 2021 rates: $29.50 to $35. (775)962-5293, 12555 SR 322, Pioche, NV 89043

ECHO CANYON (Public State Park) From Jct of US-93 & SR-322, E 4 mi on SR-322 to SH-86, S 8 mi (L). 33 Avail. 2021 rates: $15. (775)962-5103

SPRING VALLEY (Public State Park) From Jct of Hwy 93 & SR-322, E 18 mi on SR-322 (E). 37 Avail. 2021 rates: $15. (775)962-5102

RENO — C1 *Washoe*

A SPOTLIGHT Introducing Reno/Sparks' colorful attractions appearing at the front of this state section.

RENO/SPARKS See also Carson City, Dayton & Verdi, NV; Truckee, CA.

BORDERTOWN CASINO & RV RESORT

good sam park **Ratings: 9/9★/9.5** (RV Park) From Jct of US-395 & Exit 83: Go 1/4 mi NW on Frontage Rd (L). Elev 5000 ft.**FAC:** paved rds. Avail: 50 paved, patios, 48 pull-thrus, (24x70), back-ins (23x50), 50 full hkups (30/50 amps), cable, WiFi @ sites, dump, laundry, groc, LP gas, restaurant. **REC:** hunting nearby. Pets OK. Partial handicap access. No tents. Big rig sites, 28 day max stay, eco-friendly. 2021 rates: $50, Military discount. ATM.
(775)677-0169 Lat: 39.66960, Lon: -119.99990
19575 US Highway 395 N, Reno, NV 89508
Bordertowncasinorv.com
See ad page 584

GRAND SIERRA RESORT AND CASINO RV PARK

good sam park **Ratings: 9/8.5/7** (RV Park) From Jct of I-80 & I-580 (US 395 exit 15): Go 1/2 mi S US 395, then 1/2 mi E on Glendale Ave, then 1/4 mi S on 2nd St (R). Elev 5000 ft.

FAC: paved rds. 165 Avail: 86 paved, 79 gravel, 94 pull-thrus, (30x65), back-ins (28x40), accepts full hkup units only, 165 full hkups (30/50 amps), WiFi @ sites, laundry, restaurant. **REC:** heated pool, hot tub, Truckee River: fishing, kayaking/canoeing, boating nearby, hunting nearby, rec open to public. Pets OK. Partial handicap access. No tents. Big rig sites, 14 day max stay, eco-friendly. 2021 rates: $35 to $75, Military discount. ATM.
(775)789-2147 Lat: 39.523234, Lon: -119.776834
2500 E 2nd St, Reno, NV 89595
www.grandsierraresort.com
See ad opposite page

KEYSTONE RV PARK
Ratings: 6.5/7/7 (RV Park) From Jct of I-80 & Keystone Ave (Exit 12): Go 1/4 mi S on Keystone Ave, then 500 ft W on to 4th St (R). Elev 4500 ft.**FAC:** paved rds. (102 spaces). Avail: 70 paved, back-ins (23x40), 70 full hkups (30/50 amps), seasonal sites, cable, WiFi @ sites, rentals, dump, laundry. Pet restrict (Q). Partial handicap access. No tents, eco-friendly. 2021 rates: $48.59 to $51.98.
(775)324-5000 Lat: 39.5265724, Lon: -119.8309026
1455 W 4th St, Reno, NV 89503
www.keystonervpark.com
See ad page 584

RIVER WEST RESORT **Ratings: 6.5/8/7** (RV Park) Avail: 27 full hkups (30/50 amps). 2021 rates: $53.50 to $63.50. (775)322-2281, 1300 West 2nd St, Reno, NV 89503

SHAMROCK RV PARK
Ratings: 10/10★/9.5 (RV Park) Avail: 60 full hkups (30/50 amps). 2021 rates: $50 to $65. (775)329-5222, 260 E Parr Blvd, Reno, NV 89512

SILVER SAGE RV PARK
Ratings: 7.5/8/7 (RV Park) From Jct of US-395, I-80 (Exit 64) Moana Lane: Go W on Moana Lane 1/2 mi to S Virginia St, then N 1/4 mi on S Virginia St (R). Elev 4458 ft.

FAC: paved rds. (43 spaces). Avail: 30 paved, back-ins (23x50), 30 full hkups (30/50 amps), seasonal sites, cable, WiFi @ sites, laundry, controlled access. Pets OK. Partial handicap access. No tents, eco-friendly. 2021 rates: $41.75 to $46.16, Military discount.
(888)823-2002 Lat: 39.496786, Lon: -119.79900
2760 S Virginia St, Reno, NV 89502
silversagervparkreno.com
See ad opposite page, 583

Travel Services

CAMPING WORLD OF RENO As the nation's largest retailer of RV supplies, accessories, services and new and used RVs, Camping World is committed to making your total RV experience better. **SERVICES:** RV appliance, MH mechanical, sells outdoor gear, restrooms. RV Sales. RV supplies, RV accessible. Hours: 9am - 6pm.
(844)905-1048 Lat: 39.451067, Lon: -119.775523
9125 S Virginia St, Reno, NV 89511
www.campingworld.com

RV Tech Tips - Foam Sweet Foam: Here's a handy tip to keep your cups and best china from rattling about while going down the road in your motorhome. Take a 2-inch thick piece of plastic foam sheet, cut to size to fit your cupboard shelf. and place cups upside down on it. Space them just far enough apart that they don't touch. Using a ballpoint pen or marker, trace around the cup (including the handles) to make a template. Then use a sharp knife to cut entirely through the template markings you have made. Place the plastic foam sheet on your shelf and insert cups. No more rattles. It's also very convenient to lift them in and out for use.

Things to See and Do

BORDERTOWN CASINO Live sports book and gaming. Restaurant with food and drink specials. Open 24 hrs. Elev 5000 ft. Partial handicap access. RV accessible. Restrooms. Food. Hours: 24 hrs. ATM.
(800)443-4383 Lat: 39.66960, Lon: -119.99990
19575 US Highway 395 N, Reno, NV 89508
bordertowncasinorv.com
See ad page 584

GRAND SIERRA RESORT AND CASINO Casino, Hotel & Spa. Restaurants with Fine & Casual Dining, Bars & Lounges.Convention Space & Entertainment. Elev 5000 ft. Partial handicap access. RV accessible. Restrooms. Food. Hours: 24 hrs. ATM.
(775)789-2147 Lat: 39.5200, Lon: -119.77600
2500 E 2nd St, Reno, NV 89595
www.grandsierraresort.com
See ad opposite page

SEARCHLIGHT — F5 *Clark*

LAKE MOHAVE/COTTONWOOD COVE CAMPGROUND (Public National Park) From Jct of SR-95 & CR-164, E 14 mi on CR-164/Cottonwood Rd (E). Avail: 145 full hkups (30 amps). 2021 rates: $10. (702)297-1464

SILVER SPRINGS — C1 *Lyon*

FORT CHURCHILL (Public State Park) From town, S 8 mi on Hwy 95A to Fort Churchill Rd, W 1 mi (L). 20 Avail: Pit toilets. 2021 rates: $15. (775)577-2345

LAHONTAN SRA (Public State Park) From town, W 18 mi on US-50 (L). Entrance fee required. 29 Avail. 2021 rates: $15. (775)577-2226

SMITH VALLEY — C1 *Lyon*

WALKER RIVER RESORT RV PARK **Ratings: 8/8.5★/8.5** (Campground) 128 Avail: 72 full hkups, 56 W, 56 E (30/50 amps). 2021 rates: $64 to $70. Apr 01 to Oct 31. (775)465-2573, 700 Hudson Way, Smith Valley, NV 89430

SPARKS — C1 *Washoe*

A SPOTLIGHT Introducing Reno/Sparks' colorful attractions appearing at the front of this state section.

SPARKS MARINA RV PARK
Ratings: 10/10★/10 (RV Park) From jct I-80 & Exit 20(Sparks Blvd): Go 1 mi N on Sparks Blvd to Prater Way, then 1/2 mi W on Prater Way to Marina Gateway, then 1/2 mi S on Marina Gateway to Lincoln Way, then 400 feet W on Lincoln Way (R). Elev 4500 ft.-**FAC:** paved rds. Avail: 204 paved, 121 pull-thrus, (30x65), back-ins (30x39), accepts full hkup units only, 204 full hkups (30/50 amps), cable, WiFi @ sites, laundry, groc, LP gas. **REC:** heated pool, hot tub, boating nearby, hunting nearby. Pet restrict (B/Q) $. Partial handicap access. No tents. Big rig sites, 27 day max stay, eco-friendly. 2021 rates: $39 to $94, Military discount.
(775)851-8888 Lat: 39.5375145, Lon: -119.7243844
1200 E Lincoln Way, Sparks, NV 89434
www.sparksmarinarvpark.com
See ad this page

VICTORIAN RV PARK
Ratings: 10/10★/9.5 (RV Park) Avail: 43 full hkups (30/50 amps). 2021 rates: $61.29 to $81.82. (800)955-6405, 205 Nichols Blvd, Sparks, NV 89431

VERDI — C1 *Washoe*

GOLD RANCH CASINO & RV RESORT **Ratings: 10/10★/9.5** (RV Park) Avail: 105 full hkups (30/50 amps). 2021 rates: $43 to $60. (775)345-8880, 320 Gold Ranch Road, Verdi, NV 89439

WELLS — A4 *Elko*

ANGEL LAKE RV PARK **Ratings: 6/9.5★/6.5** (Campground) Avail: 40 full hkups (30/50 amps). 2021 rates: $38 to $40. (775)752-2745, 124 S Humboldt Ave, Wells, NV 89835

MOUNTAIN SHADOWS RV PARK **Ratings: 6/9★/8** (Campground) Avail: 31 full hkups (30/50 amps). 2021 rates: $35.91. (775)752-3525, 807 Humboldt Ave, Wells, NV 89835

WEST WENDOVER — B5 *Elko*

WENDOVER KOA JOURNEY **Ratings: 6.5/8/7** (Campground) 57 Avail: 22 full hkups, 34 W, 34 E (30 amps). 2021 rates: $52.20. (775)664-3221, 651 North Camper Dr, West Wendover, NV 89883

WINNEMUCCA — B2 *Humboldt*

NEW FRONTIER RV PARK
Ratings: 9/9.5★/9.5 (RV Park) Avail: 56 full hkups (30/50 amps). 2021 rates: $39 to $44. (775)621-5275, 4360 Rim Rock Rd, Winnemucca, NV 89445

YERINGTON — C1 *Lyon*

WEED HEIGHTS RV PARK **Ratings: 5.5/9★/5.5** (Campground) 62 Avail: 52 full hkups, 10 W, 10 E (30 amps). 2021 rates: $30. (775)463-4634, 25 Austin Dr, Yerington, NV 89447

ZEPHYR COVE — C1 *Douglas*

ZEPHYR COVE RESORT RV PARK & CAMPGROUND **Ratings: 8/8/7.5** (Campground) Avail: 93 full hkups (30/50 amps). 2021 rates: $62 to $105. (775)589-4980, 760 Hwy 50, Zephyr Cove, NV 89448

Thank you for using our 2022 Guide. Now you have all the latest information about RV parks, campgrounds and RV resorts across North America!

Getty Images/iStockphoto

New Hampshire

DID YOU KNOW?

The first of its kind in the world, the Mount Washington Cog Railway began ferrying passengers to the mountain's summit in 1869.

NH

New Hampshire combines towering, picturesque mountains, crystal lakes and pristine coastal beaches with small towns and a welcoming atmosphere. The nation's fifth-smallest state excels in scenic beauty.

Small Shore with More

New Hampshire has less than 20 miles of shoreline facing the Atlantic, but its biggest coastal town, Portsmouth, enjoys major historical significance. In the 1600s, it was a key landing point for English settlers. Portsmouth is a classic New England seaport, with views of ships sailing in the harbor. Step into the town's past with a visit to the Strawbery Banke Museum, an outdoor living history museum depicting life on the waterfront in the 1600s and beyond. The downtown area is a cozy place to stroll with restaurants, galleries and shops.

Wondrous White Mountains

Take a drive along the Kancamagus Highway to see the stunning scenery of New Hampshire's White Mountains. Stop to explore the epic Sabbaday Falls, which cascades over a 45-foot drop, and the Rocky Gorge Scenic Area. Just off the byway, Franconia Notch State Park encompasses unbelievable beauty. The catwalks in the Flume Gorge take visitors through a verdant wonderland, past waterfalls and moss-covered cliffs. For dizzying views of the undulating hills, take a trip on the aerial tramway to the top of Cannon Mountain.

Crystal Waters

Lake Winnipesaukee, the state's largest lake, may also be its most scenic body of water. Boating, fishing and watersports are popular pursuits. Paddlers and anglers can take their pick from Winnipesaukee and the other ample ponds and lakes that dot the state. With views of moose and virgin forests, the East Inlet is an especially picturesque spot.

Apple Cider Donuts

Nothing says fall like apple cider donuts. Cider makers use freshly pressed juice to give these donuts a slightly tangy flavor. The acidity from the cider also produces softer, chewier donuts. Sample these sweet delights along the apple cider donut trail, a 300-mile route starting at Mackintosh Fruit Farm in Londonberry.

VISITOR CENTER

TIME ZONE
Eastern Standard

ROAD & HIGHWAY INFORMATION
603-271-6862
nh.gov/dot/traveler

FISHING & HUNTING INFORMATION
603-271-3421
www.wildlife.state.nh.us/licensing

BOATING INFORMATION
603-293-2037
wildlife.state.nh.us/boating

NATIONAL PARKS
nps.gov/nh

STATE PARKS
nhstateparks.org

TOURISM INFORMATION
New Hampshire Division of Travel and Tourism
603-271-2665
visitnh.gov

TOP TOURISM ATTRACTIONS
1) Mount Washington Auto Road
2) Castle in the Clouds
3) Hampton Beach

MAJOR CITIES
Manchester, Nashua, Concord (capital), Derry, Dover

good sam park

Featured Good Sam Parks

NEW HAMPSHIRE

When you stay with Good Sam, you can expect the highest degree of cleanliness and friendliness, and better yet, you get **10% off** overnight campground fees.

If you're not already a Good Sam member you can purchase your membership at one of these locations:

BROOKLINE
Field & Stream RV Park

CONTOOCOOK
Sandy Beach RV Resort

JEFFERSON
Jefferson Campground

LANCASTER
Riverside Camping & RV Resort

LITTLETON
Crazy Horse Family Campground

MEREDITH
Twin Tamarack Family Camping & RV Resort

NEW BOSTON
Friendly Beaver Campground

NEWPORT
Crow's Nest Campground

RAYMOND
Pine Acres Resort

SOUTH HAMPTON
Tuxbury Pond RV Resort

TAMWORTH
Tamworth Camping Area

Getty Images/iStockphoto

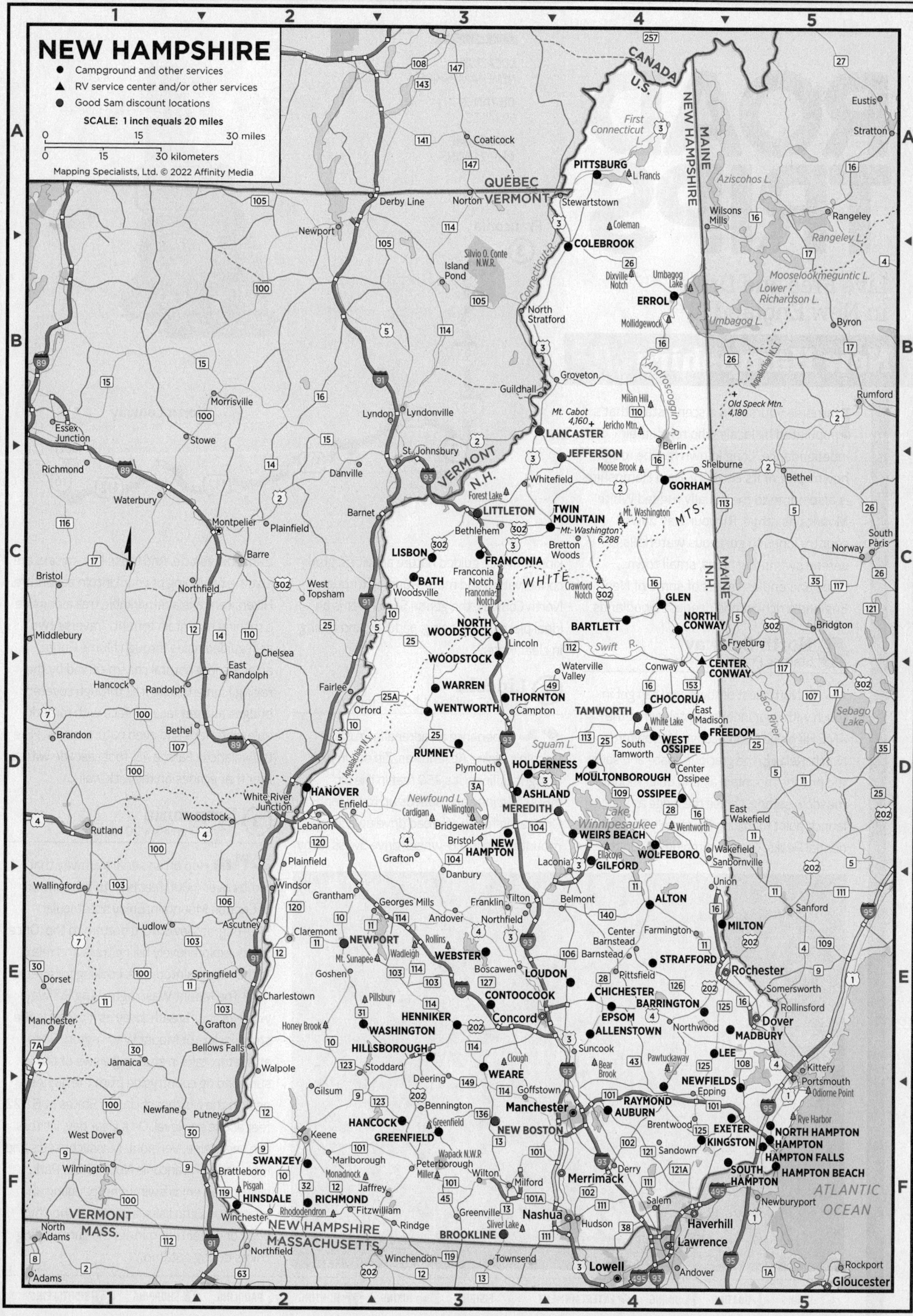
NEW HAMPSHIRE
Campground and other services
RV service center and/or other services
Good Sam discount locations
SCALE: 1 inch equals 20 miles
0 15 30 miles
0 15 30 kilometers
Mapping Specialists, Ltd. © 2022 Affinity Media
NH
CANADA
U.S.
QUÉBEC
VERMONT
N.H.
NEW HAMPSHIRE
MAINE
MASS.
MASSACHUSETTS
WHITE MTS.
ATLANTIC OCEAN
PITTSBURG
COLEBROOK
ERROL
LANCASTER
JEFFERSON
GORHAM
LITTLETON
TWIN MOUNTAIN
LISBON
FRANCONIA
BATH
GLEN
NORTH CONWAY
BARTLETT
NORTH WOODSTOCK
WOODSTOCK
CENTER CONWAY
WARREN
THORNTON
WENTWORTH
CHOCORUA
TAMWORTH
WEST OSSIPEE
FREEDOM
RUMNEY
HOLDERNESS
MOULTONBOROUGH
HANOVER
ASHLAND
OSSIPEE
MEREDITH
WEIRS BEACH
NEW HAMPTON
WOLFEBORO
GILFORD
ALTON
MILTON
NEWPORT
WEBSTER
STRAFFORD
Rochester
LOUDON
CHICHESTER
CONTOOCOOK
BARRINGTON
HENNIKER
Concord
EPSOM
Dover
WASHINGTON
ALLENSTOWN
MADBURY
HILLSBOROUGH
LEE
WEARE
NEWFIELDS
Manchester
RAYMOND
AUBURN
HANCOCK
NEW BOSTON
EXETER
NORTH HAMPTON
GREENFIELD
KINGSTON
HAMPTON
SWANZEY
HAMPTON FALLS
SOUTH HAMPTON
HAMPTON BEACH
Merrimack
HINSDALE
RICHMOND
Nashua
Haverhill
BROOKLINE
Lawrence
Lowell
Gloucester
Portsmouth
Keene
Laconia
Montpelier
Derby Line
Newport
St. Johnsbury
Coaticook
Stewartstown
Berlin
Conway
Plymouth
Lebanon
Claremont
Peterborough
Brattleboro
Rutland
Kittery
Rangeley
Mt. Washington 6,288
Lake Winnipesaukee
Squam L.
Newfound L.
First Connecticut L.
Umbagog L.
Connecticut R.
Androscoggin R.

ROAD TRIPS

Live Free and Drive in New England

New Hampshire

LOCATION
NEW HAMPSHIRE

DISTANCE
59 MILES

DRIVE TIME
1 HR 21 MINS

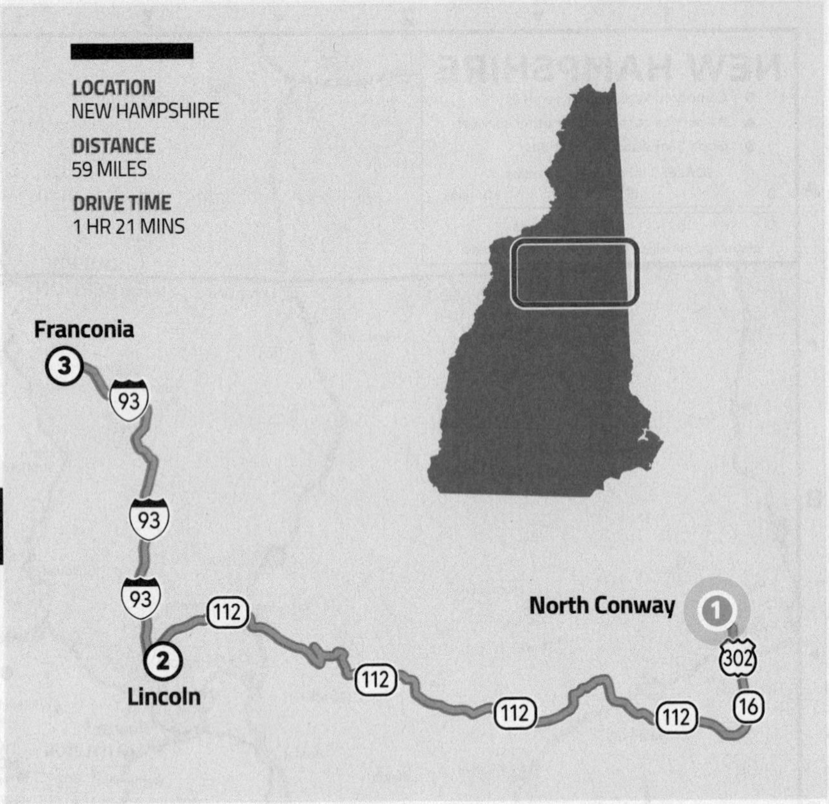

Immerse yourself in a scenic state that's populated by locals who relish their independence. Long known for the rough-hewn spirit of its citizenry, New Hampshire is also home to the equally rugged White Mountains range. RV your way down country lanes to gorgeous waterfalls, serene swimming holes, small towns, cities and endless miles of some of New England's richest and deepest woodlands.

1 North Conway
Starting Point

Northwest of town, you can get in touch with your inner mountaineer at the AMC Highland Center Lodge at Crawford Notch. Relax in the gracious space and savor the pristine mountain air and quiet mountain meadow setting. Or use the lodge as your launch point for hiking the state's Presidential Peaks. Go rock climbing, set up the kids with free guided nature activities, study conservation and more. Running through North Conway, the gentle Saco River is an ideal place for canoeing, paddling and tubing in clear water.

2 Lincoln
Drive 42 miles ▪ 1 hour, 1 minute

Experience an adrenaline rush at Lincoln's Alpine Adventures. Zip down one of eight ziplines; it's 250 feet in the air, 1,600 feet long and speeds up to 60 mph. Or strap in for an off-road drive up a steep mountaintop in a 6-wheel-drive Swiss Army transport vehicle. And these hair-raisers are just the beginning of your Lincoln adventure. Hikers can take a remarkable trek alongside a rushing mountain torrent. Traverse two self-guided miles through Flume Gorge, an awesome natural chasm carved by the raging Flume Brook. Trek through covered bridges and get face-to-face with remarkable waterfalls and even natural caves. Hike to Avalanche Falls, a 45-foot cascade with a roar that echoes on the rock walls.

3 Franconia
Drive 17 miles ▪ 20 minutes

Hop on an aerial tramway that climbs over 4,000 feet high to the summit of Cannon Mountain. Enjoy spectacular 360-degree views from bottom to top. Once there, explore lovely hiking trails and relax at the mountaintop café. Looking for a retro ride? The Mount Washington Cog Railway will take your breath away as it ascends the steep incline of Mount Washington. Once at the top, take in stunning views of the surrounding countryside from the highest peak in the Northeast United States at 6,822 feet above sea level. On a clear day, visitors can see Maine, Vermont, Massachusetts and New York. In Franconia Notch State Park, visitors can enjoy swimming, paddling and boating on Echo Lake, a postcard-worthy body of water that mirrors the surrounding colors during autumn.

Getty Images/iStockphoto

BIKING BOATING DINING ENTERTAINMENT FISHING HIKING HUNTING PADDLING SHOPPING SIGHTSEEING

New Hampshire SPOTLIGHTS

The Granite State Adds a Rugged Edge to New England

In New Hampshire, charming New England landscapes give way to rugged mountains and sprawling lakes. Experience it all with a trip to the Granite State and find out why locals embrace the motto, "Live Free or Die."

THE WALLS OF FLUME GORGE RISE AS HIGH AS 90 FEET IN SOME PLACES.

Flume Gorge extends 800 feet through Franconia Notch State Park.

Getty Images/iStockphoto

Franconia Notch

Franconia beckons visitors to explore its gorgeous landscapes. This charming town rests on the edge of Franconia Notch State Park, a veritable smorgasbord of rugged outdoor adventure.

Fine State Park

Discover a place whose history rivals its beauty. Franconia Notch State Park lies in the heart of White Mountain National Forest and is essentially a mountain pass crossed by Interstate 93, which winds between the Kinsman and Franconia mountain ranges. The Notch is immortalized in literary history, thanks to Nathaniel Hawthorne and Daniel Webster, who described the Great Stone Face belonging to the Old Man of the Mountain. Learn more about this legend at the Old Man of the Mountain Historic Site, where the famed geologic "profile" once gazed out over the landscape.

Old Man Take a Look

The rock face itself collapsed several years ago, but visitors can enjoy a recreated version of the Old Man at Profile Plaza and tour the museum and gift shop. If you're up for a walk that leads to stunning views, head to the Flume Gorge. Explore the granite walls that envelope cascading water and are home to lush ferns, mosses and flowers. A wooden walkway guides visitors through the gorge.

Final Furnace

Discover New Hampshire's last standing blast furnace at the Besaw Iron Furnace Interpretive Center. The octagonal stone stack is the last portion of a 200-year-old iron smelter and was built of local granite. See the park from great heights on an aerial tramway ride at Cannon Mountain. As the site of the nation's first aerial passenger tramway, the Cannon Mountain feature is an eight-minute trip through the sky to the 4,200-foot-high summit. From the tram station, take a walking trail to an observation tower and views of New Hampshire's neighbors — New York, Vermont, Maine and Canada.

Franconia Snowfall

You prefer the white stuff? Winter in Franconia means skiing, and the area boasts 55 trails and slopes for skiers of all skill levels. Between runs, pop over to the New England Ski Museum, which features exhibits that trace the history of skiing over thousands of years. Included are Olympian Bode Miller's medals. Wind down from a busy day or spend a leisurely afternoon at Echo Lake Beach.

Hampton Beach

New Hampshire makes the most of its 17 miles of Atlantic Ocean beach front. Mild weather and calming ocean breezes characterize Hampton Beach, a relaxing getaway on the southern edge of the state,

LOCAL FAVORITE

Sweet Onion Pie

The Granite State is known for the slogan, "Live Free or Die." Visitors might be saying, "Live Free with Pie" after sampling a slice of this regional onion delight. *Recipe by Carole Sawyer.*

INGREDIENTS

- ☐ 1 cup finely crushed round butter crackers
- ☐ ½ stick melted butter
- ☐ 1 cup sweet onions (such as Vidalia), thinly sliced
- ☐ 2 Tbsp butter
- ☐ ¾ cup milk
- ☐ 2 eggs
- ☐ ¾ tsp salt
- ☐ A dash of black pepper
- ☐ ¼ cup sharp cheddar cheese, shredded

DIRECTIONS

Mix crackers and melted butter. Press into glass pie plate that has been lightly sprayed with non-stick spray. Sauté onions in 2 tablespoons butter until the onions are clear. Spoon into the crust. Beat eggs and milk and pour over onions. Cover with cheese. Bake at 350 degrees for 30 minutes until a knife inserted in the center comes out clean.

View of brilliant autumn foliage in White Mountain National Forest from Kancamagus Highway scenic overlook.

less than an hour north of Boston. The seaside hamlet once bore the name Atlantic City of New England.

Take a Dip

For a pristine mashup of sand and sea that's perfect for swimming, sunbathing, fishing and camping, Hampton Beach State Park is the place. Families are the focus of many attractions in Hampton Beach; the Hampton Beach Playground has entertained little ones since the 1920s, and it is also home to the annual Children's Festival, where kids and kids at heart enjoy magic shows and a giant costume parade.

Harvest From the Sea

Don't forget some amazing food. Hampton Beach loves a good party, and the Hampton Beach Seafood Festival draws crowds to taste the finest fare that area restaurants have to offer. Other summer attractions here include free concerts at Seashell Stage, the Beach Master Sand Sculpting Competition, and several talent shows. Fireworks are a weekly occurrence in the summer, too.

White Mountains

Get a glimpse of New England's rugged side in the White Mountains. Crammed with snow-capped peaks, verdant valleys and over a thousand miles of hiking trails, this spectacular slice of New Hampshire was made for every outdoor explorer. Traversing the famed Appalachian Trail, riding the world's first cog railway, skiing down powder mountains and conquering the highest point in the northeast are just some of the bucket list activities you can tick off here.

Taken for Granite

Sprawling across the region is the White Mountains National Forest, encompassing 800,000 acres of lush greenery, sparkling streams and rugged ranges. In the heart of it all is the charming town of Lincoln. Located 65 miles north of Concord on Interstate 93, Lincoln is a popular gateway to this national forest and ideal jumping-off point for your outdoor excursions.

Heart of the Mountains

Lincoln sits in the center of it all. Most people make Lincoln their base camp for exploring the White Mountains, but this charismatic town is just as worthy of your time as the dramatic landscapes that surround it. A great local hang-out is Gordi's Fish & Steak House. Owned and operated by two former Olympic athletes, this restaurant welcomes skiers.

Flying High

Get above it all. Take a ride on the Cannon Mountain Aerial Tramway to see soaring peaks from a birds-eye view. If you drive 30 minutes east, you'll wind up at the Mount Washington Cog Railway, the world's first mountain-climbing cog railway. Hop on to reach the summit of Mount Washington, the highest peak in the northeast U.S. At the top, enjoy views that stretch to Canada and the Atlantic Ocean.

A Profusion of Colors

During fall, the White Mountains' vast forests undergo an amazing change. Take a scenic drive to see a hypnotizing array of red, orange and yellow leaves waving in the breeze along country roads and mountain highways. Keep your eyes open for covered bridges, too.

FOR MORE INFORMATION

Visit New Hampshire, 603-271-2665, www.visitnh.gov

Franconia Notch, 603-823-5661, www.franconianotch.org

Hampton Beach, 603-926-4541, www.hamptonbeach.com

White Mountains New Hampshire, 800-346-3687, www.visitwhitemountains.com

New Hampshire

ALLENSTOWN — E4 *Merrimack*

BEAR BROOK (Public State Park) From jct US 3 & Hwy 28: Go 3 mi NE on Hwy 28, then follow signs. 101 Avail. 2021 rates: $25. May 06 to Oct 29. (603)485-9869

ALTON — E4 *Belknap*

TURTLE KRAAL RV PARK **Ratings: 8.5/9.5★/8.5** (RV Park) Avail: 40 full hkups (30/50 amps). 2021 rates: $60. May 01 to Nov 01. (603)855-2377, 14 Fox Trot Loop, Alton, NH 03809

ASHLAND — D3 *Belknap*

AMES BROOK CAMPGROUND **Ratings: 10/10★/9.5** (Campground) 47 Avail: 44 full hkups, 3 W, 3 E (30/50 amps). 2021 rates: $52 to $55. May 12 to Oct 14. (603)968-7998, 104 Winona Rd, Ashland, NH 03217

AUBURN — F4 *Rockingham*

CALEF LAKE CAMPGROUND **Ratings: 6/8.5★/9** (Campground) Avail: 39 full hkups (30 amps). 2021 rates: $46 to $55. May 06 to Oct 10. (603)483-8282, 593 Chester Rd (Hwy 121), Auburn, NH 03032

BARRINGTON — E4 *Strafford*

AYERS LAKE FARM CAMPGROUND & COTTAGES (Campground) (Rebuilding) Avail: 10 full hkups (30/50 amps). 2021 rates: $55 to $65. May 20 to Oct 12. (603)335-1110, 497 Washington St (US 202), Barrington, NH 03825

BARRINGTON SHORES CAMPGROUND **Ratings: 8/7/8** (Campground) 16 Avail: 2 full hkups, 14 W, 14 E (30 amps). 2021 rates: $55 to $65. May 08 to Sep 27. (603)664-9333, 7 Barrington Shores Drive, Barrington, NH 03825

BARTLETT — C4 *Carroll*

CRAWFORD NOTCH/DRY RIVER CAMPGROUND (Public State Park) From town: Go 12 mi NW on US 302. 20 Avail. 2021 rates: $25. Apr 27 to Dec 03. (603)374-2272

BATH — C3 *Grafton*

TWIN RIVER CAMPGROUND & COTTAGES **Ratings: 9/9★/9.5** (RV Park) Avail: 20 full hkups (30/50 amps). 2021 rates: $39 to $47. May 15 to Oct 15. (603)747-3640, 4 Twin River Lane, Bath, NH 03740

BROOKLINE — F3 *Hillsborough*

FIELD & STREAM RV PARK
good sam park
Ratings: 8.5/9.5★/10 (Campground) Avail: 26 full hkups (30/50 amps). 2021 rates: $55. (603)673-4677, 7 Dupaw-Gould Rd, Brookline, NH 03033

CENTER CONWAY — D4 *Carroll*

Travel Services

CAMPING WORLD OF CONWAY As the nation's largest retailer of RV supplies, accessories, services and new and used RVs, Camping World is committed to making your total RV experience better. **SERVICES:** tire, RV appliance, MH mechanical, staffed RV wash, restrooms. RV Sales. RV supplies, LP gas, RV accessible. Hours: 9am to 7pm.
(888)841-9646 Lat: 43.99544, Lon: -71.063472
1571 E. Main Street, Center Conway, NH 03813
www.campingworld.com

CARBON MONOXIDE SAFETY REMINDER: Teach everybody how to recognize carbon monoxide symptoms. Carbon monoxide symptoms are similar to flu symptoms, but without the fever. Symptoms include: dizziness, vomiting, nausea, muscular twitching, intense headache, throbbing in the temples, weakness and sleepiness, inability to think coherently. If you or anyone else experiences any of these symptoms get to fresh air immediately. If the symptoms persist seek medical attention/call 911. Shut the vehicle or generator down and do not operate it until it has been inspected and repaired by a professional.

CHICHESTER — E4 *Merrimack*

Travel Services

CAMPING WORLD CHICHESTER/NEW HAMPSHIRE As the nation's largest retailer of RV supplies, accessories, services and new and used RVs, Camping World is committed to making your total RV experience better. **SERVICES:** RV, tire, RV appliance, MH mechanical, staffed RV wash, restrooms. RV Sales. RV supplies, LP gas, emergency parking, RV accessible. Hours: 9am - 7pm.
(888)485-7284 Lat: 43.244849, Lon: -71.406518
165 Dover Road, Chichester, NH 03258
www.campingworld.com

CHOCORUA — D4 *Carroll*

CHOCORUA CAMPING VILLAGE KOA **Ratings: 8.5/7/10** (Campground) 81 Avail: 61 full hkups, 20 W, 20 E (30/50 amps). 2021 rates: $52 to $105. May 01 to Oct 16. (603)323-8536, 893 White Mountain Hwy (NH Rt 16), Tamworth, NH 03886

COLEBROOK — B4 *Coos*

COLEMAN (Public State Park) From jct US 3 & Hwy 26: Go 6-3/4 mi E on Hwy 26, then 5-1/2 mi N on Diamond Pond Rd. Avail: 25 E. 2021 rates: $25 to $29. May 10 to Oct 13. (603)237-5382

CONCORD — E3 *Merrimack*

CONCORD See also Alton, Auburn, Barrington, Contoocook, Epsom, Henniker, Hillsboro, Gilford, Loudon, New Boston, Raymond, Strafford, Weare & Webster.

CONTOOCOOK — E3 *Merrimack*

SANDY BEACH RV RESORT
good sam park
Ratings: 8/6.5/8 (RV Park) Avail: 91 full hkups (30/50 amps). 2021 rates: $52 to $65. May 05 to Oct 10. (888)563-7040, 677 Clement Hill Rd, Contoocook, NH 03229

CONWAY — D4 *Carroll*

A SPOTLIGHT Introducing the White Mountains' colorful attractions appearing at the front of this state section.

EPSOM — E4 *Merrimack*

EPSOM VALLEY CAMPGROUND **Ratings: 5.5/7.5★/7** (Campground) Avail: 28 full hkups (30 amps). 2021 rates: $40. May 18 to Oct 15. (603)736-9758, 990 Suncook Valley Hwy, Epsom, NH 03234

LAZY RIVER FAMILY CAMPGROUND **Ratings: 5.5/5.5/5** (Campground) 57 Avail: 6 full hkups, 51 W, 51 E (30 amps). 2021 rates: $35. May 15 to Oct 15. (603)798-5900, 427 Goboro Rd, Epsom, NH 03234

ERROL — B4 *Coos*

UMBAGOG LAKE
(Public State Park) From jct Hwy 16 & Hwy 26: Go 7-3/4 mi E on Hwy 26. **FAC:** 60 Avail: 27 paved, 33 grass, 27 full hkups, tent sites, rentals, dump, fire rings, firewood. **REC:** Umbagog Lake: fishing, playground, rec open to public. Pets OK. 2021 rates: $30 to $35. May 06 to Nov 13.
(603)482-7795 Lat: 44.702596, Lon: -71.051161
235 East Route 26, Errol, NH 03579
www.nhstateparks.org

EXETER — F5 *Rockingham*

GREEN GATE CAMPGROUND **Ratings: 9/8★/9** (Campground) Avail: 40 full hkups (30/50 amps). 2021 rates: $55 to $59. May 01 to Oct 01. (603)772-2100, 185 Court St, Exeter, NH 03833

FRANCONIA — C3 *Grafton*

FRANCONIA NOTCH/LAFAYETTE CAMPGROUND (Public State Park) No N'bound access. N'bound on I-93: turn around at Tramway exit 2, then go back 2-1/2 mi S on I-93. S'bound: At I-93 (Lafayette Place/Campground exit). 98 Avail. 2021 rates: $25. (603)823-8800

FRANSTED FAMILY CAMPGROUND **Ratings: 8/8.5★/9.5** (Campground) 36 Avail: 18 full hkups, 18 W, 18 E (30/50 amps). 2021 rates: $45 to $60. May 15 to Oct 12. (603)823-5675, 974 Profile Rd Rte 18, Franconia, NH 03580

Slow down. For most vehicles, fuel efficiency begins to drop rapidly at 60 mph. Driving within the speed limit can improve fuel efficiency by up to 23 percent.

FREEDOM — D4 *Carroll*

DANFORTH BAY CAMPING & RV RESORT **Ratings: 9.5/9.5★/10** (Campground) 195 Avail: 128 full hkups, 67 W, 67 E (30/50 amps). 2021 rates: $49 to $92. (603)539-2069, 196 Shawtown Rd, Freedom, NH 03836

THE BLUFFS RV RESORT **Ratings: 10/9.5★/10** (RV Park) Avail: 13 full hkups (30/50 amps). 2021 rates: $57 to $66. Apr 18 to Nov 02. (603)539-2069, 196 Shawton Rd, Freedom, NH 03836

NH

GILFORD — D4 *Belknap*

ELLACOYA (Public State Park) From Jct of I-93 & I-393/Rtes 4 & 202 (exit 15E), E 3 mi on I-393/4/202 to Rte 106, N 17.5 mi to Rte 3/11 Bypass, NE 5 mi to Rte 11, SE 3.5 mi (L). Avail: 37 full hkups (20/30 amps). 2021 rates: $47. May 13 to Oct 09. (603)293-7821

GUNSTOCK MOUNTAIN RESORT **Ratings: 8/8/9** (Campground) 217 Avail: 16 full hkups, 71 W, 71 E (30/50 amps). 2021 rates: $50 to $55. (603)293-4341, 719 Cherry Valley Rd, Gilford, NH 03249

GLEN — C4 *Carroll*

GREEN MEADOW CAMPING AREA **Ratings: 7/8/8.5** (Campground) 48 Avail: 14 full hkups, 34 W, 34 E (30/50 amps). 2021 rates: $38 to $52. May 24 to Oct 14. (603)383-6801, 37 Green Meadow Campground Rd, Glen, NH 03838

YOGI BEAR'S JELLYSTONE PARK/GLEN ELLIS **Ratings: 8/9.5★/10** (Campground) 210 Avail: 100 full hkups, 110 W, 110 E (30/50 amps). 2021 rates: $75 to $105. May 26 to Oct 13. (603)383-4567, 83 Glen Ellis Campground Rd, Glen, NH 03838

GORHAM — C4 *Coos*

MOOSE BROOK (Public State Park) From west jct Hwy 16 & US 2: Go 1-1/4 mi W on US 2, then 1/2 mi N on Jimtown Rd. 29 Avail. 2021 rates: $25. May 06 to Oct 31. (603)466-3860

TIMBERLAND CAMPGROUND **Ratings: 9/8/9** (Campground) 76 Avail: 57 full hkups, 19 W, 19 E (30/50 amps). 2021 rates: $42 to $49. May 10 to Oct 20. (603)466-3872, 809 State Route 2, Shelburne, NH 03581

WHITE BIRCHES CAMPING PARK **Ratings: 8.5/8.5★/7.5** (Campground) 27 Avail: 20 full hkups, 7 W, 7 E (30/50 amps). 2021 rates: $44. May 01 to Oct 25. (603)466-2022, 218 State Rte 2, Shelburne, NH 03581

GREENFIELD — F3 *Hillsborough*

GREENFIELD (Public State Park) From Jct of SR-31 & SR-136, W 1 mi on SR-136, follow signs (R). 252 Avail. 2021 rates: $25. May 06 to Oct 29. (603)547-3497

Go to GoodSam.com/Trip-Planner for Trip Routing.

New Hampshire Privately Owned Campground Information Updated by our Good Sam Representatives

Steve & Debbie Rice

Life adventuring as friends since meeting in seventh grade, our first date in a VW Microbus (before the Summer of Love) foretold the destiny of the long highway that lay ahead. Full-timing for eight years, we've accumulated miles of smiles. Peace!

HAMPTON — F5 *Rockingham*

TIDEWATER CAMPGROUND

Ratings: 8/10★/9.5 (Campground) From Jct of I-95 & Rte 101 (Exit 2), Go 2.5 mi E on Rte 101 to US 1, then 0.2 mi S (R). **FAC:** paved/gravel rds. (186 spaces). 48 Avail: 40 gravel, 8 grass, 4 pull-thrus, (25x60), back-ins (28x60), 48 full hkups (30/50 amps), seasonal sites, WiFi @ sites, tent sites, shower$, groc, fire rings, firewood, controlled access. **REC:** pool, boating nearby, playground. Big rig sites, eco-friendly. 2021 rates: $57. May 15 to Oct 15.
(603)926-5474 Lat: 42.93121, Lon: -70.84587
160 Lafayette Rd, Hampton, NH 03842
tidewatercampgroundnh.com
See ad this page

HAMPTON BEACH — F5 *Rockingham*

HAMPTON BEACH (Public State Park) From Jct of I-95 & Rte 101 (exit 2), E 3 mi on Rte 101 to Rte 1A, S 2 mi (L). 3 day min stay. Note: No Pets April 1st-Sept. 15th. Avail: 28 full hkups (20/30 amps). 2021 rates: $50. May 10 to Oct 30. (603)926-8990

HAMPTON FALLS — F5 *Rockingham*

WAKEDA CAMPGROUND

Ratings: 7.5/9★/9.5 (Campground) From Jct of I-95 & Rte 107 (exit 1), Go 0.5 mi E on Rte 107 to US-1, then 1.7 mi N to Rte 88, then 3.7 mi W (L). **FAC:** paved rds. (377 spaces). 121 Avail: 5 paved, 90 gravel, 26 grass, 9 pull-thrus, (22x86), back-ins (30x60), 80 full hkups, 41 W, 41 E (30/50 amps), seasonal sites, WiFi, tent sites, rentals, shower$, dump, laundry, groc, LP bottles, fire rings, firewood. **REC:** boating nearby, playground. Pets OK. Partial handicap access. Big rig sites, eco-friendly. 2021 rates: $51 to $59, Military discount. May 15 to Oct 01.
(603)772-5274 Lat: 42.95631, Lon: -70.90453
294 Exeter Rd, Rt 88, Hampton Falls, NH 03844
www.wakedacampground.com
See ad this page

HANCOCK — F3 *Hillsborough*

SEVEN MAPLES CAMPGROUND **Ratings: 8.5/9.5★/10** (Campground) 53 Avail: 12 full hkups, 41 W, 41 E (30/50 amps). 2021 rates: $54 to $63. May 01 to Oct 13. (603)525-3321, 24 Longview Rd, Hancock, NH 03449

HANOVER — D2 *Grafton*

STORRS POND RECREATION AREA (Public) From jct I-89 & I-91 in VT: Go 5 mi N on I-91 (exit 13-Hanover, NH-Dartmouth College), then turn E and cross the Connecticut River into Hanover, NH (street becomes Wheelock St), 1 mi E on Wheelock St, 1 mi N on Hwy 10, then 1 mi E on Reservoir. 11 Avail: 11 W, 11 E. 2021 rates: $40. May 15 to Sep 01. (603)643-2134

HENNIKER — E3 *Merrimack*

KEYSER POND CAMPGROUND **Ratings: 7/7.5/9.5** (Campground) 48 Avail: 17 full hkups, 31 W, 31 E (50 amps). 2021 rates: $42 to $55. May 15 to Oct 31. (603)428-7741, 1739 Old Concord Rd, Henniker, NH 03242

MILE-AWAY CAMPGROUND **Ratings: 8.5/7.5/8.5** (Campground) Avail: 59 full hkups (30/50 amps). 2021 rates: $45. (603)428-7616, 479 Old W Hopkinton Rd, Henniker, NH 03242

HILLSBORO — E3 *Hillsborough*

OXBOW CAMPGROUND **Ratings: 7/8★/9** (Campground) Avail: 33 full hkups (30/50 amps). 2021 rates: $50 to $57. May 01 to Oct 31. (603)464-5952, 8 Oxbow Rd, Deering, NH 03244

HINSDALE — F2 *Cheshire*

HINSDALE CAMPGROUND AT THICKET HILL VILLAGE **Ratings: 7.5/9/8.5** (Campground) 21 Avail: 14 full hkups, 7 W, 7 E (30/50 amps). 2021 rates: $42.50 to $50. Apr 17 to Oct 31. (603)336-6240, 29 Pine St, Hinsdale, NH 03451

HOLDERNESS — D3 *Belknap*

OWLS LANDING CAMPROUND **Ratings: 7/6/7.5** (Campground) 23 Avail: 12 full hkups, 11 W, 11 E (30 amps). 2021 rates: $40 to $65. May 22 to Oct 15. (603)279-6266, 245 US Rte 3, Holderness, NH 03245

JEFFERSON — C4 *Coos*

JEFFERSON CAMPGROUND

Ratings: 8/8.5★/8 (Campground) 28 Avail: 15 full hkups, 13 W, 13 E (30/50 amps). 2021 rates: $42 to $48. May 17 to Oct 15. (603)586-4510, 1468 Presidential Highway (Route 2), Jefferson, NH 03583

LANTERN RESORT MOTEL & CAMPGROUND **Ratings: 8.5/9.5★/10** (Campground) 49 Avail: 19 full hkups, 30 W, 30 E (30/50 amps). 2021 rates: $65 to $70. May 15 to Oct 14. (603)586-7151, 571 Presidential Hwy (Rt 2), Jefferson, NH 03583

KINGSTON — F4 *Rockingham*

MILL BROOK RV PARK **Ratings: 8.5/UI/10** (RV Park) Avail: 15 full hkups (30/50 amps). 2021 rates: $44 to $50. May 10 to Oct 06. (603)642-7112, 99 Route 125, Kingston, NH 03848

LANCASTER — B3 *Coos*

MOUNTAIN LAKE CAMPING RESORT **Ratings: 10/10★/10** (Campground) 74 Avail: 71 full hkups, 3 W, 3 E (30/50 amps). 2021 rates: $55 to $98. May 15 to Oct 15. (603)788-4509, 485 Prospect St (Rt 3), Lancaster, NH 03584

RIVERSIDE CAMPING & RV RESORT

Ratings: 9/10★/9.5 (RV Park) Avail: 40 full hkups (30/50 amps). 2021 rates: $54 to $59. May 01 to Oct 15. (603)631-7433, 94 Bridge Street, Lancaster, NH 03584

LEE — E4 *Strafford*

FERNDALE ACRES CAMPGROUND **Ratings: 7/8.5★/8** (Campground) Avail: 31 full hkups (30 amps). 2021 rates: $48. May 15 to Sep 15. (603)659-5082, 130 Wednesday Hill Rd, Lee, NH 03861

LISBON — C3 *Grafton*

LITTLETON/FRANCONIA NOTCH KOA **Ratings: 10/9.5★/9.5** (Campground) 39 Avail: 33 full hkups, 6 W, 6 E (30/50 amps). 2021 rates: $54 to $85. May 15 to Oct 12. (603)838-5525, 2154 Rte 302, Lisbon, NH 03585

Set your clocks. Time zones are indicated in the front of each state and province.

LITTLETON — C3 *Grafton*

CRAZY HORSE FAMILY CAMPGROUND

Ratings: 9/10★/10 (Campground) From Jct of I-93 & Rte 135 (Exit 43), Go 0.1 mi SW on Rte 135 to Rte 135/18, then 1 mi W to Hilltop Rd, then 1.5 mi NW (R).

FAMILY CAMPING AT ITS BEST-ALL YEAR
Voted Best NH Campground in 2019 & 2020 with access to a 12-mile reservoir/lake. Enjoy fishing, canoeing, lake or pool swimming, hiking nearby and easy access to ALL White Mountain Attractions. Pet, Big Rig & Tent Friendly!

FAC: all weather rds. (175 spaces). 93 Avail: 63 gravel, 30 dirt, 15 pull-thrus, (32x64), back-ins (32x50), 55 full hkups, 38 W, 38 E (30/50 amps), seasonal sites, cable, WiFi @ sites, tent sites, rentals, shower$, dump, laundry, groc, LP gas, fire rings, firewood. **REC:** pool, pond, fishing, boating nearby, playground, hunting nearby. Pets OK. Big rig sites, eco-friendly. 2021 rates: $48, Military discount.
(603)444-2204 Lat: 44.32219, Lon: -71.84888
788 Hilltop Rd, Littleton, NH 03561
www.crazyhorsenh.com
See ad page 598

LOUDON — E3 *Merrimack*

CASCADE CAMPGROUND **Ratings: 9/8.5★/7** (Campground) Avail: 105 full hkups (30/50 amps). 2021 rates: $42. May 01 to Oct 10. (603)224-3212, 379 Route 106 South, Loudon, NH 03307

MADBURY — E5 *Strafford*

OLD STAGE CAMPGROUND **Ratings: 8/9.5★/8** (Campground) 50 Avail: 30 full hkups, 20 W, 20 E (30 amps). 2021 rates: $50. May 01 to Oct 02. (603)742-4050, 46 Old Stage Rd, Madbury, NH 03823

MEREDITH — D4 *Belknap*

CLEARWATER CAMPGROUND **Ratings: 8/9.5★/10** (Campground) 43 Avail: 19 full hkups, 24 W, 24 E (30/50 amps). 2021 rates: $34 to $64. May 15 to Oct 12. (603)279-7761, 26 Campground Rd, Meredith, NH 03253

HARBOR HILL CAMPING AREA **Ratings: 9.5/8.5★/10** (Campground) 61 Avail: 56 full hkups, 5 W, 5 E (30/50 amps). 2021 rates: $49 to $56. May 22 to Oct 12. (603)279-6910, 189 NH Rte 25, Meredith, NH 03253

MEREDITH WOODS 4 SEASON CAMPING AREA **Ratings: 10/9★/10** (Campground) Avail: 25 full hkups (30/50 amps). 2021 rates: $42 to $64. (603)279-5449, 551 NH Rte 104, Meredith, NH 03253

TWIN TAMARACK FAMILY CAMPING & RV RESORT

Ratings: 8.5/9.5★/9.5 (Campground) 117 Avail: 51 full hkups, 66 W, 66 E (30/50 amps). 2021 rates: $45. May 17 to Oct 14. (603)279-4387, 41 Twin Tamarack Rd, New Hampton, NH 03256

MILTON — E4 *Strafford*

YOGI BEAR'S JELLYSTONE PARK CAMP-RESORT LAKES REGION **Ratings: 8/8.5★/10** (Campground) Avail: 94 full hkups (30/50 amps). 2021 rates: $64.90 to $130. May 15 to Oct 10. (603)652-9022, 111 Mi-Te-Jo Rd, Milton, NH 03851

MOULTONBOROUGH — D4 *Carroll*

LONG ISLAND BRIDGE CAMPGROUND

Ratings: 8.5/9.5★/10 (Campground) From Jct of Rtes 3 & 25 (in Meredith), NE 7 mi on Rte 25 to Moultonboro Neck Rd, S 7 mi (L).

WINNIPESAUKEE BEACH SIDE
Winnipesaukee beachfront sites! We are only a stone's throw away from many attractions of the Lake's Region and the incredible White Mountains. Whether you relax, swim, hike or take in the sights, you'll be forever changed!

FAC: all weather rds. (96 spaces). Avail: 38 gravel, 5 pull-thrus, (24x45), back-ins (24x45), 18 full hkups, 20 W, 20 E (30/50 amps), seasonal sites, cable, WiFi @ sites, tent sites, rentals, shower$, dump, laundry, fire rings, firewood, controlled access. **REC:** Lake Winnipesaukee: swim, fishing, boating nearby, playground, hunting nearby. Pet restrict (B/Q). Partial handicap access, 21 day max stay, eco-friendly. 2021 rates: $47 to $55. May 15 to Oct 15. no cc.
(603)253-6053 Lat: 43.66676, Lon: -71.34689
29 Long Island Rd, Moultonborough, NH 03254
longislandbridgecampgroundnh.com
See ad this page

Find Good Sam member specials at CampingWorld.com

NEW BOSTON — F3 *Hillsborough*

FRIENDLY BEAVER CAMPGROUND

good sam park **Ratings: 9/10★/9.5** (Campground) From Jct of Rtes 77 & 136 & 13 (in town), Go 100 ft S on Rte 13 to Old Coach Rd, then 2 mi W (R).

NEW ENGLAND'S #1 FAMILY CAMPGROUND
With activities every day of the summer, themed weekends, 3 outdoor pools, heated indoor pool, 2 large children's playgrounds & separate adult & children's rec halls, you'll never be bored at Friendly Beaver. Open year-round.

FAC: gravel rds. (288 spaces). Avail: 81 gravel, 5 pull-thrus, (30x45), back-ins (30x45), 10 full hkups, 71 W, 71 E (30/50 amps), seasonal sites, WiFi @ sites, $, tent sites, rentals, dump, mobile sewer, laundry, groc, fire rings, firewood. **REC:** heated pool, wading pool, boating nearby, playground, hunting nearby. Pet restrict (B). Partial handicap access. Big rig sites, eco-friendly. 2021 rates: $60 to $87, Military discount. ATM.
(603)487-5570 Lat: 42.97494, Lon: -71.721739
Old Coach Rd., New Boston, NH 03070
www.friendlybeaver.com
See ad this page

NEW HAMPTON — D3 *Belknap*

ADVENTURE BOUND CAMPING **Ratings: 7.5/7/8.5** (Campground) 184 Avail: 19 full hkups, 165 W, 165 E (30/50 amps). 2021 rates: $76.50 to $100. May 22 to Oct 10. (603)968-9000, 35 Jellystone Park, New Hampton, NH 03256

NEWFIELDS — F5 *Rockingham*

GREAT BAY CAMPING **Ratings: 9.5/9.5★/9.5** (Campground) Avail: 33 full hkups (30/50 amps). 2021 rates: $40 to $45. May 15 to Oct 01. (603)778-0226, 56-60 Route 108, Newfields, NH 03856

NEWPORT — E2 *Sullivan*

CROW'S NEST CAMPGROUND

good sam park **Ratings: 8.5/8.5★/9** (Campground) 72 Avail: 27 full hkups, 45 W, 45 E (30/50 amps). 2021 rates: $40 to $55. May 15 to Oct 10. (603)863-6170, 529 S Main St, Newport, NH 03773

NORTH CONWAY — C4 *Carroll*

BEACH CAMPING AREA **Ratings: 7.5/8★/8.5** (Campground) Avail: 90 full hkups (20/30 amps). 2021 rates: $49 to $54. May 15 to Oct 15. (603)447-2723, 776 White Mountain Hwy/Rte 16, North Conway, NH 03818

EASTERN SLOPE CAMPING AREA **Ratings: 8.5/UI/8** (RV Park) 188 Avail: 120 full hkups, 68 W, 68 E (30/50 amps). 2021 rates: $52.99 to $69.99. May 15 to Oct 17. (603)447-5092, 584 White Mountain Hwy/NH Rt 16, Conway, NH 03818

NORTH HAMPTON — F5 *Rockingham*

SEACOAST CAMPING & RV **Ratings: 8.5/10★/10** (Campground) Avail: 87 full hkups (30/50 amps). 2021 rates: $44 to $55. May 15 to Oct 01. (603)964-5730, 115 Lafayette Rd, North Hampton, NH 03862

NORTH WOODSTOCK — C3 *Grafton*

LOST RIVER VALLEY CAMPGROUND **Ratings: 6.5/8.5★/8.5** (Campground) 53 Avail: 8 full hkups, 45 W, 45 E (30/50 amps). 2021 rates: $58 to $68. May 15 to Oct 12. (603)745-8321, 951 Lost River Road, North Woodstock, NH 03262

OSSIPEE — D4 *Carroll*

BEAVER HOLLOW CAMPGROUND **Ratings: 9/6.5/9** (Campground) Avail: 50 full hkups (30/50 amps). 2021 rates: $50. May 15 to Oct 12. (603)539-4800, 700 Rte 16, Ossipee, NH 03864

WESTWARD SHORES COTTAGES & RV RESORT **Ratings: 7.5/9.5★/9** (RV Resort) 49 Avail: 43 full hkups, 6 W, 6 E (30/50 amps). 2021 rates: $93 to $111. May 15 to Oct 15. (603)539-6445, 110 Nichols Road, Ossipee, NH 03890

PITTSBURG — A4 *Coos*

HIDDEN ACRES CAMPGROUND **Ratings: 5/7★/9** (RV Park) 36 Avail: 36 W, 36 E (20/30 amps). 2021 rates: $36 to $38. (603)331-1912, 29 Hidden Acres Rd, Pittsburg, NH 03592

LAKE FRANCIS (Public State Park) From town: Go 7 mi N on US-3. 45 Avail: 9 W, 9 E. 2021 rates: $25 to $35. May 06 to Nov 13. (603)538-6965

Thank you for being one of our best customers!

RAMBLEWOOD CABINS & CAMPGROUND **Ratings: 7.5/NA/9** (RV Park) 30 Avail: 30 W, 30 E (20/30 amps), Pit toilets. 2021 rates: $30 to $40. (603)538-6948, 59 Ranblewood Rd, Pittsburg, NH 03592

RAYMOND — F4 *Rockingham*

PAWTUCKAWAY (Public State Park) From jct Hwy 101 (exit 5) & Hwy 156: Go 2 mi N on Hwy 156, then 2 mi NW on Mountain Rd. 192 Avail. 2021 rates: $25 to $30. May 30 to Oct 10. (603)895-3031

PINE ACRES RESORT

good sam park **Ratings: 8.5/8.5★/9** (Campground) 106 Avail: 19 full hkups, 87 W, 87 E (30/50 amps). 2021 rates: $61 to $81. Apr 15 to Oct 15. (888)563-7040, 74 Freetown Rd, Raymond, NH 03077

RICHMOND — F2 *Cheshire*

SHIR-ROY CAMPING AREA Ratings: 8.5/9.5★/8.5 (Campground) Avail: 80 full hkups (30/50 amps). 2021 rates: $43 to $48. May 25 to Oct 10. (603)239-4768, 136 Athol Rd, Richmond, NH 03470

RUMNEY — D3 *Grafton*

RIVERBROOK CAMPGROUND & RV PARK **Ratings: 9.5/10★/9.5** (Campground) Avail: 60 full hkups (30/50 amps). 2021 rates: $55 to $70. (603)786-2333, 1120 Mt Moosilauke Hwy, Rumney, NH 03266

SOUTH HAMPTON — F5 *Rockingham*

TUXBURY POND RV RESORT

good sam park **Ratings: 8.5/9★/9** (RV Park) Avail: 60 full hkups (30/50 amps). 2021 rates: $68 to $91. May 01 to Oct 10. (888)563-7040, 88 Whitehall Rd, South Hampton, NH 03827

STRAFFORD — E4 *Strafford*

STRAFFORD/LAKE WINNIPESAUKEE SOUTH KOA **Ratings: 9.5/9.5★/10** (Campground) Avail: 54 full hkups (30/50 amps). 2021 rates: $69 to $140. May 10 to Oct 14. (603)332-0405, 79 First Crown Point Rd, Strafford, NH 03884

SWANZEY — F2 *Cheshire*

SWANZEY LAKE CAMPING AREA **Ratings: 5.5/7.5/8** (Campground) 43 Avail: 35 full hkups, 8 W, 8 E (20/30 amps). 2021 rates: $42. Apr 15 to Nov 01. (603)352-9880, 88 E Shore Rd, Swanzey, NH 03446

TAMWORTH — D4 *Carroll*

TAMWORTH CAMPING AREA

good sam park **Ratings: 7/8.5★/9** (Campground) From Jct of Hwys 25W & 16, Go 0.5 mi N on Hwy 16 to Depot Rd, W 3 mi (L).
FAC: gravel rds. (100 spaces). Avail: 72 gravel, back-ins (35x50), 18 full hkups, 54 W, 49 E (30/50 amps), seasonal sites, cable, WiFi, tent sites, rentals, shower$, dump, laundry, LP bottles, fire rings, firewood, controlled access. **REC:** Swift River: swim, fishing, boating nearby, shuffleboard, playground, hunting nearby. Pets OK. Big rig sites, eco-friendly. 2021 rates: $53 to $58. May 15 to Oct 15.
(603)323-8031 Lat: 43.84639, Lon: -71.25764
194 Depot Rd, Tamworth, NH 03886
tamworthcamping.com
See ad this page

THORNTON — D3 *Grafton*

PEMI RIVER CAMPGROUND **Ratings: 6.5/9★/8.5** (Campground) 60 Avail: 45 full hkups, 15 W, 15 E (30/50 amps). 2021 rates: $50 to $55. May 01 to Oct 15. (603)726-7015, 2458 US Rte 3, Thornton, NH 03285

NH

TWIN MOUNTAIN — C3 *Coos*

ALONG THE RIVER CAMPGROUND **Ratings: 7.5/9★/9.5** (Campground) 50 Avail: 36 full hkups, 14 W, 14 E (30/50 amps). 2021 rates: $55. May 24 to Oct 10. (603)846-1026, 373 Rte 302 West, Twin Mountain, NH 03595

AMMONOOSUC CAMPGROUND **Ratings: 7/9★/8** (Campground) 17 Avail: 10 full hkups, 7 W, 7 E (20/30 amps). 2021 rates: $40. (603)846-5527, 149 US-3, Twin Mountain, NH 03595

BEECH HILL CAMPGROUND & CABINS Ratings: 7.5/9★/9 (Campground) 74 Avail: 24 full hkups, 50 W, 50 E (30/50 amps). 2021 rates: $40 to $52. May 15 to Oct 15. (603)846-5521, 970 Rte 302W, Twin Mountain, NH 03595

TROUVAILLE - COTTAGES AND RV PARK **Ratings: 9.5/NA/10** (RV Park) Avail: 18 full hkups (30 amps). 2021 rates: $45 to $50. May 01 to Oct 15. (603)846-5574, 554 Rte 3 S, Twin Mountain, NH 03595

TWIN MOUNTAIN/MT. WASHINGTON KOA **Ratings: 10/10★/10** (Campground) 60 Avail: 49 full hkups, 11 W, 11 E (30/50 amps). 2021 rates: $44.04 to $89.95. May 14 to Oct 11. (603)846-5559, 372 Rte 115, Twin Mountain, NH 03595

WARREN — D3 *Grafton*

MOOSE HILLOCK CAMPGROUND **Ratings: 8.5/8.5★/9.5** (Campground) 158 Avail: 105 full hkups, 53 W, 53 E (30/50 amps). 2021 rates: $45 to $99. May 16 to Oct 14. (603)764-5294, 96 Batchelder Brook Rd - Rte 118 N, Warren, NH 03279

SCENIC VIEW CAMPGROUND **Ratings: 8/9★/9** (Campground) 62 Avail: 26 full hkups, 31 W, 31 E (30/50 amps). 2021 rates: $53 to $64. May 16 to Oct 10. (603)764-9380, 18 Gingerbread Lane, Warren, NH 03279

WASHINGTON — E2 *Sullivan*

PILLSBURY (Public State Park) From town: Go 4 mi N on Hwy 31. 14 Avail: Pit toilets. 2021 rates: $23. May 20 to Oct 15. (603)863-2860

We appreciate your business!

WEARE — E3 *Hillsborough*

↓ AUTUMN HILLS CAMPGROUND **Ratings: 8/8.5★/8.5** (Campground) Avail: 46 full hkups (20/30 amps). 2021 rates: $45 to $56. May 01 to Oct 18. (603)529-2425, 285 S Stark Hwy, Weare, NH 03281

↓ **COLD SPRINGS CAMP RESORT Ratings: 10/10★/10** (RV Resort) 100 Avail: 96 full hkups, 4 W, 4 E (30/50 amps). 2021 rates: $79 to $89. May 01 to Oct 10. (603)529-2528, 62 Barnard Hill Rd, Weare, NH 03281

WEBSTER — E3 *Merrimack*

↓ COZY POND CAMPING RESORT **Ratings: 9/8.5/9** (Campground) Avail: 26 full hkups (30/50 amps). 2021 rates: $49 to $57. May 08 to Oct 12. (603)428-7701, 541 Battle St, Webster, NH 03303

TRAVELING WITH YOUR PET: Keep cool. Humans don't wear fur coats in July, but that's what our dogs must endure during the heat of summer. Shield all pets from hot temperatures, and remember that older canines and dogs with darker hair are more vulnerable to summer heat. Canine cooling jackets and cooling bandanas are widely available to help dogs stay comfortable in hot weather.

WEIRS BEACH — D4 *Belknap*

← PAUGUS BAY CAMPGROUND **Ratings: 7.5/9.5★/9** (Campground) 27 Avail: 3 full hkups, 24 W, 24 E (30 amps). 2021 rates: $50 to $54. May 15 to Oct 15. (603)366-4757, 96 Hilliard Rd, Weirs Beach, NH 03246

WENTWORTH — D3 *Grafton*

↓ PINE HAVEN CAMPGROUND **Ratings: 8.5/8/9** (Campground) 56 Avail: 20 full hkups, 36 W, 36 E (30/50 amps). 2021 rates: $47 to $56. May 15 to Oct 15. (603)786-2900, 29 Pinehaven Campground Rd, Wentworth, NH 03282

TRAVELING WITH YOUR PET: Check in with the vet. A pre-departure vet exam can spot health problems and ensure your pet is current on vaccines required by pet-friendly parks. Parvovirus, distemper, rabies and bordatella inoculations are the most common, but they may recommend others for geographically specific conditions like leptospirosis and Lyme disease. Pets with chronic immune-system illnesses can apply for vaccine waivers. File all records in the RV. Vaccination certificates may be required, especially at international border crossings.

WEST OSSIPEE — D4 *Carroll*

WHITE LAKE (Public State Park) From jct Hwy 16 & Hwy 25: Go 1-1/2 mi N on Hwy 16. 153 Avail. 2021 rates: $25 to $30. May 13 to Oct 09. (603)323-7350

WOLFEBORO — D4 *Carroll*

↑ WOLFEBORO CAMPGROUND **Ratings: 5.5/8.5★/8** (Campground) Avail: 20 full hkups (30/50 amps). 2021 rates: $38. May 15 to Oct 15. (603)569-9881, 61 Haines Hill Rd, Wolfeboro, NH 03894

WOODSTOCK — C3 *Grafton*

↓ LINCOLN/WOODSTOCK KOA **Ratings: 9/10★/9.5** (Campground) 90 Avail: 42 full hkups, 48 W, 48 E (30/50 amps). 2021 rates: $56 to $100. May 01 to Oct 18. (800)562-9736, 1000 Eastside Rd, Woodstock, NH 03293

Our rating system is fair and thorough. We know the kinds of things that are important to you - like clean restrooms and showers, attractive, secure, well-tended grounds, and extras like swimming pools. We give the first rating for development of facilities, the second for cleanliness and physical characteristics of restrooms and showers, and the third for visual appearance.

Getty Images/iStockphoto

DID YOU KNOW?

Atlantic City's 5.5-mile boardwalk is not only the oldest in America, it's also the longest in the world.

NJ

YOU ARE HERE

New Jersey

The Garden state blooms with recreation possibilities. Munch on cotton candy on the crowded Jersey Shore, then escape to the Pine Barrens. Hike mountains in the north, then gaze across the water at the Big Apple skyline.

A Shore Thing

The fabled Jersey Shore comprises 141 miles of glorious Atlantic surf and sand. Experience the shore's pristine natural state at Island Beach State Park, where swimming and surf fishing abound. Inland, the Division of Fish and Wildlife helps anglers hit the jackpot by stocking many rivers and lakes with trout. Top picks include the state's largest lake, Lake Hopatcong in the north, and the Big Flat Brook, Rockaway River and Pequest River.

Get Away from the Bustle

The Delaware Water Gap National Recreation Area on the northern border is a one-stop shop for the great outdoors, with hunting, fishing, boating, bicycling and more. Here, the pristine Middle Delaware National Scenic River meanders through wooded mountains, creating a 70,000-acre natural playground. Jutting into the Atlantic Ocean, the Sandy Hook unit of the Gateway National Recreation Area is another amazing option.

Serenity Now!

Seventy-two miles of the Appalachian Trail snake through Jersey. Hikers won't want to miss the section that runs through High Point State Park along the Kittatinny Mountain Ridge. Hike to the top of High Point Memorial, a striking granite obelisk, for seemingly infinite views of the surrounding Pocono and Catskill mountains. Visitors to New Jersey's tranquil Pine Barrens will discover a forested getaway. Cyclists can explore scenic woodlands, cranberry bogs and cascading waterways along the 42-mile Pine Barrens River Ramble.

New Jersey Pork Roll

The pork roll has been a beloved breakfast food for over a century. Also called Taylor ham, this processed meat is made from salty ground pork and a mixture of spices. It's similar to Spam and almost always eaten in a sandwich with egg and cheese. Get your fix at bagel shops, diners and delis across the state.

VISITOR CENTER

TIME ZONE
Eastern Standard

ROAD & HIGHWAY INFORMATION
866-511-6538
state.nj.us/njcommuter

FISHING & HUNTING INFORMATION
609-292-2965
www.njfishandwildlife.com

BOATING INFORMATION
732-842-5171
njsp.org/marine-services

NATIONAL PARKS
nps.gov/nj

STATE PARKS
nj.gov/dep/parksandforests/parks

TOURISM INFORMATION
New Jersey Travel and Tourism
609-599-6540
visitnj.org

TOP TOURISM ATTRACTIONS
1) Atlantic City Boardwalk
2) Ocean City Boardwalk
3) Six Flags Great Adventure & Safari

MAJOR CITIES
Newark, Jersey City, Paterson, Elizabeth, Edison, Trenton (capital)

good sam park

Featured Good Sam Parks

NEW JERSEY

When you stay with Good Sam, you can expect the highest degree of cleanliness and friendliness, and better yet, you get **10% off** overnight campground fees.

If you're not already a Good Sam member you can purchase your membership at one of these locations:

BLAIRSTOWN
TripleBrook Camping Resort

CAPE MAY COURT HOUSE
King Nummy Trail Campground

COLUMBIA
Delaware River Family Campground

DOROTHY
Country Oaks Campground

EGG HARBOR CITY
Holly Acres Campground

FLANDERS
Fla-Net Park

GREEN CREEK
Acorn Campground

JACKSON
Indian Rock RV Park
Timberland Lake Campground
Tip Tam Camping Resort

MAYS LANDING
Mays Landing Campground

OCEAN VIEW
Echo Farms RV Resort
Lake & Shore RV

PORT REPUBLIC
Chestnut Lake RV Campground

SWAINTON
Sea Pines RV Resort & Campground

TUCKERTON
Atlantic Shore Pines Campground

Getty Images/iStockphoto

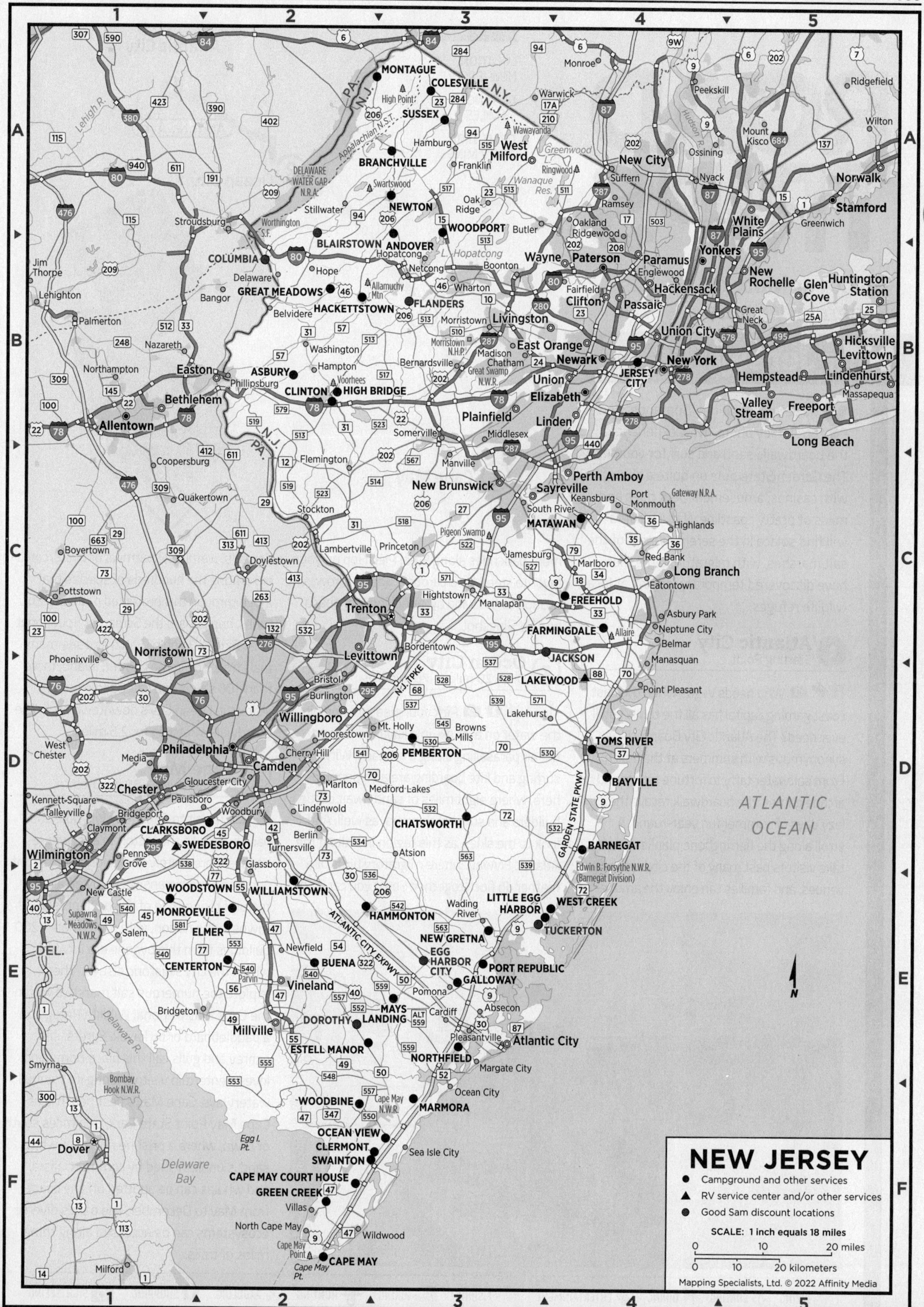
NEW JERSEY
Campground and other services
RV service center and/or other services
Good Sam discount locations
SCALE: 1 inch equals 18 miles
0 10 20 miles
0 10 20 kilometers
Mapping Specialists, Ltd. © 2022 Affinity Media
ATLANTIC OCEAN
MONTAGUE
COLESVILLE
SUSSEX
BRANCHVILLE
NEWTON
WOODPORT
BLAIRSTOWN
ANDOVER
COLUMBIA
GREAT MEADOWS
HACKETTSTOWN
FLANDERS
ASBURY
CLINTON
HIGH BRIDGE
MATAWAN
FREEHOLD
FARMINGDALE
JACKSON
LAKEWOOD
TOMS RIVER
BAYVILLE
PEMBERTON
CHATSWORTH
BARNEGAT
CLARKSBORO
SWEDESBORO
WOODSTOWN
WILLIAMSTOWN
MONROEVILLE
ELMER
CENTERTON
BUENA
HAMMONTON
NEW GRETNA
LITTLE EGG HARBOR
WEST CREEK
TUCKERTON
EGG HARBOR CITY
PORT REPUBLIC
GALLOWAY
MAYS LANDING
DOROTHY
ESTELL MANOR
NORTHFIELD
WOODBINE
MARMORA
OCEAN VIEW
CLERMONT
SWAINTON
CAPE MAY COURT HOUSE
GREEN CREEK
CAPE MAY
West Milford
New City
Norwalk
Stamford
White Plains
Yonkers
Paterson
Paramus
Hackensack
New Rochelle
Glen Cove
Huntington Station
Clifton
Passaic
Wayne
Livingston
Union City
East Orange
Newark
Jersey City
New York
Hempstead
Hicksville
Levittown
Lindenhurst
Union
Elizabeth
Valley Stream
Freeport
Long Beach
Plainfield
Linden
Perth Amboy
Sayreville
New Brunswick
Long Branch
Trenton
Levittown
Willingboro
Philadelphia
Camden
Chester
Wilmington
Norristown
Allentown
Bethlehem
Easton
Vineland
Millville
Atlantic City
Dover
Delaware Bay
Stroudsburg
Garden State Pkwy
Atlantic City Expwy
N.J. Tpke
Delaware Water Gap N.R.A.
Appalachian N.S.T.
Edwin B. Forsythe N.W.R. (Barnegat Division)
Cape May N.W.R.
Bombay Hook N.W.R.
Supawna Meadows N.W.R.
Morristown N.H.P.
Great Swamp N.W.R.
Gateway N.R.A.
Pigeon Swamp
Delaware R.
Hudson R.
Lehigh R.
DEL.
PA.
N.J.
N.Y.

 See map page 605

ROAD TRIPS

Discover More on a Legendary Shore

New Jersey

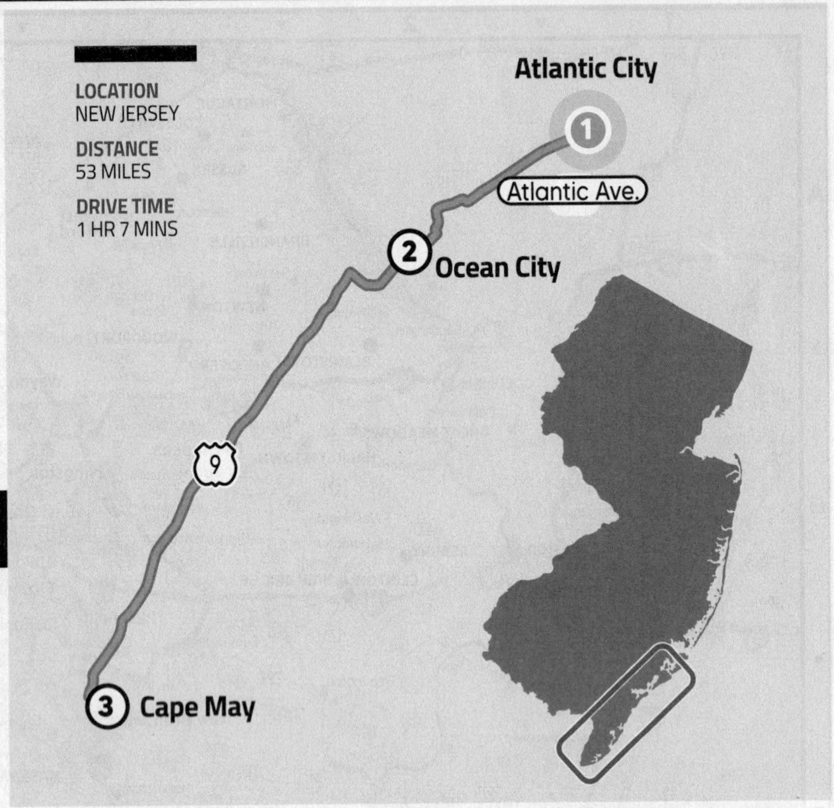

You've seen it on the "Sopranos" and on "Jersey Shore." Now experience the boardwalk, sand and surf for yourself. The Garden State puts on quite a show, with casinos, amusement park rides and miles of pretty coastline. Nature lovers will find solace in the serene waters of the salt marshes, with migratory birds that have discovered temporary lodging at local wildlife refuges.

1 Atlantic City
Starting Point

Who needs Vegas when the east coast gaming capital has all the thrills you'll ever need? The Atlantic City Boardwalk is synonymous with summers at the beach. From saltwater taffy to fortune tellers and arcade games, the boardwalk recalls the lazy days of summer fun year-round. A stroll along the herringbone planks will also take visitors past many of the city's gaming venues, and families can enjoy the amusement park rides along Steel Pier. Hop on your favorite steed for a carousel ride or throw caution to the wind by launching into space on The Slingshot.

2 Ocean City
Drive 20 miles • 28 minutes

Pick your pleasure and hit the water on a jet ski, in a kayak or take to the air parasailing along the beach. Windsurfing and kite boarding are also popular here, where eight miles of sand await castle builders and sun worshippers, as well. And look to the skies, as this region lies along the Atlantic Flyway, where migratory birds of a feather do flock together. See if you can spot pelicans, warblers, sparrows or oystercatchers among the hundreds of species that move through this protected pathway. For thrills, hop aboard the Screamer Speedboat Thrill Ride & Dolphin Watch and see mammals frolicking in the current. Inland, more than 100 shops and cafes serve hungry visitors in Ocean City's downtown area. The boardwalk stretches for 2.5 miles.

Getty Images/iStockphoto

3 Cape May
Drive 33 miles • 39 minutes

A visit to Cape May will take you back in time to the Victorian age, where houses were stately and colorful, and front porches were expansive. Enjoy an architectural tour of one of the best-preserved towns in the nation, with more than 1,200 buildings from this bygone era located within the city's historic district. Then explore the numerous salt marshes within the Cape May National Wildlife Refuge on a paddleboard or by kayak. Egrets, ibis, osprey and gulls call this place home and love to entertain visitors along its tranquil waterways. Cape May's best beach is at Cape May Point State Park, two miles south of town, where a pristine ribbon of white sand is unblemished by commercialism, and whales can be spotted off the coast from May to December. The park's diverse ecosystems can be accessed along three miles of trails.

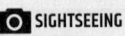

BIKING · BOATING · DINING · ENTERTAINMENT · FISHING · HIKING · HUNTING · PADDLING · SHOPPING · SIGHTSEEING

New Jersey SPOTLIGHTS

Pick Good Times in the Garden State

This state seamlessly blends quiet rustic escapes with big city thrills. Spend the day birdwatching at Cape May Point State Park, then roll the dice during the evening in an Atlantic City casino. Dine at one of the pizza joints that put Tony Soprano on the map.

ATLANTIC CITY INSPIRED THE POPULAR BOARD GAME, MONOPOLY.

Summer on the Atlantic City Boardwalk and Steel Pier, with Ferris Wheel.

Atlantic City

This coastal playground is the stuff of legend. From its beginnings in the prohibition era to its modern high-rise casinos, Atlantic City rises to the occasion. These three fabulous stops will show you what makes Atlantic City the capital of East Coast fun.

On the Boardwalk

Take a stroll down Atlantic City's neon-lit, 4-mile long boardwalk to experience the magic of this iconic town. Built in 1870, Atlantic City's esplanade reaped kudos as the world's first boardwalk where, back in the day, the rich would parade their wealth and status. The now-ubiquitous term, "boardwalk," is named for businessman Alexander Boardman. In response to disgruntled hoteliers, frustrated by guests returning from the beach with sand on their shoes, Boardman came up with the idea of placing an 8-foot-wide stretch of planks that would lead from the town to the beach.

Going Gaming

The jingle of slots and cheers at the blackjack table may be alluring, but nothing beats the sound of surf. Fortunately, it's never hard to score a primo spot on the beach. In recent years, developers have invested billions of dollars into revitalizing the boardwalk, as seedy knots of old buildings have been replaced by big, bold architectural statements.

Vegas on the Atlantic

When it comes to razzmatazz, the Hard Rock Hotel & Casino — formerly the Trump Taj Mahal — entertains guests with slots, table games and sports betting. The beach bar serves customers on a patio overlooking the Atlantic ocean. A comedy club and arena host world-famous performers.

Cape May

Cape May is one of the Garden State's most historic and charming resort towns. Established in 1620, at the tip of New Jersey, Cape May unfurls for 20 miles offshore between the Atlantic Ocean and Delaware Bay. Along sweeping arcs of sand fronted by gingerbread Victorian homes, traditional beachside pleasures hold sway. Steeped in nostalgia, much of the town life centers on the Washington Street Mall, dotted with quaint boutiques, galleries, antique stores, cafes and restaurants. Vibrant festivals celebrate the town's rich history and passion for local seafood. The state's thriving wine industry is represented by the excellent Willow Creek Winery.

Architectural Legacy

One of the best ways to appreciate Cape May's history and rich architectural heritage — consisting of more than 600 preserved Victorian homes — is to join a 90-minute trolley tour offered by the Mid-Atlantic Center for the Arts (MAC), Cape May's premier preservation organization. The Emlen Physick Estate is the town's premier site, famed as an exemplar of Stick Style architecture. Docents conduct informative 45-minute tours that detail the home's authentic period

LOCAL FAVORITE

Flo's Sloppy Joes

From Italian subs to pork rolls, New Jersey has spawned many delicious sandwiches. Jersey even has its own version of the Sloppy Joe. *Recipe by Kathy and Tom Heffron.*

INGREDIENTS

- ☐ 2 green peppers, diced
- ☐ 1 medium onion, diced
- ☐ 3 lbs of hamburger
- ☐ 2 lbs of ground round
- ☐ 2 bottles of chili sauce
- ☐ 2 small bottles of ketchup
- ☐ Toasted hamburger buns (or any buns of your choice)

DIRECTIONS

Brown the onion and green pepper until soft. Add hamburger and ground round. Cook thoroughly and then drain the grease. Add chill sauce and ketchup. Mix together. Simmer for 30 to 40 minutes. Serve on hamburger buns. Serves 8.

Once a popular shorefront hotel, St. Mary by the Sea is a Catholic retreat center on Cape May Point.

furnishings, artifacts and antiques. It's worth climbing the narrow steps to the top of the Cape May Lighthouse, the second-tallest operating lighthouse in the nation, to admire the glorious panoramas of the coastline.

On Land

Two miles south of town, in Cape May Point State Park, whales can be spotted off the coast from May to December. The park is also home to one of the state's finest beaches, a pristine ribbon of white sand. Nature lovers can explore the park's diverse ecosystems along three miles of hiking trails. The 1.6-mile novice loop trail meanders through idyllic woodlands, carpeted with wildflowers, picturesque beaches and fecund marshlands with scenic lookouts and boardwalks. Cape May is one of the country's top birding spots, with more than 400 species during the spring and fall migration seasons. Serious birders won't want to miss the Cape May Migratory Bird Refuge, a 212-acre sanctuary rated as one of the East Coast's finest birding areas.

On the Water

Cape May's placid waters and white sand beaches are the Jersey Shore's finest. Popular with locals, Sunset Beach at Cape May Point boasts picturesque swimming coves. Dolphin watching cruises are a popular summertime activity in the Delaware Bay Estuary, a sanctuary for myriad marine life species, including humpback whales, Atlantic bottlenose dolphins, manta rays, hammerheads, harbor porpoise, and seals. Numerous outfitters offer boat tours.

Liberty Harbor

Since New York City and Jersey were established, the body of water that separates them has supported thriving trade and commerce on a global scale. In its heyday, the New York Harbor was lined with dozens of docks, piers and ports that dominated the local economy. Today, this harbour reflects the stunning skyline of Manhattan, which includes One World Trade Center. To get the most out of this water wonderland, access the water from Jersey City on Liberty Harbor.

Liberty State Park

Less than a mile across the water from Ellis Island on the New Jersey Mainland, Liberty State Park gives visitors a pleasant getaway from the bustle of urban life. Tourists can visit the Liberty Science Center, which hosting an array of fun and interactive exhibits for visitors of all ages. The park also is home to the Empty Sky 9/11 Memorial, commemorating the fateful 2001 attack of the World Trade Center in Manhattan across the harbor.

FOR MORE INFORMATION

Visit New Jersey, 609-599-6540, www.visitnj.org

Cape May Chamber of Commerce, 609-884-5508, www.capemaychamber.com

Casino Reinvestment Development Authority, 609-348-7100, www.atlanticcitynj.com

Visit Liberty State Park, www.visitnj.org/article/liberty-state-park

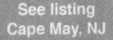

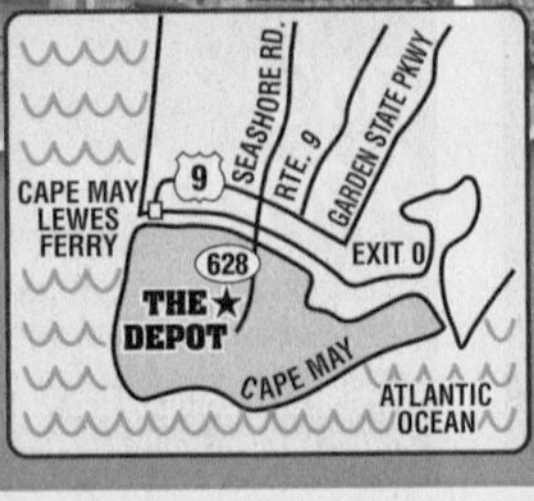

New Jersey

ANDOVER — B3 *Sussex*

PANTHER LAKE CAMPING RESORT **Ratings: 8/8★/9** (Campground) 117 Avail: 34 full hkups, 83 W, 83 E (30/50 amps). 2021 rates: $65 to $85. Apr 15 to Oct 31. (973)347-4440, 6 Panther Lake Rd, Andover, NJ 07821

ASBURY — B2 *Warren*

JUGTOWN MOUNTAIN CAMPSITES **Ratings: 6/8.5★/7** (Campground) 55 Avail: 55 W, 55 E (30/50 amps). 2021 rates: $41 to $45. (908)735-5995, 1074 Hwy 173, Asbury, NJ 08802

BARNEGAT — D4 *Ocean*

BROOKVILLE CAMPGROUND

Ratings: 5.5/8★/8 (Campground) From North: Jct of Garden State Pkwy & Exit 69 (CR 532), W 3.5 mi on CR 532 to Brookville Rd (CR 611), S 1.1 mi to Jones Rd, E 0.4 mi (E); or From South: Jct of Garden State Pkwy & Exit 67 (SR-72), NW 5.3 mi on SR-72 to CR-554, E 0.9 mi to Brookville Rd (CR 611), N 0.8 mi to Jones Rd, E 0.4 mi (E). **FAC:** gravel rds. (80 spaces). Avail: 43 gravel, back-ins (30x50), 43 full hkups (30 amps), seasonal sites, tent sites, dump, fire rings, firewood. **REC:** pool, Brookville Lake: fishing, boating nearby, playground. Pets OK. 2021 rates: $55. Apr 15 to Oct 30. no cc.
(609)698-3134 Lat: 39.778808, Lon: -74.300572
224 Jones Road - 109, Barnegat, NJ 08005
brookvillecampgrounds.com
See ad this page

LONG BEACH RV RESORT **Ratings: 8.5/9.5★/9** (RV Park) 11 Avail: 11 W, 11 E (30/50 amps). 2021 rates: $60 to $96. Apr 01 to Nov 01. (609)698-5684, 30 Route 72, Barnegat, NJ 08005

BAYVILLE — D4 *Ocean*

CEDAR CREEK CAMPGROUND **Ratings: 8/8.5★/8** (Campground) 105 Avail: 70 full hkups, 35 W, 35 E (30/50 amps). 2021 rates: $56 to $67. (732)269-1413, 1052 Atlantic City Blvd, Bayville, NJ 08721

BLAIRSTOWN — B3 *Warren*

TRIPLEBROOK CAMPING RESORT

good sam park

Ratings: 8.5/9★/9.5 (Campground) From Jct of I-80 & CR-521 (exit 12/Hope), S 1.2 mi on CR-521 to CR-609, W 3.2 mi to Nightingale Rd, N 1.2 mi to Honey Run Rd, E 0.5 mi, follow signs (L). **FAC:** paved/gravel rds. (208 spaces). 93 Avail: 50 gravel, 43 grass, 2 pull-thrus, (40x50), back-ins (40x60), 18 full hkups, 75 W, 75 E (30/50 amps), seasonal sites, WiFi @ sites, $, tent sites, rentals, dump, mobile sewer, laundry, groc, LP gas, fire rings, firewood, controlled access. **REC:** pool, hot tub, pond, fishing, boating nearby, shuffleboard, playground, hunting nearby. Pet restrict (B/Q). Partial handicap access. Big rig sites, eco-friendly. 2021 rates: $57 to $70. Apr 17 to Oct 20. ATM.
(908)459-4079 Lat: 40.91205, Lon: -75.01910
58 Honey Run Rd, Blairstown, NJ 07825
triplebrook.com
See ad this page

BRANCHVILLE — A3 *Sussex*

HARMONY RIDGE CAMPGROUND **Ratings: 7/8★/7.5** (Campground) 55 Avail: 55 W, 55 E (30 amps). 2021 rates: $50. (973)948-4941, 23 Risdon Dr, Branchville, NJ 07826

KYMER'S CAMPING RESORT **Ratings: 8/8.5/9** (Campground) 150 Avail: 40 full hkups, 110 W, 110 E (30 amps). 2021 rates: $52 to $58. Apr 01 to Oct 31. (973)875-3167, 69 Kymer Rd, Branchville, NJ 07826

STOKES

(Public State Park) From jct CR-519 & US-206: Go 3 mi NW on US-206. **FAC:** Avail: 82 dirt, tent sites, rentals, pit toilets, fire rings, firewood. **REC:** Stony Lake: swim, fishing, kayaking/canoeing, playground, hunting nearby. 2021 rates: $20 to $25. Apr 01 to Oct 31. no cc.
(973)948-3820 Lat: 41.18448, Lon: -74.797027
NULL, Branchville, NJ 07826
www.state.nj.us

FAMILY CAMPING TIPS: Choose a destination oriented camping spot. Make your plans well in advance, and expect a crowd. Break up long drives. Pack according to your space and needs. Relax, have fun, enjoy yourself.

BUENA — E2 *Atlantic*

BUENA VISTA CAMPGROUND (Campground) (Rebuilding) 385 Avail: 106 full hkups, 279 W, 279 E (20/30 amps). 2021 rates: $50 to $60. Apr 01 to Oct 31. (856)697-5555, 775 Harding Hwy, Box A-2, Buena, NJ 08310

CAPE MAY — F2 *Cape May*

BEACHCOMBER CAMPING RESORT **Ratings: 8.5/9★/10** (Campground) 200 Avail: 180 full hkups, 20 W, 20 E (30/50 amps). 2021 rates: $50 to $96. Apr 10 to Nov 03. (609)886-6035, 462 Seashore Rd, Cape May, NJ 08204

HOLLY SHORES CAMPING RESORT **Ratings: 9.5/9.5★/10** (Campground) 171 Avail: 164 full hkups, 7 W, 7 E (30/50 amps). 2021 rates: $49 to $93. Apr 06 to Nov 04. (877)494-6559, 491 US Route 9 , Cape May, NJ 08204

SEASHORE CAMPSITES & RV RESORT **Ratings: 9/9★/9.5** (Campground) 215 Avail: 88 full hkups, 127 W, 127 E (30/50 amps). 2021 rates: $89 to $96. Apr 15 to Oct 31. (888)478-8799, 720 Seashore Rd, Cape May, NJ 08204

SUN OUTDOORS CAPE MAY **Ratings: 8.5/8.5★/10** (Campground) 263 Avail: 95 full hkups, 168 W, 168 E (20/50 amps). 2021 rates: $52 to $131. Apr 01 to Oct 31. (609)884-3567, 669 Rte 9, Cape May, NJ 08204

THE DEPOT TRAVEL PARK

Ratings: 7.5/10★/10 (Campground) From Jct of Garden State Pkwy & SR-109 (Exit 0), NW 0.6 mi on SR-109 to US-9, W 0.4 mi to Seashore Rd, changes to Broadway (Rte 626), S 1.8 mi (R).

A SHORT WALK TO CAPE MAY BEACHES!
Closest campground to Cape May beaches and all the attractions that make Cape May one of the most popular places to vacation in southern New Jersey! We have the facilities to provide you with a relaxing and affordable stay.

FAC: paved rds. (240 spaces). Avail: 150 grass, 2 pull-thrus, (30x60), back-ins (30x45), 113 full hkups, 37 W, 37 E (30/50 amps), seasonal sites, cable, WiFi @ sites, tent sites, rentals, dump, laundry, LP gas, firewood, controlled access. **REC:** boating nearby, playground. Pets OK. Partial handicap access, eco-friendly. 2021 rates: $44 to $79. May 01 to Nov 01. ATM, no cc.
(609)884-2533 Lat: 38.94340, Lon: -74.92953
800 Broadway, West Cape May, NJ 08204
thedepottravelpark.com
See ad opposite page

CAPE MAY COUNTY — F2 *Cape May*

A SPOTLIGHT Introducing Cape May's wonderful attractions appearing at the front of this state section.

CAPE MAY COURT HOUSE — F2 *Cape May*

ADVENTURE BOUND CAMPING RESORTS-CAPE MAY **Ratings: 8/8.5★/8.5** (Campground) 150 Avail: 13 full hkups, 137 W, 137 E (30/50 amps). 2021 rates: $69 to $89. Apr 01 to Oct 10. (609)465-4440, 240 W Shellbay Ave, Cape May Court House, NJ 08210

AVALON CAMPGROUND Ratings: 9/8.5★/9.5 (Campground) 37 Avail: 14 full hkups, 23 W, 23 E (30/50 amps). 2021 rates: $49 to $80. Apr 14 to Oct 15. (609)624-0075, 1917 Rte 9 N, Cape May Court House, NJ 08210

BIG TIMBER LAKE RV CAMPING RESORT **Ratings: 9/9★/9.5** (Campground) 121 Avail: 120 full hkups, 1 W, 1 E (30/50 amps). 2021 rates: $80 to $108. Apr 15 to Oct 21. (800)206-3232, 116 Swainton-Goshen Rd, Cape May Court House, NJ 08210

KING NUMMY TRAIL CAMPGROUND

good sam park

Ratings: 6.5/10★/9 (Campground) 39 Avail: 4 full hkups, 35 W, 35 E (30/50 amps). 2021 rates: $60 to $85. Apr 15 to Oct 27. (888)563-7040, 205 S Delsea Dr, Cape May Court House, NJ 08210

SHELLBAY FAMILY CAMPING RESORT **Ratings: 9/9.5★/9** (Campground) 50 Avail: 10 full hkups, 40 W, 40 E (30/50 amps). 2021 rates: $60. May 15 to Sep 30. (609)465-4770, 227 W Shellbay Ave, Cape May Court House, NJ 08210

CENTERTON — E2 *Salem*

PARVIN (Public State Park) From Jct of SR-47 & CR-540, W 5 mi on Almond Rd. (L). 54 Avail. 2021 rates: $20 to $25. Apr 01 to Oct 31. (856)358-8616

CHATSWORTH — D3 *Burlington*

WADING PINES CAMPING RESORT **Ratings: 7.5/8.5★/8.5** (Campground) 184 Avail: 40 full hkups, 144 W, 144 E (30/50 amps). 2021 rates: $45 to $80. Apr 01 to Nov 01. (888)726-1313, 85 Godfrey Bridge Rd, Chatsworth, NJ 08019

We've listened to thousands of RVers like you, so we know exactly how to rate campgrounds. Got feedback? Call us! 877-209-6655.

New Jersey Privately Owned Campground Information Updated by our Good Sam Representatives

Bruce & Dianne Richardson

We love our latest life chapter traveling this beautiful country with our fur babies, Lexi (German shepherd) and Bear (mini Labradoodle)! Every day is an adventure and an opportunity to make friends and beautiful memories. Our 11 grandchildren love facetiming with us.

CLARKSBORO — D2 *Gloucester*

PHILADELPHIA SOUTH/CLARKSBORO KOA **Ratings: 9/9.5★/9.5** (Campground) Avail: 71 full hkups (30/50 amps). 2021 rates: $64 to $86. (856)423-6677, 117 Timberlane Road, Clarksboro, NJ 08020

CLERMONT — F3 *Cape May*

DRIFTWOOD RV RESORT & CAMPGROUND **Ratings: 9.5/9.5★/9.5** (Campground) 35 Avail: 30 full hkups, 5 W, 5 E (30/50 amps). 2021 rates: $55 to $115. Apr 16 to Oct 18. (877)600-6121, 1955 Route 9, Clermont, NJ 08210

DRIFTWOOD TOO CAMPING RESORT **Ratings: 10/9.5★/10** (Campground) Avail: 20 full hkups (30/50 amps). 2021 rates: $55 to $72. Mar 05 to Nov 30. (609)624-9015, 1142 Rte 83, Cape May Court House, NJ 08210

CLINTON — B2 *Hunterdon*

SPRUCE RUN SRA (Public State Park) From Jct of I-78 & Hwy 31 (Clinton exit), N 3.2 mi on Hwy 31 to Van Syckels Rd, W 1 mi (L). 67 Avail. 2021 rates: $20 to $25. Apr 01 to Oct 31. (908)638-8572

COLESVILLE — A3 *Sussex*

HIGH POINT (Public State Park) From town: Go 3 mi N on Hwy-23. 50 Avail. 2021 rates: $20 to $25. Apr 01 to Oct 31. (973)875-4800

COLUMBIA — B2 *Warren*

CAMP TAYLOR CAMPGROUND **Ratings: 6.5/9★/8.5** (Campground) 60 Avail: 60 W, 60 E (30/50 amps). 2021 rates: $37 to $47. Apr 15 to Oct 24. (908)496-4333, 85 Mt. Pleasant Rd, Columbia, NJ 07832

DELAWARE RIVER FAMILY CAMPGROUND
good sam park
Ratings: 7.5/7.5/8.5 (Campground) 48 Avail: 48 W, 48 E (30/50 amps). 2021 rates: $58 to $69. Apr 01 to Oct 31. (908)475-4517, 100 Rt 46, Columbia, NJ 07832

WORTHINGTON (Public State Park) From jct Hwy 80 & River Rd: Go 6-3/4 mi N on River Rd/Old Mine Rd. (L). 52 Avail. 2021 rates: $20 to $25. Apr 01 to Dec 31. (908)841-9575

DOROTHY — E2 *Atlantic*

COUNTRY OAKS CAMPGROUND
good sam park
Ratings: 9/9.5★/10 (Campground) From Jct of Rte 50 & Rte 40 (in May's Landing), S 1.1 mi on Rte 50 to Rte 669 (11th Ave), SW 5.5 mi to S Jersey (turn before RR tracks), NW 1.2 mi (R). **FAC:** gravel rds. (140 spaces). Avail: 45 gravel, patios, 15 pull-thrus, (30x70), back-ins (32x40), 43 full hkups, 2 W, 2 E (30/50 amps), seasonal sites, cable, WiFi @ sites, tent sites, rentals, dump, laundry, groc, LP gas, fire rings, firewood, controlled access. **REC:** pool, wading pool, playground. Pets OK. Big rig sites, eco-friendly. 2021 rates: $58 to $65. Apr 15 to Oct 15.
(609)476-2143 Lat: 39.41626, Lon: -74.83604
13 S Jersey Avenue, Dorothy, NJ 08317
countryoakscampground.com
See ad this page

EGG HARBOR CITY — E3 *Atlantic*

EGG HARBOR LAKE CAMPGROUND (Public) From Jct of US 322 & SR-50 (CR-563), N 7.7 mi on SR-50 (CR-563) (R). 40 Avail: 40 W, 40 E (30 amps). 2021 rates: $51. May 27 to Oct 01. (609)965-0330

HOLLY ACRES CAMPGROUND
good sam park
Ratings: 8.5/10★/7.5 (Campground) Avail: 60 full hkups (30/50 amps). 2021 rates: $42 to $59. Apr 15 to Oct 31. (609)965-5055, 218 Frankfurt Ave, Egg Harbor City, NJ 08215

New to RVing? Visit Blog.GoodSam.com for tips on everything camping and RVing.

ELMER — E2 *Salem*

ADVENTURE BOUND CAMPING RESORT TALL PINES **Ratings: 8/9★/8.5** (Campground) 51 Avail: 31 full hkups, 20 W, 20 E (30/50 amps). 2021 rates: $119 to $130. Apr 01 to Oct 31. (856)451-7479, 49 Beal Rd, Elmer, NJ 08318

ESTELL MANOR — E3 *Cumberland*

PLEASANT VALLEY FAMILY CAMPGROUND **Ratings: 8.5/9★/9** (Campground) Avail: 14 full hkups (30/50 amps). 2021 rates: $65. Apr 15 to Oct 15. (609)625-1238, 60 South River Rd, Mays Landing, NJ 08319

FARMINGDALE — C4 *Monmouth*

ALLAIRE (Public State Park) From town, S 3 mi on CR-524 (L); or I-195 exit 31A. 45 Avail. 2021 rates: $20 to $25. (732)938-2371

FLANDERS — B2 *Morris*

FLA-NET PARK
good sam park
Ratings: 7/7/7 (RV Park) 12 Avail: 10 full hkups, 2 W, 2 E (30/50 amps). 2021 rates: $45 to $60. (973)347-4467, 10 Flanders Netcong Rd, Flanders, NJ 07836

FREEHOLD — C4 *Monmouth*

PINE CONE RESORT **Ratings: 8.5/8.5★/9.5** (Campground) 85 Avail: 44 full hkups, 41 W, 41 E (30/50 amps). 2021 rates: $55 to $65. (732)462-2230, 340 Georgia Rd., Freehold, NJ 07728

TURKEY SWAMP PARK (Public) From Jct of I-195 & Jackson Mills Rd (exit 22), N 2.5 mi on Jackson Mills Rd to Georgia Rd, W 0.9 mi to park entrance. 64 Avail: 64 W, 64 E (20/30 amps). 2021 rates: $35 to $39. (732)462-7286

GALLOWAY — E3 *Atlantic*

POMONA RV PARK **Ratings: 9/9★/9.5** (Campground) Avail: 65 full hkups (30/50 amps). 2021 rates: $56 to $66. (609)965-2123, 536 S. Pomona Rd, Galloway, NJ 08240

SHADY PINES RV RESORT **Ratings: 9.5/9★/9.5** (RV Park) 28 Avail: 27 full hkups, 1 W, 1 E (30/50 amps). 2021 rates: $60 to $72. (609)652-1516, 443 S 6th Ave, Galloway Township, NJ 08205

GREAT MEADOWS — B2 *Warren*

JENNY JUMP (Public State Park) From jct US 46 & Hwy 611: Go 5 mi NW on Hwy 611 to Far View Rd. 22 Avail. 2021 rates: $20 to $25. Apr 01 to Oct 31. (908)459-4366

GREEN CREEK — F2 *Cape May*

ACORN CAMPGROUND
good sam park
Ratings: 8/8★/8 (Campground) 90 Avail: 25 full hkups, 65 W, 65 E (20/30 amps). 2021 rates: $65. May 20 to Sep 08. (888)563-7040, 419 Delsea Dr S, Green Creek, NJ 08210

HACKETTSTOWN — B2 *Warren*

STEPHENS (Public State Park) From town: Go 2 mi N on Willow Grove Rd. 40 Avail. 2021 rates: $20 to $25. Apr 01 to Oct 31. (908)852-3790

HAMMONTON — E2 *Atlantic*

WHARTON/ATSION FAMILY CAMPGROUND (Public State Park) From Jct of Rtes 30 & 206, N 7 mi on Rte 206 to Atsion Rd (R). 50 Avail. 2021 rates: $20 to $25. (609)268-0444

WHARTON/GODFREY BRIDGE CAMPGROUND (Public State Park) From jct US 30 & CR 542: Go 15 mi NE on CR 542 & CR 563. 34 Avail: Pit toilets. 2021 rates: $3 to $5. (609)561-0024

HIGH BRIDGE — B2 *Hunterdon*

VOORHEES (Public State Park) From town, N 2 mi on Hwy 513 (L). 47 Avail: Pit toilets. 2021 rates: $20 to $25. Apr 01 to Oct 31. (908)638-8572

JACKSON — C3 *Monmouth*

BUTTERFLY CAMPING RESORT **Ratings: 9/9★/9.5** (Campground) 92 Avail: 45 full hkups, 47 W, 47 E (30/50 amps). 2021 rates: $62 to $76. Apr 05 to Oct 16. (732)928-2107, 360 Butterfly Rd, Jackson, NJ 08527

INDIAN ROCK RV PARK
good sam park
Ratings: 8.5/8/8.5 (Campground) Avail: 50 full hkups (30/50 amps). 2021 rates: $75 to $95. (732)928-0034, 920 West Veterans Hwy, Jackson, NJ 08527

TIMBERLAND LAKE CAMPGROUND
good sam park
Ratings: 7/8.5★/9 (Campground) 140 Avail: 65 full hkups, 75 W, 75 E (30/50 amps). 2021 rates: $55 to $65. (732)928-0500, 1335 Reed Rd, Cream Ridge, NJ 08514

TIP TAM CAMPING RESORT
good sam park
Ratings: 9/9★/9.5 (Campground) 48 Avail: 36 full hkups, 12 W, 12 E (30/50 amps). 2021 rates: $51 to $69. Apr 15 to Oct 31. (732)363-4036, 301 Brewers Bridge Rd, Jackson, NJ 08527

JERSEY CITY — B4 *Hudson*

LIBERTY HARBOR MARINA & RV PARK
Ratings: 7.5/9.5★/6.5 (RV Park) From Jct of NJ Tpk I-95, (North or South), to Exit 14C (Holland Tunnel exit) I-78 E, 8.7 mi on I-78 E to Marin Blvd, (Last Signal/Exit before Holland Tunnel), S 1.3 mi (R).

CLOSEST RV PARK TO NEW YORK CITY
View the Statue of Liberty from your site. NY Waterway Ferry leaves from park. Enjoy the beauty of Manhattan's skyline. Close to PATH train, ferries and Hudson Bergen Light Rail. OPEN YEAR ROUND!

FAC: paved rds. 70 Avail: 16 paved, 54 gravel, back-ins (18x45), 50 W, 50 E (30/50 amps), WiFi @ sites, tent sites, dump, mobile sewer, laundry, restaurant, controlled access. **REC:** Hudson River: fishing, marina, kayaking/canoeing, boating nearby. Pets OK. Partial handicap access, eco-friendly. 2021 rates: $110 to $120.
(201)516-7500 Lat: 40.71222, Lon: -74.04333
11 Marin Blvd, Jersey City, NJ 07302
www.libertyharborrv.com
See ad page 638

JERSEY SHORE — C6 *Lycoming*

JERSEY SHORE AREA See also Barnegat, Egg Harbor City, Galloway, Little Egg Harbor, Ocean View, Port Republic, Tuckerton & West Creek.

LAKEWOOD — D4 *Ocean*

Travel Services

CAMPING WORLD OF LAKEWOOD/NEW JERSEY As the nation's largest retailer of RV supplies, accessories, services and new and used RVs, Camping World is committed to making your total RV experience better. **SERVICES:** RV, tire, MH mechanical, staffed RV wash, restrooms. RV Sales. RV supplies, RV accessible. Hours: 9am to 7pm.
(888)875-0398 Lat: 40.04927, Lon: -74.22071
1359 US Hwy 9 (River Ave), Lakewood, NJ 08701
www.campingworld.com

LITTLE EGG HARBOR — E3 *Ocean*

BAKER'S ACRES **Ratings: 8/8.5★/9** (Campground) 70 Avail: 19 full hkups, 51 W, 51 E (30/50 amps). 2021 rates: $45 to $60. May 01 to Oct 31. (609)296-2664, 230 Willets Ave, Little Egg Harbor, NJ 08087

MARMORA — F3 *Cape May*

WHIPPOORWILL CAMPGROUND **Ratings: 9/10★/9** (Campground) 50 Avail: 40 full hkups, 10 W, 10 E (30/50 amps). 2021 rates: $81.50. Apr 01 to Oct 31. (609)390-3458, 810 S Shore Rd, Marmora, NJ 08223

MATAWAN — C4 *Middlesex*

CHEESEQUAKE (Public State Park) From Jct of Garden State Pkwy & Matawan Rd (exit 120), follow signs (E) 11 ft height restriction for vehicles entering camping area. 53 Avail. 2021 rates: $20 to $25. Apr 01 to Oct 31. (732)566-2161

RV Tech Tips - Battery Cable Connections: Some vehicles require the negative battery cable to be disconnected when being towed to prevent the dash lights from draining the battery. There are electronic devices and switches available to prevent this problem, but they can be costly and have their own potential problems. One solution is to replace the battery cable bolt with a quick-release seat binder bolt from a bicycle shop. These bolts generally come in two lengths; the shorter one will work the best. With the seat binder bolt installed, the disconnect and reconnect that used to take minutes, has been reduced to seconds.

MAYS LANDING — E3 *Atlantic*

MAYS LANDING CAMPGROUND
Ratings: 9/9★/8.5 (Campground) Avail: 58 full hkups (30/50 amps). 2021 rates: $44 to $78. Apr 01 to Oct 31. (888)563-7040, 1079 12th Ave, Mays Landing, NJ 08330

MONROEVILLE — E2 *Salem*

OLD CEDAR CAMP **Ratings: 9/8.5★/9** (Campground) 97 Avail: 84 full hkups, 13 W, 13 E (30/50 amps). 2021 rates: $38 to $40. Apr 20 to Oct 08. (856)358-4881, 274 Richwood Rd, Monroeville, NJ 08343

MONTAGUE — A3 *Sussex*

ROCKVIEW VALLEY CAMPGROUND AND RESORT **Ratings: 5.5/5.5/7.5** (Campground) 30 Avail: 30 W, 30 E (20/30 amps). 2021 rates: $40 to $50. May 01 to Oct 15. (973)293-3383, 59 River Rd, Montague, NJ 07827

NEW GRETNA — E3 *Burlington*

BASS RIVER (Public State Park) N-bnd: From Jct Garden State Pkwy & SR-9 (exit 50), N 2.5 mi on SR-9 to Greenbush Rd (in town), N 1.5 mi to Stage Rd (R); or S-bnd: From Jct Garden State Pkwy & Greenbush Rd (exit 52), S 1.5 mi on Greenbush to Stage Rd, N 0.5 mi (L). 176 Avail. 2021 rates: $20 to $25. (609)296-1114

TIMBERLINE LAKE CAMPING RESORT **Ratings: 7.5/7.5/8.5** (Campground) 30 Avail: 3 full hkups, 27 W, 27 E (30/50 amps). 2021 rates: $60 to $70. May 01 to Oct 15. (609)296-7900, 365 Rte. 679, New Gretna, NJ 08224

NEWTON — A3 *Sussex*

SWARTSWOOD (Public State Park) From Jct of CH-519 & CH-622, W 4.2 mi. Turn left onto Rt 619 1/2 mi S. 65 Avail. 2021 rates: $20 to $25. Apr 01 to Oct 31. (973)383-5230

THE GREAT DIVIDE CAMPGROUND **Ratings: 8.5/9.5★/9.5** (Campground) 27 Avail: 20 full hkups, 7 W, 7 E (20/30 amps). 2021 rates: $70 to $100. May 01 to Oct 14. (973)383-4026, 68 Phillips Rd, Newton, NJ 07860

NORTHFIELD — E3 *Atlantic*

BIRCH GROVE PARK & FAMILY CAMPGROUND (CITY PARK) (Public) From jct US-322 & US-9: Go 2 mi S on US-9, then 1/4 mi W on Hwy 662 (Mill Rd), then 1/8 mi N on Burton Rd. 50 Avail. 2021 rates: $25 to $35. Apr 01 to Sep 30. (609)641-3778

OCEAN VIEW — F3 *Cape May*

ECHO FARMS RV RESORT
Ratings: 8.5/8.5★/9 (RV Park) Avail: 15 full hkups (30/50 amps). 2021 rates: $71 to $82. Apr 15 to Oct 31. (888)563-7040, 3066 US Rt 9, Ocean View, NJ 08230

Get the GOOD SAM CAMPING APP

FRONTIER CAMPGROUND **Ratings: 6.5/9★/8.5** (Campground) 76 Avail: 13 full hkups, 63 W, 63 E (30/50 amps). 2021 rates: $60 to $110. Apr 15 to Oct 13. (609)390-3649, 84 Tyler Rd, Ocean View, NJ 08230

LAKE & SHORE RV
Ratings: 9/8.5★/9 (Membership Park) Avail: 75 full hkups (30/50 amps). 2021 rates: $70. (888)563-7040, 515 Corson Tavern Road, Ocean View, NJ 08230

OCEAN VIEW RESORT CAMPGROUND Ratings: 9.5/10★/9.5 (Campground) Avail: 475 full hkups (30/50 amps). 2021 rates: $49.80 to $110. Apr 01 to Oct 08. (609)624-1675, 2555 Rte 9 N, Ocean View, NJ 08230

SEA GROVE CAMPING RESORT Ratings: 9/9★/9 (Campground) 60 Avail: 50 full hkups, 10 W, 10 E (30/50 amps). 2021 rates: $42 to $70. Apr 01 to Nov 01. (609)624-3529, 2665 Route 9, Ocean View, NJ 08230

TAMERLANE CAMPGROUND **Ratings: 8.5/8★/7.5** (Campground) Avail: 20 full hkups (30/50 amps). 2021 rates: $48. Apr 01 to Oct 01. (609)624-0767, 2241 US-9, Ocean View, NJ 08230

PEMBERTON — D3 *Burlington*

BRENDAN T BYRNE (Public State Park) From town, SW 17 mi on Rte 70, follow signs (L). 82 Avail. 2021 rates: $20 to $25. Mar 30 to Oct 31. (609)726-1191

PORT REPUBLIC — E3 *Atlantic*

ATLANTIC BLUEBERRY RV PARK **Ratings: 8.5/10★/9.5** (Campground) 61 Avail: 3 full hkups, 58 W, 58 E (30/50 amps). 2021 rates: $55.95 to $58.95. Apr 01 to Oct 30. (609)652-1644, 283 Clarks Landing Rd, Port Republic, NJ 08241

CHESTNUT LAKE RV CAMPGROUND
Ratings: 8/8.5★/9 (Membership Park) 143 Avail: 75 full hkups, 68 W, 68 E (30/50 amps). 2021 rates: $58 to $85. Apr 22 to Oct 17. (888)563-7040, 631 Chestnut Neck Rd, Port Republic, NJ 08241

SUSSEX — A3 *Sussex*

PLEASANT ACRES FARM RV RESORT **Ratings: 8.5/7/7** (Campground) Avail: 130 full hkups (30/50 amps). 2021 rates: $75 to $85. Apr 01 to Oct 31. (888)611-0923, 61 Dewitt Rd, Sussex, NJ 07461

WOODLAND TRAILS CAMPGROUND **Ratings: 6.5/8.5★/8.5** (Campground) Avail: 10 full hkups (30/50 amps). 2021 rates: $90 to $150. May 01 to Oct 31. (973)702-8167, 7 Babtown Road, Sussex, NJ 07461

SWAINTON — F2 *Cape May*

SEA PINES RV RESORT & CAMPGROUND
Ratings: 8.5/8★/8 (Membership Park) 228 Avail: 70 full hkups, 158 W, 158 E (30/50 amps). 2021 rates: $65 to $85. May 11 to Oct 08. (888)563-7040, 1535 Rte 9, Swainton, NJ 08210

SWEDESBORO — E2 *Gloucester*

Travel Services

CAMPING WORLD OF SWEDESBORO/BRIDGEPORT As the nation's largest retailer of RV supplies, accessories, services and new and used RVs, Camping World is committed to making your total RV experience better. **SERVICES:** tire, staffed RV wash, restrooms. RV Sales. RV supplies, LP gas, emergency parking, RV accessible. Hours: 9am - 7pm. (888)920-9140 Lat: 39.768010, Lon: -75.354239 602 Heron Dr, Swedesboro, NJ 08085 www.campingworld.com

TOMS RIVER — D4 *Ocean*

SURF N STREAM CAMPGROUND **Ratings: 8/8★/8** (Campground) 75 Avail: 60 full hkups, 15 W, 15 E (30/50 amps). 2021 rates: $58 to $78. (732)349-8919, 1801 Ridgeway Rd, Toms River, NJ 08757

TUCKERTON — E3 *Ocean*

ATLANTIC SHORE PINES CAMPGROUND
Ratings: 8/10★/9.5 (Campground) 88 Avail: 45 full hkups, 43 W, 43 E (30/50 amps). 2021 rates: $63 to $70. Apr 01 to Nov 01. (609)296-9163, 450 Ishmael Rd, Tuckerton, NJ 08087

WEST CREEK — E4 *Ocean*

SEA PIRATE CAMPGROUND **Ratings: 8.5/10★/9.5** (Campground) 81 Avail: 58 full hkups, 23 W, 23 E (30/50 amps). 2021 rates: $81.39 to $91.39. May 12 to Oct 09. (609)296-7400, 148 Main Street, West Creek, NJ 08092

WILLIAMSTOWN — E2 *Glouster*

HOSPITALITY CREEK CAMPGROUND **Ratings: 9/9★/9** (Campground) 55 Avail: 29 full hkups, 26 W, 26 E (30/50 amps). 2021 rates: $110 to $200. Apr 20 to Oct 07. (856)629-5140, 117 Coles Mill Rd, Williamstown, NJ 08094

WOODBINE — F2 *Cape May*

BELLEPLAIN (Public State Park) From Jct of Cnty Rtes 550/557, NW 1.4 mi on CR-550 (L). 169 Avail. 2021 rates: $20 to $25. (609)861-2404

WOODPORT — A3 *Morris*

MAHLON DICKERSON RESERVATION (MORRIS COUNTY PARK) (Public) From jct I-80 (exit 34) & Hwy 15: Go 5 mi N on Hwy 15, then 4 mi E on Weldon Rd. 18 Avail: 18 W, 18 E (30/50 amps). 2021 rates: $20. Mar 01 to Nov 30. (973)697-3140

WOODSTOWN — E1 *Salem*

FOUR SEASONS FAMILY CAMPGROUND **Ratings: 9/8.5/8** (Campground) 217 Avail: 165 full hkups, 52 W, 52 E (30/50 amps). 2021 rates: $70. (856)769-3635, 158 Woodstown-Daretown Rd, Pilesgrove, NJ 08098

We shine ""Spotlights'' on interesting cities and areas.

Getty Images/iStockphoto

DID YOU KNOW?

New Mexico's first wine grapes were planted by monks back in 1629, making it the oldest wine-making state in the country.

NM

YOU ARE HERE

New Mexico

The scenery, food and culture found in the Land of Enchantment can cast a spell on visitors. Immerse yourself in the magic of Native American, Spanish and Mexican history found throughout the diverse region.

Cities From the Past

Santa Fe has roots that stretch back to Spanish colonization, and its architecture and culture bear traces of that distant past. Per city ordinance, modern buildings must conform to an adobe style, giving the city a look that aligns with its heritage. New and old intermingle seamlessly. Traditional Native American arts markets stand beside modern galleries. Street vendors sell tamales on sidewalks beside fine restaurants.

Sands That Stretch into Infinity

Stand in a sea of sand that stretches to the horizon. Head to White Sands National Monument, where an expanse of rolling dunes fills a 275-square-mile patch of the Tularosa Basin. Take a driving tour, hike it or hit the sands on a sled to experience its beauty.

Albuquerque Icons

As high as Denver and surrounded by beauty, Albuquerque is the state's biggest city and filled with iconic sites. See spots where the hit TV show, "Breaking Bad," was filmed and take a dive into Americana on the Route 66 corridor. Visit the Old Town area or see modern museums. Take the tram up to Sandia Peak for an 11,000-square-mile panoramic view.

Make Elephant Memories

Like an oasis in the desert, this popular desert watering hole will fulfill your appetite for boating and fishing. For recreation on the water, Elephant Butte Lake and Navajo Lake state parks are popular choices. Paddlers seeking serene waters and natural beauty will find both at Abiquiu Lake or the Gila River, each one offering unparalleled landscapes.

New Mexico Carne Adovada Pork

Marinated for 24 hours and slowly braised in a red chile bath, carne adovada pork is a local delicacy that can be enjoyed any time of day. Fold the fiery red meat into burritos, add it in omelets or eat it on its own with a side of beans and rice. You won't find these great flavors anywhere else.

VISITOR CENTER

TIME ZONE
Mountain Standard

ROAD & HIGHWAY INFORMATION
800-432-4269
dot.state.nm.us

FISHING & HUNTING & BOATING INFORMATION
wildlife.state.nm.us

NATIONAL PARKS
nps.gov/nm

STATE PARKS
emnrd.state.nm.us/SPD/

TOURISM INFORMATION
New Mexico Tourism Department
505-827-7400
newmexico.org

TOP TOURISM ATTRACTIONS
1) White Sands National Monument
2) Carlsbad Caverns National Park
3) Georgia O'Keeffe Museum

MAJOR CITIES
Albuquerque, Las Cruces, Rio Rancho, Santa Fe (capital), Roswell

good sam park

Featured Good Sam Parks

NEW MEXICO

When you stay with Good Sam, you can expect the highest degree of cleanliness and friendliness, and better yet, you get **10% off** overnight campground fees.

If you're not already a Good Sam member you can purchase your membership at one of these locations:

ALAMOGORDO
Boot Hill RV Resort
White Sands Manufactured Home and RV Community

ALBUQUERQUE
Balloon View RV Park
Coronado Village RV Resort
Enchanted Trails RV Park & Trading Post
Isleta Lakes & RV Park
Route 66 RV Resort

BERNARDO
Kiva RV Park & Horse Motel

CARLSBAD
Bonnie & Clyde's Getaway RV Park
Bud's Place RV Park & Cabins
Carlsbad RV Park & Campground
Sun West Mobile City

CHAMA
Rio Chama RV Park
Sky Mountain Resort RV Park

CLOVIS
Clovis Point RV Stables & Storage
Clovis RV Park
Traveler's World RV Park

DEMING
Little Vineyard RV Resort
Roadrunner RV Park of Deming

ELEPHANT BUTTE
Cedar Cove RV Park
Cedar Cove RV Park Too
Elephant Butte Lake RV Resort

GALLUP
USA RV Park

GRANTS
Bar S RV Park
Blue Spruce RV Park
Lavaland RV Park

KIRTLAND
Homestead RV Park

LAS CRUCES
Hacienda RV Resort
Sunny Acres RV Park

MORIARTY
Cuervo Mountain RV Park and Horse Hotel

RIO RANCHO
Stagecoach Stop RV Park

ROSWELL
Town & Country RV Park

RUIDOSO
Eagle Creek RV Resort
Midtown Mountain Campground & RV Park
Twin Spruce RV Park

SANTA FE
Rancheros de Santa Fe Campground
Roadrunner RV Park
Santa Fe Skies RV Park

SANTA ROSA
Santa Rosa Campground

SILVER CITY
Rose Valley RV Ranch & Casitas

TRUTH OR CONSEQUENCES
Cielo Vista RV Park

TUCUMCARI
Blaze-in-Saddle RV Park & Horse Hotel
Mountain Road RV Park

10/10★/10 GOOD SAM PARK

ALBUQUERQUE
Route 66 RV Resort
(505)352-8000

What's This?

An RV park with a 10/10★/10 rating has scored perfect grades in amenities, cleanliness and appearance ("See Understanding the Campground Rating System" on pages 8 and 9 for an explanation of the trusted Good Sam Rating System). Stay in a 10/10★/10 park on your next trip for a nearly flawless camping experience.

Getty Images/iStockphoto

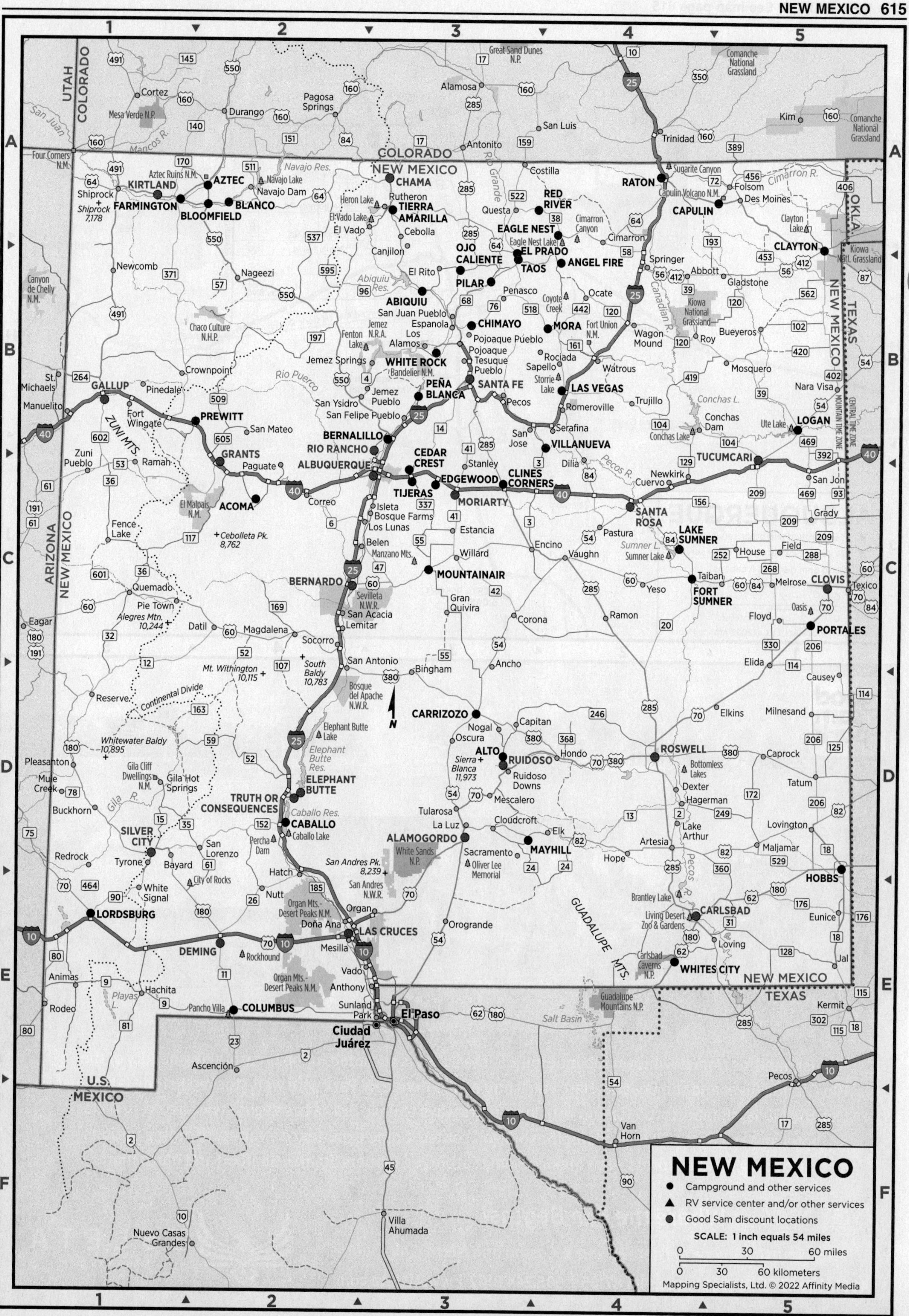
NEW MEXICO
Campground and other services
RV service center and/or other services
Good Sam discount locations
SCALE: 1 inch equals 54 miles
0 30 60 miles
0 30 60 kilometers
Mapping Specialists, Ltd. © 2022 Affinity Media
NM
UTAH
COLORADO
ARIZONA
NEW MEXICO
TEXAS
OKLA.
U.S.
MEXICO
CENTRAL TIME ZONE
MOUNTAIN TIME ZONE
Cortez
Mesa Verde N.P.
Durango
Pagosa Springs
Alamosa
Great Sand Dunes N.P.
San Luis
Antonito
Trinidad
Kim
Comanche National Grassland
Four Corners N.M.
Shiprock
Shiprock 7,178
KIRTLAND
FARMINGTON
Aztec Ruins N.M.
AZTEC
BLOOMFIELD
BLANCO
Navajo Lake
Navajo Dam
Navajo Res.
CHAMA
Heron Lake
Rutheron
El Vado Lake
El Vado
TIERRA AMARILLA
Cebolla
Canjilon
Costilla
Questa
RED RIVER
EAGLE NEST
Eagle Nest Lake
Cimarron Canyon
Cimarron
RATON
Sugarite Canyon
Capulin Volcano N.M.
CAPULIN
Folsom
Des Moines
Clayton Lake
CLAYTON
Kiowa Natl. Grassland
Newcomb
Nageezi
Chaco Culture N.H.P.
El Rito
OJO CALIENTE
EL PRADO
TAOS
ANGEL FIRE
PILAR
Abiquiu Res.
ABIQUIU
San Juan Pueblo
Espanola
Penasco
Coyote Creek
Ocate
Springer
Abbott
Gladstone
Kiowa National Grassland
Roy
Bueyeros
Fenton Lake
Jemez N.R.A.
Los Alamos
CHIMAYO
MORA
Fort Union N.M.
Wagon Mound
Pojoaque Pueblo
Pojoaque
Tesuque Pueblo
Rociada
Sapello
Storrie Lake
Watrous
Mosquero
Jemez Springs
WHITE ROCK
Bandelier N.M.
Crownpoint
St. Michaels
GALLUP
Pinedale
Manuelito
Fort Wingate
ZUNI MTS.
PREWITT
Rio Puerco
San Ysidro
Jemez Pueblo
PEÑA BLANCA
SANTA FE
Pecos
LAS VEGAS
Romeroville
Trujillo
Nara Visa
Conchas L.
Conchas Dam
Conchas Lake
Ute Lake
LOGAN
San Felipe Pueblo
San Mateo
BERNALILLO
RIO RANCHO
San Jose
Serafina
VILLANUEVA
Zuni Pueblo
Ramah
GRANTS
Paguate
ALBUQUERQUE
CEDAR CREST
Stanley
Dilia
Pecos R.
TUCUMCARI
Newkirk
Cuervo
San Jon
EDGEWOOD
CLINES CORNERS
TIJERAS
MORIARTY
El Malpais N.M.
ACOMA
Correo
Isleta
Bosque Farms
Los Lunas
SANTA ROSA
Grady
Fence Lake
Cebolleta Pk. 8,762
Belen
Estancia
Encino
Pastura
LAKE SUMNER
Sumner L.
Sumner Lake
House
Field
Manzano Mts.
Willard
Vaughn
Taiban
FORT SUMNER
Melrose
CLOVIS
Texico
Quemado
Pie Town
Alegres Mtn. 10,244
BERNARDO
MOUNTAINAIR
Sevilleta N.W.R.
San Acacia
Lemitar
Gran Quivira
Yeso
Ramon
Oasis
Floyd
PORTALES
Eagar
Datil
Magdalena
Socorro
Corona
Elida
Causey
South Baldy 10,783
San Antonio
Mt. Withington 10,115
Ancho
Bingham
Reserve
Continental Divide
Bosque del Apache N.W.R.
CARRIZOZO
Elkins
Milnesand
Elephant Butte Lake
Elephant Butte Res.
Nogal
Capitan
Oscura
Whitewater Baldy 10,895
Gila Cliff Dwellings N.M.
Gila Hot Springs
Pleasanton
Mule Creek
Buckhorn
Gila R.
ELEPHANT BUTTE
TRUTH OR CONSEQUENCES
ALTO
Sierra Blanca 11,973
RUIDOSO
Ruidoso Downs
Hondo
ROSWELL
Caprock
Bottomless Lakes
Dexter
Hagerman
Tatum
Caballo Res.
CABALLO
Caballo Lake
Tularosa
Mescalero
La Luz
Cloudcroft
Elk
Lake Arthur
Lovington
SILVER CITY
Redrock
Tyrone
Bayard
San Lorenzo
Percha Dam
ALAMOGORDO
White Sands N.P.
Sacramento
Oliver Lee Memorial
MAYHILL
Hope
Artesia
Maljamar
City of Rocks
White Signal
Hatch
San Andres Pk. 8,239
San Andres N.W.R.
Pecos R.
HOBBS
LORDSBURG
Nutt
Organ Mts.-Desert Peaks N.M.
Organ
Doña Ana
LAS CRUCES
Orogrande
GUADALUPE MTS.
Brantley Lake
Living Desert Zoo & Gardens
CARLSBAD
Eunice
DEMING
Rockhound
Mesilla
Vado
Loving
Carlsbad Caverns N.P.
WHITES CITY
Jal
Animas
Hachita
Playas L.
Rodeo
Anthony
Pancho Villa
COLUMBUS
Sunland Park
El Paso
Ciudad Juárez
Guadalupe Mountains N.P.
Salt Basin
Kermit
Ascención
Pecos
Van Horn
Villa Ahumada
Nuevo Casas Grandes

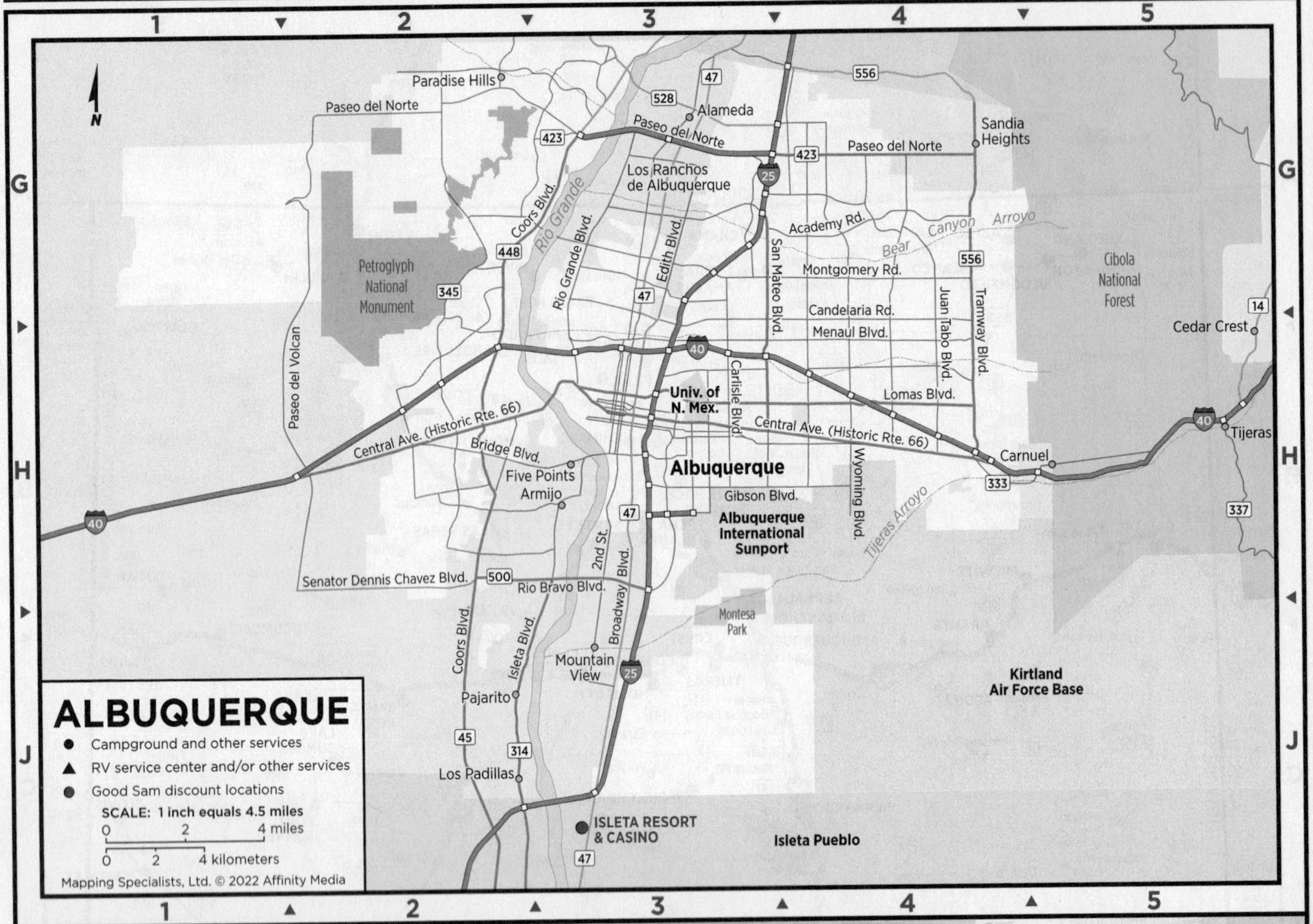

See listing Albuquerque, NM

ROAD TRIPS

Enchantment in Beautiful Cities and Tall Mountains

New Mexico

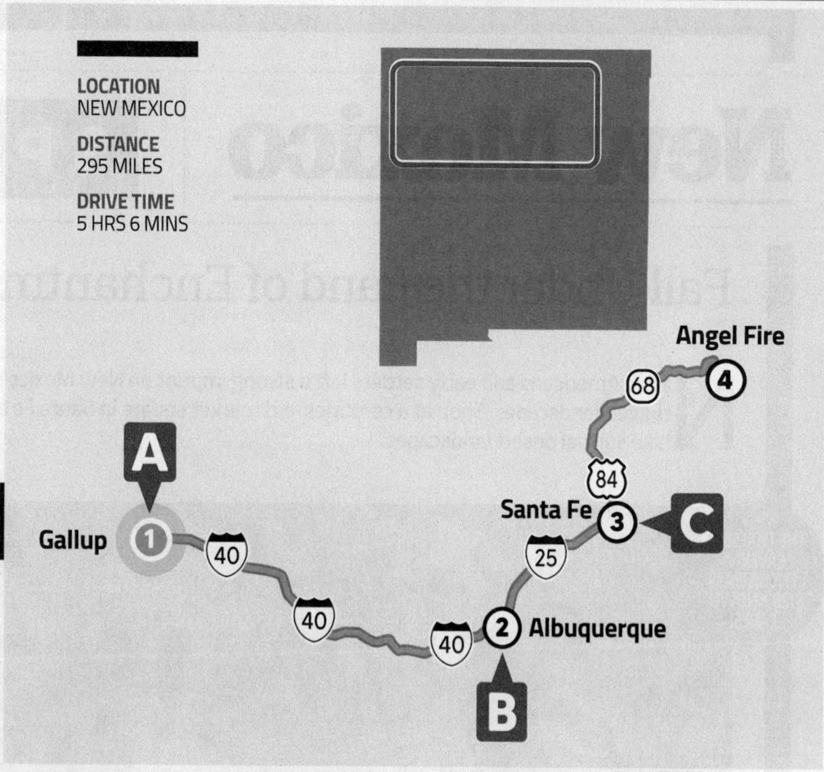

Rightly billed as the "Land of Enchantment," New Mexico brings together an intoxicating blend of culture, history, and unique outdoors fun. It's the kind of place where you can soar in a hot air balloon at sunrise, visit a living history museum in the afternoon, and spend evenings exploring galleries and boutiques.

1 Gallup
Starting Point

Brimming with natural beauty and rich Native American history, this desert town was once a top stop on historic Route 66. These days, it's home to an astonishing variety of cultural events and recreational opportunities. Throughout the summer months, the Nightly Indian Dances fill the town's Courthouse Square with the sounds of traditional drums and dancing, while the local trading posts feature one-of-a-kind creations from the area's many Native American artisans. East of town, the Zuni Mountains and the High Desert Trail System serve up endless miles of single-track mountain biking opportunities.

RECOMMENDED STOPOVER
A USA RV PARK
GALLUP, NM (505) 863-5021

2 Albuquerque
Drive 138 Miles ▪ 2 Hours, 4 Minutes

As the setting of the TV series Breaking Bad, you might have a slightly troubling impression of this vibrant, multicultural city, but despite its fictional reputation, ABQ is home to some top-notch attractions, world-class museums, and unique outdoors fun. Get the lay of the land with a ride on the nearly 4,000-foot Sandia Peak Aerial Tramway, before exploring the miles of hiking and mountain biking trails that cover the surrounding mountains. For more on the singular cultures that have called the region home, head to the National Hispanic Cultural Center and the Indian Pueblo Cultural Center.

RECOMMENDED STOPOVERS
B ENCHANTED TRAILS RV PARK & TRADING POST
ALBUQUERQUE, NM (505) 831-6317
B ROUTE 66 RV RESORT
ALBUQUERQUE, NM (505) 352-8000

Getty Images/iStockphoto

3 Santa Fe
Drive 65 Miles ▪ 1 Hour, 3 Minutes

Learn about this city's unique history at the Palace of the Governors, centrally located in Santa Fe Plaza. The oldest public building in the country, this beloved adobe structure is now home to a fascinating history museum and a must-see market featuring jewelry and other crafts made by local Native American artisans.

RECOMMENDED STOPOVER
C SANTA FE SKIES RV PARK
SANTA FE, NM (505) 473-5946

4 Angel Fire
Drive 92 Miles ▪ 1 Hour, 59 Minutes

Named for the brilliant red and orange glow that splashes across the nearby peaks at sunset, this small mountain town boasts a bevy of outdoors activities. Most of the fun begins at the Angel Fire Resort, a sprawling ski center that's home to miles of hiking and mountain biking trails during the summer months. Experienced riders can even bring their bikes on the ski lift for a quick trip to the summit of Agua Fria Peak. The ride down is ranked among the top 10 routes in the country. For more pulse-pounding fun, join the resort's popular zipline adventure tour. The ziplines range from 120 feet to 1,600 feet..

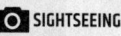

BIKING BOATING DINING ENTERTAINMENT FISHING HIKING HUNTING PADDLING SHOPPING SIGHTSEEING

New Mexico SPOTLIGHTS

Fall Under the Land of Enchantment's Spell

Native Americans and early settlers left a strong imprint on New Mexico's rugged landscapes. Shop at a centuries-old market square in Santa Fe and hike surreal desert landscapes.

THE CARLSBAD CAVERNS ENCOMPASS 120 KNOWN CAVES.

The Giant Dome and Twin Dome stalagmites in the Carlsbad Caverns.

Getty Images/iStockphoto

Carlsbad

Natural beauty abounds where the Pecos River snakes through the Chihuahuan Desert. The Guadalupe Mountains stretch along the distant horizon. While Carlsbad Caverns Natural Park is the biggest attraction, there is so much more to explore, from the arts to history to outdoor adventures.

Cool Cave

Experience the subterranean wonders of Carlsbad Caverns National Park. Prepare to be amazed by the main show cavern, which is filled with a stunning arrangement of stalactites. The Big Room is notable as North America's largest underground chamber, one of the largest in the entire world. In this cavern, you'll find the Giant Dome stalagmite, which towers 62 feet. Self-guided or narrated tours are available. Participate in an awe-inspiring event by watching the evening bat flight, as thousands of bats emerge from the underworld at sunset, filling the skies.

Albuquerque

Blending Native American and Spanish heritage with a legacy of Wild West cowboy culture, Albuquerque is one of the most interesting and diverse cities in the country. In a single day, you can explore traditional cuisines, authentic handcrafted art, and exciting, family-friendly attractions that bring the outdoors to your doorstep. Not to mention, ABQ boasts an average of more than 300 sunny days throughout the year making it the perfect destination for four-season fun. Take a seat at a local restaurant and enjoy pepper-infused flavors.

Bird's-eye Views

To get the lay of the land, first-time visitors should head straight to the Sandia Peak Tramway, a 15-minute aerial tram that ferries guests almost 4,000 feet to the crest of the Sandia Mountains. In addition to the stunning 360-degree view at the top, there are numerous hiking and biking trails to explore, as well as a restaurant, and winter-time skiing. The incredible backdrop is the perfect introduction to the Land of Enchantment. And in case you're in search of an even more elevated experience, ABQ is also known as the "Hot Air Ballooning Capital of the World." During the International Balloon Fiesta each October, hundreds of balloons take to the skies in an incredible display of artistic vision and out-of-this-world fun. The nine-day event includes competitions, entertainment, and of course plenty of balloon rides. But don't worry, even if your visit is out of season, sunrise and sunset ballooning experiences are available year-round.

Cultural Touchstones

Step back in time with a visit to Old Town, where ABQ's history comes to life. Founded

LOCAL FAVORITE

Jalapeno Popper Casserole

Chiles have been growing in New Mexico for over 400 years and are a staple ingredient in many local dishes. *Recipe by Brian and Elise Miller.*

INGREDIENTS

- ☐ 2 8-oz packages of cream cheese, softened
- ☐ 1 cup sour cream
- ☐ 2 cups Mexican Cheddar Jack shredded cheese, divided (or cheddar cheese)
- ☐ 1 lb bacon, cooked and crumbled
- ☐ 6 jalapeno peppers, deseeded and diced
- ☐ 2 1 lb bags of tater tots
- ☐ 6 green onions, thinly sliced

DIRECTIONS

Preheat oven to 425°F. Line a 13 x 9 dish with tater tots. Bake for 15 minutes. While the tots are baking, cook bacon, blot fat away and crumble into small pieces. Dice the peppers (wear plastic gloves) and slice the onions. In a medium bowl, combine cream cheese, sour cream, 1.5 cups of cheddar cheese and bacon. Save a little bit of bacon and onions for later. Stir to thoroughly combine ingredients.

Spread the jalapeno mixture over the top of the tater tots. Top with the remaining 1/2 cup of shredded cheese. Sprinkle the extra bacon

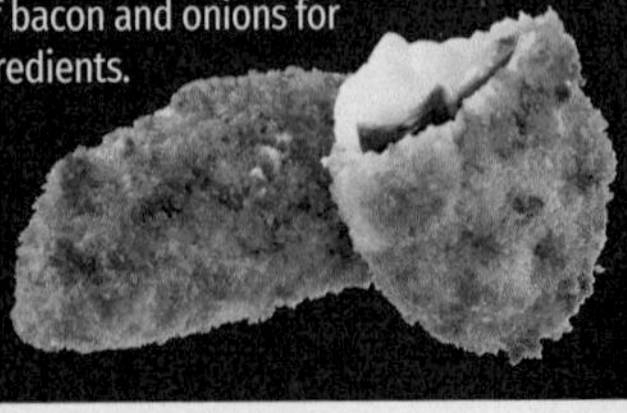

in 1706, the neighborhood now features the Albuquerque Museum (formerly the Albuquerque Museum of Art and History), the New Mexico Museum of Natural History and Science, the American International Rattlesnake Museum, and hidden gems like the Turquoise Museum, where you can view rare specimens from around the world. Old Town is also home to fantastic shopping and gallery opportunities. With more than 100 shops ranging from chic boutiques to handcrafted jewelers, there's something for everyone in this easily walkable area.

Traditional Flavors

Based on native ingredients and boasting recipes older than America itself, New Mexican cuisine is firmly rooted in tradition. And nothing is more traditional here than the ubiquitous local chile. Flavoring everything from soups, to stews, you'll likely hear the question "red or green?" at almost every meal during your stay. Pick one, or enjoy them both, just make sure to take some home — red and green chile to go is one of the state's most popular tourist items.

Angel Fire

Located just east of Taos, Angel Fire is a mountain playground for active travelers. The biggest draw is Angel Fire Resort, which attracts legions of skiers and snowboarders in the winter months, but it's also worth visiting in the spring and summer in the warm sun, especially if you're interested in hiking, mountain biking, golfing, fishing or hunting.

Awe-Inspiring Attractions

Scenic trails and winding roads will take you to popular spots around the area. Popular attractions include the Enchanted Circle Byway, an 84-mile loop that circles Wheeler Peak. Don't miss the Vietnam Veterans Memorial State Park, whose centerpiece is a majestic memorial chapel established by the parents of a young man killed in 1968 when his unit came under ambush.

Adrenaline Boosts

Hiking and mountain biking are big here. In fact, the Angel Fire Bike Park is the largest mountain biking park in the Rockies. Get ready for a day of cardio as you navigate the trails. Nearby, Carson National Forest is home to the 22-mile-long South Boundary Trail, another mountain biking hot spot. For an adrenaline rush, Angel Fire's Zipline Adventure is a three-hour tour that features six ziplines (from 120 to 1,600 feet in length) at the summit, including a tandem zipline over the forest, dishing out Rocky Mountain and Moreno Valley views.

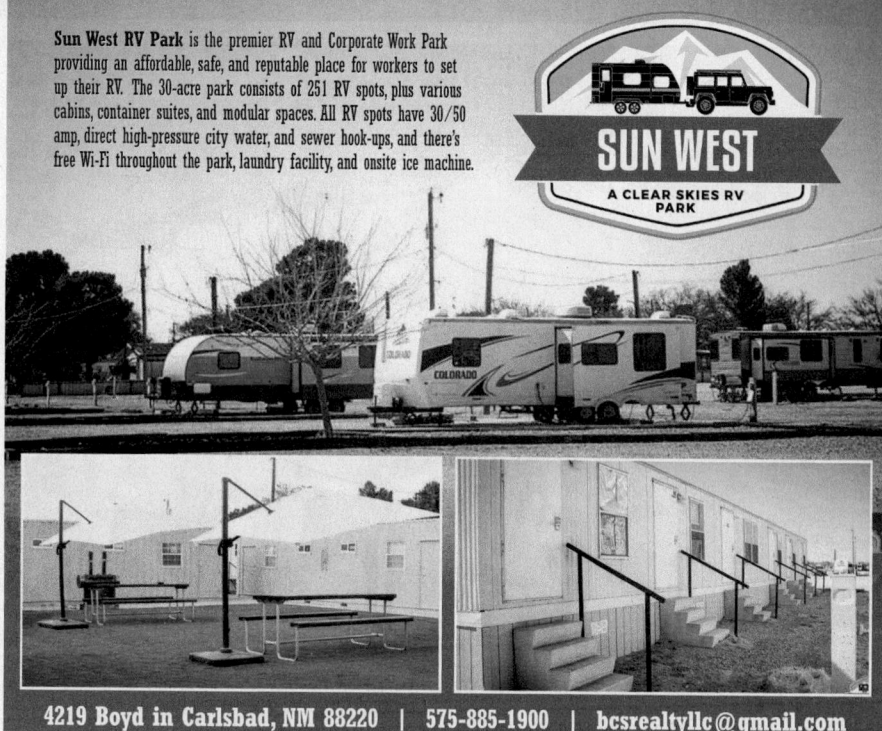

SPOTLIGHTS

Hiking past conical rocks in the surreal Kasha-Katuwe Tent Rocks National Monument near Santa Fe.

Santa Fe

Long considered one of the world's great art cities, Santa Fe is home to more than 250 galleries, as well as an extensive collection of museums and cultural institutions. But that's not all that awaits you in this bustling capital city. Outdoors adventures, incredible history, and a mouthwatering culinary tradition combine to truly set this Southwestern gem apart. No wonder they call it "The City Different."

Art on Display

Begin your artistic adventures at the eastside Museum Hill neighborhood, home to four of the city's top attractions — the Museum of Indian Arts & Culture, the Wheelwright Museum of the American Indian, the Museum of Spanish Colonial Art, and the renowned Museum of International Folk Art. Essentially next door to one another, it's the perfect introduction to the region's creative culture. The nearby Georgia O'Keeffe Museum, a nonprofit institution dedicated to the works and world of the iconic artist, is another must-see. The museum's impressive collection includes almost all of her unmistakable landscapes, flower and skull paintings. For an immersive experience, head to Meow Wolf, Santa Fe's most innovative art space. Doubling as a music venue, it's a hands-on leap into the artistic unknown.

Step Back in Time

From there, you can walk in the footsteps of Santa Fe's earliest settlers with a visit to the Palace of the Governors, a 400-year-old adobe structure located in the downtown plaza district. As the oldest continuously occupied public building in the country, the site is brimming with history and visitors can expect a deep dive into the political and cultural history of the state. The rest of the plaza is equally enchanting. Known as "the heart of Santa Fe," the central square is home to Native American artisans, performers, restaurants, boutiques and more.

Outdoors Paradise

Mere minutes from downtown, the Sangre de Cristo Mountains offer a heavenly backdrop for all manner of outdoors adventure. Beginning hikers and bikers should make time to explore the popular Dale Ball trails, a system that winds for nearly 25 miles through the foothills surrounding town, while more experienced hikers can head straight for the Nambe Lake Trail, a 6-mile route through the mountains' alpine wilderness. About 45 minutes from downtown, the Slot Canyon Trail at Kasha-Katuwe Tent Rocks National Monument is a local favorite boasting breathtaking views and an otherworldly landscape. The cone-shaped rocks were formed by volcanic activity.

FOR MORE INFORMATION

New Mexico Tourism Department, 800-827-7400, www.newmexico.org

Visit Albuquerque, 800-284-2282, www.visitalbuquerque.com

Angel Fire Fun, 575-377-3232, angelfirefun.com

Carlsbad True, www.carlsbadnmtrue.com

Tourism Santa Fe, 800-777-2489, www.santafe.org

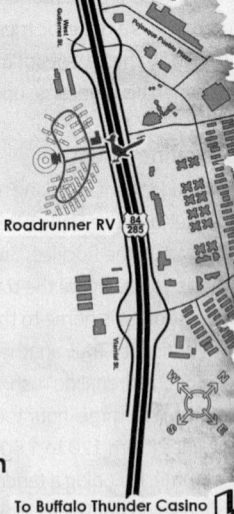

New Mexico

ABIQUIU — B3 *Rio Arriba*

ABIQUIU LAKE - COE/RIANA (Public Corps) From town: Go 7 mi N on US 84, then 1-1/2 mi W on Hwy 96. 52 Avail: 13 W, 13 E (50 amps). 2021 rates: $12 to $16. Apr 15 to Oct 15. (505)685-4371

ACOMA — C2 *Cibola*

SKY CITY RV PARK, CASINO & CULTURAL CENTER **Ratings: 8/9★/7.5** (RV Park) Avail: 42 full hkups (30/50 amps). 2021 rates: $22. (888)759-2489, I-40, Exit 102, Acoma, NM 87034

ALAMOGORDO — D3 *Otero*

ALAMOGORDO WHITE SANDS KOA **Ratings: 8.5/9★/8** (Campground) 42 Avail: 36 full hkups, 6 W, 6 E (30/50 amps). 2021 rates: $36 to $45. (575)437-3003, 412 24th St, Alamogordo, NM 88310

BOOT HILL RV RESORT

good sam park **Ratings: 9/10★/10** (RV Park) S-bnd: From Jct of NM State Hwy 54/70 in Tularosa, South 5.8 mi on Hwy 54/70 (L); or N-bnd: From N Jct of 54/70 & Hwy 82 in Alamogordo, N 3.7 mi to Dog Ranch Rd, Go East/Right and make an immediate left into park. (L). **FAC:** all weather rds. (50 spaces). Avail: 40 all weather, 18 pull-thrus, (32x83), back-ins (30x70), 40 full hkups (30/50 amps), seasonal sites, WiFi @ sites, rentals, laundry, restaurant. **REC:** hunting nearby. Pet restrict (B). Partial handicap access. No tents. Big rig sites, eco-friendly. 2021 rates: $34.50 to $43.50.
(575)439-6224 Lat: 32.99759, Lon: -105.98949
1 Dog Ranch Rd, Alamogordo, NM 88310
www.boothillrv.com
See ad this page

MILITARY PARK HOLLOMAN FAMCAMP (HOLLOMAN AFB) (Public) From Jct of US-70 & Mesquite Rd (10 mi SW of town), left 500 ft on Mesquite Rd. Avail: 35 full hkups (30/50 amps). 2021 rates: $20. (575)572-5369

OLIVER LEE MEMORIAL

(Public State Park) From S Jct of US-70 & US-54, S 8.8 mi on US-54 to CR-16, E 4 mi (E). Elev 4400 ft.**FAC:** paved rds. Avail: 42 gravel, back-ins (30x40), 19 W, 19 E (30/50 amps), tent sites, dump, fire rings. **REC:** Dog Canyon Stream:. Pets OK. Partial handicap access, 14 day max stay. 2021 rates: $8 to $18.
(575)437-8284 Lat: 32.74795, Lon: -105.91522
409 Dog Canyon Rd, Alamogordo, NM 88310
www.emnrd.state.nm.us

WHITE SANDS MANUFACTURED HOME AND RV COMMUNITY

good sam park **Ratings: 9/9.5★/7.5** (RV Area in MH Park) N-bnd: From S Jct of US-54 & US-70/82, NE 1.2 mi on US-54/70/82 - White Sands Blvd (R); or S-bnd: From N Jct of US-54/70 & US-82, S 3.8 mi on US-54/70/82 - White Sands Blvd (L). Elev 4200 ft.**FAC:** paved rds. (86 spaces). 59 Avail: 29 paved, 30 gravel, patios, 29 pull-thrus, (23x50), back-ins (26x50), 59 full hkups (30/50 amps), cable, WiFi @ sites, laundry. **REC:** pool, playground. Pets OK. Partial handicap access. No tents. 2021 rates: $44.27. no reservations.
(575)437-8388 Lat: 32.88579, Lon: -105.95703
607 S White Sands Blvd, Alamogordo, NM 88310
www.whitesandscommunity.com
See ad this page

ALBUQUERQUE — C3 *Bernalillo*

ALBUQUERQUE See also Cedar Crest, Rio Rancho & Tijeras.

ALBUQUERQUE CENTRAL KOA JOURNEY **Ratings: 9/8.5/8.5** (Campground) 140 Avail: 100 full hkups, 40 W, 40 E (30/50 amps). 2021 rates: $52 to $79. (505)296-2729, 12400 Skyline Rd NE, Albuquerque, NM 87123

AMERICAN RV RESORT **Ratings: 10/9.5★/10** (RV Resort) Avail: 183 full hkups (30/50 amps). 2021 rates: $35 to $150. (888)481-3353, 13500 Central Ave SW, Albuquerque, NM 87121

Pre-Drive Safety Checklist: Create a step-by-step, pre-trip safety interior and exterior checklist. Conduct a final walk-around visual inspection before driving to or away from your camping site.

BALLOON VIEW RV PARK

good sam park **Ratings: 8/8/5** (RV Park) S-bnd: From jct of I-25 & Exit 231 to Osuna Rd NE: Go 2 mi W on Osuna Rd NE to Edith Blvd NE, then 1/2 mi N on Edith Blvd NE, then 1/4 mi E on Tyler Rd NE (R); or N-bnd: From jct I-25 & Exit 230 to Osuna: Go 2-1/2 mi W on Osuna Rd to Edith Blvd, then N on Edith 1/4 mi to Tyler (R). Elev 5200 ft.**FAC:** gravel rds. (87 spaces). Avail: 27 gravel, patios, 13 pull-thrus, (25x40), back-ins (25x40), mostly side by side hkups, 27 full hkups (30/50 amps), cable, WiFi @ sites, laundry. **REC:** pool. Pet restrict (B). No tents. 2021 rates: $45.
(505)345-3716 Lat: 35.15630, Lon: -106.61886
500 Tyler Rd NE, Albuquerque, NM 87113
www.balloonviewrv.com
See ad this page

CORONADO VILLAGE RV RESORT

good sam park **Ratings: 9.5/10★/8.5** (RV Area in MH Park) From Jct of I-25 & Exit 233: Go 3/4 mi S on West Service Rd (R). Elev 5050 ft.

OVERSIZED PRIVATE SHADED SITES

Enjoy a resort lifestyle, spectacular clubhouse, pristine shower/restroom facilities, unlimited activities, pool, indoor spa, fitness center, 7 acres of lush green park for you and your furry friends to explore.

FAC: paved rds. (321 spaces). Avail: 13 all weather, patios, back-ins (25x60), 13 full hkups (30/50 amps), seasonal sites, WiFi, laundry, controlled access. **REC:** heated pool, hot tub, playground. Pet restrict (S/B/Q). No tents. Big rig sites. 2021 rates: $45.
(505)823-2515 Lat: 35.178269, Lon: -106.585647
8401 Pan American Freeway NE, Albuquerque, NM 87113
coronadovillagerv.com
See ad this page

ENCHANTED TRAILS RV PARK & TRADING POST

good sam park **Ratings: 9/9★/8** (RV Park) From jct of I-40 & Atrisco Vista Blvd/Exit 149 (W side of town), exit to N frntg rd, then go 1-1/2 mi (R). Elev 5672 ft.**FAC:** paved/gravel rds. Avail: 135 gravel, 127 pull-thrus, (25x80), back-ins (20x50), 115 full hkups, 20 W, 20 E (30/50 amps), WiFi @ sites, dump, laundry, LP gas. **REC:** heated pool, hot tub. Pets OK. Partial handicap access. No tents. Big rig sites, eco-friendly. 2021 rates: $34 to $37, Military discount.
(505)831-6317 Lat: 35.05987, Lon: -106.81025
14305 Central Ave NW, Albuquerque, NM 87121
enchantedtrails.com
See ad page 623

HIGH DESERT RV PARK **Ratings: 8/9★/6** (RV Park) Avail: 25 full hkups (30/50 amps). 2021 rates: $34.60 to $41.50. (505)839-9035, 13000 Frontage Rd SW, Albuquerque, NM 87121

ISLETA LAKES & RV PARK

good sam park **Ratings: 9/9.5★/9.5** (RV Park) From jct of I-25 & exit 215 (Hwy 47): Go 1/4 mi S to Isleta Lakes Rd (TR-15), then 1/2 mi W (E). Elev 4916 ft.

WHERE THE FUN BEGINS!

Enjoy the natural beauty of the Southwest. Our 50 full-service RV sites are equipped with all the necessities + WIFI, convenience store, lakes & fishing. Golf, Casino, bowling, family fun nearby. Free shuttle to all the fun!

FAC: paved/gravel rds. Avail: 50 gravel, patios, 42 pull-thrus, (30x60), back-ins (30x45), 50 full hkups (30/50 amps), WiFi @ sites, dump, laundry, groc, restaurant, controlled access. **REC:** pool $, Isleta Lake: fishing, golf, playground, rec open to public. Pet restrict (B). Partial handicap access. No tents. Big rig sites. 2021 rates: $37.10 to $50. ATM, no reservations.
(505)244-8102 Lat: 34.94548, Lon: -106.67424
4051 Hwy 47 SE, Albuquerque, NM 87105
www.isleta.com
See ad page 616

MILITARY PARK KIRTLAND FAMCAMP (KIRTLAND AFB) (Public) From I-25, Exit 222/Gibson Blvd SE, go to Truman St SE, then left on Randolph Rd SE (name changes to Kirtland Rd SE) to Wyoming St, then left to Ave F, follow signs (RVs should use Truman Gate). Avail: 72 full hkups (30/50 amps). 2021 rates: $25. (505)846-0337

RV parks in remote locations are sometimes unable to provide all amenities, like 30/50-amp service. Don't let that stop you - the tradeoff is a once-in-a-lifetime trip to some of the most beautiful wilderness areas on the planet!

Read RV topics at blog.GoodSam.com

New Mexico Privately Owned Campground Information Updated by our Good Sam Representatives

Mike & Elaine Ewing

Mike is a master electrician who built and flipped homes. Elaine worked with General Motors for 36 years before we hung up our spurs and started living the dream. We married in 1979, purchased our first RV nine months later and have enjoyed the RV lifestyle ever since.

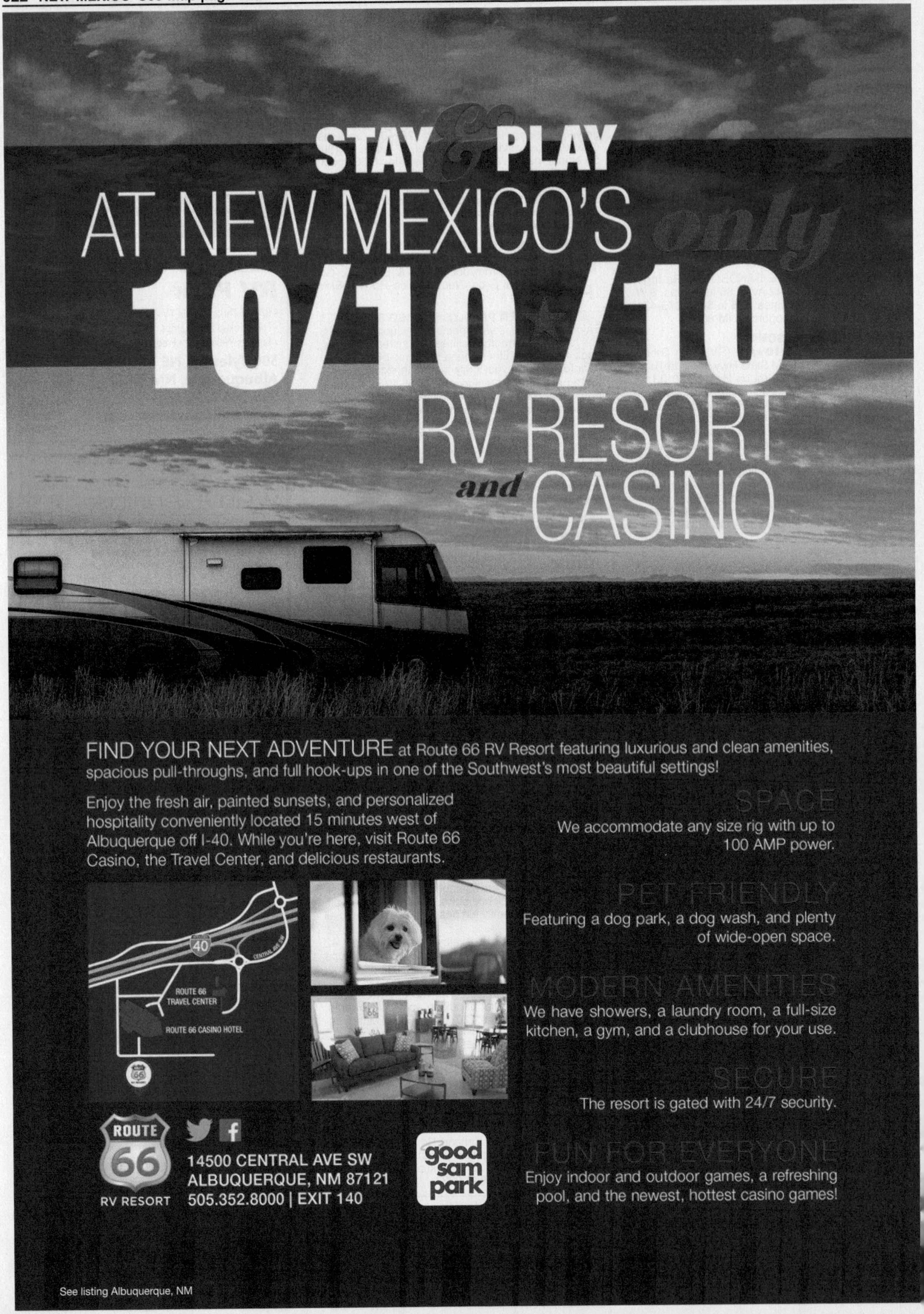
STAY & PLAY
AT NEW MEXICO'S only
10/10/10
RV RESORT
and CASINO
FIND YOUR NEXT ADVENTURE at Route 66 RV Resort featuring luxurious and clean amenities, spacious pull-throughs, and full hook-ups in one of the Southwest's most beautiful settings!
Enjoy the fresh air, painted sunsets, and personalized hospitality conveniently located 15 minutes west of Albuquerque off I-40. While you're here, visit Route 66 Casino, the Travel Center, and delicious restaurants.
40
CENTRAL AVE SW
ROUTE 66 TRAVEL CENTER
ROUTE 66 CASINO HOTEL
SPACE
We accommodate any size rig with up to 100 AMP power.
PET FRIENDLY
Featuring a dog park, a dog wash, and plenty of wide-open space.
MODERN AMENITIES
We have showers, a laundry room, a full-size kitchen, a gym, and a clubhouse for your use.
SECURE
The resort is gated with 24/7 security.
FUN FOR EVERYONE
Enjoy indoor and outdoor games, a refreshing pool, and the newest, hottest casino games!
ROUTE 66 RV RESORT
14500 CENTRAL AVE SW
ALBUQUERQUE, NM 87121
505.352.8000 | EXIT 140
good sam park
See listing Albuquerque, NM

ALBUQUERQUE (CONT)

← ROUTE 66 RV RESORT
good sam park **Ratings: 10/10★/10** (RV Resort) From I-40 & exit 140: Go west 0.2 mi on South Frontage Rd (L) Note: entrance is west of and behind casino. Elev 5200 ft.

ENJOY THE NEW ROUTE 66 RV RESORT!
Our 10/10*/10 rated Resort is just minutes west of Albuquerque on historic Route 66. A perfect destination with luxury amenities, gorgeous pool & spa, Route 66 Casino Hotel, Vegas-style gaming, restaurants & entertainment.
FAC: paved rds. Avail: 100 paved, patios, 57 pull-thrus, (45x85), back-ins (45x65), 100 full hkups (30/50 amps), WiFi @ sites, laundry, LP gas, fire rings, firewood, restaurant, controlled access. **REC:** heated pool, hot tub. Pets OK. Partial handicap access. No tents. Big rig sites, 28 day max stay, eco-friendly. 2021 rates: $50 to $60, Military discount. ATM.
(505)352-8000 Lat: 35.02693, Lon: -106.95236
I40 Exit 140, Albuquerque, NM 87121
rt66rvresort.com
See ad opposite page

↑ STAGECOACH STOP RV PARK
good sam park **Ratings: 10/9.5★/10** (RV Park) From Albuquerque, Go North on I 25 to Exit 242(Hwy 550): Go W 2.4 mi on Hwy 550 to Hwy 528, S 0.6 mi to Montoya, E 0.1 mi on Montoya to Christopher Way (behind McDonalds), N 0.1 mi to Gabby Way, E 0.1 mi (R). Elev 5300 ft.**FAC:** paved rds. (85 spaces). Avail: 45 paved, 45 pull-thrus, (27x60), 45 full hkups (30/50 amps), cable, WiFi @ sites, dump, laundry. **REC:** heated pool, hot tub. Pet restrict (B). Partial handicap access. No tents. Big rig sites, eco-friendly. 2021 rates: $42 to $52, Military discount.
(505)867-1000 Lat: 35.32323, Lon: -106.57075
3650 State Hwy 528 NE, Rio Rancho, NM 87144
www.stagecoachstoprv.com
See primary listing at Rio Rancho and ad this page

→ TURQUOISE TRAIL CAMPGROUND & RV PARK
Ratings: 6.5/9★/8.5 (Campground) From Jct I-40 & Exit 175 (Cedar Crest/Hwy 14): Go 4 mi N on Hwy 14 (L). Elev 7200 ft.**FAC:** gravel rds. Avail: 57 gravel, 36 pull-thrus, (26x70), back-ins (28x60), 47 full hkups, 10 W, 10 E (30/50 amps), WiFi @ sites, tent sites, rentals, shower$, dump, laundry. **REC:** playground. Pet restrict (B/Q). Partial handicap access. Big rig sites, eco-friendly. 2021 rates: $31.95 to $37.95, Military discount.
(505)281-2005 Lat: 35.14287, Lon: -106.36741
22 Calvary Rd, Cedar Crest, NM 87008
www.turquoisetrailcampground.com
See primary listing at Cedar Crest and ad this page

Travel Services

← CAMPING WORLD OF ALBUQUERQUE As the nation's largest retailer of RV supplies, accessories, services and new and used RVs, Camping World is committed to making your total RV experience better. **SERVICES:** RV, tire, RV appliance, MH mechanical, sells outdoor gear, sells firearms, staffed RV wash, restrooms. RV Sales. RV supplies, LP gas, RV accessible. Hours: 9am to 7pm .
(888)630-8978 Lat: 35.059254, Lon: -106.810134
14303 Central Ave N.W. Suite B, Albuquerque, NM 87121
www.campingworld.com

Things to See and Do

↓ ISLETA FUN CONNECTION Twenty-four lanes of fun with bowling, billiards, arcade, prize counter, snack bar and bar. Family fun, corporate gatherings or bowling leagues are welcome. Elev 4850 ft. Restrooms. Food. Hours: . ATM.
(505)724-3866 Lat: 34.93841, Lon: -106.66547
11000 Broadway SE, Albuquerque, NM 87105
www.isleta.com
See ad page 616

↓ ISLETA GOLF CLUB 27 hole championship golf course. Elev 4916 ft. RV accessible. Restrooms. Food. Hours: 8am to 4pm. ATM.
(505)848-1900 Lat: 34.93822, Lon: -106.67068
11001 Broadway SE, Albuquerque, NM 87105
isleta.com
See ad page 616

↓ ISLETA RESORT & CASINO 100,000sq ft hotel & casino; relaxing indoor/outdoor pool, restaurants/cocktail lounges, 2,500 seat theatre for entertainment & events, 18 hole golf, FUN Center with bowling, laser tag, billiards, bar & free shuttle service from RV Park Elev 4916 ft. Partial handicap access. RV accessible. Restrooms. Food. Hours: . ATM. No CC.
(505)724-3800 Lat: 34.94553, Lon: -106.67432
11000 Broadway SE, Albuquerque, NM 87105
www.isleta.com
See ad page 616

← ROUTE 66 CASINO HOTEL Hotel and Casino with unique themes, wall to wall entertainment and award winning food. Kids Quest and Cyber Quest. Elev 5292 ft. Partial handicap access. RV accessible. Restrooms. Food. Hours: Open 24 hrs. ATM.
(866)352-7866 Lat: 35.02693, Lon: -106.95236
14500 Central Ave SW, Albuquerque, NM 87121
www.rt66casino.com
See ad opposite page

ALTO — D3 *Lincoln*

↑ BONITO HOLLOW RV PARK & CAMPGROUND **Ratings: 5.5/8.5/8.5** (Campground) 51 Avail: 34 full hkups, 17 W, 17 E (30/50 amps). 2021 rates: $39 to $44. Mar 22 to Oct 15. (575)336-4325, 221 Hwy 37, Alto, NM 88312

↗ LITTLE CREEK RV PARK **Ratings: 7.5/9★/7.5** (RV Park) Avail: 29 full hkups (30/50 amps). 2021 rates: $38. Apr 01 to Oct 31. (575)336-4044, 290 State Hwy 220, Alto, NM 88312

↖ RUIDOSO MOTORCOACH RANCH **Ratings: 8/9.5★/10** (RV Resort) Avail: 29 full hkups (30/50 amps). 2021 rates: $95 to $105. Mar 01 to Oct 31. (575)336-4556, 358 State Hwy 220 , Alto, NM 88312

ANGEL FIRE — B4 *Colfax*

↖ ANGEL FIRE RV RESORT **Ratings: 10/10★/10** (RV Resort) Avail: 102 full hkups (30/50 amps). 2021 rates: $50 to $80. (855)421-0308, 27500 Hwy 64, Angel Fire, NM 87710

AZTEC — A2 *San Juan*

↗ NAVAJO LAKE/COTTONWOOD (Public State Park) From town, E 10 mi on Hwy 64 to Hwy 511, NE 8 mi to Hwy 173, W 1.1 mi to CR-4280, NW 2.7 mi (R). Avail: 24 E (20/30 amps). 2021 rates: $8 to $18. (505)632-2278

↖ TICO TIME RV RIVER RESORT **Ratings: 8.5/8.5★/9.5** (RV Park) Avail: 61 full hkups (30/50 amps). 2021 rates: $60 to $94. (970)903-0681, 20 Road 2050, Aztec, NM 87410

BERNALILLO — B3 *Bernalillo*

← CORONADO CAMPGROUND (Public) From jct of NM 528 & Hwy 550: Go 3/4 mi SE on Hwy 550, then 500 feet N on Kuaua Rd. (R). 23 Avail: 23 W, 23 E (30/50 amps). 2021 rates: $14 to $22. (505)980-8256

BERNARDO — C2 *Socorro*

← KIVA RV PARK & HORSE MOTEL
good sam park **Ratings: 7.5/9★/8.5** (Campground) Avail: 18 full hkups (30/50 amps). 2021 rates: $35. (505)861-0693, 21 Old Highway 60 West, Bernardo, NM 87006

BLANCO — A2 *San Juan*

↗ NAVAJO LAKE/SIMS MESA (Public State Park) From Jct of US-64 & Hwy 527, NW 9.2 mi to CR-636, W 4.9 mi to CR-490, NW 2.9 mi, W 1.8 mi. Avail: 20 E (30 amps). 2021 rates: $8 to $18. (505)632-2278

BLOOMFIELD — A2 *San Juan*

↗ MOORE'S RV PARK & CAMPGROUND **Ratings: 9/9.5★/9** (Campground) Avail: 35 full hkups (30/50 amps). 2021 rates: $45. (505)632-8339, 1900 E Blanco Blvd, Bloomfield, NM 87413

→ NAVAJO LAKE/PINE RIVER (Public State Park) From Jct of US-64 & SR-511, N 15 mi on SR-511 (R). 54 Avail: 8 full hkups, 8 W, 8 S, 46 E (20/30 amps). 2021 rates: $8 to $18. May 15 to Sep 15. (505)632-2278

CABALLO — D2 *Sierra*

↓ CABALLO LAKE (Public State Park) From jct of I-25 & Hwy 187 (exit 59): Go 3/4 mi N on Hwy 187. (R). 170 Avail: 7 full hkups, 108 W, 108 E (30/50 amps). 2021 rates: $8 to $18. (575)743-3942

↓ **CABALLO LAKE RV PARK Ratings: 6/NA/9.5** (RV Park) Avail: 18 full hkups (30/50 amps). 2021 rates: $15. (575)743-0502, 14279 Hwy 187 Mile Marker 22, Caballo, NM 87931

↓ LIL ABNERS RV PARK, GENERAL STORE & BAIT **Ratings: 5/NA/6** (RV Park) Avail: 14 full hkups (30/50 amps). 2021 rates: $20. (575)743-0153, 14422 Hwy 187, Caballo, NM 87931

↓ PERCHA DAM (Public State Park) From town, S 6.2 mi on I-25, follow signs (R). 50 Avail: 1 full hkups, 29 W, 29 E (30/50 amps). 2021 rates: $8 to $18. (575)743-3942

CAPULIN — A5 *Union*

➔ CAPULIN RV PARK **Ratings: 6/7.5★/6.5** (Campground) 32 Avail: 29 full hkups, 3 W, 3 E (30/50 amps). 2021 rates: $30. (575)278-2921, 7 S Santa Fe Ave, Capulin, NM 88414

CARLSBAD — E4 *Eddy*

A SPOTLIGHT Introducing Carlsbad Caverns' colorful attractions appearing at the front of this state section.

BONNIE & CLYDE'S GETAWAY RV PARK
good sam park **Ratings: 6/NA/10** (RV Park) From jct US 285 & Hwy 524: Go 1/4 mi N on Hwy 524/Seven Rivers Hwy (L). Elev 3295 ft.-**FAC:** all weather rds. (40 spaces). Avail: 30 all weather, back-ins (34x45), accepts full hkup units only, 30 full hkups (30/50 amps), seasonal sites, WiFi @ sites, laundry. **REC:** pond, fishing, playground. Pets OK. No tents. 2021 rates: $45, Military discount.
(575)988-5692 Lat: 32.48512, Lon: -104.32676
4154-2 Seven Rivers Highway, Carlsbad, NM 88220
See ad this page

BRANTLEY LAKE (Public State Park) From Jct of US-285 & US-62/180, N 12.3 mi on US-285 to Capitan Reef Rd/CR-30, E 4 mi on Captain Reef Rd/CR-30 (L). 51 Avail: 3 full hkups, 48 W, 48 E (30/50 amps). 2021 rates: $8 to $18. (575)457-2384

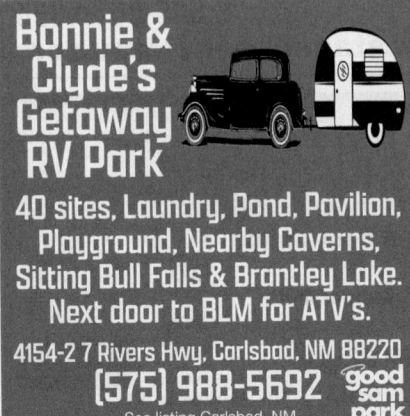

BUD'S PLACE RV PARK & CABINS
good sam park **Ratings: 7/10★/8** (RV Park) From Jct of Canal St & NM-524/W Lea St: Go W 1.5 mi on NM 524/ W Lea St to Standpipe Rd, then S 0.2 mi (L); or From Jct of US 285 & NM 524 (N of Carlsbad): Go SW 7 mi on NM 524 to Standpipe Rd (S 6th St), then S 0.2 mi (L). Elev 3294 ft.**FAC:** gravel rds. (91 spaces). Avail: 46 gravel, 46 pull-thrus, (30x70), 46 full hkups (30/50 amps), seasonal sites, WiFi @ sites, rentals, laundry, fire rings, firewood. **REC:** pond, fishing, playground. Pets OK. Partial handicap access. No tents. Big rig sites, eco-friendly. 2021 rates: $33.33 to $47.62, Military discount.
(575)200-1865 Lat: 32.41170, Lon: -104.25501
900 Standpipe Rd, Carlsbad, NM 88220
clearskiesrvparks.com
See ad page 619

CARLSBAD KOA HOLIDAY **Ratings: 9/9.5★/9** (RV Park) Avail: 57 full hkups (30/50 amps). 2021 rates: $47.89 to $66.89. (575)457-2000, 2 Manthei Rd, Carlsbad, NM 88220

CARLSBAD RV PARK & CAMPGROUND
good sam park **Ratings: 9/8★/9** (Campground) Avail: 20 full hkups (30/50 amps). 2021 rates: $52.50. (888)878-7275, 4301 National Parks Hwy, Carlsbad, NM 88220

SUN WEST MOBILE CITY
good sam park **Ratings: 7/NA/5.5** (RV Park) From Jct of US 180/US 62 & Boyd Rd: Go N 4 blocks on Boyd Rd (L), or (Sbnd: towards El Paso)From US 180 & Hidalgo St. (next to Happy's Restaurant), go West 0.2 mi on Hidalgo to Boyd Dr, S 0.25 mi (R). Elev 3294 ft.**FAC:** all weather rds. (250 spaces). Avail: 200 gravel, back-ins (24x70), 200 full hkups (30/50 amps), seasonal sites, cable, WiFi @ sites, laundry. Pets OK. No tents. 2021 rates: $36.19, Military discount.
(575)885-1900 Lat: 32.36841, Lon: -104.23769
4219 Boyd Dr, Carlsbad, NM 88220
clearskiesrvparks.com
See ad page 619

CARRIZOZO — D3 *Lincoln*

VALLEY OF FIRES REC AREA (BLM) (Public Corps) From jct US 54 & US 380: Go 3 mi NW on US 380. Avail: 14 E. 2021 rates: $12 to $18. (575)648-2241

CEDAR CREST — C3 *Bernalillo*

TURQUOISE TRAIL CAMPGROUND & RV PARK
Ratings: 6.5/9★/8.5 (Campground) From Jct of I-40 & Exit 175 (Cedar Crest/Hwy 14): Go 4 mi N on Hwy 14 (L). Elev 7200 ft.**FAC:** gravel rds. Avail: 57 gravel, 36 pull-thrus, (26x70), back-ins (28x60), 47 full hkups, 10 W, 10 E (30/50 amps), WiFi @ sites, tent sites, rentals, shower$, dump, laundry. **REC:** playground. Pet restrict (B/Q). Partial handicap access. Big rig sites, eco-friendly. 2021 rates: $31.95 to $37.95, Military discount.
(505)281-2005 Lat: 35.14287, Lon: -106.36741
22 Calvary Rd, Cedar Crest, NM 87008
turquoisetrailcampground.com
See ad previous page

CHAMA — A3 *Rio Arriba*

LITTLE CREEL RV PARK & RUSTIC CABINS **Ratings: 6.5/7/7** (RV Park) Avail: 53 full hkups (30/50 amps). 2021 rates: $30 to $50. (855)756-2382, 2631 State Hwy 84/64, Chama, NM 87520

RIO CHAMA RV PARK
good sam park **Ratings: 7/8.5★/9** (RV Park) From Jct of US-84 & Hwy 17: Go 2 mi N on Hwy 17 (R). Elev 7860 ft.**FAC:** gravel rds. Avail: 88 gravel, 59 pull-thrus, (24x70), back-ins (21x40), 74 full hkups, 14 W, 14 E (30/50 amps), WiFi @ sites, tent sites, dump, fire rings, firewood, controlled access. **REC:** Rio Chama River: fishing, hunting nearby. Pet restrict (B/Q). Big rig sites. 2021 rates: $32 to $54, Military discount. May 01 to Oct 01.
(575)756-2303 Lat: 36.90905, Lon: -106.57687
182 N St Hwy 17, Chama, NM 87520
See ad this page

SKY MOUNTAIN RESORT RV PARK
good sam park **Ratings: 8/9.5★/9.5** (RV Park) Avail: 46 full hkups (30/50 amps). 2021 rates: $42 to $50. May 15 to Oct 15. (575)756-1100, 2743 S US Hwy 84/64, Chama, NM 87520

CHIMAYO — B3 *Rio Arriba*

SANTA CRUZ LAKE REC AREA (BLM) (Public Corps) From jct Hwy 76 & Hwy 596: Go S on Hwy 596. 30 Avail: Pit toilets. 2021 rates: $7 to $9. (575)758-8851

CLAYTON — A5 *Union*

CLAYTON LAKE (Public State Park) From town, N 10 mi on Hwy 370 (L). 26 Avail: 16 W, 9 E (30/50 amps). 2021 rates: $8 to $18. (575)374-8808

CLAYTON RV PARK **Ratings: 6.5/7/6** (Campground) 65 Avail: 53 full hkups, 12 W, 12 E (30/50 amps). 2021 rates: $34 to $36. (575)374-9508, 903 S 5th St & Aspen, Clayton, NM 88415

CLINES CORNERS — C3 *Torrance*

CLINES CORNERS TRAVEL CENTER & RV PARK **Ratings: 6.5/NA/5** (RV Park) Avail: 36 full hkups (30/50 amps). 2021 rates: $39.99 to $42.69. (575)472-5488, 1 Yacht Club Dr, Clines Corners, NM 87070

CLOVIS — C5 *Curry*

CLOVIS POINT RV STABLES & STORAGE
good sam park **Ratings: 7/9.5★/7.5** (RV Park) Avail: 72 full hkups (30/50 amps). 2021 rates: $35. (575)760-4180, 961 Co Rd H, Clovis, NM 88101

CLOVIS RV PARK
good sam park **Ratings: 7.5/10★/7.5** (RV Park) From jct US 60/84 & US 70 (Prince St.): Go 2-1/4 mi E on Prince St (R). Elev 4200 ft.**FAC:** paved/gravel rds. 58 Avail: 29 gravel, 29 dirt, 5 pull-thrus, (25x75), back-ins (25x45), 58 full hkups (30/50 amps), cable, WiFi @ sites, tent sites, laundry, LP gas. **REC:** pond. Pets OK. Partial handicap access. Big rig sites, eco-friendly. 2021 rates: $36 to $38, Military discount.
(575)742-5035 Lat: 34.42928, Lon: -103.19644
3009 N Prince St, Clovis, NM 88101
clovisrvpark.co
See ad this page

TRAVELER'S WORLD RV PARK
good sam park **Ratings: 8/10★/9** (RV Park) Avail: 30 full hkups (30/50 amps). 2021 rates: $37. (575)763-8153, 1361 US Hwy 60/84, Clovis, NM 88101

COLUMBUS — E2 *Luna*

PANCHO VILLA (Public State Park) From Jct of SR-11 & SR-9, W 0.1 mi on SR-9 (L). 79 Avail: 75 W, 75 E (30 amps). 2021 rates: $8 to $18. May 01 to Aug 31. (575)531-2711

DEMING — E2 *Grant*

CITY OF ROCKS (Public State Park) From town, NW 24 mi on US-180 to SH-61, NE 3.3 mi, N 1.4 mi (L). 50 Avail: 9 W, 9 E (30/50 amps). 2021 rates: $8 to $18. (575)536-2800

DREAM CATCHER RV PARK **Ratings: 5.5/7.5/6.5** (Membership Park) Avail: 85 full hkups (30/50 amps). 2021 rates: $25 to $32. (575)544-4004, 4400 E Pine St, Deming, NM 88030

LITTLE VINEYARD RV RESORT
good sam park **Ratings: 9/10★/8.5** (RV Park) From Jct of I-10 & Pine St (exit 85), SW 1.4 mi on Pine St (R). Elev 4300 ft.

AN OASIS IN THE DESERT
Welcome to southwest New Mexico! EZ Big Rig pull-thrus & year round indoor pool & hot tub. The perfect home base to explore historic Deming & the region. State parks, museums, vineyards, golf & day trips to area attractions.

FAC: gravel rds. (144 spaces). Avail: 100 gravel, 100 pull-thrus, (32x70), 100 full hkups (30/50 amps), seasonal sites, cable, WiFi @ sites, dump, laundry, LP gas. **REC:** heated pool, hot tub, playground. Pet restrict (B/Q). No tents. Big rig sites, eco-friendly. 2021 rates: $37.
(575)546-3560 Lat: 32.26908, Lon: -107.72642
2901 E Pine St, Deming, NM 88030
littlevineyardrvresort.com
See ad opposite page

LOW-HI RV RANCH **Ratings: 6/7.5★/6.5** (Campground) 45 Avail: 42 full hkups, 3 W, 3 E (30/50 amps). 2021 rates: $30 to $34. (575)546-4058, 1795 O'Kelly Rd SE, Deming, NM 88030

ROADRUNNER RV PARK OF DEMING
good sam park **Ratings: 7.5/7.5/5.5** (RV Park) Avail: 58 full hkups (30/50 amps). 2021 rates: $28.31. (575)546-6960, 2849 E Pine St, Deming, NM 88030

ROCKHOUND (Public State Park) From town, S 4 mi on Hwy 11 to SR-141, E 7 mi, follow signs (E). Avail: 23 E (20/30 amps). 2021 rates: $8 to $18. (575)546-6182

EAGLE NEST — A4 *Colfax*

ANGEL NEST RV & RETREAT **Ratings: 6/7.5/6** (Campground) Avail: 27 full hkups (30/50 amps). 2021 rates: $39.38 to $44. May 01 to Nov 01. (575)377-0533, Hwy 64 & Marina Way, Eagle Nest, NM 87718

EDGEWOOD — C3 *Santa Fe*

➔ ROUTE 66 RV PARK **Ratings: 4.5/7/5** (RV Park) Avail: 63 full hkups (30/50 amps). 2021 rates: $32 to $85. (505)281-0893, 1981 Old US 66, Edgewood, NM 87015

EL PRADO — B3 *Taos*

TAOS MONTE BELLO RV PARK **Ratings: 6.5/9/8** (RV Park) 19 Avail: 16 full hkups, 3 W, 3 E (30/50 amps). 2021 rates: $35 to $46.13. (575)751-0774, 24819 US Hwy 64 W, El Prado, NM 87529

ELEPHANT BUTTE — D2 *Sierra*

CEDAR COVE RV PARK

good sam park **Ratings: 8/10★/10** (RV Park) Avail: 140 full hkups (30/50 amps). 2021 rates: $40 to $50. (575)744-4472, Hwy 195, 48 Cedar Cove Rd, Elephant Butte, NM 87935

CEDAR COVE RV PARK TOO

good sam park **Ratings: 6/9.5★/10** (RV Park) From jct I-25 N/US-85 N & I-25 Bus Loop (Exit 79): Go 1/2 mi S on I-25 Bus Loop/N Date St, then 1-1/2 mi N on NM-181, then 3/4 mi W on Warm Springs Blvd/NM-171 (L). Elev 4465 ft.

YOUR DESERT GATEWAY TO ADVENTURE

Our beautiful RV park getaway has room for all your toys! BLM property adjacent - ATV trails, birding, hiking trails & beautiful views. Just 2 miles to NM's largest lake, Elephant Butte Lake, the adventure begins here!

FAC: paved rds. Avail: 71 gravel, 10 pull-thrus, (36x75), back-ins (30x50), 71 full hkups (30/50 amps), WiFi @ sites, . **REC:** boating nearby. Pets OK. No tents. Big rig sites. 2021 rates: $40 to $45, Military discount.

(575)744-4472 Lat: 33.18337, Lon: -107.22432
661 Warm Springs Blvd, Elephant Butte, NM 87935
cedarcovetoo.com
See ad this page

ELEPHANT BUTTE LAKE RV RESORT

good sam park **Ratings: 9.5/10★/10** (RV Resort) From Jct of I-25 & Hwy 181 (exit 83), SE 0.1 mi on Hwy 181 to Hwy 195 (follow signs for Elephant Butte State Park), SE 3.25 mi (R). Elev 4674 ft.

ABSOLUTELY BEAUTIFUL RV RESORT!

Perfect place to explore! Elephant Butte Lake State Park, fishing & watersports, Sierra del Rio Championship Golf Course, Truth or Consequences Historic Hot Springs, hiking, biking & UTVs, Geronimo Trail & snowbird paradise!

FAC: paved rds. (132 spaces). 100 Avail: 37 all weather, 63 gravel, 28 pull-thrus, (30x70), back-ins (35x60), accepts full hkup units only, 100 full hkups (30/50 amps), seasonal sites, WiFi @ sites, dump, laundry. **REC:** heated pool, hot tub, boating nearby, hunting nearby. Pets OK. Partial handicap access. No tents. Big rig sites, eco-friendly. 2021 rates: $43 to $71, Military discount. ATM.

(575)744-5996 Lat: 33.18578, Lon: -107.21793
402 Hwy 195, Elephant Butte, NM 87935
www.ebresort.com
See ad this page

Driving a big rig? Average site width and length measurements tell you which campgrounds can accommodate your Big Rig.

Things to See and Do

FIREFLY SPA AT ELEPHANT BUTTE LAKE RV RESORT The Firefly Spa is located at the Elephant Butte Lake RV Resort and offers massage, body treatments, waxing and aromatherapy using organic materials. Elev 4674 ft. Hours: .

(575)497-0047 Lat: 33.18578, Lon: -107.21793
402 Hwy 195, Elephant Butte, NM 87935
www.elephantbuttelakervresort.com
See ad this page

FORT SUMNER — C4 *De Baca*

➔ **VALLEY VIEW RV PARK**

Ratings: 4.5/NA/6 (RV Park) From Jct of Hwys 60 & 84 (in town): Go 3/4 mi E on Hwy 60/84 (R). Elev 4000 ft.**FAC:** gravel rds. Avail: 20 gravel, 11 pull-thrus, (45x90), back-ins (45x90), 20 full hkups (30/50 amps), WiFi @ sites, . **REC:** boating nearby, hunting nearby, rec open to public. Pet restrict (B). No tents. Big rig sites. 2021 rates: $20.

(575)355-2380 Lat: 34.46712, Lon: -104.23190
1435 E Sumner Ave, Fort Sumner, NM 88119
billythekidmuseumfortsumner.com
See ad this page

Dispose of old paint, chemicals, and oil properly. Don't put batteries, antifreeze, paint, motor oil, or chemicals in the trash. Use proper toxics disposal sites.

RV Park ratings you can rely on!

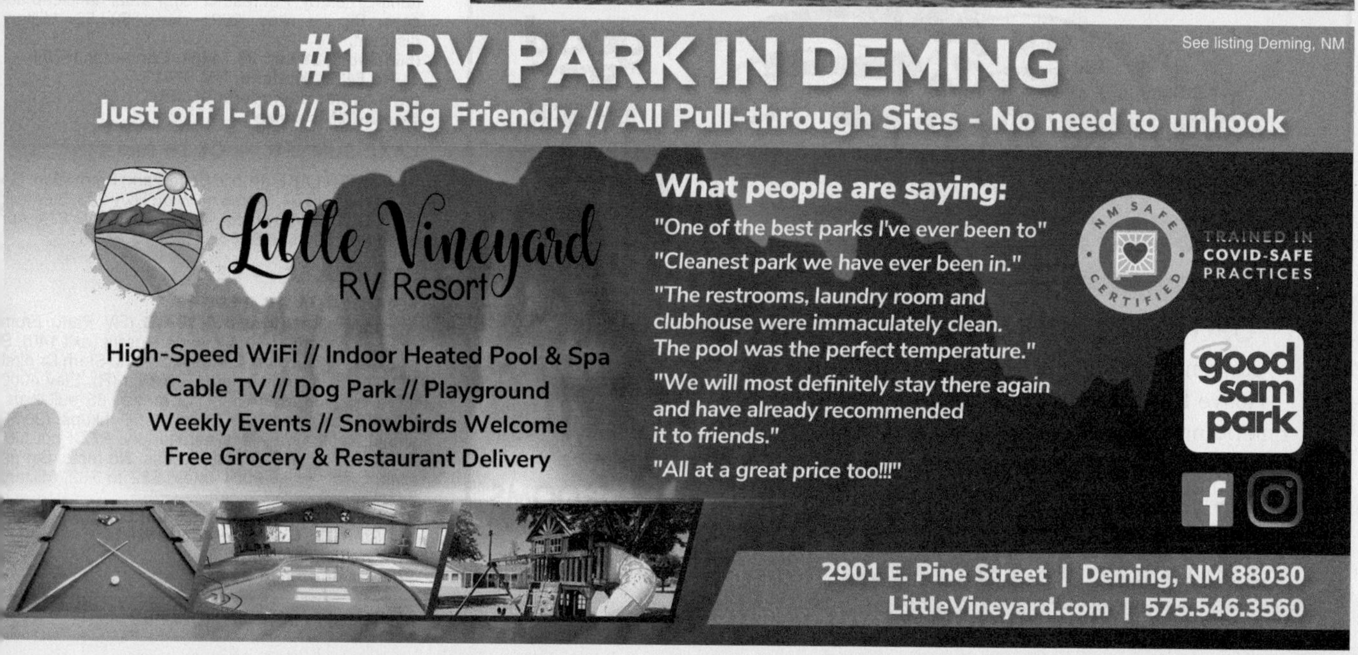

FORT SUMNER (CONT)

Things to See and Do

BILLY THE KID MUSEUM Best privately owned museum in the SW. Collection of Billy the Kid & early Western memorabilia. Elev 4000 ft. Partial handicap access. RV accessible. Restrooms. Hours: 8:30am to 5pm, vary by season. Adult fee: $5 per person.
(575)355-2380 Lat: 34.46608, Lon: -104.22885
1435 E Sumner Ave, Fort Sumner, NM 88119
billythekidmuseumfortsumner.com
See ad previous page

GALLUP — B1 *McKinley*

RED ROCK PARK (Public) E-bnd: From Jct of I-40 & Hwy 118 (exit 26), E 3.5 mi on Hwy 118 to SR-566, N 0.5 mi (L); or W-bnd: From Jct of I-40 & Hwy 118 (exit 33), W 4.2 mi on Hwy 118 to SR-566, N 0.5 mi (L). 300 Avail: 250 W, 250 E (30/50 amps). 2021 rates: $10 to $22. (505)722-3839

USA RV PARK
Ratings: 10/10★/9 (RV Park) From jct of I-40 & exit 16 (Historic Route 66/W US Hwy 66/Hwy 118/Bus Loop 40): Go 1 mi E on W US Hwy 66/Hwy 118/Bus Loop 40 (R) Note: don't rely solely on GPS. Elev 6469 ft.

NEW MEXICO UNIQUE PREMIER RV PARK
Family owned & operated park, beautifully landscaped w/ paved roads. Fine amenities including pool, Wi-Fi, sparkling restrooms & showers, gift shop & BBQ dinner. Pet friendly. Visit our Patriot Exhibit and Route 66!

FAC: paved rds. (136 spaces). Avail: 128 all weather, patios, 118 pull-thrus, (27x80), back-ins (27x75), mostly side by side hkups, 107 full hkups, 21 W, 21 E (30/50 amps), seasonal sites, cable, WiFi @ sites, tent sites, rentals, dump, laundry, groc, LP gas, restaurant. **REC:** heated pool, playground. Pet restrict (B/Q). Partial handicap access. Big rig sites, eco-friendly. 2021 rates: $39.61 to $46.20, Military discount.
(505)863-5021 Lat: 35.50738, Lon: -108.81196
2925 W Historic Hwy 66, Gallup, NM 87301
www.usarvpark.com
See ad this page

Things to See and Do

USA RV BBQ BBQ restaurant serving dinner, desserts & fountain drinks Memorial Day-Labor Day. Elev 6469 ft. May 25 to Sep 10. Food. Hours: 5:30pm to 8:30pm.
(505)863-5021 Lat: 35.50738, Lon: -108.81196
2925 W Historic Hwy 66, Gallup, NM 87301
usarvpark.com
See ad this page

USA RV GIFT SHOP Route 66 souvenirs and Native American jewelry, pottery and related collectibles. Elev 6469 ft. Hours: 8am to 10pm.
(505)863-5021 Lat: 35.50738, Lon: -108.81196
2925 W Historic Hwy 66, Gallup, NM 87301
usarvpark.com
See ad this page

GRANTS — C2 *Cibola*

BAR S RV PARK
Ratings: 7.5/9.5★/8.5 (RV Park) From jct of I-40 & Exit 79: Go 500 feet NE on Exit 79 to Pinon Dr (between Chevron & Love Truck Stop), then 1/4 mi NW (R). Elev 6575 ft.**FAC:** gravel rds. (50 spaces). Avail: 30 gravel, 30 pull-thrus, (27x70), 30 full hkups (30/50 amps), seasonal sites, cable, WiFi @ sites, laundry. **REC:** hunting nearby. Pet restrict (B). Partial handicap access. No tents. Big rig sites, eco-friendly. 2021 rates: $22 to $23, Military discount.
(505)876-6002 Lat: 35.18674, Lon: -107.90083
1860 Pinon St, Grants, NM 87021
www.barsrvpark.com
See ad this page

BLUE SPRUCE RV PARK
Ratings: 6.5/8.5★/7.5 (RV Park) From jct of I-40 & Hwy 53 (Exit 81 or 81A): Go 500 feet S on Hwy 53 (R). Elev 6460 ft.**FAC:** gravel rds. (25 spaces). Avail: 15 gravel, 12 pull-thrus, (20x65), back-ins (22x30), 9 full hkups, 6 W, 6 E (30/50 amps), seasonal sites, cable, WiFi @ sites, dump, laundry. **REC:** hunting nearby. Pet restrict (B). Partial handicap access. No tents. 2021 rates: $24.89.
(505)287-2560 Lat: 35.15159, Lon: -107.87491
1708 Zuni Canyon Rd, Grants, NM 87020
See ad this page

GRANTS KOA JOURNEY **Ratings: 7.5/9.5★/9** (Campground) 38 Avail: 36 full hkups, 2 W, 2 E (30/50 amps). 2021 rates: $48.90. Mar 01 to Nov 30. (888)562-5608, 26 Cibola Sands Loop, Grants, NM 87020

LAVALAND RV PARK
Ratings: 7/8.5★/8 (RV Park) From I-40 (exit 85): Go 100 yards S on Santa Fe Ave (R). Elev 6400 ft.**FAC:** gravel rds. (39 spaces). Avail: 19 gravel, 10 pull-thrus, (30x75), back-ins (30x65), 19 full hkups (30/50 amps), seasonal sites, WiFi @ sites, tent sites, dump, laundry. **REC:** hunting nearby. Pets OK. Partial handicap access, eco-friendly. 2021 rates: $28.25.
(505)287-8665 Lat: 35.12231, Lon: -107.83311
1901 E Santa Fe Ave, Grants, NM 87020
www.lavalandrvpark.com
See ad this page

Things to See and Do

ELKINS BREWING COMPANY Micro brewery serving local beers with flights, pints or growlers available to-go. Air conditioned bar and covered patio area. RV accessible. Restrooms. Food. Hours: 3pm to 10pm.
(505)287-5029 Lat: 35.12231, Lon: -107.83311
1901 E Santa Fe Ave, Grants, NM 87020
Elkinsbrewing.com
See ad this page

HOBBS — D5 *Lea*

MCADAMS PARK (Public) From town, NW 6 mi on NM-18 to Jack Gomez, W 0.6 mi (R). Avail: 15 full hkups (30/50 amps). 2021 rates: $18. (575)397-9291

KIRTLAND — A1 *San Juan*

HOMESTEAD RV PARK
Ratings: 7/10★/8 (RV Park) From the jct of Hwy 64 & Rd 6500: Go 1 block N on Rd 6500, then 1 block E on Rd 6432. (R). Elev 5175 ft.**FAC:** gravel rds. (64 spaces). Avail: 50 gravel, 30 pull-thrus, (30x65), back-ins (27x38), 50 full hkups (30/50 amps), seasonal sites, WiFi @ sites, tent sites, rentals, laundry. **REC:** hunting nearby. Pet restrict (B). Partial handicap access. Big rig sites. 2021 rates: $38.52, Military discount.
(505)598-9181 Lat: 36.74464, Lon: -108.35794
11 Rd 6432 , Kirtland, NM 87417
www.homesteadrvparknm.com
See ad this page

LAKE SUMNER — C4 *De Baca*

SUMNER LAKE (Public State Park) From town: Go 10 mi N on US 84, then 6 mi W on Hwy 203. 50 Avail: 16 W, 32 E (30/50 amps). 2021 rates: $8 to $18. Apr 01 to Sep 30. (575)355-2541

LAS CRUCES — E2 *Dona Ana*

HACIENDA RV RESORT
Ratings: 8.5/10★/8 (RV Park) From Jct of I-10 & Ave de Mesilla (exit 140), S 0.1 mi on Ave de Mesilla to Stern Dr (first immediate left), E 0.2 mi (R). Elev 4000 ft.**FAC:** paved rds. Avail: 113 gravel, 85 pull-thrus, (25x60), back-ins (27x36), 113 full hkups (30/50 amps), cable, WiFi @ sites, laundry. **REC:** hot tub. Pets OK. Partial handicap access. No tents. Big rig sites, eco-friendly. 2021 rates: $32 to $62, Military discount.
(888)686-9090 Lat: 32.28655, Lon: -106.78708
740 Stern Dr, Las Cruces, NM 88005
www.haciendarv.com
See ad opposite page

LAS CRUCES KOA JOURNEY **Ratings: 8/9★/8.5** (Campground) 74 Avail: 69 full hkups, 5 W, 5 E (30/50 amps). 2021 rates: $39 to $59. (575)526-6555, 814 Weinrich Rd, Las Cruces, NM 88007

LEASBURG DAM (Public State Park) From jct of I-25 & Ft Seldon Rd: Go 3/4 mi SW on Fort Seldon Rd, then 1/2 mi W on Leasburg Park Rd. (L). 23 Avail: 18 W, 18 E (30 amps). 2021 rates: $8 to $18. (575)524-4068

SIESTA RV PARK **Ratings: 6/5/5.5** (RV Park) 36 Avail: 32 full hkups, 4 W, 4 E (30/50 amps). 2021 rates: $36 to $44. (575)523-6816, 1551 Ave de Mesilla, Las Cruces, NM 88005

SUNNY ACRES RV PARK

good sam park **Ratings: 8/10★/9.5** (RV Park) From Albuquerque: From Jct of I-25 & Exit 3 (Lohman Ave/Amador), SW 2.7 mi on Lohman/Amador to Valley Dr, N 0.5 mi (L); or From W Jct of I-10 & Exit 139 (Motel Dr/SR-292), N 0.2 mi on SR-292 to Amador, E 1.2 mi to Valley Dr, N 0.5 mi (L). Elev 3889 ft.

ALL AGES - DESTINATION VACATION!

We are situated perfectly for millennials looking for outdoor adventures! Nearby Mountain biking, hiking, climbing & off roading. Also Museums & Monuments. Must plan to stay awhile to fully enjoy all our area has to offer!

FAC: gravel rds. (100 spaces). Avail: 40 gravel, patios, 16 pull-thrus, (33x85), back-ins (39x60), 40 full hkups (30/50 amps), seasonal sites, cable, WiFi @ sites, laundry. Pet restrict (B/Q). Partial handicap access. No tents, Age restrict may apply. Big rig sites. 2021 rates: $50 to $55, Military discount.

(877)800-1716 Lat: 32.31033, Lon: -106.79692
595 N Valley Dr, Las Cruces, NM 88005
www.lascrucesrvpark.com
See ad this page

LAS VEGAS — B4 *San Miguel*

LAS VEGAS KOA **Ratings: 8.5/8.5★/9** (Campground) 53 Avail: 36 full hkups, 17 W, 17 E (30/50 amps). 2021 rates: $36 to $44. (505)454-0180, 76 County Rd A 25 A, Las Vegas, NM 87701

STORRIE LAKE (Public State Park) From Jct of I-25 & exit 347 (Grand Ave) SW 0.8 mi on Grand Ave to Mountain View Dr, W 0.8 mi to 7th St (Hwy 518), N 3 mi (L). 45 Avail: 22 W, 22 E (30 amps). 2021 rates: $8 to $18. (505)425-7278

LOGAN — B5 *Quay*

UTE LAKE (Public State Park) From Jct of US-54 & Hwy 540, SW 2.4 mi on Hwy 540 (L). 161 Avail: 96 W, 98 E (30/50 amps). 2021 rates: $8 to $18. (575)487-2284

LORDSBURG — E1 *Hidalgo*

LORDSBURG KOA JOURNEY

Ratings: 8.5/8.5★/8 (Campground) From Jct of I-10 & Main St (exit 22), S 0.1 mi on Main St to Maple St, W 0.1 to Lead, S 0.2 to Park (E). Follow signs. Elev 4230 ft.**FAC:** gravel rds. Avail: 63 gravel, 63 pull-thrus, (24x60), 45 full hkups, 18 W, 18 E (30/50 amps), cable, WiFi @ sites, tent sites, rentals, dump, laundry, groc, LP gas, firewood. **REC:** pool, playground, hunting nearby. Pet restrict (B). Partial handicap access. Big rig sites. 2021 rates: $39.89 to $44.89.

(575)542-8003 Lat: 32.34105, Lon: -108.71713
1501 Lead St, Lordsburg, NM 88045
koa.com
See ad this page

MAYHILL — D3 *Otero*

DEER SPRING RV PARK **Ratings: 6.5/7.5★/7** (RV Park) Avail: 16 full hkups (30/50 amps). 2021 rates: $53.16. Apr 01 to Oct 31. (575)687-3464, 2112 Rio Penasco Rd, Mayhill, NM 88339

THE CAMP AT CLOUDCROFT **Ratings: 6.5/8★/7** (RV Park) Avail: 28 full hkups (30/50 amps). 2021 rates: $34. (575)687-3715, 2180 Rio Penasco Rd, Mayhill, NM 88339

MORA — B4 *Mora*

COYOTE CREEK (Public State Park) From Jct of Hwys 518 & 434, N 17 mi on Hwy 434; or From Jct of Hwys 121 & 434, S 18 mi on Hwy 434 (L). 35 Avail: 16 W, 16 E (30 amps). 2021 rates: $8 to $18. (575)387-2328

MORIARTY — C3 *Torrance*

CUERVO MOUNTAIN RV PARK AND HORSE HOTEL

good sam park **Ratings: 7/8.5/8** (RV Park) 54 Avail: 34 full hkups, 20 W, 20 E (30/50 amps). 2021 rates: $35 to $48. (505)316-5070, 16 Ella Dora Rd, Stanley, NM 87056

MOUNTAINAIR — C3 *Torrance*

MANZANO MOUNTAINS (Public State Park) From jct NM 55 & NM 131: Go 3-1/2 mi S on NM 131, then 1-1/4 mi W on NM 131(CR B062). (R). Avail: 9 E. 2021 rates: $8 to $18. Apr 24 to Nov 01. (505)469-7608

OJO CALIENTE — B3 *Taos*

OJO CALIENTE MINERAL SPRINGS RESORT & SPA RV PARK (Campground) (Rebuilding) 28 Avail: 28 W, 26 E (30/50 amps). 2021 rates: $42. (888)939-0007, 50 Los Banos Drive, Hwy 414, Ojo Caliente, NM 87549

PENA BLANCA — B3 *Sandoval*

COCHITI LAKE - COE/COCHITI AREA (Public Corps) From town, S 17 mi on I-25 to NM-16, NW 8.4 mi to NM-22, N 4 mi (R). Avail: 48 E (15/50 amps). 2021 rates: $12 to $20. (505)465-2557

COCHITI LAKE - COE/TETILLA PEAK (Public Corps) From town, SW on I-25 13 mi, W 3.8 mi on NM-16 to La Bajada Rd, N 10 mi (E). Avail: 36 E (30/50 amps). 2021 rates: $12 to $20. Apr 15 to Oct 15. (505)465-0274

PILAR — B3 *Taos*

ORILLA VERDE REC AREA (BLM) (Public Corps) From town, SW 5.6 mi on US-68, W 6.5 mi on Hwy 570. 41 Avail: 10 W, 10 E. 2021 rates: $15. (575)758-8851

PORTALES — C5 *Roosevelt*

OASIS (Public State Park) From Jct of US-70 & SR-467, N 5 mi on SR-467 to Oasis Rd, W 2 mi (E). 26 Avail: 2 full hkups, 20 W, 14 E (30/50 amps). 2021 rates: $8 to $18. (575)356-5331

PREWITT — B2 *Cibola*

BLUEWATER LAKE (Public State Park) From Jct of I-40 & Hwy 412 (exit 63), S 7 mi on Hwy 412, follow signs (L). Avail: 14 E (30/50 amps). 2021 rates: $8 to $18. (505)876-2391

RATON — A4 *Colfax*

NRA WHITTINGTON CENTER CAMPGROUNDS **Ratings: 6.5/7.5★/7.5** (Campground) Avail: 123 full hkups (30/50 amps). 2021 rates: $32 to $45. (575)445-3615, 34025 Hwy 64 West, Raton, NM 87740

RATON KOA JOURNEY **Ratings: 6.5/7/6.5** (Campground) 41 Avail: 31 full hkups, 10 W, 10 E (30/50 amps). 2021 rates: $34.88 to $47.88. (575)445-3488, 1330 S 2nd St, Raton, NM 87740

SUGARITE CANYON (Public State Park) From jct I-25 & Hwy 72: Go 6 mi E on Hwy 72, then 2 mi N on Hwy 526. 40 Avail: 2 full hkups, 8 W, 8 E (30 amps). 2021 rates: $8 to $18. (575)445-5607

RED RIVER — A3 *Taos*

4K RIVER RANCH **Ratings: 7/9★/7** (Campground) Avail: 74 full hkups (30/50 amps). 2021 rates: $34 to $59. May 01 to Mar 31. (575)754-2293, 1501 W Main St, Red River, NM 87558

ROAD RUNNER RV RESORT **Ratings: 8/9★/9** (RV Resort) Avail: 95 full hkups (30/50 amps). 2021 rates: $45 to $60. May 01 to Oct 15. (575)754-2286, 1371 E Main St, Red River, NM 87558

RIO RANCHO — B3 *Sandoval*

STAGECOACH STOP RV PARK

good sam park **Ratings: 10/9.5★/10** (RV Park) From jct of I-25 & Exit 242 (Hwy 550): Go W 2.4mi on Hwy 550 to Hwy 528, S 0.6 mi to Montoya, E 0.1 mi on Montoya to Christopher Way (behind McDonalds), N 0.1 mi to Gabby Way, E 0.1 mi (R). Elev 5300 ft.**FAC:** paved rds. (85 spaces). Avail: 18 paved, 18 pull-thrus, (27x60), 18 full hkups (30/50 amps), cable, WiFi @ sites, dump, laundry. **REC:** heated pool, hot tub. Pet restrict (B). Partial handicap access. No tents. Big rig sites, eco-friendly. 2021 rates: $42 to $52, Military discount.

(505)867-1000 Lat: 35.32323, Lon: -106.57075
3650 State Hwy 528 NE, Rio Rancho, NM 87144
www.stagecoachstoprv.com
See ad page 623

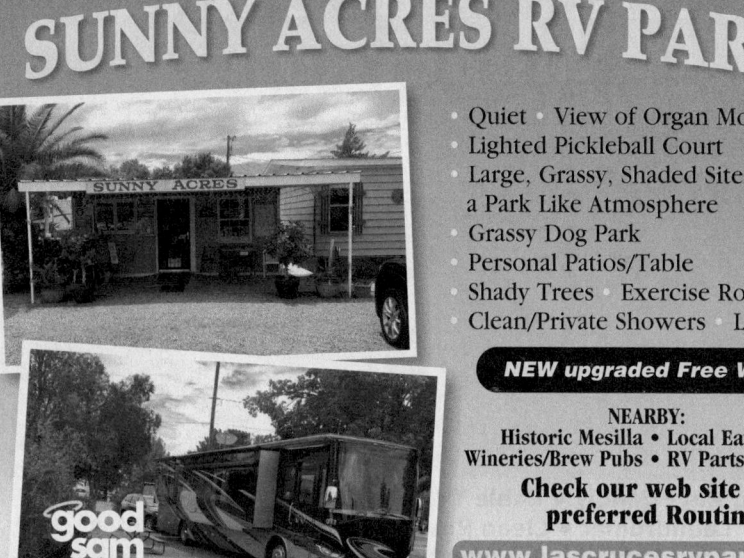

NM

ROSWELL — D4 *Chaves*

BOTTOMLESS LAKES (Public State Park) From jct of US-380 & US-285: Go 10-1/4 mi E on US-380, then 3 mi S on SR-409/Bottomless Lakes Rd (R). 32 Avail: 6 full hkups, 26 W, 26 E (30/50 amps). 2021 rates: $8 to $18. (575)624-6058

TOWN & COUNTRY RV PARK
good sam park **Ratings: 10/10★/9.5** (RV Park) Avail: 90 full hkups (30/50 amps). 2021 rates: $35. (575)624-1833, 331 W Brasher Rd, Roswell, NM 88203

TRAILER VILLAGE RV PARK **Ratings: 8/10★/9.5** (RV Park) Avail: 68 full hkups (30/50 amps). 2021 rates: $36 to $39. (575)623-6040, 1706 E 2nd St, Roswell, NM 88201

RUIDOSO — D3 *Lincoln*

EAGLE CREEK RV RESORT
good sam park **Ratings: 8/NA/9.5** (RV Park) Avail: 54 full hkups (30/50 amps). 2021 rates: $40 to $45. Apr 01 to Nov 01. (575)336-1131, 159 Ski Run Rd, Alto, NM 88312

MIDTOWN MOUNTAIN CAMPGROUND & RV PARK
good sam park **Ratings: 9/10★/9.5** (Campground) Avail: 27 full hkups (30/50 amps). 2021 rates: $39 to $59. (575)964-8555, 302 Mechem Dr, Ruidoso, NM 88345

RAINBOW LAKE CABIN & RV RESORT **Ratings: 7.5/8.5★/7.5** (RV Park) Avail: 49 full hkups (30/50 amps). 2021 rates: $38 to $45. (575)630-2267, 806 Carrizo Canyon Rd, Ruidoso, NM 88345

SLOW PLAY **Ratings: 8.5/10★/9** (RV Park) Avail: 158 full hkups (30/50 amps). 2021 rates: $44 to $55. (575)378-4990, 26514 E Hwy 70, Ruidoso Downs, NM 88346

TWIN SPRUCE RV PARK
good sam park **Ratings: 9/9.5★/9** (Campground) Avail: 111 full hkups (30/50 amps). 2021 rates: $34.95 to $46.95. (575)257-4310, 25996 US Hwy70, Ruidoso, NM 88345

SANTA FE — B3 *Sandoval*

A SPOTLIGHT Introducing Santa Fe's colorful attractions appearing at the front of this state section.

SANTA FE See also Las Vegas.

HIPICO SANTA FE **Ratings: 6.5/NA/9** (RV Park) 50 Avail: 50 W, 50 E (30/50 amps). 2021 rates: $45. (505)474-0999, 100 S. Polo Dr, Santa Fe, NM 87507

HYDE MEMORIAL (Public State Park) From Jct of Washington Ave & Hwy 475 (Artist Rd.), NE 7.5 mi on Hwy 475 (E). Entrance fee required. Avail: 7 E (30 amps), Pit toilets. 2021 rates: $8 to $18. (505)983-7175

We rate what RVers consider important.

LOS SUENOS DE SANTA FE RV RESORT & CAMPGROUND **Ratings: 7/9.5★/7.5** (RV Park) Avail: 60 full hkups (30/50 amps). 2021 rates: $38.08 to $55. (505)473-1949, 3574 Cerrillos Rd, Santa Fe, NM 87507

RANCHEROS DE SANTA FE CAMPGROUND
good sam park **Ratings: 8.5/9.5★/9** (Campground) From Jct of I-25 & Exit 290 (NM 300/Old Las Vegas Hwy): Go 1/3 mi N on US 285 to N Frntg Rd, SE (turn right) then 1 mi (L). Elev 7200 ft.

SANTA FE'S MOST SCENIC CAMPGROUND
Peaceful, wooded camping only minutes from Old Town Santa Fe & known worldwide for our scenic, natural setting. We are located on Historic Route 66, adjacent to the Santa Fe Trail & near the culture and flavor of Santa Fe.

FAC: paved/gravel rds. (124 spaces). Avail: 99 gravel, 72 pull-thrus, (24x55), back-ins (22x50), 53 full hkups, 46 W, 46 E (30/50 amps), seasonal sites, cable, WiFi @ sites, tent sites, rentals, dump, laundry, LP gas, fire rings, firewood. **REC:** pool, playground, hunting nearby. Pets OK. eco-friendly. 2021 rates: $44.95 to $58.50, Military discount.
(505)466-3482 Lat: 35.54580, Lon: -105.86404
736 Old Las Vegas Hwy, Santa Fe, NM 87505
rancheros.com
See ad this page

ROADRUNNER RV PARK
good sam park **Ratings: 8/NA/7.5** (RV Park) From jct of 84/285 & W Gutierrez St (in Pojoaque): Go 100 feet W to O'go Wii St, then 500 feet S on O'go Wii St to entrance (R). Elev 5942 ft.

FUN TIMES JUST NORTH OF SANTA FE!
Located near Buffalo Thunder & Cities of Gold Casinos as well as Poeh Cultural Center & Museum. Enjoy the amenities of a resort & casinos then return to the solitude of your campsite at night. Just off I-25 North of Santa Fe.

FAC: gravel rds. (60 spaces). Avail: 10 gravel, 10 pull-thrus, (35x60), accepts full hkup units only, 10 full hkups (30/50 amps), seasonal sites, WiFi @ sites, groc, restaurant. **REC:** heated pool, hot tub, boating nearby, rec open to public. Pets OK. No tents. Big rig sites, eco-friendly. 2021 rates: $38, Military discount. ATM.
(505)455-2626 Lat: 35.88161, Lon: -106.01367
55 O'Go Wii, Santa Fe, NM 87506
pojoaque.org
See ad page 620

SANTA FE KOA JOURNEY **Ratings: 7.5/10★/8.5** (Campground) 46 Avail: 32 full hkups, 14 W, 14 E (30/50 amps). 2021 rates: $49.45 to $95. Mar 01 to Nov 01. (505)466-1419, 934 Old Las Vegas Hwy, Santa Fe, NM 87505

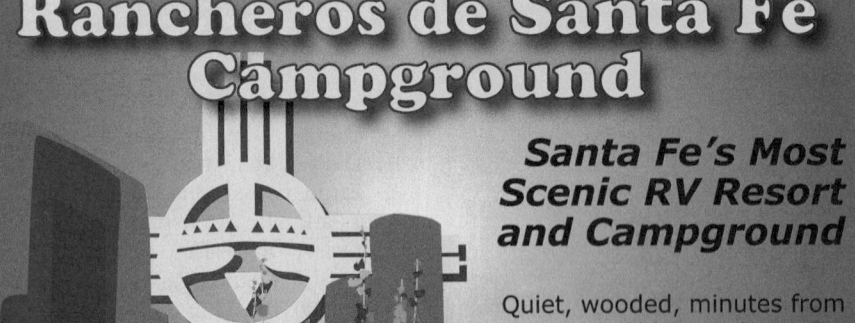

SANTA FE SKIES RV PARK
good sam park **Ratings: 8/10★/10** (RV Park) N-bnd: From Jct of I-25 & Exit 276 (SR-599) Go 1/2 mi SE on SR-599 to NM 14, continue straight across NM 14 to park on Ridge (L); or S-bnd: From Jct of I-25 & Exit 276, SE (stay left) under I-25 to NM 14, continue straight across NM 14 to park on Ridge (L). Elev 6633 ft.

PAINTERS' SUNSETS AND STARRY NIGHTS
Beautiful views & sunsets! We are at an elevation of nearly 7,000 feet with quiet serenity. Close to Santa Fe's sights & minutes from the Historic Santa Fe Plaza, miraculous Loretto Chapel, restaurants & shops. Viva Santa Fe!

FAC: paved/gravel rds. Avail: 97 gravel, patios, 53 pull-thrus, (31x75), back-ins (40x45), 97 full hkups (30/50 amps), WiFi @ sites, dump, laundry, LP gas. **REC:** hunting nearby. Pets OK. Partial handicap access. No tents. Big rig sites, eco-friendly. 2021 rates: $63 to $75, Military discount.
(505)473-5946 Lat: 35.58863, Lon: -106.04477
14 Browncastle Ranch, Santa Fe, NM 87508
www.santafeskiesrvpark.com
See ad opposite page

TRAILER RANCH RV RESORT & 55+ COMMUNITY **Ratings: 9/9.5★/9.5** (RV Park) Avail: 52 full hkups (30/50 amps). 2021 rates: $52 to $85. (505)471-9970, 3471 Cerrillos Rd, Santa Fe, NM 87507

Things to See and Do

BUFFALO THUNDER RESORT & CASINO Luxury hotel and suites. Casino has 70,000 square feet, 1,200 slot machines, dedicated poker room, race book, high limit slot area, and the large table games pit. Entertainment venue, conference center and wedding/event venue. Elev 6000 ft. Partial handicap access. RV accessible. Restrooms. Food. Hours: . ATM.
(505)455-5555 Lat: 35.86096, Lon: -105.99789
20 Buffalo Thunder Trail, Santa Fe, NM 87506
hiltonbuffalothunder.com
See ad page 620

CITIES OF GOLD CASINO & HOTEL Slots, luxury hotel, tasty buffet & sports bar. Elev 6000 ft. Partial handicap access. RV accessible. Restrooms. Food. Hours: . ATM.
(800)455-3313 Lat: 35.89003, Lon: -106.02017
10-B Cities of Gold Road, Santa Fe, NM 87506
citiesofgold.com
See ad page 620

WELLNESS & HEALING ARTS CULTURAL CENTER Pueblo of Pojoaque Wellness & Healing Arts Center open to public with some complimentary access to guests of Roadrunner RV Park. Healing Arts, Massage, Acupuncture, Classes, Aquatic Programs & Physical Therapy. Elev 7000 ft. Restrooms. Hours: 6am to 8pm. No CC.
(505)455-9355
101 Lightning Loop, Santa Fe, NM 87506
pojoaquewellness.com
See ad page 620

SANTA ROSA — C4 *Guadalupe*

SANTA ROSA CAMPGROUND
good sam park **Ratings: 8/9★/8.5** (RV Park) 91 Avail: 33 full hkups, 58 W, 58 E (30/50 amps). 2021 rates: $32 to $42. (575)472-3126, 2136 Historic Route 66, Santa Rosa, NM 88435

SANTA ROSA LAKE (Public State Park) From Jct of I-40 & 2nd St, N 1 blk on 2nd St to Eddy St, E 7 blks to 8th St, N 7.5 mi (E). Avail: 26 E (20 amps). 2021 rates: $8 to $18. (575)472-3110

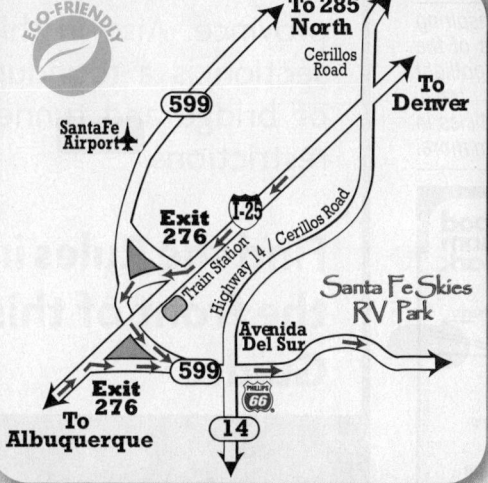

SILVER CITY — D1 *Grant*

BURRO MOUNTAIN HOMESTEAD RV PARK **Ratings: 7/8.5★/7.5** (Campground) Avail: 29 full hkups (30/50 amps). 2021 rates: $36 to $41. (575)538-2149, 665 Tyrone Rd, Silver City, NM 88061

RIDGEPARK RV **Ratings: 6.5/8.5★/10** (Campground) Avail: 39 full hkups (30/50 amps). 2021 rates: $35. (575)313-9375, 2789 Hwy 90 S, Silver City, NM 88061

ROSE VALLEY RV RANCH & CASITAS
Ratings: 8/8★/10 (RV Park) From Jct of Hwy 180 & Hwy 90, E 1.1 mi on Hwy 180 to Memory Lane, S 0.2 mi on Memory Ln (L). From Deming: Continue W on Hwy 180 to Memory Lane, S 0.2 mi on Memory Lane (L). Elev 5938 ft.**FAC:** gravel rds. (68 spaces). Avail: 52 gravel, 14 pull-thrus, (35x70), back-ins (30x58), 52 full hkups (30/50 amps), seasonal sites, WiFi @ sites, rentals, dump, laundry. Pet restrict (B). Partial handicap access. No tents. Big rig sites, eco-friendly. 2021 rates: $34 to $38, Military discount.
(575)534-4277 Lat: 32.78409, Lon: -108.25253
2040 Memory Ln, Silver City, NM 88061
rosevalleyrv.com
See ad this page

SILVER CITY KOA **Ratings: 9/10★/9** (Campground) Avail: 40 full hkups (30/50 amps). 2021 rates: $38.89 to $60.89. (575)388-3351, 11824 Hwy 180E, Silver City, NM 88022

TAOS — B3 *Taos*

TAOS VALLEY RV PARK & CAMPGROUND **Ratings: 7/9/9** (Campground) 56 Avail: 31 full hkups, 25 W, 25 E (30/50 amps). 2021 rates: $37.53 to $50.04. (575)758-4469, 120 Este Es Rd, Taos, NM 87571

TIERRA AMARILLA — A3 *Rio Arriba*

EL VADO LAKE (Public State Park) From Jct of US-84 & SR-112, W 13.5 mi on SR-112 (R). 80 Avail: 2 full hkups, 17 W, 17 E (30/50 amps). 2021 rates: $8 to $18. Apr 01 to Nov 30. (575)588-7247

HERON LAKE (Public State Park) From town, W 6 mi on SR-95 (R). Entrance fee required. Avail: 54 E (15/30 amps). 2021 rates: $8 to $18. May 15 to Sep 15. (575)588-7470

TIJERAS — C3 *Bernalillo*

HIDDEN VALLEY RV MOUNTAIN RESORT **Ratings: 6.5/7/6** (Membership Park) Avail: 50 full hkups (30/50 amps). 2021 rates: $37.63 to $50. (505)281-3363, 844-B State Hwy 333, Tijeras, NM 87059

TRUTH OR CONSEQUENCES — D2 *Sierra*

CIELO VISTA RV PARK
Ratings: 6.5/8.5★/8.5 (RV Park) Avail: 20 full hkups (30/50 amps). 2021 rates: $38. (575)894-3738, 501 S Broadway, Truth or Consequences, NM 87901

ELEPHANT BUTTE LAKE (Public State Park) From Jct of I-25 & exit 83 (SR-181), SE 0.1 mi on SR-181 to SR-195, E 4 mi, follow signs (L). 173 Avail: 8 full hkups, 144 W, 144 E (30/50 amps). 2021 rates: $8 to $18. Mar 15 to Oct 15. (575)744-5923

TUCUMCARI — B5 *Quay*

BLAZE-IN-SADDLE RV PARK & HORSE HOTEL
Ratings: 6/9★/8.5 (Campground) From jct I-40W (exit 335)/Historic Rt 66 & E Tucumcari Blvd: Go 1-1/4 mi W on Historic Rt 66/E Tucumcari Blvd (R). Elev 4030 ft.

EASY ON & OFF I-40 TUCUMCARI NM
Much to see & do! Historic Route 66 Motels in much of their original state, including the Palomino & infamous Blue Swallow-perfect photo ops! Mesalands Dinosaur, Tucumcari Historical, Route 66 Museums, etc & fabulous Sunsets!

FAC: gravel rds. (51 spaces). Avail: 43 gravel, 35 pull-thrus, (24x60), back-ins (28x65), 43 full hkups (30/50 amps), seasonal sites, WiFi @ sites, tent sites, dump, laundry, firewood. **REC:** boating nearby, hunting nearby. Pets OK. Partial handicap access. Big rig sites. 2021 rates: $32 to $34, Military discount.
(575)815-4085 Lat: 35.17177, Lon: -103.69361
2500 E Rt 66 Blvd, Tucumcari, NM 88401
www.blaze-in-saddle.com
See ad this page

CONCHAS LAKE (Public State Park) From Tucumcari, NW 32 mi on SR-104 (R). 73 Avail: 66 W, 33 E (30/50 amps). 2021 rates: $8 to $18. (575)868-2270

MOUNTAIN ROAD RV PARK
Ratings: 7/9★/9 (RV Park) From Jct of I-40 & US-54/Mountain Rd (exit 333): Go 1/2 mi N on US-54 (L). Elev 4085 ft.**FAC:** gravel rds. Avail: 58 gravel, 58 pull-thrus, (24x60), 58 full hkups (30/50 amps), cable, WiFi @ sites, tent sites, laundry. **REC:** boating nearby, playground, hunting nearby. Pets OK. Big rig sites, eco-friendly. 2021 rates: $34 to $38, Military discount.
(575)461-9628 Lat: 35.16258, Lon: -103.70305
1701 Mountain Rd, Tucumcari, NM 88401
mountainroadrvpark.com
See ad this page

TUCUMCARI KOA JOURNEY **Ratings: 8/8.5★/7** (Campground) 94 Avail: 44 full hkups, 50 W, 50 E (30/50 amps). 2021 rates: $38.35 to $50. (575)461-1841, 6299 Quay Rd AL, Tucumcari, NM 88401

VILLANUEVA — B4 *San Miguel*

VILLANUEVA (Public State Park) From Jct of I-25 & SR-3 (Villanueva State Park exit), S 13 mi on SR-3; or From Jct of I-40 & SR-3 (exit 230), N 21 mi on SR-3 (R). Avail: 12 E (20/30 amps). 2021 rates: $8 to $18. (575)421-2957

Check out those views! From awe-inspiring redwood giants to the soaring towers of the Golden Gate Bridge, we've put the Spotlight on North America's most popular travel destinations. Turn to the Spotlight articles in our State and Province sections to learn more.

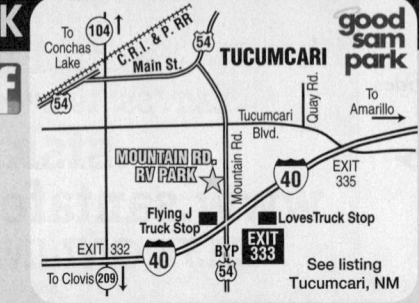

WHITE ROCK — B3 *Los Alamos*

BANDELIER NATL MON/JUNIPER (Public National Park) From town, SW 7 mi on SR-4 (L). Entrance fee required. 94 Avail. 2021 rates: $35. (505)672-3861

WHITES CITY — E4 *Eddy*

WHITE'S CITY CARLSBAD CAVERNS RV PARK **Ratings: 5/6.5/6** (Campground) 28 Avail: 8 full hkups, 20 W, 20 E (30/50 amps). 2021 rates: $45. (575)361-3665, 17 Carlsbad Caverns Hwy, Whites City, NM 88268

Got a big rig? Look for listings indicating ""big rig sites''. These campgrounds are made for you, with 12'-wide roads and 14' overhead clearance. They guarantee that 25% or more of their sites measure 24' wide by 60' long or larger, and have full hookups with 50-amp electricity.

Getty Images/iStockphoto

YOU ARE HERE

New York

DID YOU KNOW?

Experts say New York is nicknamed the Empire State because George Washington called it "the seat of the Empire."

NY

Choose between mammoth cities and lush expanses of nature in the Empire State. Everybody knows about New York City, the nation's largest city. Beyond the concrete, the state's wide-open spaces entice nature lovers.

Great Gotham!

From endless views in One World Trade Center to the lush expanse of Central Park, New York City never fails to dazzle. Study renowned artworks at the Museum of Modern Art and The Met, hear boisterous show tunes on Broadway, or sample tasty food on the go from a street vendor. In the middle of Manhattan, lush Central Park rolls out a welcoming green carpet.

Falls of Fury

For more than a century, Niagara Falls have thrilled honeymooners and adventure-seekers alike. The 2,600-foot-wide curtain of water plummets 167 feet into a misty pool, and visitors will find many ways to explore this spectacle. Niagara Falls State Park offers a number of vantage points to experience this iconic cascade from above and below. Ride on the Maid of the Mist at the foot of the falls, or walk the Cave of the Winds to feel the roar from behind the curtain. Can't get enough of raging waters? New York is home to over 2,000 waterfalls.

Long Lakes

As their name implies, the Finger Lakes stretch across the landscape like the imprints from a giants' digits. These 11 slender glacial lakes cut through picturesque rolling hills, providing a spot for angling, paddling and boating. Head to the Great Lakes for more fun. Fishing and boating count as popular activities along the shores of Lake Erie and Lake Ontario. Across the state, anglers can choose from a number of epic waterways. Fly-fishing was born in the Catskill Mountains 100 miles north of NYC.

New York Hot Dogs

New York City's teeming sidewalks are dotted with vendors who serve up steaming hot dogs. Grab a quick bite on the street or find gourmet versions of this all-American meal in some of the city's finest restaurants. For our money, it's hard to beat Feltman's of Coney Island. Enjoy the juicy meat with homemade mustard under mounds of melting cheese.

VISITOR CENTER

TIME ZONE
Eastern Standard

ROAD & HIGHWAY INFORMATION
800-THRUWAY
thruway.ny.gov

FISHING & HUNTING INFORMATION
518-402-8883
dec.ny.gov/permits/365.html

BOATING INFORMATION
518-402-8920
dec.ny.gov

NATIONAL PARKS
nps.gov/ny

STATE PARKS
parks.ny.gov

TOURISM INFORMATION
New York Department of Economic Development
800-CAL-NYS
iloveny.com

TOP TOURISM ATTRACTIONS
1) New York City
2) Adirondack Mountains
3) Niagara Falls

MAJOR CITIES
New York, Buffalo, Rochester, Yonkers, Syracuse, Albany (capital)

good sam park

Featured Good Sam Parks

NEW YORK

When you stay with Good Sam, you can expect the highest degree of cleanliness and friendliness, and better yet, you get **10% off** overnight campground fees.

If you're not already a Good Sam member you can purchase your membership at one of these locations:

ACCORD
Rondout Valley Resort

ADDISON
Sunflower Acres Family Campground

ALEXANDRIA BAY
Swan Bay Resort

BOUCKVILLE
Cider House Campground

CHAUTAUQUA
Camp Chautauqua Camping Resort

COOPERSTOWN
Cooperstown Shadow Brook Campground

COPAKE
Waubeeka Family Campground

CORINTH
Alpine Lake RV Resort

CORNING
Camp Bell Campground

DARIEN CENTER
Skyline RV Resort

FLORIDA
Black Bear Campground

GILBOA
Country Roads Campground

JAVA CENTER
Beaver Meadow Family Campground

LAKE GEORGE
King Phillips Campground
Lake George Escape Camping Resort
Lake George Riverview Campground
Ledgeview RV Park
Whippoorwill Motel & Campsites

LOCKPORT
Niagara County Camping Resort

NIAGARA FALLS
AA Royal Motel & Campground

POLAND
Adirondack Gateway Campground

PULASKI
Brennan Beach RV Resort

RANDOLPH
Pope Haven Campground

SAUGERTIES
Rip Van Winkle Campgrounds

VERONA
The Villages At Turning Stone RV Park

WARRENSBURG
Lake George Schroon Valley Resort

WILMINGTON
North Pole Resorts

WOLCOTT
Cherry Grove Campground

10/10★/10 GOOD SAM PARKS

ALEXANDRIA BAY
Swan Bay Resort
(315)482-7926

CHAUTAUQUA
Camp Chautauqua Camping Resort
(716)789-3435

FLORIDA
Black Bear Campground
(845)651-7717

LAKE GEORGE
King Phillips Campground
(518)668-5763

Lake George Riverview Campground
(518)623-9444

Ledgeview RV Park
(518)798-6621

SAUGERTIES
Rip Van Winkle Campgrounds
(845)246-8334

VERONA
The Villages At Turning Stone RV Park
(315)361-7275

What's This?

An RV park with a 10/10★/10 rating has scored perfect grades in amenities, cleanliness and appearance ("See Understanding the Campground Rating System" on pages 8 and 9 for an explanation of the trusted Good Sam Rating System). Stay in a 10/10★/10 park on your next trip for a nearly flawless camping experience.

Getty Images/iStockphoto

ROAD TRIPS

Take a Regal trip across the Empire State

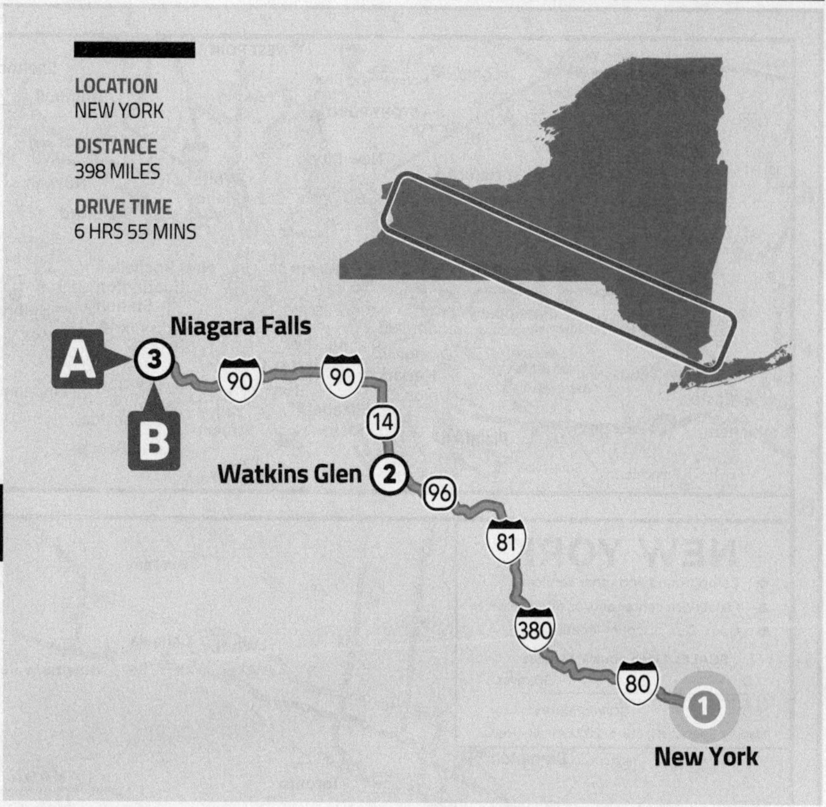

NY

New York

Go on a safari in New York's concrete jungles then head north for the great outdoors. Discover fun and fishing on the Hudson River, cruise through an iconic speedway and finish your trip at a roaring attraction. You'll love the Empire State by the time you're through.

1 New York
Starting Point

The Big Apple never disappoints. A top pick: the 102nd floor Observation Deck atop the Empire State Building for 360-degree views from the very heart of "The Big Apple." While in town, feast on a snack from a street vendor. These purveyors of vittles serve international meals on wheels. Try Ling's Sweet Mini Cakes in Chinatown. Or Gourmet Empanadas in the East Village. Korean BBQ! Tacos! Thai food! Eat on the street in NYC!

2 Watkins Glen
Drive 242 miles ▪ 4 hours, 17 minutes

Rev your engines for Watkins Glen, located on the southern shore of beautiful Seneca Lake in the heart of New York's scenic Finger Lakes Region. Watkins Glen State Park's Gorge Trail boasts 19 waterfalls along a 2.5-mile trail. The North Rim Trail (which is dog-friendly) at the State Park is open year-round and offers a neat perspective, skirting the top edge of the gorge. Southeast of town, Watkins Glen International offers a full schedule of adrenaline-pumping racing action. Watch your favorite NASCAR in action. If you want to get up close and personal with the race circuit, check out Drive the Glen, where you can drive your car on the famed road course. Get out on the water with a sail on a historic schooner on the Finger Lakes for a sightseeing cruise.

3 Niagara Falls
Drive 156 miles ▪ 2 hours, 38 minutes

Niagara Falls State Park is a window to the most legendary cascade in North America. It offers decks, boats, vista points and trails, allowing visitors up-close vantage points of the 167-foot-high American and Horseshoe falls. Nearby are adventure attractions, shopping and dining options of every kind. The Aquarium of Niagara showcases 1,500 aquatic animals from around the globe. Visit the Niagara Aerospace Museum or Old Fort Niagara, preserved as it was in the 1700s when France and Britain controlled the untamed region.

Getty Images/iStockphoto

RECOMMENDED STOPOVERS

A NIAGARA COUNTY CAMPING RESORT
LOCKPORT, NY (716) 434-3991

B AA ROYAL MOTEL & CAMPGROUND
NIAGARA FALLS, NY (716) 693-5695

BIKING BOATING DINING ENTERTAINMENT FISHING HIKING HUNTING PADDLING SHOPPING SIGHTSEEING

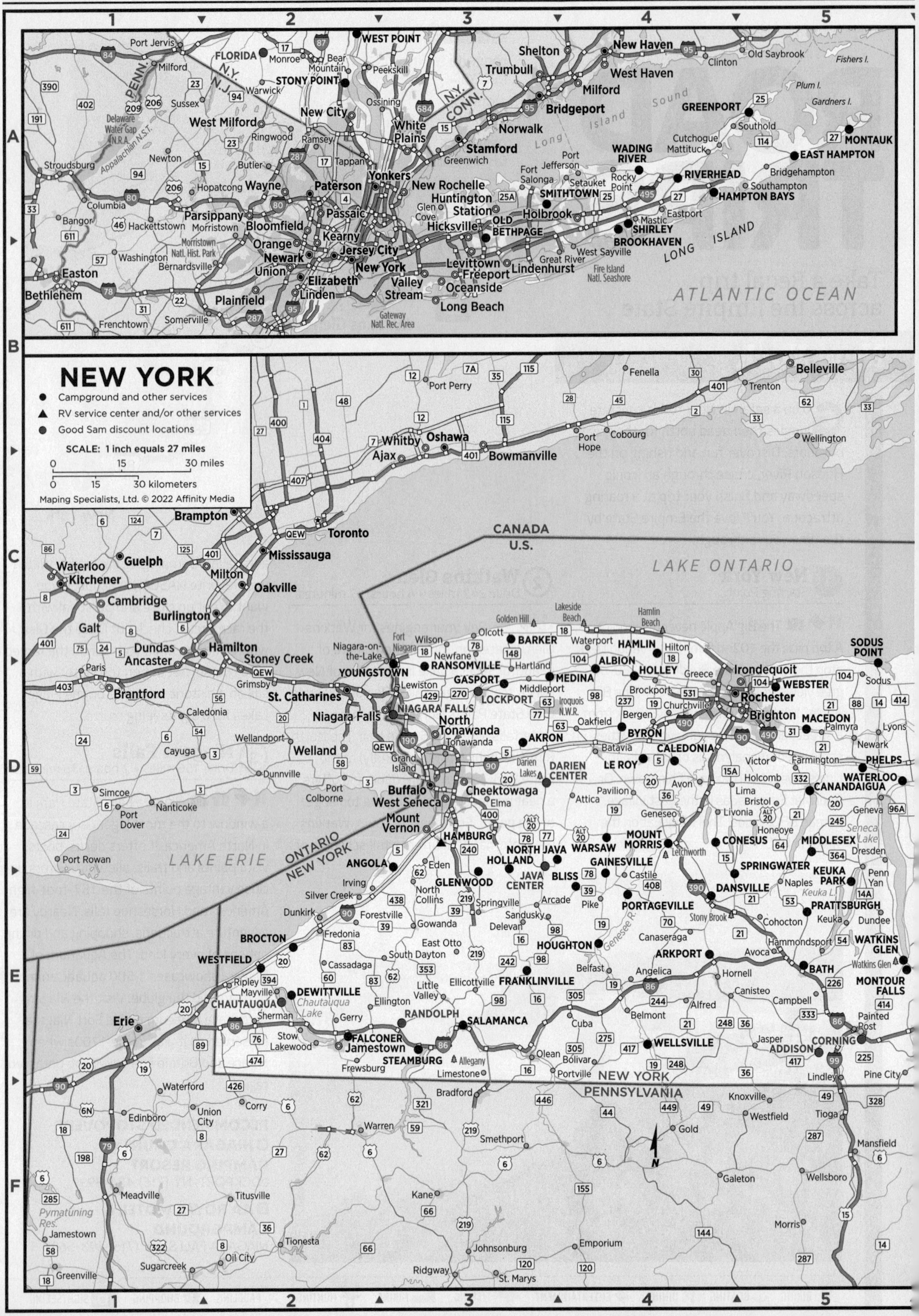
NEW YORK
Campground and other services
RV service center and/or other services
Good Sam discount locations
SCALE: 1 inch equals 27 miles
0 15 30 miles
0 15 30 kilometers
Maping Specialists, Ltd. © 2022 Affinity Media
CANADA
U.S.
LAKE ONTARIO
LAKE ERIE
ONTARIO
NEW YORK
PENNSYLVANIA
ATLANTIC OCEAN
Long Island Sound
LONG ISLAND
Port Jervis
FLORIDA
WEST POINT
STONY POINT
New City
White Plains
Yonkers
New Rochelle
Paterson
Passaic
Bloomfield
Kearny
Jersey City
New York
Newark
Elizabeth
Linden
Plainfield
Easton
Bethlehem
Stroudsburg
West Milford
Parsippany
Wayne
Stamford
Norwalk
Bridgeport
Shelton
Trumbull
New Haven
West Haven
Milford
Clinton
Old Saybrook
Fishers I.
Plum I.
Gardners I.
GREENPORT
Southold
MONTAUK
EAST HAMPTON
RIVERHEAD
WADING RIVER
SMITHTOWN
Huntington Station
Hicksville
OLD BETHPAGE
Holbrook
SHIRLEY
BROOKHAVEN
HAMPTON BAYS
Southampton
Bridgehampton
Levittown
Freeport
Lindenhurst
Oceanside
Long Beach
Valley Stream
Fire Island Natl. Seashore
Gateway Natl. Rec. Area
Belleville
Trenton
Fenella
Port Perry
Whitby
Oshawa
Ajax
Bowmanville
Port Hope
Cobourg
Wellington
Brampton
Toronto
Mississauga
Oakville
Milton
Guelph
Waterloo
Kitchener
Cambridge
Burlington
Galt
Hamilton
Dundas
Ancaster
Stoney Creek
Paris
Brantford
Grimsby
St. Catharines
Niagara Falls
Welland
Wellandport
Caledonia
Cayuga
Dunnville
Simcoe
Port Dover
Nanticoke
Port Rowan
Port Colborne
Niagara-on-the-Lake
YOUNGSTOWN
Lewiston
NIAGARA FALLS
North Tonawanda
Tonawanda
Grand Island
Buffalo
West Seneca
Cheektowaga
Mount Vernon
HAMBURG
ANGOLA
Eden
Irving
Silver Creek
Dunkirk
Fredonia
BROCTON
WESTFIELD
Ripley
Mayville
CHAUTAUQUA
DEWITTVILLE
Chautauqua Lake
Sherman
Erie
Jamestown
FALCONER
Lakewood
Frewsburg
STEAMBURG
RANDOLPH
SALAMANCA
Allegany
Olean
Limestone
Bradford
BARKER
RANSOMVILLE
GASPORT
LOCKPORT
MEDINA
ALBION
HOLLEY
HAMLIN
Brockport
Irondequoit
Rochester
WEBSTER
Brighton
SODUS POINT
MACEDON
Palmyra
Newark
Lyons
PHELPS
WATERLOO
CANANDAIGUA
BYRON
Batavia
LE ROY
CALEDONIA
AKRON
DARIEN CENTER
Attica
Geneseo
Letchworth
MOUNT MORRIS
WARSAW
NORTH JAVA
HOLLAND
GLENWOOD
JAVA CENTER
GAINESVILLE
BLISS
PORTAGEVILLE
HOUGHTON
FRANKLINVILLE
Springville
ARKPORT
Hornell
DANSVILLE
CONESUS
SPRINGWATER
MIDDLESEX
KEUKA PARK
PRATTSBURGH
BATH
WATKINS GLEN
MONTOUR FALLS
Painted Post
CORNING
ADDISON
WELLSVILLE
Belmont
Angelica
Alfred
Cuba
Bolivar
Portville
Geneva
Seneca Lake
Penn Yan
Dundee
Keuka L.
Hammondsport
Lindley
Pine City
Waterford
Corry
Union City
Edinboro
Meadville
Titusville
Warren
Kane
Smethport
Emporium
Johnsonburg
Ridgway
St. Marys
Tionesta
Oil City
Sugarcreek
Franklin
Greenville
Jamestown
Pymatuning Res.
Knoxville
Westfield
Tioga
Mansfield
Wellsboro
Galeton
Gold
Morris

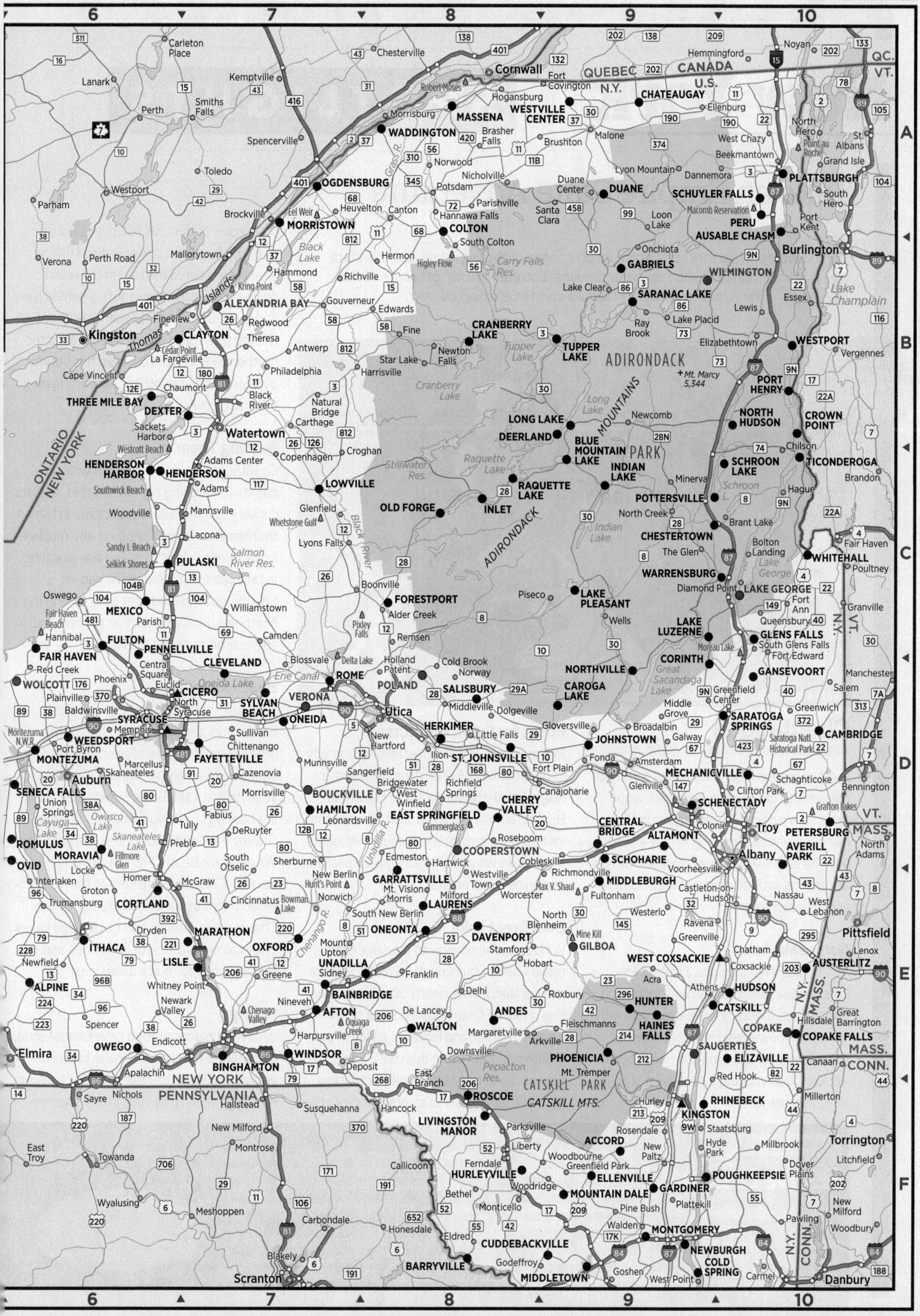

6
7
8
9
10
A
B
C
D
E
F
NY
QUEBEC
CANADA
N.Y.
U.S.
QC.
VT.
ONTARIO
NEW YORK
PENNSYLVANIA
N.Y.
VT.
MASS.
CONN.
Carleton Place
Lanark
Kemptville
Chesterville
Cornwall
Fort Covington
Hogansburg
Robert Moses
Perth
Smiths Falls
MASSENA
WESTVILLE CENTER
CHATEAUGAY
Ellenburg
Hemmingford
Noyan
North Hero
Point au Roche
St. Albans
Grand Isle
Morrisburg
WADDINGTON
Brasher Falls
Brushton
Malone
Spencerville
Norwood
Nicholville
Lyon Mountain
Dannemora
West Chazy
Beekmantown
PLATTSBURGH
South Hero
Toledo
Westport
Parham
Brockville
OGDENSBURG
Potsdam
Parishville
Duane Center
DUANE
SCHUYLER FALLS
Macomb Reservation
PERU
Port Kent
AUSABLE CHASM
Burlington
Eel Weir
MORRISTOWN
Heuvelton
Canton
Hannawa Falls
COLTON
South Colton
Santa Clara
Loon Lake
Onchiota
Verona
Perth Road
Mallorytown
Black Lake
Hammond
Hermon
Higley Flow
Carry Falls Res.
GABRIELS
WILMINGTON
Kring Point
Richville
Islands
ALEXANDRIA BAY
Gouverneur
Edwards
Lake Clear
SARANAC LAKE
Ray Brook
Lake Placid
Lewis
Essex
Lake Champlain
Fineview
Kingston
Thomas
Redwood
Theresa
Fine
CLAYTON
Cedar Point
La Fargeville
Antwerp
CRANBERRY LAKE
TUPPER LAKE
Tupper Lake
Elizabethtown
WESTPORT
Vergennes
Cape Vincent
Philadelphia
Star Lake
Newton Falls
Harrisville
ADIRONDACK
Mt. Marcy 5,344
PORT HENRY
Chaumont
THREE MILE BAY
Black River
Natural Bridge
Carthage
Cranberry Lake
Long Lake
MOUNTAINS
DEXTER
Sackets Harbor
Westcott Beach
Watertown
Croghan
LONG LAKE
Newcomb
NORTH HUDSON
CROWN POINT
DEERLAND
BLUE MOUNTAIN LAKE
PARK
Chilson
HENDERSON HARBOR
HENDERSON
Adams Center
Copenhagen
Stillwater Res.
Raquette Lake
INDIAN LAKE
SCHROON LAKE
TICONDEROGA
Southwick Beach
Adams
LOWVILLE
RAQUETTE LAKE
Minerva
Schroon L.
Hague
Brandon
Woodville
Mannsville
Glenfield
OLD FORGE
INLET
POTTERSVILLE
Whetstone Gulf
North Creek
Brant Lake
Lacona
Lyons Falls
Black River
Indian Lake
CHESTERTOWN
Bolton Landing
Fair Haven
Sandy I. Beach
Selkirk Shores
Salmon River Res.
The Glen
WHITEHALL
Poultney
PULASKI
WARRENSBURG
Lake George
Diamond Point
LAKE GEORGE
Boonville
Piseco
LAKE PLEASANT
Oswego
Fair Haven Beach
MEXICO
Williamstown
FORESTPORT
Alder Creek
Fort Ann
Granville
Parish
Wells
LAKE LUZERNE
Queensbury
Hannibal
FULTON
Pixley Falls
Remsen
Camden
GLENS FALLS
South Glens Falls
Moreau Lake
Fort Edward
FAIR HAVEN
PENNELLVILLE
Red Creek
Central Square
CLEVELAND
Blossvale
Delta Lake
Holland Patent
Cold Brook
Norway
CORINTH
Great Sacandaga Lake
NORTHVILLE
GANSEVOORT
Manchester
Phoenix
Euclid
Oneida Lake
Erie Canal
ROME
POLAND
CAROGA LAKE
Greenfield Center
Salem
WOLCOTT
Plainville
CICERO
North Syracuse
SYLVAN BEACH
VERONA
SALISBURY
Middle Grove
Baldwinsville
SYRACUSE
Memphis
ONEIDA
Utica
Middleville
Dolgeville
SARATOGA SPRINGS
Greenwich
Montezuma N.W.R.
WEEDSPORT
Sullivan
Chittenango
New Hartford
HERKIMER
Little Falls
Gloversville
Broadalbin
Galway
Saratoga Natl. Historical Park
CAMBRIDGE
MONTEZUMA
Port Byron
FAYETTEVILLE
JOHNSTOWN
Marcellus
Munnsville
Ilion
ST. JOHNSVILLE
Fonda
Fort Plain
Amsterdam
MECHANICVILLE
Schaghticoke
Auburn
Skaneateles
Cazenovia
Sangerfield
Bridgewater
Richfield Springs
Canajoharie
Glenville
Clifton Park
Bennington
SENECA FALLS
Union Springs
Morrisville
BOUCKVILLE
West Winfield
CHERRY VALLEY
SCHENECTADY
Grafton Lakes
Cayuga Lake
Owasco Lake
Fabius
HAMILTON
EAST SPRINGFIELD
Leonardsville
Glimmerglass
Colonie
Troy
PETERSBURG
Tully
DeRuyter
CENTRAL BRIDGE
ALTAMONT
ROMULUS
Skaneateles Lake
Preble
Roseboom
COOPERSTOWN
Albany
AVERILL PARK
North Adams
MORAVIA
Fillmore Glen
South Otselic
Sherburne
Unadilla R.
Edmeston
Hartwick
Cobleskill
SCHOHARIE
OVID
Locke
New Berlin
GARRATTSVILLE
Westville Town
Richmondville
MIDDLEBURGH
Voorheesville
Interlaken
Homer
McGraw
Hunt's Point
Mt. Vision
Max V. Shaul
Fultonham
Castleton-on-Hudson
Groton
Cincinnatus
Bowman Lake
Norwich
Morris
Milford
Worcester
Nassau
West Lebanon
Trumansburg
CORTLAND
Chenango R.
South New Berlin
LAURENS
North Blenheim
Westerlo
Ravena
Dryden
MARATHON
ONEONTA
DAVENPORT
Mine Kill
Greenville
Pittsfield
ITHACA
OXFORD
Mount Upton
Stamford
GILBOA
Chatham
Lenox
Newfield
LISLE
Greene
UNADILLA
Sidney
Hobart
WEST COXSACKIE
Coxsackie
AUSTERLITZ
Franklin
Acra
ALPINE
Whitney Point
BAINBRIDGE
Delhi
Roxbury
Athens
HUDSON
Newark Valley
Chenango Valley
Nineveh
AFTON
De Lancey
ANDES
HUNTER
CATSKILL
Spencer
Harpursville
Oquaga Creek
WALTON
Margaretville
Fleischmanns
HAINES FALLS
COPAKE
Hillsdale
Great Barrington
COPAKE FALLS
OWEGO
Endicott
Arkville
Elmira
BINGHAMTON
WINDSOR
Deposit
Downsville
PHOENICIA
SAUGERTIES
ELIZAVILLE
Canaan
Apalachin
NEW YORK
East Branch
Pepacton Res.
Mt. Tremper
CATSKILL PARK
Red Hook
Sayre
Nichols
Hallstead
ROSCOE
CATSKILL MTS.
Hurley
RHINEBECK
Millerton
Susquehanna
Hancock
LIVINGSTON MANOR
KINGSTON
Staatsburg
Parksville
Rosendale
New Milford
Hyde Park
Torrington
East Troy
Towanda
Montrose
ACCORD
Liberty
New Paltz
Millbrook
Litchfield
Callicoon
Ferndale
Woodbourne
Greenfield Park
HURLEYVILLE
ELLENVILLE
POUGHKEEPSIE
Dover Plains
Woodridge
GARDINER
Wyalusing
Meshoppen
Bethel
MOUNTAIN DALE
Plattekill
New Milford
Carbondale
Honesdale
Monticello
Pine Bush
Eldred
Walden
MONTGOMERY
Pawling
Woodbury
CUDDEBACKVILLE
NEWBURGH
Blakely
Godeffroy
COLD SPRING
BARRYVILLE
Goshen
Carmel
Scranton
MIDDLETOWN
West Point
Danbury

New York SPOTLIGHTS

Take an Empire State Adventure

The words "New York" often conjure up images of the Big Apple, but this state has a lot more to it than concrete canyons. Escape to rustic getaways in the north, or thrill to the thunder of Niagara on the Canadian border.

CHAUTAUQUA LAKE IS THE HIGHEST NAVIGABLE LAKE IN THE U.S.

Getty Images/iStockphoto

Lake Chautauqua ranks high as a destination for walleye and bass fishing.

Chautauqua

Located around Lake Chautauqua about 10 miles south of Lake Erie, the Chautauqua region is a rustic summer playground for campers who love boating, fishing and hiking. The area's small-towns also pack ample attractions, including compelling museums and art galleries.

Namesake Lake

At 17 miles long and up to 2 miles wide, Chautauqua Lake is dotted with recreation possibilities, including several marinas with speed and power boat rentals, as well as concessions for kayaking and paddleboarding. Conclude your day with a meal at an area restaurant.

Roost for Culture Vultures

Explore museums like the National Comedy Center, Lucille Ball-Desi Arnaz Museum, or Roger Tory Peterson Institute of Natural History, all in Jamestown. Visit Chautauqua Institution, a destination for summer learning that draws globally recognized speakers, performers and artists.

On a Great Lake

Windswept beaches with dramatic cliffs make Chautauqua County's Lake Erie shore memorable. In fact, nearly 50 miles of Lake Erie make up Chautauqua County's northwestern border, and fantastic vacation possibilities abound along this coast. Erie is the warmest and most biologically productive of the Great Lakes and accounts for roughly 50 percent of the total fish population in all of the five Great Lakes; walleye fishing here is considered the best in the world, while *Bassmaster* magazine has named New York's stretch of the Erie shoreline as one of the top three bass fishing lakes in all of the northern U.S. Visitors can reap this bounty by taking a charter into the lake and reeling in hefty catches.

Hauling Them In

Chautauqua Lake is no slouch when it comes to catching big ones, either. Anglers converge on the lake to participate in fishing tournaments for walleye, bass and muskellunge. Guide fishing trips also are available. In fact, *Bassmaster* magazine named Chautauqua the 23rd best Bass Lake in the Northeast. Find your spot on the lake and spend time exploring the water.

Beachcombing

Grab your sunblock, pack up the kids' beach toys and head out to one of the area's long stretches of unspoiled shoreline. You'll find ample sandy beaches and volleyball at Lake Erie's Sunset Bay. Seeking beach glass? You'll find lots at Point Gratiot Park and a popular splash pad at Wright Park Beach. Plan a Lake Erie beach vacation, or watch the sunset from a driftwood perch at Barcelona Harbor Beach. Chautauqua, Findley and Cassadaga Lakes offer calmer waters for little ones and village settings for quick diversions.

Hiking

In several places around Lake Chautauqua, abandoned rail corridors have been converted into safe off-road trails for walking, running, hiking, bicycling, cross-country

LOCAL FAVORITE

Festive Lasagna

With the largest population of Italian Americans, it's not hard to find lasagna in the Empire State. Try this recipe for a tasty twist. *Recipe by Julie Cathers.*

INGREDIENTS

- ☐ 1 lb. ground turkey
- ☐ 1 large can green chilis
- ☐ 1 can diced tomatoes
- ☐ 1 can black beans, rinsed
- ☐ 1 can sliced mushrooms
- ☐ 1 tsp cumin
- ☐ 1 tsp chili powder
- ☐ 8 oz shredded cheddar cheese
- ☐ 4 flour tortillas

DIRECTIONS

Brown the turkey and drain grease. Remove seeds and cut up green chilis. Put beans, tomatoes, mushrooms and spices in the bottom of a 10" Dutch oven. Put 1 tortilla on top, then keep layering with turkey and cheese between and on top of the tortillas.

Put 10 charcoal briquettes underneath and 15 on top of the lid. Bake for about 45 minutes or until the lasagna is hot and melted. Serve with sour cream, avocado, salsa and tortilla chips.

Chautauqua's craft breweries produce a wide variety of beers, making it a top draw for hops lovers.

skiing, bird watching (over 170 species identified) and horseback riding. These recreation corridors provide access to scenic woodlands, wetlands and flowering meadows, offering trail users opportunities to observe the plants, animals and birds found in areas otherwise remote from highways and roads. The trails are available for outdoor recreational activities and environmental study for the public at large.

Rolling on the Water

Take a trip back in time and embark on the steam-powered Chautauqua Belle. The vessel chugs across the lake daily, giving travelers a taste of what travel was like in the 1800s. All steamship adventures include a narration explaining the lake's role in the region's history and development. The stern-wheeler accommodates 120 passengers with open space on the upper deck as well as tables and chairs.

Brewing Blast

Check out the area's beer scene. The Southern Tier Brewing Co. Empty Pint Pub & Distillery produces more than 100,000 barrels of beer annually, and the company lavishes painstaking attention on each bottle. Find out for yourself at the Empty Pint, the taproom for the state-of-the-art production brewery in Lakewood. The sprawling outdoor beer garden is open seasonally and shoppers can also purchase packed beer to go. Enjoy delicious sandwiches and tacos to accompany your beverage.

Treetop Exploration

Travel back in time to your childhood with a visit to Mountain Adventures, where a series of nets, ropes and platforms challenge climbers to new heights. Explorers wear a harness to ensure safety while climbing to the treetops.

Chautauqua Creativity

Chautauqua has long been a haven for artists seeking inspiration in western New York's wide-open spaces and lush woods. Tour the county's many galleries and collections to sample local, regional and nationally recognized artists. Embark on Art Trail and Open Studio & Gallery Tours to make new creative discoveries. Visit places where masterpieces were made and walk the vineyards, towns hills and lake shores that fuel the inspiration of photographers, painters, potters, sculptors, artists, jewelers and stained-glass artists.

See Spectacles

Chautauqua is chock-full of jaw-dropping natural attractions. See giant rocks at Panama Rock Scenic Park, just south of town. The rugged rock faces of this natural attraction have dazzled explorers for generations. At Jamestown's Audubon Community Nature Center, visitors can see the vibrant nature that inspired Roger Tory Peterson, the naturalist who illustrated so much wildlife in the 20th century. Explore the center's 600-acre wildlife sanctuary with six miles of easy hiking trails through fields, woods, and wetlands with observations towers and handicap accessible overlook. The Audubon Community Nature Center hosts a variety of events for adults and families throughout the year.

Call Toll Free: (800) 646-2066 for Reservations Or Book Online Today
Liberty Harbor Rv
The Closest Rv Park to New York City
15 Minutes
From New York City
What You Will Find At Our Park:
✓ 70 sites (water and electric)
✓ Dump station / Honeywagon Service
✓ Full restrooms with hot showers
✓ Laundry room
✓ Subway & Ferry to NYC
✓ Bus tours daily to New York City
✓ Restaurant/Bar on premises
✓ FREE Wi-Fi
✓ 12 Tent sites Available
✓ 24 hour security and on-site manager
✓ View of New York Skyline, Statue of Liberty, Ellis Island, Liberty Science Center and Liberty State Park from your campsite
RESERVE ONLINE
11 Luis Munoz Marin Blvd. Jersey City, NJ 07302
*Open Year Round
Phone: 201.516.7500
Email: info@libertyharborrv.com
www.libertyharborrv.com
See listing Jersey City, NJ

SPOTLIGHTS

New York

The most populous city in America bursts with possibilities. The Big Apple serves up every kind of urban experience. At the center of it all is Manhattan, with its gargantuan skyscrapers, incredible museums, and lively public spaces.

Overlooking the Hudson River, One World Trade Center is the tallest building in the Western Hemisphere.

Top of the Rock Observation Deck

If you want some fantastic views (and photos) of Manhattan, make your way to the observation deck of 30 Rockefeller Plaza, known as the Top of the Rock. There are three decks in total, spanning floors 67, 69 and 70, two of which are completely outdoors. The visit starts with an exhibit on the mezzanine level, with artifacts and informational displays about the Rockefeller Center, followed by an elevator ride up to the Radiance Wall, a glass installation created by Swarovski. From here, make your way to the Breezeway, with its interactive color displays. The best views are on the top floor, with no obstructive enclosures or glass.

Monumental Magic

As the tallest building in the Western Hemisphere, the tower, officially known as One World Trade Center, is a bucket-list destination that includes hands-on exhibits and interactive tours that put the Big Apple's other landmarks at your fingertips. Seeking to burn off some calories? A walk or jog across the Brooklyn Bridge's 1.3-mile pedestrian walkway is a fantastic way to see the Big Apple.

At the Met

Easily the city's most celebrated museums, the Metropolitan Museum of Art (AKA the Met) features one of the most impressive collections of art anywhere in the world. Works here exceed two million pieces, spread across three buildings. The main building sits right on the edge of Central Park and is one of the largest art galleries on earth, displaying works from around the world ranging from Old Master paintings to Egyptian Antiquities. There's also a second location, The Cloisters, which features medieval art and tapestries in an appropriately designed building, complete with its own cloistered gardens. The newest part of the museum, the Met Breuer, focuses on contemporary and modern art.

The New York Metropolitan Museum of Art is the largest art museum in the U.S.

Museum of Modern Art (MoMA)

The foremost modern art museum in the United States, the MoMA is home to one of the world's finest collections of modern and contemporary art, with masterpieces by the likes of Picasso, Gaugin, Matisse, Rousseau, Van Gogh, and Jackson Pollock. Pieces of note include The Starry Night by Van Gogh, Matisse's The Dance I, and Rousseau's The Dream. The library here is also particular impressive, with a huge collection of books and periodicals about art from 1880 to the present.

Lady Liberty

As one of the most recognizable figures in the world, The Statue of Liberty is a national treasure and a symbol of inspiration and hope. It was Édouard de Laboulaye, French jurist, poet, author and anti-slavery activist, who proposed the idea of presenting this monumental gift from the people of France. Standing more than 150 feet tall, the Statue of Liberty has come to define New York Harbor. Erected in the late 19th century, the world-famous sculpture of a woman dressed in flowing robes and holding aloft a bright torch stands on Liberty Island and faces incoming ships. Welcoming newcomers to the United States, the Statue of Liberty is an enduring American symbol of freedom and tolerance. The statue and island are accessible to the public only by boat; tours usually start at the Battery in Lower Manhattan. Some of the best photos can be had straight from the boat, and it's worth paying extra to go inside the iconic statue. Note that tickets to access Lady Liberty's Crown are limited, but if you're lucky to get one, it's worth

NY

BlackBearCampground.com
Registration Office/ Campground Store
FULL-SERVICE CAMPGROUND NEAR NEW YORK CITY
Large RVs Welcome • Full Hookups • Extended Stays
30 & 50-Amp Service • Back-In & Pull-Thru Sites • Paved Roads
Free Wi-Fi & Cable • Family Friendly • Store with supplies & RV Parts
Clean, Heated Restrooms & Showers • 24-Hour Laundromat
Seasonal Outdoor Heated Swimming Pool • Family Picnic Areas
Children's Playground with NEW Equipment • Campfire Events
Heated & Air-Conditioned Pavilion/Gameroom • Library
Planned Activities • Arts & Crafts • Pool Table • Ping Pong
Disc Golf Course • Mini Golf • Basketball • Shuffleboard
Volleyball • Horseshoes • Special Events • Nature Trails
Fire Rings & Picnic Tables • Fishing Pond • Pets Permitted
Helpful & Knowledgeable Staff • Resident Management
Nearby Attractions include
West Point U.S. Military Academy, Legoland New York Resort, Bethel Woods, Woodbury Common Premium Outlets, Orange County Fair Speedway, Appalachian Trail, Wineries, Distilleries, Craft Breweries, & more!
Phone for reservations and COVID-19 restrictions
(845) 651-7717
P.O. Box 82 (197 Wheeler Rd.), Florida, NY 10921
info@blackbearcampground.com
OPEN ALL YEAR*
*on a limited basis
good sam park
2022 Top Rated 10/10★/10
See listings Florida & New York City, NY
VISA
MasterCard
DISCOVER
Black Bear
CAMPGROUND

climbing the 146 steps to see stellar views of the harbor below.

Central Park

The lungs of New York City, Central Park is a popular hangout spot for locals and visitors alike. It's home to meandering pathways, ponds and plenty of trees, making it ideal for cycling, jogging, and just taking a stroll. With 843 acres of green lawns, cultivated gardens, meandering streams and dramatic rock work, this rustic getaway in the heart of Manhattan sets the standard for urban green spaces. Take in the sweeping views from the newly restored Park landmark, the Belvedere. Stop and enjoy a concert in the park.

Located on the east side of Central Park, Wollman Rink is open from late October to early April.

Refreshing Reservoir

The Jacqueline Kennedy Onassis Reservoir in Central Park offers gorgeous views south from the northern edge of the reservoir. Near mid-park, the 20-acre lake is used for boating in the summer and ice skating in the winter. On the south end, the pond is one of Central Park's seven natural bodies of water. It has become a serene escape, just feet from Fifth Avenue. And don't miss the Conservatory Garden, a six-acre formal garden. Divided into three smaller gardens, each with a distinct style, Italian, French and English. Other highlights inside the park include the Central Park Carousel and the Delacorte Theater (where you can check out theatrical performances in summer months).

Times Square

In the heart of Midtown Manhattan, Times Square is a major tourist destination that's best-known as the site of the city's annual New Year's Eve ball drop. It's equally celebrated for its bright digital billboards and is a fun and vibrant place to hang out and people watch day or night, throughout the year. You can also buy last-minute Broadway theater tickets here at rock-bottom prices (though you may have to wait in line for a bit). Billed as the "Crossroads of the World," it's crowded with tourists, performers, pizza joints and hot dog carts, but there's no better introduction to the high-energy streets of the City that Never Sleeps. From there, lovers of art and artifacts can see some of the world's greatest collections at museums like the American Museum of Natural History, the Museum of Modern Art and the Whitney Museum.

The Ellis Island Registration Building on New York Harbor preserves the space that processed immigrants.

The 9/11 Memorial & Museum

Located at the former site of the Twin Towers, the 9/11 Memorial & Museum stands tribute to the lives lost at the World Trade Center, both on September 11th, 2001 and the bombing of 1993. The memorial here honors those who died in both series of attacks, with the name of each of the fallen inscribed on bronze parapets. The museum is dedicated to telling the story of 9/11 with a range of exhibits that include interactive displays and artifacts from the attack.

Ellis Island

Take a ferry tour to Ellis Island, part of the Statue of Liberty National Monument, located in New York Harbor about a mile west of the southern tip of Manhattan. This legendary complex was the epicenter for immigrants who made the courageous voyage to the U.S. between 1892 and 1954. More than 12 million people were evaluated in the labyrinthine rooms and hallways of Ellis Island's processing center. The signature Ellis Island Museum of Immigration experience includes up-close views of the Statue of Liberty, followed by poignant, often heart-wrenching accounts of the immigrants' journeys.

Empire State Building

Standing at 1,454 feet (102 stories), the Empire State Building is one of New York City's most enduring icons. Defining the skyline, this majestic structure speaks to the glory that is Manhattan. Sublime panoramas can be found on the outdoor deck that wraps around the entire circumference of the 86th-

• NIAGARA FALLS •

AA ROYAL MOTEL & CAMPGROUND

good sam park

Only 9 miles to Niagara Falls USA

GUIDED TOURS DIRECTLY FROM CAMPGROUND

Quiet, yet Convenient to All Niagara Falls Attractions!

BEST PARK & BEST RATES

BIG RIGS WELCOME

All Sites Paved
Both Shaded & Open

FREE WI-FI AT SITE

- Full Hookups
- 30/50 Amp
- Large Pull-Thru Sites
- Laundry · Restrooms
- Firewood · Fire Rings

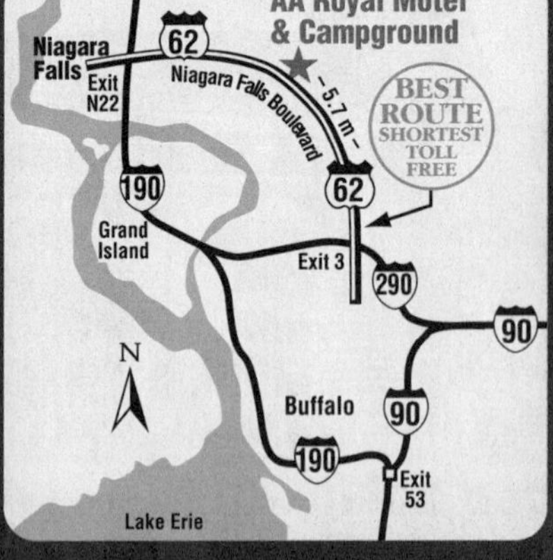

See listing Niagara Falls, NY

OPEN ALL YEAR

716-693-5695 • 716-693-0502

Cell: 716-417-5909

3333 Niagara Falls Blvd. • North Tonawanda, NY 14120

Lat 43.07530 • Lon -78.86127

mike@royalmotelandcampground.com

www.royalmotelandcampground.com

SPOTLIGHTS

More than 100 colorful LED lights placed throughout the Niagara Gorge illuminate the falls during evenings.

floor observatory and on the 102nd-floor indoor deck.

Niagara Falls

Niagara Falls has to be seen to be believed. The 167-high torrent of water that plunges with thundering impact into the Niagara River is a spectacle of sight and sound. The fall's mist is thick enough to drench visitors who get close, a visceral reminder of the sheer force of the roaring cascade. The falls are situated on the border between Ontario and New York, and the Empire State side of Niagara Falls gives visitors lots of viewpoints to view this amazing spectacle. Grab a picnic basket and find a spot overlooking one of North America's most popular spectacles.

Goat Island

Occupying land between the American Falls and Horseshoe Falls, this historic island is named for a herd of goats that grazed here in the 18th century. These days, the island offers commanding views of the Niagara River rapids, as well as access to Luna Island and the Three Sisters Islands. A picnic area provides the perfect opportunity to fuel up amidst all of the sightseeing.

Whirlpool State Park

The thundering Falls aren't the only sight that'll get your heart pumping in Niagara Falls: the downstream Class V rapids known as the Niagara Whirlpool are a thrill to experience, too. Take in views of the rapids at a picnic table along the top level of the park. Take a powerboat tour on these raging waters.

Fort Niagara State Park

On a clear day, you can gaze all the way to the Toronto skyline from a picnic table at this Lake Ontario shoreline park. Adjacent to the Old Fort Niagara Historic Site, this park also offers woodland hiking trails, playgrounds and historic markers. There are 400-some picnic tables — so your odds of finding a super scenic spot to spread out are good!

Lake George

The magnificent Lake George area in the foothills of the southern Adirondacks brims with countless outdoor activities, including river tubing and rafting, kayaking and boating. Throw in some hiking, biking, swimming and horseback riding for more family fun and you've got a great vacation destination.

Adirondack Adventure

Lake George itself is 32 miles long and nearly 3 miles wide and is dotted with 245 islands. The Village of Lake George at the southern end of the lake is ideally located to be the focal point for any Adirondack adventure.

Day Trips

Day tripping in the area is an ideal way to explore the many exciting attractions, with historical, cultural, and shopping adventures around every curve in the road. Family activities include Railroads on Parade, the Saratoga Race Course, Natural Stone Bridge and Caves Park, and Six Flags Great Escape and Splashwater Escape and Hurricane.

Chilling on the Beach

Of course, Lake George has many, many beaches and more than a few come with both a view and a show. You won't need a single dollar for admission to the shore at Million Dollar Beach State Park because it's free (there is a fee for parking). So, too, are the panoramic scenes of Lake George and the Adirondacks. An added bonus are the fireworks displays over the lake during summer.

FOR MORE INFORMATION

New York Dept. of Economic Development, 800-CALL-NYS, www.iloveny.com
Tour Chautauqua, 866-908-4569, www.tourchautauqua.com
New York City, 800-NYC-VISIT, www.nycgo.com
Welcome to Niagara Falls, 877-FALLS-US, www.niagarafallsusa.com
Visit Lake George, 877-FALLS-US, www.visitlakegeorge.com

The Maid of the Mist tour boat ferries visitors from the American side to the foot of Niagara Falls.

NY

New York

ACCORD — F9 *Ulster*

RONDOUT VALLEY RESORT
Ratings: 8.5/9★/8.5 (Membership Park) Avail: 75 full hkups (30/50 amps). 2021 rates: $78 to $88. Apr 01 to Nov 01. (888)563-7040, 105 Mettacahonts Rd, Accord, NY 12404

ADDISON — E5 *Steuben*

SUNFLOWER ACRES FAMILY CAMPGROUND
Ratings: 7.5/9/8 (Campground) 50 Avail: 17 full hkups, 33 W, 33 E (30/50 amps). 2021 rates: $38 to $43. May 01 to Oct 15. (607)523-7756, 1488 Sunflower Blvd, Addison, NY 14801

AFTON — E7 *Chenango*

KELLYSTONE PARK **Ratings: 4.5/5.5/8** (Campground) Avail: 20 full hkups (30/50 amps). 2021 rates: $42 to $44. Apr 15 to Oct 13. (607)639-1090, 51 Hawkins Rd, Nineveh, NY 13813

AKRON — D3 *Erie*

SLEEPY HOLLOW LAKE **Ratings: 8/10★/9** (Campground) 40 Avail: 40 W, 40 E (30/50 amps). 2021 rates: $47 to $54. May 01 to Oct 15. (716)542-4336, 13800 Siehl Rd, Akron, NY 14001

ALBION — D4 *Orleans*

LAKESIDE BEACH (Public State Park) From town, N 8 mi on SR-98 to W end Lake Ontario State Pkwy, W 2.2 mi (R). Avail: 268 E (20 amps). 2021 rates: $15 to $27. May 06 to Oct 16. (585)682-4888

ALEXANDRIA BAY — B7 *Jefferson*

1000 ISLANDS CAMPGROUND **Ratings: 7.5/9.5★/9.5** (Campground) Avail: 60 full hkups (30/50 amps). 2021 rates: $38 to $64. May 15 to Oct 15. (315)686-2600, 42099 NY 12, Alexandria Bay, NY 13607

GRASS POINT (Public State Park) From Jct of I-81 & SR-12, SW 1 mi on SR-12 (R). Avail: 78 E (20 amps). 2021 rates: $15 to $31. May 17 to Sep 25. (315)686-4472

KEEWAYDIN (Public State Park) From Jct SR-26 & SR-12, W 1 mi on SR-12 (R). 48 Avail. 2021 rates: $19 to $25. May 22 to Sep 06. (315)482-3331

KRING POINT (Public State Park) From Jct of I-81 & Rte 12, NE 14 mi on Rte 12 to Kring Point Rd, W 2 mi (L). Avail: 9 E. 2021 rates: $18 to $34. May 01 to Oct 11. (315)482-2444

SWAN BAY RESORT
Ratings: 10/10★/10 (RV Park) From jct I-81N & Rte 411: Go 8.6 mi N on I-81 to exit 50N, then go right to Rte 12 East, then go .9 mi (L). **FAC:** paved rds. (215 spaces). Avail: 165 paved, patios, 26 pull-thrus, (40x80), back-ins (40x80), 165 full hkups (30/50 amps), seasonal sites, WiFi @ sites, rentals, dump, laundry, groc, LP bottles, fire rings, firewood, controlled access. **REC:** heated pool, St Lawrence River: swim, fishing, marina, kayaking/canoeing, boating nearby, playground. Pets OK. Partial handicap access. No tents. Big rig sites, eco-friendly. 2021 rates: $55 to $129, Military discount. May 01 to Oct 31. ATM.
(315)482-7926 Lat: 44.298963, Lon: -75.963537
43615 NY (State Route) 12, Alexandria Bay, NY 13607
www.swanbayresort.com/goodsam
See ad this page

WELLESLEY ISLAND (Public State Park) From business center: Go 6 mi S on Hwy 12, then cross 1000 Island Bridge (Toll). 429 Avail. 2021 rates: $18 to $36. May 01 to Oct 11. (315)482-2722

ALPINE — E6 *Schuyler*

COOL-LEA CAMP **Ratings: 6.5/8/9** (Campground) 47 Avail: 25 full hkups, 22 W, 22 E (30/50 amps). 2021 rates: $42 to $70. May 15 to Oct 15. (607)594-3500, 2620 Cool-Lea Camp Dr, Alpine, NY 14805

ALTAMONT — D9 *Albany*

THATCHER/THOMPSON'S LAKE (Public State Park) From town, W 4 mi on Hwy 156, SE 2 mi on Hwy 157 (L). 140 Avail. 2021 rates: $15 to $19. May 01 to Oct 12. (518)872-1674

ANDES — E8 *Delaware*

LITTLE POND
(Public State Park) From town, NW 14 mi on Rte 17 (L). **FAC:** paved rds. Avail: 67 dirt, back-ins (15x35), tent sites, dump, fire rings, firewood. **REC:** Little Pond: swim, fishing, kayaking/canoeing, playground. Pets OK. Partial handicap access, 14 day max stay. 2021 rates: $22 to $27. May 17 to Oct 13.
(845)439-5480 Lat: 42.188935, Lon: -74.785804
549 Little Pond State Campground Rd, Andes, NY 13731
www.dec.ny.gov

ANGOLA — D3 *Erie*

EVANGOLA (Public State Park) From town, SW 1 mi on NY-5, follow signs (R). Avail: 37 E (30/50 amps). 2021 rates: $15 to $27. Apr 12 to Oct 30. (716)549-1802

ARKPORT — E4 *Allegany*

SUN VALLEY CAMPSITES **Ratings: 8/8/9** (Campground) 68 Avail: 33 full hkups, 35 W, 35 E (30/50 amps). 2021 rates: $44 to $49. May 01 to Oct 18. (607)545-8388, 10740 Poags Hole Rd, Arkport, NY 14807

AUSABLE CHASM — A10 *Clinton*

AUSABLE CHASM CAMPGROUND **Ratings: 6/10★/8** (Campground) 80 Avail: 40 full hkups, 40 W, 40 E (30/50 amps). 2021 rates: $45 to $50. May 27 to Oct 14. (518)834-9990, 634 Rt 373, Ausable Chasm, NY 12911

AUSTERLITZ — E10 *Columbia*

WOODLAND HILLS CAMPGROUND **Ratings: 7/8/9** (Campground) 72 Avail: 42 full hkups, 30 W, 30 E (30/50 amps). 2021 rates: $47 to $67. May 15 to Oct 10. (518)392-3557, 386 Fog Hill Rd, Austerlitz, NY 12017

AVERILL PARK — D10 *Rensselaer*

ALPS FAMILY CAMPGROUND **Ratings: 8/9.5★/9.5** (Campground) 36 Avail: 18 full hkups, 18 W, 18 E (30 amps). 2021 rates: $35. May 01 to Oct 15. (518)674-5565, 1928 State Route 43, Averill Park, NY 12018

BAINBRIDGE — E7 *Broome*

GENERAL CLINTON PARK (Public) From I-88 (exit 8) & SR-206: Go .5mi NW on SR-206, then 1.5mi NE on SR-7 (R). 50 Avail: 50 W, 50 E (30/50 amps). 2021 rates: $25. May 01 to Oct 31. (607)967-3781

OQUAGA CREEK (Public State Park) From Jct of Hwy 17 & Rte 8 exit 84 (at Deposit), N 3 mi on Rte 8 to CR-20, N 9 mi (L). 95 Avail. 2021 rates: $15 to $19. May 13 to Oct 09. (607)467-4160

TALL PINES CAMPGROUND AND RIVER ADVENTURES **Ratings: 9/10★/10** (Campground) 68 Avail: 44 full hkups, 24 W, 24 E (30/50 amps). 2021 rates: $40.60 to $54.51. May 03 to Oct 14. (607)563-8271, 100 Tall Pines Lane, Bainbridge, NY 13733

BARKER — C3 *Niagara*

GOLDEN HILL (Public State Park) From Jct of Rtes 18 & 269 (County Line Rd), N 1 mi on County Line Rd to Lower Lake Rd, W 1 mi (R). 59 Avail: 12 W, 32 E (30/50 amps). 2021 rates: $15 to $31. Apr 29 to Oct 15. (716)795-3885

BARRYVILLE — F8 *Sullivan*

KITTATINNY CAMPGROUNDS **Ratings: 4.5/6/7.5** (Campground) 10 Avail: 10 W, 10 E (15/20 amps). 2021 rates: $44 to $51. Apr 15 to Oct 15. (845)557-8611, 3854 SR-97, Barryville, NY 12719

BATH — E5 *Steuben*

CAMPERS HAVEN **Ratings: 7.5/7/8** (Campground) 60 Avail: 40 full hkups, 20 W, 20 E (30/50 amps). 2021 rates: $51. Apr 15 to Oct 15. (607)776-0328, 6832 CR-15 Knight Settlement Rd, Bath, NY 14810

HAMMONDSPORT-BATH KOA **Ratings: 9/10★/10** (Campground) 106 Avail: 74 full hkups, 32 W, 32 E (30/50 amps). 2021 rates: $74 to $112. May 01 to Oct 31. (800)562-5304, 7531 County Route 13, Bath, NY 14810

YOGI BEAR'S JELLYSTONE PARK AT FINGER LAKES **Ratings: 8.5/10★/10** (Campground) 35 Avail: 1 full hkups, 34 W, 34 E (20/30 amps). 2021 rates: $50 to $56. May 01 to Oct 15. (607)776-7185, 5932 County Route 11, Bath, NY 14810

BINGHAMTON — E7 *Broome*

CHENANGO VALLEY (Public State Park) From Jct of I-88 & SR-369, NE 5 mi on SR-369 (L). 184 Avail: (50 amps). 2021 rates: $15 to $27. May 10 to Oct 13. (607)648-5251

BLISS — E4 *Wyoming*

FAUN LAKE **Ratings: 7/9★/8** (Membership Park) 23 Avail: 23 W, 23 E (30 amps). 2021 rates: $28. May 01 to Oct 15. (585)322-7300, 5124 Pleasant Valley Rd, Bliss, NY 14024

BLUE MOUNTAIN LAKE — C9 *Hamilton*

ADIRONDACK/LAKE DURANT (Public State Park) From jct Hwy 30 & Hwy 28: Go 3 mi E on Hwy 28. 61 Avail. 2021 rates: $20 to $25. May 20 to Oct 10. (518)352-7797

BOUCKVILLE — D7 *Madison*

CIDER HOUSE CAMPGROUND
Ratings: 8.5/9★/10 (Campground) Avail: 40 full hkups (30/50 amps). 2021 rates: $30 to $45. May 20 to Oct 01. (315)825-8477, 3570 Canal Rd, Bouckville, NY 13310

BROCTON — E2 *Chautauqua*

LAKE ERIE (Public State Park) From Jct of I-90 & SR-380 (exit 60), N 0.75 mi on SR-380 to SR-5, E 9 mi (R). Avail: 33 E (20 amps). 2021 rates: $15 to $21. May 14 to Oct 10. (716)792-9214

BROOKHAVEN — A4 *Suffolk*

SOUTHHAVEN COUNTY PARK (Public) From Long Island Expwy (I-495, exit 68S): Go S on William Floyd Pkwy to 4th traffic light, then W on Victory Ave, then 1/2 mi N on River Rd. 150 Avail. (631)854-1414

"Full hookups" in a campground listing means there are water, electric and sewer hookups at the sites.

BUFFALO — D3 *Erie*

CAMP CHAUTAUQUA CAMPING RESORT
Ratings: 10/10★/10 (Campground) From Jct of I-86/SR-17 & SR-394 (exit 8): Go 2 mi N on SR-394 (R). **FAC:** all weather rds. (250 spaces). Avail: 100 all weather, 69 pull-thrus, (35x70), back-ins (35x70), 75 full hkups, 25 W, 25 E (30/50 amps), seasonal sites, cable, WiFi @ sites, tent sites, dump, mobile sewer, laundry, groc, LP gas, fire rings, firewood, controlled access. **REC:** heated pool, wading pool, Lake Chautauqua: swim, fishing, marina, boating nearby, playground. Pets OK. Partial handicap access. Big rig sites, eco-friendly. 2021 rates: $57 to $72. ATM.
(716)789-3435 Lat: 42.16918, Lon: -79.43985
3900 W Lake Rd, Stow, NY 14785
www.campchautauqua.com
See primary listing at Chautauqua and ad page 637

BYRON — D4 *Genesee*

SOUTHWOODS RV RESORT **Ratings: 9.5/9.5★/10** (Campground) Avail: 112 full hkups (30/50 amps). 2021 rates: $41 to $46. May 01 to Oct 31. (585)548-9002, 6749 Townline Rd, Byron, NY 14422

CALEDONIA — D4 *Livingston*

GENESEE COUNTRY CAMPGROUND **Ratings: 7.5/9/8.5** (Campground) 38 Avail: 38 W, 38 E (30/50 amps). 2021 rates: $29 to $31. May 01 to Oct 31. (585)538-4200, 40 Flint Rd, Caledonia, NY 14423

CAMBRIDGE — D10 *Washington*

LAKE LAUDERDALE CAMPGROUND **Ratings: 5.5/6.5/8** (Campground) 15 Avail: 8 full hkups, 7 W, 7 E (30/50 amps). 2021 rates: $40 to $45. May 01 to Oct 15. (518)677-8855, 744 CR-61, Cambridge, NY 12816

CANANDAIGUA — D5 *Ontario*

BRISTOL WOODLANDS CAMPGROUND **Ratings: 6.5/9★/7** (Campground) 23 Avail: 21 full hkups, 2 W, 2 E (30/50 amps). 2021 rates: $42 to $46. May 01 to Oct 20. (585)229-2290, 4835 South Hill Rd, Canandaigua, NY 14424

KOA CANANDAIGUA/ROCHESTER KAMPGROUND **Ratings: 9.5/9.5★/9.5** (Campground) Avail: 73 full hkups (30/50 amps). 2021 rates: $63 to $70. Apr 01 to Nov 01. (585)398-3582, 5374 Canandaigua Farmington Town Line Rd, Canandaigua, NY 14425

CAROGA LAKE — D9 *Fulton*

ADIRONDACK/CAROGA LAKE (Public State Park) From town, S 1 mi on Hwy 29A (R). Campground is on E-side of Caroga Lake. Entrance fee required. 105 Avail. 2021 rates: $20 to $25. May 20 to Sep 04. (518)835-4241

CATSKILL — E9 *Greene*

TREETOPIA CAMPGROUND **Ratings: 8.5/10★/9** (Campground) Avail: 10 full hkups (30/50 amps). 2021 rates: $60. May 15 to Oct 15. (518)943-4513, 1446 Leeds Athens Rd, Catskill, NY 12414

CENTRAL BRIDGE — D9 *Schoharie*

HIDE-A-WAY CAMPSITES **Ratings: 6/8.5★/8** (Campground) 33 Avail: 33 W, 33 E (30/50 amps). 2021 rates: $33 to $35. May 15 to Oct 15. (518)868-9975, 107 Janice Ln, Central Bridge, NY 12035

CHATEAUGAY — A9 *Franklin*

HIGH FALLS PARK **Ratings: 6.5/6/8** (Campground) 43 Avail: 22 full hkups, 21 W, 21 E (20/30 amps). 2021 rates: $40. May 01 to Oct 15. (518)497-3156, 34 Cemetery Rd (Jerdon Rd), Chateaugay, NY 12920

CHAUTAUQUA — E2 *Chautauqua*

A SPOTLIGHT Introducing Chautauqua Lake Region's colorful attractions appearing at the front of this state section.

CAMP CHAUTAUQUA CAMPING RESORT
Ratings: 10/10★/10 (Campground) From Jct of I-86/SR-17 & SR-394 (exit 8), N 2 mi on SR-394 (R). **FAC:** all weather rds. (250 spaces). Avail: 100 all weather, patios, 69 pull-thrus, (35x70), back-ins (35x70), 75 full hkups, 25 W, 25 E (30/50 amps), seasonal sites, cable, WiFi @ sites, tent sites, dump, mobile sewer, laundry, groc, LP gas, fire rings, firewood, controlled access. **REC:** heated pool, wading pool, Lake Chautauqua: swim, fishing, boating nearby, playground. Pets OK. Partial handicap access. Big rig sites, eco-friendly. 2021 rates: $57 to $72. ATM.
(716)789-3435 Lat: 42.16918, Lon: -79.43985
3900 W Lake Rd, Stow, NY 14785
campchautauqua.com
See ad page 637

CHERRY VALLEY — D8 *Otsego*

BELVEDERE LAKE RESORT **Ratings: 6.5/7/8.5** (Campground) 18 Avail: 18 W, 18 E (30/50 amps). 2021 rates: $45 to $50. May 01 to Oct 04. (607)264-8182, 270 Gage Rd, Cherry Valley, NY 13320

CHESTERTOWN — C9 *Warren*

RANCHO PINES CAMPGROUND **Ratings: 7.5/8.5★/9** (Campground) Avail: 17 full hkups (30 amps). 2021 rates: $39. May 20 to Oct 10. (518)494-3645, 2854 Schroon River Rd, Chestertown, NY 12817

RIVERSIDE PINES CAMPSITES **Ratings: 6.5/8/7** (Campground) Avail: 14 full hkups (30 amps). 2021 rates: $55. May 15 to Oct 13. (518)494-2280, 1 Carl Turner Rd, Chestertown, NY 12817

CICERO — D6 *Onondaga*

Travel Services

GANDER RV OF CICERO/SYRACUSE Your new hometown outfitter offering the best regional gear for all your outdoor needs. Your adventure awaits. **SERVICES:** gunsmithing svc, archery svc, sells outdoor gear, sells fishing gear, sells firearms. RV Sales. RV supplies, LP gas, dump, emergency parking. Hours: 9am to 8pm.
(855)917-0869 Lat: 43.180929, Lon: -76.114818
5864 Carmenica Drive, Cicero, NY 13039
rv.ganderoutdoors.com

CLAYTON — B6 *Jefferson*

CEDAR POINT (Public State Park) From Jct of SR-12 & SR-12E, SW 6 mi on SR-12E (R). 165 Avail: 30 full hkups, 30 W, 30 S, 88 E (20/30 amps). 2021 rates: $15 to $27. May 06 to Oct 08. (315)654-2522

MERRY KNOLL 1000 ISLANDS CAMPGROUND **Ratings: 9.5/9.5★/9.5** (Campground) Avail: 12 full hkups (30/50 amps). 2021 rates: $49. May 01 to Oct 15. (315)686-3055, 38115 RT 12E, Clayton, NY 13624

CLEVELAND — D7 *Oneida*

WHISPERING WOODS CAMPGROUND **Ratings: 7/9★/8** (Campground) 22 Avail: 6 full hkups, 16 W, 16 E (30/50 amps). 2021 rates: $48 to $53. May 01 to Oct 13. (315)675-8100, 965 Stone Barn Rd, Cleveland, NY 13042

COLD SPRING — F9 *Putnam*

FAHNESTOCK (CLARENCE FAHNESTOCK) (Public State Park) From jct US 9 & Hwy 301: Go 8 mi E on Hwy 301. (L). 80 Avail. 2021 rates: $15 to $19. (845)225-7207

COLTON — A8 *St Lawrence*

HIGLEY FLOW (Public State Park) From Potsdam, S 14 mi on Rte 56 to Cold Brook Dr, W 2.5 mi (R). Avail: 56 E (15/30 amps). 2021 rates: $15 to $31. May 15 to Sep 06. (315)262-2880

CONESUS — D4 *Livingston*

CONESUS LAKE CAMPGROUND **Ratings: 8.5/9★/9** (Campground) 61 Avail: 10 full hkups, 51 W, 50 E (30/50 amps). 2021 rates: $55 to $65. May 15 to Oct 15. (585)346-2267, 5609 E Lake Rd, Conesus, NY 14435

COOPERSTOWN — D8 *Otsego*

COOPERSTOWN BEAVER VALLEY CABINS & CAMPSITES **Ratings: 8.5/10★/9** (Campground) 46 Avail: 13 full hkups, 23 W, 23 E (30 amps). 2021 rates: $40 to $62. May 20 to Oct 14. (607)293-7324, 138 Towers Rd, Milford, NY 13807

COOPERSTOWN FAMILY CAMPGROUND **Ratings: 8/8/9.5** (Campground) 66 Avail: 26 full hkups, 40 W, 26 S, 40 E (30/50 amps). 2021 rates: $55 to $58. May 15 to Oct 15. (607)293-7766, 230 Petkewec Rd, Cooperstown, NY 13326

COOPERSTOWN KOA **Ratings: 8.5/9.5★/9.5** (Campground) 62 Avail: 44 full hkups, 18 W, 18 E (30/50 amps). 2021 rates: $53 to $59. May 01 to Oct 14. (315)858-0236, 565 Ostrander Rd, Richfield Springs, NY 13439

COOPERSTOWN SHADOW BROOK CAMPGROUND
Ratings: 9/10★/10 (Campground) 69 Avail: 27 full hkups, 42 W, 42 E (30/50 amps). 2021 rates: $57 to $78. May 06 to Oct 15. (607)264-8431, 2149 County Hwy 31, Cooperstown, NY 13326

HARTWICK HIGHLANDS CAMPGROUND **Ratings: 10/9.5★/9.5** (Campground) 49 Avail: 47 full hkups, 2 W, 2 E (30/50 amps). 2021 rates: $50 to $55. May 15 to Oct 12. (607)547-1996, 131 Burke Hill Rd, Milford, NY 13807

MEADOW-VALE CAMPSITES **Ratings: 8.5/9★/9** (Campground) 36 Avail: 36 W, 36 E (30/50 amps). 2021 rates: $42 to $46. May 12 to Oct 09. (607)293-8802, 505 Gilbert Lake Rd, Mount Vision, NY 13810

COPAKE — E10 *Columbia*

COPAKE CAMPING RESORT **Ratings: 9.5/9.5★/9.5** (Campground) Avail: 120 full hkups (30/50 amps). 2021 rates: $69 to $104. May 09 to Oct 12. (518)329-2811, 2236 County Route 7, Copake, NY 12516

WAUBEEKA FAMILY CAMPGROUND
Ratings: 8.5/10★/9.5 (Campground) Avail: 96 full hkups (30/50 amps). 2021 rates: $54.99 to $74.99. May 01 to Oct 15. (518)261-1791, 133 Farm Rd , Copake, NY 12516

COPAKE FALLS — E10 *Columbia*

TACONIC/COPAKE FALLS AREA (Public State Park) From Jct of SR-22 & Rte 344, E 1 mi on Rte 344 (L). 36 Avail. 2021 rates: $15 to $22. May 01 to Nov 28. (518)329-3993

CORINTH — D9 *Saratoga*

ALPINE LAKE RV RESORT
Ratings: 8.5/7/8.5 (Campground) 150 Avail: 130 full hkups, 20 W, 20 E (30/50 amps). 2021 rates: $75 to $110. May 01 to Oct 10. (888)563-7040, 78 Heath Rd, Corinth, NY 12822

CORNING — E5 *Steuben*

CAMP BELL CAMPGROUND
Ratings: 9/9★/9 (Campground) From Jct of I-86 & SR-333 (exit 41), E 0.5 mi on SR-333 to SR-415, N 0.75 mi (L). **FAC:** all weather rds. (96 spaces). Avail: 57 grass, 16 pull-thrus, (25x55), back-ins (35x50), 57 W, 57 E (30/50 amps), seasonal sites, cable, WiFi @ sites, tent sites, rentals, dump, mobile sewer, laundry, groc, LP gas, fire rings, firewood. **REC:** heated pool, playground, hunting nearby, rec open to public. Pets OK. Partial handicap access, eco-friendly. 2021 rates: $36 to $50, Military discount. May 01 to Oct 22.
(800)587-3301 Lat: 42.23565, Lon: -77.18454
8700 SR 415, Campbell, NY 14821
campbellcampground.com
See ad next page

FERENBAUGH CAMPGROUND **Ratings: 7.5/7/8.5** (Campground) 104 Avail: 18 full hkups, 86 W, 86 E (30/50 amps). 2021 rates: $60 to $75. May 01 to Oct 30. (607)962-6193, 4248 SR 414, Corning, NY 14830

CORTLAND — E6 *Cortland*

YELLOW LANTERN KAMPGROUND **Ratings: 7.5/7.5/7.5** (Campground) 115 Avail: 50 full hkups, 65 W, 65 E (30/50 amps). 2021 rates: $50 to $55. Apr 01 to Oct 30. (607)756-2959, 1770 State Route 13 N, Cortland, NY 13045

CRANBERRY LAKE — B8 *St Lawrence*

ADIRONDACK/CRANBERRY LAKE (Public State Park) From town: Go 1-1/2 mi off Hwy 3. 173 Avail. 2021 rates: $20 to $25. May 20 to Oct 10. (315)848-2315

CROWN POINT — B10 *Essex*

ADIRONDACK/CROWN POINT (Public) From town, N 4 mi on Rtes 9 & 22N, E 4 mi on Bridge Rd, follow signs (R). 66 Avail. 2021 rates: $18 to $23. May 20 to Oct 09. (518)597-3603

CUDDEBACKVILLE — F9 *Orange*

DEERPARK/NEW YORK CITY NW KOA **Ratings: 8/9/8** (Campground) 165 Avail: 68 full hkups, 97 W, 97 E (30/50 amps). 2021 rates: $50 to $95. (845)754-8388, 108 Guymard Turnpike, Cuddebackville, NY 12729

Drop in at one of our social media stomping grounds on Facebook, Twitter or the Good Sam Blog to mingle with thousands of fellow RVers. Learn about new RV destinations, share some hard-earned RV advice and make new friends - all with a few clicks of the mouse.

DANSVILLE — E4 *Livingston*

SKYBROOK CAMPGROUND **Ratings: 5/8.5★/7.5** (Campground) 230 Avail: 5 full hkups, 225 W, 225 E (20/30 amps). 2021 rates: $33 to $38. May 01 to Oct 01. (585)335-6880, 10816 McCurdy Rd, Dansville, NY 14437

STONY BROOK (Public State Park) From jct I-390 & Hwy 36: Go 2 mi S on Hwy 36. (L). 88 Avail. 2021 rates: $15 to $20. Apr 29 to Oct 10. (585)335-8111

DARIEN CENTER — D3 *Genesee*

DARIEN LAKES (Public State Park) From Jct of US-20 and Harlow Rd, N 0.25 mi on Harlow Rd (R). Avail: 141 E (20/30 amps). 2021 rates: $12 to $27. May 06 to Oct 15. (585)547-9242

SKYLINE RV RESORT

good sam park **Ratings: 9/9★/10** (Campground) From Jct of US-20 & SR-238, SE 3 mi on SR-238 to Town Line Rd, N 0.5 mi (R). **FAC:** all weather rds. (325 spaces). Avail: 57 all weather, 29 pull-thrus, (35x60), back-ins (35x50), accepts full hkup units only, 57 full hkups (30/50 amps), seasonal sites, WiFi @ sites, shower$, dump, mobile sewer, LP gas, fire rings, firewood, controlled access. **REC:** heated pool, pond, fishing, kayaking/canoeing, shuffleboard, playground. Pet restrict (B/Q). No tents. Big rig sites, eco-friendly. 2021 rates: $50 to $59, Military discount. May 02 to Oct 13.
(585)591-2021 Lat: 42.88498, Lon: -78.30741
10933 Town Line Rd, Darien Center, NY 14040
www.skylinervresort.com
See ad this page

DAVENPORT — E8 *Delaware*

CRAZY ACRES CAMPGROUND **Ratings: 8.5/8.5★/8.5** (Campground) Avail: 70 full hkups (30/50 amps). 2021 rates: $50 to $55. Apr 15 to Oct 31. (607)278-5293, 263 Beaver Spring Rd, Davenport, NY 13750

DEERLAND — B8 *Hamilton*

ADIRONDACK/FORKED LAKE (Public State Park) From business center: Go 3 mi W off Hwy-30 (access by foot or boat only). 80 Avail: Pit toilets. 2021 rates: $18 to $23. May 20 to Sep 05. (518)624-6646

DEWITTVILLE — E2 *Chautauqua*

CHAUTAUQUA LAKE KOA **Ratings: 9/10★/10** (Campground) 79 Avail: 69 full hkups, 10 W, 10 E (30/50 amps). 2021 rates: $55 to $92. May 01 to Oct 15. (716)386-3804, 5652 Thum Rd, Dewittville, NY 14728

DEXTER — B7 *Jefferson*

BLACK RIVER BAY CAMPGROUND **Ratings: 6/5.5/8** (Campground) 40 Avail: 12 full hkups, 28 W, 28 E (30/50 amps). 2021 rates: $38 to $40. May 01 to Oct 15. (315)639-3735, 16129 Foster Park Rd, Dexter, NY 13634

DUANE — A9 *Franklin*

ADIRONDACK/MEACHAM LAKE (Public State Park) From town, S 21 mi on Hwy 30 (L). 223 Avail. 2021 rates: $20 to $25. May 20 to Oct 09. (518)483-5116

EAST HAMPTON — A5 *Suffolk*

CEDAR POINT (SUFFOLK COUNTY PARK) (Public) From town: Go E on Hwy 27 (Montauk Hwy), then N on Stephens Hands Path to Old Northwest Rd, then follow signs to Alewive Brook Rd. 190 Avail. (631)852-7620

EAST SPRINGFIELD — D8 *Otsego*

GLIMMERGLASS (Public State Park) From town, E 3 mi on Mainstreet to CR-31, N 7 mi (L). 37 Avail. 2021 rates: $15 to $25. May 13 to Oct 09. (607)547-8662

ELIZAVILLE — E10 *Columbia*

BROOK N WOOD FAMILY CAMPGROUND **Ratings: 9/9.5★/9.5** (Campground) 105 Avail: 96 full hkups, 9 W, 9 E (30/50 amps). 2021 rates: $54 to $59. Apr 25 to Oct 17. (518)537-6896, 1947 County Rt 8, Elizaville, NY 12523

ELLENVILLE — F9 *Ulster*

JELLYSTONE PARK (TM) AT BIRCHWOOD ACRES **Ratings: 9.5/10★/10** (Campground) 69 Avail: 51 full hkups, 18 W, 18 E (30/50 amps). 2021 rates: $62 to $115. May 01 to Oct 12. (888)726-4073, 85 Martinfeld Road, Greenfield Park, NY 12345

FAIR HAVEN — C6 *Cayuga*

FAIR HAVEN BEACH (Public State Park) From city, N 2 mi on park rd (E). Avail: 46 E (15 amps). 2021 rates: $18 to $28. Apr 11 to Oct 19. (315)947-5205

HOLIDAY HARBOR CAMPGROUND & MARINA **Ratings: 3.5/UI/5.5** (Campground) 24 Avail: 1 full hkups, 23 W, 23 E (30/50 amps). 2021 rates: $26 to $33. Apr 15 to Oct 15. (315)947-5244, 9415 Blind Sodus Bay Rd, Red Creek, NY 13143

FALCONER — E2 *Chautauqua*

TOP-A-RISE CAMPGROUND **Ratings: 7/8/9.5** (Campground) Avail: 21 full hkups (30/50 amps). 2021 rates: $35 to $45. Apr 15 to Oct 15. (716)287-3222, 4267 Dean School Road, Falconer, NY 14733

FAYETTEVILLE — D7 *Onondaga*

GREEN LAKES (Public State Park) From I-481 Exit 5E, W 2.9 mi on CH-53, S 2.4 mi on CH-55, W 2.3 mi on SH-290. Avail: 42 E (20/30 amps). 2021 rates: $18 to $36. May 13 to Oct 09. (315)637-6111

County names help you follow the local weather report.

FLORIDA — A2 *Orange*

BLACK BEAR CAMPGROUND
Ratings: 10/10★/10 (Campground) From Jct of SR-17 & SR-94 (exit 126), SW 4.7 mi on SR-94 to Bridge St, W 2 blks to CR 41, 1.5 mi (L).

COUNTRY SETTING

Escape to Florida, NY where you will be in a quiet country setting, just 8 miles from Legoland Resort & near other top tourism & historical sites. Visit nearby wineries & breweries or stay & enjoy relaxing in our campground!

FAC: paved rds. Avail: 154 all weather, 25 pull-thrus, (30x75), back-ins (30x60), 154 full hkups (30/50 amps), WiFi @ sites, laundry, groc, LP bottles, fire rings, firewood. **REC:** heated pool, pond, fishing, boating nearby, shuffleboard, playground, hunting nearby. Pet restrict (B/Q). Partial handicap access. No tents. Big rig sites, eco-friendly. 2021 rates: $80 to $100, Military discount.
(845)651-7717 Lat: 41.32242, Lon: -74.37340
197 Wheeler Rd, Florida, NY 10921
blackbearcampground.com
See ad page 640

FORESTPORT — C8 *Oneida*

KAYUTA LAKE CAMPGROUND **Ratings: 8.5/5.5/9** (Campground) 70 Avail: 15 full hkups, 40 W, 40 E (30/50 amps). 2021 rates: $57. May 15 to Oct 15. (315)831-5077, 10892 Campground Rd, Forestport, NY 13338

FRANKLINVILLE — E3 *Cattaraugus*

TRIPLE R CAMPING RESORT & TRAILER SALES Ratings: 10/10★/10 (Campground) Avail: 63 full hkups (30/50 amps). 2021 rates: $77 to $95. Apr 15 to Oct 15. (716)676-3856, 3491 Bryant Hill Rd, Franklinville, NY 14737

FULTON — C6 *Oswego*

NORTH BAY CAMPGROUND (Public) From Jct of SR-3 & SR-481, W 1.3 mi on SR-3 to Phillips St, S 0.1 mi (E). 42 Avail: 42 W, 31 E (20/30 amps). 2021 rates: $20 to $23. May 15 to Sep 15. (315)592-2256

GABRIELS — B9 *Franklin*

ADIRONDACK/BUCK POND (Public State Park) From town, NE 0.5 mi on CR-30 (L). 116 Avail. 2021 rates: $20 to $25. May 20 to Sep 05. (518)891-3449

GAINESVILLE — D4 *Wyoming*

WOODSTREAM CAMPSITE **Ratings: 7.5/7/9** (Campground) 110 Avail: 15 full hkups, 95 W, 94 E (30/50 amps). 2021 rates: $47. May 01 to Oct 15. (585)493-5643, 5440 School Rd, Gainesville, NY 14066

GANSEVOORT — D10 *Saratoga*

ADIRONDACK GATEWAY CAMPGROUND **Ratings: 8.5/9.5★/9.5** (RV Park) 119 Avail: 15 full hkups, 104 W, 104 E (30/50 amps). 2021 rates: $51 to $65. May 01 to Oct 15. (518)792-0485, 427 Fortsville Rd, Gansevoort, NY 12831

SARATOGA RV PARK **Ratings: 9/9.5★/10** (Campground) Avail: 57 full hkups (30/50 amps). 2021 rates: $50.95 to $59.95. May 15 to Oct 15. (518)798-1913, 4894 Rte 50, Gansevoort, NY 12831

GARDINER — F9 *Ulster*

YOGI BEAR'S JELLYSTONE PARK AT LAZY RIVER **Ratings: 9.5/9/10** (Campground) Avail: 181 full hkups (30/50 amps). 2021 rates: $58 to $208.80. Apr 16 to Nov 01. (845)255-5193, 50 Bevier Rd, Gardiner, NY 12525

GARRATTSVILLE — E8 *Otsego*

ADVENTURE BOUND COOPERSTOWN **Ratings: 8.5/9★/8** (Campground) 177 Avail: 23 full hkups, 134 W, 134 E (30 amps). 2021 rates: $34 to $59. May 09 to Oct 13. (607)965-8265, 111 E Turtle Lake Rd, Garrattsville, NY 13342

GASPORT — D3 *Niagara*

NIAGARA HARTLAND RV RESORT **Ratings: 7.5/8★/8.5** (Campground) Avail: 30 full hkups (30/50 amps). 2021 rates: $47. May 15 to Oct 15. (800)571-4829, 2383 Hartland Rd, Gasport, NY 14067

GILBOA — E9 *Schoharie*

COUNTRY ROADS CAMPGROUND
Ratings: 8/7.5/8 (Campground) 53 Avail: 33 full hkups, 20 W, 20 E (30/50 amps). 2021 rates: $45 to $48. May 15 to Oct 12. (518)827-6397, 144 Peaceful Rd, Gilboa, NY 12076

NICKERSON PARK CAMPGROUND **Ratings: 8.5/10★/9.5** (Campground) 169 Avail: 68 full hkups, 18 W, 18 E (30/50 amps). 2021 rates: $54 to $61. May 01 to Oct 15. (607)588-7327, 378 Stryker Rd, Gilboa, NY 12076

GLENS FALLS — C10 *Warren*

MOREAU LAKE (Public State Park) From Jct of US-87 & Rte 9 (exit 17S), S 0.25 mi on Rte 9 to Old Saratoga Rd, 0.5 mi (R). 148 Avail. 2021 rates: $18 to $22. May 06 to Oct 13. (518)793-0511

GLENWOOD — E3 *Erie*

SPRAGUE BROOK PARK (Public) From Jct of SR 39 & SR 240, N 6 mi on SR 240 to Foute Rd, E 0.3 mi on Foute Rd to second entrance (L) Checks or money orders only. Avail: 72 E (20 amps). 2021 rates: $23 to $30. (716)592-2804

GREENPORT — A5 *Suffolk*

MCCANN'S CAMPGROUND (Public) From Jct of CR-48 & Moores Ln, S 0.5 mi on Moores Ln (L). 15 Avail: 15 W, 15 E (20/30 amps). 2021 rates: $35. May 01 to Oct 31. (631)477-0043

HAINES FALLS — E9 *Greene*

CATSKILL/NORTH-SOUTH LAKE (Public State Park) From Jct of Rte 23A & CR-18, NE 3 mi on CR-18 (E). 219 Avail. 2021 rates: $22 to $27. May 20 to Oct 23. (518)589-5058

HAMBURG — D3 *Erie*

Travel Services

GANDER RV & OUTDOORS OF HAMBURG/BUFFALO Your new hometown outfitter offering the best regional gear for all your outdoor needs. Your adventure awaits. **SERVICES:** tire, RV appliance, MH mechanical, sells outdoor gear, sells firearms, staffed RV wash, restrooms. RV Sales. RV supplies, LP gas, dump, emergency parking, RV accessible. Hours: 9am - 7pm. (888)668-8973 Lat: 42.735545, Lon: -78.840574
5533 Camp Road, Hamburg, NY 14075
rv.ganderoutdoors.com

HAMILTON — D7 *Madison*

LEBANON RESERVOIR CAMPGROUND **Ratings: 7/7.5/9.5** (Campground) Avail: 70 full hkups (30/50 amps). 2021 rates: $48 to $54. May 15 to Oct 15. (315)824-2278, 6277 Reservoir Rd, Hamilton, NY 13346

HAMLIN — C4 *Monroe*

HAMLIN BEACH (Public State Park) From business center: Go 4 mi N on Hwy 19, then 2 mi W on Lake Ontario Pkwy. 264 Avail. 2021 rates: $24 to $26. May 13 to Oct 16. (585)964-2462

HAMPTON BAYS — A4 *Suffolk*

SEARS BELLOWS (SUFFOLK COUNTY PARK) (Public) From Sunrise Hwy (Hwy 27, exit 65N): Go N on Bellows Pond Rd. 40 Avail. 2021 rates: $30 to $40. (631)852-8290

HENDERSON — C6 *Jefferson*

SOUTHWICK BEACH (Public State Park) From I-81 & CR-193 Jct (exit 40), W 4 mi. (E). Entance Fee Required. Avail: 41 E (30 amps). 2021 rates: $18 to $30. May 08 to Oct 11. (315)846-5338

WESTCOTT BEACH (Public State Park) From town, W 8 mi on Arsenal St/NY SR-3 (R). Avail: 83 E (20/30 amps). 2021 rates: $18 to $28. May 15 to Sep 06. (315)938-5083

HENDERSON HARBOR — C6 *Jefferson*

SUN OUTDOORS ASSOCIATION ISLAND **Ratings: 9/9★/8.5** (Campground) Avail: 260 full hkups (30/50 amps). 2021 rates: $42 to $102. May 15 to Oct 12. (888)709-1174, 15530 Snowshoe Rd, Henderson, NY 13650

THE "WILLOWS" ON THE LAKE RV PARK & RESORT **Ratings: 7.5/8★/9** (Campground) Avail: 40 full hkups (30/50 amps). 2021 rates: $48 to $50. Apr 15 to Oct 15. (315)938-5977, 11609 SR 3, Adams, NY 13605

HERKIMER — D8 *Herkimer*

HERKIMER DIAMOND KOA RESORT **Ratings: 8.5/9.5/9.5** (Campground) 96 Avail: 50 full hkups, 46 W, 46 E (30/50 amps). 2021 rates: $73 to $95. Apr 15 to Oct 31. (315)891-7355, 4626 SR 28N, Herkimer, NY 13350

Directional arrows indicate the campground's position in relation to the nearest town.

HOLLAND — D3 *Erie*

THREE VALLEY RESORT **Ratings: 6/4.5/6.5** (Membership Park) 25 Avail: 20 full hkups, 5 W, 5 E (30 amps). 2021 rates: $40. Apr 15 to Sep 15. (716)537-2372, 9766 Olean Rd/Rt 16, Holland, NY 14080

HOLLEY — D4 *Orleans*

HICKORY RIDGE GOLF & RV RESORT **Ratings: 9/9★/9** (RV Park) 127 Avail: 124 full hkups, 3 W, 3 E (30/50 amps). 2021 rates: $48 to $64. May 01 to Oct 31. (585)638-0220, 15870 Lynch Rd, Holley, NY 14470

RED ROCK PONDS RV RESORT **Ratings: 9.5/9★/10** (Campground) Avail: 45 full hkups (30/50 amps). 2021 rates: $55 to $70. May 01 to Oct 18. (585)638-2445, 16097 Canal Rd, Holley, NY 14470

HOUGHTON — E4 *Allegany*

HOUGHTON/LETCHWORTH KOA **Ratings: 9/9.5★/9.5** (Campground) 62 Avail: 48 full hkups, 14 W, 14 E (30/50 amps). 2021 rates: $61 to $76. May 01 to Oct 15. (585)567-4211, 7632 Centerville Rd, Houghton, NY 14744

NY

HUDSON — E10 *Columbia*

LAKE TAGHKANIC (Public State Park) From business center: Go 11 mi S on Hwy-82. 60 Avail. 2021 rates: $15 to $22. May 08 to Oct 17. (518)851-3631

HUNTER — E9 *Greene*

CATSKILL/DEVIL'S TOMBSTONE (Public State Park) From Jct of Hwy 214 & SR-23A, S 4 mi on Hwy 214 (E). 24 Avail: Pit toilets. 2021 rates: $16 to $21. May 19 to Sep 07. (845)688-7160

HURLEYVILLE — F8 *Sullivan*

MORNINGSIDE CAMPGROUND (Public) From Jct of Rte 17 & Exit 107, N 5 mi on CR-161 to Rte 42, N 2 mi to Brickman Rd, W 2 mi (R). Avail: 60 full hkups (30 amps). 2021 rates: $20 to $35. May 22 to Oct 12. (845)434-5877

INDIAN LAKE — C9 *Hamilton*

ADIRONDACK/LEWEY LAKE (Public State Park) From town, S 12 mi on Hwy 30 (R). 206 Avail. 2021 rates: $20 to $25. May 20 to Oct 09. (518)648-5266

INLET — C8 *Hamilton*

ADIRONDACK/LIMEKILN LAKE CAMPGROUND (Public State Park) From jct Hwy 28 & Limekiln Lake Rd: Go 1-1/3 mi S on Limekiln Lake Rd. (E). 271 Avail. 2021 rates: $20 to $25. May 20 to Sep 04. (315)357-4401

ITHACA — E6 *Tompkins*

PINECREEK CAMPGROUND **Ratings: 7.5/7.5/7.5** (Campground) 125 Avail: 58 full hkups, 67 W, 58 S, 67 E (30/50 amps). 2021 rates: $48 to $58. May 01 to Oct 15. (607)273-1974, 28 Rockwell Rd, Newfield, NY 14867

ROBERT H TREMAN (Public State Park) From Jct of SR-13 & Rte 327, W 0.25 mi on Rte 327 (L). Avail: 11 E (15 amps). 2021 rates: $18 to $28. Apr 17 to Nov 22. (607)273-3440

SPRUCE ROW CAMPGROUND & RV PARK **Ratings: 7.5/9★/9** (Campground) 90 Avail: 23 full hkups, 67 W, 67 E (20/30 amps). 2021 rates: $40 to $50. May 01 to Oct 12. (607)387-9225, 2271 Kraft Rd, Ithaca, NY 14850

TAUGHANNOCK FALLS (Public State Park) From business center: Go 8 mi N on Hwy-89. Avail: 10 E. 2021 rates: $18 to $28. Apr 17 to Oct 17. (607)387-6739

JAMESTOWN — E2 *Chautauqua*

HIDDEN VALLEY CAMPING AREA **Ratings: 9/10★/9.5** (Campground) 50 Avail: 50 W, 50 E (30/50 amps). 2021 rates: $42 to $64. Apr 15 to Oct 15. (716)569-5433, 299 Kiantone Rd, Jamestown, NY 14701

JAVA CENTER — D3 *Wyoming*

BEAVER MEADOW FAMILY CAMPGROUND
Ratings: 8.5/9★/9.5 (Campground) 107 Avail: 107 W, 107 E (30/50 amps). 2021 rates: $45 to $60. May 08 to Oct 14. (585)457-3101, 1455 Beaver Meadow Rd, Java Center, NY 14082

CASCADE COVE
EXCLUSIVE COMPLIMENTARY ACCESS FOR PARK GUESTS!
10/10★/10: RATED IN THE TOP 1% OF U.S. CAMPGROUNDS SINCE 1966!
VACATION DONE RIGHT
• 2-OUTDOOR, HEATED POOLS AND SPA CLUSTER
• CASCADE COVE SPRAY PAD
• "BIG RIG FRIENDLY" CAMPSITES
• 6-LIGHTED PICKLEBALL COURTS
• PAVED ROADS THROUGHOUT PARK
• PULL-THRU & BACK-IN SITES
• ADULT FITNESS CENTER
• AWARD-WINNING DOG PARK
• FREE WI-FI–45 OUTSIDE ACCESS POINTS
• ADIRONDACK-STYLE FAMILY LODGE
• INDOOR HEATED POOL
• LIVE FAMILY ENTERTAINMENT (Summer only)
• FREE PADDLE BOATS (Summer only)
• 24 ON-SITE RV RENTALS
• 2-INDOOR MOVIE THEATERS
• 30 & 50 AMPS, WATER, SANITARY & CABLE TV ON ALL 390 CAMPSITES
• FREE TROLLEY SHUTTLE TO OUTLETS/RESTAURANTS+
• MUNICIPAL TROLLEY SERVICE TO LAKE GEORGE VILLAGE ($)
• RESERVATIONS SUGGESTED
+ Available Summer season and most weekends
LAKE GEORGE RV PARK
FUN IN SITE!
888.572.6490
74 State Rte 149, Lake George, NY
Just off Exit 20 of I-87, near popular attractions, restaurants, and shops.
LakeGeorgeRVPark.com
See listing Lake George, NY

JOHNSTOWN — D9 *Fulton*

ROYAL MOUNTAIN CAMPSITES **Ratings: 6.5/8.5/9** (Campground) 20 Avail: 20 W, 20 E (30/50 amps). 2021 rates: $35. Apr 15 to Oct 15. (877)725-9838, 4948 Hwy 29, Johnstown, NY 12095

KEUKA PARK — E5 *Yates*

KEUKA LAKE (Public State Park) From Jct of Hwy 54A & Hwy 14A, SW 6 mi on Hwy 54A to Pepper Rd, S 0.25 mi (R). Pets need rabies certification. 150 Avail. 2021 rates: $18 to $30. May 01 to Oct 18. (315)536-3666

KINGSTON — F9 *Ulster*

Travel Services

CAMPING WORLD OF KINGSTON As the nation's largest retailer of RV supplies, accessories, services and new and used RVs, Camping World is committed to making your total RV experience better. **SERVICES:** tire, RV appliance, MH mechanical, staffed RV wash, restrooms. RV Sales. RV supplies, LP gas, emergency parking, RV accessible. Hours: 9am to 7pm. (877)466-0233 Lat: 41.945873, Lon: -74.03013
124 New York 28/Onteora Trail, Kingston, NY 12401
www.campingworld.com

LAKE GEORGE — C10 *Warren*

ADIRONDACK CAMPING VILLAGE **Ratings: 9/9.5★/9.5** (Campground) 150 Avail: 87 full hkups, 63 W, 63 E (30/50 amps). 2021 rates: $47 to $86. May 15 to Sep 15. (518)668-5226, 43 Finkle Farm Rd, Lake George, NY 12845

ADIRONDACK/HEARTHSTONE POINT (Public State Park) From town, N 2 mi on SR-9N (R). 251 Avail. 2021 rates: $22 to $27. May 20 to Sep 11. (518)668-5193

ADIRONDACK/LAKE GEORGE BATTLEGROUND (Public State Park) From town, S 0.3 mi on US-9 (L). 68 Avail. 2021 rates: $22 to $27. May 05 to Oct 12. (518)668-3348

KING PHILLIPS CAMPGROUND

good sam park **Ratings: 10/10★/10** (RV Park) From Jct of I-87 & US-9N (exit 21), N 0.2 mi on US-9N to US-9, S 0.8 mi to Bloody Pond Rd, E 0.1 mi (R).

CONVENIENTLY LOCATED TO ATTRACTIONS
Your outdoor adventure begins here, in the middle of all the fun that the Lake George area has to offer: Trolley Stop & Bike Trails take you to Village & Beaches, Great Escape, Outlet Shopping and all premier area attractions

FAC: all weather rds. (222 spaces). Avail: 97 all weather, patios, 16 pull-thrus, (35x60), back-ins (35x44), 80 full hkups, 17 W, 17 E (30/50 amps), seasonal sites, cable, WiFi @ sites, tent sites, dump, laundry, groc, LP gas, fire rings, firewood, controlled access. **REC:** pool, boating nearby, shuffleboard, playground. Pets OK. Big rig sites, eco-friendly. 2021 rates: $49 to $74, Military discount. May 01 to Oct 31.
(518)668-5763 Lat: 43.39415, Lon: -73.69948
14 Bloody Pond Rd, Lake George, NY 12845
www.kingphillipscampground.com
See ad next page

LAKE GEORGE CAMPSITES **Ratings: 8/6.5/6.5** (Campground) 122 Avail: 58 full hkups, 64 W, 64 E (30/50 amps). 2021 rates: $55 to $65. May 01 to Oct 15. (518)798-6218, 1053 Rte 9, Queensbury, NY 12804

LAKE GEORGE ESCAPE CAMPING RESORT

good sam park **Ratings: 9/9/9.5** (Campground) 500 Avail: 298 full hkups, 202 W, 202 E (30/50 amps). 2021 rates: $72 to $125. May 15 to Oct 15. (888)563-7040, 175 E Schroon River Rd, Diamond Point, NY 12824

LAKE GEORGE RIVERVIEW CAMPGROUND

good sam park **Ratings: 10/10★/10** (Campground) From Jct of I-87 & Diamond Pt Rd (exit 23), W 0.25 mi on Diamond Pt Rd to US-9, N 0.2 mi (R).

THE PERFECT SETTING FOR YOUR FAMILY
Our Campsites are placed to take advantage of the beautiful Schroon River or the beauty of the Adirondack Mountains. Whether you prefer a riverfront, a beachfront, or even a spacious site under the majestic pines.

FAC: all weather rds. (170 spaces). Avail: 115 all weather, 65 pull-thrus, (30x50), back-ins (26x45), 99 full hkups, 16 W, 16 E (30/50 amps), seasonal sites, cable, WiFi @ sites, tent sites, dump, laundry, groc, LP gas, fire rings, firewood, controlled access. **REC:** heated pool, Schroon River: swim, fishing, kayaking/canoeing, boating nearby, playground, hunting nearby. Pets OK. Big rig sites, eco-friendly. 2021 rates: $54 to $75, Military discount. May 15 to Oct 15.
(518)623-9444 Lat: 43.48995, Lon: -73.76002
3652 SR 9, Lake George, NY 12845
lakegeorgeriverview.com
See ad next page

LAKE GEORGE RV PARK

Ratings: 10/10★/10 (RV Park) From Jct of I-87 & US-9 (exit 20), N 0.5 mi on US-9 to SR-149, E 0.5 mi (R).

AWARD WINNING FAMILY CAMPING RESORT
Rated in top 1% of all US campgrounds since 1966. Experience the best amenities, service and location in the Adirondack region. Indoor heated pool, trolley shuttle, spacious landscaped sites, BIG RIG and dog friendly.

FAC: paved rds. (368 spaces). Avail: 356 all weather, 280 pull-thrus, (30x60), back-ins (30x56), 356 full hkups (50 amps), seasonal sites, cable, WiFi @ sites, rentals, dump, laundry, groc, LP gas, fire rings, firewood, restaurant, controlled access. **REC:** heated pool, wading pool, hot tub, pond, fishing, boating nearby, shuffleboard, playground. Pets OK. Partial handicap access. No tents. Big rig sites, eco-friendly. 2021 rates: $89 to $165. May 14 to Oct 12. ATM.
(518)379-3775 Lat: 43.36922, Lon: -73.69109
74 SR-149, Lake George, NY 12845
www.lakegeorgervpark.com
See ad opposite page

LEDGEVIEW RV PARK

good sam park **Ratings: 10/10★/10** (RV Park) Avail: 120 full hkups (30/50 amps). 2021 rates: $65 to $75. May 05 to Oct 10. (518)798-6621, 321 SR-149, Lake George, NY 12845

MOOSE HILLOCK CAMPING RESORT NY Ratings: 10/10★/10 (Campground) Avail: 250 full hkups (30/50 amps). 2021 rates: $69 to $109. May 13 to Oct 13. (518)792-4500, 10366 St Rt - 149, Fort Ann, NY 12827

SCHROON RIVER ESCAPE LODGE & RV RESORT **Ratings: 7/7/8** (Membership Park) 153 Avail: 79 full hkups, 74 W, 74 E (30 amps). 2021 rates: $54 to $64. May 01 to Oct 13. (518)623-3954, 969 E Schroon River Rd, Diamond Point, NY 12824

WHIPPOORWILL MOTEL & CAMPSITES

good sam park **Ratings: 9/10★/10** (Campground) 51 Avail: 14 full hkups, 32 W, 32 E (30/50 amps). 2021 rates: $44 to $50. May 15 to Sep 20. (518)668-5565, 1784 SR-9, Lake George, NY 12845

LAKE LUZERNE — C9 *Warren*

ADIRONDACK/LUZERNE (Public) From Jct of Rte 9N & I-87, SW 6.5 mi on Rte 9N (L). 174 Avail. 2021 rates: $22 to $27. May 20 to Sep 11. (518)696-2031

LAKE PLACID — B9 *Essex*

LAKE PLACID See also North Hudson & Wilmington.

LAKE PLEASANT — C9 *Hamilton*

ADIRONDACK/LITTLE SAND POINT (Public) E-bnd: From Jct of Hwy 8 & Old Piseco Rd (at S end of lake), E 5 mi on Old Piseco Rd (R); or W-bnd: From Jct of Hwy 8 & Old Piseco Rd, W 3 mi on Old Piseco Rd (L). Entrance fee required. 78 Avail. 2021 rates: $20 to $25. May 20 to Sep 11. (518)548-7585

ADIRONDACK/MOFFITT BEACH (Public State Park) From town, E 2.5 mi on Hwy 8 (L). 261 Avail. 2021 rates: $22 to $27. May 20 to Oct 09. (518)548-7102

ADIRONDACK/POINT COMFORT (Public State Park) From business center: Go 10 mi SW on Hwy 8, then 3/4 mi N on CR 24. 76 Avail: Pit toilets. 2021 rates: $20 to $25. May 20 to Sep 05. (518)548-7586

LAURENS — E8 *Otsego*

GILBERT LAKE (Public State Park) From Jct of I-88 & SR-205, N 10 mi on SR-205 to CR-11A, W to CR-12, NW 4 mi (R). 135 Avail. 2021 rates: $15 to $27. May 13 to Oct 09. (607)432-2114

LE ROY — D4 *Genesee*

JAM AT THE RIDGE **Ratings: 7.5/7/7.5** (Campground) 95 Avail: 52 full hkups, 43 W, 43 E (30/50 amps). 2021 rates: $59. (585)768-4883, 8101 Conlon Rd, Le Roy, NY 14482

TIMBERLINE LAKE PARK **Ratings: 6.5/6/6** (Campground) Avail: 21 full hkups (30/50 amps). 2021 rates: $50. May 01 to Oct 15. (585)768-6635, 8150 Vallance Rd, Le Roy, NY 14482

LISLE — E7 *Broome*

GREENWOOD PARK (Public) From Jct of I-81 & SR-26 (exit 8), S 3.7 SR-26 to Cnty Cherry Hill Rd, W 4 mi to Caldwell Hill Rd, N 3 mi to Greenwood Rd, 1 mi (L). Avail: 50 E (15 amps). 2021 rates: $20 to $25. May 15 to Oct 15. (607)778-2193

LIVINGSTON MANOR — F8 *Delaware*

CATSKILL/MONGAUP POND (Public State Park) From Jct of Hwy 17 & De Bruce Rd (exit 96), E 6.5 mi on De Bruce Rd to Mongaup Rd, N 3.5 mi, follow signs (E). 163 Avail. 2021 rates: $22 to $27. May 20 to Oct 10. (845)439-4233

LOCKPORT — D3 *Niagara*

NIAGARA COUNTY CAMPING RESORT

good sam park **Ratings: 7/8★/8** (Campground) From Jct of SR-104, SR-78 & Wheeler Rd (4 mi N of Lockport), E 3 mi on Wheeler Rd (L).

QUIET COUNTRY CAMPING
Minutes to Niagara Falls, Erie Canal and Lake Ontario. Cable TV & WiFi, cottage and cabin rentals. Pet and family friendly! Come relax & enjoy some quiet time & all that the nearby area has to offer!

FAC: gravel rds. (240 spaces). Avail: 50 grass, 47 pull-thrus, (30x50), back-ins (30x46), 50 W, 50 E (30/50 amps), seasonal sites, cable, WiFi @ sites, tent sites, rentals, dump, mobile sewer, groc, fire rings, firewood, controlled access. **REC:** Bedford Beach Lake: swim, fishing, kayaking/canoeing, boating nearby, playground. Pet restrict (Q). eco-friendly. 2021 rates: $53 to $55, Military discount. May 10 to Oct 13.
(716)434-3991 Lat: 43.23201, Lon: -78.62844
7369 Wheeler Rd, Lockport, NY 14094
www.niagaracamping.com
See ad page 651

LONG LAKE — B9 *Hamilton*

ADIRONDACK/LAKE EATON (Public State Park) From town, NW 2 mi on Hwy 30 (L). Avail: 135 E. 2021 rates: $20. May 20 to Oct 09. (518)624-2641

ADIRONDACK/LAKE HARRIS (Public State Park) From town, W 3 mi on Rte 28N (L). 89 Avail. 2021 rates: $18 to $23. May 20 to Sep 11. (518)582-2503

LOWVILLE — C7 *Lewis*

WHETSTONE GULF (Public State Park) From town, S 6 mi on SR-26 (R). Avail: 19 E (15/30 amps). 2021 rates: $15 to $27. May 22 to Sep 07. (315)376-6630

MACEDON — D5 *Wayne*

TWILIGHT ON THE ERIE RV RESORT **Ratings: 8/9★/9** (RV Resort) Avail: 92 full hkups (30/50 amps). 2021 rates: $56 to $62. Apr 15 to Oct 31. (315)986-7337, 1100 Marina Parkway , Macedon, NY 14502

MARATHON — E7 *Cortland*

COUNTRY HILLS CAMPGROUND **Ratings: 6.5/9.5★/9** (Campground) Avail: 13 full hkups (30/50 amps). 2021 rates: $39. Apr 26 to Oct 15. (607)849-3300, 1165 Muckey Rd, Marathon, NY 13803

MASSENA — A8 *St Lawrence*

MASSENA INTERNATIONAL KAMPGROUND **Ratings: 7/8.5★/8.5** (Campground) Avail: 98 full hkups (30/50 amps). 2021 rates: $40 to $44. May 01 to Oct 25. (315)769-9483, 84 CR 42A, Massena, NY 13662

MECHANICVILLE — D10 *Rensselaer*

ADVENTURE BOUND CAMPING AT DEER RUN **Ratings: 9.5/7.5/9** (Campground) 161 Avail: 138 full hkups, 23 W, 23 E (30 amps). 2021 rates: $47 to $89. Apr 18 to Oct 18. (518)664-2804, 200 Deer Run Dr (SR-67), Schaghticoke, NY 12154

MEDINA — D3 *Orleans*

MEDINA/WILDWOOD LAKE KOA **Ratings: 8.5/9/9** (Campground) 178 Avail: 40 full hkups, 138 W, 138 E (30/50 amps). 2021 rates: $71.91 to $130. May 01 to Oct 12. (585)735-3310, 2711 County Line Rd, Medina, NY 14103

MEXICO — C6 *Oswego*

J & J CAMPGROUND **Ratings: 6.5/8.5★/7** (Campground) Avail: 20 full hkups (30/50 amps). 2021 rates: $32. (315)963-1108, 291 Tubbs Rd, Mexico, NY 13114

Park policies vary. Ask about the cancellation policy when making a reservation.

See listings Lake George, NY
2 GREAT LAKE GEORGE ADVENTURES
LET OUR FAMILY TAKE CARE OF YOURS
EXIT 21
KING PHILLIPS CAMPGROUND
OUTDOOR ADVENTURES
KING PHILLIP'S
KPC
CAMPGROUND
LAKE GEORGE NEW YORK
EXCITEMENT & FUN
* CLOSEST FULL SERVICE CAMPGROUND TO LAKE GEORGE VILLAGE (1.5 MI)
* CENTRAL TO ALL ATTRACTIONS
* E-Z ACCESS I-87 EXIT 21
* BIG RIG PULL THRUS 50/30/20
* CABLE TV & FREE WIFI
* ON TROLLEY ROUTE TO ATTRACTIONS
* ON BIKE TRAIL TO LAKE GEORGE VILLAGE
MAKE YOUR RESERVATION NOW!
(518) 668-5763
WWW.KINGPHILLIPSCAMPGROUND.COM
RESERVATIONS@KINGPHILLIPSCAMPGROUND.COM
good sam park
2022 Top Rated 10/10★/10
WiFi
NEW DELUXE RIVERSIDE & BEACH SITES!!
2020 Travelers' Choice
Tripadvisor
LAKE GEORGE Riverview CAMPGROUND
EXIT 23
LAKE GEORGE RIVERVIEW
ESCAPE TO THE WILDERNESS
PEACEFUL & QUIET
* 4 MI TO LAKE GEORGE VILLAGE
* E-Z ACCESS I-87 EXIT 23
* WATERFRONT CAMPSITES
* KAYAK/TUBE/BOAT RENTALS
* ON TROLLEY ROUTE
* SHOPPING IN WALKING DISTANCE
* BIG RIG PULL THRU 50/30/20A
* CABLE TV & FREE WIFI
* TENTS & POP-UPS WELCOME
MAKE YOUR RESERVATION NOW!
(518) 623-9444
WWW.LAKEGEORGERIVERVIEW.COM
RESERVATIONS@LAKEGEORGERIVERVIEW.COM
good sam park
2022 Top Rated 10/10★/10
AAA

MEXICO (CONT)

YOGI BEAR'S JELLYSTONE PARK CAMP-RESORT AT MEXICO **Ratings: 8/7.5/9** (Campground) 110 Avail: 14 full hkups, 95 W, 95 E (30/50 amps). 2021 rates: $42 to $86. Apr 26 to Oct 20. (315)963-7096, 601 CR-16, Mexico, NY 13114

MIDDLEBURGH — E9 *Schoharie*

MAX V SHAUL (Public State Park) From town, S 5 mi on Hwy 30 (R). 30 Avail. 2021 rates: $15 to $19. May 19 to Oct 10. (518)827-4711

MIDDLESEX — D5 *Yates*

FLINT CREEK CAMPGROUND **Ratings: 6.5/7.5/7** (Campground) 55 Avail: 40 full hkups, 15 W, 15 E (30 amps). 2021 rates: $55. May 01 to Oct 31. (585)554-3567, 1455 Phelps Rd, Middlesex, NY 14507

MIDDLETOWN — F9 *Orange*

KORN'S CAMPGROUNDS (Public) From jct Rt 17 (exit 118) & Rt 17M: Go 1-1/4 mi NW on 17M, then 3 mi SW on Prosperous Valley Rd, then 200 yards W on Brola Rd, then 250 yards W on Meyer Rd. 98 Avail: 98 W, 98 E (30 amps). 2021 rates: $50. May 01 to Oct 15. (845)386-3433

MONTAUK — A5 *Suffolk*

HITHER HILLS (Public State Park) From town, W 3 mi on Old Montauk Hwy (L). 168 Avail. 2021 rates: $35 to $70. Apr 15 to Nov 20. (631)668-2554

MONTEZUMA — D6 *Seneca*

HEJAMADA CAMPGROUND & RV PARK **Ratings: 7/6/6.5** (Campground) 109 Avail: 20 full hkups, 89 W, 89 E (30/50 amps). 2021 rates: $44 to $60. May 01 to Oct 15. (315)776-5887, 748 McDonald Rd, Port Byron, NY 13140

MONTGOMERY — F9 *Orange*

WINDING HILLS PARK (Public) From Jct of I 87 & 17K, W 12 mi to Old Rt 17K (follows signs), N 0.3 mi (R) Caution: Maximum length 35'. Note: Three day minimum stay holiday weekends. Avail: 30 E (30 amps). 2021 rates: $20 to $40. May 20 to Oct 10. (845)457-4918

MONTOUR FALLS — E5 *Schuyler*

MONTOUR MARINA & CAMPGROUND (Public) From Jct of SR-14 & Marina Dr (in town), N 0.5 mi on Marina Dr (L). Avail: 20 full hkups (30/50 amps). 2021 rates: $40 to $55. May 01 to Oct 15. (607)210-4124

MORAVIA — D6 *Cayuga*

FILLMORE GLEN (Public State Park) From Jct of Hwy 90 & SR-38, N 3 mi on SR-38 (R). Avail: 9 E (30/50 amps). 2021 rates: $15 to $27. May 03 to Oct 13. (315)497-0130

MORRISTOWN — A7 *St Lawrence*

JACQUES CARTIER (Public State Park) From Jct of Rtes 37 & 12, S 2 mi on Rte 12 to unnamed rd, W 100 ft, follow signs (L). Avail: 33 E (15 amps). 2021 rates: $15 to $31. May 15 to Sep 12. (315)375-6371

MOUNT MORRIS — D4 *Livingston*

LETCHWORTH (Public State Park) From Jct of Hwys 36 & 39, S 2 mi on Hwy 36 to park rd (park entrance), S 5.5 mi (L). Avail: 68 E (20/30 amps). 2021 rates: $24 to $26. May 05 to Oct 15. (585)493-3600

MOUNTAIN DALE — F9 *Sullivan*

MOUNTAINDALE CAMPGROUND (Public) From Jct of Rte 17 & Rockhill (exit 109), N 8 mi on Cr-58 to Mountain Dale, E 2 mi to Park Hill Rd., E 1 mi. 115 Avail: 115 W, 70 S, 115 E (30 amps). 2021 rates: $33.90. May 01 to Sep 24. (845)434-7337

NEW YORK CITY — B2 *New York*

A SPOTLIGHT Introducing New York City's colorful attractions appearing at the front of this state section.

BLACK BEAR CAMPGROUND

good sam park

Ratings: 10/10★/10 (Campground) About 1 hr NW on I-87 to Exit 16 (US-17W), then 13 mi W on US-17 to Exit 124, then 5 1/2 mi SW on Hwy 17A, then R at light (Bridge St), then 1 1/2 mi W on CR-41. **FAC:** paved rds. Avail: 154 all weather, 25 pull-thrus, (30x75), back-ins (30x60), 154 full hkups (30/50 amps), WiFi @ sites, laundry, groc, LP bottles, fire rings, firewood. **REC:** heated pool, pond, fishing, boating nearby, shuffleboard, playground, hunting nearby. Pet restrict (B/Q). Partial handicap access. No tents. Big rig sites, eco-friendly. 2021 rates: $80 to $100, Military discount.
(845)651-7717 Lat: 41.32242, Lon: -74.3734
197 Wheeler Rd, Florida, NY 10921
blackbearcampground.com
See primary listing at Florida and ad page 640

LIBERTY HARBOR MARINA & RV PARK

Ratings: 7.5/9.5★/6.5 (RV Park) From jct Canal St & I-78 W/Holland Tunnel: Go 2 mi W on I-78 W/Holland Tunnel, then 500 feet S on Grove St/Manila Ave, then 400 feet E on 12th Ave, then 1-1/4 mi on Marin Blvd (R). **FAC:** paved rds. (70 spaces). 70 Avail: 16 paved, 54 gravel, back-ins (18x45), 50 W, 50 E (30/50 amps), WiFi @ sites, tent sites, dump, mobile sewer, laundry, restaurant, controlled access. **REC:** Hudson River: fishing, marina, kayaking/canoeing, boating nearby. Pets OK. Partial handicap access, eco-friendly. 2021 rates: $110 to $120.
(201)516-7500 Lat: 40.71222, Lon: -74.04333
11 Marin Blvd, Jersey City, NJ 07302
www.libertyharborrv.com
See primary listing at Jersey City, NJ and ad page 638

NEWBURGH — F9 *Orange*

NEW YORK CITY NORTH/NEWBURGH KOA **Ratings: 9/9/9.5** (Campground) 125 Avail: 81 full hkups, 44 W, 44 E (30/50 amps). 2021 rates: $46.99 to $110.99. Mar 28 to Nov 01. (845)564-2836, 119 Freetown Highway, Plattekill, NY 12568

NIAGARA FALLS — D3 *Niagara*

A SPOTLIGHT Introducing Niagara Falls' colorful attractions appearing at the front of this state section.

AA ROYAL MOTEL & CAMPGROUND

good sam park

Ratings: 7.5/8/8 (Campground) From Jct of I-90 (exit 50) & I-290, W 0.1 mi on US-62 N (Exit 3), N 5.7 mi on US-62 (R); or From Jct of I-190 N & US-62 S (exit 22), S 7.7 mi on US-62 (R). **FAC:** paved rds. Avail: 28 paved, 6 pull-thrus, (30x80), back-ins (30x50), 28 full hkups (30/50 amps), WiFi @ sites, tent sites, rentals, laundry, fire rings, firewood. Pets OK. Partial handicap access. Big rig sites. 2021 rates: $60 to $70, Military discount.
(716)693-5695 Lat: 43.07530, Lon: -78.86127
3333 Niagara Falls Blvd, North Tonawanda, NY 14120
royalmotelandcampground.com
See ad page 642

BRANCHES OF NIAGARA CAMPGROUND & RESORT **Ratings: 9.5/10★/10** (Campground) 96 Avail: 73 full hkups, 23 W, 23 E (30/50 amps). 2021 rates: $101 to $136. Apr 11 to Oct 31. (716)773-7600, 2659 Whitehaven Rd, Grand Island, NY 14072

CINDERELLA MOTEL & CAMPGROUND **Ratings: 6/9.5★/8** (Campground) Avail: 21 full hkups (30/50 amps). 2021 rates: $40 to $50. Apr 01 to Oct 31. (716)773-2872, 2797 Grand Island Blvd, Grand Island, NY 14072

NIAGARA FALLS KOA **Ratings: 9/10★/10** (Campground) 131 Avail: 21 full hkups, 48 W, 48 E (30/50 amps). 2021 rates: $75 to $155. Apr 01 to Oct 31. (716)773-7583, 2570 Grand Island Blvd, Grand Island, NY 14072

NIAGARA FALLS NORTH/LEWISTON KOA **Ratings: 8.5/9★/9** (Campground) 93 Avail: 18 full hkups, 75 W, 75 E (30/50 amps). 2021 rates: $56 to $69. Apr 15 to Oct 15. (800)562-8715, 1250 Pletcher Rd, Youngstown, NY 14174

NIAGARA'S LAZY LAKES **Ratings: 8.5/9.5/10** (Membership Park) 265 Avail: 50 full hkups, 215 W, 215 E (30/50 amps). 2021 rates: $68. May 01 to Nov 01. (800)874-2957, 4312 Church Rd, Lockport, NY 14094

Don't forget to show your Good Sam Membership card when you check in. Stay at any of the Good Sam RV Parks & Campgrounds in the U.S. and Canada and save 10% on the regular nightly RV site rate! No Blackout Dates! Visit GoodSam.com for more details.

NORTH HUDSON — B10 *Essex*

CAMP TIN BOX **Ratings: 9/10★/9.5** (Campground) 130 Avail: 95 full hkups, 35 W, 35 E (30/50 amps). 2021 rates: $70 to $81. May 01 to Oct 15. (518)532-7493, 4035 Blue Ridge Rd , North Hudson, NY 12855

NORTH JAVA — D4 *Wyoming*

JELLYSTONE PARK (TM) OF WESTERN NEW YORK **Ratings: 9/10★/9** (Campground) Avail: 222 full hkups (30/50 amps). 2021 rates: $58 to $147. May 03 to Oct 14. (877)469-7590, 5204 Youngers Road, North Java, NY 14113

NORTHVILLE — D9 *Fulton*

ADIRONDACK/NORTHAMPTON BEACH (Public State Park) From business center: Go 1-1/2 mi S on Hwy 30, then SE. 223 Avail. 2021 rates: $22 to $27. May 20 to Oct 10. (518)863-6000

ADIRONDACK/SACANDAGA (Public State Park) From Amsterdam, N 35 mi on Rte 30 (L). Entrance fee required. 143 Avail. 2021 rates: $20 to $25. May 20 to Sep 04. (518)924-4121

OGDENSBURG — A7 *St Lawrence*

LISBON BEACH AND CAMPGROUND (Public) From jct Hwy 812 & Hwy 37: Go 5 mi E on Hwy 37. Avail: 56 E Pit toilets. 2021 rates: $24 to $34. May 01 to Oct 15. (315)393-5374

OLD BETHPAGE — B3 *Nassau*

BATTLE ROW CAMPGROUND (NASSAU COUNTY PARK) (Public) From jct I-495 (exit 48) & Round Swamp Rd: Go 1-3/4 mi SE on Round Swamp Rd, then 1 block E on Bethpage-Sweethollow Rd, then 1 block S on Claremont Rd. 52 Avail: 52 W, 52 E (30/50 amps). 2021 rates: $10 to $20. (516)572-8690

OLD FORGE — C8 *Herkimer*

ADIRONDACK/NICKS LAKE (Public State Park) From business center: Go 2 mi SE on Hwy-28. 112 Avail. 2021 rates: $22 to $27. May 20 to Oct 10. (315)369-3314

OLD FORGE CAMPING RESORT **Ratings: 7.5/7/8.5** (RV Park) 132 Avail: 54 full hkups, 78 W, 78 E (30/50 amps). 2021 rates: $55 to $75. (800)226-7464, 3347 SR 28, Old Forge, NY 13420

SINGING WATERS CAMPGROUND **Ratings: 6/9.5★/9** (Campground) 88 Avail: 59 full hkups, 9 W, 9 E (30 amps). 2021 rates: $55 to $60. (315)369-6618, 1334 NY 28, Old Forge, NY 13420

ONEIDA — D7 *Madison*

VERONA BEACH (Public State Park) From jct I-90 & Hwy-13: Go 7 mi NW on Hwy-13. 45 Avail. 2021 rates: $18 to $30. May 13 to Oct 09. (315)762-4463

ONEONTA — E8 *Otsego*

DEER HAVEN CAMPGROUND & CABINS **Ratings: 7.5/9.5★/9** (Campground) Avail: 25 full hkups (30/50 amps). 2021 rates: $45 to $50. May 25 to Oct 12. (607)433-9654, 180 Deer Haven Lane, Oneonta, NY 13820

SUSQUEHANNA TRAIL CAMPGROUND **Ratings: 6/5/6.5** (Campground) Avail: 24 full hkups (30 amps). 2021 rates: $50. Apr 01 to Nov 01. (607)432-1122, 4292 State Hwy 7, Oneonta, NY 13820

OVID — D6 *Seneca*

SNED-ACRES FAMILY CAMPGROUND **Ratings: 7/8/7** (Campground) 43 Avail: (30/50 amps). 2021 rates: $36.50 to $38.50. (607)869-9787, 6590 S Cayuga Lake Rd, Ovid, NY 14521

OWEGO — E6 *Tioga*

HICKORIES PARK (Public) From Jct of SR-17C & Hickories Park Rd (exit 65), S 0.5 mi on Hickories Park Rd (E). 120 Avail: 75 full hkups, 12 W, 12 E (20/30 amps). 2021 rates: $25 to $30. (607)687-1199

OXFORD — E7 *Chenango*

BOWMAN LAKE (Public State Park) From town, W 6.3 mi on SR-220, N 1.3 mi Bowman Rd. (R). 48 Avail. 2021 rates: $15 to $19. May 20 to Sep 11. (607)334-2718

PENNELLVILLE — C6 *Oswego*

PLEASANT LAKE CAMPGROUND **Ratings: 6.5/5/8** (Campground) 36 Avail: 31 full hkups, 5 W, 5 E (30 amps). 2021 rates: $44. May 01 to Oct 13. (315)668-2074, 65 Wigwam Dr, Pennellville, NY 13132

PERU — A10 *Clinton*

AUSABLE POINT (Public) From Plattsburgh, S 12 mi on US-9 (L). 123 Avail. 2021 rates: $22 to $27. May 17 to Oct 13. (518)561-7080

IROQUOIS RV PARK & CAMPGROUND **Ratings: 8.5/8.5★/8.5** (Campground) Avail: 72 full hkups (30/50 amps). 2021 rates: $38 to $40. May 01 to Oct 01. (518)643-9057, 270 Bear Swamp Rd, Peru, NY 12972

PETERSBURGH — D10 *Rensselaer*

AQUA VISTA CAMPGROUND **Ratings: 5.5/5.5/6** (Campground) 65 Avail: 65 W, 65 E (30 amps). 2021 rates: $40 to $49.50. May 01 to Sep 30. (518)658-3659, 72 Armsby Rd, Petersburgh, NY 12138

BROKEN WHEEL CAMPGROUND **Ratings: 6.5/6/9** (Campground) 40 Avail: 40 W, 40 E (30/50 amps). 2021 rates: $33. May 01 to Oct 15. (518)658-2925, 61 Broken Wheel Rd, Petersburgh, NY 12138

PHELPS — D5 *Ontario*

CHEERFUL VALLEY CAMPGROUND **Ratings: 6.5/8/8** (Campground) 75 Avail: 19 full hkups, 56 W, 56 E (30/50 amps). 2021 rates: $50 to $69. May 01 to Oct 15. (315)781-1222, 1412 Route 14, Phelps, NY 14532

JUNIUS PONDS CABINS & CAMPGROUND **Ratings: 10/9★/9.5** (Campground) Avail: 52 full hkups (30/50 amps). 2021 rates: $46 to $55. Apr 15 to Oct 15. (315)781-5120, 1475 W Townline Rd, Phelps, NY 14532

PHOENICIA — E9 *Ulster*

CATSKILL/KENNETH L WILSON (Public State Park) Nbound: From Jct of Hwy 87 & exit 19/Kingston exit (in Kingston), W 20 ft at traffic circle to Rte 28, NW 21 mi to Rte 212 (in Mt Tremper), E 0.5 mi to Rte 40/Wittenberg, E 5 mi (R). 76 Avail. 2021 rates: $22 to $27. May 12 to Oct 12. (845)679-7020

CATSKILL/WOODLAND VALLEY (Public State Park) From town, W 0.5 mi on Rte 28 to Woodland Valley Rd, S 5 mi (L). 70 Avail. 2021 rates: $20 to $25. May 20 to Oct 10. (845)688-7647

PLATTSBURGH — A10 *Clinton*

CUMBERLAND BAY (Public State Park) From Jct. US Hwy 9 & Rte 314, E .5 Mi on Rte 314. Avail: 13 E (20/30 amps). 2021 rates: $15 to $29. May 10 to Oct 13. (518)563-5240

PLATTSBURGH RV PARK **Ratings: 8/8★/8.5** (RV Park) Avail: 75 full hkups (30/50 amps). 2021 rates: $35 to $42. May 15 to Oct 15. (518)563-3915, 7182 Rt 9, Plattsburgh, NY 12901

POLAND — D8 *Oneida*

ADIRONDACK GATEWAY CAMPGROUND

good sam park

Ratings: 8.5/10★/9.5 (Campground) From Jct of I-90 & SR-8 (exit 31), NE 17.4 mi on SR-8 to Hall Rd, E 0.4 mi to Burt Rd, N 0.3 mi (R). **FAC:** gravel rds. (74 spaces). Avail: 35 grass, 10 pull-thrus, (40x70), back-ins (50x70), 30 full hkups, 5 W, 5 E (30/50 amps), seasonal sites, WiFi, tent sites, rentals, dump, laundry, fire rings, firewood. **REC:** heated pool, pond, fishing, kayaking/canoeing, playground. Pets OK. Big rig sites, eco-friendly. 2021 rates: $38 to $41, Military discount. May 15 to Oct 13.
(315)826-5335 Lat: 43.26618, Lon: -74.98141
244 Burt Rd, Cold Brook, NY 13324
www.adirondackgatewaycampground.net
See ad this page

WEST CANADA CREEK CAMPSITES **Ratings: 8/9★/9** (Campground) 55 Avail: 45 full hkups, 10 W, 10 E (30/50 amps). 2021 rates: $44 to $60. May 01 to Oct 15. (315)826-7390, 12275 SR-28, Poland, NY 13431

PORT HENRY — B10 *Essex*

BULWAGGA BAY CAMPGROUND & RV PARK (Public) From center of town: Go 1/4 mi S on Hwy 9N/22, then 500 feet E on Bulwagga Rd (follow signs). Avail: 160 E (30/50 amps). 2021 rates: $40 to $50. May 01 to Sep 30. (518)546-7500

PORT HENRY CHAMP BEACH CAMPGROUND & RV PARK (Public) From center of town (Hwy 9N/22): Go 100 yards E on Dock St, then 1/4 mi N on Hwy 9N/22, then 1/8 mi E on Beach Rd (curve to the right). 100 Avail: 100 W, 100 E (30/50 amps). 2021 rates: $30 to $50. May 06 to Oct 08. (518)546-7123

PORTAGEVILLE — E4 *Wyoming*

ADVENTURE BOUND CAMPING RESORT - FOUR WINDS **Ratings: 6/6.5/7.5** (Campground) 124 Avail: (30/50 amps). 2021 rates: $79 to $94. Apr 01 to Oct 15. (585)493-2794, 7350 Tenefly Rd, Portageville, NY 14536

POTTERSVILLE — C9 *Warren*

ADIRONDACK/EAGLE POINT (Public State Park) From town, N 2 mi on SR-9 (R). 72 Avail. 2021 rates: $22 to $27. May 17 to Sep 07. (518)494-2220

POUGHKEEPSIE — F9 *Dutchess*

MILLS NORRIE (Public State Park) From Jct of CR-41 & US-9, N 3.4 mi on US-9 to Old Post Rd, W 0.1 mi (L). 46 Avail. 2021 rates: $15 to $19. Apr 29 to Oct 22. (845)889-4646

PRATTSBURGH — E5 *Steuben*

FINGER LAKES CAMPGROUND **Ratings: 8.5/9★/9.5** (Campground) 23 Avail: 23 W, 23 E (30/50 amps). 2021 rates: $40 to $60. May 01 to Oct 15. (607)326-0077, 10378 Presler Rd, Prattsburgh, NY 14873

PULASKI — C6 *Oswego*

BRENNAN BEACH RV RESORT

good sam park

Ratings: 8.5/8/9.5 (Campground) Avail: 170 full hkups (50 amps). 2021 rates: $63 to $88. May 01 to Oct 15. (888)563-7040, 80 Brennan Beach, Pulaski, NY 13142

SELKIRK SHORES (Public State Park) From Jct of SR-13 & SR-3, S 1.5 mi on SR-3 (R). Avail: 85 E (15 amps). 2021 rates: $15 to $19. May 13 to Oct 16. (315)298-5737

STREAMSIDE RV PARK & GOLF COURSE **Ratings: 4.5/NA/8.5** (Campground) Avail: 21 full hkups (30/50 amps). 2021 rates: $30. Apr 15 to Oct 15. (315)298-6887, 800 Tinker Tavern, Pulaski, NY 13142

RANDOLPH — E3 *Cattaraugus*

POPE HAVEN CAMPGROUND

good sam park

Ratings: 8.5/7.5/8.5 (Campground) 37 Avail: 32 full hkups, 5 W, 5 E (30/50 amps). 2021 rates: $46. May 01 to Oct 15. (716)358-4900, 11948 Pope Rd, Randolph, NY 14772

RANSOMVILLE — D3 *Niagara*

NIAGARA WOODLAND CAMPGROUND **Ratings: 7.5/6/6.5** (Campground) 30 Avail: 10 full hkups, 20 W, 20 E (30/50 amps). 2021 rates: $50. May 10 to Oct 20. (716)791-3101, 3435 New Rd, Ransomville, NY 14131

RAQUETTE LAKE — C8 *Hamilton*

ADIRONDACK/BROWN TRACT POND (Public State Park) From business center: Go 2 mi NW on Town Rd. 90 Avail. 2021 rates: $18 to $23. (315)354-4412

ADIRONDACK/EIGHTH LAKE (Public State Park) From town: Go 5 mi W on Hwy-28. 126 Avail. 2021 rates: $22 to $27. May 17 to Oct 13. (315)354-4120

ADIRONDACK/GOLDEN BEACH (Public State Park) From town, E 2 mi on SR-28 (L). 205 Avail. 2021 rates: $20 to $25. May 20 to Sep 05. (315)354-4230

RHINEBECK — F9 *Dutchess*

INTERLAKE RV PARK & SALES **Ratings: 10/9.5★/10** (Campground) 79 Avail: 61 full hkups, 18 W, 18 E (30/50 amps). 2021 rates: $50 to $62. Apr 15 to Oct 19. (845)266-5387, 428 Lake Dr, Rhinebeck, NY 12572

RIVERHEAD — A4 *Suffolk*

INDIAN ISLAND (SUFFOLK COUNTY PARK) (Public) From jct Hwy 24 & CR 105: Go E on CR 105 past golf course. 150 Avail. 2021 rates: $25. (631)852-3232

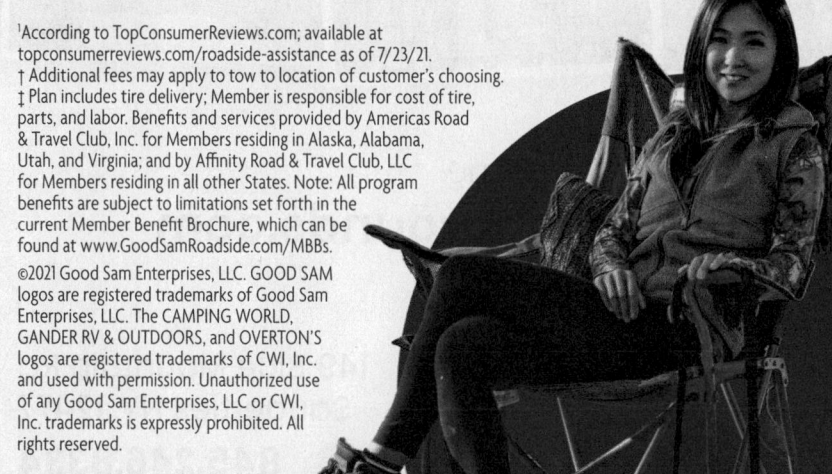

ROCHESTER — D5 *Monroe*

ROCHESTER See also Byron, Caledonia, Canandaigua, Conesus, Le Roy & Macedon.

ROME — D7 *Oneida*

↑ DELTA LAKE (Public State Park) From town, N 6 mi on Hwy 46 (L). 101 Avail. 2021 rates: $15 to $33. May 09 to Sep 01. (315)337-4670

ROMULUS — D6 *Seneca*

↓ SAMPSON (Public State Park) From Jct of Hwy 5/20 & Rte 96A, S 11 mi on Rte 96A (R); or From town, S 4 mi on Rte 14 to Rte 5/20, E 1 mi to Rte 96A, S 11 mi (R). Note: All sites closed Sept. 22-30, 2013. Avail: 245 E (30 amps). 2021 rates: $15 to $31. Apr 22 to Nov 08. (315)585-6392

ROSCOE — F8 *Delaware*

← RUSSELL BROOK CAMPSITE **Ratings: 7/9.5★/8** (Campground) 60 Avail: 60 W, 60 E (30/50 amps). 2021 rates: $50 to $60. May 01 to Oct 31. (607)498-5416, 731 Russell Brook Rd, Roscoe, NY 12776

NY

SALAMANCA — E3 *Cattaraugus*

ALLEGANY/QUAKER AREA (Public State Park) From Hwy-17 (Exit 18): Go S on Hwy-280, then E on Park Rd 3. 189 Avail. 2021 rates: $18 to $30. Mar 27 to Nov 25. (716)354-2182

ALLEGANY/RED HOUSE AREA (Public State Park) From Hwy 17 (exit 19): Go E on Allegany State Park Rd 2, then S on Allegany State Park Rd 1. 130 Avail. 2021 rates: $18 to $30. Apr 01 to Nov 01. (716)354-9121

SALISBURY — D8 *Herkimer*

→ SPRUCE CREEK CAMPGROUND **Ratings: 6.5/9/9** (RV Park) 60 Avail: 17 full hkups, 3 W, 40 E (30/50 amps). 2021 rates: $42 to $47. Apr 01 to Oct 31. (315)429-3650, 2342 SR 29, Salisbury, NY 13454

SARANAC LAKE — B9 *Franklin*

↑ ADIRONDACK/MEADOWBROOK (Public State Park) From town, N 4 mi on Rte 86 (L). 62 Avail. 2021 rates: $18 to $23. May 20 to Sep 04. (518)891-4351

SARATOGA SPRINGS — D10 *Saratoga*

↗ SARATOGA ESCAPE LODGES & RV RESORT **Ratings: 7.5/6.5/9.5** (Campground) 99 Avail: 99 W, 99 E (30 amps). 2021 rates: $54 to $64. May 15 to Oct 01. (518)893-0537, 265 Brigham Rd, Greenfield Center, NY 12833

← WHISPERING PINES CAMPSITES **Ratings: 7.5/7/7.5** (Campground) 70 Avail: 46 full hkups, 24 W, 24 E (30/50 amps). 2021 rates: $40 to $55. May 01 to Oct 31. (855)687-2267, 550 Sand Hill Rd, Greenfield Center, NY 12833

SAUGERTIES — E9 *Ulster*

↖ BLUE MOUNTAIN CAMPGROUND **Ratings: 9/9.5★/8.5** (Campground) Avail: 12 full hkups (30/50 amps). 2021 rates: $59. (845)246-7564, 3783 NY 32, Saugerties, NY 12477

↖ **RIP VAN WINKLE CAMPGROUNDS**

good sam park **Ratings: 10/10★/10** (Campground) From Jct of I-87 & SR-212 (exit 20), W 2.4 mi on SR-212 to CR-35, N 0.5 mi (L).

RELAX IN NEW YORK'S CATSKILL MTS.

Leave your worries behind in the City & enjoy the beauty & serenity of the Catskill Mountains! There are fun activities for the entire family or just relax by the campfire & enjoy the peace & quite of being away from it all!

FAC: all weather rds. (176 spaces). Avail: 106 all weather, 34 pull-thrus, (40x75), back-ins (40x60), 100 full hkups, 6 W, 6 E (30/50 amps), seasonal sites, cable, WiFi @ sites, tent sites, rentals, dump, laundry, groc, LP gas, fire rings, firewood, controlled access. **REC:** heated pool, Plattekill River: swim, fishing, playground. Pets OK. Partial handicap access. Big rig sites, eco-friendly. 2021 rates: $69, Military discount. Apr 01 to Oct 15.

(845)246-8334 Lat: 42.09249, Lon: -74.01863
149 Blue Mountain Rd (CR-35), Saugerties, NY 12477
www.ripvanwinklecampgrounds.com
See ad next page

SCHENECTADY — D9 *Schenectady*

↗ FROSTY ACRES RV & CAMPING RESORT **Ratings: 7/8.5/9** (RV Park) Avail: 51 full hkups (30/50 amps). 2021 rates: $35 to $48. May 15 to Oct 12. (518)864-5352, 1560 Skyline Dr, Schenectady, NY 12306

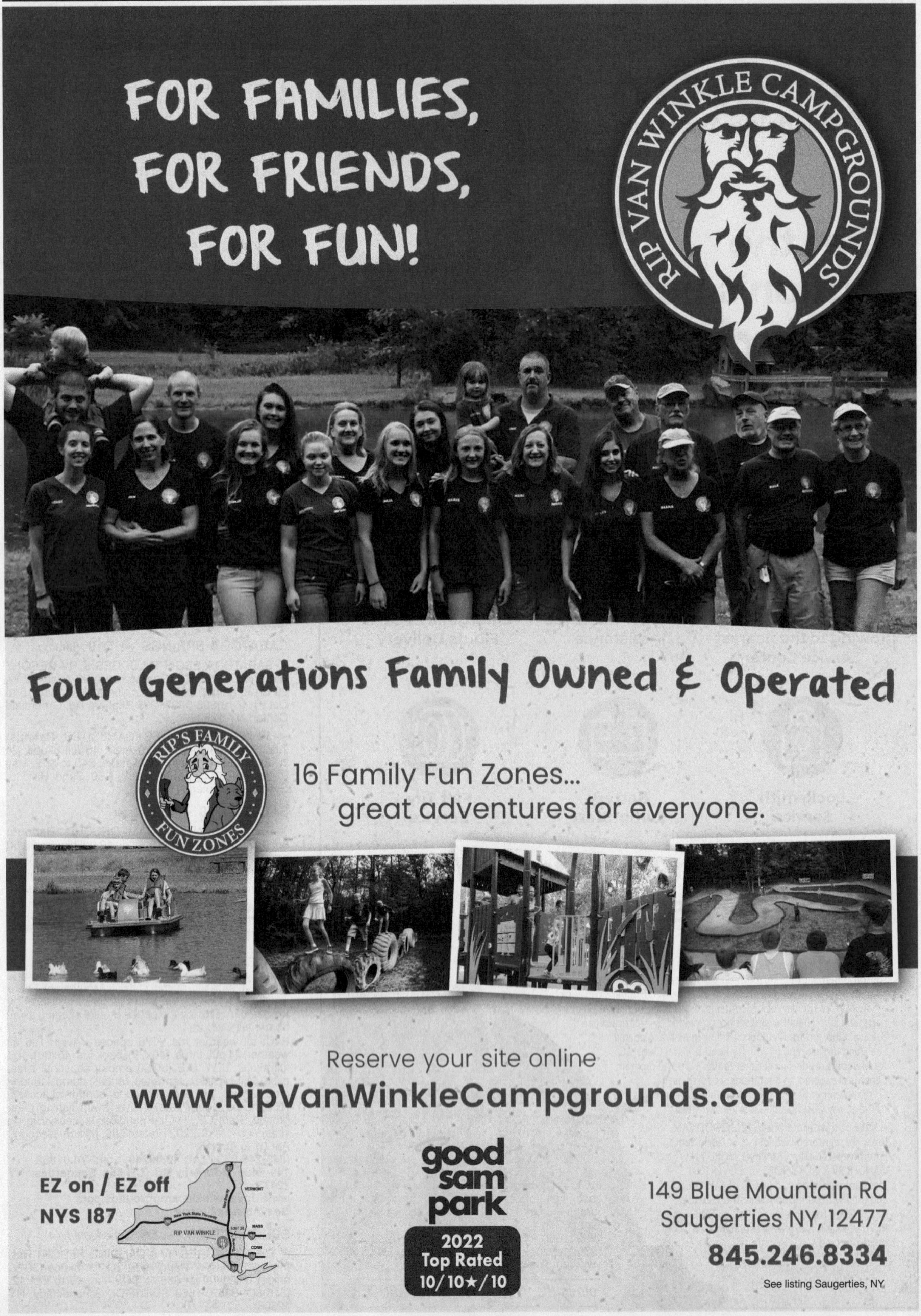
FOR FAMILIES,
FOR FRIENDS,
FOR FUN!
RIP VAN WINKLE CAMPGROUNDS
Four Generations Family Owned & Operated
RIP'S FAMILY FUN ZONES
16 Family Fun Zones...
great adventures for everyone.
Reserve your site online
www.RipVanWinkleCampgrounds.com
EZ on / EZ off
NYS I87
VERMONT
New York State Thruway
RIP VAN WINKLE
EXIT 20
MASS
CONN
good sam park
2022
Top Rated
10/10★/10
149 Blue Mountain Rd
Saugerties NY, 12477
845.246.8334
See listing Saugerties, NY.

SCHOHARIE — D9 *Schoharie*

TWIN OAKS CAMPGROUND Ratings: 9/9★/9 (Campground) 50 Avail: 49 W, 49 E (30/50 amps). 2021 rates: $37 to $50. May 15 to Oct 12. (518)827-5641, 142 Twin Oaks Ln, Schoharie, NY 12157

SCHROON LAKE — C9 *Essex*

ADIRONDACK/SHARP BRIDGE (Public State Park) From jct US 9 & Frontier Town Rd: Go 1 mi N on Hwy 9. (R). 40 Avail. 2021 rates: $18 to $23. May 20 to Sep 04. (518)532-7538

SCHUYLER FALLS — A10 *Clinton*

MACOMB RESERVATION (Public State Park) From town, S 0.25 mi on Hwy 22B to Norrisville Rd, W 3 mi to Campsite Rd, S 0.5 mi (R). Avail: 34 E (15 amps). 2021 rates: $15 to $25. May 22 to Oct 11. (518)643-9952

SENECA FALLS — D6 *Seneca*

CAYUGA LAKE/EAST CAMP (Public State Park) From Jct of I-90 & SR-414 (Exit 41),S 0.25 mi on SR-414 to Rte 318, E 4.2 mi to Jct of Rtes 5 & 20, E 5 mi on Rte 5 to Rte 90, S 4 mi (L). 267 Avail: (30 amps). 2021 rates: $15 to $25. May 02 to Oct 14. (315)568-5163

RIVERS CROSSING CAMPGROUND & MARINA **Ratings: 7.5/5.5/8.5** (Campground) Avail: 33 full hkups (30/50 amps). 2021 rates: $45 to $50. May 01 to Oct 14. (315)365-3000, 508 Rt 89, Savannah, NY 13146

SHIRLEY — A4 *Suffolk*

SMITH POINT (SUFFOLK COUNTY PARK) (Public) From Long Island Expwy (I-495, exit 68): Go S on William Floyd Pkwy to the end on Fire Island. 220 Avail. 2021 rates: $25. (631)852-1313

SMITHTOWN — A3 *Suffolk*

BLYDENBURGH (SUFFOLK COUNTY PARK) (Public) From Jct of Hwys 347 & 454, W 1.5 mi on Hwy 454 (R). 20 Avail. 2021 rates: $30 to $40. (631)854-4949

SODUS POINT — D5 *Wayne*

SOUTH SHORE RV PARK **Ratings: 6.5/UI/9** (RV Park) Avail: 20 full hkups (30/50 amps). 2021 rates: $50 to $75. (315)483-8649, 7867 Lake Road, Sodus Point, NY 14555

SPRINGWATER — E5 *Livingston*

HOLIDAY HILL CAMPGROUND **Ratings: 8.5/9★/9.5** (Campground) 25 Avail: 20 full hkups, 5 W, 5 E (30 amps). 2021 rates: $40 to $50. May 01 to Oct 11. (800)719-2267, 7818 Marvin Hill Rd, Springwater, NY 14560

ST JOHNSVILLE — D8 *Fulton*

CRYSTAL GROVE DIAMOND MINE & CAMPGROUND **Ratings: 5/5.5/7** (Campground) 20 Avail: 20 W, 20 E (15/30 amps). 2021 rates: $45. Apr 15 to Oct 15. (518)568-2914, 161 CR-114, St Johnsville, NY 13452

ST JOHNSVILLE CAMPSITE & MARINA (CITY PARK) (Public) From I-90 (Canajoharie exit): Cross Mohawk River and go 10 mi W on Hwy 5, then 1/4 mi S on Bridge St to Marina Dr. 21 Avail. May 01 to Nov 01. (518)568-7406

STEAMBURG — E3 *Cattaraugus*

ONOVILLE MARINA PARK (Public) From I-86 (exit 17): Go 9-1/4 mi S on West Perimeter Rd. 70 Avail: 70 W, 70 E (30 amps). 2021 rates: $27. (716)354-2615

STONY POINT — A2 *Suffolk*

HARRIMAN STATE PARK/BEAVER POND (Public State Park) From jct SR-202 & Palisades Interstate Pkwy: Go 5 mi N on Palisades Interstate Pkwy, then 2 mi W on Willow Grove Rd/ Kanawauke Rd (E). 137 Avail. 2021 rates: $15 to $22. Apr 22 to Oct 09. (845)947-2792

SYLVAN BEACH — D7 *Oneida*

TA-GA-SOKE CAMPGROUNDS **Ratings: 6.5/5/8** (Campground) 22 Avail: 15 full hkups, 7 W, 7 E (30/50 amps). 2021 rates: $43 to $50. Apr 26 to Oct 14. (800)831-1744, 7820 Higginsvilee Rd, Blossvale, NY 13308

THE LANDING CAMPGROUND **Ratings: 7/6/7** (Campground) Avail: 25 full hkups (30/50 amps). 2021 rates: $42 to $47. Apr 30 to Oct 01. (315)245-9951, 2796 Kellogg Road, Blossvale, NY 13308

TREASURE ISLE RV PARK **Ratings: 7.5/6/9.5** (Campground) Avail: 10 full hkups (30/50 amps). 2021 rates: $42 to $52. Apr 26 to Oct 13. (315)245-5228, 3132 Haskins Rd, Blossvale, NY 13308

SYRACUSE — D6 *Onondaga*

Travel Services

CAMPING WORLD OF SYRACUSE As the nation's largest retailer of RV supplies, accessories, services and new and used RVs, Camping World is committed to making your total RV experience better. **SERVICES:** RV, tire, RV appliance, MH mechanical, staffed RV wash, restrooms. RV Sales. RV supplies, LP gas, dump, emergency parking, RV accessible. Hours: 9am to 7pm.
(888)803-3193 Lat: 43.109200, Lon: -76.283231
7030 Interstate Island Road, Syracuse, NY 13209
www.campingworld.com

THREE MILE BAY — B6 *Jefferson*

LONG POINT (Public State Park) From Jct of SR-12E & SR-57, S 12 mi on SR-57, becomes State Park Rd (L). Pets need rabies certification. Avail: 29 E (15 amps). 2021 rates: $15 to $29. May 15 to Sep 06. (315)649-5258

TICONDEROGA — C10 *Essex*

ADIRONDACK/PARADOX LAKE (Public State Park) From Exit 28 on Rte 87, E 4 mi on Rte 74 (L). 58 Avail. 2021 rates: $18 to $23. May 20 to Sep 05. (518)532-7451

ADIRONDACK/PUTNAM POND (Public State Park) From Jct of SR-9N/22 & SR-74, W 6 mi on SR-74 (L). Entrance fee required. 63 Avail. 2021 rates: $18 to $23. May 20 to Oct 10. (518)585-7280

ADIRONDACK/ROGERS ROCK (Public State Park) From town: Go 7 mi SW on Hwy-9N. 332 Avail. 2021 rates: $22 to $27. May 20 to Oct 10. (518)585-6746

BROOKWOOD RV RESORT **Ratings: 6.5/9.5★/8.5** (Campground) Avail: 16 full hkups (30/50 amps). 2021 rates: $46 to $49. May 15 to Oct 15. (518)585-4462, 133 State Route 9N, Ticonderoga, NY 12883

TUPPER LAKE — B9 *Franklin*

ADIRONDACK/FISH CREEK POND (Public State Park) From town, E 12 mi on Rte 30 (L). Entrance fee required. 355 Avail. 2021 rates: $22 to $27. Apr 08 to Oct 23. (518)891-4560

ADIRONDACK/ROLLINS POND (Public) From Jct of SR-3 & SR-30 (in town), E 12 mi on SR-30 (L). 287 Avail. 2021 rates: $20 to $25. May 20 to Sep 05. (518)891-3239

UNADILLA — E7 *Delaware*

DELAWARE VALLEY/UNADILLA KOA **Ratings: 8.5/9/8.5** (Campground) 38 Avail: 38 W, 38 E (30/50 amps). 2021 rates: $52. May 01 to Oct 15. (607)369-9030, 242 Union Church Road, Franklin, NY 13775

UTICA — D8 *Oneida*

UTICA See also Bouckville, Cooperstown, Forestport, Herkimer, Poland, Salisbury, Sylvan Beach & Verona.

VERONA — D7 *Oneida*

THE VILLAGES AT TURNING STONE RV PARK
Ratings: 10/10★/10 (RV Park) From Jct of I-90 (exit 33) & SR-365, W 1 mi on SR-365 (R).

ADVENTURE ABOUNDS IN VERONA, NY
Enjoy nature's playground at this top-rated New York park. Hike and bike acres of terrain, swim, and enjoy themed weekends the whole season through. Entire world-class resort experience is just 5 minute shuttle ride away!

FAC: paved rds. (175 spaces). Avail: 155 paved, 50 pull-thrus, (50x60), back-ins (50x50), 155 full hkups (30/50 amps), seasonal sites, cable, WiFi @ sites, dump, laundry, groc, LP gas, fire rings, firewood. **REC:** heated pool, wading pool, hot tub, pond, fishing, golf, playground. Pets OK. Partial handicap access. No tents. Big rig sites, eco-friendly. 2021 rates: $45 to $60. May 03 to Oct 15.
(315)361-7275 Lat: 43.10667, Lon: -75.60643
5065 SR 365, Verona, NY 13478
www.turningstone.com
See ad next page

Things to See and Do

TURNING STONE RESORT CASINO Casino type games, restaurants, golf course. Rv park Partial handicap access. RV accessible. Restrooms. Food. Hours: 24 hours. ATM.
(800)771-7711 Lat: 43.11591, Lon: -75.59235
5218 Patrick Rd, Verona, NY 13478
www.turningstone.com
See ad next page

WADDINGTON — A8 *St Lawrence*

COLES CREEK (Public State Park) From Jct of SR-345 & SR-37, NE 4 mi on SR-37 (L). Avail: 154 E (30 amps). 2021 rates: $18 to $34. May 13 to Sep 10. (315)388-5636

WADING RIVER — A4 *Suffolk*

WILDWOOD (Public State Park) From Jct of I-495 & SR-46 (exit 68N), N 8 mi on SR-46 to SR-25A, E 3 mi to Sound Rd, E 0.5 mi to Hulse Landing Rd, N 0.3 mi (R). Avail: 80 full hkups (30 amps). 2021 rates: $18 to $34. Apr 01 to Oct 10. (631)929-4314

Take RV-ing Up A Notch
good sam park
2022 Top Rated 10/10★/10
With 175 paved sites, free wireless Internet, 2.5 miles of nature trails, paddleboats, fishing, a heated pool, hot tub, tennis, volleyball, basketball and horseshoes, you'll be bringing the family back to the Villages at Turning Stone year after year. Experience family-friendly fun in a picturesque outdoor setting just a short shuttle ride away from Turning Stone Resort Casino.
Village Office: 315.361.7275
Open May – October • Verona, NY
See listing Verona, NY
The Villages at TURNING STONE

WALTON — E8 *Delaware*

BEAR SPRING MOUNTAIN (Public) From town, SE 4.5 mi on Rte 206, S 1 mi on E Trout Brook Rd (R). 41 Avail. 2021 rates: $18 to $23. May 20 to Sep 05. (607)865-6989

WARRENSBURG — C9 *Warren*

LAKE GEORGE SCHROON VALLEY RESORT
good sam park
Ratings: 7.5/7.5/9 (Campground) 64 Avail: 25 full hkups, 39 W, 39 E (30/50 amps). 2021 rates: $74 to $81. May 10 to Oct 15. (888)563-7040, 1730 Schroon River Rd, Warrensburg, NY 12885

SCHROON RIVER CAMPSITES **Ratings: 5.5/5/6** (Campground) Avail: 50 full hkups (30 amps). 2021 rates: $57 to $62. May 15 to Oct 04. (518)623-2171, 686 Schroon River Rd, Warrensburg, NY 12885

WARSAW — D4 *Wyoming*

DREAM LAKE CAMPGROUND **Ratings: 6.5/7/9** (Campground) 58 Avail: 6 full hkups, 52 W, 52 E (30/50 amps). 2021 rates: $55 to $56. May 01 to Oct 25. (585)786-5172, 4391 Old Buffalo Rd, Warsaw, NY 14569

WATERLOO — D5 *Seneca*

WATERLOO HARBOR CAMPGROUND **Ratings: 8/8.5★/9** (Campground) 30 Avail: 14 full hkups, 15 W, 16 E (30/50 amps). 2021 rates: $45 to $60. May 01 to Oct 15. (315)539-8848, 1278 Waterloo-Geneva Road, Waterloo, NY 13165

WATKINS GLEN — E5 *Schuyler*

CLUTE MEMORIAL PARK & CAMPGROUND (WARREN W CLUTE) (Public) From Jct of Hwys 14 & 414 (in town), N 0.5 mi on Hwy 414 (R). For GPS aided location use "Boat Launch Road.". Avail: 70 full hkups (30/50 amps). 2021 rates: $65. May 01 to Oct 13. (607)535-4438

WATKINS GLEN (Public State Park) From Jct of Rtes 14 & CR-409, W 2.6 mi to Whites Hollow Rd, S .2 mi. Avail: 54 E (30/50 amps). 2021 rates: $18 to $30. May 08 to Oct 12. (607)535-4511

WATKINS GLEN/CORNING KOA CAMPING RESORT **Ratings: 9.5/10★/10** (Campground) 174 Avail: 147 full hkups, 27 W, 27 E (30/50 amps). 2021 rates: $72 to $146. Apr 18 to Oct 26. (800)562-7430, 1710 Route 414 S, Watkins Glen, NY 14891

WEBSTER — D5 *Monroe*

WEBSTER PARK (Public) From town, N 3 mi on Webster Rd. to Lake Rd, W 1.5 mi (L). Avail: 40 E (30 amps). 2021 rates: $30 to $50. May 01 to Oct 31. (585)872-5326

WEEDSPORT — D6 *Cayuga*

RIVER FOREST PARK **Ratings: 5.5/6/8** (Campground) 50 Avail: 50 W, 50 E (30 amps). 2021 rates: $40 to $48. May 01 to Oct 12. (315)834-9458, 9439 Riverforest Rd, Weedsport, NY 13166

WELLSVILLE — E4 *Allegany*

TROUT RUN CAMP RESORT **Ratings: 9.5/8.5/9** (Campground) Avail: 131 full hkups (30/50 amps). 2021 rates: $65 to $75. Apr 15 to Nov 30. (585)596-0500, 2137 Stannards Rd, Wellsville, NY 14895

WEST COXSACKIE — E9 *Greene*

Travel Services

GANDER RV OF ALBANY Your new hometown outfitter offering the best regional gear for all your outdoor needs. Your adventure awaits. **SERVICES:** RV appliance, MH mechanical, sells outdoor gear, restrooms. RV Sales. RV supplies, LP gas, RV accessible. Hours: 9am - 6pm.
(833)583-1660 Lat: 42.36063, Lon: -73.81679
12634 Rte 9 W, West Coxsackie, NY 12192
rv.ganderoutdoors.com

WEST POINT — A2 *Orange*

MILITARY PARK ROUND POND REC AREA (U.S. MILITARY ACADEMY) (Public) From Jct of I-87 & US-6 (Exit 16), N 2.5 mi on US-6 to NY-293, N 5.5 mi to Round Pond Rd, follow signs. 28 Avail: 28 W, 28 E (30/50 amps). 2021 rates: $28 to $36. Apr 01 to Oct 30. (845)938-2503

WESTFIELD — E2 *Chautauqua*

WESTFIELD-LAKE ERIE KOA **Ratings: 9/10★/8.5** (Campground) 112 Avail: 50 full hkups, 62 W, 62 E (30/50 amps). 2021 rates: $60 to $70. Apr 18 to Nov 01. (800)562-3973, 8001 Rte 5 (East Lake Road), Westfield, NY 14787

WESTPORT — B10 *Essex*

BARBER HOMESTEAD PARK **Ratings: 8.5/10★/9** (Campground) 20 Avail: 15 full hkups, 5 W, 5 E (30/50 amps). 2021 rates: $36 to $44. May 25 to Oct 12. (518)962-8989, 68 Barber Ln, Westport, NY 12993

WESTVILLE CENTER — A9 *Franklin*

BABBLING BROOK RV PARK **Ratings: 7.5/9.5★/9** (Campground) Avail: 51 full hkups (30/50 amps). 2021 rates: $38 to $43. Apr 15 to Oct 15. (518)358-4245, 1623 County Route 4, Fort Covington, NY 12937

WHITEHALL — C10 *Washington*

CHAMPS RV RESORT **Ratings: 5/7/6** (RV Park) Avail: 17 full hkups (30/50 amps). 2021 rates: $35 to $55. May 15 to Oct 15. (518)499-5055, 1 Main Street, Whitehall, NY 12887

WILMINGTON — B9 *Essex*

ADIRONDACK/WILMINGTON NOTCH (Public State Park) From town, W 3.5 mi on Rte 86 (R). Entrance fee required. 54 Avail. 2021 rates: $18 to $23. May 06 to Oct 09. (518)946-7172

LAKE PLACID/WHITEFACE MT KOA **Ratings: 8.5/9★/8.5** (Campground) Avail: 30 full hkups (30/50 amps). 2021 rates: $58 to $75. (518)946-7878, 77 Fox Farm Rd, Wilmington, NY 12997

NORTH POLE RESORTS
good sam park
Ratings: 9/10★/10 (Campground) N-bnd: From Jct of I-87 & SR-73 (Exit 30), NW 16 mi on SR-73 to SR-9N, 10 mi N on SR-9N to SR-86, W 5 mi on SR-86 to Jct 431, continue on SR-86 W 0.2 mi (L); or S-bnd: From Jct of I-87 & SR-9N (Exit 34), S 16 mi on SR-9N to SR-86, W 5 mi on SR-86 to Jct 431, continue on SR-86 W 0.2 mi (L).

ON THE BANKS OF THE AUSABLE RIVER
Located in the Adirondack Mountains, at the base of Whiteface Mountain and near Lake Placid with a variety of accommodations and amenities. We offer an ideal place to enjoy fishing, hiking, biking, canoeing or relaxing.
FAC: all weather rds. 113 Avail: 95 gravel, 18 grass, 40 pull-thrus, (30x80), back-ins (26x66), 85 full hkups, 28 W, 28 E (30/50 amps), cable, WiFi @ sites, tent sites, rentals, dump, laundry, groc, LP gas, fire rings, firewood. **REC:** heated pool, Ausable River: fishing, kayaking/canoeing, boating nearby, playground. Pet restrict (Q) $. Big rig sites, eco-friendly. 2021 rates: $69 to $85. Apr 25 to Oct 25. ATM.
(518)946-7733 Lat: 44.38643, Lon: -73.82225
5644 NYS RT 86, Wilmington, NY 12997
northpoleresorts.com
See ad this page

WINDSOR — E7 *Broome*

FOREST LAKE CAMPGROUND **Ratings: 6.5/9★/9.5** (Campground) Avail: 17 full hkups (30/50 amps). 2021 rates: $50. May 01 to Oct 15. (607)655-1444, 574 Ostrander Rd, Windsor, NY 13865

LAKESIDE CAMPGROUND **Ratings: 8.5/9★/8.5** (Campground) 50 Avail: 39 full hkups, 11 W, 11 E (30/50 amps). 2021 rates: $48.95. May 01 to Oct 15. (607)655-2694, 336 Hargrave Rd, Windsor, NY 13865

PINE CREST CAMPGROUND **Ratings: 5/8/8.5** (Campground) 10 Avail: 4 full hkups, 6 W, 6 E (30/50 amps). 2021 rates: $40 to $48. (607)655-1515, 280 State Rte 79, Windsor, NY 13865

WOLCOTT — D6 *Wayne*

CHERRY GROVE CAMPGROUND
good sam park
Ratings: 10/9.5★/9.5 (Campground) From Jct of SR-104 & Ridge Rd (E of town), W 300 ft on Ridge Rd (R). **FAC:** all weather rds. (105 spaces). Avail: 25 all weather, 20 pull-thrus, (30x75), back-ins (30x50), 25 full hkups (30/50 amps), seasonal sites, WiFi @ sites, $, tent sites, rentals, dump, laundry, LP gas, fire rings, firewood. **REC:** pool, boating nearby, shuffleboard, playground. Pet restrict (B/Q). Big rig sites, eco-friendly. 2021 rates: $45 to $65. Apr 15 to Oct 15.
(315)594-8320 Lat: 43.22414, Lon: -76.78472
12669 Ridge Rd, Wolcott, NY 14590
www.cherrygrovecampground.com
See ad this page

LAKE BLUFF CAMPGROUND **Ratings: 8.5/9/10** (Campground) 59 Avail: 27 full hkups, 32 W, 32 E (30/50 amps). 2021 rates: $49 to $58. Apr 15 to Oct 15. (315)587-4517, 7150 Garner Rd, Wolcott, NY 14590

YOUNGSTOWN — D3 *Niagara*

FOUR MILE CREEK (Public State Park) From town: Go 4 mi E on Hwy-18. Avail: 131 E (30 amps). 2021 rates: $18 to $34. May 01 to Oct 27. (716)745-3802

RV MYTH #1: ""Recreational vehicles are expensive.'' This is not necessarily true. Oh, yes, you can pay a million or more dollars for one, but that is far from normal and represents an extremely small market. RVs are available in many sizes, configurations and affordable prices. Additionally, the running capital cost of a unit is only the difference between the purchase price and the current value.

DID YOU KNOW?

In 1903, the Wright brothers completed the first successful airplane flight in the dunes of Kitty Hawk.

Getty Images/iStockphoto

YOU ARE HERE

NC

North Carolina

Walk on sandy shores where humans learned to fly. Hike across mountains that seem to defy gravity. Experiences like these attract travelers to the Tar Heel State, while vibrant towns and cities make visitors extend their stay.

Chill Out in Charlotte

Charlotte's got something for everyone. Diverse generations can enjoy this generous city, the largest in the state, thanks to its museums, craft breweries, up-and-coming food establishments and proximity to the great outdoors. The heart of the NASCAR racing world beats here, with the NASCAR Hall of Fame and Charlotte Motor Speedway attracting throngs of racing fans. For a relaxed change of pace, head to Asheville, known for mountain views, a vibrant art scene and small-town friendliness. Stop at the Biltmore Estate, which wows visitors with opulent architecture and dazzling furniture.

Fantastic Forest

Covering more than 500,000 acres, the Pisgah National Forest is a favorite Tar Heel State playground. A drive along one of the nation's most scenic roadways, the Blue Ridge Parkway, offers amazing beauty and recreation at every turnoff. Hike or bike along the hundreds of miles of trails, be dazzled by dozens of waterfalls and enjoy Mother Nature's waterpark at Sliding Rock. If you desire coastal views, head east to the Outer Banks, where scenic beaches stretch for miles and wild ponies roam the shores.

Breathe in the Smokies

Great Smoky Mountains National Park occupies much of Western North Carolina, giving recreation seekers an opportunity to explore majestic peaks. Enjoy the rich history and scenic beauty of this vast wonderland while watching for wildlife. Black bears, elk, coyote and deer roam the woodlands and meadows.

VISITOR CENTER

TIME ZONE
Eastern Standard

ROAD & HIGHWAY INFORMATION
877-511-4662
ncdot.gov/travel

FISHING & HUNTING INFORMATION
888-248-6834
ncwildlife.org/licensing/licenses-and-regulations

BOATING INFORMATION
919-707-0030
mdwfp.com/law-enforcement/boating-rules-regs

NATIONAL PARKS
nps.gov/nc

STATE PARKS
ncparks.gov

TOURISM INFORMATION
North Carolina Department of Travel and Tourism
800-VISITNC
visitnc.com

TOP TOURISM ATTRACTIONS
1) Great Smoky Mountains National Park
2) Biltmore Estate
3) Wright Brothers National Memorial

MAJOR CITIES
Charlotte, Raleigh (capital), Greensboro, Durham, Winston-Salem

North Carolina Fried Green Tomatoes

You've seen the movie, now try the cuisine. Featuring tomatoes coated in a delicious batter, this juicy meal gives you a hefty dose of Southern flavor. And it's vegetarian, to boot. Imagine the satisfying crunch of onion rings and the juicy goodness of tomatoes. But don't take our word for it – try it yourself in places like Relish Craft Kitchen & Bourbon Bar in Raleigh.

good sam park Featured Good Sam Parks

NORTH CAROLINA

When you stay with Good Sam, you can expect the highest degree of cleanliness and friendliness, and better yet, you get **10% off** overnight campground fees.

If you're not already a Good Sam member you can purchase your membership at one of these locations:

ABERDEEN
Oasis of North Carolina
Pine Lake RV Resort

ADVANCE
Forest Lake Preserve

ASHEVILLE
Asheville Bear Creek RV Park
Scenic RV Resort

BEAUFORT
Beaufort Waterway RV Park

BRYSON CITY
Smoky Mountain Meadows Campground

CAPE CARTERET
Goose Creek Resort
Waterway RV Park

CHARLOTTE
Camping World Racing Resort

CHEROKEE
Fort Wilderness Campground and RV Park
Happy Holiday Campground

FOUR OAKS
Four Oaks Lodging & RV Resort
Raleigh Oaks RV Resort & Cottages

FRANKLIN
Franklin RV Park & Campground
The Great Outdoors RV Resort

FRISCO
Frisco Woods Campground

HATTERAS
Hatteras Sands Campground

HENDERSONVILLE
Jaymar Travel Park
Lakewood RV Resort
Town Mountain Travel Park

HUBERT
Deep Creek RV Resort & Campground

LENOIR
Green Mountain Park Resort

LITTLETON
Lake Gaston RV & Camping Resort

MAGGIE VALLEY
Stonebridge RV Resort

MARBLE
Peachtree Cove RV Park
Valley River RV Resort

MARION
Buck Creek RV Park

MOCKSVILLE
Lake Myers RV & Camping Resort

MOREHEAD CITY
Whispering Pines RV Park

MORGANTON
Riverside Golf & RV Park

MOUNT AIRY
Mayberry Campground

PINNACLE
Greystone RV Park

ROANOKE RAPIDS
The RV Resort at Carolina Crossroads

ROBBINSVILLE
Stecoah Valley RV Resort

RODANTHE
Camp Hatteras RV Resort & Campground

STATESVILLE
Midway Campground & RV Resort

STELLA
White Oak Shores Camping & RV Resort

SURF CITY
Lanier's Campground

SWANNANOA
Mama Gertie's Hideaway Campground

UNION GROVE
Van Hoy Farms Family Campground

WADE
Fayetteville RV Resort & Cottages

WASHINGTON
Tranter's Creek Resort & Campground
Twin Lakes RV Resort

WHITTIER
Flaming Arrow Campground

WILLIAMSTON
Green Acres Family Campground

WILSON
Kamper's Lodge

10/10★/10 GOOD SAM PARKS

FOUR OAKS
Raleigh Oaks RV Resort & Cottages
(919)934-3181

FRANKLIN
The Great Outdoors RV Resort
(828)349-0412

MARBLE
Valley River RV Resort
(828)385-4220

WADE
Fayetteville RV Resort & Cottages
(910)484-5500

What's This?

An RV park with a 10/10★/10 rating has scored perfect grades in amenities, cleanliness and appearance ("See Understanding the Campground Rating System" on pages 8 and 9 for an explanation of the trusted Good Sam Rating System). Stay in a 10/10★/10 park on your next trip for a nearly flawless camping experience.

Getty Images/iStockphoto

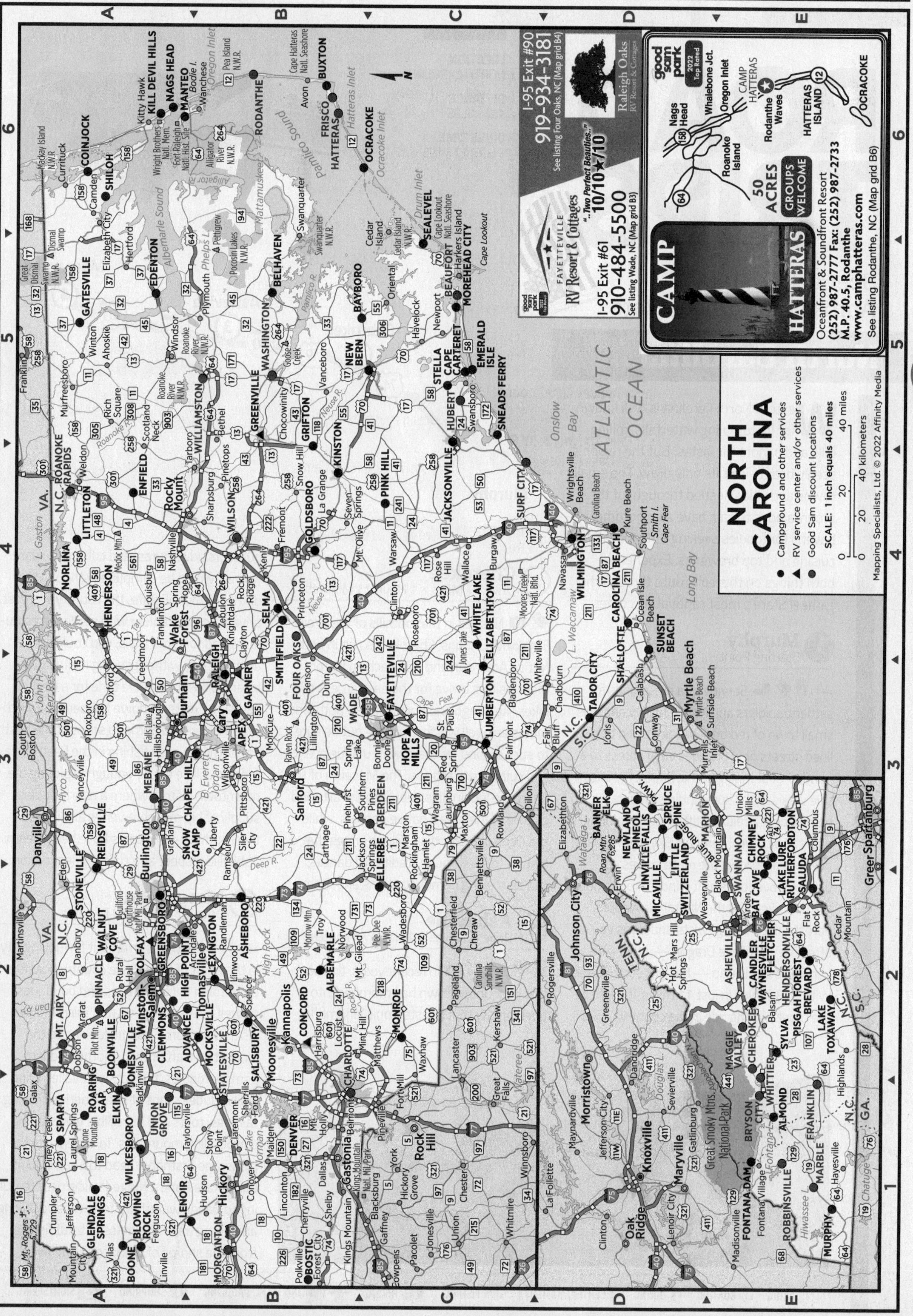
NORTH CAROLINA
Campground and other services
RV service center and/or other services
Good Sam discount locations
SCALE: 1 inch equals 40 miles
0 20 40 miles
0 20 40 kilometers
Mapping Specialists, Ltd. © 2022 Affinity Media
ATLANTIC OCEAN
FAYETTEVILLE RV Resort & Cottages
"Two Perfect Beauties..." 10/10★/10
I-95 Exit #61 910-484-5500
See listing Wade, NC (Map grid B3)
Raleigh Oaks RV Resort & Cottages
I-95 Exit #90 919-934-3181
See listing Four Oaks, NC (Map grid B4)
CAMP HATTERAS
Oceanfront & Soundfront Resort
(252) 987-2777 Fax: (252) 987-2733
M.P. 40.5, Rodanthe
www.camphatteras.com
See listing Rodanthe, NC (Map grid B6)
50 ACRES
GROUPS WELCOME
good sam park 2022 Top Rated
NC

 See map page 661

ROAD TRIPS

Scenic Cruising Across the Tarheel State

North Carolina

LOCATION
NORTH CAROLINA

DISTANCE
187 MILES

DRIVE TIME
3 HRS 17 MINS

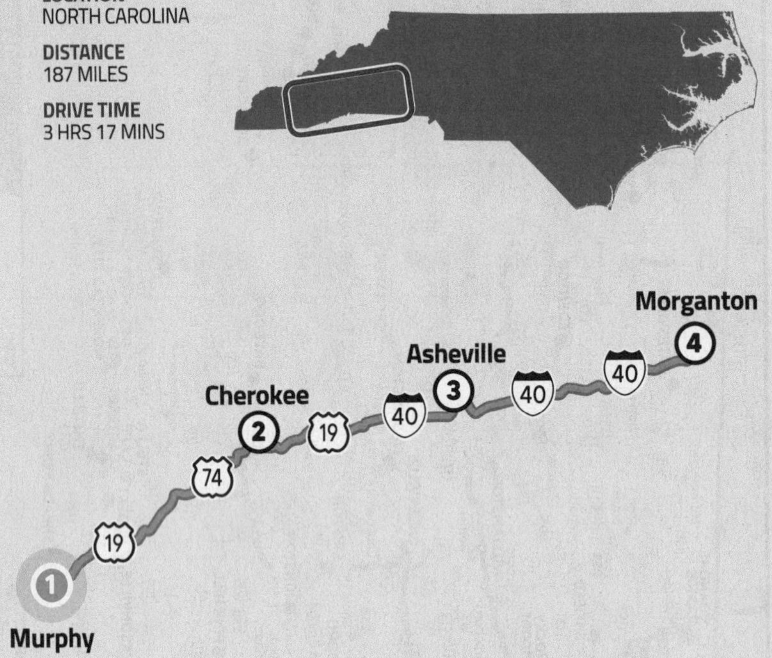

Western North Carolina is well known for its tumbling waterfalls, rolling hills and panoramic vistas. But the region's scenic beauty isn't its only draw. The small towns and cities nestled throughout the mountainous terrain have also become havens for foodies seeking out innovative cuisine and top breweries. Experience both things on this epic route through the Tarheel State's most captivating corner.

1 Murphy
Starting Point

Serving as a crossroads for settlers, soldiers and Native Americans, this small town of red brick buildings and tree-lined streets now provides easy access to a number of stunning scenic drives. For expansive views of the surrounding mountains, it's hard to beat a relaxing afternoon exploring the little-known Cherohala Skyway. At just over 40 miles long, the route serves up plenty of overlooks as it winds through both the Cherokee and the Nantahala National Forests. If it's biking twists and turns you're after, the Tail of the Dragon — otherwise known as Deals Gap — has got you covered. With 318 curves in just 11 miles, it might be the most exciting ride in the country.

2 Cherokee
Drive 57 Miles ▪ 1 Hour, 11 Minutes

Nestled in the foothills of the Great Smoky Mountains, Cherokee is rich in both Native American and Appalachian history. Most visitors arrive for the easy access to hikes like Mingo and Soco Falls — both landmarks are well worth a visit — but be sure to stick around for the town's unique events and cultural attractions. The Museum of the Cherokee Indian digs deep into the arts and culture of the area's native peoples, while the Oconaluftee Indian Village brings that history to life through traditional dances, canoe-making demonstrations and more.

3 Asheville
Drive 63 Miles ▪ 1 Hour, 7 Minutes

In recent years, this easy-going mountain town has morphed into a bustling city that boasts iconic landmarks, outdoors adventures, and culture to spare. No visit would be complete without a tour of the Biltmore Estate, the country's largest private home. Replete with gardens, restaurants and forested trails, you could spend an entire day without seeing it all. Nature lovers will want to save time for a float or paddling excursion down the serene French Broad River, also home to some of the best small-mouth bass fishing in the East, while foodies will be happy enough exploring the downtown district where a nearly endless supply of hip microbreweries and innovative southern-style cafes have helped earn Asheville respect as a culinary destination.

4 Morganton
Drive 67 Miles ▪ 59 Minutes

This small but fun-loving city in the heart of Blue Ridge country boasts a downtown full of galleries and boutiques, as well as three highly rated microbreweries that welcome visitors looking to try innovative craft brews. Another hidden gem for foodies, the Catawba Valley Wine Trail includes stops at five wineries offering tastings, tours and incredible views of the surrounding mountains. To experience the landscape firsthand, head to South Mountains State Park, a rugged wilderness featuring towering waterfalls, forty miles of hiking and biking trails and miles of trout fishing from the shores of the Jacob Fork River.

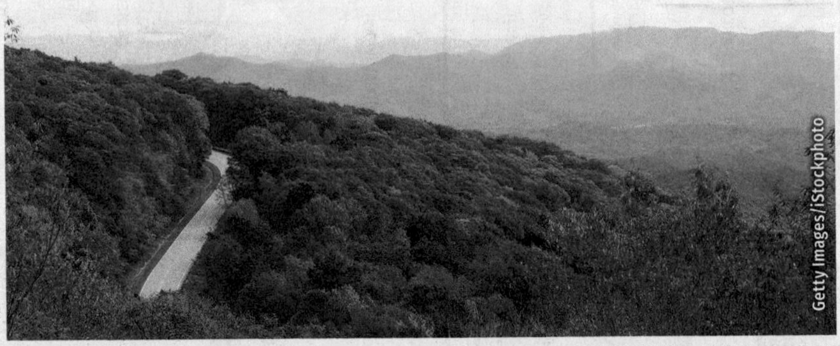

Getty Images/iStockphoto

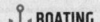

BIKING BOATING DINING ENTERTAINMENT FISHING HIKING HUNTING PADDLING SHOPPING SIGHTSEEING

North Carolina SPOTLIGHTS

A Slew of Sweet Tarheel Getaways

These stunning North Carolina destinations cover the gamut from quirky towns to epic mountain ranges. Plan a North Carolina trip from coastal plains to rugged highlands.

ASHEVILLE WAS THE BIRTHPLACE OF THE WORLD'S FIRST PRONE KAYAK.

Blue Ridge Parkway Tunnel near Asheville North Carolina during autumn.

Getty Images/iStockphoto

Asheville

Known for its laid-back vibe, artistic locals and breathtaking natural beauty, Asheville has quickly become a haven for those looking to blend outdoors adventures with easygoing city life. Home to some of the best hiking east of the Mississippi, one of the country's most historic mansions, and a seemingly never-ending array of breweries, restaurants and quirky cafes, you'll be hard-pressed to see it all it one visit. Of course, you could always do like the locals do and simply sit back, relax and soak it in at your own pace. Either way, don't be surprised to find a little something for everyone at this Blue Ridge getaway.

Mansion on the Hill

As stunning today as it was when it was built over a hundred years ago, the Biltmore is one of America's true architectural gems. For one, it's the largest privately-owned home in the country, featuring 250 rooms, priceless antiques and incredible artwork. Both self-guided and audio tours of the estate are available. What's more, the property surrounding the sprawling Gilded Age mansion is equally as inspiring. Miles of forested nature trails wind through the 8,000-acre property, while a series of ornate gardens emphasize the changing seasons and pristine natural landscape. The Biltmore is also home to one of the country's most widely visited wineries and tickets include a complimentary tasting with an expert host. It's the perfect way to relax after an afternoon exploring one of Asheville's most iconic attractions.

Hike Your Heart Out

Nestled between the Great Smoky Mountains and the Blue Ridge Mountains, Asheville is the perfect jumping-off point for outdoors adventure. There are a number of urban trails that leave from the downtown district and wind past the city's historic sites and green spaces, but to really experience the area's natural wonders, head to the Blue Ridge Parkway, one of America's most scenic roads. From there, you can pull off at any number of trailheads. The 1.2-mile hike to Craggy Pinnacle is a local favorite. Close to town and easy enough for beginners, it offers 360-degree views of the mountain.

> "THE BILTMORE IS HOME TO ONE OF THE COUNTRY'S MOST WIDELY VISITED WINERIES."

LOCAL FAVORITE

Barbecue Ribs

North Carolina barbecue is cooked at low temperatures for a long time, allowing heat and smoke to flavor the meat to perfection. It's often served with a vinegar-based sauce. *Recipe by Jason Siegel.*

INGREDIENTS

Marinade
- ☐ 2 racks of pork ribs, membrane removed
- ☐ Virgil's root beer
- ☐ 4 ancho chilis, diced
- ☐ 3 caps liquid smoke

Rub
- ☐ 1 Tbsp ancho chili powder
- ☐ 1 Tbsp brown sugar
- ☐ 4 Tbsp tomato bouillon powder
- ☐ 3 Tbsp black pepper
- ☐ 4 Tbsp ground cumin
- ☐ 2 Tbsp dry mustard
- ☐ 3 Tbsp cayenne pepper
- ☐ 3 Tbsp ground dried chipotle pepper
- ☐ 4 Tbsp McCormick mesquite seasoning

Sauce
- ☐ ⅓cup Worcestershire sauce
- ☐ ⅓ cup spicy teriyaki sauce
- ☐ 3 Tbsp melted butter

DIRECTIONS

Marinate ribs in root beer, ancho chili and liquid smoke for 12 hours. Combine rub ingredients and rub ribs thoroughly. Smoke with hickory and white oak at 225°F for 1.5 hours. Make sauce by mixing Worcestershire sauce, spicy teriyaki sauce and melted butter. Wrap ribs in tin foil and baste liberally with sauce. Barbecue ribs for another 1.5 hours.

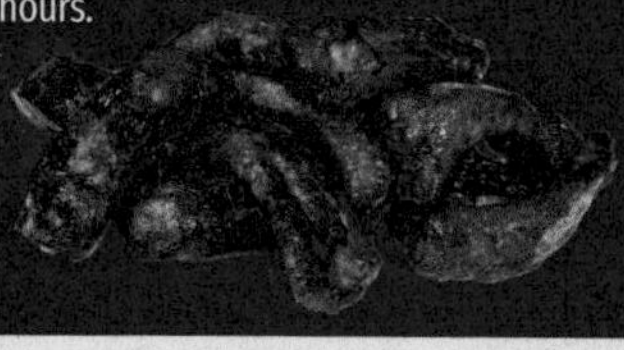

NC

Asheville's Finest Home Away From Home

Minutes Away from Biltmore Estate
Our Discount Code Saves
$13 Per Ticket

Just 5 Min from downtown Asheville & Civic Center; 1/2 Mile from Farmer's Market; Shopping Malls & Golf Nearby; 15 Min from Asheville Regional Airport

FREE Wi-Fi & CABLE

- Heated Swimming Pool
- Over 100 Full Hookup Sites • All Paved • All Level
- Heated Restrooms • Laundry
- Patios • Picnic Tables • Playground • Cable TV
- All Groups Welcome • Rally Friendly
- Beautiful Clubhouse w/Kitchen (Capacity of up to 175)
- On Site RV, Truck and Auto Repair
- Near Folk Art Center, Public Golf, Arts & Crafts Center
- Must Bring Your Own Above-Ground Fire Pit

ECO-FRIENDLY

10% KOA DISCOUNT

AAA

See listing Asheville, NC

EASY ACCESS I-40 & I-26,
5.5 MI. FROM BLUE RIDGE PARKWAY
NO ARRIVALS AFTER 10:00PM

MUST ENTER SOUTH BEAR CREEK RD. IN GPS

81 SOUTH Bear Creek Rd., Asheville, NC 28806
Reservations (828) 253-0798
www.ashevillebearcreek.com

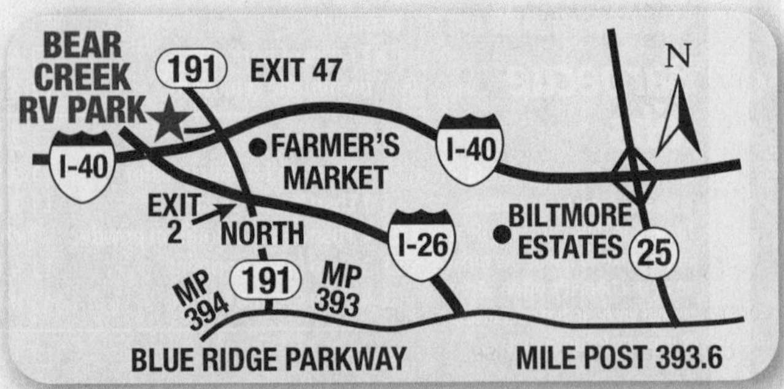

SPOTLIGHTS

Floating Fun

Slicing a path through the west side of town, the French Broad River is the beating heart of Asheville. Considered the third-oldest river in the world, its long sloping course helped form the Appalachian Mountains and drew the first settlers to the region, but these days it's the place to go for all sorts of water sports. Tubing the quiet stretch along Hominy Creek is a popular Asheville pastime, while fly-fishing, paddleboarding and whitewater rafting are all available through various outfitters in town. If you prefer to keep your feet on dry land, try a bike tour of the scenic Carrier Park that follows along the river shoreline.

Foodies Rejoice

From farm-to-table cooking, to cutting edge breweries, Asheville is well-known as one of the South's top foodie destinations. For Appalachian-inspired fare, it's hard to beat Rhubarb, a downtown staple helmed by a five-time finalist for the James Beard award, as well as local favorites like Blackbird, Buchon, and Tupelo Honey. For a more in-depth look at the region's culinary roots, your best bet is to join one of the popular cheese, beer, or wild food-foraging tours. Originating at nearby farms or farmers markets, you'll get a from-the-ground-up look at what makes "Foodtopia" so special. Of course, no trip to Asheville would be complete without a sampling of its many top-notch local beers. With more breweries per capita than almost anywhere else in the U.S., there are tours and tastings aplenty, including the fun-filled Pubcycle, a hybrid party bus that uses pedal power to transport guests between breweries.

Natural Waterslide

When summer hits, locals cool off by riding down the chilly waters of Sliding Rock in Pisgah National Forest. The 55- to 60-degree water makes for a refreshing time. Plus, many waterfalls are located nearby, including Looking Glass Falls. If you're seeking something a bit more extreme, take a canyoneering trip with Green River Adventures and rappel down Bradley Falls, deep in the Green River Gorge. After learning the fundamentals of rappelling, take a practice run on a 30-foot vertical wall before you tackle the 200-foot descent. Certified guides guide you all the way.

Leisure Cruising

If you prefer a trip down the river without working up a sweat, take a cruise. French Broad Boatworks will take you on a guided scenic tour down the river in a locally crafted wooden drift boat, complete with your personal paddler. In addition to sunrise and sunset tours, there's a birding trip and the River Arts District Tour that concludes with dinner and drinks at the riverside Smoky Park Supper Club.

Fun Among the Trees

The Adventure Center of Asheville offers adrenaline-pumping adventures high above the ground, just five minutes from downtown. Get an eyeful of expansive views of the Asheville skyline from Asheville Zipline Canopy Adventures or hop on one of the top-end mountain bikes and cruise down thrilling trails. The on-site trail system was created and groomed for the KOLO Bike Park. If you prefer climbing to riding, head up into the trees at Asheville Treetops Adventure Park, an elevated obstacle course with five levels of difficulty. For little ones, the KidZip is America's first zipline adventure designed for children under 10. Experience a true thrill rush as you zoom at high speeds through the trees.

NC

SPOTLIGHTS

The light on the 156-foot-tall Bodie Lighthouse still functions to protect boaters in the dark waters. There are 200 steps leading to the top.

Seeing Grandpa

Located northeast of Asheville, Grandfather Mountain is one of the most popular ecotourism adventures in the state. Considered one of the most biologically diverse mountains on the planet, the mountain has been designated by the United Nations as an International Biosphere Reserve. For explorers, the mountain is worthy side trip from Asheville. Visitors will feel a genuine rush as they cross the Mile High Swinging Bridge, located one mile above sea level and dishing out 360-degree views. Photographers will catch sight of bears, otters, cougars, eagles and deer in natural habitats. Hikers can tackle rugged back-country trails or stroll gentle nature paths. The onsite restaurant and many scenic picnic areas help you refuel.

Botony on Display

A carefully tended wilderness preserve, Grandfather Mountain is home to many rare North American wildflowers, with displays of such naturalized plants as native azaleas, rhododendrons, mosses and lichens, heathers and other beautiful species. Parts of the mountain are steep and rocky, but much is accessible to anyone seeking dramatic mountain vistas and wildlife habitat areas.

Reach New Heights on Mount Mitchell

Eager to hike in high altitudes? From Asheville, travel 28 miles north on the Blue Ridge Parkway to Mount Mitchell State Park. At 6,684 feet, the namesake mountain tops every other summit east of the Mississippi River. Start your visit at the museum, open from May through October. Here, you can learn about the mountain's natural and cultural history, including the effort by scholar Elisha Mitchell in the 1850s to prove the peak's standing as the tallest.

Outer Banks/ Cape Hatteras

Just off the North Carolina coast, the barrier islands known as the Outer Banks offer up over 100 miles of soft sand and welcoming small towns. Steeped in unique history and brimming with an easygoing vibe that makes getting around a breeze, you'll quickly discover why these once-remote islands have become a mainstay of East Coast summers. From windswept views to wild horses, there's nowhere else quite like it.

Historic Heights

Known as the "Graveyard of the Atlantic," the perilous waters off the coast of Cape Hatteras, on one of the southernmost islands of the Outer Banks, have long been a threat to seafarers of all stripes. Which is what makes the Cape Hatteras Lighthouse so special. Completed in 1870, the iconic blank-and-white brick lighthouse was once the tallest in the world and is now one of the most popular attractions in the state. The 360-degree views from the top are

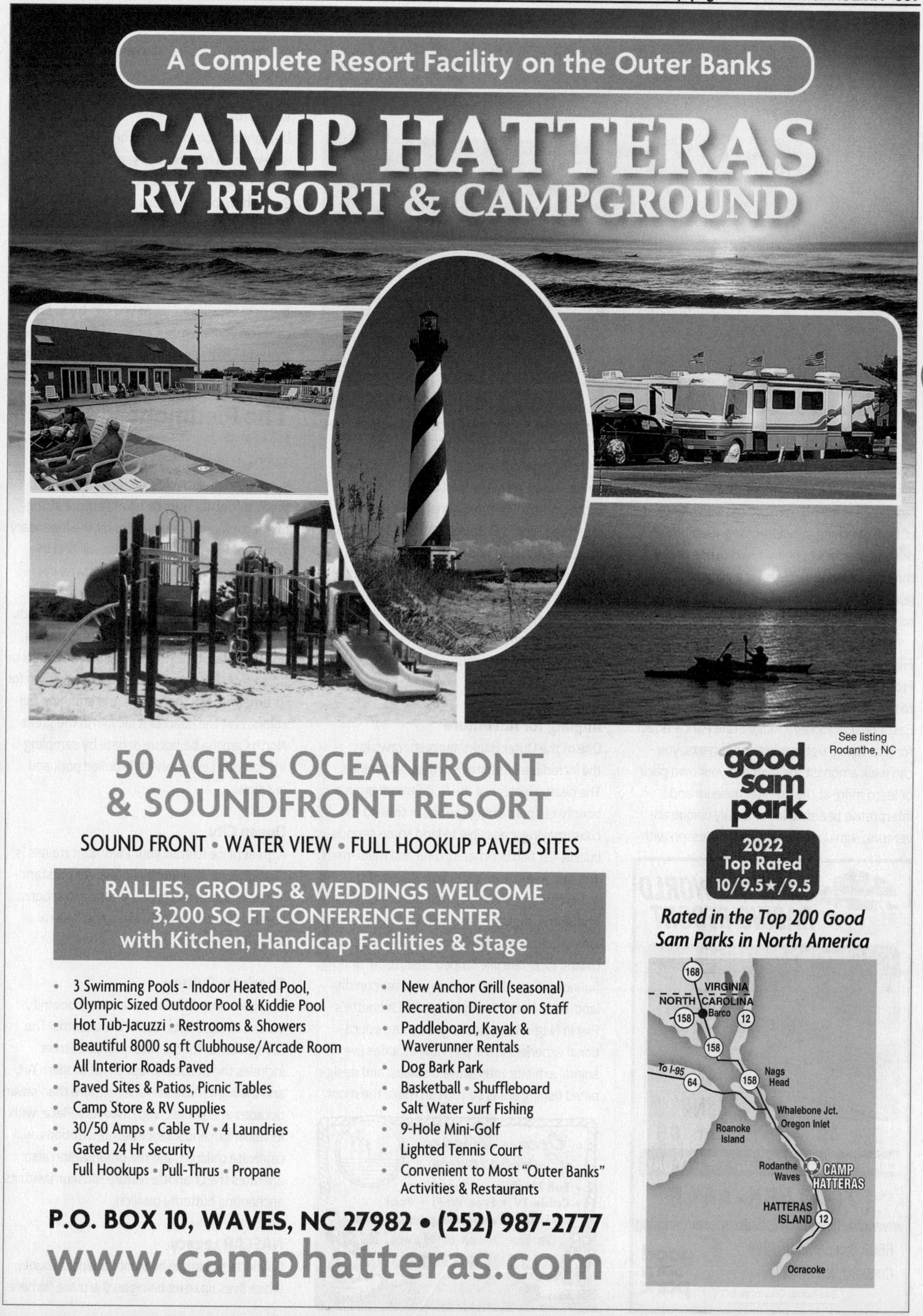
A Complete Resort Facility on the Outer Banks
CAMP HATTERAS
RV RESORT & CAMPGROUND
50 ACRES OCEANFRONT
& SOUNDFRONT RESORT
SOUND FRONT • WATER VIEW • FULL HOOKUP PAVED SITES
RALLIES, GROUPS & WEDDINGS WELCOME
3,200 SQ FT CONFERENCE CENTER
with Kitchen, Handicap Facilities & Stage
• 3 Swimming Pools - Indoor Heated Pool, Olympic Sized Outdoor Pool & Kiddie Pool
• Hot Tub-Jacuzzi • Restrooms & Showers
• Beautiful 8000 sq ft Clubhouse/Arcade Room
• All Interior Roads Paved
• Paved Sites & Patios, Picnic Tables
• Camp Store & RV Supplies
• 30/50 Amps • Cable TV • 4 Laundries
• Gated 24 Hr Security
• Full Hookups • Pull-Thrus • Propane
• New Anchor Grill (seasonal)
• Recreation Director on Staff
• Paddleboard, Kayak & Waverunner Rentals
• Dog Bark Park
• Basketball • Shuffleboard
• Salt Water Surf Fishing
• 9-Hole Mini-Golf
• Lighted Tennis Court
• Convenient to Most "Outer Banks" Activities & Restaurants
P.O. BOX 10, WAVES, NC 27982 • (252) 987-2777
www.camphatteras.com
See listing
Rodanthe, NC
good sam park
2022
Top Rated
10/9.5★/9.5
Rated in the Top 200 Good Sam Parks in North America
168
VIRGINIA
NORTH CAROLINA
158
Barco
12
158
To I-95
64
158
Nags Head
Whalebone Jct.
Oregon Inlet
Roanoke Island
Rodanthe
Waves
CAMP HATTERAS
HATTERAS ISLAND
12
Ocracoke

SPOTLIGHTS

The wild horses of the Outer Banks are protected by the National Park Service. It is illegal to get within 50 feet.

spectacular, though visitors will have to endure a 12-story climb to get there. The surrounding landscape is equally remarkable with plenty of bird-watching, as well as long stretches of pristine beaches to enjoy. Head to one of the three nearby nature trails for a glimpse of the flora and fauna that make this coastal environment so unique.

High-flying Fun

From there, head north to Nags Head, home to the tallest active sand dune system on the East Coast at Jockey's Ridge State Park. Perfect for kite-flying, sightseeing and sunsets, you can walk amongst the dunes at your own pace or learn more at the on-site museum and interpretive boardwalk. For a truly unique adventure, sign up for a hang-gliding lesson with one of the park's vendors. The area is known for having some of the best wind conditions in the country. For more aerial fun, there's the must-see Wright Brothers National Memorial at nearby Kill Devil Hills. The site of the first powered airplane flight in 1903, the memorial is now dedicated to inspiring an interest in aviation, science, and technology through hands-on exhibits and interactive simulators. You can even walk the actual routes of the brothers' historic flights.

Angling for Adventure

One of the Outer Banks' biggest draws is the incredible offshore fishing opportunities. The nearby waters of the Gulf Stream bring a bounty of sportfishing species in toward the coast making it possible to land some serious bucket-list fish like marlin, tuna and mahi-mahi. You can organize an excursion at one of the many charter companies that dot the coast. Primetime angling is also available in the sound where guides can direct you to the best spots to land local fare like striped bass, drum and flounder. If you'd rather keep your feet on dry land, head to the newly renovated Jennette's Pier in Nags Head. Redesigned as an educational experience, the pier now includes live animal exhibits, interactive displays, and designated fishing areas so you can make the most of your stay. Croaker, mackerel and bluefish are common catches.

Wild Horses

Descended from mustangs brought by Spanish explorers hundreds of years ago, the wild horses that roam the beaches of the Outer Banks have become icons of beauty and freedom. It's illegal to get closer than 50 feet to the wild herds, but viewing them from afar is still a magical experience. There are a number of beach safari companies that can take you to the best viewing areas, or you can try to find them on your own, but either way, seeing the majestic creatures in their natural habitat is a one-of-a-kind experience.

The Piedmont

The Piedmont region of North Carolina is synonymous with NASCAR, golfing and great barbecue. Throttle up adventure at the Charlotte Motor Speedway or hit the legendary greens of Pinehurst. Snowbirds will find the state's largest cities and college towns overflowing with museums, cultural attractions, and historic sites. Outdoor adventure abounds in the rolling landscape, with rivers to paddle and mountain trails to explore on foot, wheel or horseback. Hanging Rock State Park, known for its amazing rock formations and stunning fall colors, is at the heart of it all. Join in the great North Carolina barbecue debate by sampling the famous Lexington-style pulled pork and red slaw.

Queen City

A great place to start your Piedmont travels is Charlotte, an elegant city known for outstanding restaurants and great cultural attractions. It's also home to an NFL team and several NASCAR-related attractions.

Charlotte Culture

Nowhere does Charlotte wear its modernity on its streets like its resident museums. The Levine Center for the Arts on Tryon Street includes the Bechtler Museum of Modern Art, and the Mint Museum reflects more than seven decades of art collecting. Discovery Place, with its aquarium and science demonstrations, will captivate children, and the organization also operates the Charlotte Nature Museum with its enchanting butterfly pavilion.

NASCAR Legacy

Charlotte sits in the heart of Cabarrus County, which lives up to its billing as the place "Where

Racing Lives." Home to legendary Charlotte Motor Speedway, zMAX Dragway and Kannapolis, the region also is hometown of driver Dale Earnhardt Sr., so it's easy to see why NASCAR fans head to the area on more than just race days. Visitors can tour the NASCAR Hall of Fame in Charlotte to see how the sport evolved from informal stock car competitions to the billion-dollar juggernaut that it is today. Interactive exhibits give visitors a chance to experience the thrill of high-speed racing. Visit nearby NASCAR team shops to stock up on memorabilia and glean insights into the inner workings of top NASCAR comptetitors.

Charlotte is the "city of trees." Civic leaders plan to achieve 50 percent coverage under canopies by 2050.

Petty Experience

Visitors can get a real taste of racing action with the Richard Petty Driving Experience at Charlotte Motor Speedway. Slip behind the wheel of a 600 horsepower stock car or ride-along with a professional driver at speeds up to 160 mph around the 1.5-mile steep-banked oval. For spectators, the motorsports complex hosts all manner of racing competitions through the year, headlined by the Coca-Cola 600 on Memorial Day.

Life in the Colonial Era

In the 1700s, colonists named the town after Charlotte of Mecklenburg-Strelitz, queen consort to British King George III. Charlotte Museum of History is home to the 5,000-foot Hezekiah Alexander Rock House. Built in 1774, it's the oldest remaining building in Mecklenburg County. On the eve of the American Revolution, local backcountry farmers calling themselves "Regulators" took arms against the Loyalist militia at Alamance Battleground near Burlington. Battle reenactments along with infantry and artillery drills are held regularly.

Charlotte Pigskins

Are you ready for some football? When it's game time, head to Bank of America Stadium for fun with fellow fans. The Carolina Panthers NFL Team is young by league standards — founded in 1995 — but they hold on to age-old feasting traditions. Tailgaters can choose a regular space as low as $11 or get a premium tailgating site for more than $100. RV parking is available at Cedar Yard Station, located immediately east of the Interstate 77 and Morehead Street interchange.

Tantalizing Tailgate Treat

Seeking inspiration for tailgating? The Pantherfanz Tailgating club has made a fine art of whipping up snacks for game day. Carolina Panthers fan and club member Dan "12th Man" Ortel proudly shared his sizzling 12th Man Hot Wings recipe. This dish serves as the perfect appetizer.

Charlotte Plant Life

Follow the paths that lead to colorful gardens at the University of North Carolina Charlotte Botanical Gardens, a purposeful collection of plants grown for more than just their beauty. Holding curated collections of plants for inventory, education, conservation and research, they are dedicated to sharing the world of plants with people. This is also a great place to learn about planting techniques for home gardeners.

Cast a Line

The Piedmont Region may be land-locked, but there are still plenty of water activities to dive into. State parks like Mayo River and Haw River allow paddling, fishing and swimming. Kerr Lake State Recreation Area boasts

SPOTLIGHTS

Charlotte is NASCAR central. The Charlotte Motor Speedway and NASCAR Hall of Fame are located here.

50,000 acres and is one of the best fishing lakes in the state. Head to Guilford Mackintosh Park & Marina, nestled along the banks of Lake Mackintosh in Burlington and is popular for canoeing, kayaking, fishing, paddling, biking and hiking.

Hunt and Hike in the Triad

Hunters can expect big game like whitetail deer, wild turkey and black bear in the Piedmont region. Smaller game includes bobcat, beaver and feral hogs along with various birds and waterfowl. The Piedmont Trail is reserved for hikers only and features Bog Turtles, white-tailed deer, stands of cedars and wild fruit bushes. Greensboro Watershed Trails are not loops but include walks along the lake, woodlands and creeks. In the Uwharrie National Forest, hikers can walk among towering Longleaf pines.

Loving Lake Norman

Although a power company built the Cowans Ford Dam across the Catawba River to generate electrical energy, the resulting lake northwest of Charlotte attracts nature lovers and fishing enthusiasts. Indeed, anglers come to Lake Norman from around the world for their chance at a record-winning catfish, crappie, largemouth bass, striped bass, and yellow and white perch. It's the site of several fishing tournaments throughout the year. For a scenic stroll around the lake's beautiful shoreline, follow the white blazes (red blazes for a shortcut) for this 6.2-mile moderate Lake Shore Trail hike. For a much shorter, easy stroll, ideal for children, wheelchair users, or stroller accessibility, the Dragonfly Trail is just 0.15 miles and paved. Nature displays with interactive panels teach walkers a bit about local plants and animals. It's a great day for both hikers and anglers.

Pilot Mountain State Park

Known as "Jomeokee," or "the Great Guide," to the area's early Saura (also known as the Cheraw) Indians, Pilot Mountain served as an unmistakable beacon and navigational landmark to guide Native Americans and European hunters traversing the area. Today, an extensive trail network includes the moderate but short Kid's Track Trail, with fun activities for children along the way, and easy access to the top of Little Pinnacle, where, on clear days, you'll capture enviable Instagram pinnacle posts. The popular Mountains-to-Sea Trail, a 1,200-mile network of footpaths from the Great Smoky Mountains in western North Carolina to the Outer Banks in the far east, passes through the Pilot Mountain State Park on three trails: Corridor, Mountain and Grindstone.

Edible Experiences

The Piedmont Triangle is home to some tasty innovations. Winston-Salem is where Krispy Kreme donuts created their most famous product — the glazed donut. Another Winston-Salem creation is Texas Pete Louisiana Hot Sauce, first released in the 1940s and still a hot seller today. Lexington is the self-proclaimed BBQ Capital of the World, with more BBQ joints per capita than any place else in the world. Cheerwine, not a wine but a cherry flavored soda, was developed in Salisbury in 1917.

Delightful Durham Dishes

Durham is home to James Beard Award–winning chef Andrea Reusing's restaurant, appropriately named The Durham. Enjoy the evolving, fresh menu serving flavorful fare sourced primarily from North Carolina farms, fisheries and ranches. Delight in delicious dishes like Durham Paella with black rice, wild shrimp, Pamlico Sound clam and crispy pig tail.

Durham Drinks

Head to Alley Twenty Six for a night of guaranteed fun. Durham's most awarded cocktail bar is located just two blocks from the Durham Performing Arts Center. It's an ideal spot for an upscale snack and a refreshing gin and tonic.

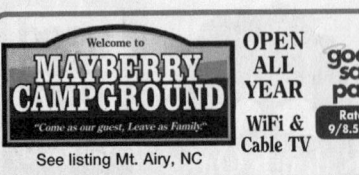

Mateo Bar de Tapas is a chic place for lunch and dinner with its banana pudding pie dulce, 14-inch pan paella with choices of shrimp, chorizo, sofrito, mussels and more.

West Point on the Eno River in Durham is a 404-acre park with a stunning waterfall.

Tarheel Wine Tasting

An easy drive from Winston-Salem, and just west of Interstate 77 in Wilkes and Yadkin counties, discover the wineries on the Swan Creek Wine Trail. Four wineries will welcome you with varietal wines and blends, framed by mountain landscapes and rolling vineyards. Shadow Springs Vineyard is located in the heart of the Yadkin Valley and offers RV parking. Windsor Run Cellars Vineyard, Winery & Distillery in Hamptonville focuses on estate reds, whites, meads and fortified wines. WRC Distillery crafts spirits from their estate grapes and meads. Laurel Gray Vineyards dates back to 1773 and is committed to sustainable farming operations and producing award winning wines.

Artistry, Attractions & Exhibitions

Durham is not only a historical haven, but a starting point for an adventure. Brimming with an abundance of natural beauty, activists, artists and scholars, Durham is home to immigrant-owned galleries as well as the Durham Performing Arts Center, a former 1960s bank turned posh mid-century designed hotel. The Greensboro & Winston-Salem region is home to furniture and is the site of a massive pottery community. Discover a pottery paradise in Seagrove, strewn with artisans and handcrafted wares. Start at the North Carolina Pottery Center where the tradition continues with education and exhibitions.

Bethabara

Learn about the journey of a unique religious group by visiting Historic Bethabara Park in Winston-Salem. The first North Carolina Moravians settled here in 1753, the founding site of Forsyth County. The Park features costumed guides leading visitors through a 1788 furnished church. You can view a restored French/Indian War fort and restored medicinal garden. Greenways and path traverse the 175-acre preserve.

West End History

The West End Historic District in downtown Winston-Salem is worth a visit. From its beginnings as a regional spa resort and an upscale community of wealthy tobacco and textile families, Winston-Salem's West End is now a dining and shopping mecca for the city and a perfect place to explore on foot. Built around one of the first electric streetcar lines in the country, the West End boasted "Millionaires' Row," where the Reynolds and Hanes families kept homes bought with manufacturing fortunes. Featuring homes built between 1890 and 1930, the neighborhood is known to have the largest and most-varied concentration of front porch designs. Take time to tour the Wake Forest campus, adjacent to the 129-acre Reynolda gardens, with its postcard-worthy Waterfall Bridge.

High Point History

To the east, the town of High Point also preserves the past. At High Point Museum & Historical Park, visitors can explore the history of region and learn how pioneers eked out an existence in the countryside. Changing exhibits provide a look at lifestyles through the years. Tour the Blacksmith Shop, as well as the clutch of Haley Houses located in the Historical Park.

Restaurants and Retailers

Occupying the former Watts and Yuille tobacco warehouses, Brightleaf Square housed some of the region's most noted and acclaimed restaurants and retailers. Offering cutting edge fashion, rare books and specialty shops, the atmosphere is quintessential Durham – artsy and funky.

Growing Seeds

The Seeds Educational Garden in Durham teaches respect for life, the earth and others through gardening and growing food. This urban sanctuary focuses on promoting principles and practices of sustainable agriculture and organic gardening.

SPOTLIGHTS

View from the Newfound Gap overlook revealing the vast wilderness of Great Smoky Mountains National Park.

Great Smoky Mountains

Spanning more than 800 square miles along the border between North Carolina and Tennessee, Great Smoky Mountains National Park is an iconic American destination and a haven for outdoors lovers everywhere. Boasting untold numbers of picturesque waterfalls, hundreds of miles of trails, and some of the highest peaks east of the Mississippi River, there's an almost endless array of activities to enjoy. Toss in a little small-town Southern hospitality and you've got all the makings of a getaway to remember.

Hike Your Heart Out

Start your visit with a stop at the Oconaluftee Visitor Center, just north of the town of Cherokee. There you'll find supplies, maps, and park rangers who can offer expert advice on the best trails for each season. The 3.2-mile Oconaluftee River Trail, which leaves from behind the center, is an easy-going introduction to the landscape, while nearby hikes like Mingus Creek Trail offer up views of historic Appalachian homesteads. For the best views, however, take scenic U.S. Route 441 toward the Newfound Gap. From there, you can access trailheads to Clingmans Dome (the highest point in the park), as well as the Appalachian Trail. Try the 8-mile roundtrip Charlies Bunion trail for some of the best views in the Southeast.

Waterfall Watching

Found on nearly every river and stream in the park, waterfalls have become synonymous with the Smokies. On the North Carolina side, there's plenty of picturesque options like the scenic Deep Creek Trail that winds between Indian Creek Falls, Juney Whank Falls and Tom Branch Falls, or the quick, half-mile hike to Mingo Falls, the tallest in the southern Appalachians. However, the most popular cascades are across state lines in Tennessee where Grotto, Rainbow, and Laurel Falls draw hundreds of thousands of hikers and photographers every year. Experienced adventurers should try the 8-mile roundtrip hike to Ramsey Cascades, the tallest and one of the most spectacular in the park. The trail ascends more than 2,000 feet in 4 miles, but you'll be treated to top-notch wildlife viewing and long stretches of stunning, old-growth forest along the way.

Historic Homesteads

Adjacent to the Oconaluftee Visitor Center is the Mountain Farm Museum, a collection of preserved log structures built in the late 19th century. Boasting a farmhouse, a barn, a blacksmith's shop and more, the museum's self-guided tour offers visitors a first-hand look at how Appalachian homesteaders lived over a hundred years ago. Other historic sites are also scattered throughout the area's top hikes. The Little Cataloochee Trail in the rugged Cataloochee Valley is known for its resident elk herd, as well as the rustic churches, schools and homes that dot the landscape. On the Tennessee side, head to Cades Cove, an 11-mile driving loop that passes 100-year-old log cabins, churches and cemeteries, as well as pull-offs to trailheads like the Abrams Falls Trail.

Perfect Paddling

Along the southern edge of the national park, sprawling Fontana Lake is the perfect backdrop

The churning Class III rapids of Nantahala Falls give kayakers a run for their money. For a greater challenge, the Cheoah River dishes out Class IV rapids.

for all your canoeing, kayaking and boating needs. With 238 miles of shoreline, there are plenty of inlets and coves to explore, not to mention the 480-foot Fontana Dam, the tallest concrete dam east of the Rockies and an awe-inspiring structure.

Wondrous Whitewater

If it's heart-pounding fun you're after, it's hard to beat a whitewater rafting excursion on the nearby Nantahala River. One of the most scenic and accessible rivers in the country, the Nantahala boasts an almost continuous circuit of family-friendly Class III rapids that surge through a beautiful gorge and other striking surrounds. Top off your stay with a thrilling zip-lining course at the Nantahala Outdoor Center.

Smoky Locomotives

Tired of hiking? Take a ride on a historic train. In 1883, the Great Smoky Mountain Railroad was constructed, stretching from Knoxville, Tennessee, to Dillsboro, North Carolina, before reaching Andrews in 1890. Nowadays, the railroad is one of the region's top tourist attractions. The distinctive steam-powered trains depart from the historic depot in Bryson City and traverse the fecund valleys and river gorges of western North Carolina. Special BBQ and Brews trains welcome passengers to enjoy slow-cooked barbecue and beers from local breweries.

South Coast

The beaches along the South Coast of North Carolina are some of the most beautiful yet overlooked in the state. This is a water lover's paradise with kayaking, sailing, paddleboarding, boating and fishing. There are also lighthouses, museums and carnivorous plants to keep you on your toes. Sink those toes into sandy beaches and marvel at gorgeous sunsets.

Where Life is Beachy

Oak Island has 19 miles of waving sea grass, boisterous waves and resounding ocean surf. Visit the last lighthouse built in the state on Caswell Beach before ambling over to explore Fort Caswell, a military fort built in 1825.

Topsail Island

Topsail Island is home to a sea turtle sanctuary where loggerhead, green, Ridley and leatherback turtles reside. And this is the best place on

SPOTLIGHTS

Top Sail Beach stretches for 26 miles and faces the Atlantic Ocean. The coast is a sea turtle sanctuary.

the Atlantic Coast for finding conch shells. The Missiles and More Museum tells the stories of Operation Bumble Bee, the Navy's secret WWII guided missile program along with the history of nearly a dozen disreputable pirates. At Holden Beach, you can book a fishing charter or take a boat tour through the Intracoastal Waterway. At the beach, you can rent a kayak, jet skies, or a pontoon boat for nautical fun. Nearby, the Fisher State Recreation Area serves up six miles of beach and trails through salt marsh.

Revel in the Water

The South Coast offers exciting aquatic activities like jet skiing, hang gliding and peddle boating; even wave running, kayaking and stand-up paddle boarding, which is one of the most popular water sports in the country. Sign up for a scuba diving adventure or relax as you watch for whales.

Explore the Trails

The Carolina Beach State Park has nearly nine miles of hiking trails with forests, marshes and the 50-foot Sugarloaf sand dune just waiting to be explored. Check out Oak Toe Trail with a briny marsh overlook and views of Cape Fear River. Sand Live Oak Trail weaves among time-worn sand dunes, and Flytrap Trail edges along wetlands where carnivorous plants reside.

Exotic Plant Life

Located on three-quarters of an acre, the Stanley Rehder Carnivorous Plant Garden gives you the fascinating yet goose-bumpy experience of watching as insectivorous plants like Venus Flytrap, Pitcher Plant and Sundews lure, trap and digest their insect meals. (Close-toed shoes are suggested.)

Aquarium Fun

Close to North Carolina's South Coast, the Crystal Coast features a slew of nautical attractions for the whole family. At Pine Knoll Shores, those traveling with kids won't want to miss the North Carolina Aquarium, which is home to an abundance of marine life, including favorites like sharks, stingrays and sea turtles. Visitors can watch river otters play or touch a stingray. At the Loggerhead Odyssey exhibit, guests can watch turtle hatchlings take their first steps. The Living Shipwreck features three intricately recreated famous shipwreck sites. The exhibits demonstrate how sunken vessels form the nucleus of a complex marine ecosystem.

Sunken Treasure

The aquarium's wrecks detail some of the violent maritime history of the Crystal Coast. The first is a replicated version of U-352, a German submarine sunk off the coast of Cape Lookout by the U.S. Coast Guard during World War II. The second showcases the flip-side of German U-boat activity along the North Carolina coast during the war: a replicated version the Caribsea freighter ship, torpedoed by U-158 near the Cape in 1942. And the third replication is the crown jewel of the entire collection: *Queen Anne's Revenge*, Blackbeard's pirate ship. For all the terror it inspired on the high seas, its end was fairly pedestrian. It ran aground in Beaufort Inlet in 1718, likely when the crew was attempting carry out hull maintenance.

One of the Best Beaches

Just east of Pine Knoll Shores at Atlantic Beach, sunbathers, surfers and sand-castle aficionados can enjoy free access to what's been routinely selected as one of the best beaches in the country.

▸ FOR MORE INFORMATION

VisitNC.com, 800-VISITNC, VisitNC.com
Explore Asheville, 828-258-6129, ww.exploreasheville.com
North Carolina's Piedmont, 800-VISITNC, www.visitnc.com/piedmont
Great Smoky Mountains, 865-436-1200, www.nps.gov/grsm
Outer Banks, 877-629-4386, www.outerbanks.org
South Coast North Carolina, 800-VISITNC, www.visitnc.com/coast

North Carolina

ABERDEEN — C3 *Moore*

OASIS OF NORTH CAROLINA
good sam park **Ratings: 7/9★/9.5** (Campground) 27 Avail: 23 full hkups, 4 E (30/50 amps). 2021 rates: $40 to $55. (910)266-8372, 15340 Palmer Rd, Marston, NC 28363

PINE LAKE RV RESORT
good sam park **Ratings: 8/8★/7.5** (Campground) From S Jct of NC-211 & US-15/501, S 9.6 mi on US-15/501 to Hill Creek Rd, E 1.9 mi (R) Note: Do not rely on GPS. **FAC:** gravel rds. Avail: 95 dirt, 78 pull-thrus, (28x50), back-ins (28x60), 89 full hkups, 6 W, 6 E (30/50 amps), WiFi @ sites, rentals, dump, laundry, fire rings, firewood, controlled access. **REC:** pool, Pine Lake: fishing, kayaking/canoeing, boating nearby, playground. Pet restrict (B). No tents, eco-friendly. 2021 rates: $40, Military discount.
(910)281-3319 Lat: 34.98546, Lon: -79.41577
32482 Hillcreek Rd, Wagram, NC 28396
www.pinelakervresorts.com
See ad page 671

ADVANCE — B2 *Davie*

FOREST LAKE PRESERVE
good sam park **Ratings: 8.5/7/8.5** (Membership Park) Avail: 138 full hkups (30/50 amps). 2021 rates: $59 to $80. (888)563-7040, 192 Thousand Trails Dr, Advance, NC 27006

ALBEMARLE — B2 *Stanly*

MORROW MOUNTAIN
(Public State Park) From Jct Hwy 24/27/73 & SR-740, E 3 mi on SR-740 to Morrow Mtn Rd, S 5 mi (E). **FAC:** paved rds. Avail: 106 gravel, 1 pull-thrus, (15x40), back-ins (15x33), 22 E tent sites, rentals, dump, firewood. **REC:** pool $, Lake Tillery: fishing, kayaking/canoeing, rec open to public. Partial handicap access, 14 day max stay. 2021 rates: $15 to $25. no cc.
(704)982-4402 Lat: 35.373724, Lon: -80.073477
49104 Morrow Mtn Rd, Albemarle, NC 28001
www.ncparks.gov

ALMOND — E1 *Swain*

TUMBLING WATERS CAMPGROUND & TROUT POND **Ratings: 5.5/8.5★/7.5** (Campground) Avail: 12 full hkups (30 amps). 2021 rates: $40. Mar 01 to Dec 01. (828)479-3814, 1612 Panther Creek Rd, Almond, NC 28702

APEX — B3 *Wake*

JORDAN LAKE/CROSSWINDS (Public State Park) From Jct of US 64 & SR-1008, N 0.3 mi on SR-1008 (R). 182 Avail: 134 W, 134 E (20/30 amps). 2021 rates: $15 to $25. (919)362-0586

JORDAN LAKE/PARKERS CREEK (Public State Park) From Jct of US-64 & SR-1008, W 2.2 mi on US-64 (R). 250 Avail: 120 W, 120 E (20/30 amps). 2021 rates: $15 to $25. (919)362-0586

JORDAN LAKE/POPLAR POINT (Public State Park) From Jct of US-64 & SR-1008, S 0.5 mi on SR-1008 (R). 579 Avail: 363 W, 363 E (20/30 amps). 2021 rates: $15 to $25. Mar 15 to Nov 30. (919)362-0586

JORDAN LAKE/VISTA POINT (Public State Park) From town: Go 12 mi W on US 64 to Griffins Crossroads, then 3 mi S on Pea Ridge Rd. 50 Avail. 2021 rates: $15 to $25. (919)362-0586

ASHEBORO — B2 *Randolph*

DEEP RIVER CAMPGROUND & RV PARK **Ratings: 8.5/8.5★/8** (Campground) Avail: 10 full hkups (30/50 amps). 2021 rates: $50. (336)629-4069, 814 McDowell Country Trail, Asheboro, NC 27203

HOLLY BLUFF FAMILY CAMPGROUND **Ratings: 8/6/7** (Campground) Avail: 42 full hkups (30/50 amps). 2021 rates: $35 to $37. (336)857-2761, 4846 NC Hwy 49 S, Asheboro, NC 27205

ASHEVILLE — E2 *Buncombe*

A SPOTLIGHT Introducing Asheville's colorful attractions appearing at the front of this state section.

ASHEVILLE See also Bat Cave, Candler, Chimney Rock, Hendersonville, Marion, Swannanoa & Waynesville.

ASHEVILLE BEAR CREEK RV PARK
good sam park **Ratings: 9.5/10★/9.5** (RV Park) From Jct of I-40 & NC-191(exit 47): Go W on NC-191 to S Bear Creek Rd, then W 6/10 mi on S Bear Creek Rd (L); or From Jct of I-26 of & NC-191(exit 31): Go N 1-1/10 mi on NC-191 to S Bear Creek Rd, then W 6/10 mi on S Bear Creek Rd (L) Note: no arrivals after 10 pm please.

BILTMORE HOUSE, SCENIC VIEWS & MORE
We're only minutes from the Biltmore & you can get a discount code from us! Stay on our BIG concrete sites. Free WIFI, mountain views. Enjoy a day of sightseeing. Then swim, unwind & get ready for another day of exploring!

FAC: paved rds. (114 spaces). Avail: 94 paved, 23 pull-thrus, (30x60), back-ins (30x60), 94 full hkups (30/50 amps), seasonal sites, cable, WiFi @ sites, laundry, LP gas. **REC:** heated pool, boating nearby, playground. Pet restrict (B/Q). Partial handicap access. No tents. Big rig sites, eco-friendly. 2021 rates: $60, Military discount.
(828)253-0798 Lat: 35.55749, Lon: -82.60465
81 South Bear Creek Rd, Asheville, NC 28806
ashevillebearcreek.com
See ad page 664

BLUE RIDGE PKWY/MOUNT PISGAH (Public National Park) From Jct of I-26 & Hwy 191, S 2 mi on Hwy 191 to Blue Ridge Pkwy, S 14 mi at MP-408.6 (R). 62 Avail. 2021 rates: $16 to $19. May 08 to Oct 24. (828)648-2644

CAMPFIRE LODGINGS **Ratings: 8/9.5★/10** (Campground) Avail: 17 full hkups (30/50 amps). 2021 rates: $55 to $80. (828)658-8012, 116 Appalachian Village Rd, Asheville, NC 28804

SCENIC RV RESORT
good sam park (Membership Park) Avail: 1 full hkups (30/50 amps). (888)563-7040, 45 Scenic Drive, Asheville, NC 28805

WILSON'S RIVERFRONT RV PARK **Ratings: 5.5/7.5/6.5** (Campground) Avail: 15 full hkups (30/50 amps). 2021 rates: $45 to $50. (828)254-4676, 225 Amboy Rd, Asheville, NC 28806

BANNER ELK — D3 *Watauga*

GRANDFATHER CAMPGROUND **Ratings: 6.5/8.5★/9** (Campground) 69 Avail: 59 full hkups, 10 W, 10 E (30/50 amps). 2021 rates: $42. (800)788-2582, 125 Profile View Dr, Banner Elk, NC 28604

BAT CAVE — E2 *Henderson*

CREEKSIDE MOUNTAIN CAMPING **Ratings: 7.5/6/8** (Campground) 22 Avail: 10 full hkups, 12 W, 12 E (30 amps). 2021 rates: $38.95. (800)248-8118, 28 Chimney View Road, Bat Cave, NC 28710

BAYBORO — B5 *Pamlico*

RIVERS EDGE FAMILY CAMPGROUND **Ratings: 7/8.5★/9** (Campground) Avail: 20 full hkups (30/50 amps). 2021 rates: $60 to $70. (252)559-3603, 149 Tempe Gut Rd, Bayboro, NC 28515

BEAUFORT — C5 *Carteret*

BEAUFORT WATERWAY RV PARK
good sam park **Ratings: 7/9★/8.5** (Campground) From jct US 70 & SR-101: Go 15 mi E on SR-101, then 1/2 mi N on Core Creek Road (L) Two-night minimum stay on RV sites. **FAC:** gravel rds. Avail: 22 gravel, patios, 6 pull-thrus, (30x80), back-ins (30x70), 22 full hkups (30/50 amps), cable, WiFi @ sites, rentals, laundry, fire rings, firewood, controlled access. **REC:** Atlantic Intracoastal Waterway: fishing, boating nearby. Pet restrict (Q). Partial handicap access. No tents, Age restrict may apply. Big rig sites, eco-friendly. 2021 rates: $79 to $99, Military discount.
(252)728-4500 Lat: 34.826655, Lon: -76.690256
333 Core Creek Road, Beaufort, NC 28516
Beaufortwaterwayrvpark.com
See ad this page

BELHAVEN — B5 *Beaufort*

RIVERSIDE CAMPGROUND **Ratings: 6.5/9★/8** (Campground) Avail: 50 full hkups (30/50 amps). 2021 rates: $30. (252)945-9012, 272 Riverside Campground Rd, Belhaven, NC 27810

BLOWING ROCK — A1 *Watauga*

BLUE RIDGE PKWY/JULIAN PRICE (Public National Park) From town, S 4 mi on Blue Ridge Pkwy at MP-297 (R). 78 Avail. 2021 rates: $16 to $19. May 08 to Oct 24. (828)963-5911

BOONE — A1 *Watauga*

BOONE KOA **Ratings: 9/10★/9** (Campground) 95 Avail: 76 full hkups, 19 W, 19 E (30/50 amps). 2021 rates: $48 to $75. May 01 to Oct 31. (828)264-7250, 123 Harmony Mtn Ln, Boone, NC 28607

FLINTLOCK CAMPGROUND **Ratings: 7.5/10★/8** (Campground) 88 Avail: 68 full hkups, 20 W, 20 E (30/50 amps). 2021 rates: $40 to $45. Apr 01 to Nov 07. (888)850-9997, 171 Flintlock Campground Dr, Boone, NC 28607

HONEY BEAR CAMPGROUND & NATURE CENTER **Ratings: 4.5/6.5/6.5** (Campground) Avail: 30 full hkups (30/50 amps). 2021 rates: $39 to $43. May 15 to Oct 31. (828)963-4586, 229 Honeybear Campground Rd., Boone, NC 28607

BOONVILLE — A2 *Yadkin*

HOLLY RIDGE FAMILY CAMPGROUND **Ratings: 8/7.5/7.5** (Campground) Avail: 90 full hkups (30/50 amps). 2021 rates: $50. (336)367-7756, 5140 River Rd, Boonville, NC 27011

BOSTIC — B1 *Rutherford*

YOGI BEAR'S JELLYSTONE PARK CAMP RESORT-GOLDEN VALLEY **Ratings: 8.5/9.5★/9.5** (RV Resort) Avail: 126 full hkups (30/50 amps). 2021 rates: $49 to $171. (828)417-0086, 182 Jellystone Pkwy , Bostic, NC 28018

BREVARD — E2 *Transylvania*

ADVENTURE VILLAGE AND LODGINGS **Ratings: 7.5/8/8** (Campground) Avail: 30 full hkups (30/50 amps). 2021 rates: $44.30. (828)862-5411, 15 Adventure Ridge Rd, Brevard, NC 28712

BRYSON CITY — E1 *Swain*

DEEP CREEK TUBE CENTER & CAMPGROUND **Ratings: 7/7.5/9** (Campground) 36 Avail: 32 full hkups, 4 W, 4 E (30/50 amps). 2021 rates: $40 to $58. Apr 01 to Oct 31. (828)488-6055, 1090 W Deep Creek Rd, Bryson City, NC 28713

GREAT SMOKY MTN/DEEP CREEK (Public National Park) From town, N 3 mi on Deep Creek Rd (R). 92 Avail. 2021 rates: $21. Mar 30 to Oct 28. (865)436-1200

Find it fast! Use our alphabetized index of campgrounds and parks.

SAVE! Camping World coupons can be found at the front and back of this Guide!

BRYSON CITY (CONT)

SMOKY MOUNTAIN MEADOWS CAMPGROUND
good sam park
Ratings: 7/8.5★/9 (Campground) 28 Avail: 21 full hkups, 7 W, 7 E (30/50 amps). 2021 rates: $40 to $50. Apr 01 to Oct 31. (828)488-3672, 755 E Alarka Rd, Bryson City, NC 28713

BUXTON — B6 *Dare*

CAPE HATTERAS NATL SEASHORE/CAPE POINT (Public National Park) From town, SW 3 mi on SR-12 (R). 202 Avail. 2021 rates: $20. Mar 30 to Dec 01. (252)473-2111

CANDLER — E2 *Buncombe*

ASHEVILLE WEST KOA **Ratings: 8/9★/8** (Campground) 67 Avail: 42 full hkups, 25 W, 25 E (30/50 amps). 2021 rates: $48.60 to $79.31. (800)562-9015, 309 Wiggins Rd, Candler, NC 28715

CAPE CARTERET — C5 *Onslow*

GOOSE CREEK RESORT
good sam park
Ratings: 8/8★/8.5 (RV Park) 46 Avail: 31 full hkups, 15 W, 15 E (30/50 amps). 2021 rates: $84 to $96. (888)563-7040, 350 Red Barn Rd, Newport, NC 28570

WATERWAY RV PARK
good sam park
Ratings: 8.5/8/7.5 (RV Park) Avail: 10 full hkups (30/50 amps). 2021 rates: $94. (888)563-7040, 850 Cedar Point Blvd, Cedar Point, NC 28584

CAROLINA BEACH — D4 *New Hanover*

CAROLINA BEACH (Public State Park) From Jct of US-421 & Dow Rd, W 0.8 mi on Dow Rd (R). Avail: 9 full hkups. 2021 rates: $15 to $20. (910)458-8206

CHAPEL HILL — B3 *Orange*

SPRING HILL RV PARK
Ratings: 6/NA/9 (RV Park) From Jct of I-40 & NC-54 (Exit 273A), W 3 mi on NC-54 (go under bridge and exit right) continue 3.8 mi to Jones Ferry Rd exit, SW 0.9 mi to Old Greensboro Rd, W 4 mi to Spring Hill Rd, N 0.2 mi on gravel rd along W side of church (E) Note: do not use GPS. **FAC:** all weather rds. (68 spaces). Avail: 20 all weather, 5 pull-thrus, (30x100), back-ins (40x75), accepts full hkup units only, 20 full hkups (30/50 amps), seasonal sites, cable, WiFi @ sites, LP gas. **REC:** playground. Pets OK. No tents. 2021 rates: $50.
(919)967-4268 Lat: 35.89999, Lon: -79.16934
110 Coachmen Road, Chapel Hill, NC 27516
springhillpark.com
See ad page 671

CHARLOTTE — B1 *Mecklenburg*

A SPOTLIGHT Introducing Piedmont's colorful attractions appearing at the front of this state section.

CHARLOTTE See also Fort Mill, SC.

CAMPING WORLD RACING RESORT
good sam park
Ratings: 9/9.5★/8 (Campground) From Jct of I-77 & I-85, N 11 mi on I-85 to Bruton Smith Blvd (Exit 49), E 1.4 mi (L) Note: Entrance at zMax Dragway sign at Charlotte Motor Speedway.

WALK TO CHARLOTTE MOTOR SPEEDWAY
Full-service RV camping area, available for all events held at Charlotte Motor Speedway, zMax Dragway & The Dirt Track. Open all year for daily camping on non-event days. Big Rigs Welcome! Less than 2 miles from I-85!

FAC: paved rds. Avail: 380 all weather, 69 pull-thrus, (30x100), back-ins (30x50), 380 full hkups (30/50 amps), WiFi @ sites, tent sites, dump, laundry, LP bottles, firewood. **REC:** boating nearby, playground. Pets OK. Partial handicap access. Big rig sites. 2021 rates: $30 to $35, Military discount.
(704)455-4445 Lat: 35.35896, Lon: -80.69059
6600 Bruton Smith Blvd, Concord, NC 28027
www.charlottemotorspeedway.com/camping
See ad page 668

You have high expectations, so we point out campgrounds, service centers and tourist attractions with elevations over 2,500 feet.

CAROWINDS CAMP WILDERNESS RESORT **Ratings: 9.5/9★/9** (Campground) Avail: 97 full hkups (30/50 amps). 2021 rates: $48 to $89. (704)587-9116, 14609 Best Day Blvd., Charlotte, NC 28273

MCDOWELL NATURE PRESERVE (Public) From Jct of I-77 & Carowinds Blvd, NW 2 mi on Carowinds Blvd to Hwy 49, S 4 mi (R). 56 Avail: 56 W, 56 E (30/50 amps). 2021 rates: $19 to $33. (980)314-1128

CHEROKEE — E2 *Jackson*

CHEROKEE CAMPGROUND & CRAIG'S LOG CABINS **Ratings: 6.5/7.5/7** (Campground) 22 Avail: 19 full hkups, 3 W, 3 E (30/50 amps). 2021 rates: $35 to $55. May 01 to Oct 15. (828)497-9838, 91 Paintown Rd, Cherokee, NC 28719

CHEROKEE/GREAT SMOKIES KOA (Campground) (Rebuilding) 219 Avail: 171 full hkups, 48 W, 48 E (30/50 amps). 2021 rates: $45.52 to $134.90. (828)497-9711, 92 KOA Kampground Rd, Cherokee, NC 28719

FORT WILDERNESS CAMPGROUND AND RV PARK
good sam park
Ratings: 8.5/7.5/7.5 (Campground) Avail: 77 full hkups (30/50 amps). 2021 rates: $40 to $60. (828)497-9331, 284 Fort Wilderness Rd, Whittier, NC 28789

GREAT SMOKY MTN/BALSAM MOUNTAIN (Public National Park) From town: Go 4 mi N on US 441, 12 mi E on Blue Ridge Pkwy to MP 458, then 8 mi N on Balsam Mtn. Rd. 46 Avail. 2021 rates: $17.50. May 18 to Oct 07. (423)436-1200

GREAT SMOKY MTN/SMOKEMONT (Public National Park) From Jct of US-19 & US-441 (Newfound Gap Rd), N 9 mi on US-441 (R). 142 Avail. 2021 rates: $21 to $25. (828)497-9270

HAPPY HOLIDAY CAMPGROUND
good sam park
Ratings: 9/9★/9 (Campground) 289 Avail: 233 full hkups, 56 W, 56 E (30/50 amps). 2021 rates: $48 to $60. (828)497-9204, 1553 Wolfetown Rd (US-19), Cherokee, NC 28719

RIVER VALLEY CAMPGROUND **Ratings: 6.5/9★/9** (Campground) Avail: 120 full hkups (30/50 amps). 2021 rates: $42 to $44. Apr 01 to Nov 01. (828)497-3540, 2978 Big Cove Rd, Cherokee, NC 28719

TIMBERLAKE CAMPGROUND **Ratings: 6.5/8★/8** (Campground) 44 Avail: 44 W, 35 E (30/50 amps). 2021 rates: $45 to $47. May 01 to Nov 01. (828)497-7320, 3270 Conley's Creek Rd, Whittier, NC 28789

YOGI IN THE SMOKIES **Ratings: 7.5/8.5★/8** (Campground) 115 Avail: 65 full hkups, 50 W, 50 E (30/50 amps). 2021 rates: $45 to $81. Mar 15 to Nov 01. (828)497-9151, 317 Galamore Bridge Rd, Cherokee, NC 28719

CHIMNEY ROCK — E3 *Rutherford*

HICKORY NUT FALLS FAMILY CAMPGROUND **Ratings: 6.5/7/7.5** (Campground) Avail: 15 full hkups (30/50 amps). 2021 rates: $65 to $75. Apr 01 to Nov 30. (828)625-4014, 639 Main St., Chimney Rock, NC 28720

CLEMMONS — A2 *Forsyth*

TANGLEWOOD PARK (Public) From Jct of I-40 & Harper Rd (Exit 182), S 0.3 mi on Harper Rd to Hwy 158 (Clemmons Rd), W 0.3 mi (L). Avail: 44 full hkups (30/50 amps). 2021 rates: $31. Mar 01 to Dec 02. (336)703-6400

COINJOCK — A6 *Currituck*

OUTER BANKS WEST KOA Ratings: 8.5/9.5★/9 (RV Resort) Avail: 152 full hkups (30/50 amps). 2021 rates: $42.72 to $250. Apr 01 to Nov 28. (252)453-2732, 1631 Waterlily Rd, Coinjock, NC 27923

COLFAX — A2 *Forsyth*

Travel Services

CAMPING WORLD OF COLFAX As the nation's largest retailer of RV supplies, accessories, services and new and used RVs, Camping World is committed to making your total RV experience better. **SERVICES:** RV, MH mechanical, staffed RV wash, restrooms. RV Sales. RV supplies, LP gas, dump, RV accessible. Hours: 9am to 7pm.
(888)248-8159 Lat: 36.094589, Lon: -79.997827
8615 Triad Drive, Colfax, NC 27235
www.campingworld.com

CONCORD — B2 *Cabarrus*

Travel Services

CAMPING WORLD OF CONCORD As the nation's largest retailer of RV supplies, accessories, services and new and used RVs, Camping World is committed to making your total RV experience better. **SERVICES:** tire, RV appliance, MH mechanical, restrooms. RV Sales. RV supplies, LP gas, dump, RV accessible. Hours: 9am to 7pm.
(877)784-9173 Lat: 35.36043, Lon: -80.69294
6700 Bruton Smith Blvd, Concord, NC 28027
www.campingworld.com

Things to See and Do

CHARLOTTE MOTOR SPEEDWAY NASCAR, Sprint Cup, Nationwide & Camping World Truck Series Racing. Also Host: Three of the Nation's Largest Car Shows, Stock Car Racing & Driving Schools. Call for available Tours & rates Partial handicap access. RV accessible. Restrooms. Food. Hours: 9am to 5pm. ATM.
(800)455-3267 Lat: 35.35246, Lon: -80.68806
5555 Concord Parkway South, Concord, NC 28027
www.charlottemotorspeedway.com
See ad page 668

DENVER — B1 *Catawba*

CROSS COUNTRY CAMPGROUND **Ratings: 8.5/7.5/8** (Campground) Avail: 160 full hkups (30/50 amps). 2021 rates: $45. (704)483-5897, 6254 Hwy 150 East, Denver, NC 28037

EDENTON — A5 *Chowan*

ROCKY HOCK CAMPGROUND **Ratings: 7/7.5★/8** (Campground) Avail: 11 full hkups (30/50 amps). 2021 rates: $40. (252)221-4695, 1008 David's Red Barn Ln, Edenton, NC 27932

ELIZABETHTOWN — C3 *Bladen*

JONES LAKE (Public State Park) From town, N 4 mi on Hwy 242 (L). 20 Avail: 1 W, 1 E (20 amps). 2021 rates: $15 to $25. (910)588-4550

ELKIN — A1 *Surry*

BYRD'S BRANCH CAMPGROUND & COUNTRY STORE **Ratings: 7/9★/9** (Campground) 14 Avail: 9 full hkups, 5 W, 5 E (30/50 amps). 2021 rates: $35 to $45. (336)366-9955, 225 Martin Byrd Rd, Elkin, NC 28621

ELLERBE — C2 *Richmond*

CAMP HENNING AT ELLERBE SPRINGS **Ratings: 6/NA/9** (RV Park) Avail: 14 full hkups (30/50 amps). 2021 rates: $37. (910)652-5600, 2537 North US Hwy 220, Ellerbe, NC 28338

EMERALD ISLE — C5 *Carteret*

HOLIDAY TRAV-L-PARK RESORT FOR CAMPERS **Ratings: 9.5/10★/9.5** (Campground) 188 Avail: 159 full hkups, 29 W, 29 E (30/50 amps). 2021 rates: $85 to $155. Mar 13 to Nov 30. (252)354-2250, 9102 Coast Guard Rd, Emerald Isle, NC 28594

ENFIELD — A4 *Halifax*

ENFIELD/ROCKY MOUNT KOA **Ratings: 6.5/7.5/8** (Campground) 29 Avail: 17 full hkups, 12 W, 12 E (30/50 amps). 2021 rates: $48 to $59. (252)445-5925, 18562 NC Hwy 481, Enfield, NC 27823

FAYETTEVILLE — C3 *Cumberland*

LAZY ACRES CAMPGROUND **Ratings: 7.5/9.5★/8.5** (RV Park) 64 Avail: 61 full hkups, 3 W, 3 E (30/50 amps). 2021 rates: $46 to $48. (910)425-9218, 821 Lazy Acres St, Fayetteville, NC 28306

MILITARY PARK SMITH LAKE ARMY RV PARK (FORT BRAGG) (Public) From jct of I-95 & Bypass I-295 (exit 58): Go 7 mi on Bypass I-295, then right .025 mi on Ramsey St (Hwy 401), then left 1.5 mi on Andrews Rd, then left 0.25 mi on McArthur Rd, then right 0.5 mi on Honeycutt Rd, then left on Smith Lake Rd. Avail: 30 full hkups (30/50 amps). 2021 rates: $23 to $25. (910)396-5979

FLETCHER — E2 *Henderson*

RUTLEDGE LAKE RV RESORT **Ratings: 10/9.5★/10** (Campground) Avail: 80 full hkups (30/50 amps). 2021 rates: $48 to $60. (828)654-7873, 125 Jillian Trail, Fletcher, NC 28732

FONTANA DAM — E1 *Graham*

FONTANA VILLAGE CAMPGROUND (Public) From jct of NC-143 & NC-28: Go W 12 mi on NC-28, then S .3 mi on Woods Rd (E). 10 Avail: 10 W, 10 E (30 amps). 2021 rates: $30 to $40. Apr 01 to Oct 31. (828)498-2211

FOUR OAKS — B4 *Johnston*

FOUR OAKS LODGING & RV RESORT

good sam park **Ratings: 8/8.5★/8** (Campground) S-bnd: From Jct of I-95 & US 301/701/NC 96 (Exit 90): on exit ramp stay left in break in island on US-301S, go S 0.2 mi (R); or N-bnd: From Jct of I-95 & US-301/701/NC96 (Exit 90): Go W 0.2 mi on US-701 to US-301, then S 0.3 mi (L). **FAC:** all weather rds. (28 spaces). Avail: 18 gravel, 6 pull-thrus, (25x80), back-ins (22x70), 18 full hkups (30/50 amps), seasonal sites, cable, WiFi @ sites, tent sites, rentals, dump, laundry, groc, LP gas, fire rings, firewood. **REC:** playground. Pet restrict (B). Partial handicap access, eco-friendly. 2021 rates: $50, Military discount.
(919)963-3596 Lat: 35.45765, Lon: -78.39428
4606 US Hwy 301 South, Four Oaks, NC 27524
www.fouroaksrvresort.com
See ad page 670

RALEIGH OAKS RV RESORT & COTTAGES

good sam park **Ratings: 10/10★/10** (RV Resort) From Jct of I-95 & US-701 (exit 90), S 0.4 mi on US-701 (L).

TOTALLY RENOVATED RALEIGH LOCATION
Easy I-95 access: NC #90. Near Carolina Premium Outlets. Free waffle breakfast daily, free WiFi & Cable. Playground, Mini-golf, 150 HUGE, level RV sites, 21+ cottages, 2 pools, spa, fitness center & 18 private bath suites.

FAC: all weather rds. (150 spaces). Avail: 58 all weather, 58 pull-thrus, (35x80), 58 full hkups (30/50 amps), seasonal sites, cable, WiFi @ sites, rentals, laundry, LP gas, fire rings, firewood. **REC:** pool, hot tub, boating nearby, playground, hunting nearby. Pets OK. Partial handicap access. No tents. Big rig sites, eco-friendly. 2021 rates: $50 to $73, Military discount.
(919)934-3181 Lat: 35.45131, Lon: -78.38793
527 US Hwy 701S, Four Oaks, NC 27524
raleighoaksrvresort.com
See ad pages 661, 669

FRANKLIN — E1 *Macon*

A SPOTLIGHT Introducing the Great Smoky Mountains of North Carolina's colorful attractions appearing at the front of this state section.

FRANKLIN See also Almond, Bryson City, Cherokee, Lake Toxaway, Sylva & Whittier, NC; Dillard, GA.

CARTOOGECHAYE CREEK CAMPGROUND **Ratings: 5/7.5★/5** (RV Park) Avail: 36 full hkups (30/50 amps). 2021 rates: $32 to $34. Apr 01 to Nov 01. (828)524-8553, 91 No Name Rd, Franklin, NC 28734

CULLASAJA RIVER RV PARK **Ratings: 7.5/9★/7.5** (Campground) Avail: 20 full hkups (30/50 amps). 2021 rates: $35 to $40. (800)843-2795, 6269 Highlands Rd, Franklin, NC 28734

FRANKLIN RV PARK & CAMPGROUND

good sam park **Ratings: 7.5/9.5★/10** (RV Park) Avail: 27 full hkups (30/50 amps). 2021 rates: $52 to $74. Apr 15 to Nov 15. (828)349-6200, 230 Old Addington Bridge Rd, Franklin, NC 28734

OLD CORUNDUM MILLSITE CAMPGROUND **Ratings: 6.5/7/6.5** (Campground) Avail: 25 full hkups (30/50 amps). 2021 rates: $37 to $40. Apr 01 to Oct 31. (828)524-4663, 80 Nickajack Rd, Franklin, NC 28734

PINES RV PARK & CABINS **Ratings: 7/8★/8.5** (Campground) 46 Avail: 35 full hkups, 11 W, 11 E (30/50 amps). 2021 rates: $32 to $38. (828)524-4490, 4724 Murphy Rd, Franklin, NC 28734

THE GREAT OUTDOORS RV RESORT

good sam park **Ratings: 10/10★/10** (RV Park) N-bnd: From Jct of US 64 & US 441/23: Go N 6.2 mi on US 441 to Echo Valley Rd, W 200 ft (R); or S-bnd: From Jct of US 74 & US 23/441 (Exit 81A): Go S 13.8 mi on US 23/441 to Echo Valley Rd, W 200 ft (R). **FAC:** paved rds. Avail: 63 all weather, patios, back-ins (35x60), 63 full hkups (30/50 amps), cable, WiFi @ sites, rentals, laundry, groc, LP gas, fire rings, firewood. **REC:** pool, boating nearby, hunting nearby. Pet restrict (B). Partial handicap access. No tents. Big rig sites, eco-friendly. 2021 rates: $58 to $64, Military discount.
(828)349-0412 Lat: 35.23335, Lon: -83.34779
321 Thumpers Trail, Franklin, NC 28734
gorvresort.com
See ad page 673

FRISCO — B6 *Dare*

CAPE HATTERAS NATL SEASHORE/FRISCO (Public National Park) From center of town on Hwy 12: Go 2 mi E following signs. 127 Avail. 2021 rates: $20. Mar 30 to Dec 01. (252)473-2111

FRISCO WOODS CAMPGROUND

good sam park **Ratings: 8.5/10★/9.5** (Campground) 241 Avail: 202 full hkups, 39 W, 39 E (30/50 amps). 2021 rates: $45 to $84. Mar 01 to Dec 01. (252)995-5208, 53124 Hwy 12, Frisco, NC 27936

GARNER — B3 *Wake*

Travel Services

CAMPING WORLD OF GARNER/RALEIGH As the nation's largest retailer of RV supplies, accessories, services and new and used RVs, Camping World is committed to making your total RV experience better. **SERVICES:** tire, RV appliance, MH mechanical, restrooms. RV Sales. RV supplies, LP gas, RV accessible. Hours: 9am to 7pm.
(888)795-3805 Lat: 35.681296, Lon: -78.532253
2300 US 70 E, Garner, NC 27529
www.campingworld.com

GATESVILLE — A5 *Gates*

MERCHANTS MILLPOND (Public State Park) From town: Go 6 mi NE on Hwy 1403. 20 Avail. 2021 rates: $15 to $25. (252)357-1191

GLENDALE SPRINGS — A1 *Ashe*

RACCOON HOLLER CAMP & RV PARK **Ratings: 7/9★/9** (Campground) 80 Avail: 47 full hkups, 33 W, 33 E (30/50 amps). 2021 rates: $35 to $50. Apr 15 to Oct 28. (336)982-2706, 493 Raccoon Hollow Rd, Jefferson, NC 28640

GOLDSBORO — B4 *Wayne*

CLIFFS OF THE NEUSE (Public State Park) From Jct of US-70 & SR-111, S 8 mi on US-70 to CR-1743 (E). 32 Avail. 2021 rates: $15 to $20. Mar 15 to Nov 30. (919)778-6234

GREENSBORO — A2 *Guilford*

GREENSBORO KOA **Ratings: 9/9★/8** (RV Park) Avail: 55 full hkups (30/50 amps). 2021 rates: $60 to $86. (336)274-4143, 1896 Trox St, Greensboro, NC 27406

HAGAN STONE CITY PARK (Public) From Jct of I-85 & US-421, S 6 mi on US-421 to Hagan-Stone Park Rd, W 2 mi (R). 70 Avail: 70 W, 70 E (30/50 amps). 2021 rates: $25. (336)674-0472

GREENVILLE — B5 *Pitt*

Travel Services

CAMPING WORLD OF GREENVILLE As the nation's largest retailer of RV supplies, accessories, services and new and used RVs, Camping World is committed to making your total RV experience better. **SERVICES:** tire, MH mechanical, sells outdoor gear, sells firearms, staffed RV wash, restrooms. RV Sales. RV supplies, LP gas, dump, emergency parking, RV accessible. Hours: 9am - 7pm.
(844)968-7499 Lat: 35.582484, Lon: -77.379545
111 Red Banks Rd, Greenville, NC 27858
www.campingworld.com

GRIFTON — B4 *Lenoir*

CONTENTNEA CREEKSIDE RV & TRAIL PARK (Public) From Jct of US 264 (E) & NC Hwy 11, S 20 mi on Hwy 11 to S Highland Dr, S 3 mi on Highland Dr (across bridge) to Contentnea Dr, E 0.5 mi (L). Avail: 13 full hkups (20/30 amps). 2021 rates: $10. (252)524-5168

HATTERAS — B6 *Dare*

HATTERAS SANDS CAMPGROUND

good sam park **Ratings: 10/10★/9** (Campground) Avail: 85 full hkups (30/50 amps). 2021 rates: $52.25 to $96.25. Apr 01 to Nov 01. (888)987-2225, 57316 Eagle Pass Rd, Hatteras, NC 27943

HENDERSON — A4 *Vance*

KERR LAKE/BULLOCKSVILLE (Public) From Jct of I-85 & SR-1244 (Manson Exit), NW 2.5 mi on SR-1244 to SR-1366, NW 4 mi (R). 59 Avail: 28 W, 28 E (30 amps). 2021 rates: $15 to $25. Apr 01 to Sep 30. (252)438-7791

KERR LAKE/HENDERSON POINT (Public) From Jct of I-85 & SR-39, N 20 mi on SR-39 to CR-1356, NE 2 mi to CR-1359 (R). Avail: 43 E (30 amps). 2021 rates: $15 to $25. Apr 01 to Sep 30. (252)438-7791

KERR LAKE/HIBERNIA (Public) From Jct of I-85 & SR-39, N 12 mi on SR-39 to CR-1347, NE 4 mi (E). Avail: 46 E (30 amps). 2021 rates: $15 to $25. Apr 01 to Oct 31. (252)438-7791

KERR LAKE/NUTBUSH BRIDGE (Public) From Jct of I-85 & Satterwhite Point Rd (exit 217), W 3 mi on Satterwhite Point Rd to Nutbush Bridge Rd, S 2 mi (R). 79 Avail: 60 W, 60 E (30 amps). 2021 rates: $15 to $25. (252)438-7791

KERR LAKE/SATTERWHITE POINT (Public) From Jct of I-85 & Satterwhite Point Rd, W 4 mi on Satterwhite Point Rd (L). Avail: 63 E (30 amps). 2021 rates: $15 to $25. (252)438-7791

HENDERSONVILLE — E2 *Henderson*

JAYMAR TRAVEL PARK

good sam park **Ratings: 9/10★/9.5** (RV Area in MH Park) From Jct of I-26 & US-64 (exit 49A), E 2.7 mi on US-64 (L). **FAC:** paved rds. (111 spaces). Avail: 36 all weather, patios, 12 pull-thrus, (30x100), back-ins (25x48), 36 full hkups (30/50 amps), seasonal sites, cable, WiFi @ sites, laundry. **REC:** boating nearby, shuffleboard. Pet restrict (Q). No tents, Age restrict may apply. Big rig sites. 2021 rates: $40 to $45. Apr 20 to Nov 05. no cc.
(828)685-3771 Lat: 35.36902, Lon: -82.40796
140 Jaymar Park Dr, Hendersonville, NC 28792
www.jaymartravelpark.com
See ad page 666

NC

LAKEWOOD RV RESORT

good sam park **Ratings: 9.5/10★/10** (RV Park) From Jct of I-26 & Upward Rd (exit 53), E 0.2 mi on Upward Rd (unmarked) to Ballenger Rd (Left), NE 0.2 mi (Right) to main entrance (R).

NC'S 55-PLUS PREMIER RV RESORT
Finally, a community that understands and celebrates the active senior. Located just 30 minutes from Asheville, NC. Come visit us today--your new home away from home in the heart of the beautiful Blue Ridge Mountains.

FAC: paved rds. (78 spaces). Avail: 40 gravel, patios, 26 pull-thrus, (30x75), back-ins (30x60), 40 full hkups (30/50 amps), seasonal sites, cable, WiFi @ sites, rentals, dump, laundry, LP gas. **REC:** heated pool, pond, fishing, boating nearby. Pet restrict (B/Q). Partial handicap access. No tents, Age restrict may apply. Big rig sites, eco-friendly. 2021 rates: $55 to $66, Military discount.
(828)697-9523 Lat: 35.30124, Lon: -82.40148
15 Timmie Ln, Flat Rock, NC 28731
www.lakewoodrvresort.com
See ad page 665

RED GATES RV PARK **Ratings: 7/9★/10** (Campground) Avail: 18 full hkups (30/50 amps). 2021 rates: $45. Apr 01 to Nov 01. (828)685-8787, 148 Red Gates Ln, Hendersonville, NC 28792

TOWN MOUNTAIN TRAVEL PARK

good sam park **Ratings: 7/10★/9** (Campground) Avail: 14 full hkups (30/50 amps). 2021 rates: $45 to $49. (828)697-6692, 48 Town Mountain Rd, Hendersonville, NC 28792

Travel Services

CAMPING WORLD OF HENDERSONVILLE/ASHEVILLE As the nation's largest retailer of RV supplies, accessories, services and new and used RVs, Camping World is committed to making your total RV experience better. **SERVICES:** RV, tire, RV appliance, MH mechanical, sells outdoor gear, staffed RV wash, restrooms. RV Sales. RV supplies, LP gas, dump, RV accessible. Hours: 9am to 7pm.
(888)762-4539 Lat: 35.40494, Lon: -82.51602
2918 North Rugby Rd., Hendersonville, NC 28791
www.campingworld.com

HIGH POINT — B2 *Guilford*

OAK HOLLOW FAMILY CAMPGROUND

(Public) From Jct of I-85 Bus & US 311 Bypass (Exit 66) to Johnson St, S 0.3 mi to Oakview Rd, E 0.4 mi to Centennial St, N 0.1 mi (L). **FAC:** paved/gravel rds. 103 Avail: 60 paved, 43 gravel, back-ins (25x50), 103 full hkups (30/50 amps), cable, WiFi @ sites, tent sites, laundry, controlled access. **REC:** pool, Oak Hollow Lake: fishing, marina, kayaking/canoeing, boating nearby, golf, playground, rec open to public. Pets OK. Partial handicap access, 21 day max stay, eco-friendly. 2021 rates: $45.
(336)883-3492 Lat: 36.00881, Lon: -80.00196
3415 N Centennial St, High Point, NC 27265
www.highpointnc.gov/OakHollowCampground
See ad page 670

HOPE MILLS — C3 *Cumberland*

Travel Services

CAMPING WORLD OF HOPE MILLS/FAYETTEVILLE As the nation's largest retailer of RV supplies, accessories, services and new and used RVs, Camping World is committed to making your total RV experience better. **SERVICES:** tire, RV appliance, MH mechanical, restrooms. RV Sales. RV supplies, LP gas, dump, emergency parking, RV accessible. Hours: 9am - 7pm. (888)409-8312 Lat: 34.947729, Lon: -78.928682 5117 U.S. Hwy 301 S., Hope Mills, NC 28348 www.campingworld.com

HUBERT — C5 *Onslow*

DEEP CREEK RV RESORT & CAMPGROUND **Ratings: 9/9.5★/9.5** (RV Park) From jct Hwy 172 & Hwy 24: Go E 1 1/2 miles on Hwy 24, then S 1/4 mi on Waterfront Rd (L). **FAC:** paved/gravel rds. (98 spaces). Avail: 20 gravel, 13 pull-thrus, (40x70), back-ins (40x70), 20 full hkups (30/50 amps), seasonal sites, WiFi @ sites, tent sites, laundry, groc, LP bottles, controlled access. **REC:** pool, Queens Creek: fishing, kayaking/canoeing, boating nearby, shuffleboard, hunting nearby. Pet restrict (B). Partial handicap access, Age restrict may apply. Big rig sites, eco-friendly. 2021 rates: $50, Military discount.
(910)330-9333 Lat: 34.712962, Lon: -77.211342
181 Waterfront Road, Hubert, NC 28539
deepcreekrvresort.com
See ad page 674

HAWKINS CREEK CAMPGROUND **Ratings: 6.5/8★/9** (Campground) Avail: 20 full hkups (30/50 amps). 2021 rates: $35. (910)340-4131, 252 Reid Acres Ln, Hubert, NC 28539

JACKSONVILLE — C5 *Onslow*

CABIN CREEK CAMPGROUND AND MOBILE HOME PARK **Ratings: 7/8.5★/8** (Campground) Avail: 30 full hkups (30/50 amps). 2021 rates: $32.50 to $39. (910)346-4808, 3200 Wilmington Hwy, Jacksonville, NC 28540

MILITARY PARK ONSLOW BEACH CAMPSITES & RECREATION AREA (CAMP LEJEUNE MCB) (Public) From jct US-17 & Hwy 24, E to main gate, S 5 mi on Holcomb blvd to Sneads Ferry Rd, left 6 mi to Beach Rd (L). Avail: 38 full hkups (30/50 amps). 2021 rates: $37. Apr 01 to Nov 01. (910)440-7502

JONESVILLE — A1 *Yadkin*

HOMETOWN RV PARK **Ratings: 7/9★/8** (RV Park) Avail: 57 full hkups (30/50 amps). 2021 rates: $55 to $65. Feb 01 to Nov 30. (336)258-2138, 100 Dwayne St, Jonesville, NC 28642

KILL DEVIL HILLS — A6 *Dare*

OBX CAMPGROUND **Ratings: 6.5/9.5★/9.5** (RV Park) Avail: 50 full hkups (30/50 amps). 2021 rates: $50 to $70. (252)564-4741, 126 Marshy Ridge Rd., Kill Devil Hills, NC 27948

KINSTON — B4 *Lenoir*

NEUSEWAY NATURE PARK & CAMPGROUND (Public) From Jct of US 70 & NC 11, NE 1 mi on NC 11, 0.1 mi on River Bank Rd (L). Avail: 32 full hkups (30/50 amps). 2021 rates: $15. (252)939-3367

LAKE LURE — E3 *Rutherford*

RIVER CREEK CAMPGROUND **Ratings: 5/6.5/7** (Campground) 10 Avail: 9 full hkups, 1 W, 1 E (30/50 amps). 2021 rates: $35. Feb 01 to Nov 15. (828)287-3915, 217 River Creek Dr, Rutherfordton, NC 28139

LAKE TOXAWAY — E2 *Transylvania*

MOUNTAIN FALLS LUXURY MOTORCOACH RESORT **Ratings: 10/10★/10** (Condo Park) Avail: 107 full hkups (30/50 amps). 2021 rates: $125 to $170. (828)966-9350, 20 Resorts Blvd, Lake Toxaway, NC 28747

RIVERBEND RV PARK **Ratings: 8/9★/9** (RV Park) Avail: 21 full hkups (30/50 amps). 2021 rates: $55. (828)966-4214, Hwy 281 N, 1400 Blue Ridge Rd 1, Lake Toxaway, NC 28747

LENOIR — B1 *Caldwell*

GREEN MOUNTAIN PARK RESORT **Ratings: 8/6.5/8.5** (Membership Park) Avail: 220 full hkups (30/50 amps). 2021 rates: $81 to $95. Apr 01 to Nov 15. (888)563-7040, 2495 Dimmette Rd, Lenoir, NC 28645

LEXINGTON — B2 *Davidson*

CROSS WINDS FAMILY CAMPGROUND Ratings: 9.5/9.5★/9.5 (Campground) Avail: 96 full hkups (30/50 amps). 2021 rates: $45 to $48. (336)853-4567, 160 Campground Ln, Linwood, NC 27299

HIGH ROCK LAKE/MARINA & CAMPGROUND **Ratings: 8/7.5/7.5** (RV Park) Avail: 26 full hkups (30/50 amps). 2021 rates: $50. (336)798-1196, 1013 Wafford Circle, Lexington, NC 27292

LINVILLE FALLS — D3 *Burke*

BLUE RIDGE PKWY/LINVILLE FALLS (Public National Park) From Jct of US-40 & US-221, N 20 mi on US-221 to Blue Ridge Pkwy, N 1 mi at MP-316.3 (R). 20 Avail. 2021 rates: $16 to $19. May 08 to Oct 24. (828)298-5330

LINVILLE FALLS CAMPGROUND, RV PARK & CABINS **Ratings: 7/10★/9** (Campground) Avail: 14 full hkups (30/50 amps). 2021 rates: $40 to $50. Apr 15 to Nov 15. (828)765-2681, 717 Gurney Franklin Rd, Linville Falls, NC 28647

LITTLE SWITZERLAND — D3 *McDowell*

BLUE RIDGE PKWY/CRABTREE FALLS (Public National Park) From Jct of I-40 & SR-221, N 11 mi on SR-221 to SR-226, NW 7 mi to Parkway Rd, S 8 mi at MP-339.5 (R). 22 Avail. 2021 rates: $16. May 01 to Oct 31. (828)271-4779

LITTLETON — A4 *Warren*

LAKE GASTON RV & CAMPING RESORT **Ratings: 7/6.5/8.5** (Membership Park) 7 Avail: 4 full hkups, 3 W, 3 E (30/50 amps). 2021 rates: $64 to $74. Apr 01 to Nov 01. (888)563-7040, 561 Fleming Dairy Rd, Littleton, NC 27850

LUMBERTON — C3 *Robeson*

LUMBERTON/I-95 KOA JOURNEY **Ratings: 8.5/9★/7.5** (Campground) Avail: 75 full hkups (30/50 amps). 2021 rates: $58.88 to $67.88. (910)739-4372, 465 Kenric Rd, Lumberton, NC 28360

MAGGIE VALLEY — E2 *Haywood*

STONEBRIDGE RV RESORT **Ratings: 9/9.5★/8.5** (RV Park) From W Jct of I-40 & US-276 (Exit 20), S 5.5 mi on US-276 (Jonathan Creek Rd) to US-19, W 1.7 mi (R). Elev 3200 ft. **FAC:** paved/gravel rds. (230 spaces). 130 Avail: 100 gravel, 30 grass, 85 pull-thrus, (25x60), back-ins (20x50), 130 full hkups (30/50 amps), seasonal sites, cable, WiFi @ sites, tent sites, rentals, laundry, groc, LP gas, fire rings, firewood. **REC:** pool, Johnathan Creek: fishing, boating nearby, playground. Pet restrict (B). Partial handicap access. Big rig sites, eco-friendly. 2021 rates: $50 to $65, Military discount. ATM.
(828)926-1904 Lat: 35.51754, Lon: -83.05923
1786 Soco Rd, Maggie Valley, NC 28751
www.stonebridgecampgrounds.com
See ad page 673

MANTEO — A6 *Dare*

THE REFUGE ON ROANOKE ISLAND **Ratings: 6/9★/9** (RV Park) Avail: 15 full hkups (30/50 amps). 2021 rates: $50 to $70. (252)473-1096, 2881 NC Hwy 345, Wanchese, NC 27981

MARBLE — E1 *Cherokee*

PEACHTREE COVE RV PARK **Ratings: 8/9.5★/9.5** (RV Park) 26 Avail: 19 full hkups, 7 W, 7 E (30/50 amps). 2021 rates: $45 to $60. (828)557-2722, 68 Old Peachtree Rd, Marble, NC 28905

VALLEY RIVER RV RESORT **Ratings: 10/10★/10** (RV Park) Jct US-64 & US-19/US-74, N 3.2 on US-19/US-74 then left on Regal Rd (R). **FAC:** paved rds. (93 spaces). Avail: 68 paved, patios, 25 pull-thrus, (40x65), back-ins (40x60), 68 full hkups (30/50 amps), seasonal sites, cable, WiFi @ sites, laundry, LP gas, fire rings, firewood. **REC:** pool, pond, fishing, boating nearby. Pet restrict (Q). Partial handicap access. No tents. Big rig sites, eco-friendly. 2021 rates: $40 to $60, Military discount.
(828)385-4220 Lat: 35.12161, Lon: -84.00114
65 Old Tomotla Road, Marble, NC 28905
www.valleyriverrv.com
See ad page 672

Making campground reservations? Remember to ask about the cancellation policy when making your reservation.

MARION — D3 *McDowell*

BUCK CREEK RV PARK **Ratings: 9.5/9★/10** (RV Park) From Jct of I-40 & NC-226 (exit 86), NW 6 mi on NC 226/US 221 to US-70, W 1.8 mi to NC-80, N 1.9 mi to Tom's Creek Rd, E .01 mi (L).

FRIENDLY PARK NEAR BLUE RIDGE PKWY
So Much to Explore Nearby - Linville Falls, Blue Ridge Parkway, Biltmore House - all within easy drives. Then come home & cool off in our Swimming Holes, walk our trails, relax in a shady site or sun in our open meadows.

FAC: all weather rds. (74 spaces). Avail: 40 all weather, 5 pull-thrus, (30x62), back-ins (30x60), 40 full hkups (30/50 amps), seasonal sites, cable, WiFi @ sites, laundry, fire rings, firewood. **REC:** Buck Creek: swim, fishing, boating nearby. Pets OK. No tents. Big rig sites, eco-friendly. 2021 rates: $54 to $73, Military discount. Apr 01 to Nov 01.
(828)724-4888 Lat: 35.71869, Lon: -82.07405
2576 Tom's Creek Rd, Marion, NC 28752
buckcreekrvparknc.com
See ad page 673

HIDDEN CREEK CAMPING RESORT **Ratings: 7.5/8.5/8.5** (Campground) Avail: 37 full hkups (30/50 amps). 2021 rates: $57 to $68. (828)652-7208, 1210 Deacon Dr, Marion, NC 28752

LAKE JAMES (Public State Park) From town: Go 5 mi NE on Hwy 126. 33 Avail. 2021 rates: $15 to $20. Mar 01 to Nov 30. (828)584-7728

MOUNTAIN STREAM RV PARK **Ratings: 7/9★/10** (RV Park) Avail: 27 full hkups (30/50 amps). 2021 rates: $50 to $69. Feb 05 to Dec 01. (828)724-9013, 6954 Buck Creek Rd, Marion, NC 28752

TOM JOHNSON CAMPING WORLD'S MOUNTAIN RESORT **Ratings: 7.5/8.5★/8.5** (RV Park) Avail: 347 full hkups (30/50 amps). 2021 rates: $40 to $55. (800)225-7802, 348 Resistoflex Rd, Marion, NC 28752

Travel Services

TOM JOHNSON CAMPING Located at the foot of the Blue Ridge Mountains, Tom Johnson's offers folding trailers to luxury coaches along with a large RV service center. **SERVICES:** tire, RV appliance, MH mechanical, staffed RV wash, restrooms. RV Sales. RV supplies, LP gas, dump, emergency parking, RV accessible. Hours: 9am to 6pm. (877)958-4264 Lat: 35.69128, Lon: -82.05900 1885 US Hwy 70 W, Marion, NC 28752 www.campingworld.com

MEBANE — A3 *Alamance*

JONES STATION RV PARK **Ratings: 7.5/9.5★/10** (RV Park) Avail: 21 full hkups (30/50 amps). 2021 rates: $45. (919)568-0153, 2710 Jones Dr., Mebane, NC 27302

Travel Services

SOUTHSIDE STORAGE RV storage in Mebane, NC, convenient to Greensboro, Durham, Chapel Hill and all towns in between. Amenities include 51 spaces with power, 31 without, plus a power station, water fill station and air compressor. Coded 24-hour access. **RV Storage:** outdoor, secured fencing, electric gate, easy reach keypad, 24/7 access, well-lit facility, well-lit roads, well-lit perimeter, security cameras, level gravel/paved spaces, power to charge battery, water, compressed air, office. **SERVICES:**. Hours: 24 hours. Special offers available for Good Sam Members (336)269-8277 Lat: 36.083162, Lon: -79.315153 805 Gibson Rd, Mebane, NC 27302 sssnc.com

MICAVILLE — D3 *Yancey*

PATIENCE PARK/TOE RIVER (Public) From Jct of Hwys 19E & 80S, S 4 mi on Hwy 80 to Blue Rock Rd, E 2 mi (L). 86 Avail: 86 W, 65 S, 86 E (20/30 amps). 2021 rates: $30 to $40. Apr 01 to Oct 31. (828)675-5104

MOCKSVILLE — B2 *Davie*

LAKE MYERS RV & CAMPING RESORT **Ratings: 8/5.5/7.5** (RV Park) 144 Avail: 75 full hkups, 69 W, 69 E (20/30 amps). 2021 rates: $67 to $88. (888)563-7040, 2862 US 64 West, Mocksville, NC 27028

Replace clogged air filters. A clogged air filter can cut a vehicle's fuel efficiency by 10 percent.

MONROE — C2 *Union*

CANE CREEK PARK/UNION COUNTY (Public) From Jct of US-74 & Hwy 200 (Skyway Dr in Monroe), S 12.8 mi on Hwy 200 to Potter Rd, E 3.2 mi to Cane Creek Rd, S 1.6 mi (E). 108 Avail: 49 full hkups, 59 W, 49 S, 59 E (30 amps). 2021 rates: $18.75 to $30. (704)283-3885

MOREHEAD CITY — C5 *Carteret*

WATERS EDGE RV PARK **Ratings: 6/9.5★/8** (Campground) Avail: 42 full hkups (30/50 amps). 2021 rates: $70. (252)247-0494, 1463 Hwy 24, Newport, NC 28570

WHISPERING PINES RV PARK
good sam park
Ratings: 8/9.5★/8 (RV Park) Avail: 75 full hkups (30/50 amps). 2021 rates: $63 to $73. (888)563-7040, 25 Whispering Pines, Newport, NC 28570

MORGANTON — B1 *Burke*

RIVERSIDE GOLF & RV PARK
good sam park
Ratings: 6/NA/6 (Campground) Avail: 15 full hkups (30/50 amps). 2021 rates: $45. (828)433-6464, 611 Independence Blvd, Morganton, NC 28655

STEELE CREEK PARK **Ratings: 7.5/6.5/7.5** (Campground) Avail: 190 full hkups (30/50 amps). 2021 rates: $40 to $50. Apr 01 to Oct 31. (828)433-5660, 7081 NC-181 N, Morganton, NC 28655

MOUNT AIRY — A2 *Surry*

BEECHNUT FAMILY CAMPGROUND **Ratings: 6.5/8/8.5** (Campground) 33 Avail: 19 full hkups, 14 W, 14 E (30/50 amps). 2021 rates: $45 to $50. Apr 01 to Oct 31. (336)504-5012, 315 Beechnut Lane, Mount Airy, NC 27030

MAYBERRY CAMPGROUND
good sam park
Ratings: 9/8.5★/9 (Campground) From Jct of I-74 & Hwy 601 (Exit 11) SW 0.3 mi on Hwy 601 to South McKinney Road, SE 0.3 mi to Rustic Village Trail, NE 0.2 mi (E). **FAC:** all weather rds. (138 spaces). Avail: 118 all weather, 53 pull-thrus, (32x73), back-ins (30x60), 118 full hkups (30/50 amps), seasonal sites, cable, WiFi @ sites, tent sites, laundry, firewood. **REC:** pond, fishing, playground, hunting nearby. Pets OK. Partial handicap access. Big rig sites, eco-friendly. 2021 rates: $40, Military discount.
(336)789-6199 Lat: 36.45433, Lon: -80.63666
114 Byron Bunker Lane, Mount Airy, NC 27030
www.mayberrycampground.com
See ad page 670

VETERAN'S MEMORIAL PARK **Ratings: 2/NA/4** (Campground) 62 Avail: 50 full hkups, 6 W, 12 E (30/50 amps). 2021 rates: $35. (336)786-2236, 691 W. Lebanon Street, Mount Airy, NC 27030

MURPHY — E1 *Cherokee*

MURPHY/PEACE VALLEY KOA **Ratings: 8.5/8.5★/8** (Campground) 58 Avail: 49 full hkups, 9 W, 9 E (30/50 amps). 2021 rates: $38 to $54. (828)837-6223, 117 Happy Valley Rd, Marble, NC 28905

RIVERS EDGE MOUNTAIN RV RESORT **Ratings: 5.5/8/8.5** (Condo Park) Avail: 19 full hkups (30/50 amps). 2021 rates: $49 to $69. (828)361-4517, 1750 Hilltop Rd, Murphy, NC 28906

NAGS HEAD — A6 *Dare*

CAPE HATTERAS NATL SEASHORE/OREGON INLET (Public National Park) From town, S 10 mi on Hwy 12 (L). 120 Avail. 2021 rates: $28. Mar 30 to Dec 01. (252)473-2111

NEW BERN — C5 *Craven*

NEW BERN KOA **Ratings: 9.5/9.5★/9.5** (Campground) 84 Avail: 80 full hkups, 4 W, 4 E (30/50 amps). 2021 rates: $55 to $135. (800)562-3341, 1565 B St, New Bern, NC 28560

NEWLAND — D3 *Avery*

MOUNTAIN RIVER FAMILY CAMPGROUND **Ratings: 7.5/9.5★/10** (Campground) Avail: 48 full hkups (30/50 amps). 2021 rates: $54 to $65. Apr 01 to Oct 30. (828)765-4810, 8555 South US Hwy 19E, Newland, NC 28657

NORLINA — A4 *Warren*

KERR LAKE/COUNTY LINE (Public) From Jct of I-85 & SR-1244 (Manson exit), NW 6 mi on SR-1244 to SR-1200, N 3 mi to SR-1203, NW 3 mi (E). Avail: 36 E (30 amps). 2021 rates: $15 to $25. Apr 01 to Sep 30. (252)438-7791

KERR LAKE/KIMBALL POINT (Public) From Jct of I-85 & SR-1244, (Manson Exit), NW 6 mi on SR-1244 to SR-1200, N 5 mi to SR-1204, NW 2 mi (E). Avail: 47 E (30 amps). 2021 rates: $15 to $25. Apr 01 to Oct 31. (252)438-7791

OCRACOKE — B6 *Hyde*

CAPE HATTERAS NATL SEASHORE/OCRACOKE (Public National Park) From town, E 3 mi on Hwy 12 (R). 136 Avail. 2021 rates: $28. Mar 30 to Dec 01. (252)473-2111

OUTER BANKS — B6 *Dare*

A SPOTLIGHT Introducing Outer Banks' colorful attractions appearing at the front of this state section.

OUTER BANKS See also Buxton, Frisco, Hatteras, Kill Devil Hills, Manteo & Rodanthe.

PINEOLA — D3 *Avery*

DOWN BY THE RIVER CAMPGROUND **Ratings: 8.5/8.5★/9.5** (Campground) Avail: 29 full hkups (30/50 amps). 2021 rates: $38 to $59. May 01 to Oct 31. (828)733-5057, 292 River Campground Rd, Pineola, NC 28662

PINK HILL — C4 *Duplin*

CABIN LAKE COUNTY PARK (Public) From the Jct of NC 41 and NC 111 (Beulaville), N 4.5 mi on NC 111 to Cabin Lake Rd, E 0.7 mi on Cabin Lake Rd (R). 13 Avail: 13 W, 13 E (20/30 amps). 2021 rates: $25. (910)298-3648

PINNACLE — A2 *Surry*

GREYSTONE RV PARK
good sam park
Ratings: 8.5/10★/10 (RV Park) Avail: 10 full hkups (30/50 amps). 2021 rates: $72. (336)368-5588, 1164 Pilot Knob Park Rd, Pinnacle, NC 27043

PILOT MOUNTAIN (Public State Park) From Winston-Salem, N 24 mi on US-52 (R). 49 Avail. 2021 rates: $15 to $25. Mar 15 to Nov 30. (336)325-2355

PISGAH FOREST — E2 *Transylvania*

LAND OF WATERFALLS RV PARK **Ratings: 5.5/NA/9.5** (RV Park) Avail: 11 full hkups (30/50 amps). 2021 rates: $50 to $60. (828)270-3539, 15 La Salle Drive, Pisgah Forest, NC 28768

RALEIGH — B3 *Durham*

RALEIGH See also Four Oaks.

FALLS LAKE/HOLLY POINT (Public State Park) From jct Hwy 50 & Hwy 98: Go 1/2 mi E on Hwy 98, then N on Ghoston Rd, then N on New Light Rd. (E). 153 Avail: 89 W, 89 E. 2021 rates: $15 to $25. (919)676-1027

FALLS LAKE/ROLLINGVIEW (Public) From Jct of Hwy 50 & Hwy 98, W 7 mi on Hwy 98 to Baptist Rd, N 3 mi (E). 80 Avail: 80 W, 80 E (15/30 amps). 2021 rates: $15 to $25. (919)676-1027

NORTH CAROLINA STATE FAIRGROUNDS (Public) From Jct of I-40 & Wade Ave (Exit 289), E 2 mi on Wade Ave to Blue Ridge Rd, S 0.5 mi to Trinity Rd, W 0.5 mi to Youth Center Dr, S 0.1 mi (R). Avail: 300 full hkups (30/50 amps). 2021 rates: $30 to $35. Nov 01 to Sep 01. (919)612-6767

WILLIAM B UMSTEAD (Public State Park) From town, NW 6 mi on US-70 (R). 28 Avail. 2021 rates: $15 to $25. Mar 15 to Dec 01. (919)571-4170

REIDSVILLE — A2 *Rockingham*

LAKE REIDSVILLE PARK (Public) From Jct of US 29N & US 29 Business, N 3 mi on US 29 Business to Waterworks Rd, W 1 mi (L). 74 Avail: 28 full hkups, 46 W, 46 E (30/50 amps). 2021 rates: $13 to $20. (336)349-4738

ROANOKE RAPIDS — A4 *Halifax*

THE RV RESORT AT CAROLINA CROSSROADS
good sam park
Ratings: 9.5/10★/9.5 (RV Park) From Jct of I-95 & Hwy 125 (exit 171), S 0.2 mi on Hwy 125 to Carolina Crossroads Blvd, (main entrance to Carolina Crossroads), N 0.9 mi (R). **FAC:** all weather rds. (84 spaces). Avail: 54 paved, patios, 54 pull-thrus, (44x65), 54 full hkups (30/50 amps), seasonal sites, cable, WiFi @ sites, rentals, dump, laundry, LP gas. **REC:** heated pool, hot tub, boating nearby, playground, hunting nearby. Pets OK. Partial handicap access. No tents. Big rig sites, eco-friendly. 2021 rates: $50, Military discount.
(252)538-9776 Lat: 36.40351, Lon: -77.63116
415 Wallace Fork Rd, Roanoke Rapids, NC 27870
033b649.netsolhost.com
See ad page 669

ROARING GAP — A1 *Alleghany*

STONE MOUNTAIN (Public State Park) From jct US 21 & Hwy 1002: Go 7 mi SW on Hwy 1002 to John P. Frank Pkwy. 90 Avail: 41 W, 41 E. 2021 rates: $15 to $25. (336)957-8185

ROBBINSVILLE — E1 *Graham*

STECOAH VALLEY RV RESORT
good sam park
Ratings: 7/NA/8.5 (RV Park) Avail: 31 full hkups (30/50 amps). 2021 rates: $45. May 01 to Oct 31. (239)707-3469, 415 Hyde Town Rd, Robbinsville, NC 28771

RODANTHE — B6 *Dare*

CAMP HATTERAS RV RESORT & CAMPGROUND
good sam park
Ratings: 10/9.5★/9.5 (RV Park) S-bnd: From Jct of US-158/64/264 & NC-12, S 24.7 mi on NC-12 (L); or N-bnd: From Jct of Ocracoke/Hatteras Ferry & NC-12, N 34.3 mi on NC-12 (R) (Mile Post 40.5). **FAC:** paved rds. Avail: 403 paved, patios, 12 pull-thrus, (30x60), back-ins (32x60), 403 full hkups (30/50 amps), cable, WiFi @ sites, tent sites, rentals, laundry, groc, LP gas, firewood, controlled access. **REC:** heated pool, wading pool, hot tub, Atlantic Ocean: swim, fishing, kayaking/canoeing, boating nearby, shuffleboard, playground. Pets OK $. Partial handicap access. Big rig sites, eco-friendly. 2021 rates: $49 to $151, Military discount.
(252)987-2777 Lat: 35.57815, Lon: -75.46606
24798 Hwy 12, Mile Post 40.5, Rodanthe, NC 27968
www.camphatteras.com
See ad pages 661, 667

CAPE HATTERAS KOA **Ratings: 8/9/8.5** (Campground) 268 Avail: 104 full hkups, 139 W, 139 E (30/50 amps). 2021 rates: $90 to $220. (252)987-2307, 25099 NC Hwy 12, Rodanthe, NC 27968

OCEAN WAVES CAMPGROUND
Ratings: 9/9★/9 (Campground) S-bnd: From Jct US-158/164/264 & NC-12: Go 25-1/4 mi S on NC-12, in Waves (L); or N-bnd: From Okracoke/Hatteras Ferry: Go 33-3/4 mi N on NC-12 (R). **FAC:** paved rds. Avail: 68 paved, back-ins (32x65), 68 full hkups (30/50 amps), cable, WiFi @ sites, tent sites, laundry, groc. **REC:** pool, Atlantic Ocean: swim, fishing, kayaking/canoeing, boating nearby, playground. Pets OK. Partial handicap access. Big rig sites, eco-friendly. 2021 rates: $62 to $67. Mar 15 to Nov 15.
(252)987-2556 Lat: 35.57164, Lon: -75.46723
25313 Hwy 12, Rodanthe, NC 27982
www.oceanwavescampground.com
See ad page 668

ST CLAIR LANDING CAMPGROUND **Ratings: 4/7/7.5** (Campground) 23 Avail: 6 full hkups, 17 W, 17 E (30 amps). 2021 rates: $50 to $60. Apr 01 to Dec 01. (252)987-2850, 25028 Hwy NC 12, Rodanthe, NC 27968

RUTHERFORDTON — E3 *Rutherford*

4 PAWS KINGDOM CAMPGROUND & DOG RETREAT **Ratings: 8.5/9.5★/10** (RV Park) Avail: 40 full hkups (30/50 amps). 2021 rates: $40 to $118. Mar 15 to Dec 01. (828)287-7324, 335 Lazy Creek Dr, Rutherfordton, NC 28139

SALISBURY — B2 *Rowan*

CAROLINA ROSE CAMPGROUND **Ratings: 8.5/7/7.5** (Campground) 69 Avail: 46 full hkups, 23 W, 23 E (30/50 amps). 2021 rates: $50. (704)633-7301, 185 Jim Neely Dr. (Hwy 601 N), Salisbury, NC 28144

DAN NICHOLAS PARK (Public) From I-85 (exit 79), follow signs (L) ; or From I-85 (exit 75), follow signs (L). 70 Avail: 67 W, 67 E (30/50 amps). 2021 rates: $17 to $24. (704)216-7803

SALUDA — E2 *Henderson*

ORCHARD LAKE CAMPGROUND **Ratings: 7.5/8/8.5** (Campground) Avail: 53 full hkups (30/50 amps). 2021 rates: $50. Apr 01 to Nov 01. (828)749-3901, 460 Orchard Lake Rd, Saluda, NC 28773

SEALEVEL — C5 *Carteret*

CEDAR CREEK CAMPGROUND & MARINA **Ratings: 7/6/6** (Campground) 16 Avail: 16 W, 16 E (30 amps). 2021 rates: $40 to $45. Apr 01 to Nov 30. (252)225-9571, 111 Canal Dr, Sealevel, NC 28577

SELMA — B4 *Johnston*

NORTHPOINTE RV RESORT **Ratings: 9.5/10★/9** (RV Park) 72 Avail: 67 full hkups, 5 W, 5 E (30/50 amps). 2021 rates: $33 to $55. (919)965-5923, 428 Campground Rd, Selma, NC 27576

SHALLOTTE — D4 *Brunswick*

SHALLOTTE See also Sunset Beach & Tabor City, NC; Longs & Myrtle Beach, SC.

S & W CAMPGROUND Ratings: 6/NA/8.5 (Campground) Avail: 5 full hkups (30/50 amps). 2021 rates: $45 to $55. (910)754-8576, 532 Holden Beach Rd SW, Shallotte, NC 28470

SHAWBORO — A6 *Currituck*

SHAWBORO See also Coinjock & Shiloh, NC; Virginia Beach, VA.

SHILOH — A6 *Camden*

NORTH RIVER CAMPGROUND **Ratings: 10/9★/9** (Campground) Avail: 70 full hkups (30/50 amps). 2021 rates: $50. (252)336-4414, 256 Garrington Island Rd, Shawboro, NC 27973

SMITHFIELD — B4 *Johnston*

SMITHFIELD See also Four Oaks & Selma.

HIDDEN HAVEN RV PARK (RV Park) (Too New to Rate) Avail: 144 full hkups (30/50 amps). 2021 rates: $50. (919)965-3131, 3241 Hwy 70 East, Smithfield, NC 27576

SNEADS FERRY — C5 *Onslow*

SEAHAVEN MARINE RV PARK **Ratings: 4.5/NA/7** (RV Park) Avail: 42 full hkups (30/50 amps). 2021 rates: $60 to $80. (910)333-5773, 148 Old Ferry Road, Sneads Ferry, NC 28460

SNOW CAMP — B3 *Alamance*

CANE CREEK CAMPGROUND & RV PARK **Ratings: 4.5/NA/8.5** (Campground) 45 Avail: 18 full hkups, 27 W, 27 E (30/50 amps), Pit toilets. 2021 rates: $30 to $35. (336)376-8324, 1256 Longest Acre Rd, Snow Camp, NC 27349

SPARTA — A1 *Alleghany*

BLUE RIDGE PKWY/DOUGHTON PARK (Public National Park) From Jct of SR-18 & Blue Ridge Pkwy, N 8 mi on Blue Ridge Pkwy at MP-239 (E). 25 Avail. 2021 rates: $16. May 01 to Oct 31. (336)372-8877

SPRUCE PINE — D3 *Avery*

BEAR DEN FAMILY CAMPGROUND AND CREEKSIDE CABINS **Ratings: 8/9★/9** (Campground) 71 Avail: 67 full hkups, 4 W, 4 E (30/50 amps). 2021 rates: $49 to $57. Mar 15 to Nov 30. (828)765-2888, 600 Bear Den Mtn Rd, Spruce Pine, NC 28777

STATESVILLE — B1 *Iredell*

LAKE NORMAN (Public State Park) From town: Go 10 mi S on Hwy 1569. 33 Avail. 2021 rates: $15 to $20. Mar 15 to Nov 30. (704)528-6350

MIDWAY CAMPGROUND & RV RESORT
Ratings: 9.5/9.5★/9.5 (Campground) E-bnd: From Jct of I-77 & I-40: Go E 9.6 mi on I-40 to Exit 162/Cool Springs/US-64, W 0.1 mi on US-64 to Campground Rd, then E 0.2 mi (L); or W-bnd: From Jct of I-40 & Exit 162/Cool Springs/US-64: Go W 0.2 mi on US-64 to Campground Rd, then E 0.2 mi (L). **FAC:** all weather rds. (59 spaces). Avail: 37 gravel, patios, 28 pull-thrus, (30x60), back-ins (30x50), 31 full hkups, 6 W, 6 E (30/50 amps), seasonal sites, cable, WiFi @ sites, tent sites, rentals, dump, laundry, groc, LP gas, fire rings, firewood, controlled access. **REC:** pool, pond, fishing, boating nearby, playground, rec open to public. Pet restrict (B). Big rig sites. 2021 rates: $50 to $60, Military discount. ATM.
(704)546-7615 Lat: 35.86609, Lon: -80.70650
114 Midway Dr, Statesville, NC 28625
www.midwaycampground.com
See ad page 671

Travel Services

GANDER RV OF STATESVILLE Your new hometown outfitter offering the best regional gear for all your outdoor needs. Your adventure awaits. **SERVICES:** RV, tire, RV appliance, MH mechanical, sells outdoor gear, staffed RV wash, restrooms. RV Sales. RV supplies, LP gas, dump, RV accessible. Hours: 9am to 7pm.
(877)874-4502 Lat: 35.766688, Lon: -80.860638
1220 Morland Drive, Statesville, NC 28677
rv.ganderoutdoors.com

STELLA — C5 *Cataret*

WHITE OAK SHORES CAMPING & RV RESORT
Ratings: 7/9★/9.5 (Campground) 100 Avail: 75 full hkups, 25 W, 25 E (30/50 amps). 2021 rates: $65 to $92. (888)563-7040, 400 Wetherington Landing Rd, Stella, NC 28582

STONEVILLE — A2 *Rockingham*

DAN RIVER CAMPGROUND AND RIVER ADVENTURES **Ratings: 9/8.5★/9** (Campground) 36 Avail: 28 full hkups, 8 W, 8 E (30/50 amps). 2021 rates: $41 to $51. (336)427-8530, 724 Webster Rd, Stoneville, NC 27048

SUNSET BEACH — D4 *Brunswick*

BRUNSWICK BEACHES CAMPING RESORT **Ratings: 8/9★/8.5** (Campground) 56 Avail: 43 full hkups, 13 W, 13 E (30/50 amps). 2021 rates: $50 to $65. (855)579-2267, 7200 KOA Dr, Sunset Beach, NC 28468

SURF CITY — C4 *Pender*

A SPOTLIGHT Introducing The South Coast's colorful attractions appearing at the front of this state section.

SURF CITY See also Hubert, Jacksonville, Sneads Ferry & Wilmington.

LANIER'S CAMPGROUND
Ratings: 9/9★/8 (Campground) From Jct of Hwy 17 & 50, S 4.3 mi on Hwy 50 (E Ocean Rd) to Little Kinston Rd, S 0.6 mi to Spot Lane, W 0.4 mi (E). **FAC:** paved/gravel rds. (447 spaces). Avail: 115 gravel, patios, 4 pull-thrus, (40x90), back-ins (25x60), 86 full hkups, 29 W, 29 E (30/50 amps), WiFi @ sites, tent sites, rentals, dump, laundry, groc, LP gas, fire rings, firewood, restaurant, controlled access. **REC:** pool, Intercoastal Waterway to Atlantic Ocean: swim, fishing, kayaking/canoeing, boating nearby, playground. Pet restrict (B). Partial handicap access. Big rig sites, eco-friendly. 2021 rates: $40 to $95, Military discount. ATM.
(910)328-9431 Lat: 34.43169, Lon: -77.56998
1161 Spot Lane, Holly Ridge, NC 28445
www.LaniersCampground.com
See ad page 674

SWANNANOA — E2 *Buncombe*

MAMA GERTIE'S HIDEAWAY CAMPGROUND
Ratings: 9/10★/10 (Campground) From Jct of I-40 & Patton Cove Rd (exit 59), S 0.5 mi on Patton Cove Rd (L). **FAC:** paved rds. 44 Avail: 2 paved, 42 all weather, patios, 23 pull-thrus, (30x60), back-ins (30x60), 37 full hkups, 7 W, 7 E (30/50 amps), cable, WiFi @ sites, tent sites, rentals, dump, laundry, LP gas, fire rings, firewood. **REC:** boating nearby. Pets OK. Partial handicap access. Big rig sites, eco-friendly. 2021 rates: $62 to $135, Military discount.
(828)686-4258 Lat: 35.58622, Lon: -82.40493
15 Uphill Rd, Swannanoa, NC 28778
www.mamagerties.com
See ad page 666

SWANSBORO — C5 *Carteret*

DEEP CREEK RV RESORT & CAMPGROUND
Ratings: 9/9.5★/9.5 (RV Park) From jct Hammock Rd & Hwy 24: Go 4-3/4 mi NW on Hwy 24, then 1/4 mi S on Waterfront Rd (L). **FAC:** paved/gravel rds. (98 spaces). Avail: 20 gravel, 13 pull-thrus, (40x70), back-ins (40x70), 20 full hkups (30/50 amps), seasonal sites, WiFi @ sites, tent sites, laundry, LP bottles, controlled access. **REC:** pool, Queens Creek: fishing, kayaking/canoeing, boating nearby, hunting nearby. Pet restrict (B). Age restrict may apply. Big rig sites, eco-friendly. 2021 rates: $50, Military discount.
(910)330-9333 Lat: 34.712962, Lon: -77.211342
181 Waterfront Rd, Hubert, NC 28539
deepcreekrvresort.com
See primary listing at Hubert and ad page 674

SYLVA — E2 *Jackson*

FORT TATHAM RV RESORT & CAMPGROUND **Ratings: 8/8.5★/7.5** (RV Park) Avail: 27 full hkups (30/50 amps). 2021 rates: $57 to $68. Apr 01 to Oct 31. (828)586-6662, 175 Tathams Creek Rd, Sylva, NC 28779

MOONSHINE CREEK CAMPGROUND **Ratings: 6.5/10★/9.5** (Campground) Avail: 50 full hkups (30/50 amps). 2021 rates: $59 to $69. Apr 01 to Nov 01. (828)586-6666, 2486 Dark Ridge Rd, Sylva, NC 28779

TABOR CITY — D3 *Columbus*

CARROLL WOODS RV PARK AT GRAPEFULL SISTERS VINEYARD **Ratings: 8/8.5★/9.5** (RV Park) Avail: 44 full hkups (30/50 amps). 2021 rates: $41 to $55. (910)653-5538, 95 Dots Drive, Tabor City, NC 28463

YOGI BEARS JELLYSTONE PARK AT DADDY JOE'S **Ratings: 10/10★/10** (Campground) Avail: 156 full hkups (30/50 amps). 2021 rates: $50 to $90. (877)668-8586, 626 Richard Wright Rd, Tabor City, NC 28463

UNION GROVE — A1 *Iredell*

VAN HOY FARMS FAMILY CAMPGROUND
Ratings: 9/8/9 (RV Park) 54 Avail: 42 full hkups, 12 W, 12 E (30/50 amps). 2021 rates: $45 to $60. (704)539-5493, 738 Jericho Rd., Harmony, NC 28634

WADE — B3 *Cumberland*

A SPOTLIGHT Introducing Piedmont's colorful attractions appearing at the front of this state section.

FAYETTEVILLE RV RESORT & COTTAGES
Ratings: 10/10★/10 (RV Resort) From Jct of I-95 & Exit 61 (Wade-Stedman Rd), E 0.3 mi on Wade-Stedman Rd (L).

PERFECT HALF WAY NORTH SOUTH I-95
Top Resort: 10/10/10. Easy I-95 access: NC #61. Near Fort Bragg; special military & LONG-TERM rates. Huge FHU 50-amp sites, Charming cottages. Fitness center, 2 pools, playground, free Wi-Fi & Cable. Free waffle breakfast.

FAC: all weather rds. (110 spaces). Avail: 45 all weather, 43 pull-thrus, (35x90), back-ins (30x55), 45 full hkups (30/50 amps), seasonal sites, cable, WiFi @ sites, rentals, laundry, groc, LP gas, fire rings, firewood. **REC:** pool, hot tub, boating nearby, playground, hunting nearby. Pets OK. Partial handicap access. No tents. Big rig sites, eco-friendly. 2021 rates: $45 to $72, Military discount.
(910)484-5500 Lat: 35.15698, Lon: -78.70762
6250 Wade-Stedman Rd, Wade, NC 28395
fayettevillervresort.com
See ad pages 661, 669

WALNUT COVE — A2 *Stokes*

HANGING ROCK (Public State Park) From town, W 5 mi on SR-1001 (Moore's Spring Rd), follow signs (R). 73 Avail. 2021 rates: $15 to $20. (336)593-8480

WASHINGTON — B5 *Pitt*

TRANTER'S CREEK RESORT & CAMPGROUND
Ratings: 9/10★/9.5 (Campground) Avail: 60 full hkups (30/50 amps). 2021 rates: $39 to $52.50. (252)948-0850, 6573 Clarks Neck Rd, Washington, NC 27889

TWIN LAKES RV RESORT
Ratings: 8/8/9 (Campground) 76 Avail: 60 full hkups, 16 W, 16 E (30/50 amps). 2021 rates: $44 to $81. (888)563-7040, 1618 Memory Lane, Chocowinity, NC 27817

WAYNESVILLE — E2 *Haywood*

WAYNESVILLE See also Asheville, Brevard, Bryson City, Candler, Cherokee, Lake Toxaway, Maggie Valley, Sylva & Whittier, NC; Cosby, Gatlinburg & Hartford, TN.

CREEKWOOD FARM RV PARK **Ratings: 9/9.5★/10** (RV Park) Avail: 122 full hkups (30/50 amps). 2021 rates: $50 to $89. (828)926-7977, 4696 Jonathan Creek Rd, Waynesville, NC 28785

GREAT SMOKY MTN/CATALOOCHEE (Public National Park) From Jct of I-40 & US-276, SW 0.5 mi on US-276 to Cove Creek Rd, follow signs (R). 27 Avail. 2021 rates: $25. Mar 14 to Oct 31. (865)436-1200

PRIDE RV RESORT **Ratings: 9/9.5★/9.5** (Membership Park) Avail: 130 full hkups (30/50 amps). 2021 rates: $55 to $72. (800)926-8191, 4394 Jonathan Creek Rd, Waynesville, NC 28785

WINNGRAY FAMILY CAMPGROUND **Ratings: 6/8★/7** (Campground) Avail: 67 full hkups (30/50 amps). 2021 rates: $44. (828)926-3170, 26 Winngray Ln, Waynesville, NC 28785

RV SPACE-SAVING TIPS: Self-adhesive wall hooks can be added to the inside of kitchen cabinets to organize and hang cooking utensils. Use self-adhesive strips to attach organizers/PVC pipes to inside of medicine cabinet for storing toiletries and toothbrushes. Use elastic and staples to keep the first aid supplies in one place and secure in the cabinet. Add slide-out surfaces and drawers where possible, for quick and easy clean ups.

WHITE LAKE — C4 *Bladen*

CAMP CLEARWATER FAMILY CAMPGROUND **Ratings: 8.5/9★/8.5** (Campground) Avail: 111 full hkups (30/50 amps). 2021 rates: $40 to $150. (910)862-3365, 2038 White Lake Dr, White Lake, NC 28337

WHITTIER — E2 *Jackson*

FLAMING ARROW CAMPGROUND
good sam park **Ratings: 8/8.5★/9** (Campground) Avail: 51 full hkups (30/50 amps). 2021 rates: $48. (877)497-6161, 283 Flaming Arrow Dr, Whittier, NC 28789

TUCKASEEGEE RV RESORT **Ratings: 8/9.5★/9** (RV Park) Avail: 43 full hkups (30/50 amps). 2021 rates: $42 to $45. (828)497-3598, 78 Wilmont Rd, Whittier, NC 28789

WILKESBORO — A1 *Wilkes*

W KERR SCOTT DAM - COE/BANDIT'S ROOST PARK (Public Corps) From Jct of US-421 & SR-268, W 6 mi on SR-268 to Jess Walsh Rd, N 0.5 mi (E). 85 Avail: 85 W, 85 E (50 amps). 2021 rates: $24. Apr 01 to Oct 30. (336)921-3190

W KERR SCOTT DAM - COE/WARRIOR CREEK PARK (Public Corps) From town, W 7.5 mi on SR-268 (R). 61 Avail: 61 W, 61 E (30/50 amps). 2021 rates: $20 to $24. Apr 15 to Oct 14. (336)921-2177

Find Good Sam member specials at GanderOutdoors.com

WILLIAMSTON — B5 *Martin*

FARM COUNTRY CAMPGROUND **Ratings: 4/9★/7** (Campground) Avail: 45 full hkups (30/50 amps). 2021 rates: $35. (252)789-8482, 2301 Eds Grocery Rd, Williamston, NC 27892

GREEN ACRES FAMILY CAMPGROUND
good sam park **Ratings: 7.5/8★/8** (Campground) 90 Avail: 29 full hkups, 61 W, 61 E (30/50 amps). 2021 rates: $31 to $35. (252)792-3939, 1679 Green Acres Rd, Williamston, NC 27892

PIERCE RV PARK **Ratings: 5/NA/7.5** (RV Park) Avail: 28 full hkups (30/50 amps). 2021 rates: $35. (252)799-0111, 2295 Garrett Rd, Williamston, NC 27892

TREESIDE MH AND RV PARK (RV Park) (Rebuilding) Avail: 20 full hkups (30/50 amps). 2021 rates: $40. (252)943-1699, 1028 Roberts Lane, Williamston, NC 27892

WILMINGTON — D4 *New Hanover*

MILITARY PARK FORT FISHER AIR FORCE RECREATION AREA (SEYMOUR JOHNSON AFB) (Public) From Wilmington, S 20 mi on S Fort Fisher Blvd/Hwy 421S then follow Fort Fisher Rec Area signs. 24 Avail: 16 full hkups, 8 E (30/50 amps). 2021 rates: $20 to $30. (910)500-6465

WILMINGTON KOA **Ratings: 9.5/9.5★/9** (Campground) 69 Avail: 63 full hkups, 6 W, 6 E (30/50 amps). 2021 rates: $55 to $160. (888)562-5699, 7415 Market Street, Wilmington, NC 28411

WILSON — B4 *Wilson*

KAMPER'S LODGE
good sam park **Ratings: 8/8★/8** (Campground) N-bnd: Jct I-95 & US 301 (Exit 107), N 18 mi on US 301 (L); or S-bnd: I-95 & US 64 (Exit 138), E 3 mi on US 64 to US 301 S, S 17 mi (R). **FAC:** gravel rds. (51 spaces). Avail: 15 gravel, patios, 15 pull-thrus, (30x70), 15 full hkups (30/50 amps), seasonal sites, WiFi @ sites, rentals, laundry, LP gas, fire rings, firewood. **REC:** pool, pond, boating nearby, playground. Pets OK. No tents. Big rig sites, eco-friendly. 2021 rates: $35, Military discount.
(252)237-0905 Lat: 35.74475, Lon: -77.87302
3465 US Hwy 301N, Wilson, NC 27893
kamperslodge.com
See ad page 670

WINSTON-SALEM — A2 *Forsyth*

WINSTON-SALEM See also Advance, High Point & Pinnacle.

SNOWBIRD TIP: Imagine your perfect destination. RV parks reflect our personalities, lifestyles and budgets. Eastern RV parks offer a more urban experience and conveniences, while parks out west typically have more elbow room. Research before reserving to find your ideal spot.

NC

good sam
RV Rentals
Experience more for less.
Coleman
List or Rent, it's 5%.
That's **up to 75% less in fees** than the competition.
LEARN MORE AT **RVRENTALS.COM**

DID YOU KNOW?
At the International Peace Garden, you can walk from the U.S. to Canada and back.
YOU ARE HERE
Getty Images/iStockphoto

North Dakota

ND

The vast stretches of North Dakota contain untold treasures in history and adventure. Embark on the same paths Lewis and Clark traversed. See the Badlands that inspired Teddy Roosevelt to create the National Park Service.

Compelling Communities

You've seen the movie and TV show that bear its name, now experience the quirkiness and fun of this region. Fargo sits on the banks of the Red River, forming the state's eastern border with Minnesota. Uncover the city's Scandinavian origins at the Hjemkomst Center, view outstanding Native American works at the Plains Art Museum or take a journey back in time at the Bonanzaville pioneer village. If you're visiting in September, head west along Interstate 94 to Bismarck for the United Tribes Technical College International Powwow, a renowned dance and drum competition.

Let's Get Along

Stretching across almost four-square miles and straddling the U.S. border with Canada, the International Peace Garden showcases a wide variety of trees and plants. It was created to celebrate the friendship between the two nations and features a tower, flower clock, conservatory and trails. There's even a wildlife refuge with deer, moose and other wildlife.

The Good Badlands

Named after the legendary political figure who explored the region, Theodore Roosevelt National Park ranks as one of the most popular destinations in the state. Drive through its 70,000-acre expanse to experience the haunting beauty of the Badlands, winding rivers and jagged canyons. Slow down and you may even see free-roaming bison grazing in the distance. Popular stops within the colorful park include the Painted Canyon and Roosevelt's restored Maltese Cross Cabin.

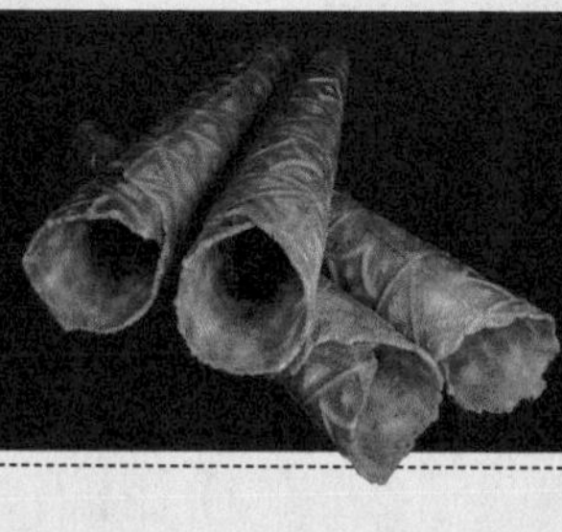

North Dakota Krumkake

When Norwegians settled in North Dakota, they didn't forget to bring the sweet stuff from the old country. Krumkake is a waffle cookie that takes the shape of a thin, curved cake. Some have compared it to a hybrid of a waffle and ice cream cone, but let's not overthink it. This is the wholesome Midwestern dessert you've always craved.

VISITOR CENTER

TIME ZONE
Mountain/Central Standard

ROAD & HIGHWAY INFORMATION
866-696-3511
dot.nd.gov

FISHING & HUNTING INFORMATION
800-406-6409
gf.nd.gov/licensing

BOATING INFORMATION
701-328-6300
mdwfp.com/law-enforcement/boating-rules-regs

NATIONAL PARKS
nps.gov/nd

STATE PARKS
parkrec.nd.gov/Parks/parks.html

TOURISM INFORMATION
North Dakota Tourism Division
800-435-5663
ndtourism.com

TOP TOURISM ATTRACTIONS
1) Theodore Roosevelt National Park
2) North Dakota Heritage Center & State Museum
3) International Peace Garden

MAJOR CITIES
Fargo, Bismarck (capital), Grand Forks, Minot, West Fargo

good sam park

Featured Good Sam Parks

NORTH DAKOTA

When you stay with Good Sam, you can expect the highest degree of cleanliness and friendliness, and better yet, you get **10% off** overnight campground fees.

If you're not already a Good Sam member you can purchase your membership at one of these locations:

CASSELTON
Governors' RV Park Campground

DICKINSON
North Park RV Campground

JAMESTOWN
Jamestown Campground

MEDORA
Red Trail Campground

MENOKEN
A Prairie Breeze RV Park

MINOT
Roughrider RV Resort

NORTH DAKOTA
Campground and other services
RV service center and/or other services
Good Sam discount locations
SCALE: 1 inch equals 42 miles
0 25 50 miles
0 25 50 kilometers
Mapping Specialists, Ltd. © 2022 Affinity Media
ND
CANADA
U.S.
MANITOBA
SASKATCHEWAN
SASK.
MONTANA
MINNESOTA
MINN.
N. DAK.
S. DAK.
NORTH DAKOTA
SOUTH DAKOTA
CENTRAL TIME ZONE
MOUNTAIN TIME ZONE
PEMBINA
WALHALLA
CAVALIER
LANGDON
GRAFTON
GRAND FORKS
LARIMORE
ARVILLA
HILLSBORO
DEVILS LAKE
DUNSEITH
BOTTINEAU
MINOT
NEW ROCKFORD
FESSENDEN
VALLEY CITY
CASSELTON
WEST FARGO
FARGO
Moorhead
JAMESTOWN
KATHRYN
LISBON
LAMOURE
NAPOLEON
BISMARCK
MANDAN
MENOKEN
HENSLER
GARRISON
RIVERDALE
HAZEN
BEULAH
PARSHALL
GLEN ULLIN
ELGIN
KILLDEER
DICKINSON
MEDORA
WATFORD CITY
WILLISTON
Theodore Roosevelt Natl. Park (North Unit)
Theodore Roosevelt Natl. Park (South Unit)
Theodore Roosevelt N.P. (Elkhorn Ranch Unit)
Little Missouri National Grassland
Sheyenne Natl. Grassland
Cedar River Natl. Grassland
Grand River National Grassland
International Peace Garden
Geographic Center of North America
Red River of the North
Missouri R.
L. Sakakawea
L. Oahe
James R.
Sheyenne R.
Souris R.
Yellowstone R.
Little Missouri R.
Heart R.
Cannonball R.
Knife R.
Bois de Sioux R.
Glendive
Wibaux
Beach
Sidney
Fairview
Culbertson
Plentywood
Baker
Ekalaka
Lemmon
Mobridge
Aberdeen
Wahpeton
Breckenridge
Crookston
Estevan
Emerson
Morden

ROAD TRIPS

Lakes and Magic Await in the Heart of the Peace Garden State

North Dakota

LOCATION
NORTH DAKOTA

DISTANCE
249 MILES

DRIVE TIME
4 HRS 27 MINS

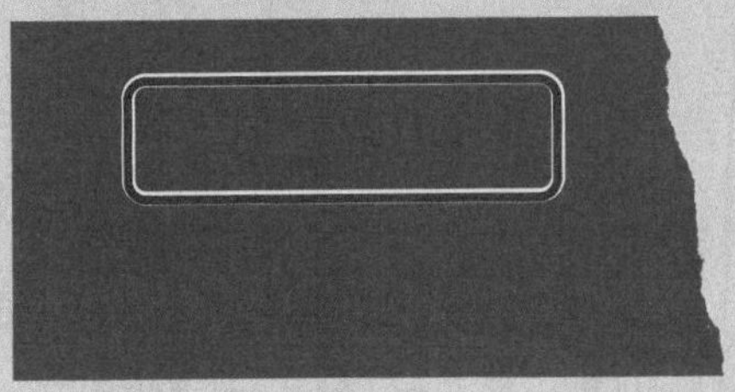

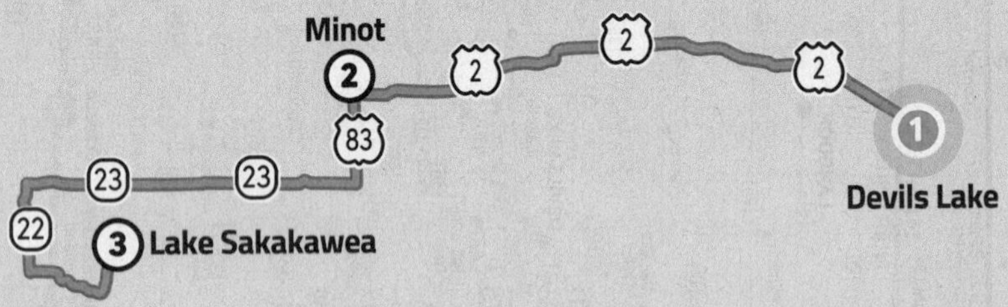

Explore beautiful lakes on your next visit to North Dakota. From boating to hunting to world-class fishing, the possibilities for outdoors adventure are nearly endless, but as a vacation destination they remain largely off the beaten track. On this route from Devils Lake to Lake Sakakawea, you'll have the chance to enjoy unspoiled natural beauty and top-notch attractions while still feeling like you've got the place to yourself. Hurry, because it won't be long before the secrets out on some of the best fishing and sailing in the lower 48.

1 Devils Lake
Starting Point

Attention anglers: Devils Lake is a hotbed of trophy-sized walleye, northern pike, white bass and, most significantly, perch. Producing perch catches that regularly reach over two pounds, the lake has been billed as the "Perch Capital of the World" and often ranks among the top five fishing lakes in the country. You'll likely spend most of your days on the water, but hikers, birdwatchers and hunters should make time for the wildlife preserves nestled on the lake's shore. Grahams Island State Park and Sully Hill National Game Preserve are popular year-round refuges for migrating waterfowl, as well as bison and elk. End your stay at the lake's namesake town, where friendly cafes, local history museums and a rollicking casino dominate the downtown.

2 Minot
Drive 121 miles ▪ 1 hour, 54 minutes

Ready for enchantment? The "Magic City" of Minot beckons visitors looking for quirky culture and one-of-a-kind festivals. The Scandinavian Heritage Park offers the chance to discover the region's Nordic roots through museum exhibits and full-scale reproductions of traditional buildings. The 60-foot-tall Stave Church and the replica 18th-century stabbur, or farmhouse, are especially popular. If you're lucky enough to visit during late September, you won't want to miss the festivities at the Norsk Høstfest, North America's largest Scandinavian festival, which boasts music, food and more from entertainers around the world. In July, the North Dakota State Fair takes over with world-class country musicians, rodeos and motorsports.

3 Lake Sakakawea
Drive 128 miles ▪ 2 hours, 33 minutes

Lake Sakakawea is the largest man-made reservoir in the nation, with a length of 180 miles long and more miles of shoreline than California's Pacific Coast. A true boater's paradise, you can rent or launch your own craft from one of the many marinas, though anglers should head to the state park on the lake's southern shores, where the boat launches offer access to some of the lake's best salmon spots. Walleye and northern pike are also frequent catches. From sailing to windsurfing, the prairie winds mean perfect conditions for a day on the water, but if you'd rather stay on dry land, there are also miles of hiking and biking trails to enjoy. The Shoreline, North Country and Overlook trails offer varying degrees of difficulty and some equally stunning views.

Getty Images/iStockphoto

BIKING · BOATING · DINING · ENTERTAINMENT · FISHING · HIKING · HUNTING · PADDLING · SHOPPING · SIGHTSEEING

North Dakota SPOTLIGHTS

See the Best of the Badlands Here

From the banks of the Red River to the tortured terrain of the Badlands, the Peace Garden State encompasses a world of history and scenery. Visit the places that struck awe in Teddy Roosevelt and play a few rounds on a golf course carved out of the Badlands.

BISON, HORSES, AND MULE DEER LIVE IN THEODORE ROOSEVELT NATL. PARK.

Theodore Roosevelt National Park protects the rugged Badlands of North Dakota.

Medora

Before he became president, Teddy Roosevelt spent years exploring the western states, and Medora held a special place in his heart. In the 1880s Teddy invested in ranch land here and fell in love with the Wild West. The town also captured the heart of the French Marquis de Mores and he named it in honor of his wife. Today, you can visit the western-inspired 26-room Chateau de Mores. Medora is also home to one of the most popular musicals in the country along with stunning views of the Badlands you'll never tire of.

Singin' Cowboys

Get ready for the "the rootin'-tootinest, boot-scootinest show in all the Midwest." The Medora Musical is and a favorite state event. This outdoor performance offers a glimpse of life during the heyday of the Wild West. There's storytelling, singing, dancing, a special visit by a Teddy Roosevelt impersonator, and real horses to boot, with the awe-inspiring Badlands providing the show's epic backdrop. Kick the evening off with a Pitch-fork Steak Fondue dinner at the Tjaden Terrace.

Tantalizing Waterway

Enjoy lush landscapes in the Scully Creek State Park Little Missouri River, North Dakota's only designated Scenic River. Grab a paddle to canoe or kayak along this 274-mile-long tributary, or cast a line out for catfish and sauger. Bike, hike or saddle-up for 150-miles of adventure along the Maah Daah Hey Trail, some of the best single track in the world. Translated from the language of the Mandian Indians, Maah Daah Hey translates to "an area that will be around for a long time."

Teddy Rode Here

Ready to get rugged? Medora is the gateway to the 700,000-acre Theodore Roosevelt National Park, where you can hike through

ND

SPOTLIGHTS

Built in an ornate Scandinavian style, the Gol Stave Church Museum honors the traditions of the area's settlers.

the wilderness to the Petrified Forest or visit Wind Canyon, a perfect sunset-viewing spot. Coal Vein Trail offers a trip through small gorges, along rugged butte edges and through aromatic juniper trees. Pay a visit to Roosevelt's Maltese Cross Cabin, the cozy log house where he stayed during his time in the Badlands. Ready to hit the greens? Bully Pulpit Golf Course, winding through the Badlands, is ranked as one of America's 100 greatest public courses.

Cowboy Culture

At the North Dakota Cowboy Hall of Fame, visitors can explore the history and heritage of cowboys, Native Americans, rodeos, ranching life and cattle drives; it's an up-close experience with Cowboy Culture. Learn about Hall of Fame honorees and the parts they played in settling and taming the rugged prairie.

Grand Forks

Go Green in Grand Forks. Home to the University of North Dakota, Grand Forks cultivates outstanding parks and gardens. Outdoor recreation isn't far from the downtown area. The Greenway consists of 2,200 acres lining the Red River and the Red Lake River as they flow through Grand Forks and East Grand Forks. This urban space offers recreational, cultural, historical and natural resource opportunities. You can hike, walk, run, roller blade, bike, bird, canoe, kayak, fish or golf, all in the heart of town. Now fully completed, the Greenway includes an all-season trail system.

Shopping, Sports and Art

You'll never run short of shopping in this town. Browse big box stores in Grand Forks and unique downtown boutiques. Cheer on championship sports teams at Ralph Engelstad Arena or Grammy-winning entertainers at the Alerus Center. Check out a Picasso hanging in the North Dakota Museum of Art or say hello to Dali at the Empire Arts Center Gallery. Check out racing action at the exciting River City Speedway. See stock car races and NLRA action. Kids will love Splasher's of the South Seas, an indoor waterpark that simulates a tropical environment.

North Dakota Dam

More water fun awaits at Larimore Dam, just 30 miles west of Grand Forks. The area offers fishing, nature trails, bike paths, 144 campsites, a sandy swimming beach, basketball and volleyball courts, a baseball diamond, horseshoes, an adjacent nine-hole golf course and winter sledding. The arboretum contains more than 500 different trees in a lush 26-acre expanse that is amazingly rich in color.

Minot by Way of Scandinavia

Did you know that some of North Dakota's early settlers were immigrants from Scandinavia? To learn more, visit the Scandinavian Heritage Park in Minot. You'll feel whisked away to Nordic lands while gazing at the immense Gol Stave Church Museum.

Minot Knows How to Party

Get ready to feast on herring and Swedish meatballs. Each fall, Minot hosts the Norsk Høstfest festival, where you can explore a Viking village, sample Nordic foods and celebrate all things Scandinavian. The festival includes top entertainers as well as exquisite Scandinavian crafts and cultural activities. Enjoy delicacies found only in the Scandinavian culture, from veal in dill to crispy waffles with cloudberries. *Skol!*

FOR MORE INFORMATION

North Dakota Tourism Division, 800-435-5663, www.ndtourism.com

Visit Grand Forks, 800-866-4566, www.visitgrandforks.com

Medora Convention & Visitors Bureau, 701-623-4830, www.medorand.com

Visit Minot, 701-857-8206, www.visitminot.com

> "IN FALL, MINOT HOSTS THE NORSK HØSTFEST FESTIVAL, WHERE YOU CAN EXPLORE A VIKING VILLAGE."

LOCAL FAVORITE

Buffalo Burgers on Focaccia with Pesto and Roasted Peppers

No trip to the Dakotas is complete without sampling this specialty. Combine savory buffalo with bread for a hearty meal. *Recipe adapted from* Best Ever RV Recipes.

INGREDIENTS

- ☐ 1 lb ground buffalo meat
- ☐ Garlic salt and Worcestershire sauce, to taste
- ☐ 3-4 slices provolone cheese
- ☐ Focaccia bread
- ☐ Olive oil
- ☐ Prepared basil pesto
- ☐ Roasted red bell peppers, sliced

DIRECTIONS

Form 3 or 4 burgers from ground buffalo meat. Cook on the barbecue about 5 minutes on each side, sprinkling with the garlic salt and Worcestershire sauce. When almost done, top with provolone cheese and let the cheese melt slightly.

Meanwhile, cut the bread, brush the cut sides with olive oil and lightly toast on the grill. Place the burgers on the bread and top with some pesto and a few slices of red pepper.

North Dakota

ARVILLA — B6 *Grand Forks*

TURTLE RIVER (Public State Park) From town, W 22 mi on Hwy 2, follow signs (R). 125 Avail: 70 W, 30 E (30 amps). 2021 rates: $10 to $30. (701)594-4445

BEULAH — C3 *Mercer*

BEULAH BAY CAMPGROUND (Public) From jct Hwy-49 & Hwy-200: Go 15 mi N on Hwy-49, follow signs. 100 Avail: 24 full hkups, 12 E. 2021 rates: $20 to $25. May 11 to Sep 16. (701)873-5852

BISMARCK — C3 *Burleigh*

BISMARCK KOA CAMPGROUND **Ratings: 9/9.5★/10** (Campground) 98 Avail: 79 full hkups, 19 W, 19 E (30/50 amps). 2021 rates: $42 to $53. (701)222-2662, 3720 Centennial Rd, Bismarck, ND 58503

GENERAL SIBLEY PARK (Public) From Jct of I-94 & SH-810, SW 5.2 mi, S 4 mi on Washington St. Avail: 115 E (30/50 amps). 2021 rates: $25. May 25 to Sep 06. (701)222-1844

HILLCREST ACRES RV PARK **Ratings: 6/8★/7.5** (RV Park) 57 Avail: 46 full hkups, 11 E (30/50 amps). 2021 rates: $40 to $45. Apr 01 to Nov 15. (701)255-4334, 5700 E Main Ave, Bismarck, ND 58501

BOTTINEAU — A3 *Bottineau*

LAKE METIGOSHE (Public State Park) From town: Go 14 mi NE on County Rd, then E on Hwy-43. 130 Avail. 2021 rates: $10 to $25. (701)263-4651

TOMMY TURTLE PARK (Public) From ND Hwy 5 & Jay St: Go 1 blk N on Jay St (L). Avail: 16 full hkups (30 amps). 2021 rates: $20. May 01 to Oct 15. (701)228-3030

CASSELTON — C6 *Cass*

GOVERNORS' RV PARK CAMPGROUND
good sam park **Ratings: 8/9★/5** (Campground) Avail: 44 full hkups (30/50 amps). 2021 rates: $41 to $54. Apr 01 to Nov 01. (888)847-4524, 2050 Governors' Dr, Casselton, ND 58012

CAVALIER — A5 *Pembina*

ICELANDIC
(Public State Park) From jct Hwy-5 & Hwy-18: Go 5 mi W on Hwy-5. **FAC:** Avail: 159 dirt, tent sites, rentals, dump, fire rings, firewood. **REC:** Lake Renwick: swim, fishing, rec open to public. Pets OK. 2021 rates: $12 to $30.
(701)265-4561 Lat: 48.77861, Lon: -97.76167
13571 Highway 5, Cavalier, ND 58220
www.parkrec.nd.gov

DEVILS LAKE — B5 *Ramsey*

GRAHAMS ISLAND (Public State Park) From town, W 10 mi on Hwy 19 to 72nd Ave./CR 0322, S 5 mi (across bridge) (E). Avail: 101 E (30/50 amps). 2021 rates: $10 to $30. (701)766-4015

DICKINSON — C2 *Stark*

NORTH PARK RV CAMPGROUND
good sam park **Ratings: 8/9.5★/8.5** (Campground) From Jct I-94 (exit 61) & 3rd Ave/Hwy 22: Go 1/2 mi N on 3rd Ave/Hwy 22, then 1/2 mi E on 21st St, then 500 ft N on 5th Ave (R). Elev 2536 ft.**FAC:** gravel rds. (102 spaces). Avail: 70 gravel, 39 pull-thrus, (24x90), back-ins (30x120), mostly side by side hkups, 70 full hkups (30/50 amps), seasonal sites, WiFi @ sites, tent sites, dump, laundry. **REC:** boating nearby, hunting nearby. Pet restrict (B). Partial handicap access. Big rig sites, eco-friendly. 2021 rates: $42, Military discount.
(701)227-8498 Lat: 46.90662, Lon: -102.77717
2320 Buckskin Dr, Dickinson, ND 58601
www.campnorthpark.com
See ad this page

PATTERSON LAKE RECREATION AREA (CITY PARK) (Public) From I-94 (exit 59): Go 3 mi W on Old Hwy 10, then 1 mi S. Avail: 22 full hkups. 2021 rates: $18 to $26. May 30 to Sep 05. (701)456-2056

DUNSEITH — A4 *Rolette*

INTERNATIONAL PEACE GARDEN (Public) From town, N 13 mi on US-281 (L). 36 Avail: 20 W, 29 E (15/30 amps). 2021 rates: $20 to $30. Jun 01 to Sep 30. (701)263-4390

ELGIN — D3 *Grant*

SHEEP CREEK DAM (Public) From Jct of SR-49 & SR-21, S 1 mi on SR-49 (becomes gravel, 68th St.), S 4.3 mi (R). 10 Avail: Pit toilets. May 01 to Oct 31. (701)584-2354

FARGO — C6 *Cass*

LINDENWOOD PARK (Public) From Jct of I-94 & US-81 (exit 351), N 0.25 mi on US-81 to 17th Ave, E 8 blks (R). 47 Avail: 47 W, 47 E (20 amps). 2021 rates: $30. May 01 to Oct 15. (701)232-3987

Travel Services

CAMPING WORLD OF FARGO As the nation's largest retailer of RV supplies, accessories, services and new and used RVs, Camping World is committed to making your total RV experience better. **SERVICES:** restrooms. RV Sales. RV supplies, RV accessible. Hours: 9am - 6pm, closed Sun.
(701)639-4296 Lat: 46.87555, Lon: -96.86243
2249 Main Ave E, Fargo, ND 58078
rv.campingworld.com

FESSENDEN — B4 *Wells*

FESSENDEN CITY PARK (Public) From Jct of Hwys 52 & 15, E 0.5 mi on Hwy 15 (L). 8 Avail: 8 S, 8 E (30/50 amps). 2021 rates: $10 to $15. May 01 to Oct 01. (701)547-3101

GARRISON — B3 *McLean*

FORT STEVENSON (Public State Park) From Jct of SR-37 & CR-15, S 3 mi on CR-15 (E). Entrance fee required. 145 Avail: 100 W, 100 E (30/50 amps). 2021 rates: $10 to $30. (701)337-5576

LAKE SAKAKAWEA - COE/DOUGLAS CREEK BAY (Public Corps) 17-1/2 mi W on Hwy 37 (Emmett), then 5 mi S, 4 mi E on CR. 20 Avail: Pit toilets. (701)654-7411

LAKE SAKAKAWEA - COE/EAST TOTTEN TRAIL (Public Corps) From jct Hwy 37 & US 83: Go 5 mi S on US 83. Avail: 30 E Pit toilets. 2021 rates: $12 to $18. May 14 to Sep 30. (701)654-7411

GLEN ULLIN — C3 *Morton*

GLEN ULLIN MEMORIAL PARK (Public) From town, W 0.5 mi on CR-139/Hwy 10 (L). 26 Avail: (30 amps), Pit toilets. 2021 rates: $15 to $25. (701)348-3683

GRAFTON — A6 *Walsh*

LEISTIKOW PARK CAMPGROUND (CITY PARK) (Public) From jct I-29 (exit 176) & Hwy 17: Go 10 mi W on Hwy 17, then 6 blocks N on Cooper Ave, then 1 mi W on Fifth St. Avail: 50 full hkups. 2021 rates: $25. (701)352-1842

GRAND FORKS — B6 *Grand Forks*

GRAND FORKS CAMPGROUND Ratings: 7.5/9.5★/8.5 (Campground) 128 Avail: 106 full hkups, 22 W, 22 E (30/50 amps). 2021 rates: $45. Apr 01 to Nov 01. (701)772-6108, 4796 S. 42nd St, Grand Forks, ND 58201

MILITARY PARK GRAND FORKS FAMCAMP (GRAND FORKS AFB) (Public) From Grand Forks, W 15 mi on US-2 to Grand Forks Air Force main gate exit, then 1.6 mi on Eielson St (R). Avail: 21 full hkups (30/50 amps). 2021 rates: $20. May 01 to Oct 01. (701)747-3688

HAZEN — C3 *Mercer*

HAZEN BAY RECREATION AREA (Public) From jct Hwy 200 & CR 27: Go 15 mi N on CR 27. 135 Avail: 69 full hkups, 32 W, 39 E. 2021 rates: $10 to $23. May 15 to Sep 15. (701)748-6948

LEWIS & CLARK RV PARK (Public) From Jct of Hwy 200 & Main St, follow signs, S 0.2 mi on Main St (L). Avail: 28 full hkups (30/50 amps). 2021 rates: $10 to $20. May 01 to Sep 15. (701)748-2267

HENSLER — C3 *Oliver*

CROSS RANCH (Public State Park) From Jct of I-94 & Hwy 25 (exit 147), N 18.5 mi on Hwy 25 (road curves west), N 5 mi on County Rd, E 3 mi on County Rd, N 2 mi (R). Avail: 7 E (30 amps). 2021 rates: $10 to $25. (701)794-3731

HILLSBORO — C6 *Traill*

HILLSBORO CAMPGROUND & RV PARK **Ratings: 4.5/UI/6** (Campground) Avail: 74 full hkups (30/50 amps). 2021 rates: $40. (701)636-5205, 201 6th St SW, Hillsboro, ND 58045

JAMESTOWN — C5 *Stutsman*

FRONTIER FORT CAMPGROUND **Ratings: 5/5.5/4.5** (Campground) 60 Avail: 52 full hkups, 8 E (30/50 amps). 2021 rates: $25 to $27. Apr 01 to Nov 15. (701)252-7492, 1838 3rd Ave SE, Jamestown, ND 58401

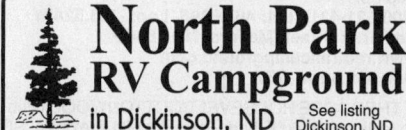

JAMESTOWN CAMPGROUND
good sam park **Ratings: 8/9★/9** (Campground) 38 Avail: 30 full hkups, 8 W, 8 E (30/50 amps). 2021 rates: $30 to $40. May 01 to Oct 01. (701)252-6262, 3605 80th Ave SE, Jamestown, ND 58401

JAMESTOWN DAM/LAKESIDE MARINA CAMPGROUND (Public) From town, N 3.5 mi on SR-20 to 30th St., W 0.5 mi (L). 48 Avail: 48 W, 48 E (20/30 amps). 2021 rates: $9 to $14. May 25 to Sep 06. (701)252-1183

KATHRYN — C5 *Barnes*

LITTLE YELLOWSTONE PARK (BARNES COUNTY PARK) (Public) From jct Hwy 1 & Hwy 46: Go 6 mi E on Hwy 46. Avail: 16 E (20/30 amps), Pit toilets. 2021 rates: $15 to $20. May 01 to Oct 31. (701)762-4450

KILLDEER — C2 *Dunn*

LITTLE MISSOURI (Public State Park) From town: Go 17 mi N on Hwy-22. Avail: 30 E. 2021 rates: $8 to $16. May 01 to Oct 31. (701)764-5256

LAMOURE — D5 *LaMoure*

LAMOURE COUNTY MEMORIAL PARK (Public) From Jct of CR-34 & CR-63, N 1 mi on CR-63 (R). Avail: 90 E (20 amps). 2021 rates: $7. May 15 to Nov 15. (701)883-5856

LANGDON — A5 *Cavalier*

LANGDON CITY PARK CAMPGROUND (Public) From Jct of SR-1 & SR-5, W 0.4 mi on SR-5, N 2 blks 7th St. (E). Avail: 13 E (30/50 amps). 2021 rates: $20. May 01 to Oct 30. (701)256-2155

ND

LARIMORE — B5 *Grand Forks*

LARIMORE DAM RECREATION AREA CAMPGROUND (Public) Westbound from Jct I-29 (Exit 141) & US-2: Go 23 mi W on US-2, then 2 mi S & W on CR-4A/18th Ave NE (R). Eastbound from Jct Hwy 18 & US 2: Go 2 mi E o n US 2, then 2 mi S & W on CR-4A//18th Ave NE (R). 144 Avail: 144 W, 144 E (30/50 amps). 2021 rates: $25. May 01 to Oct 01. (701)343-2078

LISBON — D5 *Ransom*

SANDAGER CAMPGROUND (Public) From jct Hwy 32 & Hwy 27 (in Lisbon); go 3 blks N on Hwy 32 (Main St); then 4 blks W on 2nd Ave West; then 1 blk NE on Ash St; then 1 blk NW on 1st Ave; then L on Parkway Dr & follow signs. Avail: 16 full hkups (30/50 amps). 2021 rates: $12 to $20. Apr 15 to Nov 01. (701)683-3010

MANDAN — C3 *Morton*

FORT ABRAHAM LINCOLN (Public State Park) From town, S 7 mi on Hwy 1806 (E). Avail: 55 E (30 amps). 2021 rates: $10 to $30. (701)667-6340

MEDORA — C1 *Billings*

A SPOTLIGHT Introducing Medora's colorful attractions appearing at the front of this state section.

MEDORA CAMPGROUND **Ratings: 6.5/7.5/7.5** (Campground) 158 Avail: 148 full hkups, 10 W, 10 E (30/50 amps). 2021 rates: $38 to $58. May 15 to Oct 02. (800)633-6721, 3370 Pool Dr, Medora, ND 58645

RED TRAIL CAMPGROUND

good sam park **Ratings: 6.5/9★/7** (Campground) E-bnd only: From I-94 (Exit 24): Go 2 mi SE on Bus I-94/Pacific Ave, then 1/4 mi SW (R) on E River Rd, S to Red Trail St (L). W-bnd: From I-94 (Exit 27): Go 1 1/2 mi W on Bus I-94/Pacific Ave, then 1/4 mi SW (L) on E River Rd S to Red Trail St (L) Do not rely on GPS. **FAC:** paved/gravel rds. 120 Avail: 6 paved, 114 gravel, 4 pull-thrus, (28x60), back-ins (28x60), 59 full hkups, 61 W, 61 E (30/50 amps), cable, WiFi @ sites, tent sites, dump, laundry, groc. **REC:** playground, hunting nearby. Pets OK. Partial handicap access. Big rig sites, eco-friendly. 2021 rates: $38 to $53. May 15 to Sep 30.
(800)621-4317 Lat: 46.90896, Lon: -103.52471
Red Trail Street, Medora, ND 58645
www.redtrailcampground.com
See ad page 687

THEODORE ROOSEVELT/COTTONWOOD (Public National Park) E-bnd: From Jct I-94 & exit 24, SE 1.4 mi on service rd to park access rd, N 5.5 mi (L); or W-bnd: From Jct I-94 & exit 27, SW 1 mi on service rd to park access rd, N 5.5 mi (R). 76 Avail. 2021 rates: $7 to $14. (701)623-4730

MENOKEN — C3 *Burleigh*

A PRAIRIE BREEZE RV PARK

good sam park **Ratings: 5/9★/8** (Campground) From Jct of I-94 & Exit 170 (Menoken exit): Go 1000 ft S on Rd to Menoken (R). **FAC:** gravel rds. Avail: 42 gravel, 42 pull-thrus, (30x80), mostly side by side hkups, 42 full hkups (30/50 amps), WiFi @ sites, tent sites, dump, laundry. **REC:** boating nearby, hunting nearby. Pets OK. Partial handicap access. Big rig sites. 2021 rates: $30 to $35. Apr 01 to Nov 01. no cc.
(701)224-8215 Lat: 46.83446, Lon: -100.54261
2810 158th St NE, Menoken, ND 58558
See ad this page

MINOT — B3 *Ward*

MILITARY PARK MINOT FAMCAMP (MINOT AFB) (Public) From jct US-2W & S Broadway/US-83N: Go N 12 mi on US-83N, then W on Missile Ave, follow signs (L). 6 Avail: 6 W, 6 E (30 amps). 2021 rates: $15. (701)723-3648

ROUGHRIDER RV RESORT

good sam park **Ratings: 8/9.5★/9** (Campground) From Jct of US-83 & US 2/US-52: Go 4 mi W on US-2/52, then 1/2 mi N on paved CR-17 (54th St) (R). **FAC:** gravel rds. Avail: 118 gravel, 87 pull-thrus, (21x55), back-ins (22x55), 118 full hkups (30/50 amps), WiFi @ sites, tent sites, shower$, dump, laundry, LP bottles, fire rings, firewood. **REC:** Souris River: fishing, playground. Pet restrict (B). eco-friendly. 2021 rates: $45, Military discount.
(701)852-8442 Lat: 48.24165, Lon: -101.37107
500 54th St NW, Minot, ND 58703
www.roughriderrvresort.com
See ad this page

NAPOLEON — D4 *Logan*

BEAVER LAKE (Public State Park) From town, S 17 mi on Hwy 3 to CR-Burnstad (R). Avail: 25 E (50 amps). 2021 rates: $17 to $25. (701)452-2752

NEW ROCKFORD — B4 *Eddy*

NORTH RIVERSIDE PARK (Public) At Jct of Hwys 15 & 281 (L). Avail: 13 E (15 amps). 2021 rates: $5. May 01 to Sep 30. (701)947-2461

PARSHALL — B2 *Mountrail*

PARSHALL BAY REC AREA (Public) From Jct of SR-23 & SR-37, S 2 mi on SR-37 to 37th St., W & S 4 mi, W 5.7 mi 36th St. Avail: 50 E (30/50 amps). 2021 rates: $14 to $26. May 15 to Sep 15. (701)862-3362

PEMBINA — A6 *Pembina*

FORT DAER CAMPGROUND (Public) From Canadian border, S 2 mi on I-29 (E). Avail: 12 full hkups (20 amps). 2021 rates: $15. May 31 to Sep 15. (701)825-6819

RIVERDALE — C3 *McLean*

LAKE SAKAKAWEA (Public State Park) From Jct of Hwys 83 & 200, W 9 mi on Hwy 200 to W-side of Garrison Dam & park grounds (R). 192 Avail: 192 W, 192 E (30/50 amps). 2021 rates: $12 to $30. (701)487-3315

LAKE SAKAKAWEA - COE/DOWNSTREAM (Public Corps) From town, W 1 mi on Hwy 200 to rd next to dam, follow signs (E). Avail: 101 E (30/50 amps). 2021 rates: $22. May 14 to Sep 08. (701)654-7411

LAKE SAKAKAWEA - COE/WOLF CREEK (Public Corps) From Jct of Tourist Rte/Missouri Dr & Hwy 200, E 1 mi on Hwy 200, follow sign (E). Avail: 101 W, Pit toilets. 2021 rates: $12. May 15 to Sep 14. (701)654-7411

VALLEY CITY — C5 *Barnes*

LAKE ASHTABULA - COE/EAST ASHTABULA CROSSING CAMPGROUND (Public Corps) From town, N 14 mi on CR-21 (R). Avail: 32 E (30 amps). 2021 rates: $26 to $52. May 01 to Sep 30. (701)845-2970

LAKE ASHTABULA - COE/EGGERTS LANDING (Public Corps) From town, N 12 mi on CR-21 (L). Avail: 37 E (30 amps). 2021 rates: $26. May 01 to Sep 30. (701)845-2970

LAKE ASHTABULA - COE/MEL RIEMAN (Public Corps) From town, N 1 mi on CR-21 to Valley Rd (CR-19), NW 9 mi (L). Avail: 15 E (20/30 amps). 2021 rates: $26. May 01 to Sep 30. (701)845-2970

Follow the arrow. The arrow in each listing indicates where the facility is located in relation to the listed town.

WALHALLA — A5 *Pembina*

WALHALLA RIVERSIDE PARK (Public) From Jct of SR-32 & Mountain Ave, S 0.2 mi on Mountain Ave (E). 35 Avail: 35 W, 35 E (20 amps). 2021 rates: $25. May 15 to Sep 05. (701)549-3289

WATFORD CITY — B2 *McKenzie*

THEODORE ROOSEVELT/JUNIPER (Public National Park) From town, S 15 mi on US-85 to park access rd, W 5 mi (L). 50 Avail. 2021 rates: $7 to $14. (701)842-2333

WEST FARGO — C6 *Cass*

RED RIVER VALLEY FAIR CAMPGROUND (Public) From jct I-94 (exit 343) & Hwy 10: Go 1/4 mi E on Hwy 10, then 1/4 mi S on CR 28. 91 Avail: 75 full hkups, 16 E (30 amps). 2021 rates: $20 to $30. Apr 30 to Oct 31. (701)282-2200

WILLISTON — B1 *Williams*

LEWIS & CLARK (Public State Park) From town, E 18 mi on Hwy 1804 to park access road, S 3 mi (L). Avail: 80 E (20/30 amps). 2021 rates: $10 to $30. (701)859-3071

RV Tech Tips - Dirty Water Down the Drain: When cleaning and treating your RV's roof, work on 3-foot square sections at a time. To be able to rinse the wash pads with a freshwater hose while keeping the sides of the motorhome clean from dirty water (which can leave behind streaks), put together a wash tub with a drain hose over the side to bring the dirty water down to ground level. Drill a hole near the bottom of one side of a plastic tub and applied silicone caulk on a 3/4-inch male hose thread (MHT) by 1/2-inch MPT garden hose adapter held together with a 1/2-inch galvanized hex lock nut. After the silicone has dried, attach the garden drain hose. Just be sure to secure the freshwater hose so it stays on the roof.

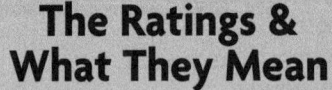

The Ratings & What They Mean

Turn to "Understanding the Rating System" section at the front of this Guide to get information on how we rate and inspect parks with our handy three number system!

The **FIRST NUMBER** represents Development of Facilities

The **SECOND NUMBER** represents Cleanliness and Physical Characteristics of Restrooms and Showers (plus, a Star is awarded to parks who receive maximum points for cleanliness!)

The **THIRD NUMBER** represents Visual Appearance/Environmental Quality

Getty Images/iStockphoto

YOU ARE HERE

Ohio

DID YOU KNOW?

You'll find Elvis Presley's car and John Lennon's sunglasses in Cleveland's Rock and Roll Hall of Fame.

You'll find it all in Ohio. Bustling cities, family farms, storied professional sports teams, lush landscapes and even rock 'n' roll have a special place in this Midwestern state. Welcome to the "heart of it all."

Major Metros

Are you ready to rock? Cleveland is home to the Rock & Roll Hall of Fame, a jaw-dropping display of memorabilia, costumes and instruments from some of music's superstars. If you're a sports nut, cheer on the Indians, Browns and Cavaliers at a home game — these teams boast fantastic histories of heartbreaks and triumphs. Continue your sports safari by touring the Pro Football Hall of Fame in nearby Canton. Learn about league legends like "Papa Bear" Halas, "Broadway Joe" Namath and "Mean Joe" Greene.

Columbus Crushes It

Did you know that Ohio's biggest city was Columbus? This town packs all the pleasures you'd expect in a major metro area. Short North Arts District, a hip neighborhood overflowing with art venues, markets and eateries, attracts visitors. In Cincinnati, feast on local delicacies like Cincinnati chili and goetta, a German-inspired meat and grain sausage. Cincy's sports offerings include football's Bengals and Major League Baseball's Reds, a team that once counted Pete Rose — also known as "Charlie Hustle" — as one of its stars.

Parks and Rec

You'll find lots of rugged trails in the Buckeye State. Take a hike in Cuyahoga Valley National Park, which straddles the Cuyahoga River. Follow 125 miles of trails, admire the majestic Brandywine Falls or paddle the river's current. Before you go, enjoy a scenic trip on the Cuyahoga Valley Scenic Railroad and keep your eyes peeled for bald eagles and blue herons along the way.

Ohio Barberton Chicken

Mix up your chicken game with Barberton chicken, named after the Ohio community where it was originated. Also known as Serbian fried chicken, this is a regional specialty that has tantalized Ohioans for generations. A whole chicken is cut into pieces that are then dredged in flour, then eggs and finally in a mixture of breadcrumbs, salt and pepper before they are deep-fried in lard.

VISITOR CENTER

TIME ZONE
Eastern Standard

ROAD & HIGHWAY INFORMATION
614-466-7170
ohgo.com

FISHING & HUNTING INFORMATION
800-WILDLIFE
wildlife.ohiodnr.gov

BOATING INFORMATION
614-265-6480
watercraft.ohiodnr.gov

NATIONAL PARKS
nps.gov/oh

STATE PARKS
parks.ohiodnr.gov

TOURISM INFORMATION
Ohio Tourism Division
800-BUCKEYE
ohio.org

TOP TOURISM ATTRACTIONS
1) Cedar Point Amusement Park and Resort
2) Rock and Roll Hall of Fame and Museum
3) Pro Football Hall of Fame

MAJOR CITIES
Columbus (capital), Cleveland, Cincinnati, Toledo, Akron

Bike the Buckeye State

Grab a bike and hop on the Ohio and Erie Canal Towpath Trail, which runs 85 miles south from the Cleveland lakeshore along a historic canal built in the 1800s. Back on the northern shore, you'll find 200 miles of coastline along Lake Erie with lots of walking and bike paths. Take a drive along the Lake Erie Coastal Ohio Trail scenic byway for epic views of Erie. Several state parks and public beaches provide outdoor recreation in this scenic location.

Angling on Erie

Off Ohio's north shore, Lake Erie teems with perch, walleye and more. To the south, about 60 miles east of Cleveland, one of the state's largest lakes, Mosquito Lake, is a favorite for anglers and boaters. For something different, check out Punderson Lake, formed by a glacier that left a deep crater. Its deep, cold waters provide an exceptional trout habitat. Paddlers won't want to miss the Hocking River, known for the stunning scenery of its banks.

Mountains High, Rivers Wide

The rollicking foothills of the Appalachian Mountains and the lush landscapes of Wayne National Forest make southeastern Ohio a popular region for outdoor recreation. Put yourself in the scenery with a hike in Hocking Hills State Park, where you'll find unique sandstone formations, picturesque waterfalls and abundant wildlife.

Gateway to Freedom

Cincinnati served a special role for escaped slaves in the years leading up to the Civil War. Because the Cincinnati was so close to the border of Kentucky —a slave state before the Civil War — the city became a crucial stop on the Underground Railroad during the 1800s. This nationwide network of safe houses and routes was used to help slaves get to free territory. The city also was home famous abolitionists, including Levi Coffin and John Rankin. Visitors can explore this incredible history in the National Underground Railroad Freedom Center in downtown Cincinnati. The town also is the home to the Mt. Airy Forest, where visitors will find Everybody's Treehouse. The ADA-accessible structure gives explorers a unique perspective of these lush woods from high in the treetops.

Ash Cave Waterfalls form a delicate curtain in Hocking Hills State Park 58 miles southeast of Columbus.

Ashtabula's Treasures

In northeast Ohio on the shores of Lake Erie, Ashtabula is a hilly region packed with recreation. Get on board a fishing charter for walleye and perch in Lake Erie. Cyclists can hit the Western Reserve Greenway Bike Trail, a 44-mile paved rail-trail that traverses Ashtabula and Trumbull Counties. The trail runs past farms and through wooded areas. During the summer, the thick canopy provides shade for riders. Interpretive signs along the way detail the area's history.

Alum Creek

Just north of Columbus, Alum Creek State Park boasts lots of watery fun. There are five boat ramps around the lake and boats with unlimited horsepower are permitted on the lake. Alum Creek Lake has a jagged shore that provides excellent fishing opportunities. Game fish found in the lake include large mouth and small mouth bass, bluegill, crappie, sunfish, channel catfish and more.

good sam park

Featured Good Sam Parks

OHIO

When you stay with Good Sam, you can expect the highest degree of cleanliness and friendliness, and better yet, you get **10% off** overnight campground fees.

If you're not already a Good Sam member you can purchase your membership at one of these locations:

AKRON
Cherokee Park Campground
Countryside Campground

ARCHBOLD
Sauder Village Campground

AURORA
Roundup Lake Campground

BERLIN
Berlin RV Park & Campground
Scenic Hills RV Park

CHILLICOTHE
Sun Valley Campground

CONNEAUT
Evergreen Lake Park

10/10★/10 GOOD SAM PARKS

DELAWARE
Cross Creek Camping Resort
(740)549-2267

NEW PARIS
Arrowhead Campground
(937)996-6203

MOUNT EATON
Evergreen Park RV Resort
(888)359-6429

What's This?

An RV park with a 10/10★/10 rating has scored perfect grades in amenities, cleanliness and appearance ("See Understanding the Campground Rating System" on pages 8 and 9 for an explanation of the trusted Good Sam Rating System). Stay in a 10/10★/10 park on your next trip for a nearly flawless camping experience.

DELAWARE
Cross Creek Camping Resort

GALLOWAY
Alton RV Park

GRAFTON
American Wilderness Campground

JEFFERSON
Kenisee Lake

LEBANON
Olive Branch Campground

MASON
Kings Island Camp Cedar

MOUNT EATON
Evergreen Park RV Resort

NAVARRE
Baylor Beach Park Water Park & Campground

NEW PARIS
Arrowhead Campground

NEW PHILADELPHIA
Wood's Tall Timber Resort

PORT CLINTON
Cedarlane RV Resort
The Resort at Erie Landing

RACINE
Kountry Resort Campground

SANDUSKY
Camp Sandusky

SEVILLE
Maple Lakes Recreational Park

SOUTH BLOOMINGVILLE
Pine Creek Horseman's Camp

STREETSBORO
Woodside Lake Park

SWANTON
Bluegrass Campground

TORONTO
Austin Lake RV Park & Cabins

WILMINGTON
Thousand Trails Wilmington

ZANESVILLE
Wolfies Campground

Getty Images/iStockphoto

OH

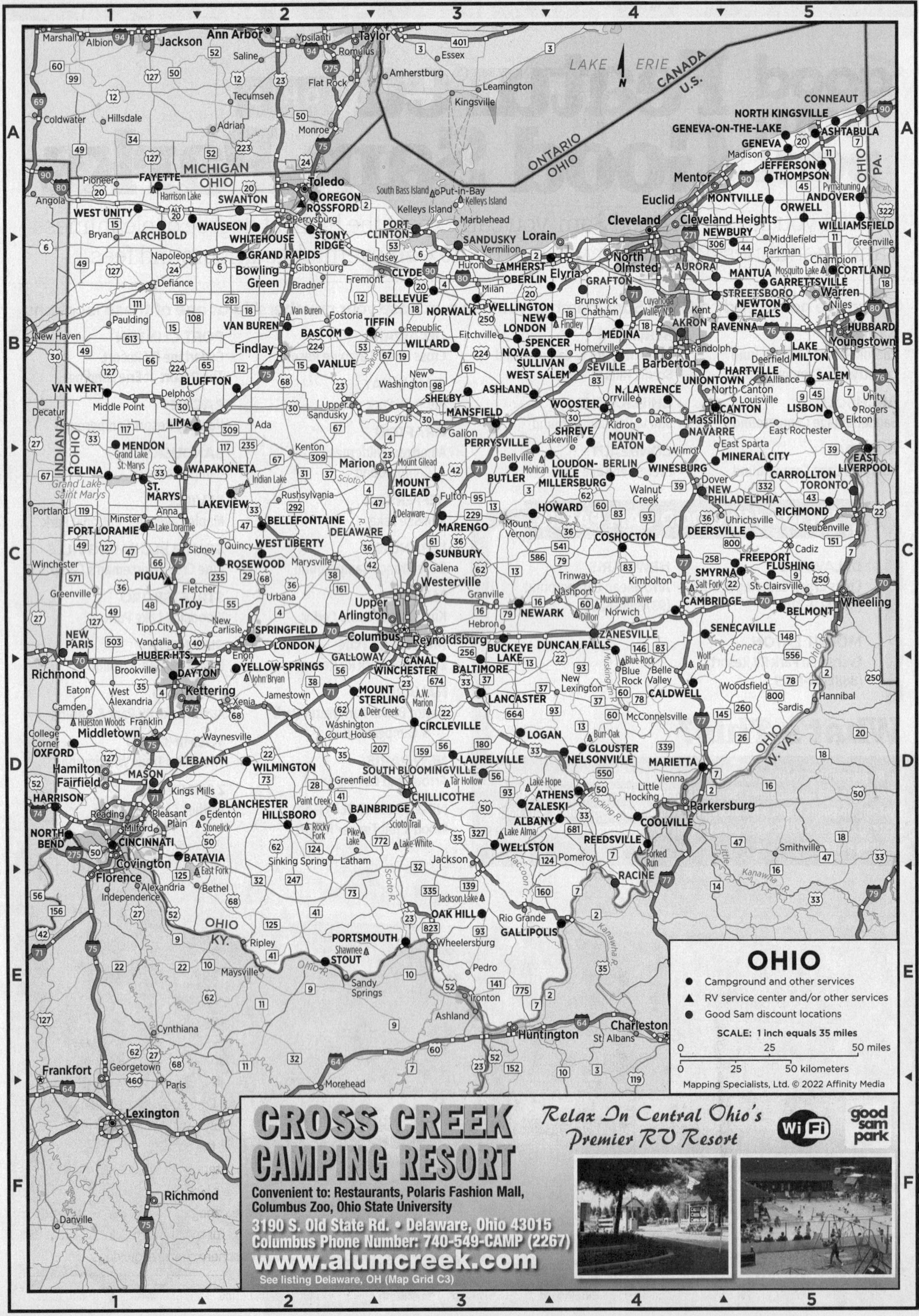
OHIO
Campground and other services
RV service center and/or other services
Good Sam discount locations
SCALE: 1 inch equals 35 miles
0 25 50 miles
0 25 50 kilometers
Mapping Specialists, Ltd. © 2022 Affinity Media
LAKE ERIE
CANADA
U.S.
ONTARIO
OHIO
MICHIGAN
INDIANA
PA.
W. VA.
KY.
CONNEAUT
NORTH KINGSVILLE
GENEVA-ON-THE-LAKE
ASHTABULA
GENEVA
JEFFERSON
THOMPSON
MONTVILLE
ANDOVER
ORWELL
WILLIAMSFIELD
NEWBURY
AURORA
MANTUA
CORTLAND
GARRETTSVILLE
STREETSBORO
NEWTON FALLS
RAVENNA
HUBBARD
LAKE MILTON
HARTVILLE
SALEM
CANTON
LISBON
EAST LIVERPOOL
CARROLLTON
TORONTO
RICHMOND
MINERAL CITY
NAVARRE
FAYETTE
OREGON
ROSSFORD
SWANTON
WEST UNITY
WAUSEON
ARCHBOLD
WHITEHOUSE
STONY RIDGE
GRAND RAPIDS
PORT CLINTON
SANDUSKY
CLYDE
BELLEVUE
NORWALK
AMHERST
OBERLIN
GRAFTON
WELLINGTON
NEW LONDON
MEDINA
SPENCER
NOVA
SULLIVAN
WEST SALEM
SEVILLE
VAN BUREN
BASCOM
TIFFIN
WILLARD
VANLUE
BLUFFTON
VAN WERT
ASHLAND
SHELBY
MANSFIELD
WOOSTER
N. LAWRENCE
UNIONTOWN
LIMA
MENDON
CELINA
WAPAKONETA
ST. MARYS
LAKEVIEW
PERRYSVILLE
SHREVE
MOUNT EATON
LOUDONVILLE
MILLERSBURG
BERLIN
WINESBURG
NEW PHILADELPHIA
BUTLER
MOUNT GILEAD
HOWARD
MARENGO
DEERSVILLE
FREEPORT
FLUSHING
SMYRNA
COSHOCTON
FORT LORAMIE
BELLEFONTAINE
WEST LIBERTY
DELAWARE
SUNBURY
ROSEWOOD
PIQUA
CAMBRIDGE
BELMONT
NEWARK
SENECAVILLE
SPRINGFIELD
LONDON
ZANESVILLE
DUNCAN FALLS
BUCKEYE LAKE
NEW PARIS
HUBER HTS.
DAYTON
YELLOW SPRINGS
GALLOWAY
CANAL WINCHESTER
BALTIMORE
LANCASTER
CALDWELL
MOUNT STERLING
CIRCLEVILLE
LOGAN
GLOUSTER
NELSONVILLE
MARIETTA
OXFORD
LEBANON
WILMINGTON
LAURELVILLE
SOUTH BLOOMINGVILLE
HARRISON
MASON
BLANCHESTER
CHILLICOTHE
BAINBRIDGE
ATHENS
ZALESKI
ALBANY
COOLVILLE
HILLSBORO
NORTH BEND
CINCINNATI
BATAVIA
WELLSTON
REEDSVILLE
RACINE
OAK HILL
GALLIPOLIS
PORTSMOUTH
STOUT
Cleveland
Columbus
Toledo
Akron
Youngstown
Wheeling
Parkersburg
Huntington
Charleston
Lexington
Frankfort

ROAD TRIPS

Big Coasters and Cool Guitars Highlight This Buckeye Journey

Ohio

LOCATION
OHIO

DISTANCE
124 MILES

DRIVE TIME
2 HRS 13 MINS

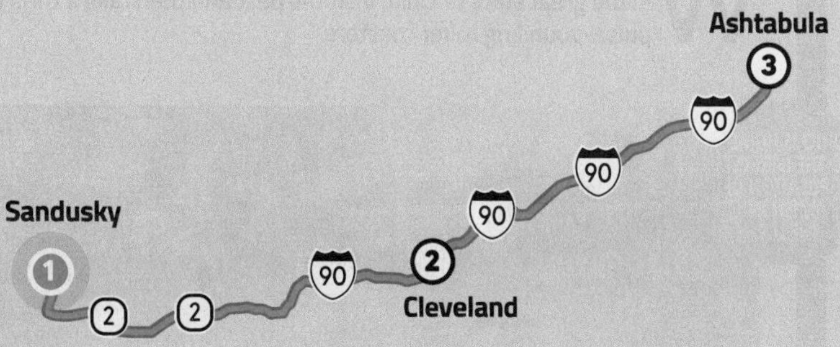

Ohio's Lake Erie coast bustles with fun and adventure. From adrenaline-pumping amusement park rides to hefty fish that tip the scales in a big way, Ohio has a few surprises in store. Take this trip along the state's north coast to learn about all that Ohio offers.

1 Sandusky
Starting Point

Sandusky is a great base for boating and fishing, owing to its prime location on the banks of Lake Erie, which teems with walleye, bass, rainbow trout and perch. Prefer land-based thrills? Cedar Point is one of the most famous amusement parks in the United States. Cedar Point offers 71 fantastic rides suitable to thrill-seekers of all ages and levels of daring, including six roller coasters over 200 feet high. The Top Thrill Dragster, the second-tallest coaster in the world, is a white-knuckle ride that thrills even the most jaded coaster buffs. Other wildly popular attractions include Kalahari, one of the world's largest indoor water parks, and the Ghostly Manor Thrill Center, which boasts a haunted house, escape room and a virtual reality feature.

2 Cleveland
Drive 66 miles ▪ 1 hour, 11 minutes

Would you like to see one of the notorious Fender Stratocasters played by rock star Jimi Hendrix during the wild 1960s? How about one of the lavish suits Elvis wore during his amazing career? It's all at the Rock 'n' Roll Hall of Fame on the shores of Lake Erie. Exhibits and artifacts will acquaint you with the musical pioneers who made earth-shaking contributions to music. If you prefer a different kind of wildlife, cruise over to the Cleveland Metroparks Zoo divided in several areas, including the Australian Adventure, Waterfowl Lake and Rainforest. It's like no zoo you'll ever experience. At the Cleveland Botanical Garden, visitors can stroll through the 18,000-square-foot Eleanor Armstrong Smith glasshouse, which encompasses ecosystems modeled on the Costa Rican Rainforest and Madagascar desert. Peruse magnificent and rare flowers during the garden's annual OrchidMania event from January to March.

Getty Images/iStockphoto

3 Ashtabula
Drive 58 miles ▪ 1 hour, 2 minutes

Explore this hilly region to get away from it all and discover new adventures. Get onboard a fishing charter for walleye and perch in Lake Erie. Cyclists can hit the Western Reserve Greenway Bike Trail, a 44-mile paved rail-trail that traverses Ashtabula and Trumbull Counties. The trail runs past farms and through wooded areas. During the summer, the thick canopy provides shade for riders. Interpretive signs along the way detail the area's history. The region is home to 19 covered bridges, and the area's wineries are praised for their flavorful vintages and casual atmosphere. Some allow dogs.

BIKING · BOATING · DINING · ENTERTAINMENT · FISHING · HIKING · HUNTING · PADDLING · SHOPPING · SIGHTSEEING

OH

Ohio SPOTLIGHTS

Beat it to the Buckeye State for History and Thrills

What do rock 'n' roll and Amish culture have in common? They both thrive in the great state of Ohio. Visit the past and then take a thrill ride on pulse-pounding roller coasters.

OHIO IS HOME TO THE LARGEST POPULATION OF AMISH IN THE U.S.

Getty Images/iStockphoto

Amish farms attract visitors seeking freshly baked goods and produce.

Amish Country

Home to the second-largest Amish community in the world, Holmes County, Ohio, is a haven for plain living, hearty food, and traditional arts and crafts. From horse-drawn buggy rides to handmade goods, a visit here is like stepping back to a simpler time. It's also one of the most scenic corners of the state, with endlessly rolling hills and long stretches of farmland that harken back to an America of yesteryear. For a quaint, relaxing getaway, Amish Country stands alone as one of the best destinations in the Buckeye State.

Living History

Introduce yourself to the history and culture of Amish people at the Amish & Mennonite Heritage Center in the small town of Berlin. Opened in 1981, the Center includes one of the region's most popular attractions: a 10ft by 265ft. circular mural known as Behalt. The hand-painted cyclorama is a tribute to the triumphs and trials that led the plain living people to the area and gives deep insight into how and why the Amish live the way they do. Guided tours are available and feature access to the museum grounds, including a restored pioneer barn house, schoolhouse, wagons, and more. The nearby Schrock's Heritage Village offers a family-friendly look at the Amish way of life through a collection of shops and attractions found nowhere else. Enjoy handmade cinnamon rolls at the Olde World Bakery, artisan baskets at the Craft Mall, or tour a working Amish home and farm.

Hearty Home Cooking

The town of Millersburg is not just the county's biggest city, it's also the perfect place to experience Amish Country's famed home cooking. From the fruit pies at Miller's Bakery to the country-style breakfasts at the Berlin Farmstead, the focus here is on simple, local food cooked with love. Other standouts include Mrs. Yoder's Kitchen, Der Dutchman, and the 40-year-old Amish Door Restaurant. For an even closer look at the area's artisanal food traditions, try a visit to a local cheesemaker, many of whom offer a front-row seat to the process. Heini's Cheese Chalet and Guggisberg Cheese in Sugarcreek are two local favorites that offer tours, samples, and plenty of sweet treats to go along with your visit. Round out your foodie adventure with one of the famous fry pies at the End of the Commons General Store in Mesopotamia. Built in 1840, it's the oldest in the state and a true treasure.

Old World Outings

No trip to Amish Country would be complete without exploring the landscape on an authentic horse-drawn buggy tour. Available at many of the farms and heritage centers throughout the region, tours often include stopovers at bakeries, farms, or other cultural highlights. Of course, you can easily explore the serene landscape on your own as well. The long stretches of quiet backroads are perfect for cycling and horseback riding. The Holmes County Trail, a converted rail trail that runs for over 23 miles, is the area's hidden gem. Wide enough to accommodate buggies, it's paved and graded, offering a gently backdrop for bike rides past pristine forests and picturesque swamplands.

Franklin Park Conservatory and Botanical Gardens preserve beautiful flora and fauna near Columbus.

Fun Festivities

Thirty minutes east of Millersburg, the village of Sugarcreek has more than a few claims to fame. Known as "Little Switzerland," it's home to a vast array of charming shops and eateries, most of which are decked out in a playful Swiss architectural style, a nod to the area's earliest settlers. It's also home to the World's Largest Cuckoo Clock, built in 1972, whose characters still come alive every hour. The town's most popular attraction, however, is the Ohio Swiss Festival, which takes place each fall and draws visitors from across the state. Featuring Swiss cheese eating contests, stone-throwing events, parades, and more, it's a one-of-a-kind celebration.

Columbus

Columbus shines as an important regional destination for arts, sports, leisure, education and shopping. The renovated Arena District is now hailed as a paradigm for a planned urban environment with warehouses transformed into commercial and residential enclaves that respect the neighborhood's turn-of-the-century industrial architecture. A 20,000-seat arena, hip restaurants, cutting edge boutiques, upmarket hotels and sleek office spaces attract a vibrant and entrepreneurial population.

Premier Sites

As the state capitol, many of Columbus's attractions are historical in nature. The Ohio Historical Center and Ohio Village house a collection of over a million artifacts spanning archaeology and history. Exhibits examine the first Ohioans with displays on prehistoric Native American art and investigate Ohio's natural world, including its plants, animals, climate, geology and geography. Ohio Village is a fascinating recreation of a typical 19th-century county seat town, complete with special events, such as ice cream socials. Recent rotating exhibits include a retrospective on polemical Presidential elections and Ohio's role as a key swing state. It's worth taking a look at the historic Ohio Statehouse, a masterpiece of 19th-century Greek Revival architecture.

Local Color

Dating to 1876, the open-air North Market features over thirty unique merchants purveying fresh and prepared foods—bratwurst, falafel, spring rolls, fresh produce—which can be enjoyed at the market or to go. On Saturdays, during growing season, there is an atmospheric farmers market. Throughout its history, fishmongers, farmers, butchers and bakers have sold their goods here, and it is the only one of four original public markets remaining in Columbus. In 1992 it moved to its current space. Franklin Park Conservatory is the site of the largest cast-iron statue in the world. Created for the 1904 World's Fair in St. Louis, the imposing male statue depicts Vulcan, the god of the forge.

On Land

While it's not surrounded by scenic mountains or lakes, Columbus does have a surprising number of scenic and picturesque places to hike or walk nearby. Known for its mostly paved "Scioto Mile," the Scioto Greenway extends 12 miles through many parts of Columbus and is a wonderful place to hike, walk, run, skate or bike. Suitable for all levels, the trail affords sweeping views of the Columbus skyline. The Camp Chase Trail is a shared recreation path with bikers, runners and walkers, and extends nearly 16 miles to the rural outskirts of central Ohio. Opened in 1958, just a short drive from downtown, Scioto Downs is one of the nation's most prestigious thoroughbred and harness tracks. The track is famous for the Jug Preview, the final preparation for horses that race in the historic Little Brown Jug in Delaware, Ohio.

On the Water

The slow-moving Scioto and Olentangy Rivers meet just outside the downtown area and are perfect for kayaking and canoeing. Olentangy Paddle guides small groups on kayaking and canoeing excursions down these placid waterways. Smaller tributaries, such as Alum Creek and Big Walnut Creek, snake their way through the city. The Wyandot Lake

SPOTLIGHTS

Getty Images/iStockphoto

The Marblehead Lighthouse is oldest navigational beacon in continuous operation on the Geat Lakes.

Amusement and Water Park is one of the Midwest's most popular water parks and is attached to the acclaimed Columbus Zoo and Aquarium. The 23-acre facility runs the gamut of water-themed attractions, including 45 rides, water slides, a Ferris wheel, and an antique carousel. Don't miss Zuma Falls, a zigzagging 455-foot descent experienced in inner tubes.

Rich History

Throughout its history, Columbus has seen its fair share of challenges and setbacks. Initially laid out in 1812 and incorporated in 1816, it continued to grow thanks to its connection to the Ohio and Erie Canal and later, railroads. It was not the original capital, but its central location in the heart of Ohio and between the Scioto and Olentangy Rivers helped develop its status as a shipping port. By the late 1880s, there were almost two hundred factories in operation and brewing companies established by the German immigrant population. Since the late 1980s, the city has won numerous accolades for its attention to renovation.

LOCAL FAVORITE

Dad's Bar-B-Que Beef

Fall in Ohio brings football fans out to root for the Bengals, Browns or Buckeyes. It's also a great season for savory beef. *Recipe by Sheree Griswold.*

INGREDIENTS

- ☐ A 5-6 lb boneless chuck roast
- ☐ 1 cup ketchup
- ☐ 1 cup barbecue sauce
- ☐ 1 cup water
- ☐ 1 large chopped onion
- ☐ 2 ½ tsp vinegar
- ☐ 2 tsp Worcestershire sauce
- ☐ Granulated garlic, pepper, salt and a seasoning salt all to taste

DIRECTIONS

Place roast in a cast iron Dutch oven. Mix all ingredients and pour over roast. Cover and slow cook over an open fire for about 5 hours. Stir and break up meat as it cooks. Shred meat and serve on onion rolls.

Nothing beats that southern flavor!

Sandusky

Pulse-pounding fun awaits on the shores of Lake Erie. Home to one of the world's premier amusement parks, the northern Ohio town sits on a peninsula jutting into Lake Erie, with plenty of swimming, fishing and boating on offer. Toss in a unique maritime history and easy island-hopping adventures for a once-in-a-lifetime Buckeye getaway.

Killer Coasters

Thrill-seekers have a home at Cedar Point, one of the country's largest and most popular amusement parks. More than 3 million visitors head to the park each year to enjoy over 71 rides, including 18 roller coasters, as well as marinas, sports complexes and a mile-long beach. The Top Thrill Dragster, the second-tallest coaster in the world, is a ride that thrills even the most jaded coaster buffs.

Haul in the Big Ones

Lake Erie presents endless possibilities for boating and fishing. Hop on the 20-minute Jet Express ferry to Kelleys Island to enjoy laid-back vibes and long stretches of public beaches. From there, you can kayak, swim and fish the bountiful waters just offshore where catfish, perch, bass and walleye regularly bite. Put-in-Bay, the southernmost of the Bass Islands, is another must-see Erie Island and the perfect destination for those looking to fish.

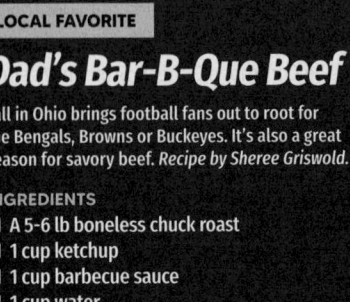

Luminous Lighthouse

At the tip of a rocky peninsula jutting into Sandusky Bay, Marblehead Lighthouse State Park is home to the oldest continuously operated lighthouse on the Great Lakes. Picturesque and popular, the park is a perfect destination for picnics, nature hikes or a tour that climbs the 77 steps to the top of the beacon. Take the ferry to the north for seven miles to visit Kelleys Island State Park. Wander six miles of nature trails and marvel at the famed "glacial grooves."

FOR MORE INFORMATION

Ohio Tourism Division, 800-282-5393, www.ohio.org

Holmes County Chamber of Commerce & Tourism Bureau, 877-643-8824, www.visitamishcountry.com

Greater Columbus Convention & Visitors Bureau, 866-397-2657, experiencecolumbus.com

Sandusky County Convention and Visitors Bureau, 800-255-8070, sanduskycounty.org

Ohio

AKRON — B4 *Summit*

AKRON See also Aurora, Hartville, Medina, Navarre, North Lawrence, Seville, Streetsboro, Uniontown & Wooster.

CHEROKEE PARK CAMPGROUND
good sam park **Ratings: 7/8.5★/7** (Campground) 30 Avail: 30 W, 30 E (30/50 amps). 2021 rates: $38. May 01 to Oct 20. (330)673-1964, 3064 State Route 43, Mogadore, OH 44260

COUNTRYSIDE CAMPGROUND
good sam park **Ratings: 8.5/9.5★/9** (Campground) From Jct of US-224 & SR-43, N 2.4 mi on Sr-43 (L). **FAC:** paved/gravel rds. (86 spaces). Avail: 25 gravel, 8 pull-thrus, (28x74), back-ins (25x50), 25 full hkups (30 amps), seasonal sites, WiFi @ sites, $, tent sites, rentals, dump, laundry, groc, LP gas, fire rings, firewood, controlled access. **REC:** heated pool, Mogadore Reservoir: fishing, boating nearby, playground. Pet restrict (B). eco-friendly. 2021 rates: $42 to $46. May 01 to Oct 15.
(330)628-1212 Lat: 41.06194, Lon: -81.34738
2687 State Route 43, Mogadore, OH 44260
countrysidecampgrounds.com
See ad this page

Travel Services

CAMPING WORLD OF AKRON As the nation's largest retailer of RV supplies, accessories, services and new and used RVs, Camping World is committed to making your total RV experience better. **SERVICES:** RV, tire, RV appliance, MH mechanical, staffed RV wash, restrooms. RV Sales. RV supplies, LP gas, emergency parking, RV accessible. Hours: 9am to 7pm.
(888)586-5558 Lat: 40.978922, Lon: -81.486322
1005 Interstate Parkway, Akron, OH 44312
www.campingworld.com

ALBANY — D4 *Athens*

LAKE SNOWDEN
(Public) From jct US 50/32 & CR 681: Go 1 mi N on US 50/32. **FAC:** (125 spaces). Avail: 120 grass, 90 E seasonal sites, tent sites, dump, laundry, fire rings, firewood. **REC:** Lake Snowden: swim, fishing, kayaking/canoeing, boating nearby, shuffleboard, rec open to public. Pets OK $. Partial handicap access. 2021 rates: $24 to $33.
(740)698-6373 Lat: 39.240722, Lon: -82.190778
5900 US Rt 50, Albany, OH 45710
www.lakesnowden.com

AMHERST — A4 *Lorain*

SERVICE PLAZA-VERMILION VALLEY (Public) From town, E 2 mi on Ohio Tpke at MP-139.5 (R). Overnight rest area (Between Exits 135 & 142). Avail: 10 E. 2021 rates: $20. (440)234-2081

ANDOVER — A5 *Ashtabula*

BAY SHORE FAMILY CAMPING **Ratings: 7.5/9★/9** (Campground) 140 Avail: 124 full hkups, 16 W, 16 E (30 amps). 2021 rates: $46 to $58. Apr 15 to Oct 16. (440)293-7202, 7124 Pymatuning Lake Rd, Andover, OH 44003

JEFFCO LAKES RESORTS **Ratings: 7/6.5/6.5** (Campground) Avail: 100 full hkups (30 amps). 2021 rates: $35 to $55. May 01 to Oct 15. (440)293-7485, 6758 Hayes Rd, Andover, OH 44003

PYMATUNING (Public State Park) From town, E 1.5 mi on SR-85 to Lake Rd, S 4 mi (L). 373 Avail: 18 full hkups, 334 E (20/30 amps). 2021 rates: $21 to $34. (440)293-6030

WILDWOOD ACRES FAMILY CAMPGROUND **Ratings: 6/NA/8.5** (Campground) 52 Avail: 52 W, 52 E (30 amps), Pit toilets. 2021 rates: $30 to $35. Apr 17 to Oct 18. (440)293-6838, 6091 Marvin Rd, Andover, OH 44003

ARCHBOLD — A1 *Fulton*

SAUDER VILLAGE CAMPGROUND
good sam park **Ratings: 9/9.5★/8.5** (Campground) From Jct of I-80 (OH Tpke) & Exit 25/SR-66: Go S 3.9 mi on SR-66 to SR-2, E 0.25 mi (R) Register at Sauder Heritage Inn. **FAC:** paved rds. Avail: 77 gravel, 11 pull-thrus, (34x75), back-ins (40x60), 55 full hkups, 22 W, 22 E (50 amps), WiFi @ sites, tent sites, dump, laundry, fire rings, firewood, restaurant. **REC:** pool, pond, fishing, shuffleboard, playground, rec open to public. Pets OK. Partial handicap access. Big rig sites, eco-friendly. 2021 rates: $29 to $52, Military discount. Apr 15 to Oct 31.
(800)590-9755 Lat: 41.54320, Lon: -84.30272
22611 SR 2, Archbold, OH 43502
saudervillage.org
See ad this page

Things to See and Do

HISTORIC SAUDER VILLAGE Historic rural village. May 01 to Oct 27. Partial handicap access. RV accessible. Restrooms. Food. Hours: 10am to 5pm Tues - Sat , Sun 12-4. Adult fee: $20.
(800)590-9755 Lat: 41.54320, Lon: -84.30272
22611 SR 2, Archbold, OH 43502
www.saudervillage.org
See ad this page

MUSEUM AT SAUDER VILLAGE Historic Village, Museum, Sauder Heritage Inn, Barn Restaurant, Bakery, Campground & Retail Shops. Museum dedicated to Ohio's history. Jun 02 to Oct 30. Partial handicap access. RV accessible. Restrooms. Food. Hours: 10am to 5pm W- Sa. Adult fee: $20 .
(800)590-9755 Lat: 41.54320, Lon: -84.30272
22611 SR 2, Archbold, OH 43502
www.saudervillage.org
See ad this page

OLD BARN RESTAURANT AT SAUDER VILLAGE Pioneer themed restaurant, buffet and menu service. Partial handicap access. RV accessible. Restrooms. Food. Hours: 11am to 8pm.
(800)590-9755 Lat: 41.54320, Lon: -84.30272
22611 SR 2, Archbold, OH 43502
www.saudervillage.org
See ad this page

ASHLAND — B3 *Ashland*

HICKORY LAKES CAMPGROUND **Ratings: 7.5/8★/8** (Campground) 60 Avail: 60 W, 60 E (30/50 amps). 2021 rates: $46. Apr 15 to Sep 30. (419)869-7587, 23 Township Rd 1300, West Salem, OH 44287

ASHTABULA — A5 *Ashtabula*

HIDE-A-WAY LAKES CAMPGROUND **Ratings: 7.5/7.5★/8.5** (Campground) 50 Avail: 5 full hkups, 45 W, 45 E (30/50 amps). 2021 rates: $48 to $55. May 01 to Oct 23. (440)992-4431, 2034 South Ridge Rd W, Ashtabula, OH 44004

ATHENS — D4 *Athens*

STROUDS RUN (Public State Park) From jct US 33 (Columbus Rd exit) & N Lancaster Rd: Go E on N Lancaster Rd, which becomes Columbia Ave then Strouds Run Rd (CR 20). 78 Avail: Pit toilets. 2021 rates: $19. (740)594-2628

AURORA — B4 *Portage*

ROUNDUP LAKE CAMPGROUND
good sam park **Ratings: 8.5/8★/8** (Campground) 58 Avail: 33 full hkups, 25 W, 25 S (30/50 amps). 2021 rates: $44 to $54. May 01 to Oct 31. (330)562-9100, 3392 SR-82, Mantua, OH 44255

BAINBRIDGE — D2 *Pike*

PAINT CREEK (Public State Park) From Jct of SR-41 & US-50, W 5 mi on US-50 (R). Avail: 199 E (30/50 amps). 2021 rates: $24 to $28. (866)644-6727

PIKE LAKE (Public State Park) From Jct of US-50 & Potts Hill Rd, SE 4 mi on Potts Hill Rd to Pike Lake Rd, S 3 mi (L). Avail: 80 E (30/50 amps), Pit toilets. 2021 rates: $18 to $22. (740)493-2212

BALTIMORE — D3 *Fairfield*

RIPPLING STREAM CAMPGROUND **Ratings: 6/8.5★/8** (RV Area in MH Park) 21 Avail: 21 W, 21 E (20/30 amps). 2021 rates: $30. Apr 01 to Oct 31. (740)862-6065, 3640 Reynoldsburg-Baltimore Rd, Baltimore, OH 43105

BASCOM — B2 *Seneca*

MEADOWBROOK PARK (Public) From Jct of SR-635 & SR-18, E 1 mi on SR-18 (R). 225 Avail: 225 W, 225 E (30 amps). 2021 rates: $35. Apr 15 to Oct 31. (419)937-2242

BATAVIA — D1 *Hamilton*

EAST FORK (Public State Park) From Jct of I-275E & SR-32E, E 10 mi on SR-32E to Half Acre Rd, S 1.5 mi to Old SR-32E, E 0.1 mi (R). 399 Avail: 23 full hkups, 376 E (30 amps). 2021 rates: $28. (513)734-6521

BELLEFONTAINE — C2 *Logan*

BACK 40 **Ratings: 5.5/7/8** (Campground) 30 Avail: 30 W, 30 E (30 amps). 2021 rates: $37 to $40. May 01 to Oct 31. (937)468-2267, 959 CR 111 E, Rushsylvania, OH 43347

OHIO STATE EAGLES RECREATION PARK **Ratings: 4.5/4/7** (Campground) 22 Avail: 22 W, 22 E (30/50 amps). 2021 rates: $35. Apr 01 to Nov 01. (937)593-1565, 5118 US 68N, Bellefontaine, OH 43311

BELLEVUE — B3 *Huron*

GOTTA GETAWAY RV PARK **Ratings: 8/9★/9** (RV Park) 47 Avail: 47 W, 47 E (30/50 amps). 2021 rates: $39 to $46. May 01 to Oct 31. (419)483-3177, 4888 US Hwy 20E, Bellevue, OH 44811

BELMONT — C5 *Belmont*

BARKCAMP (Public State Park) From Jct of I-70 & SR-149 (exit 208), S 1 mi on SR-149, E 1 mi Fox Trail Rd. Avail: 123 E (20/30 amps). 2021 rates: $21 to $23. (740)484-4064

BERLIN — C4 *Holmes*

A SPOTLIGHT Introducing Amish Country's colorful attractions appearing at the front of this state section.

BERLIN See also Canton, Coshocton, Loudonville, Millersburg, Mount Eaton, Navarre, New Philadelphia, North Lawrence, Shreve, Winesburg & Wooster.

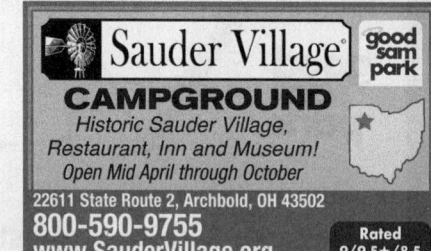

OH

Ohio Privately Owned Campground Information Updated by our Good Sam Representatives

James & Mary Margrave

We've been involved in the RV lifestyle for over 20 years, and for the past 5 years or so, we've done it full time. We love being around our fellow RVers, who are great people. And we love seeing the great variety in the parks on our travels.

BERLIN (CONT)

BERLIN RV PARK & CAMPGROUND

good sam park **Ratings: 7.5/9.5★/9.5** (Campground) W-bnd: From Jct of I-77 & SR-39 (Exit 83), W 18 mi on SR-39 (L); or E-bnd: From Jct of US 62 (SR-39), E 4.5 mi on US 62 (SR-39) (R). **FAC:** all weather rds. Avail: 72 all weather, 39 pull-thrus, (30x65), back-ins (30x50), 66 full hkups, 6 W, 6 E (30/50 amps), WiFi @ sites, tent sites, dump, laundry, fire rings, firewood. **REC:** playground. Pets OK. Partial handicap access. Big rig sites, eco-friendly. 2021 rates: $29 to $48, Military discount. Apr 01 to Dec 01.
(330)674-4774 Lat: 40.55285, Lon: -81.83573
5898 State Route 39, Millersburg, OH 44654
www.berlinrvpark.com
See ad page 697

SCENIC HILLS RV PARK

good sam park **Ratings: 8.5/NA/9.5** (RV Park) Avail: 112 full hkups (30/50 amps). 2021 rates: $40 to $50. Apr 01 to Nov 01. (330)893-3607, 4483 Township Hwy 367, Millersburg, OH 44654

BLANCHESTER — D2 *Clinton*

STONELICK (Public State Park) From Jct of SR-133 & SR-727, S 3 mi on SR-727, follow signs (L). Avail: 108 E (50 amps). 2021 rates: $26. Apr 01 to Oct 31. (866)644-6727

BLUFFTON — B2 *Hancock*

TWIN LAKES PARK **Ratings: 8.5/8/8** (Campground) 41 Avail: 6 full hkups, 35 W, 35 E (30/50 amps). 2021 rates: $45 to $55. (419)477-5255, 3506 TR-34, Bluffton, OH 45817

BUCKEYE LAKE — C3 *Licking*

BUCKEYE LAKE COLUMBUS EAST KOA **Ratings: 9/9★/8** (Campground) 178 Avail: 148 full hkups, 30 W, 30 E (30/50 amps). 2021 rates: $45 to $90. Apr 01 to Oct 31. (740)928-0706, 4460 Walnut Rd, Buckeye Lake, OH 43008

BUTLER — C3 *Richland*

RIVER TRAIL CROSSING RV PARK **Ratings: 6/5/7.5** (Campground) 31 Avail: 20 full hkups, 11 W, 11 E (30/50 amps). 2021 rates: $38 to $42. May 01 to Oct 15. (419)883-3888, 1597 SR-97, Butler, OH 44822

CALDWELL — D4 *Noble*

WOLF RUN (Public State Park) From Jct of I-77 & Belle Valley exit (Rte 821), S 0.5 mi on Rte 821 to Rte 215, NE 0.9 mi to Wolf Run Rd, N 0.3 mi (R). Avail: 71 E (50 amps), Pit toilets. 2021 rates: $25. Apr 01 to Nov 01. (740)732-5035

CAMBRIDGE — C4 *Guernsey*

SALT FORK (Public State Park) From Jct of I-77 & US-22, E 7 mi on US-22, N 2 mi on SH-285. 212 Avail: 40 full hkups, 172 E (50 amps). 2021 rates: $24 to $37. (740)432-1508

SPRING VALLEY CAMPGROUND **Ratings: 7/8/9.5** (Campground) 139 Avail: 103 full hkups, 36 W, 36 E (50 amps). 2021 rates: $32 to $38. (740)439-9291, 8000 Dozer Rd, Cambridge, OH 43725

CANAL WINCHESTER — D3 *Franklin*

JACKSON LAKE CAMPGROUND PARK **Ratings: 7/5.5/7** (RV Park) Avail: 38 full hkups (30/50 amps). 2021 rates: $52 to $56. (614)837-2656, 3715 Cedar Hill Rd. NW, Canal Winchester, OH 43110

CANTON — B4 *Stark*

BEAR CREEK RESORT RANCH KOA **Ratings: 8.5/9.5★/9** (Campground) 83 Avail: 77 full hkups, 6 W, 6 E (30/50 amps). 2021 rates: $48 to $80. (330)484-3901, 3232 Downing St SW, East Sparta, OH 44626

CARROLLTON — C5 *Carroll*

ABC COUNTRY CAMPING & CABINS **Ratings: 6/8.5★/7** (Campground) 30 Avail: 30 W, 30 E (30/50 amps). 2021 rates: $40. May 01 to Oct 15. (330)735-3220, 4105 Fresno Rd NW, Carrollton, OH 44615

PETERSBURG MARINA AND CAMPGROUNDS (Public) From town: Go 4 mi S on Hwy-332, then W on CR-22. 88 Avail: 14 full hkups, 74 E. (330)627-4270

CELINA — C1 *Mercer*

KOZY KAMP GROUND **Ratings: 7.5/8/9** (Campground) 100 Avail: 9 full hkups, 91 W, 91 E (30/50 amps). 2021 rates: $45. Apr 15 to Oct 15. (419)268-2275, 5134 Its It Rd, Celina, OH 45822

Always do a Pre-Drive Safety Check!

CHILLICOTHE — D3 *Ross*

GREAT SEAL (Public State Park) From town, N 3 mi on US-23 to Delano Rd, E 3.5 mi to Marietta Rd, S 0.5 mi (L). 15 Avail: Pit toilets. 2021 rates: $16 to $20. Mar 01 to Dec 31. (740)887-4818

SCIOTO TRAIL (Public State Park) From jct US-35 & US-23: Go 10 mi S on US-23, then 1/2 mi E on SR 372, then 2 mi E on Stoney Creek Rd, then ½ mi on Lake Rd (E). Avail: 55 E (30/50 amps), Pit toilets. 2021 rates: $16 to $24. (740)887-4818

SUN VALLEY CAMPGROUND

good sam park **Ratings: 7/9★/9** (Campground) From Jct of US 35 & CR-550, take CR-550 exit, go W 2 mi on CR-550 (R). **FAC:** all weather rds. (56 spaces). 32 Avail: 25 gravel, 7 grass, patios, 9 pull-thrus, (24x100), back-ins (20x78), 14 full hkups, 18 W, 18 E (30/50 amps), seasonal sites, WiFi @ sites, tent sites, dump, fire rings, firewood. **REC:** pond, fishing, playground. Pets OK. Big rig sites. 2021 rates: $45 to $60, Military discount. no cc.
(740)775-3490 Lat: 39.38219, Lon: -83.08528
10105 CR-550, Chillicothe, OH 45601
www.SunValleyCampground.net
See ad opposite page

CINCINNATI — D1 *Hamilton*

CINCINNATI In OH, see also Lebanon, North Bend & Wilmington. In IN, see also Batesville, Florence & Rising Sun. In KY, see also Corinth, Dry Ridge & Walton.

WINTON WOODS CAMPGROUND (GREAT PARKS OF HAMILTON COUNTY) (Public) From Jct of I-275 & Winton Rd (Exit 39), S 3.5 mi on Winton Rd, L on Lakeview Drive, follow signs (R). 105 Avail: 37 full hkups, 68 E (30/50 amps). 2021 rates: $25 to $65.50. (513)851-2267

CIRCLEVILLE — D3 *Pickaway*

A W MARION (Public State Park) From Jct of Hwy 188 & SR-22, E 4 mi on SR-22 to East Ringold Southern Rd, N 1 mi to Warner Huffer Rd, E 0.5 mi (L). Avail: 28 E (30 amps), Pit toilets. 2021 rates: $18 to $22. Apr 01 to Oct 31. (740)869-3124

CLEVELAND — A4 *Cuyahoga*

CLEVELAND See also Medina & Streetsboro.

AMERICAN WILDERNESS CAMPGROUND

good sam park **Ratings: 7/8.5★/9.5** (Campground) From jct I-80 & I-480 & SR 10, SW 2.2 mi on SR 10 to SR 83, S 7.3 on SR 83 (L). **FAC:** gravel rds. (166 spaces). Avail: 56 gravel, 23 pull-thrus, (38x95), back-ins (30x78), 56 W, 56 E (30/50 amps), seasonal sites, tent sites, rentals, dump, mobile sewer, laundry, groc, fire rings, firewood, controlled access. **REC:** American Wilderness Lakes: swim, fishing, boating nearby, playground. Pets OK. Partial handicap access, eco-friendly. 2021 rates: $42 to $48, Military discount. May 01 to Oct 15.
(440)926-3700 Lat: 41.23325, Lon: -82.02297
17273 Avon Belden Rd SR 83, Grafton, OH 44044
americanwildernesscampground.com
See primary listing at Grafton and ad page 692

CLYDE — B3 *Sandusky*

LEAFY OAKS CAMPGROUND **Ratings: 8/8.5★/9** (Campground) 41 Avail: 15 full hkups, 26 W, 26 E (30/50 amps). 2021 rates: $28 to $49. Apr 15 to Oct 15. (419)639-2887, 6955 State Route 101 N, Clyde, OH 43410

COLUMBUS — C3 *Franklin*

COLUMBUS See also Baltimore, Canal Winchester, Delaware, Galloway, Marengo & Sunbury.

CROSS CREEK CAMPING RESORT

good sam park **Ratings: 10/10★/10** (RV Resort) From I-71, go W 3 mi on SR 36/37 to Lackey Old State Rd, go S 3.2 mi (R). **FAC:** paved rds. (200 spaces). Avail: 158 all weather, patios, 46 pull-thrus, (40x65), back-ins (35x65), 136 full hkups, 22 W, 22 E (30/50 amps), seasonal sites, WiFi @ sites, tent sites, rentals, dump, laundry, groc, LP gas, fire rings, firewood. **REC:** pool, boating nearby, playground, hunting nearby, rec open to public. Pet restrict (B/Q). Partial handicap access. Big rig sites, eco-friendly. 2021 rates: $40 to $80. ATM.
(740)549-2267 Lat: 40.231675, Lon: -82.986603
3190 S Old State Rd, Delaware, OH 43015
www.alumcreek.com
See primary listing at Delaware and ad this page, 694

CONNEAUT — A5 *Ashtabula*

EVERGREEN LAKE PARK

good sam park **Ratings: 8/9★/9** (Campground) From Jct of I-90 & SR-7 (exit 241), N 0.5 mi on SR-7 to Gateway Ave, W 0.1 mi to Center Rd, S 0.4 mi (R). **FAC:** paved/gravel rds. (280 spaces). 60 Avail: 52 gravel, 8 grass, patios, 30 pull-thrus, (35x63), back-ins (35x52), 12 full hkups, 48 W, 48 E (50 amps), seasonal sites, WiFi @ sites, tent sites, rentals, dump, mobile sewer, laundry, groc, LP gas, fire rings, firewood, controlled access. **REC:** pond, swim, fishing, boating nearby, shuffleboard, playground. Pets OK. Partial handicap access. Big rig sites, eco-friendly. 2021 rates: $34 to $39, Military discount. May 01 to Oct 15. ATM.
(440)599-8802 Lat: 41.92657, Lon: -80.57098
703 Center Rd, Conneaut, OH 44030
evergreenlakecampground.com
See ad page 786

COOLVILLE — D4 *Athens*

CARTHAGE GAP CAMPGROUND **Ratings: 7.5/8.5★/7.5** (Campground) Avail: 15 full hkups (30/50 amps). 2021 rates: $40 to $45. Apr 15 to Oct 31. (740)667-3072, 22575 Brimstone Rd, Coolville, OH 45723

CORTLAND — B5 *Trumbull*

MOSQUITO LAKE (Public State Park) From Jct of SR-46 & SR-305, W 2 mi on SR-305 (R). Avail: 218 E (30 amps). 2021 rates: $20 to $26. (330)638-5700

COSHOCTON — C4 *Coshocton*

COSHOCTON KOA **Ratings: 8/8.5★/8.5** (Campground) 46 Avail: 37 full hkups, 9 W, 9 E (50 amps). 2021 rates: $69 to $79. (740)502-9245, 24688 County Road 10, Coshocton, OH 43812

LAKE PARK CAMPGROUNDS (Public) From Jct of US-36 & SR-83, N 0.5 mi on SR-83 (L). Avail: 69 E (20/30 amps). 2021 rates: $20 to $27. Apr 01 to Nov 30. (740)622-7528

DAYTON — D1 *Greene*

DAYTON See also Lebanon, Springfield & Wilmington.

ENON BEACH CAMPGROUND

Ratings: 8/6/6.5 (Campground) From Jct of I-70 & I-675 take I-70, E 3 mi to Exit 47 (Enon exit), NE 1.3 mi, on exit rd to Donnellsville/Enon, S 0.2 mi on Enon Rd. (R). **FAC:** paved rds. (117 spaces). Avail: 69 paved, 15 pull-thrus, (40x54), back-ins (40x36), 15 full hkups, 54 W, 54 E (30/50 amps), seasonal sites, tent sites, dump, laundry, LP bottles, fire rings, firewood. **REC:** wading pool, Enon Lake: swim, fishing, boating nearby, playground, hunting nearby, rec open to public. Pet restrict (B). eco-friendly. 2021 rates: $35 to $50. no cc.
(937)882-6431 Lat: 39.89004, Lon: -83.93584
2401 Enon Rd, Springfield, OH 45502
www.enonbeach.com
See primary listing at Springfield and ad this page

MILITARY PARK WRIGHT-PATTERSON BASS LAKE FAMCAMP (WRIGHT-PATTERSON AFB) (Public) From I-70 (exit 41) & SR-235: Go S 1.3 mi on SR-235, then 2.6 mi left on Chambersburg Rd, then 0.7 mi right on Broad St (turns into SR-444), then pass through main gate, then 0.4 mi right on Schuster Rd, then 0.25 mi on Skeel Ave, follow signs. 51 Avail: 40 full hkups, 11 W, 11 E (30/50 amps). 2021 rates: $22 to $25. (937)271-2535

DEERSVILLE — C5 *Harrison*

TAPPAN LAKE PARK (Public) From Jct of US-36 & US-250, E 15 mi on US-250 to CR-55, W 3.5 mi (R). Avail: 25 full hkups (30 amps). 2021 rates: $38 to $68. (740)922-3649

DELAWARE — C3 *Delaware*

ALUM CREEK (Public State Park) From Jct of I-71 & Hwy 37, W 3 mi on Hwy 37 to CR-10, S 3 mi (L). 286 Avail: 24 full hkups, 262 E (50 amps). 2021 rates: $26 to $38. (740)548-4631

CROSS CREEK CAMPING RESORT

good sam park **Ratings: 10/10★/10** (Campground) From I-71, go W 3 mi on SR 36/37 to Lackey Old State Rd, go S 3.2 mi (R).

TWO TIME NATIONAL AWARD WINNER
Twenty minutes North of Columbus. I-71 Exit 131. Close to world-famous Columbus Zoo, Ohio State University, Muirfield & next to Alum Creek Marina. 120 restaurants & Polaris Fashion Place 10 minutes away. Meet me at the Creek!

FAC: paved rds. (200 spaces). Avail: 158 all weather, patios, 46 pull-thrus, (40x65), back-ins (35x65), 136 full hkups, 22 W, 22 E (30/50 amps), seasonal sites, WiFi @ sites, tent sites, rentals, dump, laundry, groc, LP gas, fire rings, firewood. **REC:** pool, boating nearby, playground, hunting nearby, rec open to public. Pet restrict (B/Q). Partial handicap access. Big rig sites, eco-friendly. 2021 rates: $40 to $80, Military discount. ATM.
(740)549-2267 Lat: 40.231675, Lon: -82.986603
3190 S Old State Rd, Delaware, OH 43015
www.alumcreek.com
See ad this page, 694

DELAWARE (Public State Park) From town, N 5 mi on US-23 (R). Avail: 211 E (20 amps). 2021 rates: $24 to $28. Apr 01 to Dec 31. (740)363-4561

DUNCAN FALLS — C4 *Muskingum*

BLUE ROCK (Public State Park) From Jct of SR-60 & CR-45 (Cutler Lake Rd, S of Duncan Falls), E 6 mi on CR-45 (R). Avail: 77 E Pit toilets. 2021 rates: $18. May 01 to Oct 31. (866)644-6727

EAST LIVERPOOL — C5 *Columbiana*

BEAVER CREEK (Public State Park) From jct SR 7 & US 30: Go 4-1/2 mi N on SR 7, then 1-1/3 mi E on Bell School Rd, then 1-1/4 mi N on Echo Dell Rd. (E). Avail: 6 E (15/20 amps). 2021 rates: $24. May 01 to Oct 31. (330)385-3091

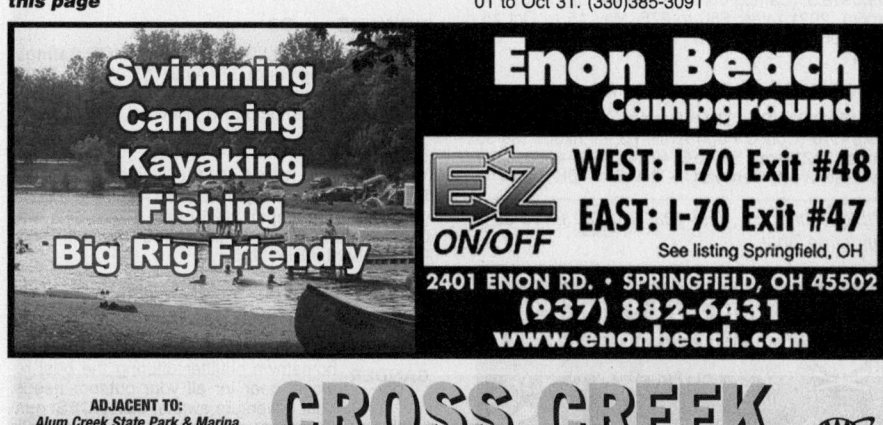

FAYETTE — A1 *Fulton*

HARRISON LAKE (Public State Park) From Jct of Hwy 66 & US-20, SW 2 mi on Hwy 66 to CR-M, W 1.5 mi (R). Avail: 149 E (50 amps). 2021 rates: $16 to $26. (419)237-2593

FINDLAY — B2 *Hancock*

FINDLAY See also Bluffton, Tiffin, Van Buren & Vanlue.

FLUSHING — C5 *Belmont*

ZION RETREAT & RV PARK **Ratings: 8/9.5★/7.5** (Campground) Avail: 55 full hkups (30/50 amps). 2021 rates: $50. (740)968-0955, 334 E. High Street, Flushing, OH 43977

FORT LORAMIE — C1 *Shelby*

LAKE LORAMIE (Public State Park) From Jct of SR-119 & SR-66, S 1 mi on SR-66 (L). Avail: 160 E (50 amps). 2021 rates: $27. Apr 01 to Oct 31. (937)295-2011

FREEPORT — C5 *Belmont*

CLENDENING LAKE CAMPGROUND (Public) From town, N 3 mi on SR-800 to SR-799, E 2 mi (L). 55 Avail: 4 full hkups, 51 E (30 amps). 2021 rates: $44. Apr 01 to Sep 30. (740)658-3691

GALLIPOLIS — E4 *Gallia*

GALLIA COUNTY JUNIOR FAIRGROUNDS (Public) From town, W 4 mi on US-35 (L). Avail: 200 full hkups (30/50 amps). 2021 rates: $20. (740)446-4120

GALLOWAY — C3 *Franklin*

ALTON RV PARK
Ratings: 7/9.5★/8 (RV Park) Avail: 25 full hkups (30/50 amps). 2021 rates: $50. (614)878-9127, 6552 W Broad St, Galloway, OH 43119

GARRETTSVILLE — B5 *Portage*

KOOL LAKES FAMILY RV PARK **Ratings: 6.5/6.5/5.5** (Campground) 70 Avail: 5 full hkups, 65 W, 65 E (30/50 amps). 2021 rates: $35. May 01 to Oct 15. (440)548-8436, 12990 Nelson Ledge Road (SR282), Garrettsville, OH 44231

GENEVA — A5 *Ashtabula*

GENEVA (Public State Park) From Jct of I-90 & SR-534 (exit 218), N 7 mi on SR-534 (L). 100 Avail: 4 full hkups, 89 E (20/30 amps). 2021 rates: $26 to $35. Apr 01 to Nov 30. (440)466-8400

KENISEE'S GRAND RIVER CAMPGROUND **Ratings: 7.5/9★/9.5** (Campground) Avail: 10 full hkups (30/50 amps). 2021 rates: $48. May 01 to Oct 15. (440)466-2320, 4680 Route 307E, Geneva, OH 44041

WILLOW LAKE CAMPGROUND **Ratings: 7/9.5★/8.5** (Campground) Avail: 44 full hkups (50 amps). 2021 rates: $50 to $75. May 15 to Oct 15. (440)466-0150, 3935 N Broadway, Geneva, OH 44041

GENEVA-ON-THE-LAKE — A5 *Ashtabula*

HEARTHSIDE GROVE LAKE ERIE **Ratings: 9/9.5★/10** (Condo Park) Avail: 63 full hkups (30/50 amps). 2021 rates: $99 to $149. (440)261-4063, 6300 Lake Rd West, Geneva-On-The-Lake, OH 44041

Things change ... last year's rates serve as a guideline only.

INDIAN CREEK CAMPING RESORT **Ratings: 8.5/10★/9** (Campground) 108 Avail: 96 full hkups, 12 W, 12 E (30/50 amps). 2021 rates: $82 to $88. (888)726-7802, 4710 Lake Rd East, Geneva-On-The-Lake, OH 44041

GLOUSTER — D4 *Morgan*

BURR OAK (Public State Park) From Jct of SR-78 & SR-13, N 4 mi on SR-13 to CR-107, E 2 mi (E). Avail: 17 E. 2021 rates: $15 to $25. (740)767-3570

GRAFTON — B4 *Lorain*

AMERICAN WILDERNESS CAMPGROUND
Ratings: 7/8.5★/9.5 (Campground) From I480 to SR 10 exit onto SR 83, go S 7.3 mi on SR-83 to campground on left. **FAC:** gravel rds. (166 spaces). Avail: 56 gravel, 23 pull-thrus, (38x95), back-ins (30x78), 56 W, 56 E (30/50 amps), seasonal sites, tent sites, rentals, dump, mobile sewer, laundry, groc, fire rings, firewood, controlled access. **REC:** American Wilderness Lakes: swim, fishing, kayaking/canoeing, boating nearby, playground. Pets OK. Partial handicap access, eco-friendly. 2021 rates: $42 to $48, Military discount. May 01 to Oct 15.
(440)926-3700 Lat: 41.23325, Lon: -82.02297
17273 Avon Belden Rd, SR 83, Grafton, OH 44044
americanwildernesscampground.com
See ad page 692

GRAND RAPIDS — B2 *Wood*

MARY JANE THURSTON (Public State Park) From Jct US 6 & SR 65, N 3.5 mi on SR 65 enter on (L). Avail: 4 E. 2021 rates: $24. (419)832-7662

HARRISON — D1 *Hamilton*

MIAMI WHITEWATER FOREST CAMPGROUND (GREAT PARKS OF HAMILTON COUNTY) (Public) From Jct of I-74 & Dry Fork Rd, E 0.5 mi on Dry Fork Rd to West Rd, S 0.5 mi (L). Avail: 46 E (30 amps). 2021 rates: $32 to $40. Mar 01 to Dec 09. (513)851-2267

HARTVILLE — B4 *Stark*

CUTTY'S SUNSET CAMPING RESORT **Ratings: 8.5/9.5★/8.5** (RV Park) 80 Avail: 60 full hkups, 20 W, 20 E (50 amps). 2021 rates: $53 to $65. May 01 to Oct 15. (800)533-7965, 8050 Edison St NE, Louisville, OH 44641

HILLSBORO — D2 *Highland*

ROCKY FORK (Public State Park) From town, E 3.5 mi on SR-124 to N Shore Dr, NE 1 mi (R). 170 Avail: 44 full hkups, 99 E (30 amps). 2021 rates: $19 to $35. (937)393-4284

SHADY TRAILS FAMILY CAMPGROUND **Ratings: 7.5/8.5★/7.5** (Campground) Avail: 17 full hkups (30/50 amps). 2021 rates: $25 to $30. Apr 01 to Oct 31. (937)393-5618, 11145 Sunset Lane, Hillsboro, OH 45133

HOWARD — C3 *Knox*

KOKOSING VALLEY CAMP & CANOE **Ratings: 6.5/6/8** (Campground) 55 Avail: 55 W, 55 E (30 amps). 2021 rates: $35. May 01 to Oct 15. (740)599-7056, 25860 Coshocton Rd., Howard, OH 43028

HUBBARD — B5 *Trumbull*

CHESTNUT RIDGE PARK & CAMPGROUND **Ratings: 7/8★/8** (Campground) 50 Avail: 2 full hkups, 48 W, 48 E (30 amps). 2021 rates: $40 to $42. May 01 to Sep 30. (330)534-2352, 6486 Chestnut Ridge Rd, Hubbard, OH 44425

HUBER HEIGHTS — D1 *Miami*

Travel Services

GANDER RV OF HUBER HEIGHTS Your new hometown outfitter offering the best regional gear for all your outdoor needs. Your adventure awaits. **SERVICES:** gunsmithing svc, archery svc, sells outdoor gear, sells fishing gear, sells firearms, restrooms. RV Sales. RV supplies, LP gas, dump, emergency parking, RV accessible. Hours: 9am - 8pm.
(833)231-8340 Lat: 39.872226, Lon: -84.145756
8001 Old Troy Pike, Huber Heights, OH 45424
rv.ganderoutdoors.com

JEFFERSON — A5 *Ashtabula*

KENISEE LAKE
Ratings: 8.5/8.5★/9 (Membership Park) Avail: 62 full hkups (30/50 amps). 2021 rates: $54 to $67. Apr 22 to Oct 19. (888)563-7040, 2021 Mill Creek Road, Jefferson, OH 44047

MILLBROOK OUTDOOR RESORT **Ratings: 6.5/7.5/8** (Membership Park) 20 Avail: 6 full hkups, 14 W, 14 E (20/30 amps). 2021 rates: $10. Apr 15 to Oct 31. (440)484-4000, 4051 State Route 46 S, Jefferson, OH 44047

LAKE MILTON — B5 *Mahoning*

LAKE MILTON/BERLIN KOA **Ratings: 7.5/8.5★/8.5** (Campground) Avail: 26 full hkups (30/50 amps). 2021 rates: $60.89 to $77.89. May 01 to Oct 15. (330)538-2194, 15487 Creed Rd, Lake Milton, OH 44429

LAKEVIEW — C2 *Logan*

INDIAN LAKE (Public State Park) From Jct of US-33 & SR-235, N 2 mi on SR-235 (R). 450 Avail: 43 full hkups, 407 E (30/50 amps). 2021 rates: $25 to $37. Apr 01 to Oct 31. (937)843-3553

LANCASTER — D3 *Fairfield*

LAKEVIEW PARK **Ratings: 8/8★/8** (Campground) Avail: 45 full hkups (30/50 amps). 2021 rates: $43. (740)653-4519, 2715 Sugar Grove Rd, Lancaster, OH 43130

LAURELVILLE — D3 *Ross*

TAR HOLLOW (Public State Park) From Jct of SR-180 & SR-327, S 8 mi on SR-327 to Tar Hollow Rd, W 0.25 mi (R). Avail: 70 E (20 amps), Pit toilets. 2021 rates: $19 to $26. (740)887-4818

LEBANON — D1 *Warren*

LEBANON/CINCINNATI NE KOA **Ratings: 8.5/8.5★/7.5** (Campground) 110 Avail: 86 full hkups, 24 W, 24 E (30/50 amps). 2021 rates: $60 to $70. (513)932-7717, 760 Franklin Rd., Lebanon, OH 45036

OLIVE BRANCH CAMPGROUND
Ratings: 9/9.5★/10 (Campground) From Jct of I-71 & Wilmington Rd (exit 36), E 0.3 mi on Wilmington Rd (R). **FAC:** gravel rds. (137 spaces). Avail: 53 gravel, 16 pull-thrus, (50x60), back-ins (35x60), 53 full hkups (30/50 amps), seasonal sites, WiFi @ sites, tent sites, rentals, dump, laundry, groc, LP gas, fire rings, firewood. **REC:** pool, pond, fishing, boating nearby, playground, hunting nearby. Pet restrict (B/Q). Big rig sites, eco-friendly. 2021 rates: $42 to $47, Military discount.
(513)932-2267 Lat: 39.42967, Lon: -84.07194
6985 Wilmington Rd, Oregonia, OH 45054
www.olivebranchcg.com
See ad this page

LIMA — B2 *Allen*

SUN VALLEY FAMILY CAMPGROUND **Ratings: 8/8.5★/8.5** (Campground) Avail: 15 full hkups (30/50 amps). 2021 rates: $40 to $50. Apr 01 to Oct 31. (419)648-2235, 9779 Faulkner Rd, Harrod, OH 45850

LISBON — B5 *Columbiana*

GUILFORD LAKE (Public State Park) From jct of SR 45 & US 30, W 1.9 mi on US 30 to SR 172, 5.6mi N on SR 172 to Teagarden RD, 0.5 mi to Camp Blvd slight right onto Lakeside Dr (R). Avail: 41 E (30 amps). 2021 rates: $35. (330)222-1712

LOGAN — D3 *Hocking*

HOCKING HILLS (Public State Park) From town, S 12 mi on SR-664 (L). 169 Avail: 47 full hkups, 109 E (30/50 amps). 2021 rates: $22 to $30. (740)385-6842

HOCKING HILLS KOA **Ratings: 8.5/10★/10** (RV Park) 57 Avail: 24 full hkups, 33 W, 33 E (30/50 amps). 2021 rates: $76 to $115. Apr 01 to Oct 31. (800)562-0251, 29150 Pattor Rd, Logan, OH 43138

LOUDONVILLE — C4 *Ashland*

CAMP TOODIK FAMILY CAMPGROUND, CABINS & CANOE LIVERY **Ratings: 8/6.5/8** (Campground) 108 Avail: 7 full hkups, 95 W, 95 E (30 amps). 2021 rates: $40. May 01 to Oct 31. (419)994-3835, 7700 Township Road 462, Loudonville, OH 44842

MOHICAN (Public State Park) From town, S 3 mi on SR-3 (R). Entrance fee required in the summertime. 186 Avail: 51 full hkups, 100 E (50 amps). 2021 rates: $23 to $40. (419)994-5125

MOHICAN ADVENTURES CAMPGROUND & CABINS **Ratings: 8/9.5★/8** (Campground) Avail: 194 full hkups (30/50 amps). 2021 rates: $45. Apr 01 to Dec 07. (419)994-2267, 3058 SR-3, Loudonville, OH 44842

Save 10% at Good Sam Parks 365 days a year with no blackout dates!!

MOHICAN RESERVATION CAMPGROUNDS & CANOEING **Ratings: 6/8.5★/7** (Campground) 126 Avail: 126 W, 126 E (30/50 amps). 2021 rates: $30 to $35. Apr 01 to Nov 01. (800)766-2267, 23270 CR-3175, Loudonville, OH 44842

MOHICAN WILDERNESS **Ratings: 6.5/7.5/8.5** (Campground) 140 Avail: 140 W, 140 E (30 amps). 2021 rates: $40 to $46. May 01 to Oct 31. (740)599-6741, 22462 Wally Rd, Glenmont, OH 44628

RIVER RUN FAMILY CAMPGROUND **Ratings: 7/5.5/7.5** (Campground) 151 Avail: 64 W, 151 E (30 amps). 2021 rates: $44 to $50. May 01 to Oct 31. (419)994-5257, 3070 CR-3175, Loudonville, OH 44842

SMITH'S PLEASANT VALLEY CAMPGROUND & CABINS **Ratings: 5/6.5/7.5** (Campground) 151 Avail: 151 W, 151 E (30/50 amps). 2021 rates: $50. Apr 15 to Oct 31. (419)994-4024, 16325 CR-23, Loudonville, OH 44842

WALLY WORLD CAMPING RESORT **Ratings: 8/8★/8** (Membership Park) 175 Avail: 5 full hkups, 170 W, 170 E (30 amps). 2021 rates: $1. (419)994-4828, 16121 CR 23, Loudonville, OH 44842

MANSFIELD — B3 *Ashland*

CHARLES MILL LAKE PARK (Public) From jct I-71 & US-30, E 3 mi on US-30 to SR-603, S 1/2 mi to SR-430 (L). Avail: 225 E (30/50 amps). 2021 rates: $38 to $68. (419)368-6885

MALABAR FARM (Public State Park) At jct of SR 39 and SR 703, S 4 mi, then W 0. 9 mi on Pleasant Valley RD, then SW 0.9mi on Bromfield Rd. 15 Avail. 2021 rates: $19. (419)892-2784

MANTUA — B5 *Portage*

SERVICE PLAZA-BRADY'S LEAP (Public) From town: Go 6 mi E on OH Tpke at MP-197 (R). Avail: 9 E (30 amps). 2021 rates: $20. (440)234-2081

MARENGO — C3 *Morrow*

CARDINAL CENTER CAMPGROUND **Ratings: 8.5/9.5★/8** (RV Park) 400 Avail: 200 full hkups, 200 W, 200 E (30/50 amps). 2021 rates: $42 to $55. (419)253-0800, 616 SR 61, Marengo, OH 43334

MARIETTA — D4 *Washington*

WASHINGTON COUNTY FAIR PARK (Public) From jct I-77 & Hwy 821: Go 2-1/2 mi S on Hwy 821, then 6 blocks S on Hwy 60 to Washington County Fairgrounds. 100 Avail: 100 W, 100 E (30/50 amps), Pit toilets. 2021 rates: $35. (740)373-1347

MASON — D1 *Warren*

KINGS ISLAND CAMP CEDAR

good sam park

(RV Resort) (Not Visited) From jct US-42 & OH-741/Kings Mills Rd: Go 3-1/2 mi S on OH-741/Kings Mills Rd, then 381 ft N on Kings Island Dr (E).

NEW LUXURY RV RESORT IN CINCINNATI

Kings Island Camp Cedar opened in July and features flat, paved sites with full hook-ups. You'll be treated to an expansive pool and water oasis, multiple dining options plus a massive lodge, Kings Island perks and more.

FAC: paved rds. Avail: 184 paved, patios, 26 pull-thrus, (35x56), back-ins (35x50), 184 full hkups (30/50 amps), WiFi @ sites, rentals, laundry, fire rings, firewood, restaurant, controlled access. **REC:** heated pool, wading pool, shuffleboard, playground. Pets OK. Partial handicap access. No tents. Big rig sites. 2021 rates: $109 to $142.80.
(513)701-9635 Lat: 39.358490179, Lon: -84.258120916
5158 Kings Island Drive, Mason, OH 45040
www.VisitCampCedar.com
See ad page 692

MEDINA — B4 *Medina*

PIER-LON PARK **Ratings: 8/8.5★/8.5** (Campground) 150 Avail: 50 full hkups, 100 W, 100 E (50 amps). 2021 rates: $44.50 to $54.50. Apr 15 to Oct 15. (330)667-2311, 5960 Vandemark Rd, Medina, OH 44256

MENDON — B1 *Mercer*

RIVER TRAIL CAMPGROUND II **Ratings: 9/7/6.5** (RV Park) Avail: 41 full hkups (30/50 amps). 2021 rates: $37 to $40. Apr 15 to Oct 15. (419)795-1400, 7712 Deep Cut Rd, Mendon, OH 45862

Want to know how we rate? Our campground inspection guidelines are detailed in the front pages of the Guide.

MILLERSBURG — C4 *Holmes*

TIMBERCREST CAMP AND RV PARK **Ratings: 6/9★/8** (Campground) 54 Avail: 40 full hkups, 2 W, 12 E (30/50 amps). 2021 rates: $45 to $50. Apr 01 to Oct 31. (330)893-2720, 5552 State Route 515, Millersburg, OH 44654

MINERAL CITY — C4 *Tuscarawas*

ATWOOD LAKE PARK (Public) From jct I-77 & SR-212 (exit 93): Go 11 mi E on SR-212, then 1-1/2 mi E on CR-93 (E). 346 Avail: 142 full hkups, 47 W, 157 E (30/50 amps). 2021 rates: $46 to $59. (330)343-6780

MONTVILLE — A5 *Geauga*

HIDDEN LAKES FAMILY CAMPGROUND **Ratings: 6.5/6/7** (Campground) 43 Avail: 43 W, 43 E (30 amps). 2021 rates: $45 to $60. May 01 to Oct 03. (440)968-3400, 17147 Gar Hwy 6 (SR-6), Montville, OH 44064

MOUNT EATON — B4 *Wayne*

EVERGREEN PARK RV RESORT

good sam park

Ratings: 10/10★/10 (RV Park) E-bnd: From Jct of US-250 & SR 241, S 0.4 mi on US-250 (R); or From Jct of I-77 & US-250, NW 12.6 mi on US-250 (L).

IN THE HEART OF OHIO AMISH COUNTRY

Visit our Premier Top-Rated RV Resort! Enjoy local Amish cheeses, Lehman's Vintage Hardware, Amish crafted furniture, Amish home-style cooking and more! All this within minutes of our stunning Evergreen Park RV Resort!

FAC: paved rds. Avail: 87 paved, 48 pull-thrus, (30x65), back-ins (30x55), 87 full hkups (30/50 amps), cable, WiFi @ sites, tent sites, rentals, dump, laundry, LP gas, fire rings, firewood. **REC:** heated pool, hot tub, shuffleboard, playground. Pet restrict (B). Partial handicap access. Big rig sites, eco-friendly. 2021 rates: $65. ATM.
(888)359-6429 Lat: 40.69114, Lon: -81.69488
16359 Dover Rd, Dundee, OH 44624
www.evergreenparkrvresort.com
See ad page 696

MOUNT GILEAD — C3 *Morrow*

MOUNT GILEAD (Public State Park) From jct I-71 (exit 151) & SR-95: Go 6 mi W on Hwy 95 (R). 59 Avail: 22 full hkups, 37 E (50 amps), Pit toilets. 2021 rates: $19 to $23. (419)946-1961

YOGI BEAR'S JELLYSTONE PARK AT DOGWOOD VALLEY **Ratings: 8.5/9★/8** (Campground) 125 Avail: 30 full hkups, 95 W, 95 E (30/50 amps). 2021 rates: $57 to $100. May 01 to Oct 15. (419)946-5230, 4185 Township Rd 99 (McKibben), Mount Gilead, OH 43338

MOUNT STERLING — D2 *Pickaway*

DEER CREEK (Public State Park) From town, S 5 mi on SR-207 to Yankeetown Rd, E 2 mi (E). Avail: 232 E (20 amps). 2021 rates: $25 to $29. (740)869-3124

NAVARRE — B4 *Stark*

BAYLOR BEACH PARK WATER PARK & CAMPGROUND

good sam park

Ratings: 7.5/9.5★/10 (Campground) From Jct of US 250 & US 62: Go 2 mi E on US 62 (at jct US 62 & Hwy 93). (L).

FAC: paved rds. Avail: 60 all weather, 33 pull-thrus, (30x60), back-ins (30x90), 20 full hkups, 40 W, 40 E (50 amps), WiFi @ sites, dump, mobile sewer, fire rings, firewood, controlled access. **REC:** Baylor Beach Park: swim, fishing, playground, rec open to public. Pet restrict (B/Q). Partial handicap access. No tents. Big rig sites, 14 day max stay, eco-friendly. 2021 rates: $41 to $49, Military discount. May 01 to Oct 15.
(330)767-3031 Lat: 40.68690, Lon: -81.59941
8777 Manchester SW, Navarre, OH 44662
www.baylorbeachpark.com
See ad page 697

Things to See and Do

BAYLOR BEACH WATERPARK 2 acre manmade lake, sand bottom, grassy beaches. 90 ft. Slide & 4 kid slides, diving boards, log rolls, picnicking, grills, concessions, mini-golf, paddle boats, sand volleyball, playground. Shelters available for rent. May 26 to Sep 01. Partial handicap access. RV accessible. Restrooms. Food. Hours: 11am to 7pm. Adult fee: $8 to $12.
(330)767-3031 Lat: 40.68686, Lon: -81.59955
8777 Manchester SW, Navarre, OH 44662
www.baylorbeachpark.com
See ad page 697

NELSONVILLE — D4 *Hocking*

HOCKING HILLS JELLYSTONE **Ratings: 7.5/9.5★/7** (Campground) 79 Avail: 20 full hkups, 45 W, 45 E (30/50 amps). 2021 rates: $72 to $95. Apr 01 to Dec 05. (740)385-6720, 22245 SR-278 S.W., Nelsonville, OH 45764

NEW LONDON — B3 *Huron*

NEW LONDON RESERVOIR PARK AND CAMPGROUND (Public) From Jct of Hwys 162 & 60, W. 8 mi on Hwy 162, S 1 mi on Euclid Rd. 114 Avail: 57 W, 57 S, 99 E (30/50 amps). 2021 rates: $20 to $35. Apr 26 to Oct 27. (419)929-8609

NEW PARIS — C1 *Darke*

ARROWHEAD CAMPGROUND

good sam park

Ratings: 10/10★/10 (RV Park) From Jct of I-70 West & US 127 (exit 10): Go N 6.8 mi to OH 722,W 6.4 mi to OH 121, N 2 mi to Thomas Rd, W on Thomas 1mi (L) or From Jct of I-70 East & US 40(exit 156B INDIANA): Go E 1.1 mi on US 40 to OH 320 N 1.5 mi to OH 121, N 8 mi to Thomas Rd W 1 mi (L). **FAC:** all weather rds. (131 spaces). Avail: 26 all weather, patios, 10 pull-thrus, (35x70), back-ins (30x40), 26 full hkups (30/50 amps), seasonal sites, WiFi @ sites, tent sites, rentals, dump, laundry, LP gas, fire rings, firewood. **REC:** pool, pond, fishing, playground. Pet restrict (B). Big rig sites, eco-friendly. 2021 rates: $44 to $56, Military discount. Apr 15 to Oct 27.
(937)996-6203 Lat: 39.94380, Lon: -84.74400
1361 Thomas Rd, New Paris, OH 45347
arrowhead-campground.com
See ad page 378

NATURAL SPRINGS RESORT **Ratings: 8.5/8/8** (Campground) 123 Avail: 93 full hkups, 30 W, 30 E (30/50 amps). 2021 rates: $46 to $68. Apr 13 to Nov 01. (888)330-5771, 500 S. Washington Street, New Paris, OH 45347

OH

NEW PHILADELPHIA — C4 *Tuscarawas*

WOOD'S TALL TIMBER RESORT

good sam park

Ratings: 9.5/9.5★/10 (RV Park) Avail: 60 full hkups (30/50 amps). 2021 rates: $47 to $62. May 01 to Nov 01. (330)602-4000, 1921 Tall Timber Rd. NE, New Philadelphia, OH 44663

NEWARK — C3 *Licking*

NEWARK See also Baltimore, Buckeye Lake, Howard & Zanesville.

HIDDEN HILL CAMPGROUND **Ratings: 4/7/6.5** (Campground) 25 Avail: 12 full hkups, 13 W, 13 E (30/50 amps). 2021 rates: $35. Apr 15 to Oct 15. (740)763-2750, 3246 Lopers Rd NE, Newark, OH 43055

LAZY RIVER AT GRANVILLE CAMPGROUND **Ratings: 9.5/10★/10** (RV Park) 165 Avail: 137 full hkups, 28 W, 28 E (30/50 amps). 2021 rates: $43 to $100. (740)366-4385, 2340 Dry Creek Rd NE, Granville, OH 43023

NEWBURY — B5 *Geauga*

PUNDERSON (Public State Park) From Jct of SR-44 & SR-87, W 2 mi on SR-87 (L). 187 Avail: 20 full hkups, 167 E (30 amps). 2021 rates: $25. (440)564-1195

NEWTON FALLS — B5 *Trumbull*

RIDGE RANCH FAMILY CAMPGROUND **Ratings: 6/5/7** (Campground) 59 Avail: 23 full hkups, 22 W, 36 E (30/50 amps). 2021 rates: $35 to $45. May 01 to Oct 15. (330)898-8080, 5219 SR 303 NW, Newton Falls, OH 44444

NORTH BEND — D1 *Hamilton*

INDIAN SPRINGS CAMPGROUND **Ratings: 8/9.5★/9** (Campground) Avail: 20 full hkups (30/50 amps). 2021 rates: $55. (888)550-9244, 3306 State Line Rd, North Bend, OH 45052

NORTH KINGSVILLE — A5 *Ashtabula*

VILLAGE GREEN CAMPGROUNDS (Public) From Jct of I-90 & exit 235 (Rte-193), N 3 mi on Rte-193 (R). 72 Avail: 60 W, 60 E (20/30 amps). 2021 rates: $18 to $20. Apr 15 to Oct 15. (440)224-0310

NORTH LAWRENCE — B4 *Stark*

CLAY'S PARK RESORT **Ratings: 8/10★/9** (Campground) 150 Avail: 24 full hkups, 126 W, 126 E (30/50 amps). 2021 rates: $75 to $115. Apr 23 to Nov 07. (330)854-6691, 12951 Patterson St. NW, North Lawrence, OH 44666

We appreciate your business!

NORWALK — B3 *Huron*

INDIAN TRAIL CAMPGROUND Ratings: 7/8.5/9 (Campground) 46 Avail: 10 full hkups, 36 W, 36 E (30/50 amps). 2021 rates: $46 to $50. Apr 25 to Oct 15. (419)929-1135, 1400 US-250S, New London, OH 44851

NOVA — B3 *Ashland*

CLEVELAND/SANDUSKY JELLYSTONE CAMP-RESORT **Ratings: 7/8★/8.5** (Campground) 45 Avail: 30 full hkups, 15 W, 15 E (30/50 amps). 2021 rates: $60 to $70. May 01 to Oct 18. (419)652-2267, 40 C Twp Rd 1031, Nova, OH 44859

OAK HILL — E3 *Jackson*

JACKSON LAKE (Public State Park) In Jackson County Jct of SR 279/SR 93,W 1.3 mi to CR 8/Tommy Been Rd, N 0.7 mi on Tommy Been Rd (R). Avail: 34 E (50 amps), Pit toilets. 2021 rates: $35. (740)682-6197

OBERLIN — B4 *Lorain*

SCHAUN ACRES CAMPGROUND **Ratings: 6.5/6.5/7** (Campground) 30 Avail: 30 W, 30 E (30 amps). 2021 rates: $35 to $40. May 01 to Oct 01. (440)775-7122, 51390 Rt 303, Oberlin, OH 44074

OREGON — A2 *Lucas*

MAUMEE BAY (Public State Park) From Jct of I-280 & SR-2, E 6.5 mi on SR-2 to N Curtice Rd, N 2.5 mi to Cedar Point Rd, W 1 mi (R). Avail: 252 E (30 amps). 2021 rates: $25 to $29. Mar 31 to Sep 30. (419)836-7758

ORWELL — A5 *Ashtabula*

PINE LAKES CAMPGROUND **Ratings: 6.5/7.5/8.5** (Campground) 140 Avail: 140 W, 140 E (30/50 amps). 2021 rates: $45. May 10 to Oct 07. (440)437-6218, 3001 Hague Rd., Orwell, OH 44076

OXFORD — D1 *Butler*

HUESTON WOODS (Public State Park) From town go S 2 mi on Hwy 27 to Todd Road, (R) on Butler Israel. Follow signs. Avail: 248 E (30 amps). 2021 rates: $26. (513)523-6347

PERRYSVILLE — C3 *Ashland*

PLEASANT HILL LAKE PARK (Public) From Jct of I-71 & SR-39, E on SR-39 to SR-95, W 10 mi (L). 220 Avail: 20 full hkups, 20 S, 200 E (15/30 amps). 2021 rates: $35 to $68. (419)938-7884

PIQUA — C1 *Miami*

Travel Services

PORT CLINTON — A3 *Ottawa*

CEDARLANE RV RESORT

Ratings: 8.5/9★/10 (Campground) W-bnd: From W Jct of SR-53N & SR-2, E 6.3 mi on SR-53N/SR-2 to E Jct of SR-53N/SR-2 (Catawba Island exit), N 4.5 mi on SR-53N (L); or E-bnd: From E Jct of SR-2 & SR-53N (Catawba Island exit), N 4.5 mi on SR-53N (L).

FAMILY FUN MINUTES FROM CEDAR POINT
Quality Family Time at our Highly Rated Park! 20 min. from Cedar Point. Enjoy 3 Pools, Splash Pad and Tiki Lounge! We are Family and Pet Friendly! Near Lake Erie Islands/Ferries -Visit Island Adventures Family Fun Center too!

FAC: paved/gravel rds. (285 spaces). 67 Avail: 55 gravel, 12 grass, 41 pull-thrus, (30x60), back-ins (30x60), 25 full hkups, 42 W, 42 E (30/50 amps), seasonal sites, WiFi @ sites, tent sites, rentals, dump, mobile sewer, laundry, groc, LP gas, fire rings, firewood, controlled access. **REC:** heated pool, wading pool, boating nearby, playground. Pets OK. Partial handicap access. Big rig sites, eco-friendly. 2021 rates: $53 to $70, Military discount. May 01 to Oct 15.
(419)797-9907 Lat: 41.564488, Lon: -82.832034
2766 NE Catawaba Rd (Rte 53N), Port Clinton, OH 43452
www.cedarlanervresort.com
See ad page 698

EAST HARBOR (Public State Park) From Jct of SR-2 & SR-269N, N 6 mi on SR-269N (R). 563 Avail: 51 full hkups, 352 E (20/50 amps). 2021 rates: $29. (419)734-5857

KELLEYS ISLAND (Public State Park) From Newman's dock on Kelley's Island, E 0.5 mi on Water St to Division St, N 2 mi (R). 124 Avail: 35 full hkups, 46 E (50 amps). 2021 rates: $33. May 01 to Oct 30. (419)746-2546

MIDDLE BASS ISLAND (Public State Park) Take ferry from Port Clinton to Middle Bass Island. 20 Avail: Pit toilets. 2021 rates: $20. May 01 to Oct 15. (866)644-6727

SOUTH BASS ISLAND (Public State Park) Take ferry from Catawba Island to S Bass Island, N 0.5 mi on Langram Rd to Meechan Rd, E 0.25 mi to Catawba Ave, N 0.1 mi (R). 70 Avail: 10 full hkups, 51 E (20/30 amps). 2021 rates: $34. Apr 01 to Oct 01. (419)734-4424

TALL TIMBERS CAMPGROUND **Ratings: 7/9★/8** (Campground) 79 Avail: 79 W, 79 E (30/50 amps). 2021 rates: $52 to $58. May 01 to Oct 31. (419)732-3938, 340 Christy Chapel Rd, Port Clinton, OH 43452

THE RESORT AT ERIE LANDING

Ratings: 8.5/9.5★/10 (RV Resort) Avail: 10 full hkups (30/50 amps). 2021 rates: $54.99 to $64.99. Apr 15 to Oct 15. (419)734-2460, 4495 W Darr-Hopfinger Rd, Port Clinton, OH 43452

PORTSMOUTH — E3 *Scioto*

LAZY VILLAGE CAMPGROUND & RV PARK **Ratings: 6.5/7.5/7.5** (Campground) 52 Avail: 52 W, 52 E (30/50 amps). 2021 rates: $40. (740)858-2409, 13610 US-52, West Portsmouth, OH 45663

SHAWNEE (Public State Park) From town, W 10.2 mi on SR-52, N 6 mi on SR-125. Avail: 112 E (20/30 amps). 2021 rates: $16 to $25. (740)858-4561

RACINE — E4 *Meigs*

KOUNTRY RESORT CAMPGROUND

Ratings: 7.5/7/8.5 (Membership Park) 56 Avail: 25 full hkups, 31 W, 31 E (30/50 amps). 2021 rates: $39. (740)992-6488, 44705 Resort Rd, Racine, OH 45771

RAVENNA — B5 *Portage*

COUNTRY ACRES CAMPGROUND **Ratings: 8/8.5★/8.5** (Campground) 51 Avail: 35 full hkups, 16 W, 16 E (50 amps). 2021 rates: $40 to $54. Apr 15 to Oct 15. (330)358-2774, 9850 Minyoung Rd, Ravenna, OH 44266

WEST BRANCH (Public State Park) From Jct of SR-14 & SR-5, E 3.7 mi on SR-5 to Rock Springs Rd, S 0.2 mi to Park Entrance Rd, E 2 mi (E). 198 Avail: 29 full hkups, 155 E (50 amps). 2021 rates: $20 to $34. (330)296-3239

REEDSVILLE — D4 *Meigs*

FORKED RUN (Public State Park) From Jct of Hwys 681 & 124, S 3 mi on Hwy 124 (R). Avail: 81 E (50 amps). 2021 rates: $16 to $24. (740)378-6206

RICHMOND — C5 *Jefferson*

JEFFERSON LAKE (Public State Park) From Jct of Hwy 152 & SR-43, NW 2.5 mi on SR-43 to CR-54, N 5 mi (L). Avail: 5 E Pit toilets. 2021 rates: $17. May 01 to Sep 30. (330)222-1712

ROSEWOOD — C2 *Champaign*

KISER LAKE (Public State Park) At jct of SR 29/SR 235, S 0. 75 mi on SR 235 to Possom Hollow Rd,E 1.5 mi on Possom Hollow Rd, to Kiser Lake Rd, N 1.3 mi (End). Avail: 10 E (30 amps), Pit toilets. 2021 rates: $17 to $39. (937)362-3565

ROSSFORD — A2 *Wood*

Travel Services

SALEM — B5 *Columbiana*

TIMASHAMIE FAMILY CAMPGROUND **Ratings: 6/7.5/6.5** (RV Park) Avail: 40 full hkups (30/50 amps). 2021 rates: $50. Apr 01 to Oct 31. (330)525-7054, 28251 Georgetown Rd, Salem, OH 44460

SANDUSKY — B3 *Erie*

A SPOTLIGHT Introducing Sandusky's and Lake Erie Shores' colorful attractions appearing at the front of this state section.

SANDUSKY See also Bellevue, Clyde, Oberlin & Port Clinton.

CAMP SANDUSKY

Ratings: 8.5/9★/7.5 (Campground) From Jct of SR-2 & SR-101, N 0.1 mi on SR-101 (R) No pets in tents.

JUST 7 MILES FROM CEDAR POINT
100 RV sites - a short drive to Cedar Point. Upgraded WiFi. City water/sewer. 2 swimming pools. Over 100 Amish-built cabins. 50 tent sites. Deluxe playground. Bunny Farm. Sand volleyball. Pancake breakfast.

FAC: paved/gravel rds. 115 Avail: 100 gravel, 15 grass, 22 pull-thrus, (25x60), back-ins (25x50), 100 full hkups, 15 W, 15 E (30/50 amps), WiFi @ sites, tent sites, rentals, dump, laundry, fire rings, firewood. **REC:** heated pool, boating nearby, playground. Pets OK. Partial handicap access. Big rig sites, eco-friendly. 2021 rates: $32 to $95, Military discount. May 06 to Oct 21.
(419)626-1133 Lat: 41.42068, Lon: -82.75615
3518 Tiffin Ave, Sandusky, OH 44870
www.campsandusky.com
See ad page 698

CRYSTAL ROCK CAMPGROUND **Ratings: 7/8.5★/8.5** (Campground) 70 Avail: 28 full hkups, 42 W, 42 E (30/50 amps). 2021 rates: $45 to $55. Apr 15 to Nov 01. (419)684-7177, 710 Crystal Rock Ave, Sandusky, OH 44870

HURON RIVER VALLEY RESORT MARINA & CAMPGROUND **Ratings: 7/7/8** (Campground) 38 Avail: 38 W, 38 E (30/50 amps). 2021 rates: $52. May 01 to Oct 10. (419)433-4118, 9019 River Rd, Huron, OH 44839

LIGHTHOUSE POINT **Ratings: 9.5/9.5★/10** (Campground) Avail: 145 full hkups (30/50 amps). 2021 rates: $115 to $190. May 06 to Oct 30. (419)627-2198, 1 Cedar Point Rd., Sandusky, OH 44870

SANDUSKY/BAYSHORE ESTATES KOA **Ratings: 7.5/9.5★/8** (Campground) 148 Avail: 79 full hkups, 49 W, 20 E (30/50 amps). 2021 rates: $76.53 to $114.66. May 01 to Oct 31. (800)962-3786, 2311 Cleveland Rd E, Sandusky, OH 44870

SENECAVILLE — C4 *Guernesy*

SENECA LAKE PARK (Public) From Jct of I-77 & SR-313 (exit 37), E 6 mi on SR-313 to SR-574, S 1.8 mi (L). 167 Avail: 41 full hkups, 126 W, 126 E (30/50 amps). 2021 rates: $38 to $68. Apr 01 to Oct 31. (740)685-6013

SEVILLE — B4 *Medina*

MAPLE LAKES RECREATIONAL PARK

Ratings: 9/9.5★/9 (Campground) 68 Avail: 62 full hkups, 6 W, 6 E (30/50 amps). 2021 rates: $60. Apr 15 to Oct 01. (330)336-2251, 4275 Blake Rd, Seville, OH 44273

SHELBY — B3 *Crawford*

SHELBY-MANSFIELD KOA RESORT **Ratings: 8.5/10★/10** (RV Resort) Avail: 60 full hkups (30/50 amps). 2021 rates: $40 to $109. May 01 to Oct 15. (888)562-5607, 6787 Baker 47, Shelby, OH 44875

SHREVE — B4 *Holmes*

WHISPERING HILLS JELLYSTONE RV PARK **Ratings: 8.5/9.5★/8.5** (Campground) 190 Avail: 60 full hkups, 130 W, 130 E (30/50 amps). 2021 rates: $39 to $99. Apr 15 to Oct 31. (800)992-2435, 8248 State Route 514, Big Prairie, OH 44611

SMYRNA — C5 *Harrison*

PIEDMONT MARINA MILL LAKE & CAMPGROUND (Public) From Jct of I-70 & SR-800, N 10 mi on SR-800 (R). 44 Avail: 26 full hkups, 18 W, 18 E (30 amps). 2021 rates: $52. (740)658-1029

SOUTH BLOOMINGVILLE — D3 *Hocking*

PINE CREEK HORSEMAN'S CAMP

Ratings: 6/9.5★/9 (Campground) 38 Avail: 38 W, 38 E (30/50 amps). 2021 rates: $52.50. (740)478-2520, 23937 Big Pine Road, South Bloomingville, OH 43152

SPENCER — B4 *Medina*

SUNSET LAKE CAMPGROUND **Ratings: 5.5/4.5/6** (Campground) 109 Avail: 25 full hkups, 84 W, 84 E (30/50 amps). 2021 rates: $32. May 01 to Oct 15. (330)667-2686, 5566 Root Rd, Spencer, OH 44275

SPRINGFIELD — C2 *Clark*

BUCK CREEK (Public State Park) From Jct of I-70 & exit 62 (Rte 40), W 3 mi on Rte 40 to North Bird, N 1 mi, follow signs (E). Avail: 89 E (30 amps). 2021 rates: $20 to $28. (937)322-5284

ENON BEACH CAMPGROUND

Ratings: 8/6/6.5 (Campground) W-bnd: From Jct of I-70 & Exit 48: Go NW 0.1 mi on Enon Rd (L) or E-bnd: From Jct of I-70 & Exit 47 (Enon exit): Go NE 1.3 mi on exit rd to Donnelsville/ Enon exit, S 0.2 mi on Enon Rd (R).

THE FEEL OF SAND BETWEEN YOUR TOES

Sunbathe on our sandy beach, swim in a clear, spring-fed lake (chlorine-free), or just cool off in our wading area, designated for non-swimmers. Kayaks, canoes & fishing boats welcome (motorboats are not permitted).

FAC: paved rds. (117 spaces). Avail: 69 paved, 15 pull-thrus, (40x54), back-ins (40x36), 15 full hkups, 54 W, 54 E (30/50 amps), seasonal sites, tent sites, dump, laundry, LP bottles, fire rings, firewood. **REC:** wading pool, Enon Lake: swim, fishing, boating nearby, playground, hunting nearby, rec open to public. Pet restrict (B). eco-friendly. 2021 rates: $35 to $50.

(937)882-6431 Lat: 39.89004, Lon: -83.93584
2401 Enon Rd, Springfield, OH 45502
www.enonbeach.com
See ad page 701

TOMORROW'S STARS RV RESORT **Ratings: 8/8.5★/8.5** (RV Park) Avail: 130 full hkups (30/50 amps). 2021 rates: $45 to $50. (937)324-2267, 6716 East National Road, South Charleston, OH 45368

ST MARYS — C1 *Auglaize*

GRAND LAKE ST MARYS (Public State Park) From town, W 1 mi on SR-703 (L). 198 Avail: 34 full hkups, 154 E (50 amps). 2021 rates: $19 to $27. (419)394-3611

STEUBENVILLE — C5 *Jefferson*

STEUBENVILLE See also Toronto.

STONY RIDGE — A2 *Wood*

TOLEDO EAST/STONY RIDGE KOA **Ratings: 8/8★/7.5** (Campground) 58 Avail: 27 full hkups, 31 W, 31 E (30/50 amps). 2021 rates: $45.52 to $60.87. Apr 01 to Oct 31. (419)837-6848, 24787 Luckey Rd, Perrysburg, OH 43551

STOUT — E2 *Adams*

SANDY SPRINGS CAMPGROUND **Ratings: 4.5/9★/8.5** (Campground) 30 Avail: 30 W, 30 E (30/50 amps). 2021 rates: $35 to $43. (701)640-7858, 27719 US Hwy 52, Stout, OH 45684

STREETSBORO — B4 *Portage*

WOODSIDE LAKE PARK

good sam park

Ratings: 8.5/10★/9 (Campground) From Jct Ohio I-80 (exit 187 Streetsboro) & I-480, W .3 mi on I-480, right exit at Frost Rd, 3 mi E on Frost Rd to Elliman, 200 yards S on Elliman (R).

NEAR CLEVELAND, AKRON & AURORA

*Gleaming lake with sandy beach and inflatables *Wooded 100-acre campground *Quiet family camping with Swimming, Fishing, Hiking, Biking, Paddle Boating & MORE! A truly spectacular place to enjoy your next camping vacation.

FAC: gravel rds. (250 spaces). 85 Avail: 28 gravel, 57 grass, 14 pull-thrus, (25x70), back-ins (30x45), 85 full hkups (30/50 amps), seasonal sites, WiFi @ sites, $, tent sites, rentals, dump, laundry, groc, LP gas, fire rings, firewood. **REC:** Woodside Lake: swim, fishing, playground, rec open to public. Pets OK. Partial handicap access. Big rig sites, eco-friendly. 2021 rates: $51 to $61, Military discount. Apr 15 to Oct 31.

(866)241-0492 Lat: 41.25914, Lon: -81.30288
2486 Frost Rd, Streetsboro, OH 44241
woodsidelake.com
See ad this page

SULLIVAN — B4 *Ashland*

RUSTIC LAKES **Ratings: 8/5.5/6.5** (Campground) 19 Avail: 5 full hkups, 14 W, 14 E (30/50 amps). 2021 rates: $35 to $38. May 01 to Oct 15. (440)647-3804, 44901 New London Eastern Rd, Sullivan, OH 44880

SUNBURY — C3 *Columbus*

SUNBURY/COLUMBUS NORTH KOA **Ratings: 10/10★/10** (Campground) Avail: 116 full hkups (50 amps). 2021 rates: $50 to $104. May 01 to Nov 01. (740)625-6600, 8644 Porter Central Rd, Sunbury, OH 43074

SWANTON — A2 *Lucas*

BIG SANDY CAMPGROUND **Ratings: 7/8.5★/8.5** (Campground) 50 Avail: 6 full hkups, 44 W, 44 E (30/50 amps). 2021 rates: $40 to $50. Apr 26 to Nov 01. (419)826-8784, 4035 S Berkey Southern, Swanton, OH 43558

BLUEGRASS CAMPGROUND

good sam park

Ratings: 8/9.5★/8.5 (Campground) 10 Avail: 3 full hkups, 7 W, 7 E (30/50 amps). 2021 rates: $34 to $41. Apr 01 to Oct 30. (419)875-5110, 5751 Waterville-Swanton Rd, Swanton, OH 43558

THOMPSON — A5 *Geauga*

THOMPSON GRAND RIVER VALLEY KOA **Ratings: 9/9.5★/9.5** (Campground) 30 Avail: 27 full hkups, 3 W, 3 E (50 amps). 2021 rates: $52.56 to $72.05. May 01 to Oct 31. (440)298-1311, 6445 Ledge Rd, Thompson, OH 44086

TIFFIN — B3 *Seneca*

CLINTON LAKE CAMPING

Ratings: 6/8.5★/8.5 (Campground) From Jct US-224 & SR-67: Go 1/4 mi E on SR-67, then 5 mi N on CR-43, then 1-1/10 mi W on Twp Rd 122 (Center Rd) (L). **FAC:** gravel rds. (160 spaces). Avail: 35 grass, 10 pull-thrus, (30x40), back-ins (30x40), 35 W, 35 E (30 amps), seasonal sites, tent sites, dump, mobile sewer, groc, fire rings, firewood. **REC:** Clinton Lake: swim, fishing, playground. Pets OK. Partial handicap access. 2021 rates: $28.50. May 01 to Oct 15.

(419)585-3331 Lat: 41.12664, Lon: -83.06924
4990 E Twp Rd-122, Republic, OH 44867
See ad this page

WALNUT GROVE CAMPGROUND **Ratings: 6.5/8.5★/7.5** (Campground) 120 Avail: 24 full hkups, 96 W, 96 E (30/50 amps). 2021 rates: $25 to $60. May 01 to Oct 31. (419)448-0914, 7325 S Twp Rd 131, Tiffin, OH 44883

TOLEDO — A2 *Lucas*

TOLEDO See also Bowling Green, Stony Ridge, Swanton & Whitehouse, OH; Monroe, Ottawa Lake & Petersburg, MI.

TORONTO — C5 *Jefferson*

AUSTIN LAKE RV PARK & CABINS

good sam park

Ratings: 9.5/10★/10 (Campground) From Jct of Hwy 22 & SR-43 (Carrollton-Wintersville exit), N 4 mi on SR-43 to SR-152, NE 4 mi to Twp Hwy 285A, SW 1.5, follow signs (L). Do not use GPS the last 20 miles. **FAC:** paved/gravel rds. (250 spaces). Avail: 51 all weather, patios, 1 pull-thrus, (34x70), back-ins (50x75), 51 full hkups (50 amps), seasonal sites, WiFi @ sites, tent sites, rentals, shower$, dump, mobile sewer, laundry, groc, LP gas, fire rings, firewood, controlled access. **REC:** Austin Lake: swim, fishing, kayaking/canoeing, playground, hunting nearby, rec open to public. Pets OK. Partial handicap access. Big rig sites, eco-friendly. 2021 rates: $60 to $75. May 01 to Oct 31.

(740)544-5253 Lat: 40.48642, Lon: -80.73744
1002 Twp Road 285A, Toronto, OH 43964
austinlakepark.com
See ad this page

UNIONTOWN — B4 *Stark*

AKRON CANTON JELLYSTONE PARK **Ratings: 8/9★/8** (RV Park) Avail: 89 full hkups (30/50 amps). 2021 rates: $74 to $114. May 01 to Oct 15. (330)877-9800, 12712 Hoover Ave NW, Uniontown, OH 44685

VAN BUREN — B2 *Hancock*

ADVENTURE BOUND PLEASANT VIEW **Ratings: 7/6.5/7** (Campground) 160 Avail: 80 full hkups, 80 W, 80 E (30/50 amps). 2021 rates: $76 to $84. (419)299-3897, 12611 Allen Township Rd 218, Van Buren, OH 45889

VAN BUREN (Public State Park) From Jct of I-75 & Hwy 613, E 1 mi on Hwy 613 to State Park Rd, S 1 mi (R). Avail: 16 E (50 amps), Pit toilets. 2021 rates: $16 to $24. (419)832-7662

Thank You to our active and retired military personnel. Look for military parks within the state listings section of your 2022 Guide.

VAN WERT — B1 *Van Wert*

HUGGY BEAR CAMPGROUND **Ratings: 8/8/8** (Campground) 175 Avail: 95 full hkups, 80 W, 80 E (30/50 amps). 2021 rates: $38 to $41. Apr 15 to Oct 15. (419)968-2211, 9065 Ringwald Rd, Middle Point, OH 45863

TIMBERWOODS CAMPING RESORT **Ratings: 7.5/5.5/7** (Campground) Avail: 17 full hkups (30/50 amps). 2021 rates: $35 to $40. Apr 01 to Nov 01. (419)238-1124, 10856 A Liberty Union Rd, Van Wert, OH 45891

VANLUE — B2 *Hancock*

HERITAGE SPRINGS CAMPGROUND **Ratings: 7/8★/8** (Campground) 25 Avail: 15 full hkups, 10 W, 10 E (30/50 amps). 2021 rates: $40 to $45. Apr 17 to Oct 18. (419)387-7738, 13891 Twp Rd 199, Vanlue, OH 45890

WAPAKONETA — C1 *Auglaize*

WAPAKONETA KOA **Ratings: 9/10★/8.5** (Campground) 55 Avail: 43 full hkups, 12 W, 12 E (30/50 amps). 2021 rates: $48 to $77. Mar 15 to Nov 15. (419)738-6016, 14719 Cemetary Rd, Wapakoneta, OH 45895

WAUSEON — A2 *Fulton*

SUNNY'S CAMPGROUND SHADY RECREATION AREA **Ratings: 7/8★/8.5** (Campground) 110 Avail: 8 full hkups, 102 W, 102 E (30/50 amps). 2021 rates: $35 to $39. Apr 28 to Oct 07. (419)337-3101, 12399 C.R. 13, Wauseon, OH 43567

WELLINGTON — B4 *Lorain*

CLAREMAR TWIN LAKES CAMPING RESORT **Ratings: 7/UI/8.5** (RV Park) 200 Avail: 200 W, 200 E (30/50 amps). 2021 rates: $44 to $109. May 01 to Oct 15. (440)647-3318, 47571 New London Eastern Rd, New London, OH 44851

FINDLEY (Public State Park) From Jct of Hwys 18 & 58, S 2.5 mi on Hwy 58 (L). 257 Avail: 15 full hkups, 91 E (50 amps). 2021 rates: $22 to $28. (440)647-4490

OH

WELLSTON — D3 *Vinton*

LAKE ALMA (Public State Park) From town, N 1 mi on Hwy 93 to Hwy 349, NE 1 mi (R). Avail: 71 E (30/50 amps), Pit toilets. 2021 rates: $16 to $24. Mar 31 to Sep 30. (740)384-4474

WEST LIBERTY — C2 *Logan*

OAK CREST CAMPGROUND **Ratings: 6/7★/7.5** (Campground) 40 Avail: 10 full hkups, 30 W, 30 E (30 amps). 2021 rates: $40 to $45. May 01 to Oct 31. (937)593-7211, 4226 Twp Rd 187, West Liberty, OH 43357

WEST SALEM — B4 *Wayne*

TOWN & COUNTRY CAMP RESORT **Ratings: 7/8.5/6.5** (RV Park) Avail: 20 full hkups (50 amps). 2021 rates: $35 to $40. Apr 01 to Nov 01. (419)853-4550, 7555 Shilling Rd, West Salem, OH 44287

WEST UNITY — A1 *Williams*

SERVICE PLAZA-INDIAN MEADOW (Public) From town, W on OH Tpke, at MP-20.8 (R). Overnight rest area (Between Exits 13 & 15). Avail: 10 E. 2021 rates: $20. (440)234-2081

WHITEHOUSE — A2 *Lucas*

TWIN ACRES CAMPGROUND **Ratings: 6.5/8★/9** (Campground) 63 Avail: 8 full hkups, 55 W, 55 E (30/50 amps). 2021 rates: $30 to $49. May 01 to Oct 15. (419)877-2684, 12029 Waterville-Swanton Rd (Rte 64), Whitehouse, OH 43571

WILLARD — B3 *Huron*

AUBURN LAKE PARK **Ratings: 6/7.5★/8** (Campground) 32 Avail: 32 W, 32 E (30/50 amps). 2021 rates: $34. Apr 15 to Oct 15. (419)492-2110, 6881 S.R. 103 East, Tiro, OH 44887

WILLIAMSFIELD — A5 *Ashtabula*

ANDOVER/PYMATUNING LAKE KOA **Ratings: 8/8.5★/8.5** (Campground) Avail: 103 full hkups (30/50 amps). 2021 rates: $45 to $55. Apr 01 to Nov 01. (440)273-3431, 7652 S Pymatuning Lake Rd, Williamsfield, OH 44093

WILMINGTON — D2 *Clinton*

BEECHWOOD ACRES CAMPING RESORT **Ratings: 9/9★/10** (RV Park) Avail: 58 full hkups (30/50 amps). 2021 rates: $50 to $65. Apr 15 to Oct 31. (937)289-2202, 855 Yankee Rd, Wilmington, OH 45177

CAESAR CREEK (Public State Park) From town, E 8 mi on SR-73 to SR-380, N 3 mi to Center Rd, W 1 mi (E). Avail: 287 E (30/50 amps). 2021 rates: $29 to $30. (937)488-4595

COWAN LAKE (Public State Park) From town, S 3 mi on US-68 to Dalton Rd, W 1.5 mi (L). Avail: 237 E (50 amps). 2021 rates: $20 to $29. (937)382-1096

THOUSAND TRAILS WILMINGTON

good sam park **Ratings: 8/9★/8.5** (Membership Park) 68 Avail: 68 W, 68 E (30 amps). 2021 rates: $65 to $75. Apr 17 to Oct 21. (888)563-7040, 1786 State Route 380, Wilmington, OH 45177

WINESBURG — C4 *Holmes*

AMISH COUNTRY CAMPSITES **Ratings: 5/8.5★/8** (Campground) 60 Avail: 60 W, 60 E (30 amps). 2021 rates: $30. Apr 01 to Nov 15. (330)359-5226, 1930 US 62 NE, Winesburg, OH 44690

WOOSTER — B4 *Wayne*

MEADOW LAKE PARK **Ratings: 6.5/NA/7.5** (Campground) 105 Avail: 105 W, 105 E (30/50 amps). 2021 rates: $40 to $45. May 01 to Nov 01. (330)435-6652, 8970 Canaan Center Rd, Wooster, OH 44691

Don't miss a thing! Check out the Table of Contents for everything the Guide has to offer.

YELLOW SPRINGS — D2 *Greene*

JOHN BRYAN (Public State Park) From Jct of SR-343 & SR-370, S 1 mi on SR-370 (L). Avail: 10 E (50 amps), Pit toilets. 2021 rates: $18 to $22. (937)767-1274

ZALESKI — D3 *Vinton*

LAKE HOPE (Public State Park) From Jct of SR-50 & Hwy 278, N 4 mi on Hwy 278, follow signs (L). Avail: 46 E (15/30 amps). 2021 rates: $16 to $24. (740)596-4938

ZANESVILLE — C4 *Muskingum*

DILLON (Public State Park) From Jct of SR-16 & SR-146, E 7 mi on SR-146 to Clay Littick Dr, S 1 mi to park entrance (R). Avail: 183 E (50 amps). 2021 rates: $26. (740)453-4377

MUSKINGUM RIVER (Public State Park) From town, N 6 mi on Hwy 60 to Powellson Rd, E 11 mi to Lock & Dam #11, follow signs (L). Avail: 20 W (15 amps), Pit toilets. 2021 rates: $18. (740)453-4377

WOLFIES CAMPGROUND

good sam park **Ratings: 9/9.5★/10** (Campground) From Jct of I-70 & SR-146 W (Exit 155, Eastbound - coming from Columbus direction - continue at bottom of the ramp onto Elberon and turn towards SR-146), W 0.25 mi on SR-146, N 0.75 mi on OH-666, N 0.75 mi on Lewis Dr (OH-666), first right past Riverside Park, (Buckeye Dr), E 0.2 mi on Buckeye Dr (L). **FAC:** gravel rds. Avail: 51 gravel, 22 pull-thrus, (30x65), back-ins (30x62), 51 full hkups (30/50 amps), WiFi @ sites, tent sites, rentals, dump, laundry, groc, LP bottles, fire rings, firewood. **REC:** heated pool, boating nearby, playground, hunting nearby. Pets OK. Big rig sites, eco-friendly. 2021 rates: $42.25 to $44.50, Military discount.
(740)454-0925 Lat: 39.96466, Lon: -81.98933
101 Buckeye Dr, Zanesville, OH 43701
www.wolfiescampground.com
See ad this page

Refer to the Table of Contents in front of the Guide to locate everything you need.

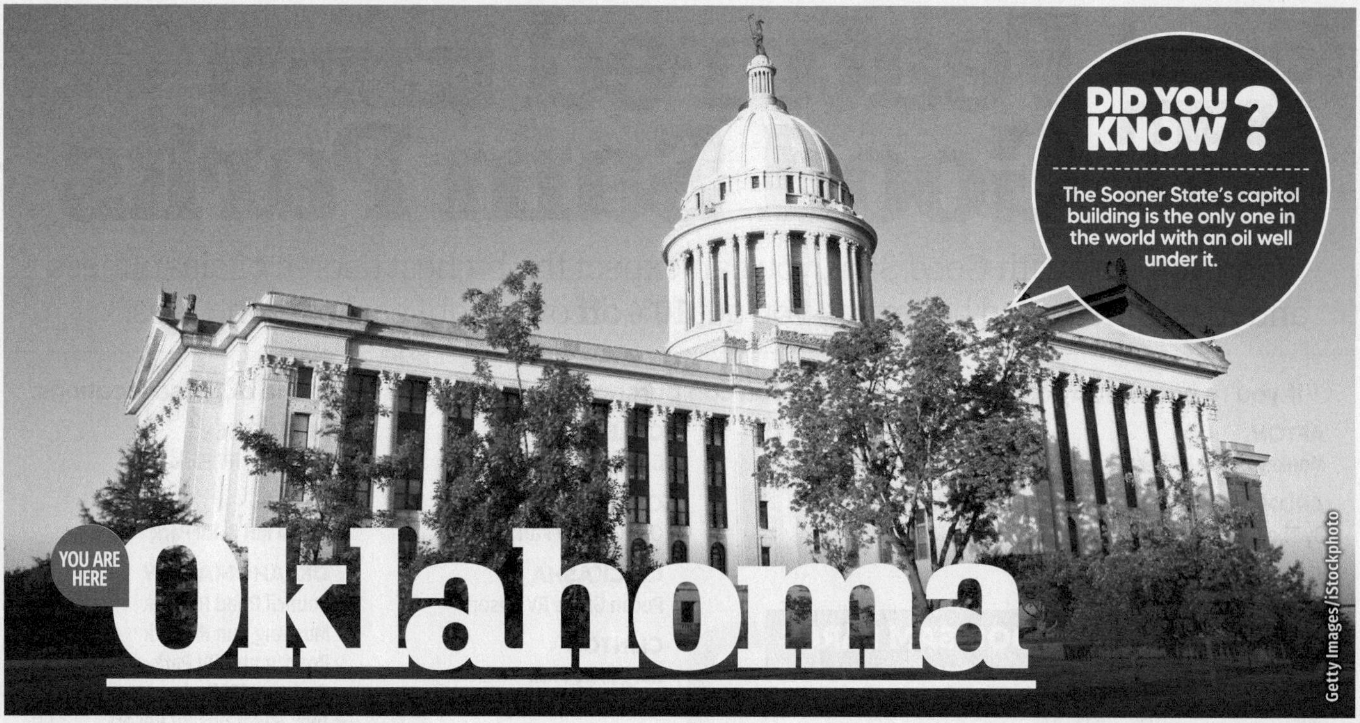

YOU ARE HERE

Oklahoma

DID YOU KNOW?

The Sooner State's capitol building is the only one in the world with an oil well under it.

Getty Images/iStockphoto

Put on your cowboy boots and saunter over to the Sooner State, where Old West history abides with Native American heritage. Oklahoma's terrain is just as varied, with its golden prairies, rugged mountains and cypress swamps.

Cowboy Culture

The state capital is also the most vibrant city in Oklahoma. In the heart of the state, Oklahoma City is home to cattle auctions at Stockyards City and relics of the Old West at the National Cowboy & Western Heritage Museum. About 100 miles to the northeast, Tulsa invites you to see a stunning array of Native American and Western art at the Gilcrease Museum. Nearby, there's also the Philbrook Museum of Art, an Italian Renaissance-styled villa teeming with art from all over the globe. Tour the town to see one of the finest collections of art deco building design in the nation.

Discovery Time

The legendary Talimena National Scenic Byway leads visitors on an adventure-filled trip through the eastern half of Oklahoma. Instead of eccentric roadside attractions, this 54-mile path takes you on a trip past rolling mountains and historic communities.

Get Your Kicks

You've heard of the Mother Road, right? You'll find Route 66's longest uninterrupted stretch in the Sooner State. Cruise this iconic road for the Oklahoma Route 66 Museum and the Route 66 Vintage Iron motorcycle museum.

Bring Your Boat

Boaters can choose from more than 200 lakes for fishing and watersports adventure. Embark on a scenic sailing trip on Lake Hefner or charter a yacht in Lake Murray to visit charming communities on the water's edge. You can also rent motorized personal watercraft.

Oklahoma Chicken Fried Steak

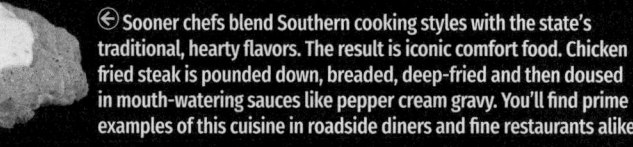

Sooner chefs blend Southern cooking styles with the state's traditional, hearty flavors. The result is iconic comfort food. Chicken fried steak is pounded down, breaded, deep-fried and then doused in mouth-watering sauces like pepper cream gravy. You'll find prime examples of this cuisine in roadside diners and fine restaurants alike.

VISITOR CENTER

TIME ZONE
Central Standard

ROAD & HIGHWAY INFORMATION
405-522-8000
ok.gov/odot

FISHING & HUNTING INFORMATION
405-521-3851
wildlifedepartment.com

BOATING INFORMATION
800-652-6552
travelok.com/lakes_and_boating

NATIONAL PARKS
nps.gov/ok

STATE PARKS
travelok.com/state-parks

TOURISM INFORMATION
Oklahoma Tourism and Recreation Department
800-652-6552
travelok.com

TOP TOURISM ATTRACTIONS
1) Oklahoma City National Memorial
2) Oklahoma Route 66 Museum
3) Turner Falls Park

MAJOR CITIES
Oklahoma City (capital), Tulsa, Norman, Broken Arrow, Lawton

Featured Good Sam Parks

OKLAHOMA

When you stay with Good Sam, you can expect the highest degree of cleanliness and friendliness, and better yet, you get **10% off** overnight campground fees.

If you're not already a Good Sam member you can purchase your membership at one of these locations:

AFTON
Monkey Island RV Resort

ARDMORE
By The Lake RV Park Resort

BARTLESVILLE
Riverside RV Park

BEGGS
Tulsa RV Ranch

CALERA
Do Drop Inn RV Resort

CHANDLER
Oak Glen RV Park

CHICKASHA
Pecan Grove RV Resort

CLINTON
Hargus RV Park
Water-Zoo Campground

DUNCAN
Duncan Mobile Village

ELK CITY
Elk Creek RV Park
Route 66 RV Park

EUFAULA
Little Turtle RV & Storage

GUTHRIE
Cedar Valley RV Park

LAWTON
Buffalo Bob's RV Park

MCALESTER
Valley Inn RV Park

MIAMI
Miami MH & RV Park

OKLAHOMA CITY
Council Road RV Park
Mustang Run RV Park
Roadrunner RV Park
Rockwell RV Park
Twin Fountains RV Resort

POTEAU
Long Lake Resort & RV Park

THACKERVILLE
Fun Town RV Park at WinStar
Red River Ranch RV Resort

TULSA
Cherry Hill MH & RV Community
Mingo RV Park

WEATHERFORD
Wanderlust Crossings RV Park

10/10★/10 GOOD SAM PARKS

ARDMORE
By The Lake RV Park Resort
(580)798-4721

THACKERVILLE
Fun Town RV Park at WinStar
(580)276-8900

CALERA
Do Drop Inn RV Resort
(580)965-3600

What's This?

An RV park with a 10/10★/10 rating has scored perfect grades in amenities, cleanliness and appearance ("See Understanding the Campground Rating System" on pages 8 and 9 for an explanation of the trusted Good Sam Rating System). Stay in a 10/10★/10 park on your next trip for a nearly flawless camping experience.

Getty Images/iStockphoto

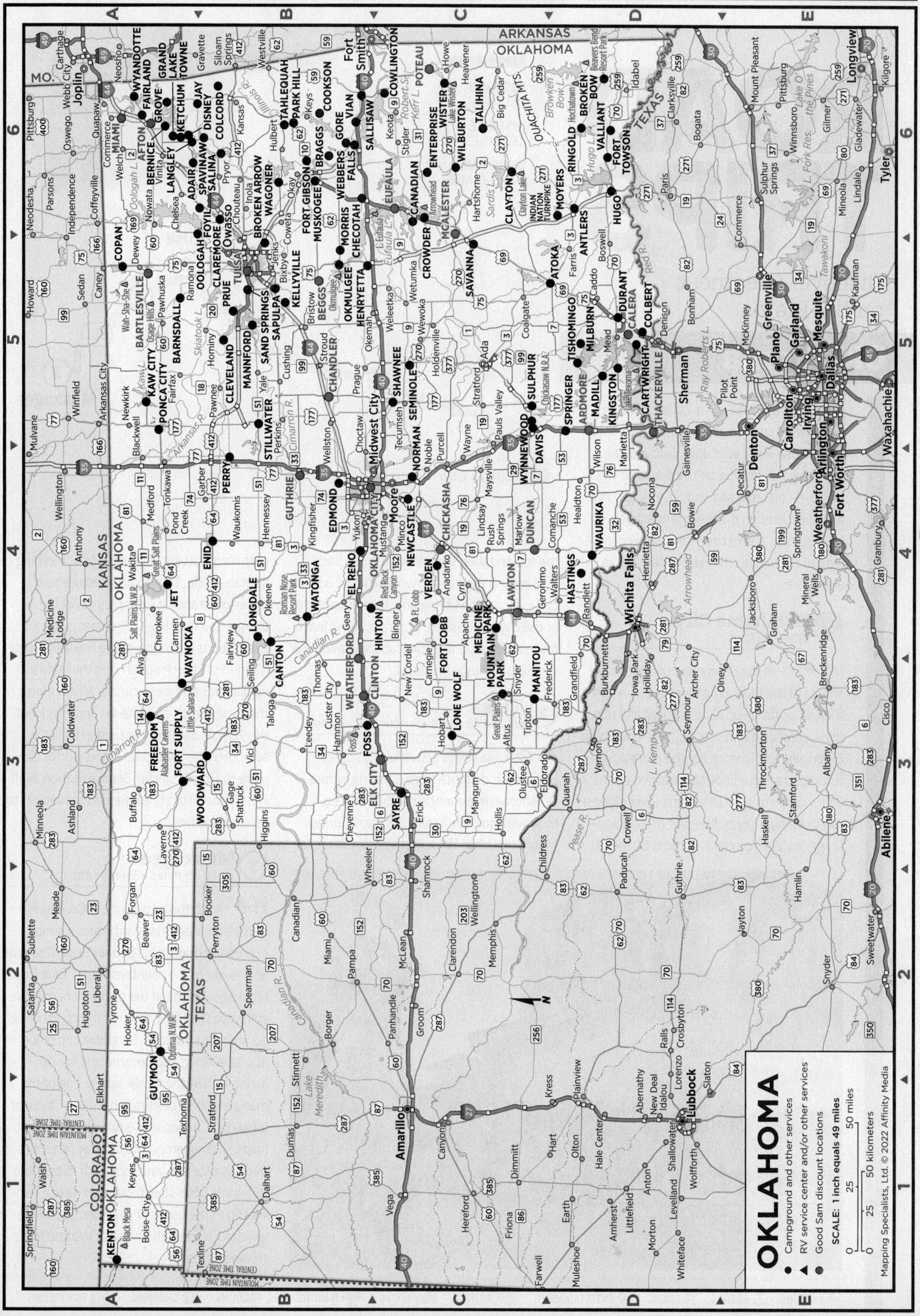
OKLAHOMA
Campground and other services
RV service center and/or other services
Good Sam discount locations
SCALE: 1 inch equals 49 miles
Mapping Specialists, Ltd. © 2022 Affinity Media

ROAD TRIPS

Discover Greatness on the Plains

Oklahoma

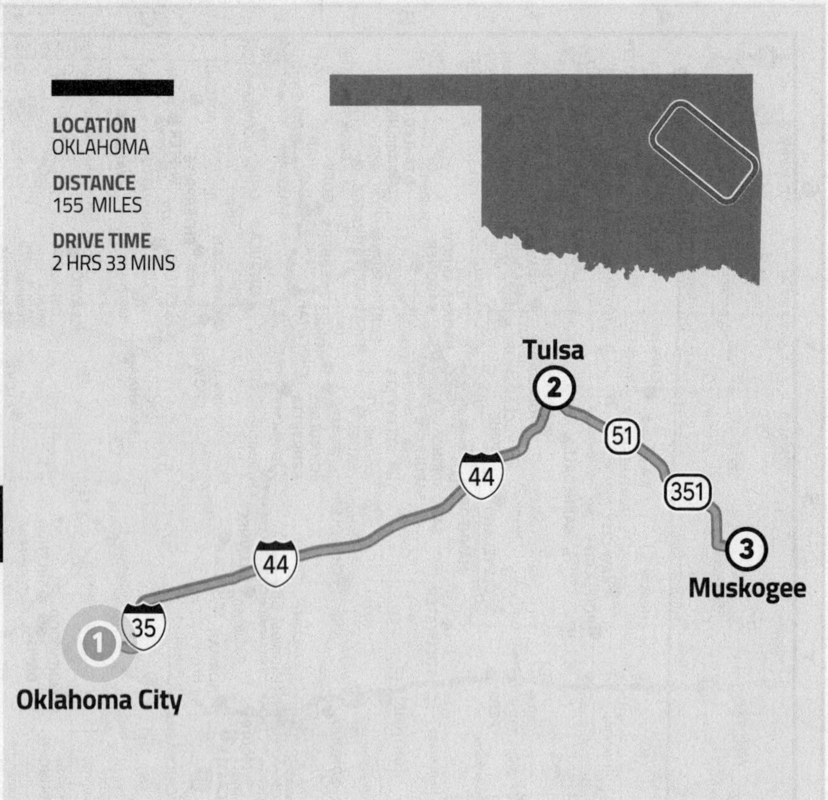

Back in the 1800s, so-called "Sooners" rushed to grab all the land they could find. Those were wild days, but you can still have a wild time on the plains of Oklahoma — on land, sea and air. You can ride a zipline through dramatic landscapes, go for a spin on a bike tour, take a skydiving leap of faith, relax in myriad state parks and more.

1 Oklahoma City
Starting Point

In the Boathouse District on the shores of the Oklahoma River, you can rent a kayak or stand-up paddle-board and ride the current as it drifts through the Bricktown Entertainment District. For the more adventurous, strap on a body harness and zipline your way across the Oklahoma River along a six-story-high sky trail as part of the SandRidge Sky Zip. You can also climb 80 feet to the top and then slide down the Sky Slide. Tool around the downtown district on a bicycle; if you didn't bring one, take advantage of the city's bike-share program. Don't leave town without visiting the National Cowboy & Western Heritage Museum.

2 Tulsa
Drive 106 miles ▪ 1 hour, 39 minutes

Tulsa offers beautiful cityscapes just a short distance from amazing nature. Downtown has every amenity, but it's a truly wild world in Tulsa's 300-acre Turkey Mountain Urban Wilderness area. Hike miles of trails of varying difficulty. For something human-made, take an architecture tour to see outstanding examples of Art Deco design. See the style in churches, schools, gas stations and homes. The Boston Avenue Methodist Church epitomizes the style's bold angles and sleek curves. Motor along the local stretch of Route 66 and check out the 76-tall statue of the Golden Driller, a symbol of the "oil capital of the world." Explore the iconic Sinclair Service Station, built in a "home-like" style intended to blend in to its surroundings.

Aurkawl

3 Muskogee
Drive 49 miles ▪ 54 minutes

In the turbulent 1960s, country music star Merle Haggard wrote a song expressing pride in his Sooner State Roots as an answer to the counterculture. "Okie from Muskogee" climbed the country charts. "We still wave Old Glory down at the courthouse," according to the tune. So grab a cup of joe at a local diner, and become an Okie-for-a-day with all the locals. Join in one of the many seasonal celebrations at the Castle of Muskogee, a medieval-style structure that hosts Halloween events, holiday festivities, Renaissance fairs and more. For even more laid-back, Okie-style recreation, take a fishing trip to the banks of the Arkansas River, which runs through town. Land some hefty channel catfish.

BIKING BOATING DINING ENTERTAINMENT FISHING HIKING HUNTING PADDLING SHOPPING SIGHTSEEING

Oklahoma

SPOTLIGHTS

Spend Your Next RV Adventure in the Sooner State

Steeped in Native American heritage and cowboy culture, Oklahoma embraces visitors with cultural experiences and outdoor adventure. Learn the customs of the vibrant Chickasaw nation and marvel at Frank Lloyd Wright's architectural genius in Bartlesville.

THE ARBUCKLE MOUNTAINS ARE AMONG THE OLDEST U.S. PEAKS.

The 77-foot-tall Turner Falls on Honey Creek in Oklahoma's Arbuckle Mountains.

Chickasaw Nation

After arriving in Oklahoma more than 150 years ago after the Trail of Tears, the Chickasaw Nation put down roots and flourished in the Sooner State. About 90 miles south of Oklahoma City on Interstate 35, the Chickasaw Nation is set amid a landscape brimming with rippling waters and rolling hills. Explore a compelling cultural heritage that opens a new reality. From stomp dances to sacred forests, don't skip out on this must-see corner of the Sooner State.

Awesome Attractions

Native American traditions are kept alive at the Chickasaw Cultural Center in the town of Sulphur. Occupying 184 acres, the center offers one of the most extensive tribal cultural experiences in the country, including a traditional village, stomp dances, reenactments, films, artifacts and immersive exhibits. A true testament to the creativity and resilience of the Chickasaw people, the center also hosts frequent events for the public and boasts a restaurant that serves up traditional dishes such as pashofa, a Chickasaw corn soup.

Native American Nerve Center

Although Oklahoma City is the capital of the Sooner State, the town of Tishomingo serves as the capital of the Chickasaw Nation. History comes alive at the Chickasaw National Capitol Building, which was built in 1898 and now serves as a museum focused on the tribe's fight for independence. Next door, the Council House Museum displays a collection of pottery, jewelry and more.

Make it to Lake Murray

Directly south of the Chickasaw Nation off Interstate 35 lies crystal-clear water and family-friendly beaches. Lake Murray has been billed the most beautiful lake in Oklahoma. Small but picturesque, it's the perfect place to spend the day boating, swimming or fishing and is renowned as one of the state's best lakes for landing small and largemouth bass. Anglers should also visit the Blue River, east of Tishomingo, for the chance to land the waters' world-famous trout. Home to a number of annual fishing derbies, the Blue is truly an outdoor lover's playground.

Hike the Sooner Way

Directly south of Sulfur, an outdoor playground entices eager explorers. The Chickasaw National Recreation Area boasts more than 30 miles of trails along with a nature center. Take an educational tour or hit Lake of the Arbuckles in the Arbuckle Mountains, a hot spot for fishing and water sports. Marvel at the sight of 77-foot-tall Turner Falls or try a trail ride on horseback.

On the Border

Lake Texoma, on the border with Texas, is another local favorite and one of the largest lakes in the state. Striped bass are the most sought-after catches, but crappie and catfish are also on the menu. Boating, sailing and water sports round out the bountiful offerings at this popular getaway.

OK

LOCAL FAVORITE

Crockpot Beef

From cattle ranching to rodeos, Oklahoma is your destination for cowboy experiences. Spend time at a working ranch and then fuel up with this mouthwatering pot roast.

INGREDIENTS

- ☐ 2 lbs chuck roast
- ☐ 1 stick unsalted butter
- ☐ 1 pack dry ranch seasoning
- ☐ 1 pack dry au jus seasoning
- ☐ 6-8 whole pepperoncini peppers
- ☐ 1 medium yellow onion
- ☐ 8 oz package of mushrooms

DIRECTIONS

Chop onions and slice mushrooms. Add all ingredients together and cook in a crockpot on low setting for 5 to 6 hours. You can also cook in an aluminum pan on a grill, but over indirect heat only. Serve on hamburger buns or thicken the gravy and serve over noodles or mashed potatoes for a complete entree.

FUN TOWN RV
PARK AT WINSTAR
Nestled in the foothills of southern Oklahoma,
less than 200 yards from the world's biggest casino,
Fun Town RV Park at WinStar is the preferred option
for guests who want to enjoy the resort experience
from the comfort of their home away from home.
good sam park
2022
Top Rated
10/10★/10
WINSTAR WORLD CASINO AND RESORT
EXIT 1, I-35 • TX/OK BORDER • 580.276.8900
See listing Thackerville, OK

SPOTLIGHTS

Diverse plant life thrives above water in the Crystal Bridge Tropical Conservatory in Oklahoma.

Oklahoma City

The Spirit of the Old West never really left Oklahoma City. Take a trip to Oklahoma City, where you'll find culture, cuisine and attractions you'd expect to find in any metropolitan city. But you'll also find a rugged and cultured past with plenty of museums that bring that past to life. Oklahoma City is rich in cowboy culture and is known as the horse show capital of the world.

Zip Across a River

Find high-flying fun on the banks of the Oklahoma River. In the Boat-house District, you can rent a kayak or stand-up paddleboard and ride the current as it drifts through the Bricktown Entertainment District. For the more adventurous, strap on a body harness and zipline your way across the Oklahoma River along a six-story-high sky trail as part of the SandRidge Sky Zip. You can also climb 80 feet to the top and then slide down the Sky Slide. Tool around the downtown district on a bicycle; if you didn't bring one, take advantage of the city's bike-share program. Just swipe your card and ride, then return the bike to a designated kiosk.

Magical Museums

Oklahoma's museums offer windows into an often-turbulent past. You can visit a museum dedicated solely to a distinctive country instrument at the American Banjo Museum. Take wing at the Pigeon Museum and pay homage to the American homing pigeon. Other interesting museums include the Oklahoma Museum of Telephone History and the Oklahoma State Firefighters Museum.

Rolling on the Rails

Learn how Oklahoma City served as a vital nexus for railroads at the Oklahoma Railway Museum. There are freight cars, passenger cars and a real steam engine on display. Even Thomas the Tank engine, a kids' favorite, drops by from time to time. There's a museum devoted to skeletons known as the Museum of Osteology, and you won't want to miss the American Indian Cultural Center and Museum. There are currently 38 federally recognized American Indian tribes associated with Oklahoma.

OKC's Tragedy

On April 19, 1995, Oklahoma City suffered its darkest day when the Alfred P. Murrah Building was bombed by a domestic terrorist. Today, you can visit the Oklahoma City National Memorial and Museum to see how the city has come out of the dark while remembering the past.

Four Legs, One Rider

Oklahoma City is a true testament to the American West and is home to more national and international equine events than any other city in the world. You can catch a rodeo with roping and riding or a more elegant event with trotting, top hats and tails. If you never travel without your horses, this is the place you'll want to visit.

Oklahoma Fun

Oklahoma City is proud of its heritage and enjoys showing off with rollicking and educational festivals. Paseo's First Friday Gallery Walk is a monthly open house for the galleries in the Paseo District, which is home to more than 20 art galleries. The second Friday of every month is dedicated to the Plaza's Live on the Plaza. Retail shops and restaurants stay open late, and vendors, street entertainers and live music round out the event. The second weekend in June brings two world-renowned festivals to the city. The Dead Center Film Festival has been deemed one of the Top 20 Coolest Film Festivals in the World. The Red Earth Native American Cultural Festival celebrates Native American art and heritage.

Cool Conservancy

With so many things to do, you'll want to make time to visit the Myriad Botanical Gardens and Crystal Bridge Conservancy. This is one of Oklahoma City's most beloved public spaces. There is a children's garden, an off-leash dog park and

OK

The Oklahoma City National Memorial marks the time when a bomb claimed 168 lives.

Council road RV PARK

good sam park

EZ On/Off
Free WiFi

See listing Oklahoma City, OK

- BIG RIG SITES • 30/50 Amps
- Long, Shaded Pull-Thrus
- Free Wi-Fi • Cable TV
- Laundry • LP • Open Year Round
- Handicap Restrooms • Storm Shelter

CLOSE TO:

Adjoining Nature/Hiking Trail,
Bricktown, Riverboat & Trolley,
OKC Memorial,
Shopping, Restaurants,
Stockyard City,
36 Holes of Public
Golf Courses, OKC Airport

I-40 at Exit 142
8108 S.W. 8th St.
Oklahoma City, OK 73128

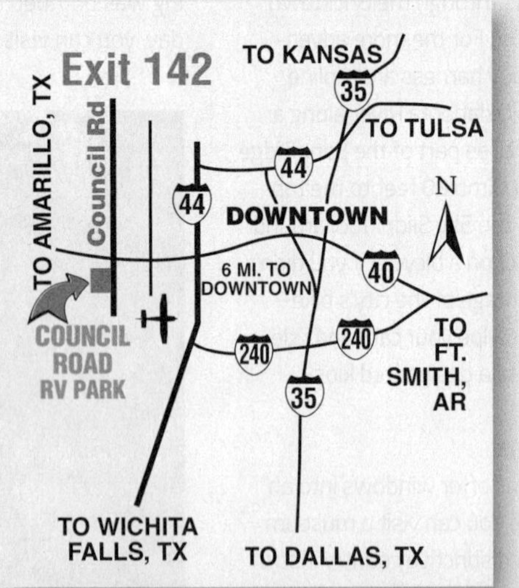

PETS WELCOME

866-589-2103
(405) 789-2103
LAT: 35.45685 LON: 97.65566

HUNT BROTHERS PIZZA
Now Serving Hunt Brothers Pizza and Hot Wings

www.councilroadrvpark.com

SPOTLIGHTS

An estimated 2,500 bison roam the 39,650-acre Tallgrass Prairie Preserve in Pawhuska.

splash fountains, as well as paths for walking and jogging. This is a must-see and offers a place to find solitude.

Oklahoma Legacy

Learn more about the city and the state of Oklahoma at the Capitol Building or at the Oklahoma History Center. An affiliate of the Smithsonian Institute, the center is located right across from the capital building. Its learning center sprawls 215,000 square feet, housing a number of hands-on audio/video and computer activities for all ages. On the grounds is a walking tour called the Red River Journey. On display are remains of the steamboat Heroine, a paddleboat that sank in the Red River in 1838 during a trip to deliver vital supplies to soldiers.

Bartlesville

Founded in 1897 in what was then known as Native American Territory, Bartlesville has been at the heart of Oklahoma history for over a hundred years. These days, it's a surprisingly cosmopolitan city with enough art, architecture and unique attractions to draw visitors from across the Midwest. Nestled against the picturesque Osage Hills, it's also the perfect jumping off point for exploring "Green Country," the state's vibrant northeast corner. If you're looking for family-friendly fun with a touch of sophistication, you'll love this hidden gem.

One-of-a-Kind Skyline

Once the tallest building in downtown Bartlesville, the Price Tower was designed in 1929 by the famed architect Frank Lloyd Wright, who originally planned for it to be built in New York City. However, nearly 30 years later, a local businessman brought in Wright to construct the tower as his company headquarters and the copper and concrete structure has been wowing visitors and locals alike ever since. Guided tours of the iconic building are available daily and include a visit to the 19th floor offices of H.C. Price, the skyscraper's original owner. There are also galleries, an upscale restaurant and panoramic views.

Heritage Trail

For more on the region's architectural history, pick up one of the self-guided Heritage Trail Walking Tour booklets available at the city Visitor's Center. With detailed descriptions of over 72 local sites, it's the perfect introduction to Prairie Style design.

Pioneering Food Prep

Combine your visit to Bartlesville with a stop at the Pioneer Woman's Mercantile in nearby Pawhuska. The "Merc" is just 30 minutes away and features a restaurant that serves up comfort foods and desserts made by Ree Drummonds, star of the Food Network's popular show, "The Pioneer Woman." Browse the shop stocked with her signature goods. The drive to Tulsa is a little longer, at 45 minutes.

FOR MORE INFORMATION

Oklahoma Tourism and Recreation Department, 800-652-6552, www.travelok.com

Chickasaw Nation, 580-436-2603, www.chickasaw.net

Visit Bartlesville, 800-364-8708, www.visitbartlesville.com

Oklahoma City, 800-225-5652, www.visitokc.com

OK

Oklahoma

ADAIR — B6 *Mayes*

HORSESHOE INN & CAMPGROUND (Campground) (Rebuilding) 17 Avail: 9 full hkups, 8 W, 8 E (30/50 amps). 2021 rates: $25 to $45. (918)809-3341, 3296 E. 4675 Road, Adair, OK 74330

AFTON — A6 *Ottawa*

GRAND COUNTRY RV PARK **Ratings: 5/NA/7.5** (RV Park) Avail: 10 full hkups (30/50 amps). 2021 rates: $30 to $35. (918)314-9508, 55015 E 270 Rd, Afton, OK 74331

MONKEY ISLAND RV RESORT

good sam park **Ratings: 10/10★/9.5** (RV Resort) From jct of I-44 & US 59/60 (Exit 302), go S 5.5 mi on US 59 to jct of US 59 & OK 125, then S 3.0 mi. on OK 125, to jct of OK 125 & E 280, then E .1 mi on E 280 (L). **FAC:** paved rds. Avail: 72 paved, patios, 34 pull-thrus, (45x85), back-ins (40x60), 72 full hkups (30/50 amps), WiFi @ sites, rentals, dump, laundry, LP gas, fire rings. **REC:** pool, boating nearby, shuffleboard, playground. Pets OK. Partial handicap access. No tents. Big rig sites, eco-friendly. 2021 rates: $38 to $48, Military discount.
(918)257-6400 Lat: 36.613228, Lon: -94.869668
56140 E. 280 Road, Afton, OK 74331
monkeyislandrv.com
See ad this page

ANTLERS — D6 *Pushmataha*

PINE CREEK LAKE - COE/LITTLE RIVER PARK (Public Corps) From town: Go 29 mi E on Hwys-7 & 3, then 3/4 mi SE on paved county road. Avail: 30 E Pit toilets. 2021 rates: $14 to $23. Mar 01 to Oct 31. (580)876-3720

Check out a campground's ad. In it you might find a locator map, photos, and a lot more information about the park to help you find just the right place to stay.

Oklahoma Privately Owned Campground Information Updated by our Good Sam Representatives

Mike & Elaine Ewing

Mike is a master electrician who built and flipped homes. Elaine worked with General Motors for 36 years before we hung up our spurs and started living the dream. We married in 1979, purchased our first RV nine months later and have enjoyed the RV lifestyle ever since.

ARDMORE — D5 *Carter*

BY THE LAKE RV PARK RESORT

good sam park **Ratings: 10/10★/10** (RV Resort) Avail: 128 full hkups (30/50 amps). 2021 rates: $45 to $49. (580)798-4721, 1031 Lodge Road, Ardmore, OK 73401

CEDARS EDGE RV PARK **Ratings: 6/8.5★/6.5** (Campground) Avail: 10 full hkups (30/50 amps). 2021 rates: $25. (580)226-2266, 3433 Highway 70 E, Ardmore, OK 73401

LAKE MURRAY

(Public State Park) From Jct of I-35 & Exit 24 (Scenic 77), E 2.7 mi on Scenic 77 (E). **FAC:** paved/gravel rds. 329 Avail: 169 paved, 160 gravel, 87 pull-thrus, (24x65), back-ins (24x50), 329 full hkups (30/50 amps), tent sites, rentals, shower$, dump, groc, LP bottles, firewood, restaurant. **REC:** pool, Lake Murray: swim, fishing, marina, kayaking/canoeing, boating nearby, golf, shuffleboard, playground. Pets OK. Partial handicap access, 14 day max stay. 2021 rates: $22 to $27. ATM, no reservations.
(580)223-4044 Lat: 34.13331, Lon: -97.10784
13528 Scenic Hwy 77, Ardmore, OK 73401
www.travelok.com

ATOKA — C5 *Atoka*

BOGGY DEPOT (Public State Park) From Jct of US-75 & SR-7 (Not Boggy Depot Rd), W 11 mi on SR-7 to park access/cnty rd, S 4 mi (L). 106 Avail: 6 full hkups, 20 W, 20 E (30/50 amps). 2021 rates: $20 to $30. (580)889-5625

MCGEE CREEK (Public State Park) From Jct of US-69 & SR-3 (in town), E 17 mi on SR-3 to McGee Creek Lake Rd, N 3 mi (R). 41 Avail: 41 W, 41 E (30/50 amps). 2021 rates: $22. (580)889-5822

BARNSDALL — A5 *Osage*

BIRCH LAKE - COE/BIRCH COVE (Public Corps) From town, S 1.5 mi on 8th St., follow signs (R). 85 Avail: 85 W, 85 E (30 amps). 2021 rates: $20. Apr 01 to Oct 30. (918)396-3170

BARTLESVILLE — A5 *Washington*

BELL RV VILLAGE **Ratings: 6.5/NA/6.5** (RV Park) Avail: 30 full hkups (30/50 amps). 2021 rates: $39. (918)214-8773, 1001 NE Washington Avenue, Bartlesville, OK 74006

OSAGE HILLS (Public State Park) E-bnd: From S Jct of US-60 & Hwy 99, N 6 mi on Hwy 99 to US-60, E 8 mi to park access rd, S 2 mi (L); or W-bnd: From Jct of US-75 & US-60, W 16 mi on US-60 to park access rd, S 2 mi (L). 20 Avail: 20 W, 20 E (30/50 amps). 2021 rates: $22. (918)336-4141

RIVERSIDE RV PARK

good sam park **Ratings: 9/9.5★/8.5** (RV Park) Avail: 72 full hkups (30/50 amps). 2021 rates: $35. (918)336-6431, 1211 SE Adams Blvd., Bartlesville, OK 74003

BEGGS — B5 *Okmulgee*

TULSA RV RANCH

good sam park **Ratings: 8/9.5★/9** (RV Park) Avail: 97 full hkups (30/50 amps). 2021 rates: $35 to $40. (918)267-9000, 2538 US-75, Beggs, OK 74421

BERNICE — A6 *Delaware*

GRAND LAKE/BERNICE (Public State Park) From Jct of I-44 & Afton exit (US-59), SE 6.4 mi on US-59 to SR-125, S 4.1 mi to State Park Rd, W 1.8 mi (R). 33 Avail: 33 W, 33 E (30 amps). 2021 rates: $27. (918)257-8330

BRAGGS — B6 *Muskogee*

GREENLEAF (Public State Park) From Jct of US-62 & Hwy 10, S 15 mi on Hwy 10, 3 mi S of town (L). 100 Avail: 24 full hkups, 76 W, 76 E (30/50 amps). 2021 rates: $20 to $27. (918)487-5196

BROKEN ARROW — B5 *Wagoner*

NEWT GRAHAM LOCK - COE/BLUFF LANDING (Public Corps) From town, E 12.7 mi on 71 St (L). 21 Avail: 21 W, 21 E (30 amps). 2021 rates: $15. May 01 to Sep 30. (918)682-4314

BROKEN BOW — D6 *McCurtain*

BEAVERS BEND (Public State Park) From Jct of US-70 & US-259, N 6 mi on US-259 to Hwy 259-A, E 5 mi (R). 393 Avail: 393 W, 393 E (20/30 amps). 2021 rates: $20 to $27. (580)494-6300

CREEKSIDE RV PARK **Ratings: 5.5/9★/9** (RV Park) Avail: 42 full hkups (30/50 amps). 2021 rates: $40. (580)306-7875, 2983 N. US Hwy 259, Broken Bow, OK 74728

CALERA — D5 *Bryan*

DO DROP INN RV RESORT

good sam park **Ratings: 10/10★/10** (RV Resort) From jct US-75 & W Main St: Go 2-1/2 mi S on US-75, then 4-1/2 mi W on Platter Rd, then 1/2 mi S on Platter Dike Rd (R).

DO DROP INN RV RESORT AND CABINS
A 10/10/10 elite park minutes from Choctaw Casino & Lake Texoma. Ideal for big rigs, rallies & reunions. Clubhouse, H/S WiFi, laundry, cafe, pool & spa, cabins, kayak rentals. UNSURPASSED HOSPITALITY & SERVICE!

FAC: all weather rds. (43 spaces). Avail: 13 all weather, patios, 13 pull-thrus, (25x55), 13 full hkups (30/50 amps), seasonal sites, WiFi @ sites, rentals, dump, laundry, LP gas, fire rings, firewood, restaurant. **REC:** pool, hot tub, boating nearby, hunting nearby. Pets OK. Partial handicap access. No tents. Big rig sites, eco-friendly. 2021 rates: $42 to $49, Military discount.
(580)965-3600 Lat: 33.903636, Lon: -96.540888
560 Platter Dike Rd, Calera, OK 74730
www.dodropinn.com
See ad opposite page

LAKE TEXOMA - COE/PLATTER FLATS (Public Corps) From town, W 7.5 mi on Smiser Rd, follow signs (L). 83 Avail: 63 W, 63 E (30/50 amps). 2021 rates: $12 to $22. Apr 01 to Sep 30. (580)434-5864

CANADIAN — C6 *Pittsburg*

LAKE EUFAULA/ARROWHEAD (Public State Park) From Jct of US-69 & SR 113 (at Canadian), E 0.1 mi on SR 113 (L). Avail: 20 full hkups (30/50 amps). 2021 rates: $22 to $30. (918)339-2204

CANTON — B4 *Blaine*

CANTON LAKE - COE/BIG BEND (Public Corps) From town, W 2 mi on Hwy 51 to paved cnty rd, N 4 mi (R). 105 Avail: 86 W, 86 E (30 amps). 2021 rates: $15 to $22. Apr 13 to Sep 30. (580)886-3576

CANTON LAKE - COE/CANADIAN (Public Corps) From town, W 1 mi on Hwy 51 to Hwy 58A, NW 1.7 mi (stay left at fork in rd) (L). 120 Avail: 120 W, 120 E (30/50 amps). 2021 rates: $18 to $22. (580)886-3454

CANTON LAKE - COE/SANDY COVE (Public Corps) From town, W 0.5 mi on SR-51 to Rte 58A, N 5.2 mi (stay rt at Y in rd) (L). Avail: 35 E (30 amps). 2021 rates: $20. Apr 01 to Sep 30. (580)274-3576

CARTWRIGHT — D5 *Bryan*

LAKE TEXOMA - COE/BURNS RUN EAST (Public Corps) From town, W 4.5 mi on SR-91, follow signs (L). 47 Avail: 44 W, 44 E (30 amps). 2021 rates: $15 to $24. (580)965-4660

CHANDLER — B5 *Lincoln*

OAK GLEN RV PARK

good sam park **Ratings: 7.5/8.5★/8.5** (RV Park) Avail: 14 full hkups (30/50 amps). 2021 rates: $27 to $29. (405)258-2994, 347203 East Highway 66, Chandler, OK 74834

CHECOTAH — B6 *McIntosh*

CHECOTAH/LAKE EUFAULA WEST KOA **Ratings: 8.5/9.5★/8.5** (Campground) Avail: 53 full hkups (30/50 amps). 2021 rates: $47.50 to $57.50. (918)473-6511, I-40 & Pierce Road (exit 255), Checotah, OK 74426

EUFAULA LAKE - COE/GENTRY CREEK (Public Corps) From town, W 9 mi on US-266, follow signs (L). Avail: 15 E (30 amps). 2021 rates: $14 to $19. Apr 01 to Sep 29. (918)799-5843

LAKE EUFAULA (Public State Park) S-bnd: From Jct of I-40 & Hwy 150 (exit 259), S 6 mi on Hwy 150 (L); or N-bnd: From Jct of US-69 & Hwy 150 (S of town), NW 3 mi on Hwy 150 (R). 99 Avail: 34 full hkups, 65 W, 65 E (30/50 amps). 2021 rates: $22 to $31. (918)689-5311

TERRA STARR RV PARK **Ratings: 7.5/7/6** (Campground) 280 Avail: 126 full hkups, 154 W, 154 E (30/50 amps). 2021 rates: $24 to $25. (918)689-7094, 420589 E 1147 Rd, Checotah, OK 74426

CHICKASHA — C4 *Grady*

PECAN GROVE RV RESORT

good sam park **Ratings: 8.5/10★/8.5** (RV Park) From jct of I-44 (H.E. Bailey Turnpike) & US-81/US-277: Go S 1/4 mi on US-81/US-277, then W 1/4 mi on W Almar Dr. (R). **FAC:** paved rds. (110 spaces). Avail: 30 gravel, patios, 9 pull-thrus, (45x107), back-ins (45x72), 30 full hkups (30/50 amps), seasonal sites, WiFi @ sites,

rentals, laundry, LP gas. Pet restrict (B/Q). Partial handicap access. No tents. Big rig sites, eco-friendly. 2021 rates: $35 to $40, Military discount.
(405)320-5690 Lat: 35.0205, Lon: -97.939519
600 W. Almar Drive, Chickasha, OK 73018
pecangrovervresort.com
See ad this page

CLAREMORE — B6 *Rogers*

CLAREMORE EXPO RV PARK (Public) From Jct of I-44 (Will Rogers Tpke) & SR-20 (Exit 255), W 2.8 mi on SR-20 (L). Avail: 44 full hkups (30 amps). 2021 rates: $12 to $37. (918)342-5357

OOLAGAH LAKE - COE/SPENCER CREEK (Public Corps) From town, S 4 mi on Hwy 66 to Cnty Rd, W 5 mi, N 2 mi (E). Avail: 29 E (30 amps). 2021 rates: $16 to $20. Apr 01 to Sep 30. (918)341-3690

TULSA NE WILL ROGERS DOWNS KOA **Ratings: 8/9.5/9** (RV Park) Avail: 182 full hkups (30/50 amps). 2021 rates: $39 to $42. (800)562-7635, 20900 S 4200 Rd, Claremore, OK 74019

CLAYTON — C6 *Pushmataha*

CLAYTON LAKE (Public State Park) From town, S 6 mi on US-271 (R). 30 Avail: 30 W, 30 E (30/50 amps). 2021 rates: $20 to $25. (918)569-7981

CLEVELAND — B5 *Pawnee*

KEYSTONE LAKE - COE/COWSKIN BAY SOUTH (Public Corps) From town, S 14 mi on US-64 to cnty rd (Westport exit), W 1.5 mi (E). Note: 30' RV length limit. 30 Avail: Pit toilets. 2021 rates: $10. May 15 to Sep 01. (918)865-2621

KEYSTONE LAKE - COE/WASHINGTON IRVING SOUTH (Public Corps) From town, W 12 mi on US-64 to Bear Glen Rd, left, cross over expwy to frntg rd, left 0.25 mi to cnty rd, W 1 mi (E). Avail: 38 E (30 amps). 2021 rates: $10 to $17. (918)865-2621

Be prepared! You can be the king of the road, but you still need to be safe. Be sure to use the valuable information provided in the Bridge, Tunnel & Ferry Regulations and Rules of the Road pages located in the front of the Guide.

CLINTON — B3 *Custer*

HARGUS RV PARK

good sam park **Ratings: 6/8★/7.5** (RV Park) From jct of I-40 & Exit 65A (Neptune Dr): Go S 1/4 mi on Neptune Dr. (R). **FAC:** all weather rds. Avail: 65 gravel, 9 pull-thrus, (38x65), back-ins (25x55), 65 full hkups (30/50 amps), WiFi @ sites, tent sites, laundry. **REC:** playground. Pets OK. Partial handicap access, eco-friendly. 2021 rates: $33, Military discount.
(580)323-1664 Lat: 35.498589, Lon: -98.977019
1410 Neptune Dr, Clinton, OK 73601
See ad this page

WATER-ZOO CAMPGROUND

good sam park **Ratings: 9/8/8.5** (RV Park) I-40W & Neptune Dr (exit 65A): Go S 1/4 mi on Neptune Dr then W on Blvd of Champions, then left at traffic circle on Blvd of Champions. RV Park is SE of the Water Park & Hotel. (L). **FAC:** paved rds. Avail: 35 paved, patios, 33 pull-thrus, (38x80), back-ins (38x45), 35 full hkups (30/50 amps), cable, WiFi @ sites, tent sites, . **REC:** heated pool $, wading pool, rec open to public. Pets OK. Partial handicap access. Big rig sites. 2021 rates: $43.99.
(580)323-9966 Lat: 35.496806, Lon: -98.984673
1900 Boulevard of Champions, Clinton, OK 73601
www.water-zoo.com
See ad this page

COLBERT — D5 *Bryan*

LAKE TEXOMA - COE/BURNS RUN WEST (Public Corps) From town, W 5.5 mi on Hwy 91, follow signs (R). 117 Avail: 105 W, 105 E (30 amps). 2021 rates: $22 to $26. May 15 to Sep 30. (903)965-4922

RIVER VIEW RV & RECREATIONAL PARK **Ratings: 8.5/10★/9.5** (RV Park) Avail: 25 full hkups (30/50 amps). 2021 rates: $40. (580)296-8439, 300 S Dickson Drive, Colbert, OK 74733

COLCORD — B6 *Delaware*

NATURAL FALLS (Public State Park) From Siloam Springs, W 6 mi on US-412 (L). 44 Avail: 7 full hkups, 37 W, 37 E (30/50 amps). 2021 rates: $20 to $27. (918)422-5802

COOKSON — B6 *Cherokee*

TENKILLER FERRY LAKE - COE/SNAKE CREEK (Public Corps) From town, S 6 mi on Hwy 82-100 to access rd, W 1 mi on Snake Creek Cove Rd (R). Avail: 111 E (30/50 amps). 2021 rates: $16 to $20. (918)487-5252

COPAN — A5 *Osage*

COPAN LAKE - COE/POST OAK PARK (Public Corps) From Jct Hwy 75 & 10, W 3.5 mi on Hwy 10 (R). Avail: 19 E (30 amps). 2021 rates: $20 to $22. Apr 01 to Oct 31. (918)532-4334

COPAN LAKE - COE/WASHINGTON COVE (Public Corps) From Jct Hwy 75 & 10, W 2 mi on Hwy 10, follow signs, N 1.5 mi (L). 101 Avail: 60 W, 101 E (30 amps). 2021 rates: $20 to $25. Apr 01 to Oct 31. (918)532-4129

COWLINGTON — C6 *Le Flore*

ROBERT S. KERR RESERVOIR - COE/COWLINGTON POINT (Public Corps) From town, S 10.5 mi on US-59, W 4 mi on CR D1172/CR E1170, follow signs (R). 35 Avail: 32 W, 32 E (30 amps). 2021 rates: $10 to $15. Apr 26 to Sep 25. (918)775-4475

ROBERT S. KERR RESERVOIR - COE/SHORT MOUNTAIN COVE (Public Corps) From town, S 12 mi on US-59 to cnty rd, W 1.5 mi, follow signs (L). Avail: 33 E (30 amps). 2021 rates: $11 to $15. Apr 26 to Sep 25. (918)775-4475

CROWDER — C6 *Pittsburg*

EUFAULA LAKE - COE/CROWDER POINT (Public Corps) From town, S 2 mi on US-69, follow signs (L). 45 Avail. 2021 rates: $7. Mar 01 to Oct 31. (918)484-5135

DAVIS — C5 *Murray*

SMOKIN' JOE'S RIB RANCH AND RV PARK **Ratings: 6/9★/8** (RV Park) Avail: 10 full hkups (30/50 amps). 2021 rates: $35. (580)369-5015, 3165 Jollyville Road, Davis, OK 73030

TURNER FALLS PARK (Public) From Jct of I-35 & SR-77 (exit 51), S 1.2 mi on SR-77 (R). Entrance fee required. Caution: Steep grade to camping area. Avail: 32 full hkups (30/50 amps). 2021 rates: $25. (580)369-2988

DISNEY — A6 *Mayes*

GRAND LAKE/CHEROKEE (Public State Park) From Jct of SR-28 & SR-82, E 2 mi on SR-28 (L). 124 Avail: 18 W, 34 E (20/30 amps). 2021 rates: $22 to $30. (918)435-8066

CARBON MONOXIDE SAFETY REMINDER: Routinely inspect generator and propane tank connections for leaks and breaks. Check carbon monoxide/smoke detectors regularly. Change batteries as needed. Turn off all appliances after use. Never use a propane stove for heat. Have an emergency exit plan. Know where emergency exits are. Know how to quickly disconnect all power sources. Know the symptoms of carbon monoxide poisoning: headache, dizziness, weakness, nausea, vomiting, confusion and drowsiness. If you suspect carbon monoxide poisoning, get outside to fresh air immediately. Call 911. Don't block exhaust vents - beware snow, tall grass, other RVs and obstructions. Don't open windows/roof vents in areas that may contain carbon monoxide.

DUNCAN — C4 *Stephens*

CHISHOLM TRAIL RV PARK **Ratings: 7/9.5★/7** (RV Park) Avail: 78 full hkups (30/50 amps). 2021 rates: $30. (580)252-7300, 3000 S. Hwy 81, Duncan, OK 73533

DUNCAN MOBILE VILLAGE

good sam park **Ratings: 6/8/6** (RV Area in MH Park) Avail: 35 full hkups (30/50 amps). 2021 rates: $35. (580)255-1348, 1702 Green Meadow Drive, Duncan, OK 73533

DURANT — D5 *Bryan*

CHOCTAW RV PARK - DURANT KOA

Ratings: 10/10★/10 (RV Park) From Jct of US-70 & US-69: Go S 3-1/2 mi on US-69 to Choctaw Road, then E 1/4 mi to Enterprise Dr, then N 1 block. (R). **FAC:** paved rds. Avail: 77 paved, patios, 77 pull-thrus, (30x80), 77 full hkups (30/50 amps), cable, WiFi @ sites, dump, laundry, groc, LP gas, firewood, restaurant. **REC:** heated pool, pond, playground. Pets OK. Partial handicap access. No tents. Big rig sites, eco-friendly. 2021 rates: $45 to $55.
(800)562-6073 Lat: 33.959965, Lon: -96.412093
3650 Enterprise Blvd., Durant, OK 74701
www.koa.com/campgrounds/durant
See ad opposite page

LAKE TEXOMA - COE/JOHNSON CREEK (Public Corps) From town, W 10 mi on US-70, follow signs (R). 54 Avail: 54 W, 54 E (30/50 amps). 2021 rates: $20 to $40. Mar 31 to Sep 05. (580)924-7316

LAKE TEXOMA - COE/LAKESIDE (Public Corps) From town, W 10 mi on US-70 to Streetman Rd, S 4 mi (E). 137 Avail: 137 W, 137 E (30/50 amps). 2021 rates: $20 to $22. Mar 31 to Sep 30. (580)920-0176

Things to See and Do

CHOCTAW CASINO & RESORT 4300 slot machines, table games, poker. 716 hotel rooms, spa, 12 restaurants, tropical pools, 3000 seat theatre, convention center, bowling alley, movie theatre, 70 game arcade, RV Park. Partial Handicap, RV Access, 24/7, ATM. Partial handicap access. RV accessible. Restrooms. Food. Hours: 24 Hours and 7 days a week. ATM.
(888)652-4628 Lat: 33.954184, Lon: -96.412111
3735 Choctaw Rd, Durant, OK 74701
www.choctawcasinos.com
See ad opposite page

EDMOND — B4 *Oklahoma*

ARCADIA LAKE - COE/SCISSORTAIL (Public Corps) From jct I-35 & Hwy 66: Go 2-1/2 mi E on Hwy 66. Avail: 38 E. 2021 rates: $19 to $35. (405)396-8026

EL RENO — B4 *Canadian*

EL RENO WEST KOA **Ratings: 8.5/10★/7.5** (RV Park) 49 Avail: 12 full hkups, 37 W, 37 E (30/50 amps). 2021 rates: $37.80 to $42. (405)884-2595, 301 S Walbaum Rd, Calumet, OK 73014

ELK CITY — C3 *Beckham*

ELK CITY See also Clinton & Sayre.

EASTRIDGE RV PARK **Ratings: 6.5/8.5★/6.5** (RV Park) Avail: 25 full hkups (30/50 amps). 2021 rates: $30. (580)339-1411, 102 Allee Drive, Elk City, OK 73644

ELK CREEK RV PARK

good sam park **Ratings: 8.5/10★/8.5** (RV Park) From jct of I-40 (exit 38) & S. Main: Go N 500 ft on S. Main to 20th St, then E 500 ft on 20th St. (L). **FAC:** paved rds. (78 spaces). Avail: 63 gravel, 53 pull-thrus, (21x65), back-ins (21x60), 63 full hkups (30/50 amps), seasonal sites, cable, WiFi @ sites, tent sites, dump, laundry. **REC:** boating nearby. Pets OK. Partial handicap access, eco-friendly. 2021 rates: $36 to $39, Military discount.
(580)225-7865 Lat: 35.3929, Lon: -99.401552
317 E 20th St, Elk City, OK 73644
elkcreekrvpark.com
See ad this page

Show Your Good Sam Membership Card!

KOA ELK CITY/CLINTON **Ratings: 8/9★/8** (Campground) Avail: 51 full hkups (30/50 amps). 2021 rates: $42.35 to $45.65. (800)562-4149, 21167 Route 66 North, Foss, OK 73647

ROUTE 66 RV PARK

good sam park **Ratings: 7/9★/8.5** (RV Park) Avail: 82 full hkups (30/50 amps). 2021 rates: $35 to $38. (580)225-0960, 100 S. Pioneer, Elk City, OK 73644

ENID — B4 *Garfield*

HIGH POINT MOBILE HOME & RV PARK **Ratings: 7.5/9.5★/8** (RV Area in MH Park) Avail: 30 full hkups (30/50 amps). 2021 rates: $34. (580)234-1726, 2700 N. Van Buren #93, Enid, OK 73703

ENTERPRISE — C6 *Haskell*

EUFAULA LAKE - COE/BROOKEN COVE (Public Corps) From town, N 4 mi on SR-71, follow signs (L). Avail: 73 E (30/50 amps). 2021 rates: $19 to $20. Apr 01 to Sep 29. (918)799-5843

EUFAULA LAKE - COE/DAM SITE SOUTH (Public Corps) From town: Go 16 mi E on Hwy 9, then 4 mi N on Hwy 71. Avail: 44 E. 2021 rates: $12 to $20. Apr 01 to Sep 29. (918)484-5135

EUFAULA LAKE - COE/PORUM LANDING (Public Corps) From town, N 6 mi on US-69 to Texanna Rd (exit 150), follow signs (R). Avail: 45 E (30/50 amps). 2021 rates: $14 to $20. Apr 01 to Sep 29. (918)799-5843

EUFAULA — C6 *McIntosh*

EUFAULA LAKE - COE/BELLE STARR (Public Corps) From town, N 5 mi on US-69 to Texanna Rd, E 2 mi, follow signs (R). 111 Avail: 111 W, 111 E (30/50 amps). 2021 rates: $18 to $20. Apr 01 to Sep 29. (918)799-5843

EUFAULA LAKE - COE/HIGHWAY 9 LANDING (Public Corps) From town, E 8 mi on Hwy 9, follow signs (L). Avail: 65 E (30/50 amps). 2021 rates: $10 to $20. Mar 31 to Sep 28. (918)799-5843

LITTLE TURTLE RV & STORAGE

good sam park **Ratings: 9.5/10★/10** (RV Park) From jct of I-40 (exit 264) & US-69: Go S 6-1/2 mi on US-69, then E 300 yds OK-150/Texanna Rd, then S 300 yds Old US-69. (L). **FAC:** gravel rds. Avail: 120 paved, patios, 51 pull-thrus, (35x80), back-ins (35x60), 120 full hkups (30/50 amps), WiFi @ sites, tent sites, dump, laundry, LP gas. **REC:** pool, Eufaula Lake: fishing, boating nearby, playground. Pets OK. Partial handicap access. Big rig sites, eco-friendly. 2021 rates: $43 to $53.
(918)618-2140 Lat: 35.359768, Lon: -95.573590
114161 N Highway 69, Eufaula, OK 74432
littleturtlerv.com
See ad next page

XTREME RV RESORT **Ratings: 10/10★/10** (RV Resort) Avail: 100 full hkups (30/50 amps). 2021 rates: $45 to $50. (918)707-5636, 935 Lakeshore Drive, Eufaula, OK 74432

YOGI BEAR'S JELLYSTONE PARK EUFAULA **Ratings: 8.5/9★/9.5** (RV Resort) Avail: 17 full hkups (30/50 amps). 2021 rates: $35 to $99. (918)689-9644, 610 Lakeshore Drive, Eufaula, OK 74432

Find new and exciting itineraries in our ""Road Trip'' article at the front of each state and province.

FAIRLAND — A6 *Ottawa*

GRAND LAKE/TWIN BRIDGES (Public State Park) E-bnd: From Jct of I-44 & Afton exit (US-60), E 11.9 mi on US-60 (L); or W-bnd: From Wyandotte, W 3 mi on US-60 (R). 63 Avail: 63 W, 63 E (30/50 amps). 2021 rates: $22. (918)542-6969

FORT COBB — C4 *Caddo*

FORT COBB (Public State Park) From Jct of Hwys 9 & 146, N 1 mi on Hwy 146 to local rd, N 4.3 mi, past golf course (R). 292 Avail: 8 full hkups, 284 W, 284 E (20/30 amps). 2021 rates: $20 to $27. (405)643-2249

FORT GIBSON — B6 *Muskogee*

FORT GIBSON LAKE - COE/WILDWOOD (Public Corps) From town, S 1 mi on Hwy 80-A to Hwy 80, W 4 mi (R). Avail: 30 E (30/50 amps). 2021 rates: $16 to $20. (918)682-4314

HARBOR RV PARK **Ratings: 5/10★/7** (RV Park) Avail: 10 full hkups (30/50 amps). 2021 rates: $25 to $30. (918)478-3300, 1217 S. Scott St., Fort Gibson, OK 74434

FORT SUPPLY — A3 *Woodward*

FORT SUPPLY LAKE - COE/SUPPLY PARK (Public Corps) From town, S 1.5 mi on access rd (E). Avail: 96 E (30/50 amps). 2021 rates: $17 to $24. Mar 01 to Sep 30. (580)766-2001

FORT TOWSON — D6 *Choctaw*

RAYMOND GARY (Public State Park) From town, E 0.5 mi on US-70 to SR-209, S 2 mi (E). 19 Avail: 10 full hkups, 9 W, 9 E (30/50 amps). 2021 rates: $22 to $30. (580)873-2307

FOSS — B3 *Custer*

FOSS (Public State Park) From Jct of I-40 & SR-44 (exit 53), N 6.3 mi on SR-44 to SR-73W, W 0.2 mi (R). 108 Avail: 10 full hkups, 98 W, 98 E (30/50 amps). 2021 rates: $22 to $30. May 01 to Oct 30. (580)592-4433

Do you know how to read each part of a listing? Check the How to Use This Guide in the front.

FOYIL — B6 *Rogers*

OOLOGAH LAKE - COE/BLUE CREEK (Public Corps) From town, N 10 mi on US-66 to 1st cnty rd, W 2.3 mi to EW-40, N 1.2 mi to EW-39, W 1.5 mi, follow signs (E). Avail: 25 E (30 amps). 2021 rates: $14 to $18. Apr 01 to Sep 30. (918)341-4244

FREEDOM — A3 *Woodward*

ALABASTER CAVERNS (Public State Park) From Jct of US-64 & Hwy 50, S 9 mi on Hwy 50 to Hwy 50A, E 0.5 mi (L). 11 Avail. 2021 rates: $22. (580)621-3381

GORE — B6 *Cherokee*

MARVAL RESORT **Ratings: 8.5/9.5★/9.5** (Campground) 80 Avail: 45 full hkups, 35 E (30/50 amps). 2021 rates: $49 to $99. (800)340-4280, 445140 E 1011 Rd., Gore, OK 74435

TENKILLER FERRY LAKE - COE/CHICKEN CREEK (Public Corps) From town, S 3 mi on SR 100-82 to cnty rd, NW 2 mi (E). Avail: 103 E (30/50 amps). 2021 rates: $13 to $18. Apr 01 to Sep 30. (918)487-5252

TENKILLER FERRY LAKE - COE/STRAYHORN LANDING (Public Corps) From town, N 8 mi on Hwy 100 to Hwy 10A, N 1.5 mi to paved access rd, E 0.25 mi (R). Avail: 40 E (30 amps). 2021 rates: $16 to $20. Apr 01 to Sep 30. (918)487-5252

GRAND LAKE TOWNE — A6 *Craig*

WATER'S EDGE RV & CABIN RESORT **Ratings: 9/9★/10** (RV Park) Avail: 91 full hkups (30/50 amps). 2021 rates: $26 to $49. (918)782-1444, 446711 E 350 Rd, Vinita, OK 74301

GROVE — A6 *Delaware*

CEDAR OAKS RV PARK **Ratings: 8/9.5★/9.5** (RV Park) Avail: 123 full hkups (30/50 amps). 2021 rates: $32 to $38. (800)880-8884, 1550 83rd St NW, Grove, OK 74344

EAGLES LANDING RESORT & RECREATION **Ratings: 8/9.5★/8.5** (Membership Park) Avail: 130 full hkups (30/50 amps). 2021 rates: $35 to $45. (918)786-6196, 25301 US Hwy 59 N, Grove, OK 74344

GRAND LAKE/HONEY CREEK (Public State Park) From Jct of I-44 & US-59, S 15 mi on US-59 to State Park Rd, W 0.8 mi (E). 49 Avail: 49 W, 49 E (30/50 amps). 2021 rates: $22 to $27. (918)786-9447

GUTHRIE — B4 *Logan*

CEDAR VALLEY RV PARK

good sam park

Ratings: 7/8/9 (RV Park) Avail: 25 full hkups (30/50 amps). 2021 rates: $39.99. (405)282-4478, 725 Masters Dr, Guthrie, OK 73044

GUYMON — A2 *Texas*

CORRAL DRIVE IN RV PARK **Ratings: 8.5/9.5★/9** (RV Park) Avail: 47 full hkups (30/50 amps). 2021 rates: $40 to $45. (580)338-3748, 825 W Hwy 54, Guymon, OK 73942

HASTINGS — D4 *Jefferson*

WAURIKA LAKE - COE/KIOWA PARK I (Public Corps) From town, NW 8 mi on Hwy 5 to cnty rd, N 3 mi, follow signs (R). 166 Avail: 166 W, 166 E (30/50 amps). 2021 rates: $16 to $20. May 01 to Sep 30. (580)963-9031

WAURIKA LAKE - COE/WICHITA RIDGE NORTH (Public Corps) From town: Go 4 mi N on county road. 27 Avail: Pit toilets. 2021 rates: $14 to $18. (580)963-2111

HENRYETTA — B5 *Okmulgee*

HIGHWAY 75 RV PARK & STORAGE **Ratings: 6/7.5/6.5** (RV Park) Avail: 48 full hkups (30/50 amps). 2021 rates: $45 to $50. (918)752-8733, 13705 Coalton Road, Henryetta, OK 74437

HINTON — C4 *Caddo*

RED ROCK CANYON (Public State Park) From Jct of I-40 & US-281 (exit 101), S 5 mi on US-281 (L) Caution: Steep decline and winding road to campground area. 73 Avail: 3 full hkups, 44 W, 44 E (30/50 amps). 2021 rates: $22 to $25. (405)542-6344

HUGO — D6 *Choctaw*

HUGO LAKE - COE/KIAMICHI PARK (Public Corps) From town, E 5 mi on US-70 to N4285, N 1 mi (E). Avail: 84 E (30/50 amps). 2021 rates: $14 to $22. Mar 31 to Sep 29. (580)326-3345

HUGO LAKE - COE/VIRGIL POINT (Public Corps) From town, E 10 mi on US-70 to SR-147, N 2.6 mi to SH 147, W 1 mi, follow signs (E). 52 Avail: 52 W, 52 E (30/50 amps). 2021 rates: $17 to $19. Apr 01 to Sep 30. (580)326-3345

JAY — B6 *Delaware*

PINE ISLAND RV RESORT **Ratings: 8.5/8/7** (Membership Park) 120 Avail: 100 full hkups, 20 W, 20 E (30/50 amps). 2021 rates: $50. (918)786-9071, 32501 S 571, Jay, OK 74346

JET — A4 *Alfalfa*

GREAT SALT PLAINS (Public State Park) From Jct of US-64 & Hwy 38 (in town), N 9 mi on Hwy 38 (L). 64 Avail: 64 W, 64 E (30/50 amps). 2021 rates: $22 to $30. (580)626-4731

KAW CITY — A5 *Kay*

KAW LAKE - COE/COON CREEK (Public Corps) From Jct of US-77 & Hwy 11, E 5.7 mi on Hwy 11 to N Enterprise Rd., N 2 mi to Furguson Rd., E 2 mi (R). Avail: 54 E (15 amps). 2021 rates: $16 to $18. Mar 01 to Nov 30. (580)762-5611

KAW LAKE - COE/SARGE CREEK (Public Corps) From town, N 4 mi on US-77 to Hwy 11, E 13.8 mi (R). Avail: 53 E (15 amps). 2021 rates: $20. Mar 30 to Sep 28. (580)762-5611

KAW LAKE - COE/WASHUNGA BAY (Public Corps) From town, N 4 mi on US-177 to Hwy 11, E 17 mi to park access rd, N 4.5 mi (R). Avail: 24 E (15 amps). 2021 rates: $20. May 01 to Sep 15. (580)762-5611

KELLYVILLE — B5 *Creek*

HEYBURN LAKE - COE/HEYBURN PARK (Public Corps) From town, W 9.4 mi on US-66 to S 337W Ave., N 4 mi to W 141st St., E 2.6 mi. 46 Avail: 46 W, 46 E (30/50 amps). 2021 rates: $20. Apr 01 to Oct 31. (918)247-6601

KENTON — A1 *Cimarron*

BLACK MESA (Public State Park) N-bnd: From Kenton, E 4.5 mi on SR-325 to D0073 Rd, S 3.2 mi (E); or S-bnd: From Jct of SR-325 & US-56 (in Boise City), NW 19.5 mi on SR-325 to N0080 Rd., W 6 mi (E). 29 Avail: 29 W, 29 E (20/30 amps). 2021 rates: $22 to $27. (580)426-2222

KETCHUM — A6 *Mayes*

PELICAN LANDING RESORT & CAMPGROUND **Ratings: 7.5/5.5/6.5** (Membership Park) 45 Avail: 25 full hkups, 20 S (30/50 amps). 2021 rates: $40. (918)782-3295, 32100 Hwy 85, Ketchum, OK 74349

KINGSTON — D5 *Bryan*

LAKE TEXOMA (Public State Park) In town, from Jct of US-70 & SR-32, E 5 mi on US-70 (R). 129 Avail: 88 full hkups, 41 W, 41 E (30/50 amps). 2021 rates: $22 to $27. (580)564-2566

LAKE TEXOMA - COE/BUNCOMBE CREEK (Public Corps) From town, W 2 mi on SR-32 to Enos Rd, S 4 mi to Shay Rd, W 3 mi, follow signs (E). Avail: 54 E (30 amps). 2021 rates: $16 to $20. (580)564-2901

LAKE TEXOMA - COE/CANEY CREEK (Public Corps) From town, S 5 mi on Muncrief Rd, follow signs. Avail: 41 E (30 amps). 2021 rates: $18 to $22. May 01 to Sep 30. (580)564-2632

LANGLEY — A6 *Mayes*

CROOKED CREEK RV PARK **Ratings: 7/NA/9.5** (RV Park) Avail: 34 full hkups (30/50 amps). 2021 rates: $35. (918)770-6111, 2036 N. 3rd St., Langley, OK 74350

LAWTON — C4 *Comanche*

BUFFALO BOB'S RV PARK

Ratings: 9/8.5/8 (RV Park) Avail: 10 full hkups (30/50 amps). 2021 rates: $50. (580)699-3534, 1508 S.E. Tower Rd., Lawton, OK 73501

LAKE ELLSWORTH (Public) From Jct of I-44 & US-277, W 4 mi on US-277 to Bonafield Rd, N 1 mi (R). Avail: 41 E (20/30 amps). 2021 rates: $7 to $12. (580)529-2663

LAKE LAWTONKA CITY PARK (Public) From Jct of I-44 & Hwy 49, W 3.7 mi on Hwy 49 to Hwy 58, N 2 mi (L). Avail: 41 E (20 amps). 2021 rates: $7 to $12. (580)529-2663

WICHITA MTNS. WILDLIFE REFUGE/CAMP DORIS (Public National Park) From jct US 62 & Hwy 115: Go 4 mi N on Hwy 115. Avail: 23 E. 2021 rates: $10 to $20. (580)429-3222

LONE WOLF — C3 *Kiowa*

QUARTZ MOUNTAIN NATURE PARK (Public State Park) From Jct of Hwys 9 & 44 (in town), S 9 mi on Hwy 44 to access rd Hwy 44A (at sign), W 1 mi (R). 119 Avail: 19 full hkups, 100 W, 100 E (20/30 amps). 2021 rates: $10 to $23. (580)563-2238

LONGDALE — B4 *Blaine*

CANTON LAKE - COE/LONGDALE (Public Corps) From town, W 2 mi on cnty rd (E). 35 Avail: Pit toilets. 2021 rates: $13. (580)886-2989

MADILL — D5 *Marshall*

LITTLE GLASSES RESORT & MARINA **Ratings: 5/5/7.5** (RV Resort) 80 Avail: 39 full hkups, 41 W, 41 E (30 amps). 2021 rates: $19 to $28. (580)795-2068, 13443 Parrot Head Lane, Madill, OK 73446

MANITOU — C3 *Tillman*

LAKE FREDERICK (Public) From Jct of US-183 & Hwy 5-C, E 5 mi on Hwy 5-C to N2290, N 0.5 mi (E). 52 Avail: 40 W, 52 E (30/50 amps). 2021 rates: $6 to $9. (580)335-1553

MANNFORD — B5 *Creek*

KEYSTONE LAKE - COE/NEW MANNFORD RAMP (Public Corps) From town, N 1 mi on cnty rd, follow signs (R). Avail: 44 E (30 amps). 2021 rates: $8 to $21. Apr 01 to Oct 31. (918)865-2621

YOGI BEAR'S JELLYSTONE PARK AT KEYSTONE LAKE **Ratings: 7.5/9★/8.5** (RV Park) Avail: 96 full hkups (30/50 amps). 2021 rates: $35 to $99. May 15 to Sep 03. (918)865-2845, 29365 OK-51, Mannford, OK 74044

MCALESTER — C5 *Pittsburg*

EUFAULA LAKE - COE/ELM POINT (Public Corps) From town, NE 13 mi on Hwy 31 (L). Avail: 14 E (30 amps), Pit toilets. 2021 rates: $7 to $11. Mar 01 to Oct 31. (918)484-5135

VALLEY INN RV PARK

Ratings: 6.5/8/8.5 (RV Park) Avail: 17 full hkups (30/50 amps). 2021 rates: $35. (918)426-5400, 2400 S Main St, McAlester, OK 74501

MEDICINE PARK — C4 *Comanche*

MILITARY PARK LAKE ELMER THOMAS REC AREA (FORT SILL) (Public) From jct US-62 & I-44, go NW to Medicine Park (exit 45), then 6 mi W on Hwy 49. Avail: 45 full hkups (30/50 amps). 2021 rates: $30. (580)250-4040

MIAMI — A6 *Ottawa*

MIAMI MH & RV PARK

Ratings: 6.5/9★/7 (RV Area in MH Park) Avail: 16 full hkups (30/50 amps). 2021 rates: $30. (918)542-2287, 2001 E Steve Owens Blvd #18, Miami, OK 74354

MILBURN — D5 *Johnston*

BLUE RIVER RV PARK **Ratings: 6/NA/6** (RV Park) Avail: 10 full hkups (30/50 amps). 2021 rates: $35 to $45. (580)443-5912, 4700 OK Hwy 78 East, Milburn, OK 73450

MORRIS — B5 *Okmulgee*

MORRIS RV PARK **Ratings: 6.5/NA/6.5** (RV Park) Avail: 10 full hkups (30/50 amps). 2021 rates: $45 to $50. (918)641-4504, 17220 Hwy 62 , Morris, OK 74445

MOUNTAIN PARK — C3 *Jackson*

GREAT PLAINS (Public State Park) From Jct of US-62 & US-183, N 7 mi on US-183 to E1570, (at sign), W 1 mi (R). 52 Avail: 14 full hkups, 38 W, 38 E (30/50 amps). 2021 rates: $22 to $30. (580)569-2032

MOYERS — D6 *Pushmataha*

K RIVER CAMPGROUND **Ratings: 4/6.5/6** (Campground) 46 Avail: 17 full hkups, 29 W, 29 E (30/50 amps). 2021 rates: $35 to $40. (580)298-2442, 415209 E 1842 Road, Moyers, OK 74557

MUSKOGEE — B6 *Muskogee*

FORT GIBSON LAKE - COE/DAM SITE (Public Corps) From town, E 6 mi on Hwy 251-A (R). Avail: 48 E (30 amps). 2021 rates: $15 to $20. Apr 01 to Oct 31. (918)683-6618

MEADOWBROOK RV PARK

Ratings: 3.5/NA/6.5 (RV Park) From jct US-62/Hwy 16 & US-69: Go S 1 mi on US-69. **FAC:** paved/gravel rds. (64 spaces). Avail: 24 paved, patios, 23 pull-thrus, (34x70), back-ins (25x45), accepts full hkup units only, 24 full hkups (30/50 amps), seasonal sites, . Pet restrict (B). No tents. Big rig sites. 2021 rates: $20. no cc.
(918)681-4574 Lat: 35.740447, Lon: -95.401348
1300 S 32nd Street (US-69), Muskogee, OK 74401
See ad this page

WEBBERS FALLS POOL - COE/SPANIARD CREEK (Public Corps) From town, S 8 mi on US-64 to Elm Grove Rd, E 5 mi (L). 36 Avail: 35 W, 35 E (30 amps). 2021 rates: $14 to $15. (918)487-5252

NEWCASTLE — C4 *McClain*

A' AAA ADULT RV PARK **Ratings: 5/NA/7.5** (RV Park) Avail: 15 full hkups (30/50 amps). 2021 rates: $25 to $50. (405)387-3334, 3300 SW 24th Street, Newcastle, OK 73065

NORMAN — C4 *Cleveland*

LAKE THUNDERBIRD (Public State Park) From Jct of I-35 & Hwy 9E (exit 108A), E 15 mi on Hwy 9E (L); or From Jct of I-40 & Choctaw Rd (exit 166), S 10.8 mi on Choctaw Rd to Alameda Dr, E 1 mi (E). 200 Avail: 30 full hkups, 131 W, 131 E (20/30 amps). 2021 rates: $20 to $28. (405)360-3572

OKLAHOMA CITY — B4 *Oklahoma*

A SPOTLIGHT Introducing Oklahoma City's colorful attractions appearing at the front of this state section.

OKLAHOMA CITY See also Newcastle.

COUNCIL ROAD RV PARK

Ratings: 7/10★/7 (RV Park) From jct of I-40 & Council Rd (Exit 142): Go S 1/4 mi on Council Rd, then W 1 block on SW 8th St (L). **FAC:** paved/gravel rds. (102 spaces). Avail: 66 gravel, patios, 66 pull-thrus, (25x60), 66 full hkups (30/50 amps), seasonal sites, cable, WiFi @ sites, dump, laundry, LP gas. Pet restrict (B). Partial handicap access. No tents. Big rig sites. 2021 rates: $40, Military discount. no reservations.
(405)789-2103 Lat: 35.45394, Lon: -97.655151
8108 SW 8th St, Oklahoma City, OK 73128
councilrdrvpark.com
See ad page 714

OK

OKLAHOMA CITY (CONT)

MILITARY PARK TINKER FAMCAMP (TINKER AFB) (Public) From jct of I-40W & Sooner Rd (exit 156A): Go 3 mi S on Sooner Rd, then 1 mi on SE 59th St to Gott Gate, then right 200 yds (L). Avail: 28 full hkups (30/50 amps). 2021 rates: $20. (405)734-2847

MUSTANG RUN RV PARK
Ratings: 9.5/10★/8 (RV Park) Avail: 61 full hkups (30/50 amps). 2021 rates: $49. (405)577-6040, 11528 W I-40 Service Road, Yukon, OK 73099

OKLAHOMA CITY EAST KOA **Ratings: 9.5/9.5★/9.5** (Campground) Avail: 51 full hkups (30/50 amps). 2021 rates: $50 to $72. (800)562-5076, 6200 S Choctaw Rd., Choctaw, OK 73020

ROADRUNNER RV PARK
Ratings: 8/9.5★/8 (RV Park) Avail: 82 full hkups (30/50 amps). 2021 rates: $42 to $45. (405)677-2373, 4740 S I-35 Service Rd, Oklahoma City, OK 73129

ROCKWELL RV PARK
Ratings: 8.5/10★/8.5 (RV Park) From Jct of I-40 & Rockwell Ave (exit 143), S 0.03 mi on Rockwell Ave (L) on SE corner of Rockwell & I-40.

EZ ON/OFF I 40 EXIT 143 INDOOR POOL
New dog park/wash. Minutes to downtown OKC, Fairgrounds, Cowboy Hall of Fame, Firefighters Museum, Bombing Memorial. Indoor pool, exercise center, handicap accessible storm shelter, private showers, hot tub. Outdoor cinema.

FAC: paved/gravel rds. (170 spaces). Avail: 51 gravel, 51 pull-thrus, (28x70), 51 full hkups (30/50 amps), seasonal sites, cable, WiFi @ sites, tent sites, rentals, laundry, LP bottles. **REC:** heated pool, hot tub, Crystal Lake: fishing, kayaking/canoeing, shuffleboard. Pets OK. Partial handicap access. Big rig sites, eco-friendly. 2021 rates: $43 to $48, Military discount.
(405)787-5992 Lat: 35.458429, Lon: -97.634299
720 S Rockwell Ave, Oklahoma City, OK 73128
www.rockwellrvpark.com
See ad page 715

TWIN FOUNTAINS RV RESORT
Ratings: 9.5/10★/9.5 (RV Resort) Avail: 50 full hkups (30/50 amps). 2021 rates: $49.50 to $55. (405)475-5514, 2727 NE 63rd St, Oklahoma City, OK 73111

Travel Services

AIRSTREAM OF OKLAHOMA New or preowned Airstreams. Also offer service and parts. **SERVICES:** RV appliance, MH mechanical, staffed RV wash, restrooms. RV Sales. RV supplies, RV accessible. Hours: 9am - 6pm, closed Sun.
(405)463-2679 Lat: 35.605050, Lon: -97.502130
13241 Broadway Extension, Oklahoma City, OK 73114
www.airstreamofok.com

CAMPING WORLD OF OKLAHOMA CITY As the nation's largest retailer of RV supplies, accessories, services and new and used RVs, Camping World is committed to making your total RV experience better. **SERVICES:** tire, RV appliance, sells outdoor gear, staffed RV wash, restrooms. RV Sales. RV supplies, LP gas, emergency parking, RV accessible. Hours: 9am - 7pm.
(888)460-6964 Lat: 35.605682, Lon: -97.49993
13111 N Broadway Ext, Oklahoma City, OK 73114
www.campingworld.com

Laundry & dishwasher detergent liquids contain up to 80 percent water. It costs energy and packaging to bring this water to the consumer. When there is a choice - choose dry powders.

GANDER RV OF OKLAHOMA CITY Your new hometown outfitter offering the best regional gear for all your outdoor needs. Your adventure awaits. **SERVICES:** sells outdoor gear, restrooms. RV Sales. RV accessible. Hours: 9am - 7pm, closed Sun.
(877)839-4463 Lat: 35.416938, Lon: -97.319709
4901 S Anderson Rd, Oklahoma City, OK 73150
rv.ganderoutdoors.com

MOTLEY RV REPAIR Repair of all types of RVs including motorhomes and bumper pulls. Large inventory of repair parts. **SERVICES:** RV, RV appliance, restrooms. RV supplies, emergency parking, RV accessible, waiting room. Hours: 8am to 6pm .
(405)789-4848 Lat: 35.463607, Lon: -97.660261
8300 W Reno Ave, Oklahoma City, OK 73127
www.motleyrvrepair.com
See ad previous page

OKMULGEE — B5 *Okfuskee*

DRIPPING SPRINGS (Public State Park) From Jct of US-75 & SR-56, W 6.5 mi on SR-56 (L). 76 Avail: 76 W, 76 E (30 amps). 2021 rates: $20 to $23. Apr 15 to Oct 15. (918)756-5971

OKMULGEE (Public State Park) From jct US 75 & Hwy 56: Go 5 mi W on Hwy 56. 48 Avail: 1 full hkups, 47 W, 47 E. 2021 rates: $20 to $23. (918)756-5971

OOLOGAH — B5 *Rogers*

OOLOGAH LAKE - COE/HAWTHORN BLUFF (Public Corps) From town, E 2 mi on SR-88 (L). Avail: 41 E (30 amps). 2021 rates: $16 to $20. Apr 01 to Sep 30. (918)443-2319

OOLOGAH LAKE - COE/REDBUD BAY (Public Corps) From town, S 4 mi on SR-88 (L). 30 Avail: 30 W, 30 E (30/50 amps), Pit toilets. 2021 rates: $16. Apr 01 to Oct 31. (918)443-2250

PARK HILL — B6 *Cherokee*

CHEROKEE LANDING (Public State Park) From Jct of Hwy 62 & Hwy 82 (S of Tahlequah), S 11 mi on Hwy 82 (R). Note: 40' RV length limit. 93 Avail: 93 W, 93 E (20/50 amps). 2021 rates: $22 to $30. (918)457-5716

PERRY — B4 *Noble*

PERRY LAKE RV PARK (CITY PARK) (Public) From jct of I-35 & OK-77 (exit 185): Go W 1/2 mi on OK-77, then S 1 mi on CR-80 (R). Avail: 10 full hkups (30/50 amps). 2021 rates: $25. Apr 01 to Nov 01. (580)336-4684

PONCA CITY — A5 *Kay*

KAW LAKE - COE/BEAR CREEK COVE (Public Corps) From Jct of Hwy 77 & Main St, E 8.3 mi on E River Rd., S 3.7 mi N Bear Creek Rd. (E). 22 Avail: 22 W, 22 E (15 amps). 2021 rates: $15. May 01 to Sep 15. (580)762-5611

KAW LAKE - COE/OSAGE COVE (Public Corps) From town, E 11 mi on Lake Rd to park access rd, S 0.1 mi (E). Avail: 97 E (15 amps). 2021 rates: $20. Mar 01 to Sep 28. (580)762-5611

KAW LAKE - COE/SANDY PARK (Public Corps) From town, E 11 mi on Lake Rd to park access rd, N .5 mi (E). Avail: 12 E (30 amps), Pit toilets. 2021 rates: $16. Apr 01 to Oct 31. (580)762-5611

LAKE PONCA (Public) From Jct of US 60 & US 77, N 0.4 mi on US 77 to Lake Rd, E 3 mi on Lake Rd to Prentice, N 0.4 mi on Prentice (L). 30 Avail: 12 W, 12 E (30/50 amps). 2021 rates: $8 to $12. (580)767-0400

POTEAU — C6 *Le Flore*

LONG LAKE RESORT & RV PARK
Ratings: 7.5/9★/9.5 (RV Park) From jct US 271 & US 59: Go 2-1/4 mi S on US-59 (L) Entrance to the park is on the hill. **FAC:** paved/gravel rds. 41 Avail: 34 paved, 7 all weather, 11 pull-thrus, (30x80), back-ins (28x45), 41 full hkups (30/50 amps), WiFi, tent sites, rentals, dump, firewood, controlled access. **REC:** Long Lake/Terrell Lake: swim, fishing, kayaking/canoeing, playground, rec open to public. Pets OK. Partial handicap access. Big rig sites. 2021 rates: $35 to $40, Military discount.
(918)647-8140 Lat: 35.003075, Lon: -94.643825
35740 Hwy 59 South, Poteau, OK 74953
longlakeresort.com
See ad this page

Traveling with Fido? Many campground listings indicate pet-friendly amenities and pet restrictions.

Travel Services

CAMPING WORLD OF POTEAU As the nation's largest retailer of RV supplies, accessories, services and new and used RVs, Camping World is committed to making your total RV experience better. **SERVICES:** RV, tire, RV appliance, MH mechanical, restrooms. RV Sales. RV supplies, LP gas, dump, RV accessible. Hours: 9am - 7pm, closed Sun.
(877)886-6503 Lat: 35.026502, Lon: -94.648119
34203 US Hwy 59 S, Poteau, OK 74953
www.campingworld.com

PRUE — B5 *Osage*

WALNUT CREEK (Public State Park) E-bnd: From Jct of SR-99 & Osage Prue Rd, SE 10 mi on Osage Prue Rd to area #2 (R); or W-bnd: From Jct of US-64/412 & 209 W Ave/Prue Rd (6 mi W of Sand Springs), W 13 mi on Prue Rd to area #2 (L). 140 Avail: 8 full hkups, 71 W, 71 E (20/30 amps). 2021 rates: $20 to $30. Apr 01 to Nov 30. (918)865-3362

RINGOLD — D6 *McCurtain*

PINE CREEK LAKE - COE/LOST RAPIDS (Public Corps) From Jct of Indian Nation Tpke & Hwy 3 (Antler exit), E 30 mi on Hwy 3, follow signs (R). Avail: 17 E (30 amps). 2021 rates: $12 to $17. Apr 01 to Sep 29. (580)876-3720

SALINA — B6 *Mayes*

GRAND LAKE/SNOWDALE (Public State Park) From Jct of I-44 & US-69, SW 12 mi on US-69 to SR-20, E 8 mi to park access rd, N 0.25 mi (L). 17 Avail: 17 W, 17 E (20/30 amps). 2021 rates: $22 to $27. (918)434-2651

SALLISAW — B6 *Haskell*

BRUSHY LAKE (Public) From Jct of I-40 & US-59, (Exit 308), N 1.3 mi on US-59 to Maple St, N 6.5 mi on Maple St to Park Rd, S 0.8 mi (E). 23 Avail: 23 W, 23 E (30/50 amps). 2021 rates: $15. (918)775-6241

SALLISAW/FORT SMITH WEST KOA **Ratings: 9/10★/9.5** (Campground) 44 Avail: 39 full hkups, 5 W, 5 E (30/50 amps). 2021 rates: $43.89 to $65.89. (800)562-2797, 1900 KOA Power Drive, Sallisaw, OK 74955

SAND SPRINGS — B5 *Osage*

KEYSTONE (Public State Park) From Jct of US-64 & Hwy 151, S 1 mi on Hwy 151 (R); or From Jct of Hwys 51 & 48, E 8 mi on Hwy 51 to Hwy 151, N 0.5 mi (R). Avail: 72 full hkups (30/50 amps). 2021 rates: $22 to $25. (918)865-4991

KEYSTONE LAKE - COE/APPALACHIA BAY (Public Corps) From town, W 12 mi on US-64 to frontage rd, W 0.25 mi to 3760 Rd, S 1 mi (E). 18 Avail: Pit toilets. 2021 rates: $8. Apr 01 to Oct 31. (918)865-2621

KEYSTONE LAKE - COE/SALT CREEK NORTH (Public Corps) From town, E 1 mi on US-51, follow signs (L). Avail: 12 E (30/50 amps). 2021 rates: $10 to $17. May 01 to Sep 10. (918)865-2621

SAPULPA — B5 *Creek*

HEYBURN LAKE - COE/SHEPPARD POINT (Public Corps) From Jct of I-44 & SR-33 (exit 211), W 7 mi on SR-33 to park access rd, S 2.4 mi, E 1.7 mi on W 141st St. (R). Avail: 21 E (30 amps). 2021 rates: $20. Apr 01 to Oct 31. (918)247-4551

SAVANNA — C5 *Pittsburg*

MILITARY PARK MURPHYS MEADOW (MCALESTER ARMY AMMUNITION PLANT) (Public) From McAlester, S 8 mi on US-69. 17 Avail: 11 full hkups, 6 W, 6 E (30/50 amps). 2021 rates: $14. (918)420-7484

SAYRE — C3 *Beckham*

BOBCAT CREEK RV PARK **Ratings: 7.5/NA/9** (RV Park) Avail: 15 full hkups (30/50 amps). 2021 rates: $35. (580)210-9877, 2005 NE Hwy 66, Sayre, OK 73662

SAYRE RV PARK (Public) From jct US 40 & US 283: Go 1/2 mi N on US 283. Avail: 80 E (30/50 amps). (580)928-2260

SEMINOLE — C5 *Seminole*

STUCKEY'S TRAVEL CENTER & RV PARK **Ratings: 6/7/7** (RV Park) Avail: 28 full hkups (30/50 amps). 2021 rates: $20 to $30. (405)303-2200, 11242 N Hwy 99, Seminole, OK 74868

Shop at Camping World and SAVE with coupons. Check the front of the Guide for yours!

SHAWNEE — C5 *Pottawatomi*

HEART OF OKLAHOMA EXPO CENTER RV PARK (Public) From jct of I-40 & US-177 (exit 181): Go SE 3-1/2 mi on US-177 (L). 795 Avail: 366 full hkups, 429 W, 429 E (30/50 amps). 2021 rates: $25. (405)275-7020

SPAVINAW — B6 *Mayes*

GRAND LAKE/SPAVINAW (Public State Park) From Jct of SR-20 & SR-82 (N of town), S 3 mi on SR-82 (L). 26 Avail: 26 W, 26 E (20/30 amps). 2021 rates: $22 to $27. (918)435-8066

SPRINGER — D5 *Carter*

COOL BREEZE RV PARK & CINEMA **Ratings: 7.5/9.5★/8.5** (RV Resort) Avail: 36 full hkups (30/50 amps). 2021 rates: $40. (580)798-4957, 16677 US Hwy 77, Springer, OK 73458

STILLWATER — B5 *Payne*

LAKE CARL BLACKWELL (Public) From town, W 7 mi on Hwy 51 to Hwy 51C, N 2 mi (E). 242 Avail: 242 W, 242 E (20/30 amps). 2021 rates: $10 to $20. (405)372-5157

SULPHUR — C5 *Murray*

ARBUCKLE RV RESORT **Ratings: 9.5/8.5/9.5** (RV Park) Avail: 30 full hkups (30/50 amps). 2021 rates: $35 to $40. (580)622-6338, 774 Charles Cooper Memorial Dr, Sulphur, OK 73086

CHICKASAW/BUCKHORN (Public National Park) From town: Go 5 mi S on US 177, then 3 mi W. Avail: 43 E. 2021 rates: $16 to $24. (580)622-7234

CHICKASAW/ROCK CREEK (Public National Park) 1 mi W of North entrance. 106 Avail. 2021 rates: $14 to $30. (580)622-3165

CHICKASAW/THE POINT (Public National Park) From Hwy 7 west of town: Go 5 mi S on access road. 23 Avail: 23 W, 23 E. 2021 rates: $16 to $22. (580)622-7234

TAHLEQUAH — B6 *Cherokee*

TENKILLER FERRY LAKE - COE/CARTERS LANDING (Public Corps) From town, E 7 mi on Hwy 82, E 5 mi to Carters Landing Rd, E 1.3 mi (E). 31 Avail. 2021 rates: $7 to $11. (918)487-5252

TENKILLER FERRY LAKE - COE/COOKSON BEND (Public Corps) From town, N 15 mi on Hwy 100 to Cookson Rd, W 2 mi (E). Avail: 64 E (30/50 amps). 2021 rates: $14 to $19. Apr 01 to Sep 30. (918)487-5252

TENKILLER FERRY LAKE - COE/ELK CREEK LANDING (Public Corps) From town, N 5 mi on SR 82 (L). Avail: 19 E (30 amps). 2021 rates: $7 to $16. Apr 01 to Sep 30. (918)487-5252

TENKILLER FERRY LAKE - COE/PETTIT BAY (Public Corps) From Jct of US-62 & OK-82, S 4 mi on OK-82 to Indian Rd, S 2 mi to paved rd, E 1 mi (E). 92 Avail: 7 full hkups, 67 E (30/50 amps). 2021 rates: $12 to $20. (918)487-5252

TENKILLER FERRY LAKE - COE/SIZEMORE LANDING (Public Corps) From town, N 6 mi on Hwy 100 to 10A, W 2 mi to Indian Rd, N 11 mi to Sizemore, E 1 mi (E). 32 Avail: Pit toilets. 2021 rates: $5. (918)487-5252

TALIHINA — C6 *Le Flore*

TALIMENA (Public National Park) From Jct of US-271 & SR-63, N 7 mi on US-271 (R). 10 Avail: 10 W, 10 E (20/30 amps). 2021 rates: $22 to $27. (918)567-2052

THACKERVILLE — D5 *Love*

A SPOTLIGHT Introducing Chickasaw Nation's colorful attractions appearing at the front of this state section.

FUN TOWN RV PARK AT WINSTAR

good sam park **Ratings: 10/10★/10** (RV Park) From jct of I-35 (exit 1) & US 77 N: Go NE 1-1/2 mi on Casino Ave, then E 1/2 mi on Vegas Rd, then N 1 blk on Merle Wolfe Rd. (L).

FUN TOWN RV PARK AT WINSTAR

Nestled in the southern foothills, 200 yards from the world's biggest casino, Fun Town RV Park at WinStar is the best option for guests wanting to enjoy the resort experience from the comfort of their home away from home.

FAC: paved rds. Avail: 152 paved, 41 pull-thrus, (30x80), back-ins (30x50), 152 full hkups (30/50 amps), WiFi @ sites, tent sites, dump, laundry. **REC:** pool, hot tub, golf, playground. Pet restrict (Q). Partial handicap access. Big rig sites. 2021 rates: $20 to $60, Military discount. ATM.

(580)276-8900 Lat: 33.752316, Lon: -97.126142
21902 Merle Wolfe Rd, Thackerville, OK 73459
www.winstarworldcasino.com/rv-park
See ad page 712

RED RIVER RANCH RV RESORT

good sam park **Ratings: 7/7/7** (RV Park) Avail: 100 full hkups (30/50 amps). 2021 rates: $40. (800)568-7837, 19691 US 77, Thackerville, OK 73459

Things to See and Do

WINSTAR WORLD CASINO AND RESORT Largest casino in the world with eight themed gaming plazas, 500,000 sq ft of gaming, restaurants, and event center. Partial handicap access. RV accessible. Restrooms. Food. Hours: 24 Hours and 7 days per week. ATM.

(800)622-6317 Lat: 33.757785, Lon: -97.132039
777 Casino Ave., Thackerville, OK 73459
www.WinstarWorldCasino.com
See ad page 712

TISHOMINGO — D5 *Johnston*

HWY 22 RV PARK **Ratings: 6/7/5.5** (Campground) Avail: 10 full hkups (30/50 amps). 2021 rates: $30. (580)371-7447, 1551 W Main St, Tishomingo, OK 73460

TULSA — B5 *Tulsa*

TULSA See also Beggs & Mannford.

CHERRY HILL MH & RV COMMUNITY

good sam park **Ratings: 8/9.5★/8.5** (RV Area in MH Park) Avail: 76 full hkups (30/50 amps). 2021 rates: $35 to $40. (918)446-9342, 4808 S Elwood Ave, Tulsa, OK 74107

EXPO-SQUARE RV PARK (Public) From Jct of I-44 & exit 229 (Yale Ave), N 3 mi on Yale Ave to 15th St, W 0.5 mi, Gate 5 Entrance (L). Avail: 172 full hkups (30/50 amps). 2021 rates: $40. (918)744-1113

MINGO RV PARK

good sam park **Ratings: 8/10★/8** (RV Park) Avail: 75 full hkups (30/50 amps). 2021 rates: $40. (918)832-8824, 801 N Mingo Rd, Tulsa, OK 74116

Travel Services

CAMPING WORLD OF TULSA As the nation's largest retailer of RV supplies, accessories, services and new and used RVs, Camping World is committed to making your total RV experience better **SERVICES:** RV appliance, MH mechanical, staffed RV wash, restrooms. RV Sales. RV supplies, LP gas, dump, emergency parking, RV accessible. Hours: 9am - 7pm.
(877)881-3213 Lat: 36.129655, Lon: -95.877457
9005 E Skelly Dr, Tulsa, OK 74129
www.campingworld.com

VALLIANT — D6 *McCurtain*

PINE CREEK LAKE - COE/PINE CREEK COVE (Public Corps) From town: Go 8 mi N on county road. 41 Avail: 41 W, 41 E. 2021 rates: $14 to $23. Apr 01 to Sep 29. (580)933-4215

VERDEN — C4 *Caddo*

LAKE CHICKASHA (Public) From Main St, N 2 mi on cnty rd to sign, W 2 mi on cnty rd to sign, N 1 mi on cnty rd (L). 50 Avail: 50 W, 50 E (30 amps). 2021 rates: $10 to $15. (405)412-6545

VIAN — B6 *Sequoyah*

TENKILLER (Public State Park) From Jct of I-40 & Hwy 100 (exit 287), NE 11 mi on Hwy 100 (L). 85 Avail: 37 full hkups, 48 W, 48 E (20/30 amps). 2021 rates: $22 to $30. (918)489-5641

WAGONER — B6 *Wagoner*

ARKANSAS RIVER - COE/AFTON LANDING (Public Corps) From town, W 4.5 mi on Hwy 51 to access rd, follow signs (L). 22 Avail: 20 W, 20 E (30 amps). 2021 rates: $15. (918)682-4314

FORT GIBSON LAKE - COE/BLUE BILL POINT (Public Corps) From town, N 4 mi on US-69 to park access rd, NE 3 mi (E). Avail: 40 E (30/50 amps). 2021 rates: $11 to $20. (918)476-6638

FORT GIBSON LAKE - COE/FLAT ROCK CREEK (Public Corps) From town, N 8 mi on US-69 to Flat Rock Rd, SE 6.5 mi, follow signs (E). Avail: 30 E (30 amps). 2021 rates: $14 to $20. Apr 01 to Sep 30. (918)474-6766

FORT GIBSON LAKE - COE/ROCKY POINT (Public Corps) From town, N 3 mi on US-69 to White Horn Cove Rd, follow signs (E). Avail: 63 E (30/50 amps). 2021 rates: $14 to $20. Apr 01 to Sep 30. (918)462-2042

FORT GIBSON LAKE - COE/TAYLOR FERRY SOUTH (Public Corps) From town, E 4 mi on SR-51 to cnty rd, S 0.5 mi to park access rd, E 1 mi (E). Avail: 89 E (30/50 amps). 2021 rates: $14 to $20. (918)485-4792

SEQUOYAH (Public State Park) From Jct of US-69 & Hwy 51 (in Wagoner), E 11 mi on Hwy 51 (R). 252 Avail: 152 full hkups, 100 W, 100 E (30/50 amps). 2021 rates: $22 to $35. (918)772-2046

SEQUOYAH BAY (Public State Park) From town, S 5 mi on Hwy 16 to Grey Oaks Rd, E 5 mi (E). 124 Avail: 124 W, 124 E (30/50 amps). 2021 rates: $20 to $28. (918)683-0878

WATONGA — B4 *Blaine*

ROMAN NOSE (Public State Park) From Jct of Hwy 33 & US-281/Hwy 8, N 5 mi on Hwy 8 to Hwy 8A, NW 2 mi (L). 47 Avail: 12 full hkups, 35 W, 35 E (30/50 amps). 2021 rates: $22 to $30. (800)892-8690

WAURIKA — D4 *Jefferson*

WAURIKA LAKE - COE/CHISHOLM TRAIL RIDGE (Public Corps) From town, NW 5 mi on Hwy 5, N 3 mi on CR (Advent Rd), W 1 mi to park entrance (L). Avail: 95 E (30 amps). 2021 rates: $14 to $16. May 01 to Sep 30. (580)439-8040

WAURIKA LAKE - COE/MONEKA PARK NORTH (Public Corps) From town: Go 4 mi W on Hwy-5, then 1 mi N on blacktop road. 38 Avail: Pit toilets. 2021 rates: $14 to $18. Mar 01 to Oct 31. (580)963-2111

WAYNOKA — A3 *Woods*

LITTLE SAHARA (Public State Park) From town, S 4 mi on US-281 (R). 86 Avail: 86 W, 86 E (20/30 amps). 2021 rates: $22 to $27. (580)824-1471

WEATHERFORD — B3 *Custer*

WANDERLUST CROSSINGS RV PARK

good sam park **Ratings: 9/9.5★/10** (RV Park) Avail: 50 full hkups (30/50 amps). 2021 rates: $40 to $45. (580)772-2800, 1038 Airport Rd , Weatherford, OK 73096

WEBBERS FALLS — B6 *Muskogee*

WEBBERS FALLS POOL - COE/BREWERS BEND (Public Corps) From town, W 2 mi on US-64 to cnty rd, N 5 mi (R). 42 Avail: 32 W, 32 E (30 amps). 2021 rates: $15. May 01 to Sep 30. (918)487-5252

WILBURTON — C6 *Latimer*

ROBBERS CAVE (Public State Park) From Jct of US-270 & Hwy 2, N 5 mi on Hwy 2 (R). 175 Avail: 22 full hkups, 67 W, 67 E (30/50 amps). 2021 rates: $22 to $30. (918)465-2565

WISTER — C6 *Le Flore*

LAKE WISTER (Public State Park) From Jct of US-270 E & 271, S 2 mi on US-270 to Quarry Island (off of dam), follow signs (R). 118 Avail: 118 W, 118 E (20/30 amps). 2021 rates: $22 to $30. (918)655-7212

WOODWARD — B3 *Woodward*

BOILING SPRINGS (Public State Park) E-bnd: From Jct of Hwys 15 & 34 (in town), N 1.4 mi on Hwy 34 to Hwy 34C, E 5 mi (E); or W-bnd: From Jct of Hwys 15 & 50 (Mooreland), N 1 mi on Hwy 50 to Hwy 50B, W 5 mi (E). 40 Avail: 40 W, 40 E (30/50 amps). 2021 rates: $22 to $30. (580)256-7664

WYANDOTTE — A6 *Ottawa*

WHISPERING WOODS RV PARK **Ratings: 7.5/9/9.5** (RV Park) 45 Avail: 45 W, 45 E (30/50 amps). 2021 rates: $15 to $25. (918)666-9200, 70220 East Highway 60, Wyandotte, OK 74370

WYNNEWOOD — C5 *Garvin*

CROSSROADS RV PARK **Ratings: 6/8.5★/8** (RV Park) Avail: 42 full hkups (30/50 amps). 2021 rates: $35. (405)238-4133, 25981 N CR 3250, Wynnewood, OK 73098

Check out 10/10/10 Good Sam Parks on the Good Sam Park page.*

RV DRIVING TIPS: Adjust your vehicle's environment so that it helps you to stay alert. Keep the temperature cool, with open windows or air conditioning in the summer and minimal amounts of heat in the winter. Avoid listening to soft, sleep-inducing music and switch radio stations frequently.

OK

Getty Images/iStockphoto

YOU ARE HERE

Oregon

DID YOU KNOW?

The Siskiyou National Forest in southwest Oregon is home to the only Bigfoot trap in the world.

Prepare for the ultimate Pacific Northwest adventure. Oregon combines wine tasting, pioneering history and rugged landscapes into a cocktail of adventure. This is where a raw coastline gives way to chic wineries.

Bouquet of Beauty

Portland, known as the City of Roses, is ahead of the curve when it comes to hip hangouts, forward-looking art and colorful characters. The locals are known for bringing their unconventional approach to cuisine, which has given birth to a delicious and diverse food scene. Get ready to have your taste buds blown away at artisanal food shops, farm-to-table restaurants and more than 75 craft breweries.

Salem Soars

Salem, the state's capital, distills the essence of Oregon. Here, you'll discover the Oregon State Capitol, the Hallie Ford Museum of Art and the Elsinore Theatre. In Eugene, catch a glimpse of future track and field stars at the newly renovated Hayward Field, and sip award-winning pinot noir at nearby wineries in the Willamette Valley.

Cool Crater

A volcano that collapsed about 8,000 years ago resulted in America's deepest lake. Crater Lake National Park sits within the Cascade Mountains in southern Oregon and plummets 1,949 feet. Follow the trails around the banks to explore old-growth forests and ascend the nearby slopes to get a bird's-eye view of the water. During winter, the best way to experience the frozen landscape is by going skiing or snowshoeing along the 31-mile rim.

Feeling Their Roots

Native American tribes flourished in Oregon for centuries before the Lewis and Clark expedition reached the region's

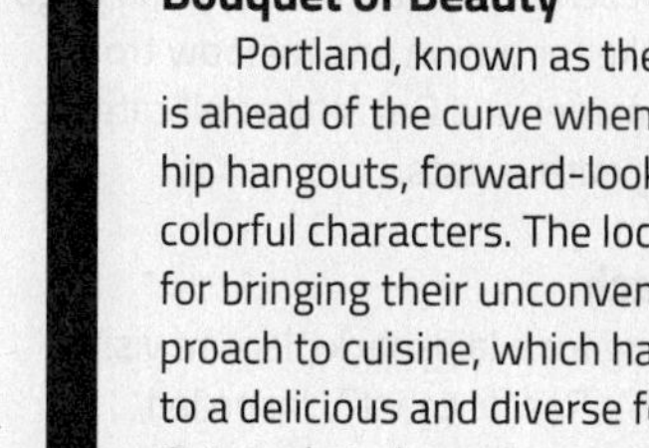

Oregon Dungeness Crab

Every day, Oregon's fishing boats return to port with big hauls of Dungeness crab. Travelers can partake in this bounty at fine restaurants and crab shacks along the coast. Enjoy the tender, juicy crab meat soaked in hot butter along with lemon. It's the ultimate Pacific Northwest foodie experience.

OR

VISITOR CENTER

TIME ZONE
Pacific/Mountain Standard

ROAD & HIGHWAY INFORMATION
800-977-6368
tripcheck.com

FISHING & HUNTING INFORMATION
503-947-6000
myodfw.com

BOATING INFORMATION
503-378-8587
oregon.gov/OSMB/boater-info

NATIONAL PARKS
nps.gov/or

STATE PARKS
oregonstateparks.org

TOURISM INFORMATION
Oregon Tourism Commission
800-547-7842
traveloregon.com

TOP TOURISM ATTRACTIONS
1) Mount Hood
2) Crater Lake National Park
3) Columbia River Gorge National Scenic Area

MAJOR CITIES
Portland, Salem (capital), Eugene, Gresham, Hillsboro

Pacific shore in 1805. Gain insight into this history at Pendleton's Tamástslikt Cultural Institute. Discover artifacts and demonstrations at the Museum at Warm Springs.

Follow Oregon Trails

Hike Oregon's famous trails to discover jaw-dropping vistas and amazing discoveries. Most famously trudged is the 382-mile Oregon Coast Trail, which weaves through Sahara-like dunes, old-growth forests and the famed Cannon Beach. The Trail of Ten Falls loop hike in Silver Falls State Park takes hikers to several cascading waterfalls, while the trek to the Gold Butte Lookout in the Willamette National Forest ends with 360-degree views of the Cascade Range. If you'd rather pedal past volcanic foothills and alpine lakes, head to Columbia River Gorge and Mount Hood National Forest for miles upon miles of mountain biking trails.

Raise a Glass to Oregon

Among Oregon's many vintages, its world-famous Pinot Noir stands tall. Olde Stone Village in McMinnville is the perfect destination for a wine-tasting trip. With more than 250 wineries within 20 miles of town, the question is not "where can I find a tasting room?" but instead — "how do I choose?" Put together an itinerary and sample some vintages. And if you prefer to set out on foot, downtown McMinnville is with one of the loveliest stroll-friendly communities you're likely to find anywhere. It boasts more than a dozen wine-tasting rooms scattered amongst its galleries, gift boutiques, antique shops, pubs and top-quality restaurants.

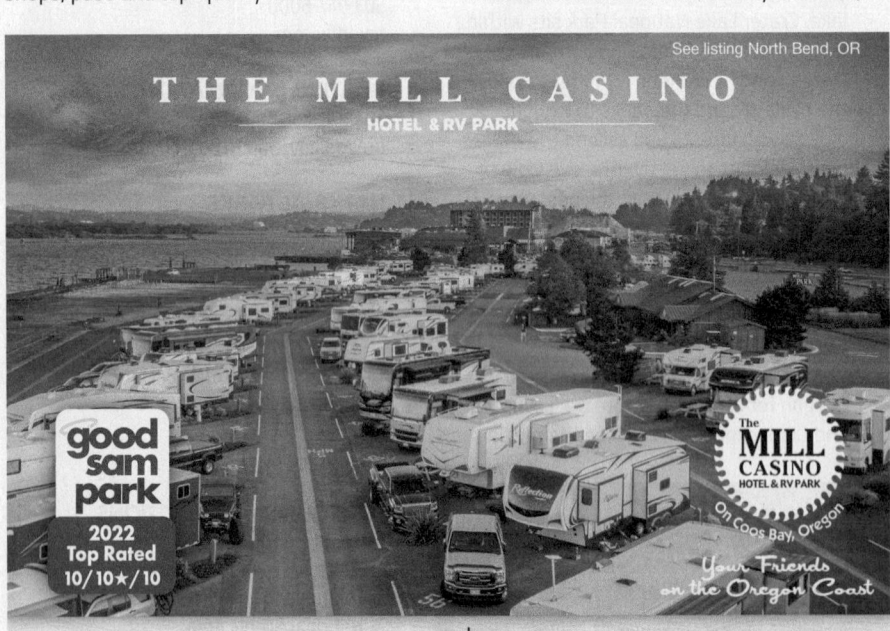

With a depth of 1,949 feet, Crater Lake is the deepest lake in the U.S. Wizard Island sits near its west bank.

The cuisine offerings include international fare from Spain, France and Peru and local options from the Bayous of Louisiana to the Coast of Oregon. The Thursday farmers market is one of the best anywhere. Lovers of flying machines will enjoy exploring the Evergreen Aviation & Space Museum in town.

Oregon Under a Roof

Learn about the state's history with a visit to the Oregon Historical Society's museum. Because of its location along the Pacific Ocean, Oregon's waterways have played a pivotal role in the state's history; learn more at the Oregon Maritime Museum. The Oregon Museum of Science and Industry is a treat, especially for families with children who will enjoy the hands-on exhibits. While not a monument in the proper sense of the word, Portland's biggest bookstore certainly is monumental. Filling a city block, Powell's City of Books offers up a maze of books.

Ride the Rapids

Ready to cast a line for hefty fish? South of Bend, fishing enthusiasts can venture into the Deschutes River for steelhead or go to East Lake for brown and rainbow trout. Sparks, Hosmer and Davis lakes all cater to fly-fishing enthusiasts.

Gold Beach

Looking for a laid-back place to visit on Oregon's Pacific coast? Unspoiled, pet-friendly sand beaches stretch for miles north and south of the town of Gold Beach. The rocky headlands are favorites with photographers, tide pool buffs and clammers. The beaches are seeded with thousands of glass floats from February through April.

Ancient Trees

East of the Oregon coast, in the lush Rogue River-Siskiyou National Forest, hikers can walk under the limbs of 500-year-old Myrtle trees, including one of the world's largest Green Myrtlewood specimens. Crafts made from the wood are popular in local galleries and shops.

Ride the Coast

From Gold Beach, the Oregon Coast Highway is one of the most scenic drives in the Pacific Northwest, with the California Redwoods and the Cape Blanco Lighthouse — the westernmost point in Oregon — within an hour's drive north or south.

Featured Good Sam Parks

OREGON

When you stay with Good Sam, you can expect the highest degree of cleanliness and friendliness, and better yet, you get **10% off** overnight campground fees.

If you're not already a Good Sam member you can purchase your membership at one of these locations:

ALBANY
Blue Ox RV Park

BAKER CITY
Mt View RV on the Oregon Trail

BANDON
Bandon By the Sea RV Park

BEND
Bend Sunriver RV
Bend/Sisters Garden RV Resort
Scandia RV Park

BOARDMAN
Boardman Marina & RV Park

BROOKINGS
AtRivers Edge RV Resort

BURNS
Burns RV Park

CANNON BEACH
Cannon Beach RV Resort

CANYONVILLE
Seven Feathers RV Resort

CHILOQUIN
Waterwheel RV Park and Campground

CLOVERDALE
Pacific City RV Camping Resort

COOS BAY
Bay Point Landing

CRESCENT
Big Pines RV Park

CRESCENT LAKE
Shelter Cove Resort and Marina

CROOKED RIVER RANCH
Crooked River Ranch RV Park

DEPOE BAY
Sea & Sand RV Park

EUGENE
Eugene Kamping World RV Park
Eugene Mobile Village & RV Park
Eugene Premier RV Resort

FAIRVIEW
Portland Fairview RV Park

FLORENCE
Heceta Beach RV Park
Pacific Pines RV Park & Storage
South Jetty RV & Camping Resort
Woahink Lake RV Resort

10/10★/10 GOOD SAM PARKS

BEND
Bend/Sisters Garden RV Resort
(541)516-3036

CANNON BEACH
Cannon Beach RV Resort
(800)847-2231

CANYONVILLE
Seven Feathers RV Resort
(541)839-3599

COOS BAY
Bay Point Landing
(541)351-9160

MCMINNVILLE
Olde Stone Village RV Resort
(503)472-4315

NORTH BEND
The Mill Casino Hotel & RV Park
(800)953-4800

SALEM
Hee Hee Illahee RV Resort
(503)463-6641

WESTFIR
Casey's Riverside RV Park
(541)782-1906

WILSONVILLE
Pheasant Ridge RV Resort
(503)682-7829

What's This?

An RV park with a 10/10★/10 rating has scored perfect grades in amenities, cleanliness and appearance ("See Understanding the Campground Rating System" on pages 8 and 9 for an explanation of the trusted Good Sam Rating System). Stay in a 10/10★/10 park on your next trip for a nearly flawless camping experience.

Getty Images/iStockphoto

GOLD BEACH
Turtle Rock RV Resort

GRANTS PASS
Jack's Landing RV Resort
Moon Mountain RV Resort
Rogue Valley Overniters

HERMISTON
Hat Rock Campground

LAKESIDE
Osprey Point RV Resort

LAKEVIEW
Junipers Reservoir RV Resort
Wild Goose Meadows RV Park

LANGLOIS
Cypress Hills RV Campground

LINCOLN CITY
Lincoln City Premier RV Resort
Logan Road RV Park

MCMINNVILLE
Olde Stone Village RV Resort

NEWPORT
Port Of Newport Marina & RV Park

NORTH BEND
The Mill Casino Hotel & RV Park

O'BRIEN
Lone Mountain Resort

PACIFIC CITY
Cape Kiwanda RV Resort & Marketplace
Hart's Camp Airstream Hotel & RV Park

PENDLETON
Wildhorse Resort & Casino RV Park

PHOENIX
Holiday RV Park

PORT ORFORD
Port Orford RV Village

PORTLAND
Columbia River RV Park
Jantzen Beach RV Park

REEDSPORT
Loon Lake Lodge & RV Resort

SALEM
Hee Hee Illahee RV Resort
Phoenix RV Park
Salem Premier RV Resort

SEASIDE
Circle Creek RV Resort
Seaside RV Resort

SILVERTON
Silver Spur RV Park & Resort

SOUTH BEACH
Whaler's Rest RV & Camping Resort

STANFIELD
Pilot RV Park

SUNNY VALLEY
Sunny Valley RV Park and Campground

SUTHERLIN
Hi-Way Haven RV Park & Drive In Movie

TILLAMOOK
Netarts Bay Garden RV Resort
Tillamook Bay City RV Park

TROUTDALE
Sandy Riverfront RV Resort

UMATILLA
Umatilla Marina & RV Park

WELCHES
Mt Hood Village Resort

WESTFIR
Casey's Riverside RV Park

WILSONVILLE
Pheasant Ridge RV Resort

WOODBURN
Portland Woodburn RV Park

YACHATS
Sea Perch RV Resort

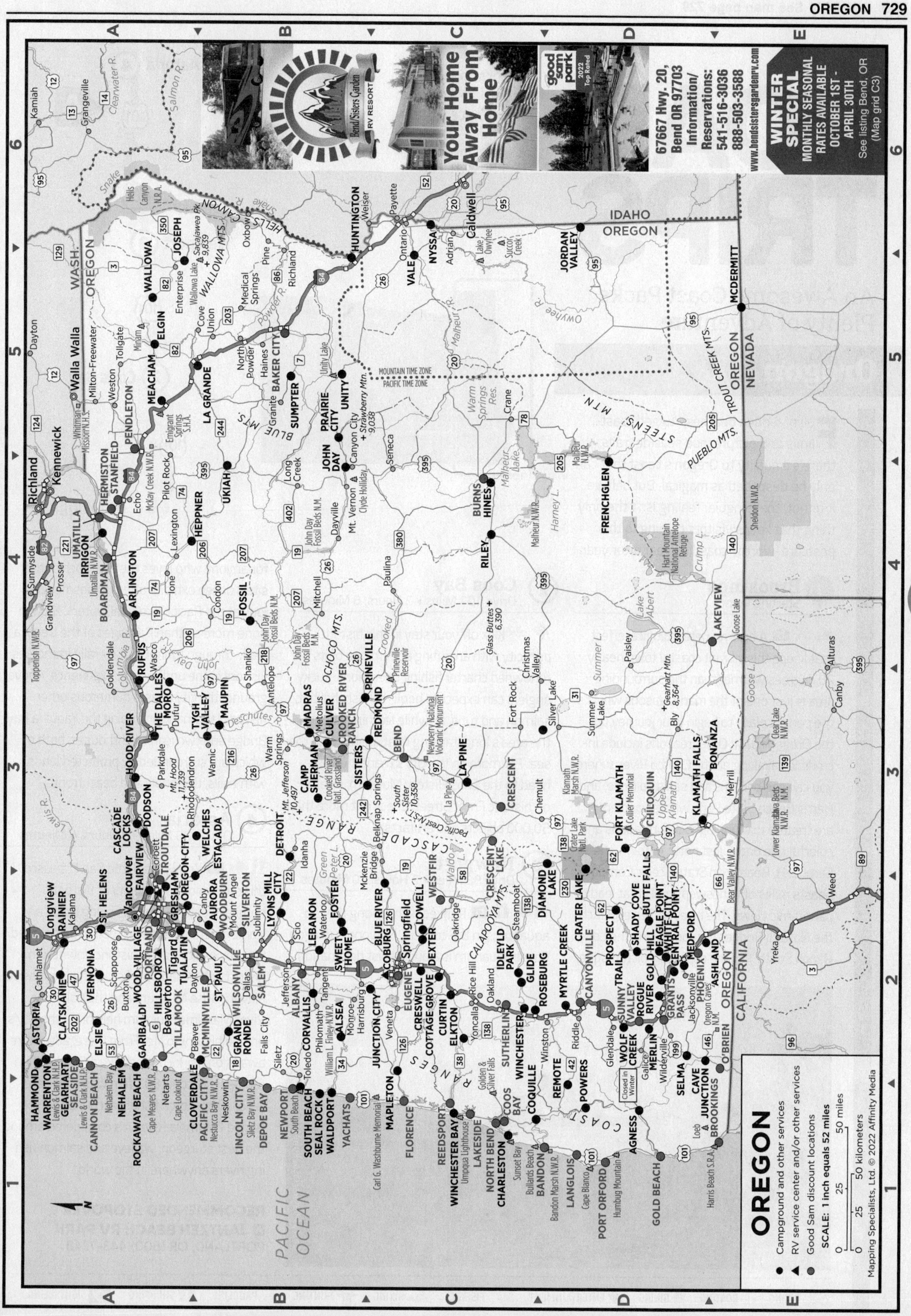
OREGON
Campground and other services
RV service center and/or other services
Good Sam discount locations
SCALE: 1 inch equals 52 miles
0 25 50 miles
0 25 50 kilometers
Mapping Specialists, Ltd. © 2022 Affinity Media
PACIFIC OCEAN
IDAHO
OREGON
WASH.
CALIFORNIA
NEVADA
MOUNTAIN TIME ZONE
PACIFIC TIME ZONE
Bend/Sisters Garden RV RESORT
Your Home Away From Home
good sam park 2022 Top Rated
67667 Hwy. 20, Bend OR 97703
Information/ Reservations:
541-516-3036
888-503-3588
www.bendsistersgardenrv.com
WINTER SPECIAL
MONTHLY SEASONAL RATES AVAILABLE
OCTOBER 1ST - APRIL 30TH
See listing Bend, OR (Map grid C3)
OR

ROAD TRIPS

An Awesome Coast Packs Plenty of Adventure

Oregon

LOCATION
OREGON

DISTANCE
338 MILES

DRIVE TIME
7 HRS 20 MINS

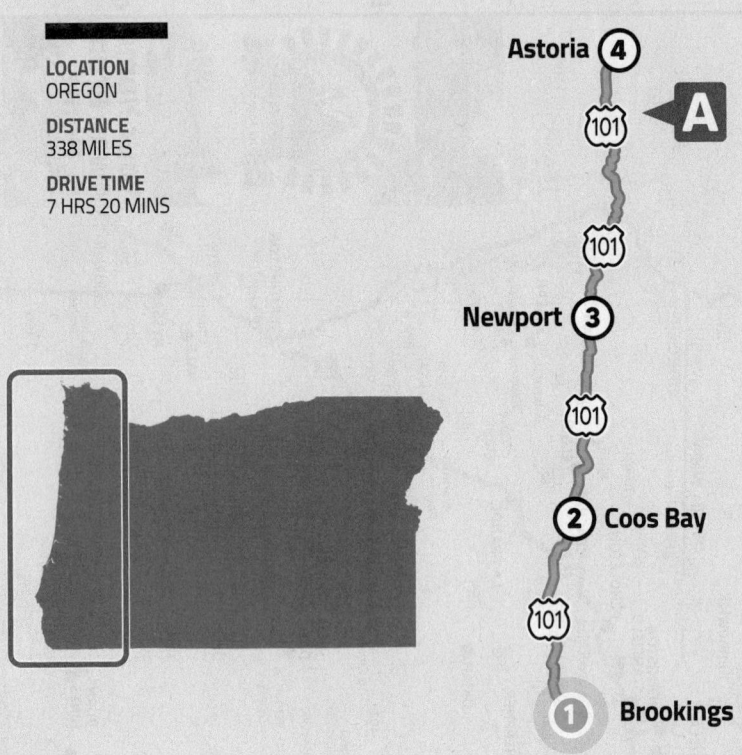

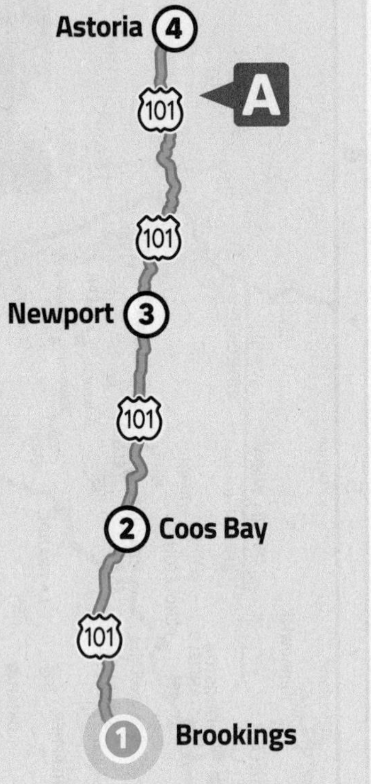

Full of hidden beaches, rugged coastlines and picturesque seaside trails, there's a quality to Oregon's coast that can only be described as magical. But believe it or not, that singular feeling isn't the only thing that keeps visitors coming to this postcard-worthy coastline year after year.

1 Brookings
Starting Point

A bizarre meteorological effect that keeps this vibrant coastal town nearly 20 degrees warmer than the surrounding area is just one of the many reasons why it's the perfect place to begin your journey up the Oregon coast. Other reasons include incredible kayaking on the Chetco River, where you can see pelicans and seals up close, and Harris Beach State Park, where paddlers are treated to stunning rock formations and colorful tide pools. Just north of town, the Samuel H. Boardman State Scenic Corridor boasts miles of windswept trails that lead to panoramic views. The hikes to Secret Beach, the Natural Bridges viewpoint, and the Lone Ranch South Trail are especially picturesque.

2 Coos Bay
Drive 107 Miles ▪ 2 Hours, 6 Minutes

Kick off your stay in this historic port city with an outing aboard one of its renowned charter fishing operations. Lucky anglers can expect to hook rockfish, halibut, salmon and tuna, all while learning about the area's longstanding relationship with the sea. For more on the city's maritime past, head to the Coos History Museum, located on historic Front Street. Check out more than 50,000 objects and artifacts.

3 Newport
Drive 98 Miles ▪ 2 Hours, 10 Minutes

Ranked high among the top aquariums in the country, Newport's Oregon Coast Aquarium is a bucket-list destination for anyone who loves the sea. Each of the site's dozen exhibits offers a mesmerizing look at the Pacific's coastal waters, though none more so than Passages of the Deep, a walk-through tunnel that literally immerses visitors in the underwater experience. Above ground, the city boasts numerous other historic landmarks including the Yaquina Bay Bridge and two iconic lighthouses, both of which are surrounded by protected lands with trails, tide pools and beachfronts.

4 Astoria
Drive 133 Miles ▪ 3 Hours, 4 Minutes

Known as "Little San Francisco," this storybook community of Victorian homes, weather-beaten fishing boats and iconic eateries has to be seen to be believed. Start by exploring the historic downtown district, where landmarks like the impressive Flavel House Museum and the Columbia River Maritime Museum help bring the city's unique history to life. From there, adventure awaits on quirky outings like a Goonies film tour — the iconic 80's film was shot here — or a top-notch fishing excursion on the famed Columbia River. It's considered among the best sturgeon, walleye and salmon fishing rivers anywhere in the world.

RECOMMENDED STOPOVER
A JANTZEN BEACH RV PARK
PORTLAND, OR (800) 443-7248

Getty Images/iStockphoto

BIKING · BOATING · DINING · ENTERTAINMENT · FISHING · HIKING · HUNTING · PADDLING · SHOPPING · SIGHTSEEING

Oregon SPOTLIGHTS

Cabernets and Coastlines: See the Best of the West

The Beaver State serves up world-class wines and wild recreation in equal measure. Sample a pinot noir in the Willamette Valley or go rafting on Class IV rapids on the Rogue River. Slow things down with a beachcombing trip to the coast for sea stack spotting.

THERE ARE MORE THAN 1,400 NAMED LAKES IN OREGON.

People kayaking on Elk lake in Central Oregon in the Cascade Mountains.

Central Oregon

From endless horizons of the high desert to the thunderous roar of deep glacial rivers, to the majestic peaks of the Cascade mountains, there are few places in the country as blessed with a multitude of landscapes as Central Oregon. Coupled with the region's near perfect weather – there are upwards of 300 days of sunshine a year – and you've got all the makings of a true outdoors lover's paradise.

Beautiful Bend

This relatively small city acts as the area's metropolitan hub and is the perfect place to start your adventure. Known as BeerTown USA, Bend boasts more than 30 craft breweries, as well as a thriving food and art scene. It's also home to hundreds of miles of hiking and mountain biking trails. A short drive away along the stunning Cascades Lakes Scenic Byway, you'll find Mt. Bachelor, one of the country's largest ski areas. Featuring more than a hundred runs and one of the longest winter seasons in America, Mt. Bachelor is among the state's most popular attractions. In the summer, off-season activities include hiking, mountain biking, and ziplining. About 10 miles south of town, Lava River Cave descends for nearly a mile into the earth offering visitors a self-guided glimpse into the region's geologic past. Just be sure to wear a jacket. Even in the height of summer, the temperature underground tops out at around 40 degrees Fahrenheit.

Wild Waterfront

Consistently ranked among the top fly-fishing destinations in the country, Central Oregon is a must-visit locale for anglers looking to land the big one. The region's most famous river, the Deschutes, boasts over 250 miles of fishable real estate, from its headwaters at Little Lava Lake to its confluence with the Columbia River. There are numerous outfitters in and around Bend to help you organize everything from a morning session on a quiet stream to a multi-day rainbow trout excursion. Locals in the know however, often head to the banks of the nearby Metolius River, said to be among the most beautiful and challenging anywhere in the West. Both bull trout and rainbows are abundant in the river's meandering water. If it's a thrill-ride you're after, the Deschutes is also home to family-friendly whitewater rafting and tubing excursions. Ranging from Class I to Class III rapids, the river is acces-

OR

"BROUGHT YOUR ROD? THE DESCHUTES RIVER BOASTS OVER 250 MILES OF FISHABLE WATER."

LOCAL FAVORITE

Sour Cream Cake

Oregon's robust dairy industry might just inspire you to create a rich and fluffy treat. You can increase the deliciousness of this cake only by adding a scoop of vanilla bean ice cream on the side. *Recipe by Carol Jacobs.*

INGREDIENTS

- ☐ 1 package yellow cake mix
- ☐ 1 small vanilla instant pudding
- ☐ 4 eggs
- ☐ ½ cup oil
- ☐ 1 tsp vanilla
- ☐ ½ cup water
- ☐ 1 cup sour cream
- ☐ ¾ cup sugar
- ☐ 2 tsp cinnamon

DIRECTIONS

In a bowl, mix all ingredients except the cinnamon and sugar. In a separate small bowl, mix the cinnamon and sugar. In greased and floured 9" x 12" pan, layer ingredients: ⅓ batter; ⅔ topping; ⅔ batter; ⅓ topping. Bake 40 minutes at 350 degrees.

See listing
Redmond, OR
EXPO CENTER
RV PARK
CENTRAL OREGON'S #1 CHOICE FOR RV CAMPING
The Expo Center RV Park is located in the heart of Central Oregon within a short distance of the Northwest's finest fishing, dining, hiking, boating, and skiing. We are also adjacent to municipal Juniper Golf Course. The majestic Cascade Mountains are located right out your RV door!
Amenities:
• 105 Full Service RV Sites
• 10 Tent Sites • Pull-Thru Sites
• Big Rig Access • Restrooms (plumbed)
• Showers • Laundry • Picnic Tables
• BBQs • Pets Allowed
• Large Field Area for Pets
• Family Friendly
OPEN YEAR ROUND
Hookups & Connectivity:
• Electric (50/30/20 AMP)
• Water • Sewer
Attend an Event During Your Stay at Our Premier Expo Center Just Next Door!
REDMOND
541-585-1569
Online reservations & event calendar:
expo.deschutes.org

SPOTLIGHTS

Part of the Cascade Range, the Three Sisters are volcanic peaks that each rise higher than 10,000 feet.

sible to experts and beginners alike and guides are often extremely knowledgeable about the area's unique natural history.

Mountain Views

Just west of Bend, the Three Sisters Wilderness beckons hikers, bikers and rock climbers looking to take their adventures to the next level. Featuring three volcanic mountains – the "sisters" that give the wilderness its name – the area is chock full of scenic trails and one-of-a-kind vistas. Start at the Three Sisters Loop, a 50-mile trail that winds past lava fields, alpine meadows, lush forests, and more. It can easily be broken up into various day hikes that will take you to the area's top landmarks. For more experienced hikers, summiting the South Sister is a bucket-list endeavor. The twelve-mile roundtrip hike ascends nearly 5,000 feet, but the majestic views from the summit are well-worth the trek. For a different kind of landscape, head to Smith Rock State Park where the sun baked sights of the high desert are on full display. Sheer canyons and otherworldly geologic formations appear around nearly every turn on the 7-mile Summit Loop trail. Be sure to keep an eye out for the stunning golden eagles that nest along the route.

Hands-on Museums

For a deep dive into how the unique environments and historic people of Central Oregon came to be, head to the High Desert Museum, just south of downtown. A Smithsonian-affiliated institution, the museum uses indoor and outdoor exhibits, living history demonstrations, and plenty of hands-on fun to offer an immersive look at the wildlife, culture, and art that define the region. The Museum at Warm Springs is another nearby gem. Located on the Warm Springs Indian Reservation, it's home to an outstanding collection Native American artifacts, as well as multimedia presentations depicting the Wasco peoples' traditional dances, celebrations, and songs.

Loving the Lava Lands

Nestled within Newberry National Volcanic Monument, the Lava Lands were formed after a volcanic eruption approximately 7,000 years ago, leaving behind an ocean of jagged lava rock. Because of its striking resemblance to the moon's surface, the area was even used by NASA as a training ground in the 1960s. Today, you can still play astronaut here at the Lava Lands Visitor Center, an interpretive hub shedding insight on the 56,700 acres of lava flows, sparkling lakes and geological wonders. Embark on the Trail of the Molten Land and Trail of the Whispering Pines to get a closer look of the lava rocks. Summit Lava Butte by foot or shuttle for 360-degree views of the desolate landscape. You can also take a helicopter tour to see the lava fields from a whole new perspective.

Mount Jefferson Wilderness

Get more peak thrills in Mount Jefferson Wilderness. Situated where the Willamette, Deschutes and Mount Hood national forests meet, this 107,000-acre oasis is dominated by Mount Jefferson, the shield volcano of Three Fingered Jack and five glaciers. The possibilities are endless here, thanks to 190 miles of trails, 40 of which are part of the gorgeous Pacific Crest National Scenic Trail. Eager anglers can also reel in boatloads of trout from over 150 lakes in the region.

Hills That Thrill

The real star here lies within the Painted Hills Unit, approximately 9 miles northwest of Mitchell. Striped in red, tan, orange and black, the jaw-dropping Painted Hills are popular subjects for photographers. Come at sunrise or sunset to see the sun bask the hills in dreamy hues. Up the road, Wheeler High School welcomes you to dig up your own fossils and take home what you find.

OR

67667 Hwy. 20, Bend OR 97703 • Information/Reservations: 541-516-3036 • 888-503-3588

bendsistersgardenrv@gmail.com • www.bendsistersgardenrv.com

See listing Bend, OR

WINTER SPECIAL • MONTHLY SEASONAL RATES • AVAILABLE OCTOBER 1ST - APRIL 30TH

SPOTLIGHTS

With plenty of bike paths, Eugene consistently ranks as one of America's "Most Bicycle Friendly Cities."

Eugene To Salem

Follow this fun-filled corridor for delicious wines, trails that snake through lush forests and a college football scene that rivals anything else in the United States. Situated in the vast Willamette Valley, the region encapsulates everything that makes Oregon great, from superb cities to excellent outdoor adventure.

Wonders of Western Oregon

This beautiful expanse of Western Oregon is bounded by the Coast Range in the west, Cascades in the east and Calapooya Mountains in the south. The Willamette Valley is characterized by its agricultural fields, rolling lowlands, hilly belts and the Willamette River, which runs through the entire region. The best season to visit is summer, as temperatures hit a toasty 80 degrees. Early fall also is an excellent time to come, as crisp country air makes for great hiking.

Rocking Rivalry

South of Portland, the town of Eugene is a college athletics hot spot. Home to the University of Oregon, Eugene draws sports fans with year-round intercollegiate competition — including NCAA football with the Oregon Ducks home team. The excitement reaches a fever pitch when the Ducks take on the Oregon State Beavers, who hail from Corvallis to the north. Eugene also entices culture vultures with the Jordan Schnitzer Museum of Art and the Museum of Natural and Cultural History.

On Track to Win

Surprisingly, this corner of the world is the place to go to see the nation's best track and field competitors. Hayward Field, located in Eugene, has a storied history. Currently undergoing a major renovation, it is scheduled to reopen soon and begin setting the scene for new records. After seeing impressive athletes, you'll be ready to be impressed by wildlife. Get an up-close view of the raptors of the Pacific Northwest with a visit to the Cascades Raptor

OR

See listing Salem, OR

SPOTLIGHTS

The National Arbor Day Foundation has named Salem "Tree City U.S.A." for the last 30 years. Pictured: cherry blossom trees around the state capitol.

Center. You'll find as many as 50 beautiful birds on display; however, these birds weren't brought here just for show. Instead, the Raptor Center specializes in rehabilitating injured wildlife and provides a home for those that cannot be re-released to the wild.

Superior Suds

Pushed by a hearty spirit of innovation, microbreweries flourish across the region. Stop by one to see what's on tap and to learn about the craft behind the beer. When you're not enjoying suds, head to the Eugene Saturday Market to enjoy a taste of the region. Artisans display their colorful wares and baskets overflow with the locally grown produce this region is known for. Food trucks tempt with an array of treats. With views of the Willamette River and open green spaces, Eugene's Riverfront Park is a popular gathering spot. Especially beloved is the carousel with an intricately handcrafted parade of animals.

Willamette Valley Water

The Willamette River attracts vacationers to its banks for fishing, boating and paddling. Trout and steelhead flourish in these cool waters. Head to the hills to find one of Oregon's best trout streams, just east of Eugene. The McKenzie River attracts more than anglers, as paddlers also enjoy the scenery around these rippling waters. The largest lake in the Willamette Valley is Fern Ridge, with 9,000 acres of surface area. The warm coves and inlets are the prime spots for bass, bluegill, crappie and catfish.

Two-Wheel Trails

Bicyclists will find trails for every level. The Willamette River Trail runs 29 miles between Eugene and Springfield, with views of parks and rivers along the way. To enjoy splendid scenery on foot, head to the McKenzie River National Recreation Trail. This trail takes you over hardened lava flows, past cascading waterfalls, and through stands of old-growth conifers. The sapphire Tamolich Blue Pool is a shocking shade of azure that nicely complements the green of the verdant forests.

Willamette Wine

With more than 500 wineries, Willamette is a must-visit spot for wine lovers. The unique maritime climate here has transformed the valley into one of the top pinot noir-producing regions in the world. Other varieties made here include pinot gris, pinot blanc, chardonnay, Riesling, Syrah, cabernet sauvignon and merlot. Chock-full of luxury inns, quaint bed-and-breakfasts, tasting rooms and fine dining restaurants, Willamette Valley wine country is the answer if you're yearning for a weekend getaway or weeklong escape. Honeywood Winery, Cubanisimo Vineyards and Orchard Heights Winery are all within the Salem vicinity, while King Estate Winery and Sweet Cheeks Winery are within easy reach from Eugene. Coming from Portland? Stop by popular Northern Willamette Valley wineries in places like Forest Grove, Hillsboro, Gaston and Yamhill. In the Willamette National Forest, to the east of Eugene, the Koosah Falls on the McKenzie River dazzles visitors.

Cruise the Capital

Laid-back Salem is a welcome change from some of the region's bigger cities. Boasting an easygoing culture and teeming with gorgeous green spaces, museums and historic sites, Salem provides a welcome break from busy city life and invites you to take things at your own pace. Start your visit with a free tour of the Oregon State Capitol and climb up 121 stairs to meet the Oregon Pioneer, an 8.5-ton bronze statue coated in gold leaf.

OR

SPOTLIGHTS

The Umatilla National Forest in northwest Oregon encompasses 1.4 million acres of wooded land.

Home to Terrific Truffles

Find out why truffles are prized among foodies. The lure of the truffle is so large that Eugene spends 10 days celebrating it. Each January, the Oregon Truffle Festival invites visitors to go on organized truffle hunts, sample savory dishes, and learn about this magnificent fungi. Each June, Salem bursts into bloom with the World Beat Festival, which includes over 125 music, dance and theatrical performances, representing 70 countries from around the world. Watch dragon boats whizz by, stroll the vendor area to find handcrafted wares from around the world, or sample an international buffet of foods.

Land of the Oregon Trail

The half-million settlers who made the westward journey along the Oregon Trail in the 1800s faced several hardships. The 2,170-mile journey from Missouri to Oregon is often romanticized, but in reality, the five-month-long expedition was a perilous endeavor. One in 10 travelers from the 1840s to 1860s never made it to their final destination and the rest endured everything from disease and starvation to snakebites. Still, their spirit lives on in Oregon along this stunning corridor. Prepare to experience pioneer history and explore timeless landscapes.

Umatilla Insights

Your Oregon Trail adventure starts in Umatilla. Situated along the Columbia River, this old gold rush town puts wildlife and outdoor activities at your doorstep. Go to the Umatilla National Wildlife Refuge to view deer, badgers and burrowing owls and then look out for woodpeckers, bluebirds and sapsuckers in Blue Mountain Scenic Corridor and State Park. The McNary Wildlife Nature Area is another popular wildlife viewing spot thanks to its large populations of migrating birds. Ready for a workout? You can burn some serious calories by hiking, cycling and whitewater rafting in the 1.4 million-acre Umatilla National Forest.

Cowboy Culture Rules

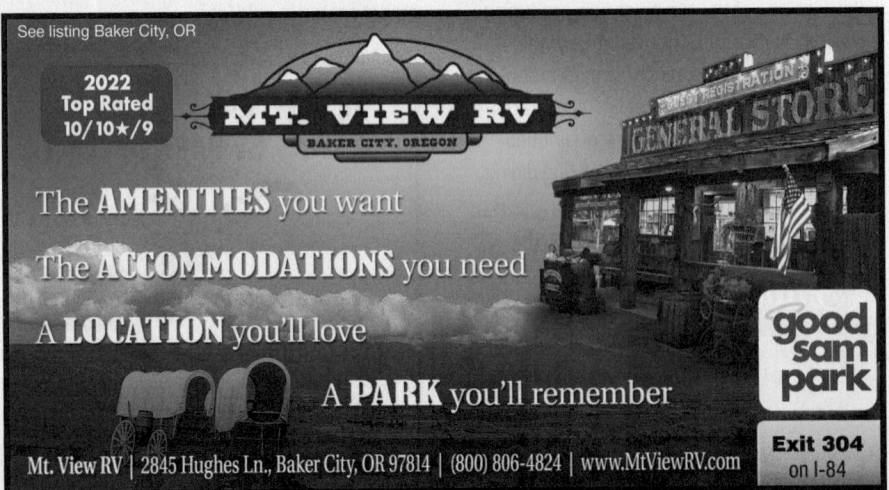

Pendleton reverently preserves the cowboy way of life. Rodeos, country music and traditional crafts continue to be part of everyday life here. You can see for yourself in September at the Pendleton Round-Up, a weeklong festival of steer roping, barrel racing and parades. Blend in with the locals by getting a custom cowboy hat at Mountain Peaks Hat Company and handmade boots from Staplemans Boots and Leather. Stop by Hamley and Co. between fittings to see saddles made using traditional methods and Pendleton Woolen Mills to learn about the city's famous weaving techniques.

Feel the Frontier Vibe in Pendleton

Relics of the town's often-turbulent history are found everywhere. Housed in a restored train depot, the Heritage Station Museum retraces Umatilla County's history using an authentic pioneer homestead, fully restored Union Pacific Railroad caboose and other intriguing artifacts. The Pendleton Underground Tour shows you the city's seedy side by leading you down tunnels which once hid brothels, gambling dens and bars. You can also learn how pioneers impacted the lives of local tribes at the Tamastslikt Cultural Institute and view Native American art at Crow's Shadow Institute for the Arts.

Going for the Gold

Once a bustling gold rush outpost, Baker City transports you to a bygone era with its preserved Victorian architecture. Wander through the downtown area to find 100 buildings listed on the National Registry of Historic Places and then swing by the luxurious Geiser Grand Hotel to admire its stained-glass ceiling, crystal chandeliers and other extravagant furnishings from the 19th century. Check out more original items from this time period at the Adler House Museum. The Baker Heritage Museum displays one of the most impressive rock and mineral collections in the western United States as well. Baker City also opens the doors to outdoor adventures like hiking, fishing and whitewater rafting thanks to its proximity to the Snake River, Hells Canyon and the Anthony Lakes Mountain Resort.

Oregon Trail Tales

Learn about pioneers at the Oregon Trail Interpretive Center, less than 10 miles from Baker. Living history exhibits, life-size displays and multimedia presentations bring the Oregon Trail to life and give you an idea of what the treacherous journey was like for pioneers. Walk through a wagon train and then go outside to explore four miles of interpretive trails.

Getty Images/iStockphoto

The Snake River runs through Hells Canyon on Oregon's eastern border. Pictured: The Brownlee Dam.

Displays of Determination

Visitors here are in for an immersive experience. Utilizing life-size displays, films and live theater presentations, this Center tells the story of explorers, miners and settlers of the frontier west. The 500-acre site includes remnants of the historic Flagstaff Gold Mine, actual ruts carved by pioneer wagons, and magnificent vistas of the historic route. Several events and programs allow visitors to walk in the shoes of intrepid pioneers. The popular "Wagons Ho! Experience the Oregon Trail" exhibit tests the pioneering skills of participants. Dress up as a settler and see if you've got what it takes to pack a prairie schooner with all the supplies and gear needed to make the long trek west.

Cool Your Heels

Feel like taking a break? About 45 minutes southeast of Baker City, Farewell Bend State Recreation Area straddles the Oregon/Idaho border on the banks of the Snake River. Here, the Brownlee Reservoir delivers prime fishing, water skiing, boating and wildlife watching opportunities.

Driving Delights

The High Desert Discovery Scenic Byway leads motorists through scenic terrain. Connecting Burns to Fields, this 127-mile stretch of road takes you to a world where sagebrush-filled desert and rolling mountains dominate. Spend the night at The Narrows RV Park near Burns and use it as a base camp for touring the 69-mile Diamond Loop Tour Route.

OR

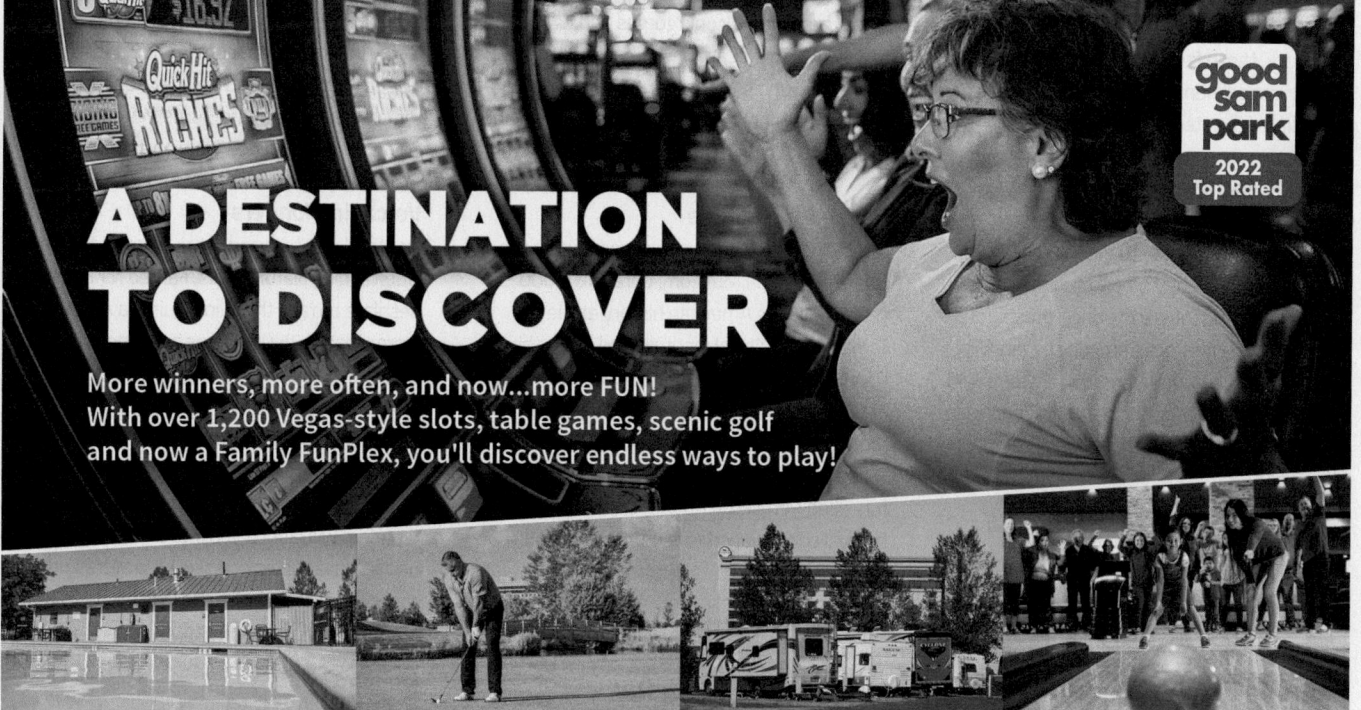

SPOTLIGHTS

Oregon's dry side: The Alvord Desert formed out of a dry lake bed that is about 12 miles long and 7 miles wide and only receives an average of 7 inches of rain per year.

Something Wild Lives Here

Along the way, make sure you stop and explore the Malheur National Wildlife Refuge. Pack your binoculars because this patch of lakes and wetlands is hailed as one of the best bird-watching spots in the Pacific Northwest. You'll even see enormous populations of snow geese and waterfowl engulf the sky in darkness during the spring. Further down the path is the Diamond Craters Outstanding Natural Area. Formed 25,000 years ago from molten lava and liquid rock, these fascinating lava fields house a peculiar assortment of lava tubes, jagged spires and collapsed craters.

Fun in Frenchglen

Travel south on the beautiful High Desert Discovery Scenic Byway to get to Frenchglen. The village has a lengthy history in the cattle industry and was where the once-prosperous French-Glenn Livestock Company began. Visit the Pete French Round Barn to see where wild horses were trained. Visit the 1924 Frenchglen Hotel, with rustic accommodations.

Cast a Line, Aim a Gun

Fly-fishing conditions are outstanding in Frenchglen. The nearby Donner und Blitzen River, called the "Blitzen" by locals, teems with wild redband trout, mountain whitefish, long-nose dace and mottled sculpin. Hunting is also an option as mule deer, Rocky Mountain elk and pronghorn antelope thrive here.

High Up in the Steens

The Steens Mountain Wilderness is home to solitude and outdoor thrills. Lace-up your hiking boots and follow the Little Blitzen Gorge Trail to reach the region's iconic gorges and waterfalls, or the Pike Creek Canyon Trail to view colorful rock outcroppings. Consider tackling the multi-day Steens Mountain Gorges Loop if you want to see everything this wilderness has to offer.

Haven for Heritage

After, dive into the town's storied past at the Heritage Station Museum, unravel 10,000 years of Native American history at the Tamastslikt Cultural Institute and go on the Pendleton Underground Tour to follow a maze of tunnels once used to hide gambling dens, brothels and other illegal activities. If you're visiting in September, be sure to check out the fun-filled Pendleton Round-Up, a weeklong festival consisting of rodeos, parades and concerts.

The High Desert Discovery

Immerse yourself in the awe-inspiring landscapes traversed by early pioneers by cruising down the High Desert Discovery Scenic Byway. Spanning 127 miles from Burns to Fields, this breathtaking road trip weaves through a diverse array of scenery, charming communities and historic sites. Before embarking on your journey, take some time in Burns to browse Native American art including pottery pieces, jewelry and ceremonial sand paintings at the Oards Indian Art Museum. Although the town was named after Scottish poet Robert Burns, the area is home to the Burns Piute Tribe, who hold a reservation powwow each October.

Volcanic Wonders

Not far down the road is the Diamond Craters Outstanding Natural Area. Famed for its black, desolate terrain, these intriguing lava fields were created 25,000 years ago when molten lava oozed across a dry lakebed. Before this layer solidified, another layer of liquid rock was unleashed, forming some of the country's most distinctive basalt rock formations. Today, a drive through this amazing backdrop of geological wonders will launch you into a world of lava domes, lava tubes, massive pit craters and craggy spires. Several trails lead hikers to the amazing geological formations.

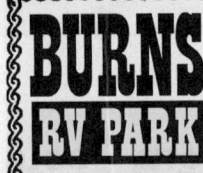

Tall Town

Travel west across the desert to the community of Lakeview, touted as the "Tallest Town in Oregon" for its elevation of 4,798 feet. Sitting at the foot of the Warner Mountains, Lakeview boasts a slew of natural wonders that make it a sleeper hit among Oregon tourism destinations. Nearby, check out the Crack in the Ground, a fissure formed between cooling lava flows around 1,100 years ago. At two miles long and 70 feet deep, the chasm entices hikers with a trail that runs along it's bottom. During hot summer days, this hike can be a welcome respite from the heat, as the temperature within the trench can be as much as 20 degrees below the surface temperature. Northwest of town, on the crest of the Warner Mountain Range at 8,222 feet, the Drake Peak Lookout serves up amazing views of the surrounding peaks. Once a forest service lookout, the site is now available to the public.

Getty Images/iStockphoto

Portland's iconic sign was Installed in 1940. The nose of the white stag lights up in red during the holidays.

Derrick Cave

More geological wonders await visitors at Derrick Cave, a lava tube 30 feet high, 50 feet wide and a quarter mile long. Located near Crack in the Ground, this subterranean chamber is collapsed in two places. One provides the access point and the other serves as a "skylight." Equally compelling is Devil's Garden Wilderness study area, which includes two spatter cones known as "the blowouts." Geological history continues to unfold in the 2,000-year-old Lake Chewaucan Lake Bed. About a mile north of town, the Old Perpetual Geyser erupts 60 feet every 90 seconds. The wonder is found near Hunter's Hot Springs, whose waters are reputed to have healing properties. Nothing beats sinking into a hot spring after a long day of traveling for a nice soak.

Off-Road Fun

Ready for some desert adventure? From Fields, you can join the 143-mile East Steens Tour Route north for a soul-stirring montage of Oregon's stunning basin country. The Alvord Desert playa is one of the largest playas in Oregon and is ground zero for motorcycling, ATV riding, land sailing, glider flying and camping. Bring your toys and cut loose.

Soothing Water

Just off East Steens Road, a mosaic of small lakes provide sanctuary to a variety of wildlife. Bighorn sheep and the speedy pronghorn antelope (capable of cruising at 60 miles per hour) can be spotted. If you need R&R, there are several hot springs located near the town of Crane. Just outside of town lie the Crystal Crane Hot Springs, which offers a hot springs pond and private bathhouses. Rent an event space to hold a one-of-a-kind get-together here.

Metro Portland

The compact city of Portland, Oregon offers all the accoutrements of a big city (think fantastic dining and shopping), plus plenty of green space and gardens for those who prefer a more sylvan vibe. The Portland metropolitan area also makes a great base for exploring Oregon's beaches, forests, and wine regions, all within a short drive from town.

Foodie City

In the past couple of decades, Portland has earned a name for itself as a culinary city. But don't expect tons of Michelin-starred spots; while Portland has its share of fine dining, the best food options here are far from hoity toity. In fact, one of the most popular ways to dine out in Portland is by hitting up one of its many food cart "pods," old parking lots that have been converted into outdoor food courts, many with covered, heated outdoor seating, toilets, ATMs, and even beer and wine service. In the true Pacific Northwest spirit, Portland also has a strong tradition of coffee roasting, from famous Stumptown and Nossa Familia, to lesser known (but no less delicious) options such as Coava and Case Study Coffee Roasters. And what better to enjoy with coffee than donuts from Portland's most famous donut producer, Voodoo Doughnuts, known for its odd flavor combinations (topped with things like bubble gum and Captain Crunch cereal).

City of Gardens

Portland is known as the City of Roses, and one of its prettiest attractions is the Portland International Rose Test Garden inside the city's sprawling

OR

JANTZEN BEACH RV P•A•R•K

PORTLAND'S ISLAND DESTINATION!

Located on the mighty Columbia River in the beautiful Portland area. The park has the quiet open, fresh-air feel of the country, with all the conveniences and attractions of nearby Portland. There is so much to see and do you'll never want to leave.

· Heated Swimming Pool · Exercise Room · Game Room · Playground
· Clubhouse · Basketball Court · Horseshoes · Free Wi-Fi · Free Cable TV
· Grassy Picnic Areas · 20/30/50 Amp Hookups · 60' Pull-thrus · Paved Sites
· Water & Sewer Connections · Spotless Restrooms & Showers
· Full Laundry Facilities · Open Year Round · Pets Welcome
· Walking Distance to Tax Free Shopping and Restaurants

Seasonal sites available from November through April

Ask us about our RV Property in Phoenix, AZ

NEAR Rose Garden · Zoo · University · Convention Center

good sam park

2022 Top Rated 10/10★/9.5

AAA

FREE WIFI

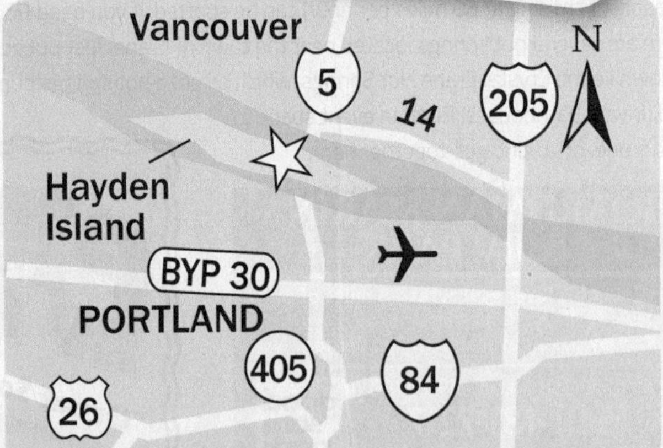

www.jantzenbeachrv.com

(503) 289-7626 • (800) 443-7248

1503 N. Hayden Is. Dr., Portland, OR 97217
One half mile west of I-5 (exit 308)

See listing Portland, OR

Two sides of Oregon: The skyline reflected on the Willamette River and a kayak ready for action on a dock.

Washington Park. Dating back to 1917, this 4.5-acre garden features around 10,000 rose bushes representing 650 varieties of roses and views out over downtown Portland. Also in Washington Park, just across from the Rose Test Garden, the Portland Japanese Garden sits on 5.5 hilly acres. This serene greenspace offers numerous smaller gardens with beautifully landscaped grounds dotted with trees and shrubs, koi ponds, and stone decorative features, plus a teahouse serving Japanese snacks.

Linger in Lan Su

One of the newer gardens in Portland, the Lan Su Chinese Garden was built in the Ming Dynasty style and features pathways meandering past decorative plants and across water features. As with the Japanese Garden, the Lan Su Chinese Garden also has a delightful teahouse.

Portland Shopping

Portland has a strong tradition of independent artistry, and it's a great place to pick up unusual jewelry pieces, clothes, and home décor items. Popular shopping districts include SE Hawthorne Boulevard, which has tons of little boutiques and vintage clothing stores (particularly between 32nd and 45th Avenues) and NW 23rd Ave, where high-end shops dominate. Book lovers won't want to miss Powell's City of Books downtown, the world's largest new-and-used independent bookstore (it takes up a whole city block), while Andy and Bax Outdoor Store is a must for lovers of the great outdoors, with an ample selection of camping gear plus tons of military surplus material. If you visit Portland on a weekend, don't miss the Portland Saturday Market, which runs from the end of February through Christmas Eve and offers booth upon booth of handcrafted items, plus great food carts and regular live entertainment. Best of all, Oregon is a sales tax-free state!

Nearby Nature

While Portland offers tons of fantastic activities within its compact city limits, it's also a great base for getting to many of Oregon's phenomenal natural attractions. The most popular close-to-Portland area for nature lovers is undoubtedly the Columbia River Gorge, which runs east from Portland along the Columbia River (which forms a natural border between the states of Oregon and Washington). The most popular site in this area is Multnomah Falls, the tallest waterfall in Oregon. While it's easily viewed from the parking lot, those wanting a bit of exercise can hike around a mile up to the top for fantastic views. To the west of Portland, the Oregon Coast is not your typical beach destination. Not only is it generally not very warm, meaning you're unlikely to see much swimming and sunbathing outside of a short window in the height of summer, it is remarkably beautiful. One of the closest beaches to Portland, Cannon Beach, is particularly worth visiting for its cute shops and restaurants as well as its iconic stone formation, Haystack Rock.

Gateway to Wine Country

If you like wine, you'll feel right at home in the Portland Metro area. The city has plenty of wineries and wine shops of its own—quirky Pairings Portland Wine Shop is particularly worth a visit—and it's just a short drive from some of the Pacific Northwest's most celebrated wineries. To the south of Portland, the Willamette

OR

A group of gray whales frequently visit Depoe Bay, making it the "whale-watching capital" of the world.

Valley is a must-visit region for Pinot fans, and produces some excellent wines thanks to its cool, relatively humid climate and rolling hills. Some of the highest concentrations of wineries can be found in cities and towns such as McMinnville, Newberg, Dundee, and Yamhill. Also within day-tripping distance of Portland, Hood River is home to and its surrounding region produces a wide range of red and white varietals, from Syrah to Riesling.

Oregon's Central Coast

The central Oregon Coast is a gorgeous blend of charming towns and wild stretches of coast. Buckle up and prepare for a beautiful ride; the wild landscape along the windswept shores is ever-changing, from the vastness of the Pacific to the denseness of the lush woodlands. Each scenic overlook offers up a different scenic snapshot. Public parks and beaches can be found every few minutes, offering up recreational opportunities of all types. When you're ready for a taste of the coast, stop to stroll around one of the charming seaside villages, like Yachats and Florence.

Lincoln City

Beachcombers can explore this town's seven miles of plush, sandy beach. Go clam digging, play in tide pools, work on your tan, or catch a dazzling sunset from shore. If you're in town during June, build a kite and fly it at the Summer Kite Festival. From mid-October to May, local artists participate in Finders Keepers, which involves the placement of thousands of beautifully crafted glass floats on the beach for you to find. You can also check out regular glass-blowing demonstrations and create masterpieces at the Jennifer Sears Glass Art Studio year-round.

Lake of the Devil

Ready to play in the water? Outside of Lincoln City, Devil's Lake is a popular spot for water play, with one of the world's shortest rivers (the D River, a mere 120 feet long) connecting it to the Pacific. Instead of massive expanses of waters, Oregon's tiny tide pools just might provide the most interesting way to have fun on the water.

Depoe Bay

See the world's largest mammals swim past from the Whale Watching Center near Depoe Bay. While whales can be spotted from the Oregon Coast any time of year, winter is especially magical as thousands of migrating whales pass by on their way to Mexico. This free facility provides prime viewing platforms and educates guests. Depoe Bay is also great for fishing. Nearby reefs support thriving populations of striped perch, rockfish and lingcod, while the offshore waters abound with salmon, albacore tuna and halibut.

Bubbling Cauldron

It's a massive cauldron formed by collapsed sea caves. Located about 5 miles south of Depoe Bay lies Devil's Punchbowl State Natural Area. The wild waters whirl like a washing machine. Further, into the sea, waves entice surfers to ride on the water.

Newport's Undersea Wonders

See aquatic wildlife from the perspective of a fish. Head to the Oregon Coast Aquarium and the Hatfield Marine Science Center in Newport. Walk through a clear underwater tunnel, with sharks, stingray and fish swimming overhead. Touch sea anemone and explore tide pools, get an up-close view of an octopus, or watch the sea otters romp.

Sweet and Savory

Attention foodies and wine lovers! Put the Newport Seafood & Wine Festival on your calendar. Held each February, it attracts 25,000 visitors annually to sample food and wines. Yaquina Bay's South Beach area fills with tents from as many as 150 vendors, representing the best regional vineyards, eateries and artisans. Sample Newport's signature crab, sip wines from across the West Coast and enjoy the sounds of live music. In May, rhododendrons burst into bloom along the Oregon Coast.

Cozy Town

Alluring scenery is part of Newport's charm. Meander along the waterfront to meet crowds of barking sea lions. The area is also home to the Yaquina Head Lighthouse, the tallest lighthouse in Oregon at 93 feet. Back near the shore, walk around the tide pools teeming with

LOGAN ROAD RV PARK · CONFEDERATED TRIBES OF SILETZ INDIANS

Logan Road RV Park

4800 NE Logan Road | Lincoln City, OR 97367

www.loganroadrvpark.com

1-877-564-2678

Only a few blocks from Chinook Winds Casino Resort & the Pacific Ocean with Beach Access!

good sam park · Wi Fi · PET FRIENDLY · AAA

See listing Lincoln City, OR

Daily, &Weekly Stays Available!*

Two Blocks from US 101

- 51 Sites (Back-in & Pull-Thru Available)
- Full Hookups
- Free Cable and Wi-Fi Access (Netflix ok)
- Bathroom & Shower Facilities
- Propane station & Pet Area
- *Call for Extended Stay Availability
- Lincoln City's only west of Hwy 101 RV Park
- 5 Minutes from Chinook Winds Golf Course
- 24/7 - Surveillance
- Gazebo and Barbecue Area
- 10 Minutes from Lincoln City Outlets
- Coin-Op Laundry Room

Registered guests have free access to Chinook Winds Casino Resort Hotel Pool & Spa along with free 24 hour shuttle to and from their site to Chinook Winds Casino Resort where, "*It is Better at the Beach*"!

OR

SPOTLIGHTS

The Ocean has spoken: Water thunders into 20-foot-deep Thor's Well on Cape Perpetua on Oregon's Coast.

starfish, sea anemones and crustaceans at Yaquina Head Outstanding Natural Area.

Mo's Magic

Savor a hot bowl of seafood goodness. Mo's Seafood and Chowder famous concoctions have put that restaurant on the map. Or shop at Local Ocean Seafoods, a restaurant and fish market that serves up scrumptious seafood with a stellar view. South of town, the stunning Yaquina Bay Bridge crosses beautiful Yaquina Bay. The bridge's abundant Art Deco and Modern design motifs are sure to please architecture buffs.

Hard Rock

Some of the Oregon coast's must-see sites are vertical columns of rocks on the beach caused by wave erosion. The largest of the area's sandstone-supported sea stacks, Elephant Rock — named for its uncanny resemblance to an elephant — is flanked by dark igneous surf-pounded rocks that rise some 20 feet above the ocean. This wild and foreboding setting forms a rich habitat and prime nesting ground for myriad sea bird species including cormorants, brown pelicans, bald eagles, gannets and gulls. Set aside some time to stroll past these amazing giants.

Waldport Wonders

Visitors to this town can drop a line in the Alsea River, which runs from the coastal mountains and enters the Pacific at Alsea Bay. Nab salmon, steelhead, trout and more. Paddlers seeking a calm, inland experience can enjoy the waters of Beaver Creek at Brian Booth State Park, also close by. Known for its tranquility, this park lets visitors experience an Oregon landscape that differs from the wind-swept coast.

Do Drift Creek

Take one of the most popular hikes in the Siuslaw National Forest. The Drift Creek Falls Trail leads hikers through coastal forest of fern, alder and maple. The destination is an impressive 240-foot suspension bridge that spans the dramatic Drift Creek Falls. You can view the cascading 75-foot waterfall (best seen in the spring or fall after seasonal rains) from above (on the bridge) or take the trail to the base of the falls where there's a picnic table carved from a tree.

Yield for Yachats

You can relax in Yachats, a romantic town nestled on the shore, with the Coast Range peaks forming a dramatic backdrop. Time slows down here, giving you a chance to revel in beachfront strolls, bird-watching, fishing, golfing and winter storm watching. Art galleries, shops and delicious seafood restaurants round out your experience.

Thrilling Views

Cape Perpetua Scenic Area lies two miles to the south. This is the highest overlook accessible by car on the Oregon Coast at over 800 feet above sea level. Part of the Siuslaw National Forest, this area is worth a visit for its postcard-worthy sights — powerful waves colliding with the shore, soaring trees peeking through coastal fog and headlands as far as the eye can see. The Yachats 804 Trail is a popular hiking choice, running almost 2 miles along the rocky shore.

Hobbits Hangout

Take a little side trip to Middle Earth on your coastal odyssey. The Hobbit Trail takes hikers through woodlands filled with lichen-covered trees and lush ferns. At one point, you'll pass through a hobbit-size tunnel before emerging

An estimated 2,000 sea lions populate the Pacific Coast of Oregon, many of them gathering at the Sea Lion Caves in Florence. Sea lions can weigh up to 800 pounds.

onto a secluded beach. Look closely at the dunes — you might see carved troll-like faces staring back at you.

Fantastic Florence

Welcoming visitors to the Port of Siuslaw, Florence's Old Town has a quaint vibe. Local galleries, shops and cafes make this a great spot, all while enjoying views of ships in the harbor. For over 100 years, Florence's Rhododendron Festival has celebrated these spring blossoms each May. This event includes a car show, 5K race, street fair, carnival and the crowning of "Queen Rhododendra." Venture to Haceta Head Lighthouse for stellar views.

Sea Lions on the Loose

The Sea Lion Caves attraction has surprised and delighted visitors since 1932. This huge grotto along the Pacific Ocean provides shelter for hundreds of sea lions. Visitors ride an elevator 200 feet down to sea level to observe these massive creatures in their natural habitat.

Light Trail

The hike to the Heceta Head Lighthouse. The Heceta Head Lighthouse is the brightest on the state's coast and is known as an architectural gem. The trail to the lighthouse ascends a few hundred feet, but it's worth it for the views down the state's south coast.

Cool Coastal Adventures

The Oregon shore packs plenty of outdoor adventure. Take a walk along a windy beach and take the time to appreciate the natural beauty. Here, the ocean is too cold for proper swimming, but the magical sound of waves lapping the sands will let you know you are someplace special. If the tide is out, take the opportunity to explore the flora and fauna of the tide pools. Head out for a whale watching excursion to get closer views of these giant mammals.

Grand Chowder

Locals along this coast say they have the best chowder in the world, and they may be on to something. This region is known as Oregon's "Chowder Belt." Warm up with a heaping bowl of clams and potatoes swimming in a creamy broth. If you're up for catching your entrée, try your hand at crabbing. Almost anyone can nab these crustaceans. Rent some crab rings, and ask a local expert where to go. Before long, you'll be hauling in heaping piles of Dungeness crab, known for its savory flavor. All you'll need is some heat and some butter for a delicious meal.

Succulent Oysters

Awesome oysters await your taste buds in this region. In 1852, a schooner became stranded near Yaquina Bay during strong storms. As the crew ventured out, they discovered bountiful oyster beds in the bay. Within a decade, two oyster companies were formed, bringing settlers to the region. To this day, oysters are a staple in restaurants along the coast, allowing visitors to sample this regional delicacy. Shipping oysters out from the coast became a big industry in the 1800s. Towns like Newport grew, with booming marinas along the shore.

Nicely Newport

Today, Newport's historic Bayfront is a thriving gathering spot, with colorful storefronts just beyond the boardwalk. Aside from tourists, Bayfront also attracts sea lions, whose barks fill the air, never letting you forget you're close to the sea. Go beachcombing and watch the mischievous mammals in their habitat.

SPOTLIGHTS

Two Siberian huskies frolic on Cannon Beach as Haystack Rock looms 235 feet tall in the distance.

Oregon's North Coast

Captain William Clark was one of the first Americans to see Oregon's Pacific Coast in 1805. After traveling almost 5,000 miles with fellow explorer Meriweather Lewis, the pair settled on a camp in an area now known as Astoria. The Lewis and Clark Expedition had taken the men across the northern Plains, over the Rockies and to the Pacific Ocean. There's little doubt that the party was overjoyed at the sight of the Pacific water.

Magical Mile 0

From Oregon's northwest corner, start with Mile 0 of Oregon's legendary Highway 101, and head south for a spellbinding tour of the Oregon Coast. Northern Oregon's long stretch of Highway 101 is chock-full of epic views and charming seaside towns, stretching from Astoria to Neotsu. At several points, bridges take motorists across inlets and bays, adding to the scenic experience.

Awesome Astoria

With gorgeous Victorian homes and rolling hills, Astoria has earned the nickname, "Little San Francisco of the Pacific Northwest." This was the first permanent settlement west of the Rockies, thanks to its prime location along the Columbia River and the Pacific. High above the city, the Astoria Column rises 600 feet above sea level, paying homage to these settlers. Take a journey on the 1913 Astoria Riverfront Trolley for a tour of the town and a step back in time. Of course, Astoria's history was shaped by the waterways nearby, and the Columbia River Maritime Museum shares stories of ships and sailors and the forces they encountered in this mighty waterway.

Pioneering Explorers

You don't have to look for history. Visit the reconstructed Fort Clatsop just south of town to see where Lewis and Clark spent a winter. Launch your kayak or canoe from Netul Landing on the Lewis and Clark River, just as the explorers did. Fish the Columbia River for big salmon.

Astoria Sets Sail

The Astoria Regatta in September is one of the city's premier events. Started in 1894, this event began as a way for the town to welcome the return of local fishermen, with their bounty of freshly caught seafood. Eventually, the event grew into a formal celebration, involving parades, concerts, coronations and a bevy of family fun. The crowning event is the Highwater Boat Parade. Watch from the shores as all kinds of vessels sail by.

Down by the Seaside

For a good, old-fashioned coastal vacation experience, check out the town of Seaside, with one of the most renowned boardwalks on Oregon's northern coast. Take a stroll on the Seaside Promenade, locally known as the Prom. Watch colorful kites dance in the skies above the waves, while cooling off with a dripping ice cream cone. Here, you'll find the Lewis and Clark statue, marking the last stop of their expedition. In August, the Seaside Beach Volleyball Tournament brings top players to the sands for fantastic competition.

See a Towering Haystack

Cannon Beach has gained a reputation as an artist colony, but it's also a destination of natural beauty. And after exploring it, you'll understand why National Geographic named it one of the world's 100 most beautiful places. Devote a good chunk of time on your itinerary for Haystack Rock on the shore. For centuries, this unusual sea stack has intrigued and inspired visitors. Rising 235 feet above the sandy shore, Haystack Rock is a prime location to explore the region's wildlife. During low tide, you can make the trek out to the rock for close-up selfies.

Castles in the Sand

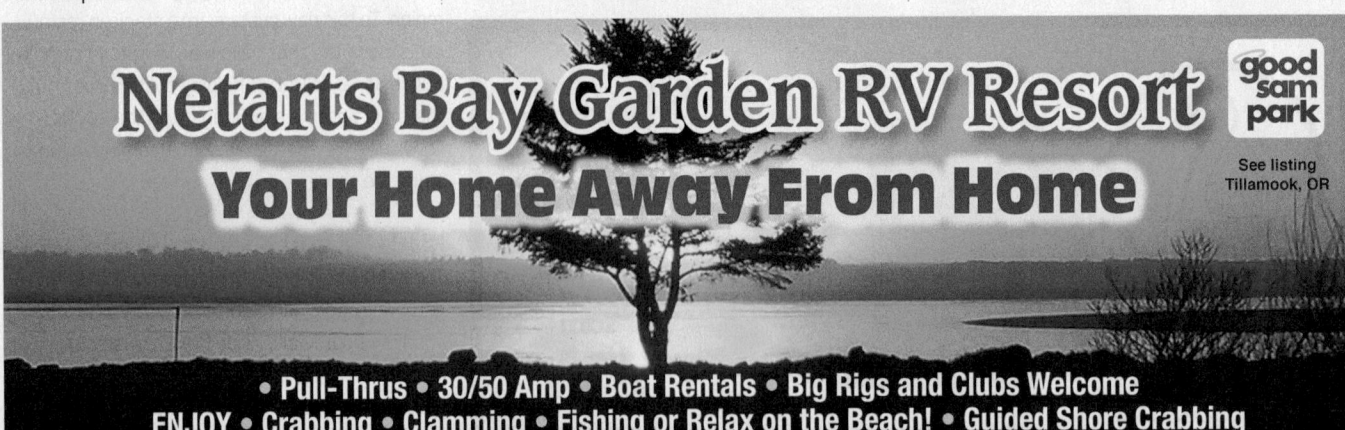

Test your building skills at the Cannon Beach Sandcastle Contest. Dozens of teams of professional sand sculpture artists, amateur groups and families construct remarkable creations in the sand during the fun-filled event.

Excellent Ecola

For many folks, Ecola State Park is a coastal highlight. Take a drive through the lush rainforests, and then emerge to find the panoramic views of the Pacific Ocean. With a lighthouse in the distance and surfers riding the waves, Ecola is the epitome of coastal Oregon.

Go to Garibaldi

Discover a bustling port, marina and community of 1,000 residents on the northern tip of Tillamook Bay. Garibaldi also is the perfect place to watch the world go by. Stroll the marina and see fishermen haul up Dungeness crab, lingcod and rockfish. Board the Oregon Coast Scenic Railroad, a historic steam train that chugs along Tillamook Bay. Hop in a kayak and paddle out in search of bald eagles and purple martins. Take a charter to the deep sea for halibut, tuna, sea trout and more.

Say, "Cheese"

The Tillamook Creamery, situated in the town of Tillamook, has a grand reputation. The creamery is a popular stop on the northern Oregon Coast, with more than one million people visiting each year to sample the wares, see the production lines and learn about the dairy farms that make these flavorful products possible. Despite the heavy foot traffic, cheese fans should be assured of the painstaking measures that Tillamook goes through to ensure quality. Many of the cheeses are aged for as long as three years. If you are a fan of Monterey Jack cheese, it should be noted that Tillamook Monterey Jack has won the best in its class at the United States Championship Cheese Contest.

Have Kayak, Will Paddle

The Nehalem River, which crosses through forests and marshlands, is excellent for paddling. The Tillamook Water Trail includes the Nehalem and four other waterways, offering paddling adventures in diverse habitats. Located in Fort Stevens State Park, Coffenbury Lake is a spot that will please anglers and boaters.

Roll Around the Loop

The Three Capes Scenic Loop is a 40-mile journey that begins in downtown Tillamook before leading to scenic overlooks. Pull off at Oceanside or Cape Lookout to gaze at the panoramic views where the ocean meets the sands. Set out for a hike at the Cape Lookout Trail, which gives hikers views of whales swimming by during the migration season.

Wonderful Oregon Waterways

Anglers will find salmon grounds along the northern Oregon Coast, including the Tillamook Bay, the Nestucca River and the Nehalem River. Trout, steelhead and more abound in the region's cool interior waters. Instead of using a rod to capture your dinner, grab a shovel and a bucket. Clamming can be enjoyed in Tillamook Bay and Netarts Bay.

The Tillamook Cheese Factory offers tours that show how cheese is made. Ice cream is served to guests.

Pacific City

Just south of Netarts, Pacific City is a quaint little town with beautiful, wide beaches flanked by large cliffs and is home to Bob Straub State Park, an excellent spot for beachside bird-watching. Visitors to this area's pristine shores can hunt for a variety of treasures, including sand dollars, hermit crabs and driftwood. A bike path runs through downtown Pacific City, giving visitors easy access to shopping and dining.

Oregon's South Coast

Oregon's Wild South Coast is a land of wild rivers, rugged coastlines and uncrowded beaches. Stretching 130 miles from Winchester Bay to the California border, the Beaver State's southern coast offers all of the beauty found along the northern shores with fewer crowds. Getaway from it all with a journey along Highway 101.

Wonderful Winchester Bay

Winchester Bay hums with outdoor activities catering to everyone from thrill-seekers to bird-watchers. Anglers can expect to catch chinook salmon, steelhead, rainbow trout and largemouth bass, while bird-watchers can spot bald eagles, hawks and more. Nearby, the Oregon Dunes National Recreation Area is an off-road paradise for ATV riders and sandboarding enthusiasts.

Umpqua Lights Up

For unbeatable scenery, hike a mile around Lake Marie and continue to the Umpqua River Lighthouse. Known for the red and white beams that emanate from the structure's top, this 19th-century lighthouse can be

OR

SPOTLIGHTS

Coos County is a top Oregon kayaking spot. Many come to the South Slough National Estuarine Reserve.

admired from the outside or inside. Tour the 65-foot tower and enjoy whale watching from the Umpqua River Whale Watching Station, near the lighthouse, from November to May.

Cool Times at Coos Bay

The town of Coos Bay tells the history of the Oregon coast's rise with several historic sites. Here, the Coos River enters the ocean, forming Coos Bay. The Oregon International Port of Coos Bay is the biggest harbor suitable for large ships between San Francisco Bay and Puget Sound, making it the second-busiest maritime commerce center in the state. Today, visitors can explore this thriving port with a visit to the Coos Bay Boardwalk. Eat freshly caught seafood at one of the local dives, or make a stop at the Cranberry Sweets & More candy shop is a must!

Shore Acres: A Feast for the Eyes

Come to Shore Acres State Park for magically manicured environments. Once the estate of a lumber baron, the park now offers 5 acres of flower gardens, a lily pond and a secluded ocean cove for visitors to explore. One of the most distinctive roadside attractions along Highway 101 is Prehistoric Gardens, a real coastal rainforest habitat that's crawling with life-size replicas of dinosaurs. See Tyrannosaurus rex, a triceratops and more lurking amid giant ferns and towering trees.

Fun on the Fairway

Bring your clubs to Bandon Dunes Golf Resort, ranked as one of the nation's best courses. It might be hard to keep your eye on the ball due to the stunning natural landscape, visible just beyond the fairways and greens. The Pacific Ocean is in view just beyond the tidy greens and the wild, rolling dunes.

Nature's Beauty in Bandon

Bandon brings visitors face-to-face with every sort of outdoor adventure imaginable. Pull up Dungeness crab and hook salmon, halibut and tuna from the bay. On the beach, go horseback riding or paddle in a kayak out for close-up views of birds, fish and otters. Just across the river is Bullards Beach State Park, a haven for wildlife and home to the Coquille River Lighthouse. Riders of fat bikes — bikes with wide tires and rims for sandy terrain — can take the six-mile ride from Bandon's South Jetty to China Creek in Bandon State Park. The course entails cruising through sea caves and past sea stacks on the beach.

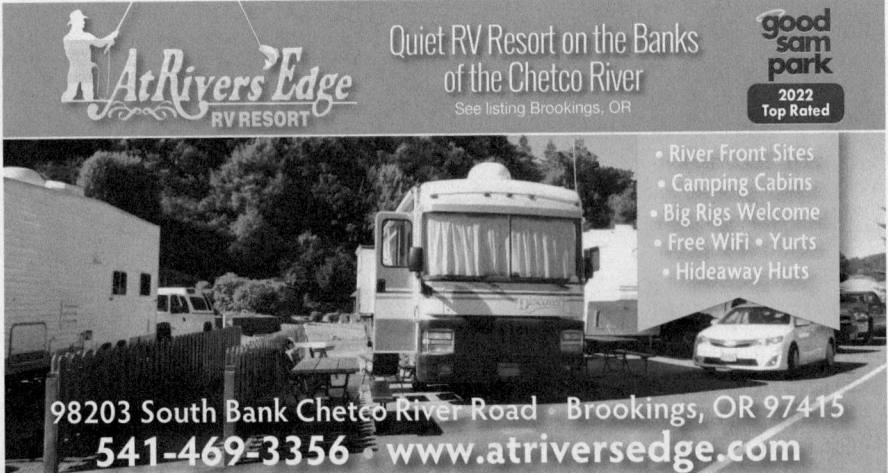

Cape Blanco Bursts with Views

As the westernmost part of Oregon, Cape Blanco State Park will wow with its spellbinding cliffs, unusual rock formations, woodland backdrops and the iconic lighthouse. Over 8 miles of trails lead you to jaw-dropping ocean vistas. If you're lucky, you may even spot a colony of sea lions on the offshore rocks below. The 59-foot Cape Blanco Lighthouse sits atop a 200-foot chalky white cliff and is open for visits.

Port Orford

History buffs and art enthusiasts won't want to miss Port Orford. This quirky town supports an active artist community with eight galleries displaying an exquisite array of local artwork. Budding historians can dive into Port Orford's seafaring past at the free museum within Port Orford Heads State Park or the Port Orford Lifeboat Station museum, which houses a restored lifeboat along with various artifacts.

Gold Beach Gourmet

Your adventures in the wilderness are sure to leave you parched. Quench your thirst at Arch Rock Brewing Company, an award-winning microbrewery that's won five gold medals at beer competitions around the world. Stop by their tasting room and sip their famous pale ale, lager and porter.

Brookings Is Oregon's Banana Belt

You'll find some of the best weather and coastal views in Brookings. Nicknamed

"Oregon's Banana Belt," this part of the Beaver State experiences warmer temperatures than the rest of the state. This phenomenon has transformed Brookings into the biggest producer of Easter lilies in the country. Admire the region's floral beauty at Azalea Park, a 33-acre space blanketed with native azaleas. The best photo ops can be found along the Samuel H. Boardman State Scenic Corridor, a linear park comprising 12 ocean-hugging miles of craggy bluffs and secluded shores. Watch as the water swirls around the Natural Bridges.

Brookings is famous for the rocks found along the coastline. See ocean vistas at the House Rock Viewpoint.

Choice Chetco

Looking for more panoramic views of the Pacific Ocean? You can't do much better than Chetco Point Park. The park sits on a hundred-foot-high plateau that's surrounded on three sides by the Pacific Ocean. This is a great place to whale watch or simply take in views of the horizon. Drive up the Chetco River to see another photogenic area. Alfred A. Loeb State Park sits on the banks of the waterway upstream, before it empties into the Pacific Ocean.

Southern Oregon

An intricate tapestry of wild rivers, stark desert, rugged mountains, lush forests and gushing waterfalls, Southern Oregon is a place of magical contrasts. Outdoor enthusiasts will feel like kids in a candy store — from traversing endless hiking trails and paddling through roaring whitewater to discovering underground worlds and exploring the deepest lake in the country, this diverse region promises adventures of epic proportions. But it's not just outdoorsy stuff here. Theater aficionados can attend an internationally renowned Shakespeare festival, history buffs can meander through old gold rush towns and foodies can sip their way through a wealth of award-winning wineries and microbreweries.

Discover Southern Oregon

Southern Oregon is a large area that comprises numerous cities, towns, valleys, national parks and more. In the southeast corner, you'll find Klamath Falls, Oregon's deserts and Lava Beds National Monument, just over the California border. The bustling city of Ashland and the popular ski area of Mount Ashland are located just 63 miles west of Klamath Falls, 285 miles south of Portland, and 295 miles north of Sacramento. Drive half an hour north from Ashland and you'll wind up in Medford, a popular base for exploring the Rogue Valley and Applegate Valley. Applegate Valley is home to historic Jacksonville and Grants Pass, the perfect place to start your Rogue River expeditions.

Main Artery

Most of this region is connected by Interstate 5. To get to Crater Lake National Park, take Highway 62 if you're coming from Medford, and Highway 97 to 62 if you're coming from Klamath Falls. Arriving from the north? Leave Interstate 5 south of Eugene and follow Highway 58 to 97 to 138. Winters at Crater Lake are long and snowy, averaging 43 feet of snow annually at park headquarters. Temperatures max out in the 30s during winter and into the 70s during summer. If you're coming from May to September, expect warm, sunny days and crisp, cool evenings.

America's Deepest Lake

Crater Lake is a site you need to see to believe. Over 7,700 years ago, Mount Mazama erupted and collapsed in on itself. This caused a gigantic

At 1,943 feet, Crater Lake is the deepest lake in the U.S. Wizard Island is named after a sorcerer's hat.

caldera measuring 6 miles wide. As time passed, the caldera filled with rain and snowmelt, thus creating Crater Lake. With a lake bed at 1,949 feet below the surface, Crater Lake is the deepest lake in the United States and continues to dazzle tourists, artists and outdoor adventurers with its sharp blue waters and dazzling Cascade mountain backdrop. In the summer, enjoy hiking and camping in old-growth forests, take your boat out on the lake, or cruise along Rim Drive to see the park's epic landscapes from the comfort of your car. It's an otherworldly landscape.

Cool Klamath

Not far from Crater Lake National Park is Klamath Falls, a hub for outdoor recreation. Seasoned hikers will want to tackle the famed 100-mile OC&E Woods Line State Trail, while bird-watchers won't want to miss seeing herons, hawks, owls and over 350 other bird species in the Klamath Basin, one of the best birding destinations in America.

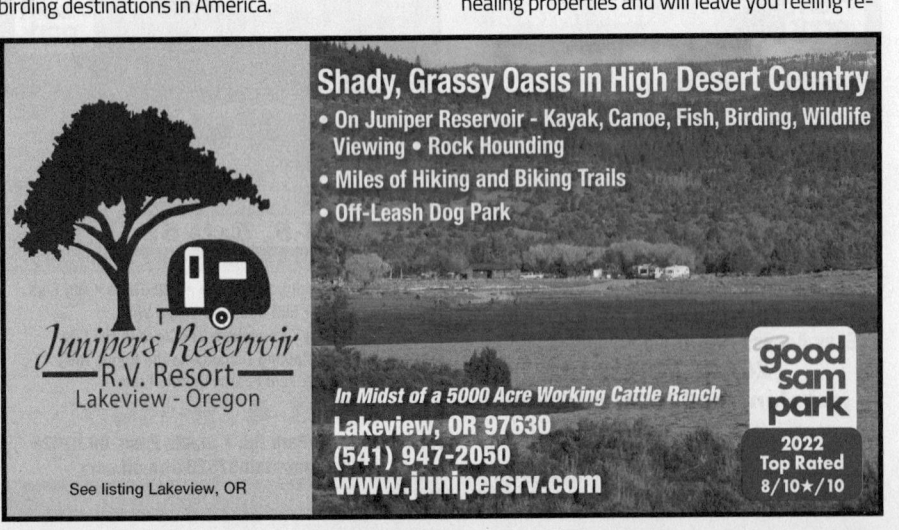

Hunting and Fishing Haven

The Klamath region is also a bird hunter's paradise as millions of ducks, geese and swans pass through this area every year. Thanks to loads of wooded areas and high desert, big-game hunters can snag everything from deer and elk to cougar and coyote. It won't be hard to bag a black bear either as Southern Oregon has the most black bears in the Lower 48. Anglers dreaming of champion-sized trout will find those here too — specifically in Upper Klamath Lake, Lake of the Woods and Odell Lake.

Aim for Ashland

Known as the cultural capital of Southern Oregon, Ashland will impress with its fine attractions, renowned eateries and the internationally acclaimed Oregon Shakespeare Festival. In need of some physical or mental soothing? Indulge in a rejuvenating soak at Lithia Springs Resort or Jackson Wellsprings. The mineral-rich waters here are said to have healing properties and will leave you feeling relaxed and calm. Check out 100-acre Lithia Park, an urban paradise with emerald lawns, tennis courts, picnic areas and dazzling landscaping. Just steps away from the festival's theaters, the park follows Ashland Creek through rugged woodlands. Visitors also can explore the park's Japanese garden and rose garden.

Wonderful Wines

Speaking of wine, Ashland is just a stone's throw away from a handful of wineries such as Belle Fiore Estate and Winery, Dana Campbell Vineyards, Weisinger Family Winery and Trium Wines. Stop by to sample varieties like cabernet sauvignon, merlot, chardonnay and sauvignon blanc, and take in the breathtaking mountain backdrop while you're enjoying the fine flavors. Wine buffs who can't get enough vino will want to go north to Grants Pass, the gateway to the Applegate Valley Wine Trail. Boasting 18 wineries, fertile valleys and dramatic hillsides, this wine trail is a feast for the eyes and taste buds.

Bard on Stage

Theater fans from all over flock to Ashland for the Tony award-winning Oregon Shakespeare Festival. Held every year from mid-February to the end of October, this 8½-month festival has been going strong for almost 85 years and offers performances six days a week (the theater takes a break on Mondays). The festival takes place on three stages (Allen Elizabethan Theatre, Angus Bowmer Theatre and the Thomas Theatre), and puts on 11 different plays to almost 400,000 people throughout the course of the season. See some of the world's top actors recite lines from the Bard.

Beer Blast

If you're more into craft beer, Medford is the destination for you. Savor a pint at top brewing companies like Opposition, Portal, Bricktown and Medford. While you're here, catch a memorable performance at the Craterian Theater, check out old locomotives at the Medford Railroad Park, or try delicious cheeses and chocolates at the Artisan Corridor located in Central Point.

Eclectic Tunes
In the summer, catch dozens of concerts at Jacksonville's Britt Music and Arts Festival. Held in a naturally formed amphitheater and featuring international artists in the classical, jazz, blues, folk, bluegrass, pop and country realm, this festival entices music lovers with incredible performances, bewitching scenery and a relaxed, easygoing atmosphere.

Located close to the Oregon Shakespeare Festival in Ashland, Lithia Park is a rustic retreat.

Preserved Gold Rush Towns
Just 7 miles west of Medford and 15 miles northwest of Ashland is the old mining town of Jacksonville. Gold was unearthed here in 1851, which led to loads of fortune-hungry miners settling in the Rogue Valley. The gold rush transformed Jacksonville into a prosperous town with saloons, gambling halls, supply shops, banks and a variety of businesses established by 1852. Today, many of Jacksonville's original buildings still stand (there are over 100 on the National Register of Historic Places), allowing you to immerse yourself in a bygone era.

Victorian Gem
Explore the Victorian-style Cornelius Beekman House, the former estate of one of Jacksonville's most wealthy families. Take a stroll through the cemetery containing some of the oldest pioneer gravesites in the entire state. Learn more about the town's history and legends by joining a trolley tour or ghost tour, and stay the night at a historic inn. You can even pretend to be a pioneer for the day by panning for gold in the nearby Applegate River (take Highway 138 outside of Jacksonville). Experience the joy of finding shiny gold and bring your treasure home.

Bygone Oregon
Dive deeper into Oregon's past at Pottsville Historical Museum. Not far from Merlin, this museum features thousands of items related to the state's heritage including legislative halls, local logging woods, steam engines, tractors, old mining equipment, and even a stagecoach that ran between Kerby and Crescent City back in the day.

Take to the Water
You've come to the right place if you're searching for heart-stopping action. Flowing through Grants Pass, the Rogue River promises thrilling, world-class rafting with Class I to IV rapids. Book a four-day excursion to battle monster whitewater, or make a day trip and paddle through the spellbinding "Wild and Scenic" section of the river. For the ultimate rush, take a 36-mile jetboat ride through the stunning Hellgate Canyon. The river is also famed for its trophy chinook salmon, king salmon and steelhead trout. Fishing can be done year-round, but anglers say the best months for steelhead fly-fishing are December through March. For chinook salmon, cast your line in April, May or June.

OR

Grants Pass
A place where the modern and the historic coalesce within a beautiful setting, Grants Pass is an all-things-to-all-people kind of town. Billed as the region's white-water rafting capital, the Rogue River (preserved as a National Wild and Scenic River) snakes through town and provides on-the-water adventures for every mood and moment. For an adrenaline rush and spectacular scenery, visitors can take a 36-mile jet boat trip (two hours) through the dramatic Hellgate Canyon.

Hellgate Canyon on Oregon's Rogue River is known for its serpentine course and steep cliff walls.

Zipline Fun
Zoom over the rugged terrain at high speeds with Rogue Valley ZipLine Adventure. The private park's progressive zipline tours whisk riders over amazing landscapes with stellar views of Crater Lake, Mt. McLoughlin and Table Rocks. Certified guides help guests through the five-zipline course, which can take more than three hours. Mix it up with the Zip, Dip and Sip Tour for a full day of fun. After ziplining, go rafting through Class I and IV rapids of the Rogue River and finish the day with a tasting at the Del Rio Vineyards and Winery.

Autumn colors transform the foliate — including the vineyards — into crimson and gold spectacles.

Animal Rescue

Injured wild animals receive the care they need at Wildlife Images Rehabilitation & Education Center in Grants Pass. The non-profit establishment has an on-site hospital for mammals, birds and reptiles as well as educational programs for visitors. Take a tour and see the residents — including bears, cougars and wolves — while learning about the area's fauna.

Awesome Umpqua

Get more of your adrenaline going on the Umpqua River. Located between Crater Lake and Roseburg, Umpqua is one of the best whitewater rafting destinations in the nation. The most popular rafted stretches offer countless Class III and a few Class IV rapids scattered in between. Raft or kayak along the North Umpqua to weave through dramatic canyons and thick forests, or take it easier in South Umpqua by fishing and viewing wildlife like bald eagles, black-tailed deer, beavers, otters and more. Back on land, the Timber Trail dishes out thrills for mountain bikers.

Below Oregon

For a change of scenery, head underground to the Oregon Caves National Monument and Preserve. Nestled in the Siskiyou Mountains, this geological wonder is packed with stalactites, stalagmites and other jaw-dropping formations. Take a ranger-led tour to learn about geology, fossils and the bats that live inside the caves. Take a three-hour off-trail caving tour to challenge your spelunking skills.

Trails Above the Caves

On the ground above the cave, six trails snake through the countryside with beautiful views of the Siskiyou Mountains. Most of the trails weave in and out of the boundary of the monument preserve. The Cliff Nature Trail leads hikers over marble outcrops, through fir forests and to panoramic views of the Illinois Valley. Take the Big Tree Trail for a great afternoon hike. This steep climb brings hikers to the widest-girthed Douglas-fir tree in Oregon.

Wine Regions

Tour amazing vineyards, sample stellar flavors and enjoy the scenic beauty with a visit to the Beaver State's vintners. With wineries along the majestic Columbia River Gorge and through the fertile Willamette Valley, you'll never run out of abundant scenery and small towns to explore. While Oregon might not be the first state that comes to mind when you think of wine producers, the state's latitude provides the long days of sunshine and crisp nights wine grapes need to mature with perfectly balanced flavors. Find out for yourself at an Oregon tasting room.

Wonderful Wine

Overall, Oregon is home to over 700 wineries producing 70 varieties of grapes, with different regions focused on different variations, including Bordeaux, pinot noir and chardonnay. You'll find 18 American Viticultural Areas (AVAs) running in the valleys between the coastal mountain ranges and the interior ranges and along the Columbia River.

Uncork Wine Month

During May, winemakers and tasters descend on Oregon to celebrate the wine industry. Tasting rooms, restaurants, and vineyards roll out the red carpet, welcoming visitors with unique opportunities to experience Oregon's wines. Local restaurants mark the occasion with special wine flights and concoct divine pairings featuring local wines, while regional wine tastings feature stellar vintages from as many as 40 local vineyards.

Water Fun Instead of Wine Tasting

Several rivers and lakes beckon adventure seekers, tempting visitors to put down the wine glass and pick up the fishing rod or paddle. The Columbia River Gorge is an obvious choice, as the massive river cuts through the Cascade Mountains. Breathtaking waterfalls abound, as do opportunities for paddling and fishing. While boaters can enjoy cruising the wide, flat waters of the main channel, paddlers might find more rollicking adventures in one of the creeks and rivers that cascade down the mountains into the valleys. Anglers can find bass, trout, salmon, steelhead, walleye and more in the Columbia River, its tributaries, and the regional lakes.

Two Wheels or Two Boots

Scenic hiking and biking trails wind through wine country. Hit one of the hundreds of hiking trails. Don't miss Multnomah Falls, located just 30 minutes outside of Portland. A dramatic wisp of water plunges over 600 feet with two falls. A graceful bridge takes you to an overlook. Look up to see the massive first cascade, and then turn around to peer at the plummet below. Bicyclists will want to hit the Willamette Valley Scenic Bikeway or the Historic Columbia River Highway State Trail, both of which cross right through bountiful wine regions. Choose your speed as you coast along country roads.

Getting Away From It All

You'll find wine-tasting opportunity in the state's largest city (Portland) as well as in several small towns. Head to Portland if urban action is your desire. Portland has an eclectic character, reflected in its motto, "Keep Portland weird." Here, you'll find dynamic nightlife and a hip foodie scene, while places like the Japanese Garden and the International Rose Test Garden provide more tranquility.

Tip a Glass in These Towns

For a small town that packs a big viticulture punch, head to McMinnville in the Willamette Valley. The downtown historic district oozes charm, transporting you back to simpler times. Stroll the local shops and galleries or grab a meal in a cozy café. In the Rogue Valley of

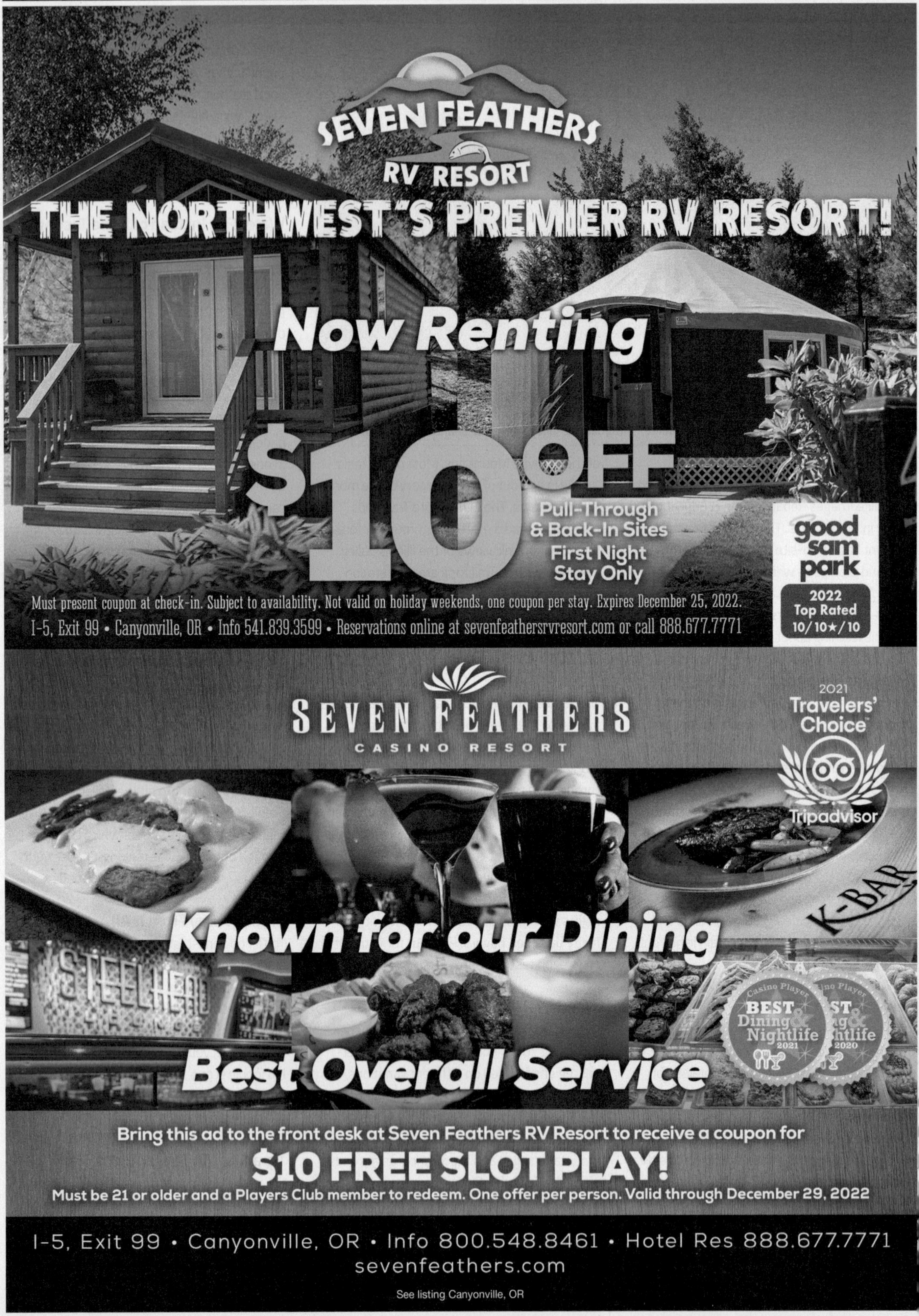
SEVEN FEATHERS
RV RESORT
THE NORTHWEST'S PREMIER RV RESORT!
Now Renting
$10 OFF
Pull-Through
& Back-In Sites
First Night
Stay Only
good sam park
2022
Top Rated
10/10★/10
Must present coupon at check-in. Subject to availability. Not valid on holiday weekends, one coupon per stay. Expires December 25, 2022.
I-5, Exit 99 • Canyonville, OR • Info 541.839.3599 • Reservations online at sevenfeathersrvresort.com or call 888.677.7771
SEVEN FEATHERS
CASINO RESORT
2021
Travelers' Choice
Tripadvisor
K-BAR
STEELHEAD
Known for our Dining
Casino Player
BEST
Dining & Nightlife
2021
2020
Best Overall Service
Bring this ad to the front desk at Seven Feathers RV Resort to receive a coupon for
$10 FREE SLOT PLAY!
Must be 21 or older and a Players Club member to redeem. One offer per person. Valid through December 29, 2022
I-5, Exit 99 • Canyonville, OR • Info 800.548.8461 • Hotel Res 888.677.7771
sevenfeathers.com
See listing Canyonville, OR

Just 30 minutes outside of Portland, Multnomah Falls is a 611-foot-tall roaring cascade of icy water.

Southern Oregon, Ashland is a gorgeous retreat, offering views of the surrounding mountains and an artsy vibe. Visit during the Oregon Shakespeare Festival (held March through October) for a taste of culture.

Eugene Genius

Head south in the valley and you'll eventually find yourself in Eugene, the second-largest city in Oregon and home to the University of Oregon. This compact town offers plenty of interesting things to see and do, including the University of Oregon's Museum of Natural and Cultural History, which focuses on the anthropological and natural history of the region. The Native Plant Courtyard contains flora that represents each of Oregon's regions. During the weekend, visit the Eugene Saturday Market, which offers local crafts and food carts, plus plenty of live entertainment.

Terrific Trees

Can't get enough of Oregon greenery? Head southeast of Eugene to the 209-acre Mt. Pisgah Arboretum, which is a living tree museum featuring riverside paths through evergreen forests and wildflower meadows on the slopes of Mt. Pisgah. Each fall, the Arboretum hosts the Mushroom Festival, with over 400 varieties of wild fungus starring in the celebration.

Get Moving

Burn off those wine-and-cheese calories on the trail. Eugene is home to the Spencer Butte, a 1.7-mile loop hike that's at the edge of the city. The steep hike takes you to a summit with stellar views of the surrounding area. For a forested setting, Hendricks Park features a rhododendron garden with some flowers towering over 6 feet.

Mountainous Country

The Klamath, Cascade and Coastal mountain ranges converge in the beautiful Umpqua Valley. If you look closer though, you'll realize this isn't a valley at all. Sprawling 65 miles from north to south, the Umpqua is actually a vast collection of hills and river drainages. Locals refer to it as the "Hundred Valleys of the Umpqua," which paints a more accurate picture of the area.

Dropping a Line

Ready to take a break from all that tasting? Swap your wine glass for a fishing rod and journey to the fabled waters of the Umpqua River. Made up of the South Umpqua, North Umpqua and Main Umpqua, this river is one of Oregon's top fly-fishing spots with salmon and steelhead ready for the taking throughout the year. Hikers will want to traverse the North Umpqua Trail, a 79-mile path that snakes along the river's edge.

Buzzing With Wineries

In the valley's north end, Elkton enjoys a concentration of four wineries, producing everything from Riesling to Pinot Noir to Baco Noir. It's estimated that the area has the highest number of wineries per capita, and visitors are welcome to tour the region to explore the local vintages.

Crashing Currents

Witness "Colliding Rivers" when you follow the waterway about 48 miles south. The nickname describes the contact point between the north-flowing Little River and a south-flowing segment of the North Umpqua River. The two rivers merge at a nearly head-on angle, resulting in a turbulent confluence of two strong currents. The Colliding Rivers Information Center, housed in the Glide Ranger Station, offers insights into the geological history of the region and the people who have made the area their home.

FOR MORE INFORMATION

Oregon Tourism Commission, 800-547-7842, www.traveloregon.com
Oregon Coast Visitors Association, 888-628-2101, www.visittheoregoncoast.com
Central Oregon, 800-800-8334, www.visitcentraloregon.com
Eugene/Cascades Coast, 800-547-5445, www.eugenecascadescoast.org
Travel Salem, 503-581-4325, www.travelsalem.com
Oregon National Historic Trail, 505-988-6098, www.nps.gov/oreg
Travel Portland, 77-678-5263, www.travelportland.com
Travel Southern Oregon, 541-708-1994, www.southernoregon.org
Oregon Wine Board, 503-228-8336, www.oregonwine.org

Travelers enjoy a glass of red wine after a day of fun in Oregon's vineyard-rich Willamette Valley.

OR

Oregon

AGNESS — D1 *Curry*

AGNESS RV PARK **Ratings: 8/9★/8.5** (Campground) Avail: 44 full hkups (30/50 amps). 2021 rates: $26 to $34. (541)247-2813, 4215 Agness Rd, Agness, OR 97406

ALBANY — B2 *Linn*

ALBANY See also Salem.

ALBANY-CORVALLIS KOA **Ratings: 8.5/8.5/8** (Campground) 77 Avail: 55 full hkups, 22 W, 22 E (30/50 amps). 2021 rates: $45 to $49. (800)562-8526, 33775 Oakville Rd SW, Albany, OR 97321

BLUE OX RV PARK

Ratings: 10/9★/9 (RV Park) From jct I-5 & Hwy 20 (exit 233): Go 1/8 mi E on Hwy 20, then 500 ft N on Price Rd (R). **FAC:** paved rds. (149 spaces). Avail: 30 paved, 29 pull-thrus, (29x66), back-ins (30x70), 30 full hkups (30/50 amps), seasonal sites, cable, WiFi @ sites, laundry, LP gas. **REC:** heated pool, boating nearby. Pets OK. Partial handicap access. No tents. Big rig sites. 2021 rates: $45.52 to $48.93, Military discount.
(541)926-2886 Lat: 44.63279, Lon: -123.05064
4000 Blue Ox Drive SE, Albany, OR 97322
theblueoxrvpark.com
See ad page 737

KNOX BUTTE RV PARK **Ratings: 9/9★/9** (RV Park) Avail: 16 full hkups (30/50 amps). 2021 rates: $47. (541)928-9033, 125 Expo Parkway NE, Albany, OR 97322

ALSEA — B2 *Benton*

SALMONBERRY CAMPGROUND (BENTON COUNTY PARK) (Public) From town, W 26 mi on Alsea Hwy/Hwy 34 (L). Avail: 13 E (30/50 amps). 2021 rates: $22 to $32. May 01 to Nov 01. (541)766-6871

ARLINGTON — A4 *Gilliam*

PORT OF ARLINGTON RV & MARINA PARK (Public) From Jct of I-84 & Arlington Exit (137), N 1.1 mi on Arlington Port Rd (L). Avail: 11 full hkups (30 amps). 2021 rates: $30. (541)454-2868

ASHLAND — D2 *Jackson*

ASHLAND See also Eagle Point, Gold Hill, Phoenix & White City, OR; Hornbrook, CA.

ASHLAND'S CREEKSIDE CAMPGROUND & RV PARK **Ratings: 9/9★/8** (Campground) 20 Avail: 6 full hkups, 14 W, 14 E (30 amps). 2021 rates: $37 to $48. (541)488-1785, 5310 Hwy 66, Ashland, OR 97520

RV Park ratings you can rely on!

EMIGRANT LAKE RECREATION AREA (JACKSON COUNTY PARK) (Public) From Jct of I-5 & SR-66, SE 5 mi on SR-66 (L). Avail: 32 full hkups (50 amps). 2021 rates: $30. (541)774-8183

GRIZZLY PARK AT HOWARD PRAIRIE LAKE (JACKSON COUNTY PARK) (Public) From town, E 28 mi on Dead Indian Memorial Rd to Hyatt Prairie Rd, S 2 mi (R). 21 Avail: Pit toilets. 2021 rates: $18. (541)774-8183

HYATT LAKE CAMPGROUND (BLM) (Public Corps) From Jct of I-5 & SR-66, E 16 mi on SR-66, Green Springs Hwy to East Hyatt Lake Rd, N 4 mi (L). 56 Avail. 2021 rates: $12 to $15. May 15 to Oct 01. (541)618-2200

KLUM LANDING (JACKSON COUNTY PARK) (Public) From town, E 19 mi on Dead Indian Memorial Rd. to Hyatt Prairie Rd, S 2 mi (R). 30 Avail. 2021 rates: $20. May 13 to Sep 30. (541)774-8183

THE POINT RV CAMPGROUND (JACKSON COUNTY PARK) (Public) From jct I-5 (exit 14) and Hwy 66: Go 4 mi SE on Hwy 66, 3.5 mi to Emigrant Lake turnoff (L). Avail: 32 full hkups (50 amps). 2021 rates: $30. (541)774-8183

WILLOW POINT PARK (Public) From town, E 28 mi on Dead Indian Memorial Lake to Hyatt Prairie Rd, S 2 mi (R). 41 Avail: Pit toilets. 2021 rates: $18. Apr 22 to Oct 30. (541)774-8183

ASTORIA — A2 *Clatsup*

ASTORIA See also Cannon Beach, Gearhart, Hammond, Seaside & Warrenton, OR; Chinook, Ilwaco, Long Beach, Ocean Park & Seaview, WA.

LEWIS & CLARK RV PARK & GOLF **Ratings: 8/9★/9** (RV Park) Avail: 35 full hkups (30/50 amps). 2021 rates: $36 to $44. (503)338-3386, 92294 Youngs River Rd, Astoria, OR 97103

AURORA — B2 *Marion*

AURORA ACRES RV RESORT **Ratings: 9/9★/7.5** (RV Park) Avail: 14 full hkups (30/50 amps). 2021 rates: $37 to $42. (503)855-0664, 21599 Dolores Way NE, Aurora, OR 97002

BAKER CITY — B5 *Baker*

A-FRAME RV PARK **Ratings: 7/8★/7.5** (RV Park) 25 Avail: 22 full hkups, 3 W, 3 E (30/50 amps). 2021 rates: $38 to $41. (541)523-3236, 42534 N Cedar Rd, Baker City, OR 97814

MT VIEW RV ON THE OREGON TRAIL

Ratings: 10/10★/9 (RV Park) From Jct of I-84 & Campbell St (exit 304), W 1.5 mi on Campbell St to 10th St, N 1 mi to Hughes Ln, E 1000 ft (R) After turning in, office is 300 feet straight ahead. Elev 3405 ft.

YOUR HUB FOR OREGON TRAIL ADVENTURE
EZ off I-84 to enjoy exploring sites along the Oregon Trail & Nat'l Scenic Byways. Feel the thrill of Hells Canyon on a jetboat tour, visit Ghost Towns or experience the small-town charm of Baker City & all it has to offer!

FAC: paved rds. (97 spaces). Avail: 77 paved, 45 pull-thrus, (26x70), back-ins (28x65), 73 full hkups, 4 W, 4 E (30/50 amps), seasonal sites, cable, WiFi @ sites, $, tent sites, dump, laundry, groc, LP gas. **REC:** heated pool, hot tub, playground. Pets OK. Partial handicap access. Big rig sites, eco-friendly. 2021 rates: $50 to $55, Military discount.
(541)523-4824 Lat: 44.79564, Lon: -117.84140
2845 Hughes Ln, Baker City, OR 97814
www.mtviewrv.com
See ad page 738

BANDON — D1 *Coos*

BANDON BY THE SEA RV PARK

Ratings: 8/9★/9.5 (RV Park) Avail: 50 full hkups (30/50 amps). 2021 rates: $52 to $67. (541)347-5155, 49612 Hwy 101 S, Bandon, OR 97411

BULLARDS BEACH

(Public State Park) From Jct of US-101 & Hwy 42S (N end of town), N 2.3 mi on US-101, at MP-259 1/4 (L). **FAC:** paved rds. Avail: 185 paved, back-ins (28x64), 103 full hkups, 82 W, 82 E (30/50 amps), tent sites, rentals, dump, firewood. **REC:** Coquille River: fishing, boating nearby. Pet restrict (Q). Partial handicap access, 10 day max stay. 2021 rates: $29 to $31.
(800)551-6949 Lat: 43.15195, Lon: -124.39527
56487 Hwy 101 N, Bandon, OR 97411
oregonstateparks.org

COQUILLE RIVER RV PARK **Ratings: 6/10★/8.5** (RV Park) 43 Avail: 43 W, 43 E (30/50 amps). 2021 rates: $40 to $60. (541)207-1730, 83202 North Bank Lane, Bandon, OR 97411

BAY CITY — B2 *Tillamook*

BAY CITY See also Cannon Beach, Cloverdale, Garibaldi, Pacific City, Rockaway Beach & Tillamook.

BEND — C3 *Deschutes*

A SPOTLIGHT Introducing Central Oregon's colorful attractions appearing at the front of this state section.

BEND See also Crooked River Ranch & Redmond.

BEND SUNRIVER RV

Ratings: 7.5/7/7.5 (Membership Park) 40 Avail: 40 W, 40 E (30/50 amps). 2021 rates: $45 to $70. (888)563-7040, 17480 S Century Dr, Bend, OR 97707

BEND/SISTERS GARDEN RV RESORT

Ratings: 10/10★/10 (RV Resort) From Jct of US Hwy 97 & US Hwy 20 (Exit 135A): Go W 14 ¾ mi on US Hwy 20 (L). Elev 3200 ft.

VACATION YEAR ROUND IN BEND!!
Mild summers, snow-capped mountains, spectacular fall color & bright blue skies. Snow-skiing & sledding. Great rainbow trout fishing, whitewater rafting, rock climbing, antiquing, golfing, shopping, dining and so much more!!!

FAC: paved rds. (99 spaces). Avail: 96 paved, patios, 66 pull-thrus, (30x70), back-ins (30x45), 96 full hkups (30/50 amps), seasonal sites, cable, WiFi @ sites, rentals, laundry, groc, LP gas, fire rings, firewood. **REC:** heated pool, hot tub, Branch Water Lake: fishing, boating nearby, playground, hunting nearby. Pet restrict (Q). Partial handicap access. No tents. Big rig sites, eco-friendly. 2021 rates: $44 to $71, Military discount.
(541)516-3036 Lat: 44.25039, Lon: -121.48825
67667 Hwy 20, Bend, OR 97703
www.bendsistersgardenrv.com
See ad pages 729, 734

CROWN VILLA RV RESORT **Ratings: 9/10★/9** (RV Park) Avail: 113 full hkups (30/50 amps). 2021 rates: $45 to $120. (888)991-5349, 60801 Brosterhous Rd, Bend, OR 97702

EXPO CENTER RV PARK

(Public) From jct Hwy 97 & Hwy 20 (N end of Bend): Go 12 mi NE on Hwy 97 to Airport Way (Exit 124), then go 1/2 mi SE on Airport Way to park (R). Elev 3096 ft.**FAC:** paved rds. Avail: 105 paved, patios, 50 pull-thrus, (28x70), back-ins (20x55), 105 full hkups (30/50 amps), tent sites, laundry. **REC:** boating nearby. Pets OK. Partial handicap access. Big rig sites. 2021 rates: $35. ATM.
(541)585-1569 Lat: 44.23328, Lon: -121.18745
4690 SW 19th St, Redmond, OR 97756
expo.deschutes.org/rv
See primary listing at Redmond and ad page 732

SCANDIA RV PARK

Ratings: 9/9.5★/9 (RV Park) N-bnd: From Jct of Hwy 97 & Bus 97 (S of town), N 1 mi on Bus 97 (L); or W-bnd: From Jct of Hwy 20 (From Burns) & Bus 97, S 2.2 mi on Bus 97 (R). Elev 3400 ft.**FAC:** paved rds. (111 spaces). Avail: 46 paved, 14 pull-thrus, (25x60), back-ins (24x60), accepts full hkup units only, 46 full hkups (30/50 amps), seasonal sites, cable, WiFi @ sites, laundry. **REC:** boating nearby, rec open to public. Pet restrict (B). Partial handicap access. No tents. Big rig sites, eco-friendly. 2021 rates: $44 to $66, Military discount.
(541)382-6206 Lat: 44.03025, Lon: -121.31153
61415 S 3rd St (US BUS 97), Bend, OR 97702
www.scandiarv.com
See ad page 733

THE CAMP **Ratings: 7/10★/9** (RV Park) Avail: 21 full hkups (30/50 amps). 2021 rates: $55 to $95. (541)382-2335, 305 NE Burnside Ave, Bend, OR 97701

TUMALO (Public State Park) From Jct of US-20 & US-97 (N of town), NW 3.7 mi on US-20 to Cook Ave (MP 14 3/4), SW 1.1 mi (L). Avail: 23 full hkups (30 amps). 2021 rates: $33. (800)452-5687

BLUE RIVER — C2 *Lane*

HOLIDAY FARM RV RESORT **Ratings: 8/9.5★/9** (Condo Park) Avail: 16 full hkups (30/50 amps). 2021 rates: $45. (541)822-3726, 54432 McKenzie Hwy, Blue River, OR 97413

PATIO RV PARK **Ratings: 7.5/UI/7.5** (RV Park) Avail: 24 full hkups (30/50 amps). 2021 rates: $34 to $41. (541)822-3596, 55636 McKenzie River Dr, Blue River, OR 97413

Like Us on Facebook.

BOARDMAN — A4 *Morrow*

BOARDMAN MARINA & RV PARK

good sam park **Ratings: 8.5/8.5★/10** (Public) From Jct of I-84 & Exit 164 (Main St), N 0.8 mi on Main St over RR tracks Bridge, stay left at fork (R). **FAC:** paved rds. Avail: 63 paved, patios, 15 pull-thrus, (31x80), back-ins (30x50), 63 full hkups (30/50 amps), WiFi @ sites, tent sites, dump, laundry, fire rings, firewood. **REC:** Columbia River: swim, fishing, marina, kayaking/canoeing, boating nearby, playground, rec open to public. Pets OK. Partial handicap access. Big rig sites, 14 day max stay. 2021 rates: $45, Military discount.
(541)481-7217 Lat: 45.84338, Lon: -119.70760
1 W Marine Dr, Boardman, OR 97818
boardmanparkandrec.com
See ad page 741

BONANZA — D3 *Klamath*

GERBER RESERVOIR (BLM) (Public Corps) From town: Go 11 mi E on E Langell Valley Rd, then 8.5 mi N on Gerber Rd (R). 50 Avail: Pit toilets. 2021 rates: $7. (541)883-6916

BROOKINGS — E1 *Curry*

A SPOTLIGHT Introducing Oregon's South Coast's colorful attractions appearing at the front of this state section.

ALFRED A. LOEB (Public State Park) From Jct of US-101 & N Bank Chetco River Rd, NE 8 mi on N Bank Chetco River Rd (R). 48 Avail: 48 W, 48 E (20 amps). 2021 rates: $22 to $24. (800)551-6949

ATRIVERS EDGE RV RESORT

good sam park **Ratings: 9/9.5★/9.5** (RV Park) From Jct of US-101 & S Bank Chetco River Rd (S end of Chetco River Bridge): Go E 1.5 mi on S Bank Chetco River Rd (L). Caution: S-bnd, enter S Bank Chetco Rd from R turn.

PARK YOUR RV BY THE CHETCO RIVER
AtRivers Edge offers a true resort feel from our beautiful multi-purpose building, remodeled restrooms, game field, paved sites, landscaping. At the river - fish, swim your dogs, launch a kayak. Relax by a riverbank fire pit.

FAC: paved rds. (110 spaces). 80 Avail: 30 paved, 50 all weather, patios, 18 pull-thrus, (24x60), back-ins (30x50), 80 full hkups (30/50 amps), seasonal sites, cable, WiFi @ sites, rentals, shower$, laundry, LP gas, firewood. **REC:** Chetco River: fishing, kayaking/canoeing, boating nearby. Pet restrict (Q). Partial handicap access. No tents. Big rig sites, eco-friendly. 2021 rates: $51 to $55, Military discount.
(541)469-3356 Lat: 42.07092, Lon: -124.25274
98203 S. Bank Chetco River Rd., Brookings, OR 97415
www.atriversedge.com
See ad page 750

DRIFTWOOD RV PARK **Ratings: 9/10★/8.5** (RV Park) Avail: 66 full hkups (30/50 amps). 2021 rates: $45 to $49. (541)469-9089, 16011 Lower Harbor Rd, Brookings, OR 97415

HARRIS BEACH (Public State Park) From Jct of US-101 & N Bank Chetco Bridge, N 2.2 mi on US-101 to Harris Beach State Park Rd (L). 90 Avail: 65 full hkups, 25 W, 25 E (30 amps). 2021 rates: $30 to $32. (800)452-5687

PORT OF BROOKINGS HARBOR BEACHFRONT RV PARK (Public) N-bnd: From OR border: Go N 3.8 mi on US-101 to Benham Ln, then W 0.6 mi to Boat Basin Rd, then N 0.2 mi (L); or S-bnd: From S end of Chetco River Bridge on US-101: Go W 1 mi on Lower Harbor Rd to Boat Basin Rd, N 0.2 mi (R). 85 Avail: 76 full hkups, 9 W, 9 E (30/50 amps). 2021 rates: $36 to $51. (541)469-5867

PORTSIDE BROOKINGS RV PARK **Ratings: 9/9.5★/8.5** (RV Park) Avail: 15 full hkups (30/50 amps). 2021 rates: $45 to $60. (541)469-6616, 16219 Lower Harbor Rd, Brookings, OR 97415

RIVERSIDE RV RESORT **Ratings: 8/7/8.5** (RV Park) Avail: 12 full hkups (30/50 amps). 2021 rates: $36 to $49. (541)469-4799, 97666 N Bank Chetco River Rd, Brookings, OR 97415

BURNS — C4 *Harney*

BURNS See also Frenchglen.

BURNS RV PARK

good sam park **Ratings: 9/9★/9.5** (RV Park) From Jct of US-20/395 & Hwy 78 (in town), NE 1 mi on US-20/395, NE city limits (R). Elev 4150 ft.**FAC:** all weather rds. Avail: 52 all weather, patios, 20 pull-thrus, (30x75), back-ins (40x60), 48 full hkups, 4 W, 4 E (30/50 amps), cable, WiFi @ sites, tent sites, rentals, dump, laundry, groc. **REC:** hunting nearby. Pet restrict (Q). Big rig sites, eco-friendly. 2021 rates: $41 to $46.54, Military discount.
(541)573-7640 Lat: 43.59789, Lon: -119.04924
1273 Seneca Dr, Burns, OR 97720
burnsrvpark.net
See ad page 740

BUTTE FALLS — D2 *Jackson*

WILLOW LAKE RESORT (Public) From Butte Falls: Go 8 mi SE on Fish Lake Road (R). 63 Avail: 19 full hkups, 12 W, 12 E (30 amps). 2021 rates: $20 to $30. Apr 15 to Oct 31. (541)774-8183

CAMP SHERMAN — B3 *Jefferson*

CAMP SHERMAN RV PARK **Ratings: 7/8★/8** (RV Park) 21 Avail: 11 full hkups, 10 W, 10 E (30/50 amps). 2021 rates: $38 to $45. (541)595-6514, 25635 SW Forest Service Rd. #1419, Camp Sherman, OR 97730

CANNON BEACH — A2 *Clatsop*

CANNON BEACH See also Astoria, Garibaldi, Gearhart, Hammond, Rockaway Beach, Seaside & Warrenton, OR; Chinook, WA.

CANNON BEACH RV RESORT

good sam park **Ratings: 10/10★/10** (Public) From Jct of US-26 & US-101 (N of town): Go S 4 mi on US-101 to 2nd Cannon Beach exit (L) (MP-29.5), then E 200 ft (L). Avail: 99 full hkups (30/50 amps). 2021 rates: $49 to $71. (800)847-2231

CANYONVILLE — D2 *Douglas*

CHARLES V STANTON PARK AND CAMPGROUND (DOUGLAS COUNTY PARK) (Public) From town: Go 1 mi N on Hwy 99. From I-5 northbound take exit 99. From I-5 southbound take exit 101. Avail: 20 full hkups. 2021 rates: $19 to $29. (541)957-7001

SEVEN FEATHERS RV RESORT

good sam park **Ratings: 10/10★/10** (RV Resort) S-Bnd: From Jct of I-5 (exit 99) to Quintioosa Blvd (R); N-Bnd: From Jct of I-5 & exit 99, Go N on Frontage Rd, then under freeway 0.2 mi to Quintioosa Blvd (L).

FIRST CLASS RV RESORT WITH CASINO
In the 'Land of Umpqua' we are nestled in a canyon of Douglas fir and pines where their fragrance lingers long after quiet hours. We are located off I-5 at exit 99 in Canyonville. Casino, dining, wine tasting tours, spa, pool

FAC: paved rds. Avail: 191 paved, patios, 104 pull-thrus, (30x60), back-ins (30x55), accepts full hkup units only, 191 full hkups (30/50 amps), WiFi @ sites, rentals, dump, laundry, groc, LP gas, restaurant. **REC:** heated pool, hot tub, Jordan Creek: playground, rec open to public. Pet restrict (Q). Partial handicap access. No tents. Big rig sites, 28 day max stay, eco-friendly. 2021 rates: $69 to $79, Military discount. ATM.
(541)839-3599 Lat: 42.94232, Lon: -123.29254
325 Quintioosa Blvd, Canyonville, OR 97417
www.sevenfeathersrvresort.com
See ad page 756

Things to See and Do

SEVEN FEATHERS CASINO RESORT 24 hour casino with slots, table games, Bingo, Keno, Poker, non-smoking casino area, 5 restaurants, 298 guest room hotel, pool, hot tubs, fitness center, River Rock Spa & Salon, live entertainment, and Good Sam 10-10-10 rated RV Resort. Partial handicap access. RV accessible. Restrooms. Food. Hours: 24 hours. ATM.
(800)548-8461 Lat: 42.94082, Lon: -123.28526
146 Chief Miwaleta Ln, Canyonville, OR 97417
www.sevenfeathers.com
See ad page 756

CASCADE LOCKS — A3 *Hood River*

CASCADE LOCKS KOA **Ratings: 9/8★/7** (Campground) 81 Avail: 69 full hkups, 12 W, 12 E (30/50 amps). 2021 rates: $46.11 to $53.89. Mar 20 to Oct 13. (800)562-8698, 841 NE Forest Lane, Cascade Locks, OR 97014

CASCADE LOCKS MARINE PARK CAMPGROUND (Public) From Jct of I-84 & Wanapa St (Cascade Locks exit), E 0.5 mi on Wanapa St (L) Caution: 12' vertical clearance at entrance to park. 15 Avail: 11 W, 11 E. 2021 rates: $25 to $35. (541)374-8619

Go to GoodSam.com/Trip-Planner for Trip Routing.

CAVE JUNCTION — D2 *Josephine*

COUNTRY HILLS RESORT **Ratings: 4.5/5/8.5** (Campground) 20 Avail: 20 W, 20 E (30/50 amps). 2021 rates: $32 to $36. (541)592-3406, 7901 Caves Highway, Cave Junction, OR 97523

LAUGHING ALPACA CAMPGROUND AND RV PARK **Ratings: 6.5/8.5★/6.5** (Campground) Avail: 13 full hkups (30 amps). 2021 rates: $35 to $40. (541)592-2656, 28288 Redwood Hwy, Cave Junction, OR 97523

CENTRAL POINT — D2 *Jackson*

SOUTHERN OREGON RV PARK (Public) From Exit 33 on I-5: Go .2 mi E on Pine St to Penninger Rd, then 1 m NW on Penninger Rd to park (R). Avail: 92 full hkups (30/50 amps). 2021 rates: $38 to $40. (541)423-8115

CHARLESTON — C1 *Coos*

BASTENDORFF BEACH PARK (COOS COUNTY PARK) (Public) From town, SW 10 mi on Cape Arago Rd, follow signs (R). 74 Avail: 74 W, 74 E (30 amps). 2021 rates: $20 to $30. (541)888-5353

CHARLESTON MARINA & RV PARK - PORT OF COOS BAY **Ratings: 8.5/8.5★/8** (Public) From Jct of US-101 & Commercial Ave (in Coos Bay), follow Ocean Beaches/Charleston signs: Go W 9 mi to Boat Basin Rd, then N 0.2 mi to Kingfisher Rd, then NE 0.1 mi on Kingfisher Rd (L). Avail: 100 full hkups (30/50 amps). 2021 rates: $38.41 to $42.56. (541)888-2548

OCEANSIDE BEACHFRONT RV RESORT **Ratings: 8/9★/8.5** (Campground) Avail: 64 full hkups (30/50 amps). 2021 rates: $40 to $92. (541)888-2598, 90281 Cape Arago Hwy, Coos Bay, OR 97420

SUNSET BAY (Public State Park) From Jct of US-101 & Charleston Harbor (beaches) exit (in Coos Bay or North Bend), W 11.7 mi on Cape Arago Hwy/Charleston Harbor Hwy to W-end Charleston Bridge MP-12 (L). 63 Avail: 29 full hkups, 34 W, 34 E (30 amps). 2021 rates: $29 to $31. (800)452-5687

CHILOQUIN — D3 *Klamath*

COLLIER MEMORIAL (Public State Park) From Jct US-97 & SR-62: Go 8 mi N on US-97 at MP 243 3/4 (R). Avail: 46 full hkups (30/50 amps). 2021 rates: $29. Apr 15 to Oct 01. (541)783-2471

WATERWHEEL RV PARK AND CAMPGROUND

good sam park **Ratings: 9/9.5/9** (RV Park) 27 Avail: 9 full hkups, 18 W, 18 E (30/50 amps). 2021 rates: $42. Mar 01 to Dec 01. (541)783-2738, 200 Williamson River Dr, Chiloquin, OR 97624

CLATSKANIE — A2 *Columbia*

CLATSKANIE RIVER INN & RV PARK **Ratings: 9/NA/8** (RV Park) Avail: 10 full hkups (30/50 amps). 2021 rates: $55. (503)728-9000, 600 East Columbia River Hwy, Clatskanie, OR 97016

CLOVERDALE — B2 *Tillamook*

CAMPER COVE GARDEN RV PARK & CAMPGROUND **Ratings: 4.5/7★/8.5** (Campground) 25 Avail: 11 full hkups, 14 W, 14 E (30/50 amps). 2021 rates: $36. (503)398-5334, 19620 Hwy 101 South, Cloverdale, OR 97112

PACIFIC CITY RV CAMPING RESORT

good sam park **Ratings: 7.5/7/7** (Membership Park) 25 Avail: 25 W, 25 E (30/50 amps). 2021 rates: $55 to $82.73. (888)563-7040, 30000 Sandlake Rd, Cloverdale, OR 97112

COBURG — C2 *Lane*

Travel Services

CAMPING WORLD OF COBURG/EUGENE As the nation's largest retailer of RV supplies, accessories, services and new and used RVs, Camping World is committed to making your total RV experience better. **SERVICES:** RV, tire, RV appliance, staffed RV wash, restrooms. RV Sales. RV supplies, LP gas, dump, emergency parking, RV accessible. Hours: 9am - 7pm.
(877)465-6570 Lat: 44.131750, Lon: -123.052515
90855 Roberts Road, Coburg, OR 97408
www.campingworld.com

COOS BAY — C1 *Coos*

COOS BAY See also Bandon, Charleston, Lakeside, North Bend & Reedsport.

ALDER ACRES RV PARK **Ratings: 9/10★/9.5** (RV Park) Avail: 30 full hkups (30/50 amps). 2021 rates: $45. (541)269-0999, 1800 28th Ct, Coos Bay, OR 97420

OR

COOS BAY (CONT)

BAY POINT LANDING

Ratings: 10/10★/10 (RV Park) From jct US Hwy 101 & Commercial St (in Coos Bay): Go 1/4 mi NW on Commercial St, then 1 block S on 7th, then 1/4 mi W on Central, then 2-3/4 mi NW on Ocean Blvd, then 1/2 mi W on Newmark, then 1-1/2 mi SW on Cape Arago (R). **FAC:** all weather rds. Avail: 142 all weather, patios, 24 pull-thrus, (41x70), back-ins (39x70), 142 full hkups (30/50 amps), cable, WiFi @ sites, rentals, laundry, LP gas, fire rings, firewood. **REC:** heated pool, Coos Bay: fishing, kayaking/canoeing, boating nearby, playground. Pet restrict (Q). No tents. Big rig sites. 2021 rates: $49 to $140, Military discount.
(541)351-9160 Lat: 43.372709, Lon: -124.291570
92443 Cape Arago Hwy, Coos Bay, OR 97420
baypointlanding.com
See ad this page

THE MILL CASINO HOTEL & RV PARK

Ratings: 10/10★/10 (RV Park) From Jct of Newmark St & US-101: Go N .3 mi on Hwy 101 (R). **FAC:** paved rds. Avail: 102 paved, patios, 70 pull-thrus, (28x62), back-ins (27x40), accepts full hkup units only, 102 full hkups (30/50 amps), cable, WiFi @ sites, rentals, laundry, LP gas, restaurant. **REC:** heated pool, hot tub, Coos Bay: fishing, boating nearby, hunting nearby. Pets OK. Partial handicap access. No tents. Big rig sites, 28 day max stay, eco-friendly. 2021 rates: $50 to $75, Military discount. ATM.
(800)953-4800 Lat: 43.39483, Lon: -124.21910
2665 Tremont Ave, North Bend, OR 97459
www.themillcasino.com
See Primary Listing at North Bend and ad page 726

Travel Services

ALDER ACRES RV PARK STORAGE Secure RV, car and boat storage. Some storage spaces have electricity. Most are pull-through. **RV Storage:** outdoor, secured fencing, electric gate, easy reach keypad, limited access, security cameras, level gravel/paved spaces, power to charge battery, water, compressed air, office. **SERVICES:**. RV supplies, dump. Hours: 5am to 10pm.
Special offers available for Good Sam Members
(888)400-7275 Lat: 43.38081, Lon: -124.24672
1800 28th Ct, Coos Bay, OR 97420
alderacres.com

Things to See and Do

OREGON'S ADVENTURE COAST Coos Bay area information - cities of Coos Bay, North Bend and Charleston. Partial handicap access. RV accessible. Restrooms.. Hours: 9am to 5pm.
(541)269-0215 Lat: 43.36822, Lon: -124.21263
50 Central Ave, Coos Bay, OR 97420
www.oregonsadventurecoast.com

COQUILLE — C1 *Coos*

LAVERNE COUNTY PARK (COOS COUNTY PARK) (Public) From town, N 1 mi on SR-42 to Fairview Rd, N 13 mi (R). 46 Avail: 46 W, 46 E (20 amps). 2021 rates: $20. (541)396-2344

CORVALLIS — B2 *Benton*

BENTON OAK RV PARK (BENTON COUNTY PARK) (Public) From Jct of Hwy 34 & Hwy 20 W (in town): Go SW 3.3 mi on Hwy 20 to 53rd St, then N 1.3 mi (L). 100 Avail: 28 full hkups, 72 W, 72 E (30/50 amps). 2021 rates: $35 to $39.50. (541)766-6259

COTTAGE GROVE — C2 *Lane*

ARMITAGE PARK CAMPGROUND (LANE COUNTY PARK) (Public) From Jct Belt Line Rd & Coburg Rd: Go 1-1/2 mi N on Coburg Rd (L). Avail: 37 full hkups (30/50 amps). 2021 rates: $30 to $33. (541)682-2000

COTTAGE GROVE LAKE - COE/PINE MEADOWS CAMPGROUND (Public Corps) From Jct of I-5 & London Rd (Cottage Grove-exit 172), S 3.5 mi on London Rd to Reservoir Rd, SE 3 mi (R). 92 Avail. 2021 rates: $14 to $22. May 14 to Sep 13. (541)942-8657

DORENA RESERVOIR - COE/SCHWARZ PARK (Public Corps) From jct I-5 (exit 174): Go 4 mi SE on Row River Rd(R). 76 Avail. 2021 rates: $20 to $40. Apr 29 to Sep 11. (541)942-1418

VILLAGE GREEN RESORT & RV PARK **Ratings: 8/NA/6** (RV Park) Avail: 11 full hkups (30 amps). 2021 rates: $38.78. (541)942-2491, 725 Row River Rd, Cottage Grove, OR 97424

CRATER LAKE — D3 *Klamath*

CRATER LAKE See also Chiloquin, Crescent, Crescent Lake, Diamond Lake, Eagle Point, Fort Klamath, Idleyld Park, Klamath Falls, Prospect, Shady Cove & White City.

MAZAMA CAMPGROUND (Public National Park) From Jct of SR-62 & SR-230, NE 25 mi on SR-62 to park access rd, N 0.1 mi to Ranger pay station (R). 214 Avail. 2021 rates: $31. Jun 12 to Sep 28. (541)594-2255

CRATER LAKE NATIONAL PARK — D3 *Klamath*

CRATER LAKE NATIONAL PARK See also Diamond Lake, Fort Klamath, Prospect.

CRESCENT — C3 *Klamath*

BIG PINES RV PARK

Ratings: 8.5/9.5★/10 (RV Park) Avail: 60 full hkups (30/50 amps). 2021 rates: $42. Mar 20 to Oct 31. (541)433-2785, 135151 Hwy 97N, Crescent, OR 97733

CRESCENT LAKE — C3 *Klamath*

CRESCENT JUNCTION RV PARK **Ratings: 7/8.5★/8** (RV Park) Avail: 16 full hkups (30/50 amps). 2021 rates: $25 to $30. May 01 to Oct 31. (541)433-5300, 20030 Crescent Lake Hwy, Crescent Lake, OR 97733

SHELTER COVE RESORT AND MARINA

Ratings: 6.5/7★/8 (Campground) Avail: 74 E (30/50 amps). 2021 rates: $55 to $85. (541)433-2548, 27600 W Odell Lake Rd, Crescent Lake, OR 97733

CRESWELL — C2 *Lane*

MEADOWLARK RV PARK **Ratings: 8.5/9.5★/8** (RV Park) Avail: 12 full hkups (30/50 amps). 2021 rates: $54. (541)525-3348, 298 E Oregon Ave, Creswell, OR 97426

CROOKED RIVER RANCH — B3 *Jefferson*

CROOKED RIVER RANCH RV PARK

Ratings: 9/9.5★/9.5 (RV Park) From Jct of US 97 & Lower Bridge Way (Milepost 115 1/4) in Terrebonne: Go W 2.2 mi on Lower Bridge Way to NW 43 RD St, then N 1.8 mi on Lower Bridge to Chinook Dr, then NW 3.3 mi on Chinook Drive to park signs (R). Elev 2569 ft.**FAC:** paved/gravel rds. Avail: 83 gravel, patios, 16 pull-thrus, (24x60), back-ins (24x60), 63 full hkups, 20 W, 20 E (30/50 amps), WiFi @ sites, tent sites, shower$, dump, laundry, groc, restaurant. **REC:** heated pool, boating nearby, golf, playground, rec open to public. Pet restrict (B). Partial handicap access. Big rig sites. 2021 rates: $38 to $42, Military discount.
(541)923-1441 Lat: 44.427300, Lon: -121.238746
14875 Hayes Rd, Crooked River Ranch, OR 97760
www.crookedriverranch.com
See ad page 733

CULVER — B3 *Jefferson*

CENTRAL OREGON KOA **Ratings: 8.5/9★/9** (Campground) 48 Avail: 30 full hkups, 18 W, 18 E (30/50 amps). 2021 rates: $33 to $59. (541)546-3046, 2435 SW Jericho Ln, Culver, OR 97734

THE COVE PALISADES (Public State Park) From Jct of US-26 & US-97 (S-end of Jordan Rd), S 6.6 mi on US-97 to Iris Ln (MP-103 1/2), W 2.4 mi to SW Feather Dr, NW 1.1 mi to Fisch/Frazier Rd, N 1.5 mi to Jordan Rd (State Park sign), W 6 mi (L). Avail: 85 full hkups (30/50 amps). 2021 rates: $30 to $32. Feb 15 to Dec 15. (800)452-5687

CURTIN — C2 *Douglas*

PASS CREEK RV PARK AND CAMPGROUND (DOUGLAS COUNTY PARK) (Public) From I-5 (exit 163): Go 1/4 mi N on W Marginal Rd. Avail: 30 full hkups. 2021 rates: $17 to $25. (541)957-7001

DEPOE BAY — B1 *Lincoln*

FOGARTY CREEK RV PARK **Ratings: 7/9.5★/8.5** (RV Park) Avail: 12 full hkups (30/50 amps). 2021 rates: $55. (541)764-2228, 3340 N Hwy 101, Depoe Bay, OR 97341

SEA & SAND RV PARK

Ratings: 8/9.5★/9.5 (RV Park) S-bnd: From Jct of US 101 & Hwy 18 (N of Lincoln City), S 13.5 mi on US 101 (R); or N-bnd: From town, N 3.6 mi on US-101 (make U turn, turn about, at Lancer St), S 0.1 mi (R). Note: Up to 40 ft max allowed. **FAC:** all weather rds. (106 spaces). Avail: 85 gravel, 16 pull-thrus, (26x40), back-ins (28x40), 85 full hkups (30/50 amps), seasonal sites, cable, WiFi @ sites, shower$, dump, laundry, groc, fire rings, firewood. **REC:** Pacific Ocean: fishing, boating nearby. Pet restrict (B/Q). Partial handicap access. No tents, 14 day max stay, eco-friendly. 2021 rates: $47 to $82, Military discount.
(541)764-2313 Lat: 44.861083, Lon: -124.03831
4985 N Hwy 101, Depoe Bay, OR 97341
seaandsandrvpark.com
See ad page 746

DETROIT — B3 *Marion*

DETROIT LAKE (Public State Park) From Jct of Hwy 22 & Forest Ave (in town), W 1.8 mi on Hwy 22 to MP-48 1/2 (L). 175 Avail: 107 full hkups, 68 W, 68 E (30 amps). 2021 rates: $29 to $31. Mar 15 to Oct 31. (800)551-6949

DEXTER — C2 *Lane*

DEXTER SHORES RV PARK **Ratings: 7.5/8★/8.5** (RV Park) 20 Avail: 14 full hkups, 6 W, 6 E (30/50 amps). 2021 rates: $34 to $38. (541)937-3711, 39140 Dexter Rd, Dexter, OR 97431

DIAMOND LAKE — D3 *Douglas*

DIAMOND LAKE RESORT & RV PARK **Ratings: 7.5/8.5★/8.5** (RV Park) Avail: 100 full hkups (30/50 amps). 2021 rates: $46 to $49. May 15 to Oct 15. (541)793-3318, 3500 Diamond Lake Loop, Diamond Lake, OR 97731

DODSON — A3 *Hood River*

AINSWORTH (Public State Park) From Jct of I-84 & Historic Hwy (exit 35), S 0.6 mi on Historic Hwy (L). Avail: 40 full hkups (30/50 amps). 2021 rates: $26. Mar 09 to Oct 31. (503)695-2261

EAGLE POINT — D2 *Jackson*

MEDFORD OAKS RV PARK & CABINS **Ratings: 9/8.5/9** (Campground) 39 Avail: 13 full hkups, 26 W, 26 E (30/50 amps). 2021 rates: $30 to $35. (541)826-5103, 7049 Hwy 140, Eagle Point, OR 97524

ELGIN — A5 *Umatilla*

HU-NA-HA RV PARK (Public) From jct Hwy 82 & Cedar St (in town): Go 1/2 mi E on Cedar St (L). Avail: 45 full hkups (30/50 amps). 2021 rates: $25.15 to $35. (541)786-1662

ELKTON — C2 *Douglas*

ELKTON RV PARK **Ratings: 8.5/8★/8.5** (RV Park) 42 Avail: 36 full hkups, 6 W, 6 E (30/50 amps). 2021 rates: $40. (541)584-2832, 450 River Dr, Elkton, OR 97436

ELSIE — A2 *Clatsop*

CLATSOP STATE FOREST/HENRY RIERSON SPRUCE RUN CAMPGROUND (Public State Park) From Jct of US-26 & Spruce Run Rd, S 5 mi on Lower Nehalem Rd (E). 32 Avail: Pit toilets. 2021 rates: $20. May 17 to Sep 16. (503)325-9306

ENTERPRISE — A5 *Wallowa*

ENTERPRISE See also Wallowa.

ESTACADA — B3 *Clackamas*

MILO MCIVER (Public State Park) From Jct of Hwys 224 & 211 (in town), SW 1 mi on Hwy 211 to S Hayden Rd, W 1.3 mi to S Springwater Rd, NW 1.2 mi (R). 44 Avail: 44 W, 44 E (20/30 amps). 2021 rates: $26. Mar 15 to Oct 31. (800)551-6949

PROMONTORY PARK CAMPGROUND (Public) From town, SE 7 mi on SR-224 (R). 46 Avail. 2021 rates: $27. May 15 to Sep 12. (503)630-7229

EUGENE — C2 *Lane*

A SPOTLIGHT Introducing Eugene's colorful attractions appearing at the front of this state section.

EUGENE See also Albany, Cottage Grove, Creswell, Dexter, Junction City & Westfir.

DEERWOOD RV PARK **Ratings: 7.5/9.5★/10** (RV Park) Avail: 65 full hkups (30/50 amps). 2021 rates: $49.95 to $57.25. (541)988-1139, 35059 Seavey Loop Rd, Eugene, OR 97405

EUGENE KAMPING WORLD RV PARK
Ratings: 9/9.5★/9.5 (Campground) From Jct of I-5 & Van Duyn Rd (exit 199): Go W 0.3 mi on Van Duyn Rd/E Pearl St to S Stuart Way, then S 0.2 mi (E). **FAC:** paved rds. (110 spaces). Avail: 60 paved, 55 pull-thrus, (22x65), back-ins (22x40), 47 full hkups, 13 W, 13 E (30/50 amps), seasonal sites, WiFi @ sites, tent sites, dump, laundry, groc, LP gas. **REC:** boating nearby, playground. Pet restrict (B). eco-friendly. 2021 rates: $47 to $49, Military discount.
(541)343-4832 Lat: 44.13420, Lon: -123.05683
90932 S Stuart Way, Coburg, OR 97408
www.eugenekampingworld.com
See ad page 737

EUGENE MOBILE VILLAGE & RV PARK
Ratings: 7/7/7 (RV Area in MH Park) Avail: 19 full hkups (30/50 amps). 2021 rates: $60. (541)747-2257, 4750 Franklin Blvd, Eugene, OR 97403

EUGENE PREMIER RV RESORT
Ratings: 10/10★/9.5 (RV Resort) From Jct of I-5 & Van Duyn Rd (exit 199): Go E 300 ft on Van Duyn Rd (R). **FAC:** paved rds. (193 spaces). Avail: 79 paved, patios, 52 pull-thrus, (33x80), back-ins (25x52), 79 full hkups (30/50 amps), seasonal sites, cable, WiFi @ sites, rentals, dump, laundry, groc, LP gas. **REC:** heated pool, hot tub, pond, fishing, kayaking/canoeing, boating nearby, playground. Pets OK. Partial handicap access. No tents. Big rig sites, eco-friendly. 2021 rates: $69.50 to $104, Military discount.
(541)686-3152 Lat: 44.13462, Lon: -123.04842
33022 Van Duyn Rd, Coburg, OR 97408
www.premierrvresorts.com
See ad page 737

RICHARDSON PARK (LANE COUNTY PARK) (Public) From Jct of Beltline Rd & Hwy 99, N 0.6 mi on Hwy 99 to Clearlake Rd, W 8.5 mi (L). 94 Avail: 94 W, 94 E (30/50 amps). 2021 rates: $25. Apr 15 to Oct 15. (541)682-2000

SHAMROCK RV & MHP VILLAGE **Ratings: 6.5/8★/6** (RV Park) 10 Avail: 10 W, 10 E (30 amps). 2021 rates: $37. (541)747-7473, 4531 Franklin Blvd, Eugene, OR 97403

FAIRVIEW — A2 *Multnomah*

PORTLAND FAIRVIEW RV PARK
Ratings: 10/8/9.5 (RV Park) Avail: 65 full hkups (30/50 amps). 2021 rates: $58 to $72. (888)563-7040, 21401 NE Sandy Blvd, Fairview, OR 97024

Travel Services

CHINOOK RV STORAGE Covered & uncovered storage facility with security including 24 Hr Digital Camera Surveillance, 6' fencing/ barbed wire plus 20' electrified perimeter fence, personalized gate access. **SERVICES:** . Hours: 8am to 6pm.
(503)661-2345 Lat: 45.55403, Lon: -122.42577
23000 NE Marine Dr, Fairview, OR 97024
chinookrvstorage.com
See ad page 743

FLORENCE — C1 *Lane*

A SPOTLIGHT Introducing Oregon's Central Coast's colorful attractions appearing at the front of this state section.

CARL G WASHBURNE (Public State Park) From Jct of US-101 & Hwy 126 (in town), N 15 mi on US-101 to MP-176 (R). 55 Avail: 41 full hkups, 14 W, 14 E (20 amps). 2021 rates: $31 to $33. (541)547-3416

DARLINGS MARINA AND RV RESORT **Ratings: 5.5/6.5/7** (Campground) 23 Avail: 12 full hkups, 11 W, 11 E (30/50 amps). 2021 rates: $38 to $50. (541)997-2841, 4879 Darlings Loop, Florence, OR 97439

HARBOR VISTA CAMPGROUND (LANE COUNTY PARK) (Public) From Jct of US-101 & Hwy 126 (in town), N 1.6 mi on US-101 to 35th St, W 1 mi to Rhododenron Dr, N 0.5 mi to N Jetty Rd, W 0.1 mi to Harbor Vista (L). 44 Avail: 44 W, 44 E (30/50 amps). 2021 rates: $25 to $27.50. (541)682-2000

HECETA BEACH RV PARK
Ratings: 8/9.5★/10 (Campground) Avail: 50 full hkups (30/50 amps). 2021 rates: $48 to $56. (541)997-7664, 4636 Heceta Beach Rd, Florence, OR 97439

JESSIE M HONEYMAN (Public State Park) From Jct of US-101 & Hwy 126 (in town), S 3 mi on Hwy 101 (R). 168 Avail: 47 full hkups, 121 W, 121 E (30/50 amps). 2021 rates: $31 to $33. (800)452-5687

PACIFIC PINES RV PARK & STORAGE
Ratings: 9/10★/9.5 (RV Park) Avail: 31 full hkups (30/50 amps). 2021 rates: $51.67. (541)997-1434, 4044 Hwy 101, Florence, OR 97439

PORT OF SIUSLAW CAMPGROUND & MARINA (Public) From Jct of 101 & Hwy 126: Go S 0.3 mi on Hwy 101 to Nopal (follow brown port signs), then SE 0.2 mi to Harbor St, then E 0.2 mi (E). 104 Avail: 78 full hkups, 23 W, 23 E (30/50 amps). 2021 rates: $32.48 to $39.20. (541)997-3040

SOUTH JETTY RV & CAMPING RESORT
Ratings: 7.5/7.5/8 (Membership Park) 20 Avail: 20 W, 20 E (30/50 amps). 2021 rates: $55 to $70. (888)563-7040, 5010 South Jetty Rd, Florence, OR 97439

WOAHINK LAKE RV RESORT
Ratings: 9.5/9.5★/10 (RV Park) Avail: 65 full hkups (30/50 amps). 2021 rates: $58.41. (541)997-6454, 83570 Hwy 101 S, Florence, OR 97439

FORT KLAMATH — D3 *Klamath*

CRATER LAKE RESORT **Ratings: 7/8★/8** (RV Park) 12 Avail: 5 full hkups, 7 W, 7 E (30/50 amps). 2021 rates: $45 to $55. (541)381-2349, 50711 Hwy 62, Fort Klamath, OR 97626

FOSSIL — B4 *Wheeler*

BEAR HOLLOW PARK (WHEELER COUNTY PARK) (Public) From Town, SE 10 mi on Hwy 19 (R). 20 Avail: Pit toilets. 2021 rates: $5 to $10. (541)763-2010

SHELTON WAYSIDE PARK (WHEELER COUNTY PARK) (Public) From Town, SE 13 mi on Hwy 19 (R). 34 Avail: Pit toilets. 2021 rates: $15 to $20. Apr 15 to Nov 01. (541)763-2010

FOSTER — B2 *Linn*

RIVER BEND PARK (LINN COUNTY PARK) (Public) From Jct of US-228 & Hwy 20 (Sweet Home), 6.3 mi on Hwy 20 to MP 36.4 (L) Online resv. 85 Avail: 74 W, 74 E (30/50 amps). 2021 rates: $26 to $32. (541)967-3917

FRENCHGLEN — D4 *Harney*

PAGE SPRINGS (BLM) (Public Corps) From town: Go 3 mi E on N Steens Mountain Loop Rd (R). 36 Avail: Pit toilets. 2021 rates: $8. (541)573-4400

STEENS MOUNTAIN WILDERNESS RESORT **Ratings: 7.5/10★/9.5** (RV Park) 50 Avail: 38 full hkups, 12 W, 12 E (30/50 amps). 2021 rates: $39 to $44. Mar 01 to Dec 10. (541)493-2415, 35678 Resort Ln, Frenchglen, OR 97736

GARIBALDI — A2 *Tillamook*

BARVIEW JETTY COUNTY PARK (TILLAMOOK COUNTY PARK) (Public) From Jct of SR-6 & US-101, N 14 mi on US-101 to Cedar St, W 0.25 mi (R). Avail: 73 full hkups (30/50 amps). 2021 rates: $16 to $38. (503)322-3522

HARBORVIEW INN & RV PARK **Ratings: 7.5/9.5★/9** (RV Park) Avail: 31 full hkups (30/50 amps). 2021 rates: $35 to $55. (503)322-3251, 302 South 7th Street, Garibaldi, OR 97118

PORT OF GARIBALDI RV PARK **Ratings: 7.5/8★/7** (Public) Front the Jct of US Hwy 1010 and 7th St (in Garibaldi): Go .2 mi S to Biak Ave, then 100 yards E on Biak to park (L). Avail: 48 full hkups (30/50 amps). 2021 rates: $38 to $42. (503)322-3292

THE OLD MILL RV PARK & EVENT CENTER **Ratings: 8/9.5★/8.5** (Campground) 80 Avail: 64 full hkups, 16 W, 16 E (30/50 amps). 2021 rates: $40 to $55.90. (503)322-0322, 210 S 3rd St, Garibaldi, OR 97118

GEARHART — A2 *Clatsop*

BUD'S RV PARK & CAMPGROUND **Ratings: 7/9.5★/8** (Campground) Avail: 10 full hkups (30/50 amps). 2021 rates: $44.99 to $61.99. (503)738-6855, 4412 Hwy 101N, Gearhart, OR 97138

GLIDE — C2 *Douglas*

SUSAN CREEK (BLM) (Public Corps) From east of town limits: Go 12-1/2 mi E on Hwy 138 (North Umpqua Hwy). 29 Avail. 2021 rates: $20. May 15 to Sep 15. (541)440-4930

GOLD BEACH — D1 *Curry*

GOLD BEACH See also Agness, Brookings & Port Orford.

ANGLER'S TRAILER VILLAGE & RV PARK **Ratings: 6/9★/7** (RV Park) Avail: 17 full hkups (30/50 amps). 2021 rates: $35. (541)247-7922, 95706 Jerry's Flat Rd, Gold Beach, OR 97444

FOUR SEASONS RV RESORT **Ratings: 8.5/8.5/9** (RV Park) Avail: 28 full hkups (30/50 amps). 2021 rates: $39 to $54. (541)247-4503, 96526 N Bank Rogue River Rd, Gold Beach, OR 97444

HONEY BEAR BY THE SEA RV RESORT **Ratings: 7.5/8★/9** (Campground) 90 Avail: 64 full hkups, 26 S, 26 E (30/50 amps). 2021 rates: $39.90 to $59.90. (541)247-2765, 34161 Ophir Rd, Gold Beach, OR 97444

INDIAN CREEK RV PARK **Ratings: 8/8★/9** (RV Park) Avail: 50 full hkups (30 amps). 2021 rates: $25 to $40. (541)247-7704, 94680 Jerry's Flat Rd, Gold Beach, OR 97444

KIMBALL CREEK BEND RV RESORT **Ratings: 8/8.5★/9** (RV Park) 33 Avail: 22 full hkups, 11 W, 11 E (30/50 amps). 2021 rates: $35.50 to $53.50. (541)247-7580, 97136 North Bank Rogue River Rd, Gold Beach, OR 97444

OCEANSIDE RV PARK **Ratings: 6.5/8.5★/7** (RV Park) 84 Avail: 27 full hkups, 57 W, 57 E (30 amps). 2021 rates: $51.03 to $60.03. (541)247-2301, 94040 S Jetty Rd, Gold Beach, OR 97444

TURTLE ROCK RV RESORT
Ratings: 8.5/9.5★/9.5 (RV Park) From Jct of Hwy 101 & S end of Rogue River Bridge, S 2.3 mi on Hwy 101 to Hunter Creek Loop, E 0.2 mi (R). **FAC:** gravel rds. Avail: 80 gravel, 22 pull-thrus, (31x60), back-ins (40x45), accepts full hkup units only, 80 full hkups (30/50 amps), cable, WiFi @ sites, tent sites, rentals, dump, laundry, groc, LP gas, fire rings, firewood, restaurant. **REC:** Hunter Creek: swim, kayaking/canoeing, boating nearby. Pet restrict (Q). Partial handicap access. Big rig sites, eco-friendly. 2021 rates: $37 to $83, Military discount.
(541)247-9203 Lat: 42.38902, Lon: -124.41698
28788 Hunter Creek Loop, Gold Beach, OR 97444
www.turtlerockresorts.com
See ad page 750

GOLD HILL — D2 *Jackson*

MEDFORD/GOLD HILL KOA JOURNEY **Ratings: 8/10★/6.5** (Campground) 40 Avail: 20 full hkups, 20 W, 20 E (30/50 amps). 2021 rates: $43 to $46. (541)855-7710, 12297 Blackwell Rd, Central Point, OR 97502

ROCK POINT RV PARK **Ratings: 7/NA/8** (RV Park) Avail: 12 full hkups (30/50 amps). 2021 rates: $39. (541)855-4300, 97 Rogue River Hwy, Gold Hill, OR 97525

GRAND RONDE — B2 *Polk*

WANDERING SPIRIT RV PARK & PARK MODEL SALES **Ratings: 7.5/8/6.5** (RV Park) Avail: 15 full hkups (30/50 amps). 2021 rates: $50. (503)879-5700, 28800 Salmon River Hwy, Grand Ronde, OR 97347

GRANTS PASS — D2 *Josephine*

GRANTS PASS See also Cave Junction, Gold Hill, Rogue River, Sunny Valley & White City.

GRANTS PASS KOA JOURNEY **Ratings: 7.5/8.5★/9** (RV Park) Avail: 38 full hkups (30/50 amps). 2021 rates: $49 to $70. (541)479-7974, 699 Jumpoff Joe Creek Rd, Grants Pass, OR 97526

GRIFFIN PARK (Public) From Jct of US-199 & Riverbanks Rd, N 6 mi on Riverbanks Rd to Griffin Rd, E 0.1 mi (L). Avail: 14 full hkups (30/50 amps). 2021 rates: $35 to $45. (541)474-5285

JACK'S LANDING RV RESORT
Ratings: 8/9.5★/9.5 (RV Park) From Jct of I-5 and Hwy 99 (exit 58/6th St),Go S 0.4 mi on Hwy 99/6th St to Hillcrest, then E 0.1 mi to 7th St, then N 0.3 mi to NE Morgan Ln, then E 0.1 mi on NE Morgan Ln (E). **FAC:** paved rds. (54 spaces). Avail: 15 paved, patios, 15 pull-thrus, (23x80), accepts full hkup units only, 15 full hkups (50 amps), seasonal sites, cable, WiFi @ sites, laundry. **REC:** boating nearby. Pet restrict (B/Q). Partial handicap access. No tents. Big rig sites. 2021 rates: $45.
(541)472-1144 Lat: 42.46175, Lon: -123.31839
247 NE Morgan Ln, Grants Pass, OR 97526
www.jackslandingrvresort.com
See ad page 751

GRANTS PASS (CONT)

JOSEPHINE COUNTY FAIRGROUNDS RV PARK (Public) From: Jct of I-5 & US-199/Redwood Hwy (Exit 55), Go 4.5 mi W on US-199/Redwood Hwy (R). 40 Avail: 30 full hkups, 10 W, 10 E (30/50 amps). 2021 rates: $20 to $25. (541)476-3215

MOON MOUNTAIN RV RESORT

Ratings: 8/9★/9.5 (RV Park) From Jct of I-5 & Hwy 199 (exit 55): Go SW .02 mi on Hwy 199 to Agness Ave, then S .02 mi to Foothill Blvd (Veer R to Pearce Park Rd), then E 1.4 mi (L). **FAC:** paved rds. (51 spaces). Avail: 11 paved, 11 pull-thrus, (20x60), 11 full hkups (30/50 amps), seasonal sites, cable, WiFi @ sites, dump, laundry, LP gas. **REC:** boating nearby, hunting nearby. Pet restrict (B/Q). Partial handicap access. No tents, eco-friendly. 2021 rates: $45, Military discount.
(541)479-1145 Lat: 42.43649, Lon: -123.27260
3298 Pearce Park Rd, Grants Pass, OR 97526
www.moonmountainrv.com
See ad page 751

RIVERPARK RV RESORT **Ratings: 8/8.5★/9.5** (Campground) Avail: 47 full hkups (30/50 amps). 2021 rates: $36 to $52. (541)479-0046, 2956 Rogue River Hwy, Grants Pass, OR 97527

ROGUE VALLEY OVERNITERS

Ratings: 9/10★/9 (RV Park) From Jct of I-5 & 6th St (exit 58), Go S 0.2 mi on 6th St (R); or From Jct of US-199 & Hwy 99 (S end of town), Go N 2.3 mi on US-199/Hwy 99 (7th St) to Morgan Ln, then W 400 ft to 6th St, then S 500 ft (R). **FAC:** paved rds. (93 spaces). 30 Avail: 8 paved, 22 all weather, 17 pull-thrus, (24x70), back-ins (23x38), 30 full hkups (30/50 amps), seasonal sites, cable, WiFi @ sites, dump, laundry. **REC:** boating nearby, hunting nearby. Pet restrict (B). No tents. Big rig sites. 2021 rates: $40.70.
(541)479-2208 Lat: 42.45912, Lon: -123.32296
1806 NW 6th St, Grants Pass, OR 97526
www.roguevalleyoverniters.com
See ad page 752

SCHROEDER PARK (Public) From Jct of I-5 & US-199, W 2 mi on US-199 to Willow Ln, N 2.3 mi (E). Avail: 22 full hkups (30/50 amps). 2021 rates: $30 to $35. (541)474-5285

WHITEHORSE PARK (Public) From Jct of I-5 & Exit 58: Go SE 0.3 mi to 6th St, then S 1.7 mi to SW G St, then W 8 mi (SW G St. turns into Upper/Lower River Rd.) (L). Avail: 8 full hkups (20 amps). 2021 rates: $30 to $35. (541)474-5285

GRESHAM — A2 *Multnomah*

OXBOW REGIONAL PARK (Public) From Jct of I-205 & Division St, E 13 mi on Division St, follow signs (L). Entrance fee required. GATE LOCKED AT SUNSET; OPENS AT 6:30AM. 74 Avail. 2021 rates: $22. (503)663-4708

HAMMOND — A2 *Clatsop*

ASTORIA/WARRENTON SEASIDE KOA **Ratings: 8/8/9.5** (Campground) Avail: 300 full hkups (30/50 amps). 2021 rates: $35 to $98. (800)562-8506, 1100 NW Ridge Rd, Hammond, OR 97121

FORT STEVENS (Public State Park) S-bnd: From Jct of US-101 & A1T US-101, SW 1 mi on A1T US-101 to Ridge Rd, W 3.5 mi (R); or N-bnd: From Jct of US-101 & Fort Stevens State Park Rd, NW 4.6 mi on Fort Stevens State Park Rd (L). 476 Avail: 174 full hkups, 302 W, 302 E (20/50 amps). 2021 rates: $32 to $34. (503)861-1671

HEPPNER — B4 *Morrow*

ANSON WRIGHT PARK (MORROW COUNTY PARK) (Public) From Jct of I-84 & SR-207, SW 26 mi on SR-207/ Jct 74, S 36.5 mi (R). 47 Avail: 20 full hkups, 3 W, 3 E (20 amps). 2021 rates: $18.70 to $28.60. May 20 to Oct 31. (541)989-9500

CUTSFORTH PARK (MORROW COUNTY PARK) (Public) From town, S 1 mi on SR-207 to Willow Creek Rd, SE 22 mi (R). Avail: 20 full hkups (20 amps). 2021 rates: $22 to $28.60. May 10 to Nov 13. (541)989-9500

HERMISTON — A4 *Umatilla*

HERMISTON See also Boardman, Irrigon, Stanfield & Umatilla, OR; Kennewick, WA.

HAT ROCK CAMPGROUND

Ratings: 7.5/8.5★/8 (Campground) 21 Avail: 4 full hkups, 17 W, 17 E (30/50 amps). 2021 rates: $30 to $35. (541)567-4188, 82284 Hat Rock Rd, Hermiston, OR 97838

HILLSBORO — A2 *Washington*

Travel Services

CAMPING WORLD OF HILLSBORO As the nation's largest retailer of RV supplies, accessories, services and new and used RVs, Camping World is committed to making your total RV experience better. **SERVICES:** RV, RV appliance, restrooms. RV Sales. RV supplies, LP gas, RV accessible. Hours: 9am to 7pm.
(877)268-9232 Lat: 45.496731, Lon: -122.914244
6503 SE Alexander St, Hillsboro, OR 97123
www.campingworld.com

HINES — C4 *Harney*

BOSCH'S BIG BEAR LODGE & RV PARK **Ratings: 7.5/NA/8** (RV Park) Avail: 10 full hkups (30/50 amps). 2021 rates: $30 to $45. (541)573-2727, 171 Hines Logging Rd, Hines, OR 97738

HOOD RIVER — A3 *Hood River*

HOOD RIVER See also Cascade Locks, OR; Stevenson, Trout Lake & White Salmon, WA.

TOLL BRIDGE PARK (HOOD RIVER COUNTY PARK) (Public) From Jct of Hwy 35 & I-84, S 17 mi on Hwy 35, to Toll Bridge Rd, W 0.4 mi (R). 64 Avail: 20 full hkups, 44 W, 44 E (30 amps). 2021 rates: $30 to $35. May 01 to Oct 31. (541)352-5522

TUCKER PARK (Public) From Jct of I-84 & US-30 (exit 62, W of town), E 1 mi on US-30 (Cascade St) to 13th/Tucker Rd, S .6 mi (left, then right), S .5 mi to 12th St., W 1 mi to Brookside Dr., S 2.9 mi to Dee Hwy, SW .4 mi. 88 Avail. 2021 rates: $25 to $35. May 01 to Oct 31. (541)386-4477

VIENTO (Public State Park) From town, W 8 mi on I-84 (exit 56) (R). 56 Avail: 56 W, 56 E (20 amps). 2021 rates: $24. May 01 to Oct 31. (541)374-8811

HUNTINGTON — B5 *Baker*

FAREWELL BEND (Public State Park) From Jct of I-84 & Bus US-30 (exit 353), N 1 mi on Bus US-30 (R). 91 Avail: 91 W, 91 E (20/30 amps). 2021 rates: $26. (800)551-6949

OASIS ON THE SNAKE (RV Park) (Rebuilding) 44 Avail: 34 full hkups, 10 W, 10 E (30/50 amps). 2021 rates: $35 to $38. Mar 01 to Nov 30. (541)262-3833, 6170 Hwy 201 N, Huntington, OR 97907

IDLEYLD PARK — C2 *Douglas*

ELK HAVEN RV RESORT **Ratings: 6/9★/8** (RV Park) Avail: 10 full hkups (30/50 amps). 2021 rates: $35. (888)552-0166, 22020 N Umpqua Hwy, Idleyld Park, OR 97447

UMPQUA'S LAST RESORT WILDERNESS RV PARK & CAMPGROUND **Ratings: 6.5/8★/8.5** (Campground) Avail: 20 full hkups (30/50 amps). 2021 rates: $28 to $45. (541)498-2500, 115 Elk Ridge Lane, Idleyld Park, OR 97447

IRRIGON — A4 *Morrow*

OREGON TRAIL RV PARK **Ratings: 7/9.5★/7** (RV Park) Avail: 12 full hkups (30/50 amps). 2021 rates: $35. (541)571-0661, 1200 NE Washington Ave, Irrigon, OR 97844

JOHN DAY — B4 *Grant*

CLYDE HOLLIDAY (Public State Park) From Jct of US-26 & US-395 (in town), W 7 mi on US-26, MP 155 1/4 (L). 31 Avail: 31 W, 31 E (30/50 amps). 2021 rates: $26. Mar 01 to Nov 30. (541)932-4453

GRANT COUNTY RV PARK (Public) From Jct of 395 & 26 (center of town), E 0.1 mi on Hwy 26 to Bridge St, N 0.3 mi (R). Avail: 25 full hkups (30/50 amps). 2021 rates: $30. (541)575-1900

JORDAN VALLEY — D6 *Malheur*

SUNNYRIDGE RV PARK (RV Park) (Rebuilding) Avail: 40 full hkups (30/50 amps). 2021 rates: $42. (541)586-2870, 41 Delar Way, Jordan Valley, OR 97910

JOSEPH — A5 *Wallowa*

HELLS CANYON REC AREA/COPPERFIELD PARK (Public) From town, S 0.1 mi on SR-82 to Imnaha Hwy, E 8.1 mi to Wallowa Mountain Loop NFD 39, SE 55.4 mi to SH-86, NE 7.3 mi. 59 Avail: 59 W, 59 E (30 amps). 2021 rates: $8 to $16. (844)472-7275

HELLS CANYON REC AREA/HELLS CANYON PARK (Public) From town, S 0.1 mi on SR-82 to Imnaha Hwy, E 8.1 mi to NF-39, Wallowa Mountain Loop, SE 55.4 mi to SH-86, NE 7.3 mi to NF-454, N (across river) 4 mi. 27 Avail: 24 W, 24 E (30 amps). 2021 rates: $8 to $16. (541)785-7209

HELLS CANYON REC AREA/MCCORMICK PARK (Public) From town, S 0.1 mi on SR-82 to Imnaha Hwy, E 8.1 mi to NF-39, Wallowa Mountain Loop, SE 55.4 mi to SH-86, NE 7.3 mi to SH-71, S 7.5 mi (across river). 28 Avail: 28 W, 28 E (30 amps). 2021 rates: $8 to $16. (541)785-7209

WALLOWA LAKE (Public State Park) From Jct of Hwy 82 (Main St) & Joseph St (in town), S 6 mi on Hwy 82 (R). Avail: 121 full hkups (30/50 amps). 2021 rates: $32. (800)452-4185

JUNCTION CITY — C2 *Lane*

GUARANTY RV PARK **Ratings: 9/NA/9** (RV Park) Avail: 55 full hkups (30/50 amps). 2021 rates: $40 to $45. (541)998-7000, 93668 Hwy 99, Junction City, OR 97448

KLAMATH FALLS — D3 *Klamath*

KLAMATH FALLS See also Chiloquin.

KLAMATH FALLS KOA JOURNEY **Ratings: 8.5/9.5★/8.5** (Campground) 55 Avail: 39 full hkups, 16 W, 16 E (30/50 amps). 2021 rates: $45.89 to $67.89. (541)884-4644, 3435 Shasta Way, Klamath Falls, OR 97603

LAKE OF THE WOODS RESORT **Ratings: 6/7/7** (Campground) 22 Avail: 12 full hkups, 10 W, 10 E (30/50 amps). 2021 rates: $25 to $60. (541)949-8300, 950 Harriman Route, Klamath Falls, OR 97601

MILITARY PARK KINGSLEY CAMPGROUND (KINGSLEY FIELD) (Public) From jct of US-97 & Joe Wright Rd: Go 2.3 mi E on Joe Wright Rd, then right on Airport Way to the main gate, then stay on McConnell Circle, then left on Arnold Ave, then Gentile St (L). Avail: 5 full hkups (30 amps). 2021 rates: $15. (541)885-6609

ROCKY POINT RESORT **Ratings: 5.5/5.5/7.5** (Campground) 25 Avail: 15 full hkups, 10 W, 10 E (30 amps). 2021 rates: $37 to $46. Mar 15 to Nov 30. (541)356-2287, 28121 Rocky Point Rd, Klamath Falls, OR 97601

LA GRANDE — B5 *Union*

GRANDE HOT SPRINGS RV RESORT **Ratings: 8.5/10★/9.5** (RV Park) Avail: 96 full hkups (30/50 amps). 2021 rates: $50 to $55. (541)963-5253, 65182 Hot Lake Ln, La Grande, OR 97850

LA GRANDE RENDEZVOUS RV RESORT **Ratings: 6/9★/7** (RV Park) Avail: 12 full hkups (30/50 amps). 2021 rates: $40 to $47. (541)962-0909, 2632 Bearco Loop, La Grande, OR 97850

LA PINE — C3 *Deschutes*

LAPINE (Public State Park) From Jct of US-97 & La Pine State Recreational Area Rd (MP-160 1/2, N of town), W 5.2 mi on La Pine SRA Rd (E). 129 Avail: 82 full hkups, 47 W, 47 E (30/50 amps). 2021 rates: $26 to $29. (800)551-6949

LAKESIDE — C1 *Coos*

NORTH LAKE RV RESORT & MARINA **Ratings: 7.5/9★/10** (Campground) 50 Avail: 17 full hkups, 33 W, 33 E (30/50 amps). 2021 rates: $37 to $56. Mar 21 to Nov 15. (541)759-3515, 2090 N Lake Rd, Lakeside, OR 97449

OSPREY POINT RV RESORT

Ratings: 9/9★/9 (RV Park) Avail: 99 full hkups (30/50 amps). 2021 rates: $35 to $50. (541)759-2801, 1505 N Lake Rd., Lakeside, OR 97449

LAKEVIEW — D4 *Lake*

GOOSE LAKE (Public State Park) From town, S 15 mi on US-395 to New Pine Creek, W 1 mi (R). 48 Avail: 48 W, 48 E (20 amps). 2021 rates: $24. May 01 to Oct 31. (541)783-2471

JUNIPERS RESERVOIR RV RESORT

Ratings: 8/10★/10 (RV Park) From jct US-395 & Hwy 140W (in town): Go 10 mi W on Hwy 140 to MP 86.5 (R). Elev 4899 ft.

RV OASIS IN MIDST OF CATTLE RANCH

A family-owned RV park set amongst shade trees, on a 5,000-acre working cattle ranch. A 200-acre reservoir provides recreation for the entire family with fishing, paddling & birding. Many birds & other wildlife reside here!

FAC: gravel rds. (40 spaces). Avail: 36 gravel, 36 pull-thrus, (30x80), 21 full hkups, 15 W, 15 E (30/50 amps), WiFi @ sites, tent sites, rentals, dump, laundry. **REC:** Junipers Reservoir: swim, fishing, kayak-

Set your clocks. Time zones are indicated in the front of each state and province.

ing/canoeing. Pets OK. Partial handicap access. Big rig sites. 2021 rates: $40 to $48, Military discount. May 01 to Oct 15.
(541)947-2050 Lat: 42.185078, Lon: -120.533022
91029 Hwy 140 W, Lakeview, OR 97630
www.junipersrv.com
See ad page 752

LAKE COUNTY FAIRGROUNDS & RV (Public) From Jct of Hwy 395 & Hwy 140 (in town), W .8 mi on Hwy 140 (R). 14 Avail: 14 W, 14 E (30 amps). 2021 rates: $12 to $18. Apr 15 to Nov 01. (541)947-2925

WILD GOOSE MEADOWS RV PARK
Ratings: 7.5/8.5★/7.5 (RV Park) Avail: 26 full hkups (30/50 amps). 2021 rates: $35 to $37. (541)947-4968, 18020 Hwy 395 North, Lakeview, OR 97630

LANGLOIS — D1 *Curry*

CYPRESS HILLS RV CAMPGROUND
Ratings: 8.5/10★/10 (RV Park) Avail: 12 full hkups (30/50 amps). 2021 rates: $49. (541)348-1040, 48203 Highway 101, Langlois, OR 97450

LEBANON — B2 *Linn*

GILL'S LANDING RV PARK (Public) Hwy 20 & Grant St (in town) E 0.6 mi on Grant St (R). Avail: 20 full hkups (30/50 amps). 2021 rates: $35 to $40. (541)258-4918

WATERLOO CAMPGROUND (Public) From Jct of Hwys 20 & 34 (in town), E 5.78 mi on Hwy 20 to Waterloo turnoff, N 1 mi on Gross (R). 120 Avail: 100 W, 100 E (20/30 amps). 2021 rates: $24 to $29. (541)967-3917

LINCOLN CITY — B2 *Lincoln*

LINCOLN CITY See also Cloverdale, Depoe Bay, Newport & Pacific City.

CHINOOK BEND RV RESORT **Ratings: 6/8/6.5** (Membership Park) 94 Avail: 81 full hkups, 8 W, 13 E (30/50 amps). 2021 rates: $53.86 to $59.40. (800)203-6364, 2920 Siletz Hwy, Lincoln City, OR 97367

COYOTE ROCK RV RESORT & MARINA **Ratings: 5/8/8.5** (Campground) 41 Avail: 26 full hkups, 15 W, 15 E (30/50 amps). 2021 rates: $29.70 to $39.60. (541)996-6824, 1676 Siletz River Hwy, Lincoln City, OR 97367

DEVIL'S LAKE (Public State Park) From Jct of US-101 & N 6th St/Vinyard Church exit (in town), E 0.2 mi on N 6th St/Vinyard Church (R). 33 Avail: 28 full hkups, 5 W, 5 E (20/50 amps). 2021 rates: $32 to $34. (541)994-2002

DEVILS LAKE RV PARK **Ratings: 8.5/9.5★/9.5** (RV Park) Avail: 20 full hkups (30/50 amps). 2021 rates: $54.95 to $61.05. (541)994-3400, 4041 NE West Devils Lake Rd, Lincoln City, OR 97367

LINCOLN CITY KOA JOURNEY **Ratings: 7/9★/9** (Campground) 51 Avail: 26 full hkups, 25 W, 25 E (30/50 amps). 2021 rates: $33.53 to $59.24. (800)562-3316, 5298 NE Park Lane, Otis, OR 97368

LINCOLN CITY PREMIER RV RESORT
Ratings: 9/10★/9.5 (RV Resort) N-Bnd: From Jct of Hwy 101 & 51st St (S of town): Go N 0.2 mi on Hwy 101 (R); or S-Bnd: From Jct of Hwy 101 & E Devils Lake Rd (outlet mall): Go S 2.5 mi on Hwy 101 (L). **FAC:** paved rds. Avail: 92 paved, patios, 7 pull-thrus, (23x45), back-ins (23x45), 92 full hkups (30/50 amps), cable, WiFi @ sites, laundry, LP gas. **REC:** hot tub, boating nearby. Pets OK. Partial handicap access. No tents, eco-friendly. 2021 rates: $57.94 to $69.93, Military discount.
(541)996-2778 Lat: 44.93457, Lon: -124.02222
4100 SE Hwy 101, Lincoln City, OR 97367
www.premierrvresorts.com
See ad page 744

LOGAN ROAD RV PARK
Ratings: 10/10★/9.5 (RV Park) From Jct of Hwy 101 & Logan Rd (North of town): Go W & N on Logan Rd 1 mi (R).

EVERYTHING IS BETTER AT THE BEACH
Lincoln City's only RV Park west of Hwy 101, just two blocks from Oregon's only oceanfront Casino. Free 24-hour shuttle service. Full hookups with cable, Wi-Fi & pet area. Close to the beach & includes pool & spa access.

FAC: paved rds. (51 spaces). Avail: 36 paved, 17 pull-thrus, (20x40), back-ins (21x40), 36 full hkups (30/50 amps), seasonal sites, cable, WiFi @ sites, laundry, LP gas, restaurant. **REC:** heated pool, hot tub, boating nearby, golf. Pet restrict (Q). Partial handicap access. No tents, 28 day max stay. 2021 rates: $47.59 to $54.38, Military discount.
(877)564-2678 Lat: 45.00083, Lon: -124.00428
4800 NE Logan Rd, Lincoln City, OR 97367
www.loganroadrvpark.com
See ad page 745

WAPITI RV PARK **Ratings: 4.5/7/7.5** (Campground) 40 Avail: 40 W, 40 E (30 amps). 2021 rates: $35. (541)996-2240, 2188 S Drift Creek Rd, Lincoln City, OR 97367

Things to See and Do

CHINOOK WINDS CASINO RESORT Full-service Casino and Hotel with meeting rooms, events venues, slots and table games, play palace, arcade, health club, pool, whirlpool, restaurants and an 18-hole golf course. Partial handicap access. RV accessible. Restrooms. Food. Hours: 24 hours. ATM.
(888)244-6665 Lat: 44.998096, Lon: -124.009215
1777 NW 44th St, Lincoln City, OR 97367
www.chinookwindscasino.com
See ad page 745

CHINOOK WINDS GOLF RESORT 79 acre, 18-hole golf course includes a pro-shop, the only indoor driving range on the Oregon Coast, fitness center, Aces Sports Bar & Grill and meeting rooms. Restrooms. Food. Hours: .
(541)994-8442 Lat: 45.00100, Lon: -123.99440
3245 NE 50th St, Lincoln City, OR 97367
www.chinookwindscasino.com
See ad page 745

LOWELL — C2 *Lane*

FALL CREEK SRA/CASCARA CAMPGROUND (Public State Park) From I-5 (exit 189A): Go 13 mi E on Hwy 58 to Lowell exit, then N across bridge, then follow signs, then 8 mi on Big Fall Creek Rd, then right 1 mi on Peninsula Rd. 39 Avail: Pit toilets. 2021 rates: $19. May 01 to Sep 30. (541)937-1173

LYONS — B2 *Linn*

JOHN NEAL MEMORIAL PARK (LINN COUNTY PARK) (Public) From Jct of Hwy 22 & Mehama-Lyons exit, S 1 mi on Mehama-Lyons to Hwy 226, E 1.5 mi to 13th St, follow signs (R). 21 Avail. 2021 rates: $26. Apr 26 to Sep 24. (541)967-3917

MADRAS — B3 *Jefferson*

MADRAS See also Crooked River Ranch & Culver.

JEFFERSON COUNTY FAIRGROUNDS (JEFFERSON COUNTY PARK) (Public) From the jct of Hwy 97 and Fairgrounds Rd (south end of Madras): Go 1/2 blk W on Fairgrounds Rd. Avail: 65 full hkups (30/50 amps). 2021 rates: $20 to $25. (541)475-6288

LAKE SIMTUSTUS RV PARK **Ratings: 9/9★/9** (RV Park) Avail: 49 full hkups (30/50 amps). 2021 rates: $40 to $53. (541)475-1085, 2750 NW Pelton Dam Rd, Madras, OR 97741

PELTON PARK (Public) From North jct. US 97 & US 26: Go 9-1/2 mi NW on US 26, then 3-3/4 mi S on Pelton Dam Rd. 67 Avail: 35 W, 35 E. Apr 22 to Sep 25. (541)325-5292

MAPLETON — C2 *Lane*

WHITTAKER CREEK RECREATION SITE (BLM) (Public Corps) From town, W 12.5 mi on Hwy 126 to Siuslaw River Rd, S 2 mi (R). 31 Avail: Pit toilets. 2021 rates: $10. May 23 to Sep 21. (541)683-6600

MAUPIN — B3 *Wasco*

MAUPIN CITY PARK (Public) From Jct of Hwy 197 & Bakeoven Rd exit, SE 0.1 mi on Bakeoven Rd (L). Avail: 25 full hkups (20/30 amps). 2021 rates: $30 to $42. (541)395-2252

MCDERMITT — E5 *Malhuer*

MITCHELLS STATELINE RV PARK **Ratings: 3/7★/4** (RV Park) Avail: 16 full hkups (30 amps). 2021 rates: $40. (541)522-8133, 4112 Stateline Rd, McDermitt, OR 89421

MCMINNVILLE — B2 *Yamhill*

A SPOTLIGHT Introducing the Wine Regions' colorful attractions appearing at the front of this state section.

OLDE STONE VILLAGE RV RESORT
Ratings: 10/10★/10 (RV Resort) From Jct of Hwy 99W & E Hwy 18 bypass (S of McMinnville): Go NE 4.2 mi on Hwy 18 bypass to MP-48.25 (L).

THE HEART OF OREGON'S WINE COUNTRY
Walk to the Evergreen Aviation Museum, home of the 'Spruce Goose', tour dozens of local wineries, the Spirit Mountain Casino, or relax on our manicured grounds. Explore McMinnville's charm, antique shopping and great food.

FAC: paved rds. Avail: 71 paved, patios, 33 pull-thrus, (30x65), back-ins (30x65), 71 full hkups (30/50 amps), cable, WiFi @ sites, laundry. **REC:** heated pool, boating nearby, playground. Pet restrict (B/Q). Partial handicap access. No tents. Big rig sites, eco-friendly. 2021 rates: $65, Military discount.
(503)472-4315 Lat: 45.20376, Lon: -123.13595
4155 NE Three Mile Lane, McMinnville, OR 97128
www.oldestonevillage.com
See ad page 754

MEACHAM — A5 *Umatilla*

EMIGRANT SPRINGS (Public State Park) N-bnd: From Jct of I-84 & Exit 234, NW 0.5 mi on exit rd (L); or S-bnd: From Jct of I-84 & Exit 233, S 0.5 mi on exit rd (R). 17 Avail: 16 full hkups, 1 W, 1 E (20/30 amps). 2021 rates: $24 to $26. (541)983-2277

MEDFORD — D2 *Jackson*

A SPOTLIGHT Introducing Southern Oregon's colorful attractions appearing at the front of this state section.

MEDFORD See also Ashland, Eagle Point, Gold Hill, Grants Pass, Phoenix, Rogue River, Shady Cove & White City.

CANTRALL BUCKLEY PARK (JACKSON COUNTY PARK) (Public) From town, SW 8 mi on SR-238 to Hamilton Rd, S 1 mi (R). 30 Avail. 2021 rates: $16. Mar 25 to Oct 15. (541)774-8183

Travel Services

CAMPING WORLD OF MEDFORD As the nation's largest retailer of RV supplies, accessories, services and new and used RVs, Camping World is committed to making your total RV experience better. **SERVICES:** restrooms. RV Sales. RV supplies, RV accessible. Hours: 9am - 6pm.
(844)959-4065 Lat: 42.36000, Lon: -122.87740
938 Chevy Way, Medford, OR 97504
rv.campingworld.com

GANDER RV OF MEDFORD Your new hometown outfitter offering the best regional gear for all your outdoor needs. Your adventure awaits. **SERVICES:** sells outdoor gear, restrooms. RV Sales. RV supplies, RV accessible. Hours: 9am - 6pm.
(833)411-0799 Lat: 42.28443, Lon: -122.83004
3800 S Pacific Hwy, Medford, OR 97501
rv.ganderoutdoors.com

MERLIN — D2 *Josephine*

ALMEDA (Public) From Jct I-5 & Merlin/Galice Rd, exit 61: Go 19 mi W on Merlin/Galice Rd. (R). 2 Avail: Pit toilets. 2021 rates: $40 to $45. (541)474-5285

INDIAN MARY PARK (Public) From Jct of I-5 & Merlin-Galice Rd (Merlin exit 61), W 10.9 mi on Merlin-Galice Rd (R). 50 Avail: 40 full hkups, 10 W, 10 E (30/50 amps). 2021 rates: $35. (541)474-5285

MILL CITY — B2 *Marion*

FISHERMEN'S BEND RECREATION SITE (BLM) (Public Corps) From town, W 1.5 mi on Hwy 22 (L). 51 Avail: 21 full hkups, 30 E (50 amps). 2021 rates: $16 to $28. Apr 01 to Oct 31. (503)897-2406

MORO — A3 *Sherman*

SHERMAN COUNTY RV PARK
(Public) From Jct of US-97 & 1st St: Go .5 mi SE on 1st St (1st St becomes Lone Rock Rd) (L). **FAC:** gravel rds. (32 spaces). Avail: 31 gravel, 16 pull-thrus, (21x65), back-ins (25x50), 31 full hkups (30/50 amps), WiFi @ sites, tent sites, laundry. **REC:** playground, hunting nearby. Pets OK. 7 day max stay. 2021 rates: $20 to $25. no cc.
(541)565-3127 Lat: 45.47768, Lon: -120.71821
66067 Lone Rock Rd, Moro, OR 97039
www.co.sherman.or.us/govt_parks.asp#rvpark
See ad page 733

MYRTLE CREEK — D2 *Douglas*

ON THE RIVER GOLF & RV RESORT **Ratings: 5.5/7/8.5** (RV Park) Avail: 25 full hkups (30/50 amps). 2021 rates: $40 to $50. (800)521-5556, 111 Whitson Ln, Myrtle Creek, OR 97457

OR

NEHALEM — A2 *Tillamook*

NEHALEM BAY (Public State Park) From Jct US-101 & Hwy 53 (S of town): Go 2-1/2 mi N on US-101, then 1-1/2 mi W on McCarney Rd MP-43 3/4 (E). 265 Avail: 265 W, 265 E (20/30 amps). 2021 rates: $31. (503)368-5154

NEWPORT — B1 *Lincoln*

NEWPORT See also Depoe Bay, Lincoln City, Seal Rock, South Beach & Waldport.

BEVERLY BEACH (Public State Park) From Jct of US-20 & US-101 (in town), N 6.3 mi on US-101 to MP-134 (R). 129 Avail: 53 full hkups, 76 W, 76 E (30/50 amps). 2021 rates: $31 to $34. (800)551-6949

HARBOR VILLAGE RV PARK & MHP (RV Park) (Phone Update) Avail: 38 full hkups (30/50 amps). 2021 rates: $40. (541)265-5088, 923 SE Bay Blvd, Newport, OR 97365

PACIFIC SHORES MOTORCOACH RESORT **Ratings: 10/10★/10** (Condo Park) Avail: 85 full hkups (30/50 amps). 2021 rates: $80 to $160. (541)265-3750, 6225 N Coast Hwy 101, Newport, OR 97365

PORT OF NEWPORT ANNEX RV PARK (Public) S-bnd: From Jct of US-101 & US-20, S 1.7 mi on US-101 to Marine Science Center exit (at S end of bridge), NE 0.5 mi on S OSU Dr (L); or N-bnd: From Jct of US-101 & 32nd (1st light), E 0.1 mi on 32nd to Ferry Slip, N 0.4 mi to Marine Science Rd, E 0.1 mi (L). Avail: 52 full hkups (30/50 amps). 2021 rates: $49.64 to $50.80. (541)867-3321

PORT OF NEWPORT MARINA & RV PARK

Ratings: 9.5/9.5★/9 (Public) S-bnd: From Jct of US-101 & US-20, S 1.7 mi on US-101 to Marine Science Center exit (at S end of bridge), NE 0.5 mi on S OSU Dr (L); or N-bnd: From Jct of US-101 & 32nd (1st light), E 0.1 mi on 32nd to Ferry Slip, N 0.4 mi to Marine Science Rd, E 0.1 mi (L). **FAC:** paved rds. Avail: 92 paved, 45 pull-thrus, (27x60), back-ins (27x40), 92 full hkups (30/50 amps), cable, WiFi @ sites, dump, laundry, groc, restaurant. **REC:** Yaquina Bay: swim, fishing, marina, kayaking/canoeing, boating nearby. Pet restrict (Q) $. Partial handicap access. No tents. Big rig sites, eco-friendly. 2021 rates: $62.34 to $69.26, Military discount. ATM.
(541)867-3321 Lat: 44.62115, Lon: -124.04874
2120 SE Marine Science Dr, Newport, OR 97365
www.portofnewport.com
See ad page 746

SOUTH BEACH (Public State Park) From Jct of US-20 & US-101 (in town), S 3 mi on US-101 to MP-143.5 (R). 227 Avail: 227 W, 227 E (20/30 amps). 2021 rates: $31. (800)551-6949

NORTH BEND — C1 *Coos*

OREGON DUNES KOA **Ratings: 7.5/10★/8.5** (Campground) Avail: 67 full hkups (30/50 amps). 2021 rates: $49 to $82. (541)756-4851, 68632 Hwy 101, North Bend, OR 97459

THE MILL CASINO HOTEL & RV PARK

Ratings: 10/10★/10 (RV Park) From Jct of Newmark St & US-101: Go N 0.3 mi on Hwy 101 (R).

BAYFRONT SITES, WALK TO OUR CASINO
Our top-rated Good Sam park offers all the amenities from trash pickup to off-leash dog park. Walk or ride free shuttle to our Casino for gaming, dining, pool, fitness center & more. Enjoy great Hospitality, Service & Views!

FAC: paved rds. Avail: 102 paved, patios, 70 pull-thrus, (28x62), back-ins (27x40), accepts full hkup units only, 102 full hkups (30/50 amps), cable, WiFi @ sites, rentals, laundry, LP gas, restaurant. **REC:** heated pool, hot tub, Coos Bay: fishing, boating nearby, hunting nearby. Pets OK. Partial handicap access. No tents. Big rig sites, 28 day max stay, eco-friendly. 2021 rates: $50 to $75, Military discount. ATM.
(800)953-4800 Lat: 43.39483, Lon: -124.21910
2665 Tremont Ave, North Bend, OR 97459
www.themillcasino.com
See ad page 726

Things to See and Do

THE MILL CASINO-HOTEL Casino with hotel, gaming, entertainment, restaurants, lounge, pool, hot tubs, fitness center & RV park. Partial handicap access. RV accessible. Restrooms. Food. Hours: 24 hrs. ATM.
(800)953-4800 Lat: 43.39483, Lon: -124.21910
3201 Tremont Ave, North Bend, OR 97459
www.themillcasino.com
See ad page 726

NYSSA — C6 *Malheur*

LAKE OWYHEE (Public State Park) From town, SW 12 mi on SR-201 to Owyhee Ave, S 25 mi (E). 51 Avail: 51 W, 51 E (30 amps). 2021 rates: $24. Apr 15 to Oct 31. (800)452-5687

O'BRIEN — E2 *JOSEPHINE*

LONE MOUNTAIN RESORT

Ratings: 9.5/9.5★/10 (Campground) From Jct Hwy 199/Redwood Hwy & SR 46 (in Cave Junction): Go S 7.08 mi on Hwy 199 to Lone Mountain Rd, then W 500 ft (L). **FAC:** paved rds. (44 spaces). Avail: 28 all weather, 12 pull-thrus, (24x75), back-ins (30x50), 28 full hkups (30/50 amps), seasonal sites, WiFi @ sites, rentals, shower$, laundry, firewood. **REC:** pond, swim, hunting nearby. Pets OK. Partial handicap access. No tents. Big rig sites. 2021 rates: $35 to $50, Military discount.
(541)596-2878 Lat: 42.06699, Lon: -123.70828
169 Lone Mountain Rd, O'Brien, OR 97534
www.lonemountainresort.com
See ad page 751

ONTARIO — C6 *Malheur*

ONTARIO See also Caldwell & Homedale, ID.

OREGON CITY — A2 *Clackamas*

CLACKAMETTE RV PARK (Public) From Jct of I 205 & 99E (Exit 9), N 0.1 mi on McLoughlin/99E (L). 36 Avail: 36 W, 36 E (30 amps). 2021 rates: $25 to $30. (503)496-1201

PACIFIC CITY — B2 *Tillamook*

CAPE KIWANDA RV RESORT & MARKETPLACE

Ratings: 10/9.5★/9.5 (RV Park) 73 Avail: 65 full hkups, 8 W, 8 E (30/50 amps). 2021 rates: $36.95 to $68. (503)965-6230, 33305 Cape Kiwanda Dr., Pacific City, OR 97135

HART'S CAMP AIRSTREAM HOTEL & RV PARK

Ratings: 7.5/8.5★/8 (RV Park) Avail: 16 full hkups (30/50 amps). 2021 rates: $39 to $69. (503)965-7006, 33145 Webb Park Rd, Pacific City, OR 97135

WEBB COUNTY CAMPGROUND (Public) From town: Go 1 mi N on 3 Capes to Cape Kiwanda. 38 Avail. 2021 rates: $15.65 to $32.42. (503)965-5001

WHALEN ISLAND COUNTY CAMPGROUND (Public) From town, NW 5 mi on Resort Dr (L). 33 Avail. 2021 rates: $15.65 to $26.83. (503)965-6085

PENDLETON — A5 *Umatilla*

A SPOTLIGHT Introducing Land of the Oregon Trails's colorful attractions appearing at the front of this state section.

PENDLETON See also Hermiston & Stanfield.

PENDLETON KOA **Ratings: 9/8.5★/9.5** (RV Park) Avail: 34 full hkups (30/50 amps). 2021 rates: $38 to $58. (541)276-1041, 1375 SE 3rd St., Pendleton, OR 97801

WILDHORSE RESORT & CASINO RV PARK

Ratings: 9.5/10★/9 (RV Park) From Jct of I-84 & Hwy 331 (exit 216), N 0.8 mi on Hwy 331 (R).

A DESTINATION TO DISCOVER
Full-service RV Park & Tipi Village for family time that's action-packed or relaxed. Pull-thru & back-in sites w/ 30/50 amp FHU. Heated pool, hot tub, laundry, showers, restrooms, free WiFi and shuttle to casino/golf course.

FAC: paved rds. 100 Avail: 52 paved, 48 gravel, patios, 56 pull-thrus, (30x60), back-ins (30x50), 100 full hkups (30/50 amps), WiFi @ sites, tent sites, rentals, dump, laundry, groc, LP gas, restaurant. **REC:** heated pool, hot tub, golf, hunting nearby. Pets OK. Partial handicap access. Big rig sites. 2021 rates: $37 to $65, Military discount. ATM.
(800)654-9453 Lat: 45.64816, Lon: -118.67534
46510 Wildhorse Blvd, Pendleton, OR 97801
www.wildhorseresort.com
See ad page 739

Things to See and Do

WILDHORSE FAMILY FUNPLEX Bowling Lanes, 5 screen theater, children's entertainment center, food court and the Arcade with wide variety of over 35 family-friendly games, accommodating up to 52 simultaneous players. Partial handicap access. RV accessible. Restrooms. Food. Hours: 11am to 12 midnight.
(800)654-9453 Lat: 45.64816, Lon: -118.67534
46510 Wildhorse Blvd, Pendleton, OR 97801
wildhorseresort.com
See ad page 739

WILDHORSE GOLF COURSE 18 holes nestled in the foothills of Oregon's Blue Mountains. RV accessible. Restrooms. Food. Hours: 7am to 6pm. Adult fee: $55.00. ATM.
(800)654-9453 Lat: 45.91103, Lon: -119.17135
46510 Wildhorse Blvd, Pendleton, OR 97801
www.wildhorseresort.com
See ad page 739

WILDHORSE RESORT & CASINO Over 1,200 slot machines, plus your favorite table games and bingo. Tower hotel with convention space, fine dining, buffet & lounge and movie theater Partial handicap access. RV accessible. Restrooms. Food. Hours: open 24 Hrs. ATM.
(800)654-9453 Lat: 45.64816, Lon: -118.67534
46510 Wildhorse Blvd, Pendleton, OR 97801
www.wildhorseresort.com
See ad page 739

PHOENIX — D2 *Jackson*

HOLIDAY RV PARK

Ratings: 10/9.5★/9.5 (RV Park) Avail: 60 full hkups (30/50 amps). 2021 rates: $50. (800)452-7970, 201 N Phoenix Rd, Phoenix, OR 97535

PORT ORFORD — D1 *Curry*

CAMP BLANCO RV PARK **Ratings: 7/8.5★/8** (RV Park) Avail: 15 full hkups (30/50 amps). 2021 rates: $40. (541)332-6175, 2011 Oregon St. (US-101), Port Orford, OR 97465

CAPE BLANCO (Public State Park) From Jct of US-101 & Madrona Ave (N end of town), N 3.7 on US-101 to Cape Blanco Rd, W 5 mi (L). 52 Avail: 52 W, 52 E (30/50 amps). 2021 rates: $24. (800)551-6949

HUMBUG MOUNTAIN (Public State Park) From Jct of US-101 & Jackson St (S end of town), S 6 mi on US-101, at MP-307 (L). 39 Avail: 39 W, 39 E (30 amps). 2021 rates: $24. (541)332-6774

PORT ORFORD RV VILLAGE

Ratings: 8.5/10★/9.5 (RV Park) Avail: 33 full hkups (30/50 amps). 2021 rates: $40. (541)332-1041, 2855 Port Orford Loop Rd, Port Orford, OR 97465

PORTLAND — A2 *Multnomah*

A SPOTLIGHT Introducing Metro Portland's colorful attractions appearing at the front of this state section.

PORTLAND See also Aurora, Cascade Locks, Fairview, McMinnville, Salem, Silverton, Troutdale, Tualatin, Welches, Wilsonville & Woodburn, OR; Cougar, Kalama, Kelso, Stevenson, Vancouver & Woodland, WA.

COLUMBIA RIVER RV PARK

Ratings: 9/10★/9.5 (RV Park) From Jct of I-5 & Exit 307 (follow E Marine Dr. signs), E 1.5 mi on Marine Dr to 13th Ave, S 100 ft (R). **FAC:** paved rds. (198 spaces). Avail: 46 paved, patios, 38 pull-thrus,

(25x60), back-ins (22x60), 46 full hkups (30/50 amps), seasonal sites, cable, WiFi @ sites, laundry. **REC:** boating nearby. Pet restrict (S/B/Q). Partial handicap access. No tents, Age restrict may apply. Big rig sites, eco-friendly. 2021 rates: $46 to $52.
(503)285-1515 Lat: 45.59972, Lon: -122.65307
10649 NE 13th Ave, Portland, OR 97211
www.columbiariverrv.com
See ad opposite page

JANTZEN BEACH RV PARK
good sam park **Ratings: 10/10★/9.5** (RV Park) From Jct of I-5 & Jantzen Beach (exit 308/N of Portland), take exit rd to N Hayden Island Dr, W 0.3 mi (R).

ACCESS TO PORTLAND & VANCOUVER
Located on the mighty Columbia River across the bridge from Portland or Vancouver, relax in the quiet, open, fresh-air environment and walk to shopping or dining. A short drive to enjoy Portland & Vancouver attractions.
FAC: paved rds. (169 spaces). Avail: 69 paved, 9 pull-thrus, (27x68), back-ins (30x50), 69 full hkups (30/50 amps), seasonal sites, cable, WiFi @ sites, laundry. **REC:** heated pool, wading pool, boating nearby, playground. Pet restrict (B). Partial handicap access. No tents. Big rig sites, eco-friendly. 2021 rates: $55, Military discount.
(800)443-7248 Lat: 45.61613, Lon: -122.68609
1503 N Hayden Island Dr, Portland, OR 97217
www.jantzenbeachrv.com
See ad page 742

OLDE STONE VILLAGE RV RESORT
good sam park **Ratings: 10/10★/10** (RV Park) From Jct of I-405 and I-5 in Portland: Go SW 22 mi on I-5 and OR-99W S/Pacific Hwy to N Springbrook Rd in Newberg, then go SW 5 1/2 mi on 99W Bypass/Newberg Dundee Bypass to OR-18/OR99W S, then go SW 3 1/4 mi to OR-18W, then continue 4 3/4 mi SW on OR-18 to park (R). **FAC:** paved rds. Avail: 71 paved, patios, 33 pull-thrus, (30x65), back-ins (30x65), 71 full hkups (30/50 amps), cable, WiFi @ sites, laundry. **REC:** heated pool, boating nearby, playground. Pet restrict (B/Q). Partial handicap access. No tents. Big rig sites, eco-friendly. 2021 rates: $54, Military discount.
(503)472-4315 Lat: 45.20376, Lon: -123.13595
4155 NE Three Mile Lane, McMinnville, OR 97128
www.oldestonevillage.com
See primary listing at McMinnville and ad page 754

POWERS — D1 *Coos*

POWERS COUNTY PARK (COOS COUNTY PARK) (Public) From Jct of Hwy 42 & Powers Hwy exit, W 17 mi on Powers Hwy (R). 40 Avail: 40 W, 40 E (20/30 amps). 2021 rates: $20. (541)439-2791

PRAIRIE CITY — B5 *Grant*

DEPOT RV PARK (Public) From Jct of State Hwy 26 & Main St, S 0.5 mi on Main St (L). Avail: 20 full hkups (30 amps). 2021 rates: $20. May 01 to Oct 31. (541)820-3605

PRINEVILLE — B3 *Crook*

CROOK COUNTY RV PARK (CROOK COUNTY PARK) (Public) From Jct of US-26 & Main St (in town), Go S 0.8 mi on Main St (L). Avail: 81 full hkups (30/50 amps). 2021 rates: $40. (800)609-2599

OCHOCO LAKE CAMPGROUND (CROOK COUNTY PARK) (Public) From jct US-26 & Main St (in town): Go 7 mi NE on US-26 (R). 22 Avail. 2021 rates: $20. Apr 01 to Oct 31. (541)447-1209

PRINEVILLE RESERVOIR (Public State Park) From Jct of US-26 & Hwy 126 (in town), E 1 mi on US-26 to Combs Flat Rd, S 1.3 mi to Prineville Reservoir Rec Area Rd, SE 14.4 mi (E). 44 Avail: 22 full hkups, 22 W, 22 E (30/50 amps). 2021 rates: $31 to $33. (541)447-4363

PRINEVILLE RESERVOIR RESORT (Campground) (Rebuilding) 65 Avail: 65 W, 65 E (15/30 amps). 2021 rates: $29 to $31. May 01 to Sep 08. (541)447-4363, 19600 SE Juniper Canyon Rd, Prineville, OR 97754

PROSPECT — D2 *Jackson*

CRATER LAKE RV PARK **Ratings: 7/9.5★/8** (RV Park) Avail: 48 full hkups (30/50 amps). 2021 rates: $37.50. (541)560-3399, 46611 Hwy 62, Prospect, OR 97536

RAINIER — A2 *Columbia*

HUDSON-PARCHER PARK (COLUMBIA COUNTY PARK) (Public) From town, W 2 mi on Hwy 30 to Larson Rd, S 0.3 mi, follow signs (R). Avail: 25 full hkups (20 amps). 2021 rates: $28. (503)366-3984

REDMOND — C3 *Deschutes*

EXPO CENTER RV PARK
(Public) From Jct of Hwy 97 & SW Airport Way (south end of town) Exit 124/Yew, E on Airport Way 0.2 mi to SW 19th St, S 0.4 mi (L) NOTE: For GPS use 4690 SW 19th St. Redmond OR 97756. Elev 3096 ft.

RV IN THE HEART OF CENTRAL OREGON
Expo Center RV Park is just a short distance from the Northwest's finest fishing, dining, hiking, boating and skiing. We're also next door to Juniper Municipal Golf Course & the majestic Cascades are right out your RV door!
FAC: paved rds. Avail: 105 paved, patios, 50 pull-thrus, (28x70), back-ins (20x55), 105 full hkups (30/50 amps), tent sites, laundry. **REC:** boating nearby. Pets OK. Partial handicap access. Big rig sites. 2021 rates: $35. ATM.
(541)585-1569 Lat: 44.23328, Lon: -121.18745
4690 SW 19th St, Redmond, OR 97756
expo.deschutes.org/p/rv-park
See ad page 732

Things to See and Do

EXPO CENTER Rodeos, Horse Shows, Dog Shows, BMX, the Fair, conferences, weddings - venues small and large at the Expo Center. Elev 3096 ft. Partial handicap access. RV accessible. Restrooms. Food. Hours: . ATM.
(541)548-2711 Lat: 44.24025, Lon: -121.18413
3800 SW Airport Rd, Redmond, OR 97756
expo.deschutes.org
See ad page 732

REEDSPORT — C1 *Douglas*

COHO RV PARK & MARINA **Ratings: 7.5/8.5★/7.5** (RV Park) Avail: 23 full hkups (30/50 amps). 2021 rates: $40. (541)271-5411, 1580 Winchester Ave, Reedsport, OR 97467

LOON LAKE CAMPGROUND (BLM) (Public Corps) From town: Go 12 mi E on Hwy 38, then 7 mi S on Loon Lake Rd (R). 61 Avail. 2021 rates: $18 to $36. May 22 to Sep 30. (541)599-2254

LOON LAKE LODGE & RV RESORT
good sam park **Ratings: 7/8/9** (Campground) Avail: 34 full hkups (30/50 amps). 2021 rates: $43 to $65. Apr 15 to Oct 31. (541)599-2244, 9011 Loon Lake Rd, Reedsport, OR 97467

OREGON COAST RV RESORT **Ratings: 6/7.5/8.5** (RV Park) 80 Avail: 60 full hkups, 20 W, 20 E (30 amps). 2021 rates: $47 to $55. (541)271-4020, 75381 US Hwy 101, Reedsport, OR 97467

WILLIAM M TUGMAN (Public State Park) 8 mi S on US 101 on Eel Lake. 93 Avail: 93 W, 93 E. 2021 rates: $26. (541)271-4118

REMOTE — D2 *Coos*

REMOTE OUTPOST RV PARK & CABINS **Ratings: 9.5/9★/9.5** (Campground) Avail: 26 full hkups (30/50 amps). 2021 rates: $50. (541)572-5105, 23146 Hwy 42, Remote, OR 97458

RILEY — C4 *Harney*

CHICKAHOMINY CAMPGROUND (BLM) (Public Corps) From town: Go 8 mi W on Hwy 20 to park access road (green sign on right), then 1/4 mi N (R). 28 Avail: Pit toilets. 2021 rates: $8. (541)573-4400

ROCKAWAY BEACH — A2 *Tillamook*

PARADISE COVE RESORT & MARINA **Ratings: 5/7.5/6.5** (Membership Park) 80 Avail: 71 full hkups, 9 W, 9 E (30/50 amps). 2021 rates: $34 to $78. (360)466-4468, 32455 US Hwy 101 North, Rockaway Beach, OR 97136

ROGUE RIVER — D2 *Jackson*

BRIDGEVIEW RV RESORT **Ratings: 8.5/8.5★/9** (RV Park) Avail: 20 full hkups (30/50 amps). 2021 rates: $35 to $45. (541)582-5980, 8880 Rogue River Hwy, Grants Pass, OR 97527

VALLEY OF THE ROGUE (Public State Park) From Jct of I-5 & State Park Rd (exit-45B), W 0.2 mi on State Park Rd. 150 Avail: 95 full hkups, 55 W, 55 E (30/50 amps). 2021 rates: $29 to $31. (541)582-1118

ROSEBURG — C2 *Douglas*

ROSEBURG See also Canyonville, Idleyld Park, Myrtle Creek, Remote & Sutherlin.

PASS CREEK RV PARK & CAMPGROUND (DOUGLAS COUNTY PARK) (Public) From Cottage Grove: S on I-5 to Curtin (Exit 163) (R). Avail: 29 full hkups (30 amps). 2021 rates: $25 to $29. (541)942-3281

RISING RIVER RV PARK **Ratings: 9.5/9.5★/10** (RV Park) Avail: 40 full hkups (30/50 amps). 2021 rates: $47. (541)679-7256, 5579 Grange Rd, Roseburg, OR 97471

TWIN RIVERS VACATION PARK **Ratings: 6.5/7.5/8.5** (RV Park) 34 Avail: 30 full hkups, 4 W, 4 E (30/50 amps). 2021 rates: $35 to $55. (541)673-3811, 433 River Forks Park Rd, Roseburg, OR 97471

WHISTLER'S BEND COUNTY PARK & CAMPGROUND (Public) From town, NE 12 mi on Hwy 138 to Whistler's Park Rd, NW 3 mi (E). 52 Avail: 12 full hkups, 14 W (50 amps). 2021 rates: $17. (541)673-4863

RUFUS — A3 *Sherman*

JOHN DAY RIVER - COE/LEPAGE PARK (Public Corps) From Jct of I-84 & exit 114, S 200 ft on exit 114 (E). 22 Avail: 22 W, 22 E (50 amps). 2021 rates: $22 to $25. Mar 31 to Oct 30. (541)506-4807

SALEM — B2 *Marion*

A SPOTLIGHT Introducing Salem's colorful attractions appearing at the front of this state section.

SALEM See also Albany, Aurora, McMinnville, Silverton & Woodburn.

HEE HEE ILLAHEE RV RESORT
good sam park **Ratings: 10/10★/10** (RV Park) From Jct of I-5 & Hwy 99E/Portland Rd (Exit 258): Go N 1/4 mi on Hwy 99E/Portland Rd to Astoria St, then NW 1/4 mi (L).

SALEM'S 10/10*/10 PREFERRED RESORT
In the heart of the Willamette Valley, EZ-ON/EZ-OFF I-5, come enjoy our resort with upgraded fiber internet circuit for real Wi-Fi or enjoy our relaxing spa, fitness center, game & meeting room or swim in our seasonal pool.
FAC: paved rds. (139 spaces). Avail: 36 paved, 36 pull-thrus, (30x75), accepts full hkup units only, 36 full hkups (30/50 amps), seasonal sites, cable, WiFi @ sites, laundry, LP gas. **REC:** heated pool, hot tub, boating nearby, playground. Pet restrict (S/B/Q). Partial handicap access. No tents. Big rig sites, eco-friendly. 2021 rates: $62.04, Military discount.
(503)463-6641 Lat: 44.99105, Lon: -122.99185
4751 Astoria Street NE, Salem, OR 97305
heeheeillahee.com
See ad page 736

PHOENIX RV PARK
good sam park **Ratings: 9/10★/10** (RV Park) From jct of I-5 & Market St (Exit 256): Go E 1/4 mi on Market to Lancaster Dr, then N 1 1/2 mi on Lancaster Dr to Silverton Rd, then E 1/10 mi on Silverton Rd (R). **FAC:** paved rds. (107 spaces). Avail: 30 paved, patios, 21 pull-thrus, (32x60), back-ins (30x40), 30 full hkups (30/50 amps), seasonal sites, cable, WiFi @ sites, laundry, LP gas. **REC:** boating nearby, playground. Pet restrict (B/Q). Partial handicap access. No tents. Big rig sites, eco-friendly. 2021 rates: $55.90, Military discount.
(503)581-2497 Lat: 44.96928, Lon: -122.98095
4130 Silverton Rd NE, Salem, OR 97305
phoenixrvpark.com
See ad page 735

SALEM CAMPGROUND & RV'S **Ratings: 5/6/3.5** (Campground) 51 Avail: 26 full hkups, 25 W, 25 E (30/50 amps). 2021 rates: $40 to $50. (800)826-9605, 3700 Hagers Grove Rd SE, Salem, OR 97317

SALEM PREMIER RV RESORT
good sam park **Ratings: 10/10★/9.5** (RV Resort) N bnd: From Jct of I-5 & SR-22/99E Bus/Mission St (exit 253): Go W 3.8 mi on SR-22/99E Bus, then 4.3 mi on SR-22 (L) NOTE: Stay on SR-22 at Marion St. OR S bnd: From Jct of I-5 Salem Parkway/99E (exit260A): Go SW 4.5 mi on Salem Pkwy/Commercial St/99E to Marion St/22W, then W 4.3 mi (L). **FAC:** paved rds. (188 spaces). Avail: 148 paved, patios, 96 pull-thrus, (25x60), back-ins (26x50), 148 full hkups (30/50 amps), seasonal sites, cable, WiFi @ sites, tent sites, rentals, dump, laundry, groc, LP gas. **REC:** heated pool, hot tub, Rickreall Creek: fishing, boating nearby, playground. Pet restrict (Q). Partial handicap access. Big rig sites, eco-friendly. 2021 rates: $57.50 to $63.50, Military discount.
(503)364-7714 Lat: 44.93074, Lon: -123.12385
4700 Salem-Dallas Hwy NW, Salem, OR 97304
www.premierrvresorts.com
See ad page 738

SILVER FALLS (Public State Park) From Jct of SR-22 & SR-214 (MP-6 1/2, E of Salem), E 16.4 mi on SR-214, MP-25 (R). 52 Avail: 52 W, 52 E (30/50 amps). 2021 rates: $29. (800)452-5687

OR

SEAL ROCK — B1 *Lincoln*

SEAL ROCKS RV COVE **Ratings: 5/7.5★/7.5** (Campground) Avail: 45 full hkups (30/50 amps). 2021 rates: $43 to $75. (541)563-3955, 1276 NW Cross St, Seal Rock, OR 97376

SEASIDE — A2 *Clatsop*

CIRCLE CREEK RV RESORT

good sam park **Ratings: 9/10★/9.5** (RV Park) Avail: 44 full hkups (30/50 amps). 2021 rates: $60 to $75. (503)738-6070, 85658 Hwy 101, Seaside, OR 97138

SEASIDE RV RESORT

good sam park **Ratings: 7.5/7/7.5** (Membership Park) Avail: 20 full hkups (30/50 amps). 2021 rates: $49 to $67. (888)563-7040, 1703 12th Ave, Seaside, OR 97138

SELMA — D2 *Josephine*

LAKE SELMAC PARK (Public) From Jct of US-199/Redwood Hwy & Deer Creek Rd (in town): Go S 0.6 mi on US-199 to Lakeshore Dr, then E 2 mi to Reeve's Creek Rd (R). 36 Avail: 34 full hkups, 2 W, 2 E (30/50 amps). 2021 rates: $30 to $35. (541)474-5285

SHADY COVE — D2 *Jackson*

FLY CASTERS RV PARK & RESORT **Ratings: 9/8★/9.5** (RV Park) Avail: 32 full hkups (30/50 amps). 2021 rates: $43 to $55. (541)878-2749, 21655 Crater Lake Hwy 62, Shady Cove, OR 97539

ROGUE RIVER RV PARK **Ratings: 7.5/8.5★/8** (RV Park) Avail: 30 full hkups (30/50 amps). 2021 rates: $42 to $59. (800)775-0367, 21800 Hwy 62, Shady Cove, OR 97539

SILVERTON — B2 *Marion*

SILVER SPUR RV PARK & RESORT

good sam park **Ratings: 9.5/10★/10** (RV Park) Avail: 100 full hkups (30/50 amps). 2021 rates: $46 to $60. (503)873-2020, 12622 Silverton Rd NE, Silverton, OR 97381

SISTERS — C3 *Deschutes*

SISTERS See also Bend, Camp Sherman, Crooked River Ranch, Culver & Redmond.

SISTERS CREEKSIDE CAMPGROUND (Public) From town: Go E 0.25 mi on US-20 to South Locust St, then S 500 ft (L). Avail: 28 full hkups (30/50 amps). 2021 rates: $46 to $76. Apr 15 to Oct 31. (541)323-5218

SOUTH BEACH — B1 *Lincoln*

WHALER'S REST RV & CAMPING RESORT

good sam park **Ratings: 8/7.5/8.5** (Membership Park) Avail: 70 full hkups (30/50 amps). 2021 rates: $50 to $70. (888)563-7040, 50 SE 123rd, South Beach, OR 97366

ST HELENS — A2 *Columbia*

BAYPORT RV PARK & CAMPGROUND (PORT OF COLUMBIA COUNTY PARK) (Public) From Jct of Hwy 30 & Bennett RD: Go SE 200 ft on Bennett Rd to Old Portland Rd, then NE 1/2 mi (R). 23 Avail: 23 W, 23 E (30/50 amps). 2021 rates: $30. (503)397-2888

ST PAUL — B2 *Marion*

CHAMPOEG (Public State Park) From Jct of I-5 & Donald/Aurora (exit 278), W 3.6 mi on Ehlen Rd to Newberg Rd, NW 2.3 mi (R). 75 Avail: 8 full hkups, 67 W, 67 E (30/50 amps). 2021 rates: $29 to $31. (800)551-6949

STANFIELD — A4 *Umatilla*

PILOT RV PARK

good sam park **Ratings: 9/9.5★/9.5** (RV Park) From Jct of I-84 & Hwy 395 (Exit 188): Go N 0.1 mi on Hwy 395 (L).

EZ OFF I-84 - ON THE OREGON TRAIL!

Close to Pendleton & Hermiston plus great fishing on the Umatilla & Columbia Rivers. Shopping, dining & wine tasting nearby! Rest & unwind in an immaculate park with large shade trees, lots of grass & paved sites! Stop in!

FAC: paved rds. (48 spaces). Avail: 10 paved, patios, 7 pull-thrus, (30x75), back-ins (30x55), 10 full hkups (30/50 amps), seasonal sites, cable, WiFi @ sites, laundry. **REC:** boating nearby, hunting nearby. Pets OK. Partial handicap access. No tents. Big rig sites. 2021 rates: $45 to $50, Military discount.

(541)449-1189 Lat: 45.76518, Lon: -119.20718
2125 Hwy 395 South, Stanfield, OR 97875
www.pilotrvpark.com
See ad page 741

SUMPTER — B5 *Baker*

SUMPTER PINES RV PARK **Ratings: 5.5/8★/6.5** (RV Park) 25 Avail: 17 full hkups, 8 W, 8 E (30/50 amps). 2021 rates: $32. Apr 01 to Oct 30. (541)894-2328, 640 S Mill St, Sumpter, OR 97877

SUNNY VALLEY — D2 *Josephine*

SUNNY VALLEY RV PARK AND CAMPGROUND

good sam park **Ratings: 8.5/10★/9.5** (RV Park) 30 Avail: 4 full hkups, 26 W, 26 E (30/50 amps). 2021 rates: $30 to $37.50. Mar 01 to Nov 01. (541)479-0209, 140 Old Stage Rd, Sunny Valley, OR 97497

SUTHERLIN — C2 *Douglas*

HI-WAY HAVEN RV PARK & DRIVE IN MOVIE

good sam park **Ratings: 9/9★/10** (RV Park) Avail: 41 full hkups (30/50 amps). 2021 rates: $42 to $60. (541)459-4557, 609 Fort McKay Rd, Sutherlin, OR 97479

UMPQUA RV PARK **Ratings: 8/9★/8.5** (RV Park) Avail: 15 full hkups (30/50 amps). 2021 rates: $40. (541)459-4423, 1916 Recreation Ln, Sutherlin, OR 97479

SWEET HOME — B2 *Linn*

SUNNYSIDE PARK (LINN COUNTY PARK) (Public) From Jct of Hwy 20 & 18th Ave (in town), E 5.2 mi on Hwy 20 to Quartzville Rd, NE 1.4 mi (R). 165 Avail: 133 W, 133 E (20/30 amps). 2021 rates: $26 to $32. May 01 to Oct 30. (541)967-3917

WHITCOMB CREEK PARK (Public) From town: Go 3 mi E on US-20, then 9 mi N on Quartzville Rd (R). 39 Avail: Pit toilets. 2021 rates: $22. Apr 25 to Nov 01. (541)967-3917

THE DALLES — A3 *Wasco*

DESCHUTES RIVER STATE REC AREA (Public State Park) From town, E 12 mi on I-84 to Columbia River Hwy (exit 97), E 5 mi (R). 63 Avail: 34 W, 34 E (20 amps). 2021 rates: $10 to $24. (541)739-2322

MEMALOOSE (Public State Park) Access from W-bnd only: From Jct of I-84 & State Park Rest Area off Ramp (milepost 73 1/4), proceed thru rest area to park (E); or E-Bnd: From Jct of I-84 & Exit 76, proceed under freeway and return, continue W 3 mi on I-84 (R). Avail: 43 full hkups (30 amps). 2021 rates: $24 to $31. Mar 15 to Oct 31. (541)478-3008

TILLAMOOK — A2 *Tillamook*

A SPOTLIGHT Introducing Oregon's North Coast's colorful attractions appearing at the front of this state section.

TILLAMOOK See also Cloverdale, Garibaldi, Pacific City & Rockaway Beach.

CAPE LOOKOUT (Public State Park) S-bnd: From Jct of US-101 & 3rd St (in town), SW 12 mi on Whiskey Creek Rd (R); or N-bnd: From Jct of US-101 & Sand Lake/Cape Lookout Rd (N of Beaver), NW 10.5 mi on Sand Lake/Cape Lookout Rd (L). Avail: 38 full hkups (30 amps). 2021 rates: $34. (800)842-3182

KILCHIS RIVER COUNTY CAMPGROUND (TILLAMOOK COUNTY PARK) (Public) From city, N 0.5 mi on US-101 to cnty rd (Alderbrook Rd), NE 7 mi (E). 63 Avail. 2021 rates: $16 to $27. May 01 to Sep 30. (503)842-6694

MISTY RIVER RV PARK & GLAMPING **Ratings: 6.5/8.5★/8** (RV Park) Avail: 28 full hkups (30/50 amps). 2021 rates: $39 to $49. (503)842-2750, 11300 Wilson River Hwy, Tillamook, OR 97141

NETARTS BAY GARDEN RV RESORT

good sam park **Ratings: 9/9.5★/9.5** (RV Park) From Jct of US-101 & 3rd St/Netarts Hwy (in Tillamook): Go W 5.8 mi on 3rd St (Netarts Hwy) to Bilyeu Ave, then SW 0.2 mi (R).

ON THE COAST & AWAY FROM THE CROWDS

Enjoy the seclusion of Netarts Bay & all it has to offer - come for fall fishing, crabbing & beachcombing, or just relaxing by the fire! We'll even cook your crabs for you! Boat rentals & guided shore crabbing available.

FAC: paved rds. 83 Avail: 4 paved, 79 all weather, patios, 11 pull-thrus, (24x55), back-ins (24x40), 83 full hkups (30/50 amps), WiFi @ sites, laundry, fire rings, firewood, restaurant. **REC:** Netarts Bay: fishing, boating nearby, hunting nearby, rec open to public. Pet restrict (Q). No tents, eco-friendly. 2021 rates: $39 to $50, Military discount.

(503)842-7774 Lat: 45.42655, Lon: -123.93851
2260 Bilyeu Ave W, Tillamook, OR 97141
www.netartsbay.com
See ad page 748

PORT OF TILLAMOOK BAY RV PARK (Public) From jct Hwy 6 & US 101: Go 2 mi S on US 101. 52 Avail. 2021 rates: $15. (503)842-7152

TILLAMOOK BAY CITY RV PARK

good sam park **Ratings: 8/9★/8** (RV Park) From Jct of US-101 & Hwy 6 (in town): Go N 4.5 mi on US-101 to Alderbrook Rd (MP-61 1/2), then E 0.2 mi (R).

YOUR GATEWAY ON THE OREGON COAST!

From here, you can visit many of Oregon's gems! Go crabbing on the coast, visit the famous (& yummy) attractions such as Tillamook Creamery or State treasures such as Cape Meares Lighthouse & Scenic Viewpoint. We have it all!

FAC: all weather rds. (43 spaces). 37 Avail: 30 gravel, 7 grass, 18 pull-thrus, (25x60), back-ins (25x60), 30 full hkups, 7 W, 7 E (30/50 amps), seasonal sites, cable, WiFi @ sites, rentals, shower$, dump, laundry, firewood. **REC:** boating nearby, playground. Pet restrict (Q). No tents. Big rig sites, eco-friendly. 2021 rates: $40 to $46.

(503)377-2124 Lat: 45.51115, Lon: -123.87536
7805 Alderbrook Rd, Tillamook, OR 97141
tillamookbaycityrvpark.com
See ad page 749

TILLAMOOK STATE FOREST/GALES CREEK CAMPGROUND (Public State Park) From the town of Tillamook: Go 23 mi E on Hwy 6, then N on North Fork Rd. 19 Avail: Pit toilets. 2021 rates: $20. May 15 to Oct 01. (503)357-2191

TILLAMOOK STATE FOREST/JONES CREEK CAMPGROUND (Public State Park) From the town of Tillamook: Go 23 mi E on Hwy 6, then N on North Fork Rd. 28 Avail: Pit toilets. 2021 rates: $20. May 24 to Sep 16. (503)842-2545

TRASK RIVER COUNTY CAMPGROUND (TILLAMOOK COUNTY PARK) (Public) From town, E 11.8 mi on Trask River Cnty Rd (R). 82 Avail: Pit toilets. 2021 rates: $22 to $32. (503)842-4559

TRAIL — D2 *Jackson*

JOSEPH H STEWART RECREATION AREA (Public State Park) From Jct of I-5 & SR-62 (exit 30 Crater Lake Hwy), NE 34 mi on SR-62 (L). 150 Avail: 150 W, 150 E (20/30 amps). 2021 rates: $24. Mar 01 to Oct 31. (541)560-3334

ROGUE ELK (JACKSON COUNTY PARK) (Public) From Jct of I-5 & Crater Lake Hwy 62, NE 27 mi on Crater Lake Hwy 62 (L). 38 Avail: 16 W, 16 E (30 amps). 2021 rates: $20 to $24. Mar 15 to Oct 14. (541)774-8183

TROUTDALE — A2 *Multnomah*

SANDY RIVERFRONT RV RESORT

good sam park **Ratings: 9.5/9★/9.5** (RV Park) From jct I-84 & NE 238th Dr (Exit16): Go 1/4 mi S on NE 238th Dr, then 3-1/2 mi E on NE Halsey St (L). Do not use GPS or Exit 18. **FAC:** paved rds. (113 spaces). Avail: 40 paved, 25 pull-thrus, (24x60), back-ins (24x60), accepts full hkup units only, 40 full hkups (30/50 amps), seasonal sites, cable, WiFi @ sites, laundry. **REC:** Sandy River: swim, fishing, boating nearby. Pet restrict (S/B/Q). Partial handicap access. No tents. Big rig sites, eco-friendly. 2021 rates: $52.20 to $59.81.

(503)665-6722 Lat: 45.53779, Lon: -122.37879
1097 E Historic Columbia River Hwy, Troutdale, OR 97060
sandyrv.com
See ad page 743

TUALATIN — A2 *Washington*

ROAMER'S REST RV PARK **Ratings: 9/9.5★/9** (RV Park) Avail: 20 full hkups (30/50 amps). 2021 rates: $62. (503)692-6350, 17585 SW Pacific Hwy, Tualatin, OR 97062

TYGH VALLEY — B3 *Wasco*

HUNT PARK-WASCO COUNTY FAIRGROUNDS (WASCO COUNTY PARK) (Public) From Jct of US-197 & SR-216, W 0.25 mi on SR-216 to Fairgrounds Rd, SW 2 mi, follow signs (L). 120 Avail: 120 W, 120 E (20 amps). 2021 rates: $20. (541)483-2288

UKIAH — B4 *Umatilla*

UKIAH-DALE/FOREST WAYSIDE (Public State Park) From Jct of US-395 & CR-244, S 1.5 mi on US-395 (L). 27 Avail. 2021 rates: $10. Apr 18 to Oct 14. (800)551-6949

UMATILLA — A4 *Umatilla*

UMATILLA MARINA & RV PARK

Ratings: 7.5/8.5★/9 (Public) From Jct of I-82 & Brownell Ave (Exit 1), N 0.4 mi on Brownell to Third, W 0.3 mi to Quincy St, N 100 ft (R). **FAC:** all weather rds. Avail: 26 all weather, 12 pull-thrus, (37x60), back-ins (37x60), 26 full hkups (30/50 amps), WiFi @ sites, tent sites, dump, fire rings, firewood. **REC:** Columbia River: swim, fishing, marina, kayaking/canoeing, boating nearby, hunting nearby. Pets OK. Big rig sites, 14 day max stay. 2021 rates: $40, Military discount.
(541)922-3939 Lat: 45.92352, Lon: -119.32990
1710 Quincy Ave, Umatilla, OR 97882
www.umatilla-city.org/marina
See ad page 740

UNITY — B5 *Baker*

UNITY LAKE (Public State Park) From town: Go 5 mi N on Hwy-7. 35 Avail: 35 W, 35 E (30/50 amps). 2021 rates: $26. Apr 01 to Oct 31. (541)932-4453

VALE — C5 *Malheur*

BULLY CREEK PARK (MALHEUR COUNTY PARK) (Public) From town, NW 7 mi on Graham Blvd to Bully Creek Rd, NW 3 mi (L). Avail: 40 E (20/30 amps). 2021 rates: $15. Apr 15 to Nov 15. (541)473-2969

VALE TRAILS RV PARK **Ratings: 6.5/9★/8** (RV Park) 25 Avail: 21 full hkups, 4 W, 4 E (30/50 amps). 2021 rates: $45. (541)473-3879, 511 11th St, Vale, OR 97918

VERNONIA — A2 *Columbia*

ANDERSON PARK (Public) From Jct of SR-47 & Jefferson St, S 2 blks on Jefferson St (E). Avail: 20 full hkups (30 amps). 2021 rates: $30. (503)429-5291

BIG EDDY PARK (Public) From town, N 7 mi on SR-47 (L). Avail: 14 full hkups (20/30 amps). 2021 rates: $25 to $30. (503)397-2353

L.L. "STUB" STEWART (Public State Park) From Jct of Hwy 26 & Hwy 47 (30 mi NW of Portland), N 3.55 mi on Hwy 47 (R). Avail: 78 full hkups (30/50 amps). 2021 rates: $33. (503)324-0606

WALDPORT — B1 *Lincoln*

BEACHSIDE (Public State Park) From Jct of US-101 & Hwy 34 (N of town), S 3.5 mi on US-101 (R). 32 Avail: 32 W, 32 E (20/30 amps). 2021 rates: $31. Mar 15 to Oct 31. (800)551-6949

MCKINLEY'S RV PARK & MARINA **Ratings: 8.5/9★/9.5** (RV Park) Avail: 53 full hkups (30/50 amps). 2021 rates: $40 to $55. (541)563-4656, 850 Hwy 34, Waldport, OR 97394

WALDPORT/NEWPORT KOA **Ratings: 8.5/8.5/9** (Campground) Avail: 69 full hkups (30/50 amps). 2021 rates: $47.50 to $93.50. (541)563-2250, 1330 NW Pacific Coast Hwy, Waldport, OR 97394

WALLOWA — A5 *Wallowa*

WALLOWA RIVER RV PARK **Ratings: 6.5/9★/9** (RV Park) Avail: 25 full hkups (30/50 amps). 2021 rates: $35. (541)886-7002, 503 Whiskey Creek Rd, Wallowa, OR 97885

WARRENTON — A2 *Clatsop*

KAMPERS WEST RV PARK **Ratings: 8/8/7** (Campground) 109 Avail: 102 full hkups, 7 W, 7 E (30 amps). 2021 rates: $48. (503)861-1814, 1140 NW Warrenton Dr, Warrenton, OR 97146

WELCHES — B3 *Clackamas*

MT HOOD VILLAGE RESORT

Ratings: 8/10★/10 (Campground) 285 Avail: 185 full hkups, 100 W, 100 E (30/50 amps). 2021 rates: $60 to $90. (888)563-7040, 65000 E Hwy 26, Welches, OR 97067

WESTFIR — C2 *Lane*

CASEY'S RIVERSIDE RV PARK

Ratings: 10/10★/10 (RV Park) Avail: 56 full hkups (30/50 amps). 2021 rates: $38 to $49. (541)782-1906, 46443 Westfir Rd, Westfir, OR 97492

WHITE CITY — D2 *Jackson*

LAKEWOOD RV PARK **Ratings: 6.5/8.5/8.5** (RV Park) Avail: 10 full hkups (30/50 amps). 2021 rates: $40. (541)830-1957, 2564 Merry Lane, White City, OR 97503

WILSONVILLE — B2 *Washington*

PHEASANT RIDGE RV RESORT

Ratings: 10/10★/10 (RV Park) From Jct of I-5 & SW Elligsen Rd/N Wilsonville (exit 286): Go E 0.5 mi on SW Elligsen Rd (L).

SECLUDED BUT CONVENIENT TO SO MUCH!
Enjoy our quiet surroundings in the beautiful Willamette Valley while being conveniently located to Portland, local wineries, Mt. Hood & much more. The kiddos can enjoy Bullwinkle's Family Fun Center, only 5 minutes away!

FAC: paved rds. (130 spaces). Avail: 80 paved, 50 pull-thrus, (30x60), back-ins (32x65), 80 full hkups (30/50 amps), seasonal sites, cable, WiFi @ sites, laundry, LP gas. **REC:** heated pool, hot tub, boating nearby. Pets OK. Partial handicap access. No tents. Big rig sites, eco-friendly. 2021 rates: $61.25 to $75, Military discount.
(503)682-7829 Lat: 45.33588, Lon: -122.76201
8275 SW Elligsen Rd, Wilsonville, OR 97070
pheasantridge.com
See ad page 744

Travel Services

CAMPING WORLD OF WILSONVILLE As the nation's largest retailer of RV supplies, accessories, services and new and used RVs, Camping World is committed to making your total RV experience better. **SERVICES:** RV, tire, RV appliance, staffed RV wash, restrooms. RV supplies, LP gas, emergency parking, RV accessible. Hours: 9am to 6pm.
(800)446-9039 Lat: 45.325091, Lon: -122.769802
26875 SW Boones Ferry Rd., Wilsonville, OR 97070
www.campingworld.com

WINCHESTER — C2 *Douglas*

JOHN P AMACHER PARK & CAMPGROUND (DOUGLAS COUNTY PARK) (Public) From Jct of I-5 & Old Hwy 99 (Exit 129), S 0.25 mi on Old Hwy 99 (R). Avail: 20 full hkups (20 amps). 2021 rates: $15 to $23. May 01 to Sep 30. (541)957-7001

WINCHESTER BAY — C1 *Douglas*

UMPQUA LIGHTHOUSE (Public State Park) From Jct of US-101 & Winchester Bay/Salmon Harbor exit, S 0.8 mi on US-101 to Old Hwy 101/Lighthouse Rd, W 0.5 mi (L). 20 Avail: 12 full hkups, 8 W, 8 E (20/30 amps). 2021 rates: $29 to $31. (541)551-6949

WINCHESTER BAY RV RESORT (Public) From Jct of US-101 & Salmon Harbor Dr (Winchester Bay exit): Go 1/4 mi SW Salmon Harbor Dr (R). Avail: 138 full hkups (30/50 amps). 2021 rates: $28 to $44. (541)271-0287

WINDY COVE A RV PARK & CAMPGROUND (Public) From Jct of Hwy 101 & Salmon Harbor Dr: Go 1/4 mi SW on Salmon Harbor Dr (L). 28 Avail: 24 full hkups, 4 E (30 amps). 2021 rates: $17 to $25. (541)271-4138

WINDY COVE B RV PARK & CAMPGROUND (Public) From Jct of Hwy 101 & Salmon Harbor Dr: Go 1/4 mi SW on Salmon Harbor Dr (L). Avail: 40 full hkups (30 amps). 2021 rates: $17 to $25. (541)271-5634

WOLF CREEK — D2 *Josephine*

WOLF CREEK CAMPGROUND (Public) From Jct of I-5 & Wolf Creek (Exit 76): Go SW onto Old State Hwy 99S, then SW 0.3 mi to Front St., then W 0.2 mi to Main St, then S 0.3 mi (L). 14 Avail: 14 W, 14 E (30 amps), Pit toilets. 2021 rates: $25. May 01 to Sep 30. (541)474-5285

WOOD VILLAGE — A2 *Multnomah*

Travel Services

CAMPING WORLD OF WOOD VILLAGE/PORTLAND As the nation's largest retailer of RV supplies, accessories, services and new and used RVs, Camping World is committed to making your total RV experience better. **SERVICES:** RV appliance, MH mechanical, sells outdoor gear, restrooms. RV Sales. RV supplies, dump, emergency parking, RV accessible. Hours: 9am to 7pm.
(877)268-7319 Lat: 45.542589, Lon: -122.416176
24000 NE Sandy Blvd, Wood Village, OR 97060
www.campingworld.com

OR

WOODBURN — B2 *Marion*

PORTLAND WOODBURN RV PARK

Ratings: 10/9.5★/8.5 (RV Park) From Jct of I-5 & Hwy 214/ Hwy 219 (exit 271): Go W 0.1 mi on Hwy 214/ Hwy 219 to Arney Rd, then N 100 ft to stop sign, then E 0.1 mi (L).

EASY OFF & ON I-5 - SO MUCH NEARBY!
Relax in our quiet park & enjoy what the area has to offer. Walk to premium outlet shopping! Woodburn Drag strip & Wooden Shoe Tulip Festival are a short drive! Nearby Oregon wineries abound! There is so much to see & do!

FAC: paved rds. (148 spaces). Avail: 77 paved, 40 pull-thrus, (25x60), back-ins (24x40), 77 full hkups (30/50 amps), seasonal sites, cable, WiFi @ sites, laundry, groc. **REC:** heated pool, boating nearby, playground. Pet restrict (B/Q). Partial handicap access. No tents. Big rig sites, eco-friendly. 2021 rates: $55, Military discount.
(503)981-0002 Lat: 45.15336, Lon: -122.88222
115 N Arney Rd, Woodburn, OR 97071
woodburnrv.com
See ad page 744

YACHATS — B1 *Lane*

SEA PERCH RV RESORT

Ratings: 9/10★/9.5 (RV Resort) From Jct of Hwy 126 & US 101 (in Florence): Go N 17 mi on US 101 to MP-171 (L). **FAC:** paved rds. Avail: 28 paved, patios, back-ins (28x60), accepts full hkup units only, 28 full hkups (30/50 amps), WiFi @ sites, laundry, firewood. **REC:** Pacific Ocean:. Pet restrict (Q). Partial handicap access. No tents. Big rig sites, eco-friendly. 2021 rates: $95 to $125, Military discount.
(541)547-3505 Lat: 44.23045, Lon: -124.10976
95480 Hwy 101 S - MP 171, Yachats, OR 97498
www.seaperchrvresort.com
See ad page 747

We give you what you want. First, we surveyed thousands of RVers just like you. Then, we developed our exclusive Triple Rating System for campgrounds based on the results. That's why our rating system is so good at explaining the quality of facilities and cleanliness of campgrounds.

YOU ARE HERE

Pennsylvania

DID YOU KNOW?

Designed by Frank Lloyd Wright in 1935, the iconic Fallingwater house is built above a waterfall and still has its original furnishings.

Pennsylvania encompasses some of America's most significant heritage sites as well as stunning landscapes. On its 46,000-square-mile territory, you can encounter both Amish communities and modern cities.

Where the Past Meets Present

Democracy took root in Philadelphia in 1776 when Thomas Jefferson wrote the Declaration of Independence. It eventually became the country's first UNESCO World Heritage City. In Independence National Historical Park, you'll find the Liberty Bell, Independence Hall and the National Constitution Center.

Pittsburgh Soars

Basking in a storied past, Pittsburgh never fails to embrace innovation and creativity. The Andy Warhol Museum and Carnegie Museums house world-class treasures. You'll also uncover Chihuly glass sculptures scattered throughout the Phipps Conservatory and Botanical Gardens. Head east for a delicious visit to Hershey, home to the world-famous chocolate company of the same name. See how the sweet stuff is made at Hershey's Chocolate World.

Appalachian Trailheads

A 229-mile segment of the Appalachian Trail runs through the southwest corner of Pennsylvania. Seasoned hikers can sample the iconic trail from several trailheads, including those found at Boiling Springs, Duncannon and the Greater Waynesboro Area.

Stunning Scenery

Horticulture thrives in the Keystone State. The Longwood Gardens in Kennett Square will impress with their conservatory and 40 gardens planted and designed in traditional English, French and Italian styles. In the Valley Forge region, the Morris Arboretum houses over 12,000 plants from around the world.

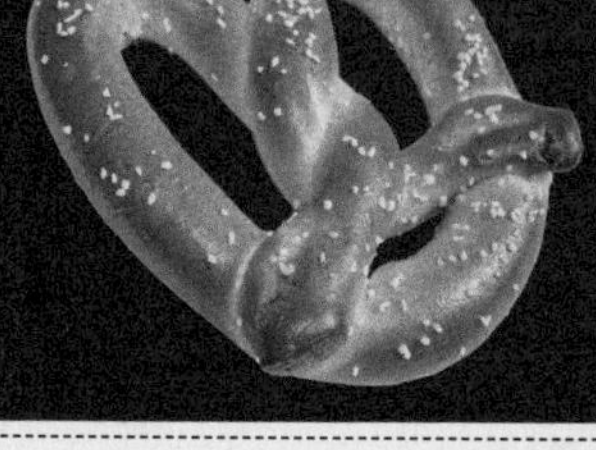

Pennsylvania Pretzels

When German immigrants settled in Pennsylvania, they brought a recipe for a knot-shaped bread snack that burst with salty flavor. Today, Pennsylvania leads the world in making both hard and soft pretzels, and visitors can sample a range of twisted treats in salty and sweet flavors throughout the state. Check out Snyder's of Hanover, Auntie Anne's in Philadelphia and the Philly Soft Pretzel Factory throughout the region.

VISITOR CENTER

PA

TIME ZONE
Eastern Standard

ROAD & HIGHWAY INFORMATION
877-511-7366
penndot.gov

FISHING & HUNTING INFORMATION
877-707-4085
fishandboat.com/license

BOATING INFORMATION
717-705-7800
fishandboat.com

NATIONAL PARKS
nps.gov/pa

STATE PARKS
dcnr.pa.gov/StateParks

TOURISM INFORMATION
Pennsylvania Tourism
800-847-4872
visitpa.com

TOP TOURISM ATTRACTIONS
1) Hersheypark
2) Fallingwater
3) Gettysburg National Military Park

MAJOR CITIES
Philadelphia, Pittsburgh, Allentown, Erie, Reading, Harrisburg (capital)

Colonel Denning State Park

Just 17 miles from Carlisle, the scenic woodlands, forests, rivers and streams of Colonel Denning State Park are a magnet for outdoor enthusiasts. Framed by majestic mountains, the park features more than 18 miles of hiking, biking and riding trails for all levels and sensibilities. The challenging 2.5-mile (one-way) Flat Rock Trail involves some rock scrambling and a steep ascent to a peak elevation of 1,987 feet. Nimble hikers are rewarded with breathtaking panoramas of the valley, especially during fall, when leaf peepers coo over the kaleidoscopic show of gold and crimson leaves.

Soldier Stories

A celebration and an homage to America's men and women in uniform, the superb U.S. Army Heritage and Education Center in Carlisle is worth a morning's exploration for anyone with even just a fleeting interest in military history. With more than 16 million military items, including 350,000 military history volumes and the world's largest collection of Civil War photography and personal journals, the center turns the spotlight on the lives and experiences of American soldiers. Several interactive simulation exhibits include a shooting range, a 700-foot parachute drop into enemy territory and the chance to take control of a Vietnam-era Huey helicopter. The outdoor Army Heritage Trail (set aside two hours) features full-scale recreations of military sites from the colonial era to the present, including an extensive maze-like trench system from WWI, tanks, helicopters, WWII barracks and winter cabins from the Civil War. Learn about the the lives of soldiers in combat zones.

In Philadelphia, the Swann Memorial Fountain honors the major rivers that run through the region.

Pretty Poconos

Bordered by the Delaware Water Gap National Recreation Area to the east, Lake Wallenpaupack to the north and the Poconos Mountains to the west, this region is a four-season paradise for lovers of outdoor recreation. Paddling, hiking, biking, skiing and hunting abound. The Delaware Water Gap is known nationally for its scenic vistas, as well as opportunities for rafting and tubing. The boardwalk trail that leads to 130-foot Dingmans Falls is a great introduction to the park's hiking and biking opportunities.

Hiking and Biking Paradise

Camelback Mountain Resort is famed for its skiing and snowboarding, and the Big Pocono State Park that surrounds it is a great spot for hiking and biking in warmer months. Skytop, known for its historic 1920s retreat hotel, also offers a wealth of outdoor adventuring. The many lakes, ponds and rivers that sculpted the mountainous region are open for fishing and swimming, and outfitters are available in most towns to help guide you through rafting and boating excursions.

Dingmans Falls drops 80 feet in Delaware Gap National Recreation Area near Pennsylvania's eastern border.

Football Fame

Each of the small towns in eastern Pennsylvania region has a distinct charm and character. The town of Jim Thorpe is brimming with Victorian homes built by the coal mining barons of an earlier era. It's also home to the Lehigh Gorge Scenic Railway, which follows winding tracks through the rugged region and offers striking views of the Lehigh Gorge State Park. The narrated trip features views of mountains and wildlife. Originally named Mauch Chunk, the town adapted the name of the local football legend who played for Carlisle Indian Industrial School and went on to win gold in the 1912 Olympics.

Gnarly NASCAR Action

If hiking and cycling aren't enough to get your adrenaline pumping, head to Long Pond, home of the Pocono Raceway. There are NASCAR and IndyCar events held throughout the summer season, highlighted by the Pocono 400 in early June. There's nothing quite like seeing the greatest drivers in the country tangle with the track's tough turns on the famed "Tricky Triangle," so nicknamed because of its triangular layout. Take the kids to Tricky's Kit Kamp, which features games, play structures and special entertainment. The Tricky Triangle Club hosts driver Q&As. Infield camping and trackside camping accommodate RVs.

Featured Good Sam Parks

PENNSYLVANIA

When you stay with Good Sam, you can expect the highest degree of cleanliness and friendliness, and better yet, you get **10% off** overnight campground fees.

If you're not already a Good Sam member you can purchase your membership at one of these locations:

ALTOONA
Wright's Orchard Station Campground

BENTON
Whispering Pines Camping Estates

BOWMANSVILLE
Sun Valley RV Resort

CHAMPION
Mountain Pines Campground

COVINGTON
Tanglewood Camping

DOVER
Gettysburg Farm RV Campground

EAST STROUDSBURG
Timothy Lake North RV Park
Timothy Lake South RV Park

ERIE
Presque Isle Passage RV Park & Cabin Rentals

GETTYSBURG
Drummer Boy Camping Resort
Round Top Campground

HARRISBURG
Harrisburg East Campground & Storage

HOLTWOOD
Tucquan Park Family Campground

KIRKWOOD
Oma's Family Campground

LAKE CITY
Camp Eriez

LANCASTER
Circle M Camping Resort
Country Acres Campground
Flory's Cottages & Camping

LAPORTE
Pioneer Campground

LEBANON
Hershey RV & Camping Resort

LEHIGHTON
StonyBrook RV Resort

LENHARTSVILLE
Robin Hill Campground

LEWISTOWN
Waterside Campground & RV Park

MANHEIM
PA Dutch Country RV Resort
Pinch Pond Family Campground

MOUNT COBB
Clayton Park RV Escape

NEW HOLLAND
Spring Gulch Resort Campground

PINE GROVE
Twin Grove RV Resort & Cottages

PORTERSVILLE
Bear Run Campground

RAVINE
Echo Valley Campground

SCOTRUN
Four Seasons Campgrounds
Scotrun RV Resort

SHARTLESVILLE
Appalachian RV Campground

STROUDSBURG
Mountain Vista Campground

TUNKHANNOCK
Cozy Creek Family Campground

WASHINGTON
Pine Cove Beach Club & RV Resort

WINFIELD
Little Mexico Campground

WOODLAND
Woodland Campground

10/10★/10 GOOD SAM PARK

LEHIGHTON
StonyBrook RV Resort
(570)386-4088

What's This?

An RV park with a 10/10★/10 rating has scored perfect grades in amenities, cleanliness and appearance ("See Understanding the Campground Rating System" on pages 8 and 9 for an explanation of the trusted Good Sam Rating System). Stay in a 10/10★/10 park on your next trip for a nearly flawless camping experience.

Getty Images/iStockphoto

PA

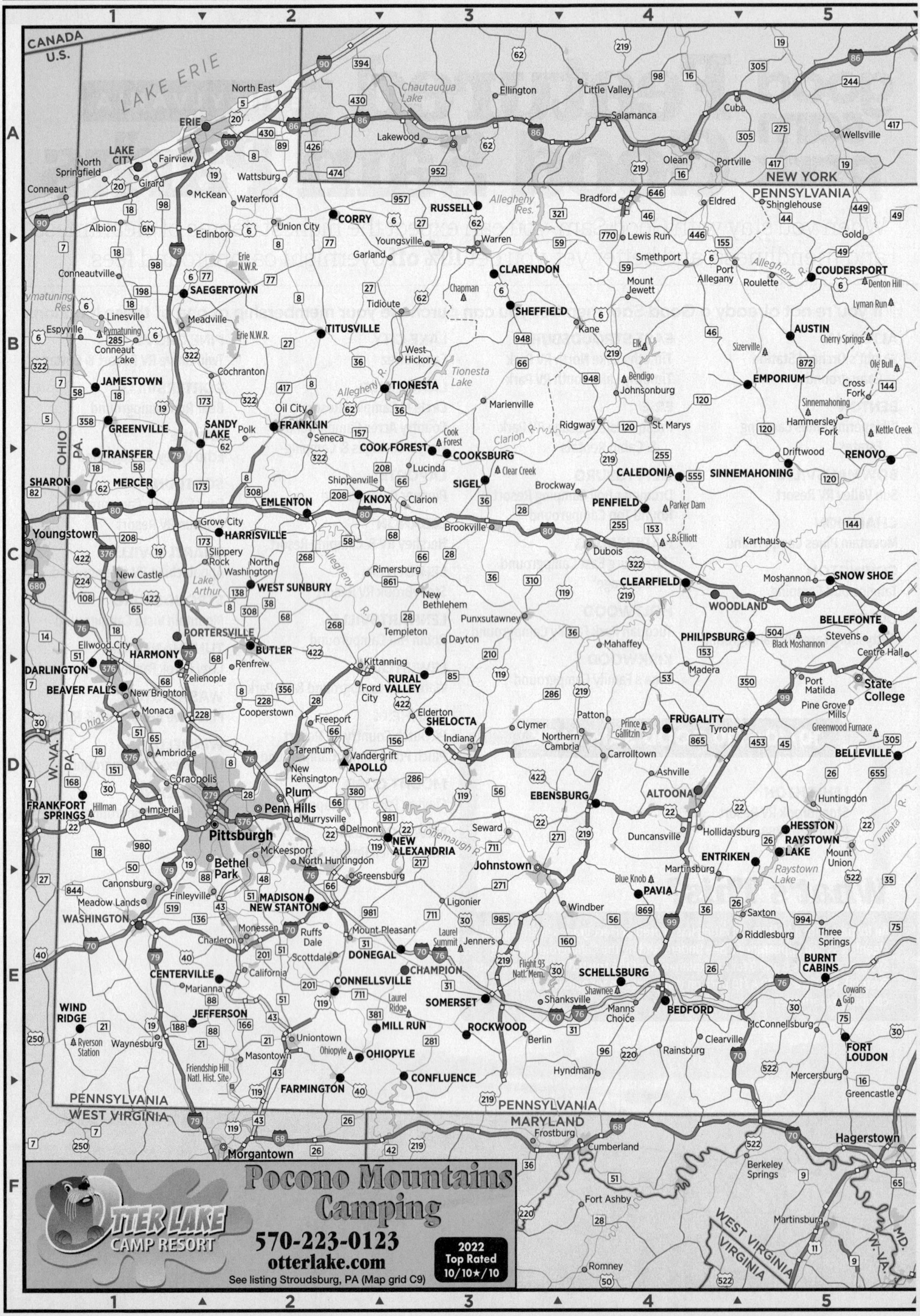
CANADA
U.S.
LAKE ERIE
NEW YORK
PENNSYLVANIA
OHIO
PA.
W. VA.
PA.
MARYLAND
WEST VIRGINIA
VIRGINIA
MD.
W. VA.
North East
ERIE
LAKE CITY
North Springfield
Fairview
Girard
Conneaut
Wattsburg
McKean
Waterford
Albion
Edinboro
Union City
CORRY
RUSSELL
Chautauqua Lake
Ellington
Little Valley
Salamanca
Lakewood
Cuba
Olean
Portville
Wellsville
Bradford
Eldred
Shinglehouse
Gold
Lewis Run
Smethport
Port Allegany
Roulette
COUDERSPORT
Denton Hill
Lyman Run
Youngsville
Warren
Garland
Allegheny Res.
CLARENDON
Chapman
SHEFFIELD
Kane
Mount Jewett
Conneautville
SAEGERTOWN
Erie N.W.R.
Pymatuning Res.
Linesville
Espyville
Pymatuning
Conneaut Lake
Meadville
Tidioute
TITUSVILLE
West Hickory
Tionesta Lake
TIONESTA
Cochranton
JAMESTOWN
Oil City
FRANKLIN
Seneca
GREENVILLE
SANDY LAKE
Polk
TRANSFER
MERCER
SHARON
Youngstown
Cook Forest
COOK FOREST
COOKSBURG
Lucinda
Marienville
Clear Creek
Shippenville
KNOX
Clarion
SIGEL
EMLENTON
Clarion R.
Ridgway
Bendigo
Johnsonburg
Elk
St. Marys
AUSTIN
Cherry Springs
Sizerville
Ole Bull
EMPORIUM
Cross Fork
Sinnemahoning
Hammersley Fork
Kettle Creek
Driftwood
RENOVO
SINNEMAHONING
CALEDONIA
Brockway
PENFIELD
Parker Dam
S.B. Elliott
Dubois
Brookville
Grove City
HARRISVILLE
Slippery Rock
North Washington
New Castle
Lake Arthur
WEST SUNBURY
Rimersburg
New Bethlehem
Punxsutawney
Karthaus
Moshannon
SNOW SHOE
CLEARFIELD
Mahaffey
WOODLAND
BELLEFONTE
Stevens
Black Moshannon
Centre Hall
PHILIPSBURG
Madera
State College
Port Matilda
Pine Grove Mills
Greenwood Furnace
Ellwood City
HARMONY
PORTERSVILLE
BUTLER
Renfrew
DARLINGTON
BEAVER FALLS
New Brighton
Zelienople
Monaca
Ohio R.
Cooperstown
Templeton
Dayton
Kittanning
Ford City
RURAL VALLEY
Elderton
SHELOCTA
Indiana
Freeport
Tarentum
Vandergrift
APOLLO
New Kensington
Plum
Penn Hills
Murrysville
Ambridge
Coraopolis
FRANKFORT SPRINGS
Hillman
Imperial
Pittsburgh
Bethel Park
McKeesport
North Huntingdon
Greensburg
Delmont
NEW ALEXANDRIA
Conemaugh R.
Clymer
Northern Cambria
Patton
Prince Gallitzin
FRUGALITY
Tyrone
Carrolltown
Ashville
ALTOONA
EBENSBURG
Duncansville
Hollidaysburg
BELLEVILLE
Huntingdon
HESSTON
RAYSTOWN LAKE
ENTRIKEN
Martinsburg
Raystown Lake
Mount Union
Juniata R.
Seward
Johnstown
Blue Knob
PAVIA
Windber
Saxton
Riddlesburg
Three Springs
Canonsburg
Finleyville
Meadow Lands
MADISON
NEW STANTON
WASHINGTON
Monessen
Charleroi
Ruffs Dale
Mount Pleasant
Scottdale
Ligonier
Laurel Summit
Jenners
DONEGAL
CHAMPION
Flight 93 Natl. Mem.
SCHELLSBURG
Shawnee
BURNT CABINS
Cowans Gap
CENTERVILLE
Marianna
California
CONNELLSVILLE
Laurel Ridge
SOMERSET
Shanksville
Manns Choice
BEDFORD
McConnellsburg
WIND RIDGE
JEFFERSON
MILL RUN
ROCKWOOD
Berlin
Clearville
FORT LOUDON
Ryerson Station
Waynesburg
Uniontown
Ohiopyle
OHIOPYLE
Rainsburg
Masontown
Friendship Hill Natl. Hist. Site
Hyndman
Mercersburg
Greencastle
FARMINGTON
CONFLUENCE
Frostburg
Cumberland
Hagerstown
Morgantown
Berkeley Springs
Fort Ashby
Martinsburg
Romney

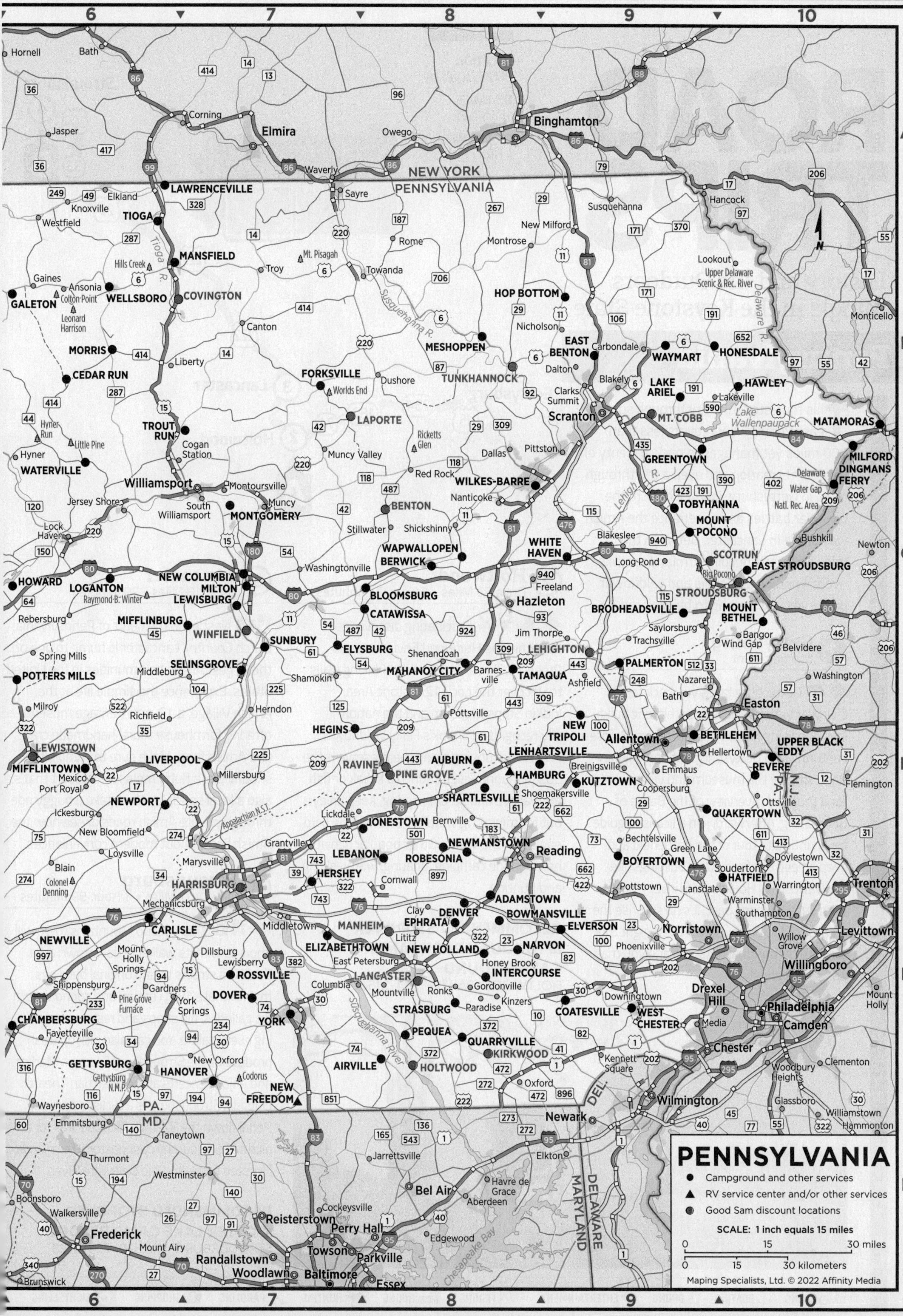
PENNSYLVANIA
Campground and other services
RV service center and/or other services
Good Sam discount locations
SCALE: 1 inch equals 15 miles
0 15 30 miles
0 15 30 kilometers
Maping Specialists, Ltd. © 2022 Affinity Media
NEW YORK
PENNSYLVANIA
MARYLAND
DELAWARE
DEL.
N.J.
PA.
MD.
Binghamton
Elmira
Corning
Hornell
Bath
Owego
Waverly
Sayre
LAWRENCEVILLE
TIOGA
MANSFIELD
WELLSBORO
COVINGTON
GALETON
MORRIS
CEDAR RUN
TROUT RUN
WATERVILLE
Williamsport
MONTGOMERY
HOWARD
LOGANTON
NEW COLUMBIA
MILTON
LEWISBURG
MIFFLINBURG
WINFIELD
SUNBURY
SELINSGROVE
POTTERS MILLS
LEWISTOWN
MIFFLINTOWN
LIVERPOOL
NEWPORT
HARRISBURG
CARLISLE
NEWVILLE
CHAMBERSBURG
GETTYSBURG
HANOVER
YORK
DOVER
ROSSVILLE
NEW FREEDOM
FORKSVILLE
LAPORTE
BENTON
MESHOPPEN
TUNKHANNOCK
HOP BOTTOM
EAST BENTON
Scranton
WAYMART
HONESDALE
LAKE ARIEL
HAWLEY
MT. COBB
GREENTOWN
MATAMORAS
MILFORD
DINGMANS FERRY
TOBYHANNA
MOUNT POCONO
SCOTRUN
EAST STROUDSBURG
STROUDSBURG
BRODHEADSVILLE
MOUNT BETHEL
WILKES-BARRE
WHITE HAVEN
WAPWALLOPEN
BERWICK
BLOOMSBURG
CATAWISSA
ELYSBURG
Hazleton
LEHIGHTON
PALMERTON
MAHANOY CITY
TAMAQUA
HEGINS
NEW TRIPOLI
Allentown
BETHLEHEM
Easton
UPPER BLACK EDDY
REVERE
QUAKERTOWN
LENHARTSVILLE
HAMBURG
KUTZTOWN
AUBURN
RAVINE
PINE GROVE
SHARTLESVILLE
JONESTOWN
LEBANON
HERSHEY
NEWMANSTOWN
ROBESONIA
Reading
BOYERTOWN
HATFIELD
ADAMSTOWN
DENVER
EPHRATA
MANHEIM
BOWMANSVILLE
ELVERSON
ELIZABETHTOWN
NEW HOLLAND
NARVON
LANCASTER
INTERCOURSE
STRASBURG
COATESVILLE
WEST CHESTER
PEQUEA
QUARRYVILLE
KIRKWOOD
AIRVILLE
HOLTWOOD
Norristown
Philadelphia
Camden
Chester
Trenton
Levittown
Willingboro
Wilmington
Newark
Baltimore
Towson
Frederick
Bel Air

ROAD TRIPS

History and the Outdoors Mingle in the Keystone State

Pennsylvania

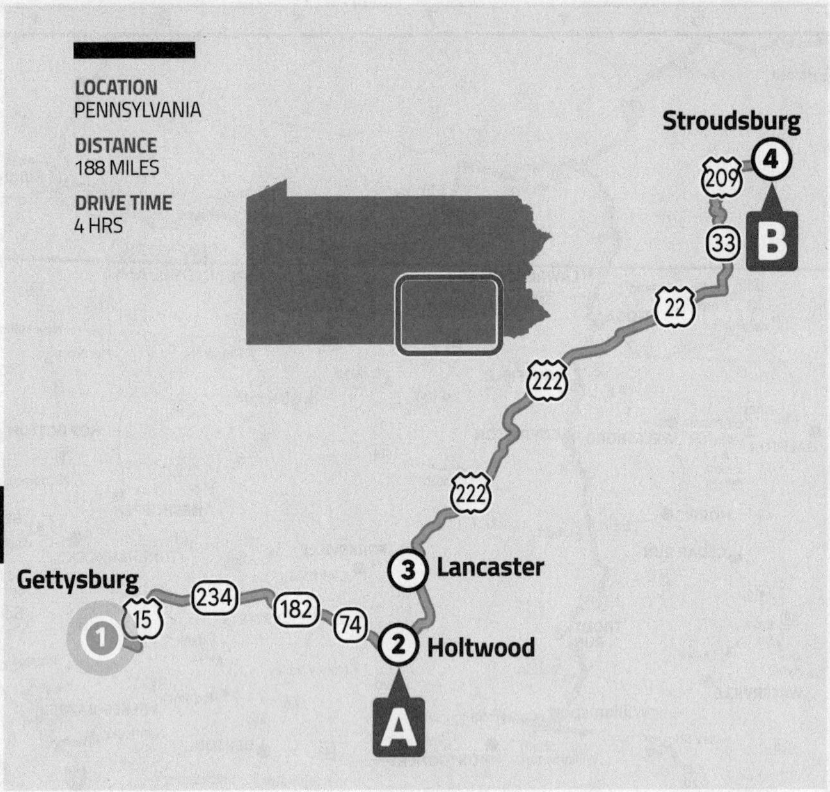

This four-stop itinerary through southeast Pennsylvania covers less than 200 miles yet manages to pack in plenty of outdoor recreation and even a trip through time. In Gettysburg, journey back to the Civil War battles and experience the Amish way of life in Lancaster. Between the rolling hills and bucolic farmland are wild rivers, winding bike trails and wildflower preserves just waiting to be explored.

① Gettysburg
Starting Point

Gettysburg takes you back to the Civil War with its battlefields, historic buildings and living history presentations. Before venturing into Gettysburg National Military Park, stop by the museum and visitor center for a thorough overview of the Battle of Gettysburg. Afterward, join a licensed guide for an intimate tour of the battlefield and keep an eye out for historic buildings like the David Wills House and Shriver House. With such a bloody past, it's no surprise the area is said to be haunted. Take a night tour through paranormal hotspots and you may just spot a ghost.

② Holtwood
Drive 63 Miles ▪ 1 Hour, 32 Minutes

Fascinating discoveries lie within the Holtwood Environmental Preserve. Traverse 39 miles of hiking trails to uncover the Lock 12 Historic Area, Indian Steps Museum and the nationally recognized Shenk's Ferry Wildflower Preserve. Running along the preserve is the Susquehanna River. Launch a kayak or fish for walleye and bass. In spring, keep an eye out for migrating warblers and nesting bald eagles on the water. Other popular activities here include camping, boating, water-skiing and hunting.

RECOMMENDED STOPOVER
A TUCQUAN PARK FAMILY CAMPGROUND
HOLTWOOD, PA (717) 284-2156

③ Lancaster
Drive 18 Miles ▪ 29 Minutes

Nestled in the heart of Pennsylvania Dutch Country, Lancaster is home to one of the largest Amish communities in the United States. Experience the simple life at the Amish Village, a 12-acre heritage museum offering farmhouse tours, handmade crafts and Amish food. Make sure to sample the shoofly pie, a fluffy molasses dessert that's also a local specialty. Next, take a buggy ride through private Amish roads or see how the Amish live without modern conveniences.

④ Stroudsburg
Drive 107 Miles ▪ 1 Hour, 59 Minutes

This Pocono Mountains town will impress with its walkable downtown area. Stroll the streets to find original buildings from the late 18th century and spend time in art galleries, hip shops and restaurants pleasing every palate. You can also pick up fresh produce at the Stroudsburg Farmers Market and enjoy concerts at the Sherman Theater. Outside, Stroudsburg is a cyclist's paradise. Pedal down the 32-mile McDade Trail for a picturesque journey past pastoral farmlands, forested areas and the Delaware River.

RECOMMENDED STOPOVER
B OTTER LAKE CAMP RESORT
STROUDSBURG, PA (570) 223-0123

Getty Images/iStockphoto

BIKING · BOATING · DINING · ENTERTAINMENT · FISHING · HIKING · HUNTING · PADDLING · SHOPPING · SIGHTSEEING

Pennsylvania SPOTLIGHTS

Unlocking Keystone State Recreation

Take Pennsylvania at your own speed. Enjoy leisurely buggy rides through Amish communities in Lancaster County or send your pulse racing with a kayak trip on the Allegheny River in Pittsburgh. Explore legendary battlefields and pivotal moments in Colonial history.

64 MEDALS OF HONOR WERE AWARDED TO SOLDIERS IN GETTYSBURG.

A row of cannons lined up in Gettysburg National Military Park.

Gettysburg

The turning point of the American Civil War occurred in July of 1863 in the small southeast Pennsylvania town of Gettysburg. Here, more than 150,000 Union and Confederate troops clashed, and over 50,000 soldiers fell in bloody combat. Today, the gently rolling hills commemorate these dark days with several museums and parks both in town and in the surrounding countryside. Encompassing almost 6,000 acres south of town, Gettysburg National Military Park preserves the battlefield itself and provides solemn spaces for remembrance. However, Gettysburg is more than a historic site. Visitors will find a delightful town at the center of Pennsylvania's scenic Fruit Belt region, which provides ample opportunity for relaxation and recreation.

Going to Gettysburg

Sitting just north of Pennsylvania's border with Maryland, Gettysburg is almost halfway between Pittsburgh and Philadelphia. Popular tourist areas of Lancaster (known as Dutch Country) and Hershey (home to the famed chocolate plant and theme park) are conveniently located nearby. Washington, D.C., and Baltimore, Maryland, sit approximately 90 minutes southeast of Gettysburg. Most visitors arrive via U.S. Route 30, which connects Interstates 81 and 83. Weather varies greatly around the year, with hot, humid summers and cold, snowy winters. During the spring and fall seasons, come prepared for changing weather conditions and be prepared for a lot of walking.

History Abounds

Check out the different ways to get around in the park. Exploring the grounds on horseback offers a unique perspective (you'll feel like a Civil War officer). A hike up Little Round Top provides a poignant overview of the battlefield, while scrambling around the rocks at Devil's Den can bring the battle to life. Nearby, the Blue Ridge Mountains offer stunning backdrops to Caledonia, Pine Grove Furnace and Mont Alto state parks, where you can enjoy golfing, fishing, hunting, hiking, boating, biking and swimming. The mountain streams provide great habitat for trout, while numerous lakes are teeming with bass and perch. Nearby, Michaux State Forest is a good pick for deer and small game hunting. Trails for horse-riding and ATVs snake through the area. Drop a line in one of the stocked trout streams for a hearty dinner.

Fruit Belt Fun

Located in Adams County, Gettysburg is surrounded by quirky and compelling attractions. Considered the state's Fruit Belt, the rolling green hills that proliferate in the region form a patchwork of orchards and vineyards. Tour the Gettysburg Wine and Fruit Trail to get a taste of the region by sampling local ciders, wines and brews. Visit Lincoln Square to enjoy the vibrant vibe of downtown Gettysburg, home to art galleries,

PA

LOCAL FAVORITE

Ground Beef Sauerbraten

German settlers arrived in Pennsylvania during the early 18th century, bringing their rich culinary history. *Recipe by Janina Shoemaker.*

INGREDIENTS

- ☐ 1-1½ lbs ground beef
- ☐ 1 cup carrot, shredded
- ☐ 1 Tbsp onion, minced
- ☐ ¼ cup milk
- ☐ 3 Tbsp olive oil
- ☐ ¾ cup beef bouillon
- ☐ ¼ cup lemon juice
- ☐ 8 gingersnap cookies, finely crushed
- ☐ ½ tsp ground clove
- ☐ Salt and pepper

DIRECTIONS

Combine ground beef, carrot, onion, milk, salt and pepper. Mix well and form into a dozen or so meatballs. Brown the meatballs in olive oil and then place them in a bowl.

Mix together beef bouillon, lemon juice, crushed gingersnap cookies and ground clove. Add to the remaining oil in the skillet and stir until it becomes a smooth sauce.

Add meatballs back in, cover with lid and cook over low heat for 15 minutes. Serve with hot buttered egg noodles, green beans, rice, boiled potatoes or sweet-sour red cabbage.

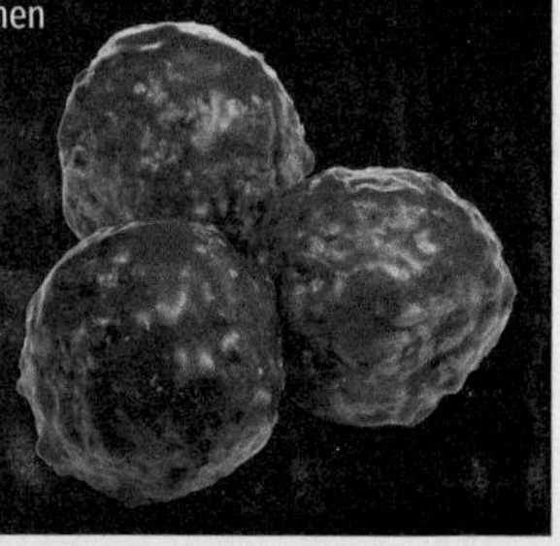

Hershey's Chocolate World features demonstrations on how the company's iconic confections are made.

enticing shops and local restaurants. You'll find historic taverns and pubs side-by-side with hip cafes offering the latest vegetarian and vegan dishes.

Ghostly Gettysburg

Living in the shadow of a bloody battle, Gettysburg is considered by some to be the most haunted town in America. Explore these tales of the paranormal with a ghost tour or candlelight walk. A tour of the Museum of Haunted Objects in town will acquaint you with some of the world's most spooky curios. Feel the spirit of haunted dolls and witchy Ouija boards. Many of the area's reported ghosts are said to be Civil War combatants wandering the battlefield. You'll also find plenty of civilian ghosts.

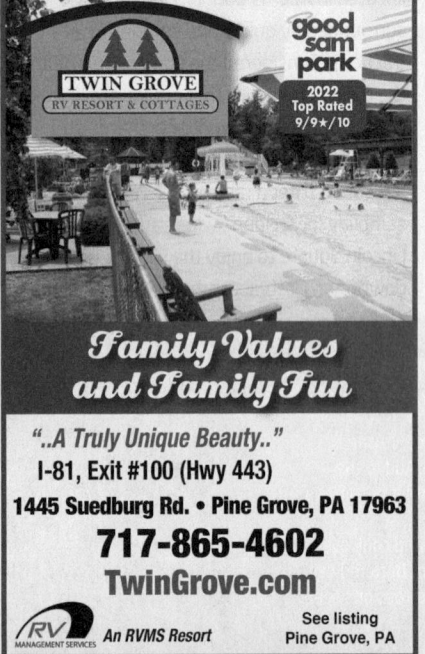

Gallivanting Around Gettysburg

Each spring, the hills of Adams County become white and pink as the blossoms on fruit trees begin to bloom, filling the air with a sweet scent. Gettysburg's Apple Blossom Festival is held each May to commemorate the arrival of spring, while the National Apple Harvest Festival celebrates the bounty of fruit each October. Crafts, music, vendors and, of course, food abound. For history buffs, there are several events marking the region's role in the Civil War. The largest is the annual Gettysburg Civil War Battle Reenactment, put on each July by the Gettysburg Anniversary Committee. Hear the boom of cannons as soldiers march in period regalia. Gettysburg National Military Park annually recognizes Dedication Day on November 19 to commemorate President Lincoln's Gettysburg Address. See a Lincoln impersonator read the historic text.

Soldier Stories

Gettysburg National Military Park is the top draw in the region. Tour the battlefield and museum to gain insight into the strategies that led to the fighting. You can also pay your respects at the Gettysburg National Cemetery or at one of the many memorials that dot the sprawling park. Several ranger-led tours and living history programs help put you in the boots of the combatants. Back in the town of Gettysburg, several Civil War-era homes preserve the lives of locals who were affected by the battle. Stop by the David Wills House, where President Lincoln stayed during his Gettysburg Address visit. Check out the Shriver House, whose attic once served as a sniper's nest for a confederate sharpshooter; historic reenactors on-site shed light on this dramatic episode. Another piece of the region's history can be explored at the National Apple Museum in nearby Biglerville.

Hershey

The aroma of cocoa and sugar waft through the streets of Hershey, America's one and only chocolate town. It was here where Milton Hershey launched his world-famous company in the early 20th century. Since then, the town has become a chocolate paradise, complete with a chocolate amusement park, chocolate tours and even chocolate spas where you can slather yourself with the sweet stuff. Satisfy your candy cravings and then venture outside the town to tour historic attractions and hike parts of the famed Appalachian Trail.

The Sweetest Place on Earth

Milton S. Hershey built his famous confection company here in 1905 and the town has been a delicious nirvana for chocolate lovers ever since. Learn how Hershey created his iconic brand at the Hershey Story Museum and then taste all sorts of treats at Hershey's Chocolate World, where you can make your own candy bar and see the entire chocolate-making process from start to finish. Learn about the Milton Hershey School, which provided an education for orphans. Afterward, skip across the street to Hersheypark for rip-roaring roller coasters, classic family rides, and of course, more chocolate. You can also go to the Hershey Gardens to explore 23 acres with 11 themed gardens and an atrium.

Lazy River Rides

When the sun's out, grab your paddle and head to Swatara Creek. The tranquil waterway runs along the edge of town and offers kayaking and canoeing trips of various lengths. Just 20 minutes away, Harrisburg is home to the Pride of the Susquehanna Riverboat. Board one of America's last paddle-wheel riverboats and enjoy a sightseeing tour with 360-degree views of Harrisburg and the Susquehanna River. The river's calm waters also make it an excellent spot for kayaking, fishing or pontoon boating. If you prefer to admire the water from land, hop on a bike and cycle down the Capital Area Greenbelt, a 21-mile trail weaving through Wildwood Park, Riverfront Park and other scenic landmarks.

The elegant Waterville Bridge spans Swatara Creek on the Appalachian Trail east of Harrisburg.

Adventures Above and Below Ground

The 2.7-mile hike to Hawk Rock lets you traverse a section of the Appalachian Trail and finishes with panoramic views. Over in Boyd Big Tree Preserve, you'll find a 12-mile trail system with treks ranging from easy to challenging. Detweiler Park also has diverse ecosystems you can wander through, including meadows and deciduous forests. After a walk in the great outdoors, trade your hiking poles for golf clubs and tee off at championship-level courses like Hershey Country Club and Spring Creek Golf Course. If you're keen to see wildlife, stop by ZooAmerica to come face-to-face with mountain lions, wolves, alligators and over 200 other animals from across North America. Geological wonders are also nearby in the Indian Echo Caverns. Take a guided underground tour to explore limestone stalactites over 440 million years old.

Sweet Relaxation

Savor IPAs, stouts and other refreshing delights along the Brew Barons Beer Trail, an interactive craft beer adventure consisting of over 20 breweries and tasting locations in Hershey and Harrisburg. Before sipping your way through the region, download the corresponding beer trail app and make sure to check into each brewery to win great prizes. Notewor-

PA

thy stops include the Appalachian Brewing Company, Rotunda Brew Pub and Tröegs Independent Brewing. When you're done tasting all the local brews, treat yourself to a luxury spa day. The Spa at The Hotel Hershey and MeltSpa by Hershey are ready to pamper you with massages, facials and chocolate body treatments.

Family Fun

From street festivals to sports games, there's always something exciting happening in Hershey. Catch a Broadway musical at the Hershey Theatre or sing along to a live music concert at Hersheypark Stadium. You can attend sporting events year-round too. Watch the Hershey Bears battle on the ice from October to June and the Harrisburg Senators hit home runs between April to September. During the holiday season, stroll through Hersheypark's Christmas Candylane to gaze at 5 million twinkling lights. You'll even get the chance to meet Santa and all nine of his reindeer.

Ride into the Past

Car enthusiasts won't want to miss the AACA Museum, a Smithsonian-affiliated museum housing more than a hundred antique vehicles and retro buses. Over at Hershey's Chocolate World, step into a vintage trolley bus and hear Milton Hershey's inspiring story as you ride around town.

The Brew Barons Beer Trail connects 20 breweries and tasting locations in Hershey and Harrisburg.

Civil War Past

Continue your historical journey in Harrisburg, where the National Civil War Museum uses artifacts and photographs to show Northern and Southern perspectives. The city is home to the Pennsylvania State Capitol Building too. Free tours give you access to the palace's ornate décor while shedding light on centuries of Commonwealth history. Lavish mansions-turned-museums are also just a stone's throw away, including the Fort Hunter Mansion and John Harris-Simon Cameron Mansion. Both historic homes were key in shaping Harrisburg's history and are open seasonally for guided tours.

Lancaster County

Lancaster County may evoke images of farmers in straw hats and horse-drawn buggies, but there's a lot more to this part of Pennsylvania Dutch Country than pastoral landscapes. Lancaster has evolved into a hip and happening city, packed with art galleries, craft breweries and world-class restaurants that have received praise from the New York Times. The scenery is also unparalleled, with rivers and rolling hills serving up outdoor adventures.

An Amish horse and buggy trots to a country store in Lancaster County.

Discover Amish Country

In the early 18th century, the first Amish settlers came to America to escape religious persecution in Europe. Today, Pennsylvania Dutch Country is home to one of the largest Amish communities in the country. The Amish way of life has not changed much in the past 300 years. Families dress in modest garments and choose to live without modern conveniences like electricity, cars and the Internet. Experience Amish life for yourself at the Amish Village, a 12-acre heritage museum complete with farmhouse tours, barn animals and stores filled with Amish-made crafts and souvenirs. You can also take a buggy ride through private Amish roads and tour a nine-room Amish house known as the Amish Country Homestead. Learn about Amish customs in a homey and informative setting.

Grab a Paddle and Cast a Line

Angling and kayaking opportunities are plentiful thanks to the region's proximity to the Susquehanna River. You can find numerous access points along the 53-mile water trail, as well as campgrounds like Otter Creek and Susquehannock State Park. Locals have great success hooking walleyes and smallmouths around the Bainbridge and Holtwood sections of the river. Catfish live in large numbers in Lake Aldred, and trout can be found in East Drumore's Conowingo Creek.

Nature's Calling

Get out and play in Lancaster County's lush green hills. Hikers can stretch their legs along nine trails in Lancaster County Central Park and take in scenic views of the Conestoga River in Windolph Landing Nature Preserve. The Tucquan Glen and Pyfer Nature Preserves are also excellent spots to view blooming wildflowers. If you're feeling adventurous, speed down zipline tracks at Refreshing Mountain Retreat & Adventure Center or meet rescued wolves in natural woodlands at the Wolf Sanctuary of Pennsylvania. Learn how these social animals select their pack leaders.

PA

The painstaking art of quilting by hand with needle and thread is still practiced in Lancaster.

Vibrant City Life

The city of Lancaster has blossomed into a hip culture hub in recent years. The culinary scene is gaining quite the reputation — foodies insist you try the wood-fired pizza at Luca, Trinidadian dishes at Callaloo and the Horse Fries at the Horse Inn, which come smothered in sausage, provolone, parmesan, garlic and heavy cream. Walk off all the food by browsing specialty items at the Lancaster Central Market and shopping at retro boutiques like Space, The Scarlet Willow and Redeux Vintage. You'll find plenty of art in town as well. Gallery Row on Prince Street houses six galleries, including the Freiman Stoltzfus Gallery and CityFolk Gallery. The Lancaster Museum of Art is also a popular place to discover local and regional artists.

Fun Festivals and Unique Fairs

Whether you're in the mood for craft beer or music concerts, you'll find all sorts of special events right up your alley. Experience the magic of the holidays with carriage rides and carolers at the Marietta Candlelight Tour of Homes. In February, check out ice sculptures at the Lititz Ice Walk, and then warm up with good tunes at the Lancaster Roots & Blues Festival, an indoor event taking over multiple venues across three blocks. Listen to more music at New Holland's Spring Gulch Folk Festival. Held every May, this laid-back event rounds up an eclectic mix of Americana performers for four days of music. In the summer, raise your glass at the Lancaster Craft Beer Festival. Spend the day sampling brews from over 50 independent breweries, listening to live music and mingling with other craft beer enthusiasts.

Turn the Clocks Back

Spending time in Amish communities isn't the only way to experience a simpler way of life. Hop in your car and cruise through rolling pastures, where farm silos, stone houses and 29 covered bridges dot the countryside. In the city, stroll past Victorian and Colonial-era architecture. Keep an eye out for the Griest skyscraper at Penn Square, designed in the Italian Renaissance Revival style by C. Emlen Urban in 1924. You'll also find the Lancaster Marriott Hotel here. The historic Beaux Arts building once housed the Watt & Shand department store. At the corner of Vine and South Queen streets is the Thaddeus Stevens and Lydia Hamilton Smith Historic Site, an Underground Railroad hideout and soon-to-be museum.

Lovely Lititz

Just 6 miles north of Lancaster, Lititz, nicknamed the Pretzel Town, is one of Pennsylvania's most alluring communities. Founded in 1756, the town's architectural gems have changed little since they were built 200 years ago. The Linden Hall School, established in 1794, ranks as the oldest girl's school in the nation, while the Julius Sturgis Pretzel Bakery is the oldest bakery of its ilk (founded in 1861). The pretzels that come out of its ovens today are as delicious as ever.

Twisted and Tasty Tours

Lighthearted and hands-on 20-minute tours of the Pretzel Bakery include lessons in bread making as well as a peek inside the centuries-old ovens and irresistibly aromatic bake shop. The Wilbur Chocolate Store tells the history of the company that invented "Wilbur Buds." In the modern candy kitchen, you can watch the brand's signature chocolates being created.

Wheatland

The elegant Federal-style mansion where U.S. President James Buchanan resided for over 20 years can be visited on a guided tour led by knowledgeable costumed docents. Built in 1828 by a local lawyer named William Jenkins, Wheatland was bought by Buchanan in 1848 as his main residence. The mansion served as the Democratic headquarters during Buchanan's 1856 presidential campaign; it was on Wheatland's front lawn that he gave his campaign address to local villagers.

Pittsburgh and Countryside

Once known for its steel industry, Pittsburgh has blossomed into a hub of culture and recreation. The second-largest city in Pennsylvania also boasts a fantastic dining scene. While the town itself is full of things to see and do, it's also a great base for exploring the nearby area and its myriad waterways.

Downtown Pittsburgh gleams at the confluence of the Allegheny, Monongahela and Ohio Rivers.

Pittsburgh Perfection

You won't run out of things to do in Pittsburgh. Shedding its past as a hub of steel production, the city is stingingly green, with four large parks within the city limits, including beautiful Schenley Park. Other major attractions include the sprawling Carnegie Museum of Natural History, known for its stunning dinosaur skeletons, as well as the Andy Warhol Museum, dedicated to the works of the renowned 20th-century pop artist. The ToonSeum is one of the few cartoon museums in the U.S., while the 42-story Cathedral of Learning is the largest educational building in this hemisphere. The eye-catching, Gothic-revival building is the centerpiece of the University of Pittsburgh.

Three Rivers

Pittsburgh's identity has been shaped in large part by its waterways. The Allegheny and Monongahela Rivers converge to become the Ohio River, all right in the heart of the city. Plenty of people go boating and kayaking around this confluence, and visitors who want to get great views of the city should look into taking a boat tour. For silly fun, consider a Just Ducky Tour, which features a duck-inspired hybrid land-and-water vehicle. For anglers, there are lots of places to go fishing not far from town. These include the gargantuan Cross Creek Lake, known for its bass fishing, North Park Lake (boat rentals are also available here) and Highland Park Dam, right on the Allegheny.

Recreation on Land

Hikers, bikers and runners have lots of room to work up a sweat on the trails that run in and out of town. The North Shore Riverfront Park & Trail gets lots of foot traffic, and there are a fair few restaurants to stop at for a snack along the way. Running along the banks of the majestic waterways, Three Rivers Heritage Trail offers 24 miles of pathways in total. There's also the Rachel Carson Trail, which traverses 35 miles of rugged terrain, while Ohiopyle State Park, south of town, offers all sorts of outdoor recreation opportunities, including the three-mile-long Meadow Run Trail to the towering Cucumber Falls. Take a ride on Pittsburgh's funicular near the city's south side to see dazzling views.

From Gritty to Great

Once a hub of steel manufacturing, the city has shed its industrial past and today is a center of technology and bioscience, with lots of restaurants, bars and cultural attractions. It also has four distinct seasons (but gets a fair amount of rainfall) and a strong urban identity. While the generational makeup of the city is fairly balanced, there's certainly a large student population here, with colleges and universities galore, including the well-regarded Carnegie Mellon University.

Steel Town Celebrations

Pittsburgh knows how to throw a party. Gourmand types won't want to miss Restaurant Week's Winter Celebration in January, which features superb cuisine and local restaurant specials. A few months later comes the Pittsburgh Fringe Festival in April, three days devoted to the performing arts. Summer festivities include the Three Rivers Arts Festival in June, the Pittsburgh International Jazz Festival in June and Bloomfield Little Italy Days in August. During fall, visitors can join a Haunted Pittsburgh Ghost Tour and learn about the spirits that haunt the city. Learn a few spooky ghost stories along the way.

PA

SPOTLIGHTS

Knights, Wizards and Minstrels

In October, the Pittsburgh the Renaissance Festival in August focuses on recreating the merriment of times of yore. Along with a smattering of Halloween festivities, October brings with it the Head of the Ohio boat race, one of the largest regattas in the U.S.

Pittsburgh's Back Pages

During the French and Indian War, British troops established Fort Pitt in what is now downtown Pittsburgh. The fort had an advantage due to its strategic location at the joining of the three rivers. The need for weapons during the War of 1812 led the city to become a steel center, and by the early 20th century, Pittsburgh was responsible for producing around half of the steel in the country. Recently, Pittsburgh has reinvented itself in the information age: A tech boom has taken the city by storm, with firms that specialize in artificial intelligence, robotics and biomedicine establishing headquarters in the city. Trendy restaurants have opened their doors to welcome the techies as well as visitors. In town, enjoy a blend of traditional cuisine and adventurous fare.

Playing Ball in Pittsburgh

Sports are a big deal here, and there are three major league teams in the city: the Pittsburgh Steelers (NFL), the Pittsburgh Pirates (MLB) and the Pittsburgh Penguins (NHL). All share common colors of black and gold, in honor of the city's flag. Pittsburgh is the only city in the country where sports teams share the same colors. Visit the statue commemorating the "Immaculate Reception," the famous catch by Steelers running back Franco Harris that helped catapault the team to greatness.

Parks in Pittsburgh

After catching Steelers games at Heinz Field or watching the Pirates play at PNC Park, sports fans may want to head out to the Western Pennsylvania Sports Museum at the Senator John Heinz History Center.

Whitewater Near Pittsburgh

Southeast of Pittsburgh, The Middle Yough River features class I and II rapids, which yield more placid conditions for kayaking, fishing and gentle rafting/floats. Cyclists can also pedal 11 miles east along a picturesque trail that traces the banks of the river.

Falling Water

Visit an iconic home with a design that seems to blend with the surrounding nature. Head 67 miles southeast to Laurel Highlands to see Frank Lloyd Wright's Falling Water, considered an iconic architectural treasure. Cantilevered over a waterfall, the house was built in 1936 for a local Pittsburgh department store owner, Edgar J. Kaufman. A jewel of 20th-century aesthetics, the home defied conventional architectural styles when it was built and still stands as an engineering marvel.

Kentuck Knob

Many Frank Lloyd Wright purists state a preference for nearby Kentuck Knob, also known as the Hagan House. Completed in 1956, the crescent-shaped structure is noted for its intimate design. Like Fallingwater, Kentuck Knob uses native materials to blend in with its surroundings.

Pocono Mountains

Thrill-seekers and scenery lovers flock to the Pocono Mountains in Northeast Pennsylvania for good reasons. The area is known to the locals as just "the Poconos." It has 150 lakes, nearly a dozen waterfalls, adrenaline-pumping ziplines, scenery-rich hiking, challenging biking and legendary NASCAR action. There are wineries and breweries, you-pick farms and even the world's largest country store. All four seasons are represented at this dynamic paradise, which should be a mainstay on your bucket list.

The sun sets over the serene Pocono Mountains after another summer day of outdoor recreation.

Pocono Power

The Pocono Raceway puts the region on the NASCAR map. Known as the "Tricky Triangle," the track challenges drivers with its three sharp turns, while the straightaway allows drivers to top 200 mph. Take the kids to Tricky's Kit Kamp, which features games, play structures and special entertainment. The Tricky Triangle Club hosts driver Q&As. Infield camping and trackside camping accommodate RVs.

Lush Forests

Take a hike in gorgeous woods. Check out the Delaware State Forest's 82-acre Tarkill Forest Demonstration Area, which was established in 1948 as a textbook example of multiuse forestry; a self-guided nature trail provides glimpses of a compelling ecosystem. Also on offer are boating, hunting and horseback riding along 26 miles of designated riding trails, along with biking and ATV trails (for all skill levels).

Poconos Paddling

Launch into the habitats of the Upper Delaware Scenic and Recreational River to experience one of the most ecologically rich rivers in the Northeast. Here, you can canoe through rapids, marvel at the ever-changing scenery from rolling hills to quaint riverside villages or partake of excellent fishing in crystal-clear streams.

Brews and Antiques

Buy a piece of the past in the Poconos. Shop for stunning antiques, take a tour of wineries and microbreweries, and bask in the welcoming atmosphere. In Carbon County, visitors can explore the railroad heritage at several fascinating sites.

Cool Camelback

Strap on skis and snowboards at Camelback Mountain Resort. In addition, the Big Pocono State Park that surrounds it is a great spot for hiking and biking in warmer months. Skytop, known for its historic 1920s retreat hotel, also offers a wealth of outdoor adventures. Many lakes, ponds and rivers here are open for fishing and swimming, and outfitters are available in most towns to help guide you through rafting and boating excursions.

Railroad Memories

Take a train ride into the past. Themed tours in the town of Honesdale, the "Birthplace of the American Railroad," show off this community's historic ties to railway transportation, which ultimately linked America's East and West. The town of Stroudsburg greets visitors with one-of-a-kind shopping experiences, including a local arts scene and a host of festivals. A visit to the Columns Museum in Pike County will transport you into the past.

Museum of Wonder

Masker Museum in Promised Land State Park features an informative series of natural history displays and artifacts, as well as interactive children's activities, a bird observation area, outdoor bird feeding stations and a native plant garden. Promised Land's lake lures water sport enthusiasts with prime conditions for recreational canoeing, kayaking and fishing.

FOR MORE INFORMATION

Pennsylvania Department of Community and Economic Development, 800-847-4872, www.visitpa.com

Destination Gettysburg, 717-334-6274, www.destinationgettysburg.com

Hershey Entertainment & Resorts, 800-437-7439, www.hersheypa.com

Discover Lancaster, 800-723-8824, www.discoverlancaster.com

Pittsburgh Convention and Visitors Bureau, 800-359-0758, www.visitpittsburgh.com

Pocono Mountains Visitors Bureau, 800-762-6667, www.800poconos.com

PA

RV SPACE-SAVING TIP: Line your trashcans with multiple bags at once and keep the roll in the bottom of the wastebasket for easy refills. Also, you could even reuse the same bag, if it hasn't gotten too soiled, by simply dumping the trash and leaving the existing bag in it for multiple uses.

Pennsylvania Privately Owned Campground Information Updated by our Good Sam Representative

Bruce & Dianne Richardson

We love our latest life chapter traveling this beautiful country with our fur babies, Lexi (German shepherd) and Bear (mini Labradoodle)! Every day is an adventure and an opportunity to make friends and beautiful memories. Our 11 grandchildren love facetiming with us.

Pennsylvania

ADAMSTOWN — E8 *Lancaster*

DUTCH COUSIN CAMPGROUND **Ratings: 8/9.5★/9.5** (Campground) Avail: 54 full hkups (30/50 amps). 2021 rates: $52. (717)336-6911, 446 Hill Rd, Denver, PA 17517

SHADY GROVE CAMPGROUND **Ratings: 9/10★/9** (Campground) Avail: 41 full hkups (30/50 amps). 2021 rates: $59 to $69. (717)484-4225, 65 Poplar Dr, Denver, PA 17517

SILL'S FAMILY CAMPGROUND **Ratings: 9/10★/10** (Campground) Avail: 87 full hkups (30/50 amps). 2021 rates: $53 to $59. (717)484-4806, 1906 Bowmansville Rd, Mohnton, PA 19540

AIRVILLE — E8 *York*

OTTER CREEK CAMPGROUND **Ratings: 6/8.5/7** (Campground) 34 Avail: 34 W, 34 E (30/50 amps). 2021 rates: $35 to $42. Apr 15 to Oct 27. (717)862-3628, 1101 Furnace Rd, Airville, PA 17302

ALLENTOWN — D9 *Lehigh*

ALLENTOWN See also Bethlehem, Boyertown, Hatfield, Kutztown, Lehighton, Lenhartsville, New Tripoli, Palmerton, Revere, Quakertown & Upper Black Eddy, PA; Asbury, NJ.

ALTOONA — D4 *Blair*

WRIGHT'S ORCHARD STATION CAMPGROUND
good sam park
Ratings: 7.5/9.5★/9 (Campground) Avail: 36 full hkups (30/50 amps). 2021 rates: $44 to $47. May 01 to Oct 31. (814)695-2628, 2381 Plank Rd, Duncansville, PA 16635

APOLLO — D2 *Westmoreland*

Travel Services

CAMPING WORLD OF APOLLO/PITTSBURGH
CAMPING WORLD
As the nation's largest retailer of RV supplies, accessories, services and new and used RVs, Camping World is committed to making your total RV experience better. **SERVICES:** RV, RV appliance, MH mechanical, staffed RV wash, restrooms. RV Sales. RV supplies, RV accessible. Hours: 9am to 7pm.
(888)610-7672 Lat: 40.581790, Lon: -79.594542
537 PA-356, Apollo, PA 15613
www.campingworld.com

Lend a hand. During the busy season park services are stretched to the max! Please do your best to keep your area ""ship-shape''.

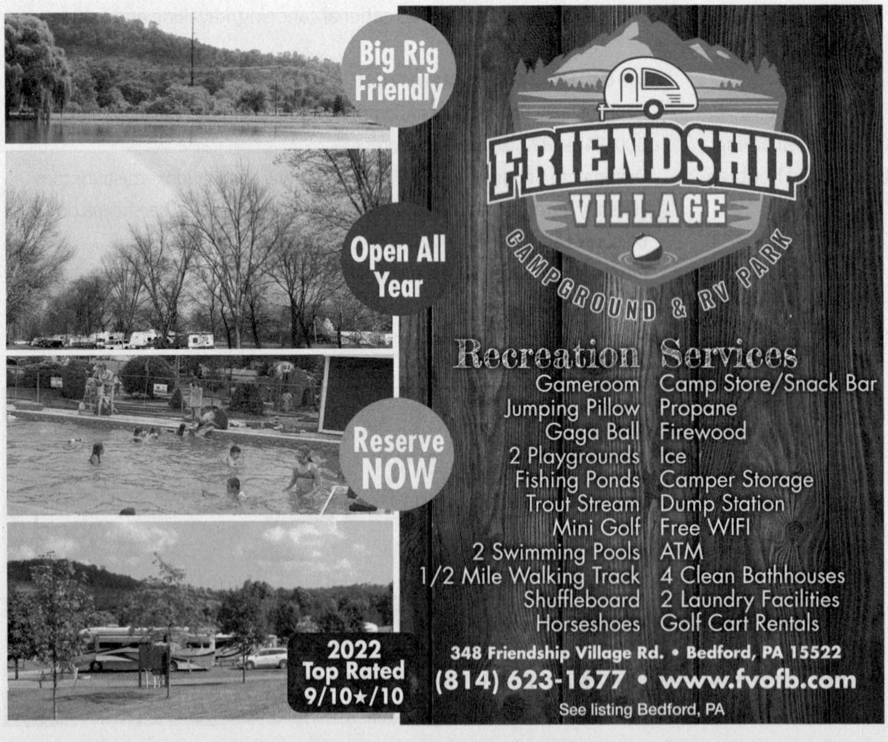

AUBURN — D8 *Schuylkill*

CHRISTMAS PINES CAMPGROUND **Ratings: 8/9★/9.5** (Campground) 26 Avail: 26 W, 26 E (30/50 amps). 2021 rates: $40. Apr 10 to Oct 20. (570)366-8866, 450 Red Church Rd, Auburn, PA 17922

AUSTIN — B5 *Potter*

AUSTIN CAMPGROUND AT NELSON RUN **Ratings: 5.5/9★/9** (Campground) 29 Avail: 29 W, 29 E (30/50 amps). 2021 rates: $36 to $45. (814)647-8777, 364 Nelson Run Rd, Austin, PA 16720

BEAVER FALLS — D1 *Beaver*

HARTS CONTENT CAMPGROUND **Ratings: 8/8.5★/8** (Campground) 45 Avail: 12 full hkups, 23 W, 23 E (30/50 amps). 2021 rates: $30. Apr 15 to Oct 15. (724)846-0005, 496 Glendale Rd, Beaver Falls, PA 15010

BEDFORD — E4 *Bedford*

FRIENDSHIP VILLAGE CAMPGROUND & RV PARK
Ratings: 9/10★/10 (Campground) From Jct I-76(exit 146) & US 220: Go 300 yds N on Bus US 220, then 1-1/2 mi S on US 220, then 1-1/2 mi NW on US 30, then 1/2 mi NE on Friendship Village Rd (E). **FAC:** paved/gravel rds. (285 spaces). Avail: 220 gravel, 86 pull-thrus, (40x70), back-ins (30x60), 193 full hkups, 27 W, 27 E (30/50 amps), seasonal sites, cable, WiFi @ sites, tent sites, rentals, dump, laundry, groc, LP gas, fire rings, firewood. **REC:** pool, Friendship Village Lake: fishing, kayaking/canoeing, shuffleboard, playground, hunting nearby. Pets OK. Partial handicap access. Big rig sites, eco-friendly. 2021 rates: $48 to $62, Military discount. ATM.
(814)623-1677 Lat: 40.04475, Lon: -78.519008
348 Friendship Village Rd, Bedford, PA 15522
www.fvofb.com
See ad this page

MERRITT POND CAMPGROUND **Ratings: 4/NA/7.5** (Campground) Avail: 18 full hkups (30/50 amps). 2021 rates: $40 to $45. Apr 15 to Oct 15. (814)623-1507, 193 Flying Dutchman Rd, Bedford, PA 15522

NATURE'S GETAWAY RV PARK **Ratings: 7.5/7.5★/6.5** (Campground) 25 Avail: 25 W, 25 E (30/50 amps). 2021 rates: $35 to $55. Apr 15 to Oct 31. (814)733-4380, 147 Sleepy Hollow Rd, Schellsburg, PA 15559

BELLEFONTE — C5 *Centre*

BELLEFONTE/STATE COLLEGE KOA **Ratings: 9/10★/9.5** (Campground) 96 Avail: 92 full hkups, 4 W, 4 E (30/50 amps). 2021 rates: $44 to $134. Apr 10 to Nov 15. (814)355-7912, 2481 Jacksonville Rd, Bellefonte, PA 16823

BELLEVILLE — D5 *Huntingdon*

GREENWOOD FURNACE
(Public State Park) From Jct of SR-26 & SR-305: Go 5 mi E on SR-305 (R). **FAC:** gravel rds. 49 Avail: 1 paved, 48 gravel, back-ins (12x35), 45 E (30/50 amps), tent sites, dump, firewood. **REC:** Greenwood Lake: swim, fishing, playground, rec open to public. Pet restrict (Q). Partial handicap access, 14 day max stay. 2021 rates: $15 to $24. Apr 10 to Nov 15. no cc, no reservations.
(814)667-1800 Lat: 40.648192, Lon: -77.757760
Belleville, PA 17004
www.dcnr.state.pa.us

BENTON — C8 *Columbia*

RICKETTS GLEN (Public State Park) From Jct SR-487 & SR-118: Go 4 mi N on SR-487 (R). Heavy trailer units access the park from SR-487 N from Dushore. 119 Avail. 2021 rates: $15 to $24. (570)477-5675

WHISPERING PINES CAMPING ESTATES
good sam park
Ratings: 9/9.5★/10 (Campground) From Jct Hwy 487 & Hwy 239 (in Benton): Go 4 mi E on Hwy 239, then 1 mi S on N Bendertown Rd (R). **FAC:** gravel rds. (55 spaces). Avail: 20 gravel, back-ins (30x60), 20 full hkups (30/50 amps), seasonal sites, WiFi @ sites, tent sites, rentals, shower$, laundry, groc, fire rings, firewood. **REC:** heated pool, pond, fishing, kayaking/canoeing, boating nearby, playground, hunting nearby. Pet restrict (Q). Partial handicap access. Big rig sites, eco-friendly. 2021 rates: $55 to $60, Military discount.
(570)925-6810 Lat: 41.179447, Lon: -76.318985
1557 North Bendertown Rd, Stillwater, PA 17878
www.wpce.com
See ad this page

BERWICK — C8 *Columbia*

BODNAROSA MOTEL & CAMPGROUND **Ratings: 7.5/10★/10** (Campground) Avail: 34 full hkups (30/50 amps). 2021 rates: $38. (570)520-4070, 1175 Salem Boulevard (US 11), Berwick, PA 18603

BETHLEHEM — D9 *Northampton*

EVERGREEN LAKE **Ratings: 7.5/8.5★/8.5** (Campground) 96 Avail: 25 full hkups, 71 W, 71 E (30/50 amps). 2021 rates: $45 to $71. Apr 15 to Oct 15. (610)837-6401, 2375 Benders Dr, Bath, PA 18014

BLOOMSBURG — C7 *Columbia*

INDIAN HEAD RECREATIONAL CAMPGROUNDS **Ratings: 4.5/7/6.5** (Campground) 135 Avail: 26 full hkups, 109 W, 100 E (30/50 amps). 2021 rates: $41 to $46. May 01 to Oct 31. (570)784-6150, 340 Reading St, Bloomsburg, PA 17815

BOWMANSVILLE — E8 *Lancaster*

SUN VALLEY RV RESORT

good sam park **Ratings: 8.5/10★/10** (Campground) Avail: 9 full hkups (30/50 amps). 2021 rates: $49 to $60. Apr 01 to Oct 31. (888)563-7040, 451 E. Maple Grove Rd, Narvon, PA 17507

BOYERTOWN — D9 *Bucks*

LAZY K CAMPGROUND **Ratings: 6/8.5★/9** (Campground) 37 Avail: 37 W, 37 E (30 amps). 2021 rates: $40. (610)367-8576, 109 Washington Rd, #106, Bechtelsville, PA 19505

BRODHEADSVILLE — C9 *Monroe*

CHESTNUT LAKE CAMPGROUND **Ratings: 7.5/6.5/8** (Campground) 45 Avail: 35 full hkups, 10 W, 10 E (30/50 amps). 2021 rates: $48 to $58. (570)992-6179, 117 Chestnut Lake Rd, Brodheadsville, PA 18322

SILVER VALLEY CAMPSITES **Ratings: 9/8.5★/8.5** (Campground) Avail: 17 full hkups (30/50 amps). 2021 rates: $50.50 to $56.50. (570)992-4824, 146 Silver Valley Circle, Saylorsburg, PA 18353

BURNT CABINS — E5 *Fulton*

BURNT CABINS GRIST MILL & FAMILY CAMPGROUND **Ratings: 7.5/8/7** (Campground) Avail: 34 full hkups (30/50 amps). 2021 rates: $32 to $38. (717)987-3244, 582 Grist Mill Rd, Burnt Cabins, PA 17215

BUTLER — C2 *Butler*

BUTTERCUP WOODLANDS CAMPGROUND Ratings: 9.5/10★/9 (Campground) Avail: 26 full hkups (30/50 amps). 2021 rates: $50. Apr 15 to Oct 15. (724)789-9340, 854 Evans City Rd, Renfrew, PA 16053

SMITH GROVE CAMPGROUND **Ratings: 7.5/7/8.5** (Campground) 15 Avail: 15 W, 15 E (30 amps). 2021 rates: $37. Apr 15 to Oct 15. (724)285-3600, 1085 Herman Rd, Butler, PA 16002

CALEDONIA — C4 *Franklin*

CALEDONIA (Public State Park) From town: Go 4 mi E on US-30, then 1 block N on SR-233 (L). Avail: 43 E (30/50 amps). 2021 rates: $15 to $20. Mar 01 to Dec 15. (717)352-2161

CARLISLE — E6 *Cumberland*

DEER RUN CAMPING RESORT **Ratings: 8.5/10★/9** (Campground) 75 Avail: 50 full hkups, 20 W, 25 E (30/50 amps). 2021 rates: $45 to $68. Apr 01 to Oct 31. (717)486-8168, 111 Sheet Iron Roof Rd, Gardners, PA 17324

MOUNTAIN CREEK CAMPGROUND **Ratings: 8.5/10★/9** (Campground) 123 Avail: 22 full hkups, 101 W, 101 E (30/50 amps). 2021 rates: $44 to $69. Mar 15 to Nov 20. (717)486-7681, 349 Pine Grove Rd, Gardners, PA 17324

RV Tech Tips - Get a Charge Out of This Nifty Battery Water Filler. The placement of batteries in some motorhomes can make them difficult to service. Here's an easy, fool-proof tool that works for any battery, regardless of location. Purchase a one-gallon or smaller garden pump sprayer. Remove the wand attachment, leaving the hose and trigger assembly. Add distilled water to the sprayer's tank, pump a few times to add air pressure and squirt the water into each battery cell with no mess or overfill.

CATAWISSA — C7 *Columbia*

J & D CAMPGROUND **Ratings: 9/10★/10** (Campground) Avail: 109 full hkups (30/50 amps). 2021 rates: $55. Apr 27 to Oct 11. (570)356-7700, 973 Southern Dr, Catawissa, PA 17820

KNOEBELS LAKE GLORY CAMPGROUND **Ratings: 5.5/6/8.5** (Campground) 144 Avail: 96 full hkups, 38 W, 38 E (30/50 amps). 2021 rates: $52 to $57. Apr 15 to Nov 01. (570)356-7392, 96 Eisenhower Rd, Catawissa, PA 17820

CEDAR RUN — B6 *Lycoming*

PETTECOTE JUNCTION CAMPGROUND **Ratings: 7/9.5★/9.5** (Campground) 23 Avail: 23 W, 23 E (30/50 amps). 2021 rates: $46 to $51. Apr 01 to Oct 31. (570)353-7183, 400 Beach Rd, Cedar Run, PA 17727

CENTERVILLE — E2 *Cumberland*

PINE GROVE FURNACE (Public State Park) From Jct of I-81 & SR-233: Go 8 mi S on SR-233 (E). Avail: 52 E (30/50 amps). 2021 rates: $15 to $24. Mar 25 to Dec 15. (717)486-7174

CHAMBERSBURG — E6 *Franklin*

TWIN BRIDGE CAMPGROUND **Ratings: 6.5/8.5★/8.5** (Campground) 135 Avail: 135 W, 135 E (30/50 amps). 2021 rates: $40 to $45. Apr 15 to Oct 31. (717)369-2216, 1345 Twin Bridge Rd, Chambersburg, PA 17202

CHAMPION — E3 *Fayette*

MOUNTAIN PINES CAMPGROUND

good sam park **Ratings: 9/9★/9** (Campground) Avail: 93 full hkups (30/50 amps). 2021 rates: $49 to $79. Apr 15 to Oct 31. (724)455-3300, 1662 Indian Creek Valley Rd, Champion, PA 15622

CLARENDON — B3 *Warren*

CHAPMAN (Public State Park) From Jct of US-6 & Chapman Dam Rd: Go 5 mi SW on Chapman Dam Rd/Railroad (E). Avail: 57 E (30/50 amps). 2021 rates: $15 to $20. Apr 15 to Dec 15. (814)723-0250

CLEARFIELD — C4 *Clearfield*

SIMON B ELLIOTT (Public State Park) At Jct of I-80 & SR-153/Exit 18 (R). 24 Avail. 2021 rates: $15 to $24. May 25 to Oct 31. (814)765-0630

COATESVILLE — E9 *Chester*

HIDDEN ACRES CAMPGROUND **Ratings: 7.5/8★/9** (Campground) 100 Avail: 22 full hkups, 78 W, 78 E (30/50 amps). 2021 rates: $42 to $52. Apr 15 to Oct 15. (610)857-0662, 103 Hidden Acres Rd, Coatesville, PA 19320

CONFLUENCE — E3 *Fayette*

YOUGH LAKE - COE/TUB RUN CAMPGROUND (Public Corps) From town: Go 4-1/2 mi S on Hwy 281, then 1 mi E on Tub Run Rd (L). Avail: 30 E (30/50 amps). 2021 rates: $30 to $60. May 16 to Aug 30. (814)395-3242

CONNELLSVILLE — E2 *Fayette*

UNIONTOWN KOA AT RIVER'S EDGE **Ratings: 9/8.5★/9.5** (Campground) Avail: 100 full hkups (30/50 amps). 2021 rates: $47 to $89. (724)628-4880, 1101 Riveredge Rd, Connellsville, PA 15425

COOK FOREST — C3 *Clarion*

DEER MEADOW CAMPGROUND **Ratings: 8.5/NA/9.5** (Campground) 150 Avail: 59 full hkups, 91 W, 91 E (30/50 amps). 2021 rates: $42 to $59. May 22 to Sep 07. (814)927-8125, 2761 Forest Rd, Cooksburg, PA 16217

KALYUMET CAMPGROUND **Ratings: 9/10★/10** (Campground) 95 Avail: 73 full hkups, 22 W, 22 E (30/50 amps). 2021 rates: $60 to $71. May 01 to Oct 31. (814)744-9622, 8630 Miola Rd, Lucinda, PA 16235

COOKSBURG — C3 *Clarion*

COOK FOREST (Public State Park) From Jct of SR-66 & SR-36: Go 7 mi S on SR-36 (L). 210 Avail: 19 full hkups, 60 E (30/50 amps). 2021 rates: $15 to $20. May 25 to Oct 10. (814)744-8407

CORRY — A2 *Erie*

HARECREEK CAMPGROUND **Ratings: 9/8.5★/9** (Campground) Avail: 20 full hkups (30/50 amps). 2021 rates: $45. (814)664-9684, 375 Sciota St. , Corry, PA 16407

Always do a Pre-Drive Safety Check!

COUDERSPORT — B5 *Potter*

ALLEGHENY RIVER CAMPGROUND **Ratings: 8/9★/10** (Campground) 80 Avail: 49 full hkups, 31 W, 31 E (30/50 amps). 2021 rates: $48 to $72. Apr 12 to Oct 20. (814)544-8844, 1737 US Route 6 W, Roulette, PA 16746

CHERRY SPRINGS (Public State Park) From Jct of US-6 & W Branch Rd: Go 14 mi SW on Branch Rd, then 1 block to SR-44 at park (R). 30 Avail: Pit toilets. 2021 rates: $15 to $20. Apr 10 to Nov 01. (814)435-5010

POTTER COUNTY FAMILY CAMPGROUND **Ratings: 5/5.5/7.5** (Campground) 65 Avail: 25 full hkups, 40 W, 40 E (30/50 amps). 2021 rates: $25 to $28. (814)274-5010, 3075 E Second St (Rt 6), Coudersport, PA 16915

COVINGTON — B6 *Tioga*

TANGLEWOOD CAMPING

good sam park **Ratings: 8/9★/9** (Campground) 58 Avail: 5 full hkups, 53 W, 53 E (30/50 amps). 2021 rates: $46 to $56. May 01 to Oct 31. (570)549-8299, 787 Tanglewood Rd, Covington, PA 16917

DARLINGTON — D1 *Beaver*

CRAWFORD'S CAMPING PARK **Ratings: 7.5/8★/7** (Campground) Avail: 52 full hkups (30/50 amps). 2021 rates: $30. Apr 15 to Oct 15. (724)846-5964, 251 Hogson Rd, Darlington, PA 16115

DENVER — E8 *Lancaster*

HICKORY RUN CAMPGROUND **Ratings: 7.5/8★/8.5** (Campground) 165 Avail: 36 full hkups, 129 W, 129 E (30/50 amps). 2021 rates: $42 to $52. Apr 01 to Nov 01. (800)458-0612, 285 Greenville Rd, Denver, PA 17517

DINGMANS FERRY — C10 *Pike*

DINGMANS CAMPGROUND **Ratings: 3/9★/6** (Campground) 35 Avail: 35 W, 35 E (30/50 amps). 2021 rates: $42 to $44. Apr 01 to Oct 15. (570)828-1551, 1006 Rte 209, Dingmans Ferry, PA 18328

DONEGAL — E3 *Westmoreland*

DONEGAL CAMPGROUND **Ratings: 7/7.5★/7** (Campground) 30 Avail: 25 full hkups, 5 W, 5 E (30/50 amps). 2021 rates: $40 to $44. Mar 15 to Dec 15. (724)593-7717, 106 Yeckel Dr, Rt 31, Donegal, PA 15628

KOOSER (Public State Park) From town, NW 11 mi on Hwy 31W (L). Avail: 28 E (30 amps). 2021 rates: $15 to $24. Apr 15 to Oct 15. (814)445-8673

LAUREL HIGHLANDS CAMPLAND **Ratings: 9.5/9.5★/7.5** (RV Park) Avail: 34 full hkups (30/50 amps). 2021 rates: $50 to $55. (724)593-6325, 1001 Clubhouse Dr., Donegal, PA 15628

DOVER — E7 *York*

GETTYSBURG FARM RV CAMPGROUND

good sam park **Ratings: 8/7/8.5** (Campground) 110 Avail: 61 full hkups, 49 W, 49 E (30/50 amps). 2021 rates: $65 to $83. Apr 12 to Oct 31. (888)563-7040, 6200 Big Mount Rd, Dover, PA 17315

EAST BENTON — B9 *Lackawanna*

LACKAWANNA (Public State Park) From I-81 (exit 199): Go 3 mi W on Hwy 524, then N on Hwy 407. Avail: 61 E (30/50 amps). 2021 rates: $15 to $24. Apr 13 to Oct 21. (570)945-3239

EAST STROUDSBURG — C10 *Monroe*

TIMOTHY LAKE NORTH RV PARK

good sam park **Ratings: 8/7.5/7.5** (Campground) 200 Avail: 169 full hkups, 31 W, 31 E (30/50 amps). 2021 rates: $85 to $89. May 01 to Oct 31. (888)563-7040, 6837 Timothy Lake Rd, East Stroudsburg, PA 18301

TIMOTHY LAKE SOUTH RV PARK

good sam park **Ratings: 9.5/9★/9** (Campground) Avail: 277 full hkups (30/50 amps). 2021 rates: $85 to $89. (888)563-7040, 2043 Allegheny Lane, East Stroudsburg, PA 18301

EBENSBURG — D4 *Cambria*

WOODLAND PARK
Ratings: 7/5.5/6.5 (Campground) From jct US 219 & US 22: Go 1-1/4 mi W on US 22, then 1/4 mi S on Campground Rd (E). **FAC:** gravel rds. (200 spaces). Avail: 80 gravel, 7 pull-thrus, (30x50), back-ins (30x40), 80 full hkups (30/50 amps), seasonal sites, WiFi @ sites, tent sites, shower$, laundry, groc, LP gas, fire rings, firewood. **REC:** pond, fishing, boating nearby, playground, hunting nearby. Pets OK. eco-friendly. 2021 rates: $28 to $36. Apr 15 to Oct 15.
(814)472-9857 Lat: 40.447168, Lon: -78.785871
220 Campground Rd, Ebensburg, PA 15931
See ad this page

ELIZABETHTOWN — E7 *Lancaster*

ELIZABETHTOWN/HERSHEY KOA **Ratings: 9/10★/9.5** (Campground) 158 Avail: 147 full hkups, 11 W, 11 E (30/50 amps). 2021 rates: $58.95 to $136. Apr 15 to Oct 30. (800)562-4774, 1980 Turnpike Rd, Elizabethtown, PA 17022

HERSHEY ROAD CAMPGROUND **Ratings: 9.5/10★/10** (RV Resort) Avail: 121 full hkups (30/50 amps). 2021 rates: $75 to $145. (844)476-6737, 1590 Hershey Rd., Elizabethtown, PA 17022

ELVERSON — E9 *Berks*

FRENCH CREEK (Public State Park) From Jct of I-76 & & SH 345: Go 4-1/2 mi N on SH 345 (R). Avail: 60 E (30/50 amps). 2021 rates: $15 to $24. (610)582-9680

ELYSBURG — C7 *Northumberland*

KNOEBELS AMUSEMENT PARK AND CAMPGROUND **Ratings: 6.5/7/6.5** (Campground) 478 Avail: 478 W, 478 E (30/50 amps). 2021 rates: $59 to $62. Apr 15 to Nov 01. (800)487-4386, 391 Knoebels Blvd, Rt 487, Elysburg, PA 17824

EMLENTON — C2 *Venango*

GASLIGHT CAMPGROUND **Ratings: 8.5/9.5★/9** (Campground) Avail: 40 full hkups (30/50 amps). 2021 rates: $40. Apr 01 to Oct 31. (724)867-6981, 6297 Emlenton Clintonville Rd, Emlenton, PA 16373

EMPORIUM — B5 *Cameron*

SIZERVILLE (Public State Park) From Jct of US-120 & Rte 155: Go 7 mi N on Rte 155 (R). Avail: 18 E (20/50 amps). 2021 rates: $15 to $24. Apr 15 to Dec 15. (814)486-5605

ENTRIKEN — D5 *Huntingdon*

TROUGH CREEK (Public State Park) From Jct of Hwy 26 & Hwy 994: Go 6 mi E on Hwy 994 (E). Avail: 23 E (20/30 amps), Pit toilets. 2021 rates: $15 to $24. Apr 15 to Dec 15. (814)658-3847

EPHRATA — E8 *Lancaster*

STARLITE CAMPING RESORT **Ratings: 8/9.5★/10** (Campground) 100 Avail: 50 full hkups, 50 W, 50 E (30/50 amps). 2021 rates: $48 to $53. May 01 to Oct 31. (717)733-9655, 1500 Furance Hill Rd, Stevens, PA 17578

ERIE — A2 *Erie*

ERIE See also Corry & Lake City.

CAMP SHERWIN YMCA (Public) From jct I-90 (exit 16) & Hwy 98: Go 3-1/4 mi N on Hwy 98, then 1-1/4 mi W on Hwy 5 (R). 24 Avail: 16 full hkups, 8 W, 8 E (30/50 amps). 2021 rates: $42 to $55. (814)774-9416

LAMPE MARINA CAMPGROUND (Public) From Jct I-79(exit 183A) & Hwy 5/Hwy 290/W 12th St: Go 3-1/4 mi E on 12th St, then 1-1/2 mi N on E Bayfront Pkwy/Port Access Road (E). 42 Avail: 42 W, 42 E (30/50 amps). 2021 rates: $35 to $40. May 01 to Oct 31. (814)454-5830

PRESQUE ISLE PASSAGE RV PARK & CABIN RENTALS
Ratings: 9/10★/9 (Campground) Avail: 76 full hkups (30/50 amps). 2021 rates: $50 to $70. Apr 01 to Oct 30. (814)458-0782, 6300 Sterrettania Rd (Hwy 832), Erie, PA 16415

SARA'S CAMPGROUND **Ratings: 7.5/9.5★/8** (Campground) Avail: 58 full hkups (30/50 amps). 2021 rates: $35 to $40. Apr 01 to Oct 31. (814)833-4560, 50 Peninsula Dr, Erie, PA 16505

SPARROW POND FAMILY CAMPGROUND & RECREATION CENTER **Ratings: 9/9.5★/10** (Campground) 106 Avail: 100 full hkups, 6 W, 6 E (30/50 amps). 2021 rates: $58 to $75. Apr 15 to Oct 15. (814)796-6777, 11103 RT. 19 N, Waterford, PA 16441

FARMINGTON — E2 *Fayette*

BENNER'S MEADOW RUN CAMPING AND CABINS **Ratings: 8.5/8.5★/8.5** (Campground) 38 Avail: 28 full hkups, 3 W, 10 E (30/50 amps). 2021 rates: $43 to $53. Apr 25 to Oct 20. (724)329-4097, 315 Nelson Rd, Farmington, PA 15437

FORKSVILLE — B7 *Sullivan*

WORLDS END (Public State Park) From town: Go 2 mi S on SR-154 (E). Avail: 32 E (30/50 amps). 2021 rates: $15 to $24. Apr 07 to Dec 07. (570)924-3287

FORT LOUDON — E5 *Franklin*

COWANS GAP (Public State Park) From Jct of US-30 & SR-75: Go 4 mi N on SR-75, then 3 mi W on Richmond Furnace Rd (L). Avail: 149 E (30/50 amps). 2021 rates: $15 to $20. Apr 10 to Dec 15. (717)485-3948

FRANKFORT SPRINGS — D1 *Beaver*

RACCOON CREEK (Public State Park) From Jct SR-18 & Hwy 168: Go 7 mi N on SR-18, then 1 Blk W on Cabin Rd (R). Avail: 65 E (50 amps). 2021 rates: $15 to $24. Apr 15 to Oct 15. (724)899-2200

FRANKLIN — B2 *Venango*

TWO MILE RUN COUNTY PARK (Public) From jct of SR 8 & US 322: Go 1/2 mi W on US 322, then 6 mi N on SR 417, then 1/2 mi E on Cherrytree Rd, then 3/4 mi S on Beach Rd. 72 Avail: 12 full hkups, 28 E (30/50 amps). 2021 rates: $15 to $25. (814)676-6116

FRUGALITY — D4 *Cambria*

PRINCE GALLITZIN (Public State Park) From Jct of SR-53 & SR-253: Go 3-1/2 mi N on SR-53, then 4-3/4 mi W on SR-1021/Beaver Valley Rd, then 1/4 mi SE on Crooked Run Campground Rd (E). 398 Avail: 26 W, 157 E (30/50 amps). 2021 rates: $15 to $24. Apr 15 to Oct 25. (814)674-1000

GALETON — B6 *Potter*

LYMAN RUN (Public State Park) From Jct of US-6 & Hwy 2002/W Branch Rd: Go 5-1/4 mi W on 2002/W Branch Rd, then 2-3/4 mi NW on Lyman Run Rd (R). Avail: 28 E (30/50 amps). 2021 rates: $17 to $24. Apr 15 to Dec 15. (814)435-5010

OLE BULL (Public State Park) From Jct of US-6 & Hwy 144: Go 18 mi S on Hwy 144 (L). Avail: 56 E (30/50 amps). 2021 rates: $15 to $24. (814)435-5000

GETTYSBURG — E6 *Adams*

ARTILLERY RIDGE CAMPING RESORT & GETTYSBURG HORSE PARK **Ratings: 9/9★/9.5** (Campground) 130 Avail: 113 full hkups, 17 W, 17 E (30/50 amps). 2021 rates: $69 to $106. (717)334-1288, 610 Taneytown Rd (Rte 134), Gettysburg, PA 17325

DRUMMER BOY CAMPING RESORT
Ratings: 9/8/9.5 (Campground) 173 Avail: 161 full hkups, 12 W, 12 E (30/50 amps). 2021 rates: $62 to $106. (888)563-7040, 1 Rocky Grove Rd, Gettysburg, PA 17325

GETTYSBURG BATTLEFIELD KOA KAMPGROUND **Ratings: 9/10★/9.5** (Campground) 72 Avail: 54 full hkups, 18 W, 18 E (30/50 amps). 2021 rates: $43 to $106.60. Apr 01 to Nov 01. (717)642-5713, 20 Knox Rd, Gettysburg, PA 17325

GETTYSBURG CAMPGROUND **Ratings: 9.5/9.5★/9.5** (Campground) 229 Avail: 111 full hkups, 118 W, 118 E (30/50 amps). 2021 rates: $69 to $109. Apr 03 to Nov 22. (717)334-3304, 2030 Fairfield Rd, Gettysburg, PA 17325

GRANITE HILL CAMPING RESORT **Ratings: 7.5/8★/8** (Campground) 302 Avail: 112 full hkups, 190 W, 190 E (30/50 amps). 2021 rates: $60 to $90. Apr 01 to Nov 15. (717)642-8749, 3340 Fairfield Rd, Gettysburg, PA 17325

ROUND TOP CAMPGROUND
Ratings: 9/8.5★/8.5 (Campground) 167 Avail: 147 full hkups, 20 W, 20 E (30/50 amps). 2021 rates: $58 to $110. Apr 02 to Oct 31. (888)563-7040, 180 Knight Rd, Gettysburg, PA 17325

Things to See and Do

DESTINATION GETTYSBURG Official tourism bureau for Gettysburg, PA. Information available on camping, housing, restaurants and places of interest in the area. Restrooms.. Hours: 8:30am to 5pm. No CC.
(800)337-5015 Lat: 39.829483, Lon: -77.242126
571 W Middle St., Gettysburg, PA 17325
www.destinationgettysburg.com

GREENTOWN — C9 *Pike*

IRONWOOD POINT RECREATION AREA **Ratings: 6/NA/8.5** (Campground) 14 Avail: 14 W, 14 E (30/50 amps), Pit toilets. 2021 rates: $48 to $54. Apr 30 to Oct 15. (570)857-0880, 155 Burns Hill Rd, Greentown, PA 18426

LEDGEDALE RECREATION AREA **Ratings: 4/8★/7** (Campground) 15 Avail: 15 W, 15 E (30 amps). 2021 rates: $46 to $50. Apr 25 to Oct 17. (570)689-2181, 153 Ledgedale Rd, Greentown, PA 18426

PROMISED LAND (Public State Park) From Jct of I-84 & SR-390 (old exit 7/new exit 26): Go 5 mi S on SR-390(R). 513 Avail: 12 full hkups, 189 E (30/50 amps). 2021 rates: $15 to $24. Apr 01 to Dec 15. (570)676-3428

GREENVILLE — B1 *Mercer*

FARMA FAMILY CAMPGROUND **Ratings: 9/8.5★/9** (Campground) Avail: 20 full hkups (30/50 amps). 2021 rates: $52 to $70. May 01 to Sep 30. (724)253-4535, 87 Hughey Rd, Greenville, PA 16125

HAMBURG — D8 *Berks*

Travel Services

GANDER RV OF HAMBURG Your new hometown outfitter offering the best regional gear for all your outdoor needs. Your adventure awaits. **SERVICES:** RV, tire, sells outdoor gear, staffed RV wash, restrooms. RV Sales. RV supplies, LP gas, RV accessible. Hours: 9am - 6pm.
(833)739-1030 Lat: 40.56064, Lon: -75.99634
20 Industrial Dr, Hamburg, PA 19526
rv.ganderoutdoors.com

HANOVER — E7 *York*

CODORUS (Public State Park) From Jct of SR-116 & SR-216, E 2.5 mi on SR-216 to Dubs Church Rd, S 1 mi (R). Avail: 112 E (30/50 amps). 2021 rates: $15 to $20. Apr 13 to Nov 01. (717)637-2816

Travel Services

CAMPING WORLD OF HANOVER As the nation's largest retailer of RV supplies, accessories, services and new and used RVs, Camping World is committed to making your total RV experience better. **SERVICES:** tire, RV appliance, MH mechanical, staffed RV wash, restrooms. RV Sales. RV supplies, LP gas, RV accessible. Hours: 9am - 7pm.
(888)899-0663 Lat: 39.755834, Lon: -76.953714
2100 Baltimore Pike, Hanover, PA 17331
www.campingworld.com

HARMONY — D1 *Butler*

INDIAN BRAVE CAMPGROUND **Ratings: 7/8.5★/8.5** (Campground) Avail: 13 full hkups (30/50 amps). 2021 rates: $50. Apr 15 to Oct 15. (724)452-9204, 159 Perry Hwy (US 19), Harmony, PA 16037

Park owners and staff are rightly proud of their business. Let them know how much you enjoyed your stay.

HARRISBURG — E7 *Dauphin*

HARRISBURG See also Carlisle, Dover, Elizabethtown, Hershey, Jonestown, Lebanon, Liverpool, Manheim & York.

HARRISBURG EAST CAMPGROUND & STORAGE
Ratings: 9/10★/9 (Campground) From Jct of I-76(exit 247) & I-283: Go 1-1/2 mi N on I-283 (to exit 2), then 1/4 mi W on PA-441/Lindle Rd, then 3/4 mi S on Eisenhower Blvd, then 1/4 mi E on Campground Rd(E). **FAC:** paved/gravel rds. (67 spaces). Avail: 42 gravel, 42 pull-thrus, (35x60), 42 full hkups (30/50 amps), seasonal sites, cable, WiFi @ sites, tent sites, dump, laundry, LP gas, fire rings, firewood. **REC:** heated pool, boating nearby, playground, hunting nearby. Pets OK. Big rig sites, eco-friendly. 2021 rates: $74 to $104, Military discount.
(717)939-4331 Lat: 40.232193, Lon: -76.798443
1134 Highspire Rd, Harrisburg, PA 17111
www.hbgeastcampground.com
See ad page 776

Travel Services

CAMPING WORLD OF HARRISBURG As the nation's largest retailer of RV supplies, accessories, services and new and used RVs, Camping World is committed to making your total RV experience better. **SERVICES:** RV, tire, RV appliance, MH mechanical, sells outdoor gear, staffed RV wash, restrooms. RV Sales. RV supplies, LP gas, dump, RV accessible. Hours: 9am - 7pm.
(888)851-5320 Lat: 40.334081, Lon: -76.732335
7501 Allentown Blvd., Harrisburg, PA 17112
www.campingworld.com

HARRISVILLE — C2 *Butler*

YOGI BEAR'S JELLYSTONE PARK AT KOZY REST **Ratings: 9/10★/9.5** (Campground) 99 Avail: 94 full hkups, 5 W, 5 E (30/50 amps). 2021 rates: $76 to $119. Apr 15 to Oct 31. (724)735-2417, 449 Campground Rd, Harrisville, PA 16038

HATFIELD — E9 *Montgomery*

VILLAGE SCENE RV PARK **Ratings: 7.5/8.5★/8** (RV Park) Avail: 35 full hkups (30/50 amps). 2021 rates: $46. (215)362-6030, 2151 Koffel Rd, Hatfield, PA 19440

HAWLEY — B10 *Pike*

WILSONVILLE RECREATION AREA **Ratings: 6/7/7.5** (Campground) 103 Avail: 103 W, 103 E (30 amps). 2021 rates: $32 to $36. Apr 29 to Oct 16. (570)226-4382, 113 Ammon Dr, Hawley, PA 18428

HEGINS — D7 *Schuylkill*

CAMP-A-WHILE **Ratings: 8.5/9.5★/8.5** (Campground) Avail: 31 full hkups (30/50 amps). 2021 rates: $45 to $48. Apr 15 to Oct 25. (570)682-8696, 1921 E Main St, Hegins, PA 17938

HERSHEY — E7 *Dauphin*

A SPOTLIGHT Introducing Hershey's colorful attractions appearing at the front of this state section.

HERSHEY See also Denver, Elizabethtown, Ephrata, Harrisburg, Jonestown, Lancaster, Lebanon, Liverpool, Manheim, Newmanstown, Pine Grove, Robesonia & York.

HERSHEYPARK CAMPING RESORT **Ratings: 8.5/9.5★/8.5** (Campground) 299 Avail: 125 full hkups, 124 W, 124 E (30/50 amps). 2021 rates: $59 to $149. (717)534-8999, 1200 Sweet St., Hummelstown, PA 17036

PINCH POND FAMILY CAMPGROUND
Ratings: 9/10★/10 (Campground) From Jct US 422 & Hwy 743 (in Hershey): Go 3/4 mi S on Hwy 743, then 12-1/4 mi E on US 322, then 3 mi S on Hwy 72(1 mi past I-76), then 1/2 mi W on Cider Press Rd, then 1 mi N on Pinch Rd(R). **FAC:** paved/gravel rds. (190 spaces). Avail: 125 gravel, 56 pull-thrus, (35x60), back-ins (30x55), 111 full hkups, 14 W, 14 E (30/50 amps), seasonal sites, cable, WiFi @ sites, $, tent sites, rentals, dump, laundry, groc, LP gas, fire rings, firewood, controlled access. **REC:** pool, pond, fishing, playground, hunting nearby. Pets OK. Partial handicap access. Big rig sites, eco-friendly. 2021 rates: $50.
(800)659-7640 Lat: 40.229546, Lon: -76.45227
3075 Pinch Rd, Manheim, PA 17545
pinchpond.com
See primary listing at Manheim and ad page 779

Say you saw it in our Guide!

HESSTON — D5 *Huntingdon*

PLEASANT HILLS CAMPGROUND **Ratings: 9/9.5★/8** (Campground) Avail: 12 full hkups (30/50 amps). 2021 rates: $45 to $55. Apr 15 to Oct 15. (814)658-3986, 12733 Pleasant Hills Dr, Hesston, PA 16647

HOLTWOOD — E8 *Lancaster*

MUDDY RUN RECREATION PARK (EXELON ENERGY) **Ratings: 7/8.5★/8** (Campground) 88 Avail: 88 W, 88 E (30/50 amps). 2021 rates: $32.50. Mar 30 to Oct 31. (717)284-5850, 172 Bethesda Church Rd , Holtwood, PA 17532

TUCQUAN PARK FAMILY CAMPGROUND
Ratings: 9/9.5★/9 (Campground) From jct Hwy 272 & Hwy 372: Go 5 mi W on Hwy 372, then 2 mi N on River Rd (R).

SEE LANCASTER, BE CLOSE TO NATURE
Located in the Susquehanna River hills, southwest of Lancaster, we are adjacent to the Tucquan Glen Nature Preserve. Hiking, river fun and other great outdoor activities make us a perfect family camping experience.
FAC: gravel rds. (144 spaces). 80 Avail: 64 gravel, 16 grass, 41 pull-thrus, (30x60), back-ins (25x40), 80 full hkups (30/50 amps), seasonal sites, WiFi @ sites, tent sites, rentals, dump, laundry, groc, LP gas, fire rings, firewood. **REC:** pool, pond, fishing, boating nearby, playground, hunting nearby. Pets OK. Partial handicap access. Big rig sites, eco-friendly. 2021 rates: $47 to $51, Military discount.
(717)284-2156 Lat: 39.857869, Lon: -76.330519
917 River Rd, Holtwood, PA 17532
camptucquanpark.com
See ad page 777

HONESDALE — B9 *Wayne*

HONESDALE/POCONOS KOA **Ratings: 9/9.5★/9** (Campground) Avail: 55 full hkups (30/50 amps). 2021 rates: $53 to $93. Mar 01 to Oct 31. (570)253-0424, 50 Countryside Lane, Honesdale, PA 18431

PONDEROSA PINES FAMILY CAMPGROUND **Ratings: 7.5/8.5★/7.5** (Campground) 45 Avail: 4 full hkups, 41 W, 41 E (30 amps). 2021 rates: $51 to $60. Apr 18 to Oct 19. (570)253-2080, 31 Ponderosa Dr, Honesdale, PA 18431

HOP BOTTOM — B9 *Susquehanna*

SHORE FOREST CAMPGROUND **Ratings: 8/9.5★/8** (Campground) 42 Avail: 25 full hkups, 17 W, 17 E (30/50 amps). 2021 rates: $35 to $55. Apr 15 to Oct 31. (570)289-4666, 121 The Driveway, Hop Bottom, PA 18824

HOWARD — C6 *Centre*

BALD EAGLE (RUSSEL P. LETTERMAN CAMPGROUND) (Public State Park) From jct I-80 (exit 158) & Hwy 150: Go 9 mi N on Hwy 150. Avail: 88 E (30/50 amps). 2021 rates: $15 to $20. Apr 15 to Dec 15. (814)625-2775

INTERCOURSE — E8 *Lancaster*

BEACON HILL CAMPING **Ratings: 7/9.5★/9.5** (RV Park) Avail: 34 full hkups (30/50 amps). 2021 rates: $47 to $55. Apr 15 to Oct 29. (717)768-8775, 128 Beacon Hill Dr., Ronks, PA 17572

JAMESTOWN — B1 *Crawford*

PYMATUNING (Public State Park) From Jct of US-322 & SR-58: Go 5 mi W on US-322 (R). 645 Avail: 38 full hkups, 343 E (30/50 amps). 2021 rates: $15 to $24. Apr 15 to Oct 28. (724)932-3142

JEFFERSON — E2 *Greene*

FIREHOUSE RV CAMPGROUND **Ratings: 5.5/6/7.5** (RV Park) Avail: 25 full hkups (30/50 amps). 2021 rates: $40. (724)833-1955, 1483 Jefferson Rd, Jefferson, PA 15344

JONESTOWN — D7 *Lebanon*

JONESTOWN AOK CAMPGROUND **Ratings: 8/8.5★/7.5** (Campground) Avail: 14 full hkups (30/50 amps). 2021 rates: $45. (717)865-2526, 145 Old Route 22, Jonestown, PA 17038

JONESTOWN/HERSHEY KOA **Ratings: 7.5/9★/8.5** (Campground) Avail: 54 full hkups (30/50 amps). 2021 rates: $57 to $70. (800)562-2609, 11 Lickdale Rd, Jonestown, PA 17038

Be prepared! Bridge, Tunnel & Ferry Regulations and Rules of the Road can be found in the front of the Guide.

KIRKWOOD — E8 *Lancaster*

OMA'S FAMILY CAMPGROUND
Ratings: 7.5/8.5★/9.5 (Campground) From Jct of Hwy 372 & Hwy 472: Go 7 1/4 mi SE on Hwy 472 (L). **FAC:** all weather rds. (87 spaces). Avail: 42 all weather, back-ins (25x40), 42 full hkups (30/50 amps), seasonal sites, WiFi @ sites, rentals, LP bottles, fire rings, firewood. **REC:** boating nearby, playground, hunting nearby. Pet restrict (Q). No tents, eco-friendly. 2021 rates: $50 to $60, Military discount.
(717)529-2020 Lat: 39.83814, Lon: -76.05786
2085 Kirkwood Pike, Kirkwood, PA 17536
omasfamilycampground.com
See ad this page

KNOX — C2 *Clarion*

WOLFS CAMPING RESORT **Ratings: 8/8.5★/9** (Campground) Avail: 100 full hkups (30/50 amps). 2021 rates: $35 to $60. Apr 15 to Oct 31. (814)797-1103, 308 Timberwolf Run, Knox, PA 16232

KUTZTOWN — D9 *Berks*

PINE HILL RV PARK **Ratings: 8/9★/8.5** (RV Park) Avail: 88 full hkups (30/50 amps). 2021 rates: $54 to $58. Apr 01 to Nov 01. (610)285-6776, 268 Old Rte 22, Kutztown, PA 19530

LAKE ARIEL — B9 *Wayne*

SECLUDED ACRES CAMPGROUND **Ratings: 7/8★/6** (Campground) 31 Avail: 31 W, 31 E (30/50 amps). 2021 rates: $35 to $40. Apr 24 to Oct 15. (570)226-9959, 150 Marty's Main St, Lake Ariel, PA 18436

LAKE CITY — A1 *Erie*

CAMP ERIEZ
Ratings: 7.5/9★/8.5 (Campground) 15 Avail: 15 W, 15 E (30/50 amps). 2021 rates: $50. May 01 to Oct 31. (814)774-8381, 9356 W Lake Rd, Lake City, PA 16423

LANCASTER — E8 *Lancaster*

A SPOTLIGHT Introducing Lancaster County's colorful attractions appearing at the front of this state section.

LANCASTER See also Adamstown, Airville, Bowmansville, Coatesville, Denver, Elizabethtown, Ephrata, Hershey, Holtwood, Intercourse, Jonestown, Kirkwood, Lebanon, Manheim, Narvon, New Holland, Newmanstown, Pequea, Quarryville, Robesonia, Strasburg, West Chester & York.

CIRCLE M CAMPING RESORT
Ratings: 7.5/9★/9 (Campground) 13 Avail: 8 full hkups, 5 W, 5 E (30/50 amps). 2021 rates: $58 to $94. Apr 15 to Oct 31. (888)563-7040, 2111 Millersville Rd, Lancaster, PA 17603

COUNTRY ACRES CAMPGROUND
Ratings: 9.5/9.5★/9.5 (Campground) From Jct US 30 & Hwy 896: Go 2-1/2 mi E on US 30, then 300 ft N on Leven Rd (L). **FAC:** all weather rds. Avail: 105 all weather, 27 pull-thrus, (36x60), back-ins (30x40), 88 full hkups, 17 W, 17 E (30/50 amps), cable, WiFi @ sites, tent sites, rentals, dump, laundry, groc, fire rings, firewood, controlled access. **REC:** pool, wading pool, shuffleboard, playground, hunting nearby. Pets OK. Partial handicap access. Big rig sites, 14 day max stay, eco-friendly. 2021 rates: $42 to $71. Mar 21 to Dec 17.
(717)687-8014 Lat: 40.015154, Lon: -76.146276
20 Leven Rd, Gordonville, PA 17529
www.countryacrescampground.com
See ad page 781

Thank you for being one of our best customers!

LANCASTER (CONT)

FLORY'S COTTAGES & CAMPING
Ratings: 8/9.5★/9 (Campground) From Jct US 30 & Hwy 896: Go 1-1/2 mi E on US 30, then 1/2 mi N on Ronks Rd (R).

'WHERE THE AMISH ARE OUR NEIGHBORS'
Whether you're here to kick back and enjoy our amenities, or pack up for the day to explore the area, we would love to be the place you call 'home' during your peaceful getaway to Amish Country.
FAC: gravel rds. (71 spaces). Avail: 62 gravel, 1 pull-thrus, (30x100), back-ins (30x60), 62 full hkups (30/50 amps), seasonal sites, cable, WiFi @ sites, rentals, dump, laundry, groc. **REC:** playground, hunting nearby. Pets OK. No tents. Big rig sites, eco-friendly. 2021 rates: $45 to $67.
(717)687-6670 Lat: 40.025031, Lon: -76.167475
99 North Ronks Rd, Ronks, PA 17572
www.floryscamping.com
See ad page 778

MILL BRIDGE VILLAGE AND CAMPRESORT **Ratings: 8.5/8.5★/8.5** (Campground) 81 Avail: 50 full hkups, 31 W, 31 E (30/50 amps). 2021 rates: $46 to $73. (717)687-8181, 101. S. Ronks Rd, Ronks, PA 17572

OLD MILL STREAM CAMPGROUND
Ratings: 8/10★/9.5 (Campground) W-bnd: From Jct of US 30 & Hwy 896: Go 1-1/4 mi W on US 30 (R); E-bnd: From Jct of US 30 & US 222: Go 4-1/2 mi E on US 30 (L). **FAC:** paved/gravel rds. Avail: 157 gravel, 8 pull-thrus, (30x60), back-ins (30x50), 147 full hkups, 10 W, 10 E (30/50 amps), cable, WiFi @ sites, tent sites, rentals, dump, laundry, groc, LP gas, fire rings, firewood. **REC:** Old Mill Stream: fishing, playground. Pet restrict (Q). Partial handicap access. Big rig sites, 14 day max stay, eco-friendly. 2021 rates: $48 to $71, Military discount. ATM.
(717)299-2314 Lat: 40.026926, Lon: -76.218411
2249 Lincoln Hwy (US 30E), Lancaster, PA 17602
www.dutchwonderland.com/old-mill-stream-campground
See ad page 780

PINCH POND FAMILY CAMPGROUND
Ratings: 9/10★/10 (Campground) From the Jct of SR 741 & SR 283, N. 2 mi. On SR 741 to SR 722, E. 9.9 mi on SR 722 to Pinch Rd., W 1.5 mi (R). **FAC:** paved/gravel rds. (190 spaces). Avail: 125 gravel, 56 pull-thrus, (35x60), back-ins (30x55), 111 full hkups, 14 W, 14 E (30/50 amps), seasonal sites, cable, WiFi @ sites, $, tent sites, rentals, dump, laundry, groc, LP gas, fire rings, firewood, controlled access. **REC:** pool, pond, fishing, playground, hunting nearby. Pets OK. Partial handicap access. Big rig sites, eco-friendly. 2021 rates: $50.
(800)659-7640 Lat: 40.229546, Lon: -76.45227
3075 Pinch Rd., Manheim, PA 17545
pinchpond.com
See primary listing at Manheim and ad page 779

New to RVing? Visit Blog.GoodSam.com for tips on everything camping and RVing.

Things to See and Do

DUTCH WONDERLAND AMUSEMENT PARK
Its Family Time, 35 rides, attractions and shows. Hours for park vary, please call. Apr 27 to Dec 29. Partial handicap access. RV accessible. Restrooms. Food. Hours: 10am to 6pm. Adult fee: $49.99. ATM.
(866)386-2839 Lat: 40.026926, Lon: -76.218411
2249 Lincoln Hwy (US-30E), Lancaster, PA 17602
www.dutchwonderland.com
See ad page 780

LAPORTE — B7 *Sullivan*

PIONEER CAMPGROUND
Ratings: 9.5/9★/10 (Campground) From Jct US 220 & Hwy 42 (in Laporte): Go S 2 mi on US 220(R). **FAC:** all weather rds. (73 spaces). Avail: 41 all weather, back-ins (45x60), 41 W, 41 E (30/50 amps), seasonal sites, WiFi @ sites, tent sites, rentals, dump, mobile sewer, laundry, groc, LP gas, fire rings, firewood. **REC:** heated pool, playground, hunting nearby. Pets OK. eco-friendly. 2021 rates: $53 to $56, Military discount. Apr 15 to Dec 15.
(570)946-9971 Lat: 41.399686, Lon: -76.505367
307 Pioneer Trail, Muncy Valley, PA 17758
pioneercampground.com
See ad this page

LAWRENCEVILLE — A6 *Tioga*

COWANESQUE LAKE - COE/TOMPKINS REC AREA (Public Corps) From jct Hwy 49 & US 15: Go 1/4 mi N on US 15, then 3 mi W on Bliss Rd. 83 Avail: 52 full hkups, 31 W, 31 E (30/50 amps). 2021 rates: $36 to $40. May 15 to Sep 29. (570)835-5281

LEBANON — D8 *Lebanon*

HERSHEY RV & CAMPING RESORT
Ratings: 9/9.5★/9.5 (Campground) 235 Avail: 199 full hkups, 36 W, 36 E (30/50 amps). 2021 rates: $75 to $121. Apr 11 to Oct 26. (888)563-7040, 493 South Mt. Pleasant Rd, Lebanon, PA 17042

LEHIGHTON — C9 *Carbon*

LIZARD CREEK CAMPGROUND **Ratings: 8/8★/8** (Campground) 45 Avail: 40 full hkups, 5 W, 5 E (30 amps). 2021 rates: $58 to $97. Apr 08 to Oct 31. (570)386-2911, 2489 W Lizard Creek Rd, Lehighton, PA 18235

STONYBROOK RV RESORT
Ratings: 10/10★/10 (RV Park) Avail: 42 full hkups (30/50 amps). 2021 rates: $69 to $139. (570)386-4088, 1435 Germans Rd, Lehighton, PA 18235

LENHARTSVILLE — D8 *Berks*

BLUE ROCKS FAMILY CAMPGROUND **Ratings: 8/10★/9** (Campground) 115 Avail: 17 full hkups, 98 W, 98 E (20/30 amps). 2021 rates: $50 to $63. Apr 01 to Nov 01. (866)478-5267, 341 Sousley Rd, Lenhartsville, PA 19534

ROBIN HILL CAMPGROUND
Ratings: 8.5/8.5★/8.5 (Campground) 72 Avail: 49 full hkups, 23 W, 23 E (30/50 amps). 2021 rates: $66. Apr 01 to Oct 31. (888)563-7040, 149 Robin Hill Rd, Lenhartsville, PA 19534

LEWISBURG — C7 *Union*

LEWISBURG See also Bloomsburg, Catawissa, Elysburg, Loganton, Mifflinburg, Milton, Montgomery, New Columbia, Selinsgrove, Sunbury & Winfield.

RAYMOND B WINTER (Public State Park) From Jct of Hwy 192 & Rte 15: Go 18 mi W on Hwy 192 (R). Avail: 48 E (50 amps). 2021 rates: $15 to $24. Apr 15 to Dec 15. (570)966-1455

LEWISTOWN — D6 *Mifflin*

WATERSIDE CAMPGROUND & RV PARK
Ratings: 8.5/8.5★/9 (Campground) From Jct Hwy 103 (in Lewistown) & US 22: Go 2-1/2 mi SW on US 22(W 4th St), then 2 mi SE on Loop Rd, then 1/2 mi S on Locust Rd (E). **FAC:** paved/gravel rds. (236 spaces). Avail: 32 gravel, back-ins (30x60), 32 full hkups (30/50 amps), seasonal sites, cable, WiFi, tent sites, rentals, shower$, dump, laundry, groc, LP gas, fire rings, firewood, controlled access. **REC:** heated pool, Juniata River: fishing, kayaking/canoeing, boating nearby, playground, hunting nearby. Pet restrict (Q). Partial handicap access. Big rig sites, eco-friendly. 2021 rates: $55.50 to $67.50, Military discount.
(717)248-3974 Lat: 40.558808, Lon: -77.598925
475 Locust Rd, Lewistown, PA 17044
watersidecampground.com
See ad this page

Things to See and Do

BOAT RIDE - HISTORIC PENNSYLVANIA CANAL A narrated boat ride on the Pennsylvania Canal. May 25 to Oct 31. Restrooms. Hours: 10am to 11:30am. Adult fee: $5 .
(717)248-3974 Lat: 40.558808, Lon: -77.598925
475 Locust Rd , Lewistown, PA 17044
www.watersidecampground.com
See ad this page

LIVERPOOL — D7 *Perry*

FERRYBOAT CAMPSITES **Ratings: 6.5/8★/7** (Campground) 65 Avail: 62 full hkups, 3 W, 3 E (30/50 amps). 2021 rates: $55 to $62. Apr 15 to Oct 31. (800)759-8707, 32 Ferry Ln, Liverpool, PA 17045

LOGANTON — C6 *Clinton*

HOLIDAY PINES CAMPGROUND **Ratings: 6/5.5/7** (Campground) 52 Avail: 30 full hkups, 22 W, 22 E (30/50 amps). 2021 rates: $38 to $43. Apr 01 to Dec 01. (570)725-2267, 16 Pine Tree Lane, Loganton, PA 17747

MADISON — E2 *Westmoreland*

MADISON/PITTSBURGH SE KOA **Ratings: 8.5/9★/7.5** (Campground) Avail: 35 full hkups (30/50 amps). 2021 rates: $48 to $61. (800)562-4034, 764 Waltz Mill Rd, Ruffs Dale, PA 15679

MAHANOY CITY — D8 *Schuylkill*

LOCUST LAKE (Public State Park) From Jct of US-209 & Brockton: Go 3 mi N on Moss Glen Rd, then 500 yds W on Locust Lake Rd (R). Avail: 80 E (50 amps). 2021 rates: $15 to $24. Mar 23 to Oct 19. (570)467-2404

MANHEIM — E8 *Lancaster*

PA DUTCH COUNTRY RV RESORT
Ratings: 7.5/9★/8.5 (Campground) Avail: 144 full hkups (30/50 amps). 2021 rates: $56.25 to $62. Apr 09 to Oct 31. (888)563-7040, 185 Lehman Rd, Manheim, PA 17545

PINCH POND FAMILY CAMPGROUND
Ratings: 9/10★/10 (Campground) From Jct of I-76 & Hwy 72 (exit 266): Go 1 mi S on Hwy 72, then 1/2 mi W on Cider Press Rd, then 1 mi N on Pinch Rd(R).

CLOSE TO HERSHEY AND LANCASTER
Located in the foothills of northern Lancaster County, halfway between Hershey and Pennsylvania Dutch Country. Our facilities include a 30' x 60' swimming pool, a large fishing pond and a new, large indoor video game room.
FAC: paved/gravel rds. (190 spaces). Avail: 125 gravel, 56 pull-thrus, (35x60), back-ins (30x55), 111 full hkups, 14 W, 14 E (30/50 amps), seasonal sites, cable, WiFi @ sites, $, tent sites, rentals, dump, laundry, groc, LP gas, fire rings, firewood, controlled access. **REC:** pool, pond, fishing, playground, hunting nearby. Pets OK. Partial handicap access. Big rig sites, eco-friendly. 2021 rates: $50.
(800)659-7640 Lat: 40.229546, Lon: -76.45227
3075 Pinch Rd, Manheim, PA 17545
pinchpond.com
See ad page 779

MANSFIELD — B6 *Tioga*

JELLYSTONE PA WILDS **Ratings: 8.5/9★/8.5** (Campground) Avail: 74 full hkups (30/50 amps). 2021 rates: $49 to $89. Apr 15 to Oct 31. (570)662-2923, 130 Bucktail Rd, Mansfield, PA 16933

MATAMORAS — B10 *Pike*

TRI-STATE RV PARK **Ratings: 6/6/6** (RV Park) Avail: 20 full hkups (30/50 amps). 2021 rates: $47. (570)491-4948, 401 Shay Lane, Matamoras, PA 18336

MERCER — C1 *Mercer*

MERCER/GROVE CITY KOA **Ratings: 9/9.5★/9.5** (Campground) 138 Avail: 136 full hkups, 2 W, 2 E (30/50 amps). 2021 rates: $47 to $84. Apr 01 to Oct 31. (724)748-3160, 1337 Butler Pike, Mercer, PA 16137

ROCKY SPRINGS CAMPGROUND **Ratings: 9/9★/10** (Campground) Avail: 24 full hkups (30/50 amps). 2021 rates: $57 to $63. May 01 to Oct 20. (724)662-1568, 84 Rocky Springs Rd, Mercer, PA 16137

RV VILLAGE CAMPING RESORT **Ratings: 8.5/7/9** (Campground) 131 Avail: 11 full hkups, 120 W, 120 E (30/50 amps). 2021 rates: $38. Apr 01 to Oct 31. (724)662-4560, 235 Skyline Dr, Mercer, PA 16137

MESHOPPEN — B8 *Susquehanna*

→ SLUMBER VALLEY CAMPGROUND **Ratings: 7.5/7.5/7.5** (Campground) 40 Avail: 3 full hkups, 37 W, 37 E (30/50 amps). 2021 rates: $42 to $62. Apr 15 to Oct 15. (570)833-5208, 248 Meshoppen Creek Rd, Meshoppen, PA 18630

MIFFLINBURG — C7 *Union*

↑ HIDDEN VALLEY CAMPING RESORT **Ratings: 8/7.5/8.5** (Campground) 86 Avail: 39 full hkups, 47 W, 47 E (30/50 amps). 2021 rates: $50 to $60. Apr 14 to Oct 26. (570)966-1330, 162 Hidden Valley Lane, Mifflinburg, PA 17844

MIFFLINTOWN — D6 *Juniata*

↘ BUTTONWOOD CAMPGROUND **Ratings: 9/10★/10** (Campground) Avail: 175 full hkups (30/50 amps). 2021 rates: $55 to $85. Apr 15 to Oct 31. (717)436-8334, 1515 E River Road, Mifflintown, PA 17059

MILFORD — C10 *Pike*

↗ RIVER BEACH CAMPSITES **Ratings: 6/8/7.5** (Campground) 35 Avail: 35 W, 35 E (30 amps). 2021 rates: $82.50 to $94.60. Mar 15 to Oct 31. (800)356-2852, 378 US 6 & 209, Milford, PA 18337

MILL RUN — E3 *Fayette*

↗ MILL RUN YOGI BEAR'S JELLYSTONE CAMP RESORT **Ratings: 10/10★/10** (Campground) Avail: 245 full hkups (30/50 amps). 2021 rates: $75 to $105. (800)439-9644, 839 Mill Run Rd, Mill Run, PA 15464

MILTON — C7 *Northumberland*

↓ MILTON JELLYSTONE PARK **Ratings: 8.5/10★/9.5** (Campground) 150 Avail: 39 full hkups, 111 W, 111 E (30/50 amps). 2021 rates: $55 to $70. (570)524-4561, 670 Hidden Paradise Rd, MIlton, PA 17847

MONTGOMERY — C7 *Lycoming*

↓ RIVERSIDE CAMPGROUND **Ratings: 8/8★/7** (Campground) Avail: 40 full hkups (30/50 amps). 2021 rates: $50 to $65. (570)547-6289, 125 S Main St, Montgomery, PA 17752

MORRIS — B6 *Tioga*

↑ TWIN STREAMS CAMPGROUND **Ratings: 7.5/9★/9** (Campground) 55 Avail: 32 full hkups, 23 W, 23 E (30/50 amps). 2021 rates: $40 to $45. Apr 10 to Dec 10. (570)353-7251, 2143 Rte 287, Morris, PA 16938

MOUNT BETHEL — C10 *Northampton*

→ DRIFTSTONE CAMPGROUND **Ratings: 8/9.5★/9** (Campground) 110 Avail: 110 W, 110 E (30/50 amps). 2021 rates: $58 to $62. May 16 to Oct 11. (888)355-6859, 2731 River Rd, Mount Bethel, PA 18343

MOUNT COBB — B9 *Lackawanna*

← **CLAYTON PARK RV ESCAPE**
good sam park
Ratings: 9/9.5★/9.5 (Campground) Avail: 12 full hkups (30/50 amps). 2021 rates: $59 to $69. May 01 to Oct 15. (570)698-6080, 26 Eagle Eye Dr, Lake Ariel, PA 18436

MOUNT POCONO — C9 *Monroe*

MOUNT POCONO See also Bethlehem, Brodheadsville, East Stroudsburg, Greentown, Lake Ariel, Mount Bethel, Mount Cobb, Palmerton, Scotrun, Stroudsburg, Tobyhanna & White Haven, PA; Blairstown & Columbia, NJ.

↗ MOUNT POCONO CAMPGROUND **Ratings: 8.5/9.5★/10** (Campground) Avail: 18 full hkups (30/50 amps). 2021 rates: $50 to $55. May 01 to Oct 31. (570)839-8950, 30 Edgewood Rd, Mount Pocono, PA 18344

NARVON — E8 *Lancaster*

↘ LAKE IN WOOD RESORT **Ratings: 10/10★/10** (RV Resort) Avail: 125 full hkups (30/50 amps). 2021 rates: $62 to $97. Apr 01 to Nov 01. (717)445-5525, 576 Yellow Hill Rd, Narvon, PA 17555

NEW ALEXANDRIA — D3 *Westmoreland*

↘ KEYSTONE (Public State Park) From town: Go 4 mi W on Derry Rd, then 3-3/4 mi N on SH-981. Avail: 65 E (30/50 amps). 2021 rates: $17 to $24. Apr 07 to Oct 21. (724)668-2939

Canada -- know the rules, regulations and tips before crossing the border. This is listed at the beginning of the country.

NEW COLUMBIA — C7 *Union*

← WILLIAMSPORT SOUTH/NITTANY MOUNTAIN KOA **Ratings: 8.5/10★/9** (Campground) 141 Avail: 99 full hkups, 42 W, 42 E (30/50 amps). 2021 rates: $48 to $99. Apr 08 to Oct 23. (570)568-5541, 2751 Millers Bottom Rd, New Columbia, PA 17856

NEW HOLLAND — E8 *Lancaster*

↘ LANCASTER/NEW HOLLAND KOA **Ratings: 8/8.5★/9.5** (Campground) Avail: 90 full hkups (30/50 amps). 2021 rates: $48.46 to $106.14. Apr 01 to Nov 30. (717)354-7926, 354 Springville Rd, New Holland, PA 17557

↑ RED RUN CAMPGROUND **Ratings: 8.5/8★/8.5** (Campground) 82 Avail: 82 W, 82 E (30 amps). 2021 rates: $46 to $50. Apr 01 to Nov 01. (717)445-4526, 877 Martin Church Rd, New Holland, PA 17557

↓ **SPRING GULCH RESORT CAMPGROUND**
good sam park
Ratings: 9/10★/9.5 (Campground) Avail: 165 full hkups (30/50 amps). 2021 rates: $58 to $92. Apr 01 to Oct 31. (888)563-7040, 475 Lynch Rd, New Holland, PA 17557

NEW STANTON — E2 *Westmoreland*

↘ **FOX DEN ACRES CAMPGROUND**
Ratings: 8.5/8★/10 (Campground) From Jct I-76/PA Tpk(exit 75) & I-70 W: Go 1/2 mi W on 1-70(exit 57), then 2 mi N on N Center Ave, then 1 Bk W on Wilson Fox Rd (L). **FAC:** all weather rds. (201 spaces). Avail: 131 all weather, 30 pull-thrus, (30x75), back-ins (30x60), 131 full hkups (30/50 amps), seasonal sites, cable, WiFi @ sites, tent sites, shower$, groc, LP gas, fire rings, firewood. **REC:** pool, wading pool, Fox Lake: fishing, playground. Pets OK. Partial handicap access. Big rig sites, eco-friendly. 2021 rates: $36. May 01 to Oct 31.
(724)925-7054 Lat: 40.238588, Lon: -79.594703
390 Wilson Fox Rd, New Stanton, PA 15672
www.foxdenacres.com
See ad page 782

NEW TRIPOLI — D9 *Lehigh*

↑ ALLENTOWN-LEHIGH VALLEY KOA **Ratings: 8.5/9★/9** (Campground) 65 Avail: 33 full hkups, 32 W, 32 E (30/50 amps). 2021 rates: $48 to $67. Apr 01 to Nov 01. (610)298-2160, 6750 KOA Dr, New Tripoli, PA 18066

NEWMANSTOWN — D8 *Lebanon*

→ SHADY OAKS FAMILY CAMPGROUND **Ratings: 8/8.5/8.5** (Campground) 34 Avail: 10 full hkups, 24 W, 24 E (30/50 amps). 2021 rates: $42 to $48. (717)949-3177, 40 Round Barn Road, Newmanstown, PA 17073

NEWPORT — D6 *Perry*

↗ LITTLE BUFFALO (Public State Park) From jct US 22 & SR 34: Go 3 mi S on SR 34, then 3 mi W on Little Buffalo Rd, then 1/2 m N on Blackhill Rd (E). Avail: 28 E (50 amps). 2021 rates: $15 to $24. Apr 01 to Oct 21. (717)567-9255

NEWVILLE — E6 *Cumberland*

↑ COLONEL DENNING (Public State Park) From town: Go 8 mi N on Hwy 233 (R). Avail: 32 E (30/50 amps), Pit toilets. 2021 rates: $15 to $20. Apr 17 to Dec 12. (717)776-5272

↑ **DOGWOOD ACRES CAMPGROUND Ratings: 8/9.5★/10** (Campground) 36 Avail: 18 full hkups, 18 W, 18 E (30/50 amps). 2021 rates: $55 to $66. Apr 01 to Oct 31. (717)776-5203, 4500 Enola Rd, Newville, PA 17241

OHIOPYLE — E2 *Somerset*

↓ OHIOPYLE (Public State Park) From Jct of PA Tpke (old exit 9/new exit 91) & SR-381: Go 25 mi S on SR-381(E). Avail: 34 E (30/50 amps). 2021 rates: $15 to $42. Apr 01 to Dec 15. (724)329-8591

PALMERTON — D9 *Carbon*

↗ DON LAINE CAMPGROUND **Ratings: 8.5/8★/8.5** (Campground) 65 Avail: 59 full hkups, 6 W, 6 E (30/50 amps). 2021 rates: $38 to $48. May 01 to Nov 01. (610)381-3381, 790 57 Dr, Palmerton, PA 18071

PAVIA — E4 *Bedford*

↑ BLUE KNOB (Public State Park) From town: Go 1 mi W on SR-869, then 3 mi N on Monument Rd (L). Avail: 50 E (30/50 amps). 2021 rates: $15 to $20. Apr 06 to Oct 15. (814)276-3576

We shine ""Spotlights'' on interesting cities and areas.

PENFIELD — C4 *Clearfield*

↑ PARKER DAM (Public State Park) From Jct of I-80 & SR-153 (exit 18): Go 5-1/2 mi N on SR-153, then 2-1/4 mi E on Mud Run Rd(E). Avail: 81 E (30/50 amps). 2021 rates: $15 to $24. Apr 15 to Dec 15. (814)765-0630

PEQUEA — E8 *Lancaster*

↑ PEQUEA CREEK CAMPGROUND **Ratings: 5.5/6/7** (Campground) 44 Avail: 44 W, 44 E (30/50 amps). 2021 rates: $35 to $42. Apr 15 to Oct 15. (717)284-4587, 86 Fox Hollow Rd, Pequea, PA 17565

PHILADELPHIA — E10 *Allegheny*

PHILADELPHIA See also Hatfield & Quakertown, PA; Clarksboro, Monroeville, Williamstown & Woodstown, NJ.

PHILIPSBURG — C5 *Centre*

BLACK MOSHANNON (Public State Park) From Jct Hwy 504 & North Run Rd: Go 1/2 mi SE on North Run Road (R). 73 Avail: 11 full hkups, 55 E. 2021 rates: $15 to $20. (814)342-5960

PINE GROVE — D8 *Lebanon*

↗ **TWIN GROVE RV RESORT & COTTAGES**
good sam park
Ratings: 9/9★/10 (Campground) From Jct I-81 & Hwy 443 (exit 100): Go 5 mi W on Hwy 443 (Suedberg Rd) (R).

FAMILY FUN IN THE AMISH COUNTRYSIDE
Best Family Resort in Central PA/I-80, PA exit #100. 250 RV sites & 62 cottages on 104 wooded acres. Free WiFi & Cable. Game arcade, Ferris Wheel, Large Carousel, 2 pools w/slides, pets OK. 4 pavilions for group activities.

FAC: paved/gravel rds. (223 spaces). Avail: 100 gravel, 70 pull-thrus, (30x80), back-ins (30x50), 100 full hkups (30/50 amps), seasonal sites, cable, WiFi @ sites, tent sites, rentals, laundry, groc, LP gas, fire rings, firewood, restaurant, controlled access. **REC:** pool, Swatara Creek: boating nearby, shuffleboard, playground, hunting nearby, rec open to public. Pet restrict (Q). Partial handicap access. Big rig sites, eco-friendly. 2021 rates: $47 to $78, Military discount. ATM.
(717)865-4602 Lat: 40.51303, Lon: -76.51501
1445 Suedburg Rd, Pine Grove, PA 17963
twingrove.com
See ad page 776

PITTSBURGH — D2 *Allegheny*

A SPOTLIGHT Introducing Pittsburgh's colorful attractions appearing at the front of this state section.

PITTSBURGH See also Beaver Falls, Butler, Champion, Connellsville, Darlington, Donegal, Farmington, Harmony, Harrisville, Jefferson, Madison, Mill Run, New Stanton, Portersville, Rural Valley, Shelocta, Somerset & Washington.

POCONO MOUNTAINS — C9 *Monroe*

A SPOTLIGHT Introducing Pocono Mountains' colorful attractions appearing at the front of this state section.

PORTERSVILLE — C1 *Butler*

→ **BEAR RUN CAMPGROUND**
good sam park
Ratings: 9/10★/9.5 (Campground) From jct I-79 (exit 96) & Hwy 488: Go 50 yds E on Hwy 488, then 1/2 mi N on Badger Hill Rd (R).

VISIT PITTSBURGH, ENJOY FAMILY FUN
We are convenient to Pittsburgh, either by I-79 or public transportation & even closer to nature at adjacent Lake Moraine. Grove City Premium Outlets, are just up I-79. Or just enjoy many fun-filled family camping activities

FAC: paved rds. (215 spaces). 59 Avail: 21 paved, 38 gravel, 19 pull-thrus, (35x60), back-ins (25x40), 31 full hkups, 28 W, 28 E (30/50 amps), seasonal sites, WiFi @ sites, tent sites, rentals, shower$, dump, laundry, groc, LP gas, fire rings, firewood, controlled access. **REC:** heated pool, Lake Arthur: swim, fishing, kayaking/canoeing, boating nearby, playground. Pet restrict (B/Q). Partial handicap access. Big rig sites, eco-friendly. 2021 rates: $42 to $93, Military discount. Apr 15 to Oct 30. ATM.
(724)368-3564 Lat: 40.92984, Lon: -80.126231
184 Badger Hill Rd, Portersville, PA 16051
www.bearruncampground.com
See ad page 782

→ ROSE POINT PARK CABINS & CAMPING **Ratings: 9.5/10★/9.5** (Campground) 32 Avail: 25 full hkups, 7 W, 7 E (30/50 amps). 2021 rates: $45 to $70. (724)924-2415, 8775 Old Route 422, New Castle, PA 16101

PA

PORTERSVILLE (CONT)

Things to See and Do

BEAR RUN CAMPGROUND CANOE & KAYAK RENTAL Canoe & Kayak rentals at Bear Run Campground to enjoy Lake Arthur at Moraine State Park. Apr 15 to Oct 30. Partial handicap access. Restrooms. Hours: 9am to 7pm . Adult fee: $34 to $42. ATM.
(724)368-3564 Lat: 40.92984, Lon: -80.126231
184 Badger Hill Rd, Portersville, PA 16051
www.bearruncampground.com
See ad page 782

POTTERS MILLS — D6 *Centre*

POE PADDY (Public State Park) From town: Go 6 mi NW on US-322, then 14 mi NE on Sand Mt Rd (R). Avail: 2 E (30/50 amps), Pit toilets. 2021 rates: $17 to $24. Apr 15 to Dec 15. (814)349-2460

POE VALLEY (Public State Park) From town: Go 6 mi NW on Hwy 322, then 11 mi N on Sand Mt Rd (R). Avail: 31 E (50 amps). 2021 rates: $15 to $24. Apr 15 to Dec 01. (814)349-2460

SEVEN MOUNTAINS CAMPGROUND & CABINS **Ratings: 6/8★/8** (Campground) 34 Avail: 20 full hkups, 14 W, 14 E (30/50 amps). 2021 rates: $47 to $72. (814)364-1910, 101 Seven Mountains Campground Rd, Spring Mills, PA 16875

QUAKERTOWN — D9 *Bucks*

QUAKERTOWN See also Bethlehem, Boyertown, Hatfield, Kutztown, New Tripoli, Revere & Upper Black Eddy, PA; Asbury, NJ.

LITTLE RED BARN CAMPGROUND **Ratings: 8.5/8★/7.5** (Campground) 52 Avail: 52 W, 52 E (30/50 amps). 2021 rates: $42 to $50. Apr 01 to Nov 01. (215)536-3357, 367 Old Bethlehem Rd, Quakertown, PA 18951

TOHICKON FAMILY CAMPGROUND **Ratings: 7/5.5/7** (Campground) 61 Avail: 17 full hkups, 44 W, 44 E (30/50 amps). 2021 rates: $54. Apr 01 to Oct 31. (215)536-7951, 8308 Covered Bridge Rd, Quakertown, PA 18951

QUARRYVILLE — E8 *Lancaster*

YOGI BEAR'S JELLYSTONE PARK/LANCASTER SOUTH/QUARRYVILLE **Ratings: 9/10★/9.5** (Campground) Avail: 175 full hkups (30/50 amps). 2021 rates: $47 to $158. Apr 18 to Nov 02. (717)610-4505, 340 Blackburn Rd, Quarryville, PA 17566

RAVINE — D8 *Schuylkill*

ECHO VALLEY CAMPGROUND
Ratings: 8.5/9.5★/8.5 (Campground) From Jct I-81 & Mollystown Rd/T634(residential rd), (exit 104): Go R off ramp & follow signs. **FAC:** gravel rds. (125 spaces). Avail: 110 gravel, 15 pull-thrus, (30x60), back-ins (30x40), 110 full hkups (30/50 amps), seasonal sites, WiFi @ sites, $, tent sites, rentals, dump, laundry, groc, LP bottles, fire rings, firewood. **REC:** pool, Black Creek: playground, hunting nearby. Pet restrict (B/Q). Partial handicap access. Big rig sites, eco-friendly. 2021 rates: $37 to $51.
(570)695-3659 Lat: 40.598182, Lon: -76.391087
52 Camp Rd, Tremont, PA 17981
www.echovalleycamp.com
See ad this page

RAYSTOWN LAKE — D5 *Huntingdon*

HERITAGE COVE RESORT **Ratings: 10/9.5★/10** (Campground) Avail: 97 full hkups (30/50 amps). 2021 rates: $55 to $70. May 01 to Oct 31. (814)635-3386, 1172 River Rd, Saxton, PA 16678

LAKE RAYSTOWN RESORT & LODGE RVC OUTDOOR DESTINATION **Ratings: 8.5/8★/8.5** (Campground) 220 Avail: 220 W, 220 E (30/50 amps). 2021 rates: $30 to $89. Apr 15 to Oct 31. (814)658-3500, 3101 Chipmunk Crossing, Entriken, PA 16638

RENOVO — C5 *Clinton*

HYNER RUN (Public State Park) From Town of Renovo: Go 6-1/4 mi E on US-20/Bucktail Trail Rd (L). Avail: 21 E. 2021 rates: $15 to $28. Apr 10 to Dec 15. (570)923-6000

KETTLE CREEK (Public State Park) From town: Go 6 mi W on Rte 120, then 7 mi N on Rte 4001 (L). Avail: 53 E (30/50 amps). 2021 rates: $15 to $28. Apr 01 to Dec 15. (570)923-6004

REVERE — D10 *Bucks*

COLONIAL WOODS FAMILY CAMPING RESORT **Ratings: 8.5/9.5★/8** (Campground) 108 Avail: 108 W, 108 E (30/50 amps). 2021 rates: $52 to $58. Apr 04 to Nov 01. (610)847-5808, 545 Lonely Cottage Dr, Upper Black Eddy, PA 18972

ROBESONIA — D8 *Lebanon*

ADVENTURE BOUND CAMPING RESORT AT EAGLES PEAK **Ratings: 8.5/9.5★/10** (Campground) Avail: 83 full hkups (30/50 amps). 2021 rates: $120 to $162. Apr 01 to Nov 01. (610)589-4800, 397 Eagles Peak Rd., Robesonia, PA 19551

ROCKWOOD — E3 *Somerset*

HICKORY HOLLOW CAMPGROUND **Ratings: 8.5/10★/10** (Campground) Avail: 35 full hkups (30/50 amps). 2021 rates: $45 to $60. Apr 15 to Oct 31. (814)926-4636, 176 Big Hickory Rd, Rockwood, PA 15557

ROSSVILLE — E7 *York*

GIFFORD PINCHOT (Public State Park) From town: Go 3-3/4 mi S on SH 177 (E). 291 Avail: 17 full hkups, 131 E (30/50 amps). 2021 rates: $15 to $24. Apr 10 to Oct 30. (717)292-4112

RURAL VALLEY — D3 *Armstrong*

SILVER CANOE CAMPGROUND **Ratings: 9/9.5★/9.5** (Campground) Avail: 37 full hkups (30/50 amps). 2021 rates: $45. (724)783-6000, 140 Silver Canoe Campground Ln, Rural Valley, PA 16249

RUSSELL — A3 *Warren*

RED OAK CAMPGROUND **Ratings: 8.5/9.5★/8.5** (Campground) 75 Avail: 25 full hkups, 50 W, 50 E (30/50 amps). 2021 rates: $45 to $66. (814)757-8507, 225 Norman Rd, Russell, PA 16345

SAEGERTOWN — B1 *Crawford*

WOODCOCK LAKE PARK (Public) From Jct of I-79 & Rte 198 (Conneautville/Saegertown exit): Go 8-1/2 mi E on Rte 198, then 1 mi S on Schultz Rd, then follow Woodcock Creek Lake signs in town(R). Avail: 75 E (30 amps). 2021 rates: $22 to $27. May 27 to Sep 05. (814)333-7372

SANDY LAKE — B2 *Mercer*

GODDARD PARK VACATIONLAND **Ratings: 8.5/8.5★/9.5** (Campground) 120 Avail: 91 full hkups, 29 W, 29 E (30/50 amps). 2021 rates: $40 to $53. Apr 15 to Oct 15. (724)253-4645, 867 Georgetown Rd, Sandy Lake, PA 16145

SCHELLSBURG — E4 *Bedford*

SHAWNEE (Public State Park) From Jct of US-30 & SR-96: Go 1 mi S on SR-96 (L). 199 Avail: 15 full hkups, 98 E (30/50 amps). 2021 rates: $15 to $24. Apr 14 to Dec 25. (814)733-4218

SCOTRUN — C9 *Monroe*

FOUR SEASONS CAMPGROUNDS
Ratings: 9/10★/10 (Campground) From jct I-80 & Hwy 715 (exit 299): Go 500 ft N on Hwy 715, then 1-3/4 mi N on Hwy 611, then 1/4 mi NW (bear left) on Scotrun Ave, then 1/2 mi W on Babbling Brook (R). **FAC:** paved/gravel rds. (109 spaces). Avail: 24 gravel, 19 pull-thrus, (30x65), back-ins (30x55), 24 full hkups (30/50 amps), seasonal sites, cable, WiFi @ sites, tent sites, laundry, groc, LP gas, fire rings, firewood, controlled access. **REC:** pool, wading pool, boating nearby, shuffleboard, playground. Pets OK. Big rig sites, eco-friendly. 2021 rates: $57 to $68. Apr 28 to Oct 10.
(570)629-2504 Lat: 41.06411, Lon: -75.33314
249 Babbling Brook Rd, Scotrun, PA 18355
Fourseasonscampgrounds.com
See ad page 783

SCOTRUN RV RESORT
Ratings: 7.5/9★/8 (Campground) 38 Avail: 13 full hkups, 25 W, 25 E (30/50 amps). 2021 rates: $52. (888)563-7040, 224 Ermine Way, Scotrun, PA 18355

SCRANTON — B9 *Lackawanna*

SCRANTON See also Greentown, Hawley, Honesdale, Hop Bottom, Lake Ariel, Mount Cobb, Tobyhanna, Tunkhannock & Waymart.

SELINSGROVE — D7 *Snyder*

PENN AVON CAMPGROUND **Ratings: 5.5/10★/9** (Campground) Avail: 35 full hkups (30/50 amps). 2021 rates: $51. Apr 01 to Oct 31. (570)374-9468, 22 Penn Avon Trail, Rte 204, Selinsgrove, PA 17870

SHARON — C1 *Mercer*

SHENANGO LAKE - COE/SHENANGO PUBLIC USE AREA (Public Corps) From jct I-80 & Hwy 18: Go 6-1/2 mi N on Hwy 18. Avail: 106 E (30 amps). 2021 rates: $19 to $34. May 16 to Aug 31. (724)646-1124

SHARTLESVILLE — D8 *Berks*

APPALACHIAN RV CAMPGROUND
Ratings: 8.5/9.5★/9 (Campground) 115 Avail: 55 full hkups, 60 W, 60 E (30/50 amps). 2021 rates: $46 to $74. Apr 01 to Oct 31. (888)563-7040, 60 Motel Drive, Shartlesville, PA 19554

MOUNTAIN SPRINGS CAMPING RESORT **Ratings: 8.5/8.5★/8.5** (Campground) 99 Avail: 45 full hkups, 54 W, 54 E (30/50 amps). 2021 rates: $42 to $49. Apr 01 to Oct 31. (610)488-6859, 3450 Mountain Rd, Hamburg, PA 19526

PENNSYLVANIA DUTCH CAMPGROUND **Ratings: 7.5/UI/8** (Campground) Avail: 31 full hkups (30/50 amps). 2021 rates: $57.50 to $67.50. (610)488-6268, 136 Campsite Rd, Bernville, PA 19506

SHEFFIELD — B3 *Warren*

WHISPERING WINDS CAMPGROUND **Ratings: 8/8★/9** (Campground) 27 Avail: 21 full hkups, 6 E (30/50 amps). 2021 rates: $35 to $49. (814)968-4377, 277 Tollgate Rd, Sheffield, PA 16347

SHELOCTA — D3 *Armstrong*

WHEEL-IN CAMPGROUND **Ratings: 6.5/9.5★/9.5** (Campground) 43 Avail: 19 full hkups, 24 W, 24 E (30/50 amps). 2021 rates: $41 to $46. Apr 15 to Oct 15. (724)354-3693, 113 Wheel In Campground Rd, Shelocta, PA 15774

SIGEL — C3 *Jefferson*

CAMPERS PARADISE CAMPGROUND **Ratings: 7.5/9.5★/9** (Campground) 50 Avail: 18 full hkups, 32 W, 32 E (30 amps). 2021 rates: $48 to $52. (814)752-2393, 37 Steele Dr, Sigel, PA 15860

CLEAR CREEK (Public State Park) From Jct I-80 & SR-949 (old exit 12/new exit 73), N 12 mi (L). Avail: 40 E (30/50 amps). 2021 rates: $15 to $20. (814)752-2368

SINNEMAHONING — C5 *Cameron*

SINNEMAHONING (Public State Park) From Jct of Rte 120 & Rte 872: Go 8 mi N on Rte 872 (R). Avail: 35 E (30/50 amps). 2021 rates: $15 to $24. Apr 14 to Dec 15. (814)647-8401

SNOW SHOE — C5 *Centre*

SNOW SHOE PARK (CITY PARK) (Public) From jct I-80 (exit 147) & SR-144: Go 1/2 mi N on SR-144. Avail: 95 full hkups. 2021 rates: $45 to $65. Apr 15 to Oct 15. (814)387-6299

SOMERSET — E3 *Somerset*

LAUREL HILL (Public State Park) From town: Go 10 mi W on SR-31, then 2 mi S on state Jimtown Rd, then 3 mi W on park access rd (R). Avail: 173 E (30/50 amps). 2021 rates: $15 to $24. Apr 01 to Oct 21. (814)445-7725

PIONEER PARK CAMPGROUND **Ratings: 9/10★/9.5** (Campground) 185 Avail: 168 full hkups, 17 W, 17 E (30/50 amps). 2021 rates: $46 to $68. Apr 10 to Oct 20. (814)445-6348, 273 Trent Rd., Somerset, PA 15501

STATE COLLEGE — D5 *Centre*

STATE COLLEGE See also Bellefonte, Lewistown & Potters Mills.

STRASBURG — E8 *Lancaster*

WHITE OAK CAMPGROUND **Ratings: 8/10★/8.5** (Campground) 106 Avail: 97 full hkups, 9 W, 9 E (30/50 amps). 2021 rates: $54 to $65. (717)687-6207, 3156 White Oak Road, Quarryville, PA 17566

STROUDSBURG — C10 *Monroe*

STROUDSBURG See also Bethlehem, Brodheadsville, East Stroudsburg, Greentown, Mount Bethel, Mount Pocono, Palmerton, Scotrun, Tobyhanna, Upper Black Eddy & White Haven, PA; Asbury, Blairstown, Branchville, Columbia, Delaware, Flanders & Newton, NJ.

DELAWARE WATER GAP - POCONO MOUNTAIN KOA **Ratings: 8.5/9.5★/9.5** (Campground) 127 Avail: 56 full hkups, 71 W, 71 E (30/50 amps). 2021 rates: $65 to $125. (570)223-8000, 227 Hollow Rd, East Stroudsburg, PA 18302

MOUNTAIN VISTA CAMPGROUND
good sam park **Ratings: 9/10★/10** (Campground) 95 Avail: 85 full hkups, 10 W, 10 E (30/50 amps). 2021 rates: $52 to $73. May 01 to Oct 20. (570)223-0111, 415 Taylor Drive, East Stroudsburg, PA 18301

OTTER LAKE CAMP RESORT
Ratings: 10/10★/10 (Campground) From Jct I-80 & US-209 (exit 309): Go 3 mi N on US 209/Seven Bridges Rd, then enter roundabout, (take 2nd exit, follow signs for Bus US-209), then 1/2 mi N on Hwy 1019/Seven Bridges Rd, then 1 blk E on Bus US 209, then 7-1/2 mi NW on Marshalls Creek Rd (L).

YEAR ROUND POCONO MOUNTAIN RESORT!
Family camping at top-rated camp resort in Poconos. 300 wooded acres. 60-acre private lake with Sandy Beach, Boating and No-license Fishing. All age Activities. Indoor & Outdoor pool with Splash Pad, Archery & Sport Courts!

FAC: paved rds. (300 spaces). Avail: 157 all weather, 27 pull-thrus, (30x60), back-ins (30x50), 118 full hkups, 39 W, 39 E (30/50 amps), seasonal sites, cable, WiFi @ sites, tent sites, dump, laundry, groc, LP gas, fire rings, firewood, controlled access. **REC:** heated pool, wading pool, hot tub, Otter Lake: swim, fishing, kayaking/canoeing, shuffleboard, playground, hunting nearby. Pets OK. Partial handicap access, eco-friendly. 2021 rates: $60 to $68. ATM.
(570)223-0123 Lat: 41.14028, Lon: -75.15222
1639 Marshalls Creek Rd, East Stroudsburg, PA 18302
otterlake.com
See ad pages 772, 783

SUNBURY — C7 *Northumberland*

FANTASY ISLAND CAMPGROUND **Ratings: 8.5/8.5★/9** (Campground) Avail: 20 full hkups (30/50 amps). 2021 rates: $45 to $50. Apr 15 to Oct 15. (570)286-1307, 401 Park Dr, Sunbury, PA 17801

TAMAQUA — D8 *Schuylkill*

ROSEMOUNT CAMPING RESORT **Ratings: 8/9.5★/9.5** (Campground) 66 Avail: 26 full hkups, 40 W, 40 E (30/50 amps). 2021 rates: $42 to $50. Apr 15 to Oct 15. (570)668-2580, 285 Valley Rd, Tamaqua, PA 18252

TIOGA — A6 *Tioga*

HAMMOND LAKE - COE/IVES RUN RECREATION AREA (Public Corps) From jct US-15 & Hwy 287: Go 6 mi S on PA-287, then 3/4 mi E on Ives Run Ln, then 1/2 mi NE on Tioga-Hammond Dam Rd (E). Avail: 131 full hkups (30 amps). 2021 rates: $20 to $40. May 01 to Oct 30. (570)835-5281

TIONESTA — B3 *Forest*

TIONESTA LAKE - COE/KELLETTVILLE REC AREA (Public Corps) From town: Go 7 mi N on 62-N, then 10 mi E on SR-666 (R). 20 Avail. 2021 rates: $12. Apr 15 to Sep 30. (814)755-3512

TIONESTA LAKE - COE/TIONESTA REC AREA CAMPGROUND (Public Corps) From Jct of SR-36 & Elm St: Go 1 mi S on Elm St (E). 123 Avail: 123 W, 123 E (50 amps). 2021 rates: $35. May 23 to Sep 05. (814)755-3512

YOUGHIOGHENY RIVER - COE/OUTFLOW CAMPING AREA (Public Corps) From Jct of SR-36 & Elm St (in town): Go 1 mi S on Elm St (E). 51 Avail: 4 W, 33 E (30/50 amps). 2021 rates: $15 to $42. May 20 to Sep 11. (814)395-3242

RV DRIVING TIPS: Don't get too comfy. Although today's RV cockpits are designed for maximum driver comfort, you should drive with your head up, your shoulders back and your lower back against the seat back. Legs should not be fully extended, but flexed at about a 45-degree angle. Don't use cruise control; keep your body involved in the driving.

TITUSVILLE — B2 *Venango*

OIL CREEK FAMILY CAMPGROUND **Ratings: 7/8.5★/8.5** (Campground) 54 Avail: 22 full hkups, 32 W, 32 E (30 amps). 2021 rates: $35 to $37. Apr 15 to Oct 31. (814)827-1023, 340 Shreve Rd, Titusville, PA 16354

TOBYHANNA — C9 *Monroe*

HEMLOCK CAMPGROUND & COTTAGES **Ratings: 8.5/9★/9.5** (Campground) 26 Avail: 12 full hkups, 10 W, 10 E (30 amps). 2021 rates: $63. Apr 15 to Oct 15. (570)894-4388, 559 Hemlock Dr, Tobyhanna, PA 18466

TOBYHANNA (Public State Park) From Jct of I-380 & old exit 7/new exit 8 (SR-423): Go 3 mi N on SR-423(L). Avail: 26 E (50 amps). 2021 rates: $15 to $24. Apr 15 to Oct 21. (570)894-8336

TRANSFER — C1 *Mercer*

ADVENTURE BOUND CAMPING RESORTS SHENANGO **Ratings: 9.5/9.5★/9.5** (Campground) Avail: 34 full hkups (30/50 amps). 2021 rates: $75 to $85. May 01 to Oct 15. (724)962-9800, 559 E Crestview Dr , Transfer, PA 16154

TROUT RUN — B7 *Lewis*

SHESHEQUIN CAMPGROUND **Ratings: 5.5/9.5★/9** (Campground) 59 Avail: 59 W, 59 E (30/50 amps). 2021 rates: $38. Apr 01 to Oct 31. (570)995-9230, 389 Marsh Hill Rd, Trout Run, PA 17771

TUNKHANNOCK — B8 *Wyoming*

COZY CREEK FAMILY CAMPGROUND
good sam park **Ratings: 8.5/9.5★/9.5** (Campground) Avail: 80 full hkups (30/50 amps). 2021 rates: $39.95 to $68. (570)836-4122, 30 Vacation Lane, Tunkhannock, PA 18657

UPPER BLACK EDDY — D10 *Bucks*

RINGING ROCKS FAMILY CAMPGROUND **Ratings: 8/9★/9** (Campground) 28 Avail: 28 W, 28 E (30 amps). 2021 rates: $46 to $52. Apr 01 to Oct 31. (610)982-5552, 75 Woodland Dr, Upper Black Eddy, PA 18972

WAPWALLOPEN — C8 *Luzerne*

MOYER'S GROVE CAMPGROUND **Ratings: 7/8.5★/7.5** (Campground) 92 Avail: 43 full hkups, 49 W, 49 E (30/50 amps). 2021 rates: $36 to $48. (800)722-1912, 309 Moyers Grove Rd, Wapwallopen, PA 18660

WASHINGTON — E1 *Washington*

PINE COVE BEACH CLUB & RV RESORT
good sam park **Ratings: 9/9★/10** (RV Park) From Jct of I-70 & Rte 481 (exit 35): Go 1/4 mi N on Rte 481 (L). **FAC:** paved/gravel rds. (57 spaces). Avail: 38 gravel, back-ins (38x60), 38 full hkups (30/50 amps), seasonal sites, cable, WiFi @ sites, laundry, fire rings, firewood, controlled access. **REC:** pool, wading pool, Pine Cove Lake: fishing, playground, rec open to public. Pets OK. Partial handicap access. No tents. Big rig sites. 2021 rates: $50 to $65, Military discount. Apr 01 to Sep 30.
(724)239-2900 Lat: 40.128104, Lon: -79.955795
1495 Rte 481, Charleroi, PA 15022
www.pinecovebeachclub.com
See ad page 781

WASHINGTON/PITTSBURGH SW KOA KAMPGROUND **Ratings: 9/9★/8.5** (Campground) Avail: 50 full hkups (30/50 amps). 2021 rates: $50 to $70. Mar 15 to Dec 01. (800)562-0254, 7 KOA Rd, Washington, PA 15301

WATERVILLE — C6 *Lycoming*

HAPPY ACRES RESORT **Ratings: 8/6.5/8** (RV Park) 53 Avail: 36 full hkups, 17 W, 17 E (30/50 amps). 2021 rates: $45 to $50. (570)753-8000, 3332 Little Pine Creek Rd, Waterville, PA 17776

LITTLE PINE (Public State Park) From Jct US-220 Bypass & SR-44 (in Jersey Shore): Go 10 mi N on SR-44, then 3 mi N on cnty rd(R). Avail: 72 E (50 amps). 2021 rates: $15 to $24. Apr 07 to Dec 15. (570)753-6000

WAYMART — B9 *Wayne*

KEEN LAKE CAMPING & COTTAGE RESORT **Ratings: 8.5/10★/10** (Campground) 151 Avail: 88 full hkups, 63 W, 63 E (30/50 amps). 2021 rates: $54 to $99. Apr 29 to Oct 11. (570)488-6161, 155 Keen Lake Rd, Waymart, PA 18472

We appreciate your business!

WELLSBORO — B6 *Tioga*

CANYON COUNTRY CAMPGROUND **Ratings: 7.5/9★/9.5** (Campground) 45 Avail: 28 full hkups, 17 W, 17 E (30/50 amps). 2021 rates: $47 to $49. Apr 15 to Oct 31. (570)724-3818, 130 Wilson Rd, Wellsboro, PA 16901

COLTON POINT (Public State Park) From Jct of US-6 & SR-287: Go 8 mi W on US-6, then 6 mi S on Colton Rd, follow signs (E). 16 Avail: Pit toilets. 2021 rates: $15 to $20. May 11 to Oct 21. (570)724-3061

HILLS CREEK (Public State Park) From Jct US-6 & SR-660: Go 8-1/2 mi N on Charleston Rd/Hills Creek Lake Rd, then 1/2 mi E on Spill Way Rd, then 1/2 mi N on Kelly's Swamp Ln (L). 78 Avail: 16 full hkups, 22 E (30/50 amps). 2021 rates: $15 to $28. Apr 13 to Oct 21. (570)724-4246

LEONARD HARRISON (Public State Park) From Jct of US-6 & SR-660: Go 10-1/2 mi W on West Ave/SR-660 (L). Avail: 7 E (50 amps). 2021 rates: $15 to $24. Apr 13 to Oct 21. (570)724-3061

STONY FORK CREEK CAMPGROUND **Ratings: 8/9.5★/9.5** (Campground) 54 Avail: 26 full hkups, 28 W, 28 E (30/50 amps). 2021 rates: $42 to $47. (570)724-3096, 658 Stony Fork Creek Rd, Wellsboro, PA 16901

WEST CHESTER — E9 *Chester*

PHILADELPHIA/WEST CHESTER KOA **Ratings: 9/8.5★/8.5** (Campground) 63 Avail: 48 full hkups, 15 W, 15 E (30/50 amps). 2021 rates: $60.75 to $102.90. Apr 01 to Oct 31. (610)486-0447, 1659 Embreeville Rd, Coatesville, PA 19320

WEST SUNBURY — C2 *Butler*

PEACEFUL VALLEY CAMPGROUND **Ratings: 9/10★/9** (Campground) 55 Avail: 45 full hkups, 10 W, 10 E (30/50 amps). 2021 rates: $42 to $65. May 01 to Oct 23. (724)894-2421, 231 Peaceful Valley Rd, West Sunbury, PA 16061

WHITE HAVEN — C9 *Carbon*

HICKORY RUN (Public State Park) From Jct of I-80 & Rte 534 (old exit 41/new exit 274): Go 6 mi E on Rte 534(R). 368 Avail: 16 full hkups, 102 E (30/50 amps). 2021 rates: $15 to $24. Apr 10 to Oct 25. (570)443-0400

LEHIGH GORGE CAMPGROUND **Ratings: 9/8.5★/8** (Campground) Avail: 30 full hkups (30/50 amps). 2021 rates: $50 to $56. Apr 15 to Nov 30. (570)443-9191, 4585 State St, White Haven, PA 18661

PA

WILKES-BARRE — C8 *Luzerne*

FRANCES SLOCUM (Public State Park) From jct I-81 (exit 170B) & Hwy 309: Go 7 mi N on Hwy 309, then 4 mi E on Carverton Rd, then 1 mi N on Eighth St, then 1 mi W on Mt. Olivet Rd. Avail: 53 E (30/50 amps). 2021 rates: $15 to $20. Apr 10 to Oct 25. (570)696-3525

WIND RIDGE — E1 *Greene*

RYERSON STATION (Public State Park) From town: Go 2 mi SW on SR-3022 (Bristoria Rd), then 1-1/4 mi E on Rte 3022(E). Avail: 19 E (30/50 amps), Pit toilets. 2021 rates: $15 to $24. (724)428-4254

WINFIELD — C7 *Snyder*

LITTLE MEXICO CAMPGROUND
good sam park **Ratings: 8.5/8.5★/9** (Campground) 116 Avail: 88 full hkups, 28 W, 28 E (30/50 amps). 2021 rates: $50 to $65. (570)374-9742, 1640 Little Mexico Rd, Winfield, PA 17889

WOODLAND — C4 *Clearfield*

WOODLAND CAMPGROUND
good sam park **Ratings: 8/9.5★/9.5** (Campground) Avail: 47 full hkups (30/50 amps). 2021 rates: $46. Apr 01 to Nov 15. (814)857-5388, 314 Egypt Rd, Woodland, PA 16881

YORK — E7 *York*

BEN FRANKLIN RV PARK **Ratings: 7/9★/9** (Campground) 47 Avail: 37 full hkups, 10 W, 10 E (30/50 amps). 2021 rates: $40. (717)744-8237, 1350 Woodberry Rd, York, PA 17408

According to the Wall Street Journal, 100 billion plastic shopping bags are consumed in the United States annually. Consider toting your own reusable shopping bags instead of using plastic.

Getty Images/iStockphoto

DID YOU KNOW?

The haunted house that inspired the film "The Conjuring" is located in Harrisville and open for overnight stays.

YOU ARE HERE

Rhode Island

Go anywhere in Rhode Island and you're never more than an hour away from the Atlantic Ocean. No wonder this small state bears the "Ocean State" nickname. The vast Narragansett Bay is a great starting point.

Big Cities in a Small State

You'll find the great city of Providence, the state capital, at the northern shore of Narragansett Bay. Known as the Renaissance City, Providence celebrates its resurgent downtown area along the riverways. Gondola tours and a nightly Waterfire show during the warm months make the Riverwalk a flavorful promenade. For seaside fun, a stop at Newport is a must. This upscale beach town is known for its annual folk and jazz festivals, which fill the salty skies with infectious melodies.

Trails by the Sea

Walk one of the trails on Newport's coast to discover some of Rhode Island's best scenery. The 10-mile Ocean Drive and 3.5-mile Cliff Walk showcase endless Atlantic views. "Oooh" and "ahh" over the many luxurious mansions that line the shores. A trip out to Block Island offers additional rugged views, and the Mohegan Bluffs are not to be missed. Rising 200-feet above the crashing waves, the cliffs serve as epic viewpoints.

Cruise on the Coast

More than 400 miles of coastline tantalize visitors to Rhode Island's Atlantic shores. Misquamicut State Beach is the place to go with kids in tow, thanks to all of the fun recreation nearby (bumper boats, carnival rides and more). For a pristine getaway, head to Goosewing Beach, where the Nature Conservancy protects 75 acres of rolling dunes and natural shores. Narragansett Town Beach is the place to hit the surf. No matter where you go, don't miss the chance to grab a classic New England lobster roll.

Rhode Island Calamari

Who can refuse a steaming plate of juicy calamari? Made from squid freshly caught from the Atlantic Ocean, this dish's battered rings and tentacles get a flavor boost from garlic, butter and pickled cherry peppers, which supply a vinegar kick. It's no wonder that calamari was named the official state appetizer of Rhode Island in 2014.

VISITOR CENTER

TIME ZONE
Eastern Standard

ROAD & HIGHWAY INFORMATION
888-401-4511
dot.ri.gov

FISHING & HUNTING INFORMATION
401-222-6800
dem.ri.gov/programs/managementservices/licenses/wildfees.php

BOATING INFORMATION
401-222-6800
dem.ri.gov/programs/managementservices

NATIONAL PARKS
nps.gov/ri

STATE PARKS
riparks.com

TOURISM INFORMATION
Rhode Island Tourism Division
800-556-2484
visitrhodeisland.com

TOP TOURISM ATTRACTIONS
1) Newport Mansions
2) Slater Mill Historic Site
3) International Tennis Hall of Fame

MAJOR CITIES
Providence (capital), Warwick, Cranston, Pawtucket, East Providence

RI

good sam park Featured Good Sam Parks

RHODE ISLAND

When you stay with Good Sam, you can expect the highest degree of cleanliness and friendliness, and better yet, you get **10% off** overnight campground fees.

If you're not already a Good Sam member you can purchase your membership at one of these locations:

WESTERLY
Timber Creek RV Resort

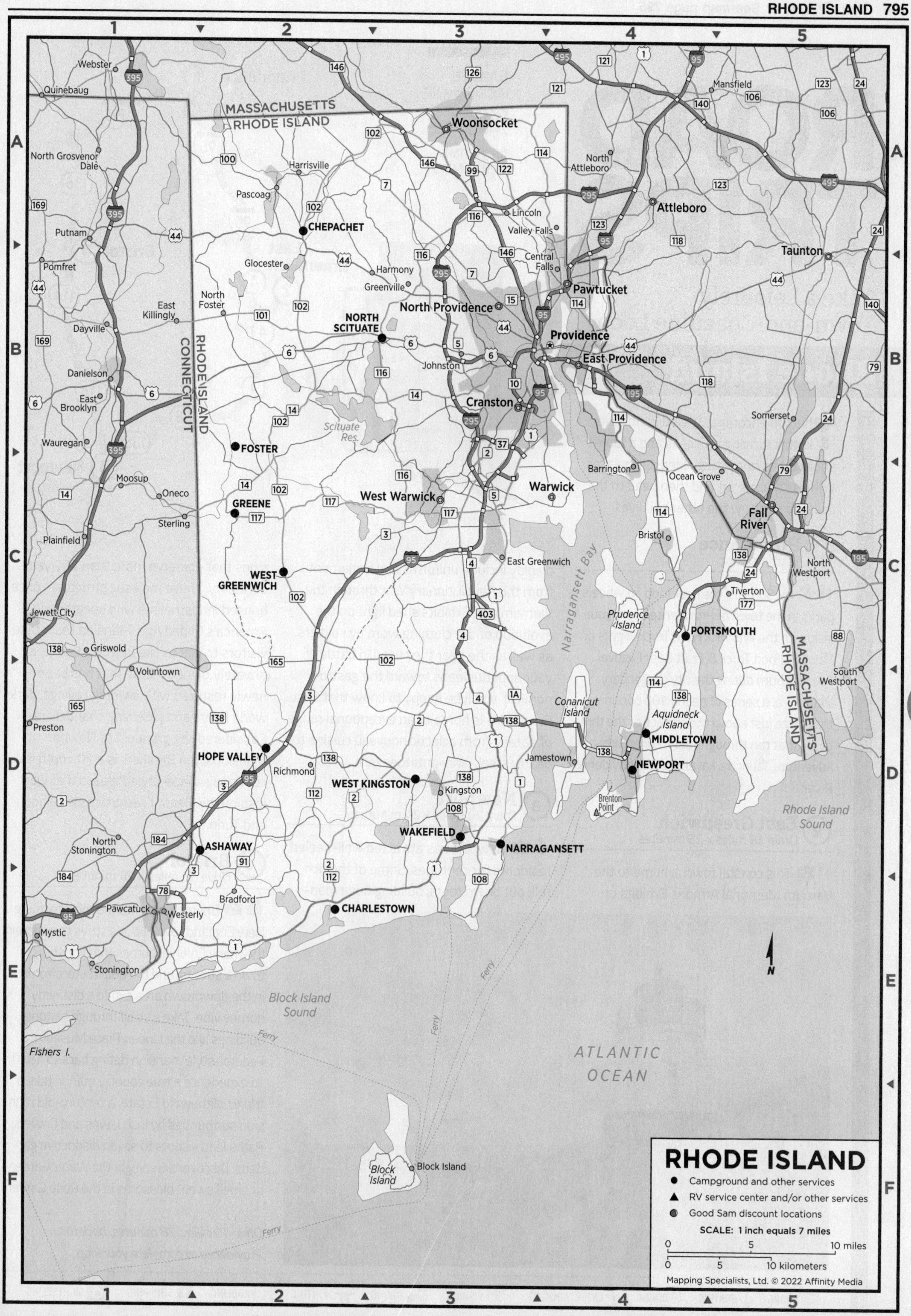
MASSACHUSETTS
RHODE ISLAND
CONNECTICUT
RHODE ISLAND
RHODE ISLAND
MASSACHUSETTS
Webster
Quinebaug
North Grosvenor Dale
Putnam
Pomfret
Dayville
Danielson
East Brooklyn
Wauregan
Moosup
Oneco
Sterling
Plainfield
Jewett City
Griswold
Voluntown
Preston
North Stonington
Pawcatuck
Westerly
Mystic
Stonington
East Killingly
North Foster
Harrisville
Pascoag
CHEPACHET
Glocester
Harmony
Greenville
NORTH SCITUATE
Johnston
FOSTER
GREENE
WEST GREENWICH
HOPE VALLEY
Richmond
ASHAWAY
Bradford
CHARLESTOWN
WEST KINGSTON
Kingston
WAKEFIELD
NARRAGANSETT
Scituate Res.
Woonsocket
Lincoln
Valley Falls
Central Falls
Pawtucket
North Providence
Providence
East Providence
Cranston
West Warwick
Warwick
East Greenwich
North Attleboro
Attleboro
Mansfield
Taunton
Somerset
Barrington
Ocean Grove
Bristol
Fall River
North Westport
Tiverton
South Westport
Prudence Island
PORTSMOUTH
Aquidneck Island
MIDDLETOWN
NEWPORT
Conanicut Island
Jamestown
Brenton Point
Narragansett Bay
Rhode Island Sound
Block Island Sound
ATLANTIC OCEAN
Fishers I.
Block Island
Block Island
Ferry
N
RHODE ISLAND
Campground and other services
RV service center and/or other services
Good Sam discount locations
SCALE: 1 inch equals 7 miles
0 5 10 miles
0 5 10 kilometers
Mapping Specialists, Ltd. © 2022 Affinity Media

RI

ROAD TRIPS

Take a Leisurely Town-and-Coastline Loop

Rhode Island

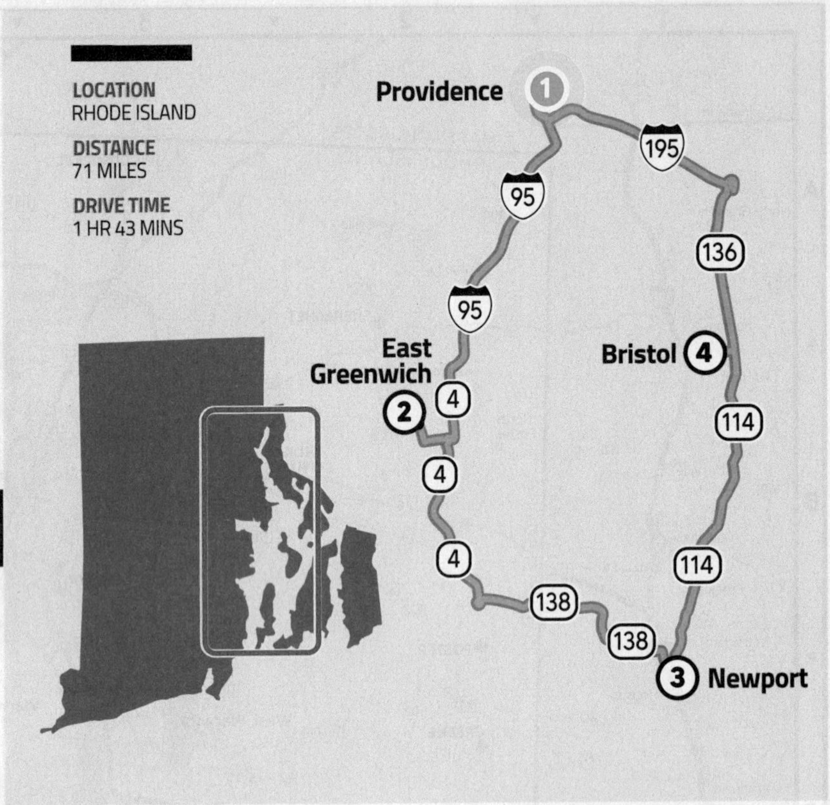

This trip encompasses a dynamic city with a thriving art scene and a fabled shore that's home to guilded age palaces. Witness blazing art and then head to the coast to see how the other half lives.

1 Providence
Starting Point

Some of the best food on wheels parks in the town of Providence. Time your visit with the Warwick Food Truck Nights or PawSox Food Truck & Craft Beer Festival. Feel the burn during the city's legendary WaterFire, a series of nearly 100 bonfires that blaze just above the surface of the three rivers that run through town. For an urban adventure, launch a kayak on the Providence River.

2 East Greenwich
Drive 18 miles ▪ 25 minutes

This coastal town is home to the Varnum Memorial Armory. Exhibits on display include uniforms and armament from the Revolutionary War through the Vietnam era. Exhibits shed light on the evolution of the clothing worn by soldiers as well as the gear they used in battle. If your appetite leans toward the gastronomical, you'll be happy to know that East Greenwich is home to an exceptional range of eaters, from eclectic nouveau cuisine to hearty steak-and-potatoes fare.

3 Newport
Drive 20 miles ▪ 24 minutes

Newport has attracted well-heeled residents for centuries. Some of the rich folk put down roots, building huge mansions that preserve more than 200 years of history. These majestic structures once housed industrialists who spearheaded America's Gilded Age. Mansion tours take visitors to places like Belcourt Castle, a privately owned estate that has been newly restored with swirling ceilings, dark-wood floors and gleaming chandeliers. Considered the grandest of Newport Mansions, the Breakers is a 70-room Italian Renaissance-style Palazzo that was inspired by elegant residences in Genoa and Turin.

4 Bristol
Drive 15 miles ▪ 26 minutes

Bristol neatly fits the role charming New England town. Locals strive to maintain the many Colonial homes that line the town's streets, and the quaint storefronts in the downtown area exude a distinctly homey vibe. Take a stroll through historic buildings like the Linden Place Museum, a Federal-style mansion dating back to 1810. To experience a true country manor, take a trip to Blithewold Estate, a century-old mansion surrounded by lush lawns and flowers. Paths lead visitors to seven distinctive gardens. Discover serenity in the Water Garden or smell sweet blossoms in the Rose Garden.

Drive 18 miles, 28 minutes, back to Providence to complete your loop.

BIKING BOATING DINING ENTERTAINMENT FISHING HIKING HUNTING PADDLING SHOPPING SIGHTSEEING

Rhode Island SPOTLIGHTS

The Ocean State Packs Big Possibilities for Travel

As the saying goes, "good things come in small packages." Rhode Island, the smallest state in the U.S., boasts a surprisingly long menu of attractions, from the Gilded Age mansions overlooking the Atlantic to the hot art installations on display in Providence. Expect big things from Rhode Island.

NEWPORT HAS HOSTED SEVERAL AMERICA'S CUP SAILING REGATTAS.

Getty Images/iStockphoto

Sunset over the Claiborne Pell Newport Bridge, which crosses Narragansett Bay.

Bristol

On the shores of Narragansett Bay, Bristol has made a name for itself as the "most patriotic town in America." Visitors will notice American flags displayed throughout town, but there's more to this delightful community than patriotic spirit.

Magical Estate

Beyond the tree-lined streets of downtown Bristol, visitors will find a wealth of fun attractions. A great place to start is Blithewold, a sprawling estate built overlooking Narragansett Bay. Built in 1908, the residence bears a striking resemblance to a 17th-century English country manor. The mansion's 45 rooms contain family treasures passed down over the generations, including Baccarat crystal, Gorham silver, more than 30 sets of fine china, several Tiffany lamps and dolls, along with objects collected in their travels. The gardens alone are worth a visit. Occupying 33 acres, the landscaping here includes a water garden, an enclosed garden, display gardens, a rock garden, and a rose garden.

Newport

In Newport, the finer things in life are right at your fingertips. From teeing off at Scottish links-style golf courses to wandering through the lavish Gilded Age mansions, this New England town serves luxury and elegance on a silver platter.

Gilded Age Glamor

Peppered near the eastern shore is a cluster of National Historic Landmarks known as the Gilded Age mansions. Get a taste of old-fashioned opulence and see where the Vanderbilt family spent their summers by touring The Breakers, a 70-room Italian Renaissance-style palazzo, and the Marble House, which was inspired by the Petit Trianon in Versailles. For a different perspective, stroll the 3.5-mile Cliff Walk to see the estates overlooking crashing waves.

Providence

There's so much to see during your visit to Rhode Island's capital city. Admire the marble dome of the capital city's statehouse before visiting the Rhode Island School of Design (RISD, pronounced "Riz-Dee" by locals) Museum and admire its 91,000 pieces of work. If it's a nice of a day, head over to Benefit Street and admire the largest concentration of Colonial buildings in the U.S. Hungry? Enjoy a meal at Federal Hill, Providence's own "Little Italy." On Saturday nights during the summer, sightseers can catch the WaterFire displays that light up the river.

FOR MORE INFORMATION

Rhode Island Tourism Division, 800-556-2484, visitrhodeisland.com

Explore Bristol, www.explorebristolri.com

Discover Newport, 800-326-6030, www.discovernewport.org

Providence Warwick, 401-456-0200, www.goprovidence.com

RI

LOCAL FAVORITE

Cream Chipped Beef Biscuits

They say the world's first diners appeared in Rhode Island in the 1800s. Celebrate this innovation by putting a twist on a diner staple: the biscuit. *Recipe by Sarah Tomlin.*

INGREDIENTS

- ☐ 1 can of refrigerated biscuits (8 per pkg)
- ☐ 2 2-oz pkgs of Buddig beef, cut or torn into 1" pieces
- ☐ 3 Tbsp flour
- ☐ 3 Tbsp butter
- ☐ 2 cups of milk
- ☐ Salt and pepper to taste

DIRECTIONS

Prepare the biscuits. Some folks use a Dutch oven or cast-iron skillet.
In a skillet over medium heat, lightly cook/warm the beef pieces. Push to the side of the pan. Stir in the butter until melted, then add in the flour, salt and pepper. (I personally go heavy on the pepper for this!)
Gradually add the milk, stirring constantly, until gravy comes to a boil. Reduce heat to low (or if cooking over a campfire, move skillet away from direct flame to the side).
Continue to cook and stir often, until thickened. Generally, 4-5 minutes.
Serve ladled over warm biscuits.

Rhode Island

ASHAWAY — D2 *Washington*

ASHAWAY RV RESORT **Ratings: 9.5/9.5★/9.5** (RV Park) Avail: 200 full hkups (30/50 amps). 2021 rates: $85 to $95. Apr 15 to Oct 15. (401)377-8100, 235 Ashaway Road, Ashaway, RI 02808

CHARLESTOWN — E2 *Washington*

BURLINGAME
(Public State Park) From town: Go 4 mi S on US-1 (R). **FAC:** paved/gravel rds. 692 Avail: 36 pull-thrus, (30x60), back-ins (15x35), tent sites, rentals, dump, groc, LP bottles, firewood, controlled access. **REC:** pond, swim, fishing, kayaking/canoeing, playground, hunting nearby. Pet restrict (Q). Partial handicap access, 14 day max stay. 2021 rates: $14 to $20. Apr 12 to Oct 14. no cc.
(401)322-7337 Lat: 41.362176, Lon: -71.699328
1 Burlingame State Park, Charlestown, RI 02813
www.riparks.com

CHARLESTOWN BREACHWAY CAMPGROUND (Public State Park) From Jct of Rte 1A & Charlestown Beach Rd: Go 4-1/2 mi S on Charlestown Beach Rd (E). 75 Avail. 2021 rates: $14 to $20. Apr 15 to Oct 31. (401)364-7000

CHEPACHET — A2 *Providence*

BOWDISH LAKE CAMPING AREA **Ratings: 5.5/UI/4** (Campground) 125 Avail: 22 full hkups, 103 W, 103 E (30/50 amps). 2021 rates: $40 to $110. May 20 to Oct 13. (401)568-8890, 40 Safari Rd, Chepachet, RI 02814

GEORGE WASHINGTON MEMORIAL CAMPING AREA (Public State Park) From Jct of US-44 & Rte 102: Go 5 mi W on US-44 (R). 57 Avail: Pit toilets. 2021 rates: $14 to $35. Apr 12 to Oct 31. (401)568-2085

FOSTER — B2 *Providence*

GINNY-B CAMPGROUND Ratings: 7.5/6.5/8 (Campground) 75 Avail: 15 full hkups, 60 W, 60 E (20/30 amps). 2021 rates: $41. May 01 to Sep 30. (401)397-9477, 7 Harrington Rd, Foster, RI 02825

GREENE — C2 *Kent*

HICKORY RIDGE FAMILY CAMPGROUND **Ratings: 5.5/UI/7** (Campground) Avail: 20 full hkups (30/50 amps). 2021 rates: $50 to $65. (401)397-7474, 584 Victory Hwy, Greene, RI 02827

HOPE VALLEY — D2 *Washington*

WHISPERING PINES CAMPGROUND **Ratings: 7.5/UI/8.5** (Campground) 85 Avail: 31 full hkups, 54 W, 54 E (30/50 amps). 2021 rates: $45 to $65. Apr 15 to Oct 15. (401)539-7011, 41 Saw Mill Rd, Hope Valley, RI 02832

Rhode Island Privately Owned Campground Information Updated by our Good Sam Representatives

Brian & Nancy Astorino

We both retired from Corporate America and took off in our fifth-wheel, LORA (Living Our Retirement Adventures) to see this great country. Pyper, our Goldendoodle, travels with us. We're excited to experience this journey with Good Sam.

MIDDLETOWN — D4 *Newport*

MEADOWLARK RV PARK **Ratings: 7/NA/7** (Campground) 63 Avail: 41 full hkups, 22 W, 22 E (30 amps). 2021 rates: $40 to $80. Apr 01 to Dec 01. (401)846-9455, 132 Prospect Ave, Middletown, RI 02842

NARRAGANSETT — D3 *Washington*

FISHERMENS MEMORIAL (Public State Park) From Jct of US-1 & SR-108: Go 3-1/2 mi S on SR-108 (R). 147 Avail: 147 W, 147 E (20/30 amps). 2021 rates: $20 to $35. Apr 12 to Oct 30. (401)789-8374

NEWPORT — D4 *Newport*

MILITARY PARK CARR POINT REC FACILITIES (NEWPORT NS) (Public) From jct of Hwy 24 & Hwy 114: Go 1.7 mi S on Hwy 114, then on Stringham Rd, then 1.5 mi left on Burma Rd (R). 6 Avail: 6 W, 6 E (30/50 amps). 2021 rates: $20 to $24. May 01 to Oct 31. (401)841-7355

NORTH SCITUATE — B3 *Providence*

HOLIDAY ACRES CAMPING RESORT **Ratings: 8/8.5★/8** (Campground) 85 Avail: 18 full hkups, 67 W, 67 E (30/50 amps). 2021 rates: $44 to $50. (401)934-0780, 593 Snake Hill Rd, North Scituate, RI 02857

PORTSMOUTH — C4 *Newport*

MELVILLE PONDS CAMPGROUND & RV PARK **Ratings: 8/9.5★/10** (Campground) Avail: 56 full hkups (30/50 amps). 2021 rates: $48 to $100. Apr 15 to Nov 01. (401)682-2424, 181 Bradford Ave, Portsmouth, RI 02871

WAKEFIELD — D3 *Washington*

WORDEN POND FAMILY CAMPGROUND **Ratings: 5.5/8.5★/8** (Campground) 19 Avail: 19 W, 19 E (30/50 amps). 2021 rates: $50. May 01 to Oct 15. (401)789-9113, 416 A Worden Pond Rd, Wakefield, RI 02879

WEST GREENWICH — C2 *West Greenwich*

OAK EMBERS **Ratings: 5.5/6/5.5** (Campground) 67 Avail: 4 full hkups, 62 W, 62 E (30/50 amps). 2021 rates: $45 to $50. May 01 to Oct 31. (401)397-4042, 219 Escoheag Hill Rd, West Greenwich, RI 02817

WEST KINGSTON — D3 *Washington*

WAWALOAM CAMPGROUND **Ratings: 8/9.5★/9.5** (Campground) 115 Avail: 30 full hkups, 85 W, 85 E (30/50 amps). 2021 rates: $50 to $65. May 01 to Oct 31. (401)294-3039, 510 Gardiner Rd, West Kingston, RI 02892

WESTERLY — D1 *Washington*

TIMBER CREEK RV RESORT
(RV Resort) (Seasonal Stay Only) 0 Avail: (30/50 amps). (888)563-7040, 118 Dunns Corner Rd, Westerly, RI 02891

RV SPACE-SAVING TIPS: Get crafty by using the insides of your doors/cabinets to store items used often, which cuts down on clutter and makes cleaning a breeze. A shoe organizer can easily be attached to the inside of a closet door for organizing shoes and other small items. Emergency flashlights are made more accessible when you install broom holders to the inside of a cabinets to put your flashlights within easy reach.

CLEAN RESTROOMS GET A STAR

Campgrounds that receive the maximum 5 points for restroom cleanliness (toilets, showers, floors, walls and sinks/counters/mirrors) achieve a star beside their total restroom rating.

Rated 10/10★/10

SPOTLIGHT ON TOP RV & CAMPING DESTINATIONS

We've put the Spotlight on popular RV & camping travel destinations. Turn to the Spotlight articles in our State and Province sections to learn more.

Getty Images/iStockphoto

DID YOU KNOW?

Hilton Head Island is home to a mysterious 4,000-year-old circle of shells known as the Sea Pines Shell Ring.

YOU ARE HERE

South Carolina

From epic fishing lakes to bustling ocean shores, South Carolina is a treat for visitors. The Palmetto State is the place to go for hospitable Southern culture.

Charleston Turns Up the Charm

Founded during the colonial era, Charleston is a charming window into the past. South Carolina's most romantic city has an old-world charm that comes to life in the clip-clop of horses hooves on the cobblestone streets. History tours, outdoor recreation and seaside fun make Charleston a destination like no other.

Reach New Heights in the South

In South Carolina's western region, the Blue Ridge Mountains entice recreation seekers for hiking, boating and fishing. The 3000-acre Table Rock State Park is a great place to hit the trails, taking hikers to cascading falls and stunning overlooks. Nearby, Devils Fork State Park overlooks picturesque Lake Jocassee, with waters reflecting the surrounding green hills. Watersports are tops here.

The Gorgeous Grand Strand

Much of South Carolina's Atlantic Coast consists of smooth, sandy shores, providing ample room for beachcombers. Whether you prefer action-packed Myrtle Beach, where throngs of people go for fun in the sun, or the calm natural beauty of Isle of Palms, you can find the right spot for your preferences.

Golfing Galore

South Carolina is a treasure trove of golf courses. Hit the links on one of the state's 300-plus courses, including many designed by legends. Bicyclists will also hit the jackpot in the Palmetto State, with the renowned bike paths found on exquisite Hilton Head Island. For a fun mix of nature and small-town charm, the 20-mile Swamp Rabbit Trail in Greenville runs along the scenic Reedy River to Travelers Rest.

South Carolina Oysters

Native Americans roasted oysters over open fires centuries before Europeans arrived to settle the New World along the Atlantic coast. Today, beach-goers keep the tradition alive with gatherings that yield juicy, flavorful oysters. Sample some grilled oysters at local restaurants and taste a timeless flavor that never fails to satisfy.

VISITOR CENTER

TIME ZONE
Eastern Standard

ROAD & HIGHWAY INFORMATION
877-511-4672
511sc.org

FISHING & HUNTING INFORMATION
803-734-3833
dnr.sc.gov

BOATING INFORMATION
803-734-3447
dnr.sc.gov/boating

NATIONAL PARKS
nps.gov/sc

STATE PARKS
southcarolinaparks.com

TOURISM INFORMATION
South Carolina Department of Parks Recreation and Tourism
803-734-0124
discoversouthcarolina.com

TOP TOURISM ATTRACTIONS
1) Historic Charleston
2) Myrtle Beach
3) Columbia

MAJOR CITIES
Columbia (capital), Charleston, North Charleston, Mount Pleasant, Greenville

SC

good sam park Featured Good Sam Parks

SOUTH CAROLINA

When you stay with Good Sam, you can expect the highest degree of cleanliness and friendliness, and better yet, you get **10% off** overnight campground fees.

If you're not already a Good Sam member you can purchase your membership at one of these locations:

CHARLESTON
Oak Plantation Campground

CROSS HILL
Moon Landing RV Park & Marina

DILLON
Camp Pedro Campground

FAIR PLAY
Carolina Landing RV Resort

GREENVILLE
Springwood RV Park

HARDEEVILLE
Camp Lake Jasper RV Resort

HILTON HEAD ISLAND
Hilton Head Harbor RV Resort & Marina

HOLLYWOOD
Lake Aire RV Park & Campground

LEXINGTON
Barnyard RV Park

LIBERTY HILL
Wateree Lake RV Park and Marina

MYRTLE BEACH
Apache Family Campground & Pier
Briarcliffe RV Resort

NORTH MYRTLE BEACH
Barefoot RV Resort

PENDLETON
Clemson RV Park at the Grove

PLUM BRANCH
Lake Thurmond RV Park

SPARTANBURG
Spartanburg/Cunningham RV Park

ST GEORGE
Jolly Acres RV Park & Storage

SUMMERTON
Taw Caw Campground & Marina

SWANSEA
River Bottom Farms Family Campground

WALTERBORO
New Green Acres RV Park

WINNSBORO
Broad River Campground & RV Park

YEMASSEE
The Oaks at Point South RV

10/10★/10 GOOD SAM PARK

HILTON HEAD ISLAND
Hilton Head Harbor RV Resort & Marina
(843)681-3256

What's This?

An RV park with a 10/10★/10 rating has scored perfect grades in amenities, cleanliness and appearance ("See Understanding the Campground Rating System" on pages 8 and 9 for an explanation of the trusted Good Sam Rating System). Stay in a 10/10★/10 park on your next trip for a nearly flawless camping experience.

Getty Images/iStockphoto

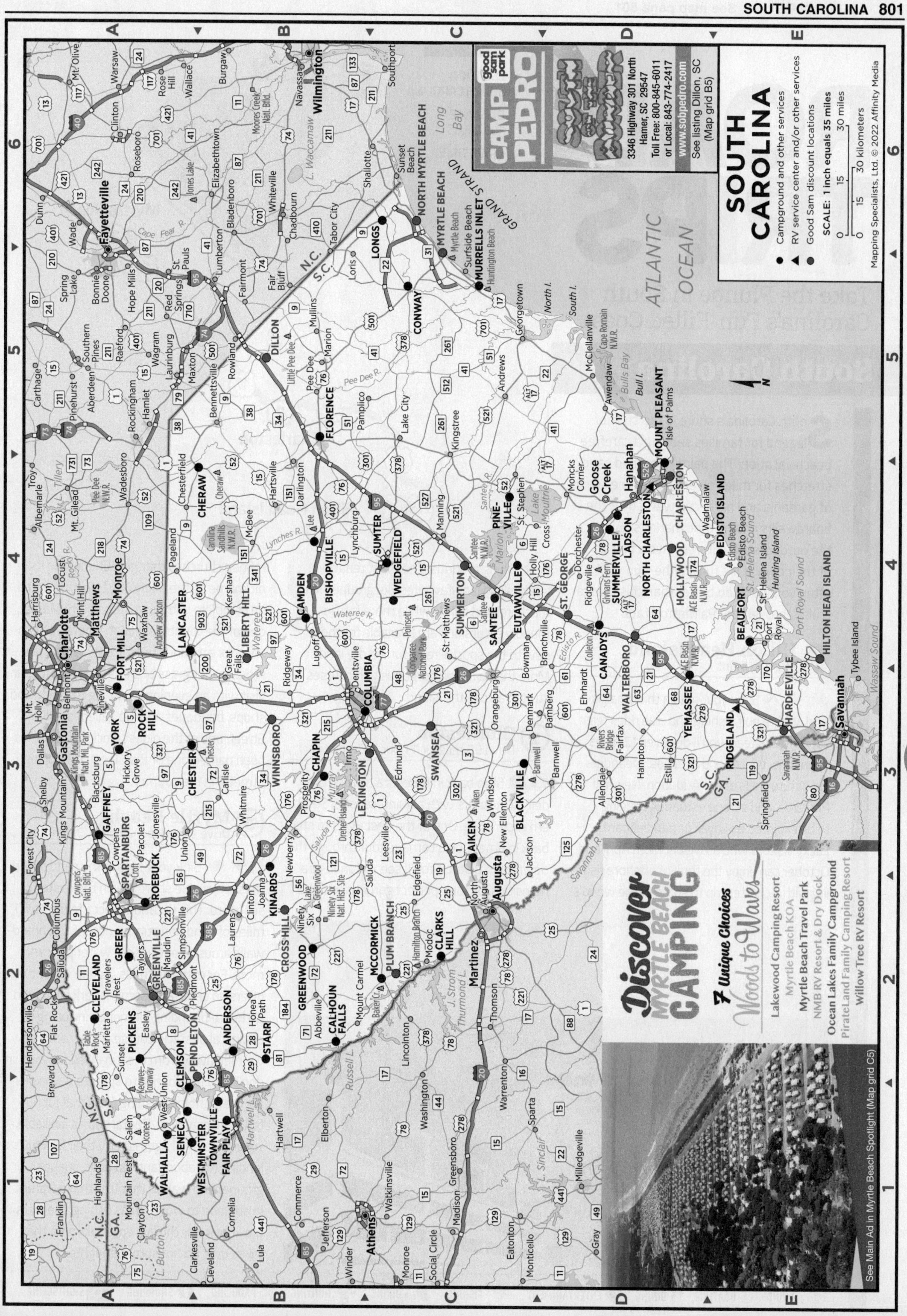
good sam park
CAMP PEDRO
3346 Highway 301 North
Hamer, SC 29547
Toll Free: 800-845-6011
or Local: 843-774-2417
www.sobpedro.com
See listing Dillon, SC
(Map grid B5)
SOUTH CAROLINA
Campground and other services
RV service center and/or other services
Good Sam discount locations
SCALE: 1 inch equals 35 miles
0 15 30 miles
0 15 30 kilometers
Mapping Specialists, Ltd. © 2022 Affinity Media
ATLANTIC OCEAN
Discover
MYRTLE BEACH
CAMPING
7 Unique Choices
Woods to Waves
Lakewood Camping Resort
Myrtle Beach KOA
Myrtle Beach Travel Park
NMB RV Resort & Dry Dock
Ocean Lakes Family Campground
PirateLand Family Camping Resort
Willow Tree RV Resort
See Main Ad in Myrtle Beach Spotlight (Map grid C5)
SC

ROAD TRIPS

Take the Plunge in South Carolina's Fun-Filled Coast

South Carolina

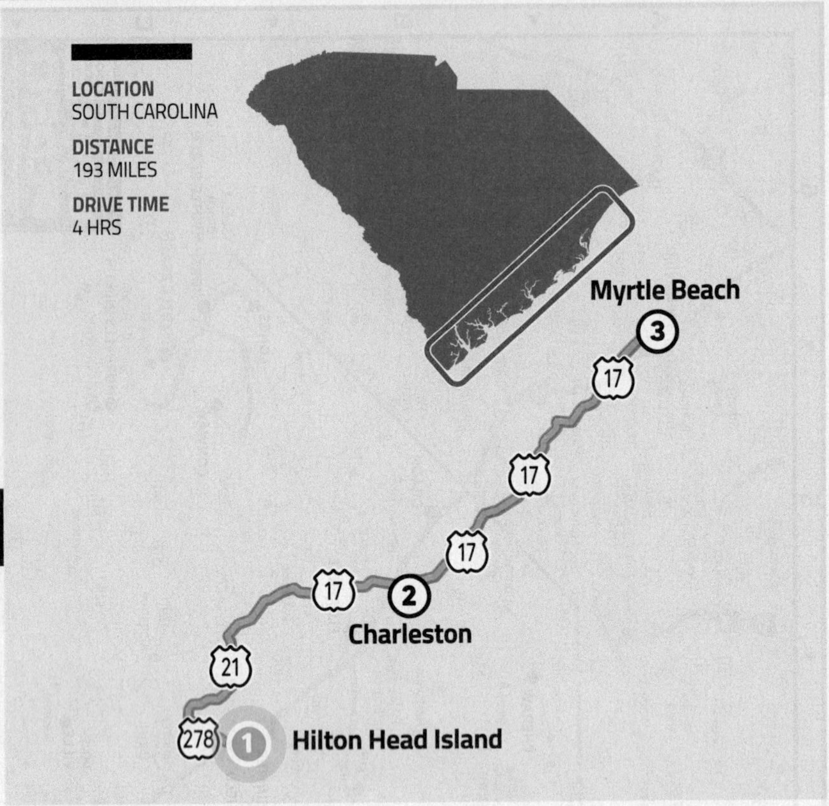

South Carolina's shore is the stuff of legend for families seeking a carefree beach vacation. The palm tree-lined sand stretches for miles on end, while the scent of gardenia and barbecue wafts over the boardwalks and historic markets. Even the outdoors adventures have a flair all of their own. If it's fun-in-the-sun you're after, you won't do better than this coastal cruise through the Palmetto State.

1 Hilton Head Island
Starting Point

Slow your roll on this small island, where golf, fishing and bike rides reign supreme. Instead, you'll discover 12 miles of pristine, white sand beaches, meandering nature trails at the Audubon-Newhall Preserve, and serene estuaries begging to be explored by kayak or paddleboard. Lucky visitors who arrive between April and October can enjoy the thrill of offshore fishing with a charter trip to some of the world's best fishing grounds. The most tenacious anglers can land favorites like grouper, king mackerel and shark, while more family-friendly excursions are available for those new to the sport. Prefer fun on dry land? More than a dozen gorgeous golf courses stretch across the island.

2 Charleston
Drive 98 miles ▪ 1 hour, 57 minutes

Step back in time as a historic city delights visitors with a quintessential Southern experience. One of the best ways to step back in time is on a carriage tour through the downtown district. You'll see Victorian-era mansions, picture-perfect gardens and the refined churches that give Charleston its nickname as the "Holy City." No tour would be complete without a stop at City Market, one of the country's oldest, where you can shop for arts and crafts like the area's famous sweet grass baskets. Round out your visit with an evening exploring the high-end shops, boutiques and hip galleries of King Street, one of the oldest blocks in town. It's been named one of the "Top 10 Shopping Streets" in the country.

3 Myrtle Beach
Drive 95 miles ▪ 2 hours, 3 minutes

Sink your toes in the sand of the most enjoyable shoreline on the eastern seaboard. This vacation mecca features 60 miles of sand and sun, an oceanfront boardwalk, amusement rides, a water park and more. For extreme thrills, Zipline Adventures offers an aerial amusement park filled with 50 heart-pounding elements, including a diabolical obstacle course. If you can drag yourself away from the fun-filled downtown, don't skip the chance to spend a day exploring the eight long fishing piers that jut out from the coastline. Rental gear is available, so anglers of all ages can try their luck at landing the abundant sea bass, snapper, grouper and wahoo that troll these waters. In addition to world-class fishing, the piers are known for the live entertainment that takes over on hot summer nights.

Getty Images/iStockphoto

BIKING · BOATING · DINING · ENTERTAINMENT · FISHING · HIKING · HUNTING · PADDLING · SHOPPING · SIGHTSEEING

South Carolina SPOTLIGHTS

Spend Lazy Days in the Palmetto State

In the Palmetto State, you'll find Southern charm on ocean shores. Bring your golf clubs and sense of adventure to a state where the fairways and ocean shores seem to stretch forever. Sample outstanding barbecue and reel in the big ones.

THE MAGNOLIA PLANTATION & GARDENS WAS FOUNDED IN 1676.

Getty Images/iStockphoto

Peakocks wander sprawling Magnolia Plantation and Gardens in Charleston.

Charleston

With its elegant old buildings, some dating back more than two centuries, and its lovely location right on the Atlantic Ocean, historic Charleston is one of the most charming spots in the South. Along with an elegant collection of antebellum, Georgian and Victorian structures, visitors will find great restaurants, clean beaches and natural areas, as well as a variety of fun festivities throughout the year.

Awesome Antebellum

Charleston is chock-full of interesting attractions, from historic antebellum homes to fascinating history museums. The oldest unrestored plantation home in the U.S., Drayton Hall is a great showpiece of Palladian architecture, while the Magnolia Plantation features some of the prettiest gardens in town. The Charleston Museum is one of the most important sites in the region. Here, you'll find a variety of Revolutionary and Civil War memorabilia, including an armory stocked with a fine selection of old guns and swords. The museum's Natural History Gallery showcases prehistoric fossils and the Lowcountry History Hall features displays of Native American artifacts from the area.

Angle for Big Trophies

Charleston offers some great inland fishing, with plenty of spots to angle for redfish, trout and flounder. Popular areas include Lake Moultrie and the Cooper River. Cape Romain National Wildlife Refuge is also a popular spot for fishing, as well as shrimping and crabbing and oysters and clams can be harvested here during the cooler season.

Paddle Power

Kayaking is also popular in the Charleston area, owing largely to the abundance of peaceful salt marshes in the region, and there are plenty of outfitters around town that offer rentals and instruction. By the same token, there are plenty of boat operators offering maritime excursions; if you're lucky, you might even spot Atlantic bottlenose dolphins.

Hike Charleston

If you want to get out into nature, you'll have plenty of chances in the Charleston area. Bulls Island, located in the Cape Romain National Wildlife Refuge, boasts two short trails: the mile-long Middens Trail and the two-mile Turkey Walk Trail. If you want to get outside but would prefer a less active adventure, consider a visit to the 1755 Middleton Place House Museum, which

> "CHARLESTON OFFERS SOME GREAT INLAND FISHING ANGLE FOR REDFISH, TROUT AND FLOUNDER."

SC

LOCAL FAVORITE

Orange-Glazed Pork Chops

The sweet combination of salty pork and citrus jelly in this sunny recipe will have your taste buds dancing the South Carolina Shag. *Recipe by John and Deanne Grant.*

INGREDIENTS

- ☐ 4 loin pork chops, ½ inch thick
- ☐ Salt and pepper to taste
- ☐ 2 Granny Smith apples peeled and thinly sliced
- ☐ 1 29 oz can of sweet potatoes in heavy syrup, drained
- ☐ 1 10 oz jar of orange marmalade jelly
- ☐ ½ cup honey mustard

DIRECTIONS

Cut 4 large rectangles of heavy-duty aluminum foil. Place 1 pork chop in the center of each foil sheet and sprinkle with salt and pepper. Place an equal number of sliced apples around each chop. Place a portion of sweet potatoes on top of each chop. In a small bowl, combine orange marmalade and honey mustard, mix well and spoon on an equal portion over each chop. Wrap each foil sheet around each serving to create a packet. Place packets on the grill or in the coals and embers of an open fire for 40 minutes turning every 10 minutes.

The pavilion at Folly Beach Pier attracts top-name entertainers. The pier is part of a 12-square-mile barrier island off Charleston that has six miles of beaches.

features the oldest landscaped garden in the United States. Historical reenactments are big here, with costumed actors showing off old-time crafts and trades, and you'll find a virtual menagerie here, from cows and chickens to water buffalo and cashmere goats.

History by the Sea

History comes to life in Charleston, and the beautiful city is filled with glorious old buildings, some of which are now museums. These include the Edmondston-Alston, a Greek Revival city mansion filled with antique furniture, and the Aiken-Rhett House, which has changed little since its last refurbishment in 1858. Other beautiful homes worthy of a visit include the Nathaniel Russel House, with its elliptical spiral staircase and gold-leaf molding and the art-filled Calhoun Mansion, which has equally impressive Japanese water gardens in its backyard. Perhaps the most famous historical building is Boone Hall, one of the oldest working plantations in the country; it's best known for its mile-long driveway that's flanked with towering oak trees, earning it the moniker, "The Avenue of Oaks."

History Preserved in Georgetown

North of Charleston along the coast, the city of Georgetown entices history buffs. Georgetown is an old port city of nearly 300 years and looks the part with colonial-style brick buildings and ancient live oaks arching over the streets. Indigo and Carolina Gold rice were its main exports; the Rice Museum is in the Old Market Building on Front Street. Georgetown is the third oldest city in South Carolina, the second oldest in Beaufort. Lowcountry planters built so many gorgeous homes in Beaufort that it was promoted as the "wealthiest town of its size in America."

Party Time

Charleston puts on no shortage of events throughout the year, most of which offer entertainment for all ages. Food celebrations include the Lowcountry Oyster Festival (the largest oyster fest on Earth), held in January, and the Charleston Wine + Food Festival, featuring around 100 food and wine offerings.

Charleston Chic

In March, Charleston Fashion Week turns Marion Square into a temporary hothouse for fashion, while the Spoleto Festival in late May and early June showcases performing arts across genres. Later in the summer, the MOJA Arts Festival celebrates arts and culture from the African diaspora, with music, theater and dance from Africa and the Caribbean.

Scenic Side Trips

To the east of Charleston lies the vast and fertile, which spans 110,000 acres and five counties. The lake was conceived in the 1940s as part of President Franklin Delano Roosevelt's New Deal Rural Electrification project; the Santee River was dammed to provide hydroelectricity to the surrounding areas. Known statewide for its epic fishing opportunities and rich wildlife, the region summons outdoor enthusiasts and budding naturalists regardless of

Pleasure craft sail past the lighthouse at Hilton Head Harbor, one of six marinas on Hilton Head Island.

the season. Fringing the lake, Santee State Park and the Santee National Wildlife Refuge offer hiking and biking along myriad trails while public boat ramps allow for on-the-water fun.

Santee State Park

With its dense forests, beaches and swamps braided with scenic trails, the 2,500-acre Santee State Park invites hiking, biking, boating, hunting, wildlife watching and swimming. The park's longest novice trail (hiking and biking) extends for 7.5-miles and meanders through a mixed pine and hardwood forest draped with Spanish moss and affords signature views of the cypress-fringed lake. From the parking area, the one-mile Sinkhole Pond Trail traverses a varied habitat, including pine forest and swamp, and introduces one of the park's unique features, a limestone sinkhole pond.

Nature Trails

Three short nature trails come ablaze with colorful wildflowers in the spring. Hikers also will see lots of animals, including deer, rabbits and snakes. Platforms located near the trails and wetland areas allow for prime time viewing of osprey, great blue herons, painted buntings and other songbirds that converge during summer nesting season. Santee is also a popular spot for swimming and paddling. The park's beaches also provide boating and fishing access. Sun worshipers will find plenty of spots to soak in rays.

Santee National Wildlife Refuge

When it comes to biodiversity, the 15,000-acre Santee National Wildlife Refuge packs a punch. Majestic forests of hardwoods and pines interspersed with marsh, wetlands, impoundments and croplands provide sanctuary to many bird, reptile and mammal species. Alligators can be spotted at Alligator Alley.

Dingle Pond Days

At Dingle Pond, a one-mile trail with an observation tower and boardwalk provides sanctuary to several wetland species. The Santee Refuge also throws some archaeological interest into the mix. The Santee Indian mound — a burial or temple mound that dates to 1200-1500 A.D. — ranks as the farthest-eastern known manifestation of Mississippian culture.

Fort Watson

In the Revolutionary War, the British built Fort Watson atop the mound. In 1781, the fort was taken by Marion's Brigade. This American unit was led by Francis Marion, nicknamed the Swamp Fox.

Big Fish

Any South Carolina angler will tell you that Lake Marion is the place to be. Synonymous with big fish and abundant wildlife, the lake's shallow swamps and black water ponds provide fertile ground for many species. Lake Marion is the site of several milestones. The state fishing record for largemouth bass was set here (16.2 pounds) and some of the lake's other famed catches include a 58-pound channel catfish and a 55-pound striped bass.

Reeling It In

Anglers of all persuasions gather at more than 16 boat ramps constructed on the lake and revel in optimum conditions for hooking white perch, crappie, channel catfish, Arkansas blue catfish and bream. If you want to partake, you'll need to purchase a South Carolina fishing license, which can be obtained in local bait shops and sporting goods stores.

Hilton Head Island

From atop the Harbour Town Lighthouse, you can see Hilton Head Island spread out below you, with undulating hills and magnificent beaches bordering the jewel-toned Atlantic. Hilton Head Island is a preeminent getaway, where relaxation comes easy. You can find it in each crash of a wave along the sandy shores. You'll also find a bounty of recreational opportunities, live entertainment venues and upscale shopping and dining experiences. While today's Hilton Head Island would be barely recognizable to its early inhabitants, their influence has left a mark in the rich Lowcountry culture that shines through in the history, cuisine, crafts and music. Spend time exploring the legacy left behind by early inhabitants.

A Picturesque Place to Play

With 24 championship golf courses, Hilton Head Island is a golfing paradise. From greens designed by grand architects to greens with grand views, Hilton Head Island has a course that will wow any golfer. But, if golf

SPOTLIGHTS

Part of the Grand Strand, the Myrtle Beach shore is lined with amusement parks, hotel sand attractions.

isn't your game, don't worry. You'll find premier racquetball, pickleball and tennis courts that will appeal to everyone from new players to advanced pros. Courts and courses aren't the only thing hidden within Hilton Head Island's manicured landscapes. Over 50 miles of biking trails crisscross the island. Take a trail that follows the coast or cut inland course that passes through untamed marshland.

A Beach for Every Personality

Twelve miles of beaches welcome visitors; each area has an ambiance all its own. Coligny Beach Park is a favorite of families. Small kids will love splashing around in the interactive fountains, while parents relax in the Adirondack chairs. If you have an itch to hit the waves, Folly Field Beach is the place to play. To find your own quiet place in the sands, head to Fish Haul Creek Park or Burkes Beach Access. Wherever you land, you will find watersports to enjoy. Take a slow kayak tour of a harbor, head out for a sunset dolphin cruise, or grab a pole for some deep-sea fishing.

A Walk on the Wild Side

Explore the quiet side of Hilton Head Island with a visit to Pinckney Island National Wildlife Refuge. Take your camera to catch the perfect shot of the migratory birds, alligators and deer that are often spotted in this 4,000-acre preserve. Get your fill of flora and fauna at Sea Pines Forest Preserve, where you can tour fields of wildflowers, seaside marshes and the Shell Ring archeological site.

Hit the Hilton Head Family Fun

If you're travelling with small children you'll want to visit the Sandbox, an interactive children's museum home to state-of-the-art exhibits and educational play centers. Highlights include a "Track The T-Rex" climbing wall, a child-sized flight simulator and magnetic sandbox.

Gullah Culture

Learn about the Gullah people, who arrived at Hilton Head as slaves and went on to create their own distinctive culture. The Gullah Museum of Hilton Head Island offers several exhibits dedicated to this vibrant people, as well as displays of the handmade baskets that put them on the map.

Myrtle Beach

Home to 60 miles of white sand, an entertainment-packed boardwalk and celebrity-designed golf courses, Myrtle Beach has come a long way from its beginnings as a quiet summer retreat. Today, the bustling vacation destination promises excitement under the sun for families, retirees and everyone in between.

Grand Strand Escapades

The Grand Strand is destination fun. The coastal strip spans 60 miles from the North Carolina border to Pawleys Island, with Myrtle Beach smack in the middle. This sandy expanse is where you can enjoy all your favorite beach activities – from sunbathing and swimming to surfing and sailing. The Strand is also where you'll find the Oceanfront Boardwalk and Promenade, a 1.2-mile walkable stretch filled with resorts, restaurants and souvenir shops. Spend your days playing carnival games, taking in spectacular views from the SkyWheel and

CampMyrtleBeach.com
Discover
MYRTLE BEACH CAMPING
KOA
RESORT
1-843-448-3421
Lakewood
Camping Resort
1-877-525-3966
Myrtle Beach Travel Park
1-800-255-3568
NMB RV RESORT
DRY DOCK
MARINA
1-844-777-5727
Ocean Lakes
FAMILY CAMPGROUND
1-800-876-4306
PIRATELAND
FAMILY CAMPING RESORT
1-800-443-2267
Willow Tree
RV Resort & Campground
1-866-207-2267
Woods to Waves

watching live music acts at the Plyler Park Promenade stage. Other attractions include the science-focused WonderWorks indoor amusement park, Ripley's Believe It or Not Odditorium, and Myrtle Beach Zipline Adventures.

Relax on the Water

If you've ever wanted to try a watersport, now is your chance. Thrill-seekers can whiz through waves on a water scooter or go scuba diving to see angelfish, sea turtles and countless other marine creatures. Those who prefer to take it easy can join a dolphin-watching tour, parasail over the open ocean or kayak through inland waterways. Fishing is exceptional here too. Take a deep-sea charter for a chance to catch black sea bass, flounder and king mackerel, or try inland fishing in the Intracoastal Waterway. You can also cast a line from many piers in town, including Apache Pier, Second Avenue Pier and Cherry Grove Pier.

Shopping and Shows

Shop till you drop at two Tanger Outlets. Flip through the racks to find incredible deals on premium brands like Coach, Nike and Ralph Lauren. For an upscale shopping experience, head to Market Common for a blend of luxury names and specialty boutiques. Situated in North Myrtle Beach, Barefoot Landing is a shopping, dining and entertainment hub. Eclectic shops line the complex so pop in to browse everything from magic trick sets and fossils to comic books and classic rock memorabilia. Load up on souvenirs and then stay for the lively nightlife. The award-winning House of Blues is a go-to spot for live music, while the Alabama Theatre is known for its musicals and comedy shows.

Fill Up at Food Festivals

Gourmet food events fill out Myrtle Beach's event calendar. Gobble up the region's most famous delicacy at the World Famous Blue Crab Festival (May) and attend a shrimp cookoff at the Little River ShrimpFest (October). Also in October is the Loris Bog-Off Festival, where chicken bog, a Southern specialty, can be enjoyed alongside arts and crafts, live entertainment and fireworks. In between the food festivals are cultural offerings like the Myrtle Beach International Film Festival (April) and Carolina Country Music Fest (June). The city also hosts many family-friendly events. Take the kids to Conway Riverfest (June) for games and raft races or the Aynor Harvest Hoedown Festival (September), which features a parade, street dance and over a hundred craft booths.

One of the 90 golf courses in Myrtle Beach. Many of the links were created by top course designers.

Hit the Links and Trails

Two state parks offer the perfect escape from the boardwalk's extravagance. Located just 300 yards from the beach, Myrtle Beach State Park hosts nature tours along its wooded trails. Bike paths, equestrian trails and campgrounds are also available. Over in Huntington Beach State Park is the best bird-watching on the East Coast so don't forget to bring your binoculars. The park is home to over 300 bird species, as well as pelicans, alligators and sea turtles. Some of the world's top golf courses are just a stone's throw away. You'll find links catering to every skill level with some greens designed by legends like Arnold Palmer, Jack Nicklaus and Greg Norman. Locals say their favorite public courses to play are Barefoot Golf Resort, Dunes Golf & Beach Club, and Caledonia Golf & Fish Club.

Great American Sculptures

Myrtle Beach doesn't have many historical attractions (it didn't become a city until 1957), but it does possess plenty of museums and art galleries. The most popular one is the Brookgreen Gardens. Over 2,000 works by America's greatest sculptors are displayed across botanical gardens and three galleries. Paintings are also showcased in the Rainey Sculpture Pavilion. Admire the natural and human-made wonders and then stop by the South Carolina Hall of Fame. Tucked away in the Myrtle Beach Convention Center, this free museum provides an insightful window into the past by spotlighting citizens who have made significant contributions to the state.

More on the Shore

More exciting attractions await at Broadway at the Beach. Challenge the kids to a game of mini golf, make a splash in Myrtle Beach Water Park, strike a pose at Old Tyme Portraits and play with more than 100 interactive exhibits at WonderWorks. Finish your action-packed day by watching Legends in Concert, a celebrity tribute show, or taking a paddleboat ride under the Broadway bridges.

The spiral fountain in Finlay Park in Columbia. The fountain sits close to the Columbia Historic District.

live oak trees and antebellum mansions can be found throughout the region, creating some picture-perfect backdrops for photos.

South of the Border

Stopping by the South of the Border complex to refill gas tanks and stomachs has long been a tradition on this stretch of I-95 in South Carolina near the North Carolina border. Started in 1949 as a small beer garden, South of the Border has grown into a full-fledged entertainment attraction, with dozens of restaurants, shops and attractions. When you catch sight of the 200-foot Sombrero Observation Tower shining brightly above the interstate, you'll know that it's time to stop at South of the Border and enjoy one of the most distinctive roadside attractions you'll ever visit.

The Midlands

In between South Carolina's mountains and beaches, you'll find an area known as the Midlands. Don't overlook this magical mid-state region, where the rolling hills meet rollicking riverways. Columbia, the state capital, is the heart of the Midlands, with a rich history dating to the Colonial days and Civil War Era. Today, South Carolina's largest city rolls out the welcome mat with family-friendly attractions and natural beauty. Iconic

Ready, Set, Ride!

Through the 1800s, South Carolinians headed to the small town of Aiken, seeking health and relaxation in the sunny, dry climate. Pine trees and natural springs set a beautiful backdrop for outdoor adventures. Horse racing became a part of that recreational allure and today's visitors can enjoy the same ambiance and activities. Catch the stampede of hooves at the steeplechase or saddle up for a relaxing ride of your own through the Hitchcock Woods, a 2,100-acre urban forest with several beautiful trails.

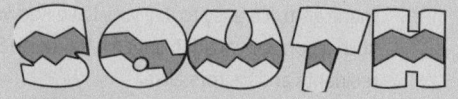

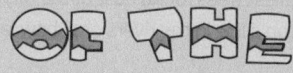

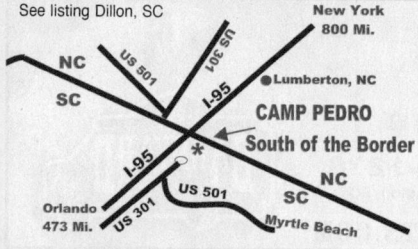

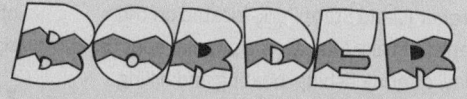

See map page 801

SPOTLIGHTS

Congaree National Park preserves the largest tracts of old growth bottomland hardwood forest in the U.S.

Make a Splash in the Midlands

The 200-mile Saluda River rolls through the Midlands, providing a variety of adventurous playscapes. Experienced kayakers won't want to miss the exhilarating rapids found near downtown Columbia, while calmer waters can be enjoyed further out. The Saluda River's waters flow into Lake Murray, creating a 50,000-acre watersport paradise. Dreher Island State Park, located on the banks of Lake Murray, is a popular spot to play, offering fishing, boating and hiking. Lake Murray is chock full of bass, crappie and perch, making it a prime spot for anglers to reel in a big one.

Cherished Natural Landscapes

One of the best places to experience the Midlands landscapes is at Congaree National Park, which preserves a bottomland forest. The Congaree and Wateree Rivers twist through the old growth woodlands, meandering around bald cypress trees. Under the towering canopy of trees, the animals play, including deer, otters, alligators and more. Take your pick of trails to explore on land, or head to the waterways to paddle through the park. The 15-mile Cedar Creek Canoe Trail water trail travels amid some of the tallest trees found east of the Mississippi. Drop a line in the rivers or oxbow lakes.

Upcountry

The Blue Ridge Mountains of western South Carolina give Upcountry its name, as towering peaks rise above the horizon. Aside from their natural beauty, these undulating hills set the stage for outdoor adventures in the Palmetto State. Small mountain towns transport you back in time, with covered bridges, roadside fruit stands and mom-and-pop cafes. Energetic urban areas also entice, including the region's largest city, Greenville. The Falls Park on the Reedy is a must-see gathering spot downtown.

Lovely Lake Jocassee

Although you can take your pick from any number of pristine lakes in Upcountry, Lake Jocassee is considered one of the best. Crystal clear spring waters flow from the mountainsides to create this stunningly beautiful 7,600-acre lake. Take a boating tour to see the lakeside waterfalls, cool off in the chilly waters, or go scuba diving for an underwater view. Devils Fork State Park is a perfect basecamp, with boating ramps, nature trails and more.

Cool Off at Lake Keowee

Directly to the north of Jocassee and separated by a small isthmus, Lake Kewoee is equally spectacular. When viewed on a map or from the air, Lake Keowee in northwestern South Carolina is often said to resemble a Christmas tree. Long, narrow and fringed with shoreline that's frayed with thousands of branching inland coves, the lake is actually a long and deep valley, one which was flooded after the construction of three massive hydroelectric dams over the course of the 1960s and 70s. Standing on the shores of this marvelous man-made gem, it's easy to see why Lake Keowee is such a popular vacation spot for Palmetto State residents and visitors alike.

Lake or Recreation

Spread across more than 18,000 acres and sporting more than 300 miles of shoreline, the lake is a popular destination for anglers, boaters, kayakers, bird watchers and backcountry hikers. To the north rise the rocky summits of Sassafras Mountain and Pinnacle Mountain — the nearest of the Blue Ridge peaks — creating a stunning alpine backdrop. And the comparatively big city of Greenville is less than an hour's drive away to the east, meaning the luxury and amenity of world-class dining, shopping and entertainment options remains close at hand.

Historical Insights

Anyone with an ear for history won't want to miss the Oconee Heritage Center or the Museum of the Cherokee, both located in Walhalla. The first one is housed in a historic tobacco warehouse that was built in 1892. Collections tell the history of Oconee County across a range of narratives, including the arrival of European settlers, the expansion of the railroad and the rise of textile manufacturing. The latter, meanwhile, is only open on Saturdays, and features a small collection of ancient Native American artifacts. Highlights include centuries-old dugout canoes

Fall colors on the shores of Pinnacle Lake at Table Rock State Park in Pickens. The park is a popular hiking spot.

Big Energy

In Seneca, history buffs will need to pencil in some time at the World of Energy Museum, Lunney Museum and Bell Gallery, as well as spend some time strolling around Ram Cat Alley, a community district which is listed on the National Register of Historic Places. At the World of Energy Museum, visitors learn the history and science behind the production of hydroelectric power in Oconee County, as well as about the Lake Keowee Dam, Little River Dam and Jocassee Dam.

Pendleton

Pendleton District is a picturesque backdrop for exploration and recreation. Whether it's a hike to a mountain-fed stream, an outdoor family adventure or an opportunity to learn more about the area's rich history and culture, you will find it here.

Falls in the Cherokee Foothills

Go Chasing Waterfalls South Carolina's longest scenic byway winds 118 miles through the Blue Ridge Mountains, creating the ultimate Upcountry road trip. The Cherokee Foothills National Scenic Byway connects several of the state's beloved state parks, including Devils Fork, Table Rock and Caesars Head.

Sullivan's Travels

Learn about a dramatic chapter in the Revolution War at on Sullivan's Island. The Battle of Sullivan's Island was fought here in 1776 when defenders of partially completed Fort Sullivan under Col. William Moultrie defeated a British naval squadron, whose cannon balls couldn't destroy the soft but sturdy palmetto-log walls of the fort. The red coats attempted an amphibious landing, but the fort's defenders repelled the invaders. The British eventually withdrew and did not return until 1780, when the second Siege of Charleston captured the city. The fort, as now constructed, was completed in 1809. Its interior has been restored to reflect American seacoast defenses from the Revolutionary War through World War II. Located near the fort is a National Park visitor center and an "African Passages" exhibit.

Make a Splash on the Wild Side

The Chattooga National Wild & Scenic River tumbles its way across Upcountry, along the borders of North Carolina, South Carolina and Georgia. It creates one of the best whitewater rivers in the Southeast as it drops 2,600 feet in elevation in a mere 50-mile stretch. Experienced paddlers can find heart-pounding rapids, while guided rafting trips are perfect for novices. Along its rolling pathway, you'll find a number of spots to wade in the waters.

FOR MORE INFORMATION

Charleston Area CVB, 800-774-0006, www.explorecharleston.com
Visit Hilton Head Island, 800-523-3373, www.hiltonheadisland.org
The Midlands Region, 803-734-0124, discoversouthcarolina.com/midlands
Visit Myrtle Beach, 800-356-3016, www.visitmyrtlebeach.com
Welcome to Upcountry South Carolina, 864-233-2690, Upcountry.com
Lake Marion: Clarendon County Chamber of Commerce, 803-435-4405, www.clarendoncounty.com
South of the Border, 800-845-6011, www.thesouthoftheborder.com
Discover Lake Keowee, 888-348-7388, www.discoverkeowee.com

SC

South Carolina

AIKEN — C3 *Aiken*

AIKEN (Public State Park) From Jct of US 78 & State Park Rd (NW side of town): Go 5 mi N on State Park Rd, then 300 feet NW on Old Tory Trail (R). 25 Avail: 25 W, 25 E (30 amps). 2021 rates: $15 to $20. (803)649-2857

ANDERSON — B2 *Anderson*

ANDERSON/LAKE HARTWELL KOA **Ratings: 8.5/8.5★/8** (Campground) 30 Avail: 25 full hkups, 5 W, 5 E (30/50 amps). 2021 rates: $41.50 to $71.50. (800)562-5804, 200 Wham Rd, Anderson, SC 29625

HARTWELL LAKE - COE/SPRINGFIELD (Public Corps) From Jct of SC Hwy 28 By-Pass & SC Hwy 24: Go 4-1/2 mi W on SC Hwy 24, then 4 mi S on SC Hwy 187, then 1/4 mi W on CR (L). 79 Avail: 79 W, 79 E (50 amps). 2021 rates: $26 to $52. Apr 01 to Oct 31. (888)893-0678

LAKE HARTWELL RV RESORT AND CABINS **Ratings: 7/9★/8** (Campground) 20 Avail: 8 full hkups, 12 W, 12 E (30/50 amps). 2021 rates: $45 to $65. (864)287-3223, 400 Ponderosa Point, Townville, SC 29689

SADLERS CREEK (Public State Park) From Jct of I-85 & SC-24 (Exit 11): Go 5 mi E on SC-24, then 7 mi S on SC-187, then 1 mi W on Sadlers Creek Rd (E). 52 Avail: 52 W, 52 E (30 amps). 2021 rates: $20 to $25. (864)226-8950

BEAUFORT — E4 *Beaufort*

HUNTING ISLAND (Public State Park) From E Jct of US 21 & SC-802 (SE of Beaufort): Go 17 mi SE on US 21 (L). 102 Avail: 102 W, 102 E (30/50 amps). 2021 rates: $18 to $45. (843)838-2011

TUCK IN THE WOOD CAMPGROUND **Ratings: 6.5/8.5★/8.5** (Campground) Avail: 74 full hkups (30/50 amps). 2021 rates: $43 to $48. (843)838-2267, 22 Tuc In De Wood Ln, St Helena Island, SC 29920

BISHOPVILLE — B4 *Lee*

LEE STATE NATURAL AREA (Public State Park) From Jct of I-20 & Road 22 (Exit 123): Go 1 mi N on Road 22 (L). 25 Avail: 25 W, 25 E (30 amps). 2021 rates: $15 to $30. (803)428-5307

BLACKVILLE — C3 *Barnwell*

BARNWELL (Public State Park) From Jct of US 78 & SC-3: Go 2-1/2 mi SW on SC-3 (R). 25 Avail: 8 full hkups, 17 W, 17 E (30/50 amps). 2021 rates: $14 to $19. (803)284-2212

So you're the one with ""pooch'' duty? Please make a clean sweep of it! Your fellow RVers will appreciate it!

CALHOUN FALLS — B2 *Abbeville*

CALHOUN FALLS (Public State Park) From Jct of SC-72 & SC-81: Go 1 mi N on SC-81 (L). 86 Avail: 86 W, 86 E (20/30 amps). 2021 rates: $23 to $27. (864)447-8267

CAMDEN — B4 *Kershaw*

MILITARY PARK WATEREE REC AREA (SHAW AFB) (Public) From jct of I-20W & Camden (Hwy 521) exit: Go N on Hwy 21, then left 9 mi on Hwy 97, then left on Baron DeKalb Rd (R). Avail: 22 full hkups (30/50 amps). 2021 rates: $20 to $22. (877)928-8372

CANADYS — D4 *Colleton*

COLLETON (Public State Park) From Jct of I-95 & SC-61 (Exit 68): Go 2-3/4 mi SE on SC-61, then 3/4 mi N on US 15 (L). 25 Avail: 25 W, 25 E (30 amps). 2021 rates: $15 to $17. (843)538-8206

CHAPIN — B3 *Lexington*

DREHER ISLAND

(Public State Park) From Jct of I-26 & RD 48/Columbia Ave (Exit 91): Go 2 mi SW on RD 48/Columbia Ave, then 1/4 mi NW on US 76, then 3-1/4 mi SW on St Peters Church Rd, then 3 mi W on Dreher Island Rd, then 2-1/2 mi SE on State Park Rd (E). **FAC:** paved rds. Avail: 97 paved, 8 pull-thrus, (15x70), back-ins (15x40), 97 W, 97 E (30 amps), tent sites, rentals, dump, groc, firewood, controlled access. **REC:** Lake Murray: fishing, marina, kayaking/canoeing, playground, hunting nearby. Pets OK. Partial handicap access, 14 day max stay. 2021 rates: $23 to $30.
(803)364-4152 Lat: 34.085592, Lon: -81.406417
3677 Stare Park Rd, Prosperity, SC 29127
southcarolinaparks.com

CHARLESTON — D4 *Charleston*

A SPOTLIGHT Introducing Charleston's colorful attractions appearing at the front of this state section.

CHARLESTON See also Hollywood, Ladson & Mount Pleasant.

LAKE AIRE RV PARK & CAMPGROUND

Ratings: 8.5/9★/9.5 (RV Park) From jct I-26 & US-17: Go 14 mi S on US-17S, then 1/2 mi SW on SC-162 (L). **FAC:** gravel rds. (92 spaces). Avail: 61 gravel, 43 pull-thrus, (30x75), back-ins (30x60), 35 full hkups, 26 W, 26 E (30/50 amps), seasonal sites, WiFi @ sites, tent sites, dump, laundry, LP gas, fire rings, firewood. **REC:** pool, Lake Rantowles: fishing, kayaking/canoeing, boating nearby, playground, hunting nearby. Pet restrict (Q). Partial handicap access. Big rig sites, eco-friendly. 2021 rates: $47 to $55, Military discount.
(843)571-1271 Lat: 32.77822, Lon: -80.14984
4375 Hwy 162, Hollywood, SC 29449
www.lakeairerv.com
See primary listing at Hollywood and ad page 805

MILITARY PARK JB CHARLESTON RV PARK (JB CHARLESTON) (Public) From jct of I-26 S & Ashley Phosphate Rd (exit 209): Go right 0.5 mi on Ashley Phosphate Rd, then left on Stall Rd, then right on Midland Park Rd, then through gate, follow signs (R). 44 Avail: 40 full hkups, 4 W, 4 E (30/50 amps). 2021 rates: $23. (843)963-1672

MILITARY PARK SHORT STAY REC AREA (JB CHARLESTON) (Public) S-bnd: From jct of I-26 & US-17 Alt (exit 199): Go 18 mi E on US-17 Alt, then 1.5 mi N on US-52, then left .025 mi on Powerhouse Rd, then right on Old Black Creek Rd, then left on Shorty Stay Rd (E). Avail: 85 full hkups (30/50 amps). 2021 rates: $19 to $28. (843)743-2608

OAK PLANTATION CAMPGROUND

Ratings: 9.5/9.5★/10 (Campground) 220 Avail: 166 full hkups, 54 W, 54 E (30/50 amps). 2021 rates: $52 to $66. (843)766-5936, 3540 Savannah Hwy, Charleston, SC 29455

THE CAMPGROUND AT JAMES ISLAND COUNTY PARK

(Public) From jct of I-26 & US 17 (exit 221A): Go 2 mi W on US 17, then 1-1/2 mi S on SC 171, then 1-1/2 mi W on SC 700, then 1-3/4 mi S on Riverland Dr (R). **FAC:** paved rds. Avail: 124 gravel, 15 pull-thrus, (35x90), back-ins (25x65), 118 full hkups, 6 W, 6 E (30/50 amps), WiFi @ sites, tent sites, rentals, dump, laundry, groc, LP gas, fire rings, firewood, controlled access. **REC:** pool $, Lake at James Island County Park: fishing, kayaking/canoeing, boating nearby, playground, rec open to public. Pets OK. Partial handicap access. Big rig sites, 28 day max stay, eco-friendly. 2021 rates: $55 to $66, Military discount.
(843)795-4386 Lat: 32.73549, Lon: -79.99193
871 Riverland Dr, Charleston, SC 29412
CharlestonCountyParks.com
See ad page 804

CHERAW — B4 *Chesterfield*

CHERAW (Public State Park) From SW Jct of SC-9 & US 52: Go 3-1/2 mi S on US 52 (R). 17 Avail: 17 W, 17 E (30 amps). 2021 rates: $17 to $31. (843)537-9656

CHESTER — B3 *Chester*

CHESTER (Public State Park) From SW Jct of US 321 & SC-72: Go 1-1/2 mi SW on SC-72 (L). 25 Avail: 25 W, 25 E (50 amps). 2021 rates: $15 to $17. (803)385-2680

CLARKS HILL — C2 *McCormick*

J. STROM THURMOND LAKE - COE/MODOC (Public Corps) From town: Go 13 mi S on SR-28, then 4 mi NW on Hwy 22 (L). Avail: 69 E (30/50 amps). 2021 rates: $18 to $52. Mar 31 to Sep 30. (864)333-2272

CLEMSON — A1 *Pickens*

HARTWELL LAKE - COE/TWIN LAKES (Public Corps) From Jct of SC Hwy 123 & US-76: Go 3-1/2 mi SE on US-76, then 3 mi SW on CR-56 (R). 99 Avail: 99 W, 99 E (50 amps). 2021 rates: $24 to $52. (888)893-0678

CLEVELAND — A2 *Greenville*

PALMETTO COVE RV PARK **Ratings: 8/NA/8.5** (RV Park) Avail: 140 full hkups (30/50 amps). 2021 rates: $33. Apr 01 to Nov 15. (864)836-6221, 521 Table Rock Rd, Cleveland, SC 29635

SOLITUDE POINTE CABINS & RV PARK **Ratings: 8.5/9.5★/10** (RV Park) 14 Avail: 13 full hkups, 1 W, 1 E (30/50 amps). 2021 rates: $65. (864)836-4128, 102 Table Rock Road, Cleveland, SC 29635

COLUMBIA — B3 *Lexington*

COLUMBIA See also Lexington, Swansea & Winnsboro.

BARNYARD RV PARK

Ratings: 8.5/10★/10 (RV Park) From Jct of I-26 (exit 111A) & US-1, W 3 mi on US-1S (R); or From Jct of I-20 (exit 58) & US-1, E (N-bnd) 2 mi on US-1 (L) Note: behind Barnyard Flea Market. **FAC:** paved rds. (129 spaces). Avail: 27 gravel, patios, 27 pull-thrus, (30x85), 27 full hkups (30/50 amps), seasonal sites, cable, WiFi @ sites, dump, laundry, LP gas. **REC:** pond, playground. Pets OK. Partial handicap access. No tents. Big rig sites, eco-friendly. 2021 rates: $42.49, Military discount.
(803)957-1238 Lat: 33.97712, Lon: -81.15610
201 Oak Dr, Lexington, SC 29073
www.barnyardrvpark.com
See primary listing at Lexington and ad page 810

MILITARY PARK WESTON LAKE REC AREA & RV PARK (FORT JACKSON) (Public) From town, E 12 mi on SC-262 (Leesburg Rd), follow signs. Avail: 33 full hkups (30/50 amps). 2021 rates: $35. (803)751-5253

SESQUICENTENNIAL (Public State Park) From Jct of I-20 & US 1 (Exit 74): Go 3 mi NE on US 1 (R); or From Jct of I-77 & US 1 (Exit 17): Go 2-1/4 mi NE on US 1 (R). 84 Avail: 84 W, 84 E (30 amps). 2021 rates: $19 to $27. (803)788-2706

Travel Services

CAMPING WORLD OF COLUMBIA As the nation's largest retailer of RV supplies, accessories, services and new and used RVs, Camping World is committed to making your total RV experience better. **SERVICES:** RV, RV appliance, MH mechanical, staffed RV wash, restrooms. RV Sales. RV supplies, LP gas, RV accessible. Hours: 9am to 7pm.
(888)486-5676 Lat: 34.053732, Lon: -81.127153
3634 Fernandina Rd, Columbia, SC 29210
www.campingworld.com

CONWAY — C5 *Horry*

BUCKSPORT PLANTATION MARINA & RV RESORT **Ratings: 5.5/7.5/7.5** (RV Park) Avail: 15 full hkups (30/50 amps). 2021 rates: $57 to $67. (843)397-5556, 135 Bucksport Rd, Conway, SC 29527

CAROLINA PINES RV RESORT **Ratings: 10/10★/10** (RV Resort) Avail: 580 full hkups (30/50 amps). 2021 rates: $66 to $95. (888)420-4092, 5800 Highway 90, Conway, SC 29526

CROSS HILL — B2 *Laurens*

LAKE GREENWOOD MOTORCOACH RESORT **Ratings: 9.5/8.5★/10** (Condo Park) Avail: 54 full hkups (50 amps). 2021 rates: $49 to $69. (864)992-4700, 463 Cane Creek Rd, Cross Hill, SC 29332

MOON LANDING RV PARK & MARINA
Ratings: 8/9★/7 (Campground) 11 Avail: 10 full hkups, 1 W, 1 E (30/50 amps). 2021 rates: $45. (864)998-4292, 4105 Watts Bridge Rd, Cross Hill, SC 29332

DILLON — B5 *Dillon*

A SPOTLIGHT Introducing The Midlands' colorful attractions appearing at the front of this state section.

BASS LAKE RV CAMPGROUND **Ratings: 6/8.5★/7.5** (Campground) 54 Avail: 43 full hkups, 11 W, 11 E (30/50 amps). 2021 rates: $42.50. (843)774-9100, 1149 Bass Lake Place, Dillon, SC 29536

CAMP PEDRO CAMPGROUND
Ratings: 9.5/8.5★/9.5 (RV Park) From Jct of I-95 (Exit 1A in NC) & US-301, 0.1 mi on US 301 (L). **FAC:** paved rds. Avail: 92 paved, 51 pull-thrus, (40x100), back-ins (40x40), 92 full hkups (30/50 amps), WiFi @ sites, rentals, dump, laundry, groc, LP gas, restaurant, controlled access. **REC:** heated pool, wading pool, playground, rec open to public. Pets OK. No tents. Big rig sites. 2021 rates: $38.15 to $49.05, Military discount. ATM.
(843)774-2411 Lat: 34.49757, Lon: -79.30655
3346 Hwy 301N, Hamer, SC 29547
www.sobpedro.com
See ad pages 801, 809

LITTLE PEE DEE (Public State Park) From Jct of I-95 & SC-34 (Exit 190): Go 3-1/4 mi E on SC-34, then 8-1/4 mi S on SC-57, then 2 mi N on State Park Rd (R). 32 Avail: 32 W, 32 E (30 amps). 2021 rates: $16 to $20. (843)774-8872

Things to See and Do

SOUTH OF THE BORDER Tourist complex with variety of restaurants, shops, arcades & hotel/motel convention center. Also features mini-golf, MX Training area & Observation Tower. Partial handicap access. RV accessible. Restrooms. Food. Hours: 9am to 9pm. ATM.
(843)774-2411 Lat: 34.49757, Lon: -79.30655
3346 Highway 301 North, Hamer, SC 29547
www.thesouthoftheborder.com
See ad pages 801, 809

EDISTO ISLAND — E4 *Colleton*

EDISTO BEACH (Public State Park) From Jct of Hwy 17 & SC-174: Go 21-1/2 mi S on SR-174 (L). 112 Avail: 112 W, 112 E (30/50 amps). 2021 rates: $21 to $55. (843)869-2756

EUTAWVILLE — C4 *Orangeburg*

ROCKS POND CAMPGROUND & MARINA **Ratings: 6/5.5/8** (Campground) Avail: 71 full hkups (30/50 amps). 2021 rates: $35 to $40. (803)492-7711, 108 Campground Rd, Eutawville, SC 29048

FAIR PLAY — B1 *Oconee*

CAROLINA LANDING RV RESORT
Ratings: 8.5/8/8.5 (Membership Park) 122 Avail: 61 full hkups, 61 W, 61 E (30/50 amps). 2021 rates: $49. (888)563-7040, 120 Carolina Landing Drive, Fair Play, SC 29643

LAKE HARTWELL (Public State Park) From Jct of I-85 & SC-11 (exit 1), N 0.7 mi on SC-11 (L). 115 Avail: 115 W, 115 E (30 amps). 2021 rates: $26 to $30. (864)972-3352

FLORENCE — B5 *Florence*

FLORENCE RV PARK **Ratings: 8/8.5★/9** (Campground) 60 Avail: 51 full hkups, 9 W, 9 E (30/50 amps). 2021 rates: $53.76. (843)665-7007, 1115 E Campground Rd, Florence, SC 29506

SWAMPFOX CAMPGROUND **Ratings: 6/8/7** (Campground) 29 Avail: 26 full hkups, 3 W, 3 E (30/50 amps). 2021 rates: $54. (843)665-9430, 1600 Gateway Road, Florence, SC 29501

FORT MILL — A3 *York*

CHARLOTTE/FORT MILL KOA **Ratings: 8.5/10★/6.5** (Campground) 85 Avail: 80 full hkups, 5 W, 5 E (30/50 amps). 2021 rates: $53.99 to $105. (803)547-5416, 940 Gold Hill Rd, Fort Mill, SC 29708

CROWN COVE RV PARK **Ratings: 7/9★/8.5** (RV Park) Avail: 20 full hkups (30/50 amps). 2021 rates: $53 to $80. (803)547-3500, 8332 Regent Pkwy, Fort Mill, SC 29715

GAFFNEY — A3 *Cherokee*

SPARTANBURG NORTHEAST/GAFFNEY KOA **Ratings: 8.5/9.5★/9** (Campground) 105 Avail: 99 full hkups, 6 W, 6 E (30/50 amps). 2021 rates: $39.50 to $65. (800)562-0362, 160 Sarratt School Rd, Gaffney, SC 29341

GREENVILLE — A2 *Greenville*

A SPOTLIGHT Introducing Upcountry's colorful attractions appearing at the front of this state section.

GREENVILLE See also Cleveland, Greer, Roebuck & Spartanburg, SC; Saluda, NC.

PARIS MOUNTAIN (Public State Park) From the Jct of US 276 & SC 253/SC 291 (State Park Rd): Go 1/4 mi E on SC 291, then 2-1/2 mi NE on SC 253, then 1/2 mi N on S23-334 (L). 26 Avail: 26 W, 26 E (30 amps). 2021 rates: $25 to $28. (864)244-5565

SPRINGWOOD RV PARK
Ratings: 7.5/9.5★/8.5 (RV Park) From the Jct of I-85 (Exit 44) & US-25/White Horse Rd: Go 2 3/4 mi S on White Horse Rd, then 1/2 mi S on Donaldson Rd (R). **FAC:** paved rds. (158 spaces). Avail: 30 gravel, patios, 8 pull-thrus, (30x65), back-ins (30x45), 30 full hkups (30/50 amps), seasonal sites, WiFi @ sites, laundry. **REC:** boating nearby. Pet restrict (B/Q). No tents. Big rig sites. 2021 rates: $48, Military discount.
(864)277-9789 Lat: 34.76017, Lon: -82.38466
810 Donaldson Rd, Greenville, SC 29605
springwoodrvpark.com
See ad page 811

GREENWOOD — B2 *Abbeville*

LAKE GREENWOOD (Public State Park) From Jct of SC-246 & SC-34: Go 3-1/2 mi E on SC-34, then 1-3/4 mi N on Island Ford Rd (E); or From Jct of SC-246 & SC-702: Go 5 S on SC-702 (L). 125 Avail: 125 W, 125 E (50 amps). 2021 rates: $23 to $24. (864)543-3535

GREER — A2 *Greenville*

GSP RV PARK **Ratings: 6.5/NA/9** (RV Park) Avail: 37 full hkups (30/50 amps). 2021 rates: $50. (864)655-4399, 894 Robinson Rd, Greer, SC 29651

HARDEEVILLE — E3 *Jasper*

CAMP LAKE JASPER RV RESORT
Ratings: 9.5/10★/10 (RV Park) From jct of I-95 (exit 8) and Hwy 278: Go E 1/4 mi on Hwy 278, then 1 mi N on Medical Center Drive, then 1 mi E on Red Dam Rd (R).

GATEWAY TO HILTON HEAD ISLAND I-95
Located off I-95-Exit 8. Lakeside sites, big rig pull-thrus, full amenities: high speed Wi-Fi, laundry, pool, store, dog park. Minutes from Hilton Head Island, historic Beaufort & Savannah. Hike, Paddle, Play, Tour, Relax!

FAC: paved rds. (103 spaces). 53 Avail: 35 all weather, 18 gravel, patios, 24 pull-thrus, (38x85), back-ins (38x90), 53 full hkups (30/50 amps), seasonal sites, cable, WiFi @ sites, laundry, LP bottles, fire rings, firewood, controlled access. **REC:** heated pool, Lake Jasper: fishing, kayaking/canoeing, boating nearby, hunting nearby. Pet restrict (Q). Partial handicap access. No tents. Big rig sites, eco-friendly. 2021 rates: $55 to $65, Military discount.
(843)784-5200 Lat: 32.322997, Lon: -81.038788
44 Camp Lake Drive, Hardeeville, SC 29927
www.camplakejasper.com
See ad page 806

HILTON HEAD ISLAND — E4 *Beaufort*

A SPOTLIGHT Introducing Hilton Head Island's colorful attractions appearing at the front of this state section.

HILTON HEAD ISLAND See also Beaufort & Hardeeville, SC; Rincon, Savannah & Tybee Island, GA.

CAMP LAKE JASPER RV RESORT
Ratings: 9.5/10★/10 (RV Resort) From jct Bus 278 & US Hwy-78: Go 21 mi W on US Hwy-278, then 1/8 mi NE on John Smith Rd, then 1/2 mi N on Brickyard Rd, then 1 mi NE on Red Dam Rd, then 50 feet NW on Camp Lake Dr (L). **FAC:** paved rds. (103 spaces). 53 Avail: 35 all weather, 18 gravel, 24 pull-thrus, (38x85), back-ins (38x90), 53 full hkups (30/50 amps), seasonal sites, cable, WiFi @ sites, laundry, LP bottles, fire rings, firewood, controlled access. **REC:** heated pool, Lake Jasper: fishing, kayaking/canoeing, boating nearby, hunting nearby. Pet restrict (Q). No tents. Big rig sites. 2021 rates: $55 to $65, Military discount.
(843)784-5200 Lat: 32.322997, Lon: -81.038788
44 Camp Lake Drive, Hardeeville, SC 29927
www.camplakejasper.com
See primary listing at Hardeeville and ad page 806

HILTON HEAD HARBOR RV RESORT & MARINA
Ratings: 10/10★/10 (Condo Park) Avail: 200 full hkups (30/50 amps). 2021 rates: $79 to $149. (843)681-3256, 43A Jenkins Island Rd, Hilton Head Island, SC 29926

HILTON HEAD ISLAND MOTORCOACH RESORT **Ratings: 10/10★/10** (Condo Park) Avail: 250 full hkups (30/50 amps). 2021 rates: $90 to $140. (800)722-2365, 133 Arrow Rd, Hilton Head Island, SC 29928

HOLLYWOOD — D4 *Charleston*

LAKE AIRE RV PARK & CAMPGROUND
Ratings: 8.5/9★/9.5 (Campground) From W Jct of I-526 & US-17: Go 7-1/2 mi S on US-17S, then 1/4 mi SW on SC-162 (L). **FAC:** gravel rds. (92 spaces). Avail: 61 gravel, 43 pull-thrus, (30x75), back-ins (30x60), 35 full hkups, 26 W, 26 E (30/50 amps), seasonal sites, WiFi @ sites, tent sites, dump, laundry, LP gas, fire rings, firewood. **REC:** pool, Lake Rantowles: fishing, kayaking/canoeing, boating nearby, playground, hunting nearby. Pet restrict (Q). Partial handicap access. Big rig sites, eco-friendly. 2021 rates: $47 to $55, Military discount.
(843)571-1271 Lat: 32.77822, Lon: -80.14984
4375 Hwy 162, Hollywood, SC 29449
www.lakeairerv.com
See ad page 805

KINARDS — B3 *Newberry*

NEWBERRY SC/I-26 KOA **Ratings: 9/9.5★/9** (RV Park) 43 Avail: 34 full hkups, 9 W, 9 E (30/50 amps). 2021 rates: $42 to $55. (864)697-1214, 567 Fairview Church Rd, Kinards, SC 29355

LADSON — D4 *Charleston*

CHARLESTON KOA **Ratings: 8.5/8.5★/8** (Campground) 140 Avail: 90 full hkups, 50 W, 50 E (30/50 amps). 2021 rates: $56 to $66. (800)562-5812, 9494 Hwy 78, Ladson, SC 29456

LANCASTER — A4 *Lancaster*

ANDREW JACKSON (Public State Park) From Jct of SC-9 & US 521 N: Go 8 mi N on US 521 (R). 25 Avail: 25 W, 25 E (20/30 amps). 2021 rates: $18 to $25. (803)285-3344

SC

LEXINGTON — C3 *Lexington*

A SPOTLIGHT Introducing The Midlands' colorful attractions appearing at the front of this state section.

BARNYARD RV PARK
Ratings: 8.5/10★/10 (RV Park) From Jct of I-26 & US-1 (Exit 111A), go 3 mi on US-1S (R); or From Jct of I-20 & US-1 (exit 58), E (N-bnd) 3 mi on US-1 (L) Note: behind Barnyard Flea Market. **FAC:** paved rds. (129 spaces). Avail: 27 gravel, patios, 27 pull-thrus, (30x85), 27 full hkups (30/50 amps), seasonal sites, cable, WiFi @ sites, dump, laundry, LP gas. **REC:** pond, playground. Pets OK. Partial handicap access. No tents. Big rig sites, eco-friendly. 2021 rates: $42.49, Military discount.
(803)957-1238 Lat: 33.97712, Lon: -81.15610
201 Oak Dr, Lexington, SC 29073
www.barnyardrvpark.com
See ad page 810

Keep one Guide at home, and one in your RV! To purchase additional copies, call 877-209-6655.

LEXINGTON (CONT)

EDMUND RV PARK
Ratings: 7/8★/7 (RV Park) From Jct I-20 & SC-6 (Exit 55), S 7.3 mi on SC-6 to SC-302, SW 0.2 mi (R). **FAC:** paved/dirt rds. (125 spaces). Avail: 65 grass, 65 pull-thrus, (30x60), 65 full hkups (30/50 amps), seasonal sites, WiFi @ sites, laundry. Pet restrict (B). No tents, eco-friendly. 2021 rates: $30, Military discount. no cc.
(803)955-4010 Lat: 33.85839, Lon: -81.20519
5920 Edmund Hwy, Lexington, SC 29073
See ad previous page

Things to See and Do

THE BARNYARD FLEA MARKETS Flea Market with over 500 vendors, everything under cover, restaurant, church service, candy store and hair salon. Adjacent to Barnyard RV Park. Partial handicap access. RV accessible. Restrooms. Food. Hours: Sat 7am to 4:30pm; Sun 8am to 4:30pm. ATM. No CC.
(803)957-6570 Lat: 33.97712, Lon: -81.15610
4414 Augusta Rd, Lexington, SC 29073
www.barnyardfleamarkets.com
See ad page 810

LIBERTY HILL — B4 *Kershaw*

WATEREE LAKE RV PARK AND MARINA
Ratings: 8.5/8.5★/8.5 (RV Park) 30 Avail: 24 full hkups, 6 W, 6 E (30/50 amps). 2021 rates: $40 to $45. (803)273-3013, 2367 Dolan Lane, Liberty Hill, SC 29074

LONGS — C6 *Horry*

WILLOWTREE RV RESORT & CAMPGROUND
Ratings: 10/10★/10 (RV Park) From Jct of SC-9 & SC-905: Go 1-3/4 mi N on SC-905, then 1-1/2 mi N on Old Buck Creek Rd (R).

MYRTLE BEACH'S HIDDEN JEWEL
Fully paved sites with SPACIOUS lawns, patios, fire rings, charcoal grills & picnic tables. Full amenities. Lakefront cottages with a picturesque lake view! Near the Grand Strand. Minutes to the beach, miles from the masses.

FAC: paved rds. (106 spaces). Avail: 88 paved, patios, 65 pull-thrus, (50x100), back-ins (50x80), 88 full hkups (30/50 amps), seasonal sites, WiFi @ sites, rentals, dump, laundry, LP gas, fire rings, firewood, controlled access. **REC:** heated pool, wading pool, hot tub, Lake Willowtree: swim, fishing, kayaking/canoeing, boating nearby, shuffleboard, playground, hunting nearby. Pet restrict (B). Partial handicap access. No tents. Big rig sites, eco-friendly. 2021 rates: $58 to $81.
(866)207-2267 Lat: 33.97509, Lon: -78.71985
520 Southern Sights Drive, Longs, SC 29568
willowtreervr.com
See ad pages 801, 807

MCCORMICK — C2 *McCormick*

BAKER CREEK (Public State Park) From Jct of SC-28 & US 378: Go 3-1/2 mi SW on US 378, then 1 mi N on park access rd (L). 50 Avail: 50 W, 50 E (30 amps). 2021 rates: $18. Mar 01 to Sep 30. (864)443-2457

HAMILTON BRANCH (Public State Park) From jct US SC-23 & US-221/SC-28: Go 1-1/2 mi N on US 221/SC-28 (L) Note: 40' RV length limit. 173 Avail: 173 W, 173 E (30/50 amps). 2021 rates: $21 to $27. (864)333-2223

HICKORY KNOB STATE RESORT PARK (Public State Park) From Jct of SC-28 & US 378: Go 5-3/4 mi SW on US 378, then 1-1/2 mi N on Hwy 7 (L). 44 Avail: 44 W, 44 E (30 amps). 2021 rates: $18 to $25. (800)491-1764

J. STROM THURMOND LAKE - COE/HAWE CREEK (Public Corps) From Jct of US-221 & US-378: Go 6 mi SW on US-378, then 4 mi S on Park Rd (E). Avail: 34 E (30/50 amps). 2021 rates: $24 to $26. Apr 01 to Sep 30. (864)333-1147

MOUNT PLEASANT — D4 *Charleston*

MT PLEASANT/CHARLESTON KOA **Ratings: 9/9★/9** (Campground) 94 Avail: 79 full hkups, 15 W, 15 E (30/50 amps). 2021 rates: $69 to $150. (843)849-5177, 3157 Hwy 17 N, Mount Pleasant, SC 29466

MURRELLS INLET — C5 *Georgetown*

HUNTINGTON BEACH (Public State Park) From Jct of SC-707 & US 17: Go 4 mi SW on US 17 (L). 131 Avail: 24 full hkups, 107 W, 107 E (30 amps). 2021 rates: $21 to $62. (843)237-4440

MYRTLE BEACH — C5 *Horry*

A SPOTLIGHT Introducing Myrtle Beach's colorful attractions appearing at the front of this state section.

APACHE FAMILY CAMPGROUND & PIER
Ratings: 9/9.5★/9 (Campground) From Jct of US-501 & SC 22: Go 28 mi E on SC 22, then 1-3/4 mi S on Kings Rd (L).

THE PIER -- OCEANFRONT CAMPGROUND
Hosting families on the Grand Strand for over 40 years. Full amenities, store, restaurant/lounge, planned activities, live entertainment & the Apache Pier; the East Coast's longest wooden fishing pier, open 365 days a year.

FAC: paved/gravel rds. (994 spaces). Avail: 227 grass, 31 pull-thrus, (30x60), back-ins (31x45), 227 full hkups (30/50 amps), cable, WiFi @ sites, tent sites, rentals, dump, laundry, groc, LP gas, firewood, restaurant, controlled access. **REC:** pool, wading pool, Atlantic Ocean: swim, fishing, kayaking/canoeing, boating nearby, playground. Pets OK. Partial handicap access. Big rig sites, eco-friendly. 2021 rates: $42 to $84, Military discount. ATM.
(800)553-1749 Lat: 33.76320, Lon: -78.78140
9700 Kings Rd, Myrtle Beach, SC 29572
www.apachefamilycampground.com
See ad page 808

BRIARCLIFFE RV RESORT
Ratings: 10/9.5★/9.5 (RV Resort) Avail: 161 full hkups (30/50 amps). 2021 rates: $50 to $70. (843)272-2730, 10495 N Kings Hwy, Myrtle Beach, SC 29572

HIDEAWAY RV RESORT **Ratings: 9/9.5★/9** (RV Resort) Avail: 101 full hkups (30/50 amps). 2021 rates: $70 to $95. (843)444-2119, 5790 Dick Pond Rd, Myrtle Beach, SC 29588

LAKEWOOD CAMPING RESORT
Ratings: 9.5/9★/9.5 (Campground) From Jct of US-501 & SC 544: Go 14-1/2 mi SE to Bus US-17, then 1/2 mi NE on Bus US-17 (R). **FAC:** paved rds. (2000 spaces). 1055 Avail: 40 paved, 1015 grass, patios, 40 pull-thrus, (30x60), back-ins (30x55), 1025 full hkups, 30 W, 30 E (30/50 amps), cable, WiFi @ sites, tent sites, rentals, dump, laundry, groc, LP gas, firewood, restaurant, controlled access. **REC:** heated pool, wading pool, hot tub, Atlantic Ocean: swim, fishing, kayaking/canoeing, boating nearby, shuffleboard, playground. Pet restrict (B/Q). Partial handicap access. Big rig sites, eco-friendly. 2021 rates: $33 to $102. ATM.
(877)525-3966 Lat: 33.63380, Lon: -78.95564
5901 S Kings Hwy, Myrtle Beach, SC 29575
www.lakewoodcampingresort.com
See ad pages 801, 807

MYRTLE BEACH (Public State Park) From Jct of US 501 & Bus US 17-S: Go 4-1/4 mi S on Bus US 17-S (L). 300 Avail: 66 full hkups, 234 W, 234 E (30/50 amps). 2021 rates: $21 to $52. (843)238-5325

MYRTLE BEACH KOA
Ratings: 9.5/8.5/9 (Campground) From jct of US-501 & US-17: Go 1 mi E on US-50, then 1 mi SE on 3rd Ave S, then 1/4 mi S on Bus US-17/Kings Hwy to 5th Ave S, then 1/4 mi NW (L).

IN THE HEART OF MYRTLE BEACH
Enjoy fun activities including splash pad, big bouncer, pet park, outdoor cinema & more. RV, cabin, tent sites or deluxe cabins with all the comforts of home. Hop on our beach shuttle or take a short stroll to the oceanfront.

FAC: paved rds. (420 spaces). 353 Avail: 120 gravel, 90 grass, 143 dirt, 71 pull-thrus, (24x60), back-ins (24x56), 272 full hkups, 81 W, 81 E (30/50 amps), seasonal sites, cable, WiFi @ sites, tent sites, rentals, dump, laundry, groc, LP gas, fire rings, firewood, restaurant, controlled access. **REC:** heated pool, wading pool, pond, fishing, playground. Pets OK $. Partial handicap access, eco-friendly. 2021 rates: $52 to $170, Military discount. ATM.
(800)562-7790 Lat: 33.68416, Lon: -78.89663
613 5th Ave S, Myrtle Beach, SC 29577
www.myrtlebeachkoa.com
See ad pages 801, 807

MYRTLE BEACH TRAVEL PARK
Ratings: 9/10★/10 (Campground) From Jct of US-501 & SC 22: Go 28 mi E on SC 22, then 3/4 mi S on Kings Rd (L).

ENJOY OCEANFRONT CAMPING
Choose from beach sites or shaded sites all with easy access to the beautiful Atlantic Ocean. Modern facilities include store, restaurant, game room, 10* bath houses, rentals & more plus a variety of activities for ALL ages.

FAC: paved/gravel rds. (1188 spaces). 700 Avail: 410 grass, 290 dirt, 535 pull-thrus, (30x55), back-ins (30x45), 695 full hkups, 5 W, 5 E (30/50 amps), seasonal sites, cable, WiFi @ sites, tent sites, rentals, dump, laundry, groc, LP gas, firewood, restaurant, controlled access. **REC:** heated pool, wading pool, Atlantic Ocean: swim, fishing, kayaking/canoeing, boating nearby, playground. Pets OK. Partial handicap access, eco-friendly. 2021 rates: $47 to $92, Military discount. ATM.
(800)255-3568 Lat: 33.77719, Lon: -78.77321
10108 Kings Rd, Myrtle Beach, SC 29572
myrtlebeachtravelpark.com
See ad pages 801, 807

NMB RV RESORT AND DRY DOCK MARINA
Ratings: 10/10★/10 (RV Resort) From jct of SC90 & Robert Edge Pkwy: Go 1/2 mi E on SC90, then 1/4 mi SW on Sandridge Rd, then 1/4 mi S on Old Crane Road (E).

LUXURY. RV RESORT. DRY DOCK.
Looking for a One of a Kind Resort with Something for All? Supersized Paved Sites, 38 Wet Slips, Boat & Jet Ski Rentals, Pool/Water-slide & Tiki Bar. Greater Grand Strand's Newest Luxury EVERYTHING! More Sites Coming Soon!

FAC: paved rds. Avail: 242 paved, patios, 16 pull-thrus, (50x75), back-ins (50x65), 235 full hkups, 7 W, 7 E (30/50 amps), cable, WiFi @ sites, tent sites, dump, laundry, fire rings, firewood, restaurant, controlled access. **REC:** pool, hot tub, Intracoastal Waterway: swim, fishing, marina, kayaking/canoeing, boating nearby, playground. Pet restrict (B). Partial handicap access. Big rig sites, eco-friendly. 2021 rates: $48 to $105. ATM.
(844)777-5727 Lat: 33.849774, Lon: -78.669705
260 Old Crane Road, Little River, SC 29566
www.nmbrvresort.com
See ad pages 801, 807

OCEAN LAKES FAMILY CAMPGROUND
Ratings: 10/10★/10 (Campground) From Jct of US-31 & SC-544: Go 6-1/2 mi E on SC-544 to Ocean Lake Dr (E).

RANKED IN THE TOP 1% OF 8,000 PARKS
Our oceanfront camping resort features outstanding amenities, activities and customer service. Rent or camp: all pull-thru, concrete pads, inclusive rates - people, pets, full hook-ups, Wi-Fi. ARVC's 6 Time Park of the Year.

FAC: paved rds. (3430 spaces). 859 Avail: 665 paved, 194 all weather, patios, 859 pull-thrus, (35x55), 859 full hkups (30/50 amps), cable, WiFi @ sites, tent sites, rentals, laundry, groc, LP gas, restaurant, controlled access. **REC:** heated pool, wading pool, Atlantic Ocean: swim, fishing, kayaking/canoeing, boating nearby, shuffleboard, playground. Pet restrict (B). Partial handicap access. Big rig sites, eco-friendly. 2021 rates: $40 to $102. ATM.
(800)341-6659 Lat: 33.62819, Lon: -78.96142
6001 S Kings Hwy, Myrtle Beach, SC 29575
www.oceanlakes.com
See ad pages 801, 807

PIRATELAND FAMILY CAMPING RESORT
Ratings: 9.5/10★/9.5 (Campground) From Jct of US-501 & SC 544: Go 13-1/2 mi SE to Bus US-17, then 1-1/4 mi NE on Bus US-17 (R).

OCEANFRONT, PLUS 510' LAZY RIVER
The absolute best in oceanfront camping; we have it all! Arrr Mateys, enjoy our waterpark, lazy river, pools, splash pad, paddle boat, kayaks, golf cart rentals, arcade, snack bar, mini golf, camp store, laundry, wifi & more.

FAC: paved rds. (1408 spaces). 758 Avail: 85 paved, 573 grass, 100 dirt, patios, 48 pull-thrus, (24x60), back-ins (25x50), 758 full hkups (30/50 amps), cable, WiFi @ sites, tent sites, rentals, laundry, groc, LP gas, controlled access. **REC:** heated pool, wading pool, hot tub, Atlantic Ocean: swim, fishing, kayaking/canoeing, boating nearby, playground. Pets OK. Partial handicap access. Big rig sites, eco-friendly. 2021 rates: $37 to $110. ATM.
(800)443-2267 Lat: 33.64136, Lon: -78.94659
5401 S Kings Hwy, Myrtle Beach, SC 29575
www.pirateland.com
See ad pages 801, 807

WILLOWTREE RV RESORT & CAMPGROUND
Ratings: 10/10★/10 (RV Park) From jct of SC-22W & SC-31N: Go 7-1/2 mi N on SC-31N, then 5-3/4 mi N on SC-9N, then 1-3/4 mi N on SC-905, then 1-1/2 mi N on Old Buck Creek Rd (R). **FAC:** paved rds. (106 spaces). Avail: 88 paved, patios, 65 pull-thrus, (50x100), back-ins (50x80), 88 full hkups (30/50 amps), seasonal sites, WiFi @ sites, rentals, dump, laundry, LP gas, fire rings, firewood, controlled access. **REC:** heated pool, wading pool, hot tub, Lake Willowtree: swim, fishing, kayaking/canoeing, boating nearby, shuffleboard, playground,

hunting nearby. Pet restrict (B). Partial handicap access. No tents. Big rig sites, eco-friendly. 2021 rates: $58 to $81.
(866)207-2267 Lat: 33.97505, Lon: -78.71937
520 Southern Sights Drive, Longs, SC 29568
willowtreervr.com
See primary listing at Longs and ad pages 801, 807

Travel Services

CAMPING WORLD OF MYRTLE BEACH As the nation's largest retailer of RV supplies, accessories, services and new and used RVs, Camping World is committed to making your total RV experience better. **SERVICES:** RV, tire, RV appliance, MH mechanical, sells outdoor gear, restrooms. RV Sales. RV supplies, LP gas, emergency parking, RV accessible. Hours: 9am to 7pm.
(877)304-7880 Lat: 33.643865, Lon: -78.972576
2295 Dick Pond Road (Hwy 544), Myrtle Beach, SC 29575
www.campingworld.com

Things to See and Do

MYRTLE BEACH CAMPGROUNDS Association of seven Myrtle Beach Campgrounds which promotes tourism in the area. Hours: . No CC. **(843)916-2013**
3023 Church St, Myrtle Beach, SC 29577
www.campmyrtlebeach.com
See ad pages 801, 807

NORTH CHARLESTON — D4 *Charleston*

Travel Services

CAMPING WORLD OF CHARLESTON As the nation's largest retailer of RV supplies, accessories, services and new and used RVs, Camping World is committed to making your total RV experience better. **SERVICES:** RV, tire, MH mechanical, staffed RV wash, restrooms. RV Sales. RV supplies, LP gas, dump, emergency parking, RV accessible. Hours: 9am to 7pm.
(888)586-5446 Lat: 32.95618, Lon: -80.042877
8155 Rivers Ave, North Charleston, SC 29406
www.campingworld.com

NORTH MYRTLE BEACH — C6 *Horry*

BAREFOOT RV RESORT
good sam park **Ratings: 10/10★/8.5** (RV Park) Avail: 51 full hkups (30/50 amps). 2021 rates: $50 to $77. (843)663-4000, 920 37th Ave S, North Myrtle Beach, SC 29582

PENDLETON — B2 *Anderson*

CLEMSON RV PARK AT THE GROVE
good sam park **Ratings: 8.5/9.5★/8.5** (RV Park) Avail: 243 full hkups (30/50 amps). 2021 rates: $39 to $59. (864)228-2858, 150 Dalton Dr, Pendleton, SC 29670

PICKENS — A2 *Pickens*

KEOWEE-TOXAWAY (Public State Park) From Jct of SC-183 & US 178: Go 9 mi N on US 178, then 8-1/2 mi SW on SC-11 (R). 10 Avail: 10 W, 10 E (30 amps). 2021 rates: $16 to $18. (864)868-2605

TABLE ROCK (Public State Park) From Jct of SC-183 & US 178: Go 9 mi N on US 178, then 4 mi E on SC-11, then 1 mi N on park entrance rd (R). 94 Avail: 94 W, 94 E (30 amps). 2021 rates: $25. (864)878-9813

PINEVILLE — C4 *Berkeley*

ANGELS LANDING FAMILY CAMPGROUND **Ratings: 8/8★/8.5** (RV Park) Avail: 26 full hkups (30/50 amps). 2021 rates: $44.50 to $49.50. (843)351-4274, 1556 Viper Rd, Pineville, SC 29468

PLUM BRANCH — C2 *McCormick*

LAKE THURMOND RV PARK
good sam park **Ratings: 7.5/9★/9** (RV Park) Avail: 35 full hkups (30/50 amps). 2021 rates: $35 to $40. (864)484-6365, 678 Fishing Village Rd, Plum Branch, SC 29845

RIDGELAND — E3 *Jasper*

Travel Services

GANDER RV OF RIDGELAND Your new hometown outfitter offering the best regional gear for all your outdoor needs. Your adventure awaits. **SERVICES:** RV appliance, MH mechanical, sells outdoor gear, restrooms. RV Sales. RV supplies, LP gas, RV accessible, waiting room. Hours: 9am - 6pm.
(844)976-3787 Lat: 32.47379, Lon: -80.97207
401 Sycamore Dr, Ridgeland, SC 29936
rv.ganderoutdoors.com

ROCK HILL — A3 *York*

EBENEZER PARK
(Public) From Jct of I-77 (exit 82C) & SR-161: Go W (towards York) 0.8 mi on SC-161 to Mt Gallant Rd, NE 6 mi to Boatshore Rd, N 0.4 mi (E). **FAC:** paved/gravel rds. Avail: 66 gravel, 4 pull-thrus, (28x63), back-ins (30x50), 66 full hkups (30/50 amps), WiFi @ sites, tent sites, fire rings, firewood, controlled access. **REC:** Lake Wylie: swim, fishing, kayaking/canoeing, boating nearby, playground, rec open to public. Pets OK. Partial handicap access, 14 day max stay, eco-friendly. 2021 rates: $31.
(803)366-6620 Lat: 35.02205, Lon: -81.04297
4490 Boatshore Rd, Rock Hill, SC 29732
www.yorkcountygov.com/212/Ebenezer-Park
See ad page 676

ROEBUCK — A2 *Spartanburg*

PINE RIDGE CAMPGROUND **Ratings: 9/10★/9** (Campground) Avail: 30 full hkups (30/50 amps). 2021 rates: $44 to $116. (864)576-0302, 199 Pineridge Campground Rd, Roebuck, SC 29376

SANTEE — C4 *Clarendon*

SANTEE See also Eutawville, Pineville, St George & Summerton.

PALMETTO SHORES RV RESORT **Ratings: 8.5/9★/9.5** (RV Park) Avail: 63 full hkups (30/50 amps). 2021 rates: $60 to $88. (803)478-6336, 5215 Dingle Pond Rd, Summerton, SC 29148

SANTEE (Public State Park) From Jct of I-95 & SC-6 (Exit 98): Go 1-1/4 mi NW on SC-6, then 4-1/2 mi N on State Park Rd (R). 158 Avail: 158 W, 158 E (15/30 amps). 2021 rates: $16 to $40. (803)854-2408

SANTEE LAKES KOA **Ratings: 7.5/8.5★/8.5** (Campground) 120 Avail: 70 full hkups, 50 W, 50 E (30/50 amps). 2021 rates: $55 to $86. (803)478-2262, 1268 Gordon Rd, Summerton, SC 29148

SENECA — A1 *Oconee*

CROOKED CREEK RV PARK **Ratings: 9/9★/8.5** (RV Park) Avail: 97 full hkups (30/50 amps). 2021 rates: $33 to $57. (864)882-5040, 777 Arvee Ln, West Union, SC 29696

HIGH FALLS COUNTY PARK (Public) From town: Go 9-3/4 mi W on US-76, the 5 mi N on SR-183 (L). 91 Avail: 91 W, 91 E (20/30 amps). 2021 rates: $15 to $30. Mar 01 to Nov 01. (864)882-8234

SOUTH COVE (Public) From Jct of Hwy 123/76 & Hwy 28: Go 1-1/2 mi N on Hwy 28 (R). 88 Avail: 88 W, 88 E (20/30 amps). 2021 rates: $15 to $30. (864)882-5250

SPARTANBURG — A2 *Spartanburg*

SPARTANBURG See also Gaffney, Greenville, Greer & Roebuck.

CROFT STATE NATURAL AREA (Public State Park) From Jct of SC-295 & SC-56: Go 2-1/4 mi S on SC-56, then 1/4 mi E on Dairy Ridge Rd (R). 50 Avail: 50 W, 50 E (30/50 amps). 2021 rates: $14 to $24. (864)585-1283

SPARTANBURG/CUNNINGHAM RV PARK
good sam park **Ratings: 8.5/9.5★/9** (RV Park) From Jct of I-85 (exit 70) & I-26: Go NW 0.5 mi on I-26 (exit 17) to New Cut Rd, then W 1 mi on New Cut Rd, then SW 0.3 mi on Blackstock Rd, then W 0.5 mi on Campground Rd (R). **FAC:** gravel rds. (100 spaces). Avail: 50 gravel, 50 pull-thrus, (31x60), 50 full hkups (30/50 amps), seasonal sites, WiFi @ sites, tent sites, dump, laundry, LP gas, firewood. **REC:** pool, boating nearby, playground, rec open to public. Pets OK. Partial handicap access, eco-friendly. 2021 rates: $47, Military discount.
(864)576-1973 Lat: 34.98549, Lon: -82.04153
600 Campground Rd, Spartanburg, SC 29303
www.cunninghamrvpark.com
See ad page 811

Travel Services

CAMPING WORLD OF SPARTANBURG As the nation's largest retailer of RV supplies, accessories, services and new and used RVs, Camping World is committed to making your total RV experience better. **SERVICES:** RV, tire, RV appliance, MH mechanical, staffed RV wash, restrooms. RV Sales. RV supplies, LP gas, dump, emergency parking, RV accessible. Hours: 9am to 7pm.
(877)871-9365 Lat: 35.100786, Lon: -82.026699
114 Best Drive, Spartanburg, SC 29303
www.campingworld.com

ST GEORGE — D4 *Dorchester*

JOLLY ACRES RV PARK & STORAGE
good sam park **Ratings: 8/9★/9** (RV Park) From jct I-95 & Hwy 78 (exit 77): Go 5 mi E on Hwy 78, then 1/2 mi N on Horne Taylor Rd (L). **FAC:** all weather rds. 38 Avail: 9 paved, 29 gravel, 36 pull-thrus, (35x78), back-ins (30x60), 31 full hkups, 7 W, 7 E (30/50 amps), WiFi @ sites, dump, laundry, LP gas. **REC:** pond, fishing, boating nearby, playground, hunting nearby. Pet restrict (B). Partial handicap access. No tents. Big rig sites, eco-friendly. 2021 rates: $36 to $39, Military discount.
(843)563-8303 Lat: 33.17987, Lon: -80.51405
289 Horne Taylor Rd, St George, SC 29477
www.syrrrun.com
See ad page 804

STARR — B2 *Anderson*

BIG WATER MARINA AND RV PARK **Ratings: 7/8/7** (RV Park) 10 Avail: 10 W, 10 E (30/50 amps). 2021 rates: $35 to $50. (864)226-3339, 320 Big Water Rd, Starr, SC 29684

SUMMERTON — C4 *Clarendon*

TAW CAW CAMPGROUND & MARINA
good sam park **Ratings: 6.5/7/7** (Campground) 15 Avail: 2 full hkups, 13 W, 13 E (30/50 amps). 2021 rates: $47. (803)478-2171, 1328 Joyner Drive, Summerton, SC 29148

SUMMERVILLE — D4 *Dorchester*

GIVHANS FERRY (Public State Park) From jct I-26 & SC-27 (Exit 187): Go 9-1/2 mi S on SR-27, then 3 mi W on SR-61, then 1/4 mi N on Givhans Ferry Rd (L) Note: 40' RV length limit. 25 Avail: 6 full hkups, 7 W, 7 E (30 amps). 2021 rates: $14 to $21. (843)873-0692

SUMTER — C4 *Sumter*

MILITARY PARK FALCON'S NEST FAMCAMP (SHAW AFB) (Public) From jct I-95 & US-378 (exit 135): Go 25 mi W on US-378 to Shaw AFB truck gate, then left 0.75 mi on Patrol Rd, then follow signs (R). Avail: 30 full hkups (30/50 amps). 2021 rates: $20. (803)895-0450

SWANSEA — C3 *Lexington*

RIVER BOTTOM FARMS FAMILY CAMPGROUND
good sam park **Ratings: 9/9★/10** (Campground) S-bnd: From Jct of I-77 & US 321 S (Exit 71), S 15 mi on US 321 to SC3, SW 6.5 mi on SC-3 to SC-178, NW 0.5 mi on 178 to Cedar Creek Rd, W 0.7 mi (L); N-bnd: From Jct of US-321 & SC 178 (S of Swansea), W 6.3 mi on SC 178 to Cedar Creek Rd, W 0.7 mi (L). **FAC:** gravel rds. 62 Avail: 8 gravel, 54 grass, 24 pull-thrus, (33x63), back-ins (35x61), 52 full hkups, 10 W, 10 E (30/50 amps), WiFi @ sites, tent sites, rentals, dump, laundry, fire rings, firewood. **REC:** pool, Edisto River: fishing, boating nearby, playground. Pet restrict (B). Partial handicap access. Big rig sites, eco-friendly. 2021 rates: $38 to $45, Military discount.
(803)568-4182 Lat: 33.66797, Lon: -81.19844
357 Cedar Creek Rd, Swansea, SC 29160
www.riverbottomfarms.com
See ad page 810

SC

TOWNVILLE — B1 *Anderson*

HARTWELL LAKE - COE/CONEROSS PARK (Public Corps) From town: Go 2 mi NE on Hwy 24, then 1 mi N on Hwy 184, then 1 mi NE on Coneross Creek Rd (E). 105 Avail: 93 W, 93 E (50 amps). 2021 rates: $20. May 01 to Sep 29. (888)893-0678

HARTWELL LAKE - COE/OCONEE POINT (Public Corps) From town: Go 2 mi W on SR-24, then 3-1/2 mi N on CR-184, then 2-1/2 mi SE on CR-21 (L). 70 Avail: 70 W, 70 E (50 amps). 2021 rates: $28 to $56. May 01 to Sep 29. (888)893-0678

WALHALLA — A1 *Oconee*

DEVILS FORK (Public State Park) From Jct of SC-130 & SC-11: Go 1-1/2 mi E on SC-11, then 3-1/3 mi N on Jocassee Lake Rd (E). 59 Avail: 59 W, 59 E (30 amps). 2021 rates: $23 to $42. (864)944-2639

OCONEE (Public State Park) From Jct of SC-11 & SR-28: Go 9-3/4 mi NW on SC-28, then 2-1/2 mi NE on SC-107 (R). 140 Avail: 140 W, 140 E (20/30 amps). 2021 rates: $21 to $23. (864)638-5353

WALTERBORO — D4 *Colleton*

NEW GREEN ACRES RV PARK

good sam park **Ratings: 8/8★/8** (Campground) From jct of I-95 & SC-63 (exit 53): Go 1/4 mi W on SC-63, then 1/4 mi N on Campground Rd (R). **FAC:** gravel rds. (106 spaces). 86 Avail: 26 gravel, 60 grass, patios, 86 pull-thrus, (40x125), 45 full hkups, 41 W, 41 E (30/50 amps), seasonal sites, cable, WiFi @ sites, tent sites, dump, laundry, LP gas. **REC:** pool, playground, hunting nearby. Pet restrict (B). Big rig sites, eco-friendly. 2021 rates: $33 to $38, Military discount.
(800)474-3450 Lat: 32.88375, Lon: -80.71646
396 Campground Rd, Walterboro, SC 29488
www.newgreenacres.com
See ad page 804

WEDGEFIELD — C4 *Sumter*

POINSETT (Public State Park) From Jct of US 76/ US 378 & SC-261: Go 10-1/2 mi S on SC-261, then 1-1/2 mi W on S-43-63 (R). 24 Avail: 24 W, 24 E (30 amps). 2021 rates: $16 to $22. (803)494-8177

WESTMINSTER — B1 *Oconee*

CHAU RAM PARK (Public) From town: Go 2-1/2 mi W on US-76, then 1 mi S on Chau Ram Park Rd (L). 28 Avail: 28 W, 28 E (30/50 amps). 2021 rates: $25. Mar 01 to Nov 01. (877)685-2537

Had a great stay? Let us know by emailing us Parks@goodsam.com

WINNSBORO — B3 *Fairfield*

BROAD RIVER CAMPGROUND & RV PARK

good sam park **Ratings: 6.5/8★/8** (RV Park) From jct I-20 (Exit 68) & SC-215: Go 16 mi NW on SC-215 (L). **FAC:** gravel/dirt rds. (150 spaces). Avail: 15 gravel, 10 pull-thrus, (35x65), back-ins (35x50), 15 full hkups (30/50 amps), seasonal sites, WiFi @ sites, laundry, fire rings, firewood. **REC:** boating nearby, playground, hunting nearby. Pet restrict (Q). Partial handicap access. No tents. Big rig sites. 2021 rates: $44, Military discount.
(803)749-9100 Lat: 34.21812, Lon: -81.21391
16842 State Hwy 215 South, Winnsboro, SC 29180
broadrivercampground.com
See ad page 810

LAKE WATEREE (Public State Park) From Jct of I-77 & Rd 41 (exit 41), E 2.6 mi on Rd 41 to US-21, N 2.1 mi to River Rd 101, E 5.1 mi (L). Note: 40' RV length limit. 72 Avail: 72 W, 72 E (30 amps). 2021 rates: $17 to $22. (803)482-6401

How much will it all cost? Use this as a guide: Rates shown are the minimum and maximum for two adults in one RV at the time of inspection (excluding any additional fees for items not at the site). Remember, these rates serve as guidelines only. It's always best to call ahead for the most current rate information.

YEMASSEE — D3 *Hampton*

POINT SOUTH/YEMASSEE KOA JOURNEY **Ratings: 8.5/9★/8.5** (Campground) 58 Avail: 28 full hkups, 30 W, 30 E (30/50 amps). 2021 rates: $59 to $95. (843)726-5733, 14 Campground Rd, Yemassee, SC 29945

THE OAKS AT POINT SOUTH RV

good sam park **Ratings: 7/9★/7.5** (Campground) 77 Avail: 74 full hkups, 3 W, 3 E (30/50 amps). 2021 rates: $68.20 to $78. (888)563-7040, 1292 Campground Rd, Yemassee, SC 29945

YORK — A3 *York*

KINGS MOUNTAIN (Public State Park) From Jct of I-85 & Hwy 216 (Exit 2 in NC): Go 7 mi SE on NC/ SC 216 (L). 115 Avail: 115 W, 115 E (30 amps). 2021 rates: $17 to $19. (803)222-3209

CLEANING YOUR RV: When you're finished with the exterior cleaning, it's time for waxing. There are products that claim to wax and wash at the same time, while on the other end of the product list are paste waxes that require an electric buffing tool and lots of grunt work. Bottom line - the easier it is the least amount of time the coating will last. Put in the work and you will have a shiny vehicle much longer.

YOU ARE HERE

South Dakota

DID YOU KNOW?

Jewel Cave is the third-longest cave in the world with over 120 miles of passages surveyed.

Larger-than-life statutes loom over beautiful hills. Badlands cut harsh grooves into rugged landscapes. Spires of rock reach into the sky. In South Dakota, visitors can walk the landscapes revered by Native Americans.

Go Slow in Rapid City

The vibrant town of Rapid City near the Black Hills boasts cultural attractions along with outstanding dining. Explore vibrant murals along Art Alley, learn about the region's geography and people at the Journey Museum or stop for a local brew at Lost Cabin Beer Co. or Independent Ale House. Get ready to meet U.S. leaders in town. Known as the "City of Presidents," Rapid City's streets feature life-size bronze statues of former U.S. chief executives, from Washington to Obama. And of course, Mount Rushmore National Memorial is a perennial bucket list item for many travelers.

Formidable Warrior

Get the full story of South Dakota History. Crazy Horse Memorial celebrates the namesake leader who beat General Custer. The work-in-progress sculpture of the Lakota icon on horseback will eventually stand at 641 feet tall, making it the world's largest mountain sculpture. Peruse exhibits at the adjacent Indian Museum of North America; this repository of history offers profound insight into the history and culture of Native Americans.

Crawling and Creeping

On your way back to Rapid City, you might also want to pay a visit to Reptile Gardens, which nicely rounds out the trio of animal attractions in the immediate area. The star of the show here is the resident Komodo dragon, followed closely by a rare saltwater crocodile, but the enclosures feature a large selection of other snakes, birds and, of course, lizards in an exotic setting.

South Dakota Chislic

This funny-sounding dish packs some serious flavor. Brought to the Rushmore State by Crimean immigrants in the late 1800s, chislic consists of cubes of meat on a skewer roasted over a fire or barbecue grill. Sides of dipping sauces and crackers complete the experience. Order it at a South Dakota restaurant or hold your own chislic cookout. You can't go wrong with this South Dakota delight.

VISITOR CENTER

TIME ZONE
Mountain/Central Standard

ROAD & HIGHWAY INFORMATION
866-697-3511
sddot.com

FISHING & HUNTING INFORMATION
605-223-7660
gfp.sd.gov/hunt
gfp.sd.gov/fish

BOATING INFORMATION
605-223-7660
gfp.sd.gov/boating

NATIONAL PARKS
nps.gov/sd

STATE PARKS
gfp.sd.gov/parks

TOURISM INFORMATION
South Dakota Department of Tourism
800-732-5682
travelsd.com

TOP TOURISM ATTRACTIONS
1) Mount Rushmore National Memorial
2) Badlands National Park
3) Crazy Horse Memorial

MAJOR CITIES
Sioux Falls, Rapid City, Aberdeen, Brookings, Watertown, Pierre (capital)

SD

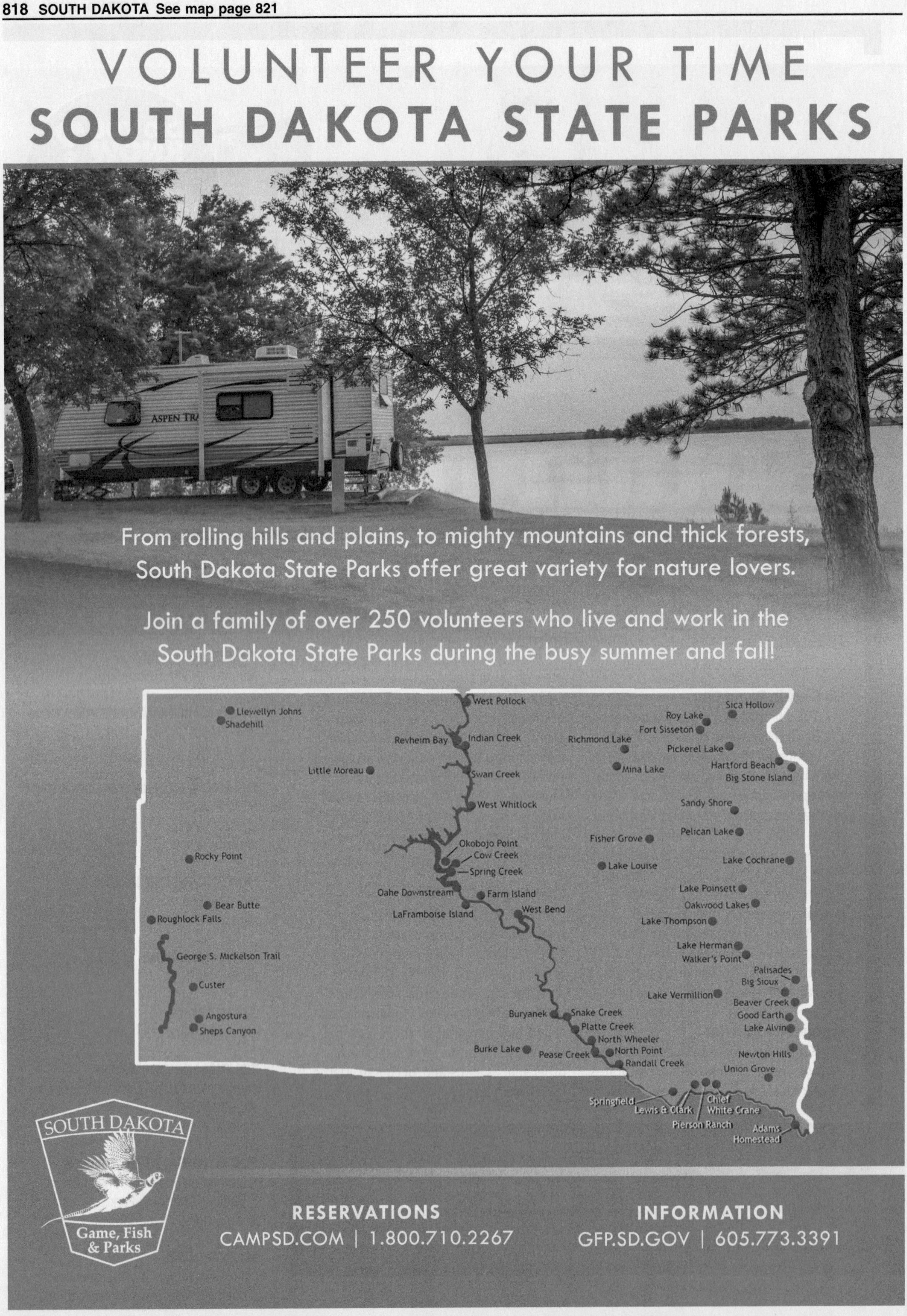
VOLUNTEER YOUR TIME
SOUTH DAKOTA STATE PARKS
ASPEN TR
From rolling hills and plains, to mighty mountains and thick forests, South Dakota State Parks offer great variety for nature lovers.
Join a family of over 250 volunteers who live and work in the South Dakota State Parks during the busy summer and fall!
Llewellyn Johns
Shadehill
West Pollock
Revheim Bay
Indian Creek
Little Moreau
Swan Creek
West Whitlock
Rocky Point
Okobojo Point
Cow Creek
Spring Creek
Oahe Downstream
Farm Island
LaFramboise Island
West Bend
Bear Butte
Roughlock Falls
George S. Mickelson Trail
Custer
Angostura
Sheps Canyon
Buryanek
Snake Creek
Platte Creek
North Wheeler
Burke Lake
Pease Creek
North Point
Randall Creek
Roy Lake
Sica Hollow
Fort Sisseton
Richmond Lake
Pickerel Lake
Mina Lake
Hartford Beach
Big Stone Island
Sandy Shore
Fisher Grove
Pelican Lake
Lake Louise
Lake Cochrane
Lake Poinsett
Oakwood Lakes
Lake Thompson
Lake Herman
Walker's Point
Palisades
Big Sioux
Lake Vermillion
Beaver Creek
Good Earth
Lake Alvin
Newton Hills
Union Grove
Springfield
Lewis & Clark
Chief White Crane
Pierson Ranch
Adams Homestead
SOUTH DAKOTA
Game, Fish & Parks
RESERVATIONS
CAMPSD.COM | 1.800.710.2267
INFORMATION
GFP.SD.GOV | 605.773.3391

In Mitchell, the Corn Palace is decorated annually with colorful murals made from corn, grain and grass.

Dinosaur Park

If you're looking for a taste of South Dakota's incredible prehistory, head to Dinosaur Park. The attraction has been free to the public since 1936. Set atop a scenic ridge, the park is home to sweeping vistas that stretch for upwards of 100 miles as well as a rich history of archeological discovery. Dinosaur statues loom over the landscape, adding a whimsical touch to the scenery. Dinosaur bones from the Late Jurassic and Early Cretaceous periods have been discovered here.

Pheasant Season

South Dakota ranks as one of the top pheasant hunting destination in the United States. With almost five million acres of varied terrain and plenty of private lodges, it's easy to bag these birds, along with waterfowl, turkey and more. Check the Welcome page for information about obtaining hunting licenses.

Going Deep

Take a break from the hustle and bustle by going underground. Sitting Bull Crystal Caverns, for its part, features anything but sweeping panoramic vistas. Here, visitors descend deep underground for guided tours of the world's largest natural displays of dogtooth spar crystal. Other highlights of the tour include a subterranean lake and underground domes known as the French Chandelier Room, Crystal Palace and Rainbow Arch.

Ride the Black Hills

Let someone else do the driving. The 1880 Train is another great way to see a vast swath of the Black Hills. Departing from Hill City, this sightseeing train tour is pulled by a vintage steam engine and covers a scenic 20-mile round-trip route. The 1880 Train departs from each town at various points throughout the day, so this can be a great way to pencil in a trip to the National Presidential Wax Museum, located just outside of nearby Keystone. The museum features life-sized wax figures of every President in American history.

The Mighty I-90

Starting your travels from the east? Along Interstate 90, South Dakota's largest city, Sioux Falls, is abounding with Midwestern friendliness and family fun. Stay active by exploring the miles of walking and biking trails that traverse the city. Head to Falls Park to check out the namesake waterfall, or visit the compelling SculptureWalk.

Magical Montrose

In nearby Montrose, the Porter Sculpture Park entertains and amuses, with massive outdoor artworks dotting the countryside. These quirky creations were made by sculptor Wayne Porter, a self-taught artist whose works attracts visitors from across the country. Porter's found-object structures tell compelling stories.

Great Times in the Badlands

Some of South Dakota's most stunning vistas are found in Badlands National Park near the state's southwest corner, where eerie, sandy pinnacles jut skyward above the surrounding grasslands. Take the Badlands Loop Road for a brief tour of this unique landscape. Better yet, take a hike: Several trails present different views.

Veggie Venue

Mitchell, in the southwest corner of the state, is nothing if not charming. Its quiet streets, mom-and-pop cafes and humbly-historic attractions are perfect for anyone seeking an escape from the hustle and bustle of big city life. The Corn Palace (built in 1892) sits at the center of the community, attracting some 500,000 tourists annually. Each year since its construction, the Palace's outer walls are redecorated in new massive murals made entirely from colored corn, grain and grass. The Palace hosts a full schedule of industry trade shows, banquets and state championship basketball tournaments.

good sam park Featured Good Sam Parks

SOUTH DAKOTA

When you stay with Good Sam, you can expect the highest degree of cleanliness and friendliness, and better yet, you get **10% off** overnight campground fees.

If you're not already a Good Sam member you can purchase your membership at one of these locations:

ABERDEEN
Wylie Park Campground & Storybook Land

CANTON
Gate City Events & Lodging

CHAMBERLAIN
Oasis Campground

CUSTER
Beaver Lake Campground
Buffalo Ridge Camp Resort
Fort Welikit Family Campground

DEADWOOD
Custer Crossing Campground
Fish'N Fry Campground & RV Park
Whistler Gulch Campground & RV Park

HILL CITY
Black Hills Trailside Park Resort
Firehouse Campground
Horse Thief Campground and Resort
Rafter J Bar Ranch Camping Resort

HOT SPRINGS
Sunrise Ridge Campground

INTERIOR
Badlands Motel & Campground

KEYSTONE
Rushmore View RV Park

MITCHELL
Betts Campground
Dakota Campground
R & R Campground & RV Park

MURDO
American Inn & RV Park

PRESHO
New Frontier Campground & RV Park

RAPID CITY
Happy Holiday RV Resort
Heartland RV Park & Cabins
Lake Park Campground & Cottages
Rapid City RV Park and Campground
Rapid City South RV Park
Rushmore Shadows Resort
Southern Hills RV Park & Campground

SIOUX FALLS
Red Barn RV Park
Sioux Falls Yogi Bear
Tower Campground

SPEARFISH
Chris' Camp & RV Park
Elkhorn Ridge RV Resort & Cabins

STURGIS
No Name City Luxury Cabins & RV Park
Sturgis RV Park
Suzie's Camp

SUMMIT
County Line RV Park & Campground

WALL
Sleepy Hollow Campground

10/10★/10 GOOD SAM PARKS

RAPID CITY
Heartland RV Park & Cabins
(605)255-5460

Rushmore Shadows Resort
(800)231-0425

What's This?

An RV park with a 10/10★/10 rating has scored perfect grades in amenities, cleanliness and appearance ("See Understanding the Campground Rating System" on pages 8 and 9 for an explanation of the trusted Good Sam Rating System). Stay in a 10/10★/10 park on your next trip for a nearly flawless camping experience.

Getty Images/iStockphoto

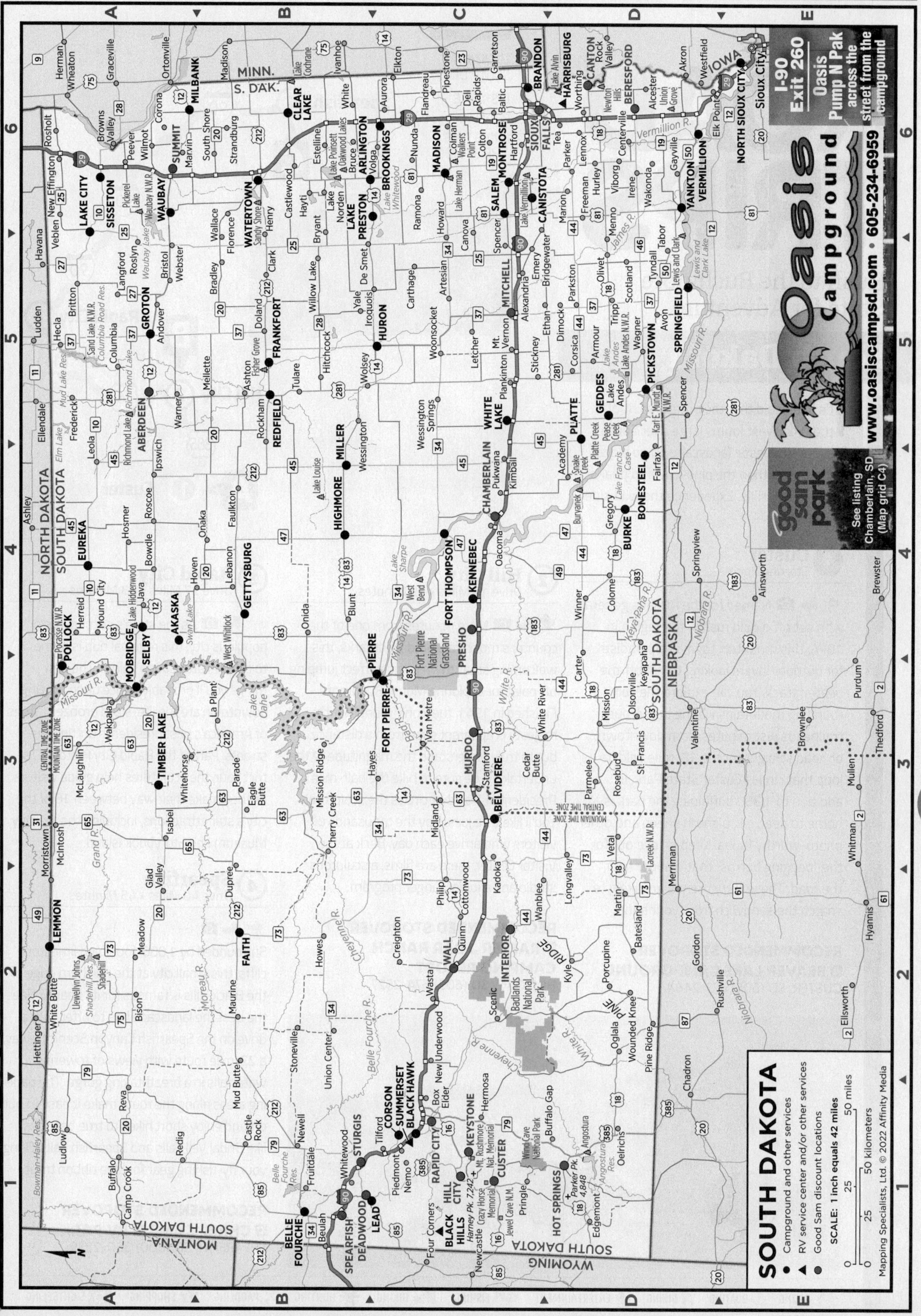
SOUTH DAKOTA
Campground and other services
RV service center and/or other services
Good Sam discount locations
SCALE: 1 inch equals 42 miles
0 25 50 miles
0 25 50 kilometers
Mapping Specialists, Ltd. © 2022 Affinity Media
good sam park
See listing Chamberlain, SD (Map grid C4)
Oasis Campground
605-234-6959
www.oasiscampsd.com
I-90 Exit 260
Oasis Pump N Pak across the street from the campground
NORTH DAKOTA
SOUTH DAKOTA
MINN.
S. DAK.
IOWA
NEBRASKA
WYOMING
MONTANA
CENTRAL TIME ZONE
MOUNTAIN TIME ZONE
LEMMON
MOBRIDGE
ABERDEEN
WATERTOWN
BROOKINGS
HURON
MITCHELL
SIOUX FALLS
PIERRE
FORT PIERRE
CHAMBERLAIN
RAPID CITY
STURGIS
SPEARFISH
DEADWOOD
LEAD
CUSTER
HOT SPRINGS
YANKTON
VERMILLION
NORTH SIOUX CITY
Sioux City
SD

ROAD TRIPS

Rush to the Rushmore State for Adventure

South Dakota

LOCATION
SOUTH DAKOTA

DISTANCE
89 MILES

DRIVE TIME
1 HR 37 MINS

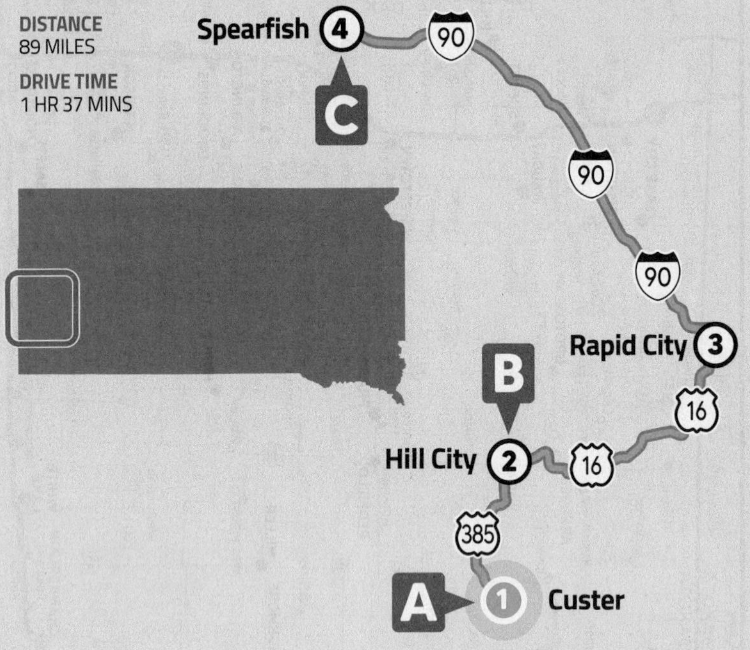

It's been said that the outlaw spirit of the Wild West looms large over South Dakota's majestic landscape. In no place is that truer than the pine-covered peaks of the Black Hills. Experience the wild side for yourself.

1 Custer
Starting Point

Named for the famous general who set off a gold rush in the region in 1874, this mountain town is a paradise for outdoor lovers looking to get off the beaten track. You can explore the surrounding mountains via the numerous trailheads just minutes from downtown, or head straight for the 18-mile wildlife loop that circles Custer State Park. In addition to 1,350 buffaloes, the park is home to deer, elk, bighorn sheep and other photo-worthy fauna. Keep an eye out for the "begging burros" that wander near the road. These furry friends are likely to snatch the sandwich from your hand.

RECOMMENDED STOPOVER
A BEAVER LAKE CAMPGROUND
CUSTER, SD (605) 673-2464

2 Hill City
Drive 14 Miles • 19 Minutes

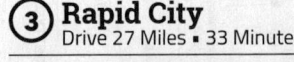

Mere minutes from one of the country's most treasured landmarks, this welcoming small town is the perfect jumping off point for exploring Mount Rushmore. Finished in 1941, the iconic monument's majesty is apparent even from a distance, but to truly understand the magnitude of the undertaking, be sure to hike the half-mile Presidential Trail that circles the sculpture. You'll likely be joined by the thousands of visitors who arrive each day. Back at the Visitor Center, there are films, a sculptor's studio and a junior ranger program.

RECOMMENDED STOPOVER
B RAFTER J BAR RANCH CAMPING RESORT
HILL CITY, SD (605) 574-2527

3 Rapid City
Drive 27 Miles • 33 Minutes

As the state's second-most populous city, this regional hub is home to cultural attractions galore. The first things you'll probably notice upon arriving downtown are the life-sized bronze statues of America's past presidents dotting the streets. Part of the Rapid City Historic District Tour, the sculptures help guide visitors as they make their way between 16 of the city's star attractions, including the Journey Museum and Storybook Island.

4 Spearfish
Drive 48 Miles • 45 Minutes

Surrounded by 1,000-foot-high limestone cliffs, this small city at the northern edge of the Black Hills is famous for its beauty. See the best the landscape has to offer with a drive on the Spearfish Canyon Scenic Byway, a 22-mile route with views of towering waterfalls in a breathtaking gorge. The parking areas along the route make it easy to pull off and enjoy short hikes to true beauties like Bridal Veil Falls and Spearfish Falls. Bring your fly-fishing gear for blue ribbon trout.

RECOMMENDED STOPOVER
C CHRIS' CAMP & RV PARK
SPEARFISH, SD (800) 350-2239

Getty Images/iStockphoto

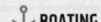

BIKING BOATING DINING ENTERTAINMENT FISHING HIKING HUNTING PADDLING SHOPPING SIGHTSEEING

South Dakota SPOTLIGHTS

High Rolling in the Rushmore State

South Dakota's Black Hills are the stuff of legend. But while many tourists make a beeline to Mount Rushmore, smart travelers know that equally spectacular treasures are found throughout the state, from the Badlands to the banks of the Missouri River.

NINE NATIVE AMERICAN TRIBES CALL SOUTH DAKOTA HOME.

Overlooking the Missouri River, the Dignity statue shimmers with the wind. Klemdy

Chamberlain/Oacoma

This Rushmore State destination perfectly blends fishing and hunting, antiques and scenic beauty. These twin towns, separated by the Mighty Missouri River, offer campers a peaceful haven with wandering wildlife, spectacular sunsets, galleries and showrooms, golfing, shopping and a towering sculpture to welcome you to the area. Travel like Lewis and Clark, who camped here in 1804, and call the place home for a few days or weeks.

Rugged Landscapes

Follow in the footsteps of the dynamic duo who helped blaze the trail for western settlement in the U.S. The Lewis and Clark Interpretive Center on Interstate 90, (at the Chamberlain rest area between exits 263 and 265) includes a replica of the 55-foot keelboat piloted by the explorers as they navigated the waterways across the continent during their famous journey, which lasted from 1803 to 1805. Visitors also will find interpretive panels that provide convenient history lessons.

Woman in the Wind

A statue named Dignity invariably catches the eyes of visitors. Built in 2016 to celebrate the state's centennial, this stainless steel, 50-foot statue of a Native American woman represents the courage and wisdom of the Lakota people. The statue has earned the nickname Colossus of Chamberlain, and her quilt is built with more than 100 blue diamond shapes that move with the wind. Deepen your knowledge of Native American heritage in Chamberlain with a visit to the Akta Lakota Museum and Cultural Center.

River of Plenty

Take your pick of fun activities along the wide Missouri River. Navigate the waters on your boat or rent a pontoon with the family. There is plenty of room to go fast and just as much room for those that don't like the speed. If you didn't bring your boat, you can rent canoes, kayaks, paddleboards and pontoons in town, or if you'd prefer to stay on land, throw a line in the water to tempt the walleye from the bank. If you seek help, you can even hire a fishing guide to make sure you take home a trophy. Sometimes it's nice to just watch the sunset over the river from the fishing piers. Take your lawn chair, sit back and relax as the day unfolds before your eyes.

Outdoor Splendor

Enjoy the abundant picturesque natural scenery by bike or foot. Several hiking and biking trails surround the area. Prefer tech-related adventures? Turn on your GPS and go geocaching. A local community of geocaching enthusiasts have left many good finds in the area.

'Fore!' and More

Golf is a popular pastime in these parts. Arnold Palmer and Ed Seay's 1991 design at Dakota Dunes was a major draw for a decade, but don't miss swinging the club

SD

LOCAL FAVORITE

Biscuits on a Stick

Biscuits were a cowboy staple in the Old West. Put them on a stick for more flavor possibilities. *Recipe by Debra Meadows.*

INGREDIENTS

- ☐ 2 cans of plain biscuits
- ☐ Non-stick cooking spray (as needed)
- ☐ 1 cup (2 sticks) melted butter
- ☐ Selection of toppings like mixed cinnamon and sugar, chocolate sauce, cooked and crumbled Bacon, jams, candy bar pieces or other sweet or savory toppings as desired.
- ☐ Whipped cream (optional)

DIRECTIONS

Melt butter and place in a shallow bowl or plate. Place toppings on various plates and bowls, or in shakers and squeeze bottles. Open biscuit cans and separate individual biscuits. Using clean hands, shape and roll each piece of dough into rope shape. Wrap dough around a wooden dowel, cleaned wood stick, or campfire cooking tool. You may spray the implement with non-stick spray if desired or needed for easy removal. Toast slowly over fire until golden brown. Remove from stick and roll in melted butter, then use choice of toppings.

Getty Images/iStockphoto

Custer State Park's Sylvan Lake is a popular spot for swimming, rock climbing, fishing and paddling.

at Chamberlain Country Club — nine holes of pure fun. And if you're into bird-watching, then you're in luck, because locals report seeing everything from bald eagles to Canada geese. Over 400 species have been spotted here.

Stop to Shop

From specialty shops, vintage items to tourist attractions and convenience stores, you'll find everything you want while enjoying the scenic beauty on the banks of the river. Every June, shoppers come from miles around to look, ogle and often purchase from the 90-mile-long Scavenger's Journey yard sale, which stretches from Kadoka to Mt. Vernon (Chamberlain-Oacoma sits about 58 miles east of Mt. Vernon). Need some java? Duck into Al's Oasis in Oacoma, famous for cheap cups of Joe, delicious pie and adjoining stores. It's one of the Midwest's favorite stops, welcoming travelers from across the U.S.

Relic of an Early Resident

Paleontologists flock to the area each summer for an annual dig in the wake of a remarkable discovery. It all started in 1992, when town officials recorded the discovery of the fossil remains of a 78-million-year-old sea lizard known as a "mosasaur" that was unearthed just east of downtown Chamberlain. This 16-foot prehistoric find gave credence to the theory that this area of South Dakota was once a virtual "Jurassic Park."

Custer

In Custer, the best of the Black Hills is just minutes away. Spend less time driving and more time photographing bison herds, admiring famous faces and getting lost in swaths of ponderosa pines. Make memories in the great outdoors and then participate in Old West traditions at the Gold Discovery Days, and the Buffalo Roundup and Arts Festival.

Wild Parks

Go on safari in Custer State Park. Recognized as one of the Ten Best Wildlife Destinations in the World, this 71,000-acre preserve in the Black Hills is home to over 1,300 North American bison. Get a close-up view of these mighty creatures by driving along the 18-mile Wildlife Loop State Scenic Byway. Along the way, you'll encounter other wildlife such as mule deer, mountain goats, coyotes and prairie dogs. Keep an eye out for the "begging burros," wild donkeys that aren't afraid to come right up to your window and beg for snacks.

Beat it to the Badlands

Keep basking in the beauty of the Badlands on the George S. Mickelson Trail. Weaving through spruce and ponderosa pine forests, this 109-mile trail features small slopes and over 100 converted railroad bridges, making it easily accessible for hikers, bikers and horseback riders.

Abundant Streams and Lakes

It's always fishing season, so cast a line in 14 mountain lakes and hundreds of streams. Reel in brown trout in hot spots like Battle Creek, Beaver Creek and Iron Creek. Bismarck Lake, Center Lake, Legion Lake and Sylvan Lake are great for rainbow trout, while the Cheyenne River and Stockade Lake are stocked with bass. Paddling is another great way to enjoy the waterways. Rent a kayak from Sylvan Lake and Legion Lake and set off in search of wildlife and rugged scenery.

Getty Images/iStockphoto

In Mount Rushmore National Memorial, the Avenue of Flags represents all U.S. states and territories.

Prairie Biodiversity

You'll find one of the world's longest and most complex cave systems in Wind Cave National Park. Go beneath the surface to see rare boxwork formations and then hike around the 33,970-acre wildlife sanctuary above ground. For more caving excursions, make your way to Jewel Cave National Monument, the third-longest cave on the planet. Take a guided tour to learn how the cave was formed while admiring sparkling crystals and gypsum strands. The Black Hills is also a prime destination for hunting. Wild turkeys roam the area in large numbers and big game can be found in the rolling hills and high mountains. Elk hunting is reserved for locals, but it is still possible to hunt deer and antelope as long as you have a license.

Black Hills Culture

Brimming with Native American heritage and Old West spirit, Custer immerses you in a culture that's unique to the Black Hills. Bring out the cowboy or cowgirl in you by horseback riding through grassland prairie. Outfitters like Hollingsworth Horses and Rockin' R Rides offer guided trail rides and overnight camping trips. You can even stay at a working ranch to get the full Western experience. For a glimpse into the past, visit the 1881 Courthouse Museum. Showcasing Native American artifacts, old mining tools and other relics, this museum tells the story of the Black Hills beginning in 1874.

Annual Roundups and Rallies

Befriend local motorheads at action-packed car events throughout the year. Tesla owners can join the Sound of Silence Tesla Rally, an annual road trip in May exploring the southern Black Hills' most stunning drives. In June, the Off-Road Rally promises thrilling ATV adventures along hundreds of miles of trails, while September's Studebaker Car Show displays modified and restored vehicles from different decades.

Dakota Fourth

In the area during Independence Day? Attend the Old Time Country Fourth of July for the largest parade in the Black Hills. Gold Discovery Days is also in the same month, a three-day event celebrating the discovery of gold in Custer. Take part in the gold nugget hunt and stick around for the quilt show, bed races and stick horse rodeo. If you can, try to time your stay with the Buffalo Roundup and Arts Festival. Penciled for the end of September, this unique event lets you watch herders round up buffalo in Custer State Park.

Hill City

Perfectly situated to be the hub of your Black Hills vacation, Hill City is rich in history, small in size and big on hospitality. The downtown core pulses with activity thanks to wineries, art galleries and Old West attractions. A short drive from town quickly reveals the most famous site in all of South Dakota: Mount Rushmore National Memorial.

Historic Hill City

The second-oldest town in the Black Hills has flourished as the central location to significant attractions. Hill City is a favorite destination and often referred to as the "Heart of the Black Hills." A great place to start is the Museum at Black Hills Institute in downtown Hill City, which features a mix of geological and archeological artifacts that tell the story of the area. The main highlight here is "Stan," a massive Tyrannosaurus Rex skeleton that towers over awed visitors.

Shrine of Democracy

Mount Rushmore National Memorial features the 60-foot faces of George Washington, Thomas Jefferson, Abraham Lincoln and Theodore Roosevelt, who collectively represents the birth, growth, development and preservation of the U.S. Get a close-up view of the colossal sculptures by walking along the Presidential Trail, offering awe-inspiring views of the 60-foot faces carved 500 feet up a stone mountain.

Mountain Monument

Nearby, Crazy Horse Memorial has progressed through many changes since its 1948 dedication. Once complete, this tribute to the Lakota leader will be the largest mountain carving in South Dakota and the world. When it's finished, it will be 641 feet long and 563 feet high,cutting a dramatic form against the horizon. The memorial pays tribute to the legendary 19th-century Lakota hero who strove to preserve the living heritage of his people. The Indian Museum of North America is also situated here, so stop

SD

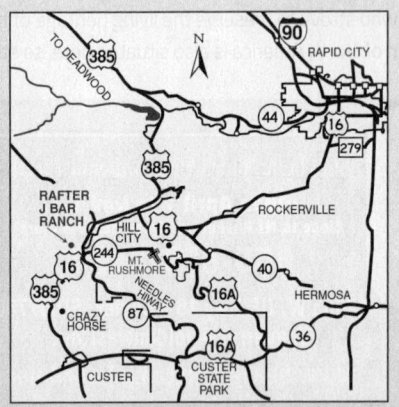

The 1880 Train steams along the Black Hills Central Railroad on a sightseeing tour near Hill City.

by to view a compelling collection of indigenous art and artifacts.

History & Nostalgia on the Railroad

The 1880 Train is a two-hour 20-mile round trip between Hill City and Keystone. The Black Hills Central Railroad is the oldest continuously operating tour railroad in the nation. Step aboard the 1880 Train and enjoy a narrated trip between Hill City and Keystone on a century-old steam engine. Explore the railroad's history and watch a model train in action at the South Dakota State Railroad Museum. Tour historic buildings and see how fish are cultivated.

Spearfish

Spearfish gives you easy access to the adventures and beauty of the Northern Black Hills of South Dakota. This year-round playground for outdoor adventure puts you in the middle of rock climbing, hiking, magnificent canyon waterfalls within a micropolitan community. Cruise along the Spearfish Canyon Scenic Byway to experience the best of the northern Black Hills, or hang out at the craft breweries, art galleries and antique shops in town. Spearfish serves as a relaxing getaway as well as a jumping-off point for outdoor adventures.

Roaring waters of Spearfish Falls

Located in the heart of Spearfish Canyon near the Savoy area, this natural wonderland is home to breathtaking, multi-tiered waterfalls, lush forest and even ice displays — depending on the time of year. There are many pull-offs on the side of the road for great views.

Flowing Falls

Bridal Veil Falls is the most accessible waterfall in the canyon and the 60-foot cascade can be easily seen from the road. Hiking is not allowed here, but there is an observation platform that offers fantastic photo opportunities. If you do want to hike, continue on the byway until you reach the Savoy area. There you'll find a trail that takes you from the Latchstring Inn restaurant to the raging waters of Spearfish Falls. The last wonder on the circuit is Roughlock Falls, a multitiered waterfall resting along Little Spearfish Canyon.

Freshwater Fishing

With the freestone river sitting in a gorgeous canyon and two of the largest streams in the region, Spearfish Canyon is a favorite among anglers. Cast a line in Spearfish Creek to snag wild brook, brown and rainbow trout. Next, head west to Iron Creek Lake for yellow perch and more rainbow trout. Located upstream from Cheyenne Crossing, Hanna Creeks and Little Spearfish are worth visiting too for their good numbers of brook trout. Crow Creek is the biggest stream in the Black Hills and another great spot for catching wild brown trout. Between catches, check out the D.C. Booth Historic National Fish Hatchery, one of the oldest fish hatcheries in the country.

Outdoor Adventure

Whether you love hiking or climbing, Spearfish is the destination for folks who love to explore on foot. Enjoy a leisurely or challenging trek to the top of Lookout Mountain, and create your own adventure on the Eagle Cliff Trails by following a combination of 21 intertwining loop and dead-end paths. You can also climb to the summit of Crow Peak if you're up for a challenge. The 1,600-foot ascent isn't easy, but the 360-degree views of Spearfish Valley and Eastern Wyoming are well worth it at the end of the long hike.

Hunting Mecca

The Mount Rushmore State boasts prime hunting, allowing hunters to enjoy a big success rate every year. Perhaps the most sought-after animals in the Black Hills are elk. The area north of the town is prime hunting ground for antelope and mountain lions, while the Black Hills in the south support an abundance of deer and wild turkey. Small game available for the taking includes prairie dogs, coyotes and jackrabbits.

Bridal Veil Falls forms a 60-foot-high curtain in Spearfish Canyon, a popular spot for flyfishing.

Bikes and Cars

Spearfish is a mecca for mountain biking, with hundreds of miles of rocky tracks as well as paved trails. Race against other cyclists at the Gold Rush Gravel Grinder in June. For motorized transportation, check out sweet rides at the Black Hills Corvette Classic each July and shop for everything from art to furniture at the annual Festival in the Park in July. After dark, the fun keeps going. For an enjoyable evening, attend the Downtown Friday Nights block party for live music, family-friendly activities and delicious food vendors all summer long.

Spearfish Suds

With a vibrant culture and youthful community, Spearfish is home to three craft breweries serving hand-crafted brews. What better way to end a day of adventure in the Northern Hills than a local, cold beer? Head to Spearfish Brewing Company for a classic American lager and hefty burger. The taproom also produces craft ales and features a rotating lineup of locally made kombucha. Up the street is Sawyer, a brewery serving hoppy IPAs and wood-fired pizzas, with a beautiful creekside view. Crow Peak is right beside it and well known for its diverse lineup of lagers, ales and stouts. Get a tasting flight to start, or order local favorites the Pile O'Dirt Porter and Canyon Cream Ale.

Signature Spearfish

Culture is a cornerstone of life in this outdoor mecca. Every second Friday from June until Labor Day, Spearfish offers Downtown Friday Nights on Historic Main Street. Live music, food, vendors and entertainment.

Spearfish Treasure

And yes, there really is gold in "them there hills." Jewelry made from gold mined right from the Black Hills is available all around in Spearfish. This is but one example of the unique shopping experiences that visitors can discover. Art galleries and unique stores with locally made rugs, wines and gourmet foods make shopping in downtown Spearfish a stellar retail experience.

South Dakota's Petrified Forest

While you're in the area, get a glimpse of arboreal life from prehistory. At South Dakota's Petrified Forest of the Black Hills, a museum opened in 1929 near Rapid City, the earth has preserved a cypress swamp 120 million years old. This was the time of dinosaurs — when the Black Hills didn't exist and the entire area was a flat, tropical swamp. The wetlands areas were similiar to the cypress swamps found in the American South.

Frozen in Time

Visitors can walk the mile loop trail to see and touch these ancient trees. The fiber of their wood is still visible in the petrified logs, and a stack of "wood" made up of pieces gathered from other parts of the property resembles a cord of wood stacked for winter. In addition to the logs, the museum offers a very interesting film on the history of geology in this area.

FOR MORE INFORMATION

South Dakota Department of Tourism, 800-732-5682, www.travelsouthdakota.com

Chamberlain Convention and Visitors Bureau, 605-234-4416, www.chamberlainsd.com

Visit Custer, 605-673-2244, www.visitcuster.com

Hill City Area Chamber of Commerce, 800-888-1798, www.hillcitysd.com

Petrified Forest of the Black Hills, 605-787-4884, blackhillsbadlands.com/business/petrified-forest-black-hills

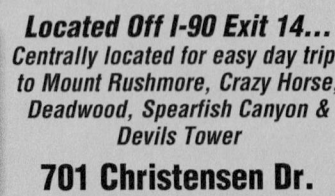

Visit Spearfish, 800-344-6181, www.visitspearfish.com

South Dakota

ABERDEEN — A5 *Brown*

MELGAARD PARK
(Public) From Jct of Hwy 12 & State St: Go 1 mi S on State St (E). **FAC:** paved rds. Avail: 15 paved, 4 pull-thrus, (15x45), back-ins (15x45), 15 E (50 amps), tent sites, dump. **REC:** pool, playground. Pets OK. Partial handicap access. 2021 rates: $32. Apr 01 to Oct 31. no cc, no reservations.
(605)626-7015 Lat: 45.446306, Lon: -98.477806
1790 S Lloyd St, Aberdeen, SD 57401
www.aberdeen.sd.us

MINA LAKE RECREATION AREA
(Public State Park) From Aberdeen: Go 11 mi W on Hwy 12, follow signs (R). Entrance fee required. **FAC:** paved rds. Avail: 38 gravel, back-ins (16x55), 38 E (20/30 amps), tent sites, rentals, dump. **REC:** Mina Lake: swim, fishing, playground, rec open to public. Pets OK. Partial handicap access, 14 day max stay. 2021 rates: $22 to $26.
(800)710-2267 Lat: 45.446704, Lon: -98.74082
402 Park Ave, Mina, SD 57451
gfp.sd.gov/state-parks
See ad page 818

RICHMOND LAKE STATE RECREATION AREA
(Public State Park) From Jct of US-12 & US-281, W 5 mi on US-12 to park access rd, NW 6 mi (L). Entrance fee required. **FAC:** paved rds. Avail: 24 gravel, 1 pull-thrus, (20x50), back-ins (20x50), 22 E (30/50 amps), tent sites, rentals, dump. **REC:** Richmond Lake: swim, fishing, kayaking/canoeing, boating nearby, playground, rec open to public. Pets OK. Partial handicap access, 14 day max stay. 2021 rates: $22 to $26.
(800)710-2267 Lat: 45.5399, Lon: -98.61109
37908 Youth Camp Rd, Aberdeen, SD 57401
gfp.sd.gov/state-parks
See ad page 818

WYLIE PARK CAMPGROUND & STORYBOOK LAND
Ratings: 9/9.5★/10 (Campground) From Jct US-12 & US-281: Go 2 1/4 mi N on US-281, then 1/4 mi W on Seratoma Pkwy (L). **FAC:** paved rds. Avail: 107 paved, patios, 29 pull-thrus, (34x60), back-ins (35x60), 69 full hkups, 38 W, 38 E (30/50 amps), WiFi @ sites, tent sites, rentals, dump, laundry, groc, fire rings, firewood. **REC:** Wylie Lake: swim, fishing, kayaking/canoeing, playground, rec open to public. Pets OK. Partial handicap access. Big rig sites. 2021 rates: $37. Apr 01 to Nov 01. ATM.
(888)326-9693 Lat: 45.48910, Lon: -98.52437
2312 24th Ave NW, Aberdeen, SD 57401
www.aberdeen.sd.us/242/Wylie-Park-Storybook-Land
See ad this page

Things to See and Do

STORYBOOK / LAND OF OZ THEME PARKS
210-acre park featuring picnic facilities, lake & swimming beach, recreational trails, wildlife exhibits, Story Book Land, Land of Oz, train,-Roller Coaster,carousel,balloon rides, paddle boat & canoe rentals. Admission free to Theme Park. Apr 15 to Oct 15. RV accessible. Restrooms. Food. Hours: 10am to 9pm.
(605)626-7015 Lat: 45.49118, Lon: -98.52192
2202 24th Ave NW, Aberdeen, SD 57401
www.aberdeen.sd.us/storybookland
See ad this page

Get the GOOD SAM CAMPING APP

AKASKA — A4 *Walworth*

D & S CAMPGROUND & LODGE **Ratings: 5/8★/6** (Campground) 43 Avail: 34 full hkups, 9 W, 9 E (30/50 amps). 2021 rates: $50. May 01 to Dec 01. (605)229-1739, 103 Swan Creek Rd, Akaska, SD 57420

SWAN CREEK RECREATION AREA
(Public State Park) From Gettysburg: W 9 mi on 142nd St. (E). Entrance fee required. **FAC:** paved rds. Avail: 26 paved, back-ins (14x60), 26 E (20/30 amps), tent sites, dump. **REC:** Missouri River: fishing, boating nearby, rec open to public. Pets OK. Partial handicap access, 14 day max stay. 2021 rates: $16 to $20.
(800)710-2267 Lat: 45.319177, Lon: -100.3
16157A West Whitlock Rd c/o West Whitlock, Gettysburg, SD 57442
gfp.sd.gov/state-parks
See ad page 818

ARLINGTON — B6 *Brookings*

LAKE POINSETT RECREATION AREA
(Public State Park) From town, N 12 mi on Hwy 81 to CR-2, E 2 mi (E) Entrance fee required. **FAC:** paved rds. Avail: 114 gravel, 22 pull-thrus, (14x50), back-ins (14x60), 114 E (30 amps), tent sites, rentals, dump. **REC:** Lake Poinsett: swim, fishing, boating nearby, playground, rec open to public. Pets OK. Partial handicap access, 14 day max stay. 2021 rates: $22 to $26.
(800)710-2267 Lat: 44.534183, Lon: -97.083956
45617 S Poinsett Dr, Arlington, SD 57212
gfp.sd.gov/state-parks
See ad page 818

BADLANDS NATIONAL PARK — C2 *Jackson*

BADLANDS NATIONAL PARK See also Interior & Wall.

BELLE FOURCHE — B1 *Butte*

ROCKY POINT RECREATION AREA
(Public State Park) From Belle Fourche: Go 8 mi E on SD-212. **FAC:** gravel rds. Avail: 62 gravel, back-ins (15x65), 56 E (20/30 amps), tent sites, rentals, dump. **REC:** Belle Fourche Reservoir: swim, fishing, kayaking/canoeing, boating nearby, playground, rec open to public. Pets OK. Partial handicap access, 14 day max stay. 2021 rates: $22 to $26.
(800)710-2267 Lat: 44.709733, Lon: -103.710709
18513 Fisherman's Rd, Belle Fourche, SD 57717
gfp.sd.gov/state-parks
See ad page 818

BELVIDERE — C3 *Jackson*

BELVIDERE EAST/EXIT 170 KOA **Ratings: 7/8.5★/9.5** (Campground) 38 Avail: 26 full hkups, 12 W, 12 E (30/50 amps). 2021 rates: $53.97 to $70.97. May 01 to Oct 15. (800)562-2134, 24201 SD Hwy 63, Midland, SD 57552

Read RV topics at blog.GoodSam.com

BERESFORD — D6 *Union*

UNION GROVE
(Public State Park) From Jct of SR-46 & I-29, S 11 mi on I-29 to exit 38, S 2 mi (L) Note: Entrance fee required. **FAC:** paved rds. Avail: 25 gravel, 9 pull-thrus, (20x40), back-ins (20x40), 25 E (20/30 amps), tent sites, dump. **REC:** Brule Creek: playground, rec open to public. Pets OK. 14 day max stay. 2021 rates: $22 to $26.
(800)710-2267 Lat: 42.920242, Lon: -96.785322
30828-471st Ave, Beresford, SD 57004
gfp.sd.gov/state-parks
See ad page 818

Travel Services

BIG TOY STORAGE Indoor and outdoor secured RV and Boat Storage **RV Storage:** indoor, outdoor, secured fencing, electric gate, easy reach keypad, 24/7 access, well-lit facility, well-lit roads, well-lit perimeter, security cameras, level gravel/paved spaces, power to charge battery. **SERVICES:**. Hours: 24 hr. Special offers available for Good Sam Members
(605)366-2620 Lat: 43.12724, Lon: -96.79148
47076 294th St., Beresford, SD 57004
www.i-29bigtoystorage.com

BLACK HAWK — C1 *Meade*

THREE FLAGS RV PARK **Ratings: 6.5/9★/7** (Campground) 41 Avail: 23 full hkups, 18 W, 18 E (30/50 amps). 2021 rates: $36 to $55. Apr 01 to Oct 30. (605)787-7898, 9484 Three Flags Ln, Black Hawk, SD 57718

County names help you follow the local weather report.

SD

BLACK HILLS — C1 *Lawrence*

Things to See and Do

GEORGE S MICKELSON TRAIL (SRA) The trail is 109 miles long and contains more than 100 converted railroad bridges and 4 rock tunnels. Its gentle slopes and easy access allow people of all ages and abilities to enjoy the beauty of the Black Hills. Restrooms. Food. Hours: Dawn to Dusk. Adult fee: $4.00 daily. No CC.
(800)710-2267 Lat: 44.28262, Lon: -103.4586
11361 Nevada Gulch Rd, Lead, SD 57501
gfp.sd.gov/parks
See ad page 818

BONESTEEL — D4 *Gregory*

WHETSTONE BAY - COE/WHETSTONE BAY REC AREA (Public Corps) From town: Go 1/4 mi W on US-18, then 10 mi N on CR-1806 (R). 10 Avail: Pit toilets. 2021 rates: $11 to $15. (605)487-7046

BRANDON — C6 *Minnehaha*

BIG SIOUX RECREATION AREA
(Public State Park) From Jct of I-90 & SR-11 (Exit 406), S 3 mi on SR-11/Splitrock Blvd to S. Sioux Blvd, NW 0.2 mi to Park St, W 0.3 mi to Park Entrance (R) Note: Entrance fee required. **FAC:** gravel rds. Avail: 49 gravel, back-ins (18x75), 49 E (20/30 amps), tent sites, rentals, dump. **REC:** Big Sioux River: fishing, kayaking/canoeing, boating nearby, playground, rec open to public. Pets OK. Partial handicap access, 14 day max stay. 2021 rates: $15 to $26.
(800)710-2267 Lat: 43.57267, Lon: -96.59472
410 W Park Ave, Brandon, SD 57005
www.gfp.sd.gov/state-parks
See ad page 818

BROOKINGS — C6 *Brookings*

OAKWOOD LAKES
(Public State Park) From Jct of I-29 & SR-30, W 10 mi on SR-30, follow signs (R). Entrance fee required. **FAC:** paved rds. Avail: 145 gravel, 3 pull-thrus, (15x35), back-ins (15x35), 145 E (20/30 amps), tent sites, rentals, dump. **REC:** Oakwood Lakes: swim, fishing, kayaking/canoeing, playground, rec open to public. Pets OK. Partial handicap access, 14 day max stay. 2021 rates: $22 to $26. no cc.
(800)710-2267 Lat: 44.449753, Lon: -96.981982
20247 Oakwood Dr, Bruce, SD 57220
gfp.sd.gov/state-parks
See ad page 818

Directional arrows indicate the campground's position in relation to the nearest town.

SEXAUER PARK & CAMPGROUND (Public) From Jct of I-29 & Hwy 14 (6th St): Go 2 mi W on Hwy 14, then 1/2 on Western Ave (R). Avail: 18 E (20 amps). 2021 rates: $20. May 15 to Oct 15. (605)692-2708

BURKE — D4 *Gregory*

BURKE LAKE (SRA)
(Public State Park) From Burke: Go 2 mi E on US-18. **FAC:** gravel rds. Avail: 15 gravel, back-ins (18x46), tent sites, pit toilets. **REC:** Burke Lake: swim, fishing, kayaking/canoeing, hunting nearby, rec open to public. Pets OK. 14 day max stay. 2021 rates: $11 to $26.
(800)710-2267 Lat: 43.183192, Lon: -99.260023
29145 Burke Lake Rd, Burke, SD 57523
gfp.sd.gov/state-parks
See ad page 818

CANISTOTA — C6 *McCook*

LAKE VERMILLION RECREATION AREA
(Public State Park) From Jct of I-90 & CR-E30 (exit 374), S 5 mi on CR-E30 to Lake Vermillion Rd (L) Note: Entrance fee required. **FAC:** paved rds. Avail: 94 gravel, 18 pull-thrus, (14x70), back-ins (14x70), 94 E (20/30 amps), tent sites, rentals, dump. **REC:** Lake Vermillion: swim, fishing, kayaking/canoeing, boating nearby, playground, rec open to public. Pets OK. Partial handicap access, 14 day max stay. 2021 rates: $15 to $26.
(800)710-2267 Lat: 43.5947, Lon: -97.185173
26140 451st Ave, Canistota, SD 57012
gfp.sd.gov/state-parks
See ad page 818

CANTON — D6 *Lincoln*

GATE CITY EVENTS & LODGING
Ratings: 5/NA/9.5 (RV Park) Avail: 19 full hkups (30/50 amps). 2021 rates: $35. (605)214-4604, 47947 W. 5th Street, Canton, SD 57013

NEWTON HILLS
(Public State Park) 6 mi S of Canton, off CR-135: From Jct of I-29 & CR-140 (exit 56), E 12 mi on CR-140 to CR-135, N 0.25 mi (L). Entrance fee required. **FAC:** gravel rds. Avail: 126 gravel, back-ins (14x60), 126 E (20/30 amps), tent sites, rentals, dump. **REC:** Lake Lakota: swim, fishing, boating nearby, playground, rec open to public. Pets OK. Partial handicap access, 14 day max stay. 2021 rates: $16 to $26.
(800)710-2267 Lat: 43.219041, Lon: -96.570193
28767 482nd Ave, Canton, SD 57013
www.gfp.sd.gov/state-parks
See ad page 818

Travel Services

ROD'S RV, BOAT, & TRAILER STORAGE Enclosed RV, Boat & Trailer facility with additional storage available in open, uncovered gravel lot. **RV Storage:** indoor, outdoor, secured fencing, electric gate, easy reach keypad, 24/7 access, well-lit facility, well-lit roads, well-lit perimeter, security cameras, level gravel/paved spaces, power to charge battery, water, compressed air. **SERVICES:**. Hours: 24-7. No CC. Special offers available for Good Sam Members (605)728-5960 Lat: 43.30224, Lon: -96.60904 28189 West Ave., Canton, SD 57013

CHAMBERLAIN — C4 *Brule*

A SPOTLIGHT Introducing Chamberlain/Oacoma's colorful attractions appearing at the front of this state section.

OASIS CAMPGROUND
Ratings: 8.5/10★/9 (Campground) From Jct of I-90 & Exit 260: Go 100 ft N on Douglas Ave, then 1/4 mi E on Bus-90/Hwy 16 (R).

OASIS CAMPGROUND
We invite you to stay & relax at the Oasis Campground, one of South Dakota's greatest locations. Complete with scenic views of Missouri River and history, art & culture to explore! Across from Oasis Pump N Pak.

FAC: gravel rds. 75 Avail: 61 gravel, 14 grass, 34 pull-thrus, (30x65), back-ins (30x65), 75 full hkups (30/50 amps), WiFi @ sites, tent sites, rentals, dump, laundry, fire rings, firewood. **REC:** heated pool, Missouri: boating nearby, playground, hunting nearby. Pet restrict (B) $. Partial handicap access. Big rig sites. 2021 rates: $45.95, Military discount. Apr 15 to Nov 01.
(800)675-6959 Lat: 43.80205, Lon: -99.38755
605 East SD Hwy16, Oacoma, SD 57365
oasiscampsd.com
See ad pages 821, 824

Things to See and Do

OASIS PUMP N PAK Service station, convenience store, sells fishing & hunting licenses & ammunition, plus a casino across from Oasis Campground. RV accessible. Restrooms. Food. Hours: 24 Hours. ATM.
(605)234-5325 Lat: 43.80281, Lon: -99.38435
802 East Hwy 16, Oacoma, SD 57365
www.oasiscampsd.com
See ad pages 821, 824

CLEAR LAKE — B6 *Deuel*

CLEAR LAKE CITY PARK (Public) From Jct of SR-22 & SR-15: Go 1 mi N on SR-15 (L). 18 Avail: 18 W, 18 E (20 amps). 2021 rates: $15. (605)874-2121

LAKE COCHRANE RECREATION AREA
(Public State Park) From Clear Lake, E 10 mi on Hwy 22, follow signs (R). Entrance fee required. **FAC:** paved rds. Avail: 30 gravel, back-ins (17x60), 30 E (20/30 amps), tent sites, rentals, dump. **REC:** Lake Cochrane: swim, fishing, kayaking/canoeing, golf, playground, hunting nearby, rec open to public. Pets OK. Partial handicap access, 14 day max stay. 2021 rates: $26.
(800)710-2267 Lat: 44.714191, Lon: -96.478932
3454 Edgewater Dr, Gary, SD 57237
gfp.sd.gov/state-parks
See ad page 818

ULVEN PARK (Public) From town: Go 1/4 mi E on SR-22 (R). Avail: 10 E (20 amps). 2021 rates: $15. (605)874-2121

CORSON — C1 *Minnehaha*

PALISADES
(Public State Park) From Jct I-90 & Brandon (Exit 406): Go 10 mi N on Cnty Rd 11. Follow signs(R). Entrance fee required. **FAC:** paved rds. Avail: 34 gravel, back-ins (20x60), 34 E (20/30 amps), tent sites, rentals, . **REC:** Split Rock Creek: fishing, kayaking/canoeing, playground, rec open to public. Pets OK. Partial handicap access, 14 day max stay. 2021 rates: $16 to $26.
(800)710-2267 Lat: 43.687645, Lon: -96.517166
25491-485th Ave, Garretson, SD 57030
gfp.sd.gov/state-parks
See ad page 818

CUSTER — C1 *Custer*

A SPOTLIGHT Introducing Custer's colorful attractions appearing at the front of this state section.

CUSTER See also Hill City, Hot Springs, Keystone & Rapid City.

BEAVER LAKE CAMPGROUND
Ratings: 9/10★/10 (Campground) From Jct US 385 & US 16 (in town): Go 3.5 mi W on US 16 (L). Elev 5600 ft.

19 PINE-FILLED ACRES IN CUSTER
Enjoy sounds of the breeze through tall pines, birds singing, calm surroundings in a safe, small town atmosphere. Try a spacious RV or tent site or simple to deluxe cabins.

FAC: gravel rds. Avail: 88 gravel, 29 pull-thrus, (40x60), back-ins (35x60), 66 full hkups, 22 W, 22 E (30/50 amps), cable, WiFi @ sites, tent sites, rentals, dump, mobile sewer, laundry, groc, LP gas, fire rings, firewood. **REC:** heated pool, playground, hunting nearby. Pets OK. Partial handicap access. Big rig sites, eco-friendly. 2021 rates: $34 to $60, Military discount. Apr 01 to Nov 01.
(605)673-2464 Lat: 43.73967, Lon: -103.65685
12005 US Hwy 16, Custer, SD 57730
www.beaverlakecampground.net
See ad this page, 825, 834

Show Your Good Sam Membership Card!

BIG PINE CAMPGROUND **Ratings: 7.5/10★/10** (Campground) 62 Avail: 35 full hkups, 27 W, 27 E (30/50 amps). 2021 rates: $46. May 20 to Oct 01. (800)235-3981, 12084 Big Pine Road, Custer, SD 57730

BROKEN ARROW HORSE & RV CAMPGROUND **Ratings: 7/9.5★/10** (RV Park) 43 Avail: 32 full hkups, 11 W, 11 E (30/50 amps). 2021 rates: $46 to $49. May 01 to Oct 01. (605)517-1964, 25446 Sidney Park Rd, Custer, SD 57730

BUFFALO RIDGE CAMP RESORT
Ratings: 9/10★/10 (Campground) From Jct US-16/385 & 16-A: Go 3/4 mi W on US-16 to U.S. 385; Go S 2 blocks on U.S. 385 (R). Elev 5380 ft.**FAC:** all weather rds. Avail: 116 all weather, patios, 106 pull-thrus, (30x65), back-ins (16x75), 116 full hkups (30/50 amps), WiFi @ sites, tent sites, rentals, dump, laundry, groc, fire rings, firewood. **REC:** heated pool, hot tub, Lake Sylvan: swim, fishing, kayaking/canoeing, boating nearby, playground, hunting nearby. Pet restrict (Q). Partial handicap access. Big rig sites, eco-friendly. 2021 rates: $36 to $90, Military discount. May 13 to Oct 02.
(605)673-4664 Lat: 43.757462, Lon: -103.610689
245 Centennial Dr., Custer, SD 57730
www.custerhospitality.com
See ad opposite page

CUSTER CRAZY HORSE CAMPGROUND **Ratings: 6.5/8.5★/7** (Campground) 119 Avail: 70 full hkups, 49 W, 49 E (30/50 amps). 2021 rates: $40 to $50. (605)517-9016, 1116 N 5th St, Custer, SD 57730

CUSTER MOUNTAIN CABINS & CAMPGROUND **Ratings: 6.5/8.5★/7.5** (Campground) 30 Avail: 21 full hkups, 9 E (30/50 amps). 2021 rates: $40 to $48. May 01 to Nov 30. (800)239-5505, 12503 Hwy 16A, Custer, SD 57730

CUSTER/BLUE BELL
(Public State Park) From Custer: Go 8 mi E on US-16A (to Visitor's Ctr), then continue 7 mi E on US-16A, then 3 mi S on SD-87 (L). Entrance fee required. Elev 5000 ft.**FAC:** paved rds. Avail: 31 paved, back-ins (20x45), 31 E (30/50 amps), tent sites, rentals, laundry, groc, restaurant. **REC:** rec open to public. Pets OK. Partial handicap access, 14 day max stay. 2021 rates: $15 to $30. May 01 to Oct 31.
(800)710-2267 Lat: 43.705415, Lon: -103.5
13329 US Hwy 16A, Custer, SD 57730
www.gfp.sd.gov/state-parks
See ad page 818

CUSTER/CENTER LAKE
(Public State Park) From Custer: Go 10 mi E on US-16A, then 4 mi N on SD-87. (R). Elev 4686 ft.**FAC:** paved rds. Avail: 71 gravel, back-ins (20x50), tent sites, pit toilets. **REC:** Center Lake: swim, fishing, kayaking/canoeing, playground, rec open to public. Pets OK. Partial handicap access, 14 day max stay. 2021 rates: $19. May 01 to Sep 30.
(800)710-2267 Lat: 43.807161, Lon: -103.4
13329 US Hwy 16A, Custer, SD 57730
gfp.sd.gov/state-parks
See ad page 818

CUSTER/GAME LODGE
(Public State Park) From Custer: Go 15 mi E on US-16A to Visitor Center, then continue 1 mi E on US-16A (R). Elev 4250 ft.**FAC:** paved rds. Avail: 59 paved, back-ins (20x60), 59 E (20/30 amps), tent sites, rentals, dump, laundry, restaurant. **REC:** pond, swim, fishing, playground, hunting nearby, rec open to public. Pets OK. Partial handicap access, 14 day max stay. 2021 rates: $16 to $26.
(800)710-2267 Lat: 43.760274, Lon: -103.4
13389 US 16 Scenic, Custer, SD 57730
gfp.sd.gov/state-parks
See ad page 818

CUSTER/GRACE COOLIDGE
(Public State Park) From Custer: E 14.5 mi on US-16A (R). Elev 4250 ft.**FAC:** paved rds. Avail: 20 paved, back-ins (20x35), 20 E (30 amps), tent sites, restaurant. **REC:** Grace Coolidge Creek: swim, fishing, hunting nearby, rec open to public. Pets OK. Partial handicap access, 14 day max stay. 2021 rates: $30. May 17 to Oct 13.
(800)710-2267 Lat: 43.778816, Lon: -103.402240
13329 US Hwy 16A, Custer, SD 57730
gfp.sd.gov/state-parks
See ad page 818

Check the air pressure on your tires and inflate any that are lower than the pressure recommended in the owner's manual. Properly inflated tires can increase fuel efficiency by 3.3 percent.

CUSTER/LEGION LAKE
(Public State Park) From Custer: Go 9 mi E on US-16A (L). Elev 5000 ft.**FAC:** paved rds. Avail: 26 gravel, back-ins (20x50), 26 E (20/30 amps), tent sites, rentals, . **REC:** Legion Lake: swim, fishing, kayaking/canoeing, rec open to public. Pets OK. Partial handicap access, 14 day max stay. 2021 rates: $16 to $26. May 17 to Oct 13.
(800)710-2267 Lat: 43.762262, Lon: -103.50000
13329 US Hwy 16A, Custer, SD 57730
gfp.sd.gov/state-parks
See ad page 818

CUSTER/STOCKADE LAKE
(Public State Park) From Custer: E 3 mi on US-16A (R). Elev 5280 ft.**FAC:** gravel rds. Avail: 67 gravel, back-ins (20x50), 56 E (20/30 amps), tent sites, rentals, . **REC:** Stockade Lake: swim, fishing, kayaking/canoeing, playground, hunting nearby, rec open to public. Pets OK. Partial handicap access, 14 day max stay. 2021 rates: $30. May 17 to Oct 07.
(800)710-2267 Lat: 43.769500, Lon: -103.532556
13329 US Hwy16A, Custer, SD 57730
gfp.sd.gov/state-parks
See ad page 818

CUSTER/SYLVAN LAKE
(Public State Park) From Custer: Go 6 mi N on Hwy 89 (R). Elev 6200 ft.**FAC:** paved rds. Avail: 39 gravel, back-ins (20x30), 39 E (20/30 amps), tent sites, restaurant. **REC:** Sylvan Lake: swim, fishing, kayaking/canoeing, hunting nearby, rec open to public. Pets OK. Partial handicap access, 14 day max stay. 2021 rates: $30. May 17 to Sep 30.
(800)710-2267 Lat: 43.843695, Lon: -103.60000
13329 US Hwy 16A, Custer, SD 57730
gfp.sd.gov/state-parks
See ad page 818

FORT WELIKIT FAMILY CAMPGROUND
Ratings: 8/10★/10 (Campground) 65 Avail: 61 full hkups, 4 W, 4 E (30/50 amps). 2021 rates: $45 to $50. May 01 to Oct 15. (605)673-3600, 24992 Sylvan Lake Rd, Custer, SD 57730

HERITAGE VILLAGE CAMPGROUND **Ratings: 6.5/9★/7.5** (Campground) Avail: 35 full hkups (30/50 amps). 2021 rates: $22 to $26. May 01 to Sep 18. (605)673-5005, 24827 Village Ave, Crazy Horse, SD 57730

Things to See and Do

CUSTER STATE PARK Headquarters for Custer State Park RV accessible. Restrooms. Hours: 8am to 5pm. No CC.
(605)255-4515 Lat: 43.77404, Lon: -103.52295
13329 US Hwy 16A, Custer, SD 57730
www.custerstatepark.com
See ad page 818

DEADWOOD — B1 *Lawrence*

DEADWOOD See also Black Hawk, Lead, Rapid City, Spearfish & Sturgis.

CHRIS' CAMP & RV PARK
Ratings: 9.5/9.5★/9.5 (Campground) From jct Deadwood St & Pioneer Way: Go 1-1/4 mi NE on Pioneer Way, then 7 mi N on US-85N, then 4-1/2 mi W on Colorado Blvd, then 3/4 mi S on Christensen Dr (R). Elev 3600 ft.**FAC:** paved/gravel rds. 135 Avail: 95 gravel, 40 grass, 68 pull-thrus, (20x50), back-ins (24x75), 103 full hkups, 32 W, 32 E (30/50 amps), cable, WiFi @ sites, tent sites, rentals, shower$, dump, laundry, groc, fire rings, firewood. **REC:** heated pool, wading pool, playground, hunting nearby. Pets OK. Partial handicap access. Big rig sites, eco-friendly. 2021 rates: $43 to $58, Military discount. Apr 15 to Oct 15. ATM, no cc.
(800)350-2239 Lat: 44.47092, Lon: -103.82711
701 Christensen Dr, Spearfish, SD 57783
www.chriscampground.com
See primary listing at Spearfish and ad this page, 828

CUSTER CROSSING CAMPGROUND
Ratings: 5.5/9★/9 (Campground) Avail: 20 E (30/50 amps). 2021 rates: $38 to $70. (605)584-1009, 22036 US Hwy 385, Deadwood, SD 57732

FISH'N FRY CAMPGROUND & RV PARK
Ratings: 8.5/8.5★/8.5 (Campground) 59 Avail: 29 full hkups, 19 W, 19 E (30/50 amps). 2021 rates: $38 to $42. May 15 to Sep 16. (605)578-2150, 21390 US Hwy 385, Deadwood, SD 57732

RV Park ratings you can rely on!

HIDDEN VALLEY CAMPGROUND **Ratings: 8/10★/9.5** (Campground) 32 Avail: 5 full hkups, 27 W, 27 E (30/50 amps). 2021 rates: $35 to $40. May 15 to Sep 10. (605)578-1342, 21423 US Hwy 385, Deadwood, SD 57732

STEEL WHEEL CAMPGROUND & TRADING POST **Ratings: 7.5/10★/8** (Campground) 33 Avail: 27 full hkups, 4 E (30/50 amps). 2021 rates: $30 to $42. (605)578-9767, 21399 US Hwy 385, Deadwood, SD 57732

WHISTLER GULCH CAMPGROUND & RV PARK
Ratings: 9.5/9.5★/9 (Campground) Avail: 123 full hkups (30/50 amps). 2021 rates: $47 to $55. May 01 to Sep 30. (800)704-7139, 235 Cliff St , Deadwood, SD 57732

WILD BILL'S CAMPGROUND, SALOON & GRILL **Ratings: 6/8★/8** (Campground) 49 Avail: 25 full hkups, 10 W, 24 E (30/50 amps). 2021 rates: $29 to $38. May 15 to Sep 15. (605)578-2800, 21372 US Hwy 385, Deadwood, SD 57732

EUREKA — A4 *McPherson*

EUREKA CITY PARK (Public) From Jct of 47 & SD-10: Go 3/4 mi N on 18th St/327th Ave, then 1 blk W on E Ave (L). Avail: 18 E (30/50 amps). 2021 rates: $15. (605)284-2441

FAITH — B2 *Meade*

FAITH CITY PARK (Public) From Jct of US-212 & Main St: Go 4 blks S on Main St (L). 12 Avail: 12 W, 12 E (30 amps). 2021 rates: $10. (605)967-2261

FORT PIERRE — C3 *Stanley*

COW CREEK RECREATION AREA
(Public State Park) From Fort Pierre: Go 15 mi NW on Hwy 1804. Entrance fee required. **FAC:** gravel rds. Avail: 46 gravel, back-ins (18x60), 31 E (20/30 amps), tent sites, rentals, dump. **REC:** Oahe Reservoir: swim, fishing, rec open to public. Pets OK. 14 day max stay. 2021 rates: $16 to $20.
(800)710-2267 Lat: 44.55568, Lon: -100.4762
28229 Cow Creek Rd, Pierre, SD 57501
gfp.sd.gov/state-parks
See ad page 818

OAHE DOWNSTREAM RECREATION AREA
(Public State Park) From Fort Pierre: Go 5 mi N on Hwy 1806. **FAC:** paved rds. 205 Avail: 160 paved, 45 gravel, 1 pull-thrus, (20x60), back-ins (20x50), 205 E (20/30 amps), WiFi @ sites, tent sites, rentals, dump. **REC:** Missouri River: swim, fishing, marina, playground, rec open to public. Pets OK. Partial handicap access, 14 day max stay. 2021 rates: $23.
(800)710-2267 Lat: 44.436944, Lon: -100.3998
20439 Marina Loop Rd, Fort Pierre, SD 57532
gfp.sd.gov/state-parks
See ad page 818

RIVER VIEW RV PARK **Ratings: 8.5/9.5★/9.5** (RV Park) Avail: 52 full hkups (30/50 amps). 2021 rates: $32 to $42. Mar 01 to Dec 01. (605)280-6266, 910 Verendrye Dr, Fort Pierre, SD 57532

FORT THOMPSON — C4 *Buffalo*

LAKE SHARPE - COE/LEFT TAILRACE CAMPGROUND (Public Corps) From town: Go 2 mi S on Hwy 47-W (L). Avail: 81 E (30/50 amps), Pit toilets. 2021 rates: $8 to $14. May 15 to Sep 12. (605)245-2255

Like Us on Facebook.

SD

FRANKFORT — B5 *Spink*

FISHER GROVE
(Public State Park) From Redfield: Go 7 mi E on US-212, N .5 mi. Entrance fee required. **FAC:** paved rds. Avail: 22 gravel, 4 pull-thrus, (14x75), back-ins (14x65), 22 E (30 amps), tent sites, dump. **REC:** James River: fishing, kayaking/canoeing, playground, rec open to public. Pets OK. 14 day max stay. 2021 rates: $19 to $23.
(800)710-2267 Lat: 44.88346, Lon: -98.35471
17290 Fishers Lane, Frankfort, SD 57440
gfp.sd.gov/state-parks
See ad page 818

GEDDES — D5 *Charles Mix*

PEASE CREEK RECREATION AREA
(Public State Park) From Jct of Hwy 50 & Main St (in Lake Andes), W 8.5 mi on Hwy 50 to SD-1804, S 1.1 mi to 292nd St, W 1 mi to 373rd Ave, S 1 mi to park entrance (R). Note: Park Entrance fee required. **FAC:** gravel rds. Avail: 28 gravel, back-ins (35x60), 23 E (20/30 amps), tent sites, dump. **REC:** Lake Francis Case: fishing, kayaking/canoeing, boating nearby, playground, rec open to public. Pets OK. Partial handicap access, 14 day max stay. 2021 rates: $22 to $26.
(800)710-2267 Lat: 43.140208, Lon: -98.731855
37270-293rd St, Geddes, SD 57342
gfp.sd.gov/state-parks
See ad page 818

GETTYSBURG — B4 *Potter*

WEST WHITLOCK RECREATION AREA
(Public State Park) From Gettysburg: Go 18 mi W on US-212. **FAC:** gravel rds. Avail: 105 gravel, back-ins (22x75), 105 E (20/30 amps), WiFi @ sites, tent sites, rentals, dump. **REC:** Lake Oahe: swim, fishing, kayaking/canoeing, boating nearby, playground, rec open to public. Pets OK. Partial handicap access, 14 day max stay. 2021 rates: $16 to $26.
(800)710-2267 Lat: 45.0481, Lon: -100.2661
16157A West Whitlock Rd., Gettysburg, SD 57442
gfp.sd.gov/state-parks
See ad page 818

GROTON — A5 *Brown*

GROTON CITY PARK (Public) From Jct of US-12 & SR-37: Go 3 blks E on US-12, then 4 blks S on Main St (L). Avail: 5 full hkups (20 amps). 2021 rates: $20. May 01 to Nov 30. (605)397-8422

From fishing along the Cape to boating on the Great Lakes, we've put the Spotlight on North America's most popular travel destinations. Turn to the Spotlight articles in our State and Province sections to learn more.

HARRISBURG — D6 *Lincoln*

Things to See and Do

LAKE ALVIN RECREATION AREA This 59 acre park is best known for its beach facilities and excellent fishing. Anglers can expect to snag walleye, northern pike, crappie, sunfish, perch, catfish and bullheads. Hours: 9am to 5pm. Adult fee: $6.00 per vehicle. No CC.
(800)710-2267 Lat: 43.442555, Lon: -96.609
27225 480th Ave, Harrisburg, SD 57032
gfp.sd.gov/state-parks
See ad page 818

HIGHMORE — B4 *Hyde*

CITY PARK EAST (Public) From Jct of US-14 & SD-47, S 0.5 mi on SD-47 to 2nd St, E 2 blks (L). Avail: 10 E (20 amps). 2021 rates: $8. (605)852-2716

HILL CITY — C1 *Pennington*

A SPOTLIGHT Introducing Hill City's colorful attraction appearing at the front of this state section.

BLACK HILLS TRAILSIDE PARK RESORT
good sam park
Ratings: 6.5/9.5★/7.5 (Campground) At South city limit of Hill City on US-16/385. (East side). Elev 5000 ft.**FAC:** gravel rds. Avail: 35 gravel, 2 pull-thrus, (30x55), back-ins (24x45), 35 full hkups (30/50 amps), cable, WiFi @ sites, tent sites, rentals, dump, fire rings, firewood. **REC:** Spring Creek: boating nearby, playground, hunting nearby. Pets OK. Partial handicap access. Big rig sites, eco-friendly. 2021 rates: $54 to $75, Military discount. May 01 to Oct 30.
(605)574-9079 Lat: 43.92564, Lon: -103.57831
24024 Hwy 16/385, Hill City, SD 57745
trailsideparkresort.com
See ad this page

FIREHOUSE CAMPGROUND
good sam park
Ratings: 6/9.5★/7.5 (RV Park) Avail: 23 full hkups (30/50 amps). 2021 rates: $40 to $55. May 01 to Oct 01. (605)786-2350, 23856 Hwy 385, Hill City, SD 57745

HORSE THIEF CAMPGROUND AND RESORT
good sam park
Ratings: 9/10★/9 (Campground) 66 Avail: 51 full hkups, 15 W, 15 E (30/50 amps). 2021 rates: $39.80 to $63. May 15 to Oct 01. (605)574-2668, 24391 SD Hwy 87, Hill City, SD 57745

LARSSONS CROOKED CREEK RESORT **Ratings: 9/10★/9.5** (Campground) 84 Avail: 56 full hkups, 28 W, 28 E (30/50 amps). 2021 rates: $59 to $169. May 15 to Oct 05. (605)574-2418, 24184 US 385 S, Hill City, SD 57745

MT RUSHMORE KOA AT PALMER GULCH **Ratings: 8.5/9.5★/9.5** (Campground) 352 Avail: 225 full hkups, 125 W, 125 E (30/50 amps). 2021 rates: $71 to $127. May 01 to Oct 01. (800)562-8503, 12620 Hwy 244, Hill City, SD 57745

RAFTER J BAR RANCH CAMPING RESORT
good sam park
Ratings: 8.5/10★/10 (Campground) From south city limits of Hill City: Go 3.0 mi S on US-16/385 (R). Elev 5280 ft.

RAFTER J BAR RANCH CAMPING RESORT
A Black Hills premier camping resort near Mt. Rushmore & other attractions. Enjoy our VERIZON + AT & T 4G coverage across park! 5 Pristine & picturesque camping areas! Only a few minutes to Mount Rushmore & Custer State Park!

FAC: paved/gravel rds. Avail: 180 gravel, patios, 60 pull-thrus, (40x80), back-ins (15x60), 135 full hkups, 13 W, 13 E (30/50 amps), WiFi @ sites, rentals, dump, laundry, groc, LP gas, fire rings, firewood. **REC:** heated pool, hot tub, Spring Creek: fishing, boating nearby, playground, hunting nearby. Pet restrict (B). Partial handicap access. No tents. Big rig sites, eco-friendly. 2021 rates: $63 to $98, Military discount. May 05 to Sep 25.
(605)574-2527 Lat: 43.89461, Lon: -103.59104
12325 Rafter J Rd. , Hill City, SD 57745
www.rafterj.com
See ad page 826

Things to See and Do

RAFTER J BAR RANCH GIFT SHOP Large store carries: Black Hills Gold Jewelry, T-shirts, Sioux Indian Pottery, Souvenirs, Clothing, Camping Supplies, Toys, Gifts, Ice Cream & Snack Bar. Also, limited Groceries. May 01 to Oct 01. RV accessible. Restrooms. Food. Hours: 8am to 7pm. ATM.
(605)574-2527 Lat: 43.89461, Lon: -103.59104
12325 Rafter J Rd, Hill City, SD 57745
www.rafterj.com
See ad page 826

HOT SPRINGS — D1 *Fall River*

ANGOSTURA RECREATION AREA
(Public State Park) From Hot Springs: SE 10 mi on US-18/385 (R). Entrance fee required. Elev 3200 ft.**FAC:** paved rds. Avail: 166 gravel, back-ins (15x55), 160 E (30/50 amps), tent sites, rentals, dump, restaurant. **REC:** Angostura Reservoir: swim, fishing, marina, boating nearby, playground, rec open to public. Pets OK. Partial handicap access, 14 day max stay. 2021 rates: $22 to $26.
(800)710-2267 Lat: 43.345873, Lon: -103.42202
13157 N. Angostura Rd, Hot Springs, SD 57747
gfp.sd.gov/state-parks
See ad page 818

COLD BROOK LAKE - COE (Public Corps) From Jct of Hwy 385 & N River Street (N end of town): Go 1/4 mi NW on Co Rd 18-B, then 1/4 mi W on Cold Brook Ave, then 1/2 mi E on Evans St, then 1-3/4 mi NW on Larive Lake Rd (L). 13 Avail: Pit toilets. 2021 rates: $8. (605)745-5476

COTTONWOOD SPRINGS LAKE - COE/COTTONWOOD SPRINGS CAMPGROUND (Public Corps) From town: Go 5 mi W on US-18, then 2 mi N on CR-17 (R). 18 Avail. 2021 rates: $10. (605)745-5476

HIDDEN LAKE CAMPGROUND & RESORT **Ratings: 7/9.5★/9.5** (RV Resort) Avail: 22 full hkups (30/50 amps). 2021 rates: $45. Apr 15 to Nov 01. (605)745-4042, 27291 Evans St, Hot Springs, SD 57747

HOT SPRINGS KOA **Ratings: 8.5/10★/8** (Campground) 45 Avail: 29 full hkups, 16 W, 16 E (30/50 amps). 2021 rates: $48.55 to $70.49. (605)745-6449, 27585 SD Hwy 79, Hot Springs, SD 57747

SHEPS CANYON RECREATION AREA
(Public) From jct US-385 & Hwy 71 (at Hot Springs): Go 6 mi S on Hwy 71; then 5 mi E on Sheps Canyon Rd. **FAC:** gravel rds. Avail: 22 gravel, back-ins (15x80), WiFi @ sites, tent sites, rentals, dump. **REC:** Angostura Reservoir: swim, fishing, kayaking/canoeing, boating nearby, rec open to public. Pets OK. Partial handicap access. 2021 rates: $22 to $26.
(800)710-2267 Lat: 43.32550, Lon: -103.44579
28150 S Boat Ramp Rd, Hot Springs, SD 57747
gfp.sd.gov/state-parks
See ad page 818

SUNRISE RIDGE CAMPGROUND
good sam park
(RV Park) (Rebuilding) Avail: 27 full hkups (30/50 amps). 2021 rates: $40 to $48. May 25 to Oct 03. (605)745-4397, 27288 Wind Cave Rd, Hot Springs, SD 57747

WIND CAVE/ELK MOUNTAIN (Public National Park) From town: Go 7 mi N on US-385 (L). 48 Avail. 2021 rates: $9 to $18. (605)745-4600

HURON — C5 *Beadle*

MEMORIAL PARK CAMPGROUND (Public) From Jct of Hwy 37 & Hwy 14: Go 3/4 mi E on Hwy 14, then 1/4 N on Jersey Ave (L). Avail: 24 full hkups (30/50 amps). 2021 rates: $25. Apr 01 to Nov 30. (605)353-8533

SOUTH DAKOTA STATE FAIRGROUNDS & PARK (Public) From Jct of Hwy 37 & Hwy 14: Go 1/2 mi S on Dakota Ave, then 1 mi W on 3rd St SW (R). 1256 Avail: 50 full hkups, 1206 E (30/50 amps). 2021 rates: $20 to $25. (800)529-0900

INTERIOR — C2 *Jackson*

BADLANDS MOTEL & CAMPGROUND
good sam park
Ratings: 7/9★/8.5 (Campground) From Jct I-90 (Exit 131) & Hwy 240: Go 9 mi S on Hwy 240, then 2 mi S on Hwy 377. (R). Don't rely on GPS, call. **FAC:** gravel rds. Avail: 57 gravel, 57 pull-thrus, (28x75), mostly side by side hkups, 22 full hkups, 12 W, 12 E (30/50 amps), WiFi @ sites, tent sites, rentals, dump, laundry, groc, fire rings, firewood, restaurant. **REC:** pool, playground, hunting nearby. Pets OK. Partial handicap access, eco-friendly. 2021 rates: $35.60 to $49.80, Military discount. Apr 15 to Oct 01.
(605)433-5335 Lat: 43.72909, Lon: -101.97857
900 SD Hwy 377, Interior, SD 57750
www.badlandsinteriorcampground.com
See ad this page

BADLANDS/CEDAR PASS (Public National Park) From Jct I-90 (exit 131) & Hwy 240: Go 8-1/2 S on Hwy 240, then 1/2 mi S on SR 377 (L). Avail: 21 E (30/50 amps). 2021 rates: $22 to $37. (605)433-5460

We've listened to thousands of RVers like you, so we know exactly how to rate campgrounds. Got feedback? Call us! 877-209-6655.

BADLANDS/WHITE RIVER KOA **Ratings: 8.5/10★/9.5** (Campground) 69 Avail: 39 full hkups, 30 W, 30 E (30/50 amps). 2021 rates: $47 to $120. May 01 to Sep 30. (800)KOA-3897, 20720 SD Highway 44, Interior, SD 57750

MINUTEMAN RV PARK & LODGING **Ratings: 6/7.5★/6.5** (Campground) 33 Avail: 16 full hkups, 17 W, 17 E (30/50 amps). 2021 rates: $37 to $40. Apr 20 to Oct 15. (605)433-5451, 21295 SD Hwy 240, Philip, SD 57567

KENNEBEC — C4 *Lyman*

KENNEBEC KOA **Ratings: 8.5/10★/8.5** (Campground) 41 Avail: 28 full hkups, 13 W, 13 E (30/50 amps). 2021 rates: $58 to $79. May 01 to Oct 31. (605)869-2300, 307 S Hwy 273, Kennebec, SD 57544

KEYSTONE — C1 *Custer*

KEMP'S KAMP **Ratings: 6.5/9★/7.5** (Campground) 37 Avail: 14 full hkups, 23 W, 23 E (30/50 amps). 2021 rates: $25 to $55. May 10 to Oct 01. (605)666-4654, 1022 Old Hill City Road, Keystone, SD 57751

RUSHMORE VIEW RV PARK

good sam park **Ratings: 7/9★/8** (Campground) From jct Hwy 16 & Hwy 16A: Go 2-1/2 mi S on Hwy 16A to center of Keystone & the Magneson Grand Rushmore View & RV (L). Elev 4386 ft.**FAC:** gravel rds. Avail: 23 gravel, 9 pull-thrus, (24x60), back-ins (30x60), 23 full hkups (30/50 amps), WiFi @ sites, tent sites, rentals, dump, laundry, groc, LP bottles, restaurant. **REC:** Grizzley Creek: fishing, boating nearby. Pets OK. Partial handicap access. Big rig sites. 2021 rates: $49 to $69, Military discount. May 01 to Oct 15. ATM.
(605)666-4638 Lat: 43.88909, Lon: -103.42449
522 S. Hwy 16A, Keystone, SD 57751
www.rushmoreviewinn.com
See ad this page

SPOKANE CREEK CABINS & CAMPGROUND **Ratings: 7/7.5/8** (Campground) 29 Avail: 15 full hkups, 14 W, 14 E (20/30 amps). 2021 rates: $41 to $46.50. May 15 to Sep 10. (605)666-4609, 24631 Iron Mountain Rd, Keystone, SD 57751

LAKE CITY — A6 *Marshall*

FORT SISSETON

(Public State Park) 10 mi SW of Lake City off US Hwy 10. **FAC:** paved rds. Avail: 14 gravel, back-ins (12x70), 10 E (20/30 amps), WiFi @ sites, tent sites, rentals, . **REC:** Kettle Lake: fishing, kayaking/canoeing, hunting nearby, rec open to public. Pets OK. Partial handicap access, 14 day max stay. 2021 rates: $22 to $26. Oct 01 to Apr 30.
(800)710-2267 Lat: 45.659398, Lon: -97.528266
11907 434th Ave, Lake City, SD 57247
gfp.sd.gov/state-parks
See ad page 818

ROY LAKE

(Public State Park) From Lake City: Go 3 mi SW on SD-10. **FAC:** paved rds. Avail: 100 gravel, 6 pull-thrus, (20x75), back-ins (20x60), 100 E (30/50 amps), tent sites, rentals, dump, groc, restaurant. **REC:** Roy Lake: swim, fishing, kayaking/canoeing, boating nearby, playground, rec open to public. Pets OK. Partial handicap access, 14 day max stay. 2021 rates: $22 to $26.
(800)710-2267 Lat: 45.709611, Lon: -97.448000
11545 Northside Dr, Lake City, SD 57247
gfp.sd.gov/state-parks
See ad page 818

LAKE PRESTON — B6 *Kingsbury*

LAKE THOMPSON RECREATION AREA

(Public State Park) From Jct of Hwy 14 & Main St (in Lake Preston), W 3.8 mi on Hwy 14 to 438th Ave, S 4 mi to park entrance. Entrance fee required. **FAC:** gravel rds. Avail: 103 gravel, 21 pull-thrus, (16x72), back-ins (16x72), 103 E (20/30 amps), tent sites, rentals, dump. **REC:** Lake Thompson: swim, fishing, boating nearby, playground, rec open to public. Pets OK. Partial handicap access, 14 day max stay. 2021 rates: $15 to $26.
(800)710-2267 Lat: 44.32346, Lon: -97.43463
21176 Flood Club Rd, Lake Preston, SD 57249
gfp.sd.gov/state-parks
See ad page 818

LEAD — C1 *Lawrence*

RECREATIONAL SPRINGS RESORT **Ratings: 6/8.5★/8.5** (Campground) 50 Avail: 20 full hkups, 30 W, 30 E (30/50 amps). 2021 rates: $40 to $55. (605)584-1228, 11201 US Highway 14A, Lead, SD 57754

LEMMON — A2 *Perkins*

LLEWELLYN JOHNS RECREATION AREA

(Public State Park) From Lemmon: Go 12 mi S on Hwy 73. **FAC:** gravel rds. Avail: 10 gravel, back-ins (12x50), 10 E (20/30 amps), tent sites, pit toilets. Pets OK. 14 day max stay. 2021 rates: $22 to $26.
(800)710-2267 Lat: 45.775402, Lon: -102.17742
Hwy 73, Lemmon, SD 57638
gfp.sd.gov/state-parks
See ad page 818

SHADEHILL RECREATION AREA

(Public State Park) From Lemmon: Go 12 mi S on Hwy 73 (R). Entrance fee required. **FAC:** gravel rds. Avail: 56 gravel, 3 pull-thrus, (20x100), back-ins (20x70), 56 E (20/30 amps), tent sites, rentals, dump. **REC:** Shadehill Reservoir: swim, fishing, kayaking/canoeing, boating nearby, playground, rec open to public. Pets OK. Partial handicap access, 14 day max stay. 2021 rates: $16 to $26.
(800)710-2267 Lat: 45.761144, Lon: -102.21849
19150 Summerville Rd, Shadehill, SD 57638
gfp.sd.gov/state-parks
See ad page 818

MADISON — C6 *Lake*

LAKE HERMAN

(Public State Park) From Madison: Go W 2 mi on Hwy 34 to Lake Rd, S 2 mi (E). **FAC:** paved rds. Avail: 72 gravel, 6 pull-thrus, (15x50), back-ins (15x50), 72 E (20/30 amps), tent sites, rentals, dump. **REC:** Lake Herman: swim, fishing, kayaking/canoeing, playground, hunting nearby, rec open to public. Pets OK. Partial handicap access, 14 day max stay. 2021 rates: $22 to $26.
(800)710-2267 Lat: 43.992878, Lon: -97.160427
23409 State Park Dr, Madison, SD 57042
gfp.sd.gov/state-parks
See ad page 818

WALKER'S POINT RECREATION AREA

(Public State Park) From Madison: Go 9 mi SE on Hwy 19 to Walker's Point Rd, E 2 mi, N 1.5 mi on township road (R). **FAC:** paved rds. Avail: 43 gravel, 8 pull-thrus, (20x60), back-ins (26x60), 43 E (20/30 amps), tent sites, rentals, dump. **REC:** Madison Lake: fishing, kayaking/canoeing, boating nearby, playground, rec open to public. Pets OK. Partial handicap access, 14 day max stay. 2021 rates: $22 to $26.
(800)710-2267 Lat: 43.956806, Lon: -97.028615
6431 Walker's Point Dr, Madison, SD 57042
gfp.sd.gov/state-parks
See ad page 818

MILBANK — A6 *Grant*

HARTFORD BEACH

(Public State Park) From Milbank: Go 15 mi N on Hwy 15. Entrance fee required. **FAC:** paved rds. Avail: 87 gravel, back-ins (15x70), 87 E (20/30 amps), tent sites, rentals, dump. **REC:** Big Stone Lake: swim, fishing, boating nearby, playground, rec open to public. Pets OK. Partial handicap access, 14 day max stay. 2021 rates: $26.
(800)710-2267 Lat: 45.402196, Lon: -96.673074
13672 Hartford Beach Rd, Corona, SD 57227
gfp.sd.gov/state-parks
See ad page 818

MILLER — B4 *Hand*

CRYSTAL PARK (Public) From Jct of Hwy 14 & 7th St exit, W 3 blks on 7th St (R). Avail: 32 E (20 amps). May 01 to Sep 30. (605)853-2705

LAKE LOUISE RECREATION AREA

(Public State Park) From Miller, go 14 mi NW on US-14. Entrance fee required. **FAC:** paved rds. 39 Avail: 28 paved, 11 gravel, back-ins (14x50), 39 E (20/30 amps), tent sites, rentals, dump. **REC:** Lake Louise: swim, fishing, playground, rec open to public. Pets OK. Partial handicap access, 14 day max stay. 2021 rates: $15 to $26.
(800)710-2267 Lat: 44.620547, Lon: -99.140554
35250 191st St, Miller, SD 57362
gfp.sd.gov/state-parks
See ad page 818

MITCHELL — C5 *Davison*

BETTS CAMPGROUND

good sam park **Ratings: 9/9.5★/9.5** (Campground) From Jct of I-90 & Exit 325 (Betts Rd), S 0.2 mi on Betts Rd (R). **FAC:** gravel rds. Avail: 66 gravel, 39 pull-thrus, (25x65), back-ins (35x65), 58 full hkups, 8 W, 8 E (30/50 amps), WiFi @ sites, tent sites, rentals, dump, laundry, groc, fire rings, firewood. **REC:** pool, playground. Pets OK. Partial handicap access. Big rig sites, eco-friendly. 2021 rates: $32 to $35, Military discount. Apr 15 to Oct 15.
(605)996-8983 Lat: 43.69179, Lon: -98.14728
25473 403rd Ave, Mitchell, SD 57301
www.bettscampground.com
See ad this page

We rate what RVers consider important.

DAKOTA CAMPGROUND

good sam park **Ratings: 9/9.5★/9** (Campground) From Jct of I-90 & Exit 330, S 0.2 mi on 408th Ave/Ohlman St to Spruce St, W 0.1 mi on Spruce St (R). **FAC:** gravel rds. Avail: 54 gravel, 12 pull-thrus, (30x70), back-ins (30x70), 42 full hkups, 12 W, 12 E (30/50 amps), WiFi @ sites, tent sites, rentals, dump, laundry, fire rings, firewood. **REC:** pool, boating nearby, playground, hunting nearby. Pets OK. Partial handicap access. Big rig sites, eco-friendly. 2021 rates: $30 to $34, Military discount. Apr 01 to Nov 30.
(605)996-9432 Lat: 43.68765, Lon: -98.04991
1800 W Spruce, Mitchell, SD 57301
www.dakotacampground.net
See ad this page

LAKE MITCHELL CAMPGROUND (Public) From Jct of I-90 & SR-37 (Exit 330): Go 3 mi N on SR-37, then 1/2 mi N on Main St (L). Avail: 50 full hkups (30/50 amps). 2021 rates: $37. Apr 15 to Oct 31. (605)995-8450

MITCHELL (CONT)

MITCHELL KOA **Ratings: 7.5/9★/8.5** (Campground) 56 Avail: 26 full hkups, 30 W, 30 E (30/50 amps). 2021 rates: $34 to $49. May 01 to Oct 31. (800)562-1236, 41255 SD Hwy 38, MItchell, SD 57301

R & R CAMPGROUND & RV PARK

good sam park **Ratings: 8/10★/7.5** (Campground) From Jct I-90 (exit 332) & Burr St: Go 1000 ft N on Burr St to first right turn, then 1000 ft E & S to campground entrance (behind Super 8 motel).

VISIT THE WORLD'S ONLY CORN PALACE
Conveniently located off the freeway en route to the Black Hills. Enjoy a visit to the Corn Palace decorated with thousands of bushels of corn, grains and native grasses and features light-up domes in downtown Mitchell.

FAC: paved/gravel rds. 40 Avail: 5 paved, 35 gravel, 35 pull-thrus, (30x70), back-ins (30x70), 40 full hkups (30/50 amps), cable, WiFi @ sites, tent sites, rentals, dump, laundry, groc, fire rings, firewood. **REC:** heated pool, boating nearby, playground. Pet restrict (B). Partial handicap access. Big rig sites. 2021 rates: $36 to $40, Military discount. May 01 to Sep 30.
(605)996-8895 Lat: 43.69431, Lon: -98.01131
1700 S Burr St., Mitchell, SD 57301
www.mitchellsuper8.com
See ad previous page

RONDEE'S RV PARK **Ratings: 8.5/9.5★/8** (Campground) Avail: 35 full hkups (30/50 amps). 2021 rates: $30 to $35. May 01 to Sep 30. (605)996-0769, 911 E Kay Ave, Mitchell, SD 57301

MOBRIDGE — A3 *Corson*

INDIAN CREEK RECREATION AREA

(Public State Park) From Mobridge: Go 2 mi SE on US-12. **FAC:** gravel rds. Avail: 123 gravel, 2 pull-thrus, (15x70), back-ins (15x70), 123 E (20/30 amps), tent sites, rentals, dump. **REC:** Lake Oahe: swim, fishing, marina, kayaking/canoeing, playground, hunting nearby, rec open to public. Pets OK. Partial handicap access, 14 day max stay. 2021 rates: $20.
(800)710-2267 Lat: 45.522137, Lon: -100.3868
12905 - 288th Ave, Mobridge, SD 57631
www.gfp.sd.gov/state-parks
See ad page 818

MONTROSE — C6 *McCook*

PIONEER CAMPGROUND (Public) From Jct of I-90 & 451st Ave: Go 2 mi N on 451st Ave (L). 40 Avail: 40 W, 40 E (30/50 amps). 2021 rates: $25. May 01 to Nov 01. (605)480-1999

MOUNT RUSHMORE — C1 *Pennington*

HEARTLAND RV PARK & CABINS

good sam park **Ratings: 10/10★/10** (RV Park) From Mount Rushmore: Go 2-3/4 mi NE on US-16A/Hwy 244, then 19-1/2 mi E on Hwy 40, then 1/4 mi S on Hwy 79 (R). Elev 3300 ft.**FAC:** all weather rds. Avail: 215 all weather, 215 pull-thrus, (30x80), 215 full hkups (30/50 amps), WiFi @ sites, tent sites, rentals, dump, laundry, LP gas, fire rings, firewood. **REC:** heated pool, hot tub, playground, hunting nearby. Pets OK. Partial handicap access. Big rig sites. 2021 rates: $29.99 to $79.99, Military discount.
(605)255-5460 Lat: 43.81876, Lon: -103.20265
24743 Hwy 79, Hermosa, SD 57744
www.heartlandrvpark.com
See primary listing at Rapid City and ad opposite page

RUSHMORE SHADOWS RESORT

good sam park **Ratings: 10/10★/10** (Membership Park) From Mount Rushmore: Go 1-1/2 mi NE on Hwy 244, then 4-1/2 mi NE on US-16A (through Keystone), then 7 mi NE on US-16. (L). Elev 4425 ft.**FAC:** paved rds. 198 Avail: 45 paved, 153 all weather, 56 pull-thrus, (30x60), back-ins (28x60), 198 full hkups (30/50 amps), WiFi @ sites, tent sites, dump, laundry, groc, fire rings, firewood, controlled access. **REC:** heated pool, hot tub, playground. Pets OK. Partial handicap access. Big rig sites, eco-friendly. 2021 rates: $75, Military discount. May 01 to Oct 15.
(800)231-0425 Lat: 43.97309, Lon: -103.32716
23680 Busted Five Ct, Rapid City, SD 57702
www.midwestoutdoorresorts.com
See primary listing at Rapid City and ad page 819

MURDO — C3 *Jones*

AMERICAN INN & RV PARK

good sam park **Ratings: 5/8.5★/9** (Campground) 51 Avail: 20 full hkups, 31 W, 31 E (30/50 amps). 2021 rates: $28 to $38. May 25 to Sep 30. (605)669-2461, 305 5th Street, Murdo, SD 57559

NORTH SIOUX CITY — E6 *Union*

SIOUX CITY NORTH KOA **Ratings: 9/10★/8.5** (Campground) 83 Avail: 76 full hkups, 7 W, 7 E (30/50 amps). 2021 rates: $49.03 to $87.19. (605)232-4519, 675 Streeter Dr, North Sioux CIty, SD 57049

PICKSTOWN — D5 *Charles Mix*

FORT RANDALL DAM - COE/RANDALL CREEK CAMPGROUND

(Public Corps) From Pickstown: Go 1 mi W on US-281. **FAC:** paved rds. Avail: 132 gravel, back-ins (12x55), 132 E (30/50 amps), tent sites, rentals, dump. **REC:** Missouri River: swim, fishing, kayaking/canoeing, playground, hunting nearby, rec open to public. Pets OK. 14 day max stay. 2021 rates: $23.
(800)710-2267 Lat: 43.051021, Lon: -98.555139
136 Randall Creek Rd, Pickstown, SD 57367
gfp.sd.gov
See ad page 818

NORTH POINT RECREATION AREA

(Public State Park) From Pickstown: Go 1 mi NW on US-281, follow signs (L) Entrance fee required. **FAC:** paved rds. Avail: 115 gravel, back-ins (15x70), 115 E (20/30 amps), tent sites, rentals, dump. **REC:** Lake Francis Case: swim, fishing, marina, boating nearby, golf, playground, rec open to public. Pets OK. Partial handicap access, 14 day max stay. 2021 rates: $26.
(800)710-2267 Lat: 43.083064, Lon: -98.550327
38180-297th St, Lake Andes, SD 57356
gfp.sd.gov/state-parks
See ad page 818

PIERRE — C3 *Hughes*

FARM ISLAND RECREATION AREA

(Public State Park) From Pierre: Go 4 mi E on Hwy 34 (R). Entrance fee required. **FAC:** paved rds. Avail: 90 gravel, back-ins (16x70), 90 E (20/30 amps), tent sites, rentals, dump. **REC:** Missouri River: swim, fishing, kayaking/canoeing, playground, hunting nearby, rec open to public. Pets OK. Partial handicap access, 14 day max stay. 2021 rates: $26.
(800)710-2267 Lat: 44.345921, Lon: -100.3
1301 Farm Island Rd, Pierre, SD 57501
gfp.sd.gov/state-parks
See ad page 818

GRIFFIN PARK (Public) From Jct of US-83 & Sioux St: Go 5 blks E on Sioux St, then 2 blks S to Washington (E). Avail: 16 E (20 amps). 2021 rates: $10 to $16. (605)773-2527

Exclusive! According to our research, restroom cleanliness is of the utmost importance to RVers. Of course, you knew that already. The cleanest campgrounds have a star in their restroom rating!

OKOBOJO POINT RECREATION AREA

(Public State Park) From Pierre: Go 17 mi NW on Hwy 1804. **FAC:** gravel rds. Avail: 18 gravel, back-ins (15x60), tent sites, . **REC:** Lake Oahe: swim, fishing, kayaking/canoeing, boating nearby, rec open to public. Pets OK. 14 day max stay. 2021 rates: $16. no cc.
(800)710-2267 Lat: 44.57596, Lon: -100.4955
19425 Okobojo Point Dr, Fort Pierre, SD 57532
gfp.sd.gov/state-parks
See ad page 818

WEST BEND RECREATION AREA

(Public State Park) From Pierce: Go 26 mi E on Hwy 34 then 9 mi S on unnamed CR. Follow signs. (L) Entrance fee required. **FAC:** paved rds. Avail: 120 gravel, back-ins (16x65), 108 E (20/30 amps), WiFi @ sites, tent sites, rentals, dump. **REC:** Lake Sharpe Reservoir: fishing, boating nearby, playground, rec open to public. Pets OK. Partial handicap access, 14 day max stay. 2021 rates: $16 to $26.
(800)710-2267 Lat: 44.170744, Lon: -99.721022
22154 West Bend Rd, Harrold, SD 57536
gfp.sd.gov/state-parks
See ad page 818

Things to See and Do

SOUTH DAKOTA DEPT OF GAME, FISH & PARKS Home to breathtaking scenery, abundant wildlife, and exciting geological wonders, South Dakota offers visitors a range of things to do and see.

ENJOY BIKING IN OUR STATE PARKS!
We have the George S Mickelson Trail, trails that can be used for Fat Tire bikes, strider bikes, normal bikes. We even have fun bikes like banana bikes, tricycles and more!

Partial handicap access. Hours: 8am to 5pm. Adult fee: $15 to $185. No CC.
(800)710-2267 Lat: 44.365360, Lon: -100.344990
523 East Capitol, Joe Foss Bldg, Pierre, SD 57501
gfp.sd.gov
See ad page 818

PLATTE — D5 *Charles Mix*

BURYANEK RECREATION AREA

(Public State Park) From Platte: Go 20 mi NW on Hwy 44. **FAC:** gravel rds. Avail: 44 gravel, back-ins (14x67), 41 E (20/30 amps), tent sites, rentals, dump. **REC:** Lake Francis Case: swim, fishing, kayaking/canoeing, playground, hunting nearby, rec open to public. Pets OK. Partial handicap access, 14 day max stay. 2021 rates: $19 to $23.
(800)710-2267 Lat: 43.415231, Lon: -99.173167
27450 Buryanek Rd, Burke, SD 57523
gfp.sd.gov/state-parks
See ad page 818

NORTH WHEELER RECREATION AREA

(Public State Park) From Platte: Go 16 mi S on Hwy 1804. **FAC:** gravel rds. Avail: 25 gravel, back-ins (12x65), 25 E (20/30 amps), tent sites, pit toilets. **REC:** Lake Francis Case: fishing, boating nearby, rec open to public. Pets OK. 14 day max stay. 2021 rates: $11 to $15. no cc.
(800)710-2267 Lat: 43.17173, Lon: -98.82555
29084 N Wheeler Rd, Geddes, SD 57342
gfp.sd.gov/state-parks
See ad page 818

PLATTE CREEK RECREATION AREA

(Public State Park) From Jct of Hwy 45 & Hwy 44: Go 8 mi W on Hwy 44, then 10 mi S on Hwy 1804 (R). Entrance fee required. **FAC:** paved rds. Avail: 36 gravel, back-ins (18x60), 36 E (20/30 amps), tent sites, dump. **REC:** Lake Francis Case: swim, fishing, kayaking/canoeing, boating nearby, playground, rec open to public. Pets OK. Partial handicap access, 14 day max stay. 2021 rates: $20.
(800)710-2267 Lat: 43.298531, Lon: -98.997652
35910-282nd St, Platte, SD 57369
gfp.sd.gov/state-parks
See ad page 818

SNAKE CREEK RECREATION AREA

(Public State Park) From Platte: Go 14 mi W on Hwy 44 (L). Entrance fee required. **FAC:** paved rds. Avail: 115 gravel, 7 pull-thrus, (18x51), back-ins (18x40), 111 E (20/30 amps), tent sites, rentals, dump, groc, restaurant. **REC:** Lake Francis Case: swim, fishing, marina, boating nearby, playground, rec open to public. Pets OK. Partial handicap access, 14 day max stay. 2021 rates: $22 to $26.
(800)710-2267 Lat: 43.389979, Lon: -99.119491
35316 SD Hwy 44, Platte, SD 57369
gfp.sd.gov/state-parks
See ad page 818

POLLOCK — A3 *Campbell*

WEST POLLOCK RECREATION AREA
(Public State Park) From Pollock: Go 3 mi SW on Hwy 1804. **FAC:** gravel rds. Avail: 29 gravel, back-ins (16x75), 29 E (20/30 amps), tent sites, dump. **REC:** Lake Oahe: fishing, kayaking/canoeing, boating nearby, playground, rec open to public. Pets OK. 14 day max stay. 2021 rates: $20.
(800)710-2267 Lat: 45.88432, Lon: -100.3356
12905-288th Ave, Mobridge, SD 57601
gfp.sd.gov/state-parks
See ad page 818

PRESHO — C4 *Lyman*

NEW FRONTIER CAMPGROUND & RV PARK
good sam park
Ratings: 8/10★/9 (Campground) From jct I-90 (Exit 226) & US-183: Go 1/4 mi W on I-90 Service Road. (R).

QUIET NIGHTS REST UNDER THE STARS
Conveniently located between Sioux Falls and the Black Hills, enjoy Western hospitality, a clean camp, and a quiet nights rest under a peaceful Prairie sky!
FAC: gravel rds. Avail: 86 gravel, 60 pull-thrus, (24x60), back-ins (18x75), 86 full hkups (30/50 amps), WiFi @ sites, tent sites, rentals, dump, laundry, LP gas, fire rings, firewood. **REC:** Brakke Dam/Fate Dam: boating nearby, playground, hunting nearby. Pets OK. Partial handicap access. Big rig sites, eco-friendly. 2021 rates: $47.50 to $67.50, Military discount. Apr 01 to Nov 01.
(605)895-2604 Lat: 43.90314, Lon: -100.05262
502 E Hwy 16, Presho, SD 57568
www.newfrontiercampground.com
See ad this page

RAPID CITY — C1 *Meade*

A SPOTLIGHT Introducing Rapid City's colorful attractions appearing at the front of this state section.

RAPID CITY See also Black Hawk, Deadwood, Hill City, Keystone & Sturgis.

HAPPY HOLIDAY RV RESORT
good sam park
Ratings: 9/9★/7.5 (Campground) From Jct I-90 & Exit 61 (Elkvale Rd): Go 8.8 mi S on Elkvale Rd (turns into Catron Blvd/US-16 Truck BYP) to US 16, then 2.2 mi S on US-16. (L). Elev 3200 ft.**FAC:** paved/gravel rds. Avail: 190 gravel, patios, 146 pull-thrus, (22x54), back-ins (23x50), 148 full hkups, 42 W, 42 E (30/50 amps), WiFi @ sites, tent sites, rentals, dump, laundry, groc, LP gas, fire rings, firewood. **REC:** heated pool, playground. Pets OK $. Partial handicap access. 2021 rates: $35 to $55, Military discount.
(605)342-7365 Lat: 43.99030, Lon: -103.26870
8990 S Hwy 16, Rapid City, SD 57702
happyholidayrvresort.com
See ad this page

HEARTLAND RV PARK & CABINS
good sam park
Ratings: 10/10★/10 (RV Park) From Jct I-90 (Exit 61) & US-16 truck rte/Hwy 79: Go 5 1/4 mi S & W on US-16 truck rte/Hwy 79 (N Elk Vale Rd), then 12.5 mi S on Hwy 79 mile marker 59 (R). Elev 3300 ft.

COME FOR THE NIGHT STAY FOR THE FUN
Wine tasting, Bingo, breakfasts & music are just some of the great entertainment in the beautiful onsite events center. Our Pickleball/basketball court is sure to please the athletes. Easy access to all the local attractions.
FAC: all weather rds. Avail: 215 all weather, 215 pull-thrus, (30x80), 215 full hkups (30/50 amps), WiFi @ sites, tent sites, rentals, dump, laundry, LP gas, fire rings, firewood. **REC:** heated pool, hot tub, playground, hunting nearby. Pets OK. Partial handicap access. Big rig sites. 2021 rates: $29.99 to $79.99, Military discount.
(605)255-5460 Lat: 43.81876, Lon: -103.20265
24743 Hwy 79, Hermosa, SD 57744
www.heartlandrvpark.com
See ad this page

LAKE PARK CAMPGROUND & COTTAGES
good sam park
Ratings: 8.5/10★/9.5 (Campground) 29 Avail: 23 full hkups, 6 W, 6 E (30/50 amps). 2021 rates: $47 to $78. (605)341-5320, 2850 Chapel Ln, Rapid City, SD 57702

LAZY JD RV PARK **Ratings: 3.5/8.5★/6.5** (Campground) Avail: 22 full hkups (30/50 amps). 2021 rates: $35. May 01 to Oct 01. (605)787-7036, 12336 Erickson Ranch Rd, Piedmont, SD 57769

The best things happen outdoors. Start your adventure today at GanderOutdoors.com

MILITARY PARK ELLSWORTH AFB FAMCAMP (ELLSWORTH AFB) (Public) From jct US-90 & Commercial Gate Rd (exit 63): Go on Commercial Gate Rd which becomes Ellsworth St, then turn right on Lemay (merges into N Ellsworth Rd), then turn left on Lincoln (R). 63 Avail: 51 full hkups, 12 E (30/50 amps). 2021 rates: $10 to $30. (605)385-6699

RAPID CITY KOA **Ratings: 8.5/10★/9.5** (Campground) 139 Avail: 89 full hkups, 42 W, 50 E (30/50 amps). 2021 rates: $49.25 to $81. Apr 15 to Oct 15. (800)562-8504, 3010 E Hwy 44, Rapid City, SD 57703

RAPID CITY RV PARK AND CAMPGROUND
good sam park
Ratings: 9.5/10★/8 (Campground) Avail: 72 full hkups (30/50 amps). 2021 rates: $51.98 to $57.75. Apr 15 to Oct 15. (605)342-2751, 4110 S Hwy 16 / Mt Rushmore Rd, Rapid City, SD 57701

RAPID CITY SOUTH RV PARK
good sam park
Ratings: 6.5/9★/8 (Campground) 70 Avail: 50 full hkups, 20 W, 20 E (30/50 amps). 2021 rates: $44.36 to $51.98. May 01 to Sep 30. (605)343-6319, 2200 Ft Hayes Dr, Rapid City, SD 57702

RUSHMORE SHADOWS RESORT
good sam park
Ratings: 10/10★/10 (Membership Park) From Jct I-90 (Exit 61) & US-16 Truck/Hwy 79: Go 9 mi S & W on US-16 Truck, then 6-1/2 mi W on US-16 W (R). Elev 4313 ft.

ON THE ROAD TO MOUNT RUSHMORE
15 minutes to Rapid City, Keystone, Hill City, Mount Rushmore & Custer State Park. Full RV hook-ups, cabins & spots for tents. Plenty of pine trees and lots of family fun! Private, secure & quiet. Perfect for your base camp!
FAC: paved rds. 198 Avail: 45 paved, 153 all weather, 56 pull-thrus, (30x60), back-ins (28x60), 198 full hkups (30/50 amps), WiFi @ sites, tent sites, dump, laundry, groc, fire rings, firewood, controlled access. **REC:** heated pool, hot tub, playground. Pets OK. Partial handicap access. Big rig sites, eco-friendly. 2021 rates: $75, Military discount. May 01 to Oct 15.
(800)231-0425 Lat: 43.97309, Lon: -103.32716
23680 Busted Five Court, Rapid City, SD 57702
midwestoutdoorresorts.com
See ad page 819

SOUTHERN HILLS RV PARK & CAMPGROUND
good sam park
Ratings: 8/9.5★/8.5 (RV Park) From I-90 & Elk Vale Rd (US-16 Truck bypass): Go 5.4 mi S to Hwy 79, then go 14 mi S on Hwy 79 to mile marker 61 (R). **FAC:** all weather rds. Avail: 38 all weather, patios, 32 pull-thrus, (43x73), back-ins (43x73), 38 full hkups (30/50 amps), WiFi @ sites, tent sites, laundry. **REC:** hunting nearby. Pet restrict (Q). Big rig sites, eco-friendly. 2021 rates: $44, Military discount. May 01 to Sep 30.
(605)939-7609 Lat: 43.84580, Lon: -103.20218
24549 Hwy 79, Hermosa, SD 57744
southernhillsrvparkandcampground.com
See ad this page

WHISPERING PINES CAMPGROUND **Ratings: 7.5/7/8.5** (Campground) 44 Avail: 24 full hkups, 20 W, 20 E (30/50 amps). 2021 rates: $35 to $45. May 15 to Sep 15. (605)341-3667, 22700 Silver City Rd, Rapid City, SD 57702

REDFIELD — B5 *Spink*

HAV-A-REST CAMPGROUND (Public) From W Jct US-212 & US-281: Go 1/2 mi NW on US-212; then 1/2 mi E on W 4th Ave (L). 19 Avail: 19 W, 19 E (30/50 amps). 2021 rates: $20. Apr 01 to Nov 01. (605)472-4552

Park policies vary. Ask about the cancellation policy when making a reservation.

SALEM — C6 *McCook*

DAKOTA SUNSETS RV PARK & CAMPGROUND **Ratings: 8/9.5★/10** (Campground) 54 Avail: 47 full hkups, 7 W, 7 E (30/50 amps). 2021 rates: $36 to $43. Apr 15 to Oct 31. (605)425-9085, 25495 US-81, Salem, SD 57058

Driving a big rig? Average site width and length measurements tell you which campgrounds can accommodate your Big Rig.

SELBY — A4 *Walworth*

LAKE HIDDENWOOD RECREATION AREA (Public State Park) From Selby: Go 5 mi NE on US 12/83. Avail: 7 E (20/30 amps), Pit toilets. 2021 rates: $15. (800)710-2267

SIOUX FALLS — C6 *Minnehaha*

SIOUX FALLS See also Canton.

RED BARN RV PARK
good sam park **Ratings: 7.5/8.5★/8.5** (Campground) Avail: 73 full hkups (30/50 amps). 2021 rates: $45. Apr 01 to Nov 01. (605)368-2268, 47003 272nd St, Tea, SD 57064

SIOUX FALLS KOA **Ratings: 9/9.5★/8** (Campground) 79 Avail: 63 full hkups, 16 W, 16 E (30/50 amps). 2021 rates: $44 to $83. May 01 to Oct 15. (605)332-9987, 1401 E Robur Dr, Sioux Falls, SD 57104

SIOUX FALLS YOGI BEAR
good sam park **Ratings: 9/10★/9.5** (Campground) 112 Avail: 98 full hkups, 14 W, 14 E (30/50 amps). 2021 rates: $40 to $72. Apr 01 to Nov 30. (605)332-2233, 26014 478th Ave, Brandon, SD 57005

Join in the fun. Like us on FACEBOOK!

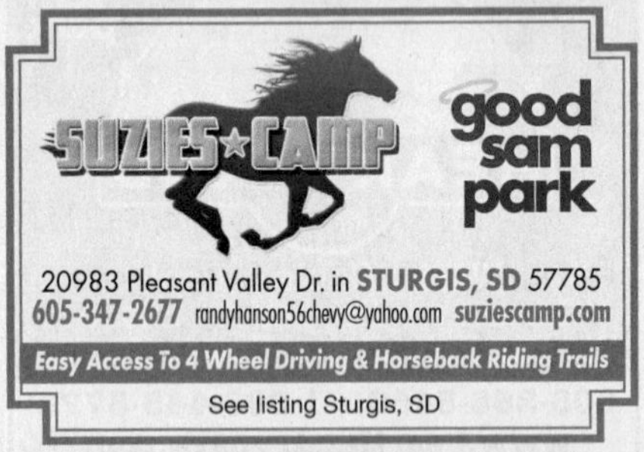

TOWER CAMPGROUND
good sam park **Ratings: 8/9.5★/8.5** (RV Park) N Bnd: From Jct I-29 (exit 78) & 26th St: Go 1/2 mi W on 26th St, then 1 mi N on Marion Rd, then 1/3 mi E on W 12th St/SD-42 (R). S Bnd: From Jct I-29 (exit 80) & W Madison St: Go 1/2 mi W on Madison St, then 1 mi S on S Ebenezer, then 1/3 mi E on W 12th St/SD-42 (R). **FAC:** paved/gravel rds. 119 Avail: 87 paved, 32 gravel, 18 pull-thrus, (50x60), back-ins (50x50), 119 full hkups (30/50 amps), cable, WiFi @ sites, dump, laundry, LP bottles, fire rings, firewood. **REC:** boating nearby, playground, hunting nearby. Pet restrict (B). Partial handicap access. No tents. Big rig sites, eco-friendly. 2021 rates: $49.50 to $55, Military discount.
(605)332-1173 Lat: 43.54361, Lon: -96.78177
4609 W. 12th St, Sioux Falls, SD 57106
www.towercampground.com
See ad this page

W.H. LYON FAIRGROUNDS CAMPGROUND (Public) From Jct of I-29 & Exit 80 (Madison St), E 0.2 mi on Madison St to Fairground Rd, S 0.3 mi (R) or From Jct of I-29 & Exit 79 (W 12th St), E 0.2 mi on W 12th St to Lyons Blvd, N 0.2 mi to fairground entrance (R). 251 Avail: 115 full hkups, 82 W, 136 E (30/50 amps). 2021 rates: $30. Apr 15 to Oct 31. (605)367-7178

Travel Services

CAMPING WORLD OF SIOUX FALLS As the nation's largest retailer of RV supplies, accessories, services and new and used RVs, Camping World is committed to making your total RV experience better. **SERVICES:** RV, MH mechanical, restrooms. RV Sales. RV supplies, RV accessible. Hours: 9am to 7pm.
(888)796-8743 Lat: 43.607029, Lon: -96.704229
1601 E Robur Dr, Sioux Falls, SD 57104
www.campingworld.com

Things to See and Do

GOOD EARTH STATE PARK An important cultural and historical site as well as a unique nature retreat. The site itself is one of the oldest sites of long-term human habitation in the U.S. Hours: Tues-Sat 9-5, Sun 1-5. Adult fee: $6.00 per vehicle. No CC.
(800)710-2267 Lat: 43.475595, Lon: -96.5942
26924 480th Avenue, Sioux Falls, SD 57018
gfp.sd.gov/state-parks
See ad page 818

SISSETON — A6 *Roberts*

CAMP DAKOTAH **Ratings: 7.5/8.5★/8.5** (Campground) Avail: 26 full hkups (30/50 amps). 2021 rates: $35 to $40. (605)698-7388, 11885 460th Ave, Sisseton, SD 57262

SICA HOLLOW
(Public State Park) From Sisseton: Go 15 mi NW on Hwy 10. **FAC:** gravel rds. Avail: 8 grass, 8 pull-thrus, (50x100), pit toilets. **REC:** rec open to public. Pets OK. No tents, 14 day max stay. 2021 rates: $18.
(800)710-2267 Lat: 45.7421, Lon: -97.242668
44950 Park Rd, Sisseton, SD 57262
gfp.sd.gov/state-parks
See ad page 818

SPEARFISH — B1 *Lawrence*

A SPOTLIGHT Introducing Spearfish's colorful attractions appearing at the front of this state section.

CHRIS' CAMP & RV PARK
good sam park **Ratings: 9.5/9.5★/9.5** (Campground) From Jct US-85 N & I-90: Go 4 mi E on I-90 (Exit 14), then 1/2 mi W on Bus I-90, then 3/4 mi S on Christensen Dr (R). Elev 3600 ft.

A START TO A GREAT VACATION
We welcome big rigs to sleeping bags. We are a full-service campground with all amenities including 3 bath houses, 2 laundry rooms, 3 heated pools, a pet farm and tour planning. See you soon!

FAC: paved/gravel rds. 135 Avail: 95 gravel, 40 grass, 68 pull-thrus, (20x50), back-ins (24x75), 103 full hkups, 32 W, 32 E (30/50 amps), cable, WiFi @ sites, tent sites, rentals, shower$, dump, laundry, groc, fire rings, firewood. **REC:** heated pool, wading pool, playground, hunting nearby. Pets OK. Partial handicap access. Big rig sites, eco-friendly. 2021 rates: $43 to $58, Military discount. Apr 15 to Oct 15. ATM, no cc.
(800)350-2239 Lat: 44.47092, Lon: -103.82711
701 Christensen Dr, Spearfish, SD 57783
www.chrisscampground.com
See ad pages 828, 831

JOIN GoodSamRoadside.com

ELKHORN RIDGE RV RESORT & CABINS
good sam park **Ratings: 10/9.5★/10** (RV Park) Avail: 186 full hkups (50 amps). 2021 rates: $49 to $77. (605)722-1800, 20189 US Hwy 85, Spearfish, SD 57783

SPEARFISH CITY CAMPGROUND (Public) From Jct of I-90 & Jackson Blvd (exit 12): Go 1/2 mi SW on Jackson Blvd, then 3/4 mi S on Canyon St across bridge (L). Avail: 57 full hkups (30/50 amps). 2021 rates: $25 to $45. May 09 to Sep 30. (605)642-1340

SPEARFISH KOA **Ratings: 7.5/9.5★/7.5** (Campground) 84 Avail: 50 full hkups, 34 W, 34 E (30/50 amps). 2021 rates: $45.89 to $89.19. Apr 01 to Oct 31. (800)562-0805, 41 W Hwy 14, Spearfish, SD 57783

SPRINGFIELD — D5 *Bon Homme*

SPRINGFIELD RECREATION AREA
(Public State Park) From Springfield: Go 1 mi E on Hwy 37 (R) Entrance fee required. **FAC:** gravel rds. Avail: 20 gravel, 2 pull-thrus, (15x52), back-ins (15x48), 19 E (20/30 amps), tent sites, rentals, dump. **REC:** Missouri River: fishing, kayaking/canoeing, boating nearby, playground, rec open to public. Pets OK. 14 day max stay. 2021 rates: $19 to $23.
(800)710-2267 Lat: 42.85588, Lon: -97.88458
1412 Boat Basin Dr, Springfield, SD 57062
gfp.sd.gov/state-parks
See ad page 818

STURGIS — B1 *Meade*

STURGIS See also Black Hawk, Deadwood, Lead, Rapid City & Spearfish.

BEAR BUTTE
(Public State Park) From Jct of Hwy 79 & Junction Ave (in Sturgis): Go 3 3/4 mi E on Hwy 79/34, then continue 3 1/4 mi N on Hwy 79 (L). Entrance fee required. Elev 3181 ft.**FAC:** gravel rds. Avail: 19 gravel, back-ins (30x49) (20/30 amps), tent sites, pit toilets. **REC:** Bear Butte Lake: swim, fishing, kayaking/canoeing, hunting nearby, rec open to public. Pets OK. 14 day max stay. 2021 rates: $11 to $18.
(800)710-2267 Lat: 44.46128, Lon: -103.43513
20250 Hwy 79, Sturgis, SD 57785
www.gfp.sd.gov/state-parks
See ad page 818

NO NAME CITY LUXURY CABINS & RV PARK
good sam park **Ratings: 9/9★/8** (Campground) From Jct US-14A & I-90: Go 4 mi SE on I-90 (Exit 34), then 3/4 mi E on Pleasant Valley Dr/Service Rd (R). Elev 3600 ft.**FAC:** all weather rds. 42 Avail: 16 gravel, 26 grass, 16 pull-thrus, (24x100), back-ins (24x50), 16 full hkups, 26 W, 26 E (30/50 amps), cable, WiFi @ sites, tent sites, rentals, dump, laundry, LP gas, restaurant. **REC:** pool, hot tub, boating nearby, playground, hunting nearby. Pet restrict (B). Partial handicap access. Big rig sites. 2021 rates: $35 to $45, Military discount. ATM.
(605)347-8891 Lat: 44.36337, Lon: -103.46594
20899 Pleasant Valley Dr, Sturgis, SD 57785
www.nonamecity.com
See ad this page

RUSH NO MORE RV RESORT & CAMPGROUND **Ratings: 9/10★/10** (Campground) 125 Avail: 113 full hkups, 12 W, 12 E (30/50 amps). 2021 rates: $41.99 to $54.99. (605)347-2916, 21137 Brimstone Pl, Sturgis, SD 57785

STURGIS RV PARK
good sam park **Ratings: 8.5/10★/9.5** (Campground) From Jct I-90 (exit 32) and Jct Ave: Go 1-1/2 mi N on Jct Ave; then 1/4 mi W on Woodland Dr (R). Elev 3407 ft.**FAC:** paved/gravel rds. 158 Avail: 72 paved, 86 all weather, 80 pull-thrus, (30x80), back-ins (27x50), 158 full hkups (30/50 amps), WiFi @ sites, tent sites, rentals, dump, laundry. Pets OK. Partial handicap access. Big rig sites, eco-friendly. 2021 rates: $45, Military discount. May 15 to Sep 30.
(605)720-1501 Lat: 44.41814, Lon: -103.51245
1175 W Woodland Dr, Sturgis, SD 57785
www.sturgisdowntownrvpark.com
See ad this page

Wasn't that a beautiful campground you visited ten years ago? But can you remember where it was? Use our "Find-it-Fast" index, located in the back of the Guide. It's an alphabetical list, by state, of every private and public park and campground in the Guide.

SUZIE'S CAMP
Ratings: 6/9.5★/6.5 (Campground) From jct US-14A & I-90: Go 4 mi SE on I-90 (Exit 34), then 1 mi E on Pleasant Valley Dr/Service Rd (R). Elev 3600 ft.- **FAC:** paved/gravel rds. Avail: 48 grass, 35 pull-thrus, (25x80), back-ins (25x40), 48 full hkups (30/50 amps), WiFi @ sites, tent sites, rentals, dump, mobile sewer, laundry. **REC:** boating nearby, hunting nearby. Pets OK. Big rig sites. 2021 rates: $40 to $45.
(605)347-2677 Lat: 44.36233, Lon: -103.4672
20983 Pleasant Valley Dr, Sturgis, SD 57785
www.suziescamp.com
See ad opposite page

SUMMERSET — C1 *Meade*

Travel Services

CAMPING WORLD OF SUMMERSET/RAPID CITY As the nation's largest retailer of RV supplies, accessories, services and new and used RVs, Camping World is committed to making your total RV experience better. **SERVICES:** RV, tire, RV appliance, MH mechanical, staffed RV wash, restrooms. RV Sales. RV supplies, LP gas, dump, emergency parking, RV accessible. Hours: 9am to 7pm.
(888)419-9105 Lat: 44.181962, Lon: -103.328575
10400 Recreational Drive, Summerset, SD 57718
www.campingworld.com

RV Tech Tips - Precision Fifth-Wheel Hitching: If, like many fellow fifth-wheel owners, you often have trouble gauging how high to position the front of your trailer for a smooth hitch-up process, try this RV Tech Tip. After unhitching pull the tow vehicle forward a couple of feet and measure the distance between the truck bed and the pin plate with a tape measure. When preparing to hitch up, set the tape to the same height, stand it on the truck bed and raise or lower the front of the trailer until the pin plate is even with the end of the tape. The distance remains the same each time, so there's no guesswork.

SUMMIT — A6 *Roberts*

COUNTY LINE RV PARK & CAMPGROUND
Ratings: 7/9.5★/9 (Campground) 58 Avail: 54 full hkups, 4 W, 4 E (30/50 amps). 2021 rates: $23 to $38. (605)398-6355, 907 Maple St, Summit, SD 57266

TIMBER LAKE — A3 *Dewey*

LITTLE MOREAU RECREATION AREA
(Public State Park) From Timber Lake: Go 6 mi S on Hwy 20. **FAC:** gravel rds. Avail: 5 gravel, back-ins (16x50), tent sites, pit toilets. **REC:** Moreau & Little Moreau Rivers: fishing, boating nearby, rec open to public. Pets OK. 14 day max stay. 2021 rates: $22 to $26.
(800)710-2267 Lat: 45.349193, Lon: -101.0845
6 miles South of Timberlake off SD 20, Timber Lake, SD 57656
gfp.sd.gov/state-parks
See ad page 818

VERMILLION — D6 *Clay*

LION'S PARK (Public) From Jct of Hwy 19 (W Cherry St) and Hwy 50 (N edge of town): Go 1/2 mi S on Hwy 19, then 1/2 mi E on W Cherry St (R). Avail: 5 E. 2021 rates: $5. (605)677-7064

WALL — C2 *Pennington*

SLEEPY HOLLOW CAMPGROUND
Ratings: 7.5/10★/8.5 (Campground) From Jct I-90 (Exit 110): Go 1/2 mi N on Glenn, then 1/4 mi W on 4th Ave (R). **FAC:** gravel rds. Avail: 59 gravel, 59 pull-thrus, (24x65), 37 full hkups, 22 W, 22 E (30/50 amps), cable, WiFi @ sites, tent sites, dump, laundry, groc, fire rings, firewood. **REC:** boating nearby, playground, hunting nearby. Pet restrict (B). Big rig sites, eco-friendly. 2021 rates: $45 to $60, Military discount. Apr 15 to Oct 31.
(605)279-2100 Lat: 43.99471, Lon: -102.24374
118 4th Ave. West, Wall, SD 57790
www.sleepyhollowcampgroundsd.com
See ad this page

WATERTOWN — B6 *Codington*

MEMORIAL PARK (CODINGTON COUNTY CAMPGROUND) (Public) From Jct of Hwy 212 & Hwy 81: Go 7 mi W on Hwy 212, then 2-1/2 mi N on Hwy 139 (R). 95 Avail: 34 full hkups, 60 W, 60 E (30/50 amps). 2021 rates: $22 to $24. May 01 to Sep 30. (605)882-6290

PELICAN LAKE RECREATION AREA
(Public State Park) From Watertown: Go 4 mi W on US-212, then 1 1/2 mi S on 450th Ave. Entrance fee required. **FAC:** paved rds. Avail: 76 gravel, back-ins (15x75), 76 E (20/30 amps), tent sites, rentals, dump. **REC:** Pelican Lake: swim, fishing, kayaking/canoeing, boating nearby, playground, rec open to public. Pets OK. Partial handicap access, 14 day max stay. 2021 rates: $16 to $26.
(800)710-2267 Lat: 44.852222, Lon: -97.208449
17450 450TH Ave, Watertown, SD 57201
gfp.sd.gov/state-parks
See ad page 818

SANDY SHORE RECREATION AREA
(Public State Park) From Jct of US-212 & US-20: Go 5 mi W on US-212, follow signs (R). Entrance fee required. **FAC:** paved rds. Avail: 17 grass, back-ins (15x40), 15 E (30/50 amps), tent sites, . **REC:** Lake Kampeska: swim, fishing, kayaking/canoeing, boating nearby, playground, rec open to public. Pets OK. 14 day max stay. 2021 rates: $22 to $26.
(800)710-2267 Lat: 44.893844, Lon: -97.240953
1100 South Lake Dr, Watertown, SD 57201
gfp.sd.gov/state-parks
See ad page 818

STOKES-THOMAS LAKE CITY PARK & CAMPGROUND (Public) From jct US-81 & Hwy-20: Go 3 mi NW on Hwy-20 to S Lake Dr. 72 Avail: 72 W, 72 E (30/50 amps). 2021 rates: $21. May 01 to Sep 30. (605)882-6264

RV SPACE-SAVING TIPS: Get crafty by using the insides of your doors/cabinets to store items used often, which cuts down on clutter and makes cleaning a breeze. A shoe organizer can easily be attached to the inside of a closet door for organizing shoes and other small items. Emergency flashlights are made more accessible when you install broom holders to the inside of a cabinets to put your flashlights within easy reach.

WAUBAY — A6 *Day*

PICKEREL LAKE
(Public State Park) From Waubay: Go 14 mi N on DAY CR-1 (R). Entrance fee required. **FAC:** paved rds. Avail: 69 gravel, 5 pull-thrus, (25x60), back-ins (25x60), 66 E (30/50 amps), tent sites, rentals, dump. **REC:** Pickerel Lake: swim, fishing, kayaking/canoeing, boating nearby, playground, rec open to public. Pets OK. Partial handicap access, 14 day max stay. 2021 rates: $26.
(800)710-2267 Lat: 45.485552, Lon: -97.248139
12980-446th Ave, Grenville, SD 57239
gfp.sd.gov/state-parks
See ad page 818

WHITE LAKE — C5 *Aurora*

CIRCLE K CAMPGROUND **Ratings: 7.5/9★/6.5** (Campground) Avail: 35 full hkups (30/50 amps). 2021 rates: $40 to $45. (605)249-2295, 1500 S. Main Street, White Lake, SD 57383

YANKTON — D6 *Yankton*

CHIEF WHITE CRANE RECREATION AREA
(Public State Park) From Yankton: Go 4 mi W on Hwy 52, then 4 mi S on Toe Rd (E). **FAC:** paved rds. Avail: 146 paved, back-ins (15x75), 144 E (30/50 amps), tent sites, rentals, dump. **REC:** Lake Yankton: fishing, kayaking/canoeing, playground, rec open to public. Pets OK. Partial handicap access, 14 day max stay. 2021 rates: $22 to $26.
(800)710-2267 Lat: 42.851249, Lon: -97.460067
31323 Toe Rd, Yankton, SD 57078
gfp.sd.gov/state-parks
See ad page 818

LEWIS & CLARK LAKE - COE/COTTONWOOD (Public Corps) From town: Go 5 mi W on Hwy 52, then 1 mi S on Toe Rd. Avail: 77 E. 2021 rates: $16 to $18. (877)444-6777

LEWIS & CLARK RECREATION AREA
(Public State Park) From Yankton: Go 4 mi W on Hwy 52. (L) Entrance fee required. **FAC:** paved rds. Avail: 418 paved, back-ins (15x60), 418 E (30/50 amps), WiFi @ sites, tent sites, rentals, dump, restaurant. **REC:** Lewis & Clark Lake: swim, fishing, marina, boating nearby, golf, playground, rec open to public. Pets OK. Partial handicap access, 14 day max stay. 2021 rates: $22 to $26.
(800)710-2267 Lat: 42.867723, Lon: -97.521526
43349 SD Hwy 52, Yankton, SD 57078
gfp.sd.gov/state-parks
See ad page 818

PIERSON RANCH RECREATION AREA
(Public State Park) From Yankton: Go 4 mi W on Hwy 52. (L) Entrance fee required. **FAC:** paved rds. Avail: 67 paved, back-ins (15x75), 67 E (30/50 amps), tent sites, rentals, dump. **REC:** Lewis & Clark Lake: swim, fishing, kayaking/canoeing, boating nearby, playground, rec open to public. Pets OK. Partial handicap access, 14 day max stay. 2021 rates: $22 to $26.
(800)710-2267 Lat: 42.871111, Lon: -97.485556
31144 Toe Rd, Yankton, SD 57442
gfp.sd.gov/state-parks
See ad page 818

YANKTON/MISSOURI RIVER KOA **Ratings: 9/10★/9** (Campground) Avail: 56 full hkups (30/50 amps). 2021 rates: $42 to $51. (605)260-1010, 807 Bill Baggs Rd, Yankton, SD 57078

Pre-Drive Safety INTERIOR Checklist: Secure all loose items; Ensure stove burners and oven are in off position; Securely latch cabinet and closet doors; Close roof vents and windows; Turn OFF air conditioner/heat pump/furnace; Turn OFF refrigerator and securely latch doors; Turn OFF water pump; Turn OFF interior RV lights; Fully retract slides and secure.

SD

good sam
RV Rentals
Experience
more for less.
Coleman
List or Rent, it's 5%.
That's up to 75% less in fees than the competition.
LEARN MORE AT RVRENTALS.COM

Getty Images/iStockphoto

DID YOU KNOW?

The Great Smoky Mountains are known as the "Salamander Capital of the World," with 30 species found in the park.

YOU ARE HERE

Tennessee

Tennessee's rugged mountains, rollicking cities and homey small towns cast a spell on visitors. Explore cities rich with musical history and hear sounds from hit makers of the past and future. Experience Appalachian culture.

Where Hits Are Made

Tennessee played a huge role in the evolution of both country music and rock 'n' roll in two of its largest cities, Nashville and Memphis. Nashville swings with a country twang, which is showcased at the Grand Ole Opry and the historic Ryman Auditorium. Many live-music venues that feature rising stars in more intimate settings. Memphis, on the old hand, rolls to a soulful melody. Explore the roots of rhythm and blues and rock n' roll with a stroll along Beale Street, where music still fills the streets, and a visit to Elvis's beloved home, Graceland.

One National Park Smokes the Rest

Great Smoky Mountains National Park is America's most popular national park, and it's easy to see why. Take a scenic drive for views of the endless mist-filled peaks, hike along one of the many trails to catch the rush of a waterfall taking a plunge, or watch for wildlife in verdant woodlands and rolling fields. Over 800 miles of trails can be explored throughout the park, as well as a number of spectacular waterways, offering prime locals for fishing, swimming, tubing, and paddling. Explore the northeast's backcountry, where you can find the observation point of Clingmans Dome. Part of the Southern Appalachian range, the dome forms the park's highest vantage point at 6,643 feet. Walk a 375-foot-long ramp to the observation tower.

Bring Your Fishing Gear

Here's an angling experience found nowhere else. Tennessee is home to the Eastern U.S.'s only native species of trout, the Southern Appalachian brook

Tennessee Ham

Slices of country ham grace plates in Tennessee year-round, not just during the holidays. Can you blame Volunteer State cooks for serving up this classic dish on the regular? In Tennessee, diners can enjoy ham in flavors that range from traditional seasoning to maple. Establishments like Rice's Country Hams in Juliet raise ham to an art form. Give your palette something it will genuinely appreciate.

VISITOR CENTER

TIME ZONE
Eastern Standard

ROAD & HIGHWAY INFORMATION
615-741-2848
tn.gov/tdot

FISHING & HUNTING INFORMATION
615-781-6500
tn.gov/twra/license-sales

BOATING INFORMATION
800-648-8798
tn.gov/twra/boating.html

NATIONAL PARKS
nps.gov/tn

STATE PARKS
tnstateparks.com

TOURISM INFORMATION
Tennessee Department of Tourism
800-462-8366
tnvacation.com

TOP TOURISM ATTRACTIONS
1) Grand Ole Opry
2) Graceland
3) Great Smoky Mountains

MAJOR CITIES
Memphis, Nashville (capital), Knoxville, Chattanooga, Clarksville

trout. Anglers can find this elusive fish in tiny mountain creeks in the Great Smokies. Take a hike away from the beaten path for prime opportunities. This landlocked state offers plenty of waterside fun at its many lakes and reservoirs. With 800 miles of shoreline, Norris Lake's turquoise waters entice boaters.

Trails Through Majesty

Brought your two-wheeler? Bicyclists have the opportunity to hit the Cades Code Loop in Great Smoky Mountains National Park before this popular roadway opens to vehicles two mornings a week during specified months. Take in views of mountains and meadows, while watching for roaming bears and deer. Of course, hiking is a popular activity in a state as rollicking as Tennessee. Many renowned trails, including the Appalachian Trail, are found in the Great Smokies. Travelers can also find adventures in popular spots such as Fall Creek Falls, Rock Island, and Cumberland Mountain State Parks.

Mountain of Majesty

Take your vacation to new heights. Just six miles from Chattanooga, along Tennessee's southern border, Lookout Mountain provides the backdrop for some of the city's most beloved attractions: the historic Incline Railway, Ruby Falls and Rock City Gardens. In addition to its family-friendly activities, this scenic area ripples with American Civil War and Native American historical touchstones. It was at Lookout Mountain that the Last Battle of the Cherokee was fought in 1794 during the Nickajack Expedition (the long-running battle between American frontiersmen and the Chickamauga Cherokee), as well as the 1863 Battle of Lookout Mountain during the Civil War.

Getty Images/iStockphoto

Spruce Flat Falls is one of many stunning waterfalls accessible by hiking trails in the Great Smoky Mountains.

A Steep Ride

In operation since 1895, the Lookout Mountain Incline Railway is the self-proclaimed "steepest passenger railway in the world." A rite of passage for locals and visitors, a trip on "America's Most Amazing Mile" affords sweeping views (on a clear day) of Chattanooga and the Great Smoky Mountains 100 miles away.

See Ruby Falls

When it comes to tourist brochure spin, there's no shortage of hyperbole attached to Ruby Falls. Considered one of the most incredible falls on the Earth, the 145-foot waterfall (located 1,100 feet inside Lookout Mountain) ranks as the nation's largest underground waterfall and deepest commercial caves. The iconic falls have been etched in the popular consciousness since the mid-20th century, when seemingly every barn roof in the South was emblazoned with the advertising slogan, "See Ruby Falls." The slogan wasn't lost on Johnny Cash and Roy Orbison, who cowrote the popular hit, "See Ruby Fall," in 1969 after a visit to the falls.

Rocking Out

With its stellar views of seven states (if the weather cooperates), Rock City completes Lookout Mountain's triumvirate of attractions. A captivating 4,100-foot walking trail traverses the mountain's lofty sandstone formations, surreal caves and kaleidoscopic gardens, which brim with more than 400 native plant species. A series of ancient rock displays based on classic fairy tales enchant young children.

Bluff View

Perched high atop a bluff overlooking the Tennessee River, an easy stroll from downtown Chattanooga, the historic Bluff View Art District is a center for the town's artistic creativity. Experience experimental gastronomy, acclaimed performance art, and innovative arts and crafts.

Chock Full of Wildlife

Outdoor fun awaits in Tennessee. Hunters can find lots of big deer in Wildlife Management Areas such as Catoosa and Yanahli. Not far from the Mississippi River is Reelfoot Lake State Park, renowned for its duck hunting. Fish year-round, thanks to great weather, plenty of lakes and over 50 rivers. Reel in bass from the colossal Pickwick Lake or Dale Hollow Lake, one of the top bass fisheries in the U.S. Douglas Lake and Lake Barkley are known for exceptional crappie fishing.

Getty Images/iStockphoto

At 6,643 feet, Clingman's Dome is the highest vantage point in Great Smoky Mountains National Park.

Featured Good Sam Parks

TENNESSEE

When you stay with Good Sam, you can expect the highest degree of cleanliness and friendliness, and better yet, you get **10% off** overnight campground fees.

If you're not already a Good Sam member you can purchase your membership at one of these locations:

BRISTOL
Shadrack Campground

CAMDEN
Birdsong Resort & Marina Lakeside RV & Tent Campground

CHATTANOOGA
Chattanooga Holiday Travel Park
Raccoon Mountain Campground and Caverns

CLARKSVILLE
Clarksville RV Park

CROSSVILLE
Bean Pot Campground

GATLINBURG
Greenbrier Campground
Smoky Bear Campground and RV Park
Twin Creek RV Resort

GREENEVILLE
Lazy Llama Campground

HARTFORD
Pigeon River Campground

HOHENWALD
Natchez Trace Wilderness Preserve

JACKSON
Parkway Village MH and RV Community

KNOXVILLE
Volunteer Park Family Campground

LENOIR CITY
Soaring Eagle Campground & RV Park

MADISON
Old Hickory MH Community

MEMPHIS
Cook's Lake RV Resort & Campground
Memphis Graceland RV Park & Campground

MIDDLETON
Cherokee Landing Campground

MONTEREY
Belle Ridge Campground

NASHVILLE
Nashville Shores Lakeside Resort
Two Rivers Campground

NEWPORT
Triple Creek Campground

PARKERS CROSSROADS
Parkers Crossroads RV Park

PIGEON FORGE
Clabough's Campground
Creekside RV Park
Gateway to the Smokies RV Park & Campground
King's Holly Haven RV Park
Mill Creek Resort
Pine Mountain RV Park by the Creek
Riveredge RV Park & Cabin Rentals

PIONEER
Rock Ridge Retreat at Royal Blue

SAVANNAH
Green Acres RV Park

SEVIERVILLE
Duvall in the Smokies RV Campground & Cabins
Riverside RV Park & Resort
Two Rivers Landing RV Resort

SMYRNA
Nashville I-24 Campground

SOUTH PITTSBURG
Sasquatch Farm RV Park & Campground

TRACY CITY
Bigfoot Adventure RV Park & Campground

10/10★/10 GOOD SAM PARKS

GATLINBURG
Smoky Bear Campground and RV Park
(865)436-8372

Twin Creek RV Resort
(865)436-7081

SEVIERVILLE
Two Rivers Landing RV Resort
(866)727-5781

What's This?

An RV park with a 10/10★/10 rating has scored perfect grades in amenities, cleanliness and appearance ("See Understanding the Campground Rating System" on pages 8 and 9 for an explanation of the trusted Good Sam Rating System). Stay in a 10/10★/10 park on your next trip for a nearly flawless camping experience.

Getty Images/iStockphoto

TN

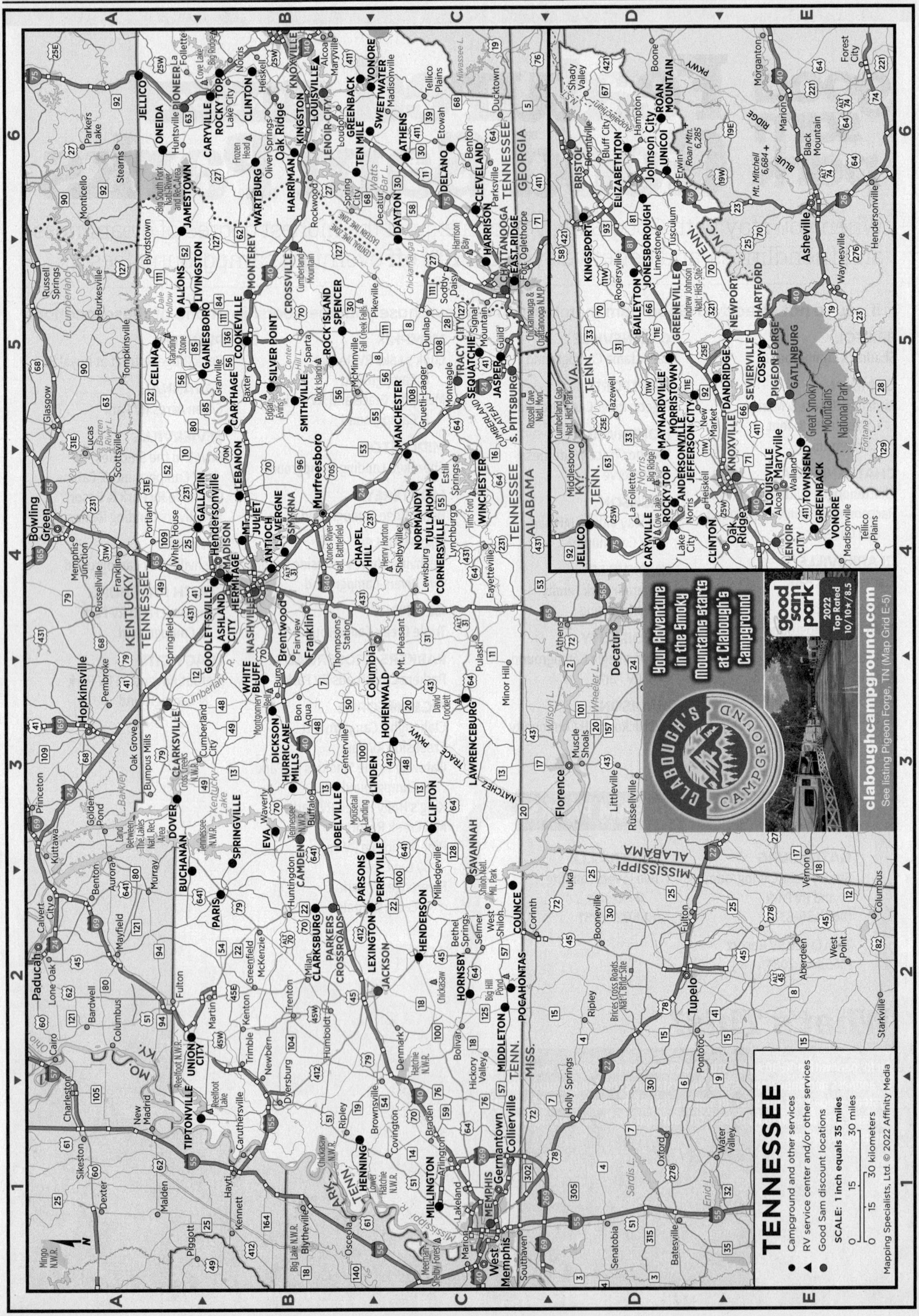
TENNESSEE
Campground and other services
RV service center and/or other services
Good Sam discount locations
SCALE: 1 inch equals 35 miles
Mapping Specialists, Ltd. © 2022 Affinity Media
Your Adventure in the Smoky Mountains starts at Clabough's Campground
CLABOUGH'S CAMPGROUND
good sam park
2022 Top Rated 10/10★/8.5
claboughcampground.com
See listing Pigeon Forge, TN (Map Grid E-5)

ROAD TRIPS

Savor Smoky Mountain Scenery on a High-Altitude Adventure

Tennessee

LOCATION
TENNESSEE

DISTANCE
38 MILES

DRIVE TIME
1 HR 15 MINS

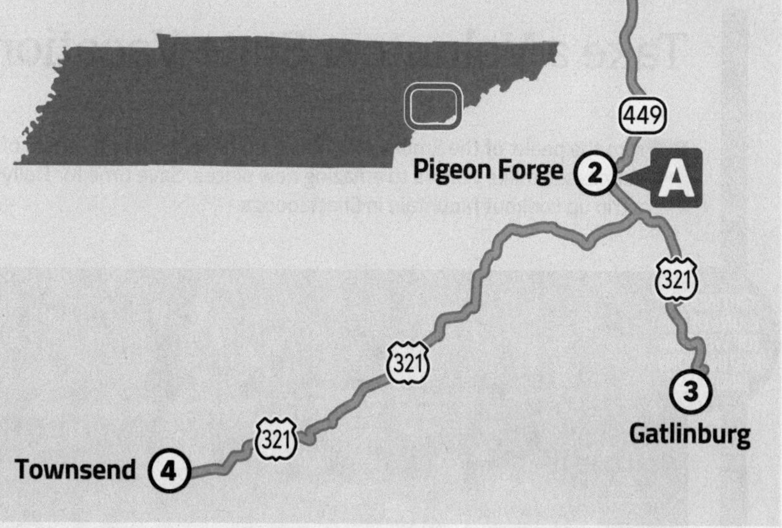

Sky-high mountains and down-home attractions make this a special trip. As you wind your way through the lush foothills of the Great Smoky Mountains, you'll experience spectacular caves, high-flying thrills and stellar entertainment at one of the world's great theme parks. And with a special focus on family-friendly fun, you can rest easy knowing there's a little something for everyone. From moonshine to mountains and everything in between, the Volunteer State steps up.

1 Sevierville
Starting Point

Enter the Forbidden Caverns for an adventure that's out of this world. On the one-hour walking tour, you'll see towering rock chimneys, glistening grottoes and crystal-clear streams, as well as learn the incredible history of the cave as a shelter for Native Americans during hunting parties. For some aboveground fun, there's always rafting the Class IV rapids on the Pigeon River, or fishing and boating the day away on nearby Douglas Lake. You can't take the incredible landscape with you, but you can come close at the headquarters of the Sevier Distilling Company, a homegrown operation that specializes in a modern take on moonshine.

2 Pigeon Forge
Drive 7 Miles ▪ 13 Minutes

Pigeon Forge is a larger-than-life wonderland of theme parks, quirky stores and compelling museums. There are over-the-top stores and attractions on nearly every corner, but Dollywood, the Southern living-themed amusement park, steals the show. Featuring dozens of thrilling rides, including the innovative SkyZip, a multistation zipline adventure that sends visitors soaring above the trees, as well as water parks, arts and crafts, and performance venues, it's a one-stop shop for all things entertainment. History buffs can step back in time at the Titanic Museum, which features interactive exhibits that re-create life aboard the doomed ship.

RECOMMENDED STOPOVER
A RIVEREDGE RV PARK & CABIN RENTALS
PIGEON FORGE, TN (866) 777-6127

3 Gatlinburg
Drive 7 Miles ▪ 16 Minutes

At the doorstep of the Smoky Mountains, Gatlinburg dishes out adventure. For a bird's-eye view of the breathtaking scenery, try the 2.1-mile Ober Gatlinburg Aerial Tramway, a cable car ride that leaves from the heart of downtown Gatlinburg, or the "chondola" — part chairlift, part gondola — ride to Anakeesta's magical Firefly Village. Both rides deliver guests at mountaintop amusement parks featuring ziplines, coasters, water slides and more.

4 Townsend
Drive 24 Miles ▪ 46 Minutes

Take a deep dive into the history and heritage of southern Appalachian culture. At the Great Smoky Mountains Heritage Center, you can wander through a restored pioneer village and take part in music, art and food events. For a break from the crowds in the national park, spend a day exploring the impossibly picturesque Little River. Home to plentiful trout and other wildlife, the cool, clean waters are an angler's dream.

Getty Images/iStockphoto

TN

BIKING BOATING DINING ENTERTAINMENT FISHING HIKING HUNTING PADDLING SHOPPING SIGHTSEEING

Tennessee SPOTLIGHTS

Take a Volunteer State Vacation

From the peaks of the Smoky Mountains to the legendary theaters of Nashville, Tennessee takes visitors to amazing new places. Save time for Dollywood and a trip up Lookout Mountain in Chattanooga.

GATLINBURG IS ONE OF THE TOP WEDDING DESTINATIONS IN THE U.S.

Gatlinburg's 407-foot-tall Space Needle offers views of the Smokies.

Gatlinburg

Surrounded on all sides by mountain ridges, Gatlinburg is a small town with big opportunities for outdoor adventure. Situated at the foot of the Great Smoky Mountains, the surrounding area boasts hiking, skiing, whitewater rafting and one-of-a-kind vistas. But there's more to the "Crown Jewel of the Smokies" than just the great outdoors.

Set Out for Adventure

Camping, fishing and picnicking are possible across the sprawling park, and the experienced guides and rangers at the visitor centers can help you get the most out of your trip.

Above it All

There's no better way to get the lay of the land in Gatlinburg than a trip on the aerial tramway that connects downtown to the Ober Gatlinburg Amusement Park and Ski Area. Running every 20 minutes throughout the day, the 2.1-mile ride offers breathtaking views of the Smoky Mountains and Gatlinburg's downtown skyline. The tramway deposits riders at a recreation center featuring an ice skating rink, waterslides and more.

Sharks and Sights

The small town is also known for its assortment of unique attractions, including the Ripley's Aquarium of the Smokies, which features underwater shark-viewing tunnels and other exotic sea creatures. A ride up the 407-foot-tall Gatlinburg Space Needle offers stellar views.

Great Smoky Mountains Natl. Park

Known for its soaring, mist-shrouded peaks, Great Smoky Mountains National Park is one of the most visited national parks in the nation. The park sits just 11 miles south of Pigeon Forge and it straddles the ridgeline of the Smokies, at the tail end of the Appalachian Mountains (the world's oldest mountain range). The park's 814 square miles of pristine forest were designated in 1936. Spanning Tennessee and North Carolina, the park's unfathomable scale encompasses more than 4,000 species of plants, some 2,000 black bears and over 30 different species of salamanders — mind-blowing diversity for an area of roughly 800 square miles.

Through the Haze

You'll find lots of recreation possibilities within 521,000 acres of preserved wilderness. Over 800 miles of hiking trails afford spectacular views across rolling mountains

"RIPLEY'S AQUARIUM OF THE SMOKIES, FEATURES UNDERWATER SHARK-VIEWING TUNNELS."

LOCAL FAVORITE

Rustic Tomato Tart

The Volunteer State grows some of the world's best tomatoes and this recipe showcases them beautifully. Serve this tart as a side dish, as a main course or as a stunning appetizer. *Recipe by Alisa M.*

INGREDIENTS

- ☐ 1 refrigerated pie crust, rolled out
- ☐ 3 Tbsp basil pesto
- ☐ 4 large, ripe tomatoes, sliced
- ☐ 2 Tbsp olive oil
- ☐ ¾ cup good quality hard cheese such as Romano, shredded
- ☐ 1 egg white, beaten
- ☐ Salt and pepper to taste

DIRECTIONS

Brush the pie crust with the pesto. Layer sliced tomatoes around the crust leaving a 3-4-inch border. Sprinkle with salt and pepper and the cheese. Fold the edges of the crust up toward the center. The center of the tart will not be covered. Brush the crust with the egg white and drizzle with olive oil. Bake on a cookie sheet or foil at 350 degrees for 20 minutes, or until the crust is brown and the center is bubbly. Let cool for several minutes, slice and serve warm.

and deciduous forests bathed in milky haze; the "smoke" is plant respiration produced on a scale and range that would equal a rainforest. With over 2,100 miles of waterways throughout the park, the fishing here is excellent, and thrill-seekers can revel in the park's exhilarating whitewater rafting opportunities and an array of snow sports during the winter. A large number of family-friendly biking trails crisscross the park. One of the most popular biking trails, the Cades Cove Loop, orbits the park's eponymous 19th-century settlement and yields prime wildlife viewing.

The low mists that hang over the Smoky Mountains give the famous range its name.

Backcountry Beauty

The park attracts big crowds, but you don't have to get lost in the shuffle. To get away, head out to the northeast's backcountry, where the lofty peaks of Mount LeConte offer breathtaking hiking. Here, the observation point of Clingmans Dome, part of the Southern Appalachian range, forms the park's highest vantage point at 6,643 feet. Walk a 375-foot-long ramp to the observation tower.

Magnificent Mount

Mount LeConte offers one of the most popular (and easiest) hikes in the park. This 2.5-mile round-trip paved path bisects a series of beautiful cascades before reaching its breathtaking climax at the 60-foot-high Laurel Falls, one of the many accessible waterfalls within the park.

Smoky Mountain Strikes

More than 2,000 miles of streams course through the park, giving anglers an abundance of fishing opportunities from the remote, headwater trout waterways to large, cool water smallmouth bass streams. The Horseshoe at Cades Cove, Little River and LeConte Creek are local favorites for hooking pristine rainbow trout, while guides in town can help organize excursions to the area's secret spots. For family-friendly thrills, try battling the white water in the area's steep canyons. Pigeon River is your best bet, with everything from Class IV rapids fun to gentle float trips.

Pigeon Forge

Make Pigeon Forge your launchpad for all your Great Smoky Mountains excursions. From fly-fishing in abundant streams to trekking the Appalachian Trail, this friendly resort city puts epic outdoor adventures right at your fingertips. Get your fill of Mother Nature and then stick around for amusement park thrills, car shows and Southern feasts.

Dollywood Delights

Dolly Parton's Dollywood combines dozens of thrilling rides, stellar entertainment and Smoky Mountain heritage all in a single amusement park. Feel the adrenaline rush through your veins on the Lightning Rod, the world's fastest wooden roller coaster. Watch local craftsmen show off their blacksmithing skills and listen to live artists perform country and rock 'n' roll hits. Country music fans will enjoy top artists who perform here while train buffs can enjoy a spin on the Dollywood Express. Dolly fans can view one-of-a-kind memorabilia in the Chasing Rainbows Museum, while bird enthusiasts can come face-to-face with bald eagles in the 30,000-square-foot Eagle Mountain Sanctuary.

TN

MILL CREEK RESORT
CABINS, CAMPING, & PARK MODELS

Pigeon Forge's Best-Kept Resort Secret...

2 miles from Dollywood and the Great Smoky Mountains

- Pool, Wading Pool
- Clubhouse • 2 Playgrounds
- Full Hookups • Cable/Wi-Fi
- Cabin/Park Model Rentals
- Shuffleboard Court
- Basketball Court
- On-Site Store
- Horseshoes
- Laundry Room
- Bathhouse

good sam park

865-428-3498
millcreekresortpf.com

Trolley Stop
449 W. Mill Creek Rd.
Pigeon Forge, TN 37863

Pine Mountain
RV Park by the Creek

♦♦♦♦♦ Facility

- Located on Pine Mountain Rd. at Traffic Light #6
- 2 blocks from the Pigeon Forge Parkway
- Large Splash Pool
- Concrete Pads
- Water/Sewer/Electric Hookups
- 30 & 50 Amp Service
- Cable TV Hookup
- Wireless High-Speed Internet Access

good sam park

For Reservations & Information, Please Call: (877) 753-9994
pinemountainrvpark.com

Trolley Stop
411 Pine Mountain Rd.
Pigeon Forge, TN 37863

RIVERBEND Campground

Big Rigs Welcome
Long Concrete Sites
30/50 Amps
Free Cable & Wi-Fi
Laundry, Fishing
River Sites

1/2 mile off Parkway – Stoplight #1
Away from noise of traffic and alongside a cool mountain stream.

865-453-1224
riverbendcampground.com

2479 Riverbend Loop #1
Pigeon Forge, TN 37863

Riveredge RV PARK & CABIN RENTALS

"Pigeon Forge Camping At Its Finest!"

Conveniently located at the South End of Pigeon Forge

- Splash Pad
- Heated Outdoor Pool, Kiddie Pool, Hot Tub
- Kids Playground • Free Wi-Fi
- 1 BR & 2 BR Cabin & Camping Cabin Rentals
- All Sites Full Hookups with Cable
- Indoor Arcade
- 5-Star Bath Houses

good sam park

866-777-6127
stayriveredge.com

Trolley Stop
4220 Huskey St.
Pigeon Forge, TN 37863

TN

Camping in Pigeon Forge, Tennessee

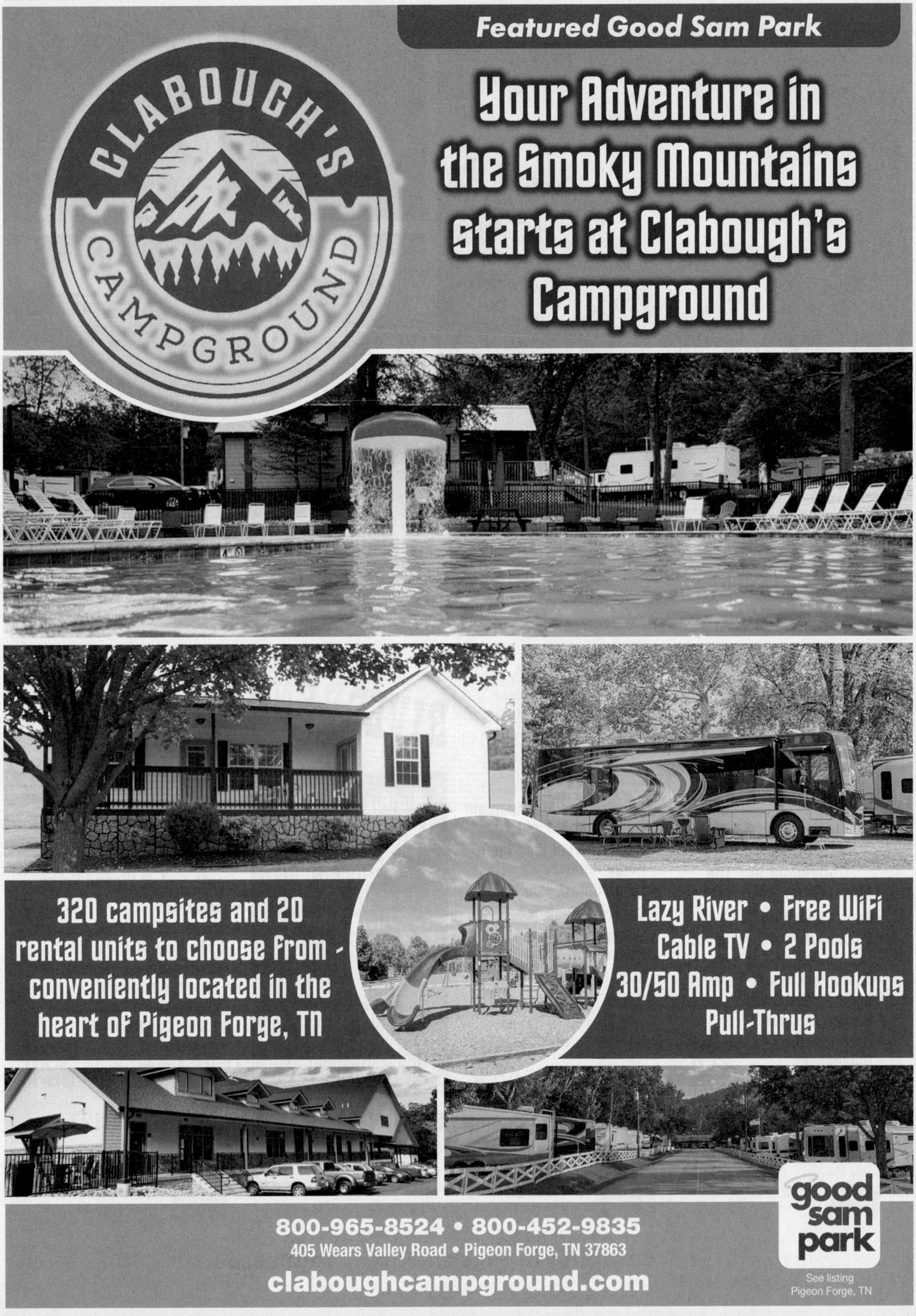
Featured Good Sam Park
CLABOUGH'S CAMPGROUND
Your Adventure in the Smoky Mountains starts at Clabough's Campground
320 campsites and 20 rental units to choose from - conveniently located in the heart of Pigeon Forge, TN
Lazy River • Free WiFi
Cable TV • 2 Pools
30/50 Amp • Full Hookups
Pull-Thrus
800-965-8524 • 800-452-9835
405 Wears Valley Road • Pigeon Forge, TN 37863
claboughcampground.com
good sam park
See listing
Pigeon Forge, TN

SPOTLIGHTS

Built in 1830, the historical Old Grist Mill on the banks of the Pigeon River still operates.

Festival of Nations

The park is also home to some of Tennessee's most popular festivals. Every March, it hosts the Festival of Nations, a multicultural celebration combining food, dance and art from around the world. Held in April, the Barbecue & Trout Bluegrass Festival lets attendees enjoy free daily concerts with heaps of saucy pulled pork, ribs and barbecue chicken.

Heart-pumping Rapids

Grab a paddle and go whitewater rafting on the Big Pigeon River. Rafting companies like Smoky Mountain Outdoors provide training, equipment and guides so there's no experience necessary. Fishing is another popular pastime thanks to more than 2,000 miles of streams in Great Smoky Mountains National Park. Catch wild trout in the upper section of Abrams Creek and reel in smallmouth bass in lower elevation streams such as the Little Pigeon River's East Prong and the streams leading into Fontana Lake. The Smoky Mountain Trout Tournament occurs every spring, so sign up if you want to show off your angling skills.

Land of the Smokies

The Great Smoky Mountains' historic areas, endless trails and famed bluish haze draw more than 10 million visitors a year, making it the most-visited national park in America. Hikers can trek over a hundred trails, including a 70-mile section of the Appalachian Trail. Blooming wildflowers and cascading waterfalls line the paths. Deer, foxes and beavers may even make an appearance. For spectacular views, drive to Clingman's Dome. Resting at the park's highest point, this observation tower offers 360-degree panoramas.

Southern Hospitality

Locals can't wait to share their heritage and way of life with you. Dating back to 1830, the Historic Old Mill in Old Mill Square is listed on the National Register of Historic Places. Snap a photo of its famous waterwheel and then shop for pottery, crafts and local specialty products. When you've worked up an appetite, dine on classic Southern fare like corn chowder and fried chicken at the Old Mill Farmhouse Kitchen. In the evening, head to the Hatfield & McCoy Dinner Feud for singing, dancing and comedy acts. Shows are served alongside homestyle feasts so make sure you come hungry. If Dollywood wasn't enough, visit The Island in Pigeon Forge for more amusement park fun. Get a fantastic view of the mountains while riding the Ferris wheel and check out over 40 unique boutiques stocked with everything from artisanal beef jerky and moonshine to farmhouse décor and souvenir T-shirts.

Considered the first wing coaster, the Wild Eagle takes passengers on a high-speed ride above Dollywood.

Eclectic Events

Hosting car shows, cookoffs and craft expos, Pigeon Forge events cater to every interest and hobby. Pack your May calendar with the Chuck Wagon Cookoff, a weekend competition where cooks whip up hearty dishes in mobile kitchens. In the same month, you can view stunning handmade quilts at A Mountain Quiltfest and celebrate the region's rich musical heritage at the Music in the Mountains Spring Parade.

Four-Wheel Fun

Automotive events are held year-round. In spring, check out the Corvette Expo, Pigeon Forge Spring Rod Run and Grand National F-100 Ford Show to view an impressive collection of vintage rides.

Basic Buildings

Hidden away in the Great Smoky Mountains is one of the country's finest collections of historic log buildings. There are over 90 structures preserved in the national park and you can access them by car or foot. Follow the 11-mile Cades Cove Loop Road to uncover old churches, log cabins and even a working gristmill and then go to Elkmont to explore an abandoned resort town from the 1920s. More historic sites can be seen along the Roaring Fork Motor Nature Trail, as well as in Cataloochee and Oconaluftee.

FOR MORE INFORMATION

Tennessee Department of Tourist Development, 615-741-2159, www.tnvacation.com

Gatlinburg CVB, 800-588-1817, www.gatlinburg.com

Great Smoky Mountain National Park, 865-436-1200, www.nps.gov/grsm

Pigeon Forge Department of Tourism, 800-251-9100, www.mypigeonforge.com

Know the name? Then you can use our special ""Find-it-Fast'' index to locate your campground on the map. The index arranges private and public campgrounds alphabetically, by state. Next to the name, you'll quickly find the name of the town the park is in, plus the Listing's page number.

Tennessee

ALLONS — A5 *Clay*

DALE HOLLOW LAKE - COE/WILLOW GROVE CAMPGROUND (Public Corps) From town: Go 2 mi NW on SR-52, then 1-1/2 mi NE on Hwy 1209, then 6 mi NW on Hwy 294 (E). 62 Avail: 62 W, 62 E (50 amps). 2021 rates: $23 to $30. May 15 to Sep 01. (931)823-4285

ANDERSONVILLE — D4 *Anderson*

ANDERSON COUNTY PARK (Public) From jct TN 61 & US 41: Go 2 mi E on TN 61, then 1-1/2 mi N on Norris Park Rd, then 4-3/4 mi N on Park Rd (E). 53 Avail: 53 W, 53 E (30/50 amps). 2021 rates: $21. Mar 01 to Dec 01. (865)494-9352

LOYSTON POINT CAMPGROUND **Ratings: 5/9★/8** (Campground) Avail: 33 E (30 amps). 2021 rates: $32 to $35. (865)494-9369, 730 Loyston Point Rd, Andersonville, TN 37705

ANTIOCH — B4 *Davidson*

J PERCY PRIEST LAKE - COE/ANDERSON ROAD CAMPGROUND (Public Corps) From Jct of US-41 & Bell Rd: Go 1-1/2 mi N on Bell Rd, then 1 mi E on Smith Springs Rd, then 1-1/2 mi N on Anderson Rd (L). 36 Avail: 10 W, 10 E (15 amps). 2021 rates: $20 to $30. May 16 to Oct 29. (615)361-1980

ASHLAND CITY — B4 *Cheatham*

CHEATHAM LOCK AND DAM - COE/LOCK A CAMPGROUND (Public Corps) From jct Ashland City: Go W 8 mi on US 12 to Cheap Hill, then W 4 mi on Cheatham Dam Rd. 38 Avail: 38 W, 38 E (50 amps). 2021 rates: $22 to $26. Apr 01 to Oct 30. (615)792-3715

ATHENS — C6 *McMinn*

OVER-NITER RV PARK **Ratings: 6.5/8.5★/7.5** (RV Park) Avail: 10 full hkups (30/50 amps). 2021 rates: $29. (423)507-0069, 316 John J Duncan Parkway, Athens, TN 37303

BAILEYTON — D5 *Greene*

BAILEYTON KOA **Ratings: 9/10★/9.5** (Campground) Avail: 71 full hkups (30/50 amps). 2021 rates: $42 to $55. (423)234-4992, 7485 Horton Hwy, Baileyton, TN 37745

BRISTOL — D6 *Sullivan*

LAKEVIEW RV RESORT **Ratings: 8.5/7.5/8.5** (RV Park) Avail: 150 full hkups (30/50 amps). 2021 rates: $47 to $67. (423)538-5600, 4550 Hwy 11E, Bristol, TN 37618

OBSERVATION KNOB PARK (Public) From jct TN 394 & US 421: Go 6-1/2 mi S on US 421, then 1-1/4 mi N on Knob Park Rd (E). 56 Avail: 56 W, 56 E (30 amps). 2021 rates: $25. Apr 01 to Nov 01. (423)878-1881

SHADRACK CAMPGROUND
good sam park
Ratings: 7.5/9.5★/6.5 (Campground) From Jct I-81 & SR-394 (exit 69): Go 5-1/2 mi S on SR-394, then 2 mi E on US-19 (US-11E) (R). **FAC:** gravel rds. 218 Avail: 180 gravel, 38 grass, back-ins (20x40), 168 full hkups, 50 W, 50 E (30/50 amps), WiFi @ sites, tent sites, rentals, dump, laundry, fire rings, firewood. **REC:** Beaver Creek: fishing. Pets OK. Partial handicap access, eco-friendly. 2021 rates: $32 to $40, Military discount.
(423)217-1181 Lat: 36.52906, Lon: -82.24979
2537 Volunteer Pkwy, Bristol, TN 37620
www.shadrackcampground.com
See ad this page

THUNDER MOUNTAIN CAMPGROUND **Ratings: 2.5/7/6** (Campground) 134 Avail: 110 full hkups, 24 W, 24 E (30/50 amps). 2021 rates: $20 to $40. Apr 10 to Aug 20. (423)946-2380, 250 North Raceway Villa Drive, Bristol, TN 37620

BUCHANAN — A3 *Benton*

LITTLE EAGLE RV PARK **Ratings: 7/9★/7** (RV Park) Avail: 10 full hkups (30/50 amps). 2021 rates: $35. (731)642-4669, 14652 Hwy 79 N, Buchanan, TN 38222

PARIS LANDING
(Public State Park) From Jct of US-641 & US-79, E 16.9 mi on US-79 (L). **FAC:** paved rds. 45 Avail: 30 paved, 15 gravel, 3 pull-thrus, (30x80), back-ins (20x30), 45 W, 45 E (30 amps), tent sites, rentals, dump, laundry, fire rings, firewood, restaurant. **REC:** pool $, wading pool, Kentucky Lake: swim, fishing, marina, kayaking/canoeing, boating nearby, golf, playground. Pets OK. Partial handicap access, 14 day max stay, eco-friendly. 2021 rates: $25.
(731)641-4465 Lat: 36.43934, Lon: -88.08320
16055 Hwy 79N, Buchanan, TN 38222
tnstateparks.com/parks/paris-landing

CAMDEN — B3 *Benton*

BIRDSONG RESORT & MARINA LAKESIDE RV & TENT CAMPGROUND
good sam park
Ratings: 8/9★/7 (Campground) From Jct of I-40 & SR 191/Birdsong Rd (Exit 133): Go N 9.1 mi on SR 191 to Marina Rd, then go E 0.4 mi (L). **FAC:** paved rds. (74 spaces). Avail: 62 paved, 7 pull-thrus, (22x65), back-ins (22x45), 54 full hkups, 8 W, 8 E (30/50 amps), seasonal sites, tent sites, rentals, dump, mobile sewer, laundry, LP bottles, firewood. **REC:** pool, Kentucky Lake: fishing, marina, kayaking/canoeing, boating nearby, playground, rec open to public. Pets OK. Partial handicap access, eco-friendly. 2021 rates: $45, Military discount.
(731)584-7880 Lat: 35.96973, Lon: -88.04623
255 Marina Rd, Camden, TN 38320
www.birdsongresort.com
See ad this page

CARTHAGE — B5 *Jackson*

CORDELL HULL LAKE - COE/DEFEATED CREEK (Public Corps) From town: Go 4 mi W on Hwy 25, then 2 mi N on Hwy 80, then 2 mi E on Hwy 85, then 1-1/2 mi S on Marina Ln (R). Avail: 155 E (30/50 amps). 2021 rates: $25 to $30. Mar 16 to Oct 30. (615)774-3141

CARYVILLE — B6 *Campbell*

COVE LAKE (Public State Park) From Jct of I-75 & Hwy 25W (exit 134), N 0.8 mi on Hwy 25W (L). 98 Avail: 98 W, 98 E (30 amps). 2021 rates: $25. (423)566-9701

CELINA — A5 *Clay*

DALE HOLLOW LAKE - COE/DALE HOLLOW DAM (Public Corps) From town: Go 3 mi E on SR-53 (R). Avail: 78 E (50 amps). 2021 rates: $23 to $30. Apr 07 to Oct 23. (877)444-6777

CHAPEL HILL — C4 *Marshall*

HENRY HORTON STATE RESORT PARK (Public State Park) From Jct of I-65 & SR-99 (exit 46), E 12 mi on SR-99 to Jct with US-31A, S 0.4 mi (R). Avail: 56 E (30/50 amps). 2021 rates: $30. (931)364-2222

CHATTANOOGA — C5 *Hamilton*

CHATTANOOGA See also Athens, Cleveland, Dayton, Jasper & Pikeville, TN; Fort Payne, AL; Adairsville, Calhoun, Ellijay & Rossville, GA.

CHATTANOOGA HOLIDAY TRAVEL PARK
good sam park
Ratings: 9.5/10★/9.5 (Campground) From jct I-75 & US-41 N (exit 1): Go 1/2 mi W on US-41 N, then 3/4 mi S on Mack Smith Rd (R).

CHATTANOOGA KEEPS GETTING BETTER!
And so do we! Our family-friendly park offers groomed shady sites. Visit downtown's freshwater/saltwater aquarium. See Rock City on Lookout Mountain and re-live Civil War history. Rallies welcome. Easy on/off I-75.

FAC: all weather rds. (140 spaces). Avail: 60 gravel, 57 pull-thrus, (30x60), back-ins (35x60), 60 full hkups (30/50 amps), seasonal sites, cable, WiFi @ sites, tent sites, rentals, dump, laundry, LP gas, fire rings, firewood. **REC:** pool, boating nearby, shuffleboard, playground. Pets OK. Partial handicap access. Big rig sites, eco-friendly. 2021 rates: $51 to $68, Military discount.
(800)693-2877 Lat: 34.98624, Lon: -85.211008
1709 Mack Smith Rd, Chattanooga, TN 37412
www.travelparkchattanooga.com
See ad opposite page

CHESTER FROST PARK (HAMILTON COUNTY PARK) (Public) From Jct of I-75 & Hwy 153: Go 8 mi W on Hwy 153, then 10 mi N on Hixson Pike, then 1/5 mi NE on Gold Point Cir (use 2nd Cir) (L). 200 Avail: 180 W, 180 E (30/50 amps). 2021 rates: $21.15 to $30. Apr 01 to Oct 30. (423)842-3306

HAWKINS POINTE PARK, STORE & MORE
good sam park
Ratings: 6.5/NA/7.5 (RV Park) From jct I-24 (TN) & US 27: Go 6-1/2 mi E on I-24 to (exit 185A), then 1 mi S on I-75 (exit 1), then 1/4 mi W on US 41 (N/Ringold Rd), then 3/4 mi S on Mack Smith Rd, then 1 block E on Emerson Circle (L). **FAC:** paved rds. Avail: 50 paved, 32 pull-thrus, (24x75), back-ins (20x55), accepts full hkup units only, 50 full hkups (50 amps),

WiFi @ sites, dump. **REC:** boating nearby. Pets OK. Partial handicap access. No tents. Big rig sites. 2021 rates: $45 to $70.
(706)820-6757 Lat: 34.979311, Lon: -85.209864
182 Emerson Circle, Rossville, GA 30741
hawkinspointe.com
See primary listing at Rossville, GA and ad this page

RACCOON MOUNTAIN CAMPGROUND AND CAVERNS **Ratings: 9/10★/9** (Campground) Avail: 56 full hkups (30/50 amps). 2021 rates: $45 to $70. (423)821-9403, 319 W Hills Dr, Chattanooga, TN 37419

SASQUATCH FARM RV PARK & CAMPGROUND **Ratings: 7.5/8.5★/8.5** (RV Park) From Downtown Chattanooga: Go 27 mi W on I-24 W to US-72 W in Kimball, then 2 mi S on US-72 W, then 11-3/4 mi W on SH 156, then 3 mi S on Browns Trace Road (L). **FAC:** gravel rds. (50 spaces). Avail: 50 gravel, back-ins (40x75), 50 full hkups (30/50 amps), WiFi @ sites, tent sites, dump, LP gas, fire rings, firewood. **REC:** Man Made: swim, fishing, kayaking/canoeing, boating nearby. Pets OK. Big rig sites. 2021 rates: $55, Military discount.
(423)919-9852 Lat: 35.002586, Lon: -85.5555
2985 Browns Trace Road, South Pittsburgh, TN 37380
www.sasquatchfarm.com
See primary listing at South Pittsburg and ad opposite page

Travel Services

CAMPING WORLD OF CHATTANOOGA As the nation's largest retailer of RV supplies, accessories, services and new and used RVs, Camping World is committed to making your total RV experience better. **SERVICES:** RV, tire, RV appliance, MH mechanical, staffed RV wash, restrooms. RV Sales. RV supplies, LP gas, emergency parking, RV accessible. Hours: 9am to 7pm.
(877)295-2202 Lat: 34.989034, Lon: -85.194508
6728 Ringgold Road, Chattanooga, TN 37412
www.campingworld.com

CLARKSBURG — B2 *Carroll*

NATCHEZ TRACE/PIN OAK RV CAMPGROUND (Public State Park) From jct I-40 & SR-114 (exit 116): Go 11-1/2 mi S on SR-114 (R). Avail: 77 full hkups (20/30 amps). 2021 rates: $11 to $25. (800)250-8616

CLARKSVILLE — A3 *Montgomery*

CLARKSVILLE RV PARK **Ratings: 10/10★/9.5** (Campground) 47 Avail: 36 full hkups, 11 W, 11 E (30/50 amps). 2021 rates: $39 to $42. (931)648-8638, 1270 Tylertown Rd, Clarksville, TN 37040

CLEVELAND — C6 *Bradley*

CHATTANOOGA NORTH KOA **Ratings: 8.5/9★/8.5** (Campground) 58 Avail: 44 full hkups, 14 W, 14 E (30/50 amps). 2021 rates: $41.20 to $65.92. (800)562-9039, 648 Pleasant Grove Road, Cleveland, TN 37353

CLIFTON — C3 *Wayne*

CLIFTON RV PARK & MARINA **Ratings: 6.5/7.5★/6** (Campground) Avail: 14 full hkups (30/50 amps). 2021 rates: $49.99 to $55. (931)676-5225, 111 Harbor Dr, Clifton, TN 38425

CLINTON — B6 *Anderson*

CLINTON/KNOXVILLE NORTH KOA **Ratings: 9/9★/8.5** (Campground) 32 Avail: 27 full hkups, 5 W, 5 E (30/50 amps). 2021 rates: $48.03 to $55.33. (865)494-9386, 2423 N Charles G Seivers Blvd, Clinton, TN 37716

COOKEVILLE — B5 *Putnam*

OLD MILL CAMP & GENERAL STORE **Ratings: 6.5/9★/10** (Campground) Avail: 22 full hkups (50 amps). 2021 rates: $35 to $40. (931)268-0045, 4801 Blackburn Fork Rd, Cookeville, TN 38501

CORNERSVILLE — C4 *Marshall*

TEXAS T CAMPGROUND **Ratings: 6.5/8.5★/8** (Campground) Avail: 41 full hkups (30/50 amps). 2021 rates: $42.50 to $48.44. (931)293-2500, 2499 Lynnville Hwy, Cornersville, TN 37047

""Full hookups'' in a campground listing means there are water, electric and sewer hookups at the sites.

COSBY — E5 *Cocke*

GREAT SMOKY MTN/COSBY (Public National Park) From Jct of I-40 & Foothills Pkwy: Go 7 mi W on Foothills Pkwy, then 2 mi S on US-321 (R). 18 Avail. 2021 rates: $17.50. Apr 03 to Nov 01. (865)487-2683

IMAGINATION MOUNTAIN CAMP-RESORT **Ratings: 8.5/8.5/9** (Campground) 32 Avail: 26 full hkups, 6 W, 6 E (30/50 amps). 2021 rates: $48 to $75. Mar 15 to Dec 01. (423)487-5534, 4946 Hooper Hwy, Cosby, TN 37722

SMOKY MOUNTAIN PREMIER (GATLINBURG EAST/SMOKY MOUNTAIN KOA) **Ratings: 10/9★/9.5** (RV Park) Avail: 70 full hkups (30/50 amps). 2021 rates: $46 to $91. (844)557-6778, 4874 Hooper Hwy, Cosby, TN 37722

COUNCE — C2 *Hardin*

PICKWICK LANDING (Public State Park) From Jct of SR-128 & SR-57, E 0.5 mi on SR-57 to Hardin Dock Rd, N 0.9 mi (L). 48 Avail: 48 W, 48 E (30/50 amps). 2021 rates: $24.10. (731)689-3129

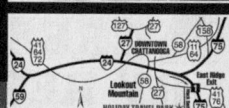

CROSSVILLE — B5 *Cumberland*

BEAN POT CAMPGROUND **Ratings: 9/9★/9** (Campground) 49 Avail: 41 full hkups, 8 W, 8 E (30/50 amps). 2021 rates: $35. (931)484-7671, 23 Bean Pot Campground Loop, Crossville, TN 38571

BRECKENRIDGE LAKE RESORT **Ratings: 6.5/7.5/7.5** (Membership Park) 66 Avail: 27 full hkups, 39 W, 39 E (30/50 amps). 2021 rates: $10 to $36. (931)788-1873, 395 Oak Park Circle, Crossville, TN 38572

CROSSVILLE KOA **Ratings: 8.5/9★/9.5** (Campground) Avail: 50 full hkups (30/50 amps). 2021 rates: $54.73 to $82.17. (931)707-5349, 6575 Hwy 70E, Crossville, TN 38555

CUMBERLAND MOUNTAIN (Public State Park) From Jct of I-40 & US-127 (exit 317), S 7 mi on US-127 (R). 145 Avail: 145 W, 145 E (20/50 amps). 2021 rates: $32 to $35. (931)484-6138

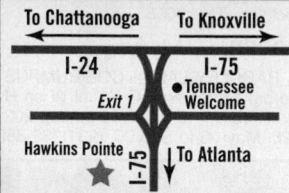

TN

CROSSVILLE (CONT)

DEER RUN RV RESORT **Ratings: 9/9.5★/10** (RV Park) Avail: 84 full hkups (30/50 amps). 2021 rates: $47. (931)484-3333, 3609 Peavine Firetower Rd, Crossville, TN 38571

SPRING LAKE RV RESORT **Ratings: 9/9.5★/9.5** (Campground) Avail: 60 full hkups (30/50 amps). 2021 rates: $39 to $42. (877)707-1414, 255 Fairview Drive, Crossville, TN 38571

DANDRIDGE — D5 *Jefferson*

ANCHOR DOWN RV RESORT **Ratings: 10/10★/10** (RV Resort) Avail: 171 full hkups (30/50 amps). 2021 rates: $59 to $79. Mar 01 to Dec 01. (877)784-4446, 1703 Highway 139, Dandridge, TN 37725

DAYTON — C6 *Rhea*

BLUE WATER RESORT **Ratings: 9.5/9.5★/9.5** (RV Park) Avail: 38 full hkups (30/50 amps). 2021 rates: $49 to $59. (423)775-3265, 220 Bluewater Campground Rd, Dayton, TN 37321

DELANO — C6 *Polk*

HIWASSEE/OCOEE SCENIC RIVER (Public State Park) From north jct Hwy 30 & US 411: Go 6 mi S on US 411 to Hwy 163, then 1 mi SE on Spring Creek Rd. 47 Avail. 2021 rates: $15. (423)263-0050

DICKSON — B3 *Dickson*

TANBARK CAMPGROUND **Ratings: 5.5/7/5.5** (Campground) Avail: 10 full hkups (30/50 amps). 2021 rates: $34. (615)441-1613, 125 S. Spradlin Rd., Dickson, TN 37055

DOVER — A3 *Henry*

BARKLEY LAKE - COE/BUMPUS MILLS (Public Corps) From town: Go 4 mi W on Hwy 120 (L). 15 Avail: 15 W, 15 E (20/30 amps). 2021 rates: $24 to $26. May 06 to Sep 05. (931)232-8831

LBL NATIONAL RECREATION AREA/GATLIN POINT (Public National Park) From town, W 5 mi on US-79 to The Trace (Hwy 453), N 7 mi to CR-227, E 4 mi, follow signs (E) Backcountry cmaper use permit required. 17 Avail: (30 amps), Pit toilets. 2021 rates: $10. (270)924-2000

LBL NATIONAL RECREATION AREA/PINEY CAMPGROUND (Public National Park) From town, W 9.5 mi on US-79 to Fort Henry Rd (CR-230), N 2 mi, follow signs (L). 384 Avail: 44 full hkups, 283 E (30/50 amps). 2021 rates: $12 to $32. Mar 01 to Nov 30. (800)525-7077

DYERSBURG — B1 *Dyer*

DYERSBURG See also Caruthersville & Portageville, MO.

EAST RIDGE — C5 *Hamilton*

RV CAMPGROUND AT CAMP JORDAN PARK (Public) From jct I-75 & US 41 (Ringgold Rd): Go 1/4 mi E on US 41, then 1 mi N on Camp Jordan Pkwy (R). 58 Avail: 58 W, 58 E (30 amps). 2021 rates: $20 to $25. (423)551-0538

ELIZABETHTON — D6 *Carter*

WATAUGA DAM CAMPGROUND **Ratings: 5.5/9★/8.5** (Campground) 27 Avail: 2 full hkups, 25 W, 25 E (30 amps). 2021 rates: $29. Mar 15 to Nov 15. (423)543-0233, 744 Wilbur Dam Rd, Elizabethton, TN 37643

EVA — B3 *Benton*

NATHAN BEDFORD FORREST (Public State Park) From Jct of US-70 & SR-191, N 10.3 mi on SR-191 (E). 37 Avail: 37 W, 37 E (30/50 amps). 2021 rates: $21 to $25. (731)584-6356

GAINESBORO — B5 *Jackson*

CORDELL HULL LAKE - COE/SALT LICK CREEK (Public Corps) From town: Go 4 mi W on Hwy 25, then 2 mi N on Hwy 80, then 8 mi E on Hwy 85, then 1 mi S on Smith Bend Rd to park access rd (E). Avail: 145 E (30/50 amps). 2021 rates: $20 to $25. Apr 16 to Sep 30. (931)678-4718

GALLATIN — B4 *Sumner*

BLEDSOE CREEK (Public State Park) From Jct of US-31 & SR-25, E 6 mi on SR-25 to Ziegler Fort Rd, S 1.3 mi (L). 57 Avail: 57 W, 57 E (30/50 amps). 2021 rates: $20 to $25. (615)452-3706

OLD HICKORY LAKE - COE/CAGES BEND (Public Corps) From Jct of US-31E & Cages Bend Rd: Go 3-1/2 mi S on Cages Bend Rd (L). 42 Avail: 42 W, 42 E (30/50 amps). 2021 rates: $25 to $29. Apr 14 to Oct 10. (615)824-4989

GATLINBURG — E5 *Cocke*

A SPOTLIGHT Introducing Gatlinburg's colorful attractions appearing at the front of this state section.

ADVENTURE BOUND CAMPING RESORT-GATLINBURG **Ratings: 8/7/7.5** (Campground) 200 Avail: 90 full hkups, 110 W, 110 E (30/50 amps). 2021 rates: $49 to $89. Apr 01 to Nov 01. (865)436-4434, 4609 E Pkwy (Hwy 321 S), Gatlinburg, TN 37738

CAMP LECONTE LUXURY OUTDOOR RESORT **Ratings: 10/10★/10** (Campground) Avail: 18 full hkups (30/50 amps). 2021 rates: $55 to $85. Mar 01 to Dec 07. (865)436-8831, 1739 East Parkway, Gatlinburg, TN 37738

GREAT SMOKY MTN/ELKMONT (Public National Park) From Jct of US-441 S & Little River Rd: Go 8 mi W on Little River Rd (L). 172 Avail. 2021 rates: $25 to $27. May 15 to Oct 31. (865)436-1271

GREENBRIER CAMPGROUND

good sam park **Ratings: 8.5/10★/9.5** (Campground) From Jct of US-441 & US-321N/SR-73, E 6 mi on US-321N/SR-73 to SR-416, N 250 yds (L). **FAC:** gravel rds. Avail: 119 gravel, 4 pull-thrus, (28x60), back-ins (28x50), 119 full hkups (30/50 amps), cable, WiFi @ sites, tent sites, rentals, laundry, groc, LP bottles, fire rings, firewood. **REC:** Little Pigeon River: swim, fishing, playground. Pets OK. Partial handicap access. Big rig sites, eco-friendly. 2021 rates: $66 to $89, Military discount. Mar 01 to Dec 31.
(865)430-7415 Lat: 35.74440, Lon: -83.41335
2353 E Pkwy, Gatlinburg, TN 37738
www.greenbriercampground.com
See ad page 845

OUTDOOR RESORTS AT GATLINBURG **Ratings: 10/9★/10** (Condo Park) Avail: 18 full hkups (30/50 amps). 2021 rates: $60 to $65. (865)436-5861, 4229 E Pkwy (Hwy 321N), Gatlinburg, TN 37738

SMOKY BEAR CAMPGROUND AND RV PARK

good sam park **Ratings: 10/10★/10** (RV Park) E-bnd: From Jct of I-40 & US 321S (exit 435), S 17.2 mi on US 321S (R); or W-bnd: From Jct of I-40 & US 73S (Exit 440), S 2.3 mi on US 73S to US 321S, S 11.6 mi (R). **FAC:** paved rds. 44 Avail: 10 paved, 34 all weather, 9 pull-thrus, (30x80), back-ins (30x70), 44 full hkups (30/50 amps), WiFi @ sites, tent sites, rentals, laundry, fire rings, firewood. **REC:** heated pool, hot tub, playground. Pets OK. Partial handicap access. Big rig sites, eco-friendly. 2021 rates: $57 to $62, Military discount. Mar 15 to Jan 04.
(865)436-8372 Lat: 35.76258, Lon: -83.30222
4857 East Parkway, Gatlinburg, TN 37738
www.smokybearcampground.com
See ad this page

TWIN CREEK RV RESORT

good sam park **Ratings: 10/10★/10** (RV Park) From Jct of US-441 & US-321N (traffic light #3 in downtown Gatlinburg), E 2 mi on US-321N/East Parkway (R). **FAC:** paved rds. Avail: 85 paved, patios, 17 pull-thrus, (30x55), back-ins (30x60), 85 full hkups (30/50 amps), cable, WiFi @ sites, rentals, laundry, groc, fire rings, firewood. **REC:** heated pool, wading pool, hot tub, Dudley Creek: fishing, playground. Pet restrict (B/Q). No tents. Big rig sites, eco-friendly. 2021 rates: $80 to $84, Military discount. Mar 29 to Dec 01.
(865)436-7081 Lat: 35.72597, Lon: -83.48291
1202 E Parkway, Gatlinburg, TN 37738
twincreekrvresort.com
See ad this page

GOODLETTSVILLE — B4 *Robertson*

GRAND OLE RV RESORT & MARKET **Ratings: 8/9.5★/8** (RV Park) Avail: 105 full hkups (30/50 amps). 2021 rates: $39.50. (615)420-6036, 708 N Main St, Goodlettsville, TN 37072

NASHVILLE NORTH KOA **Ratings: 9.5/9★/8.5** (RV Park) 82 Avail: 72 full hkups, 10 W, 10 E (30/50 amps). 2021 rates: $65 to $97. (615)859-0348, 1200 Louisville Highway (31 W), Goodlettsville, TN 37072

GREAT SMOKY MOUNTAIN NATIONAL PARK — E5 *Blount*

GREAT SMOKY MOUNTAIN NATIONAL PARK See also Cosby, Dandridge, Gatlinburg, Newport, Pigeon Forge, Sevierville & Townsend, TN; Bryson City, Cherokee & Whittier, NC.

GREENBACK — B6 *Loudon*

LOTTERDALE COVE CAMPGROUND (Public) From jct US 411 & East Coast Tellico Parkway: Go 4-1/2 mi N on East Coast Tellico Parkway (E). 25 Avail: 25 W, 25 E (30/50 amps). 2021 rates: $36. Mar 15 to Nov 15. (865)856-7284

GREENEVILLE — D5 *Greene*

DAVY CROCKETT BIRTH PLACE (Public State Park) From Jct of US 11E & S Heritage, SE 0.7 mi on S. Heritage to Old SR-34, E 0.6 mi to Davy Crockett Rd, SW and follow signs for next 2 mi. 71 Avail: 54 full hkups, 17 W, 17 E (30/50 amps). 2021 rates: $16 to $35. (423)257-2167

KINSER PARK (GREENE COUNTY PARK) (Public) From jct US 321 & Hwy 70: Go 5 mi S on Hwy 70, then 5 mi E on Allens Bridge Rd. 132 Avail: 132 W, 132 E (30 amps). 2021 rates: $25. Mar 29 to Oct 01. (423)639-5912

LAZY LLAMA CAMPGROUND

good sam park **Ratings: 7.5/9.5★/8.5** (Campground) Avail: 10 full hkups (30/50 amps). 2021 rates: $38 to $45. (423)823-2100, 405 Chuckey Ruritan Road South, Chuckey, TN 37641

Explore America's Top RV Destinations! Turn to the Spotlight articles in our State and Province sections to learn more.

HARRIMAN — B6 *Roane*

CANEY CREEK RV RESORT & MARINA **Ratings: 10/8.5/9** (RV Park) Avail: 40 full hkups (30/50 amps). 2021 rates: $56.69 to $62.98. (865)882-4042, 3615 Roane State Hwy, Harriman, TN 37748

HARRISON — C5 *Hamilton*

HARRISON BAY (Public State Park) From Jct of SR-153 & SR-58, N 8.2 mi on SR-58 to Harrison Bay Rd, NW 1.5 mi to park entrance, NW 1.5 mi (E). 168 Avail: 128 W, 128 E (30/50 amps). 2021 rates: $35 to $37. (423)344-6214

HARTFORD — E5 *Cocke*

PIGEON RIVER CAMPGROUND
Ratings: 9/9.5★/9.5 (Campground) From Jct of I-40 & Hartford Road (Exit 447): Go N 1 mi on Hartford Rd (L). Do not follow GPS directions. **FAC:** gravel rds. Avail: 12 gravel, patios, back-ins (30x50), 12 full hkups (30/50 amps), WiFi @ sites, tent sites, rentals, laundry, fire rings, firewood. **REC:** heated pool, Pigeon River: swim, fishing, kayaking/canoeing, boating nearby, playground, rec open to public. Pets OK. eco-friendly. 2021 rates: $55 to $65, Military discount. Mar 01 to Oct 31.
(888)820-8771 Lat: 35.817328, Lon: -83.158706
3375 Hartford Rd, Hartford, TN 37753
campinginthesmokymountains.com
See ad opposite page

Things to See and Do

SMOKY MOUNTAIN OUTDOORS WHITEWATER RAFTING Whitewater rafting and scenic float trips on the Pigeon River from a 12 acre riverside outpost. Mar 01 to Sep 15. Partial handicap access. RV accessible. Restrooms. Food. Hours: 11am to 6pm . Adult fee: $55.00. ATM.
(800)771-7238 Lat: 35.817328, Lon: -83.158706
3299 Hartford Road, Hartford, TN 37753
www.smokymountainrafting.com
See ad opposite page

HENDERSON — C2 *Chester*

CHICKASAW (Public State Park) From Jct of US-45 & SR-100, W 7.6 mi on SR-100 (L). 52 Avail: 52 W, 52 E (20/30 amps). 2021 rates: $25 to $35. (731)989-5141

HENNING — B1 *Lauderdale*

FORT PILLOW STATE HISTORIC AREA (Public State Park) From jct US 51 & Hwy 87: Go 17 mi W on 87, then 1 mi N on Hwy 207. 30 Avail: 6 W, 21 E (20/50 amps). 2021 rates: $25 to $35. (731)738-5581

HERMITAGE — B4 *Wilson*

J PERCY PRIEST LAKE - COE/SEVEN POINTS CAMPGROUND (Public Corps) From town: Go 10 mi E on I-40, then 3/4 mi S on exit 221B (Old Hickory Blvd), then 1 mi E on Bell Rd, then 1-1/2 mi S on New Hope Rd, then 1-1/2 mi E on Stewart Ferry Pike (R). 58 Avail: 58 W, 58 E (30/50 amps). 2021 rates: $26 to $30. Mar 01 to Oct 30. (615)889-1975

HOHENWALD — C3 *Lewis*

FALL HOLLOW CAMPGROUND, B & B AND RESTAURANT **Ratings: 5/6.5/7.5** (Campground) Avail: 23 full hkups (30/50 amps). 2021 rates: $30 to $40. (931)796-1480, 1329 Columbia Hwy, Hohenwald, TN 38462

NATCHEZ TRACE PKWY/MERIWETHER LEWIS CAMPGROUND (Public National Park) From Hohenwald: Go 8 mi E on Hwy 20 at MP-385.9 (E). 32 Avail. (800)305-7417

NATCHEZ TRACE WILDERNESS PRESERVE
Ratings: 7.5/9★/8.5 (Membership Park) 216 Avail: 85 full hkups, 131 W, 131 E (30/50 amps). 2021 rates: $52 to $56. (888)563-7040, 1363 Napier Rd, Hohenwald, TN 38462

HORNSBY — C2 *Hardeman*

BIG BUCK CAMPING RESORT **Ratings: 8/7.5/8.5** (Membership Park) 96 Avail: 55 full hkups, 41 W, 41 E (30/50 amps). 2021 rates: $30 to $35. (731)658-2246, 205 Sparks Rd, Hornsby, TN 38044

HURRICANE MILLS — B3 *Humphreys*

BUFFALO I-40 KOA **Ratings: 8.5/9★/8** (Campground) 45 Avail: 36 full hkups, 9 W, 9 E (30/50 amps). 2021 rates: $37 to $70. (931)296-1306, 473 Barren Hollow Rd, Hurricane Mills, TN 37078

Save 10% at Good Sam Parks!

LORETTA LYNN'S RANCH & FAMILY CAMPGROUND **Ratings: 9.5/9★/9.5** (Campground) Avail: 35 full hkups (30/50 amps). 2021 rates: $37.50 to $42.50. (931)296-7700, 8000 Highway 13S, Hurricane Mills, TN 37078

JACKSON — C2 *Madison*

JACKSON RV PARK (MHP) **Ratings: 5.5/NA/4.5** (RV Area in MH Park) Avail: 15 full hkups (30/50 amps). 2021 rates: $40. (731)234-2009, 2223 Hollywood Dr, Jackson, TN 38305

PARKWAY VILLAGE MH AND RV COMMUNITY
Ratings: 9/NA/8.5 (RV Area in MH Park) Avail: 52 full hkups (30/50 amps). 2021 rates: $40. (731)423-3331, 1243 Whitehall St, Jackson, TN 38301

Travel Services

GANDER RV OF JACKSON Your new hometown outfitter offering the best regional gear for all your outdoor needs. Your adventure awaits. **SERVICES:** gunsmithing svc, archery svc, sells outdoor gear, sells fishing gear, sells firearms, restrooms. RV Sales. RV supplies, LP gas, RV accessible. Hours: 9am to 7pm.
(877)510-7785 Lat: 35.660814, Lon: -88.870185
1523 Vann Dr, Jackson, TN 38305
rv.ganderoutdoors.com

JAMESTOWN — A6 *Fentress*

CHEROKEE RIDGE CAMPGROUND **Ratings: 7/6/5.5** (Campground) 27 Avail: 17 full hkups, 10 W, 10 E (30 amps). 2021 rates: $27 to $35. (931)879-7696, 150 Laurel Creek Campground Rd, Jamestown, TN 38556

EAST FORK RESORT & STABLES **Ratings: 6.5/7/7.5** (Campground) 125 Avail: 28 full hkups, 53 W, 97 E (30/50 amps). 2021 rates: $25 to $35. Apr 01 to Nov 01. (931)879-1176, 3598 S York Hwy, Jamestown, TN 38556

MAPLE HILL RV PARK & CABINS **Ratings: 6/8/8** (Campground) Avail: 19 full hkups (30/50 amps). 2021 rates: $35. (931)879-3025, 1386 North York Hwy (US 127), Jamestown, TN 38556

PICKETT CCC MEMORIAL (Public State Park) From Jct of US-127/Jamestown Bypass & SR-154, NE 12 mi on SR-154 to park access rd, NW 1 mi (L). CAUTION: Maximum length 25 ft. 31 Avail: 31 W, 31 E (30 amps). 2021 rates: $25. (931)879-5821

TRUE WEST CAMPGROUND, STABLES AND MERCANTILE **Ratings: 6/9★/9** (Campground) 33 Avail: 7 full hkups, 26 W, 26 E (30/50 amps). 2021 rates: $30 to $35. (931)752-8272, 3341 Leatherwood Ford Rd, Jamestown, TN 38556

JASPER — C5 *Marion*

SHELLMOUND RV RESORT & CAMPGROUND **Ratings: 6.5/7★/8.5** (Campground) 47 Avail: 47 W, 47 E (30/50 amps). 2021 rates: $31 to $36. Feb 01 to Jan 15. (423)942-9857, 2735 TVA Rd, Jasper, TN 37347

JEFFERSON CITY — D5 *Grainger*

CHEROKEE DAM CAMPGROUND **Ratings: 6/8.5★/9** (Campground) 36 Avail: 36 W, 36 E (30/50 amps). 2021 rates: $27 to $29. Mar 15 to Nov 15. (865)361-2151, 2805 N Highway 92, Jefferson City, TN 37760

JELLICO — A6 *Campbell*

INDIAN MOUNTAIN (Public State Park) From jct I-75 (exit #160 & US 25 NW: Follow signs 3 mi N to park. 47 Avail: 47 W, 47 E (30/50 amps). 2021 rates: $32 to $35. (423)784-7958

JOHNSON CITY — D6 *Washington*

JOHNSON CITY See also Bristol, Elizabethton, Greeneville, Jonesborough, Kingsport & Unicoi.

JONESBOROUGH — D6 *Washington*

JONESBOROUGH/CHEROKEE NF KOA **Ratings: 9.5/10★/9.5** (Campground) Avail: 37 full hkups (30/50 amps). 2021 rates: $45 to $70. Mar 01 to Dec 15. (423)753-5359, 3937 Hwy 81 South, Jonesborough, TN 37659

RIVERVIEW CAMPGROUND **Ratings: 7.5/9★/9** (Campground) Avail: 32 full hkups (30/50 amps). 2021 rates: $38 to $4,800. (423)753-2577, 408 Hwy 107, Jonesborough, TN 37659

Looking for places the ""locals'' frequent? Make friends with park owners and staff to get the inside scoop!

KINGSPORT — D5 *Sullivan*

WARRIORS PATH (Public State Park) From Jct of I-81 & SR-36 (exit 59), N 1.3 mi on SR-36 to Hemlock Rd, E 1.8 mi (L). 94 Avail: 94 W, 94 E (30/50 amps). 2021 rates: $25. (423)239-8531

KINGSTON — B6 *Roane*

RILEY CREEK CAMPGROUND (Public) From Jct. I-40 & Hwy 58, S 5.6 mi to Old Hood Rd., E .5 mi (R). 20 Avail: 20 W, 20 E (30 amps). 2021 rates: $35. Mar 15 to Nov 15. (865)250-6152

KNOXVILLE — B6 *Knox*

KNOXVILLE See also Andersonville, Clinton, Cosby, Dandridge, Gatlinburg, Harriman, Hartford, Jefferson City, Lenoir City, Newport, Pigeon Forge, Pioneer, Rocky Top, Sevierville, Sweetwater & Townsend.

RACCOON VALLEY RV PARK **Ratings: 7/9★/8** (Campground) Avail: 68 full hkups (30/50 amps). 2021 rates: $23 to $30. (865)947-9776, 908 Raccoon Valley Rd NE, Heiskell, TN 37754

SOUTHLAKE RV PARK **Ratings: 7.5/7.5/5.5** (Campground) 40 Avail: 35 full hkups, 5 W, 5 S (30/50 amps). 2021 rates: $30 to $38. (865)573-1837, 3730 Maryville Pike, Knoxville, TN 37920

VOLUNTEER PARK FAMILY CAMPGROUND
Ratings: 9/8.5★/9 (Campground) From Jct of I-75 & Raccoon Valley Rd (exit 117), W 0.2 mi on Raccoon Valley Rd (L). **FAC:** paved/gravel rds. (125 spaces). 85 Avail: 30 paved, 55 gravel, 35 pull-thrus, (24x50), back-ins (24x50), 73 full hkups, 12 W, 12 E (30/50 amps), seasonal sites, cable, WiFi @ sites, tent sites, dump, laundry, LP gas, fire rings, firewood. **REC:** pool, wading pool, boating nearby, playground. Pet restrict (Q). eco-friendly. 2021 rates: $35 to $57, Military discount.
(865)938-6600 Lat: 36.10271, Lon: -84.02594
9514 Diggs Gap Rd, Heiskell, TN 37754
www.volunteerpark.com
See ad next page

Travel Services

MAN CAVE STORAGE A premier concierge storage for RVs, boats & campers. Indoor, covered & outdoor storage options as well as full professional detailing along with minor repairs, maintenance, provisioning & campsite set-up. **RV Storage:** indoor, outdoor, covered canopy, secured fencing, electric gate, easy reach keypad, 24/7 access, well-lit facility, well-lit roads, well-lit perimeter, security cameras, on-site staff, level gravel/paved spaces, temp controlled, battery charger, power to charge battery, water, compressed air, office. **SERVICES:** tire, RV appliance, MH mechanical, staffed RV wash, restrooms. RV supplies, LP gas, dump. Hours: 8am to 6pm. No CC. Special offers available for Good Sam Members
(865)766-5367 Lat: 36.0681213, Lon: -83.9313462
3908 Fountain Valley Dr, Knoxville, TN 37918
mancavestorage.com

LA VERGNE — B4 *Robertson*

J PERCY PRIEST LAKE - COE/POOLE KNOBS (Public Corps) From Jct Hwy 41 & Hwy 266: Go 1-1/2 mi N on Hwy 41, then 3/4 mi NE on Fergus Rd, then 4 mi N on Jones Mill Rd (L). Avail: 46 E (50 amps). 2021 rates: $20 to $40. May 01 to Oct 31. (615)459-6948

LAWRENCEBURG — C3 *Lawrence*

DAVID CROCKETT (Public State Park) From Jct of US-43 & US-64, W 1.4 mi on US-64 (R). 97 Avail: 97 W, 97 E (20/50 amps). 2021 rates: $20 to $35. (931)762-9408

You have high expectations, so we point out campgrounds, service centers and tourist attractions with elevations over 2,500 feet.

LEBANON — B4 *Wilson*

CEDARS OF LEBANON (Public State Park) From Jct of I-40 & US-231 (exit 238), S 6.4 mi on US-231 (L). 117 Avail: 117 W, 117 E (30/50 amps). 2021 rates: $25 to $35. (615)443-2769

NASHVILLE EAST/LEBANON KOA **Ratings: 7.5/9.5★/9.5** (RV Park) 53 Avail: 28 full hkups, 25 W, 25 E (30/50 amps). 2021 rates: $39.10 to $55.30. (615)449-5527, 2100 Safari Camp Rd, Lebanon, TN 37090

LENOIR CITY — B6 *Loudon*

LAZY ACRES RV PARK **Ratings: 6.5/8.5/6.5** (Campground) 37 Avail: 27 full hkups, 10 W, 10 E (30/50 amps). 2021 rates: $35 to $50. (865)986-3539, 7502 Jackson Bend Rd, Lenoir City, TN 37772

MELTON HILL DAM CAMPGROUND **Ratings: 5/8★/9** (Campground) 47 Avail: 9 full hkups, 38 W, 38 E (30/50 amps). 2021 rates: $27 to $29. Mar 15 to Nov 15. (865)361-0436, 201 Campground Rd, Lenoir City, TN 37771

SOARING EAGLE CAMPGROUND & RV PARK
good sam park
Ratings: 8.5/9.5★/9 (Campground) Avail: 77 full hkups (30/50 amps). 2021 rates: $34 to $40. (865)376-9017, 3152 Buttermilk Rd West, Lenoir City, TN 37771

YARBERRY CAMPGROUND **Ratings: 5/9.5★/8.5** (Campground) 34 Avail: 34 W, 34 E (30/50 amps). 2021 rates: $31 to $36. (865)986-3993, 4825 Yarberry Rd, Lenoir City, TN 37772

LEXINGTON — C2 *Henderson*

BEECH LAKE FAMILY CAMPING RESORT **Ratings: 6.5/9★/8.5** (Campground) 50 Avail: 50 W, 50 E (30/50 amps). 2021 rates: $28 to $35. Apr 01 to Nov 30. (731)968-9542, 495 Beech Lake Campground Road, Lexington, TN 38351

LINDEN — C3 *Perry*

MOUSETAIL LANDING (Public State Park) From jct US 412 & TN 13: Go 11-3/4 mi W on US 412, then 2-3/4 mi NE on TN 438, then 1/2 mi NW on Campground Rd (E) Caution: Steep grade in park. 20 Avail: 1 full hkups, 19 W, 19 E (30/50 amps). 2021 rates: $25. (731)847-0841

LIVINGSTON — B5 *Overton*

DALE HOLLOW LAKE - COE/LILLYDALE CAMPGROUND (Public Corps) From town: Go 2 mi NW on SR-52, then 1-1/2 mi NE on Hwy 1209, then 6 mi NW on Hwy 294 (E). Avail: 109 E (30/50 amps). 2021 rates: $19 to $33. May 06 to Sep 11. (931)823-4155

DALE HOLLOW LAKE - COE/OBEY RIVER PARK (Public Corps) From town: Go 3 mi SW on SR-111 (R). Avail: 131 E (30/50 amps). 2021 rates: $19 to $30. Apr 11 to Oct 15. (931)864-6388

STANDING STONE (Public State Park) From Jct of Hwys 111 & 52 (in Livingston), W 8.7 mi on Hwy 52 to SR-136, S 0.5 mi (L). Note: 45' RV length limit. 36 Avail: 36 W, 36 E (30/50 amps). 2021 rates: $25 to $35. (931)823-6347

LOBELVILLE — B3 *Lobelville*

BUFFALO RIVER RESORT **Ratings: 4.5/5.5/6.5** (Campground) Avail: 24 full hkups (30/50 amps). 2021 rates: $44.50. (931)593-2000, 3520 Highway 13 North, Lobelville, TN 37097

LOUISVILLE — E4 *Blount*

Travel Services

CAMPING WORLD OF LOUISVILLE/KNOXVILLE As the nation's largest retailer of RV supplies, accessories, services and new and used RVs, Camping World is committed to making your total RV experience better. **SERVICES:** RV, tire, RV appliance, MH mechanical, staffed RV wash, restrooms. RV Sales. RV supplies, LP gas, RV accessible. Hours: 9am to 7pm.
(888)387-3452 Lat: 35.854903, Lon: -83.962671
4223 Airport Highway, Louisville, TN 37777
www.campingworld.com

MADISON — B4 *Davidson*

OLD HICKORY MH COMMUNITY
good sam park
(RV Area in MH Park) (Seasonal Stay Only) 0 Avail: (30/50 amps). (615)868-9674, 500 Cheyenne Boulevard #306, Madison, TN 37115

It's the law! Rules of the Road and Towing Laws are updated each year. Be sure to consult this chart to find the laws for every state on your traveling route.

MANCHESTER — C5 *Coffee*

CEDAR POINT CAMPGROUND **Ratings: 5.5/7.5/9** (Campground) 13 Avail: 13 W, 13 E (30/50 amps). 2021 rates: $32 to $35. Apr 01 to Oct 31. (931)857-3705, 1659 Cedar Point Rd, Manchester, TN 37355

MANCHESTER KOA **Ratings: 9.5/10★/9.5** (Campground) Avail: 39 full hkups (30/50 amps). 2021 rates: $55 to $90. (800)562-7785, 586 Campground Rd, Manchester, TN 37355

OLD STONE FORT STATE ARCHAEOLOGICAL PARK (Public State Park) From Jct of I-24 & Hwy 53 (exit 110), W 0.8 mi on Hwy 53 to US-41, N 0.7 mi (L). CAUTION: Must drive over narrow bridge (11 ft wide) to get to campground. 10 ton wt limit for 2 axles, 18 ton for 3 axles. 51 Avail: 51 W, 51 E (30 amps). 2021 rates: $25. (931)723-5073

MAYNARDVILLE — D4 *Union*

BIG RIDGE (Public State Park) From Jct of I-75 & Hwy 61 (Exit 122), E 11.6 mi on Hwy 61 (L). Note: 35' RV length limit. 50 Avail: 50 W, 48 E (30/50 amps). 2021 rates: $25 to $27. (865)992-5523

MEMPHIS — C1 *Shelby*

MEMPHIS See also Marion & West Memphis, AR; Coldwater, Horn Lake & Southaven, MS.

AGRICENTER INTERNATIONAL RV PARK
(Public) From Jct of I-40 & Germantown Rd (W-bnd-exit 16A, E-bnd-exit 16B), S 4.7 mi on Germantown Pkwy to Timbercreek Rd, W 0.1 mi (follow signs to RV park in complex) (L). **FAC:** paved rds. 300 Avail: 175 gravel, 125 grass, 300 pull-thrus, (20x70), mostly side by side hkups, 175 full hkups, 125 W, 125 E (30/50 amps), WiFi @ sites, dump, laundry. **REC:** pond, fishing. Pets OK. Partial handicap access. No tents. 2021 rates: $35, Military discount. ATM.
(901)355-1977 Lat: 35.12758, Lon: -89.80566
7777 Walnut Grove Rd, Memphis, TN 38120
www.agricenter.org/rvpark
See ad page 856

COOK'S LAKE RV RESORT & CAMPGROUND
good sam park
Ratings: 10/7/8.5 (Campground) Avail: 50 full hkups (30/50 amps). 2021 rates: $55. (901)570-3595, 4249 N Watkins, Memphis, TN 38127

ELVIS PRESLEY BLVD RV PARK **Ratings: 6/5.5/5** (Campground) Avail: 10 full hkups (30/50 amps). 2021 rates: $35 to $40. (901)332-3633, 3971 Elvis Presley Blvd, Memphis, TN 38116

OFF SEASON RVING TIP: Find out which campground sections are open. With fewer campers to contend with, many campgrounds limit off-season camping to a smaller area of the campground. You may find your favorite area off-limits or without hookups.

EZ DAZE RV PARK

Our Southern Hospitality and Dedication to Excellence will make your stay at EZ Daze RV Park like staying at a fine resort

Only 5 minutes from Memphis, Tennessee

- Graceland-Elvis home
- Beale Street- Home of the Blues
- Sun Studio-Birthplace of Rock"n"Roll
- Bass Pro Shop-at the Pyramid
- Peabody Hotel-Twice daily Duck March
- Memphis Zoo
- Memphis Botanic Garden
- Tanger Outlet Mall

Casinos only 20 minutes away!

Southaven Storage Now Open with RV Storage

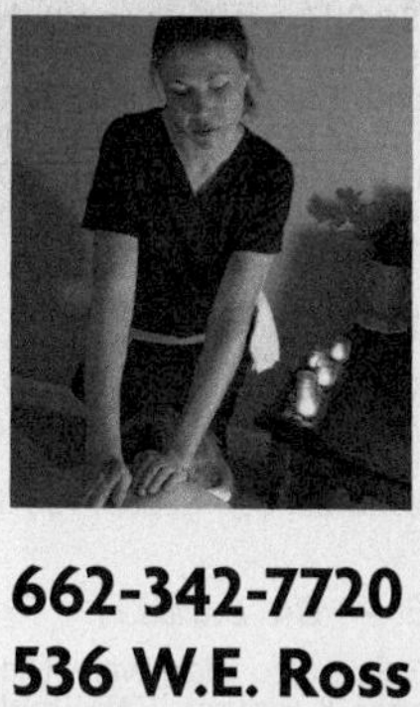

MASSAGE ROOM ON SITE!
Call or text ahead for appointment with
Jeannie South
901-216-6353

good sam park
2022 Top Rated

662-342-7720 • reservationsezdaze@yahoo.com
536 W.E. Ross Pkwy. (I-55, Exit 287) Southaven, MS 38671

See listing Southaven, MS

www.ezdazervpark.com

TN

MEMPHIS (CONT)

EZ DAZE RV PARK
good sam park **Ratings: 10/10★/9** (RV Park) From jct I-55 & I-240 in Memphis: Go 9-1/2 mi S on I-55 (exit 287), then 1/4 mi W on Church Rd, then 1/2 mi N on Pepper Chase Dr., then 1/4 mi W on W E Ross Pkwy (R). **FAC:** paved rds. (136 spaces). Avail: 50 paved, patios, 47 pull-thrus, (25x75), back-ins (25x60), 50 full hkups (30/50 amps), seasonal sites, cable, WiFi @ sites, laundry, LP gas. **REC:** pool, boating nearby, playground. Pet restrict (B). Partial handicap access. No tents. Big rig sites, eco-friendly. 2021 rates: $57 to $72, Military discount.
(662)342-7720 Lat: 34.94186, Lon: -89.99883
536 W.E. Ross Pkwy, Southaven, MS 38671
www.ezdazervpark.com
See primary listing at Southaven, MS and ad previous page, 528

Making campground reservations? Remember to ask about the cancellation policy when making your reservation.

MEMPHIS GRACELAND RV PARK & CAMPGROUND
good sam park **Ratings: 9.5/9★/8** (Campground) 74 Avail: 61 full hkups, 13 W, 13 E (30/50 amps). 2021 rates: $46 to $52. (866)571-9236, 3691 Elvis Presley Blvd, Memphis, TN 38116

SOUTHAVEN RV PARK
good sam park **Ratings: 7.5/9.5★/8** (Campground) From jct I-55 and I-240 in town: Go 6 mi S on I-55, then 1/2 mi E on Stateline R (L). **FAC:** paved rds. (44 spaces). Avail: 10 paved, patios, 10 pull-thrus, (20x65), 10 full hkups (30/50 amps), cable, WiFi @ sites, laundry. **REC:** boating nearby. Pet restrict (B). No tents. 2021 rates: $45, Military discount.
(662)393-8585 Lat: 34.9925, Lon: -89.9945
270 Stateline Rd, Southaven, MS 38671
www.southavenrvpark.com
See primary listing at Southaven, MS and ad page 854

T. O. FULLER (Public State Park) From Jct of I 55 & Mallory Ave (Exit 9), E 450 ft on Mallory Ave to Riverport Rd, S 5 mi to Plant Rd (L). 45 Avail: 45 W, 45 E (30/50 amps). 2021 rates: $21 to $35. (901)543-7581

TOM SAWYER'S RV PARK
good sam park **Ratings: 7.5/9★/8** (RV Park) From jct I-40 & I-240: Go 6-1/4 mi W on I-40, then 2-1/2 mi S (exit 280) on Martin Luther King Dr. (becomes South Loop Drive), then 1/4 mi S on 8th St (over levy) (L). **FAC:** paved/gravel rds. (121 spaces). 110 Avail: 47 paved, 63 all weather, 103 pull-thrus, (30x130), back-ins (30x60), 110 full hkups (30/50 amps), seasonal sites, WiFi @ sites, tent sites, laundry, firewood, controlled access. **REC:** Mississippi River: fishing, kayaking/canoeing, boating nearby. Pet restrict (B). Big rig sites. 2021 rates: $40 to $55.
(870)735-9770 Lat: 35.12999, Lon: -90.16714
1286 S 8th St, West Memphis, AR 72301
tomsawyersrvpark.com
See primary listing at West Memphis, AR and ad this page

MIDDLETON — C2 *Hardeman*

CHEROKEE LANDING CAMPGROUND
good sam park **Ratings: 6/3/8** (Membership Park) 292 Avail: 21 full hkups, 271 W, 271 E (30 amps). 2021 rates: $48.29. Apr 01 to Oct 25. (888)563-7040, 1385 Old Stateline Rd, Saulsbury, TN 38067

MILLINGTON — C1 *Shelby*

MEEMAN-SHELBY FOREST (Public State Park) From Jct of US-51 & Hwy 388, N 6.9 mi on Hwy 388 (N Watkins Rd) to Locke Cuba Rd, W 0.7 to Bluff Rd, N 0.8 mi (L). 49 Avail: 49 W, 49 E (20/30 amps). 2021 rates: $25 to $27. (800)471-5293

MONTEREY — B5 *Putnam*

BELLE RIDGE CAMPGROUND
good sam park **Ratings: 9/10★/10** (Campground) Avail: 50 full hkups (30/50 amps). 2021 rates: $44 to $49. (931)241-4341, 15341 Crossville Hwy, Monterey, TN 38574

MORRISTOWN — D5 *Hamblen*

CHEROKEE PARK (HAMBLEN COUNTY PARK) (Public) From town: Go 3 mi N on Hwy 25E, then 1 mi NE on Cherokee Park Rd (L). 74 Avail: 74 W, 74 E (30 amps). 2021 rates: $15 to $20. (423)586-0325

PANTHER CREEK (Public State Park) W-bnd: From Jct of I-81 & Hwy 160 (exit 12), NW 10 mi on Hwy 160 to US-11E, NE 1.2 mi to Hwy 342, NW 2.4 mi (R); or E-bnd: From Jct of I-40 & US-11E (exit 394), NE 29.5 mi on US-11E thru Talbott to Hwy 342, NW 2.2 mi (R) Max RV length 35 ft. 50 Avail: 8 full hkups, 42 W, 42 E (30/50 amps). 2021 rates: $25 to $35. (423)587-7046

MOUNT JULIET — B4 *Wilson*

OLD HICKORY LAKE - COE/CEDAR CREEK (Public Corps) From Jct of US-70 & Nonaville Rd: Go 5 mi N on Nonaville Rd (R). 59 Avail: 59 W, 59 E (15/50 amps). 2021 rates: $30 to $35. Apr 14 to Oct 10. (615)754-4947

NASHVILLE — B4 *Davidson*

NASHVILLE See also Clarksville, Dickson, Goodlettsville, Lebanon & Smyrna, TN; Franklin, KY.

FOUR CORNERS RV RESORT **Ratings: 10/10★/9** (RV Resort) Avail: 118 full hkups (30/50 amps). 2021 rates: $69 to $94. (629)236-2600, 4029 LaVergne Couchville Pike, Antioch, TN 37013

➚ NASHVILLE RV RESORT AND CABINS **Ratings: 8.5/9★/9** (Campground) 237 Avail: 174 full hkups, 63 W, 63 E (30/50 amps). 2021 rates: $65 to $99. (615)889-4225, 2572 Music Valley Drive, Nashville, TN 37214

← NASHVILLE SHORES LAKESIDE RESORT
good sam park **Ratings: 9.5/9★/10** (RV Park) From Jct of I-40 & Old Hickory Blvd (Exit 221 & 221B), S 0.5 mi on Old Hickory Blvd to Bell Rd, W 0.5 mi (L). **FAC:** paved rds. Avail: 100 paved, patios, 31 pull-thrus, (30x60), back-ins (30x55), 100 full hkups (30/50 amps), cable, WiFi @ sites, rentals, laundry, fire rings, firewood, restaurant, controlled access. **REC:** pool $, wading pool, Percy Priest Lake: fishing, marina, kayaking/canoeing, boating nearby, shuffleboard, playground, rec open to public. Pets OK. No tents. Big rig sites, 14 day max stay, eco-friendly. 2021 rates: $60 to $85, Military discount. Feb 01 to Dec 01. ATM.
(615)889-7434 Lat: 36.15874, Lon: -86.60826
4001 Bell Road, Nashville, TN 37076
www.nashvilleshores.com
See ad opposite page

➚ TWO RIVERS CAMPGROUND
good sam park **Ratings: 8.5/10★/9** (RV Park) E-bnd: From Jct of I-40 & Briley Pkwy (Exit 204), N 16.4 mi on Briley Pkwy to McGavock Pike (exit 12), W 0.2 mi to Music Valley Dr, N 1.2 mi (L); or W-bnd: From Jct of I-40 & Briley Pkway (Exit 215), N 5.3 mi on Briley Pkwy to McGavock Pike (exit 12), W 0.2 mi to Music Valley Dr, N 1.2 mi (L).

11 MI. TO DOWNTOWN NASHVILLE!
Music City USA - home of country music & the Grand Ole Opry. Visit historic landmarks & battlefields, enjoy great golf & water fun, fine dining, world-famous 'Honky Tonks' & Opryland Hotel! Join us for a fun vacation!
FAC: paved/gravel rds. Avail: 104 gravel, patios, 11 pull-thrus, (24x54), back-ins (30x54), 78 full hkups, 26 W, 26 E (30/50 amps), cable, WiFi @ sites, dump, laundry, groc. **REC:** pool, boating nearby, playground. Pets OK. No tents, eco-friendly. 2021 rates: $46.80 to $55.80, Military discount. ATM.
(615)883-8559 Lat: 36.23431, Lon: -86.70369
2616 Music Valley Drive, Nashville, TN 37214
www.tworiverscampground.com
See ad opposite page

Travel Services

➚ **CAMPING WORLD OF NASHVILLE** As the nation's largest retailer of RV supplies, accessories, services and new and used RVs, Camping World is committed to making your total RV experience better. **SERVICES:** RV, tire, RV appliance, MH mechanical, staffed RV wash, restrooms. RV Sales. RV supplies, LP gas, RV accessible. Hours: 9am to 7pm.
(877)827-2398 Lat: 36.160974, Lon: -86.664267
2618 Music Valley Dr., Nashville, TN 37214
www.campingworld.com

➚ **GANDER RV OF NASHVILLE** Your new hometown outfitter offering the best regional gear for all your outdoor needs. Your adventure awaits. **SERVICES:** restrooms. RV Sales. RV supplies, RV accessible. Hours: 9am to 7pm.
(888)847-0095 Lat: 36.23289, Lon: -86.70312
2614 Music Valley Dr, Nashville, TN 37214
rv.ganderoutdoors.com

NEWPORT — E5 *Cocke*

← NEWPORT/SMOKY MOUNTAIN KOA **Ratings: 8.5/9★/9** (Campground) Avail: 68 full hkups (30/50 amps). 2021 rates: $48. (800)562-9016, 240 KOA Lane, Newport, TN 37821

↓ TRIPLE CREEK CAMPGROUND
good sam park **Ratings: 7.5/8.5/10** (Campground) Avail: 25 full hkups (30/50 amps). 2021 rates: $45 to $50. (423)465-3060, 141 Lower Bogard Rd, Newport, TN 37821

NORMANDY — C4 *Coffee*

→ BARTON SPRINGS CAMPGROUND **Ratings: 5/8.5/8.5** (Campground) 30 Avail: 30 W, 30 E (30/50 amps). 2021 rates: $37.04 to $39.29. Mar 15 to Nov 15. (931)857-3777, 158 Barton Springs Rd, Normandy, TN 37360

We give campgrounds one rating for development, a second for restrooms and a third for visual appearance and environmental quality. That's the Triple Rating System.

ONEIDA — A6 *Scott*

BIG SOUTH FORK NAT'L RIVER & REC AREA/ BANDY CREEK CAMPGROUND (Public National Park) From jct US 27 & Hwy 297: Go 15 mi W on Hwy 297. 96 Avail: 96 W, 96 E (30 amps). 2021 rates: $20 to $32. (423)569-9778

PARIS — B2 *Henry*

➚ PARIS LANDING/KENTUCKY LAKE KOA **Ratings: 9/10★/9** (Campground) 45 Avail: 24 full hkups, 21 W, 21 E (30/50 amps). 2021 rates: $39 to $57. Mar 01 to Nov 10. (731)642-6895, 6290 East Antioch Road, Buchanan, TN 38222

PARKERS CROSSROADS — B2 *Henderson*

↑ PARKERS CROSSROADS RV PARK
good sam park **Ratings: 8.5/9★/8.5** (Campground) Avail: 36 full hkups (30/50 amps). 2021 rates: $41.51. (731)249-9988, 22580 Highway 22N, Yuma, TN 38390

PARSONS — B3 *Decatur*

→ PERRYVILLE MARINA & CAMPGROUND **Ratings: 4.5/NA/6.5** (Campground) Avail: 70 full hkups (30/50 amps). 2021 rates: $50. Mar 16 to Feb 28. (731)847-2444, 108 Perryville Marina Ln, Parsons, TN 38363

PERRYVILLE — C3 *Decatur*

BEECH BEND PARK (DECATUR COUNTY PK) (Public) From jct US 412/Hwy 20 & Hwy 100: Go 1-1/2 mi S on Hwy 100. 56 Avail: 56 W, 56 E. 2021 rates: $19. (731)847-4252

PIGEON FORGE — E5 *Sevier*

A SPOTLIGHT Introducing Pigeon Forge's colorful attractions appearing at the front of this state section.

↓ ALPINE HIDEAWAY CAMPGROUND **Ratings: 8/10★/9** (Campground) Avail: 45 full hkups (30/50 amps). 2021 rates: $48. (865)428-3285, 251 Spring Valley Road, Pigeon Forge, TN 37863

➚ CAMP MARGARITAVILLE RV RESORT & LODGE **Ratings: 9.5/10★/10** (RV Resort) Avail: 159 full hkups (30/50 amps). 2021 rates: $59 to $149. (865)429-0070, 149 Cates Lane, Pigeon Forge, TN 37863

↓ CAMP RIVERSLANDING **Ratings: 9.5/10★/9** (RV Park) Avail: 114 full hkups (30/50 amps). 2021 rates: $50 to $70. (800)848-9097, 304 Day Springs Road, Pigeon Forge, TN 37863

→ CLABOUGH'S CAMPGROUND
good sam park **Ratings: 10/10★/8.5** (Campground) From Jct of US-441 & Wears Valley Rd (US 321): Go W 0.5 mi on Wears Valley Rd (US-321) to Sequoia Rd S 0.1 mi (E).

YOUR SMOKY ADVENTURE STARTS HERE!
Convenient to Pigeon Forge, Gatlinburg & Sevierville, at Clabough's you are just minutes away from shopping, attractions & restaurants to suit every age & interest! And we offer great amenities right here in our campground!
FAC: paved rds. (320 spaces). Avail: 290 all weather, patios, 70 pull-thrus, (30x70), back-ins (25x50), 290 full hkups (30/50 amps), seasonal sites, cable, WiFi @ sites, tent sites, rentals, laundry, groc, firewood, restaurant. **REC:** heated pool, Walden's Creek: fishing, playground, hunting nearby. Pet restrict (Q). Partial handicap access. Big rig sites, eco-friendly. 2021 rates: $39 to $72. ATM.
(800)965-8524 Lat: 35.79956, Lon: -83.58604
405 Wears Valley Rd, Pigeon Forge, TN 37863
www.claboughcampground.com
See ad pages 842, 846, 848

↑ CREEKSIDE RV PARK
good sam park **Ratings: 9.5/9.5★/9.5** (Campground) Avail: 107 full hkups (30/50 amps). 2021 rates: $52 to $58. Mar 01 to Jan 01. (865)428-4801, 2475 Henderson Springs Rd, Pigeon Forge, TN 37863

↓ FOOTHILLS RV PARK & CABINS
Ratings: 9/9.5★/8.5 (RV Park) From Jct. of US 441 & Wears Valley Road (US 321), S 3 mi on US 441 to Cates Lane, (200 ft before reaching traffic light #10), E 0.1 mi to Huskey St, S 750 ft (L). **FAC:** paved rds. Avail: 32 paved, patios, back-ins (25x42), 32 full hkups (30/50 amps), cable, WiFi @ sites, rentals, laundry, fire rings, firewood. **REC:** heated pool. Pets OK. Partial handicap access. No tents, eco-friendly. 2021 rates: $42 to $52. Apr 01 to Nov 01.
(865)428-3818 Lat: 35.77356, Lon: -83.53658
4235 Huskey St, Pigeon Forge, TN 37863
foothillsrvparkandcabins.com
See ad page 846

↓ GATEWAY TO THE SMOKIES RV PARK & CAMPGROUND
good sam park **Ratings: 9.5/10★/9** (RV Park) From jct US-441 & Conner Hgts Rd: Go 1/4 mi W on Conner Hgts Rd (R). **FAC:** paved rds. 68 Avail: 24 paved, 44 gravel, back-ins (38x60), 68 full hkups (30/50 amps), cable, WiFi @ sites, tent sites, rentals, laundry, groc, fire rings, firewood. **REC:** pool, wading pool, playground. Pets OK. Partial handicap access, eco-friendly. 2021 rates: $44 to $57, Military discount. Apr 01 to Nov 15.
(865)428-4490 Lat: 35.770461, Lon: -83.543061
210 Conner Heights Rd, Pigeon Forge, TN 37863
www.gatewaytothesmokies.com
See ad page 846

← KING'S HOLLY HAVEN RV PARK
good sam park **Ratings: 9/9.5★/9.5** (Campground) From Jct of US-441 & US-321, SW 1 mi on US-321 (L). **FAC:** paved rds. Avail: 161 all weather, patios, 12 pull-thrus, (25x60), back-ins (28x55), 161 full hkups (30/50 amps), cable, WiFi @ sites, laundry, fire rings. **REC:** pool, Waldens Creek: fishing, playground. Pets OK. Partial handicap access. No tents. Big rig sites, eco-friendly. 2021 rates: $37 to $46.
(888)204-0247 Lat: 35.79576, Lon: -83.59064
647 Wears Valley Rd, Pigeon Forge, TN 37863
www.hollyhavenrvpark.com
See ad page 846

↓ MILL CREEK RESORT
good sam park **Ratings: 10/10★/9.5** (RV Park) From South city limits at Jct US-441 & Conner Hgts Rd: Go 1/2 mi W on Conner Hgts Rd, then 100 yards N on Mill Creek Rd. **FAC:** paved rds. 71 Avail: 14 paved, 57 all weather, 16 pull-thrus, (28x50), back-ins (28x40), 71 full hkups (30/50 amps), cable, WiFi @ sites, rentals, laundry, groc, fire rings, firewood. **REC:** pool, wading pool, shuffleboard, playground. Pets OK. No tents, eco-friendly. 2021 rates: $44, Military discount.
(865)428-3498 Lat: 35.77205, Lon: -83.54616
449 W Mill Creek Rd, Pigeon Forge, TN 37863
millcreekresortpf.com
See ad page 846

↑ PIGEON FORGE RV RESORT **Ratings: 9.5/10★/9** (RV Park) Avail: 158 full hkups (30/50 amps). 2021 rates: $49.34 to $84.80. (865)428-5841, 1111 Wears Valley Rd, Pigeon Forge, TN 37863

↓ PIGEON FORGE/GATLINBURG KOA **Ratings: 9/10★/9.5** (Campground) 187 Avail: 179 full hkups, 8 W, 8 E (30/50 amps). 2021 rates: $35 to $102. (865)453-7903, 3122 Veterans Blvd, Pigeon Forge, TN 37863

Replace clogged air filters. A clogged air filter can cut a vehicle's fuel efficiency by 10 percent.

TN

good sam park
2022
Top Rated
10/9.5★/9.5
Riveredge RV Park

PIGEON FORGE (CONT)

PINE MOUNTAIN RV PARK BY THE CREEK
good sam park **Ratings: 10/10★/9.5** (RV Park) From Jct of US-441 & Pine Mountain Rd (traffic light #6 in Pigeon Forge), SE 0.4 mi on Pine Mountain Rd (L). **FAC:** paved rds. Avail: 61 paved, patios, 25 pull-thrus, (35x45), back-ins (35x60), 61 full hkups (30/50 amps), cable, WiFi @ sites, rentals, laundry, fire rings, firewood. **REC:** heated pool, hot tub, Mill Creek: fishing. Pet restrict (S/B). Partial handicap access. No tents. Big rig sites, eco-friendly. 2021 rates: $45 to $85, Military discount.
(877)753-9994 Lat: 35.789986, Lon: -83.566389
411 Pine Mountain Rd, Pigeon Forge, TN 37863
pinemountainrvpark.com
See ad page 846

RIVERBEND CAMPGROUND
Ratings: 8/NA/7.5 (Campground) From Jct of US-441 & US-321, N 0.3 mi on US-441 to Henderson Chapel Rd (Stoplight No. 1), W 0.3 mi on Henderson Chapel Rd to Riverbend Loop SW 0.4 mi (L). **FAC:** paved rds. 120 Avail: 100 paved, 20 gravel, 42 pull-thrus, (24x60), back-ins (25x60), 120 full hkups (30/50 amps), cable, WiFi @ sites, laundry, firewood. **REC:** Little Pigeon River: fishing, hunting nearby. Pets OK. No tents. Big rig sites. 2021 rates: $40, Military discount. Mar 15 to Nov 30.
(865)453-1224 Lat: 35.80957, Lon: -83.58787
2479 Riverbend Loop 1, Pigeon Forge, TN 37863
www.riverbendcampground.com
See ad page 846

RIVEREDGE RV PARK & CABIN RENTALS
good sam park **Ratings: 10/9.5★/9.5** (RV Park) From Jct 321 & 441 (Stoplight #3): Go 3 mi S on 441 (Parkway), then E on Cates Ln for .1 mi, then S on Huskey St (rear entrance to park).

PREMIERE SMOKY MOUNTAIN RV CAMPING
Stay at our conveniently located campground in Pigeon Forge - only 15 minutes from the Great Smoky Mountains National Park. Get the best camping experience at our luxury cabins and RV campsites and make memories at Riveredge

FAC: paved rds. 171 Avail: 5 paved, 166 all weather, patios, back-ins (27x55), 171 full hkups (30/50 amps), cable, WiFi @ sites, rentals, laundry, groc, fire rings, firewood. **REC:** heated pool, wading pool, hot tub, playground. Pets OK. Partial handicap access. No tents. Big rig sites, eco-friendly. 2021 rates: $59 to $89, Military discount.
(866)777-6127 Lat: 35.77388, Lon: -83.53718
4220 Huskey St, Pigeon Forge, TN 37863
www.stayriveredge.com
See ad opposite page, 846

UP THE CREEK RV CAMP **Ratings: 7/NA/10** (Campground) Avail: 61 full hkups (30/50 amps). 2021 rates: $51 to $75. Mar 11 to Dec 02. (865)453-8474, 1919 Little Valley Rd, Pigeon Forge, TN 37868

YOGI BEAR'S JELLYSTONE PARK OF PIGEON FORGE/GATLINBURG **Ratings: 10/10★/9.5** (RV Park) Avail: 81 full hkups (30/50 amps). 2021 rates: $39 to $69. (865)453-8117, 3404 Whaley Dr, Pigeon Forge, TN 37863

Things to See and Do

PIGEON FORGE DEPARTMENT OF TOURISM
Promotion & Marketing agency of Pigeon Forge. Hours: 8:30am to 5pm. No CC.
(800)251-9100
1950 Parkway, Pigeon Forge, TN 37863
www.mypigeonforge.com
See ad page 846

PIKEVILLE — C5 *Bledsoe*

MOUNTAIN GLEN RV PARK & CAMPGROUND **Ratings: 8/9.5★/9** (Campground) Avail: 42 full hkups (30/50 amps). 2021 rates: $34 to $42. (877)716-4493, 6182 Brockdell Rd, Pikeville, TN 37367

PIONEER — A6 *Campbell*

EAGLE ROCK RESORT & CAMPGROUND (Campground) (Too New to Rate) 53 Avail: 49 full hkups, 4 W, 4 E (30/50 amps). 2021 rates: $55 to $65. (423)566-4999, 805 Luther Siebers Blvd, Pioneer, TN 37847

RIDE ROYAL BLUE ATV RESORT & CAMPGROUND **Ratings: 5/8.5/7** (Campground) 26 Avail: 16 full hkups, 10 W, 10 E (30/50 amps). 2021 rates: $44 to $58.50. (423)784-9445, 6307 Stinking Creek Rd, Pioneer, TN 37847

Find it fast! Use our alphabetized index of campgrounds and parks.

ROCK RIDGE RETREAT AT ROYAL BLUE
good sam park **Ratings: 7.5/9.5★/10** (RV Resort) Avail: 19 full hkups (30/50 amps). 2021 rates: $100. (678)751-8174, 116 Rock Ridge Lane, Pioneer, TN 37847

THE RIDGES AT ROYAL BLUE **Ratings: 5.5/9.5★/9.5** (Campground) Avail: 30 full hkups (30/50 amps). 2021 rates: $50 to $65. (423)784-1700, 6949 Stinking Creek Rd, Pioneer, TN 37847

POCAHONTAS — C2 *Hardeman*

BIG HILL POND (Public State Park) From town: Go 5 mi E on Hwy 57. 28 Avail. 2021 rates: $8 to $25. (731)645-7967

ROAN MOUNTAIN — D6 *Carter*

ROAN MOUNTAIN (Public State Park) From Jct of US-19E & SR-143, S 4.5 mi on SR-143 (R). 87 Avail: 87 W, 87 E (30/50 amps). 2021 rates: $35. (423)547-3900

ROCK ISLAND — B5 *Warren*

ROCK ISLAND (Public State Park) From Jct of US-70S & SR 136 (in town), N 1.2 mi on SR 136 to SR-287, NW 2.2 mi (R). 50 Avail: 4 full hkups, 46 W, 46 E (30/50 amps). 2021 rates: $32. (931)686-2471

ROCKY TOP — D4 *Anderson*

MOUNTAIN LAKE MARINA & CAMPGROUND **Ratings: 7/9★/7.5** (Campground) Avail: 81 full hkups (30/50 amps). 2021 rates: $35 to $45. (865)630-1221, 136 Campground Rd, Rocky Top, TN 37769

NORRIS DAM (Public State Park) From Jct of I-75 & US-441 (exit 128), S 3 mi on US-441 (L) Caution: Steep, winding curves to campground (Self contained units only in winter). 75 Avail: 75 W, 75 E (30/50 amps). 2021 rates: $25. (865)426-7461

SAVANNAH — C2 *Hardin*

GREEN ACRES RV PARK
good sam park **Ratings: 9.5/9.5★/9.5** (Campground) From Jct of US-64 & SR-128 in Savannah: Go S 5.9 mi on SR-128 (L). **FAC:** paved/gravel rds. Avail: 49 all weather, 13 pull-thrus, (30x120), back-ins (30x65), 49 full hkups (30/50 amps), cable, WiFi @ sites, laundry, groc, fire rings, firewood. **REC:** pool, boating nearby, playground. Pet restrict (B). No tents. Big rig sites, eco-friendly. 2021 rates: $40, Military discount.
(731)926-1928 Lat: 35.141069, Lon: -88.251168
215 Ziffle Circle, Savannah, TN 38372
www.greenacresrvparktn.com
See ad this page

SEQUATCHIE — C5 *Marion*

SOUTH CUMBERLAND/FOSTER FALLS CAMPGROUND (Public State Park) From jct Old TN 28 & Sequatchie Mountain Rd: Go 2-3/4 mi S on Old TN 28, then 7-1/2 mi NW on US 41, then 3/4 mi W on Foster Falls Rd (E). 26 Avail. 2021 rates: $18. (931)924-2980

SEVIERVILLE — E5 *Sevier*

COVE CREEK RV RESORT **Ratings: 8.5/9.5★/8.5** (Campground) Avail: 95 full hkups (30/50 amps). 2021 rates: $44 to $80. (865)429-7716, 3293 Wears Valley Rd, Sevierville, TN 37862

DOUGLAS HEADWATER CAMPGROUND **Ratings: 5.5/8.5★/9** (Campground) 61 Avail: 61 W, 61 E (30/50 amps). 2021 rates: $27 to $29. Mar 15 to Nov 15. (865)361-1379, 1680 Boat Launch Rd, Sevierville, TN 37876

DOUGLAS TAILWATER CAMPGROUND **Ratings: 4.5/9★/9** (Campground) 57 Avail: 57 W, 57 E (30/50 amps). 2021 rates: $27 to $29. Mar 15 to Nov 15. (865)361-1522, 829 Riverview Way, Kodak, TN 37764

DUVALL IN THE SMOKIES RV CAMPGROUND & CABINS
good sam park **Ratings: 8/9★/10** (RV Park) Avail: 29 full hkups (30/50 amps). 2021 rates: $62 to $70. Mar 01 to Jan 02. (865)440-2082, 1518 Dolly Parton Parkway, Sevierville, TN 37862

HONEYSUCKLE MEADOWS RV PARK **Ratings: 8/NA/9.5** (Campground) Avail: 36 full hkups (30/50 amps). 2021 rates: $35 to $45. (865)453-1041, 3958 Wears Valley Rd, Sevierville, TN 37862

PIGEON FORGE LANDING RV RESORT **Ratings: 9.5/10★/10** (RV Resort) Avail: 149 full hkups (30/50 amps). 2021 rates: $55 to $120. (865)446-1500, 455 Lonesome Valley Road, Sevierville, TN 37862

Always do a Pre-Drive Safety Check!

RIPPLIN' WATERS CAMPGROUND & CABIN RENTAL **Ratings: 8.5/9.5★/8** (Campground) Avail: 128 full hkups (30/50 amps). 2021 rates: $38 to $43. (865)453-4169, 1930 Winfield Dunn Parkway, Sevierville, TN 37876

RIVERSIDE RV PARK & RESORT
good sam park **Ratings: 10/10★/9.5** (Campground) From Jct of I-40 & Hwy 66 (exit 407): Go S 4 mi on Hwy 66 to Boyds Creek Rd, W 500 ft (R). **FAC:** all weather rds. (330 spaces). Avail: 285 all weather, patios, 123 pull-thrus, (25x80), back-ins (25x45), 285 full hkups (30/50 amps), seasonal sites, WiFi @ sites, rentals, laundry, LP gas, firewood. **REC:** pool, Little Pigeon River: fishing, kayaking/canoeing, boating nearby, playground, hunting nearby. Pets OK. Partial handicap access. No tents. Big rig sites, eco-friendly. 2021 rates: $46 to $48, Military discount.
(865)453-7299 Lat: 35.92821, Lon: -83.58670
4280 Boyds Creek Highway, Sevierville, TN 37876
www.riversidecamp.com
See ad this page

SUN OUTDOORS SEVIERVILLE PIGEON FORGE Ratings: 9/10★/9.5 (RV Resort) Avail: 230 full hkups (30/50 amps). 2021 rates: $52.28 to $89.86. (800)758-5267, 1004 Parkway, Sevierville, TN 37862

THE RIDGE OUTDOOR RESORT **Ratings: 10/10★/10** (RV Resort) Avail: 143 full hkups (30/50 amps). 2021 rates: $45.99 to $124.99. (888)559-2267, 1250 Middle Creek Rd, Sevierville, TN 37862

Follow the arrow. The arrow in each listing indicates where the facility is located in relation to the listed town.

SEVIERVILLE (CONT)

TWO RIVERS LANDING RV RESORT
Ratings: 10/10★/10 (RV Resort) From Jct of I 40 & Hwy 66 (Exit 407), S 3 mi on Hwy 66 to Knife Works Ln, W 0.1 mi to Business Center Circle (R). **FAC:** paved rds. Avail: 55 paved, patios, back-ins (30x65), 55 full hkups (30/50 amps), cable, WiFi @ sites, laundry. **REC:** pool, French Broad River: fishing, kayaking/canoeing, boating nearby, playground, hunting nearby. Pet restrict (B). Partial handicap access. No tents. Big rig sites, eco-friendly. 2021 rates: $75 to $85.
(866)727-5781 Lat: 35.93486, Lon: -83.58674
2328 Business Center Circle, Sevierville, TN 37876
tworiversrvresort.com
See ad previous page

SILVER POINT — B5 *Putnam*

CENTER HILL LAKE - COE/FLOATING MILL PARK (Public Corps) From Jct of I-40 & Hwy 56 (exit 273): Go 5 mi S on Hwy 56 to Hurricane Dock Rd (R). Avail: 57 E (30/50 amps). 2021 rates: $22 to $30. May 02 to Sep 24. (931)858-4845

CENTER HILL LAKE - COE/LONG BRANCH (Public Corps) From Jct of I-40 & exit 268: Go 4-1/2 mi S on exit rd (R). 60 Avail: 60 W, 60 E (50 amps). 2021 rates: $26 to $30. May 02 to Sep 24. (615)548-8002

SMITHVILLE — B5 *DeKalb*

CENTER HILL LAKE - COE/RAGLAND BOTTOM (Public Corps) From town: Go 8 mi E on US-70 (L). Avail: 29 E (30/50 amps). 2021 rates: $26 to $30. May 02 to Sep 24. (931)761-3616

EDGAR EVINS (Public State Park) From Jct of I-40 & SR-96 (Center Hill Dam exit 268), S 7.2 mi on SR-96 (L). Caution: Interior roads have steep inclines throughout park. 60 Avail: 60 W, 60 E (30/50 amps). 2021 rates: $20 to $35. (931)858-2446

SMYRNA — B4 *Rutherford*

NASHVILLE I-24 CAMPGROUND
Ratings: 9/10★/8 (Campground) E-bnd: From Jct of I-24 & Hwy 266 (E-bnd: exit 66B; or W-bnd: exit 66), NE 1.6 mi on Hwy 266 to Old Nashville Hwy, SE 1.7 mi to Rocky Fork Rd, W 0.1 mi (R). **FAC:** paved/gravel rds. (140 spaces). Avail: 50 gravel, 35 pull-thrus, (25x50), back-ins (25x50), mostly side by side hkups, 42 full hkups, 8 W, 8 E (30/50 amps), seasonal sites, WiFi @ sites, tent sites, rentals, dump, laundry, groc, LP gas, firewood. **REC:** pool, boating nearby, playground, hunting nearby. Pet restrict (B/Q). eco-friendly. 2021 rates: $35 to $39, Military discount.
(615)459-5818 Lat: 35.96631, Lon: -86.53040
1130 Rocky Fork Rd, Smyrna, TN 37167
nashvillei24kampground.com
See ad page 857

SOUTH PITTSBURG — C5 *Marion*

SASQUATCH FARM RV PARK & CAMPGROUND
Ratings: 7.5/8.5★/8.5 (RV Park) From jct US 41A & SH 156: Go 15 mi S on SH 156, then 3 mi S on Browns Trace Rd (R). **FAC:** gravel rds. Avail: 50 gravel, back-ins (40x75), 50 full hkups (30/50 amps), WiFi @ sites, tent sites, dump, LP gas, fire rings, firewood. **REC:** Man Made: swim, fishing, kayaking/canoeing, boating nearby. Pets OK. Big rig sites. 2021 rates: $55, Military discount.
(423)919-9852 Lat: 35.002586, Lon: -85.85555
2985 Browns Trace Road, South Pittsburg, TN 37380
www.sasquatchfarm.com
See ad page 850

SPENCER — B5 *Van Buren*

FALL CREEK FALLS (Public State Park) From Pikeville, W 12 mi on SR-30 to Hwy 284, SW 4 mi (R). 66 Avail: 66 W, 66 E (30/50 amps). 2021 rates: $20 to $35. (423)881-5298

SPRINGVILLE — B3 *Benton*

BUCHANAN RESORT **Ratings: 7.5/8/8** (Campground) 25 Avail: 25 W, 25 E (30/50 amps). 2021 rates: $35. Mar 15 to Nov 15. (731)642-2828, 785 Buchanan Resort Rd, Springville, TN 38256

SWEETWATER — C6 *Loudon*

SWEETWATER VALLEY KOA
Ratings: 9.5/10★/10 (Campground) From Jct of I-75 & Hwy 322 (exit 62), W 0.8 mi on Hwy 322 to Murray's Chapel Rd, S 0.4 mi (L). **FAC:** paved rds. (77 spaces). 61 Avail: 43 paved, 18 gravel, 61 pull-thrus, (30x60), 55 full hkups, 6 W, 6 E (30/50 amps), seasonal sites, cable, WiFi @ sites, tent sites, rentals, dump, laundry, groc, LP gas, fire rings, firewood. **REC:** pool, pond, fishing, playground. Pets OK. Partial handicap access. Big rig sites, eco-friendly. 2021 rates: $43 to $76.94, Military discount.
(800)562-9224 Lat: 35.62253, Lon: -84.50581
269 Murrays Chapel Rd, Sweetwater, TN 37874
koa.com
See ad this page

TEN MILE — B6 *Meigs*

FOOSHEE PASS CAMPGROUND (MEIGS COUNTY PARK) (Public) From Jct TN-58 & TN-68: Go 2-3/4 mi W on TN-68, then 1-1/2 mi N on Hwy 304, then 1-1/2 W on Hwy 475, then 1/2 mi N on Sandy Bottoms Ln (E). 52 Avail: 52 W, 52 E (30 amps). 2021 rates: $14 to $17. Apr 15 to Sep 01. (423)334-4842

TIPTONVILLE — B1 *Obion*

REELFOOT LAKE (Public State Park) E-bnd: From Jct of Hwys 78 & 21 (in Tiptonville), E 5.2 mi on Hwy 21 (L); or W-bnd: From Jct of US-51 & Hwy 21 (Troy exit), W 15.5 mi on Hwy 21 (R). 100 Avail: 100 W, 100 E (30/50 amps). 2021 rates: $25 to $35. (731)253-9652

TOWNSEND — E5 *Blount*

BIG MEADOW FAMILY CAMPGROUND
Ratings: 9.5/10★/10 (RV Park) From Jct of US-321 & Hwy 73, NE 0.2 mi on US-321 to Cedar Creek Rd, W 300 ft (R).

TRIP ADVISOR TRAVELER'S CHOICE 2021
Family owned & operated for 26 years, we have all the comforts you want, plus a dog park for your fur-baby! Play in our Splash pad or Little River. Close to Great Smoky Mtns, Pigeon Forge, Gatlinburg and Tail of the Dragon.

FAC: all weather rds. Avail: 71 paved, patios, 52 pull-thrus, (30x75), back-ins (29x55), 71 full hkups (30/50 amps), cable, WiFi @ sites, laundry, LP gas, firewood, controlled access. **REC:** Little River: swim, fishing, playground. Pets OK. Partial handicap access. No tents. Big rig sites, eco-friendly. 2021 rates: $75 to $77.
(865)448-0625 Lat: 35.68179, Lon: -83.73348
8215 Cedar Creek Road, Townsend, TN 37882
www.bigmeadowcampground.com
See ad this page

GREAT SMOKY MTN/CADES COVE (Public National Park) From Jct of US-411 & Little River Rd: Go 26 mi W on Little River Rd (L); or From Jct of US-411 & US-441: Go 13 mi S on US-441 to Little River Rd (R). 131 Avail. 2021 rates: $25. May 15 to Oct 31. (865)436-2472

LAZY DAZE CAMPGROUND **Ratings: 7.5/8.5/8** (Campground) Avail: 39 full hkups (30/50 amps). 2021 rates: $60 to $75. (865)448-6061, 8429 State Hwy 73, Townsend, TN 37882

LITTLE ARROW OUTDOOR RESORT **Ratings: 10/10★/9.5** (Campground) Avail: 80 full hkups (30/50 amps). 2021 rates: $52 to $90. (865)448 6363, 118 Stables Dr, Townsend, TN 37882

MOUNTAINEER CAMPGROUND **Ratings: 7.5/7.5★/7** (Campground) 40 Avail: 29 full hkups, 11 W, 11 E (30/50 amps). 2021 rates: $50 to $60. Mar 01 to Nov 30. (865)448-6421, 8451 State Hwy 73, Townsend, TN 37882

WHISPERING RIVER RESORT **Ratings: 9/9.5★/9.5** (RV Park) Avail: 48 full hkups (30/50 amps). 2021 rates: $47. (865)981-4300, 5050 Old Walland Hwy, Walland, TN 37886

TRACY CITY — C5 *Grundy*

BIGFOOT ADVENTURE RV PARK & CAMPGROUND
Ratings: 7/9.5★/9.5 (Campground) From jct I-24 & US 41 (Exit 134): Go 3-1/4 mi N on US 41, then 2-3/4 mi NW on Summerfield Rd, then 1-1/2 mi E on Clouse Hill Rd, then 1 mi N on Brawley Rd (E). **FAC:** gravel rds. (45 spaces). Avail: 40 gravel, 40 pull-thrus, (30x70), 34 full hkups, 4 W, 4 E (30/50 amps), seasonal sites, WiFi @ sites, tent sites, rentals, dump, fire rings, firewood, controlled access. **REC:** pond, fishing, rec open to public. Pets OK. eco-friendly. 2021 rates: $50 to $60, Military discount.
(931)488-8652 Lat: 35.303243, Lon: -85.770993
514 Brawley Rd, Tracy City, TN 37387
www.bigfootadventuretn.com
See ad opposite page

SAVE! Camping World coupons can be found at the front and back of this Guide!

TULLAHOMA — C4 *Coffee*

MILITARY PARK ARNOLD FAMCAMP (ARNOLD AFB) (Public) From jct I-24 E & Wattendorf Memorial Hwy (exit 117): Go right 4.5 mi on Wattendorf Memorial Hwy, then left on Hap Arnold Rd, then right on Northshore Rd (L). 36 Avail: 36 W, 36 E (30/50 amps). 2021 rates: $15 to $20. (931)454-6084

UNICOI — D6 *Unicoi*

WOODSMOKE CAMPGROUND
Ratings: 6/8.5★/9 (Campground) W-bnd: From Jct of I-26 & SR-173 (Exit 32) left at the Jct. (under I-26) 0.1 mi to Greenoak Dr, SW 0.1 mi (R) E-bnd: From Jct of I-26 & SR-173 (Exit 32) right at the Jct. 300 ft to Greenoak Dr, SW 0.1 mi (R) Note: RV maximum length 40 ft. **FAC:** gravel rds. (32 spaces). Avail: 27 gravel, back-ins (24x60), 27 full hkups (30/50 amps), seasonal sites, WiFi @ sites, tent sites, fire rings, firewood. **REC:** hunting nearby. Pet restrict (Q). Partial handicap access, eco-friendly. 2021 rates: $41. Mar 15 to Nov 30.
(423)743-2116 Lat: 36.20775, Lon: -82.35573
215 Woodsmoke Drive, Unicoi, TN 37692
www.woodsmokecampground.com
See ad page 853

UNION CITY — A2 *Obion*

AAA RV PARK **Ratings: 5/8★/5** (RV Park) Avail: 20 full hkups (30/50 amps). 2021 rates: $35. (731)446-4514, 2029 Phebus Lane, Union City, TN 38261

VONORE — C6 *Monroe*

NOTCHY CREEK CAMPGROUND (Public) From jct US 411 & CR 435: Go 2 mi S on CR 435, then 1/2 mi SW on Niles Ferry Rd, then 1 mi SE on Povo Rd, then 2 mi E on Corntassle Rd (E). 51 Avail: 51 W, 51 E (30/50 amps). 2021 rates: $36. Mar 15 to Nov 15. (423)884-6280

TOQUA CAMPGROUND (Public) From jct US 411 & TN 360: Go 3 mi SE on TN 360 (E). Avail: 19 full hkups (30/50 amps). 2021 rates: $41. Mar 15 to Nov 15. (423)884-3317

WARTBURG — B6 *Morgan*

FROZEN HEAD (Public State Park) From Hwy 27 in Harriman: Go N on Hwy 27, then 2 mi E on Hwy 62, then 4 mi N on Flat Fork Rd to park entrance. 20 Avail. 2021 rates: $15 to $35. (423)346-3318

WHITE BLUFF — B3 *Dickson*

MONTGOMERY BELL (Public State Park) W-bnd: From Jct of I-40 & Hwy 96 (exit 182), NW 10.6 mi on Hwy 96 to US-70, E 3.7 mi (R); or E-bnd: From Jct of I-40 & Hwy 46 (exit 172), N 5.2 mi on Hwy 46 to Bus US-70, E 6 mi (R). 94 Avail: 94 W, 40 S, 94 E (30/50 amps). 2021 rates: $35. (615)797-9052

WINCHESTER — C4 *Franklin*

TIMS FORD (Public State Park) From jct TN 50 & TN 130: Go 5 mi SW on TN 50, then 4-3/4 mi W on TN 476, then 1/2 mi SW on Tims Ford Dr (E). 52 Avail: 4 full hkups, 48 W, 48 E (30 amps). 2021 rates: $25 to $32. (931)962-1183

TWIN CREEKS RV RESORT **Ratings: 9/10★/10** (RV Resort) Avail: 30 full hkups (30/50 amps). 2021 rates: $75 to $110. (931)229-4095, 216 Anchors-A Way, Winchester, TN 37398

Want to know how we rate? Our campground inspection guidelines are detailed in the front pages of the Guide.

TN

good sam
Roadside Assistance
Get the Nation's best RV Roadside Assistance
RANKED #1
TopConsumerReviews.com[1]
★★★★★
Unlimited Distance Towing to the nearest Service Center†
24-Hour Roadside Assistance
Emergency Fuel & Fluids Delivery
Locksmith Service
Battery Jump-Start
Flat Tire Service‡
Visit GoodSamRoadside.com/Guide
Call 888-884-8830
[1]According to TopConsumerReviews.com; available at topconsumerreviews.com/roadside-assistance as of 7/23/21. † Additional fees may apply to tow to location of customer's choosing. ‡ Plan includes tire delivery; Member is responsible for cost of tire, parts, and labor. Benefits and services provided by Americas Road & Travel Club, Inc. for Members residing in Alaska, Alabama, Utah, and Virginia; and by Affinity Road & Travel Club, LLC for Members residing in all other States. Note: All program benefits are subject to limitations set forth in the current Member Benefit Brochure, which can be found at www.GoodSamRoadside.com/MBBs.
©2021 Good Sam Enterprises, LLC. GOOD SAM logos are registered trademarks of Good Sam Enterprises, LLC. The CAMPING WORLD, GANDER RV & OUTDOORS, and OVERTON'S logos are registered trademarks of CWI, Inc. and used with permission. Unauthorized use of any Good Sam Enterprises, LLC or CWI, Inc. trademarks is expressly prohibited. All rights reserved.

YOU ARE HERE

Texas

One of the largest states in the union boasts the biggest personality, with larger-than-life history, music and culture to spare. Get out there and explore the wide-open spaces that have made Texas the suff of legend.

Big Texas Towns

Choose from a wide array of great cities in Texas. Wanting some culture with a side of barbecue? Texas's largest city, Houston, should be your pick. Seeking something quirky with some food truck fare? Head to the state's capital, Austin. Feeling a little Old West and seeking a savory steak? Dallas is your place. Wanting a unique cityscape with a Tex-Mex meal? Don't miss San Antonio.

Red Rocks and More

See the Lone Star State's answer to the Grand Canyon. Palo Duro Canyon State Park serves up a landscape that is definitively Texas, while also being uniquely unlike anywhere else in the state. The second largest behind the Grand Canyon, this 60-mile canyon reaches depths of 800 feet. Red rock walls and hoodoos contrast the blue skies. Over 30 miles of trails allow you to explore the park by foot, on wheels, or on horseback.

Currents of Fun

The San Marcos River runs with gem-colored, crystal-clear waters surrounded by the lush landscapes of the beautiful Hill Country region. Grab an inner tube and hit the cool waters for a true treat. Texas has 367 miles of shoreline along the Gulf of Mexico, providing prime places to play in the waves. Padre Island National Seashore, Port Aransas and Mustang Island State Park are popular picks.

Texas-size Wonders

As the song says, "The stars at night are big and bright/deep in the heart of

Texas Tex-Mex Fajitas

Texans take pride in this hearty Lone Star dish. Watch as long, savory slices of beef sizzle on an iron skillet surrounded by peppers and onions. When it cools off, wrap it in a tortilla, blend it with a tamale, add salsa or eat it keto style. It's a feast that can be customized to your liking and chased with a tall cerveza.

VISITOR CENTER

TIME ZONE
Standard/Central Standard

ROAD & HIGHWAY INFORMATION
800-558-9368
txdot.gov

FISHING, HUNTING, & BOATING INFORMATION
800-792-1112
tpwd.texas.gov/fishboat/boat

NATIONAL PARKS
nps.gov/tx

STATE PARKS
tpwd.texas.gov/state-parks

TOURISM INFORMATION
Texas Tourism
512-463-2000
traveltex.com

TOP TOURISM ATTRACTIONS
1) The Alamo
2) The San Antonio River Walk
3) Houston Space Center

MAJOR CITIES
Houston, San Antonio, Dallas, Austin (capital), Fort Worth

Texas." Imagine hiking to a perch up in the mountains for views of the surrounding desert lands. Imagine watching unimaginable varieties of colorful birds stop for a rest in the waters of the Rio Grande. These experiences and more can be found in Big Bend National Park. Located in the Chihuahuan Desert of west Texas along the Mexico border, this massive park offers scenic drives, hot spring pools and 150 miles of hiking trails.

An early morning view along the Rio Grande looking towards Santa Elena Canyon in Big Bend National Park.

Lone Star Breezes

Feeling the Texas heat? Take a dip in Krause Springs, located west of Austin in Spicewood. The 115-acre recreation site is privately owned but open to the public, as it has been since 1955. Explore the 32 springs, many of which feed a manmade pool. Of course, Austin, the capital city of the Lone Star State, shouldn't be missed. The home of the University of Texas, this metropolis is renowned for music, great food and freewheeling culture. To the southwest lies Bandera, and if you listen, you might hear the faint jingle of spurs in the so-called Cowboy Capital of the World.

Tuneful Texans

Over the decades, music legends launched dazzling careers in the small town of Luckenbach in Hill Country. Here, "everybody's somebody," and the town still embraces the adventurous spirit kindled when it started as a trading post in 1849. Country music icon Willie Nelson, who had some of his first performances here, brings thousands to Luckenbach for his Fourth of July Picnic every year.

Find Fun Here

Throughout the year, Texas hums with top-tier fairs, festivals and concerts. No matter where (or when) you find yourself setting up camp in the Lone Star State, fun festivals won't be far away. March brings South by Southwest, one of the largest events in the country, to Austin. Also known as SXSW, the festival serves up the latest and greatest from all walks of popular entertainment and culture — from music to TV. Other popular events around the state include BorderFest in Hidalgo, the Art Car Parade in Houston and the annual State Fair of Texas in Dallas.

Prairie Past

Find a treasure trove of history in San Antonio. Founded in 1718 by Spanish missionaries, this is one of the oldest cities in the country. It's packed with historic sites and old architecture, including a quintet of 18th-century missions. Two of the most popular are Mission San Jose (built in 1720) and the legendary Alamo (site of the Battle of the Alamo in 1836). Today, the city is home to the River Walk, a pedestrian thoroughfare that runs along the banks of the San Antonio River. Stores, cultural spots and shops line the walkway, giving visitors ample opportunity to shop and dine. Boat tours are available on the river.

Cattle Drives

The town of Fort Worth is home to Stockyards National Historic District. This 98-acre district was once a booming livestock market in the 1860s. Today, it's home to original brick walkways, wooden corrals, a working rodeo and an old opry. Buy an authentic pair of leather boots here or simply watch all the cowboy action.

good sam park Featured Good Sam Parks TEXAS

When you stay with Good Sam, you can expect the highest degree of cleanliness and friendliness, and better yet, you get **10% off** overnight campground fees.

If you're not already a Good Sam member you can purchase your membership at one of these locations:

ABILENE
Abilene RV Park
Buck Creek RV Park
Ridgeview RV Resort
Whistle Stop RV Resort

ALAMO
Alamo Palms RV Resort
Alamo Rec-Veh Park/MHP
Alamo Rose RV Resort
Casa Del Valle RV Resort
Trophy Gardens
Winter Ranch RV Resort

ALPINE
La Vista RV Park
Lost Alaskan RV Park

ALVARADO
Texas Ranch RV Resort

ALVIN
St. Ives RV Resort

ALVORD
A + RV Park

AMARILLO
Amarillo Best Wonderland RV Resort
Big Texan RV Ranch
Fort Amarillo RV Resort
Oasis RV Resort
Overnite RV Park

AUBREY
Shady Creek RV Park and Storage

AUSTIN
Oak Forest RV Resort

BANDERA
Bandera Crossing Riverfront RV Park
Bandera Pioneer RV River Resort

BASTROP
Basin RV Resort-Bastrop
Hwy 71 RV Park

BAYTOWN
Bayou Bend RV Resort
Houston East RV Resort

BEAUMONT
Beaumont RV & Marina
Gulf Coast RV Resort
Hidden Lake RV Park

10/10★/10 GOOD SAM PARKS

ABILENE
Ridgeview RV Resort
(325)999-9631

Whistle Stop RV Resort
(325)704-5252

AMARILLO
Oasis RV Resort
(888)789-9697

AUBREY
Shady Creek RV Park and Storage
(972)347-5384

BASTROP
Basin RV Resort-Bastrop
(512)321-7500

BELTON
Basin RV Resort
(254)393-1450

BULLARD
Bushman's RV Park
(903)894-8221

CASTROVILLE
Alsatian RV Resort & Golf Club
(830)931-9190

GALVESTON
Jamaica Beach RV Resort
(409)632-0200

GLADEWATER
Shallow Creek RV Resort
(888)984-4513

HIGHLANDS
San Jacinto Riverfront RV Park
(281)426-6919

HOUSTON
Advanced RV Resort
(713)433-6950

KATY
Katy Lake RV Resort
(281)492-0044

KERRVILLE
Buckhorn Lake Resort
(830)895-0007

LONGVIEW
Fernbrook Park
(903)643-8888

MISSION
Bentsen Palm Village RV Resort
(956)585-5568

NEW CANEY
Forest Retreat RV Park
(281)354-9888

ROANOKE
Northlake Village RV Park
(817)430-3303

SANTO
Coffee Creek RV Resort & Cabins
(940)769-2277

THE WOODLANDS
Rayford Crossing RV Resort
(281)298-8008

WEATHERFORD
Oak Creek RV Park
(817)594-0200

What's This?

An RV park with a 10/10★/10 rating has scored perfect grades in amenities, cleanliness and appearance ("See Understanding the Campground Rating System" on pages 8 and 9 for an explanation of the trusted Good Sam Rating System). Stay in a 10/10★/10 park on your next trip for a nearly flawless camping experience.

Getty Images/iStockphoto

TX

BELTON
Basin RV Resort

BIG SPRING
Whip In RV Park

BOERNE
Cascade Caverns & Campground

BRACKETTVILLE
Fort Clark Springs RV Park

BRIDGEPORT
Bay Landing RV

BROOKSHIRE
Houston West RV Park
Summer Breeze USA Katy

BROWNSVILLE
Breeze Lake RV Campground
Sunset Palms RV & MHP
Tropical Trails RV Resort

BROWNWOOD
Riverside Park RV

BRYAN
Hardy's Landing
Hardy's Resort
Hidden Creek RV Resort

BUCHANAN DAM
Freedom Lives Ranch RV Resort

BULLARD
Bushman's RV Park

BULVERDE
Texas 281 RV Park

BURLESON
Mockingbird Hill Mobile Home & RV Park

CADDO MILLS
Dallas NE Campground

CAMPBELL
Stinson RV Park

CANTON
Canton Creek RV Park
Canton I-20 RV Park
Mill Creek Ranch Resort

CANUTILLO
Gaslight Square Mobile Estates

CANYON
Palo Duro RV Park

CANYON LAKE
Summit Vacation & RV Resort

CARTHAGE
Carthage RV Campground

CASTROVILLE
Alsatian RV Resort & Golf Club

CLEVELAND
East Fork RV Resort

COLORADO CITY
Lone Wolf Creek RV Village

COLUMBUS
Colorado River RV Resort

COMFORT
RV Park USA

CONCAN
Parkview Riverside RV Park
Riverbend On The Frio

CORPUS CHRISTI
Colonia Del Rey RV Park
Hatch RV Park
Padre Palms RV Park

COTULLA
Cotulla/Nueces River KOA

CROCKETT
Crockett Family Resort Cottages, Marina & RV Park

DALHART
Corral RV Park

DONNA
Victoria Palms Resort

EDNA
Brackenridge Recreation Complex - Brackenridge Park & Campground
Brackenridge Recreation Complex-Texana Park & Campground
Twin Lakes RV Park

EL PASO
Mission RV Park
Mission Trail Mobile Home & RV Village

FENTRESS
Leisure Resort

FORT DAVIS
MacMillen RV Park

FORT STOCKTON
Hilltop RV Park

FORT WORTH
Cowtown RV Park
Lakeview RV & MH Community

FREDERICKSBURG
Fredericksburg RV Park
The Vineyards At Fredericksburg RV Park

FREEPORT
Blue Water RV Resort

GALVESTON
Jamaica Beach RV Resort
Sandpiper RV Resort

GARLAND
Lakeshore RV Resort

GEORGETOWN
Berry Springs RV Park
East View RV Ranch
New Life RV Park

GLADEWATER
Shallow Creek RV Resort

GLEN ROSE
Dinosaur Valley RV Park

GONZALES
Gone Fishin RV Park
Texas Freedom RV Village

GORDONVILLE
Lake Texoma RV

GRANBURY
Bennett's RV Ranch

GRAND PRAIRIE
Loyd Park Camping Cabins & Lodge
Traders Village RV Park

GRAPEVINE
The Vineyards Campground & Cabins

HARLINGEN
Fig Tree RV Resort
Lakewood RV Resort
Palm Gardens MHP & RV Resort
Paradise Park RV Resort
Park Place Estates
Sunshine RV Resort
Tropic Winds RV Resort

HIGHLANDS
San Jacinto Riverfront RV Park

HONEY GROVE
Hidden Grove RV Resort

HOUSTON
Advanced RV Resort
Houston Central RV Park
Sheldon Lake RV Resort
Traders Village RV Park

JACKSBORO
Hidden Lake RV Ranch & Safari

JARRELL
Valley View RV Park

JOHNSON CITY
Roadrunner RV Park

JUNCTION
10/83 RV Park
Tree Cabins RV Resort

KATY
Katy Lake RV Resort

KERRVILLE
Buckhorn Lake Resort
Take-It-Easy RV Resort
Triple T RV Resort

KILLEEN
Elm Grove MH Community

KINGSVILLE
CM Nature's Own RV Resort

LA FERIA
Kenwood RV Resort
VIP-La Feria RV Park

LA GRANGE
Colorado Landing RV Park

LAKEHILLS
Medina Lake RV

LAMPASAS
Boone RV Park

LEAGUE CITY
Safari Mobile Home & RV Community

LINN
Lazy Palms Ranch RV Park

LONGVIEW
Fernbrook Park
North Point RV Park

LOS FRESNOS
Palmdale RV Resort

LUBBOCK
Camelot Village RV Park
Lubbock RV Park

MAGNOLIA
Royal Palms RV Resort

MANSFIELD
Texan RV Ranch

MARBLE FALLS
Sunset Point On Lake LBJ

MCALLEN
McAllen Mobile Park

MERCEDES
Llano Grande Lake Park Resort & Country Club MHP
Paradise South RV Resort

MIDLAND
Midland RV Campground

MINEOLA
Mineola Civic Center & RV Park

MINGUS
Cactus Rose RV Park

MISSION
Americana RV Resort MHP
Bentsen Palm Village RV Resort
Bluebonnet RV Resort
El Valle Del Sol/de La Luna RV & MHC
J Five RV & Mobilehome Park
Seven Oaks Resort

MURCHISON
Stay A While RV Park

NEW BRAUNFELS
New Braunfels RV and MH Park
River Ranch RV Resort

NEW CANEY
Forest Retreat RV Park
Grand Texas RV Resort

ODESSA
Baron Mobile Estates & RV Park (MHP)

PEARLAND
Cullen RV Resort

PHARR
Texas Trails RV Resort
Tip O Texas RV Resort
Tropic Star RV Resort

PITTSBURG
The Bluffs RV Park

PLAINVIEW
The Hitchin' Post RV Park and Cabins

POINT
Lake Tawakoni RV

POOLVILLE
West Gate RV Park

PORT ARANSAS
Island RV Resort
Pioneer Beach Resort
Tropic Island Resort

PORTLAND
Sea Breeze RV Community Resort

QUANAH
Ole Towne Cotton Gin RV Park

RIESEL
Brazos Trail RV Park

RIVIERA
Seawind RV Resort On the Bay

ROANOKE
Northlake Village RV Park

ROCKPORT
Ancient Oaks RV Park
Big Fish RV Park
Reel Chill RV Resort

SAN ANGELO
Concho Pearl RV Estates
Spring Creek Marina & RV Park
Braunig Lake RV Resort
Mission City RV Park
Stone Creek RV Park
Tejas Valley RV Park

SAN BENITO
Fun N Sun RV Resort

SAN LEON
Summer Breeze USA Kemah

SAN MARCOS
Pecan Park Riverside RV Park

SANTO
Coffee Creek RV Resort & Cabins

SCHULENBURG
Schulenburg RV Park

SHERMAN
Lazy L RV Park

SILSBEE
Thompson Lake RV Resort

SLATON
Twin Pine RV Park

SOMERSET
A Country Breeze RV Park

STONEWALL
Peach Country RV Park

SWEETWATER
Bar J Hitchin Post RV

TERRELL
Bluebonnet Ridge RV Park & Cottages

TEXARKANA
Shady Pines RV Park
Texarkana RV Park

THE WOODLANDS
Rayford Crossing RV Resort
Woodland Lakes RV Park

TOMBALL
Corral RV Resort

TYLER
Tyler Oaks RV Resort
We RV Champions of Tyler

UVALDE
Little RV Spot
Quail Springs RV Park

VAN HORN
Van Horn RV Park
Wild West RV Park

VERNON
Rocking "A" RV Park

VICTORIA
Coleto Lake RV Resort

VIDOR
Boomtown USA RV Resort

VON ORMY
Alamo River Ranch RV Park

WACO
Flat Creek Farms RV Resort

WEATHERFORD
Hooves N' Wheels RV Park & Horse Motel
Oak Creek RV Park

WEIMAR
Whispering Oaks RV Park

WESLACO
Country Sunshine RV Resort
Leisure World RV Resort
Snow To Sun RV Resort
Southern Comfort RV Resort
Trails End RV Resort

WHITNEY
Lake Whitney RV

WICHITA FALLS
Wichita Falls RV Park

WILLIS
Lake Conroe RV

WINNIE
Winnie Inn & RV Park

WOLFFORTH
Mesa Verde RV Park

YOAKUM
Shade Tree RV Park

ZAPATA
Amigo Inn & RV Park
Stinson RV Park & Storage

Getty Images/iStockphoto

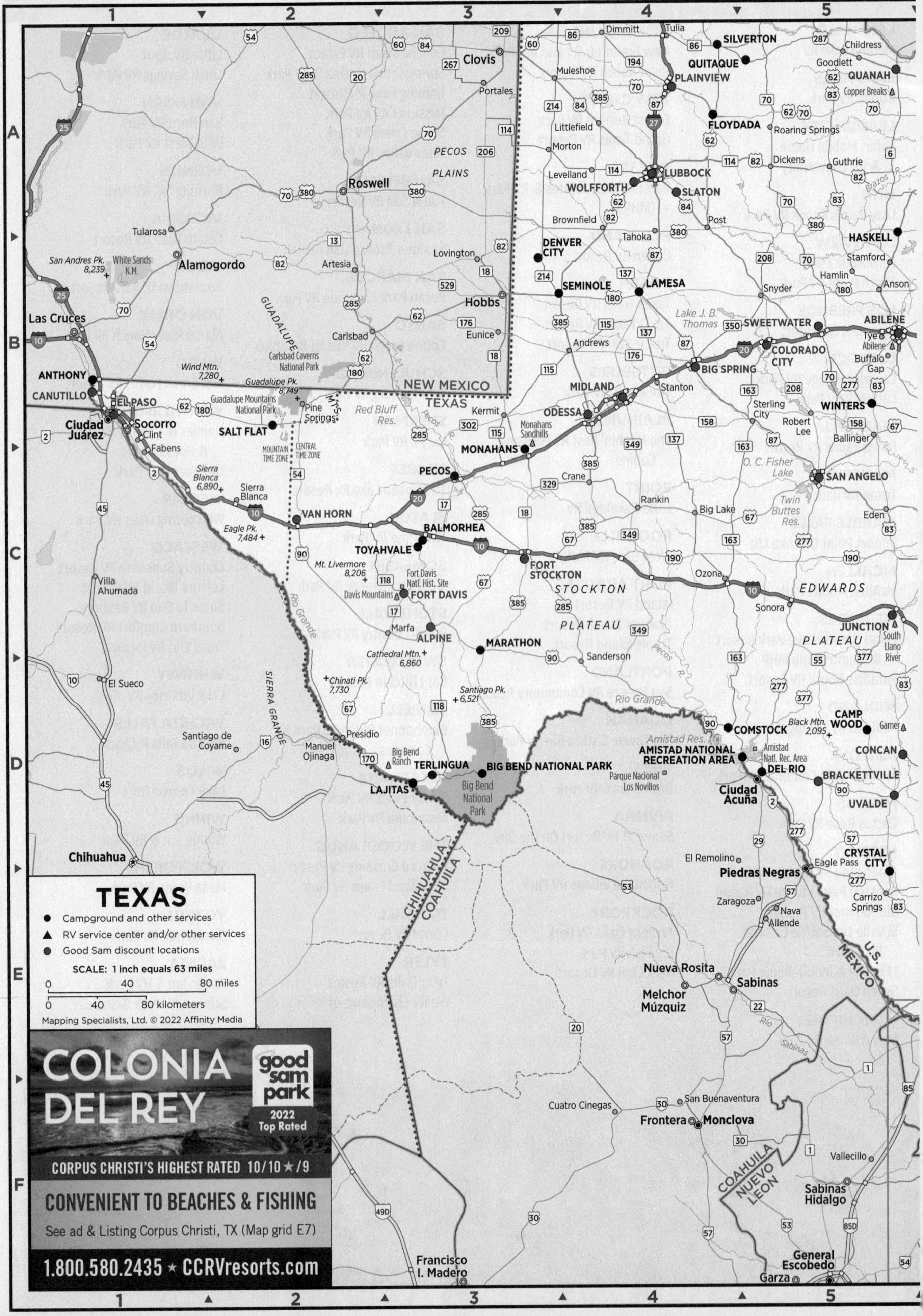
TEXAS
Campground and other services
RV service center and/or other services
Good Sam discount locations
SCALE: 1 inch equals 63 miles
0 40 80 miles
0 40 80 kilometers
Mapping Specialists, Ltd. © 2022 Affinity Media
1
2
3
4
5
A
B
C
D
E
F
NEW MEXICO
TEXAS
CHIHUAHUA
COAHUILA
NUEVO LEON
U.S.
MEXICO
Clovis
Portales
Roswell
PECOS PLAINS
Tularosa
Alamogordo
San Andres Pk. 8,239
White Sands N.M.
Las Cruces
Artesia
Lovington
Hobbs
Eunice
Carlsbad
Carlsbad Caverns National Park
GUADALUPE MTS.
Wind Mtn. 7,280
Guadalupe Pk. 8,749
Guadalupe Mountains National Park
Pine Springs
ANTHONY
CANUTILLO
EL PASO
Ciudad Juárez
Socorro
Clint
Fabens
SALT FLAT
MOUNTAIN TIME ZONE
CENTRAL TIME ZONE
Sierra Blanca 6,890
Sierra Blanca
Eagle Pk. 7,484
VAN HORN
Villa Ahumada
El Sueco
Santiago de Coyame
Chihuahua
Rio Grande
SIERRA GRANDE
Dimmitt
Tulia
SILVERTON
QUITAQUE
PLAINVIEW
Muleshoe
Littlefield
Morton
FLOYDADA
Levelland
WOLFFORTH
LUBBOCK
SLATON
Brownfield
Post
Tahoka
DENVER CITY
SEMINOLE
LAMESA
Andrews
MIDLAND
ODESSA
Stanton
BIG SPRING
Kermit
Monahans Sandhills
MONAHANS
Red Bluff Res.
PECOS
Crane
Rankin
BALMORHEA
TOYAHVALE
Mt. Livermore 8,206
Fort Davis Natl. Hist. Site
Davis Mountains
FORT DAVIS
Marfa
ALPINE
Cathedral Mtn. 6,860
Chinati Pk. 7,730
MARATHON
Santiago Pk. 6,521
FORT STOCKTON
STOCKTON PLATEAU
Sanderson
Presidio
Manuel Ojinaga
Big Bend Ranch
TERLINGUA
LAJITAS
BIG BEND NATIONAL PARK
Big Bend National Park
Childress
Goodlett
QUANAH
Copper Breaks
Roaring Springs
Dickens
Guthrie
Brazos R.
HASKELL
Stamford
Hamlin
Anson
Snyder
Lake J. B. Thomas
SWEETWATER
ABILENE
Tye
Abilene
COLORADO CITY
Buffalo Gap
Sterling City
Robert Lee
WINTERS
Ballinger
O. C. Fisher Lake
SAN ANGELO
Twin Buttes Res.
Big Lake
Eden
Ozona
EDWARDS PLATEAU
Sonora
JUNCTION
South Llano River
Pecos R.
Rio Grande
COMSTOCK
Black Mtn. 2,095
CAMP WOOD
Garner
Amistad Res.
AMISTAD NATIONAL RECREATION AREA
Amistad Natl. Rec. Area
CONCAN
DEL RIO
BRACKETTVILLE
Parque Nacional Los Novillos
Ciudad Acuña
UVALDE
El Remolino
Eagle Pass
CRYSTAL CITY
Piedras Negras
Zaragoza
Carrizo Springs
Nava
Allende
Nueva Rosita
Sabinas
Melchor Múzquiz
Rio Sabinas
San Buenaventura
Cuatro Cinegas
Frontera
Monclova
Vallecillo
Sabinas Hidalgo
General Escobedo
Garza
Francisco I. Madero

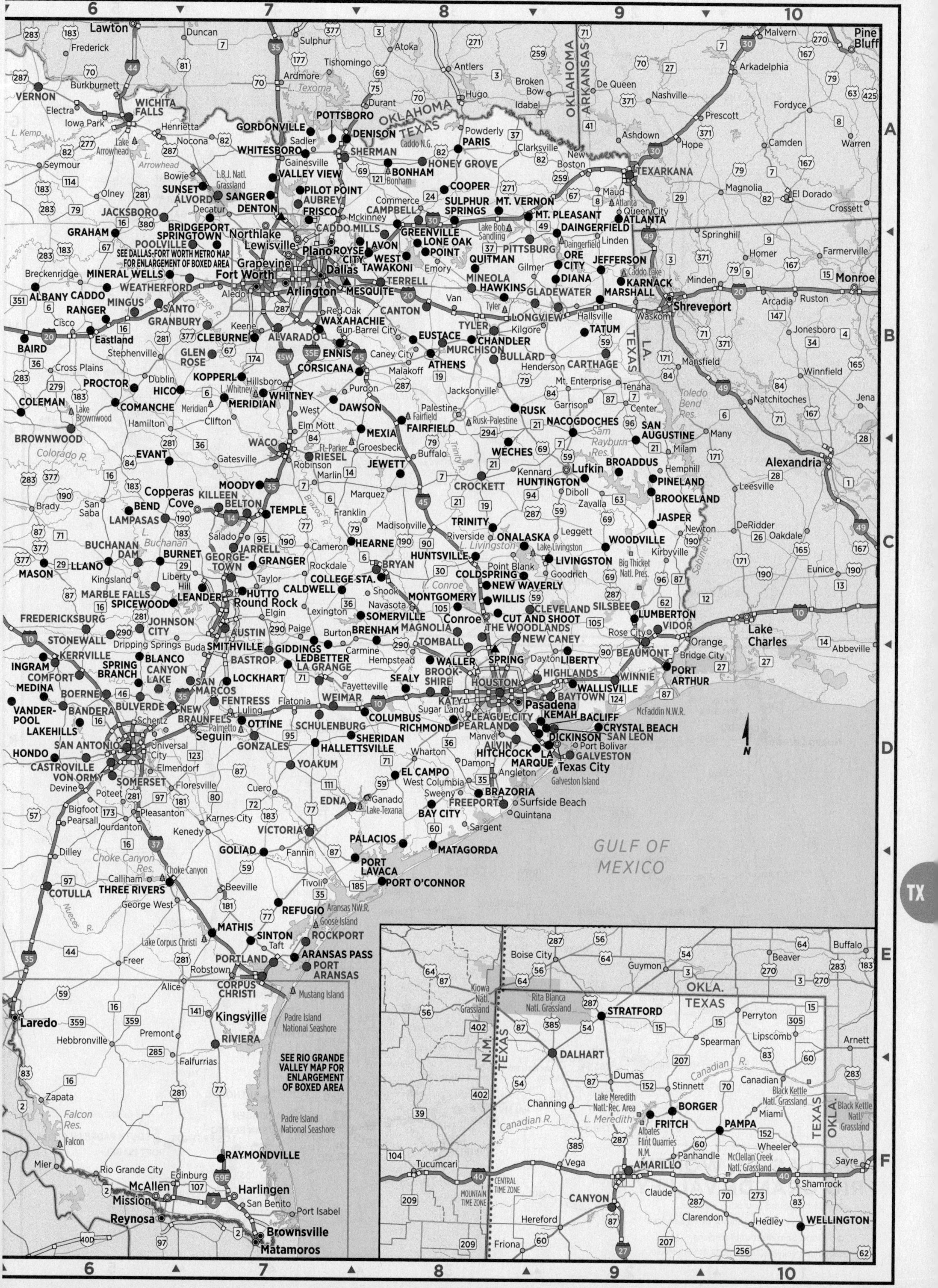

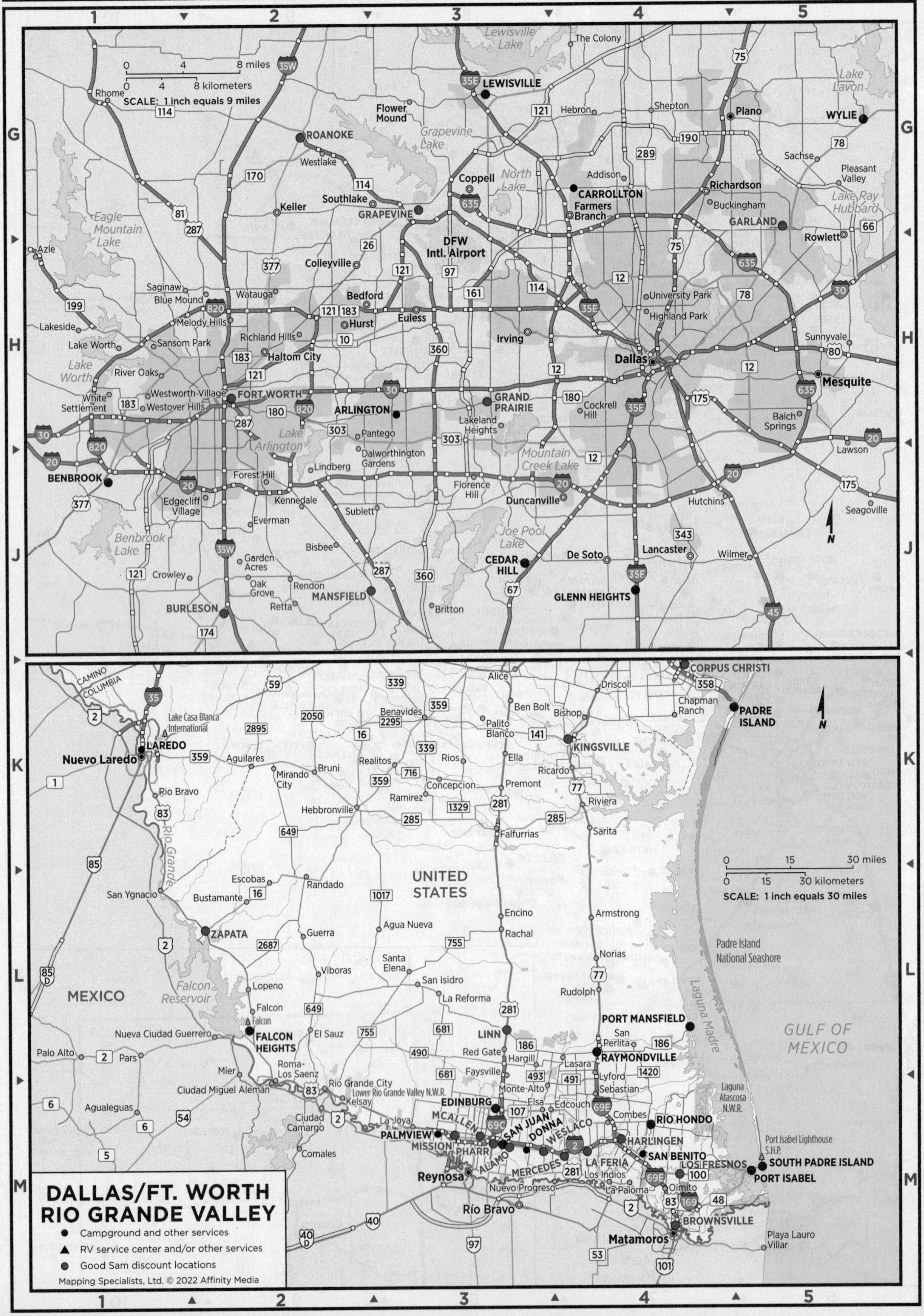
DALLAS/FT. WORTH
RIO GRANDE VALLEY
Campground and other services
RV service center and/or other services
Good Sam discount locations
Mapping Specialists, Ltd. © 2022 Affinity Media
SCALE: 1 inch equals 9 miles
0 4 8 miles
0 4 8 kilometers
SCALE: 1 inch equals 30 miles
0 15 30 miles
0 15 30 kilometers
1
2
3
4
5
G
H
J
K
L
M
Lewisville Lake
The Colony
LEWISVILLE
Lake Lavon
Rhome
Flower Mound
Hebron
Shepton
Plano
WYLIE
ROANOKE
Grapevine Lake
Westlake
Sachse
Pleasant Valley
North Lake
Addison
Coppell
CARROLLTON
Richardson
Southlake
Keller
Farmers Branch
Buckingham
Lake Ray Hubbard
GRAPEVINE
Eagle Mountain Lake
GARLAND
Rowlett
DFW Intl. Airport
Azle
Colleyville
Saginaw
Watauga
Bedford
University Park
Blue Mound
Highland Park
Melody Hills
Hurst
Euless
Lakeside
Richland Hills
Irving
Sunnyvale
Lake Worth
Sansom Park
Haltom City
Dallas
Lake Worth
River Oaks
Mesquite
White Settlement
Westworth Village
FORT WORTH
GRAND PRAIRIE
Westover Hills
ARLINGTON
Cockrell Hill
Balch Springs
Lake Arlington
Lakeland Heights
Pantego
Dalworthington Gardens
Lindberg
Mountain Creek Lake
Lawson
BENBROOK
Forest Hill
Florence Hill
Edgecliff Village
Kennedale
Duncanville
Hutchins
Sublett
Seagoville
Everman
Joe Pool Lake
Benbrook Lake
Bisbee
Lancaster
Garden Acres
CEDAR HILL
De Soto
Wilmer
Crowley
Oak Grove
Rendon
MANSFIELD
GLENN HEIGHTS
BURLESON
Retta
Britton
CAMINO COLUMBIA
Alice
CORPUS CHRISTI
Driscoll
Lake Casa Blanca International
Benavides
Ben Bolt
Bishop
Chapman Ranch
PADRE ISLAND
Palito Blanco
LAREDO
KINGSVILLE
Nuevo Laredo
Aguilares
Bruni
Realitos
Rios
Ella
Mirando City
Ricardo
Concepcion
Premont
Rio Bravo
Ramirez
Riviera
Hebbronville
Falfurrias
Sarita
Rio Grande
UNITED STATES
Escobas
San Ygnacio
Bustamante
Randado
Encino
Armstrong
ZAPATA
Guerra
Agua Nueva
Rachal
Padre Island National Seashore
Santa Elena
Norias
Viboras
MEXICO
San Isidro
Lopeno
Falcon Reservoir
La Reforma
Rudolph
Laguna Madre
Falcon
PORT MANSFIELD
Nueva Ciudad Guerrero
FALCON HEIGHTS
El Sauz
LINN
San Perlita
GULF OF MEXICO
Palo Alto
Pars
Red Gate
Hargill
RAYMONDVILLE
Mier
Roma-Los Saenz
Lasara
Faysville
Lyford
Ciudad Miguel Aleman
Rio Grande City
Lower Rio Grande Valley N.W.R.
Monte Alto
Sebastian
Laguna Atascosa N.W.R.
Kelsay
Agualeguas
Elsa
Edcouch
EDINBURG
Combes
Ciudad Camargo
La Joya
RIO HONDO
MCALLEN
SAN JUAN
DONNA
Port Isabel Lighthouse S.H.P.
PALMVIEW
WESLACO
HARLINGEN
MISSION
PHARR
SAN BENITO
ALAMO
SOUTH PADRE ISLAND
Comales
MERCEDES
LA FERIA
LOS FRESNOS
Reynosa
PORT ISABEL
Los Indios
Nuevo Progreso
Olmito
La Paloma
Río Bravo
BROWNSVILLE
Playa Lauro Villar
Matamoros

ROAD TRIPS

Get a True Taste of Texas at a Lone Star Crossroads

Texas

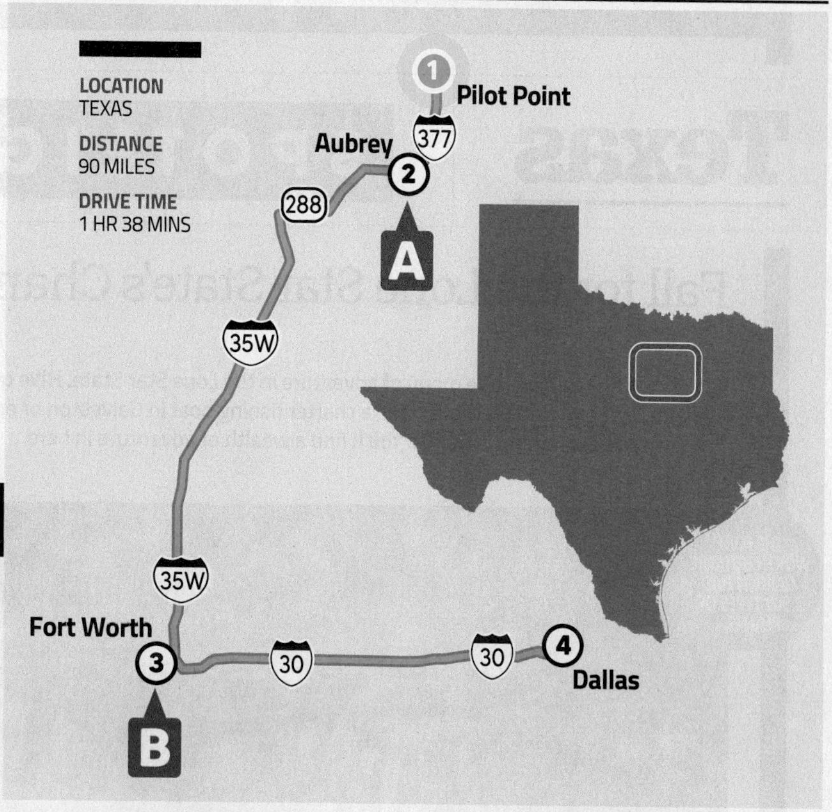

One of the fastest growing metro areas in the country, Dallas-Fort Worth is quickly becoming a cosmopolitan mecca. But that doesn't mean it's lost its down-home Texas flavor. See for yourself on this rollicking road trip from Pilot Point to the "Big D," where you'll experience everything from fun-loving lakefronts to old-time cattle drives and the vibrant cultural attractions of the modern West.

1 Pilot Point
Starting Point

Nestled on the shores of Lake Ray Roberts, this welcoming small town is the perfect introduction to the easy-going atmosphere of north Texas. You'll find plenty of equestrian, hiking and biking trails along the waterfront, as well as swimming beaches and excellent smallmouth bass, crappie and catfish angling from the pier.

2 Aubrey
Drive 7 Miles ▪ 10 Minutes

A few minutes due south, this historic town sits at the heart of Texas horse country. Brimming with old-fashioned charm, the downtown boasts a handful of cute cafes and locally-owned boutiques, but the real draw is nearby Lewisville Lake, where locals cool off during the hot summer months. With 233 miles of shoreline, there are endless opportunities to enjoy life on the water, including swimming, boating and top-notch bass fishing.

RECOMMENDED STOPOVER
A SHADY CREEK RV PARK AND STORAGE
AUBREY, TX (972) 347-5384

3 Fort Worth
Drive 51 Miles ▪ 53 Minutes

Nothing screams Texas quite like a visit to Fort Worth's iconic Stockyard National Historic District. Featuring a twice-daily cattle drive, the Cowboy Hall of Fame, live country music, authentic saloons and a year-round weekend rodeo, it's a one-stop-shop for all things Western. It's also just one of Fort Worth's many must-see attractions. After soaking in some serious cowboy culture, head to the city's burgeoning arts district where five world-class art and history museums await, before making off to Sundance Square, where you'll find historic murals, water gardens, and a moving tribute to President John F. Kennedy.

RECOMMENDED STOPOVER
B NORTHLAKE VILLAGE RV PARK
ROANOKE, TX (817) 430-3303

4 Dallas
Drive 32 Miles ▪ 35 Minutes

A cultural bonanza that gets bigger every year, the "Big D" is home to an all-star array of museums, attractions and unique neighborhoods waiting to be explored. Start your visit atop the Reunion Tower GeO-Deck, an observation tower 570 feet in the sky that offers unbeatable views of the sprawling cityscape. Once you've got the lay of the land, you're ready to take to the streets of West End for a shopping spree, or to wander the saloons and southern-style barbecue joints in historic Deep Ellum. If it's history you're after, the Sixth Floor Museum at Dealey Plaza focuses on JFK's assasination, while the George W. Bush Presidential Library and Museum offers a deep dive on the nation's 43rd commander in chief.

Getty Images/iStockphoto

BIKING BOATING DINING ENTERTAINMENT FISHING HIKING HUNTING PADDLING SHOPPING SIGHTSEEING

Texas SPOTLIGHTS

Fall for the Lone Star State's Charms

You'll find a Texas-size menu of adventure in the Lone Star State. Hike trails in Big Bend National Park, take a charter fishing boat in Galveston or embark on a shopping trip in Dallas. You'll find a wealth of adventure in here.

THE FORT WORTH BOTANIC GARDEN HAS 2,500 TYPES OF PLANTS.

Getty Images/iStockphoto

A waterfall in the Fort Worth Botanic Garden's Japanese Garden.

Dallas and Fort Worth

Dallas and Fort Worth are right beside each other, but they couldn't be more worlds apart. In Fort Worth, cattle drives, saloons and rodeos harken back to the Old West, while Dallas' high-end shopping centers, multicultural restaurants and vibrant nightlife scene offer every metropolitan delight imaginable. Whether you're craving urban adventures or seeking a glimpse into the past, you'll get to experience the best of both worlds in the heart of the Lone Star State.

World-class Museums

History, science and art come alive in Dallas' renowned galleries and museums. Gain insight into John F. Kennedy's assassination by sifting through over 60,000 artifacts at The Sixth Floor Museum at Dealey Plaza. At the Perot Museum of Nature and Science, experience a simulated earthquake and view gigantic dinosaur fossils. The city is also home to the country's largest contiguous urban arts district. Head to the Nasher Sculpture Center to admire works by the likes of Picasso and Henry Moore, and then visit the Dallas Museum of Art which houses over 22,000 pieces spanning 5,000 years of history.

Fort Worth Fun

More artistic treasures are waiting in Fort Worth. In the Cultural District, you'll find masterpieces by Michelangelo and Caravaggio at the Kimbell Art Museum, pop art from Andy Warhol in the Modern Art Museum of Fort Worth and paintings by Georgia O'Keeffe at the Amon Carter Museum of American Art. The National Cowgirl Museum also pays homage to the great women of the American West, with interactive exhibits, theater presentations and intriguing artifacts.

City Retreats

Escape the hustle and bustle of the city in the Lake and Garden District, situated just 5 miles from downtown Dallas. White Rock Lake is located here and provides 1,015 acres of green surroundings. Get out on the water by paddleboard or kayak and keep an eye out for nearly 300 bird species such as herons and egrets. If you brought your rod and tackle box, drop a line around the lake's

"WHITE ROCK LAKE PROVIDES 1,015 ACRES OF LUSH NATURE."

LOCAL FAVORITE

Winston's Long Horn Chili

Lone Star State chili purists declare that their regional specialty should be meaty, spicy and without beans. But if you're feeling like a maverick, this version has a few unique twists including sausage, beer and the option of adding beans. *Recipe by Robert Arnhold.*

INGREDIENTS

- ☐ 1 lb ground round
- ☐ 1 lb hot Italian sausage
- ☐ 1 large Vidalia sweet onion
- ☐ 1 green pepper
- ☐ 2 jalapeno peppers
- ☐ 1 clove of garlic crushed and minced
- ☐ 1 14.5 oz can diced tomatoes, well drained.
- ☐ 1 8 oz can tomato sauce
- ☐ 4 oz beef broth or stock
- ☐ 4 oz beer, preferably Texas Shiner or Southern Star
- ☐ 2 Tbsp chili powder
- ☐ 1 Tbsp smoked paprika
- ☐ Salt and pepper to taste
- ☐ 1 tsp crushed red chili flakes (or to taste)
- ☐ 1 tsp dried or 1 Tbsp. fresh oregano
- ☐ 2 cans of red or kidney beans (optional)

DIRECTIONS

In a stock pot, brown the meats and set aside. Rough chop and sauté all vegetables until just beginning to soften and then fold in the spices. Add in the meat, sauces, broth and beer. Simmer uncovered for one hour. Add in beans if desired and then cook on very low heat, uncovered, for at least another two hours.

TX

SPOTLIGHTS

The distinctive Reunion Tower, nicknamed "The Ball" by locals, gleams with other buildings in the Dallas skyline in the dawn light as the Trinity River flows past.

reeds and creeks to catch largemouth bass and crappie. For more angling, head to Benbrook Lake on the Fort Worth side to catch hybrid striped bass, carp and catfish. Other nearby fishing spots include Lewisville Lake, Lake Fork and Lake Palestine.

Explore by Foot

Start your day with a run or cycle on the 3.5-mile Katy Trail. The paved path connects several Dallas districts and runs along an old railway line. You can also enjoy fantastic views of the Dallas skyline while strolling Klyde Warren Park. Take a Dallas walking tour to get acquainted with some of the town's top attractions.

Great Gardens

Need a breath of fresh air? Venture into the enchanting gardens of Dallas and Fort Worth. Perched along White Rock Lake, the Dallas Arboretum and Botanical Garden wows visitors with its 19 dazzling garden displays. If you're here from late February to early April, see over 500,000 vibrant spring blooms during Dallas Blooms, the biggest outdoor floral festival in the Southwest. When it's time for a break from the city, unwind at the Fort Worth Water Gardens. Boasting an array of beautifully designed fountains and pools, this tranquil oasis is the perfect place to relax. Flower lovers will want to visit the Fort Worth Botanic Garden, home to 23 gardens and 2,500 types of plants. It's a lush getaway for folks seeking the town's natural side.

Hike the Town

There are plenty of hiking trails outside the downtown core. Located 20 minutes away, the Cedar Ridge Nature Preserve offers 9 miles of trails ranging from easy to challenging. The Great Trinity Forest possesses the country's largest urban hardwood forest. Trek along the paths around the Trinity River Audubon Center to reach quiet wetlands and birding spots.

Lively Urban Spaces

Sundance Square in downtown Fort Worth is an entertainment district packed with live theaters, galleries and over 30 restaurants. Although Dallas is an urban center with restaurants from around the globe, you'll also find plenty of local specialties, including barbecue and Tex Mex cuisine. In Dallas, the AT&T Performing Arts Center offers theater and dance programming, while the AT&T Stadium is home to the Dallas Cowboys.

Music in Dallas

There's plenty of toe-tapping nightlife in Dallas. The Deep Ellum district is a former industrial center steeped in music history, thanks to the likes of jazz and blues artists like Blind Lemon Jefferson and Huddie William "Lead Belly" Ledbetter. Today, Deep Ellum is still the place to be for music lovers, who will find trendy clubs, hip dining spots and a shopping area where one-of-a-kind finds are the norm. The Lower Greenville area is another hip locale, featuring a vast array of bars, restaurants and shops.

TX

SPOTLIGHTS

Parades, Festivals and Fairs

Fill your calendar with fun annual events. In the spring, admire over 50,000 blossoms at Dallas Blooms, watch acclaimed movies at the Dallas International Film Festival, and enjoy countless plays and exhibitions during the Dallas Arts Month. The Taste of Dallas in June offers something delicious for every foodie, while the Riverfront Jazz Festival during Labor Day weekend features performances by the world's top jazz artists. Dallas is also big on parades. Come see for yourself at the Martin Luther King Jr. Parade (January), St. Patrick's Day Festival (March) and Dallas Holiday Parade (December).

Way of the Old West

Over in Fort Worth, saddle up for mock gunfight shows, rib-eating contests and live Western music on the National Day of the American Cowboy. You can also satisfy your need for speed at year-round NASCAR and IndyCar events at the Texas Motor Speedway.

Return to the Wild West

The Old West lives on in Fort Worth's Stockyards National Historic District. Experience the world's only twice-daily cattle drive at 11:30 a.m. and 4 p.m. You can also watch cowboys in action during the weekly Stockyards Championship Rodeo. The Texas Cowboy Hall of Fame is located here so stop by to learn about the men and women who have helped preserve the state's Western heritage. Round out your visit with a concert at Billy Bob's Texas, which claims to be the largest honky-tonk on the planet, and shop for quality cowboy gear at Stockyards Station, Fincher's White Front Western Wear and M.L. Leddy's.

Galveston's Kemah Boardwalk has lots of rides, restaurants and attractions close to Trinity Bay.

Galveston

Half sun-drenched beach playground, half historic town, Galveston makes every visit a memorable one. Well-preserved Victorian architecture and fascinating museums shed light on Texas' storied past, while 32 miles of shoreline let you enjoy every beach activity under the sun. Whether you're here for a weekend getaway or waiting to depart for a Caribbean cruise, you'll find time in Galveston is always time well spent.

Family Fun

Take the family to Moody Gardens, where three glass pyramids open the doors to different worlds. Come face-to-face with sharks and other marine creatures in the Aquarium Pyramid and then step inside the Rainforest Pyramid to meet animals from South America, Asia and beyond. You can also view interactive exhibits in the Discovery Museum and play at the on-site zipline and ropes course.

Perfect Pier

The Galveston Island Historic Pleasure Pier is just 5 miles away. Packed with rides, carnival games and Texas' first Bubba Gump Shrimp Co., this amusement park will keep the young and young at heart entertained all day long. Add the Schlitterbahn Waterpark to your itinerary too. The 26-acre park houses adrenaline-pumping slides, wave pools and lazy rivers, making it the perfect place to cool off on scorching days.

Gulf Coast Recreation

Enjoy all your favorite watersports at more than a couple dozen beaches. If you've ever wanted to try surfing, sign up for a class and ride waves near the Pleasure Pier. Stewart Beach is one of the most popular strips of sand with showers, concessions and volleyball courts, while East Beach is known for its concerts and festivals during the summer months. Fishing is phenomenal here too. Snap up flounder in Seawall Park and then reel in sand trout, bull reds and croaker from the Street Fishing Pier on 61st Street and Galveston Fishing Pier at 91st Street. You can also take a fishing charter out to the sea to catch sport fish such as mackerel and dorado.

At 113 miles long, Padre Island is the longest Barrier Island in the world and a magnet for beach lovers.

Watch for Birds

Galveston is a bird-watcher's paradise with multiple spots on the Great Texas Coastal Birding Trail. Hundreds of native and migrating bird species can be seen around the island's wetlands, beaches and wooded areas. Keep an eye out for great blue herons, roseate spoonbills and wood storks in the Brazoria National Wildlife Refuge, and view numerous types of waterfowl in Anahuac National Wildlife Refuge. Galveston Island State Park is another top birding spot. Hike or cycle along 4 miles of trails to catch glimpses of mallard ducks and 300 other species.

Historic Charms on the Strand

Known as The Strand, Galveston's downtown takes you on a trip back in time. Lined with Victorian and Greek Revival-style buildings, this five-block radius houses shops, galleries and restaurants, along with historical gems like the Grand 1894 Opera House, 1859 Ashton Villa and 1895 Moody Mansion. Admire the architecture and look for placards highlighting significant landmarks. During your stroll through town, look out for La King's Confectionary, an old-fashioned candy shop specializing in hand-pulled saltwater taffy. You'll also want to meander through the Galveston Downtown Cultural Arts District for films, art exhibits and more. The Galveston Symphony Orchestra puts on classical music concerts and Island ETC offers a robust lineup of theater performances. There are plenty of art galleries as well — browse works by local artists in places such as The Heard Gallery, Galveston Arts Center, and René Wiley Gallery.

Events to Look Forward To

Get to know Galveston better at its seasonal events. Kick off the year by sampling local flavors at Galveston Restaurant Week and watching towering floats parade through town during Mardi Gras. In May, the Galveston Historical Foundation organizes tours through privately owned historical homes. The three-day Texas Crab Festival occurs in the same month – stop by for a crab gumbo cookoff, crab races and musical performances. Things heat up in the summer with Independence Day festivities and the AIA Sandcastle Competition, where over 60 teams compete for the esteemed Golden Bucket Award. In the fall, the Galveston Island Shrimp Festival promises cookoffs, parades and fun runs, while the Lone Star Rally draws thousands of motorheads with car shows and free concerts.

Museums and Mansion Tours

Some of Galveston's historic homes are open for you to explore. Take a tour of Bishop's Palace, a National Historic Landmark adorned with bronze dragons and stained-glass windows. You can also go inside Moody Mansion, a 20-room estate once home to one of Texas' most influential families. Learn more about the state's past by studying artifacts and artwork at The Bryan Museum and discover one of the southwest's largest restored railroad collections at the Galveston Railroad Museum.

Port Aransas

Known as Port A to locals, this laid-back town on Mustang Island's northern tip is where you want to spend a relaxing weekend. Hang out at the beach and partake in your favorite outdoor activities on the

See listing Port Aransas, Texas

Island RV Resort

THE PREMIER TEXAS GULF OF MEXICO DESTINATION!

Enjoy an exceptional Gulf of Mexico getaway at our RV park on the Texas Gulf Coast. Featuring an exceptional island location that abounds with recreation & entertainment, world class sport fishing, beautiful beaches, golf, birding centers and much more!

ACCOMMODATIONS INCLUDE:

- Complimentary Wi-Fi
- Cable TV
- Salt Water Pool & Spa
- Shower Cabanas
- Paved Streets & Sites
- Recreation Hall
- LP Gas
- All Pull-Thru Sites & Full Hook-Ups

good sam park

361-749-5600
www.islandrvresort.com
700 6th St. Port Aransas, TX 78373

Seagull taking wing on an uncrowded beach on Mustang Island near Port Aransas on the Gulf of Mexico.

world's longest stretch of undeveloped barrier island. Fishing is especially fantastic, so catch something fresh and have it cooked to order at a waterfront restaurant. The town itself is compact enough to travel around by foot or bike, yet manages to pack in plenty of activities and attractions.

A Bird-watcher's Paradise

Port Aransas is home to six sites along the Great Texas Coastal Birding Trail, so get ready to view hundreds of native and migrating species. Nestled in the wooded wetlands of Mustang Island, the Joan and Scott Holt Paradise Pond is a hidden hot spot full of colorful songbirds and neotropical migratory birds — see the day's sightings at the chalkboard by the entrance. The Port Aransas Nature Preserve and Leonabelle Turnbull Birding Center let you view shorebirds from boardwalks and observation platforms, while the UTMSI Wetlands Education Center offers guided tours through a wildlife-rich salt marsh.

Waves of Fun

Dubbed the Fishing Capital of Texas, this easygoing beach town offers rewards for every type of angler. Drop bait in the shallow waterways surrounding Mustang Island to catch flounder, trout and redfish, or cast a line 24/7 from the south jetty and four lighted public fishing piers. For a deep-sea adventure, set off into the Gulf of Mexico to wrestle with marlin, tuna and kingfish. At the end of the day, bring your catch to a harborfront restaurant and have them prepare it for you just the way you like. Port Aransas also hosts more than 20 fishing tournaments, including the famous Deep Sea Roundup.

Super Seashore

Drive 20 miles south to reach Padre Island National Seashore, the longest stretch of undeveloped barrier island on the planet. Spend your day hunting for shells, cycling beside waves or traversing the Grasslands Nature Trail beside the park entrance. You can even watch sea turtles hatch and scuttle to the sea if you time your visit right.

Take Life at a Slower Pace

Port Aransas may be small, but it still has fun activities at every turn. Cruise through streets in a golf cart and swing by the Port Aransas Art Center to discover works by local artists. You can also catch a play at the Port Aransas Community Theatre and even start a boat-building project at Farley Boat Works. Just a stone's throw away is Palmilla Beach Resort and Golf Club, a nine-hole course designed by legendary golfer Arnold Palmer.

South Texas Tropics

With images of sun-drenched beaches and swaying palms, this vibrant southern tip of Texas is a triangle of coastal plains roughly bounded by the Rio Grande, San Antonio River and the Gulf of Mexico. It's one of the top birdwatching spots in the country and home to the world's largest undeveloped barrier island. Step inside the lush terrain to hear birds sing, see baby turtles hatch and catch a bounty of bass. Between the sprawling expanses of wilderness, you'll uncover 20 lively counties all eager to show you their version of the good life.

The Valley of Birds

The Rio Grande has become a bucket list spot for birders, having become popular with bird and butterfly chasers alike. The World Birding Center has nine designated sites in the area, each showcasing a unique habitat. Go to Mission's Bentsen-Rio Grande Valley to come face-to-face with the rare green jay and flocks of migrating hawks; McAllen's Quinta Mazatlan is the place to spot sparrows and hummingbirds. The Estero Llano Grande in Weslaco welcomes you into the Indigo Blind, a tropical zone that houses the park's most elusive birds, like white-tipped doves and Altamira Orioles. Other fantastic birding locations include the Roma Bluffs, Edinburg Scenic Wetlands, Brownsville's Resaca de la Palma, and the South Padre Island Birding and Nature Center.

Birds, Blooms & Bass

Anglers are drawn to Falcon State Park for

Boats moored at the Port Aransas Marina. The town is renowned as the "Fishing Capital of Texas."

SPOTLIGHTS

Bird watchers flock to the Gulf Coast region to spot a variety of species, including this crested caracara falcon.

some of the best freshwater fishing lakes in South Texas. Largemouth bass anglers tend to be successful during the spring, fall and winter months. Take your boat out on the 84,000-acre Falcon International Reservoir to nab largemouth bass and channel catfish. Lake Casa Blanca is right next door and supports largemouth and hybrid striped bass along with catfish and crappie. The state park offers fishing gear rentals in case you forget to bring yours. On the coast, book a deep-sea charter from South Padre Island if you want to fish for monster grouper, tuna and blue marlin.

The Last Great Habitat

Established in 1946 to provide habitat for wintering waterfowl and other migratory birds, Laguna Atascosa is a world-renowned birding destination. Feeding stations at the visitor center attract gorgeous green jays, northern cardinals, woodpeckers and more. This 45,000-acre expanse supports an abundance of birds and mammals including the endangered ocelot.

A Slice of Paradise

Take in the gulf's breeze, sandy beaches and precious marine wildlife at this shimmering oasis. Just north of Laguna Atascosa lies the longest remaining undeveloped stretch of barrier island in the world. Covering 130,000 acres, the Padre Island National Seashore will captivate you with its rolling dunes and vast prairies.

▸ FOR MORE INFORMATION

Texas Economic Development and Tourism, 512-463-2000, www.traveltex.com

Visit DFW, 817-756-9434, www.visitdfw.com

Galveston Island CVB, 888-GAL-ISLE, www.galveston.com

Hill Country of Texas, 512-763-0051, www.texashillcountry.com

Port Aransas Chamber of Commerce and Tourism Bureau, 800-45-COAST, www.portaransas.org

South Padre Island/South Texas Tropics, 800-767-2373, www.sopadre.com

Tour San Marcos, 512-393-5930, www.toursanmarcos.com

TX

Texas

ABILENE — B5 *Taylor*

ABILENE See also Baird.

ABILENE

(Public State Park) From Jct of Hwy 83/84 & FM-89 S side of Abilene (Buffalo Gap Rd), SW 13.9 mi on FM-89, follow signs (L) (Entrance fee). **FAC:** paved rds. Avail: 64 gravel, patios, back-ins (25x50), 3 full hkups, 12 W, 49 E (30/50 amps), tent sites, rentals, dump, groc, fire rings, firewood, controlled access. **REC:** pool, Lake Abilene: swim, fishing, kayaking/canoeing, playground. Pets OK. Partial handicap access, 14 day max stay. 2021 rates: $12 to $24.
(325)572-3204 Lat: 32.240731, Lon: -99.879139
150 Park Rd 32, Tuscola, TX 79562
tpwd.texas.gov

ABILENE KOA **Ratings: 9/9.5★/8.5** (Campground) Avail: 40 full hkups (30/50 amps). 2021 rates: $53 to $55. (325)672-3681, 4851 W Stamford St, Abilene, TX 79603

ABILENE RV PARK
good sam park
Ratings: 9.5/9.5★/8 (RV Park) E-bnd: From Jct of I-20 & Exit 292B, E 1.1 mi on S service rd (R); or W-bnd: From Jct of I-20 & Exit 294, Exit 294 & cross over frwy to S service rd, W 1 mi (L). **FAC:** all weather rds. (66 spaces). Avail: 54 gravel, 54 pull-thrus, (20x56), 54 full hkups (30/50 amps), seasonal sites, WiFi @ sites, rentals, laundry, groc. **REC:** pool, boating nearby. Pet restrict (B/Q). No tents. 2021 rates: $42, Military discount.
(325)672-2212 Lat: 32.434380, Lon: -99.622542
6195 E Hwy 80, Abilene, TX 79601
abilenetexasrvpark.com
See ad this page

BUCK CREEK RV PARK
good sam park
Ratings: 6.5/8★/8 (RV Park) Avail: 50 full hkups (30/50 amps). 2021 rates: $31 to $35. (325)672-2825, 12445 Buck Creek Rd., Abilene, TX 79601

RIDGEVIEW RV RESORT
good sam park
Ratings: 10/10★/10 (RV Resort) From jct Hwy 351 & I-20: Go 1/8 mi SE on I-20 & take Exit 290, then 3/4 mi SE on I-20 Service Rd. (Stamford Rd) (R). **FAC:** paved rds. (147 spaces). Avail: 35 all weather, 13 pull-thrus, (37x85), back-ins (50x37), 35 full hkups (30/50 amps), seasonal sites, WiFi @ sites, laundry. **REC:** pool, wading pool, boating nearby, playground. Pets OK. Partial handicap access. No tents. Big rig sites. 2021 rates: $40 to $55, Military discount.
(325)999-9631 Lat: 32.467095, Lon: -99.685776
2233 E. Stamford Rd, Abilene, TX 79601
www.ridgeviewrvresort.com
See ad this page

TYE RV PARK **Ratings: 6/10★/6.5** (RV Park) Avail: 20 full hkups (30/50 amps). 2021 rates: $35. (325)691-0398, 441 N Access Rd, Tye, TX 79563

WHISTLE STOP RV RESORT
good sam park
Ratings: 10/10★/10 (RV Resort) Avail: 66 full hkups (30/50 amps). 2021 rates: $45 to $55. (325)704-5252, 695 East Stamford St, Abilene, TX 79601

ALAMO — M3 *Hidalgo*

A SPOTLIGHT Introducing South Texas Tropics' colorful attractions appearing at the front of this state section.

ACACIA RV & MH PARK **Ratings: 7.5/8.5★/8** (RV Park) Avail: 79 full hkups (30/50 amps). 2021 rates: $35. (956)884-0202, 89 E. Business Hwy 83, Alamo, TX 78516

ALAMO PALMS RV RESORT
good sam park
Ratings: 9/9★/8.5 (RV Area in MH Park) Avail: 244 full hkups (30/50 amps). 2021 rates: $54. (888)563-7040, 1341 W US Hwy 83, Alamo, TX 78516

Texas Privately Owned Campground Information Updated by our Good Sam Representatives

David & Connie Karr

After 25 years as business owners, we decided to sell our house and have been full-time RVers for the last 17 years. Our great experiences and travels have allowed us to relate with our park owners. We are native West Texans, living and working in the territory that we love.

David & Sally Harmon

When David met Sally in 1996, she told him she wanted to see America by road. Her dream came true after they got married in 1997, traveling full-time in an RV for seven years. Both are now delighted to be traveling again as part of the Good Sam family.

ALAMO REC-VEH PARK/MHP
good sam park **Ratings: 9.5/9★/8** (RV Park) From Jct of US-83 (Expwy) & FM-907 (Alamo Rd) exit, W 0.3 mi on N frntg rd (R). **FAC:** paved rds. (463 spaces). Avail: 243 paved, patios, back-ins (30x60), 243 full hkups (30/50 amps), WiFi @ sites, laundry, controlled access. **REC:** heated pool, hot tub, pond, fishing, shuffleboard. Pets OK. Partial handicap access. No tents, Age restrict may apply. Big rig sites, eco-friendly. 2021 rates: $45.
(956)787-8221 Lat: 26.19333, Lon: -98.12822
1320 W Frontage Road, Alamo, TX 78516
www.alamorecvehpark.com
See ad opposite page

ALAMO ROSE RV RESORT
good sam park **Ratings: 10/8.5★/8.5** (RV Resort) From Jct of US-83 (Expwy) & FM-907 exit, S 1.5 mi on FM-907 (L). **FAC:** paved rds. (435 spaces). Avail: 274 paved, patios, back-ins (30x55), 274 full hkups (30/50 amps), WiFi @ sites, $, laundry, controlled access. **REC:** heated pool, hot tub, shuffleboard. Pets OK. Partial handicap access. No tents, Age restrict may apply, eco-friendly. 2021 rates: $45, Military discount.
(956)783-2600 Lat: 26.16925, Lon: -98.12385
938 S Alamo Rd, Alamo, TX 78516
www.rvresorts.com
See ad opposite page

CASA DEL VALLE RV RESORT
good sam park **Ratings: 10/9★/9.5** (RV Park) From Jct of US-83 (Expwy) & FM-907 (N Rudy Villarreal Rd): Go 1.1 mi N on FM-907 (R). **FAC:** paved rds. (368 spaces). Avail: 138 paved, patios, back-ins (30x70), 138 full hkups (30/50 amps), seasonal sites, WiFi @ sites, rentals, laundry, controlled access. **REC:** heated pool, hot tub, shuffleboard. Pets OK. Partial handicap access. No tents, Age restrict may apply. Big rig sites, eco-friendly. 2021 rates: $21 to $39, Military discount.
(956)783-5008 Lat: 26.20633, Lon: -98.11859
1048 N Alamo Road, Alamo, TX 78516
rhprvresorts.com
See ad page 881

TROPHY GARDENS
good sam park **Ratings: 9/9★/8.5** (RV Resort) From Jct of US-83 Expwy & FM-907 exit, N 0.8 mi on FM-907 to SH-495, E 0.3 mi (L). **FAC:** paved rds. (699 spaces). Avail: 300 paved, patios, back-ins (35x60), 300 full hkups (30/50 amps), WiFi, rentals, laundry, controlled access. **REC:** heated pool, hot tub, golf, shuffleboard. Pets OK. Partial handicap access. No tents, Age restrict may apply. Big rig sites, eco-friendly. 2021 rates: $45, Military discount.
(956)787-7717 Lat: 26.20469, Lon: -98.11395
800 State Hwy 495, Alamo, TX 78516
www.rvresorts.com
See ad opposite page

WINTER RANCH RV RESORT
good sam park **Ratings: 9.5/8.5★/8.5** (RV Resort) From Jct of US-83 (Expwy) & Tower Rd exit, N 0.8 mi on Tower Rd to SH-495, W 0.2 mi (R). **FAC:** paved rds. (688 spaces). Avail: 400 paved, patios, back-ins (30x60), 400 full hkups (30/50 amps), WiFi @ sites, $, rentals, laundry, controlled access. **REC:** heated pool, hot tub, golf, shuffleboard. Pets OK. Partial handicap access. No tents, Age restrict may apply. Big rig sites, eco-friendly. 2021 rates: $45, Military discount.
(956)781-1358 Lat: 26.20343, Lon: -98.11079
600 SH-495, Alamo, TX 78516
www.rvresorts.com
See ad this page

The Ratings & What They Mean

Rated 10/10★/10

Turn to "Understanding the Rating System" section at the front of this Guide to get information on how we rate and inspect parks with our handy three number system!

ALBANY — B6 *Shackelford*

FORT GRIFFIN STATE HISTORIC PARK (Public State Park) From Jct of US-180 & US-283, N 13.5 mi on US-283 (L) Entrance fee. 28 Avail: 8 full hkups, 20 W, 20 E (30 amps). 2021 rates: $15 to $22. (325)762-3592

ALPINE — C3 *Brewster*

B C RANCH RV PARK **Ratings: 6/7.5★/6.5** (RV Park) Avail: 20 full hkups (30/50 amps). 2021 rates: $33. (432)837-5883, 45560 N Hwy 118, Alpine, TX 79830

LA VISTA RV PARK
good sam park **Ratings: 6.5/9★/8.5** (RV Park) Avail: 14 full hkups (30/50 amps). 2021 rates: $32 to $35. (432)364-2293, 46501 State Hwy 118 S, Alpine, TX 79830

LOST ALASKAN RV PARK
good sam park **Ratings: 9.5/10★/10** (RV Park) From Jct of US-90 & Hwy 118: Go 1-1/2 mi N on Hwy 118 (L). Elev 4435 ft.**FAC:** paved rds. (98 spaces). Avail: 61 gravel, 61 pull-thrus, (32x95), 61 full hkups (30/50 amps), seasonal sites, WiFi @ sites, tent sites, laundry, LP gas. **REC:** pool, playground. Pets OK. Partial handicap access. Big rig sites, eco-friendly. 2021 rates: $35.95 to $49.95, Military discount.
(432)837-1136 Lat: 30.394985, Lon: -103.678981
2401 N Hwy 118, Alpine, TX 79830
lostalaskan.com
See ad this page

Travel Services

ROAM N' RIVER RV, boat and equipment storage facility. Offers open, covered and covered + electricity. All are gravel bottom flooring, stalls are metal and steel. Elev 4475 ft. **RV Storage:** 3-sided enclosed spaces, secured fencing, electric gate, easy reach keypad, 24/7 access, well-lit facility, security cameras, on-site staff, level gravel/paved spaces, level dirt/grass spaces, battery charger, power to charge battery, compressed air, office. **SERVICES:**. Hours: 24/7. Special offers available for Good Sam Members
(541)591-4659 Lat: 30.357592, Lon: -103.686741
2412 Covey Lane, Alpine, TX 79830

ALVARADO — B7 *Johnson*

TEXAS RANCH RV RESORT
good sam park **Ratings: 10/10★/8.5** (RV Resort) From jct I-35 & US 67: Go 3-1/2 mi E on US 67, then make a U-turn (R). **FAC:** all weather rds. (163 spaces). Avail: 60 all weather, patios, 35 pull-thrus, (37x72), back-ins (35x70), 60 full hkups (30/50 amps), seasonal sites, cable, WiFi @ sites, laundry, LP gas. **REC:** pool, pond, fishing, playground. Pet restrict (B). No tents. Big rig sites. 2021 rates: $60.
(817)295-5594 Lat: 32.418654, Lon: -97.168131
9101 E. US 67, Alvarado, TX 76009
txranchresort.com
See ad page 896

Travel Services

CAMPING WORLD OF ALVARADO As the nation's largest retailer of RV supplies, accessories, services and new and used RVs, Camping World is committed to making your total RV experience better. **SERVICES:** MH mechanical, sells outdoor gear, restrooms. RV Sales. RV supplies, LP gas, RV accessible. Hours: 9am - 7pm.
(888)327-0151 Lat: 32.428134, Lon: -97.235377
5201 S I-35 W, Alvarado, TX 76009
www.campingworld.com

Find Good Sam member specials at GanderOutdoors.com

EXCLUSIVE! Every listing includes a special "arrow" symbol. This valuable tool shows you where the facility is located (N, S, E, W, NE, NW, SE, SW) in relation to the town.

TX

Don't miss the best part! Look in the front of most state/province sections for articles that focus on areas of special interest to RVers. These ""Spotlights" tell you about interesting tourist destinations you might otherwise miss.

ALVIN — D8 *Brazoria*

MEADOWLARK RV PARK **Ratings: 5/NA/8.5** (RV Park) Avail: 38 full hkups (30/50 amps). 2021 rates: $45. (281)331-5992, 2607 W South St, Alvin, TX 77511

ST. IVES RV RESORT
good sam park
Ratings: 9/9.5★/9 (RV Resort) From jct Hwy 35 & FM 2917: Go 4-3/4 mi S on FM 2917 (L). **FAC:** gravel rds. Avail: 72 gravel, 54 pull-thrus, (45x100), back-ins (45x75), 72 full hkups (30/50 amps), WiFi @ sites, laundry, controlled access. **REC:** pool, pond. Pet restrict (B/Q). Partial handicap access. No tents. Big rig sites. 2021 rates: $55.
(832)717-9393 Lat: 29.295222, Lon: -95.224624
4959 FM 2917, Alvin, TX 77511
stivesrvresort.com
See ad this page

ALVORD — A7 *Wise*

A + RV PARK
good sam park
Ratings: 8/9.5★/9 (RV Park) From Jct of US 287 (Alvord exit) & Bus 287 (Franklin St): Go 1/4 mi N on Bus 287 N. (R). **FAC:** gravel rds. Avail: 47 gravel, 47 pull-thrus, (30x70), 47 full hkups (30/50 amps), WiFi @ sites, tent sites, dump, laundry, LP gas. **REC:** pond, fishing. Pet restrict (B). Partial handicap access, Age restrict may apply. Big rig sites. 2021 rates: $40, Military discount.
(940)427-9621 Lat: 33.34791, Lon: -97.68293
667 E Franklin St, Alvord, TX 76225
properties.camping.com/A-Plus-RV-Park
See ad this page

AMARILLO — F9 *Potter*

AMARILLO See also Canyon.

AMARILLO BEST WONDERLAND RV RESORT
good sam park
Ratings: 6.5/8.5★/7.5 (RV Park) Avail: 11 full hkups (30/50 amps). 2021 rates: $38. (806)383-1700, 2001 Dumas Dr, Amarillo, TX 79107

AMARILLO KOA **Ratings: 8.5/9.5★/8** (Campground) 82 Avail: 59 full hkups, 23 W, 23 E (30/50 amps). 2021 rates: $54.67 to $62. (806)335-1792, 1100 Folsom Rd, Amarillo, TX 79108

BIG TEXAN RV RANCH
good sam park
Ratings: 9.5/9.5★/9 (RV Park) From Jct of I-40 (exit 74) & Whitaker Rd: Go 1/2 mi W on N Service Rd (R). Elev 3670 ft.

FREE LIMO RIDE TO THE BIG TEXAN
Large pull-thrus and easy interior roads. No rig is too big! Easy access off I-40 plus free coffee in the morning. Heated indoor pool, hot tub and sauna. Our friendly staff is ready to welcome you!

FAC: paved rds. (156 spaces). Avail: 81 gravel, 80 pull-thrus, (30x90), back-ins (30x80), 81 full hkups (30/50 amps), seasonal sites, cable, WiFi @ sites, tent sites, dump, laundry. **REC:** heated pool, hot tub, playground. Pet restrict (B). Big rig sites. 2021 rates: $44, Military discount.
(806)373-4962 Lat: 35.19449, Lon: -101.77150
1414 Sunrise Dr, Amarillo, TX 79104
amarilloranch.com
See ad this page

FORT AMARILLO RV RESORT
good sam park
Ratings: 9/10★/9.5 (RV Park) From jct I-40 (exit 64) & Loop 335: Go 1/4 mi N on W Loop 335, then 1-1/4 W on Rt 66/ Amarillo Blvd W (L). Elev 3670 ft.

TOP-RATED PARK JUST OFF I-40
You'll enjoy our western setting, indoor heated pool, fitness room, stream-fed fishing pond, illuminated walking paths & breathtaking sunsets! Huge pull-thrus with free WiFi. Be sure to shop at Lizzie Mae's Mercantile.

FAC: paved/gravel rds. (105 spaces). Avail: 70 gravel, patios, 70 pull-thrus, (30x75), 70 full hkups (30/50 amps), seasonal sites, WiFi @ sites, laundry, LP gas. **REC:** heated pool, pond, fishing, playground. Pet restrict (B/Q). Partial handicap access. No tents. Big rig sites, eco-friendly. 2021 rates: $45, Military discount.
(806)331-1700 Lat: 35.19122, Lon: -101.95817
10101 Amarillo Blvd W, Amarillo, TX 79124
fortrvparks.com
See ad this page

OASIS RV RESORT
good sam park
Ratings: 10/10★/10 (RV Park) From Jct I-40 (Exit 60) & Arnot Rd: Go 1/2 mi S on Arnot Rd. (L).

OASIS RV RESORT IN AMARILLO TEXAS
Amarillo's highest rated RV Resort located in friendly Amarillo with easy access off Interstate 40 at exit 60. Resort style pool & spa, event center, spacious concrete sites, paved roads, cottages, game room & gift shop.

FAC: paved rds. (178 spaces). Avail: 149 paved, patios, 147 pull-thrus, (39x75), back-ins (39x50), 149 full hkups (30/50 amps), seasonal sites, cable, WiFi @ sites, rentals, dump, laundry, LP gas. **REC:** pool, hot tub, playground. Pets OK. Partial handicap access. No tents. Big rig sites. 2021 rates: $49 to $65, Military discount.
(888)789-9697 Lat: 35.18388, Lon: -102.00949
2715 Arnot Rd, Amarillo, TX 79124
www.myrvoasis.com
See ad this page

Each privately owned campground has been rated three times. The first rating is for development of facilities. The second one is for cleanliness and physical characteristics of restrooms and showers. The third is for campground visual appearance and environmental quality.

OVERNITE RV PARK
Ratings: 6/9★/7.5 (RV Park) From Jct of I-40 (Exit 75) & Lakeside Dr: Go 1/4 mi N on Lakeside Dr (Loop 335) (L). Elev 3670 ft. **FAC:** all weather rds. (85 spaces). Avail: 55 gravel, 55 pull-thrus, (32x65), 55 full hkups (30/50 amps), seasonal sites, laundry. **REC:** playground. Pets OK. No tents. Big rig sites. 2021 rates: $48, Military discount.
(806)373-1431 Lat: 35.19636, Lon: -101.74266
900 S Lakeside Dr, Amarillo, TX 79118
www.overnitervpark.com
See ad opposite page

Travel Services

CAMPING WORLD OF AMARILLO As the nation's largest retailer of RV supplies, accessories, services and new and used RVs, Camping World is committed to making your total RV experience better. **SERVICES:** gunsmithing svc, archery svc, sells outdoor gear, sells fishing gear, sells firearms. RV Sales. RV supplies, LP gas, emergency parking. Hours: 9am to 7pm.
(844)219-0819 Lat: 35.188595, Lon: -101.9575459
10300 I-40 Frontage Road, Amarillo, TX 79124
www.campingworld.com

GANDER RV OF AMARILLO Your new hometown outfitter offering the best regional gear for all your outdoor needs. Your adventure awaits. Elev 3670 ft. **SERVICES:** RV, RV appliance, MH mechanical, restrooms. RV Sales. RV supplies, RV accessible. Hours: 9am to 6pm, 11am to 5pm Sunday.
(877)610-0034 Lat: 35.16752, Lon: -101.86811
4341 Canyon Expressway, Amarillo, TX 79110
rv.ganderoutdoors.com

Things to See and Do

LIZZIE MAE'S MERCANTILE Located inside Fort Amarillo RV Resort, 3,000 sq ft gifts and home decor. Unique specialty gift store in a warm cabin setting. RV accessible. Restrooms. Hours: 8:30am to 5pm.
(806)331-1700 Lat: 35.19109, Lon: -101.95605
10101 Amarillo Blvd W, Amarillo, TX 79124
www.lizziemaes.net
See ad opposite page

THE BIG TEXAN Home of the free 72oz steak. World Famous Steak House & Brewery on Route 66. Partial handicap access. Food. Hours: 7am to 10:30pm.
(806)372-6000 Lat: 35.19306, Lon: -101.75504
7701 I-40 East, Amarillo, TX 79118
www.bigtexan.com
See ad opposite page

AMISTAD NATIONAL REC AREA — D5 *Val Verde*

AMISTAD NRA/277 NORTH (Public National Park) From Del Rio, N 11 mi on US-277, follow signs 0.5 mi (E). 17 Avail: Pit toilets. 2021 rates: $6. (830)775-7491

AMISTAD NRA/SAN PEDRO (Public National Park) From Jct of US-90 & Hwy 277, W 3 mi on US-90 to Spur Rd 454, N 0.5 mi, follow signs (R). 30 Avail: Pit toilets. 2021 rates: $4. (830)775-7491

ANTHONY — B1 *El Paso*

ROAD HOST RV **Ratings: 6/8.5★/8** (RV Park) Avail: 92 full hkups (30/50 amps). 2021 rates: $40. (915)603-3105, 901 S Leisure Fun Rd, Anthony, TX 79821

Travel Services

CAMPING WORLD OF ANTHONY/EL PASO As the nation's largest retailer of RV supplies, accessories, services and new and used RVs, Camping World is committed to making your total RV experience better. **SERVICES:** RV, tire, RV appliance, sells firearms, staffed RV wash, restrooms. RV Sales. RV supplies, LP gas, emergency parking, RV accessible. Hours: 9am - 6pm.
(888)618-4803 Lat: 31.973965, Lon: -106.599314
8805B N. Desert Blvd., Anthony, TX 79821
www.campingworld.com

ARANSAS PASS — E7 *San Patricio*

ARANSAS BAY RV RESORT **Ratings: 9.5/9.5★/9** (RV Park) Avail: 90 full hkups (30/50 amps). 2021 rates: $45. (830)423-4322, 501 N Avenue A, Aransas Pass, TX 78336

RANSOM ROAD RV PARK **Ratings: 9/9.5★/9** (RV Park) Avail: 128 full hkups (30/50 amps). 2021 rates: $52 to $56. (361)758-2715, 240 East Ransom Rd. #129, Aransas Pass, TX 78336

SOUTHERN OAKS LUXURY RV RESORT **Ratings: 9.5/9★/9** (RV Park) Avail: 234 full hkups (30/50 amps). 2021 rates: $60 to $70. (361)758-1249, 1850 Hwy 35 Bypass, Aransas Pass, TX 78336

ARLINGTON — H3 *Tarrant*

ARLINGTON See also Alvarado, Burleson, Fort Worth, Glenn Heights, Grand Prairie, Grapevine, Mansfield & Waxahachie.

DALLAS/ARLINGTON KOA **Ratings: 8.5/9.5★/8** (RV Park) Avail: 70 full hkups (30/50 amps). 2021 rates: $60 to $95. (817)277-6600, 2715 S Cooper, Arlington, TX 76015

TREETOPS RV RESORT **Ratings: 8.5/8/9.5** (RV Park) Avail: 35 full hkups (30/50 amps). 2021 rates: $81 to $90. (800)747-0787, 1901 W Arbrook Blvd, Arlington, TX 76015

ATHENS — B8 *Henderson*

TEXAN RV PARK **Ratings: 8/9.5★/9** (RV Park) Avail: 27 full hkups (30/50 amps). 2021 rates: $42 to $47. (903)677-3326, 9024 US Hwy 175 W, Athens, TX 75751

ATLANTA — A9 *Cass*

ATLANTA (Public State Park) From Jct of US-59 & FM-96, W 7.1 mi on FM-96 to FM-1154, N 1.7 mi to Park Rd 42 (E) (Entrance free). 58 Avail: 14 full hkups, 44 W, 44 E (30/50 amps). 2021 rates: $14 to $16. (903)796-6476

AUBREY — A7 *Denton*

SHADY CREEK RV PARK AND STORAGE
Ratings: 10/10★/10 (RV Park) From E jct US 377 & US 380: Go 6-1/4 mi E on US 380, then 1 mi N on FM 1385 (L).

TOP RATED *DALLAS* RESORT
With all the amenities you've come to expect, paved streets, pool, dog park, WiFi & more. Convenient to restaurants, shopping and all that Dallas & Fort Worth has to offer, you will want to stay awhile! Call today.
FAC: paved rds. (261 spaces). Avail: 133 all weather, patios, back-ins (35x65), 133 full hkups (30/50 amps), seasonal sites, WiFi @ sites, laundry, LP gas. **REC:** pool, pond, fishing, playground. Pet restrict (B). Partial handicap access. No tents. Big rig sites. 2021 rates: $60 to $70, Military discount.
(972)347-5384 Lat: 33.23544, Lon: -96.89525
1893 FM 1385, Aubrey, TX 76227
www.shadycreekrvpark.com
See ad page 875

THE RETREAT AT SHADY CREEK (RV Park) (Too New to Rate) Avail: 115 full hkups (30/50 amps). 2021 rates: $60 to $70. (972)347-5384, 15038 Fishtrap Rd, Aubrey, TX 76227

AUSTIN — C7 *Travis*

AUSTIN See also Bastrop, Hutto, Leander & Spicewood.

AUSTIN LONE STAR RV RESORT **Ratings: 9.5/9.5★/9** (RV Park) Avail: 50 full hkups (30/50 amps). 2021 rates: $60 to $122. (512)444-6322, 7009 S I-35, Austin, TX 78744

EMMA LONG METROPOLITAN PARK (Public) From town, W 6.5 mi on RR-2222 to City Park Rd, S 6 mi (E) Entry fee required. 36 Avail: 20 W, 20 E (30 amps). 2021 rates: $10 to $25. (512)346-1831

GEICO REV LINE PARK **Ratings: 9/9.5★/7.5** (RV Park) 75 Avail: 25 full hkups, 50 W, 50 E (30/50 amps). 2021 rates: $45 to $68. (512)655-6226, 9201 Circuit of the Americas Blvd., Austin, TX 78617

LA HACIENDA SUN RV RESORT **Ratings: 9.5/10★/10** (RV Park) Avail: 181 full hkups (30/50 amps). 2021 rates: $52 to $68. (512)266-8001, 5220 Hudson Bend Rd, Austin, TX 78734

MCKINNEY FALLS (Public State Park) From Jct of I-35 & Wm Cannon Dr (exit 228), E 3.3 mi on Wm Cannon Dr to McKinney Falls Pkwy, N 1.1 mi (L) (Entrance fee). 81 Avail: 81 W, 81 E (30/50 amps). 2021 rates: $20 to $24. (512)243-1643

OAK FOREST RV RESORT
Ratings: 9.5/9★/9 (RV Park) Avail: 26 full hkups (30/50 amps). 2021 rates: $65 to $71. (512)813-2908, 8207 Canoga Ave, Austin, TX 78724

BACLIFF — D9 *Galveston*

GORDY ROAD RV PARK **Ratings: 8.5/10★/7.5** (RV Park) Avail: 93 full hkups (30/50 amps). 2021 rates: $40. (281)549-6734, 715 Gordy Road, Bacliff, TX 77518

KEMAH RV RESORT **Ratings: 9/7/7.5** (RV Park) Avail: 94 full hkups (30/50 amps). 2021 rates: $35 to $49. (281)559-2362, 675 Miles Rd, Bacliff, TX 77518

BAIRD — B6 *Callahan*

SUNDANCE RV PARK **Ratings: 6.5/10★/7.5** (RV Park) Avail: 10 full hkups (30/50 amps). 2021 rates: $45. (325)266-4499, 1055 W I-20, Baird, TX 79504

BALMORHEA — C3 *Reeves*

SADDLEBACK MOUNTAIN RV PARK **Ratings: 4/NA/7.5** (RV Park) Avail: 46 full hkups (30/50 amps). 2021 rates: $20. (432)448-1550, 2899 CR 303, Balmorhea, TX 79718

BANDERA — D6 *Bandera*

AL'S HIDEAWAY CABINS & RV PARK **Ratings: 8/9★/8.5** (Campground) Avail: 10 full hkups (30/50 amps). 2021 rates: $35 to $45. (863)781-9408, 299 Willow Springs, Pipe Creek, TX 78063

ANTLER OAKS LODGE AND RV RESORT **Ratings: 8.5/8.5/9.5** (RV Park) Avail: 98 full hkups (30/50 amps). 2021 rates: $59. (830)796-8111, 3862 Hwy 16 North, Bandera, TX 78003

BANDERA CROSSING RIVERFRONT RV PARK
(RV Park) (Too New to Rate) Avail: 98 full hkups (30/50 amps). 2021 rates: $45. (830)288-2200, 4300 TX-16N, Bandera, TX 78003

Don't take any chances when it comes to cleanliness. We rate campground restrooms and showers for cleanliness and physical characteristics such as supplies and appearance.

TX

BANDERA (CONT)

BANDERA PIONEER RV RIVER RESORT
good sam park **Ratings: 9/9.5★/8** (Campground) From Jct of Hwys 16 & 173, S 1 blk on Hwy 173 (L). **FAC:** paved rds. Avail: 167 grass, 66 pull-thrus, (18x60), back-ins (18x35), mostly side by side hkups, 167 full hkups (30/50 amps), cable, WiFi @ sites, rentals, dump, laundry. **REC:** pool, hot tub, Medina River: swim, fishing, kayaking/canoeing, shuffleboard, playground, hunting nearby. Pet restrict (B). No tents, eco-friendly. 2021 rates: $38 to $43, Military discount.
(830)796-3751 Lat: 29.72375, Lon: -99.06957
1202 Maple St, Bandera, TX 78003
pioneerriverresort.com
See ad previous page

HOLIDAY VILLAGES OF MEDINA **Ratings: 8.5/8.5★/8.5** (Membership Park) Avail: 30 full hkups (30/50 amps). 2021 rates: $25. (830)796-8141, 234 Private Road 1501, Bandera, TX 78003

MANSFIELD PARK (BANDERA COUNTY PARK) (Public) From Jct of Hwys 173 & 16, N 1.5 mi on Hwy 16 (R). 28 Avail: 28 W, 28 E (30 amps). 2021 rates: $15. (830)796-8448

SKYLINE RANCH RV PARK **Ratings: 8/9.5★/9.5** (RV Park) Avail: 130 full hkups (30/50 amps). 2021 rates: $38 to $43. (830)796-4958, 2231 Hwy 16 N, Bandera, TX 78003

TWIN ELM GUEST RANCH & 2 E RV PARK **Ratings: 9.5/9.5★/8.5** (RV Park) Avail: 30 full hkups (30/50 amps). 2021 rates: $40. (830)796-3628, 810 FM 470, Bandera, TX 78003

BASTROP — D7 *Bastrop*

BASIN RV RESORT-BASTROP
good sam park **Ratings: 10/10★/10** (RV Park) W-Bnd: From Jct of Hwys W 21/71 & Hasler Blvd Exit, cross under freeway, E 0.3 mi on S frntg rd move to & stay in right lane (R) E-Bnd: From Jct of US 71 & Hasler/Childress Exit, E 1.3 mi on S frntg rd (move to & stay in right lane) (R). **FAC:** paved rds. (66 spaces). Avail: 17 paved, patios, 2 pull-thrus, (40x65), back-ins (40x60), 17 full hkups (30/50 amps), seasonal sites, WiFi @ sites, rentals, laundry, groc, LP gas, fire rings, firewood, controlled access. **REC:** pool, Colorado River: swim, fishing, kayaking/canoeing, playground. Pet restrict (B). Partial handicap access. No tents. Big rig sites. 2021 rates: $48 to $66, Military discount.
(512)321-7500 Lat: 30.10411, Lon: -97.32418
98 Hwy 71 West, Bastrop, TX 78602
basinrvresort.com/bastrop-tx
See ad this page

BASTROP (Public State Park) From Jct of SR-71, 95 & 21, NE 0.6 mi on SR-21 (R); or From Hwy-71 Loop 150, NW 0.7 mi on Hwy 71 (R) (Entrance fee). 54 Avail: 35 full hkups, 19 W, 19 E (20/50 amps). 2021 rates: $20 to $25. (512)321-2101

HWY 71 RV PARK
good sam park **Ratings: 9.5/10★/8.5** (RV Park) Avail: 55 full hkups (30/50 amps). 2021 rates: $30 to $50. (512)321-7275, 931 Union Chapel Rd, Cedar Creek, TX 78612

Are you using a friend's Guide? Want one of your own? Call 877-209-6655.

BAY CITY — D8 *Matagorda*

RIVERSIDE PARK (Public) From Jct of Hwys 35 & 60, S 3 mi on Hwy 60 to FM-2668, SW 2 mi (R). Avail: 40 full hkups (30/50 amps). 2021 rates: $20 to $25. (979)245-0340

BAYTOWN — D9 *Chambers*

BAYOU BEND RV RESORT
good sam park **Ratings: 10/10★/9** (RV Resort) From jct I-10 & Hwy 146: Go west 1 1/2 mi on service road (R). **FAC:** paved rds. Avail: 118 paved, back-ins (30x60), 118 full hkups (30/50 amps), cable, WiFi @ sites, rentals, laundry, controlled access. **REC:** pool, playground. Pet restrict (B). Partial handicap access. No tents. Big rig sites, eco-friendly. 2021 rates: $45.
(281)867-7702 Lat: 29.820747, Lon: -94.905888
10220 I-10 East Freeway, Baytown, TX 77521
www.bayoubendrvresort.com
See ad this page

CEDAR GROVE PARK RV RESORT **Ratings: 10/9.5★/10** (RV Resort) Avail: 266 full hkups (30/50 amps). 2021 rates: $45 to $60. (832)269-3960, 4419 N Hwy 146, Baytown, TX 77520

CRYSTAL LAKE RV RESORT **Ratings: 10/9.5★/7** (RV Resort) Avail: 166 full hkups (30/50 amps). 2021 rates: $40 to $55. (281)303-8777, 5511 S FM 565 Rd, Baytown, TX 77523

HOUSTON EAST RV RESORT
good sam park **Ratings: 9.5/10★/10** (RV Park) W-bnd: From Jct of I-10 & Hwy 146 (Exit 798): Go E 1.4 mi on S Frntg Rd (R) or E-bnd: From Jct of I-10 & Exit 797, E 1.5 mi on S. Frntg Rd (L). **FAC:** paved rds. (146 spaces). Avail: 116 paved, 50 pull-thrus, (30x61), back-ins (30x70), 116 full hkups (30/50 amps), seasonal sites, cable, WiFi @ sites, rentals, laundry, LP gas, firewood, controlled access. **REC:** pool. Pet restrict (B/Q). Partial handicap access. No tents, Age restrict may apply. Big rig sites, eco-friendly. 2021 rates: $49 to $59, Military discount.
(281)383-3618 Lat: 29.82250, Lon: -94.87500
11810 I-10 E, Baytown, TX 77523
houstoneastrvresort.com
See ad pages 876, 901

MONT BELVIEU RV RESORT **Ratings: 10/9.5★/10** (RV Resort) Avail: 242 full hkups (30/50 amps). 2021 rates: $54.44 to $78.89. (832)902-2200, 6103 S FM 565, Baytown, TX 77523

BEAUMONT — D9 *Jefferson*

BEAUMONT RV & MARINA
good sam park **Ratings: 7.5/8.5★/6** (RV Park) Avail: 81 full hkups (30/50 amps). 2021 rates: $45. (409)838-9066, 560 Marina St, Beaumont, TX 77703

EAST LUCAS RV PARK **Ratings: 6/6.5/7.5** (RV Park) Avail: 12 full hkups (30/50 amps). 2021 rates: $27 to $30. (409)899-9209, 2590 E Lucas Dr, Beaumont, TX 77703

GULF COAST RV RESORT
good sam park **Ratings: 10/10★/9** (RV Park) Avail: 125 full hkups (30/50 amps). 2021 rates: $45. (866)410-7801, 5175 Brooks Rd., Beaumont, TX 77705

HIDDEN LAKE RV PARK
good sam park **Ratings: 8.5/10★/9.5** (RV Park) Avail: 70 full hkups (30/50 amps). 2021 rates: $50. (409)840-9691, 6860 S. Major Dr. (FM 364), Beaumont, TX 77705

BELTON — C7 *Bell*

BASIN RV RESORT
good sam park **Ratings: 10/10★/10** (RV Park) From jct I-14 (US 190) & FM 2410: Go 2-1/2 mi W on FM 2410 (R). **FAC:** paved rds. (90 spaces). Avail: 70 all weather, patios, 7 pull-thrus, (42x70), back-ins (42x56), 70 full hkups (30/50 amps), seasonal sites, WiFi @ sites, laundry, LP bottles, controlled access. **REC:** pool, boating nearby. Pet restrict (B/Q). Partial handicap access. No tents. Big rig sites. 2021 rates: $44.95 to $49.95.
(254)393-1450 Lat: 31.056929, Lon: -97.586284
10502 FM 2410, Belton, TX 76513
basinrv-park.com
See ad this page

BELTON LAKE - COE/LIVE OAK RIDGE (Public Corps) 2 mi N on Hwy-317, then 2 mi W & N on FM-439, then N on FM-2271 to N side of Belton Dam. 48 Avail: 48 W, 48 E (30/50 amps). 2021 rates: $20 to $24. (254)780-1738

BELTON LAKE - COE/WESTCLIFF (Public Corps) From jct Hwy 317 & FM 439: Go 4-1/2 mi W on FM 439, then 1 mi N on Sparta Rd, then 1 mi NE on Westcliff Rd. 26 Avail: 26 W, 26 E (50 amps). 2021 rates: $24. (254)939-9828

STILLHOUSE HOLLOW LAKE - COE/DANA PEAK (Public Corps) From town, W 5 mi on US-190 to FM-2410, SW 6 mi to Comanche Gap Rd, S 5 mi (E). Avail: 20 E (30/50 amps). 2021 rates: $24 to $40. Mar 02 to Sep 29. (254)698-4282

STILLHOUSE HOLLOW LAKE - COE/UNION GROVE (Public Corps) From town, W 4 mi on US-190 to FM-1670, S 3 mi to FM-2484, W 5 mi (R). 30 Avail: 30 W, 30 E (50 amps). 2021 rates: $24 to $40. (254)947-0072

BENBROOK — J1 *Tarrant*

BENBROOK LAKE - COE/HOLIDAY PARK (Public Corps) From town, S 6 mi on US-377 to Pearl Ranch Dr/S Lakeview Dr, E 2 mi (E). 79 Avail: 74 W, 79 E (30/50 amps). 2021 rates: $28. (817)292-2400

BEND — C6 *San Saba*

COLORADO BEND (Public State Park) From town: Go 4 mi S on gravel road (unmarked CR 442). Note: Maximum length 30'. Entrance fee required. 15 Avail: Pit toilets. 2021 rates: $15. (512)389-8900

BIG BEND NATIONAL PARK — D3 *Brewster*

BIG BEND/COTTONWOOD (Public National Park) From park headquarters (Panther Junction): Go 35 mi SW of park hdqtrs. 24 Avail: Pit toilets. 2021 rates: $14. (432)477-1121

BIG BEND/RIO GRANDE VILLAGE (Public National Park) From Jct of US-90 & US-385 (in Marathon), S 40 mi on US-385 to park entrance, S 29 mi to park hdqtrs at Panther Jct, SE 20 mi (E). Entrance fee required. 100 Avail. 2021 rates: $14. (432)477-1121

RIO GRANDE RV PARK & CAMPGROUND (Public National Park) From Jct of US-90 & US-385 (in Marathon), S 40 mi to park entrance, S 29 mi to park hdqtrs at Panther Junction, SE 20 mi (E). Entrance fee required. Register at Rio Grande Village Store/Service Station. Avail: 25 full hkups (30 amps). 2021 rates: $35. (432)477-2293

BIG SPRING — B4 *Howard*

WHIP IN RV PARK
good sam park **Ratings: 7/8.5/7.5** (RV Park) Avail: 10 full hkups (30/50 amps). 2021 rates: $35. (432)393-5242, 7000 S Service Rd I-20, Big Spring, TX 79720

BLANCO — D6 *Blanco*

BLANCO (Public State Park) From Jct of US-281 & RR-165 (Loop 163, in town), S 0.3 mi on US-281 (R). CAUTION: 24,000 lb weight limit bridge at campground entrance (Entrance fee). 29 Avail: 17 full hkups, 12 W, 12 E (30/50 amps). 2021 rates: $20 to $25. (830)833-4333

BOERNE — D6 *Bexar*

ALAMO FIESTA RV RESORT **Ratings: 9.5/9.5★/8** (RV Park) Avail: 21 full hkups (30/50 amps). 2021 rates: $55 to $80. (830)249-4700, 33000 IH-10 W, Boerne, TX 78006

CASCADE CAVERNS & CAMPGROUND
good sam park **Ratings: 7/9★/7.5** (Campground) From Jct of I-10 & Exit 543 (Cascade Caverns Rd), then follow signs on Cascade Caverns Rd 2.6 mi (R). **FAC:** paved/gravel rds. (56 spaces). Avail: 45 gravel, 25 pull-thrus, (20x60), back-ins (20x60), 45 full hkups (30/50 amps), seasonal sites, WiFi @ sites, tent sites, dump, laundry. Pet restrict (Q). eco-friendly. 2021 rates: $50, Military discount. no reservations.
(830)755-8080 Lat: 29.76339, Lon: -98.68066
226 Cascade Caverns Rd, Boerne, TX 78015
www.cascadecaverns.com
See ad opposite page

TOP OF THE HILL RV RESORT **Ratings: 9/9.5★/9** (RV Park) Avail: 10 full hkups (30/50 amps). 2021 rates: $40 to $50. (830)537-3666, 12 Green Cedar Rd, Boerne, TX 78006

Things to See and Do

CASCADE CAVERNS 100 foot waterfall - guided tours. RV accessible. Restrooms. Hours: 9am to 5pm. Adult fee: $19.95 kids under 12 $12.95 under 4 free.
(830)755-8080 Lat: 29.76339, Lon: -98.68066
226 Cascade Caverns Rd, Boerne, TX 78015
www.cascadecaverns.com
See ad this page

BONHAM — A8 *Fannin*

BONHAM (Public State Park) From Jct of SR-56 & SR-78, S 1.4 mi on SR-78 to FM-271, E 1.9 mi (L). 14 Avail: 14 W, 14 E (30/50 amps). 2021 rates: $20 to $24. (903)583-5022

BORGER — F9 *Hutchinson*

HUBER PARK (Public) At Jct of SR-207 (S Main St) & Cedar St (E). 10 Avail: 10 W, 10 E (30 amps), Pit toilets. (806)273-0975

BRACKETTVILLE — D5 *Kinney*

FORT CLARK SPRINGS RV PARK
Ratings: 8/8.5★/8 (RV Park) Avail: 85 full hkups (30/50 amps). 2021 rates: $23.50 to $25.50. (830)563-9340, 80 Scales Road, Brackettville, TX 78832

BRAZORIA — D8 *Brazoria*

BRAZORIA LAKES RV RESORT **Ratings: 10/9.5★/10** (RV Resort) Avail: 266 full hkups (30/50 amps). 2021 rates: $49 to $77. (979)798-1000, 109 Stephen F. Austin Trail, Brazoria, TX 77422

BRENHAM — C8 *Washington*

ARTESIAN PARK RV CAMPGROUND **Ratings: 6.5/9.5/7** (RV Park) Avail: 18 full hkups (30/50 amps). 2021 rates: $28 to $33. (979)836-0680, 8601 Hwy 290 W, Brenham, TX 77833

BRIDGEPORT — A7 *Wise*

BAY LANDING RV
Ratings: 7.5/7.5/8.5 (Membership Park) 204 Avail: 49 full hkups, 155 W, 155 E (30/50 amps). 2021 rates: $44 to $48. (888)563-7040, 2305 US Hwy 380 W, Bridgeport, TX 76426

BROADDUS — C9 *San Augustine*

JACKSON HILL PARK & MARINA (Public Corps) From town, SW 4 mi on Hwy 147 to FR-2851, W 1 mi (E). 48 Avail: (30/50 amps), Pit toilets. 2021 rates: $30. Jan 01 to Sep 30. (936)872-9266

BROOKELAND — C9 *Jasper*

BROOKELAND/LAKE SAM RAYBURN KOA **Ratings: 7/8.5/8** (RV Park) Avail: 81 full hkups (30/50 amps). 2021 rates: $46 to $57. (800)562-1612, 505 CR 212, Brookeland, TX 75931

SAM RAYBURN RESERVOIR - COE/MILL CREEK (Public Corps) From town, W 1 mi on Spur 165 (E). 110 Avail: 110 W, 110 E (30/50 amps). 2021 rates: $26 to $28. (409)384-5716

SAM RAYBURN RESERVOIR - COE/TWIN DIKES (Public Corps) From town, N 15 mi on US-96 to RR-255, W 5 mi (R). 25 Avail: 9 full hkups, 10 W, 10 E (30/50 amps). 2021 rates: $14 to $28. Mar 01 to Sep 03. (409)384-5716

BROOKSHIRE — D8 *Waller*

HOUSTON WEST RV PARK
Ratings: 9/10★/9.5 (RV Park) Avail: 189 full hkups (30/50 amps). 2021 rates: $44 to $46. (281)375-5678, 35303 Cooper Rd., Brookshire, TX 77423

SPOTLIGHT ON
TOP RV & CAMPING DESTINATIONS

We've put the Spotlight on popular RV & camping travel destinations. Turn to the Spotlight articles in our State and Province sections to learn more.

SUMMER BREEZE USA KATY
Ratings: 10/9★/9.5 (RV Park) From jct Koomey Rd & I-10: Go 2 mi W on I-10 (R).

RV RESORT & WATERPARK W OF HOUSTON
RV Resort in Brookshire features a Tropical Village themed water park, huge interactive playground, and a giant outdoor hot tub. Resort has all paved roads & sites, club house & fitness center. Close to Houston attractions.

FAC: paved rds. (99 spaces). Avail: 95 paved, patios, 43 pull-thrus, (40x75), back-ins (35x50), 95 full hkups (30/50 amps), seasonal sites, WiFi @ sites, laundry, LP gas, fire rings. **REC:** pool, wading pool, hot tub, playground, rec open to public. Pet restrict (B/Q). Partial handicap access. No tents. Big rig sites. 2021 rates: $65 to $105, Military discount.
(713)358-8430 Lat: 29.781892, Lon: -95.999104
1019 Wilpitz Rd, Brookshire, TX 77423
SUMMERBREEZEUSA.COM
See ad page 902

BROWNSVILLE — M4 *Cameron*

4 SEASONS MHP & RV RESORT **Ratings: 9.5/9★/8.5** (RV Area in MH Park) Avail: 81 full hkups (30/50 amps). 2021 rates: $38. (956)831-4918, 6900 Coffee Port Rd, Brownsville, TX 78521

BREEZE LAKE RV CAMPGROUND
Ratings: 9.5/9★/8.5 (RV Area in MH Park) Avail: 90 full hkups (30/50 amps). 2021 rates: $36 to $39. (956)831-4427, 1710 N Vermillion Ave, Brownsville, TX 78521

HONEYDALE MOBILE HOME & RV PARK **Ratings: 7/8.5★/7** (RV Area in MH Park) Avail: 25 full hkups (30/50 amps). 2021 rates: $50. (956)982-2230, 505 Honeydale Rd, # 22, Brownsville, TX 78520

PALM RESACA MOBILE HOME PARK **Ratings: 9.5/9.5★/8.5** (RV Area in MH Park) Avail: 13 full hkups (30/50 amps). 2021 rates: $40 to $50. (956)546-7423, 100 Tangerine Blvd, Brownsville, TX 78521

RIVER BEND RESORT & GOLF CLUB **Ratings: 9.5/9★/9.5** (Membership Park) Avail: 22 full hkups (30/50 amps). 2021 rates: $28 to $45. (956)548-0194, 4541 US Hwy 281, Brownsville, TX 78520

SUNSET PALMS RV & MHP
Ratings: 9/9.5★/8 (RV Area in MH Park) Avail: 113 full hkups (30/50 amps). 2021 rates: $36. (956)831-4852, 1129 N Minnesota Ave., Brownsville, TX 78521

TROPICAL TRAILS RV RESORT
Ratings: 10/10★/9.5 (RV Resort) Avail: 240 full hkups (30/50 amps). 2021 rates: $50 to $75. (855)684-2887, 3605 FM 511, Brownsville, TX 78526

WINTER HAVEN RESORT **Ratings: 10/9★/8.5** (RV Area in MH Park) Avail: 29 full hkups (30/50 amps). 2021 rates: $40. (956)831-7755, 3501 Old Port Isabel Rd, Brownsville, TX 78526

BROWNWOOD — B6 *Brown*

LAKE BROWNWOOD (Public State Park) From Jct of US 67/84 & SR 279 N (in town), N 14.4 mi on SR 279 N to PR-15, E 4.8 mi (E) (Entrance fee). 66 Avail: 20 full hkups, 46 W, 46 E (30/50 amps). 2021 rates: $20 to $25. (325)784-5223

RIVERSIDE PARK RV
Ratings: 5.5/9★/7 (RV Park) From jct of Hwy 377 & Riverside Park Dr: Go 1/4 mi N on Riverside Park Dr (R). **FAC:** paved rds. Avail: 26 paved, 24 pull-thrus, (40x100), back-ins (30x65), 26 full hkups (30/50 amps), WiFi @ sites, laundry. **REC:** Pecan Bayou: fishing, boating nearby, playground. Pet restrict (B). No tents. Big rig sites. 2021 rates: $39, Military discount.
(325)642-5033 Lat: 31.730272, Lon: -98.975627
320 Riverside Park Dr, Brownwood, TX 76801
www.riversideparkrv.com
See ad this page

THE HIDEOUT GOLF CLUB & RESORT **Ratings: 9.5/9.5★/9** (RV Resort) Avail: 16 full hkups (30/50 amps). 2021 rates: $10. (325)784-4653, 185 Hideout Lane, Brownwood, TX 76801

BRYAN — C8 *Brazos*

AGGIELAND RV PARK **Ratings: 8.5/8.5★/7.5** (RV Park) Avail: 20 full hkups (30/50 amps). 2021 rates: $40. (979)703-7937, 3203 Colson Road, Bryan, TX 77808

We appreciate your business!

HARDY'S LANDING
(RV Park) (Too New to Rate) From jct Hwy 21 & Hwy 6: Go 7 mi NE on Hwy 6, then 2-1/4 mi SW on OSR Rd (L). **FAC:** paved rds. (99 spaces). Avail: 39 all weather, 5 pull-thrus, (48x65), back-ins (30x48), 39 full hkups (30/50 amps), seasonal sites, cable, WiFi @ sites, laundry, LP gas. **REC:** pond, fishing, boating nearby. Pet restrict (B/Q). Partial handicap access. No tents. Big rig sites. 2021 rates: $45, Military discount.
(979)286-3344 Lat: 30.670581, Lon: -96.494958
6385 W OSR Rd, Bryan, TX 77807
hardyslanding.com
See ad page 890

HARDY'S RESORT
(RV Resort) (Too New to Rate) From jct Hwy 21 & Hwy 6 E Frontage Rd: Go 1/8 mi NW on Hwy 6 E Frontage Rd, then 1/8 mi E on Colson Road (L).

RESORT IN THE HEART OF AGGIELAND
Spectacular RV Resort just minutes away from Texas A & M, Kyle Field, George Bush Presidential Library, Lake Bryan, & Aggieland Safari Park. First class amenities including pool and lots of recreation.

FAC: paved rds. Avail: 103 paved, patios, 33 pull-thrus, (45x65), back-ins (45x55), 103 full hkups (30/50 amps), cable, WiFi @ sites, laundry, LP gas, fire rings. **REC:** pool, pond, fishing, boating nearby. Pet restrict (B/Q). Partial handicap access. No tents. Big rig sites, eco-friendly. 2021 rates: $50.
(979)703-1201 Lat: 30.702932, Lon: -96.360485
3414 Colson Road, Bryan, TX 77808
hardysresort.com
See ad page 890

HIDDEN CREEK RV RESORT
Ratings: 10/9.5★/10 (RV Resort) From jct Hwy 6 & State Hwy 21 East: Go 1-1/4 mi E on State Hwy 21 East (R).

BRYAN/COLLEGE STATION'S BEST RESORT
Have a luxurious camping experience in one of our 98 RV sites or 6 cabins. From our resort style pool to our cabins, we strive to provide guests with a stay that is more than ordinary. Enjoy attractions and Aggie football.

FAC: paved rds. Avail: 98 paved, patios, 14 pull-thrus, (30x60), back-ins (30x60), 98 full hkups (30/50 amps), cable, WiFi @ sites, rentals, laundry, groc, LP gas, controlled access. **REC:** pool, hot tub, pond, fishing, playground. Pet restrict (B/Q). Partial handicap access. No tents, Age restrict may apply. Big rig sites. 2021 rates: $52 to $68, Military discount.
(979)778-1200 Lat: 30.712289, Lon: -96.343781
5780 State Hwy 21 East, Bryan, TX 77808
www.hiddencreekrv.com
See ad page 891

BUCHANAN DAM — C6 *Burnet*

FREEDOM LIVES RANCH RV RESORT
Ratings: 8.5/9★/8.5 (RV Park) Avail: 28 full hkups (30/50 amps). 2021 rates: $45. (512)793-2171, 9606 W RR 1431, Buchanan Dam, TX 78609

TX

BULLARD — B8 *Smith*

BUSHMAN'S RV PARK
good sam park **Ratings: 10/10★/10** (RV Park) From Jct of FM 344 & US 69: Go 1-1/2 mi S on US 69. (L).

RV RESORT - WINERY - RESTAURANT
Top Rated RV Resort with gorgeous indoor swimming pool and hot tub, fitness center, convenience store and fishing lake. Three miles from the legendary Kiepersol Winery and Restaurant.
FAC: paved rds. Avail: 95 paved, 25 pull-thrus, (40x70), back-ins (30x65), 95 full hkups (30/50 amps), WiFi @ sites, tent sites, laundry, groc, LP bottles, firewood, controlled access. **REC:** pool, hot tub, pond, fishing, boating nearby, playground. Pets OK. Partial handicap access. Big rig sites, eco-friendly. 2021 rates: $42, Military discount.
(903)894-8221 Lat: 32.11974, Lon: -95.30060
51152 S. US Hwy 69N, Bullard, TX 75757
www.bushmansrvpark.com
See ad page 918

Get the GOOD SAM CAMPING APP

Things to See and Do

KIEPERSOL ESTATES VINEYARDS & WINERY
Texas winery and distillery featuring estate-grown wine, rum, bourbon, and vodka. Wine tastings and facility tours. Fine dining restaurant serving lunch and dinner. Bed and Breakfast. Partial handicap access. Restrooms. Hours: 11am to 7pm, Tues thru Sat.
(903)894-8995 Lat: 32.154453, Lon: -95.284742
4120 FM 344 E, Tyler, TX 75703
kiepersol.com
See ad page 918

BULVERDE — D6 *Comal*

TEXAS 281 RV PARK
good sam park **Ratings: 9/9★/9** (RV Park) From Jct of SR-46 & US-281: Go 3/4 mi S on US-281, then crossover & back N 1/4 mi (R). **FAC:** paved rds. Avail: 160 paved, patios, 47 pull-thrus, (28x65), back-ins (28x40), 160 full hkups (30/50 amps), WiFi @ sites, laundry. **REC:** shuffleboard, hunting nearby. Pet restrict (B). No tents. Big rig sites, eco-friendly. 2021 rates: $44, Military discount.
(830)980-2282 Lat: 29.78960, Lon: -98.42121
33300 Hwy 281 N, Bulverde, TX 78163
www.texas281rvpark.com
See ad this page

BURLESON — J2 *Johnson*

JELLYSTONE PARK AT THE RUSTIC CREEK RANCH **Ratings: 9.5/9.5★/8** (Campground) Avail: 264 full hkups (30/50 amps). 2021 rates: $45 to $100. (817)426-5037, 2301 S I-35 West, Burleson, TX 76028

MOCKINGBIRD HILL MOBILE HOME & RV PARK
good sam park **Ratings: 8/9★/9** (RV Area in MH Park) S-Bound I-35W (Exit 35): Go 2-1/2 mi S on W Frontage Rd (R). N-Bound I-35W (Exit 32): Go 1-1/4 mi N on W Frontage Rd (L). **FAC:** paved rds. (120 spaces). Avail: 20 paved, patios, 20 pull-thrus, (25x70), 20 full hkups (30/50 amps), seasonal sites, WiFi @ sites, laundry. Pet restrict (B). Partial handicap access. No tents. Big rig sites. 2021 rates: $45, Military discount.
(817)295-3011 Lat: 32.50145, Lon: -97.29320
1990 S Burleson Blvd #20, Burleson, TX 76028
www.mockingbirdrvpark.com
See ad this page

BURNET — C6 *Burnet*

BIG CHIEF RV & CABIN RESORT **Ratings: 8/9★/9.5** (RV Park) Avail: 72 full hkups (30/50 amps). 2021 rates: $30 to $55. (512)793-4746, 1420 FM 690, Burnet, TX 78611

INKS LAKE (Public State Park) From Jct of US-281 & Hwy 29, W 9 mi on Hwy 29 to Park Rd 4, S 3 mi (R) (Entrance fee). 174 Avail: 174 W, 125 E (20/50 amps). 2021 rates: $16 to $23. (512)793-2223

Things change ... last year's rates serve as a guideline only.

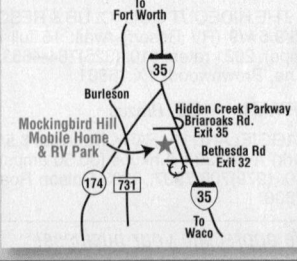

CADDO — B6 *Palo Pinto*

POSSUM KINGDOM (Public State Park) From Jct of US-180 & PR-33, N 14.3 mi on PR-33, on Possum Kingdom Lake (E) (Entrance fee). 114 Avail: 114 W, 61 E (20/50 amps). 2021 rates: $12 to $20. (940)549-1803

CADDO MILLS — B8 *Hunt*

DALLAS NE CAMPGROUND
good sam park **Ratings: 9/9.5★/9** (Campground) Avail: 71 full hkups (30/50 amps). 2021 rates: $45.95 to $70. (903)527-3615, 4268 FM 36 S, Caddo Mills, TX 75135

CALDWELL — C7 *Burleson*

BRAZOS VALLEY RV PARK **Ratings: 10/9.5★/10** (RV Park) Avail: 30 full hkups (30/50 amps). 2021 rates: $40. (979)200-3007, 2190 Hwy 21 East, Caldwell, TX 77836

CAMP WOOD — D5 *Uvalde*

WES COOKSEY PARK (Public) From town, S 3 mi on Hwy 55 (R). 30 Avail: 12 full hkups, 18 W, 18 E (50 amps). 2021 rates: $16. (830)597-3223

CAMPBELL — A8 *Hunt*

STINSON RV PARK
good sam park **Ratings: 7/10★/9** (RV Park) Avail: 79 full hkups (30/50 amps). 2021 rates: $40 to $50. (903)455-7878, 3641 East I-30, Campbell, TX 75422

CANTON — B8 *Van Zandt*

CANTON See also Athens, Malakoff, Mineola, Murchison, Point & Terrell.

CANTON CREEK RV PARK
good sam park **Ratings: 8.5/8.5/8.5** (RV Park) Avail: 10 full hkups (30/50 amps). 2021 rates: $40 to $45. (903)865-6000, 32891 TX-64, Wills Point, TX 75169

CANTON I-20 RV PARK
good sam park **Ratings: 9/8.5★/9.5** (RV Park) From Jct of I-20 & Exit 519, E 0.25 mi on South access rd (R). **FAC:** all weather rds. (45 spaces). Avail: 24 gravel, 24 pull-thrus, (40x80), 24 full hkups (30/50 amps), seasonal sites, WiFi @ sites, laundry, firewood. **REC:** pool. Pet restrict (B). No tents. Big rig sites. 2021 rates: $40, Military discount.
(903)873-8561 Lat: 32.61606, Lon: -95.97761
24481 IH-20, Wills Point, TX 75169
www.cantonI20rvpark.com
See ad this page

FIRST MONDAY TRADE DAYS RV PARK (Public) From Jct of I-20 & Exit 527/TX 19, S 1.1 mi to Hwy 64, W 1.5 mi to Edgewood Rd, E 0.7 mi (R). 334 Avail: 240 full hkups, 94 W, 94 E (30/50 amps). 2021 rates: $25 to $40. (903)567-6556

MILL CREEK RANCH RESORT
good sam park **Ratings: 9.5/10★/10** (RV Park) From Jct I-20 (Exit 527) & Hwy 19 (Trade Days Blvd): Go 1/4 mi S on Hwy 19 (L).

YOUR MEMORIES BEGIN HERE
Embrace nature, enjoy 1st class amenities & gracious hospitality at East Texas' BEST RV & Cottage Resort destination. Explore 200 tranquil acres with designer pools, stocked fishing ponds & activities for all. Top-Rated Park.
FAC: paved rds. Avail: 100 paved, 74 pull-thrus, (32x100), back-ins (33x50), 100 full hkups (30/50 amps), WiFi @ sites, rentals, laundry, groc, LP bottles, fire rings, firewood, controlled access. **REC:** pool, hot tub, pond, fishing, playground. Pets OK. Partial handicap access. No tents. Big rig sites. 2021 rates: $45 to $65, Military discount.
(877)927-3439 Lat: 32.57360, Lon: -95.85264
1880 N. Trade Days Blvd, Canton, TX 75103
www.millcreekranchresort.com
See ad this page

ROLLING OAKS RV PARK **Ratings: 6/9★/7** (RV Park) Avail: 29 full hkups (30/50 amps). 2021 rates: $32 to $57. (903)502-5555, 20445 Interstate 20, Canton, TX 75103

WAGON TRAIN RV PARK **Ratings: 7/9★/9.5** (RV Park) Avail: 16 full hkups (30/50 amps). 2021 rates: $32 to $35. (903)963-1333, 7869 Interstate 20 S Access Rd., Canton, TX 75103

CANUTILLO — B1 *El Paso*

GASLIGHT SQUARE MOBILE ESTATES
good sam park **Ratings: 8.5/9★/8** (Campground) Avail: 23 full hkups (30/50 amps). 2021 rates: $40. (915)877-2238, 500 Talbot Ave, Canutillo, TX 79835

CANYON — F9 *Randall*

PALO DURO CANYON (Public State Park) From Jct of US-87 & SR-217, E 12.2 mi on SR-217 (E); or From Jct of I-27 & SR-217, E 10 mi on SR-217 (E) (2 mi - 10% Grade Down to sites) (Entrance fee). 97 Avail: 97 W, 97 E (20/50 amps). 2021 rates: $24 to $26. (806)488-2227

PALO DURO RV PARK
good sam park **Ratings: 7/9★/7** (RV Park) Avail: 64 full hkups (30/50 amps). 2021 rates: $40. (806)488-2548, 5707 4th Ave, Canyon, TX 79015

CANYON LAKE — D6 *Comal*

CANYON LAKE - COE/CRANES MILL (Public Corps) From Jct of I-35 & Hwy 306, W 14 mi on Hwy 306 to FM-2673, S (following Guadalupe River crossing) to park entrance (E). 30 Avail: 30 W, 30 E (50 amps). 2021 rates: $30. (830)964-3341

MILITARY PARK JOINT BASE SAN ANTONIO CANYON LAKE REC PARK (JBSA-FORT SAM HOUSTON) (Public) From town: Go 8 mi E on FM2673 E, then 2-1/2 mi N on S Access Rd, then continue 1-1/4 mi N on FM306, then 1 mi W on Jacobs Creek Rd (R). 37 Avail: 25 full hkups, 12 W, 12 E (30/50 amps). 2021 rates: $18 to $20. (800)280-3466

MYSTIC QUARRY **Ratings: 9/9★/9.5** (RV Resort) Avail: 52 full hkups (30/50 amps). 2021 rates: $45 to $71. (830)964-3330, 13190 FM 306, Canyon Lake, TX 78133

SUMMIT VACATION & RV RESORT
good sam park **Ratings: 9.5/9★/9.5** (RV Resort) From Jct FM-306 & FM-2673: Go 1-1/2 mi S on FM-2673, then 1-1/2 mi E on River Rd (R). **FAC:** paved rds. (106 spaces). Avail: 94 gravel, 18 pull-thrus, (45x80), back-ins (45x60), 94 full hkups (30/50 amps), seasonal sites, WiFi @ sites, rentals, dump, laundry, fire rings, controlled access. **REC:** pool, wading pool, hot tub, Guadalupe River: swim, fishing, kayaking/canoeing, boating nearby, shuffleboard, playground, hunting nearby. Pet restrict (B). No tents. Big rig sites, eco-friendly. 2021 rates: $39 to $69, Military discount.
(830)964-2531 Lat: 29.83273, Lon: -98.16363
13105 River Road, New Braunfels, TX 78132
www.summitresorttexas.com
See ad this page

YOGI BEAR'S JELLYSTONE PARK HILL COUNTRY **Ratings: 9.5/9★/8.5** (Campground) Avail: 78 full hkups (30/50 amps). 2021 rates: $54 to $83. (830)256-0088, 12915 FM 306, Canyon Lake, TX 78133

CARROLLTON — G4 *Dallas*

SANDY LAKE MH & RV RESORT **Ratings: 9/9.5★/7.5** (RV Park) Avail: 30 full hkups (30/50 amps). 2021 rates: $65 to $70. (972)242-6808, 1915 Sandy Lake Rd, Carrollton, TX 75006

CARTHAGE — B9 *Panola*

CARTHAGE RV CAMPGROUND
good sam park **Ratings: 9.5/10★/8.5** (RV Park) From Jct of North US 59/US 79 & Lasalle Pkwy (Loop 59), SE 2 mi (R). **FAC:** paved/gravel rds. Avail: 64 paved, 59 pull-thrus, (35x65), back-ins (27x60), 64 full hkups (30/50 amps), cable, WiFi @ sites, tent sites, rentals, dump, laundry, LP gas. **REC:** pool, pond, fishing, boating nearby. Pets OK. Partial handicap access. Big rig sites. 2021 rates: $37 to $46.50, Military discount.
(903)693-6640 Lat: 32.179255, Lon: -94.327241
1294 NE Loop 59, Carthage, TX 75633
carthagervcampground.com
See ad this page

OFF SEASON RVING TIP: Prepare to handle the elements: During the regular camping season, weather is usually a minimal concern. During the off-season, however, ignoring the weather forecast may lead to damage and danger. Keep an eye on the weather to watch for freezing temperatures or precipitation. If the temperature will be dropping much below 32 degrees, you may need to winterize your rig before exposing it to the elements. Never fear, you can still camp as long as you take plenty of drinking water and flush the grey and black tanks with RV antifreeze. Make sure you have ways to stay warm inside your rig by testing your heating system before the trip and taking extra blankets.

CASTROVILLE — D6 *Medina*

ALSATIAN RV RESORT & GOLF CLUB
good sam park **Ratings: 10/10★/10** (RV Resort) From Jct Hwy 90 & CR 4516: Go 2.5 mi on CR 4516 (R). **FAC:** paved rds. Avail: 67 paved, patios, 23 pull-thrus, (41x110), back-ins (41x80), 67 full hkups (30/50 amps), WiFi @ sites, rentals, laundry, LP gas, controlled access. **REC:** heated pool, hot tub, pond, fishing, golf, hunting nearby. Pets OK. Partial handicap access. No tents. Big rig sites, eco-friendly. 2021 rates: $40 to $95, Military discount.
(830)931-9190 Lat: 29.36310, Lon: -98.94100
1581 CR 4516, Castroville, TX 78009
www.alsatianresort.com
See ad this page

CASTROVILLE REGIONAL PARK (Public) From jct US-90 & Athens St: Go 1/4 mi S on Athens St, then 1/4 mi W on Lisbon St (E). Avail: 40 full hkups (30/50 amps). 2021 rates: $45. (830)931-4070

Things to See and Do

ALSATIAN RV RESORT AND GOLF COURSE
Par 71, 18 hole golf course. Full driving range & practice facility. Club house with pro shop & restaurant. Partial handicap access. Restrooms. Food. Hours: 7am to 7pm . Adult fee: $25 to $50. ATM.
(830)931-3100 Lat: 29.36050, Lon: -98.93370
1339 County Road 4516, Castroville, TX 78009
www.alsatiangolfclub.com
See ad this page

CEDAR HILL — J3 *Dallas*

CEDAR HILL (Public State Park) From Jct of I-20 & FM-1382 (exit 457), S 3.7 mi on FM-1382 (R) (Entrance fee). 350 Avail: 150 full hkups, 200 W, 200 E (30/50 amps). 2021 rates: $25 to $30. (972)291-3900

CHANDLER — B8 *Henderson*

FLAT CREEK MARINA AND RV **Ratings: 7/9★/6.5** (RV Park) 50 Avail: 47 full hkups, 3 W, 3 E (30/50 amps). 2021 rates: $40 to $45. (903)849-6356, 20758 Twin Oaks Drive, Chandler, TX 75758

CLEBURNE — B7 *Johnson*

CLEBURNE (Public State Park) From Jct of US-67 & SR-171/174, SW 6 mi on US-67 to PR-21, S 6 mi (R). CAUTION: Bridge weight limit 15000 lbs single or tandem axle (Entrance fee). 59 Avail: 28 full hkups, 31 W, 31 E (20/50 amps). 2021 rates: $16 to $30. (817)645-4215

CLEVELAND — C8 *Liberty*

EAST FORK RV RESORT
good sam park **Ratings: 10/9.5★/9** (RV Park) Avail: 79 full hkups (30/50 amps). 2021 rates: $49 to $55. (281)593-2053, 1626 Hwy 59 S, Cleveland, TX 77327

Got a big rig? Look for listings indicating ""big rig sites''. These campgrounds are made for you, with 12'-wide roads and 14' overhead clearance. They guarantee that 25% or more of their sites measure 24' wide by 60' long or larger, and have full hookups with 50-amp electricity.

COLDSPRING — C8 *San Jacinto*

BROWDER'S MARINA RV PARK & CAMPGROUND **Ratings: 6/7/8** (Campground) 56 Avail: 41 full hkups, 15 W, 15 E (30/50 amps). 2021 rates: $37 to $42. (936)653-3278, 1333 FM 3278, Coldspring, TX 77331

ROCK'N E RV PARK **Ratings: 7.5/9.5★/9.5** (Campground) Avail: 10 full hkups (30/50 amps). 2021 rates: $40. (936)653-2727, 5221 FM 222, Coldspring, TX 77331

WOLF CREEK PARK (Public) From Coldspring, turn left on Hwy 156, go 1 mi. to Hwy 224, turn right. Park is 5 mi. on the right. (R). 103 Avail: 46 full hkups, 57 W, 57 E (50 amps). 2021 rates: $25 to $35. Mar 01 to Nov 30. (936)653-4312

COLEMAN — B6 *Coleman*

HORDS CREEK LAKE - COE/FLATROCK (Public Corps) From town, W 8 mi on FM 53 to Dam Rd, S 2 mi (R). 56 Avail: 10 full hkups, 46 W, 46 E (20/30 amps), Pit toilets. 2021 rates: $16 to $44. May 01 to Sep 20. (325)625-2322

HORDS CREEK LAKE - COE/LAKESIDE PARK (Public Corps) From town, W 8 mi on Hwy 153 to Hords Creek Lake, follow signs (E). 88 Avail: 31 full hkups, 57 W, 57 E (15/50 amps). 2021 rates: $16 to $26. (325)625-2322

PRESS MORRIS (Public) From town, N 14 mi on US-283 to FM-1274, W 2 mi (R). 27 Avail: 9 full hkups, 18 W, 18 E (30 amps). 2021 rates: $10 to $20. (915)382-4635

TX

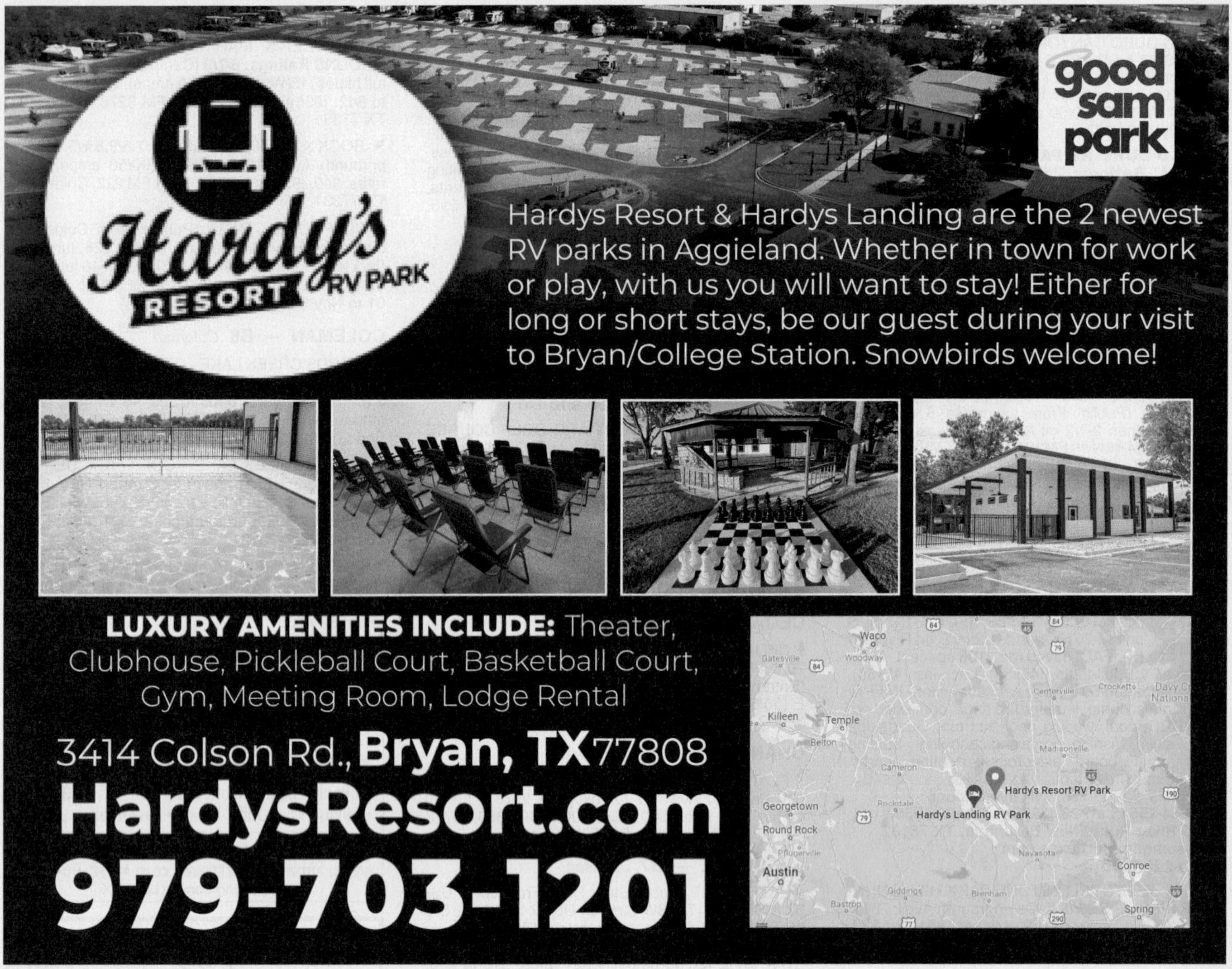
good sam park
Hardy's RESORT RV PARK
Hardys Resort & Hardys Landing are the 2 newest RV parks in Aggieland. Whether in town for work or play, with us you will want to stay! Either for long or short stays, be our guest during your visit to Bryan/College Station. Snowbirds welcome!
LUXURY AMENITIES INCLUDE: Theater, Clubhouse, Pickleball Court, Basketball Court, Gym, Meeting Room, Lodge Rental
3414 Colson Rd., Bryan, TX 77808
HardysResort.com
979-703-1201
Waco
Killeen
Temple
Belton
Georgetown
Round Rock
Austin
Madisonville
Centerville
Crockett
Hardy's Resort RV Park
Hardy's Landing RV Park
Navasota
Conroe
Spring

good sam park
Hardy's LANDING RV PARK
Luxurious Texas RV Park - We Accommodate All RV Sizes!
Huge spacious lots, FREE Laundry, Texas A&M Rellis Campus & Lake Bryan 2 Miles Away
6385 W OSR Rd. Bryan, TX 77807 • 979-286-3344 • HardysLanding.com
See listing Bryan, TX

COLLEGE STATION — C8 *Brazos*

KARSTENS RV RESORT **Ratings: 9/8.5★/8** (RV Park) Avail: 10 full hkups (30/50 amps). 2021 rates: $40 to $70. (979)774-7799, 6685 Elmo Weedon , College Station, TX 77845

COLORADO CITY — B5 *Mitchell*

LAKE COLORADO CITY (Public State Park) From Jct of I-20 & FM-2836 (exit 210), S 5.3 mi on FM-2836 (L) 15,000 # per axle or Tandem Bridge on FM 2836S (Entrance fee). 112 Avail: 112 W, 78 E (30/50 amps). 2021 rates: $15 to $22. (325)728-3931

LONE WOLF CREEK RV VILLAGE
good sam park **Ratings: 7.5/9★/7** (RV Park) Avail: 10 full hkups (30/50 amps). 2021 rates: $30. (325)728-9310, 1591 S Highway 208, Colorado City, TX 79512

COLUMBUS — D8 *Colorado*

COLORADO RIVER RV RESORT
good sam park **Ratings: 8.5/10★/7.5** (Membership Park) 121 Avail: 91 full hkups, 30 W, 30 E (30/50 amps). 2021 rates: $50 to $52. (888)563-7040, 1062 Thousand Trails Lane, Columbus, TX 78934

COMANCHE — B6 *Comanche*

PROCTOR LAKE - COE/COPPERAS CREEK (Public Corps) From town, NE 5 mi on US-377 to FM-2861, N 2.5 mi (R). 67 Avail: 67 W, 67 E (30/50 amps). 2021 rates: $16 to $38. (254)879-2498

PROCTOR LAKE - COE/PROMONTORY (Public Corps) From town, N 12 mi on Hwy 16 to FM-2318, E 5 mi (E). 57 Avail: 56 W, 57 E (30/50 amps). 2021 rates: $16 to $38. Apr 01 to Sep 30. (254)893-7545

RV SPACE-SAVING TIPS: Install an over-the-counter trashcan for the bathroom to save space and for easy clean up that isn't going to get knocked over. Keep a handheld vacuum handy (ideally attached to the wall/ceiling in the bathroom or closet) for quick and easy clean-up for after a sandy day at the beach or after the kids or grandkids eat lunch.

COMFORT — D6 *Kendall*

RV PARK USA
good sam park **Ratings: 8/9.5★/8.5** (RV Park) From Jct of I-10 & Hwy 87 (exit 523), exit to SW side (R). **FAC:** all weather rds. Avail: 67 gravel, patios, 12 pull-thrus, (25x70), back-ins (25x45), 67 full hkups (30/50 amps), cable, WiFi @ sites, tent sites, rentals, laundry. **REC:** hunting nearby. Pet restrict (B). Partial handicap access. Big rig sites, eco-friendly. 2021 rates: $45, Military discount.
(830)995-2900 Lat: 29.97996, Lon: -98.90713
108 Blueridge, Comfort, TX 78013
www.rvparkusa.com
See ad this page

COMSTOCK — D4 *Val Verde*

SEMINOLE CANYON STATE PARK & HISTORIC SITE (Public State Park) From Jct of US-90 & Hwy 163 (in town), W 8.6 mi on US-90 (L) (Entrance fee). 31 Avail: 31 W, 23 E (30 amps). 2021 rates: $10 to $20. (432)292-4464

CONCAN — D5 *Uvalde*

BECS STORE & RV PARK **Ratings: 8/9.5★/9.5** (RV Park) Avail: 50 full hkups (30/50 amps). 2021 rates: $45 to $65. (830)232-5477, 29015 N US Hwy 83, Concan, TX 78838

CAMP RIVER VIEW **Ratings: 8/9★/9** (Campground) 73 Avail: 35 full hkups, 38 W, 38 E (30/50 amps). 2021 rates: $55 to $60. (830)232-5412, 1636 CR 350, Concan, TX 78838

GARNER (Public State Park) From Jct of Hwy 127 & US-83, N 8.3 mi on US-83 to FM-1050, E 0.2 mi (R) (Entrance fee). 347 Avail: 51 full hkups, 296 W, 172 E (20/50 amps). 2021 rates: $20 to $35. (830)232-6132

Got something to tell us? We welcome your comments and suggestions regarding the ratings for a particular campground, or our rating system in general. Please email them to: Parks@goodsam.com

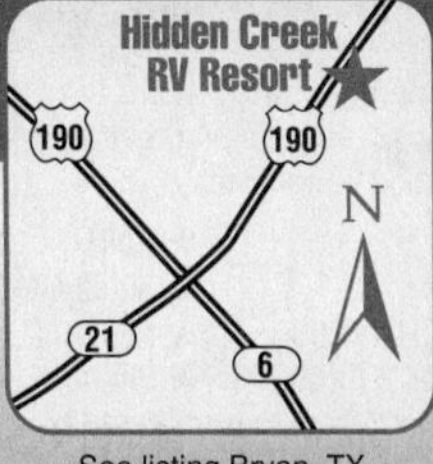

RV SPACE-SAVING TIPS: Hang a fruit and veggie hammock/basket. Use magnetic strips for hanging knives and scissors. Use dish cradles for storing dishes. Install a shelf system above your kitchen and/or toilet. This allows for extra storage space for light items, such as toilet paper, paper towels, bath towels, etc.

TRAVELING WITH YOUR PET: Know the rules. Visit GoodSam.com/campgrounds-rv-parks for pet restrictions at RV parks you're considering for your trip. Always call and ask before visiting. If you are allowed to bring a commonly prohibited breed, like a Pit Bull, Doberman or Rottweiler, go the extra mile to be an exemplary canine citizen.

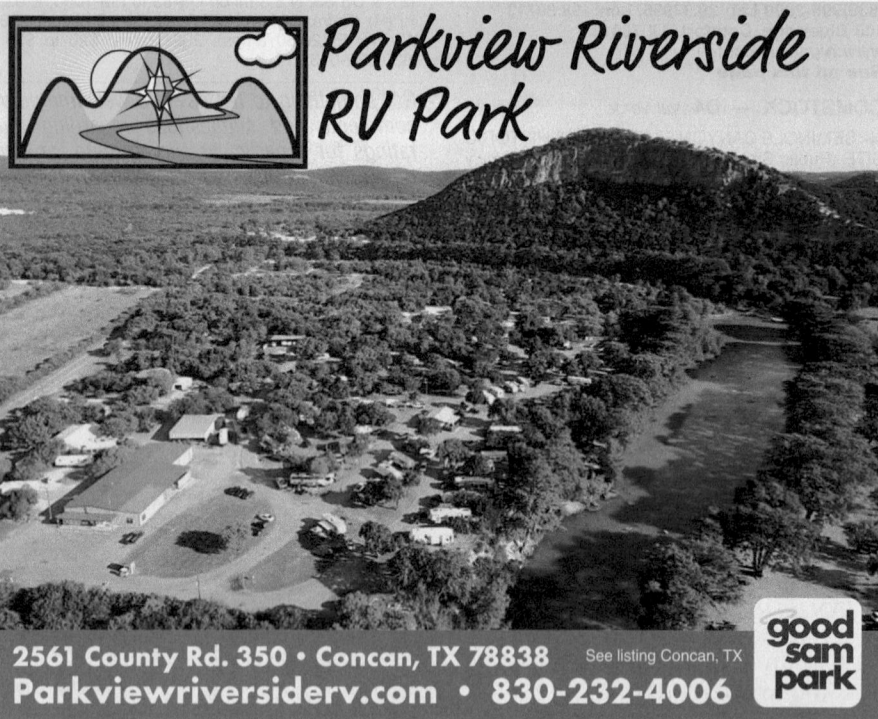

CONCAN (CONT)

PARKVIEW RIVERSIDE RV PARK

good sam park **Ratings: 9/9.5★/9** (RV Park) From Jct of Hwy 83 & Hwy 1050 (North of Concan), E 1.1mi on Hwy 1050 to CR-350, S 1.5 mi (R).

WINTER TRAVELERS SPECIAL

Enjoy our beautiful riverfront park in the heart of the Texas Hill Country. Moderate winter temperatures. Golf stay and play packages available at a top ranked golf course only 5 min away. Adjacent to Garner State Park.

FAC: paved rds. 99 Avail: 12 paved, 87 gravel, 17 pull-thrus, (28x65), back-ins (35x55), 99 full hkups (30/50 amps), WiFi @ sites, rentals, dump, laundry, groc, LP gas, fire rings, firewood. **REC:** Frio River: swim, fishing, kayaking/canoeing, boating nearby, hunting nearby. Pets OK. Partial handicap access. No tents. Big rig sites, eco-friendly. 2021 rates: $50 to $71, Military discount. ATM.
(830)232-4006 Lat: 29.58256, Lon: -99.72801
2561 County Road 350, Concan, TX 78838
parkviewriversiderv.com
See ad this page

RIVERBEND ON THE FRIO

good sam park **Ratings: 7/9.5★/8** (Campground) 40 Avail: 10 full hkups, 30 W, 30 E (30/50 amps). 2021 rates: $52 to $77. (830)232-6616, 32710 N Hwy 83, Concan, TX 78838

COOPER — A8 *Delta*

COOPER LAKE-DOCTORS CREEK UNIT (Public State Park) From Jct of Hwy 19/154 & 154, W 2.3 mi on Hwy 154 to FM 1529, S 1.6 mi (R); or From Jct of Hwy 19 & FM 1529, W 5.3 mi on FM 1529 (R) (Entrance fee). 39 Avail: 39 W, 39 E (30 amps). 2021 rates: $18. (903)395-3100

COOPER LAKE-SOUTH SULPHUR UNIT (Public State Park) From Jct of SR-19/SR-154 & FM-71, W 4.2 mi on FM-71 to FM-3505, N 1.4 mi on FM-3505 (E) (Entrance fee). 82 Avail: 82 W, 82 E (30 amps). 2021 rates: $20. (903)945-5256

CORPUS CHRISTI — E7 *Nueces*

CORPUS CHRISTI See also Aransas Pass, Port Aransas, Portland & Rockport.

COLONIA DEL REY RV PARK

good sam park **Ratings: 10/10★/9** (RV Park) From Jct of I-37 & Hwy 358 (Padre Island Dr), SE 15.7 mi on Hwy 358 to Waldron Rd exit, S 0.8 mi (L).

CORPUS CHRISTI'S FINEST RV PARK

Come explore the Beautiful Texas Coastal Bend! We are located only 5 miles from Sandy Padre Island. The best vacation spot on the TX Gulf Coast. Beaches, fine dining, shopping, golf courses and many more activities.

FAC: paved rds. (208 spaces). 34 Avail: 25 paved, 9 all weather, patios, 34 pull-thrus, (25x70), 34 full hkups (30/50 amps), seasonal sites, cable, WiFi @ sites, dump, laundry. **REC:** pool. Pet restrict (B). No tents. Big rig sites, eco-friendly. 2021 rates: $45 to $55.
(800)580-2435 Lat: 27.65783, Lon: -97.28857
1717 Waldron Rd, Corpus Christi, TX 78418
www.ccrvresorts.com
See ad this page, 868

GREYHOUND RV PARK **Ratings: 7.5/9.5★/7.5** (RV Park) Avail: 40 full hkups (30/50 amps). 2021 rates: $50. (361)289-2076, 5402 Leopard St, Corpus Christi, TX 78408

HATCH RV PARK
good sam park **Ratings: 8.5/9.5★/7.5** (RV Park) From Jct of I-37 & Nueces Bay Blvd (exit 1B in town), Go S 0.6 mi to Up River Rd then E on Up River Rd 2 blocks (R). **FAC:** paved rds. (127 spaces). 117 Avail: 10 paved, 85 gravel, 22 grass, patios, 32 pull-thrus, (22x80), back-ins (24x65), 117 full hkups (30/50 amps), seasonal sites, WiFi @ sites, laundry, LP gas, firewood. **REC:** pool, hot tub. Pets OK. No tents. Big rig sites, eco-friendly. 2021 rates: $48, Military discount.
(361)883-9781 Lat: 27.79367, Lon: -97.42455
3101 Up River Rd., Corpus Christi, TX 78408
www.hatchrv.com
See ad opposite page

MARINA VILLAGE MOBILE HOME & RV COMMUNITY **Ratings: 6.5/7/6** (RV Area in MH Park) Avail: 228 full hkups (30/50 amps). 2021 rates: $50. (361)937-2560, 229 NAS Drive, Corpus Christi, TX 78418

MILITARY PARK CORPUS CHRISTI RV PARK (CORPUS CHRISTI NAS) (Public) From town: Go 4 mi SW on TX-286 S, then 9 mi S on TX-358 E, then 1 mi E on Lexington Blvd, then 1 mi S on Ocean Dr (E). 92 Avail: 80 full hkups, 12 W, 12 E (30/50 amps). 2021 rates: $15 to $20. (361)961-1293

PADRE BALLI PARK (Public) From Jct of JFK Bridge & P-22, SW 3.5 mi on P-22 (L). 54 Avail: 54 W, 54 E (30 amps). 2021 rates: $25. (361)949-8121

PADRE PALMS RV PARK
good sam park **Ratings: 9.5/9.5★/8.5** (RV Park) From Jct of I-37 & Hwy 358 (Padre Island Dr), SE 15.5 mi on Hwy 358 to NAS Dr/CCAD exit, NE 0.4 mi to Skipper Ln, E 0.3 mi (R). **FAC:** paved rds. (84 spaces). 59 Avail: 34 paved, 25 grass, 59 pull-thrus, (17x70), mostly side by side hkups, 59 full hkups (30/50 amps), seasonal sites, cable, WiFi @ sites, dump, laundry. **REC:** pool, Laguna Madre: fishing, shuffleboard. Pet restrict (B). No tents, eco-friendly. 2021 rates: $55.
(361)937-2125 Lat: 27.67281, Lon: -97.27090
131 Skipper Lane, Corpus Christi, TX 78418
www.ccrvresorts.com
See ad opposite page

PUERTO DEL SOL RV PARK **Ratings: 7.5/8★/6.5** (RV Park) Avail: 53 full hkups (30/50 amps). 2021 rates: $45 to $55. (361)882-5373, 5100 Timon Blvd, Corpus Christi, TX 78402

SHADY GROVE RV PARK **Ratings: 7/9.5★/8.5** (RV Park) Avail: 35 full hkups (30/50 amps). 2021 rates: $50. (361)937-1314, 2919 Waldron Rd, Corpus Christi, TX 78418

CORSICANA — B7 *Navarro*

AMERICAN RV PARK **Ratings: 8/9★/7.5** (RV Park) Avail: 38 full hkups (30/50 amps). 2021 rates: $38. (903)872-0233, 4345 W Hwy 31, Corsicana, TX 75110

COTULLA — E6 *La Salle*

COTULLA/NUECES RIVER KOA
good sam park **Ratings: 8.5/9.5★/9** (RV Park) Avail: 150 full hkups (30/50 amps). 2021 rates: $45. (830)879-4181, 153 RV Park Rd, Cotulla, TX 78014

CROCKETT — C8 *Houston*

CROCKETT FAMILY RESORT COTTAGES, MARINA & RV PARK
good sam park **Ratings: 8/8/8** (Campground) Avail: 91 full hkups (30/50 amps). 2021 rates: $36 to $49. (936)544-8466, 75 Dogwood Lane West, Crockett, TX 75835

CRYSTAL BEACH — D9 *Galveston*

BOLIVAR PENINSULA RV PARK **Ratings: 6/7.5★/7.5** (RV Park) Avail: 90 full hkups (30/50 amps). 2021 rates: $45 to $60. (409)684-0939, 1685 Hwy 87, Crystal Beach, TX 77650

LAZY PELICAN RV PARK **Ratings: 6/NA/7.5** (RV Park) Avail: 35 full hkups (30/50 amps). 2021 rates: $45 to $55. (409)684-9909, 996 Sea Spray Dr, Crystal Beach, TX 77650

LITTLE SCHIPPERS RV PARK **Ratings: 7.5/NA/8** (RV Park) Avail: 23 full hkups (30/50 amps). 2021 rates: $65 to $130. (409)502-2542, 1811 Hwy 87, Crystal Beach, TX 77550

CRYSTAL CITY — E5 *Zavala*

CROSS S RV PARK **Ratings: 7.5/9.5★/8** (RV Park) Avail: 59 full hkups (30/50 amps). 2021 rates: $39 to $47. (830)374-9933, 3780 US-83, Crystal City, TX 78839

CUT AND SHOOT — C8 *Montgomery*

QRV CONROE **Ratings: 9/9★/9.5** (RV Park) Avail: 92 full hkups (30/50 amps). 2021 rates: $55 to $70. (936)264-2854, 3043 Waukegan Rd, Cut and Shoot, TX 77306

DAINGERFIELD — B9 *Morris*

DAINGERFIELD (Public State Park) From Jct of US-259 & SR-11/49, E 2.3 mi on SR-49 (R) (Entrance fee). Avail: 40 full hkups (30/50 amps). 2021 rates: $20 to $25. (903)645-2921

DALHART — E9 *Dallum*

CORRAL RV PARK
good sam park **Ratings: 8/9.5★/8.5** (RV Park) Avail: 65 full hkups (30/50 amps). 2021 rates: $32.50. (806)249-2798, 1202 Liberal, Dalhart, TX 79022

DALLAS — H4 *Dallas*

A SPOTLIGHT Introducing Dallas' colorful attractions appearing at the front of this state section.

DALLAS See also Alvarado, Alvord, Arlington, Aubrey, Caddo Mills, Canton, Carrollton, Fort Worth, Frisco, Glenn Heights, Granbury, Grand Prairie, Grapevine, Greenville, Lone Oak, Mansfield, Pilot Point, Poolville, Roanoke, Royse City, Terrell, Waxahachie, Weatherford, Whitney.

DAWSON — B7 *Bosque*

NAVARRO MILLS LAKE - COE/LIBERTY HILL (Public Corps) From town, NW 4 mi on FM-709 (R). 92 Avail: 14 full hkups, 78 W, 78 E (30/50 amps). 2021 rates: $18 to $40. (254)578-1431

NAVARRO MILLS LAKE - COE/PECAN POINT (Public Corps) From jct Hwy 31 & FM 667: Go 4 mi NW on FM 667, then 2-1/2 mi SW on FM 744, then 2 mi S on 1578, then at dead end 1/4 mi W. 33 Avail: 5 W, 5 E (50 amps), Pit toilets. 2021 rates: $12 to $14. Apr 01 to Sep 30. (254)578-1431

NAVARRO MILLS LAKE - COE/WOLF CREEK (Public Corps) From town, NE 3.5 mi on SR-31 to FM-667, NW 3 mi to FM-639, SW 2 mi (E). 72 Avail: 60 W, 50 E (30 amps). 2021 rates: $16 to $30. Apr 01 to Sep 30. (254)578-1431

DEL RIO — D5 *Val Verde*

AMERICAN CAMPGROUND **Ratings: 7/9★/7.5** (RV Park) Avail: 88 full hkups (30/50 amps). 2021 rates: $40. (830)734-6008, 10348 US Hwy 90 W, Del Rio, TX 78840

BROKE MILL RV PARK **Ratings: 9/10★/9** (RV Park) Avail: 80 full hkups (30/50 amps). 2021 rates: $37 to $42. (830)422-2961, 6069 W. US Hwy 90, Del Rio, TX 78840

LONESOME DOVE RV RANCH **Ratings: 6.5/NA/7.5** (RV Park) Avail: 20 full hkups (30/50 amps). 2021 rates: $28. (830)774-1823, 4832 Hwy 90 W, Del Rio, TX 78840

MILITARY PARK LAUGHLIN AFB FAMCAMP (LAUGHLIN AFB) (Public) From town: Go 5 mi SE on Dr Fermin Calderon Blvd, then 2 mi on TX-317 Spur N, then 3/4 mi on Arnold Blvd, then 2 blocks S on Liberty Dr (R). Avail: 20 full hkups (30/50 amps). 2021 rates: $25. (830)298-5830

DENISON — A7 *Grayson*

EISENHOWER (Public State Park) From Jct of US-75 & SR-91 (exit 72), NW 1.7 mi on SR-91 to FM-1310, W 1.8 mi (E) (Entrance fees). 154 Avail: 50 full hkups, 92 W, 45 E (30/50 amps). 2021 rates: $12 to $23. (903)465-1956

RED RIVER - COE/DENISON DAMSITE (Public Corps) From Jct of Hwy 75 & Hwy 91, N 1.8 mi on Hwy 91 to Denison Dam, follow signs (R). 30 Avail: 30 W, 30 E (30 amps). 2021 rates: $20. Apr 01 to Oct 31. (903)465-4990

DENTON — A7 *Denton*

Travel Services

CAMPING WORLD OF DENTON As the nation's largest retailer of RV supplies, accessories, services and new and used RVs, Camping World is committed to making your total RV experience better. **SERVICES:** RV appliance, MH mechanical, staffed RV wash, restrooms. RV Sales. RV supplies, LP gas, RV accessible. Hours: 9am to 7pm.
(844)969-0813 Lat: 33.246169, Lon: -97.177463
5209 I-35 North, Denton, TX 76207
www.campingworld.com

DENVER CITY — B3 *Yoakum*

YOAKUM COUNTY PARK (Public) From town, N 7 mi on SR-214 (R). 15 Avail: 10 W, 10 E (20 amps). 2021 rates: $14. (806)592-3166

DIANA — B9 *Upshur*

LAKE O THE PINES - COE/BRUSHY CREEK (Public Corps) From town, NW 4 mi on Hwy-49 to Hwy-729, W 3.5 mi to Hwy-726, S 4.9 mi (R). 49 Avail: 49 W, 49 E (30 amps). 2021 rates: $28 to $44. Mar 01 to Sep 30. (903)755-2637

DICKINSON — D9 *Galveston*

GALVESTON BAY RV RESORT AND MARINA **Ratings: 10/9★/9.5** (RV Resort) Avail: 168 full hkups (30/50 amps). 2021 rates: $55 to $80. (281)339-5550, 10000 San Leon Drive, Dickinson, TX 77539

MARQUEE ON THE BAY RV RESORT **Ratings: 8.5/9★/9.5** (RV Park) Avail: 77 full hkups (30/50 amps). 2021 rates: $40. (281)339-1260, 9900 San Leon Drive, Dickinson, TX 77539

USA RV RESORTS LAKE COVE **Ratings: 10/9.5★/9** (RV Resort) Avail: 94 full hkups (30/50 amps). 2021 rates: $49. (281)337-6817, 2601 Wyoming, Dickinson, TX 77539

DONNA — M3 *Hidalgo*

BIG VALLEY RV RESORT **Ratings: 9.5/9★/8.5** (RV Park) Avail: 219 full hkups (30/50 amps). 2021 rates: $38. (956)464-4159, 109 W Business Hwy 83, Donna, TX 78537

BIT-O-HEAVEN RV & MOBILE HOME PARK **Ratings: 9/9★/7.5** (RV Area in MH Park) Avail: 315 full hkups (50 amps). 2021 rates: $45. (956)464-5191, 1051 W Bus Hwy 83, Donna, TX 78537

CASA DEL SOL MH & RV RESORT **Ratings: 9.5/9★/8** (RV Park) Avail: 180 full hkups (30/50 amps). 2021 rates: $50 to $60. (956)464-2272, 400 N Val Verde Rd, Donna, TX 78537

MAGNOLIA VILLAGE MHP & RV PARK **Ratings: 7.5/7.5/7** (RV Park) Avail: 10 full hkups (30/50 amps). 2021 rates: $45. (956)464-2421, 3707 E. Hwy Business 83, Donna, TX 78537

VICTORIA PALMS RESORT
good sam park **Ratings: 10/9.5★/9** (RV Park) Avail: 728 full hkups (30/50 amps). 2021 rates: $55 to $76. (888)563-7040, 602 N Victoria Rd, Donna, TX 78537

EASTLAND — B6 *Eastland*

EASTLAND RV PARK **Ratings: 6/8★/7** (RV Park) Avail: 20 full hkups (30/50 amps). 2021 rates: $45 to $50. (254)433-1359, 202 CR 237, Eastland, TX 76448

WANDERING OAKS RV PARK **Ratings: 6.5/9.5★/8** (RV Park) Avail: 48 full hkups (30/50 amps). 2021 rates: $40. (254)433-9090, 10502 IH 20, Eastland, TX 76448

EDINBURG — M3 *Hidalgo*

ORANGE GROVE RV PARK **Ratings: 8.5/9★/8** (RV Park) Avail: 125 full hkups (30/50 amps). 2021 rates: $50. (956)383-7931, 5005 E State Hwy 107, Edinburg, TX 78542

RV Tech Tips - Hands Free Washing: Make your exterior shower and compartment hands free. The shower offers hot and cold water, but using it requires holding the showerhead with one hand while washing with the other. To make the shower hands-free, use an old hose holder, form it around the bumper and mount an adjustable rod onto the frame. You can then place the showerhead on the rod and wash up using both hands.

EDNA — D7 *Jackson*

BRACKENRIDGE RECREATION COMPLEX - BRACKENRIDGE PARK & CAMPGROUND
good sam park
Ratings: 8/9★/9.5 (Public) From Jct of US-59 & Hwy 111, E 7.5 mi on Hwy 111 (R). **FAC:** paved rds. 134 Avail: 102 paved, 32 gravel, 16 pull-thrus, (35x50), back-ins (30x40), 98 full hkups, 36 W, 36 E (30/50 amps), WiFi @ sites, tent sites, rentals, dump, laundry, groc, fire rings, firewood, controlled access. **REC:** Lake Texana: swim, fishing, kayaking/canoeing, playground, rec open to public. Pet restrict (B/Q). Partial handicap access. Big rig sites, eco-friendly. 2021 rates: $30 to $35.
(361)782-5456 Lat: 28.94214, Lon: -96.53978
891 Brackenridge Pkwy, Edna, TX 77957
www.brackenridgepark.com
See ad this page

BRACKENRIDGE RECREATION COMPLEX-TEXANA PARK & CAMPGROUND
good sam park
Ratings: 7.5/9★/9.5 (Public) From Jct 111 & 59: Go 7 mi E on Hwy 111 to Brackenridge Pkwy (L). **FAC:** paved rds. Avail: 141 paved, back-ins (30x50), 63 full hkups, 78 W, 78 E (30/50 amps), WiFi, tent sites, rentals, dump, groc, fire rings, firewood, controlled access. **REC:** Lake Texana: swim, fishing, kayaking/canoeing, playground, rec open to public. Pet restrict (B/Q). Partial handicap access, eco-friendly. 2021 rates: $30 to $35.
(361)782-5718 Lat: 28.95706, Lon: -96.543812
46 Park Road 1, Edna, TX 77957
www.brackenridgepark.com
See ad this page

FIVE COATS RV PARK **Ratings: 6.5/NA/7.5** (Campground) Avail: 46 full hkups (30/50 amps). 2021 rates: $40. (361)782-5109, 87 FM 234 South, Edna, TX 77957

TWIN LAKES RV PARK
good sam park
Ratings: 6/NA/8 (RV Park) Avail: 70 full hkups (30/50 amps). 2021 rates: $40. (361)782-1431, 397 Private Rd 3190, Edna, TX 77957

Things to See and Do

BRACKENRIDGE MAIN EVENT CENTER The Brackenridge Main Event Center is a multi-purpose facility that hosts a wide variety of events, situated on 188 acres adjacent to Brackenridge Park & Campground. Partial handicap access. RV accessible. Restrooms. Food. Hours: . ATM.
(361)782-7272 Lat: 28.95313, Lon: -96.54257
284 Brackenridge Parkway, Edna, TX 77957
www.brackenridgepark.com
See ad this page

Refer to the Table of Contents in front of the Guide to locate everything you need.

EL CAMPO — D8 *Wharton*

CREEKSIDE RV RANCH & HORSE HOTEL **Ratings: 5.5/8.5★/6.5** (RV Park) Avail: 10 full hkups (30/50 amps). 2021 rates: $50. (713)289-4717, 1621 County Rd 406, El Campo, TX 77437

EL PASO — B1 *El Paso*

EL PASO See also Anthony & Canutillo.

EL PASO ROADRUNNER RV PARK **Ratings: 7/9★/7** (RV Park) Avail: 73 full hkups (30/50 amps). 2021 rates: $41.95. (915)598-4469, 1212 Lafayette, El Paso, TX 79907

HUECO TANKS STATE HISTORIC SITE (Public State Park) From Jct of US-62/180 (Montana St) & FM-659/Zargoza (E edge of town), E 8.5 mi on US-62/180 to RR-2775, N 8 mi (E) (Entrance fee). 20 Avail: 20 W, 20 E (50 amps). 2021 rates: $12 to $16. (800)792-1112

MILITARY PARK FORT BLISS RV PARK (FORT BLISS) (Public) From town: Go 2 mi E on I-10E, then 3 mi N on US-54 E, then take exit 25 toward Ellerthorpe Ave, then left onto Gerlich St and continue on Gateway Blvd (R). Avail: 133 full hkups (30/50 amps). 2021 rates: $18 to $20. (915)568-4693

MISSION RV PARK
good sam park
Ratings: 9.5/9.5★/8 (RV Park) From Jct I-10 & Exit 35: Go 1/4 mi N on Eastlake, then 1 1/3 mi W on Rojas, then 1 Block S (past the trailer park) on RV Drive (L). Elev 3770 ft.**FAC:** paved rds. (188 spaces). Avail: 80 gravel, patios, 72 pull-thrus, (24x70), back-ins (33x40), 80 full hkups (30/50 amps), seasonal sites, cable, WiFi @ sites, tent sites, dump, laundry, LP gas. **REC:** heated pool, hot tub, playground. Pet restrict (B). Big rig sites, eco-friendly. 2021 rates: $32 to $44, Military discount.
(915)859-1133 Lat: 31.70105, Lon: -106.28031
1420 RV Dr., El Paso, TX 79928
missionrvparklp.com
See ad opposite page

MISSION TRAIL MOBILE HOME & RV VILLAGE
good sam park
(RV Park) (Rebuilding) Avail: 15 full hkups (30/50 amps). 2021 rates: $35. (915)859-0202, 8479 Alameda Ave, El Paso, TX 79907

ENNIS — B7 *Ellis*

BARDWELL - COE/LAKE HIGH VIEW (Public Corps) From Jct of I-45 & US-287 Bypass/Exit 247, W 4.5 mi on US-287 to Bardwell Lake exit/Hwy 34, SW 2.5 mi on Hwy 34 to High View Park Rd, SE 0.2 mi to park entrance. 39 Avail: 39 W, 39 E (30/50 amps). 2021 rates: $14 to $16. (972)875-5711

Don't miss a thing! Check out the Table of Contents for everything the Guide has to offer.

BARDWELL LAKE - COE/MOTT PARK (Public Corps) From town, SW 5.5 mi on SH-34 (over bridge), SE 1.7 mi on FM-985. 33 Avail: 33 W, 33 E (30/50 amps). 2021 rates: $14 to $16. Apr 01 to Sep 30. (972)875-5711

BARDWELL LAKE - COE/WAXAHACHIE CREEK (Public Corps) From Jct of I-45 & US-287 Bypass (exit 247), W 4.5 mi on US-287 to Bardwell Lake exit/Hwy 34, SW 3 mi on Hwy 34 to Bozek Rd, NW 1.5 mi (E). 58 Avail: 58 W, 58 E (30/50 amps). 2021 rates: $16 to $18. Apr 01 to Sep 30. (972)875-5711

EUSTACE — B8 *Henderson*

PURTIS CREEK (Public State Park) From Jct US-175 & FM-316, N 3.4 mi on FM-316 (L) (Entrance fee). 59 Avail: 59 W, 59 E (20/30 amps). 2021 rates: $20. (903)425-2332

EVANT — C6 *Coryell*

BUENA VISTA WILDLIFE SAFARI AND RV PARK **Ratings: 8.5/9.5★/9** (RV Park) Avail: 35 full hkups (30/50 amps). 2021 rates: $35 to $45. (254)791-5441, 1830 S. US Hwy 281, Evant, TX 76525

FAIRFIELD — B8 *Freestone*

FAIRFIELD LAKE (Public State Park) From Jct of US-84 & FM-488 (in town), NE 1.7 mi on FM-488 to FM-2570, N 1.2 mi to FM-3285, E 3 mi (E) (Entrance fee). 130 Avail: 130 W, 96 E (20/30 amps). 2021 rates: $15 to $20. (903)389-4514

FALCON HEIGHTS — L2 *Zapata*

FALCON (Public State Park) From Jct of US-83 & FM-2098, SW 2.6 mi on FM-2098 to Park Rd 46, N 1 mi (L). Entrance fee required. 98 Avail: 31 full hkups, 67 W, 31 E (50 amps). 2021 rates: $10 to $18. (956)848-5327

FENTRESS — D7 *Caldwell*

LEISURE RESORT
good sam park
Ratings: 7.5/8/9 (RV Park) From Jct of I-10 & SR-80 (exit 628), N 11.8 mi on SR-80 to FM-20, S 0.3 mi to CR-125, E 0.4 mi, follow signs (E); or From Jct of I-35 & Exit 205, SE 13.3 mi on SR-80 to FM-20, S 0.3 mi to CR-125, E 0.4 mi, follow signs (E). **FAC:** paved/gravel rds. (117 spaces). 93 Avail: 66 paved, 27 gravel, 46 pull-thrus, (22x90), back-ins (27x65), 48 full hkups, 45 W, 45 E (30/50 amps), seasonal sites, tent sites, rentals, shower$, dump, laundry, firewood, controlled access. **REC:** pool, San Marcos River: swim, fishing, boating nearby, playground, rec open to public. Pets OK. Partial handicap access. Big rig sites. 2021 rates: $49 to $70, Military discount.
(512)213-0112 Lat: 29.74770, Lon: -97.77580
745 S Main, Fentress, TX 78622
www.leisurecamp.net
See ad page 916

FLOYDADA — A4 *Floyd*

FLOYDADA OVERNIGHT RV PARK (Public) From jct Hwy 207/62 & US 70: Go 1 mi NW on US 70 to park entrance. Avail: 24 E (30 amps), Pit toilets. (806)983-2834

FORT DAVIS — C3 *Jeff Davis*

DAVIS MOUNTAIN RV PARK (RV Park) (Too New to Rate) Avail: 24 full hkups (30/50 amps). 2021 rates: $30. (432)249-0327, 43125 N. Hwy 17, Fort Davis, TX 79734

DAVIS MOUNTAINS (Public State Park) From N Jct of Hwys 17 & 118, W 2.8 mi on Hwy 118 (L) (Entrance fee). 126 Avail: 26 full hkups, 67 W, 34 E (20/50 amps). 2021 rates: $15 to $25. (432)426-3337

MACMILLEN RV PARK
good sam park
Ratings: 6/9★/8 (Campground) Avail: 28 full hkups (30/50 amps). 2021 rates: $35. (432)426-2056, 43424 TX-17, Fort Davis, TX 79734

FORT STOCKTON — C3 *Pecos*

FORT STOCKTON RV PARK **Ratings: 8/9★/9.5** (Campground) Avail: 90 full hkups (30/50 amps). 2021 rates: $40. (432)395-2494, 3604 KOA Rd, Fort Stockton, TX 79735

HILLTOP RV PARK
good sam park
Ratings: 7.5/8.5★/9 (RV Park) Avail: 66 full hkups (30/50 amps). 2021 rates: $35. (432)336-6090, 4076 IH-10 West, Fort Stockton, TX 79735

Save 10% at Good Sam Parks 365 days a year with no blackout dates!!

Here at Mission RV Park, we offer a clean park in a quiet country setting that is only minutes from shopping, restaurants and recreation. We invite you to come out and stay with us. Along with our pleasant hospitality, we promise you rest, relaxation and enjoyment on our 15.5 acres of aged shade trees.

See listing El Paso, TX

- Full Hookups
- 30/50 Amp Services
- Volleyball Court
- Basketball Court
- Laundry Rooms
- Playground For Children
- Clubhouse
- Large Swimming Pool • Spa
- Free WiFi • Cable
- Night Patrol Supervision

(915) 859-1133 • I-10 Exit 35 • 1420 R.V. Drive 79928

MissionRVParklp.com

TX

Enjoy the scenery as you travel North America. We exclusively rate campgrounds for their visual appearance and environmental quality, and represent their score, 1 through 10, as the third rating in our Triple Rating System.

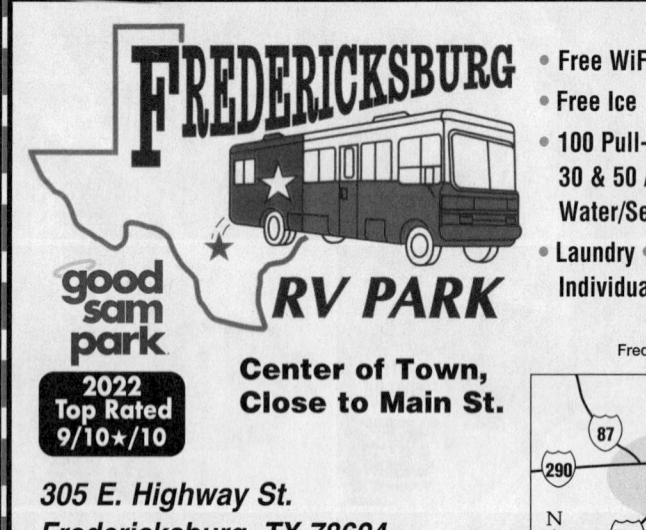

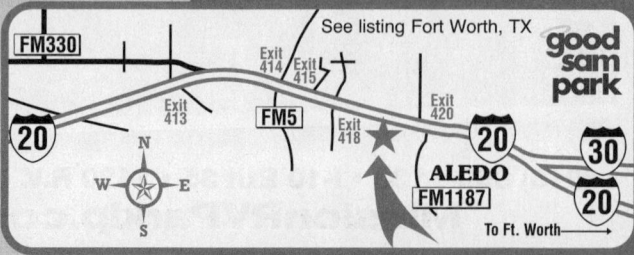

FORT WORTH — H2 *Tarrant*

A SPOTLIGHT Introducing Fort Worth's colorful attractions appearing at the front of this state section.

FORT WORTH See also Alvarado, Alvord, Arlington, Aubrey, Caddo Mills, Canton, Carrollton, Dallas, Denton, Frisco, Glenn Heights, Granbury, Grand Prairie, Grapevine, Greenville, Lone Oak, Mansfield, Pilot Point, Poolville, Roanoke, Royse City, Terrell, Waxahachie, Weatherford, Whitney.

BENBROOK LAKE - COE/BEAR CREEK (Public Corps) From town, S 6.2 mi on US-377 to FM-1187, E 1.4 mi to CR-1125 (Ben Day Murrin Rd), N 1.7 mi (L). 46 Avail: 2 full hkups, 44 W, 44 E (30/50 amps), Pit toilets. 2021 rates: $28. Apr 01 to Sep 30. (817)292-2400

COWTOWN RV PARK
good sam park **Ratings: 9/9.5★/9** (RV Park) From Jct I-20 (exit 418) & Ranch House Rd: Go 1 mi E on S Frontage Rd. (R). **FAC:** paved/gravel rds. (168 spaces). 33 Avail: 25 paved, 8 gravel, 33 pull-thrus, (27x65), 33 full hkups (30/50 amps), seasonal sites, cable, WiFi @ sites, dump, laundry, LP gas. **REC:** pool, playground. Pet restrict (B/Q). Partial handicap access. No tents. Big rig sites. 2021 rates: $42, Military discount.
(817)441-7878 Lat: 32.72986, Lon: -97.61420
7000 I-20 East, Aledo, TX 76008
www.cowtownrvpark.com
See ad this page

LAKEVIEW RV & MH COMMUNITY
good sam park **Ratings: 6.5/NA/7** (RV Park) Avail: 10 full hkups (30/50 amps). 2021 rates: $55. (800)767-7756, 4793 E Loop 820 South, Fort Worth, TX 76119

Travel Services

CAMPING WORLD OF FORT WORTH As the nation's largest retailer of RV supplies, accessories, services and new and used RVs, Camping World is committed to making your total RV experience better. **SERVICES:** restrooms. RV Sales. RV supplies, LP gas, RV accessible. Hours: 9am - 7pm.
(844)996-1514 Lat: 32.804913, Lon: -97.428008
6001 Quebec St, Fort Worth, TX 76135
www.campingworld.com

FREDERICKSBURG — C6 *Gillespie*

BENDING OAK RANCH RV RESORT **Ratings: 8.5/8.5★/8** (RV Park) Avail: 54 full hkups (30/50 amps). 2021 rates: $46 to $59. (830)997-4796, 5681 US Hwy 290 East, Fredericksburg, TX 78624

FREDERICKSBURG RV PARK
good sam park **Ratings: 9/10★/10** (RV Park) From Jct of US 290 & S US 87 (Washington St): Go 3/4 mi SE on Hwy 87, then 1/2 block W on Highway St (L). **FAC:** paved rds. (105 spaces). Avail: 80 all weather, patios, 74 pull-thrus, (30x70), back-ins (25x60), 80 full hkups (30/50 amps), seasonal sites, cable, WiFi @ sites, laundry. **REC:** pond, shuffleboard, hunting nearby. Pet restrict (B). Partial handicap access. No tents. Big rig sites, eco-friendly. 2021 rates: $53 to $63, Military discount.
(830)990-9582 Lat: 30.26143, Lon: -98.87439
305 E Highway St, Fredericksburg, TX 78624
fbgrvpark.com
See ad this page

LADY BIRD JOHNSON MUNICIPAL PARK (Public) From Jct of US-290 & SR-16S: Go 3-1/2 mi S on SR 16S, then 1/4 mi W on Lady Bird Dr (E). Avail: 98 full hkups (30/50 amps). 2021 rates: $40. (830)997-4202

OAKWOOD RV RESORT **Ratings: 9/9★/8.5** (RV Park) Avail: 102 full hkups (30/50 amps). 2021 rates: $37 to $65. (830)997-9817, 78 FM 2093, Fredericksburg, TX 78624

TEXAS WINE COUNTRY JELLYSTONE PARK CAMP-RESORT **Ratings: 9/9.5★/8.5** (Campground) Avail: 50 full hkups (30/50 amps). 2021 rates: $53 to $77. (830)997-6100, 10618 E US Hwy 290, Fredericksburg, TX 78624

THE VINEYARDS AT FREDERICKSBURG RV PARK
good sam park **Ratings: 9.5/10★/9.5** (RV Park) Avail: 149 full hkups (30/50 amps). 2021 rates: $45 to $60. (830)992-1237, 2647 N US Hwy 87, Fredericksburg, TX 78624

FREEPORT — D8 *Brazoria*

BLUE WATER RV RESORT
good sam park **Ratings: 10/9.5★/10** (RV Resort) From jct FM 1495 & TX-332: Go 3-1/2 mi S on TX-332, then 11 mi E on Bluewater Hwy (L). **FAC:** paved rds. Avail: 179 paved, patios, 14 pull-thrus, (30x75), back-ins (32x65), 179 full hkups (30/50 amps), cable, WiFi @ sites, rentals, laundry, groc, controlled access. **REC:** pool, Gulf of Mexico: swim, fishing, kayaking/canoeing, boating nearby, playground. Pet restrict (Q). Partial handicap access. No tents. Big rig sites, eco-friendly. 2021 rates: $55 to $105, Military discount.
(979)239-4301 Lat: 29.05788, Lon: -95.14387
11511 Bluewater Hwy, Freeport, TX 77541
www.bluewaterrvpark.com
See ad opposite page

QUINTANA BEACH COUNTY PARK (BRAZORIA COUNTY) (Public) From Jct of Hwy 36/288 & FM-1495, SW 1.7 mi on FM-1495 to FM-723, NE 3 mi to 5th St, S 0.1 mi (E). Avail: 56 full hkups (30/50 amps). 2021 rates: $20 to $32. (800)872-7578

FRISCO — A7 *Denton*

HIDDEN COVE RV PARK & MARINA **Ratings: 7/8/9.5** (RV Park) 88 Avail: 46 full hkups, 42 W, 42 E (30/50 amps). 2021 rates: $50 to $70. (972)294-1443, 20400 Hackberry Creek Park Rd, Frisco, TX 75034

FRITCH — F9 *Hutchinson*

LAKE MEREDITH NRA/BLUE WEST (Public National Park) From Amarillo, N 35 mi on Hwy 287, E 15.5 mi on Ranch Rd. 1913, E 3.1 mi on Blue West Rd. 20 Avail: Pit toilets. (806)857-3151

GALVESTON — D9 *Galveston*

A SPOTLIGHT Introducing Galveston Island's colorful attractions appearing at the front of the state section.

DELLANERA RV PARK

(Public) From Jct of I-45 & 61st St Exit (Spur Rd 342), S 1.7 mi on 61st to Seawall Blvd, W 3.2 mi (becomes San Luis Pass Rd) (L). **FAC:** paved rds. Avail: 65 paved, patios, 21 pull-thrus, (20x55), back-ins (18x40), 65 full hkups (30/50 amps), WiFi @ sites, laundry, groc. **REC:** Gulf of Mexico: swim, fishing, kayaking/canoeing. Pets OK. Partial handicap access. No tents, eco-friendly. 2021 rates: $43.05 to $76.

(409)797-5102 Lat: 29.24207, Lon: -94.87220
10901 Termini-San Luis Pass Rd, Galveston, TX 77554
dellanerarvpark.com
See ad page 878

GALVESTON ISLAND (Public State Park) From Jct of I-45 & 61st St exit, S 1.7 mi on 61st St to Seawall Blvd (FM-3005), W 9.2 mi (becomes San Luis Pass Rd), (L) (Entrance fee). 20 Avail: 20 W, 20 E (30/50 amps). 2021 rates: $20. (409)737-1222

Do you know how to read each part of a listing? Check the How to Use This Guide in the front.

JAMAICA BEACH RV RESORT

good sam park **Ratings: 10/10★/10** (RV Resort) From Jct of I-45 & 61st St. exit (1A), S 1.7 mi to Seawall Blvd (FM-3005), W 11 mi (R).

BEAUTY ON GALVESTON ISLAND

Come enjoy a Jamaican style resort nestled among our beautiful foliage & gorgeous variety of palms! Take a splash in one of our pools or just relax as you float along our Lazy River sipping on your favorite beverage!

FAC: paved rds. Avail: 181 paved, patios, 181 pull-thrus, (31x65), 181 full hkups (30/50 amps), cable, WiFi @ sites, rentals, laundry, groc, LP gas. **REC:** heated pool, wading pool, hot tub, Gulf of Mexico: swim, fishing, kayaking/canoeing, boating nearby, playground. Pet restrict (B/Q). Partial handicap access. No tents. Big rig sites, eco-friendly. 2021 rates: $49 to $89, Military discount.

(409)632-0200 Lat: 29.178319, Lon: -94.982501
17200 FM 3005, Galveston, TX 77554
www.jbrv.net
See ad next page

SAN LUIS PASS COUNTY PARK (BRAZORIA COUNTY PARK) (Public) On CR 257 (Blue Water Hwy) at the south end of Galveston Island. Cross over toll bridge. Avail: 69 full hkups (30/50 amps). 2021 rates: $35 to $43. (800)372-7578

Keeping pets quiet and on a leash is common courtesy. ""Pet Restrictions'' which you'll find in some listings refers to limits on size, breed or quantity of pets allowed.

Jamaica Beach RV Resort
ACROSS FROM GULF OF MEXICO
• Pool • Spa
• Splash Pond
• Indoor Infinity Spa
• Playground • Propane
• Pull-Thru Sites
• Club House
• 30/50 Amp Service
• Full Hookups • Cable TV
• Mini Golf Course
• Planned Activities
• Free WiFi • Pet Area • Fishing
• Laundry • Fitness Center
• Large Outdoor Movie Theater
• Beach Pool w/Zero Entrance & Cabaña Bar
ECO-FRIENDLY
I-45
FM 3005
11 miles
61st
Seawall
Galveston Island
Gulf of Mexico
MINUTES AWAY FROM:
~Moody Gardens • The Strand • NASA • Schlitterbahn • Cruise Lines~
good sam park
2022 Top Rated 10/10★/10
17200 FM 3005
Galveston Island, Texas
866-725-5511
409-632-0200
reservations@jbrv.net
www.jbrv.net
See listing Galveston, TX

GALVESTON (CONT)

SANDPIPER RV RESORT

good sam park **Ratings: 10/9.5★/9.5** (RV Park) From I-45 in Galveston (Broadway St), continue S .5 mi on Broadway St to Seawall Blvd (curve left), E 0.3 mi on Seawall Blvd (R). **FAC:** paved rds. Avail: 40 paved, patios, 8 pull-thrus, (30x75), back-ins (30x65), 40 full hkups (30/50 amps), cable, WiFi @ sites, rentals, laundry, controlled access. **REC:** pool, hot tub, Gulf of Mexico: swim, fishing, kayaking/canoeing, playground. Pet restrict (B/Q). Partial handicap access. No tents. Big rig sites, eco-friendly. 2021 rates: $50 to $135, Military discount.
(409)765-9431 Lat: 29.30926, Lon: -94.76811
201 Seawall Blvd., Galveston, TX 77550
www.sandpiperrvresort.com
See ad page 897

ST. IVES RV RESORT

good sam park **Ratings: 9/9.5★/9** (RV Resort) From jct Spur 342 & I-45: Go 6 mi N on I-45, then 5-3/4 mi N on FM 2004S, then 11-1/4 mi W on Hwy 6, then 4-1/2 mi N on FM 2917 (R). **FAC:** gravel rds. (72 spaces). Avail: 72 gravel, 54 pull-thrus, (45x100), back-ins (45x75), 72 full hkups (30/50 amps), WiFi @ sites, laundry, controlled access. **REC:** pool. Pet restrict (B/Q). Partial handicap access. No tents. Big rig sites. 2021 rates: $55.
(832)717-9393 Lat: 29.295222, Lon: -95.224624
4959 FM 2917, Alvin, TX 77511
stivesrvresort.com
See primary listing at Alvin and ad page 884

STELLA MARE RV RESORT **Ratings: 10/9.5★/9.5** (RV Park) Avail: 195 full hkups (30/50 amps). 2021 rates: $69 to $86. (409)632-7017, 3418 Stella Mare Lane, Galveston, TX 77554

GARLAND — B7 *Dallas*

LAKESHORE RV RESORT

good sam park (RV Resort) (Too New to Rate) I-30 Westbound: Take exit 62 and go 3/4 mi W on W I-30 Service Rd (R) I-30 Eastbound: Take exit 62 and go 1/2 mi E on E I-30 Service Rd, then 1 blk S on Chaha Rd, then 300ft N on Bass Pro Dr, then take the first turn left on I-30 connection Rd, then go 1/2 mi W on W I-30 Service Rd (R).

NEW RV RESORT IN GARLAND, TX
First-class RV Resort on the shores of Lake Ray Hubbard. Concrete roads & sites, world class activity building with observation deck, beach access pool with hot tub, computer room, fitness center. Close to Dallas Attractions

FAC: paved rds. Avail: 184 paved, 70 pull-thrus, (32x65), back-ins (32x50), 184 full hkups (30/50 amps), WiFi @ sites, laundry. **REC:** Lake Ray Hubbard: swim, fishing, kayaking/canoeing, boating nearby. Pets OK. Partial handicap access. No tents. Big rig sites. 2021 rates: $79 to $99.
(469)661-3827 Lat: 32.860293, Lon: -96.551222
1233 E Interstate 30, Garland, TX 75043
lakeshorervresort.com
See ad pages 876, 901

GEORGETOWN — C7 *Travis*

BERRY SPRINGS RV PARK

good sam park **Ratings: 7.5/9★/8.5** (RV Park) N-bnd: From Jct of I-35 & Exit 265, N 1.2 mi on E Fntg Rd to Market St, E 0.3 mi (L); or S-bnd: From Jct of I-35 & Exit 266, to W Fntg Rd, (pass thru Hwy 195 intersection, stay in center ln), S 1.5 mi on W Fntg Rd, cross I-35 at double bridge, N 0.7 mi on E Fntg Rd to Market St, E 0.3 mi (L). **FAC:** paved rds. (155 spaces). Avail: 35 gravel, patios, 35 pull-thrus, (36x80), 35 full hkups (30/50 amps), seasonal sites, WiFi @ sites, laundry. Pet restrict (Q). No tents. Big rig sites. 2021 rates: $40, Military discount.
(512)864-2724 Lat: 30.69271, Lon: -97.64938
131 Market St, Georgetown, TX 78626
www.berryspringsrv.com
See ad this page

EAST VIEW RV RANCH

good sam park **Ratings: 8/8.5★/8.5** (RV Park) Avail: 50 full hkups (30/50 amps). 2021 rates: $42. (512)931-2251, 552 Eastview Dr, Georgetown, TX 78626

We make finding the perfect campground easier. Just use the ""Find-it-Fast" index in the back of the Guide. It's a complete, state-by-state, alphabetical listing of our private and public park listings.

NEW LIFE RV PARK

good sam park **Ratings: 9.5/9.5★/9** (RV Park) Avail: 12 full hkups (30/50 amps). 2021 rates: $45. (512)931-2073, 1200 County Rd 152, Georgetown, TX 78626

STONE OAK RANCH RV RESORT **Ratings: 10/9.5★/9.5** (RV Resort) Avail: 227 full hkups (30/50 amps). 2021 rates: $59 to $65. (512)710-4343, 25101 Ronald W Reagan Blvd, Georgetown, TX 78633

GIDDINGS — D7 *Robertson*

GIDDINGS RV PARK **Ratings: 8/9★/7.5** (RV Park) Avail: 50 full hkups (30/50 amps). 2021 rates: $39. (979)325-0412, 1850 West Austin Street, Giddings, TX 78942

GLADEWATER — B8 *Gregg*

ANTIQUE CAPITAL RV PARK **Ratings: 9.5/10★/9.5** (RV Park) Avail: 50 full hkups (30/50 amps). 2021 rates: $38.50. (903)845-7378, 500 S Loop 485, Gladewater, TX 75647

SHALLOW CREEK RV RESORT

good sam park **Ratings: 10/10★/10** (RV Park) From Jct of I-20 (exit 583) & SR 135: Go 1-1/2 mi N on SR 135 (R).

EAST TEXAS PINEY WOODS BEST
In the Longview area and Gladewater's Antique District, enjoy sparkling pool, hot tub and splashpad. Nearby activities & Lonestar Speedway will round out your stay. Reserve now for this Top Rated Destination.

FAC: paved rds. (63 spaces). Avail: 43 paved, patios, 16 pull-thrus, (31x90), back-ins (35x70), 43 full hkups (30/50 amps), seasonal sites, cable, WiFi @ sites, dump, laundry, LP gas, fire rings. **REC:** pool, hot tub, pond, fishing, golf, playground. Pet restrict (B/Q). Partial handicap access. No tents, Age restrict may apply. Big rig sites. 2021 rates: $40.
(888)984-4513 Lat: 32.45467, Lon: -94.93566
5261 Hwy 135 N, Gladewater, TX 75647
www.shallowcreek.com
See ad this page

GLEN ROSE — B7 *Somervell*

DINOSAUR VALLEY (Public State Park) From Jct of US-67 & FM-205 (Park Rd 59), W 2.8 mi on FM-205 (Park Rd 59), NW 0.4 mi on Park Rd 59 (E) (Entrance fee). 44 Avail: 44 W, 44 E (30 amps). 2021 rates: $25. (254)897-4588

DINOSAUR VALLEY RV PARK

good sam park **Ratings: 10/9.5★/8.5** (RV Park) Avail: 80 full hkups (30/50 amps). 2021 rates: $49. (888)996-3466, 1099 Park Road 59, Glen Rose, TX 76043

OAKDALE PARK **Ratings: 9.5/9.5★/8** (RV Park) Avail: 120 full hkups (30/50 amps). 2021 rates: $39.95 to $49.95. (254)897-2321, 1019 NE Barnard Street, Glen Rose, TX 76043

GLENN HEIGHTS — J4 *Dallas*

DALLAS HI HO RV PARK

Ratings: 6/8.5/7 (RV Park) From Jct of I-20 & I-35 E: Go 5 mi S on I-35 E (exit 412), then 2-1/2 mi W on Bear Creek Rd (L). **FAC:** paved/gravel rds. (125 spaces). Avail: 12 gravel, 12 pull-thrus, (19x55), 12 full hkups (30/50 amps), seasonal sites, WiFi @ sites, dump, laundry. **REC:** playground. Pets OK. Partial handicap access. No tents. 2021 rates: $35.
(972)223-4834 Lat: 32.56060, Lon: -96.85996
200 W. Bear Creek Rd, Glenn Heights, TX 75154
www.hihorvpark.com
See ad page 893

Check out 10/10★/10 Good Sam Parks on the Good Sam Park page.

GOLIAD — E7 *Goliad*

COLETO CREEK PARK & RESERVOIR (Public) From Fannin, NE 4 mi on US-59 to Coleto Park Rd, N 0.3 mi (R). 79 Avail: 79 W, 79 E (20/50 amps). 2021 rates: $40 to $45. (361)575-6366

GOLIAD STATE HISTORIC SITE (Public State Park) From Jct of US-59 & US-183/77A, S 0.8 mi on US-183/77A (R) (Entrance fee). 34 Avail: 20 full hkups, 14 W, 14 E (20/50 amps). 2021 rates: $20 to $25. (361)645-3405

GONZALES — D7 *Gonzales*

GONE FISHIN RV PARK

good sam park **Ratings: 6.5/9★/6** (RV Park) 47 Avail: 42 full hkups, 5 W, 5 E (30/50 amps). 2021 rates: $35. (210)306-8444, 595 County Rd 90b, Gonzales, TX 78629

GONZALES INDEPENDENCE PARK (Public) From town, S 1 mi on US-183 (R). Avail: 21 full hkups (20/30 amps). 2021 rates: $30. (830)672-1324

LAKE WOOD REC AREA (Public) From town, W 4 mi on US-90A to FM-2091, S 3 mi (E). Avail: 16 full hkups (30/50 amps). 2021 rates: $28 to $32. (830)672-2779

TEXAS FREEDOM RV VILLAGE

good sam park **Ratings: 7.5/9.5★/9.5** (RV Park) Avail: 96 full hkups (30/50 amps). 2021 rates: $35. (830)519-9005, 5784 US Hwy 90A East, Gonzales, TX 78629

GORDONVILLE — A7 *Grayson*

BIG MINERAL RESORT, MARINA AND CAMPGROUND (Public) From town, W 14 mi on US-82, N 10 mi on SR-901, follow signs (R). 100 Avail: 23 full hkups, 77 W, 77 E (30 amps). 2021 rates: $19 to $27. (903)523-4287

CEDAR MILLS RV RESORT & MARINA **Ratings: 8.5/9★/8** (RV Park) Avail: 25 full hkups (30/50 amps). 2021 rates: $28 to $40. (903)523-4222, 500 Harbour View Rd Dr, Gordonville, TX 76245

LAKE TEXOMA - COE/JUNIPER POINT (Public Corps) From town, N 5 mi on US-377, follow signs (R). 69 Avail: 44 W, 44 E (30/50 amps). 2021 rates: $22 to $24. May 01 to Sep 05. (903)523-4022

LAKE TEXOMA RV

good sam park **Ratings: 8/7/8** (RV Park) 220 Avail: 195 full hkups, 25 W, 25 E (30/50 amps). 2021 rates: $50 to $60. (888)563-7040, 209 Thousand Trails Rd, Gordonville, TX 76245

GRAHAM — B6 *Young*

KINDLEY PARK (Public) From town, W 6.8 mi on US-380 (L). Avail: 10 E (20 amps). 2021 rates: $10. (940)549-3324

Before you head north, know the rules and regulations for crossing the border into Canada. Read all about it in our Crossing into Canada section.

TX

GRANBURY — B7 *Hood*

BENNETT'S RV RANCH
good sam park **Ratings: 8.5/10★/9.5** (RV Park) From jct Hwy 144 & US 377: Go 3-1/2 mi NE on US 377 (L). **FAC:** paved rds. (44 spaces). Avail: 25 paved, 11 pull-thrus, (30x57), back-ins (30x68), 25 full hkups (50 amps), seasonal sites, cable, WiFi @ sites, laundry. **REC:** boating nearby, playground. Pet restrict (B/Q). Partial handicap access. No tents. Big rig sites. 2021 rates: $40, Military discount.
(817)279-7500 Lat: 32.45020, Lon: -97.73984
3101 Old Granbury Rd, Granbury, TX 76049
www.bennettsrv.com
See ad this page

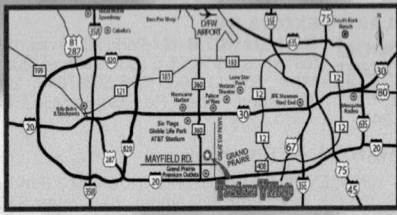

GRAND PRAIRIE — H3 *Dallas*

LOYD PARK CAMPING CABINS & LODGE
good sam park **Ratings: 8/9.5★/9** (Public) From Jct of I-20 (exit 453 B) & SR 360: Go 4 3/4 mi S on SR 360, then 1/2 mi E on Ragland Rd. (R).

DALLAS FORT WORTH METROPLEX
On the west shore of Joe Pool Lake with more Texas tranquility than you can handle! Lakefront cabins and huge private campsites. Close to the major DFW attractions with easy access from I-20 and SH 360.

FAC: paved rds. Avail: 221 paved, patios, back-ins (50x65), 115 full hkups, 106 W, 106 E (30/50 amps), WiFi @ sites, tent sites, rentals, dump, groc, fire rings, firewood, controlled access. **REC:** Joe Pool Lake: swim, fishing, kayaking/canoeing, boating nearby, playground. Pets OK. Partial handicap access. 2021 rates: $25 to $50.
(972)237-4120 Lat: 32.61313, Lon: -97.06939
City of Grand Prairie , 3401 Ragland Rd, Grand Prairie, TX 75052
loydpark.com
See ad page 877

TRADERS VILLAGE RV PARK
good sam park **Ratings: 10/10★/8.5** (RV Park) From Jct of I-20 & Great Southwest Parkway (exit 454), N 1 mi on Great Southwest Parkway to Mayfield Rd, W 0.2 mi (R).

SHOP FROM OVER 3,000 VENDORS
Conveniently located off I-20 & Hwy 360, this Top-Rated RV Park is adjacent to Traders Village, the nation's largest Flea Market with rides, live music, and special events. Big rig friendly featuring a pool, WIFI, and store.

FAC: paved rds. (126 spaces). Avail: 51 paved, patios, 48 pull-thrus, (21x60), back-ins (25x40), 51 full hkups (30/50 amps), seasonal sites, WiFi @ sites, tent sites, dump, laundry, groc, LP gas. **REC:** pool, shuffleboard, playground. Pet restrict (S/B/Q). Partial handicap access. 2021 rates: $60, Military discount. ATM.
(972)647-8205 Lat: 32.69158, Lon: -97.04872
2602 Mayfield Rd, Grand Prairie, TX 75052
tradersvillagervpark.com/grand-prairie
See ad this page

Things to See and Do

TRADERS VILLAGE 154 acre flea market with special events, entertainment, rides and concerts. Festivals and special events are planned year-round. $4 per car parking fee. Partial handicap access. RV accessible. Restrooms. Food. Hours: 8am to 9pm. ATM. No CC.
(972)647-2331 Lat: 32.69274, Lon: -97.04868
2602 Mayfield Rd, Grand Prairie, TX 75052
www.tradersvillage.com/grand-prairie
See ad this page

GRANGER — C7 *Williamson*

GRANGER LAKE - COE/TAYLOR (Public Corps) From town, S 6.1 mi on Hwy 95, E 5 mi on FM-1331 (L). 48 Avail: 48 W, 48 E (30 amps). 2021 rates: $22 to $26. Apr 01 to Sep 30. (512)859-2668

GRANGER LAKE - COE/WILLIS CREEK (Public Corps) From Jct of SR-95 & CR-346, E 4 mi on CR-346 (E). 27 Avail: 27 W, 27 E (30 amps). 2021 rates: $22 to $26. (512)859-2668

GRANGER LAKE - COE/WILSON H FOX (Public Corps) From I-35: E on Hwy 79 to Hwy 95, N 5.9 mi on Hwy 95, E 6.5 mi on FM-1331 to entrance of Granger Dam, N to park (L). 49 Avail: 44 W, 49 E (30/50 amps). 2021 rates: $22 to $36. (512)859-2668

RETREAT AT 971 RV PARK **Ratings: 8.5/9.5★/8.5** (RV Park) Avail: 12 full hkups (30/50 amps). 2021 rates: $40 to $45. (512)677-6998, 12801 FM971, Granger, TX 76530

GRAPEVINE — G3 *Tarrant*

THE VINEYARDS CAMPGROUND & CABINS
good sam park **Ratings: 9.5/9.5★/10** (Public) From E Jct Hwy 121 & Hwy 26 (Northwest Hwy): Go 2-1/2 mi SW on Hwy 26, then 1 mi N on Dooley Rd (L).

RELAX ON SHORES OF GRAPEVINE LAKE
Our nationally acclaimed campground is well-known for its peaceful setting, lovely grounds, lakefront views and accommodating staff. Spacious pull-thrus & cozy furnished cabins offer something for everyone.

FAC: paved rds. Avail: 93 paved, patios, 30 pull-thrus, (40x85), back-ins (40x70), 93 full hkups (30/50 amps), WiFi @ sites, rentals, laundry, groc, fire rings, firewood, controlled access. **REC:** Lake Grapevine: swim, fishing, kayaking/canoeing, boating nearby, playground. Pets OK. Partial handicap access. No tents. Big rig sites. 2021 rates: $54 to $74, Military discount.
(888)329-8993 Lat: 32.95549, Lon: -97.07394
1501 N Dooley, Grapevine, TX 76051
www.vineyardscampground.com
See ad page 874

GREENVILLE — B8 *Hunt*

1770 WEST I-30 RV PARK **Ratings: 7/NA/6.5** (RV Park) Avail: 50 full hkups (30/50 amps). 2021 rates: $50. (903)554-5640, 1770 W I-30, Greenville, TX 75402

EAST TEXAS RV PARK **Ratings: 6/5.5/6** (Campground) Avail: 10 full hkups (30/50 amps). 2021 rates: $30. (903)454-8900, 2935 SH 69S, Greenville, TX 75402

HALLETTSVILLE — D7 *Lavaca*

HALLETTSVILLE CITY PARK (Public) From town, N 0.9 mi on North Main St, follow signs (R). 17 Avail: 17 W, 17 E (20 amps). 2021 rates: $10. (361)798-3246

K C RV PARK **Ratings: 7/9★/7** (RV Park) Avail: 59 full hkups (30/50 amps). 2021 rates: $30. (361)798-2311, 321 U.S. Hwy 77 South, Hallettsville, TX 77964

OUTBACK RV CAMPGROUND **Ratings: 6.5/8.5★/7** (RV Park) Avail: 48 full hkups (30/50 amps). 2021 rates: $25. (361)798-4645, 1641 N Texana, Hallettsville, TX 77964

HARLINGEN — M4 *Cameron*

HARLINGEN See also Alamo, Brownsville, Donna, La Feria, Los Fresnos, Mercedes, Raymondville, Rio Hondo, San Benito & Weslaco.

CAREFREE VALLEY MHP & RV RESORT **Ratings: 7.5/7/6** (RV Park) Avail: 34 full hkups (30/50 amps). 2021 rates: $30. (956)335-9396, 4506 N Bus 77, Harlingen, TX 78552

EASTGATE RV & MH PARK **Ratings: 8.5/8.5★/7** (RV Area in MH Park) Avail: 110 full hkups (30/50 amps). 2021 rates: $42. (800)499-3137, 2801 E Harrison Ave, Harlingen, TX 78550

FIG TREE RV RESORT
good sam park **Ratings: 9.5/9★/8.5** (RV Park) From Jct of W US-83 (Expwy) & Altas Palmas exit, W 0.3 mi on N frntg rd (R). **FAC:** paved rds. (197 spaces). Avail: 100 grass, patios, back-ins (35x50), 100 full hkups (30/50 amps), seasonal sites, WiFi @ sites, laundry, controlled access. **REC:** heated pool, hot tub, shuffleboard. Pet restrict (S/B/Q). Partial handicap access. No tents, Age restrict may apply, eco-friendly. 2021 rates: $40.
(956)423-6699 Lat: 26.18678, Lon: -97.77838
15257 N. 83 Expressway, Harlingen, TX 78552
FigTreeRVResort.com
See ad this page

LAKEWOOD RV RESORT
good sam park **Ratings: 9.5/9★/8** (RV Park) Avail: 166 full hkups (30/50 amps). 2021 rates: $52. (888)563-7040, 4525 Graham Rd, Harlingen, TX 78552

PALM GARDENS MHP & RV RESORT
good sam park **Ratings: 9/9★/8.5** (RV Area in MH Park) Avail: 66 full hkups (30/50 amps). 2021 rates: $45. (956)423-7670, 3401 W Bus 83, Harlingen, TX 78552

PARADISE PARK RV RESORT
good sam park **Ratings: 9/9★/8** (RV Area in MH Park) Avail: 255 full hkups (30/50 amps). 2021 rates: $54. (888)563-7040, 1201 N Expwy 77, Harlingen, TX 78552

PARK PLACE ESTATES
good sam park **Ratings: 9.5/9★/9** (RV Resort) From Jct of US-83/77 (Expwy) & Bus 83 exit, W 1.8 mi on Bus 83 (L). **FAC:** paved rds. (847 spaces). Avail: 687 grass, patios, back-ins (38x45), 687 full hkups (30/50 amps), cable, WiFi @ sites, rentals, laundry, controlled access. **REC:** heated pool, hot tub, shuffleboard. Pet restrict (Q). Partial handicap access. No tents, Age restrict may apply, eco-friendly. 2021 rates: $45, Military discount.
(956)428-4414 Lat: 26.18071, Lon: -97.74650
5401 W Bus 83, Harlingen, TX 78552
www.rvresorts.com
See ad opposite page

SUNSHINE RV RESORT
good sam park **Ratings: 9.5/9★/8.5** (RV Park) Avail: 527 full hkups (30/50 amps). 2021 rates: $54 to $58. (888)563-7040, 1900 Grace Ave, Harlingen, TX 78550

TROPIC WINDS RV RESORT
good sam park **Ratings: 9/9★/8.5** (RV Park) Avail: 400 full hkups (30/50 amps). 2021 rates: $52. (888)563-7040, 1501 North Loop 499, Harlingen, TX 78550

HASKELL — B5 *Haskell*

HASKELL MUNICIPAL RV PARK (Public) From Jct of US-277 & US-380, E 0.2 mi on US-380 to Ave B, S S 0.3 mi (E). First night free. Avail: 36 full hkups (20/30 amps). 2021 rates: $16. (940)864-2333

HAWKINS — B8 *Wood*

LAKE HAWKINS RV PARK (Public) From Jct of Hwy 14 & US-80, W 3 mi on US-80 to CR-3440, N 1 mi (R). 41 Avail: 12 full hkups, 29 W, 29 E (30/50 amps). 2021 rates: $25. (903)769-4545

HEARNE — C7 *Robertson*

BRAZOS TRAIL RV PARK
(RV Spaces) From jct Franklin St & North Market St: Go 1/2 mi N on North Market St (L). **FAC:** paved rds. Avail: 31 paved, back-ins (24x50), accepts full hkup units only, 31 full hkups (30/50 amps), WiFi @ sites, . Pets OK. No tents. 2021 rates: $35. ATM.
(979)977-7275 Lat: 30.890078, Lon: -96.599941
901 North Market Street, Hearne, TX 77859
brazostrailrvpark.com
See ad page 920

HICO — B7 *Hamilton*

BOSQUE RIVER RV PARK (Public) From jct US 281 & FM 1602: Go 1/2 mi E on FM 1602, then 1/2 mi N on Elm St (L). Avail: 21 full hkups (30/50 amps). 2021 rates: $25 to $35. (254)796-4620

HIGHLANDS — D8 *Harris*

HOUSTON LEISURE RV RESORT **Ratings: 8.5/5/7.5** (RV Park) Avail: 15 full hkups (30/50 amps). 2021 rates: $44 to $49. (281)426-3576, 1601 South Main Street, Highlands, TX 77562

SAN JACINTO RIVERFRONT RV PARK
good sam park **Ratings: 10/10★/10** (RV Park) Avail: 30 full hkups (30/50 amps). 2021 rates: $60 to $95. (281)426-6919, 540 S. Main, Highlands, TX 77562

HITCHCOCK — D9 *Galveston*

TEXAS RV PARK **Ratings: 8/9.5★/9** (RV Park) Avail: 62 full hkups (30/50 amps). 2021 rates: $35 to $50. (409)440-8722, 5605 FM 2004, Hitchcock, TX 77563

HONDO — D6 *Medina*

QUIET TEXAS RV PARK **Ratings: 7.5/NA/10** (RV Park) Avail: 30 full hkups (30/50 amps). 2021 rates: $50. (830)931-5777, 3316 Avenue U South, Hondo, TX 78861

HONEY GROVE — A8 *Fannin*

HIDDEN GROVE RV RESORT
good sam park **Ratings: 7.5/9.5★/9** (RV Park) Avail: 64 full hkups (30/50 amps). 2021 rates: $45 to $60. (855)723-4140, 19300 E US Highway 82, Honey Grove, TX 75446

HOUSTON — D8 *Harris*

HOUSTON See also Alvin, Baytown, Brookshire, Cleveland, Crystal Beach, Cut and Shoot, Dickinson, Galveston, Highlands, Hitchcock, Katy, Kemah, La Marque, League City, Liberty, Magnolia, Montgomery, New Caney, Pearland, Richmond, San Leon, Sugar Land, The Woodlands, Tomball, Waller, Wallisville & Willis.

ADVANCED RV RESORT
good sam park **Ratings: 10/10★/10** (RV Park) From jct I-610 & Hwy 288: Go 5-1/2 mi S on US 288, then 1/2 mi SE on Beltway 8 Frontage Rd (R). **FAC:** paved rds. Avail: 230 paved, patios, 121 pull-thrus, (30x65), back-ins (30x35), 230 full hkups (30/50 amps), cable, WiFi @ sites, dump, laundry, LP gas, controlled access. **REC:** heated pool, hot tub. Pet restrict (B/Q). Partial handicap access. No tents. Big rig sites, eco-friendly. 2021 rates: $64 to $69, Military discount.
(713)433-6950 Lat: 29.59623, Lon: -95.38083
2850 S Sam Houston Pkwy E, Houston, TX 77047
www.advancedrvresort.com
See ad page 903

ALLSTAR RV RESORT **Ratings: 10/9.5★/9** (RV Park) Avail: 118 full hkups (30/50 amps). 2021 rates: $48.89 to $72.22. (713)981-6814, 10650 SW Plaza Ct., Houston, TX 77074

EASTLAKE RV RESORT **Ratings: 10/10★/10** (RV Resort) Avail: 241 full hkups (30/50 amps). 2021 rates: $54 to $106. (832)243-6919, 11802 Lockwood Road, Houston, TX 77044

ERIC & JAYS RV RESORT **Ratings: 10/9.5★/9.5** (RV Resort) Avail: 114 full hkups (30/50 amps). 2021 rates: $65 to $79. (713)206-0779, 2935 Lockcrest St, Houston, TX 77047

FALLBROOK RV RESORT **Ratings: 10/10★/10** (RV Resort) Avail: 186 full hkups (30/50 amps). 2021 rates: $52.22 to $77.78. (832)598-2752, 3102 Fallbrook Dr, Houston, TX 77038

HIGHWAY 6 RV RESORT **Ratings: 10/9.5★/9.5** (RV Resort) Avail: 218 full hkups (30/50 amps). 2021 rates: $54 to $91. (832)230-1531, 14350 Schiller Rd., Houston, TX 77082

HOUSTON CENTRAL RV PARK
good sam park **Ratings: 8/8/7.5** (Campground) Avail: 34 full hkups (30/50 amps). 2021 rates: $40 to $50. (281)442-3700, 1620 Peach Leaf St, Houston, TX 77039

JETSTREAM RV RESORT AT NASA **Ratings: 10/10★/8.5** (RV Resort) Avail: 202 full hkups (30/50 amps). 2021 rates: $65. (713)609-1019, 14450 Ellington Park Dr, Webster, TX 77598

KING PARKWAY MH COMMUNITY **Ratings: 7.5/NA/8.5** (RV Area in MH Park) Avail: 10 full hkups (30/50 amps). 2021 rates: $25. (281)458-1806, 8903 C.E. King Parkway, Houston, TX 77044

LAKEVIEW RV RESORT **Ratings: 10/9.5★/10** (RV Resort) Avail: 373 full hkups (30/50 amps). 2021 rates: $63.33 to $78.89. (713)723-0973, 11991 S. Main St, Houston, TX 77035

NORTHLAKE RV RESORT **Ratings: 10/10★/10** (RV Resort) Avail: 230 full hkups (30/50 amps). 2021 rates: $53.33 to $78.89. (281)209-1770, 1919 Humble-Westfield Road, Houston, TX 77073

OAK HOLLOW RV PARK **Ratings: 7/NA/9** (RV Park) Avail: 90 full hkups (30/50 amps). 2021 rates: $52. (281)960-2250, 16730 County Rd 127, Pearland, TX 77581

SAFARI MOBILE HOME & RV COMMUNITY
good sam park **Ratings: 7.5/8.5★/7** (RV Area in MH Park) From jct I-69 & I-45: Go 24 mi S on I-45, then 1-1/2 mi SW on Calder Dr (exit 22) (R). **FAC:** paved rds. (133 spaces). Avail: 50 gravel, 11 pull-thrus, (25x80), back-ins (25x45), 50 full hkups (30/50 amps), WiFi @ sites, $, laundry. **REC:** pool. Pets OK. No tents, eco-friendly. 2021 rates: $40, Military discount.
(281)332-4131 Lat: 29.47160, Lon: -95.10545
2935 Calder Dr, League City, TX 77573
www.safarirvpark.com
See primary listing at League City and ad page 907

SHELDON LAKE RV RESORT
good sam park **Ratings: 8/9★/6** (RV Park) Avail: 55 full hkups (30/50 amps). 2021 rates: $50. (281)456-9703, 16925 Crosby Freeway, Houston, TX 77049

SOUTH MAIN RV PARK **Ratings: 8/9★/7** (RV Park) Avail: 106 full hkups (30/50 amps). 2021 rates: $50. (713)667-0120, 10100 South Main, Houston, TX 77025

SOUTHLAKE RV RESORT **Ratings: 9/9.5★/10** (RV Resort) Avail: 122 full hkups (30/50 amps). 2021 rates: $62.22 to $77.78. (832)804-8088, 13701 Hycohen Road, Houston, TX 77047

TX

SUMMER BREEZE USA KATY
A World Class Destination RV Resort
good sam park
• Conveniently located off I-10
• Tropical Themed Waterpark!
• 99 Concrete Pad Sites From 45ft-75ft w/FHU
• Free High Speed Fiber Optic WiFi
• Basketball Court-Covered Pavilion
• Clubhouse W/Fitness Center!
• Golf Car Rentals
• Laundry Facility
• Onsite Store w/Blue Bell Ice Cream & Vending Machines
• Oversized Hot Tub
• Resort Style Pool w/slide!
• RV Park Models
• State-of-the-Art Playground
• Picnic Tables
RV RESORT
Summer
BREEZE
See listing Brookshire, TX
1019 Wilpitz Rd.
Brookshire, TX 77423
713.358.8430
SUMMERBREEZEUSA.COM

HOUSTON (CONT)

ST. IVES RV RESORT
good sam park **Ratings: 9/9.5★/9** (RV Resort) From jct I-610 & I-45: Go 10 mi S on I-45, then 7-1/4 mi W on Dixie Farm Rd, then 15 mi S on Hwy 35, then 4-3/4 mi S on FM 2917 (L). **FAC:** gravel rds. (72 spaces). Avail: 72 gravel, 54 pull-thrus, (45x100), back-ins (45x75), 72 full hkups (30/50 amps), WiFi @ sites, laundry, controlled access. **REC:** pool. Pet restrict (B/Q). Partial handicap access. No tents. Big rig sites. 2021 rates: $55.
(832)717-9393 Lat: 29.295222, Lon: -95.224624
4959 FM 2917, Alvin, TX 77511
stivesrvresort.com
See primary listing at Alvin and ad page 884

TRADERS VILLAGE RV PARK
good sam park **Ratings: 10/10★/9** (RV Park) From Jct of I-10 & Eldridge Rd (exit 753A), N 7.8 mi on Eldridge Rd (L); or From N Jct of I-45 & Beltway 8/Sam Houston Tollway (exit 60), W 12.6 mi on Beltway 8/Sam Houston Tollway to US-290, NW 2.2 mi to Eldridge Rd, S 0.6 mi (R).

STAY & SHOP THOUSANDS OF DEALERS
America's #1 Flea Market with thousands of vendors and millions of deals. Enjoy festivals and special events while staying at our Top Rated RV Park. Great amenities include a Swimming Pool, Rec Hall, and Free WiFI.

FAC: paved rds. (284 spaces). Avail: 179 paved, 140 pull-thrus, (20x68), back-ins (32x40), 179 full hkups (30/50 amps), seasonal sites, WiFi @ sites, dump, laundry, LP gas, controlled access. **REC:** pool, shuffleboard, playground. Pet restrict (B/Q). Partial handicap access. No tents, eco-friendly. 2021 rates: $42.95. ATM.
(281)890-5500 Lat: 29.89511, Lon: -95.60785
7979 N Eldridge, Houston, TX 77041
tradersvillagervpark.com
See ad this page

USA RV RESORT HOUSTON **Ratings: 9.5/10★/8** (RV Resort) Avail: 157 full hkups (30/50 amps). 2021 rates: $67 to $88. (832)781-4777, 12187 Sagedowne Ln, Houston, TX 77089

WESTLAKE RV RESORT **Ratings: 10/10★/10** (RV Resort) Avail: 196 full hkups (30/50 amps). 2021 rates: $60 to $91. (281)463-8566, 18602 Clay Rd., Houston, TX 77084

Things to See and Do

TRADERS VILLAGE 106 acres of bargain hunters paradise, thousands of dealers, thrill rides and festival foods. Plus special events & live entertainment. Partial handicap access. RV accessible. Restrooms. Food. Hours: 10am to 5pm (Sat & Sun). ATM.
(281)890-5500 Lat: 29.89472, Lon: -95.60785
7979 N Eldridge Rd, Houston, TX 77041
tradersvillage.com/houston
See ad this page

HUNTINGTON — C9 *Angelina*

SAM RAYBURN RESERVOIR - COE/HANKS CREEK (Public Corps) From town, NE 0.5 mi on Hwy 147 to FR-2109, N 8 mi to FR-2801, E 2 mi (R). 47 Avail: 47 W, 47 E (30/50 amps). 2021 rates: $26 to $28. (409)384-5716

HUNTSVILLE — C8 *Walker*

HUNTSVILLE (Public State Park) From Jct of I-45 & Park Rd 40 (exit 109), W 1.2 mi on Park Rd 40 (E) (Entrance fee). 160 Avail: 23 full hkups, 137 W, 77 E (30/50 amps). 2021 rates: $15 to $25. (936)295-5644

HUTTO — C7 *Williamson*

REDBUD RANCH RV RESORT **Ratings: 10/10★/10** (RV Park) Avail: 124 full hkups (30/50 amps). 2021 rates: $60 to $85. (512)265-8000, 211 Benelli Drive, Hutto, TX 78634

JACKSBORO — A6 *Jack*

FORT RICHARDSON STATE HISTORICAL PARK (Public State Park) S-bnd: From Jacksboro town square, S 1 mi on US-281 (R); or N-bnd: From jct of US-380 & US-281 (S of town), NW 1.6 mi on US-281 (L) (Entrance fee). 41 Avail: 4 full hkups, 37 W, 37 E (20/50 amps). 2021 rates: $20 to $25. (940)567-3506

HIDDEN LAKE RV RANCH & SAFARI
good sam park **Ratings: 7.5/8★/6.5** (RV Park) From jct Hwy 148 & US 281: Go 5-1/4 mi NW on US 281, then 1/2 mi E on Lowrance Rd (L). **FAC:** gravel rds. (36 spaces). Avail: 30 gravel, 2 pull-thrus, (24x55), back-ins (24x35), 30 full hkups (30/50 amps), seasonal sites, WiFi @ sites, tent sites, rentals, laundry, fire rings, controlled access. **REC:** pond, fishing, playground, rec open to public. Pet restrict (B). 2021 rates: $40 to $50.
(940)567-6900 Lat: 33.252520, Lon: -98.237350
3100 Lowrance Rd., Jacksboro, TX 76458
www.hiddenlakervranch.com
See ad this page

JARRELL — C7 *Williamson*

VALLEY VIEW RV PARK
good sam park **Ratings: 8/10★/9.5** (RV Park) Sbnd: From jct I-35 & Exit 275: Go 1/2 mi S on I-35 W Service Rd (R) Nbnd: From jct I-35 & Exit 277: Go 1 mi N on I-35 E Service Rd, then 1/8 mi W on CR 313 (I-35 turnaround), then 1/2 mi N on I-35 W Service Rd (R). **FAC:** paved rds. (189 spaces). Avail: 129 all weather, patios, 43 pull-thrus, (32x70), back-ins (32x60), 129 full hkups (30/50 amps), seasonal sites, cable, WiFi @ sites, laundry. Pet restrict (S/B/Q). No tents. Big rig sites. 2021 rates: $49, Military discount.
(512)887-9168 Lat: 30.834012, Lon: -97.601096
13483 N I-35, Jarrell, TX 76537
vvrvpark.com
See ad page 885

JASPER — C9 *Jasper*

DOUBLE HEART RV PARK **Ratings: 7/8.5/7** (RV Park) Avail: 12 full hkups (30/50 amps). 2021 rates: $30 to $35. (409)489-1515, 14600 TX SH 63 W, Jasper, TX 75951

MARTIN DIES JR (Public State Park) From Jct of US-96 & US-190 (in town), W 10.8 mi on US-190 (L) (Entrance fee). 173 Avail: 173 W, 122 E (30/50 amps). 2021 rates: $14 to $20. (409)384-5231

STEINHAGEN LAKE - COE/SANDY CREEK (Public Corps) From town, W 15 mi on US-190 to FM-777, S 1.5 mi to CR-150, W 2.2 mi (E). 71 Avail: 69 W, 71 E (30/50 amps). 2021 rates: $10 to $18. (409)429-3491

JEFFERSON — B9 *Marion*

LAKE O' THE PINES - COE/ALLEY CREEK (Public Corps) From town, NW 4 mi on Hwy 49 to Hwy 729, W 12 mi (L). 49 Avail: 49 W, 49 E (15/50 amps). 2021 rates: $28 to $44. Mar 01 to Sep 30. (903)755-2637

How can we make a great Travel Guide even better? We ask YOU! Please share your thoughts with us. Drop us a note and let us know if there's anything we haven't thought of.

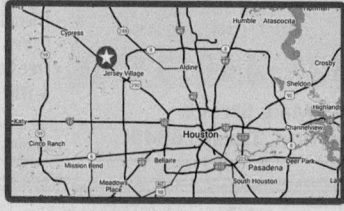

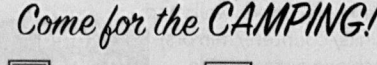

TX

JEFFERSON (CONT)

← LAKE O' THE PINES - COE/BUCKHORN CREEK (Public Corps) From town, NW 4 mi on Hwy 49 to Hwy 729, W 3.5 mi to Hwy 726, S 2.4 mi (R). 57 Avail: 57 W, 57 E (30/50 amps). 2021 rates: $26 to $42. (903)665-8261

← LAKE O' THE PINES - COE/JOHNSON CREEK (Public Corps) From town, NW 4 mi on Hwy 49 to Hwy 729, W 8 mi, follow signs (L). 65 Avail: 62 W, 31 E (30/50 amps). 2021 rates: $26 to $32. (903)755-2435

JEWETT — C8 *Leon*

↖ LAKE LIMESTONE CAMPGROUND & MARINA **Ratings: 5.5/7.5/6.5** (Campground) Avail: 42 full hkups (30/50 amps). 2021 rates: $40 to $45. (903)626-4119, 100 Private Road 5888A, Jewett, TX 75846

JOHNSON CITY — C6 *Blanco*

→ PEDERNALES FALLS (Public State Park) From Jct of US-281/290 & Ranch Rd 2766 (in town), E 9.2 mi on Ranch Rd 2766 (L) (Entrance fee). 69 Avail: 69 W, 69 E (30 amps). 2021 rates: $20. (830)868-7304

↓ **ROADRUNNER RV PARK**

good sam park **Ratings: 8/9★/8** (RV Park) From Jct US-290 & US-281 (in town): Go 3/4 mi S on US-290/281 (L). N Bnd: From S jct US 290 & US 281, Go 5 mi N on US 281 (R). **FAC:** paved rds. (72 spaces). Avail: 52 paved, 42 pull-thrus, (15x65), back-ins (15x65), 52 full hkups (30/50 amps), seasonal sites, WiFi @ sites, rentals, laundry. **REC:** hunting nearby. Pet restrict (B/Q). No tents. Big rig sites. 2021 rates: $45, Military discount.
(830)255-7650 Lat: 30.26895, Lon: -98.39752
501 US Hwy 281 South, Johnson City, TX 78636
www.rrvtx.com
See ad this page

JUNCTION — C5 *Kimble*

↖ **10/83 RV PARK**

good sam park **Ratings: 9/9.5★/9** (Campground) From Jct of I-10 & US-377 (exit 456): Go 1/2 mi S on US-377 (R). **FAC:** paved/gravel rds. Avail: 52 gravel, patios, 51 pull-thrus, (32x70), back-ins (32x35), 42 full hkups, 10 W, 10 E (30/50 amps), cable, WiFi @ sites, tent sites, dump, laundry, fire rings, firewood, controlled access. **REC:** pool, North Llano River: swim, fishing, playground, hunting nearby. Pets OK. Big rig sites, eco-friendly. 2021 rates: $41.11, Military discount.
(325)446-3138 Lat: 30.50130, Lon: -99.77870
2145 Main St, Junction, TX 76849
See ad this page

↖ PECAN VALLEY RV PARK & FARM **Ratings: 6/9★/8.5** (Campground) Avail: 20 full hkups (30/50 amps). 2021 rates: $42. (325)446-3065, 6720 W Ranch Rd 1674, Junction, TX 76849

↓ SOUTH LLANO RIVER (Public State Park) From Jct of Bus Loop 481 & US-377 (in town), S 5.2 mi on US-377 to Park Rd 73, NE 2 mi (R) (Entrance fee). 58 Avail: 58 W, 58 E (30 amps). 2021 rates: $20. (325)446-3994

↓ **TREE CABINS RV RESORT**

good sam park **Ratings: 7/10★/8.5** (RV Park) From I-10 & FM 2169 (exit 457); Go 1 mi S on W FM 2169, then continue straight across Loop 481 to Cedar Creek Rd (R). **FAC:** gravel rds. Avail: 39 gravel, 25 pull-thrus, (30x60), back-ins (30x60), 39 full hkups (30/50 amps), WiFi @ sites, tent sites, rentals, laundry, fire rings, firewood. **REC:** South Llano River: swim, fishing, kayaking/canoeing, hunting nearby. Pets OK. Partial handicap access. Big rig sites. 2021 rates: $40, Military discount.
(325)446-3388 Lat: 30.48384, Lon: -99.75996
210 Cedar Creek Road, Junction, TX 76849
treecabinsrvresort.com
See ad this page

KARNACK — B9 *Harrison*

↗ CADDO LAKE (Public State Park) From Jct of SR-43 & FM-2198, E 0.4 mi on FM-2198 (L) CAUTION: Low branches. Entrance fee required. 46 Avail: 8 full hkups, 38 W, 18 E (30/50 amps). 2021 rates: $10 to $20. (903)679-3351

KATY — D8 *Fort Bend*

→ **KATY LAKE RV RESORT**

good sam park **Ratings: 10/10★/10** (RV Park) From jct I-10 & Fry Rd: Go 2 mi N on Fry Rd, then 1/4 mi W on Morton Rd (R). From jct H-99 & Morton Rd: Go 2-1/2 mi E on Morton Rd (L).

RELAX IN THE HEART OF WEST HOUSTON
Enjoy 18 acres surrounding a 6-acre lake nestled in the heart of Houston. Experience the peaceful, easy, laid-back lake life atmosphere. Located within 10 min. of a wide variety of restaurants, shopping, and medical services.

FAC: paved rds. Avail: 209 paved, patios, 64 pull-thrus, (30x66), back-ins (30x45), 209 full hkups (30/50 amps), cable, WiFi @ sites, rentals, laundry, LP gas, controlled access. **REC:** heated pool, hot tub, Katy Lake: fishing. Pet restrict (B/Q). Partial handicap access. No tents. Big rig sites, eco-friendly. 2021 rates: $49 to $79, Military discount.
(281)492-0044 Lat: 29.81524, Lon: -95.72398
20222 Morton Rd, Katy, TX 77449
www.katylakervresort.com
See ad pages 876, 901

Travel Services

← **CAMPING WORLD OF KATY/HOUSTON** As the nation's largest retailer of RV supplies, accessories, services and new and used RVs, Camping World is committed to making your total RV experience better. **SERVICES:** RV, tire, RV appliance, MH mechanical, sells outdoor gear, sells firearms, staffed RV wash, restrooms. RV Sales. RV supplies, LP gas, dump, emergency parking, RV accessible. Hours: 9am to 7pm.
(877)240-6487 Lat: 29.776994, Lon: -95.854341
27905 A Katy Freeway, Katy, TX 77494
www.campingworld.com

KEMAH — D9 *Galveston*

← BRICKHOUSE RV RESORT **Ratings: 9.5/9.5★/7.5** (RV Resort) Avail: 95 full hkups (30/50 amps). 2021 rates: $49 to $59. (281)334-0333, 1029 Marina Bay Drive, Kemah, TX 77565

↗ USA RV RESORTS MARINA BAY **Ratings: 10/10★/9** (RV Park) Avail: 209 full hkups (30/50 amps). 2021 rates: $49 to $97. (281)334-9944, 925 FM 2094, Kemah, TX 77565

OFF SEASON RVING TIPS - Extend your adventure. Though you may find RV parks limited in amenities during the off-season, you will find them brimming with opportunities to enjoy camping in a whole different way. The following tips will help you plan your first off-season camping trip: #1 Find out which campground sections and loops are open. #2 Off season amenities: Ask what's available. #3 Prepare for limited access to shower houses and restrooms. #4 Off season power: Plan for limited utility hookups. #5 Prepare to handle the elements.

KERRVILLE — D6 *Kerr*

BUCKHORN LAKE RESORT

good sam park **Ratings: 10/10★/10** (RV Park) From Jct of I-10 & Exit 501 (FM-1338/Goat Creek Rd) - on the NW corner of N access rd & Goat Creek Rd, N 50 yds on Goat Creek Rd (L).

SIMPLY THE FINEST RV RESORT IN TX

Buckhorn Lake Resort is the perfect place to stay while exploring the Texas Hill Country. We're just a short drive to many charming towns including Fredericksburg, Bandera, Boerne, Luckenbach and San Antonio. Top Rated.

FAC: paved rds. Avail: 145 paved, patios, 41 pull-thrus, (32x90), back-ins (32x65), 145 full hkups (30/50 amps), cable, WiFi @ sites, rentals, laundry, groc. **REC:** heated pool, hot tub, Goat Creek: fishing, boating nearby, playground, hunting nearby. Pet restrict (Q). Partial handicap access. No tents. Big rig sites, eco-friendly. 2021 rates: $46 to $57, Military discount.
(830)895-0007 Lat: 30.119915, Lon: -99.198363
2885 Goat Creek Rd, Kerrville, TX 78028
www.buckhornlake.com
See ad this page

BY THE RIVER RV PARK & CAMPGROUND **Ratings: 9/9★/8.5** (Campground) Avail: 59 full hkups (30/50 amps). 2021 rates: $40 to $53. (830)367-5566, 175 Riverview Rd, Kerrville, TX 78028

JOHNSON CREEK RV RESORT & PARK **Ratings: 10/10★/10** (RV Park) Avail: 83 full hkups (30/50 amps). 2021 rates: $46 to $52. (830)367-3300, 4279 Junction Hwy, Ingram, TX 78025

KERRVILLE KOA **Ratings: 9.5/9★/8** (RV Park) 40 Avail: 34 full hkups, 6 W, 6 E (30/50 amps). 2021 rates: $42 to $46. (830)895-1665, 2400 Goat Creek Rd, Kerrville, TX 78028

KERRVILLE-SCHREINER PARK (Public) From Jct of I-10 & Hwy 16 (exit 508), S 0.4 mi on Hwy 16 to Loop 534, SE 4.2 mi to Hwy 173, S 0.2 mi (L). 120 Avail: 40 full hkups, 62 W, 62 E (30/50 amps). 2021 rates: $23 to $28. (830)257-7300

OLD RIVER ROAD RV RESORT **Ratings: 10/9.5★/9.5** (RV Resort) Avail: 240 full hkups (30/50 amps). 2021 rates: $40 to $60. (830)634-2993, 310 Calvin Ranch Rd, Kerrville, TX 78028

TAKE-IT-EASY RV RESORT

good sam park **Ratings: 9/10★/9** (RV Park) From Jct of I-10 & FM-783 (exit 505), S 2.4 mi on FM-783/Harper Rd to Hwy 27, E 0.3 mi (R). **FAC:** paved rds. (169 spaces). 81 Avail: 5 paved, 76 gravel, patios, 13 pull-thrus, (24x60), back-ins (25x45), 81 full hkups (30/50 amps), seasonal sites, cable, WiFi @ sites, laundry. **REC:** heated pool, hot tub, shuffleboard, hunting nearby. Pet restrict (Q). Partial handicap access. No tents, Age restrict may apply, eco-friendly. 2021 rates: $50, Military discount. no cc.
(830)257-6636 Lat: 30.05650, Lon: -99.15975
703 Junction Hwy, Kerrville, TX 78028
www.takeiteasy.net
See ad next page

TRIPLE T RV RESORT

good sam park **Ratings: 9/10★/9** (RV Park) From Jct of I-10 & Exit 508 (Hwy 16/Sidney Baker St.), S 0.4 mi on Hwy 16 to Veterans Hwy, (Loop 534), SW 4.2 mi to Hwy 173 (Bandera Hwy), S 5.1 mi (R). **FAC:** paved/gravel rds. Avail: 54 gravel, 34 pull-thrus, (24x75), back-ins (24x60), 54 full hkups (30/50 amps), WiFi @ sites, dump, laundry, controlled access. **REC:** pool, wading pool, hunting nearby. Pets OK. No tents. Big rig sites, eco-friendly. 2021 rates: $45 to $50, Military discount.
(830)634-3000 Lat: 29.94826, Lon: -99.10933
3900 Bandera Hwy, Kerrville, TX 78028
tripletrvresort.com
See ad this page

YOGI BEAR'S GUADALUPE RIVER CAMP RESORT **Ratings: 10/9.5★/9** (RV Park) Avail: 160 full hkups (30/50 amps). 2021 rates: $42 to $140. (830)460-3262, 2605 Junction Hwy, Kerrville, TX 78028

Things to See and Do

KERRVILLE CONVENTION & VISITORS BUREAU Tourist information. Free WiFi. Monday thru Friday 8:30am to 5pm. Saturday 9:00am to 3:00pm & Sunday 10:00am to 3:00pm Partial handicap access. Restrooms. Hours: 8:30am to 5pm.
(830)792-3535 Lat: 30.06741, Lon: -99.11572
2108 Sidney Baker, Kerrville, TX 78028
www.kerrvilletexascvb.com
See ad page 864

KILLEEN — C7 *Bell*

ELM GROVE MH COMMUNITY

good sam park **Ratings: 7.5/NA/8.5** (RV Area in MH Park) Avail: 24 full hkups (30/50 amps). 2021 rates: $42. (254)690-3838, 1704 MLK Jr Blvd, Killeen, TX 76543

MILITARY PARK BELTON LAKE OUTDOOR REC AREA (FORT HOOD) (Public) From town: Go 12 mi E on FM-439 E, then 4 mi N on Sparta Rd, then 1 mi E on Cottage Rd (R). 52 Avail: 10 full hkups, 42 W, 42 E (30 amps). 2021 rates: $18 to $22. (254)287-2523

MILITARY PARK WEST FORT HOOD TRAVEL CAMP (FORT HOOD) (Public) From town: Go 3 mi W on US-190 Bus W, then 3 mi W on I-14, then 1/2 mi S on Clark Rd (R). Avail: 82 full hkups (30/50 amps). 2021 rates: $14 to $21. (254)288-9926

Don't miss out on great savings - find Camping World coupons at the front and back of this Guide!

Need RV repair or service? Camping World has many certified and trained technicians, warranty-covered repairs, workmanship and a price match guarantee. Find out more at CampingWorld.com

KINGSVILLE — K4 *Kleberg*

CM NATURE'S OWN RV RESORT

good sam park **Ratings: 9.5/10★/9.5** (RV Park) From Jct of US-77 & FM-1356 (Gen Cavazos Rd), S 1.9 mi on US-77 (R). **FAC:** paved rds. (115 spaces). 50 Avail: 25 paved, 25 all weather, 50 pull-thrus, (25x85), 50 full hkups (30/50 amps), seasonal sites, WiFi @ sites, laundry, controlled access. **REC:** pool, hot tub, playground. Pet restrict (B). Partial handicap access. No tents. Big rig sites, eco-friendly. 2021 rates: $44.
(361)488-9425 Lat: 27.46773, Lon: -97.85565
5151 S Hwy 77, Kingsville, TX 78363
naturesownrvresort.com
See ad this page

MILITARY PARK ROCKING K RV PARK (KINGSVILLE NAS) (Public) From town: Go 1/2 mi S on S Hwy 77, then 1-1/4 mi E on E Caesar Ave, then 1/2 mi S on Nimitz Ave (R). Avail: 15 full hkups (30/50 amps). 2021 rates: $18. (361)516-6191

KOPPERL — B7 *Bosque*

WHITNEY LAKE - COE/PLOWMAN CREEK (Public Corps) From town, S 1 mi on Hwy 56 (L). 32 Avail: 32 W, 32 E (30 amps). 2021 rates: $20. (254)622-3332

LA FERIA — M4 *Cameron*

KENWOOD RV RESORT

good sam park **Ratings: 9.5/9.5★/8** (RV Park) From Jct of US-83 Expwy & La Feria/FM-506 exit, N 300 ft on FM-506 (L). **FAC:** paved rds. (278 spaces). Avail: 178 grass, patios, back-ins (28x45), 178 full hkups (30/50 amps), seasonal sites, WiFi @ sites, rentals, laundry, controlled access. **REC:** heated pool, hot tub, shuffleboard. Pets OK. Partial handicap access. No tents, Age restrict may apply, eco-friendly. 2021 rates: $22 to $41.
(956)797-1851 Lat: 26.16737, Lon: -97.82467
1201 North Main #1, La Feria, TX 78559
rhprvresorts.com
See ad page 881

VIP-LA FERIA RV PARK

good sam park **Ratings: 9.5/9.5★/8.5** (RV Park) From Jct of US-83 Expwy & La Feria/FM-506, exit to S frntg rd, E 0.4 mi (R). **FAC:** paved rds. (360 spaces). 256 Avail: 4 paved, 252 grass, patios, 125 pull-thrus, (30x60), back-ins (32x60), 256 full hkups (30/50 amps), seasonal sites, cable, WiFi @ sites, $, laundry, controlled access. **REC:** heated pool, hot tub. Pet restrict (S/B/Q). Partial handicap access. No tents, Age restrict may apply. Big rig sites, eco-friendly. 2021 rates: $38 to $41.
(956)797-1401 Lat: 26.16514, Lon: -97.81802
600 E Expressway 83, La Feria, TX 78559
viplaferia.com
See ad this page

LA GRANGE — D7 *Fayette*

COLORADO LANDING RV PARK

good sam park **Ratings: 9.5/9.5★/10** (RV Park) From Jct of US-77 & Bus SR-71 (downtown La Grange), S 0.4 mi on US-77 to Cedar St, W 0.1 mi (E).

HUGE BEAUTIFUL SITES ON THE RIVER
Large shaded pull-thru sites in a peaceful setting by the Colorado River. Beautiful swimming pool, river fishing, free WiFi and cable TV. In historic La Grange Texas, where giant live oak trees drape the streets.

FAC: paved rds. Avail: 98 gravel, 18 pull-thrus, (30x70), back-ins (40x90), 98 full hkups (30/50 amps), cable, WiFi @ sites, tent sites, laundry, LP gas. **REC:** pool, Colorado River: fishing, playground. Pet restrict (B). Partial handicap access. Big rig sites. 2021 rates: $45, Military discount.
(979)968-9465 Lat: 29.89613, Lon: -96.87387
64 East Bluffview, La Grange, TX 78945
www.coloradolanding.com
See ad opposite page

OAK THICKET PARK (Public) From Jct of Hwy 159 & FM-955 (in town), W 4.4 mi on Hwy 159 (L). 20 Avail: 20 W, 20 E (30/50 amps). 2021 rates: $22 to $27. (979)249-3504

LA MARQUE — D9 *Galveston*

BIG STATE RV PARK **Ratings: 7/NA/7** (RV Park) Avail: 62 full hkups (30/50 amps). 2021 rates: $25 to $35. (409)797-4850, 2401 Maxwell St, La Marque, TX 77568

OASIS RV PARK **Ratings: 8/7.5/7.5** (RV Park) Avail: 107 full hkups (30/50 amps). 2021 rates: $50. (409)935-7101, 1903 Gulf Fwy, La Marque, TX 77568

USA RV RESORTS LA MARQUE **Ratings: 10/10★/7.5** (RV Resort) Avail: 169 full hkups (30/50 amps). 2021 rates: $54. (409)316-4558, 4313 FM 2004, La Marque, TX 77568

LAJITAS — D3 *Brewster*

MAVERICK RANCH RV PARK AT LAJITAS GOLF RESORT & SPA **Ratings: 10/10★/8.5** (RV Park) Avail: 100 full hkups (30/50 amps). 2021 rates: $49 to $64. (432)424-5180, 102 Maverick Ranch Rd, Lajitas, TX 79852

LAKEHILLS — D6 *Bandera*

LAKE MEDINA RV RESORT **Ratings: 9.5/9.5★/9.5** (RV Park) 95 Avail: 93 full hkups, 2 W, 2 E (30/50 amps). 2021 rates: $42 to $49. (830)751-2640, 1218 Leibold's Point, Lakehills, TX 78063

MEDINA LAKE RV

good sam park **Ratings: 8/9★/7.5** (Membership Park) 387 Avail: 220 full hkups, 167 W, 167 E (30/50 amps). 2021 rates: $60. (888)563-7040, 215 Spettle Rd., Lakehills, TX 78063

LAMESA — B4 *Dawson*

FORREST PARK (Public) At Jct of Hwy 137 & S 9th St (R) (Free camping limited to 4 days). 10 Avail: 10 W, 10 E (30 amps). 2021 rates: $20. (806)872-2124

LAMPASAS — C6 *Lampasas*

BOONE RV PARK

good sam park **Ratings: 8/10★/8.5** (RV Park) Avail: 12 full hkups (30/50 amps). 2021 rates: $40. (512)556-5171, 1907 S Hwy 281, Lampasas, TX 76550

LAREDO — K1 *Webb*

LAKE CASA BLANCA INTERNATIONAL (Public State Park) At jct US 59 & Loop 20. Entrance fee required. 66 Avail: 10 full hkups, 56 W, 56 E. 2021 rates: $18 to $21. (956)723-3826

LAVON — B7 *Collin*

LAVON LAKE - COE/LAVONIA (Public Corps) From town, E 3 mi on Hwy 78 to CR-486 Lake Rd, W 0.5 mi, follow signs (E). Avail: 38 full hkups (30 amps). 2021 rates: $30. (972)442-3141

RV Tech Tips - A Handy Solution to Open a Gas Cap: Often the simple act of opening the gas cap on your tow vehicle can be bothersome. Cut a notch to fit the raised area on the gas cap on one end of a 6-inch long piece of PVC pipe, drill a hole at the top of the pipe and slide a wooden dowel in the hole to act as a handle. Now, opening the cap is a cinch.

LEAGUE CITY — D8 *Galveston*

SAFARI MOBILE HOME & RV COMMUNITY
good sam park
Ratings: 7.5/8.5★/7 (RV Area in MH Park) From jct I-45 & Calder Dr (exit 22): Go 1-1/2 mi SW on Calder Dr (R). **FAC:** paved rds. (133 spaces). Avail: 50 gravel, 11 pull-thrus, (25x80), back-ins (25x45), 50 full hkups (30/50 amps), WiFi @ sites, $, laundry. **REC:** pool. Pets OK. Partial handicap access. No tents, eco-friendly. 2021 rates: $40, Military discount.
(281)332-4131 Lat: 29.47160, Lon: -95.10545
2935 Calder Dr, League City, TX 77573
safarirvpark.com
See ad this page

SPACE CENTER RV PARK **Ratings: 9.5/10★/7.5** (RV Park) Avail: 105 full hkups (30/50 amps). 2021 rates: $44.99 to $59.99. (281)554-8800, 301 Gulf Fwy South, League City, TX 77573

USA RV RESORTS WILLOW LAKE **Ratings: 10/10★/8.5** (RV Resort) Avail: 150 full hkups (30/50 amps). 2021 rates: $59 to $79. (281)724-2020, 1316 State Hwy 3, League City, TX 77573

LEANDER — C7 *Williamson*

LEANDER/NW AUSTIN KOA **Ratings: 10/9★/9** (RV Park) Avail: 58 full hkups (30/50 amps). 2021 rates: $65 to $79. (512)259-7200, 2689 Hero Way, Leander, TX 78641

LEDBETTER — D7 *Fayette*

LAKE SOMERVILLE/NAILS CREEK (Public State Park) From jct US 290 & FM 1697: Go 11 mi W on FM 1697, then 4 mi NE on FM 180. Entrance fee required. 43 Avail. 2021 rates: $12. (979)289-2392

LEWISVILLE — G3 *Denton*

LEWISVILLE LAKE PARK CAMPGROUND (Public) From Jct I-35 E & Exit 454A (Highland Village): Go 1 mi E on Lake Park Rd., then 1/8 mi N on Kingfisher Dr. (L). 92 Avail: 92 W, 92 E (30/50 amps). 2021 rates: $16 to $18. (972)219-3742

LIBERTY — D9 *Liberty*

HIGHWAY 90 RV RESORT **Ratings: 6.5/8.5★/6.5** (RV Park) Avail: 13 full hkups (30/50 amps). 2021 rates: $30 to $40. (936)641-5148, 710 E Main, Liberty, TX 77575

LINN — L3 *Hidalgo*

LAZY PALMS RANCH RV PARK
good sam park
Ratings: 8/9★/7 (Membership Park) Avail: 225 full hkups (30/50 amps). 2021 rates: $21 to $23. (956)383-1020, 35100 Lazy Palms Dr, Linn, TX 78541

VALLEY GATEWAY RV PARK **Ratings: 7/7.5/6** (RV Park) Avail: 96 full hkups (30/50 amps). 2021 rates: $25. (956)381-1883, 34961 N Hwy 281, Edinburg, TX 78542

LIVINGSTON — C9 *Polk*

LAKE LIVINGSTON (Public State Park) From Jct of US-59 & FM-1988 (exit 436A, exit S), W 3.7 mi on FM-1988 to FM-3126, N 0.4 mi (L) (Entrance fee). 147 Avail: 78 full hkups, 69 W, 69 E (20/50 amps). 2021 rates: $18 to $28. (936)365-2201

LAKE TOMBIGBEE CAMPGROUND **Ratings: 5.5/8.5★/8.5** (Campground) 71 Avail: 47 full hkups, 24 W, 24 E (30/50 amps). 2021 rates: $20 to $30. (936)563-1221, 1427 Campground Rd, Livingston, TX 77351

RAINBOW'S END RV PARK **Ratings: 9/8.5/8.5** (RV Park) Avail: 90 full hkups (30/50 amps). 2021 rates: $33.50 to $37.50. (936)327-1279, 140 Escapees Dr, Livingston, TX 77351

SERINITY PINES RV PARK **Ratings: 6.5/NA/8** (RV Park) Avail: 32 full hkups (30/50 amps). 2021 rates: $45. (936)967-0101, 4700 Hwy 190 W, Livingston, TX 77351

WOODSY HOLLOW CAMPGROUND & RV RESORT **Ratings: 9/8/7** (Campground) Avail: 10 full hkups (30/50 amps). 2021 rates: $40. (936)365-2267, 248 Woodsy Hollow, Goodrich, TX 77335

LLANO — C6 *Llano*

LLANO RIVER GOLF & RV RESORT (Public) From Jct of Hwy 16/71 (Bessemer Ave) & TX 29, S 0.6 mi on Hwy 16/71 to Ranch Rd 152 (Main St), W 1.8 mi (R). Avail: 25 full hkups (30/50 amps). 2021 rates: $27. (325)247-5100

ROBINSON CITY PARK (Public) From jct Hwy 16 & RR 152: Go 2 mi W on RR 152. Avail: 25 full hkups (30 amps). 2021 rates: $20. (325)247-4158

LOCKHART — D7 *Caldwell*

LOCKHART (Public State Park) From town, S 1 mi on US-183 to FM-20, SW 2 mi to Prk Rd 10, S 1 mi (L) (Entrance fee). 20 Avail: 10 full hkups, 10 W, 10 E (20/30 amps). 2021 rates: $20 to $24. (512)398-3479

LONE OAK — B8 *Hunt*

WIND POINT PARK **Ratings: 8/7.5/8** (Campground) Avail: 104 full hkups (30/50 amps). 2021 rates: $34 to $41. (903)634-9463, 6553 State Park Road 55, Lone Oak, TX 75453

LONGVIEW — B9 *Gregg*

FERNBROOK PARK
good sam park
Ratings: 10/10★/10 (RV Park) From Jct of I-20 (exit 591) & FM 2011: Go 2 mi SE on FM 2011. (L). **FAC:** paved rds. Avail: 128 paved, 32 pull-thrus, (34x77), back-ins (34x65), 128 full hkups (30/50 amps), cable, WiFi @ sites, laundry, LP gas. **REC:** pool, playground. Pet restrict (B/Q). Partial handicap access. No tents. Big rig sites. 2021 rates: $45 to $50.
(903)643-8888 Lat: 32.41547, Lon: -94.76741
2073 FM 2011, Longview, TX 75603
www.fernbrookpark.com
See ad this page

NORTH POINT RV PARK
good sam park
Ratings: 7/9★/7 (RV Park) From jct Loop 281 & US 259: Go 5 mi N on US 259. (R). **FAC:** gravel rds. Avail: 39 paved, 22 pull-thrus, (24x55), back-ins (27x45), 39 full hkups (30/50 amps), cable, WiFi @ sites, laundry. Pet restrict (B). Partial handicap access. No tents. Big rig sites. 2021 rates: $35 to $42.
(903)663-6400 Lat: 32.6130236, Lon: -94.7544920
7552 US Highway 259 N, Longview, TX 75605
www.northpointrvpark.net
See ad this page

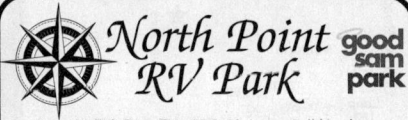

TX

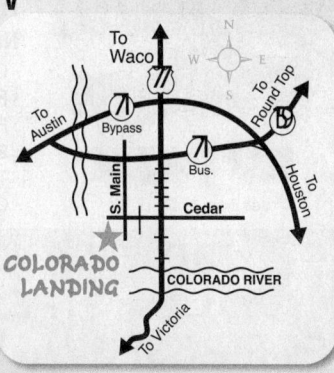

LOS FRESNOS — M4 *Cameron*

PALMDALE RV RESORT
Ratings: 9.5/10★/8.5 (RV Park) Avail: 120 full hkups (30/50 amps). 2021 rates: $49. (956)399-8694, 30910 State Highway 100, Los Fresnos, TX 78566

LUBBOCK — A4 *Lubbock*

LUBBOCK See also Slaton & Wolfforth.

BUFFALO SPRINGS LAKE (Public) From Jct of Loop 289 & E 50th St, E 4.5 mi on E 50th St, S .8 mi on CR 3100, High Meadow Rd. 2.8 mi around lake (R) Entrance fee required. 74 Avail: 34 full hkups, 40 W, 40 E (30/50 amps). 2021 rates: $20 to $25. (806)747-3353

CAMELOT VILLAGE RV PARK
Ratings: 8.5/9★/10 (RV Area in MH Park) From jct Loop 289W & 34th St exit: Go 500 feet W on 34th St. (L). Elev 3240 ft.**FAC:** paved rds. (213 spaces). Avail: 10 paved, patios, 6 pull-thrus, (35x80), back-ins (35x70), 10 full hkups (30/50 amps), seasonal sites, WiFi, laundry. **REC:** pool. Pets OK. No tents. Big rig sites. 2021 rates: $44, Military discount.
(806)792-6477 Lat: 33.56308, Lon: -101.94703
6001 34th St, Lubbock, TX 79407
www.camelotvillagelubbock.com
See ad this page

LUBBOCK KOA **Ratings: 8.5/8.5/9** (Campground) Avail: 40 full hkups (30/50 amps). 2021 rates: $44 to $49. (806)762-8653, 5502 CR-6300, Lubbock, TX 79416

LUBBOCK RV PARK
Ratings: 9.5/10★/8 (RV Park) From Jct I-27 & Exit 9: Go 1/2 mi S on W Service Rd (R). Elev 3240 ft.**FAC:** paved rds. (98 spaces). Avail: 39 paved, 39 pull-thrus, (25x70), 39 full hkups (30/50 amps), seasonal sites, WiFi @ sites, laundry, LP gas. **REC:** heated pool, playground. Pet restrict (Q). Partial handicap access. No tents. Big rig sites. 2021 rates: $40, Military discount.
(806)747-2366 Lat: 33.64890, Lon: -101.83646
4811 N I-27, Lubbock, TX 79403
www.lubbockrvpark.com
See ad this page

THE RETREAT RV RESORT **Ratings: 10/NA/8** (RV Park) Avail: 15 full hkups (30/50 amps). 2021 rates: $42 to $67. (806)368-8613, 7516 Interstate 27, Lubbock, TX 79404

Travel Services

CAMPING WORLD OF LUBBOCK As the nation's largest retailer of RV supplies, accessories, services and new and used RVs, Camping World is committed to making your total RV experience better. **SERVICES:** RV, tire, RV appliance, sells firearms, staffed RV wash, restrooms. RV Sales. RV supplies, LP gas, RV accessible. Hours: 9am to 7pm.
(877)349-1343 Lat: 33.528257, Lon: -101.855962
1701 S. Loop 289, Lubbock, TX 79423
www.campingworld.com

LUMBERTON — C9 *Hardin*

VILLAGE CREEK (Public State Park) From US 96 (Dana St exit): Go 1/2 mi E on Dana St, then 1/2 block S on Village Creek Pkwy, then 1/2 mi E on Alma Dr. (Entrance fee). 25 Avail: 25 W, 25 E. 2021 rates: $15. (409)755-7322

MAGNOLIA — C8 *Montgomery*

MAGNOLIA FOREST RV PARK **Ratings: 8.5/9★/10** (RV Park) Avail: 91 full hkups (30/50 amps). 2021 rates: $45 to $65. (281)259-9700, 30427 Nichols Sawmill Rd, Magnolia, TX 77355

ROYAL PALMS RV RESORT
Ratings: 10/10★/8.5 (RV Resort) Avail: 101 full hkups (30/50 amps). 2021 rates: $55. (281)746-1032, 25103 Decker Prairie Rosehill Rd., Magnolia, TX 77355

MANSFIELD — J3 *Johnson*

DODGE CITY RV PARK **Ratings: 8/8.5/7.5** (RV Park) Avail: 10 full hkups (30/50 amps). 2021 rates: $40. (817)477-4433, 4126 CR 616, Alvarado, TX 76009

TEXAN RV RANCH
Ratings: 9.5/10★/9 (RV Park) From Jct of I-20 & US-287: Go 10 1/2 mi S on US-287, then 1/4 mi SW on Lone Star Rd (FM 157) (R). **FAC:** paved rds. (159 spaces). Avail: 51 gravel, 18 pull-thrus, (27x70), back-ins (25x65), 51 full hkups (30/50 amps), seasonal sites, cable, WiFi @ sites, rentals, dump, laundry, groc, LP gas. **REC:** pool, boating nearby, playground. Pet restrict (B/Q). Partial handicap access. No tents. Big rig sites. 2021 rates: $55, Military discount.
(817)473-1666 Lat: 32.53450, Lon: -97.10996
1961 Lone Star Rd, Mansfield, TX 76063
texanrvranch.com
See ad pages 876, 901

MARATHON — C3 *Brewster*

MARATHON MOTEL & RV PARK **Ratings: 6.5/8★/8** (RV Park) 24 Avail: 19 full hkups, 5 W, 5 E (30/50 amps). 2021 rates: $35. (432)386-4241, 703 West Hwy 90, Marathon, TX 79842

MARBLE FALLS — C6 *Burnet*

MARBLE FALLS See also Austin, Buchanan Dam, Burnet, Johnson City & Spicewood.

SUNSET POINT ON LAKE LBJ
Ratings: 9.5/10★/10 (RV Park) Avail: 60 full hkups (30/50 amps). 2021 rates: $59 to $101. (830)798-8199, 2322 N Wirtz Dam Rd, Marble Falls, TX 78654

MARSHALL — B9 *Harrison*

MARSHALL See also Longview & Tatum, TX; Greenwood, LA.

COUNTRY PINES RV PARK **Ratings: 4.5/5.5/5.5** (RV Park) Avail: 50 full hkups (30/50 amps). 2021 rates: $30 to $33. (903)935-4278, 5935 Hwy 59N, Marshall, TX 75670

MASON — C6 *Mason*

FORT MASON CITY PARK (Public) From Jct of US 87 & SR 29, S 1.2 mi on US 87 (L). Avail: 24 full hkups (30/50 amps). 2021 rates: $25. (325)347-2064

MATAGORDA — D8 *Matagorda*

MATAGORDA BAY NATURE PARK (Public) From jct TX-60 & FM 2031: Go 6 mi S on FM 2031 (R). Avail: 70 full hkups (30/50 amps). 2021 rates: $40 to $58. (979)863-7120

MATHIS — E7 *Live Oak*

LAKE CORPUS CHRISTI (Public State Park) From Jct of I-37 & SR-359 (exit 36), SW 5.8 mi on SR-359 to Park Rd 25, NW 1.4 mi (L) (Entrance fee). 108 Avail: 26 full hkups, 82 W, 23 E (30/50 amps). 2021 rates: $10 to $25. (361)547-2635

MUSTANG HOLLOW CAMPGROUND **Ratings: 8/8.5★/8.5** (Campground) 135 Avail: 131 full hkups, 4 W, 4 E (30/50 amps). 2021 rates: $36 to $39. (361)547-5201, 101 C.R. 371, Mathis, TX 78368

SUNRISE BEACH RV (Public) From jct I-37 & Hwy 359: Go 5-1/2 mi SW on Hwy 359, then 1-1/2 mi W on Park Rd 25, then 1 block S on FM 1068. (Entrance fee). Avail: 93 full hkups (50 amps). 2021 rates: $16 to $20. (361)547-3004

TOTEM POLE RV PARK **Ratings: 7.5/8★/5.5** (RV Park) Avail: 102 full hkups (30/50 amps). 2021 rates: $35. (361)356-7400, 10754 North IH-37, Mathis, TX 78368

WILDERNESS LAKES RV RESORT **Ratings: 9/9★/8.5** (RV Resort) Avail: 120 full hkups (50 amps). 2021 rates: $36 to $44. (361)547-9995, 22552 Park Rd 25, Mathis, TX 78368

MCALLEN — M3 *Hidalgo*

CITRUS VALLEY MH & RV PARK **Ratings: 8/8.5★/7** (RV Park) Avail: 150 full hkups (30/50 amps). 2021 rates: $40. (956)383-8189, 2901 Hwy 107 West, McAllen, TX 78504

MCALLEN MOBILE PARK

good sam park

Ratings: 9/9★/8.5 (RV Area in MH Park) From Jct of US-281 & Nolana Loop (Hwy 3461) exit, W 1.5 mi on Nolana Loop/Hwy 3461 to FM-2061/McColl Rd, N 0.5 mi (R). **FAC:** paved rds. (410 spaces). 188 Avail: 132 paved, 56 grass, patios, 50 pull-thrus, (25x45), back-ins (25x45), 188 full hkups (30/50 amps), seasonal sites, WiFi @ sites, laundry, controlled access. **REC:** heated pool, hot tub, shuffleboard. Pet restrict (S/Q). Partial handicap access. No tents, eco-friendly. 2021 rates: $40 to $45. no cc.
(956)682-3304 Lat: 26.2367024, Lon: -98.2067242
4900 N McColl Rd , McAllen, TX 78504
mcallenmobilepark.com
See ad this page

SUNLIGHT TRAVEL TRAILER PARK **Ratings: 8/8.5★/6** (RV Park) Avail: 110 full hkups (30/50 amps). 2021 rates: $40. (956)682-7721, 4821 W Business 83, McAllen, TX 78501

MEDINA — D6 *Bandera*

HILL COUNTRY RESORT AND EVENT CENTER **Ratings: 9/8★/8** (RV Park) Avail: 68 full hkups (30/50 amps). 2021 rates: $37. (830)589-7475, 17740 State Hwy 16 N, Medina, TX 78055

MEDINA HIGHPOINT RESORT **Ratings: 9.5/9.5★/9.5** (Campground) Avail: 48 full hkups (30/50 amps). 2021 rates: $60 to $65. (800)225-0991, 23195 Hwy 16 N, Medina, TX 78055

MERCEDES — M4 *Hidalgo*

LLANO GRANDE LAKE PARK RESORT & COUNTRY CLUB MHP

good sam park

Ratings: 10/9.5★/9.5 (RV Area in MH Park) Avail: 570 full hkups (30/50 amps). 2021 rates: $35 to $61. (956)565-2638, 2215 East West Blvd, Mercedes, TX 78570

PARADISE SOUTH RV RESORT

good sam park

Ratings: 9.5/9★/8 (RV Park) Avail: 200 full hkups (30/50 amps). 2021 rates: $51. (888)563-7040, 9099 N. Mile 2 West Road, Mercedes, TX 78570

MERIDIAN — B7 *Bosque*

MERIDIAN (Public State Park) From Jct of SH-6 & Hwy 22, SW 2.4 mi on Hwy 22 (R) Note: Water & Elec. sites max. of 20 ft length. (Entrance fee). 31 Avail: 8 full hkups, 15 W, 7 E (30 amps). 2021 rates: $15 to $25. (254)435-2536

Set your clocks. Time zones are indicated in the front of each state and province.

MESQUITE — B7 *Dallas*

Travel Services

GANDER RV OF MESQUITE Your new hometown outfitter offering the best regional gear for all your outdoor needs. Your adventure awaits. **SERVICES:** MH mechanical, staffed RV wash, restrooms. RV Sales. RV supplies, LP gas, RV accessible. Hours: 9am - 7pm. (888)385-1084 Lat: 32.816233, Lon: -96.640373 2764 Interstate 30, Mesquite, TX 75150 rv.ganderoutdoors.com

MEXIA — B8 *Limestone*

FORT PARKER (Public State Park) From Jct of SR-14 & US-84, S 6.5 mi on SR-14 to Park Rd 28 (R) (Entrance fee). 34 Avail: 24 W, 24 E (30 amps). 2021 rates: $12 to $20. (254)562-5751

MIDLAND — B4 *Midland*

MIDESSA/ODESSA KOA **Ratings: 9/9★/8** (RV Park) Avail: 62 full hkups (30/50 amps). 2021 rates: $45. (800)864-3204, 4220 S County Rd 1290, Odessa, TX 79765

MIDLAND RV CAMPGROUND

good sam park

Ratings: 7.5/9.5★/7 (RV Park) Avail: 21 full hkups (30/50 amps). 2021 rates: $40. (432)697-0801, 2134 South Midland Dr, Midland, TX 79703

MINEOLA — B8 *Wood*

MINEOLA CIVIC CENTER & RV PARK

good sam park

Ratings: 6/9★/6.5 (RV Park) 221 Avail: 194 full hkups, 27 W, 27 E (30/50 amps). 2021 rates: $34 to $39. (903)569-6115, 1150 N. Newsom , Mineola, TX 75773

MINERAL WELLS — B6 *Palo Pinto*

COUNTRY LIVING RETREAT **Ratings: 7.5/9★/8** (RV Park) Avail: 23 full hkups (30/50 amps). 2021 rates: $35. (940)452-7970, 3299 S US Highway 281, Mineral Wells, TX 76067

LAKE MINERAL WELLS (Public State Park) E-bnd: From Jct of US-281 & US-180, E 3.9 mi on US-180 (L); or W-bnd: From Jct of I-20 & Exit 406 (S Bowie Dr), N 2.1 mi on Bowie Dr to Hwy 180, W 14 mi (R) (Entrance fee). 88 Avail: 88 W, 77 E (30/50 amps). 2021 rates: $14 to $26. (940)328-1171

MINGUS — B6 *Palo Pinto*

CACTUS ROSE RV PARK

good sam park

Ratings: 8/9.5★/8 (RV Park) 18 Avail: 17 full hkups, 1 W, 1 E (30/50 amps). 2021 rates: $36 to $48. (254)693-5976, 115 W I-20, Mingus, TX 76463

MISSION — M3 *Hidalgo*

AMERICANA RV RESORT MHP

good sam park

Ratings: 9/9★/8.5 (RV Park) Avail: 100 full hkups (30/50 amps). 2021 rates: $35 to $41. (956)581-1705, 1840 S Bentsen Palm Dr, Palmview, TX 78572

BENTSEN PALM RV PARK **Ratings: 9/8.5★/8.5** (RV Park) Avail: 84 full hkups (30/50 amps). 2021 rates: $45. (956)585-0541, 3501 North Bentsen Palm Drive, Mission, TX 78574

Like Us on Facebook.

MISSION (CONT)

BENTSEN PALM VILLAGE RV RESORT
Ratings: 10/10★/10 (RV Resort) From Jct of US-83 Expwy & Conway, go S 4 mi on Conway,to Military, go W 3 mi on Military to Bentsen Palm Dr, go S 1/4mi on Bentsen Palm Dr (L). **FAC:** paved rds. Avail: 230 paved, patios, 86 pull-thrus, (41x80), back-ins (30x65), 230 full hkups (30/50 amps), cable, WiFi @ sites, rentals, laundry, controlled access. **REC:** heated pool, hot tub, Rio Grande River: fishing, kayaking/canoeing. Pet restrict (Q). Partial handicap access. No tents, Age restrict may apply. Big rig sites, eco-friendly. 2021 rates: $49 to $69.
(956)585-5568 Lat: 26.18841, Lon: -98.37857
2500 S Bentsen Palm Drive, Mission, TX 78572
www.bentsenpalm.com
See ad this page

BLUEBONNET RV RESORT
Ratings: 9/9★/8 (RV Resort) Eastbound: From jct of US 83 Expressway/I-2 & Bentsen Palm Dr: Go 1.2 mi N (R) or Westbound from the Jct of US 83 Expressway & Lahoma exit: Go 1 block W on N Frontage Rd, then 1.2 mi N on Bentsen Palm Dr (R). **FAC:** paved rds. (332 spaces). Avail: 250 grass, patios, back-ins (25x50), 250 full hkups (30/50 amps), seasonal sites, WiFi, laundry, controlled access. **REC:** heated pool, shuffleboard. Pet restrict (Q). Partial handicap access. No tents, Age restrict may apply, eco-friendly. 2021 rates: $39, Military discount.
(956)585-7630 Lat: 26.250054, Lon: -98.367388
3366 N Bentsen Palm Dr, Mission, TX 78574
www.rvresorts.com
See ad previous page

CANYON LAKE RV RESORT **Ratings: 8.5/9.5★/8** (RV Park) Avail: 212 full hkups (30/50 amps). 2021 rates: $40 to $50. (956)580-4545, 4770 N. Mayberry Rd., Mission, TX 78573

CHIMNEY PARK RV RESORT **Ratings: 9/9★/8** (RV Park) Avail: 215 full hkups (30/50 amps). 2021 rates: $34 to $57. (956)585-5061, 4224 S Conway, Mission, TX 78572

CIRCLE T FAMILY COMMUNITY **Ratings: 8/9★/6.5** (RV Park) Avail: 270 full hkups (30/50 amps). 2021 rates: $40. (956)585-5381, 1820 Clay Tolle, Mission, TX 78572

We rate what RVers consider important.

EL VALLE DEL SOL/DE LA LUNA RV & MHC
Ratings: 9/9★/8.5 (RV Park) Avail: 97 full hkups (30/50 amps). 2021 rates: $35. (956)585-5704, 2500 E Bus 83, Mission, TX 78572

ELDORADO ACRES RV PARK **Ratings: 9.5/9.5★/7.5** (RV Park) Avail: 84 full hkups (30/50 amps). 2021 rates: $40. (956)581-6718, 610 N FM 492, Palmview, TX 78574

J FIVE RV & MOBILEHOME PARK
Ratings: 7.5/9★/7.5 (RV Area in MH Park) Avail: 55 full hkups (50 amps). 2021 rates: $30. (956)682-7495, 3907 N Taylor Road, Mission, TX 78573

MISSION BELL TRADEWINDS RV RESORT & MHP **Ratings: 8.5/9★/7.5** (RV Park) Avail: 356 full hkups (30/50 amps). 2021 rates: $41 to $51. (956)585-4833, 1711 E Bus Highway 83, Mission, TX 78572

MISSION WEST RV PARK **Ratings: 9/9★/8** (RV Park) Avail: 200 full hkups (30/50 amps). 2021 rates: $45. (956)585-5551, 511 E Loop 374, Palmview, TX 78572

OLEANDER ACRES MH & RV PARK **Ratings: 8/8★/6.5** (RV Park) Avail: 197 full hkups (30/50 amps). 2021 rates: $40 to $50. (956)585-9093, 2421 S Conway, Mission, TX 78572

PATRIOT POINTE **Ratings: 9/9★/7** (RV Area in MH Park) Avail: 54 full hkups (50 amps). 2021 rates: $40. (956)585-6861, 1740 E Bus Hwy 83 C-1, Mission, TX 78572

PLEASANT VALLEY RESORT **Ratings: 9.5/9.5★/8.5** (RV Park) Avail: 135 full hkups (30/50 amps). 2021 rates: $50 to $55. (956)580-2940, 7320 West Expressway 83, Mission, TX 78572

RETAMA VILLAGE (Planned RV Community) (RV Homes/Park Models/Lots for Sale only) 0 Avail. (956)530-3252, 2204 Seagull Ln, Mission, TX 78572

SEVEN OAKS RESORT
Ratings: 9.5/9.5★/9 (RV Park) From Jct of US-83 Expwy & Los Ebanos Rd exit, S 0.5 mi on Los Ebanos Rd to One Mile South Rd, W 0.5 mi to Inspiration Rd, S 0.5 mi to entrance (L). **FAC:** paved rds. (231 spaces). 131 Avail: 30 paved, 91 all weather, 10 grass, patios, back-ins (35x90), 131 full hkups (30/50 amps), seasonal sites, WiFi @ sites, rentals, laundry. **REC:** heated pool, hot tub, shuffleboard. Pet restrict (B). No tents, Age restrict may apply. Big rig sites, eco-friendly. 2021 rates: $44 to $57. no cc.
(956)581-0068 Lat: 26.19976, Lon: -98.35258
801 S Inspiration Rd #222, Mission, TX 78572
www.sevenoaksresort.com
See ad previous page

SHARYLAND VILLAS RV AND MHP **Ratings: 8/7.5★/6** (RV Park) Avail: 29 full hkups (30/50 amps). 2021 rates: $38. (956)585-0966, 3417 N Shary Road, Mission, TX 78573

SLEEPY VALLEY RESORT **Ratings: 9/9★/8** (RV Park) Avail: 50 full hkups (30/50 amps). 2021 rates: $40. (956)581-1871, 2301 N Abram Rd, Mission, TX 78572

SPLIT RAIL RV PARK **Ratings: 9/9.5★/9** (RV Park) Avail: 50 full hkups (30/50 amps). 2021 rates: $38. (956)585-8135, 513 N Los Ebanos, Mission, TX 78572

MONAHANS — C3 *Ward*

MONAHANS SANDHILLS (Public State Park) From town, E 6 mi on I-H 20 to Park Rd 41 (exit 86), N 0.25 mi (E) (Entrance fee). 26 Avail: 26 W, 26 E (30/50 amps). 2021 rates: $15. (432)943-2092

MONTGOMERY — C8 *Montgomery*

LAKE CONROE/HOUSTON NORTH KOA **Ratings: 9.5/9/8.5** (RV Park) Avail: 159 full hkups (30/50 amps). 2021 rates: $48 to $64. (936)582-1200, 19785 Hwy 105W, Montgomery, TX 77356

MOODY — C7 *McLennan*

MOTHER NEFF (Public State Park) From jct Hwy 317 & FM 107: Go 6-1/2 mi W on FM 107, then 1-3/4 mi S on Hwy 236, then W on Park Rd 14. Entrance fee required. Avail: 20 full hkups (30/50 amps). 2021 rates: $12 to $25. (254)853-2389

MOUNT PLEASANT — A8 *Titus*

CAMP LANGSTON RV RESORT **Ratings: 9/9★/7.5** (RV Park) Avail: 54 full hkups (30/50 amps). 2021 rates: $50. (903)572-5935, 50 County Road 3227, Mount Pleasant, TX 75455

LAKE BOB SANDLIN (Public State Park) From Jct of US-271 & FM-127 (W of town), SW 10.5 mi on FM-127 to FM-21, S 1.1 mi (L); or N-bnd: From Jct of US-271 & SR-11, W 5.2 mi on SR-11 to FM-21, NW 4.8 mi (R) (Entrance fee). 75 Avail: 75 W, 75 E (30 amps). 2021 rates: $18. (903)572-5531

MOUNT PLEASANT KOA **Ratings: 9/10★/8** (RV Park) Avail: 62 full hkups (30/50 amps). 2021 rates: $39.95 to $45.95. (903)572-5005, 2322 Greenhill Rd, Mount Pleasant, TX 75455

MOUNT VERNON — A8 *Franklin*

WALLEYE PARK AT LAKE CYPRESS SPRINGS (Public) From Jct of I-30 & Exit 146/Hwy 37, S 0.9 mi to FM 21, E 1.5 mi to FM 2723, S 2.8 mi to FM 3122, E 1.5 mi to SE 4220, S 0.9 mi on SE 4220 (L) (Entrance fee). 84 Avail: 84 W, 84 E (30/50 amps). 2021 rates: $20 to $50. (903)537-4536

MURCHISON — B8 *Henderson*

STAY A WHILE RV PARK
Ratings: 7.5/9★/9.5 (RV Park) Avail: 150 full hkups (30/50 amps). 2021 rates: $39. (903)469-4477, 10101 State Hwy 31 East, Murchison, TX 75778

NACOGDOCHES — B9 *Nacogdoches*

FAIRWAY RV PARK **Ratings: 7/9★/8** (RV Park) Avail: 11 full hkups (30/50 amps). 2021 rates: $30. (936)462-9900, 5393 US Hwy 59 South, Nacogdoches, TX 75964

WESTERN PINES RV PARK **Ratings: 5.5/NA/6.5** (RV Park) Avail: 12 full hkups (30/50 amps). 2021 rates: $35 to $45. (936)645-6352, 5001 NW Stallings Dr, Nacogdoches, TX 75964

NEW BRAUNFELS — D6 *Comal*

CANYON LAKE - COE/POTTERS CREEK (Public Corps) From Jct of I-35 & FM-306, W 26 mi on FM-306 to Potters Creek Rd, S 2.3 mi (E). 114 Avail: 114 W, 98 E (50 amps), Pit toilets. 2021 rates: $30. (830)964-3341

HILL COUNTRY COTTAGE AND RV RESORT **Ratings: 9/9★/9.5** (RV Resort) Avail: 100 full hkups (30/50 amps). 2021 rates: $62 to $74. (830)625-1919, 131 Rueckle Rd, New Braunfels, TX 78130

NEW BRAUNFELS RV AND MH PARK
Ratings: 8/9★/6.5 (RV Park) Avail: 110 full hkups (30/50 amps). 2021 rates: $50 to $60. (830)310-4647, 2136 N I-35, New Braunfels, TX 78130

RIO GUADALUPE RESORT **Ratings: 8/8.5★/8** (RV Park) Avail: 58 full hkups (30/50 amps). 2021 rates: $50 to $95. (830)964-3613, 14130 River Rd, New Braunfels, TX 78132

RIVER RANCH RV RESORT
Ratings: 9/10★/8 (RV Park) S-Bnd I-35 (Exit 188) & Bus 35/46: Go 1/4 mi S on Bus 35/46, then 1 block East on Guadalupe River Turnaround (R). N-Bnd I-35 (Exit 187) & Seguin Ave: Go 1 block W on Seguin Ave, then 1/4 mi N on Business 35, then 1 Block E on Guadalupe River Turnaround (R). **FAC:** paved rds. Avail: 53 paved, patios, 3 pull-thrus, (27x55), back-ins (28x43), 53 full hkups (30/50 amps), cable, WiFi @ sites, laundry. **REC:** Guadalupe River: swim, fishing, kayaking/canoeing, boating nearby. Pet restrict (S/B/Q). Partial handicap access. No tents. Big rig sites. 2021 rates: $45 to $75, Military discount.
(830)625-7788 Lat: 29.69412, Lon: -98.10605
420 North Business I-35, New Braunfels, TX 78130
www.riverranchtexas.com
See ad this page

Travel Services

CAMPING WORLD OF NEW BRAUNFELS/SAN ANTONIO As the nation's largest retailer of RV supplies, accessories, services and new and used RVs, Camping World is committed to making your total RV experience better. **SERVICES:** RV, tire, RV appliance, MH mechanical, sells outdoor gear, sells firearms, staffed RV wash, restrooms. RV Sales. RV supplies, LP gas, dump, RV accessible. Hours: 9am - 7pm.
(877)240-7221 Lat: 29.762147, Lon: -98.017535
3891 South I.H. 35, New Braunfels, TX 78130
www.campingworld.com

NEW CANEY — C8 *Montgomery*

FOREST RETREAT RV PARK
Ratings: 10/10★/10 (RV Park) Avail: 32 full hkups (30/50 amps). 2021 rates: $55. (281)354-9888, 21711 MCCleskey Rd, New Caney, TX 77357

GRAND TEXAS RV RESORT
good sam park **Ratings: 10/9.5★/8.5** (RV Resort) Avail: 41 full hkups (30/50 amps). 2021 rates: $45 to $65. (281)806-3036, 22846 State Highway 242, New Caney, TX 77357

LONE STAR LAKES RV PARK
Ratings: 9.5/9.5★/9 (RV Park) From Jct of US-59 & FM 1485: Go S 0.9 mi on S-bnd Frntg Rd (R). **FAC:** paved/gravel rds. (101 spaces). Avail: 13 paved, patios, 13 pull-thrus, (20x70), 13 full hkups (30/50 amps), seasonal sites, WiFi @ sites, laundry, LP gas, fire rings. **REC:** pool, Lake Redmond: fishing, playground. Pet restrict (B). No tents. Big rig sites. 2021 rates: $42.
(281)399-8977 Lat: 30.14612, Lon: -95.22481
20980 US Hwy 59, New Caney, TX 77357
lonestarlakesrvpark.com
See ad opposite page

NEW WAVERLY — C8 *Walker*

HILLCREST RV PARK **Ratings: 5/5/4.5** (RV Park) Avail: 10 full hkups (30/50 amps). 2021 rates: $10 to $15. (936)767-4101, 5260 Hwy 150W, New Waverly, TX 77358

ODESSA — B4 *Ector*

ODESSA See also Midland.

BARON MOBILE ESTATES & RV PARK (MHP)
good sam park **Ratings: 5.5/9★/7.5** (RV Park) Avail: 15 full hkups (30/50 amps). 2021 rates: $45. (432)332-4976, 1147 Gary Terrace, Odessa, TX 79764

PARK PLACE RV PARK **Ratings: 9.5/10★/7.5** (RV Park) Avail: 150 full hkups (30/50 amps). 2021 rates: $75. (432)582-1962, 9249 West Murphy Street, Odessa, TX 79763

ONALASKA — C8 *Polk*

LAKE LIVINGSTON/ONALASKA KOA **Ratings: 9.5/8.5/10** (RV Park) Avail: 95 full hkups (30/50 amps). 2021 rates: $44.89 to $90.89. (936)646-3824, 15152 US Hwy 190 West, Onalaska, TX 77360

ORE CITY — B9 *Upshur*

LAKE O' THE PINES - COE/CEDAR SPRINGS (Public Corps) From jct US-259 & Hwy-155: Go 1/2 mi E on Hwy-155. 28 Avail: Pit toilets. (903)665-2336

OTTINE — D7 *Gonzales*

PALMETTO (Public State Park) From Jct of I-10 & US-183, S 2.4 mi on US-183 to Park Rd 11, W 2 mi (R) (Entrance fee). 18 Avail: 1 full hkups, 17 W, 17 E (30/50 amps). 2021 rates: $18 to $20. (830)672-3266

PADRE ISLAND — K5 *Nueces*

PADRE ISLAND NATL SEASHORE/MALAQUITE (Public National Park) From JFK Causeway, S 10 mi on PR-22 (E). Entrance fee required. 48 Avail. 2021 rates: $14. (361)949-8068

PALACIOS — D8 *Matagorda*

SERENDIPITY BAY RV RESORT CABINS & MARINA **Ratings: 9/9.5★/9** (RV Park) Avail: 150 full hkups (30/50 amps). 2021 rates: $48 to $60. (361)972-5454, 1001 Main St, Palacios, TX 77465

PALMVIEW — M3 *Hidalgo*

BENTSEN GROVE RESORT MHP **Ratings: 9.5/9.5★/9** (RV Park) Avail: 300 full hkups (30/50 amps). 2021 rates: $32 to $41. (956)585-7011, 1645 S Bentsen Palm Drive, Palmview, TX 78572

GOLDEN GROVE RV PARK **Ratings: 6/8★/6** (RV Park) Avail: 11 full hkups (30/50 amps). 2021 rates: $35. (956)585-9910, 2545 S Bentsen Palm Dr, Palmview, TX 78572

PAMPA — F10 *Gray*

RECREATION PARK, CITY OF PAMPA (Public) From Jct of US-60 & US-70, E 2.3 mi on US-60 to Rodeo Dr, N 0.1 mi (L). 25 Avail: 25 W, 25 E (30 amps). 2021 rates: $15 to $20. (806)669-1044

PARIS — A8 *Lamar*

PAT MAYSE LAKE - COE/PAT MAYSE WEST (Public Corps) From Jct of Hwy 271 & FM-906, W 4 mi on FM-906 to FM-197, W 3 mi to CR-35810, S 1 mi to CR-35800, E to park (L). 88 Avail: 88 W, 83 E (30 amps). 2021 rates: $12 to $18. May 01 to Oct 31. (903)732-4956

Find Good Sam member specials at CampingWorld.com

PAT MAYSE LAKE - COE/SANDERS COVE (Public Corps) From Jct of US-271 & FM-906, W 0.75 mi on FM-906 to CR-35920, SW 0.75 mi to park (E). 85 Avail: 85 W, 85 E (30 amps), Pit toilets. 2021 rates: $18 to $22. Mar 01 to Oct 31. (903)732-4955

PEARLAND — D8 *Brazoria*

CULLEN RV RESORT
good sam park **Ratings: 9.5/9.5★/9** (RV Resort) From jct Hwy 288 & Bailey Ave: Go 2-3/4 mi E on Bailey Ave, then 300 feet S on Joe Dr (R). **FAC:** paved rds. Avail: 97 paved, patios, 20 pull-thrus, (30x80), back-ins (35x70), 97 full hkups (30/50 amps), WiFi @ sites, laundry, controlled access. **REC:** pool, hot tub, pond, fishing. Pets OK. Partial handicap access. No tents. Big rig sites. 2021 rates: $50.
(832)554-6966 Lat: 29.529234, Lon: -95.34189
3802 Joe Dr, Pearland, TX 77584
cullenrvresort.com
See ad this page

PECOS — C3 *Reeves*

TRAPARK RV PARK **Ratings: 4/5/5** (Membership Park) Avail: 10 full hkups (30/50 amps). 2021 rates: $30 to $32. (432)447-2137, 3100 Moore St, Pecos, TX 79772

PHARR — M3 *Hidalgo*

TEXAS TRAILS RV RESORT
good sam park **Ratings: 10/8.5★/9** (RV Resort) S-bnd: US-281 & Bus 281 (Owassa Rd exit), W 0.3 mi on Owassa Rd (L) or N-bnd: US-83 & US-281, N 1.8 mi on US-281 to Edinburgh (Owassa Rd exit), N 0.8 mi on E Frntg Rd to Owassa Rd, W 0.3 mi (L). **FAC:** paved rds. (866 spaces). Avail: 684 paved, patios, back-ins (30x60), 684 full hkups (30/50 amps), WiFi @ sites, rentals, laundry, controlled access. **REC:** heated pool, hot tub, shuffleboard. Pet restrict (Q). Partial handicap access. No tents, Age restrict may apply. Big rig sites, eco-friendly. 2021 rates: $45, Military discount.
(956)787-6538 Lat: 26.24652, Lon: -98.18207
501 W Owassa Rd., Pharr, TX 78577
www.rvresorts.com
See ad this page

Find new and exciting itineraries in our ""Road Trip'' article at the front of each state and province.

TIP O TEXAS RV RESORT
good sam park **Ratings: 10/9★/8.5** (RV Resort) N-bnd: From Jct of US-83 Expwy & US-281/ Pharr South exit, N 1 mi on US-281 Frontg Rd (N Cage Blvd) to Sioux Rd E 0.2 mi (L) S-bnd: From Jct of US-281 & Sioux Rd exit, E 0.2 mi on Sioux Rd (L). **FAC:** paved rds. (846 spaces). Avail: 500 paved, patios, back-ins (25x55), 500 full hkups (50 amps), WiFi @ sites, rentals, laundry, controlled access. **REC:** heated pool, hot tub, shuffleboard. Pet restrict (B/Q). No tents, Age restrict may apply, eco-friendly. 2021 rates: $45, Military discount.
(956)787-9959 Lat: 26.22010, Lon: -98.17546
101 E Sioux Rd, Pharr, TX 78577
www.rvresorts.com
See ad this page

Thank You to our active and retired military personnel. Look for military parks within the state listings section of your 2022 Guide.

TX

PHARR (CONT)

TROPIC STAR RV RESORT
good sam park **Ratings: 9/9★/9** (RV Resort) From Jct of US-83 Expwy & US-281, S 2.1 mi on US-281/Cage Blvd (L). **FAC:** paved rds. (1182 spaces). Avail: 550 paved, patios, 15 pull-thrus, (30x55), back-ins (30x60), 550 full hkups (30/50 amps), seasonal sites, WiFi, rentals, laundry, controlled access. **REC:** heated pool, hot tub, golf, shuffleboard. Pet restrict (Q). Partial handicap access. No tents, Age restrict may apply. Big rig sites, eco-friendly. 2021 rates: $45, Military discount.
(956)787-5957 Lat: 26.17627, Lon: -98.18530
1401 S Cage Blvd., Pharr, TX 78577
www.rvresorts.com
See ad previous page

PILOT POINT — A7 *Denton*

SHARK TOOTH RV RANCH **Ratings: 6/NA/7.5** (RV Park) Avail: 30 full hkups (30/50 amps). 2021 rates: $30. (940)600-2749, 11670 Massey Road, Pilot Point, TX 76258

PINELAND — C9 *San Augustine*

POWELL PARK CAMPING RESORT & MARINA (Public Corps) From town, NW 10 mi on FR-83 to FR-705, S 12 mi (L). 68 Avail: 19 W, 19 E (30/50 amps). 2021 rates: $20 to $34. (409)584-2624

SAM RAYBURN RESERVOIR - COE/RAYBURN (Public Corps) From town, NW 10 mi on FR-83 to FR-705, S 11 mi to FR-3127, W 1.5 mi (L). 29 Avail: 24 W, 24 E (30/50 amps). 2021 rates: $14 to $28. Mar 01 to Dec 31. (409)384-5716

SAM RAYBURN RESERVOIR - COE/SAN AUGUSTINE (Public Corps) From town, NW 6 mi on FR-83 to FR-1751, S 4 mi (E). 94 Avail: 94 W, 94 E (30 amps). 2021 rates: $26. (409)384-5716

PITTSBURG — B8 *Camp*

BAREFOOT BAY MARINA AND RESORT **Ratings: 8/9.5★/9** (RV Park) Avail: 79 full hkups (30/50 amps). 2021 rates: $40 to $50. (903)856-3643, 5244 FM 1520, Pittsburg, TX 75686

THE BLUFFS RV PARK
good sam park **Ratings: 5.5/NA/7.5** (RV Park) Avail: 27 full hkups (30/50 amps). 2021 rates: $39. (469)363-1212, 3160 FM 21, Pittsburg, TX 75686

PLAINVIEW — A4 *Hale*

THE HITCHIN' POST RV PARK AND CABINS
good sam park **Ratings: 9/9.5★/8.5** (RV Park) From jct I-27 & Exit 51: Go 1/2 mi N on E service Rd (R) (I 27 E Frontage Rd at Exit 51). Elev 3302 ft.**FAC:** all weather rds. Avail: 79 all weather, 10 pull-thrus, (45x75), back-ins (45x60), 79 full hkups (30/50 amps), cable, WiFi @ sites, tent sites, rentals, laundry, LP gas, fire rings, firewood. **REC:** playground. Pet restrict (Q). Big rig sites. 2021 rates: $40, Military discount.
(806)789-3066 Lat: 34.225069, Lon: -101.717842
4018 N. Interstate 27, Plainview, TX 79072
thehitchinpostrvpark.com
See ad this page

POINT — B8 *Rains*

LAKE TAWAKONI RV
good sam park **Ratings: 7/7.5/7.5** (Membership Park) Avail: 159 full hkups (30 amps). 2021 rates: $49. (888)563-7040, 1246 Rains CR1470, Point, TX 75472

POOLVILLE — B7 *Parker*

WEST GATE RV PARK
good sam park **Ratings: 8/9.5★/8** (RV Park) Avail: 15 full hkups (30/50 amps). 2021 rates: $35 to $45. (817)523-2240, 10850 Texas Route 199, Poolville, TX 76487

PORT ARANSAS — E7 *Nueces*

A SPOTLIGHT Introducing Port Aransas' colorful attractions appearing at the front of this state section.

I.B. MAGEE BEACH PARK (Public) E on Hwy 361 to Port Aransas. Leave ferry, stay on Cotter St to park (E). 75 Avail: 75 W, 75 E (30 amps). 2021 rates: $25. (361)749-6117

ISLAND RV RESORT
good sam park **Ratings: 8.5/9.5★/8.5** (RV Park) From Jct of Hwy 361 (Ave G) & Hwy 361 (Alistar Rd), NW 0.25 mi on Hwy 361/Ave G (L); or From ferry landing & Hwy 361 (Cut-Off Rd), S 0.6 on Hwy 361 (R).

PREMIER TEXAS GULF RESORT
Enjoy your exceptional island getaway at our RV park with lots of recreation & entertainment, world class sport fishing, beautiful beaches, golf, birding centers & Gulf of Mexico fun!

FAC: paved rds. Avail: 200 paved, patios, 200 pull-thrus, (24x60), mostly side by side hkups, 200 full hkups (30/50 amps), cable, WiFi @ sites, LP gas. **REC:** pool, wading pool, hot tub, boating nearby. Pet restrict (B/Q). Partial handicap access. No tents, eco-friendly. 2021 rates: $60 to $70.
(361)749-5600 Lat: 27.83097, Lon: -97.07168
700 6th St, Port Aransas, TX 78373
www.islandrvresort.com
See ad page 879

MUSTANG ISLAND (Public State Park) From Corpus Christi: From Jct of Hwy 361 & Park Rd 22, N 4.9 mi on Hwy 361 (R); or From Port Aransas: From Jct of Ave G & Hwy 361, S 17.4 mi on Hwy 361 (L) (Entrance fee). 48 Avail: 48 W, 48 E (50 amps). 2021 rates: $20. (361)749-5246

PIONEER BEACH RESORT
good sam park **Ratings: 10/10★/9** (RV Park) Avail: 361 full hkups (30/50 amps). 2021 rates: $51 to $69. (361)749-6248, 120 Gulfwind Drive, Port Aransas, TX 78373

PORT A RV RESORT **Ratings: 10/9.5★/8** (RV Park) Avail: 184 full hkups (30/50 amps). 2021 rates: $75 to $85. (361)416-1405, 2600 Hwy 361, Port Aransas, TX 78373

TROPIC ISLAND RESORT
good sam park **Ratings: 10/10★/8.5** (RV Resort) Avail: 136 full hkups (30/50 amps). 2021 rates: $55 to $75. (361)749-6128, 315 Cut Off Rd, Port Aransas, TX 78373

PORT ARTHUR — D9 *Nueces*

ACCESS RV PARK **Ratings: 8.5/9★/7.5** (RV Park) Avail: 83 full hkups (30/50 amps). 2021 rates: $49. (409)729-8000, 2565 95th St, Port Arthur, TX 77640

SEA RIM (Public State Park) From town: Go 10 mi S on Hwy 87 to Sabine Pass Battleground, then 10 mi SW on Hwy 87 (Entrance fee). 90 Avail: 15 W, 15 E (30/50 amps), Pit toilets. 2021 rates: $10 to $20. (409)971-2559

PORT ISABEL — M5 *Cameron*

PORT ISABEL PARK CENTER MHP **Ratings: 9/8.5★/6.5** (RV Park) Avail: 235 full hkups (30/50 amps). 2021 rates: $46 to $70. (956)943-7340, 702 Champion Ave, Port Isabel, TX 78578

PORT LAVACA — E7 *Calhoun*

LIGHTHOUSE BEACH RV PARK (Public) From Jct of Hwy 35 & Smith Rd (E side of town), SE 1 blk on Smith Rd (L). Avail: 55 full hkups (30/50 amps). 2021 rates: $30 to $35. (361)552-5311

TEXAS LAKESIDE RV RESORT **Ratings: 10/10★/10** (RV Park) Avail: 178 full hkups (30/50 amps). 2021 rates: $61 to $76. (361)551-2267, 2499 W Austin St, Port Lavaca, TX 77979

PORT MANSFIELD — L4 *Willacy*

R & R RV PARK **Ratings: 7.5/8★/7** (RV Park) Avail: 52 full hkups (30/50 amps). 2021 rates: $35. (956)944-2253, 901 Mansfield Drive , Port Mansfield, TX 78598

THE PARK @ PORT MANSFIELD **Ratings: 6.5/8★/7.5** (RV Park) Avail: 64 full hkups (30/50 amps). 2021 rates: $40. (956)746-1530, 1300 Mansfield Rd, Port Mansfield, TX 78598

PORT O'CONNOR — E8 *Calhoun*

R & R RV RESORT & CASITAS **Ratings: 10/10★/9** (RV Resort) Avail: 81 full hkups (30/50 amps). 2021 rates: $55 to $85. (361)920-2267, 2350 Harrison Ave, Port O'Connor, TX 77982

PORTLAND — E7 *San Patricio*

SEA BREEZE RV COMMUNITY RESORT
good sam park **Ratings: 9/9.5★/9** (RV Park) From Jct of US-181 & FM-893/Moore Ave exit, NW 1 mi on FM-893/Moore Ave to Marriott St, SW 0.5 mi to Doyle, S 0.2 mi (R).

EASY ACCESS TO CORPUS CHRISTI
Great location near Corpus Christi attractions like the USS Lexington & Texas State Aquarium. Our park is located on the Nueces Bay. Come stay in one of our long pull-thrus and enjoy our clean pool & Texas shape whirlpool.

FAC: gravel rds. (164 spaces). Avail: 104 gravel, patios, 42 pull-thrus, (22x60), back-ins (22x40), 102 full hkups, 1 W, 1 E (30/50 amps), seasonal sites, WiFi @ sites, dump, laundry. **REC:** heated pool, Corpus Christi Bay: fishing, kayaking/canoeing, boating nearby. Pet restrict (B/Q) $. No tents, eco-friendly. 2021 rates: $65 to $70, Military discount.
(361)643-0744 Lat: 27.88515, Lon: -97.34420
1026 Seabreeze Lane, Portland, TX 78374
seabreezerv.com
See ad this page

POTTSBORO — A7 *Grayson*

LAKE TEXOMA - COE/PRESTON BEND (Public Corps) From town, N 9 mi on Hwy 120, follow signs (R). 24 Avail: 23 W, 24 E (30 amps). 2021 rates: $22 to $24. Apr 01 to Sep 29. (903)786-8408

PROCTOR — B6 *Comanche*

PROCTOR LAKE - COE/SOWELL CREEK (Public Corps) From town, E 12 mi on US-377 to FM-1476, W 2.2 mi to recreation road 6, S 0.5 mi to park entrance (R). Avail: 61 full hkups (30/50 amps). 2021 rates: $16 to $18. (254)879-2322

Join in the fun. Like us on FACEBOOK!

Thank you for being one of our best customers!

QUANAH — A5 *Hardeman*

COPPER BREAKS (Public State Park) S-bnd: From Jct of US-287 & SR-6/Main St., S 12 mi on SR-6 (R); or N-bnd: From Jct of US-70 & SR-6, N 8 mi on SR-6 (L) (Entrance fee). 35 Avail: 35 W, 35 E (30/50 amps). 2021 rates: $12 to $20. (940)839-4331

OLE TOWNE COTTON GIN RV PARK
good sam park **Ratings: 9/9★/8.5** (RV Park) From jct US 287 & FM 2363/Goodlett Rd: Go 1 block N on Goodlett Rd. (L) Location is 9 mi NW of Quanah. **FAC:** all weather rds. (60 spaces). Avail: 42 gravel, patios, 20 pull-thrus, (28x85), back-ins (27x60), 42 full hkups (30/50 amps), seasonal sites, cable, WiFi @ sites, tent sites, laundry, groc. **REC:** pool, hunting nearby. Pet restrict (B). Partial handicap access. Big rig sites. 2021 rates: $35 to $45, Military discount.
(940)674-2477 Lat: 34.33514, Lon: -99.88112
230 Market St, Quanah, TX 79252
www.oletowncottonginrvpark.com
See ad this page

QUITAQUE — A5 *Briscoe*

CAPROCK CANYONS (Public State Park) From Jct of SR-86 & FM-1065, N 3.1 mi on FM-1065 (L) (Entrance fee). 44 Avail: 44 W, 35 E (30/50 amps). 2021 rates: $14 to $22. (806)455-1492

QUITMAN — B8 *Wood*

GOVERNOR JIM HOGG CITY PARK (Public) From jct Hwy 154 & Hwy 37 (at courthouse square): Go 6 blocks S on Hwy 37. Avail: 19 full hkups (30/50 amps). 2021 rates: $20. (903)763-2223

RANGER — B6 *Eastland*

HORSESHOE RV PARK **Ratings: 3.5/4.5/6** (RV Park) Avail: 30 full hkups (30/50 amps). 2021 rates: $40. (254)631-9209, 1424 W Loop 254, Ranger, TX 76470

LA MANCHA LAKE RESORT **Ratings: 6.5/NA/7** (RV Park) Avail: 12 full hkups (30/50 amps). 2021 rates: $45 to $65. (254)647-3651, 402 CR 567, Eastland, TX 76448

RAYMONDVILLE — F7 *Willacy*

GATEWAY MHP & RV PARK **Ratings: 8.5/8.5★/8** (RV Park) Avail: 291 full hkups (30/50 amps). 2021 rates: $40. (956)689-6658, 400 FM 3168, Raymondville, TX 78580

REFUGIO — E7 *Refugio*

JETER RV PARK (Public) From jct US 77 & Hwy 774: Go 200 yds W on Hwy 774. Avail: 14 full hkups (30/50 amps). 2021 rates: $35. (512)526-5361

RICHMOND — D8 *Fort Bend*

BRAZOS BEND (Public State Park) From Jct of US-59 & FM-2759, S 1.9 mi on FM-2759 to FM-762, S 14.5 mi (L) (Entrance fee). 71 Avail: 71 W, 71 E (30/50 amps). 2021 rates: $20 to $25. (979)553-5101

RIVERBEND RV PARK **Ratings: 7/8★/6.5** (RV Park) Avail: 156 full hkups (30/50 amps). 2021 rates: $35. (281)343-5151, 1055 Agnes Rd, Richmond, TX 77469

SHILOH RV PARK **Ratings: 5.5/8.5/5.5** (RV Park) Avail: 111 full hkups (30/50 amps). 2021 rates: $30. (281)344-2888, 5539 FM 762, Richmond, TX 77469

RIESEL — C7 *McLennan*

BRAZOS TRAIL RV PARK
good sam park **Ratings: 7.5/10★/8** (RV Park) From jct FM 1860 & Hwy 6: Go 1 mi S on Hwy 6, then 1 Blk W on Rice Road (L). **FAC:** gravel rds. (100 spaces). Avail: 82 gravel, 82 pull-thrus, (32x60), 82 full hkups (30/50 amps), seasonal sites, WiFi @ sites, tent sites, dump, laundry, LP gas. **REC:** pond, fishing. Pets OK. Partial handicap access. Big rig sites. 2021 rates: $40 to $45.
(254)277-7275 Lat: 31.460810, Lon: -96.925739
219 Rice Road, Riesel, TX 76682
brazostrailrvpark.com
See ad page 920

RIO GRANDE VALLEY — F7 *Starr*

RIO GRANDE VALLEY See also Alamo, Brownsville, Donna, Edinburg, Harlingen, La Feria, McAllen, Mercedes, Mission & Weslaco.

RIO HONDO — M4 *Cameron*

TWIN PALMS RV RESORT **Ratings: 9/8★/7.5** (RV Park) Avail: 71 full hkups (30/50 amps). 2021 rates: $50. (956)748-0800, 107 E Colorado, Rio Hondo, TX 78583

RIVIERA — E7 *Kleberg*

SEAWIND RV RESORT ON THE BAY
good sam park **Ratings: 9/8.5★/9** (Public) From Jct of US-77 & FM-628 (N of town), E 9.8 mi on FM-628 (L). **FAC:** paved rds. Avail: 184 paved, patios, 25 pull-thrus, (35x70), back-ins (30x60), 184 full hkups (30/50 amps), WiFi @ sites, dump, laundry. **REC:** Baffin Bay: fishing, shuffleboard, playground. Pet restrict (B/Q). Partial handicap access. No tents. Big rig sites, eco-friendly. 2021 rates: $40, Military discount.
(361)297-5738 Lat: 27.31681, Lon: -97.67923
1066 E FM 628, Riviera, TX 78379
www.seawindrv.com
See ad page 906

ROANOKE — G2 *Denton*

NORTHLAKE VILLAGE RV PARK
good sam park **Ratings: 10/10★/10** (RV Park) From Jct I-35W (exit 70) & Hwy 114: Go 1 mi E on Hwy 114, then 1/4 mi N on Cleveland-Gibbs Rd (E).

QUIET COUNTRY LIVING NEAR DALLAS
Beautiful sites with paved patios and easy access, close to all that DFW has to offer. Only 3 minutes to Texas Motor Speedway and 15 minutes to Fort Worth and Denton. Book your long or short term stay now.
FAC: paved rds. (176 spaces). Avail: 80 all weather, patios, back-ins (30x60), 80 full hkups (30/50 amps), seasonal sites, WiFi @ sites, laundry, LP gas. **REC:** pool. Pet restrict (B/Q). Partial handicap access. No tents. Big rig sites. 2021 rates: $60 to $70, Military discount.
(817)430-3303 Lat: 33.03099, Lon: -97.25084
13001 Cleveland-Gibbs Rd #79, Roanoke, TX 76262
www.northlakevillagerv.com
See ad page 873

ROCKPORT — E7 *Aransas*

ANCIENT OAKS RV PARK
good sam park **Ratings: 9.5/10★/9.5** (Campground) From Jct of Bus Hwy 35 & FM-1069, SW 0.7 mi on Bus Hwy 35 (L). **FAC:** paved rds. 125 Avail: 38 paved, 87 grass, 125 pull-thrus, (24x60), 125 full hkups (30/50 amps), cable, WiFi @ sites, tent sites, rentals, dump, laundry. **REC:** heated pool, hot tub, pond, fishing, boating nearby, shuffleboard, playground. Pet restrict (B/Q). Partial handicap access. Big rig sites, eco-friendly. 2021 rates: $45 to $50.
(361)729-5051 Lat: 28.01259, Lon: -97.06348
1222 Business Hwy 35 S, Rockport, TX 78382
ancientoaksrvpark.com
See ad next page

BAY VIEW RV RESORT **Ratings: 7.5/8.5★/7** (RV Park) Avail: 225 full hkups (30/50 amps). 2021 rates: $45. (361)400-6000, 5451 Hwy 35 N, Rockport, TX 78382

BIG FISH RV PARK
good sam park **Ratings: 7/NA/8** (RV Park) Avail: 53 full hkups (30/50 amps). 2021 rates: $40. (361)727-9211, 450 S. Hwy 35 Bypass, Rockport, TX 78382

CIRCLE W RV RANCH **Ratings: 9/8★/7.5** (RV Park) Avail: 300 full hkups (30/50 amps). 2021 rates: $47 to $55. (361)729-1542, 1401 Smokehouse Rd, Rockport, TX 78382

COASTAL BREEZE RV RESORT **Ratings: 10/9.5★/9** (RV Resort) Avail: 198 full hkups (30/50 amps). 2021 rates: $60 to $90. (361)444-4131, 3025 FM 1781, Rockport, TX 78382

COPANO BAY RV RESORT **Ratings: 9.5/9★/8** (RV Park) Avail: 144 full hkups (30/50 amps). 2021 rates: $59. (361)790-9373, 3101 FM 1781, Rockport, TX 78382

COVE HARBOR COACH RESORT **Ratings: 10/NA/10** (RV Resort) Avail: 42 full hkups (30/50 amps). 2021 rates: $65 to $75. (361)480-0180, 2620 TX 35 Business S, Rockport, TX 78382

FULTON OAKS PARK **Ratings: 7/8.5★/7** (RV Park) Avail: 10 full hkups (30/50 amps). 2021 rates: $35. (361)729-4606, 1301 Lone Star Rd, Fulton, TX 78358

GOOSE ISLAND (Public State Park) From Jct of SR-35 & Park Rd 13, E 1.4 mi on Park Rd 13 (R) (Entrance fee). 101 Avail: 101 W, 101 E (30/50 amps). 2021 rates: $18 to $22. (361)729-2858

LAGOON'S RV RESORT **Ratings: 9/9.5★/9.5** (RV Resort) Avail: 360 full hkups (30/50 amps). 2021 rates: $50. (361)729-7834, 600 Enterprise Blvd, Rockport, TX 78382

MAJESTIC OAK RV RESORT **Ratings: 9.5/9.5★/9.5** (RV Park) Avail: 151 full hkups (30/50 amps). 2021 rates: $65 to $75. (361)727-0034, 298 TX-188, Rockport, TX 78382

MAMAW'S COASTAL HIDEAWAY (RV Park) (Under Construction) Avail: 17 full hkups (30/50 amps). 2021 rates: $45. (361)263-7568, 379 Rattlesnake Point Rd., Rockport, TX 78374

RV parks in remote locations are sometimes unable to provide all amenities, like 30/50-amp service. Although these inconveniences can lower a park's facility rating, the tradeoff is a once-in-a-lifetime trip to some of the most beautiful wilderness areas on the planet!

ROCKPORT (CONT)

↖ REEL CHILL RV RESORT
good sam park **Ratings: 10/9.5★/9.5** (RV Park) From jct FM 188 & Hwy 35 Bypass: Go 3 mi E on Hwy 35 Bypass (R). **FAC:** paved rds. Avail: 136 paved, patios, 59 pull-thrus, (36x85), back-ins (36x75), 136 full hkups (30/50 amps), WiFi @ sites, laundry. **REC:** pool, boating nearby, hunting nearby. Pet restrict (Q). Partial handicap access. No tents. Big rig sites. 2021 rates: $65 to $80.
(361)345-1088 Lat: 28.00173, Lon: -97.09811
1368 Hwy 35 Bypass, Rockport, TX 78382
reelchillrvresort.com
See ad previous page

↓ ROCKPORT RETREAT RV RESORT **Ratings: 9.5/8.5★/9.5** (RV Resort) Avail: 50 full hkups (30/50 amps). 2021 rates: $45 to $50. (361)500-9975, 175 Nell Street, Rockport, TX 78382

↑ SANDOLLAR RV RESORT **Ratings: 8/8.5★/7.5** (RV Park) Avail: 109 full hkups (30/50 amps). 2021 rates: $40 to $44. (361)729-2381, 919 N Fulton Beach Rd, Rockport, TX 78382

↑ WILDERNESS OAKS RV RESORT **Ratings: 9.5/8.5★/7.5** (RV Park) Avail: 151 full hkups (30/50 amps). 2021 rates: $41 to $61. (361)729-2307, 4851 Hwy 35 North, Rockport, TX 78382

↑ WOODY ACRES MOBILE HOME & RV RESORT **Ratings: 8.5/9★/8** (RV Area in MH Park) Avail: 260 full hkups (30/50 amps). 2021 rates: $39.95. (361)729-5636, 1202 West Mesquite St., Fulton, TX 78358

ROYSE CITY — B8 *Rockwall*

↗ BRUSHY CREEK RANCH RV RESORT **Ratings: 5.5/NA/6.5** (RV Park) Avail: 20 full hkups (30/50 amps). 2021 rates: $30 to $40. (903)413-6383, 359 Brushy Creek Ranch Road, Royse City, TX 75189

RUSK — B8 *Cherokee*

← COUNTRY ESTATES RV PARK
Ratings: 7/7/6.5 (RV Park) From Jct of US 69 & US 84, W 2.3 mi on US 84 (L). **FAC:** paved rds. 42 Avail: 23 gravel, 19 grass, 4 pull-thrus, (20x60), back-ins (20x60), 42 full hkups (30/50 amps), WiFi @ sites, laundry. **REC:** hunting nearby. Pet restrict (B). No tents. Big rig sites. 2021 rates: $45, Military discount. no cc.
(903)683-9684 Lat: 31.79735, Lon: -95.17611
1639 W. 6th St, Rusk, TX 75785
See ad this page

SALT FLAT — B2 *Hudspeth*

→ GUADALUPE MOUNTAINS/PINE SPRINGS (Public National Park) From El Paso, E 110 mi on Hwy 62/180 (L) Or From Carlsbad NM, SW 60 mi on Hwy 62/180 (R). 19 Avail. 2021 rates: $15. (915)828-3251

SAN ANGELO — C5 *Tom Green*

↑ CONCHO PEARL RV ESTATES
good sam park **Ratings: 9/NA/9** (RV Park) From jct US 87 & FM 2105: Go 4-1/2 mi E on FM 2105, then 3/4 mi S on SH 208 (R). **FAC:** all weather rds. Avail: 46 all weather, 30 pull-thrus, (45x80), back-ins (45x80), accepts full hkup units only, 46 full hkups (30/50 amps), WiFi @ sites, laundry, groc. Pet restrict (B/Q). No tents. Big rig sites. 2021 rates: $38.99 to $42.99, Military discount.
(325)650-0788 Lat: 31.515676, Lon: -100.436516
5193 South Hwy 208 (Armstrong), San Angelo, TX 76903
conchopearlrvpark.com
See ad this page

↗ MILITARY PARK GOODFELLOW AFB REC CAMP (GOODFELLOW AFB) (Public) From town: go 3-1/4 mi S on US-67 S, then 2-1/2 mi E on TX-306 Loop E, then 3 mi S on Knickerbocker Rd (R). 30 Avail: 20 full hkups, 10 W, 10 E (30/50 amps). 2021 rates: $15 to $20. (325)944-1012

↗ SAN ANGELO KOA **Ratings: 9/10★/8** (Campground) Avail: 52 full hkups (30/50 amps). 2021 rates: $35.95 to $48.95. (800)562-7519, 6699 Knickerbocker Rd, San Angelo, TX 76904

↖ SAN ANGELO/BALD EAGLE CREEK (Public State Park) From town, NW 8 mi on US-87 to FM-2288, S 1 mi, follow signs (L) (Entrance fee). 20 Avail: 11 W, 11 E (30 amps). 2021 rates: $20. (325)949-4757

SAN ANGELO/LAKEVIEW (Public State Park) From jct US 67 & US 87: Go 9 mi N on US 87, then 1-1/4 mi S on FM 2288. (Entrance fee). 22 Avail. 2021 rates: $10. (325)949-4757

SAN ANGELO/NORTH CONCHO (Public State Park) From Grape Creek, S 1.5 mi on FM-2288 (L). Entrance fee required. 35 Avail: 35 W, 35 E (30 amps). 2021 rates: $20. (325)949-4757

← SAN ANGELO/RED ARROYO-SOUTH SHORE ENTRANCE (Public State Park) From Jct of US-67 & US-87, SW 3 mi on US-67 to RR 853/Arden Rd, W 1.5 mi to FM-2288, NE 0.8 mi to Park Rd, follow signs (R) (Entrance fee). 40 Avail: 40 W, 40 E (30/50 amps). 2021 rates: $20. (325)949-4757

↗ SPRING CREEK MARINA & RV PARK
good sam park **Ratings: 7.5/NA/8.5** (RV Park) From Jct of US-67 & US 87/277: Go 2 mi S on US-87, then 6 mi SW on Knickerbocker Rd, then 1 1/2 mi W on Fisherman's Rd (end). **FAC:** gravel rds. (83 spaces). Avail: 56 gravel, 45 pull-thrus, (40x68), back-ins (35x50), 56 full hkups (30/50 amps), seasonal sites, cable, WiFi @ sites, $, rentals, laundry, groc, LP gas, fire rings, firewood, controlled access. **REC:** Lake Nasworthy: swim, fishing, marina, kayaking/canoeing, boating nearby, playground, hunting nearby, rec open to public. Pet restrict (B). Partial handicap access. No tents. Big rig sites. 2021 rates: $50 to $61, Military discount.
(325)944-3850 Lat: 31.37582, Lon: -100.51290
2680 Camper Rd, San Angelo, TX 76904
www.springcreekmarinarv.com
See ad this page

SAN ANTONIO — D6 *Bexar*

SAN ANTONIO See also Boerne, Bulverde, Castroville, Somerset & Von Ormy.

← ADMIRALTY RV RESORT **Ratings: 10/10★/9** (RV Park) Avail: 192 full hkups (30/50 amps). 2021 rates: $56.67 to $84.44. (210)647-7878, 1485 N Ellison Dr., San Antonio, TX 78251

↓ ALAMO RIVER RANCH RV PARK
good sam park **Ratings: 8/9.5★/9.5** (RV Park) From jct Loop 410 & I-35: Go 4 mi S on I-35 (exit 141), then 300 feet S on I-35 frontage, then 1/2 mi W on Benton City Rd, then 3/4 mi S on Quintana Rd, then 3/4 mi W on Trawalter Ln (L). **FAC:** gravel rds. Avail: 72 gravel, 40 pull-thrus, (50x70), back-ins (50x65), 62 full hkups, 10 W, 10 E (30/50 amps), WiFi @ sites, tent sites, rentals, dump, laundry, fire rings, firewood, controlled access. **REC:** Medina River: swim, fishing, kayaking/canoeing, playground. Pet restrict (B/Q). Partial handicap access. Big rig sites, eco-friendly. 2021 rates: $55, Military discount.
(210)622-5022 Lat: 29.29893, Lon: -98.65340
12430 Trawalter Lane, Von Ormy, TX 78073
alamoriver.com
See primary listing at Von Ormy and ad opposite page

ALSATIAN RV RESORT & GOLF CLUB
good sam park **Ratings: 10/10★/10** (RV Resort) From jct Hwy 90 & CR 4516: Go 2.5 mi on CR 4516 (R). **FAC:** paved rds. Avail: 67 paved, patios, 23 pull-thrus, (41x110), back-ins (41x80), 67 full hkups (30/50 amps), WiFi @ sites, rentals, laundry, LP gas, controlled access. **REC:** heated pool, hot tub, pond, fishing, golf, hunting nearby. Pets OK. Partial handicap access. No tents. Big rig sites, eco-friendly. 2021 rates: $40 to $95, Military discount.
(830)931-9190 Lat: 29.36310, Lon: -98.94100
1581 CR 4516, Castroville, TX 78009
www.alsatianresort.com
See primary listing at Castroville and ad page 889

BLAZING STAR LUXURY RV RESORT **Ratings: 10/10★/9.5** (RV Resort) Avail: 229 full hkups (30/50 amps). 2021 rates: $62 to $83. (888)838-7186, 1120 W Loop 1604 N, San Antonio, TX 78251

BRAUNIG LAKE RV RESORT
good sam park **Ratings: 9.5/9★/8** (RV Park) Avail: 266 full hkups (30/50 amps). 2021 rates: $54 to $66. (210)633-3170, 13550 Donop Rd, Elmendorf, TX 78112

GREENLAKE RV RESORT **Ratings: 10/10★/9.5** (RV Resort) Avail: 231 full hkups (30/50 amps). 2021 rates: $47.78 to $81.11. (210)467-9178, 10842 Green Lake St., San Antonio, TX 78223

GREENTREE VILLAGE RV PARK MHP **Ratings: 9.5/9★/9.5** (RV Area in MH Park) Avail: 201 full hkups (30/50 amps). 2021 rates: $45. (210)655-3331, 12015 O'Conner Rd, San Antonio, TX 78233

MILITARY PARK FORT SAM HOUSTON RV PARK (JBSA FORT SAM HOUSTON) (Public) From town: Go 2 mi N on I-37N, then 1/2 mi on I-35 Frontage Rd, then 1/2 N on Walters St, then 1/2 mi on Wilson Way, then 1 mi N on Garden Rd, then 2 mi NE on William Hardee Rd (E). Avail: 74 full hkups (30/50 amps). 2021 rates: $25. (210)221-5502

MILITARY PARK LACKLAND FAMCAMP (JBSA-LACKLAND AFB) (Public) From town: Go 4 mi SW on I-35 S, then 6 mi W on US-90 W, then merge onto US 90 Access Rd for 3 mi, then 1 mi on W Military Dr, then left onto Luke Blvd, then left onto Kenly Ave, then right onto Pepperell St (E). Avail: 41 full hkups (30/50 amps). 2021 rates: $25 to $27. (210)671-5179

MISSION CITY RV PARK
good sam park **Ratings: 9/10★/9.5** (RV Park) From I-35 & AT & T Ctr Pkwy: Go 1/2 mi S on AT & T Ctr Pkwy, then 1 mi E on Gembler Rd (R). **FAC:** paved rds. 189 Avail: 41 paved, 148 gravel, patios, 58 pull-thrus, (30x60), back-ins (30x60), 189 full hkups (30/50 amps), WiFi @ sites, laundry, groc, firewood, controlled access. **REC:** heated pool. Pet restrict (B). Partial handicap access. No tents. Big rig sites, eco-friendly. 2021 rates: $50 to $70.
(210)337-6501 Lat: 29.43622, Lon: -98.41461
1011 Gembler Rd., San Antonio, TX 78219
missioncityrv.com
See ad opposite page

MISSION TRAILS RV RESORT **Ratings: 4/6.5/5** (RV Park) Avail: 70 full hkups (30/50 amps). 2021 rates: $40. (210)928-8285, 3500 Orkney Ave, San Antonio, TX 78223

SAN ANTONIO / ALAMO KOA **Ratings: 8.5/10★/9** (Campground) 300 Avail: 145 full hkups, 155 W, 155 E (30/50 amps). 2021 rates: $48 to $78. (210)224-9296, 602 Gembler Rd, San Antonio, TX 78219

STONE CREEK RV PARK
good sam park **Ratings: 9.5/9★/8.5** (Campground) From Jct of I-35 & Exit 177, S 0.4 mi on W Frntg Rd (R). **FAC:** paved rds. (231 spaces). Avail: 91 gravel, patios, 90 pull-thrus, (33x60), back-ins (34x44), 91 full hkups (30/50 amps), seasonal sites, cable, WiFi @ sites, rentals, dump, laundry, LP gas. **REC:** pool, hot tub, hunting nearby. Pet restrict (B). Partial handicap access. No tents. Big rig sites, eco-friendly. 2021 rates: $47 to $55, Military discount.
(830)609-7759 Lat: 29.61815, Lon: -98.26480
18905 IH-35 N, Schertz, TX 78154
www.stonecreekrvpark.com
See ad this page

E2. C5. F1. It's not a cipher; it's our easy-to-use map grid. Draw a line horizontally from the letter, vertically from the number, in the map border. ""X" will mark a spot near your destination.

TEJAS VALLEY RV PARK
good sam park **Ratings: 9.5/10★/9.5** (RV Park) From jct W Loop 1604 S & Potranco Rd (FM 1957): Go 2-3/4 mi W on Potranco Rd. (L). **FAC:** paved rds. 117 Avail: 45 all weather, 72 gravel, 68 pull-thrus, (35x60), back-ins (30x30), 117 full hkups (30/50 amps), cable, WiFi @ sites, rentals, dump, laundry, LP gas. **REC:** pool. Pet restrict (B/Q). Partial handicap access. No tents. Big rig sites, eco-friendly. 2021 rates: $30 to $50, Military discount.
(210)679-7715 Lat: 29.425803, Lon: -98.754030
13080 Potranco Rd, San Antonio, TX 78253
www.tejasvalleyrvpark.com
See ad this page

TRAVELERS WORLD RV RESORT **Ratings: 9/10★/9** (RV Park) Avail: 165 full hkups (30/50 amps). 2021 rates: $61 to $67. (210)532-8310, 2617 Roosevelt Ave, San Antonio, TX 78214

SAN AUGUSTINE — C9 *San Augustine*

MISSION DOLORES CAMPGROUND (Public) From Jct of SR-21W & SR-147/S Broadway (in town), S 0.5 mi on SR-147/S Broadway (L); or From Jct of US-96 & SR-147, E 1.1 mi on SR-147 (R). Avail: 32 full hkups (30 amps). 2021 rates: $24. (936)275-3815

SAN BENITO — M4 *Cameron*

FUN N SUN RV RESORT
good sam park **Ratings: 9/9★/8.5** (RV Area in MH Park) Avail: 700 full hkups (30/50 amps). 2021 rates: $46 to $52. (888)563-7040, 1400 Zillock Rd, San Benito, TX 78586

SAN JUAN — M3 *Hidalgo*

SAN JUAN GARDENS **Ratings: 9/8.5★/7.5** (RV Park) Avail: 30 full hkups (50 amps). 2021 rates: $35. (956)781-1082, 900 E US Business Hwy 83, San Juan, TX 78589

JOIN GoodSamRoadside.com

SAN LEON — D9 *Galveston*

SUMMER BREEZE USA KEMAH
good sam park **Ratings: 9/10★/8** (RV Park) From jct Hwy 146 & FM 517: Go 2-3/4 mi E on FM 517 (L). **FAC:** paved rds. Avail: 97 paved, 33 pull-thrus, (25x60), back-ins (25x38), 97 full hkups (30/50 amps), WiFi @ sites, rentals, laundry, controlled access. **REC:** pool, hot tub, boating nearby. Pet restrict (B/Q). Partial handicap access. No tents. 2021 rates: $50 to $65, Military discount.
(713)335-9588 Lat: 29.489083, Lon: -94.955289
2630 FM 517, San Leon, TX 77539
summerbreezeusa.com/kemah
See ad page 904

TROPICAL GARDENS RV PARK & RESORT **Ratings: 8/8.5★/8.5** (RV Park) Avail: 91 full hkups (30/50 amps). 2021 rates: $30 to $40. (281)339-1729, 609 24th St., San Leon, TX 77539

USA RV RESORTS BIG SPOT **Ratings: 10/10★/6.5** (RV Resort) Avail: 162 full hkups (30/50 amps). 2021 rates: $49 to $59. (832)864-2930, 2241 E Bayshore Dr., San Leon, TX 77539

Save 10% at Good Sam Parks!

TX

SAN MARCOS — D7 *Hays*

PECAN PARK RIVERSIDE RV PARK
good sam park **Ratings: 9.5/9.5★/9.5** (RV Park) From Jct I-35 (exit 205) & Hwy 80: Go 2 mi SE on Hwy 80 (1 mi past Blanco River Bridge), then 1 block S on Old Bastrop Hwy, then 1/2 mi E on Martindale Rd. (R).

ENJOY SAN MARCOS RIVER FUN
Relax in our scenic, peaceful location along the San Marcos River under the shade of our huge pecan trees. Fishing, snorkeling, & tubing. Swim in our heated pool. Our mild winters make us a prime snowbird destination.

FAC: paved/gravel rds. (145 spaces). Avail: 75 gravel, patios, 33 pull-thrus, (35x75), back-ins (30x60), 75 full hkups (30/50 amps), seasonal sites, cable, WiFi @ sites, laundry, LP gas, fire rings, firewood, controlled access. **REC:** heated pool, hot tub, San Marcos River: swim, fishing, kayaking/canoeing, playground. Pet restrict (B). No tents. Big rig sites, eco-friendly. 2021 rates: $45 to $69, Military discount.
(512)396-0070 Lat: 29.86323, Lon: -97.88964
50 Squirrel Run, San Marcos, TX 78666
www.pecanpark.com
See ad this page

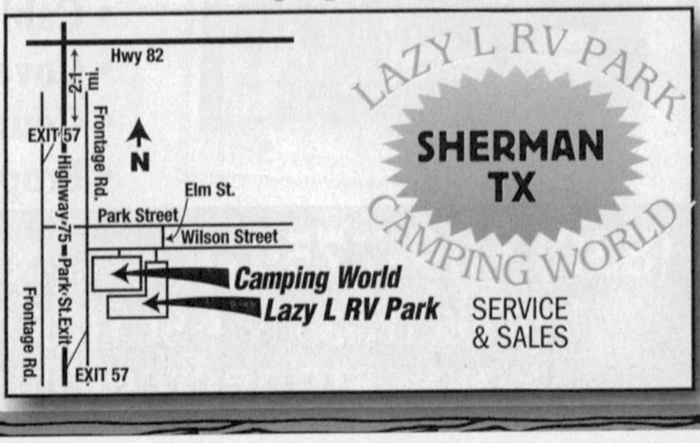

SANGER — A7 *Denton*

RAY ROBERTS LAKE/ISLE DU BOIS UNIT (Public State Park) From Jct of I-35 & FM-455 (exit 467), E 11 mi on FM-455 (L); or From Jct of US-377 & FM-455, W 3.1 mi on FM-455 (R) (Entrance fee). 115 Avail: 115 W, 115 E (20/50 amps). 2021 rates: $25 to $26. (940)686-2148

SANTO — B6 *Palo Pinto*

COFFEE CREEK RV RESORT & CABINS
good sam park **Ratings: 10/10★/10** (RV Park) Avail: 97 full hkups (30/50 amps). 2021 rates: $45. (940)769-2277, 13429 S Hwy 281, Santo, TX 76472

SCHULENBURG — D7 *Fayette*

SCHULENBURG RV PARK
good sam park **Ratings: 8/10★/9.5** (RV Park) N-bnd: From Jct of US-90 & US-77, N 0.5 mi on US-77 (L); or S, E & W-bnd: From Jct of I-10 & US-77 (exit 674), S 0.2 mi on US-77 (R). **FAC:** paved/gravel rds. Avail: 49 gravel, 45 pull-thrus, (32x60), back-ins (30x60), 49 full hkups (30/50 amps), WiFi @ sites, tent sites, laundry. **REC:** pond, fishing. Pet restrict (B/Q). Partial handicap access. Big rig sites, eco-friendly. 2021 rates: $47.05, Military discount.
(979)743-4388 Lat: 29.68995, Lon: -96.90304
65 North Kessler Ave, Schulenburg, TX 78956
www.schulenburgrvpark.com
See ad this page

SEALY — D8 *Austin*

STEPHEN F AUSTIN (Public State Park) From Jct of I-10 & FM-1458 (exit 723), N 2 mi on FM-1458 to Park Rd 38, SW 0.8 mi (E) (Entrance fee). Avail: 40 full hkups (30 amps). 2021 rates: $25. (979)885-3613

SEMINOLE — B4 *Andrews*

GAINES COUNTY PARK (Public) From town, N 8 mi on US-385 (L). 18 Avail: 18 W, 18 E (30 amps). 2021 rates: $4. (432)758-4002

SHERIDAN — D7 *Colorado*

SPLASHWAY WATERPARK & CAMPGROUND **Ratings: 9/9.5★/10** (Campground) Avail: 188 full hkups (30/50 amps). 2021 rates: $36 to $67. (979)234-7718, 5211 Main St., Sheridan, TX 77475

SHERMAN — A7 *Grayson*

LAZY L RV PARK
good sam park **Ratings: 9/9.5★/7.5** (RV Park) From Jct US-75/(Exit 57) & Park St: Go 1/8 mi E on Park St, then 2 blocks S on Elm St, then 100 ft W on Wilson St (L). **FAC:** paved/gravel rds. (97 spaces). Avail: 47 gravel, 43 pull-thrus, (24x60), back-ins (24x60), 47 full hkups (30/50 amps), seasonal sites, cable, WiFi @ sites, dump, laundry. **REC:** pool. Pet restrict (B). Partial handicap access. No tents. Big rig sites. 2021 rates: $34.50 to $36.50, Military discount.
(903)870-7772 Lat: 33.61458, Lon: -96.60621
310 W Wilson, Sherman, TX 75090
www.thelazylrvpark.com
See ad this page

Travel Services

CAMPING WORLD OF SHERMAN As the nation's largest retailer of RV supplies, accessories, services and new and used RVs, Camping World is committed to making your total RV experience better. **SERVICES:** tire, RV appliance, MH mechanical, restrooms. RV Sales. RV supplies, LP gas, RV accessible. Hours: 9am - 7pm. (888)209-5502 Lat: 33.61478, Lon: -96.60730
2005 S Sam Rayburn Fwy, Sherman, TX 75090
www.campingworld.com

SILSBEE — C9 *Hardin*

THOMPSON LAKE RV RESORT
good sam park **Ratings: 8/9.5★/8.5** (RV Park) From jct Hwy 92 & Hwy 418: Go 1-3/4 mi SE on Hwy 418, then 1/2 mi E on E Ave G, then 1 Blk N on US Hwy 96 W Frontage Rd, then 1 Blk NW on Red Cloud Park Dr, then 1 Blk W on Thompson Lake Dr (R). **FAC:** paved rds. (155 spaces). 130 Avail: 45 paved, 45 gravel, 40 grass, back-ins (45x60), 130 full hkups (30/50 amps), seasonal sites, WiFi @ sites, laundry. **REC:** Thompson Lake: swim, fishing, playground. Pet restrict (B). Partial handicap access. No tents. Big rig sites. 2021 rates: $40 to $45.
(409)385-0231 Lat: 30.352520, Lon: -94.146543
1506 Thompson Lake Drive, Silsbee, TX 77656
thompsonlakervresort.com
See ad this page

SILVERTON — A4 *Briscoe*

LAKE MACKENZIE PARK (Public) From jct Hwy-86 & Hwy-207: Go 7 mi N on Hwy-207. 61 Avail: 25 W, 25 E (30 amps). 2021 rates: $12 to $35. (806)633-4335

SINTON — E7 *San Patricio*

ROB & BESSIE WELDER PARK (Public) From Jct of US-77 & US-181, N 1.4 mi on US-181 (R). Avail: 60 full hkups (30/50 amps). 2021 rates: $25. (361)437-6795

SLATON — A4 *Lubbock*

TWIN PINE RV PARK

good sam park **Ratings: 8/9.5★/9.5** (RV Park) Avail: 28 full hkups (30/50 amps). 2021 rates: $38. (866)708-3311, 1202 N Hwy 84, Slaton, TX 79364

SMITHVILLE — D7 *Bastrop*

BUESCHER (Public State Park) From Jct of SR-71 & FM-153, NE 0.5 mi on FM-153 (L). Caution: low tree clearance (Entrance fee). 52 Avail: 52 W, 32 E (20/30 amps). 2021 rates: $14 to $17. (512)237-2241

SOMERSET — D6 *Bexar*

A COUNTRY BREEZE RV PARK

good sam park **Ratings: 7/9★/9** (RV Park) From S jct Loop 1604 & I-35: Go 1 mi SW on I-35 (exit 139), then 2-1/4 mi S on Kinney Rd, then 1/2 mi E on Briggs Rd, then 1/4 mi S on Benton City Rd. **FAC:** gravel rds. Avail: 46 paved, patios, 16 pull-thrus, (45x70), back-ins (45x70), 46 full hkups (30/50 amps), laundry. Pet restrict (B). No tents. Big rig sites, eco-friendly. 2021 rates: $56, Military discount.
(210)624-2665 Lat: 29.22954, Lon: -98.68193
19575 Benton City Rd, Somerset, TX 78069
www.acountrybreezervpark.com
See ad this page

SOMERVILLE — C8 *Burleson*

BIG CREEK RESORT MARINA & CAMPGROUND (Public) From jct Hwy-36 & FM-60: Go 4 mi W on FM-60, then 3-1/2 mi S on Park Road 4. Avail: 120 full hkups (30/50 amps). 2021 rates: $30 to $45. (979)596-1616

LAKE SOMERVILLE/BIRCH CREEK (Public State Park) From Jct of FM 1361 & US 36 (in town), NW 3.4 mi on Hwy 36 to FM-60, SW 7 mi to Park Rd 57, S 4.1 mi (E) (Entrance fee). 100 Avail: 100 W, 100 E (30/50 amps). 2021 rates: $10 to $20. (979)535-7763

OVERLOOK PARK (Public Corps) From town, S 2 mi on Hwy 36 to FM-1948, E 0.2 mi to LBJ Dr, N 0.5 mi to park entrance (L). 165 Avail: 165 W, 165 E (30 amps). 2021 rates: $25 to $30. (979)596-1622

SOMERVILLE LAKE - COE/ROCKY CREEK (Public Corps) From town, S 2 mi on Hwy 36 to FM-1948, E 5 mi (R). 157 Avail: 153 W, 157 E (30/50 amps). 2021 rates: $24 to $28. (979)596-1622

SOMERVILLE LAKE - COE/YEGUA CREEK (Public Corps) From town, S 2 mi on Hwy 36 to FM-1948, E 3 mi (R). 66 Avail: 66 W, 66 E (50 amps). 2021 rates: $26 to $28. Jan 01 to Sep 30. (979)596-1622

SOUTH PADRE ISLAND — M5 *Cameron*

SOUTH PADRE ISLAND See also Brownsville, Los Fresnos & Port Isabel.

ISLA BLANCA PARK (CAMERON COUNTY PARK) (Public) From Hwy 100, E across Causeway, S 0.3 mi on Park Rd 100 (E). Avail: 600 full hkups (30/50 amps). 2021 rates: $40 to $70. (956)761-5494

SOUTH PADRE KOA **Ratings: 9.5/9.5★/9** (RV Park) Avail: 179 full hkups (30/50 amps). 2021 rates: $54 to $91. (800)562-9724, 1 Padre Blvd, South Padre Island, TX 78597

SPICEWOOD — C6 *Travis*

OPEN AIR RESORTS **Ratings: 9.5/10★/9** (RV Resort) Avail: 120 full hkups (30/50 amps). 2021 rates: $55 to $101. (512)559-4284, 25928 Haynie Flat Road, Spicewood, TX 78669

SPRING — D8 *Harris*

Travel Services

CAMPING WORLD OF SPRING As the nation's largest retailer of RV supplies, accessories, services and new and used RVs, Camping World is committed to making your total RV experience better. **SERVICES:** sells outdoor gear, sells fishing gear, sells firearms, restrooms. RV Sales. RV supplies, RV accessible. Hours: 9am - 6pm.
(844)324-6799 Lat: 30.04788, Lon: -95.42826
19302 Interstate 45, Spring, TX 77373
rv.campingworld.com

SPRING BRANCH — D6 *Comal*

GUADALUPE RIVER (Public State Park) From Jct of US-281 & SR-46, W 7.3 mi on SR-46 to Park Rd 31, N 3 mi (E) (Entrance fee). 85 Avail: 85 W, 85 E (30/50 amps). 2021 rates: $20 to $24. (830)438-2656

SPRINGTOWN — B7 *Parker*

VALLEY ROSE RV PARK **Ratings: 8/9★/6.5** (RV Park) Avail: 50 full hkups (30/50 amps). 2021 rates: $40. (817)583-5372, 1515 Hwy 199, Springtown, TX 76082

STONEWALL — C6 *Gillespie*

PEACH COUNTRY RV PARK

good sam park **Ratings: 8/9★/9** (RV Park) Avail: 44 full hkups (30/50 amps). 2021 rates: $55 to $60. (830)644-2233, 14781 Hwy 290 East, Stonewall, TX 78671

STRATFORD — E9 *Sherman*

STAR OF TEXAS RV PARK AND HORSE HOTEL (RV Spaces) Avail: 60 full hkups (30/50 amps), Pit toilets. 2021 rates: $30. (806)366-7827, 5680 Texas Highway 15, Stratford, TX 79084

SUGAR LAND — D8 *Fort Bend*

USA RV PARK SUGAR LAND **Ratings: 6/UI/5.5** (RV Park) Avail: 100 full hkups (30/50 amps). 2021 rates: $35. (281)343-0626, 20825 Southwest Frwy, Sugar Land, TX 77479

SULPHUR SPRINGS — A8 *Hopkins*

SHADY LAKE RV PARK **Ratings: 6/8★/6.5** (RV Park) Avail: 12 full hkups (30/50 amps). 2021 rates: $40. (903)885-8885, 2306 Tx Hwy 19S, Sulphur Springs, TX 75482

SUNSET — A7 *Montage*

CAMPER'S PARADISE RV PARK **Ratings: 9/8.5★/7.5** (RV Park) Avail: 50 full hkups (30/50 amps). 2021 rates: $35. (940)872-2429, 4242 US Highway 287, Sunset, TX 76270

SWEENY — D8 *Brazoria*

STONEBRIDGE RV PARK & RESORT **Ratings: 9.5/9★/8** (RV Park) Avail: 102 full hkups (30/50 amps). 2021 rates: $35 to $45. (979)245-1200, 15804 Hwy 35 N, Sweeny, TX 77480

SWEETWATER — B5 *Nolan*

BAR J HITCHIN POST RV

good sam park **Ratings: 8.5/10★/8.5** (RV Park) From jct I20 and exit 242: Go 1 Blk N on CR142 (L).

I-20 STOP IN SWEETWATER TEXAS
With easy access off I-20, Bar J is a great place to stop, kick the dust off your boots and sit a spell. Large pull-thrus with Great amenities. Sweetwater is home of the world famous Rattlesnake Roundup held each Spring.

FAC: all weather rds. Avail: 50 all weather, 33 pull-thrus, (30x80), back-ins (30x60), 50 full hkups (30/50 amps), WiFi @ sites, laundry. Pet restrict (S/B). Partial handicap access. No tents. Big rig sites. 2021 rates: $44, Military discount.
(325)236-3889 Lat: 32.4527934, Lon: -100.4428972
50 N Hopkins Rd, Sweetwater, TX 79556
www.barjhitchinpostrv.com
See ad this page

LAKE SWEETWATER (Public) From Jct of I-20 & Exit 249, S 5 mi on FM-1856 to FM-2035, E 0.5 mi (E). 39 Avail: 32 W, 32 E (30 amps). 2021 rates: $6 to $20. Mar 15 to Oct 01. (325)235-1223

TATUM — B9 *Rusk*

AMAZING TEXAS RV RESORT & CAMPGROUND **Ratings: 8/8/7.5** (RV Park) Avail: 150 full hkups (30/50 amps). 2021 rates: $30 to $40. (903)836-4444, 17506 FM 782 N, Tatum, TX 75691

MARTIN CREEK LAKE (Public State Park) From Jct of SR-149 & SR-43, SW 3.7 mi on SR-43 to CR-2183, S 0.7 mi to CR-2181D, SW 0.1 mi (E) (Entrance fee). 58 Avail: 58 W, 58 E (30/50 amps). 2021 rates: $13 to $17. (903)836-4336

TEMPLE — C7 *Bell*

BELAIRE JUNCTION **Ratings: 9/10★/9** (RV Park) Avail: 117 full hkups (30/50 amps). 2021 rates: $49. (254)314-8033, 13103 NE HK Dodgen Loop, Temple, TX 76502

TEMPLE (CONT)

BELTON LAKE - COE/CEDAR RIDGE (Public Corps) From Jct of Hwy 317 & Hwy 36, NW 2 mi on Hwy 36 to Cedar Ridge Rd, S 1 mi (E). 64 Avail: 64 W, 64 E (30/50 amps). 2021 rates: $24 to $40. (254)986-1404

TERLINGUA — D3 *Brewster*

BIG BEND RESORT & ADVENTURES RV PARK **Ratings: 6.5/8.5★/7.5** (RV Park) Avail: 110 full hkups (30/50 amps). 2021 rates: $44 to $49. (432)371-2218, 1 Main St, Terlingua, TX 79852

We shine ""Spotlights'' on interesting cities and areas.

TERRELL — B8 *Kaufman*

BLUEBONNET RIDGE RV PARK & COTTAGES
Ratings: 9.5/10★/10 (RV Park) From Jct of I-20 (exit 506) & FM-429: Go 1/2 mi N on FM-429 (L).

TOP RATED PARK EAST OF DALLAS

Easy On & Off I-20, this Top Rated RV Resort is located on 64 acres with a country setting. Park features 90' long pull thru concrete sites, a gorgeous family pool, country store, and a 5 acre fishing lake.

FAC: paved rds. (150 spaces). 64 Avail: 30 paved, 34 gravel, patios, 44 pull-thrus, (33x90), back-ins (33x60), 64 full hkups (30/50 amps), seasonal sites, cable, WiFi @ sites, laundry, groc, LP gas. **REC:** pool, hot tub, pond, fishing, playground. Pet restrict (B/Q). Partial handicap access. No tents, Age restrict may apply. Big rig sites. 2021 rates: $45, Military discount.
(972)524-9600 Lat: 32.69096, Lon: -96.20029
16543 FM 429, Terrell, TX 75161
www.bluebonnetrv.com
See ad this page

TEXARKANA — A9 *Bowie*

FOREST LAKE RV PARK & EVENTS **Ratings: 8.5/10★/8** (RV Park) Avail: 35 full hkups (30/50 amps). 2021 rates: $35. (903)832-0128, 915 Farm Rd 2148 S, Texarkana, TX 75501

MILITARY PARK ELLIOTT LAKE RECREATION AREA (RED RIVER ARMY DEPOT) (Public) From I-30 (exit 207) & Main Gate: Go 2 blocks on Texas St, then right onto Ave K and follow signs for 7 mi to campground (L). Avail: 45 full hkups (30/50 amps). 2021 rates: $15. (903)334-2254

SHADY PINES RV PARK
Ratings: 9/10★/10 (RV Park) Avail: 38 full hkups (30/50 amps). 2021 rates: $50. (903)832-1268, 10010 W 7th St, Texarkana, TX 75501

TEXARKANA RV PARK
Ratings: 8.5/10★/8.5 (RV Park) From jct I30 & US 369: Go 4 mi S on US 369, then 1 mi SW on US 59 (R). **FAC:** paved/gravel rds. Avail: 98 gravel, 59 pull-thrus, (24x70), back-ins (24x63), 98 full hkups (30/50 amps), cable, WiFi @ sites, rentals, laundry, controlled access. **REC:** pool, pond, fishing. Pets OK. Partial handicap access. No tents. Big rig sites. 2021 rates: $40, Military discount.
(903)306-1364 Lat: 33.385542, Lon: -94.111844
5000 US Hwy 59 S, Texarkana, TX 75501
www.txarkanarvpark.com
See ad this page

Traveling with Fido? Many campground listings indicate pet-friendly amenities and pet restrictions.

WRIGHT PATMAN LAKE - COE/CLEAR SPRINGS CAMPGROUND (Public Corps) From town, S 10 mi on Hwy 59S to FM-2148, N 3 mi to Clear Springs Park, W 2 mi (E). 115 Avail: 103 W, 41 S, 103 E (30/50 amps). 2021 rates: $14 to $32. (903)838-8636

WRIGHT PATMAN LAKE - COE/PINEY POINT (Public Corps) From town: Go 12 mi SW on US 59 to first park road past Sulphur River bridge. Follow signs. 65 Avail: 45 W, 45 E (30 amps). 2021 rates: $14 to $55. Mar 01 to Nov 30. (877)444-6777

WRIGHT PATMAN LAKE - COE/ROCKY POINT (Public Corps) From town, S 10 mi on US-59 (R). 124 Avail: 15 full hkups, 109 W, 109 E (30/50 amps). 2021 rates: $24 to $55. (877)444-6777

THE WOODLANDS — C8 *Montgomery*

RAYFORD CROSSING RV RESORT
Ratings: 10/10★/10 (RV Resort) Avail: 45 full hkups (30/50 amps). 2021 rates: $59 to $96. (281)298-8008, 29321 S. Plum Creek Dr, Spring, TX 77386

WOODLAND LAKES RV PARK
Ratings: 8/8.5★/9 (RV Park) Avail: 25 full hkups (30/50 amps). 2021 rates: $65. (936)273-6666, 17110 Fire House Rd, Conroe, TX 77385

THREE RIVERS — E6 *Live Oak*

CHOKE CANYON/CALLIHAM UNIT (Public State Park) From Jct of US-281 & Hwy 72, W 10.9 mi on Hwy 72 to Park Rd 8, N 1 mi (E). 40 Avail: 40 W, 40 E (50 amps). 2021 rates: $22. (361)786-3868

TOMBALL — D8 *Montgomery*

CORRAL RV RESORT
Ratings: 8.5/8.5★/9 (RV Park) From jct Hwy 249 & Alice Rd: Go 1-1/4 mi E on Alice Rd, then 1/2 mi N on S Cherry St (L). **FAC:** paved rds. 210 Avail: 110 paved, 100 gravel, 82 pull-thrus, (40x90), back-ins (40x70), 210 full hkups (30/50 amps), cable, WiFi @ sites, laundry, LP gas. Pet restrict (S/B/Q). No tents. Big rig sites. 2021 rates: $43 to $47, Military discount. ATM.
(281)351-2761 Lat: 30.083217, Lon: -95.611879
1402 South Cherry Street #37, Tomball, TX 77375
corralrvresort.com
See ad this page

TOYAHVALE — C3 *Reeves*

BALMORHEA (Public State Park) From I-10 & SR-17 (exit 209), SW 6.8 mi on SR-17 (L) (Entrance fee). 33 Avail: 33 W, 33 E (30/50 amps). 2021 rates: $15 to $20. (432)375-2370

TRINITY — C8 *Trinity*

MARINA VILLAGE RESORT **Ratings: 7.5/7/8.5** (Membership Park) 270 Avail: 189 full hkups, 81 W, 81 E (30/50 amps). 2021 rates: $10. (936)594-0149, 176 E Westwood Dr, Trinity, TX 75862

TYLER — B8 *Smith*

TYLER See also Bullard, Chandler, Gladewater & Murchison.

JELLYSTONE PARK AT WHISPERING PINES **Ratings: 9.5/10★/9.5** (RV Park) 100 Avail: 97 full hkups, 3 W, 3 E (30/50 amps). 2021 rates: $50 to $90. (903)858-2405, 5583 FM 16E, Tyler, TX 75706

TYLER (Public State Park) From Jct of I-20 & FM-14 (exit 562), N 2 mi on FM-14 (L) (Entrance fee). 77 Avail: 57 full hkups, 20 W, 20 E (30/50 amps). 2021 rates: $22 to $30. (903)597-5338

TYLER OAKS RV RESORT
Ratings: 10/9.5★/9.5 (RV Resort) Avail: 27 full hkups (30/50 amps). 2021 rates: $38 to $43. (430)235-2030, 10855 US 69 N, Tyler, TX 75706

WE RV CHAMPIONS OF TYLER
Ratings: 8.5/8.5★/8.5 (RV Park) Avail: 10 full hkups (30/50 amps). 2021 rates: $39 to $45. (903)592-6065, 15537 State Highway 64 W, Tyler, TX 75704

Get ready for your next camping trip at CampingWorld.com

Travel Services

↑ **CAMPING WORLD OF TYLER** As the nation's largest retailer of RV supplies, accessories, services and new and used RVs, Camping World is committed to making your total RV experience better. **SERVICES:** MH mechanical, staffed RV wash, restrooms. RV Sales. RV supplies, LP gas, emergency parking, RV accessible. Hours: 9am to 7pm.
(877)848-0413 Lat: 32.428844, Lon: -95.362610
11271 US Highway 69 N, Tyler, TX 75706
www.campingworld.com

↓ **GANDER RV OF TYLER** Your new hometown outfitter offering the best regional gear for all your outdoor needs. Your adventure awaits. **SERVICES:** gunsmithing svc, archery svc, sells outdoor gear, sells fishing gear, sells firearms, restrooms. RV Sales. RV supplies, LP gas, dump, emergency parking, RV accessible. Hours: 9am to 8pm.
(844)288-3445 Lat: 32.2467, Lon: -95.3051
151 Market Square Blvd, Tyler, TX 75703
rv.ganderoutdoors.com

UVALDE — D5 *Uvalde*

LITTLE RV SPOT
good sam park **Ratings: 7/NA/8** (RV Park) Avail: 22 full hkups (30/50 amps). 2021 rates: $35 to $40. (210)606-5328, 1574 Westward Trail, Uvalde, TX 78801

PARKVIEW RIVERSIDE RV PARK
good sam park **Ratings: 9/9.5★/9** (RV Park) From Jct of Hwy 83 & Hwy 90 in Uvalde: Go 29 3/4 mi N on Hwy 83, then 1 mi E on Hwy 1050 (north of Concan), then 1 1/2 mi S on CR-350 (R). **FAC:** paved rds. 99 Avail: 12 paved, 87 gravel, 17 pull-thrus, (28x65), back-ins (35x55), 99 full hkups (30/50 amps), WiFi @ sites, rentals, dump, laundry, groc, LP gas, fire rings, firewood. **REC:** Frio River: swim, fishing, kayaking/canoeing, boating nearby, hunting nearby. Pets OK. Partial handicap access. No tents. Big rig sites, eco-friendly. 2021 rates: $50 to $71, Military discount. ATM.
(830)232-4006 Lat: 29.58256, Lon: -99.72801
2561 County Road 350, Concan, TX 78838
parkviewriversiderv.com
See primary listing at Concan and ad page 892

→ **QUAIL SPRINGS RV PARK**
good sam park **Ratings: 7.5/9★/9.5** (RV Park) From Jct of US-83 & US-90 (in Uvalde), E 2.2 mi on US-90 (R). **FAC:** paved rds. (83 spaces). Avail: 53 gravel, patios, 35 pull-thrus, (30x60), back-ins (30x55), 53 full hkups (30/50 amps), seasonal sites, cable, WiFi @ sites, laundry. **REC:** hunting nearby. Pet restrict (B). No tents, Age restrict may apply. Big rig sites, eco-friendly. 2021 rates: $37.
(830)278-8182 Lat: 29.22854, Lon: -99.75597
2727 E Main St, Uvalde, TX 78801
www.quailspringsrvpark.com
See ad this page

VALLEY VIEW — A7 *Cook*

RAY ROBERTS LAKE/JOHNSON BRANCH (Public State Park) From Jct of I-35 & Exit 483 (FM-3002), E 6.6 mi on FM-3002 (R) (Entrance fee). 104 Avail: 104 W, 104 E (20/50 amps). 2021 rates: $25 to $26. (940)637-2294

VAN HORN — C2 *Culberson*

← OASIS RV **Ratings: 6.5/6/4** (Campground) Avail: 27 full hkups (30/50 amps). 2021 rates: $30. (432)283-1160, 1201 W Broadway, Van Horn, TX 79855

← SOUTHERN STAR RV PARK **Ratings: 7.5/9★/8** (RV Park) Avail: 46 full hkups (30/50 amps). 2021 rates: $35. (432)283-2420, 1605 W Broadway, Van Horn, TX 79855

VAN HORN RV PARK
good sam park **Ratings: 9/10★/9.5** (Campground) From Jct of I-10 (Exit 140-A) & US-90: Go 1/4 mi S on US-90, then E onto Kampers Lane (L). Elev 4042 ft.**FAC:** gravel rds. (94 spaces). Avail: 92 gravel, 92 pull-thrus, (30x75), 92 full hkups (30/50 amps), seasonal sites, cable, WiFi @ sites, tent sites, rentals, dump, laundry, groc, LP gas, restaurant. **REC:** pool, pond, fishing, playground, hunting nearby. Pets OK. Partial handicap access. Big rig sites, eco-friendly. 2021 rates: $43, Military discount.
(432)283-2728 Lat: 31.03056, Lon: -104.82601
#10 Kampers Lane, Van Horn, TX 79855
www.vanhorntexasrvpark.com
See ad this page

→ **WILD WEST RV PARK**
good sam park **Ratings: 6.5/10★/7.5** (RV Park) Avail: 46 full hkups (30/50 amps). 2021 rates: $30. (432)283-2225, 404 E Broadway, Van Horn, TX 79855

Things to See and Do

↓ **VAN HORN RV PARK CAFE** Dine in, take out or delivery to your door nightly from 5:30pm to 8pm. Breakfast 7:30am-9:30am. Elev 4042 ft. Oct 01 to Apr 30. Partial handicap access. Restrooms. Food. Hours: 7am to 9am 5.30pm to 8pm.
(432)283-2728 Lat: 31.03109, Lon: -104.82599
10 Kampers Lane, Van Horn, TX 79855
www.vanhorntexasrvpark.com
See ad this page

VANDERPOOL — D6 *Bandera*

↑ LOST MAPLES STATE NATURAL AREA (Public State Park) From S Jct of Hwys 337 & 187, N 4.8 mi on Hwy 187 (L) (Entrance fee). 30 Avail: 30 W, 30 E (30 amps). 2021 rates: $20. (830)966-3413

VERNON — A6 *Wilbarger*

ROCKING "A" RV PARK
good sam park **Ratings: 9/9.5★/8.5** (Campground) Avail: 50 full hkups (30/50 amps). 2021 rates: $40. (940)552-2821, 3725 Harrison St, Vernon, TX 76384

VICTORIA — D7 *Victoria*

↓ **COLETO LAKE RV RESORT**
good sam park **Ratings: 9.5/9.5★/10** (RV Resort) From jct US Hwy 59 & Coleto Park Rd, go W .5 mi (L). **FAC:** all weather rds. (171 spaces). Avail: 121 all weather, patios, 21 pull-thrus, (30x90), back-ins (30x55), 121 full hkups (30/50 amps), seasonal sites, cable, WiFi @ sites, rentals, laundry, LP gas. **REC:** pool, pond, fishing, playground. Pet restrict (B/Q). Partial handicap access. No tents. Big rig sites, eco-friendly. 2021 rates: $43 to $48, Military discount.
(361)582-0222 Lat: 28.71528, Lon: -97.17719
500 Coleto Park Road, Victoria, TX 77905
www.coletolakervpark.com
See ad this page

↓ DAD'S RV PARK **Ratings: 8.5/10★/7.5** (RV Park) Avail: 114 full hkups (30/50 amps). 2021 rates: $50. (361)573-1231, 203 Hopkins Street, Victoria, TX 77901

GATEWAY TO THE GULF RV PARK **Ratings: 9/9.5★/8** (RV Park) Avail: 118 full hkups (30/50 amps). 2021 rates: $40. (361)570-7080, 9809 US Hwy 59 North, Victoria, TX 77905

↓ QRV VICTORIA **Ratings: 10/10★/9.5** (RV Park) Avail: 104 full hkups (30/50 amps). 2021 rates: $61.11 to $65.56. (361)485-1598, 1402 S Laurent St., Victoria, TX 77901

↑ RV PARK OF VICTORIA **Ratings: 8/8/8** (RV Park) Avail: 156 full hkups (30/50 amps). 2021 rates: $32. (361)580-2424, 13202 N Navarro (US-77), Victoria, TX 77904

VIDOR — C9 *Orange*

← **BOOMTOWN USA RV RESORT**
good sam park **Ratings: 9.5/10★/8** (RV Park) Avail: 61 full hkups (30/50 amps). 2021 rates: $50 to $85. (409)769-6105, 23030 IH-10, Vidor, TX 77662

VON ORMY — D6 *Bexar*

↑ **ALAMO RIVER RANCH RV PARK**
good sam park **Ratings: 8/9.5★/9.5** (RV Park) From I-35 & Loop 1604 (exit 140), go N 150' to Quintana Rd, then go S over the RR tracks, then go E under 1604, 3/4 mi to Trawalter the 3/4 mi to end (L). **FAC:** gravel rds. Avail: 72 gravel, 40 pull-thrus, (50x70), back-ins (50x65), 62 full hkups, 10 W, 10 E (30/50 amps), WiFi @ sites, tent sites, rentals, dump, laundry, fire rings, firewood, controlled access. **REC:** Medina River: swim, fishing, kayaking/canoeing, playground. Pet restrict (B/Q). Partial handicap access. Big rig sites, eco-friendly. 2021 rates: $55, Military discount.
(210)622-5022 Lat: 29.29893, Lon: -98.65340
12430 Trawalter Ln, Von Ormy, TX 78073
alamoriver.com
See ad page 915

TX

WACO — C7 *McLennan*

WACO See also Riesel & Whitney.

EXTRACO EVENT CENTER (Public) From I-35 (exit 331 New Rd): Go NW on New Rd, then SW on Bosque Blvd. Follow signs. 315 Avail: 17 full hkups, 235 W, 46 E (30 amps). 2021 rates: $12 to $15. (254)776-1660

FLAT CREEK FARMS RV RESORT
good sam park **Ratings: 6/8.5★/9** (RV Park) From jct I-35 & Exit 328: Go 1 Block N on E service rd, then 1-3/4 mi NE on Greig Dr (R). **FAC:** paved/gravel rds. (72 spaces). Avail: 20 gravel, 20 pull-thrus, (30x70), 20 full hkups (30/50 amps), seasonal sites, WiFi @ sites, laundry. **REC:** Flat Creek Lake: fishing, boating nearby. Pets OK. No tents. Big rig sites. 2021 rates: $45 to $60.
(254)662-9858 Lat: 31.46913, Lon: -97.14141
1633 Greig Dr, Waco, TX 76706
flatcreekfarmsrvresort.com
See ad this page

LAKE WACO RV PARK & MARINA **Ratings: 6/NA/7** (RV Park) 71 Avail: 54 full hkups, 17 W, 17 E (30/50 amps). 2021 rates: $35 to $45. (254)717-1901, 3201 Overflow Road, Waco, TX 76712

RIVERVIEW CAMPGROUND **Ratings: 7.5/8/7.5** (RV Park) Avail: 60 full hkups (30/50 amps). 2021 rates: $40. (254)662-0475, 988 Riverview Rd, Waco, TX 76706

WACO LAKE - COE/AIRPORT (Public Corps) From Jct of I-35 & Lake Shore Dr exit, W to Steinbeck Bend Rd, N to Airport Rd, E 2 mi (L). 46 Avail: 22 full hkups, 24 W, 24 E (50 amps). 2021 rates: $26 to $30. (254)756-5359

WACO LAKE - COE/MIDWAY (Public Corps) From Jct of I-35 & Hwy 6, W 5 mi on Hwy 6 to Midway Park exit, 0.5 mi on service rd. (E). 37 Avail: 32 W, 11 S, 32 E (30/50 amps). 2021 rates: $26 to $30. (254)756-5359

WACO LAKE - COE/SPEEGLEVILLE (Public Corps) From Jct of I-35 & Hwy 6, W 7 mi on Hwy 6 to Speegleville Rd, N 2 mi to Overflow Rd (R). 30 Avail: 30 W, 30 E (50 amps). 2021 rates: $26. Mar 01 to Oct 31. (254)756-5359

WALLER — D8 *Waller*

LONE STAR JELLYSTONE PARK **Ratings: 8.5/9/9** (Campground) 150 Avail: 145 full hkups, 5 W, 5 E (30/50 amps). 2021 rates: $64 to $66. (979)826-4111, 34843 Betka Rd, Waller, TX 77484

WALLISVILLE — D9 *Chambers*

RIO RV PARK **Ratings: 7.5/9★/7.5** (RV Park) Avail: 47 full hkups (30/50 amps). 2021 rates: $40 to $65. (281)782-1704, 25128 I-10 East, Wallisville, TX 77597

WAXAHACHIE — B7 *Ellis*

NORTHSIDE RV RESORT **Ratings: 8/9.5★/9.5** (RV Park) Avail: 66 full hkups (30/50 amps). 2021 rates: $55 to $65. (972)908-0040, 200 East Butcher Road, Waxahachie, TX 75165

WEATHERFORD — B7 *Parker*

HOOVES N' WHEELS RV PARK & HORSE MOTEL
good sam park **Ratings: 8/9★/9.5** (RV Park) Avail: 10 full hkups (30/50 amps). 2021 rates: $45 to $55. (817)599-4686, 4128 Granbury Hwy, Weatherford, TX 76087

OAK CREEK RV PARK
good sam park **Ratings: 10/10★/10** (RV Park) Avail: 72 full hkups (30/50 amps). 2021 rates: $50. (817)594-0200, 7652 W I-20, Weatherford, TX 76088

WEATHERFORD/FORT WORTH WEST KOA **Ratings: 8.5/10★/8.5** (RV Park) Avail: 11 full hkups (30/50 amps). 2021 rates: $35 to $39. (817)594-8801, 2205 Tin Top Rd, Weatherford, TX 76087

WECHES — C8 *Houston*

MISSION TEJAS (Public State Park) From Jct of SR-21 & FM-227, NE 1.4 mi on SR-21 to Park Rd 44 (L) (Entrance fee). 14 Avail: 14 W, 12 E (20/30 amps). 2021 rates: $10 to $15. (936)687-2394

WEIMAR — D7 *Colorado*

WHISPERING OAKS RV PARK
good sam park **Ratings: 8/8.5★/9.5** (RV Park) W-bnd: From Jct of I-10 & Hatterman Ln (exit 689), W 200 ft on N Frntg Rd (L); or E-bnd: From Jct of I-10 & Hatterman Ln (exit 689), E 100 ft on N Frntg Rd (R).

EASY ACCESS ON/OFF I-10 AT EXIT 689
Beautifully landscaped RV Park 40 miles W of Houston. Big Rig Friendly. Large level pull-thru sites, paved roads, free WiFi, propane, convenience store & cabins. RV Inspections & Mobile Service on-site.

FAC: paved rds. Avail: 49 gravel, 42 pull-thrus, (30x85), back-ins (30x43), 46 full hkups, 3 W, 3 E (30/50 amps), WiFi @ sites, tent sites, rentals, dump, laundry, groc, LP gas, fire rings, firewood. **REC:** playground. Pets OK. Big rig sites, eco-friendly. 2021 rates: $41, Military discount.
(979)732-9494 Lat: 29.69271, Lon: -96.64751
2965 Hwy 90, Weimar, TX 78962
whisperingoaksrvpark.com
See ad page 903

WELLINGTON — F10 *Collingsworth*

COLLINGSWORTH COUNTY PIONEER'S PARK (Public) From town, N 7 mi on US-83 (L). 30 Avail: 30 W, 30 E (30/50 amps). 2021 rates: $15 to $20. (806)447-5408

WESLACO — M3 *Hidalgo*

1015 RV PARK **Ratings: 9/9★/7.5** (RV Park) Avail: 88 full hkups (30/50 amps). 2021 rates: $40. (956)968-7516, 1402 S International Blvd., Weslaco, TX 78596

COUNTRY SUNSHINE RV RESORT
good sam park **Ratings: 9.5/9★/8.5** (RV Area in MH Park) Avail: 191 full hkups (30/50 amps). 2021 rates: $51. (888)563-7040, 1601 S Airport Dr, Weslaco, TX 78596

LEISURE WORLD RV RESORT
good sam park (RV Resort) (Not Visited) Avail: 133 full hkups (30/50 amps). 2021 rates: $40. (888)563-7040, 400 E 18th St, Weslaco, TX 78596

MAGIC VALLEY RV PARK MHP **Ratings: 9.5/8.5★/7.5** (RV Area in MH Park) Avail: 83 full hkups (30/50 amps). 2021 rates: $40 to $46. (956)968-8242, 2300 E Bus Hwy 83, Weslaco, TX 78596

SNOW TO SUN RV RESORT
good sam park **Ratings: 9/10★/8.5** (RV Area in MH Park) From Jct of Expwy 83 & FM-1015 (International Blvd), N 1.1 mi on International Blvd (L). **FAC:** paved rds. (489 spaces). 152 Avail: 32 paved, 120 grass, patios, back-ins (25x50), 152 full hkups (30/50 amps), seasonal sites, WiFi @ sites, rentals, laundry, controlled access. **REC:** heated pool, hot tub, shuffleboard. Pet restrict (B/Q). Partial handicap access. No tents, Age restrict may apply, eco-friendly. 2021 rates: $23 to $38, Military discount.
(956)968-0322 Lat: 26.17868, Lon: -97.96058
1701 N International Blvd, Weslaco, TX 78599
rhprvresorts.com
See ad page 881

SOUTHERN COMFORT RV RESORT
good sam park **Ratings: 9.5/8.5★/8.5** (RV Area in MH Park) Avail: 100 full hkups (30/50 amps). 2021 rates: $54. (888)563-7040, 1501 S Airport Drive, Weslaco, TX 78596

TRAILS END RV RESORT
good sam park (RV Resort) (Not Visited) 71 full hkups (50 amps). 2021 rates: $30. (888)563-7040, 2001 S Texas Blvd, Weslaco, TX 78596

WEST TAWAKONI — B8 *Hunt*

VETERAN'S MEMORIAL CITY PARK (Public) From Jct TX Hwy 34 & TX Hwy 276 (in Quinlan W of W Tawakoni), E 5 mi (L). Avail: 11 full hkups (30/50 amps). 2021 rates: $20. (903)274-7180

WHITESBORO — A7 *Grayson*

MILITARY PARK SHEPPARD REC ANNEX AT LAKE TEXOMA (SHEPPARD AFB) (Public) From town: Go 11 mi N on US-377, then 1-3/4 mi W on FR-901, then N onto Rock Creek Rd and follow signs to Sheppard Annex. Caution: road is narrow and has curves. (E). 41 Avail: 25 full hkups, 16 W, 16 E (30/50 amps). 2021 rates: $20 to $25. (903)523-4613

WHITNEY — B7 *Bosque*

LAKE WHITNEY (Public State Park) From Jct of I-35 & SR-22 (exit 368A), W 15 mi on SR-22 to FM-933, N 0.6 mi to FM-1244, SW 2.2 mi (E) (Entrance fee). 145 Avail: 43 full hkups, 94 W, 31 E (50 amps). 2021 rates: $10 to $24. (254)694-3793

LAKE WHITNEY RV
good sam park **Ratings: 6.5/7/8** (Membership Park) 232 Avail: 151 full hkups, 81 W, 81 E (30/50 amps). 2021 rates: $54 to $66. (888)563-7040, 417 Thousand Trails Dr, Whitney, TX 76692

WHITNEY LAKE - COE/CEDRON CREEK (Public Corps) From town, N 3 mi on Hwy 933 to FM-1713, 2 mi to Cedron Rd, S 0.5 mi (follow signs). 58 Avail: 57 W, 58 E (30/50 amps). 2021 rates: $16 to $20. Apr 01 to Sep 30. (254)622-3332

WHITNEY LAKE - COE/LOFERS BEND EAST (Public Corps) From town, SW 6 mi on Hwy 22 (R). 74 Avail: 74 W, 69 E (15/30 amps). 2021 rates: $12 to $20. Apr 01 to Sep 30. (254)622-3332

WHITNEY LAKE - COE/MCCOWN VALLEY (Public Corps) From town, N 2.4 mi on SR-933 to FM-1713, SW 4.4 mi (L). 47 Avail: 47 W, 47 E (30/50 amps). 2021 rates: $20 to $22. Apr 01 to Sep 30. (254)622-3332

WHITNEY RESORTS **Ratings: 7/8★/6.5** (Membership Park) Avail: 76 full hkups (30/50 amps). 2021 rates: $28 to $32. (254)694-4023, 255 Sun Country Dr, Whitney, TX 76692

WICHITA FALLS — A6 *Clay*

COYOTE RANCH RESORT **Ratings: 10/10★/9** (RV Park) Avail: 73 full hkups (30/50 amps). 2021 rates: $59 to $79. (940)767-6700, 14145 US Hwy 287 N, Wichita Falls, TX 76310

LAKE ARROWHEAD (Public State Park) From Jct of US-287/281 & US-281/79 (S of town), S 5.8 mi on US -281 to FM-1954, E 7.2 mi to Pk Rd 63 (E); or From Jct of US-287 & FM-2393, S 6.7 mi on FM-2393 to FM-1954, SE 3.2 mi (L) (Entrance fee). 67 Avail: 67 W, 48 E (50 amps). 2021 rates: $12 to $22. (940)528-2211

WICHITA FALLS RV PARK
Ratings: 9.5/10★/9.5 (RV Park) Avail: 59 full hkups (30/50 amps). 2021 rates: $45 to $55. (800)252-1532, 2944 Seymour Hwy, Wichita Falls, TX 76301

WICHITA RIVER BEND RV PARK (Public) From Jct of I-44 & US-277, N 1.5 mi on I-44, exit at Tourist Bureau, S 0.2 mi on frntg rd (E). 28 Avail: 28 W, 28 E (30/50 amps). 2021 rates: $17. (940)761-7491

WILLIS — C8 *Montgomery*

LAKE CONROE RV
Ratings: 8.5/10★/9 (Membership Park) Avail: 290 full hkups (30/50 amps). 2021 rates: $52 to $55. (888)563-7040, 11720 Thousand Trails Rd, Willis, TX 77318

WATERS EDGE **Ratings: 7/7/8** (RV Park) Avail: 20 full hkups (30/50 amps). 2021 rates: $10. (936)856-2949, 12922 Longstreet Rd, Willis, TX 77318

WINNIE — D9 *Chambers*

WINNIE INN & RV PARK
Ratings: 7.5/NA/7 (RV Park) Avail: 22 full hkups (30/50 amps). 2021 rates: $35. (409)296-2947, 205 Spur 5, Winnie, TX 77665

Always do a Pre-Drive Safety Check!

WINTERS — B5 *Runnels*

ELM CREEK RESERVOIR (Public) From town, E 5 mi on Hwy 153 (L). 14 Avail: 14 W, 14 E (30 amps). 2021 rates: $9 to $12. (325)754-4424

WOLFFORTH — A4 *Lubbock*

MESA VERDE RV PARK
Ratings: 9.5/9.5★/9 (RV Park) From Jct W Loop 289 & US 62/82 (Lubbock): Go 5 mi SW on US 62/82 (Exit FM 179), then 1-1/4 mi N on E Service Rd (R). Elev 3312 ft.**FAC:** paved rds. Avail: 78 gravel, 21 pull-thrus, (35x65), back-ins (35x70), 78 full hkups (30/50 amps), cable, WiFi @ sites, laundry, LP bottles. **REC:** pool. Pet restrict (B/Q). Partial handicap access. No tents. Big rig sites. 2021 rates: $44, Military discount.
(806)773-3135 Lat: 33.51413, Lon: -101.99806
503 E Hwy 62, Wolfforth, TX 79382
rvlubbock.com
See ad page 908

WOODVILLE — C9 *Jasper*

STEINHAGEN LAKE - COE/MAGNOLIA RIDGE (Public Corps) From town, E 15 mi on US-190 to FM-92, N 1.5 mi to park entrance rd, E 1 mi (E). 38 Avail: 36 W, 36 E (30/50 amps). 2021 rates: $10 to $18. (409)429-3491

Camping World RV & Outdoors ProCare, service you can trust from the RV experts.

WYLIE — G5 *Collin*

LAVON LAKE - COE/EAST FORK (Public Corps) From town, E 2.5 mi on Hwy 78 to CR-434, N 0.05 mi to Sky View Dr, W 0.5 mi (R). Avail: 50 E (50 amps). 2021 rates: $30. (972)442-3141

YOAKUM — D7 *Lavaca*

HUB CITY RV PARK (Public) From Jct of Hwy 95/US-77A & FM-3475 (NE of Yoakum), SE 1.3 mi on FM-3475 (R). Avail: 30 full hkups (30/50 amps). 2021 rates: $8 to $18. (361)293-5682

SHADE TREE RV PARK
Ratings: 6/8.5★/8 (RV Park) Avail: 14 full hkups (30/50 amps). 2021 rates: $35. (361)293-3540, 10363 FM 682, Yoakum, TX 77995

ZAPATA — L2 *Zapata*

AMIGO INN & RV PARK
Ratings: 7/9★/9 (RV Park) Avail: 61 full hkups (30/50 amps). 2021 rates: $45. (956)765-3095, 209 Lake Shore Drive, Zapata, TX 78076

STINSON RV PARK & STORAGE
Ratings: 7.5/9★/8 (RV Park) Avail: 50 full hkups (30/50 amps). 2021 rates: $40. (956)765-5162, 3299 S US Hwy 83, Zapata, TX 78076

Say you saw it in our Guide!

TX

good sam
Extended Service Plan

You make the priceless memories. We'll pay for the pricey repair bills.

We know that time spent traveling with your family is precious. When your RV needs a mechanical repair, let us pick up the bill, so that you can get back on the road and back to spending time with your family.

Program Benefits:

- No waiting for reimbursement, we pay the shop directly.
- Take your vehicle to the repair shop of your choice.
- Choose the deductible and payment schedule that works for you, and lock in your rate for up to 3 years.
- Trip Interruption: If your RV is not usable due to a covered loss, we'll help cover costs for meals and lodging for $100 a day, for up to 5 days per repair visit.
- Rental Car Reimbursement: If you can't drive your vehicle due to a covered loss, we'll help cover costs for a rental car for $60 a day, for up to 5 days per repair visit.

Rental car benefit is not available on 5th wheel and travel trailer coverage.

Visit **GoodSamESP.com/Guide**

Call **866-601-2317**

To qualify, towable RVs must be 15 model years or newer. Cars, trucks, SUVs, and gas Motorhomes must be 15 model years or newer with less than 100,000 miles, and rear engine diesel Motorhomes must be 15 model years or newer with less than 120,000 miles. Coverage is renewable up to 18 model years or 150,000 miles. All program benefits are subject to limitations set forth in the current Terms & Conditions.

The Good Sam Extended Service Plan is not available to residents of New York or Indiana. If you are a resident of New York or Indiana, please call 1-866-524-7842 as other products may be available to you.

The Good Sam Extended Service Plan, which was designed for Good Sam by Affinity Brokerage, LLC, a Colorado surplus lines brokerage (Lic. #185640), is available exclusively for active members of Good Sam. Membership is required for eligibility in this program. Termination of your membership in Good Sam during the policy period may result in termination of The Good Sam Extended Service Plan. The cost of Good Sam Membership is the responsibility of the certificate holder and will be available at the then current rate. The Good Sam Extended Service Plan is available to U.S. residents only.

YOU ARE HERE
Utah
DID YOU KNOW?
Utah residents eat more Jell-O per capita than any other state. They also celebrate National Jell-O week in February.
tty Images/iStockphoto

Utah

From Arches National Park to Zion, Utah's stunning landscapes and welcoming towns make it one of the most attractive destinations in the Southwest. Visit in person to see what makes the Beehive State truly buzz.

Superb Cities of the Southwest

The Salt Lake Tabernacle may be Salt Lake City's main attraction, but the town has many other attractions in store for eager travelers. Dig into seasonal, locally sourced plates at Pago's and feast on a mean Mole Coloradito at the Red Iguana. Authentic Tuscan fare is served at Valter's Osteria, while craft beer flows endlessly at Avenues Proper, Epic Brewing Company and Red Rock Brewery. Walk off your delicious meals by shopping at over 90 stores at City Creek Shopping Center.

Park City Powder

Ski buffs speak with reverence when describing the powdery snow on the slopes of the Park City Mountain. Located just 35 minutes from Salt Lake City International Airport, this historic silver mining town spoils skiers with a world-class resort that's home to over 300 trails, 41 lifts and eight terrain parks. During winter, stop by the Utah Olympic Park for a heart-pumping bobsled ride.

Get Wet in the Desert

River riders will discover one of the most exciting stretches of the Colorado River near the town of Moab. Thrill-seeking rafters can take on the raging waters in Westwater and Cataract Canyons, while families can enjoy a leisurely float in Fisher Towers. Calmer sections of the Colorado can also be explored by canoe, kayak or paddleboard.

Fast Flats

Land speed records have been smashed on the Bonneville Salt Flats, one of North America's most interesting

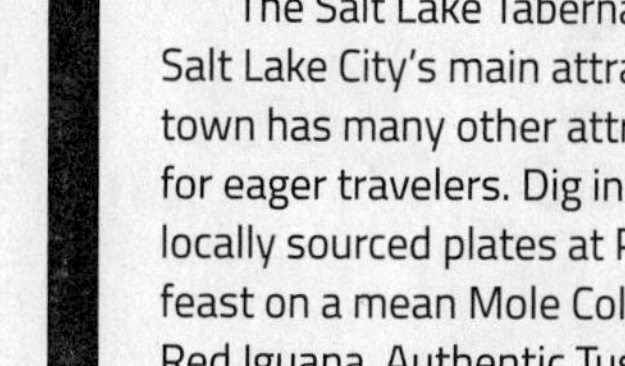

Utah Funeral Potatoes

Don't let the name fool you. The warm, cheesy flavors that burst from this dish will make you feel alive. Dig into a hefty helping of comfort food that consists of cubed potatoes, cheese, onions, cream soup or sauce, sour cream, and a topping of butter and corn flakes or crushed potato chips. Make this dish the star attraction of potlucks, family events and casual get-togethers.

VISITOR CENTER

TIME ZONE
Mountain Standard

ROAD & HIGHWAY INFORMATION
866-511-8824
udot.utah.gov

FISHING & HUNTING INFORMATION
801-538-4700
wildlife.utah.gov

BOATING INFORMATION
801-538-BOAT
stateparks.utah.gov/activities/boating

NATIONAL PARKS
nps.gov/ut

STATE PARKS
stateparks.utah.gov

TOURISM INFORMATION
Utah Office of Tourism
800-200-1160
visitutah.com

TOP TOURISM ATTRACTIONS
1) Bryce Canyon National Park
2) Arches National Park
3) Latter-day Saints Temple Square

MAJOR CITIES
Salt Lake City (capital), West Valley City, Provo, West Jordan, Orem

 See map page 926

environments. This white salt-coated surface sprawls for 30,000 acres and hosts land speed racing events every summer. Wildlife such as bison and antelope can be viewed in Antelope Island State Park, and the densest concentration of Jurassic-era dinosaur bones await at the Cleveland Lloyd Dinosaur Quarry in the heart of the state.

Mormon Origins

Mormon settlers reached the Salt Lake Valley in 1847, and since their arrival, this religion has become part of the tapestry of the state. Today, 60 percent of the state's population are members of the Latter-day Saints Church. Mormon heritage is on full display at Salt Lake City's Temple Square. Featuring the Salt Lake Temple, Tabernacle, Family History Library and a dozen other attractions, this 35-acre area in the downtown core weaves history with stunning architecture and art.

Legacy of the Native Americans

Native Americans flourished throughout the state long before American settlers arrived. Gain insight into the state's first occupants at Fremont Indian State Park in central Utah near Interstate 70. Home to the largest Fremont Native American village ever discovered, this park lets you view the remains of ancient pit houses and ponder petroglyphs adorning rock walls.

Bagging Beehive State Game

Outside of Utah's parks and monuments, hunters can take advantage of thriving populations of mule deer, elk, antelope, pheasant, duck and more.

The National Park Five

Experience Utah's Mighty 5 National Parks. Trek through a wonderland of sandstone towers and over 2,000 arches in Arches National Park. Watch the sun's rays dance on sharp, brilliantly colored hoodoos at Bryce Canyon National Park. Capture stunning photos of Zion National Park's famous rock formations. In Canyonlands National Park, bike down challenging dirt roads and be rewarded with panoramic vistas. If you want to beat the crowds, head to Capitol Reef National Park for vibrant cliffs all to yourself.

Hiking in Utah's Bryce Canyon National Park, known for its orange-hued rock formations and stunning overlooks.

Buzzing Beehive

Utah has established a name for itself in theater, art and film, and you can experience all of it at the state's many festivals. Park City's Sundance Film Festival showcases independent films, while the Utah Shakespeare Festival in Cedar City puts on performances from June to October. In Salt Lake City, view works by renowned artists at the Utah Arts Festival, and learn how to enhance your artistic skills at the Craft Lake City DIY Festival. Racing fans will want to swing by St. George in March for the Skywest Airlines Mini Indy.

good sam park

Featured Good Sam Parks

UTAH

When you stay with Good Sam, you can expect the highest degree of cleanliness and friendliness, and better yet, you get **10% off** overnight campground fees.

If you're not already a Good Sam member you can purchase your membership at one of these locations:

BLANDING
Blanding RV Park
Blue Mountain RV and Trading

BRYCE CANYON
Bryce Canyon Pines Store & Campground & RV Park
Red Canyon Village

CANNONVILLE
Bryce Valley Ranch RV and Horse Park

CEDAR CITY
Cedar Breaks RV Park
Iron Springs Adventure Resort

COALVILLE
Holiday Hills RV Park

DRAPER
Mountain Shadows RV Park & MHP

ESCALANTE
Canyons Of Escalante RV Park
Escalante Cabins & RV Park
Yonder Escalante

FILLMORE
Wagons West RV Park and Campground

FOUNTAIN GREEN
Standing Bear RV Park

GLENDALE
Bauer's Canyon Ranch RV Park
Bryce-Zion Campground

GREEN RIVER
iCamp
Shady Acres RV Park

HEBER CITY
Mountain Valley RV Resort

HURRICANE
WillowWind RV Park

KANAB
Crazy Horse RV Resort
Grand Plateau RV Resort at Kanab

LAYTON
Circle L Mobile Home Community

LOA
Fremont River RV Park

MOAB
Spanish Trail RV Park

MONUMENT VALLEY
Goulding's Monument Valley Campground & RV Park

NEPHI
Jones High Country RV Camp

OGDEN
Century RV Park & Campground

PROVO
Lakeside RV Campground

ST GEORGE
McArthur's Temple View RV Resort

TREMONTON
Aspen Grove RV Park

VERNAL
Fossil Valley RV Park

VIRGIN
Zion River Resort RV Park & Campground

10/10★/10 GOOD SAM PARKS

HEBER CITY
Mountain Valley RV Resort
(435)657-6100

KANAB
Grand Plateau RV Resort at Kanab
(435)610-2500

What's This?

An RV park with a 10/10★/10 rating has scored perfect grades in amenities, cleanliness and appearance ("See Understanding the Campground Rating System" on pages 8 and 9 for an explanation of the trusted Good Sam Rating System). Stay in a 10/10★/10 park on your next trip for a nearly flawless camping experience.

Getty Images/iStockphoto

UT

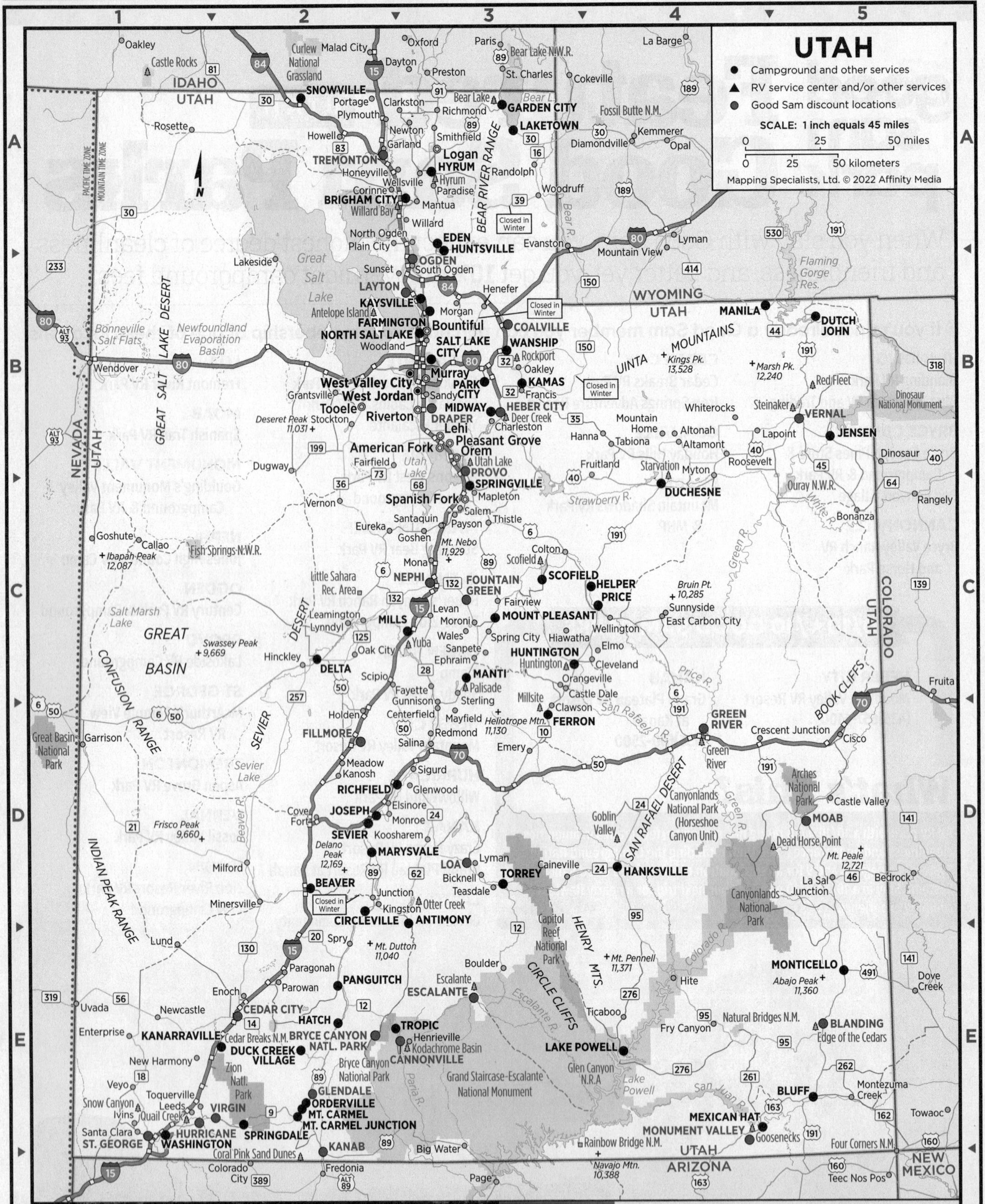
UTAH
Campground and other services
RV service center and/or other services
Good Sam discount locations
SCALE: 1 inch equals 45 miles
0 25 50 miles
0 25 50 kilometers
Mapping Specialists, Ltd. © 2022 Affinity Media
IDAHO
UTAH
WYOMING
NEVADA
COLORADO
ARIZONA
NEW MEXICO
PACIFIC TIME ZONE
MOUNTAIN TIME ZONE
SNOWVILLE
TREMONTON
BRIGHAM CITY
Logan
HYRUM
GARDEN CITY
LAKETOWN
BEAR RIVER RANGE
EDEN
HUNTSVILLE
OGDEN
LAYTON
KAYSVILLE
FARMINGTON
Bountiful
NORTH SALT LAKE
SALT LAKE CITY
COALVILLE
WANSHIP
KAMAS
HEBER CITY
PARK CITY
MIDWAY
Murray
West Valley City
West Jordan
Tooele
Riverton
DRAPER
Lehi
Pleasant Grove
American Fork
Orem
PROVO
SPRINGVILLE
Spanish Fork
Great Salt Lake
GREAT SALT LAKE DESERT
Bonneville Salt Flats
Newfoundland Evaporation Basin
Wendover
UINTA MOUNTAINS
Kings Pk. 13,528
Marsh Pk. 12,240
MANILA
DUTCH JOHN
Flaming Gorge Res.
VERNAL
JENSEN
Dinosaur National Monument
DUCHESNE
Roosevelt
Ouray N.W.R.
Strawberry R.
Deseret Peak 11,031
Ibapah Peak 12,087
Fish Springs N.W.R.
Mt. Nebo 11,929
NEPHI
FOUNTAIN GREEN
SCOFIELD
HELPER
PRICE
MOUNT PLEASANT
Bruin Pt. 10,285
MILLS
DELTA
Little Sahara Rec. Area
GREAT BASIN
CONFUSION RANGE
Swasey Peak 9,669
Salt Marsh Lake
SEVIER DESERT
Sevier Lake
Great Basin National Park
MANTI
HUNTINGTON
FERRON
Heliotrope Mtn. 11,130
FILLMORE
GREEN RIVER
BOOK CLIFFS
Crescent Junction
Cisco
Fruita
RICHFIELD
JOSEPH
SEVIER
MARYSVALE
Frisco Peak 9,660
INDIAN PEAK RANGE
Delano Peak 12,169
BEAVER
CIRCLEVILLE
ANTIMONY
LOA
TORREY
HANKSVILLE
SAN RAFAEL DESERT
Canyonlands National Park (Horseshoe Canyon Unit)
Arches National Park
Castle Valley
MOAB
Dead Horse Point
Mt. Peale 12,721
Canyonlands National Park
Capitol Reef National Park
HENRY MTS.
Mt. Pennell 11,371
Mt. Dutton 11,040
PANGUITCH
ESCALANTE
MONTICELLO
Abajo Peak 11,360
CEDAR CITY
HATCH
BRYCE CANYON NATL. PARK
TROPIC
CANNONVILLE
KANARRAVILLE
DUCK CREEK VILLAGE
Cedar Breaks N.M.
Kodachrome Basin
CIRCLE CLIFFS
LAKE POWELL
Glen Canyon N.R.A.
Grand Staircase-Escalante National Monument
Natural Bridges N.M.
BLANDING
Edge of the Cedars
Zion Natl. Park
GLENDALE
ORDERVILLE
MT. CARMEL
MT. CARMEL JUNCTION
VIRGIN
HURRICANE
SPRINGDALE
ST. GEORGE
WASHINGTON
KANAB
Coral Pink Sand Dunes
Rainbow Bridge N.M.
Navajo Mtn. 10,388
MEXICAN HAT
MONUMENT VALLEY
Goosenecks
BLUFF
Four Corners N.M.
Closed in Winter

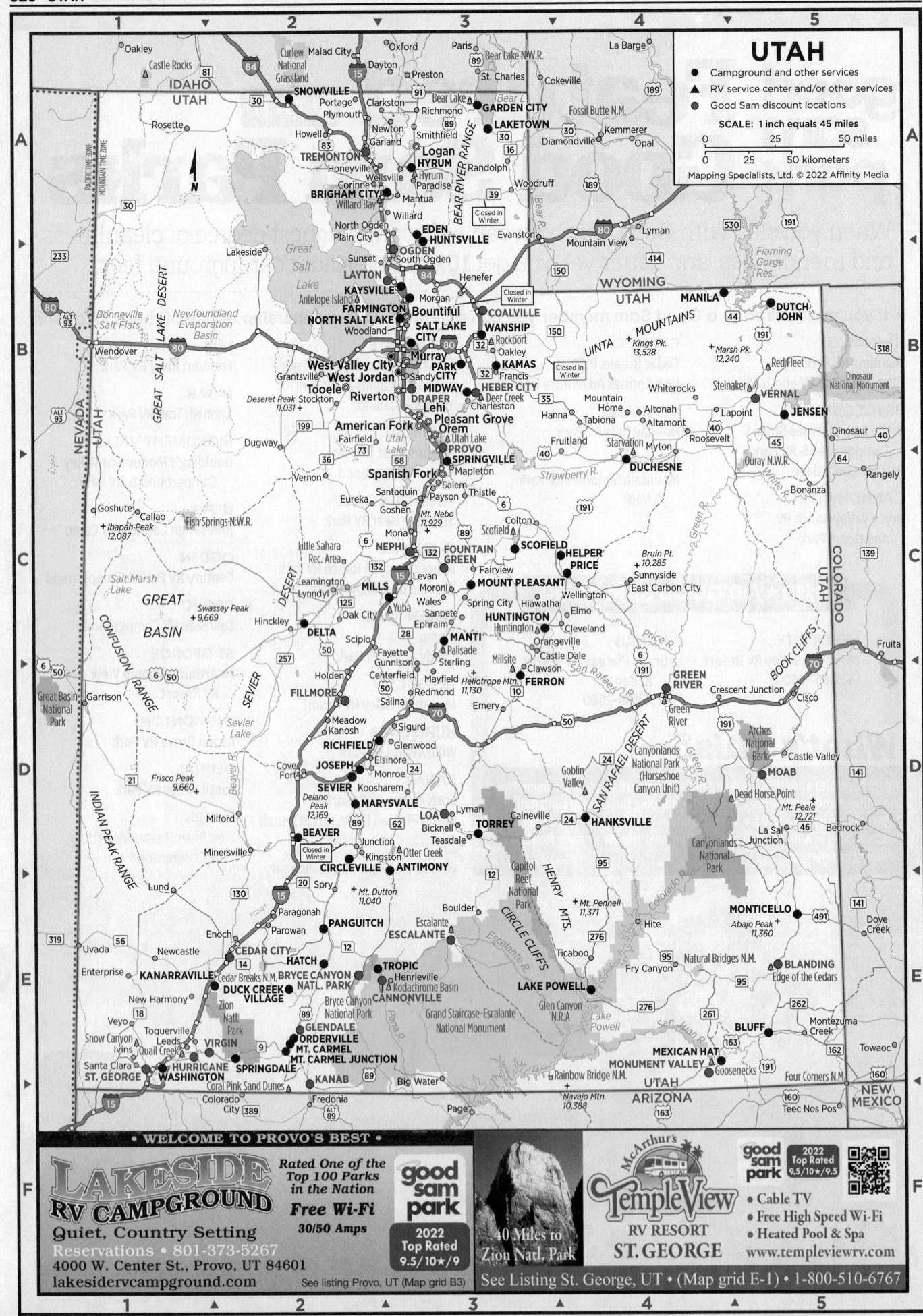

ROAD TRIPS

See Iconic National Parks on this Scenic Journey

Utah

LOCATION
UTAH

DISTANCE
336 MILES

DRIVE TIME
6 HRS 14 MINS

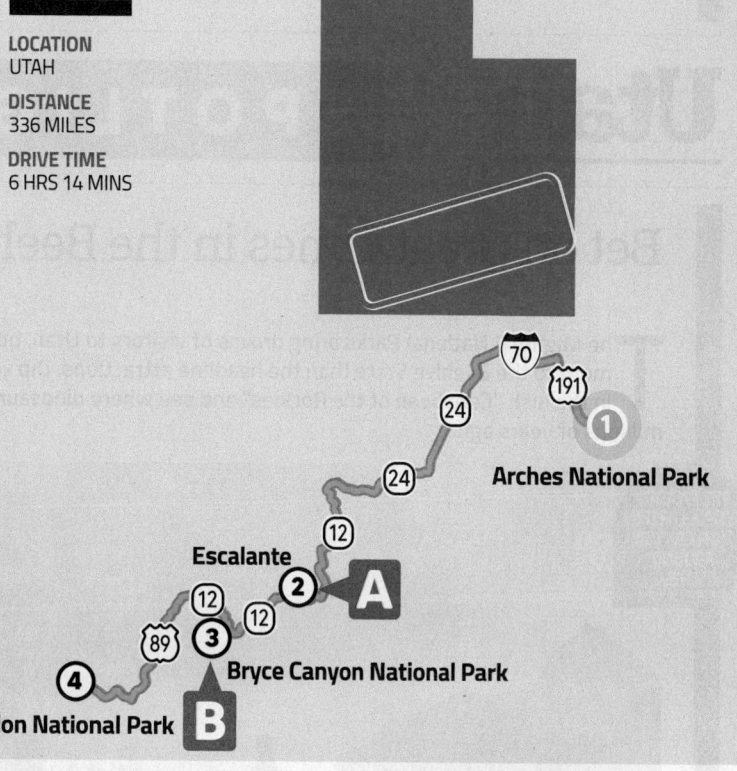

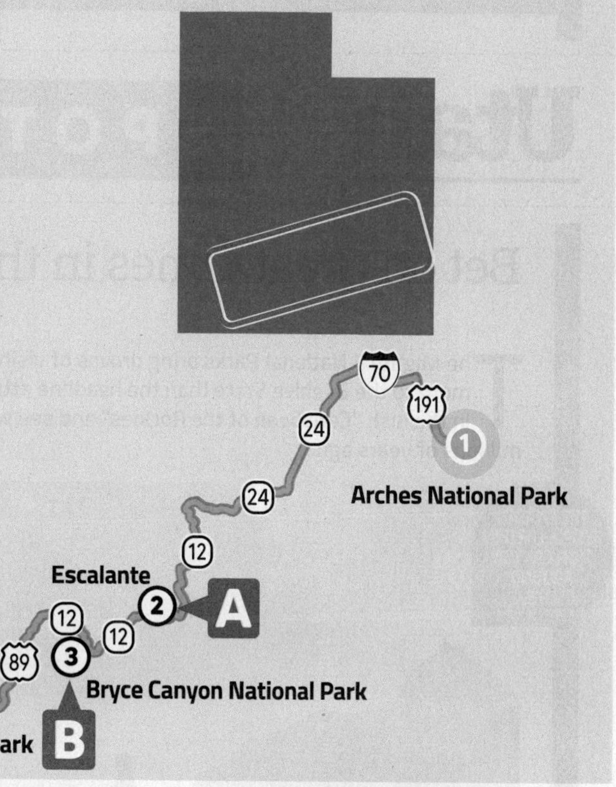

Utah's landscapes have to be seen to be believed. Experience wind-carved stone arches and impressive canyons enclosed by red rock walls that are covered with ancient petroglyphs. Hike among hoodoos, or bicycle around the rim of giant chasms. See land folded like an enormous paper fan, exemplifying the inordinate pressure needed to create a 100-mile rift in the earth's crust.

1 Arches National Park
Starting Point

Rock arches stand tall and mammoth rock "fins" reach to the sky in a national park masterpiece. Hike, bike or drive through this spectacular park, where sandstone rock formations with names like Fiery Furnace and The Three Gossips stand, along with over 2,000 natural stone arches, the handiwork of thousands of years of wind and rain. In nearby Moab, mountain bike fanatics prepare for adventurous rides. These cyclists start their treks in town, then head out to Canyonlands National Park to tackle precarious backcountry trails, like White Rim Drive or Confluence Overlook Trail.

2 Escalante
Drive 215 miles ▪ 3 hours, 57 minutes

The Escalante-Grand Staircase National Monument is a desert playground, where hikers and Jeep enthusiasts revel in wonder. Navajo sandstone has been carved into tight canyons with cascading waterfalls, slickrock domes and surprising grottoes. Follow Hole-In-The-Rock Road to witness a true pioneer miracle, where Mormon missionaries moved wagons and stock down a slot in the sandstone, lowering them over 2,000 feet to the Colorado River way back in 1879.

RECOMMENDED STOPOVER
A YONDER ESCALANTE
ESCALANTE, UT (435) 826-4440

3 Bryce Canyon National Park
Drive 49 miles ▪ 57minutes

In Bryce Canyon, the eerie sandstone hoodoos reflect sunlight in golden-orange hues, creating one of the most exciting light shows in nature. Photographers love these striated pinnacles of rock, which give a performance that changes dramatically every hour. From vantage points throughout the park, visitors can soak in the spectacle.

RECOMMENDED STOPOVER
B BRYCE CANYON PINES STORE & CAMPGROUND & RV PARK
BRYCE CANYON, UT (800) 892-7923

4 Zion National Park
Drive 72 miles ▪ 1 hour, 20 minutes

Zion National Park provides an amazing menu for hikers, with trails that run through narrow chasms and over scenic ridges. Crowds have discovered this desert gem, but most do not venture past two popular trails. Stick with Canyon Overlook Trail for an astonishing view of the park's monolithic domes and green valleys. Then hike the Lower Emerald Pools Trail to discover quiet pools and waterfalls.

UT

Utah

SPOTLIGHTS

Bet on Great Times in the Beehive State

The Mighty 5 National Parks bring droves of visitors to Utah, but there's more to the Beehive State than the headline attractions. Dip your toes in the lush "Caribbean of the Rockies" and see where dinosaurs roamed millions of years ago.

THE ANASAZI PEOPLE LIVED IN ZION CANYON AROUND 1500 B.C.

Enjoying scenery on the Canyon Overlook Trail in Zion National Park during sunset.

Logan

Logan welcomes visitors to enjoy life at a slower pace. Nestled in a high mountain valley, there's hiking, biking and fishing galore, while the charming downtown hosts enough cultural attractions to fit a college town twice its size. Come for the natural wonders and stay for the world-class performances; there's a little something for everyone in the heart of Cache Valley.

The Hills Are Alive

Discover an abundance of nature just outside the city limits. Five minutes east of town, the Bear River Mountains greet adventurers with a combination of wildflower prairies and tall peaks surrounded by rugged cliffs. Home to moose, elk and deer, they constitute the perfect place for day hikes of all levels. Driving the Logan Canyon National Scenic Byway is a great way to explore the mountains by car, while still getting the chance to take in breathtaking summit and canyon views.

Utah Gets Tropical

You won't hear steel drums, but you may feel like you've just ventured into the Bahamas. Further to the east on the byway, motorists will reach Bear Lake State Park, which, because of its clear, turquoise water, has earned the title "The Caribbean of the Rockies." The lake is an ideal destination for families with boating, fishing, swimming and camping, as well as a surrounding forest that's home to over a hundred miles of trails to keep you busy throughout the day.

St. George

Travelers from all walks of life are drawn to St. George. Snowbirds come for the warm weather, vacationers flock to the top-rated golf courses and outdoor adventurers make the city their base camp for exploring Zion National Park. Whatever type of traveler you are, you can be sure red rock mesas, canyon waterfalls and soaring cliffs will provide the ultimate backdrop for all your excursions.

Gateway to Zion National Park

An hour's drive is all it takes to get to Zion National Park. Packed with vast canyons, jagged spires and hanging gardens, this 148,000-acre park has countless highlights so it's best to spend a few days exploring. If heights don't bother you, hike up rocky ridges on Angels Landing or Observation Point trail to get to expansive vistas. The 1-mile Canyon Overlook Trail is a much easier trek, yet still rewards you with sweeping panoramas of the valley floor. The Narrows Riverside Walk, Emerald Pools and Weeping Rock are short trails geared toward families, while the 6.5-mile Zion Canyon Scenic Drive gives you a close-up view of the Grotto and Great White Throne from the comfort of your car.

All About the Bass

Many of Utah's top bass fishing spots are just a stone's throw away from St. George. Snap up fish in big numbers from Sand

LOCAL FAVORITE

Fred's 5 Star Chili Cheese Sauce

This warm sauce is perfect for camping in the rugged landscapes of the Beehive State. Use it as a dip, a salad topping (try it on taco salads) or on a baked potato. *Recipe by Fred Douthit.*

INGREDIENTS

- ☐ 1 can chili
- ☐ 1 can refried beans
- ☐ 1 cup salsa
- ☐ 1 cup sour cream
- ☐ 1 cup of shredded cheese

DIRECTIONS

In a large saucepan, combine the first 4 ingredients while heating over low heat. Use a mixer to puree the ingredients as they warm. You want the mix to be just warm enough to melt the cheese, which you add last.

Once the cheese has melted, it is ready for use. It can be used warm or cold.

This recipe makes approximately 3 pints of finished sauce. Leftovers can be kept in the refrigerator for several days or frozen and thawed for later use. If frozen, stir the sauce before serving.

Hollow Reservoir, Gunlock Reservoir, Lake Powell and Quail Lake. Besides bass, Lake Powell contains channel catfish and walleye, Gunlock Reservoir has plenty of catfish, and Sand Hollow Reservoir is great for bluegill. Quail Lake also has trout around the beginning and end of the year. Launch a kayak from any of these destinations if you want to admire the desert landscape from the water. More paddling opportunities can be found in Kolob Reservoir and Ivins Reservoir.

Adventures for the Bold and Brave

Hikers will find endless possibilities in Snow Canyon State Park. Famed for its sculpted canyons and sand dunes, this desert playground features an extensive network of trails ranging from easy to challenging. Trek the moderate Three Ponds Trail to reach a narrow canyon or the White Rocks Trail for sweeping views of the West Canyon. For the best mountain biking, head to Gooseberry Mesa where single tracks wind through the hills. You can also boulder to your heart's content in Moe's Valley and Black Rocks Canyon, both of which offer dozens of routes amid dramatic scenery. If you're into paleontology, visit the Dinosaur Discovery Site at Johnson Farm to follow thousands of fossilized footprints from the Early Jurassic Period.

Provo

Nestled in the foothills of Mount Timpanogos (11,749 feet) — the second-highest summit of the Wasatch Mountains (only Mount Nebo is higher) — Provo is the home of Brigham Young University with a vibrant student population along with myriad museums, cultural events and spectator sports. While many visitors head straight to the university's attractions, Provo's historic downtown is well worth a stroll, with eclectic shops and family-owned restaurants.

As Seen in Movies

Framed by the Wasatch Mountains, Provo provides plenty of opportunities to interact with the landscape. Just a short drive away, Sundance Mountain Resort — founded by Robert Redford — offers novice and intermediate hiking and biking trails amidst spectacular scenery. Some of the Wasatch Mountains' most popular trails are within minutes of Provo. Try the family-friendly, 1.4-mile Bridal Veil Falls and the 3.4-mile Stewart Falls which culminate with the namesake waterfall. At Timpanogos Cave National Monument, a 1.5-mile trail rewards with colorful limestone caves. Near town, Uinta National Forest has abundant hiking, biking and horseback riding trails.

Majestic Mountains

A stunning wall of mountains forms the backdrop for the 96,600-acre Utah Lake State Park, home to Utah's largest freshwater lake. Anglers cast for channel catfish, walleye, white bass, black bass and several species of panfish. With water temperatures hovering around 75 degrees, the lake provides excellent opportunities for boating, canoeing, paddleboarding and swimming. The Provo River Parkway Trail leads from the edge of the park into Provo Canyon. For families, the iconic 17-acre Splash Summit Waterpark offers multiple play areas, including a 500,000-gallon wave pool, waterslides, and a rope swing.

FOR MORE INFORMATION

Utah Office of Tourism, 800-200-1160, www.visitutah.com
Cache Valley Visitors Bureau (Logan), 435-755-1890, www.explorelogan.com
St. George Area Tourism Office, 435-634-5747, www.visitstgeorge.com
Visit Provo, 800-222-UTAH, www.utahvalley.com

UT

FAMILY CAMPING TIPS: Choose a destination oriented camping spot. Make your plans well in advance, and expect a crowd. Break up long drives. Pack according to your space and needs. Relax, have fun, enjoy yourself.

Utah Privately Owned Campground Information Updated by our Good Sam Representatives

Steve & Diane Doherty

The RV Lifestyle has allowed us to foster our love of travel and outdoor adventure. We have visited all 50 States plus Puerto Rico. Over the past 6 years, we have traveled 11 states as Good Sam Reps. We have enjoyed working with the campground owners to help them share their story.

Utah

ANTIMONY — D3 *Garfield*

OTTER CREEK (Public State Park) From town: Go 5 mi N on Hwy 22. Elev 6400 ft.**FAC:** Avail: 53 paved, 15 W, 15 E tent sites, dump, groc, fire rings, firewood. **REC:** Otter Creek Reservoir: swim, fishing, kayaking/canoeing, rec open to public. Pets OK. Partial handicap access. 2021 rates: $20 to $30. no cc. **(435)624-3268 Lat: 38.15313, Lon: -112.00261 Antimony, UT 84712 www.stateparks.utah.gov**

BEAVER — D2 *Beaver*

BEAVER CAMPERLAND **Ratings: 5/6.5/5** (Campground) Avail: 41 full hkups (30/50 amps). 2021 rates: $36 to $41. (877)438-2808, 1603 S Camperworld Rd, Beaver, UT 84713

BEAVER CANYON CAMPGROUND **Ratings: 4/7.5/7** (Campground) Avail: 20 full hkups (20/30 amps). 2021 rates: $30. May 01 to Nov 01. (435)438-5654, 1419 E. 200 North, Beaver, UT 84713

BEAVER KOA **Ratings: 9/9.5★/8.5** (Campground) 62 Avail: 53 full hkups, 9 W, 9 E (30/50 amps). 2021 rates: $45 to $57. (435)438-2924, 1428 N Manderfield Rd (Hwy 357), Beaver, UT 84713

MINERSVILLE RESERVOIR (BEAVER COUNTY PARK) (Public) From jct I-15 & Hwy-21: Go 11 mi W on Hwy-21. Avail: 29 E. 2021 rates: $10 to $20. (801)438-5472

BLANDING — E5 *San Juan*

BLANDING RV PARK
good sam park **Ratings: 6.5/8.5★/8.5** (Campground) From Jct of Center St & Main St (Hwy 191), S 0.9 mi on Hwy 191 (L). Elev 6200 ft.**FAC:** gravel rds. (60 spaces). Avail: 55 gravel, 39 pull-thrus, (30x40), back-ins (30x35), 55 full hkups (30/50 amps), WiFi @ sites, tent sites, dump, laundry, groc, LP bottles, firewood. **REC:** hunting nearby. Pets OK. Partial handicap access. 2021 rates: $30. ATM.
(435)678-2991 Lat: 37.61321, Lon: -109.47804 861 S Main St, Blanding, UT 84511
See ad this page

BLUE MOUNTAIN RV AND TRADING
good sam park **Ratings: 7.5/10★/9** (RV Park) From Jct of Center St & Main St (Hwy 191): Go S 1.9 mi on Hwy 191 (R). Elev 5955 ft.**FAC:** gravel rds. Avail: 42 gravel, 19 pull-thrus, (30x75), back-ins (30x40), 42 full hkups (30/50 amps), WiFi @ sites, tent sites, laundry, groc, firewood. **REC:** hunting nearby. Pets OK. Partial handicap access. Big rig sites, eco-friendly. 2021 rates: $34 to $84, Military discount. Mar 15 to Nov 01.
(435)678-7840 Lat: 37.59758, Lon: -109.47888 1930 S Main Street, Blanding, UT 84511 www.bluemountainrvpark.com
See ad this page

BLUFF — E5 *San Juan*

CADILLAC RANCH RV PARK **Ratings: 5.5/8★/8** (RV Park) 15 Avail: 14 full hkups, 1 W, 1 E (30/50 amps). 2021 rates: $33. (435)672-2262, 630 E Main, Bluff, UT 84512

COTTONWOOD RV PARK **Ratings: 6.5/9★/9.5** (Campground) 23 Avail: 22 full hkups, 1 W, 1 E (30/50 amps). 2021 rates: $38 to $40. Mar 05 to Nov 05. (435)672-2287, 32 W Main St, Bluff, UT 84512

BRIGHAM CITY — A3 *Box Elder*

BRIGHAM CITY PERRY SOUTH KOA **Ratings: 8.5/9★/9** (Campground) Avail: 44 full hkups (30/50 amps). 2021 rates: $40.89 to $67.89. (435)723-5503, 1040 West 3600 South, Perry, UT 84302

GOLDEN SPIKE RV PARK **Ratings: 8/9.5★/8.5** (RV Park) Avail: 38 full hkups (30/50 amps). 2021 rates: $49. (435)723-8858, 905 W 1075 S, Brigham City, UT 84302

BRYCE CANYON — E2 *Garfield*

BRYCE CANYON PINES STORE & CAMPGROUND & RV PARK
good sam park **Ratings: 7/9★/8.5** (Campground) From Jct of US-89 & Hwy 12, E 9.7 mi on Hwy 12 (R); or From Bryce Cyn Nat'l Park, NW 3.8 mi on Hwy 12 (L). Elev 7600 ft.**FAC:** gravel rds. Avail: 30 gravel, 16 pull-thrus, (30x40), back-ins (26x50), 30 full hkups (30/50 amps), WiFi, tent sites, rentals, laundry, groc, LP bottles, fire rings, firewood. **REC:** hunting nearby. Pets OK. eco-friendly. 2021 rates: $50.50 to $60. Apr 01 to Nov 01.
(800)892-7923 Lat: 37.71169, Lon: -112.21724 MP 10 Hwy 12, Bryce Canyon National Park, UT 84764 www.brycecanyonmotel.com/bryce-campgrounds
See ad this page

BRYCE CANYON/NORTH CAMPGROUND (Public National Park) From Jct of Hwy 12 & Hwy 63: Go 4 mi S on Hwy 63 (E). 52 Avail. 2021 rates: $30. (435)834-5322

BRYCE CANYON/SUNSET CAMPGROUND (Public National Park) From visitors center: Go 6 mi S on Hwy 63 (R). 80 Avail. 2021 rates: $30. Apr 15 to Oct 15. (435)834-5322

RED CANYON VILLAGE
good sam park **Ratings: 6.5/8.5★/7** (RV Park) From Jct of Hwys 89 & 12, E 1 mi on Hwy 12 (L). Elev 6700 ft.**FAC:** paved rds. Avail: 21 gravel, patios, 15 pull-thrus, (30x70), back-ins (28x50), 21 full hkups (30/50 amps), WiFi @ sites, rentals, dump, laundry, fire rings, firewood. Pets OK. No tents. Big rig sites, eco-friendly. 2021 rates: $39, Military discount. Apr 15 to Oct 15.
(435)676-2243 Lat: 37.74898, Lon: -112.36197 3279 E. Hwy 12, Panguitch, UT 84759 www.redcanyonvillage.com
See ad this page

RUBY'S INN RV PARK & CAMPGROUND **Ratings: 9/9.5★/9.5** (Campground) 170 Avail: 163 full hkups, 7 W, 7 E (30/50 amps). 2021 rates: $41.95 to $68.95. Apr 01 to Oct 30. (435)834-5301, 300 S Main, Bryce Canyon City, UT 84764

Things to See and Do

RED CANYON TRAIL RIDES Trail Rides at Bryce Canyon Pines; half hour, hour, half day, and full day rides available. Surrounded by beautiful red rock mountains, Ponderosa Pine trees, and hidden water- holes. Apr 01 to Nov 01. Hours: 8am to 5pm. Adult fee: $25 to $125 . ATM.
(435)834-5441 Lat: 37.710149, Lon: -112.210346 Highway 12 Mile Marker 10, Bryce, UT 84764 redacanyontrailrides.com
See ad this page

BRYCE CANYON NATIONAL PARK — E2 *Garfield*

BRYCE CANYON NATIONAL PARK See also Bryce Canyon, Cannonville, Duck Creek Village, Escalante, Hatch, Panguitch & Tropic.

Had a great stay? Let us know by emailing us Parks@goodsam.com

CANNONVILLE — E3 *Garfield*

BRYCE VALLEY RANCH RV AND HORSE PARK
good sam park
Ratings: 7/10★/9.5 (RV Park) From jct Main St & SR 12: Go 1 mi W on SR 12 (R). **FAC:** gravel rds. Avail: 130 gravel, 53 pull-thrus, (30x85), back-ins (30x45), 130 full hkups (30/50 amps), WiFi @ sites, tent sites, dump, laundry, groc, LP gas, fire rings, firewood. **REC:** playground, hunting nearby. Pets OK. Partial handicap access, eco-friendly. 2021 rates: $45 to $65, Military discount. Mar 01 to Oct 31.
(435)679-8228 Lat: 37.584234, Lon: -112.0587322
940 N Hwy 12, Cannonville, UT 84718
www.brycervandhorsepark.com
See ad this page

CANNONVILLE/BRYCE VALLEY KOA **Ratings: 8/10★/9.5** (Campground) 57 Avail: 37 full hkups, 20 W, 20 E (30/50 amps). 2021 rates: $39 to $95. Mar 15 to Oct 30. (435)679-8988, 250 N Red Rocks Dr, Cannonville, UT 84718

KODACHROME BASIN (Public State Park) From jct Hwy 12 & Main St (cnty rd): Go 7-1/4 mi S on Unnamed Cnty Rd, follow signs (E). Avail: 15 full hkups (15 amps). 2021 rates: $20 to $40. (435)679-8562

CAPITOL REEF NATIONAL PARK — D3 *Wayne*

CAPITOL REEF NATIONAL PARK See also Torrey.

CEDAR CITY — E2 *Iron*

BNB SWISS RV PARK **Ratings: 6/NA/7** (RV Park) Avail: 17 full hkups (30/50 amps). 2021 rates: $45. (435)559-3018, 436 S Cross Hollow Rd, Cedar City, UT 84720

CEDAR BREAKS NATL MON/POINT SUPREME (Public National Park) From Jct Rte 14 & Rte 148: Go 4 mi N on Rte 148 (R). 25 Avail. 2021 rates: $20. Jun 15 to Sep 15. (435)586-9451

CEDAR BREAKS RV PARK
good sam park
Ratings: 7/9★/8.5 (RV Park) From Jct of I-15 & Main St (exit 62), S 1.7 mi on Main St (L). Elev 5800 ft.**FAC:** paved/gravel rds. (53 spaces). Avail: 46 gravel, patios, 42 pull-thrus, (25x60), back-ins (25x65), 46 full hkups (30/50 amps), seasonal sites, WiFi @ sites, rentals, laundry, LP gas. **REC:** hunting nearby. Pets OK. Partial handicap access. No tents. Big rig sites. 2021 rates: $45 to $69, Military discount.
(435)586-2550 Lat: 37.70767, Lon: -113.06207
1700 N Main St, Cedar City, UT 84721
cedarbreaksrv.com
See ad this page

CEDAR CITY KOA KAMPGROUND **Ratings: 9/9.5★/8** (Campground) Avail: 64 full hkups (30/50 amps). 2021 rates: $40.84 to $68.58. (435)586-9872, 1121 N Main St, Cedar City, UT 84720

CEDAR CITY RV PARK **Ratings: 8/NA/6.5** (Campground) Avail: 10 full hkups (30/50 amps). 2021 rates: $50 to $65. (435)586-1234, 50 W 200 North, Cedar City, UT 84720

IRON SPRINGS ADVENTURE RESORT
good sam park
Ratings: 8/9.5★/9.5 (RV Resort) Avail: 39 full hkups (30/50 amps). 2021 rates: $54.99. (435)708-0101, 3196 North Iron Springs Rd, Cedar City, UT 84720

CIRCLEVILLE — D2 *Piute*

CIRCLEVILLE RV PARK & KOUNTRYSTORE **Ratings: 7.5/8.5★/8.5** (RV Park) 34 Avail: 28 full hkups, 5 W, 5 E (30/50 amps). 2021 rates: $38. May 01 to Nov 15. (435)577-2437, 35 S Hwy 89, Circleville, UT 84723

COALVILLE — B3 *Summit*

ECHO ISLAND RANCH **Ratings: 8/9.5★/9** (Membership Park) 154 Avail: 146 full hkups, 8 W, 8 E (30/50 amps). 2021 rates: $62.42. (435)336-2100, 340 S 500 W , Coalville, UT 84017

HOLIDAY HILLS RV PARK
good sam park
Ratings: 7/8★/7 (RV Park) Avail: 32 full hkups (30/50 amps). 2021 rates: $36. (435)336-4421, 500 West 100 South, Coalville, UT 84017

DELTA — C2 *Millard*

ANTELOPE VALLEY RV PARK **Ratings: 7.5/9.5★/8** (RV Park) Avail: 87 full hkups (30/50 amps). 2021 rates: $40 to $45. (435)864-1813, 776 W Main St, Delta, UT 84624

We appreciate your business!

DRAPER — B3 *Salt Lake*

MOUNTAIN SHADOWS RV PARK & MHP
good sam park
Ratings: 9.5/10★/8.5 (Campground) From Jct of I-15 & 12300 South St (Draper exit 291), E 150 ft on 12300 South St to MinuteMan Dr (frntg rd), S 1.2 mi (L). Elev 4100 ft.**FAC:** paved rds. (101 spaces). 49 Avail: 37 paved, 12 gravel, 42 pull-thrus, (17x62), back-ins (20x50), mostly side by side hkups, 49 full hkups (30/50 amps), seasonal sites, WiFi @ sites, tent sites, dump, laundry, groc, LP gas. **REC:** heated pool, hot tub, boating nearby, playground, hunting nearby. Pets OK. Partial handicap access. Big rig sites, eco-friendly. 2021 rates: $54.95 to $69.95, Military discount.
(801)571-4024 Lat: 40.51053, Lon: -111.88960
13275 S Minuteman Dr, Draper, UT 84020
www.mountain-shadows.com
See ad this page

Travel Services

CAMPING WORLD OF DRAPER/SALT LAKE CITY As the nation's largest retailer of RV supplies, accessories, services and new and used RVs, Camping World is committed to making your total RV experience better. Elev 4100 ft. **SERVICES:** RV, tire, RV appliance, restrooms. RV Sales. RV supplies, emergency parking, RV accessible. Hours: 9am to 7pm.
(888)533-8913 Lat: 40.512612, Lon: -111.890673
13153 S Minuteman Dr., Draper, UT 84020
www.campingworld.com

DUCHESNE — C4 *Duchesne*

LAKESIDE PARK **Ratings: 6.5/7.5★/8** (Membership Park) 27 Avail: 20 full hkups, 1 W, 6 E (30/50 amps). 2021 rates: $38 to $42. (435)823-2244, 8850 S 26500 W, Duchesne, UT 84021

STARVATION (Public State Park) From jct Hwy 191 & Hwy 40: Go 1/2 mi W on Hwy 40, then 4 mi NW on 2220 West St (Starvation Rd) (E). 259 Avail: 4 full hkups, 57 W, 57 E (30/50 amps). 2021 rates: $15 to $28. (435)738-2326

DUCK CREEK VILLAGE — E2 *Kane*

PINEWOODS RESORT RV PARK **Ratings: 9/10★/9** (RV Park) Avail: 10 full hkups (30/50 amps). 2021 rates: $46 to $56. Apr 01 to Dec 01. (435)682-2512, 1460 E Duck Creek Ridge Rd, Duck Creek Village, UT 84762

DUTCH JOHN — B5 *Daggett*

DUTCH JOHN RESORT **Ratings: 7.5/9★/8.5** (RV Park) Avail: 56 full hkups (30/50 amps). 2021 rates: $35 to $65. (435)885-3191, 1050 South Boulevard, Dutch John, UT 84023

EDEN — A3 *Weber*

NORTH FORK PARK (WEBER COUNTY PARK) (Public) From jct Hwy 166 & Hwy 162: Go 2-1/2 mi W on Hwy 162, then 1/2 mi N on 3500 E (Hwy 162), then 1/4 mi W on E 4100 N (Hwy 162), then 1-1/2 mi N on N 3300 E (Hwy 162) (E). 181 Avail. 2021 rates: $20. (801)625-3850

ESCALANTE — E3 *Garfield*

CANYONS OF ESCALANTE RV PARK
good sam park
Ratings: 7/9.5★/9.5 (RV Park) From Jct of Hwy 12 & Center St (in town): Go S 1/2 mi on Hwy 12 (L). Elev 5800 ft.**FAC:** gravel rds. Avail: 28 gravel, 26 pull-thrus, (20x45), back-ins (30x60), 28 full hkups (30/50 amps), WiFi @ sites, tent sites, rentals, laundry, firewood, restaurant. **REC:** hunting nearby. Pets OK. Partial handicap access, eco-friendly. 2021 rates: $36 to $46, Military discount. Mar 01 to Oct 31.
(435)826-4959 Lat: 37.77019, Lon: -111.60963
495 W Main St, Escalante, UT 84726
www.canyonsofescalantervpark.com
See ad next page

County names help you follow the local weather report.

UT

ESCALANTE (CONT)

ESCALANTE CABINS & RV PARK
Ratings: 8/10★/9.5 (RV Park) Avail: 60 full hkups (30/50 amps). 2021 rates: $39 to $58. (435)826-4433, 680 W Main St, Escalante, UT 84726

ESCALANTE PETRIFIED FOREST (Public State Park) From jct Center St & Hwy 12: Go 1-3/4 mi S on Hwy 12, then 1/2 mi NW on park access road (E). 26 Avail. 2021 rates: $20 to $28. (435)826-4466

YONDER ESCALANTE
Ratings: 8.5/10★/8.5 (RV Park) From Jct of Hwy 12 & Center St (in Escalante), W 1.8 mi on Hwy 12 (R). Elev 5800 ft.

OUTDOOR EXPLORATION AT ITS FINEST!
Yonder Escalante is in the Heart of Southern Utah's Red Canyon Country and is the perfect base camp for adventure! We offer it all from RV sites, to Glamping in beautiful tiny cabins and Airstream rentals.
FAC: gravel rds. Avail: 67 gravel, 20 pull-thrus, (30x70), back-ins (16x50), 40 full hkups, 27 W, 27 E (30/50 amps), WiFi @ sites, rentals, dump, laundry, groc, LP gas, fire rings, firewood. **REC:** heated pool, hot tub, hunting nearby. Pets OK. Partial handicap access. No tents, eco-friendly. 2021 rates: $64 to $109. Mar 15 to Nov 15.
(435)826-4440 Lat: 37.781997, Lon: -111.631874
2020 W Hwy 12, Escalante, UT 84726
stayyonder.com
See ad previous page

FARMINGTON — B3 *Davis*

LAGOON RV PARK & CAMPGROUND **Ratings: 6.5/9★/7.5** (Campground) 145 Avail: 86 full hkups, 59 W, 59 E (30/50 amps). 2021 rates: $50 to $62. May 05 to Oct 31. (800)748-5246, 375 N Lagoon Dr, Farmington, UT 84025

FERRON — D3 *Sanpete*

MILLSITE (Public State Park) From jct Hwy 10 & Ferron Canyon Rd: Go 4 mi W on Ferron Canyon Rd. Avail: 10 E. 2021 rates: $20 to $25. (435)384-2552

FILLMORE — D2 *Millard*

FILLMORE KOA **Ratings: 9/9.5★/10** (Campground) 46 Avail: 39 full hkups, 7 W, 7 E (30/50 amps). 2021 rates: $45 to $53. Mar 01 to Nov 15. (435)743-4420, 905 South Hwy 99, Fillmore, UT 84631

WAGONS WEST RV PARK AND CAMPGROUND
Ratings: 7/9.5★/7.5 (Campground) From jct I-15 (exit 163) & Bus Loop I-15: Go 4 mi N on I-15 to (exit 167/Main St), then 1 mi S on Main St. Elev 5071 ft.**FAC:** paved/gravel rds. (61 spaces). Avail: 51 gravel, 36 pull-thrus, (24x120), back-ins (18x32), 51 full hkups (30/50 amps), seasonal sites, cable, WiFi @ sites, tent sites, rentals, dump, laundry, LP gas, fire rings, firewood. **REC:** hunting nearby. Pets OK. eco-friendly. 2021 rates: $40 to $45, Military discount.
(435)743-6188 Lat: 38.98065, Lon: -112.32391
545 N Main St, Fillmore, UT 84631
www.wagonswestrv.weebly.com
See ad this page

FLAMING GORGE NATIONAL REC AREA — B5 *Daggett*

FLAMING GORGE NATIONAL RECREATION AREA See also Dutch John, Manila & Vernal.

FOUNTAIN GREEN — C3 *Sanpete*

STANDING BEAR RV PARK
Ratings: 5.5/10★/6 (RV Park) Avail: 60 full hkups (30/50 amps). 2021 rates: $39. May 01 to Sep 30. (801)628-2884, 22700 N 990 E. Hwy 132, Fountain Green, UT 84632

GARDEN CITY — A3 *Rich*

BEAR LAKE TRAIL SIDE KOA JOURNEY **Ratings: 8/10★/7.5** (RV Park) Avail: 36 full hkups (30/50 amps). 2021 rates: $37 to $141. May 15 to Oct 15. (435)946-3454, 145 North 300 West, Garden City, UT 84028

BEAR LAKE VENTURE PARK **Ratings: 8/9/8.5** (RV Park) Avail: 52 full hkups (30/50 amps). 2021 rates: $45 to $70. May 15 to Oct 31. (435)946-8780, 2201 N Bear Lake Blvd, Garden City, UT 84028

BEAR LAKE/MARINA SIDE KOA HOLIDAY **Ratings: 8/9/9.5** (Campground) Avail: 94 full hkups (30 amps). 2021 rates: $58 to $148. Apr 01 to Nov 01. (435)946-3454, 485 N Bear Lake Blvd, Garden City, UT 84028

BEAVER MOUNTAIN SKI RESORT & RV PARK
Ratings: 4.5/8/5.5 (Campground) From jct Hwy 30 & US 89: Go 12 mi W on US 89, then 1-1/4 mi N on Hwy 243. Elev 7228 ft.**FAC:** paved rds. Avail: 24 paved, back-ins (22x50), mostly side by side hkups, 17 full hkups, 7 W, 7 E (20/30 amps), WiFi @ sites, tent sites, rentals, fire rings. Pets OK. 2021 rates: $20 to $35. May 30 to Oct 03.
(435)563-5677 Lat: 41.96969, Lon: -111.54008
40000 E. Hwy 89, Garden City, UT 84028
www.skithebeav.com
See ad this page

GLENDALE — E2 *Kane*

BAUER'S CANYON RANCH RV PARK
Ratings: 7.5/9★/8 (RV Park) 25 Avail: 20 full hkups, 5 W, 5 E (30/50 amps). 2021 rates: $44. Mar 01 to Nov 01. (435)648-2564, 90 W Center St, Glendale, UT 84729

BRYCE-ZION CAMPGROUND
Ratings: 7.5/9.5★/8 (Campground) From Jct of US-89 & Hwy 9, N 16 mi on US-89(L). Elev 6500 ft.**FAC:** gravel rds. Avail: 59 gravel, 51 pull-thrus, (26x44), back-ins (22x44), 20 full hkups, 39 W, 39 E (30/50 amps), WiFi @ sites, tent sites, rentals, dump, laundry, groc, fire rings, firewood, restaurant. **REC:** heated pool, Virgin River: fishing, playground, hunting nearby. Pets OK. eco-friendly. 2021 rates: $45 to $50, Military discount. May 01 to Sep 30.
(435)648-2490 Lat: 37.38529, Lon: -112.57596
175 E Koa Road, Glendale, UT 84729
brycezioncampground.net
See ad this page

GREEN RIVER — D4 *Emery*

GOBLIN VALLEY (Public State Park) From jct I-70 & Hwy 24: Go 25 mi S on Hwy 24, then 5 mi W at Temple Mtn. turnoff, then 7 mi S on gravel road (E). 14 Avail. 2021 rates: $30. (435)275-4584

GREEN RIVER (Public State Park) From jct I-70 & Exit 158 (bus loop): Go 2 mi E on bus loop, then 1/2 mi S on Green River Blvd (L); or From jct I-70 & Exit 162 (bus loop): Go 2 mi W on bus loop, then 1/2 mi S on Green River Blvd (L). 78 Avail. 2021 rates: $21 to $30. (435)564-3633

GREEN RIVER KOA **Ratings: 8.5/10★/9** (Campground) Avail: 53 full hkups (30/50 amps). 2021 rates: $55 to $85. (800)562-5734, 235 South 1780 East, Green River, UT 84525

ICAMP
Ratings: 7/9.5★/7 (Campground) 34 Avail: 28 full hkups, 6 W, 6 E (30/50 amps). 2021 rates: $36.89. (435)564-8372, 610 S Green River Blvd, Green River, UT 84525

SHADY ACRES RV PARK
Ratings: 8.5/10★/10 (Campground) 99 Avail: 88 full hkups, 11 W, 11 E (30/50 amps). 2021 rates: $46.99 to $55. (800)537-8674, 690 E Main St, Green River, UT 84525

HANKSVILLE — D4 *Wayne*

DUKES SLICKROCK CAMPGROUND & RV PARK **Ratings: 7/7/7** (Campground) Avail: 34 full hkups (30/50 amps). 2021 rates: $35 to $40. Mar 01 to Oct 31. (435)542-3235, 275 East 100 North, Hanksville, UT 84734

HATCH — E2 *Garfield*

THE RIVERSIDE RANCH RV PARK MOTEL & CAMPGROUND **Ratings: 7.5/9★/9** (RV Park) 36 Avail: 24 full hkups, 12 W, 12 E (30/50 amps). 2021 rates: $49 to $55. Apr 11 to Oct 25. (435)720-4464, 594 Hwy 89, Hatch, UT 84735

HEBER CITY — B3 *Wasatch*

DEER CREEK SRA (Public State Park) From Jct of Hwys 40 & 189, S 9.6 mi on Hwy 189 (R). Avail: 30 full hkups (20/30 amps). 2021 rates: $20 to $30. May 01 to Oct 30. (435)654-0171

JORDANELLE (Public State Park) From jct US-40 & Mayflower Rd (exit 8): Go 1 mi E on Mayflower Rd (E). 142 Avail: 14 full hkups, 88 W, 88 E (20/30 amps). 2021 rates: $30 to $35. (435)649-9540

MOUNTAIN VALLEY RV RESORT
Ratings: 10/10★/10 (RV Resort) From Jct of SR 40 & SR 189 (in town), S 1.0 mi on SR 40 (R). Elev 5778 ft.

VISIT US AT OUR 10/10*/10 RESORT
Located in the beautiful Heber Valley, home to blue ribbon fishing on the Provo River & over 90 holes of championship golf. Big rig friendly, cabins & tent sites. 2 beautiful pools! Your vacation for lasting memories.
FAC: paved rds. (193 spaces). Avail: 133 paved, patios, 125 pull-thrus, (30x75), back-ins (25x45), 133 full hkups (30/50 amps), seasonal sites, cable, WiFi @ sites, tent sites, rentals, dump, laundry, LP gas, controlled access. **REC:** heated pool, hot tub, boating nearby, playground, hunting nearby. Pets OK. Partial handicap access. Big rig sites, eco-friendly. 2021 rates: $45 to $88, Military discount.
(435)657-6100 Lat: 40.481377, Lon: -111.401861
2120 South Hwy 40, Heber City, UT 84032
mountainvalleyrv.com
See ad opposite page

RIVERS EDGE AT DEER PARK **Ratings: 9/9★/8.5** (RV Park) Avail: 33 full hkups (50 amps). 2021 rates: $55. (435)654-4049, 7000 N Old Hwy 40, Heber City, UT 84032

HELPER — C4 *Carbon*

CASTLE GATE RV PARK & CAMPGROUND **Ratings: 8.5/10★/9** (RV Park) Avail: 92 full hkups (30/50 amps). 2021 rates: $51 to $69. (435)472-2267, 1020 Spring Glen Rd, Helper, UT 84526

HUNTINGTON — C3 *Emery*

HUNTINGTON (Public State Park) From jct SR-10 & SR-31: Go 1-3/4 mi N on SR-10, then 1/4 mi W on park access road (L). 25 Avail: 3 full hkups, 22 W, 22 E (30 amps). 2021 rates: $25 to $28. (435)687-2491

HUNTSVILLE — B3 *Weber*

WEBER MEMORIAL PARK (WEBER COUNTY PARK) (Public) From jct of Hwy 162 & Hwy 39 E: Go 8-1/2 mi E on Hwy 39 E, then 1-1/4 mi E on Camsey Rd. 58 Avail. 2021 rates: $20. (801)625-3850

HURRICANE — E1 *Washington*

QUAIL CREEK (Public State Park) From jct I-15 & Hwy 9 (exit 16): Go 2-1/4 mi E on Hwy 9, then 2 mi N on Quail Creek Road (SR-317) (R). 22 Avail. 2021 rates: $15. (435)879-2378

QUAIL CREEK RV PARK **Ratings: 7/9.5★/8.5** (RV Park) Avail: 40 full hkups (30/50 amps). 2021 rates: $38 to $59. (435)359-2299, 8 Crimson Ridge Dr, Hurricane, UT 84737

ST GEORGE KOA **Ratings: 8/8.5★/7** (RV Park) Avail: 127 full hkups (30/50 amps). 2021 rates: $41.50 to $45.50. (888)563-7040, 5800 N Hwy 91, Hurricane, UT 84737

WILLOWWIND RV PARK

good sam park **Ratings: 9/10★/9.5** (RV Park) E-bnd: From Jct of I-15 & Hwy 9 (Exit 16), E 8 mi on Hwy 9 to 1150 West, S 0.1 mi (L); or W-bnd: From Jct of SR-9 & SR-17, 3.8 mi on SR-9 to S 1150 W, L 0.1 mi on S 1150 W (L). Elev 3200 ft.

PUT'ER IN PARK

Great home base for Zion, Bryce, Grand Canyon & Sand Hollow Parks! Big rigs, full hook-ups, tents, restrooms & showers. Laundry, free cable & Wi-fi. ATV trails, groceries, banks, movies, restaurants, gasoline & Walgreen's.

FAC: paved rds. (176 spaces). Avail: 136 paved, patios, 13 pull-thrus, (25x66), back-ins (27x60), 136 full hkups (30/50 amps), seasonal sites, cable, WiFi @ sites, laundry, LP gas. **REC:** boating nearby, hunting nearby. Pet restrict (B). Partial handicap access. No tents. Big rig sites. 2021 rates: $60 to $80, Military discount.

(435)635-4154 Lat: 37.17520, Lon: -113.30953
80 S 1150 W, Hurricane, UT 84737
www.willowwindrvpark.com
See ad this page

ZIONS GATE RV PARK **Ratings: 6.5/9.5★/7** (Membership Park) Avail: 92 full hkups (30/50 amps). 2021 rates: $39 to $44. (801)903-9326, 150 North 3700 West, Hurricane, UT 84737

Travel Services

GANDER RV OF HURRICANE Your new hometown outfitter offering the best regional gear for all your outdoor needs. Your adventure awaits. **SERVICES:** sells outdoor gear, restrooms. RV Sales. RV supplies, RV accessible. Hours: 9am - 6pm, closed Sun.
(855)496-0620 Lat: 37.17726, Lon: -113.31118
1210 W State St, Hurricane, UT 84737
rv.ganderoutdoors.com

HYRUM — A3 *Cache*

HYRUM (Public State Park) On north shore of Hyrum Lake. 31 Avail. 2021 rates: $25 to $30. (435)245-6866

JENSEN — B5 *Uintah*

DINOSAUR NATL MON/GREEN RIVER CAMPGROUND (Public National Park) From jct US-40 & Hwy 149: Go 8-1/4 mi N on Hwy 149 (L). 80 Avail. 2021 rates: $18. Apr 07 to Oct 21. (970)374-3000

JOSEPH — D2 *Sevier*

FLYING U COUNTRY STORE, RV PARK & CAMPGROUND **Ratings: 4.5/6/6** (Campground) Avail: 18 full hkups (30/50 amps). 2021 rates: $35. (866)527-4758, 45 South State St, Joseph, UT 84739

KAMAS — B3 *Summit*

KNOTTY PINE RESORT **Ratings: 9/10★/8** (RV Resort) 75 Avail: 71 full hkups, 4 W, 4 E (30/50 amps). 2021 rates: $44 to $57. Apr 01 to Oct 31. (435)783-4349, 5175 E Highway 35, Kamas, UT 84036

KANAB — E2 *Kane*

CRAZY HORSE RV RESORT

good sam park **Ratings: 9/10★/9.5** (Campground) From Jct of Hwy 89 and 300 South (in town), E .5 mi on 300 South (L). Elev 5000 ft.**FAC:** gravel rds. (108 spaces). Avail: 75 gravel, 30 pull-thrus, (25x60), back-ins (25x60), mostly side by side hkups, 75 full hkups (30/50 amps), WiFi @ sites, tent sites, dump, laundry, groc, LP gas, fire rings, firewood. **REC:** heated pool, boating nearby, playground, hunting nearby. Pets OK. eco-friendly. 2021 rates: $47.95 to $49.95, Military discount.

(435)644-2782 Lat: 37.02589, Lon: -112.30996
625 E 300 South, Kanab, UT 84741
www.crazyhorservkanabut.com
See ad next page

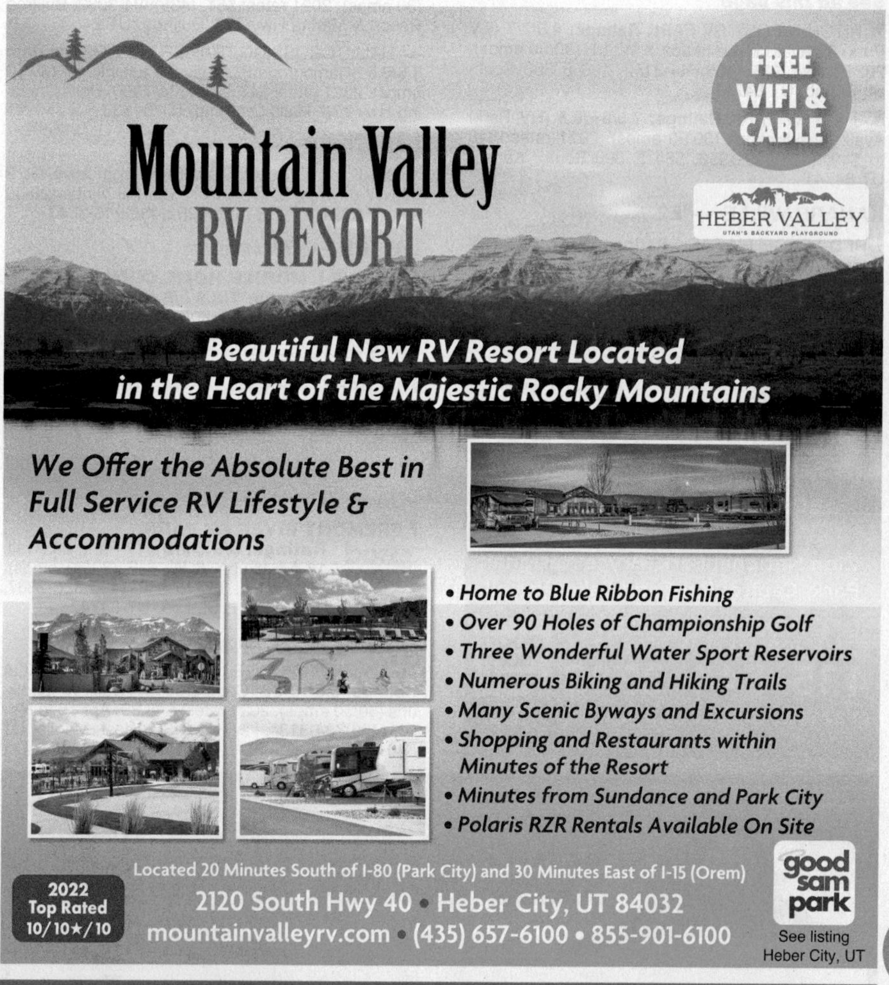
FREE WIFI & CABLE
Mountain Valley
RV RESORT
HEBER VALLEY
UTAH'S BACKYARD PLAYGROUND
Beautiful New RV Resort Located in the Heart of the Majestic Rocky Mountains
We Offer the Absolute Best in Full Service RV Lifestyle & Accommodations
• Home to Blue Ribbon Fishing
• Over 90 Holes of Championship Golf
• Three Wonderful Water Sport Reservoirs
• Numerous Biking and Hiking Trails
• Many Scenic Byways and Excursions
• Shopping and Restaurants within Minutes of the Resort
• Minutes from Sundance and Park City
• Polaris RZR Rentals Available On Site
Located 20 Minutes South of I-80 (Park City) and 30 Minutes East of I-15 (Orem)
2022 Top Rated 10/10★/10
2120 South Hwy 40 • Heber City, UT 84032
mountainvalleyrv.com • (435) 657-6100 • 855-901-6100
good sam park
See listing Heber City, UT

UT

STAY IN HURRICANE, UTAH
GATEWAY TO ZION
good sam park
WALK TO EVERYTHING. HEAR NOTHING.
PULL THRUS - PET FRIENDLY - TENT SITES
LAUNDRY - FREE UPGRADED CABLE & WIFI
WILLOWWIND
RV PARK
HURRICANE, UTAH
435.635.4154
WILLOWWINDRVPARK.COM
See listing Hurricane, UT

KANAB (CONT)

GRAND PLATEAU RV RESORT AT KANAB

good sam park **Ratings: 10/10★/10** (RV Park) From jct US 89A & US 89: Go 3-1/4 mi E on US 89, then 1/4 mi N on Vermilion Dr (E). Elev 4970 ft.

YOUR BASE CAMP FOR ADVENTURE!

Nestled in the middle of 3 National Parks, several state parks and numerous National Monuments. Kanab is the place for outdoor exploration whether by foot, on horseback or 4 wheeling! Relax in the pool after a day of fun!

FAC: all weather rds. Avail: 80 all weather, patios, 30 pull-thrus, (30x70), back-ins (30x70), 80 full hkups (30/50 amps), WiFi @ sites, rentals, laundry, LP gas. **REC:** heated pool, hot tub, boating nearby, playground, hunting nearby. Pets OK. Partial handicap access. No tents. Big rig sites, eco-friendly. 2021 rates: $49 to $63. no cc.

(435)610-2500 Lat: 37.029003, Lon: -112.471699
2550 East Hwy 89, Kanab, UT 84741
www.gprvresort.com
See ad this page

HITCH-N-POST RV PARK **Ratings: 4.5/7/7** (RV Park) 32 Avail: 31 full hkups, 1 W, 1 E (30/50 amps). 2021 rates: $43. (435)644-2142, 196 E 300 South St, Kanab, UT 84741

J & J RV PARK **Ratings: 7.5/9★/8.5** (RV Park) Avail: 42 full hkups (30/50 amps). 2021 rates: $45 to $49. (435)899-1956, 584 E 300 South, Kanab, UT 84741

KANARRAVILLE — E2 *Iron*

RED LEDGE RV PARK **Ratings: 5.5/7.5/6.5** (RV Resort) Avail: 20 full hkups (30/50 amps). 2021 rates: $30 to $32. (435)586-9150, 15 N Main St (Hwy 91), Kanarraville, UT 84742

KAYSVILLE — B3 *Davis*

CHERRY HILL CAMPING RESORT **Ratings: 8.5/9.5★/9** (Campground) 94 Avail: 82 full hkups, 12 W, 12 E (30/50 amps). 2021 rates: $46 to $51. (801)451-5379, 1325 S Main, Kaysville, UT 84037

Travel Services

CAMPING WORLD OF KAYSVILLE As the nation's largest retailer of RV supplies, accessories, services and new and used RVs, Camping World is committed to making your total RV experience better. Elev 4352 ft. **SERVICES:** RV, RV appliance, MH mechanical, restrooms. RV Sales. RV supplies, LP gas, dump, emergency parking, RV accessible. Hours: 9am to 7pm.
(888)652-9944 Lat: 41.045884, Lon: -111.9595
780 N 900 W, Kaysville, UT 84037
www.campingworld.com

LAKE POWELL — E4 *Kane*

BULLFROG RV PARK & CAMPGROUND **Ratings: 5.5/8.5★/7.5** (Campground) Avail: 24 full hkups (30 amps). 2021 rates: $51. (435)684-3032, Bullfrog Resort & Marina Hwy 276, Bullfrog, UT 84533

HALLS CROSSING TRAILER VILLAGE **Ratings: 5/6/6.5** (Campground) Avail: 24 full hkups (30/50 amps). 2021 rates: $47. (435)684-7000, Halls Crossing Hwy 276, Halls Crossing, UT 84533

LAKETOWN — A3 *Rich*

BEAR LAKE (Public State Park) From town: Go 2 mi NW on Hwy 30 (R). Avail: 103 full hkups (20/30 amps). 2021 rates: $15 to $25. (435)946-3343

LAYTON — B3 *Morgan*

CIRCLE L MOBILE HOME COMMUNITY

good sam park **Ratings: 7/8.5★/8.5** (RV Park) Avail: 64 full hkups (30/50 amps). 2021 rates: $45. (801)544-8945, 231 North Main, Layton, UT 84041

MILITARY PARK HILL FAMCAMP (HILL AFB) (Public) From jct I-15 (exit 331) & Hwy 232: Go N on Hwy 232 (Hill Field Rd), then through the gate, then turn left (L). 47 Avail: 28 full hkups, 19 W, 19 E (30/50 amps). 2021 rates: $15 to $22. (801)775-3250

LOA — D3 *Wayne*

FREMONT RIVER RV PARK

good sam park **Ratings: 6/9.5★/8** (RV Park) 24 Avail: 18 full hkups, 6 W, 6 E (30/50 amps). 2021 rates: $37 to $42. (435)836-2267, 265 S 100 E St, Loa, UT 84747

MANILA — B4 *Daggett*

FLAMING GORGE CAMPING RESORT KOA **Ratings: 8.5/10★/9** (Campground) Avail: 40 full hkups (30/50 amps). 2021 rates: $48.89. Apr 15 to Nov 01. (435)784-3184, Hwy 43 & 3rd West, Manila, UT 84046

MANTI — C3 *Sanpete*

PALISADE (Public State Park) From jct US-89 & Palisade Dr: Go 2 mi E on Palisade Dr (E). 71 Avail: 29 full hkups, 1 W, 1 E (30/50 amps). 2021 rates: $25 to $35. (435)835-7275

MARYSVALE — D2 *Piute*

BIG ROCK CANDY MOUNTAIN RV **Ratings: 6.5/8/7** (RV Park) 29 Avail: 26 full hkups, 3 W, 3 E (30/50 amps). 2021 rates: $38. May 01 to Nov 01. (435)326-2031, 4479 Hwy 89, Marysvale, UT 84750

LIZZIE & CHARLIE'S RV/ATV PARK **Ratings: 6/8★/5.5** (RV Park) Avail: 82 full hkups (30/50 amps). 2021 rates: $41. Apr 01 to Oct 30. (435)326-4213, 995 Main, Marysvale, UT 84750

ROSE RANCH RESORT **Ratings: 6/9★/8.5** (RV Park) Avail: 21 full hkups (30/50 amps). 2021 rates: $38. May 01 to Oct 15. (435)326-2022, 1240 N Hwy 89 , Marysvale, UT 84750

SOUTH-FORTY RV PARK **Ratings: 6.5/9★/8.5** (RV Park) Avail: 77 full hkups (30/50 amps). 2021 rates: $43. Apr 01 to Oct 15. (435)326-4404, 1170 N Highway 89, Marysvale, UT 84750

MEXICAN HAT — E4 *San Juan*

VALLE'S RV PARK **Ratings: 2/UI/3.5** (Campground) Avail: 6 full hkups (20/30 amps). 2021 rates: $35. (435)683-2226, 268 E Main St, Mexican Hat, UT 84531

MIDWAY — B3 *Wasatch*

WASATCH MOUNTAIN (Public State Park) S-bnd: From jct US 40 & SR 113/SR 222: Go 6-1/2 mi W on SR 222 (L) N-bnd: From jct US 189 & SR 113: Go 4 mi N on SR 113, then 3-1/4 mi N on SR-222 (L). 120 Avail: 61 full hkups, 59 W, 59 E (20/50 amps). 2021 rates: $20 to $40. (435)654-1791

MILLS — C3 *Juab*

YUBA (Public State Park) From town: Go 5 mi S on I-15 to exit 202, then 5 mi S on local paved road (L). 217 Avail: 48 W, 48 E. 2021 rates: $25 to $35. (435)758-2611

MOAB — D5 *Grand*

ACT CAMPGROUND **Ratings: 7.5/10★/9** (RV Park) Avail: 21 full hkups (30/50 amps). 2021 rates: $49 to $67. Mar 01 to Oct 31. (435)355-0355, US 191 at Mill Creek, Moab, UT 84532

ARCHES/DEVILS GARDEN (Public National Park) From Jct of I-70 & US-191: Go 28 mi S on US-191, then 18 mi E on park access rd (R). 49 Avail. 2021 rates: $25. (435)719-2299

ARCHVIEW RV PARK & CAMPGROUND **Ratings: 7.5/9★/9** (RV Park) Avail: 77 full hkups (30/50 amps). 2021 rates: $53 to $109. Mar 01 to Oct 31. (877)396-3630, 13701 North Highway 191, Moab, UT 84532

CANYONLANDS CAMPGROUND **Ratings: 8.5/9★/9** (RV Park) 88 Avail: 70 full hkups, 18 W, 18 E (30/50 amps). 2021 rates: $65 to $80. Mar 01 to Nov 07. (800)522-6848, 555 S Main St, Moab, UT 84532

DEAD HORSE POINT (Public State Park) From jct US-191 & SR-313: Go 21-1/2 mi SW on SR-313 (E). Avail: 21 E (50 amps). 2021 rates: $35. (435)259-2614

MOAB KOA **Ratings: 9/9★/8.5** (Campground) 135 Avail: 115 full hkups, 20 W, 20 E (30/50 amps). 2021 rates: $44 to $126. Mar 01 to Nov 10. (435)241-7890, 3225 S Hwy 191, Moab, UT 84532

MOAB RIM CAMPARK **Ratings: 5.5/8.5/8** (Campground) 30 Avail: 25 full hkups, 5 W, 5 E (30/50 amps). 2021 rates: $44 to $62. (435)259-5002, 1900 S Hwy 191, Moab, UT 84532

MOAB VALLEY RV RESORT **Ratings: 9/9.5★/9** (RV Park) Avail: 85 full hkups (30/50 amps). 2021 rates: $58.56 to $94.16. (435)259-4469, 1773 N Hwy 191, Moab, UT 84532

O.K. RV PARK & CANYONLANDS STABLES **Ratings: 7/10★/9.5** (RV Park) Avail: 38 full hkups (30/50 amps). 2021 rates: $49 to $59. (435)259-1400, 3310 Spanish Valley Dr, Moab, UT 84532

SLICKROCK CAMPGROUND RV & TENT CAMPING RESORT **Ratings: 8.5/9.5★/7.5** (Campground) 126 Avail: 115 full hkups, 11 W, 11 E (30/50 amps). 2021 rates: $65 to $75. Mar 01 to Oct 31. (435)259-7660, 1301 N Hwy 191, Moab, UT 84532

SPANISH TRAIL RV PARK

good sam park **Ratings: 9/10★/9** (RV Park) From Jct of Center & Main St (Hwy 191), S 4.4 mi on Hwy 191 (R). Elev 4200 ft.

NEAR TWO NATIONAL PARKS!
Let Moab be your base camp for world famous mountain biking, hiking, four-wheel driving, or river expeditions of any length and experience level.
FAC: gravel rds. Avail: 81 gravel, patios, 70 pull-thrus, (30x60), back-ins (30x40), 81 full hkups (30/50 amps), cable, WiFi @ sites, dump, laundry, groc. **REC:** heated pool, hot tub, hunting nearby. Pets OK. Partial handicap access. No tents. Big rig sites, eco-friendly. 2021 rates: $58 to $88, Military discount.
(800)787-2751 Lat: 38.52799, Lon: -109.50435
2980 S Hwy 191, Moab, UT 84532
spanishtrailrvpark.com
See ad opposite page

MONTICELLO — E5 *San Juan*

CANYONLANDS/THE NEEDLES CAMPGROUND (Public National Park) From town: Go 15 mi N on US-191, then 38 mi W on Hwy 211 (E). 26 Avail. 2021 rates: $20. (435)719-2313

MOUNTAIN VIEW RV PARK **Ratings: 6.5/10★/8** (RV Park) Avail: 25 full hkups (30/50 amps). 2021 rates: $38 to $45. Apr 01 to Nov 30. (435)587-2974, 632 N Main, Monticello, UT 84535

OLD WEST RV PARK **Ratings: 6.5/9★/6.5** (RV Park) Avail: 16 full hkups (30/50 amps). 2021 rates: $35 to $40. Mar 15 to Oct 31. (435)459-1327, 348 S Main St, Monticello, UT 84535

WESTERNER RV PARK **Ratings: 7/9.5★/8** (RV Park) Avail: 25 full hkups (30/50 amps). 2021 rates: $45 to $50. Mar 15 to Nov 07. (435)587-2762, 532 S Main St., Monticello, UT 84535

MONUMENT VALLEY — E4 *San Juan*

GOULDING'S MONUMENT VALLEY CAMPGROUND & RV PARK
good sam park
Ratings: 9/9★/10 (RV Park) Avail: 66 full hkups (30/50 amps). 2021 rates: $55 to $68. (435)359-0047, 1000 Main St, Monument Valley, UT 84536

MONUMENT VALLEY KOA **Ratings: 7.5/10★/9.5** (RV Park) Avail: 52 full hkups (30/50 amps). 2021 rates: $50 to $75. (800)562-3424, Milepost 2, Highway 163, Monument Valley, UT 84536

MOUNT CARMEL — E2 *Kane*

EAST ZION RIVERSIDE RV PARK **Ratings: 5.5/NA/4.5** (Campground) Avail: 10 full hkups (30/50 amps). 2021 rates: $35. (888)848-6358, 4530 S State Street, Mount Carmel, UT 84755

HI-ROAD BASECAMP CAMPGROUND **Ratings: 5/6.5/7** (Campground) Avail: 13 full hkups (30/50 amps). 2021 rates: $45 to $49. (877)290-5756, 12120 W Hwy 9, Mount Carmel, UT 84755

MOUNT CARMEL MOTEL & RV PARK **Ratings: 4/7★/6.5** (RV Park) Avail: 10 full hkups (30/50 amps). 2021 rates: $40. Mar 15 to Oct 31. (435)648-2323, 3000 S State, Mount Carmel, UT 84755

ZION PONDEROSA RANCH RESORT **Ratings: 8.5/9.5★/8** (RV Park) Avail: 13 full hkups (30/50 amps). 2021 rates: $119 to $149. Mar 05 to Nov 30. (800)293-5444, 5 Miles up North Fork Rd, Orderville, UT 84758

MOUNT CARMEL JUNCTION — E2 *Kane*

CORAL PINK SAND DUNES (Public State Park) S-bnd: From jct Hwy 9 & US-89: Go 4 mi S on US-89, then 12 mi S on Cnty Rd (L); or N-bnd: From jct US-89A & US-89: Go 8-1/4 mi N on US-89, then 9-1/2 mi W on Hancock Rd, then 3-1/4 mi S on Cnty Rd (L). 17 Avail. 2021 rates: $20. (801)322-3770

MOUNT PLEASANT — C3 *Sanpete*

PLEASANT CREEK RANCH **Ratings: 9/10★/8.5** (Membership Park) 76 Avail: 66 full hkups, 10 W, 10 E (30/50 amps). 2021 rates: $41 to $53. Apr 01 to Oct 31. (801)903-9752, 2903 S 1700 E, Mount Pleasant, UT 84647

NEPHI — C3 *Juab*

JONES HIGH COUNTRY RV CAMP
good sam park
Ratings: 7/9.5★/6.5 (RV Park) Avail: 48 full hkups (30/50 amps). 2021 rates: $30. (435)623-2624, 899 S Main, Nephi, UT 84648

OASIS (BLM) (Public Corps) From jct Hwy 132 & Hwy 148: Go 9 mi N on Hwy 148, then 4 mi W on county road, then 5 mi SW on park road. 115 Avail. 2021 rates: $18. (435)433-5960

WHITE SANDS (BLM) (Public Corps) From jct Hwy-132 & Hwy-148: Go 9 mi NW on Hwy-148, then 4 mi W on paved county road, then 1 mi SW on paved road, then 1 mi N on dirt road. 99 Avail: Pit toilets. 2021 rates: $18. (435)433-5960

NORTH SALT LAKE — B3 *Davis*

PONY EXPRESS RV RESORT **Ratings: 10/9★/8.5** (RV Park) Avail: 110 full hkups (30/50 amps). 2021 rates: $48 to $78. (801)355-1550, 1012 West Recreation Way, North Salt Lake, UT 84054

OGDEN — B3 *Weber*

CENTURY RV PARK & CAMPGROUND
good sam park
Ratings: 9.5/9.5★/9 (RV Park) From Jct of I-15 & 2100 South St (exit 343), W 0.1 mi on 2100 South St to Century Ln, S 0.1 mi (L). Do not use GPS. Elev 4300 ft.**FAC:** paved rds. (150 spaces). 80 Avail: 34 paved, 46 gravel, 80 pull-thrus, (26x65), mostly side by side hkups, 80 full hkups (30/50 amps), seasonal sites, cable, WiFi @ sites, tent sites, dump, laundry, groc. **REC:** heated pool, hot tub, boating nearby, shuffleboard, playground. Pets OK. Big rig sites, eco-friendly. 2021 rates: $37.32 to $52.25, Military discount.
(801)731-3800 Lat: 41.22753, Lon: -112.01303
1483 W 2100 S, Ogden, UT 84401
See ad this page

FORT BUENAVENTURA CAMPGROUND (WEBER COUNTY PARK) (Public) From jct of 25th St & Lincoln Ave: Go N 1 blk on Lincoln Ave, then W 7/10 mi on 24th St, then S 1 blk on A Ave and E 6/10 mi on Capitol. 15 Avail. 2021 rates: $20. May 01 to Nov 30. (801)399-8099

WILLARD BAY (Public State Park) From jct I-15 & Exit 357 (SR-315): Go 100 ft W on SR-315, then 1/2 mi S on park access rd (E). Avail: 60 full hkups (20/30 amps). 2021 rates: $20 to $30. (435)734-9494

ORDERVILLE — E2 *Kane*

CLIFFSIDE CABINS AND RV PARK **Ratings: 6/10★/7** (RV Park) Avail: 10 full hkups (30/50 amps). 2021 rates: $50. (435)868-1020, 600 North State St, Orderville, UT 84758

PANGUITCH — E2 *Garfield*

BEAR PAW FISHING RESORT & RV PARK **Ratings: 3/7.5★/6** (RV Resort) Avail: 16 full hkups (20 amps). 2021 rates: $35. Apr 22 to Oct 09. (435)676-2650, 905 S Hwy 143, Panguitch, UT 84759

BEAR VALLEY RV & CAMPGROUND **Ratings: 7/10★/9** (RV Park) Avail: 36 full hkups (30/50 amps). 2021 rates: $43. (435)676-2500, 900 East SR 20, Panguitch, UT 84759

HENRIES HITCH-N-POST RV RESORT **Ratings: 8/10★/8.5** (RV Park) Avail: 41 full hkups (30/50 amps). 2021 rates: $39 to $45. (435)749-0534, 420 N Main, Panguitch, UT 84759

PANGUITCH KOA **Ratings: 8/10★/8** (Campground) 32 Avail: 24 full hkups, 8 W, 8 E (30/50 amps). 2021 rates: $51 to $68. Apr 01 to Oct 07. (435)676-2225, 555 S Main Street, Panguitch, UT 84759

PARADISE RV PARK & CAMPGROUND **Ratings: 5/5.5/4.5** (RV Park) 49 Avail: 43 full hkups, 6 W, 6 E (30/50 amps). 2021 rates: $23 to $25. (435)676-8348, 2153 Hwy 89, Panguitch, UT 84759

Things to See and Do

GARFIELD COUNTY OFFICE OF TOURISM
Maps, brochures and information for Bryce Canyon Country. Elev 6640 ft. Partial handicap access. RV accessible. Restrooms. Hours: 9am to 5pm. No CC.
(800)444-6689 Lat: 37.82217, Lon: -112.43571
55 S Main, Panguitch, UT 84759
BryceCanyonCountry.com/RV
See ad page 924

PARK CITY — B3 *Summit*

PARK CITY RV RESORT **Ratings: 7/8.5/7.5** (RV Resort) 51 Avail: 24 full hkups, 27 W, 27 E (30/50 amps). 2021 rates: $45 to $65. (435)649-2535, 2200 Rasmussen Rd, Park City, UT 84098

PRICE — C4 *Carbon*

LEGACY INN & RV PARK **Ratings: 5/9★/5** (RV Park) Avail: 30 full hkups (30/50 amps). 2021 rates: $34 to $49. (435)637-2424, 145 N Carbonville Rd, Price, UT 84501

PROVO — B3 *Utah*

A SPOTLIGHT Introducing Provo's colorful attractions appearing at the front of this state section.

PROVO See also Draper, Heber City & Springville.

LAKESIDE RV CAMPGROUND
good sam park
Ratings: 9.5/10★/9 (Campground) S-bnd: From Jct of I-15 & Center St (exit 265), W 2.2 mi on Center St (R); or N-bnd: From Jct of I-15 & Center St (exit 265), W 2.2 mi on Center St (R). Elev 4491 ft.

CLEAN & GREEN IS OUR MOTTO!
A lawn on every site & ample shade. Close to everything, but in a country setting. Relax by the pool or fish the Provo River. A short drive to historic Mormon Temple Square, Bridal Veil Falls, Timpanogos Cave & Park City.
FAC: paved/gravel rds. (125 spaces). Avail: 100 gravel, 100 pull-thrus, (22x65), mostly side by side hkups, 100 full hkups (30/50 amps), seasonal sites, cable, WiFi @ sites, tent sites, dump, laundry, groc, LP gas, firewood. **REC:** heated pool, Provo River: fishing, playground, hunting nearby. Pets OK. eco-friendly. 2021 rates: $41.95 to $45.95, Military discount.
(801)373-5267 Lat: 40.23561, Lon: -111.72813
4000 West Center St, Provo, UT 84601
lakesidervcampground.com
See ad pages 926, 929

UTAH LAKE (Public State Park) From jct I-15 & Center St (exit 265B): Go 3 mi W on Center St (E). Avail: 63 full hkups (20/30 amps). 2021 rates: $30. May 15 to Oct 01. (801)375-0731

RICHFIELD — D2 *Sevier*

RICHFIELD'S KOA RV PARK & KAMPGROUND **Ratings: 9/10★/9.5** (Campground) Avail: 100 full hkups (30/50 amps). 2021 rates: $46.99 to $88.99. Mar 01 to Oct 31. (435)896-6674, 590 W 600 S, Richfield, UT 84701

SALT LAKE CITY — B3 *Salt Lake*

SALT LAKE CITY See also Coalville, Draper, Farmington, Heber City, Kamas, Kaysville, Layton, North Salt Lake, Ogden, Park City, Provo & Springville.

EAST CANYON (Public State Park) W-bnd: From jct I-84 & SR-65 (exit 115): Go 8-3/4 mi SW on SR-65, then 1-1/4 mi W on SR-66 (L), E-bnd: From jct I-84 & SR-66 (exit 103): Go 12 mi SE on SR-66 (R). 33 Avail: 17 full hkups, 16 W, 16 E (30/50 amps). 2021 rates: $24 to $28. (801)829-6866

SNOWBIRD TIP: Imagine your perfect destination. RV parks reflect our personalities, lifestyles and budgets. Eastern RV parks offer a more urban experience and conveniences, while parks out west typically have more elbow room. Research before reserving to find your ideal spot.

UT

SALT LAKE CITY (CONT)

SALT LAKE CITY KOA
Ratings: 10/10★/9 (RV Park) W-bnd: From Jct of I-15 & I-80 (exit 308), W 1.7 mi on I-80 to Redwood Rd exit (exit 118), N 0.3 mi on Redwood Rd to N Temple, E 0.3 mi to 1460 West, N on 1460 West 100 ft. (R) E-bnd: From Jct of I-80 & exit 115 (N Temple), E 3 mi on N Temple (follow signs) to 1460 West, N on 1460 West 100 ft (R). Elev 4300 ft.**FAC:** paved rds. (183 spaces). Avail: 153 paved, patios, 153 pull-thrus, (26x60), 153 full hkups (30/50 amps), seasonal sites, cable, WiFi @ sites, tent sites, rentals, dump, laundry, groc, LP gas, firewood, restaurant. **REC:** heated pool, hot tub, Jordan River: playground. Pets OK. Partial handicap access. Big rig sites, eco-friendly. 2021 rates: $59.99 to $89.99, Military discount. ATM.
(801)328-0224 Lat: 40.77185, Lon: -111.93217
1400 W N Temple, Salt Lake City, UT 84116
www.slckoa.com
See ad previous page

SCOFIELD — C3 *Carbon*

SCOFIELD (Public State Park) From jct US-6 & Hwy-96: Go 13 mi S on Hwy-96. 69 Avail: 1 full hkups, 36 W, 36 E (20 amps). 2021 rates: $15 to $30. (435)448-9449

SEVIER — D2 *Sevier*

FREMONT INDIAN (Public State Park) From town: Go 7 mi SW on I-70. 22 Avail. 2021 rates: $15 to $30. (435)527-4631

SNOWVILLE — A2 *Box Elder*

EARP AND JAMES HITCHING POST **Ratings: 5/7.5★/6** (Campground) Avail: 41 full hkups (20/30 amps). 2021 rates: $30 to $35. (435)872-8273, 490 West Main, Snowville, UT 84336

SPRINGDALE — E2 *Washington*

ZION CANYON CAMPGROUND & ZION CAMPFIRE LODGE **Ratings: 8.5/9.5★/9** (RV Park) 133 Avail: 122 full hkups, 11 W, 11 E (30/50 amps). 2021 rates: $69 to $109. Mar 01 to Dec 01. (435)772-3237, 479 Zion Park Blvd, Springdale, UT 84767

ZION/SOUTH CAMPGROUND (Public National Park) From jct I-15 & Hwy 17: Go 7 mi S on Hwy 17, then 20 mi E on Hwy 9 (R). 117 Avail. 2021 rates: $20. Mar 01 to Dec 02. (435)772-3256

ZION/WATCHMAN (Public National Park) From jct I-15 & Hwy 17: Go 7 mi S on Hwy 17, then 20 mi E on Hwy 9 (R). Avail: 95 E (30/50 amps). 2021 rates: $20 to $30. Feb 28 to Nov 30. (435)772-3256

SPRINGVILLE — C3 *Utah*

SPRINGVILLE/PROVO KOA **Ratings: 9.5/9.5★/8.5** (RV Park) Avail: 168 full hkups (30/50 amps). 2021 rates: $59 to $74. (801)491-0700, 1550 North 1750 West, Springville, UT 84663

Clean Green! Vinegar and baking soda can be used to clean almost anything. Mix in a little warm water with either of these and you've got yourself an all-purpose cleaner.

ST GEORGE — E1 *Washington*

ST GEORGE See also Hurricane, Leeds & Virgin, UT; Beaver Dam, AZ.

DESERT CANYONS RV PARK RESORT **Ratings: 7/10★/9** (RV Resort) Avail: 72 full hkups (30/50 amps). 2021 rates: $50 to $90. (435)216-7950, 3692 E Desert Ct, St George, UT 84790

MCARTHUR'S TEMPLE VIEW RV RESORT
Ratings: 9.5/10★/9.5 (RV Park) From Jct of I-15 & Bluff St (exit 6), N 0.2 mi on Bluff St to Main St, NE 0.3 mi (R). Elev 2700 ft.

ZION, BRYCE AND MORE!
Located in the heart of St. George & convenient to everything! Stay with us while seeing Zion, Bryce & more. With a friendly staff, best wireless internet & most amenities of any RV Resort in Utah, you will love it here!

FAC: paved rds. (270 spaces). Avail: 163 all weather, patios, 20 pull-thrus, (30x60), back-ins (33x48), 163 full hkups (30/50 amps), seasonal sites, cable, WiFi @ sites, dump, laundry. **REC:** heated pool, hot tub, shuffleboard, hunting nearby. Pet restrict (B). Partial handicap access. No tents. Big rig sites, eco-friendly. 2021 rates: $49.95 to $59.95, Military discount.
(800)510-6765 Lat: 37.09155, Lon: -113.58302
975 S Main St, St George, UT 84770
www.templeviewrv.com
See ad this page, 926

SNOW CANYON (Public State Park) From jct I-15 & Exit 6 (Bluff St): Go 3-1/2 mi N on Bluff St, then 3-3/4 mi NW on Snow Canyon Pkwy, then 3/4 mi N on Snow Canyon Dr (E). 24 Avail: 14 W, 14 E (20/30 amps). 2021 rates: $20 to $25. (435)628-2255

Travel Services

CAMPING WORLD OF ST GEORGE As the nation's largest retailer of RV supplies, accessories, services and new and used RVs, Camping World is committed to making your total RV experience better. Elev 2700 ft. **SERVICES:** tire, RV appliance, MH mechanical, staffed RV wash, restrooms. RV Sales. RV supplies, LP gas, RV accessible. Hours: 8am to 7pm; closed Sunday.
(888)380-7185 Lat: 37.081673, Lon: -113.584727
1500 South Hilton Drive, St George, UT 84770
www.campingworld.com

GANDER RV OF ST GEORGE Your new hometown outfitter offering the best regional gear for all your outdoor needs. Your adventure awaits. **SERVICES:** sells outdoor gear, restrooms. RV Sales. RV supplies, RV accessible. Hours: 9am - 6pm, closed Sun.
(855)496-0620 Lat: 37.08750, Lon: -113.57640
341 W Sundland Dr, St George, UT 84790
rv.ganderoutdoors.com

MCARTHUR'S TEMPLE VIEW RV STORAGE Spacious dry storage lot for RVs and Trailers located at McArthur's Temple View RV Resort. Elev 2700 ft. **RV Storage:** outdoor, secured fencing, limited access, well-lit perimeter, level gravel/paved spaces, office. **SERVICES:** restrooms. Hours: 7:30am to 8pm. Special offers available for Good Sam Members
(800)510-6765 Lat: 37.09155, Lon: -113.58302
975 S Main St, St George, UT 84770
templeviewrv.com

TORREY — D3 *Wayne*

CAPITOL REEF/FRUITA CAMPGROUND (Public National Park) From Jct of SR-12 & SR-24: Go 10 mi E on SR-24 to park access rd, follow signs (R). 64 Avail. 2021 rates: $20. (435)425-3791

SAND CREEK RV PARK & CAMPGROUND **Ratings: 5.5/8★/8** (RV Park) 18 Avail: 15 full hkups, 3 E (30/50 amps). 2021 rates: $42 to $45. Mar 14 to Oct 31. (435)425-3577, 540 W SR 24, Torrey, UT 84775

WONDERLAND RV PARK **Ratings: 8/10★/10** (RV Park) 36 Avail: 33 full hkups, 3 W, 3 E (30/50 amps). 2021 rates: $44 to $54. Apr 01 to Nov 01. (435)425-3665, 44 South Hwy 12, Torrey, UT 84775

TREMONTON — A2 *Box Elder*

ASPEN GROVE RV PARK
Ratings: 9/10★/10 (RV Park) Avail: 54 full hkups (30/50 amps). 2021 rates: $48 to $62. (435)339-6003, 700 West Main St, Tremonton, UT 84337

TROPIC — E2 *Garfield*

BRYCE PIONEER VILLAGE RV PARK **Ratings: 6/10★/8** (RV Park) Avail: 12 full hkups (30/50 amps). 2021 rates: $55. Apr 01 to Oct 31. (435)679-8546, 80 South Main, Tropic, UT 84776

VERNAL — B5 *Uintah*

DINOSAURLAND KOA **Ratings: 9/9.5★/8.5** (Campground) 60 Avail: 52 full hkups, 8 W, 8 E (30/50 amps). 2021 rates: $51.75 to $94.51. Apr 01 to Oct 31. (435)789-2148, 930 N Vernal Ave, Vernal, UT 84078

FOSSIL VALLEY RV PARK
Ratings: 6.5/9.5★/8 (RV Park) Avail: 51 full hkups (30/50 amps). 2021 rates: $43 to $51. (435)789-6450, 999 W Hwy 40, Vernal, UT 84078

RED FLEET (Public State Park) From jct Main St & Vernal Ave: Go 10 mi N on SR-191, then 2 mi E on Red Fleet Rd (E). 21 Avail: 4 full hkups, 3 W, 3 E (30 amps). 2021 rates: $15 to $25. (435)789-4432

STEINAKER (Public State Park) From jct Main & Vernal Ave (SR-191): Go 5-1/2 mi N on SR-191, then 1-3/4 mi SW on Steinaker Park Rd (E). 27 Avail: 8 full hkups, 8 W, 8 E (20/30 amps). 2021 rates: $15 to $28. Apr 14 to Oct 15. (435)789-4432

VIRGIN — E2 *Washington*

ZION RIVER RESORT RV PARK & CAMPGROUND
Ratings: 10/10★/9.5 (RV Park) N-bnd: From Jct of I-15 & Hwy 9 (exit 16), E 18.9 mi on Hwy 9 to MP 19 (R); or S-bnd: From Jct of I-15 & Hwy 17 (exit 27), S 6 mi on Hwy 17 to Hwy 9, E 6.3 mi to MP 19 (R). Elev 3582 ft.**FAC:** paved rds. 112 Avail: 74 paved, 38 all weather, 47 pull-thrus, (30x65), back-ins (25x35), 112 full hkups (30/50 amps), cable, WiFi @ sites, tent sites, rentals, shower$, laundry, groc, LP gas, fire rings, firewood. **REC:** heated pool, hot tub, Virgin River: swim, fishing, playground, hunting nearby. Pet restrict (B/Q). Partial handicap access. Big rig sites, eco-friendly. 2021 rates: $41 to $82, Military discount.
(888)822-8594 Lat: 37.20310, Lon: -113.17744
551 E State Route 9, Virgin, UT 84779
www.zionriverresort.com
See ad this page

WANSHIP — B3 *Summit*

ROCKPORT LAKE SRA (Public State Park) From jct I-80 & Hwy 32 (exit 155): 4-3/4 mi S on Hwy 32 (L). 110 Avail: 34 W, 34 E (20/30 amps). 2021 rates: $24 to $50. Apr 15 to Nov 01. (435)336-2241

WASHINGTON — E1 *Washington*

SOUTHERN UTAH RV RESORT **Ratings: 8/9.5★/9.5** (RV Resort) Avail: 80 full hkups (30/50 amps). 2021 rates: $50 to $65. (435)669-2242, 720 E Merit Way, Washington, UT 84780

ZION NATIONAL PARK — E2 *Washington*

ZION NATIONAL PARK See also Cedar City, Glendale, Hurricane, Kanab, Mount Carmel, Springdale & Virgin.

Dealing with Extreme Weather Conditions: When flooding conditions are encountered, seek higher ground. If a section of roadway is flooded, do not drive through it. If you must cross it, observe other vehicles to determine depth of water. Be sure there are no downed electrical lines in the water. Depending on type of RV you are traveling in, a safe still water maximum depth must be established. That figure should not exceed much more than about half the height of your wheel/tire radius. E.g., a 22.5'' wheel with an 80-series tire, would be about 14'' or so. A 15'' wheel with a 70-series tire may be about 10''. Drive slowly and do not stop. In addition to water depth, the roadway below may be eroded or starting to collapse. If the water is moving at any speed across the roadway the vehicle could easily lose control. Items in the water can pose an additional hazard. Do not camp in low elevation locations. Avoid areas near any mountain washes. If a flood watch is upgraded to a warning, hold up in the highest ground you can find. Early warning is one of the best defenses when facing severe weather events. Monitor your local weather broadcasts. Consider getting an automatic ""First Alert'' or ""NOAA Radio'' to keep you safe and informed.

Getty Images/iStockphoto

YOU ARE HERE

Vermont

DID YOU KNOW?

According to local legend, a sea monster named Champ roams the waters of Lake Champlain.

Vermont sparkles with New England charm. Drive across one of the covered bridges that dot the state, settle into small-town life with a visit to a farmers market or explore the scenic beauty found in all directions.

Lakes and Rivers

Lake Champlain, straddling the state's western border with New York, is a prized spot for summertime vacationers seeking water sports, boating and fishing. Elsewhere, the Missisquoi River on the Canadian border and the Connecticut River on the New Hampshire border give travelers more paddling and angling options. Trout, walleye and bass thrive in these cool currents.

Sneaky Smuggler's Notch

This scenic Green Mountain Byway leads visitors past remarkable mountain scenery on an 11-mile journey between Stowe and Waterbury. In autumn, enjoy the epic scenery of the state's famed fall foliage. Make a stop at Smugglers' Notch State Park, once part of a smuggling route out of Canada and now one of the state's most popular recreation areas, offering scenic overlooks and mountain biking trails.

Stowe for All Seasons

Savor the seasons in beautiful Stowe. During winter, fresh snow attracts skiers to the surrounding slopes. In the summer and fall months, Stowe entices mountain bikers to navigate its network of well-maintained, interconnected trails in places like Candy Hill Forest.

Beautiful Burlington

In the northwest, the large city of Burlington sits on the shores of Lake Champlain and serves up a bounty of attractions in a compact space. Travelers are drawn away from the sparkling waters by the Church Street Marketplace and the South End Arts District.

Vermont Maple Creemee

Vermont is renowned for tasty dairy products and sweet syrup. The maple creemee combines the best of both worlds and puts it in a cone. Oozing with the silky consistency of soft-serve ice cream, this dessert puts maple syrup into an ice cream base. The result is a sweet, cool flavor explosion that will make you forget the heat and humidity of summer.

VISITOR CENTER

TIME ZONE
Eastern Standard

ROAD & HIGHWAY INFORMATION
802-917-2458
vtrans.vermont.gov

FISHING & HUNTING INFORMATION
802-828-1190
vtfishandwildlife.com

BOATING INFORMATION
802-828-1000
www.boat-ed.com/vermont

NATIONAL PARKS
nps.gov/vt

STATE PARKS
vtstateparks.com

TOURISM INFORMATION
Vermont Department of Tourism and Marketing
800-VERMONT
vermontvacation.com

TOP TOURISM ATTRACTIONS
1) Ben & Jerry's
2) Lake Champlain
3) Church Street Marketplace

MAJOR CITIES
Burlington, Essex, South Burlington, Colchester, Rutland City, Montpelier (capital)

VT

good sam park

Featured Good Sam Parks

VERMONT

When you stay with Good Sam, you can expect the highest degree of cleanliness and friendliness, and better yet, you get **10% off** overnight campground fees.

If you're not already a Good Sam member you can purchase your membership at one of these locations:

ANDOVER
Horseshoe Acres

COLCHESTER
Lone Pine Campsites

DANVILLE
Sugar Ridge RV Village & Campground

EAST THETFORD
Rest N' Nest Campground

LYNDONVILLE
Kingdom Campground

ST JOHNSBURY
Moose River Campground

10/10★/10 GOOD SAM PARK

DANVILLE
Sugar Ridge RV Village & Campground
(802)684-2550

What's This?

An RV park with a 10/10★/10 rating has scored perfect grades in amenities, cleanliness and appearance ("See Understanding the Campground Rating System" on pages 8 and 9 for an explanation of the trusted Good Sam Rating System). Stay in a 10/10★/10 park on your next trip for a nearly flawless camping experience.

Getty Images/iStockphoto

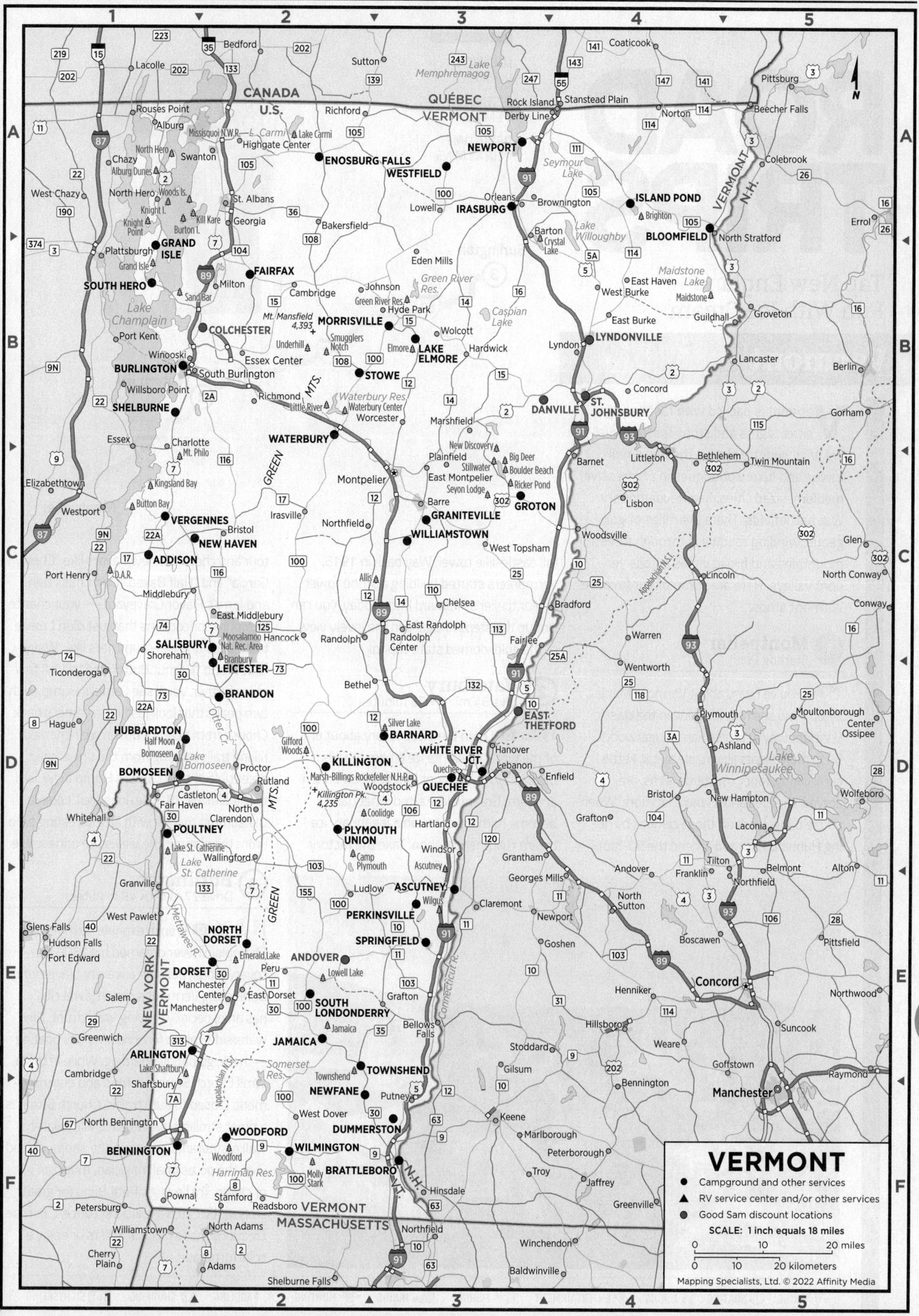
VERMONT
Campground and other services
RV service center and/or other services
Good Sam discount locations
SCALE: 1 inch equals 18 miles
0 10 20 miles
0 10 20 kilometers
Mapping Specialists, Ltd. © 2022 Affinity Media
CANADA
U.S.
QUÉBEC
VERMONT
NEW YORK
N.H.
MASSACHUSETTS
Lake Champlain
Lake Memphremagog
Seymour Lake
Lake Willoughby
Maidstone Lake
Caspian Lake
Green River Res.
Waterbury Res.
Lake Bomoseen
Lake St. Catherine
Somerset Res.
Harriman Res.
Lake Winnipesaukee
Connecticut R.
Otter Cr.
Mettawee R.
GREEN MTS.
Appalachian N.S.T.
Mt. Mansfield 4,393
Killington Pk. 4,235
ENOSBURG FALLS
WESTFIELD
NEWPORT
IRASBURG
ISLAND POND
BLOOMFIELD
GRAND ISLE
SOUTH HERO
FAIRFAX
COLCHESTER
MORRISVILLE
LAKE ELMORE
STOWE
BURLINGTON
SHELBURNE
WATERBURY
LYNDONVILLE
DANVILLE
ST. JOHNSBURY
GROTON
GRANITEVILLE
WILLIAMSTOWN
VERGENNES
NEW HAVEN
ADDISON
SALISBURY
LEICESTER
BRANDON
HUBBARDTON
BOMOSEEN
BARNARD
EAST THETFORD
WHITE RIVER JCT.
KILLINGTON
QUECHEE
POULTNEY
PLYMOUTH UNION
ASCUTNEY
PERKINSVILLE
SPRINGFIELD
NORTH DORSET
DORSET
ANDOVER
SOUTH LONDONDERRY
JAMAICA
ARLINGTON
TOWNSHEND
NEWFANE
DUMMERSTON
WOODFORD
WILMINGTON
BRATTLEBORO
BENNINGTON
Concord
Manchester
Bedford
Lacolle
Sutton
Coaticook
Pittsburg
Rock Island
Stanstead Plain
Derby Line
Norton
Beecher Falls
Rouses Point
Alburg
Missisquoi N.W.R.
Lake Carmi
Highgate Center
Richford
North Hero
Swanton
Chazy
Alburg Dunes
Colebrook
West Chazy
Woods Is.
St. Albans
Knight I.
Kill Kare
Knight Point
Burton I.
Georgia
Bakersfield
Orleans
Brownington
Lowell
Brighton
Errol
Barton
Crystal Lake
North Stratford
Plattsburgh
Grand Isle
Milton
Eden Mills
Sand Bar
Cambridge
Johnson
Green River Res.
Hyde Park
East Haven
West Burke
Maidstone
Groveton
Guildhall
East Burke
Port Kent
Underhill
Smugglers Notch
Wolcott
Elmore
Hardwick
Lyndon
Winooski
Essex Center
South Burlington
Lancaster
Berlin
Willsboro Point
Richmond
Little River
Waterbury Center
Worcester
Concord
Marshfield
Gorham
Essex
Charlotte
Mt. Philo
Barnet
Littleton
Bethlehem
Twin Mountain
New Discovery
Big Deer
Plainfield
Stillwater
Boulder Beach
East Montpelier
Montpelier
Seyon Lodge
Ricker Pond
Elizabethtown
Kingsland Bay
Barre
Lisbon
Button Bay
Westport
Bristol
Irasville
Northfield
Woodsville
Glen
West Topsham
Port Henry
D.A.R.
Lincoln
North Conway
Middlebury
Allis
Chelsea
Bradford
Conway
East Middlebury
East Randolph
Moosalamoo Nat. Rec. Area
Hancock
Randolph
Randolph Center
Warren
Fairlee
Shoreham
Branbury
Ticonderoga
Wentworth
Bethel
Hague
Half Moon
Silver Lake
Plymouth
Moultonborough
Center Ossipee
Bomoseen
Gifford Woods
Ashland
Hanover
Lebanon
Enfield
Proctor
Rutland
Marsh-Billings Rockefeller N.H.P.
Woodstock
Castleton
Fair Haven
North Clarendon
Bristol
New Hampton
Wolfeboro
Coolidge
Hartland
Grafton
Whitehall
Laconia
Lake St. Catherine
Wallingford
Windsor
Camp Plymouth
Grantham
Tilton
Ascutney
Andover
Franklin
Belmont
Alton
Granville
Georges Mills
Northfield
Ludlow
North Sutton
Claremont
Wilgus
Newport
West Pawlet
Glens Falls
Hudson Falls
Fort Edward
Goshen
Boscawen
Pittsfield
Emerald Lake
Peru
Lowell Lake
Manchester Center
East Dorset
Grafton
Henniker
Northwood
Salem
Manchester
Bellows Falls
Hillsboro
Suncook
Greenwich
Weare
Stoddard
Lake Shaftsbury
Townshend
Gilsum
Goffstown
Cambridge
Shaftsbury
Raymond
Putney
Bennington
West Dover
Keene
North Bennington
Marlborough
Peterborough
Woodford
Molly Stark
Troy
Jaffrey
Hinsdale
Pownal
Stamford
Readsboro
Greenville
Petersburg
North Adams
Northfield
Williamstown
Winchendon
Cherry Plain
Adams
Baldwinville
Shelburne Falls
1
2
3
4
5
A
B
C
D
E
F
VT

ROAD TRIPS

Tap New England Fun With Ice Cream

Vermont

LOCATION
VERMONT

DISTANCE
61 MILES

DRIVE TIME
1 HR 43 MINS

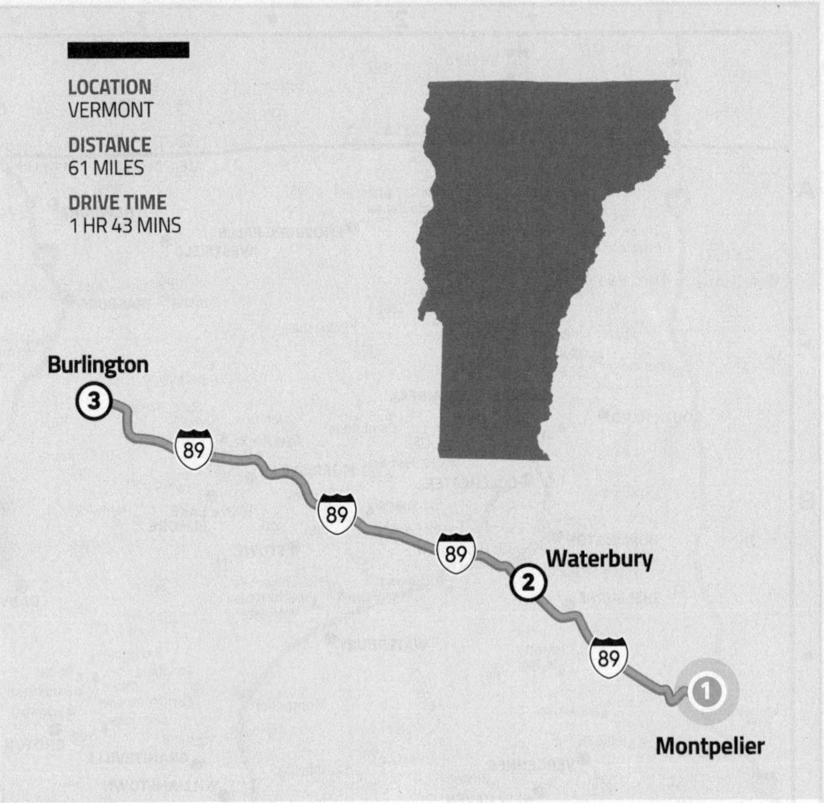

Vermont is packed with fascinating sites, sights and stops for RV travelers. Visit country stores, thriving small towns and luxury boutiques in progressive, medium-sized cities. See Revolutionary War battlefields. There are miles of gorgeous, winding roadways through forested mountains and broad vistas across verdant valleys. Here are some of our favorite Vermont stops.

1 Montpelier
Starting Point

You've heard about Vermont Maple syrup, now see how it's done in the classic Vermont way at Morse Farm Sugarworks. Shop more treats like maple sugar, kettle corn, candy, fancy mustards, jams, preserves, cheeses and a whole lot more. When you're done, work off those calories by hiking Hubbard Park and ascend the 50-foot-tall castle-like tower. Way back in 1915, Vermonters started building a stone tower in Montpelier's Hubbard Park. Today, you can trot up the steps and take in the lovely view of the gold-domed state capitol.

2 Waterbury
Drive 34 miles • 55 minutes

Learn the sweet story about one of the world's favorite ice cream brands. Back in 1978, Vermont buddies Ben Cohen and Jerry Greenfield started what has become nothing less than a legendary ice cream cult phenomenon. Take the factory tour and check out new flavors like "Cherry Garcia" and "Half Baked." Don't miss Ben and Jerry's Flavor Graveyard — your chance to mourn concoctions that just didn't make taste buds tingle — bummers like "Wavy Gravy" and "Peanut Butter and Jelly." A few miles further, you'll see Camel's Hump, with two peaks that look just like a camel's back. Choose from nearly a dozen well-marked hiking trails ranging from the universally accessible 1-mile Camel's Hump View Trail to the difficult 19-mile-long trail. Look for the summit marker with an interesting typo. From the summit the views are unbeatable.

3 Burlington
Drive 27 miles • 48 minutes

French explorer Samuel de Champlain never dreamed his 1609 discovery would become a watery playground. Burlington, Vermont's crown jewel city, has an especially thriving waterfront. Dine waterside, take a ferry ride, try sail boating — heck, go paddleboarding. While in town, stroll Church Street for food and entertainment. Closed to auto traffic, Church Street is a great strolling marketplace with wall-to-wall restaurants and specialty shops, spiced with the occasional magician, musician or clown. Try Leunig's Petit Bijou for great croissants. Catch a rollicking concert, peruse creations made by local artists or enjoy a colorful parade.

Getty Images/iStockphoto

BIKING BOATING DINING ENTERTAINMENT FISHING HIKING HUNTING PADDLING SHOPPING SIGHTSEEING

Vermont SPOTLIGHTS

Treat Yourself to Treats in the Green Mountain State

Don't believe the stereotypes. There's more to Vermont than tasty ice cream, picturesque church steeples and gorgeous lakes and mountains. Take a New England vacation with more variety than a Ben & Jerry's menu.

LONE ROCK POINT ON LAKE CHAMPLAIN FORMED IN THE CAMBRIAN ERA.

Getty Images/iStockphoto

Lone Rock Point is part of a stretch of cliff-walled shoreline on Lake Champlain.

Burlington

Nestled on the shores of scenic Lake Champlain, this small yet bustling city is like a microcosm of greater New England — charming, quaint and historic. Settled in 1783, this picturesque locale has been drawing northeasterners for over two hundred years, and still today it's easy to see why. Whether you're looking for a relaxing downtown shopping experience or four seasons of outdoors fun, you can find it all in the "Queen City."

Vibrant Downtown

At the center of Burlington's outsized food and arts scenes is the six-block pedestrian mall known as the Church St. Marketplace. Buzzing with energy, it's where almost every visit to the city begins. You can start yours by wandering between the many quirky vintage clothing shops, galleries and bookstores, before settling into one of the cute cafes that line the cobblestone streets. Local food is a focus in Vermont and many of the restaurants fill their menus with produce from the city's famed Farmer's Market.

One-of-a-kind Waterfront

At nearly 500 square miles, Lake Champlain is among the largest lakes in the country and holds a special place in the heart of every Vermonter. For the perfect introduction to New England-style lake life, head to Burlington's Waterfront Park where you can hike, bike, sail and paddle, all while enjoying views of the Adirondack Mountains in New York.

Montpelier

The smallest state capital by population, Montpelier packs a big punch of food, fun and scenery. The golden dome of the capitol building rises high over the unassuming skyline of this classic New England town, with streets lined by friendly restaurants.

Waterbury

The most popular thing to do in Waterbury is to take a tour of the Ben & Jerry's ice cream factory. See how ice cream is made and get a scoop of your favorite flavor at their full-service ice cream parlor. Just a few miles from Ben & Jerry's is the Cabot Creamery store. Here, you can indulge in a huge selection of Vermont artisanal cheeses. After, stop by the Lake Champlain chocolate store and café to satisfy your sweet tooth with chocolate truffles and hand-whipped fudge.

FOR MORE INFORMATION

Vermont Department of Tourism and Marketing, 800-VERMONT, vermontvacation.com

Burlington Vermont, 877-686-5253, www.vermont.org/experiences/burlington

Montpelier Alive, 802-223-9604, www.montpelieralive.com

Discover Waterbury Vermont, www.discoverwaterbury.com

LOCAL FAVORITE

Home Churned Strawberry Ice Cream

Vermont natives really enjoy a great bowl of ice cream. Double the fun of this cool treat by having each camper take a turn with the churning. *Recipe by Macy Payne.*

INGREDIENTS

- ☐ 2 ½ cups sugar
- ☐ 2 ½ cups fresh strawberries diced and mashed
- ☐ 2 ½ cups half and half
- ☐ 5 ¼ cup heavy cream
- ☐ 5 tsp vanilla flavoring
- ☐ 3 drops pink or red food coloring (optional)

DIRECTIONS

Combine sugar and the mashed strawberries, mix well. Mix strawberry mixture with the rest of ingredients in a mixing bowl and stir well. Transfer to an ice cream maker canister and churn.

VT

Vermont

ADDISON — C1 *Addison*

DAR (Public State Park) From Jct of Rte 22A & Rte 17 (in town), W 7 mi on Rte 17 (R). 47 Avail. 2021 rates: $18 to $27. May 27 to Sep 04. (802)759-2354

Clean Green! Vinegar and baking soda can be used to clean almost anything. Mix in a little warm water with either of these and you've got yourself an all-purpose cleaner.

Vermont Privately Owned Campground Information Updated by our Good Sam Representatives

Steve & Debbie Rice

Life adventuring as friends since meeting in seventh grade, our first date in a VW Microbus (before the Summer of Love) foretold the destiny of the long highway that lay ahead. Full-timing for eight years, we've accumulated miles of smiles. Peace!

ANDOVER — E2 *Windsor*

HORSESHOE ACRES
good sam park
Ratings: 8.5/9★/9 (Campground) 50 Avail: 12 full hkups, 38 W, 38 E (30/50 amps). 2021 rates: $38.50 to $53. May 01 to Oct 18. (802)875-2960, 1978 Weston-Andover Rd, Andover, VT 05143

ARLINGTON — E2 *Bennington*

CAMPING ON THE BATTENKILL **Ratings: 7.5/9★/9** (Campground) 78 Avail: 12 full hkups, 43 W, 43 E (30/50 amps). 2021 rates: $42 to $50. May 01 to Oct 15. (802)375-6663, 48 Camping on the Battenkill, Arlington, VT 05250

ASCUTNEY — E3 *Windsor*

ASCUTNEY (Public State Park) From Jct of I-91 & exit 8 (US-5), N 2 mi on US-5 to VR-44A, NW 1 mi (L). 38 Avail. 2021 rates: $18 to $27. May 22 to Oct 15. (802)674-2060

GETAWAY MOUNTAIN CAMPGROUND **Ratings: 7.5/8★/8** (Campground) 18 Avail: 13 full hkups, 5 W, 5 E (30/50 amps). 2021 rates: $30 to $33. May 01 to Oct 27. (802)674-2812, 3628 Rte 5S, Ascutney, VT 05030

RUNNING BEAR CAMPING AREA **Ratings: 7.5/4.5/5.5** (Campground) 44 Avail: 20 full hkups, 24 W, 24 E (30/50 amps). 2021 rates: $39 to $45. Apr 15 to Oct 15. (802)674-6417, 6248 US Rte 5, Ascutney, VT 05030

BARNARD — D3 *Windsor*

SILVER LAKE (Public State Park) From town, N 0.25 mi on Town Rd (R). 39 Avail. 2021 rates: $18 to $29. May 29 to Sep 04. (802)234-9451

BENNINGTON — F1 *Bennington*

GREENWOOD LODGE & CAMPSITES
Ratings: 7/9.5★/9 (Campground) From Jct of Rte 7 & Rte 9 (in Bennington): Go 8 mi E on Rte 9 to 204 Prospect Access, then 1/4 mi up gravel driveway to Greenwood Dr (L). From Jct of I-91 & Rte 9 (exit 2): Go 32 mi W on Rte 9 to 204 Prospect Access, then 1/4 mi up gravel driveway to Greenwood Dr (L). **FAC:** gravel rds. Avail: 40 gravel, 8 pull-thrus, (35x76), back-ins (30x74), 23 W, 23 E (30/50 amps), WiFi @ sites, tent sites, dump, fire rings, firewood. **REC:** pond, swim, kayaking/canoeing, boating nearby. Pet restrict (B). Partial handicap access, eco-friendly. 2021 rates: $41 to $43. May 20 to Oct 20.
(802)442-2547 Lat: 42.87546, Lon: -73.077923
311 Greenwood Drive, Woodford, VT 05201
www.campvermont.com/greenwood
See ad this page

PINE HOLLOW CAMPGROUND **Ratings: 7/9★/9** (Campground) 50 Avail: 27 full hkups, 23 W, 23 E (30/50 amps). 2021 rates: $42 to $52. May 01 to Oct 31. (802)823-5569, 342 Pine Hollow Rd, Pownal, VT 05261

BLOOMFIELD — A4 *Essex*

MAIDSTONE (Public State Park) From Bloomfield, S 5 mi on SR-102 to Maidstone State Forest Hwy, SW 6 mi (E). 34 Avail. 2021 rates: $18 to $29. May 27 to Sep 04. (802)676-3930

BOMOSEEN — D1 *Rutland*

BOMOSEEN (Public State Park) From Jct of US-A & Town Rd (exit 3), N 5 mi on Town Rd (R). 55 Avail. 2021 rates: $18 to $29. May 25 to Sep 07. (802)265-4242

LAKE BOMOSEEN KOA **Ratings: 8/8.5★/8.5** (Campground) 99 Avail: 61 full hkups, 38 W, 38 E (30/50 amps). 2021 rates: $53 to $73. May 01 to Oct 12. (802)273-2061, 18 Campground Dr, Bomoseen, VT 05732

BRANDON — D2 *Rutland*

SMOKE RISE CAMPGROUND **Ratings: 9.5/9★/9** (Campground) Avail: 89 full hkups (30/50 amps). 2021 rates: $45. May 15 to Oct 15. (802)247-6984, 2145 Grove St (Rte 7), Brandon, VT 05733

BRATTLEBORO — F3 *Windham*

FORT DUMMER (Public State Park) From Jct of I-91 & Exit 1 (CR-5), N 0.1 mi on CR-5 to Fairgrounds Rd, E 0.5 mi to S Main St (Old Guilford Rd), S 1 mi (E). 50 Avail. 2021 rates: $18 to $27. May 27 to Sep 04. (802)254-2610

The best things happen outdoors. Start your adventure today at GanderOutdoors.com

BURLINGTON — B1 *Chittenden*

BURLINGTON See also Colchester, Fairfax, Shelburne, South Hero & Stowe, VT; Ausable Chasm, Peru, Plattsburgh & Westport, NY.

NORTH BEACH CAMPGROUND
(Public) From Jct of I-89 & US-2 (exit 14W), W 2 mi on US-2 (Main St) to Battery St, N 0.5 mi to Sherman St, W 0.1 mi to North Ave, N 1.5 mi to Institute Rd, W 0.3 mi (E). **FAC:** paved/gravel rds. Avail: 68 gravel, back-ins (23x50), 29 full hkups, 39 W, 39 E WiFi @ sites, tent sites, shower$, dump, laundry, fire rings, firewood, controlled access. **REC:** Lake Champlain: swim, playground. Pets OK. Partial handicap access, 14 day max stay. 2021 rates: $41 to $45. May 01 to Oct 15.
(802)862-0942 Lat: 44.49488, Lon: -73.23605
60 Institute Rd, Burlington, VT 05408
enjoyburlington.com

COLCHESTER — B2 *Chittenden*

LONE PINE CAMPSITES
good sam park
Ratings: 9/10★/10 (Campground) From Jct of I-89 & US 7 (Exit 16), Go 3.2 mi NW on US 7 to Jct of Rte 2A & Bay Rd, then 1 mi W on Bay Rd (R). **FAC:** paved rds. (280 spaces). 150 Avail: 10 gravel, 140 grass, patios, 10 pull-thrus, (30x60), back-ins (39x66), 78 full hkups, 72 W, 72 E (30/50 amps), seasonal sites, cable, WiFi @ sites, $, tent sites, rentals, shower$, dump, mobile sewer, laundry, groc, LP gas, fire rings, firewood. **REC:** heated pool, boating nearby, playground. Pet restrict (Q). Partial handicap access. Big rig sites, eco-friendly. 2021 rates: $43 to $93, Military discount. May 01 to Oct 15.
(802)878-5447 Lat: 44.55551, Lon: -73.18538
52 Sunset View Rd, Colchester, VT 05446
lonepinecampsites.com
See ad this page

MALLETTS BAY CAMPGROUND **Ratings: 7.5/6/7.5** (Campground) 45 Avail: 34 full hkups, 11 W, 11 E (30/50 amps). 2021 rates: $52 to $55. May 01 to Oct 15. (802)863-6980, 88 Malletts Bay Campground Rd, Colchester, VT 05446

DANVILLE — B3 *Caledonia*

SUGAR RIDGE RV VILLAGE & CAMPGROUND
good sam park
Ratings: 10/10★/10 (Campground) 100 Avail: 82 full hkups, 18 W, 18 E (30/50 amps). 2021 rates: $48.50 to $55. May 10 to Oct 17. (802)684-2550, 24 Old Stagecoach Rd, Danville, VT 05828

DORSET — E2 *Bennington*

DORSET RV PARK
Ratings: 8.5/9★/9.5 (Campground) From Jct of US-7 & SR-30 (exit 4), NW 6 mi on Rte 30 (L); or From Jct of Historic Rte 7A & SR-30 (in Manchester Center), NW 4.3 mi on SR-30 (L). **FAC:** all weather rds. (40 spaces). Avail: 33 all weather, 5 pull-thrus, (32x103), back-ins (35x50), 31 full hkups, 2 W, 2 E (30/50 amps), seasonal sites, cable, WiFi @ sites, tent sites, rentals, dump, mobile sewer, laundry, groc, LP gas, fire rings, firewood. **REC:** shuffleboard, playground. Pets OK. Partial handicap access. Big rig sites, eco-friendly. 2021 rates: $45 to $49. May 01 to Oct 31.
(802)867-5754 Lat: 43.23342, Lon: -73.08048
1567 Rte 30, Dorset, VT 05251
www.dorsetrvpark.com
See ad this page

DUMMERSTON — F3 *Windham*

BRATTLEBORO NORTH KOA **Ratings: 9/10★/9** (Campground) 40 Avail: 21 full hkups, 19 W, 19 E (30/50 amps). 2021 rates: $40 to $79.94. Apr 17 to Oct 22. (800)562-5909, 1238 US Rte 5, East Dummerston, VT 05346

EAST THETFORD — D3 *Orange*

REST N' NEST CAMPGROUND
good sam park
Ratings: 9/9★/9.5 (Campground) From Jct of I-91 & Rte 113 (exit 14), Go 0.1 E mi on Rte 113 to Latham Rd, then N 0.25 mi (R). **FAC:** all weather rds. (80 spaces). Avail: 54 all weather, 7 pull-thrus, (44x92), back-ins (35x50), 37 full hkups, 17 W, 17 E (30/50 amps), seasonal sites, WiFi @ sites, tent sites, rentals, dump, mobile sewer, laundry, groc, LP gas, fire rings, firewood. **REC:** heated pool, pond, swim, boating nearby, playground. Pet restrict (Q). Big rig sites, eco-friendly. 2021 rates: $43 to $50. Apr 24 to Oct 12.
(802)785-2997 Lat: 43.81570, Lon: -72.21069
300 Latham Rd, East Thetford, VT 05043
www.restnnest.com
See ad opposite page

ENOSBURG FALLS — A2 *Franklin*

LAKE CARMI (Public State Park) From town, W 3 mi on Rte 105 to Rte 236, N 3 mi (L). 138 Avail. 2021 rates: $18 to $29. May 18 to Oct 09. (802)933-8383

FAIRFAX — B2 *Franklin*

MAPLE GROVE CAMPGROUND **Ratings: 6.5/8.5★/9.5** (Campground) Avail: 13 full hkups (30/50 amps). 2021 rates: $28 to $40. May 01 to Oct 12. (802)849-6439, 1627 Main St., Fairfax, VT 05454

GRAND ISLE — B1 *Grand Isle*

GRAND ISLE (Public State Park) From town: Go 1 mi S on US-2. 115 Avail. 2021 rates: $18 to $29. May 11 to Oct 15. (802)372-4300

GRANITEVILLE — C3 *Washington*

LAZY LIONS CAMPGROUND **Ratings: 7.5/8/9** (Campground) Avail: 30 full hkups (20/30 amps). 2021 rates: $45. May 15 to Oct 15. (802)479-2823, 281 Middle Road, Graniteville, VT 05654

GROTON — C3 *Washington*

BIG DEER (Public State Park) From Jct US-302 & SR-232, NW 5.3 mi on SR-232 to Boulder Beach Rd, NE 1.5 mi (L). 22 Avail. 2021 rates: $18 to $27. May 30 to Sep 04. (802)584-3822

NEW DISCOVERY (Public State Park) From Jct of US-2 & SR-232, S 5 mi on SR-232 (L). 39 Avail. 2021 rates: $18 to $27. May 29 to Oct 09. (802)426-3042

RICKER POND (Public State Park) From town: Go 2 mi W on US-302, then 2-1/2 mi N on Hwy-232. 26 Avail. May 27 to Oct 09. (802)584-3821

STILLWATER (Public State Park) From Jct US-302 & SR-232, N 5.5 mi on SR-232 to Boulder Beach Rd, NE 0.5 mi (R). 59 Avail. 2021 rates: $18 to $29. May 18 to Sep 04. (802)584-3822

HUBBARDTON — D1 *Rutland*

HALF MOON (Public State Park) From Jct of US-4 & SR-30, N 14 mi on SR-30 to Hubbardton Rd, S 1.5 mi to Black Pond Rd, E 2 mi (L). 52 Avail. 2021 rates: $18 to $29. May 25 to Oct 12. (802)273-2848

IRASBURG — A3 *Orleans*

TREE CORNERS FAMILY CAMPGROUND **Ratings: 9/9.5★/9.5** (Campground) 81 Avail: 56 full hkups, 25 W, 25 E (30/50 amps). 2021 rates: $49.29 to $52.47. May 15 to Oct 15. (802)754-6042, 95 Rte 58 West, Irasburg, VT 05845

ISLAND POND — A4 *Essex*

BRIGHTON (Public State Park) From town, E 2 mi on SR-105 to Lakeshore Dr, S 0.75 mi (L). 54 Avail. 2021 rates: $18 to $29. May 27 to Sep 04. (802)723-4360

LAKESIDE CAMPING AREA **Ratings: 8.5/9.5★/8.5** (Campground) Avail: 100 full hkups (30/50 amps). 2021 rates: $56 to $66. May 15 to Sep 08. (802)723-6649, 1348 Rte 105 E Brighton Rd, Island Pond, VT 05846

JAMAICA — E2 *Windham*

JAMAICA (Public State Park) In town, N 0.8 mi on Depot St (L). 41 Avail. 2021 rates: $18 to $29. May 07 to Oct 09. (802)874-4600

KILLINGTON — D2 *Rutland*

GIFFORD WOODS (Public State Park) From town, E 10 mi on US-4 to VT-100, N 0.5 mi (L). 21 Avail. 2021 rates: $18 to $29. May 18 to Oct 15. (802)775-5354

LAKE ELMORE — B3 *Lamoille*

ELMORE (Public State Park) From Jct of SR-100 & SR-12, SE 5 mi on SR-12 (R). 44 Avail. 2021 rates: $18 to $29. May 27 to Oct 09. (802)888-2982

LEICESTER — D2 *Addison*

COUNTRY VILLAGE CAMPGROUND **Ratings: 7.5/8.5★/8.5** (Campground) 36 Avail: 36 W, 36 E (30 amps). 2021 rates: $35. May 01 to Sep 30. (802)247-3333, 40 US-Rte 7, Leicester, VT 05733

Find it fast! To locate a town on a map, follow these easy instructions: Look for the map grid code after the town heading in the listing section and match it to the letters and numbers on the map borders. Draw a line horizontally from the letter and vertically from the number. You'll find the town near the intersection of the two lines.

LYNDONVILLE — B4 *Caledonia*

KINGDOM CAMPGROUND
good sam park **Ratings: 8/10★/9** (Campground) Avail: 66 full hkups (30/50 amps). 2021 rates: $49.50. May 07 to Oct 13. (802)626-1151, 972 Lynburke Rd, Lyndonville, VT 05850

MORRISVILLE — B3 *Lamoille*

MOUNTAIN VIEW CAMPGROUND **Ratings: 8/UI/9** (Campground) Avail: 46 full hkups (30/50 amps). 2021 rates: $46 to $60. May 01 to Oct 12. (802)888-2178, 3154 Vermont Rte 15 E, Morrisville, VT 05661

NEW HAVEN — C2 *Addison*

RIVERS BEND CAMPGROUND **Ratings: 7/8.5★/9.5** (Campground) 50 Avail: 50 W, 50 E (20/30 amps). 2021 rates: $49 to $57. May 15 to Oct 15. (802)388-9092, 722 Rivers Bend Rd, New Haven, VT 05472

NEWFANE — F2 *Windham*

KENOLIE VILLAGE **Ratings: 7/7.5/7.5** (Campground) 30 Avail: 30 W, 30 E (30/50 amps). 2021 rates: $33.75 to $35. Apr 01 to Oct 31. (802)365-7671, 16 Kenolie Campground, Newfane, VT 05345

NEWPORT — A3 *Orleans*

PROUTY BEACH CAMPGROUND (Public) From jct I-91 (exit 27) & Hwy 191: Go 2 mi toward Newport, 1st traffic light continue straight, R at 2nd set of lights on to Union St. Avail: 52 full hkups. 2021 rates: $39 to $45. May 04 to Oct 08. (802)334-7951

NORTH DORSET — E2 *Bennington*

EMERALD LAKE (Public State Park) From town, N 3 mi on US-7 (L). 66 Avail. 2021 rates: $18 to $29. May 27 to Oct 09. (802)362-1655

PERKINSVILLE — E3 *Windsor*

CROWN POINT CAMPING AREA **Ratings: 7.5/9★/8.5** (Campground) 67 Avail: 20 full hkups, 47 W, 47 E (30 amps). 2021 rates: $48 to $65. May 01 to Oct 15. (802)263-5555, 131 Bishop Camp Rd, Perkinsville, VT 05151

PLYMOUTH UNION — D2 *Windsor*

COOLIDGE (Public State Park) From town, E 17 mi on US-4 to SR-100, S 5 mi to SR-100A, NE 2 mi to Coolidge State Park Rd (R). Steep entrance. 26 Avail. 2021 rates: $18 to $29. May 27 to Oct 09. (802)672-3612

POULTNEY — D1 *Rutland*

LAKE ST CATHERINE (Public State Park) From Jct of US-4 & SR-30 (exit 4), S 10 mi on SR-30 (R). 50 Avail. 2021 rates: $18 to $29. May 27 to Sep 04. (802)287-9158

QUECHEE — D3 *Windsor*

QUECHEE (Public State Park) From Jct of I-89 & US 4 (exit 1), W 3 mi on US 4 (L). 45 Avail. 2021 rates: $18 to $29. May 18 to Oct 15. (802)295-2990

SALISBURY — C2 *Addison*

LAKE DUNMORE KAMPERSVILLE **Ratings: 8/6.5/8.5** (Campground) 87 Avail: 60 full hkups, 27 W, 27 E (30/50 amps). 2021 rates: $50.50 to $68. Apr 01 to Dec 01. (802)352-4501, 1457 Lake Dunmore Road, Salisbury, VT 05769

SHELBURNE — B1 *Chittenden*

SHELBURNE CAMPING AREA **Ratings: 7.5/8.5★/8.5** (Campground) 66 Avail: 30 full hkups, 36 W, 36 E (30/50 amps). 2021 rates: $52. (802)985-2540, 4385 Shelburne Rd, Shelburne, VT 05482

SOUTH HERO — B1 *Grand Isle*

APPLE ISLAND RESORT **Ratings: 10/10★/10** (RV Resort) Avail: 220 full hkups (30/50 amps). 2021 rates: $70 to $100. May 01 to Oct 20. (802)372-3800, 71 US Rte 2, South Hero, VT 05486

SOUTH LONDONDERRY — E2 *Windham*

BALL MOUNTAIN LAKE - COE/WINHALL BROOK (Public Corps) From town: Go 2-1/2 mi S on Hwy 100, then E on Windhall Station Rd. Avail: 88 E. 2021 rates: $20 to $26. May 18 to Oct 08. (802)874-4881

SPRINGFIELD — E3 *Windsor*

TREE FARM CAMPGROUND **Ratings: 6.5/9★/9** (Campground) 63 Avail: 38 full hkups, 25 W, 25 E (30/50 amps). 2021 rates: $40. May 15 to Oct 31. (802)885-2889, 53 Skitchewaug Trail, Springfield, VT 05156

ST JOHNSBURY — B4 *Caledonia*

MOOSE RIVER CAMPGROUND
good sam park **Ratings: 9/10★/9.5** (Campground) Avail: 25 full hkups (30/50 amps). 2021 rates: $43 to $65. May 01 to Oct 16. (802)748-4334, 2870 Portland St, St Johnsbury, VT 05819

STOWE — B2 *Lamoille*

GOLD BROOK CAMPGROUND **Ratings: 6/8★/8.5** (Campground) 63 Avail: 26 full hkups, 37 W, 37 E (30/50 amps). 2021 rates: $41 to $51. May 15 to Oct 15. (802)253-7683, 1900 Waterbury Rd, Stowe, VT 05672

SMUGGLERS NOTCH (Public State Park) From Jct of SR-100 & SR-108 (in town), NW 6 mi on SR-108 (R). 20 Avail. 2021 rates: $18 to $29. May 18 to Oct 13. (802)253-4014

TOWNSHEND — E2 *Windham*

TOWNSHEND (Public State Park) From jct Hwy 30 & Town Rd: Go 3 mi N on Town Rd. Note: One vehicle per site. 30 Avail. 2021 rates: $18 to $27. May 27 to Sep 04. (802)365-7500

VERGENNES — C1 *Addison*

BUTTON BAY (Public State Park) From town, S 0.5 mi on SR-22A to Panton Rd, W 1.2 mi to Basin Rd, NW 5.5 mi to Lake Rd, S 1 mi (L). 53 Avail. 2021 rates: $18 to $29. May 27 to Oct 09. (802)475-2377

WATERBURY — B2 *Washington*

LITTLE RIVER (Public State Park) From town, W 2 mi on US-2, follow signs (R). 81 Avail. 2021 rates: $18 to $29. May 18 to Oct 21. (802)244-7103

WESTFIELD — A3 *Orleans*

BARREWOOD CAMPGROUND **Ratings: 6/5.5/7.5** (Campground) 24 Avail: 8 full hkups, 16 W, 16 E (20/30 amps). 2021 rates: $38 to $42. (802)744-6340, 2998 VT Rte 100, Westfield, VT 05874

WHITE RIVER JCT — D3 *Windsor*

QUECHEE PINE VALLEY KOA **Ratings: 9.5/9.5★/10** (Campground) 92 Avail: 46 full hkups, 46 W, 46 E (30/50 amps). 2021 rates: $63 to $95. May 01 to Oct 20. (802)296-6711, 3700 Woodstock Rd, White River Jct, VT 05001

WILLIAMSTOWN — C3 *Orange*

LIMEHURST LAKE CAMPGROUND **Ratings: 9/8.5/10** (Campground) 32 Avail: 25 full hkups, 7 W, 7 E (30/50 amps). 2021 rates: $45 to $50. May 01 to Oct 15. (802)433-6662, 4104 VT Rte 14, Williamstown, VT 05679

WILMINGTON — F2 *Windham*

MOLLY STARK (Public State Park) From Jct of I-91 & SR-9, exit 2 (in Brattleboro), W 15 mi on SR-9 (L); or From Wilmington, E 3 mi on SR-9 (R). 23 Avail. 2021 rates: $18 to $27. May 27 to Oct 09. (802)464-5460

WOODFORD — F2 *Bennington*

WOODFORD (Public State Park) From Jct of US-7 & SR-9, E 10 mi on SR-9 (R). 76 Avail. 2021 rates: $18 to $29. May 27 to Oct 09. (802)447-7169

County names are provided after the city names. If you're tracking the weather, this is the information you'll need to follow the reports.

VT

JamesDeMers

YOU ARE HERE

Virginia

DID YOU KNOW?

Eight U.S. presidents were born in the Old Dominion State, including George Washington, Thomas Jefferson and Woodrow Wilson.

The Old Dominion State exudes history and scenic beauty. This is a place where Civil War battles raged, major leaders cut their teeth and trailblazers opened new frontiers. Virginia is sure to exceed your expectations.

D.C. Adjacent

Located next to Washington, D.C., Arlington rivals D.C. in history and monuments. Visit the final resting place of John F. Kennedy and the Tomb of the Unknowns at the Arlington National Cemetery. You can even take a guided tour of the Pentagon as long as you book in advance.

Walk Through History

In Richmond, the Liberty Trail is a walk into history. Follow the self-guided walking path to historic sites including the Virginia State Capitol, Edgar Allan Poe Museum, Hollywood Cemetery and the oldest church in town. Don't leave without seeing funky street art in the Carytown neighborhood and smelling the roses in the Lewis Ginter Botanical Garden.

Ponies on Parade

Assateague Island National Seashore hosts a stunning variety of wildlife. Situated in both Maryland and Virginia, this 37-mile barrier island lets you come face-to-face with shorebirds, dolphins, whales and wild ponies. Beyond the resident creatures, you'll find sandy beaches and maritime forests to roam. Go horseback riding, crabbing and kayaking.

Water Recreation and Walking

Virginia Beach has no shortage of ocean adventures. Paddle down peaceful waterways, sail the high seas and stop by the Cape Henry Lighthouse resting just outside First Landing State Park. Finish your day with a leisurely stroll on Virginia Beach's 3-mile-long boardwalk and capture a photo with the bronze King Neptune statue along the way.

Virginia Brunswick Stew

Early residents of Virginia's Brunswick County pulled together local ingredients to make a hearty stew that satisfied hungry bellies. The tomato-based mixture consists of chicken, lima beans, okra and corn. Cooks of their day discovered that you didn't have to go far to get great flavor, and you'll reach the same conclusion after polishing off a bowl of this comforting concoction.

VISITOR CENTER

TIME ZONE
Eastern Standard

ROAD & HIGHWAY INFORMATION
800-FOR-ROAD
virginiadot.org

FISHING & HUNTING INFORMATION
866-721-6911
dgif.virginia.gov/licenses

BOATING INFORMATION
866-721-6911
dgif.virginia.gov/boating

NATIONAL PARKS
nps.gov/va

STATE PARKS
dcr.virginia.gov/state-parks

TOURISM INFORMATION
Virginia Tourism Corporation
804-545-5600
virginia.org

TOP TOURISM ATTRACTIONS
1) Busch Gardens
2) Colonial Williamsburg
3) Presidential Estates

MAJOR CITIES
Virginia Beach, Norfolk, Chesapeake, Arlington, Richmond (capital)

Founding Spark of America

Visit Colonial National Historical Park and walk in the footsteps of movers and shakers that shaped a nation. Wander around Jamestown, the first permanent British colony in the New World, to view a recreated fort, Powhatan village and replica ships. The park also encompasses the Yorktown Battlefield where the last major American Revolution battle was fought.

Take a Shine to Shenandoah

Shenandoah National Park protects a big slice of the Blue Ridge Mountains. The park encompasses cascading waterfalls, rolling peaks and panoramic vistas. Experience all the park has to offer by cruising along the scenic Skyline Drive or trekking 101 miles of the legendary Appalachian Trail. A bird's-eye view of the entire landscape can be enjoyed at Mary's Rock and at the top of Hawksbill Mountain, the park's highest peak at 4,050 feet. The largest caverns in the eastern United States are just west of Skyline Drive. The Luray Caverns offers guided tours so you can go deep beneath the surface and enter cathedral-sized rooms overflowing with stalactites and stalagmites.

Stunning scenery in Shenandoah National Park along Skyline Drive near Hawksbill Mountain.

Appalachia Region

Home to hundreds of miles of hiking, biking and ATV trails, as well as one-of-a-kind natural wonders, the Appalachia region of southwest Virginia entices thrill seekers looking to push their limits in the fun-filled Appalachian Mountains. Visitors looking to enjoy the area's cultural heritage will discover a full menu of treasures. Some of the country's most revered and authentic American musical traditions were born and are still thriving in the region's communities.

Appalachian Living

The small town of Pennington Gap, connected to the advanced Stone Mountain Trail system, is a charming example of life in Appalachia, with a homey theater, low-key restaurants and annual festivals. Guide shops in towns like Grundy, Coeburn and St. Paul are great places to organize an ATV excursion, and experts there can keep you up to date on safety gear and regulations while out in the wild.

Hitting the Trail

Hiking and mountain biking are welcome on most of the Appalachian's trails and can be a great way to get up close and personal to geologic formations like the Devil's Bathtub and Natural Tunnel State Park, as well as the nearby Clinch River. These hikes, which include swimming holes, waterfalls and fishing spots, are favorite pastimes in the warm summer months, so make sure that you get there early.

Wetlands and Hemlocks

The mostly low Lakeshore Trail winds through wetlands and hemlock forests on its way to the 45-acre Bark Camp Lake, where locals enjoy swimming, boating and fishing for largemouth bass, catfish and trout. For those looking to relax, there's nothing better than a float down the Clinch River, one of the most dynamic and biologically diverse waterways in the nation.

Appalachian Melodies

Connecting four cities and 50 towns along 330 miles of backcountry roads, the Crooked Road Heritage Music Trail began in 2003 as a way to celebrate southwest Virginia's storied musical traditions. With everything from small-town venues to yearly festivals along the route, Crooked Road offers a deep dive into a unique musical heritage that combines old-time string bands, gospel, blues and bluegrass. For a glimpse into the daily lives of the many pioneers who helped create the area's cultural heritage, try the Southwest Virginia Museum Historical State Park. Exhibits focus on the 19th century's coal, iron and railroad industries and include restored homes.

good sam park

Featured Good Sam Parks

VIRGINIA

When you stay with Good Sam, you can expect the highest degree of cleanliness and friendliness, and better yet, you get **10% off** overnight campground fees.

If you're not already a Good Sam member you can purchase your membership at one of these locations:

ASHLAND
Americamps RV Resort

BASSETT
Cahill's Lily Pad Campground

BRACEY
Lake Gaston Americamps

CHESAPEAKE
Chesapeake Campground

COLONIAL BEACH
Harbor View RV Park
Monroe Bay Campground

DUMFRIES
Prince William Forest RV Campground

FRONT ROYAL
North Fork Resort

GLOUCESTER
Chesapeake Bay RV Resort

GREENWOOD
Misty Mountain Camp Resort

HAYMARKET
Greenville Farm Family Campground

KEELING
Paradise Lake and Campground

LEXINGTON
Lee Hi Campground

MADISON
Madison Vines RV Resort & Cottages

MILFORD
R & D Family Campground

MINERAL
Christopher Run Campground

MOUNT JACKSON
Shenandoah Valley Campground - Mt Jackson

PETERSBURG
Camptown Campground
Picture Lake Campground
South Forty RV Campground

POWHATAN
Cozy Acres Campground/RV Park

QUINBY
Virginia Landing RV Campground

RUSTBURG
Lynchburg RV

SPOUT SPRING
Paradise Lake Family Campground

SUFFOLK
Davis Lakes RV Park and Campground

TOANO
Colonial Pines Campground at Williamsburg Christian Retreat Center

TOPPING
Grey's Point Camp

URBANNA
Bethpage Camp-Resort

VERONA
Shenandoah Valley Campground

VIRGINIA BEACH
Holiday Trav-L-Park
North Landing Beach RV Resort & Cottages

WILLIAMSBURG
American Heritage RV Park
Anvil Campground
Williamsburg RV Campground Thousand Trails

WINCHESTER
Candy Hill Campground

WYTHEVILLE
Deer Trail Park & Campground
Fort Chiswell RV Park

10/10★/10 GOOD SAM PARKS

VIRGINIA BEACH
North Landing Beach RV Resort & Cottages
(757)426-6241

WILLIAMSBURG
American Heritage RV Park
(888)530-2267

What's This?

An RV park with a 10/10★/10 rating has scored perfect grades in amenities, cleanliness and appearance ("See Understanding the Campground Rating System" on pages 8 and 9 for an explanation of the trusted Good Sam Rating System). Stay in a 10/10★/10 park on your next trip for a nearly flawless camping experience.

Getty Images/iStockphoto

VA

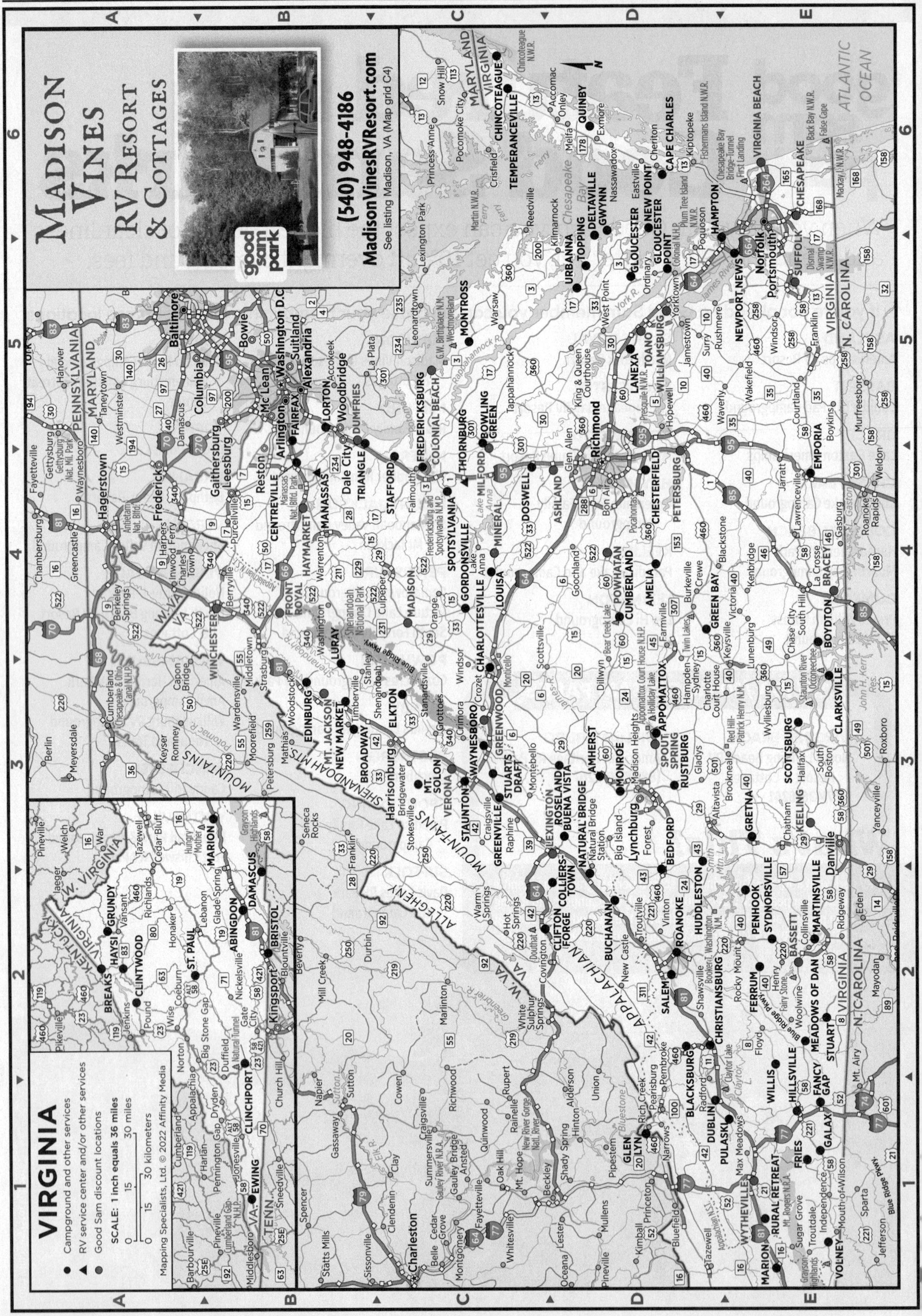
VIRGINIA
Campground and other services
RV service center and/or other services
Good Sam discount locations
SCALE: 1 inch equals 36 miles
Mapping Specialists, Ltd. © 2022 Affinity Media
Madison Vines RV Resort & Cottages
good sam park
(540) 948-4186
MadisonVinesRVResort.com
See listing Madison, VA (Map grid C4)
ATLANTIC OCEAN

ROAD TRIPS

Journeys Through American History

Virginia

LOCATION
VIRGINIA

DISTANCE
193 MILES

DRIVE TIME
3 HRS 33 MINS

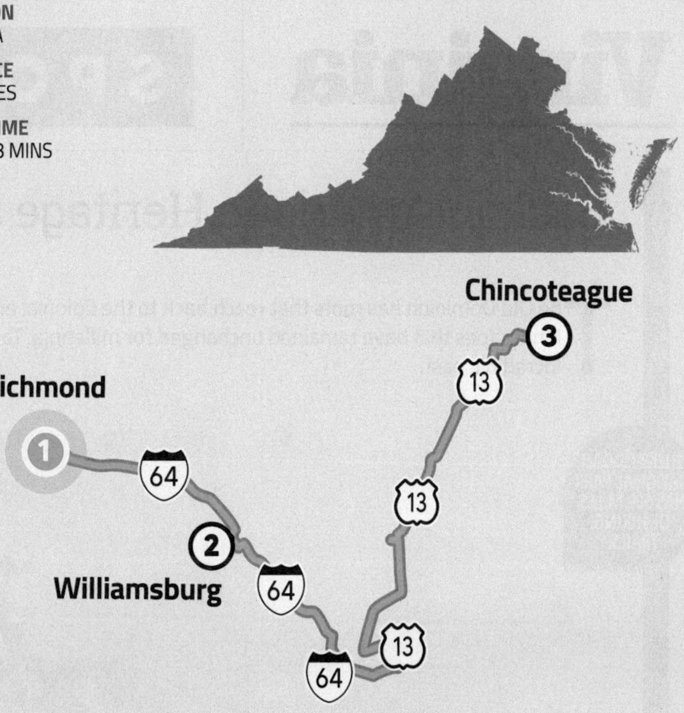

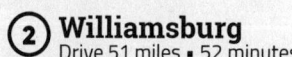

This road trip from a historic center of the Old South to the picturesque beauty of the barrier islands includes first-class dining, rich history and the chance to hike, bike and kayak among picture-perfect landscapes. Enjoy monuments, museums, and miles of sand dunes as you plot a course along the unforgettable shores of Old Dominion.

1 Richmond
Starting Point

Civil War history meets outdoor fun in this dynamic town. Start your visit at the American Civil War Center at Historic Tredegar, where you'll have the chance to experience the war from three perspectives — Union, Confederate and African American — as you visit the White House of the Confederacy. Learn about military strategy used by the war's generals and discover the inner thoughts of critical players in one of our country's most troubled periods. Thrill-seekers should head straight to the banks of the James River, where you can raft or kayak your way down the country's only Class IV urban whitewater. On dry land, the James River Park System and the trails of Pocahontas State Park are popular among hikers and mountain bikers.

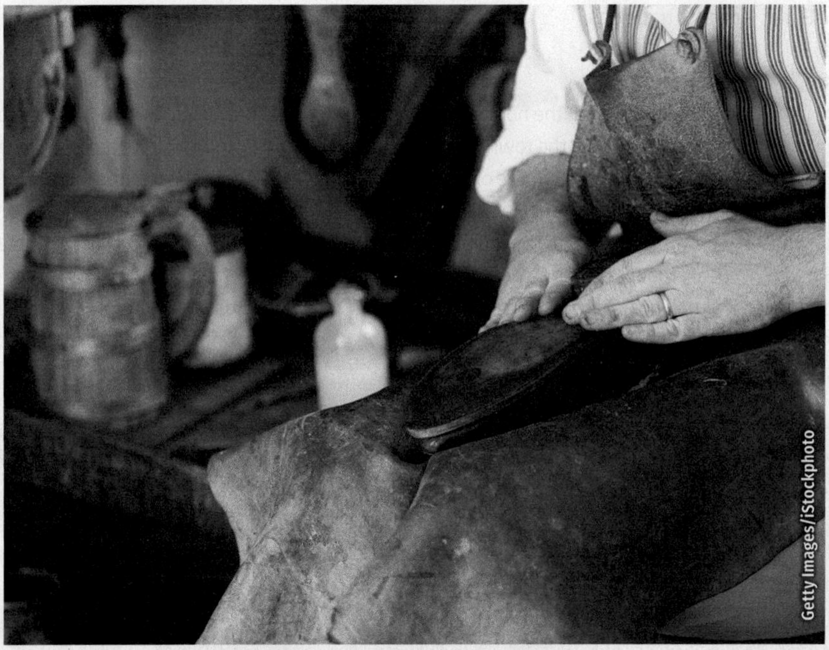
Getty Images/iStockphoto

2 Williamsburg
Drive 51 miles ▪ 52 minutes

In Colonial Williamsburg, explore 88 historic buildings, including authentic homes and reconstructed trade shops and taverns. Costumed interpreters never break character here, so you'll feel as if you've been transported back in time. Swing by Busch Gardens Williamsburg theme park for the ultimate adrenaline rush. Ride thrilling roller coasters like the winding Loch Ness Monster or the diabolical Griffin. Dine in European-themed restaurants or enjoy fun family-friendly entertainment and live performances throughout the year.

3 Chincoteague
Drive 142 miles ▪ 2 hours, 41 minutes

The island town of Chincoteague is home to one of the most unique natural wonders you'll ever see. Each July, a herd of wild ponies is shepherded across the narrow channel between Chincoteague Island and its island neighbor to the north, where the ponies graze each year. Thousands arrive to watch the annual swim, but if you can't time it right, the Chincoteague Pony Centre offers year-round rides and shows. A favorite among birders, Chincoteague National Wildlife Refuge offers stunning insights.

VA

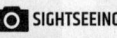

BIKING BOATING DINING ENTERTAINMENT FISHING HIKING HUNTING PADDLING SHOPPING SIGHTSEEING

Virginia SPOTLIGHTS

Bask in American Heritage and Rugged Landscapes

The Old Dominion has roots that reach back to the Colonial era — and rugged landscapes that have remained unchanged for millennia. Take a trip into an incredible past.

SHENANDOAH NATIONAL PARK HAS 500 MILES OF HIKING TRAILS.

Standing atop Little Stony Man waiting for sunset in Shenandoah National Park.

Getty Images/iStockphoto

Blue Ridge Parkway/ Shenandoah Valley

Two scenic Virginia destinations beckon travelers to the Old Dominion. Add the Blue Ridge Parkway and Shenandoah Valley to your travel itinerary on your next trip to Virginia.

Back on the Blue Ridge

Known as "America's Favorite Drive," the Blue Ridge Parkway has been the most popular destination in the National Park System nearly every year since 1946, and it's easy to see why. Free of truck traffic and tracing the Appalachian Mountain ridgeline for hundreds of miles, the scenic route is brimming with mesmerizing vistas that stretch as far as the eye can see. Photogenic historic sites and charming small towns that are home to some of America's most distinctive arts and crafts traditions.

See the Rocks

Just six miles from the northern entrance to the parkway, near the town of Waynesboro, a hike to Humpback Rocks offers the perfect introduction to the spectacular landscape. The two-mile hike to the mountain's rocky peak, though steep, is short and accessible for beginning hikers. Along the trail, you'll pass historic 1890s farmhouses that have been repurposed as open-air exhibits of life in the Virginia mountains. The hike culminates with an outcropping that provides 360-degree views of the hazy, azure skyline that gives the Blue Ridge Mountains their name.

Shenandoah Valley

Once lauded as America's first frontier, the Shenandoah Valley is home to distinctive small towns, expansive vistas and some of the country's most revered historic sites. From museums to music festivals to marathon hikes, the "Big Valley" is a four-season destination that encompasses nearly 200 miles of unmatched beauty and rural charm. There's a surprise around every corner.

River Fun

The Shenandoah River, which meanders the length of the valley floor, is a popular paddling and recreation corridor that boasts smooth water and grassy banks. Outfitters in Luray and other points along the river are on hand to help arrange kayaks, canoes, inner tubes and rafting trips along different stretches of the waterway. Anglers, too, can try their hand at the trout and bass that call the river home.

Shenandoah Vintages

The Wisteria Farm and Vineyard in Stanley uses only Virginia-grown grapes to produce whites and reds that are quickly becoming favorites of the region's wine lovers. In addition to tours and tastings, you can bring a picnic and wander the lush grounds of the scenic farm at your leisure. Barren Ridge Vineyards and Peaks of Otter Winery are also favorite vineyard visits that offer tours and tastings.

LOCAL FAVORITE

Ground Beef Casserole

Originally a French dish, casseroles first appeared in America in the 1700s on the tables of Virginia households. Sample a classic version of this meal with a hefty helping of beef. *Recipe by Cynthia Hershey.*

INGREDIENTS

- ☐ 1 lb ground beef
- ☐ 4 oz package egg noodles
- ☐ ¼ cup chopped onion
- ☐ 1 can condensed cream of celery soup
- ☐ 5 oz can evaporated milk
- ☐ ¼ lb American cheese
- ☐ Salt and pepper, to taste

DIRECTIONS

Boil the noodles and rinse in cool water. In a skillet, brown the beef and onions, drain any excess grease. To the skillet add milk, soup, salt and pepper and simmer. Mix in the noodles. Layer by pouring half the mixture into a baking dish; top with half the cheese, layer remaining beef noodle mixture; top with remaining cheese. Bake at 350 degrees for 20 minutes.

Rocky Outcrops and Waterfalls

The choices are endless when it comes to hiking in the area, with high rock outcroppings that dish out stellar views in nearly every direction. There are plenty of treks that lead to spectacular waterfalls, too. Explore a dramatic gorge on the way to White Rock Falls, capture photos from the top or base of Crabtree Falls or enjoy a refreshing shower under the Apple Orchard Falls in the summer.

The Best of Bluegrass

Did you know the Blue Ridge Parkway region has produced more bluegrass musicians per capita than any other place? You can dive into the region's rich music heritage at the Blue Ridge Music Center in Galax. Learn about the history of the music genre through films and interactive exhibits and stay for live performances by local artists. The Blue Ridge Folklife Festival also takes place on the fourth Saturday of October and has been celebrating music and folk traditions for nearly half a century.

Magnificent Mabry

No trip along Blue Ridge Parkway is complete without a visit to Mabry Mill. This structure once operated as a sawmill, gristmill and community center for the Meadows of Dan region. Today, it's a gathering place for musicians and dancers on Sunday afternoons. Walk on the trail near the mill to find historical exhibits.

Cool Carvins Cove

Set aside some time at Carvins Cove Natural Reserve. Ranked as the second-largest municipal park in the nation, this vast expanse is threaded with 60 miles of trails for biking and hiking as well as a large reservoir for fishing.

Historic Triangle

Brimming with living history museums, fascinating monuments and Colonial towns, the Historic Triangle of southeast Virginia transports you to America's pivotal historic moments. Start your journey in Jamestown to explore North America's first permanent English settlement. Following northeast along the Colonial Parkway will take you to the triangle's apex, Williamsburg, a Colonial town that roiled with revolutionary fervor in the 1770s. Go southeast along the same parkway and you'll wind up in Yorktown, the spot where American forces won a pivotal battle against the British Empire. Visitors will acquire a new appreciation of the pivotal moments in America's history.

A statue in Colonial Williamsburg honors Thomas Jefferson, author of the Declaration of Independence.

Colonial Roads Take You Home

Let southeast Virginia's Colonial Parkway take you on your trip through the past. The north tip of the Historic Triangle (Williamsburg) is only an hour's drive east from Richmond on Interstate 64. You can start your American Revolution adventure here, or carry on to the Colonial Parkway. If you're coming up from the south through Norfolk, Interstate 64 is your best bet for heading straight to Williamsburg. Veer off to the east on U.S. Route 17 if you'd rather begin in Yorktown. Plan to visit in May, June or September, when temperatures aren't too hot, because you'll be doing plenty of walking and reenacting at Colonial Williamsburg, a 300-acre living history museum. This is a great trip for kids, because it mixes fun with lots of history lessons.

Lifestyles of the Colonial

Start your Historic Triangle adventure in the place where it all began: Historic Jamestowne, located on the James River near the Atlantic. This living history museum immerses you in 17th-century Virginian life, thanks to recreated British ships, a Powhatan Native American village and more.

Powhatan Village

Begin by watching "1607: A Nation Takes Root," a film that reenacts the landing, and then visit exhibition galleries for an in-depth overview of Jamestown's beginnings. Afterward, make your way to the Powhatan Indian Village to gain insight into the indigenous way of life. Learn about Pocahontas, the Native American woman who played a pivotal role in the

VA

SPOTLIGHTS

A Powhatan village in Historic Jamestowne serves as a window into the region's indigenous past.

colony's success. Demonstrations show how the Powhatans made food, tools, cordage and more. Walk past the village, and you'll stumble upon replicas of the Susan Constant, Godspeed and Discovery, the first ships to arrive in Virginia and start the permanent English colony.

Ship Ahoy

Step aboard the moored vessels to learn how sailors piloted the ships during their journey and to see what shipboard life was like. Costumed interpreters add to the experience, and visitors will even get to try steering with a whipstaff — the predecessor to the steering wheel — or tiller. Learn about the struggles and dangers faced by the passengers on the vessel. Finish your journey at the recreated James Fort.

European Settlement

Featuring an Anglican church, court of guard, storehouse, governor's house and many thatched-roof houses, this fort takes you back in time to 1610-1614. Exhibits educate visitors about the trials endured by settlers who braved the tough conditions of the New World. During your stay, you'll get to put on armor, play games, try your hand at farming and watch interpreters make wood and leather goods. See how settlers defended themselves from attack.

Williamsburg: Window to the Past

Colonial Williamsburg is a sprawling "city" boasting an entire neighborhood of original buildings, replicas of colonial homes and reconstructed trade shops and taverns. Experience what life was like in the 1770s as you tour 88 authentic colonial buildings and 90 acres of picturesque gardens. While you're here, see where Patrick Henry gave his famous "give me liberty or give me death" speech. Walk in the footsteps of Thomas Jefferson and other revolutionaries who strove for independence.

Bringing the Past to Life

Costumed interpreters add authenticity to the streetscapes, as shopkeepers, marching soldiers, tavern patrons and farm families never break character. Here, you'll also find the DeWitt Wallace Decorative Arts Museum. Meander through its halls to see an impressive array of British and American antiques from the 17th to 19th century. Featuring everything from ceramics and furniture to firearms and art, this museum gives you an even deeper glimpse into vibrant colonial life.

Famous Faces

During your visit, you can see famous figures such as Benjamin Franklin walk the streets as the Revolutionary War gains steam. Hear fiery speakers` exhort the crowd and watch the local militia march out to face the British. Colonial Williamsburg offers evening programs that focus on witch trials and ghosts.

Dose of Adrenaline

After exploring Colonial Williamsburg, pop into the present and head to nearby Busch Gardens Theme Park for the ultimate adrenaline rush. Ride pulse-pounding roller coasters, savor phenomenal dining options and take part in fun events.

International Fare

If you're here in the spring, attend the Busch Gardens Food and Wine Festival. Not far away is Water Country USA, the largest waterpark in the mid-Atlantic. Cool off during the hot summer months on over 40 slides and water rides.

Battlefield of Yorktown

Nestled along the York River, visit the site of the 1781 Siege of Yorktown, in which forces led by General George Washington vanquished the British army. Today, it's part of the Colonial National Historic Park, with the Yorktown Victory Center and Yorktown Battlefield open to the public. Within the Yorktown Battlefield is the visitor center, which plays the 16-minute "Siege at York-town" film. Peruse the museum showcasing George Washington's field tent and other intriguing artifacts from the battle.

Under Siege

Outside, take a guided or self-guided tour to see the siege lines and visit the place where terms of surrender were accepted. Another popular attraction here is the American Revolution Museum at Yorktown. Home to dynamic exhibits, films and outdoor living history, this museum covers colonial beginnings leading up to the creation of the Constitution. Play with interactive exhibits, watch artillery demonstrations or drill with wooden muskets in the outdoor living history section.

There's Wildlife, Too

Uncover the wild side of the Historic Triangle at College Landing Park in Williamsburg. Set on the shores of College Creek, the park is threaded with trails that wind through lush marshlands and a lookout tower; watch for a variety of birds as you stroll through the landscape.

Paddle the Powhatan

Near Jamestown, you can paddle to your heart's content in Powhatan Creek Park and enjoy stunning views of Jamestown along the way. Cast a line from your boat or from one of five fishing piers to catch spotted sea trout, black sea bass, bluefish, catfish, largemouth bass and more. You can also take in the area's spellbinding landscapes at a slower pace by cycling the 23-mile Colonial Parkway. If you want to take it even slower, play 18 leisurely holes or practice your swing at the handfuls of golf courses nearby. Near Yorktown, boaters can hit the current on the York River, stretching 34 miles and feeding into Chesapeake Bay.

Indulge in Art and Shopping

The Historic Triangle is home to riveting living history museums, but there's so much more to this part of the Virginia peninsula. Gaze at the world's largest collection of Southern furniture and impressive British ceramics at Williamsburg's DeWitt Wallace Decorative Arts Museum.

Art on Tap

The town also houses one of the biggest collections of American folk art in the world. The Abby Aldrich Rockefeller Folk Art Museum showcases exquisite portraits, quilts, toys and more from the 18th, 19th and early 20th centuries. Take a break from the history lessons by shopping at Williamsburg Premium Outlets. Boasting top names like Nike, Banana Republic, Coach, Gap and J. Crew, this outlet mall offers incredible deals on quality clothes and accessories.

Fuel for the Mind and Stomach

You can feast like American revolutionaries did thanks to an overload of delicious eateries. Stop by a replica of George Washington's favorite seafood joint, Christiana Campbell's Tavern, and devour their signature crab cakes just like the former president did. Dine like 18th-century royalty at the King's Arms Tavern, Colonial Williamsburg's most elegant restaurant. Costumed waiters serve up early American cuisine such as game pie, venison, rabbit and duck braised in port-wine sauce, while serenading guests with live traditional music. Festival season kicks off in spring with everything from art displays and concerts to garden tours and wine tastings.

The Virginia Shoreline

That relaxing beach vacation you've been dreaming of isn't as far away as you think. Set where Chesapeake Bay meets the Atlantic Ocean, Coastal Virginia has all the makings of a dream holiday. Balmy beaches, two state parks, blue crab feasts, rich history and an overload of entertainment options come together to spoil adventurers, fun-seeking families and city slickers looking for an escape.

A Sunny Escape Close to Home

Located in the southeast corner of Virginia, this coastal paradise runs from Norfolk down to the North Carolina border. It's not hard to get here, as major hubs like Washington, D.C., Raleigh, Durham and Baltimore are all within 240 miles. If you're coming from the west, the best highways to take include Interstate 64, U.S. Route 460 or U.S. Route 58. Arriving from the north? Take the Chesapeake Bay Bridge-Tunnel for an unforgettable drive. This 23-mile engineering marvel connects the Virginia mainland to its eastern shore, and offers sweeping views overlooking Chesapeake Bay. The region enjoys approximately 200 days of sunshine a year and boasts a year-round average temperature of 60 degrees.

Wild Encounters

Take a walk on the wild side in Back Bay National Wildlife Refuge. Boasting 9,100 acres of woodland, marsh, dunes and beach, this complex of barrier islands supports a diverse range of animals. Stroll along its many scenic trails to see foxes, deer, bobcats, sea turtles and bald eagles.

SPOTLIGHTS

Wild horses on Assateague Island relax during sunrise. Horses from the island are herded and sold.

Bordering the refuge is Little Island Park, an excellent spot for viewing diving ducks and Atlantic bottle-nosed dolphins. Sunseekers can enjoy swimming, volleyball, tennis and canoeing in nearby Lotus Garden, too.

Wild Diversity

The Chesapeake Bay supports more than 3,600 species of plants and animals, including 348 species of finfish, 173 species of shellfish, over 2,700 plant species and more than 16 species of underwater grasses. Rockfish are a staple in the bay and there are plenty of ways to reel them in. Launch your boat from various ramps, take a private charter or drop your hook from the local fishing piers.

Broaden Your Horizons

Beachgoers aren't the only ones who will have fun here. Lined with restaurants, shops, hotels, street performers and a Ferris wheel, the 3-mile Virginia Beach Boardwalk brings fun with every step. Along the way, visit the Military Aviation Museum, Virginia Museum of Contemporary Art (MOCA), and the Virginia Aquarium & Marine Science Center. Snap a photo with the iconic King Neptune statue on 31st Street.

Find Your Beach

What many people don't know is that Virginia Beach is actually made up of three beach areas. Each offers a completely different experience. The most famous is the "resort area." Here, you'll find the city's most popular stretch of shoreline and attraction-packed boardwalk. Those who want to escape the hustle and bustle can seek peace in the quiet, shallow beaches along Chesapeake Bay. Top spots here include Cape Charles Beach, Ocean View and Huntington Park Beach.

Coastal Getaway

A popular excursion is to sign up for a tram tour from Little Island Park in Sandbridge along the West Dike Trail and through Back Bay National Wildlife Refuge before culminating at False Cape State Park in Virginia Beach's southeast corner. One of the last undisturbed coastal environments on the East Coast, this stunning mile-wide barrier split between Back Bay and the Atlantic Ocean comprises 6 miles of pristine beaches, 9 miles of hiking/biking trails and an environmental educational center.

The Chincoteague Wild Pony Swim

If you're in town during late July, it's worth making the journey to Chincoteague Island for the legendary Chincoteague Wild Pony Swim and Auction. Local firefighters gather wild ponies from Assateague Island and herd them across the channel — yes, ponies can swim — to Chincoteague Island. From there, the horses are paraded down Main Street and then auctioned off at the carnival grounds. With a population of only about 3,000, the island boasts a small-town feel. Seven miles long and three miles wide, the island packs a lot of recreation in a small space. Fishing, biking and hiking are plentiful on the island, and more adventurous souls and try hang gliding (accompanied by a professional hang-gliding pilot, of course).

Seaside Treasures

Located amid Norfolk's bustling docks, the stellar Nauticus Museum features the USS Wisconsin, a World War II-era battleship that saw action in the South Pacific. Walk the decks of this formidable vessel on a self-guided tour, or take a guided journey topside for a glimpse of maritime history. Just 1 mile north, the Chrysler Museum of Art is hailed as one of North America's most prestigious art museums. Chrysler's dazzling collection includes works by Renoir, Rubens, Picasso, Cézanne, Matisse, Warhol and Pollock, as well as a decorative-arts collection with art nouveau furnishings and glass objects spanning the 6th century B.C. to the present. Don't miss the glorious Tiffany glassworks, French art glass and English cameo.

▸ **FOR MORE INFORMATION**

Virginia Tourism Corporation Tourism, 804-545-5500, www.virginia.org

Blue Ridge Parkway Association, 828-670-1924, www.blueridgeparkway.org

Historic Triangle, www.virginia.org/getawayHistoricTriangle

Eastern Shore of Virginia Tourism, 757-331-1660 www.esvatourism.org

Virginia

ABINGDON — B2 *Washington*

WASHINGTON COUNTY PARK (Public) From Jct US-81 & VA-75 S/Cummings St: Go 8-1/2 mi S on VA-75 S, then 3/4 mi SE on County Park Rd/663/664, then 1/4 mi W on County Park Rd (R). Avail: 3 full hkups (30 amps). 2021 rates: $25. Apr 01 to Oct 15. (276)628-9677

AMELIA — D4 *Amelia*

AMELIA FAMILY CAMPGROUND **Ratings: 7/UI/7.5** (Campground) 80 Avail: 50 full hkups, 20 W, 20 E (30/50 amps). 2021 rates: $40 to $45. (804)561-3011, 9720 Military Rd, Amelia, VA 23002

AMHERST — D3 *Amherst*

BLUE RIDGE PKWY/OTTER CREEK (Public National Park) From Jct of US-501 & Blue Ridge Pkwy, N 3 mi on Blue Ridge Pkwy (R). 24 Avail. 2021 rates: $20. May 01 to Nov 30. (828)271-4779

APPOMATTOX — D3 *Appomattox*

APPOMATTOX See also Monroe, Rustburg & Spout Spring.

HOLLIDAY LAKE (Public State Park) From town: Go 9 mi E on Hwy-24, then 6 mi SE on Hwy-626 & 692. 29 Avail: 29 W, 29 E (30/50 amps). 2021 rates: $35 to $40. (434)248-6308

PARKVIEW RV PARK
Ratings: 6/NA/7 (RV Park) Take 2nd Appomattox exit on US 460-Bypass (from either direction) then at Jct of US 460 & Hwy 24, N 1 block on Hwy 24E, E 1 block on Clover Lane (R). **FAC:** paved rds. Avail: 33 paved, 30 pull-thrus, (30x70), back-ins (30x60), accepts full hkup units only, 33 full hkups (30/50 amps), WiFi @ sites, . **REC:** hunting nearby. Pet restrict (B). No tents. Big rig sites. 2021 rates: $52. no cc.
(434)665-8418 Lat: 37.36987, Lon: -78.82317
174-A Clover Lane, Appomattox, VA 24522
See ad this page

ASHLAND — D4 *Hanover*

AMERICAMPS RV RESORT
Ratings: 9.5/10★/9 (Campground) From Jct of I-95 & I-295, N 4 mi on I-95 to Jct of exit 89 (Lewistown Rd/Rte 802) & Rte 802, E 0.1 mi on Rte 802 to Air Park Rd, S 0.75 mi (L).

IDEAL HISTORIC RICHMOND LOCATION
Easy I-95 access: VA #89. Huge, FHU 50-amp level pull-thru sites. Propane. Updated bathhouses & fitness center. Free WiFi & Cable, free waffle breakfast. New rally room, kitchen and coffee bar. Hospitality Galore!

FAC: paved rds. (200 spaces). 150 Avail: 9 paved, 141 gravel, 118 pull-thrus, (30x68), back-ins (30x60), 150 full hkups (30/50 amps), seasonal sites, cable, WiFi @ sites, dump, laundry, groc, LP gas, fire rings, firewood, controlled access. **REC:** pool, wading pool, playground, hunting nearby. Pets OK. Partial handicap access. No tents. Big rig sites, 14 day max stay, eco-friendly. 2021 rates: $47 to $95.17, Military discount.
(804)798-5298 Lat: 37.70995, Lon: -77.44720
11322 Air Park Rd, Ashland, VA 23005
americamps.com
See ad page 960

Travel Services

AIRSTREAM OF VIRGINIA Selling new and pre-owned Airstreams. Also offer Airstream service and parts. **SERVICES:** RV, RV appliance, MH mechanical, sells outdoor gear, staffed RV wash, restrooms. RV Sales. RV supplies, LP gas, RV accessible. Hours: 9am - 6pm.
(855)570-4398 Lat: 37.733651, Lon: -77.451817
10300 NorthLake Park Dr, Ashland, VA 23005
www.airstreamofva.com

MCGEORGE'S RV - A CAMPING WORLD COMPANY Professional RV outfitters,with an extensive parts & accessories store. RV brands include Keystone, Heartland, and Forest River. **SERVICES:** RV, tire, RV appliance, MH mechanical, sells outdoor gear, staffed RV wash, restrooms. RV Sales. RV supplies, LP gas, dump, RV accessible. Hours: 8am to 6pm.
(888)461-5687 Lat: 37.72465, Lon: -77.45166
11525 Sunshade Ln., Ashland, VA 23005
www.mcgeorgerv.com

BASSETT — E2 *Patrick*

CAHILL'S LILY PAD CAMPGROUND
Ratings: 8/10★/8.5 (Campground) Avail: 117 full hkups (30/50 amps). 2021 rates: $50 to $70. (276)647-4005, 319 TB Stanley Hwy, Bassett, VA 24055

PHILPOTT LAKE - COE/GOOSE POINT (Public Corps) From town, W 8 mi on Hwy 57 to Rte 822, N 4 mi (E). 63 Avail: 53 W, 53 E (50 amps). 2021 rates: $20 to $25. Apr 01 to Oct 30. (276)629-1847

BEDFORD — D3 *Bedford*

BLUE RIDGE PKWY/PEAKS OF OTTER (Public National Park) From town, on Blue Ridge Pkwy at MP-86 (L). Elev 2565 ft.**FAC:** paved rds. Avail: 24 gravel, tent sites, restrooms only, dump, fire rings, restaurant. **REC:** Abbott Lake: fishing. Pets OK. Partial handicap access, 21 day max stay. 2021 rates: $20. May 15 to Oct 24.
(540)586-7321 Lat: 37.44315, Lon: -79.609471
10454 Peaks Rd, Bedford, VA 24523
www.blueridgeparkway.org

BLACKSBURG — D2 *Montgomery*

NEW RIVER JUNCTION CAMPGROUND **Ratings: 5.5/5.5/5.5** (Campground) 16 Avail: 16 W, 16 E (30 amps). 2021 rates: $45. May 01 to Sep 30. (540)639-6633, 2591 Big Falls Rd, Blacksburg, VA 24060

BOWLING GREEN — C5 *Caroline*

BOWLING GREEN See also Ashland, Colonial Beach, Doswell, Fredericksburg & Milford.

MILITARY PARK CHAMPS CAMP RV PARK (FORT AP HILL) (Public) S-bnd: From jct I-95 & US-17 (Bowling Green/Ft AP Hill exit), E 6 mi on US-17 to VA-2, S 14 mi to US-301, NE 2 mi; or N-bnd: From jct I-95 & VA-207, N 12 mi on VA-27 to Bowling Green, N 2 mi. Avail: 30 full hkups (30/50 amps). 2021 rates: $30 to $35. (804)633-8244

BOYDTON — E4 *Mecklenburg*

JOHN H. KERR DAM & RESERVOIR - COE/BUFFALO (Public Corps) From town, W 6 mi on US-58 to SR-732, N 5 mi (E). 11 Avail: 11 W, 11 E (50 amps). 2021 rates: $26 to $52. May 01 to Sep 30. (434)374-2063

JOHN H. KERR DAM & RESERVOIR - COE/NORTH BEND (Public Corps) From Jct of US-58 & Rte 4, S 6 mi on Rte 4/Buggs Allen Rd to CR-678, W 1 mi (L). 210 Avail: 137 W, 137 E (30/50 amps). 2021 rates: $20 to $52. Apr 01 to Oct 31. (434)738-0059

JOHN H. KERR DAM & RESERVOIR - COE/RUDDS CREEK (Public Corps) From town, W 3 mi on Hwy 58 (L). 70 Avail: 69 W, 70 E (50 amps), Pit toilets. 2021 rates: $26 to $52. Apr 01 to Oct 31. (434)738-6827

BRACEY — E4 *Mecklenburg*

LAKE GASTON AMERICAMPS
Ratings: 8.5/10★/9.5 (Campground) From Jct of I-85 & Rte 903 (exit 4), E 5.4 mi on Rte 903 (R).

LOCATED ON BEAUTIFUL LAKE GASTON
A great place to bring the whole family, lots of planned activities & fun things to do! Bring your boat & fishing gear to enjoy Lake Gaston, a 35-mile stocked lake. We have group facilities and an adult activity center.

FAC: paved/gravel rds. (475 spaces). 124 Avail: 11 paved, 93 gravel, 20 dirt, 8 pull-thrus, (25x55), back-ins (25x40), 10 full hkups, 114 W, 114 E (30/50 amps), seasonal sites, WiFi @ sites, tent sites, rentals, dump, mobile sewer, laundry, groc, LP gas, fire rings, firewood, controlled access. **REC:** pool, wading pool, Lake Gaston: swim, fishing, boating nearby, playground, hunting nearby. Pets OK. eco-friendly. 2021 rates: $49 to $66, Military discount.
(434)636-2668 Lat: 36.56216, Lon: -78.07183
9 Lakeside Lane, Bracey, VA 23919
www.lakegastonamericamps.com
See ad page 946

Find it fast! To locate a town on a map, follow these easy instructions: Look for the map grid code after the town heading in the listing section and match it to the letters and numbers on the map borders. Draw a line horizontally from the letter and vertically from the number. You'll find the town near the intersection of the two lines.

BREAKS — A2 *Dickenson*

BREAKS INTERSTATE PARK (Public) From Jct of SR-768 & SR-80, W 0.5 mi on SR-80 (R). 138 Avail: (30/50 amps). 2021 rates: $19 to $28. Mar 30 to Nov 10. (276)865-4413

BRISTOL — B2 *Washington*

SUGAR HOLLOW PARK AND CAMPGROUND (Public) From I-81 (exit 7): Go 1 mi N on US 11 (Robert E. Lee Hwy) (L). 50 Avail: 50 W, 50 E (30/50 amps). 2021 rates: $20 to $27. Apr 15 to Oct 31. (276)645-7275

BROADWAY — B3 *Rockingham*

HARRISONBURG/SHENANDOAH VALLEY KOA **Ratings: 8.5/9.5★/9** (Campground) 62 Avail: 41 full hkups, 21 W, 21 E (30/50 amps). 2021 rates: $55 to $140. (540)896-8929, 12480 Mountain Valley Road, Broadway, VA 22815

BUCHANAN — D2 *Botetourt*

MIDDLE CREEK CAMPGROUND **Ratings: 6.5/7/5.5** (Campground) 60 Avail: 15 full hkups, 45 W, 45 E (30/50 amps). 2021 rates: $40 to $45. (540)254-2550, 1164 Middle Creek Road, Buchanan, VA 24066

BUENA VISTA — D3 *Rockbridge*

GLEN MAURY PARK (Public) From Jct of I-81 & US-60 (Buena Vista exit 188A), E 3.5 mi on US-60 to US-501S, S 2 mi to 10th St, W 0.25 mi, follow signs (R). 52 Avail: 22 full hkups, 30 W, 30 E (20/30 amps). 2021 rates: $27 to $30. (540)261-7321

CAPE CHARLES — D6 *Northampton*

CAPE CHARLES/CHESAPEAKE BAY KOA & SUNSET BEACH HOTEL Ratings: 9.5/10★/10 (RV Park) Avail: 177 full hkups (30/50 amps). 2021 rates: $65 to $329. Apr 01 to Nov 15. (757)331-1776, 32246 Lankford Highway, Cape Charles, VA 23310

Find 'em fast. Our advertisers often include extra information or provide a detailed map in their ads to help you find their facilities quickly and easily.

Virginia Privately Owned Campground Information Updated by our Good Sam Representatives

Grady Dagnan & Liz Chambers

We are "The Grady Bunch" from Tennessee, circa 1993. Four kids and five grands later, and we still love camping. After long careers in marketing/advertising and nursing, we partnered with Good Sam. We love helping RV parks and campgrounds.

CAPE CHARLES (CONT)

CHERRYSTONE FAMILY CAMPING RESORT
Ratings: 8.5/10★/9.5 (RV Resort) From Jct of Chesapeake Bay Bridge Tunnel (N end) & US-13, N 11.1 mi on US-13 to SR-680, W 1.5 mi (E).

WE'VE GOT IT ALL AND THEN SOME!
Best family camping resort in the Mid-Atlantic region! Over 300 acres of natural beauty on the Chesapeake shore. Planned activities, boat rentals, five pools, cafe/lounge. No RV, no problem. Deluxe cabin rentals to RV rentals

FAC: paved/gravel rds. (459 spaces). 439 Avail: 72 paved, 237 gravel, 130 grass, 115 pull-thrus, (30x70), back-ins (30x60), 248 full hkups, 191 W, 191 E (30/50 amps), seasonal sites, WiFi @ sites, $, tent sites, rentals, dump, mobile sewer, laundry, groc, LP gas, firewood, restaurant, controlled access. **REC:** pool, wading pool, Chesapeake Bay: swim, fishing, kayaking/canoeing, boating nearby, playground, hunting nearby, rec open to public. Pet restrict (B/Q). Partial handicap access. Big rig sites, eco-friendly. 2021 rates: $60 to $295, Military discount. ATM.
(757)331-3063 Lat: 37.28557, Lon: -76.01077
1511 Townfield Dr, Cape Charles, VA 23310
www.cherrystone.com
See ad page 953

KIPTOPEKE (Public State Park) From Jct of US-13 & N end of The Chesapeake Bay Bridge Tunnel, N 3 mi on US-13 to Rte 704, W 0.5 mi (E). Avail: 86 full hkups (30/50 amps). 2021 rates: $28 to $47. (757)331-2267

CENTREVILLE — B4 *Fairfax*

BULL RUN REGIONAL PARK (Public) From Jct of Rtes 28 & 29, S 3 mi on Rte 29 to Bull Run Post Office Rd, S 1.1 mi to Bull Run Dr, S 2 mi (R). Entrance fee required. 97 Avail: 32 full hkups, 29 W, 57 E (30/50 amps). 2021 rates: $36 to $55. (703)631-0550

CHARLOTTESVILLE — C3 *Albemarle*

CHARLOTTESVILLE KOA **Ratings: 9/9.5★/8** (Campground) 43 Avail: 40 full hkups, 3 W, 3 E (30/50 amps). 2021 rates: $46 to $145. Mar 13 to Nov 08. (434)296-9881, 3825 Red Hill Rd, Charlottesville, VA 22903

The best things happen outdoors. Start your adventure today at GanderOutdoors.com

CHESAPEAKE — E6 *Chesapeake City*

CHESAPEAKE CAMPGROUND
Ratings: 9/9/8 (Campground) 59 Avail: 13 full hkups, 46 W, 46 E (30/50 amps). 2021 rates: $36 to $43. (757)485-0149, 693 S George Washington Hwy, Chesapeake, VA 23323

MILITARY PARK STEWART CAMPGROUNDS (NSA NORFOLK NORTHWEST ANNEX) (Public) From jct I-64 & VA-168, S 16 mi on VA-168 to Ballahock Rd, W 3 mi to Relay Rd, S through gate to Milepost Rd, right to Wilderness Rd, follow signs. Avail: 14 full hkups (30/50 amps). 2021 rates: $18. (757)421-8104

NORTHWEST RIVER PARK & CAMPGROUND (Public) From Jct Rt 168 & Hillcrest Pkwy E (Exit 86), S .25 mi to Battlefield Blvd, S on Battlefield Blvd to Indian Cree Rd, S .4 mi on Indian Creek Rd (R). 66 Avail: 66 W, 66 E (30/50 amps). 2021 rates: $21 to $26. Apr 01 to Nov 30. (757)382-6411

CHESTERFIELD — D4 *Chesterfield*

POCAHONTAS (Public State Park) From Jct of I-95 & Hwy 10, W 7 mi on Hwy 10 to Beach Rd, S 4 mi (R). 113 Avail: 113 W, 113 E (30/50 amps). 2021 rates: $30. (804)796-4255

CHINCOTEAGUE ISLAND — C6 *Accomack*

CHINCOTEAGUE ISLAND KOA Ratings: 9/10★/9.5 (Campground) Avail: 124 full hkups (30/50 amps). 2021 rates: $65 to $211. Apr 01 to Nov 30. (757)336-3111, 6742 Maddox Blvd., Chincoteague Island, VA 23336

PINE GROVE CAMPGROUND & WATERFOWL PARK **Ratings: 6/8★/7** (Campground) 100 Avail: 60 full hkups, 40 W, 40 E (30/50 amps). 2021 rates: $40 to $49. Apr 01 to Dec 01. (757)336-5200, 5283 Deep Hole Rd, Chincoteague Island, VA 23336

TOM'S COVE PARK Ratings: 8.5/8.5★/8.5 (Campground) 520 Avail: 240 full hkups, 280 W, 280 E (30/50 amps). 2021 rates: $56.15 to $67.63. Mar 01 to Nov 30. (757)336-6498, 8128 Beebe Rd, Chincoteague Island, VA 23336

CHRISTIANSBURG — D2 *Montgomery*

BLUE RIDGE PKWY/ROCKY KNOB (Public National Park) From town, on Blue Ridge Parkway at MP-167 (R). 28 Avail. 2021 rates: $20. May 24 to Nov 02. (540)745-9664

CLARKSVILLE — E3 *Mecklenburg*

IVY HILL CAMPGROUND DAY USE AREA (Public Corps) From town, S 10 mi on US-15 to NC-1501, E 7 mi to VA-825, N 3 mi (E). 25 Avail: Pit toilets. 2021 rates: $10 to $12. Apr 01 to Oct 30. (434)738-6143

JOHN H. KERR DAM & RESERVOIR - COE/LONGWOOD (Public Corps) From town, S 4 mi on US-15 (R). 65 Avail: 33 W, 33 E (50 amps). 2021 rates: $20 to $52. Apr 01 to Oct 31. (434)374-2711

OCCONEECHEE (Public State Park) From town: Go 1 mi E on US-58. 48 Avail: 39 W, 39 E Pit toilets. 2021 rates: $24 to $35. (804)374-2210

CLIFTON FORGE — C2 *Alleghany*

DOUTHAT (Public State Park) From Jct of I-64 & SR-629 (exit 27), N 5 mi on SR-629 (R). 87 Avail: 23 full hkups, 45 W, 45 E (30 amps). 2021 rates: $30 to $40. May 01 to Sep 30. (540)862-8100

CLINCHPORT — B2 *Scott*

NATURAL TUNNEL (Public State Park) From Jct of US-23 & SR-871, E 1 mi on SR-871 (R). 34 Avail: 34 W, 34 E (20/50 amps). 2021 rates: $35 to $40. (276)940-2674

CLINTWOOD — A2 *Dickenson*

JOHN W FLANNAGAN RESERVOIR - COE/CRANESNEST (Public Corps) From town: Go 2 mi E on Hwy 83, then 3 mi W on FR. 37 Avail. 2021 rates: $16. (276)835-9544

COLLIERSTOWN — D2 *Rockbridge*

LAKE A WILLIS ROBERTSON REC AREA (ROCKBRIDGE COUNTY PARK) (Public) From Jct of I-81 & US 60 (Exit 51), NW 2 mi on US 60 to US 11, SW 1 mi to SR-251, W 11 mi to SR-770, W 1.4 mi (R). 53 Avail: 53 W, 53 E (30 amps). 2021 rates: $30. Apr 01 to Oct 30. (540)463-4164

Reducing your speed to 55 mph from 65 mph may increase your fuel efficiency by as much as 15 percent; cut it to 55 from 70, and you could get a 23 percent improvement.

COLONIAL BEACH — C5 *Westmoreland*

HARBOR VIEW RV PARK
Ratings: 7.5/8/9.5 (Membership Park) Avail: 100 full hkups (30/50 amps). 2021 rates: $52. Apr 01 to Dec 01. (888)563-7040, 15 Harbor View Circle, Colonial Beach, VA 22443

MONROE BAY CAMPGROUND
Ratings: 6.5/8.5★/7.5 (Campground) From Jct of Hwy 3 & Hwy 205: N 4 mi on Hwy 205 to Hwy 628 (Monroe Bay Circle), E 2 mi on Hwy 628 (Monroe Bay Circle) (E). **FAC:** paved/gravel rds. (310 spaces). Avail: 60 gravel, 30 pull-thrus, (25x50), back-ins (25x50), 12 full hkups, 48 W, 48 E (30/50 amps), seasonal sites, WiFi, tent sites, dump, LP gas, firewood, restaurant. **REC:** Monroe Bay: swim, fishing, kayaking/canoeing, boating nearby, playground. Pets OK. 2021 rates: $40 to $50, Military discount. Apr 01 to Nov 01. ATM.
(804)224-7418 Lat: 38.23932, Lon: -76.96856
1412 Monroe Bay Circle, Colonial Beach, VA 22443
monroebaymarina.com
See ad this page

CUMBERLAND — D4 *Cumberland*

BEAR CREEK LAKE (Public State Park) From town: Go 1/2 mi E on US-60, then 4-1/2 mi W on Hwy-622 & 629. 37 Avail: 37 W, 37 E (20/30 amps). 2021 rates: $25 to $35. Mar 01 to Dec 07. (804)492-4410

DAMASCUS — B2 *Washington*

LAUREL CREEK RV PARK **Ratings: 3.5/NA/7.5** (Campground) Avail: 16 full hkups (30/50 amps). 2021 rates: $35. (423)440-3042, 812 Orchard Hill Rd, Damascus, VA 24236

DELTAVILLE — D6 *Middlesex*

BUSH PARK CAMPING RESORT **Ratings: 8.5/8/8** (RV Park) Avail: 35 full hkups (30/50 amps). 2021 rates: $65 to $75. Apr 01 to Nov 15. (804)776-6750, 724 Bushy Park Rd, Wake, VA 23176

CROSS RIP CAMPGROUND AND RESORT **Ratings: 5/8★/7** (Campground) 32 Avail: 32 W, 32 E (30/50 amps). 2021 rates: $40 to $50. May 01 to Nov 15. (619)987-1582, 503 Cross Rip Road, Deltaville, VA 23043

DOSWELL — C4 *Hanover*

KINGS DOMINION CAMP WILDERNESS KOA **Ratings: 8.5/9.5★/9** (Campground) 232 Avail: 90 full hkups, 142 W, 142 E (30/50 amps). 2021 rates: $39 to $86. (804)876-3006, 10061 Kings Dominion Blvd, Doswell, VA 23047

DUBLIN — D1 *Pulaski*

CLAYTOR LAKE (Public State Park) From Jct of I-81 & SR-660 (exit 101), S 2 mi on SR-660/State Park Rd (E). 103 Avail: 39 W, 39 E (20/30 amps). 2021 rates: $25 to $40. (540)643-2500

DUMFRIES — B5 *Prince William*

PRINCE WILLIAM FOREST RV CAMPGROUND
Ratings: 9/10★/9 (RV Park) From Jct of I-95 & SR-234 (exit 152B/Manassas), NW 2.5 mi on SR-234 (L). **FAC:** paved rds. Avail: 71 paved, 54 pull-thrus, (24x45), back-ins (24x75), 36 full hkups, 35 W, 35 E (30/50 amps), WiFi @ sites, tent sites, dump, laundry, LP gas, fire rings, firewood. **REC:** pool, boating nearby, playground, hunting nearby. Pet restrict (B). Partial handicap access, eco-friendly. 2021 rates: $38 to $65, Military discount.
(888)737-5730 Lat: 38.60398, Lon: -77.35073
16058 Dumfries Rd, Dumfries, VA 22025
www.princewilliamforestrvcampground.com
See ad page 205

EDINBURG — B3 *Shenandoah*

CREEKSIDE CAMPGROUND **Ratings: 6/9/7.5** (Campground) Avail: 25 full hkups (30/50 amps). 2021 rates: $37 to $50. (540)984-4299, 108 Palmyra Rd, Edinburg, VA 22824

ELKTON — C3 *Madison*

SHENANDOAH/BIG MEADOWS (Public National Park) From town, E 9 mi on Rte 211 to Skyline Dr, S 19 mi (MP-51), follow signs (R). Entrance fee required. 168 Avail. 2021 rates: $17 to $20. Apr 26 to Nov 30. (540)999-3500

Park policies vary. Ask about the cancellation policy when making a reservation.

SHENANDOAH/LEWIS MOUNTAIN (Public National Park) From town, E 7 mi on Rte 33 to Skyline Dr, N 7 mi, follow signs to MP-57 (R). Entrance fee required. 31 Avail. 2021 rates: $15. May 01 to Dec 31. (540)999-3500

SHENANDOAH/LOFT MOUNTAIN (Public National Park) From town, E 5 mi on Rte 250 to Skyline Dr, N 25 mi, follow signs (R). Entrance fee required. 155 Avail. 2021 rates: $15. May 13 to Oct 30. (540)999-3500

EMPORIA — E4 *Greensville*

YOGI BEAR'S JELLYSTONE PARK CAMP-RESORT EMPORIA **Ratings: 9/9★/9** (Campground) 50 Avail: 44 full hkups, 6 W, 6 E (30/50 amps). 2021 rates: $42 to $56. (434)634-3115, 2940 Sussex Dr, Emporia, VA 23847

EWING — B1 *Lee*

CUMBERLAND GAP NATL HIST PARK/WILDERNESS ROAD (Public National Park) From Jct of US-25E & US-58, E 1.5 mi on US-58 (L). Avail: 41 E (30/50 amps). 2021 rates: $14 to $20. (606)248-2817

FAIRFAX — B5 *Fairfax*

BURKE LAKE PARK (FAIRFAX COUNTY PARK) (Public) From Jct of I-495 & exit 54, W 1.8 mi Braddock Rd. to Burke Lake Rd, S 4.5 mi, (L). 100 Avail. 2021 rates: $28 to $31. Apr 18 to Oct 26. (703)323-6600

LAKE FAIRFAX PARK (Public) From Jct of I-495 & Rte 7 (Exit 47A), W 6.5 mi on Rte 7 to Rte 606, S 0.1 mi to Lake Fairfax Dr, turn left (E). Avail: 57 E (20/50 amps). 2021 rates: $40 to $50. Mar 22 to Sep 07. (703)471-5415

FANCY GAP — E1 *Carroll*

FANCY GAP / BLUE RIDGE PARKWAY KOA **Ratings: 9/9.5★/9.5** (Campground) Avail: 65 full hkups (30/50 amps). 2021 rates: $40 to $65. Mar 01 to Nov 15. (800)562-1876, 47 Fox Trail Loop, Fancy Gap, VA 24328

UTT'S CAMPGROUND **Ratings: 7/8★/8** (Campground) Avail: 38 full hkups (30/50 amps). 2021 rates: $32. May 01 to Nov 01. (276)728-7203, 574 Campground Road, Fancy Gap, VA 24328

FERRUM — E2 *Franklin*

DEER RUN CAMPGROUND **Ratings: 7/8★/6.5** (Campground) 65 Avail: 14 full hkups, 51 W, 51 E (30 amps). 2021 rates: $35 to $45. May 23 to Nov 01. (276)930-1235, 28 Fawn Road, Ferrum, VA 24088

PHILPOTT LAKE - COE/HORSESHOE POINT (Public Corps) From town, SE 7 mi on Rte 767 to Henry Rd, NW 3 mi to Horse Point Rd, W 4 mi (E). 49 Avail: 15 W, 15 E (50 amps). 2021 rates: $20 to $25. May 01 to Sep 29. (276)629-2703

PHILPOTT LAKE - COE/SALTHOUSE BRANCH (Public Corps) From town, W 2.5 mi on Henry Rd to Knob Church Rd/Salthouse Branch Rd, SW 2 mi (E). 58 Avail: 44 W, 44 E (50 amps). 2021 rates: $20 to $25. Mar 22 to Oct 31. (540)365-7005

FREDERICKSBURG — C4 *Spotsylvania*

FREDERICKSBURG See also Dumfries, Milford, Spotsylvania & Stafford.

FREDERICKSBURG/WASHINGTON DC SOUTH KOA **Ratings: 9/10★/8.5** (Campground) 85 Avail: 77 full hkups, 8 W, 8 E (30/50 amps). 2021 rates: $65.10 to $89.54. (800)562-1889, 7400 Brookside Lane, Fredericksburg, VA 22408

Travel Services

GANDER RV OF FREDERICKSBURG Your new hometown outfitter offering the best regional gear for all your outdoor needs. Your adventure awaits. **SERVICES:** gunsmithing svc, archery svc, sells outdoor gear, sells fishing gear, sells firearms. RV Sales. RV supplies. Hours: 9am to 8pm.
(844)913-7505 Lat: 38.291436, Lon: -77.524529
3708 Plank Road, Fredericksburg, VA 22407
www.ganderoutdoors.com

FRIES — E1 *Grayson*

FRIES NEW RIVER TRAIL RV PARK **Ratings: 6.5/8.5★/9** (RV Park) Avail: 14 full hkups (30/50 amps). 2021 rates: $45. (276)744-7566, 26 Dalton Rd, Fries, VA 24330

FRONT ROYAL — B4 *Warren*

NORTH FORK RESORT
Ratings: 9/8.5★/8.5 (Membership Park) 470 Avail: 440 full hkups, 30 W, 30 E (30/50 amps). 2021 rates: $55. (540)636-2995, 301 North Fork Rd, Front Royal, VA 22630

SKYLINE RANCH RESORT **Ratings: 8.5/8★/9** (Membership Park) Avail: 120 full hkups (30/50 amps). 2021 rates: $60 to $70. (540)635-4169, 751 Mountain Rd, Front Royal, VA 22630

GALAX — E1 *Grayson*

COOL BREEZE CAMPGROUND **Ratings: 7.5/9★/8** (Campground) Avail: 51 full hkups (30/50 amps). 2021 rates: $36 to $45. Apr 01 to Nov 01. (276)236-0300, 2330 Edmonds Road, Galax, VA 24333

OLD CRANKS CAMPGROUND & RV PARK **Ratings: 3/7.5/6** (Campground) Avail: 15 full hkups (30/50 amps). 2021 rates: $33. (276)236-5114, 407 Railroad Avenue, Galax, VA 24333

GLEN LYN — D1 *Giles*

KAIROS WILDERNESS RESORT **Ratings: 7/9.5★/9** (Campground) Avail: 42 full hkups (30/50 amps). 2021 rates: $45. (540)235-2777, 1 Shumate Falls Rd, Glen Lyn, VA 24093

GLOUCESTER — D5 *Gloucester*

CHESAPEAKE BAY RV RESORT
Ratings: 7.5/9.5★/9 (RV Resort) Avail: 195 full hkups (30/50 amps). 2021 rates: $63 to $85. (888)563-7040, 12014 Trails Ln, Gloucester, VA 23061

GLOUCESTER POINT — D5 *Gloucester*

GLOUCESTER POINT See also Deltaville, Gloucester, Gwynn, Hampton, New Point, Newport News, Toano, Topping & Williamsburg.

GLOUCESTER POINT FAMILY CAMPGROUND **Ratings: 9/9/9** (Campground) Avail: 116 full hkups (30/50 amps). 2021 rates: $47 to $106. (804)642-4316, 3149 Campground Rd, Hayes, VA 23072

GORDONSVILLE — C4 *Orange*

SHENANDOAH CROSSING, A BLUEGREEN RESORT **Ratings: 8.5/9★/9.5** (Membership Park) Avail: 111 full hkups (30/50 amps). 2021 rates: $50 to $100. (540)832-9400, 174 Horseshoe Cir, Gordonsville, VA 22942

GREEN BAY — D4 *Prince Edward*

TWIN LAKES (Public State Park) From town, SW 4 mi on US-360 to SR-613, N 2 mi to SR-629, E 1 mi (E). 22 Avail: 22 W, 22 E (20/30 amps). 2021 rates: $35 to $40. Mar 27 to Dec 07. (434)392-3435

GREENVILLE — C3 *Augusta*

STONEY CREEK RESORT CAMPGROUND **Ratings: 7.5/7/6** (Membership Park) 138 Avail: 80 full hkups, 58 W, 58 E (30/50 amps). 2021 rates: $50 to $65. (540)337-1510, 277 Lake Dr, Greenville, VA 24440

GREENWOOD — C3 *Albemarle*

MISTY MOUNTAIN CAMP RESORT
Ratings: 8.5/9.5★/10 (Campground) From Jct of I-64 (exit 107/Crozet) & US-250 (13 mi W of Charlottesville), W 0.7 mi on US-250 (L).

SCENIC 50 ACRE DESTINATION RESORT
Relax at the foot of the Blue Ridge Mtns near historic Charlottesville, Virginia. Explore AT, wine and beer trails, historical landmarks. Gather at our bonfire for s'mores or music amphitheater. Big Rig friendly. Cabins.

FAC: paved/gravel rds. (93 spaces). Avail: 92 gravel, patios, 45 pull-thrus, (30x100), back-ins (30x60), 57 full hkups, 35 W, 35 E (30/50 amps), seasonal sites, cable, WiFi @ sites, tent sites, rentals, dump, laundry, groc, LP gas, fire rings, firewood. **REC:** pool, pond, fishing, boating nearby, playground, hunting nearby, rec open to public. Pet restrict (Q). Partial handicap access. Big rig sites, eco-friendly. 2021 rates: $40 to $65, Military discount.
(888)647-8900 Lat: 38.03953, Lon: -78.73961
56 Misty Mountain Rd, Greenwood, VA 22943
www.mistymountaincampresort.com
See ad opposite page

GRETNA — E3 *Pittsylvania*

LEESVILLE LAKE CAMPGROUND **Ratings: 8/9.5★/9.5** (Campground) Avail: 24 full hkups (30/50 amps). 2021 rates: $50 to $60. (434)818-1177, 3129 Gallows Road, Gretna, VA 24557

GRUNDY — A2 *Buchanan*

SOUTHERN GAP OUTDOOR ADVENTURE RV PARK **Ratings: 7.5/9★/8** (RV Park) Avail: 19 full hkups (30/50 amps). 2021 rates: $45 to $50. (276)244-1111, 1124 Chipping Sparrow Rd, Grundy, VA 24614

GWYNN — D6 *Mathews*

GWYNN'S ISLAND RV RESORT & CAMPGROUND **Ratings: 7/9.5★/8.5** (RV Park) 30 Avail: 7 full hkups, 23 W, 23 E (30/50 amps). 2021 rates: $48 to $152. Apr 01 to Oct 31. (888)639-3805, 551 Buckchase Rd., Gwynn, VA 23066

HAMPTON — D5 *Hampton*

THE COLONIES RV & TRAVEL PARK AT FORT MONROE **Ratings: 6.5/8.5★/8** (Campground) 23 Avail: 13 full hkups, 10 W, 10 E (30/50 amps). 2021 rates: $58 to $63. (757)722-2200, 501 Fenwick Rd, Hampton, VA 23651

HAYMARKET — B4 *Prince William*

GREENVILLE FARM FAMILY CAMPGROUND
Ratings: 7/8/7.5 (Campground) From Jct of I-66 & US-15 (Exit 40), N 4 mi on US-15 to Rte 234 (Sudley Rd), SE 0.1 mi on Sudley Rd to Rte 601 (Shelter Lane), NE 1.3 mi on Shelter Lane (L). **FAC:** paved/gravel rds. Avail: 125 gravel, 67 pull-thrus, (25x70), back-ins (20x50), 30 full hkups, 95 W, 95 E (30/50 amps), tent sites, dump, laundry, LP gas, fire rings, firewood. **REC:** pool, wading pool, pond, fishing, playground. Pets OK. Partial handicap access. Big rig sites, 14 day max stay, eco-friendly. 2021 rates: $45 to $55, Military discount.
(703)754-7944 Lat: 38.87638, Lon: -77.61081
14004 Shelter Lane, Haymarket, VA 20169
www.greenvillecampground.com
See ad page 205

HAYSI — A2 *Dickenson*

JOHN W FLANNAGAN RESERVOIR - COE/LOWER TWIN CAMPGROUND (Public Corps) From town: Go 3 mi SW on Hwy-63, then 1/2 mi S on Hwy-614, then 2 mi NW on Hwy-739, then W on Hwy-611. Avail: 15 E. 2021 rates: $14 to $16. May 11 to Oct 17. (270)835-9544

HILLSVILLE — E1 *Carroll*

LAKE RIDGE RV RESORT **Ratings: 8.5/9.5★/8.5** (Campground) 138 Avail: 101 full hkups, 37 W, 37 E (30/50 amps). 2021 rates: $34 to $57. (276)766-3703, 8736 Double Cabin Road, Hillsville, VA 24343

HUDDLESTON — D3 *Bedford*

SMITH MOUNTAIN LAKE (Public State Park) From jct Hwy 43 & Hwy 626: Go 14 mi SW on Hwy 626. 24 Avail: 24 W, 24 E. 2021 rates: $24 to $35. (540)297-6066

KEELING — E3 *Pittsylvania*

PARADISE LAKE AND CAMPGROUND
Ratings: 8.5/9★/8 (Campground) Avail: 30 full hkups (30/50 amps). 2021 rates: $39.49 to $41.59. (434)836-2620, 593 Keeling Drive, Keeling, VA 24566

LANEXA — D5 *New Kent*

ROCKAHOCK CAMPGROUND & RESORT RV PARK **Ratings: 8.5/8.5★/9** (Campground) 150 Avail: 137 full hkups, 13 W, 13 E (30/50 amps). 2021 rates: $28 to $78. (804)966-8362, 1428 Outpost Rd, Lanexa, VA 23089

LEXINGTON — D3 *Rockbridge*

LEE HI CAMPGROUND
Ratings: 6.5/8.5/6.5 (Campground) From Jct of I-81 and US 11 (Exit 195), S 0.75 mi on US 11 (L). **FAC:** paved/gravel rds. (50 spaces). Avail: 40 gravel, 8 pull-thrus, (24x60), back-ins (24x45), 34 full hkups, 6 W, 6 E (30/50 amps), seasonal sites, WiFi, $, tent sites, dump, laundry, groc, LP bottles, firewood, restaurant. **REC:** hunting nearby. Pets OK. Big rig sites. 2021 rates: $37.50. ATM.
(540)463-3478 Lat: 37.83161, Lon: -79.37811
2516 North Lee Hwy, Lexington, VA 24450
www.leehi.com
See ad next page

LEXINGTON (CONT)

Things to See and Do

IHOP RESTAURANT AT LEE HI TRAVEL PLAZA Restaurant Open Sunday through Thursday 5 am to midnight, Friday & Saturday 5 am to 2 am. RV accessible. Restrooms. Food. Hours: 24 hours. ATM.
(540)463-3478 Lat: 37.82771, Lon: -79.37402
2516 North Lee Hwy, Lexington, VA 24450
leehi.com/ihop
See ad this page

LORTON — B5 *Fairfax*

POHICK BAY REGIONAL PARK (Public) From Jct of I-95 & US1 (Ft. Belvoir exit 161), N 1.9 mi to Gunston Rd, SE 2 mi to park entrance (L). 96 Avail: 10 full hkups, 14 W, 86 E (30/50 amps). 2021 rates: $36 to $55. (703)339-6104

LOUISA — C4 *Louisa*

SMALL COUNTRY CAMPGROUND (Campground) (Rebuilding) 169 Avail: 142 full hkups, 27 W, 27 E (30/50 amps). 2021 rates: $45 to $59. (540)967-2431, 4400 Byrd Mill Rd, Louisa, VA 23093

LURAY — B3 *Page*

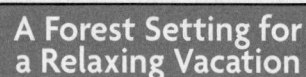

LURAY KOA **Ratings: 9/9.5★/10** (RV Park) Avail: 78 full hkups (30/50 amps). 2021 rates: $50 to $105. Mar 15 to Nov 15. (540)743-7222, 3402 Kimball Rd, Luray, VA 22835

OUTLANDERS RIVER CAMP **Ratings: 6.5/9★/9.5** (Campground) Avail: 42 full hkups (30/50 amps). 2021 rates: $45 to $65. (540)743-5540, 4253 US Hwy 211 W, Luray, VA 22835

YOGI BEAR'S JELLYSTONE PARK CAMP-RESORT LURAY **Ratings: 8.5/10★/9.5** (Campground) 172 Avail: 132 full hkups, 40 W, 40 E (30/50 amps). 2021 rates: $40 to $130. Apr 05 to Dec 01. (540)300-1697, 2250 US Hwy 211 E, Luray, VA 22835

LYNCHBURG — D3 *Lynchburg City*

LYNCHBURG See also Appomattox, Gretna, Monroe, Natural Bridge, Rustburg & Spout Spring.

MADISON — C4 *Madison*

MADISON VINES RV RESORT & COTTAGES (Campground) (Rebuilding) From Jct of I-64 & US 29 (Exit 118), N 28 mi on US 29 (L).

EXPLORE & RELAX ALL IN ONE PLACE
Centrally located in the Shenandoah Valley between Historic Fredericksburg & Shenandoah Natl Park. In the foothills of the Blue Ridge Mts, vintners are plentiful, history abounds & nature beckons you to sit a spell.

FAC: paved/gravel rds. (64 spaces). Avail: 57 gravel, 16 pull-thrus, (30x65), back-ins (30x37), 49 full hkups, 8 W, 8 E (30/50 amps), seasonal sites, WiFi @ sites, rentals, dump, laundry, groc, LP gas, fire rings, firewood, controlled access. **REC:** pool, pond, fishing, boating nearby, playground. Pets OK. No tents, eco-friendly. 2021 rates: $47 to $51.50, Military discount.
(540)948-4186 Lat: 38.35417, Lon: -78.28205
110 Campground Lane, Madison, VA 22727
madisonvinesrvresort.com
See ad this page, 948

MANASSAS — B4 *Manassas*

Travel Services

CAMPING WORLD OF MANASSAS/ARLINGTON As the nation's largest retailer of RV supplies, accessories, services and new and used RVs, Camping World is committed to making your total RV experience better. **SERVICES:** RV, RV appliance, staffed RV wash, restrooms. RV Sales. RV supplies, RV accessible. Hours: 9am to 7pm.
(855)597-2899 Lat: 38.799446, Lon: -77.523614
10850 Balls Ford Rd, Manassas, VA 20109
www.campingworld.com

MARION — E1 *Smyth*

HUNGRY MOTHER (Public State Park) From Jct of I-81 & US-11 (exit 47), W 1 mi on US-11 to SR-16, N 4 mi (L). CAUTION: 35 ft max length on road through park. 70 Avail: 30 full hkups, 40 W, 40 E (30/50 amps). 2021 rates: $25 to $45. (276)781-7400

MARTINSVILLE — E2 *Henry*

INDIAN HERITAGE RV PARK **Ratings: 7/9.5★/7.5** (RV Park) Avail: 36 full hkups (30/50 amps). 2021 rates: $45. (276)632-9500, 184 Tensbury Dr, Martinsville, VA 24112

MEADOWS OF DAN — E2 *Patrick*

MEADOWS OF DAN CAMPGROUND **Ratings: 6.5/9★/8.5** (Campground) Avail: 26 full hkups (30/50 amps). 2021 rates: $36.50. (866)952-2292, 2182 Jeb Stuart Hwy, Meadows of Dan, VA 24120

MILFORD — C4 *Caroline*

HIDDEN ACRES FAMILY CAMPGROUND **Ratings: 6.5/6.5/6.5** (Campground) 99 Avail: 48 full hkups, 51 W, 51 E (30/50 amps). 2021 rates: $44 to $47. (804)633-7592, 17391 Richmond Turnpike, Milford, VA 22514

R & D FAMILY CAMPGROUND **Ratings: 8/9.5★/9** (Campground) From jct I-95 & SR-30 (Exit 98): Go 4 mi E on SR-30, then 13 mi N on US-301/SR-2 (Richmond Tpke), then 4-1/2 mi SE on SR-721/Sparta Rd (L). **FAC:** gravel rds. Avail: 45 gravel, 17 pull-thrus, (25x65), back-ins (25x40), 45 full hkups (30/50 amps), WiFi @ sites, tent sites, rentals, dump, mobile sewer, laundry, LP gas, fire rings, firewood. **REC:** pool, boating nearby, hunting nearby. Pet restrict (B/Q). 2021 rates: $40, Military discount.
(804)633-9515 Lat: 37.98732, Lon: -77.26550
22085 Sparta Rd (Rt 721), Milford, VA 22514
rdfamilycampground.homestead.com
See ad this page

MINERAL — C4 *Louisa*

CHRISTOPHER RUN CAMPGROUND **Ratings: 7/9.5★/9** (Campground) 130 Avail: 33 full hkups, 97 W, 97 E (30/50 amps). 2021 rates: $35 to $50. Apr 01 to Oct 31. (540)894-4744, 6478 Zachary Taylor Hwy., Mineral, VA 23117

MONROE — D3 *Amherst*

LYNCHBURG / BLUE RIDGE PARKWAY KOA **Ratings: 9/10★/10** (Campground) Avail: 40 full hkups (30/50 amps). 2021 rates: $55 to $90. Apr 01 to Nov 01. (434)299-5228, 6252 Elon Rd, Monroe, VA 24574

MONTROSS — C5 *Westmoreland*

WESTMORELAND (Public State Park) From Montross, N 5 mi on SR-3 to SR-347 and entrance (R). 116 Avail: 42 W, 42 E (20/30 amps). 2021 rates: $25 to $40. Mar 06 to Dec 07. (804)493-8821

MOUNT JACKSON — B3 *Shenandoah*

SHENANDOAH VALLEY CAMPGROUND - MT JACKSON **Ratings: 9.5/9.5★/9.5** (Campground) Avail: 43 full hkups (30/50 amps). 2021 rates: $39 to $51. Apr 01 to Nov 30. (540)477-3080, 168 Industrial Park Road, Mount Jackson, VA 22842

MOUNT SOLON — C3 *Augusta*

NATURAL CHIMNEYS PARK & CAMPGROUND (AUGUSTA COUNTY PARK) (Public) From Jct of SR-747 & SR-731, NW 0.5 mi on SR-731 (R). 145 Avail: 6 full hkups, 34 W, 34 E (30/50 amps). 2021 rates: $19 to $36. May 01 to Oct 31. (540)350-2510

NATURAL BRIDGE — D2 *Rockbridge*

NATURAL BRIDGE-LEXINGTON KOA **Ratings: 8.5/8.5/8.5** (Campground) 70 Avail: 45 full hkups, 25 W, 25 E (30/50 amps). 2021 rates: $37 to $77. (540)291-2770, 214 Killdeer Lane, Natural Bridge, VA 24578

YOGI BEAR'S JELLYSTONE PARK CAMP RESORT AT NATURAL BRIDGE **Ratings: 9/8.5★/9** (Campground) 183 Avail: 162 full hkups, 18 W, 18 E (30/50 amps). 2021 rates: $51 to $87. Apr 01 to Nov 15. (540)291-2727, 16 Recreation Lane, Natural Bridge Station, VA 24579

NEW MARKET — B3 *Shenandoah*

ENDLESS CAVERNS RV RESORT **Ratings: 8/10★/8** (Campground) Avail: 150 full hkups (30/50 amps). 2021 rates: $45 to $65. Apr 01 to Nov 15. (540)896-2283, 1800 Endless Caverns Rd, New Market, VA 22844

NEW POINT — D6 *Mathews*

NEW POINT RV RESORT & MARINA **Ratings 8/9★/9.5** (Campground) Avail: 111 full hkups (30/50 amps). 2021 rates: $39 to $106. Apr 15 to Nov 15. (888)669-6472, 846 Sand Bank Rd, New Point, VA 23125

NEWPORT NEWS — E5 *City of Newport News*

A SPOTLIGHT Introducing the Historic Triangle's colorful attractions appearing at the front of this state section.

NEWPORT NEWS PARK CAMPGROUND (Public) From jct of I-64 & SR-105 (exit 250B): Go E 0.1 mi on SR-105 to SR-143/Jefferson Ave, W 1 mi (R). 188 Avail: 125 W, 165 E (30/50 amps). 2021 rates $36. (800)203-8322

Travel Services

CAMPING WORLD OF HAMPTON ROADS As the nation's largest retailer of RV supplies, accessories, services and new and used RVs, Camping World is committed to making your total RV experience better. **SERVICES:** RV, sells outdoor gear, staffed RV wash, restrooms. RV Sales. RV supplies, RV accessible. Hours: 9am to 7pm.
(877)815-9589 Lat: 37.09458, Lon: -76.48645
11963 Jefferson Ave, Newport News, VA 23606
www.campingworld.com

PENHOOK — E2 *Pittsylvania*

SMITH MOUNTAIN CAMPGROUND Ratings: 5.5/8.5★/9.5 (Campground) 37 Avail: 27 full hkups, 10 W, 10 E (30/50 amps). 2021 rates: $55 to $60. (434)927-4198, 155 Liberty Rd, Penhook, VA 24137

PETERSBURG — D4 *Dinwiddie*

CAMPTOWN CAMPGROUND

good sam park **Ratings: 7/8.5★/9** (Campground) Avail: 12 full hkups (30/50 amps). 2021 rates: $40. (804)469-4569, 22819 Camptown Dr, Petersburg, VA 23803

PICTURE LAKE CAMPGROUND

good sam park **Ratings: 8.5/9★/9** (Campground) From Jct of I-85 & US 460 (Exit 61), E 0.4 mi on US 460 to US 1, S 1.8 mi (R).

THE BEST MEMORIES ARE MADE CAMPING

A great camping experience for the whole family near Richmond. New Premiere area with 40x60 ft sites FHU. Cabin Rentals. Surrounded by Civil War History, adjacent to VA Motorsports Park. A Cruise America RV rental location.

FAC: paved/gravel rds. (214 spaces). 166 Avail: 15 paved, 151 gravel, 69 pull-thrus, (35x60), back-ins (32x50), 166 full hkups (30/50 amps), seasonal sites, WiFi @ sites, tent sites, rentals, dump, mobile sewer, laundry, groc, LP gas, fire rings, firewood. **REC:** pool, Picture Lake: fishing, kayaking/canoeing, boating nearby, playground, rec open to public. Pet restrict (B). Big rig sites, eco-friendly. 2021 rates: $48 to $60, Military discount.

(804)861-0174 Lat: 37.16432, Lon: -77.51302
7818 Boydton Plank Rd, Dinwiddie, VA 23803
www.picturelakecampground.com
See ad this page

SOUTH FORTY RV CAMPGROUND

good sam park **Ratings: 9/7/8.5** (Campground) 40 Avail: 34 full hkups, 6 W, 6 E (30/50 amps). 2021 rates: $48 to $53. (877)732-8345, 2809 Courtland Rd, Petersburg, VA 23805

SAVE! Camping World coupons can be found at the front and back of this Guide!

POWHATAN — D4 *Powhatan*

COZY ACRES CAMPGROUND/RV PARK

good sam park **Ratings: 9/10★/9.5** (Campground) From Jct of US Rte 522 & US Rte 60, W 3.9 mi on US Rte 60 to SR-627 (Ridge Rd), S 1.8 mi to entrance rd (R). **FAC:** paved/gravel rds. (116 spaces). Avail: 104 gravel, patios, 85 pull-thrus, (35x70), back-ins (30x70), 95 full hkups, 9 W, 9 E (30/50 amps), seasonal sites, WiFi, tent sites, rentals, dump, laundry, groc, LP gas, fire rings, firewood, controlled access. **REC:** pool, wading pool, pond, fishing, boating nearby, playground, hunting nearby. Pet restrict (Q). Big rig sites, eco-friendly. 2021 rates: $49 to $80, Military discount. Apr 01 to Nov 15.

(804)598-2470 Lat: 37.53920, Lon: -78.01364
2177 Ridge Road, Powhatan, VA 23139
cozyacres.com
See ad this page

PULASKI — D1 *Pulaski*

GATEWOOD PARK & RESERVOIR (Public) From Jct of Hwy 81 & Rte 99 (Exit 94), W 3.8 mi on Count Pulaski Dr./Main st. to Magazine St, NE 0.1 mi to Mt Olivet Rd (Rte 710), W 2.3 mi to Gatewood Ave, NW 6 mi (R). 35 Avail: 35 W, 35 E (30/50 amps). 2021 rates: $15 to $30. Apr 06 to Dec 01. (540)980-2561

QUINBY — D6 *Accomack*

VIRGINIA LANDING RV CAMPGROUND

good sam park **Ratings: 5/8★/8** (Membership Park) 23 Avail: 23 W, 23 E (30/50 amps). 2021 rates: $49.50 to $62.70. Apr 01 to Oct 31. (888)563-7040, 40226 Upshur Neck Road, Quinby, VA 23423

RICHMOND — D4 *Richmond City*

RICHMOND See also Ashland, Doswell & Petersburg.

ROANOKE — D2 *Roanoke*

ROANOKE See also Buchanan & Salem.

BLUE RIDGE PKWY/ROANOKE MOUNTAIN (Public National Park) From Jct of US-220 & Blue Ridge Pkwy, N 1 mi on Blue Ridge Pkwy to Mill Mt Rd., W 1.5 mi at MP-120.4 (E). 30 Avail. 2021 rates: $16. May 01 to Oct 31. (540)342-3051

EXPLORE PARK (Public) From jct I-81 & I-581S/220S: Go 11-3/4 mi S on I-581S/220S, then 5-3/4 mi NE on Blue Ridge Parkway to MP 115, then 1/2 mi on Roanoke River Parkway (E). Avail: 6 E (30 amps). 2021 rates: $25. (540)427-1800

Lend a hand. During the busy season park services are stretched to the max! Please do your best to keep your area ""ship-shape"".

VA

ROANOKE (CONT)

Travel Services

GANDER RV OF ROANOKE Your new hometown outfitter offering the best regional gear for all your outdoor needs. Your adventure awaits. **SERVICES:** RV, tire, RV appliance, MH mechanical, gunsmithing svc, archery svc, sells outdoor gear, sells fishing gear, sells firearms, staffed RV wash, restrooms. RV Sales. RV supplies, LP gas, dump, emergency parking, RV accessible. Hours: 9am to 8pm.
(877)464-5709 Lat: 37.359481, Lon: -79.961082
8198 Gander Way, Roanoke, VA 24019
rv.ganderoutdoors.com

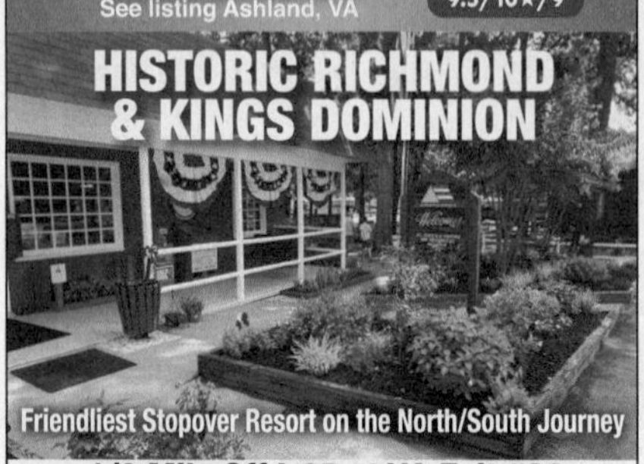

ROSELAND — D3 *Nelson*

DEVILS BACKBONE CAMP **Ratings: 6.5/9.5★/8.5** (RV Park) Avail: 25 full hkups (30/50 amps). 2021 rates: $35 to $65. (540)817-6061, 200 Mosbys Run, Roseland, VA 22967

RURAL RETREAT — E1 *Wythe*

RURAL RETREAT FISHING LAKE & CAMPGROUND (Public) From Jct of I-81 & CR-79 (Exit 60), S 4 mi on Exit 60 to CR-677, W 2 mi (L). 74 Avail: 54 W, 54 E (30/50 amps). 2021 rates: $18 to $28. Apr 01 to Oct 01. (276)223-6022

RUSTBURG — D3 *Campbell*

LYNCHBURG RV
good sam park **Ratings: 7/8.5★/8** (Membership Park) 30 Avail: 15 full hkups, 15 W, 15 E (30 amps). 2021 rates: $57.92 to $68.45. Apr 27 to Oct 20. (888)563-7040, 405 Mollies Creek Road, Gladys, VA 24554

SALEM — D2 *Roanoke*

CAMPGROUND AT DIXIE CAVERNS
Ratings: 6.5/UI/6 (Campground) From jct I-81 (exit 132/Dixie Caverns) & Rte 647: Go 1/4 mi SE on Rte 647, then 1/4 mi SW on US-11/460/Main St (R). **FAC:** paved/gravel rds. Avail: 62 gravel, 32 pull-thrus, (24x55), back-ins (25x55), 62 full hkups (30/50 amps), cable, WiFi @ sites, tent sites, dump, LP gas, firewood. **REC:** boating nearby, rec open to public. Pets OK. 2021 rates: $34.
(540)380-2085 Lat: 37.25268, Lon: -80.17545
5757 W Main St, Salem, VA 24153
www.dixiecaverns.com
See ad this page

Things to See and Do

DIXIE CAVERNS, ANTIQUE MALL, GIFTS, ROCK SHOP & SOUVENIRS The only scenic underground caverns in SW Virginia, with antique mall, rock shop, RV campground & souvenirs. Open 7 days, discount to caverns for campers. RV accessible. Restrooms. Hours: 9am to 6pm. Adult fee: $14.
(540)380-2085 Lat: 37.25231, Lon: -80.17448
5757 W Main St, Salem, VA 24153
www.dixiecaverns.com
See ad this page

SCOTTSBURG — E3 *Halifax*

STAUNTON RIVER (Public State Park) From Town, Ne 7.3 mi. on Us-360, SE 2.4 mi. on Scottsburg Rd., SE 7.8 mi. MacDonald Rd. 14 Avail: 14 W, 14 E (20/30 amps). 2021 rates: $25 to $35. Mar 02 to Dec 07. (434)572-4623

SPOTSYLVANIA — C4 *Spotsylvania*

WILDERNESS PRESIDENTIAL RESORT **Ratings: 8/9.5★/8.5** (Membership Park) 439 Avail: 235 full hkups, 204 W, 204 E (30 amps). 2021 rates: $50 to $60. (540)972-7433, 9220 Plank Rd, Spotsylvania, VA 22553

SPOUT SPRING — D3 *Appomattox*

PARADISE LAKE FAMILY CAMPGROUND
good sam park **Ratings: 8/8.5★/9.5** (Campground) W-bnd: From Appomattox, Jct of SR-24 & US 460, W 6 mi on US 460 to West Lake Rd, S 1 mi (E); or E-bnd: From Lynchburg, Jct of US-29 & US 460 (S Lynchburg), E 10.2 mi on US 460 to West Lake Rd, S 1 mi (E). **FAC:** paved/gravel rds. (91 spaces). Avail: 81 gravel, patios, 26 pull-thrus, (30x60), back-ins (30x45), 52 full hkups, 29 W, 29 E (30/50 amps), seasonal sites, WiFi, tent sites, dump, mobile sewer, laundry, groc, LP gas, fire rings, firewood, controlled access. **REC:** pool, Paradise Lake: swim, fishing, kayaking/canoeing, boating nearby, playground, hunting nearby. Pet restrict (Q). Partial handicap access. Big rig sites, eco-friendly. 2021 rates: $48 to $51, Military discount. ATM.
(434)993-3332 Lat: 37.33841, Lon: -78.93726
1105 West Lake Rd, Spout Spring, VA 24593
www.paradise-lake.com
See ad this page

ST PAUL — A2 *Russell*

RIDGE RUNNER CAMPGROUND **Ratings: 5/9.5★/5.5** (Campground) Avail: 10 full hkups (30/50 amps). 2021 rates: $40. May 01 to Dec 31. (276)455-0550, 4111 Russell Creek Rd, St Paul, VA 24283

STAFFORD — C4 *Stafford*

AQUIA PINES CAMP RESORT **Ratings: 8.5/8.5★/8** (Campground) Avail: 100 full hkups (30/50 amps). 2021 rates: $61.30 to $72.10. (540)659-3447, 3071 Jefferson Davis Hwy, Stafford, VA 22554

STAUNTON — C3 *Augusta*

A SPOTLIGHT Introducing Blue Ridge Parkway/Shenandoah Valley's colorful attractions appearing at the front of this state section.

WALNUT HILLS CAMPGROUND AND RV PARK
good sam park **Ratings: 8.5/9.5/9** (Campground) 126 Avail: 63 full hkups, 63 W, 63 E (30/50 amps). 2021 rates: $26 to $68. (540)337-3920, 484 Walnut Hills Rd, Staunton, VA 24401

STUART — E2 *Patrick*

FAIRY STONE (Public State Park) From N jct US 58 & Hwy 8: go 4 mi N on Hwy 8, then 8 mi E on Hwy 57 (Fairystone Park Hwy), then 3/4 mi N on Hwy 346. 50 Avail: 50 W, 50 E. 2021 rates: $20 to $35. (276)930-2424

STUARTS DRAFT — C3 *Waynesboro*

SHENANDOAH ACRES FAMILY CAMPGROUND **Ratings: 8.5/9.5★/9.5** (Campground) 150 Avail: 48 full hkups, 102 W, 102 E (30/50 amps). 2021 rates: $47 to $65. (888)709-1172, 348 Lake Rd, Stuarts Draft, VA 24477

SUFFOLK — E5 *Isle of Wight*

DAVIS LAKES RV PARK AND CAMPGROUND
good sam park **Ratings: 9/10★/10** (RV Park) Avail: 54 full hkups (30/50 amps). 2021 rates: $60 to $66. (757)539-1191, 200 Byrd St, Suffolk, VA 23434

SYDNORSVILLE — E2 *Franklin*

GOOSE DAM CAMPGROUND (Public) From Jct of US-220 & Hwy 40, S 8 mi on US-220 to Hwy 724 (Goose Dam Rd), W 1 mi (R). Avail: 25 full hkups (20/30 amps). 2021 rates: $14 to $18. (540)483-2100

TEMPERANCEVILLE — C6 *Accomack*

TALL PINES HARBOR WATERFRONT CAMPGROUND **Ratings: 9/10★/10** (Campground) 170 Avail: 147 full hkups, 23 W, 23 E (30/50 amps). 2021 rates: $50 to $94. Mar 01 to Nov 01. (757)824-0777, 8107 Tall Pines Ln, Temperanceville, VA 23442

THORNBURG — C4 *Spotsylvania*

Travel Services

GANDER RV OF THORNBURG Your new hometown outfitter offering the best regional gear for all your outdoor needs. Your adventure awaits. **SERVICES:** RV, RV appliance, MH mechanical, restrooms. RV Sales. RV supplies, LP gas, dump, RV accessible. Hours: 9am to 7pm.
(888)258-5755 Lat: 38.12431, Lon: -77.51210
6101 Mallard Rd, Thornburg, VA 22565
rv.ganderoutdoors.com

TOANO — D5 *James City*

TOANO See also Deltaville, Gloucester, Gloucester Point, Lanexa, Newport News, Topping, Urbanna & Williamsburg.

COLONIAL PINES CAMPGROUND AT WILLIAMSBURG CHRISTIAN RETREAT CENTER
good sam park **Ratings: 8.5/9/9.5** (Campground) From Jct of I-64 & SR-30 (Exit 227), N 0.6 mi on SR-30 to SR-601/Barnes Rd, S (Left) 1 mi on SR-601/Barnes Rd (R). **FAC:** gravel rds. Avail: 22 gravel, back-ins (35x55), 22 full hkups (30/50 amps), WiFi @ sites, tent sites, rentals, dump, laundry, fire rings, firewood. **REC:** pool, wading pool, boating nearby, playground. Pets OK. Partial handicap access, eco-friendly. 2021 rates: $34 to $44.
(757)566-2256 Lat: 37.419954, Lon: -76.843081
9275 Barnes Rd (Rt 601), Toano, VA 23168
www.wcrc.info
See ad this page

TOPPING — D5 *Middlesex*

GREY'S POINT CAMP
good sam park **Ratings: 9/10★/10** (RV Park) Avail: 155 full hkups (30/50 amps). 2021 rates: $55 to $110. Apr 01 to Nov 15. (888)563-7040, 3601 Greys Point Rd, Topping, VA 23169

TRIANGLE — B5 *Prince William*

PRINCE WILLIAM FOREST PARK/OAK RIDGE CAMPGROUND (Public National Park) From Jct of I-95 & SR-619 (Exit 150), W 0.25 mi on SR-619 to park entrance rd, NW to Scenic Dr (R). Entrance fee required. 67 Avail. 2021 rates: $20. Mar 01 to Nov 30. (703)221-7181

URBANNA — D5 *Middlesex*

BETHPAGE CAMP-RESORT
good sam park **Ratings: 9/10★/9.5** (RV Resort) Avail: 300 full hkups (30/50 amps). 2021 rates: $55 to $150. Apr 01 to Nov 15. (888)563-7040, 679 Brown's Lane, Urbanna, VA 23175

VERONA — C3 *Augusta*

SHENANDOAH VALLEY CAMPGROUND
good sam park **Ratings: 8.5/9★/9.5** (Campground) From Jct of I-81 & Rte 612 (exit 227), W 1 mi on Rte 612 to US-11, N 0.5 mi to Rte 781, W 1.2 mi (L). **FAC:** paved/gravel rds. Avail: 132 gravel, 90 pull-thrus, (25x50), back-ins (35x40), 44 full hkups, 88 W, 88 E (30/50 amps), cable, WiFi @ sites, $, tent sites, rentals, dump, mobile sewer, laundry, groc, LP gas, fire rings, firewood. **REC:** heated pool, wading pool, hot tub, Middle River: swim, fishing, kayaking/canoeing, playground. Pets OK. Partial handicap access, eco-friendly. 2021 rates: $47 to $61, Military discount. Apr 01 to Nov 01. ATM.
(540)248-2267 Lat: 38.22324, Lon: -79.00636
296 Riner Ln, Verona, VA 24482
campsvc.com
See ad page 951

VIRGINIA BEACH — E6 *Virginia Beach*

A SPOTLIGHT Introducing the Virginia Shoreline's colorful attractions appearing at the front of this state section.

VIRGINIA BEACH See also Cape Charles, Chesapeake & Hampton.

FIRST LANDING (Public State Park) From Jct of I-64 & US-13N (North Hampton Blvd, exit 282), E 4.5 mi on 13N to Shore Dr (Rte 60), E 4.5 mi (R). 183 Avail: 108 W, 108 E (20/50 amps). 2021 rates: $30 to $46. Mar 01 to Dec 04. (757)412-2300

HOLIDAY TRAV-L-PARK
good sam park **Ratings: 8.5/10★/9** (RV Park) From Jct of I-64 (exit 284) & I-264, E 10.5 mi on I-264 to Birdneck Rd (exit 22), S 3 mi to General Booth Blvd, SW 0.3 mi (R). **FAC:** paved rds. 687 Avail: 80 paved, 265 gravel, 200 grass, 142 dirt, 589 pull-thrus, (30x50), back-ins (30x50), 368 full hkups, 319 W, 319 E (30/50 amps), cable, WiFi @ sites, tent sites, rentals, dump, mobile sewer, laundry, groc, LP gas, fire rings, firewood. **REC:** heated pool, boating nearby, playground. Pet restrict (B/Q). Partial handicap access. Big rig sites, eco-friendly. 2021 rates: $30 to $92. ATM.
(866)850-9630 Lat: 36.80546, Lon: -75.99196
1075 General Booth Blvd, Virginia Beach, VA 23451
www.campingvb.com
See ad page 954

MILITARY PARK LITTLE CREEK MWR RV PARK (JOINT EXPEDITIONARY BASE LITTLE CREEK-FORT STORY) (Public) From jct of I-64 & US-13 (Northhampton Blvd exit 282): Go E on US-13 (Northhampton Blvd exit 282), then left on Diamond Springs Rd, then 1 mi E on Shore Dr, then left to Gate 3, follow signs. Avail: 45 full hkups (30/50 amps). 2021 rates: $27. (757)462-7282

NORTH BAY SHORE CAMPGROUND **Ratings: 8/8.5★/8.5** (Campground) 62 Avail: 8 full hkups, 54 W, 54 E (30/50 amps). 2021 rates: $55 to $85. (757)426-7911, 3257 Colechester Road, Virginia Beach, VA 23456

NORTH LANDING BEACH RV RESORT & COTTAGES
good sam park **Ratings: 10/10★/10** (RV Resort) From Jct I-64 (Exit 286) & Indian River Rd, SE 12 mi to Princess Anne Rd, S 12.8 mi on Princess Anne Rd (R).

TOTAL RENOVATION! PRIVATE BEACH
Great South Virginia Beach Resort w/800 foot sandy beach. New amenities; 100 HUGE, FHU level RV sites, 90+ Studio/1-bed/2-bed cottages, Pool, spa, fitness center, 30 private bath suites, mini-golf, free WiFi & Cable TV.

FAC: all weather rds. (160 spaces). Avail: 122 all weather, 87 pull-thrus, (45x70), back-ins (40x60), 122 full hkups (30/50 amps), seasonal sites, cable, WiFi @ sites, rentals, dump, laundry, groc, LP gas, fire rings, firewood, controlled access. **REC:** pool, hot tub, North Landing River: swim, fishing, marina, kayaking/canoeing, boating nearby, playground, hunting nearby. Pets OK. Partial handicap access. No tents. Big rig sites, eco-friendly. 2021 rates: $35 to $119, Military discount. ATM.
(757)426-6241 Lat: 36.55768, Lon: -76.00685
161 Princess Anne Rd, Virginia Beach, VA 23457
northlandingbeach.com
See ad page 954

VIRGINIA BEACH KOA **Ratings: 9/9★/8** (Campground) 191 Avail: 126 full hkups, 65 W, 65 E (30/50 amps). 2021 rates: $69 to $115.57. (800)562-4150, 1240 General Booth Blvd., Virginia Beach, VA 23451

VOLNEY — E1 *Grayson*

GRAYSON HIGHLANDS (Public State Park) From Jct of I-81 & SR-16 exit, S 25 mi on SR-16 to US-58, W 8 mi (E). 69 Avail: 36 W, 36 E (20/30 amps), Pit toilets. 2021 rates: $25 to $35. (276)579-7092

WAYNESBORO — C3 *Augusta*

WAYNESBORO NORTH 340 CAMPGROUND
Ratings: 9.5/9.5★/9 (Campground) From Jct of I-64 & US-340 (exit 96), N 7 mi on US-340 (R); or From Jct of I-81 & SR-612 (exit 227), E 9.6 mi on SR-612 to US-340, S 2 mi (L). **FAC:** paved rds. (165 spaces). 140 Avail: 20 paved, 80 gravel, 40 grass, 68 pull-thrus, (28x70), back-ins (30x55), 140 full hkups (30/50 amps), seasonal sites, WiFi @ sites, tent sites, dump, laundry, groc, fire rings, firewood. **REC:** pool, playground. Pet restrict (Q) $. Big rig sites. 2021 rates: $40.
(540)943-9573 Lat: 38.12856, Lon: -78.84436
1125 Eastside Hwy (US-340), Waynesboro, VA 22980
www.waynesboron340campground.com
See ad page 951

WILLIAMSBURG — D5 *James City*

WILLIAMSBURG See also Gloucester, Gloucester Point, Lanexa, Newport News & Toano.

AMERICAN HERITAGE RV PARK
good sam park **Ratings: 10/10★/10** (RV Park) From Jct of I-64 & Rte 607 (exit 231A), SW 0.5 mi on Rte 607 to Maxton Ln on left, S 0.2 mi (L). **FAC:** paved rds. Avail: 145 paved, patios, 70 pull-thrus, (30x60), back-ins (30x60), 145 full hkups (30/50 amps), cable, WiFi @ sites, tent sites, rentals, dump, laundry, groc, LP gas, fire rings, firewood. **REC:** pool, boating nearby, playground. Pets OK. Big rig sites, eco-friendly. 2021 rates: $59.25 to $94.99, Military discount. ATM.
(888)530-2267 Lat: 37.37708, Lon: -76.76866
146 Maxton Lane, Williamsburg, VA 23188
americanheritagervpark.com
See ad page 952

ANVIL CAMPGROUND
good sam park **Ratings: 10/10★/9.5** (Campground) From Jct of I-64 & Rte 143 (Camp Peary-exit 238), S 0.1 mi on Rte 143 to Rochambeau Dr, NW 1.4 mi to Rte 645 (Airport Rd), SW 1.8 mi to Rte 603 (Mooretown Rd), SE 0.3 mi (R); or From Jct of US-60 & Rte 645, NE 0.1 mi on Rte 645 to Rte 603, SE 0.3 mi (R). **FAC:** paved rds. Avail: 48 all weather, 9 pull-thrus, (30x65), back-ins (25x50), 48 full hkups (30/50 amps), cable, WiFi @ sites, tent sites, rentals, dump, mobile sewer, laundry, groc, fire rings, firewood. **REC:** pool, boating nearby, playground. Pets OK. Big rig sites, eco-friendly. 2021 rates: $49.99 to $79.99, Military discount.
(757)565-2300 Lat: 37.30793, Lon: -76.72878
5243 Mooretown Rd, Williamsburg, VA 23188
www.anvilcampground.com
See ad page 952

COLONIAL KOA **Ratings: 9/9.5★/9.5** (Campground) 175 Avail: 143 full hkups, 32 W, 32 E (30/50 amps). 2021 rates: $39.95 to $109. Mar 01 to Dec 20. (800)562-1733, 4000 Newman Rd, Williamsburg, VA 23188

MILITARY PARK KINGS CREEK RV CAMPGROUND (NAVAL WEAPONS STATION YORKTOWN) (Public) From jct I-64 of SR-199 NE (exit 242): Go 2.5 mi E on SR-199 which turns into SR-641, then through the gate, then on Sanda Ave to 4th street, follow signs (L). Avail: 50 full hkups (50 amps). 2021 rates: $35. (757)887-7418

WILLIAMSBURG KOA **Ratings: 9/10★/9.5** (Campground) 83 Avail: 76 full hkups, 7 W, 7 E (30/50 amps). 2021 rates: $39.95 to $120. Mar 01 to Dec 15. (800)562-1733, 4000 Newman Rd, Williamsburg, VA 23188

WILLIAMSBURG RV CAMPGROUND THOUSAND TRAILS
good sam park **Ratings: 9/8/7** (Membership Park) 123 Avail: 118 full hkups, 5 W, 5 E (30/50 amps). 2021 rates: $64 to $78. (888)563-7040, 4301 Rochambeau Dr, Williamsburg, VA 23188

WILLIS — E2 *Floyd*

DADDY RABBIT'S CAMPGROUND **Ratings: 5/6.5/6.5** (Campground) 54 Avail: 8 full hkups, 46 W, 46 E (20 amps). 2021 rates: $25 to $30. Apr 15 to Oct 31. (540)789-4150, 2015 Union School Rd SW, Willis, VA 24380

WINCHESTER — B4 *Frederick*

CANDY HILL CAMPGROUND
good sam park **Ratings: 8.5/9★/9** (Campground) S-bnd: From Jct of I-81 & US 11/37 (Exit 317), SW 4.1 mi on Rte 37 to US 50, W 0.25 mi to Ward Ave, S 0.25 mi (E); or N-bnd: From Jct of N I-81 & Rte 37 (Exit 310), N 5.2 mi on Rte 37 to US 50, W 0.25 to Ward Ave, S 0.25 mi (E). **FAC:** paved/gravel rds. 86 Avail: 47 paved, 39 gravel, 25 pull-thrus, (30x60), back-ins (35x50), 78 full hkups, 8 W, 8 E (30/50 amps), cable, WiFi @ sites, tent sites, rentals, dump, laundry, groc, LP gas, fire rings, firewood. **REC:** pool, wading pool, playground, rec open to public. Pets OK. Big rig sites, eco-friendly. 2021 rates: $45 to $75. ATM.
(540)662-5198 Lat: 39.18746, Lon: -78.20373
165 Ward Ave, Winchester, VA 22602
www.candyhill.com
See ad this page

WYTHEVILLE — E1 *Wythe*

WYTHEVILLE See also Fries, Galax & Hillsville.

DEER TRAIL PARK & CAMPGROUND
good sam park **Ratings: 8/8.5★/9** (Campground) 60 Avail: 35 full hkups, 25 W, 25 E (30/50 amps). 2021 rates: $42 to $59. (276)228-3636, 599 Gullion Fork Rd, Wytheville, VA 24382

FORT CHISWELL RV PARK
good sam park **Ratings: 8.5/10★/9** (RV Park) From jct I-81/77 & US-52 (exit 80): Go 1/2 mi S on US-52 (L). **FAC:** paved/gravel rds. 110 Avail: 8 paved, 102 gravel, 91 pull-thrus, (30x60), back-ins (30x60), 110 full hkups (30/50 amps), cable, WiFi @ sites, laundry, groc, LP gas. **REC:** heated pool, hunting nearby. Pets OK. Partial handicap access. No tents. Big rig sites, eco-friendly. 2021 rates: $40 to $50, Military discount.
(276)637-6868 Lat: 36.94028, Lon: -80.94322
312 Ft. Chiswell Rd, Max Meadows, VA 24360
properties.camping.com/fort-chiswell-rv-campground/Overview
See ad page 951

PIONEER VILLAGE CAMPGROUND **Ratings: 6/7/8** (Campground) Avail: 82 full hkups (30/50 amps). 2021 rates: $35 to $40. Apr 01 to Nov 30. (276)637-3777, 3627 East Lee Hwy, Max Meadows, VA 24360

WYTHEVILLE KOA CAMPGROUND **Ratings: 9/8.5★/9** (Campground) Avail: 92 full hkups (30/50 amps). 2021 rates: $59 to $75. (276)228-2601, 231 KOA Rd, Wytheville, VA 24382

VA

Getty Images/iStockphoto

DID YOU KNOW?

In the San Juan Islands, as many as 450 islands can appear during low tide.

YOU ARE HERE

Washington

Washington is a feast for travelers. Home to thousand-year-old trees, windswept beaches and volcanoes crowned with glaciers, the Evergreen State gives new meaning to "the great outdoors."

The Wine of Washington

The rich, fertile soil and an ideal climate of southeast Washington bring wine lovers to Walla Walla and other towns in the area. You can unlock the secrets of wine making and sample premium vintages at famous wine estates such as Seven Hills, Three Rivers and Woodward Canyon.

Supersonic Seattle

Seattle invites visitors to sample new food experiences and make amazing cultural discoveries. Indulge in everything from hearty bowls of chowder to flaky Russian pastries at the legendary Pike Place Market. Just a stone's throw away is the very first Starbucks location and the historic waterfront with popular attractions like the Ye Olde Curiosity Shop, Seattle Aquarium and Seattle Great Wheel. Don't leave the city without visiting the colossal troll sculpture in the artsy Fremont district and admiring sweeping skyline views from the top of the Space Needle.

Rainier Reigns

The tallest mountain on the Washington and the Cascade Range, and Mount Rainier attracts recreation seekers and scenery lovers. Draped in dense forest and glaciers, Mount Rainer is an active volcano soaring over 14,000 feet into the sky. Drive the Road to Paradise to easily reach high elevations and traverse a network of trails and climbing routes at the top. Carve some time out to explore the massive thousand-year-old trees in the Grove of Patriarchs and admire panoramic views of the Puget Sound basin near the Paradise Visitor Center.

VISITOR CENTER

TIME ZONE
Pacific Standard

ROAD & HIGHWAY INFORMATION
800-695-7623
wsdot.com/traffic

FISHING & HUNTING INFORMATION
360-902-2464
wdfw.wa.gov/licensing

BOATING INFORMATION
360-902-8555
boat.wa.gov

NATIONAL PARKS
nps.gov/wa

STATE PARKS
parks.wa.gov

TOURISM INFORMATION
Washington Tourism Alliance
800-544-1800
experiencewa.com

TOP TOURISM ATTRACTIONS
1) Olympic National Park
2) Space Needle
3) Mount Rainier National Park

MAJOR CITIES
Seattle, Spokane, Tacoma, Vancouver, Bellevue, Olympia (capital)

Washington Cherry Pie

Fans of the TV show "Twin Peaks" may recall the big slices of cherry pie enjoyed by agent Cooper, played by Kyle MacLachlan. You'll find the delicious pie in roadside diners and restaurants across the state, thanks to the ample local harvests of cherries. Start your pie odyssey at the breakfast bar at Twede's Café in North Bend, which served as the Double R Diner in the aforementioned TV show.

Cape of Good Views

Come to Cape Disappointment State Park for jaw-dropping coastal scenery. Eight miles of trails lead to secluded coves and the west coast's oldest functioning lighthouse. The park also marks the end of the Lewis and Clark expedition. You can learn more about the epic journey and find a vantage point for humpback whale spotting from the Lewis and Clark Interpretive Center.

Tantalizing Trails

Washington is a hiker's paradise, with trails of every variety to choose from. Boasting more than 400 miles of trails winding through alpine lakes and rugged peaks, the North Cascades National Park east of Seattle packs bucket list hikes. Pro tip: Take the Horseshoe Basin Trail, which covers a glacier and 15 waterfalls.

A Wilderness of Lakes

The Alpine Lakes Wilderness Area encompasses 394,000 acres in the Central Cascades. This region takes its name from the 700 mountain lakes dotted around the mountainous peaks and forested valleys of the Cascades. Forty-seven trailheads leading into the wilderness fan out more than 615 miles of trails. Part of the famous Pacific Crest Trail traverses this region, and picture-perfect Bridal Veil Falls and Lake Serene are also tucked inside. Nearby Mt. Baker-Snoqualmie National Forest and Wenatchee National Forest invite their guests to take a deep breath of alpine air.

High Times in Skykomish

Skykomish, a gateway community to the Alpine Lakes Wilderness Area is known for its railroad history and its four-seasons of outdoor recreation, including hundreds of hiking trails. More than a dozen or so towns and communities are nestled along the route known as the Cascades Loop. Among them is Chelan, a resort town located on the tip of Lake Chelan.

Coulee Corridor

Spanning around 150 miles from the town of Connell up to Omak, Eastern Washington's Coulee Corridor Scenic Byway is a picturesque expanse of varied landscape that follows the Columbia River's prehistoric flood path. The corridor gets its name from coulees, channels that emerged from post-glacial floods, which are found throughout the expansive landscape.

Morning sunlight creates a rainbow in the spray of Sol Duc Falls in Olympic National Park in Washington.

Connel to Moses Lake

Many travelers start their explorations of the corridor in Connel, a small historic community dating back to 1883. From Connel, it's a short drive up to the town of Moses Lake, certainly worth a stopover for its numerous opportunities for outdoor recreation, ranging from a nine-hole golf course to several hikes. Boaters won't want to miss the Moses Lake Water Trail, which traverses the town's 18-mile-long namesake. Other local highlights include the mineral-rich Soap Lake, a two-mile-long body of water that is believed to have therapeutic benefits.

An Olympian Park

If you're looking to hike, bike, hunt or camp, you'd be well served to dive into the sprawling confines of Olympic National Park. Encompassing more than a million acres, the park is home to snowcapped peaks, ancient glaciers, and thick old-growth rain forests. There are four different visitor centers, 16 different campgrounds, thousands of miles of hiking trails and lots of opportunities for mountaineering and wildlife viewing.

Vancouver (the American One)

If you're driving up from the south, the first city you will hit is Vancouver, just across the Columbia River from Portland, Oregon. This quaint little city is a great place to begin your Washington discoveries. Discover a charming and compact downtown with lots of independent restaurants, microbreweries and coffee shops. There's also a lovely waterfront with a mix of restaurants and residences, not to mention the five-mile-long Waterfront Renaissance Trail, popular with runners and cyclists.

Fine Fort

Those with an interest in history won't want to miss the Fort Vancouver National Historic Site, the site of the original Hudson's Bay Company Columbia Department trading post. This 336-acre expanse on the banks of the Columbia includes a historic village featuring a blacksmith, a trading shop and even an old-fashioned kitchen. On nice days, visitors can explore the lovely trails around the fort, including the Vancouver Land Bridge.

good sam park

Featured Good Sam Parks

WASHINGTON

When you stay with Good Sam, you can expect the highest degree of cleanliness and friendliness, and better yet, you get **10% off** overnight campground fees.

If you're not already a Good Sam member you can purchase your membership at one of these locations:

AIRWAY HEIGHTS
Northern Quest RV Resort

BELLINGHAM
Bellingham RV Park

BIRCH BAY
Birch Bay Resort -Thousand Trails

BOW
Mount Vernon RV Campground

BURLINGTON
Friday Creek

CASTLE ROCK
Toutle River RV Resort

CENTRALIA
Midway RV Park

CHEHALIS
Chehalis Resort

CLARKSTON
Granite Lake Premier RV Resort
Hells Canyon RV Resort & Marina

CLE ELUM
Whispering Pines RV Park & RV Parts Store

COLBERT
Wild Rose RV Park

CONCRETE
Grandy Creek RV Campground KOA

CONNELL
Coyote Run RV Park

COSMOPOLIS
River Run RV Park

CUSICK
Kalispel RV Resort

DEER PARK
Deer Park RV Resort

ELECTRIC CITY
Coulee Playland Resort

10/10★/10 GOOD SAM PARKS

AIRWAY HEIGHTS
Northern Quest RV Resort
(833)702-2082

DEER PARK
Deer Park RV Resort
(509)276-1555

LIBERTY LAKE
Liberty Lake RV Campground
(509)868-0567

PROSSER
Wine Country RV Park
(509)786-5192

RICHLAND
Horn Rapids RV Resort
(866)557-9637

SPOKANE
North Spokane RV Campground
(509)315-5561

What's This?

An RV park with a 10/10★/10 rating has scored perfect grades in amenities, cleanliness and appearance ("See Understanding the Campground Rating System" on pages 8 and 9 for an explanation of the trusted Good Sam Rating System). Stay in a 10/10★/10 park on your next trip for a nearly flawless camping experience.

Getty Images/iStockphoto

Getty Images/iStockphoto

ELLENSBURG
E & J RV Park
Yakima River RV Park

ELMA
Elma RV Park

EVERETT
Maple Grove RV Resort

FALL CITY
Tall Chief RV & Camping Resort

GOLDENDALE
Stargazers RV Resort

GRAYLAND
Kenanna RV Park

HOODSPORT
Glen Ayr Resort
Skokomish Park At Lake Cushman
The Waterfront At Potlatch Resort & RV Park

HOQUIAM
Hoquiam River RV Park

IONE
Cedar RV Park

ISSAQUAH
Issaquah Village RV Park

KELSO
Brookhollow RV Park

KETTLE FALLS
Grandview Inn Motel & RV Park

LA CONNER
La Conner
La Conner Marina & RV Park

LEAVENWORTH
Leavenworth RV Campground

LIBERTY LAKE
Liberty Lake RV Campground

MANSON
Mill Bay Casino RV Park

MONROE
Thunderbird Resort

MONTESANO
Friends Landing RV Park

MOSES LAKE
Grant County Fairgrounds & RV Park
MarDon Resort on Potholes Reservoir

MOUNT VERNON
Mount Vernon RV Park

NEWPORT
Little Diamond

OCEAN CITY
Oceana Campground

OCEAN PARK
Cedar To Surf Campground
Ocean Park Resort

OLYMPIA
Washington Land Yacht Harbor RV Park & Event Center

OMAK
12 Tribes Resort Casino RV Park
Carl Precht Memorial RV Park

OTHELLO
O'Sullivan Sportsman Resort (Camping Resort)

PACKWOOD
Rainier Wings / Packwood RV Park

PORT ANGELES
Elwha Dam RV Park

POULSBO
Cedar Glen RV Park
Eagle Tree RV Park

PROSSER
Wine Country RV Park

PUYALLUP
Majestic RV Park

QUINCY
Crescent Bar

RICHLAND
Horn Rapids RV Resort
Wright's Desert Gold Motel & RV Park

SEAVIEW
Long Beach

SILVER CREEK
Paradise Thousand Trails Resort

SKAMOKAWA
Vista Park

SPOKANE
North Spokane RV Campground

STANWOOD
Cedar Grove Shores RV Park

WARDEN
Sage Hills Golf Club & RV Resort

WESTPORT
American Sunset RV & Tent Resort

WHITE SALMON
Gorge Base Camp RV Park

WILBUR
Country Lane Campground & RV Park
Goose Creek RV Park & Campground

WINTHROP
Riverbend RV Park of Twisp
Silverline Resort

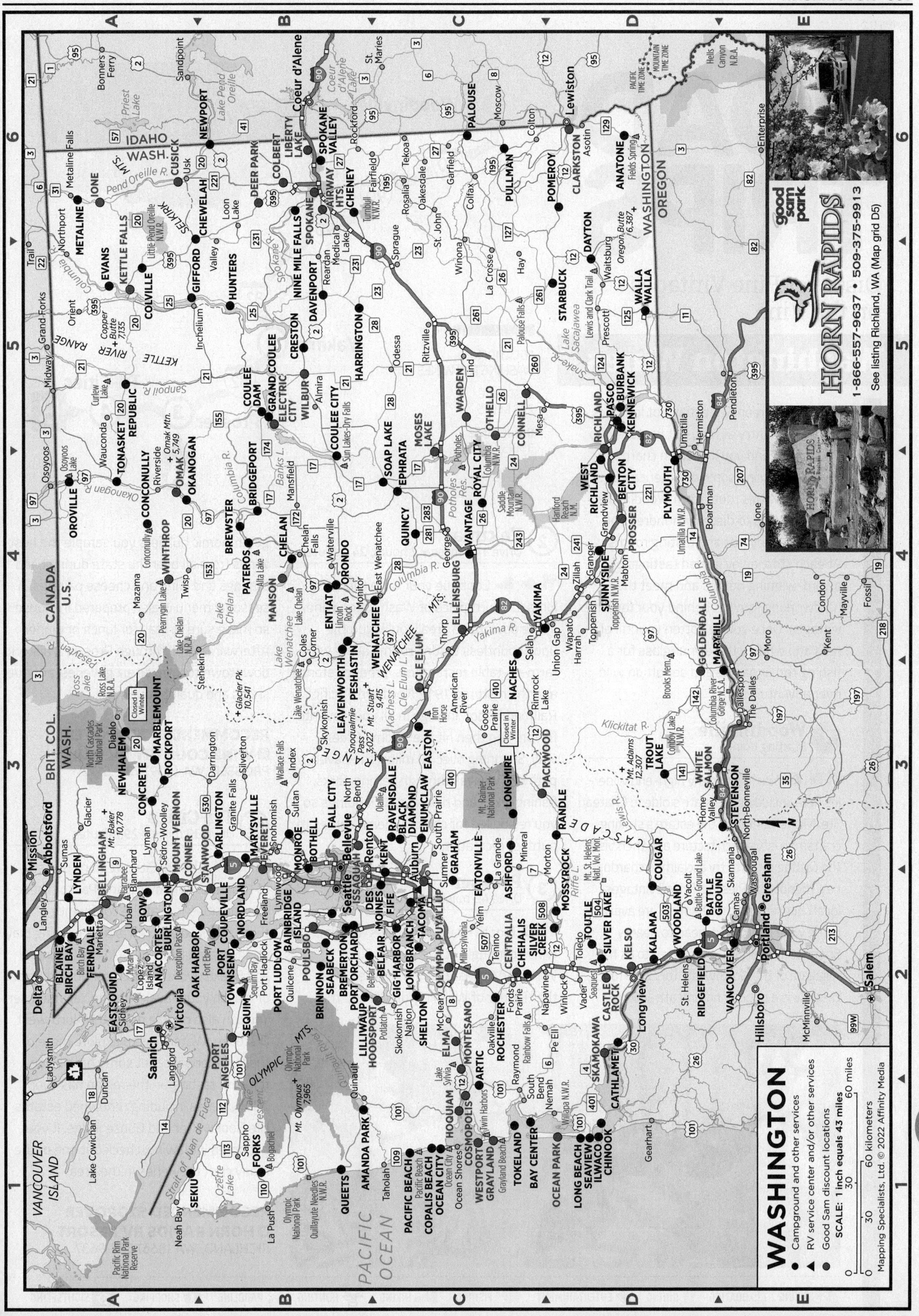
WASHINGTON
Campground and other services
RV service center and/or other services
Good Sam discount locations
SCALE: 1 inch equals 43 miles
0 30 60 miles
0 30 60 kilometers
Mapping Specialists, Ltd. © 2022 Affinity Media
good sam park
HORN RAPIDS
1-866-557-9637 • 509-375-9913
See listing Richland, WA (Map grid D5)
CANADA
U.S.
BRIT. COL.
WASH.
IDAHO
OREGON
PACIFIC OCEAN
VANCOUVER ISLAND
Strait of Juan de Fuca
Olympic National Park
North Cascades National Park
Mt. Rainier National Park
SEATTLE
SPOKANE
TACOMA
OLYMPIA
YAKIMA
WENATCHEE
ELLENSBURG
RICHLAND
KENNEWICK
PASCO
WALLA WALLA
VANCOUVER
Portland
Lewiston
Coeur d'Alene
Victoria

WA

ROAD TRIPS

Discover Fine Vintages on the Vine

Washington Wines

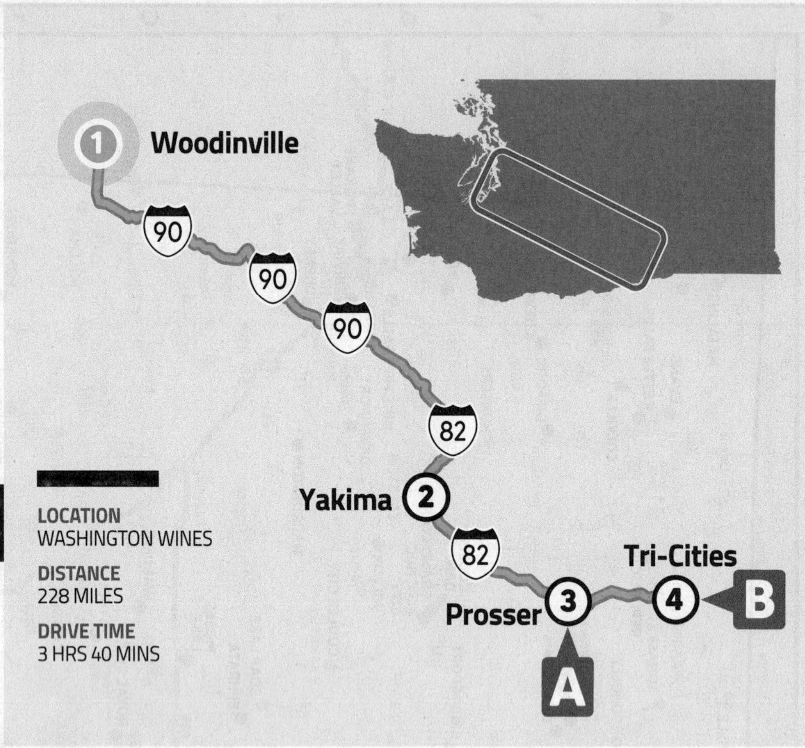

LOCATION
WASHINGTON WINES

DISTANCE
228 MILES

DRIVE TIME
3 HRS 40 MINS

The Evergreen State may not look like wine country at first, but venture into the interior and you'll unearth charming towns producing some of America's best vino. Follow this route from Woodinville to Walla Walla to discover hundreds of wineries, vineyards and tasting rooms. At each stop, enjoy guided tastings of award-winning bottles and meet the hardworking families behind your favorite vintages. Once you've gotten your fill of reds and whites, trade your glass for a fishing rod or paddle and set off on wild river adventures.

1 Woodinville
Starting point

You'll find many high-end wineries here, including the state's oldest: Chateau Ste. Michelle. Admire the estate's striking craftsman-style architecture and then visit the tasting room to try acclaimed chardonnay, merlot and Riesling. Prized vintages, local cheeses and merchandise are available in the wine shop. Next, head to nearby Snoqualmie Falls. Often referred to as the "Niagara of the Northwest," this 286-foot cascade is a popular natural attraction.

2 Yakima
Drive 149 miles • 2 hours, 24 minutes

Continue your wine tour in Yakima, the birthplace of Washington wine. In the downtown area, you'll stumble upon countless tasting rooms along with farm-to-table restaurants, produce stands and the restored 1912 Northern Pacific Railroad Depot. Indulge in all your favorite flavors and then hit the Yakima Greenway. Spanning over 10 miles, the paved pathway weaves through serene parks, fishing lakes and river access landings so you're spoiled for choice when it comes to outdoor recreation.

3 Prosser
Drive 49 miles • 47 minutes

Mouth-watering dishes and fine wines comingle at the Walter Clore Wine and Culinary Center. Named after the "Father of Washington Wines," this gastronomic hub lets you sample the best wines from all over the state during blind tastings and wine and cheese pairings. A seasonal menu is also prepared in-house so make sure to stay for lunch or dinner. Afterward, stroll through Prosser's historic downtown to browse art galleries, antique shops and quaint boutiques.

RECOMMENDED STOPOVER
A WINE COUNTRY RV PARK
PROSSER, WA (509) 786-5192

4 Tri-Cities
Drive 30 miles • 29 minutes

The Tri-Cities region consists of Richland, Kennewick and Pasco. These communities rest at the confluence of three rivers so you can expect exciting play on the water. Drop a line in the Columbia and Snake rivers to catch salmon and trout or launch your kayak into the Yakima River. You can also paddle down the Northwest Discovery Water Trail to explore more of these waterways. Set some time aside for wine tasting — the region has over 200 wineries including renowned estates like Bookwalter and Goose Ridge. If you get bored with wine, check out one of the many craft breweries in the area.

RECOMMENDED STOPOVER
B HORN RAPIDS RV RESORT
RICHLAND, WA (866) 557-9637

Getty Images/iStockphoto

BIKING BOATING DINING ENTERTAINMENT FISHING HIKING HUNTING PADDLING SHOPPING SIGHTSEEING

Washington SPOTLIGHTS

Adventure Never Gets Old in the Evergreen State

Take your pick between urban and outdoor experiences. These destinations showcase Washington at its most spectacular. Whether you plan on hitting the trail or the tasting room, Washington overwhelms the senses.

THE SPACE NEEDLE HAS HAD 1.3 MILLION GUESTS.

The space needle stands 605 feet with 360-degree views of Seattle.

Getty Images/iStockphoto

Greater Seattle

Effortlessly blending urban cool with an easy-going, outdoorsy mentality, Seattle is the beating heart of the Pacific Northwest — the region's largest city and its cultural capital. Boasting a nearly endless supply of unique attractions and nearby natural wonders, it's also the perfect jumping off point for exploring the scenic coast and one-of-a-kind parks that lie beyond the urban landscape.

Out-of-this-World Landmarks

Built for the 1962 World's Fair, the flying saucer-inspired Space Needle has become synonymous with the Seattle skyline. These days, you can take a super-fast elevator to the observation platform at the top, where spectacular views of the downtown district, the Cascade Mountains, and Puget Sound await. Once you've got the lay of the land, head to the Pike Place Market where the spirit of Seattle truly comes alive. Renowned for its daring throw-and-catch fishmongers, the hundred year old market is also home to bookstores, antique shops, and quirky boutiques. You could easily spend a day wandering between the hundreds of vendors, listening to the top-notch street musicians, and enjoying the many restaurants and cafes that turn the market's offerings into innovative menu items. For a pick-me-up, grab a cup of joe from the original Starbucks Coffee store located at 1912 Pike Place.

Wondrous Waterfront

Nestled on the shores of glistening Puget Sound, the lure of the sea is never far away in Seattle. Thankfully, sightseeing excursions are easy to come by via the many ferries that leave from downtown. The 35-minute ride to Bainbridge Island or the slightly longer route on the Bremerton Ferry make for easily accessible day trips, while specially-crafted sailboat outings or the narrated Locks Cruise to Lake Union offer more in-depth opportunities to experience the area's waterways. Anglers can join one of the many salmon fishing charters throughout the Sound, or head inland to hotspots like Lake Washington and Green Lake where Cutthroat trout, bass, and Coho salmon are abundant. For something a bit more thrilling, book a whitewater rafting trip on the Skykomish River about an hour east of the city center.

Arts & Culture

Thanks to its rainy day reputation, many of the Emerald City's indoor attractions have become must-sees in their own right. Art

> "HEAD TO THE VIBRANT PIKE PLACE MARKET, WHERE THE SPIRIT OF SEATTLE TRULY COMES ALIVE."

LOCAL FAVORITE

Chris's Chipotle Hummus Recipe

Chickpeas recently enjoyed a surge in popularity among farmers in the Pacific Northwest, and that's good news for folks who love making their own hummus. *Recipe by Chris Schlieter.*

INGREDIENTS

- ☐ 2 15-oz cans of chickpeas (or garbanzo beans), one drained, one with liquid
- ☐ zest and juice from 1 Lemon
- ☐ 1 chipotle pepper
- ☐ 2-3 tbsp Tahini paste
- ☐ ¼ teaspoon garam masala
- ☐ 2 tablespoons olive oil

DIRECTIONS

Starting with the chickpeas, add all ingredients to your blender. Start with low speed (or pulsing) to chop and mix ingredients, then process at high speed until desired consistency is reached (pausing to stir or let mix settle as needed). Processing time is approximately 1 minute with a high-powered blender.

A powerful blender will produce a smooth texture. You can use a food processor if you prefer a coarse texture. Can be dressed up with pine nuts or roasted red peppers.

WA

SPOTLIGHTS

Reflection Lake Trail cuts through a meadow of wildflowers outside of Mount Rainier.

lovers will relish in the plentiful museum options including the remarkably diverse Seattle Art Museum. Focused on the region's Nature American traditions, the museum's Northwest Gallery is not to be missed. Across town, the Frye Art Museum focuses on contemporary pieces, while the innovative Henry Art Gallery houses a constantly-changing array of works by emerging artists. For something a bit more playful, head to the Museum of Pop Culture, where science fiction, music and film dominate the innovative and colorful exhibits. Learn about Seattle's contribution to rock 'n' roll music. Located at the foot of the Space Needle, the museum is adjacent to the Seattle Children's Museum, and Chihuly Garden and Glass, a unique glimpse into the work of one of the world's finest glassblowers.

Deep Dive Into History

Once a major travel and trade hub during the gold rush, Seattle packs an amazing history. Go deep to the Seattle Underground, a warren of underground passageways that were originally the ground level of Seattle before streets were elevated in the early 20th century. Take tours of the tunnels throughout the year.

Outdoors Adventures

Northwest of downtown, Discovery Park is a nature lover's paradise without leaving the city limits. Boasting 12 miles of trails that wind past meadows, beaches, and bluffs, this urban treasure is a must-visit for first-timers and the perfect place for a picnic. About thirty minutes east of the city, Mount Si is another getaway that's not to be missed. The mountain's popular, 4-mile trail is steep at times, but offers up incredible views of Seattle, the Snoqualmie Valley, and Mount Rainier in the distance.

Seattle Salad Days

In the wild and woolly days of the Klondike Gold Rush during the late 1800s, Seattle was a busy stop on the way to Alaska. The Seattle Unit of Klondike Gold Rush National Historical

Park offers a self-guided experience that includes a walking tour of Pioneer Square and on-site exhibits detailing the journey and hardships experienced by gold miners hoping to strike it rich.

Taking Wing

Seattle has long held a central role in the nation's aerospace industry, and the Museum of Flight is a must-see destination for aviation buffs. Permanent exhibits feature World War I aircraft, World War II fighters and the story of Boeing's early years. Reach beyond the skies and into the stars in the Spaceflight Academy exhibit, which presents the science of space aviation and offers guests a look inside a fuselage trainer.

Mount Rainier & Mount St. Helens

The natural world seems larger than life in the Evergreen State, especially in Mount Rainier and Mount St. Helens. These titanic peaks are shrouded in myth and majesty, enticing hikers to exploring their seemingly endless slopes. Hikers will find endless trails here.

Peak Experiences

Located 65 miles southeast of Seattle, Mount Rainier soars 14,411 feet into the sky, and its distinctive silhouette is plastered on every license plate in Washington. The daunting mountain leaves visitors open-mouthed with its cathedral-like groves of ancient trees, cascading waterfalls and the biggest glacial system in the continental United States. Drive 50 miles south to Mount St. Helens, where the largest landslide in recorded history occurred after a volcanic eruption in 1980. From roaming through lava tubes to a multifaceted landscape that's still recovering today, this unique site lets you witness Mother Nature's sheer power while spoiling you with myriad outdoor adventures.

Conquer Washington's highest peak

Mount Rainier is an active volcano covered in glaciers, old-growth forests and wildflower meadows. Get to the summit by riding the Mount Rainier Gondola and soak up panoramic views of the Cascade Range on your way up. You can also admire the landscape from the comfort of your car. Drive down the White Pass or Chinook scenic byways and look out the window to see river valleys, snowcapped peaks and charming mountain villages.

Rainier by Foot

Another way to experience this Washington icon is by following some of the more than 260 miles of maintained trails in Mount Rainier National Park. The most famous is Wonderland Trail, a 93-mile multiday journey that takes you around the entire mountain. Just as renowned is the family-friendly Grove of the Patriarchs Trail, which leads you to huge trees well over a thousand years old. If you're keen to encounter wildlife, stroll the Sourdough Ridge Trail at sunrise to spot endearing marmots. Equally stunning is the Reflection Lakes Trail, famous for beautiful water and wildflowers.

Where Fish Always Bite

The waterways clustered around Mount Rainier are revered for their robust fish populations. Mineral Lake is considered one of the best trout fishing lakes in western Washington, so cast a line from there from late April to late September to score big. Silver Lake houses everything from largemouth bass to catfish and is replenished with approximately 30,000 rainbow trout every April. Local anglers also recommend the Tieton River if you want to catch whitefish and Carbon River for winter salmon or

TOUTLE RIVER
RV RESORT
Make Us Your Headquarters to Visit the Mount St. Helens Area
Conveniently located off I-5 @ exit 52
• Big Rig Friendly pull thru sites with 50 Amp Service
• Tent Area • Heated Pool & Spa Seasonal
• Cedar Barrel Saunas
• Full Size Basketball & Volleyball Courts
• Movie Pavilion Seasonal
• General Store with Large Variety of RV Supplies & Groceries
• Professional Dog Bath & Doggie Social Deck
• 10★ Restrooms & Showers
• Family & Pet Friendly
good sam park
2022 Top Rated 10/10★/9
150 Happy Trails in CASTLE ROCK, WA 98611
360-274-8373 • GreatRVResort.com
See listing Castle Rock, WA

SPOTLIGHTS

The crater from Mt. Saint Helens' 1980 eruption is on full display at the Johnston Ridge Observatory.

steelhead. Other popular fishing spots include the Nisqually River, Skate Creek, Leech Lake and Packwood Lake.

Whole Lava Adventures

You'll find more adventures at Rainier's counterpart, which stands 8,366 feet and packs a powerful history. The south end of Mount St. Helens is home to Ape Cave, the third-longest lava tube in North America. This natural wonder was formed thousands of years ago by a lava stream and randomly discovered by a logger in 1947. It was named after the St. Helens Apes, the Boy Scouts who were the first to explore the cave entirely in the 1950s. You can follow in their footsteps by traversing the 1.5-mile round-trip Lower Ape Cave Trail or the tougher Upper Ape Cave Trail. The trip it not recommended for folks who have claustrophobia.

Lava Canyon

Nearby is the Lava Canyon Trail, a 5-mile loop weaving through waterfalls and a deep gorge. What makes this trail fascinating is that it gives you an idea of how powerful the 1980 eruption was. The gorge it passes was once filled by sediment and then completely cleaned out by mudflows during the blast.

Windy Views

Beyond the south side is another 200 miles of trails. In the east, stop by Windy Ridge Viewpoint to see the crater up close and trek along Norway Pass for stunning wildflower fields and sweeping mountain views. In the west, hike Hummocks Trail to reach a dramatic landscape of ash, rock and mud, which was created by the massive eruption. Climbing to the top of the mountain is also possible as long as you have a permit. This, of course, is only recommended for serious hikers.

Festivals With Wide Appeal

There's a lot more than outdoor recreation going on in this alpine region. Discover local filmmakers by attending screenings and workshops at the Rainier Independent Film Festival, held every May in the Ashford Valley. In the summer, savor a variety of Washington wines at the Mount Rainier Wine Festival. You can also board the Washington Wine Express during three fall weekends to enjoy wine tastings and a scenic ride through Mount Rainier's southern foothills. For a taste of Scotland, check out the Pacific Northwest Scottish Highland Games in the area for Highland dancing, bagpiping and food vendors serving haggis.

Blast from the Past

Mount St. Helens blew its top on May 18, 1980, leaving charred terrain, billows of ash and a horseshoe-shaped crater over a mile wide. Fast forward nearly 40 years and the area has transformed into an ecological wonderland with a growing wildlife population and pink lupines blanketing the pumice plains. You can learn more about the eruption and recovery of the blast zone at the Mount St. Helens Visitors Center. Located just off Highway 504, this information point features a massive step-in model of the volcano and live feed showing Mount St. Helens' current volcano seismicity. Outside, you'll find a vantage point with stunning panoramic views of the surrounding mountains.

See the Stars

The Johnston Ridge Observatory is 50 miles east in the heart of the blast zone. Take a seat in its theater to watch footage of the blast and then view rock samples from nearby lava flows. Afterward, follow the half-mile Eruption Trail behind the building to see the lava dome, crater and landslide deposit with your own eyes.

Olympic Peninsula

Bounded by the Pacific Ocean to the west, Hood Canal to the east and Strait of Juan de Fuca to the north, the 3,600-square-mile Olympic Peninsula buzzes with magic that few wilderness areas can match. The region's mystique owes to the temperate rainforest overflowing with emerald moss and misty old-growth trees. The sense of enchantment is fueled by the dramatic sea stacks sprinkled along the rugged coast. The freshest seafood around and delightful communities rich in maritime history have something to do with the vibe, too. Whether you come for a weekend getaway or weeklong adventure, this northwest pocket of the Evergreen State will delight you with its raw landscape and limitless outdoor pursuits.

Highlights of Olympic National Park

Few places hold UNESCO World Heritage and International Biosphere Reserve status, but

WA

SPOTLIGHTS

An elk grazes in a meadow in the lush Hoh Rainforest in Olympic National Park in the Olympic Peninsula.

Olympic National Park, which occupies much of the peninsula's interior, has managed to pull off both. With glacier-tipped peaks, over 70 miles of coastline and swaths of ancient trees, this natural marvel sets the scene for wild adventures year-round.

Forest Fun

The Hoh Rain Forest is a great place to start your journey. Hike the Hall of Mosses or Spruce Nature trails to uncover an ultralush world teeming with old-growth forests, jade-colored ferns and herds of Roosevelt elk. In search of peace and quiet? Head to the "One Square Inch of Silence," deemed the quietest place in America by Emmy-winning acoustic ecologist Gordon Hempton.

Heart O' the Hills

Hurricane Ridge is another bucket list-worthy spot and can be easily reached by driving up the Hurricane Ridge Road. At the top, you'll come across the Cirque Rim Trail. Follow it to a scenic overlook, where you can take in astounding views of the San Juan Islands and even Vancouver Island on a clear day. The area is also a popular winter sports getaway, so trade your hiking poles for skiing ones when the snow starts to fall.

Home of Big Fish

The fishing in 1,441-square-mile Olympic National Park isn't just good, it's extraordinary. Home to 600 lakes and 4,000 miles of fishable waters, this coastal wilderness makes it easy to catch 37 species of native fish. Anglers agree Lake Crescent is the most beautiful place to reel in epic catches. Extremely large and just as deep, this glacial-carved lake boasts phenomenal visibility of up to 60 feet and produces fish often measuring more than 20 inches. Paddle crystal-clear waters to catch and release the Beardslee trout.

Salmon and Cutthroat, Oh My!

Washington's third-largest natural lake, Lake Ozette supports an abundance of cutthroat trout, while the Hoh River is a hot spot for chinook salmon, coho salmon and steelhead trout. The Elwha River is a renowned fly-fishing destination too, so cast a line to reel in rainbow trout. If you prefer to dig for your dinner, scour the beaches around Hood Canal and Kalaloch for clams.

Rugged Beaches and Deep Forests

There's a lot of ground to cover and so many diverse landscapes to discover in the Olympic Peninsula. One of the best ways to see almost all of it is by cycling the Olympic Discovery Trail. Spanning 130 miles from Port Townsend to La Push, this year-round bike path shows you the highlights of the North Olympic Peninsula while passing rustic farms, historic towns, serene lakes and dense forest.

Beachcombing

Go from bike to foot and stick your toes in the sand at Ruby Beach on the west coast. At low tide, peek in the tide pools to find starfish and sea snails. Afterward, go for a stroll on the Dungeness Spit on the north coast, the longest natural sand spit in North America. Extending almost 6 miles into the Juan de Fuca Strait, this stretch of sand allows you to get up close to harbor seals while providing awe-inspiring views of the Olympic Mountains. Walk to the very tip to reach the New Dungeness Lighthouse and spot 250 species of birds.

A Flattering Cape

More wildlife can be encountered in Cape Flattery. Located at the peninsula's northwest end, where the Strait of Juan de Fuca meets the Pacific, this bird-watching paradise serves up views of eagles, falcons and more from four observation decks and a cedar boardwalk.

Coastal Communities

The most populated areas in the Olympic Peninsula are clustered around the northeast and include Sequim, Port Angeles and Port Townsend. Small-town charm is a running theme throughout all of them, with ample maritime history and delicious local fare added to the mix. In Port Angeles, take the Underground Heritage Tour to wander old storefronts and tunnels beneath the surface, and then dine on freshly caught seafood at Kokopelli Grill or the Crab House restaurant. Port Townsend is one of the few Victorian seaports on the National Register of Historic Places, so spend some time exploring its preserved homes and the Jefferson Museum of Art & History.

Getty Images/iStockphoto

A rock formation stands like a sentinal on Ruby Beach in the Olympic Peninsula National Park

Twilight Time

Sequim and the Dungeness Valley in the northeast also produce a wide variety of organic produce and artisanal goods that can be sampled at regional festivals and farmers markets. Visiting Forks in the west is a must if you love the "Twilight" series of books and films. The historic timber town was used as the setting for Stephenie Meyer's best-selling series and welcomes fans with Forever Twilight in Forks, a four-day festival in September featuring actors from the films about teen vampires.

Mark Your Calendar

Port Angeles has been satisfying seafood cravings for almost two decades with the Dungeness Crab & Seafood Festival. Dig into an old-fashioned crab feast at the Crab Central Pavilion, and then check out the chowder cook-off, grab-a-crab derby and cooking demos with famous chefs. Swap crab for shrimp at Hood Canal ShrimpFest. The Memorial Day weekend event dishes out local spot shrimp alongside live music, craft booths and belt sander races. The Juan de Fuca Festival takes place the same weekend in Port Angeles. Four stages host more than a hundred musicians so swing by for great tunes and family-friendly activities under the summer sky.

Lovely Lavender

Sequim's lavender fields rival those in Provence, France, and you can see them in full bloom at the Lavender Festival every July. The town also hosts the Irrigation Festival, Washington's oldest continuing festival celebrating the region's flourishing agricultural industry. The May event promises nonstop fun thanks to a carnival, parade and fireworks shows.

Spokane and the Inland Empire

As the second-largest city in the Evergreen State, Spokane reigns as the eastern Washington's cultural and commercial hub. One of the big attractions for visitors is the wild and untamed Spokane River. The city's rich Native American history finds expression in numerous sites and monuments, and several days can be spent exploring the lively downtown, awash with good restaurants, bars, cafes and clutch of museums. Along the river, numerous parks are woven with paved hiking/biking trails. The city's proximity to Lake Coeur d'Alene and several Idaho ski areas makes it an ideal launch pad for exploring the northern Idaho Rocky Mountains.

On Land

Walkers, joggers and cyclists ply the Spokane River Centennial Trail, which starts at Nine Mile Falls, west of the city. At Riverside State Park, six miles northwest of downtown Spokane, 10,000 acres of protected forest and trails are a magnet for outdoor enthusiasts, with hiking and biking trails through gorgeous

WA

UNHITCH
AND UNWIND.
Earning a flawless 10/10★/10 Good Sam rating is impressive, but we're not resting on our laurels. In addition to offering an extensive list of RV resort amenities, at Northern Quest RV Resort your entertainment options are endless. Sitting just a stone's throw from Forbes Four-Star, AAA Four Diamond-rated Northern Quest Resort & Casino, you can enjoy 24/7 slots and table games, big-name acts, premier dining, upscale shopping, a luxury spa, an on-site movie theatre, and kids' activities.
NORTHERN QUEST
RV RESORT
A BUD SURLES
SIGNATURE RESORT
Reserve today at NQRVResort.com
COUGAR
good sam park
2022
Top Rated
10/10★/10
KALISPEL
Forbes
NQRVRESORT.COM | 833.702.2082 | SPOKANE, WA
See listing Airway Heights, WA

SPOTLIGHTS

The Washington Water Power Building and Monroe Street Bridge along the Spokane in Spokane.

scenery. Among the park's highlights is the Bowl and Pitcher, a deep gorge with massive boulders at a bend in the river. The popular trail parallels the river for 37 miles to the Idaho state line where it connects to the Idaho Centennial Trail for a final leg into Coeur d'Alene (a total of 61 miles of pathway).

On the Water

Summertime transforms the Spokane area into a freshwater playground. Creeks and rivers cut through the hills that rise above the city and within an hour's drive of downtown, there are 76 lakes. The famous Spokane River is a 111-mile-long tributary of the Columbia River which runs right through the heart of the city. From Spokane, you can head in any direction to swim, boat, fly fish, paddle board, kayak, canoe and raft.

Local Color

The Spokane area is home to some of the most beautiful public gardens in the Northwest. At Manito Park, the classically proportioned Duncan Garden is a formal Renaissance-style garden designed after those of 17th-century Europe. The adjacent Gaiser Conservatory brims with exotic tropical plants, a rose garden, a lilac garden and a kaleidoscopic perennial garden that peaks in June. The peaceful Nishinomiya Japanese Garden features willows, brilliant azaleas, and a strolling pond garden. The John A. Finch Arboretum houses a botanical and tree garden with over 2,000 labeled ornamental trees, shrubs, and flowers; it is breathtaking in the fall.

Festivals and Events

The city's most anticipated summer event, Hoopfest, is the largest 3-on-3 basketball tournament in the world and draws thousands of spectators. The Gathering at the Falls Powwow is an annual celebration of Native American arts and culture, past and present. Throughout June, the Spokane Pride Parade and Rainbow Festival features parades, shows, pop-up events and music that honor LGBT communities around the world.

Premier Sites

By far, Spokane's most impressive museum, the Northwest Museum of Arts & Culture, presents world-class exhibitions on regional subjects. Created for the 1974 World's Fair Expo, the 100-acre Riverfront Park is Spokane's beloved front yard. Formerly occupied with railroad tracks and depots, the park's genesis propelled the city's rebirth. Locals and visitors flock to enjoy a range of family-friendly activities, including summertime concerts and ice-skating in the winter. Public artworks and points of interest abound, including the eye-catching Rotary Fountain and one of the nation's most beautiful carousels, the restored 1909 Looff Carousel, with hand-carved horses. Some 15 miles north of Spokane, Cat Tales Zoological Park allows visitors to get up close and view tigers and other big cats. Children can pet a baby tiger at the petting zoo.

Spokane Past

Native Americans lived along the Spokane River for thousands of years. When the first explorers and fur traders arrived in 1807, they established a trading post — Spokan House (originally spelled with no letter e)— downriver from Spokane Falls and battled with Native Americans for beaver pelts. Today, the Spokane House Interpretive Site presents an overview of the early fur trade in the Spokane/Inland Empire region through exhibits, maps, and interactive displays. With the arrival of the Northern Pacific Railroad in 1881, the town of Spokane Falls became the region's economic powerhouse. The city's stature lasted less than a decade. In the summer of 1889, a fire destroyed the commercial district. Within two years, the city had fully recovered and moved onwards, adding an 'e' to its name in the process.

Tri-Cities

With 300 days of sunshine per year and a dry, desert-like climate, the Tri-Cities region looks quite different from the rest of Washington. But rest assured, this region delivers everything you know and love about the Evergreen State. Spend your vacation hooking big fish, roaming vast green spaces and feasting on locally grown fare. The cities of Richland, Pasco and Kennewick have your urban needs covered. All you need to do is bring your sense of adventure.

Wonderful Weather

The Cascade Mountains to the west serve as a natural guard against weather patterns

WA

TRI-CITIES LARGEST RV PARK
HORN RAPIDS
Business Center
RV Resort
HORN RAPIDS
BIG-RIG
FRIENDLY
• 225+ BEAUTIFULLY LANDSCAPED SITES
• WiFi & CABLE
• 20-30-50- AMP SERVICE
• LARGE PULL-THRU SITES
• SWIMMING POOL/SPA
• STORE/DELI/RV SUPPLIES/PROPANE
• REC. HALL W/ KITCHEN
• DAILY, WEEKLY, EXTENDED STAY SITES
BE SURE TO ASK ABOUT
SPECIAL RATES, WINE TASTING TOURS & GOLF PACKAGES
good sam park
2022
Top Rated
10/10★/10
See listing
Richland, WA
WWW.HORNRAPIDSRVRESORT.COM

WA

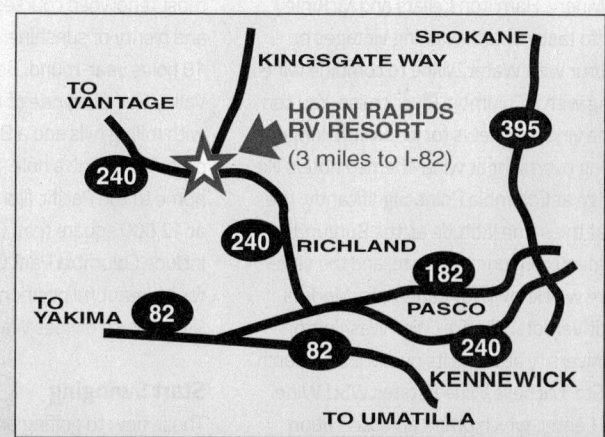

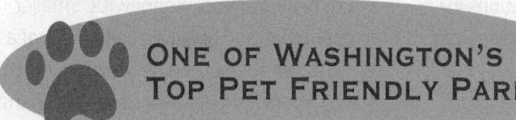

Visitors enjoy a pinot noir poured at a winery in the vineyard-rich Tri Cities area in eastern Washington.

from the rainier, western portion of the state—keeping out heavy precipitation and creating the kind of balmy summers and mild winters more commonly found further to the southeast.

Grape Expectations

This part of southeast Washington likes to call itself the "Heart of Washington Wine Country," a well-deserved title, considering the area has over 200 wineries within a 50-mile radius. Yakima Valley, Prosser, Red Mountain and Walla Walla have all been blessed with excellent soil and warm temperatures, allowing them to produce a wide range of vintages. Set aside some time to tour these wine makers.

Tantalizing Tastes

Pop in the rustic tasting rooms at Barnard Griffin Winery, Hamilton Cellars and McKinley Springs to taste award-winning vintages or book a tour with Water2Wine to combine wine sampling with a Columbia River cruise. You can enjoy the vineyard views for just a little longer by staying overnight at wine-themed hotels like The Lodge at Columbia Point. Significantly, the area is at the same latitude as the Burgundy and Bordeaux regions of France, and the vineyards are well known for Cabernets, Merlots and Petit Verdots. The Tri-Cities Washington State University also has its own wine research center, Ste. Michelle Wine Estates WSU Wine Science Center, which offers an observation deck for visitors who want to look in on the research. Learn all about the science that takes wines from grapevine to stem glass, and find out how vintners coax maximum flavor from grapes. Get a new appreciation for these beautiful beverages.

Play in the Land of Three Rivers

Major rivers flow through the Tri-Cities, so grab your fishing rod and make a beeline to the banks. Drop a line in the Columbia River to catch an abundance of Chinook and coho salmon or head a bit north and nab rainbow and kokanee trout in large reservoirs such as Moses Lake and Banks Lake. The Snake River is also a hot spot for steelhead trout from October to March. If paddling is more your thing, launch your kayak into the Yakima River Delta to reach the dramatic White Bluffs or set off on the Northwest Discovery Water Trail to explore more of the Clearwater, Snake and Columbia rivers. Other popular paddling destinations include Lake Sacajawea and Potholes State Park.

Perfect Your Golf Game

The Tri-Cities boast some of Washington's most renowned courses with mild winters and plenty of sunshine, allowing you to play 18 holes year-round. Book a tee time at Wine Valley Golf Club, one of the most scenic courses with rolling hills and a Blue Mountains backdrop. Try to sink a hole-in-one at Canyon Lakes, home to the Pacific Northwest's largest green at 12,000 square feet. Other popular courses include Columbia Park Golf Course — notable for its beautiful position next to the Columbia River, which divides Washington and Oregon.

Start Swinging

Those new to golfing or in search of professional guidance will appreciate the 28-acre Pasco Golfland, with a driving range, and chipping and putting greens. Sun Willows golf course in central Pasco is a particularly popular public option. Designed by legendary golf architect Robert Muir Graves, it features five scenic lakes and a full driving range. In Richland, Columbia Point weaves a moderately challenging course from a mix of sandy terrain and manicured greens — all on the banks of the Columbia River.

Tri-Cities Nature

Beyond the links are a world of nature preserves, treeless mountains and lush valleys. Hike to the summit of Badger Mountain for captivating vistas of the Yakima and Columbia River valleys and trek along the Candy Mountain Trail to see a landscape blanketed in wildflowers. Bird-watching is also excellent in the Chamna Natural Preserve.

From Local Fields to Delicious Meals

The fertile valleys of this region produce more than 200 kinds of fruits, vegetables and grains. Local chefs love incorporating the freshest produce into their culinary creations, so come to the Tri-Cities hungry and ready to feast. Kennewick, Pasco and Richland all have their own farmers markets, too. The one in Pasco is the largest open-air farmers market in Washington and packed to the brim with luscious berries, freshly picked corn and artisanal products. The Prosser Farmers Market is the place to go for gourmet cheeses, while Bill's Berry Farm allows you to pick your own strawberries.

Prime Pasco

Pasco, on the northern shores of the Columbia River, is in many ways a mirror image of its south bank neighbor, Kennewick. Smaller in population and boasting even more of a small-town image than Kennewick or Richland, Pasco offers a similar assortment of charming riverside walks and parks, as well a healthy mix of wineries and tasting bars. History buffs can choose to whittle away a few hours combing through the eclectic, small-town history items on display in Franklin County Historical Museum.

FOR MORE INFORMATION

Washington State Tourism, 800-544-1800, www.experiencewa.com
Visit Seattle, 866-732-2695, www.visitseattle.org
Visit Rainier, www.visitrainier.com
Mount St. Helens, 360-274-7750, www.mountsthelens.com
Olympic Peninsula, 360-274-7750, olympicpeninsula.org
Visit Spokane, 888-SPOKANE www.visitspokane.com
Tri-Cities Visitor and Convention Bureau, 800-254-5824, www.visittri-cities.com

Washington

AIRWAY HEIGHTS — B6 *Spokane*

NORTHERN QUEST RV RESORT

good sam park **Ratings: 10/10★/10** (RV Resort) From Jct of I-90 and US-2 at exit 277: Go 4-1/2 mi W on US-2, then 1 mi N on S Hayford Rd, then 1/4 mi W on Sprague Ave, then exit roundabout on Kelso Way (L). **FAC:** paved rds. (67 spaces). Avail: 47 paved, patios, 29 pull-thrus, (50x80), back-ins (50x65), 47 full hkups (30/50 amps), seasonal sites, WiFi @ sites, rentals, dump, laundry, groc, LP bottles, fire rings, firewood, restaurant, controlled access. **REC:** heated pool, golf. Pet restrict (Q). Partial handicap access. No tents. Big rig sites, 14 day max stay, eco-friendly. 2021 rates: $65 to $85, Military discount. ATM.
(833)702-2082 Lat: 47.658409, Lon: -117.562623
303 South Kalispel Way, Airway Heights, WA 99001
www.nqrvresort.com
See ad page 976

Things to See and Do

NORTHERN QUEST RESORT & CASINO AAA Four-Diamond Resort with luxury amenities. 24/7 Casino has 55,000 sq ft of gaming space. 14 distinct restaurants, bars, lounges, and nightclubs. Luxury Spa with extensive services. Star-studded entertainment and concerts. Partial handicap access. RV accessible. Restrooms. Food. Hours: 24 hours. ATM.
(877)871-6772 Lat: 47.65840, Lon: -117.56262
100 North Hayford Road, Airway Heights, WA 99001
www.northernquest.com
See ad page 976

AMANDA PARK — B1 *Grays Harbor*

OLYMPIC NATIONAL PARK/GRAVES CREEK (Public National Park) From town: Go 20 mi NE on gravel access road. 30 Avail: Pit toilets. 2021 rates: $20. (360)365-3130

ANACORTES — A2 *Skagit*

ANACORTES See also Bellingham, Bow, Burlington, Ferndale, La Conner, Mount Vernon & Oak Harbor.

FIDALGO BAY RV RESORT **Ratings: 9/10★/9** (RV Resort) Avail: 119 full hkups (30/50 amps). 2021 rates: $39.78 to $70.72. (360)293-5353, 4701 Fidalgo Bay Rd, Anacortes, WA 98221

PIONEER TRAILS RV RESORT **Ratings: 7.5/8.5★/8.5** (RV Park) Avail: 150 full hkups (30/50 amps). 2021 rates: $42 to $55. (360)293-5355, 7337 Miller Rd, Anacortes, WA 98221

SPENCER SPIT (Public State Park) Board ferry at Anacortes, exit at Lopez Island, S 1 mi to Jct of Ferry Rd & Center Rd, S 1 mi on Center Rd to Cross Rd, E 0.75 mi to Port Stanley, S 0.25 mi to Bakerview Rd (E). 30 Avail. 2021 rates: $12 to $37. Mar 14 to Oct 30. (888)226-7688

SWINOMISH CASINO RV PARK **Ratings: 7.5/NA/7.5** (RV Park) Avail: 35 full hkups (30/50 amps). 2021 rates: $27 to $35. (888)288-8883, 12885 Casino Dr, Anacortes, WA 98221

WASHINGTON PARK (Public) From Jct of I-5 & Hwy 20 (exit 230), W 16 mi on Hwy 20 to 12th St, W 3.5 mi to Sunset Ave, W 1 mi (E). 68 Avail: 46 W, 46 E (20 amps). 2021 rates: $17 to $26. (360)293-1918

ANATONE — D6 *Asotin*

FIELDS SPRING (Public State Park) From Jct of Hwy 12 & 129 (in Clarkston), S 30 mi on Hwy 129 (L). 20 Avail. 2021 rates: $20 to $45. (509)256-3332

ARLINGTON — B3 *Snohomish*

LAKE KI RV RESORT & CAMP **Ratings: 6.5/8.5/7.5** (Campground) Avail: 14 full hkups (30/50 amps). 2021 rates: $35 to $45. (360)652-0619, 2904 Lakewood Rd, Arlington, WA 98223

ARTIC — C1 *Grays Harbor*

ARTIC RV PARK **Ratings: 4.5/7.5★/8** (Campground) 17 Avail: 8 full hkups, 9 W, 9 E (30/50 amps). 2021 rates: $25 to $30. May 01 to Oct 01. (360)591-8246, 893 US Hwy 101, Cosmopolis, WA 98537

Park owners and staff are rightly proud of their business. Let them know how much you enjoyed your stay.

ASHFORD — C3 *Pierce*

MOUNTHAVEN RESORT **Ratings: 5/7.5/7** (Campground) Avail: 13 full hkups (20/30 amps). 2021 rates: $59. (360)569-2594, 38210 SR 706 E, Ashford, WA 98304

BAINBRIDGE ISLAND — B2 *Kitsap*

FAY BAINBRIDGE PARK & CAMPGROUND (Public) Take ferry from Seattle to Bainbridge Island, N 5 mi on Hwy 305 to Day Rd NE, E 2 mi to Sunrise Dr NE, N 2 mi (R). 26 Avail: 26 W, 19 E. 2021 rates: $30 to $40. (206)842-3931

BATTLE GROUND — D2 *Clark*

BATTLE GROUND LAKE (Public State Park) From town, E 0.3 mi on Main St to Grace Ave, N 0.5 mi to N 229 St, E 2.5 mi (L). Avail: 6 E (20/30 amps). 2021 rates: $20 to $45. (888)226-7688

BAY CENTER — C1 *Pacific*

BAY CENTER/WILLAPA BAY KOA **Ratings: 7.5/9.5★/9** (Campground) 32 Avail: 21 full hkups, 11 W, 11 E (30/50 amps). 2021 rates: $42 to $77. Apr 01 to Dec 01. (800)562-7810, 457 Bay Center Rd, Bay Center, WA 98527

BELFAIR — C2 *Mason*

BELFAIR (Public State Park) From Jct of SR-3 & SR-300, W 3 mi on SR-300 (L). Avail: 37 full hkups (30 amps). 2021 rates: $20 to $45. (888)226-7688

POTHOLES

(Public State Park) From Jct of Sr-17 & Hwy 262 (O'Sullivan Dam Rd), W 11.8 mi on O'Sullivan Dam Rd (R). **FAC:** paved/gravel rds. Avail: 121 gravel, patios, back-ins (40x46), 60 full hkups (30 amps), tent sites, rentals, shower$, dump, mobile sewer, groc, firewood. **REC:** Potholes Reservoir: fishing, kayaking/canoeing, playground. Pets OK. Partial handicap access, 10 day max stay. 2021 rates: $20 to $45.
(888)226-7688 Lat: 46.971768, Lon: -119.348582
6762 Hwy 262E, Othello, WA 99344
www.parks.wa.gov

SUMMERTIDE RESORT & MARINA ON HOOD CANAL **Ratings: 5.5/8.5★/7** (Campground) Avail: 13 full hkups (30/50 amps). 2021 rates: $50. (360)275-9313, 15781 NE North Shore Rd, Tahuya, WA 98588

BELLEVUE — B3 *King*

BELLEVUE See also Black Diamond, Bothell, Everett, Fall City, Issaquah, Kent, Monroe & Poulsbo.

BELLINGHAM — A2 *Whatcom*

BELLINGHAM See also Anacortes, Birch Bay, Bow, Burlington, Ferndale, La Conner, Lynden, Mount Vernon & Oak Harbor, WA; Aldergrove & Surrey, BC.

BELLINGHAM RV PARK

good sam park **Ratings: 9/9.5★/8.5** (RV Park) Avail: 37 full hkups (30/50 amps). 2021 rates: $48 to $53. (888)372-1224, 3939 Bennett Dr, Bellingham, WA 98225

LARRABEE (Public State Park) From Jct of I-5 & Old Fairhaven Pkwy (exit 250), W 1.4 mi on Old Fairhaven Pkwy to 12th St, S 0.1 mi to Chuckanut Dr, S 4.1 mi (R). Avail: 26 full hkups (20/30 amps). 2021 rates: $20 to $50. (888)226-7688

BENTON CITY — D4 *Benton*

BEACH RV PARK AND CAMPGROUND **Ratings: 8.5/9.5★/7** (RV Park) Avail: 59 full hkups (30/50 amps). 2021 rates: $42. (509)588-5959, 100 Abby Ave, Benton City, WA 99320

BIRCH BAY — A2 *Whatcom*

BEACHWOOD RESORT **Ratings: 8/9★/8.5** (RV Resort) 277 Avail: 199 full hkups, 78 W, 78 E (30/50 amps). 2021 rates: $50. (888)901-2719, 5001 Bay Rd, Blaine, WA 98230

BIRCH BAY RESORT -THOUSAND TRAILS

good sam park **Ratings: 9/7.5/8** (Membership Park) Avail: 20 full hkups (30/50 amps). 2021 rates: $56 to $67. (888)563-7040, 8418 Harborview Rd, Blaine, WA 98230

BLACK DIAMOND — C3 *King*

LAKE SAWYER RESORT-SUNRISE RESORTS **Ratings: 7/6/7** (Membership Park) 75 Avail: 48 full hkups, 27 W, 27 E (30 amps). 2021 rates: $42 to $51. (360)886-2244, 30250 224th Ave SE, Black Diamond, WA 98010

Find Good Sam member specials at GanderOutdoors.com

BLAINE — A2 *Whatcom*

BIRCH BAY (Public State Park) S-bnd: From Jct of I-5 & Birch Bay/Lynden Rd (exit 270), W 3 mi on Birch Bay/Lynden Rd to Blaine Rd, S 2 mi to Bay Rd, W 1.1 mi to Jackson Rd, S 0.3 mi to Helwig Rd, W 0.5 mi (E); or N-bnd: From Jct of I-5 & Grandview Rd (exit 266), W 7 mi on Grandview Rd to Jackson Rd, N 0.8 mi (E). 167 Avail: 20 W, 20 E (20/30 amps). 2021 rates: $20 to $45. May 15 to Sep 15. (360)371-2800

BOTHELL — B3 *Snohomish*

BOTHELL See also Everett, Fall City, Issaquah, Kent, Monroe & Poulsbo.

LAKE PLEASANT RV PARK

Ratings: 9/9.5★/10 (RV Park) From Jct of I-405 and Bothell Hwy (Exit 26), Go 1-1/8 mi S on Bothell Hwy to 242nd St (L).

VALLEY SETTING - ATTRACTIONS GALORE

We're the perfect park to stay & rest or explore the Seattle area. See the Space Needle-Pike Place Mkt-Boeing-Bellevue Shops-Snoqualmie Falls. Special RV Parking while cruising or flying out. Book early-we fill up in Summer.

FAC: paved rds. (198 spaces). Avail: 119 paved, 45 pull-thrus, (27x65), back-ins (29x65), 119 full hkups (30/50 amps), seasonal sites, WiFi @ sites, dump, laundry, LP gas. **REC:** Lake Pleasant: fishing, boating nearby, playground. Pet restrict (B). Partial handicap access. No tents. Big rig sites, 14 day max stay, eco-friendly. 2021 rates: $52.
(425)487-1785 Lat: 47.777965, Lon: -122.217693
24025 Bothell Everett Hwy SE, Bothell, WA 98021
www.lakepleasantrv.com
See ad page 971

BOW — A2 *Skagit*

MOUNT VERNON RV CAMPGROUND

good sam park **Ratings: 7.5/8/6.5** (Membership Park) 20 Avail: 20 W, 20 E (20/30 amps). 2021 rates: $57. (888)563-7040, 5409 N Darrk Lane, Bow, WA 98232

BREMERTON — B2 *Kitsap*

ILLAHEE (Public State Park) From town, NE 3 mi on Sylvan Way (E). Avail: 2 full hkups. 2021 rates: $20 to $45. (360)478-6460

BREWSTER — B4 *Okanogan*

COLUMBIA COVE RV PARK (Public) From Jct of US-97 & 7th St (in town), S 0.5 mi on 7th St (L). Avail: 29 full hkups (30 amps). 2021 rates: $15 to $45. (509)689-3464

BRIDGEPORT — B4 *Douglas*

BRIDGEPORT (Public State Park) From Jct of SR-17 & park access rd: Go 3 mi NE on park access rd (L). 20 Avail: 20 W, 20 E (30 amps). 2021 rates: $20 to $50. (888)226-7688

RV Park ratings you can rely on!

Washington Privately Owned Campground Information Updated by our Good Sam Representatives

Kelly & Monica Wentz

Kelly and I went fulltime in 2017. The kids grew up and we took off. We have always loved to travel and experience new things and RVing allows us to do both. We both come from marketing backgrounds and love helping others.

WA

BRIDGEPORT (CONT)

MARINA & RV PARK (Public) From Jct of SR-17 & SR-173, NW 1.4 mi on SR-173 to Columbia St, N 0.2 mi to 7th St, N 0.1 mi (E). Avail: 21 full hkups (30/50 amps). 2021 rates: $20 to $30. (509)686-4747

BRINNON — B2 *Jefferson*

COVE RV PARK & COUNTRY STORE **Ratings: 7/7.5★/7** (Campground) Avail: 23 full hkups (30/50 amps). 2021 rates: $39. Mar 01 to Oct 31. (360)796-4723, 303075 N Hwy 101, Brinnon, WA 98320

DOSEWALLIPS (Public State Park) From town, S 1 mi on Hood Canal (US-101), at MP-307 (R). 48 Avail: 38 full hkups, 10 W, 10 E (30 amps). 2021 rates: $20 to $45. (360)796-4415

BURBANK — D5 *Walla Walla*

LAKE SACAJAWEA - COE/CHARBONNEAU PARK (Public Corps) From E Jct of US-12 & US-395, S 4 mi on US-12 to Hwy 124, E 8 mi to Sun Harbor Dr, N 1.5 mi to Charbonneau Rd, W 0.1 mi (R). Avail: 52 E (20/30 amps). 2021 rates: $12 to $30. May 18 to Sep 03. (509)547-2048

LAKE SACAJAWEA - COE/FISHHOOK PARK (Public Corps) From E Jct of US-12 & US-395, S 4 mi on US-12 to Hwy 124, E 19 mi to Fishhook Park Rd, N 4 mi (L). 41 Avail: 41 W, 41 E (20/30 amps). 2021 rates: $12 to $30. May 18 to Sep 03. (509)547-2048

BURLINGTON — A2 *Skagit*

BURLINGTON/ANACORTES KOA **Ratings: 7.5/8/8** (Campground) 96 Avail: 71 full hkups, 25 W, 25 E (30/50 amps). 2021 rates: $39.97 to $70.97. (800)562-9154, 6397 N Green Rd, Burlington, WA 98233

FRIDAY CREEK

Ratings: 3/7/5.5 (Membership Park) 27 Avail: 27 W, 27 E (30 amps). 2021 rates: $42. May 01 to Oct 01. (888)563-7040, 4474 Friday Creek Rd, Burlington, WA 98233

Travel Services

CAMPING WORLD OF BURLINGTON As the nation's largest retailer of RV supplies, accessories, services and new and used RVs, Camping World is committed to making your total RV experience better. RV Dealership located at 1535 Walton Dr, Burlington. **SERVICES:** RV, tire, RV appliance, restrooms. RV Sales. RV supplies, LP gas, dump, emergency parking, RV accessible. Hours: 9am to 7pm.
(855)212-3307 Lat: 48.485498, Lon: -122.333787
1535 Walton Dr, Burlington, WA 98233
www.campingworld.com

CASTLE ROCK — D2 *Cowlitz*

MOUNT ST HELENS KOA **Ratings: 8/9★/8.5** (Campground) 51 Avail: 28 full hkups, 23 W, 23 E (30/50 amps). 2021 rates: $35.89 to $58.89. (360)274-8522, 167 Schaffran Rd, Castle Rock, WA 98611

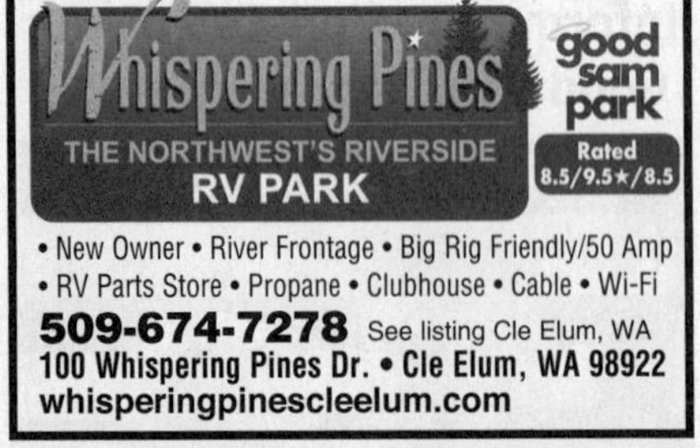

TOUTLE RIVER RV RESORT

Ratings: 10/10★/9 (RV Park) From Jct of I-5 (Exit 52) & Barnes Rd: Go W on Barnes Rd to first left, Happy Trails Rd (L).

FAMILY FRIENDLY DESTINATION FOR ALL
One of the Northwest's largest, best equipped, resorts. Great base camp for exploring-8 miles from Mt St Helens Visitor Center, day trips galore. More amenities than you can imagine!

FAC: paved rds. (306 spaces). Avail: 271 all weather, 116 pull-thrus, (35x100), back-ins (30x70), 271 full hkups (30/50 amps), seasonal sites, WiFi @ sites, tent sites, laundry, groc, LP gas, fire rings, firewood, controlled access. **REC:** heated pool, hot tub, Toutle River: playground. Pet restrict (B). Partial handicap access. Big rig sites, eco-friendly. 2021 rates: $49.
(360)274-8373 Lat: 46.32526, Lon: -122.91478
150 Happy Trails, Castle Rock, WA 98611
www.greatrvresort.com
See ad page 972

CATHLAMET — D2 *Wahkiakum*

ELOCHOMAN SLOUGH MARINA (Public) From Jct SR-4 & SR-409, NW 300 ft on SR-4 to 3rd Ave (Chester), W 0.2 mi (E). 15 Avail: 15 W, 15 E (30/50 amps). 2021 rates: $35. (360)795-3501

CENTRALIA — C2 *Lewis*

CENTRALIA See also Chehalis, Mossyrock, Olympia, Rochester & Silver Creek.

MIDWAY RV PARK

Ratings: 9/10★/9.5 (RV Park) From Jct of I-5 & Harrison Ave (exit 82): Go W 0.8 mi on Harrison Ave to Galvin Rd, then S 0.3 mi on Galvin Rd (L). **FAC:** paved rds. (62 spaces). Avail: 22 paved, patios, 20 pull-thrus, (27x66), back-ins (28x60), 22 full hkups (30/50 amps), seasonal sites, cable, WiFi @ sites, laundry, groc, LP gas, firewood. **REC:** boating nearby. Pet restrict (S/B/Q). Partial handicap access. No tents. Big rig sites, eco-friendly. 2021 rates: $52.75, Military discount.
(360)736-3200 Lat: 46.734670, Lon: -122.995321
3200 Galvin Rd, Centralia, WA 98531
www.midwayrvparkwa.com
See ad page 973

CHEHALIS — C2 *Lewis*

CHEHALIS RESORT

Ratings: 7.5/8.5★/7 (Membership Park) 292 Avail: 292 W, 292 E (30/50 amps). 2021 rates: $55 to $73. (888)563-7040, 2228 Centralia Alpha Rd, Chehalis, WA 98532

RAINBOW FALLS (Public State Park) From Jct of I-5 & Exit 77 (Hwy 6), W 16 mi on Hwy 6 (R). 48 Avail: 8 W, 8 E (20/50 amps). 2021 rates: $20 to $45. (360)291-3767

RIVERSIDE GOLF CLUB & RV PARK **Ratings: 7/NA/7.5** (RV Park) Avail: 36 full hkups (30/50 amps). 2021 rates: $50 to $70. (360)748-8182, 1451 NW Airport Rd, Chehalis, WA 98532

STAN HEDWALL PARK (Public) From Jct of I-5 & Rice Rd (exit 76), W 0.5 mi on Rice Rd (R). 29 Avail: 29 W, 29 E (30/50 amps). 2021 rates: $20. Mar 02 to Nov 30. (360)748-0271

CHELAN — B4 *Chelan*

LAKE CHELAN (Public State Park) From Jct of Woodin Ave & Alt US-97 (in town), S 3.9 mi on Alt US-97 to South Shore Rd/SR-971, W 6 mi (R). 35 Avail: 17 full hkups, 18 W, 18 E (50 amps). 2021 rates: $20 to $45. (509)687-3710

LAKESHORE RV PARK & MARINA (Public) From W Jct of US-Alt 97A & SR 150: Go 1/2 mi NW on SR 150/Manson Rd (L) Note: No dogs are allowed in park Memorial Day weekend and from July 1st thru Labor Day. Avail: 163 full hkups (30/50 amps). 2021 rates: $32 to $67. (509)682-8023

TWENTY-FIVE MILE CREEK (Public State Park) From jct US 97 & Hwy 150: Go 4 mi S on US 97, then 16 mi W on S Lakeshore Rd. 21 Avail: 13 full hkups, 8 W, 8 E. 2021 rates: $20 to $45. (888)226-7688

CHENEY — B6 *Spokane*

KLINK'S WILLIAMS LAKE RESORT **Ratings: 7.5/8.5★/8.5** (Campground) 62 Avail: 57 full hkups, 5 W, 5 E (30/50 amps). 2021 rates: $59.95 to $64.95. Apr 01 to Oct 01. (509)235-2391, 18617 W Williams Lake Rd, Cheney, WA 99004

MILITARY PARK CLEAR LAKE REC AREA (FAIRCHILD AFB) (Public) From jct I-90 & Salnave Rd (exit 264), N on Salnave Rd to Clear Lake Rd, E 1 mi, follow signs. 30 Avail: 24 full hkups, 6 W, 6 E (30/50 amps). 2021 rates: $15 to $20. Apr 30 to Sep 01. (509)299-5129

PEACEFUL PINES RV PARK & CAMPGROUND **Ratings: 7.5/9.5★/8.5** (Campground) 21 Avail: 15 full hkups, 4 W, 4 E (30/50 amps). 2021 rates: $32 to $38. (509)235-4966, 1231 W 1st St, Cheney, WA 99004

CHEWELAH — B6 *Stevens*

CHEWELAH CASINO & RV PARK **Ratings: 3.5/NA/5** (RV Park) 10 Avail: 10 W, 10 E (30/50 amps). 2021 rates: $25 to $30. Apr 15 to Oct 31. (800)322-2788, 2555 Smith Rd, Chewelah, WA 99109

CHEWELAH GOLF & COUNTRY CLUB **Ratings: 6/7.5/7.5** (Campground) Avail: 27 full hkups (30/50 amps). 2021 rates: $37. Apr 01 to Oct 31. (509)935-6807, 2537 Sand Canyon Rd, Chewelah, WA 99109

JENNE MEMORIAL PARK (Public) From town: Go 1/4 mi N on US-395. 14 Avail: 14 W, 14 E. (509)935-8311

CHINOOK — D1 *Pacific*

COLUMBIA SHORES RV PARK - K/M RESORTS **Ratings: 4/7/6** (Membership Park) 57 Avail: 57 W, 57 E (30 amps). 2021 rates: $75. (800)392-5722, 706 Hwy 101, Chinook, WA 98614

CLARKSTON — D6 *Asotin*

CHIEF TIMOTHY PARK **Ratings: 8.5/9★/9.5** (RV Park) 48 Avail: 25 full hkups, 8 W, 8 E (30 amps). 2021 rates: $38 to $42. Mar 01 to Nov 30. (509)758-9580, 13766 Hwy 12, Clarkston, WA 99403

GRANITE LAKE PREMIER RV RESORT

Ratings: 9.5/10★/10 (RV Park) From Jct of Hwy 12 & 5th St (in town): Go 1/4 mi N on 5th St (L). **FAC:** paved rds. (75 spaces). Avail: 50 paved, patios, 18 pull-thrus, (28x60), back-ins (28x57), 50 full hkups (30/50 amps), seasonal sites, WiFi @ sites, rentals, laundry. **REC:** Granite Lake: swim, fishing, kayaking/canoeing, boating nearby, hunting nearby, rec open to public. Pets OK. Partial handicap access. No tents. Big rig sites, eco-friendly. 2021 rates: $56 to $62.50, Military discount.
(509)751-1635 Lat: 46.424214, Lon: -117.043018
306 Granite Lake Dr, Clarkston, WA 99403
www.premierrvresorts.com
See ad this page

HELLS CANYON RV RESORT & MARINA

Ratings: 9.5/10★/9.5 (RV Park) Avail: 47 full hkups (30/50 amps). 2021 rates: $41.99 to $48.99. (509)758-6963, 1560 Port Drive, Clarkston, WA 99403

HILLVIEW RV PARK **Ratings: 8/10★/7** (RV Park) Avail: 10 full hkups (30/50 amps). 2021 rates: $40. (866)758-6299, 1224 Bridge St, Clarkston, WA 99403

CLE ELUM — C3 *Kittitas*

SUN COUNTRY GOLF AND RV **Ratings: 6/9.5★/8.5** (RV Park) Avail: 14 full hkups (50 amps). 2021 rates: $42 to $49. Apr 01 to Nov 01. (509)674-2226, 841 St Andrews Dr, Cle Elum, WA 98922

WHISPERING PINES RV PARK & RV PARTS STORE

Ratings: 8.5/9.5★/8.5 (Campground) W-bnd: From Jct of I-90 & Exit 84 (Cle Elum): Go 1/8 mi S (L); or E-bnd: From Jct of I-90 & Exit 84 (Cle Elum): Go 3/4 mi E on First St to Oakes Ave, then 1/2 mi S on Oakes Ave (L). **FAC:** paved rds. (81 spaces). Avail: 77 gravel, patios, 14 pull-thrus, (34x75), back-ins (30x65), 15 full hkups, 25 W, 25 E (30/50 amps), seasonal sites, WiFi @ sites, tent sites, rentals, dump, laundry, LP gas, fire rings, controlled access. **REC:** Watts Lake: swim, fishing, kayaking/canoeing, boating nearby, hunting nearby. Pets OK. Big rig sites, 29 day max stay. 2021 rates: $42 to $55, Military discount.
(509)674-7278 Lat: 47.189420, Lon: -120.936748
100 Whispering Pines Dr, Cle Elum, WA 98922
whisperingpinescleelum.com
See ad this page

COLBERT — B6 *Spokane*

WILD ROSE RV PARK

Ratings: 8/8.5★/9 (RV Park) From Jct of SR-395 & SR-2 (between MP 173-174): Go 9 mi N on SR-395 (R). **FAC:** gravel rds. (57 spaces). Avail: 34 gravel, patios, 9 pull-thrus, (32x55), back-ins (25x55), 34 full

hkups (30/50 amps), seasonal sites, WiFi @ sites, shower$, laundry. Pets OK. Partial handicap access. No tents. 2021 rates: $40. no cc.
(509)276-8853 Lat: 47.869011, Lon: -117.421890
23106 N Hwy 395, Colbert, WA 99005
See ad this page

COLVILLE — A5 *Stevens*

NORTHEAST WASHINGTON FAIRGROUNDS RV PARK (Public) From Jct of Hwy 395 & Columbia Ave., W 0.1 mi on Columbia St (E). 55 Avail: 55 W, 55 E (30 amps). 2021 rates: $25. Apr 01 to Nov 30. (509)684-2585

CONCONULLY — A4 *Okanogan*

CONCONULLY (Public State Park) At Jct of Conconully Hwy & W Broadway (L). 20 Avail: 20 W, 20 E (30/50 amps). 2021 rates: $20 to $50. Apr 01 to Oct 31. (888)226-7688

CONCRETE — A3 *Skagit*

GRANDY CREEK RV CAMPGROUND KOA
good sam park **Ratings: 7.5/8/7** (Campground) 50 Avail: 25 full hkups, 25 W, 25 E (30/50 amps). 2021 rates: $54. Mar 01 to Oct 31. (888)563-7040, 7370 Russell Rd, Concrete, WA 98237

RASAR (Public State Park) From town: Go 7 mi W on Hwy 20, then 3/4 mi S on Russell Rd, then 2 mi W on Cape Horn Rd. 38 Avail: 20 W, 20 E. 2021 rates: $20 to $45. (360)826-3942

CONNELL — C5 *Franklin*

COYOTE RUN RV PARK
good sam park **Ratings: 8.5/10★/8** (RV Park) Avail: 42 full hkups (30/50 amps). 2021 rates: $41 to $45. (509)234-0111, 351 E Hawthorn, Connell, WA 99326

COPALIS BEACH — C1 *Grays Harbor*

COPALIS BEACH RESORT-SUNRISE RESORTS **Ratings: 7/6/6.5** (Membership Park) Avail: 81 full hkups (30/50 amps). 2021 rates: $38 to $50. (360)289-4278, 14 Heath Rd, Copalis Beach, WA 98535

COSMOPOLIS — C1 *Grays Harbor*

RIVER RUN RV PARK
good sam park (RV Park) (Too New to Rate) From jct US-12 & US-101 S: Go 2-1/4 mi SE on US-101 S, then 1/10 mi S on 1st St (L). **FAC:** gravel rds. Avail: 57 all weather, 30 pull-thrus, (30x50), back-ins (30x45), 57 full hkups (30/50 amps), cable, WiFi @ sites, shower$, laundry, LP gas. **REC:** Chehalis River: boating nearby, playground, hunting nearby. Pet restrict (S/B/Q). Partial handicap access. No tents, Age restrict may apply, eco-friendly. 2021 rates: $55.
(360)581-2255 Lat: 46.960599, Lon: -123.777337
316 1st Street, Cosmopolis, WA 98537
www.stayatriverrun.com
See ad this page

COUGAR — D2 *Cowlitz*

LONE FIR RESORT **Ratings: 9/8.5★/9.5** (RV Park) Avail: 27 full hkups (30 amps). 2021 rates: $36 to $49. (360)238-5210, 16806 Lewis River Rd, Cougar, WA 98616

COULEE CITY — B4 *Grant*

COULEE CITY COMMUNITY PARK (Public) From Jct of SR-17 & SR-2, E 2 mi on SR-2 (L). Avail: 55 full hkups (30/50 amps). 2021 rates: $15 to $20. Apr 01 to Oct 31. (509)632-5331

SUN LAKES - DRY FALLS (Public State Park) From Jct of US-2 & SR-17, Go 4 mi S on SR-17 to Park Lake Rd, then 1.1 mi E on Park Lake Rd (L). Avail: 41 full hkups (30/50 amps). 2021 rates: $20 to $50. (888)226-7688

SUN LAKES PARK RESORT **Ratings: 9/7/6.5** (Campground) Avail: 144 full hkups (30/50 amps). 2021 rates: $27 to $46. Mar 30 to Oct 15. (509)632-5291, 34228 Park Lake Road NE, Coulee City, WA 99115

COULEE DAM — B5 *Lincoln*

LAKE ROOSEVELT NRA/SPRING CANYON (Public National Park) From Jct SR-155 & SR-174, E 3 mi on SR-174 (L). 87 Avail: Pit toilets. 2021 rates: $9 to $18. (509)633-9441

COUPEVILLE — B2 *Island*

FORT CASEY (Public State Park) On Whidbey Island (from town): Go 3 mi S on Hwy 20 to Keystone ferry terminal exit. Park is by terminal (L). 13 Avail: 13 W, 13 E (30/50 amps). 2021 rates: $20 to $50. (888)226-7688

CRESTON — B5 *Lincoln*

LAKE ROOSEVELT NRA/HAWK CREEK (Public National Park) From town, E 22 mi to SH-25, N 5 mi to Chase Rd., w 1.5 mi to Indian Creek Rd., NW 12.5 (E). 21 Avail: Pit toilets. 2021 rates: $9 to $18. (509)633-9441

CUSICK — A6 *Pend Oreille*

BLUESLIDE RESORT **Ratings: 5/UI/6** (Campground) 18 Avail: 16 full hkups, 2 E (30/50 amps). 2021 rates: $25 to $50. Apr 15 to Oct 15. (509)445-1327, 400041 Hwy 20, Cusick, WA 99119

KALISPEL RV RESORT
good sam park **Ratings: 8.5/10★/9.5** (RV Resort) From jct Tule Rd & Hwy 20 E: Go 1/4 mi N on Hwy 20 W (R). **FAC:** paved rds. Avail: 33 paved, back-ins (15x60), 33 full hkups (30/50 amps), cable, WiFi @ sites, tent sites, rentals, dump, laundry, groc, LP gas, fire rings, firewood, restaurant. **REC:** boating nearby, hunting nearby. Pets OK. 2021 rates: $35 to $55. ATM.
(509)447-7144 Lat: 48.347770, Lon: -117.303604
370 Qlispe River Way, Cusick, WA 99119
www.kalispelrvresort.com
See ad this page

Things to See and Do

KALISPEL CASINO Casino with 130 slots, banquet room, restaurant. Partial handicap access. RV accessible. Restrooms. Food. Hours: 10am to 10pm. ATM.
(833)881-7492 Lat: 48.349215, Lon: -117.303358
420 Qlispe River Way, Cusick, WA 99119
www.kalispelcasino.com
See ad this page

DAVENPORT — B5 *Lincoln*

LAKE ROOSEVELT NRA/FORT SPOKANE (Public National Park) From E end of town, W 21 mi on SR-25 (R). 67 Avail: Pit toilets. 2021 rates: $9 to $18. (509)633-3830

LAKE ROOSEVELT NRA/PORCUPINE BAY (Public National Park) From town, N 19 mi on SR-25 to unnamed cnty rd, NW 4 mi (R). 31 Avail: Pit toilets. 2021 rates: $9 to $18. (509)633-9441

TWO RIVERS RV & MARINA RESORT **Ratings: 8.5/5.5/6.5** (Campground) Avail: 81 full hkups (30/50 amps). 2021 rates: $35 to $45. (509)722-4029, 6828 D Hwy 25 S, Davenport, WA 99122

DAYTON — D5 *Columbia*

LEWIS & CLARK TRAIL (Public State Park) From town, W 5 mi on US-12 (R). 24 Avail. 2021 rates: $20 to $45. Apr 01 to Oct 31. (509)337-6457

TUCANNON RIVER RV PARK **Ratings: 6/8.5★/7** (RV Park) Avail: 33 full hkups (30/50 amps). 2021 rates: $35. (509)399-2056, 511 Hwy 261, Dayton, WA 99328

DEER PARK — B6 *Spokane*

DEER PARK RV RESORT
good sam park **Ratings: 10/10★/10** (RV Resort) From Jct of US-395 & Crawford St (between MP 180 & 181): Go 1-3/4 mi E on W Crawford St to N Country Club Dr, then 1 mi N on N Country Club Dr (R). **FAC:** paved rds. (127 spaces). Avail: 100 paved, patios, 11 pull-thrus, (35x120), back-ins (35x100), 100 full hkups (30/50 amps), seasonal sites, cable, WiFi @ sites, dump, laundry, LP gas, restaurant, controlled access. **REC:** heated pool, hot tub, boating nearby, golf, playground, hunting nearby. Pets OK. Partial handicap access. No tents, Age restrict may apply. Big rig sites, eco-friendly. 2021 rates: $52 to $62, Military discount.
(509)276-1555 Lat: 47.972696, Lon: -117.447336
1205 N Country Club Dr, Deer Park, WA 99006
www.g7rvresorts.com
See ad this page

DES MOINES — C2 *King*

SALTWATER (Public State Park) From Jct of I-5 & Des Moines Rd exit, W 4 mi on Des Moines Rd to SR-509, S 2 mi (R). 47 Avail. 2021 rates: $20 to $45. Apr 23 to Oct 06. (253)661-4956

EASTON — C3 *Kittitas*

LAKE EASTON (Public State Park) From I-90 (exit 70): Follow signs 1/2 mi. Avail: 45 full hkups. 2021 rates: $20 to $45. (509)656-2586

SUNRISE RESORTS AT LAKE EASTON **Ratings: 7/6/5.5** (Membership Park) 118 Avail: 58 full hkups, 60 W, 60 E (30/50 amps). 2021 rates: $35 to $53. (509)656-2255, 581 Lake Easton Rd, Easton, WA 98925

EASTSOUND — A2 *San Juan*

MORAN (Public State Park) From town: Go 5 mi E on Horseshoe Hwy. On Orcas Island. 151 Avail. 2021 rates: $20 to $45. (885)226-7688

Be prepared! Bridge, Tunnel & Ferry Regulations and Rules of the Road can be found in the front of the Guide.

EATONVILLE — C2 *Pierce*

HENLEY'S SILVER LAKE RESORT (Public) From town, W 2.2 mi on Eatonville Hwy W, NW 4.5 mi on Hwy 7. 41 Avail: 12 full hkups, 29 W, 29 E (30 amps). 2021 rates: $34. (360)832-3580

RAINBOW RV RESORT Ratings: 7.5/8★/7.5 (Campground) Avail: 18 full hkups (30 amps). 2021 rates: $37. (360)879-5115, 34217 Tanwax Ct E, Eatonville, WA 98328

ELECTRIC CITY — B5 *Grant*

COULEE PLAYLAND RESORT

good sam park

Ratings: 7/8★/6.5 (Campground) 59 Avail: 37 full hkups, 22 W, 22 E (30/50 amps). 2021 rates: $47. (509)633-2671, 401 Coulee Blvd E (Hwy 155), Electric City, WA 99123

SUNBANKS LAKE RESORT **Ratings: 7/8.5/8.5** (Campground) 80 Avail: 9 full hkups, 71 W, 71 E (30/50 amps). 2021 rates: $68. (509)633-3786, 57662 Hwy 155 N, Electric City, WA 99123

ELLENSBURG — C4 *Kittitas*

E & J RV PARK

good sam park

Ratings: 7.5/8★/6 (RV Park) Avail: 44 full hkups (30/50 amps). 2021 rates: $49.99 to $79. (509)933-1500, 901 Berry Rd, Ellensburg, WA 98926

ELLENSBURG KOA JOURNEY **Ratings: 8.5/7.5/7** (Campground) 88 Avail: 26 full hkups, 62 W, 62 E (30/50 amps). 2021 rates: $88 to $99. (509)925-9319, 32 Thorp Hwy S, Ellensburg, WA 98926

YAKIMA RIVER RV PARK

good sam park

Ratings: 6/NA/10 (Campground) 36 Avail: 16 full hkups, 20 W, 20 E (30/50 amps), Pit toilets. 2021 rates: $45. Apr 01 to Sep 30. (509)925-4734, 791 Ringer Loop Rd, Ellensburg, WA 98926

ELMA — C2 *Grays Harbor*

ELMA RV PARK

good sam park

Ratings: 8/10★/9.5 (RV Park) From Jct of SR-8 & SR-12: Go 1/8 mi S on SR-12 to unnamed street (behind gas station), then 1/8 mi W (L).

GATEWAY TO THE OLYMPIC PENINSULA

Small town hospitality abounds at Elma. Fresh cookies, coffee or tea, beautiful landscaping, easy access to Hwy 12. Big rig sites. Lovely clubhouse for groups. Nearby hiking, biking, shopping, fishing, kayaking & disc golf.

FAC: paved/gravel rds. (81 spaces). Avail: 31 gravel, 4 pull-thrus, (25x80), back-ins (25x42), 31 full hkups (30/50 amps), seasonal sites, cable, WiFi @ sites, shower$, dump, laundry, LP gas, fire rings, firewood. Pet restrict (Q). No tents. Big rig sites, eco-friendly. 2021 rates: $47 to $60, Military discount.
(866)211-3939 Lat: 47.001621, Lon: -123.387899
4730 US Hwy 12, Elma, WA 98541
www.elmarvpark.com
See ad page 973

SCHAFER (Public State Park) From town: Go 5 mi W on Hwy-410, then 10 mi N on E Satsop Rd. 10 Avail: 9 W, 9 E. 2021 rates: $20 to $45. (888)226-7688

TRAVEL INN RESORT **Ratings: 9/9★/9.5** (Membership Park) Avail: 130 full hkups (30/50 amps). 2021 rates: $75. (360)482-3877, 801 East Main St, Elma, WA 98541

Are you using a friend's Guide? Want one of your own? Call 877-209-6655.

ENTIAT — B4 *Chelan*

ENTIAT CITY PARK (Public) From Jct of Hwy 2 & US-97 alternate, S 8.3 mi on US-97 Alternate (R). 31 Avail: 29 full hkups, 2 W, 2 E (30 amps). 2021 rates: $20 to $40. (509)784-1500

ENUMCLAW — C3 *King*

ENUMCLAW EXPO CENTER RV CAMPGROUND (Public) From Jct of Hwy 410 & 284th, N 0.2 mi on 284th (L). 28 Avail: 28 W, 28 E (30/50 amps). 2021 rates: $30 to $40. (360)615-5631

MT RAINIER/WHITE RIVER (Public National Park) From town, E 38 mi on Hwy 410 to Sunrise Rd, W 5.5 mi (L). 112 Avail. 2021 rates: $20. Jun 30 to Sep 30. (360)569-2211

EPHRATA — C4 *Grant*

EPHRATA See also Coulee City, Moses Lake, Othello, Quincy & Soap Lake.

EPHRATA RV PARK & CAMPGROUND **Ratings: 9/7.5/8** (RV Park) Avail: 51 full hkups (30/50 amps). 2021 rates: $30 to $50. (800)422-8447, 5707 Hwy 28W, Ephrata, WA 98823

OASIS RV PARK & GOLF COURSE **Ratings: 8.5/8.5★/9** (Campground) 60 Avail: 28 full hkups, 32 W, 32 E (30 amps). 2021 rates: $38. (877)754-5102, 2541 Basin St SW, Ephrata, WA 98823

EVANS — A5 *Stevens*

LAKE ROOSEVELT NRA/EVANS (Public National Park) From town, S 2 mi on SR-25 (L). 43 Avail: Pit toilets. 2021 rates: $9 to $18. (509)633-9441

EVERETT — B3 *Snohomish*

HARBOUR POINTE RV PARK

(RV Park) (Seasonal Stay Only) From Jct I-5 (exit 186) & 128th St SW: Go 1-1/2 mi W on 128th St SW/Airport Rd to Hwy 99/Evergreen Way, then 4-3/4 mi N on Hwy 99/Evergreen Way. (R). **FAC:** paved rds. (60 spaces). 0 Avail: (30/50 amps), seasonal sites, cable, laundry. Pet restrict (S/B/Q). No tents, Military discount.
(425)789-1169 Lat: 47.893665, Lon: -122.253784
11501 Hwy 99, Everett, WA 98204
www.harbourpointervpark.com
See ad page 970

LAKESIDE RV PARK

(RV Park) (Seasonal Stay Only) From Jct of I-5 & 128th St SW (Exit 186): Go 1-1/2 mi W on 128th St/Airport Rd to Hwy 99/Evergreen Way, then 1/4 mi SW on Hwy 99 (L). **FAC:** paved rds. (150 spaces). Avail: 1 paved, 1 pull-thrus, (19x55), 1 full hkups (30/50 amps), seasonal sites, cable, WiFi @ sites, laundry, LP bottles. **REC:** Lakeside Lake: fishing, playground. Pet restrict (S/B/Q). Partial handicap access. No tents, eco-friendly. 2021 rates: $50, Military discount.
(425)347-2970 Lat: 47.885856, Lon: -122.260500
12321 Hwy 99 , Everett, WA 98204
www.lakesidervpark.net
See ad page 970

MAPLE GROVE RV RESORT

good sam park

Ratings: 9/10★/9.5 (RV Park) Southbound From Jct of I-5S & 128th St SW (Exit 186): Go 3/4 mi W on 128th St to Airport Rd, then 1/4 mi NW on Airport Rd to Hwy 99 (Evergreen Way), then 1/2 mi SW on Hwy 99 (L).

WELCOME TO MAPLE GROVE RV RESORT

15 min to Seattle, Bellevue & the Whidbey Island ferry. Few RV resorts rated by Good Sam can compare with the standard of our resort. We are YOUR premier RV resort when visiting Seattle, WA State and the Pacific NW.

FAC: paved rds. (99 spaces). Avail: 74 paved, 44 pull-thrus, (23x57), back-ins (23x40), accepts full hkup units only, 74 full hkups (30/50 amps), seasonal sites, cable, WiFi @ sites, laundry, LP gas. **REC:** boating nearby. Pet restrict (B/Q) $. Partial handicap access. No tents. 2021 rates: $54 to $99, Military discount.
(425)423-9608 Lat: 47.885275, Lon: -122.262034
12417 Hwy 99, Everett, WA 98204
maplegrovervresort.com
See ad page 970

FALL CITY — B3 *King*

TALL CHIEF RV & CAMPING RESORT

good sam park

Ratings: 8/8/7.5 (Membership Park) 55 Avail: 55 W, 55 E (30/50 amps). 2021 rates: $55 to $65. (888)563-7040, 29290 SE 8th St, Fall City, WA 98024

Join in the fun. Like us on FACEBOOK!

FERNDALE — A2 *Whatcom*

NOR'WEST RV PARK **Ratings: 7/8.5★/6.5** (RV Park) Avail: 14 full hkups (30/50 amps). 2021 rates: $35. (360)384-5038, 1627 Main St, Ferndale, WA 98248

THE CEDARS RV RESORT **Ratings: 9.5/9★/10** (RV Park) 123 Avail: 104 full hkups, 19 W, 19 E (30/50 amps). 2021 rates: $50 to $65. (360)384-2622, 6335 Portal Way, Ferndale, WA 98248

FIFE — C2 *Pierce*

Travel Services

CAMPING WORLD OF FIFE/TACOMA As the nation's largest retailer of RV supplies, accessories, services and new and used RVs, Camping World is committed to making your total RV experience better. **SERVICES:** tire, RV appliance, staffed RV wash, restrooms. RV supplies, emergency parking, RV accessible. Hours: 9am to 6pm.
(800)526-4165 Lat: 47.242561, Lon: -122.366169
4650 16th St. East, Fife, WA 98424
www.campingworld.com

FORKS — B1 *Clallam*

BOGACHIEL (Public State Park) From town: Go 6 mi S on US-101. 32 Avail: 6 W, 6 E. 2021 rates: $20 to $45. (360)374-6356

FORKS 101 RV PARK **Ratings: 5.5/6.5/7.5** (RV Park) Avail: 36 full hkups (30/50 amps). 2021 rates: $38 to $50. (360)374-5073, 901 S Forks Ave, Forks, WA 98331

OLYMPIC NATIONAL PARK/HOH (Public National Park) From town, S 12 mi on US-101 to Upper Hoh River Rd, E 18 mi (R). Entrance fee required. 88 Avail. 2021 rates: $20. (360)565-3130

OLYMPIC NATIONAL PARK/MORA (Public National Park) From town, N 1 mi on Hwy 101 to Mora-La Push Rd, W 9 mi to Mora, NW 2.5 mi (at 3 Rivers Resort), follow signs (L). 105 Avail. 2021 rates: $20. (360)565-3130

RIVERVIEW RV PARK **Ratings: 8/9.5★/8** (RV Park) Avail: 28 full hkups (30/50 amps). 2021 rates: $45 to $50. (360)640-4819, 33 Mora Rd, Forks, WA 98331

GIFFORD — B5 *Stevens*

LAKE ROOSEVELT NRA/GIFFORD CAMPGROUND (Public National Park) From S end of town, S 2 mi on SR-25 (R). 42 Avail: Pit toilets. 2021 rates: $9 to $18. (509)633-9441

GIG HARBOR — C2 *Pierce*

GIG HARBOR RV RESORT **Ratings: 8.5/9.5★/9** (RV Park) 103 Avail: 93 full hkups, 10 W, 10 E (30/50 amps). 2021 rates: $56 to $62. (888)709-0631, 9515 Burnham Dr, Gig Harbor, WA 98332

GOLDENDALE — D3 *Klickitat*

BROOKS MEMORIAL (Public State Park) From Jct of SR-142 & US-97 in town, N 11.5 mi on US-97 (L). Avail: 24 full hkups (50 amps). 2021 rates: $20 to $45. (509)773-4611

MARYHILL (Public State Park) From Jct of SR-14 & US-97, (S of town), S 1.6 mi on US-97 (L); or From Jct of US-97 & I-84 (in Oregon), N 1 mi on US-97 (R). Avail: 50 full hkups (30 amps). 2021 rates: $20 to $45. (888)226-7688

STARGAZERS RV RESORT

good sam park

Ratings: 8/10★/9 (RV Resort) From jct 97-N & East Simcoe Dr: Go 200 feet W on Simcoe Dr (L). **FAC:** gravel rds. (64 spaces). Avail: 43 gravel, 43 pull-thrus, (20x65), 43 full hkups (30/50 amps), seasonal sites, WiFi @ sites, tent sites, laundry, groc, fire rings. **REC:** boating nearby, playground, hunting nearby. Pets OK. Partial handicap access. Big rig sites. 2021 rates: $45.66 to $55. ATM.
(509)773-7827 Lat: 45.812383, Lon: -120.809370
800 E Simcoe Drive, Goldendale, WA 98620
stargazersrvresort.com
See ad this page

GRAHAM — C2 *Pierce*

CAMP LAKEVIEW **Ratings: 6.5/7.5/7.5** (Campground) 21 Avail: 7 full hkups, 14 W, 14 E (30/50 amps). 2021 rates: $25 to $30. (360)879-5426, 32919 Benbow Dr E, Graham, WA 98338

GRAND COULEE — B5 *Grant*

STEAMBOAT ROCK (Public State Park) From Grand Coulee: Go 10 mi S on SR-155, then 2 mi W on Steamboat Rock Rd (R). Avail: 136 full hkups (30/50 amps). 2021 rates: $20 to $50. (888)226-7688

THE KING'S COURT RV PARK **Ratings: 6/7/6** (RV Park) Avail: 32 full hkups (30/50 amps). 2021 rates: $30 to $40. (800)759-2608, 212 East Grand Coulee Ave, Grand Coulee, WA 99133

GRAYLAND — C1 *Grays Harbor*

GRAYLAND BEACH (Public State Park) From Jct of SR-105 & Cnty Line Rd (Cranberry Bch Rd), W 0.1 mi on Cranberry Bch Rd (L). 97 Avail: 55 full hkups, 38 W, 38 E (30 amps). 2021 rates: $20 to $45. (888)226-7688

KENANNA RV PARK

Ratings: 7.5/10★/9 (Campground) From Grayland, WA: Go 3 mi S on SR-105 to Kenanna RV Park Rd (R). **FAC:** gravel rds. (85 spaces). Avail: 75 grass, 75 pull-thrus, (27x65), 75 full hkups (30 amps), seasonal sites, WiFi @ sites, tent sites, rentals, shower$, laundry, LP gas, fire rings, firewood. **REC:** Pacific Ocean: fishing, kayaking/canoeing, boating nearby, playground. Pet restrict (Q). 2021 rates: $40 to $45, Military discount.
(360)267-3515 Lat: 46.75393, Lon: -124.08686
2955 SR 105, Grayland, WA 98547
kenannarv.com
See ad this page

HARRINGTON — B5 *Lincoln*

HARRINGTON HIDEAWAY RV PARK **Ratings: 5.5/8★/5.5** (RV Park) Avail: 12 full hkups (30/50 amps). 2021 rates: $30. (509)253-4788, 208 W Adams St, Harrington, WA 99134

HOODSPORT — C2 *Mason*

DOW CREEK RESORT-SUNRISE RESORTS **Ratings: 7/8.5★/9** (Membership Park) 55 Avail: 21 full hkups, 34 W, 34 E (30/50 amps). 2021 rates: $40 to $52. (360)877-5022, 2670 N Lake Cushman Rd, Hoodsport, WA 98548

GLEN AYR RESORT

Ratings: 8.5/9.5★/9 (RV Park) From Jct of US Hwy 101 & SR-119/N Lake Cushman Rd (in town): Go 1.2 mi N on US Hwy 101; Between MP 330 & 331 (L). **FAC:** all weather rds. Avail: 36 all weather, patios, 9 pull-thrus, (24x65), back-ins (27x40), 36 full hkups (30/50 amps), WiFi @ sites, rentals, laundry, LP gas, fire rings, firewood. **REC:** hot tub, Hood Canal: fishing, kayaking/canoeing, boating nearby. Pets OK. No tents. Big rig sites, eco-friendly. 2021 rates: $40 to $55, Military discount.
(360)877-9522 Lat: 47.420311, Lon: -123.132038
25381 N Hwy 101, Hoodsport, WA 98548
www.garesort.com
See ad this page

OLYMPIC NATIONAL PARK/STAIRCASE (Public National Park) From Jct of US-101 & SR-119, NW 9 mi on SR-119 to FR-24, W 7 mi (E). Entrance fee required. 49 Avail: Pit toilets. 2021 rates: $20. (360)565-3130

REST-A-WHILE RV PARK AND MARINA **Ratings: 5.5/7.5/5.5** (Campground) Avail: 70 full hkups (30/50 amps). 2021 rates: $45 to $55. (360)877-9474, 27001 N US Hwy 101, Hoodsport, WA 98548

SKOKOMISH PARK AT LAKE CUSHMAN

Ratings: 8/8★/8.5 (Campground) Avail: 30 full hkups (30 amps). 2021 rates: $42 to $54. Apr 01 to Nov 01. (360)877-5656, 7211 N Lake Cushman Rd, Hoodsport, WA 98548

THE WATERFRONT AT POTLATCH RESORT & RV PARK

Ratings: 9.5/9.5★/9.5 (RV Park) Avail: 16 full hkups (30/50 amps). 2021 rates: $40 to $66. (360)877-9422, 21660 North US Hwy 101, Shelton, WA 98584

HOQUIAM — C1 *Grays Harbor*

HOQUIAM RIVER RV PARK

Ratings: 8/9.5★/9 (RV Park) Avail: 45 full hkups (30/50 amps). 2021 rates: $47. (360)538-2870, 425 Queen Ave, Hoquiam, WA 98550

HUNTERS — B5 *Stevens*

LAKE ROOSEVELT NRA/HUNTERS (Public National Park) From town, S 1 mi on CR-292 (E). 39 Avail. 2021 rates: $9 to $18. (509)633-9441

ILWACO — D1 *Pacific*

CAPE DISAPPOINTMENT (Public State Park) From town, Go SW 3.2 mi on SR-100 (R). 215 Avail: 60 full hkups, 18 W, 18 E (20/30 amps). 2021 rates: $20 to $45. (888)226-7688

EAGLE'S NEST RESORT-SUNRISE RESORTS **Ratings: 8.5/10★/8.5** (Membership Park) Avail: 106 full hkups (30/50 amps). 2021 rates: $35 to $57. (360)642-8351, 700 W. North Head Rd, Ilwaco, WA 98624

IONE — A6 *Pend Oreille*

CEDAR RV PARK

Ratings: 6/9★/7 (RV Park) 16 Avail: 10 full hkups, 6 W, 6 E (30/50 amps). 2021 rates: $30. (509)442-2144, 4404 North Highway 31, Ione, WA 99139

ISSAQUAH — B3 *King*

ISSAQUAH See also Black Diamond, Bothell, Everett, Fall City, Gig Harbor, Kent, Monroe, Poulsbo & Puyallup.

ISSAQUAH VILLAGE RV PARK

Ratings: 9/9.5★/7.5 (RV Park) From Jct of I-90 & Front St/E Lake Sammamish Rd (exit 17): Go 1/4 mi N on Front St to 229th Ave SE, then 50 ft NE to SE 66th St (keep right), then 1/4 mi E on 66th St to 1st Ave NE, then 1/4 mi S on 1st Ave (L). **FAC:** paved rds. (56 spaces). 30 Avail: 29 paved, 1 all weather, 2 pull-thrus, (24x60), back-ins (21x60), 30 full hkups (30/50 amps), seasonal sites, cable, WiFi @ sites, dump, laundry, LP gas. **REC:** playground. Pet restrict (Q). Partial handicap access. No tents. Big rig sites, eco-friendly. 2021 rates: $65, Military discount.
(425)392-9233 Lat: 47.536959, Lon: -122.030923
650 1st Ave NE, Issaquah, WA 98027
ivrvpark.com
See ad this page

KALAMA — D2 *Cowlitz*

CAMP KALAMA RV PARK **Ratings: 5.5/9★/7** (Campground) 57 Avail: 27 full hkups, 30 W, 30 E (30/50 amps). 2021 rates: $38. (360)673-2456, 5055 N Meeker Dr, Kalama, WA 98625

KELSO — D2 *Cowlitz*

A SPOTLIGHT Introducing Mount Rainier & Mount St Helens' colorful attractions appearing at the front of this state section.

KELSO See also Castle Rock, Kalama, Silverlake, Toutle & Woodland, WA; Clatskanie, OR.

BROOKHOLLOW RV PARK

Ratings: 9/10★/10 (RV Park) From Jct of I-5 & Allen St (exit 39): Go 1 mi E on Allen St (just past mobile home park) (R).

ENJOY OUR QUIET COUNTRY SETTING!
By I-5, our BIG RIG friendly park is centrally located between Portland, OR/Vancouver, WA/Mt. Rainier/Mt. St. Helens - all a day trip away and 6 hours south of Vancouver, BC...Great Fishing in 3 nearby rivers!

FAC: paved rds. (132 spaces). Avail: 52 paved, patios, 20 pull-thrus, (35x60), back-ins (32x45), 52 full hkups (30/50 amps), seasonal sites, cable, WiFi @ sites, laundry. **REC:** Coweeman River: fishing, kayaking/canoeing, boating nearby. Pet restrict (B/Q) $. Partial handicap access. No tents. Big rig sites, eco-friendly. 2021 rates: $50 to $57.29.
(360)577-6474 Lat: 46.14472, Lon: -122.87946
2506 Allen St, Kelso, WA 98626
brookhollowrvpark.com
See ad next page, 764

KENNEWICK — D5 *Benton*

COLUMBIA SUN RV RESORT **Ratings: 10/10★/10** (RV Resort) Avail: 99 full hkups (30/50 amps). 2021 rates: $47 to $61.50. (509)420-4880, 103907 Wiser Parkway, Kennewick, WA 99338

KENT — C3 *King*

SEATTLE/TACOMA KOA **Ratings: 8.5/8/7** (Campground) 140 Avail: 126 full hkups, 14 W, 14 E (30/50 amps). 2021 rates: $34.95 to $69.95. (253)872-8652, 5801 S 212th St., Kent, WA 98032

KETTLE FALLS — A5 *Ferry*

GRANDVIEW INN MOTEL & RV PARK

Ratings: 7.5/9.5★/8.5 (RV Park) Avail: 17 full hkups (30 amps). 2021 rates: $41. (509)738-6733, 978 Hwy 395N, Kettle Falls, WA 99141

LAKE ROOSEVELT NRA/HAAG COVE (Public National Park) From Jct US-395 & Hwy 20, SW 4.22 mi on Hwy 20, S 2.3 mi on Inchelium Hwy/CH-3, E on Haag Rd. 16 Avail: Pit toilets. 2021 rates: $9 to $18. (509)633-9441

Things change ... last year's rates serve as a guideline only.

LAKE ROOSEVELT NRA/KETTLE FALLS (Public National Park) From Jct of US-395 & SR-25, W 4 mi on US-395 to unnamed cnty rd, S 2 mi (E). 76 Avail: Pit toilets. 2021 rates: $9 to $18. (509)738-6266

NORTH LAKE RV PARK AND CAMPGROUND **Ratings: 5.5/7.5★/7** (Campground) 22 Avail: 14 full hkups, 8 W, 8 E (30/50 amps). 2021 rates: $40 to $45. Apr 01 to Dec 01. (509)738-2593, 20 Roosevelt Rd, Kettle Falls, WA 99141

LA CONNER — A2 *Skagit*

LA CONNER

Ratings: 6/7/7.5 (Membership Park) 22 Avail: 22 W, 22 E (20/30 amps). 2021 rates: $36 to $55. (888)563-7040, 16362 Snee Oosh Rd, La Conner, WA 98257

LA CONNER MARINA & RV PARK

Ratings: 8/9★/8.5 (Public) From Jct of Morris St and Third St in downtown La Conner: Go 1/4 mi N on Third St to Pearle Jensen way, then 1/4 mile E on Pearle Jensen Way (R). **FAC:** paved rds. Avail: 52 paved, 5 pull-thrus, (21x73), back-ins (20x45), 52 full hkups (30 amps), WiFi @ sites, laundry, LP gas. **REC:** Swinomish Channel: fishing, marina, kayaking/canoeing, boating nearby, rec open to public. Pets OK. Partial handicap access. No tents, eco-friendly. 2021 rates: $42 to $55.
(360)466-3118 Lat: 48.398432, Lon: -122.492564
420 Pearle Jensen Way, La Conner, WA 98257
www.portofskagit.com
See ad page 964

LEAVENWORTH — B4 *Chelan*

ALPINE VIEW RV PARK & CAMPGROUND **Ratings: 4.5/9★/8** (Campground) 26 Avail: 14 full hkups, 12 W, 12 E (30/50 amps). 2021 rates: $40 to $45. (509)548-8439, 9825 Duncan Rd, Leavenworth, WA 98826

Save 10% at Good Sam Parks 365 days a year with no blackout dates!!

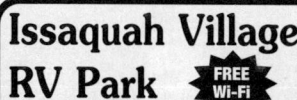

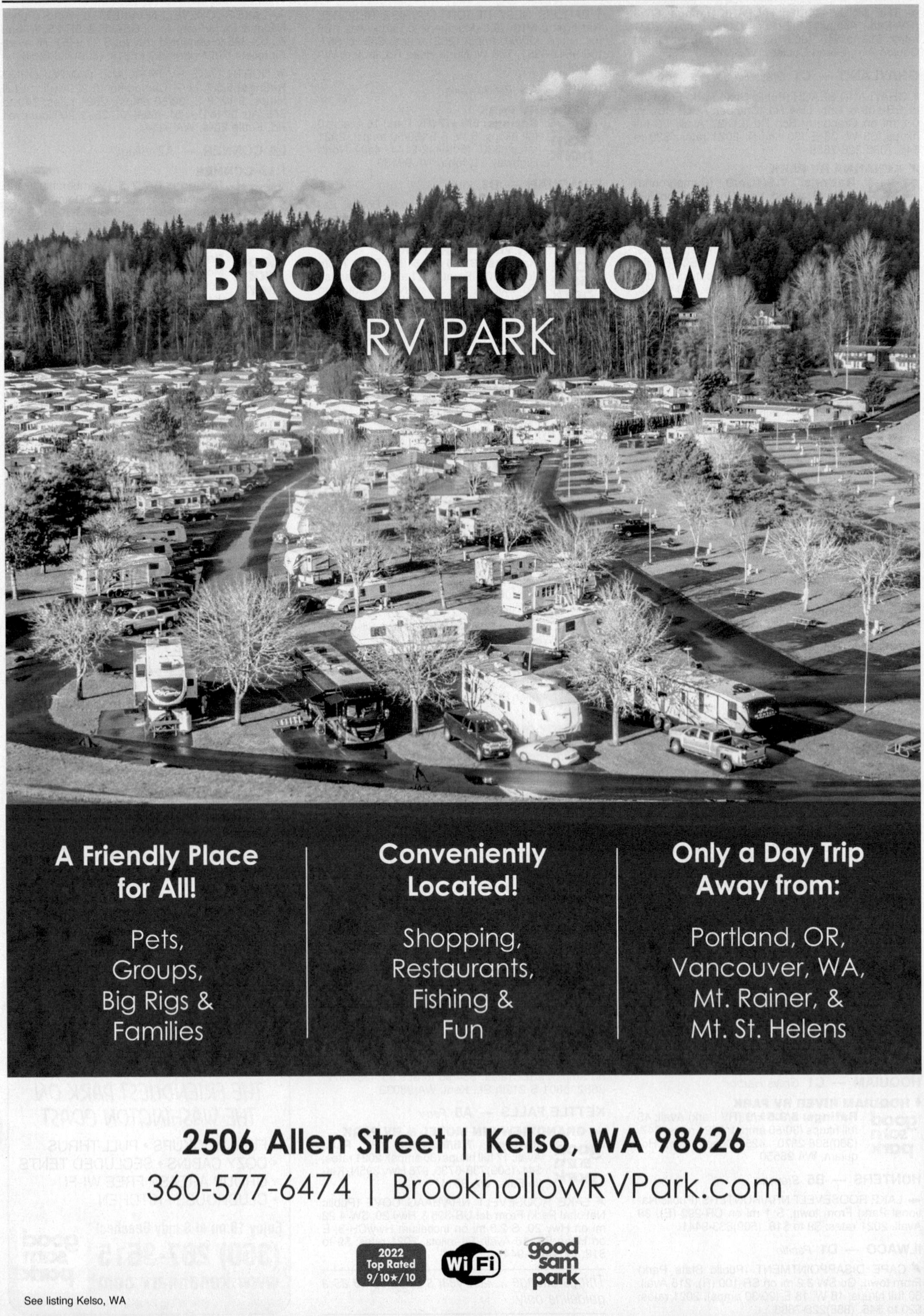

BROOKHOLLOW
RV PARK
A Friendly Place for All!
Pets, Groups, Big Rigs & Families
Conveniently Located!
Shopping, Restaurants, Fishing & Fun
Only a Day Trip Away from:
Portland, OR, Vancouver, WA, Mt. Rainer, & Mt. St. Helens
2506 Allen Street | Kelso, WA 98626
360-577-6474 | BrookhollowRVPark.com
2022 Top Rated 9/10★/10
WiFi
good sam park
See listing Kelso, WA

LEAVENWORTH (CONT)

ICICLE RIVER RV RESORT Ratings: 9/9.5★/9.5 (RV Park) 111 Avail: 107 full hkups, 4 W, 4 E (30/50 amps). 2021 rates: $50 to $65. Apr 01 to Oct 20. (509)548-5420, 7305 Icicle Rd, Leavenworth, WA 98826

LAKE WENATCHEE (Public State Park) From Leavenworth: Go 17 mi NW on Hwy 97/US-2 to SR-207, then 4 mi N (L). 42 Avail: 42 W, 42 E (30/50 amps). 2021 rates: $20 to $50. (888)226-7688

LEAVENWORTH RV CAMPGROUND
Ratings: 6.5/7.5/7.5 (Membership Park) 160 Avail: 50 full hkups, 110 W, 110 E (30/50 amps). 2021 rates: $59 to $77. (888)563-7040, 20752 Chiwawa Loop Rd, Leavenworth, WA 98826

LEAVENWORTH/PINE VILLAGE KOA CAMPGROUND **Ratings: 9/10★/9** (Campground) 134 Avail: 68 full hkups, 66 W, 66 E (30/50 amps). 2021 rates: $50 to $125. (800)562-5709, 308 Zelt Strasse Street, Leavenworth, WA 98826

LIBERTY LAKE — B6 *Spokane*

LIBERTY LAKE RV CAMPGROUND
Ratings: 10/10★/10 (RV Resort) From E Appleway Ave & N Liberty Lake Rd: Go 1/4 mi NE on E Appleway Ave (L). **FAC:** paved rds. Avail: 130 paved, patios, 58 pull-thrus, (32x90), back-ins (30x60), 120 full hkups, 10 W, 10 E (30/50 amps), cable, WiFi @ sites, dump, laundry, LP gas. **REC:** heated pool, boating nearby, playground. Pet restrict (Q). Partial handicap access. No tents. Big rig sites, eco-friendly. 2021 rates: $68 to $105.
(509)868-0567 Lat: 47.675129, Lon: -117.101085
22751 E Appleway Ave, Liberty Lake, WA 99019
www.libertylakervcampground.com
See ad page 977

Travel Services

CAMPING WORLD OF LIBERTY LAKE/SPOKANE As the nation's largest retailer of RV supplies, accessories, services and new and used RVs, Camping World is committed to making your total RV experience better. **SERVICES:** RV appliance, MH mechanical, sells outdoor gear, staffed RV wash, restrooms. RV Sales. RV supplies, LP gas, dump, emergency parking, RV accessible. Hours: 9am - 7pm.
(888)480-2175 Lat: 47.666508, Lon: -117.140086
19651 East Cataldo Ave., Liberty Lake, WA 99016
www.campingworld.com

LILLIWAUP — B2 *Mason*

MIKE'S BEACH RESORT **Ratings: 5.5/7★/6** (Campground) 14 Avail: 6 full hkups, 8 W, 8 E (30 amps). 2021 rates: $45. May 01 to Oct 31. (360)877-5324, 38470 North US Hwy 101, Lilliwaup, WA 98555

LONG BEACH — D1 *Pacific*

LONG BEACH See also Bay Center, Chinook, Grayland, Ilwaco, Ocean Park, Seaview & Tokeland, WA; Astoria, Gearhart, Hammond, Seaside & Warrenton, OR.

ANDERSENS OCEANSIDE RV RESORT AND COTTAGES **Ratings: 8.5/8.5★/9** (RV Park) Avail: 60 full hkups (30/50 amps). 2021 rates: $45 to $63. (360)642-2231, 1400 138th St, Long Beach, WA 98631

CRANBERRY RV PARK **Ratings: 6/7/6.5** (RV Park) Avail: 14 full hkups (30/50 amps). 2021 rates: $30 to $43. (360)642-2027, 1801 Cranberry Rd, Long Beach, WA 98631

DRIFTWOOD RV PARK **Ratings: 6/8.5★/8** (Campground) Avail: 26 full hkups (30 amps). 2021 rates: $39.50 to $75. (360)642-2711, 1408 Pacific Ave N, Long Beach, WA 98631

PACIFIC HOLIDAY RV RESORT-SUNRISE RESORTS **Ratings: 9/8.5★/9** (Membership Park) Avail: 89 full hkups (20/30 amps). 2021 rates: $38 to $57. (360)642-2770, 12109 Pacific Hwy, Long Beach, WA 98631

SAND CASTLE RV PARK **Ratings: 5/8★/5** (RV Park) Avail: 20 full hkups (20/30 amps). 2021 rates: $45.13. (360)642-2174, 1100 Pacific Avenue North, Long Beach, WA 98631

LONGBRANCH — C2 *Pierce*

PENROSE POINT (Public State Park) From Jct of SR-16 & SR-302:Go S 16 mi on SR-302 to Cornwall Rd, then E .5 mi to Delano Rd, then E 1 mi to 158th St, N 200 yds (E). 82 Avail. 2021 rates: $20 to $45. (888)226-7688

LONGMIRE — C3 *Pierce*

MT RAINIER/COUGAR ROCK (Public National Park) From town, N 2.3 mi on Nisqually/SH-706 to Paradise Rd (L) Note: max RV length is 35, max trailer length is 27. 183 Avail. 2021 rates: $20. May 25 to Oct 07. (360)569-2211

LONGVIEW — D2 *Cowlitz*

LONGVIEW See also Castle Rock, Kalama, Kelso, Silverlake, Toutle & Woodland, WA; Clatskanie, OR.

LYNDEN — A2 *Whatcom*

HIDDEN VILLAGE RV PARK & CAMPGROUND **Ratings: 8/7.5/6.5** (Campground) 42 Avail: 28 full hkups, 14 W, 14 E (30/50 amps). 2021 rates: $30 to $36. (800)843-8606, 7062 Guide Meridian, Lynden, WA 98264

LYNDEN KOA **Ratings: 8/9★/8.5** (Campground) 85 Avail: 39 full hkups, 46 W, 46 E (30/50 amps). 2021 rates: $34.50 to $52.50. (800)562-4779, 8717 Line Rd, Lynden, WA 98264

MANSON — B4 *Chelan*

MILL BAY CASINO RV PARK
(RV Park) (Too New to Rate) Avail: 21 full hkups (50 amps). 2021 rates: $35 to $75. (800)648-2946, 455 Wapato Lake Road, Manson, WA 98831

MARBLEMOUNT — A3 *Skagit*

NORTH CASCADES/GOODELL CREEK (Public National Park) From town, E 13 mi on SR-20 (R). 19 Avail: Pit toilets. 2021 rates: $16. (360)854-7200

MARYHILL — D3 *Klickitat*

PEACH BEACH CAMPARK **Ratings: 4/10★/8** (Campground) 80 Avail: 22 full hkups, 46 W, 46 E (30/50 amps). 2021 rates: $40 to $45. (509)773-4927, 89 Maryhill Hwy, Goldendale, WA 98620

MARYSVILLE — B3 *Snohomish*

WENBERG COUNTY PARK (Public State Park) From jct I-5 (exit 206) & Hwy 531: Go 6 mi W on Hwy 531. 68 Avail: 15 full hkups, 31 W, 31 E. 2021 rates: $22 to $40. Mar 01 to Oct 31. (360)652-7417

METALINE — A6 *Pend Oreille*

MT LINTON RV & TRAILER PARK **Ratings: 6.5/9★/5.5** (Campground) Avail: 21 full hkups (30/50 amps). 2021 rates: $30. (509)446-4553, 103 W. Metaline St, Metaline, WA 99152

MONROE — B3 *Snohomish*

THUNDERBIRD RESORT
Ratings: 7/7/7.5 (Membership Park) 13 Avail: 6 full hkups, 7 W, 7 E (30/50 amps). 2021 rates: $49 to $57. (888)563-7040, 26702 Ben Howard Rd, Monroe, WA 98272

MONTESANO — C2 *Grays Harbor*

FRIENDS LANDING RV PARK
Ratings: 6.5/8.5★/10 (Public) From the Jct of Hwy 12 and the Devonshire Rd Exit: Go 1.1 mi SW on Devonshire Rd to Katon Rd, then 1.7 mi S on Katon Rd to park (R). **FAC:** paved rds. Avail: 18 paved, back-ins (32x65), 18 W, 18 E (30 amps), WiFi @ sites, tent sites, shower$, dump, fire rings, firewood. **REC:** Chehalis River: fishing, kayaking/canoeing, boating nearby, playground, rec open to public. Pets OK. Partial handicap access, eco-friendly. 2021 rates: $45. Mar 15 to Nov 15.
(360)861-8864 Lat: 46.947075, Lon: -123.643682
300 Katon Rd, Montesano, WA 98563
www.friendslanding.org
See ad page 975

LAKE SYLVIA (Public State Park) From Jct of Hwy 12 & 3rd St: Go N 1 mi on 3rd St (E). 4 Avail: 4 W, 4 E (30/50 amps). 2021 rates: $20 to $50. (888)226-7688

MONTESQUARE RV PARK & LODGE **Ratings: 8/10★/7** (RV Park) Avail: 20 full hkups (30/50 amps). 2021 rates: $35. (369)249-8425, 525 S 1st St, Montesano, WA 98563

MOSES LAKE — C4 *Grant*

MOSES LAKE See also Ephrata, Othello & Warden.

GRANT COUNTY FAIRGROUNDS & RV PARK
(Public) From the Jct of I-90 and WA-17 (exit 179): Go 6-1/4 mi N on WA-17, then 1-1/2 mi S on Airway Drive (L). **FAC:** gravel rds. Avail: 456 grass, patios, 20 pull-thrus, (20x50), back-ins (27x45), 56 full hkups, 400 W, 400 E (30/50 amps), WiFi @ sites, dump. **REC:** boating nearby, hunting nearby. Pets OK. Partial handicap access. No tents, 7 day max stay. 2021 rates: $30 to $35. Apr 01 to Oct 15.
(509)765-3581 Lat: 47.145386, Lon: -119.310768
3953 Airway Dr NE, Moses Lake, WA 98837
www.gcfairgrounds.com
See ad this page

MARDON RESORT ON POTHOLES RESERVOIR
Ratings: 9/9★/9 (RV Park) 109 Avail: 83 full hkups, 26 W, 26 E (30/50 amps). 2021 rates: $31 to $61. (509)346-2651, 8198 Highway 262 SE, Othello, WA 99344

SUNCREST RV PARK **Ratings: 8/UI/9.5** (RV Park) Avail: 35 full hkups (30/50 amps). 2021 rates: $53. (509)765-0355, 303 Hansen Rd, Moses Lake, WA 98837

SUNRISE RESORTS PIER 4 **Ratings: 9/7.5/7** (Membership Park) 167 Avail: 148 full hkups, 19 W, 19 E (30/50 amps). 2021 rates: $30 to $60. (509)765-6319, 3400 Sage Rd, Moses Lake, WA 98837

MOSSYROCK — D2 *Lewis*

HARMONY LAKESIDE RV PARK & DELUXE CABINS **Ratings: 8.5/10★/10** (RV Park) Avail: 89 full hkups (30/50 amps). 2021 rates: $51.25 to $71.25. (877)780-7275, 563 SR-122, Silver Creek, WA 98585

IKE KINSWA (Public State Park) From Jct of US-12 & SR-122 (between MP-86 & MP-87), N 3.8 mi on SR-122 (R). 72 Avail: 41 full hkups, 31 W, 31 E (30/50 amps). 2021 rates: $20 to $50. (888)226-7688

MAYFIELD LAKE PARK (Public) From Jct of I-5 & US-12, E 17 mi on US-12 to Beach Rd, N 0.25 mi (R). 54 Avail: 54 W, 54 E (30/50 amps). 2021 rates: $35 to $39. Apr 15 to Oct 15. (360)985-2364

MOUNT VERNON — A2 *Skagit*

BAY VIEW (Public State Park) From Jct of I-5 & Exit 230 (Hwy 20), W 7 mi on Hwy 20 to Bay View-Edison Rd, N 4 mi (R). Avail: 29 full hkups (30 amps). 2021 rates: $20 to $45. (888)226-7688

BLAKES RV PARK & MARINA **Ratings: 6.5/8★/7.5** (RV Park) 49 Avail: 41 full hkups, 8 W, 8 E (30/50 amps). 2021 rates: $35 to $48. (360)445-6533, 13739 Rawlins Rd, Mount Vernon, WA 98273

MOUNT VERNON RV PARK
Ratings: 8.5/9★/9.5 (RV Park) From Jct of I-5 & Kincaid St (exit 226): Go 1/8 mi W on Kincaid St to SR-536 (Third St), then 1 mi N on SR-536 (becomes Memorial Hwy) over bridge (R). **FAC:** paved rds. (85 spaces). Avail: 16 all weather, patios, 8 pull-thrus, (24x82), back-ins (27x50), 16 full hkups (30/50 amps), seasonal sites, cable, WiFi @ sites, laundry, LP gas. **REC:** boating nearby. Pet restrict (B/Q). Partial handicap access. No tents. Big rig sites, eco-friendly. 2021 rates: $38 to $43, Military discount.
(800)385-9895 Lat: 48.423405, Lon: -122.350874
1229 Memorial Hwy, Mount Vernon, WA 98273
www.mvrvpark.com
See ad this page

NACHES — C4 *Yakima*

RIMROCK LAKE RESORT **Ratings: 5/6.5/8** (Campground) 29 Avail: 13 full hkups, 16 W, 16 E (30/50 amps). 2021 rates: $40 to $45. (509)672-2460, 37590 US Hwy 12, Naches, WA 98937

NEWHALEM — A3 *Skagit*

NORTH CASCADES/COLONIAL CREEK (Public National Park) From town, E 25 mi on SR-20. 142 Avail. 2021 rates: $16. May 21 to Sep 07. (360)854-7200

NORTH CASCADES/NEWHALEM CREEK (Public National Park) From town, E 14 mi on SR-20, across the river on a single lane bridge (R). 111 Avail. 2021 rates: $16 to $18. May 20 to Sep 08. (360)854-7200

NEWPORT — B6 *Pend Oreille*

LITTLE DIAMOND
good sam park **Ratings: 7.5/UI/7** (Membership Park) 86 Avail: 4 full hkups, 82 W, 82 E (30/50 amps). 2021 rates: $36.88 to $56.88. Apr 15 to Oct 04. (888)563-7040, 1002 McGowen Rd, Newport, WA 99156

OLD AMERICAN KAMPGROUND **Ratings: 7/10★/7** (Membership Park) Avail: 15 full hkups (30/50 amps). 2021 rates: $75. (509)447-3663, 701 N Newport Ave, Newport, WA 99156

PEND OREILLE COUNTY PARK (Public) From town, S 17 mi on Hwy 2 (R). 17 Avail: Pit toilets. 2021 rates: $10. May 27 to Sep 04. (509)447-4513

NINE MILE FALLS — B6 *Spokane*

WILLOW BAY RESORT **Ratings: 4/3/5.5** (Campground) 38 Avail: 7 full hkups, 31 W, 31 E (30/50 amps). 2021 rates: $40 to $68. Apr 01 to Oct 15. (800)445-9519, 6607 Highway 291, Nine Mile Falls, WA 99026

NORDLAND — B2 *Jefferson*

FORT FLAGLER (Public State Park) From Jct of Oak Bay Rd & Irondale Rd/Chimacum Rd (in Port Hadlock), E 0.8 mi on Oak Bay Rd to Flagler Rd, N 8.5 mi (E). Avail: 55 full hkups (30 amps). 2021 rates: $20 to $45. (360)385-1259

OAK HARBOR — B2 *Island*

DECEPTION PASS (Public State Park) From town, N 8 mi on SR-20 (L). 143 Avail: 143 W, 143 E (20/30 amps). 2021 rates: $20 to $45. (360)675-2417

FORT EBEY (Public State Park) From Mukilteo/Clinton Ferry: From Clinton (on Whidbey Island), N 32 mi on Hwy 525 (becomes Hwy 20) to Libbey Rd, W 1.5 mi to Hill Valley Dr, S 0.5 mi (E). 50 Avail: 11 W, 11 E (30 amps). 2021 rates: $20 to $45. May 15 to Sep 15. (560)678-4636

MILITARY PARK CLIFFSIDE RV PARK (WHIDBEY ISLAND NAS) (Public) From town, NW 4 mi on WA-20 to Ault Field Rd, enter at Charles Porter gate, then on Charles Porter Ave, then left 0.5 mi on Midway St, then N on Saratoga St, then left on Intruder St. Avail: 57 full hkups (30/50 amps). 2021 rates: $50 to $60. (360)257-2649

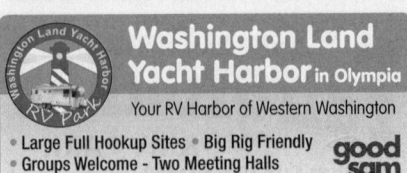

NORTH WHIDBEY RV PARK **Ratings: 8.5/9.5★/9** (RV Park) Avail: 63 full hkups (30/50 amps). 2021 rates: $40 to $46. (360)675-9597, 565 W Cornet Bay Rd, Oak Harbor, WA 98277

OCEAN CITY — C1 *Grays Harbor*

OCEAN BREEZE RV RESORT & CAMPGROUND **Ratings: 8.5/8.5★/10** (Membership Park) 250 Avail: 250 W, 250 E (30/50 amps). 2021 rates: $75. (360)289-0628, 2428 SR-109, Ocean City, WA 98569

OCEAN CITY (Public State Park) From Jct of SR-109 & SR-115, S 1 mi on SR-115 (R). Avail: 29 full hkups (30 amps). 2021 rates: $20 to $45. (360)289-3553

OCEANA CAMPGROUND
good sam park **Ratings: 5.5/9★/7** (Membership Park) 87 Avail: 14 full hkups, 73 W, 73 E (30/50 amps). 2021 rates: $48 to $50. (888)563-7040, 2733 SR 109, Ocean City, WA 98569

SCREAMIN' EAGLE CAMPGROUND & RV PARK **Ratings: 5.5/8★/7.5** (Campground) 15 Avail: 15 W, 15 E (30/50 amps). 2021 rates: $40. Feb 01 to Nov 01. (360)289-2189, 17 2nd Ave, Ocean City, WA 98569

OCEAN PARK — D1 *Pacific*

OCEAN PARK See also Bay Center, Chinook, Grayland, Ilwaco, Long Beach, Raymond, Seaview & Tokeland, WA; Hammond & Warrenton, OR.

CEDAR TO SURF CAMPGROUND
good sam park **Ratings: 7/8★/8** (RV Park) Avail: 33 full hkups (30 amps). 2021 rates: $45 to $65. (360)214-4006, 20803 Pacific Way, Ocean Park, WA 98640

OCEAN PARK RESORT
good sam park **Ratings: 7.5/9★/6.5** (Campground) Avail: 70 full hkups (30/50 amps). 2021 rates: $36 to $54. (360)665-4585, 25904 R St, Ocean Park, WA 98640

OKANOGAN — A4 *Okanogan*

LEGION RV PARK (Public) From town, N 0.8 mi on 2nd Ave/SR-215 (R). 35 Avail. 2021 rates: $3 to $12. Apr 15 to Oct 15. (509)422-3600

OKANOGAN COUNTY FAIRGROUNDS RV PARK (Public) From N end of town, N 1.75 mi on Rodeo Trail (L). 108 Avail: 64 full hkups, 44 W, 44 E (20 amps). 2021 rates: $20 to $25. May 01 to Oct 01. (509)422-1621

OLYMPIA — C2 *Thurston*

AMERICAN HERITAGE CAMPGROUND **Ratings: 7/8.5★/9.5** (Campground) 76 Avail: 24 full hkups, 52 W, 52 E (30 amps). 2021 rates: $33 to $40. (360)943-8778, 9610 Kimmie St SW, Olympia, WA 98512

MILLERSYLVANIA (Public State Park) From Jct of I-5 & Exit 95, E 2.5 mi on Maytown Rd to Tilley Rd, N 0.7 mi (L). 48 Avail: 48 W, 48 E (30 amps). 2021 rates: $20 to $45. (366)753-1519

OLYMPIA CAMPGROUND **Ratings: 6.5/8/6.5** (Campground) 67 Avail: 24 full hkups, 43 W, 43 E (20/30 amps). 2021 rates: $35 to $39. (360)352-2551, 1441 83rd Ave SW, Olympia, WA 98512

RIVERBEND CAMPGROUND OF OLYMPIA **Ratings: 7.5/8★/8.5** (Campground) 42 Avail: 15 full hkups, 27 W, 27 E (30/50 amps). 2021 rates: $40 to $45. (360)491-2534, 1040 Clubhouse Lane SE, Olympia, WA 98513

WASHINGTON LAND YACHT HARBOR RV PARK & EVENT CENTER
good sam park **Ratings: 7.5/NA/8** (RV Park) From Jct I-5 and Marvin Rd (Exit 111): Go 1 mi S on Marvin Rd SE to Steilacoom Rd SE, then 1 mi E on Steilacoom Rd (R). **FAC:** paved rds. Avail: 60 all weather, back-ins (20x60), accepts full hkup units only, 60 full hkups (30 amps), WiFi @ sites, restrooms only, dump, controlled access. **REC:** boating nearby. Pets OK. Partial handicap access. No tents, 29 day max stay. 2021 rates: $33.
(360)491-3750 Lat: 47.050561, Lon: -122.746642
9101 Steilacoom Rd SE, Olympia, WA 98513
www.washingtonlandyachtharbor.com
See ad this page

SNOWBIRD TIP: Get social and active. Winter getaways are a chance to try activities you've been curious about. From line dancing to woodworking, pickle ball to rock hounding, you'll never get bored at snowbird RV parks with jam-packed activity calendars.

Things to See and Do

WASHINGTON STATE PARKS AND RECREATION Manages and markets Washington's State Parks, Recreation Areas, Discover Pass program and Park Volunteers. Partial handicap access. RV accessible. Restrooms. Hours: 9am to 5pm.
(888)226-7688
1111 Israel Rd SW, Tumwater, WA 98501
parks.state.wa.us
See ad page 964

OMAK — A4 *Okanogan*

12 TRIBES RESORT CASINO RV PARK
good sam park **Ratings: 9/NA/8** (RV Park) Avail: 21 full hkups (30/50 amps). 2021 rates: $30 to $60. (509)422-8500, 28968 Hwy 97, Omak, WA 98841

CARL PRECHT MEMORIAL RV PARK
good sam park **Ratings: 7/8.5★/8.5** (Public) From Jct of US 97 & Hwy 155 (traffic light): Go .3 mi N on Dayton Street to Visitor's Center and Eastside Park complex and follow signs to RV park at back of complex. **FAC:** paved rds. Avail: 68 paved, 12 pull-thrus, (22x75), back-ins (24x35), 68 full hkups (30/50 amps), WiFi @ sites, tent sites, shower$, dump. **REC:** pool $, Okanogan River: swim, fishing, kayaking/canoeing, boating nearby, playground, rec open to public. Pets OK. Partial handicap access, 5 day max stay. 2021 rates: $33 to $35.
(509)826-1170 Lat: 48.410161, Lon: -119.519534
401 Omak Ave, Omak, WA 98841
www.omakcity.com
See ad this page

ORONDO — B4 *Douglas*

BEEBE BRIDGE PARK (Public) At Jct of US-97 & MP-234 (R). 46 Avail: 46 W, 46 E (20/30 amps). 2021 rates: $15 to $30. Apr 01 to Oct 31. (509)661-4551

OROVILLE — A4 *Okanogan*

BAINS RV PARK **Ratings: 6/8★/6** (RV Park) 24 Avail: 11 full hkups, 13 W, 13 E (30/50 amps). 2021 rates: $35 to $40. (509)476-4122, 5 Swann Lane, Oroville, WA 98844

OSOYOOS LAKE STATE VETERAN'S MEMORIAL PARK (Public State Park) From town, N 0.5 mi on US-97 (R). 61 Avail: 23 W, 23 E. 2021 rates: $12 to $25. Mar 01 to Oct 31. (509)476-3321

RIVER OAKS RV PARK **Ratings: 7.5/9★/9** (RV Park) Avail: 48 full hkups (30/50 amps). 2021 rates: $35 to $40. (509)476-2087, 962 Kernan Rd, Oroville, WA 98844

OTHELLO — C5 *Grant*

O'SULLIVAN SPORTSMAN RESORT (CAMPING RESORT)
good sam park **Ratings: 8.5/9★/9.5** (Membership Park) Avail: 110 full hkups (30/50 amps). 2021 rates: $50. (509)346-2447, 6897 Hwy 262 SE, Othello, WA 99344

PACIFIC BEACH — C1 *Grays Harbor*

MILITARY PARK PACIFIC BEACH RESORT & CONFERENCE CENTER (NS EVERETT) (Public) From jct I-5 & US-8/Exit 104 (Aberdeen/Port Angeles exit), W on US-8 (becomes US-8/12) thru Aberdeen to Hoquiam (becomes US-101), NW 4 mi on US-101 to Beaches sign, left on Ocean Beach Rd, NW 20 mi to Pacific Beach, camp located adjacent to Pacific Beach Resort (L). 43 Avail: 43 W, 43 E (30 amps). 2021 rates: $18 to $25. (360)276-4414

PACIFIC BEACH (Public State Park) From Jct of Hwy 109 & Main St, W 0.3 mi on Main St to 2nd St, S 0.3 mi (E). Avail: 42 E (30 amps). 2021 rates: $20 to $45. (888)226-7688

PACKWOOD — C3 *Lewis*

MT RAINIER/OHANAPECOSH (Public National Park) From town, N 7 mi on US-12 to SR-123, N 3 mi (L). 140 Avail. 2021 rates: $20. May 25 to Oct 07. (360)569-2211

RAINIER WINGS / PACKWOOD RV PARK
good sam park **Ratings: 5.5/7.5★/6** (RV Park) Avail: 77 full hkups (30/50 amps). 2021 rates: $34. (360)494-5145, 12985 Hwy 12, Packwood, WA 98361

PALOUSE — C6 *Whitman*

PALOUSE RV PARK (Public) From Jct of SR-27 & Main St (in town), W 0.2 mi on Main St (R). Avail: 10 full hkups (30/50 amps). 2021 rates: $25. (509)878-1811

PASCO — D5 *Franklin*

A SPOTLIGHT Introducing the Tri-Cities' colorful attractions appearing at the front of this state section.

PASCO See also Benton City, Kennewick, Richland & West Richland, WA; Hermiston, Umatilla, OR.

FRANKLIN COUNTY RV PARK (Public) From Jct of I-182 and Exit 9 (N Road 68): Go 1/4 mi N on Rd 68, then 1/8 mi E on Burden Blvd, then 1/4 mi S on Convention Pl, then 1/4 mi E on Homerun Rd to entrance (L). 24 Avail: 11 full hkups, 13 W, 13 E (30/50 amps). 2021 rates: $40 to $45. (509)542-5982

LAKE WALLULA - COE/HOOD PARK (Public Corps) From jct US-395 & US-12: Go 4 mi S on US-12, then 1/4 mi E on Hwy-124 (L). Avail: 46 E (30/50 amps). 2021 rates: $24 to $26. May 16 to Sep 01. (509)547-2048

PASCO TRI-CITIES KOA **Ratings: 9.5/10★/8.5** (RV Park) Avail: 42 full hkups (30/50 amps). 2021 rates: $52. (800)562-2495, 8801 St Thomas Dr, Pasco, WA 99301

Travel Services

CAMPING WORLD OF PASCO As the nation's largest retailer of RV supplies, accessories, services and new and used RVs, Camping World is committed to making your total RV experience better. **SERVICES:** restrooms. RV Sales. RV supplies, RV accessible. Hours: 9am - 6pm.
(833)783-3208 Lat: 46.278012, Lon: -119.213653
9420 Sandifur Parkway, Pasco, WA 99301
www.campingworld.com

PATEROS — B4 *Okanogan*

ALTA LAKE (Public State Park) From jct US 97 & Hwy 153: Go 1-1/4 mi W on Hwy 153, then 1-1/2 mi S on Alta Lake Rd/CR 1517. Avail: 32 full hkups. 2021 rates: $20 to $45. Apr 01 to Sep 30. (509)923-2473

PESHASTIN — B4 *Chelan*

BLU-SHASTIN RV PARK **Ratings: 8/9.5★/8.5** (Campground) Avail: 60 full hkups (30/50 amps). 2021 rates: $45. (888)548-4184, 3300 Hwy 97, Peshastin, WA 98847

PLYMOUTH — D4 *Benton*

LAKE UMATILLA - COE/JOHN DAY LOCK & DAM/PLYMOUTH PARK (Public Corps) From Jct of I-82 & SR-14, W 1 mi on SR-14 to Old State Hwy (Plymouth Rd), S 1 mi to Christy Rd, W 300 ft (L). Avail: 32 E (20/30 amps). 2021 rates: $24 to $27. Apr 01 to Oct 30. (541)506-4807

POMEROY — D6 *Columbia*

PATAHA CREEK RV PARK (Public) From Jct of US-12 & Port Way (west end of town): Go S 0.1 mi on Port Way (L). Avail: 16 full hkups (30/50 amps). 2021 rates: $35. (509)843-3740

THE LAST RESORT **Ratings: 6.5/9★/9** (RV Park) 33 Avail: 21 full hkups, 12 W, 12 E (30/50 amps). 2021 rates: $41 to $47. (509)843-1556, 2005 Tucannon Rd, Pomeroy, WA 99347

PORT ANGELES — B2 *Clallam*

A SPOTLIGHT Introducing Olympic Peninsula's colorful attractions appearing at the front of this state section.

CRESCENT BEACH & RV PARK **Ratings: 5/7/7** (RV Park) Avail: 34 full hkups (30/50 amps). 2021 rates: $50 to $53. (360)928-3344, 2860 Crescent Beach Rd, Port Angeles, WA 98363

ELWHA DAM RV PARK
Ratings: 9/10★/9.5 (RV Park) 51 Avail: 39 full hkups, 12 W, 12 E (30/50 amps). 2021 rates: $42 to $65. (360)452-7054, 47 Lower Dam Rd, Port Angeles, WA 98363

LOG CABIN RESORT **Ratings: 3.5/4.5/6** (Campground) 32 Avail: 32 W, 32 E (20/30 amps). 2021 rates: $40. May 18 to Sep 30. (360)928-3325, 3183 E Beach Rd, Port Angeles, WA 98363

OLYMPIC PENINSULA / PORT ANGELES KOA **Ratings: 8.5/9.5★/8.5** (Campground) 68 Avail: 23 full hkups, 41 W, 41 E (30/50 amps). 2021 rates: $49 to $92. (360)457-5916, 80 O'Brien Rd, Port Angeles, WA 98362

SALT CREEK REC AREA (Public) From Jct of US-101 & SR-112, W 6 mi on SR-112 to Camp Hayden Rd, N 3 mi (R). 90 Avail: 39 W, 39 E (30/50 amps). 2021 rates: $22 to $30. (360)928-3441

Refer to the Table of Contents in front of the Guide to locate everything you need.

SOL DUC HOT SPRINGS RV & CAMPGROUND **Ratings: 6/NA/7** (Campground) 82 Avail: Pit toilets. 2021 rates: $21 to $40. Mar 24 to Oct 29. (888)896-3818, 12076 Sol Duc Hot Springs Rd, Port Angeles, WA 98362

PORT LUDLOW — B2 *Jefferson*

PORT LUDLOW RV PARK **Ratings: 5.5/7/7.5** (Campground) 27 Avail: 26 full hkups, 1 W, 1 E (30 amps). 2021 rates: $35 to $40. (360)437-9377, 44 Breaker Ln, Port Ludlow, WA 98365

PORT ORCHARD — B2 *Kitsap*

MANCHESTER (Public State Park) From Jct of SR-16 & SR-160 E (Sedgwick Rd SE), E 2.5 mi on SR-160 E to Long Lake Rd SE, N 2.3 mi to Mile Hill Dr, E 1.5 mi to Colchester Dr, N 1.7 mi to Main St, W 100 ft to Beach Dr, N 2 mi to Hilldale, E 0.2 mi (E). 15 Avail: 15 W, 15 E (30 amps). 2021 rates: $20 to $45. (360)871-4065

PORT TOWNSEND — B2 *Jefferson*

FORT WORDEN (Public State Park) From town: Go 1 mi N on Hwy 20 to Kearney St, then .4 mi W to Blaine St, then E 0.2 mi to Walker/Cherry St, then N 0.8 mi to Redwood St, then NW 0.4 mi to W St, then E 0.1 mi (L). Follow signs inside park. 80 Avail: 50 full hkups, 30 W, 30 E (30/50 amps). 2021 rates: $25 to $45. (888)226-7688

JEFFERSON COUNTY FAIRGROUNDS CAMPGROUND
(Public) From Jct of Hwy 20 & Kearney St (stoplight): Go 1/4-mi N on Kearney St, then 1/8 mi W on Blaine St (19th), then 1-1/2 mi N on San Juan, then 1/8 mi W on 49th St, then 1/8 mi S on Jackman St (L). **FAC:** gravel/dirt rds. Avail: 78 grass, 58 pull-thrus, (20x40), back-ins (10x20), mostly side by side hkups, 18 full hkups, 40 W, 40 E (20/30 amps), WiFi, tent sites, dump. **REC:** boating nearby, rec open to public. Pets OK. Partial handicap access, 10 day max stay. 2021 rates: $20 to $25. no cc, no reservations.
(360)385-1013 Lat: 48.134415, Lon: -122.783013
4907 Landes St, Port Townsend, WA 98368
www.jeffcofairgrounds.com
See ad page 975

OLD FORT TOWNSEND (Public State Park) From town, S 4 mi on SR-20 to Old Fort Townsend Rd, W 0.5 mi (E). 40 Avail. 2021 rates: $20 to $45. (360)385-3595

POINT HUDSON MARINA & RV PARK (Public) From Jct of SR-20 & Ferry Landing (Water St): Go 1/2 mi N on Water St to Monroe St, then 1/8 mi W on Monroe St to Jefferson St, then 1/8 mi NE on Jefferson St (R). Avail: 40 full hkups (30/50 amps). 2021 rates: $32 to $63. (360)385-2828

POULSBO — B2 *Kitsap*

CEDAR GLEN RV PARK
Ratings: 9/9.5★/9.5 (RV Park) From Jct State Hwy 3 and State Hwy 305 (Poulsbo): Go 5 mi SE on State Hwy 305 to park office (L). **FAC:** paved rds. Avail: 38 all weather, patios, back-ins (30x75), 38 full hkups (30/50 amps), WiFi @ sites, laundry. **REC:** boating nearby. Pet restrict (B/Q). Partial handicap access. No tents. Big rig sites, eco-friendly. 2021 rates: $55.
(360)779-4305 Lat: 47.706030, Lon: -122.594494
16300 NE State Highway 305, Poulsbo, WA 98370
www.cedarglenmhp.com
See ad this page

EAGLE TREE RV PARK
Ratings: 9/9★/9 (RV Park) Avail: 53 full hkups (30/50 amps). 2021 rates: $44.86. (360)598-5988, 16280 Washington State Hwy 305, Poulsbo, WA 98370

KITSAP MEMORIAL (Public State Park) From town, N 5 mi on SR-3 to Park St, E 0.25 mi, follow signs (R). 39 Avail: 18 W, 18 E (30 amps). 2021 rates: $20 to $45. (888)226-7688

PROSSER — D4 *Benton*

WINE COUNTRY RV PARK
Ratings: 10/10★/10 (RV Park) From Jct of I-82 & Wine Country Rd (exit 80): Go 1/8 mi SE on Wine Country Rd to Merlot Dr, then 1/4 mi E (R). **FAC:** paved rds. (126 spaces). 121 Avail: 65 paved, 56 all weather, 85 pull-thrus, (29x70), back-ins (32x35), 121 full hkups (30/50 amps), seasonal sites, cable, WiFi @ sites, tent sites, rentals, shower$, laundry, groc, LP gas, fire rings. **REC:** heated pool, hot tub, playground. Pets OK. Partial handicap access. Big rig sites, eco-friendly. 2021 rates: $43 to $68, Military discount.
(509)786-5192 Lat: 46.219755, Lon: -119.783890
330 Merlot Drive, Prosser, WA 99350
www.winecountryrvpark.com
See ad this page

Canada -- know the rules, regulations and tips before crossing the border. This is listed at the beginning of the country.

PULLMAN — C6 *Whitman*

PULLMAN See also Clarkston, WA; Lewiston, ID.

PULLMAN RV PARK (Public) From Jct of US-195 & US-270, E 2.3 mi on US-270 to Spring St, N 0.5 mi (R). Avail: 19 full hkups (20/30 amps), Pit toilets. 2021 rates: $30. Apr 01 to Nov 30. (509)338-3227

PUYALLUP — C2 *Pierce*

MAJESTIC RV PARK
Ratings: 9.5/9.5★/7.5 (RV Park) From Jct of SR-167 & WA-512: Go 1 mi NW on SR-167 (L). **FAC:** paved rds. (115 spaces). Avail: 44 all weather, 1 pull-thrus, (24x70), back-ins (22x55), 44 full hkups (30/50 amps), seasonal sites, cable, WiFi @ sites, laundry, groc, LP gas. **REC:** heated pool, Clarks Creek: fishing, boating nearby. Pet restrict (B/Q). No tents. Big rig sites, eco-friendly. 2021 rates: $65.
(253)845-3144 Lat: 47.209531, Lon: -122.336874
6906 52nd Street Court E., Puyallup, WA 98371
majesticrvpark.com
See ad page 974

WASHINGTON STATE FAIR RV PARK **Ratings: 4/NA/4.5** (Campground) 295 Avail: 159 full hkups, 136 W, 136 E (30/50 amps). 2021 rates: $35 to $40. (253)845-1771, 110 9th Ave SW, Puyallup, WA 98371

Things to See and Do

WASHINGTON STATE FAIR Headquarters for Washington State Fairs in spring and fall, plus year-round venue for events such as concerts, dog shows, craft, hobby and antiques shows. RV accessible. Restrooms. Hours: 8am to 4:30pm. No CC.
(253)841-5045 Lat: 47.184282, Lon: -122.293928
110 9th Ave SW, Puyallup, WA 98371
www.thefair.com
See ad page 964

QUEETS — B1 *Jefferson*

OLYMPIC NATIONAL PARK/KALALOCH (Public National Park) From town, N 6 mi on Hwy 101 (L). 170 Avail. 2021 rates: $22. (360)565-3130

QUINCY — C4 *Grant*

CRESCENT BAR
Ratings: 8.5/7.5/8.5 (Membership Park) Avail: 13 full hkups (30/50 amps). 2021 rates: $71 to $74. Apr 15 to Oct 01. (888)563-7040, 9252 Crescent Bar Rd NW, Quincy, WA 98848

Got a different point of view? We want to know. Rate the campgrounds you visit using the rating guidelines located in front of this Guide, then compare your ratings to ours.

WA

RANDLE — D3 *Lewis*

CASCADE PEAKS FAMILY CAMPING **Ratings: 8/4/7** (Membership Park) 400 Avail: 120 full hkups, 280 W, 280 E (30/50 amps). 2021 rates: $35 to $43. (360)494-9202, 11519 US Highway 12, Randle, WA 98377

MAPLE GROVE RESORT & GOLF COURSE **Ratings: 8/8.5★/9.5** (Membership Park) 161 Avail: 54 full hkups, 107 W, 70 E (30/50 amps). 2021 rates: $75. (360)497-2742, 175 SR 131, Randle, WA 98377

RAVENSDALE — C3 *King*

KANASKAT-PALMER (Public State Park) From Jct Hwy-410 & Farman Rd (east of town): Go 11 mi NE. Avail: 18 E (30 amps). 2021 rates: $20 to $50. (888)226-7688

REPUBLIC — A5 *Ferry*

CURLEW LAKE (Public State Park) From town, E 2.5 mi on SR-20 to SR-21, N 7 mi, follow signs (L). 25 Avail: 18 full hkups, 7 W, 7 E (30 amps). 2021 rates: $20 to $45. (509)775-3592

GOLD MOUNTAIN RV PARK **Ratings: 7.5/UI/8** (RV Park) Avail: 21 full hkups (30/50 amps). 2021 rates: $34 to $36. (509)775-3700, 16330 North Hwy 21, Republic, WA 99166

WINCHESTER RV RESORT

good sam park **Ratings: 9/10★/9.5** (RV Park) Avail: 33 full hkups (30/50 amps). 2021 rates: $37. (509)775-1039, 8 West Curlew Lake Rd, Republic, WA 99166

RICHLAND — D5 *Benton*

RICHLAND See also Benton City, Kennewick, Pasco, Prosser & West Richland, WA; Hermiston & Umatilla, OR.

HORN RAPIDS RV RESORT

good sam park **Ratings: 10/10★/10** (RV Resort) From Jct of I-182 & Hwy 240W (exit 4): go 4 mi NE on Hwy 240W, then 2 mi NW on Hwy 240W to Kingsgate Wy, then 1/8 mi NE on Kingsgate Wy (R).

TRI-CITIES PREMIER CAMPING RESORT

Experience all the best the Tri-Cities has to offer: wine trails, golf courses, art galleries, world-class fishing, boating, bike trails & restaurants. Be sure to stop by the Mini-Mart and grab a snack or a meal. Book Now! **FAC:** paved rds. (225 spaces). Avail: 45 all weather, patios, 20 pull-thrus, (24x70), back-ins (30x50), 45 full hkups (30/50 amps), seasonal sites, cable, WiFi @ sites, dump, laundry, groc, LP gas. **REC:** heated pool, hot tub, boating nearby, shuffleboard, playground. Pet restrict (B). Partial handicap access. No tents. Big rig sites. 2021 rates: $55, Military discount.
(866)557-9637 Lat: 46.32740, Lon: -119.31495
2640 Kingsgate Way, Richland, WA 99354
hornrapidsrvresort.com
See ad pages 967, 978

Don't miss a thing! Check out the Table of Contents for everything the Guide has to offer.

WRIGHT'S DESERT GOLD MOTEL & RV PARK

good sam park **Ratings: 9/10★/8** (RV Park) From jct of US-395 & SR-240: Go 5 mi W on SR-240 to Columbia Park Trail, then 1/2 mi W on Columbia Park Trail under overpass (L). **FAC:** paved rds. (89 spaces). Avail: 49 paved, 15 pull-thrus, (18x60), back-ins (17x35), 49 full hkups (30 amps), seasonal sites, cable, WiFi @ sites, rentals, laundry, groc, LP gas. **REC:** pool, hot tub, boating nearby. Pets OK. No tents. 2021 rates: $35, Military discount.
(509)627-1000 Lat: 46.23912, Lon: -119.25129
611 Columbia Park Trail, Richland, WA 99352
wrightsdesertgold.com
See ad this page

RIDGEFIELD — D2 *Cowlitz*

RIDGEFIELD See also Kalama, Vancouver & Woodland, WA; Fairview, Portland & Troutdale, OR.

PARADISE POINT (Public State Park) From town, N 3 mi on I-5 to exit 16, follow sign on frntg rd (E). Avail: 18 E (30/50 amps). 2021 rates: $20 to $45. Apr 01 to Sep 30. (888)226-7688

ROCHESTER — C2 *Thurston*

OUTBACK RV PARK **Ratings: 7.5/9★/6.5** (RV Park) Avail: 13 full hkups (30/50 amps). 2021 rates: $45. (360)273-0585, 19100 Huntington St SW, Rochester, WA 98579

ROCKPORT — A3 *Skagit*

GLACIER PEAK RESORT AND WINERY **Ratings: 8.5/10★/9** (Campground) Avail: 23 full hkups (30/50 amps). 2021 rates: $40. (360)873-2250, 58468 Clark Cabin Rd, Rockport, WA 98283

HOWARD MILLER STEELHEAD PARK/SKAGIT COUNTY (Public) From Jct of Hwy 20 & SR-530, S 0.25 mi on SR-530 (L). 50 Avail: 50 W, 50 E (30/50 amps). 2021 rates: $30. (360)853-8808

ROYAL CITY — C4 *Grant*

ROYAL CITY GOLF COURSE & RV PARK (Public) From the town of Royal City: Go 3-1/2 mi E on Hwy 26, then 1/2 mi NW on Dodson Rd. Avail: 12 full hkups. 2021 rates: $20. (509)346-2052

SEABECK — B2 *Kitsap*

SCENIC BEACH (Public State Park) From Jct of SR-3 & Newberry Hill Rd exit, S 2 mi on Newberry Hill Rd to Seabeck Hwy, W 2 mi to Scenic Beach Park Rd, W 2 mi (E). 18 Avail. 2021 rates: $20 to $45. (888)226-7688

SEATTLE — B2 *King*

A SPOTLIGHT Introducing Greater Seattle's colorful attractions appearing at the front of this state section.

SEATTLE See also Black Diamond, Bothell, Everett, Fall City, Gig Harbor, Issaquah, Kent & Poulsbo.

MAPLE GROVE RV RESORT

good sam park **Ratings: 9/10★/9.5** (RV Park) Northbound: At Jct 1-5N & Hwy 525 (Exit 182): Go 3 mi N on Hwy 525 to WA-99N, then 1-1/2 mi NE on WA-99N (R). **FAC:** paved rds. (99 spaces). Avail: 74 paved, 44 pull-thrus, (23x57), back-ins (23x40), accepts full hkup units only, 74 full hkups (30/50 amps), seasonal sites, cable, WiFi @ sites, laundry, LP gas. **REC:** boating nearby. Pet restrict (B/Q). Partial handicap access. No tents. 2021 rates: $54 to $99, Military discount.
(425)423-9608 Lat: 47.885275, Lon: -122.262034
12417 Hwy 99, Everett, WA 98204
maplegrovervresort.com
See primary listing at Everett and ad page 970

JOIN GoodSamRoadside.com

SEAVIEW — D1 *Pacific*

LONG BEACH

good sam park **Ratings: 7/8.5★/7** (Membership Park) Avail: 10 full hkups (30/50 amps). 2021 rates: $54 to $75. (888)563-7040, 2215 Willows Rd, Seaview, WA 98644

SEKIU — A1 *Clallam*

OLYMPIC NATIONAL PARK/OZETTE (Public National Park) From Jct of Hoko River Rd & SR-112, SW 30 mi on Hoko River Rd (E). 15 Avail: Pit toilets. 2021 rates: $20. (360)565-3130

SEQUIM — B2 *Clallam*

DIAMOND POINT RESORT **Ratings: 6/8★/8** (Membership Park) 10 Avail: 5 full hkups, 5 W, 5 E (30 amps). 2021 rates: $75. (360)681-0590, 294 Industrial Parkway, Sequim, WA 98382

DUNGENESS REC AREA (Public) From town, E 12 mi on Rte 101 to Kitchen Dick Rd, N 3 mi, into the park (L). 66 Avail. 2021 rates: $20 to $28. (360)683-5847

GILGAL OASIS RV PARK **Ratings: 9/10★/9.5** (RV Park) Avail: 25 full hkups (30/50 amps). 2021 rates: $39 to $60. (360)452-1324, 400 S Brown Rd, Sequim, WA 98382

JOHN WAYNE'S WATERFRONT RESORT **Ratings: 6.5/9★/7.5** (RV Park) 42 Avail: 31 full hkups, 11 W, 11 E (30/50 amps). 2021 rates: $40 to $50. (360)681-3853, 2634 W Sequim Bay Rd, Sequim, WA 98382

SEQUIM BAY (Public State Park) From town, E 4 mi on Hwy 101 at MP-269 (L). Avail: 15 full hkups (30 amps). 2021 rates: $20 to $45. May 15 to Sep 15. (888)226-7688

SHELTON — C2 *Mason*

LITTLE CREEK CASINO RESORT RV PARK **Ratings: 10/10★/9.5** (RV Resort) Avail: 44 full hkups (30/50 amps). 2021 rates: $49. (800)667-7711, 91 W State Route 108, Shelton, WA 98584

POTLATCH (Public State Park) From town, S 3.2 mi on US-101, btwn MP-335 & 336 (R). Avail: 35 full hkups. 2021 rates: $20 to $45. (888)226-7688

SILVER CREEK — C2 *Lewis*

SILVER CREEK See also Castle Rock, Centralia, Chehalis, Mossyrock, Silverlake & Toutle.

PARADISE THOUSAND TRAILS RESORT

good sam park **Ratings: 7/8★/7** (Membership Park) 199 Avail: 85 full hkups, 114 W, 114 E (30/50 amps). 2021 rates: $52 to $58. Apr 25 to Sep 22. (888)563-7040, 173 Salem Plant Rd, Silver Creek, WA 98585

SILVERLAKE — D2 *Cowlitz*

SILVERLAKE See also Arlington, Bothell, Everett, Fall City, Monroe, Port Ludlow, Poulsbo & Stanwood.

MOUNT ST HELENS RV RESORT **Ratings: 5/7.5/5** (Campground) Avail: 16 full hkups (30/50 amps). 2021 rates: $18 to $33. (360)274-2701, 4220 Spirit Lake Hwy, Silverlake, WA 98645

SEAQUEST (Public State Park) From jct I-5 (exit 49) & Hwy 504: Go 6 mi E on Hwy 504. 33 Avail: 33 W, 33 E (30/50 amps). 2021 rates: $20 to $45. (888)226-7688

SILVER COVE RV RESORT **Ratings: 8/9★/10** (RV Park) Avail: 105 full hkups (30/50 amps). 2021 rates: $52 to $99. (360)967-2057, 351 Hall Rd, Silverlake, WA 98645

SILVER LAKE RESORT **Ratings: 5/6.5/7** (Campground) 18 Avail: 5 full hkups, 13 W, 13 E (30/50 amps). 2021 rates: $25 to $45. (360)274-6141, 3201 Spirit Lake Hwy, Silverlake, WA 98645

SKAMOKAWA — D2 *Wahkiakum*

VISTA PARK

good sam park **Ratings: 7.5/8.5★/8.5** (Public) From jct WA 4 & Vista Park Rd: Go 3/4 mi W on Vista Park Road (R). **FAC:** all weather rds. Avail: 42 gravel, back-ins (25x50), 15 full hkups, 27 W, 27 E (30 amps), WiFi @ sites, tent sites, rentals, dump, LP bottles, fire rings, firewood. **REC:** Columbia River: fishing, kayaking/canoeing, boating nearby, playground. Pets OK. 21 day max stay. 2021 rates: $40.
(360)795-8605 Lat: 46.271347, Lon: -123.459098
13 Vista Park Road, Skamokawa, WA 98647
www.wahport2.org
See ad this page

Save 10% at Good Sam Parks!

SOAP LAKE — C4 *Grant*

SMOKIAM CAMPGROUND (Public) From jct Hwy 28 & Hwy 17: Go 1 mi N on Hwy 17. 28 Avail. 2021 rates: $25. (509)246-1211

SMOKIAM RV RESORT **Ratings: 8.5/10★/8.5** (RV Park) Avail: 43 full hkups (30/50 amps). 2021 rates: $69 to $85. (509)246-0413, 22818 Hwy 17 North, Soap Lake, WA 98851

SPOKANE — B6 *Spokane*

A SPOTLIGHT Introducing Spokane and the Inland Empire's colorful attractions appearing at the front of this state section.

SPOKANE See also Airway Heights, Cheney, Colbert, Deer Park, Liberty Lake & Nine Mile Falls, WA; Post Falls, ID.

MILITARY PARK FAIRCHILD FAMCAMP (FAIRCHILD AFB) (Public) From jct I-90 & US Hwy 2: exit through Airway Heights, base entrance on left (RVs must use Rambo Gate). Avail: 32 full hkups (30/50 amps). 2021 rates: $20. Apr 01 to Oct 31. (509)247-5920

NORTH SPOKANE RV CAMPGROUND

Ratings: 10/10★/10 (RV Park) From Jct of I-90 and US Hwy 2: Go 5-3/4 mi N on Hwy 2/Division St to Jct US 395 and Hwy 2, then right at the V to continue 1-1/4 mi NE on Hwy 2 to park (R). **FAC:** paved rds. Avail: 92 paved, patios, 33 pull-thrus, (32x70), back-ins (30x60), 92 full hkups (30/50 amps), cable, WiFi @ sites, dump, laundry, LP gas. **REC:** heated pool, playground. Pet restrict (Q). Partial handicap access. No tents. Big rig sites, eco-friendly. 2021 rates: $60 to $90, Military discount.
(509)315-5561 Lat: 47.757010, Lon: -117.394646
10904 N Newport Hwy, Spokane, WA 99218
www.northspokanervcampground.com
See ad page 975

RIVERSIDE (Public State Park) From town, NW 6 mi on SR-291, follow signs (L). 37 Avail: 37 W, 37 E (30/50 amps). 2021 rates: $20 to $50. May 15 to Sep 15. (888)226-7688

Do you know how to read each part of a listing? Check the How to Use This Guide in the front.

SPOKANE VALLEY — B6 *Spokane*

KOA OF SPOKANE **Ratings: 8.5/8★/7.5** (Campground) 120 Avail: 100 full hkups, 20 W, 20 E (30/50 amps). 2021 rates: $49.95 to $84.95. (509)924-4722, 3025 N Barker Rd, Spokane Valley, WA 99027

PARK LANE MOTEL & RV PARK **Ratings: 6/NA/6.5** (RV Park) Avail: 12 full hkups (30/50 amps). 2021 rates: $35 to $42. (509)535-1626, 4412 E Sprague Ave, Spokane Valley, WA 99212

STANWOOD — B2 *Island*

CAMANO ISLAND (Public State Park) From town, W 3 mi on Hwy 532 to E Camano Dr (left at fork), S 6 mi (rd becomes Elger Bay Rd) to Mountain View, W 2 mi to Lowell Point Rd, S 0.6 mi (E). 88 Avail. 2021 rates: $20 to $45. (360)387-3031

CEDAR GROVE SHORES RV PARK

Ratings: 8.5/9.5★/9 (RV Park) 12 Avail: 12 W, 12 E (30/50 amps). 2021 rates: $50. (360)652-7083, 16529 W Lake Goodwin Rd, Stanwood, WA 98292

LAKE GOODWIN RESORT **Ratings: 8/8.5/7.5** (Campground) Avail: 48 full hkups (30 amps). 2021 rates: $55. (360)652-8169, 4726 Lakewood Rd, Stanwood, WA 98292

STARBUCK — D5 *Franklin*

KOA AT LYONS FERRY MARINA **Ratings: 6/7.5/7.5** (Campground) 30 Avail: 19 full hkups, 11 W, 11 E (30/50 amps). 2021 rates: $32.75 to $50.75. (800)562-5418, 102 Lyons Ferry Rd, Starbuck, WA 99359

STEVENSON — D3 *Skamania*

THE RESORT AT SKAMANIA COVES **Ratings: 6/8.5/7** (RV Park) Avail: 10 full hkups (30/50 amps). 2021 rates: $42. Apr 15 to Oct 31. (509)427-4900, 45932 Hwy 14, Stevenson, WA 98648

WIND MOUNTAIN RV PARK & LODGE **Ratings: 6/9/5** (Campground) Avail: 22 full hkups (30/50 amps). 2021 rates: $45. (509)607-3409, 50561 St Hwy 14, Stevenson, WA 98648

Check out 10/10/10 Good Sam Parks on the Good Sam Park page.*

SUNNYSIDE — D4 *Yakima*

SUNNYSIDE RV PARK **Ratings: 9.5/9★/8.5** (RV Park) Avail: 10 full hkups (30/50 amps). 2021 rates: $40. (509)837-8486, 609 Scoon Rd, Sunnyside, WA 98944

TACOMA — C2 *Pierce*

TACOMA See also Black Diamond, Eatonville, Gig Harbor, Graham, Kent, Olympia & Puyallup.

DASH POINT (Public State Park) From I-5 (exit 143): Go 4-1/2 mi W on 320th St, then 1/2 mi N on 47th Ave, then 1-1/2 mi SW on Marine View Dr (Hwy 509). Avail: 27 full hkups. 2021 rates: $20 to $45. (253)661-4955

MILITARY PARK CAMP MURRAY BEACH (CAMP MURRAY) (Public) From Jct I-5 & Exit 122: Go W on exit 122, then 1 mi N on Berkley St, then on Portland Ave go through the traffic circle to base gate, then right on Armor Dr, then left on Quartermaster Rd, then right on 41st Division Rd (E). Avail: 28 full hkups (30/50 amps). 2021 rates: $20 to $32. (253)584-5411

MILITARY PARK HOLIDAY PARK FAMCAMP (JB LEWIS) (Public) From Jct of I-5 & exit 125, S 0.25 mi on exit rd to main gate, follow signs (R). Avail: 37 full hkups (30/50 amps). 2021 rates: $25 to $28. (253)982-5488

MILITARY PARK JOINT BASE LEWIS-MCCHORD TRAVEL CAMP (FORT LEWIS) (Public) From jct I-5 & Exit 120, on exit rd to North Ft Lewis gate, then right at the first intersection signal light, then stay at Y onto NCO Beach Rd, enter Northwest Adventure Center (L). Avail: 58 full hkups (30/50 amps). 2021 rates: $28 to $35. (253)967-8282

TOKELAND — C1 *Pacific*

BAYSHORE RV PARK **Ratings: 7/8★/7.5** (RV Park) Avail: 37 full hkups (30 amps). 2021 rates: $50 to $60. (360)267-2625, 2941 Kindred Ave, Tokeland, WA 98590

TONASKET — A4 *Okanogan*

SPECTACLE LAKE RESORT **Ratings: 6.5/5/5** (Campground) 36 Avail: 32 full hkups, 4 W, 4 E (30 amps). 2021 rates: $38. Apr 01 to Oct 31. (509)223-3433, 10 McCammon Rd, Tonasket, WA 98855

TOUTLE — D2 *Cowlitz*

KID VALLEY CAMPGROUND **Ratings: 4/7/7.5** (Campground) 17 Avail: 15 full hkups, 2 W, 2 E (30/50 amps). 2021 rates: $25 to $30. (360)274-9060, 9360 Spirit Lake Highway, Toutle, WA 98649

TROUT LAKE — D3 *Klickitat*

ELK MEADOWS RV PARK **Ratings: 5.5/7★/8** (Campground) 57 Avail: 38 full hkups, 19 W, 19 E (30 amps). 2021 rates: $34 to $42. Apr 15 to Nov 15. (509)395-2400, 78 Trout Lake Creek Rd, Trout Lake, WA 98650

VANCOUVER — E2 *Clark*

VANCOUVER See also Woodland, WA; Fairview, Portland, Troutdale, Tualatin & Wilsonville, OR.

99 RV PARK **Ratings: 7.5/9★/6.5** (RV Park) Avail: 30 full hkups (30/50 amps). 2021 rates: $75. (360)573-0351, 1913 NE Leichner Rd , Vancouver, WA 98686

VANTAGE — C4 *Kittitas*

GINKGO/WANAPUM RECREATION AREA (Public State Park) From Jct of I-90 & Huntzinger Rd (exit 136), S 3 mi on Huntzinger Rd to Wanapum Recreation Area (L). Avail: 50 full hkups (30/50 amps). 2021 rates: $20 to $50. Mar 01 to Oct 31. (888)266-7688

VANTAGE RIVERSTONE RV & RETREAT **Ratings: 3.5/5/5** (Campground) 75 Avail: 40 full hkups, 35 W, 35 E (30 amps). 2021 rates: $30 to $40. (509)856-2800, 551 Main St, Vantage, WA 98950

WALLA WALLA — D5 *Walla Walla*

BLUE VALLEY RV PARK **Ratings: 9/10★/10** (RV Park) Avail: 35 full hkups (30/50 amps). 2021 rates: $45 to $50.75. (509)525-8282, 50 W George St, Walla Walla, WA 99362

RV RESORT FOUR SEASONS **Ratings: 8.5/9.5★/10** (RV Park) Avail: 69 full hkups (30/50 amps). 2021 rates: $47 to $67. (509)529-6072, 1440 The Dalles Military Rd, Walla Walla, WA 99362

WARDEN — C5 *Grant*

SAGE HILLS GOLF CLUB & RV RESORT

Ratings: 9/8.5★/9 (RV Park) Avail: 25 full hkups (30/50 amps). 2021 rates: $45 to $55. (509)349-2088, 10400 Sage Hill Rd SE, Warden, WA 98857

WENATCHEE — C4 *Chelan*

DAROGA (Public State Park) From Jct of US-2 & US-97 (at MP-219), NW 6.5 mi on US-97 (L). 28 Avail: 28 W, 28 E (20/30 amps). 2021 rates: $20 to $45. (509)664-6380

LINCOLN ROCK (Public State Park) From town, N 8.4 mi on US-2/US-97 (L). 67 Avail: 32 full hkups, 35 W, 35 E (30 amps). 2021 rates: $20 to $45. Mar 09 to Oct 15. (888)226-7688

WENATCHEE CONFLUENCE (Public State Park) From Jct of US-2 & US-97Alt exit, S 0.4 mi on US-97Alt to Euclid Ave, SE 0.4 to Olds Station Rd, W 0.25 mi (L); or From Jct of Wenatchee & Penny (Old Station exit), E 0.1 mi on Penny Rd to Chester Kim Rd, S 0.25 mi to Old Station Rd, E 0.25 mi (R). Avail: 51 full hkups (30 amps). 2021 rates: $20 to $45. Apr 01 to Sep 20. (888)226-7688

WENATCHEE RIVER COUNTY PARK (Public) From Jct of US-2 & US-97 (Wenatchee): Go 6 mi NW on US-2 (L). 39 Avail: 33 full hkups, 4 W, 4 E (30/50 amps). 2021 rates: $33 to $38. Apr 01 to Oct 31. (509)667-7503

WEST RICHLAND — D4 *Benton*

RED MOUNTAIN RV PARK **Ratings: 9.5/UI/7** (RV Park) Avail: 39 full hkups (30/50 amps). 2021 rates: $37. (509)967-9900, 7300 W Van Giesen St, West Richland, WA 99353

WESTPORT — C1 *Grays Harbor*

AMERICAN SUNSET RV & TENT RESORT
Ratings: 9.5/10★/9 (RV Park) Avail: 60 full hkups (30/50 amps). 2021 rates: $38 to $58. (360)268-0207, 1209 North Montesano St, Westport, WA 98595

PACIFIC MOTEL & RV **Ratings: 7/8★/7.5** (RV Park) Avail: 65 full hkups (30/50 amps). 2021 rates: $55. (360)268-9325, 330 S Forrest St, Westport, WA 98595

TWIN HARBORS (Public State Park) From Jct of SR-105 & SR-105 Spur, E 0.2 mi on SR-105 (R). Avail: 42 full hkups (30 amps). 2021 rates: $20 to $45. (360)268-9717

WHITE SALMON — D3 *Klickitat*

GORGE BASE CAMP RV PARK
Ratings: 8/10★/9 (RV Park) Avail: 35 full hkups (30/50 amps). 2021 rates: $62 to $68. (509)493-1111, 65271 Hwy 14, White Salmon, WA 98672

WILBUR — B5 *Lincoln*

COUNTRY LANE CAMPGROUND & RV PARK
Ratings: 8/8.5★/7.5 (RV Park) 27 Avail: 24 full hkups, 3 W, 3 E (30/50 amps). 2021 rates: $35 to $45. (509)647-0100, 14 Portland St NW, Wilbur, WA 99185

GOOSE CREEK RV PARK & CAMPGROUND
Ratings: 7.5/8★/8.5 (Campground) Avail: 23 full hkups (30/50 amps). 2021 rates: $36 to $43. Apr 01 to Oct 31. (509)647-5888, 712 SE Railroad St #22, Wilbur, WA 99185

LAKE ROOSEVELT NRA/KELLER FERRY (Public National Park) From town, N 14 mi on SR-21 (L). 55 Avail: Pit toilets. 2021 rates: $9 to $18. (509)633-9441

THE RIVER RUE RV PARK **Ratings: 6/5/9** (Campground) Avail: 21 full hkups (30/50 amps). 2021 rates: $40.50. (509)647-2647, 44892 State Route 21 N, Wilbur, WA 99185

Go to GoodSam.com/Trip-Planner for Trip Routing.

WINTHROP — A4 *Okanogan*

PEARRYGIN LAKE (Public State Park) From Jct of Hwy 20 & Riverside Ave (Main St thru town), NW 1.6 mi on Riverside Ave/Bluff St to Bear Crk Rd, E 2 mi (R). 152 Avail: 50 full hkups, 27 W, 27 E (30 amps). 2021 rates: $20 to $45. (509)996-2370

PINE NEAR RV PARK & CAMPGROUND **Ratings: 7.5/9.5★/8** (Campground) Avail: 38 full hkups (30/50 amps). 2021 rates: $35 to $57. (509)341-4062, 316 Castle Ave, Winthrop, WA 98862

RIVERBEND RV PARK OF TWISP
Ratings: 9/10★/9.5 (Campground) From town: Go 2 mi N on SR-20 (bet MP 199 & 200) (R); or From Winthrop: Go 6 mi S on SR-20 (L). **FAC:** paved rds. (69 spaces). Avail: 64 gravel, 37 pull-thrus, (26x105), back-ins (28x60), 56 full hkups, 8 W, 8 E (30/50 amps), seasonal sites, WiFi @ sites, tent sites, rentals, shower$, dump, laundry, fire rings. **REC:** Methow River: swim, fishing, kayaking/canoeing, boating nearby, playground, hunting nearby. Pets OK $. Big rig sites, eco-friendly. 2021 rates: $42 to $48, Military discount. Apr 15 to Oct 27.
(509)997-3500 Lat: 48.391426, Lon: -120.135704
19961 Hwy 20, Twisp, WA 98856
www.riverbendrv.com
See ad this page

SILVERLINE RESORT
Ratings: 7/10★/9.5 (Campground) 76 Avail: 25 full hkups, 51 W, 51 E (30/50 amps). 2021 rates: $43 to $48. Apr 20 to Oct 20. (509)996-2448, 677 Bear Creek Rd, Winthrop, WA 98862

WINTHROP/NORTH CASCADES NAT'L PARK KOA **Ratings: 7.5/9.5★/8** (Campground) 68 Avail: 29 full hkups, 28 W, 28 E (30/50 amps). 2021 rates: $71.76 to $160. Apr 15 to Nov 01. (509)996-2258, 1114 State Route 20, Winthrop, WA 98862

WOODLAND — D2 *Cowlitz*

WOODLAND See also Cougar, Kalama, Kelso & Vancouver, WA; Portland, OR.

COLUMBIA RIVERFRONT RV PARK **Ratings: 8.5/10★/9** (RV Park) Avail: 46 full hkups (30/50 amps). 2021 rates: $49 to $55. (360)225-2227, 1881 Dike Rd, Woodland, WA 98674

YAKIMA — C4 *Yakima*

SUNTIDES RV PARK & GOLF COURSE **Ratings: 8.5/9★/9.5** (RV Park) Avail: 15 full hkups (30/50 amps). 2021 rates: $50. (509)966-7883, 201 Pence Rd, Yakima, WA 98908

YAKIMA SPORTSMAN (Public State Park) From Jct of I-82 & Hwy 24 (exit 34), E 0.7 mi on Hwy 24 to Keys Rd, N 1 mi (L). Avail: 37 full hkups (30/50 amps). 2021 rates: $28 to $50. Mar 01 to Oct 31. (888)226-7688

RV Tech Tips - Foam Sweet Foam: Here's a handy tip to keep your cups and best china from rattling about while going down the road in your motorhome. Take a 2-inch thick piece of plastic foam sheet, cut to size to fit your cupboard shelf. and place cups upside down on it. Space them just far enough apart that they don't touch. Using a ballpoint pen or marker, trace around the cup (including the handles) to make a template. Then use a sharp knife to cut entirely through the template markings you have made. Place the plastic foam sheet on your shelf and insert cups. No more rattles. It's also very convenient to lift them in and out for use.

Getty Images/iStockphoto

YOU ARE HERE

West Virginia

DID YOU KNOW?

West Virginia has the most towns named after international cities, including Shanghai, Berlin, Athens, Geneva and Calcutta.

West Virginia is home to a particularly beautiful segment of the Appalachian Mountains along with a slew of charming towns. This environment has shaped the rich local culture, with a Southern charm all its own.

Doing the Charleston

As the state capital, Charleston preserves the Mountain State's past. History comes alive at the State Capitol building and the State Museum, and the nearby Clay Center hosts regular musical and theatrical performances that celebrate the state's identity. More episodes of the past can be experienced in the small town of Harpers Ferry, located at the confluence of the Shenandoah and Potomac rivers. A wealth of buildings from the 1800s still stand, and the Civil War Museum shares the tale of John Brown's raid, which escalated tensions in the years leading up to the war.

Wallace Hartman Nature Preserve

Charleston's natural beauty and ecological heritage are prized features, and the Wallace Hartman Nature Preserve in town entices guests to enjoy nature up close. More than 50 acres are traversed by hiking and biking trails, and attractions include small waterfalls along Lick Creek and its tributaries.

Wander WV

Just outside the city lies Kanawha State Park, an outdoor lover's dream destination. Cross-country skiing is a popular winter pastime, while the warmer months beckon guests to the hiking trails. Settle in for days of spotting some of the 19 species of warblers that call the 9,300-acre forest home. Licensed fishermen can drop a line in Ellison Pond for the chance to snag bluegill, bass or trout.

Old Pastime, New River

Paddling on one of West Virginia's tumultuous waterways is an exhilarating

VISITOR CENTER

TIME ZONE
Eastern Standard

ROAD & HIGHWAY INFORMATION
855-699-8511
wv511.org

FISHING & HUNTING INFORMATION
304-558-2758
wvdnr.gov/hunting/licensing.shtm

BOATING INFORMATION
304-558-2784
wvdnr.gov/lenforce/boating.shtm

NATIONAL PARKS
nps.gov/wv

STATE PARKS
wvstateparks.com

TOURISM INFORMATION
West Virginia Tourism Office
800-CALL-WVA
wvtourism.com

TOP TOURISM ATTRACTIONS
1) Monongahela National Forest
2) Harpers Ferry National Historical Park
3) New River Gorge Bridge

MAJOR CITIES
Charleston (capital), Huntington, Morgantown, Parkersburg, Wheeling

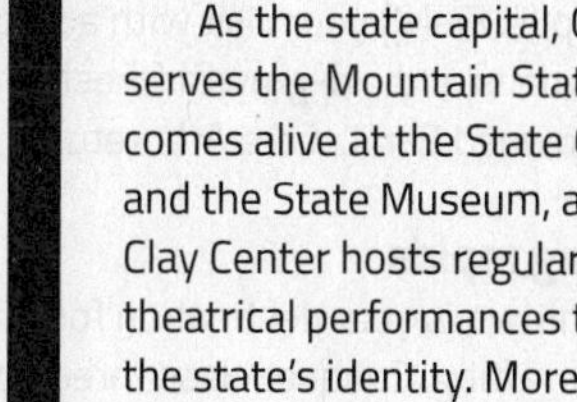

West Virginia Skillet Cornbread

Sweet, buttery and moist, cornbread delights tastebuds with its hearty flavor. In West Virginia, cooks use a seasoned cast-iron skillet to coax maximum richness from this Southern staple. Top it with whipped cream, or just eat it by itself. Nothing beats the texture of a steaming slice of cornbread served in a homey roadside diner. Savvy chefs use a dedicated skillet for cornbread and nothing else.

way to experience the Mountain State. The New River and the Gauley River are legendary for their beauty and their rapids. Anglers will also find "almost heaven" in West Virginia, thanks to the number of creeks flowing from the mountains and through the valleys. The Elk River and the Cranberry River attract anglers from across the nation with their plump trout and limitless views.

Magnificent Mountains

Take a drive to enjoy the beauty of West Virginia's mountains. The Highland Scenic Highway runs 43 miles through the Monongahela National Forest, with views of surrounding peaks. This landscape can best be experienced at Blackwater Falls State Park near Davis. The falls are named for the amber-colored waters that are stained by the tannic acid of the fallen hemlock and red spruce needles.

Fish Rich West Virginia Waterways

For anglers, West Virginia is a trout paradise. The Cranberry River and Elk River are top picks for fly-fishing. Trout-rich lakes also abound in these hills, with Summersville Lake and Stonewall Jackson Lake topping the list. At almost a million acres, the Monongahela National Forest is a hunting ground for deer, turkey and waterfowl.

Stunning Landscapes

More natural spectacles draw sightseers to Blackwater Falls State Park, home to a 62-foot waterfall surrounded by rugged rock faces and lush forest. More of the state's famed scenery can be appreciated with a drive along the Highland Scenic Highway or a bike ride along the 78-mile Greenbrier River Trail.

Local Lewisburg

Lewisburg has been a sought-after location for 250 years. Drawn by the curative powers of the local sulfur springs, the scenic area eventually became home to several luxury resorts. Explore the mysteries of the once top-secret Cold War Congressional Bunker, located under the Greenbrier luxury resort in nearby Sulphur Springs. This subterranean complex was designed to house the government's legislative branch in the event of nuclear war. Descend more than 100 feet into the Lost World Caverns to gape at the Snowy Chandelier, the largest stalactite in the U.S. If you're ready for adventure, sign up for the Wild Cave Tour, where you'll crawl and climb into the deepest and darkest depths of an otherworldly underground chamber. Get ready for great professional acting at the Green Valley Theatre, where music, live performances and literary events provide quality entertainment for all.

Whitewater rafting on the New River in West Virginia. Surfers can ride swells in some areas of the river.

Great Gauley Bridge

At the conflux of two rivers lies Gauley Bridge, a quaint town named for the toll bridge that once crossed the Gauley River. Nearby is Cathedral State Park, one of the few remaining ancient hemlock forests in the country, with trees that tower up to 90 feet tall, many of which exceed 20 feet in circumference. Cathedral Falls, one of the highest and most scenic waterfalls in West Virginia, is located along Route 60, providing a dramatic atmosphere and stunning photo opportunities with its steep, rushing waters cascading down into the rocky gorge below. There are over a dozen waterfalls along this five-mile stretch of scenic highway.

Morgantown

Home to West Virginia University since 1867, this spirited college town boasts stunning natural landscapes, sporting events and a lively nightlight scene – everything you need for a fun-filled getaway. Watch the Mountaineers sink three-pointers at WVU Coliseum and score touchdowns on Mountaineer Field. If art is more your thing, check out the stunning collection of paintings, sculptures and ceramics inside the Art Museum on campus. Finish your visit with a stroll through gardens and old-growth forest in the university-owned Earl L. Core Arboretum.

Rip-roaring rapids

Morgantown is your destination for whitewater rafting. Conquer class three and higher rapids in Cheat Canyon, Elk Creek, Teter Creek and other action-packed waterways. You can join a group tour with skilled guides or do a self-guided expedition if you're a seasoned paddler. Beneath the water's surface is a whole lot of catfish, bass, trout and bluegill. Grab your bait and tackle and snag an epic catch from Cheat Lake, Dixon Lake and Little Sandy Creek.

Dramatic Mountain Vistas

The sights are unbelievable in Coopers Rock State Forest. The Raven Rock Trail quickly reveals spectacular views of Cheat River Canyon, while the Virgin Hemlock Trail brings you to a 300-year-old hemlock grove. Mountain biking, rock climbing and camping can all be done after admiring the scenery. Licensed hunting and fishing are also permitted in the forest. You'll find more epic vistas in Dorsey's Knob Park – just head to the top of Sky Rock peak for photo opportunities of Monongalia County.

good sam park

Featured Good Sam Parks

WEST VIRGINIA

When you stay with Good Sam, you can expect the highest degree of cleanliness and friendliness, and better yet, you get **10% off** overnight campground fees.

If you're not already a Good Sam member you can purchase your membership at one of these locations:

BOWDEN
Revelles River Resort

FALLING WATERS
Leatherman's Falling Waters Campsite

FAYETTEVILLE
Rifrafters Campground

HUNTINGTON
Robert Newlon RV Park

MORGANTOWN
Sand Springs Campground

Getty Images/iStockphoto

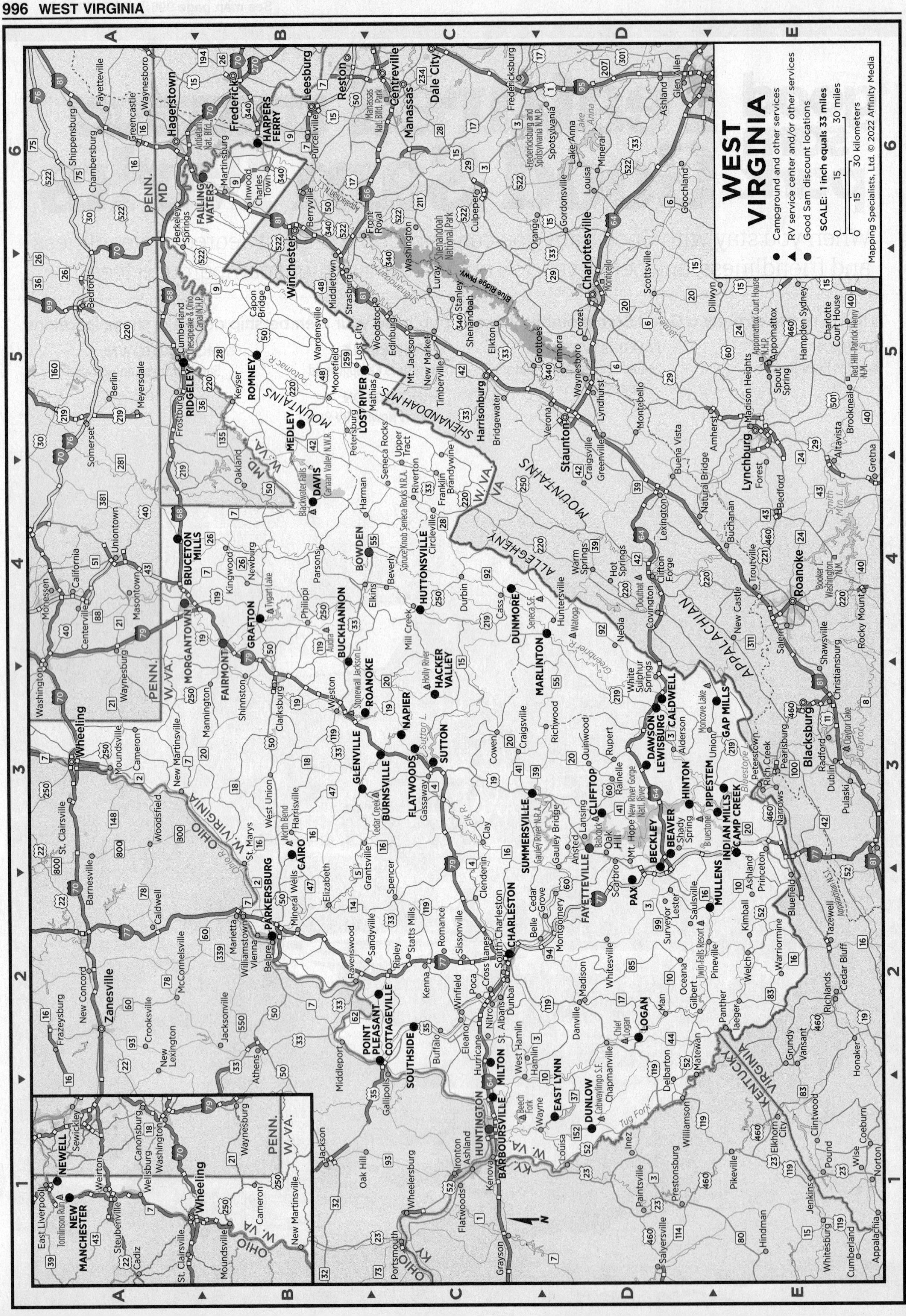
WEST VIRGINIA
Campground and other services
RV service center and/or other services
Good Sam discount locations
SCALE: 1 inch equals 33 miles
0 15 30 miles
0 15 30 kilometers
Mapping Specialists, Ltd. © 2022 Affinity Media

ROAD TRIPS

Country Roads Will Take You Home on This Trip

West Virginia

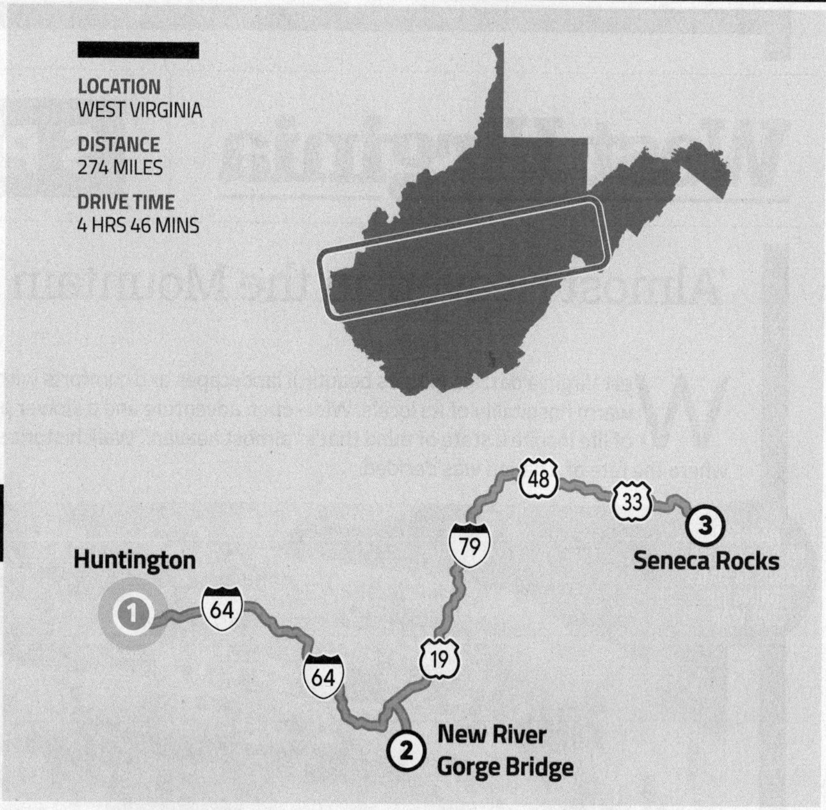

Take a trip to some of the most thrilling pastimes in North America. Whether you strap on a parachute or fasten climbing shoes, you'll find an adrenaline-pumping experience amidst the homey hospitality of Mountain State locals. At the end of the day, reward yourself with a hot dog laden with all the fixings and washed down by a hearty brew.

1 Huntington
Starting Point

Skydivers have plenty of safe landing zones in West Virginia. WV Skydivers takes advantage of these expanses, whisking would-be daredevils to 11,000-feet and letting them fall to the ground before their parachutes deploy. Participate in tandem jumps with instructors or get a solo certification. Once the adrenaline rush has worn off, enjoy a hearty treat at Hillbilly Hot Dogs, with delicious wieners and ample brews to satisfy the hungriest of thrill-seekers. Food Network star Guy Fieri raved about the robust cuisine on his show, "Diners, Drive-Ins and Dives."

2 New River Gorge Bridge
Drive 112 miles ▪ 1 hour, 58 minutes

New River Gorge Bridge rises 876-feet above its namesake river, making it a popular destination among daredevils. Come to admire the architecture of the longest single-arch bridge in North America, and then stay to Watch BASE jumpers take the leap off this iconic span. For the uninitiated, BASE stands for building, antenna, span and earth (cliff), referring to places that attract parachutists. You don't have to be a thrill-seeker to enjoy the site of risk-takers hurtling off the bridge before deploying their parachutes; simply watch the show. During Bridge Day, held each October, large numbers of daredevils take the leap. If you prefer something closer to the ground, take a kayaking trip on the New River below. Long stretches of the scenic waterway thunder with rapids and several outfitters can give you a thrill on fast-moving water. Expect exciting Class III rapids.

Getty Images/iStockphoto

3 Seneca Rocks
Drive 162 miles ▪ 2 hours, 48 minutes

Rock climbers flock here to scale the 900-foot-high Seneca Rocks. Hikers can take the trail up this rugged geological formation for amazing views of the forest below. Folks who prefer ropes and pitons can scale the rough face and choose a course that ranges from beginner and expert. Nearby outfitters can help climbers get started on the rocks. In the surrounding Monongahela National Forest, several mountain biking trails lead cyclists to scenic overlooks.

WV

BIKING BOATING DINING ENTERTAINMENT FISHING HIKING HUNTING PADDLING SHOPPING SIGHTSEEING

West Virginia SPOTLIGHTS

'Almost Heaven' in the Mountain State

West Virginia dazzles with its beautiful landscapes and comforts with the warm hospitality of its locals. Wide-open adventure and a slower pace of life inspire a state of mind that's "almost heaven." Walk historic sites where the fate of a nation was decided.

HARPER'S FERRY CHANGED HANDS 14 TIMES DURING THE CIVIL WAR.

Getty Images/iStockphoto

Harper's Ferry sits at the confluence of the Potomac and Shenandoah rivers.

Charleston

Once considered a waypoint on the road to somewhere else, West Virginia's capital city has quietly become a destination all its own. Boasting unique architecture, one-of-a-kind history and a burgeoning arts scene, Charleston has enough cultural offerings to keep visitors busy for days, while the city's location at the confluence of the Kanawha and Elk Rivers makes for some unexpected outdoors adventures.

River Walks and Trail Runs

A few minutes south of the Capitol Complex, Daniel Boone Park draws visitors looking for a break from the bustle of downtown without leaving the city limits. Featuring riverfront fishing, boating and picnicking opportunities, as well as a handful of historic buildings dating back to the early 1800s, the park is a popular getaway for locals and tourists alike. For even more outdoor fun, head to Kanawha State Forest, about seven miles south of the city center. The park boasts 25 miles of hiking and biking trails.

Harper's Ferry

Bordered by the Potomac and Shenandoah Rivers, the quaint 19th-century village of Harper's Ferry seduces visitors with its charm, history and stunning natural setting. A living history village within Harper's Ferry National Park, the town's tidy web of streets is punctuated with historic homes, Civil War-era sights and compelling stores that purvey everything from antiques, handicrafts and souvenirs to outdoor gear. Harper's Ferry's museums and landmarks commemorate abolitionist John Brown's 1859 rebellion and the town's seminal role in the Civil War.

Harper's Ferry National Park

With 2,300 acres draped across three states, Harper's Ferry National Historical Park is one of West Virginia's undisputed highlights. Incorporating Harper's Ferry living history village, the educational activities include conversations with historic reenactors playing Union soldiers, blacksmiths and more.

New River Gorge

The New River winds through a deep gorge known as the Grand Canyon of the East. Long stretches of the scenic waterway thunder with rapids and several outfitters can give you a thrill on fast-moving water. Expect water tumbling over huge boulders as the gorge narrows, along with roller coaster waves and giant holes in Class III environments. Enjoy expeditions to places like Jump Rock, Swimmer's Rapids and areas where you can go surfing on giant swells.

FOR MORE INFORMATION

West Virginia Tourism Office, 800-CALL-WVA, wvtourism.com
Charleston WV, 304-344-5075, www.charlestonwv.com
Harper's Ferry National Historical Park, 304-535-6029, www.nps.gov/hafe
New River Gorge, www.nps.gov/neri

LOCAL FAVORITE

Campfire Breakfast Bake

Whip up this wholesome breakfast before embarking on a West Virginia adventure.
Recipe by Melissa Marchon.

INGREDIENTS

- ☐ 3 lbs red potatoes, rinsed and cut into 1" cubes
- ☐ 1 yellow onion, sliced
- ☐ 1 ring of smoked sausage of choice, sliced into ½" pieces
- ☐ 2 Tbsp butter
- ☐ Salt, pepper, garlic powder and Slap Ya Mama Cajun seasoning — all to taste

DIRECTIONS

Toss all ingredients but the butter into a 9x13 foil pan and mix well so seasoning is distributed throughout. Add pats of butter to the top. Cover with foil and cook over indirect heat of the fire. After approximately 15 minutes, check doneness of potatoes and stir. Cook longer, checking frequently, until the potatoes are soft but not mushy.

Serve in bowls by itself or on tortillas with scrambled eggs and shredded cheese.

West Virginia

BARBOURSVILLE — C1 *Wayne*

BEECH FORK (Public State Park) From town I-64 (Exit 11), SE 4 mi, (follow signs total of 10 mi from I-64). 275 Avail: 53 full hkups, 186 E (30/50 amps). 2021 rates: $35 to $38. (304)528-5794

BEAVER — D3 *Raleigh*

LITTLE BEAVER (Public State Park) From US 64 & SR 307 (exit 129A), S. 2 mi on SR 307 (E). 46 Avail: 46 W, 30 E (30 amps). 2021 rates: $25 to $28. Apr 15 to Oct 31. (304)763-2494

BECKLEY — D3 *Raleigh*

BECKLEY See also Fayetteville.

BECKLEY EXHIBITION MINE CAMPGROUND (Public) From Jct of WV Tpke/I-77 & SR-3 (exit 44), E 1.7 mi on SR-3 to Ewart Ave, N 0.5 mi, follow signs (R). **FAC:** paved rds. Avail: 17 paved, back-ins (20x50), 17 full hkups (30/50 amps), . **REC:** pool $, wading pool, boating nearby, playground, hunting nearby. Pets OK. Partial handicap access. No tents. 2021 rates: $30 to $35. Apr 01 to Nov 01.
(304)256-1747 Lat: 37.78439, Lon: -81.19631
513 Ewart Ave, Beckley, WV 25801
beckley.org
See ad page 994

LAKE STEPHENS CAMPGROUND & MARINA (RALEIGH COUNTY PARK) (Public) From Jct of I-77 & SR-3 (exit 44), W 8.1 mi on SR-3 to entrance (R), then 2.5 mi to campground. Avail: 100 full hkups (30/50 amps). 2021 rates: $32 to $35. May 01 to Sep 30. (304)934-5322

Things to See and Do

BECKLEY EXHIBITION COAL MINE AND YOUTH MUSEUM Museum of WV coal mine, recreation of coal mine camp/buildings to tour. Apr 01 to Nov 01. Partial handicap access. RV accessible. Restrooms. Food. Hours: 10am to 6pm. Adult fee: $12.50 to $22.00.
(304)256-1747 Lat: 37.78439, Lon: -81.19631
513 Ewart Ave, Beckley, WV 25801
beckley.org
See ad page 994

BOWDEN — C4 *Randolph*

REVELLES RIVER RESORT **Ratings: 7.5/8★/8.5** (Campground) Avail: 46 full hkups (30/50 amps). 2021 rates: $45 to $50. (304)636-0023, 5 Faulkner Rd, Bowden, WV 26254

BRUCETON MILLS — B5 *Monongalia*

CHESTNUT RIDGE PARK & CAMPGROUND (Public) From Jct of I-68 & Old Rte 73 (Exit 15), NE 0.6 mi on Old Rte 73 to Chestnut Ridge/Sand Springs Rd, N 1.5 mi (L). 20 Avail: 20 W, 20 E (30 amps). 2021 rates: $24 to $34. (888)594-3111

COOPERS ROCK STATE FOREST (Public State Park) From town, W 9 mi on I-68 to exit 15/park access rd, S 1.25 mi (L). Avail: 25 E (30 amps). 2021 rates: $26. Apr 01 to Nov 30. (304)594-1561

BUCKHANNON — B4 *Webster*

AUDRA (Public State Park) From Jct of SR-20 & US-119: Go NE 6 mi on US-119 to Audra Park Rd, E 8 mi (R). Avail: 39 E (20 amps). 2021 rates: $28. Apr 15 to Oct 15. (304)457-1162

BURNSVILLE — C3 *Braxton*

BURNSVILLE LAKE - COE/RIFFLE RUN (Public Corps) From Jct of US-79 & exit 79, E 3.5 mi on 5th St./CH-5. Avail: 54 full hkups (30/50 amps). 2021 rates: $12 to $26. May 18 to Sep 05. (304)853-2371

CAIRO — B3 *Ritchie*

NORTH BEND (Public State Park) From town follow signs to park. 77 Avail: 28 W, 54 E (30 amps). 2021 rates: $25 to $28. Apr 15 to Oct 31. (304)643-2931

CALDWELL — D3 *Greenbrier*

GREENBRIER STATE FOREST (Public State Park) From Jct of I-64 & Rte 60/14 (exit 175), S 3.5 mi on Rte 60/14 (R). Avail: 16 E (30 amps). 2021 rates: $28. Apr 09 to Nov 30. (304)536-1944

CAMP CREEK — E3 *Mercer*

CAMP CREEK (Public State Park) From Jct of I-77 & US-19 (Exit 20), SW 0.3 mi on US-19 to Camp Creek Rd, N 1.7 mi on Camp Creek Rd (E). 26 Avail: 9 full hkups, 8 W, 17 E (30/50 amps). 2021 rates: $16 to $33. (304)425-9481

CHARLESTON — C2 *Kanawha*

CHARLESTON See also Milton.

KANAWHA STATE FOREST (Public State Park) From Jct of I-64 & US 119 (Exit 58A, Oakwood Rd), S 0.8 mi to Oakwood Rd. SE 1 mi to CR23 (Bridge Rd), NE 3 mi to Connell Rd, 2 mi (E) Note: Road is narrow & winding with switchbacks. Rigs over 26' not advisable. 44 Avail: 25 W, 25 E (20/30 amps). 2021 rates: $30. Apr 15 to Nov 30. (304)558-3500

CLIFFTOP — D3 *Fayette*

BABCOCK (Public State Park) From Jct of US-60 & SR-41, S 3.8 mi on SR-41 (R). **FAC:** paved rds. Avail: 52 grass, back-ins (20x50), 28 E (30 amps), WiFi, tent sites, rentals, dump, laundry, fire rings, firewood. **REC:** pool, Boley Lake: fishing, kayaking/canoeing, playground, hunting nearby, rec open to public. Pets OK. Partial handicap access, 14 day max stay. 2021 rates: $29. Apr 15 to Oct 31.
(304)438-3004 Lat: 38.005527, Lon: -80.949352
486 Babcock Rd, Clifftop, WV 25831
www.wvstateparks.com

COTTAGEVILLE — C2 *Jackson*

BLUE HERON LANDING RV CAMPGROUND (Campground) (Rebuilding) Avail: 47 full hkups (30/50 amps). 2021 rates: $40. (304)531-9193, 8825 Ripley Rd, Cottageville, WV 25239

DAVIS — B4 *Tucker*

BLACKWATER FALLS (Public State Park) From Jct of Rte 32 & Blackwater Falls State Pk Rd, SW 2 mi on Blackwater Falls State Pk Rd (R). Avail: 30 E (30 amps). 2021 rates: $23 to $26. Apr 15 to Oct 31. (304)259-5216

CANAAN VALLEY RESORT (Public State Park) From Jct of SR-93 & SR-32, S 10 mi on SR-32 to park entrance, W 1 mi to park pay station (R). Avail: 34 full hkups (30/50 amps). 2021 rates: $32 to $35. (304)866-4121

DAWSON — D3 *Greenbrier*

HAMPTON'S SUMMER WIND RV PARK Ratings: 5.5/7.5/8 (Campground) Avail: 24 full hkups (30/50 amps). 2021 rates: $32 to $35. May 01 to Oct 15. (304)575-9158, 2204 Lawn Rd, Meadow Bridge, WV 25976

DUNLOW — D1 *Wayne*

CABWAYLINGO STATE FOREST (Public State Park) From Huntington, S 42 mi on US Rte 152 and follow signs. 19 Avail: 11 W, 11 E (20 amps). 2021 rates: $20 to $30. Apr 01 to Oct 03. (304)385-4255

DUNMORE — C4 *Pocahontas*

SENECA STATE FOREST (Public State Park) From Jct of Hwys 92 & 28, S 5 mi on Hwy 28, NW 1.3 mi Cabin Rd. 10 Avail: Pit toilets. 2021 rates: $17. Apr 15 to Dec 01. (304)799-6213

EAST LYNN — D1 *Wayne*

EAST LYNN LAKE - COE/EAST FORK (Public Corps) From Jct of SR-152 & SR-37, E 20 mi on SR-37 (R). Avail: 167 E (30 amps). 2021 rates: $16 to $24. May 08 to Oct 11. (304)849-5000

ELKINS — C4 *Randolph*

ELKINS See also Bowden.

FAIRMONT — B4 *Marion*

Travel Services

CAMPING WORLD OF FAIRMONT As the nation's largest retailer of RV supplies, accessories, services and new and used RVs, Camping World is committed to making your total RV experience better. **SERVICES:** restrooms. RV Sales. RV supplies, RV accessible. Hours: 9am - 6pm.
(855)695-0704 Lat: 39.43692, Lon: -80.18387
2386 White Hall Blvd, Fairmont, WV 26544
rv.campingworld.com

CLIMATE CONTROL STORAGE PLUS RV and boat storage with covered and uncovered spaces. On-site water, dump station & timed electric. Easily accessible to I-79. **RV Storage:** outdoor, covered canopy, 3-sided enclosed spaces, secured fencing, electric gate, easy reach keypad, 24/7 access, well-lit facility, well-lit roads, well-lit perimeter, security cameras, level gravel/paved spaces, battery charger, power to charge battery, water, compressed air, office. **SERVICES:** restrooms. Hours: 9am to 5pm.
Special offers available for Good Sam Members
(304)534-3333 Lat: 39.433033, Lon: -80.204319
110 Van Kirk Dr, Fairmont, WV 26554
ccstorageplusllc.com

FALLING WATERS — B6 *Berkeley*

LEATHERMAN'S FALLING WATERS CAMPSITE **Ratings: 6.5/8.5★/7.5** (Campground) 43 Avail: 22 full hkups, 21 W, 21 E (30/50 amps). 2021 rates: $44 to $46. (304)274-2791, 7685 Williamsport Pike, Falling Waters, WV 25419

FAYETTEVILLE — D3 *Fayette*

RIFRAFTERS CAMPGROUND **Ratings: 7/8.5★/8.5** (Campground) From Jct of US-19 & Laurel Creek Rd (in Fayetteville), W 0.4 mi on Laurel Creek Rd (R).

CLOSE TO THE NEW RIVER GORGE
Visit Almost Heaven. Explore the New River Gorge National Park, then relax by the fire with family and friends. We offer a variety of campsites for pop ups to big rigs, rustic cabins and tent sites. Open to RVs year-round.

FAC: gravel rds. (28 spaces). 25 Avail: 11 paved, 14 gravel, 1 pull-thrus, (30x50), back-ins (30x45), 11 full hkups, 14 W, 14 E (30/50 amps), seasonal sites, cable, WiFi @ sites, tent sites, rentals, dump, laundry, fire rings, firewood. **REC:** pond, fishing, boating nearby, playground, hunting nearby. Pets OK. Partial handicap access. 2021 rates: $44 to $48, Military discount.
(304)574-1065 Lat: 38.047654, Lon: -81.125961
448 Laurel Creek Rd, Fayetteville, WV 25840
www.rifrafters.com

FLATWOODS — C3 *Braxton*

FLATWOODS KOA **Ratings: 9.5/10★/8** (RV Park) Avail: 46 full hkups (30/50 amps). 2021 rates: $47 to $50. (866)700-7284, 350 Days Dr, Sutton, WV 26601

GAP MILLS — E3 *Monroe*

MONCOVE LAKE (Public State Park) From town, N 6 mi on Hwy 8 (L). Avail: 34 E (20/30 amps). 2021 rates: $26. Apr 01 to Oct 31. (304)772-3450

GLENVILLE — B3 *Braxton*

CEDAR CREEK (Public State Park) From Jct of US-33/119 & SR-17: Go SE 4 mi on SR-17 (R). 65 Avail: 65 W, 65 E (20/30 amps). 2021 rates: $31. Apr 15 to Oct 15. (304)735-8517

WV

GRAFTON — B4 *Taylor*

TYGART LAKE (Public State Park) From Jct of US-119 & Tygart Lake access rd, S 4 mi on McVicker Rd, follow signs (E). Avail: 10 E (20 amps). 2021 rates: $22 to $25. Mar 19 to Sep 22. (304)265-6144

HACKER VALLEY — C3 *Webster*

HOLLY RIVER (Public State Park) From Jct of SR-15 & SR-20, N 12 mi on SR-20 (R). Avail: 88 E (30 amps). 2021 rates: $30. Apr 02 to Nov 30. (304)493-6353

HARPERS FERRY — B6 *Jefferson*

HARPERS FERRY/CIVIL WAR BATTLEFIELDS KOA **Ratings: 8/9★/8** (Campground) 183 Avail: 173 full hkups, 10 W, 10 E (30/50 amps). 2021 rates: $52 to $94. (800)562-9497, 343 Campground Rd, Harpers Ferry, WV 25425

HINTON — D3 *Summers*

BLUESTONE (Public State Park) From Jct of I-64 & WV-20, S 16 mi on WV-20 (R). 120 Avail: 32 W, 47 E (20/30 amps). 2021 rates: $29. Apr 15 to Oct 31. (304)466-2805

HUNTINGTON — C1 *Cabell*

HUNTINGTON See also Milton, WV; Ashland & Louisa, KY.

HUNTINGTON KOA HOLIDAY
Ratings: 9/10★/9 (Campground) W-bnd: Jct of I-64 & Mason Rd (exit 28), S 0.3 mi on Mason Rd to US-60, W 2.5 mi, N at Fox Fire Rd (NOTE: sharp right, hairpin turn). 0.25 mi on access rd (E) E-bnd: Jct of I-64 & Mall Rd (exit 20B), S 0.2 mi on Mall Rd to US-60, E (L) 5 mi on US-60 to Fox Fire Rd on left, 0.25 mi on access rd (E). **FAC:** paved rds. Avail: 110 gravel, 70 pull-thrus, (30x65), back-ins (30x55), 110 full hkups (30/50 amps), cable, WiFi @ sites, tent sites, rentals, dump, laundry, groc, LP gas, firewood. **REC:** KOA Lake: swim, fishing, kayaking/canoeing, boating nearby, playground, hunting nearby. Pets OK. Partial handicap access. Big rig sites, eco-friendly. 2021 rates: $44 to $80.
(800)562-0898 Lat: 38.43251, Lon: -82.16936
290 Fox Fire Rd, Milton, WV 25541
koa.com
See ad this page

ROBERT NEWLON RV PARK
good sam park
Ratings: 8.5/9.5★/8 (Campground) From Jct of I-64 & SR-193N/Merritts Creek Connector (Exit 18), N 3.3 mi on Merritts Creek Connector to SR-2 (Ohio River R), S 0.2 mi on SR-2 to Kyle Ln, W 0.3 mi on Kyle Ln (R). **FAC:** gravel rds. Avail: 33 gravel, 33 pull-thrus, (30x65), 33 full hkups (30/50 amps), WiFi @ sites, rentals, dump, laundry, LP gas, firewood, restaurant. **REC:** Ohio River: swim, fishing, kayaking/canoeing, boating nearby, hunting nearby, rec open to public. Pets OK. No tents. Big rig sites. 2021 rates: $36. ATM.
(304)733-1240 Lat: 38.46092, Lon: -82.31013
6090 Kyle Lane, Huntington, WV 25702
See ad this page

HUTTONSVILLE — C4 *Randolph*

KUMBRABOW STATE FOREST (Public State Park) From town, S 7 mi on US 219 to Kumbrabow Forest Rd, and follow signs. Note: RVx longer than 20' may experience difficulty. Avail: 13 W, Pit toilets. 2021 rates: $17. Apr 15 to Oct 31. (304)335-2219

INDIAN MILLS — E3 *Summers*

BLUESTONE (Public State Park) From town: Go 2 mi S on Hwy 12, then 3 mi SW on Indian Mills Rd. 81 Avail: 7 W, 15 E Pit toilets. Apr 15 to Oct 25. (304)466-3398

LEWISBURG — D3 *Greenbrier*

GREENBRIER RIVER CAMPGROUND Ratings: 7.5/9.5★/8.5 (Campground) Avail: 17 full hkups (30/50 amps). 2021 rates: $36 to $45. Apr 01 to Oct 31. (304)445-2203, 4316 Highland Tr (Hwy 63), Alderson, WV 24910

STATE FAIR OF WEST VIRGINIA CAMPGROUND
(Public State Park) From jct Rt 219 S & I-64 (Exit 169): Go 3 1/2 mi S on Rt 219 S (R). **FAC:** gravel rds. 742 Avail: 342 gravel, 400 grass, 5 pull-thrus, (35x90), back-ins (18x50), 562 full hkups, 180 W, 180 E (30/50 amps), WiFi @ sites, tent sites, dump. **REC:** boating nearby, hunting nearby, rec open to public. Pets OK. Partial handicap access. 2021 rates: $45, Military discount. Apr 01 to Nov 20.
(304)645-1090 Lat: 37.78067, Lon: -80.44501
947 Maplewood Ave, Lewisburg, WV 24901
statefairofwv.com
See ad this page

LOGAN — D2 *Logan*

CHIEF LOGAN (Public State Park) From Jct of US 119 (Corridor G) & Rte 10 (in Chapmanville), S 8 mi on Rte 10 (R). 26 Avail: 14 full hkups, 12 W, 12 E (20/30 amps). 2021 rates: $30. Mar 19 to Sep 22. (304)792-7125

LOST RIVER — B5 *Hardy*

LOST RIVER CAMPGROUND **Ratings: 5.5/8★/7.5** (Campground) Avail: 25 full hkups (30/50 amps). 2021 rates: $38. (304)897-8500, 337 Kimsey Run Rd, Lost River, WV 26810

MARLINTON — D4 *Pocahontas*

WATOGA (Public State Park) From Jct of SR-39 & SR-21, S 9 mi on SR-21, follow signs (R). Avail: 50 E (20 amps). 2021 rates: $22 to $30. (304)799-4087

MEDLEY — B5 *Grant*

JUST PLANE ADVENTURES LODGING & CAMPGROUND **Ratings: 7.5/9.5★/8.5** (Campground) Avail: 24 full hkups (30/50 amps). 2021 rates: $42. May 01 to Oct 31. (304)703-5898, 59 Just Plane Adventures Lane, Medley, WV 26710

MILTON — C2 *Cabell*

BLUE SPRUCE MH COMMUNITY **Ratings: 5/NA/5** (RV Area in MH Park) Avail: 17 full hkups (30/50 amps). 2021 rates: $35. (304)743-0103, 2208 Kirby Road, Milton, WV 25541

JIM'S CAMPING **Ratings: 6/UI/6** (Campground) 63 Avail: 59 full hkups, 2 W, 2 E (30/50 amps). 2021 rates: $40. (304)743-4560, 1794 US Route 60 West, Milton, WV 25541

MORGANTOWN — A4 *Monongalia*

MORGANTOWN See also Jefferson, PA.

MYLAN PARK
(RV Spaces) From jct I-79 & WV-7 (Exit-155): Go 2 mi W on WV-7 (Chaplin Hill Rd), then turn R on Mylan Park Ln (second entrance), then go 1/4 mi S on Mylan Park Ln (R). **FAC:** paved rds. Avail: 42 paved, back-ins (25x50), 23 full hkups, 7 W, 19 E (30/50 amps), WiFi @ sites, restrooms only, restaurant. **REC:** heated pool $, pond, fishing, hunting nearby, rec open to public. Pets OK. No tents. 2021 rates: $40. ATM.
(304)973-9733 Lat: 39.63625, Lon: -80.031683
111 Milan Park Ln, Morgantown, WV 26501
mylanpark.org
See ad this page

SAND SPRINGS CAMPGROUND
good sam park
Ratings: 8.5/8.5★/9 (Campground) From jct I-68 & Old Rte 73 (Exit 15): Go 1/2 mi NE on Old Rte 73, then 2-1/4 mi N on Sand Springs Rd (L) Do not use any type of GPS. **FAC:** gravel rds. (62 spaces). Avail: 39 gravel, 10 pull-thrus, (30x60), back-ins (30x40), 39 full hkups (30/50 amps), seasonal sites, WiFi, tent sites, shower$, laundry, groc, fire rings, firewood. **REC:** pool, boating nearby, playground, hunting nearby. Pet restrict (B). Big rig sites, eco-friendly. 2021 rates: $44 to $53.
(304)594-2415 Lat: 39.685824, Lon: -79.772035
1309 Sand Springs Road, Morgantown, WV 26508
See ad this page

Pre-Drive Safety Checklist: Create a step-by-step, pre-trip safety interior and exterior checklist. Conduct a final walk-around visual inspection before driving to or away from your camping site.

MULLENS — D2 *Wyoming*

TWIN FALLS RESORT (Public State Park) From town: Go 5 E on WV-16, then 2 mi N on WV-97, then 1/4 mi W on Black Fork Rd, then W 1-3/4 mi on Park Rd 803, then N on Park Rd 802 (R). Avail: 25 E (20/30 amps). 2021 rates: $25. (304)294-4000

NAPIER — C3 *Braxton*

BURNSVILLE LAKE - COE/BULLTOWN (Public Corps) From Jct of US-79 & US-19 (exit 67), N 10 mi on US-19. Avail: 196 E (30 amps). 2021 rates: $24 to $30. Apr 13 to Nov 24. (304)853-2371

NEW MANCHESTER — A1 *Hancock*

TOMLINSON RUN (Public State Park) From Jct of Rtes 2 & 8, NE 3 mi on Rte 8 (R); or From Jct of Rtes 30 & 8, S 5.5 mi on Rte 8 (R). Avail: 39 E (30 amps). 2021 rates: $26. Apr 01 to Oct 31. (304)564-3651

NEWELL — A1 *Hancock*

KENNEDY PARK & MARINA (Public) From Jct of US-30 & SR-2, S 2 mi on SR-2 (R). 36 Avail: 36 W, 36 E (30/50 amps). 2021 rates: $27 to $37. May 15 to Sep 15. (304)387-3063

PARKERSBURG — B2 *Wood*

MOUNTWOOD PARK (WOOD COUNTY PARK) (Public) From jct I-77 & US 50: Go 14 mi E on US 50, then N on Borland Springs Rd. Follow signs. 87 Avail: 16 full hkups, 64 W, 64 E. 2021 rates: $20 to $35. Apr 01 to Oct 31. (304)679-3694

RV MAINTENANCE CHECKLIST: Check for fluid leaks and that they are all at their desired levels. Change the engine oil and filter or put it on your checklist to have it done before your first Spring trip. Check battery connections for corrosion and clean terminals. Spray with anti-corrosive. Test batteries in all smoke detectors and CO detectors. Verify that your fire extinguisher's pressure gauge is still in the green zone. If not, have it serviced.

PAX — D2 *Fayette*

PLUM ORCHARD LAKE WILDLIFE MANAGEMENT AREA (Public) From the Pax (Exit 54) off the I-77, take CR-23 to the lake. (R). 38 Avail: Pit toilets. 2021 rates: $12. (304)469-9905

PIPESTEM — E3 *Mercer*

PIPESTEM RESORT (Public State Park) From Jct of I-77 & CR-7 (Athens exit 14), N 3.5 mi on CR-7 to SR-20, NE 13 mi (L). 50 Avail: 31 full hkups, 19 E (30/50 amps). 2021 rates: $32 to $37. (304)466-1800

POINT PLEASANT — C2 *Mason*

KRODEL PARK (Public) From Jct of SR-2 & SR-62, E 1 mi on SR-2 (L). Avail: 63 full hkups (30/50 amps). 2021 rates: $25. Apr 01 to Oct 31. (304)675-1068

RIDGELEY — B5 *Mineral*

EAGLE'S NEST CAMPGROUND **Ratings: 4.5/NA/6.5** (Campground) Avail: 72 full hkups (30/50 amps). 2021 rates: $38 to $42. May 01 to Oct 10. (304)298-4380, 1714 Patterson Creek Rd (Off Route 28), Ridgeley, WV 26753

ROANOKE — B3 *Lewis*

STONEWALL RESORT (Public State Park) From Jct of I-79 & US-19 (exit 91), E 2.7 mi on US-19 (L). Avail: 40 full hkups (30/50 amps). 2021 rates: $47 to $51. (304)269-7400

ROMNEY — B5 *Hampshire*

WAPOCOMA CAMPGROUND **Ratings: 6/8★/7.5** (Campground) 100 Avail: 88 full hkups, 12 W, 12 E (30/50 amps). 2021 rates: $31. Apr 15 to Oct 31. (304)822-5528, 145 Wapocoma Campground Rd, Romney, WV 26757

SOUTHSIDE — C2 *Mason*

CHIEF CORNSTALK WILDLIFE MANAGEMENT AREA (Public State Park) From town: Go 6 mi W on CR 29. 15 Avail: Pit toilets. (304)675-0871

Set your clocks. Time zones are indicated in the front of each state and province.

SUMMERSVILLE — C3 *Nicholas*

SUMMERSVILLE See also Fayetteville.

MOUNTAIN LAKE CAMPGROUND (Campground) (Rebuilding) 195 Avail: 195 W, 195 E (20/30 amps). 2021 rates: $28 to $58. Apr 12 to Oct 21. (877)686-6222, 1898 Summersville Airport Rd, Summersville, WV 26651

SUMMERSVILLE LAKE - COE/BATTLE RUN (Public Corps) From Jct of US-19 & SR-129, W 3.3 mi on SR-129 (R). Avail: 107 E (30 amps). 2021 rates: $30. May 01 to Oct 06. (304)872-3459

SUMMERSVILLE LAKE RETREAT **Ratings: 7/9★/9.5** (Campground) 32 Avail: 12 full hkups, 20 W, 20 E (30/50 amps). 2021 rates: $40 to $56. (304)872-5975, 278 Summersville Lake Rd, Mount Nebo, WV 26679

WV NAZARENE CAMP MUSIC PARK **Ratings: 4/8.5★/6.5** (Campground) 150 Avail: 42 full hkups, 10 W, 108 E (30/50 amps). 2021 rates: $30. Apr 01 to Oct 31. (304)872-6698, 7441 Webster Rd (Hwy 41 N), Summersville, WV 26651

SUTTON — C3 *Braxton*

SUTTON LAKE - COE/BAKERS RUN (Public Corps) From town, S 5 mi on US-19 to CR-17, E 10 mi (L). 207 Avail: 8 full hkups, 26 E (30 amps). 2021 rates: $12 to $14. Apr 23 to Nov 30. (304)765-5631

SUTTON LAKE - COE/GERALD FREEMAN (Public Corps) From town, N 3 mi on US-19 to CR-15, E 12 mi (R). Avail: 78 E (20/30 amps). 2021 rates: $20 to $30. Apr 18 to Dec 01. (304)765-7756

CLEANING YOUR RV: Use the proper cleaning products for fiberglass, rubber, windows, and for removing bugs; A long-handled telescoping pole with multiple attachments (brushes, squeegee, soft mitt for waxing, etc.) will make your job easier; This is also the right time to inspect for cracks in caulking around windows and roof mounted vents and TV antenna; Inspect inside for any evidence of water leaks.

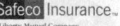

Getty Images/iStockphoto

YOU ARE HERE

Wisconsin

DID YOU KNOW?

The National Historic Cheesemaking Center makes a 90-pound wheel of Swiss cheese on the second Saturday of June.

Minnesota may boast about its large quantity of lakes, but neighboring Wisconsin is no slouch when it comes to bodies of water. Bordered to the east and north by Great Lakes, Wisconsin has over 15,000 inland lakes and produces over a quarter of the U.S. cheese supply.

Cheese and Choppers

Brawny bikes and gourmet cheese abide nicely in Milwaukee. Gearheads can rev their engines at the Harley-Davidson Museum, while art buffs can draw inspiration perusing the 2,500 masterpieces at the Milwaukee Art Museum. If you're a football fan, rush to Green Bay's Lambeau Field for a Packers game or guided stadium tour. Learn the ins and outs of cheesemaking at the National Historic Cheesemaking Center.

Make a Big Catch

Anglers have a wide menu from which to choose. Head to one of Wisconsin's many inland lakes, Lake Michigan (north coast) or Lake Superior (east coast) and the grand Mississippi River along its western border. Lake Michigan and Superior are always popular fishing spots, but locals will tell you to cast a rod in hidden gems like Altoona Lake and Fox Lake if you want all the muskie, panfish and walleye to yourself. For a different kind of fun, head to Wisconsin Dells to dip your toes in the biggest collection of water parks in the world.

Lights That Never Go Out

On a scenic peninsula that juts out between Lake Michigan and Green Bay, Wisconsin's Door County boasts unforgettable scenery. Here, lighthouse lovers will enjoy visiting the county's most majestic beacons. Looming over Sturgeon Bay is the Sturgeon Bay Canal Lighthouse. While in the area, enjoy a fish boil, a longstanding regional tradition that yields tasty food.

Wisconsin Bratwurst

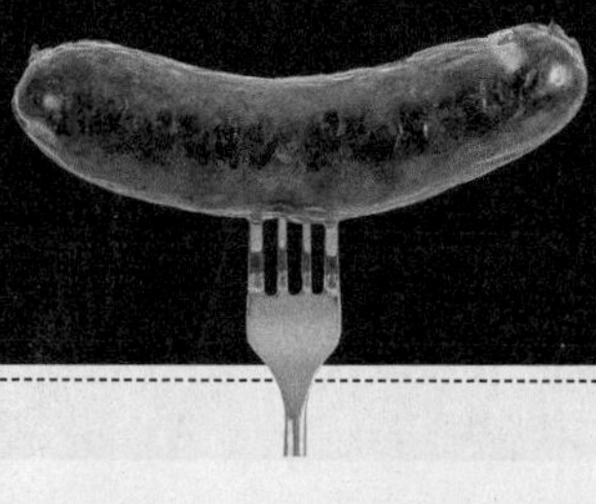

Spend enough time in the Badger State, and you're bound to catch the scent of bratwurst roasting on a grill somewhere. The German sausage is a favorite of Midwest tailgaters at Lambeau Field before a Packers football game and at American Family Field before the first pitch of a Brewers game. Sink your teeth into the juicy, flavorful sausage and you'll understand why it's so popular.

VISITOR CENTER

TIME ZONE
Central Standard

ROAD & HIGHWAY INFORMATION
866-511-9472
dot.state.wi.us

FISHING & HUNTING INFORMATION
888-936-7463
dnr.wi.gov/GoWild

BOATING INFORMATION
888-936-7463
dnr.wi.gov/topic/boat

NATIONAL PARKS
nps.gov/wi

STATE PARKS
dnr.wi.gov/topic/parks

TOURISM INFORMATION
Wisconsin Department of Tourism
800-432-8747
travelwisconsin.com

TOP TOURISM ATTRACTIONS
1) Wisconsin Dells
2) Door County
3) Harley-Davidson Museum

MAJOR CITIES
Milwaukee, Madison (capital), Green Bay, Kenosha, Racine

good sam park

Featured Good Sam Parks

WISCONSIN

When you stay with Good Sam, you can expect the highest degree of cleanliness and friendliness, and better yet, you get **10% off** overnight campground fees.

If you're not already a Good Sam member you can purchase your membership at one of these locations:

BAILEYS HARBOR
Baileys Grove Campground

BARABOO
Ho-Chunk Gaming RV Park

CHIPPEWA FALLS
O'Neil Creek Campground

DE FOREST
Madison Campground

EAGLE RIVER
Chain O' Lakes Campground

FREMONT
Yogi Bear's Jellystone Park Camp-Resort

KNOWLTON
Lake DuBay Shores Campground

LYNDON STATION
Ho-Chunk RV Resort & Campground
Yukon Trails Camping

MILTON
Blackhawk Camping Resort
Lakeland Camping Resort

MONTELLO
Buffalo Lake Camping Resort

OSSEO
Stoney Creek RV Resort

PLYMOUTH
Plymouth Rock Camping Resort

PORTAGE
Sky High Camping Resort

STURGEON BAY
Tranquil Timbers Camping Retreat

SUPERIOR
Mont du Lac Resort

WAUSAUKEE
Evergreen Park & Campground

WAUTOMA
Lake Of the Woods Campground

WEST SALEM
Neshonoc Lakeside Camp-Resort

WISCONSIN DELLS
Arrowhead Resort Campground
Sherwood Forest Camping & RV Park

WOODRUFF
Hiawatha Trailer Resort

10/10★/10 GOOD SAM PARKS

OSSEO
Stoney Creek RV Resort
(715)597-2102

SUPERIOR
Mont du Lac Resort
(218)626-3797

What's This?

An RV park with a 10/10★/10 rating has scored perfect grades in amenities, cleanliness and appearance ("See Understanding the Campground Rating System" on pages 8 and 9 for an explanation of the trusted Good Sam Rating System). Stay in a 10/10★/10 park on your next trip for a nearly flawless camping experience.

Getty Images/iStockphoto

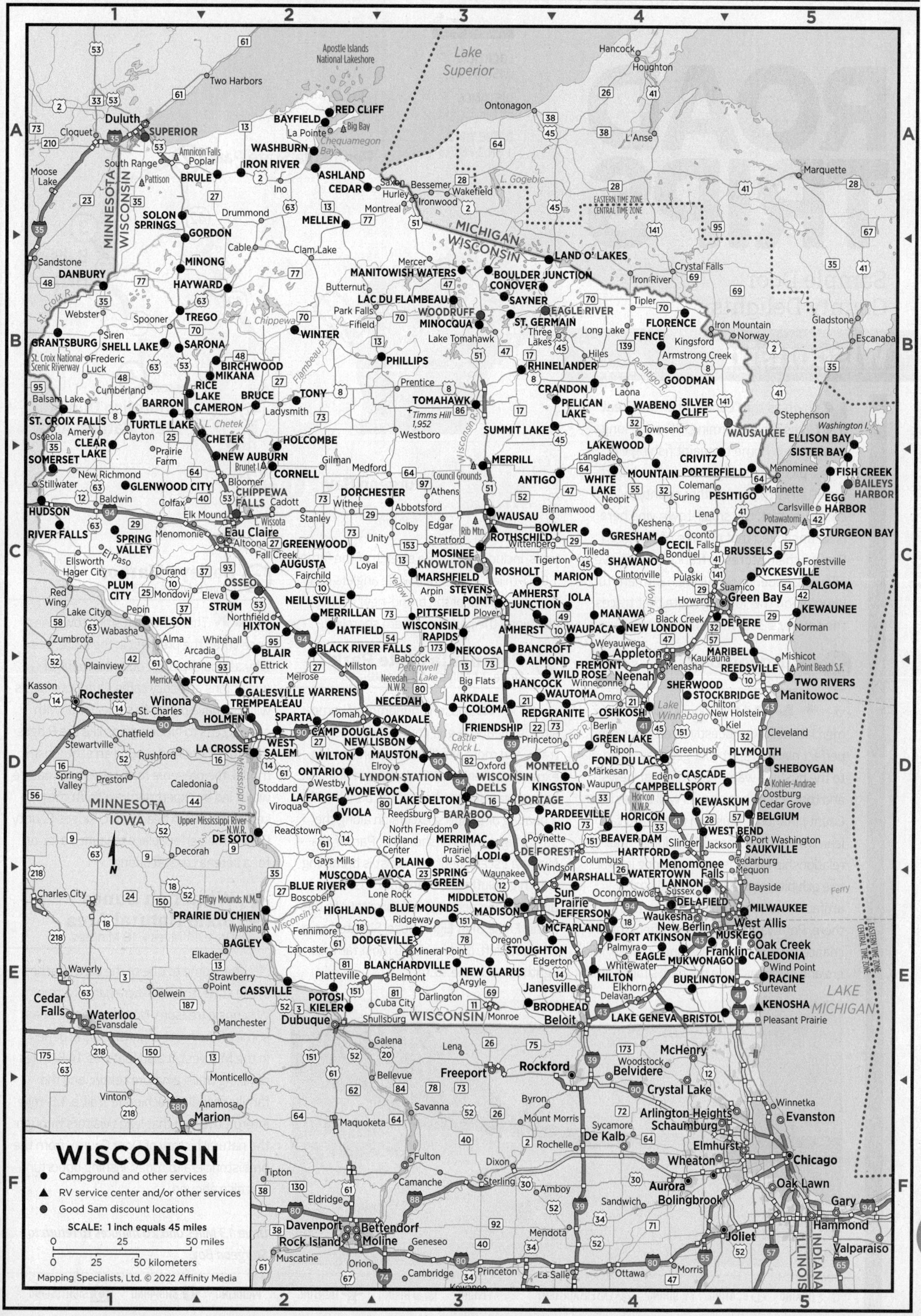
WISCONSIN
Campground and other services
RV service center and/or other services
Good Sam discount locations
SCALE: 1 inch equals 45 miles
0 25 50 miles
0 25 50 kilometers
Mapping Specialists, Ltd. © 2022 Affinity Media
Lake Superior
LAKE MICHIGAN
MINNESOTA
IOWA
ILLINOIS
INDIANA
MICHIGAN
EASTERN TIME ZONE
CENTRAL TIME ZONE
SUPERIOR
RED CLIFF
BAYFIELD
WASHBURN
IRON RIVER
BRULE
ASHLAND
CEDAR
MELLEN
SOLON SPRINGS
GORDON
MINONG
DANBURY
HAYWARD
TREGO
GRANTSBURG
SHELL LAKE
SARONA
WINTER
BIRCHWOOD
MIKANA
RICE LAKE
CAMERON
BRUCE
TONY
BARRON
TURTLE LAKE
ST. CROIX FALLS
CLEAR LAKE
CHETEK
HOLCOMBE
NEW AUBURN
CORNELL
SOMERSET
GLENWOOD CITY
CHIPPEWA FALLS
HUDSON
RIVER FALLS
SPRING VALLEY
GREENWOOD
AUGUSTA
PLUM CITY
OSSEO
STRUM
NEILLSVILLE
NELSON
HIXTON
MERRILLAN
HATFIELD
BLAIR
BLACK RIVER FALLS
FOUNTAIN CITY
GALESVILLE
WARRENS
TREMPEALEAU
HOLMEN
SPARTA
LA CROSSE
WEST SALEM
CAMP DOUGLAS
NEW LISBON
MAUSTON
WILTON
ONTARIO
LYNDON STATION
WONEWOC
LA FARGE
VIOLA
DE SOTO
PRAIRIE DU CHIEN
BAGLEY
CASSVILLE
POTOSI
KIELER
MANITOWISH WATERS
BOULDER JUNCTION
CONOVER
LAC DU FLAMBEAU
WOODRUFF
MINOCQUA
SAYNER
EAGLE RIVER
ST. GERMAIN
LAND O' LAKES
PHILLIPS
RHINELANDER
CRANDON
TOMAHAWK
PELICAN LAKE
SUMMIT LAKE
MERRILL
ANTIGO
DORCHESTER
WAUSAU
ROTHSCHILD
MOSINEE
KNOWLTON
MARSHFIELD
STEVENS POINT
PITTSFIELD
WISCONSIN RAPIDS
NEKOOSA
NECEDAH
OAKDALE
ARKDALE
COLOMA
FRIENDSHIP
WISCONSIN DELLS
LAKE DELTON
BARABOO
PORTAGE
MERRIMAC
LODI
PLAIN
SPRING GREEN
MUSCODA
AVOCA
BLUE RIVER
HIGHLAND
BLUE MOUNDS
DODGEVILLE
BLANCHARDVILLE
NEW GLARUS
MIDDLETON
MADISON
STOUGHTON
FLORENCE
FENCE
GOODMAN
WABENO
SILVER CLIFF
WAUSAUKEE
LAKEWOOD
CRIVITZ
MOUNTAIN
PORTERFIELD
WHITE LAKE
PESHTIGO
MARINETTE
BOWLER
GRESHAM
CECIL
SHAWANO
ROSHOLT
MARION
AMHERST JUNCTION
AMHERST
IOLA
MANAWA
WAUPACA
NEW LONDON
BANCROFT
ALMOND
HANCOCK
WAUTOMA
REDGRANITE
FREMONT
WILD ROSE
OSHKOSH
GREEN LAKE
MONTELLO
KINGSTON
PARDEEVILLE
RIO
DE FOREST
FOND DU LAC
CAMPBELLSPORT
HORICON
BEAVER DAM
HARTFORD
MARSHALL
WATERTOWN
JEFFERSON
MCFARLAND
FORT ATKINSON
MILTON
JANESVILLE
BRODHEAD
LAKE GENEVA
BRISTOL
KENOSHA
RACINE
BURLINGTON
EAGLE
MUKWONAGO
MUSKEGO
CALEDONIA
MILWAUKEE
DELAFIELD
LANNON
WEST BEND
KEWASKUM
CASCADE
BELGIUM
SAUKVILLE
SHEBOYGAN
PLYMOUTH
SHERWOOD
STOCKBRIDGE
REEDSVILLE
MARIBEL
TWO RIVERS
DE PERE
KEWAUNEE
ALGOMA
DYCKESVILLE
BRUSSELS
STURGEON BAY
EGG HARBOR
FISH CREEK
BAILEYS HARBOR
SISTER BAY
ELLISON BAY
OCONTO

ROAD TRIPS

Sample Door County Delights

Wisconsin

LOCATION
WISCONSIN

DISTANCE
59 MILES

DRIVE TIME
1 HR 34 MINS

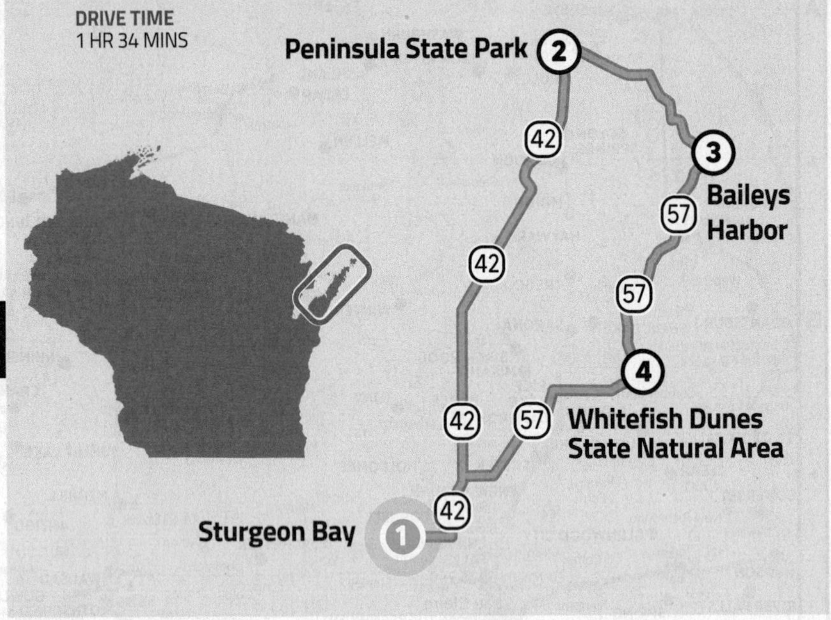

Known as the "Cape Cod of the Great Lakes," this charming, 75-mile-long peninsula is home to quaint fishing villages, picturesque lighthouses and more state parks than any other county in Wisconsin. In fact, the small-town vibe here is so unspoiled that outside of Sturgeon Bay no chain stores or franchises are even allowed. Experience the enchantment for yourself on this looping route that traces the county's 300-mile shoreline.

1 Sturgeon Bay
Starting Point

As Door County's commercial hub, this modestly sized city is the perfect place to start your getaway. Head to the bustling waterfront for great views and top-notch shopping, as well as the Door County Maritime Museum where you can learn more about the region's longstanding relationship with the sea. Featuring interactive exhibits, as well as restored boats, artifacts and boatbuilding classes. From there, Potawatomi State Park offers the chance to explore the coastline up close. Hikers and bikers will love the park's four scenic trails, including a 3-mile stretch of the famed 1,000-mile Ice Age Trail, while anglers can take advantage of the brand-new fishing pier along the park's southern shoreline.

2 Peninsula State Park
Drive 27 Miles ▪ 43 Minutes

Boasting hundreds of campsites, a theater, a golf course, beaches, bike trails, and more, you'll be hard-pressed to experience Peninsula State Park in one visit, but you can see the best of the bunch with a boating or paddling excursion along the park's eight miles of shoreline. Part of the Niagara Escarpment, the coast is brimming with high bluffs and dramatic cliffs. For a different perspective, join a bike tour to the iconic Eagle Bluff Lighthouse. Situated on a 76-foot bluff, it's one of the most famous lighthouses in the state.

Getty Images/iStockphoto

3 Baileys Harbor
Drive 8 Miles ▪ 13 Minutes

This attractive small town was once voted the prettiest in the state. See why as you explore a downtown full of quaint inns and cozy cafés. Outdoors lovers will also have plenty to smile about with easy access to hidden gems like the Ridges Sanctuary. Created around an ecotourism model, the preserve features 2-hour nature walks led by expert naturalists. At the preserve's southern beachfront, Ridges County Park is the perfect place to launch a kayak for a serene coastal outing.

4 Whitefish Dunes State Natural Area
Drive 11 Miles ▪ 18 Minutes

Home to one of the best beaches in the state, this 863-acre park is a true Wisconsin treasure. Not only does it boast some of the most expansive sand dunes in the Midwest, it also features 14.5-miles of hiking trails, a nature center, and the family-friendly Brachiopod Trail, a 1.5-mile interpretive trail that leads visitors through the natural history of Door County from the prehistoric era to today. Fishing opportunities also abound.

Drive 13 Miles and 20 minutes to return to Sturgeon Bay.

BIKING BOATING DINING ENTERTAINMENT FISHING HIKING HUNTING PADDLING SHOPPING SIGHTSEEING

Wisconsin SPOTLIGHTS

Beauty in the Badger State

Wisconsin has it all: an amazing collection of waterparks, gorgeous shores on two Great Lakes and championship major league sports teams. Take your pick of adventures and sample some great cheese along the way.

DOOR COUNTY HAS 34 NAMED OUTLYING ISLANDS.

Wisconsin's Door County is a popular destination for seeing fall colors.

Getty Images/iStockphoto

Apostle Islands

Sitting on the shores of Lake Superior, Apostle Islands National Lakeshore consists of 21 idyllic islands and 12 miles of mainland shore, making this a great spot for kayaking, canoeing, boating and swimming. The islands and the mainland are also home to more than 50 miles of official hiking trails, linking together a smattering of old lighthouses, logging camps and farm sites.

Hit the Apostle Shores

In addition to hiking, there are numerous sandy beaches that are great for walking and exploring. Some of the favorites are Little Sand Bay and Meyers Beach on the mainland, Julian Bay on Stockton Island, Long Island beaches, Raspberry Island sandspit, Lighthouse Bay on Sand Island, South Twin sandspit and Rocky Island sandspit.

Door County

This peninsula along the state's eastern shore is a hodge-podge of orchards, lighthouses and state parks, all nestled within a landscape that harkens back to a simpler time. The region is also a haven for lake lovers and watersports aficionados who arrive each summer to enjoy the more than 300 miles of pristine shoreline. Whether you're looking for fun-in-the-sun or laid-back luxury, life just seems easier in Door County.

Loads of Lighthouses

Getting its name from the 19th-century ship captains who called the waters around its northernmost point "Porte des Morts" — or "Death's Door"— it's no wonder that the coast of Door County is dotted with lifesaving beacons. The most photogenic of the bunch, the Cana Island Lighthouse, stands just off the coast and can be waded to during low tide.

Wisconsin Dells

Slip and slide to this popular Badger State attraction. Dubbed the "Water Park Capital of the World," Wisconsin Dells has more indoor and outdoor water parks per capita than anywhere else on Earth. Pair that with quirky museums, zipline tracks and three state parks, and you've got a recipe for the ultimate family vacation.

Water Park Wonderland

More than 200 water slides deliver high-speed thrills in this watery Mecca. Speed down the Scorpion's Tail and Black Anaconda at Noah's Ark, the largest water park in America with three miles of water slides. The Wilderness Resort is the size of 12 football fields, with indoor and outdoor water parks.

FOR MORE INFORMATION

Wisconsin Department of Tourism, 800-432-8747, www.travelwisconsin.com

Apostle Islands National Park, www.nps.gov/apis

Door County Visitor Bureau, 800-527-3529, www.doorcounty.com

Wisconsin Dells, 800-223-3557, www.wisdells.com

LOCAL FAVORITE

Veggie Cheese Puffs

America's DairyLand is the inspiration for these cheesy treats. Serve them warm and toasty with a chilled Milwaukee ale. ***Recipe by Debbie Hill.***

INGREDIENTS

- ☐ 1 pkg fresh English muffins (such as Bays) sliced in halves
- ☐ ½ cup each chopped black (or green) olives
- ☐ ½ cup green onions
- ☐ 1 cup chopped fresh mushrooms, peppers, finely diced tomato or other vegetables as desired
- ☐ 2 cups grated colby, cheddar or other favorite cheese
- ☐ ½ cup mayonnaise or just enough to keep mixture together
- ☐ Salt and pepper or seasoning salt to taste

DIRECTIONS

Gently stir together the olives, mayonnaise, onions, other vegetables and seasonings. Spread some of the mixture on each muffin half. Top with cheese. Broil until cheese is browning and bubbly.

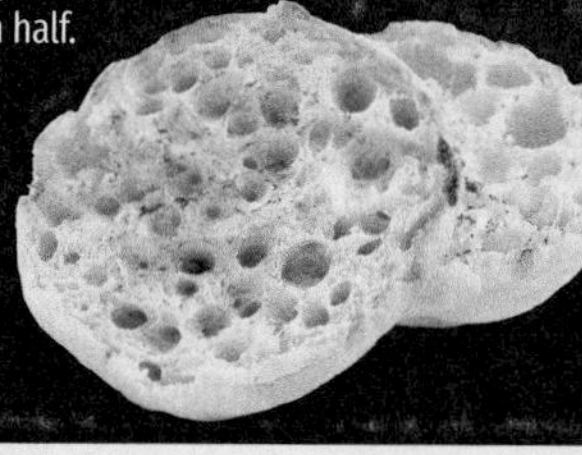

WI

Wisconsin

ALGOMA — C5 *Kewaunee*

AHNAPEE RIVER TRAILS CAMPGROUND **Ratings: 8/9★/7.5** (Campground) 16 Avail: 16 W, 16 E (30 amps). 2021 rates: $36 to $38. May 01 to Oct 15. (920)487-5777, E 6053 W Wilson Rd, Algoma, WI 54201

BIG LAKE CAMPGROUND **Ratings: 7/8★/7.5** (Campground) 37 Avail: 8 full hkups, 29 W, 29 E (20/30 amps). 2021 rates: $34 to $53. May 01 to Oct 15. (920)487-2726, 2427 Lake St, Algoma, WI 54201

TIMBER TRAIL CAMPGROUND **Ratings: 7/9★/8.5** (Campground) 40 Avail: 40 W, 40 E (30/50 amps). 2021 rates: $42 to $46. Apr 15 to Oct 15. (920)487-3707, N8326 County Rd M, Algoma, WI 54201

ALMOND — D3 *Portage*

FOUNTAIN LAKE RV PARK **Ratings: 7/9★/8.5** (Campground) Avail: 20 full hkups (50 amps). 2021 rates: $30. May 01 to Oct 01. (715)366-2954, 8599 16th Rd, Almond, WI 54909

AMHERST — C3 *Portage*

WILD WEST CAMPGROUND & CORRAL **Ratings: 6/8.5★/7** (Campground) 24 Avail: 24 W, 24 E (30 amps). 2021 rates: $45 to $60. Apr 15 to Oct 15. (715)824-5112, 9495 Hwy 54, Amherst, WI 54406

AMHERST JUNCTION — C3 *Portage*

LAKE EMILY COUNTY PARK (Public) From town, W 1 mi on Old US-18 (L). Avail: 66 E (20 amps). 2021 rates: $24. May 01 to Oct 31. (715)824-3175

ANTIGO — C4 *Langlade*

ANTIGO LAKE RV CAMPGROUND (Public) From Jct of Hwy 45 & 2nd Ave, E 0.3 mi on 2nd Ave. to Hudson St, S 0.1 mi (L). Note: 45' RV length limit. Avail: 12 full hkups (20/30 amps). 2021 rates: $20. May 01 to Oct 01. (715)623-3633

ARKDALE — D3 *Adams*

PINELAND CAMPING PARK **Ratings: 7/8.5/7** (Campground) 67 Avail: 14 full hkups, 53 W, 53 E (30/50 amps). 2021 rates: $44 to $64. Apr 15 to Dec 01. (608)564-7818, 916 Hwy 13, Arkdale, WI 54613

ASHLAND — A2 *Ashland*

KREHER RV PARK (Public) From Jct of SR-13 & US 2, E 0.2 mi on US 2 to N Prentice Ave, N 0.2 mi, follow signs (R). 33 Avail: 33 W, 33 E (30/50 amps). 2021 rates: $35. May 15 to Oct 15. (715)682-7059

Thank you for being one of our best customers!

Wisconsin Privately Owned Campground Information Updated by our Good Sam Representatives

Carey & Julia Bryant

Texas is home to us, our children and grands. Being with family and friends is our favorite, and dancing, hunting, biking, golfing and the ocean are things we want more time for! Grateful to God for new roads, new opportunities and new memories.

AUGUSTA — C2 *Eau Claire*

COON FORK PARK (EAU CLAIRE COUNTY PARK) (Public) From town: Go 1 mi E on US 12, then 4 mi N on CR CF. 108 Avail: 20 W, 57 E (30/50 amps). 2021 rates: $17 to $27. (715)839-4738

AVOCA — E3 *Iowa*

AVOCA LAKESIDE CAMPGROUND
(Public) From Jct of SR-133 & 6th St (in town), N 0.2 mi on 6th St to Clyde St, E 0.3 mi to 8th St, N 0.2 mi (R). **FAC:** paved/gravel rds. (87 spaces). Avail: 54 dirt, no slide-outs, back-ins (12x30), 54 E (30 amps), seasonal sites, tent sites, shower$, dump, fire rings, firewood. **REC:** Avoca Lake: swim, fishing, kayaking/canoeing, boating nearby, playground. Pets OK. Partial handicap access. 2021 rates: $24. Apr 15 to Nov 30. no cc.
(608)532-6831 Lat: 43.188928, Lon: -90.320512
Avoca, WI 53506
villageofavoca.com

BAGLEY — E2 *Grant*

BOULDER CREEK CAMPGROUND **Ratings: 8.5/9★/9** (Campground) 109 Avail: 25 full hkups, 84 W, 84 E (30/50 amps). 2021 rates: $29 to $59. May 01 to Oct 31. (608)996-2201, 11354 Cnty Rd X, Bagley, WI 53801

RIVER OF LAKES CAMPGROUND **Ratings: 4.5/7.5/5** (Campground) 70 Avail: 70 W, 70 E (30 amps). 2021 rates: $40.75. Apr 15 to Nov 15. (608)996-2275, 132 Packer Dr, Bagley, WI 53801

WYALUSING/WISCONSIN RIDGE (Public State Park) From town, N 10 mi on CR-X, through village of Wyalusing (L). Entrance fee required. Avail: 25 E (30 amps). 2021 rates: $18 to $33. (608)996-2261

BAILEYS HARBOR — C5 *Door*

BAILEYS GROVE CAMPGROUND
Ratings: 9/10★/10 (Campground) 79 Avail: 59 full hkups, 20 W, 20 E (30/50 amps). 2021 rates: $48 to $61. May 01 to Oct 18. (920)839-2559, 2552 Cty Rd F, Baileys Harbor, WI 54202

BAILEYS WOODS CAMPGROUND **Ratings: 5.5/7.5/7.5** (Campground) 35 Avail: 35 W, 26 E (30 amps). 2021 rates: $39 to $49. May 15 to Oct 15. (262)470-7091, 2701 County Road EE, Baileys Harbor, WI 54202

BEANTOWN CAMPGROUND **Ratings: 9/8.5★/8** (Campground) Avail: 41 full hkups (30/50 amps). 2021 rates: $49 to $54. May 01 to Oct 22. (920)839-1439, 8398 Cty Rd F, Baileys Harbor, WI 54202

BANCROFT — C3 *Portage*

VISTA ROYALLE CAMPGROUND Ratings: 8/9.5★/9.5 (Campground) 150 Avail: 50 full hkups, 100 W, 100 E (30/50 amps). 2021 rates: $52.75 to $55.92. Apr 20 to Oct 20. (715)335-6860, 8025 Isherwood Rd, Bancroft, WI 54921

BARABOO — D3 *Sauk*

BARABOO HILLS CAMPGROUND **Ratings: 8.5/9★/9.5** (Campground) 89 Avail: 17 full hkups, 72 W, 72 E (30/50 amps). 2021 rates: $57 to $61. Apr 15 to Oct 15. (608)356-8505, E10545 Terrytown Rd, Baraboo, WI 53913

DEVIL'S LAKE (Public State Park) From Jct of I-90/94 & Hwy 33, W 13 mi on Hwy 33 to Hwy 123, S 4 mi (E). Entrance fee required. Avail: 136 E (30 amps), Pit toilets. 2021 rates: $20 to $35. (608)356-8301

FOX HILL RV PARK & CAMPGROUND **Ratings: 9/9.5★/10** (Campground) 150 Avail: 128 full hkups, 22 W, 22 E (30/50 amps). 2021 rates: $46 to $181. Apr 24 to Oct 12. (608)356-5890, E 11371 N Reedsburg Rd, Baraboo, WI 53913

HO-CHUNK GAMING RV PARK
Ratings: 10/10★/9.5 (RV Park) 49 Avail: 38 full hkups, 11 W, 11 E (30/50 amps). 2021 rates: $39 to $44. Apr 15 to Oct 15. (800)746-2486, S3214 County Rd BD, Baraboo, WI 53913

SKILLET CREEK CAMPGROUND **Ratings: 5/9★/8** (Campground) 12 Avail: 8 full hkups, 4 W, 4 E (30/50 amps). 2021 rates: $44 to $57. Apr 15 to Oct 15. (608)356-4877, E11329 Hwy 159, Baraboo, WI 53913

BARRON — B1 *Barron*

STOP ON INN **Ratings: 5.5/4.5/7** (Campground) 17 Avail: 8 full hkups, 9 E (20/30 amps). 2021 rates: $35. May 01 to Oct 01. (715)637-3154, 1521 E Division Ave, Hwy 8, Barron, WI 54812

BAYFIELD — A2 *Bayfield*

APOSTLE ISLANDS AREA CAMPGROUND **Ratings: 5/7.5★/7** (Campground) 45 Avail: 36 full hkups, 9 W, 9 E (30/50 amps). 2021 rates: $39 to $50. May 26 to Oct 09. (715)779-5524, 85150 Trailer Court Rd, Bayfield, WI 54814

APOSTLE ISLANDS/PRESQUE ISLE-STOCKTON (Public National Park) Access by excursion boat (Jul & Aug) or private boat. 16 mi NE of Bayfield on Stockton Island. 21 Avail: Pit toilets. 2021 rates: $15. (715)779-3397

BIG BAY (Public State Park) Take ferry from Bayfield to Madeline Island, follow signs. Avail: 15 E (30 amps). 2021 rates: $20 to $35. (715)747-6425

LEGENDARY WATERS CAMPGROUND & MARINA **Ratings: 7/8.5★/8** (Campground) 37 Avail: 37 W, 37 E (20/50 amps). 2021 rates: $45. May 01 to Oct 15. (800)226-8478, 37600 Onigamiing Dr. , Bayfield, WI 54814

BEAVER DAM — D4 *Dodge*

DERGE PARK (DODGE COUNTY PARK) (Public) From Beaver Dam, NW 4 mi on Hwy G to Hwy CP, NE 1 mi (L). Avail: 25 E (30 amps). 2021 rates: $24. (920)887-0365

BELGIUM — D5 *Ozaukee*

HARRINGTON BEACH (Public State Park) From jct I-43 (exit 107) & CR D: Go 2-1/4 mi E on CR D, then 3/4 mi S on Sauk Trail Rd. Avail: 31 E. 2021 rates: $12 to $23. May 07 to Oct 25. (262)285-3015

BIRCHWOOD — B2 *Sawyer*

DOOLITTLE PARK (Public) From Jct of US-53 & CR-V, E 10 mi on CR-V to Hwy 48, NE 7 mi (Birchwood Village) to Main St, left 1 mi to Hinman Dr, right 0.5 mi (R). 40 Avail: 40 W, 40 E (30/50 amps). 2021 rates: $30 to $35. May 01 to Sep 30. (612)804-3457

BLACK RIVER FALLS — C2 *Jackson*

BLACK RIVER/CASTLE MOUND (Public State Park) From town, SE 1 mi on US-12 (R). Entrance fee required. Avail: 14 E (30 amps). 2021 rates: $18 to $33. (715)284-4103

BLACK RIVER/PIGEON CREEK (Public State Park) From Jct of I-94 (Exit 128) & CR-O, E 0.25 mi on CR-O to N Settlement Rd, NE 2 mi (R) Entrance fee required. Avail: 38 E Pit toilets. 2021 rates: $16 to $31. (715)284-4103

LOST FALLS CAMPGROUND **Ratings: 5.5/8.5★/7.5** (Campground) 16 Avail: 6 full hkups, 10 W, 10 E (30 amps). 2021 rates: $44 to $46. May 15 to Oct 01. (800)329-3911, N2974 E Sunnyvale Rd, Black River Falls, WI 54615

PARKLAND VILLAGE CAMPGROUND **Ratings: 7/8.5★/7** (Campground) 53 Avail: 12 full hkups, 41 W, 41 E (30/50 amps). 2021 rates: $45 to $50. Apr 15 to Nov 15. (715)284-9700, N6150 Julianna Rd 409, Black River Falls, WI 54615

BLAIR — C2 *Trempealeau*

RIVERSIDE MEMORIAL PARK (Public) From town, Hwy 95 to Park Rd, S 0.25 mi (L). 31 Avail: 31 W, 31 E (20/50 amps). 2021 rates: $25 to $30. (608)989-2517

BLANCHARDVILLE — E3 *Green*

YELLOWSTONE LAKE (Public State Park) From town, SW 9 mi on CR-F, follow signs (L). Entrance fee required. 74 Avail: 50 S, 24 E (15 amps), Pit toilets. 2021 rates: $18 to $33. (608)523-4427

BLUE MOUNDS — E3 *Dane*

BLUE MOUND (Public State Park) From Jct of US-18/151 & Blue Mound Rd, NW 1 mi on Blue Mound Rd, follow signs (R) Entrance fee required. Avail: 18 E (30/50 amps). 2021 rates: $18 to $33. (608)437-5711

BRIGHAM PARK (DANE COUNTY PARK) (Public) From Jct of US-18 & CR-F, NE 2 mi on CR-F (R). Avail: 4 E (50 amps), Pit toilets. 2021 rates: $15 to $20. (608)242-4576

BLUE RIVER — E2 *Grant*

EAGLE CAVE RESORT **Ratings: 5.5/6.5/7** (Campground) 68 Avail: 28 full hkups, 40 W, 40 E (30 amps). 2021 rates: $32. May 22 to Sep 07. (608)537-2988, 16320 Cavern Lane, Blue River, WI 53518

BOULDER JUNCTION — B3 *Vilas*

NO HIGHLAND AMERICAN LEGION/BIG LAKE (Public State Park) From the Jct of US-51 & Hwy W, N 2.5 mi on Hwy W to Hwy K, E 4.5 mi to Hwy P, N 1.5 mi (R). Entrance fee required. 68 Avail: Pit toilets. 2021 rates: $16 to $21. (715)385-3352

NO HIGHLAND AMERICAN LEGION/MUSKY LAKE (Public State Park) From Woodruff, N 6 mi on US-51 to Hwy M, NE 3 mi to Hwy N, E 3 mi, follow SF sign (L). Entrance fee required. 81 Avail. 2021 rates: $20 to $35. (715)385-2704

NO HIGHLAND AMERICAN LEGION/SOUTH TROUT LAKE (Public State Park) From Jct of US-51 & Hwy M, N 4 mi on Hwy M to Lake Shore Dr, W 0.25 mi (L). Entrance fee required. 20 Avail: Pit toilets. 2021 rates: $20 to $35. May 22 to Sep 05. (715)385-2727

NO HIGHLAND AMERICAN LEGION/UPPER GRESHAM LAKE (Public State Park) From S end of town, S 4 mi on CR-M to N Creek Rd, W 5 mi (R). Entrance fee required. 22 Avail: Pit toilets. 2021 rates: $16 to $21. May 04 to Oct 10. (715)385-2727

BOWLER — C4 *Shawano*

MOHICAN RV PARK **Ratings: 6/NA/7** (RV Park) Avail: 57 full hkups (30/50 amps), Pit toilets. 2021 rates: $29 to $39. (800)952-0195, W 12180 Cty Rd A, Bowler, WI 54416

BRISTOL — E4 *Kenosha*

HAPPY ACRES KAMPGROUND **Ratings: 7/8.5★/9** (Campground) 150 Avail: 150 W, 150 E (30/50 amps). 2021 rates: $38 to $55. May 01 to Oct 01. (262)857-7373, 22230 45th St, Bristol, WI 53104

BRODHEAD — E3 *Green*

CRAZY HORSE CAMPGROUND **Ratings: 7.5/9.5★/9** (Campground) 117 Avail: 10 full hkups, 107 W, 107 E (30/50 amps). 2021 rates: $30 to $57. May 01 to Oct 31. (608)897-2207, N3201 Crazy Horse Ln, Brodhead, WI 53520

BRUCE — B2 *Rusk*

AUDIE LAKE PARK (Public) From town, N 1 mi on SR-40 to CR-0, NW 7 mi to Fire Lane Rd, NW 3.5 mi to Perch Lake Rd, W 1 mi (L). Avail: 15 E (30 amps), Pit toilets. 2021 rates: $23. May 01 to Dec 01. (715)532-2113

BRULE — A2 *Douglas*

BRULE RIVER/BOIS BRULE (Public State Park) From jct Hwy 27 & US 2: Go 1 mi W on US 2, then 1/2 mi W & 1 mi S on Ranger Rd. 17 Avail: Pit toilets. 2021 rates: $16 to $21. (715)372-5678

BRUSSELS — C5 *Door*

DOOR COUNTY KOA **Ratings: 8.5/10★/10** (Campground) 131 Avail: 6 full hkups, 125 W, 125 E (30/50 amps). 2021 rates: $56 to $72. Apr 17 to Oct 25. (920)825-7065, 9245 Lovers Lane, Brussels, WI 54204

BURLINGTON — E4 *Walworth*

RICHARD BONG SRA/SUNRISE - SUNSET (Public State Park) From Jct of Hwys 75 & 142, W 1 mi on Hwy 142 (L). Entrance fee required. Avail: 54 E (30 amps). 2021 rates: $18 to $33. (262)878-5600

CALEDONIA — E5 *Racine*

YOGI BEAR'S JELLYSTONE PARK CAMP-RESORT **Ratings: 8.5/9.5★/9.5** (Campground) 196 Avail: 100 full hkups, 96 W, 96 E (30/50 amps). 2021 rates: $47 to $70. May 01 to Oct 15. (262)835-2565, 8425 State Rd 38, Caledonia, WI 53108

CAMERON — B1 *Barron*

BUCK 'N BEAM'S CAMPGROUND 'N BAR **Ratings: 6/8/9** (Campground) 13 Avail: 13 W, 13 E (30/50 amps). 2021 rates: $35. May 01 to Nov 01. (715)458-2990, 1277 20th St , Cameron, WI 54822

VETERANS MEMORIAL PARK (BARRON COUNTY PARK) (Public) Go 1-1/2 mi S on CR-'SS', then 1 mi E on 12-1/2 Ave. 29 Avail: 22 W, 23 E Pit toilets. 2021 rates: $10 to $15. May 01 to Oct 01. (715)354-3353

CAMP DOUGLAS — D3 *Juneau*

MILL BLUFF (Public State Park) From jct I-90 (exit 55) & US 12/16: Go 3 mi E on US 12/16. Avail: 6 E Pit toilets. 2021 rates: $16 to $31. May 27 to Sep 30. (608)337-4775

CAMPBELLSPORT — D4 *Fond du Lac*

BENSON'S CENTURY CAMPING RESORT **Ratings: 4.5/5.5/6.5** (Campground) 70 Avail: 70 W, 70 E (30/50 amps). 2021 rates: $35 to $40. May 15 to Oct 15. (920)533-8597, N3845 Hwy 67, Campbellsport, WI 53010

New to RVing? Visit Blog.GoodSam.com for tips on everything camping and RVing.

KETTLE MORAINE/NORTH LONG LAKE (Public State Park) From Jct of US-45 & Hwy 67, E 6 mi on Hwy 67 to Dundee, N 2.5 mi to Kettle Moraine Dr, follow signs (L). Entrance fee required. Avail: 16 E (30 amps). 2021 rates: $12 to $23. (920)533-8612

CASCADE — D4 *Sheboygan*

HOEFT'S RESORT & CAMPGROUND **Ratings: 6/7/7** (Campground) 30 Avail: 30 W, 30 E (30/50 amps). 2021 rates: $40. May 01 to Oct 15. (262)626-2221, W9070 Crooked Lake Dr, Cascade, WI 53011

CASSVILLE — E2 *Grant*

NELSON DEWEY (Public State Park) From Jct of Hwy 133 & Cnty Trunk VV, W 1 mi on Cnty Trunk VV (R). Entrance fee required. Avail: 18 E (20/30 amps), Pit toilets. 2021 rates: $16 to $31. Apr 01 to Nov 30. (608)725-5374

WHITETAIL BLUFF CAMP & RESORT **Ratings: 8/8/6** (RV Park) 40 Avail: 30 full hkups, 10 W, 10 E (30/50 amps). 2021 rates: $49 to $89. Apr 15 to Oct 15. (608)725-5577, 8973 Irish Ridge Rd, Cassville, WI 53806

CECIL — C4 *Shawano*

CECIL LAKEVIEW PARK (Public) In town on Hwy 22. 35 Avail: 35 W, 35 E. 2021 rates: $32 to $38. May 15 to Sep 01. (715)745-4428

CEDAR — A2 *Iron*

FRONTIER RV PARK & CAMPGROUND **Ratings: 5.5/7/7** (RV Park) 30 Avail: 22 full hkups, 8 W, 8 E (30/50 amps). 2021 rates: $32 to $40. May 15 to Oct 15. (715)893-2461, 11296 W US Hwy 2, Saxon, WI 54559

CHETEK — B2 *Barron*

CHETEK RIVER CAMPGROUND **Ratings: 7.5/9★/9** (Campground) 30 Avail: 26 full hkups, 4 W, 4 E (30 amps). 2021 rates: $50. May 01 to Sep 30. (715)924-2440, 590 24th St, Chetek, WI 54728

NORTHERN EXPOSURE RESORT & CAMPGROUND **Ratings: 6.5/8★/6.5** (Campground) 20 Avail: 20 W, 20 E (20/30 amps). 2021 rates: $40. May 01 to Oct 01. (800)731-2887, 1075 Bronstad Beach Rd, Chetek, WI 54822

SIX LAKES RESORT & RV PARK **Ratings: 7/5.5/5.5** (Campground) 45 Avail: 31 full hkups, 14 W, 14 E (30/50 amps). 2021 rates: $35 to $40. Apr 25 to Oct 01. (715)924-3680, 2535 8-7/8 Ave, Chetek, WI 54728

SOUTHWORTH MEMORIAL PARK (BARRON COUNTY PARK) (Public) From town: Go 1-1/2 mi S on CR SS, then 1 mi E on 6th Ave, then 3/4 mi N on 26-1/2 St. 30 Avail: 26 W, 30 E Pit toilets. 2021 rates: $15 to $23. May 01 to Oct 01. (715)924-1875

CHIPPEWA FALLS — C2 *Chippewa*

COUNTRY VILLA MOTEL & COUNTRY CAMPING **Ratings: 6.5/8★/8.5** (Campground) Avail: 20 full hkups (30/50 amps). 2021 rates: $38 to $44. May 01 to Nov 01. (715)288-6376, 10765 County Hwy Q, Chippewa Falls, WI 54729

LAKE WISSOTA (Public State Park) From Jct of US-124 & Hwy 29, N 3 mi on US-124 to Cnty Rd S, NE 3 mi to Cnty Rd O, E 2 mi (R). Entrance fee required. Avail: 59 E (30/50 amps), Pit toilets. 2021 rates: $18 to $33. (715)382-4574

O'NEIL CREEK CAMPGROUND

Ratings: 8/10★/8.5 (Campground) 110 Avail: 26 full hkups, 84 W, 84 E (30/50 amps). 2021 rates: $48 to $75. Apr 15 to Oct 15. (715)723-6581, 14912 105th Ave, Chippewa Falls, WI 54729

PINE HARBOR CAMPGROUND **Ratings: 6.5/7.5/8.5** (Campground) 25 Avail: 25 W, 25 E (30/50 amps). 2021 rates: $35 to $40. May 01 to Oct 15. (715)723-9865, 7181 185th St , Chippewa Falls, WI 54729

CLEAR LAKE — C1 *Polk*

CLEAR LAKE PARK (Public) From Jct of SR-63 & 7th St., N 0.5 mi on park access rd (E). 18 Avail: 11 W, 11 E (20 amps). 2021 rates: $25 to $30. May 01 to Oct 31. (715)263-2157

COLOMA — D3 *Waushara*

COLOMA CAMPERLAND **Ratings: 7.5/8★/5.5** (Campground) 19 Avail: 3 full hkups, 16 W, 16 E (30/50 amps). 2021 rates: $44 to $54. (715)228-3600, N1130 5th Rd, Coloma, WI 54930

We shine ""Spotlights" on interesting cities and areas.

CONOVER — B3 *Vilas*

BUCKATABON LODGE & LIGHTHOUSE INN **Ratings: 4.5/7/5.5** (Campground) 12 Avail: 12 W, 12 E (20 amps). 2021 rates: $40 to $50. May 01 to Nov 01. (715)479-4660, 5630 Rush Rd, Conover, WI 54519

NO HIGHLAND AMERICAN LEGION/STAR LAKE (Public State Park) From Woodruff, N 5 mi on US-51 to Hwy M, N 9 mi to Hwy K, E 12 mi to Hwy N, S 1 mi (R). Entrance fee required. 44 Avail: Pit toilets. 2021 rates: $16 to $21. (715)385-3352

ROHR'S WILDERNESS TOURS **Ratings: 5/8★/6** (Campground) Avail: 17 full hkups (20/50 amps). 2021 rates: $25 to $45. (715)547-3639, 5230 Razorback Rd, Conover, WI 54519

TORCH LAKE CAMPGROUND (Public) From County K & 45 (Conover): Go 1-1/2 mi S on 45, then right 1/2 mi W on Torch Lake Rd, then left 1/2 mi W on Torch Lake Rd, then turn left into campground (E). 20 Avail: 20 W, 20 E (30/50 amps). 2021 rates: $40. Apr 01 to Oct 31. (715)479-5160

CORNELL — C2 *Chippewa*

BRUNET ISLAND (Public State Park) From Jct of Hwy 64 & Park Rd, N 1 mi on Park Rd (E). Entrance fee required. Avail: 23 E (30 amps). 2021 rates: $18 to $33. (715)239-6888

CRANDON — B4 *Forest*

VETERAN'S MEMORIAL PARK (FOREST COUNTY PARK) (Public) From town, S 3 mi on East Shore Dr (R). Avail: 58 E (50 amps). 2021 rates: $20 to $25. May 01 to Oct 01. (715)478-2040

CRIVITZ — C4 *Marinette*

PESHTIGO RIVER CAMPGROUND **Ratings: 7.5/8.5★/6.5** (Campground) 74 Avail: 13 full hkups, 61 W, 61 E (30/50 amps). 2021 rates: $35 to $41. May 01 to Oct 15. (715)854-2986, W 7948 Airport Rd, Crivitz, WI 54114

DANBURY — B1 *Burnett*

EAGLES LANDING CAMPGROUND **Ratings: 7.5/6/6** (Campground) 45 Avail: 36 full hkups, 9 W, 9 E (30/50 amps). 2021 rates: $27. May 01 to Oct 15. (715)656-4402, 30158 Highway 35, Danbury, WI 54830

DE FOREST — D3 *Dane*

MADISON CAMPGROUND

Ratings: 9.5/10★/9.5 (Campground) 102 Avail: 92 full hkups, 8 W, 8 E (30/50 amps). 2021 rates: $59 to $69. Apr 01 to Oct 31. (608)846-4528, 4859 County Rd V, De Forest, WI 53532

TOKEN CREEK PARK (DANE COUNTY PARK) (Public) From Jct of I-90 & SR-51, N 0.5 mi on SR-51 (R). Avail: 43 E (30 amps). 2021 rates: $18 to $28. Apr 27 to Oct 12. (608)242-4576

Travel Services

GANDER RV OF DEFOREST/MADISON Your new hometown outfitter offering the best regional gear for all your outdoor needs. Your adventure awaits. **SERVICES:** tire, RV appliance, MH mechanical, gunsmithing svc, archery svc, sells outdoor gear, sells fishing gear, sells firearms, restrooms. RV Sales. RV supplies, LP gas, dump, emergency parking, RV accessible. Hours: 9am to 8pm.
(888)264-6191 Lat: 43.186169, Lon: -89.330444
6199 E Metro Dr, De Forest, WI 53532
rv.ganderoutdoors.com

DE PERE — C4 *Brown*

APPLE CREEK CAMPGROUND **Ratings: 8/8.5★/8** (Campground) 135 Avail: 135 W, 135 E (30/50 amps). 2021 rates: $47. Apr 01 to Oct 31. (920)532-4386, 3831 County Road U, De Pere, WI 54115

DE SOTO — D2 *Vernon*

MISSISSIPPI RIVER POOL 9 - COE/BLACKHAWK PARK (Public Corps) From jct Hwy 82 & Hwy 35: Go 3 mi N on Hwy 35. Avail: 73 E Pit toilets. 2021 rates: $18 to $26. Apr 15 to Oct 31. (608)648-3314

DELAFIELD — E4 *Dane*

NAGA-WAUKEE PARK (WAUKESHA COUNTY PARK) (Public) From jct I-94 & Hwy-83: Go 1/2 mi N on Hwy-83, then 1/2 mi W on Mariner Dr. 25 Avail: Pit toilets. 2021 rates: $20. Apr 01 to Nov 02. (262)548-7801

Always do a Pre-Drive Safety Check!

DODGEVILLE — E3 *Iowa*

↑ GOVERNOR DODGE (Public State Park) From town, N 3 mi on State Hwy 23 (R). Entrance fee required. Avail: 80 E (30 amps), Pit toilets. 2021 rates: $18 to $33. (608)935-2315

→ TOM'S CAMPGROUND **Ratings: 6/7/8** (Campground) 60 Avail: 60 W, 60 E (30/50 amps). 2021 rates: $30 to $34. Apr 01 to Oct 31. (608)935-5446, 2626 Spring Rd, Dodgeville, WI 53533

DORCHESTER — C3 *Clark*

→ DORCHESTER PARK (Public) From Jct of SR-29 & SR-13, N 4 mi on SR-13 to CR-A, W 0.5 mi (L). 26 Avail: 16 W, 16 E (30 amps). 2021 rates: $18 to $21. May 01 to Oct 31. (715)654-5098

DYCKESVILLE — C5 *Kewaunee*

↑ BAY SHORE PARK (Public) From Jct of I-43 & Hwy 57, NE 12 mi on Hwy 57 (L). 115 Avail: 85 W, 85 E (20/30 amps). 2021 rates: $20 to $30. Apr 20 to Oct 15. (920)448-4466

EAGLE — E4 *Waukesha*

← KETTLE MORAINE/OTTAWA LAKE REC AREA (Public State Park) From Jct of Hwys 59 & 67, N 6 mi on Hwy 67 to Hwy ZZ, W 0.1 mi (R). Entrance fee required. Avail: 49 E (30/50 amps), Pit toilets. 2021 rates: $18 to $33. (262)594-6220

EAGLE RIVER — B3 *Vilas*

→ **CHAIN O' LAKES CAMPGROUND**

good sam park

Ratings: 8/9.5★/8 (Membership Park) 75 Avail: 75 W, 75 E (20/30 amps). 2021 rates: $42 to $50. May 01 to Oct 07. (715)479-6708, 3165 Campground Rd, Eagle River, WI 54521

↑ HI-PINES EAGLE RIVER CAMPGROUND **Ratings: 6.5/9/8.5** (RV Park) 86 Avail: 19 full hkups, 67 W, 67 E (30/50 amps). 2021 rates: $31 to $55. May 01 to Oct 15. (715)479-9124, 1919 Hwy 45 N, Eagle River, WI 54521

EGG HARBOR — C5 *Door*

↑ EGG HARBOR CAMPGROUND & RV RESORT **Ratings: 9/8.5★/10** (Campground) Avail: 100 full hkups (30/50 amps). 2021 rates: $53 to $73. May 15 to Oct 23. (920)868-3278, 8164 State Hwy 42, Egg Harbor, WI 54209

↖ FRONTIER WILDERNESS CAMPGROUND **Ratings: 8/9★/9** (Campground) 50 Avail: 50 W, 50 E (30/50 amps). 2021 rates: $47 to $50. May 01 to Oct 31. (920)868-3349, 4375 Hillside Rd, Egg Harbor, WI 54209

ELLISON BAY — B5 *Door*

↗ HY-LAND COURT RV PARK **Ratings: 7/8.5★/9.5** (Campground) 54 Avail: 46 full hkups, 8 W, 8 E (30/50 amps). 2021 rates: $40 to $48. May 08 to Nov 01. (920)854-4850, 11503 Hwy 42, Ellison Bay, WI 54210

↗ WAGON TRAIL CAMPGROUND **Ratings: 7/10★/10** (Campground) 90 Avail: 12 full hkups, 78 W, 78 E (30/50 amps). 2021 rates: $50 to $62. May 08 to Oct 19. (920)854-4818, 1190 County Road ZZ, Ellison Bay, WI 54210

FENCE — B4 *Florence*

WEST BASS LAKE (FLORENCE COUNTY PARK) (Public) From Pembine, W 24 mi on Rte 8 to Hwy 101, N 7 mi to Cnty Trunk Hwy C, E 5 mi to Fire Lane Rd, N 1 mi (L). Avail: 29 E Pit toilets. 2021 rates: $8. (715)528-3207

FISH CREEK — C5 *Door*

→ FISH CREEK CAMPGROUND **Ratings: 7/8/9** (Campground) 43 Avail: 43 W, 43 E (30 amps). 2021 rates: $45 to $55. May 06 to Oct 19. (920)495-CAMP, 3709 Cty Rd F, Fish Creek, WI 54212

↑ PENINSULA (Public State Park) From town, W 100' on Hwy 42. Entrance fee required. Avail: 157 E (20/30 amps), Pit toilets. 2021 rates: $20 to $35. (920)868-3258

FLORENCE — B4 *Florence*

↙ KEYES LAKE CAMPGROUND **Ratings: 5.5/8/6.5** (RV Park) 13 Avail: 13 W, 13 E (20/30 amps). 2021 rates: $31 to $36. (715)528-4907, N4918 Hwy 101, Florence, WI 54121

FOND DU LAC — D4 *Byron*

↓ BREEZY HILL CAMPGROUND **Ratings: 8.5/9.5★/9.5** (Campground) 121 Avail: 50 full hkups, 71 W, 71 E (30/50 amps). 2021 rates: $52 to $70. Apr 15 to Oct 15. (920)477-2300, N4177 Cearns Lane, Fond du Lac, WI 54937

↙ FOND DU LAC EAST / KETTLE MORAINE KOA **Ratings: 8.5/10★/9** (Campground) 106 Avail: 12 full hkups, 94 W, 94 E (30/50 amps). 2021 rates: $46 to $68. Apr 15 to Oct 15. (888)712-9617, N5456 Division Rd, Glenbeulah, WI 53023

FORT ATKINSON — E4 *Jefferson*

↙ JELLYSTONE PARK OF FORT ATKINSON **Ratings: 8.5/8.5★/8.5** (Membership Park) 150 Avail: 150 W, 150 E (30/50 amps). 2021 rates: $52.80 to $66. May 01 to Oct 15. (920)568-4100, N551 Wishing Well Ln, Fort Atkinson, WI 53538

FOUNTAIN CITY — D1 *Buffalo*

↑ MERRICK (Public State Park) From town, N 2 mi on Hwy 35 (L). Entrance fee required. Avail: 22 E (30 amps), Pit toilets. 2021 rates: $16 to $31. (608)687-4936

FREMONT — D4 *Waupaca*

← BLUE TOP RESORT & CAMPGROUND **Ratings: 5.5/9★/10** (Campground) 26 Avail: 8 W, 26 E (20/30 amps). 2021 rates: $32 to $52. Apr 15 to Oct 31. (920)446-3343, 1460 Wolf River Dr, Fremont, WI 54940

← **YOGI BEAR'S JELLYSTONE PARK CAMP-RESORT**

good sam park

Ratings: 7.5/7.5/6.5 (Campground) 125 Avail: 29 full hkups, 96 W, 96 E (30/50 amps). 2021 rates: $56 to $104. Apr 15 to Oct 15. (888)563-7040, E6506 Hwy 110, Fremont, WI 54940

FRIENDSHIP — D3 *Adams*

CASTLE ROCK PARK (ADAMS COUNTY PARK) (Public) From jct CR J & Hwy 13 (in town): Go 3-1/2 mi S on Hwy 13, then 6 mi W on CR F, then 1/2 mi S on CR Z. 189 Avail. 2021 rates: $17 to $25. (608)339-7713

↖ PETENWELL LAKE (ADAMS COUNTY PARK) (Public) From Jct of Hwys 13 & 21, W 8 mi on Hwy 21 to CR-Z, N 6 mi to Bighorn Dr, W 1 mi (E). 125 Avail: (20/30 amps). 2021 rates: $17 to $22. (608)564-7513

↑ ROCHE A' CRI (Public State Park) From Jct of SR-21 & SR-13, S 1.5 mi on SR-13 (R). Entrance fee required. Avail: 4 E (30 amps), Pit toilets. 2021 rates: $12 to $14. (608)565-2789

GALESVILLE — D2 *Trempealeau*

↑ CHAMPION'S RIVERSIDE RESORT **Ratings: 8/8.5★/7.5** (Campground) 90 Avail: 90 W, 90 E (30/50 amps). 2021 rates: $38 to $45. Apr 15 to Oct 31. (608)582-2995, W16751 Pow Wow Ln, Galesville, WI 54630

GLENWOOD CITY — C1 *St Croix*

↓ GLEN HILLS COUNTY PARK (Public) From town, S 1.8 mi on Hwy 128 to Rustic Rd 3, S 2 mi (L). Avail: 61 E (20/30 amps), Pit toilets. 2021 rates: $20. May 01 to Oct 31. (715)265-4613

GOODMAN — B4 *Marinette*

↖ LAKE HILBERT CAMPGROUND **Ratings: 3/6/7.5** (Campground) 35 Avail: 35 W, 35 E (30 amps). 2021 rates: $28. May 02 to Oct 24. (715)336-3013, N 20470 Town Park Rd, Goodman, WI 54120

GORDON — B1 *Douglas*

← GORDON DAM PARK (Public) From Jct of US-53 & Cnty Hwy Y, W 7 mi on Cnty Hwy Y (R). Avail: 12 E (20 amps), Pit toilets. 2021 rates: $12 to $25. May 17 to Sep 11. (715)378-2219

← HAPPY OURS RV PARK **Ratings: 4/8/4.5** (RV Park) Avail: 37 full hkups (30/50 amps). 2021 rates: $30. (715)919-0909, 14627 S East Mail Rd, Gordon, WI 54838

GRANTSBURG — B1 *Burnett*

← JAMES N MCNALLY CAMPGROUND (Public) From Jct of Hwy 70/48 & S Pine St, N 0.4 mi on S Pine St to Olson St, W 0.3 mi (R). Avail: 38 full hkups (30/50 amps). 2021 rates: $25 to $30. Apr 15 to Oct 15. (715)463-2405

GREEN LAKE — D4 *Green Lake*

← GREEN LAKE CAMPGROUND **Ratings: 8/8.5/9** (Campground) 210 Avail: 19 full hkups, 191 W, 191 E (30/50 amps). 2021 rates: $67 to $82. Apr 18 to Oct 18. (920)294-3543, W 2360 Hwy 23, Green Lake, WI 54941

↙ HATTIE SHERWOOD (Public) From Jct SR-23 & CR-A, SW 1.2 mi on SR-23B, E .6 mi Lawson Dr. Avail: 27 E (20/50 amps). 2021 rates: $28. May 01 to Oct 15. (920)294-6380

GREENWOOD — C2 *Clark*

← MEAD LAKE PARK AND CAMPGROUND (CLARK COUNTY PARK) (Public) From town, N 15 mi on Hwy 73 to CR-G, W 2.5 mi to CR-0, N 2 mi to CR-MM, W 5 mi (L). Avail: 66 E (20 amps), Pit toilets. 2021 rates: $17 to $31. May 01 to Nov 01. (715)743-5140

↗ ROCK DAM (CLARK COUNTY PARK) (Public) From town, N 6 mi on CR-H to Rock Dam Rd (turns into Camp Globe Rd), continue N 3 mi (passed the TV tower) to the two curves in the rd, E 6 mi on the 2nd curve in the road (L). 150 Avail: 7 full hkups, 16 W, 16 E (20/30 amps). 2021 rates: $17 to $33. (715)743-5140

GRESHAM — C4 *Shawano*

← ANNIE'S CAMPGROUND **Ratings: 7/8.5★/8.5** (Campground) 51 Avail: 51 W, 51 E (30/50 amps). 2021 rates: $55 to $65. (715)787-3632, W12505 Roosevelt Rd, Gresham, WI 54128

→ CAPTAIN'S COVE RESORT AND COUNTRY CLUB **Ratings: 6.5/7/7.5** (Membership Park) 162 Avail: 55 full hkups, 107 W, 107 E (30/50 amps). 2021 rates: $59. May 01 to Oct 31. (715)787-3535, N 9099 Big Lake Rd, Gresham, WI 54128

HANCOCK — D3 *Waushara*

← OASIS HANCOCK **Ratings: 10/10★/9** (Campground) Avail: 100 full hkups (30/50 amps). 2021 rates: $65 to $110. May 01 to Oct 31. (715)249-3322, N4398 Elizabeth Lane, Hancock, WI 54943

→ VILLAGE OF HANCOCK CAMPGROUND (Public) From Jct of US-51 & CR-V, E 1.3 mi on CR-V to CR-GG, SE 0.75 mi (R). 30 Avail: 30 W, 30 E (20 amps), Pit toilets. 2021 rates: $7.50 to $10. (715)249-5521

HARTFORD — D4 *Washington*

→ KETTLE MORAINE/PIKE LAKE (Public State Park) From Jct of SR-83 & SR-60, E 2.8 mi on SR-60 (R). Entrance fee required. Avail: 11 E (50 amps). 2021 rates: $18 to $33. Apr 18 to Nov 01. (262)670-3400

HATFIELD — C2 *Jackson*

↗ BLACK RIVER/EAST FORK (Public State Park) From Jct of I-94 & Hwy 54, E 8 mi on Hwy 54 to S Cemetary Rd (unposted, follow signs), N 4 mi to Old Hwy 54, E 0.5 mi to campground rd, N 2 mi (E). Entrance fee required. Avail: 24 E Pit toilets. 2021 rates: $16 to $31. Apr 15 to Nov 30. (715)284-4103

↗ RUSSELL MEMORIAL PARK (CLARK COUNTY PARK) (Public) From town, SW 13 mi on Hwy 95 to CR-J, S 3 mi (L). 202 Avail: 9 full hkups, 6 W, 190 E (20/30 amps). 2021 rates: $17 to $33. May 01 to Nov 01. (715)743-5140

HAYWARD — B2 *Sawyer*

↓ CAMP NAMEKAGON **Ratings: 5.5/7.5/7.5** (Campground) Avail: 35 full hkups (30/50 amps). 2021 rates: $48. Apr 15 to Oct 15. (715)766-2277, W2108 Larson Rd, Springbrook, WI 54875

↗ HAYWARD KOA **Ratings: 8.5/10★/9.5** (Campground) 200 Avail: 52 full hkups, 148 W, 148 E (30/50 amps). 2021 rates: $55 to $78. May 01 to Oct 06. (715)634-2331, 11544 N US Hwy 63, Hayward, WI 54843

↖ LAKE CHIPPEWA CAMPGROUND **Ratings: 8/10★/8.5** (Campground) 105 Avail: 45 full hkups, 60 W, 60 E (30/50 amps). 2021 rates: $24 to $60. May 01 to Nov 01. (715)462-3672, 8380 N CR-CC, Hayward, WI 54843

↖ SUNRISE BAY CAMPGROUND **Ratings: 5.5/6.5/6** (Campground) 19 Avail: 19 W, 19 E (30 amps). 2021 rates: $35. (715)634-2213, 16269 W Jolly Fisherman Rd, Hayward, WI 54843

→ TREELAND FARM RV RESORT **Ratings: 9.5/10★/10** (RV Park) Avail: 52 full hkups (30/50 amps). 2021 rates: $44 to $69. May 01 to Oct 15. (715)462-3874, 10138 W CR-B, Hayward, WI 54843

HIGHLAND — E3 *Iowa*

↓ BLACKHAWK LAKE REC AREA (Public) From Jct of Hwy 80 & CR-BH, E 3 mi on CR-BH (E). Entrance fee required. Avail: 92 E (30 amps). 2021 rates: $15 to $25. Apr 15 to Nov 01. (608)623-2707

HIXTON — C2 *Jackson*

→ KOA HIXTON/ALMA CENTER **Ratings: 8.5/10★/7.5** (Campground) 68 Avail: 44 full hkups, 24 W, 24 E (30/50 amps). 2021 rates: $26 to $50. May 01 to Nov 01. (800)562-2680, N 9657 State Hwy 95, Alma Center, WI 54611

HOLCOMBE — C2 *Chippewa*

PINE POINT CAMPGROUND (CHIPPEWA COUNTY) (Public) From town, W 2.5 mi on CR-M (R). Avail: 48 E (50 amps). 2021 rates: $18 to $23. May 02 to Oct 31. (715)726-7882

UNCLE SALTY'S GOLF AND CAMP **Ratings: 6/NA/7.5** (RV Park) Avail: 22 full hkups (30/50 amps). 2021 rates: $45 to $55. Apr 01 to Oct 31. (715)595-6013, 27366 270th Ave, Holcombe, WI 54745

HOLMEN — D2 *La Crosse*

WHISPERING PINES CAMPGROUND **Ratings: 7.5/9★/9** (Campground) 63 Avail: 22 full hkups, 41 W, 41 E (30/50 amps). 2021 rates: $48 to $73. Apr 15 to Oct 15. (608)526-4956, N 8905 Hwy 53, Holmen, WI 54636

HORICON — D4 *Dodge*

LEDGE PARK (Public) From Jct of SR-33 & SR-28, NE 0.2 mi on SR-28 to Raaschs Hill Rd, E 2.5 mi (E). Avail: 22 E (20 amps). 2021 rates: $18 to $22. Nov 27 to Nov 17. (920)387-5450

PLAYFUL GOOSE CAMPGROUND **Ratings: 6/7.5★/5.5** (Campground) 55 Avail: 23 full hkups, 32 W, 32 E (20/30 amps). 2021 rates: $39 to $46. May 01 to Oct 12. (920)485-4744, 2001 S. Main St., Horicon, WI 53032

HUDSON — C1 *St Croix*

WILLOW RIVER (Public State Park) From town, E 3 mi on I-94 to Hwy 12, N 2 mi to CR-A, N 2 mi (L). Entrance fee required. Avail: 53 E (30/50 amps). 2021 rates: $18 to $33. (715)386-5931

IOLA — C4 *Waupaca*

IOLA PINES CAMPGROUND **Ratings: 6/7.5/7.5** (Campground) 35 Avail: 2 full hkups, 33 W, 33 E (20/30 amps). 2021 rates: $32 to $40. May 01 to Nov 30. (715)445-3489, 100 Fairway Dr, Iola, WI 54945

IRON RIVER — A2 *Bayfield*

DELTA LAKE CAMPGROUND (BAYFIELD COUNTY PARK) (Public) From jct US 2 & CR H: Go 5 mi S on CR H, then 5 mi S on Scenic Drive Rd. Avail: 34 E Pit toilets. 2021 rates: $24 to $29. (715)373-6114

MOON LAKE PARK (Public) From town, S 0.5 mi on County Trunk H (R). Avail: 26 E (20 amps). 2021 rates: $20 to $25. May 01 to Oct 15. (218)591-0905

TOP O THE MORN RESORT & CAMPGROUND **Ratings: 8/8.5★/9.5** (Campground) 16 Avail: 8 full hkups, 8 W, 8 E (30/50 amps). 2021 rates: $35 to $40. May 01 to Oct 15. (715)372-4546, 6080 Iron Lake Rd, Iron River, WI 54847

TWIN BEAR PARK (BAYFIELD COUNTY PARK) (Public) From jct US 2 & CR H: Go 7 mi S on CR H. Avail: 43 E Pit toilets. 2021 rates: $24 to $29. (715)372-8610

JEFFERSON — E4 *Jefferson*

BARK RIVER CAMPGROUND **Ratings: 6.5/7/7.5** (Campground) 15 Avail: 15 W, 15 E (30/50 amps). 2021 rates: $40. Apr 03 to Oct 26. (262)593-2421, W2340 Hanson Rd, Jefferson, WI 53549

JEFFERSON COUNTY FAIR PARK CAMPGROUND (Public) From Jct of US-26 & US-18: Go E 1/3 mi on US-18 to N Jackson Ave (L), then 3 blocks to park (L). 199 Avail: 20 full hkups, 179 W, 179 E (30/50 amps). 2021 rates: $35 to $45. (920)674-7148

KENOSHA — E5 *Kenosha*

Travel Services

CAMPING WORLD OF KENOSHA As the nation's largest retailer of RV supplies, accessories, services and new and used RVs, Camping World is committed to making your total RV experience better. **SERVICES:** gunsmithing svc, archery svc, sells outdoor gear, sells fishing gear, sells firearms, restrooms. RV Sales. RV supplies, RV accessible. Hours: 9am to 8pm.
(866)984-4807 Lat: 42.573946, Lon: -87.951243
6802 118th Ave, Kenosha, WI 53142
www.campingworld.com

KEWASKUM — D4 *Fond du Lac*

KETTLE MORAINE/MAUTHE LAKE (Public State Park) From Jct of Hwy 28 & Hwy S, N 6 mi on Hwy S to Hwy GGG, N 1 mi (E). Entrance fee required. Avail: 51 E (30 amps), Pit toilets. 2021 rates: $18 to $33. (262)626-4305

KEWAUNEE — C5 *Kewaunee*

CEDAR VALLEY CAMPGROUND **Ratings: 8/9★/9** (Campground) 100 Avail: 100 W, 100 E (20/30 amps). 2021 rates: $60 to $70. Apr 25 to Oct 10. (920)388-4983, N5098 Cedar Valley Rd, Kewaunee, WI 54216

KEWAUNEE MUNICIPAL MARINA & CAMPGROUND (Public) From jct Hwy 29 & Hwy 42: Go 1/4 mi N on Hwy 42. 36 Avail: 36 W, 36 E. (920)388-3300

KEWAUNEE RV & CAMPGROUND Ratings: 8/9.5★/9.5 (Campground) 50 Avail: 26 full hkups, 24 W, 24 E (30/50 amps). 2021 rates: $42 to $49. May 01 to Oct 01. (920)388-4851, 333 Terraqua Dr, Kewaunee, WI 54216

KIELER — E2 *Grant*

RUSTIC BARN CAMPGROUND & RV PARK **Ratings: 8/9.5★/9.5** (RV Park) Avail: 42 full hkups (30/50 amps). 2021 rates: $39.50 to $49.50. Apr 15 to Oct 31. (608)568-7797, 3854 Dry Hollow Rd, Kieler, WI 53812

KINGSTON — D4 *Green Lake*

GRAND VALLEY CAMPGROUND **Ratings: 8.5/9★/9.5** (Campground) 69 Avail: 69 W, 69 E (30/50 amps). 2021 rates: $44 to $49. Apr 01 to Dec 01. (920)394-3643, W 5855 CR-B, Dalton, WI 53926

KNOWLTON — C3 *Marathon*

LAKE DUBAY SHORES CAMPGROUND
Ratings: 8/7.5/6.5 (Campground) From Jct of I-39/US-51 & SR-34 (exit 175): Go SW 2 mi on SR-34 to DuBay Dr (turn left), then 500 ft (R). **FAC:** gravel rds. (225 spaces). Avail: 120 grass, 10 pull-thrus, (45x60), back-ins (45x50), 20 full hkups, 100 W, 100 E (30/50 amps), seasonal sites, WiFi @ sites, tent sites, rentals, dump, mobile sewer, laundry, groc, LP gas, fire rings, firewood. **REC:** Lake DuBay: swim, fishing, marina, kayaking/canoeing, playground, rec open to public. Pets OK $. Partial handicap access. Big rig sites, eco-friendly. 2021 rates: $42 to $70. Apr 15 to Oct 15.
(715)457-2484 Lat: 44.71027, Lon: -89.69600
203040 DuBay Dr., Mosinee, WI 54455
www.dubayshores.com
See ad this page

LA CROSSE — D2 *La Crosse*

GOOSE ISLAND CAMPGROUND (Public) From Jct of I-90 & WI-16 (Exit 5): Go 9 3/4 mi S on WI-16 to US-14E/US-61/WI-35, then go 1 1/2 mi on SR-35 S to CR GI (R). 239 Avail: 140 W, 239 E (30/50 amps). 2021 rates: $28 to $32.50. Apr 15 to Oct 30. (608)788-7018

PETTIBONE RESORT **Ratings: 8/7.5/8.5** (RV Park) 72 Avail: 72 W, 72 E (30/50 amps). 2021 rates: $52. Apr 15 to Nov 01. (608)782-5858, 333 Park Plaza Dr, La Crosse, WI 54601

LA FARGE — D2 *Vernon*

LA FARGE VILLAGE PARK (Public) From Jct of US-14 & SR-131, NE 16 mi on SR-131 to Adams St, E 0.2 mi, follow signs (L). Avail: 12 E (15 amps). 2021 rates: $20. Apr 01 to Dec 01. (608)625-4422

LAC DU FLAMBEAU — B3 *Vilas*

LAC DU FLAMBEAU TRIBAL CAMPGROUND & MARINA **Ratings: 5.5/8★/8** (Campground) 50 Avail: 13 full hkups, 37 W, 37 E (30 amps). 2021 rates: $37 to $40. May 01 to Sep 30. (715)588-4211, 2549 State Hwy 47N, Lac Du Flambeau, WI 54538

LAKE DELTON — D3 *Sauk*

COUNTRY ROADS MOTORHOME & RV PARK **Ratings: 7.5/9/9** (RV Park) 73 Avail: 67 full hkups, 6 W, 6 E (30/50 amps). 2021 rates: $4 to $46. Apr 15 to Oct 07. (608)253-2132, S1633 Hwy 23, Lake Delton, WI 53940

LAKE GENEVA — E4 *Walworth*

BIG FOOT BEACH (Public State Park) From Jct of Hwys 50 & 120, S 1.5 mi on Hwy 120 (L). Avail: 32 E (50 amps), Pit toilets. 2021 rates: $18 to $33. Apr 20 to Oct 15. (262)248-2528

LAKEWOOD — B4 *Oconto*

HEAVEN'S UP NORTH FAMILY CAMPGROUND **Ratings: 7.5/9★/8.5** (Campground) 36 Avail: 36 W, 36 E (20/30 amps). 2021 rates: $20 to $42. May 01 to Oct 15. (715)276-6556, 18344 Lake John Rd, Lakewood, WI 54138

MAPLE HEIGHTS CAMPGROUND **Ratings: 7.5/8★/6.5** (Campground) 32 Avail: 21 W, 32 E (30/50 amps). 2021 rates: $35 to $41. May 01 to Oct 31. (715)276-6441, 16091 E Chain Lake Rd, Lakewood, WI 54138

LAND O'LAKES — B3 *Vilas*

BORDERLINE RV PARK **Ratings: 3.5/7.5/6.5** (Campground) Avail: 26 full hkups (30/50 amps). 2021 rates: $25. May 01 to Oct 31. (715)547-6169, 6078 Hwy 45, Land O' Lakes, WI 54540

LANNON — E4 *Waukesha*

MENOMONEE PARK (WAUKESHA COUNTY PARK) (Public) From jct Hwy 74 & CR V: Go 1-1/2 mi N on CR V. 30 Avail: Pit toilets. 2021 rates: $16. Apr 01 to Nov 02. (262)548-7801

LODI — D3 *Columbia*

SMOKEY HOLLOW CAMPGROUND **Ratings: 7.5/10★/9** (Campground) 56 Avail: 56 W, 56 E (30/50 amps). 2021 rates: $30 to $88. (608)635-4806, W9935 Mc Gowan Rd, Lodi, WI 53555

LYNDON STATION — D3 *Juneau*

HO-CHUNK RV RESORT & CAMPGROUND
Ratings: 8/9★/9 (Campground) 59 Avail: 54 full hkups, 5 W, 5 E (30/50 amps). 2021 rates: $48 to $55. (608)666-2040, N 2884 28th Ave, Lyndon Station, WI 53944

RIVER BAY CAMPING RESORT & MARINA **Ratings: 8/8.5★/8.5** (Campground) 126 Avail: 42 full hkups, 84 W, 84 E (30/50 amps). 2021 rates: $50 to $60. Apr 15 to Oct 15. (608)254-7193, W1147 River Bay Rd, Lyndon Station, WI 53944

YUKON TRAILS CAMPING
Ratings: 7/8.5★/8 (Campground) 78 Avail: 78 W, 78 E (30/50 amps). 2021 rates: $60 to $68. Apr 15 to Oct 15. (888)563-7040, N2330 Cty Rd HH, Lyndon Station, WI 53944

MADISON — E3 *Dane*

LAKE FARM PARK (DANE COUNTY PARK) (Public) From Jct of US12/18 & Exit 264 (South Town Dr), S 0.75 mi on South Town Dr to Moorland Rd, E .8 mi (rd becomes Lake Farm Rd) (L). Avail: 39 E (50 amps). 2021 rates: $18 to $27. Apr 26 to Nov 03. (608)242-4576

MANAWA — C4 *Waupaca*

BEAR LAKE CAMPGROUND **Ratings: 6.5/7/6.5** (Campground) 107 Avail: 107 W, 107 E (20/30 amps). 2021 rates: $38 to $42. May 01 to Oct 15. (920)596-3308, N4715 Hwy 110 & 22, Manawa, WI 54949

MANITOWISH WATERS — B3 *Vilas*

NO HIGHLAND AMERICAN LEGION/SANDY BEACH (Public State Park) From town, SE 3.8 mi on US-51, S 4.5 mi on SR-47 to Powell Rd, N 0.25 mi to Sandy Beach (E). Entrance fee required. 30 Avail: Pit toilets. 2021 rates: $16 to $21. May 22 to Oct 10. (715)385-2727

MARIBEL — C5 *Manitowoc*

DEVILS RIVER CAMPGROUND **Ratings: 4.5/7/7** (Campground) 26 Avail: 26 W, 26 E (30 amps). 2021 rates: $34 to $40. May 01 to Oct 01. (920)863-2812, 16612 County Hwy R, Maribel, WI 54227

Had a great stay? Let us know by emailing us Parks@goodsam.com

MARION — C4 *Waupaca*

FARMER GENE'S CAMPGROUND **Ratings: 7/8.5★/7** (Campground) 180 Avail: 180 W, 180 E (30/50 amps). 2021 rates: $45 to $50. (715)754-5900, N11301 Kinney Lake Rd, Marion, WI 54950

MARSHALL — E4 *Dane*

WHISTLE STOP CAMPGROUND **Ratings: 7/9/9** (Campground) 58 Avail: 54 full hkups, 4 W, 4 E (30/50 amps). 2021 rates: $57 to $62. (608)655-3080, 114 Whistle St, Marshall, WI 53559

MARSHFIELD — C3 *Wood*

NORTH WOOD PARK (WOOD COUNTY PARK) (Public) From town, W 14 mi on Hwy 13 to CR-A, N 5 mi (L). Avail: 78 E (30/50 amps). 2021 rates: $16 to $28. May 01 to Oct 31. (715)421-8422

MAUSTON — D3 *Juneau*

CASTLE ROCK (JUNEAU COUNTY PARK) (Public) From Jct of I-90 & Rte 82 (exit 69), W 0.6 mi on Rte 82 to Rte 58, N 6.8 mi on Rte 58 to CR-G, S 5.1 mi (L). Avail: 150 E (20/30 amps). 2021 rates: $17 to $23. May 27 to Sep 04. (608)847-7089

MCFARLAND — E3 *Dane*

BABCOCK PARK (DANE COUNTY PARK) (Public) From Jct of SR-12 & SR-51, S 3 mi on SR-51 (R). Avail: 25 E (30 amps). 2021 rates: $28. Apr 27 to Oct 12. (608)242-4576

MELLEN — A2 *Ashland*

COPPER FALLS (Public State Park) From town, NE 2 mi on SR-169 (L). Entrance fee required. Avail: 24 E (30/50 amps). 2021 rates: $20 to $35. (715)274-5123

MERRILL — C3 *Lincoln*

COUNCIL GROUNDS (Public State Park) From Jct US-51 & SR-64, W 2 mi on SR-64 to SR-107N, NW 2 mi (L). Entrance fee required. Avail: 19 E (30 amps). 2021 rates: $18 to $33. (715)536-8773

MERRILLAN — C2 *Jackson*

JACKSON COUNTY/EAST ARBUTUS (Public) From Jct of US-12 & SH-54, E 5.8 mi to CH-K, N 6.4 mi to Clay School Rd, E 1.5 mi to Klima Rd., N .5 mi. Avail: 136 E (30 amps). 2021 rates: $20 to $28. (715)333-5832

JACKSON COUNTY/WEST ARBUTUS (Public) From Jct of US-12 & SH-54, E 5.8 mi to CH-K, N 7.8 mi to Hatfield, follow signs (R). Avail: 36 E (20/30 amps). 2021 rates: $20 to $28. May 15 to Sep 01. (715)333-5832

MERRIMAC — D3 *Sauk*

MERRY MAC'S CAMPGROUND **Ratings: 8/9.5★/9** (Campground) 79 Avail: 79 W, 79 E (30/50 amps). 2021 rates: $55 to $68. Apr 15 to Oct 15. (608)493-2367, E12995 Halweg Rd, Merrimac, WI 53561

MIDDLETON — E3 *Dane*

MENDOTA PARK (DANE COUNTY PARK) (Public) From Jct of I-90 & US-12, W 17 mi on US-12 to CR-M Century Ave, E 2.5 mi (R). Avail: 30 E (30 amps). 2021 rates: $28. Apr 27 to Oct 12. (608)242-4576

MIKANA — B2 *Barron*

WALDO CARLSON PARK (BARRON COUNTY PARK) (Public) From Jct of I-53 & Hwy 48, NE 12.5 mi on Hwy 48 to park access rd, E 0.5 mi (E). Avail: 29 E (30/50 amps). 2021 rates: $15 to $23. May 01 to Oct 01. (800)272-9829

MILTON — E4 *Rock*

BLACKHAWK CAMPING RESORT
(Campground) (Phone Update) 24 Avail: 24 W, 24 E (30/50 amps). 2021 rates: $55 to $82. Apr 15 to Oct 15. (888)563-7040, 3407 E Blackhawk Dr, Milton, WI 53563

LAKELAND CAMPING RESORT
Ratings: 7.5/6.5/6.5 (Campground) 111 Avail: 9 full hkups, 102 W, 102 E (30/50 amps). 2021 rates: $57 to $84. Apr 15 to Oct 15. (888)563-7040, 2803 E State Rd 59, Milton, WI 53563

MILTON KOA Ratings: 10/10★/10 (RV Park) 164 Avail: 125 full hkups, 39 W, 39 E (30/50 amps). 2021 rates: $45 to $92. Apr 25 to Oct 20. (800)469-5515, 872 E State Rd 59, Milton, WI 53563

MILWAUKEE — E5 *Milwaukee*

MILWAUKEE See also Caledonia & Mukwonago.

WISCONSIN STATE FAIR RV PARK (Public) From Jct of I-94 & 84th St exit, (exit 306) S 50 ft on 84th St (L). 103 Avail: 70 full hkups, 19 W, 33 E (30/50 amps). 2021 rates: $35 to $75. (414)266-7035

MINOCQUA — B3 *Vilas*

PATRICIA LAKE CAMPGROUND & RV PARK **Ratings: 8.5/9★/9.5** (Campground) 34 Avail: 30 full hkups, 4 W, 4 E (30/50 amps). 2021 rates: $42.50 to $45.50. May 01 to Oct 15. (715)356-3198, 8508 Camp Pinemere Rd , Minocqua, WI 54548

MINONG — B1 *Washburn*

TOTOGATIC PARK (WASHBURN COUNTY PARK) (Public) From town, NW 7 mi on CR-I (R). Avail: 69 E (15 amps), Pit toilets. 2021 rates: $17 to $25. May 01 to Oct 31. (715)635-4490

MONTELLO — D3 *Marquette*

BUFFALO LAKE CAMPING RESORT
Ratings: 8.5/10★/10 (Campground) 47 Avail: 8 full hkups, 39 W, 39 E (30/50 amps). 2021 rates: $42 to $67. Apr 15 to Oct 15. (608)297-2915, 555 Lake Ave, Montello, WI 53949

CROOKED RIVER CAMPGROUND **Ratings: 5.5/8.5/7** (Campground) 24 Avail: 4 full hkups, 20 W, 20 E (30/50 amps). 2021 rates: $40 to $65. Apr 15 to Oct 15. (608)297-7307, W 4054 11th Rd, Montello, WI 53949

KILBY LAKE CAMPGROUND **Ratings: 6/7/8** (Campground) 37 Avail: 37 W, 37 E (30/50 amps). 2021 rates: $37 to $41. Apr 15 to Oct 15. (877)497-2344, N 4492 Fern Ave, Montello, WI 53949

LAKE ARROWHEAD CAMPGROUND **Ratings: 8.5/8/8.5** (Campground) 120 Avail: 45 full hkups, 75 W, 75 E (30/50 amps). 2021 rates: $49 to $82. Apr 15 to Oct 15. (920)295-3000, W781 Fox Ct, Montello, WI 53949

WILDERNESS CAMPGROUND **Ratings: 7.5/9★/9.5** (Campground) 176 Avail: 28 full hkups, 148 W, 148 E (20/50 amps). 2021 rates: $52 to $59. Apr 14 to Oct 08. (608)297-2002, N 1499 State Hwy 22, Montello, WI 53949

MOSINEE — C3 *Marathon*

BIG EAU PLEINE COUNTY PARK (Public) From town, W 6 mi on SR-153 to Eau Pleine Parks Rd, S 3 mi (E). Avail: 70 E (20/30 amps), Pit toilets. 2021 rates: $15 to $17. May 02 to Oct 31. (715)261-1566

MOUNTAIN — C4 *Oconto*

CHUTE POND CAMPGROUND (OCONTO COUNTY PARK) (Public) From town: Go 5 mi S on Hwy-32/64. 72 Avail. 2021 rates: $25. Apr 01 to Nov 30. (715)276-6261

MUKWONAGO — E4 *Waukesha*

COUNTRY VIEW CAMPGROUND **Ratings: 7/9.5★/8** (Campground) 150 Avail: 37 full hkups, 113 W, 113 E (20/30 amps). 2021 rates: $38 to $42. May 01 to Oct 15. (262)662-3654, S 110 W 26400 Craig Ave, Mukwonago, WI 53149

MUKWONAGO PARK (WAUKESHA COUNTY PARK) (Public) From jct US-83 & US-99: Go 3 mi W on US-99. Entrance fee. 30 Avail: Pit toilets. 2021 rates: $20. Apr 01 to Nov 02. (262)548-7801

MUSCODA — E2 *Grant*

RIVERSIDE CAMPGROUND (Public) From Hwy-80 north of town, follow signs. Avail: 31 E. 2021 rates: $10 to $25. May 01 to Oct 30. (608)739-2924

VICTORIA RIVERSIDE PARK (Public) From Jct of Hwys 80 & 133, N 1 mi on Hwy 80 to River St, E 0.2 mi (R). Avail: 32 E (15 amps). 2021 rates: $10 to $25. May 15 to Oct 01. (608)604-7094

MUSKEGO — E4 *Waukesha*

MUSKEGO PARK (WAUKESHA COUNTY PARK) (Public) From jct I-43 & CR Y(Racine Ave): Go 2-1/2 mi S on CR Y, then 3/4 mi W on CR L (Janesville Rd). 17 Avail: Pit toilets. 2021 rates: $20. (262)548-7801

NECEDAH — D3 *Juneau*

BUCKHORN (Public State Park) From jct Hwy 21 & Hwy 80/CR Q: Go 3-1/4 mi S on Hwy 80/CR Q, then 4-1/2 mi E on CR G. Avail: 10 E Pit toilets. 2021 rates: $18 to $33. (608)565-2789

MOONLITE TRAILS CAMPGROUND **Ratings: 4.5/7.5/6.5** (Campground) 20 Avail: 20 W, 20 E (30/50 amps). 2021 rates: $25. Apr 15 to Nov 30. (608)565-6936, W 4641 9th St East, Necedah, WI 54646

ST JOSEPH RESORT **Ratings: 5.5/5.5/6.5** (Campground) 25 Avail: 25 W, 25 E (30/50 amps). 2021 rates: $25. May 01 to Oct 15. (608)565-7258, W 5630 Hwy 21, Necedah, WI 54646

WILDERNESS PARK (JUNEAU COUNTY PARK) (Public) From Jct of Hwy 21 & Cnty G (E edge of town), N 9 mi on Cnty G to 8th St E 4 mi (R). Avail: 107 E (20/30 amps). 2021 rates: $17 to $23. May 01 to Oct 01. (608)565-7285

NEILLSVILLE — C2 *Clark*

SHERWOOD CAMPGROUND (CLARK COUNTY PARK) (Public) From town, SE 17 mi on Hwy 73 to CR-Z, S 2 mi to Badger Ave (E). Avail: 34 E (20/30 amps), Pit toilets. 2021 rates: $8 to $14. May 01 to Nov 01. (715)743-5140

SNYDER CAMPGROUND (CLARK COUNTY PARK) (Public) From town, W 6 mi on Hwy 10 to CR-B, N 0.5 follow signs (R). Avail: 40 E (20/30 amps), Pit toilets. 2021 rates: $17 to $26. (715)743-5140

NEKOOSA — C3 *Wood*

HOMEGROUNDS RV PARK **Ratings: 5/9.5★/5.5** (RV Park) Avail: 129 full hkups (30/50 amps). 2021 rates: $30 to $45. Apr 15 to Nov 01. (888)704-6588, 1312 Akron Drive, Nekoosa, WI 54457

LAKESIDE FIRE CAMPGROUND **Ratings: 6.5/7/7** (Campground) 110 Avail: 110 W, 110 E (30/50 amps). 2021 rates: $50 to $60. Apr 15 to Oct 15. (715)886-3871, 14014 County Rd Z, Nekoosa, WI 54457

NELSON — C1 *Buffalo*

NELSON'S LANDING RV PARK **Ratings: 7/9.5★/6** (RV Park) Avail: 91 full hkups (50 amps). 2021 rates: $45 to $55. May 01 to Oct 31. (507)951-2842, E 203 Cleveland St, Nelson, WI 54756

NEW AUBURN — C2 *Chippewa*

MORRIS ERICKSON PARK (CHIPPEWA COUNTY PARK) (Public) From town: Go 8 mi NE on CR M & Hwy 40. Avail: 28 E Pit toilets. 2021 rates: $16 to $23. May 02 to Oct 31. (715)726-7880

SAND HAVEN CAMPGROUND **Ratings: 6/UI/8.5** (Campground) Avail: 21 full hkups (30/50 amps). 2021 rates: $30 to $55. (715)967-2067, 30714 152nd St, New Auburn, WI 54757

NEW GLARUS — E3 *Green*

NEW GLARUS WOODS (Public State Park) From jct Hwy 69 & CR NN: Go 1/8 mi W on CR NN. Avail: 1 E Pit toilets. 2021 rates: $18 to $33. (608)527-2335

NEW LISBON — D3 *Juneau*

RIVERSIDE PARK (Public) From Jct of I-90/94 & Hwy 80 (exit 61), W 0.6 mi on Hwy 80 to Hog Island Rd, N 0.05 mi (R). Avail: 50 E (20/30 amps). 2021 rates: $15 to $25. May 15 to Oct 15. (608)562-3534

NEW LONDON — C4 *Waupaca*

HUCKLBERRY ACRES CAMPGROUND **Ratings: 5.5/8/6.5** (Campground) 64 Avail: 64 W, 64 E (30/50 amps). 2021 rates: $40. May 01 to Oct 15. (920)982-4628, 9005 Hucklberry Rd, New London, WI 54961

WOLF RIVER TRIPS & CAMPGROUND **Ratings: 7/8/8** (Campground) 198 Avail: 64 full hkups, 134 W, 134 E (30/50 amps). 2021 rates: $48. Apr 15 to Oct 15. (920)982-2458, E8041 County Hwy X, New London, WI 54961

OAKDALE — D3 *Monroe*

GRANGER'S CAMPGROUND **Ratings: 3/8.5★/3.5** (Campground) 27 Avail: 14 full hkups, 13 W, 13 E (30 amps). 2021 rates: $30. Apr 01 to Nov 01. (608)372-4511, 566 N Oakwood St, Tomah, WI 54660

OAKDALE KOA **Ratings: 8.5/10★/8.5** (Campground) 70 Avail: 50 full hkups, 20 W, 20 E (30/50 amps). 2021 rates: $37 to $65. Apr 01 to Oct 15. (800)562-1737, 200 Jay St, Oakdale, WI 54649

OCONTO — C5 *Oconto*

HOLTWOOD (OCONTO CITY PARK) (Public) From Jct of US-41 & SR-22, S 0.5 mi on US-41 to McDonald St, W 0.1 mi to Holtwood Way, N 0.05 mi (R). 152 Avail: (30/50 amps). 2021 rates: $28 to $30. May 15 to Oct 01. (920)834-7732

NORTH BAY SHORE (Public State Park) From town: Go 9 mi NE on CR-Y. 34 Avail: 24 W, 33 E. 2021 rates: $25. (920)834-6825

ONTARIO — D2 *Vernon*

WILDCAT MOUNTAIN (Public State Park) From Jct of Hwys 131 & 33, E 1.5 mi on Hwy 33 to park office rd (L). Entrance fee required. Avail: 1 E Pit toilets. 2021 rates: $18 to $33. (888)947-2757

OSHKOSH — D4 *Winnebago*

HICKORY OAKS FLY IN & CAMPGROUND Ratings: 6.5/8★/9 (Campground) 58 Avail: 31 W, 31 E (30/50 amps). 2021 rates: $34 to $40. May 01 to Nov 01. (920)235-8076, 3485 Vinland Rd, Oshkosh, WI 54901

KALBUS' COUNTRY HARBOR **Ratings: 7/9.5★/8.5** (Campground) 72 Avail: 8 full hkups, 64 W, 64 E (30/50 amps). 2021 rates: $40 to $65. May 01 to Oct 31. (920)426-0062, 5309 Lake Rd, Oshkosh, WI 54902

OSSEO — C2 *Trempealeau*

STONEY CREEK RV RESORT

good sam park **Ratings: 10/10★/10** (Campground) 163 Avail: 132 full hkups, 31 W, 31 E (30/50 amps). 2021 rates: $43 to $80. Apr 01 to Nov 01. (715)597-2102, 50483 Oak Grove Rd, Osseo, WI 54758

PARDEEVILLE — D3 *Columbia*

DUCK CREEK CAMPGROUND **Ratings: 8/9★/8.5** (Campground) 50 Avail: 16 full hkups, 34 W, 34 E (30 amps). 2021 rates: $45 to $55. Apr 25 to Oct 12. (608)429-2425, W6560 County Rd G, Pardeeville, WI 53954

GLACIER VALLEY CAMPGROUND **Ratings: 6/7.5/8.5** (Campground) 60 Avail: 60 W, 60 E (30 amps). 2021 rates: $45 to $62. Apr 15 to Oct 15. (920)348-5488, N8129 Larson Rd, Cambria, WI 53923

INDIAN TRAILS CAMPGROUND **Ratings: 8/9★/10** (Campground) 176 Avail: 22 full hkups, 154 W, 154 E (30/50 amps). 2021 rates: $48 to $71. Apr 15 to Oct 15. (608)429-3244, W6445 Haynes Rd, Pardeeville, WI 53954

PELICAN LAKE — B4 *Oneida*

PELICAN LAKE CAMPGROUND **Ratings: 8/8★/8.5** (Campground) Avail: 10 full hkups (30/50 amps). 2021 rates: $42. May 01 to Oct 15. (715)487-4600, 2060 Cty Road Q, Pelican Lake, WI 54463

PESHTIGO — C5 *Marinette*

BADGER PARK (Public) From Jct of Hwy 41 & Emery Ave (in town), N .25 mi on Emery Ave (E). 35 Avail: 35 W, 35 E (50 amps). 2021 rates: $27. May 01 to Sep 26. (715)582-4321

PHILLIPS — B3 *Price*

SOLBERG LAKE PARK (PRICE COUNTY PARK) (Public) From town, N 2.5 mi on Old Hwy 13 to West Solberg Lake Rd, N 2.5 mi (R). Avail: 60 E (50 amps). 2021 rates: $25. (715)339-6371

PITTSVILLE — C3 *Wood*

DEXTER PARK (WOOD COUNTY PARK) (Public) From Jct of Hwys 80 & 54, W 1 mi on Hwy 54 (R). Avail: 86 E (30/50 amps). 2021 rates: $16 to $28. May 01 to Oct 31. (715)421-8422

PLAIN — D3 *Sauk*

WHITE MOUND (SAUK COUNTY PARK) (Public) From jct Hwy 23 & CR GG: Go 2 mi W on CR GG, then 1/2 mi N on Lake Rd. Avail: 37 E. 2021 rates: $5 to $10. Apr 01 to Nov 15. (608)355-4800

PLUM CITY — C1 *Pierce*

NUGGET LAKE (PIERCE COUNTY PARK) (Public) From center of town: Go 3-1/2 mi W on US 10, then 3 mi N on CR CC, then 2 mi E on CR HH. Entrance fee required. Avail: 55 E. 2021 rates: $25. Apr 01 to Nov 30. (715)639-5611

PLYMOUTH — D5 *Sheboygan*

PLYMOUTH ROCK CAMPING RESORT

good sam park **Ratings: 8/7.5/7.5** (Campground) 241 Avail: 20 full hkups, 221 W, 221 E (30/50 amps). 2021 rates: $65 to $85. Apr 15 to Oct 15. (888)563-7040, N7271 Lando St, Plymouth, WI 53073

PORTAGE — D3 *Columbia*

PRIDE OF AMERICA CAMPING RESORT **Ratings: 9/9.5★/9.5** (RV Park) 122 Avail: 66 full hkups, 56 W, 56 E (30/50 amps). 2021 rates: $54.41 to $83.14. Apr 15 to Oct 15. (800)236-6395, W7520 West Bush Rd, Pardeeville, WI 53954

SKY HIGH CAMPING RESORT

good sam park **Ratings: 8.5/10★/10** (Campground) 125 Avail: 38 full hkups, 87 W, 87 E (30/50 amps). 2021 rates: $38 to $58. (608)742-2572, N5740 Sky High Dr, Portage, WI 53901

PORTERFIELD — C5 *Marinette*

DIAMOND LAKE FAMILY CAMPGROUND **Ratings: 5.5/8/7.5** (Campground) 25 Avail: 5 full hkups, 20 W, 20 E (30/50 amps). 2021 rates: $42 to $47. May 01 to Oct 31. (715)789-2113, W5449 Loomis Rd, Porterfield, WI 54159

POTOSI — E2 *Grant*

MISSISSIPPI RIVER - POOLS 11-22 - COE/GRANT RIVER (Public Corps) From town, S 3 mi on SR-133 (L). Avail: 63 E (50 amps). 2021 rates: $14 to $20. May 01 to Oct 25. (563)582-0881

PRAIRIE DU CHIEN — E2 *Crawford*

SPORTS UNLIMITED CAMPGROUND & BARN YARD 9 GOLF COURSE **Ratings: 7.5/8.5★/8** (Campground) Avail: 30 full hkups (30/50 amps). 2021 rates: $35 to $55. Apr 15 to Oct 15. (608)326-2141, 32750 Cty Rd K, Prairie du Chien, WI 53821

RACINE — E5 *Racine*

CLIFFSIDE PARK (RACINE COUNTY PARK) (Public) From Jct of I-94 & Seven Mile Rd (Exit 326), E 4.5 mi from Seven Mile Rd to SR-32/Douglas Ave, (R) 1 mi on SR-32/Douglas to Six Mile Rd (L) go 2 mi to Michna Rd (L). Park is on the right. 92 Avail: 92 W, 92 E (30/50 amps). 2021 rates: $23. Apr 15 to Oct 15. (800)272-2463

SANDERS PARK (RACINE COUNTY PARK) (Public) From Jct of I-94 & Cnty 'KR' (exit 337), E 5.5 mi on Cnty 'KR' to Wood Rd, N 0.5 mi (R). Avail: 12 E (20/50 amps). 2021 rates: $23. Apr 15 to Oct 15. (262)886-8440

RED CLIFF — A2 *Bayfield*

BUFFALO BAY CAMPGROUND & MARINA (Public) From N end of town, N 3 mi on SR-13 (R). 34 Avail: 34 W, 34 E (30 amps). 2021 rates: $35. May 15 to Oct 15. (715)779-3712

REDGRANITE — D4 *Waushara*

FLANAGAN'S PEARL LAKE CAMPSITE **Ratings: 6/7.5/4.5** (Campground) 50 Avail: 50 W, 50 E (30/50 amps). 2021 rates: $38 to $40. Apr 15 to Oct 15. (920)566-2758, W4585 Pearl Lake Rd, Redgranite, WI 54970

REEDSVILLE — D5 *Manitowoc*

CAMP 10 **Ratings: 8/8/7.5** (Campground) 44 Avail: 44 W, 44 E (20/30 amps). 2021 rates: $42. May 01 to Oct 15. (920)754-4142, 18227 US Hwy 10, Reedsville, WI 54230

RHINELANDER — B3 *Oneida*

WEST BAY CAMPING RESORT **Ratings: 7.5/8★/8** (Membership Park) Avail: 43 full hkups (50 amps). 2021 rates: $34. May 01 to Oct 01. (715)362-3481, 4330 South Shore Dr, Rhinelander, WI 54501

RICE LAKE — B1 *Barron*

NORTHWOOD SHORES CAMPGROUND **Ratings: 8/7.5/8.5** (Campground) Avail: 11 full hkups (30/50 amps). 2021 rates: $50. May 01 to Oct 13. (715)234-1150, 1876 29-3/4 Avenue, Rice Lake, WI 54868

RIO — D3 *Columbia*

SILVER SPRINGS CAMPSITES **Ratings: 8.5/10★/9.5** (Campground) 140 Avail: 5 full hkups, 135 W, 135 E (30/50 amps). 2021 rates: $42 to $67. Apr 15 to Sep 30. (920)992-3537, N5048 Ludwig Rd, Rio, WI 53960

WILLOW MILL CAMPSITE Ratings: 8/8.5★/9.5 (RV Park) 50 Avail: 50 W, 50 E (20/30 amps). 2021 rates: $42 to $44. May 01 to Oct 01. (800)582-0393, N 5830 County Hwy SS, Rio, WI 53960

RIVER FALLS — C1 *St Croix*

HOFFMAN PARK (Public) From Jct of I-94 & Hwy 35 (Exit 3), S 8 mi on Hwy 35 to Division St, E 0.2 mi to Division St (Cty M), W 0.3 mi on Hanson, N 0.2 mi (L). Avail: 15 E (20/30 amps). 2021 rates: $20. Apr 15 to Oct 15. (715)426-3420

ROSHOLT — C3 *Portage*

COLLINS PARK (PORTAGE COUNTY PARK) (Public) From town, NE 12 mi on SR-66 to CR-I, S 1.5 mi (L). Avail: 27 E (20 amps), Pit toilets. 2021 rates: $24. May 15 to Sep 30. (715)346-1433

Time and rates don't stand still. Remember that last year's rates serve as a guideline only. Call ahead for the most current rate information.

ROTHSCHILD — C4 *Marathon*

Travel Services

GANDER RV OF ROTHSCHILD Your new hometown outfitter offering the best regional gear for all your outdoor needs. Your adventure awaits. **SERVICES:** MH mechanical, gunsmithing svc, archery svc, sells outdoor gear, sells fishing gear, sells firearms, staffed RV wash, restrooms. RV Sales. RV supplies, LP gas, dump, RV accessible. Hours: 9am to 8pm.
(877)878-8102 Lat: 44.860315, Lon: -89.636081
1560 County Road XX, Rothschild, WI 54474
rv.ganderoutdoors.com

SARONA — B1 *Washburn*

WHITETAIL RIDGE CAMPGROUND & RV PARK **Ratings: 4.5/8.5/9** (Campground) 11 Avail: 11 W, 11 E (30/50 amps). 2021 rates: $40. Apr 01 to Oct 01. (715)469-3309, N 753 Shallow Lake Rd, Sarona, WI 54870

SAUKVILLE — D5 *Ozaukee*

Travel Services

CAMPING WORLD OF SAUKVILLE/MILWAUKEE As the nation's largest retailer of RV supplies, accessories, services and new and used RVs, Camping World is committed to making your total RV experience better. **SERVICES:** tire, RV appliance, MH mechanical, staffed RV wash, restrooms. RV Sales. RV supplies, LP gas, dump, emergency parking, RV accessible. Hours: 9am - 7pm.
(888)440-5467 Lat: 43.385820, Lon: -87.924560
800 E. Green Bay Avenue, Saukville, WI 53080
www.campingworld.com

SAYNER — B3 *Vilas*

NO HIGHLAND AMERICAN LEGION/FIREFLY LAKE (Public State Park) From Boulder Junction, N 5 mi on US-51 to Hwy M, NE 3 mi to Hwy M, E 1.5 mi, follow sign (R). Entrance fee required. 71 Avail: (15 amps), Pit toilets. 2021 rates: $15 to $17. (715)385-2727

NO HIGHLAND AMERICAN LEGION/PLUM LAKE (Public State Park) From town, W 1 mi on Hwy N (R). Entrance fee required. 16 Avail: Pit toilets. 2021 rates: $20 to $35. May 22 to Sep 05. (715)385-2727

NO HIGHLAND AMERICAN LEGION/RAZORBACK LAKE (Public State Park) From town, W 2.5 mi on Hwy N to Razorback Rd, N 5 mi (R). Entrance fee required. 53 Avail: Pit toilets. 2021 rates: $16 to $20. (715)385-2727

NO HIGHLAND AMERICAN LEGION/STARRETT LAKE (Public State Park) From town, S 7.5 mi on Hwy M to N Muskellunge Rd, W 5 mi (L). Entrance fee required. 38 Avail: Pit toilets. 2021 rates: $16 to $21. May 04 to Oct 10. (715)385-2727

SHAWANO — C4 *Shawano*

PINE GROVE CAMPGROUND **Ratings: 8/8.5/9.5** (Campground) 100 Avail: 12 full hkups, 88 W, 88 E (30/50 amps). 2021 rates: $55 to $70. Apr 15 to Nov 30. (715)787-4555, N5999 Campground Rd, Shawano, WI 54166

SHAWANO LAKE PARK (SHAWNO COUNTY PARK) (Public) From town, NE 5 mi on CR-H, follow signs (R). 90 Avail: 90 W, 90 E (30 amps). 2021 rates: $25 to $30. May 15 to Oct 15. (715)524-4986

SHEBOYGAN — D5 *Sheboygan*

KOHLER-ANDRAE (Public State Park) From Jct of I-43 & exit 120 (V St), E 1 mi on V St to CR-KK, S 1 mi to Old Park Rd, E 0.25 mi (E). Entrance fee required. Avail: 52 E (30/50 amps). 2021 rates: $20 to $35. (920)451-4080

SHELL LAKE — B1 *Washburn*

RED BARN CAMPGROUND **Ratings: 4.5/6.5/7.5** (Campground) 38 Avail: 22 full hkups, 16 W, 16 E (30/50 amps). 2021 rates: $40 to $44. May 01 to Oct 10. (715)468-2575, W6820 Cty Hwy B, Shell Lake, WI 54871

SHELL LAKE CAMPGROUND (Public) From Jct of Hwy 63 & CR-B, S 0.4 mi on Hwy 63 (L). 46 Avail: 38 full hkups, 8 W, 8 E (30 amps). 2021 rates: $30 to $45. May 01 to Oct 15. (715)468-7846

SHERWOOD — D4 *Calument*

HIGH CLIFF (Public State Park) From Appleton, E 5 mi on Hwy 10 to Hwy 114, E 3 mi to State Park Rd, S 3 mi (E). Avail: 32 E (30 amps). 2021 rates: $18 to $33. (920)989-1106

We appreciate your business!

SILVER CLIFF — B4 *Marinette*

MCCASLIN MOUNTAIN CAMPGROUND **Ratings: 5/6.5/6** (Campground) 35 Avail: 35 W, 35 E (20/30 amps). 2021 rates: $25 to $35. May 15 to Dec 01. (715)757-3734, W 15720 County F, Silver Cliff, WI 54104

SISTER BAY — C5 *Door*

DOVETAIL ACRES CAMPGROUND **Ratings: 7/9.5★/7.5** (Campground) Avail: 50 full hkups (50 amps). 2021 rates: $54 to $59. May 15 to Oct 15. (920)868-6218, 10282 Hwy WI-57, Sister Bay, WI 54234

SOLON SPRINGS — A1 *Douglas*

LUCIUS WOODS (Public) From jct CR A & US 53: Go 1/4 mi S, then 1/10 mi E on Marion Ave. Avail: 13 E. 2021 rates: $20 to $25. May 17 to Sep 08. (715)378-4528

SOMERSET — C1 *St Croix*

APPLE RIVER FAMILY CAMPGROUND **Ratings: 7/7/7** (Campground) 127 Avail: 127 W, 127 E (20/50 amps). 2021 rates: $40 to $90. (715)247-3600, 345 Church Hill Rd, Somerset, WI 54025

SPARTA — D2 *La Crosse*

LEON VALLEY CAMPGROUND **Ratings: 5.5/7.5★/7.5** (Campground) 57 Avail: 57 W, 57 E (30/50 amps). 2021 rates: $40. Apr 01 to Oct 31. (608)269-6400, 9050 Jancing Ave , Sparta, WI 54656

MILITARY PARK PINE VIEW REC AREA (FORT MCCOY) (Public) From jct I-90 East & Hwy 27 (exit 25 Sparta), Left on Hwy 27 (Black River St), then right on Montgomery St (3rd set of lights), then left 7 mi on Hwy 21 (2nd stop sign), follow signs. 102 Avail: 64 full hkups, 21 W, 21 E (30/50 amps). 2021 rates: $17 to $50. (608)388-3517

SPRING GREEN — E3 *Sauk*

FIRESIDE CAMPGROUND **Ratings: 7.5/7/7** (Campground) 68 Avail: 15 full hkups, 53 W, 53 E (30/50 amps). 2021 rates: $33.50 to $43.50. Apr 06 to Nov 30. (608)583-5111, 33533 Jay Ln, Lone Rock, WI 53556

TOWER HILL (Public State Park) 3 mi SE via US-14 and Hwy-23. 11 Avail: Pit toilets. May 15 to Oct 09. (608)588-2116

WISCONSIN RIVERSIDE RESORT **Ratings: 9.5/8.5/10** (RV Park) Avail: 95 full hkups (30/50 amps). 2021 rates: $45 to $80. Apr 01 to Nov 01. (608)588-2826, S13220 Shifflet Rd, Spring Green, WI 53588

SPRING VALLEY — C1 *St Croix*

EAU GALLE LAKE - COE/HIGHLAND RIDGE (Public Corps) From Jct of I-94 & exit 24, S 2 mile on CR-B (exit 24) to CR-N, E 2 mi to CR-NN, S 2 mi (R). Avail: 35 E (50 amps). 2021 rates: $20 to $24. Apr 01 to Nov 30. (715)778-5562

ST CROIX FALLS — B1 *Polk*

INTERSTATE (Public State Park) From Jct of US-8 & SR-35, S 0.5 mi on SR-35 (R). Avail: 27 E (50 amps). 2021 rates: $18 to $33. (715)483-3747

ST GERMAIN — B3 *Vilas*

LYNN ANN'S CAMPGROUND **Ratings: 8/8.5★/9.5** (Campground) 80 Avail: 40 full hkups, 40 W, 40 E (30 amps). 2021 rates: $40 to $60. May 01 to Oct 12. (715)542-3456, 1597 S Shore, St Germain, WI 54558

STEVENS POINT — C3 *Portage*

DUBAY PARK (Public) From Jct of US-51 & Hwy 10, W 7 mi on Hwy 10 to CR-E, N 8 mi (R). Avail: 31 E (20 amps), Pit toilets. 2021 rates: $24. May 01 to Oct 31. (715)346-1433

JORDAN PARK (Public) From town, NE 4 mi on Hwy 66 to CR-Y, N 0.25 mi (L). Avail: 22 E (20 amps). 2021 rates: $24. May 01 to Oct 31. (715)346-1433

STOCKBRIDGE — D4 *Calumet*

CALUMET COUNTY PARK (Public) From town, N 2 mi on Hwy 55 to Cnty Trunk Rd, W 2 mi (E). Note: 40' RV length limit. Avail: 59 E (20/50 amps). 2021 rates: $20 to $24. Apr 01 to Nov 01. (920)439-1008

LAKEVIEW RV CAMPGROUND AND CABINS **Ratings: 7/9.5★/9.5** (Campground) 58 Avail: 58 W, 58 E (30/50 amps). 2021 rates: $52 to $55. Apr 15 to Oct 15. (920)439-1495, N4475 Ledge Rd, Chilton, WI 53014

STOUGHTON — E4 *Dane*

BADGERLAND CAMPGROUND **Ratings: 7/8.5★/10** (Campground) 49 Avail: 49 W, 49 E (30/50 amps). 2021 rates: $49 to $57. Apr 01 to Oct 30. (608)873-5800, 2671 Circle Dr, Stoughton, WI 53589

LAKE KEGONSA (Public State Park) From Jct of I-90 & CR-N (exit 147), S 1 mi on CR-N to Koshkonong Rd, W 1.5 mi to Door Creek Rd, S 1 mi. Entrance fee required. Avail: 29 E (30/50 amps). 2021 rates: $20 to $35. (608)873-9695

STRUM — C2 *Trempealeau*

CRYSTAL LAKE CAMPGROUND (Public) From Jct of I-94 & Hwy 10, W 9 mi on Hwy 10 to Woodland Dr, S 100 ft (L). 42 Avail: 21 full hkups, 21 W, 21 E (20 amps). 2021 rates: $25 to $27. May 15 to Oct 01. (715)533-2664

STURGEON BAY — C5 *Door*

HARBOUR VILLAGE RESORT **Ratings: 7.5/9/9** (Membership Park) 85 Avail: 85 W, 85 E (30/50 amps). 2021 rates: $55 to $73. May 15 to Oct 15. (920)743-0274, 5840 Hwy 42, Sturgeon Bay, WI 54235

POTAWATOMI (Public State Park) From Hwy 42/57 (in Green Bay), N 40 mi to County Trunk PD, S 1 mi (R). Entrance fee required. Avail: 25 E (30/50 amps), Pit toilets. 2021 rates: $18 to $33. (920)746-2890

TRANQUIL TIMBERS CAMPING RETREAT
good sam park
Ratings: 6.5/8★/7.5 (Campground) 63 Avail: 13 full hkups, 50 W, 50 E (30/50 amps). 2021 rates: $61 to $73. Apr 15 to Oct 15. (888)563-7040, 3668 Grondin Rd, Sturgeon Bay, WI 54235

YOGI BEAR'S JELLYSTONE PARK **Ratings: 8.5/8.5/8** (Campground) 170 Avail: 10 full hkups, 160 W, 160 E (30/50 amps). 2021 rates: $48 to $77. May 16 to Sep 10. (920)743-9001, 3677 May Rd, Sturgeon Bay, WI 54235

SUMMIT LAKE — B4 *Langlade*

JACK LAKE VETERANS MEMORIAL PARK (Public) From Jct of Hwy 45 & Cnty Trunk J, E 3 mi on Cnty Trunk J (E). Avail: 48 E (30 amps). 2021 rates: $30. May 01 to Dec 01. (715)623-6214

SUPERIOR — A1 *Douglas*

AMNICON FALLS (Public State Park) From town, E 10 mi on Hwy 2 to CR-U, N 0.5 mi (L). Entrance fee required. 26 Avail. 2021 rates: $16 to $21. (715)398-3000

MONT DU LAC RESORT
good sam park
Ratings: 10/10★/10 (RV Resort) 37 Avail: 29 full hkups, 8 W, 8 E (30/50 amps). 2021 rates: $57 to $129. (218)626-3797, 3125 South Mont du Lac Rd. , Superior, WI 54880

NORTHLAND CAMPING & RV PARK **Ratings: 7/7.5/8.5** (Campground) Avail: 60 full hkups (30/50 amps). 2021 rates: $40. May 15 to Oct 15. (715)398-3327, 6377 E State Rd 13, South Range, WI 54874

PATTISON (Public State Park) From town, S 13 mi on Hwy 35 (L). Entrance fee required. Avail: 17 E (30 amps), Pit toilets. 2021 rates: $18 to $33. (715)399-3111

TOMAHAWK — B3 *Lincoln*

OTTER LAKE RECREATION AREA (LINCOLN COUNTY PARK) (Public) From town: Go 3 mi S on US-51, then 7 mi E on CR-S, Stevenson Rd, Grundy Rd, Bear Trail Rd & Otter Lake Rd. 25 Avail: Pit toilets. 2021 rates: $15. May 02 to Oct 31. (715)536-0327

TONY — B2 *Rusk*

JOSIE CREEK PARK (Public) From town, E 1 mi on Hwy 8 to CR-X, N 2 mi (L). 24 Avail: (30 amps), Pit toilets. 2021 rates: $18 to $23. May 01 to Dec 01. (715)532-2113

TREGO — B1 *Washburn*

LOG CABIN RESORT & CAMPGROUND **Ratings: 7/7.5/7.5** (Campground) 20 Avail: 3 full hkups, 17 W, 17 E (30 amps). 2021 rates: $44 to $54. May 01 to Oct 15. (715)635-2959, N 7470 Log Cabin Dr, Trego, WI 54888

So you're the one with ""pooch'' duty? Please make a clean sweep of it! Your fellow RVers will appreciate it!

TREMPEALEAU — D2 *Trempealeau*

LAKE ROAD CAMPGROUND (Campground) (Rebuilding) 8 Avail: 8 W, 8 E (50 amps). 2021 rates: $47. Apr 15 to Oct 15. (715)831-8003, 23828 Lake Road, Trempealeau, WI 54661

PERROT (Public State Park) From town, W 3.5 mi on park rd (E). Avail: 38 E (30/50 amps), Pit toilets. 2021 rates: $18 to $33. (608)534-6409

TURTLE LAKE — B1 *Barron*

ST CROIX RV PARK **Ratings: 8/6/6.5** (Campground) 17 Avail: 17 W, 17 E (30/50 amps). 2021 rates: $27. May 01 to Oct 31. (715)986-4777, 777 Hwy 8 & 63, Turtle Lake, WI 54889

TURTLE LAKE RV PARK Ratings: 5.5/8/7.5 (Campground) Avail: 30 full hkups (30/50 amps). 2021 rates: $35. Apr 15 to Oct 15. (715)986-4140, 750 US Hwy 8 & 63S, Turtle Lake, WI 54889

TWO RIVERS — D5 *Manitowoc*

POINT BEACH (Public State Park) From town, N 4 mi on Cnty Hwy O to park access rd, E 0.3 mi (L). Entrance fee required. 131 Avail: 22 W, 58 S, 73 E (30 amps), Pit toilets. 2021 rates: $20 to $33. (920)794-7480

SCHEFFEL'S HIDEAWAY CAMPGROUND **Ratings: 7/8.5★/9.5** (Campground) 63 Avail: 36 full hkups, 27 W, 27 E (30/50 amps). 2021 rates: $37 to $44. (920)657-1270, 6511 County Rd O, Two Rivers, WI 54241

SEA GULL MARINA & CAMPGROUND **Ratings: 5/8.5★/6.5** (Campground) 40 Avail: 22 full hkups, 18 W, 18 E (30/50 amps). 2021 rates: $23 to $37. May 15 to Oct 15. (920)794-7533, 1400 Lake St, Two Rivers, WI 54241

VILLAGE INN ON THE LAKE HOTEL & RV PARK **Ratings: 8.5/9★/8** (RV Park) Avail: 24 full hkups (30/50 amps). 2021 rates: $68 to $78. (920)794-8818, 3310 Memorial Dr, Two Rivers, WI 54241

VIOLA — D2 *Vernon*

BANKER PARK (Public) At jct Hwy-131 & Hwy-56. 12 Avail. (608)627-1831

WARRENS — D2 *Monroe*

JELLYSTONE PARK WARRENS **Ratings: 8.5/9★/9.5** (RV Park) Avail: 393 full hkups (30/50 amps). 2021 rates: $50 to $85. Apr 15 to Oct 15. (888)386-9644, 1500 Jellystone Park Dr, Warrens, WI 54666

WASHBURN — A2 *Bayfield*

MEMORIAL PARK (Public) From town: Go N on Memorial Park Lane. Avail: 45 E. 2021 rates: $27 to $35. May 15 to Oct 15. (715)373-6160

THOMPSON'S WEST END PARK (Public) From Jct of Hwy 13 & 8th St, S 0.3 mi on 8th St (E). Avail: 50 E (20/50 amps). 2021 rates: $27 to $35. Apr 15 to Oct 15. (715)373-6160

WATERTOWN — E4 *Dodge*

RIVER BEND RV RESORT **Ratings: 8/9.5★/8.5** (RV Resort) 82 Avail: 82 W, 82 E (30/50 amps). 2021 rates: $55 to $85. (920)261-7505, W 6940 Rubidell Rd, Watertown, WI 53094

WAUPACA — C4 *Waupaca*

HARTMAN CREEK (Public State Park) From town, W 6 mi on Hwy 54 to Hartman Creek Rd, S 1.6 mi (L). Avail: 24 E (20/50 amps). 2021 rates: $18 to $33. Apr 02 to Nov 30. (715)258-2372

WAUPACA S'MORE FUN CAMPGROUND **Ratings: 8.5/9★/8.5** (Campground) 66 Avail: 11 full hkups, 55 W, 55 E (30/50 amps). 2021 rates: $34 to $55. May 01 to Oct 06. (715)258-8010, E2411 Holmes Rd, Waupaca, WI 54981

WAUSAU — C3 *Marathon*

MARATHON PARK (Public) From Jct of I-39/51 & Hwy 52E (exit 192), E 0.6 mi on Hwy 52E/Stewart Ave (R). Note: No fire allowed. Avail: 24 E (20/30 amps). 2021 rates: $18 to $23. May 02 to Oct 31. (715)261-1566

WAUSAUKEE — B5 *Marinette*

EVERGREEN PARK & CAMPGROUND
good sam park
Ratings: 5/9.5★/8.5 (Public) From jct WI 180 & US 141: Go 1 mi N on US 141, then 1/3 mi E on North Ave, then 178 ft SE on Harrison Ave (R). 40 Avail: 32 full hkups, 8 W, 8 E (30/50 amps). 2021 rates: $39. May 01 to Oct 15. (715)856-5341

WAUTOMA — D3 *Marquette*

LAKE OF THE WOODS CAMPGROUND
good sam park **Ratings: 7/7.5/8** (Campground) 159 Avail: 6 full hkups, 150 W, 150 E (20/30 amps). 2021 rates: $50 to $75. (888)563-7040, N9070 14th Ave, Wautoma, WI 54982

WEST BEND — D4 *Washington*

LAKE LENWOOD BEACH & CAMPGROUND **Ratings: 7/9★/8.5** (Campground) 60 Avail: 45 full hkups, 15 W, 15 E (30/50 amps). 2021 rates: $48 to $52. Apr 21 to Oct 08. (262)334-1335, 7053 Lenwood Dr, West Bend, WI 53090

WEST SALEM — D2 *La Crosse*

NESHONOC LAKESIDE CAMP-RESORT
good sam park **Ratings: 8.5/9.5★/9.5** (Campground) 102 Avail: 81 full hkups, 21 W, 21 E (30/50 amps). 2021 rates: $64 to $108. Apr 15 to Oct 15. (888)563-7040, N 5334 Neshonoc Rd , West Salem, WI 54669

VETERANS MEMORIAL CAMPGROUND (Public) From Jct of I-90 & SR 16 (exit 5): Go 3 3/4 mi N on SR 16 to CR-VP (R). 120 Avail: 56 W, 57 E (30/50 amps). 2021 rates: $20.25 to $31.50. Apr 15 to Oct 15. (608)789-8599

WHITE LAKE — C4 *Langlade*

9 MILE ALL SPORT RESORT **Ratings: 4.5/7/7** (Campground) Avail: 25 full hkups (30/50 amps). 2021 rates: $45. (715)484-8908, N5751 Hwy 55, White lake, WI 54491

WILD ROSE — D3 *Waushara*

EVERGREEN CAMPSITES & RESORT **Ratings: 9/10★/10** (Campground) 194 Avail: 78 full hkups, 116 W, 116 E (30/50 amps). 2021 rates: $49.95 to $76.95. Apr 15 to Oct 15. (920)622-3498, W5449 Archer Lane, Wild Rose, WI 54984

LUWISOMO CAMPGROUND **Ratings: 3.5/7/6.5** (Campground) 43 Avail: 38 W, 43 E (30 amps). 2021 rates: $45. May 28 to Oct 03. (920)622-3350, W5421 Aspen Rd, Wild Rose, WI 54984

WILTON — D2 *Monroe*

TUNNEL TRAIL CAMPGROUND **Ratings: 7/7.5/9** (Campground) 110 Avail: 51 W, 51 E (30/50 amps). 2021 rates: $43. May 01 to Oct 15. (608)435-6829, 26983 State Hwy 71, Wilton, WI 54670

WINTER — B2 *Sawyer*

FLAMBEAU RIVER/CONNORS LAKE (Public State Park) From Jct of US-8 & SR M, N 17 mi on SR M to Connors Lake (L). Entrance fee required. Note: 45' RV length limit. Avail: 4 E Pit toilets. 2021 rates: $12 to $14. May 21 to Sep 06. (715)332-5271

FLAMBEAU RIVER/LAKE OF THE PINES (Public State Park) From Jct of SR-13 & SR-W, NW 18 mi on SR-W to Lake of the Pines Rd, N 1.5 mi; or From Jct of Hwys 70 & W, SE 17 mi on Hwy W to Lake of the Pines Rd, N 1.5 mi (E) Entrance fee required. 30 Avail: Pit toilets. 2021 rates: $16 to $21. Apr 15 to Dec 15. (715)332-5271

TIPS FOR THE BBQ CHEF: BURGERS - Use fresh meat and mix in ingredients-onions, garlic, chopped jalapeno or bell peppers, oregano, BBQ or hot sauce-sprinkle salt and pepper just before going on the grill. Cook 3 to 5 mins per side to 140-degree internal temp. Tip: Don't press down on the patties during cooking or you'll squeeze out the delicious juices. BEEF BRISKET - Marinate a 3 to 4 lb brisket for 24 hrs. or more in Worcestershire or teriyaki sauce with garlic and black pepper. Cook for 3 to 5 mins per side on direct high heat, then indirect heat for 15-20 mins to 130-degree internal temp (medium-rare). FISH FILLETS OR STEAKS (such as salmon, striped bass, and mahi-mahi) - Cook 5 to 8 mins per side (depending on heat) or to 130 to 135-degree internal temp. BONELESS CHICKEN BREASTS - Marinate for 30 mins or more or rub both sides with a spice mix. Cook over high heat (375-400 degrees) for 4 to 5 mins per side, then indirect heat for 8 to 12 mins to 160-165 internal temp.

WISCONSIN DELLS — D3 *Adams*

WISCONSIN DELLS See also Arkdale, Bancroft, Baraboo, Coloma, DeForest, Green Lake, Hancock, Kingston, Lake Delton, Lodi, Lyndon Station, Merrimac, Montello, Necedah, Nekoosa, Oakdale, Pardeeville, Portage, Redgranite, Rio, Spring Green, Warrens, Wautoma, Wild Rose, Wilton & Wonewoc.

ARROWHEAD RESORT CAMPGROUND
good sam park **Ratings: 7.5/9★/9** (Campground) 190 Avail: 15 full hkups, 175 W, 175 E (30 amps). 2021 rates: $36 to $68. Apr 15 to Oct 15. (888)563-7040, W1530 Arrowhead Rd, Wisconsin Dells, WI 53965

BASS LAKE CAMPGROUND **Ratings: 5.5/7.5/8** (Campground) 42 Avail: 42 W, 42 E (20/30 amps). 2021 rates: $44. May 01 to Oct 01. (608)666-2311, N 1497 Southern Rd, Lyndon Station, WI 53944

BONANZA CAMPING RESORT **Ratings: 7.5/8.5★/7.5** (Campground) 150 Avail: 66 full hkups, 84 W, 84 E (30/50 amps). 2021 rates: $65 to $75. Apr 01 to Oct 20. (608)254-8124, 1770 Wisconsin Dells Pkwy, Wisconsin Dells, WI 53965

CHRISTMAS MOUNTAIN VILLAGE **Ratings: 10/9.5★/10** (RV Park) Avail: 91 full hkups (30/50 amps). 2021 rates: $55. (608)253-1000, S944 Christmas Mtn Rd, Wisconsin Dells, WI 53965

DELL PINES CAMPGROUND **Ratings: 8/9★/8.5** (Campground) 91 Avail: 54 full hkups, 37 W, 37 E (30/50 amps). 2021 rates: $41 to $59. May 01 to Oct 01. (608)356-5898, E 10562 Shady Lane Rd, Baraboo, WI 53913

DELLS CAMPING RESORT **Ratings: 6.5/8/7.5** (Campground) 29 Avail: 9 full hkups, 20 W, 20 E (20/50 amps). 2021 rates: $43 to $62. Apr 15 to Oct 15. (608)305-8404, 1130 Freedom Ct, Wisconsin Dells, WI 53935

EDGE-O-DELLS CAMPING & RV RESORT Ratings: 6.5/9.5★/9 (RV Park) 80 Avail: 26 full hkups, 54 W, 54 E (30/50 amps). 2021 rates: $34 to $119. May 01 to Sep 30. (608)253-4275, N555 US Hwys 12 and 16, Wisconsin Dells, WI 53965

HOLIDAY SHORES CAMPGROUND & RESORT **Ratings: 8/9★/9** (Campground) 79 Avail: 40 full hkups, 39 W, 39 E (30/50 amps). 2021 rates: $46 to $56. May 01 to Oct 15. (608)254-2717, 3901 River Rd, Wisconsin Dells, WI 53965

MIRROR LAKE (Public State Park) From Jct of I-90/94 & Hwy 12 (exit 92), S 0.5 mi on Hwy 12 to Fern Dell Rd, W 1.5 mi (R). Entrance fee required. Avail: 34 E (30 amps). 2021 rates: $20 to $35. (608)254-2333

ROCKY ARBOR (Public State Park) From jct I-90/94 (exit 92) & US 12: Go 200 yds W on US 12, then 2 mi W on Fern Dell Rd. Avail: 18 E. 2021 rates: $16 to $31. May 22 to Sep 04. (608)254-8001

SHANGRI-LA CAMPGROUND **Ratings: 7/9★/7.5** (RV Park) 31 Avail: 31 W, 31 E (30/50 amps). 2021 rates: $62 to $67. May 01 to Oct 15. (608)408-0898, N980 Smith Rd, Wisconsin Dells, WI 53965

SHERWOOD FOREST CAMPING & RV PARK
good sam park **Ratings: 8.5/9.5★/9.5** (Campground) 165 Avail: 54 full hkups, 76 W, 94 E (30/50 amps). 2021 rates: $32 to $63. May 05 to Oct 01. (877)474-3796, 2852 Wisconsin Dells Parkway, Wisconsin Dells, WI 53965

WANNA BEE CAMPGROUND & RV RESORT **Ratings: 7/8★/8.5** (RV Park) 57 Avail: 17 full hkups, 40 W, 40 E (30/50 amps). 2021 rates: $53 to $60. Apr 15 to Oct 15. (608)253-3122, E 10096 Trout Rd, Wisconsin Dells, WI 53965

WISCONSIN DELLS KOA **Ratings: 8.5/9.5★/9** (Campground) 73 Avail: 68 full hkups, 5 W, 5 E (30/50 amps). 2021 rates: $54.17 to $127.63. Apr 17 to Oct 25. (800)254-4177, S235 A Stand Rock Rd, Wisconsin Dells, WI 53965

YOGI BEAR'S JELLYSTONE PARK CAMP-RESORT **Ratings: 9/9/9** (Campground) 196 Avail: 61 full hkups, 135 W, 135 E (20/50 amps). 2021 rates: $50 to $70. May 08 to Sep 20. (800)462-9644, S1915 Ishnala Rd, Wisconsin Dells, WI 53965

WISCONSIN RAPIDS — C3 *Wood*

SOUTH PARK (WOOD COUNTY PARK) (Public) From Jct of Hwy 13 & CR-Z, E 3.5 mi on CR-Z to 64th St, N 1 mi (R). Avail: 54 E (30/50 amps), Pit toilets. 2021 rates: $16 to $28. May 01 to Oct 31. (715)421-8422

Keep one Guide at home, and one in your RV! To purchase additional copies, call 877-209-6655.

WONEWOC — D3 *Sauk*

CHAPPARAL CAMPGROUND & RESORT **Ratings: 8.5/9.5★/9.5** (Campground) 110 Avail: 75 full hkups, 35 W, 35 E (30/50 amps). 2021 rates: $52 to $56. Apr 15 to Oct 31. (608)464-3200, S316 Dreamland Dr, Wonewoc, WI 53968

WOODRUFF — B3 *Oneida*

ARBOR VITAE CAMPGROUND **Ratings: 6.5/8/7** (Campground) 47 Avail: 23 full hkups, 6 W, 18 E (30/50 amps). 2021 rates: $27 to $38. May 01 to Oct 15. (715)356-5146, 10545 Big Arbor Vitae Dr, Arbor Vitae, WI 54568

HIAWATHA TRAILER RESORT
good sam park **Ratings: 9/10★/9.5** (RV Park) From Jct of Hwys 51 & 47: Go E 1/3 mi on Hwy 47 to Old Hwy 51 (Balsam St), then N 1/2 mi (L). **FAC:** paved rds. (170 spaces). Avail: 20 grass, patios, 10 pull-thrus, (25x65), back-ins (21x50), 20 full hkups (30/50 amps), seasonal sites, WiFi @ sites, laundry, firewood. **REC:** Lake Arrowhead: swim, fishing, playground. Pets OK. Partial handicap access. No tents. Big rig sites, eco-friendly. 2021 rates: $42.50 to $47.50. May 01 to Oct 15.
(715)356-6111 Lat: 45.90269, Lon: -89.68811
1077 Old Hwy 51S, Woodruff, WI 54568
www.hiawathatrailerresort.com
See ad this page

INDIAN SHORES RV & COTTAGE RESORT **Ratings: 9/9★/9** (RV Park) Avail: 130 full hkups (30/50 amps). 2021 rates: $49 to $79. May 01 to Oct 31. (715)356-5552, 7750 Indian Shores Rd, Woodruff, WI 54568

NO HIGHLAND AMERICAN LEGION/BUFFALO LAKE (Public State Park) From town, S 2 mi on Hwy 47 to Hwy J, E 7.5 mi to Buffalo Lake Rd, N 1 mi (L). Entrance fee required. 49 Avail: Pit toilets. 2021 rates: $12 to $14. May 04 to Oct 10. (715)385-3352

NO HIGHLAND AMERICAN LEGION/CARROL LAKE (Public State Park) From Jct of US-51 & Hwy 47, S 2 mi on Hwy 47 to Hwy J, E 3 mi (L). Entrance fee required. 11 Avail: Pit toilets. 2021 rates: $20 to $35. (715)385-2727

NO HIGHLAND AMERICAN LEGION/CLEAR LAKE (Public State Park) From town, S 4 mi on Hwy 47 to Woodruff Rd, NE 1 mi to Clear Lake Rd, E 0.5 mi (R). Entrance fee required. 80 Avail. 2021 rates: $15 to $25. (715)385-2727

NO HIGHLAND AMERICAN LEGION/CRYSTAL-MUSKIE LAKES (Public State Park) From Woodruff, N 6 mi on US-51 to Hwy M, NE 3 mi to Hwy N, E 2 mi (L). Entrance fee required. 93 Avail. 2021 rates: $15 to $17. (715)385-2727

NO HIGHLAND AMERICAN LEGION/INDIAN MOUNDS AREA (Public State Park) From Woodruff, SE 5 mi on Hwy 47 (R). Entrance fee required. 32 Avail: Pit toilets. 2021 rates: $12 to $14. (715)385-2727

NO HIGHLAND AMERICAN LEGION/NORTH TROUT LAKE (Public State Park) From Jct of US-51 & CT-M, N 5.5 mi on CT-M (L). Entrance fee required. 41 Avail: Pit toilets. 2021 rates: $16 to $21. (715)385-2727

Be prepared! You can be the king of the road, but you still need to be safe. Be sure to use the valuable information provided in the Bridge, Tunnel & Ferry Regulations and Rules of the Road pages located in the front of the Guide.

DID YOU KNOW?

Less than 600,000 people call Wyoming home, making it the least populous state in the nation.

Getty Images/iStockphoto

YOU ARE HERE

Wyoming

Visit the Equality State and discover the rugged and untamed landscapes that have inspired movie directors for decades. The spirit of the Wild West lives on in its towns, too, with rodeos and ranches opening their doors.

Wild West Ways

The streets of Cheyenne exude an Old West vibe, with century-old hotels boasting storied pasts and live gun shows that re-create the town's rough legacy. Watch the Cheyenne Gunslingers re-enact gunfights or come face-to-face with 2,300 bison at the Terry Bison Ranch. You can also immerse yourself in rodeo exhibits and an extensive collection of antique wagons at the Frontier Days Old West Museum.

Sacred Tower

You may have seen the Devil's Tower National Monument in the film, "Close Encounters of the Third Kind," but nothing beats seeing it in person. Standing at 867 feet with sheer vertical cliffs, this 65 million-year-old geological discovery is considered sacred by Northern Plains tribes. Join a ranger-led tour to learn more about the unique site or traverse eight miles of trails to admire it from every angle. Rock climbers can scale its almost-sheer sides to earn a stunning view from the top.

Cowboy Rope in Fun

The town of Cody celebrates the legacy of the American cowboy. Set at the foot of the Absaroka Mountains in the state's northwest corner, this town carries on the traditions of the iconic riders and ropers. The Buffalo Bill Center of the West covers every aspect of this mythical region. There are five museums all under one roof, including the Big Horn Galleries, which showcase works by famous Western artists. Old West town offers enlightening trolley tours to pioneer homes and the historic district.

Wyoming Elk

Where's the beef? Expand your food repertoire with locally harvested meat that's a tasty alternative to cow meat. Wyoming restaurants serve elk steaks, elk burgers and even elk sliders. Elk has less fat and more protein than beef, so you'll know that you're getting some quality fuel for the next day's travels.

VISITOR CENTER

TIME ZONE
Mountain Standard

ROAD & HIGHWAY INFORMATION
888-WYO-ROAD
wyoroad.info

FISHING & HUNTING INFORMATION
307-777-4600
wgfd.wyo.gov/Apply-or-Buy

BOATING INFORMATION
307-777-4600
wgfd.wyo.gov/Fishing-and-Boating/Boating-and-Watercraft

NATIONAL PARKS
nps.gov/wy

STATE PARKS
wyoparks.state.wy.us

TOURISM INFORMATION
Wyoming Office of Tourism
800-225-5996
travelwyoming.com

TOP TOURISM ATTRACTIONS
1) Yellowstone National Park
2) Grand Teton National Park
3) Devils Tower National Monument

MAJOR CITIES
Cheyenne (capital), Casper, Laramie, Gillette, Rock Springs

Wide-Open Spaces galore

You won't run short of public lands in Wyoming. In all, there are 12 state parks, five national forests, four national wildlife refuges and a pair of national recreation areas. But when it comes to outdoor adventure, it's the state's pair of elite national parks that steal most of the spotlight. Yellowstone and Grand Teton are among the finest national parks in the country, offering a mix of mesmerizing geography and an abundance of activities.

Getty Images/iStockphoto

Located on Lake Jackson near Grand Teton National Park, Colter Bay blends boating with beautiful scenery.

Iconic National Park

Wyoming's biggest draw is Yellowstone National Park in the state's northwest corner. Established as the world's first national park in 1872, this two million-acre region seethes with natural hot springs and roars with gushing waterfalls. It also has the largest concentration of geysers in the world. Take a scenic drive or trek along hundreds of miles of trails to reach famous sites like the Old Faithful Geyser, Mammoth Hot Springs and the Grand Canyon of Yellowstone.

Good Times Among the Tetons

Grand Teton National Park is known for the spiky peaks that stab the sky. Start by cruising the 42-mile Scenic Loop Drive, which shows off the park's incredible scenery and wildlife. The park itself is home to more than 230 miles of marked hiking trails and lots of opportunities to fish, ride, boat, bird-watch or view wildlife. You've probably seen the park's famous mountains adorning postcards; now see it in person.

Land of Heritage

In the town of Buffalo, you can see where the notorious Hole in the Wall Gang stayed at the Historic Occidental Hotel. Venture outside of town and see their hiding place: a remote pass in the Bighorn Mountains — the so-called "hole" — where they planned heists. In Laramie and Rawlins, visit the Wyoming Territorial Prison State Historic Site and then the Wyoming Frontier Prison.

Buffalo's Best

Go a little wild in the historic Old West town of Buffalo. Resting in the foothills of the Big Horn Mountains in northern Wyoming, Buffalo is a popular destination for hunters, wilderness enthusiasts and aficionados of the cowboy way. From here, visitors can make daytrips to a variety of destinations.

Wyoming's Wild Rivers

Trout fishing can be found in Wyoming. Miles of mountain streams and clear, cool lakes provide prime habitats. Grab your fly-fishing rod, and take your pick of the Snake, the North Platte or the Big Laramie rivers. Within Yellowstone and the Grand Tetons national parks, you'll find spectacular fishing within spectacular landscapes. In eastern Wyoming, Glendo State Park and Keyhole State Park are top picks for boating and outdoor recreation.

Big Game Galore

Across the state, hunters will find public lands teeming with wildlife, including elk, moose, bear, antelope and bighorn sheep. The Bridger-Teton National Forest — the third-largest national forest in the U.S. — is a top choice near Jackson. In northeastern Wyoming, the Black Hills National Forest offers big and small game.

The Sporting Life

If you like to ski, boat, fish or hike, Buffalo serves as your gateway to a sportsman's paradise. Take the boat out on Lake DeSmet just north of the town and take advantage of clear, cool days on the water. Jet Skis and water skis are permitted on this popular lake, as is fishing.

Cowboy State Catches

Anglers can cast their lines at Healy Reservoir and in the Middle Fork of the Powder River, as well as in the mountain streams and lakes throughout Bighorn National Forest and Cloud Peak Wilderness. With a little patience, you're bound to hook one of several trout species, as well as bass, perch and bluegill.

An elk and members of its family roam a meadow as the Grand Teton Mountains loom in the distance.

Head for the Horns

The Big Horns beckon hikers and horseback riders to test its trails, which follow lakes and streams as they wind through parklands and climb mountains. The U.S. Forest Service provides detailed trail maps and tips for making the most of a hike. Area guest ranches and outfitters offer visitors the opportunity to ride at their leisure, whether for a half-day or an overnight camping trip.

Land That Tells a Story

Travel back in time 60 million years at the Dry Creek Petrified Tree Environmental Education Area, located 13 miles east of Buffalo. A mile loop interpretive trail winds its way through petrified trees, remnants of the jungle-like swamp that covered the land during this prehistoric era. Paleontologists speculate the crocodiles and large mammals made their home here.

Hunting for Photos

From the comfort of your RV seat, you can still experience the beauty of the region. Cloud Peak Skyway — US 16 — crosses the southern Big Horns and showcases views of snowcapped peaks on its 45-mile route. Equally thrilling are views of Hospital Hill, Meadow Lark Lake and Tensleep Canyon.

As the Wheel Turns

Medicine Wheel Passage, also known as US 14A, rises from the Bighorn Basin near the town of Lovell and crosses through steep canyons and alpine meadows, but the main attraction is the largest intact Native American medicine wheel in North America. The rocks and markings that created the 80-foot-diameter wheel remain intact. This spiritual site is used for tribal ceremonies to this day.

Phil's Fort

Wyoming's frontier history is preserved at Fort Phil Kearny. The fort's historic site features a museum that tells the outpost's story. Butch Cassidy's famous "Hole in the Wall" hideout is nearby; don't miss out on the tour of Outlaw Cave and Dull Knife Battlefield.

Ride 'em and Rope 'em

If you visit in the summer, you might be lucky enough to stroll around the Johnson County Fair and Rodeo, which kicks off in the last days of July. From agriculture lessons to bucking broncos, the fair is a tribute to Wyoming's farming and ranching heritage.

Featured Good Sam Parks

WYOMING

When you stay with Good Sam, you can expect the highest degree of cleanliness and friendliness, and better yet, you get **10% off** overnight campground fees.

If you're not already a Good Sam member you can purchase your membership at one of these locations:

ALPINE
Greys River Cove Resort

BOULDER
Highline Trail RV Park

BUFFALO
Deer Park
Indian Campground & RV Park

CHEYENNE
AB Camping RV Park
Restway Travel Park
Terry Bison Ranch RV Park
WYO Campground

CODY
Absaroka Bay RV Park
Chief Joseph RV Park
Ponderosa Campground
Yellowstone Valley Inn & RV Park

DUBOIS
The Longhorn Ranch Lodge and RV Resort

EVANSTON
Phillips RV Park
River's Edge RV Resort

FORT BRIDGER
Fort Bridger RV Park

GREEN RIVER
The Travel Camp

KEMMERER
Riverside RV Park

LANDER
Sleeping Bear RV Park & Campground
Twin Pines RV Park & Campground

LINGLE
Pony Soldier RV Park

MEETEETSE
Black-Footed Ferret RV Resort

RAWLINS
Western Hills Campground

SHERIDAN
Peter D's RV Park

SUNDANCE
Mountain View RV Park & Campground

THERMOPOLIS
Eagle RV Park & Campground

WHEATLAND
El Rancho Village RV & Cabins

WORLAND
Worland RV Park and Campground

Getty Images/iStockphoto

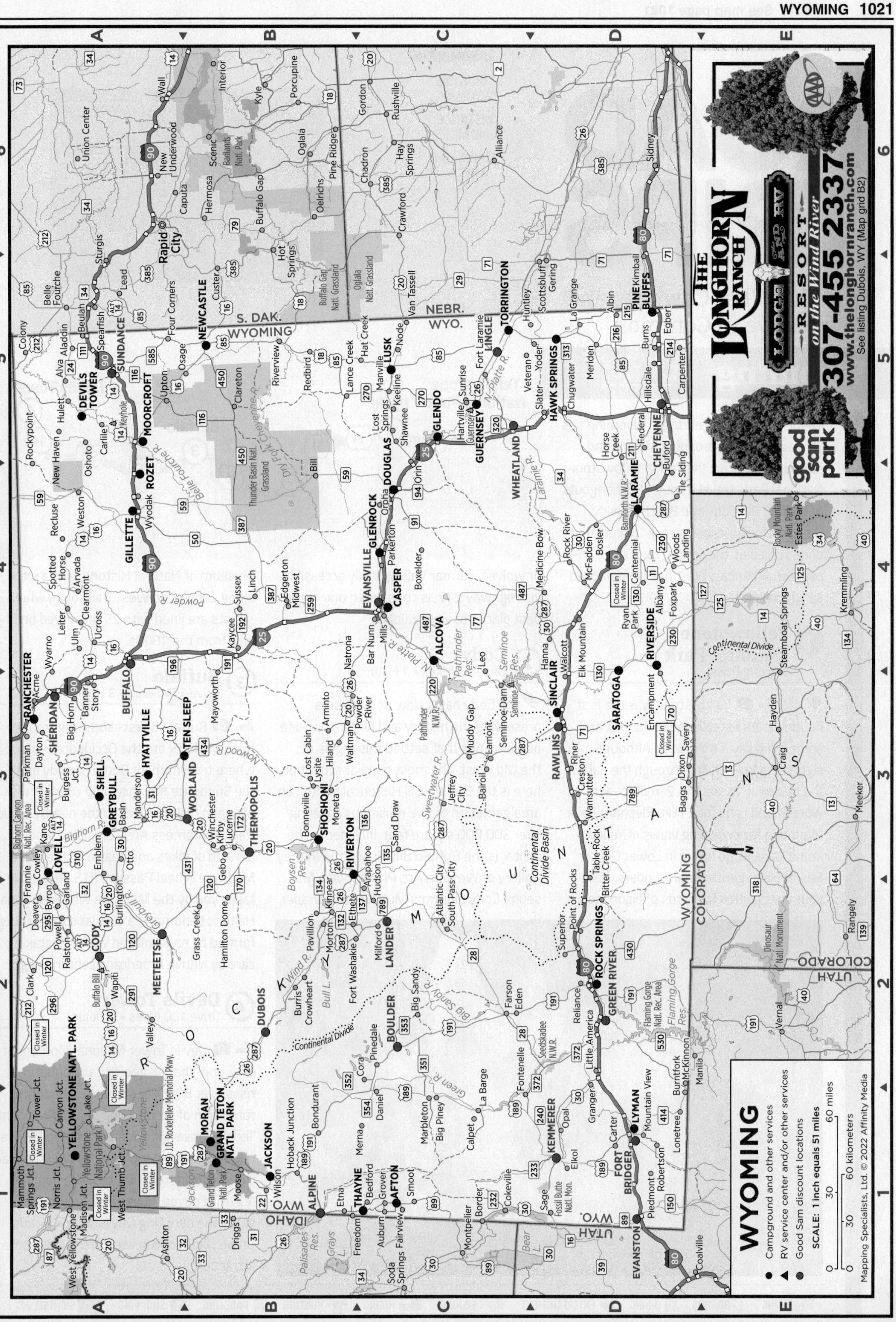
WYOMING
Campground and other services
RV service center and/or other services
Good Sam discount locations
SCALE: 1 inch equals 51 miles
0 30 60 miles
0 30 60 kilometers
Mapping Specialists, Ltd. © 2022 Affinity Media
THE LONGHORN RANCH
LODGE AND RV RESORT
on the Wind River
307-455 2337
www.thelonghornranch.com
See listing Dubois, WY (Map grid B2)
good sam park
YELLOWSTONE NATL. PARK
GRAND TETON NATL. PARK
JACKSON
DUBOIS
CODY
SHERIDAN
BUFFALO
GILLETTE
CASPER
RIVERTON
LANDER
ROCK SPRINGS
RAWLINS
LARAMIE
CHEYENNE
EVANSTON
S. DAK.
WYOMING
NEBR.
WYO.
COLORADO
UTAH
IDAHO

ROAD TRIPS

Find Out What Cowboys and Devils Have in Common

Wyoming

LOCATION
WYOMING

DISTANCE
346 MILES

DRIVE TIME
6 HRS

This trip through northern Wyoming ties together jaw-dropping historic and natural sites. Start this trip in Yellowstone National Park, travel through the hangouts of Buffalo Bill Cody and Butch Cassidy, then finish your trip at a rock "tower" that once served as the setting for a close encounter. America's West has never looked so spectacular.

1 Yellowstone National Park
Starting Point

Yellowstone was the first national park established in the U.S. and some folks say it's the best. Although sightseers love driving through the park, the best way to see this 2-million-acre wonderland is by foot. Hike Elephant Back Mountain for sweeping views of Yellowstone Lake, or go biking in Lower Geyser Basin to see geothermal wonders. Keep your eyes peeled for herds of bison, bears or wolves. Larmar Valley, easily accessible via Highway 212, is considered one of the best places to view wildlife.

2 Cody
Drive 52 Miles • 1 Hour

Cody has a slew of museums preserving the history and larger-than-life personalities that settled this region of the Old West. The most popular attraction here is the Buffalo Bill Historical Center, an amalgamation of five museums covering over 300,000 square feet. Included in the center is the Buffalo Bill Museum, Whitney Gallery of Western Art, Plains Indian Museum, Cody Firearms Museum and Draper Museum of Natural History. Take a walk along Cody's Old West Trail Town, where streets are lined with 25 preserved buildings from the 1800s.

Getty Images/iStockphoto

3 Buffalo
Drive 164 Miles • 3 Hours

Buffalo boasts some big frontier history. Check out the Occidental Hotel, where train robbers Butch Cassidy and the Sundance Kid once held court. Prefer hiking to history? Trek to the nearby Cloud Peak Wilderness Area, an alpine wonderland of lakes and peaks. To the west, Medicine Wheel Passage (U.S. Route 14A) takes you by the Medicine Wheel National Historic Landmark, a circular configuration formed by rocks placed with painstaking care by Native Americans centuries ago.

4 Devils Tower
Drive 130 Miles • 2 Hours

Devils Tower National Monument is a cone-shaped geological wonder that rises over 800 feet skyward, a daunting formation of stone. Long before President Teddy Roosevelt declared it America's first national monument, local Native American tribes considered it sacred. The popular 1.3-mile paved Tower Trail circumnavigates the daunting Devils Tower. Bonus: Brave climbers can ascend this awesome attraction.

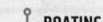

BIKING BOATING DINING ENTERTAINMENT FISHING HIKING HUNTING PADDLING SHOPPING SIGHTSEEING

Wyoming SPOTLIGHTS

Cruising Through the Cowboy State

Saddle up for a great time. Wyoming keeps the Old West spirit alive with rodeos, museums and towns dotted with historic sites. You'll also find the first national park ever established.

BIG BEASTS: MALE BISON CAN WEIGHT UP TO 2,000 POUNDS.

A male bison relaxes in a field of wildflowers in Yellowstone National Park in Wyoming.

Cody

Directly east of Yellowstone National Park, the small town of Cody attracts visitors eager to take a look into Wild West history and to experience historical attractions. The town was named for its most famous former resident, William F. Cody, better known as Buffalo Bill.

Gateway to Yellowstone

Cody makes a good base for those who want to explore Yellowstone, and it's only about a 78-mile drive from the park's Northeastern entrance. Popular attractions within the park include the iconic Old Faithful Geyser, Yellowstone Lake, the terraced Mammoth Hot Springs and the multi-hued Grand Prismatic Spring. Tours are available from Cody for those who'd rather sit back and let someone else do the driving.

Buffalo Bill Center of the West

Cody's most celebrated attraction is undoubtedly the Buffalo Bill Center of the West, a collection of five museums focused primarily on the story of the American West.

Old Trail Town

See what life was like over a century ago at Old Trail Town, a collection of around two dozen old structures dating to as early as the 1880s. Many of the buildings on the site were salvaged from other areas in the region and reassembled and restored.

Buffalo

Go a little wild in the historic Old West town of Buffalo. Resting in the foothills of the Big Horn Mountains, Buffalo is a popular destination for hunters, wilderness enthusiasts and aficionados of the cowboy way. From here, visitors can make trips historic destinations like the Bighorn Medicine Wheel.

Casper

Embracing the Wild West spirit comes naturally in Casper. Spend your days retracing the journeys of western pioneers and savor the tranquility of Wyoming's wide-open spaces. In town, you're welcome to admire Western art and let loose at action-packed rodeos.

Fish the Miracle Mile

Blue ribbon trout are yours to catch in the North Platte River. Cast a line in the Miracle Mile or Grey Reef sections of the river. You can also reel in trout from the Pathfinder Reservoir and Alcova Reservoir.

FOR MORE INFORMATION

Wyoming Travel & Tourism, 800-225-5996, www.travelwyoming.com
Discover Historic Buffalo, 800-227-5122, www.buffalowyoming.org
Visit Casper, 800-852-1889, www.visitcasper.com
Cody Yellowstone, 307-586-1574. www.codyyellowstone.org

LOCAL FAVORITE

Easy-Does-It Ribs

In true Cowboy State fashion, this recipe yields delicious ribs without too much fuss. Recipe adapted from *Best Ever RV Recipes*.

INGREDIENTS

- ☐ 4 lbs spare ribs
- ☐ 1 10 ½-oz can tomato soup
- ☐ 2 Tbsp soy sauce
- ☐ 2 Tbsp honey
- ☐ 2 Tbsp minced onion
- ☐ ½ tsp Worcestershire sauce
- ☐ ¼ tsp minced ginger

DIRECTIONS

Precook the ribs in the oven or on a grill. Combine the soup with remaining ingredients in a saucepan and simmer for about 10 minutes

Drain ribs and brush with sauce. Place ribs on a grill about 6 inches above coals and cook for about 30 minutes, turning and basting frequently.

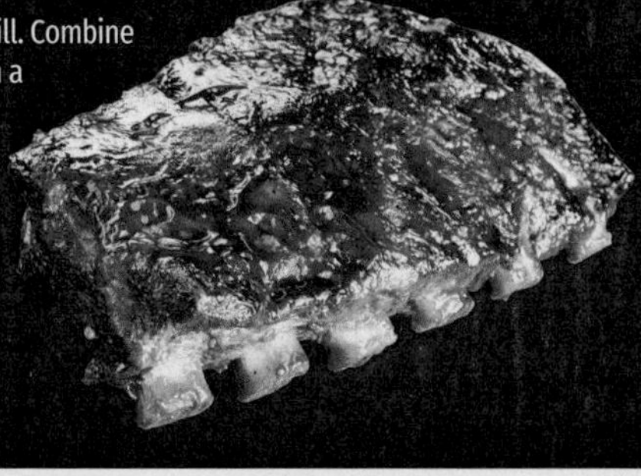

Wyoming

AFTON — C1 *Lincoln*

↓ KODIAK MOUNTAIN RESORT **Ratings: 6.5/7/9** (RV Resort) Avail: 29 full hkups (30/50 amps). 2021 rates: $49. May 15 to Oct 15. (307)885-8800, 82717 Highway 89, Afton, WY 83110

ALCOVA — C4 *Natrona*

↓ ALCOVA LAKE/FREMONT CANYON CAMPGROUND (Public) From Casper: Go 26 mi W on Hwy 220, then S on CR-406 (L). 80 Avail: Pit toilets. 2021 rates: $10. (307)235-9311

PATHFINDER NATIONAL WILDLIFE REFUGE
(Public State Park) From town, W 32 mi on Hwy 220 (follow signs) to CR-409, S 6.4 mi (R). Elev 5850 ft.**FAC:** gravel rds. Avail: 50 grass, back-ins (18x35), tent sites, pit toilets, dump, mobile sewer, groc, firewood. **REC:** Pathfinder Reservoir: fishing, kayaking/canoeing, hunting nearby. Pets OK. 14 day max stay. 2021 rates: $10. no cc, no reservations.
(307)235-9325 Lat: 42.470528, Lon: -106.852928
Alcova, WY 82620
www.natrona.net

ALPINE — B1 *Lincoln*

↑ **ALPINE VALLEY RV RESORT** (RV Park) (Not Visited) Avail: 102 full hkups (30/50 amps). 2021 rates: $75 to $140. Apr 15 to Nov 01. (307)241-5707, 118450 US 26, Alpine, WY 83128

Get the GOOD SAM CAMPING APP

↓ **GREYS RIVER COVE RESORT**
Ratings: 7/9.5★/7.5 (RV Park) From Jct US 26 & US 89 (Alpine Jct): Go S 1/2 mile (L). Elev 5650 ft.**FAC:** paved rds. Avail: 48 gravel, 18 pull-thrus, (18x75), back-ins (18x40), 48 full hkups (30/50 amps), WiFi @ sites, tent sites, laundry, fire rings, firewood, restaurant. **REC:** Snake River: fishing, kayaking/canoeing, boating nearby, hunting nearby. Pets OK. Big rig sites. 2021 rates: $90, Military discount. May 01 to Nov 01. ATM.
(307)880-2267 Lat: 43.16454, Lon: -111.01707
25 Hwy 89, Alpine, WY 83128
greysrivercove.com
See ad this page

BOULDER — C2 *Sublette*

← **HIGHLINE TRAIL RV PARK**
Ratings: 8/9.5★/9.5 (RV Park) Avail: 43 full hkups (30/50 amps). 2021 rates: $40. (307)871-0865, 8718 Hwy 191, Boulder, WY 82923

← WIND RIVER VIEW CAMPGROUND **Ratings: 4.5/6/6.5** (Membership Park) Avail: 10 full hkups (30/50 amps). 2021 rates: $31.50. May 15 to Oct 15. (307)537-5453, 8889 US Hwy 191, Boulder, WY 82923

BUFFALO — A4 *Johnson*

→ BUFFALO KOA JOURNEY **Ratings: 9/9.5★/10** (Campground) Avail: 80 full hkups (30/50 amps). 2021 rates: $50 to $100. Apr 15 to Oct 25. (307)684-5423, 87 US Highway 16 East, Buffalo, WY 82834

→ **DEER PARK**
Ratings: 9/10★/9 (Campground) From Jct of I-90 & US-16 (exit 58), W 0.7 mi on US-16 (R); or From Jct of I-25 & US-16 (exit 299), E 0.7 mi on US-16 (L). Elev 4550 ft.**FAC:** gravel rds. (67 spaces). Avail: 52 gravel, 36 pull-thrus, (25x65), back-ins (30x35), 42 full hkups, 10 W, 10 E (30/50 amps), seasonal sites, cable, WiFi @ sites, tent sites, rentals, dump, laundry, fire rings, firewood. **REC:** heated pool, boating nearby, hunting nearby. Pets OK. Big rig sites, eco-friendly. 2021 rates: $43 to $50, Military discount. May 01 to Sep 30.
(307)684-5722 Lat: 44.35643, Lon: -106.66970
146 Hwy 16E @ Deer Park Rd, Buffalo, WY 82834
deerparkrv.com
See ad opposite page

→ **INDIAN CAMPGROUND & RV PARK**
Ratings: 8.5/9.5★/9.5 (Campground) Avail: 90 full hkups (30/50 amps). 2021 rates: $49.50 to $59.50. Apr 15 to Oct 31. (307)684-9601, 660 E Hart St, Buffalo, WY 82834

Thank you for using our 2022 Guide. Now you have all the latest information about RV parks, campgrounds and RV resorts across North America!

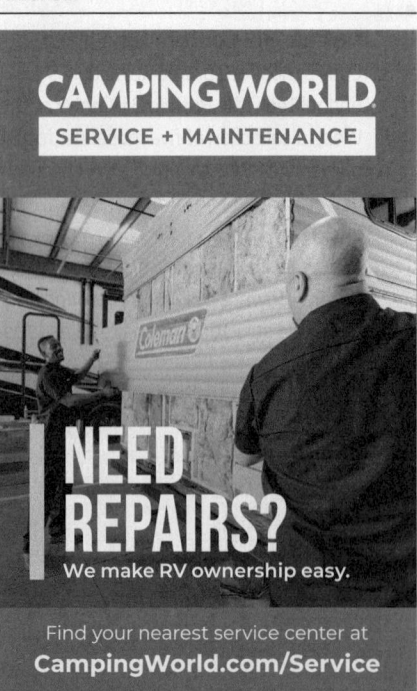

CASPER — C4 *Natrona*

CASPER See also Evansville & Glenrock.

CASPER EAST RV PARK & CAMPGROUND **Ratings: 7/8.5★/7** (Campground) 45 Avail: 40 full hkups, 5 W, 5 E (30/50 amps). 2021 rates: $44.95 to $47.95. Apr 01 to Oct 31. (307)337-1284, 2800 E Yellowstone Hwy, Casper, WY 82609

FORT CASPAR CAMPGROUND **Ratings: 7.5/9★/8.5** (Campground) Avail: 38 full hkups (30/50 amps). 2021 rates: $42. (307)234-3260, 4205 Fort Caspar Rd, Casper, WY 82604

GRAY REEF RESERVOIR (Public) From town, W 30 mi on Hwy 220 to CR-412, S 0.5 mi (R). 15 Avail: Pit toilets. 2021 rates: $10. (307)235-9311

CHEYENNE — D5 *Laramie*

AB CAMPING RV PARK

Ratings: 8/9★/8.5 (Campground) From Jct of I-80 & I-25, S 0.5 mi on I-25 to College Dr (exit 7), E 1.5 mi (R); or From Jct of I-80 & exit 364, SW 4.5 mi on College Dr (L). Elev 6100 ft.**FAC:** gravel rds. Avail: 115 gravel, patios, 82 pull-thrus, (20x60), back-ins (18x27), 89 full hkups, 26 W, 26 E (30/50 amps), cable, WiFi @ sites, tent sites, dump, laundry, LP gas, restaurant. **REC:** playground, hunting nearby. Pets OK. Big rig sites, eco-friendly. 2021 rates: $42 to $95, Military discount. Apr 01 to Oct 15.
(307)634-7035 Lat: 41.10205, Lon: -104.82174
1503 W College Dr, Cheyenne, WY 82007
campcheyenne.com
See ad this page

CHEYENNE KOA **Ratings: 8.5/10★/8.5** (Campground) 45 Avail: 28 full hkups, 16 W, 16 E (30/50 amps). 2021 rates: $48 to $160. (800)562-1507, 8800 Hutchins Dr, Cheyenne, WY 82007

CURT GOWDY (Public State Park) From jct I-80 & I-25: Go 1-3/4 mi N on I-25 (exit 5) then 1/2 mi E on Missile Dr., then 18 mi W on Hwy-210 (Happy Jack Rd.). Avail: 15 E Pit toilets. 2021 rates: $10 to $17. (307)632-7946

MILITARY PARK F.E. WARREN AFB CROW CREEK FAMCAMP (FE WARREN AFB) (Public) From Jct of I-80 & I-25, N 2 mi on I-25. Avail: 40 full hkups (30/50 amps). 2021 rates: $10 to $35. (307)773-3874

RESTWAY TRAVEL PARK

Ratings: 9/9.5★/8 (Campground) 40 Avail: 39 full hkups, 1 W, 1 E (30/50 amps). 2021 rates: $35 to $42. (307)634-3811, 4212 Whitney Rd, Cheyenne, WY 82001

TERRY BISON RANCH RV PARK

Ratings: 8/9.5★/7 (RV Park) From Jct of I-80 & I-25, S 3 mi on 511-25 Service Road East (Terry Ranch Road) (L). Elev 6200 ft.**FAC:** gravel rds. (112 spaces). Avail: 92 gravel, 72 pull-thrus, (24x70), back-ins (24x60), 72 full hkups, 20 W, 20 E (30/50 amps), seasonal sites, WiFi @ sites, tent sites, rentals, dump, laundry, groc, LP gas, firewood, restaurant. **REC:** pond, fishing, playground, hunting nearby, rec open to public. Pets OK. Partial handicap access. Big rig sites, eco-friendly. 2021 rates: $48 to $135, Military discount. ATM.
(307)634-4171 Lat: 41.00047, Lon: -104.90528
51 I-25 Service Rd E, Cheyenne, WY 82007
terrybisonranch.com
See ad this page

WYO CAMPGROUND

Ratings: 8/10★/7 (Campground) Avail: 36 full hkups (30/50 amps). 2021 rates: $40 to $80. (307)547-2244, 4066 Interstate 80 Service Rd Exit 377, Cheyenne, WY 82003

CODY — A2 *Park*

CODY See also Greybull, WY; Red Lodge, MT.

ABSAROKA BAY RV PARK

Ratings: 8/9★/8 (RV Park) Avail: 98 full hkups (30/50 amps). 2021 rates: $45. May 01 to Oct 01. (307)527-7440, 2002 Mountain View Dr., Cody, WY 82414

BUFFALO BILL/NORTH FORK (Public State Park) From town, W 13.5 mi on US-14/16/20 (L). Entrance fee & camping permit required. 60 Avail: 14 W, 14 E. 2021 rates: $10 to $17. (307)587-9227

BUFFALO BILL/NORTH SHORE BAY (Public State Park) From town: Go 9 mi W on US-14/16/20 (L). 37 Avail: 7 W, 7 E (30 amps). 2021 rates: $10 to $26. (307)587-9227

CHIEF JOSEPH RV PARK

Ratings: 6/8★/7.5 (RV Park) 16 Avail: 8 full hkups, 8 W, 8 E (30 amps). 2021 rates: $35 to $45. (307)527-5510, 4 Van Dyke Rd, Cody, WY 82414

CODY KOA HOLIDAY **Ratings: 9/10★/8** (Campground) Avail: 90 full hkups (30/50 amps). 2021 rates: $49.94 to $86.57. May 01 to Oct 01. (307)587-2369, 5561 Greybull Hwy, Cody, WY 82414

CODY TROUT RANCH CAMP RV PARK **Ratings: 8/10★/9.5** (RV Park) Avail: 38 full hkups (30/50 amps). 2021 rates: $43 to $59. Apr 01 to Sep 30. (307)578-6757, 1 Trout Ranch Rd , Cody, WY 82414

PARKWAY RV CAMPGROUND **Ratings: 5.5/6.5/7** (Campground) Avail: 25 full hkups (30/50 amps). 2021 rates: $33. (307)527-5927, 132 Yellowstone Ave, Cody, WY 82414

PONDEROSA CAMPGROUND

Ratings: 8/9.5★/8 (Campground) From Jct of Hwy 120 & US-14/16/20 (in town), W 1.3 mi on US-14/16/20-Yellowstone Park Hwy (R). Elev 5000 ft.

PERFECT HOMEBASE FOR EXPLORING CODY
Trolley tours, chuck wagon dinner & show, nightly rodeo, golf course, rafting trips, trail rides & more; let us help you plan your visit, experience the true western heritage of Cody while staying at our full-service RV park.

FAC: paved/gravel rds. 137 Avail: 87 paved, 50 gravel, 32 pull-thrus, (18x65), back-ins (21x35), 137 full hkups (30/50 amps), cable, WiFi @ sites, tent sites, rentals, dump, laundry, groc. **REC:** Shoshone River: fishing, boating nearby, playground, hunting nearby. Pets OK. Big rig sites, eco-friendly. 2021 rates: $40 to $60, Military discount. Apr 15 to Oct 15. ATM, no cc.
(307)587-9203 Lat: 44.51769, Lon: -109.07279
1815 8th St, Cody, WY 82414
codyponderosa.com
See ad opposite page

YELLOWSTONE VALLEY INN & RV PARK

Ratings: 8.5/9.5★/8.5 (RV Park) From Jct of Hwy 14/16/20 & 8th St (W edge of Cody), W 18 mi on Hwy 14/16/20 Yellowstone Hwy (L). Elev 5250 ft.**FAC:** gravel rds. Avail: 65 gravel, 54 pull-thrus, (30x62), back-ins (33x50), 65 full hkups (30/50 amps), WiFi @ sites, rentals, laundry, groc, LP gas, fire rings, firewood, restaurant. **REC:** heated pool, hot tub, Shoshone River: fishing, kayaking/canoeing, boating nearby, playground, hunting nearby. Pets OK. Partial handicap access. No tents. Big rig sites, eco-friendly. 2021 rates: $77 to $95, Military discount. May 01 to Oct 15. ATM.
(877)587-3961 Lat: 44.474738, Lon: -109.411001
3324 North Fork Hwy, Cody, WY 82414
www.yellowstonevalleyinn.com
See ad page 1030

Things to See and Do

CODY YELLOWSTONE COUNTRY All area information for Cody & Yellowstone Nat'l Park. Maps, calendars of events and things to do. Elev 5000 ft. Partial handicap access. RV accessible. Restrooms. Hours: 8am to 5pm. No CC.
(800)393-2639 Lat: 44.52569, Lon: -109.07019
836 Sheridan Ave, Cody, WY 82414
CodyYellowstone.org
See ad page 1018

DEVILS TOWER — A5 *Crook*

DEVILS TOWER NATL MON/BELLE FOURCHE (Public National Park) From Jct of US 14 & WY Hwy 24, N 7 mi on WY Hwy 24, follow signs (E) Entrance fee required. 47 Avail. 2021 rates: $20. May 01 to Oct 29. (307)467-5283

DEVILS TOWER/BLACK HILLS KOA JOURNEY **Ratings: 7.5/8/9.5** (Campground) 87 Avail: 64 full hkups, 23 W, 23 E (30/50 amps). 2021 rates: $60 to $90. May 15 to Sep 30. (800)562-5785, 60 Hwy 110, Devils Tower, WY 82714

DOUGLAS — C4 *Converse*

DOUGLAS KOA **Ratings: 9/10★/9** (Campground) Avail: 52 full hkups (30/50 amps). 2021 rates: $40 to $43. (800)562-2469, 168 Cold Spring Rd, Douglas, WY 82633

DUBOIS — B2 *Fremont*

DUBOIS/WIND RIVER KOA HOLIDAY **Ratings: 9/9★/9** (Campground) 49 Avail: 48 full hkups, 1 W, 1 E (30/50 amps). 2021 rates: $74 to $94. May 11 to Sep 30. (307)455-2238, 225 Welty St, Dubois, WY 82513

THE LONGHORN RANCH LODGE AND RV RESORT

Ratings: 8/9.5★/10 (Campground) From town, E 3 mi on Hwy 26 (L). Elev 6900 ft.

GATEWAY TO JACKSON, TETONS & YLSTN
No rig too big, riverfront sites, full hook ups, cable & WiFi. One of the highest rated parks in WY. Day trip to the National Parks then relax with us. Fishing, horseback rides, ride your ATV from your site & horse corrals.

FAC: gravel rds. Avail: 50 gravel, 24 pull-thrus, (40x85), back-ins (40x60), 50 full hkups (30/50 amps), WiFi @ sites, tent sites, rentals, dump, laundry, groc, LP gas, fire rings, firewood. **REC:** Wind River: fishing, boating nearby, playground, hunting nearby. Pets OK. Partial handicap access. Big rig sites, eco-friendly. 2021 rates: $50 to $85, Military discount. May 01 to Oct 15.
(307)455-2337 Lat: 43.51754, Lon: -109.59067
5810 US Hwy 26, Dubois, WY 82513
thelonghornranch.com
See ad pages 1021, 1030

EVANSTON — D1 *Uinta*

PHILLIPS RV PARK

Ratings: 8/9.5★/8 (Campground) From Jct of I-80 & I-80 Bus Loop (E Evanston exit 6), W 0.6 mi on I-80 Bus Loop/ Bear River Dr (L) Note: Do Not Use GPS. Elev 6748 ft.**FAC:** gravel rds. (61 spaces). 56 Avail: 48 gravel, 8 grass, 52 pull-thrus, (24x75), back-ins (25x45), 56 full hkups (30/50 amps), seasonal sites, cable, WiFi @ sites, tent sites, laundry. **REC:** play-

ground. Pets OK. Big rig sites, eco-friendly. 2021 rates: $37.50 to $40.75, Military discount. Apr 15 to Oct 15.
(307)789-3805 Lat: 41.27017, Lon: -110.94659
225 Bear River Dr, Evanston, WY 82930
www.phillipsrvpark.com
See ad this page

EVANSVILLE — C4 *Natrona*

➔ RIVER'S EDGE RV RESORT
good sam park **Ratings: 9/9.5★/10** (RV Park) From jct I-25 & Hat Six Rd (exit 182): Go 1/2 mi N on Hat Six Rd, then 1/2 mi N on Yellowstone-Cole Creek Rd, then 500 feet W on Santa Fe Circle (R). Elev 5130 ft.**FAC:** all weather rds. (94 spaces). Avail: 70 all weather, 38 pull-thrus, (35x75), back-ins (32x63), 53 full hkups, 17 W, 17 E (30/50 amps), seasonal sites, cable, WiFi @ sites, rentals, dump, laundry, firewood. **REC:** North Platte River: fishing, kayaking/canoeing, boating nearby, playground, hunting nearby. Pets OK. Partial handicap access. No tents. Big rig sites, eco-friendly. 2021 rates: $50 to $56.25, Military discount.
(307)234-0042 Lat: 42.85778, Lon: -106.21467
6820 Santa Fe Circle, Evansville, WY 82636
www.riversedgervresort.net
See ad opposite page

Travel Services

➔ RIVER'S EDGE RV & BOAT STORAGE All indoor secure RV and Boat storage **RV Storage:** indoor, easy reach keypad, 24/7 access, well-lit facility, well-lit roads, well-lit perimeter, on-site staff, power to charge battery, office. **SERVICES:** restrooms. Hours: 9am to 4pm.
good sam RV Storage
Special offers available for Good Sam Members
(307)234-0042 Lat: 42.85778, Lon: -106.21467
6820 Santa Fe Circle, Evansville, WY 82636
www.riversedgervresort.net/rv-and-boat-storage

FORT BRIDGER — D1 *Uinta*

⬇ FORT BRIDGER RV PARK
good sam park **Ratings: 7.5/9.5★/9** (Campground) From Jct of I-80 & Exit 34 (Fort Bridger/Bus Loop), S 2.2 mi on I-80 Bus Loop (turn S on street between fort entrance & trading post) (L). Elev 6700 ft.**FAC:** gravel rds. (37 spaces). Avail: 32 grass, 16 pull-thrus, (50x80), back-ins (50x80), 32 full hkups (30/50 amps), seasonal sites, WiFi @ sites, tent sites, laundry. **REC:** boating nearby, hunting nearby. Pets OK. Partial handicap access. Big rig sites, eco-friendly. 2021 rates: $45.50 to $52, Military discount.
(307)782-3150 Lat: 41.31618, Lon: -110.38860
64 Groshon Rd, Fort Bridger, WY 82933
www.fbrvpark.com
See ad this page

GILLETTE — A4 *Campbell*

➚ GREEN TREE'S CRAZY WOMAN CAMPGROUND Ratings: 7/9.5★/8 (Campground) 73 Avail: 50 full hkups, 23 W, 23 E (30/50 amps). 2021 rates: $26.40 to $40.18. (307)682-3665, 1001 W 2nd St., Gillette, WY 82716

Read RV topics at blog.GoodSam.com

GLENDO — C5 *Platte*

GLENDO (Public State Park) From Jct of I-25 & Glendo Park Rd, E 2 mi on Glendo Park Rd, follow signs (L) Entrance fee required. 568 Avail. 2021 rates: $10 to $17. (307)735-4433

GLENROCK — C4 *Converse*

PLATTE RIVER RV & CAMPGROUND **Ratings: 6/8★/7** (Campground) Avail: 20 full hkups (30/50 amps). 2021 rates: $45. (307)262-9768, 131 Shawnie Ln, Glenrock, WY 82637

GRAND TETON NATIONAL PARK — B1 *Teton*

GRAND TETON/GROS VENTRE (Public National Park) From Jackson, N 6.5 mi on Hwy 89/191 to Gros Ventre Jct, E 4.5 mi (R) Entrance fee required. Avail: 45 E. 2021 rates: $39 to $51. May 04 to Oct 14. (800)628-9988

GREEN RIVER — D2 *Sweetwater*

THE TRAVEL CAMP
Ratings: 7.5/9★/7.5 (RV Park) Avail: 34 full hkups (30/50 amps). 2021 rates: $48. (307)875-2630, 4626 4th St, Green River, WY 82935

GREYBULL — A3 *Big Horn*

CAMPBELLS GREEN OASIS CAMPGROUND **Ratings: 6/10★/8** (RV Park) 10 Avail: 9 full hkups, 1 E (30/50 amps). 2021 rates: $42. (307)765-2856, 540 12TH Ave N, Greybull, WY 82426

GREYBULL KOA HOLIDAY **Ratings: 9/10★/9.5** (Campground) 38 Avail: 33 full hkups, 3 W, 3 E (30/50 amps). 2021 rates: $42.95 to $80.95. May 01 to Oct 15. (307)250-8098, 399 N 2nd St, Greybull, WY 82426

Show Your Good Sam Membership Card!

GUERNSEY — C5 *Platte*

GUERNSEY (Public State Park) From town, W 0.5 mi on Hwy 26, N 2 mi on Hwy 319 (E) Entrance fee required. 245 Avail: 16 W, 16 E. 2021 rates: $10 to $17. (307)836-2334

LARSON PARK CAMPGROUND (Public) From town, S 1 mi on Wyoming Ave (L). 16 Avail: 16 W, 16 E (30 amps). 2021 rates: $30 to $50. Apr 15 to Oct 15. (307)836-2255

HAWK SPRINGS — D5 *Goshen*

HAWK SPRINGS STATE RECREATION AREA (Public State Park) From town: Go 3 mi S on US 85, then 3 mi E on dirt county road. 24 Avail: Pit toilets. 2021 rates: $10 to $17. (307)836-2334

HYATTVILLE — A3 *Big Horn*

MEDICINE LODGE STATE ARCHAEOLOGICAL SITE (Public State Park) From Hwy 31 in town: Go 6 mi NW on dirt local road. 28 Avail: Pit toilets. 2021 rates: $6 to $11. (307)469-2234

JACKSON — B1 *Teton*

JACKSON See also Alpine, WY; Palisades, ID.

SNAKE RIVER CABINS & RV VILLAGE Ratings: 7/9.5★/7 (Campground) Avail: 16 full hkups (30/50 amps). 2021 rates: $50 to $114. Apr 15 to Oct 15. (800)562-1878, 9705 S U S Hwy 89, Jackson, WY 83001

THE VIRGINIAN LODGE AND RV PARK **Ratings: 8.5/10★/7.5** (RV Park) Avail: 103 full hkups (30/50 amps). 2021 rates: $119 to $170. May 01 to Oct 15. (307)733-7189, 750 W Broadway, Jackson, WY 83001

JACKSON HOLE — B1 *Teton*

JACKSON HOLE See also Alpine & Jackson, WY; Palisades, ID.

KEMMERER — D1 *Lincoln*

FONTENELLE RESERVOIR CAMPGROUND (BLM) (Public Corps) From town: Go 30 mi NE on US 189. 55 Avail. 2021 rates: $7. May 20 to Oct 15. (307)828-4500

RIVERSIDE RV PARK
Ratings: 6.5/NA/8 (RV Park) From Jct of Hwys 30 & 189 (in town), N 0.5 mi on Hwy 189 to sign (Aspen Ave), S 0.3 mi to sign (Spinel St), E 0.1 mi (R). Elev 6927 ft.**FAC:** paved/gravel rds. (35 spaces). 20 Avail: 11 paved, 8 gravel, 1 grass, 11 pull-thrus, (25x57), back-ins (25x30), 20 full hkups (30/50 amps), seasonal sites, WiFi @ sites, $, dump. **REC:** Hams Fork River: fishing, kayaking/canoeing, hunting nearby. Pets OK $. No tents. 2021 rates: $35. May 15 to Oct 15. no cc.
(307)877-3416 Lat: 41.79735, Lon: -110.53495
216 Spinel St, Kemmerer, WY 83101
See ad this page

Things to See and Do

FOSSIL BASIN PROMOTION BOARD Fossil Basin Promotion Board is a group dedicated to the promotion of the rich outdoor adventures provided by both Kemmerer and Diamondville Wyoming.There is NO public visitor center. Elev 6949 ft. Hours: . No CC.
(307)828-4089
855 Fossil Dr, Kemmerer, WY 83101
fossilbasin.org
See ad page 1019

LANDER — C2 *Fremont*

MAVERICK RV PARK & CAMPGROUND **Ratings: 4.5/7.5★/5** (RV Park) Avail: 25 full hkups (30/50 amps). 2021 rates: $50. (307)332-3142, 1104 N Second St, Lander, WY 82520

SINKS CANYON (Public State Park) From town: Go 6 mi W on Hwy 131. 29 Avail: Pit toilets. 2021 rates: $10 to $17. (307)332-6333

SLEEPING BEAR RV PARK & CAMPGROUND
Ratings: 8/9.5★/9 (RV Park) From W Jct of Hwy 287 & SR-789 (in town), S 0.5 mi on Hwy 287/SR-789 (R). E edge of town on Hwy 287. Elev 5381 ft.**FAC:** gravel rds. (46 spaces). Avail: 38 gravel, 18 pull-thrus, (30x65), back-ins (25x35), 33 full hkups, 5 W, 5 E (30/50 amps), seasonal sites, WiFi @ sites, tent sites, rentals, dump, laundry, groc, LP gas, fire rings, firewood. **REC:** playground, hunting nearby, rec open to public. Pets OK. Partial handicap access, eco-friendly. 2021 rates: $32 to $46.50, Military discount.
(307)332-5159 Lat: 42.82516, Lon: -108.71869
715 E Main, Lander, WY 82520
www.sleepingbearrvpark.com
See ad page 1030

TWIN PINES RV PARK & CAMPGROUND
Ratings: 8/9★/8.5 (RV Park) From Jct of Hwy 287 & SR 789, S 8 mi on SR 789 (L). Elev 5600 ft.**FAC:** gravel rds. Avail: 20 gravel, 20 pull-thrus, (22x60), 20 full hkups (30/50 amps), WiFi @ sites, tent sites, rentals, laundry, LP bottles, firewood. **REC:** pond, boating nearby, playground, hunting nearby. Pets OK. Big rig sites, eco-friendly. 2021 rates: $45, Military discount. May 01 to Nov 01.
(800)986-4008 Lat: 42.73738, Lon: -108.64835
7345 Hwy 789, Lander, WY 82520
www.twinpinesrvpark.com
See ad page 1030

LARAMIE — D4 *Albany*

LARAMIE KOA **Ratings: 7.5/10★/7.5** (Campground) Avail: 142 full hkups (30/50 amps). 2021 rates: $38.52 to $122.85. (800)562-4153, 1271 W Baker St, Laramie, WY 82072

LINGLE — C5 *Goshen*

PONY SOLDIER RV PARK
Ratings: 6.5/9★/8 (RV Park) 53 Avail: 43 full hkups, 10 W, 10 E (30/50 amps). 2021 rates: $40.50. Apr 15 to Sep 30. (307)837-3078, 2302 US Hwy 26, Lingle, WY 82223

LOVELL — A3 *Big Horn*

BIGHORN CANYON NRA/HORSESHOE BEND (Public National Park) From Lovell, E 3 mi on 14A to SR-37, N 9.7 mi to park access rd, E 2 mi (E). 48 Avail: 19 W, 19 E. 2021 rates: $10 to $20. (307)548-2251

LOVELL CAMPER PARK (Public) From Jct of US-310 & Quebec Ave, N 0.2 mi on Quebec Ave (L). 10 Avail. (307)548-6551

LUSK — C5 *Niobrara*

BJ'S CAMPGROUND **Ratings: 6.5/9.5★/9** (Campground) Avail: 23 full hkups (30/50 amps). 2021 rates: $38.50 to $40. May 15 to Nov 01. (307)334-2314, 902 S Maple, Lusk, WY 82225

LYMAN — D1 *Uinta*

LYMAN KOA
Ratings: 8/8.5★/8 (Campground) From Jct of I-80 & Hwy 413 (exit 41), S 1 mi on Hwy 413 (R). Elev 6700 ft.**FAC:** gravel rds. 36 Avail: 18 gravel, 18 grass, 36 pull-thrus, (21x90), 18 full hkups, 18 W, 18 E (30/50 amps), WiFi @ sites, tent sites, rentals, dump, laundry, groc, fire rings, firewood. **REC:** heated pool, playground, hunting nearby. Pets OK. 2021 rates: $35 to $44. May 15 to Sep 30.
(800)562-2762 Lat: 41.35012, Lon: -110.29915
1545 N Hwy 413, Lyman, WY 82937
koa.com/campgrounds/lyman
See ad this page

MEETEETSE — A2 *Park*

BLACK-FOOTED FERRET RV RESORT
(RV Resort) (Too New to Rate) From jct WY-290 & WY-120 E: Go 3/4 mi E on WY-120, then 1/2 mi N on Phelps Way (R). Elev 5675 ft.

HOME ON THE RANGE IN MEETEETSE, WY!
The Authentic Western Town of Meeteetse is at the front porch of Yellowstone and 30 mins from Cody. Meeteetse is known for fishing, hunting and wildlife viewing. The town gives visitors a glimpse of how the West used to be.
FAC: gravel rds. Avail: 98 gravel, 12 pull-thrus, (35x100), back-ins (35x60), 98 full hkups (50 amps),

RV Park ratings you can rely on!

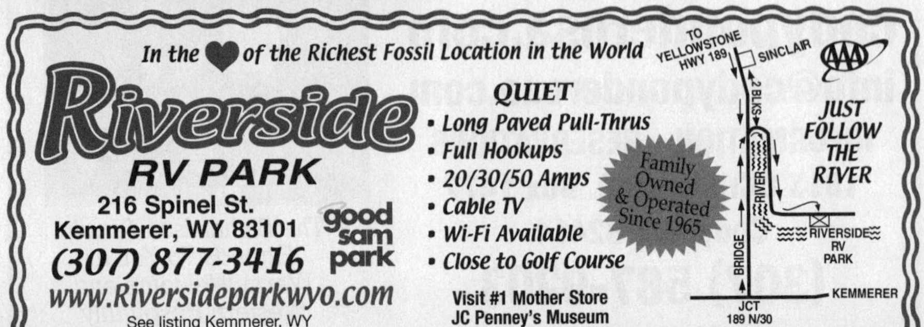

WiFi @ sites, . **REC:** hunting nearby. Pets OK. No tents. Big rig sites, eco-friendly. 2021 rates: $60 to $100.
(307)296-7187 Lat: 44.152220, Lon: -108.857860
100 Phelps Way, Meeteetse, WY 82443
bffrvresort.com
See ad opposite page

MOORCROFT — A5 *Crook*

KEYHOLE (Public State Park) From town, E 11.3 mi on I-90 to Pine Ridge Rd., N 6 mi on Pine Ridge Rd., follow signs (L). Entrance fee required. 256 Avail: 31 W, 31 E (30 amps), Pit toilets. 2021 rates: $10 to $17. (307)756-3596

MORAN — B1 *Teton*

COLTER BAY CAMPGROUND **Ratings: 4/7/6.5** (RV Park) Avail: 13 E (20/30 amps). 2021 rates: $66.60. May 21 to Sep 20. (307)543-2811, 100 Colter Bay Village Road, Moran, WY 83013

COLTER BAY VILLAGE RV PARK **Ratings: 6.5/8★/7.5** (RV Park) Avail: 112 full hkups (30/50 amps). 2021 rates: $94 to $97.68. May 27 to Sep 30. (307)543-3100, 100 Colter Bay Campground, Moran, WY 83013

HEADWATERS LODGE & CABINS @ FLAGG RANCH **Ratings: 5.5/8.5★/7.5** (Campground) Avail: 97 full hkups (30/50 amps). 2021 rates: $84. Jun 01 to Sep 30. (307)543-2861, 100 Grassy Lake Rd, Moran, WY 83013

LIZARD CREEK CAMPGROUND **Ratings: 2.5/NA/6.5** (Campground) 60 Avail. 2021 rates: $41. Jun 15 to Sep 02. (800)672-6012, 651 Lizard Creek Campground, Moran, WY 83013

SIGNAL MOUNTAIN CAMPGROUND **Ratings: 6.5/NA/7** (Campground) Avail: 24 E (20/30 amps). 2021 rates: $68.82. May 10 to Oct 13. (307)739-3300, 1 Inner Park Rd, Moran, WY 83013

NEWCASTLE — B5 *Weston*

AUTO-INN MOTEL & RV PARK Ratings: 5.5/8.5★/6.5 (RV Park) Avail: 28 full hkups (30/50 amps). 2021 rates: $35 to $45. (307)746-2734, 2503 W Main, Newcastle, WY 82701

PINE BLUFFS — D5 *Laramie*

PINE BLUFFS RV PARK **Ratings: 7.5/10★/8.5** (RV Park) Avail: 91 full hkups (30/50 amps). 2021 rates: $44. Apr 15 to Nov 01. (307)245-3222, 10 Paintbrush Rd, Pine Bluffs, WY 82082

RANCHESTER — A3 *Sheridan*

LAZY R RV CAMPGROUND & CABINS **Ratings: 4/8★/7.5** (RV Park) Avail: 22 full hkups (30/50 amps). 2021 rates: $40.68. (888)655-9284, 652 U S Hwy 14, Ranchester, WY 82839

RAWLINS — D3 *Carbon*

RAWLINS KOA **Ratings: 8/10★/8** (Campground) 44 Avail: 38 full hkups, 6 W, 6 E (30/50 amps). 2021 rates: $32 to $65. Mar 15 to Nov 15. (800)562-7559, 205 E Hwy 71, Rawlins, WY 82301

WESTERN HILLS CAMPGROUND
Ratings: 8/9.5★/8.5 (Campground) From Jct of I-80 & Spruce St (Exit 211), NE 0.3 mi on Spruce St to 23rd St, N 50 yds on 23rd St to Wagon Circle Rd, W 0.2 mi (R). Elev 6750 ft.**FAC:** gravel rds. (83 spaces). Avail: 45 gravel, 45 pull-thrus, (24x80), 45 full hkups (30/50 amps), seasonal sites, cable, WiFi @ sites, tent sites, rentals, dump, laundry, groc. **REC:** playground, hunting nearby. Pets OK. Big rig sites, eco-friendly. 2021 rates: $33 to $40, Military discount. Apr 01 to Nov 01.
(307)324-2592 Lat: 41.78523, Lon: -107.26664
2500 Wagon Circle Road, Rawlins, WY 82301
See ad this page

RIVERSIDE — D4 *Carbon*

LAZY ACRES CAMPGROUND & MOTEL **Ratings: 7/UI/8.5** (Campground) 24 Avail: 13 full hkups, 11 W, 11 E (30/50 amps). 2021 rates: $40 to $42. May 15 to Sep 30. (307)327-5968, 110 Fields Ave, Riverside, WY 82325

RV DRIVING TIPS: Adjust your vehicle's environment so that it helps you to stay alert. Keep the temperature cool, with open windows or air conditioning in the summer and minimal amounts of heat in the winter. Avoid listening to soft, sleep-inducing music and switch radio stations frequently.

RIVERTON — B3 *Fremont*

WIND RIVER RV PARK **Ratings: 7/9.5★/6.5** (RV Park) Avail: 60 full hkups (30/50 amps). 2021 rates: $36.02 to $44.55. (307)857-3000, 1618 E Park Ave, Riverton, WY 82501

ROCK SPRINGS — D2 *Sweetwater*

ROCK SPRINGS - GREEN RIVER KOA **Ratings: 7.5/9.5★/7** (Campground) 79 Avail: 50 full hkups, 29 W, 29 E (30/50 amps). 2021 rates: $48 to $68. (800)562-8699, 86 Foothill Blvd, Rock Springs, WY 82901

ROZET — A4 *Campbell*

ALL SEASONS RV PARK **Ratings: 4/8.5★/7** (RV Park) Avail: 18 full hkups (30/50 amps). 2021 rates: $40. (307)686-2552, 1000 Mcintosh Lane, Rozet, WY 82727

SARATOGA — D3 *Carbon*

DEER HAVEN RV PARK/MHP **Ratings: 5.5/NA/6.5** (RV Park) Avail: 30 full hkups (30/50 amps). 2021 rates: $45 to $55. May 01 to Oct 31. (307)326-8746, 706 N 1st St, Saratoga, WY 82331

SARATOGA LAKE CAMPGROUND (Public) From town, N 1 mi on Hwy 230/130 to Saratoga Lake Rd, E 1 mi (S). Avail: 25 E (30 amps). 2021 rates: $10 to $15. (307)326-8335

SHELL — A3 *Big Horn*

SHELL CAMPGROUND **Ratings: 5.5/8★/8** (Campground) 13 Avail: 11 full hkups, 2 E (20/30 amps). 2021 rates: $35. (307)765-9924, 102 1st St, Shell, WY 82441

SHERIDAN — A3 *Sheridan*

JACKALOPE CAMPGROUND **Ratings: 6/10★/5.5** (RV Park) Avail: 50 full hkups (30/50 amps). 2021 rates: $55. (307)673-5553, 2744 Heartland Dr, Sheridan, WY 82801

PETER D'S RV PARK
Ratings: 6.5/9.5★/8.5 (RV Park) Avail: 54 full hkups (30/50 amps). 2021 rates: $40 to $55. Apr 15 to Oct 01. (888)673-0597, 1105 Joe St, Sheridan, WY 82801

SHERIDAN/BIG HORN MOUNTAINS KOA JOURNEY **Ratings: 8/9.5★/8.5** (Campground) 65 Avail: 43 full hkups, 22 W, 22 E (30/50 amps). 2021 rates: $48.89 to $70.89. Apr 01 to Oct 31. (800)562-7621, 63 Decker Rd, Sheridan, WY 82801

SHOSHONI — B3 *Fremont*

BOYSEN (Public State Park) From Jct of US-26 & US-20, N 13 mi on US-20, follow signs (E). Entrance fee required. 277 Avail. 2021 rates: $17. (307)876-2796

SINCLAIR — D3 *Carbon*

SEMINOE (Public State Park) From town, N 34 mi on CR-351, follow signs (R) Entrance fee required. 88 Avail. 2021 rates: $10 to $17. (307)320-2234

SUNDANCE — A5 *Crook*

MOUNTAIN VIEW RV PARK & CAMPGROUND
Ratings: 9/10★/9 (Campground) 56 Avail: 42 full hkups, 14 W, 14 E (30/50 amps). 2021 rates: $39 to $66. Apr 01 to Nov 15. (307)283-2270, 117 Government Valley Rd, Sundance, WY 82729

TEN SLEEP — B3 *Washakie*

TEN SLEEP RV PARK & CABINS **Ratings: 6.5/8★/9** (Campground) Avail: 43 full hkups (30/50 amps). 2021 rates: $40 to $50. (307)366-2250, 98 2nd St, Ten Sleep, WY 82442

THAYNE — C1 *Lincoln*

FLAT CREEK RV PARK & CABINS **Ratings: 5/7.5★/7** (RV Park) 10 Avail: 7 full hkups, 3 W, 3 E (30/50 amps). 2021 rates: $46. May 01 to Nov 01. (307)883-2231, 74 Hokanson Ave., Thayne, WY 83127

STAR VALLEY RANCH RESORT **Ratings: 9.5/10★/9** (Membership Park) Avail: 35 full hkups (30/50 amps). 2021 rates: $45. May 01 to Oct 15. (307)883-2670, 3522 Muddy String Rd, Thayne, WY 83127

WOLF DEN RV PARK **Ratings: 6/9.5★/9** (RV Park) Avail: 13 full hkups (30/50 amps). 2021 rates: $48. (307)883-2226, 55 County Road 115/US Hwy 89, Thayne, WY 83127

THERMOPOLIS — B3 *Hot Springs*

EAGLE RV PARK & CAMPGROUND
Ratings: 8/10★/8.5 (RV Park) From Jct of SR-120 (Broadway) & US-20 (6th St), S 2 mi on US-20 (R). Elev 4300 ft.-**FAC:** gravel rds. (34 spaces). Avail: 26 gravel, 24 pull-thrus, (22x50), back-ins (22x50), 26 full hkups (30/50 amps), seasonal sites, cable, WiFi @ sites, tent sites, rentals, laundry, LP gas, fire rings, firewood. **REC:** playground, hunting nearby. Pets OK. eco-friendly. 2021 rates: $47.40 to $52.05, Military discount.
(307)864-5262 Lat: 43.62427, Lon: -108.220918
204 US Hwy 20 S, Thermopolis, WY 82443
www.eaglervpark.com
See ad this page

TORRINGTON — C5 *Goshen*

PIONEER PARK (Public) From Jct of US-85 & 15th St, W 0.2 mi on 15th St, follow signs (L). Avail: 10 E (20 amps). 2021 rates: $15. (307)532-5666

WHEATLAND — C5 *Platte*

ARROWHEAD RV PARK **Ratings: 5/8★/6.5** (RV Park) Avail: 16 full hkups (30/50 amps). 2021 rates: $40. (307)322-3467, 2005 16th St, Wheatland, WY 82201

EL RANCHO VILLAGE RV & CABINS
Ratings: 7/9.5★/7 (RV Park) Avail: 28 full hkups (30/50 amps). 2021 rates: $40. (307)331-9972, 26 Fish Creek Rd, Wheatland, WY 82201

LEWIS PARK (Public) From Jct of I-25 & Mariposa Pkwy (exit 78), E 0.1 mi on Mariposa Pkwy to 16th St, N 0.5 mi to Gilchrist, E 0.6 mi to 8th St, S 0.2 mi, follow signs (R). Avail: 10 full hkups (20/30 amps). (307)322-2962

MOUNTAIN VIEW RV PARK **Ratings: 6.5/10★/7.5** (RV Park) Avail: 14 full hkups (30/50 amps). 2021 rates: $40. (307)322-4858, 77 N 20th St, Wheatland, WY 82201

WORLAND — B3 *Hot Springs*

WORLAND RV PARK AND CAMPGROUND
Ratings: 7.5/9.5★/9 (RV Park) 37 Avail: 34 full hkups, 3 W, 3 E (30/50 amps). 2021 rates: $38. May 01 to Oct 01. (307)347-2329, 2313 Big Horn Ave, Worland, WY 82401

YELLOWSTONE NATIONAL PARK — A1 *Teton*

YELLOWSTONE NATIONAL PARK See also Cody & Jackson, WY; Island Park, ID; Cameron, Gardiner, Livingston & West Yellowstone, MT.

YELLOWSTONE/BRIDGE BAY (Public National Park) In town, SW 3 mi on Lake Village Rd, follow signs (R). 432 Avail. 2021 rates: $25.25. May 18 to Sep 23. (307)344-7381

YELLOWSTONE/CANYON (Public National Park) From Canyon Junction, E 0.25 mi on County Rd, follow signs (L). 270 Avail. 2021 rates: $30. May 25 to Sep 23. (307)344-7311

YELLOWSTONE/FISHING BRIDGE (Public National Park) From Lake Jct, E 1 mi on US-14/16/20, 0.5 mi E of Fishing Bridge (L) Note: Hard sided units only/. Avail: 346 full hkups (30/50 amps). 2021 rates: $47.75. May 11 to Sep 05. (307)344-7311

YELLOWSTONE/GRANT VILLAGE (Public National Park) From West Thumb Jct, S 2 mi, follow signs (L). 429 Avail. 2021 rates: $30. Jun 08 to Sep 16. (307)344-7311

YELLOWSTONE/INDIAN CREEK (Public National Park) From Mammoth Jct, S 7.5 mi, follow signs (R). Entrance fee required. 70 Avail: Pit toilets. 2021 rates: $15. Jun 08 to Sep 17. (307)344-7381

Like Us on Facebook.

YELLOWSTONE/LEWIS LAKE (Public National Park) From town, S 10 mi on Thumb Jct Rd, follow signs (R). Entrance fee required. 85 Avail: Pit toilets. 2021 rates: $15. Jun 15 to Nov 01. (307)344-7381

YELLOWSTONE/MADISON (Public National Park) From Jct of Hwys 20 & 191 (W entrance), E 14 mi on Hwy 20, follow signs (L). 149 Avail. 2021 rates: $25.25. Apr 27 to Oct 14. (307)344-7311

YELLOWSTONE/MAMMOTH (Public National Park) From Jct of Hwys 89 & 212 (N entrance), S 5 mi on Hwy 89, follow signs (R). Entrance fee required. 85 Avail. 2021 rates: $20. (307)344-7381

YELLOWSTONE/NORRIS (Public National Park) From Mammoth Jct, S 20 mi. 100 Avail. 2021 rates: $20. May 15 to Sep 27. (307)344-7381

YELLOWSTONE/PEBBLE CREEK (Public National Park) From Via Cooke City Mt entrance, SW 7 mi on Via Cooke City MT entrance rd (R). Entrance fee required. 27 Avail: Pit toilets. 2021 rates: $15. Jun 15 to Sep 30. (307)344-7381

YELLOWSTONE/SLOUGH CREEK (Public National Park) From Tower Jct, NE 6 mi on Tower Rd to gravel rd, N 2.5 mi, follow signs (L). Entrance fee required. 16 Avail: Pit toilets. 2021 rates: $15. Jun 15 to Sep 30. (307)344-7381

YELLOWSTONE/TOWER FALL (Public National Park) From Tower Jct, S 2.5 mi on Tower Canyon Rd, follow signs (R). Entrance fee required. Avail: 31 W, Pit toilets. 2021 rates: $15. May 23 to Sep 29. (307)344-7381

Get the Most Out of Your Awnings. Safeguard them from the environmental risks. If the weather looks at all iffy, check local forecasts to determine the wind's predicted direction and speed. Pay special attention to any gusty wind conditions. Don't leave extended awnings out if you're not going to be in the RV park to attend the situation. This includes automatic power-retract models. A fast-approaching squall line or a wind micro-burst can destroy an awning quicker than any retract motor can reel it in. Be sure to trim your awning to shed water. Excessive water pooling weight can exceed the awning's structural integrity. If you put your awning away in the rain, or if it was wet by any other reason, be sure to dry it out later. Extending the awning to dry and air it out will keep the fabric clean and bright. Furl your awnings if any nearby campfires are producing glowing ash that may reach your site. Proper care for your awnings can keep them looking new for years to come.

CROSSING INTO CANADA

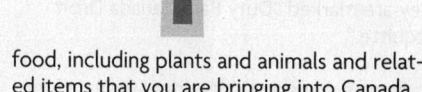

What you need to know when visiting the United States' northern neighbor

Canada's thrilling destinations, courteous citizens and beautiful scenery beckon visitors from all corners of the United States. But U.S. travelers shouldn't cross the northern border without being informed of Canada's laws regarding identification, customs, driving and importation. Visit travel.gc.ca for more information.

REQUIRED IDENTIFICATION

Upon entering Canada, U.S. citizens are required in most cases to show a passport to the Canada Border Services Agency (CBSA) as proof of identity and as a document that denotes citizenship. For U.S. citizens, proof of citizenship can also include a birth certificate, certificate of citizenship or naturalization, or a Certificate of Indian Status along with photo identification at the land border.

If you are a U.S. permanent resident, carry proof of your status, such as a U.S. Permanent Resident Card, in addition to a passport.

Citizens and permanent U.S. residents who are members of the NEXUS or FAST programs may present their membership cards to the CBSA. This identification only applies to travelers arriving by land or by the sea. NEXUS and FAST members who are U.S. permanent residents must also travel with a passport and proof of permanent residence to present to CBSA upon request.

All travelers are encouraged to visit the CBSA website, cbsa-asfc.gc.ca, for more information.

Also helpful is the U.S. Customs and Border Protection's website, cbp.gov.

BORDER RESTRICTIONS AND WHAT TO DECLARE

GOODS

As a visitor crossing the border, you can transport certain goods into Canada for your own use as "personal baggage."

Canadian law requires that you declare all food, including plants and animals and related items that you are bringing into Canada.

Personal baggage includes clothing, camping and sports equipment, cameras and personal computers. This also includes your mode of transportation.

You must declare all goods at the port of entry with the CBSA. Border Services Officers may conduct examinations of goods being imported or exported to verify the declarations.

If you declare goods when you arrive and take them back with you when you leave, you will not have to pay any duty or taxes. These goods can't be used by a resident of Canada, used on behalf of a business based in Canada, given as a gift to a Canadian resident or disposed of or left behind in Canada.

ALCOHOL

Visitors who are of legal age in the province they are entering are allowed to import a

Rainbow Bridge above the Niagara River between the United States and Canada.

maximum of 1.14 liters of liquor (40 fluid ounces), 1.5 liters of wine (53 fluid ounces or two 750 milliliter bottles), or 8.5 liters of beer or ale (287 fluid ounces) without paying any applicable duties and taxes. Any alcohol quantities above this amount will incur duties and taxes.

CIGARS AND CIGARETTES

Visitors who are 18 years or older can import 200 cigarettes, 50 cigars, 200 grams of manufactured tobacco and 200 tobacco sticks.

Visitors who include tobacco products in personal exemptions will still have to pay a minimum duty on these products unless they are marked "Duty Paid Canada Droit Acquitté."

Adults can transport duty-free 50 cigars (not of Cuban origin) or 200 cigarettes (1 carton) back to the U.S.

CANNABIS

Entering: Cannabis is legal for adults in Canada. But restrictions apply to those traveling with cannabis. It is still illegal to transport cannabis and products containing cannabis — including edible cannabis, cannabis extracts and cannabis topicals — across the Canadian border. If you are entering Canada and have cannabis with you in any form, you must declare it to the Canada Border Services Agency.

Failing to declare cannabis in your possession when attempting to cross the Canadian border is a serious criminal offense. You could be arrested and prosecuted.

Leaving: The rules that apply to entering with cannabis also apply when it comes to leaving Canada. It is illegal to take cannabis across the Canadian border. You could be charged with a criminal offense if you try to travel to other countries with any amount of cannabis in your possession. This applies to all countries, whether cannabis is legal there or not.

MONEY

If you have currency or monetary instruments equal to or greater than CAN$10,000 (or the equivalent in a foreign currency) in your possession when arriving in or departing from Canada, you must report this to the CBSA. Monetary instruments include items such as stocks, bonds, bank drafts, checks and traveler's checks.

The Canadian dollar is the currency used in all of Canada's provinces. You can exchange U.S. dollars and Canadian dollars at banks in the U.S. or Canada. To find the current exchange rate, consult the Bank of Canada, bankofcanada.ca/rates/exchange.

TRAVEL WITH MINORS

If you plan to travel to Canada with a minor who is not your own child or for whom you do not have full legal custody, CBSA may require you to present a notarized affidavit of consent from the minor's parents. CBSA strongly recommends a consent letter if they are traveling with only one parent/guardian, with friends or relatives, or with a group.

FIREARMS

When you enter Canada, you must declare all firearms and weapons to the CBSA. If you do not, they may be seized, and you could face criminal charges. Visitors to Canada cannot import prohibited weapons or devices.

Firearms are more strictly controlled in Canada than in the U.S. Violations of firearms restrictions may result in prosecution and imprisonment.

PETS

Dogs and cats may enter Canada if they are accompanied by a rabies certification. The Canadian Food Inspection Agency establishes import requirements for all animals and animal products entering Canada.

See inspection.gc.ca for more information.

▸ FOR MORE INFORMATION
Canada Border Services Agency (CBSA)
Outside Canada: 204-983-3500
or 506-636-5064
Within Canada: 800-461-9999
cbsa-asfc.gc.ca

COVID GUIDELINES FOR FULLY VACCINATED U.S. TRAVELERS

Fully vaccinated United States (U.S.) citizens and permanent residents are eligible to enter Canada for discretionary (non-essential) reasons, such as tourism. However, these individuals must:

1) Be fully vaccinated: to be considered fully vaccinated, a traveler must have received the full series of a vaccine — or combination of vaccines — accepted by the Government of Canada at least 14 days prior to entering Canada. Currently, those vaccines are manufactured by Pfizer-BioNTech, Moderna, AstraZeneca/COVISHIELD and Janssen (Johnson & Johnson).

2) Have a valid pre-arrival COVID-19 molecular test result taken in the U.S. no longer than 72 hours prior to arrival. (Antigen tests — also known as rapid tests —are not accepted). If driving or traveling by water, tests must have been taken in the U.S.

3) Be asymptomatic.

4) Submit their mandatory information via ArriveCAN (www.canada.com/arrivecan) app or website, including proof of vaccination in English or French and quarantine plan.

5) Be admissible under the Immigration and Refugee Protection Act.

6) Take a test on arrival, if selected.

▸ FOR MORE INFORMATION
travel.gc.ca/travel-covid

Getty Images/iStockphoto

DID YOU KNOW?
The town of Vulcan has a Star Trek museum with a 31-foot replica of the Enterprise spacecraft.
YOU ARE HERE
Alberta
Getty Images/iStockphoto

Few places in North America can rival Alberta when it comes to scenery. The Canadian Rockies, running along the province's southwestern border, are stars. Banff and Jasper National Parks, in particular, take top billing.

Legendary Towns

Alberta is home to a slew of cities that capture the imagination. Edmonton holds the distinction of being North America's northernmost town with a population exceeding one million. It also bursts with quirky yet rugged Canadian spirit. Start with West Edmonton Mall. Spanning the equivalent of 48 city blocks, this behemoth of an indoor shopping center offers endless retail stores, restaurants and attractions, all protected from the fierce winter winds. There's even an indoor water park for folks who want a thrill.

Sky-High Parks

Towering peaks, clear blue skies and turquoise-colored lakes and ponds characterize Alberta's parks. Banff National Park is an iconic spot, nestled in the Canadian Rockies. Over three million people come to explore this 1.6-million-acre park annually. Jasper National Park, located more than 100 miles to the north along Alberta Highway 93, is more remote but no less beautiful. This pair of iconic recreational playgrounds is laced with hiking and biking trails. Famous waterways and spectacular rock climbing keep the fun going.

Driving the Rockies

The 143-mile Icefields Parkway treats drivers to gorgeous scenery on a route through the mountains. Connecting Lake Louise and Jasper National Park, this famed roadway takes you past waterfalls, glaciers and limestone cliffs. Watch for black bears, elk and moose. The lucky few might catch sight of caribou, wolves and grizzlies.

Alberta Pierogi

Back in the 1800s, Ukrainian immigrants mastered the art of cramming an abundance of flavor into a small package. Pierogies are dough dumplings traditionally stuffed with potatoes, cheese and sauerkraut. First boiled and then fried in butter, these pockets hold in lots of heat and moisture, unleashing great taste with each bite. Add some protein to the mix by ordering a meat-filled Pierogi.

VISITOR CENTER

TIME ZONE
Mountain Standard

ROAD & HIGHWAY INFORMATION
511.alberta.ca

FISHING & HUNTING INFORMATION
800-267-6687
albertaregulations.ca/huntingregs

BOATING INFORMATION
tc.gc.ca/marinesafety

NATIONAL PARKS
pc.gc.ca/en/pn-np

PROVINCIAL PARKS
albertaparks.ca

TOURISM INFORMATION
Travel Alberta
800-ALBERTA
travelalberta.com

TOP TOURISM ATTRACTIONS
1) Banff National Park
2) Jasper National Park
3) West Edmonton Mall

MAJOR CITIES
Calgary, Edmonton (capital), Red Deer, Strathcona County, Lethbridge

good sam park

Featured Good Sam Parks

ALBERTA

When you stay with Good Sam, you can expect the highest degree of cleanliness and friendliness, and better yet, you get **10% off** overnight campground fees.

If you're not already a Good Sam member you can purchase your membership at one of these locations:

CAMROSE
Camrose RV Park

COCHRANE
Bow RiversEdge Campground

EDMONTON
Diamond Grove RV Campground
Glowing Embers RV Park & Travel Centre

GRANDE PRAIRIE
Bear Paw Par 3 Golf Course & RV Park
Camp Tamarack RV Park
Country Roads RV Park
Nitehawk Wilderness RV Park & Campground

PEACE RIVER
Rendez Vous RV Park & Storage

ROCKY MOUNTAIN HOUSE
Riverview Campground

ST ALBERT
St. Albert RV Park

STONY PLAIN
Camp 'N Class RV Park

VALLEYVIEW
Sherk's RV Park

Getty Images/iStockphoto

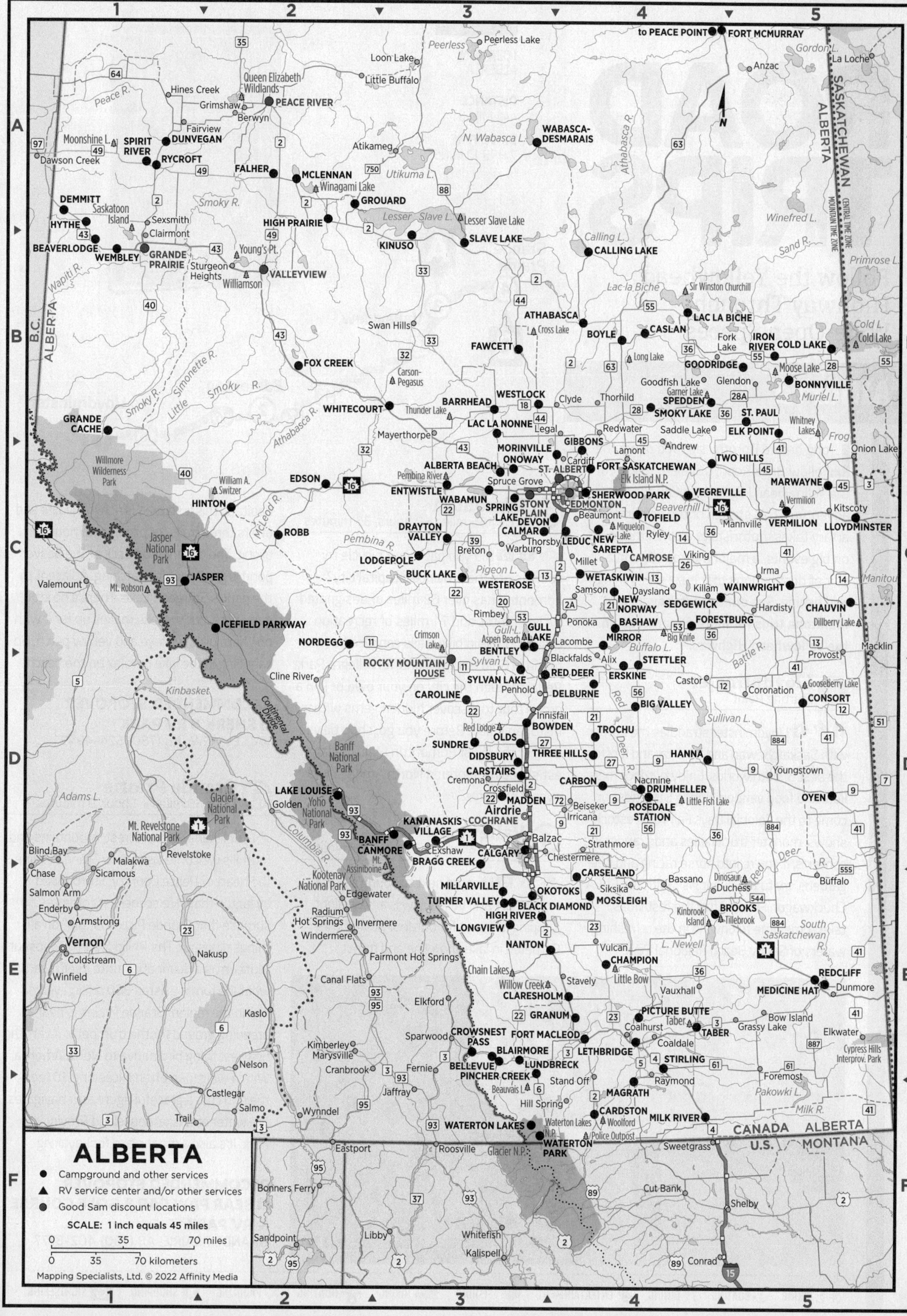
ALBERTA
Campground and other services
RV service center and/or other services
Good Sam discount locations
SCALE: 1 inch equals 45 miles
0 35 70 miles
0 35 70 kilometers
Mapping Specialists, Ltd. © 2022 Affinity Media
to PEACE POINT
FORT MCMURRAY
Peerless Lake
Loon Lake
Little Buffalo
Queen Elizabeth Wildlands
Hines Creek
Grimshaw
PEACE RIVER
Berwyn
Fairview
DUNVEGAN
SPIRIT RIVER
RYCROFT
Moonshine L.
Dawson Creek
Atikameg
WABASCA-DESMARAIS
N. Wabasca L.
Utikuma L.
FALHER
MCLENNAN
Winagami Lake
GROUARD
HIGH PRAIRIE
Lesser Slave L.
Lesser Slave Lake
SLAVE LAKE
KINUSO
DEMMITT
HYTHE
Saskatoon Island
Sexsmith
Clairmont
BEAVERLODGE
WEMBLEY
GRANDE PRAIRIE
Young's Pt.
Sturgeon Heights
Williamson
VALLEYVIEW
Smoky R.
Peace R.
Wapiti R.
Anzac
Gordon L.
La Loche
SASKATCHEWAN
ALBERTA
CENTRAL TIME ZONE
MOUNTAIN TIME ZONE
Athabasca R.
Calling L.
CALLING LAKE
Winefred L.
Sand R.
Primrose L.
Lac la Biche
Sir Winston Churchill
LAC LA BICHE
ATHABASCA
Cross Lake
BOYLE
CASLAN
Fork Lake
IRON RIVER
COLD LAKE
Cold L.
Cold Lake
Long Lake
GOODRIDGE
Moose Lake
BONNYVILLE
Swan Hills
FOX CREEK
Carson-Pegasus
FAWCETT
B.C.
ALBERTA
Simonette R.
Little Smoky R.
WHITECOURT
Thunder Lake
BARRHEAD
WESTLOCK
Clyde
Thorhild
Goodfish Lake
Glendon
Garner Lake
SPEDDEN
SMOKY LAKE
ST. PAUL
Muriel L.
GRANDE CACHE
Mayerthorpe
LAC LA NONNE
Legal
Redwater
Saddle Lake
Whitney Lakes
ELK POINT
Frog L.
Onion Lake
Willmore Wilderness Park
MORINVILLE
GIBBONS
Andrew
Lamont
ONOWAY
Cardiff
ST. ALBERT
FORT SASKATCHEWAN
TWO HILLS
ALBERTA BEACH
Pembina River
Elk Island N.P.
Spruce Grove
MARWAYNE
William A. Switzer
EDSON
ENTWISTLE
WABAMUN
SHERWOOD PARK
VEGREVILLE
Vermilion
Kitscoty
HINTON
SPRING LAKE
STONY PLAIN
DEVON
EDMONTON
Beaverhill L.
Beaumont
TOFIELD
Mannville
VERMILION
LLOYDMINSTER
McLeod R.
ROBB
DRAYTON VALLEY
CALMAR
Thorsby
Warburg
LEDUC
Miquelon Lake
NEW SAREPTA
Ryley
Jasper National Park
Pembina R.
Breton
Millet
CAMROSE
Viking
LODGEPOLE
Irma
Manitou
Valemount
Mt. Robson
JASPER
BUCK LAKE
Pigeon L.
WESTEROSE
WETASKIWIN
Samson
Daysland
Killam
WAINWRIGHT
NEW NORWAY
SEDGEWICK
Hardisty
CHAUVIN
Dillberry Lake
Rimbey
Ponoka
BASHAW
FORESTBURG
ICEFIELD PARKWAY
Crimson Lake
Gull L.
GULL LAKE
Aspen Beach
Big Knife
NORDEGG
BENTLEY
Lacombe
MIRROR
Buffalo L.
ROCKY MOUNTAIN HOUSE
Sylvan L.
Blackfalds
Alix
STETTLER
Provost
Macklin
Battle R.
Cline River
SYLVAN LAKE
RED DEER
ERSKINE
Castor
Kinbasket L.
Penhold
DELBURNE
Coronation
Gooseberry Lake
CONSORT
CAROLINE
BIG VALLEY
Continental Divide
Innisfail
Sullivan L.
Red Lodge
BOWDEN
TROCHU
Banff National Park
SUNDRE
OLDS
DIDSBURY
THREE HILLS
HANNA
Red Deer R.
Youngstown
CARSTAIRS
Cremona
CARBON
Nacmine
DRUMHELLER
Little Fish Lake
Adams L.
Glacier National Park
LAKE LOUISE
Golden
Yoho National Park
Crossfield
MADDEN
Airdrie
Beiseker
Irricana
ROSEDALE STATION
OYEN
Mt. Revelstone National Park
Revelstoke
Blind Bay
KANANASKIS VILLAGE
COCHRANE
Balzac
BANFF
CANMORE
Exshaw
CALGARY
Strathmore
Chestermere
BRAGG CREEK
Columbia R.
Mt. Assiniboine
Malakwa
Chase
Sicamous
Salmon Arm
Enderby
Armstrong
Kootenay National Park
Edgewater
MILLARVILLE
CARSELAND
Bassano
Dinosaur
Duchess
Buffalo
TURNER VALLEY
OKOTOKS
Siksika
MOSSLEIGH
BLACK DIAMOND
HIGH RIVER
Radium Hot Springs
Invermere
Windermere
LONGVIEW
Kinbrook Island
BROOKS
Tillebrook
South Saskatchewan R.
Vernon
Coldstream
Winfield
Nakusp
NANTON
Vulcan
L. Newell
Fairmont Hot Springs
Chain Lakes
CHAMPION
Little Bow
Stavely
Willow Creek
Canal Flats
CLARESHOLM
REDCLIFF
Dunmore
MEDICINE HAT
Vauxhall
Elkford
Kaslo
GRANUM
PICTURE BUTTE
Taber
Bow Island
Grassy Lake
Sparwood
CROWSNEST PASS
FORT MACLEOD
Coalhurst
TABER
Elkwater
Kimberley
Marysville
BLAIRMORE
LETHBRIDGE
Coaldale
Cypress Hills Interprov. Park
Nelson
Cranbrook
Fernie
BELLEVUE
LUNDBRECK
STIRLING
PINCHER CREEK
Raymond
Foremost
Castlegar
Beauvais L.
Stand Off
Jaffray
MAGRATH
Pakowki L.
Hill Spring
Salmo
Wynndel
CARDSTON
Milk R.
Trail
Woolford
MILK RIVER
WATERTON LAKES
Waterton Lakes N.P.
Police Outpost
CANADA
U.S.
ALBERTA
MONTANA
WATERTON PARK
Eastport
Roosville
Glacier N.P.
Sweetgrass
Bonners Ferry
Cut Bank
Shelby
Libby
Whitefish
Kalispell
Sandpoint
Conrad
1 2 3 4 5
A B C D E F

ROAD TRIPS

Follow the Yellowhead Highway Through Wide-Open Spaces

Alberta

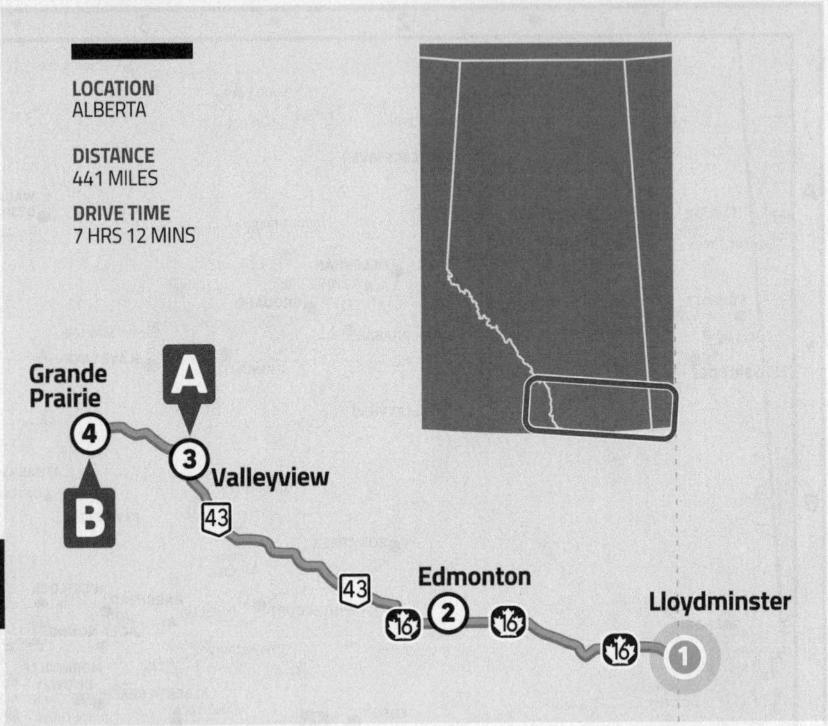

Long before Dorothy skipped down the Yellow Brick Road, travelers followed the Yellowhead Highway in Canada for adventure. This stretch of the celebrated artery takes motorists to a town that puts on big events, a major metropolis and a pair of destinations that buzz with hiking and fishing. **See our Saskatchewan and Manitoba trips for more adventures on the Yellowhead Highway.**

1 Lloydminster
Starting Point

Lloydminster straddles the border with Saskatchewan and Alberta, and it offers the best of both worlds. Enjoy outdoor markets and food vendors during Streetfest or come to the Colonial Days Fair for livestock shows, monster truck rallies and grandstand concerts. If you're into horse racing and beer gardens, try to time your visit with the CPCA Chuckwagon Finals. After the festivities, take some time to unwind in the refreshing waters of Sandy Beach Regional Park.

2 Edmonton
Drive 156 miles ▪ 2 hours, 35 minutes

Did you pack your bicycle for your visit to the province's capital city? Edmonton has over 62 miles of designated cycling routes and 71 miles of recreation trails. Mountain bike trails can also be found in Gold Bar Park and Terwillegar Park. Pedal through the city on your own or join a group tour to discover hidden gems with a historian guide. Before you go, shop till you drop at the West Edmonton Mall, the largest shopping center in North America with over 800 stores.

3 Valleyview
Drive 216 miles ▪ 3 hours, 28 minutes

Located next to Young's Point Provincial Park, Valleyview is an excellent jumping-off spot for outdoor adventures. Carpeted in lake shoreline and forest habitats, this lush area is rich in wildlife and offers three trails for hiking and mountain biking. The observation deck at the beaver pond is great for birdwatching. Adjacent to the park is Sturgeon Lake. There's no sturgeon here, but the lake makes up for it with northern pike, walleye and yellow perch. Go canoeing in the lake or relax on the beach.

RECOMMENDED STOPOVER
A SHERK'S RV PARK
VALLEYVIEW, AB (780) 524-4949

4 Grande Prairie
Drive 69 miles ▪ 1 hour, 9 minutes

Prairie, boreal forest, mountains and foothills welcome visitors to Grande Prairie, the heart of Peace Country. Surrounded by larger-than-life scenery, it comes as no surprise that Grande Prairie is "big" on all things dinosaur. The Philip J. Currie Dinosaur Museum is a destination unto itself. Learn what life forms existed 360 million years ago in the region. Grande Prairie is near a breeding ground for the trumpeter swan, the heaviest living bird native to North America. With a wingspan often exceeding 10 feet, the bird cuts a graceful figure as it navigates the water of Saskatoon Island Provincial Park. It's also a great place for kayaking.

RECOMMENDED STOPOVER
B BEAR PAW PAR 3 GOLF COURSE & RV PARK
GRANDE PRAIRIE, AB (780) 402-8777

Getty Images/iStockphoto

BIKING · BOATING · DINING · ENTERTAINMENT · FISHING · HIKING · HUNTING · PADDLING · SHOPPING · SIGHTSEEING

Alberta SPOTLIGHTS

Come to a Land of Buckaroos and Big Mountains

Alberta serves up the perfect blend of big-city sophistication and frontier escape. Explore the largest mall in North America, then roam Jasper and Banff national parks.

BONES FROM 58 DINOSAUR SPECIES WERE FOUND IN ALBERTA.

Dusk over Dinosaur Provincial Park, a UNESCO World Heritage Site.

Getty Images/iStockphoto

Dinosaur Adventures

All your Jurassic Park dreams come true in Alberta. With one of the planet's highest concentrations of dinosaur fossils, the Canadian province unleashes your inner paleontologist and opens the door to a world of exploration. Unearth over 70 million years of history and then make your own fossil discoveries in the spectacular badlands. From renowned museums to epic provincial parks, here are five essential stops for your dinosaur adventure.

Dinosaur Provincial Park

The badlands in southeastern Alberta are a hotbed for dinosaur fossils. Since the first fossil was uncovered in 1880, paleontologists have found over 4,500 dinosaur skeletons across 44 species, with some dating back as much as 75 million years. Make your own prehistoric discoveries at Dinosaur Provincial Park. The UNESCO World Heritage Site is situated about two and a half hours from Calgary and offers various guided and self-guided activities.

Guided Tours and Fossil Digs

A big chunk of the park is not open to the public, so book a tour with a park guide to access bone beds with millions of fossils. Serious dino enthusiasts can even join a guided excavation. Every year, new fossils are exposed as rain and run-off from nearby creeks wash away the top layer of soil. By participating in an authentic dinosaur dig, you'll get to learn excavation techniques from experienced paleontologists and work with a team to find fossils that have never been seen before.

Self-guided Hikes

Five trails show off the diversity of the park. Follow the Coulee Viewpoint Trail to see the dramatic badlands from a bird's-eye view, trek sandstone ridges along the Badlands Trail or take the Trail of the Fossil Hunters to reach a 1913 quarry site. The Cottonwood Flats Trail offers excellent birdwatching along a riverside while the Prairie Trail weaves through scenic prairie grassland. There are also random access hiking areas throughout the park, giving you the freedom to climb the stark hoodoos and hills.

Royal Tyrrell Museum

Located in Drumheller, the Royal Tyrrell Museum of Paleontology houses a massive collection of dinosaur skeletons with over 157,000 specimens. About 50 are on display, including Black Beauty, a 67-million-year-old t-rex, and Hell Boy, a dinosaur unearthed in 2005. The museum also lets you see what happens inside a fossil lab and offers interactive activities like simulated fossil digs and fossil casting.

Drumheller Valley

In Drumheller, the dinosaur experiences don't stop after the Royal Tyrrell Museum.

LOCAL FAVORITE

Cast Iron Protein Pancakes

The Calgary Stampede is famous for its pancake breakfasts. The tradition started in 1923 when a local rancher began serving pancakes from his camp stove during the festival. *Recipe by Donald and Melody*

INGREDIENTS

- ☐ 1 cup raw oats
- ☐ 1 scoop protein powder
- ☐ 1 egg
- ☐ ¼ cup water
- ☐ 1 ½ tsp cinnamon
- ☐ 2 packets of stevia
- ☐ 1 ½ tsp baking powder
- ☐ 1 small apple, finely chopped (optional)
- ☐ ¼ cup walnuts (optional)

DIRECTIONS

Put all dry ingredients in a jar and shake well. Spray cast iron skillet with cooking spray and preheat for about 1 minute. Add wet ingredients to jarred dry ingredients and shake until well blended. Pour mixture into skillet and cook until air bubbles form in the batter and the pancake rises. Flip pancake to brown the other side and serve. Serve with butter or syrup if desired.

SPOTLIGHTS

Make sure to stop for a photo at the World's Largest Dinosaur. Standing 86 feet tall and 151 feet long, this popular roadside attraction is more than four times larger than a real t-rex. You can even go inside and climb 106 stairs to get an aerial view of the Drumheller Valley from the dinosaur's gaping jaw. If you're traveling with little ones, bring them to the Fossil World Dinosaur Discovery Center to see animatronic dinosaurs and over 1,000 real fossils. Round out your visit with the DinoWalk, a self-guided walking tour marked with wayfinding signs around town. Each sign tells the story of more than 20 dinosaurs found in the Drumheller area.

Devil's Coulee Dinosaur and Heritage Museum

See where baby dinosaurs come from in Warner, a village 50 minutes south of Lethbridge. In 1987, young Wendy Sloboda believed she found a dinosaur eggshell by the Milk River Ridge. Paleontologist Dr. Phillip Currie confirmed the girl's theory, which led to the excavation of a Hadrosaur nesting site. At the Devil's Coulee Dinosaur and Heritage Museum, you can learn more about the ground-breaking discovery and book a tour to see where the eggs were found. Other museum highlights include a Hadrosaur nest and embryo, ancient fossils and dinosaur models.

Philip J. Currie Dinosaur Museum

Near Grand Prairie is Pipestone Creek, considered one of the richest bonebeds on the globe and where Boreonykus was discovered. Camp where dinosaurs roamed in Pipestone Creek Park and then visit the Philip J. Currie Dinosaur Museum, a venue that takes you on a 360-million-year journey from prehistoric times to the petroleum days of modern Alberta. Exhibits cover everything from flora and fauna to geology and climate. Noteworthy displays include newly identified dinosaur species in the main gallery and a recreation of the Pipestone Creek bonebed after a floodplain, which washed away hundreds of horned dinosaurs. There are also plenty of activities to enjoy. Make a fossil replica in

In Edmonton, the graceful Walterdale Bridge spans the frozen, snow-covered Saskatchewan River.

the lab, watch a movie in the Aykroyd Family Theatre or head out for a bonebed excursion with a knowledgeable guide.

Edmonton

As provincial capitals go, it's hard to beat Edmonton, the seat of government for Alberta. Known as the Gateway to the North, this friendly city features plenty of lively, urban culture. However, Edmonton's location in the heart of Canada's prairie does not go forgotten, and there are plenty of opportunities for outdoor pursuits near the dynamic city center.

Massive Mall

For many visitors, Edmonton is a shopper's paradise. The West Edmonton Mall is the largest mall on the continent, boasting 800-plus retail stores along with a water park and an amusement park. Other popular attractions include the Telus World of Science, which features a variety of interactive exhibits for kids and adults, mostly focused on science, technology and space.

Creativity on Display

Put the Muttart Conservatory on your list of Edmonton destinations. It's also worth a visit for its numerous gardens and pyramid-shaped greenhouses, while the Ukrainian Cultural Heritage Village is a living history museum that shows how settlers lived when they first came to the area in large numbers in the late 1800s.

Bodies of Wonderful Water

Get away from civilization by dropping a line in the winding North Saskatchewan River, which flows through town. Capilano Park and Laurier Park both have boat launches to the waterway that are open from April to November (weather permitting). In the northeastern part of the city, Hermitage Park allows nonmotorized boating and canoeing on the river. There are plenty of great opportunities for fishing, with stocked ponds nearby that yield rainbow trout. Fishing in the North Saskatchewan River usually requires a license, but it's free during the Alberta Family Day weekend and at the tail end of National Fishing Week in late June.

Prairie Pathways

The vast prairie surrounding Edmonton harbors lots of recreation possibilities. The 192-mile Waskahegan Trail runs right through town and out into the countryside and is popular with hikers and runners alike. The trail also goes through one of the largest urban park areas in the country: River Valley Parks, a collection of 20 parks featuring miles of hiking trails along with plenty of playgrounds, campsites and even tennis courts and swimming pools. In the northernmost reaches are all sorts of creatures, from

Near Grande Prairie, the Sulphur Gates Provincial Recreation Area attracts hikers and horseback riders.

moose, deer, elk and bison to pigmy shrews, not to mention hundreds of species of birds.

History Comes Alive

Like much of North America, the area now known as Edmonton was settled by First Nations people for millennia. It was inhabited by Europeans in 1795 and grew alongside the fur trade, with large influxes of migration toward the end of the 1800s and into the 20th century. Today, travelers wanting to learn more about the roots of the city flock to Fort Edmonton Park, the largest living history museum in the country. The park is split into different historical periods, with sections devoted to 1846, 1885, 1905 and 1920, each with era-specific activities, displays and costumed interpreters.

Superb Street Car

For a unique view of the city, hop aboard Edmonton's High Level Bridge Street Car. The bridge opened in 1913 and was outfitted with three sets of tracks on its top deck; Canadian Pacific Railway trains ran down the center and local streetcars traveled on the outside. Operated by the Edmonton Radial Railway Society, the streetcar is a restored 1912 model that runs daily between May and September, and on weekends through Thanksgiving Day (in Canada, it's mid-October).

Grande Prairie

Known as the "Swan City," Grande Prairie is a bustling and vibrant town less than 62 miles from Alberta's border with British Columbia. One of the larger towns at the southern end of the scenic aspen parkland known as Peace River Country, its picturesque landscape is best known as the nesting ground for the iconic birds

but also boasts serene provincial parks, miles of hiking trails and world-class museums that delve into the region's prehistoric past.

Dino Days

Visitors rave about the one-of-a-kind interactive exhibits at the Phillip J. Currie Dinosaur Museum just west of town. Dedicated to experiential learning, the museum features educational tours, fossil beds, augmented-reality videos and special events throughout the year, all of which bring guests closer than they've ever been to Alberta's paleontological past.

Human Heritage

History buffs can continue their deep dive at Heritage Park Historical Village, which features 14 restored buildings, including an 1896 Hudson Bay Outpost. Tours of the grounds and adjacent museum give visitors an in-depth glimpse into the challenges and joys of life for the area's early settlers.

Swan Lake

Nestled on the shores of Saskatoon Lake, the Saskatoon Island Provincial Park serves up tranquil views, calm water and the chance to see migrating trumpeter swans. This bird species earned its name for its loud, trumpet-like call, but it might be best known for its graceful ap-

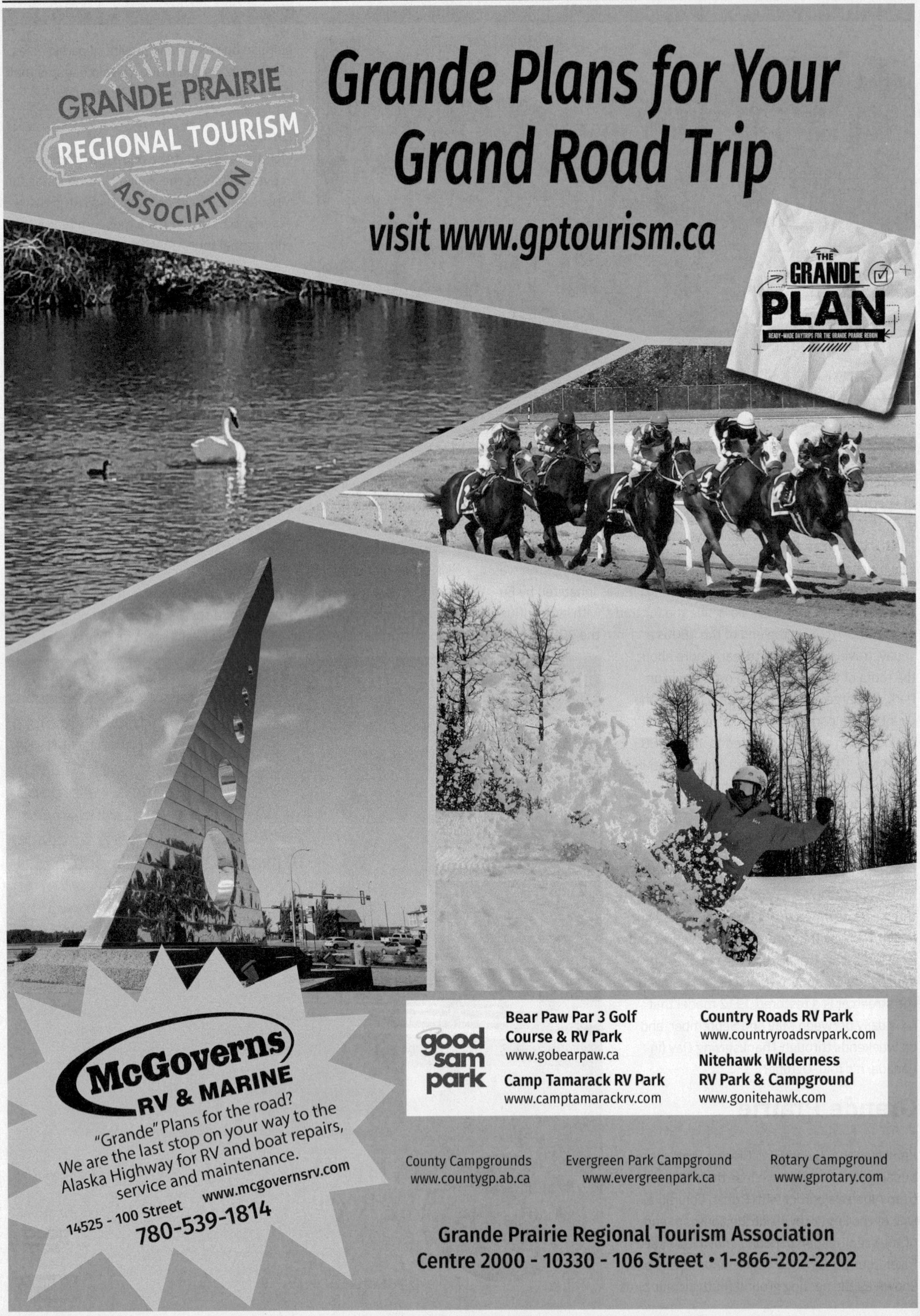
GRANDE PRAIRIE
REGIONAL TOURISM
ASSOCIATION
Grande Plans for Your Grand Road Trip
visit www.gptourism.ca
THE GRANDE PLAN
READY-MADE DAYTRIPS FOR THE GRANDE PRAIRIE REGION
McGoverns RV & MARINE
"Grande" Plans for the road?
We are the last stop on your way to the Alaska Highway for RV and boat repairs, service and maintenance.
www.mcgovernsrv.com
14525 - 100 Street
780-539-1814
good sam park
Bear Paw Par 3 Golf Course & RV Park
www.gobearpaw.ca
Camp Tamarack RV Park
www.camptamarackrv.com
Country Roads RV Park
www.countryroadsrvpark.com
Nitehawk Wilderness RV Park & Campground
www.gonitehawk.com
County Campgrounds
www.countygp.ab.ca
Evergreen Park Campground
www.evergreenpark.ca
Rotary Campground
www.gprotary.com
Grande Prairie Regional Tourism Association
Centre 2000 - 10330 - 106 Street • 1-866-202-2202

During Grande Prairie's Stompede, top rodeo riders demonstrate remarkable riding and roping skills.

pearance. The wingspans of these amazing birds can exceed 10 feet.

Trails to Natural Treasures

Running through the heart of Grande Prairie, Muskoseepi Park is an innovative and extensive 1,100-acre green space that has been a gathering place for locals since the earliest settlers. These days, there are six distinct areas of the park, including a fishing pond stocked with rainbow trout.

Days of Music and Rodeos

Grande Prairie locals have learned how to take advantage of the region's pleasantly mild summers. The result is a series of festivals that celebrate the rugged history and fun-loving mentality of today's residents. Stompede, a five-day rodeo held in June every year since 1977, sees as many as 50,000 visitors converge on the city for pro-level rodeo competition. Spectators can watch thrilling chuckwagon racing, win stuffed animals on the midway, peruse arts and crafts and enjoy tasty treats. The Bear Creek Folk Festival is another summer classic, featuring 30 artists from across the country on four stages. Despite its considerable size and scope, Bear Creek is a rare family-friendly music festival.

Eastlink Connection

The Eastlink Centre provides a mix of aquatics and field sports for every level of athlete. The broad range of equipment gives the entire family—from grandparents to grandkids—full access to this barrier-free facility. It is connected to the Coca-Cola Centre, a gymnastic club and three Grande Prairie schools. After a swim or a workout, visit some of the shops and restaurants nearby.

Ready for a Bite to Eat?

Looking for a specialty dish? You'll find whatever your palate desires in one of many Grande Prairie restaurants. Whether it's Greek, Italian, Chinese, succulent prime rib with all of the trimmings or a simple fish taco, it's available. Family-friendly options are the norm.

Dynamic History

Cree and Beaver tribes first inhabited the region, but the lucrative fur trade drew Grande Prairie's first European settlers and explorers as early as the late 1700s. By the late 1800s, a Hudson Bay Company trading post was soon established, followed by missionaries from the Roman Catholic Church. Grande Prairie became a village in 1914. Among other things, it had a local weekly newspaper, banks, a hospital, high school and a railway connection to Edmonton.

Lumber Heritage

Grande Prairie evolved into a main player in the lumber industry during the 1920s. Ironically, it was an American—John Bickell of Washington State—who began his stake in lumber with a mill at the family farm. Decades later, it would be known as Northern Plywoods, Alberta's first plywood mill.

Hail to the Queen

In 1958, Grande Prairie was officially made a city. Its milestones would be many, including hosting none other than Queen Elizabeth II, who came in 1978 for the groundbreaking of a hospital named after Her Royal Highness. The other big milestone was the discovery of the Elmworth natural gas field—the second largest in North America.

FOR MORE INFORMATION

Travel Alberta, 800-252-3782, www.travelalberta.com

Dinosaur Adventures Alberta, travelalberta.com/us/things-to-do/ attractions-entertainment/dinosaur-adventures/

Edmonton Tourism, 800-463-4667, www.exploreedmonton.com

Grande Prairie Regional Tourism Association, 866-202-2202, www.gptourism.ca

A mother trumpeter swan prepares to usher her brood of chicks from their nest to the water for a swim.

Alberta

ALBERTA BEACH — C3 *Lac Ste Anne*

ALBERTA BEACH FAMILY RV PARK & CAMPGROUND (Public) From jct Hwy 43 & Secondary Hwy 633: Go 8 km/5 mi W on Secondary Hwy 633, then 1.6 km/1 mi N on 47th St, then 1 block W. Follow signs. Avail: 87 full hkups. 2021 rates: $30 to $40. May 01 to Sep 30. (780)924-2333

ALBERTA BEACH GOLF RESORT **Ratings: 6/UI/7.5** (Campground) Avail: 30 full hkups (20/30 amps). 2021 rates: $50.45. May 01 to Sep 30. (780)924-2421, 4438 44th Street, Alberta Beach, AB T0E 0A0

ATHABASCA — B4 *Athabasca*

BLUEBERRY HILL RV PARK (RV Park) (Phone Update) Avail: 29 full hkups (15/30 amps). 2021 rates: $38. Apr 01 to Oct 01. (780)675-3733, Hwy 813, Athabasca, AB T9S 2A6

BANFF — D3 *Banff National Park*

BANFF See also Canmore.

BANFF/CASTLE MOUNTAIN (Public National Park) From Jct of TCH 1 & Hwy 1A, E 1 km on Hwy 1A (Bow Valley Pkwy) (R). 43 Avail. 2021 rates: $21.50. May 29 to Sep 15. (877)737-3783

BANFF/JOHNSTON CANYON (Public National Park) From Jct of Hwy 1A & TCH-1, W 10 mi on Hwy 1A (Bow Valley Pkwy), follow signs (L) Due to construction, park is currently closed. Expected to reopen in Spring 2020. 132 Avail. 2021 rates: $27.40. May 26 to Sep 25. (877)737-3783

BANFF/TUNNEL MOUNTAIN TRAILER COURT (Public National Park) From Hwy 1 & Lake Minnewanka exit (Banff Ave), S .06 mi on Banff Ave to Tunnel Mtn Rd, E 2 mi to entrance (R). Avail: 321 full hkups (15/30 amps). 2021 rates: $38.20. May 12 to Oct 02. (877)737-3783

BANFF/TWO JACK LAKESIDE (Public National Park) From Banff, NE 7.5 on Minnewanka Rd (L). 64 Avail. 2021 rates: $27.40. Jun 26 to Oct 04. (877)737-3783

BANFF/TWO JACK MAIN (Public National Park) From Banff, NE 8 mi on Lake Minnewanka Rd (L). 381 Avail. 2021 rates: $21.50. Jun 23 to Sep 04. (877)737-3783

BANFF/WATERFOWL LAKES (Public National Park) From Jct of TCH-1 & Hwy 93, N 35 mi on Hwy 93 (L). 116 Avail. 2021 rates: $21.97. Jun 24 to Sep 05. (877)737-3783

We've listened to thousands of RVers like you, so we know exactly how to rate campgrounds. Got feedback? Call us! 877-209-6655.

BARRHEAD — B3 *Barrhead*

THUNDER LAKE (Public Prov Park) From town, W 13 mi on Hwy 18 (E). 127 Avail: 61 S, 66 E (15/30 amps). 2021 rates: $26 to $34. Apr 15 to Oct 13. (780)674-4051

BASHAW — C4 *Camrose*

BASHAW MUNICIPAL CAMPGROUND (Public) From Jct of Hwys 21 & 53, E 0.3 mi on Hwy 53 (R). 16 Avail. 2021 rates: $20. (780)372-3911

BEAVERLODGE — B1 *Grande Prairie County No. 1*

HOMMY CAMPGROUND (GRANDE PRAIRIE COUNTY #1) (Public) From town: Go 6.5 km (4 mi) NW on Hwy 43, then 1 km (1/2 mi) E on 11th St. (R). Avail: 23 E (50 amps), Pit toilets. 2021 rates: $36. May 15 to Oct 15. (780)354-8039

BELLEVUE — E3 *Crowsnest Pass*

BEAVER MINES LAKE PRA (Public Prov Park) From town: Go 4-3/4 km/3 mi E, then 22-1/2 km/14 mi S on local roads. 76 Avail: Pit toilets. 2021 rates: $26. May 01 to Nov 30. (403)563-5395

BENTLEY — C3 *Lacombe*

BREWER'S (Public Prov Park) From jct Hwy 2 & Hwy 12: Go 9 km/5.6 mi W on Hwy 12. 300 Avail. 2021 rates: $29. May 09 to Oct 15. (403)748-1123

LAKEVIEW (Public Prov Park) From Jct of Hwys 2 & 12, W 7 mi on Hwy 12 to Aspen Beach Prov Park sign (R). 255 Avail: 77 full hkups, 151 E (15/30 amps). 2021 rates: $34 to $58. Jun 01 to Sep 21. (403)748-4066

BIG VALLEY — D4 *Stettler County No. 6*

MCKENZIE CROSSING RECREATION AREA (Public) From town, W 9.3 mi on Hwy 590 (L). 12 Avail: Pit toilets. 2021 rates: $15. (403)876-2269

BLACK DIAMOND — E3 *Foothills*

FOOTHILLS LIONS CENTENNIAL CAMPGROUND (Public) From Jct of Hwy 2 & Hwy 7, W 16 mi on Hwy 7 to Hwy 22 (Centre Ave), N 0.4 mi to 5th St, W 0.2 mi (R). 45 Avail: 45 W, 45 E (30/50 amps). 2021 rates: $40. May 01 to Oct 31. (403)933-5785

BLAIRMORE — E3 *Crowsnest*

LOST LEMON RV PARK & CAMPGROUND **Ratings: 6.5/8.5★/6.5** (Campground) 45 Avail: 30 full hkups, 5 W, 5 E (30/50 amps). 2021 rates: $42 to $50. (403)562-2932, 11001 19th Avenue, Blairmore, AB T0K 0E0

BONNYVILLE — B5 *Bonnyville*

FRANCHERE BAY PRA (Public Prov Park) From Jct of Hwy 28 & park access rd, N 8 mi on park access rd, follow signs (R). 198 Avail: 41 W, 99 E (15/30 amps). 2021 rates: $23 to $39. May 15 to Oct 12. (780)594-7856

MOOSE LAKE (Public Prov Park) From Jct of PR-28 & PR-41, N 3 mi on PR-41 to CR-660, W 7 mi (L). Avail: 47 E (15/30 amps), Pit toilets. 2021 rates: $25 to $33. May 14 to Oct 14. (780)594-7856

MURIEL LAKE MD PARK (MUNICIPAL PARK) (Public) From town, S 2 mi on SR-890 to unmarked CR, E 4 mi to unmarked CR, S 3 mi (E). Avail: 54 E (30 amps). 2021 rates: $25 to $30. May 15 to Sep 15. (780)826-4140

PELICAN POINT MD PARK (MUNICIPAL PARK) (Public) From Jct of Hwys 41 & 660, W 13 mi on Hwy 660 to Franchere Bay Prov Park, S 1.5 mi, follow signs (L); or From Edmonton: From Jct of Hwys 882 & 28, N 6 mi to Hwy 660, E 6 mi to Franchere Bay Prov Park, S 1.5 mi, Follow signs (L). 35 Avail: Pit toilets. 2021 rates: $25. May 08 to Sep 13. (780)635-3825

BOWDEN — D3 *Red Deer*

RED LODGE (Public Prov Park) From town, W 8.3 mi on Hwy 587 (R). Avail: 38 E (15/30 amps). 2021 rates: $24 to $32. May 08 to Oct 12. (403)224-2547

BOYLE — B4 *Athabasca*

LONG LAKE (Public Prov Park) From Jct SR-63 & CR-661, E 5 mi on CR-661 to CR-831, N 10 mi (R). Avail: 145 E (15/30 amps). 2021 rates: $30 to $38. Jun 01 to Oct 13. (780)576-3959

BRAGG CREEK — D3 *Rocky View*

BEAVER FLATS CAMPGROUND (Public) From jct Hwy 22 & Hwy 66: Go 29-1/2 km/18-1/2 mi SW on Hwy 66. 49 Avail: Pit toilets. 2021 rates: $26. May 16 to Sep 06. (403)949-3132

LITTLE ELBOW CAMPGROUND (Public Prov Park) From jct Hwy 22 & Hwy 66: Go 49-1/2 km/31 mi SW on Hwy 66. 64 Avail. 2021 rates: $29. Jun 01 to Sep 21. (403)949-3132

MCLEAN CREEK PRA (Public Prov Park) From jct Hwy 22 & Hwy 66: Go 14-1/2 km/9 mi SW on Hwy 66. Avail: 96 E (15/30 amps). 2021 rates: $29 to $37. (403)949-3132

PADDY'S FLAT CAMPGROUND (Public Prov Park) From Hwy 22 & Hwy 66: Go 20 km/12-1/2 mi SW on Hwy 66. 98 Avail: Pit toilets. 2021 rates: $29. May 15 to Sep 22. (403)949-3132

BROOKS — E4 *Newell*

DINOSAUR

(Public Prov Park) From town, N 5 mi on Hwy 873 to Hwy 544, E 20 mi on Hwy 544, N at Patricia Turnoff, Follow signs (R). **FAC:** gravel rds. Avail: 122 gravel, back-ins (18x24), 93 E (15/30 amps), tent sites, dump, laundry, groc, fire rings, firewood. **REC:** Red Deer River: fishing, playground, rec open to public. Pets OK. Partial handicap access, 14 day max stay. 2021 rates: $29 to $37.
(877)537-2757 Lat: 50.759636, Lon: -111.481719
NULL, Brooks, AB T1R 1C5
www.albertaparks.ca

KINBROOK ISLAND (Public Prov Park) From town, S 9 mi on Hwy 873 to access rd, W 1 mi (E). Avail: 155 E (15/30 amps). 2021 rates: $29 to $37. (403)362-2962

TILLEBROOK (Public Prov Park) From town: Go 7 km/4-1/4 mi E on Trans Canada Hwy 1. Note: 44' RV length limit. Avail: 65 E (30 amps). 2021 rates: $29 to $37. Apr 17 to Oct 13. (403)362-4525

BUCK LAKE — C3 *Westaskiwin*

BUCK LAKE (Public Prov Park) From jct Hwy 13 & Buck Lake Rd: Go 10.5 km/6-1/2 mi N on Buck Lake Rd, then 2 km/1.2 mi E on gravel road. 20 Avail: Pit toilets. 2021 rates: $24. May 01 to Oct 14. (780)586-2864

CALHOUN BAY (Public Prov Park) From jct Hwy 13 & Buck Mountain Rd: Go 5 km/3 mi N on Buck Mountain Rd (gravel) and follow signs. 38 Avail: Pit toilets. 2021 rates: $24. May 16 to Oct 15. (780)586-2864

CALGARY — D3 *Calgary*

CALGARY See also Cochrane & Okotoks.

BALZAC CAMPGROUND RV PARK & STORAGE **Ratings: 5.5/8/5.5** (RV Park) 69 Avail: 42 full hkups, 27 W, 27 E (30 amps). 2021 rates: $25 to $42.50. May 01 to Oct 31. (403)226-0097, 262195 Balzac Blvd, Balzac, AB T4B 2T3

CALAWAY RV PARK & CAMPGROUND **Ratings: 6/9.5★/7.5** (RV Park) 104 Avail: 56 full hkups, 41 E (15/30 amps). 2021 rates: $38 to $44. May 18 to Sep 03. (403)249-7372, 245033 Range Road 33, Calgary, AB T3Z 2E9

CALGARY WEST CAMPGROUND **Ratings: 8/8.5★/6** (Campground) 250 Avail: 120 full hkups, 130 W, 130 E (20/30 amps). 2021 rates: $46 to $58. Apr 15 to Oct 15. (403)288-0411, 221 101 St SW, Calgary, AB T3B 5T2

MOUNTAIN VIEW CAMPING **Ratings: 8/8/7** (Campground) 160 Avail: 144 full hkups, 16 W, 16 E (30/50 amps). 2021 rates: $43 to $62. Mar 01 to Nov 15. (403)293-6640, 244024 Range Rd 284, Calgary, AB T2M 4L5

CALLING LAKE — B4 *Opportunity No. 17*

CALLING LAKE (Public Prov Park) From town: Go 1-1/2 km/1 mi S on Hwy 813. Avail: 81 E (15/30 amps), Pit toilets. 2021 rates: $34. May 16 to Sep 03. (780)675-8213

TANASIUK ROCK ISLAND LAKE CAMPGROUND (MUNICIPAL PARK) (Public) From Hwy 813 in town: Go 40 km/25 mi N on improved road to Rock Island Lake. 51 Avail: (50 amps), Pit toilets. 2021 rates: $15. May 01 to Oct 31. (855)953-3358

CALMAR — C3 *Leduc*

JUBILEE PARK CAMPGROUND (Public) From jct Hwy 616 & Hwy 795: Go 3-1/2 km/2 mi N on Hwy 795, then 1-1/2 km/.9 mi W on Twp Rd 481, then 3/4 km/.5 mi S on Range Rd 271. Avail: 30 E (30 amps). 2021 rates: $30 to $40. May 23 to Sep 08. (780)985-2499

Driving a big rig? Average site width and length measurements tell you which campgrounds can accommodate your Big Rig.

CAMROSE — C4 *Camrose*

CAMROSE RV PARK
Ratings: 9/10★/9 (RV Park) From jct AB 21 & AB 13: Go 12 km/7-1/2 mi E on AB 13, then 160 m/ 500 ft S on Exhibition Dr, then 300 m/1/4 mi W on 42 a Ave (R). **FAC:** paved rds. (107 spaces). Avail: 67 all weather, 50 pull-thrus, (30x60), back-ins (30x60), 67 full hkups (30/50 amps), seasonal sites, WiFi @ sites, shower$, dump, laundry, fire rings, firewood. **REC:** pond, boating nearby, playground, hunting nearby. Pets OK. Partial handicap access. No tents. Big rig sites, eco-friendly. 2021 rates: $45 to $64.50. Apr 15 to Oct 31. **(780)678-2888 Lat: 53.008996, Lon: -112.791317**
4250 Exhibition Trail, Camrose, AB T4V 4Z8
camroservpark.com
See ad this page

MIQUELON LAKE (Public Prov Park) From town, E 14.25 mi on Hwy 623(L). Avail: 191 E (15/30 amps). 2021 rates: $30 to $38. (780)672-7274

CANMORE — D3 *Canmore*

BOW RIVER (Public Prov Park) From Calgary, W 89 km on Hwy 1 (R). 66 Avail: 59 W, 59 E (15/30 amps), Pit toilets. 2021 rates: $29 to $45. May 03 to Nov 10. (403)673-2163

BOW VALLEY (Public Prov Park) From Jct of Hwy 1 & Seebe-Exshaw exit, N 0.75 mi on Seebe-Exshaw Hwy/Hwy 1X (L). 167 Avail: 131 W, 131 E (15/30 amps). 2021 rates: $29 to $45. May 03 to Oct 07. (877)537-2757

LAC DES ARCS (Public Prov Park) From town, W 80 km on Hwy 1 (R). 28 Avail: Pit toilets. 2021 rates: $29. May 01 to Sep 01. (403)673-2163

SPRING CREEK RV CAMPGROUND **Ratings: 6.5/9★/6.5** (RV Park) 71 Avail: 64 full hkups, 2 W, 7 E (30/50 amps). 2021 rates: $54 to $66. (403)678-5111, 1 Spring Creek Gate, Canmore, AB T1W 0A7

THREE SISTERS CAMPGROUND (Public Prov Park) From town, W 86 km on Hwy 1 (R). 36 Avail: Pit toilets. 2021 rates: $29. Apr 12 to Nov 24. (403)673-2163

CARBON — D4 *Carbon*

CARBON MUNICIPAL CAMPGROUND (Public) From Jct of Hwys 21 & 575, E 5 mi on Hwy 575 to SR-836 (Carbon exit), S 1.5 mi (R). 59 Avail: 19 full hkups, 21 W, 21 E (30/50 amps). 2021 rates: $35 to $40. (403)572-3244

CARDSTON — F4 *Cardston*

LEE CREEK CAMPGROUND (Public) From jct Hwy 5 & Hwy 2: Go 1.1 km/3/4 mi S on Hwy 2 (Main St), 0.4km/1/4 mi W on 7 Ave W. 58 Avail: 33 full hkups, 10 W, 10 E (30 amps). 2021 rates: $24 to $30. Apr 01 to Oct 31. (403)388-4230

POLICE OUTPOST (Public Prov Park) From town: Go 6.5 mi S on Hwy 2, then 10 mi W on dirt road, then 2 mi S on dirt road (E). 46 Avail: Pit toilets. 2021 rates: $24. Apr 01 to Nov 01. (403)653-4060

CAROLINE — D3 *Clearwater*

TAY RIVER PRA (Public Prov Park) From town: Go 16 km/10 mi SW on Hwy 591. 32 Avail: Pit toilets. 2021 rates: $26. May 01 to Oct 14. (403)845-8349

CARSELAND — E4 *Wheatland*

WYNDHAM-CARSELAND (Public Prov Park) From Jct Hwys 1 & 24, S 18 mi (30 km) on Hwy 24 (R). Closed due to Flooding, expecting to reopen Spring 2015. 178 Avail: Pit toilets. 2021 rates: $29. Apr 19 to Oct 14. (403)934-3523

CARSTAIRS — D3 *Mountain View*

CARSTAIRS MUNICIPAL CAMPGROUND (Public) From jct Hwy 2 & Hwy 581: Go 4-3/4 km/3 mi W on Hwy 581, then 3 blocks N on Hwy 2A. Avail: 28 E (15/30 amps). 2021 rates: $28. Jun 01 to Oct 05. (403)990-2059

CASLAN — B4 *Athabasca*

NORTH BUCK LAKE PRA (Public Prov Park) From Hwy 663 in town: Go 4 km/2-1/2 mi N on access road. Avail: 30 E (15/30 amps), Pit toilets. 2021 rates: $26 to $33. May 15 to Oct 15. (780)519-1452

CHAMPION — E4 *Vulcan*

LITTLE BOW (Public Prov Park) From Jct PR-23 & CR-529, E 12 mi on CR-529 to park access rd, S 1 mi (R). Avail: 86 E (15/30 amps). 2021 rates: $26 to $34. Apr 17 to Oct 13. (403)897-3933

County names help you follow the local weather report.

CHAUVIN — C5 *Wainwright*

DILLBERRY LAKE (Public Prov Park) From town, S 10 mi on Hwy 17 (L). Avail: 75 E (15/30 amps). 2021 rates: $30 to $38. May 18 to Oct 12. (780)853-8221

CLARESHOLM — E4 *Willow Creek No. 26*

CLARESHOLM CENTENNIAL PARK (Public) From Jct of Hwy 2 and Secondary Hwy 520, W 0.3 mi on Hwy 520 to 4th St W, N 0.5 mi. Avail: 28 full hkups (30 amps). 2021 rates: $21 to $35. (403)625-2751

COCHRANE — D3 *Rockyview*

BOTTREL STORE AND CAMPGROUND (Public) From Jct of TCH & Hwy 22 exit (Cochrane), N 23.5 mi on Cochrane to Bottrel St, W 1.8 mi (L). 30 Avail: (30/50 amps). 2021 rates: $15. May 01 to Oct 31. (403)932-5423

BOW RIVERSEDGE CAMPGROUND
Ratings: 9/10★/9.5 (Public) From Jct of Hwy 22 & Griffin Rd, E 1.9 mi / 3km on Griffin Rd to Arena sign, W 0.2 mi / 0.3km (R). Avail: 74 full hkups (30/50 amps). 2021 rates: $50 to $60. Apr 01 to Oct 31. (403)932-4675

BURNT TIMBER (Public Prov Park) From jct Hwy 1A & Hwy 40: Go 68 km/42-1/4 mi W on Hwy 40 (Forestry Trunk Rd). 30 Avail: Pit toilets. 2021 rates: $35. May 01 to Sep 15. (587)830-2198

FALLEN TIMBER PRA-SOUTH (Public Prov Park) From jct Hwy 1A & Hwy 40: Go 54 km/33-1/2 mi NW on Hwy 40 (Forestry Trunk Rd). 55 Avail: Pit toilets. 2021 rates: $35. May 01 to Oct 13. (587)830-2198

GHOST RESERVOIR PRA (Public Prov Park) From town: Go 21-1/2 km/13-1/2 mi W on Hwy 1A. 80 Avail: Pit toilets. 2021 rates: $26. May 01 to Oct 31. (403)851-0766

NORTH GHOST PRA (Public Prov Park) From jct Hwy 1A & Hwy 40: Go 40 km/24.8 mi NW on Hwy 40 (Forestry Trunk Rd). 169 Avail: Pit toilets. 2021 rates: $35. Jun 01 to Oct 14. (403)637-2198

SPRING HILL RV PARK **Ratings: 7/10★/8** (RV Park) Avail: 58 full hkups (30/50 amps). 2021 rates: $50 to $60. (403)932-2010, 41216 Big Hill Springs Road, Cochrane, AB T4C 1A1

WAIPAROUS CREEK CAMPGROUND (Public Prov Park) From jct Hwy 1A & Hwy 40: Go 37 km/ 23 mi NW on Hwy 40 (Forestry Trunk Rd). 53 Avail: Pit toilets. 2021 rates: $35. Jun 01 to Oct 14. (587)830-2198

COLD LAKE — B5 *Bonnyville*

COLD LAKE (Public Prov Park) From town, E 2 mi on Hwy 28, follow signs (E). 103 Avail: 25 W, 78 E (15/30 amps). 2021 rates: $35 to $44. May 15 to Oct 15. (780)594-7856

COLD LAKE MUNICIPAL DISTRICT CAMPGROUND (Public) From Jct of Hwy 28 & Hwy 55, NE 1.5 mi on Hwy 28 to Cold Lake town, follow signs (R). Avail: 71 E (30 amps). 2021 rates: $30. May 08 to Sep 13. (780)639-4121

CONSORT — D5 *Division No. 4*

GOOSEBERRY LAKE CAMPGROUND (Public Prov Park) From jct Hwy 22 & Hwy 66: Go 9-1/2 km/ 6 mi SW on Hwy 66. 45 Avail: 18 W, 24 E (15/30 amps). 2021 rates: $20 to $35. May 15 to Oct 14. (403)577-3873

CROWSNEST PASS — E3 *Crowsnest Pass*

CASTLE FALLS (Public Prov Park) From town: Go 28-3/4 km/18 mi SW on local roads. 45 Avail: Pit toilets. 2021 rates: $24. May 03 to Oct 15. (403)627-1165

CASTLE RIVER BRIDGE (Public Prov Park) From town: Go 22-3/4 km/14-1/4 mi SW on local roads. Avail: 25 E (30 amps), Pit toilets. 2021 rates: $32. May 16 to Oct 15. (403)627-1165

DUTCH CREEK PRA (Public Prov Park) From town: Go 30-1/2 km/19 mi NE on Hwy 940. 45 Avail: Pit toilets. 2021 rates: $24. May 01 to Oct 14. (403)627-1165

LYNX CREEK (Public Prov Park) From town: Go 19-1/2 km/12-1/4 mi SW on local roads. 27 Avail: Pit toilets. 2021 rates: $21. Jun 01 to Oct 15. (403)627-1165

RACEHORSE PRA (Public Prov Park) From town: Go 24 km/15 mi N on Hwy 940. 38 Avail: Pit toilets. 2021 rates: $24. May 01 to Nov 30. (403)563-5395

Directional arrows indicate the campground's position in relation to the nearest town.

DELBURNE — D4 *Red Deer*

FAWN MEADOWS LODGE & RV PARK **Ratings: 4.5/9.5★/7** (Campground) Avail: 22 full hkups (30 amps). 2021 rates: $45. (403)749-2099, 2201 18th Avenue, Delburne, AB T0M 0V0

DEMMITT — A1 *Grande Prairie No. 1*

DEMMITT CAMPGROUND (Public) From Jct AB 40 & AB 43: Go 86.3 km (53 1/2 mi) W on AB 43. (R). 15 Avail: Pit toilets. 2021 rates: $20. May 15 to Oct 15. (780)356-6764

DEVON — C3 *Edmonton*

DEVON LIONS CAMPGROUND (Public) N/bnd or S/bnd -From Jct of Hwy 60 & Athabaska Dr., E 190 yds/174m on Athabaska Dr. to Superior St., N 140 yds/128m to Saskatchewan Ave, E 1.2 mi/1.9km (E). 195 Avail: 108 full hkups, 55 W, 55 E (30/50 amps). 2021 rates: $36 to $53. May 01 to Oct 15. (780)987-4777

DIDSBURY — D3 *Mountain View*

ROSEBUD VALLEY CAMPGROUND (Public) From Jct of Hwy 2 & SR-582 (exit 326), W 4 mi/6.4km on SR-582 (R). Avail: 28 E (15/30 amps). 2021 rates: $26 to $30. Apr 01 to Oct 15. (403)335-8578

DRAYTON VALLEY — C3 *Brazeau*

WILLEY WEST PARK (Public) From Jct of Hwys 39 & 22, W 2.5 mi to park entrance rd (R). 97 Avail: 7 full hkups, 88 E (15/30 amps). 2021 rates: $30 to $46. May 01 to Sep 30. (780)542-5821

DRUMHELLER — D4 *Starland*

BLERIOT FERRY (Public Prov Park) From Bleriot Ferry crossing to Hwy 837, W 300 yds (E). 28 Avail: Pit toilets. 2021 rates: $21. May 15 to Sep 15. (877)537-2757

DINOSAUR RV PARK & DINO NEST **Ratings: 6.5/8/7** (RV Park) 170 Avail: 124 full hkups, 46 W, 46 E (30 amps). 2021 rates: $53 to $63. May 01 to Oct 31. (403)823-3291, 500 N. Dinosaur Trail, Drumheller, AB T0J 0Y0

DINOSAUR TRAIL RV RESORT **Ratings: 8/8/8** (RV Park) 225 Avail: 129 full hkups, 10 W, 30 E (30/50 amps). 2021 rates: $63 to $97.20. May 01 to Sep 30. (403)823-9333, 294004 N Dinosaur Trail, Drumheller, AB T0J 0Y0

LITTLE FISH LAKE (Public Prov Park) From Jct of Hwys 10 & 573, E 13.6 mi on Hwy 573 (R). 10 Avail: Pit toilets. 2021 rates: $20. May 15 to Sep 15. (403)823-1749

RIVER GROVE CAMPGROUND & CABINS **Ratings: 7/9/7.5** (Campground) 95 Avail: 19 full hkups, 57 W, 57 E (20/30 amps). 2021 rates: $50 to $55. May 01 to Sep 16. (403)823-6655, 25 Poplar St., Drumheller, AB T0J 0Y0

THE HOODOO RV RESORT & CAMPGROUND **Ratings: 5.5/7/8** (Campground) 98 Avail: 30 full hkups, 68 W, 68 E (30 amps). 2021 rates: $35 to $43. May 01 to Oct 15. (866)923-2790, 5075 Hwy 10E, Drumheller, AB T0J 0Y0

DUNVEGAN — A1 *Fairviewe No. 136*

DUNVEGAN (Public Prov Park) From town, S 15 mi on Hwy 2 (L). Avail: 65 E (15 amps), Pit toilets. 2021 rates: $35. May 01 to Oct 15. (780)538-5350

EDMONTON — C4 *Edmonton*

A SPOTLIGHT Introducing Edmonton's colorful attractions appearing at the front of this province section.

EDMONTON See also Gibbons, Morinville, Sherwood Park, St Albert & Stony Plain.

DIAMOND GROVE RV CAMPGROUND
Ratings: 9/10★/9 (RV Resort) Avail: 242 full hkups (30/50 amps). 2021 rates: $50. (780)962-8003, 41 Century Close, Spruce Grove, AB T7X 3B3

EDMONTON (CONT)

GLOWING EMBERS RV PARK & TRAVEL CENTRE
good sam park
Ratings: 7.5/9.5/9.5 (RV Park) From Jct of Hwy AB-16A & Hwy AB-60, S 0.75 mi (1.2 km) on Hwy-60 to Twshp Rd 525A, W 0.1 mi (.2 km) (R); N-bnd on Frntg Rd 263A to entrance 1.1 mi (1.8 km) (L). Elev 2900 ft.**FAC:** all weather rds. (288 spaces). Avail: 223 all weather, 25 pull-thrus, (30x70), back-ins (25x45), 223 full hkups (30/50 amps), seasonal sites, WiFi @ sites, tent sites, shower$, dump, laundry, LP gas, restaurant. **REC:** boating nearby, playground, hunting nearby. Pets OK. Partial handicap access. Big rig sites, eco-friendly. 2021 rates: $45 to $50. ATM.
(877)785-7275 Lat: 53.53913, Lon: -113.77012
26821 100th Avenue, Acheson, AB T7X 6H8
glowingembersrvpark.com
See ad page 1039

RAINBOW VALLEY CAMPGROUND (Public) From Jct of Whitemud Fwy & 119th St, S 1 blk on 119th St to Whitemud Park (45th Ave), W 2 blks (E). Avail: 29 E (15 amps). 2021 rates: $37 to $45. Apr 15 to Oct 10. (780)434-5531

SHAKERS ACRES RV PARK **Ratings: 5.5/7/6.5** (Campground) 130 Avail: 100 full hkups, 10 W, 30 E (15/30 amps). 2021 rates: $36.75 to $52.50. May 01 to Oct 01. (877)447-3565, 21530 103Rd Ave, Edmonton, AB T5S 2C4

EDSON — C2 *Yellowhead*

FICKLE LAKE PRA (Public Prov Park) From town: Go 38-1/2 km/24 mi SW on Hwy 47. 41 Avail: Pit toilets. 2021 rates: $28. May 01 to Sep 30. (780)723-0738

WILLMORE RECREATION PARK (Public) From Jct of Hwy 16 & 63rd St, S 3 mi on 63rd St (L). 41 Avail: Pit toilets. 2021 rates: $17. May 15 to Oct 15. (780)723-7141

WOLF LAKE WEST PRA (Public Prov Park) From town: Go 30-3/4 km/19-1/4 mi E on Hwy 16, then 54-1/2 km/34 mi S on local road. 36 Avail: Pit toilets. 2021 rates: $28. May 01 to Oct 13. (780)723-0738

ELK POINT — B5 *St Paul*

WHITNEY LAKE CAMPGROUND (Public Prov Park) From town, E 15 mi on Hwy 646 (L). Avail: 33 E (15/30 amps), Pit toilets. 2021 rates: $26 to $33. May 14 to Oct 13. (780)645-6295

ENTWISTLE — C3 *Parkland*

PEMBINA RIVER (Public Prov Park) From Jct of Hwy 16 & Hwy 16A at Entwistle, NW 1 mi on Hwy 16A (R). Avail: 132 E (15/30 amps), Pit toilets. 2021 rates: $29 to $37. May 11 to Oct 12. (780)727-3643

ERSKINE — D4 *Stettler*

ROCHON SANDS (Public Prov Park) From town: Go 13-1/4 km/8-1/4 mi N on Hwy 835, then 1-1/2 km/1 mi W. 69 Avail: Pit toilets. 2021 rates: $28. May 15 to Oct 15. (403)742-4338

FALHER — A2 *Smoky River No. 130*

FALHER MUNICIPAL CAMPGROUND (Public) In town on Hwy 49. Avail: 30 E (30 amps). 2021 rates: $25 to $30. May 01 to Sep 30. (780)837-2247

FAWCETT — B3 *Westlock*

CROSS LAKE (Public Prov Park) From town, N 0.5 mi on Hwy 44 to Hwy 663, NE 13 mi (L). Avail: 130 E (15/30 amps). 2021 rates: $38. May 09 to Oct 31. (780)675-8213

FORESTBURG — C4 *Flagstaff*

BIG KNIFE (Public Prov Park) From Jct of Hwys 53 & 855, S 8.5 mi on Hwy 855 (R). 40 Avail: Pit toilets. 2021 rates: $24. May 15 to Oct 15. (403)574-2341

FORT MACLEOD — E4 *Fort Macleod*

DAISY MAY CAMPGROUND **Ratings: 8.5/6.5/8.5** (Campground) 110 Avail: 24 full hkups, 64 W, 64 E (30/50 amps). 2021 rates: $42 to $55. Apr 01 to Oct 31. (888)553-2455, 249 Lyndon Road, Fort MacLeod, AB T0L 0Z0

FORT MCMURRAY — A4 *Wood Buffalo*

GREGOIRE LAKE (Public Prov Park) From town, S 11.78 mi on Hwy 63 to Hwy 881, E 6 mi (L). 140 Avail: 68 W, 140 E (15/30 amps). 2021 rates: $35 to $43. May 01 to Oct 15. (780)743-7437

HANGINGSTONE RIVER PRA (Public Prov Park) From town, S 22 mi Hwy 63 (R). 56 Avail: Pit toilets. 2021 rates: $26. May 17 to Sep 15. (587)919-5133

FORT SASKATCHEWAN — C4 *Sturgeon*

ELK ISLAND/ASTOTIN (Public National Park) From town: Go 35 km/21-3/4 mi E on Hwy 16, then 14 km/8-1/2 mi N on Elk Island Pkwy, then W into Astotin Lake Area, then 200 meters N at first right. 75 Avail. 2021 rates: $26.06. May 01 to Oct 01. (877)737-3783

FOX CREEK — B2 *Greenview No. 16*

FOX CREEK RV CAMPGROUND (Public) From jct Hwy 43 & Kaybob Dr: Go 1 block E on Kaybob Dr, then 2 blocks N on Campground Rd. Avail: 19 full hkups (30 amps). 2021 rates: $20 to $40. (780)622-3896

IOSEGUN LAKE CAMPGROUND (TOWN PARK) (Public) From town: Go 11-1/4 km/7 mi N on Hwy 43. 52 Avail: Pit toilets. 2021 rates: $20 to $25. May 15 to Oct 15. (780)622-5503

SMOKE LAKE CAMPGROUND (PRA) (Public) From town: Go 8-3/4 km/5-1/2 mi SW on Hwy 43. 47 Avail: Pit toilets. 2021 rates: $25. May 24 to Oct 01. (780)538-5350

GIBBONS — C4 *Sturgeon*

LONGRIDERS RV PARK **Ratings: 5.5/7.5/6.5** (RV Park) Avail: 192 full hkups (30/50 amps). 2021 rates: $46 to $49. (780)923-3300, 23136 Secondary Hwy 643, Gibbons, AB T0A 1N0

GOODRIDGE — B5 *Glendon*

LAKELAND PRA (IRONWOOD LAKE CAMPGROUND) (Public Prov Park) From town: Go 20 km/12.4 mi S on Hwy 36, then 30 km/18.6 mi E. 20 Avail: Pit toilets. 2021 rates: $20. May 14 to Oct 31. (780)623-7189

GRANDE CACHE — B1 *Greenview*

GRANDE CACHE MUNICIPAL CAMPGROUND (Public) From Jct of Hwy 40 & Shand Ave, E 0.4 mi on Shand Ave to 97th St, N 0.2 mi to 104th Ave, E 0.3 mi to Memorial Dr, N 0.6 mi to Campground Dr (E). 77 Avail: 56 full hkups, 21 W, 21 E (15/30 amps). 2021 rates: $35 to $40. May 15 to Oct 15. (780)827-2404

PIERRE GREY'S LAKES PRA (Public Prov Park) From town: Go 120 km/74-1/2 mi NW on Hwy 40. Avail: 61 E (30 amps), Pit toilets. 2021 rates: $29 to $37. May 14 to Oct 15. (780)827-7393

GRANDE PRAIRIE — B1 *Grand Prairie*

A SPOTLIGHT Introducing Grande Prairie's and Dinosaurs of the Alberta Badlands' colorful attractions appearing at the front of this province section.

BEAR LAKE CAMPGROUND (Public) From Jct AB 43X and AB 2: Go 6.5 km (4 mi) N on AB 2, then 11.4 km (7 mi) W on T. Rd. 730, then 1.9 km (1 1/4) S on RR 72. 21 Avail: Pit toilets. 2021 rates: $26. May 15 to Oct 15. (780)567-4105

BEAR PAW PAR 3 GOLF COURSE & RV PARK
good sam park
Ratings: 6.5/9.5★/8.5 (Campground) From jct AB 43 and AB 40: Go 3.2 km / 2 mi S on AB 40, then 1.8 km /1 mi E on 68 Ave (Township Rd 712), then 220 m S on 100 St, then 180 m W on 67 Ave, then 100 m S on 100 St (L). **FAC:** gravel rds. Avail: 43 gravel, back-ins (25x40), 35 W, 35 E (20/30 amps), WiFi @ sites, dump, fire rings, firewood, controlled access. **REC:** boating nearby, golf, rec open to public. Pets OK. No tents, eco-friendly. 2021 rates: $30 to $37. May 01 to Oct 01.
(780)402-8777 Lat: 55.137035, Lon: -118.792775
6325 - 100th Street, Grande Prairie, AB T8V 4B5
gobearpaw.ca
See ad page 1040

CAMP TAMARACK RV PARK
good sam park
Ratings: 8/10★/9 (RV Park) From Jct Hwy 43 & Hwy 40, S 5.5 mi (9 km) on Hwy 40 (L). **FAC:** all weather rds. (89 spaces). Avail: 37 gravel, 22 pull-thrus, (34x75), back-ins (34x60), 22 full hkups, 15 W, 15 E (30/50 amps), seasonal sites, WiFi @ sites, tent sites, dump, mobile sewer, laundry, groc, LP gas, fire rings, firewood. **REC:** boating nearby, playground, hunting nearby. Pets OK. Partial handicap access. Big rig sites, eco-friendly. 2021 rates: $44 to $51. Apr 15 to Oct 15.
(877)532-9998 Lat: 55.09466, Lon: -118.81274
704063 Range Rd 62, Grande Prairie, AB T8W 5B3
www.camptamarackrv.com
See ad page 1040

COUNTRY ROADS RV PARK
good sam park
Ratings: 8/9★/9 (Campground) From Jct of 43 & 116 St, N 6.6 km (4 mi) on 116 St to Hwy 43X, W 1.2km/0.7 mi to park entrance (L); or W-bnd: From Jct of Hwy 43 & Hwy 2, W 4.4 km (2.5 mi) on Hwy 43X (L).

A WELCOME STOP ON THE ALASKA ROAD!
Easy on & off Highway 43. Spacious, private full-service Big Rig sites. Unique onsite store featuring local art, wine, honey & much more! Close to all the major stores, great restaurants & excellent service centres.

FAC: gravel rds. (115 spaces). Avail: 80 gravel, 60 pull-thrus, (36x75), back-ins (24x50), 80 full hkups (30/50 amps), seasonal sites, WiFi @ sites, tent sites, shower$, dump, laundry, groc, LP gas, fire rings, firewood, controlled access. **REC:** pond, fishing, boating nearby, playground. Pet restrict (B/Q). Partial handicap access. Big rig sites, eco-friendly. 2021 rates: $51. ATM.
(866)532-6323 Lat: 55.227726, Lon: -118.864339
63061A Twp. Rd.722, Grande Prairie, AB T8X 4K7
www.countryroadsrvpark.com
See ad pages 1038, 1040

EVERGREEN PARK CAMPGROUND
(Public) From jct AB 43 & AB 40: Go 6.5 km/4-1/2 mi S on AB 40, then 3.3 km/2 mi E on AB 668, then continue straight 0.9 km/1/2 mi, then 0.2 km/100 yds S on gravel rd (L). **FAC:** gravel rds. (77 spaces). Avail: 65 gravel, back-ins (28x70), mostly side by side hkups, 65 W, 65 E (15/30 amps), seasonal sites, WiFi @ sites, dump, laundry, fire rings, firewood, restaurant. **REC:** boating nearby. Pet restrict (B/Q). No tents. 2021 rates: $35. May 01 to Sep 30.
(780)532-4568 Lat: 55.110297, Lon: -118.752792
AB-668 West, Grande Prairie, AB T8V 3A5
www.evergreenpark.ca
See ad page 1040

GRANDE PRAIRIE ROTARY RV PARK
Ratings: 6/9★/7 (RV Park) From Jct Hwy 40 & Hwy 43 (108 St.), N 77 yds/ 70 m on Hwy 43, E 30 yds/ 27m on 107 Ave, N 140 yds, 128m on frontage rd (R). **FAC:** paved rds. Avail: 61 paved, 16 pull-thrus, (30x72), back-ins (20x40), 21 full hkups, 40 W, 40 E (30/50 amps), WiFi @ sites, dump, laundry, fire rings, firewood. **REC:** boating nearby, playground. Pets OK. Partial handicap access. No tents. 2021 rates: $42 to $46. May 01 to Sep 30.
(780)532-1137 Lat: 55.179456, Lon: -118.819687
10747 108 St, Grande Prairie, AB T8V 7T8
www.rotarycampground.com
See ad page 1040

KLESKUN HILL CAMPGROUND (Public) From Grande Prairie: Go 20 km (12 1/2 mi) NE on AB 43, then 4 km (2 1/2 mi) N on RR 41. 10 Avail. 2021 rates: $26. May 15 to Oct 15. (780)567-3685

NITEHAWK WILDERNESS RV PARK & CAMPGROUND
good sam park
Ratings: 7/9.5★/8.5 (Campground) From Jct of Hwy 43 & Hwy 40, S 11.6km/7.2 mi on Hwy 40 to Hwy 666 (Nitehawk Exit), W 3.9km/2.4 mi to Nitehawk Ski Hill (R). **FAC:** gravel rds. (78 spaces). Avail: 50 gravel, 3 pull-thrus, (32x70), back-ins (32x70), 40 full hkups, 10 W, 10 E (30/50 amps), seasonal sites, WiFi @ sites, dump, mobile sewer, laundry, fire rings, firewood, restaurant. **REC:** Wapiti River: fishing, boating nearby, playground, hunting nearby. Pet restrict (Q). No tents, eco-friendly. 2021 rates: $39 to $44.
(888)754-6778 Lat: 55.05551, Lon: -118.86213
6356 Twp Rd 702A (Hwy 666W), Grovedale, AB T8V 4B5
gonitehawk.com
See ad page 1040

Things to See and Do

GRANDE PRAIRIE REGIONAL TOURISM ASSOCIATION Visitor info centre - Regional & provincial information, maps & souvenirs. Additional information on BC, Yukon, Northwest territories. FREE city tours Tues, Wed, Thur 6:30 pm June - Aug. Partial handicap access. RV accessible. Restrooms. Hours: 8:30am to 6:30pm.
(866)202-2202 Lat: 55.18172, Lon: -118.81757
#114-11330 106th st, Grande Prairie, AB T8V 7X9
gptourism.ca
See ad page 1040

PHILIP J. CURRIE DINOSAUR MUSEUM New world class dinosaur museum located west of Grande Prairie AB. Partial handicap access. Restrooms. Food. Hours: 10am to 8pm. Adult fee: $14.
(587)771-0662 Lat: 55.168255, Lon: -119.129970
9301-112 Ave, Wembley, AB T0H 3S0
dinomuseum.ca
See ad page 1038

GRANUM — E4 *Willow Creek*

GRANVIEW RECREATIONAL PARK (Public) From Jct of Hwy 2 & Hwy 519, E 0.4 mi on Hwy 519, follow signs (R). 37 Avail: 37 W, 16 S, 37 E (30 amps). 2021 rates: $30 to $50. (403)687-3830

GROUARD — A2 *Big Lakes*

HILLIARD'S BAY (Public Prov Park) From town: Go 8 km/5 mi E on access road. Avail: 139 E (30 amps). 2021 rates: $27 to $35. May 14 to Oct 13. (780)849-7100

GULL LAKE — C3 *Lacombe*

SUMMERLAND RV PARK **Ratings: 7.5/9.5★/10** (RV Park) Avail: 30 full hkups (30/50 amps). 2021 rates: $42 to $55. May 01 to Oct 01. (403)748-4855, 40325 Rge Rd 282, Lacombe, AB T4L 2N1

HANNA — D4 *Special Area No. 2*

FOX LAKE PARK (TOWN PARK) (Public) From jct Hwy 9 & Palliser Trail at west city limits: Go 1 mi N on Palliser Trail, then 2 mi W on Fox Lake Trail. 50 Avail: 2 full hkups, 28 E (20/30 amps). 2021 rates: $25 to $36. May 15 to Sep 15. (403)854-4433

HANNA MUSEUM TRAILER PARK (TOWN PARK) (Public) From jct Hwy 9 & Pioneer Trail at east city limits: Go 2 mi on Pioneer Trail. Avail: 26 full hkups (30 amps). 2021 rates: $31.50. May 01 to Sep 30. (403)854-4433

HIGH PRAIRIE — A2 *Big Lakes*

ELKS RV PARK **Ratings: 3/6/8** (RV Park) Avail: 24 full hkups (30/50 amps). 2021 rates: $30 to $35. (780)507-0399, 74508 Hwy 749 (48th St), High Prairie, AB T0G 1E0

HIGH PRAIRIE CAMPGROUND (Public) From jct Hwy 749 & Hwy 2: Go 2.4 km/1-1/2 mi E on Hwy 2, then 90 m/100 yds N on access road. 54 Avail: 54 W, 54 E (30/50 amps). 2021 rates: $20 to $25. May 01 to Sep 30. (780)523-3724

SHAW'S POINT RESORT (Campground) (Phone Update) 250 Avail: 50 full hkups, 200 W, 200 E (20/30 amps). 2021 rates: $45 to $54. May 01 to Oct 01. (780)751-3900, 751-15A Range Rd 141, High Prairie, AB T0G 1E0

HIGH RIVER — E3 *Foothills No. 31*

GEORGE LANE MEMORIAL CAMPGROUND (HIGH RIVER CITY PARK) (Public) From Jct of Hwys 23 (12th Ave) & Hwy 2, W 2 mi on Hwy 23 (12th Ave) to 1st St SW, N 1 mi to 5th Ave, W (E). Reservations recommended. Avail: 57 E (15/30 amps). 2021 rates: $20 to $29.50. Apr 15 to Sep 30. (403)652-2529

HINTON — C2 *Yellowhead*

HINTON/JASPER KOA **Ratings: 7.5/9.5★/9.5** (RV Park) 88 Avail: 77 full hkups, 11 W, 11 E (30/50 amps). 2021 rates: $64 to $75. May 15 to Oct 01. (888)562-4714, 50409B Hwy 16, Hinton, AB T7V 1X3

ROCK LAKE (Public Prov Park) From town: Go 86 km/53-1/2 mi NW on Hwy 40. 112 Avail: Pit toilets. 2021 rates: $16. May 15 to Oct 14. (780)865-2154

WATSON CREEK PRA (Public Prov Park) From town: Go 48 km/30 mi S on Hwy 40. 38 Avail: Pit toilets. 2021 rates: $11. May 01 to Sep 30. (780)865-2154

WHITEHORSE CREEK PRA (Public Prov Park) From town: Go 71-1/4 km/44-1/2 mi S on Hwy 40 and local roads. 26 Avail: Pit toilets. 2021 rates: $11. May 01 to Sep 30. (780)865-2154

WILLIAM A SWITZER (Public Prov Park) From town, W 2 mi on Hwy 16 to Hwy 40, NW 12.75 mi (R). Avail: 39 E (30 amps). 2021 rates: $29 to $45. (780)865-5600

HYTHE — A1 *Grande Prairie County No. 1*

HYTHE MUNICIPAL CAMPGROUND (Public) From Jct of Hwy 2 & 100th St, NW 0.2 mi on Hwy-2 (R). 20 Avail: 10 full hkups, 10 E (15/30 amps). 2021 rates: $25. May 01 to Oct 31. (780)356-3888

ICEFIELD PARKWAY — C2 *Edson*

DAVID THOMPSON RESORT (RV Resort) (Phone Update) 108 Avail: 34 full hkups, 29 E (15/30 amps). 2021 rates: $42 to $52. May 15 to Sep 23. (888)810-2103, Hwy 11(David Thomson Hwy), Nordegg, AB T0M 2H0

IRON RIVER — B5 *Bonnyville No. 87*

WOLF LAKE PRA (Public Prov Park) From jct Hwy 41 & Hwy 55: Go 18-1/2 km/11-1/2 mi W on Hwy 55, then 30-3/4 km/19-1/4 mi N on access road. 65 Avail: Pit toilets. 2021 rates: $20. May 15 to Sep 14. (780)723-0738

JASPER — C1 *Edson*

JASPER/HONEYMOON LAKE (Public National Park) From town, S 32.3 mi on Hwy 93 (L). 35 Avail: Pit toilets. 2021 rates: $16.05. Jun 23 to Sep 05. (877)737-3783

JASPER/JONAS CREEK (Public National Park) From town: Go 76-3/4 km/ 48 mi on Icefields Pkwy S (Hwy 93). 25 Avail: Pit toilets. 2021 rates: $16.05. May 17 to Sep 02. (877)737-3783

JASPER/KERKESLIN (Public National Park) From Jct of Hwys 93 & 16, S 22.5 mi on Hwy 93 (R). 42 Avail: Pit toilets. 2021 rates: $16.05. Jun 20 to Sep 01. (877)737-3783

JASPER/POCAHONTAS (Public National Park) From Jct of Hwys 93 & 16, NE 22 mi on Hwy 16 to Miette Rd, S 1.25 mi (R). 140 Avail. 2021 rates: $21.97. Jun 16 to Sep 05. (877)737-3783

JASPER/SNARING RIVER (Public National Park) From town, N 6.8 mi on Hwy 16 to Snaring Rd, W 3 mi (L). 62 Avail: Pit toilets. 2021 rates: $16.05. Jun 30 to Sep 28. (877)737-3783

JASPER/WABASSO (Public National Park) From town, S 10 mi on Hwy 93A (L). Avail: 51 E (15/20 amps). 2021 rates: $21.97 to $28. May 19 to Sep 19. (877)737-3783

JASPER/WAPITI (Public National Park) From Jct of Hwy 93 & Hwy 16, S 3 mi on Hwy 93 (L). Avail: 86 E (15/30 amps). 2021 rates: $28 to $33.01. (877)737-3783

JASPER/WHISTLERS (Public National Park) From Jct of Hwys 93 & 16, S 1.5 mi on Hwy 93 (R). 780 Avail: 123 full hkups, 126 E (15/30 amps). 2021 rates: $27.40 to $38.20. May 02 to Oct 13. (877)737-3783

JASPER/WILCOX (Public National Park) From Jct of Hwy 16 & Hwy 93, S 65 mi on Hwy 93 (L). 46 Avail: Pit toilets. 2021 rates: $16.05. Jul 17 to Sep 21. (877)737-3783

KANANASKIS — D3 *Kananaskis*

INDIAN GRAVES PRA (Public Prov Park) From town: Go 38-1/2 km/24 mi W on Hwy 533, then 11-1/4 km/7 mi N on Hwy 22, then 12-3/4 km/8 mi W on Hwy 532. 32 Avail: Pit toilets. 2021 rates: $26. May 17 to Sep 28. (403)995-5554

KANANASKIS VILLAGE — D3 *Kanaskis*

BOULTON CREEK CAMPGROUND (Public) From jct Hwy 1 & Hwy 40: Go 53 km/33 mi S on Hwy 40, then 10 km/6.2 mi SW on Kananaskis Lake Trail. 161 Avail: 32 full hkups, 37 W, 37 E (15/30 amps). 2021 rates: $29 to $53. May 13 to Oct 10. (877)537-2757

DAWSON EQUESTRIAN (Public Prov Park) From jct Hwy 1 & Hwy 40: Go 8 km/5 mi S on Hwy 40, then 11.7 km/7 mi E on Hwy 68, then 5 km/3 mi S on Powderface Trail. 10 Avail: Pit toilets. 2021 rates: $26 to $33. (403)673-2163

EAU CLAIRE CAMPGROUND (Public Prov Park) From jct Hwy 1 & Hwy 40: Go 38 km/23.6 mi S on Hwy 40. 51 Avail: Pit toilets. 2021 rates: $29. May 15 to Sep 02. (403)591-7226

ELKWOOD CAMPGROUND (Public Prov Park) From jct Hwy 1 & Hwy 40: Go 53 km/33 mi S on Hwy 40, then 6 km/3-3/4 mi SW on Kananaskis Lake Trail. 130 Avail: 69 W, 69 E (30 amps). 2021 rates: $26 to $40. May 13 to Oct 10. (403)591-7226

INTERLAKES CAMPGROUND (Public Prov Park) From jct Hwy 1 & Hwy 40: Go 53 km/33 mi S on Hwy 40, then 15 km/9.3 mi SW on Kananaskis Lake Trail. 48 Avail: Pit toilets. 2021 rates: $29. May 18 to Oct 10. (403)591-7226

LOWER LAKE CAMPGROUND (Public Prov Park) From jct Hwy 1 & Hwy 40: Go 53 km/33 mi S on Hwy 40, then 10.5 km/6-1/2 mi SW on Kananaskis Lake Trail. 95 Avail: Pit toilets. 2021 rates: $29. Jun 01 to Sep 20. (403)591-7226

MOUNT KIDD RV PARK (Public) From Jct of Hwy 1 & Hwy 40, S 16 mi on Hwy 40 (R). 229 Avail: 74 full hkups, 109 W, 155 E (15/30 amps). 2021 rates: $36.15 to $53.40. (403)591-7700

SIBBALD LAKE CAMPGROUND (Public Prov Park) From jct Hwy 1 & Hwy 40: Go 8 km/5 mi S on Hwy 40, then 12 km/7-1/2 mi E on Hwy 68. 134 Avail: Pit toilets. 2021 rates: $29. Apr 29 to Oct 10. (403)673-2163

SPRAY LAKES WEST CAMPGROUND (Public Prov Park) From jct Hwy 1 & Hwy 40: Go 53 km/33 mi S on Hwy 40, then 2 km/1.3 mi SW on Kananaskis Lake Trail, then 50 km/31 mi N on Smith Dorrien/Spray Trail (gravel road). (Across 3 Sister Dam.). 50 Avail: Pit toilets. 2021 rates: $29. May 14 to Sep 14. (403)591-7226

KINUSO — B3 *Big Lakes*

SPRUCE POINT PARK (Public) From town, N 7 mi on Hwy 2, follow signs (R). Avail: 30 E (15/30 amps). 2021 rates: $30 to $38.50. May 15 to Sep 15. (780)775-2117

LAC LA BICHE — B4 *Bonnyville*

FISH'N FRIENDS BEAVER LAKE CAMPGROUND (Public) From jct Hwy 55 & Hwy 36: Go 2 km/1.2 mi S on Hwy 36, then 5 km/3 mi E on Hwy 663. Avail: 61 E (15/30 amps). 2021 rates: $23 to $29. (780)623-9222

FORK LAKE CAMPGROUND (LAC LA BICHE COUNTY PARK) (Public) From jct Hwy 55 & Hwy 867: Go 2-1/2 km/1-1/2 mi S on Hwy 867. 43 Avail: Pit toilets. 2021 rates: $18.90 to $25.20. (780)623-1747

LAKELAND PRA (PINEHURST LAKE CAMPGROUND) (Public Prov Park) From town: Go 20 km/12.4 mi S on Hwy 36, then 30 km/18.6 mi E. 126 Avail: Pit toilets. 2021 rates: $25. Jun 01 to Sep 07. (780)623-7189

LAKELAND PRA (TOUCHWOOD LAKE CAMPGROUND) (Public Prov Park) From town: Go 12-3/4 km/8 mi E on Secondary Hwy 881, then 29-1/2 km/18-1/2 mi E. 87 Avail: Pit toilets. 2021 rates: $20. May 14 to Oct 31. (780)623-7189

SEIBERT LAKE CAMPGROUND (Public Prov Park) From town: Go 9-1/2 km/6 mi W on Hwy 660, then 40 km/25 mi N on Hwy 881, then 9-1/2 km/6 mi E on Hwy 55, then 30-1/2 km/19 mi N on local road/forestry trail. 2-wheel drive recommended in dry weather only. 43 Avail: Pit toilets. 2021 rates: $20. May 14 to Oct 31. (780)623-7189

SIR WINSTON CHURCHILL (Public Prov Park) From town, N 6 mi on Hwy 881 (L). Avail: 72 E (15/30 amps). 2021 rates: $38. May 07 to Oct 13. (780)623-4144

LAC LA NONNE — B3 *Lac Ste Anne*

ELKS BEACH (Public) From Jct of Hwy 33 & Secondary Hwy 651, E 2 mi on Secondary Hwy 651 to Elks Beach Rd, S 1.5 mi (R). 334 Avail: 334 W, 334 E (15 amps). 2021 rates: $12 to $18. May 01 to Oct 10. (780)967-5029

LAKE LOUISE — D2 *Improvement District No. 9 Banff*

BANFF/LAKE LOUISE-TRAILER PARK (Public National Park) From Jct TCH 1 & Whitehorn Rd exit, W 0.7 mi on Whitehorn Rd (becomes Lake Louise Dr) to Fairview Rd, S .80 mi (E). Avail: 189 full hkups (15/30 amps). 2021 rates: $32.30. (877)737-3783

BANFF/MOSQUITO CREEK (Public National Park) At Milepost 14.5 on Banff Rte 93 (Icefields Pkwy) (L). 32 Avail: Pit toilets. 2021 rates: $17.99. Jun 01 to Oct 10. (877)737-3783

BANFF/RAMPART CREEK (Public National Park) From Jct of TCH 1 & Hwy 93, N 55 mi on Hwy 93 (Icefields Pkwy) to park access rd (E). 50 Avail: Pit toilets. 2021 rates: $17.99. May 31 to Oct 14. (877)737-3783

LEDUC — C4 *Leduc*

LEDUC LIONS CLUB RV PARK & CAMPGROUND (Public) From Jct of Hwy 2 & 50th St (Exit 519), S 2.4 mi on 50th St to Rollyview Rd, E 1.2 mi to Lions Park Rd, N 0.3 mi (L). 101 Avail: 63 full hkups, 38 E (30/50 amps). 2021 rates: $30 to $49. Apr 15 to Oct 15. (780)986-1882

LETHBRIDGE — E4 *Lethbridge*

LETHBRIDGE See also Magrath.

BRIDGEVIEW RV RESORT **Ratings: 8.5/10★/8.5** (RV Park) 176 Avail: 136 full hkups, 40 W, 40 E (30/50 amps). 2021 rates: $45 to $90. (403)381-2357, 1501 2nd Avenue, Lethbridge, AB T1J 4S5

PARK LAKE (Public Prov Park) From town, W 3 mi on Crows Nest #3 to Picture Butte exit, N 3 mi, follow signs (L). Avail: 54 E (15/30 amps), Pit toilets. 2021 rates: $27 to $35. Jun 01 to Sep 08. (403)382-4097

LLOYDMINSTER — C5 *Vermilion River*

CAMPN RV **Ratings: 7.5/9.5★/9** (Campground) Avail: 38 full hkups (30/50 amps). 2021 rates: $38 to $48. (780)875-4663, Range Rd 22 & AB-16, Lloydminster, AB T0B 0L0

LODGEPOLE — C3 *Brazeau*

BRAZEAU RESERVOIR (Public Prov Park) From town: Go 24-3/4 km/15-1/2 mi SW on Hwy 620. Avail: 20 E (30 amps), Pit toilets. 2021 rates: $26 to $33. May 01 to Oct 14. (780)894-0006

LONGVIEW — E3 *Foothills No. 31*

CATARACT CREEK (Public Prov Park) From jct Hwy 22 & Hwy 541: Go 44 km/26-1/2 mi W on Hwy 541, then 15 km/9 mi S on Hwy 940 Secondary (gravel road). 100 Avail: Pit toilets. 2021 rates: $29. May 15 to Sep 02. (403)591-7226

ETHERINGTON CREEK (Public Prov Park) From jct Hwy 22 & Hwy 541: Go 44 km/26-1/2 mi W on Hwy 541, then 7.6 km/4-1/2 mi S on Hwy 940 Secondary (gravel road). 55 Avail: Pit toilets. 2021 rates: $29. May 15 to Oct 14. (403)591-7226

GREENFORD PRA (Public Prov Park) From jct Hwy 22 & Hwy 541: Go 24 km/15 mi W on Hwy 541. 13 Avail: Pit toilets. 2021 rates: $29. May 18 to Sep 05. (403)591-7226

LUNDBRECK — E3 *Pincher Creek No. 9*

LUNDBRECK FALLS PRA (Public Prov Park) From town: Go 1-1/2 km/1 mi W on Hwy 3, then follow signs. Avail: 29 E (15/30 amps), Pit toilets. 2021 rates: $26 to $34. May 06 to Oct 15. (403)627-1165

MADDEN — D3 *Rocky View*

BEAVER DAM GOLF & RV RESORT (RV Park) (Phone Update) Avail: 71 full hkups (30/50 amps). 2021 rates: $46. Apr 15 to Oct 15. (587)436-5204, 285127 Symons Valley Rd NW, Madden, AB T0M 1L0

MAGRATH — F4 *Cardston*

COVERED WAGON RV PARK **Ratings: 7.5/9★/9** (RV Park) 34 Avail: 23 full hkups, 8 W, 11 E (30/50 amps). 2021 rates: $40 to $45. Apr 01 to Oct 31. (403)758-3572, 234 W 5th Avenue South, Magrath, AB T0K 1J0

MARWAYNE — C5 *Vermillion River*

JUBILEE REGIONAL CAMPGROUND (Public) From Jct of Hwys 16 & 897, N 10 mi on Hwy 897 (L). Avail: 16 full hkups (15/20 amps). 2021 rates: $20 to $30. Apr 01 to Oct 30. (780)847-2273

MCLENNAN — A2 *Smoky River*

WINAGAMI LAKE (Public Prov Park) From Jct of PR-2 & PR-679, E 7 mi on PR-679 (L). Avail: 52 E (15 amps), Pit toilets. 2021 rates: $27 to $35. May 01 to Oct 13. (780)751-2598

MEDICINE HAT — E5 *Cypress*

CYPRESS HILLS (Public Prov Park) From Jct of TCH 1 & DR-41, S 21 mi on DR-41 (R). 434 Avail: 20 full hkups, 80 W, 183 E (15/30 amps). 2021 rates: $24 to $54. (403)893-3833

GAS CITY CAMPGROUND (Public) From Jct of Hwy 1 W & 7th St SW, W 1 mi on 7th St SW (R). 97 Avail: 51 W, 21 S, 73 E (30/50 amps). 2021 rates: $21 to $59. Jun 01 to Sep 28. (403)529-8158

ROSS CREEK RV PARK **Ratings: 4/NA/5.5** (RV Park) 41 Avail: 19 full hkups, 22 W, 22 E (30/50 amps), Pit toilets. 2021 rates: $44 to $49. Apr 01 to Oct 15. (403)526-5809, 2990 54th St SE , Medicine Hat, AB T1B 0N2

MILK RIVER — F4 *Warner County No. 5*

EIGHT FLAGS CAMPGROUND (CITY PARK) (Public) From jct Hwy 501 & Hwy 4: Go .4 km/1/4 mi S on Hwy 4. 34 Avail. 2021 rates: $20 to $30. (403)647-3639

WRITING-ON-STONE (Public Prov Park) From town: Go 32 km/20 mi E on Hwy 501, then 10 km/6 mi S on local access road. Avail: 47 E (15/30 amps). 2021 rates: $21 to $37. (403)647-2364

MILLARVILLE — E3 *Foothills No. 31*

MESA BUTTE PRA (Public Prov Park) From jct Hwy 22 & Hwy 549 (secondary): Go 15 km/9.3 mi W on Hwy 549 (Equestrian Camping). 15 Avail: Pit toilets. 2021 rates: $36. May 15 to Sep 15. (403)949-3132

NORTH FORK PRA (Public Prov Park) From jct Hwy 22 & Hwy 549 (secondary): Go 13 km/8 mi W on Hwy 549. 34 Avail: Pit toilets. 2021 rates: $29. May 15 to Sep 15. (403)949-3132

MIRROR — C4 *Lacombe*

THE NARROWS PRA (Public Prov Park) From town: Go 3 km/1-3/4 mi S on Hwy 21, then 3 km/1-3/4 mi E and 1 km/1/2 mi N on access roads. 61 Avail: Pit toilets. 2021 rates: $22. May 15 to Oct 14. (403)742-4338

MORINVILLE — C4 *Sturgeon*

HERITAGE LAKE CAMPGROUND **Ratings: 6/5.5/5.5** (Campground) 50 Avail: 25 full hkups, 25 W, 25 E (30 amps). 2021 rates: $46 to $48. Apr 01 to Oct 31. (780)939-6040, 55529 Range Rd 254, Morinville, AB T8R 1R9

MOSSLEIGH — E4 *Vulcan*

ASPEN CROSSING **Ratings: 7/10★/9.5** (RV Park) 131 Avail: 95 full hkups, 26 W, 26 E (30/50 amps). 2021 rates: $34.50 to $70. Apr 01 to Oct 31. (866)440-3500, 203079 Range Rd 251, Mossleigh, AB T0L 1P0

NANTON — E3 *Willow Creek No. 26*

CHAIN LAKES (Public Prov Park) From Jct of Hwy 2 & Hwy 533, W 25 mi on Hwy 533 (R). Avail: 60 E (15/30 amps). 2021 rates: $26 to $34. (403)627-1165

NEW NORWAY — C4 *Camrose*

SILVER CREEK GOLF & RV RESORT **Ratings: 6/5/7.5** (Campground) 71 Avail: 31 full hkups, 32 W, 40 E (15/30 amps). 2021 rates: $35 to $52. Apr 15 to Oct 15. (780)855-3982, 45314 Highway 21 RR#2, New Norway, AB T0B 3L0

NEW SAREPTA — C4 *Leduc*

CENTENNIAL PARK CAMPGROUND (LEDUC COUNTY PARK) (Public) From jct Hwy 21 & Twp Rd 500: Go 7 km/4-1/4 mi E on Twp Rd 500. 68 Avail: 14 W, 14 E. 2021 rates: $27 to $32. May 18 to Sep 07. (780)941-2124

NORDEGG — C2 *Clearwater*

FISH LAKE (Public Prov Park) From town, W 3 mi on Hwy 11 (L). Avail: 24 E (30 amps), Pit toilets. 2021 rates: $26 to $34. May 01 to Oct 12. (403)721-3975

GOLDEYE LAKE PRA (Public Prov Park) From town, W 7 mi on Hwy 11 (R). 40 Avail. 2021 rates: $26. May 01 to Oct 14. (403)721-3975

RAM FALLS (Public Prov Park) From town: Go 64 km/40 mi S on Hwy 940. 54 Avail: Pit toilets. 2021 rates: $26. May 01 to Oct 13. (403)845-8349

THOMPSON CREEK (Public Prov Park) From town, W 54 mi on Hwy 11 (L). 56 Avail: Pit toilets. 2021 rates: $29. May 01 to Oct 14. (855)721-3975

TWO O'CLOCK CREEK (Public Prov Park) From town, W 41.5 mi on Hwy 11 (R). 20 Avail: Pit toilets. 2021 rates: $29. May 01 to Nov 26. (403)721-3975

UPPER SHUNDA CREEK CAMPGROUND (Public) From town, W 1.5 mi on Hwy 11 (R) Note: 30' RV length limit. 25 Avail: Pit toilets. 2021 rates: $22 to $25. May 01 to Sep 30. (403)845-8250

OKOTOKS — E3 *Calgary*

OKOTOKS LIONS SHEEP RIVER CAMPGROUND **Ratings: 5.5/9.5★/8.5** (RV Park) 56 Avail: 50 full hkups, 6 E (30 amps). 2021 rates: $45. May 01 to Oct 01. (403)938-4282, 99 Woodhaven Dr, Okotoks, AB T1S 2L2

OLDS — D3 *Mountain View*

O.R. HEDGES LIONS CAMPGROUND (Public) From jct Hwy 2A & Hwy 27 (46 St): Go 3 blocks W on Hwy 27 (46 St), then 5 blocks S on 50th Ave, then 1 block W on 54th St. 45 Avail: 45 W, 45 E (30 amps). 2021 rates: $22 to $35. May 01 to Oct 15. (403)556-2299

WESTWARD HO PARK & CAMPGROUND (Public) From town, W 18 mi on Hwy 27 (L). 220 Avail. 2021 rates: $25. (403)556-2568

ONOWAY — C3 *Lac Ste Anne*

MEMORY LANE CAMPGROUND **Ratings: 6.5/8/8.5** (Campground) Avail: 37 full hkups (30/50 amps). 2021 rates: $42 to $47. May 01 to Sep 30. (780)995-5555, 56309 Range Road 13, Onoway, AB T0E 1V0

We rate what RVers consider important.

OYEN — D5 *Special Area No. 3*

OYEN CENTENNIAL PARK (TOWN PARK) (Public) From jct Hwy 9 & Hwy 41: Go 3 km/1-3/4 mi S on Hwy 41, then 3 blocks on West Frontage Rd. 40 Avail: 40 W, 40 E (30 amps). 2021 rates: $30. (403)664-9711

SAOKII CAMPGROUND (Campground) (Phone Update) Avail: 44 full hkups (30 amps). 2021 rates: $35 to $44. Apr 01 to Nov 01. (403)664-1270, Hwy 41 & Hwy 9 Jct, Oyen, AB T0J 2J0

PEACE POINT — A4 *Peace Point Indian Reserve 222*

WOOD BUFFALO/PINE LAKE (Public National Park) From Fort Smith, Northwest Terr: Go 2 km/1-1/4 mi E on Hwy 5, then 57 km/35-1/4 mi S on Pine Lake Rd into Alberta, then W into Pine Lake. Approx. 55 km/34 mi N of Peace Point, AB. 36 Avail: Pit toilets. 2021 rates: $15.70. May 17 to Sep 07. (877)737-3783

PEACE RIVER — A2 *Saddle Hills*

PEACE RIVER LIONS CAMPSITE **Ratings: 6.5/5.5/4.5** (Campground) 48 Avail: 36 full hkups, 12 W, 12 E (15/30 amps). 2021 rates: $30 to $35. Apr 01 to Nov 01. (780)624-2120, 8700-100 Ave, Peace River, AB T8S 1R8

RENDEZ VOUS RV PARK & STORAGE
good sam park **Ratings: 9/9.5★/7.5** (RV Park) From jct of AB 2 N & AB 688: Go 1 km(1/2 mi) NE on AB 688, then 230 m (750 feet) NW on Sunrise Road, then 800 m (1/2 mi) W on Sunrise Road S, then 300 m (1/4 mi) N on Woods Road (R). **FAC:** all weather rds. (119 spaces). Avail: 109 all weather, 56 pull-thrus, (32x130), back-ins (32x42), 109 full hkups (30/50 amps), seasonal sites, WiFi @ sites, rentals, shower$, dump, laundry, groc, LP gas, fire rings, firewood. **REC:** pond, fishing, boating nearby, playground, rec open to public. Pet restrict (Q). Partial handicap access. No tents. Big rig sites, eco-friendly. 2021 rates: $45 to $50. ATM.
(780)618-1345 Lat: 56.207727, Lon: -117.199600
950 Woods Road, Peace River, AB T8S 1Y9
www.rvpeaceriver.com
See ad this page

STRONG CREEK PARK (MUNICIPAL PARK) (Public) From town: Go 12-3/4 km/8 mi S on Shaftsbury Trail (Secondary 684). 18 Avail: Pit toilets. (780)338-3845

PICTURE BUTTE — E4 *Lethridge*

COUNTRYSIDE CAMPGROUND & RV PARK (Campground) (Phone Update) 37 Avail: 8 S, 29 E (15/30 amps). 2021 rates: $30 to $35. Apr 01 to Oct 15. (403)732-5371, 105005 Range Road 215, Picture Butte, AB T0K 1V0

PINCHER CREEK — E3 *Pincher Creek No. 9*

BEAUVAIS LAKE (Public Prov Park) From town, W 8 mi on Hwy 507 to Hwy 775, S 5 mi (L). Avail: 53 E (15/30 amps), Pit toilets. 2021 rates: $26 to $34. (877)537-2757

RED DEER — D3 *Red Deer*

LIONS CAMPGROUND (Public) From Jct of Hwy 2 & 67th St (Exit 401), E 2.1 mi on 67th St to Riverside Dr, S 0.5 mi (L). Avail: 138 full hkups (15/30 amps). 2021 rates: $27 to $53. May 01 to Sep 30. (403)342-8183

WESTERNER CAMPGROUND **Ratings: 6.5/10★/8** (RV Park) Avail: 98 full hkups (30/50 amps). 2021 rates: $46 to $51. (403)352-8801, 4847D 19 St, Red Deer, AB T4R 2N7

REDCLIFF — E5 *Cypress*

REDCLIFF CAMPGROUND (CITY PARK) (Public) From jct Trans Canada Hwy 1 & Broadway Ave: Go 6 blocks W on Broadway to 3rd St SW. Avail: 14 E. 2021 rates: $30. May 01 to Oct 15. (403)548-9253

ROBB — C2 *Yellowhead*

FAIRFAX LAKE PRA (Public Prov Park) From jct Hwy 47 & Hwy 40: Go 45-1/2 km/28-1/2 mi SE on Hwy 40. 27 Avail: Pit toilets. 2021 rates: $11. May 01 to Sep 30. (780)865-2154

ROCKY MOUNTAIN HOUSE — D3 *Clearwater*

CANYON CREEK GOLF COURSE & CAMPING **Ratings: 5/8/8.5** (Campground) 77 Avail: 48 full hkups, 29 W, 29 E (30/50 amps). 2021 rates: $40 to $48. May 15 to Sep 30. (403)845-5001, 64043 Hwy 12, Rocky Mountain House, AB T4T 2A1

CHAMBERS CREEK PRA (Public Prov Park) From town, W 15 mi on Hwy 11 (L). 25 Avail: Pit toilets. 2021 rates: $26. May 01 to Oct 14. (403)721-3975

CLEARWATER TRADING RV PARK **Ratings: 4.5/7/4.5** (Campground) 24 Avail: 10 W, 24 E (15 amps). 2021 rates: $25 to $35. (403)722-2378, 362047 Hwy 22, Rocky Mountain House, AB T4T 2A3

CRIMSON LAKE (Public Prov Park) From town, W 5 mi on Hwy 11 to Hwy 756, N 4 mi (L). Avail: 173 E (15 amps). 2021 rates: $20 to $29. (403)845-2330

MEDICINE LAKE PRA (Public Prov Park) From town: Go 47 km/31 mi N on Hwy 22, then 8 km SE on access road. 49 Avail: Pit toilets. 2021 rates: $32. May 01 to Oct 13. (780)388-2223

NEW OLD TOWN COTTAGES & RV PARK **Ratings: 3.5/9★/7** (Campground) Avail: 19 full hkups (30 amps). 2021 rates: $36.75. Apr 01 to Oct 15. (403)844-4442, 4203 62 St, Rocky Mountain House, AB T4T 1B3

RIVERVIEW CAMPGROUND
Ratings: 8/10★/9 (Campground) 100 Avail: 65 full hkups, 35 W, 35 E (30/50 amps). 2021 rates: $46.50 to $52.50. (403)845-4422, 400009 Range Rd 7-3A, Rocky Mountain House, AB T4T 2A4

RUSTIC RIVER RESORT (Campground) (Phone Update) 200 Avail: 200 W, 200 E (30 amps). 2021 rates: $50. (403)692-9905, 80010 Township Rd 41-4, Rocky Mountain House, AB T0M 0C0

STRACHAN PRA (Public Prov Park) From town, SW 15 mi on Hwy 752 (R). 27 Avail: Pit toilets. 2021 rates: $26. May 20 to Sep 06. (403)845-8349

TWIN LAKES (Public Prov Park) From town: Go 12 km/7-1/2 mi W on Hwy 11, then 2 km/1.2 mi N on Hwy 756. 39 Avail: Pit toilets. 2021 rates: $29. May 13 to Oct 10. (403)845-2330

WILDERNESS VILLAGE RESORT **Ratings: 8/10★/9** (RV Park) 283 Avail: 283 W, 283 E (20/30 amps). 2021 rates: $88. May 01 to Oct 15. (403)845-2145, SE-14-40-08-W5, Rocky Mountain House, AB T4T 1A9

ROSEDALE STATION — D4 *Wheatland*

THE 11 BRIDGES CAMPGROUND RV AND COZY CABIN PARK **Ratings: 7/9★/7.5** (Campground) 41 Avail: 6 full hkups, 21 W, 21 E (30 amps). 2021 rates: $48 to $50. May 01 to Sep 30. (403)823-2890, 332 4th Avenue S, Rosedale Station, AB T0J 2V0

RYCROFT — A1 *Spirit River*

NARDAM RV PARK (Public) From Jct of Hwy 2 & Hwy 49: Go W 1 mi (1.6 km) on Hwy 49, then 1000 ft (300 meters) on Range Road 54 (L). Avail: 16 full hkups (15/30 amps). 2021 rates: $35. May 15 to Oct 01. (780)864-8286

SEDGEWICK — C4 *Flagstaff*

SEDGEWICK LAKE CAMPGROUND (Public) From town, N 0.5 mi on Hwy 13 (R). Avail: 26 full hkups (15/30 amps). 2021 rates: $25 to $30. May 01 to Sep 30. (780)384-2256

SHERWOOD PARK — C4 *Strathcona*

HALF MOON LAKE RESORT **Ratings: 7/9.5★/8.5** (Campground) 207 Avail: 110 full hkups, 40 W, 60 E (30 amps). 2021 rates: $55 to $65. May 16 to Oct 15. (780)922-3045, 21524 Twp Rd 520, Sherwood Park, AB T8E 1E5

SLAVE LAKE — B3 *Lesser Slave River No. 124*

MARTEN RIVER CAMPGROUND (Public Prov Park) From Jct of Hwys 2 & 88, N 20.5 mi on Hwy 88 to park access rd, SW 3 mi (E). Avail: 72 E (15/30 amps). 2021 rates: $29 to $37. Jun 01 to Sep 08. (780)849-7100

SMOKY LAKE — B4 *Smoky Lake*

HANMORE LAKE CAMPGROUND (Public) From jct Hwy 28 & Hwy 855 (Secondary): Go 17.6 km/11 mi N on Hwy 855, then 3.2 km/2 mi W on access road. 46 Avail: Pit toilets. 2021 rates: $25. (780)656-6580

SPEDDEN — B4 *Smoky Lake*

GARNER LAKE (Public Prov Park) From Hwy 28 in town: Go 4-3/4 km/3 mi N on paved road. Avail: 24 E (15/30 amps). 2021 rates: $26 to $34. May 15 to Oct 12. (780)594-7856

SPIRIT RIVER — A1 *Spirit River No. 133*

MOONSHINE LAKE (Public Prov Park) From town, W 19 mi on Hwy 49 to Hwy 725, N 3 mi (L). Avail: 110 E (15/30 amps). 2021 rates: $35. May 01 to Oct 13. (780)538-5350

SPRING LAKE — C3 *Parkland*

SPRING LAKE RV RESORT **Ratings: 7.5/8.5/8.5** (Campground) 60 Avail: 40 full hkups, 15 W, 15 E (30/50 amps). 2021 rates: $53 to $63. May 01 to Sep 30. (780)963-3993, 499 Lakeside Dr., Spring Lake, AB T7Z 2V5

ST ALBERT — C4 *Sturgeon*

ST. ALBERT RV PARK
Ratings: 7/10★/10 (RV Park) From Jct of Hwy 16 (Yellowhead Hwy) & Hwy 216 (Anthony Henday Dr): NE 1.5km/.9 mi on Hwy 216 (Anthony Henday Dr) to Ray Gibbon Dr (Exit 27), N 2.3km/1.4 mi to LeClair Way, E 0.3km/0.2 mi to Riel Dr, N 1.3km/.8 mi (E).

GREAT LOCATION WITH SO MUCH TO DO!
Clean, spacious RV sites close to everything. St. Albert is home of the largest Farmer's Market in Western Canada. We're just 15 minutes from West Edmonton Mall, cycling/walking paths & bird & nature viewing areas.

FAC: paved rds. Avail: 93 all weather, 33 pull-thrus, (30x72), back-ins (30x64), 93 full hkups (50 amps), WiFi @ sites, . **REC:** Sturgeon river: boating nearby, playground. Pet restrict (B). Partial handicap access. No tents. Big rig sites, eco-friendly. 2021 rates: $50. May 01 to Sep 30.
(888)459-1724 Lat: 53.620525, Lon: -113.651094
47 Riel Dr., St Albert, AB T8N 3Z2
www.stalbertrvpark.ca
See ad page 1038

ST PAUL — B5 *St Paul County No. 19*

ST PAUL OVERNIGHT TOWN PARK (Public) In town, from west end at jct Hwy 28 & 55th St: Go 1 block S. Avail: 24 E (30 amps). 2021 rates: $16 to $26. May 13 to Sep 03. (780)645-5313

WESTCOVE MUNICIPAL RECREATION AREA (Public) From jct Hwy 28 & 50th St: Go 8 km/5 mi N, then follow signs. Avail: 66 E (15 amps), Pit toilets. 2021 rates: $25 to $35. May 11 to Aug 28. (780)645-6688

STETTLER — D4 *West End*

BUFFALO LAKE (Public Prov Park) From town: Go 20-3/4 km/13 mi N on Hwy 56, then 6-3/4 km/4-1/4 mi W on access road. 28 Avail: Pit toilets. 2021 rates: $28. May 15 to Sep 30. (403)741-2246

OL' MACDONALD'S RESORT **Ratings: 7/7.5/7** (RV Park) 375 Avail: 200 full hkups, 60 W, 60 E (15/30 amps). 2021 rates: $44 to $58. May 15 to Sep 15. (403)742-6603, 21246 Twp Rd, 40-2, Erskine, AB T0C 1G0

STETTLER LIONS CAMPGROUND (Public) From Jct of Hwys 56 & 12, W 0.5 mi on Hwy 12 to 62nd St, S 0.3 mi (L). 66 Avail: 22 full hkups, 40 W, 40 E (30 amps). 2021 rates: $20 to $35. (403)742-4411

STETTLER ROTARY PARK (Public) From Jct of SR-12 & SR-56, S 0.3 mi on SR-56 to 45th Ave, E 0.05 mi (R). 45 Avail: 15 W, 15 E (15 amps). 2021 rates: $10 to $12. (403)740-6425

STIRLING — E4 *Warner County No. 5*

CENTENNIAL REUNION SQUARE (VILLAGE PARK) (Public) From jct Hwy 4 & Stirling turnoff: Go 3/4 km/1/2 mi S, then 3/4 km/1/2 mi W on 4th Ave. 10 Avail: 10 W, 10 E (30 amps). 2021 rates: $30. (403)756-3379

STONY PLAIN — C3 *Parkland*

CAMP 'N CLASS RV PARK
Ratings: 9/10★/10 (RV Park) Avail: 57 full hkups (30/50 amps). 2021 rates: $50 to $60. (855)455-2299, 4107 50 Street, Stony Plain, AB T7Z 1L5

STONY PLAIN LION'S CAMPGROUND **Ratings: 5.5/7/7.5** (Campground) 23 Avail: 16 full hkups, 7 W, 7 E (30/50 amps). 2021 rates: $35 to $50. Apr 15 to Oct 15. (780)963-4505, #9 Granite Drive, Stony Plain, AB T7Z 1V8

SUNDRE — D3 *Mountain View*

COYOTE CREEK GOLF & RV RESORT **Ratings: 9/10★/10** (RV Park) Avail: 40 full hkups (15/50 amps). 2021 rates: $45. (403)638-1215, 32351 Range Rd 55, Sundre, AB T0M 1X0

GREENWOOD CAMPGROUND (TOWN PARK) (Public) From jct Hwy 22 (Main Ave) & Center St: Go 2 blocks S on Center St. 31 Avail: 2 full hkups, 17 E. 2021 rates: $24 to $37. May 18 to Sep 07. (403)638-2130

WAGONS WEST RV PARK & STORAGE **Ratings: 6.5/8.5/8.5** (Campground) Avail: 31 full hkups (30 amps). 2021 rates: $40. (403)638-4402, 103 5446 Hwy 584, Site 103, Sundre, AB T0M 1X0

SYLVAN LAKE — D3 *Red Deer*

JARVIS BAY (Public Prov Park) From town, N 3 mi on Hwy 20 (L). Avail: 195 E (15/30 amps). 2021 rates: $38. May 14 to Oct 13. (403)887-5522

MEADOWLANDS RV PARK & GOLF COURSE **Ratings: 7/9★/7.5** (RV Park) Avail: 23 full hkups (30/50 amps). 2021 rates: $51. May 01 to Oct 15. (403)896-4865, 3101 50th Street, Sylvan Lake, AB T4S 0P7

TABER — E4 *Taber*

MUNICIPAL DISTRICT OF TABER PARK (Public) From jct Hwy 3 & Hwy 864: Go 2-3/4 km/1-3/4 mi N on Hwy 864. Avail: 84 E (15/30 amps). 2021 rates: $35 to $40. Apr 15 to Oct 30. (403)223-0091

THREE HILLS — D4 *Kneehill*

KEIVER'S LAKE CAMPGROUND (KNEEHILL COUNTY PARK) (Public) From Jct of Hwy 21 & Hwy 583, W 11 mi on Hwy 583 to Keiver's Rd, S 1 mi (R). 34 Avail: 24 W, 24 E. 2021 rates: $20 to $30. May 15 to Sep 30. (403)443-0380

TOFIELD — C4 *Beaver*

LINDBROOK STAR GAZER CAMPGROUND & RV PARK **Ratings: 6.5/9★/8** (RV Park) Avail: 40 E (15/50 amps). 2021 rates: $45 to $50. May 01 to Sep 30. (780)662-4439, 51123 Range Rd 200, Tofield, AB T0B 4J0

TROCHU — D4 *Kneehill*

TOLMAN BRIDGE RECREATION AREA (Public Prov Park) From town: Go 20 km/13-1/2 mi E on Hwy 585. 40 Avail: Pit toilets. 2021 rates: $21. (403)442-4211

TURNER VALLEY — E3 *Foothills No. 31*

SANDY MCNABB (Public Prov Park) From jct Hwy 22 & Hwy 546: Go 20 km/12.5 mi W on Hwy 546. Avail: 112 E (30 amps). 2021 rates: $37. May 01 to Oct 13. (403)949-3132

TURNER VALLEY MUNICIPAL CAMPGROUND (Public) From Jct of Hwy 2 & Hwy 22, S 24 mi on Hwy 22 (L). Avail: 22 E (30 amps). 2021 rates: $28 to $30. May 01 to Oct 31. (403)933-7483

TWO HILLS — C4 *Two Hills County No. 21*

SANDY LAKE RECREATION PARK (TWO HILLS COUNTY PARK) (Public) From jct Hwy 861 & Hwy 45: Go 4.8 km/3 mi E on Hwy 45, then 12.8 km/8 mi N on Hwy 831. 37 Avail: 37 W, 37 E (15 amps). 2021 rates: $25 to $30. May 01 to Sep 30. (780)768-2330

Slow down. For most vehicles, fuel efficiency begins to drop rapidly at 60 mph. Driving within the speed limit can improve fuel efficiency by up to 23 percent.

VALLEYVIEW — B2 *Greenview*

SHERK'S RV PARK
Ratings: 8.5/10★/10 (RV Park) E-bnd: From Jct of Hwy 43 & Hwy 49, S 0.8km/0.5 mi on Hwy 43 to Twp Range Rd 702, W 1.1km /0.6mi on Range Rd 702 (R).

OASIS ON ROUTE TO AND FROM ALASKA!
Easy on and off AB-Hwy 43. Perfect stop for a night or a month! Full hookups, spacious sites, quiet, friendly surroundings. Clean washrooms/laundry. WiFi. Stroll groomed trails, relax by the pond. Archery range on site

FAC: all weather rds. (56 spaces). Avail: 46 all weather, 14 pull-thrus, (35x60), back-ins (35x65), 46 full hkups (15/30 amps), seasonal sites, WiFi @ sites, tent sites, shower$, laundry, LP gas, fire rings, firewood. **REC:** pond, boating nearby, playground, hunting nearby. Pets OK. Partial handicap access, eco-friendly. 2021 rates: $47.25 to $50. May 01 to Sep 30. **(780)524-4949 Lat: 55.05491, Lon: -117.29852 22362 Township Road 702, Valleyview, AB T0H 3N0**
www.sherksrvpark.com
See ad this page

WILLIAMSON (Public Prov Park) From town, W 10.5 mi on Hwy 43 to access rd, N 1 mi (L). Avail: 31 E (15 amps), Pit toilets. 2021 rates: $27 to $35. May 01 to Oct 13. (780)538-5350

YOUNG'S POINT (Public Prov Park) From town, W 16 mi on Hwy 43 to park access rd, N 6.25 mi (E). Avail: 78 E (15/30 amps). 2021 rates: $27 to $34. May 01 to Oct 15. (780)538-5350

VEGREVILLE — C4 *Minburn*

VEGREVILLE MUNICIPAL CAMPGROUND (Public) From Jct of PR-16 & 43rd St, N 0.1 mi on 43rd St (R). Avail: 48 E (30 amps). 2021 rates: $23 to $25. May 01 to Sep 01. (780)632-6800

VERMILION — C5 *Wainwright*

VERMILION (Public Prov Park) From Jct of Hwys 16 & 41 (in town), N 1 mi on Hwy 41 to 50th Ave, W 1.5 mi on entrance rd, N 0.25 mi (R). 98 Avail: 20 full hkups, 6 W, 50 E (30 amps). 2021 rates: $26 to $47. (780)853-4372

WABAMUN — C3 *Parkland*

WABAMUN LAKE (Public Prov Park) From Jct of Hwys 16 & 30, S 0.5 mi on Hwy 30 (R) Note: 49' RV length limit. Avail: 109 E (15/30 amps). 2021 rates: $35 to $43. May 01 to Oct 31. (780)892-2702

WABASCA-DESMARAIS — A3 *Opportunity No. 17*

WABASCA LIONS CLUB CAMPGROUND (Public) From town: At 4 way stop, go 15 km/9 mi N following Mistassiniy Rd N. Avail: 20 E (15/30 amps), Pit toilets. 2021 rates: $20 to $30. May 15 to Sep 28. (780)891-2093

WAINWRIGHT — C5 *Wainwright*

DR MIDDLEMASS CAMPGROUND (Public) From Jct of Hwy 14 & 15th St, S 0.4 mi on 15th St (L). Avail: 30 full hkups (15/30 amps). 2021 rates: $35. May 15 to Oct 15. (780)842-3541

RIVERDALE MINIPARK (MUNICIPAL PARK) (Public) From jct Hwy 14 & Hwy 41: Go 17 km/10-1/2 mi N on Hwy 41. 110 Avail: 38 full hkups, 15 W, 72 E. 2021 rates: $13 to $27. May 01 to Sep 30. (780)842-2996

WATERTON LAKES — F3 *Improvement District No. 4 Waterton*

WATERTON LAKES/CRANDELL MOUNTAIN (Public National Park) From Jct PR-6 & PR-5, SW 2.5 mi on PR-5 to Red Rock Canyon Rd, NE 5 mi (L) Due to wildfires, park is currently closed and expected to open spring 2022. 129 Avail. 2021 rates: $21.50 to $38.20. May 15 to Sep 01. (877)737-3783

WATERTON PARK — F3 *Cardston*

CROOKED CREEK CAMPGROUND **Ratings: 5.5/7.5★/7.5** (Campground) 50 Avail: 6 full hkups, 28 W, 24 E (30/50 amps). 2021 rates: $39 to $42. May 01 to Oct 01. (403)653-1100, RR 292 and Hwy 5 , Waterton Park, AB T0K 2M0

WATERTON LAKES/BELLY RIVER (Public National Park) From Jct of PR-6 & PR-5, W 1 mi on PR-5/6, S 10 mi on PR-6 (R). 24 Avail. 2021 rates: $15.70 to $38.20. May 10 to Sep 10. (877)737-3783

WATERTON LAKES/TOWNSITE (Public National Park) From Jct of PR-6 & PR-5, SW 5 mi on PR-5 (R). 237 Avail: 97 full hkups, 46 E (15/30 amps). 2021 rates: $28 to $39.04. May 10 to Oct 15. (877)737-3783

WEMBLEY — B1 *Grande Prairie County No. 1*

PIPESTONE CREEK PARK (GRANDE PRAIRIE COUNTY #1) (Public) From jct Hwy 2 & access road into Wembley: Go 16 km/10 mi S following signs. Avail: 35 E (15/30 amps). 2021 rates: $26 to $36. May 15 to Oct 15. (780)766-2391

SASKATOON ISLAND (Public Prov Park) From Jct of Hwys 34 & 2, W 17 mi on Hwy 2 to Saskatoon Island Rd, N 2.5 mi (E). Avail: 55 E (15/30 amps). 2021 rates: $30 to $38. May 01 to Oct 15. (780)538-5350

WESTEROSE — C3 *Leduc*

PIGEON LAKE (Public Prov Park) From town, W 3 mi on Hwy 13 to Hwy 771, N 4 mi to Park Access Rd, E 0.5 mi (L). 387 Avail: 10 W, 242 E (15/30 amps). 2021 rates: $20 to $54. (780)586-2644

ZEINER CAMPGROUND (Public Prov Park) From town, W 3 mi on Hwy 13 to Hwy 771, NW 11 mi (R). Reservations strongly recommended. Avail: 88 E (15/30 amps). 2021 rates: $30 to $38. May 08 to Sep 14. (780)586-2644

WESTLOCK — B3 *Westlock*

MOUNTIE PARK CAMPGROUND (Public) From Jct of Hwys 44 & 18, W 1 mi on Hwy 18 (L). 21 Avail: 12 full hkups, 9 W, 9 E (15/30 amps). 2021 rates: $30 to $32. Jun 01 to Sep 30. (780)349-4444

WETASKIWIN — C4 *Wetaskiwin*

WETASKIWIN LIONS RV CAMPGROUND (Public) From Jct of Hwy 2A & Hwy 13, E 1.7 mi on Hwy 13 (R). 52 Avail: 27 full hkups, 25 W, 25 E (15/30 amps). 2021 rates: $20 to $35. May 01 to Sep 30. (780)352-7258

WHITECOURT — B3 *Lac Ste Anne*

CARSON-PEGASUS (Public Prov Park) From town, W 3 mi on Hwy 43 to Hwy 32, N 7 mi to park access rd, E 3 mi, follow signs (E). Avail: 182 E (15 amps). 2021 rates: $36 to $38. May 16 to Oct 14. (780)778-2664

EAGLE RIVER TOURISM RV PARK **Ratings: 7/9★/8** (Campground) Avail: 77 full hkups (30/50 amps). 2021 rates: $35 to $40. (587)773-2497, Hwy 43 at Hwy 32N, Whitecourt, AB T7S 1N3

SAGITAWAH RV PARK **Ratings: 6/7.5/8.5** (RV Park) 33 Avail: 33 W, 33 E (30/50 amps). 2021 rates: $32 to $44.50. Jan 15 to Dec 31. (780)778-3734, River Boat Park Rd, Whitecourt, AB T7S 1N9

WHITECOURT LIONS CAMPGROUND **Ratings: 7.5/10★/8.5** (Campground) 53 Avail: 25 full hkups, 22 W, 22 E (30/50 amps). 2021 rates: $36 to $44. Apr 15 to Oct 15. (780)778-6782, 3001 33rd Street, Whitecourt, AB T7S 1P3

RV Tech Tips - You Screen, I Screen, We All Screen: Like the screen door of many coaches, opening your door from the inside requires sliding a plastic panel to access and pull the spring-loaded handle. This can be very inconvenient at times, especially when carrying something. To eliminate the sliding of the panel and make it easier to unlock the handle, attach a nylon cord between the handle and the hinged edge of the door. After drilling a small hole in the handle, wind the cord through the hole and tie it to the handle. The other end of the cord is attached to a screw along the edge of the screen door. The string can be easily pulled down to open the door handle from inside or outside without ever needing to slide the plastic and pull the handle.

BC

DID YOU KNOW?

North of Vancouver, Capilano Suspension Bridge Park leads visitors though dense forest landscapes.

YOU ARE HERE

Getty Images/iStockphoto

British Columbia

British Columbia is Canada's gateway to the Pacific and home to some of the country's most dramatic landscapes. Jaunts to ancient rain forests, snow-blanketed peaks and sophisticated urban hubs can be packed into one trip.

World-Class Western City

The port town of Vancouver has a truly international flavor. Thanks to its multicultural population, the city overflows with authentic sushi bars, Italian eateries and Middle Eastern establishments. It's also a wonderland for outdoor recreation just a stone's throw from urban attractions. Swimming at Kitsilano Beach, strolling the Capilano Suspension Bridge, cycling along the Stanley Park Seawall and snowboarding at nearby ski resorts are just some of the fun activities that entice travelers.

Rocky Roads

The Canadian Rocky Mountains constitute one of the most scenic ranges in the world, and visitors can get outstanding views of majestic skylines from Yoho National Park. See the peaks in all their glory along with cascading waterfalls, glacial lakes and fossil beds by traversing a myriad of hiking trails or driving scenic routes around the park. In the Okanagan Valley, relax on sandy beaches, tee off at championship links and roam romantic vineyards at over 200 wineries. Boating and paddling on Lake Okanagan are also popular pursuits. In winter, ski bums will want to head straight to Whistler, renowned for its world-class slopes.

Victoria's Verve

Take one of the BC Ferries from Tsawwassen in Vancouver and take the scenic ride to Victoria on Vancouver Island. The provincial capital is known for its colonial heritage, which can be experienced at the Butchart Gardens, the Royal BC Museum and the iconic Fairmont Empress Hotel.

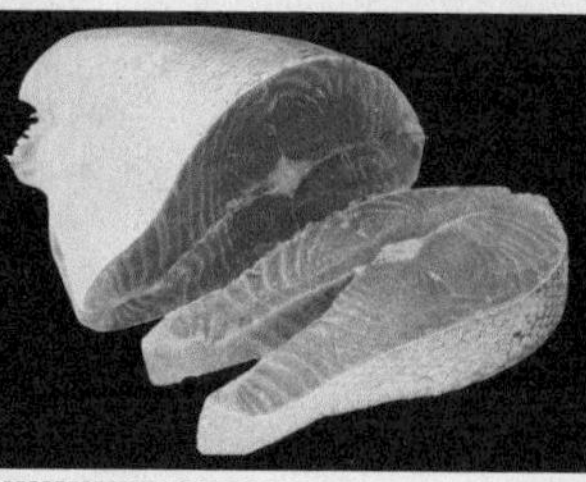

British Columbia Pacific Salmon

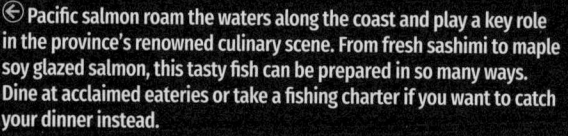

Pacific salmon roam the waters along the coast and play a key role in the province's renowned culinary scene. From fresh sashimi to maple soy glazed salmon, this tasty fish can be prepared in so many ways. Dine at acclaimed eateries or take a fishing charter if you want to catch your dinner instead.

VISITOR CENTER

TIME ZONE
Pacific Standard

ROAD & HIGHWAY INFORMATION
800-550-4997
drivebc.ca

FISHING, HUNTING & BOATING INFORMATION
800-267-6687
tc.gc.ca/eng/marinesafety/debs-obs-menu-1362.htm

NATIONAL PARKS
pc.gc.ca/en/pn-np

PROVINCIAL PARKS
gov.bc.ca/bcparks

TOURISM INFORMATION
Destination British Columbia
800-HELLOBC
hellobc.com

TOP TOURISM ATTRACTIONS
1) Stanley Park
2) Capilano Suspension Bridge
3) Pacific Rim National Park Preserve

MAJOR CITIES
Vancouver, Surrey, Burnaby, Richmond, Coquitlam, Victoria (capital)

Featured Good Sam Parks

BRITISH COLUMBIA

When you stay with Good Sam, you can expect the highest degree of cleanliness and friendliness, and better yet, you get **10% off** overnight campground fees.

If you're not already a Good Sam member you can purchase your membership at one of these locations:

BRIDESVILLE
Summit RV Resort

BURNABY
Burnaby Cariboo RV Park

CHETWYND
Westwind RV Park

CHILLIWACK
Cottonwood Meadows RV Country Club

CRESTON
Pair-A-Dice RV Park

DAWSON CREEK
Northern Lights RV Park

FAIRMONT HOT SPRINGS
Fairmont Hot Springs Resort

GOLDEN
Golden Municipal Campground

GRAND FORKS
Riviera RV Park & Campground

HOPE
Wild Rose Campground & RV Park

KELOWNA
Holiday Park Resort

LINDELL BEACH
Cultus Lake Thousand Trails RV Resort

MERRITT
Moon Shadows RV Park & Campground

PRINCE GEORGE
Bee Lazee RV Park & Campground

VALEMOUNT
Irvin's Park & Campground

WEST VANCOUVER
Capilano River RV Park

Getty Images/iStockphoto

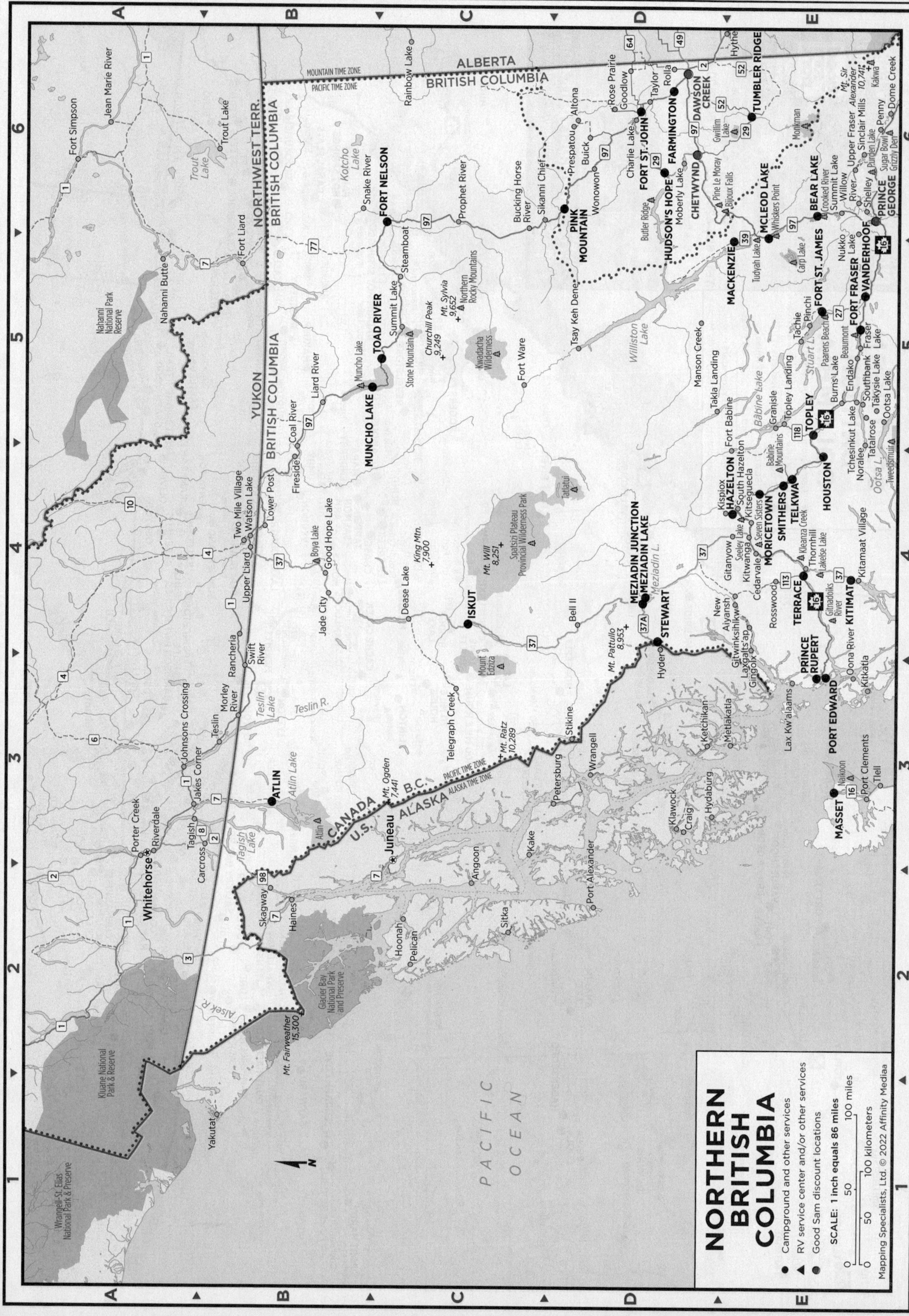
NORTHERN BRITISH COLUMBIA
Campground and other services
RV service center and/or other services
Good Sam discount locations
SCALE: 1 inch equals 86 miles
0 50 100 miles
0 50 100 kilometers
Mapping Specialists, Ltd. © 2022 Affinity Media
BC
PACIFIC OCEAN
YUKON
BRITISH COLUMBIA
NORTHWEST TERR.
ALBERTA
ALASKA
CANADA
U.S.
B.C.
MOUNTAIN TIME ZONE
PACIFIC TIME ZONE
ALASKA TIME ZONE
Whitehorse
Juneau
FORT NELSON
TOAD RIVER
MUNCHO LAKE
PINK MOUNTAIN
FORT ST. JOHN
HUDSON'S HOPE
FARMINGTON
DAWSON CREEK
CHETWYND
TUMBLER RIDGE
MACKENZIE
MCLEOD LAKE
BEAR LAKE
PRINCE GEORGE
FORT ST. JAMES
FORT FRASER
VANDERHOOF
TOPLEY
HOUSTON
TELKWA
SMITHERS
MORICETOWN
HAZELTON
MEZIADIN JUNCTION
MEZIADIN LAKE
STEWART
ISKUT
ATLIN
TERRACE
KITIMAT
PRINCE RUPERT
PORT EDWARD
MASSET
Kluane National Park & Reserve
Wrangell-St. Elias National Park & Preserve
Glacier Bay National Park and Preserve
Nahanni National Park Reserve
Spatsizi Plateau Provincial Wilderness Park
Kwadacha Wilderness
Mt. Fairweather 15,300
Mt. Ogden 7,441
Mt. Ratz 10,289
Mt. Pattullo 8,953
Mt. Will 8,251
King Mtn. 7,900
Churchill Peak 9,249
Mt. Sylvia 9,652
Mt. Sir Alexander 10,741
Williston Lake
Babine Lake
Stuart L.
Atlin Lake
Teslin Lake
Tagish Lake
Ootsa L.

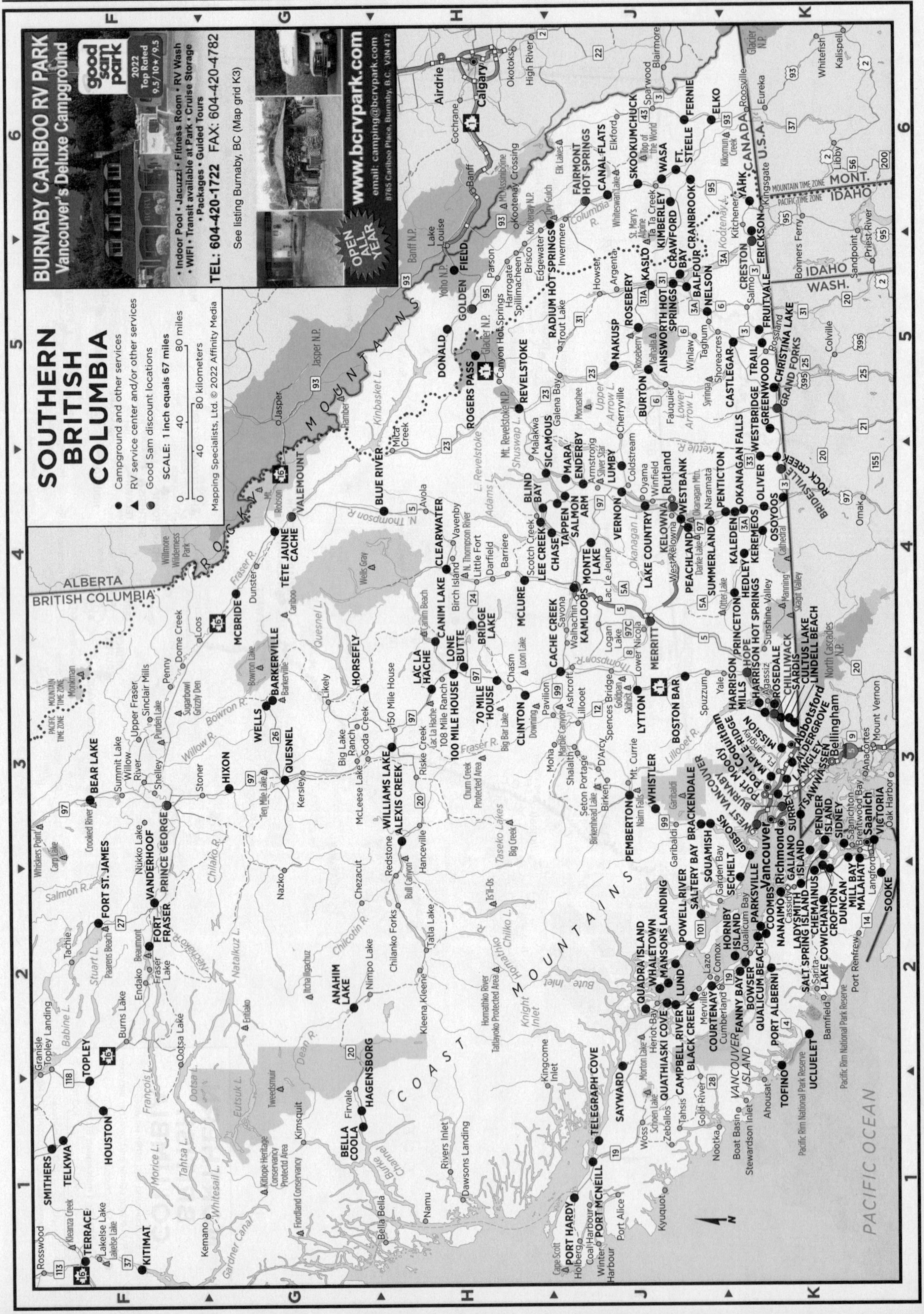
SOUTHERN BRITISH COLUMBIA
Campground and other services
RV service center and/or other services
Good Sam discount locations
SCALE: 1 inch equals 67 miles
0 40 80 miles
0 40 80 kilometers
Mapping Specialists, Ltd. © 2022 Affinity Media
BURNABY CARIBOO RV PARK
Vancouver's Deluxe Campground
• Indoor Pool • Jacuzzi • Fitness Room • RV Wash
• WiFi • Transit available at Park • Cruise Storage
• Packages • Guided Tours
TEL: 604-420-1722 FAX: 604-420-4782
See listing Burnaby, BC (Map grid K3)
good sam park
2022 Top Rated 9.5/10★/9.5
OPEN ALL YEAR
www.bcrvpark.com
email: camping@bcrvpark.com
8765 Cariboo Place, Burnaby, B.C. V3N 4T2
ALBERTA
BRITISH COLUMBIA
ROCKY MOUNTAINS
COAST MOUNTAINS
PACIFIC OCEAN
VANCOUVER ISLAND
CANADA
U.S.A.
WASH.
IDAHO
MONT.

ROAD TRIPS

Answer the Call of the Wild in the West

British Columbia

In British Columbia, big cities coexist with sprawling wilderness. Drive out of Vancouver and you'll see skyscrapers quickly give way to soaring mountain peaks and lush valleys. Continue north and the scenery just keeps getting better. Home to ancient old-growth forests and abundant rivers, this part of the province is an untamed natural playground so prepare to pull over often and explore. If you're passing through on your way to Alaska, enjoy these amazing stops.

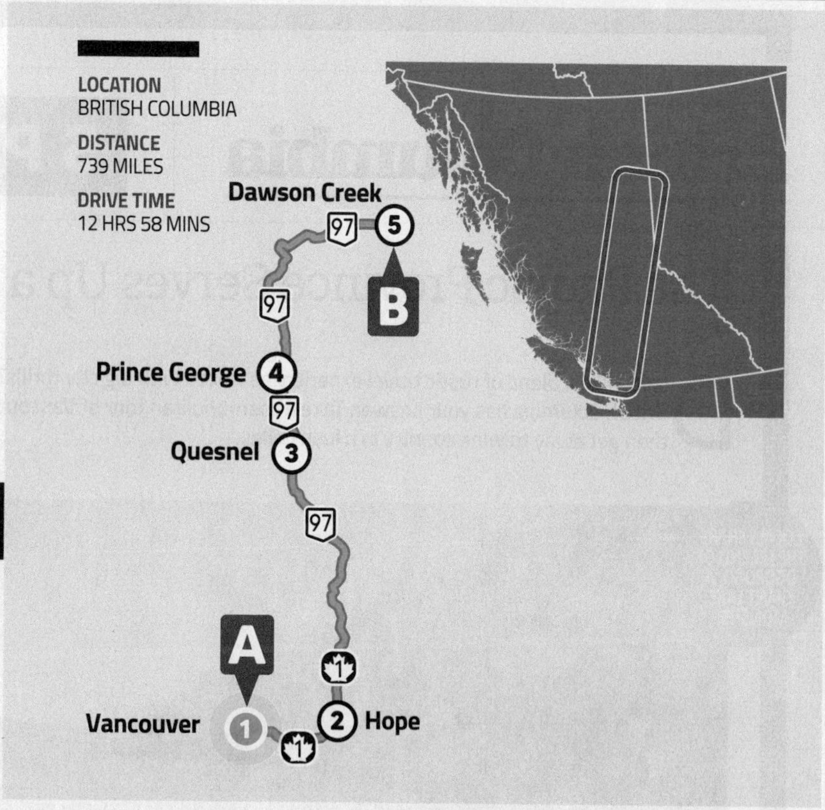

1 Vancouver
Starting point

This West Coast city bustles with cultures from around the world. From Pacific Northwest dishes and dim sum to gourmet donuts and fusion street food, you'll get to feast on all sorts of delicious delights in foodie neighborhoods like Gastown, Yaletown, Chinatown and Granville Island. Burn off the calories by kayaking around Vancouver Harbor or cycling along the Stanley Park seawall. For a challenging yet rewarding workout, climb the 1.8-mile Grouse Grind for views of the city.

RECOMMENDED STOPOVER
A BURNABY CARIBOO RV PARK
BURNABY, BC (604) 420-1722

2 Hope
Drive 94 miles ▪ 1 hour, 41 minutes

Spend some time in Hope, nestled at the edge of the Fraser Valley. Hope is a natural wonderland rich in wildlife. Reel in steelhead, salmon and sturgeon in its surrounding rivers and lakes and stay on the lookout for blue herons and eagles while you're out on the water. In town, take a self-guided tour to see the Hope Chainsaw Carvings, a collection of almost 100 sculptures crafted by local carvers. Many of them depict local wildlife such as bears, cougars and mountain sheep.

3 Quesnel
Drive 320 miles ▪ 5 hours, 35 minutes

Quesnel sits close to several waterways that entice anglers and rafters. Gear up and paddle against Class I to Class IV rapids on the Quesnel, Cariboo and Chilcotin rivers. Fishing is excellent here too. It's not uncommon for rainbow trout, bull trout and spring salmon to reach 30 pounds in the Quesnel River.

4 Prince George
Drive 75 miles ▪ 1 hour, 22 minutes

Prince George is British Columbia's fourth-largest city, but it's also about an hour away from the world's only inland temperate rainforest. Chun T'oh Whudujut Provincial Park, better known as the Ancient Forest, harbors a unique forest ecosystem that blends British Columbia's coastal rainforests with the boreal forests of the far north. Follow the Ancient Forest Trail to encounter gigantic cedar trees.

5 Dawson Creek
Drive 250 miles ▪ 4 hours, 20 minutes

Dawson Creek is the southernmost stop on the Alaska Highway and the starting point of a 1,422-mile journey to Delta Junction, Alaska. Snap a photo of the Mile 0 Post at 102nd Avenue and 10th Street, and then pop in the Alaska Highway House to find out how 30,000 soldiers and civilians built this expansive roadway in just nine months. Join a walking tour to hear about the town's fascinating WWII history and view works by local artists at the Dawson Creek Art Gallery.

RECOMMENDED STOPOVER
B NORTHERN LIGHTS RV PARK
DAWSON CREEK, BC (250) 782-9433

Getty Images/iStockphoto

BIKING · BOATING · DINING · ENTERTAINMENT · FISHING · HIKING · HUNTING · PADDLING · SHOPPING · SIGHTSEEING

British Columbia

SPOTLIGHTS

The Pacific Province Serves Up a Mix of Fun

Do you like a blend of rustic travel experiences mixed with big city thrills? British Columbia has your answer. Take a cosmopolitan tour of Vancouver, then get away to wine country in a lush valley.

LOCALS SHARE THE LEGEND OF OGOPOGO, A GIANT LAKE MONSTER.

Enjoying a warm climate, Lake Okanagan sits in the heart of BC's wine country.

Getty Images/iStockphoto

Okanagan Valley

With lush fields and rugged hills, the Okanagan Valley offers visitors some of the finest scenic drives in the country, along with an abundance of activities and attractions along the way. Located in the southern central region of the province, the rugged valley — which is highlighted by Okanagan Lake in the middle — contains the only desert in Canada. Here, many wineries and fruit farms can be found scattered throughout the countryside. Many of these wineries have traditional tasting rooms and unique restaurants on-site that serve a variety of delicious fare. So whether it's a casual lunch or an evening of fine dining, the Okanagan region wineries will not disappoint.

Harvested Goodness

Take your time and sample the bounty of the valley. Roadside fruit stands abound, offering that "just-picked" freshness. The cherry season is in full swing by the end of June and runs through the summer. Some RVers travel here and set up to can some of the local fruit. The entire family gets involved in the process right at their campsite.

Life on the Lake

Launch a vessel into Okanagan Lake to enjoy a serene and fun voyage. If you enjoy boating, this is the place to go. Whether you bring your own or rent one, the scenic lakes offer breathtaking sights. Prefer to be even closer to the water? Ride the Penticton River for a 4-mile float on a flotation device. It's free if you have your own flotation item or you can rent one for a low fee. Enjoy a sunny day on a carefree lake.

Cool It Down

Driving north on Highway 97 from Oliver to Penticton and onwards to Kelowna offers beautiful scenery as you wind your way along the mountainsides above Lake Skaha and Lake Okanagan. On your travels, don't miss stopping at Tickleberry's in Okanagan Falls for delicious ice cream treats. To the south catch the Osoyoos Desert Model Railroad. It may be the biggest model rail you have ever seen.

Vancouver Area

Mountains. Beaches. Buzzy restaurants. Canada's third largest city has it all. The best part? You can experience all three in the course of a single day. Whether you're an outdoors lover looking to conquer high peaks, or a cultural connoisseur with an eye for the next big thing, Vancouver serves up a little something for everyone. The only hard part is figuring out how to fit it all in.

Unique Neighborhoods

Diverse and multicultural, Vancouver is a city of neighborhoods, each with their own distinctive style. Among the must-see hotspots are Granville Street and the downtown district, home to hip nightlife and the one-of-a-kind Vancouver Art Museum, as well as Gastown, the city's oldest neighborhood, which brims with quirky boutiques, galleries and innovative restaurants. Join a local walking tour to learn more about the historic architecture that makes this compelling metropolis so unique.

LOCAL FAVORITE

Drunk Chicken

British Columbians embrace cuisine from across the globe. Check out this traditional Chinese dish during your Pacific Province travels. *Recipe by Caryl Chambers.*

INGREDIENTS

- ☐ ¼ cup soy sauce
- ☐ ¼ cup vegetable oil
- ☐ ¼ cup wine (rose or white)
- ☐ 2 Tbsp brown sugar
- ☐ 2 cloves garlic
- ☐ Add ginger if desired
- ☐ 2-5 lb cut up chicken

DIRECTIONS

Mix the sauce in a blender. Place the chicken in a shallow baking dish and cover with the above sauce mixture. Bake at 350 degrees for 1 1/2 hours. (Tastes even better the next day).

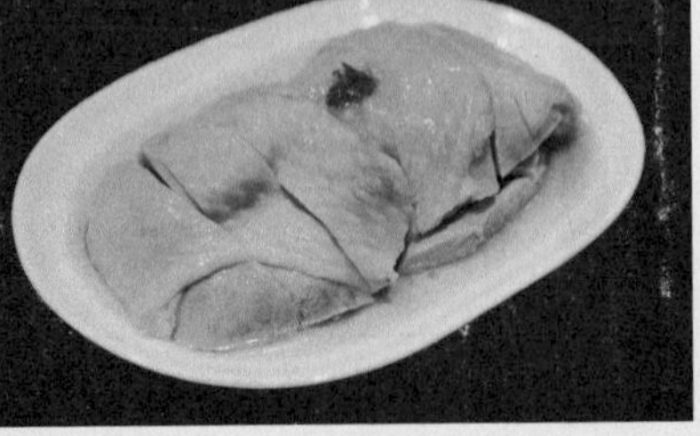

A First Nation totem pole outside of Vancouver honors the heritage of BC's indigenous people.

Chinese Heritage

Established in the 1890's, Vancouver's Chinatown is another don't-miss destination. One of the most vibrant of its kind in the world, the neighborhood is home to incredible dining and shopping, as well as hidden gems like the Dr. Sun Yat-Sen Classical Chinese Garden. Built using only 14th-century methods, no glues, screws or power tools were used in constructing the one-of-a-kind urban treasure. For more interesting outposts, try beachfront Kitsilano, the waterfront views of Lower Lonsdale and the outdoorsy West End neighborhoods.

Urban Oasis

Located on a peninsula just north of downtown, Stanley Park has been earning its reputation as one of the world's great urban parks for over 130 years. Officially opened in 1888, the 1,000-acre green space is home to 17 miles of trails that wind through dense West Coast rainforest, as well as pristine beaches, an aquarium, water park, cultural landmarks and more. To get the lay of the land, walk or bike the 5.5-mile seawall path that circles the park. Along the way, you'll discover incredible skyline views, First Nations totem poles, and easy access to all the top attractions. Other popular routes include the Cathedral Trail, which leads hikers past massive moss-covered pines, and the mile-long Beaver Lake Trail, which includes educational displays and a picturesque pond. Keep an eye out for the five pairs of bald eagles that call the area home.

Hiker's Paradise

Surrounded by scenic mountains, there's no shortage of hiking and biking in the Vancouver area. For starters, there's Pacific Spirit Regional Park at the city's western edge. Boasting 34 miles of both forested and shoreline trails, it's the perfect place to ease your way into the outdoors. Even better, many of the routes are designated for cycling and horseback riding, so you can enjoy the backdrop however you see fit. If it's more of a challenge you're after, the Grouse Grind awaits. About eight miles north of downtown, this super-steep climb — it ascends 2,800 feet in less than 2 miles — has been challenging Vancouverites for years. Thankfully, there's now a scenic sky lift to the summit, as well as restaurants and cafes that will help you refuel after a long hike. For backcountry adventures on the outskirts of town, head to Cypress Provincial Park, about 18 miles north of downtown, or Mount Seymour Provincial Park, the same distance to the east. Both offer incredible views of the city and beyond.

Waterfront Magic

Cooling off after a morning hike is easy with a day on the water. The calm waters of False Creek are perfect for an urban kayaking adventure, while a North Shore paddle from Deep Cove to the Indian Arm fjord reveals old growth forests, stunning waterfalls and endless wildlife viewing opportunities. There are plenty of outfitters in town who can help organize an outing. Anglers will revel in the many opportunities to join a charter trip fishing for king salmon, or simply do like the locals do and head to the Capilano River, about 30 minutes from Stanley Park. The waters there are abundant with the picture-perfect Coho salmon famous throughout the Pacific Northwest. Finish your trip with a one-of-a-kind whale watching excursion. Considered among the world's best locations for spotting the

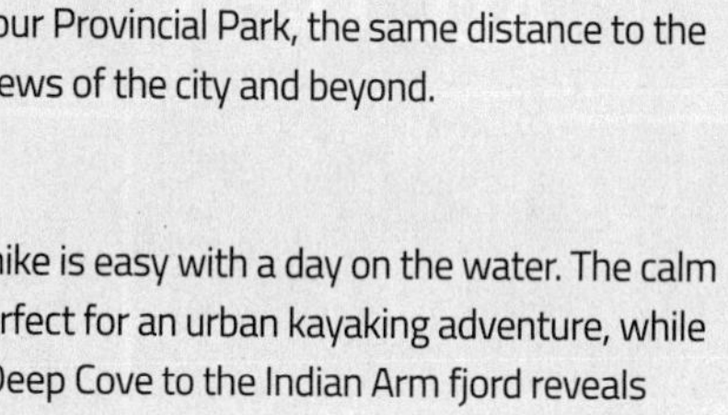
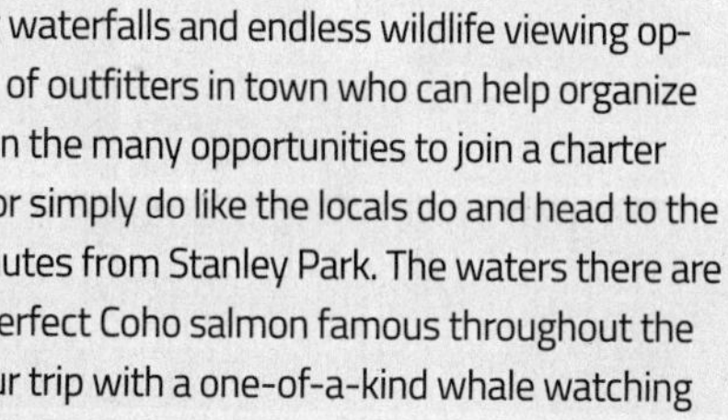

BURNABY CARIBOO RV PARK
Vancouver's Deluxe RV Park
On BC's Road to Alaska
OPEN
ALL YEAR
• Indoor Pool • Jacuzzi • Fitness Room • RV Wash • WiFi • Transit Available at Park • Cruise Storage • Packages
• Central to Vancouver's Attractions • Guided Tours Pick Up at the Park Daily • On Public Transit Route
604-420-1722
camping@bcrvpark.com
8765 Cariboo Place • Burnaby, BC V3N 4T2
From Hwy #1 (East or West)
Take Exit 37 (Gaglardi Way) turn right at the traffic light, immediately left, next right turn is our road.
From USA Interstate 5:
Take Exit 275 (Commercial/truck border crossing) onto Highway 15. From Highway 15 go West on Highway 1, take Exit 37.
good sam park
2022
Top Rated
9.5/10★/9.5
www.bcrvpark.com
AAA
See listing Burnaby, BC

BC

Shrouded in First Nation legend, Siwash Rock in Vancouver's Stanley Park stands around 50 feet tall.

incredible creatures, it's sure to be an unforgettable experience.

Vancouver Island

All cares and worries drift away in the ocean-carved region of Vancouver Island. Spanning 285 miles from the rocky bluffs of Cape Scott to the colonial capital of Victoria, this tranquil corner of British Columbia takes you away from the hustle and bustle of the big cities and plops you right at nature's doorstep. From Tofino's temperate rainforests and windswept beaches to Salt Spring Island's spas and bucolic countryside, you'll find so many destinations to rest and recharge in.

Surf's Up

Grab a board and learn how to ride waves in Tofino, the surfing capital of Canada. The town boasts 21 miles of surfable beach and an easygoing vibe to go with it. Take a stroll downtown to find hip breweries, food trucks, independent boutiques and a handful of galleries. Tofino is also nestled in the heart of the Clayoquot Sound, a UNESCO Biosphere Reserve packed to the brim with ancient trees. Follow the Meares Island Big Tree Trail to meet the Hanging Garden, a 2,000-year-old tree with a 60-foot diameter. Winter is an excellent time to visit if you'd like to watch powerful storms ravage the land and sea from the comfort of your hotel room.

Coastal Connections

With 2,000 miles of coastline and almost 10,000 lakes, the marine activities here go from mild to mind-blowingly fast. Go on a whale-watching tour in Victoria, Campbell River or Port Hardy to come face to face with pods of orcas and humpback whales. Hop in a kayak and paddle to deserted beaches and coastal rainforests in Barkley Sound, Clayoquot Sound and the Discovery Islands. The fishing here is also out of this world. Hire a charter and hook colossal salmon and halibut from secret fishing holes in Port Renfrew, Nootka Sound and Esperanza Inlet. You can also enjoy fly-fishing on the Cowichan River and go crabbing in Sooke Harbour.

Epic Trails

Outdoor adventures come in all sizes, thanks to Vancouver Island's diverse landscapes. Hit the 47-mile West Coast Trail in Pacific Rim National Park for dramatic views of the rugged west coast, or traverse Ucluelet's Wild Pacific Trail to explore old-growth forests and a historic lighthouse. Waterfalls, peculiar rock formations and hidden grottos are all easily accessible via the 29-mile Juan de Fuca Marine Trail.

Gulf Island Hospitality

The relaxation you crave can be found in every corner of the Southern Gulf Islands. Set in the Salish Sea off the shores of southeastern Vancouver Island, this region encompasses over 300 islands, with the five largest supporting local populations. The biggest is Salt Spring Island, inhabited by artisan producers who are all eager to show you their organic vineyards, microbreweries and farmers markets.

Indigenous Experiences in Victoria

Immersive galleries blend natural and human history at Victoria's Royal BC Museum. Discover traditional masks, totem poles and other cultural relics in the First Peoples Gallery and then wander down the language forest to hear greetings in 34 Indigenous BC languages. Other highlights include a recreated Kwakwaka'wakw clan house and a life-size wooly mammoth.

FOR MORE INFORMATION

Destination British Columbia,
800-435-5622, www.hellobc.com
Okanagan Valley,
hellobc.com/places-to-go/okanagan-valley
Metro Vancouver Convention and Visitors Bureau,
604-682-2222, www.tourismvancouver.com
Vancouver Island, Vancouverisland.travel

San Josef Beach is an uncrowded getaway in Cape Scott on the northwest tip of Vancouver Island.

British Columbia

100 MILE HOUSE — H3 *Bulkley-Nechako*

CARIBOO BONANZA RESORT (Campground) (Phone Update) Avail: 51 full hkups (15/30 amps). 2021 rates: $38 to $40. May 01 to Sep 30. (250)395-3766, 6384 Watson Rd, Lone Butte, BC V0K 1X3

70 MILE HOUSE — H3 *Cariboo*

GREEN LAKE/SUNSET VIEW (Public Prov Park) From town: Go 19-1/4 km/12 mi E on Green Lake South Rd. 54 Avail: Pit toilets. 2021 rates: $18. May 15 to Sep 07. (250)320-9305

AINSWORTH HOT SPRINGS — J5 *Thompson-Nicola*

WOODBURY RESORT & MARINA **Ratings: 7.5/6/7** (Membership Park) 33 Avail: 33 W, 33 E (30 amps). 2021 rates: $35 to $40. (877)353-7717, 4112 Hwy 31, Ainsworth Hot Springs, BC V0G 1A0

ALDERGROVE — K3 *Langley*

EAGLE WIND RV PARK **Ratings: 10/10★/8.5** (RV Park) Avail: 45 full hkups (30/50 amps). 2021 rates: $50 to $60. (604)856-6674, 26920 52nd Ave , Aldergrove, BC V4W 1N6

ALEXIS CREEK — H3 *Cariboo*

BULL CANYON (Public Prov Park) From town, W 5 mi on Hwy 20 (L). 20 Avail: Pit toilets. 2021 rates: $20. May 15 to Sep 15. (250)320-9305

Park policies vary. Ask about the cancellation policy when making a reservation.

ANAHIM LAKE — G2 *Kitimat-Stikine*

ANAHIM LAKE RESORT & RV PARK (RV Park) (Phone Update) 30 Avail: 30 W, 30 E (15/30 amps). 2021 rates: $37. Jun 01 to Sep 30. (800)667-7212, 2799 Reed Rd, Anahim Lake, BC V0L 1C0

ATLIN — B3 *Stikine*

BOYA LAKE (Public Prov Park) From Jct of Hwy 37 & Boya Lake Rd, E 1.5 mi on Boya Lake Rd (E). 44 Avail: Pit toilets. 2021 rates: $20. May 15 to Sep 15. (250)638-8490

BALFOUR — J5 *Thompson-Nicola*

BIRCH GROVE CAMPGROUND **Ratings: 5/8★/7.5** (Campground) Avail: 47 full hkups (30 amps). 2021 rates: $45 to $55. Apr 15 to Oct 31. (877)247-8774, 7048 Lee Rd, Nelson, BC V1L 6R9

BARKERVILLE — G3 *Cariboo*

BARKERVILLE (Public) From Jct of Hwy 26 & Hwy 97, E 50 mi on Hwy 26 (R). Avail: 5 E. 2021 rates: $14.50. Jun 01 to Oct 31. (250)994-3297

BARKERVILLE CAMPGROUNDS (LOWHEE/FOREST ROSE) **Ratings: 1.5/8.5★/7.5** (Campground) 141 Avail: 96 W, 96 E (15/30 amps). 2021 rates: $25 to $30. May 15 to Sep 29. (888)994-3332, 13500 Hwy 26, Barkerville, BC V0K 1B0

BOWRON LAKE (Public Prov Park) From town: Go 17-1/2 km/11 mi E on secondary road. 25 Avail: Pit toilets. 2021 rates: $18. May 15 to Sep 30. (800)689-9025

BEAR LAKE — F3 *Peace River*

CROOKED RIVER (Public Prov Park) From town: Go 1-1/2 km/1 mi N on Hwy 97. 65 Avail. 2021 rates: $22. May 15 to Oct 04. (250)964-3489

BELLA COOLA — G1 *Central Coast*

GNOMES HOME RV PARK AND CAMPGROUND (RV Park) (Rebuilding) 24 Avail: 15 full hkups, 5 E (15/30 amps). 2021 rates: $18 to $20. May 01 to Oct 06. (236)589-0660, 1875 Hwy 20, Hagensborg, BC V0T 1C0

TWEEDSMUIR SOUTH PARK (Public Prov Park) From Williams Lake, W 240 mi on Hwy 20 (L). 24 Avail. 2021 rates: $20. Jun 15 to Oct 15. (250)397-2523

BLACK CREEK — G3 *East Island*

PACIFIC PLAYGROUNDS RV PARK COTTAGES MARINA **Ratings: 8/7.5/9** (RV Park) Avail: 162 full hkups (30/50 amps). 2021 rates: $45 to $65. (877)239-5600, 9082 Clarkson Ave, Black Creek, BC V9J 1B3

BLIND BAY — H4 *Okanagan*

BLIND BAY RESORT **Ratings: 9/9.5★/8** (Condo Park) Avail: 13 full hkups (30/50 amps). 2021 rates: $58 to $90. (250)675-2595, 2698 Blind Bay Rd, Blind Bay, BC V0E 1H1

BLUE RIVER — H4 *Columbia*

BLUE RIVER CAMPGROUND AND RV PARK (Campground) (Phone Update) 30 Avail: 14 full hkups, 12 W, 12 E (15/30 amps). 2021 rates: $34 to $40. May 01 to Oct 15. (866)675-8203, 991 W Frontage Rd, Blue River, BC V0E 1J0

BOSTON BAR — J3 *Thompson Region*

ANDERSON CREEK CAMPGROUND **Ratings: 3.5/8/7.5** (Campground) 10 Avail: 10 W, 10 E (30 amps). 2021 rates: $35 to $40. Apr 01 to Oct 15. (604)867-9089, 48500 Tuckkwiowhum, Boston Bar, BC V0K 1C0

BOWSER — K2 *East Island*

DEEP BAY RV PARK (Campground) (Phone Update) 30 Avail: 25 full hkups, 5 W, 5 E (30 amps). 2021 rates: $43 to $49. May 01 to Sep 30. (250)757-8424, 5315 Deep Bay Dr, Bowser, BC V0R 1G0

BRACKENDALE — J3 *Squamish*

MTN FUN BASE CAMP **Ratings: 5/8/7** (Campground) Avail: 23 full hkups (30 amps). 2021 rates: $40 to $80. (604)390-4200, 1796 Depot Rd, Squamish, BC V0N 1T0

Dispose of old paint, chemicals, and oil properly. Don't put batteries, antifreeze, paint, motor oil, or chemicals in the trash. Use proper toxics disposal sites.

BRIDESVILLE — K4 *Okanagan*

SUMMIT RV RESORT

good sam park **Ratings: 6/10★/6.5** (RV Park) From jct Courtney Brown Road & BC 3: Go 3.7 km/2-1/4 mi W on BC 3 (R). Elev 4024 ft.

NEW YEAR ROUND CAMPING GETAWAY!

Great for overnight stop or long term stay! Huge 50/30 amp pull thrus off Hwy #3. Minutes from Osoyoos Tourist Area with Restaurants, Wineries & Events! Close to skiing, hiking, biking, fishing & so much more! German spoken.

FAC: all weather rds. Avail: 33 gravel, 8 pull-thrus, (30x90), back-ins (50x50), mostly side by side hkups, 33 full hkups (30/50 amps), WiFi @ sites, rentals, laundry, groc, LP gas, fire rings, firewood, controlled access. Pets OK. No tents. Big rig sites, eco-friendly. 2021 rates: $50. no cc.

(250)533-1111 Lat: 49.017450, Lon: -119.199010
6075 BC-3, Bridesville, BC V0H 1Y0
summitrvresort.com
See ad this page

BRIDGE LAKE — H4 *Cariboo*

BRIDGE LAKE PROVINCIAL PARK (Public Prov Park) From town: Go N on Hwy 24. 13 Avail: Pit toilets. 2021 rates: $18. Jun 15 to Sep 18. (250)397-2523

BURNABY — K3 *Mount Waddington*

BURNABY CARIBOO RV PARK

good sam park **Ratings: 9.5/10★/9.5** (RV Park) From Jct of Hwy 1 & Gaglardi Way (exit 37) W 9.6km/6 mi (W of Port Mann Bridge), N 91m/300 ft to traffic light, E 91m/300 ft on Cariboo Rd, N 0.3km/0.2 mi on Cariboo Rd (under overpass) to Cariboo Pl (E).

WE ARE BC'S PREMIER RV PARK!

Amazing urban forest setting with the best modern amenities. Stroll along pristine creekside trails or visit BC's largest shopping mall with over 400 stores. Easy access to all attractions and adventures; outdoor or indoor.

FAC: paved rds. Avail: 212 paved, patios, back-ins (30x45), 212 full hkups (30 amps), cable, WiFi @ sites, tent sites, dump, laundry, groc. **REC:** heated pool, hot tub, Brunette River : fishing, boating nearby, playground. Pets OK. Partial handicap access, eco-friendly. 2021 rates: $62 to $73. ATM.

(604)420-1722 Lat: 49.24864, Lon: -122.91216
8765 Cariboo Place, Burnaby, BC V3N 4T2
bcrv.com
See ad pages 1052, 1056, 1066

BURTON — J5 *West Kootenay*

BURTON HISTORICAL PARK CAMPGROUND (Campground) (Phone Update) 37 Avail: 21 W, 21 E (15/30 amps). 2021 rates: $30 to $37. May 01 to Sep 30. (844)265-4885, 145 Lakeview Park Rd, Burton, BC V0G 1E0

CACHE CREEK — J3 *Cariboo*

BROOKSIDE CAMPSITE **Ratings: 7.5/9★/8** (Campground) 48 Avail: 33 full hkups, 15 W, 15 E (30 amps). 2021 rates: $33 to $41. (250)457-6633, 1621 E Trans Canada Hwy, Cache Creek, BC V0K 1H0

JUNIPER BEACH PARK

(Public Prov Park) From town, E 12 mi on Hwy 1 (R). **FAC:** gravel rds. Avail: 32 gravel, back-ins (12x35), 32 E (30 amps), tent sites, pit toilets, dump, mobile sewer, fire rings, firewood. **REC:** Thompson River: swim, fishing, playground. Pets OK. Partial handicap access, 14 day max stay. 2021 rates: $23. Apr 27 to Oct 01. no cc, no reservations.

(250)457-6794 Lat: 50.784123, Lon: -121.081168
NULL, Cache Creek, BC V0K 1H0
www.env.gov.bc.ca/bcparks

MARBLE CANYON (Public Prov Park) From Jct of Hwy 97 & Hwy 99, W 18 mi on Hwy 99 (L). 30 Avail: Pit toilets. 2021 rates: $18. (250)320-9305

CAMPBELL RIVER — J2 *East Island*

ELK FALLS (Public Prov Park) From Jct of Hwy 19 & Hwy 28, W 2 mi on Hwy 28. 122 Avail. 2021 rates: $11 to $22. (250)474-1336

FRIENDSHIP INN MOTEL & TRAILER PARK **Ratings: 4.5/9★/7** (RV Park) Avail: 10 full hkups (30 amps). 2021 rates: $35. (250)287-9591, 3900 North Island Hwy, Campbell River, BC V9W 2J2

LOVELAND BAY (Public Prov Park) From town, W 20 km on Hwy 28 (L). 31 Avail: Pit toilets. 2021 rates: $22. Apr 30 to Sep 30. (250)850-7125

MORTON LAKE (Public Prov Park) From town, NW 17 mi on Hwy 19 (R). 24 Avail: Pit toilets. 2021 rates: $11 to $18. (250)850-7125

RIPPLE ROCK RV PARK AT BROWN'S BAY RESORT (RV Park) (Phone Update) Avail: 41 full hkups (30/50 amps). 2021 rates: $60 to $65. Apr 01 to Oct 31. (800)620-6739, 15021 Brown's Bay Rd, Campbell River, BC V9H 1N9

SALMON POINT RESORT RV PARK & MARINA **Ratings: 9/9.5★/9.5** (RV Park) Avail: 160 full hkups (30/50 amps). 2021 rates: $44 to $65. (866)246-6605, 2176 Salmon Point Rd, Campbell River, BC V9H 1E5

STRATHCONA/BUTTLE LAKE (Public Prov Park) From Jct of Hwy 19 & Hwy 28, SW 33 mi on Hwy 28 (L). 85 Avail: Pit toilets. 2021 rates: $20. Apr 01 to Oct 31. (250)474-1336

STRATHCONA/RALPH RIVER (Public Prov Park) From Jct of Hwy 19 & Hwy 28, SW 47 mi on Hwy 28 to Western Mines Rd, S 17 mi (E). 75 Avail: Pit toilets. 2021 rates: $20. Apr 01 to Oct 31. (250)248-9460

THUNDERBIRD RV PARK & COTTAGE RESORT **Ratings: 8/9.5★/7.5** (RV Park) Avail: 55 full hkups (30/50 amps). 2021 rates: $45 to $50. (250)286-3344, 2660 Spit Rd, Campbell River, BC V9W 6E3

CANAL FLATS — J6 *Columbia-Shuswap*

WHITESWAN LAKE PARK (Public Prov Park) From town, S 3 mi on Hwy 93/95 to gravel logging rd, E 13 mi (L). 114 Avail: Pit toilets. 2021 rates: $20 to $23. (250)422-3003

CANIM LAKE — H4 *Fraser-Fort George*

SOUTH POINT RESORT (Campground) (Phone Update) 25 Avail: 25 W, 25 E (15/30 amps). 2021 rates: $49. May 15 to Oct 15. (250)397-2243, 7405 Canim Lake Rd, Canim Lake, BC V0K 1J0

WELLS GRAY PARK/MANHOOD LAKE (Public Prov Park) From town: Go 1-1/2 km/1 mi S on Hwy 97, then 88 km/55 mi E on Horsefly Rd (gravel). 39 Avail: Pit toilets. 2021 rates: $23. (250)674-2194

CASTLEGAR — K5 *Kootenay West*

CASTLEGAR CABINS RV PARK & CAMPGROUND **Ratings: 5/7.5/7** (Campground) Avail: 18 full hkups (15/30 amps). 2021 rates: $40. (866)687-7275, 1725 Hwy 3, Castlegar, BC V1N 4W1

CASTLEGAR GOLF CLUB & RV PARK **Ratings: 5.5/9.5★/8** (RV Park) 20 Avail: 20 W, 20 E (15/30 amps). 2021 rates: $35 to $50. Apr 15 to Oct 15. (800)666-0324, 1602 Aaron Rd, Castlegar, BC V1N 4L6

SYRINGA PARK (Public Prov Park) From N-end of town, N 2 mi on Hwy 3A to Robson Turnoff, W 12 mi (R). 76 Avail: Pit toilets. 2021 rates: $26. Apr 27 to Sep 30. (250)837-5734

CHASE — J4 *Okanagan*

SHUSWAP LAKE (Public Prov Park) From Jct of Hwy 1 & Squilax-Anglemont Rd, NE 13 mi on Squilax-Anglemont Rd (R). 274 Avail. 2021 rates: $32. May 01 to Oct 08. (250)836-2958

SILVER BEACH PARK (Public Prov Park) From town: Go 11-1/4 km/7 mi NE on Hwy 1 to Squilax, then 64 km/40 mi NE on Squilax-Anglemont-Seymour Arm Rd. 35 Avail: Pit toilets. 2021 rates: $20. Apr 01 to Oct 31. (250)836-2958

CHEMAINUS — K2 *North Cowichan*

COUNTRY MAPLES RV RESORT **Ratings: 8/7.5/8.5** (Membership Park) 125 Avail: 116 full hkups, 9 W, 9 E (30/50 amps). 2021 rates: $52.50. (250)246-2078, 9010 Trans Canada Hwy, Chemainus, BC V0R 1K4

CHETWYND — D6 *Peace River*

GWILLIM LAKE (Public Prov Park) From town: Go 4 km/2-1/2 mi E on Hwy 97, then 56 km/35 mi S on Hwy 29. 50 Avail: Pit toilets. 2021 rates: $20. May 11 to Sep 13. (250)242-1146

MOBERLY LAKE (Public Prov Park) From Jct of Hwys 97 & 29, NW 15 mi (24 km) on Hwy 29 to park access rd, W 1.5 mi (2.4 km) (R). 109 Avail: Pit toilets. 2021 rates: $20. May 14 to Sep 13. (250)964-2243

WESTWIND RV PARK

good sam park

Ratings: 6/9.5★/7 (RV Park) From Jct of Hwy 97 & 29, N 1.2 mi on Hwy 97N (R).

EXCELLENT LOCATION TO EXPLORE FROM!
Chetwynd is a must-see on the route to Alaska. Located in the foothills of the Canadian Rockies, Chetwynd is renowned for over 60 life-size wooden chainsaw sculptures. Perfect location for site seeing. Easy on/off Hwy #97.

FAC: gravel rds. Avail: 50 gravel, 50 pull-thrus, (20x65), 50 full hkups (30 amps), WiFi @ sites, tent sites, dump, laundry, fire rings, firewood. **REC:** boating nearby, playground. Pets OK. Partial handicap access. 2021 rates: $38. May 01 to Oct 31.
(250)788-2190 Lat: 55.68752, Lon: -121.60345
4441 53rd Ave, Chetwynd, BC V0C 1J0
www.westwindrvpark.com
See ad this page

CHILLIWACK — K3 *Fraser Valley*

COTTONWOOD MEADOWS RV COUNTRY CLUB

good sam park

Ratings: 8/10★/9 (RV Park) From Jct of Hwy 1 & Lickman Rd (exit 116), S 0.2km/0.1 mi on Lickman Rd to Luckakuck Way, E 0.6km/0.4 mi (R). **FAC:** paved rds. (118 spaces). Avail: 73 gravel, 17 pull-thrus, (30x64), backins (28x65), 73 full hkups (30/50 amps), seasonal sites, cable, WiFi @ sites, tent sites, dump, laundry, controlled access. **REC:** Athelix Creek: boating nearby. Pet restrict (S/B/Q). Partial handicap access. Big rig sites, eco-friendly. 2021 rates: $57 to $63.
(604)824-7275 Lat: 49.14358, Lon: -121.99952
44280 Luckakuck Way, Chilliwack, BC V2R 4A7
www.cottonwoodrvpark.com
See ad this page

CULTUS LAKE PROVINCIAL PARK (CLEAR CREEK CAMPGROUND) (Public Prov Park) From Hwy 1 (Sardis exit): Go 11-1/4 km/7 mi S. 82 Avail. 2021 rates: $35. Apr 01 to Oct 14. (604)986-9371

CULTUS LAKE PROVINCIAL PARK (DELTA GROVE CAMPGROUND) (Public Prov Park) From Hwy 1 (Sardis exit): Go 11-1/4 km/7 mi S. 58 Avail. 2021 rates: $35. Mar 28 to Oct 13. (604)986-9371

CULTUS LAKE PROVINCIAL PARK (ENTRANCE BAY CAMPGROUND) (Public Prov Park) From Hwy 1 (Sardis exit): Go 10-1/2 km/6-1/2 mi S. 52 Avail. 2021 rates: $35. Mar 28 to Oct 13. (604)986-9371

CULTUS LAKE PROVINCIAL PARK (MAPLE BAY CAMPGROUND) (Public Prov Park) From Hwy 1 (Sardis exit): Go 12 km/7-1/2 mi S. 106 Avail. 2021 rates: $35. Apr 01 to Oct 13. (604)986-9371

CHRISTINA LAKE — K5 *Kootenay West*

CASCADE COVE RV PARK & CAMPGROUND **Ratings: 7.5/9/8.5** (Campground) Avail: 60 full hkups (15/30 amps). 2021 rates: $40 to $50. Apr 01 to Oct 31. (250)447-6662, 1211 River Rd, Christina Lake, BC V0H 1E0

CHRISTINA PINES CAMPGROUND **Ratings: 8/9.5★/7.5** (Condo Park) 80 Avail: 75 full hkups, 5 W, 5 E (30/50 amps). 2021 rates: $43 to $49.50. Apr 15 to Oct 15. (250)447-9587, 1528 Neimi Rd, Christina Lake, BC V0H 1E0

GLADSTONE/TEXAS CREEK (Public Prov Park) From town, E 15 mi on Hwy 3 to Christina Lake, N 4 mi to Eastlake Dr (E). 62 Avail. 2021 rates: $27. Apr 30 to Sep 27. (250)548-9025

CLEARWATER — H4 *Thompson*

CLEARWATER/WELLS GRAY KOA **Ratings: 8.5/7.5/8** (Campground) 93 Avail: 53 full hkups, 20 W, 20 E (30/50 amps). 2021 rates: $49.50. Jan 01 to Dec 31. (250)674-3909, 373 Clearwater Valley Rd, Clearwater, BC V0E 1N1

DUTCH LAKE RESORT & RV PARK **Ratings: 6/8.5★/7.5** (RV Park) 64 Avail: 31 full hkups, 33 W, 33 E (15/30 amps). 2021 rates: $48 to $52. Apr 01 to Oct 15. (888)884-4424, 361 Ridge Dr., Clearwater, BC V0E 1N2

NORTH THOMPSON RIVER (Public Prov Park) From town: Go 4-3/4 km/3 mi S on Hwy 5. 69 Avail: Pit toilets. 2021 rates: $23. May 01 to Sep 30. (250)320-9305

WELLS GRAY GOLF RESORT & RV PARK (Campground) (Phone Update) 60 Avail: 16 full hkups, 34 W, 34 E (30 amps). 2021 rates: $42 to $50. May 01 to Oct 15. (250)674-0009, 6624 Clearwater Valley Rd, Clearwater, BC V0E 1N1

WELLS GRAY PARK/CLEARWATER LAKE (Public Prov Park) From Jct of Hwy 5 & Clearwater Valley Rd, N 40 km on Clearwater Valley Rd (E). 39 Avail: Pit toilets. 2021 rates: $23. May 14 to Sep 30. (250)674-2194

CLINTON — H3 *Cariboo*

BIG BAR LAKE (Public Prov Park) From N end of town, N 5 mi on Hwy 97 to Big Bar Lake Rd, NW 21 mi (R). 46 Avail: Pit toilets. 2021 rates: $18. May 15 to Sep 30. (250)320-9305

COOMBS — K2 *East Island*

COOMBS COUNTRY CAMPGROUND & RV PARK (Campground) (Phone Update) 80 Avail: 38 full hkups, 24 W, 24 E (30 amps). 2021 rates: $40 to $50. May 01 to Sep 30. (258)248-9371, 2619 Alberni Hwy, Coombs, BC V0R 1M0

COURTENAY — J2 *East Island*

BATES BEACH OCEANFRONT & RV PARK **Ratings: 6.5/8.5★/7** (RV Park) Avail: 20 full hkups (15/30 amps). 2021 rates: $45 to $60. (250)334-4154, 5726 Coral Rd, Courtenay, BC V9J 1W9

MIRACLE BEACH (Public Prov Park) From town, N 14 mi on Hwy 19 to Miracle Beach Dr, E 1 mi (L). 200 Avail. 2021 rates: $33. (250)337-8020

PUNTLEDGE RV CAMPGROUND & NIM NIM INTERPRETIVE CENTRE **Ratings: 4/8.5/7.5** (RV Park) 42 Avail: 5 full hkups, 10 W, 10 E (15/30 amps). 2021 rates: $48 to $55. Apr 01 to Oct 01. (250)334-3773, 4624 Condensory Rd, Courtenay, BC V9J 1R6

SEAL BAY RV PARK & CAMPGROUND **Ratings: 7.5/9.5★/9** (RV Park) Avail: 80 full hkups (30/50 amps). 2021 rates: $47 to $50. (250)339-1837, 1901 Larch Rd, Courtenay, BC V9J 1X7

CRANBROOK — J6 *Kootenay East*

CRANBROOK/ST EUGENE KOA **Ratings: 10/9.5★/9** (Campground) Avail: 114 full hkups (30/50 amps). 2021 rates: $47.25 to $68.25. Apr 01 to Oct 31. (800)562-5403, 7777 Mission Road, Cranbrook, BC V1C 7E5

JIMSMITH LAKE (Public Prov Park) From town, S 1 mi on Hwy 3/95, 2 mi on Jimsmith Lake Rd (L). 35 Avail: Pit toilets. 2021 rates: $23. May 03 to Sep 21. (250)422-3003

MOYIE LAKE PARK (Public Prov Park) From town, S 12 mi on Hwy 3/95 (R). 111 Avail. 2021 rates: $33. May 01 to Sep 30. (250)422-3003

CRAWFORD BAY — J5 *Kootenay West*

KOKANEE CHALETS, CABINS, MOTEL & RV CAMPGROUND **Ratings: 6.5/8.5/8.5** (Campground) 33 Avail: 28 full hkups, 5 W, 5 E (20/50 amps). 2021 rates: $33 to $47. Apr 15 to Oct 15. (800)448-9292, 15981 Hwy 3A, Crawford Bay, BC V0B 1E0

""Full hookups" in a campground listing means there are water, electric and sewer hookups at the sites.

Join in the fun. Like us on FACEBOOK!

Find it fast! Use our alphabetized index of campgrounds and parks.

CRESTON — K5 *Kootenay West*

LOCKHART CREEK (Public Prov Park) From town, N 18 mi on Hwy-3A (R). 18 Avail: Pit toilets. 2021 rates: $23. May 09 to Sep 30. (250)422-3003

PAIR-A-DICE RV PARK

Ratings: 7/9.5★/8 (RV Park) From jct Hwy 3A & Hwy 3 (West side of town): Go 0.8 kms/1/2 mi E on Hwy 3 (L). **FAC:** gravel rds. (44 spaces). Avail: 40 gravel, 10 pull-thrus, (30x65), back-ins (30x45), 22 full hkups, 18 W, 18 E (30 amps), seasonal sites, cable, WiFi @ sites, tent sites, dump, laundry. **REC:** Glasser Creek: boating nearby, hunting nearby. Pet restrict (Q). Partial handicap access, eco-friendly. 2021 rates: $33 to $51.
(866)223-3423 Lat: 49.11124, Lon: -116.52311
1322 North West Blvd. (Hwy 3), Creston, BC V0B 1G6
www.pairadicepark.com
See ad this page

CROFTON — K2 *South Island*

OSBORNE BAY RESORT **Ratings: 6/7.5/8** (RV Resort) 41 Avail: 20 full hkups, 21 W, 21 E (15/30 amps). 2021 rates: $38 to $48. (800)567-7275, 1450 Charlotte St, Box 39, Crofton, BC V0R 1R0

CULTUS LAKE — K3 *Lower Mainland*

CULTUS LAKE (Public Prov Park) From Jct of TCH-1 & Sardis exit (Vedder Rd), S 5 mi on Vedder Rd to Cultus Lake Rd, S 3.5 mi, follow signs. 298 Avail. 2021 rates: $11 to $30. Mar 28 to Oct 14. (604)986-9371

SUNNYSIDE CAMPGROUND (Public) From Jct of Prov Hwy 1 & Vedder Rd, S 5 mi on Vedder Rd (across Vedder River bridge) to Jct of Cultus Lake Rd & Vedder Mountain Rd, S 2 mi on Cultus Lake Rd (R). Avail: 104 full hkups (30 amps). 2021 rates: $44 to $48. Apr 15 to Sep 30. (604)858-5253

VEDDER RIVER CAMPGROUND (Public) From town, W 3 mi on Vedder Rd to Vedder Mt Rd, W 2.5 mi to Giesbrecht Rd, N 0.5 mi (R). 67 Avail: 43 full hkups, 24 W, 24 E (30 amps). 2021 rates: $31 to $39. Jun 01 to Nov 01. (604)823-6012

DAWSON CREEK — D6 *Peace River*

MILE 0 RV PARK (Public) From AK Hwy MP-0, N 1.5 mi (2.4 km) on AK Hwy to PR-97, W 1/4 mi (.04 km) on PR-97 (R). 80 Avail: 23 full hkups, 57 W, 57 E (15/50 amps). 2021 rates: $25 to $45. May 01 to Oct 01. (250)782-2590

NORTHERN LIGHTS RV PARK

Ratings: 8.5/9.5★/7.5 (RV Park) From jct Hwy 97 N & Hwy 97 S: Go 2.6 km/1-1/2 mi W on Hwy 97 S (L).

YOUR ALASKAN ADVENTURE STARTS HERE! You made it to Mile 0 of the Alaska Highway. Now relax at the best RV Park in Dawson Creek! Spacious pull-thrus, gorgeous restrooms, excellent gathering room and lots of genuine Canadian hospitality awaits; going & returning!

FAC: all weather rds. Avail: 90 all weather, 71 pull-thrus, (30x60), back-ins (18x32), 90 full hkups (30/50 amps), WiFi @ sites, tent sites, rentals, shower$, laundry, fire rings, firewood. Pets OK. Big rig sites, eco-friendly. 2021 rates: $45 to $50.
(250)782-9433 Lat: 55.76532, Lon: -120.29120
9636 Friesen Sub, Dawson Creek, BC V1G 4T9
nlrv.com
See ad this page

ONE ISLAND LAKE (Public Prov Park) From town: Go 36-3/4 km/23 mi SE on Hwy 2, then 29-1/2 km/18-1/2 mi S on secondary road. 30 Avail: Pit toilets. 2021 rates: $20. May 21 to Sep 15. (250)242-8054

SWAN LAKE PARK (Public Prov Park) From town, SE 35 km on Hwy 2 (R). 44 Avail: Pit toilets. 2021 rates: $20. May 11 to Sep 10. (250)786-5960

TUBBY'S RV PARK & CAR WASH **Ratings: 5/9.5/7** (RV Park) Avail: 61 full hkups (30 amps). 2021 rates: $36 to $40. (250)782-2584, 1913 96th Ave # 4, Dawson Creek, BC V1G 1M2

DONALD — H5 *Division No. 14*

CAMPER'S HAVEN RV TENTING & MOTEL **Ratings: 6/9★/7.5** (Campground) Avail: 49 full hkups (15/50 amps). 2021 rates: $32 to $43. (800)563-6122, 2779 Dejordie Road , Donald, BC V0A 1H1

DUNCAN — K2 *Cowichan Valley*

RIVERSIDE RV & CAMPING **Ratings: 3.5/UI/5.5** (RV Park) 51 Avail: 35 full hkups, 16 W, 16 E (30 amps). 2021 rates: $25 to $30. (250)746-4352, #1-3065 Allenby Road, Duncan, BC V9L 6W5

ELKO — J6 *Columbia-Shuswap*

KIKOMUN CREEK (Public Prov Park) From town, W 3 mi on Hwy 3/93, W 5 mi on paved rd, follow signs (L). 171 Avail. 2021 rates: $35 to $40. May 01 to Sep 30. (250)422-3003

ENDERBY — J4 *North Okanagan*

RIVERSIDE RV PARK (Public) From Jct Hwy 97 & Regent Ave, E 0.1 mi on Regent Ave to Belvedere Rd, N 0.4 mi to Howard St, Howard St to Kate St, N 0.5 mi on Kate St to Kildonan Ave, E 0.2 mi (R). 50 Avail: 17 full hkups, 19 W, 33 E (30 amps). 2021 rates: $34 to $38. (250)838-0155

SHUSWAP FALLS RV RESORT **Ratings: 8/9.5★/9** (Condo Park) Avail: 48 full hkups (30 amps). 2021 rates: $40 to $60. Apr 15 to Oct 15. (250)838-6100, 2202 Mabel Lake Rd, Enderby, BC V0E 1V5

ERICKSON — K5 *Kootenay West*

MOUNTAIN PARK RESORT **Ratings: 6/8.5/7.5** (Campground) 40 Avail: 40 W, 40 E (15/30 amps). 2021 rates: $39 to $55. (877)428-2954, 4020 Hwy 3, Erickson, BC V0B 1K0

FAIRMONT HOT SPRINGS — J6 *Columbia Valley*

FAIRMONT HOT SPRINGS RESORT

Ratings: 10/9.5★/10 (RV Park) Avail: 177 full hkups (30/50 amps). 2021 rates: $51 to $115. (800)663-4979, 5225 Fairmont Resort Rd, Fairmont Hot Springs, BC V0B 1L1

SPRUCE GROVE RV PARK AND CAMPGROUND **Ratings: 6/7.5/8** (Campground) 118 Avail: 12 full hkups, 38 W, 38 E (30 amps). 2021 rates: $51 to $56. Apr 15 to Sep 30. (888)629-4004, 5225 Fairmont Resort Rd, Fairmont Hot Springs, BC V0B 1L1

FANNY BAY — K2 *Central Coast*

LIGHTHOUSE RV PARK **Ratings: 6.5/9★/6.5** (RV Park) Avail: 30 full hkups (30/50 amps). 2021 rates: $45 to $65. (250)335-1667, 8256 E Island Hwy S, Fanny Bay, BC V0R 1W0

FARMINGTON — D6 *Peace River*

KISKATINAW (Public Prov Park) On the Alaska Hwy at milepost 21. 28 Avail: Pit toilets. 2021 rates: $20. May 11 to Sep 13. (250)843-0092

FERNIE — J6 *Columbia-Shuswap*

FERNIE RV RESORT **Ratings: 8/9.5★/9.5** (RV Resort) Avail: 91 full hkups (30/50 amps). 2021 rates: $52 to $105. (844)343-2233, 2001 6th Avenue, Fernie, BC V0B 1M0

MOUNT FERNIE (Public Prov Park) From town, W 2 mi on Hwy 3 (R). 43 Avail. 2021 rates: $30. Jun 01 to Sep 30. (250)422-3003

FIELD — H5 *Division No. 14*

YOHO/HOODOO CREEK (Public National Park) From town: Go 22-1/2 km/14 mi W Trans Canada Hwy. 30 Avail: Pit toilets. 2021 rates: $15.70. Jun 24 to Sep 05. (877)737-3783

YOHO/KICKING HORSE (Public National Park) From Jct of TCH 1 & Yoho Valley Rd, N 1 mi on Yoho Valley Rd (L). 88 Avail. 2021 rates: $27.40. May 23 to Oct 03. (877)737-3783

FORT FRASER — F2 *Bulkley-Nechako*

BEAUMONT (Public Prov Park) From town: Go 6-1/2 km/4 mi W on Hwy 16, then 1/2 km/1/4 mi off Hwy on gravel road. 46 Avail. 2021 rates: $22. May 15 to Sep 13. (250)964-3489

FORT NELSON — C6 *Peace River*

TETSA RIVER LODGE (Campground) (Phone Update) 30 Avail: 30 W, 30 E (15 amps). 2021 rates: $35. Apr 15 to Oct 30. (250)774-1005, Mile 375 Alaska Hwy, Fort Nelson, BC V0C 1R0

TETSA RIVER REGIONAL PARK (Public) From town: Go 95-1/4 km/59-1/2 mi NW on Hwy 97 (Alaska Hwy), then 3/4 km/ 1/2 mi S on secondary road. 29 Avail: Pit toilets. 2021 rates: $20. May 01 to Sep 30. (250)774-2541

TRIPLE "G" HIDEAWAY RV PARK & RESTAURANT (Campground) (Phone Update) Avail: 130 full hkups (30 amps). 2021 rates: $45. May 01 to Sep 30. (250)774-2340, 5651 Alaska Hwy, Fort Nelson, BC V0C 1R0

FORT ST JAMES — F2 *Stikine*

PAARENS BEACH PARK (Public Prov Park) From town: Go 4-3/4 km/3 mi W on secondary road. 39 Avail: Pit toilets. 2021 rates: $22. May 15 to Sep 15. (250)964-3489

FORT ST JOHN — D6 *Peace River*

BEATTON (Public Prov Park) From town, NW 3 mi (8 km) on Hwy 97 (AK Hwy), N 5 mi on Rd 271, W 1 mi on access rd to entrance of park. 39 Avail: Pit toilets. 2021 rates: $20. May 15 to Sep 01. (250)964-2243

CHARLIE LAKE (Public Prov Park) From Jct of Prov Hwy 2 & Prov Hwy 97, NW 54 mi (74 km) on Prov Hwy 97 to park access rd (R). 57 Avail: Pit toilets. 2021 rates: $20. May 11 to Sep 13. (250)787-1894

ROSS H MACLEAN ROTARY RV PARK (Public) N-bnd: On AK Hwy at MP-52, 3.5 mi N of town (R). 69 Avail: 10 full hkups, 48 W, 48 E (30 amps). 2021 rates: $29 to $38. May 01 to Sep 30. (250)785-1700

FORT STEELE — J6 *Kootenay East*

FORT STEELE RESORT & RV PARK **Ratings: 7.5/7.5/7** (RV Park) 113 Avail: 85 full hkups, 2 W (30/50 amps). 2021 rates: $50 to $55. (250)489-4268, 10 Wardner-Fort Steele Rd, Fort Steele, BC V0B 1N0

NORBURY LAKE (Public Prov Park) From town, SE 10 mi on CR-3/Dull River Rd (Secondary Rd), follow signs (R). 46 Avail: Pit toilets. 2021 rates: $20. (250)422-3003

FRUITVALE — K5 *Thompson-Nicola*

CHAMPION LAKES (Public Prov Park) From NE end of town, NE 4 mi on Hwy 3B to Champion Lakes Rd, NW 6 mi (L). 95 Avail. 2021 rates: $25. May 17 to Sep 25. (250)825-0117

GALIANO ISLAND — K3 *Mount Waddington*

MONTAGUE HARBOUR (Public Prov Park) Accessible by car ferry only from Swartz Bay & Tsawwassen. On west coast of Galiano Island. 44 Avail: Pit toilets. 2021 rates: $13 to $25. (877)559-2115

GIBSONS — K3 *South Coast*

LANGDALE HEIGHTS RV PAR 3 GOLF RESORT **Ratings: 6.5/9★/8.5** (RV Resort) Avail: 18 full hkups (30 amps). 2021 rates: $46. Apr 01 to Oct 01. (604)886-2182, Unit 100 - 2170 Port Mellon Hwy, Unit 100, Gibsons, BC V0N 1V6

ROBERTS CREEK (Public Prov Park) From town, SE 3 mi on Hwy 101 (R). 21 Avail: Pit toilets. 2021 rates: $20. May 15 to Sep 15. (604)885-3714

GOLDEN — H5 *Columbia Valley*

GOLDEN ECO ADVENTURE RANCH **Ratings: 5/9.5★/7.5** (Campground) 94 Avail: 43 W, 43 E (30/50 amps). 2021 rates: $40 to $48. Apr 01 to Oct 08. (250)344-6825, 872 McBeath Rd, Golden, BC V0A 1H2

GOLDEN MUNICIPAL CAMPGROUND

Ratings: 7/8.5★/7.5 (Campground) From Jct of TCH 1 & Hwy 95, S 0.5 mi on Hwy 95 to 9th St, E 0.3 Kms/ 0.2 mi (L). Elev 2500 ft.

THIS IS KICKING HORSE COUNTRY!
In the heart of 6 National Parks, it's the perfect base to explore & enjoy a vast array of outdoor activities. Horseback riding, mountain climbing & biking, hiking, golfing, bird watching, white water rafting & hang gliding.
FAC: gravel rds. Avail: 35 gravel, 4 pull-thrus, (30x60), back-ins (30x50), mostly side by side hkups, 35 W, 35 E (30/50 amps), WiFi @ sites, tent sites, dump, laundry, groc, LP bottles, fire rings, firewood. **REC:** Kicking Horse River: fishing, kayaking/canoeing, playground. Pets OK. Partial handicap access, 14 day max stay, eco-friendly. 2021 rates: $38 to $50. Apr 01 to Oct 31.
(866)538-6625 Lat: 51.29700, Lon: -116.95221
1411 9th St South, Golden, BC VOA 1HO
goldenmunicipalcampground.com
See ad this page

WHISPERING SPRUCE CAMPGROUND AND RV PARK **Ratings: 5.5/8.5★/6.5** (Campground) 64 Avail: 54 full hkups, 10 W, 10 E (30 amps). 2021 rates: $49.98 to $52.40. Apr 15 to Oct 15. (250)344-6680, 1430 Golden View Rd, Golden, BC V0A 1H1

GRAND FORKS — K5 *Kootenay West*

GRAND FORKS CITY PARK (Public) From Jct of Hwy 3 & Fifth St, S 0.1 mi on Fifth St (R). 26 Avail: 26 W, 26 E (30/50 amps). 2021 rates: $34 to $61.20. May 01 to Sep 30. (250)442-5835

RIVIERA RV PARK & CAMPGROUND
good sam park **Ratings: 8/9.5★/8** (Campground) From Jct Hwy 3 & Kettle River Bridge: Go 2 km/1-1/2 mi E on Hwy 3 (R). **FAC:** gravel rds. Avail: 40 gravel, 6 pull-thrus, (25x60), back-ins (25x35), 40 full hkups (30 amps), WiFi @ sites, tent sites, shower$, dump, laundry, LP bottles, fire rings, firewood. **REC:** Kettle River: swim, fishing, kayaking/canoeing, boating nearby, playground, hunting nearby. Pets OK. Partial handicap access, eco-friendly. 2021 rates: $45 to $55. Mar 01 to Oct 31.
(250)442-2158 Lat: 49.02472, Lon: -118.41930
6331 Hwy 3 East, Grand Forks, BC V0H 1H9
grandforksrivierarvpark.com
See ad this page

GREENWOOD — K5 *Okanagan*

BOUNDARY CREEK (Public Prov Park) From town, SW 3 mi on Hwy 3 (R). 16 Avail. 2021 rates: $18. Apr 30 to Sep 27. (250)584-9025

HAGENSBORG — G1 *Skeena-Queen Charlotte*

RIP RAP CAMPSITE (RV Park) (Phone Update) 26 Avail: 8 full hkups, 5 W, 13 E (20/30 amps). 2021 rates: $25 to $32. Apr 30 to Oct 30. (250)982-2752, 1854 Hwy 20, Hagensborg, BC V0T 1H0

HARRISON HOT SPRINGS — K3 *Lower Mainland*

SASQUATCH (Public Prov Park) From town, N 4 mi on Rockwell Dr (E). 178 Avail: Pit toilets. 2021 rates: $23. Mar 29 to Oct 08. (604)986-9371

HARRISON MILLS — K3 *Fraser Valley*

KILBY (Public Prov Park) From Jct of SR-7 & School Rd, S 0.4 mi on School Rd, follow signs. 35 Avail: Pit toilets. 2021 rates: $10 to $25. (604)796-9576

HAZELTON — E4 *Bulkley Valley*

KSAN CAMPGROUND **Ratings: 6/8.5★/8.5** (Campground) Avail: 30 full hkups (15/30 amps). 2021 rates: $36 to $40. May 01 to Oct 31. (250)842-5940, 1450 River Road, Hazelton, BC V0J 1Y0

SEELEY LAKE (Public Prov Park) From town, W 4 mi on Hwy 16 (L). 20 Avail: Pit toilets. 2021 rates: $20. May 13 to Sep 15. (250)842-6546

HEDLEY — K4 *Okanagan*

STEMWINDER PARK (Public Prov Park) From town, W 2 mi on Hwy 3 (R). 28 Avail: Pit toilets. 2021 rates: $18. (250)840-8807

HIXON — G3 *Central Interior*

CANYON CREEK CAMPGROUND & RV PARK **Ratings: 7.5/9★/10** (Campground) 35 Avail: 23 full hkups, 3 W, 3 E (15/30 amps). 2021 rates: $34 to $36. May 01 to Sep 30. (250)998-4384, 39035 Hwy 97S, Hixon, BC V0K 1S0

Check out a campground's ad. In it you might find a locator map, photos, and a lot more information about the park to help you find just the right place to stay.

HOPE — K3 *Fraser Valley*

COQUIHALLA CAMPGROUND **Ratings: 5.5/8/7.5** (Campground) 108 Avail: 46 full hkups, 5 W, 5 E (30 amps). 2021 rates: $40 to $50. Mar 01 to Nov 01. (888)869-7118, 800 Kawkawa Lake Rd, Hope, BC V0X 1L0

EMORY BAR RV PARK **Ratings: 5/7.5/7** (RV Park) 35 Avail: 15 W, 15 E (30/50 amps). 2021 rates: $39. Apr 01 to Oct 31. (604)863-2423, 28775 Hwy 1, Hope, BC V0X 1L3

EMORY CREEK (Public Prov Park) From Jct Hwy 3 & TCH 1, N 11 mi on TCH 1, follow signs. 35 Avail. 2021 rates: $21. May 10 to Oct 18. (604)807-2684

HOPE VALLEY RV & CAMPGROUND **Ratings: 7.5/8.5/7** (Campground) Avail: 68 full hkups (30/50 amps). 2021 rates: $50. (604)869-9857, 62280 Flood-Hope Rd, Hope, BC V0X 1L2

MANNING PARK/LIGHTNING LAKE (Public Prov Park) From town: Go 64 km/40 mi E on Hwy 3. 143 Avail: Pit toilets. 2021 rates: $35. May 15 to Oct 12. (250)840-8822

OTHELLO TUNNELS CAMPGROUND & RV PARK **Ratings: 4.5/7/6** (Campground) 26 Avail: 14 full hkups, 12 W, 12 E (15/30 amps). 2021 rates: $47 to $49. (877)869-0543, 67851 Othello Rd, Hope, BC V0X 1L1

SKAGIT VALLEY PARK (Public Prov Park) From Jct of Hwy 3 & TCH 1, W 2 mi on TCH 1 to Skagit Valley Rd, S 27 mi, follow signs (E). 131 Avail: Pit toilets. 2021 rates: $18. Apr 27 to Oct 08. (604)986-9371

SUNSHINE VALLEY RV RESORT & CAMPING CABINS **Ratings: 9/10★/9** (Membership Park) Avail: 109 full hkups (20/50 amps). 2021 rates: $52 to $72. (604)869-0066, 14850 Alpine Blvd, Hope, BC V0X 1L5

WILD ROSE CAMPGROUND & RV PARK
good sam park **Ratings: 8.5/9.5★/9** (RV Park) 38 Avail: 36 full hkups, 2 W, 2 E (30/50 amps). 2021 rates: $42 to $52. (604)869-9842, 62030 Flood-Hope Rd, Hope, BC V0X 1L2

HORNBY ISLAND — K2 *Central Coast*

BRADSDADSLAND RESORT (Campground) (Phone Update) 50 Avail: 17 full hkups, 25 W, 25 E (15/30 amps). 2021 rates: $34.50 to $63.50. Apr 15 to Oct 15. (250)335-0757, 2105 Shingle Spit Rd, Hornby Island, BC V0R 1Z0

TRIBUNE BAY CAMPSITE (Campground) (Phone Update) 100 Avail: 78 W, 78 E (15/30 amps). 2021 rates: $43 to $48. Jun 15 to Sep 15. (250)335-2359, 5200 Shields Rd, Hornby Island, BC V0R 1Z0

HORSEFLY — G3 *Bulkley-Nechako*

HORSEFLY LAKE (Public Prov Park) From Jct of Hwy 97 & Horsefly-Quesnel Lake Rd, E 42 mi on Horsefly-Quesnel Lake Rd (R). 23 Avail. 2021 rates: $23. May 15 to Sep 15. (250)320-9305

HOUSTON — F1 *Bulkley Valley*

SHADY REST RV PARK **Ratings: 6.5/10★/8** (Campground) Avail: 26 full hkups (15/30 amps). 2021 rates: $40 to $65. May 01 to Oct 01. (250)845-2314, 3960 Drive In Road, Houston, BC V0J 1Z2

HUDSON'S HOPE — D6 *Peace River*

DINOSAUR LAKE CAMPGROUND (DISTRICT PARK) (Public) From south town limits: Go 6.4 km/4 mi S on Hwy 29, then 1.6 km/1 mi W on Peace Canyon Dam Rd. 50 Avail: Pit toilets. 2021 rates: $20 to $60. May 22 to Sep 07. (250)783-9154

ISKUT — C4 *Cassiar Mountains*

MOUNTAIN SHADOW RV PARK & CAMPGROUND (RV Park) (Phone Update) 34 Avail: 22 W, 22 E (30 amps). 2021 rates: $21 to $45. May 01 to Sep 30. (250)234-3333, Hwy 37, Km 254, Iskut, BC V0J 1K0

TATOGGA LAKE RV RESORT (Campground) (Phone Update) 35 Avail: 35 W, 35 E (15/30 amps). 2021 rates: $40. May 15 to Nov 01. (250)234-3526, KM 390 - Hwy 37, Iskut, BC V0J 1K0

KALEDEN — K4 *South Okanagan*

BANBURY GREEN RV & CAMPING RESORT **Ratings: 5/7.5★/8** (RV Resort) 67 Avail: 17 full hkups, 50 W, 50 E (15/30 amps). 2021 rates: $45 to $65. May 15 to Sep 30. (250)497-5221, 930 Pineview Drive, Kaleden, BC V0H 1K0

Save 10% at Good Sam Parks!

CAMP-ALONG RESORT **Ratings: 7/8.5★/7.5** (Campground) 20 Avail: 8 full hkups, 12 W, 12 E (15/30 amps). 2021 rates: $34 to $53. Apr 01 to Oct 01. (250)497-5584, 100 Ash Ave, Kaleden, BC V0H 1K0

KAMLOOPS — J4 *Thompson*

KAMLOOPS RV PARK **Ratings: 6.5/8/6.5** (RV Park) Avail: 82 full hkups (30/50 amps). 2021 rates: $45 to $50. (250)573-3789, 9225 Dallas Dr, Kamloops, BC V2C 6V1

LAC LE JEUNE (Public Prov Park) From town, SW 23 mi on Hwy 5 to Lac Le Jeune Rd exit, E 3 mi (R). 144 Avail. 2021 rates: $23. May 11 to Sep 23. (250)320-9305

PAUL LAKE (Public Prov Park) From Jct of Prov Hwy 5 & Paul Lake Rd, E 14 mi on Paul Lake Rd (R). 90 Avail. 2021 rates: $18. May 15 to Sep 20. (250)320-9305

KASLO — J5 *Kootenay West*

KOOTENAY/LOST LEDGE (Public National Park) From town, N 15 mi on Hwy-31 (R). 14 Avail: Pit toilets. 2021 rates: $23. (877)737-3783

MIRROR LAKE CAMPGROUND **Ratings: 5.5/7.5/8** (Campground) 67 Avail: 50 W, 50 E (15 amps). 2021 rates: $26 to $30. Apr 15 to Oct 15. (250)353-7102, 5777 Arcola Rd, Kaslo, BC V0G 1M0

SCHROEDER CREEK RESORT **Ratings: 6.5/6.5/7.5** (Campground) Avail: 30 full hkups (20/30 amps). 2021 rates: $38 to $40. Apr 01 to Oct 31. (250)353-7383, 128 Bickel Rd, Kaslo, BC V0G 1M0

KELOWNA — J4 *Central Okanagan*

BEAR CREEK PROVINCIAL PARK (Public Prov Park) From town: Go 8-3/4 km/5-1/2 mi S on Hwy 97, then 8 km/5 mi NW on Westside Rd. Avail: 122 W. 2021 rates: $35. Apr 01 to Oct 14. (250)548-0076

HOLIDAY PARK RESORT
good sam park **Ratings: 10/9.5★/9.5** (Condo Park) Avail: 34 full hkups (50 amps). 2021 rates: $55 to $81. (250)766-4255, I-415 Commonwealth Rd, Kelowna, BC V4V 1P4

KEREMEOS — K4 *Okanagan*

RIVER VALLEY RV PARK (KEREMEOS) **Ratings: 5/7/7** (Campground) 10 Avail: 5 full hkups, 5 W, 5 E (15/30 amps). 2021 rates: $35 to $40. (250)718-8018, 3491 Hwy 3, Keremeos, BC V0X 1N1

KIMBERLEY — J6 *Kimberley*

KIMBERLEY RIVERSIDE CAMPGROUND (Public) From Jct of Hwy 95A North & St Mary Lake Rd, W 2.7kms/ 1.7 mi on St Mary Lake Rd (L). 105 Avail: 80 full hkups, 25 W, 25 E (30/50 amps). 2021 rates: $36 to $60. Apr 15 to Oct 15. (877)999-2929

KITIMAT — F1 *Kitimat-Stikine*

RADLEY PARK (Public) In town on Commercial St next to Kitimat River. Follow signs. Avail: 16 E Pit toilets. 2021 rates: $16 to $27. May 15 to Sep 15. (250)632-8955

LAC LA HACHE — H3 *Cariboo*

BIG COUNTRY CAMPGROUND & RV PARK **Ratings: 7/UI/7.5** (Campground) 18 Avail: 17 full hkups, 1 W, 1 E (30/50 amps). 2021 rates: $37 to $43. May 15 to Sep 30. (250)396-4181, 4239 Caraboo Hwy 97S, Lac La Hache, BC V0K 1T0

KOKANEE BAY MOTEL & CAMPGROUND **Ratings: 5.5/6.5/7** (Campground) 36 Avail: 18 full hkups, 18 W, 18 E (15/30 amps). 2021 rates: $38 to $42. May 01 to Oct 15. (250)396-7345, 3728 Hwy 97 Cariboo Hwy, Lac La Hache, BC V0K 1T1

LAC LA HACHE (Public Prov Park) From town, N 15 mi on Hwy 97 (R). 83 Avail. 2021 rates: $18. May 15 to Sep 30. (250)320-9305

LADYSMITH — K2 *Lower Island*

RONDALYN RESORT - PARKBRIDGE **Ratings: 8/10★/9.5** (RV Resort) Avail: 62 full hkups (15/30 amps). 2021 rates: $46 to $57. (250)245-3227, 1350 Timberlands Road, Ladysmith, BC V9G 1L5

LAKE COUNTRY — J4 *Cariboo*

WOOD LAKE RV PARK AND MARINA **Ratings: 7/9.5★/7.5** (RV Park) Avail: 194 full hkups (30/50 amps). 2021 rates: $40 to $85. (250)766-1881, 2930 Woodsdale Rd, Lake Country, BC V4V 1Y1

LAKE COWICHAN — K2 *Mount Waddington*

GORDON BAY PROVINCIAL PARK (Public Prov Park) From town: Go 12-3/4 km/8 mi W on Hwy 18. 126 Avail. 2021 rates: $13 to $35. (877)559-2115

LANGLEY — K3 *Lower Mainland*

FORT CAMPING IN BRAE ISLAND REGIONAL PARK **Ratings: 8/8.5/8.5** (Campground) 156 Avail: 126 full hkups, 30 W, 30 E (30/50 amps). 2021 rates: $40 to $60. (604)888-3678, 9451 Glover Rd, Langley, BC V1M 2R9

LEE CREEK — H4 *Thompson Okanagan*

COTTONWOOD COVE RESORT **Ratings: 9.5/9.5★/9.5** (Condo Park) Avail: 110 full hkups (15/50 amps). 2021 rates: $55 to $100. May 01 to Oct 31. (250)679-2294, 2604 Squilax-Anglemont Hwy, Lee Creek, BC V0E 1M4

LINDELL BEACH — K3 *Strathcona*

CULTUS LAKE THOUSAND TRAILS RV RESORT
Ratings: 8.5/9★/8.5 (Membership Park) 164 Avail: 135 full hkups, 29 W, 29 E (15/30 amps). 2021 rates: $57 to $66. (888)563-7040, 1855 Columbia Valley Rd., Lindell Beach, BC V2R 0E1

LONE BUTTE — H3 *Cariboo*

LOON BAY RESORT (Campground) (Phone Update) 48 Avail: 18 full hkups, 30 W, 30 E (30 amps). 2021 rates: $38 to $42. May 15 to Oct 15. (250)593-4431, 7250 Texas Rd, Lone Butte, BC V0K 1X1

SHERIDAN LAKE RESORT (Campground) (Phone Update) 70 Avail: 70 W, 70 E (30 amps). 2021 rates: $38. May 15 to Oct 15. (250)593-4611, 7510 Magnussen Rd, Lone Butte, BC V0K 1X1

LUMBY — J4 *Cariboo*

MABEL LAKE (Public Prov Park) From Jct of Hwys 97 & 6, E 32 mi on Hwy 6 to Mabel Lake Rd, NE 47 mi (E). 84 Avail: Pit toilets. 2021 rates: $23. Apr 03 to Oct 12. (250)548-0076

LUND — J2 *Sunshine Coast*

LUND See also Black Creek, Campbell River & Courtenay.

SUNLUND BY-THE-SEA RV PARK & CABINS (RV Park) (Phone Update) Avail: 29 full hkups (15/30 amps). 2021 rates: $42 to $45. May 01 to Sep 30. (604)483-9220, 1496 Murray Rd, Lund, BC V0N 2G0

LYTTON — J3 *Cariboo*

SKIHIST PARK (Public Prov Park) From town, E 8 km (5 mi) on Hwy 1 (R). 58 Avail. 2021 rates: $23. May 01 to Sep 30. (250)455-2708

MACKENZIE — E5 *Peace River*

MACKENZIE MUNICIPAL CAMPGROUND (Public) From Jct of Hwys 97 & 39, N 18 mi on Hwy 39, at entrance to town (R). 36 Avail: 16 W, 16 S, 25 E (30 amps). 2021 rates: $17.85 to $28.35. May 01 to Oct 31. (250)997-3221

MALAHAT — K3 *South Island*

CEDAR SPRINGS RANCH (Campground) (Phone Update) 39 Avail: 8 full hkups, 25 W, 31 E (15/30 amps). 2021 rates: $45 to $56. Jun 01 to Sep 30. (250)478-3332, 230 Trans Canada Hwy 1, Malahat, BC V0R 2L0

MANSONS LANDING — J2 *Strathcona*

SMELT BAY PARK (Public Prov Park) Take ferry from Campbell River to Quadra Island, cross island, take ferry from Quadra Island to Cortes Island, follow signs. 24 Avail: Pit toilets. 2021 rates: $20. May 11 to Sep 30. (250)474-1336

MAPLE RIDGE — K3 *Greater Vancouver*

GOLDEN EARS (Public Prov Park) From E end of town, E 3.5 mi on Hwy 7 to 232nd St, N 2.5 mi to Fern Crescent Rd, E 2.5 mi (E). 423 Avail. 2021 rates: $23 to $35. May 13 to Oct 15. (604)466-8325

MARA — J4 *Okanagan*

WHISPERING PINES TENT & RV PARK **Ratings: 7.5/8.5★/8** (Campground) 90 Avail: 60 full hkups, 30 W, 30 E (15/30 amps). 2021 rates: $50 to $62. May 15 to Sep 15. (250)838-6775, 11 Hamilton Rd, Mara, BC V0E 2K0

MASSET — E3 *Skeena-Queen Charlotte*

NAIKOON/AGATE BEACH (Public Prov Park) From town, E 25 km on Hwy 16 to Toll Hill Rd (L). 39 Avail: Pit toilets. 2021 rates: $18. (250)626-3337

NAIKOON/MISTY MEADOWS (Public Prov Park) Take ferry from Prince Rupert to Skidgate, N 20.5 mi (45 km) on Hwy 16 (R). 30 Avail: Pit toilets. 2021 rates: $18. (250)847-7260

MCBRIDE — G4 *Cariboo*

BEAVERVIEW RV PARK & CAMPGROUND **Ratings: 5.5/8★/8** (Campground) 37 Avail: 37 W, 37 E (20/30 amps). 2021 rates: $38. May 01 to Sep 30. (250)569-2513, 2435 Hwy 16E, McBride, BC V0J 2E0

N.V. MOUNTAIN VIEW CHALETS & RV RESORT **Ratings: 6.5/9★/7.5** (RV Park) Avail: 36 full hkups (30/50 amps). 2021 rates: $27 to $41. May 15 to Nov 15. (250)569-0185, 5306 Hwy 10 East, McBride, BC V0J 2E0

MCLEOD LAKE — E6 *Fraswer-Fortt George*

CARP LAKE (Public Prov Park) From town: Go 32 km/20 mi W on gravel, secondary road. Check locally before proceeding. 102 Avail: Pit toilets. 2021 rates: $20. May 16 to Sep 01. (250)964-3489

TUDYAH LAKE PARK (Public Prov Park) From town: Go 8-3/4 km/5-1/2 mi N on Hwy 97. 36 Avail: Pit toilets. 2021 rates: $15. May 16 to Sep 30. (250)964-3489

WHISKERS POINT PARK (Public Prov Park) From town: Go 9-1/2 km/6 mi S on Hwy 97. 59 Avail. 2021 rates: $22. May 15 to Sep 10. (250)964-3489

MCLURE — H4 *Thompson*

PINEGROVE CAMPGROUND AND RV PARK **Ratings: 7/7.5★/7.5** (Campground) 25 Avail: 6 full hkups, 19 W, 19 E (30/50 amps). 2021 rates: $32 to $44. May 13 to Sep 15. (877)672-5529, 421 Walterdale Rd, General Delivery, McLure, BC V0E 2H0

MERRITT — J4 *Thompson Region*

CLAYBANKS RV PARK (Public) From Jct of Hwy 5 & Voght St (exit 290), S 2.4 mi on Voght St, follow Sani-Station signs (L). Avail: 44 full hkups (15/30 amps). 2021 rates: $20 to $35. (250)378-6441

KENTUCKY ALLEYNE (Public Prov Park) From town: Go 31-1/2 km/19-3/4 mi S on Hwy 5, then 6 km/3-3/4 mi E on secondary road. 58 Avail: Pit toilets. 2021 rates: $18. May 08 to Sep 30. (250)378-5334

MONCK (Public Prov Park) From city center, NE 11 mi on Prov Hwy 5A to Monck Park access rd, E 5 mi (R). 132 Avail. 2021 rates: $23. May 01 to Sep 30. (250)320-9305

MOON SHADOWS RV PARK & CAMPGROUND
Ratings: 7.5/9★/7.5 (RV Park) From jct Hwy 5 & Hwy 5A/97C in Merrit (exit 286): Go 1.1 km/1/2 mi W on Hwy 5A/97C (Nicola Ave) to Coldwater Rd, then 0.8 km/1/2 mi S to Pooley Ave, then 0.2 km/1/4 mi E to Neilson St, then 0.8 km/1/2 mi S (R). **FAC:** gravel rds. (79 spaces). 69 Avail: 20 gravel, 49 dirt, 13 pull-thrus, (22x60), back-ins (22x50), 69 full hkups (30/50 amps), seasonal sites, WiFi @ sites, tent sites, rentals, dump, laundry, groc, LP bottles, fire rings, firewood. **REC:** Coldwater River: swim, boating nearby, hunting nearby. Pets OK. Partial handicap access, eco-friendly. 2021 rates: $37 to $48, Military discount.
(888)344-2267 Lat: 50.08829, Lon: -120.77624
1145 Neilson St, Merritt, BC V1K 1B8
www.moonshadows.ca
See ad this page

MEZIADIN JUNCTION — D4 *Kitimat-Stikine*

KINASKAN LAKE (Public Prov Park) From Dease Lake, S 100 km/63 mi on Hwy 37 (R). 50 Avail: Pit toilets. 2021 rates: $20. May 15 to Oct 01. (250)847-7260

MEZIADIN LAKE (Public Prov Park) From Jct of Hwy 16 & Hwy 37, N 150 mi, follow signs (L). Avail: 18 E (30 amps), Pit toilets. 2021 rates: $22 to $27. May 13 to Sep 22. (250)638-8490

MEZIADIN LAKE — D4 *Kitimat-Stikine*

BELL 2 LODGE (RV Park) (Phone Update) Avail: 10 full hkups (15 amps). 2021 rates: $32 to $47. (250)275-4770, KM 249 Hwy 37, Meziadin Lake, BC V0J 3S0

MILL BAY — K3 *South Island*

BAMBERTON PROVINCIAL PARK (Public Prov Park) From town: Go 8 km/5 mi S on Hwy 1. 53 Avail: Pit toilets. 2021 rates: $11 to $20. (250)474-1336

MISSION — K3 *Greater Vancouver*

ROLLEY LAKE (Public Prov Park) From Jct of Hwy 7 (Maple Ridge) & Dewdney Trunk Rd, NW 8 mi on Dewdney Trunk Rd to Rolley Lake Rd, N 2 mi (L). 64 Avail. 2021 rates: $35. Apr 01 to Oct 15. (604)466-8325

MONTE LAKE — J4 *Thompson*

HERITAGE CAMPSITE & RV PARK (RV Park) (Phone Update) 37 Avail: 17 full hkups, 3 W, 3 E (15/30 amps). 2021 rates: $35 to $40. Apr 15 to Oct 01. (250)375-2434, 3961 Hwy 97, Monte Lake, BC V0E 2N0

MORICETOWN — E4 *Bulkley-Nechako*

MORICETOWN RV PARK **Ratings: 5/8.5★/8** (Campground) 33 Avail: 33 W, 33 E (30/50 amps). 2021 rates: $25 to $35. May 15 to Sep 15. (250)847-2133, 163 Telkwa High Rd, Smithers, BC V0J 2N1

MUNCHO LAKE — B5 *Liard*

LIARD RIVER HOT SPRINGS (Public Prov Park) From town, NE 36 mi on Hwy 97 (R). 53 Avail: Pit toilets. 2021 rates: $16 to $26. (250)776-7000

MUNCHO LAKE (Public Prov Park) From town, S 3 km on Hwy 97 (R). 30 Avail: Pit toilets. 2021 rates: $20. May 01 to Sep 15. (250)776-7000

NORTHERN ROCKIES LODGE & RV PARK (Campground) (Phone Update) 36 Avail: 6 full hkups, 24 W, 24 E (30 amps). 2021 rates: $50 to $68. (800)663-5269, Mile 462 Alaska Hwy, Muncho Lake, BC V0C 1Z0

NAKUSP — J5 *Kootenay West*

KBR CAMPGROUND (Campground) (Phone Update) 42 Avail: 27 full hkups, 9 W, 9 E (15/30 amps). 2021 rates: $30 to $45. (250)265-4212, 1701 Hwy 23N, Nakusp, BC V0G 1R0

NAKUSP HOT SPRINGS CAMPGROUND (Public) From Jct of Hwy 6 & Hwy 23, (6th Ave NW & W Broadway), N 1.6 mi on Hwy 6 to Hot Springs Rd, E 7.5 mi (E). Avail: 30 E (30 amps). 2021 rates: $26.75 to $30. May 01 to Oct 15. (866)999-4528

NAKUSP VILLAGE CAMPGROUND (Public) In town from jct Hwy 23 & 4th St NW: Go 200 meters/220 yards W on 4th St NW, then 30 meters/100 feet S on 8th Ave NW. Avail: 10 E. 2021 rates: $19 to $27. May 15 to Oct 15. (250)265-4019

THREE ISLANDS RESORT RV & CAMPING (Campground) (Phone Update) 62 Avail: 34 full hkups, 21 W, 21 E (15/30 amps). 2021 rates: $35 to $38. May 01 to Sep 30. (250)265-3023, 2384 Hwy 6, Nakusp, BC V0G 1R0

NANAIMO — K2 *East Island*

BRANNEN LAKE RV PARK & CAMPSITE **Ratings: 7/9.5★/8.5** (Campground) 45 Avail: 30 full hkups, 15 W, 15 E (30/50 amps). 2021 rates: $41 to $43. (866)756-0404, 4220 Biggs Rd, Nanaimo, BC V9T 5P9

JINGLEPOT RV PARK & CAMPGROUNDS **Ratings: 6/9.5★/6** (Campground) 40 Avail: 10 full hkups, 30 W, 30 E (30 amps). 2021 rates: $40 to $55. (250)758-1614, 4012 Jinglepot Rd, Nanaimo, BC V9T 5P9

LIVING FOREST OCEANSIDE CAMPGROUND & RV PARK **Ratings: 9/8.5/9.5** (RV Park) Avail: 206 full hkups (30/50 amps). 2021 rates: $43 to $65. (250)755-1755, 6 Maki Rd, Nanaimo, BC V9R 6N7

MOUNTAINAIRE CAMPGROUND & RV PARK **Ratings: 6.5/6.5/7.5** (Campground) 70 Avail: 57 full hkups, 13 W, 13 E (30 amps). 2021 rates: $42 to $45. (250)245-1169, 1092 Spruston Rd, Nanaimo, BC V9X 1R2

NELSON — J5 *Kootenay West*

KOKANEE CREEK (Public Prov Park) From town, NE 12 mi on Hwy 3A (R). Avail: 13 E. 2021 rates: $32 to $39. Apr 24 to Oct 05. (250)825-4293

NELSON CITY CAMPGROUND (Public) From Jct of Hwys 6 & 3A, NE 0.7 mi on Hwy 3A to Edgewood, N 0.2 mi, follow signs (E). 27 Avail: 7 full hkups, 20 W, 20 E (20/30 amps). 2021 rates: $25 to $35. May 01 to Oct 15. (250)352-7618

OKANAGAN FALLS — K4 *South Okanagan*

OKANAGAN FALLS (Public Prov Park) From town, N 1 mi on Hwy 97 to Green Lake Rd (L). 25 Avail. 2021 rates: $25. Apr 01 to Oct 12. (250)497-5423

SUN & SAND TENT & TRAILER PARK **Ratings: 6.5/9★/7** (Campground) Avail: 50 full hkups (30 amps). 2021 rates: $40 to $75. Apr 15 to Oct 15. (250)497-8289, 5356 8th Ave, Okanagan Falls, BC V0H 1R0

OLIVER — K4 *South Okanagan*

APPLE BEACH RV PARK **Ratings: 6.5/7/8.5** (RV Park) Avail: 20 full hkups (30 amps). 2021 rates: $45 to $60. (855)358-3287, 915 Bulrush Road, Oliver, BC V0H 1T2

DESERT GEM RV RESORT **Ratings: 8.5/10★/9.5** (RV Park) Avail: 50 full hkups (15/50 amps). 2021 rates: $44 to $58. (888)925-9966, 5753 Main St (Hwy 97), Oliver, BC V0H 1T0

GALLAGHER LAKE RESORT - PARKBRIDGE **Ratings: 8/9/9** (Campground) 95 Avail: 68 full hkups, 27 W, 27 E (15/30 amps). 2021 rates: $39 to $128. (250)498-3358, 8439 Hwy 97, Oliver, BC V0H 1T2

THE LAKESIDE RESORT **Ratings: 7/7.5/7.5** (Campground) 54 Avail: 54 W, 54 E (15/30 amps). 2021 rates: $35 to $63. (800)220-7330, 6707 Lakeside Dr, Oliver, BC V0H 1T4

THE ORCHARD AT OLIVER MOTEL AND RV PARK **Ratings: 7.5/10★/8** (RV Park) Avail: 19 full hkups (30/50 amps). 2021 rates: $35 to $60. (800)801-0999, 5650 Hwy 97 S, Oliver, BC V0H 1T9

OSOYOOS — K4 *South Okanagan*

BROOKVALE HOLIDAY RESORT (Campground) (Phone Update) 59 Avail: 4 full hkups, 55 W, 55 E (15/30 amps). 2021 rates: $38 to $46. May 15 to Oct 15. (250)495-7514, 1219 Lakeshore Dr, Osoyoos, BC V0H 1V6

HAYNES POINT (Public Prov Park) From town, S 1 mi on Hwy 97 to 32nd Ave (R). 41 Avail. 2021 rates: $32. Apr 01 to Oct 12. (778)437-2295

NK'MIP RV PARK **Ratings: 9.5/8.5/9** (RV Park) Avail: 310 full hkups (30/50 amps). 2021 rates: $38 to $85. (250)495-7279, 8000 45th St, Osoyoos, BC V0H 1V6

WALTON'S LAKEFRONT RESORT **Ratings: 9.5/9/9** (Condo Park) Avail: 37 full hkups (30/50 amps). 2021 rates: $70 to $85. (800)964-1148, 3207 Lakeshore Drive, Osoyoos, BC V0H 1V6

PARKSVILLE — K2 *East Island*

ENGLISHMAN RIVER FALLS (Public Prov Park) From town, W 3.5 mi on Hwy 4 to Errington Rd, S 5 mi (E). 104 Avail: Pit toilets. 2021 rates: $23. May 01 to Sep 30. (250)474-1336

FILLONGLEY (Public Prov Park) From ferry (Buckley Bay to Denman Island), E 9 mi on PR-19 (R). 10 Avail: Pit toilets. 2021 rates: $12 to $23. (250)308-4479

LITTLE QUALICUM FALLS (Public Prov Park) From Jct of Hwy 19 & Hwy 4, W 12 mi on Hwy 4 (R). 96 Avail. 2021 rates: $23. Apr 15 to Oct 14. (250)474-1336

PARADISE SEA SIDE RESORT **Ratings: 8/10★/9** (RV Park) Avail: 30 full hkups (30/50 amps). 2021 rates: $45 to $65. Mar 01 to Oct 31. (250)248-6612, 375 W Island Hwy, Parksville, BC V9P 1A1

PATHFINDER CAMP RESORTS PARKSVILLE (RV Park) (Phone Update) 106 Avail: 85 full hkups, 21 W, 21 E (20/30 amps). 2021 rates: $56 to $72. May 01 to Sep 30. (833)581-2012, 380 Martingdale Rd, Parksville, BC V9P 1R7

RATHTREVOR BEACH (Public Prov Park) From town, S 2 mi on Hwy 19A (R). 250 Avail. 2021 rates: $35. (250)474-1336

SURFSIDE RV RESORT **Ratings: 9.5/9.5★/9.5** (Membership Park) Avail: 29 full hkups (30/50 amps). 2021 rates: $40 to $85. (866)642-2001, 200 N Corfield St, Parksville, BC V9P 2H5

PEACHLAND — J4 *Central Okanagan*

TODD'S RV & CAMPING **Ratings: 4.5/6.5/6.5** (Campground) 60 Avail: 53 full hkups, 7 W, 7 E (15/50 amps). 2021 rates: $45 to $80. Apr 01 to Oct 15. (866)255-6864, 3976 Beach Ave, Peachland, BC V0H 1X1

PEMBERTON — J3 *Cariboo*

BIRKENHEAD LAKE (Public Prov Park) From Pemberton-D'Arcy Hwy, NW 11 mi on gravel rd (L). 78 Avail: Pit toilets. 2021 rates: $22. May 15 to Sep 30. (604)986-9371

NAIRN FALLS (Public Prov Park) From town, S 2 mi on Hwy 99 (L). 94 Avail: Pit toilets. 2021 rates: $22. May 08 to Sep 30. (604)986-9371

PENDER ISLAND — K3 *Cowichan Valley*

GULF ISLANDS PRIOR CENTENNIAL PARK (Public National Park) Take ferry from Swartz Bay to Pender Island, S 3 mi, follow signs (L). 17 Avail: Pit toilets. 2021 rates: $17.60. May 15 to Sep 30. (877)737-3783

PENTICTON — J4 *South Okanagan*

OKANAGAN LAKE (Public Prov Park) From town, N 20 mi on Hwy 97 (R). 176 Avail. 2021 rates: $35. Mar 27 to Oct 13. (250)548-0076

SOUTH BEACH GARDENS RV PARK **Ratings: 6.5/7.5/5.5** (Campground) Avail: 210 full hkups (15/30 amps). 2021 rates: $51 to $59. May 15 to Sep 15. (250)492-0628, 3815 Skaha Lake Rd, Penticton, BC V2A 6G8

WRIGHT'S BEACH CAMP **Ratings: 8/7.5/6.5** (Campground) 245 Avail: 238 full hkups, 7 W (30 amps). 2021 rates: $52 to $75. (250)492-7120, 4200 Skaha Lake Rd, Penticton, BC V2A 6J7

PINK MOUNTAIN — D6 *Peace River*

BUCKINGHORSE RIVER WAYSIDE (Public Prov Park) From town, W 9 mi (14 km) on Hwy 97 (AK Hwy) to MP-175 (L). 33 Avail: Pit toilets. 2021 rates: $20. May 13 to Sep 30. (250)772-4999

PORT ALBERNI — K2 *East Island*

CHINA CREEK CAMPGROUND & MARINA (Public) From jct Hwy 4 & 10th Ave: Go S on 10th Ave following signs to Bamfield Rd, then 16 km/10 mi on Bamfield Rd. 250 Avail: 70 full hkups, 100 W, 100 E. 2021 rates: $30 to $45. Apr 01 to Sep 30. (250)723-9812

SPROAT LAKE PARK (Public Prov Park) From town, NW 8 mi on SR-4 (R). 59 Avail. 2021 rates: $25. (250)474-1336

STAMP RIVER PARK (Public Prov Park) From Jct of Hwy 4 & Beaver Creek Rd, N 9 mi on Beaver Creek Rd (L). 23 Avail: Pit toilets. 2021 rates: $18. (250)474-1336

PORT EDWARD — E3 *Skeena-Queen Charlotte*

KINNIKINNICK CAMPGROUND & RV PARK (Campground) (Phone Update) 20 Avail: 8 full hkups, 12 W, 12 E (15/30 amps). 2021 rates: $29 to $40. (866)628-9449, 333 Skeena Dr, Port Edward, BC V8J 4S4

PORT HARDY — J1 *North Island*

PORT HARDY RV RESORT & LOG CABINS (RV Park) (Phone Update) Avail: 76 full hkups (30 amps). 2021 rates: $42.50. Jun 01 to Sep 14. (855)949-8118, 8080 Goodspeed Rd, Port Hardy, BC V0N 2P0

QUATSE RIVER CAMPGROUND (Public) From south city limits: Go 1-1/2 km/1 mi S on Hwy 19, then 3/4 km/1/2 mi W on Coal Harbour Rd. 41 Avail: 41 W, 41 E. 2021 rates: $30.45 to $39.90. (866)949-2395

PORT MCNEILL — J1 *North Island*

ALDER BAY RV PARK & MARINA (Campground) (Phone Update) Avail: 63 full hkups (15/30 amps). 2021 rates: $39 to $46. (888)956-4117, #1 Alder Bay Dr, Port McNeill, BC V0N 2R0

CLUXEWE RESORT (RV Park) (Phone Update) 132 Avail: 81 full hkups, 23 W, 34 E (30 amps). 2021 rates: $31 to $34. (250)949-0378, 1 Cluxewe Campground Rd, Port McNeill, BC V0N 2R0

POWELL RIVER — J2 *South Coast*

POWELL RIVER See also Courtenay, Hornby Island & Lund.

HAYWIRE BAY REGIONAL PARK (POWELL RIVER REG DISTRICT) (Public) From town: Go N on Manson Ave, then right on Cranberry St, then left on Haslam St, turn left on gravel road, then 7-1/4 km/4-1/2 mi on gravel road to park. 48 Avail. 2021 rates: $23. May 05 to Sep 29. (604)483-1097

SHELTER POINT REGIONAL PARK (Public) From Powell River: Take Texada Island ferry to Blubber Bay terminal. Follow Hwy, turn S toward Gillies Bay at only intersection. On SW coast of Texada Isl. 33-1/2 km/21 mi from ferry terminal. 52 Avail. 2021 rates: $16 to $23. (604)485-2260

WILLINGDON BEACH CAMPSITE (Public) From Ferry, N 1 mi on Marine Ave (L). 68 Avail: 41 full hkups, 17 E (30 amps). 2021 rates: $25 to $33.50. (604)485-2242

PRINCE GEORGE — F3 *Central Interior*

BEE LAZEE RV PARK & CAMPGROUND

good sam park

Ratings: 7.5/9.5★/8 (Campground) From Jct of Hwys 16 & 97, S 9.4 mi on Hwy 97, 8 mi S of Simon Fraser Bridge (L).

BE OUR GUEST

Quaint RV park right on Hwy 97 just minutes from Prince George. Features clean washrooms, laundry & swimming pool for relaxing after a day's journey or on hot summer days. Close to hiking trails & nature paths.

FAC: all weather rds. Avail: 35 all weather, 26 pull-thrus, (32x60), back-ins (34x40), 30 full hkups, 5 W, 5 E (15/30 amps), WiFi @ sites, tent sites, dump, laundry, controlled access. **REC:** heated pool, boating nearby, playground. Pet restrict (B). Partial handicap access, eco-friendly. 2021 rates: $30 to $34. May 01 to Sep 30.

(866)963-7263 Lat: 53.78196, Lon: -122.65516
15910 Hwy 97 S, Prince George, BC V2N 5Y3
beelazee.ca
See ad this page

BLUE CEDARS CAMPGROUND **Ratings: 6/8.5★/6** (Campground) 61 Avail: 38 full hkups, 23 W, 23 E (15/30 amps). 2021 rates: $42. (888)964-7271, 4433 Kimball Road, Prince George, BC V2N 5N7

PRINCE GEORGE (CONT)

HARTWAY RV PARK **Ratings: 6.5/9.5★/8** (RV Park) Avail: 42 full hkups (30/50 amps). 2021 rates: $42 to $48. (866)962-8848, 7729 Kelly Rd S, Prince George, BC V2K 2H5

MAMA YEH RV PARK **Ratings: 3/NA/6.5** (Campground) Avail: 24 full hkups (20/50 amps), Pit toilets. 2021 rates: $35 to $45. May 01 to Sep 30. (855)963-8828, 5235 White Rd, Prince George, BC V2N 5Y5

NORTHERN EXPERIENCE RV PARK **Ratings: 7/9.5★/8** (RV Park) 32 Avail: 17 full hkups, 15 W, 15 E (30 amps). 2021 rates: $33 to $42. (250)963-7577, 9180 Hwy 97 S., Prince George, BC V2N 6E2

NORTHLAND RV TRAILER PARK 2014 **Ratings: 5/6.5/6** (RV Park) 32 Avail: 17 full hkups, 15 W, 15 E (30/50 amps). 2021 rates: $40. (250)962-5010, 10180 Hart Hwy, Prince George, BC V2K 5X6

PURDEN LAKE (Public Prov Park) From town: Go 64 km/40 mi E on Hwy 16. 78 Avail. 2021 rates: $22. Jun 01 to Sep 20. (250)964-3489

SINTICH RV PARK **Ratings: 8/8.5★/7.5** (RV Park) 43 Avail: 41 full hkups, 2 W, 2 E (30/50 amps). 2021 rates: $40 to $44. (877)791-1152, 7817 Hwy 97S, Prince George, BC V2N 6P6

PRINCE RUPERT — E3 *North Coast*

PRINCE RUPERT RV CAMPGROUND (Public) From Ferry Terminal: Go 1.6 km/1 mi E on Yellowhead Hwy 16 (Park Avenue). Avail: 77 full hkups. 2021 rates: $27.61 to $47.15. Mar 01 to Dec 31. (250)627-1000

PRUDHOMME LAKE (Public Prov Park) From town, E 15 mi on Yellowhead Hwy 16 (L). 24 Avail: Pit toilets. 2021 rates: $20. May 08 to Sep 08. (250)286-9992

PRINCETON — K4 *Similkameen*

ALLISON LAKE (Public Prov Park) From town, N 17.4 mi on Hwy 5A (R). 22 Avail: Pit toilets. 2021 rates: $18. Jun 15 to Sep 15. (250)548-0076

MANNING PARK/MULE DEER (Public Prov Park) From town: Go 56 km/35 mi SW on Hwy 3. 49 Avail: Pit toilets. 2021 rates: $25. May 01 to Sep 13. (604)668-5953

MANNING/HAMPTON (Public Prov Park) From town: Go 62-1/2 km/39 mi SW on Hwy 3. 99 Avail: Pit toilets. 2021 rates: $23. May 08 to Sep 28. (250)840-8822

OTTER LAKE PARK (Public Prov Park) From Princeton, NW 47 km on Hwy 5A (at Tulameen), follow signs (R). 45 Avail. 2021 rates: $23. May 15 to Sep 27. (250)548-0076

PRINCETON GOLF CLUB AND RV SITES **Ratings: 6.5/9★/7** (Campground) Avail: 36 full hkups (15/30 amps). 2021 rates: $44 to $48. Apr 06 to Oct 15. (250)295-6123, 365 Darcy Mountain Rd, Princeton, BC V0X 1W0

PRINCETON RV PARK (PRINCETON MUNICIPAL PARK) (Public) From Jct of Hwy 3 & Bridge St (Hwy 5A), E 1.6 mi on Hwy 3 (L). 73 Avail: 43 W, 43 E (30 amps). 2021 rates: $28.57. May 01 to Sep 30. (250)295-7355

QUADRA ISLAND — J2 *Central Coast*

WE WAI KAI CAMPSITE (Campground) (Phone Update) 135 Avail: 7 full hkups, 128 E (15 amps). 2021 rates: $43 to $48. May 10 to Sep 30. (250)285-3111, 1 Rebecca Spit Rd, Quathiaski Cove, BC V0P 1N0

QUALICUM BEACH — K2 *East Island*

CEDAR GROVE RV PARK & CAMPGROUND **Ratings: 7/6.5/7** (Campground) 34 Avail: 11 full hkups, 23 W, 23 E (20/30 amps). 2021 rates: $44 to $47. Mar 01 to Sep 30. (250)752-2442, 246 Riverbend Rd, Qualicum Beach, BC V9K 2N2

QUALICUM BAY RESORT **Ratings: 7.5/9★/8.5** (RV Park) Avail: 60 full hkups (30 amps). 2021 rates: $42 to $47. (250)757-2003, 5970 West Island Hwy, Qualicum Beach, BC V9K 2N1

RIVERSIDE RESORT **Ratings: 7/8★/7.5** (RV Park) 30 Avail: 24 full hkups, 6 W, 6 E (15/30 amps). 2021 rates: $35 to $65. (250)752-9544, 3506 W Island Hwy, Qualicum Beach, BC V9K 2H4

QUATHIASKI COVE — J2 *East Island*

TSA-KWA-LUTEN LODGE & RV PARK (RV Park) (Phone Update) Avail: 13 full hkups (30/50 amps). 2021 rates: $42 to $52. Apr 26 to Sep 29. (250)830-2299, 1 Lighthouse Road, Quathiaski Cove, BC V0P 1N0

QUESNEL — G3 *Cariboo*

AIRPORT INN MOTEL & RV PARK **Ratings: 6.5/8/7.5** (RV Park) 40 Avail: 30 full hkups, 10 W, 10 E (15/30 amps). 2021 rates: $35 to $50. (855)567-5942, 3101 Hwy 97N , Quesnel, BC V2J 5Y8

LAZY DAZE RESORT **Ratings: 4/9★/8.5** (Campground) Avail: 30 full hkups (15/30 amps). 2021 rates: $35 to $40. May 01 to Sep 30. (250)992-6700, 714 Ritchie Rd, Quesnel, BC V2J 6X2

TEN MILE LAKE PARK (Public Prov Park) From town, N 10 mi on Hwy 97 (L). 108 Avail. 2021 rates: $20 to $25. May 15 to Sep 30. (250)397-2523

RADIUM HOT SPRINGS — J6 *Columbia Valley*

DRY GULCH (Public Prov Park) From town, S 5 mi on Hwy 93/95 (L). 27 Avail. 2021 rates: $25. May 01 to Sep 30. (250)422-3003

KOOTENAY/MARBLE CANYON (Public National Park) From town: Go 85-1/2 km/53-1/2 mi N on Hwy 93. 61 Avail. 2021 rates: $21.50. Jun 21 to Sep 04. (877)737-3783

KOOTENAY/MCLEOD MEADOWS (Public National Park) From town, N 16 mi on Hwy 93 (R). 80 Avail. 2021 rates: $21.50. Jun 14 to Sep 17. (877)737-3783

KOOTENAY/REDSTREAK (Public National Park) From Jct of Hwy 93/95 & Redstreak Rd, E 1.4 mi on Redstreak Rd., E 1.2 mi on Redstreak Rd (E). 232 Avail: 50 full hkups, 38 E (15/30 amps). 2021 rates: $27.40 to $38.20. May 02 to Oct 15. (877)737-3783

RIDGEVIEW RESORT **Ratings: 9.5/10★/9** (Condo Park) Avail: 29 full hkups (30/50 amps). 2021 rates: $30 to $68. Apr 01 to Oct 30. (250)347-9715, 7274 Radium Valley Rd, Radium Hot Springs, BC V0A 1M0

THE CANYON RV RESORT **Ratings: 7/9.5★/9.5** (RV Park) 75 Avail: 62 full hkups, 13 W, 13 E (30/50 amps). 2021 rates: $48 to $65. Apr 15 to Oct 30. (250)347-9564, 5012 Sinclair Creek Rd, Radium Hot Springs, BC V0A 1M0

REVELSTOKE — H5 *Columbia*

BLANKET CREEK (Public Prov Park) From town S 14 mi on Hwy 23 (L). 105 Avail. 2021 rates: $28. May 08 to Sep 30. (250)837-5734

BOULDER MOUNTAIN RESORT **Ratings: 4.5/9.5★/8.5** (Campground) 13 Avail: 7 full hkups, 6 E (30/50 amps). 2021 rates: $55 to $75. (250)837-4420, 3069 Hwy 1, Revelstoke, BC V0E 2S0

CANYON HOT SPRINGS RESORT **Ratings: 7/9.5★/8** (Campground) 62 Avail: 62 W, 62 E (15/30 amps). 2021 rates: $45 to $55. May 15 to Sep 20. (250)837-2420, 7050 Trans Canada Hwy Number 1, Revelstoke, BC V0E 2S0

LAMPLIGHTER CAMPGROUND **Ratings: 7.5/9.5★/8** (Campground) Avail: 38 full hkups (15/30 amps). 2021 rates: $40 to $50. May 01 to Sep 30. (250)837-3385, 1760 Nixon Rd, Revelstoke, BC V0E 2S0

REVELSTOKE CAMPGROUND **Ratings: 7.5/9.5★/8** (Campground) 157 Avail: 70 full hkups, 23 W, 23 E (30/50 amps). 2021 rates: $35 to $73. May 01 to Oct 01. (250)837-2085, 2411 KOA Rd, Revelstoke, BC V0E 2S0

WILLIAMSON LAKE CAMPGROUND **Ratings: 6.5/7.5/7** (Campground) 50 Avail: 18 full hkups, 9 S, 9 E (15/30 amps). 2021 rates: $37 to $43. Apr 15 to Oct 15. (250)837-8806, 1817 Williamson Lake Rd, Revelstoke, BC V0E 2S0

ROCK CREEK — K4 *South Okanagan*

KETTLE RIVER (Public Prov Park) From town, N 2 mi on Hwy 33 (R). 114 Avail. 2021 rates: $30. Apr 23 to Sep 27. (250)548-9025

KETTLE RIVER RV PARK **Ratings: 7.5/9★/7.5** (RV Park) 20 Avail: 9 full hkups, 11 W, 11 E (20/50 amps). 2021 rates: $45 to $48. Apr 01 to Oct 31. (888)441-2225, 3255 Hwy 3, Rock Creek, BC V0H 1Y0

ROGERS PASS — H5 *Fraser-Fort George*

GLACIER/ILLECILLEWAET (Public National Park) From town: Go 3-1/4 km/2 mi W on Hwy 1. 60 Avail. 2021 rates: $21.50. Jun 25 to Oct 01. (877)737-3783

GLACIER/LOOP BROOK (Public National Park) From town: Go 5-1/2 km/3-1/2 mi W on Hwy 1. 20 Avail. 2021 rates: $21.50. (877)737-3783

Always do a Pre-Drive Safety Check!

ROSEBERY — J5 *Thompson-Nicola*

MARTHA CREEK (Public Prov Park) From town, N 11 mi on Hwy 23 (L). 75 Avail: Pit toilets. 2021 rates: $28. May 06 to Sep 30. (866)937-5734

ROSEDALE — K3 *Fraser Valley*

CAMPERLAND BRIDAL FALLS **Ratings: 9.5/8/9** (Membership Park) Avail: 261 full hkups (30/50 amps). 2021 rates: $46 to $90. Apr 01 to Oct 31. (604)794-7361, 53730 Bridal Falls Rd, Rosedale, BC V0X 1X1

SALMON ARM — J4 *Okanagan*

PIERRE'S POINT CAMPGROUND **Ratings: 6/8/6.5** (Campground) 70 Avail: 10 full hkups, 40 W, 40 E (15/30 amps). 2021 rates: $45 to $85. May 01 to Oct 01. (250)253-1340, 2569 Campground Rd, Salmon Arm, BC V1E 3A1

SALMON ARM CAMPING RESORT **Ratings: 8.5/8.5/8** (Campground) Avail: 62 full hkups (30 amps). 2021 rates: $43 to $59. May 01 to Oct 01. (866)979-1659, 381 Hwy 97B, Salmon Arm, BC V1E 1X5

SALT SPRING ISLAND — K3 *Mount Waddington*

RUCKLE PARK (Public Prov Park) On Saltspring Island. Accessible by car ferry from Swartz Bay, Crofton or Tsawwassen. 8-3/4 km/5-1/2 mi E of Fulford on country road. 20 Avail: Pit toilets. 2021 rates: $20. (250)539-2115

SALTERY BAY — J2 *Central Coast*

SALTERY BAY (Public Prov Park) From Jct of Saltery Bay ferry landing & Hwy 101, W 0.75 mi on Hwy 101 (L). 42 Avail: Pit toilets. 2021 rates: $20. (250)286-9992

SARDIS — K3 *Lower Mainland*

CHILLIWACK LAKE PARK (Public Prov Park) From town, S 6 mi on Vedder Rd to Chilliwack Lake Rd, E 25.5 mi, follow signs. 146 Avail: Pit toilets. 2021 rates: $22. May 01 to Oct 13. (604)795-6169

Find Good Sam member specials at GanderOutdoors.com

SAYWARD — J2 *North Island*

SAYWARD VALLEY RESORT/FISHERBOY PARK **Ratings: 7/9★/8.5** (Campground) Avail: 34 full hkups (30/50 amps). 2021 rates: $38. (866)357-0598, 1546 Sayward Rd, Sayward, BC V0P 1R0

WHITE RIVER RESORT **Ratings: 4/6.5/8** (RV Park) 20 Avail: 12 full hkups, 8 W, 8 E (20/30 amps). 2021 rates: $38. (250)282-0117, 1673 Sayward Rd, Sayward, BC V0P 1R0

SECHELT — K2 *South Coast*

BAYSIDE CAMPGROUND & RV PARK **Ratings: 5/7.5/7.5** (Campground) 16 Avail: 8 full hkups, 8 W, 8 E (30 amps). 2021 rates: $40 to $45. (877)885-7444, 6040 Sechelt Inlet Rd, Sechelt, BC V0N 3A3

CREEKSIDE CAMPGROUND **Ratings: 5.5/6.5/6** (Campground) 32 Avail: 18 full hkups, 14 W, 14 E (15/30 amps). 2021 rates: $40 to $50. (800)565-9222, 4314 Sunshine Coast Hwy, Sechelt, BC V0N 3A1

PORPOISE BAY (Public Prov Park) From town, N 3 mi on Porpoise Bay Rd (L). 84 Avail. 2021 rates: $29. (604)885-3714

SICAMOUS — H4 *Okanagan*

CEDARS RV RESORT **Ratings: 7/7/8** (Campground) 55 Avail: 29 full hkups, 26 W, 26 E (30 amps). 2021 rates: $45. (778)212-2151, 3499 Luoma Rd, Malakwa, BC V0E 2J0

SICAMOUS KOA **Ratings: 7/9★/8** (Campground) 46 Avail: 36 full hkups, 10 W, 10 E (15/30 amps). 2021 rates: $49.89 to $81.89. May 01 to Sep 30. (800)562-0797, 3250 Oxbow Frontage Rd, Malakwa, BC V0E 2J0

YARD CREEK PARK (Public Prov Park) From town: Go 12-3/4 km/8 mi E on Hwy 1. 65 Avail: Pit toilets. 2021 rates: $20. May 21 to Sep 30. (250)836-4663

SIDNEY — K3 *South Island*

MCDONALD CREEK (Public Prov Park) From town, S 6 mi on Hwy 6 (R). 73 Avail: Pit toilets. 2021 rates: $30. May 01 to Sep 30. (866)937-5734

SKOOKUMCHUCK — J6 *Kootenay East*

PREMIER LAKE (Public Prov Park) From town, N 0.6 mi on Hwy 93/95 to Sheep Creek Rd, E 6.6 mi on Sheep Creek Rd to Premier Ridge Rd, S 2.4 mi (E). 61 Avail: Pit toilets. 2021 rates: $25. (250)422-3003

SMITHERS — F1 *Bulkley Valley*

RIVERSIDE PARK CAMPGROUND (Public) From Jct of Hwy 16 & Main St, N 0.75 mi on Main St (L). Avail: 9 E (15/30 amps). 2021 rates: $25 to $32. May 16 to Oct 10. (250)847-1600

SOOKE — K2 *South Island*

FRENCH BEACH (Public Prov Park) From town: Go 26-3/4 km/16-3/4 mi W on Hwy 14. 69 Avail: Pit toilets. 2021 rates: $26. (250)474-1336

SUNNY SHORES RESORT AND MARINA **Ratings: 5.5/7.5/6.5** (Campground) 31 Avail: 6 full hkups, 25 W, 25 E (15 amps). 2021 rates: $40. (250)642-5731, 5621 Sooke Rd, Sooke, BC V9Z 0C6

SQUAMISH — J3 *Howe Sound*

ALICE LAKE PARK (Public Prov Park) From town, N 3 mi on Hwy 99 (R). Avail: 55 E (15/30 amps). 2021 rates: $35 to $43. Mar 15 to Oct 31. (604)986-9371

PORTEAU COVE (Public Prov Park) From Horseshoe Bay, N 15 mi on Hwy 99 (L). Avail: 44 E (15/30 amps). 2021 rates: $35 to $43. (604)986-9371

STEWART — D4 *North Coast Inland*

BEAR RIVER RV PARK (RV Park) (Phone Update) Avail: 72 full hkups (30 amps). 2021 rates: $41.30 to $45.85. May 01 to Sep 30. (250)636-9205, 2200 Davis St, Stewart, BC V0T 1W0

RAINEY CREEK CAMPGROUND & RV PARK (Public) From Jct Hwy 37A Conway St & 5th Ave, N 0.2 mi on Hwy 37A to 8th Ave, W 0.4 mi (E). Avail: 62 E (30 amps). 2021 rates: $18 to $32. May 15 to Sep 15. (403)998-8546

SUMMERLAND — J4 *South Okanagan*

PEACH ORCHARD CAMPGROUND (Public) From Jct of Hwy 97 & Rosedale Ave, W 0.05 mi on Rosedale Ave, E 0.7 mi on Peach Orchard Rd (R). 123 Avail: 123 W, 123 E (30 amps). 2021 rates: $28 to $37. May 15 to Sep 15. (250)494-9649

SURREY — K3 *Lower Mainland*

HAZELMERE RV PARK **Ratings: 9/10★/9** (RV Park) 53 Avail: 28 full hkups, 25 W, 25 E (30 amps). 2021 rates: $50 to $60. (604)538-1167, 18843-8th Ave, Surrey, BC V3Z 9R9

PEACE ARCH RV PARK **Ratings: 8.5/9★/7** (RV Park) Avail: 30 full hkups (30/50 amps). 2021 rates: $47 to $57. (604)594-7009, 14601 40th Ave, Surrey, BC V3Z 1E7

TYNEHEAD RV CAMP **Ratings: 7/10★/7.5** (Campground) Avail: 43 full hkups (30 amps). 2021 rates: $59 to $64. (877)599-1161, 16275 102nd Ave, Surrey, BC V4N 2K7

TAPPEN — J4 *Cariboo*

HERALD PARK (Public Prov Park) From Trans Canada Hwy at Tappen, N 9 mi (R). 128 Avail. 2021 rates: $32. May 01 to Oct 12. (250)320-9305

TELEGRAPH COVE — J1 *North Island*

TELEGRAPH COVE MARINA & RV PARK (RV Park) (Phone Update) Avail: 48 full hkups (30 amps). 2021 rates: $35 to $52.50. (877)835-2683, 1642B Telegraph Cove Road, Telegraph Cove, BC V0N 3J0

TELEGRAPH COVE RESORT-FOREST CAMPGROUND (Campground) (Phone Update) 92 Avail: 13 full hkups, 79 W, 79 E (30 amps). 2021 rates: $34 to $41. May 01 to Oct 15. (800)200-4665, #5 Telegraph Cove Rd, Telegraph Cove, BC V0N 3J0

TELKWA — F1 *Bulkley Valley*

FORT TELKWA RV PARK **Ratings: 7/9★/7** (RV Park) Avail: 36 full hkups (30/50 amps). 2021 rates: $35 to $37. May 01 to Oct 31. (250)846-5012, 11939 Hwy 16 East, Telkwa, BC V0J 2X0

TYHEE LAKE PARK (Public Prov Park) From Jct of PR-16 & Coal Mine Rd, W 0.2 mi on PR-16 to Telkwa High Rd, N 0.2 mi to Cemetery Rd, E 0.1 mi (L). 59 Avail. 2021 rates: $27. May 10 to Sep 18. (250)847-7260

TERRACE — F1 *North Coast Inland*

FERRY ISLAND MUNICIPAL CAMPGROUND (Public) At east edge of town on Hwy 16 E. Avail: 25 E (15/30 amps), Pit toilets. 2021 rates: $20 to $25. May 06 to Sep 30. (250)615-9657

KLEANZA CREEK (Public Prov Park) From town, E 19 km on Hwy 16 (R). 34 Avail: Pit toilets. 2021 rates: $20. May 08 to Sep 06. (250)286-9992

LAKELSE LAKE (Public Prov Park) From Jct of Prov Hwy 37 & Yellowhead 16, S 20 km on Prov Hwy 37 (R). Avail: 50 E. 2021 rates: $28 to $34. May 08 to Sep 08. (250)286-9992

WILD DUCK MOTEL & RV PARK (RV Park) (Phone Update) Avail: 20 full hkups (30/50 amps). 2021 rates: $35 to $40. (250)638-1511, 5504 Hwy 16 W, Terrace, BC V8G 0C6

TETE JAUNE CACHE — G4 *Fraser-Fort George*

MOUNT ROBSON/ROBSON MEADOWS (Public Prov Park) From town: Go 19-1/4 km/12 mi E on Hwy 16. Avail: 22 E (15/50 amps). 2021 rates: $28. May 15 to Sep 30. (800)689-9025

TOAD RIVER — C5 *Liard*

STONE MOUNTAIN PARK (Public Prov Park) On the Alaska Hwy at milepost 387. 28 Avail: Pit toilets. 2021 rates: $20. May 01 to Sep 15. (250)776-7000

TOAD RIVER LODGE & RV PARK (RV Park) (Phone Update) Avail: 23 full hkups (30 amps). 2021 rates: $44. (855)878-8623, Mile 422 Alaska Hwy, Toad River, BC V0C 2X0

TOFINO — K2 *West Island*

BELLA PACIFICA CAMPGROUND (Campground) (Phone Update) 183 Avail: 38 full hkups, 8 W, 27 E (15/30 amps). 2021 rates: $49 to $78. Mar 01 to Nov 04. (250)725-3400, 400 Mackenzie Beach Road, Tofino, BC V0R 2Z0

CRYSTAL COVE BEACH RESORT (RV Park) (Phone Update) Avail: 70 full hkups (30 amps). 2021 rates: $55 to $95. (877)725-4213, 1165 Cedarwood Place, Tofino, BC V0R 2Z0

TOPLEY — F2 *Kitimat-Stikine*

RED BLUFF (Public Prov Park) From town: Go 56 km/34-3/4 mi N on secondary road to Granisle. 34 Avail: Pit toilets. 2021 rates: $20. May 15 to Sep 15. (250)697-6264

TRAIL — K5 *Thompson-Nicola*

TRAIL MUNICIPAL RV PARK (Public) In town on Hwy 3B. 31 Avail. 2021 rates: $25. May 01 to Sep 30. (250)364-1262

TSAWWASSEN — K3 *Greater Vancouver*

TSAWWASSEN RV RESORT **Ratings: 7.5/6/5.5** (RV Resort) 75 Avail: 45 full hkups, 30 W, 30 E (20/30 amps). 2021 rates: $65 to $80. (778)434-5254, 4761 Nulelum Way, Delta, BC V4M 4G9

TUMBLER RIDGE — E6 *Peace River*

DISTRICT OF TUMBLER RIDGE LIONS FLAT BED CREEK CAMPGROUND (Public) From south town limits at jct Monkman Way & Hwy 29: Go 2 km/1-1/4 mi SW on Hwy 29. 45 Avail. 2021 rates: $20. May 01 to Oct 31. (250)242-3123

MONKMAN PARK (Public Prov Park) From town: Go 10 km/6-1/4 mi E on paved local road, then 44-3/4 km/28 mi S on gravel secondary road. 20 Avail: Pit toilets. 2021 rates: $20. May 21 to Nov 15. (250)787-3407

UCLUELET — K2 *West Island*

PACIFIC RIM/GREEN POINT (Public National Park) From town: Go 12-3/4 km/8 mi N on Hwy 4 (Pacific Rim Hwy). 94 Avail. 2021 rates: $27.40 to $32.30. Mar 03 to Oct 08. (877)737-3783

SURF JUNCTION CAMPGROUND (Campground) (Phone Update) 50 Avail: 14 full hkups, 17 W, 17 E (15/30 amps). 2021 rates: $27 to $63. Apr 04 to Oct 01. (250)726-7214, 2650 Tofino-Ucluelet Hwy. , Ucluelet, BC V0R 3A0

UCLUELET CAMPGROUND (Campground) (Phone Update) 123 Avail: 27 full hkups, 10 W, 10 E (15/30 amps). 2021 rates: $38 to $67. (250)726-4355, 260 Seaplane Base Rd, Ucluelet, BC V0R 3A0

VALEMOUNT — G4 *Columbia*

CANOE RIVER CAMPGROUND **Ratings: 4.5/7/6.5** (Campground) 114 Avail: 114 W, 114 E (15/50 amps). 2021 rates: $30 to $35. Apr 01 to Oct 31. (250)566-9112, 6190 Hwy 5 South, Valemount, BC V0E 2Z0

IRVIN'S PARK & CAMPGROUND

good sam park

Ratings: 8/10★/9 (RV Park) From Jct Hwy 5 & 5th Ave, N 0.6kms/0.4 mi on Hwy 5 to Loseth Rd, E 0.2kms/0.1 mi (R). Elev 2600 ft.

SPECTACULAR SCENERY ALASKA BOUND!

Start or end your Canadian Rockies adventure at one of the nicest parks in BC! Enjoy day trips to Jasper, Mount Robson, Rearguard Falls Provincial Park or just relax at camp and take in the endless view! Perfect caravans!

FAC: all weather rds. Avail: 68 gravel, 68 pull-thrus, (32x65), 68 full hkups (30/50 amps), WiFi @ sites, tent sites, dump, laundry, LP gas, fire rings, firewood. Pets OK. Partial handicap access. Big rig sites, eco-friendly. 2021 rates: $39 to $45. Apr 01 to Oct 30. ATM.

(250)566-4781 Lat: 52.84285, Lon: -119.28320
360 Loseth Rd, Valemount, BC V0E 2Z0
irvinsrvpark.com
See ad this page

VALEMOUNT PINES GOLF CLUB & RV PARK **Ratings: 5/9★/8** (Campground) 33 Avail: 3 full hkups, 22 W, 22 E (30/50 amps). 2021 rates: $28 to $35. (250)566-4550, 1110 Hwy N #5, Valemount, BC V0E 2Z0

YELLOWHEAD RV PARK & CAMPGROUND **Ratings: 5/9★/7** (Campground) 44 Avail: 44 W, 44 E (30 amps). 2021 rates: $37 to $45. May 01 to Sep 30. (250)566-0078, 325 North Hwy #5, Valemount, BC V0E 2Z0

Things change ... last year's rates serve as a guideline only.

VANCOUVER — K3 *Lower Mainland*

A SPOTLIGHT Introducing Vancouver's colorful attractions appearing at the front of this province section.

VANCOUVER In BC, see also Aldergrove, Brackendale, Burnaby, Chemainus, Chilliwack, Crofton, Duncan, Gibsons, Ladysmith, Langley, Lindell Beach, Nanaimo, Sechelt, Surrey, Tsawwassen, Victoria & West Vancouver. In WA, see also Bellingham, Birch Bay, Ferndale & Lynden.

BURNABY CARIBOO RV PARK

good sam park **Ratings: 9.5/10★/9.5** (RV Park) From E city limits: Go 9 km/5-1/2 mi E on Hwy 1 (exit 37), then 0.4 km/1/4 mi NE on exit ramp, then 0.4 km/ 1/4 mi N on Gaglardi Way, then 100 m/100 yds E on S Cariboo Rd, then 0.4 km/1/4 mi N on Stormont Ave/N Cariboo Rd, then 200 m/200 yds SE on Cariboo Pl (E). **FAC:** paved rds. Avail: 212 paved, patios, back-ins (30x45), 212 full hkups (30 amps), cable, WiFi @ sites, tent sites, dump, laundry, groc. **REC:** heated pool, hot tub, Brunette River: fishing, boating nearby, playground. Pets OK. Partial handicap access, eco-friendly. 2021 rates: $62 to $73. ATM.
(604)420-1722 Lat: 49.24818, Lon: -122.9141
8765 Cariboo Place, Burnaby, BC V3N 4T2
bcrv.com
See primary listing at Burnaby and ad this page, 1052, 1056

CAPILANO RIVER RV PARK

good sam park **Ratings: 9.5/9.5★/8** (RV Park) From E city limits: Go 8.25mi/13.2kms on TCH 1 to Capilano Rd then 1mi/1.6 kms S to Welch St (stay in left lane), then .5 mi/ .8kms W to Bridge Rd, then 100ft/30m N to Tomahawk Ave (L). **FAC:** paved rds. (178 spaces). 158 Avail: 70 paved, 88 all weather, 1 pull-thrus, (30x60), back-ins (24x45), 92 full hkups, 66 W, 66 E (15/30 amps), seasonal sites, WiFi @ sites, tent sites, dump, laundry, controlled access. **REC:** heated pool, hot tub, Capilano River: boating nearby, playground. Pet restrict (Q). Partial handicap access, eco-friendly. 2021 rates: $54 to $85.
(604)987-4722 Lat: 49.32421, Lon: -123.13213
295 Tomahawk Ave, West Vancouver, BC V7P 1C5
www.capilanoriverrvpark.com
See primary listing at West Vancouver and ad page 1055

VANDERHOOF — F2 *Bulkley*

SOWCHEA BAY PARK (Public Prov Park) From Hwy 27: Go 4 km/2-1/2 mi W of Paaren Beach, Stuart Lake on secondary road. 30 Avail: Pit toilets. 2021 rates: $20. May 15 to Sep 05. (250)964-3489

VERNON — J4 *North Okanagan*

ELLISON (Public Prov Park) From town, SW 10 mi on Okanagan Landing Rd (R). 71 Avail. 2021 rates: $32. Jun 01 to Sep 06. (250)548-0076

SILVER STAR RV PARK **Ratings: 6/9.5★/7.5** (RV Park) 63 Avail: 42 full hkups, 21 W, 21 E (30/50 amps). 2021 rates: $50 to $60. (250)542-2808, 6310 Stickle Rd, Vernon, BC V1B 3V1

SWAN LAKE RV PARK & CAMPGROUND **Ratings: 5.5/7.5★/7** (Campground) Avail: 19 full hkups (15/30 amps). 2021 rates: $52.50 to $56. (250)545-2300, 7235 Old Kamloops Rd, Vernon, BC V1H 1W6

SWAN LAKE RV RESORT **Ratings: 10/9/9.5** (Membership Park) Avail: 50 full hkups (30/50 amps). 2021 rates: $56.70 to $70.35. Mar 15 to Oct 31. (250)558-1116, 8000 Highland Rd, Vernon, BC V1B 3W5

VICTORIA — K3 *Metchosin*

VICTORIA See also Sooke, BC; Port Angeles, WA.

FORT VICTORIA RV PARK **Ratings: 7/9.5★/7** (RV Park) 160 Avail: 150 full hkups, 10 W, 10 E (30/50 amps). 2021 rates: $65. (250)479-8112, 129 Burnett Road, Victoria, BC V9B 4P6

GOLDSTREAM PARK (Public Prov Park) From Jct of Hwy 1 & Sooke Lake Rd, N 0.4 mi on Sooke Lake Rd to Golden Gate Rd, W 0.1 mi (R). 172 Avail. 2021 rates: $13 to $35. (250)478-9414

OCEANSIDE RV RESORT - PARKBRIDGE **Ratings: 8.5/10★/10** (RV Park) Avail: 68 full hkups (30/50 amps). 2021 rates: $48 to $68. (250)544-0508, 3000 Stautw Rd, Saanichton, BC V8M 2K5

PEDDER BAY RV RESORT & MARINA **Ratings: 8/9/10** (RV Park) Avail: 68 full hkups (30/50 amps). 2021 rates: $45 to $79. (250)478-1771, 925 Pedder Bay Dr, Victoria, BC V9C 4H1

SALISH SEASIDE RV HAVEN Ratings: 7/9★/8 (RV Park) Avail: 36 full hkups (30/50 amps). 2021 rates: $59 to $125. (250)590-5995, 445 Head St, Victoria, BC V9A 5S1

WEIR'S BEACH RV RESORT **Ratings: 8.5/8.5★/9.5** (RV Park) Avail: 25 full hkups (30/50 amps). 2021 rates: $55 to $75. (866)478-6888, 5191 William Head Rd, Victoria, BC V9C 4H5

WASA — J6 *Columbia-Shuswap*

WASA LAKE PARK (Public Prov Park) From Jct of Hwy 93/95 & Hwy 3/93, N 25 mi on Hwy 93/95 (R). 104 Avail. 2021 rates: $30. May 01 to Sep 30. (250)422-3003

WELLS — G3 *Bulkley-Nechako*

CARIBOO JOY RV PARK (RV Park) (Phone Update) 30 Avail: 30 W, 30 E (20 amps). 2021 rates: $45 to $55. May 18 to Sep 20. (888)996-4653, 12566 Hwy 26, Barkerville, BC V0K 1B0

NUGGET HILLS RV PARK (Campground) (Phone Update) 22 Avail: 10 full hkups, 5 W, 2 E (15/30 amps). 2021 rates: $35 to $45. May 20 to Oct 15. (250)994-2333, 3895 Ski Hill Rd, Barkerville, BC V0K 1B0

WEST VANCOUVER — K3 *Mount Waddington*

CAPILANO RIVER RV PARK

good sam park **Ratings: 9.5/9.5★/8** (RV Park) N-bnd/ S-bnd: From Jct of Hwy 1 & Capilano Rd (Exit 14), S 1 mi on Capilano Rd to Welch St (stay in left lane), W 0.8km/0.5mi on Welch St to Bridge Rd, N 30m/100 ft to Tomahawk Ave (L). **FAC:** paved rds. (178 spaces). 158 Avail: 70 paved, 88 all weather, 1 pull-thrus, (30x60), back-ins (24x45), 92 full hkups, 66 W, 66 E (15/30 amps), seasonal sites, WiFi @ sites, tent sites, dump, laundry, LP gas, controlled access. **REC:** heated pool, hot tub, Capilano River: boating nearby, playground. Pet restrict (Q). Partial handicap access, eco-friendly. 2021 rates: $64 to $85. ATM.
(604)987-4722 Lat: 49.32421, Lon: -123.13213
295 Tomahawk Ave, West Vancouver, BC V7P 1C5
www.capilanoriverrvpark.com
See ad page 1055

WESTBANK — J4 *Central Okanagan*

WEST EAGLE CAMPGROUND **Ratings: 4.5/9★/6.5** (Campground) 50 Avail: 36 full hkups, 14 W, 14 E (30 amps). 2021 rates: $40 to $50. May 01 to Sep 30. (250)768-7426, 2325 Old Okanagan Hwy, Westbank, BC V4T 1V3

WESTBRIDGE — K4 *Thompson-Nicola*

JOHNSTONE CREEK (Public Prov Park) From town, E 7 mi on Hwy 3 (R). 16 Avail: Pit toilets. 2021 rates: $18. May 13 to Sep 20. (250)548-9025

WHALETOWN — J2 *Coastal*

GORGE HARBOUR MARINA RESORT (RV Resort) (Phone Update) 30 Avail: 6 full hkups, 24 W, 24 E (30 amps). 2021 rates: $40 to $50.50. (250)935-6433, 1374 Hunt Rd, Whaletown, BC V0P 1Z0

WHISTLER — J3 *Home Sound*

RIVERSIDE RESORT - PARKBRIDGE **Ratings: 7.5/10★/9** (RV Park) 119 Avail: 66 full hkups, 53 W, 53 E (30 amps). 2021 rates: $70 to $80. (604)905-5533, 8018 Mons Rd, Whistler, BC V0N 1B8

WHISTLER RV PARK & CAMPGROUND **Ratings: 5.5/8.5/8.5** (RV Park) Avail: 100 full hkups (30/50 amps). 2021 rates: $60 to $65. (604)905-2523, 55 Hwy 99, Whistler, BC V0N 1B1

WILLIAMS LAKE — H3 *Cariboo*

WILLIAMS LAKE STAMPEDE CAMPGROUND **Ratings: 5.5/9★/7** (Campground) Avail: 58 full hkups (30/50 amps). 2021 rates: $34 to $40. (250)398-6718, 800 South McKenzie Ave, Williams Lake, BC V2G 2V2

YAHK — K6 *Columbia-Shuswap*

YAHK PARK (Public Prov Park) From Jct of SR-95 & SR-3, N 3 mi on SR-95/3 (R). 26 Avail: Pit toilets. 2021 rates: $21. May 13 to Sep 30. (250)422-3003

Save 10% at Good Sam Parks 365 days a year with no blackout dates!!

Laundry & dishwasher detergent liquids contain up to 80 percent water. It costs energy and packaging to bring this water to the consumer. When there is a choice - choose dry powders.

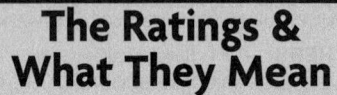

The Ratings & What They Mean

Turn to "Understanding the Rating System" section at the front of this Guide to get information on how we rate and inspect parks with our handy three number system!

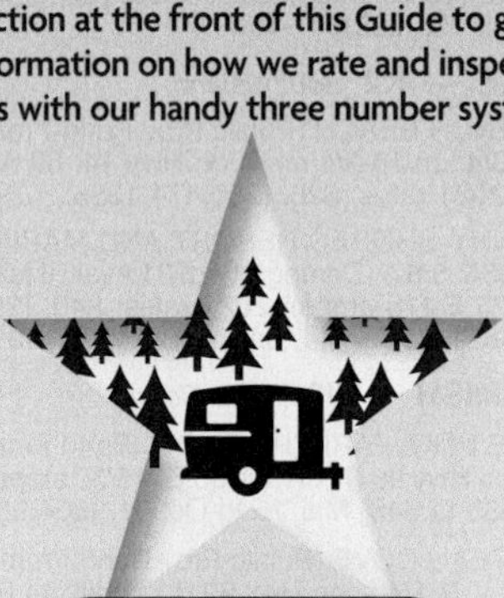

Rated 10/10★/10

The **FIRST NUMBER** represents Development of Facilities

The **SECOND NUMBER** represents Cleanliness and Physical Characteristics of Restrooms and Showers (plus, a Star is awarded to parks who receive maximum points for cleanliness!)

The **THIRD NUMBER** represents Visual Appearance/Environmental Quality

DID YOU KNOW ?
Set on the west shores of Lake Winnipeg, Gimli possesses the largest Icelandic community outside of Iceland.
YOU ARE HERE
Manitoba
Getty Images/iStockphoto

The Canadian plains stretch on endlessly, with landscapes that range from rugged hills to sweeping grasslands. Southern Manitoba is home to the large city of Winnipeg; the province is a frontier that's prime for adventures.

Wonders of Winnipeg

Winnipeg sits at the confluence of the Red and Assiniboine Rivers, allowing it to assume the natural role as the region's cultural and political capital. Museums and monuments honor the influences of the indigenous Metis people and, later, European settlers. Creativity thrives in Royal Winnipeg Ballet, the Royal Manitoba Theatre Centre and the Winnipeg Art Gallery. World-class museums detail local history and geology.

So Many City Parks

Manitoba has more than 100 parks, giving visitors a wide variety of recreation opportunities. From the easily accessible Birds Hill Provincial Park, just north of Winnipeg, to the rugged wilderness of Atikaki Wilderness Provincial Park, there's something for every visitor.

Back to the Beach

North of town, several lakeshores serve as beaches for summer vacationers. For a unique taste of the region's Icelandic history, visit the small town of Gimli. The annual Icelandic Festival of Manitoba draws visitors to the town each August to celebrate Scandinavian culture.

Haul 'em In

With more than 100,000 lakes and 30 species of fish, it's no wonder that anglers dream of casting their lines in Manitoba's waters. From December to March, ice fishermen can catch gargantuan greenback walleyes in Lake Manitoba. Other popular walleye destinations include Red River and Cranberry Portage. In the northern town of Churchill, polar bear spotting is a popular attraction.

Manitoba Imperial Cookie

These sweet treats will rule your appetite. The cookie consists of two pieces of shortbread separated by raspberry filling and coated with a white sugar glaze. As a final touch, a dollop of raspberry filling is placed on top. These cookies taste as good as they look, and coffee shops, restaurants and confectioners around town keep these in supply for diners with a sweet tooth.

VISITOR CENTER

TIME ZONE
Central Standard

ROAD & HIGHWAY INFORMATION
866-626-4862
manitoba511.ca

FISHING & HUNTING INFORMATION
800-214-6497
huntfishmanitoba.ca/go-fishing

BOATING INFORMATION
800-267-6687
tc.gc.ca/marinesafety

NATIONAL PARKS
pc.gc.ca/en/pn-np

PROVINCIAL PARKS
manitobaparks.com

TOURISM INFORMATION
Travel Manitoba
800-665-0040
travelmanitoba.com

TOP TOURISM ATTRACTIONS
1) Churchill
2) Canadian Museum for Human Rights
3) Assiniboine Park Zoo

MAJOR CITIES
Winnipeg (capital), Brandon, Steinbach, Portage la Prairie, Thompson

good sam park Featured Good Sam Parks MANITOBA

When you stay with Good Sam, you can expect the highest degree of cleanliness and friendliness, and better yet, you get **10% off** overnight campground fees.

If you're not already a Good Sam member you can purchase your membership at one of these locations:

PORTAGE LA PRAIRIE
Miller's Camping Resort

WINNIPEG
Arrowhead RV Park

Getty Images/iStockphoto

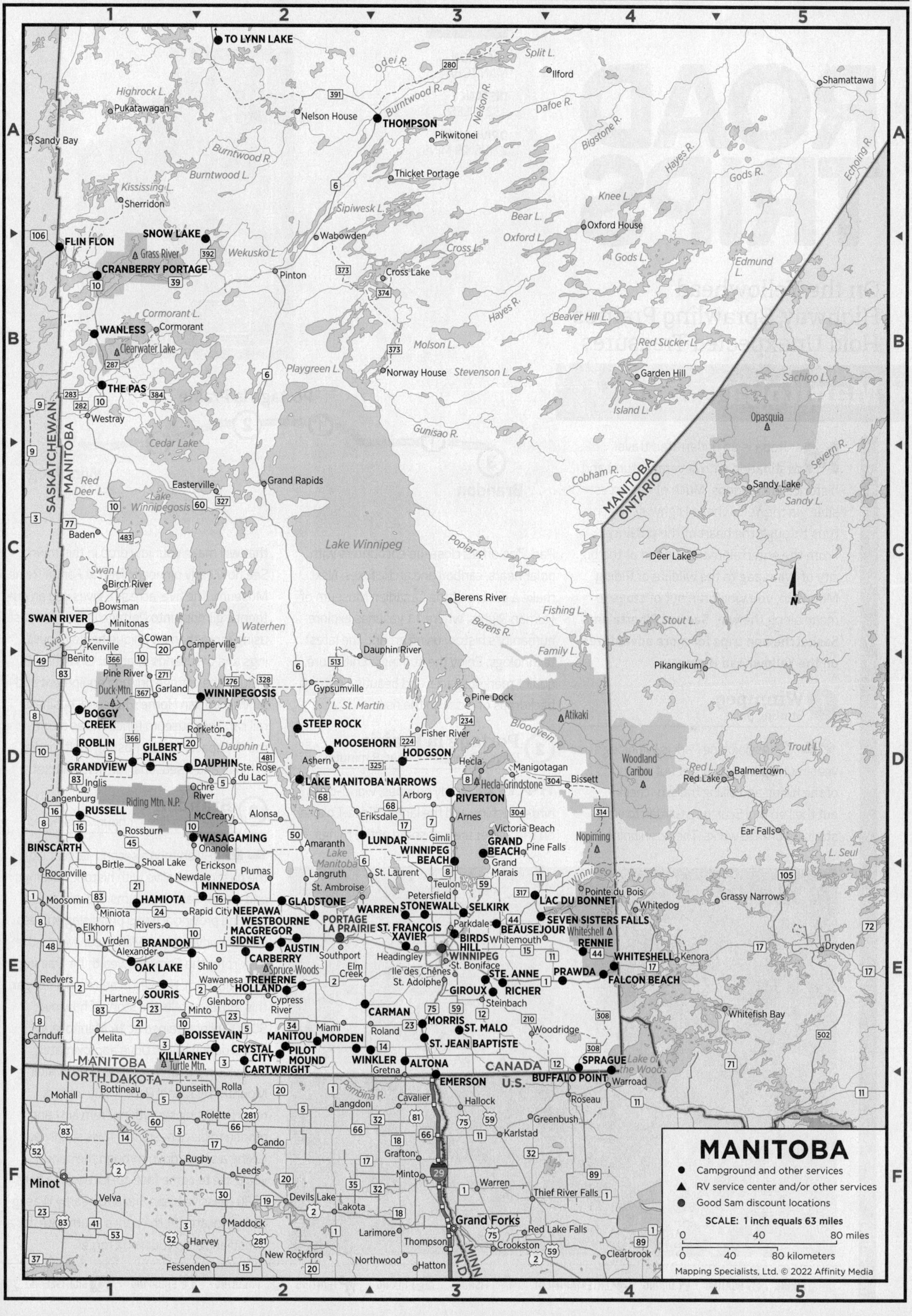
MB
TO LYNN LAKE
THOMPSON
Nelson House
Pikwitonei
Thicket Portage
Ilford
Shamattawa
Pukatawagan
Sandy Bay
Sherridon
FLIN FLON
SNOW LAKE
Grass River
CRANBERRY PORTAGE
Wabowden
Pinton
Cross Lake
Oxford House
WANLESS
Cormorant
Clearwater Lake
THE PAS
Westray
Norway House
Garden Hill
Opasquia
Grand Rapids
Easterville
Sandy Lake
Baden
Deer Lake
Lake Winnipeg
Birch River
Berens River
Bowsman
SWAN RIVER
Minitonas
Kenville
Cowan
Camperville
Benito
Dauphin River
Pikangikum
Pine River
Garland
Duck Mtn.
WINNIPEGOSIS
BOGGY CREEK
Gypsumville
Pine Dock
STEEP ROCK
Atikaki
Rorketon
Fisher River
ROBLIN
GILBERT PLAINS
GRANDVIEW
DAUPHIN
MOOSEHORN
HODGSON
Hecla
Manigotagan
Woodland Caribou
Balmertown
Red Lake
Ste. Rose du Lac
Inglis
LAKE MANITOBA NARROWS
Hecla-Grindstone
Bissett
Langenburg
Riding Mtn. N.P.
Ochre River
Arborg
RIVERTON
RUSSELL
McCreary
Alonsa
Eriksdale
Arnes
Rossburn
WASAGAMING
LUNDAR
Gimli
Victoria Beach
Nopiming
Ear Falls
BINSCARTH
Onanole
Amaranth
WINNIPEG BEACH
GRAND BEACH
Pine Falls
Birtle
Shoal Lake
Erickson
Plumas
Langruth
St. Laurent
Grand Marais
Rocanville
Newdale
St. Ambroise
Teulon
MINNEDOSA
Petersfield
Pointe du Bois
Moosomin
HAMIOTA
NEEPAWA
GLADSTONE
STONEWALL
SELKIRK
LAC DU BONNET
Whitedog
Grassy Narrows
Miniota
Rapid City
WESTBOURNE
WARREN
PORTAGE LA PRAIRIE
SEVEN SISTERS FALLS
Elkhorn
Rivers
MACGREGOR
ST. FRANÇOIS XAVIER
Parkdale
BEAUSEJOUR
Whiteshell
Virden
BRANDON
SIDNEY
BIRDS HILL
Whitemouth
Alexander
AUSTIN
Southport
Headingley
WINNIPEG
RENNIE
Dryden
OAK LAKE
CARBERRY
St. Boniface
WHITESHELL
Kenora
Shilo
Spruce Woods
Elm Creek
Ile des Chênes
Redvers
Wawanesa
TREHERNE
St. Adolphe
STE. ANNE
PRAWDA
FALCON BEACH
SOURIS
HOLLAND
GIROUX
RICHER
Hartney
Glenboro
Cypress River
Steinbach
Minto
CARMAN
Whitefish Bay
Carnduff
Melita
Miami
MORRIS
ST. MALO
Woodridge
BOISSEVAIN
MANITOU
MORDEN
Roland
ST. JEAN BAPTISTE
KILLARNEY
CRYSTAL CITY
PILOT MOUND
WINKLER
SPRAGUE
Turtle Mtn.
CARTWRIGHT
Gretna
ALTONA
Lake of the Woods
EMERSON
BUFFALO POINT
Warroad
MANITOBA
NORTH DAKOTA
CANADA
U.S.
SASKATCHEWAN
ONTARIO
Bottineau
Dunseith
Rolla
Mohall
Langdon
Cavalier
Hallock
Roseau
Rolette
Greenbush
Karlstad
Cando
Rugby
Grafton
Leeds
Minto
Minot
Warren
Thief River Falls
Velva
Devils Lake
Lakota
Grand Forks
Maddock
Larimore
Red Lake Falls
Harvey
Thompson
Crookston
New Rockford
Northwood
Clearbrook
Fessenden
Hatton
MINN
N.D.
MANITOBA
Campground and other services
RV service center and/or other services
Good Sam discount locations
SCALE: 1 inch equals 63 miles
0 40 80 miles
0 40 80 kilometers
Mapping Specialists, Ltd. © 2022 Affinity Media

ROAD TRIPS

On the Yellowhead Highway, Sprawling Prairies Hold Unexpected Treasures

Manitoba

LOCATION
MANITOBA

DISTANCE
132 MILES

DRIVE TIME
2 HRS 29 MINS

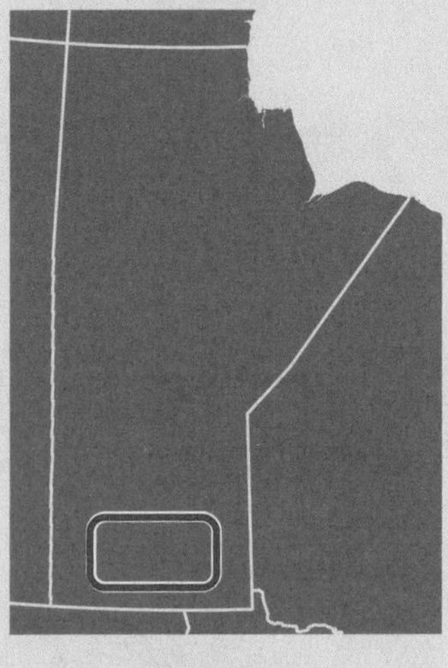

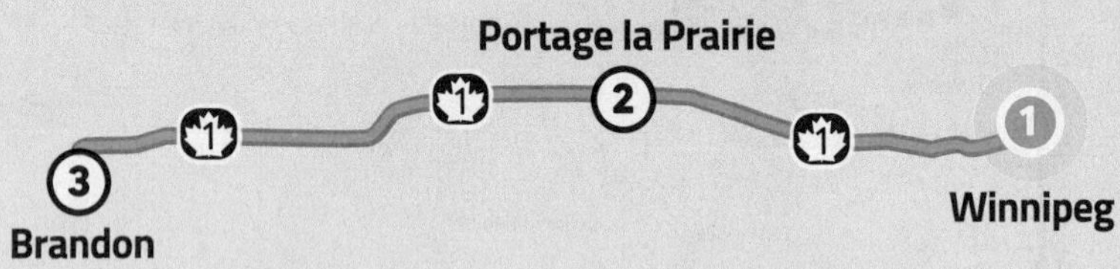

Manitoba is an underrated travel destination with several natural and historical attractions. Much of it is accessible via the Yellowhead Highway, which runs through the heart of the province. From the entertainment and fun of the big city of Winnipeg to the wildlife of Riding Mountain, you won't run out of stops to make along the way. **See our Alberta and Saskatchewan trips for more adventures on the Yellowhead Highway.**

1 Winnipeg
Starting point

Assiniboine Park is Winnipeg's year-round playground. Set out on one of the hiking and biking trails, or check out the Leo Mol Sculpture Garden to view stunning bronze works. The Assiniboine Park Zoo offers close-up encounters with polar bears, caribou and arctic foxes. Next, make a pitstop at the Canadian Museum of Human Rights, where 11 galleries explore humanity's history using art and the latest technology. Enjoy the striking architecture, quaint market spaces and beautiful natural backdrops of a city on the rise.

2 Portage la Prairie
Drive 53 miles ▪ 1 hour, 8 minutes

Sandy beaches, world-class bird-watching and the largest Coca-Cola can on the planet are just some of the things that will make your jaw drop in this town. See how early pioneers lived at Fort la Reine Museum. The five-acre site gives you an authentic glimpse into Portage la Prairie's past using more than 20 unique heritage buildings and thousands of artifacts. Highlights include the vintage printing equipment and Sir William van Horne's personal business rail car. The museum functions as a community space, too, by hosting multimedia exhibits and a seasonal farmers' market.

3 Brandon
Drive 79 miles ▪ 1 hour, 21 minutes

In Manitoba's second-largest city, the past comes alive with historic buildings and world-class museums. Travelers also will find provincial parks promising endless outdoor adventures. Make your way to the airport for the Commonwealth Air Training Plan Museum. Housed in an original hangar, this museum tells the story of how over 50,000 pilots trained at 14 Manitoba air bases during WWII. Drive approximately 60 miles north and you'll wind up in Riding Mountain National Park. Many visitors report spotting everything from lynx and moose to black bears and owls simply by taking a scenic drive through the park. If you'd like to come face-to-face with a herd of 30 massive bison, head to nearby Wasagaming, located at the park's south gate, for a Canadian safari you won't forget.

Getty Images/iStockphoto

BIKING · BOATING · DINING · ENTERTAINMENT · FISHING · HIKING · HUNTING · PADDLING · SHOPPING · SIGHTSEEING

Manitoba SPOTLIGHTS

Canada's Keystone Province is the Gateway to the Plains

Manitoba doesn't fool around when it comes to fun. See polar bears in the north, watch bison along the Yellowhead Highway and walk the footsteps of French fur traders in the capital city. See where history was made at the meeting of the Red and Assiniboine Rivers.

THE WINNIPEG JETS HOCKEY TEAM ARE TOP NHL MERCH SELLERS.

The Canadian Museum for Human Rights (right) stands out against the Winnipeg skyline.

Getty Images/iStockphoto

Grand Beach

Hit the shore in Manitoba's Grand Beach, where sand, sun and water mix nicely. Located just one hour north of Winnipeg on Highway 59, the area has enjoyed the status as one of the favorite destinations of the Keystone Province. Sitting on the northern edge of the small town of Grand Marais, Grand Beach boasts almost two miles broad, sandy beaches on the gentle shores of Lake Winnipeg.

Manitoba Boardwalk

Ready to cruise the shore? A boardwalk at the west end of the beach offers food and shopping. Bring a basket and pick the ample Saskatoon, chokecherry and blueberries that grow around the beach.

Riding Mountain

Approximately 25 miles west of Lake Manitoba lies Riding Mountain National Park. A wealth of wildlife species inhabit its lush boreal forests, grasslands, marshes and wetlands. The park is home to lynx, moose, black bears and owls.

Bison on the Broad Planes

Gigantic bison have a place to graze and ramble here. You'll find a herd of 30 of the massive mammals at nearby Wasagaming, located at the park's south gate, for a Canadian safari you won't forget. The provincial parks of Rivers, Spruce Wood, Turtle Mountain and William Lake can be easily accessed from Brandon.

Winnipeg

At the confluence of the Red and Assiniboine Rivers, the eighth-largest city in Canada pulses with a unique blend of European and First Nation cultures. Over the centuries, Winnipeg evolved from a major trading center to a vital hub for recreation and industry. Visitors can enjoy its urban pleasures or use it as a springboard for trips to the parks around the city. Visit the Canadian Museum for Human Rights, dedicated to people's struggles and triumphs around the world.

Crossing to Cool Sights

Take a trip to a district that traces its roots to early French fur traders. The Esplanade Riel Pedestrian Bridge takes visitors to St. Boniface, known as Winnipeg's French Quarter. Founded in 1818 by French fur traders, St. Boniface is the largest French-speaking community west of the Great Lakes. Lovers of big mammals should visit the northern town of Churchill in the fall, when polar bears pass through town during their migration.

FOR MORE INFORMATION

Travel Manitoba, 800-665-0040, www.travelmanitoba.com

Grand Beach Tourism, www.grandbeachtourism.com

Riding Mountain National Park, www.pc.gc.ca/en/pn-np/mb/riding

Tourism Winnipeg, 855-PEG-CITY, www.tourismwinnipeg.com

LOCAL FAVORITE

Sugar-Rubbed Steak

Add some sweet flavor to your steaks during your campout on the sprawling Canadian prairie.
Recipe by Gary and Pam Parker.

INGREDIENTS

- ☐ 1 New York or ribeye steak
- ☐ 3 tbsp sugar
- ☐ 1 tbsp salt (sea salt)
- ☐ 1 tbsp garlic powder

DIRECTIONS

Remove from the fridge and turn over. Make sure not to knock any of the rub off the steak. Apply rub on the other side. Let it sit out for thirty minutes.
While the steak is waiting, light your barbecue (charcoal works best). Set the coals three to four inches below the grill. Make sure the grill is clean and sprayed with PAM or some sort of nonstick spray. Carefully put the steak on the grill close to the coals for 2 minutes. Turn the steak over (leaving the coals close to the grill, for another 2 minutes). Lower the coals and cook for 4 minutes for medium rare.

Manitoba

ALTONA — E3 *Central*

ALTONA CENTENNIAL PARK (Public) From town, W 1 mi on 10th Ave (L). 20 Avail: 10 W, 10 E (30/50 amps). 2021 rates: $25. May 22 to Oct 31. (204)324-9005

AUSTIN — E2 *North Central*

MANITOBA AGRICULTURAL MUSEUM THREE CREEKS CAMPGROUND (Campground) (Phone Update) Avail: 62 E (30 amps). 2021 rates: $25 to $28.57. May 12 to Sep 30. (204)637-2354, Site 62105 Hwy 34, Austin, MB R0H 0C0

BEAUSEJOUR — E3 *Eastern*

GREAT WOODS PARK **Ratings: 6/7/8.5** (Campground) 150 Avail: 150 W, 150 E (30 amps). 2021 rates: $28 to $35. May 15 to Oct 01. (204)268-2814, #73 Great Woods Park Rd, Beausejour, MB R0E 0C0

BINSCARTH — D1 *Parkland*

BINSCARTH PARK & POOL (Public) From Jct of Hwy 41 & 16 (Yellowhead), N 0.4 mi on Hwy 16 (R). 45 Avail: 9 full hkups, 36 W, 36 E (30/50 amps). 2021 rates: $15 to $45. May 16 to Oct 13. (204)532-2353

BIRDS HILL — E3 *Interlake*

BIRDS HILL PARK (Public Prov Park) From Town, NE 12 mi on Hwy 59 (R). 478 Avail: 47 full hkups, 174 E (15/30 amps). 2021 rates: $17.85 to $28.35. May 01 to Oct 15. (888)482-2267

BOGGY CREEK — D1 *Division No 16*

DUCK MOUNTAIN/WELLMAN LAKE CAMPGROUND (Public Prov Park) From Jct of Hwy 10 & Secondary Hwy 366, S 15.5 mi on Secondary Rd 366 (E). 86 Avail: 34 W, 67 E (30 amps). 2021 rates: $16.80 to $28.35. May 01 to Oct 01. (888)482-2267

BOISSEVAIN — E1 *Western*

BOISSEVAIN LIONS CAMPGROUND (Public) From Jct of Hwy 10 & P Rd 348 exit, W 0.05 mi on Hwy 10 (L). 34 Avail: 22 full hkups, 12 W, 12 E (15/30 amps). 2021 rates: $15 to $18. May 01 to Aug 30. (204)534-6250

INTERNATIONAL PEACE GARDEN CAMPGROUND (Public) From Jct of Hwy 10 & secondary Rd 443, S 16 mi on Hwy 10 (R). 36 Avail: 20 W, 20 E (15/30 amps). 2021 rates: $20 to $30. May 25 to Sep 30. (888)432-6733

TURTLE MOUNTAIN/ADAM LAKE CAMPGROUND (Public Prov Park) From Jct of Hwy 10 & Secondary Hwy 443, S 15 mi on Hwy 10 (R). 105 Avail: 36 W, 81 E (30 amps). 2021 rates: $16.80 to $28.35. May 01 to Sep 01. (888)482-2267

TURTLE MOUNTAIN/MAX LAKE CAMPGROUND (Public Prov Park) From jct Hwy 10 & Hwy 3: Go 8 km/5 mi W on Hwy 3, then 11-1/4 km/7 mi S. 24 Avail. 2021 rates: $16.80. May 15 to Sep 15. (204)534-2578

WILLIAM LAKE PARK (Public Prov Park) From Jct of Hwy 10 & Secondary Rd 443, S 8 mi on Hwy 10 to Sec Hwy 341, E 4 mi to Lake William Rd, S 5 mi (E). 51 Avail. 2021 rates: $21 to $28.35. May 01 to Sep 15. (888)482-2267

BRANDON — E2 *Brandon*

BRY-MAR RV PARK AND CAMPGROUND **Ratings: 7.5/8.5★/8.5** (Campground) Avail: 51 full hkups (30 amps). 2021 rates: $35. May 01 to Oct 01. (204)573-7067, Site 520 Road 102 (Hwy 1), Douglas, MB R7A 5Y5

MEADOWLARK CAMPGROUND **Ratings: 6.5/9.5★/8** (Campground) 70 Avail: 60 full hkups, 10 W, 10 E (30/50 amps). 2021 rates: $25 to $40. Apr 15 to Oct 15. (800)363-6434, 1629 Middleton Avenue, Brandon, MB R7C 0C1

RIVERS PARK (Public Prov Park) From Jct of Hwy 25 & Hwy 250, N .5 mi on Hwy 250 to Memorial Dr. E 1.6 mi (E). 51 Avail: 20 full hkups, 18 E (30 amps). 2021 rates: $11.55 to $28.35. May 11 to Sep 01. (888)482-2267

TURTLE CROSSING **Ratings: 5.5/8/7.5** (Campground) 81 Avail: 48 full hkups, 23 W, 23 E (30/50 amps). 2021 rates: $29 to $35. (204)571-0750, 4100 Grand Valley Rd, Brandon, MB R7A 5Y3

BUFFALO POINT — E4 *Division No 1*

BUFFALO POINT RESORT **Ratings: 7.5/7.5/7.5** (Campground) 80 Avail: 11 full hkups, 14 W, 35 E (30 amps). 2021 rates: $30 to $34. May 01 to Sep 30. (204)437-2402, 1 Marina Road, Buffalo Point, MB R0A 2W0

MOOSE LAKE PARK (Public Prov Park) From town: Go 32 km/20 mi NE on Hwy 308 (16 km/10 mi paved, 16 km/10 mi gravel). Avail: 24 E (15 amps). 2021 rates: $11.55 to $28.35. May 01 to Sep 01. (888)482-2267

CARBERRY — E2 *Southwest*

FOREST HILLS CABIN RENTALS & RV PARK **Ratings: 5/9.5★/9** (Campground) 41 Avail: 41 W, 41 E (30/50 amps). 2021 rates: $30. May 01 to Oct 30. (204)834-2421, NE 19-9-14 W, Carberry, MB R0K 0H0

SPRUCE WOODS/KICHE MANITOU (Public Prov Park) From Jct of Hwys 2 & 5, N 6 mi on Hwy 5 (R). Avail: 80 E (30 amps). 2021 rates: $15.75 to $28.35. May 01 to Sep 15. (204)827-2458

CARMAN — E2 *Pembina Valley*

KING'S PARK

(Public) From jct Hwys 13, Hwy 3 & Secondary Hwy 245: Go 3/4 km/1/2 mi W on Hwy 245. **FAC:** paved rds. Avail: 38 paved, 38 E (15/30 amps), tent sites, dump, fire rings, firewood. **REC:** pool, playground. Pets OK. 2021 rates: $15 to $25. May 20 to Sep 01. no cc.
(204)745-2684 Lat: 49.504971, Lon: -98.011384
Kings Park Road, Carman, MB R0G 0J0
www.carmandufferinrecreation.com

CARTWRIGHT — E2 *Western*

HERITAGE PARK (Public) From Jct of Hwys 5 & 3, W 0.25 mi on Hwy 3 (L). Avail: 10 E (30 amps). 2021 rates: $15. May 01 to Sep 30. (204)529-2363

CRANBERRY PORTAGE — B1 *Northern*

CRANBERRY PORTAGE CAMPGROUND (Public) From Jct of Prov Hwy 10 & Portage Rd, W 0.5 mi on Portage Rd (L). 10 Avail: (20/30 amps). 2021 rates: $10 to $20. May 15 to Sep 15. (204)472-3219

GRASS RIVER/REED LAKE (Public Prov Park) From Jct of Hwy 10 & Hwy 39, E 38 mi on Hwy 39 (L). 48 Avail: Pit toilets. 2021 rates: $16.80 to $28.35. May 01 to Sep 15. (888)482-2267

MCKENZIE'S RV PARK & CAMPROUND (Campground) (Phone Update) Avail: 11 full hkups (15 amps). 2021 rates: $30. May 24 to Sep 15. (204)687-0278, 126 McLean St, Cranberry Portage, MB R0B 0H0

VIKING LODGE (Campground) (Phone Update) Avail: 18 full hkups (30 amps). 2021 rates: $29. May 15 to Sep 30. (204)472-3337, 351 Public Rd SE, Cranberry Portage, MB R0B 0H0

Explore America's Top RV Destinations! Turn to the Spotlight articles in our State and Province sections to learn more.

CRYSTAL CITY — E2 *Division No 4*

CRYSTAL CITY CAMPGROUND (Public) From jct Hwy 3 & S Railway Ave: Go 1 km/1/2 mi W on S Railway Ave (R). 12 Avail: 7 full hkups, 5 W, 5 E (15/50 amps). 2021 rates: $20. May 01 to Sep 15. (204)873-2591

DAUPHIN — D1 *Parkland*

RAINBOW BEACH CAMPGROUND (Public Prov Park) From Town, E 11 mi on Hwy 20 (L). Avail: 29 E (30 amps). 2021 rates: $11.55 to $28.35. May 01 to Sep 30. (888)482-2267

VERMILLION PARK CAMPGROUND (Public) From Jct of Hwy 5 (2nd St) & 2nd Ave (in town), W 0.1 mi on 2nd Ave (R). 191 Avail: 17 full hkups, 40 W, 60 E (30/50 amps). 2021 rates: $15 to $35. May 15 to Sep 15. (204)622-3150

EMERSON — E3 *South Central*

EMERSON PARK (Public) From jct Hwy 75 & I-29: Go E to Banks St. 22 Avail: 12 W, 12 E Pit toilets. 2021 rates: $10 to $15. May 15 to Oct 15. (204)373-2002

FALCON BEACH — E4 *Eastern*

WHITESHELL PARK/FALCON BEACH (Public Prov Park) From Town, S 0.6 mi on Hwy 1 (R). 154 Avail: 75 W, 75 S, 154 E (30/50 amps). 2021 rates: $19.95 to $28.35. May 01 to Oct 01. (888)482-2267

WHITESHELL PARK/LAKESHORE (Public Prov Park) From Town, S 0.6 mi on Hwy 1 (R). 153 Avail: 33 W, 83 E (15/30 amps). 2021 rates: $17.85 to $28.35. May 01 to Sep 30. (888)482-2267

FLIN FLON — B1 *Northern*

BAKER'S NARROWS PARK (Public Prov Park) From the Jct of Hwy 10 & Bakers Narrows (L). Avail: 71 E (30 amps). 2021 rates: $18.90 to $28.35. May 16 to Sep 01. (888)482-2267

FLIN FLON TOURIST PARK (Public) On Hwy 10A at E edge of town (R). Avail: 24 E (30 amps). 2021 rates: $9 to $11. May 01 to Sep 15. (204)687-7674

GILBERT PLAINS — D1 *Parklands*

GILBERT PLAINS CENTENNIAL PARK (Public) From jct Hwy 5 & Main St: Go 2 blocks N, then 2 blocks W on Gordon Ave W. 34 Avail: 34 W, 34 E. 2021 rates: $30. (204)548-2063

GIROUX — E3 *Southeast*

RIDGEWOOD SOUTH GOLF COURSE & CAMPGROUND (Campground) (Phone Update) Avail: 15 full hkups (30/50 amps). 2021 rates: $33 to $38. May 01 to Oct 10. (204)326-5722, Hwy 311, Giroux, MB R5G 1R7

GLADSTONE — E2 *Central*

WILLIAMS PARK (Public) From Jct of SR-16 & CR-460, N 1 mi on CR-460 (L). 47 Avail: 35 W, 47 E (15/30 amps). 2021 rates: $19 to $26. May 15 to Sep 30. (204)212-3047

GRAND BEACH — D3 *Eastern*

GRAND BEACH PARK (Public Prov Park) From Jct of Hwy 12 & Hwy 59, W 6 mi on Hwy 12 (E). Avail: 147 E (30 amps). 2021 rates: $17.85 to $28.35. May 01 to Sep 15. (888)482-2267

GRANDVIEW — D1 *Western*

DUCK MOUNTAIN/SINGUSH LAKE CAMPGROUND (Public Prov Park) From town: Go 25 km/15-1/2 mi W on Hwy 367. 13 Avail: Pit toilets. 2021 rates: $16.80 to $28.35. May 01 to Sep 01. (306)542-5500

WILSON CENTENNIAL PARK (Public) From Jct of Hwy 5 & Main St, NE 0.1 mi on Main St to Railway North Rd, W 0.3 mi (R). Avail: 20 E (30 amps). May 15 to Sep 01. (204)546-5250

HAMIOTA — E1 *Western*

HAMIOTA MUNICIPAL CAMPGROUND (Public) From Jct of Hwy 21 & Main St, E 0.5 mi on Main St (R). 55 Avail: 45 full hkups, 10 E (30 amps). 2021 rates: $25 to $30. May 01 to Oct 01. (204)764-3050

HODGSON — D3 *Interlake*

LAKE ST GEORGE CAMPGROUND (Public Prov Park) From town: Go 24 km/15 mi N on Hwy 224 to Dallas, then 40 km/25 mi N on gravel access road. 28 Avail: Pit toilets. 2021 rates: $16.80 to $28.35. May 01 to Sep 01. (888)482-2267

Refer to the Table of Contents in front of the Guide to locate everything you need.

HOLLAND — E2 *North Central*

HOLLAND AGRICULTURAL SOCIETY CAMPGROUND (Campground) (Phone Update) 63 Avail: 26 W, 37 E (15/30 amps). 2021 rates: $20 to $25. May 15 to Oct 15. (204)526-2263, Hwy 34, Holland, MB R0G 0X0

KILLARNEY — E2 *Southwest*

KERRY PARK CAMPGROUND (Campground) (Phone Update) Avail: 25 full hkups (30 amps). 2021 rates: $35. May 15 to Sep 30. (204)523-6000, 402 South Railway St, Killarney, MB R0K 1G0

KILLARNEY AGRICULTURAL SOCIETY CAMPGROUNDS (Public) From jct Hwy 18 & Hwy 3W: Go .5 km/1/3 mi W on Hwy 3. 115 Avail: (30 amps). 2021 rates: $14 to $20. (204)523-4699

LAC DU BONNET — E3 *Southeast*

CHAMPAGNE'S RV PARK **Ratings: 8/9.5★/10** (RV Park) Avail: 44 full hkups (15/30 amps). 2021 rates: $40. May 01 to Oct 01. (204)345-2414, 120 Champagne Road, Lac Du Bonnet, MB R0E 1A0

NOPIMING PARK/BERESFORD LAKE CAMPGROUND (Public Prov Park) From town: Go 70 km/43-1/2 mi SE on Hwy 304. Follow signs. 17 Avail. 2021 rates: $10.50 to $28.35. (888)482-2267

NOPIMING PARK/BIRD LAKE CAMPGROUND (Public Prov Park) From town: Go 72.5 km/45 mi N on Hwys 314 & 315. Follow signs. 29 Avail. 2021 rates: $10.50 to $28.35. (888)482-2267

NOPIMING PARK/BLACK LAKE CAMPGROUND (Public Prov Park) Travel 3 km N on Pth 11 to PR 313; drive E 20 km, then N on PR 315. 64 Avail: Pit toilets. 2021 rates: $10.50 to $28.35. (888)482-2267

NOPIMING PARK/TULABI FALLS CAMPGROUND (Public Prov Park) From town: Go 60 km/37-1/4 mi S. Follow signs. Avail: 19 E. 2021 rates: $10.50 to $28.35. (888)482-2267

LAKE MANITOBA NARROWS — D2 *Interlake*

NARROWS SUNSET LODGE (Campground) (Phone Update) 10 Avail: 10 W, 10 E (15/30 amps). 2021 rates: $35. May 15 to Oct 15. (204)768-2749, Hwy 68, Oakview, MB R0C 2K0

LUNDAR — D2 *Interlake*

LUNDAR BEACH CAMPGROUND (Public Prov Park) From Jct of Hwy 6 & Secondary Hwy 419, W 12 mi on Secondary Rd 419 (L). Avail: 32 E (30 amps). 2021 rates: $18.90 to $28.35. May 01 to Sep 15. (888)482-2267

LYNN LAKE — A2 *Northern*

ZED LAKE PARK (Public Prov Park) From town, N 13 mi on PR-394 to park access rd, SW .25 mi (E). 10 Avail: Pit toilets. 2021 rates: $11 to $28.35. May 01 to Sep 15. (204)356-2413

MACGREGOR — E2 *North Central*

MACGREGOR LIONS RV PARK (Public) Downtown, follow signs. 23 Avail: 7 full hkups, 5 W, 9 E (30 amps). 2021 rates: $8 to $20. May 01 to Oct 15. (204)685-2582

MANITOU — E2 *South Central*

STEPHENFIELD PARK (Public Prov Park) From Jct of Hwys 13, 3 & Secondary Hwy 245, W 10 mi on Hwy 245 (R). 134 Avail: 35 W, 98 E (30/50 amps). 2021 rates: $11.55 to $28.35. May 11 to Oct 13. (204)828-3366

MINNEDOSA — E2 *Central*

MINNEDOSA CAMPGROUND (Public) From N Jct of Hwys 10 & 16A, E 2.5 mi on Hwy 16A to clock tower (Downtown), follow signs to PR-262, E 0.5 mi (L). 150 Avail: 57 W, 94 E (15/30 amps). 2021 rates: $25 to $35. May 01 to Sep 15. (204)867-3450

MOOSEHORN — D2 *Interlake*

WATCHORN BAY CAMPGROUND (Public Prov Park) From Jct of Hwy 6 & Secondary Rd 237, W 7 mi on Secondary Rd 237 (E). Avail: 22 E (15/30 amps). 2021 rates: $18.90 to $28.35. May 01 to Sep 15. (888)482-2267

MORDEN — E2 *Pembina Valley*

LAKE MINNEWASTA (Public) From Jct of Hwy 3 & Hwy 432, W 1.2 mi on Hwy 3 to Colert Rd, S 0.5 mi (E). 125 Avail: 125 W, 125 E (15/30 amps). 2021 rates: $25 to $30. Jun 01 to Aug 27. (204)822-4991

We appreciate your business!

MORRIS — E3 *South Central*

BIG M CENTENNIAL PARK (Public) At jct Hwy 75 & Hwy 23 E, adjacent to fairgrounds. 25 Avail: 25 W, 25 E (15/30 amps). 2021 rates: $15. Jun 01 to Sep 30. (204)746-2169

MUSEUM CAMPGROUND (Public) At jct Hwy 75 & Hwy 23 E, adjacent to Fairgrounds. 45 Avail: 25 W, 25 E (15/30 amps). 2021 rates: $10 to $20. May 15 to Sep 30. (204)746-2169

SCRATCHING RIVER CAMPGROUND (Public) From jct Hwy 75 & Hwy 23 E: Go 3/4 km/1/2 mi E on Hwy 23 E. Avail: 4 E (15 amps), Pit toilets. 2021 rates: $8 to $10. (204)746-2531

NEEPAWA — E2 *Central*

LIONS RIVERBEND CAMPGROUND (Public) From Jct of Hwy 16 & Hwy 5, E 1 mi on Hwy 16 (L). 70 Avail: 6 W, 70 S, 55 E (15/30 amps). 2021 rates: $15 to $28. May 01 to Sep 30. (204)476-7676

OAK LAKE — E1 *Southwest*

ASPEN GROVE CAMPGROUND **Ratings: 8/8★/8** (Campground) 95 Avail: 80 full hkups, 15 W, 15 E (30/50 amps). 2021 rates: $42.50 to $44.50. May 01 to Oct 01. (204)855-2260, NW 25-9-25W, Oak Lake, MB R0M 1P0

FOUR SEASONS ISLAND RESORT (OAK ISLAND RESORT) **Ratings: 8/8/7.5** (Campground) Avail: 139 full hkups (30 amps). 2021 rates: $42. May 14 to Oct 01. (204)855-2307, Hwy 254, Oak Lake, MB R0M 1P0

PILOT MOUND — E2 *South Central*

PILOT MOUND CAMPGROUND (Public) From jct Hwy 253 & Hwy 3: Go 1 km/1/2 mi S on Hwy 3, then 1 km/1/2 mi NW on Broadway Ave, then 40 meters/130 feet N on Brown Street North (L). Avail: 23 full hkups (30 amps). 2021 rates: $30. May 01 to Sep 15. (204)245-0680

PORTAGE LA PRAIRIE — E2 *Central*

MILLER'S CAMPING RESORT

Ratings: 8.5/9.5★/10 (Campground) From town, E 6 mi on Hwy 1, follow signs (L).

HIGHEST RATED RV PARK IN MANITOBA!

One of Canada's loveliest RV parks; perfectly situated for travel on Hwy 1 & the Yellowhead. Family friendly, lots to do, exceedingly well run & very quiet. Big rig friendly, extra-long & wide sites. Beautiful pool!

FAC: all weather rds. (192 spaces). Avail: 62 gravel, 20 pull-thrus, (40x90), back-ins (40x55), 38 full hkups, 24 W, 24 E (30/50 amps), seasonal sites, WiFi @ sites, tent sites, shower$, dump, laundry, groc, LP bottles, fire rings, firewood, controlled access. **REC:** heated pool, playground. Pet restrict (Q). Partial handicap access. Big rig sites, eco-friendly. 2021 rates: $40 to $50. May 01 to Oct 01.

(204)857-4255 Lat: 49.97557, Lon: -98.136613
Hwy 1, Portage La Prairie, MB R1N 3C3
millerscampground.com
See ad this page

PRAWDA — E4 *Southeast*

PINE TREE CAMPGROUND & TRAILER PARK (Campground) (Phone Update) 13 Avail: 8 W, 8 E (15/30 amps). 2021 rates: $40 to $50. May 15 to Oct 15. (204)426-5413, Group 8, Box 11, Prawda, MB R0E 0X0

RENNIE — E4 *Eastern*

WHITESHELL PARK/BIG WHITESHELL LAKE (Public Prov Park) From Jct of Hwy 307 & Hwy 309, E 6.3 mi on Hwy 309 NE 1.1 mi on un-named rd (L). Avail: 36 E (30 amps). 2021 rates: $13.85 to $28.35. May 01 to Oct 01. (888)482-2267

WHITESHELL PARK/BRERETON LAKE (Public Prov Park) From Jct of Hwy 44 & Hwy 307, N 5.5 mi on Hwy 307 (L). Avail: 8 E (15/30 amps). 2021 rates: $13.85 to $28.35. May 11 to Oct 01. (888)482-2267

WHITESHELL PARK/WHITE LAKE (Public Prov Park) From town: Go 26 km/16 mi N on Hwy 307. 17 Avail. 2021 rates: $13.85 to $28.35. May 01 to Oct 01. (888)482-2267

RICHER — E3 *Eastern*

CRIPPLE CREEK CAMPGROUND **Ratings: 5.5/5.5/7** (Campground) 12 Avail: 10 W, 10 E (30 amps). 2021 rates: $45. Apr 26 to Sep 30. (204)771-0242, 44154 Trudeau Road, Richer, MB R0J 0N0

Don't miss a thing! Check out the Table of Contents for everything the Guide has to offer.

ROCK GARDEN CAMPGROUND **Ratings: 8/7.5/8.5** (Campground) 38 Avail: 4 full hkups, 29 W, 29 E (30 amps). 2021 rates: $36 to $46. May 01 to Oct 15. (866)422-5441, 44025 Mun. Rd 46 N, Richer, MB R0E 1S0

WILD OAKS CAMPGROUND **Ratings: 6/6/7.5** (Campground) 49 Avail: 49 W, 49 E (15/30 amps). 2021 rates: $30 to $38. May 01 to Oct 01. (204)422-6175, 45136 Pr 302, Richer, MB R0E 1S0

RIVERTON — D3 *Interlake*

BEAVER CREEK PARK (Public Prov Park) Take Hwy 8 N of Riverton then N on to Hwy 234 & follow for approx 35 km. 10 Avail: Pit toilets. 2021 rates: $16.80 to $28.35. May 15 to Sep 01. (888)4U2-CAMP

HECLA/GULL HARBOUR CAMPGROUND (Public Prov Park) From Town, NE 5 mi on Hwy 8 (E). 175 Avail: 15 W, 104 E (30 amps). 2021 rates: $17.85 to $28.35. May 01 to Sep 15. (888)482-2267

ROBLIN — D1 *Parklands*

ASESSIPPI PARK (Public Prov Park) From Jct of Hwy 16 & Hwy 83, N 12 mi on Hwy 83 to Secondary Rd 482, W 5 mi (R). Avail: 91 E (30 amps). 2021 rates: $11.55 to $28.35. May 22 to Sep 30. (888)482-2267

DUCK MOUNTAIN/CHILDS LAKE CAMPGROUND (Public Prov Park) From Jct of Hwy 5 & Secondary Hwy 366, NW 30 mi on Secondary Rd 366 to Secondary Rd 367, W 12 mi (R). 93 Avail: 8 S, 65 E (30 amps). 2021 rates: $18.90 to $28.35. May 01 to Sep 01. (888)482-2267

PYOTT'S WEST CAMPGOUND (Campground) (Phone Update) 46 Avail: 46 W, 46 E (20/30 amps). 2021 rates: $45. May 14 to Sep 30. (204)564-2308, Hwy 482, Roblin, MB R0L 1P0

RUSSELL — D1 *Western*

PEACE PARK (Public) At Jct of Hwys 16 & 83, in town (R). Avail: 20 E (15 amps). May 01 to Sep 30. (204)773-2456

SELKIRK — E3 *Interlake*

SELKIRK MUNICIPAL PARK (Public) From Jct of Hwy 9 & Queen Ave, SE 0.1 mi on Queen Ave (E). Avail: 164 E (15/30 amps). 2021 rates: $15 to $19. May 21 to Oct 15. (204)785-4958

SEVEN SISTERS FALLS — E3 *Eastern*

WHITESHELL PARK/BETULA LAKE CAMPGROUND (Public Prov Park) From town: Go 42 km/26 mi E on Hwy 307. Avail: 14 E (15/30 amps). 2021 rates: $15.75 to $28.35. May 01 to Oct 01. (888)482-2267

WHITESHELL PARK/NUTIMIK LAKE (Public Prov Park) From town: Go 33 km/21 mi E on Hwy 307. 98 Avail: 77 W, 77 E (15/30 amps). 2021 rates: $13.85 to $28.35. May 01 to Oct 01. (888)482-2267

WHITESHELL PARK/OPAPISKAW (Public Prov Park) From Town, E 26 mi on Hwy 307 (L). Avail: 40 E (15/30 amps). 2021 rates: $13.85 to $28.35. May 09 to Oct 13. (888)482-2267

WHITESHELL PARK/OTTER FALLS (Public Prov Park) From Jct of Hwy 408 & Hwy 307, E 11.3 mi on Hwy 307 (L). Avail: 40 E (15/30 amps). 2021 rates: $13.65 to $28.35. May 01 to Oct 01. (888)482-2267

SIDNEY — E2 *Central*

KEESHKEEMAQUAH CAMPGROUND & RV PARK **Ratings: 6/6.5/8** (Campground) 52 Avail: 14 full hkups, 38 W, 38 E (15/30 amps). 2021 rates: $32 to $34. May 20 to Sep 30. (204)466-2777, Hwy 1 & Service Road 70W, Sidney, MB R0H 1L0

SNOW LAKE — B2 *Northern*

WEKUSKO FALLS PARK (Public Prov Park) From town: Go 10 km/6-1/4 mi S on Hwy 392. Avail: 27 E (15/30 amps). 2021 rates: $17.85 to $28.35. May 01 to Sep 01. (888)482-2267

SOURIS — E1 *Glenwood*

VICTORIA PARK (Public) From Jct Hwy 2 & 3rd St, S 0.9 mi on 3rd St (E). 75 Avail: 75 W, 75 E (15/30 amps). 2021 rates: $18 to $27. May 01 to Oct 31. (204)483-5212

SPRAGUE — E4 *Southeast*

BIRCH POINT PARK (Public Prov Park) From town: Go 40 km/24-3/4 mi NE on Hwy 308. (Entrance fee). 26 Avail: Pit toilets. 2021 rates: $11.55 to $28.35. May 01 to Sep 01. (888)482-2267

ST FRANCOIS XAVIER — E3 *Central*

WINNIPEG WEST KOA **Ratings: 8.5/10★/8** (Campground) 96 Avail: 70 full hkups, 16 W, 26 E (30/50 amps). 2021 rates: $39 to $57. Apr 15 to Oct 15. (800)562-0378, 588 PTH 1, Jones Drive South, St Francois Xavier, MB R4L 1A1

ST JEAN BAPTISTE — E3 *Southeastern*

ST JEAN PARK (Public) From N end of town, E 0.25 mi on Park rd (L). 26 Avail: 4 W, 22 E (15/30 amps). 2021 rates: $10 to $12. Jun 01 to Oct 01. (204)758-3881

ST MALO — E3 *Eastern*

DEBONAIR CAMPGROUND **Ratings: 6/7/8** (Campground) Avail: 17 full hkups (15/30 amps). 2021 rates: $25 to $35. Apr 15 to Oct 11. (204)347-5336, 22079 Pr 403, St Malo, MB R0A 1T0

ST MALO PARK (Public Prov Park) From Jct of Hwy 59 & Beach Rd, E 0.5 mi (E). Avail: 156 E (15/30 amps). 2021 rates: $17.85 to $28.35. May 09 to Sep 07. (204)347-5283

STE ANNE — E3 *Eastern*

LILAC RESORT **Ratings: 7.5/8.5★/7.5** (Campground) 68 Avail: 44 full hkups, 14 W, 14 E (15/30 amps). 2021 rates: $27 to $57. Apr 15 to Oct 15. (866)388-6095, 911 Marker: Hwy 1 East, 37162, Ste Anne, MB R5H 1H7

STEEP ROCK — D2 *Interlake*

NORTH STEEPROCK LAKE PARK (Public Prov Park) From jct Hwy 239 & gravel road on south end of town: Go 3.9 km/6-1/4 mi N on gravel road. 31 Avail. 2021 rates: $10.50 to $28.35. (888)482-2267

STONEWALL — E3 *Interlake*

QUARRY PARK CAMPGROUND (Public) From Jct of Hwys 67 & 236, N 0.4 mi on Hwy 236 (L). 41 Avail: 41 W, 41 E (15/30 amps). 2021 rates: $26 to $36. May 01 to Sep 30. (204)467-7980

SWAN RIVER — C1 *Parklands*

GREEN ACRES CAMPGROUND (Campground) (Phone Update) 40 Avail: 30 full hkups, 10 E (20/30 amps). 2021 rates: $34 to $36. May 15 to Oct 15. (204)734-9918, 312 Centennial Drive, Swan River, MB R0L 1Z0

WHITEFISH LAKE PARK (Public Prov Park) From jct Hwy 10 & Hwy 279: Go 25-1/2 km/16 mi NW on Hwy 279. 40 Avail. 2021 rates: $13.86 to $28.35. (888)482-2267

THE PAS — B1 *Northern*

CLEARWATER LAKE PARK (Public Prov Park) From town, NW 15 mi on Hwy 287 (L). Avail: 34 E (30 amps). 2021 rates: $10.50 to $28.35. May 01 to Sep 15. (888)482-2267

KINSMEN KAMPGROUND (Public) In town, from jct Hwy 10 & Edwards Ave: Go 1 block NW on Edwards Ave, then follow signs. 54 Avail. May 01 to Oct 01. (204)623-2233

THOMPSON — A3 *Northern*

MCCREEDY CAMPGROUND (Public) From Burntwood Bridge to Hwy 6, NE 0.5 mi, follow signs (R). 51 Avail: 2 W, 29 E (15/30 amps), Pit toilets. 2021 rates: $10 to $16. May 21 to Oct 01. (204)679-6315

PAINT LAKE PARK (Public Prov Park) From Town, S 17.3 mi on Hwy 6 to SR 375, SE 3.6 mi (R). Avail: 54 E (30 amps). 2021 rates: $10.50 to $28.35. May 01 to Sep 30. (204)677-6444

TREHERNE — E2 *Central*

COTTONWOOD CAMPGROUND (Public) From Jct of Hwy 2 & Railway St, SE 0.1 mi on Railway St to Vanzile St, S 0.25 mi (R). 67 Avail: 50 full hkups, 17 W, 17 E (15/30 amps). 2021 rates: $25 to $32. May 20 to Sep 15. (204)723-5040

WANLESS — B1 *Northern*

ROCKY LAKE (Public Prov Park) From The Pas, N 30 mi on Hwy 10 to Wanless, W 1.5 mi to unnamed Rd, S 0.25 mi, follow signs (L). 35 Avail: 7 W, 7 E (15/30 amps). 2021 rates: $18 to $23. May 22 to Oct 01. (204)682-7423

WARREN — E2 *Central*

RUBBER DUCKY RESORT & CAMPGROUND **Ratings: 8/7/8.5** (RV Park) 65 Avail: 27 full hkups, 21 W, 21 E (30 amps). 2021 rates: $47 to $54. May 01 to Oct 15. (204)322-5286, 1069 Road 76.5N, Warren, MB R0C 3E0

WASAGAMING — D2 *Riding Mountain*

RIDING MTN/LAKE AUDY (Public National Park) From Jct of Hwy 10 & Lake Audy Rd, W 16 mi on Lake Audy Rd (R). 32 Avail: Pit toilets. 2021 rates: $15.70. May 01 to Oct 31. (877)737-3783

RIDING MTN/MOON LAKE (Public National Park) From Jct of Yellowhead Hwy 16 & Hwy 10, N 48 mi on Hwy 10 (R). 29 Avail: Pit toilets. 2021 rates: $15.70. May 01 to Oct 31. (877)737-3783

RIDING MTN/WASAGAMING (Public National Park) From Jct of Hwy 10 & Yellowhead Hwy 16, N 26 mi on Hwy 10 (L). 428 Avail: 86 W, 86 S, 146 E (30 amps). 2021 rates: $27.40 to $38.20. May 15 to Oct 15. (877)737-3783

WESTBOURNE — E2 *Central*

OFTY'S RIVERSIDE CAMPGROUND (Campground) (Phone Update) 26 Avail: 22 W, 22 E (15/20 amps). 2021 rates: $28 to $35. May 15 to Sep 30. (204)274-2705, PR 242N, Westbourne, MB R0H 1P0

SPORTSMAN'S CORNER CAMPGROUND (Campground) (Phone Update) 30 Avail: 30 W, 30 E (15/30 amps), Pit toilets. 2021 rates: $35. May 01 to Sep 30. (204)274-2015, 48071, Rd 81 North, Westbourne, MB R0H 0C0

WHITESHELL — E4 *Eastern Manitoba*

WHITESHELL PARK/CADDY LAKE (Public Prov Park) From town, W 5 mi on Hwy 44 (R). 26 Avail. 2021 rates: $13.65 to $28.35. May 01 to Oct 31. (888)482-2267

WHITESHELL PARK/WEST HAWK LAKE (Public Prov Park) From Jct of Hwy 17 & Hwy 44, E 500 yds (L). 122 Avail: 10 W, 36 S, 76 E (15/30 amps), Pit toilets. 2021 rates: $15.75 to $28.35. May 01 to Oct 01. (888)482-2267

WINKLER — E3 *Central*

WINKLER TOURIST PARK (Public) From Jct of Hwy 14 & Park St (exit 2nd), S 0.1 mi on Park St (R). Avail: 38 full hkups (15/30 amps). 2021 rates: $25. May 20 to Nov 22. (204)325-8212

WINNIPEG — E3 *Eastern*

ARROWHEAD RV PARK

good sam park **Ratings: 8.5/10★/9** (Campground) N-bnd from USA: From jct MB 75 & MB 210: Go 13.1 km (8 mi) E on MB 210, (cross MB 59 and follow MB 210 N) Then 650 m (1/2 mi) N on Old 59 Hwy (R). **FAC:** all weather rds. Avail: 54 all weather, 41 pull-thrus, (24x65), back-ins (20x55), 54 full hkups (30/50 amps), WiFi @ sites, $, dump, laundry, fire rings, firewood, controlled access. **REC:** boating nearby, playground, hunting nearby. Pets OK. No tents. Big rig sites, eco-friendly. 2021 rates: $40 to $50. Apr 15 to Oct 31.
(888)878-4203 Lat: 49.69691, Lon: -96.98386
1375 A Major Trail, Ile des Chenes, MB R0A 0T0
www.arrowheadrvpark.ca
See ad this page

Do you know how to read each part of a listing? Check the How to Use This Guide in the front.

TOWN & COUNTRY CAMPGROUND **Ratings: 7/UI/8** (Campground) Avail: 202 full hkups (30/50 amps). 2021 rates: $43 to $51. May 01 to Oct 31. (888)615-1995, 56001 Murdock Road, Winnipeg, MB R2C 2Z3

WINNIPEG BEACH — D3 *Interlake*

CAMP MORTON PARK (Public Prov Park) From town: Go 6 km/4 mi N on Park Rd 222. 19 Avail. 2021 rates: $16.80 to $28.35. May 01 to Sep 01. (888)482-2267

HNAUSA BEACH PARK (Public Prov Park) Follow PR 222, 22 km N of Gimli. Avail: 36 E (15/30 amps). 2021 rates: $10.50 to $28.35. (888)4U2-CAMP

NORRIS LAKE PARK (Public Prov Park) Approx 1 hour from Winnipeg, take PTH 7 N 45 km to Teulon. Then NW 20 km on PTH 17. 15 Avail. 2021 rates: $11.55 to $28.35. May 01 to Sep 15. (888)4U2-CAMP

WINNIPEG BEACH PARK (Public Prov Park) Leaving Winnipeg, go N on PTH 8 for 45 km/28 mi, turn right at PR 229 drive 5 km/3.1 mi to Winnipeg Beach. Avail: 120 full hkups (15/30 amps). 2021 rates: $25.20 to $28.35. May 01 to Oct 01. (888)4U2-CAMP

WINNIPEGOSIS — D2 *Western*

MANIPOGO PARK (Public Prov Park) From Jct of Secondary Hwy 276 & Secondary Hwy 364, N 12 mi on Secondary Hwy 276 (R). Avail: 33 E (30 amps). 2021 rates: $14.90 to $28.35. May 11 to Sep 08. (888)482-2267

WINNIPEGOSIS PARK BEACH CAMPGROUND (Public) From Jct of Hwys 20A & 20, N 35 mi on Hwy 20, follow signs (R). Avail: 16 E (30 amps). 2021 rates: $15. May 15 to Oct 01. (204)656-4791

TRAVELING WITH YOUR PET: Choose the right chow. Feeding time can be tricky on the road, especially if your pet eats an uncommon food. Consider transitioning to a more common one at least three weeks before leaving. Dehydrated pet food is helpful too; it's made on the spot with hot water, takes up less space and weighs less than cans.

NB

Getty Images/iStockphoto

DID YOU KNOW?

The Bay of Fundy has the world's highest tides, which rise at a rate of 3.3 feet per hour.

YOU ARE HERE

New Brunswick

Calling yourself the "Picture Province" raises expectations for unforgettable sweeping vistas. For New Brunswick, the scenery lives up to the nickname. Discover epic lighthouses and sweeping coasts that dazzle the eye.

St. John on the Bay

On the Bay of Fundy, an exciting city awaits your visit. St. John is the province's largest city and pulses with the province's vibrant culture. Canada's longest-running farmers market, the City Market, provides a charming introduction to the foods and crafts of this region. The region's natural beauty can be explored at Reversing Falls and King's Square. Celebrate New Brunswick's cultural heritage by exploring the small towns of the Acadia region. Here, French foods, language and culture still thrive.

Roll With the Tides

See where the world's highest tides surge. The remarkable Bay of Fundy holds the record for the world's highest tides. During low tide, you can walk along the ocean floor, looking for treasures in the tide pools. As the tides come in, the waters deepen, providing paddlers a unique landscape to explore. Nearby Fundy National Park offers over 62 miles of trails, which wind through lush forests past waterfalls and lakes.

Wonderful Waterways

You may have a hard time choosing your New Brunswick water recreation destination. There are more than 4,350 miles of shoreline and 1,000 lakes, making the province a prime destination for watersports. Paddlers won't want to miss Hopewell Rocks, where towering rock spires rise to 70 feet above the Bay of Fundy. Anglers can head to the Miramichi River for abundant salmon fishing in a stunning environment. Take a ride along the St. John River for a memorable way to experience New Brunswick.

New Brunswick Lobster

Lobster is king in New Brunswick, and you won't have any problem finding restaurants in the province that serve up the succulent crustacean. So have a cracklin' good time with a helping of hot butter and a nutcracker. You'll find fresh catches in towns like Shediac on the coast.

VISITOR CENTER

TIME ZONE
Eastern Standard

ROAD & HIGHWAY INFORMATION
506-453-3939
511.gnb.ca/en

FISHING & HUNTING INFORMATION
506-453-3826
snb.ca/erd-dnr/erd-dnr-e.html

BOATING INFORMATION
800-267-6687
tc.gc.ca/boatingsafety

NATIONAL PARKS
pc.gc.ca/en/pn-np

PROVINCIAL PARKS
www.parcsnbparks.info

TOURISM INFORMATION
Tourism New Brunswick
800-561-0123
tourismnewbrunswick.ca

TOP TOURISM ATTRACTIONS
1) Bay of Fundy
2) Irving Nature Park
3) Centennial Park

MAJOR CITIES
St. John, Moncton, Fredericton (capital), Dieppe, Riverview

good sam park Featured Good Sam Parks

NEW BRUNSWICK

When you stay with Good Sam, you can expect the highest degree of cleanliness and friendliness, and better yet, you get **10% off** overnight campground fees.

If you're not already a Good Sam member you can purchase your membership at one of these locations:

BERTRAND
Camping Colibri

FREDERICTON
Hartt Island RV Resort

HOPEWELL CAPE
Ponderosa Pines Campground

POKEMOUCHE
Camping Pokemouche

SAINT-JOHN
Hardings Point Campground

SAINT-MARTINS
Century Farm Family Campground

SHEDIAC
Ocean Surf RV Park

WOODSTOCK
Yogi Bear's Jellystone Park Camp Resorts

10/10★/10 GOOD SAM PARKS

BERTRAND
Camping Colibri
(506)727-2222

SHEDIAC
Ocean Surf RV Park
(506)532-5480

POKEMOUCHE
Camping Pokemouche
(506)727-6090

What's This?

An RV park with a 10/10★/10 rating has scored perfect grades in amenities, cleanliness and appearance ("See Understanding the Campground Rating System" on pages 8 and 9 for an explanation of the trusted Good Sam Rating System). Stay in a 10/10★/10 park on your next trip for a nearly flawless camping experience.

Getty Images/iStockphoto

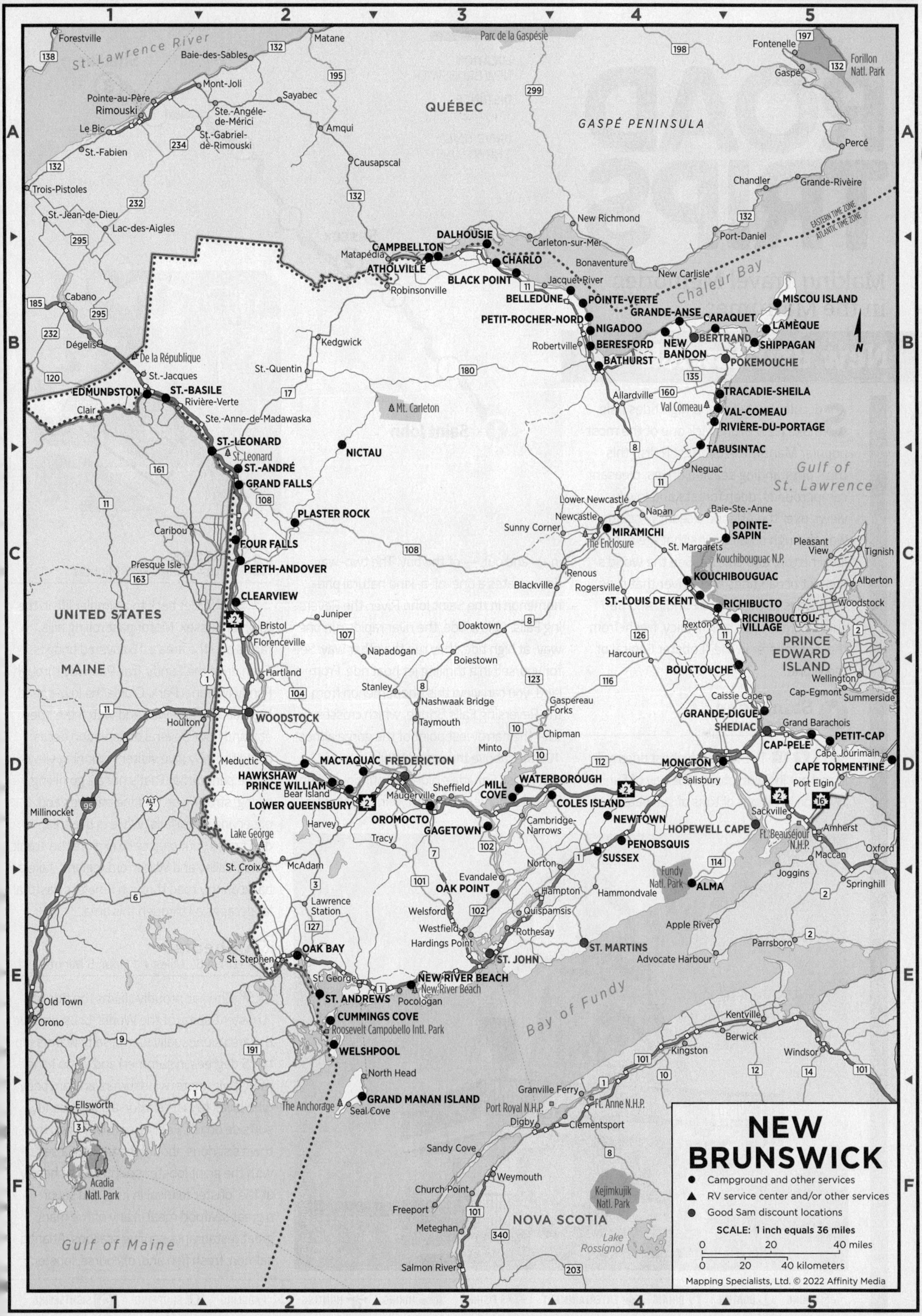
NEW BRUNSWICK
Campground and other services
RV service center and/or other services
Good Sam discount locations
SCALE: 1 inch equals 36 miles
0 20 40 miles
0 20 40 kilometers
Mapping Specialists, Ltd. © 2022 Affinity Media
QUÉBEC
GASPÉ PENINSULA
UNITED STATES
MAINE
PRINCE EDWARD ISLAND
NOVA SCOTIA
St. Lawrence River
Chaleur Bay
Gulf of St. Lawrence
Bay of Fundy
Gulf of Maine
EASTERN TIME ZONE
ATLANTIC TIME ZONE
DALHOUSIE
CAMPBELLTON
ATHOLVILLE
CHARLO
BLACK POINT
BELLEDUNE
PÔINTE-VERTE
PETIT-ROCHER-NORD
NIGADOO
BERESFORD
BATHURST
GRANDE-ANSE
NEW BANDON
CARAQUET
BERTRAND
MISCOU ISLAND
LAMÈQUE
SHIPPAGAN
POKEMOUCHE
TRACADIE-SHEILA
VAL-COMEAU
RIVIÈRE-DU-PORTAGE
TABUSINTAC
MIRAMICHI
POINTE-SAPIN
KOUCHIBOUGUAC
ST.-LOUIS DE KENT
RICHIBUCTO
RICHIBOUCTOU-VILLAGE
BOUCTOUCHE
GRANDE-DIGUE
SHEDIAC
CAP-PELE
PETIT-CAP
CAPE TORMENTINE
MONCTON
HOPEWELL CAPE
ALMA
PENOBSQUIS
SUSSEX
NEWTOWN
COLES ISLAND
WATERBOROUGH
MILL COVE
GAGETOWN
OROMOCTO
FREDERICTON
MACTAQUAC
HAWKSHAW
PRINCE WILLIAM
LOWER QUEENSBURY
WOODSTOCK
CLEARVIEW
PERTH-ANDOVER
FOUR FALLS
PLASTER ROCK
GRAND FALLS
ST.-ANDRÉ
ST.-LEONARD
NICTAU
EDMUNDSTON
ST.-BASILE
OAK POINT
ST. MARTINS
ST. JOHN
NEW RIVER BEACH
OAK BAY
ST. ANDREWS
CUMMINGS COVE
WELSHPOOL
GRAND MANAN ISLAND
Forestville
Baie-des-Sables
Matane
Parc de la Gaspésie
Mont-Joli
Sayabec
Pointe-au-Père
Rimouski
Ste.-Angèle-de-Mérici
St.-Gabriel-de-Rimouski
Le Bic
Amqui
St.-Fabien
Causapscal
Trois-Pistoles
St.-Jean-de-Dieu
Lac-des-Aigles
Cabano
Dégelis
De la République
St.-Jacques
Rivière-Verte
Clair
Ste.-Anne-de-Madawaska
St. Leonard
Matapédia
Robinsonville
Kedgwick
St.-Quentin
Mt. Carleton
Fontenelle
Gaspé
Forillon Natl. Park
Percé
Chandler
Grande-Rivière
Port-Daniel
New Richmond
Carleton-sur-Mer
Bonaventure
New Carlisle
Jacquet River
Robertville
Allardville
Val Comeau
Neguac
Lower Newcastle
Newcastle
Napan
Baie-Ste.-Anne
Sunny Corner
The Enclosure
St. Margarets
Kouchibouguac N.P.
Renous
Rogersville
Blackville
Rexton
Harcourt
Doaktown
Boiestown
Caribou
Presque Isle
Juniper
Bristol
Florenceville
Napadogan
Hartland
Stanley
Nashwaak Bridge
Taymouth
Gaspereau Forks
Chipman
Minto
Houlton
Meductic
Bear Island
Sheffield
Maugerville
Harvey
Tracy
Cambridge-Narrows
Salisbury
Lake George
McAdam
St. Croix
Millinocket
Lawrence Station
Evandale
Norton
Hampton
Hammondvale
Fundy Natl. Park
Welsford
Quispamsis
Westfield
Rothesay
Hardings Point
St. Stephen
St. George
Pocologan
New River Beach
Roosevelt Campobello Intl. Park
North Head
The Anchorage
Seal Cove
Old Town
Orono
Ellsworth
Acadia Natl. Park
Pleasant View
Tignish
Alberton
Woodstock
Wellington
Cap-Egmont
Summerside
Caissie Cape
Grand Barachois
Cape Jourimain
Port Elgin
Sackville
Ft. Beauséjour N.H.P.
Amherst
Maccan
Oxford
Joggins
Springhill
Apple River
Parrsboro
Advocate Harbour
Kentville
Berwick
Kingston
Windsor
Granville Ferry
Ft. Anne N.H.P.
Port Royal N.H.P.
Digby
Clementsport
Sandy Cove
Weymouth
Church Point
Freeport
Meteghan
Salmon River
Kejimkujik Natl. Park
Lake Rossignol

ROAD TRIPS

Making Travel Memories in the Maritimes

New Brunswick

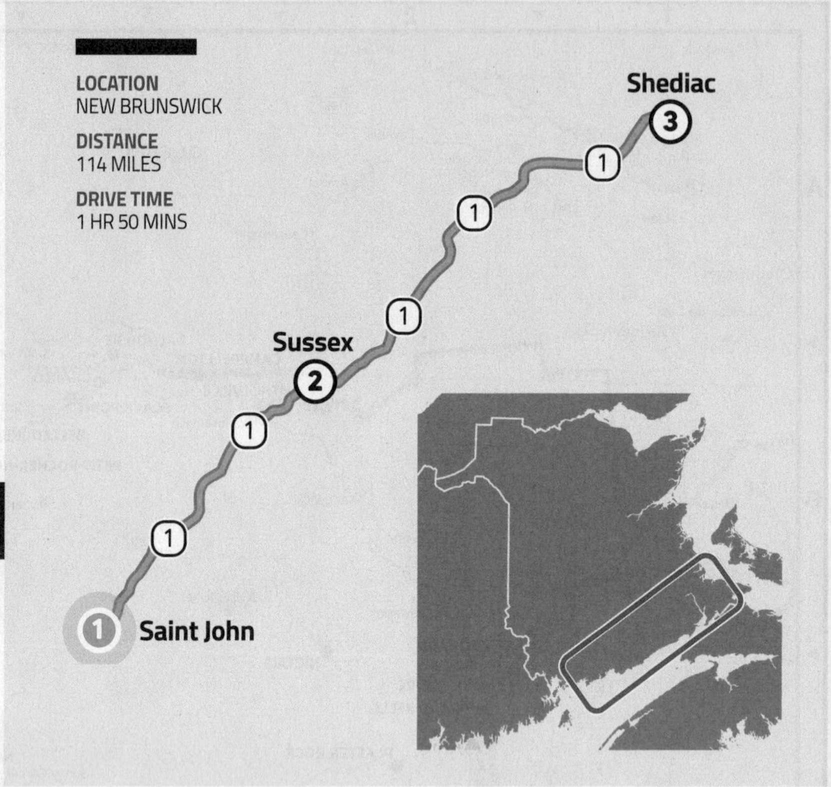

Succulent Lobster and high tides help make New Brunswick one of the most popular Maritime Provinces. Relish this trip's outstanding seaside drives, pleasant campgrounds, deep forests and lovely views over the Atlantic Ocean. Wind your way through small towns that are rich in local history and culture. See the world's highest ocean tides and a river that runs both ways at the Bay of Fundy. And be sure to crack open a rich, juicy, fresh-from-the-sea lobster in the "Lobster Capital of the World."

1 Saint John
Starting Point

The world's highest tides roll in and out in Saint John on the Bay of Fundy. Twice daily, billions of tons of seawater rush in — and out — of the bay. The two-way flow creates a one-of-a-kind natural phenomenon in the Saint John River: the Reversing Falls. At low tide, the river rapids run one way; at high tide, they run the other way. See for yourself in a thrilling jet boat ride. From land, you can view this phenomenon from the Reversing Falls Bridge, which crosses over the narrowest point of the gorge almost 100 feet above the water. While in town, don't miss Canada's oldest continuously run farmers market, the Saint John City Market.

2 Sussex
Drive 47 Miles ▪ 45 Minutes

Get back to a simpler life in the town of Sussex. Motor past rolling hills, farms and the area's 16 covered bridges. Then drive the Fundy Trail Parkway through Fundy National Park. Cruise the low-speed, high-beauty parkway and watch the tides ebb and flow. Several observation decks along the way give visitors stunning views of the panorama. That's not all: go hiking, biking, strolling on pristine beaches and observing waterfalls. While in the area, don't miss your chance to explore the scenic Dutch Valley and Waterford regions. Take a backcountry road through timeless pastoral landscapes all through this area.

3 Shediac
Drive 67 Miles ▪ 1 Hour, 5 Minutes

Shediac proudly claims the title of "Lobster Capital of the World." Lobsters love the area's unusually warm, salty waters (up to 75 degrees in summer) and so do fishermen, swimmers, windsurfers and anybody who loves to just relax on a sunny, sandy, surfside beach. Feeling peckish? Well, this town's serious about lobster. Take a selfie with the giant lobster sculpture. Eat hearty at the lobster festival in June and savor a great seafood meal in any of the many great restaurants serving scallops, Atlantic salmon, fresh fish and, of course, lobster.

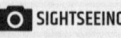

BIKING BOATING DINING ENTERTAINMENT FISHING HIKING HUNTING PADDLING SHOPPING SIGHTSEEING

NB

New Brunswick SPOTLIGHTS

See Photogenic Sights in Canada's Picture Province

New Brunswick rises to the occasion for visitors. The province has the highest tides in the world as well as gorgeous, rustic landscapes and Old World Cities. Taste succulent lobster on the coast or explore friendly farm towns nestled in the countryside.

NEW BRUNSWICK IS A MAJOR SOURCE FOR CHRISTMAS TREES.

In late September and early October, fall colors erupt throughout New Brunswick.

Getty Images/iStockphoto

Fredericton

Fredericton is the Goldilocks of Canadian towns. This New Brunswick capital is not too big, not too small and has just enough quaint charm to entice you to extend your stay. With its tree-lined riverbanks, lovely walking trails, waterfront views and brick heritage buildings, the vibrant town will captivate you with its diverse culture and riverside beauty.

Open a Chapter Into the Past

Walk into the city's vibrant past in the Garrison District. Located in the heart of downtown by the Saint John River, the Garrison is home to a wealth of heritage buildings, museums and festivals. Take a walking tour through the grounds with a historically costumed guide to explore the Soldiers' Barracks and Guard House. Watch as the Ceremonial Guard marches in downtown Fredericton daily from 10 a.m. to 6 p.m. throughout the summer.

Saint John

A magnificent waterfront and stellar urban charms put Saint John high on the list of sought-after Canadian destinations. The only city situated on the Bay of Fundy, Saint John invites you to see the world's highest tides and explore the oldest incorporated urban area in Canada. Saint John promises endless possibilities, making it a worthy destination for your next vacation. Check out Carleton Martello Tower National Historic Site, a fortification built in 1812 and used as late as 1944 during WWII.

Nature Near the City

Irving Nature Park puts explorers in a wild setting just minutes from Saint John. Covering 600 acres, including seven miles of rugged Bay of Fundy shoreline, the park encompasses six different ecosystems with eight walking trails. The park serves as a great vantage point to watch as the world's highest tides roll in and out.

Shediac

Save room for juicy lobster on your trip to Shediac. The town is known for its bountiful lobster harvests, and you can feast on fresh crustaceans from several local restaurants. Marvel at the 55-ton metal lobster in the center of town or embark on the many hiking trails outside of town with tremendous views of the coast.

Work Lobster Calories

Spent too much time cracking shells? Work off the calories from your meals by embarking on some of the warmest waters north of Virginia. Swimmers, windsurfers and boaters will enjoy Shediac Bay.

FOR MORE INFORMATION

New Brunswick, 800-561-0123, tourismnewbrunswick.ca

Fredericton Tourism, 888-888-4768, tourismfredericton.ca

Discover Saint John, 866-GO FUNDY discoversaintjohn.com

Shediac, 800-561-0123, tourismnewbrunswick.ca/story/southeast-vacation-land

LOCAL FAVORITE

Quick Chili and Squash Snack

Take advantage of New Brunswick's ample squash harvest. Enjoy a savory sweet treat with lots of veggies. *Recipe by Clinton Black.*

INGREDIENTS

- ☐ 1 large acorn squash
- ☐ 1 can of chili with beans or not
- ☐ Optional toppings: diced onions, cheese

DIRECTIONS

Heat chili in separate pot. Remove stem from squash. Cut squash from stem top to pointed end. Remove seeds with spoon. Cook in microwave 10-12 minutes or until soft.
Place in bowls.
Add chili and any optional toppings.

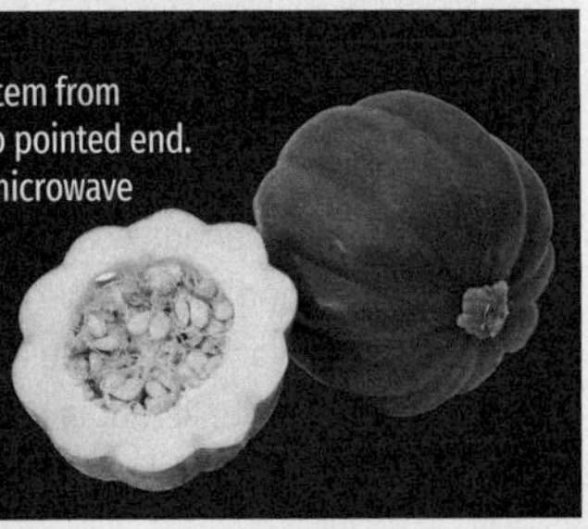

New Brunswick

ALMA — E4 *Albert*

FUNDY/CHIGNECTO (Public National Park) From town, NW 4 km (2.48 mi) on Rte 114 (R). 263 Avail: 10 full hkups, 171 W, 10 S, 171 E (30/50 amps). 2021 rates: $25.50 to $35.30. May 17 to Oct 13. (877)737-3783

FUNDY/HEADQUARTERS (Public National Park) From town, NW 0.5 km on Rte 114 (R). 139 Avail: 30 full hkups, 25 W, 25 E (30 amps). 2021 rates: $25 to $40. May 16 to Oct 13. (877)737-3783

FUNDY/POINT WOLFE (Public National Park) From Alma & Rte 114, SW 10 km (6.2 mi) on 114/ Pointe Wolfe Rd (R). 144 Avail: 24 W, 24 E. 2021 rates: $25 to $27. Jun 23 to Oct 08. (877)737-3783

ATHOLVILLE — B3 *Restigouche*

SUGARLOAF PROVINCIAL PARK (Public Prov Park) From Jct of Hwy 11 & Exit 415 (Chemin Val D'Amour Rd), W 0.4 mi (L). 76 Avail: 8 full hkups, 57 E (15/30 amps). 2021 rates: $28 to $43. May 31 to Sep 30. (506)789-2366

BATHURST — B4 *Gloucester*

BATHURST WILDLIFE CAMPING **Ratings: 5/8.5★/8.5** (Campground) Avail: 33 full hkups (30/50 amps). 2021 rates: $28 to $50. May 15 to Oct 15. (506)546-8987, 2476 Sunset Dr, Bathurst, NB E2A 7K8

BELLEDUNE — B4 *Restigouche*

JACQUET RIVER PARK (Public) From Hwy 11 (exit 351): Go 2.6 km/1-1/2 mi E on Jacquet River Rd, then 90 meters/100 yards S on Hwy 134. 31 Avail. 2021 rates: $25. Jun 01 to Sep 02. (506)237-3239

BERESFORD — B4 *Gloucester*

PARC MALYBEL **Ratings: 9/8/9.5** (Campground) 92 Avail: 58 full hkups, 9 W, 9 E (30/50 amps). 2021 rates: $44 to $59. May 15 to Sep 14. (506)545-6888, 1121 Bryar Rd, Beresford, NB E8K 1B2

BERTRAND — B4 *Gloucester*

CAMPING COLIBRI

good sam park **Ratings: 10/10★/10** (Campground) 142 Avail: 126 full hkups, 16 W, 16 E (30/ 50 amps). 2021 rates: $34 to $54. May 18 to Sep 24. (506)727-2222, 913 Boul des Acadiens Rte 11, Bertrand, NB E1W 1A5

BLACK POINT — B3 *Restigouche*

CAMPING BY THE BAY **Ratings: 4.5/8★/7.5** (Campground) Avail: 14 full hkups (20/30 amps). 2021 rates: $16 to $25. Jun 01 to Sep 08. (506)237-5291, 55 Black Point Rd, Black Point, NB E8G 1P8

New Brunswick Privately Owned Campground Information Updated by our Good Sam Representatives

Patrice Richard & Chantal Belisle

We sold everything in 2002, then traveled in Canada coast to coast, U.S. (44 states) and Mexico. We're Frenchies who switch from one culture to another. La vie est trop courte, il faut la prendre en riant. Life's too short so take it with a laugh.

BOUCTOUCHE — D5 *Kent*

BOUCTOUCHE BAIE CHALETS & CAMPING **Ratings: 9/9★/9** (Campground) 126 Avail: 73 full hkups, 19 W, 19 E (30/50 amps). 2021 rates: $33.75 to $54.75. May 16 to Sep 26. (506)743-8883, 2239 Rte 475, Saint-Edouard-de-Kent, NB E4S 4W4

CAMPBELLTON — B3 *Restigouche*

EXPERIENCE RESTIGOUCHE **Ratings: 7.5/9.5★/9** (Campground) Avail: 67 full hkups (30/50 amps). 2021 rates: $28 to $55. May 18 to Oct 01. (844)787-3701, 1 Riverview Drive, Campbellton, NB E3N 0E1

CAPE TORMENTINE — D5 *Westmorland*

CAPE TORMENTINE BEACH CG **Ratings: 7/8.5★/7** (Campground) Avail: 10 full hkups (30 amps). 2021 rates: $41.90. May 15 to Sep 30. (506)538-7229, #1Route 955, Cape Tormentine, NB E4M 2A3

MURRAY BEACH (Public Prov Park) From Cape Tormentine (Hwy 16), E 10 km (6.2 mi) on Hwy 955 (R). Avail: 57 E (15/30 amps). 2021 rates: $10 to $90. May 25 to Oct 08. (506)538-2628

CAP-PELE — D5 *Westmorland*

CAMPING PLAGE GAGNON BEACH **Ratings: 7.5/8★/8** (Campground) 100 Avail: 20 full hkups, 30 W, 30 E (30/50 amps). 2021 rates: $43.48 to $55.65. May 15 to Sep 30. (506)577-2519, 30 Chemin Plage Gagnon, Grand-Barachois, NB E4P 7Z6

SANDY BEACH TRAILER PARK **Ratings: 6.5/8★/8** (Campground) 250 Avail: 110 full hkups, 90 W, 90 E (30/50 amps). 2021 rates: $37 to $54. May 18 to Sep 20. (506)577-2218, 380 Chem Bas-Cap Pele, Cap-Pele, NB E4N 1J1

CARAQUET — B4 *Gloucester*

CAMPING COLIBRI BY THE SEA Ratings: 6/8★/8 (Campground) 100 Avail: 29 full hkups, 27 W, 32 E (30 amps). 2021 rates: $32 to $37. May 18 to Oct 04. (506)726-2696, 619 Boulevard St Pierre West, Caraquet, NB E1W 1A5

CAMPING LA MARINA **Ratings: 5/7.5/5.5** (Campground) Avail: 10 full hkups (15/30 amps). 2021 rates: $26 to $36.50. May 15 to Sep 15. (506)726-8900, 2242 Beauport, Caraquet, NB E1W 5V3

MAISON TOURISTIQUE DUGAS CAMPING **Ratings: 6/8.5★/8.5** (Campground) 35 Avail: 14 full hkups, 21 W, 21 E (15/30 amps). 2021 rates: $32 to $49. May 01 to Oct 30. (506)727-3195, 683 Blvd. St Pierre Quest, Caraquet, NB E1W 1A1

CHARLO — B3 *Restigouche*

BLUE HERON CAMPING HERON BLEU (Public) From Jct of Hwy 11 & Exit 385 (Rte 134), E 0.6 mi on Ch. Craig Rd (exit rd) to Rte 134, N 1.25 mi to Rte 280 (Cove Rd), W 600 ft, Follow Signs (L). 172 Avail: 135 full hkups, 10 W, 10 E (15/30 amps). 2021 rates: $29 to $38. May 30 to Sep 14. (506)684-7860

CLEARVIEW — C2 *Carleton*

RIVER COUNTRY CAMPGROUND **Ratings: 6.5/8★/8.5** (Campground) Avail: 15 full hkups (20/30 amps). 2021 rates: $30 to $40. May 15 to Sep 15. (506)278-3700, 69 Lahue Road, Clearview, NB E7L 1X6

COLES ISLAND — D4 *Queens*

RIVERRUN CAMPGROUND **Ratings: 6/8.5★/8** (Campground) Avail: 12 full hkups (30 amps). 2021 rates: $43.50. May 15 to Sep 03. (506)362-9198, 8976 Rte 112, Coles Island, NB E4C 2V2

TNT CAMPGROUND **Ratings: 7.5/8.5★/9** (Campground) 70 Avail: 30 full hkups, 40 W, 40 E (15/30 amps). 2021 rates: $29 to $40.25. May 09 to Sep 30. (506)362-5372, 131 Boyd Loop Rd, Coles Island, NB E4C 2W9

CUMMINGS COVE — E2 *Charlotte*

DEER ISLAND POINT CAMPGROUND

(Public) Located at Campobello-Eastport ferry dock. **FAC:** Avail: 39 gravel, 39 W, 39 E tent sites, dump, laundry, fire rings, firewood, controlled access. **REC:** playground. Pets OK. 2021 rates: $25 to $30. no cc.
(506)747-2423 Lat: 44.926444, Lon: -66.985333
195 Deer Island Point Rd, Cummings Cove, NB E5V 1W2
deerislandpointpark.com

Looking for places the ""locals" frequent? Make friends with park owners and staff to get the inside scoop!

DALHOUSIE — B3 *Restigouche*

INCH ARRAN PARK (Public) S'bnd: From jct of Hwy 11 & Exit 397 (Rte 134), E 0.5 mi on Blair Malcom Rd to Rte 134, S 5 mi to Victoria St, S 1.4 mi, (R), follow signs. N'bnd: From Jct of Hwy 11 & Exit 391A, E 1 mi on Rte 275 to Rte 134, N 1 mi on 134 to Goderich St, E 1 mi to Inch Arran, N 20 ft to entrance (R). Avail: 40 full hkups (30 amps). 2021 rates: $30 to $45. May 01 to Aug 31. (506)684-7363

EDMUNDSTON — B1 *Madawaska*

CAMPING PANORAMIC '86 Ratings: 8.5/8.5★/8.5 (Campground) Avail: 32 full hkups (30 amps). 2021 rates: $40 to $42. May 15 to Oct 15. (506)739-6544, 86, Chemin Albert , Saint-Jacques, NB E7B 1Z5

DE LA REPUBLIQUE (Public Prov Park) From Edmundston, W 5 mi on TCH 2, exit 8 (R). 150 Avail: 100 W, 100 E (15/30 amps). 2021 rates: $28 to $36. May 30 to Sep 01. (506)735-2525

FOUR FALLS — C2 *Victoria*

SPRING WATER CAMPGROUND **Ratings: 8/8★/8** (Campground) 27 Avail: 12 full hkups, 15 W, 15 E (15/30 amps). 2021 rates: $43.48. May 13 to Sep 15. (506)273-3682, 2539 Route 130, Four Falls, NB E3Z 2H3

FREDERICTON — D3 *Sunbury*

HARTT ISLAND RV RESORT

good sam park **Ratings: 10/9★/9.5** (Campground) Avail: 91 full hkups (30/50 amps). 2021 rates: $65 to $80. May 15 to Oct 15. (506)462-9400, 2475 Woodstock Rd Rte 102, Fredericton, NB E3C 1P6

WOOLASTOOK PARK **Ratings: 8/9.5★/8** (Campground) Avail: 75 full hkups (30/50 amps). 2021 rates: $45 to $83. May 15 to Oct 15. (506)472-5584, 5171 Rte 102, Upper Kingsclear, NB E3E 1P9

GAGETOWN — D3 *Queens*

COY LAKE CAMPING RV PARK **Ratings: 6.5/8.5★/8** (Campground) Avail: 10 full hkups (30/50 amps). 2021 rates: $46 to $55. May 15 to Sep 15. (506)488-2567, 1805 Rte 102, Upper Gagetown, NB E5N 1N3

GRAND FALLS — C2 *Victoria*

MULHERIN'S CAMPGROUND **Ratings: 8/8/9** (Campground) 75 Avail: 55 full hkups, 20 W, 20 E (30/50 amps). 2021 rates: $37 to $42. May 22 to Sep 08. (506)473-3050, 170 McCluskey Rd., Grand Falls, NB E3Z 1L3

RAPID BROOK CAMPING Ratings: 8/7.5/8 (Campground) Avail: 23 full hkups (30 amps). 2021 rates: $40 to $50. May 15 to Oct 01. (506)473-1036, 59 Michaud Rd, Grand Falls, NB E3Z 2K3

GRAND MANAN ISLAND — F2 *Charlotte*

THE ANCHORAGE (Public Prov Park) From ferry terminal, S 5 mi on Rte 776, follow signs (L). Avail: 29 E (15/30 amps). 2021 rates: $25 to $39. May 30 to Sep 28. (506)662-7022

GRANDE-ANSE — B4 *Gloucester*

CAMPING & MOTEL DOIRON **Ratings: 5/6/7.5** (Campground) Avail: 14 full hkups (30 amps). 2021 rates: $24 to $30. Jun 01 to Sep 30. (506)732-5316, 575 Acadie St., Grande Anse, NB E8N 1E9

MOTEL & CAMPING BAIE DES CHALEURS **Ratings: 6/7/7** (Campground) Avail: 18 full hkups (15/ 30 amps). 2021 rates: $32 to $35. May 20 to Sep 21. (506)732-2948, 480 Rue Acadie, Grande Anse, NB E8N 1E4

GRANDE-DIGUE — D5 *Kent*

BEACH VIEW CAMPING **Ratings: 6/8/7.5** (Campground) Avail: 13 full hkups (20/30 amps). 2021 rates: $42. May 20 to Sep 30. (506)576-1118, 2449 Rte 530, Grande Digue, NB E4R 5M7

HAWKSHAW — D2 *York*

SUNSET VIEW CAMPGROUND Ratings: 8.5/9★/9 (Campground) 57 Avail: 23 full hkups, 19 W, 19 E (30 amps). 2021 rates: $47 to $49. Jun 01 to Sep 15. (506)575-2592, 45 Hawkshaw Rd, Hawkshaw, NB E6G 1N8

According to the Wall Street Journal, 100 billion plastic shopping bags are consumed in the United States annually. Consider toting your own reusable shopping bags instead of using plastic.

HOPEWELL CAPE — D5 *Albert*

PONDEROSA PINES CAMPGROUND
good sam park
Ratings: 8.5/10★/9.5 (Campground) From Jct of Rte 114 & Hopewell Rock Entrance (in town), W 1 mi on Rte 114 (L). **FAC:** gravel rds. 120 Avail: 72 all weather, 48 grass, 31 pull-thrus, (30x75), back-ins (30x50), 75 full hkups, 21 W, 21 E (30/50 amps), WiFi @ sites, tent sites, rentals, dump, laundry, groc, fire rings, firewood, controlled access. **REC:** heated pool, Bay of Fundy: swim, fishing, kayaking/canoeing, playground. Pets OK. Big rig sites, 14 day max stay, eco-friendly. 2021 rates: $52 to $69. May 12 to Oct 24.
(800)822-8800 Lat: 45.81907, Lon: -64.59628
4325 Rte 114, Hopewell Cape, NB E4H 3P1
ponderosapines.ca
See ad this page

KOUCHIBOUGUAC — C4 *Kent*

SOUTH KOUCHIBOUGUAC (Public National Park) From Jct of TCH-11 & Rd 117, E 2 mi on Rd 117 (R). 311 Avail: 71 full hkups, 98 E (15 amps). 2021 rates: $27.40 to $38.20. Jun 28 to Sep 01. (877)737-3783

LAMEQUE — B5 *Gloucester*

CAMPING ILE LAMEQUE **Ratings: 6/8.5/7.5** (Campground) Avail: 40 full hkups (30 amps). 2021 rates: $37 to $40. May 31 to Sep 15. (506)344-2525, 237 Gauvin Rd, Petite Lameque, NB E8T 2N1

CHALETS ET CAMPING DES ILES JEANNOT **Ratings: 7.5/9.5★/8.5** (Campground) Avail: 17 full hkups (30/50 amps). 2021 rates: $35 to $43. May 15 to Sep 15. (506)344-2590, 110 Allee Jeaunnot Lane, Petite Lameque, NB E8T 4R8

LOWER QUEENSBURY — D2 *York*

HERITAGE COUNTRY CAMPING **Ratings: 7/7.5★/8.5** (Campground) 35 Avail: 20 full hkups, 15 W, 15 E (30 amps). 2021 rates: $35 to $44. May 15 to Sep 30. (506)363-3338, 2400 Rte 105, Lower Queensbury, NB E6L 1G3

MACTAQUAC — D2 *York*

EVERETT'S CAMPGROUND **Ratings: 6.5/8.5★/8** (Campground) 10 Avail: 10 W, 10 E (15/30 amps). 2021 rates: $35 to $40. May 15 to Sep 30. (506)461-8020, 2137 Rte 105, Lower Queensbury, NB E6L 1E6

MACTAQUAC PARK (Public Prov Park) From Jct of TCH 2 & Hwy 105 (exit 274), W 6 mi on Hwy 105 (L). Avail: 235 E (30 amps). 2021 rates: $25 to $28. May 17 to Oct 13. (506)363-4747

MILL COVE — D3 *Queens*

LAKESIDE CAMPGROUND & RECREATION PARK (Public Prov Park) From Jemseg, E 9 mi on TCH 2 (L). 128 Avail: 9 full hkups, 54 W, 54 E (15/30 amps). 2021 rates: $28 to $42. May 17 to Oct 13. (506)488-2321

MIRAMICHI — C4 *Northumberland*

ENCLOSURE CAMPGROUND **Ratings: 8/7/7.5** (Campground) 51 Avail: 11 full hkups, 31 W, 31 E (15/30 amps). 2021 rates: $32 to $40. May 15 to Oct 15. (506)622-8638, 8 Enclosure Road, Miramichi, NB E1V 3V4

SUNRISE CAMPGROUND **Ratings: 9/8.5★/8** (Campground) Avail: 62 full hkups (30 amps). 2021 rates: $39. May 20 to Oct 08. (506)778-2282, 504 Rte 11, Lower Newcastle, NB E1V 7G1

MISCOU ISLAND — B5 *Gloucester*

CAMPING LA VAGUE **Ratings: 6/9.5★/7.5** (Campground) 81 Avail: 16 full hkups, 36 W, 36 E (30 amps). 2021 rates: $36.75 to $42.75. Jun 01 to Sep 15. (506)344-8531, 3 Herring Pte Rd., Miscou Island, NB E8T 2G2

MONCTON — D4 *Westmorland*

STONEHURST GOLF COURSE & TRAILER PARK **Ratings: 9/8.5★/8** (Campground) 141 Avail: 58 full hkups, 66 W, 66 E (30/50 amps). 2021 rates: $28 to $48. May 15 to Oct 15. (855)295-7464, 47915 Homestead Rd., Berry Mills, NB E1G 3S5

NEW BANDON — B4 *Gloucester*

BACK HOME FAMILY CAMPGROUND **Ratings: 6.5/9★/8.5** (Campground) 40 Avail: 28 full hkups, 12 W, 12 E (20/50 amps). 2021 rates: $30 to $35. May 15 to Sep 19. (506)365-8920, 7195 Route 8, New Bandon, NB E9C 2B9

Check out 10/10/10 Good Sam Parks on the Good Sam Park page.*

NEW RIVER BEACH — E3 *Charlotte*

NEW RIVER BEACH (Public Prov Park) From St John, W 31 mi on Hwy 1 (L). Avail: 60 E (15 amps). 2021 rates: $10 to $90. May 18 to Oct 08. (800)561-0123

NEWTOWN — D3 *Kings*

ALL DONE RV CAMPING **Ratings: 5.5/NA/7.5** (Campground) Avail: 26 full hkups (30 amps). 2021 rates: $35. May 01 to Nov 01. (506)869-0547, 1468 Route 890 , Newtown, NB E4G 1N2

NICTAU — C2 *Victoria*

MOUNT CARLETON (Public Prov Park) From Hwy 385 (in town), N 20 mi on private rd (R). 88 Avail. 2021 rates: $28 to $43. May 30 to Sep 14. (506)235-0793

NIGADOO — B4 *Gloucester*

CAMPING HACHE **Ratings: 9/8★/7.5** (Campground) Avail: 30 full hkups (30 amps). 2021 rates: $29 to $39. May 10 to Sep 30. (506)430-2300, 264 Rue Principale, Nigadoo, NB E8K 3T3

OAK BAY — E2 *Charlotte*

OAK BAY CAMPGROUND **Ratings: 7/8.5★/8.5** (Campground) 62 Avail: 23 full hkups, 22 W, 22 E (30 amps). 2021 rates: $37 to $43. May 08 to Oct 14. (506)466-4999, 742 Rte 170, Oak Bay, NB E3L 4A4

OAK POINT — E3 *Kings*

KIWANIS OAK POINT CAMPGROUND & PARK (Public) From Jct of Hwys 7 & 102 (Westfield), N 18.6 mi on Hwy 102 (R). 66 Avail: 34 full hkups, 32 W, 32 E (15/30 amps). 2021 rates: $32 to $50. May 17 to Sep 15. (506)468-2266

OROMOCTO — D3 *Sunbury*

SUNBURY-OROMOCTO PARK **Ratings: 6.5/7/7** (Campground) 25 Avail: 13 full hkups, 12 W, 12 E (15/30 amps). 2021 rates: $37 to $40. May 15 to Sep 14. (506)357-3708, 413 Smith Rd., Oromocto, NB E2V 3S9

PENOBSQUIS — D4 *Kings*

LONE PINE PARK & CABINS **Ratings: 6.5/10★/8** (Campground) 20 Avail: 13 full hkups, 7 W, 7 E (20/30 amps). 2021 rates: $36.53. May 15 to Sep 18. (506)432-4007, 45 Lone Pine Rd, Penobsquis, NB E4E 5T3

PINE CONE CAMPING **Ratings: 9/9/8.5** (Campground) Avail: 10 full hkups (20/30 amps). 2021 rates: $41.83. May 15 to Sep 15. (506)433-4389, 12788 Rte 114 Hwy, Penobsquis, NB E4E 5L9

THREE BEARS FAMILY CAMPING & RV PARK **Ratings: 7.5/9★/8.5** (Campground) 110 Avail: 42 full hkups, 49 W, 48 E (30 amps). 2021 rates: $35 to $37. May 10 to Sep 23. (506)433-2870, 12049 Rte 114, Penobsquis, NB E4G 2Y2

PERTH-ANDOVER — C2 *Victoria*

ROBERT E BAIRD MEMORIAL PARK **Ratings: 6/7.5/7** (Campground) 24 Avail: 6 full hkups, 18 W, 18 E (20/30 amps). 2021 rates: $40 to $42. May 15 to Oct 20. (506)273-3080, 12255 Rte 105, Perth-Andover, NB E7H 3X2

PETIT-CAP — D5 *Westmorland*

SILVER SANDS CAMPGROUND **Ratings: 7/6/7** (Campground) Avail: 25 full hkups (30 amps). 2021 rates: $35 to $54. May 20 to Sep 30. (506)577-6771, 64 Chemin Du Camp, Petit Cap, NB E4N 2W2

You have high expectations, so we point out campgrounds, service centers and tourist attractions with elevations over 2,500 feet.

PETIT-ROCHER-NORD — B4 *Gloucester*

CAMPING MURRAYWOOD PARK **Ratings: 8/9★/8.5** (Campground) 83 Avail: 77 full hkups, 6 W, 6 E (30/50 amps). 2021 rates: $34.05 to $42.09. May 15 to Sep 30. (506)783-2137, 281 Route 134, Petit-Rocher-Nord, NB E8J 2E5

PLASTER ROCK — C2 *Victoria*

PLASTER ROCK TOURIST PARK (Public) From town, S 1 mi on Rte 108 (L). Avail: 11 full hkups (15 amps). 2021 rates: $30 to $34.50. Jun 17 to Aug 31. (506)356-6077

POINTE-SAPIN — C4 *Kent*

CAMPING L'ETOILE DE MER (Public) From Richucto, N 23 mi on Rte 117, exit at Kouchibouguac (R). 168 Avail: 42 W, 42 E (30/50 amps). 2021 rates: $15 to $48. May 01 to Oct 31. (506)876-2282

POINTE-VERTE — B4 *Gloucester*

CEDAR COVE CAMPGROUND **Ratings: 7.5/7.5/7** (RV Park) 91 Avail: 55 full hkups, 36 W, 36 E (30 amps). 2021 rates: $30 to $35. May 15 to Sep 15. (506)783-2648, 115 Rue Principale St, Pointe-Verte, NB E8J 2Z3

POKEMOUCHE — B4 *Gloucester*

CAMPING POKEMOUCHE
good sam park
Ratings: 10/10★/10 (Campground) 72 Avail: 45 full hkups, 23 W, 23 E (30/50 amps). 2021 rates: $40.87 to $54.69. May 15 to Sep 20. (506)727-6090, 11220, Rte 11, Pokemouche, NB E8P 1J8

PRINCE WILLIAM — D2 *York*

LAKE GEORGE FAMILY CAMPGROUND (Public) From jct Hwy 3 & Hwy 636: Go 12.8 km/8 mi N on Hwy 636. 27 Avail. 2021 rates: $30 to $40. (506)366-2933

RICHIBOUCTOU-VILLAGE — C4 *Kent*

CAMPING CAP LUMIERE BEACH **Ratings: 7.5/7.5/8** (RV Park) 80 Avail: 35 full hkups, 45 W, 45 E (30/50 amps). 2021 rates: $34.80 to $39.15. May 15 to Sep 15. (506)523-0994, 239 Ch Cap Lumiere, Richibouctou-Village, NB E4W 1C9

RICHIBUCTO — C4 *Kent*

PARC MUNICIPAL JARDINE MUNICIPAL PARK (Public) N-bnd: From Jct of Hwy 11 & Exit 57, E 500 ft to Prom Park Dr, E 0.25 mi on Prom Park Dr (E). 70 Avail: 68 full hkups, 2 W, 2 E (15/30 amps). 2021 rates: $30 to $60. May 15 to Sep 30. (506)523-7874

RIVIERE-DU-PORTAGE — B4 *Northumberland*

PLAGE TRACADIE BEACH CAMPING **Ratings: 6/7.5★/7.5** (Campground) 39 Avail: 19 full hkups, 20 W, 20 E (15/30 amps). 2021 rates: $42 to $46. May 15 to Sep 14. (506)395-4010, 5903 Route 11, Riviere-du-Portage, NB E9H 1W7

SAINT-ANDRE — C2 *Madawaska*

CAMPING PARADIS DE LA P'TITE MONTAGNE **Ratings: 8/8.5★/8.5** (RV Park) 87 Avail: 12 full hkups, 56 W, 56 E (30 amps). 2021 rates: $52 to $55. May 15 to Sep 15. (506)473-6683, 472 Chemin de la P'tite Montagne, Saint-Andre, NB E3Y 1H4

We give you what you want. First, we surveyed thousands of RVers just like you. Then, we developed our exclusive Triple Rating System for campgrounds based on the results. That's why our rating system is so good at explaining the quality of facilities and cleanliness of campgrounds.

SAINT-ANDREWS — E2 *Charlotte*

ISLAND VIEW CAMPING **Ratings: 5.5/8/8** (Campground) 48 Avail: 30 full hkups, 18 W, 18 E (30 amps). 2021 rates: $30 to $47. May 15 to Oct 15. (506)529-3787, 3406, Rte127, St Andrews, NB E5B 2V1

KIWANIS OCEAN FRONT CAMPING (Campground) (Phone Update) 60 Avail: 51 full hkups, 9 W, 9 E (30 amps). 2021 rates: $48 to $55. May 07 to Oct 15. (506)529-3439, 550 Water St, St Andrews, NB E5B 2R6

SAINT-BASILE — B1 *Madawaska*

CAMPING ST BASILE **Ratings: 7.5/8.5★/8.5** (Campground) 35 Avail: 14 full hkups, 21 W, 21 E (15/30 amps). 2021 rates: $37 to $40. May 15 to Sep 15. (506)263-1183, 14411 Rte 144, Edmundston, NB E7B 2L2

SAINT-JOHN — E3 *Saint John*

HARDINGS POINT CAMPGROUND

good sam park

Ratings: 8/9★/9 (Campground) From Jct of Hwy 7 & Exit 80 (Rte 177), E 0.75 mi on exit rd (Rte 102) to Rte 177, S 1.5 mi to Ferry Landing, take (free) Ferry (R). **FAC:** gravel rds. (175 spaces). 75 Avail: 40 gravel, 35 grass, 15 pull-thrus, (28x70), back-ins (25x65), 65 full hkups, 10 W, 10 E (30/50 amps), seasonal sites, WiFi, tent sites, shower$, dump, laundry, groc, fire rings, firewood, controlled access. **REC:** heated pool, Saint John River: swim, marina, kayaking/canoeing, playground. Pets OK. Big rig sites, eco-friendly. 2021 rates: $42 to $48. May 18 to Sep 30.
(506)763-2517 Lat: 45.352074, Lon: -66.217707
71 Hardings Point Landing Rd., Carters Point, NB E5S 1N8
hardingspointcampground.com
See ad this page

ROCKWOOD PARK **Ratings: 7/8.5★/8** (Campground) 180 Avail: 100 full hkups, 35 W, 35 E (20/30 amps). 2021 rates: $43. May 25 to Sep 30. (506)652-4050, 142 Lake Dr. South, Saint John, NB E2K 5S2

SAINT-LEONARD — C2 *Madawaska*

CAMPING ST LEONARD **Ratings: 8/8.5★/8** (Campground) 35 Avail: 30 full hkups, 5 W, 5 E (30/50 amps). 2021 rates: $40 to $50. May 29 to Sep 29. (506)423-6536, 470 Route #17, Saint-Leonard, NB E7E 2L7

SAINT-LOUIS-DE-KENT — C4 *Kent*

EVERGREEN ACRES CAMPGROUNDS **Ratings: 7/8★/8** (Campground) Avail: 40 full hkups (30 amps). 2021 rates: $30 to $35. May 15 to Sep 15. (506)876-4897, 10374 Route 134, Portage St-Louis, NB E4X 2L2

SAINT-MARTINS — E4 *St John*

CENTURY FARM FAMILY CAMPGROUND

good sam park

Ratings: 8.5/9.5★/8.5 (Campground) 80 Avail: 53 full hkups, 16 W, 16 E (30 amps). 2021 rates: $38 to $40. May 15 to Sep 30. (866)394-4400, 67 Ocean Wave Dr., St Martins, NB E5R 2E8

SHEDIAC — D5 *Westmorland*

BEAUSEJOUR CAMPING **Ratings: 7/8.5★/8.5** (Campground) 39 Avail: 25 full hkups, 14 W, 14 E (30/50 amps). 2021 rates: $39 to $60. May 01 to Oct 15. (506)532-5885, 747 Lino Rd, Shediac, NB E4P 1Z5

CAMPING OCEANIC **Ratings: 8/9/9** (Campground) Avail: 75 full hkups (30/50 amps). 2021 rates: $49.75 to $58.80. May 15 to Sep 15. (506)533-7006, 221 Chemin Ohio, Shediac, NB E4P 2J8

CAMPING PARASOL **Ratings: 7/9.5★/8** (Campground) 40 Avail: 30 full hkups, 10 W, 10 E (30/50 amps). 2021 rates: $40 to $52. May 15 to Oct 15. (506)532-8229, 205 Rue Main, Shediac, NB E4P 2A5

OCEAN SURF RV PARK

good sam park

Ratings: 10/10★/10 (Campground) Avail: 150 full hkups (30/50 amps). 2021 rates: $55 to $65. May 10 to Oct 10. (506)532-5480, 73 Belliveau Beach Rd, Pointe-Du-Chene, NB E4P 3W2

OCEAN VIEW PARK **Ratings: 7.5/8★/8** (Campground) 38 Avail: 7 full hkups, 25 W, 25 E (20/30 amps). 2021 rates: $37.40 to $39.14. May 15 to Sep 25. (506)532-3520, 1586 Rte 133, Grand-Barachois, NB E4P 8H2

PARLEE BEACH (Campground) (Phone Update) 205 Avail: 65 full hkups, 9 W, 9 E (15/30 amps). 2021 rates: $32 to $38. May 20 to Sep 06. (506)532-1500, 25 Gould Beach Rd, Pointe-du-Chene, NB E4P 4S8

SOUTH-COVE CAMPING & GOLF (Campground) (Phone Update) Avail: 11 full hkups (30/50 amps). 2021 rates: $35 to $50. May 15 to Oct 01. (506)532-6713, 55 South Cove Rd., Shediac, NB E4P 2T4

WISHING STAR CAMPGROUND **Ratings: 7.5/8.5/8** (RV Park) Avail: 40 full hkups (30/50 amps). 2021 rates: $40 to $47. May 15 to Oct 15. (506)532-6786, 218 Main St, Shediac, NB E4P 2E1

SHIPPAGAN — B5 *Gloucester*

CAMPING JANINE DU HAVRE **Ratings: 5/8★/7** (Campground) 42 Avail: 12 full hkups, 30 W, 30 E (15/30 amps). 2021 rates: $28 to $30. May 01 to Oct 31. (506)336-8884, 48 Chemin Chiasson, Shippagan, NB E8S 3A6

CAMPING SHIPPAGAN (Public) From Jct of Rtes 11 & 113, N 10 mi on Rte 113 to blvd J.D. Gauthier, W 2.5 mi (R). 101 Avail: 55 W, 55 E (15/30 amps). 2021 rates: $27 to $34.50. Jun 01 to Sep 09. (506)336-3960

SUSSEX — D4 *Kings*

SUSSEX KOA (Campground) (Phone Update) Avail: 49 full hkups (20/30 amps). 2021 rates: $37.65 to $73.77. May 25 to Sep 15. (506)432-6788, 133 Aiton Rd, Sussex, NB E4G 2V5

TABUSINTAC — B4 *Northumberland*

RIVER HAVEN CAMPGROUND **Ratings: 7.5/7.5/8** (Campground) 53 Avail: 37 full hkups, 16 W, 16 E (30/50 amps). 2021 rates: $30 to $35. May 15 to Sep 30. (506)779-4608, 119 J Mackenzie Rd., Tabusintac, NB E9H 2B8

TRACADIE-SHEILA — B4 *Gloucester*

AQUAPARC DE LA RIVIERE TRACADIE **Ratings: 8/9★/8** (Campground) Avail: 30 full hkups (15/30 amps). 2021 rates: $34 to $50. May 15 to Sep 30. (506)393-7759, 3205 Rue Alcide, Tracadie-Sheila, NB E1X 1A5

CHALETS ET CAMPING DE LA POINTE **Ratings: 8.5/8/7** (Campground) Avail: 78 full hkups (30/50 amps). 2021 rates: $32 to $45. May 15 to Sep 15. (506)393-0987, C.P. 20003 - Centre Ville, Tracadie Sheila, NB E1X 1G6

RV Tech Tips - Stable Cables for Towed Vehicles: The various cables from your motorhome to your towed vehicle can get frayed while traveling and when exiting or entering a service station that was a bit higher than the highway. The angle can cause the cables to end up crushed between the dropped receiver and the driveway. A permanent fix for this is to install two pieces of angle iron 1/4-inch higher than the bottom of the receiver, secure with the same huge bolt that secures the receiver to your tow bar. This pair of ""shelves'' keeps the cables out of harm's way. Wire ties, of course, complete the installation.

VAL-COMEAU — B4 *Gloucester*

VAL COMEAU (Public Prov Park) N-bnd: In town on Rte 11, end of peninsula (R). Avail: 120 full hkups (30 amps). 2021 rates: $27 to $50. Jun 01 to Sep 08. (506)393-7150

WATERBOROUGH — D3 *Queens*

MOHAWK CAMPING **Ratings: 6/UI/7.5** (Campground) Avail: 10 full hkups (20/30 amps). 2021 rates: $28 to $32. May 15 to Oct 15. (506)362-5250, 6249 RTe 105, Waterborough, NB E4C 2Y5

WELSHPOOL — E2 *Charlotte*

HERRING COVE (Public Prov Park) From Jct of US-1 & SR-189 (in ME), NE 6.2 mi on SR-189, cross bridge at Lubec to Hwy 774, follow signs (R). 93 Avail: (30 amps). 2021 rates: $28 to $43. May 23 to Sep 21. (506)752-7010

WOODSTOCK — D2 *Carleton*

CONNELL PARK CAMPGROUND (Public) From Jct of TCH 2 & exit 188 (Connell Rd), S 0.75 mi on Connell Rd (R). Avail: 90 full hkups (15/30 amps). 2021 rates: $25 to $32. May 17 to Sep 18. (506)325-4979

YOGI BEAR'S JELLYSTONE PARK CAMP RESORTS

good sam park

Ratings: 9.5/9.5★/9 (Campground) From Jct of TCH-2 & Exit 191 (Beardsley Rd/Woodstock Direction), N 0.25 mi on Beardsley Rd to Hemlock St, W 0.25 mi, follow signs (E). **FAC:** paved rds. Avail: 142 all weather, 60 pull-thrus, (35x80), back-ins (27x60), 142 W, 142 E (30/50 amps), WiFi @ sites, tent sites, rentals, dump, mobile sewer, laundry, groc, LP bottles, fire rings, firewood, controlled access. **REC:** heated pool, wading pool, boating nearby, playground, rec open to public. Pets OK. Partial handicap access, eco-friendly. 2021 rates: $69.50 to $72.50. Jun 01 to Sep 03.
(506)328-6287 Lat: 46.125304, Lon: -67.604006
174 Hemlock St., Lower Woodstock, NB E7M 4E5
www.jellystoneparknb.com
See ad this page

Get the GOOD SAM CAMPING APP

Getty Images/iStockphoto

DID YOU KNOW?

In St. John's, there are more bars per square foot on George Street than anywhere else in Canada.

NL

YOU ARE HERE

Newfoundland & Labrador

Newfoundland and Labrador pack big scenery, from breaching whales that make a big splash to huge icebergs that float by like ghost ships. On land, the vistas are equally rich, with rugged landscapes and tall mountains.

St. John's Speech

When you meet locals from St. John, the first thing you'll notice is their distinctive brogue. But that's not the only trait that sets this city apart. Climb Signal Hill to explore Cabot Tower, a historic structure with sweeping views of the surrounding coastline and the Atlantic Ocean. You'll also want to visit the Rooms for its impressive collection of local art. Motor about 10 miles out of town to make a stop at the Cape Spear Lighthouse, the easternmost point in North America (except for Danish-controlled Greenland). In Bonavista, see colorful row houses and a replica of Cabot's ship.

Gros Morne Dazzles

Gros Morne National Park has received international acclaim, and it's not hard to see why. The UNESCO World Heritage Site attracts hikers to its lush river valleys, sheer cliffs and rare flora and fauna. The remarkable flat-top mountains date back 500 million years and have helped geologists understand plate tectonics theory.

Where the Vikings Are

Bold Viking settlers landed on the area now known as Newfoundland in the year 1000, predating Christopher Columbus's landing by almost 500 years. Today, you can see what's left of one of their settlements at the L'Anse aux Meadows National Historic Site on the northern tip of Newfoundland. Excavated wood-framed buildings and 1,000-year-old artifacts provide incredible insight into how the Vikings lived. Costumed guides and a dramatic backdrop of cliffs, coastline and bogs round out the experience.

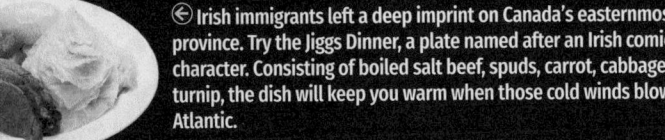

The Jiggs Dinner

Irish immigrants left a deep imprint on Canada's easternmost province. Try the Jiggs Dinner, a plate named after an Irish comic strip character. Consisting of boiled salt beef, spuds, carrot, cabbage and turnip, the dish will keep you warm when those cold winds blow off the Atlantic.

VISITOR CENTER

TIME ZONE
Newfoundland Standard

ROAD & HIGHWAY INFORMATION
709-729-2300
www.gov.nl.ca/ti/roads/home/

FISHING & HUNTING INFORMATION
709-637-2025
flr.gov.nl.ca/wildlife/permits

BOATING INFORMATION
800-267-6687
tc.gc.ca/eng/marinesafety/debs-obs-menu-1362.htm

NATIONAL PARKS
pc.gc.ca/en/pn-np

PROVINCIAL PARKS
tcii.gov.nl.ca/parks

TOURISM INFORMATION
Newfoundland and Labrador Tourism
800-563-6353
newfoundlandlabrador.com

TOP TOURISM ATTRACTIONS
1) St. John's
2) Cape St. Mary's Ecological Reserve
3) Gros Morne National Park

MAJOR CITIES
St. John's (capital), Conception Bay South, Mount Pearl, Corner Brook, Paradise

good sam park Featured Good Sam Parks

NEWFOUNDLAND AND LABRADOR

When you stay with Good Sam, you can expect the highest degree of cleanliness and friendliness, and better yet, you get **10% off** overnight campground fees.

If you're not already a Good Sam member you can purchase your membership at one of these locations:

DEER LAKE
Gateway To the North RV Park

ROBINSONS
Pirate's Haven RV Park & Chalets

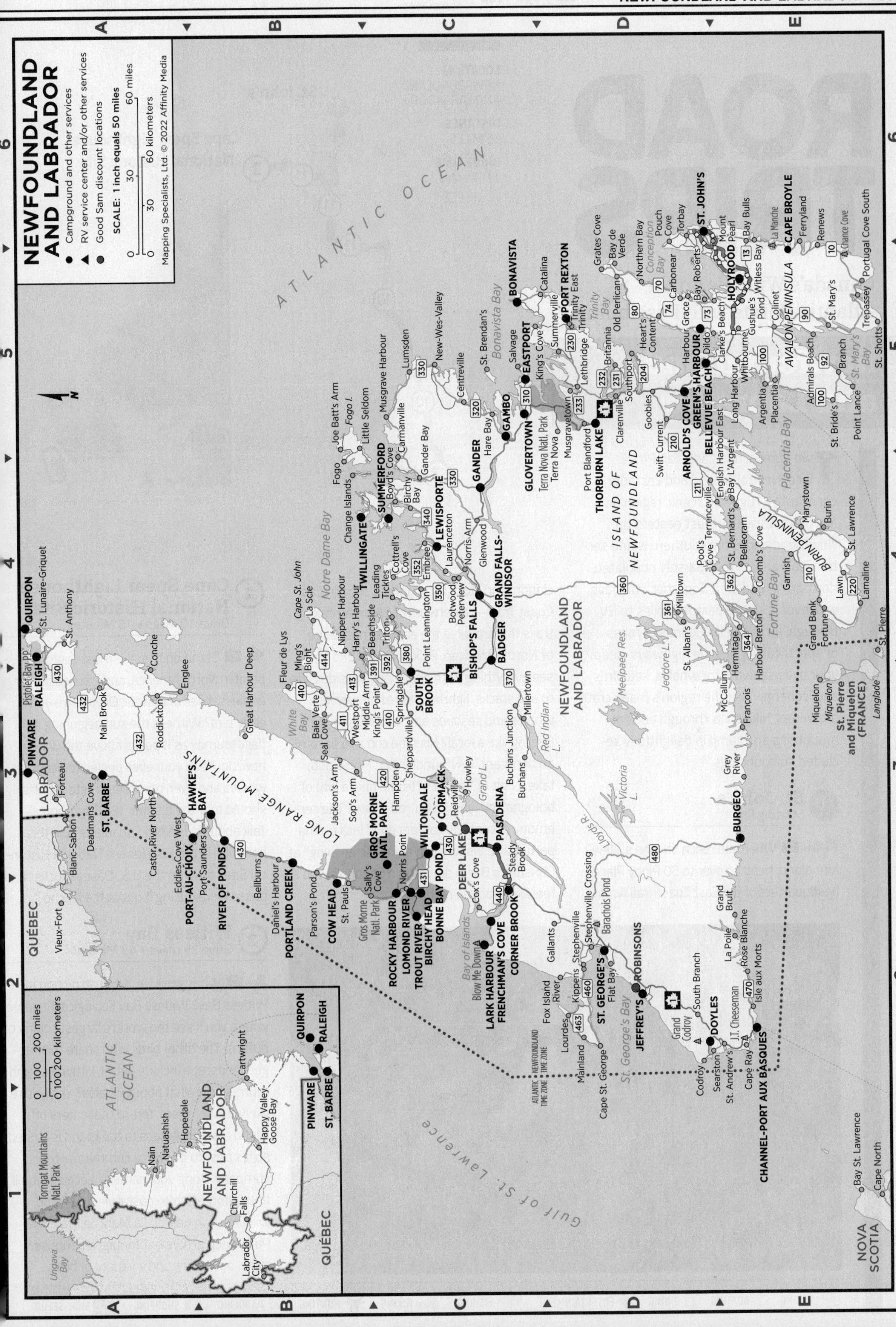
NEWFOUNDLAND AND LABRADOR
Campground and other services
RV service center and/or other services
Good Sam discount locations
SCALE: 1 inch equals 50 miles
0 30 60 miles
0 30 60 kilometers
Mapping Specialists, Ltd. © 2022 Affinity Media
ATLANTIC OCEAN
LONG RANGE MOUNTAINS
Gulf of St. Lawrence
ISLAND OF NEWFOUNDLAND
NEWFOUNDLAND AND LABRADOR
AVALON PENINSULA
BURIN PENINSULA
QUÉBEC
LABRADOR
NOVA SCOTIA
St. Pierre and Miquelon (FRANCE)
ATLANTIC TIME ZONE
NEWFOUNDLAND TIME ZONE
QUIRPON
RALEIGH
PINWARE
ST. BARBE
HAWKE'S BAY
PORT-AU-CHOIX
RIVER OF PONDS
PORTLAND CREEK
COW HEAD
GROS MORNE NATL. PARK
ROCKY HARBOUR
LOMOND RIVER
TROUT RIVER
BIRCHY HEAD
BONNE BAY POND
WILTONDALE
CORMACK
DEER LAKE
PASADENA
LARK HARBOUR
FRENCHMAN'S COVE
CORNER BROOK
ST. GEORGE'S
ROBINSONS
JEFFREY'S
DOYLES
CHANNEL-PORT AUX BASQUES
BURGEO
SOUTH BROOK
BISHOP'S FALLS
BADGER
GRAND FALLS-WINDSOR
LEWISPORTE
TWILLINGATE
SUMMERFORD
GANDER
GAMBO
GLOVERTOWN
EASTPORT
BONAVISTA
PORT REXTON
THORBURN LAKE
ARNOLD'S COVE
GREEN'S HARBOUR
BELLEVUE BEACH
HOLYROOD
ST. JOHN'S
CAPE BROYLE
Notre Dame Bay
Bonavista Bay
Trinity Bay
Conception Bay
Placentia Bay
Fortune Bay
St. Mary's Bay
Bay of Islands
St. George's Bay
White Bay
Terra Nova Natl. Park
Torngat Mountains Natl. Park
Red Indian L.
Grand L.
Meelpaeg Res.
Victoria L.
Ungava Bay

ROAD TRIPS

Canada's Window on the Atlantic Bursts with Possibilities

Newfoundland and Labrador

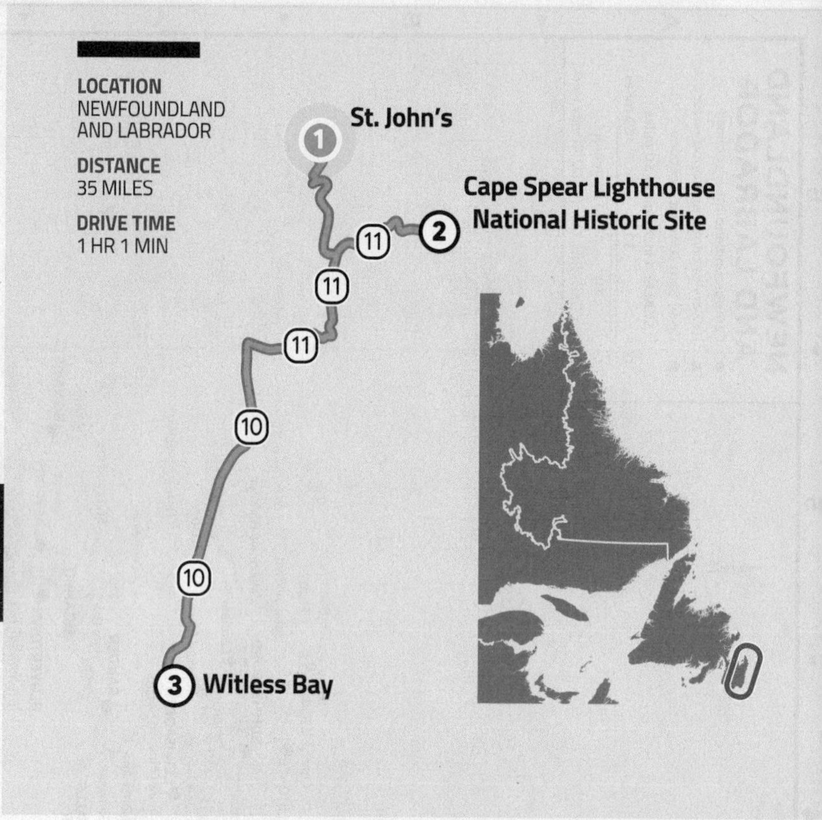

Two names, one Canadian Province. Newfoundland and Labrador constitute a ruggedly scenic region on North America's farthest eastern tip. Newfoundland is the southern island section; Labrador is the sparsely populated northern inland area. Together, you have well over 150,000 pastoral miles to RV through, including thousands of miles of spectacular coastline highways. Keep your eyes seaward for whales, sea birds and icebergs. Visit the region's many craft breweries, hike trails through ancient mountains and camp in delightfully secluded surroundings.

1 St. John's
Starting Point

When you reach St. John's, Newfoundland, head on over to 50 Pippy Place, headquarters of the East Coast Trail Association, and stock up on info about the East Coast Trail — a network of 26 breathtaking trails that traverse the easternmost edge of North American. Pick your trail and you'll see everything from enormous seaside cliffs to sea stacks, lighthouses, eco-reserves, whales and seabirds and icebergs, oh my! Feeling like a local? Kiss the cod and become an honorary Newfoundlander! Find a pub, take a belt of "screech" (rum), take a bite of bologna and, yes, kiss a cod. *Bravo!* The ceremony essentially confers good luck on the participant. Visitors can enjoy "screeching" at Christian's Bar in downtown St. John's. You'll feel like a local in no time.

2 Cape Spear Lighthouse National Historic Site
Drive 10 miles ▪ 18 Minutes

Stand on this, the most easterly point in North America, and gaze east over endless miles of Atlantic Ocean. Are you an early bird? Witness the sun beginning its daily journey as it peeks above the watery horizon. Keep your eyes peeled for icebergs, whales and even porpoises. History buffs should tour the historic 1836 lighthouse. Talk about old. While Canadians built this beautiful lighthouse (now a National Historical Site), down in the U.S., Davey Crocket and posse were duking it out at the Alamo.

3 Witless Bay
Drive 25 miles ▪ 43 Minutes

What's the No. 1 top attraction in Witless Bay? Witless Bay Ecological Reserve, where you'll see the world's largest colony of puffins. The other birds who share this rugged landscape include petrel, kittiwakes and murres. But what about whales? Yes, you're likely to spot them, too, in the waters off island reserve. Access to the island is limited so it's best to go with a commercial tour company. Bring your camera, because you'll find unforgettable coastal views — and wildlife — in nearby La Manche Provincial Park. Keep an eye out for beaver, moose, mink, butterflies and a variety of birds.

Getty Images/iStockphoto

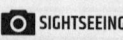

BIKING · BOATING · DINING · ENTERTAINMENT · FISHING · HIKING · HUNTING · PADDLING · SHOPPING · SIGHTSEEING

Newfoundland and Labrador

SPOTLIGHTS

Go Extreme on the Atlantic

North America's easternmost region treats visitors to unforgettable travel experiences. See icebergs floating off the coast and witness whales breaching in the Atlantic. Take a seat in a St. John's pub for an interesting initiation ceremony.

BONAVISTA IS ONE OF THE WINDIEST PLACES IN CANADA.

Fishing boats docked in Bonavista Harbour, which connects to the Atlantic Ocean.

Getty Images/iStockphoto

Bonavista

In 1497, Italian explorer John Cabot made landfall on a rocky coast on a strange new land. Five centuries later, the town of Bonavista honors the discovery of Newfoundland and Labrador in a variety of ways. Visit the replica of his tall ship and view whales and icebergs near shore. But there's much more to discover in this coastal enclave. Bonavista is a community rich in history and cultural traditions from centuries past.

Picturesque Places

Set aside time to enjoy the vibrant scenery of this community. Rows of small, colorful houses, new and old, sit alongside rocky shores, pebble beaches and picturesque fishing boats. The dense forest becomes an amazing shoreline, frequently visited by whales, seabirds, and icebergs. At the Dungeon Provincial Park, the cliffs drop away into a mammoth sinkhole with two seaward channels, the result of years of ocean erosion. In fact, throughout the peninsula, the past is recorded in the land and seascapes.

Butter Pot Provincial Park

Butter Pot Provincial Park in Newfoundland inspires visitors with stunning and rugged landscapes. Located 22 miles south of St. John's on the Trans-Canada Highway, Butter Pot is the product of millennia of carving, dragging and gouging by glaciers during the wane of the last ice age, 10,000 years ago. The result is a starkly beautiful landscape highlighted by beautifully shaped rocks that were dragged there by ice sheets.

St. John's

Homey pubs and stellar views combine to form a one-of-a-kind travel experience in this coastal town. Nestled in the steep hills of a sheltered harbor, the capital of Newfoundland is home to impressive food culture, sweeping views of the Atlantic Ocean, colorful row houses and more. Local pubs intiate visitors with a "screech" ceremony, which involves kissing a cod and taking shots of rum.

Hike the East Coast Trail

Follow a trail that is unmatched in scenery and adventure. The East Coast Trail, which runs through St. John's, is calling your name. This 335-mile-long hiking trail takes you through soaring cliffs, scenic headlands, deep fjords and a wave-driven geyser. It's also a great way to come face-to-face with wildlife. Keep your eyes peeled for whales, sea bird colonies and herds of caribou.

› **FOR MORE INFORMATION**

Newfoundland and Labrador, 800-563-6353
www.newfoundlandlabrador.com
Historic Bonavista, 709-468-7747
www.townofbonavista.com
Butter Pot Provincial Park, 800-563-6181
www.gov.nl.ca/tcii/parks/p-bup
Destination St. John's, 877-739-8899,
www.destinationstjohns.com

LOCAL FAVORITE

Shrimp Boil Foil Packets

Buy fresh shrimp from a seafood market and enjoy one of this province's most delicious exports. *Recipe by Sheryl Paul.*

INGREDIENTS

- ☐ 1 lbs pkg smoked sausage (cut into cubes)
- ☐ 1 ½ lb uncooked shrimp (preferably large)
- ☐ 6 ears corn on the cob (cut each ear in ½" or ⅓")
- ☐ 4 baby red potatoes (cubed or sliced)
- ☐ 1 Tbsp Cajun seasoning
- ☐ 1 Tbsp butter
- ☐ 2 Tbsp vegetable oil
- ☐ 2 tsp parsley
- ☐ Salt & pepper

DIRECTIONS

Using heavy-duty foil, evenly distribute corn, potatoes, shrimp and sausage among 4 pieces of foil.
Drizzle butter and vegetable oil over each foil packet.
Season with Cajun seasoning, parsley and salt and pepper to taste.
Tightly seal the foil packets by folding up the sides over the contents and tightly fold up the ends over the seam.
Grill 30-40 minutes at 400 F°. Flip once halfway through.
Be careful when opening the packets to check for doneness. The steam inside is very hot.

Newfoundland & Labrador

ARNOLD'S COVE — D5 *Avalon Region*

JACKS POND PARK **Ratings: 6.5/7.5/7.5** (Campground) 50 Avail: 50 W, 50 E (20/30 amps). 2021 rates: $21.74 to $30.44. May 15 to Sep 30. (709)463-0150, Hwy 1, Arnolds Cove, NL A0B 1A0

BADGER — C4 *Central Region*

CATAMARAN PARK **Ratings: 8/9.5★/9** (Campground) 205 Avail: 205 W, 205 E (15/30 amps). 2021 rates: $37.95. May 16 to Sep 15. (709)539-5115, Hwy 1, Badger, NL A0H 1A0

BELLEVUE BEACH — D5 *Avalon Region*

BELLEVUE BEACH CAMPGROUND **Ratings: 6/7.5/8.5** (Campground) 85 Avail: 85 W, 85 E (20/30 amps). 2021 rates: $30. May 15 to Sep 04. (709)442-4536, 239 Main Road, Bellevue, NL A0B 1B0

BIRCHY HEAD — C2 *Division No. 5*

THE WATER'S EDGE RV CAMPGROUND (Public National Park) From Hwy 430 & 431: Go 33.4 km/20 3/4 mi W on 431. 25 Avail: 25 W, 25 E (30 amps). 2021 rates: $22 to $26. May 01 to Oct 01. (709)453-2020

BISHOP'S FALLS — C4 *Central Region*

BROOKDALE COUNTRY INN & RV PARK **Ratings: 7.5/7.5/8** (Campground) 26 Avail: 24 full hkups, 2 W, 2 E (30/50 amps). 2021 rates: $30 to $40. (709)258-7377, 10 Main St, Bishops Falls, NL A0H 1C0

FALLSVIEW MUNICIPAL PARK (Public) From Jct of TCH-1 & exit 21 (Bishop's Falls), S 4 mi on Main St to Powerhouse Rd, W 0.25 mi (E). 24 Avail: 24 W, 24 E (15/30 amps). 2021 rates: $15 to $18. Jun 12 to Sep 07. (709)258-6581

BONAVISTA — C5 *Eastern Region*

PARADISE FARM TRAILER PARK (Campground) (Phone Update) 30 Avail: 30 W, 30 E (30/50 amps). 2021 rates: $35 to $40. May 15 to Sep 15. (709)468-8811, Hwy 230, Bonavista, NL A0C 1B0

BONNE BAY POND — C3 *Division No. 9*

THE JACKLADDER RV PARK AND RESTAURANT **Ratings: 7/8.5★/8** (Campground) 22 Avail: 15 full hkups, 7 W, 7 E (30/50 amps). 2021 rates: $40. May 07 to Oct 31. (709)635-5000, #6 Route 430, Bonne Bay Pond, NL A8A 3N3

BURGEO — E3 *Central Region*

SANDBANKS (Public Prov Park) In town on Hwy 480. 30 Avail. 2021 rates: $20.15. May 31 to Sep 15. (877)214-2267

Read RV topics at blog.GoodSam.com

Newfoundland & Labrador Privately Owned Campground Information Updated by our Good Sam Representatives

Patrice Richard & Chantal Belisle

We sold everything in 2002, then traveled in Canada coast to coast, U.S. (44 states) and Mexico. We're Frenchies who switch from one culture to another. La vie est trop courte, il faut la prendre en riant. Life's too short so take it with a laugh.

CAPE BROYLE — E5 *Avalon Region*

LA MANCHE (Public Prov Park) From town: Go 11.5 km/7 mi N on Hwy 10. 83 Avail: Pit toilets. 2021 rates: $30.90. May 15 to Sep 15. (877)214-2267

CHANNEL-PORT-AUX-BASQUES — E2 *Western Region*

JT CHEESEMAN (Public Prov Park) From town, E 6 km (3.6 mi) on TCH 1 (L) Daily vehicle permit fee. 92 Avail. 2021 rates: $30.90. May 15 to Sep 15. (877)214-2267

CORMACK — C3 *Western Region*

FUNLAND RESORT **Ratings: 7.5/8★/7.5** (Campground) Avail: 3 full hkups (30 amps). 2021 rates: $25 to $35. May 15 to Sep 15. (709)635-7227, 34 Veterans Dr, Cormack, NL A8A 2P8

CORNER BROOK — C2 *Humber West*

APPALACHIAN CHALETS & RV (Campground) (Phone Update) Avail: 37 full hkups (30/50 amps). 2021 rates: $33 to $38. May 20 to Oct 01. (709)632-2278, 64 Lundrigan Drive, Corner Brook, NL A2H 6G7

PRINCE EDWARD CAMPGROUNDS & RV PARK **Ratings: 7/9.5★/8** (Campground) 90 Avail: 78 full hkups, 12 W, 12 E (30/50 amps). 2021 rates: $36 to $38. Jun 23 to Sep 15. (709)637-1580, North Shore Hwy Rte 440, Corner Brook, NL A2H 6J7

COW HEAD — B2 *Western Region*

GROS MORNE/SHALLOW BAY

(Public National Park) From Cow Head, N 2 km on Main St (E). **FAC:** gravel rds. Avail: 62 grass, back-ins (20x40), tent sites, rentals, dump, fire rings, firewood. **REC:** Gulf of St Lawrence: swim, fishing, playground, rec open to public. Pets OK. Partial handicap access. 2021 rates: $18.60 to $25.50. Jun 01 to Sep 16.
(877)737-3783 Lat: 49.930833, Lon: -57.766333
Cow Head, NL A0K 4N0
www.pc.gc.ca

DEER LAKE — C2 *Western Region*

GATEWAY TO THE NORTH RV PARK

good sam park **Ratings: 9.5/10★/10** (Campground) Avail: 25 full hkups (30/50 amps). 2021 rates: $43.49. Jun 15 to Sep 15. (709)635-2693, 1 Bonne Bay Rd., Deer Lake, NL A8A 2Z4

SIR RICHARD SQUIRES MEMORIAL (Public Prov Park) From town: Go 12.7 km/8 mi NW on Hwy 430, then 27.3 km/17 mi NE on Hwy 422. 157 Avail. 2021 rates: $20.15. May 01 to Sep 01. (877)214-2267

DOYLES — D2 *Western Region*

GRAND CODROY RV CAMPING **Ratings: 6.5/9★/9.5** (Campground) 82 Avail: 38 full hkups, 36 W, 36 E (30 amps). 2021 rates: $40. May 15 to Sep 30. (877)955-2520, 5 Doyles Station Rd., Doyles, NL A0N 1J0

EASTPORT — C5 *Central Region*

HAROLD W. DUFFETT SHRINERS RV PARK Ratings: 8.5/9.5★/9 (Campground) Avail: 61 full hkups (30/50 amps). 2021 rates: $34 to $40. May 15 to Sep 30. (709)677-2438, Route 310, Eastport, NL A0G 1Z0

FRENCHMAN'S COVE — C2 *Western Region*

FRENCHMAN'S COVE (Public Prov Park) From town: Go 1 km/1/2 mi S on Hwy 210. 76 Avail: Pit toilets. 2021 rates: $30.90. May 15 to Sep 15. (709)214-2267

GAMBO — C5 *Central Region*

DAVID SMALLWOOD PARK (TOWN PARK) (Public) From jct Hwy 1 & Hwy 320: Go 7.1 km/4.3 mi N on Hwy 320. Avail: 15 E (20/30 amps). 2021 rates: $18 to $25. May 19 to Sep 05. (709)674-0122

SQUARE POND FRIENDS AND FAMILY RV PARK **Ratings: 6.5/UI/9** (Campground) 40 Avail: 40 W, 21 E (30 amps). 2021 rates: $32 to $38. May 18 to Sep 10. (709)674-7566, Hwy 1, Gambo, NL A0G 2L0

GANDER — C4 *Central Region*

COUNTRY INN MOTEL & TRAILER PARK Ratings: 6.5/8.5/8 (RV Park) 36 Avail: 36 W, 36 E (30 amps). 2021 rates: $30 to $36. May 15 to Oct 15. (877)956-4005, 315 Magee Rd., Gander, NL A1V 1W6

Show Your Good Sam Membership Card!

JONATHAN'S POND CAMPGROUND **Ratings: 5.5/8★/8** (Campground) 50 Avail: 50 W, 50 E (30 amps). 2021 rates: $20 to $26. May 19 to Sep 30. (709)651-2492, Route 330, Gander Bay Rd., Gander Bay, NL A1V 1W5

GLOVERTOWN — C5 *Central Region*

TERRA NOVA/MALADY HEAD (Public National Park) From jct TCH 1 & Hwy 310 (Eastport Peninsula exit): Go 5.7 km/3-1/2 mi E on Hwy 310/Traytown (R). 92 Avail. 2021 rates: $15.70 to $29.40. Jun 29 to Sep 18. (877)737-3783

TERRA NOVA/NEWMAN SOUND (Public National Park) From Jct of TCH 1 & Hwy 310, S 7 mi on TCH 1 (L). Avail: 202 E (20 amps). 2021 rates: $18.60 to $29.40. May 17 to Oct 09. (877)737-3783

GRAND FALLS-WINDSOR — C4 *Central Region*

SANGER MEMORIAL RV PARK (Public) From Jct of TCH-1 & exit 20 (Scott Avenue), S 1.5 mi on Scott Avenue (L). Avail: 47 full hkups (15/50 amps). 2021 rates: $31 to $33. Jun 16 to Sep 05. (709)489-7350

GREEN'S HARBOUR — D5 *Avalon Region*

GOLDEN ARM PARK **Ratings: 8.5/8/8** (Campground) Avail: 60 full hkups (20/30 amps). 2021 rates: $27. May 01 to Oct 20. (709)582-3600, RT 80, Greens Harbour, NL A0B 1X0

GROS MORNE NATIONAL PARK — C3 *Western Region*

GROS MORNE/GREEN POINT (Public National Park) From Rocky Harbour, N 12 km or Rte 430 (L). 33 Avail. 2021 rates: $15.70. (877)737-3783

HAWKE'S BAY — B3 *Western Region*

TORRENT RIVER NATURE PARK **Ratings: 4.5/8★/7.5** (Campground) 24 Avail: 24 W, 24 E (30 amps). 2021 rates: $20 to $23. Jun 01 to Sep 30. (709)248-5344, Hwy 430, Hawke's Bay, NL A0K 3B0

HOLYROOD — E5 *Division No. 1*

BUTTER POT (Public Prov Park) From town: Go 32 km/20 mi SW on Hwy 1. 175 Avail. 2021 rates: $20.15. May 15 to Sep 15. (709)214-2267

JEFFREYS — D2 *Western Region*

WISHINGWELL CAMPGROUND **Ratings: 2/6.5/7** (Campground) Avail: 32 full hkups (15/20 amps). 2021 rates: $10 to $22. May 15 to Oct 01. (709)645-2501, 520 Seaside Road Southwest, Jeffreys, NL A0N 1P0

LARK HARBOUR — C2 *Western Region*

BLOW ME DOWN (Public Prov Park) From Jct of Rtes 450 & 1, W 36 mi on Rte 450 (R). 28 Avail. 2021 rates: $20.15. Jun 01 to Sep 15. (709)214-2267

LEWISPORTE — C4 *Central Region*

NOTRE DAME (Public Prov Park) From town, W 7 mi on Lewisporte Hwy to TCH 1, E 0.7 mi (R). 100 Avail. 2021 rates: $20.15. May 15 to Sep 15. (877)214-2267

WOOLFREY'S POND TRAIL CAMPGROUND **Ratings: 7.5/8.5★/7.5** (Campground) 56 Avail: 36 W, 36 E (30/50 amps). 2021 rates: $16.50 to $27.50. May 31 to Sep 01. (709)541-2267, Church St, Lewisporte, NL A0G 3A0

LOMOND RIVER — C2 *Western Region*

LOMOND RIVER LODGE AND RV PARK **Ratings: 6.5/8.5★/8.5** (Campground) Avail: 13 full hkups (15 amps). 2021 rates: $20 to $35. May 15 to Oct 15. (877)456-6663, Route 431, Lomond River, NL A0K 3V0

TRAVELING WITH YOUR PET: Ban the barking. Dog barking is a major annoyance to RV park neighbors, but a few simple exercises can put a stop to it. For example, if your dog gets anxious when you leave the RV, start daily training sessions that have you coming and going from your RV while gradually extending your away times. Just don't leave your pet unattended too long, even well-behaved dogs will bark at outside noises. Other good tools include pheromone collars with calming scents and anti-anxiety music composed especially for dogs.

PASADENA — C3 *Western Region*

PINERIDGE CABINS & CAMPGROUND **Ratings: 8/8★/7.5** (Campground) 10 Avail: 2 full hkups, 8 W, 8 E (30 amps). 2021 rates: $33. May 15 to Sep 25. (709)686-2541, South Service Rd, Pasadena, NL A0L 1K0

PINWARE — A3 *Labrador Region*

PINWARE RIVER (Public Prov Park) From Trans-Labrador Hwy/NL-510 N at West St Modeste: Go 2.2 km SE to Pinware, then go 700 m (E). 22 Avail: Pit toilets. 2021 rates: $20.15. Jun 01 to Sep 15. (877)214-2267

PORT REXTON — D5 *Eastern Region*

LOCKSTON PATH (Public Prov Park) From town: Go 6.8 km/4 mi N on Hwy 236. 57 Avail: 20 W, 20 E. 2021 rates: $20.15. May 15 to Sep 15. (709)464-3553

PORT-AU-CHOIX — B3 *Western Region*

OCEANSIDE RV PARK **Ratings: 6/8★/7** (Campground) Avail: 26 full hkups (30 amps). 2021 rates: $30. May 24 to Sep 30. (709)861-3163, 18 Fisher Street, Route 430, Port Au Choix, NL A0K 4H0

PORTLAND CREEK — B3 *Western Region*

MOUNTAIN WATERS RESORT **Ratings: 7/9★/8.5** (RV Park) Avail: 15 full hkups (30 amps). 2021 rates: $30. Jun 01 to Oct 10. (709)898-2490, RT 430, Portland Creek, NL A0K 4G0

QUIRPON — A4 *Western Region*

VIKING RV PARK Ratings: 7.5/9.5★/9.5 (Campground) 40 Avail: 40 W, 40 E (15/30 amps). 2021 rates: $30. Jun 01 to Sep 30. (709)623-2425, Main St, Quirpon, NL A0K 2X0

RALEIGH — A4 *Western Region*

PISTOLET BAY (Public Prov Park) From Jct of Rtes 430 & 437, S 16 mi on Rte 437 (R). 30 Avail. 2021 rates: $20.15. May 01 to Sep 15. (877)214-2267

RIVER OF PONDS — B3 *Western Region*

RIVER OF PONDS PARK **Ratings: 5.5/7★/7.5** (Campground) 64 Avail: 28 W, 28 E (30 amps). 2021 rates: $17.40 to $25.45. Jun 01 to Sep 30. (709)225-3130, Hwy 430, River of Ponds, NL A0K 4M0

ROBINSONS — D2 *Division No. 4*

PIRATE'S HAVEN RV PARK & CHALETS

good sam park **Ratings: 9/10★/9** (Campground) Avail: 40 full hkups (30/50 amps). 2021 rates: $30 to $35. May 01 to Oct 15. (709)649-0601, Route 404 (229 Main Rd.), Robinsons, NL A0N 1V0

ROCKY HARBOUR — C2 *Western Region*

GROS MORNE RV CAMPGROUND & MOTEL UNITS **Ratings: 8/10★/9.5** (Campground) Avail: 51 full hkups (30/50 amps). 2021 rates: $28 to $38. May 15 to Oct 11. (877)488-3133, 10 West Link Rd, Rocky Harbour, NL A0K 4N0

GROS MORNE/BERRY HILL (Public National Park) From Rocky Harbour, N 4 km on Rte 430 (R). Avail: 25 E. 2021 rates: $18.60 to $25.50. Jun 01 to Oct 01. (877)737-3783

GROS MORNE/NORRIS POINT KOA **Ratings: 8/10★/9** (Campground) 85 Avail: 30 full hkups, 34 W, 34 E (30/50 amps). 2021 rates: $37 to $48. May 14 to Oct 14. (709)458-2229, 5 Shearakin Lane, Rocky Harbour, NL A0K 4N0

SOUTH BROOK — C3 *Central Region*

KONA BEACH CAMPGROUND RV PARK **Ratings: 6.5/8.5★/9** (Campground) 66 Avail: 22 W, 17 E (20/30 amps). 2021 rates: $22 to $30. May 19 to Sep 24. (709)657-2400, Hwy 1, South Brook, NL A0J 1S0

ST BARBE — A3 *Western Region*

ST BARBE RV PARK **Ratings: 6/9★/6.5** (RV Area in MH Park) Avail: 14 E (30 amps). 2021 rates: $30 to $40. Jun 01 to Sep 20. (709)877-2515, Main Road 430, Black Duck Cove, NL A0K 1M0

ST GEORGE'S — D2 *Western Region*

BARACHOIS POND (Public Prov Park) From town: Go 4.8 km/3 mi SE on paved road, then 14.8 km/9 mi N on Hwy 1. 150 Avail. 2021 rates: $20.15. May 15 to Sep 15. (877)214-2267

Go to GoodSam.com/Trip-Planner for Trip Routing.

ST JOHN'S — D6 *Avalon Region*

BLUE FIN RV TRAILER PARK **Ratings: 9/9/8.5** (RV Park) Avail: 55 full hkups (30/50 amps). 2021 rates: $35. May 15 to Sep 30. (709)229-5500, 22 TCH 1, Holyrood, NL A0A 2R0

PIPPY PARK CAMPGROUNDS AND TRAILER PARK (Public) From Jct of TCH & Prince Philip Pkwy, E 1.5 mi on Prince Philip Pkwy to Allandale Rd, N 0.25 mi to Nagle Pl, N 0.1 mi (R). 216 Avail: 186 full hkups, 30 W, 30 E (30/50 amps). 2021 rates: $29.20 to $45.13. May 15 to Oct 17. (709)737-3669

SUMMERFORD — C4 *Central Region*

DILDO RUN (Public Prov Park) From town: Go 15.4 km/9-1/2 mi NW on Hwy 340 (on New World Island). 55 Avail. 2021 rates: $30.90. May 25 to Sep 15. (877)214-2267

THORBURN LAKE — D5 *Eastern Region*

LAKESIDE RV RESORT **Ratings: 6.5/8.5★/9** (Campground) 90 Avail: 52 W, 52 E (15/30 amps). 2021 rates: $37. May 15 to Oct 15. (709)427-7668, Hwy 1, Clarenville, NL A5A 2C2

TROUT RIVER — C2 *Western Region*

ELEPHANTS HEAD RV PARK **Ratings: 6.5/9★/8.5** (Campground) Avail: 12 full hkups (30 amps). 2021 rates: $25 to $35. May 15 to Sep 15. (709)451-5500, 120 - 126 Old Highway Road, Trout River, NL A0K 5P0

GROS MORNE/TROUT RIVER (Public National Park) From Trout River, S 2 km on Hwy 431, follow sign (E). 44 Avail. 2021 rates: $18.60 to $25.50. Jun 01 to Sep 17. (877)737-3783

TWILLINGATE — B4 *Central Region*

PEYTON'S WOODS RV PARK AND CAMPGROUND (Campground) (Phone Update) 64 Avail: 64 W, 64 E (30/50 amps). 2021 rates: $30 to $49. May 15 to Sep 30. (709)884-2000, 35 Back Harbour Road, Twillingate, NL A0G 4M0

WILTONDALE — C3 *Western Region*

GROS MORNE/LOMOND (Public National Park) From Jct of Rtes 430 & 431, W 17km on Rte 431, NE 4 km on Lomond Rd (R). 34 Avail. 2021 rates: $18.60 to $25.50. Jun 08 to Sep 17. (877)737-3783

good sam
RV Rentals
Experience more for less.
Coleman
List or Rent, it's 5%.
That's up to 75% less in fees than the competition.
LEARN MORE AT RVRENTALS.COM

DID YOU KNOW ?
Virginia Falls in the Nahanni National Park is almost twice the height of Niagara Falls.
Getty Images/iStockphoto

YOU ARE HERE

Northwest Territories

Canada truly shows off its wild side in the Northwest Territories. From the dazzling aurora borealis to vasts forests in Canada's largest national park, the memories forged in this natural wonderland can't be rivaled.

Lights in the Sky

Canada's north is prime viewing territory for the spectacular aurora borealis. From January until March, visitors are treated to the greatest light show on Earth as the sky erupts in vibrant blues, greens, reds and yellows across the vast night sky.

Radical Rapids

The Northwest Territories constitute a paradise for paddlers. Make your way to the Nahanni National Park Reserve on the western border with the Yukon to ride swift rapids past four deep canyons and the spectacular Virginia Falls. The 255-mile Keele River to the north is another popular rafting destination, with its sweeping views of alpine tundra and the Mackenzie Mountains. You can also fish for scores of lake trout, pike and arctic grayling in Great Slave Lake, the deepest lake on the continent at an astonishing 2,014 feet. Straddling the border with Alberta, Wood Buffalo National Park is Canada's largest national park and provides a safe habitat for its namesake mammal.

Northwest Natives

Yellowknife makes up for its remoteness with a vibrant local culture. Situated on the northern banks of Great Slave Lake, hundreds of miles from the nearest major town, the rollicking city and provincial capital boasts an eccentric personality. Take a stroll downtown and you'll find dozens of art galleries and restaurants serving up everything from Japanese to Ethiopian fare. You can also learn about Inuit culture at the Prince of Wales Northern Heritage Center.

Northwest Territories Arctic Char

Arctic Char is abundant in this part of the Great White North, so get ready to eat lots of it. Part of the salmon family, this cold-water fish is traditionally eaten raw, dried or smoked. Restaurants in Yellowknife are giving it a modern twist so look out for familiar dishes like Arctic char chowder and eggs benedict.

VISITOR CENTER

TIME ZONE
Mountain Standard

ROAD & HIGHWAY INFORMATION
867-777-7343
www.dot.gov.nt.ca

FISHING, HUNTING, & BOATING INFORMATION
800-267-6687
tc.gc.ca/eng/marinesafety/debs-obs-menu-1362.htm

NATIONAL PARKS
pc.gc.ca/en/pn-np

TERRITORIAL PARKS
nwtparks.ca

TOURISM INFORMATION
Northwest Territories Tourism
800-661-0788
www.spectacularnwt.com

TOP TOURISM ATTRACTIONS
1) Nahanni National Park Reserve
2) Wood Buffalo National Park
3) Baffin Island

MAJOR CITIES
Yellowknife (NT capital), Hay City, Inuvik

NT

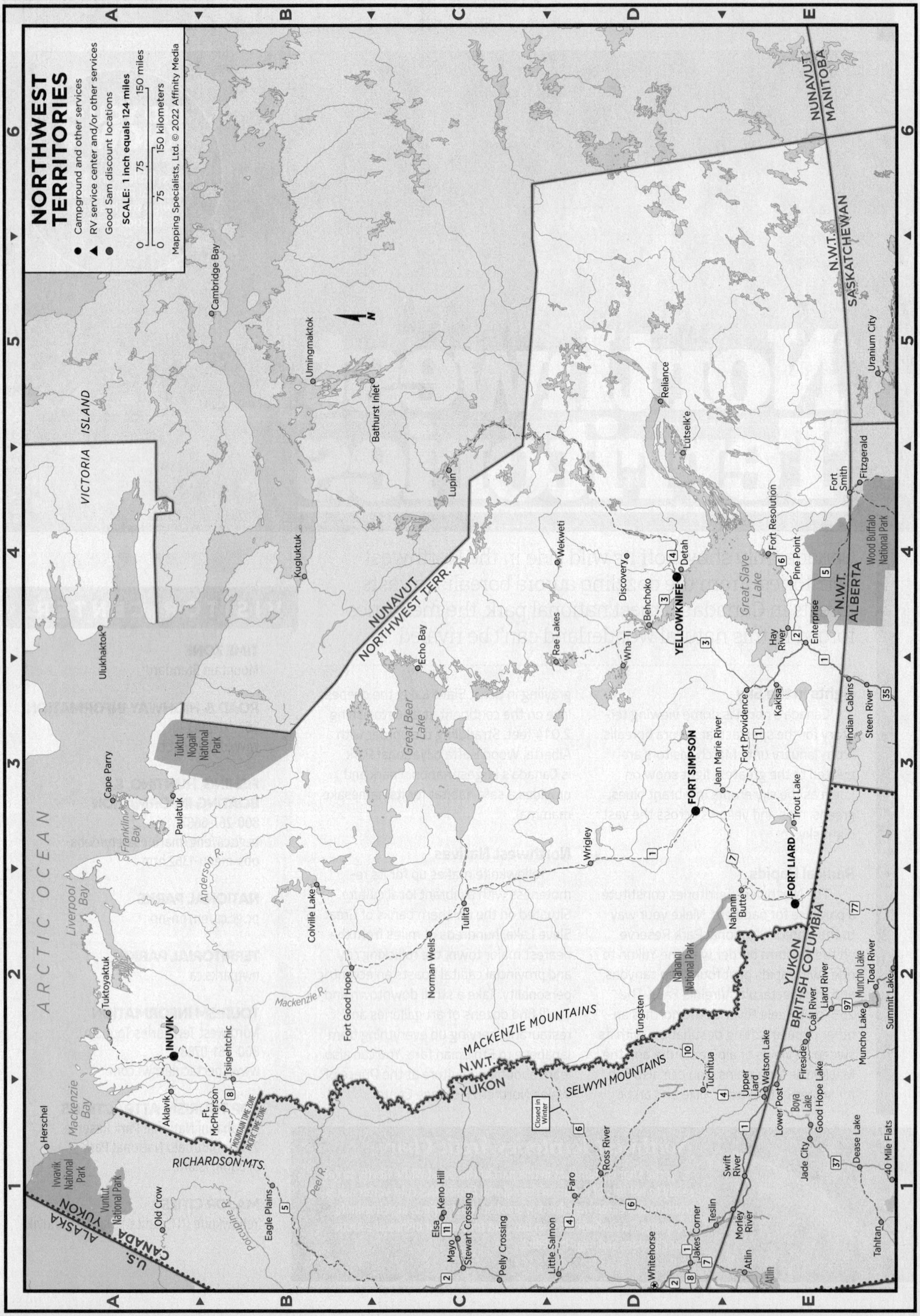
NORTHWEST TERRITORIES
Campground and other services
RV service center and/or other services
Good Sam discount locations
SCALE: 1 inch equals 124 miles
0 75 150 miles
0 75 150 kilometers
Mapping Specialists, Ltd. © 2022 Affinity Media
ARCTIC OCEAN
VICTORIA ISLAND
NUNAVUT
NORTHWEST TERR.
Cambridge Bay
Umingmaktok
Bathurst Inlet
Kugluktuk
Lupin
Ulukhaktok
Tuktut Nogait National Park
Cape Parry
Paulatuk
Franklin Bay
Anderson R.
Liverpool Bay
Tuktoyaktuk
Mackenzie Bay
INUVIK
Aklavik
Tsiigehtchic
Ft. McPherson
Herschel
Ivvavik National Park
Vuntut National Park
Old Crow
U.S. CANADA
ALASKA YUKON
RICHARDSON MTS.
MOUNTAIN TIME ZONE
PACIFIC TIME ZONE
Eagle Plains
Porcupine R.
Peel R.
Great Bear Lake
Echo Bay
Colville Lake
Fort Good Hope
Mackenzie R.
Norman Wells
Tulita
MACKENZIE MOUNTAINS
N.W.T.
YUKON
SELWYN MOUNTAINS
Closed in Winter
Wrigley
Rae Lakes
Wekweti
Discovery
Wha Ti
Behchoko
YELLOWKNIFE
Detah
Great Slave Lake
Reliance
Lutselk'e
Fort Resolution
Pine Point
Hay River
Enterprise
Kakisa
Fort Providence
Jean Marie River
FORT SIMPSON
Trout Lake
Nahanni Butte
Nahanni National Park
FORT LIARD
Tungsten
Tuchitua
Watson Lake
Upper Liard
Lower Post
Fort Smith
Fitzgerald
Wood Buffalo National Park
N.W.T.
ALBERTA
SASKATCHEWAN
NUNAVUT
MANITOBA
Uranium City
Indian Cabins
Steen River
YUKON
BRITISH COLUMBIA
Fireside
Coal River
Liard River
Muncho Lake
Toad River
Summit Lake
Boya Lake
Good Hope Lake
Jade City
Dease Lake
40 Mile Flats
Tahltan
Swift River
Teslin
Morley River
Jakes Corner
Atlin
Whitehorse
Ross River
Faro
Little Salmon
Pelly Crossing
Stewart Crossing
Mayo
Elsa
Keno Hill
A B C D E
1 2 3 4 5 6

ROAD TRIPS

Canada's Frontier Calls Out for Explorers

Northwest Territories

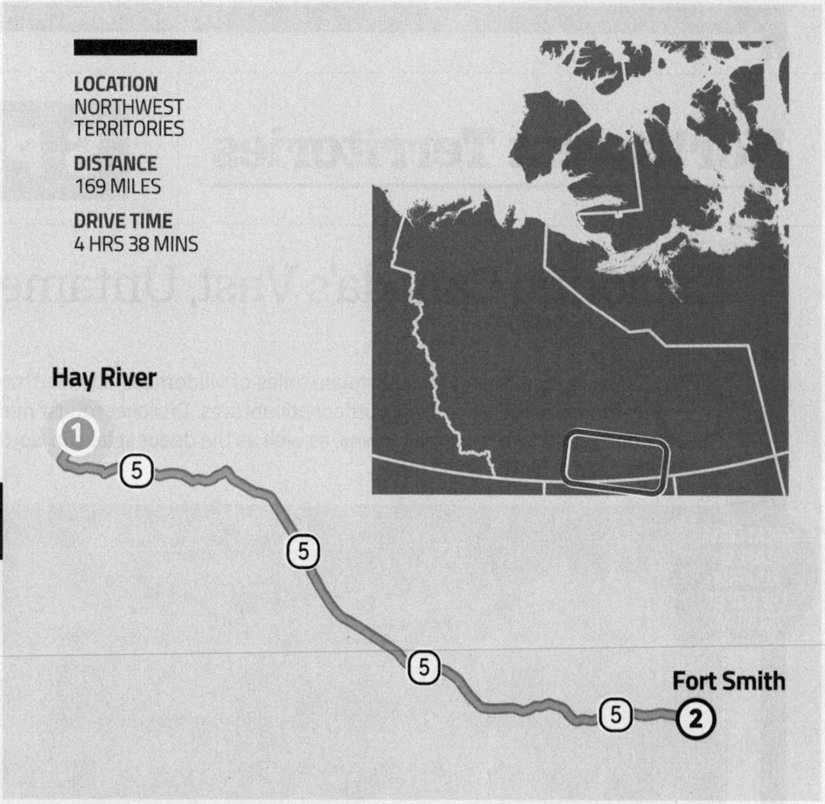

NT

Go where the buffalo roam. The world's largest herd of bison (aka, buffalo) lives in Canada's Northwest Territories and across the border in Alberta. But that's just scratching the surface. Encompassing more than 500,000 square miles and populated by roughly 44,000 people, this territory's wide-open spaces give way to undisturbed wildlife, lakes, mountains, canyons and huge tracts of wilderness.

1 Hay River
Starting Point

Come to the nexus of the frontier. Hay River is known as the "Hub of the North," where you might catch a carnival or a lobster fest. The town's namesake river empties into Great Slave Lake, the deepest lake in North America and the 10th largest lake in the world. The fishing's great, too.

While in the area, take a side trip to Alexandra Falls and Louise Falls. Alexandra Falls is a 105-foot-tall curtain of cascading water in Twin Falls Gorge Territorial Park. And don't miss Alexandra's little sister, 50-foot Louise Falls, an easy 2-mile hike through a pastoral wooded setting.

Along the Way

Untamed landscapes stretch to the horizon in Canada's largest national park. Wood Buffalo National Park was established in the 1920s as a haven for the last herds of buffalo, and those survivors have multiplied big time. The estimated 3,000 wood bison that roam the park constitute the largest free-moving, self-regulating wood bison herd left on the planet. Explore this 28,000 square-mile park — you might also see bears, wolves, moose, foxes and beavers. You may have to stop occasionally as big bison slowly cross the road, but it's worth the photo ops. On the eastern edge of the park, take a walk on the sprawling Salt Plains, where saline minerals leach from an ancient seabed. Remove your boots and stroll over smooth, crusty salt flats.

Getty Images/iStockphoto

2 Fort Smith
Drive 169 miles ▪ 4 hours, 38 minutes

Go on a wild ride. The Slave River rapids near Fort Smith offer some of the world's finest whitewater rafting and kayaking. Choose from four sets of rapids — from easy Class I to "un-runnable" Class VI. Choose your level of difficulty, strap on your personal flotation device and go. Outfitters will help you get the gear that you need for your adventure. Note: Don't exceed your kayaking abilities. When night falls, enjoy the largest Dark Sky Preserve on earth. Ever wonder what the night sky looked like *before* electric lights? Nearby Wood Buffalo Park hosts the world's largest Dark Sky Preserve in late August.

BIKING BOATING DINING ENTERTAINMENT FISHING HIKING HUNTING PADDLING SHOPPING SIGHTSEEING

 See map page 1092

Northwest Territories

SPOTLIGHTS

Exploring Canada's Vast, Untamed Terrain

Occupying more than 442,000 square miles of wilderness, the Northwest Territories serve up endless outdoor adventures. Discover robust rivers punctuated by a few small towns, as well as the deepest lake in North America, named after the Slave tribe.

GREAT SLAVE LAKE IS ROUGHLY THE SIZE OF BELGIUM.

Sailboats and houseboats moored on Great Slave Lake during a calm autumn evening.

Fort Smith

Fort Smith is a small town that serves up big helpings of fun. Adventurous kayakers can hone their skills on the rapids of the Slave River, which feeds Great Slave Lake to the north. Attend a community feast organized by the local Salt River First Nation or cheer on competitors at the traditional Hand Games Tournament. See amazing night skies during the Thebacha & Buffalo Dark Sky Festival.

See Sprawling Wilderness

Fort Smith is a gateway to Wood Buffalo National Park. Covering 17,300 square miles of lush boreal forest and salt plains of both the Northwest Territories and Alberta, it's the largest national park in Canada and a UNESCO World Heritage Site. In the summer, visitors can embark on a wealth of outdoor adventures such as hiking, fishing, kayaking, camping and canoeing. Home to 5,000 bison, the park has the world's largest free-roaming herd of these hefty mammals.

Great Slave Lake

Go fishing, houseboating and paddling on an epic body of water. The Great Slave Lake stretches across the Northwest Territories like an inland ocean, an expanse of clear blue water that breaks up the rugged terrain of softwoods and vast tundra. Home to a wide variety of fish, mammals and birds, it's North America's fifth-largest lake, with 10,502 square miles of surface area and depths reaching more than 1,000 feet. Visitors take advantage of the lake's sheer size for uncrowded fishing and boating adventures during the summer; in the winter, the lake's frozen surface makes it a perfect setting for dogsledding and cross-country skiing adventures.

Radical River

If fishing and waterfalls are high on your list, then you have no excuse to miss Hay River. This small town is located on the south shore of the lake and at the mouth of the river that shares its name. The town is a magnet for sports fishing, with arctic grayling, lake trout and northern pike enticing anglers from across the world. Just 30 miles south of Town, Louise Falls dazzles with its 66-foot-tall curtain of water.

Yellowknife

Find fun under the aurora borealis. Sitting 200 miles south of the Arctic Circle on the Canadian Shield, Yellowknife bustles with a vibrant culture. With a population close to 20,000, Yellowknife's streets are lined with hip art galleries, scintillating restaurants and a robust aboriginal culture that influences many aspects of the community. The aurora borealis shimmers brightly in the town's night skies, but the terrestrial festivals and celebrations pulse with equal dynamism.

FOR MORE INFORMATION

Northwest Territories Tourism, 800-661-0788, www.spectacularnwt.com
Town of Fort Smith, 867-872-8400, www.fortsmith.ca
Hay River Tourism, 867-874-6522, www.hayriver.com/tourism
Visit Yellowknife, 867-873-4262, visityellowknife.com

LOCAL FAVORITE

Deer Stew

In the Northwest Territories, First Nations peoples relied on deer as a major food staple. Succulent deer meat is still served in this region. *Recipe by Dennis Schmucker.*

INGREDIENTS

- ☐ 2 bags deer or turkey meat
- ☐ 2 cups lunchbox peppers
- ☐ 1 cup onion, diced
- ☐ 1 potato, diced
- ☐ 1 Tbsp seasoning salt
- ☐ 1 tsp chili powder
- ☐ 1 Tbsp Worcestershire sauce
- ☐ ¼ tsp ground red pepper (cayenne)
- ☐ 1 tsp pepper
- ☐ ¼ cup olive oil
- ☐ 4 cups water

DIRECTIONS

Combine all ingredients in a large pot. Simmer for 30 minutes and cook until vegetables are soft.

Northwest Territories

FORT LIARD — E2 *Dehcho*

BLACKSTONE TERRITORIAL PARK (Public Prov Park) From Fort Simpson, W 173 km (104 mi) on Hwy 7 (R); or from Fort Liard, E 173 km (104 mi) on Hwy 7 (L). 19 Avail. 2021 rates: $22.50. Jun 01 to Sep 01. (867)695-7515

FORT SIMPSON — D3 *Dehcho*

FORT SIMPSON TERRITORIAL PARK (Public Prov Park) N-bnd: At km/mp 480 on Hwy 1, (L). Entrance fee required. Avail: 20 E. 2021 rates: $22.50 to $28. Jun 01 to Oct 01. (867)695-7515

SAMBAA DEH FALLS TERRITORIAL PARK (Public Prov Park) From town, E 155 km on Hwy 1 (R). 20 Avail. 2021 rates: $22.50. May 18 to Sep 17. (867)695-7515

Stay at any of the Good Sam RV Parks & Campgrounds in the U.S. and Canada and save 10% on the regular nightly RV site rate! No Blackout dates! Good Sam RV Parks are inspected and rated annually-look for the exclusive Triple Rating System.

INUVIK — A2 *Inuvik*

HAPPY VALLEY TERRITORIAL PARK (Public) From town, N 1.5 km on Mackenzie Rd to Reliance St, W 100 km to Franklin St, N 0.8 km (L). Avail: 19 E (15 amps). 2021 rates: $22.50 to $28. Jun 01 to Sep 01. (867)777-3652

JA'K TERRITORIAL PARK (Public) N-bnd: At Km 267 (mile 161) on Hwy 8 (L). Avail: 6 E (15 amps). 2021 rates: $22.50 to $28. May 15 to Sep 15. (867)777-3613

YELLOWKNIFE — D4 *North Slave*

PRELUDE LAKE TERRITORIAL PARK (Public Prov Park) N-bnd: At km 22/MP-8, on Hwy 4 (L). Avail: 32 E Pit toilets. 2021 rates: $22.50. May 11 to Sep 16. (867)873-7184

REID LAKE TERRITORIAL PARK (Public Prov Park) E-bnd: At MP-38 on Hwy 4 (R). 65 Avail: Pit toilets. 2021 rates: $22.50. May 11 to Sep 16. (867)873-7317

RV SPACE-SAVING TIP: Line your trashcans with multiple bags at once and keep the roll in the bottom of the wastebasket for easy refills. Also, you could even reuse the same bag, if it hasn't gotten too soiled, by simply dumping the trash and leaving the existing bag in it for multiple uses.

How much will it all cost? Use this as a guide: Rates shown are the minimum and maximum for two adults in one RV at the time of inspection (excluding any additional fees for items not at the site). Remember, these rates serve as guidelines only. It's always best to call ahead for the most current rate information.

The Ratings & What They Mean

Rated 10/10★/10

Turn to "Understanding the Rating System" section at the front of this Guide to get information on how we rate and inspect parks with our handy three number system!

DID YOU KNOW?
A cannon goes off at noon every day from the Halifax Citadel National Historic Site.
YOU ARE HERE
Getty Images/iStockphoto

Nova Scotia

NS

Visitors to Nova Scotia can enjoy big city fun in Halifax, the largest city of the Atlantic Provinces, or explore charming coastal villages. Explore the Bay of Fundy, the Gulf of St. Lawrence and the Gulf of Maine.

Halifax Has It All

Halifax's bustling docks ship and receive goods from 150 global economies, and that adds to the city's international flavor. A walk along the waterfront boardwalk of this bustling port town offers up the best of present-day Halifax. Grab a lobster roll and take a stroll while watching the boats in the harbor. The Halifax Public Gardens provide a tranquil retreat, boasting cascades of blooms and 240 varieties of trees.

Waterway Wonders

Few Canadian provinces dish out so many options for lovers of water sports. There are more than 4,350 miles of saltwater coastline, almost 7,000 lakes and 100 rivers. You can paddle or toss in a line without stopping. Brave the waves along the coast or meander down a trickling creek. Anglers can take their pick from saltwater and freshwater locales. Head to the Highlands for epic Atlantic salmon fishing in the Margaree River or hit the coast for the chance to reel in a Giant Bluefin Tuna (with the largest weighing over 1,000 pounds).

Major National Parks

Kejimkujik National Park takes beautiful scenery to another level. Located 101 miles southwest of Halifax, this expanse unfolds in two distinct areas. The main park takes visitors inland to woodlands. Here, enchanted old-growth forests and rippling creeks form a picturesque scene. At night, the show takes to the skies, with a dazzling array of stars. Kejimkujik Seaside is a separate park, located on the coast. Get an eyeful of scenic lagoons, beaches and marshes.

Nova Scotia Scallops

Located on the Atlantic coast, the town of Digby has earned the title "Scallop Capital of the World." You'll find these tasty morsels on menus throughout the province, and local chefs have perfected the art of preparing them in a creamy sauce that's to die for. In Lunenburg, restaurants serve their Adams & Knickle deep-sea scallops with pride.

VISITOR CENTER

TIME ZONE
Atlantic Standard

ROAD & HIGHWAY INFORMATION
844-696-7737
novascotia.ca/tran

FISHING & HUNTING INFORMATION
800-670-4357
novascotia.ca/fish/sportfishing

BOATING INFORMATION
800-267-6687
tc.gc.ca/boatingsafety

NATIONAL PARKS
pc.gc.ca/en/pn-np

PROVINCIAL PARKS
parks.novascotia.ca

TOURISM INFORMATION
Tourism Nova Scotia
800-565-0000
novascotia.com

TOP TOURISM ATTRACTIONS
1) Cape Breton Island
2) Halifax
3) Bay of Fundy

MAJOR CITIES
Halifax (capital), Cape Breton, Truro, Amherst, New Glasgow

Featured Good Sam Parks

NOVA SCOTIA

When you stay with Good Sam, you can expect the highest degree of cleanliness and friendliness, and better yet, you get **10% off** overnight campground fees.

If you're not already a Good Sam member you can purchase your membership at one of these locations:

ARCADIA
Castle Lake Campground & Cottages

BADDECK
Adventures East Campground & Cottages
Baddeck Cabot Trail Campground
Bras d'Or Lakes Campground On The Cabot Trail

MARTIN'S RIVER
Rayport Campground

SMITH'S COVE
Jaggars Point Oceanfront Campground Resort

10/10★/10 GOOD SAM PARKS

BADDECK
Baddeck Cabot Trail Campground
(866)404-4199

Bras d'Or Lakes Campground On The Cabot Trail
(866)892-5253

What's This?

An RV park with a 10/10★/10 rating has scored perfect grades in amenities, cleanliness and appearance ("See Understanding the Campground Rating System" on pages 8 and 9 for an explanation of the trusted Good Sam Rating System). Stay in a 10/10★/10 park on your next trip for a nearly flawless camping experience.

Getty Images/iStockphoto

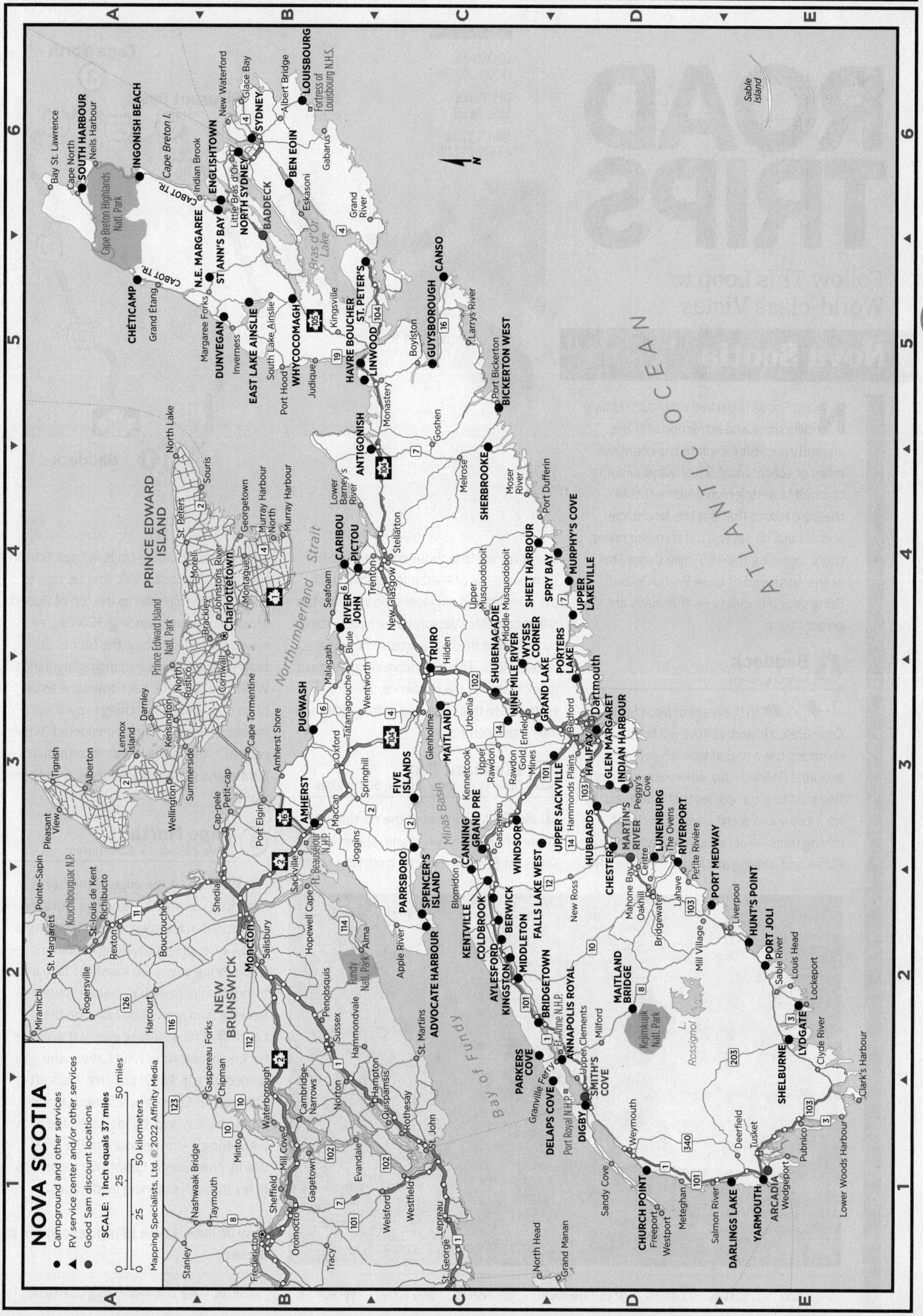
NOVA SCOTIA
Campground and other services
RV service center and/or other services
Good Sam discount locations
SCALE: 1 inch equals 37 miles
0 25 50 miles
0 25 50 kilometers
Mapping Specialists, Ltd. © 2022 Affinity Media
NEW BRUNSWICK
PRINCE EDWARD ISLAND
Northumberland Strait
Bay of Fundy
Minas Basin
ATLANTIC OCEAN
Cape Breton Highlands Natl. Park
Kejimkujik Natl. Park
Fundy Natl. Park
Prince Edward Island Natl. Park
Kouchibouguac N.P.
Sable Island
Cape Breton I.
CABOT TR.
Bras d'Or Lake
Fortress of Louisbourg N.H.S.
Port Royal N.H.P.
Ft. Anne N.H.P.
Ft. Beauséjour N.H.P.
L. Rossignol
SOUTH HARBOUR
INGONISH BEACH
CHÉTICAMP
N.E. MARGAREE
DUNVEGAN
EAST LAKE AINSLIE
WHYCOCOMAGH
ST ANN'S BAY
BADDECK
ENGLISHTOWN
NORTH SYDNEY
SYDNEY
BEN EOIN
LOUISBOURG
HAVRE BOUCHER
ST. PETER'S
LINWOOD
GUYSBOROUGH
CANSO
BICKERTON WEST
ANTIGONISH
SHERBROOKE
CARIBOU
PICTOU
RIVER JOHN
TRURO
PUGWASH
AMHERST
FIVE ISLANDS
MAITLAND
PARRSBORO
SPENCER'S ISLAND
ADVOCATE HARBOUR
SHUBENACADIE
NINE MILE RIVER
WYSES CORNER
GRAND LAKE
PORTERS LAKE
SHEET HARBOUR
SPRY BAY
MURPHY'S COVE
UPPER LAKEVILLE
Dartmouth
HALIFAX
GLEN MARGARET
INDIAN HARBOUR
UPPER SACKVILLE
HUBBARDS
CHESTER
MARTIN'S RIVER
LUNENBURG
RIVERPORT
PORT MEDWAY
HUNT'S POINT
PORT JOLI
LYDGATE
SHELBURNE
CANNING
GRAND PRE
WINDSOR
FALLS LAKE WEST
KENTVILLE
COLDBROOK
BERWICK
AYLESFORD
KINGSTON
MIDDLETON
BRIDGETOWN
ANNAPOLIS ROYAL
MAITLAND BRIDGE
PARKERS COVE
SMITH'S COVE
DELAPS COVE
DIGBY
CHURCH POINT
DARLINGS LAKE
YARMOUTH
ARCADIA
Moncton
Charlottetown
Fredericton
Saint John

ROAD TRIPS

Follow This Loop to World-class Vistas

Nova Scotia

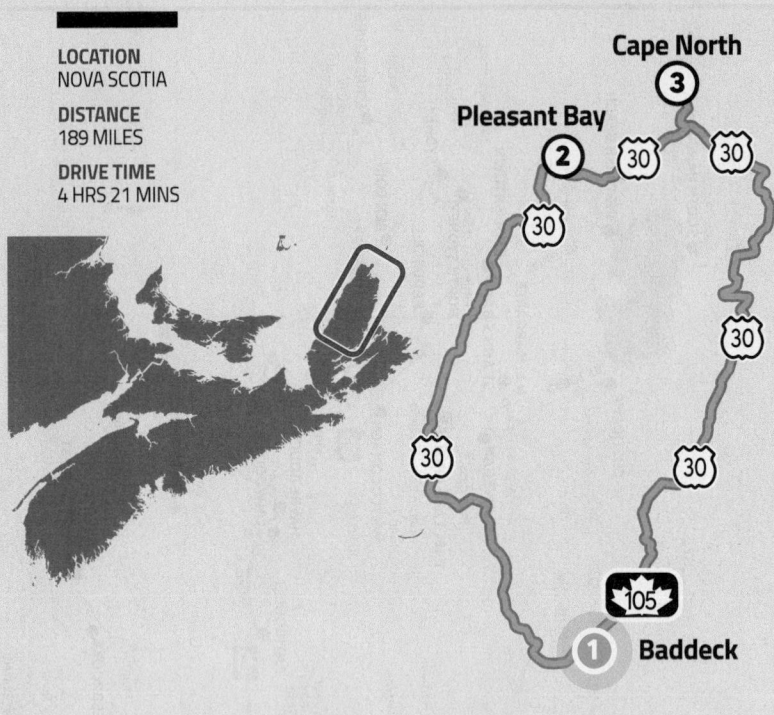

LOCATION
NOVA SCOTIA

DISTANCE
189 MILES

DRIVE TIME
4 HRS 21 MINS

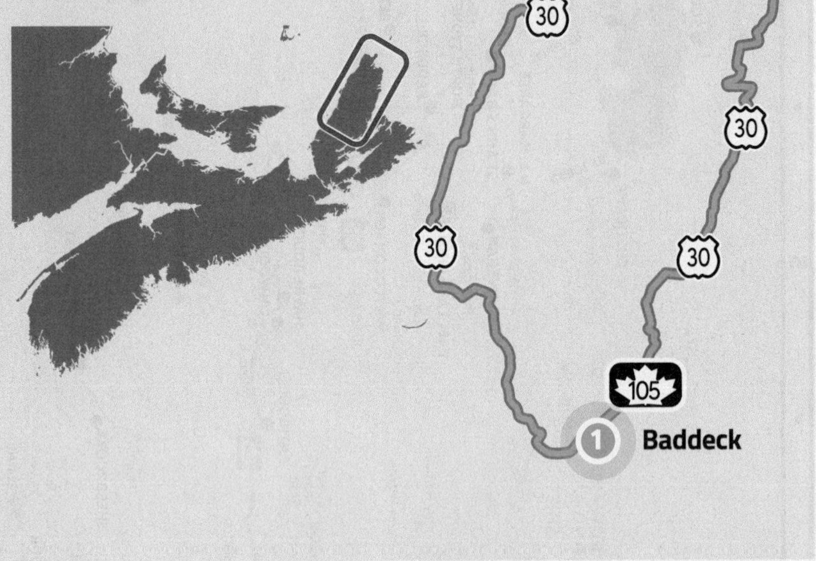

Nova Scotia is packed with outstanding diversions and attractions for the adventurous RVer. Explore the countless miles of scenic coastal highways winding through towering highlands; sightsee the little towns that dot the landscape; and set out on several outstanding hiking trails, including the 185-mile Cabot Trail at the north end of Cape Breton Island. Bring your binoculars — the views are breathtaking.

1 Baddeck
Starting Point

In the heart of Nova Scotia's Cape Breton Island, visitors will find the charming town of Baddeck. It's set on beautiful Baddeck Bay, where you can easily find boat tour companies that'll take you for a lovely and scenic cruise. Check out driving tours — via a tour company or your RV — and walking and kayak tours, too. No visit is complete without dropping into the summer home of Alexander Graham Bell the scientist and engineer who invented the telephone. "Mr. Watson, come here," uttered by Bell, were the first words communicated by telephone. This groundbreaking moment is celebrated at the residence, a National Historic Site that is packed with exhibits and interactive demos.

2 Pleasant Bay
Drive 80 miles ▪ 1 hour, 50 minutes

As you round the northwest shore of Cape Breton Island, spend time in Pleasant Bay. Explore the charming town and trek outstanding trails in Cape Breton Highlands National Park. And be sure to hike the 2.5-mile trail to the top of Roberts Mountain for outstanding 360-degree views out over the bay, the Gulf of St. Lawrence and the surrounding highlands. While you're there, set some time aside to go on a whale-watching expedition. Indeed, Pleasant Bay is considered "whale central." Stop in the Whale Interpretive Center and get a quick education on these giants.

Getty Images/iStockphoto

3 Cape North
Drive 21 miles ▪ 32 minutes

Here, at the edge of the North American continent, the views looking out on the water are spectacular. The waters below offer prime kayaking conditions — BYOK (bring your own kayak) or take a tour through wildlife-rich saltwater marshes. Seeking land recreation? Bike on the Cabot Trail for stunning views. It's named for English explorer John Cabot, who landed here in 1497, just five years after Christopher Columbus's famous landing on the New World. Cabot it credited with pioneering a shorter route to the New World. The famous Cabot Trail loops 185 miles through stunning landscapes.

Drive 88 miles, 1 hour, 59 minutes to return to Baddeck.

BIKING BOATING DINING ENTERTAINMENT FISHING HIKING HUNTING PADDLING SHOPPING SIGHTSEEING

Nova Scotia SPOTLIGHTS

Travel Through Town and Country in the Maritimes

This province offers big-city experiences in towns like Halifax as well as small-town charm in villages like Peggy's Cove. Take your pick in a maritime province known for its seafood and tall glasses of beer. See one of the most photographed lighthouses in North America.

BUILT IN 1868, THE POPULAR PEGGY'S POINT LIGHTHOUSE IS STILL ACTIVE.

Peggy's Point Lighthouse is a prime attraction on the Lighthouse Trail scenic drive.

Getty Images/iStockphoto

Digby

The fun-filled town of Digby is the ultimate waterfront community. Nestled on the Annapolis Basin near the Bay of Fundy, the small municipality of Digby has it all. During the day, travelers can go whale watching, golfing or hiking; in the evening, guests can savor a plate of scallops and other delicacies offloaded hours earlier from docking fishing boats. Although Digby has a population of only 2,152, the town buzzes with the energy of a bigger city, owing to the town's role as a hub for leisure boats and fishing trawlers.

Halifax

The largest city east of Montréal, Halifax puts eastern Canada's vibrant culture in a big-city package. From its dynamic food scene and exciting festivals to its alluring waterfront views and stunning architecture, this historic yet hip metropolis is sure to captivate you. Belly up to a beer maker who has satisfied Haligonian thirsts for more than 200 years. Alexander Keith's original 1820 brewery, located across the street from the waterfront, serves up crisp ales that are the stuff of legend among beer enthusiasts.

Peggy's Cove Calls

Drive less than an hour to the southwest to see a postcard-worthy fishing village. The charming hamlet of Peggy's Cove is home to one of the region's most beloved landmarks. Standing at the entrance to St. Margaret's Bay, the town's red and white lighthouse was built in 1915 and rises over colossal granite boulders where the ocean crashes. A traditional fishing community, Peggy's Cove is like a painting come to life of small houses nestled upon a small inlet.

Truro

This small town lives right next door to jaw-dropping natural attractions. In the center of town, the 3,000-acre Victoria Park entices visitors to descend stairs down a steep-sided gorge and see cascading waterfalls and thick hemlock groves. At the Fundy discovery site, visitors can watch as the incredible tidal bore rushes from the Bay of Fundy during the area's epic tides. Back in town, the Masstown Market sells fresh seafood, gifts and more. Take a spin on the Cobequid Trail, which welcomes hikers and bikers to follow a former railbed along a scenic coastline.

FOR MORE INFORMATION

Nova Scotia, 800-565-0000, www.novascotia.com

Digby, 902-245-2121, www.digby.ca

Destination Halifax, 877-422-9334, www.destinationhalifax.com

Town of Truro, 902-895-4484, www.truro.ca

LOCAL FAVORITE

Shrimp and Sausage Foil Packets

This delicious yet easy campfire meal features Old Bay seasoning and a flavor-packed blend of herbs and spices. Try it with Nova Scotia's distinctive cold-water shrimp. *Recipe by Carrie Richardson.*

INGREDIENTS

- ☐ 1.5 lb large shrimp, peeled and deveined
- ☐ 2 cloves garlic, minced
- ☐ 2 smoked andouille sausages, thinly sliced
- ☐ 2 ears corn, each cut crosswise into 4 pieces
- ☐ 1 lb red bliss potatoes, chopped in 1" pieces
- ☐ 2 Tbsp extra-virgin olive oil
- ☐ 1 Tbsp Old Bay seasoning
- ☐ Kosher salt
- ☐ Freshly ground black pepper
- ☐ 2 Tbsp freshly chopped parsley
- ☐ 1 lemon, sliced into thin wedges
- ☐ 4 Tbsp butter

DIRECTIONS

Preheat grill over high heat or preheat oven to 425°F.

Cut 4 sheets of foil about 12" long. Divide shrimp, garlic, sausage, corn and potatoes evenly over the foil sheets. Drizzle with olive oil. Then add Old Bay seasoning and salt and pepper to taste. Toss gently to combine. Top each portion with parsley, lemon and a tablespoon of butter.

Fold foil packets crosswise over the shrimp boil mixture to completely cover the food. Roll top and bottom edges to seal them closed. Place foil packets on the grill and cook until just cooked through, about 15 to 20 minutes.

Serve with extra Old Bay seasoning and sour cream for a delicious meal with little clean up.

Nova Scotia

ADVOCATE HARBOUR — C2 *Cumberland*

CAPE CHIGNECTO (Public Prov Park) From town: Go 2.5 km/1-1/2 mi W on Hwy 209, then 1 km/1/2 mi S on West Advocate Rd. 80 Avail: Pit toilets. 2021 rates: $26.70. May 19 to Oct 09. (902)392-2085

AMHERST — B3 *Cumberland*

AMHERST SHORE (Public Prov Park) From town, E 4 mi on Tyndal Rd/Rte 366 (R). 42 Avail. 2021 rates: $26.70. Jun 09 to Oct 09. (902)661-6002

LOCH LOMOND TENT & TRAILER PARK **Ratings: 8/10★/9.5** (Campground) 75 Avail: 47 full hkups, 28 W, 28 E (30/50 amps). 2021 rates: $32 to $36. May 15 to Sep 30. (902)667-3890, 1 Loch Lamond Lane, Amherst, NS B4H 3Y4

RV Park ratings you can rely on!

ANNAPOLIS ROYAL — D2 *Annapolis*

DUNROMIN CAMPSITE **Ratings: 9/9.5★/9.5** (Campground) 110 Avail: 53 full hkups, 57 W, 57 E (30/50 amps). 2021 rates: $40 to $50. May 15 to Oct 15. (844)292-1929, 4618 Hwy 1, Granville Ferry, NS B0S 1K0

RAVEN HAVEN BEACHSIDE FAMILY PARK (Public) From jct Hwy 101 (exit 22) & Rt 8: Go 20 km/12 mi S on Rt 8, then 5 km/3 mi W on Virginia Rd. to West Springhill. 15 Avail: 15 W, 3 E (30 amps). 2021 rates: $24 to $27. Jun 11 to Sep 01. (902)532-7320

ANTIGONISH — B4 *Antigonish*

AE WHIDDEN TRAILER COURT **Ratings: 9/9★/9** (Campground) 74 Avail: 10 full hkups, 52 W, 52 E (30/50 amps). 2021 rates: $36.62 to $47.83. May 01 to Oct 15. (877)263-3736, 4 Park Lane, Antigonish, NS B2G 1N5

ARCADIA — E1 *Yarmouth*

CASTLE LAKE CAMPGROUND & COTTAGES

good sam park

Ratings: 8.5/10★/10 (Campground) Avail: 100 full hkups (30/50 amps). 2021 rates: $45 to $75. May 24 to Oct 15. (902)749-1739, 83 Comeaus Hill Rd., Arcadia, NS B0W 1B0

AYLESFORD — C2 *Kings*

KLAHANIE KAMPING **Ratings: 7.5/9★/8** (Campground) 61 Avail: 14 full hkups, 25 W, 25 E (15/30 amps). 2021 rates: $36 to $75. May 15 to Oct 15. (902)847-9316, 1144 Victoria Rd, Aylesford, NS B0P 1C0

BADDECK — B5 *Victoria*

ADVENTURES EAST CAMPGROUND & COTTAGES

good sam park

Ratings: 9.5/10★/10 (Membership Park) 46 Avail: 38 full hkups, 8 W, 8 E (30/50 amps). 2021 rates: $38.50 to $62. May 15 to Oct 20. (800)507-2228, 9585 Hwy 105, Baddeck, NS B0E 1B0

BADDECK CABOT TRAIL CAMPGROUND

good sam park

Ratings: 10/10★/10 (Campground) W-bnd: From town, W 5 mi on TCH-105 (R); or E-bnd: From Jct of TCH-105 & Exit 7 (Cabot Trail Entrance), E 0.5 mi on TCH-105 (L). **FAC:** all weather rds. (163 spaces). Avail: 88 all weather, 44 pull-thrus, (25x80), back-ins (25x40), 41 full hkups, 47 W, 47 E (30/50 amps), seasonal sites, WiFi @ sites, tent sites, rentals, dump, laundry, groc, LP bottles, fire rings, firewood. **REC:** heated pool, Baddeck River: fishing, kayaking/canoeing, boating nearby, playground. Pets OK. Big rig sites, eco-friendly. 2021 rates: $39 to $59. May 14 to Oct 15.
(866)404-4199 Lat: 46.090520, Lon: -60.852559
9584 Hwy 105, Baddeck, NS B0E 1B0
baddeckcabottrailcampground.com
See ad this page

BRAS D'OR LAKES CAMPGROUND ON THE CABOT TRAIL

good sam park

Ratings: 10/10★/10 (Campground) From town, W 3 mi on TCH-105 (L) Between Exit 7 & 8, MM 80. **FAC:** all weather rds. Avail: 81 all weather, 8 pull-thrus, (35x85), back-ins (32x65), 81 full hkups (30/50 amps), WiFi @ sites, tent sites, rentals, dump, laundry, groc, fire rings, firewood. **REC:** pool, Bras d'Or Lake: swim, fishing, kayaking/canoeing, playground. Pets OK. Big rig sites, eco-friendly. 2021 rates: $48 to $67, Military discount. Jun 15 to Sep 30.
(866)892-5253 Lat: 46.079114, Lon: -60.819352
Box 595, 8885 Hwy 105, Baddeck, NS B0E 1B0
brasdorlakescampground.com
See ad this page

BEN EOIN — B6 *Cape Breton*

BEN EOIN BEACH RV RESORT & CAMPGROUND **Ratings: 8.5/9★/8** (Campground) 30 Avail: 30 W, 30 E (30/50 amps). 2021 rates: $50 to $58. Jun 01 to Sep 15. (902)828-3100, 6140 East Bay Hwy, Big Pond, NS B0A 1H0

BERWICK — C2 *Kings*

FOX MOUNTAIN CAMPING PARK **Ratings: 4.5/7/7.5** (Campground) Avail: 290 full hkups (15 amps). 2021 rates: $40 to $45. May 15 to Oct 30. (902)847-3747, 6128 Aylesford Road, Aylesford, NS B0P 1C0

THE PLANTATION CAMPGROUND **Ratings: 8/8.5★/8** (Campground) Avail: 62 full hkups (30/50 amps). 2021 rates: $47 to $53. May 15 to Oct 15. (888)363-8882, 210 West Steadman Rd, Berwick, NS B0P 1E0

BICKERTON WEST — C5 *Guysborough*

SALSMAN (Public Prov Park) From Goshen, S 16.3 mi on Rte 316 (R). 40 Avail. 2021 rates: $26.70. Jun 09 to Oct 09. (902)328-2999

BRIDGETOWN — C2 *Annapolis*

VALLEYVIEW

(Public Prov Park) From Bridgetown, N 3 mi on Church St, at top of mtn (R). **FAC:** gravel rds. Avail: 30 grass, back-ins (30x30), WiFi, tent sites, pit toilets, dump, fire rings, firewood. Pets OK. Partial handicap access, 14 day max stay. 2021 rates: $20. Jun 09 to Oct 09.
(902)665-2559 Lat: 44.872222, Lon: -65.316944
960 Hampton Mountain Rd, Bridgetown, NS B0S 1C0
parks.novascotia.ca

CANNING — C3 *Kings*

BLOMIDON (Public Prov Park) From town, NE 10 mi on Hwy 358 (R). 70 Avail. 2021 rates: $26.70. May 15 to Sep 05. (902)582-7319

CANSO — C5 *Guysborough*

SEABREEZE CAMPGROUND & COTTAGES **Ratings: 7/8★/8.5** (Campground) 52 Avail: 16 full hkups, 22 W, 22 E (15/30 amps). 2021 rates: $30 to $40. May 15 to Oct 15. (902)366-2352, 230 Fox Island Main Rd., Canso, NS B0H 1H0

CARIBOU — B4 *Pictou*

CARIBOU & MUNROES ISLAND (Public Prov Park) From Jct TCH-106 & Pictou Rotary, P.E.I. Ferry Rd NE 4 mi to Three Brooks Rd, 1.5 mi (L). 95 Avail. 2021 rates: $26.70. Jun 10 to Oct 10. (902)485-6134

CHESTER — D3 *Lunenburg*

GRAVES ISLAND PARK (Public Prov Park) From Chester, E 2 mi on Rte 3 to access rd, S 0.5 mi (R). 95 Avail. 33 W, 33 E. 2021 rates: $27 to $36. May 17 to Oct 14. (902)275-4425

CHETICAMP — A5 *Inverness*

CAPE BRETON HIGHLANDS/CHETICAMP (Public National Park) From jct Cabot Trail Rd & Barren Rd: Go 7 km/ 4-1/3 mi N on Cabot Trail Rd. (R). 109 Avail: 24 full hkups, 14 E (15/30 amps). 2021 rates: $25.50 to $35.30. May 18 to Oct 09. (877)737-3783

CAPE BRETON HIGHLANDS/CORNEY BROOK (Public National Park) From town: Go 8-3/4 km/5-1/2 mi N on the Cabot Trail. (No potable water). 22 Avail. 2021 rates: $23.50. May 15 to Oct 18. (877)737-3783

PLAGE SAINT PIERRE BEACH AND CAMPGROUND **Ratings: 7.5/9★/9.5** (Campground) 90 Avail: 80 full hkups, 10 W, 10 E (30/50 amps). 2021 rates: $48.50 to $52.50. May 14 to Oct 14. (902)224-2112, 635 ChetiCamp Island Rd., Cheticamp, NS B0E 1H0

CHURCH POINT — D1 *Yarmouth*

BELLE BAIE PARK **Ratings: 8/8.5★/9.5** (Campground) 56 Avail: 50 full hkups, 6 W, 6 E (30/50 amps). 2021 rates: $35 to $56. May 03 to Sep 23. (902)769-3160, RR 1, 2135 Hwy 1, Church Point, NS B0W 1M0

CHURCH POINT CAMPGROUND **Ratings: 5.5/8.5/9.5** (Campground) Avail: 28 full hkups (30 amps). 2021 rates: $35 to $50. May 21 to Oct 11. (902)769-0070, 164 Bonnenfant Rd., Church Point, NS B0W 1M0

COLDBROOK — C2 *Kings*

SHERWOOD FOREST CAMPING PARK **Ratings: 8/8.5★/8** (Campground) 35 Avail: 4 full hkups, 31 W, 31 E (20/30 amps). 2021 rates: $44 to $49. May 15 to Sep 30. (902)679-6632, 6890 Hwy 1, Coldbrook, NS B4R 1C5

DARLINGS LAKE — E1 *Yarmouth*

LAKE BREEZE CAMPGROUND & COTTAGES **Ratings: 7/7.5/8.5** (Campground) 20 Avail: 2 full hkups, 18 W, 18 E (15/30 amps). 2021 rates: $38. May 15 to Oct 15. (902)649-2332, 2560 Hwy 1, Yarmouth, NS B5A 4A5

DELAPS COVE — D1 *Annapolis*

FUNDY TRAIL CAMPGROUND & COTTAGES **Ratings: 7.5/7/8** (Campground) 17 Avail: 6 full hkups, 8 W, 8 E (20/30 amps). 2021 rates: $35 to $45. May 15 to Oct 15. (902)532-7711, 62 Deplaps Cove Road, RR #3, Granville Ferry, NS B0S 1K0

Making campground reservations? Remember to ask about the cancellation policy when making your reservation.

DIGBY — D1 *Digby*

↓ DIGBY CAMPGROUND & FUN PARK **Ratings: 7/8/8** (Campground) 39 Avail: 18 full hkups, 21 W, 21 E (20/30 amps). 2021 rates: $30 to $50. May 15 to Sep 30. (902)245-1985, 230 Victoria St, Digby, NS B0V 1A0

→ FUNDY SPRAY CAMPGROUND **Ratings: 7.5/7.5★/9** (Campground) 50 Avail: 42 full hkups, 8 W, 8 E (30/50 amps). 2021 rates: $36 to $45. May 09 to Sep 29. (902)245-4884, Route 1 100, Smiths Cove, NS B0S 1S0

← WHALE COVE CAMPGROUND **Ratings: 5.5/8/8** (Campground) 39 Avail: 22 W, 22 E (20/30 amps). 2021 rates: $36. May 01 to Oct 15. (902)834-2025, 50 Whale Cove, Digby, NS B0V 1E0

DUNVEGAN — B5 *Inverness*

↑ MACLEOD'S BEACH CAMPSITE **Ratings: 7.5/9.5★/9.5** (Campground) 97 Avail: 39 full hkups, 6 W, 6 E (30/50 amps). 2021 rates: $45 to $57. Jun 07 to Oct 06. (902)258-2433, RR 1 1485 Broad Cove Marsh Rd, Inverness, NS B0E 1N0

EAST LAKE AINSLIE — B5 *Inverness*

→ MACKINNON'S CAMPGROUNDS **Ratings: 8/9.5★/9** (Campground) Avail: 15 full hkups (30/50 amps). 2021 rates: $38. May 01 to Oct 15. (902)756-2790, RR 1 2457 Hwy 395, Whycocomagh, NS B0E 3M0

ENGLISHTOWN — B6 *Victoria*

↓ KLUSKAP RIDGE RV & CAMPGROUND **Ratings: 8.5/9.5★/8.5** (Campground) 25 Avail: 19 full hkups, 6 W, 6 E (30 amps). 2021 rates: $35 to $45. May 04 to Oct 28. (902)929-2598, 938 Englishtown Rd, Englishtown, NS B0C 1H0

FALLS LAKE WEST — C3 *Hants*

FALLS LAKE RECREATIONAL FACILITY (Public) From Hwy 101 (exit 5): Go 24.1 km/15 mi on Hwy 14 W, then R on New Ross Rd, 3.2 km/2 mi (watch for signs), then R 3.2 km/2 mi on Pioneer (dirt) Rd. From Hwy 103 (exit 8): Go N 30 km/17 mi on Hwy 14, then L on New Ross Rd 3.2 km, then R on Pioneer Rd. Avail: 15 full hkups (30 amps). 2021 rates: $22 to $35. May 17 to Dec 01. (877)325-5253

FIVE ISLANDS — C3 *Colchester*

→ DIAMOND SHORES CAMPGROUND **Ratings: 3.5/7/7** (Campground) Avail: 12 full hkups (30 amps). 2021 rates: $32. May 21 to Sep 30. (902)254-2903, 59 Seascape Lane, Five Islands, NS B0M 1N0

← FIVE ISLAND OCEAN RESORT **Ratings: 8/7/8** (RV Resort) 92 Avail: 72 full hkups, 20 W, 20 E (30/50 amps). 2021 rates: $35 to $57. May 15 to Oct 15. (902)254-2824, 482 Hwy 2, Lower Five Islands, NS B0M 1N0

← FIVE ISLANDS PARK (Public Prov Park) From Jct of TCH 104 & Hwy 2, W 30 mi on Hwy 2 to Five Islands Rd, SE 2 mi (L). 87 Avail. 2021 rates: $26.70. Jun 12 to Oct 11. (902)254-2980

GLEN MARGARET — D3 *Halifax*

→ WAYSIDE RV PARK **Ratings: 6.5/7/7.5** (Campground) 100 Avail: 52 full hkups, 38 W, 38 E (30/50 amps). 2021 rates: $40 to $45. Apr 01 to Nov 30. (902)823-2547, 10295 Peggy's Cove Rd, Glen Margaret, NS B3Z 3H1

GRAND LAKE — C3 *Halifax*

↑ LAURIE (Public Prov Park) From jct Hwy 2 & Laurie Park Rd: Go .5 km/1/3 mi N on Laurie Park Rd. (L). 63 Avail: Pit toilets. 2021 rates: $26.70. Jun 09 to Sep 11. (888)544-3434

GRAND PRE — C3 *Hants*

↑ LAND OF EVANGELINE FAMILY CAMPING RESORT (Campground) (Phone Update) 97 Avail: 51 full hkups, 32 W, 32 E (30/50 amps). 2021 rates: $40 to $47. May 15 to Oct 15. (902)542-5309, 84 Evangeline Beach Rd, Grand Pre, NS B4P 1W4

GUYSBOROUGH — C5 *Guysborough*

→ BOYLSTON (Public Prov Park) From Guysborough, E 2 mi Hwy 16 (L). 34 Avail: Pit toilets. 2021 rates: $20. Jun 09 to Sep 11. (902)533-3326

HALIFAX — D3 *Halifax*

↗ SHUBIE CAMPGROUND **Ratings: 7.5/8★/9** (Campground) 99 Avail: 10 full hkups, 62 W, 62 E (30/50 amps). 2021 rates: $44 to $59. May 18 to Oct 13. (902)435-8328, 30 John Brenton Dr., Dartmouth, NS B2X 2V5

→ WOODHAVEN RV PARK OF HALIFAX **Ratings: 8.5/8.5★/9.5** (RV Park) 167 Avail: 129 full hkups, 38 W, 38 E (30/50 amps). 2021 rates: $40 to $55. May 01 to Oct 15. (902)835-2271, 1757 Hammonds Plains Rd, Halifax, NS B4B 1P5

HAVRE BOUCHER — B5 *Antigonish*

→ HYCLASS OCEAN CAMPGROUND **Ratings: 8/8★/8** (Campground) 60 Avail: 10 full hkups, 35 W, 35 E (15/30 amps). 2021 rates: $40 to $45. May 15 to Sep 30. (866)892-3117, 11373 Hwy 4, Havre Boucher, NS B0H 1P0

HUBBARDS — D3 *Halifax*

↘ HUBBARDS BEACH CAMPGROUND & COTTAGES **Ratings: 8.5/8.5★/9.5** (Campground) 35 Avail: 33 full hkups, 2 W (15/30 amps). 2021 rates: $43 to $45. May 15 to Oct 01. (902)857-9460, 226 Shore Club Rd, Hubbards, NS B0J 1T0

HUNT'S POINT — E2 *Queens*

← FISHERMAN'S COVE RV & CAMPGROUND **Ratings: 7/8.5★/7.5** (Campground) Avail: 13 full hkups (30 amps). 2021 rates: $44.95 to $49.96. May 15 to Oct 31. (902)646-0160, 6718 Hwy 3 , Hunts Point, NS B0T 1G0

INDIAN HARBOUR — D3 *Halifax*

→ KING NEPTUNE CAMPGROUND **Ratings: 5.5/8★/7.5** (Campground) 65 Avail: 11 full hkups, 36 W, 36 E (30 amps). 2021 rates: $40 to $45. Jun 01 to Sep 30. (902)823-2582, 8536 Peggy's Cove Rd, Indian Harbour, NS B3Z 3P4

INGONISH BEACH — A6 *Victoria*

↑ CAPE BRETON HIGHLANDS/BROAD COVE (Public National Park) From jct Cabot Trail Rd & Park Headquarters Ln: Go 10.5 km/ 6-1/2 mi N on Cabot Trail Rd. (R). Avail: 83 full hkups (15/30 amps). 2021 rates: $25.50 to $35.30. May 18 to Oct 08. (877)737-3783

↑ CAPE BRETON HIGHLANDS/INGONISH BEACH (Public National Park) From town, N 4 mi on Cabot Trail to E park entrance, N 0.5 mi (L) Entrance fee. 51 Avail. 2021 rates: $27.40. May 18 to Oct 08. (877)737-3783

KENTVILLE — C2 *Kings*

↓ HIGHBURY GARDENS FAMILY CAMPING (Campground) (Phone Update) 54 Avail: 15 full hkups, 39 W, 39 E (30/50 amps). 2021 rates: $47.50 to $53. May 15 to Oct 15. (902)678-8011, 121 New Canaan Rd, Kentville, NS B4N 4K1

↓ SOUTH MOUNTAIN PARK FAMILY CAMPING & RV RESORT **Ratings: 8/10★/9** (Campground) 70 Avail: 49 full hkups, 21 W, 21 E (30 amps). 2021 rates: $34 to $49. May 15 to Oct 15. (866)860-6092, 3022 Hwy 12, Kentville, NS B4N 3X9

KINGSTON — C2 *Kings*

← YOGI BEAR'S JELLYSTONE PARK CAMP RESORT **Ratings: 8.5/9.5★/9** (Campground) 160 Avail: 68 full hkups, 92 W, 92 E (30/50 amps). 2021 rates: $43 to $93. Jun 01 to Sep 16. (888)225-7773, RR 1-43 Boo Boo Blvd, Kingston, NS B0P 1R0

LINWOOD — B5 *Antigonish*

↑ LINWOOD HARBOUR CAMPGROUND **Ratings: 8/10★/10** (Campground) Avail: 33 full hkups (30/50 amps). 2021 rates: $32 to $48. May 15 to Oct 15. (866)661-9145, 11087 Hwy 4, Linwood, NS B0H 1P0

LOUISBOURG — B6 *Cape Breton*

← LAKEVIEW TREASURES CAMPGROUND & RV PARK **Ratings: 6.5/UI/7** (Campground) 89 Avail: 32 full hkups, 57 W, 57 E (30/50 amps). 2021 rates: $40 to $46. May 15 to Oct 15. (902)733-2058, 5785 Louisbourg Hwy, Catalone, NS B1C 2G4

← RIVERDALE RV PARK **Ratings: 6.5/9.5★/8** (RV Park) Avail: 30 full hkups (30/50 amps). 2021 rates: $35. May 15 to Oct 15. (902)733-2531, 9 Riverdale St., Louisbourg, NS B1C 2H9

LUNENBURG — D3 *Lunenburg*

↗ LITTLE LAKE FAMILY CAMPGROUND **Ratings: 8/9★/7.5** (Campground) 65 Avail: 28 full hkups, 37 W, 14 E (20/50 amps). 2021 rates: $46 to $54.05. May 01 to Oct 31. (902)634-4308, 11677 Hwy 3, Lunenburg, NS B0J 2C0

↗ LUNENBURG BOARD OF TRADE CAMPGROUND **Ratings: 4.5/8★/7.5** (Campground) 55 Avail: 22 full hkups, 23 W, 23 E (30 amps). 2021 rates: $46 to $48. May 14 to Oct 08. (902)634-8100, 11 Blockhouse Hill Rd, Lunenburg, NS B0J 2C0

LYDGATE — E2 *Shelburne*

← LOCKEPORT COTTAGES & CAMPGROUND **Ratings: 7.5/8★/7.5** (Campground) 29 Avail: 23 full hkups, 6 W, 6 E (30 amps). 2021 rates: $37 to $42. May 15 to Sep 30. (902)830-7091, 3318 Hwy 3, Lydgate, NS B0T 1L0

MAHONE BAY — D3 *Lunenburg*

MAHONE BAY See also Glen Margaret, Hubbards, Indian Harbour, Lunenburg, Martin's River & Riverport.

MAITLAND — C3 *Hants*

↓ MAITLAND FAMILY CAMPGROUND **Ratings: 6.5/8★/8** (Campground) 20 Avail: 8 full hkups, 7 W, 7 E (20/30 amps). 2021 rates: $25 to $35. May 13 to Oct 08. (902)261-2267, 520 Cedar Rd, Maitland, NS B0N 1T0

MAITLAND BRIDGE — D2 *Annapolis*

↑ KEJIMKUJIK/JEREMY'S BAY (Public National Park) From Annapolis Royal, S 28.5 mi on Rte 8, near Maitland Bridge (R); or From Liverpool, N 45 mi on Rte 8, near Maitland Bridge (L). Avail: 154 E. 2021 rates: $25.50 to $29.40. May 18 to Oct 30. (877)737-3783

MARTIN'S RIVER — D3 *Lunenburg*

↑ **RAYPORT CAMPGROUND**

Ratings: 8.5/8.5★/9.5 (Campground) From Jct of Hwy 103 & Exit 10 (Rte 3), S. 0.5 mi on access rd to Rte 3, E 2 mi, Follow signs (L). **FAC:** gravel rds. (86 spaces). Avail: 26 gravel, 4 pull-thrus, (40x75), back-ins (40x45), 21 W, 21 E (30/50 amps), seasonal sites, cable, WiFi @ sites, tent sites, dump, mobile sewer, laundry, groc, LP bottles, fire rings, firewood, controlled access. **REC:** pool, Martin's River: swim, fishing, boating nearby, playground. Pets OK. eco-friendly. 2021 rates: $45 to $47. May 10 to Oct 15.
(902)627-2678 Lat: 44.48876, Lon: -64.34227
165 Shingle Mill Rd, Martin's River, NS B0J 2E0
www.rayport.ca
See ad this page

MIDDLETON — C2 *Annapolis*

→ ORCHARD QUEEN MOTEL & CAMPGROUND **Ratings: 7.5/8★/8** (Campground) Avail: 26 full hkups (30/50 amps). 2021 rates: $40 to $45. May 01 to Oct 15. (902)825-4801, 425 Main St., Middleton, NS B0S 1P0

→ VIDITO FAMILY CAMPGROUND & COTTAGES **Ratings: 8/8.5★/9** (Campground) 49 Avail: 3 full hkups, 46 W, 46 E (20/30 amps). 2021 rates: $32 to $39. May 01 to Oct 30. (902)825-4380, RR 1, 13736 Hwy 1, Middleton, NS B0P 1W0

MURPHY'S COVE — D4 *Halifax*

→ MURPHY'S CAMPING ON THE OCEAN **Ratings: 6.5/8★/8** (Campground) 48 Avail: 20 W, 20 E (20/30 amps). 2021 rates: $44 to $49.50. May 15 to Oct 15. (902)772-2700, 308 Murphy's Rd., Tangier, NS B0J 3H0

N.E. MARGAREE — B5 *Inverness*

↓ THE LAKES CAMPGROUND **Ratings: 8/8★/10** (Campground) 29 Avail: 2 full hkups, 27 W, 27 E (30 amps). 2021 rates: $35. May 15 to Oct 20. (902)248-2360, 4932 Cabot Trail, North East Margaree, NS B0E 2H0

NINE MILE RIVER — C3 *Hants*

↗ RENFREW CAMPGROUND **Ratings: 7.5/6/9** (Campground) 148 Avail: 96 full hkups, 52 W, 52 E (20/30 amps). 2021 rates: $42 to $45. May 16 to Oct 14. (902)883-1681, 824 Renfrew Road, Nine Mile River, NS B2S 2W5

Set your clocks. Time zones are indicated in the front of each state and province.

NS

NORTH SYDNEY — B6 *Cape Breton*

ARM OF GOLD CAMPGROUND Ratings: 8.5/10★/9.5 (Campground) Avail: 120 full hkups (30/50 amps). 2021 rates: $41.95 to $51.95. Jun 01 to Oct 01. (866)736-6516, 24 Church Rd., Little Bras D'Or, NS B1Y 2Y2

NORTH SYDNEY CABOT TRAIL KOA (Campground) (Phone Update) 135 Avail: 106 full hkups, 29 W, 29 E (30/50 amps). 2021 rates: $40 to $60. May 15 to Oct 15. (902)674-2145, RR 1, 3779 New Harris Rd., New Harris, NS B1X 1T1

PARKERS COVE — C2 *Annapolis*

COVE OCEANFRONT CAMPGROUND **Ratings: 8/9★/9.5** (Campground) Avail: 90 full hkups (30 amps). 2021 rates: $57.95 to $109.95. May 08 to Oct 20. (902)532-5166, 4405 Shore Rd. West, Parkers Cove, NS B0S 1K0

MOUNTAIN TOP CAMPGROUND & COTTAGES **Ratings: 7.5/8.5★/10** (Campground) Avail: 10 full hkups (30 amps). 2021 rates: $38 to $43. May 01 to Sep 30. (877)885-1185, 888 Parker Mountain Rd., Parkers Cove, NS B0S 1K0

PARRSBORO — C3 *Cumberland*

GLOOSCAP PARK AND CAMPGROUND (Public) From Jct of TCH-104 & Hwy 2 (in Glenholme), W 35 mi on Hwy 2 to Parrsboro Tourist Bureau, continue on Hwy 2 to War Memorial, left 3.5 mi (R). 47 Avail: 47 W, 47 E (15/30 amps). 2021 rates: $27 to $32. May 16 to Sep 30. (902)254-2529

PEGGY'S COVE — D3 *Halifax*

PEGGY'S COVE See also Glen Margaret, Halifax, Hubbards, Indian Harbour, Lunenburg & Martin's River.

PICTOU — B4 *Pictou*

BIRCHWOOD CAMPGROUND & CABINS **Ratings: 7/8/8** (Campground) 32 Avail: 25 full hkups, 7 W, 7 E (15/30 amps). 2021 rates: $32.15 to $36.50. May 01 to Oct 15. (902)382-8565, 2521 Hwy 376, Pictou, NS B0K 1H0

HARBOUR LIGHT TRAILER COURT & CAMPGROUND **Ratings: 8/8★/8** (Campground) 80 Avail: 60 full hkups, 20 W, 20 E (30/50 amps). 2021 rates: $32 to $36. May 10 to Oct 15. (902)485-5733, 2881 Three Brooks Road, Pictou, NS B0K 1H0

PORT JOLI — E2 *Queens*

THOMAS RADDALL (Public Prov Park) From Jct of Hwy 103 & East Port L'Hebert Rd to Thomas Raddall Rd (park entrance), E 2 mi (E). 69 Avail. 2021 rates: $26.70. May 20 to Oct 10. (902)683-2664

PORT MEDWAY — D2 *Queens*

RISSERS BEACH (Public Prov Park) From Jct of Hwy 103 & exit 15, exit to town, E 1 mi on Rte 331 (R). 99 Avail: 19 W, 19 E. 2021 rates: $26.70. May 19 to Oct 09. (902)688-2034

PORTERS LAKE — D3 *Halifax*

PORTERS LAKE (Public Prov Park) From Jct of Hwy 107 & exit 19, 3 km on Porters Lake Rd (R). 80 Avail: 10 W, 10 E. 2021 rates: $26.70. May 19 to Oct 09. (902)827-2250

PUGWASH — B3 *Colchester*

GULF SHORE CAMPING PARK **Ratings: 5/7.5/8** (Campground) 32 Avail: 17 full hkups, 15 W, 15 E (20/30 amps). 2021 rates: $46. Jun 15 to Sep 15. (902)243-2489, RR 4 2167 Gulf Shore Rd, Pugwash, NS B0K 1L0

RIVER JOHN — B4 *Pictou*

SEAFOAM CAMPGROUND **Ratings: 7.5/8/7.5** (Campground) 51 Avail: 29 full hkups, 22 W, 22 E (30 amps). 2021 rates: $39.13 to $43.48. May 15 to Sep 30. (902)351-3122, 3493 NS-6, River John, NS B0K 1N0

RIVERPORT — D3 *Lunenburg*

THE OVENS NATURAL PARK **Ratings: 6.5/7.5/7.5** (Campground) 194 Avail: 32 full hkups, 30 W, 30 E (30 amps). 2021 rates: $54 to $79. May 18 to Sep 30. (902)766-4621, 326 Feltsen South Rd, Riverport, NS B0J 2W0

Check the air pressure on your tires and inflate any that are lower than the pressure recommended in the owner's manual. Properly inflated tires can increase fuel efficiency by 3.3 percent.

SHEET HARBOUR — C4 *Buysborough*

EAST RIVER LODGE CAMPGROUND & TRAILER PARK **Ratings: 5.5/6.5/7.5** (Campground) Avail: 10 full hkups (15/30 amps). 2021 rates: $25 to $38. May 01 to Oct 30. (902)885-2057, 200 Pool Rd, Sheet Harbour, NS B0J 3B0

SHELBURNE — E2 *Shelburne*

THE ISLANDS (Public Prov Park) From Shelbourne, W 3 mi on Rte 3 (L). 70 Avail. 2021 rates: $26.70. Jun 09 to Oct 09. (902)875-4304

SHERBROOKE — C4 *Guysborough*

NIMROD'S CAMPGROUND **Ratings: 5/7.5/7** (Campground) 33 Avail: 33 W, 33 E (30/50 amps). 2021 rates: $26 to $35. May 15 to Oct 15. (902)522-2441, 159 Rte 211, Sherbrooke, NS B0J 3C0

SHUBENACADIE — C3 *Colchester*

WHISPERING WINDS FAMILY CAMPING **Ratings: 7/8★/7** (Campground) 85 Avail: 6 full hkups, 79 W, 79 E (30/50 amps). 2021 rates: $45 to $50. May 02 to Oct 15. (902)758-2177, 14201 Hwy 215, Shubenacadie, NS B0N 2H0

WILD NATURE CAMPING GROUND **Ratings: 5.5/7.5★/8.5** (Campground) Avail: 15 full hkups (30 amps). 2021 rates: $32 to $38. May 30 to Sep 30. (902)758-1631, 20961 Hwy 2, Shubenacadie, NS B0N 2H0

SMITH'S COVE — D1 *Digby*

JAGGARS POINT OCEANFRONT CAMPGROUND RESORT
good sam park
Ratings: 8/8.5★/8.5 (Campground) 55 Avail: 30 full hkups, 25 W, 25 E (15/30 amps). 2021 rates: $43.48 - $60.87. May 07 to Oct 15. (902)245-4814, 57 Cross Rd, Smiths Cove, NS B0S 1S0

SOUTH HARBOUR — A6 *Victoria*

HIDEAWAY CAMPGROUND AND OYSTER MARKET (Campground) (Phone Update) 44 Avail: 6 full hkups, 38 W, 38 E (15/30 amps). 2021 rates: $40 to $44.35. May 15 to Oct 15. (902)383-2116, 401 Shore Rd., Dingwall, NS B0C 1G0

SPENCER'S ISLAND — C2 *Colchester*

THE OLD SHIPYARD BEACH CAMPGROUND **Ratings: 7/8★/7.5** (Campground) Avail: 27 full hkups (30/50 amps). 2021 rates: $34 to $36. Jun 01 to Sep 30. (902)392-2487, 774 Spencer's Beach Rd, Spencer's Island, NS B0M 1S0

SPRY BAY — D4 *Halifax*

SPRYBAY CAMPGROUND & CABINS **Ratings: 7/9★/9** (Campground) 27 Avail: 27 W, 27 E (30/50 amps). 2021 rates: $35 to $50. May 01 to Oct 30. (902)772-2554, 19867 Hwy 7, Tangier, NS B0J 3H0

ST ANN'S BAY — B6 *Victoria*

JOYFUL JOURNEYS CAMPARK (Campground) (Phone Update) 42 Avail: 30 full hkups, 12 W, 12 E (30/50 amps). 2021 rates: $35 to $45. May 15 to Oct 20. (902)929-2267, 1762 Hwy 312, Englishtown, NS B0C 1H0

ST PETERS — B5 *Richmond*

BATTERY (Public Prov Park) From town: Go 3/4 km/1/2 mi E on Hwy 4. 56 Avail. 2021 rates: $26.70. Jun 09 to Oct 16. (902)535-3094

SYDNEY — B6 *Cape Breton*

MIRA RIVER (Public Prov Park) From Jct of Hwy 125 & Exit 8 (Rte 22), S 10 mi on Rte 22 to Brickyard Rd, E 1.2 mi (L). 156 Avail: 59 W, 59 E. 2021 rates: $27 to $36. Jun 03 to Sep 12. (902)563-3373

TRURO — C3 *Colchester*

ELM RIVER RV PARK **Ratings: 9/10★/9** (Campground) 80 Avail: 58 full hkups, 22 W, 22 E (30/50 amps). 2021 rates: $50.87 to $52.17. Apr 01 to Nov 30. (902)662-3162, 85 Elm River Parkway, Debert, NS B0M 1G0

HIDDEN HILLTOP CAMPGROUND **Ratings: 9/7.5/9** (Campground) 81 Avail: 51 full hkups, 30 W, 30 E (20/30 amps). 2021 rates: $46.52 to $56.52. May 17 to Oct 15. (866)662-3391, 2600 Hwy 4, Truro, NS B0M 1G0

SCOTIA PINE CAMPGROUND **Ratings: 9/10★/10** (Campground) 96 Avail: 71 full hkups, 9 W, 9 E (30/50 amps). 2021 rates: $41 to $62. May 01 to Oct 20. (877)893-3666, 1911 Hwy 2, Brookfield, NS B0N 1C0

UPPER LAKEVILLE — D4 *Halifax*

E AND F WEBBER'S LAKESIDE PARK **Ratings: 8/9.5★/8.5** (Campground) 38 Avail: 14 full hkups, 4 W, 4 E (15/30 amps). 2021 rates: $36.90 to $48. May 02 to Oct 09. (800)589-2282, 738 Upper Lakeville Rd, Lake Charlotte, NS B0J 1W0

UPPER SACKVILLE — D3 *Halifax*

HALIFAX WEST KOA **Ratings: 8.5/10★/9.5** (Campground) 91 Avail: 31 full hkups, 57 W, 56 E (30/50 amps). 2021 rates: $37 to $53. May 01 to Oct 31. (902)865-4342, 3070 Sackville Dr., Upper Sackville, NS B4E 3C9

WHYCOCOMAGH — B5 *Inverness*

GLENVIEW CAMPGROUND (Campground) (Phone Update) 60 Avail: 46 full hkups, 14 W, 14 E (30/50 amps). 2021 rates: $35 to $55. May 15 to Oct 31. (902)756-3198, 40 Hwy 252, Whycocomagh, NS B0E 3M0

WHYCOCOMAGH (Public Prov Park) From Whycocomagh, E 0.25 mi on Hwy 105 (L). 40 Avail: 10 W, 10 E. 2021 rates: $26.70 to $35.60. Jun 09 to Oct 16. (902)756-2448

WINDSOR — C3 *Hants*

SMILEYS (Public Prov Park) From town, E 9 mi on Rte 14 to MacKay Rd, E 0.2 mi (E). 86 Avail. 2021 rates: $26.70. Jun 10 to Sep 19. (902)757-3131

WYSES CORNER — C3 *Halifax*

DOLLAR LAKE (Public Prov Park) From town, N 20 km on Hwy 102 to Hwy 212, E 18 km on Hwy 212, follow the signs (R). 119 Avail. 2021 rates: $26.70. Jun 09 to Oct 09. (902)384-2770

YARMOUTH — E1 *Yarmouth*

CAMPER'S HAVEN CAMPGROUND & COTTAGES **Ratings: 8/8.5★/9** (Campground) 165 Avail: 53 full hkups, 75 W, 75 E (30/50 amps). 2021 rates: $35 to $48. May 18 to Oct 09. (844)742-4848, 9700 Hwy 3, Arcadia, NS B5A 5J8

ELLENWOOD LAKE (Public Prov Park) From town, NE 12 mi on Rte 340 (L). 87 Avail. 2021 rates: $27. May 20 to Sep 05. (902)761-2400

Getty Images/iStockphoto

DID YOU KNOW?

Toronto is Canada's largest city and nearly 25% of the nation's population lives within a 100-mile radius of the city.

YOU ARE HERE

Ontario

Ontario serves up an eclectic travel experience found nowhere else in Canada. Boasting big-city entertainment and scenic landscapes, this province has it all.

Major Metro

Toronto is the fourth largest city in North America, and it has all of the towering buildings and awesome attractions you'd expect from a major global metropolis. The Western Hemisphere's tallest freestanding structure, the CN Tower rises over 1,800 feet above the city, providing views of the cityscape and beyond. Get hip to the vibe at the St. Lawrence Market, a former town hall that's been converted into a bustling bazaar. The vibrant Distillery Historic District has reclaimed a former Victorian industrial area, turning into one of the city's most visited spots. World-class museums appeal to travelers of all ages, as does scenic Toronto Island Park.

Fall for Niagara

Niagara Falls attracts sightseers from across the globe to witness the falls' 176-foot-tall curtain of cascading water. Adjoining the U.S. and Canada, the falls are a significant attraction on both sides of the border, with many claiming the Canadian side offers the best views. Experience the power with the Journey Behind the Falls tour or a ride on the Hornblower Cruise.

Park Life

Beyond the cities and popular tourist attractions, visitors can explore Ontario's many vast parks. Take a splash in the breathtaking turquoise waters of Georgian Bay at Bruce Peninsula National Park or visit Canada's southernmost point in mainland Canada at Point Pelee National Park, which extends into Lake Erie. Paddlers will find a great playground in Thunder Bay on Lake Superior. Bring your kayak or stand-up paddleboard to Boulevard Lake and Mac and Kam rivers.

Ontario Sushi Pizza

No, this isn't some crazy food experiment. Sushi pizza consists of a fried rice patty topped with salmon, tuna or crab along with avocado slices, spicy mayonnaise and soy wasabi sauce. Food buffs believe a Japanese chef in Toronto invented it, but its popularity has spread steadily throughout the province. Grab a slice!

VISITOR CENTER

TIME ZONE
Eastern/Central Standard

ROAD & HIGHWAY INFORMATION
800-268-4686
511on.ca

FISHING & HUNTING INFORMATION
800-667-1940
ontario.ca/page/fishing

BOATING INFORMATION
800-267-6687
tc.gc.ca/boatingsafety

NATIONAL PARKS
pc.gc.ca/en/pn-np

PROVINCIAL PARKS
ontarioparks.com/en

TOURISM INFORMATION
Ontario Tourism Marketing Partnership
800-ONTARIO
ontariotravel.net

TOP TOURISM ATTRACTIONS
1) CN Tower
2) Niagara Falls
3) Hockey Hall of Fame

MAJOR CITIES
Toronto (capital), Ottawa (Canada's capital), Mississauga, Brampton, Hamilton

Featured Good Sam Parks

ONTARIO

When you stay with Good Sam, you can expect the highest degree of cleanliness and friendliness, and better yet, you get **10% off** overnight campground fees.

If you're not already a Good Sam member you can purchase your membership at one of these locations:

ALLISTON
Nicolston Dam Campground & Travellers Park

BAILIEBORO
Bensfort Bridge Resort

BAINSVILLE
Maplewood Acres RV Park

CHERRY VALLEY
Quinte's Isle Campark

ESSEX
Wildwood Golf & RV Resort

GRAFTON
Cobourg East Campground

HANOVER
Saugeen Springs RV Park

HAWKESTONE
Heidi's Campground

IGNACE
Davy Lake Campground

MATTAWA
Sid Turcotte Park Camping and Cottage Resort

MORRISBURG
Upper Canada Campground

NIAGARA FALLS
Campark Resorts Family Camping & RV Resort

NIAGARA FALLS
Knight's Hide-Away Park

NIAGARA FALLS
Scott's Family RV-Park Camp-ground

NIAGARA FALLS
Yogi Bear's Jellystone Park Camp-Resort

NIPIGON
Stillwater Tent & RV Park

OTTAWA
Camp Hither Hills

PELHAM
Bissell's Hideaway Resort

PUSLINCH
Emerald Lake Trailer Resort & Waterpark

SAULT STE MARIE
Glenview Cottages & RV Park

STURGEON FALLS
Glenrock Cottages & Trailer Park

THUNDER BAY
Happy Land RV Park

VINELAND
N.E.T. Camping Resort

WAWA
Wawa RV Resort & Campground

WHEATLEY
Campers Cove Campground

10/10★/10 GOOD SAM PARKS

CHERRY VALLEY
Quinte's Isle Campark
(613)476-6310

PELHAM
Bissell's Hideaway Resort
(888)236-0619

ESSEX
Wildwood Golf & RV Resort
(866)994-9699

What's This?

An RV park with a 10/10★/10 rating has scored perfect grades in amenities, cleanliness and appearance ("See Understanding the Campground Rating System" on pages 8 and 9 for an explanation of the trusted Good Sam Rating System). Stay in a 10/10★/10 park on your next trip for a nearly flawless camping experience.

Getty Images/iStockphoto

ROAD TRIPS

Go with the Flow From Niagara

Ontario

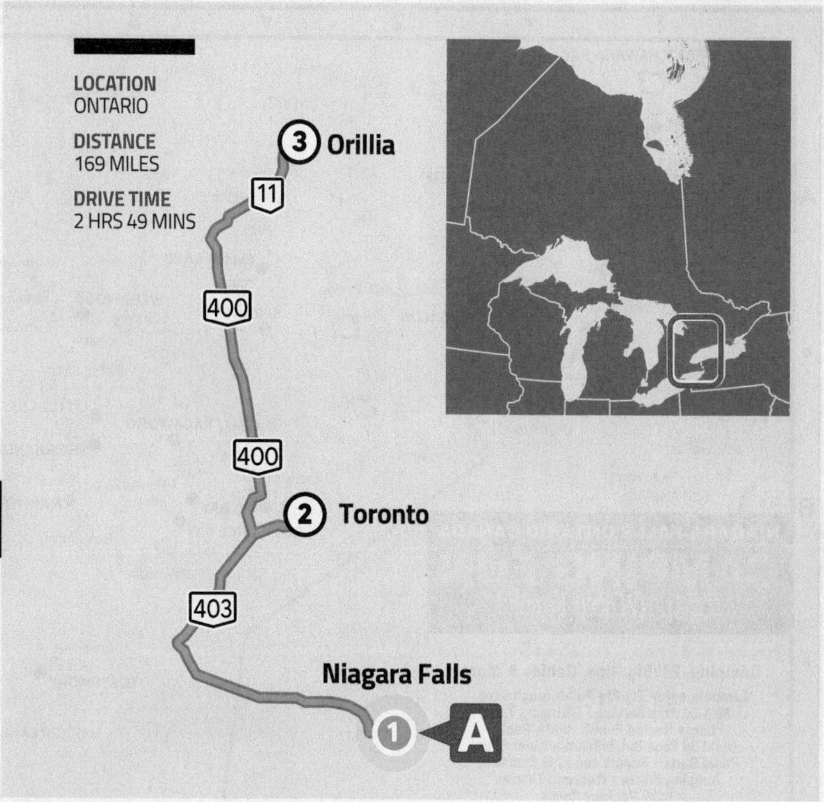

Canada's most populous province is a wonderland of epic adventures and oversized attractions. At the heart of it all is Toronto, the country's trendsetting cultural capital, but that doesn't mean that thrills outside of the city are any less exciting. On this route from Niagara Falls to the shores of Lake Simcoe, you'll discover some of the most incredible natural wonders and scenic landscapes that the Heartland Province has to offer.

1 Niagara Falls
Starting Point

Though you can no longer hear the thunderous roar of North America's most famous falls from miles away, approaching them for the first time is still an awe-inspiring spectacle. The classic way to experience the sheer power of this 165-foot marvel is on one of the wet-and-wild boat cruises that ferries visitors to the foot of the falls, but for a truly unique perspective nothing beats a "Journey Behind the Falls." This bucket list attraction allows visitors to explore 130-year-old tunnels carved in the bedrock behind the crashing cascade, before leading to a series of observation windows and platforms that look out onto one-fifth of the world's freshwater plummeting into the basin below.

RECOMMENDED STOPOVER
A CAMPARK RESORTS FAMILY CAMPING & RV RESORT
NIAGARA FALLS, ON (877) CAMPARK

2 Toronto
Drive 80 Miles ▪ 1 Hour, 19 Minutes

Vibrant and diverse, this urban gem ranks high on the list of most welcoming cities in the world. And for good reason: It's home to people of over 200 different ethnic origins. For visitors, that means plenty of international eateries, incredible shopping, and a smattering of neighborhoods each with their own distinct flavor. For the best views of this cosmopolitan mecca, head to the top of the CN Tower, the city's tallest and most recognizable attraction. At a dizzying 1,815 feet, views from the observation platform stretch as far as Niagara Falls in the distance, and often include sights of helicopters flying below you as they zoom across the cityscape.

3 Orillia
Drive 89 Miles ▪ 1 Hour, 30 Minutes

A far cry from the hustle and bustle of the big city, this easygoing getaway is a playground for outdoors lovers of all stripes. Situated on the Atherley Narrows that connects Lake Simcoe to Lake Couchiching, it's a boater's paradise with seemingly endless opportunities for waterskiing, tubing, canoeing and kayaking. It's also perfectly placed for anglers looking to land the big one. Depending on your catch of choice, the deeper waters of Lake Simcoe hold abundant lake trout and whitefish, while the shallower waters of Lake Couchiching are well-known for their bass, walleye and perch. For a special treat, hop aboard one of the area's relaxing sightseeing excursions.

Getty Images/iStockphoto

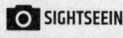

BIKING · BOATING · DINING · ENTERTAINMENT · FISHING · HIKING · HUNTING · PADDLING · SHOPPING · SIGHTSEEING

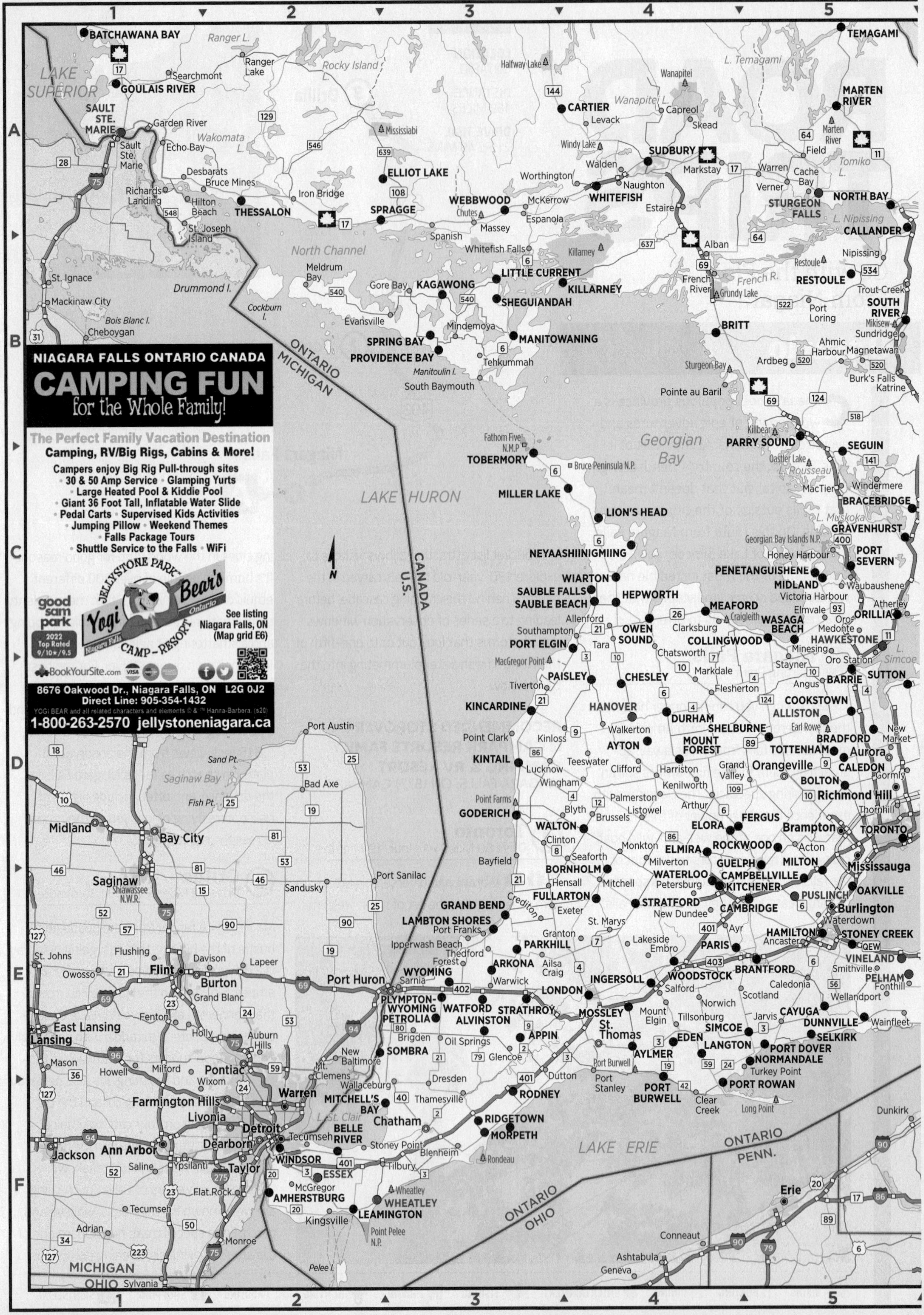
1
2
3
4
5
A
B
C
D
E
F
BATCHAWANA BAY
Ranger L.
LAKE SUPERIOR
GOULAIS RIVER
Searchmont
Ranger Lake
Rocky Island L.
Halfway Lake
L. Temagami
TEMAGAMI
Wanapitei
CARTIER
Wanapitei L.
Capreol
Levack
Skead
MARTEN RIVER
SAULT STE. MARIE
Garden River
Wakomata L.
Mississiabi
Marten River
Sault Ste. Marie
Echo Bay
Windy Lake
SUDBURY
Field
Tomiko L.
Walden
Markstay
Warren
Cache Bay
Desbarats
Bruce Mines
ELLIOT LAKE
Worthington
Naughton
Verner
Richards Landing
Hilton Beach
Iron Bridge
WEBBWOOD
McKerrow
WHITEFISH
Estaire
STURGEON FALLS
NORTH BAY
THESSALON
SPRAGGE
Chutes
Massey
Espanola
L. Nipissing
CALLANDER
St. Joseph Island
Spanish
Alban
North Channel
Whitefish Falls
Killarney
Nipissing
Restoule
Meldrum Bay
LITTLE CURRENT
French River
French R.
RESTOULE
St. Ignace
Drummond I.
Gore Bay
KAGAWONG
KILLARNEY
Grundy Lake
Trout Creek
Mackinaw City
Cockburn I.
SHEGUIANDAH
Port Loring
SOUTH RIVER
Bois Blanc I.
Evansville
Mikisew
Cheboygan
Mindemoya
BRITT
Sundridge
SPRING BAY
MANITOWANING
Ahmic Harbour
Magnetawan
PROVIDENCE BAY
Tehkummah
Sturgeon Bay
Ardbeg
Manitoulin I.
Burk's Falls
Katrine
South Baymouth
Pointe au Baril
ONTARIO
MICHIGAN
Killbear
Georgian Bay
Fathom Five N.M.P.
PARRY SOUND
SEGUIN
TOBERMORY
Oastler Lake
L. Rousseau
Bruce Peninsula N.P.
LAKE HURON
MILLER LAKE
MacTier
Windermere
BRACEBRIDGE
LION'S HEAD
L. Muskoka
GRAVENHURST
Georgian Bay Islands N.P.
NEYAASHIINIGMIING
Honey Harbour
PORT SEVERN
N
CANADA
U.S.
PENETANGUISHENE
WIARTON
MIDLAND
Waubaushene
SAUBLE FALLS
Victoria Harbour
SAUBLE BEACH
HEPWORTH
Elmvale
Atherley
MEAFORD
Oro
ORILLIA
Allenford
Craigleith
WASAGA BEACH
Southampton
OWEN SOUND
Clarksburg
HAWKESTONE
PORT ELGIN
Tara
COLLINGWOOD
Minesing
Chatsworth
Oro Station
L. Simcoe
MacGregor Point
Markdale
Stayner
PAISLEY
CHESLEY
BARRIE
SUTTON
Tiverton
Flesherton
Angus
KINCARDINE
HANOVER
COOKSTOWN
DURHAM
ALLISTON
Walkerton
SHELBURNE
Earl Rowe
New Market
Point Clark
Kinloss
AYTON
MOUNT FOREST
BRADFORD
TOTTENHAM
Aurora
KINTAIL
Teeswater
Clifford
Harriston
Grand Valley
Orangeville
CALEDON
Lucknow
Gormly
Wingham
Kenilworth
BOLTON
Richmond Hill
Point Farms
Palmerston
Arthur
Thornhill
GODERICH
Blyth
Listowel
FERGUS
Brussels
ELORA
Brampton
TORONTO
WALTON
Clinton
Monkton
ELMIRA
ROCKWOOD
Acton
Seaforth
Milverton
GUELPH
MILTON
Bayfield
BORNHOLM
WATERLOO
CAMPBELLVILLE
Mississauga
Hensall
Mitchell
Petersburg
KITCHENER
FULLARTON
PUSLINCH
OAKVILLE
Crediton
STRATFORD
CAMBRIDGE
GRAND BEND
Exeter
New Dundee
Burlington
LAMBTON SHORES
St. Marys
Waterdown
Port Franks
Ayr
Granton
HAMILTON
STONEY CREEK
Ipperwash Beach
Lakeside
Ancaster
PARKHILL
Embro
Thedford
PARIS
Forest
VINELAND
ARKONA
Ailsa Craig
BRANTFORD
Smithville
WYOMING
WOODSTOCK
PELHAM
Sarnia
INGERSOLL
Caledonia
Fonthill
Warwick
Salford
LONDON
Scotland
Welland port
PLYMPTON-WYOMING
Norwich
WATFORD
STRATHROY
MOSSLEY
CAYUGA
PETROLIA
Mount Elgin
Tillsonburg
Jarvis
ALVINSTON
St. Thomas
DUNNVILLE
Wainfleet
Brigden
SIMCOE
SELKIRK
APPIN
EDEN
Oil Springs
LANGTON
PORT DOVER
SOMBRA
Glencoe
AYLMER
NORMANDALE
Port Burwell
Turkey Point
Dresden
Dutton
Port Stanley
PORT ROWAN
PORT BURWELL
Wallaceburg
RODNEY
Clear Creek
Thamesville
Long Point
MITCHELL'S BAY
L. St. Clair
Chatham
RIDGETOWN
Dunkirk
BELLE RIVER
MORPETH
Tecumseh
Stoney Point
Blenheim
LAKE ERIE
ONTARIO
PENN.
WINDSOR
Tilbury
Rondeau
ESSEX
McGregor
Wheatley
WHEATLEY
Erie
AMHERSTBURG
LEAMINGTON
ONTARIO
OHIO
Kingsville
Point Pelee N.P.
Conneaut
Ashtabula
Geneva
Pelee I.
Port Austin
Sand Pt.
Saginaw Bay
Bad Axe
Fish Pt.
Midland
Bay City
Saginaw
Shiawassee N.W.R.
Sandusky
Port Sanilac
Flushing
Davison
Lapeer
St. Johns
Owosso
Flint
Burton
Port Huron
Grand Blanc
Fenton
East Lansing
Lansing
Holly
Auburn Hills
Mason
Howell
Milford
Pontiac
New Baltimore
Mt. Clemens
Wixom
Warren
Farmington Hills
Livonia
Detroit
Jackson
Ann Arbor
Dearborn
Taylor
Saline
Ypsilanti
Flat Rock
Tecumseh
Adrian
Monroe
MICHIGAN
OHIO
Sylvania

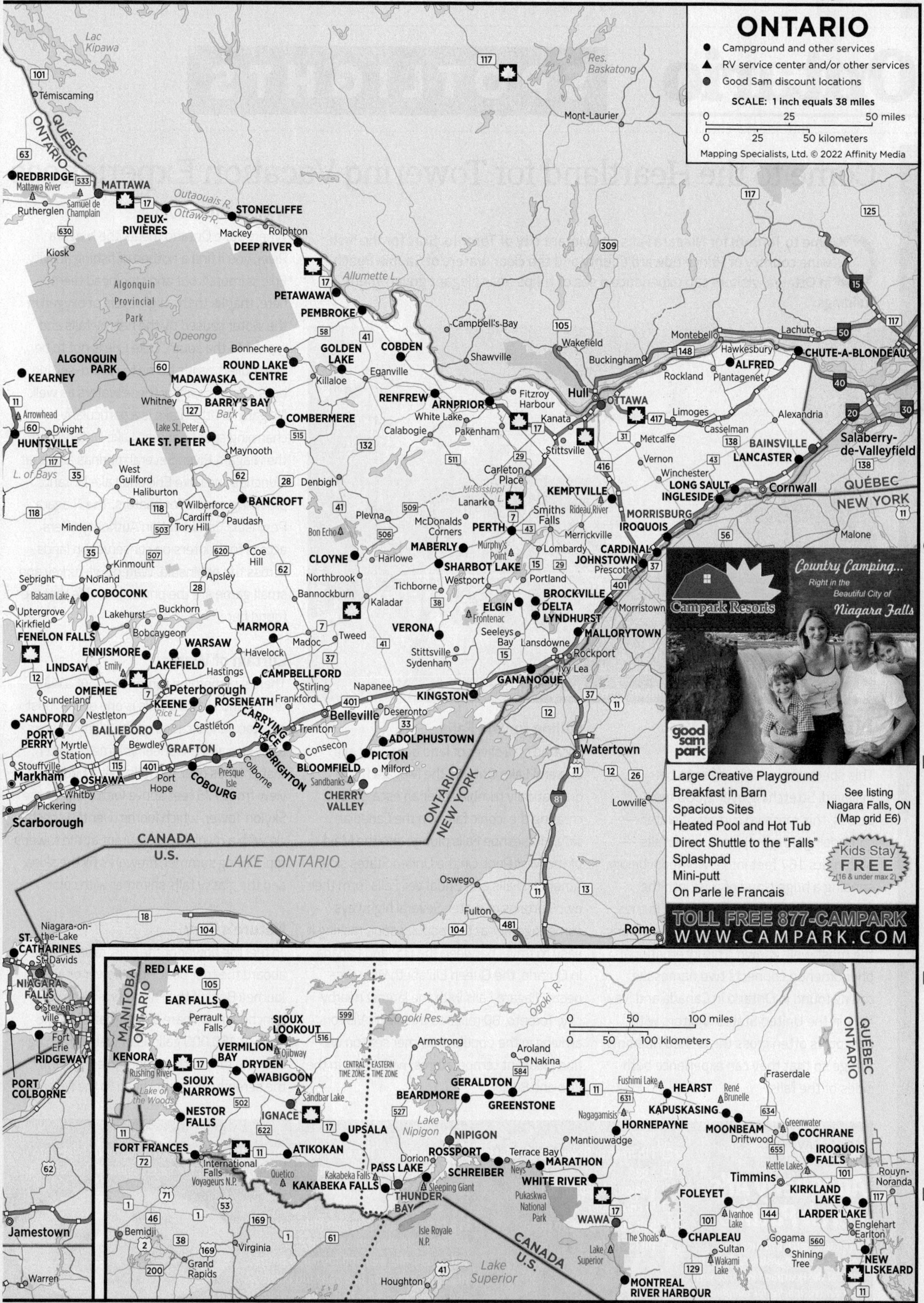
ONTARIO
Campground and other services
RV service center and/or other services
Good Sam discount locations
SCALE: 1 inch equals 38 miles
0 25 50 miles
0 25 50 kilometers
Mapping Specialists, Ltd. © 2022 Affinity Media
REDBRIDGE
MATTAWA
DEUX-RIVIÈRES
STONECLIFFE
DEEP RIVER
PETAWAWA
PEMBROKE
GOLDEN LAKE
COBDEN
ALGONQUIN PARK
KEARNEY
ROUND LAKE CENTRE
MADAWASKA
BARRY'S BAY
RENFREW
ARNPRIOR
OTTAWA
ALFRED
CHUTE-A-BLONDEAU
HUNTSVILLE
COMBERMERE
LAKE ST. PETER
BAINSVILLE
LANCASTER
Salaberry-de-Valleyfield
KEMPTVILLE
LONG SAULT
INGLESIDE
Cornwall
BANCROFT
MORRISBURG
IROQUOIS
PERTH
CLOYNE
MABERLY
SHARBOT LAKE
CARDINAL
JOHNSTOWN
COBOCONK
BROCKVILLE
ELGIN
DELTA
LYNDHURST
FENELON FALLS
MARMORA
VERONA
MALLORYTOWN
WARSAW
ENNISMORE
LINDSAY
LAKEFIELD
CAMPBELLFORD
GANANOQUE
OMEMEE
Peterborough
KEENE
ROSENEATH
KINGSTON
SANDFORD
BAILIEBORO
CARRYING PLACE
Belleville
PORT PERRY
GRAFTON
BRIGHTON
ADOLPHUSTOWN
PICTON
BLOOMFIELD
Markham
OSHAWA
COBOURG
CHERRY VALLEY
Scarborough
Watertown
LAKE ONTARIO
CANADA
U.S.
ST. CATHARINES
NIAGARA FALLS
RIDGEWAY
PORT COLBORNE
RED LAKE
EAR FALLS
SIOUX LOOKOUT
KENORA
VERMILION BAY
DRYDEN
WABIGOON
SIOUX NARROWS
NESTOR FALLS
IGNACE
FORT FRANCES
ATIKOKAN
UPSALA
KAKABEKA FALLS
PASS LAKE
THUNDER BAY
NIPIGON
ROSSPORT
SCHREIBER
BEARDMORE
GERALDTON
GREENSTONE
MARATHON
WHITE RIVER
WAWA
HEARST
KAPUSKASING
HORNEPAYNE
MOONBEAM
COCHRANE
IROQUOIS FALLS
Timmins
FOLEYET
CHAPLEAU
KIRKLAND LAKE
LARDER LAKE
NEW LISKEARD
MONTREAL RIVER HARBOUR
0 50 100 miles
0 50 100 kilometers
Campark Resorts
Country Camping...
Right in the Beautiful City of
Niagara Falls
good sam park
Large Creative Playground
Breakfast in Barn
Spacious Sites
Heated Pool and Hot Tub
Direct Shuttle to the "Falls"
Splashpad
Mini-putt
On Parle le Francais
See listing Niagara Falls, ON (Map grid E6)
Kids Stay FREE
(16 & under max 2)
TOLL FREE 877-CAMPARK
WWW.CAMPARK.COM

Ontario SPOTLIGHTS

Come to the Heartland for Towering Vacation Experiences

Come to Toronto for Niagara Falls and vibrant city of Toronto. Stay for the lush wine country of Prince Edward County and the clear waters of Sauble Beach. In Ottawa, visitors can experience a sea of tulips near elegant government buildings.

NIAGARA FALLS HAS A FLOW RATE OF 700,000 GALLONS PER SECOND.

Getty Images/iStockphoto

Several vantage points give visitors stunning views of Niagara Falls.

Niagara Falls

This spectacle must be seen to be believed. Stretching over 2,600 feet across, this massive curtain of water — comprising three separate waterfalls — plummets 167 feet into a whirlpool below, sending a huge cloud of mist into the air. While not the tallest waterfall in the world, Niagara Falls certainly ranks among the most well-known. This international phenomenon connects two namesake towns found in Ontario in Canada and New York in the United States. Visitors with passports often cross the arched Rainbow Bridge so that they can experience both sides of the falls.

Falling for the Falls

Located on a sliver of land between Lake Erie and Lake Ontario, the Niagara River dramatically rumbles over an escarpment, creating the iconic falls: On the Canadian side, Horseshoe Falls plunge into the Maid of the Mist Pool. On the United States side, American Falls and Bridal Veil Falls form their own curtains of water. Several highways come together at this popular spot, making it easy to travel between the U.S. and Canada. In Ontario, the Queen Elizabeth Way connects Niagara Falls with the largest nearby city, Toronto, 80 miles to the north. Visitors arriving in the popular summer season will find pleasant temperatures, with highs in the 70s and 80s.

A River Runs Over It

Where Lake Ontario meets the Niagara River, you'll find a hotbed of fishing activity. Epic salmon, trout and steelhead teem here, thanks to the high levels of oxygen in the water caused by the nearby falls and rapids. To the south, Lake Erie is not to be overlooked, as it's home to record-setting bass. Paddlers enjoy these waters as well. Niagara-on-the-Lake is a particularly charming spot to access Lake Ontario and the Niagara River. Several marinas and boat launches line Lake Erie and Lake Ontario, providing access for boaters. The Niagara Peninsula Conservation Authority offers access for hunters on conservation lands across the peninsula. Waterfowl, turkey and small game are the primary wildlife that are found here.

Curtain of Water

There's something romantic about a waterfall, and Niagara Falls is one of the most spectacular cascades on the planet thanks to its size and the sheer volume of water that crashes over the falls. Get a bird's-eye view from 775 feet above with a trip up the Skylon Tower, which looms over the spectacle with a revolving restaurant at the tower's top. During summer, fireworks fill the skies, and the glassy falls shimmer with color.

Nature's Fury

To feel the power of the falls, take a cruise aboard the tour boat Hornblower or a Journey Behind the Falls tour. Put on your poncho and prepare to be amazed by the sight of 150,000 gallons of water crashing over the falls each second. To escape into the serenity of nature, head to the Niagara

LOCAL FAVORITE

Allegheny Al's Perch Patties

In Ontario, perch fish fries are popular summer pastimes. Get in the spirit of the Heartland Province with your own recipe. *Recipe adapted from Best Ever RV Recipes.*

INGREDIENTS

- ☐ 1 lb fresh or frozen perch fillets
- ☐ 1 egg
- ☐ 1 onion, chopped, to taste
- ☐ ½ cup flour
- ☐ Salt and pepper, to taste
- ☐ Oil for frying

DIRECTIONS

Thaw the perch if frozen. Bring a pan of water to a boil and place perch fillets into the boiling water for no more than two minutes. Immediately drain off hot water and plunge the fish into a pan of cold water.

In a bowl, break fillets into little pieces. Add egg, chopped onion, flour and seasoning. Mix well and form into patties. Heat 1/8 inch of oil in a pan, add patties and brown each side to a golden brown.

See listing Niagara Falls, ON
Campark Resorts
FAMILY CAMPING & RV RESORT
Country Camping...
RIGHT IN THE BEAUTIFUL CITY OF
Niagara Falls
good sam park
Children Stay FREE *Up to 2
WEGO
• 3.5 miles to the Falls and Casinos
• Hot Tub
• Heated Pool
• Splash Pad
• Playgrounds & Tube Maze
• Planned Activities
• Restaurant & Ice Cream
• Pedal Cart Bikes
• Shuttles to Falls Entertainment
• Axe Throwing, Laser Tag, Escape Rooms
• 30/50 amp Big Rig Pull-Thrus
• RV Supplies & Groceries
• FREE Wireless Internet
• Mini-Putt & Nearby Golfing
• Volleyball & Basketball
• Wine Tours
1-877-CAMPARK
9387 Lundy's Lane Niagara Falls, ON, L2E 6S4
www.CAMPARK.com
info@campark.com
Create yout family memories
with Campark Resorts!

Glen Nature Reserve, featuring miles of trails through the woodlands above the river.

Fine Festivals

After a cold, snowy winter, Niagara Falls springs to life with the annual Springlicious celebration, held in early June. Queen Street fills with vendors, live entertainment and colorful carnival rides. Though Ontario's winter weather inhibits some agriculture, it gives the region a unique treat: icewine. As the crisp, frozen air begins to bite, local vineyards leave their grapes on the vines and later pluck them to make a sweet, luscious wine, found few places in the world. It's so revered, Niagara Falls celebrates with an annual Icewine Festival, held in January. In the fall, traditional wines are celebrated at the Niagara Grape & Wine Festival, which features hundreds of events over the course of 18 days.

Ontario Battleground

North of the falls, on the top of the Niagara Escarpment (a UNESCO world biosphere), Queenston Heights Park is the site of the 1812 Battle of Queenston Heights. A series of formal gardens sprawl in the shadow of a 185-foot column that commemorates Major General Sir Isaac Brock, "Savior of Upper Canada." One of Canada's great heroes of the War of 1812, Brock was killed here by a gun shot; his remains are interred at the monument's base along with his Lieutenant-Colonel, John Macdonell.

Heed the Heritage Trail

For more history, follow the Niagara Heritage Trail, which runs 33 miles along the Niagara River between Fort Erie and Niagara-on-the-Lake, connecting several historic sites. Built by the British in 1764, Fort Erie was later the site of the bloodiest battle in Canadian history during the War of 1812. Today, this story is shared through educational displays, fort tours and live reenactments. Canada's oldest museum is also found in the region. What started as a collection of taxidermy animals in 1827 has now become the Niagara Falls History Museum, featuring displays about the War of 1812 and the fascinating history of the falls and the daredevils who have tried to conquer them.

Niagara-on-the-Lake

Colorful homes and grand brick beauties dating to the 1700-1800s line the streets of Niagara-on-the-Lake. This charming village, bordered by both Lake Ontario and the Niagara River, is simply steeped with character and romance. Listen for the clip-clop of horses' hooves as horse-drawn carriages glide under the majestic shade trees. The vibrancy of the floral-lined sidewalks is matched only by the liveliness of the wares sold in cozy shops, bakeries and cafés. Continue onward to Niagara's Wine Country, a region marked by fields of grapes and welcoming wineries. From quaint houses to gleaming glass structures, you'll find diverse tasting rooms to match the diverse wines filling the cellars.

Wine and Farm to Table Dining

The Niagara Falls wine region adds to the dining options available in the area's burgeoning culinary scene. Glasses of delicious, locally sourced vintages accompany meals at restaurants that are renowned for their farm-to-table menus.

Cuisine From Around the World

International cuisine is commonplace in Niagara Falls, and options range from fresh seafood specialties to spicy Thai and Caribbean. Family-style restaurants are also on hand, along with casual dining in local pubs and grills. For a view of Niagara Falls with your meal, try a dinner cruise on an old-fashioned riverboat by signing on with Grand Sunset Cruises. The Niagara

The Niagara Parks Gardens has 2,400 roses along with other beautiful plants on 99 acres.

Belle sails the Lower Niagara river from the opening of the Niagara Gorge to Lake Ontario.

Niagara Parks Botanical Gardens

To immerse yourself in the area's flora, Niagara Parks' 99-acre Botanical Gardens is well worth a visit. North of town, on the scenic Niagara Parkway, the gardens were established in 1936. During the summer, horse and carriage rides are offered through the kaleidoscopic gardens, which brim with perennials, rhododendrons, azaleas, a formal parterre garden, herb and vegetable gardens, and a rose garden with over 2,400 roses. The garden's signature attraction is a 12-meter diameter Floral Clock comprising more than 25,000 plants. But what draws most visitors is the acclaimed Butterfly Conservatory, where 2,000 fluttering insects (with more than 50 international species), including swallowtails, fritillaries and luminous blue Morphos.

For the Birds

At Bird Kingdom, located just a short walk from Horseshoe Falls, visitors enjoy encounters with wild animals. Guests can learn about the world of exotic plants, animals, birds and reptiles. A gift shop offers a variety of plush toys. The experience culminates with an entry into the world's largest aviary, home to a 40-foot waterfall, living jungle and free-flying exotic birds.

Walk the Footsteps of Soldiers

Tours of the battlefield outline the history behind the combat and include a jaunt to the top of the hillside for superb panoramic views. With picnic pavilions, tennis courts, a children's playground and splash pool, and the highly praised Queenston Heights Restaurant, the park makes for a great half-day excursion.

Zipping, Swinging and Climbing

Unveiled in 2016, the Whirlpool Adventure Course shakes up Niagara's old-school image with a pulse-racing series of log ladders, rope swings, tightrope obstacles and ziplines suspended high above the Niagara gorge. On the Canadian side, and not for the faint of heart, the Mistrider is a 2,200-foot, white-knuckle zipline that jettisons four people at a time for some 670 meters towards the Horseshoe Falls at speeds approaching 65 miles per hour. There's a viewing platform with exhilarating views of Horseshoe Falls at the bottom.

More Fun With Water

Another major attraction in the area for family fun is Marineland, where visitors can marvel at the amazing performances by sea lions, dolphins and walruses. Educational exhibits shed light on the planet's delicate marine ecosystem. The Fallsview Indoor Waterpark is home to 16 waterslides, a giant wave pool and Beach House Rain Fortress. The Americana Waterpark Resort and Spa offers the whole family its Waves Indoor Waterpark, with features that include water slides up to three stories high, a wave pool and a retractable glass roof.

Prince Edward County

Occupying a peninsula that juts off the north shore of Lake Ontario, Prince Edward County is a scenic getaway for travelers seeking an escape into a rustic setting. Sandbanks Provincial Park in the southwest is the county's

ON

SPOTLIGHTS

natural highlight, with soaring cliffs and wide, sandy beaches that are perfect for lake swimming. Several acclaimed wineries dot the 405-square-mile region, and award-winning cheesemakers have put the town on the foodie map. Visitors can sample the town's bounty in Picton, where restaurants, galleries and museums form the nucleus of the county.

Picton is the largest community and the county seat of Prince Edward County Ontario.

Premier Attractions

Located on Picton Bay on the eastern shore, Picton is a wonderful place to stroll, with a picturesque harbor and marina overlooked by lush green spaces. One of the few remaining art deco movie houses in Ontario, the Regent Theatre first opened its doors in 1918 and continues to show films.

Seeing Wrecks

More than 50 shipwrecks have been found in the waters surrounding Prince Edward County, and the Mariners Park Museum, built around a lighthouse south of Picton in Port Milford, has become the repository for the treasures discovered during initial diving expeditions. Fascinating artifacts and relics tell the story of the region's prohibition-era rumrunners.

Wonderful Wineries

Described by locals as "Ontario's Camelot," Prince Edward County's nutrient-rich soil yields bountiful harvests. Visitors can tour lots of wineries, along with distilleries and cider and beer producers. Prince Edward County is a Designated Viticultural Area, with lots of pinot noir and chardonnay. Local wineries of note include Domaine Darius, Half Moon Bay Winery and Cape Vineyards, and there are plenty of area operators offering wine-related tours (and safe driving services) for those who want to explore the surrounding vineyards. Make a day out of your visit to the Waupoos Winery, on the shore of Lake Ontario, with a petting zoo and chocolatier on-site. Prince Edward County is home to the largest number of wineries outside of Niagara, which dot the twisted lanes of the popular Taste Trail.

Follow the Arts

Renowned for its rich cultural heritage, Prince Edward County has no shortage of artistic flair. The Arts Trail takes art lovers through the countryside lined with an eclectic mix of modern galleries to rustic barn studios.

Small Pond, Big Creativity

One of the most popular stops, the Small Pond Arts features work by local landscape and portrait artist Milé Murtanovski. Throughout the county, tradition and modernity coalesce with county fairs, art festivals, wine tastings, street dances, summer festivals and even an Innovation Centre.

Gallivant On Land

Cloaked in mystery, the Lake on the Mountain is one of Ontario's natural wonders and a great curiosity. Sitting more than 200 feet above Lake Ontario's Bay of Quinte, the turquoise lake, with a constant flow of fresh, clean water with no apparent source, defies all geological and geographical logic; the most generally accepted theory is that it is a collapsed doline, an odd feature found in areas with a limestone foundation. The lake's scenic views of Picton Bay provide a dramatic backdrop for recreational activities, including hiking and cycling within the namesake park. Sandbanks Provincial Park is home to the world's largest baymouth barrier dune formation.

Sandbanks Provincial Park is home to the world's largest baymouth barrier dune formation.

Sand Steps

A number of walking trails traverse the dune and wetland habitats and afford excellent bird-watching; the park is a bird migration hot spot in spring and fall. The 1.5-mile moderately rated Sandbanks Dunes Trail meanders through fragile dune habitat and skirts several pannes, rare wetland habitats that support myriad wildlife species and unusual flora.

Water Wonders

Point Petre Wildlife Conservation Area, an exceptional area for bird-watching, features a long pebble beach where you can swim off flat limestone ledges. Sandbanks Provincial Park provides countless opportunities for on-the-water recreation with boating and fishing

Quinte's Isle
Campark
Yes! This is Vacation Land!
Have the time of your life
Full Service
Big Rig Park
30/50 Amp Sites
Pull-Thrus
X-Large Sites
Heated Swimming Pools
Pickle Ball Courts
Mini-Golf
Nature Trails
Planned Activities
New Restaurant & Bar Overlooking Lake Ontario
Essential RV Parts
Boat Launch & Inlet to Lake Ontario
613-476-6310
237 Salmon Point Rd.
Cherry Valley, ON
info@qicampark.com
www.qicampark.com
good sam park
2022 Top Rated 10/10★/10
See listing Cherry Valley, ON

ON

Water cascading in Sauble Falls Provincial Park outside of Sauble Beach in Ontario.

on the East and West Lake for yellow pickerel, smallmouth and largemouth bass, northern pike and various pan fish. Although there are no formal canoe routes at Sandbanks, the Outlet River is ideal for those just learning to canoe and who wish to explore the marsh habitat. Sandbanks is famous for its three expansive sandy beaches that are deemed among the best in Canada; Outlet and Sandbanks beaches have shallow waters and gradual drop-offs that are ideal for families, but beware that Dunes Beach has a steep drop-off and is not recommended for children.

Party in Prince Edward County

Famed nationwide for its superb sparkling wines, wine tasting is one of the county's most popular activities. In May, Terroir on the Move is a showcase for the region's acclaimed wineries, offering participants a passport to visit six participating wineries.

Art Aplenty

Throughout June and July, the Arts in the County festival is Eastern Ontario's leading art exhibition, with more than 2,000 juried works of art by local artists. In August, the Prince Edward County Jazz Festival draws some of Canada's leading jazz musicians to perform against the stunning backdrop of the region's wine country.

Vintage History

For an insight into the region's fascinating history, take a drive along the Loyalist Parkway (Highway 33), stretching 62 miles from Trenton, along Lake Ontario, to Kingston. The historic parkway retraces the steps of the British Loyalists who settled here after fleeing the Revolutionary War. One of Picton's historic and natural treasures, Macaulay Heritage Park highlights local history through its collection of 19th-century buildings, including a carriage house, church and delightful heritage gardens. Learn the histories of early residents who thrived in the area.

Sauble Beach

Is the beach calling for you? Check out a lakeside town that has over seven miles of sand, stunning sunsets and warm summer temperatures. Discover endless windsurfing, waterskiing and swimming. Dip your toes in the sand and feel the breeze. As a bonus, this stunning beach is considered part of Canada's No. 1 freshwater beach community. Pack your beach chairs; roll up your shirt sleeves and head on over to Sauble Beach on Lake Ontario in Canada.

Hot in Huron

Sauble Beach is located on the eastern shore of Lake Huron in the southern end of the Bruce Peninsula in Ontario. You can get there on Ontario Highway 10 outside of Toronto or take the coastal Ontario Highway 21, which connects with Interstate 94 in Detroit. This route follows the lakeshore the whole way to Sauble Beach, dishing out stunning scenery along the way. The beach's location on the eastern shore of the lake means spectacular sunsets over the shimmering water is the norm. Bring your camera to the beach about an hour before the sun drops.

Hitting the Water

Of course, with all this sand, you can expect to find a lot of activities centered around the shore. Join in a beach volleyball game, or try your skill at windsurfing or waterskiing. Explore the Sauble River on kayak or paddleboard, or go fishing for rainbow trout and Chinook salmon in their spring and fall spawning runs. Paddle along the Rankin River Canoe Route, which is perfect for novices. Just a short drive away, Owen Sound, with its lively historic district, provides the amenities of an outdoorsy regional hub with even more boating opportunities.

Cool Beach Vibe

Sauble Beach locals tell visitors that the town hasn't changed a lot since the 1950s and they like it that way. There is a casual, laid-back vibe in Sauble Beach that has brought generations of visitors to the area and keeps them coming back year after year. One other thing you may not expect to find in Sauble Beach is NASCAR. Yes, Sauble Beach is home to the Sauble Speedway and hosts high-speed NASCAR action.

Sauble Beach on Lake Ontario is the second-largest freshwater beach in the world.

Mixed Adventures

While you're here, make time to play 18 holes at one of the courses in town. If you brought your ATV instead of your clubs, then check out the mixed trails at the South Bruce Peninsula ATV Club. Take the kids to the rock-climbing wall or book a boat tour to the Fishing Islands, where visitors will find a First Nations Smokehouse and first European settlement in the area.

Bruce Peninsula National Park

Less than an hour's drive from Sauble Beach, Bruce Peninsula National Park forms the core of UNESCO's Niagara Escarpment World Biosphere Reserve. Opportunities for outdoor recreation abound with hiking, biking, swimming, canoeing and wildlife spotting amidst a pristine wilderness of craggy oyster gray cliffs, dense forests and gorgeous turquoise waters that feel more Caribbean than Canadian. This glorious park is famed for its superb hiking trails, which range in difficulty from novice to advanced and connect to the Bruce Trail, a wild 586-mile path that ends in Tobermory.

Flower Pot Hikes

The most popular (easy) hikes include the three-mile jaunt to Flowerpot Island — named for the 35-foot-tall wind-carved columns that resemble giant vases — and the 2-mile Georgian Bay Trail to Indian Head Cove, a small, secluded cove framed with giant boulders. It's a perfect outdoor gym for kids. Bruce's crowning jewel is Cyprus Lake Grotto, where crystalline waters in shades of blue and green and intricate cave structures lure travelers looking to revel in the area's serene beauty.

Going Under

For more adventurous types, Bruce Peninsula is also one of the best caving and spelunking areas in the country. Ancient holes and crevices that were carved out of the Niagara Escarpment more than 7,000 years ago during the last ice age are ripe for exploration. Greig's Caves, the Grotto, Bruce's Caves and a loop trail on Flowerpot Island are among the most popular. The erie rock formations are popular spots for photographers.

Tobermory

At the northern tip of the Bruce Peninsula, quaint Tobermory exudes an end-of-the-world aura (with a whiff of the eccentric), despite the growing numbers of tourists who use the town as a base for exploring the wild and beautiful lands of the Bruce Peninsula. Beyond the small town with its stores, bars, live music venues, waterside restaurants (the sunsets here are incredible) and hotels that dot Little Tub Harbor, Tobermory caters to active travelers who are always looking to raise the bar. Enjoy a fun and relaxing time here.

Unfathomable Marine Treasure

Nestled in Bruce Peninsula's northern tip, the Fathom Five National Marine Park will pique your curiosity with 22 shipwrecks, many of which lie within reach of divers. From schooners to barges, this marine park encompasses some of the best-preserved sunken vessels in Canada's history.

FOR MORE INFORMATION

Ontario Travel, 800-668-2746, www.ontariotravel.net

Tourism Partnership of Niagara, 800-563-2557, www.visitniagaracanada.com

Prince Edward County, 800-640-4717, prince-edward-county.com

Sauble Beach Tourism Office, 519-422-1262, www.saublebeach.com

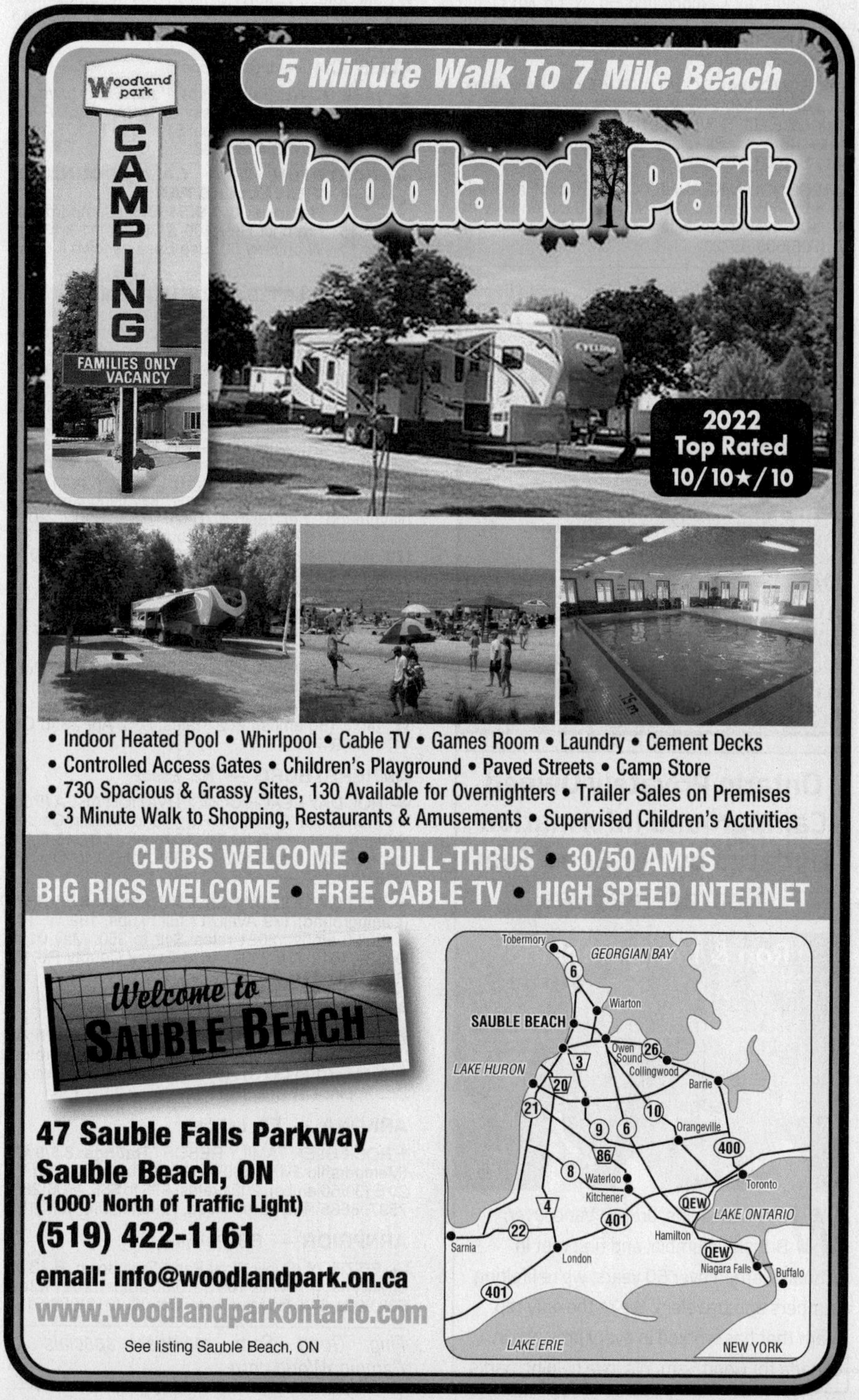

Ontario

ADOLPHUSTOWN — D8 *Lennox*

UNITED EMPIRE LOYALIST HERITAGE CENTRE & PARK (Public) E-bnd: At W-end of town, on Hwy 33 (Loyalist Parkway) (R). 66 Avail: 66 W, 66 E (30 amps). 2021 rates: $37 to $48. May 15 to Oct 08. (613)373-2196

ALFRED — B9 *Prescott-Russell*

EVERGREEN CAMPING RESORT **Ratings: 8/8.5★/8.5** (Campground) 30 Avail: 22 full hkups, 8 W, 8 E (15/50 amps). 2021 rates: $50 to $60. May 01 to Oct 01. (888)679-4059, 5279 CR 17, Alfred, ON K0B 1A0

ALGONQUIN PARK — B6 *Nipissing*

ALGONQUIN/CANISBAY LAKE (Public Prov Park) From W Park Gate, E 24 km (15 mi) on Hwy 60 to Canisbay Campground Rd, N 1.6 km (1 mi) (L). Use of generators is allowed. Avail: 66 E (15/30 amps). 2021 rates: $44.91. May 18 to Nov 14. (705)633-5572

ALGONQUIN/COON LAKE (Public Prov Park) From W Park Gate, E 38.6 km (24 mi) on Hwy 60 to Rock Lake Rd, S 5 km (3.1 mi) (R). Generators allowed. 48 Avail: Pit toilets. 2021 rates: $39.83. Jun 14 to Sep 03. (705)633-5572

ALGONQUIN/KEARNEY LAKE (Public Prov Park) From W Park Gate, E 39.4 km (24.5 mi) on Hwy 60 (R). 104 Avail. 2021 rates: $44.91. May 18 to Sep 07. (705)633-5572

Like Us on Facebook.

ALGONQUIN/KIOSK (Public Prov Park) From Jct of Hwys 17 & 630, S 19.3 km (12 mi) on Hwy 630 (E). 24 Avail. 2021 rates: $39.83. Apr 26 to Nov 14. (705)633-5572

ALGONQUIN/LAKE OF TWO RIVERS (Public Prov Park) From W Park Gate, E 33.8 km (21 mi) on Hwy 60 (L). Avail: 162 E (15/30 amps). 2021 rates: $44.91. May 18 to Nov 14. (705)633-5572

ALGONQUIN/MEW LAKE (Public Prov Park) From W Park Gate, E 33 km (20.5 mi) on Hwy 60 (L). Avail: 66 E (15/30 amps). 2021 rates: $44.91. (705)633-5572

ALGONQUIN/POG LAKE (Public Prov Park) From W Park Gate, E 37 km (23 mi) on Hwy 60 (L). Avail: 83 E (15/30 amps). 2021 rates: $44.91. May 18 to Sep 03. (705)633-5572

ALGONQUIN/ROCK LAKE (Public Prov Park) From W Park Gate, E 38.6 km (24 mi) on Hwy 60 to Rock Lake Rd, S 6.4 km (4 mi) (E). Avail: 72 E (15/30 amps). 2021 rates: $44.91. Apr 26 to Nov 14. (705)633-5572

ALGONQUIN/TEA LAKE (Public Prov Park) From W Park Gate, E 12 km (7.5 mi) on Hwy 60 (L). Generators allowed. 42 Avail. 2021 rates: $44.91. May 18 to Sep 03. (705)633-5572

ALLISTON — D5 *Simcoe*

EARL ROWE (Public Prov Park) From town, W 1 mi on Hwy 89 to Concession 7, N 0.5 mi (L). Avail: 163 E (15 amps). 2021 rates: $12.75 to $43.75. May 11 to Oct 09. (705)435-2498

NICOLSTON DAM CAMPGROUND & TRAVELLERS PARK

good sam park

Ratings: 8.5/9.5★/8.5 (Campground) From jct Hwy 400 & 89: Go 11 km/7 mi W on Hwy 89. Use Essa as town if using a GPS.

A LITTLE BIT OF HEAVEN!

Visit our gorgeous, unique campground with original historic mill buildings incorporating our office & store. Riverfront sites, great fishing & kayaking. Visit Toronto & come back to peace! Enjoy our heated pool too!

FAC: gravel rds. (88 spaces). Avail: 69 grass, 15 pull-thrus, (30x75), back-ins (30x45), 69 W, 69 E (15/30 amps), seasonal sites, WiFi @ sites, tent sites, rentals, dump, mobile sewer, laundry, groc, fire rings, firewood, controlled access. **REC:** heated pool, Nottawasaga River : swim, fishing, kayaking/canoeing, playground. Pet restrict (B/Q). eco-friendly. 2021 rates: $50 to $72, Military discount. May 01 to Oct 31.
(705)435-7946 Lat: 44.167450, Lon: -79.807160
5140 5th Line Essa, Alliston, ON L9R 1V2
nicolstondam.ca
See ad this page

ALVINSTON — E3 *Middlesex*

A W CAMPBELL CONSERVATION AREA (Public) From Jct of Hwy 402 & Hwy 79 (Nauvoo Rd), S 11.2 mi to Shiloh Line, E 1.7 mi (R). 140 Avail: 140 W, 140 E (50 amps). 2021 rates: $33. Apr 23 to Oct 11. (519)847-5357

AMHERSTBURG — F2 *Essex*

HOLIDAY BEACH CONSERVATION AREA (Public) From town, S 6 mi on Hwy 18 to Malden Center, S (right) 2 mi on CR-50 (R). 15 Avail: 15 W, 15 E (15 amps). 2021 rates: $25 to $35. Apr 19 to Oct 15. (519)736-3772

WILLOWOOD RV RESORT **Ratings: 8.5/9.5★/9** (Campground) 179 Avail: 17 full hkups, 162 W, 162 E (30/50 amps). 2021 rates: $42 to $50. May 01 to Oct 31. (519)736-3201, 4610 Essex County Rd 18, RR 1 (Pike Rd), Amherstburg, ON N9V 2Y7

APPIN — E3 *Middlesex*

SILVER DOVE ESTATES (Campground) (Phone Update) Avail: 25 full hkups (30 amps). 2021 rates: $45. May 01 to Oct 31. (519)289-2100, 4838 Switzer Dr , Appin, ON N0L 1A0

ARKONA — E3 *Lambton*

ROCK GLEN FAMILY RESORT **Ratings: 8.5/9★/9** (Membership Park) 100 Avail: 80 full hkups, 20 W, 20 E (30/50 amps). 2021 rates: $75 to $85. (800)265-7597, 8685 Rock Glen Road, Arkona, ON N0M 1B0

ARNPRIOR — B8 *Renfrew*

FITZROY (Public Prov Park) From town, E 13 mi on Hwy 17, (L). Avail: 106 E (15/30 amps). 2021 rates: $32.90 to $43.75. May 11 to Oct 09. (613)623-5159

Find Good Sam member specials at CampingWorld.com

ATIKOKAN — F7 *Rainy River*

BUNNELL PARK CAMPGROUND

(Public) From Jct of SR-622 & Saturn Ave, E 0.1 mi on Saturn Ave (R). **FAC:** paved rds. Avail: 20 grass, 2 W, 20 E (15/30 amps), tent sites, shower$, dump, fire rings, firewood. **REC:** Atikokan River: fishing. Pets OK. Partial handicap access. 2021 rates: $27.50 to $30. May 01 to Sep 30. no cc.
(807)597-1234 Lat: 48.75637, Lon: -91.58750
Atikokan, ON P0T 1C0
www.atikokan.ca

QUETICO/DAWSON TRAIL (Public Prov Park) From town, E 30 mi on Hwy 11 to access rd, S 1 mi (E). Avail: 51 E (15/30 amps). 2021 rates: $12.75 to $51.42. May 18 to Oct 09. (807)597-2735

AYTON — D4 *Grey*

RIVER PLACE PARK CAMPGROUND **Ratings: 6/10★/7** (Campground) 63 Avail: 45 full hkups, 18 W, 18 E (30 amps). 2021 rates: $59.25. May 15 to Oct 15. (519)338-3010, 232352 Concession 2 West Grey, Ayton, ON N0G 1C0

SILENT VALLEY PARK RESORT - PARK-BRIDGE **Ratings: 8.5/9.5★/9** (Campground) 57 Avail: 28 full hkups, 18 W, 14 E (15/30 amps). 2021 rates: $50 to $165. May 10 to Oct 20. (519)665-7787, 142571 Road 35, RR 3, Ayton, ON N0G 1C0

BAILIEBORO — D6 *Peterborough*

BENSFORT BRIDGE RESORT

good sam park

Ratings: 7.5/8.5★/8 (Campground) 10 Avail: 5 full hkups, 5 W, 5 E (30 amps). 2021 rates: $50 to $55. May 05 to Oct 15. (705)939-6515, 1821 CR 2, Bailieboro, ON K0L 1B0

BAINSVILLE — C10 *Stormont*

MAPLEWOOD ACRES RV PARK

good sam park

Ratings: 9/10★/9.5 (Campground) Avail: 36 full hkups (30/50 amps). 2021 rates: $49.50 to $58. May 03 to Oct 07. (613)347-2130, 21848 Concession 3 Road, Bainsville, ON K0C 1E0

BANCROFT — C7 *Hastings*

BANCROFT CAMPGROUND (Campground) (Phone Update) 28 Avail: 15 full hkups, 13 W, 13 E (15/30 amps). 2021 rates: $38 to $45. May 01 to Oct 09. (877)404-4160, 98 Bird Lake Road, Bancroft, ON K0L 1C0

SILENT LAKE (Public Prov Park) From town, S 6 mi on Hwy 28 (L). Avail: 41 E (15/30 amps). 2021 rates: $12.75 to $51.42. May 11 to Oct 09. (613)339-2807

THE HOMESTEAD TRAILER PARK (RV Area in MH Park) (Phone Update) Avail: 12 full hkups (30 amps). 2021 rates: $47. May 21 to Oct 15. (613)339-2500, 1123 Homestead Rd, Bancroft, ON K0L 1C0

BARRIE — D5 *Springwater*

BARRIE KOA **Ratings: 8.5/9.5★/8.5** (Campground) 106 Avail: 77 full hkups, 29 W, 29 E (15/50 amps). 2021 rates: $66 to $110. May 06 to Oct 15. (800)562-7397, 3138 Penetanguishene Road, Barrie, ON L4M 4Y8

BARRY'S BAY — B7 *Renfrew*

SUNNY HILL RESORT **Ratings: 8/10★/8** (Campground) 25 Avail: 24 full hkups, 1 W, 1 E (30 amps). 2021 rates: $65 to $70. May 12 to Oct 14. (800)494-6883, 531 Sunny Hill Road, Barry's Bay, ON K0J 1B0

BATCHAWANA BAY — A1 *Algoma*

PANCAKE BAY (Public Prov Park) From Sault Ste Marie, N 47 mi on Hwy 17 (L). Avail: 160 E (15/30 amps). 2021 rates: $36.75 to $51.42. May 04 to Oct 09. (705)882-2209

SUNSET SHORES RESORT **Ratings: 8/8.5★/8.5** (Campground) 13 Avail: 3 full hkups, 10 W, 10 E (30 amps). 2021 rates: $50 to $55. May 01 to Oct 31. (705)882-2231, 10243 Hwy 17N, Batchawana Bay, ON P0S 1A0

BEARDMORE — F8 *Thunder Bay*

POPLAR LODGE PARK (Public) From Jct of Hwys 11 & 580, W 7 mi on Hwy 580 (E). 125 Avail: 45 W, 45 E (30 amps). 2021 rates: $28.85 to $33.90. May 14 to Sep 06. (807)854-2335

Visit Camping World RV & Outdoors and stock up on accessories and supplies while on the road. Find your nearest location at CampingWorld.com

BELLE RIVER — F2 *Essex*

ROCHESTER PLACE GOLF CLUB & RESORT **Ratings: 8/8★/8.5** (Campground) Avail: 26 full hkups (30/50 amps). 2021 rates: $65. May 01 to Oct 31. (519)728-2361, 981-991 County Road 2, Belle River, ON N0R 1A0

BLOOMFIELD — D7 *Prince Edward*

SANDBANKS (Public Prov Park) From town, SW 3 mi on CR-10 to CR-11, W (right) 4 mi (E). Avail: 174 E (15/30 amps). 2021 rates: $28.75 to $51.42. Apr 27 to Oct 09. (613)393-3319

BOLTON — D5 *Peel*

ALBION HILLS CAMPGROUND (Public) From Bolton, N 8.8 km (5.5 mi) on Hwy 50 (L). Minimum stay of 3 ngts on holiday w/ends. 234 Avail: 99 W, 99 E (15/30 amps). 2021 rates: $33 to $38.50. May 01 to Oct 31. (905)880-0227

BORNHOLM — E4 *Perth*

WOODLAND LAKE RV RESORT **Ratings: 8.5/9.5★/8.5** (Campground) Avail: 25 full hkups (30/50 amps). 2021 rates: $46 to $56. May 01 to Oct 31. (519)347-2315, 6710 Line 46, RR 1, Bornholm, ON N0K 1A0

BRACEBRIDGE — C5 *Muskoka*

SANTA'S WHISPERING PINES CAMPGROUND **Ratings: 8.5/10★/8.5** (Campground) 147 Avail: 133 W, 133 E (15/50 amps). 2021 rates: $75 to $118. May 17 to Oct 14. (705)645-5682, 1623 Golden Beach Rd, Bracebridge, ON P1L 1W8

BRADFORD — D5 *Simcoe*

YOGI BEAR'S JELLYSTONE PARK & CAMP-RESORT **Ratings: 7.5/9/8.5** (Campground) 128 Avail: 22 full hkups, 70 W, 70 E (15/50 amps). 2021 rates: $79.95 to $146.95. May 01 to Sep 30. (905)775-1377, 3666 Simcoe Road County Road 88, Bradford, ON L3Z 2A4

BRANTFORD — E5 *Brant*

BRANT CONSERVATION AREA (Public) From Jct of Hwy 403 & Hwy 24 South, S 1.7 mi on Hwy 24 South to Robinson Rd, E 2.8 mi (L). 403 Avail: 31 full hkups, 126 W, 126 E (15/30 amps). 2021 rates: $35 to $50.50. May 01 to Oct 15. (519)752-2040

BRIGHTON — D7 *Northumberland*

BRIGHTON KOA **Ratings: 8.5/9★/8** (Campground) 75 Avail: 45 full hkups, 30 W, 30 E (20/50 amps). 2021 rates: $60 to $120. May 01 to Oct 15. (613)475-2186, 15051 Telephone Road, Brighton, ON K0K 1H0

PRESQU'ILE (Public Prov Park) From Jct of Hwy 401 (exit 509) & Hwy 30, S 3.2 mi on Hwy 30 to Hwy 2, W 0.2 mi on Hwy 2 (Main St) to Presqu'ile Parkway, S 2.4 mi (E). Avail: 160 E (30 amps). 2021 rates: $34.92 to $51.42. Apr 27 to Oct 09. (613)475-4324

BRITT — B4 *Parry Sound*

GRUNDY LAKE (Public Prov Park) From town, N 12 mi on Hwy 69 (R). Avail: 138 E (15/30 amps). 2021 rates: $12.75 to $43.75. May 13 to Oct 11. (705)383-2286

KILLBEAR (Public Prov Park) From town, N 8 mi on Hwy 69 to Hwy 559, W 12.6 mi (E). Avail: 252 E (15/30 amps). 2021 rates: $10 to $51.42. May 13 to Oct 31. (705)342-5492

STURGEON BAY (Public Prov Park) From Jct of TCH-69 & Hwy 529, NW 2 mi on Hwy 529 (L). Avail: 31 E (15/30 amps). 2021 rates: $16.81 to $50.57. May 11 to Oct 09. (705)366-2521

BROCKVILLE — C9 *Grenville*

PLEASURE PARK RV RESORT **Ratings: 7.5/8.5★/8.5** (Campground) 71 Avail: 71 W, 71 E (15/50 amps). 2021 rates: $47 to $56. May 01 to Sep 13. (613)923-5490, 80 Graham Lake Road, Mallorytown, ON K0E 1R0

ST LAWRENCE PARK (Public) In town, on Hwy 2 (R). 20 Avail: 10 W, 10 E (15 amps). 2021 rates: $33 to $39. May 15 to Sep 15. (613)345-1341

CALLANDER — B5 *Nipissing*

BAYVIEW CAMP & COTTAGES **Ratings: 7/7/8.5** (Campground) Avail: 14 full hkups (30 amps). 2021 rates: $45. May 15 to Oct 15. (705)477-8282, 35 Camp Road, Callander, ON P0H 1H0

Replace clogged air filters. A clogged air filter can cut a vehicle's fuel efficiency by 10 percent.

CAMBRIDGE — E5 *Hamilton-Wentworth*

VALENS CONSERVATION AREA (Public) From town, E 6 mi on Hwy 97 (L) Refundable entrance fee required to access this campground when office closed. (Min 2 day stay on holiday weekends). 225 Avail: 125 W, 125 E (30 amps). 2021 rates: $40 to $47. (905)525-2183

WHISTLE BARE CAMPGROUND **Ratings: 6/7.5★/7.5** (Campground) Avail: 10 full hkups (30 amps). 2021 rates: $70. Apr 23 to Nov 03. (519)623-2463, 1912 Whistle Bare Road, Cambridge, ON N1R 5S3

CAMPBELLFORD — D7 *Northumberland*

FERRIS (Public Prov Park) From Jct of Hwys 401 & 30, N 18.6 mi on Hwy 30 to Campbellford, follow signs (R). Avail: 20 E. 2021 rates: $12.75 to $51.42. May 11 to Oct 09. (705)653-3575

CAMPBELLVILLE — E5 *Halton*

TORONTO WEST KOA **Ratings: 8/8/7.5** (Campground) 48 Avail: 28 full hkups, 20 W, 20 E (30/50 amps). 2021 rates: $44 to $68. May 01 to Oct 14. (800)562-1523, 9301 2nd Line, Campbellville, ON L0P 1B0

CARDINAL — C9 *Grenville*

CARDINAL/OTTAWA SOUTH KOA **Ratings: 8.5/10★/10** (Campground) 120 Avail: 120 W, 120 E (30/50 amps). 2021 rates: $60 to $125. May 18 to Oct 11. (877)894-3140, 609 Pittston Road, Cardinal, ON K0E 1E0

CARRYING PLACE — D7 *Hastings*

CAMP BARCOVAN TENT & RV RESORT (Campground) (Phone Update) 20 Avail: 2 full hkups, 18 W, 18 E (15/30 amps). 2021 rates: $50 to $70. May 15 to Oct 15. (888)859-2369, 133 Carter Road, Carrying Place, ON K0K 1L0

CARTIER — A4 *Sudbury*

HALFWAY LAKE (Public Prov Park) From town, N 10 mi on Hwy 144 (L). Avail: 122 E (15 amps). 2021 rates: $12.75 to $51.42. May 18 to Sep 23. (705)965-2702

CAYUGA — E5 *Haldimand-Norfolk*

GRAND OAKS RV RESORT **Ratings: 8.5/10★/8** (Campground) 30 Avail: 21 W, 21 E (30 amps). 2021 rates: $51 to $69. May 01 to Oct 31. (905)772-3713, 107 Haldimand Hwy 54, Cayuga, ON N0A 1E0

CHAPLEAU — F9 *Algoma*

MISSINAIBI (Public Prov Park) From Jct of Hwy 101 & Missinaibi Lake Rd, N 55 mi on Missinaibi Lake Rd (E). 35 Avail: Pit toilets. 2021 rates: $23.75 to $51.42. May 04 to Sep 16. (705)234-2222

WAKAMI LAKE (Public Prov Park) From town, S 20 mi on Hwy 129 to Hwy 667, follow signs, E 16 mi (R). 59 Avail: Pit toilets. 2021 rates: $16.81 to $51.42. May 11 to Sep 23. (705)233-2853

CHERRY VALLEY — D7 *Prince Edward*

A SPOTLIGHT Introducing Prince Edward County's colorful attractions appearing at the front of this province section.

QUINTE'S ISLE CAMPARK

good sam park **Ratings: 10/10★/10** (Campground) From Jct of Hwys 401 & 62 (Exit 543A), S 46.6 km (29 mi) on Hwy 62 to Hwy 33, E 9.6 km (6 mi) to CR-10 (Lake St, in Picton), S 8 km (5 mi) to CR-18, SW 8 km (5 mi) to Salmon Pt Rd, S 2 km (1.25 mi) (L). Note: 3 night minimum stay on holiday weekends.

SPRING TO FALL - ALWAYS SPECTACULAR

Big rigs, small rigs, young, young at heart - something for all in this fabulous park! Amazing, friendly atmosphere on Prince Edward County Lake Ontario waterfront with nearby restaurants, wineries, family activities & more!

FAC: all weather rds. (620 spaces). Avail: 159 all weather, 94 pull-thrus, (40x90), back-ins (40x60), 159 full hkups (30/50 amps), seasonal sites, WiFi @ sites, tent sites, rentals, shower$, dump, laundry, groc, LP bottles, fire rings, firewood, controlled access. **REC:** heated pool, wading pool, Lake Ontario: swim, fishing, kayaking/canoeing, shuffleboard, playground, rec open to public. Pets OK. Partial handicap access. Big rig sites, eco-friendly. 2021 rates: $53 to $103. Apr 15 to Nov 01. ATM.

(613)476-6310 Lat: 43.87610, Lon: -77.21199
237 Salmon Point Road, Cherry Valley, ON K0K 1P0
qicampark.com
See ad page 1115

CHESLEY — D4 *Grey*

CEDAR RAIL FAMILY CAMPGROUND **Ratings: 8.5/8.5★/8.5** (Campground) 79 Avail: 31 full hkups, 48 W, 48 E (30/50 amps). 2021 rates: $42 to $61. May 01 to Oct 15. (519)363-3387, 015259 Grey Bruce Line, RR 2, Chesley, ON N0G 1L0

CHUTE-A-BLONDEAU — B10 *Ontario*

VOYAGEUR (Public Prov Park) From Jct of Hwy 417 & CR-14 (exit 5), N 0.6 mi on CR-14 (R). Avail: 110 E (15/30 amps). 2021 rates: $25.25 to $51.42. May 11 to Oct 09. (613)674-2825

CLOYNE — C7 *Frontenac*

BON ECHO (Public Prov Park) From Jct of Hwys 7 & 41 (Kaladar), N 20 mi on Hwy 41 (R). Avail: 169 E (15/30 amps). 2021 rates: $30.50 to $51.42. May 13 to Oct 16. (613)336-2228

SHERWOOD PARK CAMPGROUND (Campground) (Phone Update) 2 Avail: 2 W, 2 E (15/30 amps). 2021 rates: $50 to $61. May 01 to Oct 08. (613)336-8844, 1141 Hwy 506, RR 2, Cloyne, ON K0H 1K0

COBDEN — B8 *Renfrew*

LOGOS LAND RESORT **Ratings: 8/9.5★/8.5** (Campground) 186 Avail: 100 full hkups, 86 W, 86 E (30/50 amps). 2021 rates: $59 to $63. May 19 to Oct 11. (877)816-6605, 15906 Hwy 17, Cobden, ON K0J 1K0

COBOCONK — C6 *Kawartha Lakes*

BALSAM LAKE (Public Prov Park) From town, E 7.5 mi on Hwy 48 (R). Avail: 213 E (15/30 amps). 2021 rates: $28.75 to $43.75. May 13 to Oct 11. (705)454-3324

COBOURG — D7 *Northumberland*

VICTORIA PARK CAMPGROUND (Public) From Jct of Hwy 401 & Division St (Exit 474), S 3.2 km (2 mi) on Division St (L). Avail: 48 full hkups (30 amps). 2021 rates: $41 to $52. May 15 to Oct 08. (905)373-7321

COCHRANE — F10 *Cochrane*

KAP-KIG-IWAN (Public Prov Park) From town: Go 3/4 km/1/2 mi W on Hwy 11, then 2-1/2 km/1-1/2 mi S on 5th St. Avail: 32 E Pit toilets. 2021 rates: $28.75 to $51.42. May 18 to Sep 23. (705)544-1968

COLLINGWOOD — C5 *Grey*

CRAIGLEITH (Public Prov Park) From Jct of Hwys 24 & 26, NW 7 mi on Hwy 26 (R). Avail: 66 E (15/30 amps). 2021 rates: $36.75 to $43.75. Apr 13 to Oct 28. (705)445-4467

COMBERMERE — B7 *Renfrew*

PINE CLIFF RESORT **Ratings: 8.5/8.5★/8.5** (RV Resort) 15 Avail: 5 full hkups, 10 W, 10 E (30/50 amps). 2021 rates: $65. May 12 to Oct 14. (888)756-3014, 21 Allingham Lane, Box 99, Combermere, ON K0J 1L0

COOKSTOWN — D5 *Simcoe*

TORONTO NORTH/COOKSTOWN KOA **Ratings: 9/10★/9.5** (Campground) 97 Avail: 57 full hkups, 40 W, 40 E (30/50 amps). 2021 rates: $63 to $125. Apr 29 to Oct 21. (800)562-2691, 139 Reive Blvd, Cookstown, ON L0L 1L0

Thank you for being one of our best customers!

ON

DEEP RIVER — B7 *Renfrew*

DRIFTWOOD (Public Prov Park) From Mattawa, E 30 mi on Hwy 17 to Driftwood Rd (R). Avail: 20 E (15/30 amps). 2021 rates: $12.75 to $51.42. May 18 to Sep 16. (613)586-2553

RYAN'S CAMPSITE **Ratings: 4.5/5.5/5.5** (Campground) 50 Avail: 50 W, 50 E (15/30 amps). 2021 rates: $45. May 24 to Oct 08. (613)584-3453, 34572 Hwy 17, Deep River, ON K0J 1P0

DELTA — C8 *Grenville*

LOWER BEVERLEY LAKE PARK (Public) From Lyndhurst, N 10 mi on Hwy 33 to Hwy 42, W 2 mi (L). 235 Avail: 235 W, 10 E (15/30 amps). 2021 rates: $27.50 to $50. May 07 to Oct 11. (613)928-2881

DEUX RIVIERES — A6 *Renfrew*

ANTLER'S KINGFISHER LODGE & TRAILER PARK **Ratings: 8/7.5★/8** (Campground) 15 Avail: 12 full hkups, 3 W, 3 E (30 amps). 2021 rates: $42.48. May 12 to Oct 14. (705)747-0851, 46980 Hwy 17, RR1, Deux Rivieres, ON K0J 1R0

DRYDEN — E7 *Kenora*

AARON (Public Prov Park) From town, E 9 mi on Hwy 17 (L). Avail: 33 E (15/30 amps). 2021 rates: $34.47 to $39.55. May 20 to Sep 18. (807)938-6534

NORTHWESTERN TENT & RV PARK **Ratings: 7/8★/8** (RV Park) Avail: 43 full hkups (15/30 amps). 2021 rates: $47. Apr 15 to Oct 31. (807)223-4945, 559 Government St, Dryden, ON P8N 2Y8

DUNNVILLE — E5 *Haldimand*

BYNG ISLAND CONSERVATION AREA (Public) From Jct of Hwy 3 & Reg Rd 3, W 0.2 mi on Reg Rd 3 to Reg Rd 20, N 0.1 mi (R). 380 Avail: 134 W, 134 E (15/30 amps). 2021 rates: $27 to $46. May 01 to Oct 15. (905)774-5755

CHIPPAWA CREEK CONSERVATION AREA (Public) From Jct of Niagara Hwy 27 & Niagara Hwy 4, S 0.2 mi on Niagara Hwy 4 to CR-45, W 1.7 mi (R). 156 Avail: 39 W, 39 E (15/30 amps). 2021 rates: $32 to $42. May 17 to Oct 11. (905)386-6387

KNIGHT'S BEACH RESORT **Ratings: 8/10★/9.5** (Campground) 79 Avail: 55 full hkups, 24 W, 24 E (15/30 amps). 2021 rates: $85 to $150. May 01 to Oct 11. (905)774-4566, 2190 Lakeshore Road, Dunnville, ON N1A 2W8

ROCK POINT (Public Prov Park) From Jct of Hwy 3 & RR 3 (Dunnville), E 5.5 mi on RR 3 to Niece Rd, W 0.5 mi (L). Avail: 81 E (15/30 amps). 2021 rates: $36.75 to $43.75. May 11 to Oct 09. (905)774-6642

DURHAM — D4 *Grey*

AMAZING ROCKY PARK CAMPGROUND **Ratings: 7.5/6.5/6.5** (Campground) 22 Avail: 22 W, 22 E (15 amps). 2021 rates: $60. May 01 to Oct 14. (519)369-6450, 423059 Rocky Saugeen Road, RR 1, Durham, ON N0G 1R0

DURHAM CONSERVATION AREA (Public) From Jct of Hwy 6 & Old Durham Rd, E 1 mi on Old Durham Rd (R). 205 Avail: 94 W, 94 E (15/30 amps). 2021 rates: $30 to $39. (519)369-2074

EAR FALLS — E7 *Kenora*

PAKWASH (Public Prov Park) From town, N 13 mi on Hwy 105 (L). Avail: 26 E (15/30 amps). 2021 rates: $32.25 to $51.42. May 18 to Sep 16. (807)222-3346

New to RVing? Visit Blog.GoodSam.com for tips on everything camping and RVing.

EDEN — E4 *Elgin*

RED OAK TRAVEL PARK **Ratings: 8.5/8.5★/8.5** (Campground) 25 Avail: 25 W, 25 E (15/30 amps). 2021 rates: $40 to $50. May 01 to Oct 15. (519)866-3504, 54428 Talbot Line (Hwy 3), Eden, ON N0J 1H0

ELGIN — C8 *Leeds and Grenville*

SAND LAKE CAMPGROUND & COTTAGES **Ratings: 6/6.5/7** (Campground) 20 Avail: 6 W, 9 E (15/30 amps). 2021 rates: $63. May 07 to Oct 01. (613)359-6361, 5 Powell Bay, Elgin, ON K0G 1E0

ELLIOT LAKE — A3 *Algoma*

MISSISSAGI (Public Prov Park) From town, N 16 mi on Hwy 108/639 (R). Avail: 60 E. 2021 rates: $12.75 to $51.42. May 18 to Oct 07. (705)862-1203

WESTVIEW PARK TRAILER PARK (Public) From town, N 1 mi on Hwy 108 (R). Avail: 18 full hkups (30 amps). 2021 rates: $25 to $30. May 01 to Oct 01. (705)848-7737

ELMIRA — D4 *Wellington*

CONESTOGO LAKE CONSERVATION AREA (Public) From Jct of Hwy 86 & CR-11, NE 1.7 mi on CR-11, SE 0.7 mi on CR-145/CR-11, NE 0.5 mi on CR-11 (L). 167 Avail: 92 W, 92 E (30 amps). 2021 rates: $31 to $45. May 01 to Oct 15. (519)638-2873

ELORA — D4 *Wellington*

ELORA GORGE CONSERVATION AREA (Public) From Jct of CR-7 & CR-21, SW 0.7 mi on CR-21 (R). 400 Avail: 130 W, 150 E (15/30 amps). 2021 rates: $28 to $46. Apr 30 to Oct 16. (519)846-9742

ENNISMORE — D6 *Peterborough*

ANCHOR BAY CAMP **Ratings: 8/9.5★/8.5** (Campground) 20 Avail: 8 full hkups, 12 W, 12 E (30 amps). 2021 rates: $45 to $55. May 15 to Oct 15. (705)657-8439, 197 Anchor Bay Road, Peterborough, ON K9J 6X2

WOODLAND CAMP SITE **Ratings: 6/7.5/8** (Campground) 50 Avail: 50 W, 50 E (30 amps). 2021 rates: $50 to $65. May 07 to Oct 18. (705)933-8946, 209 Allen's Road, Lakehurst, ON K0L 1J0

ESSEX — F2 *Essex*

WILDWOOD GOLF & RV RESORT

Ratings: 10/10★/10 (Campground) From Jct of Hwy 401 & CR-19 (Manning Rd) Exit 21, S 4.7 km (2.9 mi) on CR-19 to Hwy 3, SE 4.8 km (3 mi) to N. Malden Rd, SW 9.2 km (5.7 mi) to 11th Conc Rd, W 0.6 km (0.4 mi) (R).

A PIECE OF FLORIDA IN ESSEX ONTARIO

Peaceful, relaxing atmosphere in this superior RV resort. Close to great shopping & dining & surrounded by a fantastic wine route! Add a restaurant, great golf & Caesar's Windsor Casino with Vegas-style gambling nearby.

FAC: paved rds. (365 spaces). Avail: 25 all weather, patios, 25 pull-thrus, (35x70), 25 full hkups (30/50 amps), seasonal sites, cable, WiFi @ sites, laundry, restaurant, controlled access. **REC:** heated pool, golf, playground. Pet restrict (S/B). Partial handicap access. No tents. Big rig sites, eco-friendly. 2021 rates: $75. May 01 to Oct 31. ATM.
(866)994-9699 Lat: 42.13936, Lon: -82.94960
11112 11th Concession Road , Essex, ON N0R 1J0
www.wildwoodgolfandrvresort.com
See ad this page

Things to See and Do

WILDWOOD GOLF & RV RESORT Discover a golf resort that's quite different. Apr 15 to Oct 30. Restrooms. Food. Hours: 7am to 7pm. Adult fee: $28.00. ATM.
(519)726-6176 Lat: 42.140186, Lon: -82.949382
11112 11th Concession , Essex, ON N0R 1J0
www.wildwoodgolfandrvresort.com
See ad this page

FENELON FALLS — C6 *Kawartha Lakes*

LOG CHATEAU PARK (Campground) (Phone Update) 55 Avail: 9 full hkups, 41 W, 41 E (30 amps). 2021 rates: $50. May 01 to Oct 12. (705)887-3960, 1691 C.R #121, RR 2, Fenelon Falls, ON K0M 1N0

SUNNY ACRES **Ratings: 4.5/7/6.5** (Campground) 20 Avail: 3 full hkups, 17 W, 17 E (15/30 amps). 2021 rates: $45. May 01 to Oct 08. (705)887-3416, 24 Sunny Acres Road, Fenelon Falls, ON K0M 1N0

Follow the arrow. The arrow in each listing indicates where the facility is located in relation to the listed town.

FERGUS — D5 *Wellington*

HIGHLAND PINES CAMPGROUND & RV SALES **Ratings: 8/8.5★/9** (Campground) 124 Avail: 41 full hkups, 48 W, 48 E (30/50 amps). 2021 rates: $75 to $95. May 08 to Oct 12. (519)843-2537, 8523 Wellington Rd. 19, Belwood, ON N0B 1J0

FOLEYET — F9 *Sudbury*

IVANHOE LAKE (Public Prov Park) From town, W 5 mi on Hwy 101 (L). Avail: 64 E (15/30 amps). 2021 rates: $12.75 to $51.42. May 20 to Sep 05. (705)899-2644

FORT FRANCES — F7 *Rainy River*

POINT PARK (Public) From town, E 0.5 mi on Hwy 11 (R). 30 Avail: 18 W, 18 E (30 amps). 2021 rates: $18 to $35. May 18 to Sep 01. (807)274-9893

FULLARTON — E4 *Perth*

WINDMILL FAMILY CAMPGROUND **Ratings: 8/9★/7.5** (Campground) 24 Avail: 17 full hkups, 7 W, 7 E (15/30 amps). 2021 rates: $58 to $65. May 01 to Oct 31. (519)229-8982, 2778 Perth Rd 163, Fullarton, ON N0K 1H0

GANANOQUE — D9 *Grenville*

1000 ISLANDS IVY LEA KOA **Ratings: 8/8/8.5** (Campground) 115 Avail: 76 full hkups, 24 W, 24 E (15/50 amps). 2021 rates: $69.95 to $113.95. May 05 to Oct 11. (613)659-2817, 514-1000 Islands Parkway, Lansdowne, ON K0E 1L0

IVY LEA PARK (Public Prov Park) From Jct Hwy 401 & (Hill Islands) (Exit 661), S 0.8 km (0.5 mi) on CR-137 to 1000 Islands Pkwy, W 90 m (300 ft) (L). Note: Two night min. stay on holiday weekends. 146 Avail: 41 W, 41 E (30 amps). 2021 rates: $40.50. May 17 to Oct 14. (800)437-2233

GERALDTON — F8 *Thunder Bay*

MACLEOD (Public Prov Park) From town, E 6 mi on Hwy 11 (R). Avail: 28 E (15/30 amps). 2021 rates: $12.75 to $51.42. May 18 to Sep 23. (807)854-0370

GODERICH — D3 *Huron*

FALLS RESERVE CONSERVATION AREA (Public) From Jct of Hwy 21 & CR-31, SE 6 mi on CR-31 (R). 190 Avail: 130 W, 130 E (15/30 amps). 2021 rates: $32 to $47. Apr 15 to Oct 30. (519)524-6429

POINT FARMS (Public Prov Park) From town, N 3 mi on Hwy 21 (L). Avail: 131 E (15/30 amps). 2021 rates: $12.75 to $51.42. May 13 to Oct 11. (519)524-7124

SHELTER VALLEY CAMPGROUND **Ratings: 8.5/8.5★/8** (Campground) 34 Avail: 34 W, 34 E (30/50 amps). 2021 rates: $47 to $72. May 08 to Oct 12. (519)524-4141, 36534 Huron Road, Clinton, ON N0M 1L0

GOLDEN LAKE — B7 *Renfrew*

GOLDEN LAKE PARK CAMPGROUND **Ratings: 8/8★/8** (Campground) 100 Avail: 8 full hkups, 92 W, 47 S, 47 E (20/30 amps). 2021 rates: $37 to $46. May 15 to Oct 14. (613)757-0018, 13685 Hwy 60, Golden Lake, ON K0J 1X0

GOULAIS RIVER — A1 *Algoma*

BLUEBERRY HILL MOTEL & CAMPGROUND **Ratings: 8/8.5★/9** (Campground) 28 Avail: 24 full hkups, 4 W, 4 E (30 amps). 2021 rates: $50 to $55. (800)811-4411, 2528 Hwy 17 N, Goulais River, ON P0S 1E0

GRAFTON — D7 *Northumberland*

COBOURG EAST CAMPGROUND

Ratings: 8/9.5★/9.5 (Campground) From Jct of Hwy 401 & Exit 487, S 1.6 km (1 mi) on Lyle St to Hwy 2, E 1.3 km (0.8 mi) to Benlock Rd, S 0.8 km (0.5 mi) (R). **FAC:** gravel rds. (160 spaces). Avail: 75 gravel, 24 pull-thrus, (28x65), back-ins (20x40), 8 full hkups, 45 W, 45 E (20/30 amps), seasonal sites, WiFi, tent sites, rentals, dump, mobile sewer, laundry, groc, fire rings, firewood. **REC:** pool, Shelter Valley Creek: fishing, playground, rec open to public. Pet restrict (Q). eco-friendly. 2021 rates: $41 to $45. May 01 to Oct 15.
(905)349-2594 Lat: 43.99191, Lon: -77.99983
253 Benlock Road, Grafton, ON K0K 2G0
cobourgeastcamp.com
See ad previous page

GRAND BEND — E3 *Huron*

PINERY (Public Prov Park) From town, S 4 mi on Hwy 21 (R). Min 3 ngt stay on holiday weekends. Avail: 404 E (15/30 amps). 2021 rates: $34.92 to $38. (519)243-2220

GRAVENHURST — C5 *Muskoka*

CAMP HILLBILLY ESTATES **Ratings: 9/8.5★/8** (Campground) 62 Avail: 20 full hkups, 16 W, 16 E (15/50 amps). 2021 rates: $60 to $100. May 01 to Oct 08. (705)689-2366, 1633 Hwy 11S, Kilworthy, ON P0E 1G0

GRAVENHURST/MUSKOKA KOA **Ratings: 8/10★/9.5** (Campground) 77 Avail: 10 full hkups, 67 W, 67 E (15/30 amps). 2021 rates: $52 to $63. May 15 to Oct 12. (800)562-9883, 1083 Reay Road, RR 3 , Gravenhurst, ON P1P 1R3

GREENSTONE — F8 *Thunder Bay*

WILD GOOSE LAKE CAMPGROUND **Ratings: 7/8★/8.5** (Campground) 31 Avail: 21 full hkups, 10 W, 10 E (20/30 amps). 2021 rates: $35 to $60. May 15 to Sep 30. (866)465-4404, 8 Kueng's Road, Geraldton, ON P0T 1M0

GUELPH — E5 *Wellington*

GUELPH LAKE CONSERVATION AREA (Public) From Jct of Hwy 7 West & Hwy 6 North, N 1.3 mi on Hwy 6 North to Conservation Rd, E 2.4 mi (E). 300 Avail: 108 W, 108 E (15/30 amps). 2021 rates: $35 to $42. May 01 to Oct 15. (519)824-5061

HAMILTON — E5 *Hamilton-Wentworth*

FLAMBORO VALLEY CAMPING RESORT **Ratings: 8.5/9.5★/9** (Campground) 121 Avail: 23 full hkups, 68 W, 68 E (30/50 amps). 2021 rates: $58 to $66. May 01 to Oct 15. (905)659-5053, #1158 Regional Road 97, Puslinch, ON N0B 2J0

OLYMPIA VILLAGE CAMPGROUND & RV PARK **Ratings: 7/7/7.5** (Campground) Avail: 40 full hkups (30/50 amps). 2021 rates: $53 to $64. Apr 15 to Oct 31. (905)627-1923, 1161 4th Con Road W., R.R.2, Waterdown, ON L8B 0X3

HANOVER — D4 *Grey*

SAUGEEN SPRINGS RV PARK

good sam park **Ratings: 8.5/8.5★/10** (Campground) 114 Avail: 24 full hkups, 90 W, 90 E (30 amps). 2021 rates: $45 to $98. Apr 01 to Nov 15. (519)369-5136, 173844 Mulock Road, RR3, Hanover, ON N4N 3B9

HAWKESTONE — C5 *Simcoe*

HEIDI'S CAMPGROUND

good sam park **Ratings: 9/9.5★/9.5** (Campground) From Jct of Hwy 400 & Hwy 11N, N 14.5 km (9 mi) on Hwy 11N to Oro/Medonte Line 11, (over the overpass) NW 0.16 km (0.1 mi) (R). Min stay 3 ngts on holiday w/ends.

STORYBOOK FAMILY CAMPING & MORE!
Located just off Hwy 11 between Barrie & Orillia. Long pull-thrus, indoor pool & planned activities. Close to attractions, great shopping in big box stores & a wide variety of dining options. Heidi's RV Superstore on site!

FAC: all weather rds. (242 spaces). Avail: 96 gravel, patios, 52 pull-thrus, (40x90), back-ins (30x90), 96 full hkups (30/50 amps), seasonal sites, WiFi @ sites, $, tent sites, rentals, dump, laundry, groc, LP gas, fire rings, firewood, controlled access. **REC:** heated pool, hot tub, Heidis Creek: boating nearby, playground. Pet restrict (B). Partial handicap access. Big rig sites, eco-friendly. 2021 rates: $54 to $76.50. May 01 to Oct 15.
(705)487-3311 Lat: 44.5062459, Lon: -79.4804692
3982 Hwy 11S, Oro-Medonte, ON L0L 1T0
www.heidisrv.com
See ad this page

HEARST — F9 *Cochrane*

FUSHIMI LAKE (Public Prov Park) From town, W 15 mi on Hwy 11 to Fushimi Forest Access Rd, N 10 mi (R). Avail: 39 E (30 amps). 2021 rates: $12.75 to $51.42. May 18 to Sep 03. (705)372-5909

VEILLEUX CAMPING & MARINA (Campground) (Phone Update) Avail: 15 full hkups (30 amps). 2021 rates: $44.25 to $50. May 15 to Sep 30. (705)362-5379, 20 Desgroseillers Road, Hearst, ON P0L 1N0

HEPWORTH — C4 *Grey*

WHISPERING PINES FAMILY CAMPGROUND **Ratings: 8/9★/7.5** (RV Park) 14 Avail: 14 W, 14 E (30 amps). 2021 rates: $53 to $65. May 08 to Oct 18. (519)935-2571, 719601 Hwy 6, Hepworth, ON N0H 1P0

Want to know how we rate? Our campground inspection guidelines are detailed in the front pages of the Guide.

HORNEPAYNE — F9 *Hearst*

NAGAGAMISIS (Public Prov Park) From Jct of Hwy 11 & Hwy 631, S 26 mi on Hwy 631 (L). 107 Avail. 2021 rates: $12.75 to $51.42. May 18 to Sep 23. (807)868-2254

HUNTSVILLE — C6 *Muskoka*

ARROWHEAD (Public Prov Park) From Jct of Hwy 11 (exit 226) & Muskoka Rd 3, E 0.1 mi on Muskoka Rd 3 to Arrowhead Park Rd, N 0.75 mi (E). Avail: 185 E (15/30 amps). 2021 rates: $34.47 to $51.42. (705)789-5105

DEER LAKE RV RESORT **Ratings: 8.5/10★/9** (Campground) 52 Avail: 43 W, 43 E (30 amps). 2021 rates: $47 to $66. May 15 to Oct 15. (705)789-3326, 85 Hutcheson Beach Rd, Huntsville, ON P1H 1N4

LAGOON TENT & TRAILER PARK **Ratings: 7.5/10★/8.5** (Campground) 55 Avail: 31 W, 31 E (20/30 amps). 2021 rates: $48 to $52. May 15 to Oct 15. (705)789-5011, 100 Lagoon Trailer Park Rd, Huntsville, ON P1H 2J4

SILVER SANDS TENT & TRAILER PARK **Ratings: 7.5/8.5★/7.5** (Campground) 38 Avail: 2 full hkups, 36 W, 36 E (15/30 amps). 2021 rates: $49. May 15 to Oct 15. (705)789-5383, 58 Silver Sands Rd., Huntsville, ON P1H 2J4

IGNACE — F7 *Kenora*

DAVY LAKE CAMPGROUND

good sam park **Ratings: 8.5/10★/9.5** (Campground) From Jct of Hwy 17 & Hwy 599, W 0.5 km (0.3 mi) on Hwy 17 to Davy Lake Rd, SW 0.8 km (0.5 mi) (L).

TOP-RATED GOOD SAM PARK ON ON-17!
Just off Ontario's picturesque Trans Canada Hwy; and surprisingly quiet! So easy on & off. Peaceful, Welcoming, Spacious, Beautiful camping oasis. Book at least a night on your way anywhere; you'll want to stay a lot longer!

FAC: all weather rds. (60 spaces). 45 Avail: 23 all weather, 22 grass, 18 pull-thrus, (46x100), back-ins (30x45), 21 full hkups, 13 W, 13 E (15/50 amps), seasonal sites, cable, WiFi @ sites, tent sites, rentals, dump, laundry, groc, fire rings, firewood, controlled access. **REC:** Davy Lake: swim, fishing, kayaking/canoeing, boating nearby, playground. Pets OK. Big rig sites, eco-friendly. 2021 rates: $40 to $55. May 15 to Oct 14.
(877)374-3113 Lat: 49.41009, Lon: -91.65237
400 Davy Lake Road, Ignace, ON P0T 1T0
www.davylakecampground.com
See ad this page

SANDBAR LAKE (Public Prov Park) From town, E 0.5 mi on Hwy 17 to Hwy 599, N 7 mi (L). Avail: 37 E (15/30 amps). 2021 rates: $12.75 to $43.75. May 18 to Sep 16. (807)934-2995

INGERSOLL — E4 *Oxford*

CENTENNIAL PARK (Public) From Jct of Hwy 401 & 19 (exit 218), N 0.7 mi on Hwy 19 (L) (Registration at Victoria Park Community Center). 15 Avail: 15 W, 15 E (15 amps). 2021 rates: $16.50. May 20 to Sep 01. (519)425-1181

INGLESIDE — C9 *Stormont*

FARRAN PARK (TOWNSHIP PARK) (Public) From west town limits: Go 4-1/4 km/2-3/4 mi W on Hwy 2. Avail: 46 full hkups (30/50 amps). May 13 to Oct 10. (613)537-8600

UPPER CANADA MIGRATORY BIRD SANCTUARY CAMPGROUND (Public Prov Park) From town, W 2 mi on forest service rd. (E). 69 Avail: 47 W, 47 E (30/50 amps). 2021 rates: $33 to $43. May 18 to Oct 21. (800)437-2233

We rate what RVers consider important.

IROQUOIS — C9 *South Dundas*

IROQUOIS MUNICIPAL PARK (Public Prov Park) From jct Hwy 401 & Hwy 2 (Carman Rd): Go 3/4 km/1/2 mi S on Hwy 2. 70 Avail: 70 W, 70 E Pit toilets. 2021 rates: $22.57 to $28.22. (613)652-2506

IROQUOIS FALLS — F10 *Cochrane*

CAMERON'S BEACH TRAILER PARK (Campground) (Phone Update) 16 Avail: 4 full hkups, 12 W, 12 E (30 amps). 2021 rates: $45. May 15 to Sep 15. (705)232-4905, 1011 Cameron Ave, Iroquois Falls, ON P0K 1G0

KETTLE LAKES (Public Prov Park) From town, E 24 mi on Hwy 101 to Hwy 67, N 2 mi (R). Avail: 95 E (15/30 amps). 2021 rates: $12.75 to $51.42. May 20 to Oct 11. (705)363-3511

JOHNSTOWN — C9 *Leeds and Grenville*

GRENVILLE PARK CAMPING & RV PARK **Ratings: 7.5/9★/8.5** (Campground) 64 Avail: 64 W, 64 E (15/30 amps). 2021 rates: $44 to $54. May 01 to Oct 15. (613)925-5055, 2323 County Road 2, Johnstown, ON K0E 1T1

KAGAWONG — B3 *Manitoulin*

NORM'S TENT & TRAILER PARK **Ratings: 6.5/8★/8.5** (Campground) 25 Avail: 25 W, 25 E (30 amps). 2021 rates: $34. May 15 to Oct 14. (705)282-2827, RR 1, 1125B Lakeshore Road, Kagawong, ON P0P 1J0

ON

KAKABEKA FALLS — F8 *Thunder Bay*

KAKABEKA FALLS (Public Prov Park) From Thunder Bay, W 20 mi on Hwy 11/17 (L). Avail: 90 E (15/30 amps). 2021 rates: $36.75 to $51.42. May 18 to Oct 09. (807)473-9231

KAPUSKASING — F9 *Cochrane*

RENE BRUNELLE (Public Prov Park) From Jct of Hwys 11 & 581, N 6 mi on Hwy 581 (R). Avail: 60 E (15/30 amps). 2021 rates: $12.75 to $51.42. May 18 to Sep 03. (705)367-2692

KEARNEY — B6 *Parry Sound*

GRANITE RIDGE CAMPGROUND **Ratings: 6/7.5/7.5** (Campground) 150 Avail: 15 full hkups, 135 W, 135 E (15/30 amps). 2021 rates: $60 to $64. May 18 to Sep 04. (705)636-1474, Hwy 518 East #2900, Kearney, ON P0A 1M0

KEENE — D7 *Peterborough*

SHADY ACRES - PARKBRIDGE **Ratings: 8/7.5/8.5** (Campground) 32 Avail: 2 full hkups, 30 W, 30 E (15/30 amps). 2021 rates: $50 to $70. May 08 to Oct 18. (705)295-6815, 740 Serpent Mounds Rd, Keene, ON L0L 2G0

KEMPTVILLE — C9 *Stormont*

RIDEAU RIVER (Public Prov Park) From town, NW 2.5 mi on CR-44 (becomes CR-5), NE 1 mi (R). Avail: 46 E (15 amps). 2021 rates: $12.75 to $51.72. May 13 to Sep 18. (613)258-2740

SANDY MOUNTAIN CAMP & GOLF **Ratings: 7/7.5★/8.5** (Campground) 20 Avail: 15 full hkups, 5 W, 5 E (15/30 amps). 2021 rates: $46. May 15 to Oct 15. (613)989-2058, 10152 CR 43, Mountain, ON K0E 1S0

KENORA — E6 *Kenora*

ANICINABE PARK **Ratings: 8/9.5★/9** (Campground) 80 Avail: 28 full hkups, 33 W, 33 E (15/30 amps). 2021 rates: $35 to $44. May 01 to Oct 15. (807)467-2700, 955 Golf Course Road, Kenora, ON P9N 4J1

RUSHING RIVER (Public Prov Park) From Jct of Hwys 17 & 71, S 3 mi on Hwy 71 (L). Avail: 82 E (15/30 amps). 2021 rates: $12.75 to $43.75. May 18 to Sep 16. (807)548-4351

THE WILLOWS RV PARK & CAMPGROUND **Ratings: 7.5/9★/9** (Campground) 35 Avail: 7 full hkups, 28 W, 28 E (15/50 amps). 2021 rates: $44 to $55. May 10 to Oct 15. (807)548-1821, 41 Longbow Lake Road, Longbow Lake, ON P0X 1H0

Don't miss out on great savings - find Camping World coupons at the front and back of this Guide!

KILLARNEY — B4 *Algoma*

KILLARNEY/GEORGE LAKE (Public Prov Park) From Jct of Hwys 69 & 637, W 45 mi on Hwy 637 (R). 128 Avail. 2021 rates: $10.75 to $51.42. (705)287-2900

KINCARDINE — D3 *Bruce*

AINTREE TRAILER PARK
Ratings: 8/8.5★/9 (Campground) From Jct of Hwy 21 & Hwy 9, SW 3.2 km (2 mi) on Hwy 21 to Conc #12, NW 1.9 km (1.2 mi) (L). **FAC:** gravel rds. (170 spaces). 18 Avail: 6 gravel, 12 grass, patios, 6 pull-thrus, (22x65), back-ins (30x65), 6 full hkups, 12 W, 12 E (30 amps), seasonal sites, WiFi @ sites, tent sites, shower$, dump, laundry, LP bottles, fire rings, firewood. **REC:** Lake Huron: swim, fishing, kayaking/canoeing, playground. Pets OK. eco-friendly. 2021 rates: $51 to $57. Apr 15 to Oct 11.
(877)396-8533 Lat: 44.148936, Lon: -81.667515
2435 Huron Concession 12 Road, Kincardine, ON N2Z 2X3
www.aintreepark.com
See ad this page

BLUEWATER TRAILER PARK (CITY PARK) (Public) From jct Hwy 9 & Hwy 21: Go 1/2 km/1/4 mi S on Hwy 21, then 1/2 km/1/4 mi W on Durham St. 44 Avail. 2021 rates: $35. (519)396-8698

FISHERMAN'S COVE TENT & TRAILER PARK
Ratings: 10/10★/10 (Campground) From jct Hwys 21 & 9, E 18 km (11.25 mi) on Hwy 9 to Bruce CR-1, S 2 km (1.3 mi) to Southline, SE 0.8 km (0.5 mi) (E). Note: Min 3 ngt stay on holiday weekends. **FAC:** paved rds. (530 spaces). Avail: 68 all weather, patios, 13 pull-thrus, (40x100), back-ins (40x70), 58 full hkups, 10 W, 10 E (30/50 amps), seasonal sites, WiFi @ sites, $, tent sites, rentals, shower$, dump, laundry, groc, LP bottles, fire rings, firewood, controlled access. **REC:** heated pool, hot tub, Otter Lake: swim, fishing, marina, kayaking/canoeing, shuffleboard, playground. Pet restrict (B). Partial handicap access. Big rig sites, eco-friendly. 2021 rates: $71 to $77. May 15 to Oct 01. ATM.
(519)395-2757 Lat: 44.074340, Lon: -81.4147565
13 Southline Ave, Kincardine, ON N2Z 2X5
fishermanscove.com
See ad this page

GREEN ACRES CAMPGROUND & RV PARK **Ratings: 8/9★/8.5** (Campground) 74 Avail: 61 full hkups, 13 W, 13 E (15/30 amps). 2021 rates: $50. May 01 to Oct 15. (519)395-2808, 2310 Concession 12, RR 1, Kincardine, ON N2Z 2X3

KINGSTON — D8 *Frontenac*

1000 ISLANDS/KINGSTON HOLIDAY KOA **Ratings: 9/10★/10** (Campground) 85 Avail: 51 W, 34 S, 51 E (30/50 amps). 2021 rates: $65 to $109. May 01 to Oct 15. (800)562-9178, 2039 Cordukes Road, Kingston, ON K7L 4V4

RIDEAU ACRES CAMPING RESORT **Ratings: 8/10★/9** (Campground) 245 Avail: 169 full hkups, 76 W, 76 E (30/50 amps). 2021 rates: $58 to $68. May 15 to Oct 15. (800)958-5830, 1014 Cunningham Road, Kingston, ON K7L 4V3

KINTAIL — D3 *Huron*

MACKENZIE'S TRAILER PARK **Ratings: 6/7/7** (Campground) 25 Avail: 3 full hkups, 6 W, 22 E (15/30 amps). 2021 rates: $45 to $50. May 07 to Oct 11. (519)529-7536, 85324 MacKenzie Camp Rd South, Goderich, ON N7A 3X9

KIRKLAND LAKE — F10 *Timiskaming*

ESKER LAKES (Public Prov Park) From Jct of TCH-11 & Hwy 112, N 12 mi on Hwy 112 to Hwy 66, E 9 mi to Hwy 672, N 10 mi to park access rd, E 1 mi (E). Avail: 65 E (15 amps). 2021 rates: $12.75 to $51.42. May 18 to Sep 03. (705)568-7677

KITCHENER — E4 *Waterloo*

BINGEMANS CAMPING RESORT **Ratings: 7.5/8.5★/8.5** (Campground) 343 Avail: 41 full hkups, 168 W, 168 E (15/50 amps). 2021 rates: $50 to $70. May 01 to Oct 31. (800)565-4631, 425 Bingemans Centre Drive, Kitchener, ON N2B 3X7

COUNTRY GARDENS RV PARK **Ratings: 8.5/9.5★/8** (Campground) Avail: 20 full hkups (30 amps). 2021 rates: $73. Apr 15 to Oct 31. (866)224-0503, 1335 Witmer Road, Petersburg, ON N0B 2H0

Thank You to our active and retired military personnel. Look for military parks within the state listings section of your 2022 Guide.

LAKE ST PETER — C7 *Hastings*

LAKE SAINT PETER (Public Prov Park) From Jct of Hwys 62 & 127, NW 15 mi on Hwy 127 to North Rd, N 1.5 mi (R). Avail: 26 E. 2021 rates: $12.75 to $43.75. May 11 to Oct 09. (613)338-5312

LAKEFIELD — D6 *Peterborough*

LAKEFIELD CAMPGROUND **Ratings: 6.5/7/7.5** (Campground) 23 Avail: 23 W, 23 E (15/30 amps). 2021 rates: $50 to $60. May 01 to Oct 30. (705)652-8610, 59 Hague Blvd, Lakefield, ON K0L 2H0

LAMBTON SHORES — E3 *Lambton*

OAKRIDGE FAMILY CAMPGROUND **Ratings: 8/9★/8.5** (Campground) 75 Avail: 4 full hkups, 44 W, 44 E (15/30 amps). 2021 rates: $48 to $62. May 01 to Oct 15. (519)243-2500, 9910 Northville Cres, RR1, Thedford, ON N0M 2N0

OUR PONDEROSA RV & GOLF RESORT - PARKBRIDGE **Ratings: 8/9★/8.5** (Campground) Avail: 47 full hkups (30/50 amps). 2021 rates: $50 to $240. May 01 to Nov 01. (519)786-2031, 9338 West Ipperwash Road, Lambton Shores, ON N0N 1J2

SILVER BIRCHES RV RESORT **Ratings: 7.5/9.5/7.5** (Campground) 29 Avail: 11 full hkups, 7 W, 7 E (15/30 amps). 2021 rates: $47. May 01 to Oct 31. (519)243-2480, 9537 Army Camp Rd, Lambton Shores, ON N0N 1J3

LANCASTER — C10 *Stormont*

GLENGARRY PARK (Public Prov Park) W-bnd: From Jct of Hwy 401 & Hwy 2 (Exit 814), S 0.5 km (0.3 mi) on Hwy 2 to S Service Rd, E 3.4 km (2.1 mi) (R) Note: Three night min. stay on holiday weekends. 183 Avail: 27 W, 27 E (15/30 amps). 2021 rates: $34.50 to $38.25. May 13 to Oct 10. (613)347-2595

LANGTON — E4 *Norwich*

DEER CREEK CONSERVATION AREA (Public) From town, S 3 mi on Hwy 59 to Regional Rd 45, W 0.25 mi (R). 40 Avail: 7 W, 23 E (15/30 amps), Pit toilets. 2021 rates: $34 to $46. May 01 to Oct 15. (877)990-9934

LARDER LAKE — F10 *Timiskaming*

RAVEN BEACH CAMPGROUND (Public) At Jct of Hwy 66 & E 2nd Ave (R). 70 Avail: 70 W, 70 E (30 amps). 2021 rates: $25 to $43.75. May 15 to Oct 15. (705)643-2171

LEAMINGTON — F2 *Essex*

LEISURE LAKE RESORT - PARKBRIDGE **Ratings: 8.5/8.5/8.5** (Campground) 37 Avail: 7 full hkups, 30 W, 30 E (30/50 amps). 2021 rates: $50 to $165. May 01 to Nov 01. (519)326-1255, 510 Essex Rd #31, Ruthven, ON N0P 2G0

LINDSAY — D6 *Kawartha Lakes*

DOUBLE "M" RV RESORT & CAMPGROUND **Ratings: 6.5/7/8** (Campground) 30 Avail: 2 full hkups, 28 W, 28 E (15/30 amps). 2021 rates: $55 to $60. Apr 15 to Nov 15. (705)324-9317, 101 Ridgewood Rd, Lindsay, ON K9V 4R2

RIVERWOOD PARK **Ratings: 8/9★/7.5** (Campground) 48 Avail: 10 full hkups, 38 W, 38 E (15/30 amps). 2021 rates: $53.10 to $59. May 18 to Oct 12. (705)324-1655, 78 Riverwood Park Drive, Lindsay, ON K9V 0K2

LION'S HEAD — C4 *Bruce*

LION'S HEAD BEACH PARK (Public Prov Park) From jct Hwy 6 & CR 9 at Ferndale: Go 4km/2 1/2 mi E on CR9A, then .4 km/ 1/4 mi N on Main St. Then 1 block E on Webster St. 13 Avail. 2021 rates: $27.50 to $37.50. (519)793-3522

LITTLE CURRENT — B3 *Manitoulin*

SILVER BIRCHES **Ratings: 6.5/6/6** (Campground) 10 Avail: 10 W, 10 E (30 amps). 2021 rates: $65. May 22 to Oct 11. (705)368-2669, 110 Honora Bay Road, Little Current, ON P0P 1K0

LONDON — E4 *Middlesex*

FANSHAWE CONSERVATION AREA (Public) From Jct of Hwys 401 & Airport Rd, N 4 mi on Airport Rd to Oxford St, W 2 mi to Clark Rd, N 2 mi (R). 650 Avail: 420 W, 420 E (15/30 amps). 2021 rates: $35 to $45. Apr 22 to Oct 16. (519)951-6181

From fishing along the Cape to boating on the Great Lakes, we've put the Spotlight on North America's most popular travel destinations. Turn to the Spotlight articles in our State and Province sections to learn more.

LONG SAULT — C9 *Stormont*

LONG SAULT PARKWAY/MCLAREN CAMPGROUND (Public Prov Park) From Jct of Hwy 401 & Moulinette Rd (Exit 778), S 2.6 km (1.6 mi) on Moulinette Rd to Long Sault Pkwy, W 10.5 km (6.5 mi) (L). Note: Three night min stay on holiday weekends. Avail: 113 full hkups (30/50 amps). 2021 rates: $31.07 to $43.73. May 18 to Oct 08. (613)534-8202

LONG SAULT PARKWAY/MILLE ROCHES CAMPGROUND (Public Prov Park) From Hwy 401 & Moulinette Rd (Exit 778), S 2.6 km (1.6 mi) on Moulinette Rd to Long Sault Pkwy, S 3.2 km (2 mi) on Long Sault Pkwy (R). Min. three night stay on holiday weekend. 214 Avail: 17 W, 45 E (15 amps). 2021 rates: $31.07 to $43.73. May 17 to Sep 01. (613)543-8202

LONG SAULT PARKWAY/WOODLANDS CAMPGROUND (Public Prov Park) From Hwy 401 & Moulinette Rd (Exit 778), S 2.6 km (1.6 mi) on Moulinette Rd to Long Sault Parkway, S 9 km (5.6 mi) (R). Note: Three night min. stay on holiday weekends. 181 Avail: 106 W, 106 E (15/50 amps). 2021 rates: $34.50 to $38.25. May 17 to Sep 01. (613)543-8202

LYNDHURST — C8 *Leeds and Grenville*

CHARLESTON LAKE (Public Prov Park) From Jct of Hwy 401 CR-3 (exit 659), N 12 mi on CR-3 (R). Avail: 109 E (15/30 amps). 2021 rates: $30.50 to $51.42. May 11 to Oct 09. (613)659-2065

WILSON'S TENT & TRAILER PARK **Ratings: 4.5/5/6** (Campground) 25 Avail: 15 W, 15 E (15/30 amps). 2021 rates: $35. May 01 to Sep 30. (613)928-2557, 465 Lyndhurst Rd, Lyndhurst, ON K0E 1N0

MABERLY — C8 *Lanark*

SILVER LAKE (Public Prov Park) From town, W 2 mi on Hwy 7 (R). Avail: 27 E (20 amps). 2021 rates: $12.75 to $43.75. May 17 to Sep 09. (613)268-2000

MADAWASKA — B7 *Nipissing*

RIVERLAND LODGE & CAMP (Campground) (Phone Update) 50 Avail: 50 W, 50 E (30 amps). 2021 rates: $50. May 15 to Oct 15. (613)637-5338, 25141 Hwy 60, Box 98, Madawaska, ON K0J 2C0

MALLORYTOWN — C9 *Leeds and Grenville*

1000 ISLANDS/MALLORYTOWN KOA HOLIDAY **Ratings: 8.5/10★/9.5** (Campground) 140 Avail: 35 full hkups, 105 W, 105 E (15/50 amps). 2021 rates: $76 to $109. Apr 10 to Oct 31. (800)562-9725, 1477 County Rd 2, Box 29, Mallorytown, ON K0E 1R0

HAPPY GREEN ACRES CAMPGROUND **Ratings: 8/9★/9** (Campground) 86 Avail: 67 full hkups, 7 W (15/30 amps). 2021 rates: $67 to $99. May 01 to Oct 31. (343)264-2468, 2 Green Acres Road, Mallorytown, ON K0E 1R0

MANITOWANING — B3 *Manitoulin*

MANITOULIN RESORT **Ratings: 7.5/10★/9.5** (Campground) 30 Avail: 23 W, 23 E (30 amps). 2021 rates: $50 to $53. May 09 to Sep 28. (705)859-3550, 152 Holiday Haven Road, Manitowaning, ON P0P 1N0

MARATHON — F8 *Thunder Bay*

NEYS (Public Prov Park) From town, W 16 mi on Hwy 17 (L). Avail: 61 E (15/30 amps). 2021 rates: $12.75 to $51.42. May 20 to Sep 18. (807)229-1624

MARMORA — C7 *Hastings*

HERITAGE TRAILS CAMPGROUND **Ratings: 9/9★/8.5** (Campground) 50 Avail: 19 full hkups, 31 W, 31 E (20/30 amps). 2021 rates: $79 to $87. Apr 30 to Oct 17. (800)792-0223, 178 KOA Campground Road, RR2, Marmora, ON K0K 2M0

MARTEN RIVER — A5 *Nipissing*

MARTEN RIVER (Public Prov Park) From Jct of Trans-Canada 11 & Trans-Canada 17, N 36 mi on Trans-Canada 11 (L). Avail: 105 E (15/30 amps). 2021 rates: $12.75 to $51.42. May 18 to Sep 23. (705)892-2200

MATTAWA — A6 *Nipissing*

SAMUEL DE CHAMPLAIN (Public Prov Park) From town, W 8 mi on Hwy 17 (L). Avail: 94 E (15/30 amps). 2021 rates: $12.75 to $43.75. May 18 to Oct 09. (705)744-2276

SID TURCOTTE PARK CAMPING AND COTTAGE RESORT
Ratings: 8/9★/9.5 (Campground) 52 Avail: 39 full hkups, 13 W, 13 E (15/30 amps). 2021 rates: $40 to $64. May 10 to Oct 14. (705)744-5375, 750 Mattawan St, Mattawa, ON P0H 1V0

MEAFORD — C4 *Grey*

MEAFORD MEMORIAL PARK (Public) From Jct of Hwy 26 & CR-7, N 0.1 mi on CR-7 to Aitken St, E 0.25 mi to Grant Ave, SE 0.3 mi (E). 135 Avail: 135 W, 104 S, 135 E (15/30 amps). 2021 rates: $35 to $57. May 01 to Oct 18. (800)399-6323

MIDLAND — C5 *Simcoe*

BAYFORT TENT AND TRAILER PARK (Campground) (Phone Update) 54 Avail: 15 W, 15 E (30 amps). 2021 rates: $60. May 20 to Oct 11. (705)526-8704, 3321 Ogden's Beach Road, Midland, ON L0K 1R0

SMITH'S TRAILER PARK & CAMP
Ratings: 7.5/8★/8.5 (RV Area in MH Park) From Jct of Hwy 93 & Hwy 12, E 3.2 km (2 mi) on Hwy 12 to King St, N 0.8 km (0.5 mi) (L). **FAC:** paved/gravel rds. (179 spaces). Avail: 17 grass, 7 pull-thrus, (30x70), back-ins (35x45), 7 full hkups, 10 W, 10 E (15/50 amps), seasonal sites, WiFi @ sites, shower$, dump, groc, fire rings, firewood. **REC:** heated pool, Little Lake: swim, fishing, kayaking/canoeing, shuffleboard, playground. Pet restrict (B). No tents, eco-friendly. 2021 rates: $53 to $59. May 18 to Oct 14.
(705)526-4339 Lat: 44.73645, Lon: -79.87666
736 King St, Midland, ON L4R 0B9
www.smithscamp.ca
See ad this page

MILLER LAKE — C4 *Bruce*

SUMMER HOUSE PARK
Ratings: 8.5/10★/10 (Campground) From Jct of Hwy 6 & Miller Lake Rd, E 3.2 km (2 mi) on Miller Lake Rd (L). Min 3-5 nights stay on holiday weekends. **FAC:** all weather rds. (230 spaces). Avail: 60 gravel, 15 pull-thrus, (25x65), back-ins (20x45), 34 full hkups, 26 W, 26 E (30/50 amps), seasonal sites, WiFi @ sites, $, tent sites, rentals, dump, mobile sewer, laundry, groc, LP bottles, fire rings, firewood, restaurant, controlled access. **REC:** Miller Lake: swim, fishing, marina, kayaking/canoeing, shuffleboard, playground, rec open to public. Pet restrict (B). Partial handicap access, eco-friendly. 2021 rates: $59 to $71. May 01 to Oct 18. ATM.
(519)795-7712 Lat: 45.098626, Lon: -81.402174
197 Miller Lake Shore Road, Miller Lake, ON N0H 1Z0
www.summerhousepark.ca
See ad this page

MILTON — E5 *Halton*

MILTON HEIGHTS CAMPGROUND **Ratings: 9/10★/9** (Campground) 141 Avail: 81 full hkups, 46 W, 46 E (15/50 amps). 2021 rates: $51 to $59. (905)878-6781, 8690 Tremaine Road, RR3, Milton, ON L9E 0E3

MITCHELL'S BAY — F3 *Chatham-Kent*

MITCHELL'S BAY MARINE PARK **Ratings: 7/9★/8** (RV Park) 24 Avail: 24 W, 24 E (30 amps). 2021 rates: $48 to $60. May 01 to Oct 31. (519)354-8423, 3 Allen St, Mitchell's Bay, ON N0P 1L0

MONTREAL RIVER HARBOUR — F9 *Algoma*

TWILIGHT RESORT (Campground) (Phone Update) 22 Avail: 4 full hkups, 18 W, 18 E (15 amps). 2021 rates: $60 to $85. May 01 to Oct 11. (705)882-2183, Hwy 17 N, Montreal River Harbour, ON P0S 1H0

MOONBEAM — F9 *Cochrane*

REMI LAKE TRAILER PARK (RV Area in MH Park) (Phone Update) 25 Avail: 10 full hkups, 10 W, 10 E (15/30 amps). 2021 rates: $40 to $45. May 15 to Sep 15. (705)367-2068, 80 Remi Lake Road, Moonbeam, ON P0L 1V0

TWIN LAKES CAMPING (Campground) (Phone Update) 35 Avail: 25 full hkups, 10 W, 10 E (30 amps). 2021 rates: $40 to $45. May 15 to Sep 15. (705)367-9000, 35 Hwy 581, Moonbeam, ON P0L 1V0

MORPETH — F3 *Chatham-Kent*

RONDEAU (Public Prov Park) From Jct of Hwy 401 & CR 15 (exit 101), SE 9.8 mi on CR 15 (E). Follow signs. Avail: 152 E (15/30 amps). 2021 rates: $34.91 to $51.42. Apr 06 to Oct 28. (519)674-1750

MORRISBURG — C9 *Dundas*

RIVERSIDE-CEDAR CAMPGROUND (Public Prov Park) From Jct of Hwy 401 & Upper Canada Rd (Exit 758), SE 1.6 km (1 mi) on Upper Canada Rd to CR 2, SW 1.9 km (1.2 mi) (L). Min. three night stay on holiday weekends. Avail: 148 E (15/30 amps). 2021 rates: $34.50 to $38.25. May 18 to Oct 08. (613)543-3287

UPPER CANADA CAMPGROUND
good sam park **Ratings: 8/9★/9** (Campground) 47 Avail: 47 W, 47 E (15/50 amps). 2021 rates: $43 to $52. May 07 to Sep 26. (613)543-2201, 13390 Upper Canada Road North, Morrisburg, ON K0C 1X0

The Ratings & What They Mean

Turn to "Understanding the Rating System" section at the front of this Guide to get information on how we rate and inspect parks with our handy three number system!

Rated 10/10★/10

The **FIRST NUMBER** represents Development of Facilities

The **SECOND NUMBER** represents Cleanliness and Physical Characteristics of Restrooms and Showers (plus, a Star is awarded to parks who receive maximum points for cleanliness!)

The **THIRD NUMBER** represents Visual Appearance/Environmental Quality

MOSSLEY — E4 *Middlesex*

GOLDEN POND RV RESORT **Ratings: 9.5/10★/9.5** (Campground) Avail: 25 full hkups (30/50 amps). 2021 rates: $64 to $70. Apr 01 to Dec 15. (888)990-9920, 4340 Cromarty Drive, Mossley, ON N0L 1V0

MOUNT FOREST — D4 *Wellington*

SPRING VALLEY RESORT - PARKBRIDGE **Ratings: 7.5/7.5★/7.5** (Campground) 13 Avail: 8 W, 8 E (30 amps). 2021 rates: $50 to $55. May 15 to Oct 17. (519)323-2581, 7489 Side Road 5E, Mount Forest, ON N0G 2L0

NESTOR FALLS — F6 *Rainy River*

CALIPER LAKE (Public Prov Park) From town, S 3 mi on Hwy 71 (R). Avail: 25 E (15/30 amps). 2021 rates: $30.50 to $51.42. May 16 to Sep 14. (807)484-2181

NEW LISKEARD — F10 *Timiskaming*

SUTTON BAY PARK (Campground) (Phone Update) 75 Avail: 50 full hkups, 25 W, 25 E (15/30 amps). 2021 rates: $34 to $45. May 01 to Oct 01. (705)647-8510, 841514 Waugh's Hill Road , New Liskeard, ON P0J 1P0

NEYAASHIINIGMIING — C4 *Bruce*

CAPE CROKER PARK **Ratings: 7/7.5/8** (RV Park) Avail: 22 E (20/50 amps). 2021 rates: $42 to $50.75. May 01 to Oct 15. (519)534-0571, 112 Park Road, Wiarton, ON N0H 2T0

NIAGARA FALLS — E6 *Niagara*

A SPOTLIGHT Introducing Niagara Falls' colorful attractions appearing at the front of this province section.

NIAGARA FALLS See also Cayuga, Dunnville, Hamilton, Millgrove, Milton, Pelham, Port Colborne, Ridgeway, St Catharines & Vineland, ON; Akron, Darien Center, Gasport, Holland, Holley, Java Center, Lockport, Medina, Niagara Falls, North Java & Warsaw, NY.

CAMPARK RESORTS FAMILY CAMPING & RV RESORT

Ratings: 8.5/9★/9 (Campground) S-bnd: Jct of QEW & Exit 30B, W 0.16 km (0.1 mi) to Montrose Rd, S 0.8 km (0.5 mi) to Lundy's Ln, W 2.6 km (1.6 mi) (R); N-bnd: Jct of QEW & McLeod Rd (Exit 27), W 0.5 km (0.3 mi) on McLeod Rd to Montrose Rd, N 2 km (1.3 mi) to Lundy's Ln, W 2.6 km (1.6 mi) (R). Min. 2 ngts stay holiday weekends.

NIAGARA FALLS FAMILY CAMPING RESORT
Along Lundy's Lane, just minutes from everything Niagara Falls has to offer, Campark Resorts is a preferred camping destination for families from all over the world. We are all about creating a family fun experience.

FAC: all weather rds. (350 spaces). 285 Avail: 139 gravel, 146 grass, 43 pull-thrus, (30x75), back-ins (30x49), 220 full hkups, 65 W, 65 E (30/50 amps), seasonal sites, WiFi, tent sites, rentals, dump, laundry, groc, LP bottles, fire rings, firewood, restaurant, controlled access. **REC:** heated pool, hot tub, golf, playground, rec open to public. Pets OK. Partial handicap access. Big rig sites, eco-friendly. 2021 rates: $72 to $95. May 01 to Oct 31. ATM.
(877)CAMPARK Lat: 43.08631, Lon: -79.15514
9387 Lundy's Lane, Niagara Falls, ON L2E 6S4
www.campark.com
See ad next page, 651, 1109, 1111, 1127

Be a Greener RVer: Turn off utilities at home before you hit the road and conserve water as much as possible when in the RV. Work with nature to avoid using the A/C and heater. Try to park in the shade or use your awning in the heat of the day. In the winter, park in the sun and where the wind will be resisted. Use non-toxic tank additives and cleaning supplies. Observe and follow fire rules, which can change with the weather. Don't put anything in a fire pit that will not burn. Keep campfires small to minimize ash and pollution. Recycle when possible, use less plastic cups/plates/utensils. Keep your RV well-tuned to conserve energy/reduce emissions. Always stay in marked campsites so as not to disturb the natural habitat.

KNIGHT'S HIDE-AWAY PARK

Ratings: 8.5/8★/8 (Campground) From Jct of Peace Bridge & Hwy 3, W 9.7 km (6 mi) on Hwy 3 to Gorham Rd (RR 116), N 91 m (100 yds) (R); or From Jct of QEW & RR 116 (Exit 16), S 9.7 km (6 mi) on RR 116 (L). Minimum 2 day stay on holiday weekends. **FAC:** gravel rds. (160 spaces). 80 Avail: 19 gravel, 61 grass, 19 pull-thrus, (25x75), back-ins (22x40), mostly side by side hkups, 19 full hkups, 30 W, 30 E (15/30 amps), seasonal sites, WiFi @ sites, tent sites, dump, mobile sewer, laundry, groc, fire rings, firewood, controlled access. **REC:** heated pool, boating nearby, playground. Pets OK. Partial handicap access, eco-friendly. 2021 rates: $48 to $54. May 01 to Oct 30.
(905)894-1911 Lat: 42.90575, Lon: -79.05720
1154 Gorham Road, Ridgeway, ON L0S 1N0
www.knightsfamilycamping.com
See ad this page

NIAGARA FALLS KOA

Ratings: 9/10★/10 (Campground) S-bnd: From jct of QEW & Exit 30B, W 0.16 km (0.1 mi) to Montrose Rd, S 0.8 km (0.5 mi) to Lundy's Lane, W 1.6 km (1 mi) (R); or N-bnd: From Jct of QEW & McLeod Rd (Exit 27), W 0.48 km (0.3 mi) on McLeod Rd to Montrose Rd, N 2.1 km (1.3 mi) to Lundy's Lane, W 1.6 km (1 mi) (R). **FAC:** paved rds. (163 spaces). 156 Avail: 40 paved, 116 all weather, patios, 46 pull-thrus, (30x70), back-ins (21x40), 101 full hkups, 55 W, 55 E (30/50 amps), seasonal sites, WiFi @ sites, tent sites, rentals, dump, laundry, groc, fire rings, firewood, restaurant, controlled access. **REC:** heated pool, wading pool, hot tub, boating nearby, playground. Pet restrict (B). Partial handicap access. Big rig sites, eco-friendly. 2021 rates: $90 to $175. Apr 15 to Oct 23. ATM.
(800)562-6478 Lat: 43.08892, Lon: -79.14240
8625 Lundy's Lane, Niagara Falls, ON L2H 1H5
www.niagarakoa.net
See ad page 1113

RIVERSIDE PARK MOTEL & CAMPGROUND **Ratings: 8.5/9★/10** (Campground) 78 Avail: 49 full hkups, 29 W, 29 E (15/50 amps). 2021 rates: $58 to $79. May 01 to Oct 13. (905)382-2204, 13541 Niagara Parkway, Niagara Falls, ON L2E 6S6

SCOTT'S FAMILY RV-PARK CAMPGROUND

Ratings: 8/9.5★/8 (Campground) S-Bnd: From Jct of QEW & Exit 30B, W 0.16 km (0.1 mi) to Montrose Rd, S 0.8 km (0.5 mi) to Lundy's Ln, W 1.9 km (1.2 mi) (R); N-bnd: From Jct of QEW & McLeod Rd (Exit 27), W 0.5 km (0.3 mi) on McLeod Rd to Montrose Rd, N 2.1 km (1.3 mi) to Lundy's Ln, W 1.9 km (1.2 mi) (R). **FAC:** paved/gravel rds. (265 spaces). Avail: 180 gravel, 15 pull-thrus, (35x65), back-ins (35x65), mostly side by side hkups, 90 full hkups, 70 W, 70 E (30/50 amps), seasonal sites, WiFi @ sites, tent sites, dump, laundry, groc, LP gas, fire rings, firewood, controlled access. **REC:** heated pool, boating nearby, playground. Pet restrict (B). eco-friendly. 2021 rates: $50 to $78. May 01 to Oct 31.
(905)356-6988 Lat: 43.08843, Lon: -79.14705
8845 Lundy's Lane, Niagara Falls, ON L2H 1H5
www.campingatscotts.com
See ad page 1113

YOGI BEAR'S JELLYSTONE PARK CAMP-RESORT

Ratings: 9/10★/9.5 (Campground) From Jct of QEW & McLeod Rd (Exit 27), E 182 m (200 yds) on McLeod Rd to Oakwood Dr, S 2.4 km (1.5 mi) (L). NOTE: Min. 3 day stay on summer holiday weekends.

BEST FAMILY FUN AT NIAGARA FALLS
As the closest campground to the Falls, we are also at the heart of all the attractions, restaurants & entertainment. Yogi's campground is an attraction itself! So many family fun things to do! Plan to stay long enough!

FAC: paved/gravel rds. (188 spaces). Avail: 185 gravel, patios, 73 pull-thrus, (30x80), back-ins (30x60), 122 full hkups, 30 W, 30 E (30/50 amps), seasonal sites, WiFi @ sites, $, tent sites, rentals, dump, laundry, groc, fire rings, firewood, controlled access. **REC:** heated pool, wading pool, playground. Pet restrict (B/Q). Partial handicap access. Big rig sites, 14 day max stay, eco-friendly. 2021 rates: $74 to $105. May 01 to Oct 15. ATM.
(800)263-2570 Lat: 43.050850, Lon: -79.121206
8676 Oakwood Dr, Niagara Falls, ON L2G 0J2
jellystoneniagara.ca
See ad pages 651, 1108, 1112

We shine ""Spotlights'' on interesting cities and areas.

NIPIGON — F8 *Thunder Bay*

STILLWATER TENT & RV PARK

Ratings: 7/8.5★/8.5 (Campground) 39 Avail: 8 full hkups, 31 W, 31 E (30/50 amps). 2021 rates: $40 to $49. May 15 to Oct 01. (807)887-3701, 358 Hwy 11/17, Nipigon, ON P0T 2J0

NORMANDALE — E5 *Norfolk*

HIDDEN VALLEY RV RESORT **Ratings: 7.5/8/8.5** (Campground) 26 Avail: 26 W, 26 E (30 amps). 2021 rates: $46 to $67. May 01 to Oct 31. (519)426-5666, 61 Mole Side Road, Normandale, ON N0E 1W0

NORTH BAY — A5 *Nipissing*

CHAMPLAIN TENT RV & TRAILER PARK **Ratings: 7/8★/8.5** (Campground) 43 Avail: 26 full hkups, 11 W, 17 E (15/30 amps). 2021 rates: $40. May 15 to Oct 15. (705)474-4669, 1202 Premier Road, North Bay, ON P1A 2J4

DREANY HAVEN CAMPGROUND **Ratings: 6.5/8.5★/9.5** (Campground) 10 Avail: 10 W, 10 E (15/30 amps). 2021 rates: $39 to $42. May 15 to Sep 30. (705)752-2800, 1859 Hwy 17 E , Corbeil, ON P0H 1K0

FAIRVIEW PARK CAMPING & MARINA (RV Area in MH Park) (Phone Update) 33 Avail: 22 full hkups, 4 W, 4 E (15/30 amps). 2021 rates: $39 to $45. May 15 to Oct 15. (705)474-0903, 395 Riverbend Rd, North Bay, ON P1B 8Z4

FRANKLIN MOTEL TENT & TRAILER PARK **Ratings: 6/6/7.5** (Campground) 32 Avail: 24 full hkups, 5 W, 5 E (30/50 amps). 2021 rates: $40 to $45. May 15 to Oct 15. (705)472-1360, 444 Lakeshore Drive, North Bay, ON P1A 2E1

ON

OAKVILLE — E5 *Halton*

BRONTE CREEK (Public Prov Park) From Jct of Hwy 403 (QEW) & Bronte Rd (Exit 111), NW 1.7 mi on Bronte Rd to Upper Middle Rd, SW 0.4 mi (E). Avail: 148 E (15/30 amps). 2021 rates: $30.50 to $51.42. Apr 01 to Oct 23. (905)827-6911

OMEMEE — D6 *Victoria*

EMILY (Public Prov Park) From town, E 3 mi on Hwy 7 to CR-10, N 3 mi (L). Avail: 170 E (15/30 amps). 2021 rates: $12.75 to $51.42. May 11 to Oct 09. (705)799-5170

ORILLIA — C5 *Simcoe*

BASS LAKE (Public Prov Park) From Jct of Hwys 11 & 12, W 2 mi on Hwy 12 to Bass Lake Side Rd, S 1 mi (R). Avail: 92 E (15/30 amps). 2021 rates: $13.88 to $42.75. May 11 to Sep 23. (705)326-7054

HAMMOCK HARBOUR RV PARK **Ratings: 8/7.5★/8.5** (Campground) 31 Avail: 31 W, 31 E (30 amps). 2021 rates: $50. Apr 18 to Oct 12. (705)326-7885, 4569 Concession12, Ramara , Ramara, ON L3V 0M2

MARA (Public Prov Park) From Orillia, E 3 mi on Hwy 12 S to Courtland St, S 1 mi (E). Avail: 33 E (15/30 amps). 2021 rates: $12.75 to $51.42. May 13 to Sep 05. (705)326-4451

MCRAE POINT (Public Prov Park) From Jct of Hwys 11 & 12, E 7 mi on Hwy 12 to Muley Point Rd, SE 2.5 mi (E). Avail: 166 E (15/30 amps). 2021 rates: $12.75 to $51.42. May 11 to Oct 09. (705)325-7290

OSHAWA — D6 *Durham*

DARLINGTON (Public Prov Park) From Jct of Hwy 401 & Courtice Rd (Exit 425), S 0.2 mi on Courtice Rd to Darlington Park Rd, W 1 mi (E). Avail: 135 E (15/30 amps). 2021 rates: $28.75 to $43.75. May 04 to Oct 09. (905)436-2036

Find new and exciting itineraries in our ""Road Trip'' article at the front of each state and province.

See listing Niagara Falls, ON
Ways To Stay
RV Sites
Basic & Deluxe Cabins
Tent Sites
Seasonal Stays
Day Passes
Campark
HOLIDAY RESORTS
NIAGARA FALLS, CANADA
good sam park
www.CAMPARK.com • info@campark.com

OTTAWA — B9 *Ottawa*

OTTAWA See also Alfred, Cardinal, Johnstown, Kemptville, Morrisburg & Renfrew, ON; Cantley, Cheneville, L'Ange-Gardein (Outaouais), Notre-Dame-de-la-Salette & Saint-Andre-Avellin, QC.

CAMP HITHER HILLS

good sam park **Ratings: 9/10★/9** (Campground) E-bnd: From Jct of Hwy 417 & 416S (Exit 131), S 17.7 km (11 mi) on Hwy 416S to Bankfield Rd (Exit 57), E 4.5 km (2.8 mi) to Manotick Main St, SE 0.3 km (0.2 mi) to Bridge St, NE 11 km (6.8 mi) to Bank St, NW 1.3 km (0.8 mi) (R). Min 3 ngts stay on July 1 weekend.

HIGHEST RATED RV PARK IN OTTAWA

Canada's capitol city is packed with interesting, exciting attractions. Parliament Hill, the National Gallery, Rideau Canal, the Canadian Aviation Museum, and world-famous ByWard Market are but a few of Ottawa's treasures.

FAC: paved/gravel rds. (80 spaces). Avail: 65 all weather, patios, 13 pull-thrus, (30x100), back-ins (30x90), 65 full hkups (30/50 amps), seasonal sites, WiFi @ sites, tent sites, shower$, dump, laundry, fire rings, firewood. **REC:** heated pool, boating nearby, playground. Pets OK. Partial handicap access. Big rig sites, eco-friendly. 2021 rates: $51 to $61. Apr 15 to Oct 31.
(613)822-0509 Lat: 45.29080, Lon: -75.57530
5227 Bank Street, Ottawa, ON K1X 1H2
camphitherhills.com
See ad this page

OTTAWA'S POPLAR GROVE CAMPGROUND/RV PARK **Ratings: 8/8/8.5** (Campground) 130 Avail: 120 full hkups, 10 W, 10 E (15/50 amps). 2021 rates: $49 to $54. May 01 to Oct 31. (613)821-2973, 6154 Bank St, Ottawa, ON K4P 1B4

RECREATIONLAND **Ratings: 6/5.5/7.5** (Campground) Avail: 40 full hkups (30 amps). 2021 rates: $40 to $44. Apr 15 to Oct 15. (613)833-2974, 1566 Canaan Rd, Cumberland, ON K4C 1E5

OWEN SOUND — C4 *Grey*

HARRISON PARK (Public) From Jct of Hwy 6 & 2nd Ave, S 0.5 mi on 2nd Ave (E). 104 Avail: 104 W, 104 E (15/30 amps). 2021 rates: $38.85. May 01 to Oct 24. (519)371-9734

KELSO BEACH (CITY PARK) (Public) From town: Go 3/4 km/1/2 mi W on Hwy 21, then 2-1/2 km/1-1/2 mi N on 4th Ave West. Avail: 18 full hkups. 2021 rates: $35.81. (519)371-9734

ROCKSPRINGS/OWEN SOUND KOA **Ratings: 8/8.5/8.5** (Campground) 73 Avail: 53 full hkups, 20 W, 20 E (30/50 amps). 2021 rates: $64 to $71. May 01 to Oct 13. (800)562-8675, 398235 28 Ave East, Owen Sound, ON N4K 5N8

PAISLEY — D4 *Bruce*

SAUGEEN BLUFF CONSERVATION AREA (Public) From town, N 2.5 mi on Bruce County Rd-3, follow signs (L). 200 Avail: 100 W, 100 E (15/30 amps). 2021 rates: $30.40. May 01 to Sep 15. (519)353-7206

PARIS — E5 *Brant*

PINEHURST LAKE CONSERVATION (Public) From N side of town, N 3.5 mi on Hwy 24A (R). 233 Avail: 169 W, 169 E (15/30 amps). 2021 rates: $27 to $46. May 01 to Oct 15. (519)442-4721

Join in the fun. Like us on FACEBOOK!

PARKHILL — E3 *Middlesex*

GREAT CANADIAN HIDEAWAY (Campground) (Phone Update) 55 Avail: 2 full hkups, 53 W, 53 E (15/30 amps). 2021 rates: $52. May 01 to Oct 13. (800)539-5226, 32910 Centre Road, Parkhill, ON N0M 2K0

PARRY SOUND — B5 *Parry Sound*

HORSESHOE LAKE CAMP & COTTAGES **Ratings: 7/8/8** (Campground) 24 Avail: 6 full hkups, 18 W, 18 E (30/50 amps). 2021 rates: $55 to $67.50. May 15 to Oct 15. (705)732-4928, 55 North Sandy Plains Road, Seguin, ON P2A 2W8

OASTLER LAKE (Public Prov Park) From Jct of Hwys 124 & 69, S 8 mi on Hwy 69 (L). Avail: 42 E (15 amps). 2021 rates: $12.75 to $51.42. May 11 to Oct 09. (705)378-2401

PASS LAKE — F8 *Thunder Bay*

MIRROR LAKE RESORT & CAMPGROUND **Ratings: 6/7/7.5** (Campground) 20 Avail: 20 W, 20 E (20 amps). 2021 rates: $30. May 01 to Oct 01. (807)977-2840, 3495 Hwy 11/17, Shuniah, ON P0T 2M0

SLEEPING GIANT (Public Prov Park) From Thunder Bay, E 24 mi on Hwy 11/17 to Hwy 587, S 21 mi (R). Avail: 85 E (15 amps). 2021 rates: $16.81 to $51.42. May 18 to Oct 09. (807)977-2526

PELHAM — E5 *Niagara*

BISSELL'S HIDEAWAY RESORT

good sam park **Ratings: 10/10★/10** (Campground) 200 Avail: 170 full hkups, 30 W, 30 E (30/50 amps). 2021 rates: $95 to $125. May 14 to Oct 17. (888)236-0619, 205 Metler Rd, RR1, Ridgeville, ON L0S 1M0

PEMBROKE — B7 *Renfrew*

RIVERSIDE PARK CAMPGROUND (Public) From Jct of Hwy 17 & CR 40, NW 7.8 mi on CR 40 to Pembroke St W (R). 52 Avail: 52 W, 52 E (20/30 amps). 2021 rates: $26 to $32. May 15 to Oct 11. (613)735-6821

PENETANGUISHENE — C5 *Simcoe*

AWENDA (Public Prov Park) From town, W 7 mi on Hwy 93 (R). Avail: 102 E (15/30 amps). 2021 rates: $28.75 to $43.75. May 13 to Oct 11. (705)549-2231

PERTH — C8 *Lanark*

LAST DUEL PARK & CAMPGROUND (Public) From town, E 0.1 mi on Hwy 43 (R). 47 Avail: 47 W, 47 E (30 amps). 2021 rates: $28.25 to $45.77. May 15 to Oct 15. (613)812-0020

MURPHYS POINT (Public Prov Park) From town, SE 4 mi on CR-1 to Elmgrove Rd/CR-21, S 6.6 mi (L). Avail: 27 E (15/30 amps). 2021 rates: $36.75 to $51.42. May 11 to Oct 09. (613)267-5060

PETAWAWA — B7 *Renfrew*

BLACK BEAR CAMPGROUND (Public) From Jct of Hwy 17 & Paquette Rd, NE 2.4 km (1.5 mi) on Paquette Rd to Menin Rd, N 1.6 km (1 mi) to Passchendale Rd, NE 366 m (400 yds) to Lieven Rd, E 0.6 km (0.4 mi) (L). 30 Avail: 30 W, 30 E (15 amps). 2021 rates: $25 to $35. May 01 to Oct 11. (613)687-7268

Get ready for your next camping trip at CampingWorld.com

PETROLIA — E3 *Lambton*

LORNE C. HENDERSON CONSERVATION AREA (Public Prov Park) From town: Go 2 km/1-1/4 mi W on CR 4. 145 Avail: 145 W, 145 E. (519)882-2280

PICTON — D7 *Prince Edward*

SANDBANKS RIVER COUNTRY CAMPGROUNDS **Ratings: 7.5/8/8.5** (Campground) Avail: 65 full hkups (30/50 amps). 2021 rates: $60 to $70. May 01 to Oct 15. (613)393-5645, #1854 County Road 18, Picton, ON K0K 2T0

SMUGGLERS COVE RV RESORT **Ratings: 8/8.5★/9** (Campground) 70 Avail: 35 full hkups, 35 W, 35 E (30 amps). 2021 rates: $47 to $65. May 01 to Oct 11. (613)476-4125, 3187 CR 13, RR 3, Picton, ON K0K 2T0

PLYMPTON-WYOMING — E3 *Lambton*

LAKEWOOD CHRISTIAN CAMPGROUND **Ratings: 8.5/9.5★/8.5** (Campground) 63 Avail: 60 full hkups, 3 W, 3 E (20/30 amps). 2021 rates: $45 to $60. May 01 to Oct 15. (519)899-4415, 4297 Lakeshore Rd, Plympton-Wyoming, ON N0N 1J6

PARADISE VALLEY CAMPGROUND **Ratings: 8/9★/7.5** (Campground) Avail: 27 full hkups (30 amps). 2021 rates: $55 to $70. Apr 30 to Oct 17. (519)899-4080, 4895 Lakeshore Road, Unit A100, Plympton-Wyoming, ON N0N 1J6

PORT BURWELL — F4 *Norfolk*

PORT BURWELL (Public Prov Park) From Jct of Hwys 3 & 19S, S 0.25 mi on Hwy 19S to CR-42, E 300 ft (E). Avail: 123 E (15/30 amps). 2021 rates: $30.20 to $51.42. May 13 to Oct 11. (519)874-4691

SAND HILL PARK **Ratings: 6.5/7/8** (Campground) 216 Avail: 44 full hkups, 40 W, 40 E (15/50 amps). 2021 rates: $72. May 01 to Oct 09. (519)586-3891, 930 Lakeshore Road, RR 2, Port Burwell, ON N0J 1T0

PORT COLBORNE — E6 *Niagara*

LONG BEACH CONSERVATION AREA (Public) From Jct of Hwy 3 & Reg Rd, W 4 mi on Reg Rd (L). Min 3 night stay on holiday weekends. 225 Avail: 125 W, 125 E (15/30 amps). 2021 rates: $32 to $42. May 14 to Oct 20. (905)899-3462

SHERKSTON SHORES RV RESORT **Ratings: 10/10★/10** (RV Park) 193 Avail: 153 full hkups, 40 W, 40 E (30/50 amps). 2021 rates: $66 to $143. May 01 to Oct 31. (877)482-3224, 490 Empire Road, Sherkston, ON L0S 1R0

PORT DOVER — E5 *Norfolk*

SHORE ACRES PARK **Ratings: 7.5/9.5★/9.5** (RV Park) Avail: 24 full hkups (30 amps). 2021 rates: $75 to $95. Apr 15 to Oct 15. (519)583-2222, 574 Radical Road, Port Dover, ON N0A 1N2

PORT ELGIN — C4 *Bruce*

MACGREGOR POINT (Public Prov Park) From town, S 3 mi on Hwy 21, follow signs (R). Avail: 174 E (15/30 amps). 2021 rates: $12.75 to $51.42. (519)389-9056

PORT ELGIN MUNICIPAL TOURIST CAMP (Public) In town, at Jct of Johnson Ave & Bruce St (E). Avail: 35 full hkups (30 amps). 2021 rates: $30.77. May 01 to Oct 31. (519)832-2512

PORT PERRY — D6 *Durham*

GORESKI'S LANDING - PARKBRIDGE **Ratings: 7/9★/9** (Campground) 21 Avail: 21 W, 21 E (30 amps). 2021 rates: $50 to $55. May 07 to Oct 17. (905)985-9763, 225 Platten Boulevard, Port Perry, ON L9L 1B4

PORT ROWAN — F4 *Haldimand-Norfolk*

BACKUS HERITAGE CONSERVATION AREA (Public) From town, N 2 mi on Regional Rd 42, to CR-2 (E). 160 Avail: 26 W, 98 E (15 amps). 2021 rates: $35 to $41. May 19 to Sep 03. (519)586-2201

LONG POINT (Public Prov Park) From town, S 2 mi on Hwy 59 (E). Avail: 101 E (15/30 amps). 2021 rates: $12.75 to $43.75. May 13 to Oct 11. (519)586-2133

PORT SEVERN — C5 *Muskoka Lakes*

SIX MILE LAKE (Public Prov Park) From Jct of Hwys 400 & 34 (exit 162), W 1 mi on Hwy 34 (R). Avail: 53 E (15/30 amps). 2021 rates: $16.81 to $50.57. May 11 to Oct 09. (705)756-2746

Traveling with Fido? Many campground listings indicate pet-friendly amenities and pet restrictions.

PROVIDENCE BAY — B3 *Manitoulin*

PROVIDENCE BAY TENT-TRAILER PARK **Ratings: 5/7.5/7** (Campground) 120 Avail: 120 W, 120 E (20/30 amps). 2021 rates: $42. May 01 to Oct 01. (877)269-2018, 5466 Hwy 551, Providence Bay, ON P0P 1T0

PUSLINCH — E5 *Wellington*

EMERALD LAKE TRAILER RESORT & WATERPARK

good sam park

Ratings: 9/9★/9 (RV Park) 68 Avail: 28 full hkups, 40 W, 40 E (30/50 amps). 2021 rates: $115 to $125. May 15 to Oct 15. (905)659-7923, 7248 Gore Road, RR2, Puslinch, ON N0B 2J0

RED LAKE — E7 *Kenora*

GULL ROCK LAKE LODGE (Campground) (Phone Update) 17 Avail: 14 full hkups, 3 W, 3 E (30/50 amps). 2021 rates: $63. May 15 to Oct 15. (807)728-2445, 1 Gull Rock Road, Red Lake, ON P0V 2M0

REDBRIDGE — A6 *Nipissing*

CAMP CONEWANGO CAMPGROUND (Campground) (Phone Update) 1 Avail: 1 W, 1 E (15 amps). May 15 to Oct 15. (866)802-6644, 1875 Songis Road, Redbridge, ON P0H 2A0

RENFREW — B8 *Renfrew*

RENFREW/OTTAWA WEST KOA **Ratings: 8/9★/9.5** (Campground) 62 Avail: 49 full hkups, 13 W, 13 E (30/50 amps). 2021 rates: $45 to $69. May 01 to Oct 15. (800)562-3980, 2826 Johnston Road, Renfrew, ON K7V 3Z8

SERENITY HILLS RV PARK **Ratings: 7/8.5★/8** (Campground) 75 Avail: 45 full hkups, 15 W, 15 E (15/30 amps). 2021 rates: $55. May 07 to Oct 08. (613)628-2454, 435 Castleford Road, Renfrew, ON K7V 3Z8

RESTOULE — B5 *Nipissing*

RESTOULE (Public Prov Park) From town, N 6 mi on Hwy 534 (E). Avail: 97 E (15/30 amps). 2021 rates: $25.25 to $37.35. May 18 to Oct 09. (705)729-2010

RIDGETOWN — F3 *Chatham-Kent*

CLEARVILLE PARK (Public) From Jct of Hwy 401 & CR 103 (Furnnal Rd) SE 5.8 mi on CR 103 to CR 3, SW 5.9 mi to Clearville Rd. SE 1.2 mi (E). Avail: 10 full hkups (30 amps). 2021 rates: $25.69 to $27.84. May 01 to Oct 15. (519)674-5583

RIDGEWAY — E6 *Niagara*

WINDMILL POINT PARK AND CAMPGROUND **Ratings: 7.5/8.5/8.5** (Campground) 72 Avail: 72 W, 72 E (30/50 amps). 2021 rates: $60 to $75. May 01 to Oct 15. (888)977-8888, 2409 Dominion Rd, Ridgeway, ON L0S 1N0

ROCKWOOD — D5 *Wellington*

ROCKWOOD CONSERVATION AREA (Public) From Jct of Hwys 6 & 7, NE 7 mi on Hwy 7 (R). 105 Avail: 16 full hkups, 46 W, 46 E (15/30 amps). 2021 rates: $31 to $54. May 01 to Oct 15. (519)856-9543

RODNEY — F3 *Elgin*

PORT GLASGOW TRAILER PARK (Public) From Jct of Hwy 401 & Furnival Rd (exit 129), SE 6.8 mi on Furnival Rd (L). 50 Avail: 50 W, 50 E (30 amps). 2021 rates: $23 to $25. May 01 to Oct 30. (519)785-0560

ROSENEATH — D7 *Northumberland*

GOLDEN BEACH RESORT AND TRAILER PARK **Ratings: 8.5/8.5/9** (Campground) Avail: 35 full hkups (30/50 amps). 2021 rates: $55 to $66. May 01 to Oct 31. (905)342-5366, 7100 CR 18, Roseneath, ON K0K 2X0

ROSSPORT — F8 *Thunder Bay*

RAINBOW FALLS/WHITESAND LAKE (Public Prov Park) From town, E 5 mi on Hwy 17 (L). Avail: 49 E (15/30 amps). 2021 rates: $12.75 to $43.75. May 18 to Sep 16. (807)824-2298

Know the name? Then you can use our special "Find-it-Fast" index to locate your campground on the map. The index arranges private and public campgrounds alphabetically, by state. Next to the name, you'll quickly find the name of the town the park is in, plus the Listing's page number.

ROUND LAKE CENTRE — B7 *Renfrew*

BONNECHERE (Public Prov Park) From town, NE 0.5 mi on Rte-58 (L). Avail: 24 E (15/30 amps). 2021 rates: $30.50 to $51.42. May 18 to Oct 09. (613)757-2103

SANDFORD — D6 *Durham Region*

GRANGEWAYS RV PARK & FAMILY CAMPGROUND **Ratings: 7.5/8.5★/8.5** (Campground) Avail: 45 full hkups (15/30 amps). 2021 rates: $70 to $85. May 01 to Oct 09. (877)223-5034, 9700 3rd Concession, Sandford, ON L0C 1E0

SAUBLE BEACH — C4 *Bruce*

A SPOTLIGHT Introducing Sauble Beach's colorful attractions appearing at the front of this province section.

SAUBLE BEACH RESORT CAMP **Ratings: 8/8.5★/7.5** (Campground) 100 Avail: 50 full hkups, 50 W, 50 E (30 amps). 2021 rates: $59. May 10 to Oct 09. (519)422-1101, 877 Main St, Sauble Beach, ON N0H 2G0

SAUBLE FALLS (Public Prov Park) From town, N 3 mi on Rd 21 (E). Avail: 53 E (15/30 amps). 2021 rates: $12.75 to $51.42. Apr 27 to Oct 28. (519)422-1952

WOODLAND PARK

Ratings: 10/10★/10 (Campground) From Jct of CR-8 & CR-13 (Sauble Falls Pkwy), N 0.4 km (0.25 mi) on CR-13/Sauble Falls Pkwy (R) Note: Min. 3 nights stay on holiday weekends.

ONE OF ONTARIO'S BEST RV PARKS!
Located in Sauble Beach, Canada's #1 fresh-water beach, relax & enjoy beautiful landscaped surroundings in this top-rated Canadian park; a 5-minute walk to 7 miles of sandy beach on beautiful Lake Huron. Great amenities too!

FAC: paved rds. (737 spaces). Avail: 137 paved, patios, 13 pull-thrus, (40x65), back-ins (40x65), 127 full hkups, 10 W, 10 E (30/50 amps), seasonal sites, cable, WiFi @ sites, $, tent sites, rentals, shower$, dump, laundry, groc, LP bottles, fire rings, firewood, controlled access. **REC:** heated pool, hot tub, boating nearby, playground. Pet restrict (B). Partial handicap access. Big rig sites, eco-friendly. 2021 rates: $45 to $79. May 01 to Oct 14.
(519)422-1161 Lat: 44.63431, Lon: -81.26333
47 Sauble Falls Parkway, Sauble Beach, ON N0H 2G0
www.woodlandparkontario.com
See ad page 1117

SAUBLE FALLS — C4 *Bruce*

SAUBLE FALLS TENT & TRAILER PARK **Ratings: 7/8.5/8** (Campground) 58 Avail: 11 full hkups, 47 W, 47 E (15/30 amps). 2021 rates: $50 to $60. May 01 to Sep 04. (519)422-1322, 849 Sauble Falls Parkway, South Bruce Peninsula, ON N0H 2T0

SAULT STE MARIE — A1 *Algoma*

GLENVIEW COTTAGES & RV PARK

good sam park

Ratings: 9/9★/8 (Campground) From Jct of International Bridge & Queen St W, W 259 m (850 ft) on Queen St W to Carmens Way, N 2.3 km (1.4 mi) to Second Line, E 2.1 km (1.3 mi) to Great Northern Rd/Hwy 17 N, N 8.1 km (5 mi) (L).

TWO CAMPING RESORTS TO CHOOSE FROM!
15 min. from International Bridge! 141 Acres of beautiful Ontario woodland. Large campsites, cottages, hiking trails, pool, hot tub & 10-acre natural pond. Also visit our Thunderbird Resort in Upsala ON for fabulous fishing!

FAC: all weather rds. Avail: 40 gravel, 22 pull-thrus, (35x50), back-ins (20x40), 19 full hkups, 21 W, 21 E (15/30 amps), WiFi @ sites, tent sites, rentals, dump, laundry, fire rings, firewood, controlled access. **REC:** pool, pond, fishing, boating nearby, playground. Pets OK. eco-friendly. 2021 rates: $47 to $55. May 15 to Oct 15.
(705)759-3436 Lat: 46.60153, Lon: -84.29473
2611 Great Northern Road, Hwy 17, Sault Ste Marie, ON P6A 5K7
www.glenviewcottages.com
See ad this page

SAULT STE MARIE KOA **Ratings: 8.5/9★/8** (Campground) 80 Avail: 27 full hkups, 53 W, 53 E (15/50 amps). 2021 rates: $56 to $89. May 01 to Oct 15. (800)562-0847, 501 Fifth Line East, Sault Ste Marie, ON P6A 6J8

Shop at Camping World and SAVE with coupons. Check the front of the Guide for yours!

SCHREIBER — F8 *Thunder Bay*

RAINBOW FALLS/ROSSPORT (Public Prov Park) From town, W 17 mi on Hwy 17, follow signs. Avail: 23 E (15/30 amps). 2021 rates: $12.75 to $43.75. May 18 to Oct 09. (807)824-2298

SEGUIN — C5 *Parry Sound*

PARRY SOUND KOA **Ratings: 8/8.5/8** (Campground) 64 Avail: 64 W, 64 E (15/50 amps). 2021 rates: $56 to $91. May 01 to Oct 15. (800)562-2681, 276 Rankin Lake Road, Seguin, ON P2A 0B2

SELKIRK — E5 *Haldimand-Norfolk*

HALDIMAND CONSERVATION AREA (Public) From Jct of Hwy 3 & Regional Rd 18 S 7 mi on Regional Rd 18 to Lakeshore Rd, E. 0.6 mi (R). Avail: 165 full hkups (15/30 amps). 2021 rates: $25 to $35. May 01 to Oct 15. (905)776-2700

SELKIRK (Public Prov Park) From Jct of Hwy 3 & Reg Rd 53, S 5 mi on Reg Rd 53 to Reg Rd 3, W 1 mi to Wheelers Rd, S 0.5 mi (R). Avail: 88 E (15 amps). 2021 rates: $34.47 to $51.42. May 11 to Sep 03. (905)776-2600

SHARBOT LAKE — C8 *Frontenac*

SHARBOT LAKE (Public Prov Park) From town, W 3.2 mi on Hwy 7 (L). Avail: 38 E (15 amps). 2021 rates: $12.75 to $51.42. May 11 to Sep 23. (613)335-2814

SHEGUIANDAH — B3 *Manitoulin*

BATMAN'S COTTAGES & CAMPGROUND **Ratings: 7.5/9★/10** (Campground) 62 Avail: 6 full hkups, 56 W, 56 E (30/50 amps). 2021 rates: $49 to $54. May 01 to Oct 14. (705)368-2180, 11408 Hwy 6, Sheguiandah, ON P0P 1W0

GREEN ACRES TENT & TRAILER PARK **Ratings: 6.5/8.5★/8.5** (Campground) 30 Avail: 30 W, 30 E (30 amps). 2021 rates: $49. May 14 to Oct 03. (705)368-2428, 10944 Hwy 6, Sheguiandah, ON P0P 1W0

SHELBURNE — D5 *Dufferin*

PRIMROSE PARK **Ratings: 8/9/8.5** (Campground) 60 Avail: 6 full hkups, 24 W, 24 E (15/30 amps). 2021 rates: $50 to $60. May 01 to Oct 14. (519)925-2848, 635687 Hwy 10, Mono, ON L9V 0Z8

SIMCOE — E5 *Haldimand-Norfolk*

NORFOLK CONSERVATION AREA (Public) From Simcoe, S 7 mi on Hwy 24, follow signs to township rds, S 1 mi to Lakeshore Rd (R). 164 Avail: 52 full hkups, 98 E (15 amps). 2021 rates: $26 to $36. May 01 to Oct 15. (519)428-1460

TURKEY POINT (Public Prov Park) From Jct of Hwy 24 & Reg Rd 10, S 2.5 mi on Reg Rd 10 to park access rd, E 200 yds (R). Avail: 124 E (15/30 amps). 2021 rates: $34.92 to $51.42. May 11 to Oct 09. (519)426-3239

SIOUX LOOKOUT — E7 *Kenora*

ABRAM LAKE PARK (Campground) (Phone Update) 37 Avail: 16 full hkups, 21 W, 21 E (15/30 amps). 2021 rates: $48 to $52. May 15 to Oct 15. (807)737-1247, 1041 Hwy 72, Sioux Lookout, ON P8T 1A5

OJIBWAY (Public Prov Park) From town, S 13 mi on Hwy 72 (R). Avail: 26 E (15/30 amps). 2021 rates: $12.75 to $51.42. May 18 to Sep 03. (807)223-7535

Camping World RV & Outdoors offers new and used RV sales and so much more! Find a SuperCenter near you at CampingWorld.com

SIOUX NARROWS — F6 *Kenora*

↑ LAUGHING WATER TRAILER PARK **Ratings: 7/8.5★/8.5** (Campground) 20 Avail: 6 full hkups, 14 W, 14 E (30 amps). 2021 rates: $46 to $48. May 15 to Sep 30. (800)341-1048, 30 Heithecker Lane , Sioux Narrows, ON P0X 1N0

← SIOUX NARROWS (Public Prov Park) From town, N 5 mi on Hwy 71 (R). Avail: 17 E (15/30 amps). 2021 rates: $16.81 to $50.57. May 18 to Sep 09. (807)226-5223

↓ TOMAHAWK RESORT RV PARK (Campground) (Phone Update) Avail: 29 full hkups (30/50 amps). 2021 rates: $56 to $64. May 01 to Oct 15. (800)465-1091, 101 Tomahawk Road, Sioux Narrows, ON P0X 1N0

SOMBRA — E3 *Lambton*

↑ CATHCART CAMPGROUND (Public) From town, N 2 mi on St Clair Pkwy (L). 47 Avail: 43 full hkups, 4 W, 4 S (30/50 amps). 2021 rates: $40 to $46. May 01 to Oct 31. (519)892-3342

SOUTH RIVER — B5 *Parry Sound*

← MIKISEW (Public Prov Park) From Jct of Hwy 11 & Eagle Lake Rd, W 12 mi on Eagle Lake Rd (L). Avail: 62 E (15/30 amps). 2021 rates: $12.75 to $51.42. Jun 15 to Sep 23. (705)386-7762

SPRAGGE — A3 *Algoma*

→ SERPENT RIVER CAMPGROUND **Ratings: 8.5/9.5★/10** (Campground) 23 Avail: 23 W, 23 E (15/30 amps). 2021 rates: $44.24 to $49.16. May 01 to Oct 15. (705)849-2210, 4696 Hwy 17W, Spragge, ON P0R 1K0

SPRING BAY — B3 *Manitoulin*

↗ SANTA MARIA TRAILER RESORT & COTTAGES **Ratings: 8/10★/9** (Campground) Avail: 19 full hkups (30 amps). 2021 rates: $45. May 01 to Sep 30. (705)377-5870, 249 Square Bay Road, Spring Bay, ON P0P 2B0

→ STANLEY PARK (RV Park) (Phone Update) 20 Avail: 20 W, 20 E (20/30 amps). 2021 rates: $40. May 07 to Oct 07. (705)377-4661, 1702 Monument Road, RR 1, Spring Bay, ON P0P 2B0

ST CATHARINES — E6 *Niagara*

↗ BIG VALLEY CAMPING RESORT **Ratings: 7/7.5/8.5** (Campground) Avail: 21 full hkups (30 amps). 2021 rates: $50 to $60. May 01 to Oct 31. (905)562-5616, 2211 King St. , St Catharines, ON L2R 6P7

→ JORDAN VALLEY CAMPGROUND **Ratings: 9/10★/10** (Campground) 74 Avail: 9 full hkups, 10 W, 10 E (15/30 amps). 2021 rates: $51.77 to $58.40. May 01 to Oct 15. (866)526-2267, 3902 21st St , Jordan Station, ON L0R 1S0

↓ SHANGRI-LA NIAGARA FAMILY CAMPGROUND **Ratings: 8.5/8★/8** (Campground) 79 Avail: 79 W, 79 E (30/50 amps). 2021 rates: $55 to $58. May 15 to Oct 15. (905)562-5851, 3425 17th Street , St Catharines, ON L2R 6P7

STONECLIFFE — B7 *Renfrew*

→ MORNING MIST RESORT **Ratings: 7.5/9★/8** (Campground) 21 Avail: 14 full hkups, 7 W, 7 E (30/50 amps). 2021 rates: $42 to $45. May 01 to Oct 31. (888)356-1113, 1256 Pine Valley Road, Stonecliffe, ON K0J 2K0

STONEY CREEK — E5 *Hamilton*

↘ FIFTY POINT CONSERVATION AREA (Public) From Jct of QEW & Fifty Rd (Exit 78), N 0.2 km (0.1 mi) on Fifty Rd to N Service Rd, SE 0.3 km (0.2 mi) to Lockport Way, NE 61 m (200 ft) to Baseline Rd, SE 0.3 km (0.2 mi) (L). Note: 2 nights min. stay on holiday weekends. Avail: 70 full hkups (30/50 amps). 2021 rates: $47 to $52. Apr 03 to Nov 29. (905)525-2187

STRATFORD — E4 *Perth*

↓ WILDWOOD CONSERVATION AREA (Public) From Stratford, SW 7 mi on Hwy 7 (L). 110 Avail: 110 W, 110 E (15/30 amps). 2021 rates: $39 to $49. Apr 25 to Oct 19. (866)668-2267

STRATHROY — E3 *Middlesex*

↓ TROUT HAVEN PARK **Ratings: 7.5/9.5★/8.5** (Campground) 35 Avail: 29 full hkups, 6 W, 6 E (15/50 amps). 2021 rates: $48 to $60. May 01 to Oct 31. (519)245-4070, 24749 Park St, Strathroy, ON N7G 3H5

STURGEON FALLS — A5 *Nipissing*

↓ **GLENROCK COTTAGES & TRAILER PARK**
good sam park
Ratings: 8/10★/8.5 (Campground) Avail: 21 full hkups (30/50 amps). 2021 rates: $44. May 15 to Oct 15. (866)592-1157, 100 Glenrock Road, Sturgeon Falls, ON P2B 2M5

← STURGEON FALLS KOA **Ratings: 8/10★/9.5** (Campground) Avail: 46 full hkups (30/50 amps). 2021 rates: $62 to $97. May 14 to Oct 14. (800)562-7798, 818 Lalande Road, Sturgeon Falls, ON P2B 2V4

SUDBURY — A4 *Sudbury (City)*

↓ CAROL'S CAMPSITE AND RV PARK **Ratings: 8/8.5★/8.5** (Campground) Avail: 82 full hkups (30 amps). 2021 rates: $44. May 01 to Oct 15. (705)522-5570, 2388 Richard Lake Drive, Sudbury, ON P3G 0A3

↓ MINE MILL 598/CAW CAMPGROUND **Ratings: 5/6/7** (Campground) 33 Avail: 33 W, 33 E (30 amps). 2021 rates: $45. May 15 to Oct 11. (705)522-5076, 2550 Richard Lake Drive, Sudbury, ON P3E 0A3

↑ WINDY LAKE (Public Prov Park) From town, N 35 mi on Hwy 144 N (L). Avail: 56 E (15/30 amps). 2021 rates: $16.81 to $51.42. May 18 to Sep 03. (705)966-2315

SUTTON — D5 *York*

→ SIBBALD POINT (Public Prov Park) From town, E 3 mi on Hwy 48 (L). Avail: 279 E (15/30 amps). 2021 rates: $12.75 to $51.42. May 09 to Oct 14. (905)722-8061

TEMAGAMI — A5 *Nipissing*

↓ FINLAYSON POINT (Public Prov Park) From town, S 0.6 mi on Hwy 11 to access rd, W 0.25 mi (E). Avail: 34 E (15/30 amps). 2021 rates: $22.46 to $52.55. May 17 to Sep 22. (705)569-3205

↑ HAPPY HOLIDAY CAMPGROUND AND COTTAGES (Campground) (Phone Update) 44 Avail: 27 full hkups, 17 W, 17 E (15/30 amps). 2021 rates: $48 to $53. May 15 to Oct 01. (705)569-3540, 7727 Hwy 11 North, Temagami, ON P0H 2H0

THESSALON — A2 *Algoma*

→ BROWNLEE LAKE PARK RESORT & CAMPGROUND **Ratings: 6.5/9.5★/9** (Campground) Avail: 12 full hkups (15/30 amps). 2021 rates: $37 to $42. May 20 to Oct 14. (705)842-2118, 136 Ingram Road, Thessalon, ON P0R 1L0

← THESSALON LAKESIDE PARK (Public) In town on Hwy 17B (L). 33 Avail: 4 full hkups, 29 W, 29 E (30 amps). 2021 rates: $21.63. May 01 to Oct 01. (705)842-2523

THUNDER BAY — F8 *Thunder Bay*

↓ CHIPPEWA PARK (Public) From Jct of Hwys 11/17, 11B/17B & 61, S 5.1 km (3.2 mi) on Hwy 61 to Chippewa Rd/City Rd, E 9.7 km (6 mi) on Chippewa Rd (becomes City Rd) (L). 62 Avail: 34 W, 12 E (30/50 amps). 2021 rates: $45.25. Jun 04 to Sep 06. (807)623-3912

← **HAPPY LAND RV PARK**
good sam park
Ratings: 9/10★/10 (Campground) 60 Avail: 38 full hkups, 22 E (30/50 amps). 2021 rates: $46 to $56. May 01 to Oct 14. (866)473-9003, I-4650 Hwy 11-17, Kakabeka Falls, ON P7K 0J1

→ THUNDER BAY KOA **Ratings: 8.5/10★/10** (Campground) 205 Avail: 126 full hkups, 79 W, 79 E (15/50 amps). 2021 rates: $53 to $89. Apr 15 to Oct 15. (800)562-4162, 162 Spruce River Road, Shuniah, ON P7A 0P4

→ TROWBRIDGE FALLS CAMPGROUND (Public) From Jct of Hwy 17/11 & Hodder-Copenhagen exit (NE edge of town), NW 274 m (300 yds) on Copenhagen Rd (L). 122 Avail: 36 full hkups, 28 E (15/50 amps). 2021 rates: $45.25. Jun 04 to Sep 06. (807)683-6661

TOBERMORY — C3 *Bruce*

↓ BRUCE PENINSULA/CYPRUS LAKE (Public National Park) From town, S 6 mi on Hwy 6 (L). 232 Avail: Pit toilets. 2021 rates: $15.70 to $23.50. (877)737-3783

↓ HAPPY HEARTS PARK **Ratings: 8.5/8.5★/10** (Campground) 115 Avail: 4 full hkups, 27 W, 27 E (15/50 amps). 2021 rates: $57 to $67. May 01 to Oct 15. (519)596-2455, 93 Cape Hurd Road, Tobermory, ON N0H 2R0

↓ **TOBERMORY VILLAGE CAMPGROUND & CABINS**
Ratings: 8.5/10★/10 (Campground) From S city limits, S 1.6 km (1 mi) on Hwy 6 (R). Min. 3 night stay on holiday weekends. **FAC:** all weather rds. (100 spaces). 85 Avail: 26 gravel, 59 grass, 16 pull-thrus, (30x120), back-ins (30x60), 42 full hkups, 43 W, 43 E (15/50 amps), seasonal sites, WiFi @ sites, tent sites, rentals, shower$, dump, laundry, groc, fire rings, firewood, controlled access. **REC:** heated pool, pond, boating nearby, playground, rec open to public. Pet restrict (B). Partial handicap access, eco-friendly. 2021 rates: $64 to $66. May 01 to Oct 14.
(519)596-2689 Lat: 45.23646, Lon: -81.64052
7159 Hwy 6, Tobermory, ON N0H 2R0
www.tobermoryvillagecamp.com
See ad this page

It's the law! Rules of the Road and Towing Laws are updated each year. Be sure to consult this chart to find the laws for every state on your traveling route.

TORONTO — D5 *Toronto*

TORONTO See also Alliston, Bradford, Campbellville, Cookstown, Fergus, Hamilton, Lindsay, Milton, Niagara Falls, Pelham, Port Perry, Puslinch, St Catherines, Sandford, Shelburne & Vineland, ON; Gasport, Lockport & Niagara Falls, NY.

GLEN ROUGE CAMPGROUND (Public) From Jct of Hwy 401 & (E-bnd) exit 390 (W-bnd) exit 392, E 0.6 mi on Kingston Rd (L). 114 Avail: 87 W, 87 E (15/30 amps). 2021 rates: $33 to $43.50. May 13 to Nov 01. (855)811-0111

INDIAN LINE CAMPGROUND (Public) From Jct of Hwy 401 & Hwy 427, N 5.6 km (3.5 mi) on Hwy 427 to Finch Ave, W 0.8 km (0.5 mi) (R). 247 Avail: (15/50 amps). 2021 rates: $34.50 to $50. May 01 to Oct 31. (855)811-0111

TOTTENHAM — D5 *Simcoe*

TOTTENHAM CONSERVATION AREA (Public Prov Park) From jct Hwy 9 & CR 10: Go 6.4 km/4 mi N on CR 10, then 1/2 km/1/4 mi W on Mill St. 76 Avail: (15/30 amps). 2021 rates: $25 to $30. (705)435-4030

UPSALA — F7 *Thunder Bay*

PINE POINT RESORT **Ratings: 6/7/7.5** (Campground) 28 Avail: 21 full hkups, 7 W, 7 E (30 amps). 2021 rates: $36 to $37. (807)986-1300, Lac Des Milles Lac Road South, Upsala, ON P0T 2Y0

THUNDERBIRD RESORT & CAMPGROUND
(Campground) (Not Visited) From jct ON 17 & Lac Des Mille Lacs Rd: Go 2.3 km/1-1/2 mi S on Lac Des Mille Lacs Rd, then 0.7 km/1/2 mi SE on Cushing Lake Loop Rd (E). **FAC:** gravel rds. (60 spaces). Avail: 10 grass, 10 pull-thrus, (35x75), 10 W, 10 E (30 amps), seasonal sites, WiFi, tent sites, rentals, dump, fire rings. **REC:** Lac Des Mille Lacs: swim, fishing, marina, kayaking/canoeing, boating nearby, hunting nearby. Pets OK. 2021 rates: $30 to $90. May 15 to Sep 30. no cc.
(807)986-2332 Lat: 48.940516, Lon: -90.491496
249 Cushing Lake Loop Rd, Upsala, ON P0T 2Y0
thunderbirdresort.net
See ad page 1129

UPSALA CAMPGROUND **Ratings: 3.5/6/6** (Campground) 11 Avail: 11 W, 11 E (30 amps). 2021 rates: $40. May 15 to Sep 15. (807)986-2312, 4850 Hwy 17, Upsala, ON P0T 2Y0

VERMILION BAY — E7 *Kenora*

BLUE BIRD TRAILER & CAMPSITE **Ratings: 4.5/6.5/7.5** (Campground) 30 Avail: 25 full hkups, 5 W, 5 E (30/50 amps). 2021 rates: $55. May 15 to Oct 30. (807)227-2042, 144 Myers Road, Vermilion Bay, ON P0V 2V0

BLUE LAKE (Public Prov Park) From town, N 5 mi on Hwy 647 (L). Avail: 108 E (15/30 amps). 2021 rates: $13.88 to $43.75. May 18 to Sep 16. (807)227-2601

CRYSTAL LAKE CAMPGROUND RV PARK **Ratings: 7/8.5★/8.5** (Campground) 28 Avail: 15 full hkups, 13 W, 13 E (30/50 amps). 2021 rates: $33.25 to $35.50. May 15 to Sep 15. (807)220-5467, 167 Hanslips Road , Vermilion Bay, ON P0V 2V0

VERONA — C8 *Frontenac*

DESERT LAKE FAMILY RESORT **Ratings: 6/7/7.5** (Campground) 30 Avail: 7 full hkups, 23 W, 23 E (30 amps). 2021 rates: $55 to $59. May 01 to Oct 09. (613)374-2196, 2466 Desert Lake Road, RR 1, Hartington, ON K0H 1W0

VINELAND — E5 *Niagara*

N.E.T. CAMPING RESORT
Ratings: 10/10★/9 (Campground) 101 Avail: 90 full hkups, 11 W, 11 E (30/50 amps). 2021 rates: $55 to $75. May 01 to Oct 15. (866)490-4745, 2325 Regional Road 24, Box 541, Vineland, ON L0R 2C0

WABIGOON — E7 *Kenora*

WABIGOON LAKE RV PARK **Ratings: 6.5/9★/7** (RV Park) Avail: 11 full hkups (15/50 amps). 2021 rates: $35. Apr 20 to Oct 12. (807)938-6432, 10188 Hwy 17, Wabigoon, ON P0V 2W0

Each privately owned campground has been rated three times. The first rating is for development of facilities. The second one is for cleanliness and physical characteristics of restrooms and showers. The third is for campground visual appearance and environmental quality.

WALTON — D4 *Huron*

FAMILY PARADISE CAMPGROUND **Ratings: 7.5/8★/8** (Campground) 40 Avail: 4 full hkups, 36 W, 36 E (30 amps). 2021 rates: $52 to $77. May 07 to Oct 20. (519)527-0629, 43835 Hullett-Mckillop Road, RR 4, Walton, ON N0K 1Z0

WARSAW — D6 *Peterborough*

WARSAW CAVES CONSERVATION AREA (Public Prov Park) From town: Go 4 km/2-1/2 mi N on CR 4. 52 Avail. 2021 rates: $45. May 08 to Oct 12. (705)652-3161

WASAGA BEACH — C5 *Simcoe*

CEDAR GROVE CAMPGROUND **Ratings: 5.5/8.5★/6.5** (RV Park) Avail: 75 full hkups (30 amps). 2021 rates: $65 to $75. May 01 to Oct 01. (705)429-2134, 100 Cedar Grove Parkway, Wasaga Beach, ON L9Z 1T5

GATEWAY CAMPING **Ratings: 6/7.5/7.5** (Campground) 48 Avail: 40 full hkups, 8 W, 8 E (15/30 amps). 2021 rates: $50 to $65. May 15 to Oct 15. (705)429-5862, 186 Main St, Wasaga Beach, ON L9Z 2L2

WASAGA DUNES FAMILY CAMPGROUND - PARKBRIDGE **Ratings: 7.5/8.5/8** (Campground) Avail: 4 full hkups (30/50 amps). 2021 rates: $73. May 15 to Oct 15. (705)322-3130, 4300 County Road 29, Wyevale, ON L0L 2T0

WASAGA PINES FAMILY CAMPGROUND - PARKBRIDGE **Ratings: 7.5/8.5/8.5** (Campground) 34 Avail: 10 full hkups, 24 W, 24 E (30 amps). 2021 rates: $53.11 to $73.45. May 08 to Oct 14. (705)322-2727, 1780 County Road 92, Elmvale, ON L0L 1P0

WATERLOO — E4 *Waterloo*

GREEN ACRE PARK **Ratings: 8.5/10★/8.5** (RV Park) 91 Avail: 51 full hkups, 40 W, 40 E (30/50 amps). 2021 rates: $48 to $76. Mar 01 to Dec 31. (519)885-1758, 580 Beaver Creek Road, Waterloo, ON N2J 3Z4

LAUREL CREEK CONSERVATION AREA (Public) From Jct of Hwy 86 North & Northfield Dr (CR-22), W 1 mi on CR-22 to Westmount Rd N, N 0.2 mi (L). 120 Avail: 76 W, 76 E (15/30 amps). 2021 rates: $26 to $44. May 01 to Oct 15. (519)884-6620

WATFORD — E3 *Lambton*

WARWICK CONSERVATION AREA (Public) From Jct of Hwy 402 & CR 9 (exit 44), N 0.9 mi to CR 22, W 3.5 mi (L). 181 Avail: 181 W, 181 E (30 amps). 2021 rates: $30.40. May 01 to Oct 11. (519)849-6770

WAWA — F9 *Algoma*

LAKE SUPERIOR/AGAWA BAY (Public Prov Park) On Hwy 17, 5 mi N of S Park boundary (L). Avail: 38 E (15/30 amps). 2021 rates: $32.90 to $51.42. May 02 to Oct 14. (705)856-2284

LAKE SUPERIOR/RABBIT BLANKET LAKE (Public Prov Park) From town, 17 mi S on Hwy 17 (L). Avail: 20 E (15/30 amps). 2021 rates: $32.90 to $51.42. May 16 to Oct 26. (705)856-2284

WAWA RV RESORT & CAMPGROUND
Ratings: 8.5/9★/8.5 (Campground) N-bnd: From Jct of Hwys 101 & 17 N, W 1.6 km (1 mi) on Hwy 17 N to Magpie River Rd, S 275 m (900 ft) (L).

HOSPITALITY NORTHERN ONTARIO STYLE!
On the Magpie River, we are the perfect stop along the beautiful northeastern shores of Lake Superior. Quiet & secluded, yet easy on & off Hwy 17 - Trans Canada. Enjoy a hike along our many trails or relax around our pool.
FAC: paved/gravel rds. (80 spaces). Avail: 60 gravel, 19 pull-thrus, (25x60), back-ins (30x40), 10 full hkups, 40 W, 40 E (30/50 amps), seasonal sites, WiFi @ sites, tent sites, rentals, dump, mobile sewer, laundry, fire rings, firewood, controlled access. **REC:** heated pool, hot tub, Magpie River: fishing, kayaking/canoeing, boating nearby, playground. Pets OK. eco-friendly. 2021 rates: $45 to $57. May 01 to Oct 31.
(877)256-4368 Lat: 47.98430, Lon: -84.80159
634-A Hwy 17 N, Wawa, ON P0S 1K0
wawarvresort.com
See ad this page

WEBBWOOD — A3 *Sudbury*

CHUTES (Public Prov Park) From town, N 0.5 mi on Hwy 553 (R). Avail: 79 E (15/30 amps). 2021 rates: $30.50 to $51.42. May 18 to Oct 09. (705)865-2021

WHEATLEY — F3 *Chatham-Kent*

CAMPERS COVE CAMPGROUND
Ratings: 8/10★/10 (Campground) 86 Avail: 73 full hkups, 13 W, 13 E (30/50 amps). 2021 rates: $59 to $150. May 03 to Oct 14. (519)825-4732, 21097 Campers Cove Road, Wheatley, ON N0P 2P0

LAKESIDE VILLAGE MOTEL & CAMPGROUND **Ratings: 7/8/8** (Campground) Avail: 31 full hkups (15/30 amps). 2021 rates: $46.75 to $50. May 01 to Oct 13. (519)825-4307, 2416 Talbot Trail RR1, Wheatley, ON N0P 2P0

WHEATLEY (Public Prov Park) From Jct of Hwy 3 & CR 1, E 0.6 mi on Hwy 3 to Klondike Rd S (E). Avail: 96 E (15/30 amps). 2021 rates: $16.81 to $51.42. Apr 13 to Oct 09. (519)825-4659

WHITE RIVER — F9 *Thunder Bay*

WHITE LAKE (Public Prov Park) From town, w 20 mi on Hwy 17 (L). Avail: 60 E (15/30 amps). 2021 rates: $16.81 to $51.42. May 18 to Sep 23. (807)822-2447

WHITEFISH — A4 *Sudbury (District)*

FAIRBANK (Public Prov Park) From town, N 2 mi on CR-4 (R). Avail: 40 E (30 amps). 2021 rates: $12.75 to $51.42. May 18 to Sep 03. (705)866-0530

WIARTON — C4 *Bruce*

BLUEWATER PARK CAMPGROUND (Public) From Jct of SR-6 & William St, E 0.1 mi on William St (L). 41 Avail: 41 W, 41 E (15 amps). 2021 rates: $40. May 15 to Oct 15. (519)534-1400

HOPE BAY CAMPGROUND **Ratings: 6/8/8** (Campground) 29 Avail: 13 full hkups, 8 W, 8 E (30 amps). 2021 rates: $50 to $70. May 05 to Oct 15. (519)534-1208, 2 Hope Bay Rd, South Bruce Peninsula, ON N0H 2T0

ROTH PARK FAMILY CAMPGROUND **Ratings: 7.5/7.5/8** (Campground) 54 Avail: 39 W, 39 E (15/30 amps). 2021 rates: $45 to $60. May 21 to Oct 14. (519)534-0145, 102 Parkside Avenue, South Bruce Peninsula, ON N0H 2T0

WINDSOR — F2 *Essex*

WINDSOR CAMPGROUND **Ratings: 8/8/7.5** (Campground) 110 Avail: 40 full hkups, 36 W, 36 E (30/50 amps). 2021 rates: $50 to $59.50. Apr 15 to Oct 15. (519)735-3660, 4855 9th Concession, Windsor, ON N0R 1K0

WOODSTOCK — E4 *Oxford*

PITTOCK CONSERVATION AREA (Public) From Jct of Hwy 401 (exit 230) & Sweaburg Rd, N 2 mi on Sweaburg Rd (Mill St) to Hwy 2, E 100 yds to Hwy 59, N 3.9 mi on Hwy 59 to Pittock Park Rd, NE 0.9 mi (R). Avail: 100 E (15/30 amps). 2021 rates: $35 to $45. Apr 23 to Oct 18. (519)539-5088

WILLOW LAKE CAMPGROUND & RV PARK **Ratings: 8/8.5★/9.5** (Campground) Avail: 38 full hkups (30/50 amps). 2021 rates: $58 to $75. Apr 26 to Oct 06. (519)537-7301, 595487 County Road 59, Woodstock, ON N4S 7W1

WYOMING — E3 *Lambton*

COUNTRY VIEW MOTEL & RV RESORT **Ratings: 8.5/10★/9.5** (Campground) 62 Avail: 22 full hkups, 40 W, 40 E (30/50 amps). 2021 rates: $50 to $64. Apr 15 to Oct 22. (519)845-3394, 4569 London Line, Wyoming, ON N0N 1T0

ON

YOU ARE HERE
DID YOU KNOW?
Lucy Maud Montgomery published Anne of Green Gables in 1908. You can visit the house featured in the book.

Getty Images/iStockphoto

Prince Edward Island

Slow things down on the leisurely getaway on the Atlantic. Tee off at world-class links when the sun comes up, relax on red-sand beaches in the afternoon and finish off your day with a delicious seafood feast.

Hit the Shore

Take your choice between white- and red-sand beaches at beautiful Prince Edward Island National Park, where swimming is a popular pastime. The 37-mile park is also known for the Greenwich sand dunes, a delicate ecosystem not normally found in North America. You can walk the 900-acre area by following the extensive trail system and floating boardwalk. Make sure to stop by the Greenwich Interpretation Center to uncover 10,000 years of the region's natural history.

Go to the Green Gables

The famous "Ann of Green Gables" novels were penned here, and you can experience them at Green Gables Heritage Place. From walking through the former home of author Lucy Maud Montgomery to admiring the pastoral farmland that inspired the books, you'll get to experience Anne's world and get a glimpse of life on the island in the 1800s.

Charlottetown Hot Spots

Popular activities in the capital include exploring historic buildings on Victoria Row, soaking up sweeping ocean views from Peake's Wharf and sipping craft beer at the PEI Brewing Company. Go on a beer tasting tour and sample hops across town.

A Province of Play

Get some cardio in during your visit. Swim in warm salt water and sink your feet in the "singing sands" of Basin Head Provincial Park. The 270-mile Confederation Trail is a must if you're an avid cyclist in search of scenic rides.

Prince Edward Island Mussels

Prince Edward Island has been called Canada's Food Island for a good reason. The nation's smallest province is a virtual powerhouse of seafood, fruit and vegetables. Are you having a hard time choosing your next PEI meal? Order rich, delicious mussels. The clear water surrounding the island and the nutrient-rich environment have resulted in grit-free, tender morsels that have earned worldwide acclaim.

VISITOR CENTER

TIME ZONE
Atlantic Standard

ROAD & HIGHWAY INFORMATION
902-368-5100
princeedwardisland.ca

FISHING & HUNTING INFORMATION
800-236-5196
princeedwardisland.ca/en/topic/fishing-hunting-trapping-licences

BOATING INFORMATION
800-267-6687
tc.gc.ca/boatingsafety

NATIONAL PARKS
pc.gc.ca/en/pn-np

PROVINCIAL PARKS
tourismpei.com/pei-provincial-parks

TOURISM INFORMATION
Prince Edward Island Tourism
800-463-4PEI
tourismpei.com

TOP TOURISM ATTRACTIONS
1) Confederation Trail
2) Green Gables Heritage Place
3) Prince Edward Island-National Park

MAJOR CITIES
Charlottetown (capital), Summerside, Stratford, Cornwall, Montague

good sam park Featured Good Sam Park

PRINCE EDWARD ISLAND

When you stay with Good Sam, you can expect the highest degree of cleanliness and friendliness, and better yet, you get **10% off** overnight campground fees.

If you're not already a Good Sam member you can purchase your membership at this location:

CAVENDISH
Marco Polo Land

Getty Images/iStockphoto

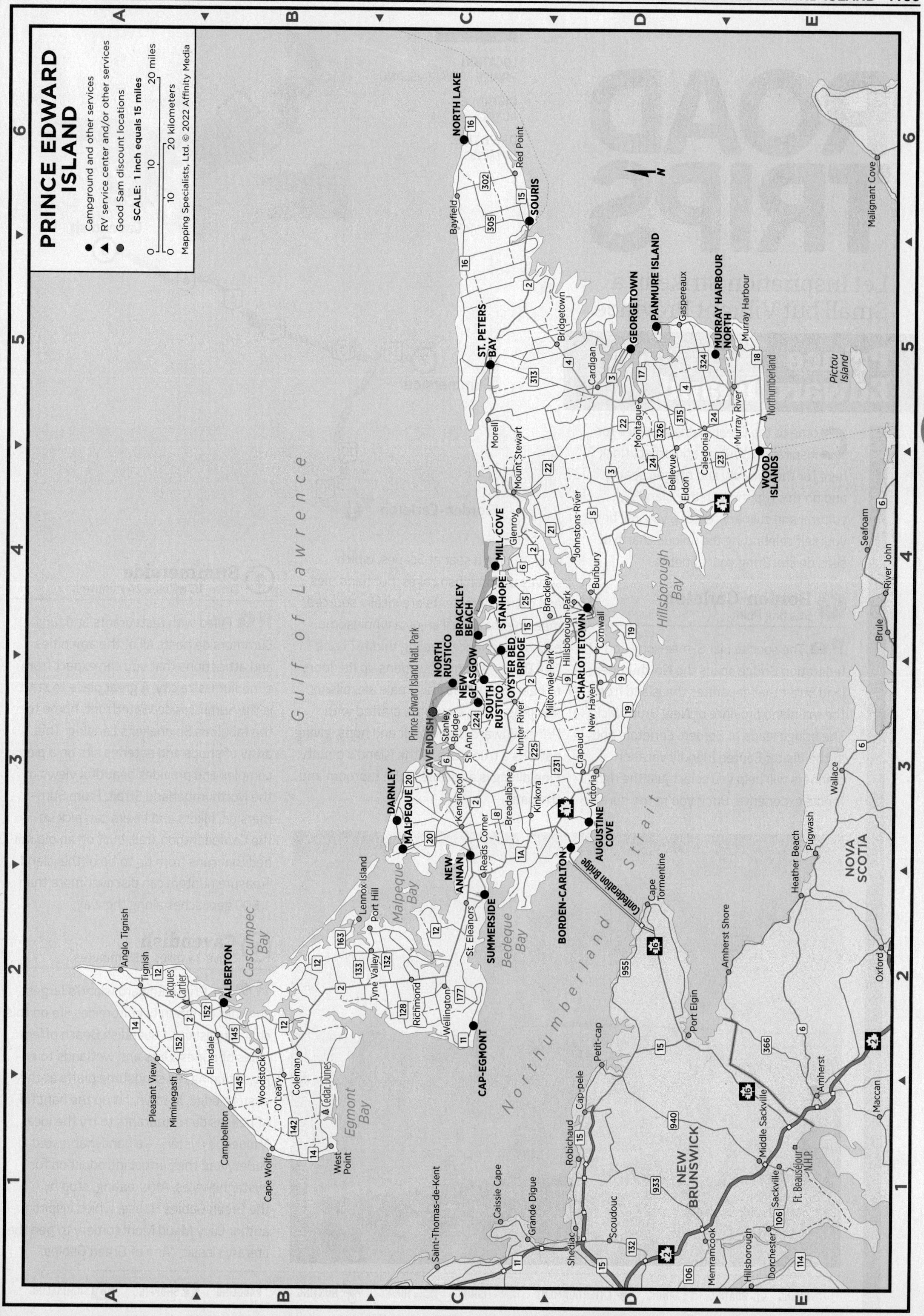
PRINCE EDWARD ISLAND
Campground and other services
RV service center and/or other services
Good Sam discount locations
SCALE: 1 inch equals 15 miles
0 10 20 miles
0 10 20 kilometers
Mapping Specialists, Ltd. © 2022 Affinity Media
Gulf of Lawrence
Northumberland Strait
Hillsborough Bay
Malpeque Bay
Bedeque Bay
Egmont Bay
Cascumpec Bay
Prince Edward Island Natl. Park
Confederation Bridge
NEW BRUNSWICK
NOVA SCOTIA
Pictou Island
NORTH LAKE
SOURIS
Red Point
Bayfield
ST. PETERS BAY
Morell
Mount Stewart
MILL COVE
Glenroy
Bridgetown
GEORGETOWN
PANMURE ISLAND
Gaspereaux
MURRAY HARBOUR NORTH
Murray Harbour
Cardigan
Montague
Murray River
Northumberland
Bellevue
Eldon
Caledonia
WOOD ISLANDS
Johnstons River
Bunbury
STANHOPE
BRACKLEY BEACH
Brackley
Hillsborough Park
CHARLOTTETOWN
Cornwall
OYSTER BED BRIDGE
NORTH RUSTICO
NEW GLASGOW
SOUTH RUSTICO
Miltonvale Park
New Haven
CAVENDISH
Stanley Bridge
St. Ann
Hunter River
Crapaud
Victoria
AUGUSTINE COVE
BORDEN-CARLTON
Kinkora
Breadalbane
DARNLEY
MALPEQUE
Kensington
NEW ANNAN
Reads Corner
SUMMERSIDE
St. Eleanors
Lennox Island
Port Hill
Tyne Valley
Richmond
Wellington
CAP-EGMONT
ALBERTON
Tignish
Anglo Tignish
Jacques Cartier
Elmsdale
Pleasant View
Miminegash
Woodstock
O'Leary
Coleman
Cedar Dunes
Campbellton
Cape Wolfe
West Point
Cape Tormentine
Saint-Thomas-de-Kent
Caissie Cape
Grande Digue
Shediac
Scoudouc
Robichaud
Cap-pele
Petit-cap
Port Elgin
Amherst Shore
Memramcook
Hillsborough
Dorchester
Sackville
Ft. Beauséjour N.H.P.
Middle Sackville
Amherst
Maccan
Oxford
Heather Beach
Pugwash
Wallace
Brule
River John
Seafoam
Malignant Cove
PE

ROAD TRIPS

Let Inspiration Strike in a Small but Vibrant Province

Prince Edward Island

LOCATION
PRINCE EDWARD ISLAND

DISTANCE
40 MILES

DRIVE TIME
59 MINS

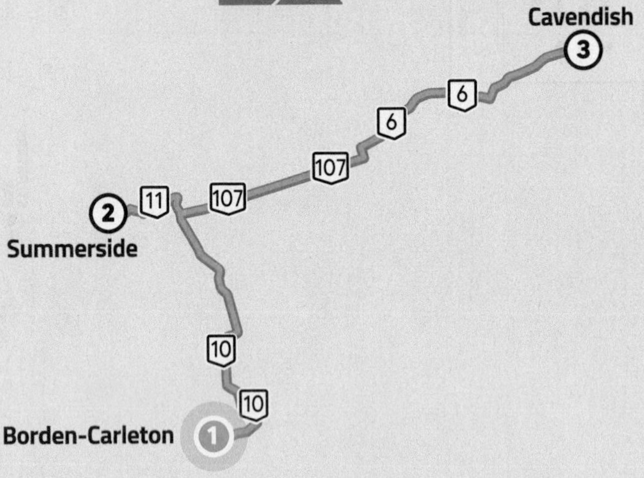

Come to the Green Gable province for inspiration. Writers and artists flock here for the serenity and rugged beauty, and on this trip through the island's cultural and culinary centers, you will find yourself celebrating the unique charm of seaside life. Bring your appetite.

1 Borden-Carleton
Starting Point

The spectacular 8-mile-long Confederation Bridge spans the Northumberland Strait that separates the island from the mainland province of New Brunswick. The bridge leads to Borden-Carleton, and at the Visitor Center, friendly vacation planners will help you select just the right foodie experience. But if you're too hungry to wait, take a seat at Scapes, which serves up fresh fish cakes, hot hand pies and more. Ingredients are locally sourced, meaning that you'll enjoy a wholesome eating experience. Feeling thirsty? Lone Oak Brewing Company opens up its doors to beer lovers who crave pale ale, pilsner and IPAs. Their brews are crafted with Prince Edward Island malt and hops, giving patrons a true taste of the island's bounty. Fine dining is available in the taproom and the patio.

Getty Images/iStockphoto

2 Summerside
Drive 16 miles ▪ 24 minutes

Filled with restaurants and fun, Summerside hosts all of the amenities and attractions that you can expect from a medium-size city. A great place to start is the Summerside Waterfront, home to the fabulous Spinnaker's Landing. This array of shops and eateries sits on a pier complex and provides beautiful views of the Northumberland Strait. From Summerside, hikers and bikers can pick up the Confederation Trail, built on an old rail bed that runs from tip to tip of the island. Treasure hunters can discover more than 1,600 geocaches along the way.

3 Cavendish
Drive 24 miles ▪ 35 minutes

Prince Edward Island's largest summer community epitomizes life on this charming island. Cavendish Beach offers miles of dunes, cliffs and wetlands to enjoy, including red sandstone bluffs at the eastern edge. In town, hit up the handful of beachside restaurants to try the local Malpeque oyster — a hand-harvested variety and the perfect introduction for oyster newbies. After eating, stop by the Green Gables House, which inspired author Lucy Maud Montgomery to pen the literary classic, "Ann of Green Gables."

BIKING · BOATING · DINING · ENTERTAINMENT · FISHING · HIKING · HUNTING · PADDLING · SHOPPING · SIGHTSEEING

Prince Edward Island SPOTLIGHTS

Reap Vacation Bounty in the 'Garden of the Gulf'

Explore sprawling farmlands, gorgeous shores and quaint towns on your trip to Canada's smallest province. See the house that inspired a bestselling novel and wander a boardwalk where lobster boats bring their hauls to the shore. See where Canada's Constitution was signed.

THE WILD FOXES OF PEI OFTEN VENTURE INTO THE PROVINCE'S CITIES.

Getty Images/iStockphoto

A kit fox surveys his surroundings in Prince Edward Island National Park.

Cavendish

Get back to simple living in a town that moves at its own slower pace. Stroll on uncrowded beaches and go shopping without big city hassles.

Beauty on the Beach

On Cavendish Beach, summertime means lounging on a towel or enjoying the water. Known for its creamy sand and red sandstone cliffs, the area is home to deep-sea fishing, horseback riding, parasailing and kayaking. Walk the Cavendish Duneland Trail to see a scenic coast. Take a ride on a nearby roller coaster then hit the links at the Cavendish Golf Club.

Prince Edward Island National Park

Travel into an iconic fictional world. This renowned national park is home to the Green Gables Heritage Place, the residence that inspired author Lucy Maude Montgomery to pen the classic novel, "Anne of Green Gables." Published in 1908, the story focuses on a precocious redheaded orphan and became a perennial bestseller; the residence it was partially based upon has been preserved in its original condition. The structure, with its distinctive gables, draws thousands of book buffs every year. Along the coast, the towering dunes of the beach form dramatic backdrops for hikers.

Charlottetown

The United States has Philadelphia, where the Declaration of Independence was signed in 1776. Canada has Charlottetown, where Canada united to become a country during the Charlottetown Conference in 1864. Stop here and where leaders set the direction of the United States' northern neighbor.

Live Through History

You can read about this history in book, or you can see it unfold live. Stroll through Charlottetown's historic district alongside the Confederation Players, a troupe of actors who tell the story of Canada's forefathers through reenactments in July and August. Amble along Peake's Wharf, walk in the footsteps of Canada's political legends and browse the dozens of waterfront shops.

Go Golfing

Golfers can pick from 20 courses in the Charlottetown area, with lush fairways and gorgeous views of the countryside. For adventurers who can't get enough of the sea, kayaks and paddleboards are perfect for traveling up the North River, the Hillsborough River and the Victoria Park coastline.

FOR MORE INFORMATION

Tourism PEI, 800-463-4734, www.tourismpei.com

Cavendish, welcomepei.com/destinations/cavendish-pei

Discover Charlottetown, 800-955-1864, www.discovercharlottetown.com

Green Gables, 902-368-4000, www.gov.pe.ca/greengables

PE

LOCAL FAVORITE

Spinach and Artichoke Dip

Enjoy Prince Edward Island's agricultural abundance with veggies that can be purchased at a local farmers market. *Recipe by John Sherwood.*

INGREDIENTS

- ☐ 14 oz bag of frozen chopped spinach, thawed/drained
- ☐ 1 cup mayonnaise
- ☐ 1 cup grated Parmesan cheese
- ☐ 1 8-oz bag of shredded mozzarella cheese
- ☐ ½ cup artichokes
- ☐ 2-3 garlic cloves
- ☐ Salt & pepper to taste

DIRECTIONS

Preheat oven to 400° F. Mix chopped thawed/drained spinach, mayo, Parmesan cheese, mozzarella in large bowl. Finely chop garlic by hand or in food processor, then add to bowl. Chop artichokes by hand or in food processor, then add to bowl. Add Salt and Pepper and mix well.

Spoon Mixture into an 8"x8" pan. Sprinkle additional salt and pepper to taste and sprinkle additional mozzarella cheese on top. Bake uncovered at 400 F° for 30-40 mins (until top is browned). Serve warm with pita chips, crackers, etc.

Prince Edward Island

ALBERTON — B2 *Prince*

JACQUES CARTIER (Public Prov Park) From Jct of Hwys 2 & 150, W 12 mi on Hwy 150 to Hwy 12, N 20 mi to Jacques Cartier Entrance, NE 0.25 mi (R). 51 Avail: 20 full hkups, 31 W, 31 E (15/30 amps). 2021 rates: $34 to $39. Jun 04 to Sep 12. (877)445-4938

AUGUSTINE COVE — D3 *Prince*

CUMBERLAND COVE CAMPGROUND **Ratings: 6/7/8** (Campground) 24 Avail: 8 W, 8 E (15 amps). 2021 rates: $33.35. Jun 01 to Sep 15. (902)855-2961, RR #1, Albany, PE C0B 1A0

BORDEN-CARLETON — D3 *Prince*

BORDEN/SUMMERSIDE KOA Ratings: 9.5/9.5★/10 (Campground) 50 Avail: 40 full hkups, 10 W, 10 E (30/50 amps). 2021 rates: $39 to $58. Jun 01 to Sep 30. (800)562-3319, 23714 TCH 1, Borden-Carleton, PE C0B 1X0

BRACKLEY BEACH — C4 *Queens*

VACATIONLAND RV PARK **Ratings: 8.5/6.5/8.5** (Campground) 124 Avail: 67 full hkups, 57 W, 57 E (30/50 amps). 2021 rates: $37.26 to $63.14. May 25 to Sep 19. (902)672-2317, 29 Vacationland Lane, Brackley Beach, PE C1A 7N9

CAP-EGMONT — C2 *Prince*

CEDAR DUNES (Public Prov Park) From Jct of Hwys 2 & 14, SW 12 mi on Hwy 14 (L). 69 Avail: 23 full hkups, 46 W, 46 E (15 amps). 2021 rates: $34 to $39. Jun 05 to Sep 13. (877)445-4938

CAVENDISH — C3 *Queens*

CAVENDISH KOA **Ratings: 8/10★/9** (Campground) 215 Avail: 137 full hkups, 75 W, 75 E (30/50 amps). 2021 rates: $44.50 to $69.75. May 25 to Oct 01. (800)562-1879, 198 Forest Hill Lane, Hunter River, PE C0A 1N0

Prince Edward Island Privately Owned Campground Information Updated by our Good Sam Representatives

Patrice Richard & Chantal Belisle

We sold everything in 2002, then traveled in Canada coast to coast, U.S. (44 states) and Mexico. We're Frenchies who switch from one culture to another. La vie est trop courte, il faut la prendre en riant. Life's too short so take it with a laugh.

CAVENDISH SUNSET CAMPGROUND **Ratings: 8/9★/8.5** (Campground) 365 Avail: 135 full hkups, 115 W, 115 E (30/50 amps). 2021 rates: $47 to $55.50. Jun 15 to Sep 03. (902)963-2440, 9095 Rte 6, Cavendish, PE C0A 1M0

MARCO POLO LAND

good sam park **Ratings: 8.5/10★/10** (Campground) From Jct of Rtes 6 & 13, S 0.5 mi on Rte 13 (L). **FAC:** all weather rds. (618 spaces). 400 Avail: 24 gravel, 376 grass, 90 pull-thrus, (35x85), back-ins (40x90), 259 full hkups, 141 W, 141 E (30/50 amps), seasonal sites, WiFi @ sites, tent sites, rentals, dump, laundry, groc, LP bottles, fire rings, firewood, restaurant, controlled access. **REC:** wading pool, pond, boating nearby, playground. Pets OK. Partial handicap access. Big rig sites, eco-friendly. 2021 rates: $40 to $60. May 25 to Oct 08. ATM.
(902)963-2352 Lat: 46.482455, Lon: -63.370724
7406 Route 13, Cavendish, PE C0A 1N0
marcopololand.ca
See ad this page

PRINCE EDWARD ISLAND/CAVENDISH (Public National Park) From town, W 2 mi off Rte 6 on Gulf Shore Pky (E). Natl Park personal use permit required. **FAC:** gravel rds. Avail: 302 grass, 80 pull-thrus, (20x40), back-ins (20x40), 83 W, 78 S, 83 E (15/20 amps), tent sites, dump, laundry, firewood. **REC:** pool, Gulf of St-Lawrence: swim, fishing, kayaking/canoeing, playground, rec open to public. Pets OK. Partial handicap access, 14 day max stay. 2021 rates: $27.40 to $35.30. Jun 11 to Sep 14.
(877)737-3783 Lat: 46.49726, Lon: -63.408291
357 Graham's Lane, New Glasgow, PE C0A 1N0
www.pc.gc.ca

RED ROCK RETREAT CAMPGROUND **Ratings: 7/7/8** (Campground) Avail: 18 full hkups (30 amps). 2021 rates: $42. May 20 to Sep 30. (902)963-3757, 230 Toronto Rd Extension , Green Gables, PE C0A 1N0

CHARLOTTETOWN — D4 *Queens*

CORNWALL KOA **Ratings: 8.5/9.5/9** (Campground) 275 Avail: 208 full hkups, 53 W, 53 E (30/50 amps). 2021 rates: $46.85 to $79.50. May 15 to Oct 12. (902)566-2421, 208 Ferry Rd., Cornwall, PE C0A 1H0

PINE HILLS RV PARK **Ratings: 9/10★/10** (Campground) 104 Avail: 66 full hkups, 38 W, 38 E (30/50 amps). 2021 rates: $40 to $56. Jun 01 to Sep 30. (877)226-2267, 1531 Brackley Pt Rd (Harrington), Charlottetown, PE C1E 1R1

Things to See and Do

PEI PROVINCIAL PARKS 8 province parks, heritage sites, day parks & golf courses. Jun 15 to Sep 15.. Hours: 9am to 5pm. No CC.
(877)445-4938
105 Rochford St, 3rd floor, Charlottetown, PE C1A 7N8
www.tourismpei.com/pei-provincial-parks

DARNLEY — C3 *Prince*

TWIN SHORES CAMPING AREA **Ratings: 9/10★/10** (Campground) Avail: 473 full hkups (30/50 amps). 2021 rates: $59 to $78. Jun 01 to Oct 01. (877)734-2267, 705 Lower Darnley Rd., Kensington, PE C0B 1M0

GEORGETOWN — D5 *Kings*

BRUDENELL RIVER (Public Prov Park) From Jct of Hwys 3 & 4, E 5 mi on Hwy 3 to Brundenel Provincial Rd S 0.1 mi (L). 43 Avail: 25 full hkups, 18 W, 18 E (15/30 amps). 2021 rates: $34 to $39. Jun 05 to Oct 12. (877)445-4938

MALPEQUE — C3 *Prince*

CABOT BEACH (Public Prov Park) Jct of Hwy 2 & 20: Go 6 mi on Rte 20 follow signs (L). 76 Avail: 33 full hkups, 43 W, 43 E (15/30 amps). 2021 rates: $34 to $39. Jun 05 to Sep 20. (877)445-4938

MILL COVE — C4 *Queens*

WINTER BAY TENT & TRAILER PARK **Ratings: 6/7.5/7** (Campground) 68 Avail: 30 full hkups, 15 W, 15 E (15/30 amps). 2021 rates: $30 to $35. May 15 to Sep 25. (902)672-2834, RR 1 95 Donaldston, Mount Stewart, PE C0A 1P0

MURRAY HARBOUR NORTH — D5 *Kings*

SEAL COVE CAMPGROUND **Ratings: 7.5/8★/9** (Campground) 66 Avail: 37 full hkups, 29 W, 29 E (30 amps). 2021 rates: $40 to $56. May 16 to Sep 21. (902)962-2745, RR 4, Murray Harbour N, Montague, PE C0A 1R0

NEW ANNAN — C3 *Prince*

CRYSTAL BEACH CAMPGROUND **Ratings: 8.5/8★/8** (Campground) 108 Avail: 82 full hkups, 26 W, 26 E (15/30 amps). 2021 rates: $38 to $50. May 16 to Sep 29. (902)436-4984, 178 Crystal Dr., New Annan, PE C1N 4J8

NEW GLASGOW — C3 *Queens*

NEW GLASGOW HIGHLANDS **Ratings: 8/9.5★/9.5** (Campground) Avail: 15 full hkups (30/50 amps). 2021 rates: $36 to $52. May 01 to Oct 31. (902)964-3232, RR3 2497 Hwy 224, Hunter River, PE C0A 1N0

NORTH LAKE — C6 *Kings*

CAMPBELL'S COVE CAMPGROUND **Ratings: 7/7/7.5** (Campground) 42 Avail: 8 full hkups, 12 W, 12 E (15/30 amps). 2021 rates: $38.26 to $45.22. May 20 to Sep 20. (902)357-2233, 538 RR #4, Elmira, PE C0A 2B0

NORTH RUSTICO — C3 *Queens*

WHITE SANDS COTTAGES & CAMPGROUND **Ratings: 6.5/7.5/7.5** (Campground) 30 Avail: 3 full hkups, 27 W, 27 E (30 amps). 2021 rates: $22 to $48. May 05 to Sep 30. (902)963-2532, 226 Cape Rd, North Rustico, PE C0A 1X0

OYSTER BED BRIDGE — C4 *Queens*

BAYSIDE RV CAMPGROUND **Ratings: 8/7.5/9** (Campground) 38 Avail: 22 full hkups, 16 W, 16 E (30 amps). 2021 rates: $35 to $40. May 30 to Sep 14. (902)621-0144, 112 Camp Rd, Oyster Bed Bridge, PE C1E 0L4

PANMURE ISLAND — D5 *Kings*

PANMURE ISLAND (Public Prov Park) From Jct of Hwys 1&4 N 12 mi on Rte 4 to Rte 17 11 mi follow signs to Rte 347 (R). 22 Avail: 22 W, 22 E (15 amps). 2021 rates: $34 to $36. Jun 05 to Sep 13. (877)445-4938

SOURIS — C6 *Kings*

RED POINT (Public Prov Park) On Rte 16, E 6 mi to Souris (R). 98 Avail: 58 full hkups, 40 W, 40 E (15/30 amps). 2021 rates: $34 to $39. Jun 04 to Sep 19. (877)445-4938

SOUTH RUSTICO — C3 *Queens*

CYMBRIA TENT & TRAILER PARK **Ratings: 8.5/7/9** (Campground) 90 Avail: 44 full hkups, 17 W, 17 E (20/30 amps). 2021 rates: $29 to $45. May 28 to Sep 08. (902)963-2458, RR 3 0729 Grandpere Point Rd, Hunter River, PE C0A 1N0

ST PETERS BAY — C5 *Kings*

ST PETERS PARK (Public) From Jct of Rtes 2 & 313: Go 1.21 km/3/4 mi W on Rte 2 (R). 81 Avail: 13 full hkups, 1 W, 1 E (30 amps). 2021 rates: $22 to $28. Jun 15 to Sep 17. (902)961-2786

STANHOPE — C4 *Queens*

PRINCE EDWARD ISLAND/STANHOPE (Public National Park) From Jct of Hwy 2 & Hwy 15: Go 15 mi N on Hwy 15, then 4-1/2 mi E on Gulf Shore Hwy (R). Natl park personal use permit required. 93 Avail: 20 full hkups, 73 W, 73 E (15/30 amps). 2021 rates: $27.40 to $35.30. Jun 16 to Sep 04. (877)737-3783

SUMMERSIDE — C2 *Prince*

LINKLETTER (Public Prov Park) From Jct Hwys 1 & 11 W 5 mi follow signs to 437 Linkletter Rd (R). 42 Avail: 25 full hkups, 17 W, 17 E (30/50 amps). 2021 rates: $34 to $39. Jun 07 to Sep 29. (877)445-4938

WOOD ISLANDS — E4 *Kings*

NORTHUMBERLAND (Public Prov Park) From ferry terminal, E 2 mi on Hwy 4 (R). 31 Avail: 20 full hkups, 11 W, 11 E (15 amps). 2021 rates: $34 to $36. Jun 05 to Sep 20. (877)445-4938

OFF SEASON RVING TIP: Off season amenities: Ask what's available. While it's obvious that you won't have access to amenities like pools, you should also note that some campgrounds close their camp stores and other useful amenities during the off-season. While urban and suburban campgrounds will have grocery stores nearby open year-round, if you are camping in a rural area, you may find yourself quite a distance from any type of store. Plan accordingly by packing plenty of groceries and firewood.

Getty Images/iStockphoto

YOU ARE HERE

Québec

DID YOU KNOW?

Hôtel de Glace is North America's only ice hotel. It's constructed every winter with 40,000 tons of snow and ice.

QC

Québec makes a dramatic departure from the other provinces. From French speakers to old-world streets, Québec has a cultural identity like nowhere else. Beyond its cities, you'll encounter gorgeous wilderness.

Quebec's Wild Side

North of Montréal, visitors can get up close and personal with North American wildlife. Take a drive through Mantigouche Wildlife Reserve to see bison, wolves, foxes and deer. The reserve has 417 lakes and 13 rivers. Many visitors are also surprised to discover Québec has a waterfall that's taller than the Niagara Falls. Standing at 272 feet tall, the Montmorency Falls is a beloved provincial treasure that offers a wealth of activities like hiking, ziplining and a gondola ride overlooking the spectacle.

Back in the Old World

Québec blends forward thinking city experiences with cityscapes that have stood for hundreds of years. Venture into the old part of Montréal to wander cobblestone streets, chic boutiques and sophisticated cafes. Located three hours northeast, Québec City invites you to explore the Petit Champlain District, one of North America's oldest neighborhoods. Take a break at La Petite Cabane à Sucre, which serves local maple syrup treats.

Paddle Power

Adventure on the water beckons paddlers to Saguenay Fjord, about 164 miles north of Québec City, for prime paddling environments. Sculpted by glaciers and spanning over 60 miles, this area is paradise if you're a kayaker. Paddle out far enough and you may even spot a family of belugas or humpback whales. Anglers, bring your gear, because fishing is another popular pastime here. Drop your rod in Lake Mistassini to catch trout and walleye or get on the St. Lawrence River to hook bass, carp and northern pike.

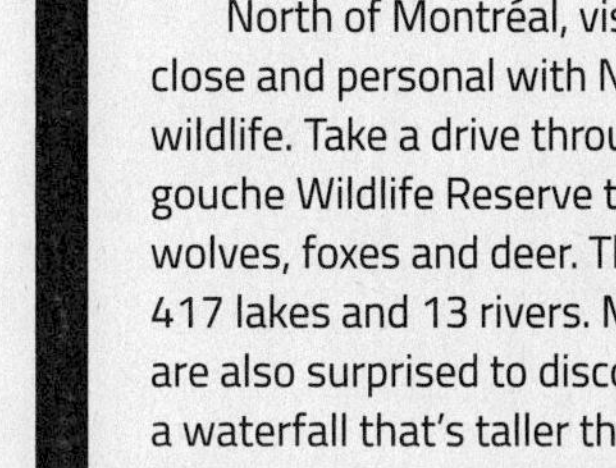

Québec Poutine

Poutine takes comfort food to another level. This delightful combination of French fries, cheese curds and gravy is served throughout the French-speaking province. In Montréal, La Banquise offers more than 30 types of poutine and is open 24 hours a day. You'll also find poutine served from food trucks and in roadside diners.

VISITOR CENTER

TIME ZONE
Eastern Standard

ROAD & HIGHWAY INFORMATION
888-355-0511
quebec511.info

FISHING & HUNTING INFORMATION
877-644-4545
quebec.ca/en/tourism-and-recreation

BOATING INFORMATION
800-267-6687
tc.gc.ca/boatingsafety

NATIONAL PARKS
pc.gc.ca/en/pn-np

PROVINCIAL PARKS
pc.gc.ca/en/voyage-travel/region/quebec

TOURISM INFORMATION
Tourisme Quebec
877-BONJOUR
bonjourquebec.com

TOP TOURISM ATTRACTIONS
1) Chateau Frontenac
2) Old Quebec
3) Plains of Abraham

MAJOR CITIES
Montréal, Quebec City (capital), Lava
Gatineau, Longueuil

good sam park Featured Good Sam Parks QUEBEC

When you stay with Good Sam, you can expect the highest degree of cleanliness and friendliness, and better yet, you get **10% off** overnight campground fees.

If you're not already a Good Sam member you can purchase your membership at one of these locations:

LEVIS
Camping Transit

MELBOURNE
Camping Melbourne Estrie

RIMOUSKI
Camping Rimouski

SAINT-ANTONIN
Camping Chez Jean

SAINT-BARTHELEMY
Camping du Vieux Moulin

SAINT-PHILIPPE
Camping la Cle des Champs RV Resort

10/10★/10 GOOD SAM PARK

SAINT-PHILIPPE
Camping la Cle des Champs RV Resort
(450)659-3389

What's This?

An RV park with a 10/10★/10 rating has scored perfect grades in amenities, cleanliness and appearance ("See Understanding the Campground Rating System" on pages 8 and 9 for an explanation of the trusted Good Sam Rating System). Stay in a 10/10★/10 park on your next trip for a nearly flawless camping experience.

Getty Images/iStockphoto

ROAD TRIPS

The Gaspé Peninsula Preserves Vast Wilderness

Québec

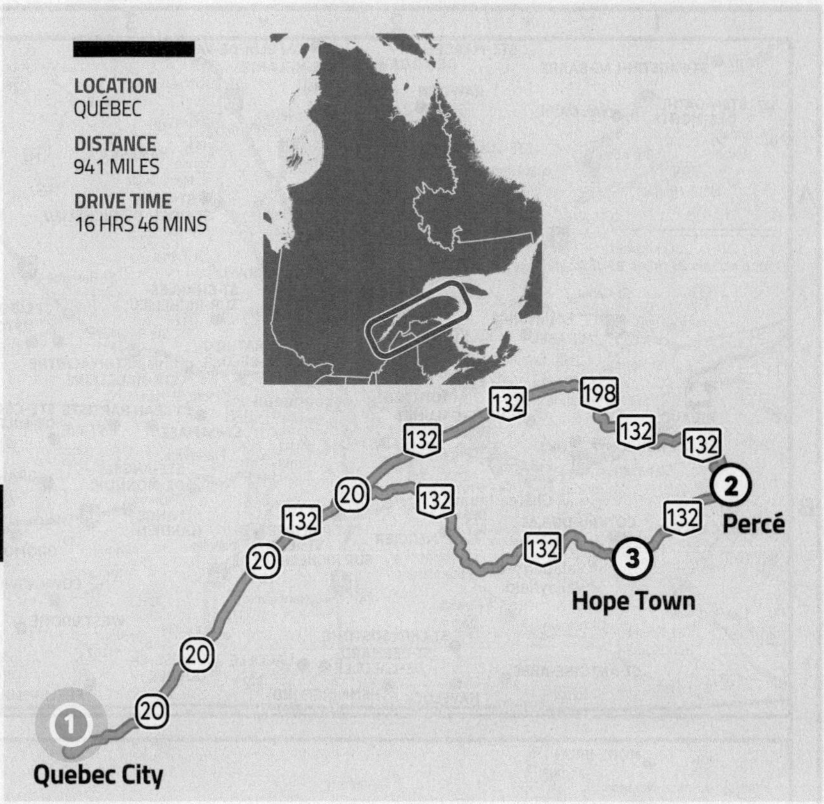

This trip begins along the banks of the St. Lawrence River in historic Québec City and leads travelers to the Gaspé Peninsula, a 11,998-square-mile expanse with rugged coasts and quaint fishing villages. Journey into the past on cobblestone streets and witness a natural attraction that has gained UNESCO status.

1 Québec City
Starting Point

Start from a French-Canadian metropolis that's a window into the region's storied past. Founded in 1535, the city's Old Town preserves several centuries-old stone buildings. Be sure to look at the Fairmont Le Château Frontenac, a hotel opened in 1893. Constructed in the elegant chateau-style design tradition of Canada's grand railway hotels, this building is considered to be the most photographed hotel in North America. Nosh on some Poutine at a cozy restaurant, then burn off those calories by following the Governeur's Walk, which leads to stunning views of the St. Lawrence River.

2 Percé
Drive 470 miles ▪ 8 hours, 16 minutes

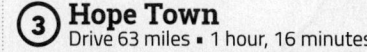

Amazing views of the rugged ocean coastline will highlight your drive along the Gaspé Peninsula. Along the coast facing the Gulf of St. Lawrence, visitors will be compelled to see the Percé Rock, a geological formation off the coast with 289-foot sheer cliffs. The 1,420-foot-long limestone monolith is named after the hole at the water level. At the UNESCO Global Geopark, travelers can observe the stunning rock from a glass platform suspended 660 feet above the ground. You can also kayak at the base of the daunting rock walls. Then take a boat excursion to nearby Bonaventure Island, home to boutiques, restaurants and cafés.

Getty Images/iStockphoto

3 Hope Town
Drive 63 miles ▪ 1 hour, 16 minutes

Use this dynamic coastal community as a launching pad for adventure in surrounding attractions. Down the coast to the west lies Bonaventure, home to Bioparc, an animal park that's home to 40 native animal species that are native to the Gaspé Peninsula. Visitors can hike an outdoor trail and help the animals at mealtime. Further west lies Miguasha National Park, site of fossils dating back 370 million years ago to the Devonian Period. See the preserved fossils then hike the shoreline, with gorgeous views of the Gulf of St. Lawrence.

Drive 408 miles, 7 hours, 14 minutes to return to your starting point of Québec City.

BIKING · BOATING · DINING · ENTERTAINMENT · FISHING · HIKING · HUNTING · PADDLING · SHOPPING · SIGHTSEEING

QC

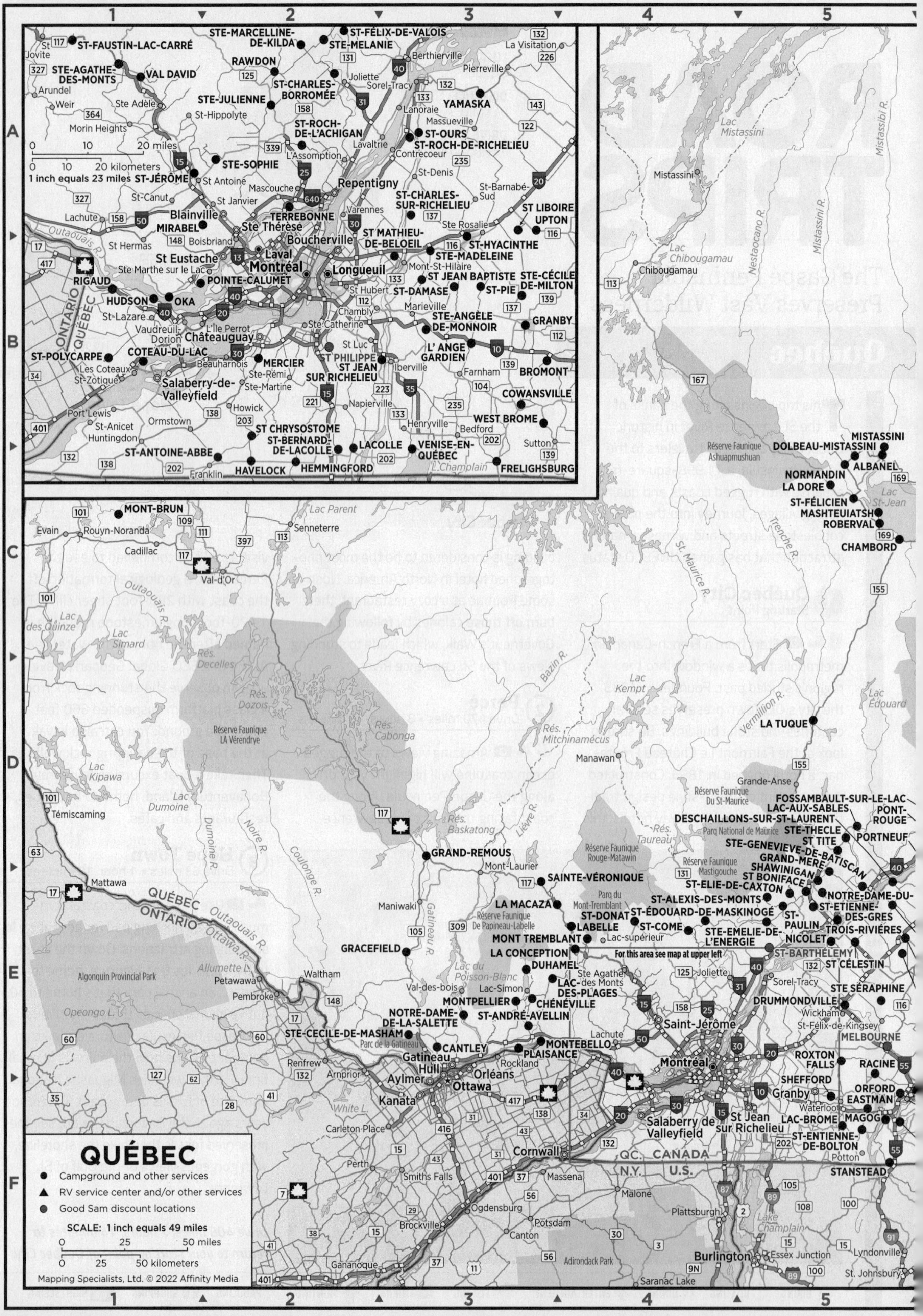
QUÉBEC
Campground and other services
RV service center and/or other services
Good Sam discount locations
SCALE: 1 inch equals 49 miles
0 25 50 miles
0 25 50 kilometers
Mapping Specialists, Ltd. © 2022 Affinity Media
1 inch equals 23 miles
0 10 20 miles
0 10 20 kilometers
For this area see map at upper left
ST-FAUSTIN-LAC-CARRÉ
STE-AGATHE-DES-MONTS
VAL DAVID
STE-MARCELLINE-DE-KILDA
ST-FÉLIX-DE-VALOIS
STE-MELANIE
RAWDON
ST-CHARLES-BORROMÉE
STE-JULIENNE
YAMASKA
ST-ROCH-DE-L'ACHIGAN
ST-OURS
ST-ROCH-DE-RICHELIEU
STE-SOPHIE
ST-JÉRÔME
Repentigny
ST-CHARLES-SUR-RICHELIEU
ST LIBOIRE
UPTON
Blainville
MIRABEL
TERREBONNE
Ste Thérèse
ST MATHIEU-DE-BELOEIL
ST-HYACINTHE
STE-MADELEINE
St Eustache
Laval
Boucherville
Montréal
Longueuil
RIGAUD
HUDSON
OKA
POINTE-CALUMET
ST JEAN BAPTISTE
STE-CÉCILE-DE-MILTON
ST-DAMASE
ST-PIE
STE-ANGÈLE-DE-MONNOIR
GRANBY
Châteauguay
ST-POLYCARPE
COTEAU-DU-LAC
MERCIER
ST PHILIPPE
ST JEAN SUR RICHELIEU
L' ANGE GARDIEN
BROMONT
Salaberry-de-Valleyfield
COWANSVILLE
WEST BROME
ST CHRYSOSTOME
ST-BERNARD-DE-LACOLLE
LACOLLE
VENISE-EN-QUÉBEC
ST-ANTOINE-ABBE
HAVELOCK
HEMMINGFORD
FRELIGHSBURG
ONTARIO
QUÉBEC
MONT-BRUN
Rouyn-Noranda
Val-d'Or
Réserve Faunique LA Vérendrye
GRAND-REMOUS
SAINTE-VÉRONIQUE
LA MACAZA
MONT TREMBLANT
LABELLE
ST-DONAT
GRACEFIELD
LA CONCEPTION
DUHAMEL
LAC-DES-PLAGES
CHÉNÉVILLE
MONTPELLIER
ST-ANDRÉ-AVELLIN
NOTRE-DAME-DE-LA-SALETTE
STE-CECILE-DE-MASHAM
CANTLEY
MONTEBELLO
PLAISANCE
Gatineau
Hull
Aylmer
Ottawa
Orléans
Kanata
Algonquin Provincial Park
Cornwall
MISTASSINI
DOLBEAU-MISTASSINI
ALBANEL
NORMANDIN
LA DORE
ST-FÉLICIEN
MASHTEUIATSH
ROBERVAL
CHAMBORD
LA TUQUE
FOSSAMBAULT-SUR-LE-LAC
LAC-AUX-SABLES
PONT-ROUGE
DESCHAILLONS-SUR-ST-LAURENT
STE-THECLE
ST TITE
PORTNEUF
STE-GENEVIEVE-DE-BATISCAN
GRAND-MERE
SHAWINIGAN
ST BONIFACE
ST-ELIE-DE-CAXTON
ST-ALEXIS-DES-MONTS
NOTRE-DAME-DU-
ST-ÉDOUARD-DE-MASKINOGÉ
ST-ETIENNE-DES-GRES
ST-COME
ST-PAULIN
TROIS-RIVIÈRES
STE-EMELIE-DE-L'ENERGIE
NICOLET
ST-BARTHÉLEMY
ST CÉLESTIN
STE SÉRAPHINE
DRUMMONDVILLE
Saint-Jérôme
MELBOURNE
ROXTON FALLS
RACINE
SHEFFORD
Granby
ORFORD
EASTMAN
MAGOG
LAC-BROME
St Jean sur Richelieu
Salaberry de Valleyfield
ST-ENTIENNE-DE-BOLTON
STANSTEAD
QC. CANADA
N.Y. U.S.
Burlington

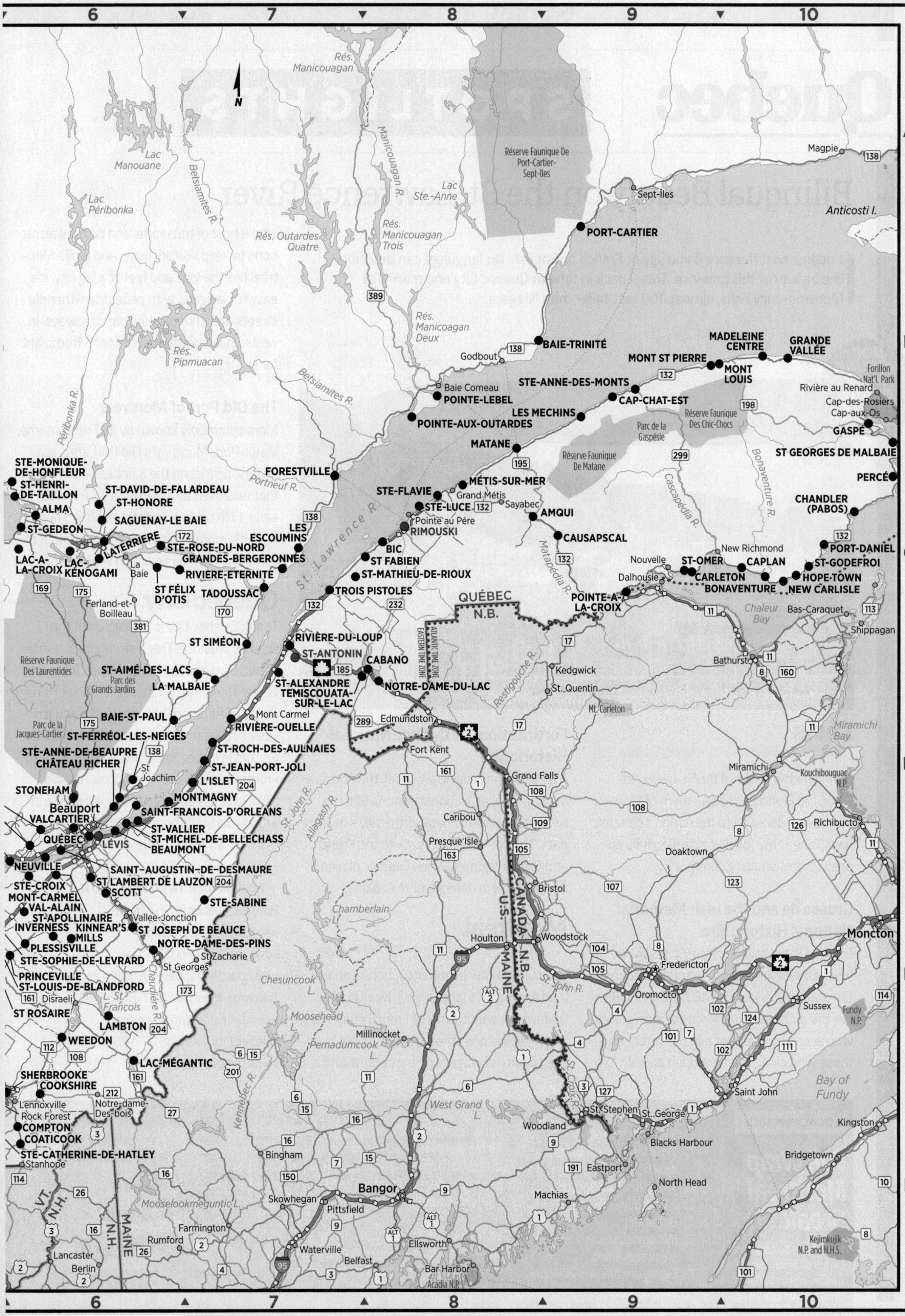

6
7
8
9
10
A
B
C
D
E
F
N
Rés. Manicouagan
Lac Manouane
Betsiamites R.
Manicouagan R.
Lac Ste.-Anne
Réserve Faunique De Port-Cartier-Sept-Iles
Magpie
138
Sept-Iles
Anticosti I.
Lac Péribonka
Rés. Outardes Quatre
Rés. Manicouagan Trois
PORT-CARTIER
389
Rés. Manicouagan Deux
Rés. Pipmuacan
BAIE-TRINITÉ
Godbout
MADELEINE CENTRE
GRANDE VALLÉE
MONT ST PIERRE
MONT LOUIS
Forillon Nat'l. Park
Betsiamites R.
Baie Comeau
POINTE-LEBEL
STE-ANNE-DES-MONTS
132
Rivière au Renard
Péribonka R.
CAP-CHAT-EST
198
Cap-des-Rosiers
Cap-aux-Os
LES MECHINS
Réserve Faunique Des Chic-Chocs
POINTE-AUX-OUTARDES
Parc de la Gaspésie
GASPÉ
MATANE
ST GEORGES DE MALBAIE
Réserve Faunique De Matane
299
Cascapédia R.
Bonaventure R.
195
STE-MONIQUE-DE-HONFLEUR
FORESTVILLE
MÉTIS-SUR-MER
PERCÉ
ST-HENRI-DE-TAILLON
Portneuf R.
ST-DAVID-DE-FALARDEAU
STE-FLAVIE
Grand Métis
Sayabec
CHANDLER (PABOS)
ST-HONORE
STE-LUCE
ALMA
AMQUI
138
Pointe au Pére
RIMOUSKI
ST-GEDEON
SAGUENAY-LE BAIE
LES ESCOUMINS
St. Lawrence R.
CAUSAPSCAL
132
172
ST-ROSE-DU-NORD
BIC
PORT-DANIEL
LATERRIERE
GRANDES-BERGERONNES
ST FABIEN
New Richmond
ST-GODEFROI
LAC-A-LA-CROIX
LAC-KENOGAMI
132
Nouvelle
ST-OMER
CAPLAN
La Baie
RIVIERE-ETERNITÉ
ST-MATHIEU-DE-RIOUX
Matapédia R.
Dalhousie
CARLETON
HOPE-TOWN
169
175
ST FÉLIX D'OTIS
TADOUSSAC
TROIS PISTOLES
BONAVENTURE
NEW CARLISLE
Ferland-et-Boilleau
232
QUÉBEC
N.B.
POINTE-A-LA-CROIX
132
11
Chaleur Bay
Bas-Caraquet
113
170
Shippagan
381
ST SIMÉON
RIVIÈRE-DU-LOUP
ATLANTIC TIME ZONE
EASTERN TIME ZONE
17
Réserve Faunique Des Laurentides
ST-ANTONIN
CABANO
Bathurst
11
185
Restigouche R.
Kedgwick
8
160
ST-AIMÉ-DES-LACS
Parc des Grands Jardins
ST-ALEXANDRE
LA MALBAIE
TEMISCOUATA-SUR-LE-LAC
NOTRE-DAME-DU-LAC
St. Quentin
Mt. Carleton
Mont Carmel
Parc de la Jacques-Cartier
175
BAIE-ST-PAUL
RIVIÈRE-OUELLE
289
Edmundston
17
11
Miramichi Bay
ST-FERRÉOL-LES-NEIGES
2
STE-ANNE-DE-BEAUPRE
138
ST-ROCH-DES-AULNAIES
Fort Kent
CHÂTEAU RICHER
ST-JEAN-PORT-JOLI
161
Miramichi
Kouchibouguac N.P.
St Joachim
L'ISLET
11
1
Grand Falls
STONEHAM
204
108
MONTMAGNY
St. John R.
Allagash R.
Beauport
SAINT-FRANCOIS-D'ORLEANS
108
VALCARTIER
Caribou
109
ST-VALLIER
126
Richibucto
QUÉBEC
LÉVIS
ST-MICHEL-DE-BELLECHASS
8
BEAUMONT
Presque Isle
11
105
NEUVILLE
SAINT-AUGUSTIN-DE-DESMAURE
163
Doaktown
STE-CROIX
ST LAMBERT DE LAUZON
204
MONT-CARMEL
SCOTT
107
Bristol
123
VAL-ALAIN
STE-SABINE
CANADA
U.S.
Chamberlain L.
ST-APOLLINAIRE
Vallee-Jonction
INVERNESS
KINNEAR'S MILLS
ST JOSEPH DE BEAUCE
Woodstock
Moncton
PLESSISVILLE
NOTRE-DAME-DES-PINS
11
Houlton
104
8
STE-SOPHIE-DE-LEVRARD
St Zacharie
95
N.B.
105
Fredericton
2
PRINCEVILLE
St Georges
Chesuncook L.
MAINE
St. John R.
1
ST-LOUIS-DE-BLANDFORD
173
Oromocto
161
Disraeli
L. St. François
Chaudière R.
ALT 2
4
102
114
ST ROSAIRE
Moosehead L.
2
124
Sussex
LAMBTON
204
Fundy N.P.
WEEDON
Millinocket
101
7
112
Pemadumcook L.
102
111
108
6
15
4
LAC-MÉGANTIC
1
St. Croix R.
201
SHERBROOKE
161
Kennebec R.
11
COOKSHIRE
212
6
3
127
Bay of Fundy
Lennoxville
Notre-dame-Des-bois
6
Saint John
Rock Forest
27
15
West Grand L.
St. Stephen
St. George
1
COMPTON
3
16
Kingston
COATICOOK
Woodland
2
16
9
Blacks Harbour
STE-CATHERINE-DE-HATLEY
Bingham
Stanhope
7
15
Bridgetown
16
191
Eastport
114
150
North Head
26
Bangor
9
10
VT.
N.H.
Mooselookmeguntic L.
Skowhegan
Pittsfield
Machias
MAINE
N.H.
3
16
Farmington
9
ALT 1
1
8
Rumford
2
ALT 1
Lancaster
26
Waterville
Ellsworth
Kejimkujik N.P. and N.H.S.
2
Berlin
2
4
95
3
Belfast
Bar Harbor
101
Acadia N.P.

QC

Quebec SPOTLIGHTS

Bilingual Beauty on the St. Lawrence River

It makes no difference if you speak French or English. No language can describe the beauty of this province. Travel back in time in Quebec City and marvel at Montmorency Falls, almost 100 feet taller than Niagara.

MONT-TREMBLANT'S COLOFUL BUILDINGS EVOKE THE SWISS ALPS.

Getty Images/iStockphoto
Mont-Tremblant doubles as a summer getaway and winter ski resort.

Lévis

Sitting on the banks of the St. Lawrence River, the French-Canadian town of Lévis opens up a doorway to the nation's dynamic past. Take in the following sites to fully appreciate this amazing community.

Grosse Île and the Irish Memorial National Historic Site

Located in the middle of the St. Lawrence River, Grosse île was a quarantine station for the port of Québec from 1832 to 1937. Relive the dramatic experiences of immigrants who set sail in hopes of a better future and those who cared for them upon arrival.

Fortifications of Québec National Historic Site

A jewel of the provincial capital, the Fortifications of Québec National Historic Site is a reminder of the richness of the city's military past. The site takes you back to the French and British regimes, when Québec played a deciding role in defense of the colony.

Montréal

The cultural capital of francophone Canada (and the region's largest city), Montréal features a beautiful mix of French influences, with cobblestone streets, beautiful old buildings, plenty of elegant dining options and a whole host of museums and cultural attractions to keep visitors busy. And while Montréal has the look and feel of a big city, it's easy to navigate, with pedestrian-friendly streets and underground passageways. In winter, head northwest to Mont-Tremblant for skiing.

The Old Port of Montréal

More commonly known by its French name, Vieux-Port, Montréal's Old Port area, is a historic district on the Saint Lawrence River that was used as a trading area from the early 17th century until the 1970s. These days it's more of a tourist area, with lots of cafes and a sandy beach on the waterway.

Québec City

Today, Québec City is the capital of the Québec province. This historic city is divided in two by steep bluffs into Upper Town and Lower Town. The Château Frontenac Hotel, Plains of Abraham battlefield site and the Québec Parliament are attractions that lure visitors in Upper Town. Within the Château Frontenac area, you'll find horse-drawn carriages, street entertainers, singers and artists, particularly at Old Québec's own open-air art gallery, Rue du Tresor.

FOR MORE INFORMATION

Bonjour Québec, 877-BONJOUR, www.bonjourquebec.com
Lévis, 418-838-6026, levis.chaudiereappalaches.com/en
Tourisme Montréal, 877-BONJOUR, www.tourisme-montreal.org
Quebec City Tourism, 877-783-1608, www.quebecregion.com

LOCAL FAVORITE

Foil Wrap Montréal Steak

Montréal is best known for Cirque de Soleil, beautiful winters and its special steak.
Recipe by Annette Joyner.

INGREDIENTS

- ☐ 8 Beef Lit'l Smokies
- ☐ 1 cup frozen hash browns, diced
- ☐ ½ cup broccoli florets
- ☐ 2 Tbsp olive oil
- ☐ Onion salt
- ☐ McCormick smoky Montreal steak seasoning
- ☐ Lipton dry onion mushroom soup and dip

DIRECTIONS

Spray large piece of aluminum foil with olive oil spray. Place potatoes on foil with smokies on top. Sprinkle a dash or two of onion seasoning on potatoes. Add olive oil and place broccoli on top. Stir a little to coat broccoli in oil. Sprinkle broccoli with Montreal steak seasoning. Season potatoes and smokies with soup mix until just covered.

Wrap well with foil and cook on the grill for about 20 minutes. You can speed up the process by microwaving the potatoes a bit beforehand. Unwrap foil carefully and enjoy!

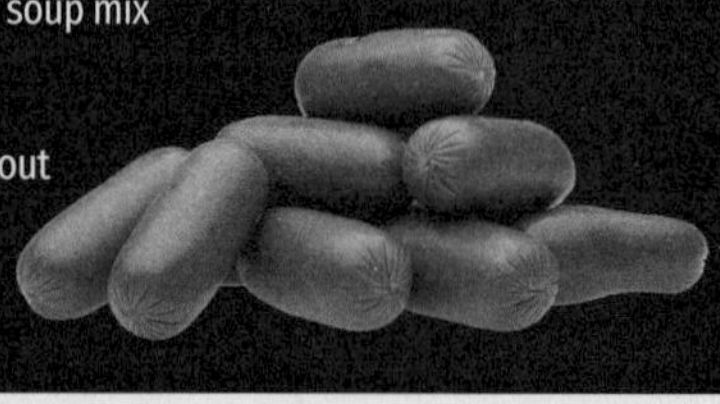

Quebec

ALBANEL — C5 *Saguenay-Lac-Saint-Jean*

CAMPING MUNICIPAL ALBANEL (Public) From center town: Go .4 km/400 m on Rte 169 (L). 72 Avail: 61 full hkups, 11 W, 11 E (15/30 amps). 2021 rates: $35 to $45. May 15 to Sep 04. (418)279-3374

ALMA — C6 *Saguenay-Lac-Saint-Jean*

CAMPING ALMA LA COLONIE (Campground) (Phone Update) 74 Avail: 48 full hkups, 26 W, 26 E (30/50 amps). 2021 rates: $40 to $50. May 15 to Sep 23. (418)662-9113, 700, chemin de la Baie-Moïse, Alma, QC G8B 5V5

DAM-EN-TERRE CENTRE DE VILLEGIATURE (Campground) (Phone Update) 239 Avail: 160 full hkups, 53 W, 53 E (30/50 amps). 2021 rates: $35.89 to $53.35. May 15 to Sep 13. (418)668-3016, 1385 Chemin De La Marina (C.P. 836), Alma, QC G8B 5W1

RESERVE FAUNIQUE DES LAURENTIDES/ CAMPING BELLE-RIVIERE (Public National Park) From jct Hwy 175 & Hwy 169: Go NW on Hwy 169 N to Laurentides Wildlife Reserve. 39 Avail. 2021 rates: $29.75. May 16 to Aug 30. (418)864-2161

AMQUI — C8 *Gaspesie*

CAMPING AMQUI (Public) From S Jct of Rte 195 & Rte 132: Go 4.8 km/3 mi W on Rte 132 (R). 102 Avail: 30 full hkups, 6 W, 66 E (30 amps). 2021 rates: $31 to $42. Jun 15 to Sep 03. (418)629-3433

BAIE-SAINT-PAUL — D6 *Quebec*

CAMPING DU GOUFFRE **Ratings: 8/10★/8.5** (Campground) 81 Avail: 64 full hkups, 17 W, 17 E (15/30 amps). 2021 rates: $45.49 to $51.75. May 10 to Sep 29. (418)435-2143, 439 St Laurent (C.P. 3164), Baie-Saint-Paul, QC G3Z 3B6

CAMPING LE GENEVRIER **Ratings: 8/9★/9** (Campground) 184 Avail: 97 full hkups, 87 W, 87 E (30/50 amps). 2021 rates: $34.79 to $59.15. May 01 to Oct 14. (418)435-6520, 1175 Monseigneur-de-Laval Blvd. (Rte 138), Baie-Saint-Paul, QC G3Z 2X4

PARC NATIONAL DES GRANDS-JARDINS (Public National Park) From jct Hwy 138 & Hwy 381: Go 21 km/13 mi N on Hwy 381 (R). 107 Avail. 2021 rates: $23.75 to $35. (418)439-1227

BAIE-TRINITE — B9 *Manicouagan*

CAMPING DOMAINE ENSOLEILLE (Campground) (Phone Update) Avail: 45 full hkups (20/30 amps). 2021 rates: $34.95 to $42. May 16 to Sep 14. (418)939-2002, 15 Rte 138 Est, Baie-Trinite, QC G0H 1A0

BEAUMONT — D6 *Chaudiere-Appalaches*

CAMPING GUILMETTE **Ratings: 9/10★/8.5** (Campground) 30 Avail: 28 full hkups, 2 W, 2 E (20/30 amps). 2021 rates: $44 to $63. May 15 to Sep 15. (418)837-6900, 152 Rue du Fleuve, Beaumont, QC G0R 1C0

BIC — C8 *Bas-Saint-Laurent*

PARC NATIONAL DU BIC/CAMPING RIOUX (Public National Park) From jct Hwy 20 & Hwy 132: Go 5.7 km/3-1/2 mi W on Hwy 132 (R). Avail: 31 E. 2021 rates: $23.25 to $37.75. (800)665-6527

BONAVENTURE — C10 *Gaspesie*

CAMPING PLAGE BEAUBASSIN (Public) From Center of Town: Go .4 km/1/4 mi E on Hwy 132, then .15 km/500 ft to Chemin Plage-De-Beaubassin, then .3 km/1000 ft E on Marina Drive (R). 234 Avail: 155 full hkups, 39 W, 77 E (15/30 amps). 2021 rates: $20 to $34. May 18 to Sep 22. (418)534-3246

BROMONT — B3 *Cantons de l'Est*

CAMPING PARC BROMONT **Ratings: 8.5/7.5/8** (Campground) 150 Avail: 82 full hkups, 68 W, 68 E (30/50 amps). 2021 rates: $30 to $85. Apr 19 to Oct 20. (450)534-2712, 24 Rue Lafontaine, Bromont, QC J2L 2S9

CAMPING VACANCES BROMONT **Ratings: 8.5/10★/8** (Campground) 308 Avail: 250 full hkups, 58 W, 58 E (30/50 amps). 2021 rates: $48 to $76. Apr 26 to Oct 20. (877)534-4434, 22 rue Bleury St, Bromont, QC J2L 1B3

GRANBY/BROMONT KOA **Ratings: 9.5/9.5★/9.5** (Campground) Avail: 120 full hkups (30/50 amps). 2021 rates: $46 to $95. Apr 15 to Oct 15. (450)534-2404, 1699 Shefford, Bromont, QC J2L 3N8

CABANO — D7 *Bas-Saint-Laurent*

CAMPING TEMILAC **Ratings: 8.5/10★/8** (Campground) 70 Avail: 55 full hkups, 15 W, 15 E (30 amps). 2021 rates: $38 to $45. May 11 to Sep 16. (418)854-7660, 33 Rue de La Plage, Cabano, QC G0L 1E0

CANTLEY — E3 *Outaouais*

CAMPING CANTLEY **Ratings: 8.5/9★/8.5** (Campground) 175 Avail: 125 full hkups, 50 W, 50 E (30/50 amps). 2021 rates: $40.50 to $51.50. May 15 to Sep 15. (819)827-1056, 100 Ch Ste Elisabeth, Cantley, QC J8V 3G4

CAP-CHAT-EST — B9 *Gaspesie*

CAMPING AU BORD DE LA MER **Ratings: 6.5/8.5/6.5** (Campground) Avail: 59 full hkups (15/30 amps). 2021 rates: $40 to $50. Jun 01 to Sep 30. (418)809-3675, 173 Notre Dame Est, Cap-Chat-Est, QC G0J 1G0

CAPLAN — C10 *Gaspesie*

CAMPING RUISSELET **Ratings: 8/UI/8** (Campground) Avail: 26 full hkups (30 amps). 2021 rates: $50. Jun 01 to Sep 05. (418)388-2138, 322 Blvd Perron Est (CP.1955), Caplan, QC G0C 1H0

CARLETON — C9 *Gaspesie*

CAMPING DE CARLETON-SUR-MER (Public) From Jct of Rte 132 & Avenue Du Phare in E part of town, S on Avenue Du Phare access road (L). 301 Avail: 153 full hkups, 67 W, 67 E (30 amps). 2021 rates: $23 to $48. Jun 01 to Sep 23. (418)364-3992

CAUSAPSCAL — C9 *Gaspesie*

CAMPING CAUSAPSCAL CHEZ MOOSE **Ratings: 7.5/9.5/8** (Campground) 56 Avail: 37 full hkups, 19 W, 19 E (20/30 amps). 2021 rates: $35 to $42. Jun 01 to Sep 04. (418)756-5621, 601 Rte 132 Ouest, Causapscal, QC G0J 1J0

CHAMBORD — C5 *Saguenay-Lac-Saint-Jean*

CAMPING PLAGE BLANCHET
(Public) From Town: Go 1.6 km/1 mi N on Rte 169, then .4 km/1/4 mi NE on Ch Du Domaine Norois (E). **FAC:** gravel rds. Avail: 80 grass, back-ins (45x55), 80 W, 41 S, 80 E (15/30 amps), dump, laundry, firewood, restaurant. **REC:** Lake St Jean: swim, fishing, playground. Pets OK. No tents. 2021 rates: $32.83 to $54.36. May 25 to Sep 09. no cc, no reservations.
(418)346-5436 Lat: 48.41928, Lon: -71.98039
121 Route 169, Chambord, QC G0W 1N0
www.campingblanchet.ca

CAMPING VAL-JALBERT (Public) From jct Rtes 155 & 169 (in town): Go 4 mi N on Rte 169 (L). 190 Avail: 85 full hkups, 21 W, 21 E (30/50 amps). 2021 rates: $29 to $45. May 16 to Sep 21. (888)675-3132

CHANDLER — C10 *Gaspesie*

PARC DU BOURG DE PABOS **Ratings: 7/8.5★/7.5** (Campground) 110 Avail: 13 full hkups, 97 W, 97 E (30/50 amps). 2021 rates: $46.29. May 11 to Sep 30. (418)689-6043, 75 De la Plage Rd., Chandler, QC G0C 2J0

CHANDLER (PABOS) — C10 *Gaspesie*

CENTRE DE PLAIN AIR LA SEIGNEURIE **Ratings: 7/9★/8** (Campground) 33 Avail: 30 full hkups, 3 W, 3 E (15/30 amps). 2021 rates: $28.50 to $42. Jun 01 to Sep 30. (418)689-3031, 99 Rte de L'Eglise, Pabos, QC G0C 2H0

CHATEAU-RICHER — D6 *Quebec*

CAMPING TURMEL ENR **Ratings: 8.5/9/8** (Campground) 55 Avail: 38 full hkups, 10 W, 10 E (30/50 amps). 2021 rates: $38.27 to $45.23. May 15 to Sep 30. (418)824-4311, 7000 Boul Ste-Anne , Chateau-Richer, QC G0A 1N0

CHENEVILLE — E3 *Outaouais*

CAMPING LA PINEDE **Ratings: 5.5/9.5★/8.5** (Campground) 19 Avail: 4 full hkups, 15 W, 15 E (20/30 amps). 2021 rates: $50. May 17 to Sep 29. (819)428-3264, 1735 De La Pinede St, Cheneville, QC J0V 1E0

COATICOOK — F6 *Cantons de l'Est*

CAMPING DU LAC LYSTER (PISKIART-LA SEQUINIERE) (Campground) (Phone Update) 70 Avail: 52 full hkups, 18 W, 18 E (15/30 amps). 2021 rates: $38 to $54. May 15 to Oct 10. (818)345-3787, 385 Chemin Sequin, Coaticook, QC J1A 2S4

COMPTON — F6 *Cantons de l'Est*

CAMPING DE COMPTON **Ratings: 9/10★/9.5** (Membership Park) 140 Avail: 48 full hkups, 49 W, 49 E (30/50 amps). 2021 rates: $54.50 to $64.50. Apr 13 to Oct 20. (800)563-5277, 24 Chemin de la Station, Compton, QC J0B 1L0

COOKSHIRE — F6 *Cantons de l'Est*

CAMPING COOP FAMILIALE DE PREVERT **Ratings: 8.5/9★/8.5** (Campground) 61 Avail: 30 full hkups, 20 W, 20 E (30/50 amps). 2021 rates: $36.53 to $49.97. May 01 to Sep 15. (819)875-3186, 530 Chemin Chute, Cookshire, QC J0B 1M0

COTEAU-DU-LAC — B1 *Monteregie*

KOA MONTREAL WEST **Ratings: 10/8.5/8** (Campground) Avail: 55 full hkups (30/50 amps). 2021 rates: $45 to $60. Apr 20 to Oct 20. (800)562-9395, 171 Rte 338, Coteau-Du-Lac, QC J0P 1B0

COWANSVILLE — B3 *Cantons de l'Est*

CAMPING DOMAINE TOURNESOL **Ratings: 8.5/10★/7.5** (Campground) 63 Avail: 52 full hkups, 3 W, 3 E (15/30 amps). 2021 rates: $37.40 to $50. Apr 14 to Oct 13. (450)263-9515, 327 Chemin Brosseau, Cowansville, QC J2K 3S7

DESCHAILLONS-SUR-SAINT-LAURENT — E5 *Centre du Quebec*

CAMPING CAP A LA ROCHE (Campground) (Phone Update) 108 Avail: 96 full hkups, 5 W, 5 E (30 amps). 2021 rates: $32.50 to $58. May 10 to Oct 19. (819)292-1212, 1820 Marie Victorin, Deschaillons-Sur-Saint-Laurent, QC G0S 1G0

DOLBEAU-MISTASSINI — C5 *Saguenay-Lac-Saint-Jean*

CAMPING DES CHUTES (Public) From Jct of Rtes 373 & 169, (in town) S 2 mi on Rte 169 (R). Avail: 40 full hkups (30 amps). 2021 rates: $22 to $32. May 16 to Sep 07. (418)276-5675

DRUMMONDVILLE — E5 *Centre du Quebec*

CAMPING DES VOLTIGEURS (Public Prov Park) From Jct of Hwy 20 & Exit 181: Go .4 km/1/4 mi S on Montplaisir (R). 281 Avail: 118 full hkups, 68 W, 163 E (30 amps). 2021 rates: $23 to $32.50. May 15 to Sep 07. (819)477-1360

CAMPING LA DETENTE **Ratings: 8/8★/7.5** (Campground) 168 Avail: 153 full hkups, 15 W, 15 E (30 amps). 2021 rates: $32 to $40. May 15 to Sep 15. (819)478-0651, 1580, Fontainebleau , Drummondville, QC J2B 8T7

DUHAMEL — E3 *Outaouais*

CENTRE TOURISTIQUE DU LAC-SIMON (Public Prov Park) From town (at Hwy 321): Go 2 km/1-1/4 mi S on Rue Principale, then 400 m/1/4 mi on Municipalite De Dunhamel (R). 326 Avail: 79 full hkups, 100 W, 100 E (15/30 amps). 2021 rates: $32.50 to $41.30. May 19 to Oct 29. (819)428-7931

Quebec Privately Owned Campground Information Updated by our Good Sam Representatives

Patrice Richard & Chantal Belisle

We sold everything in 2002, then traveled in Canada coast to coast, U.S. (44 states) and Mexico. We're Frenchies who switch from one culture to another. La vie est trop courte, il faut la prendre en riant. Life's too short so take it with a laugh.

QC

EASTMAN — F5 *Cantons de l'Est*

CAMPING LA MINE DE CUIVRE **Ratings: 7.5/8.5/7** (Campground) 74 Avail: 64 full hkups, 10 W, 10 E (15/30 amps). 2021 rates: $48. May 15 to Oct 15. (450)297-3226, 33 Chemin de la Mine de Cuivre , Eastman, QC J0E 1P0

CAMPING LEROUX **Ratings: 5/8.5★/6** (Campground) Avail: 12 full hkups (15/30 amps). 2021 rates: $55 to $66. May 10 to Oct 10. (450)297-3219, 1050 Chemin des Diligences, Eastman, QC J0E 1P0

FORESTVILLE — C7 *Manicouagan*

CAMPING LAC AUX PINS (Campground) (Phone Update) Avail: 20 full hkups (20 amps). 2021 rates: $30 to $35. May 15 to Sep 15. (418)587-5010, 1025 Rte 385, Forestville, QC G0T 1E0

FOSSAMBAULT-SUR-LE-LAC — D6 *Quebec*

PLAGE LAC SAINT-JOSEPH (Campground) (Phone Update) 203 Avail: 75 full hkups, 128 W, 128 E (30/50 amps). 2021 rates: $40.01 to $68.50. Jun 19 to Sep 01. (418)875-2242, 7001 Rte de Fossambault, Fossambault-sur-le-Lac, QC G0A 3M0

FRELIGHSBURG — C3 *Cantons de l'Est*

CAMPING DES CHUTES HUNTER **Ratings: 7/9.5★/7.5** (Campground) Avail: 140 full hkups (30 amps). 2021 rates: $45.95 to $47.95. May 10 to Oct 14. (450)298-5005, 18 Chemin des Chutes, Frelighsburg, QC J0J 1C0

CAMPING ECOLOGIQUE DE FRELIGHSBURG **Ratings: 6/9.5★/8.5** (Campground) Avail: 44 full hkups (30/50 amps). 2021 rates: $36 to $44. May 15 to Sep 15. (450)298-5259, 174 Route 237 Sud, Frelighsburg, QC J0J 1C0

GASPE — B10 *Gaspesie*

CAMPING BAIE DE GASPE **Ratings: 6/8.5★/7** (Campground) 70 Avail: 66 full hkups, 4 W, 4 E (30/50 amps). 2021 rates: $40 to $50. Jun 01 to Sep 01. (418)892-5503, 2107 Blvd. Grande Greve (Route 132), Gaspe, QC G4X 6L7

CAMPING DES APPALACHES **Ratings: 8.5/9★/8** (Campground) 60 Avail: 50 full hkups, 10 W, 10 E (15/30 amps). 2021 rates: $33 to $45. Jun 01 to Sep 30. (418)269-7775, 367 Montee Riviere Morris, Gaspe, QC G4X 5P7

CAMPING GASPE **Ratings: 7.5/8★/9** (Campground) 42 Avail: 23 full hkups, 19 W, 19 E (20/30 amps). 2021 rates: $35.23 to $40.88. Jun 01 to Oct 01. (418)368-4800, 1029 Rte. Haldimand, Gaspe, QC G4X 2H7

CAMPING GRIFFON **Ratings: 6.5/9.5★/7.5** (Campground) 75 Avail: 31 full hkups, 44 W, 44 E (15/30 amps). 2021 rates: $35 to $45. Jun 01 to Sep 30. (418)892-5938, 421 Blvd Griffon, Gaspe, QC G4X 6A1

CAMPING PARC NATURE GASPE **Ratings: 5.5/8★/5.5** (Campground) Avail: 15 full hkups (20/30 amps). 2021 rates: $32. May 01 to Oct 31. (418)361-2070, 1986 Blvd Grande Greve, Gaspe, QC G4X 6L6

FORILLON/CAMPING DES ROSIERS (Public National Park) From town, E 1.5 mi on Rte 132 to access rd (L). Avail: 42 E (15/30 amps). 2021 rates: $25.50 to $32.30. Jun 01 to Aug 18. (877)737-3783

FORILLON/PETIT GASPE (Public National Park) From village of Cap-Aux-Os: Go 4.8 km/3 mi W on Rte 132 to access rd (R). 167 Avail: 31 W, 66 E (15/30 amps). 2021 rates: $25.50 to $32.30. May 17 to Oct 13. (877)737-3783

FORT RAMSAY CAMPING & MOTELS **Ratings: 5.5/8/7.5** (Campground) 42 Avail: 21 full hkups, 21 E (30 amps). 2021 rates: $25 to $35. May 15 to Sep 30. (418)368-5094, 254 Boul Gaspe, Gaspe, QC G4X 1B1

GRACEFIELD — E3 *Outaouais*

CAMPING PIONNIER (Campground) (Phone Update) Avail: 10 full hkups (15/30 amps). 2021 rates: $30 to $40. May 10 to Oct 10. (819)463-4163, 180 Route 105, Gracefield, QC J0X 1W0

GRANBY — B3 *Cantons de l'Est*

AZTEC CAMPING **Ratings: 10/10★/10** (Campground) 499 Avail: 495 full hkups, 4 W, 4 E (30/50 amps). 2021 rates: $39.95 to $87. May 01 to Oct 15. (450)378-9410, 1680 Principale Rte 112, Granby, QC J2J 0M6

CAMPING BON-JOUR **Ratings: 8.5/10★/9.5** (Campground) 150 Avail: 134 full hkups, 16 W, 16 E (30/50 amps). 2021 rates: $35 to $60. Apr 15 to Oct 15. (450)378-0213, 1633 Principale Rte 112, Granby, QC J2G 0M7

GRANDES-BERGERONNES — C7 *Cote-Nord*

CAMPING BON DESIR (Public) From overpass Rue de la Mer in Grandes Bergeronnes: Go 4 km/2-1/2 mi E on Rte 138 (R). 67 Avail: 22 full hkups, 45 W, 45 E (30 amps). 2021 rates: $27.32 to $43.97. Jun 01 to Sep 30. (418)232-6297

GRANDE-VALLEE — B10 *Gaspesie*

CAMPING AU SOLEIL COUCHANT **Ratings: 7.5/8/8.5** (Campground) 79 Avail: 67 full hkups, 12 W, 12 E (30/50 amps). 2021 rates: $34. Jun 01 to Sep 30. (418)393-2489, 73 St Francois Xavier Est, Grande-Vallee, QC G0E 1K0

GRAND-MERE — E5 *Mauricie*

LA MAURICIE/RIVIERE-A-LA-PECHE CAMPGROUND (Public Prov Park) From Hwy 55 (exit 226): Go 16 km/10 mi N. 4-8/10 km/3 mi NW of St-Jean des Piles entrance. Park closed for 2018 year due to rebuilding. Avail: 98 E (15/50 amps). 2021 rates: $29.40 to $29.50. May 16 to Oct 13. (819)533-7272

GRAND-REMOUS — D3 *Outaouais*

RESERVE FAUNIQUE LA VERENDRYE/CAMPING LAC DE LA VIEILLE (Public National Park) From jct Hwy 105 & Hwy 117: Go 31.6 km/19-1/2 mi NW on Hwy 117 (L). Avail: 30 full hkups (30 amps). 2021 rates: $32.50 to $43.55. May 19 to Sep 05. (819)438-2017

RESERVE FAUNIQUE LA VERENDRYE/CAMPING LAC RAPIDE (Public National Park) From jct Hwy 105 & Hwy 117: Go 99.4 km/61-3/4 mi N on Hwy 117 (R). Avail: 45 W. 2021 rates: $33.65. May 16 to Sep 08. (819)435-2246

RESERVE FAUNIQUE LA VERENDRYE/CAMPING LAC SAVARY (Public National Park) From jct Hwy 105 & Hwy 117: Go 31.5 km/19-1/2 mi NW on Hwy 117 (L). Avail: 10 W. 2021 rates: $32.50. May 14 to Sep 07. (819)438-2017

HAVELOCK — C2 *Monteregie*

CAMPING GEMEAUX **Ratings: 9/8.5★/8.5** (Campground) Avail: 10 full hkups (30 amps). 2021 rates: $28 to $36. Apr 15 to Oct 15. (877)826-0193, 330 Rang St Charles, Havelock, QC J0S 2C0

DOMAINE FRONTIERE ENCHANTEE **Ratings: 7.5/8/8** (Campground) Avail: 30 full hkups (30 amps). 2021 rates: $34.80 to $43.48. May 01 to Sep 30. (450)826-4490, 474 Covey Hill Rd, Havelock, QC J0S 2C0

HEMMINGFORD — C2 *Monteregie*

CANNE DE BOIS DE HEMMINGFORD **Ratings: 7.5/8/8.5** (Campground) 98 Avail: 48 full hkups, 50 W, 50 E (15/30 amps). 2021 rates: $38 to $45. May 03 to Sep 15. (450)247-2031, 306 Rte 219 S, Hemmingford, QC J0L 1H0

HOPE TOWN — C10 *Bonaventure*

CAMPING DES ETOILES **Ratings: 7.5/9.5★/7.5** (Campground) Avail: 35 full hkups (30/50 amps). 2021 rates: $39 to $59. May 17 to Sep 11. (418)752-6553, 269 Rte 132, Hope Town, QC G0C 3C1

HUDSON — B1 *Monteregie*

CAMPING D'AOUST **Ratings: 8/8★/7.5** (Campground) 118 Avail: 43 full hkups, 65 W, 65 E (20/30 amps). 2021 rates: $45 to $50. May 15 to Oct 31. (450)458-7301, 3844 Harwood Route, Vaudreuil-Dorion, QC J7V 0G1

INVERNESS — E6 *Centre du Quebec*

CAMPING INVERNESS **Ratings: 5/8★/6.5** (Campground) Avail: 58 full hkups (15/30 amps). 2021 rates: $32 to $42. May 13 to Sep 11. (418)453-2400, 1771 Chemin Gosford Nord, Inverness, QC G0S 1K0

KINNEAR'S MILLS — E6 *Chaudiere-Appalaches*

CAMPING SOLEIL **Ratings: 9/10★/9.5** (Campground) 77 Avail: 30 full hkups, 47 W, 47 E (30 amps). 2021 rates: $45 to $52. May 10 to Sep 15. (418)424-3372, 111 des Eglises Rd, Kinnear's Mills, QC G0N 1K0

LA CONCEPTION — E4 *Laurentides*

CAMPING MONTAGNE D'ARGENT (Campground) (Rebuilding) 164 Avail: 10 full hkups, 154 W, 154 E (30 amps). 2021 rates: $47.10 to $76.81. May 17 to Oct 15. (819)686-5207, 1321, Route Montaigne d'Argent, La Conception, QC J0T 1M0

Always do a Pre-Drive Safety Check!

CAMPING PARC LA CONCEPTION - PARKBRIDGE **Ratings: 8/9★/8.5** (Campground) 119 Avail: 100 full hkups, 19 W, 19 E (20/30 amps). 2021 rates: $38 to $69. May 17 to Oct 14. (819)686-5596, 1158 Chemin Des Ormes, La Conception, QC J0T 1M0

LA DORE — C5 *Saguenay-Lac-Saint-Jean*

RESERVE FAUNIQUE ASHUAPMUSHUAN/CAMPING LAC CHIBOUBICHE (Public National Park) From Road 175 N & Hwy 169: Go 33 km on Hwy 167. 37 Avail. 2021 rates: $27.55. May 24 to Oct 28. (418)256-3806

LA MACAZA — E4 *Antoine-Labelle*

RESERVE FAUNIQUE ROUGE MATAWIN/CAMPING LAC DES SUCRERIES (Public National Park) North on Hwy 117. 26 Avail. 2021 rates: $32.50 to $36.20. May 09 to Nov 02. (819)275-1811

LA MALBAIE — D7 *Charlevoix*

CAMPING AU BORD DE LA RIVIERE **Ratings: 8/8.5★/8.5** (Campground) 85 Avail: 66 full hkups, 19 W, 19 E (15/30 amps). 2021 rates: $42 to $55. May 15 to Oct 14. (418)665-9999, 1520 Boul de Comporte, La Malbaie, QC G5A 1M8

CAMPING CHUTES FRASER **Ratings: 7/8.5★/7.5** (Campground) 92 Avail: 28 full hkups, 64 W, 64 E (30 amps). 2021 rates: $38 to $46. May 10 to Oct 20. (418)665-2151, 500 Chemin De La Vallee, La Malbaie, QC G5A 1C2

LA TUQUE — D5 *Mauricie*

LA TUQUE MUNICIPAL CAMPGROUND (Public) In town at Hwy 155 N. 294 Avail. 2021 rates: $32.80 to $45.99. (819)523-4561

LABELLE — E4 *Laurentides*

CAMPING CHUTES AUX IROQUOIS **Ratings: 8/9★/8** (Campground) 58 Avail: 17 full hkups, 41 W, 41 E (15/30 amps). 2021 rates: $44.59 to $58.50. May 10 to Sep 29. (819)686-2337, 36 du Camping, Labelle, QC J0T 1H0

LAC-A-LA-CROIX — C6 *Saguenay-Lac-Saint-Jean*

CAMPING VILLA DES SABLES (Campground) (Phone Update) 95 Avail: 45 full hkups, 50 W, 50 E (15/30 amps). 2021 rates: $55 to $65. May 28 to Sep 03. (418)345-3422, 600 Chemin 10, Rte 170 Est, Metabetchouan-Lac-a-la-Croix, QC G8G 1P1

LAC-AUX-SABLES — D5 *Mauricie*

CAMPING LAC-AUX-SABLES **Ratings: 7.5/8.5/9** (Campground) Avail: 108 full hkups (15/30 amps). 2021 rates: $50.17 to $55.60. May 17 to Oct 07. (418)336-2488, 200 rue Sainte-Marie, Lac-Aux-Sables, QC G0X 1M0

LAC-BROME — F5 *Monteregie*

CAMPING FAIRMOUNT **Ratings: 7/8.5★/7.5** (Campground) Avail: 16 full hkups (30 amps). 2021 rates: $34.50 to $42.50. May 10 to Sep 23. (450)266-0928, 127 Chemin Fairmount, Brome, QC J0E 1K0

DOMAINE DES ERABLES **Ratings: 6.5/UI/6** (Campground) 63 Avail: 22 full hkups, 32 W, 32 E (30/50 amps). 2021 rates: $39.99 to $49.99. (450)242-8888, 688 Bondville (Foster), Foster, QC J0E 1R0

LAC-DES-PLAGES — E4 *Outaouais*

CAMPING LAC DES PLAGES **Ratings: 8.5/10★/9.5** (Campground) 74 Avail: 51 full hkups, 23 W, 23 E (30 amps). 2021 rates: $50 to $57. May 17 to Oct 14. (819)426-2576, 10 Chenail du Moine, Lac-Des-Plages, QC J0T 1K0

LAC-KENOGAMI — C6 *Saguenay-Lac-Saint-Jean*

CENTRE TOURISTIQUE DU LAC KENOGAMI (Public Prov Park) From jct Hwy 175 & Hwy 169: Go 73 km/45 mi N on Hwy 169, then 10 km/6 mi E on Rand Du Lac Vert/Rang Saint Andre, then 550 m/1/4 mi SE on Rang Saint Isidore, then 11 km/7 mi SE on Route de Kenogami, then 36 m/1 blk E on Rue des Decouvreurs (E). 149 Avail: 60 full hkups, 48 E. 2021 rates: $29.75 to $33.15. Jun 08 to Sep 03. (418)344-1142

LAC-MEGANTIC — E6 *Cantons de l'Est*

CAMPING BAIE DES SABLES (Public) From town: Go 3.2 km/2 mi W on Hwy 161, then .8 km/1/2 m S on Hwy 263 (L). 345 Avail: 240 full hkups, 56 W, 56 E (30/50 amps). 2021 rates: $34 to $51. May 11 to Oct 09. (819)583-3965

LACOLLE — C2 *Monteregie*

CAMPING GREGOIRE **Ratings: 8.5/9★/9** (Campground) 104 Avail: 30 full hkups, 74 W, 74 E (30 amps). 2021 rates: $46 to $54. May 15 to Sep 15. (450)246-3385, 347 Rte 221, Lacolle, QC J0J 1J0

LAMBTON — E6 *Cantons de l'Est*

PARC NATIONAL DE FRONTENAC/BAIE-SAUVAGE (Public National Park) From jct Hwy 108 & Hwy 263: Go 9 km/6 mi SW/N on Rte 263. 101 Avail: 27 W, 45 E (15 amps). 2021 rates: $30.25 to $38.75. May 18 to Oct 08. (418)486-2300

L'ANGE GARDIEN (OUTAOUAIS) — B3 *Monteregie*

CAMPING ANGE GARDIEN **Ratings: 8.5/8/8.5** (Campground) Avail: 50 full hkups (30/50 amps). 2021 rates: $40 to $46. Apr 15 to Oct 31. (819)281-5055, 671 Lamarche Rd, L'Ange-Gardien, QC J8L 0S1

LE DOMAINE DE L'ANGE GARDIEN **Ratings: 8.5/8.5★/8** (Campground) Avail: 51 full hkups (15/30 amps). 2021 rates: $38.88 to $46.92. May 01 to Oct 31. (819)281-0299, 1031 rue Pierre-Laporte, L'Ange-Gardien, QC J8L 0E9

LATERRIERE — C6 *Saguenay-Lac-Saint-Jean*

DOMAINE DE VACANCES LA ROCAILLE (Campground) (Phone Update) 31 Avail: 16 full hkups, 15 W, 15 E (15/30 amps). 2021 rates: $28 to $45. May 31 to Sep 13. (418)678-2657, 7894 Portage des Roches Nord, Laterriere, QC G7N 2A1

LES ESCOUMINS — C7 *Manicouagan*

CAMPING LE TIPI (Campground) (Phone Update) Avail: 10 full hkups (15/30 amps). 2021 rates: $32 to $42. May 17 to Sep 02. (888)868-6666, 46 De La Reserve, Les Escoumins, QC G0T 1K0

LES MECHINS — B9 *Bas-Saint-Laurent*

CAMPING AUX PIGNONS VERTS **Ratings: 6.5/8.5★/7.5** (Campground) Avail: 41 full hkups (30 amps). 2021 rates: $27.83 to $36.53. May 04 to Oct 27. (418)729-3423, 218 Rte Bellevue est, Les Mechins, QC G0T 1T0

LEVIS — D6 *Chaudiere-Appalaches*

BOISE DE LA CHAUDIERE **Ratings: 10/9.5/8.5** (Condo Park) Avail: 70 full hkups (50 amps). 2021 rates: $35 to $135. Apr 01 to Dec 01. (418)907-2000, 264 Chemin Saint-Gregoire, Levis, QC G6Y 1E8

CAMPING AU SOUS-BOIS DU CAMPEUR **Ratings: 7.5/9.5★/8** (Campground) 72 Avail: 58 full hkups, 6 W, 6 E (15/30 amps). 2021 rates: $45 to $60. May 15 to Oct 15. (888)731-1788, 1932 Chemin Filteau, Levis, QC G7A 2N4

CAMPING BERNIERES (Campground) (Phone Update) 100 Avail: 69 full hkups, 31 W, 31 E (30/50 amps). 2021 rates: $50 to $78. May 15 to Oct 01. (418)831-8665, 1012 Oliver, Levis, QC G7A 2M9

CAMPING LA JOLIE ROCHELLE **Ratings: 8.5/10★/9.5** (RV Park) 100 Avail: 67 full hkups, 33 W, 33 E (30 amps). 2021 rates: $31 to $55. May 15 to Oct 14. (418)243-1320, 221, Petite troisième, Saint-Raphael, QC G0R 4C0

CAMPING TRANSIT
Ratings: 9.5/10★/10 (Campground) Avail: 142 full hkups (30/50 amps). 2021 rates: $40 to $69. Apr 19 to Oct 20. (418)838-0948, 600 Chemin St. Roch, Levis, QC G6Y 0W3

KOA QUEBEC CITY **Ratings: 9/10★/9** (Campground) Avail: 201 full hkups (30/50 amps). 2021 rates: $70 to $85. May 01 to Oct 11. (418)831-1813, 684 Chemin Oliver, Levis, QC G7A 2N6

MOTEL ET CAMPING ETCHEMIN **Ratings: 6/7★/7.5** (Campground) Avail: 16 full hkups (30/50 amps). 2021 rates: $55 to $60. May 01 to Oct 15. (418)839-6853, 2774 Boulevard Guillaume-Couture, Levis, QC G6W 7Y1

L'ISLET — D7 *Chaudiere-Appalaches*

CAMPING MUNICIPAL ROCHER PANET (Public) From Jct of Hwy 20 & Rte 285 (Exit 400): Go 3.7 km/2-1/2 mi N on Rte 285, then 1.3 km/3/4 mi E on Rte 132 (L). 143 Avail: 135 full hkups, 8 W, 8 E (30 amps). 2021 rates: $22 to $48. May 15 to Oct 15. (418)247-3193

We give campgrounds one rating for development, a second for restrooms and a third for visual appearance and environmental quality. That's the Triple Rating System.

MADELEINE-CENTRE — B10 *La Cote-de Gaspe*

CAMPING CHALETS MER AND MONTAGNE **Ratings: 5.5/8/7.5** (Campground) 24 Avail: 20 full hkups, 4 W, 4 E (20/30 amps). 2021 rates: $32 to $45. May 15 to Sep 30. (514)402-6174, 99 Rte Principale, Madeleine-Centre, QC G0E 1P0

MAGOG — F5 *Cantons de l'Est*

CAMPING MAGOG-ORFORD **Ratings: 8/9★/8.5** (Campground) 105 Avail: 31 full hkups, 74 W, 74 E (30 amps). 2021 rates: $36.53 to $45.23. May 01 to Oct 31. (819)843-2500, 611 Alfred Desrochers, Orford, QC J1X 6J4

DOMAINE PARC-ESTRIE - PARKBRIDGE **Ratings: 8.5/10★/8.5** (Campground) 199 Avail: 103 full hkups, 96 W, 96 E (15/30 amps). 2021 rates: $37 to $59.75. Apr 26 to Oct 26. (819)868-6944, 19 Rue du Domaine, Magog, QC J1X 5Z3

MASHTEUIATSH — C5 *Saguenay-Lac-Saint-Jean*

CAMPING PLAGE ROBERTSON (Campground) (Phone Update) 75 Avail: 58 full hkups, 17 W, 17 E (15/30 amps). 2021 rates: $22 to $45. May 22 to Oct 12. (418)275-1375, 2202 Rue Ouiatchouan, Mashteuiatsh, QC G0W 2H0

MATANE — C8 *Gaspesie*

CAMPING PARC SIROIS LA BALEINE **Ratings: 6/8/7** (Campground) Avail: 60 full hkups (15/30 amps). 2021 rates: $21.74 to $33.05. Jun 01 to Sep 29. (866)876-2242, 2345 Ave Du Phare Ouest, Matane, QC G4W 3M6

RESERVE FAUNIQUE DE MATANE ET DE DUNIERE/CAMPING ETANG A LA TRUITE (Public National Park) From jct Hwy 195 & Hwy 132: Go 30 km/18-1/2 mi NE on QC-195, then 31 km/19 mi E on Chemin de la Reserve Faunique (L). 24 Avail: 4 full hkups, 5 E (30 amps). 2021 rates: $23 to $37.40. Jun 08 to Sep 03. (418)562-3700

RESERVE FAUNIQUE DE MATANE/CAMPING JOHN (Public National Park) From jct Hwy 132 & Hwy 195: Go 1.6 km/1 mi S on Hwy 195, then 1.4 km/3/4 mi NE on Avenue Henri Dunant (L). Avail: 12 full hkups (30 amps). 2021 rates: $23 to $37.40. Jun 08 to Sep 03. (418)224-3345

MELBOURNE — E5 *Cantons de l'Est*

CAMPING MELBOURNE ESTRIE
Ratings: 8/10★/9 (Campground) 62 Avail: 42 full hkups, 16 W, 16 E (15/30 amps). 2021 rates: $31 to $47. May 10 to Sep 15. (819)826-6222, 1185 Chemin du camping, Melbourne, QC J0B 2B0

MERCIER — B2 *Nord du Quebec*

DOMAINE DU BEL AGE **Ratings: 7.5/7.5★/7.5** (Campground) Avail: 11 full hkups (30/50 amps). 2021 rates: $40 to $55. Apr 20 to Oct 31. (450)691-0306, 475 St Jean Baptiste, Mercier, QC J6R 2A9

METIS-SUR-MER — C8 *Bas-Saint-Laurent*

CAMPING ANNIE **Ratings: 8.5/9.5★/9.5** (Campground) 145 Avail: 72 full hkups, 53 W, 53 E (15/30 amps). 2021 rates: $35.67 to $49.49. May 10 to Sep 29. (418)936-3825, 394 Rte 132, Metis-Sur-Mer, QC G0J 1S0

MIRABEL — A2 *Laurentides*

CAMPING MIRABEL **Ratings: 9/9★/8** (Campground) 96 Avail: 30 full hkups, 16 W, 16 E (30/50 amps). 2021 rates: $64 to $74.50. May 01 to Oct 31. (450)475-7725, 8500 Chemin Bourgeois, Mirabel, QC J7N 2K1

MISTASSINI — C5 *Saguenay-Lac-Saint-Jean*

CAMPING ST-LOUIS (Campground) (Phone Update) Avail: 25 full hkups (15/30 amps). 2021 rates: $40 to $50. May 17 to Sep 24. (418)276-4670, 543 Rang St Louis, Dolbeau-Mistassini, QC G8L 5H6

MONT-BRUN — C1 *Abitibi-Tmiscamingue*

PARC NATIONAL AIGUEBELLE/CAMPING ABIJEVIS (Public National Park) From town: Go 11 km/6-3/4 mi N on Rang Hudon, then 2 km/1-1/4 mi W on Aiguebelle 2 (R). 94 Avail: 47 full hkups, 26 W, 26 E. 2021 rates: $27.55 to $35. May 17 to Oct 14. (819)637-2480

MONTEBELLO — E3 *Outaouais*

AUBERGE MONTEBELLO CAMPING & MARINA (Public Prov Park) From jct Hwy 148 & rue Laurier in town: Go 152 m/500 feet S on rue Laurier. 46 Avail. 2021 rates: $40 to $50. May 21 to Oct 08. (877)423-0001

MONT-LOUIS — B9 *Gaspesie*

CAMPING PARC ET MER MONT LOUIS (Public) From jct QC 198 & QC 132: Go 5.6 km/3-1/2 mi W on QC 132. 56 Avail: 39 full hkups, 13 W, 2 S, 15 E (30 amps). 2021 rates: $25 to $38. May 18 to Oct 11. (418)797-5270

MONTMAGNY — D6 *Chaudiere-Appalaches*

CAMPING COOP DES ERABLES DE MONTMAGNY **Ratings: 9/10★/9** (Campground) 144 Avail: 101 full hkups, 43 W, 43 E (30/50 amps). 2021 rates: $40 to $50. May 10 to Oct 07. (418)248-8953, 860 Boul Tache Ouest, Montmagny, QC G5V 3R8

CAMPING POINTE AUX OIES **Ratings: 9/10★/9.5** (Campground) 248 Avail: 172 full hkups, 76 W, 76 E (30/50 amps). 2021 rates: $38 to $48. May 10 to Sep 15. (418)248-9710, 45, avenue du Bassin North, Montmagny, QC G5V 4E5

MONTPELLIER — E3 *Outaouais*

RESERVE FAUNIQUE DE PAPINEAU-LABELLE/LAC ECHO (Public National Park) From jct Hwy 148 & Hwy 315: Go N on Hwy 315 to Montpellier (Accueil Mulet). 36 Avail. 2021 rates: $23.20 to $32.50. (819)454-2011

MONTREAL — B2 *Montreal*

MONTREAL See also Mercier, Mirabel, Pointe-Calumet, St-Charles-sur-Richelieu, St-Jean-Baptiste, St-Jean-sur-Richelieu, St-Mathieu-de-Beloeil, St-Ours, St-Philippe, St-Roch-de-lAchigan, St-Roch-de-Richelieu, Ste-Julienne, Ste-Madeleine & Terrebonne.

MONT-SAINT-PIERRE — B9 *Gaspesie*

CAMPING MUNICIPAL MONT SAINT PIERRE (Public) From Jct of Rte 132 & Pierre-Godefroi Coulombe St: Go S 2.3 km/1-1/4 mi on PG Coulombe St (L). 169 Avail: 53 full hkups, 9 W, 9 E (30 amps). 2021 rates: $28 to $44. Jun 11 to Sep 10. (418)797-2250

MONT-TREMBLANT — E4 *Lanaudiere*

CAMPING DE LA DIABLE **Ratings: 8/9/8** (Campground) 222 Avail: 150 full hkups, 72 W, 72 E (30/50 amps). 2021 rates: $58 to $71. (819)425-5501, 140 Regimbald St, Mont-Tremblant, QC J8E 3C5

PARC NATIONAL DU MONT-TREMBLANT/CAMPING SECTEUR DE LA DIABLE (Public National Park) From Jct of Hwy 117 & Hwy 323 (Rte Transcanadienne): Go 2 km/1-1/4 mi NW Hwy 117/Rte Transcanadienne, then 5 km/3 mi E on Montee Ryan, then continue 3.8 km/2-1-4 mi on Montee Ryan (2nd exit on roundabout), then 1.9 km/1 mi on Chemin Duplessis (2nd exit on roundabout), then 12 km/7-1/2 mi to park (R). Avail: 39 full hkups (15/30 amps). 2021 rates: $38. May 12 to Oct 09. (819)688-2281

PARC NATIONAL DU MONT-TREMBLANT/CAMPING SECTEUR DE LAC CACHE (Public National Park) From jct Hwy 117 & Hwy 323: Go 22.2 km N on QC-117, then 3 km E on Blvd du Cure Labelle (L). 24 Avail: Pit toilets. 2021 rates: $24.75 to $29.75. Jun 21 to Sep 02. (877)688-2289

NEUVILLE — D6 *Quebec*

CAMPING L'EGARE **Ratings: 6/6.5/6.5** (Campground) 47 Avail: 35 full hkups, 12 W, 12 E (30 amps). 2021 rates: $36.53 to $42. May 10 to Oct 15. (418)876-3359, 1069 Rte 138 Ouest, Neuville, QC G0A 2R0

NEW CARLISLE — C10 *Gaspesie*

CAMPING LE MOULIN ROUGE **Ratings: 6.5/5/6.5** (Campground) 30 Avail: 25 full hkups, 5 W, 5 E (20/30 amps). 2021 rates: $28 to $34. May 30 to Sep 30. (418)752-2724, 11 Green St, New Carlisle, QC G0C 1Z0

NICOLET — E5 *Bois*

CAMPING PORT ST FRANCOIS (Campground) (Rebuilding) Avail: 80 full hkups (30 amps). 2021 rates: $42 to $45. Jun 07 to Oct 15. (819)293-5091, 25 Des Bains, Nicolet, QC J3T 1P9

NORMANDIN — C5 *Saguenay-Lac-Saint-Jean*

CAMPING CHUTE A L'OURS (Public) From Jct of Rte 169 & Du Rocher Ave: Go 3.2 km/2 mi W on Du Rocher Ave, then 6.4 km/4 mi S to Rang 4, then 2.8 km/1-3/4 mi W on LS-Ovide Bouchard Rd (E). 92 Avail: 57 full hkups, 35 W, 35 E (15/50 amps). 2021 rates: $28.19 to $40.12. Jun 14 to Sep 09. (418)274-3411

Lend a hand. During the busy season park services are stretched to the max! Please do your best to keep your area ""ship-shape''.

NOTRE-DAME-DE-LA-SALETTE — E3 *Outaouais*

↑ ROYAL PAPINEAU - PARKBRIDGE (Campground) (Phone Update) 22 Avail: 18 full hkups, 4 W, 4 E (30/50 amps). 2021 rates: $38 to $59.75. May 03 to Oct 14. (819)766-2826, 237 Chemin Du Golf, Notre-Dame-De-La-Salette, QC J0X 2L0

NOTRE-DAME-DES-PINS — E6 *Chaudiere-Appalaches*

↓ CAMPING LA ROCHE D'OR - PARKBRIDGE **Ratings: 9/9.5★/9** (Campground) 171 Avail: 115 full hkups, 49 W, 49 E (30 amps). 2021 rates: $45.25 to $59.75. May 03 to Sep 22. (418)774-9191, 3005 Rte 173, Notre-Dame-Des-Pins, QC G0M 1K0

NOTRE-DAME-DU-LAC — D8 *Bas-Saint-Laurent*

→ CAMPING MUNICIPAL NOTRE DAME DU LAC (Public) From Jct of Rte 185 & exit 29 (N.D. Du Lac): Go .8 km/1/2 mi E on Rue de l'Eglise, then .9 km/1/2 mi S on Rue Commerciale (L). 90 Avail: 72 full hkups, 18 W, 18 E (15/30 amps). 2021 rates: $24.08 to $38. May 13 to Oct 09. (418)899-6820

NOTRE-DAME-DU-MONT-CARMEL — E5 *Mauricie*

↗ CAMPING LAC MORIN **Ratings: 8/8.5★/10** (Campground) 34 Avail: 28 full hkups, 6 W, 6 E (30/50 amps). 2021 rates: $45 to $58. (819)376-1479, 1430 Rang Saint-Flavien, Notre-Dame-du-Mont-Carmel, QC G0X 3J0

↘ CAMPING PARADISO **Ratings: 8/10★/9** (Campground) Avail: 85 full hkups (30/50 amps). 2021 rates: $43 to $57. May 17 to Sep 15. (819)375-1569, 1281 Rang St-Flavien, Notre-Dame-Du-Mont-Carmel, QC G0X 3J0

OKA — B1 *Laurentides*

↗ PARC NATIONAL D'OKA (Public National Park) From Jct of Hwy 640 & Hwy 344: Go 6.2 km/3-3/4 mi W on Hwy 640 (L). 842 Avail: 301 full hkups, 36 W, 57 E (15/30 amps). 2021 rates: $24.75 to $40.30. (450)479-8365

ORFORD — F5 *Cantons de l'Est*

PARC NATIONAL DU MONT-ORFORD (Public National Park) From jct I-10 & Hwy 141: Go 4 km/2-1/2 mi N on Hwy 141, then 6 km/3-3/4 mi NW on Chemin du Camping (R). 425 Avail: 120 W, 170 E. 2021 rates: $30.25 to $43.50. May 13 to Sep 05. (819)843-9855

PERCE — C10 *Gaspesie*

↑ BAIE DE PERCE (Public Prov Park) From center of town: Go 1.6 km/1 mi W on Rte 132 (L). 176 Avail: 33 W, 33 E (15 amps). 2021 rates: $32 to $40. May 31 to Sep 02. (418)782-5102

← CAMPING COTE SURPRISE **Ratings: 7/9★/8.5** (Campground) Avail: 125 full hkups (30/50 amps). 2021 rates: $46 to $56. May 01 to Oct 30. (418)782-5443, 335 Rte 132 (C.P. 296), Perce, QC G0C 2L0

← CAMPING DU PHARE A PERCE **Ratings: 6.5/9.5★/7.5** (Campground) 132 Avail: 64 full hkups, 68 W, 38 E (30/50 amps). 2021 rates: $35 to $48. May 20 to Oct 15. (877)332-5588, 385 Rte 132 Ouest, Perce, QC G0C 2L0

→ CAMPING DU VILLAGE **Ratings: 7/9★/8** (Campground) Avail: 28 full hkups (30 amps). 2021 rates: $45 to $48. Jun 01 to Sep 30. (418)782-2020, 230 Rte 132 Ouest, Perce, QC G0C 2L0

↓ CAMPING HAVRE DE LA NUIT **Ratings: 5.5/8★/6** (RV Park) Avail: 26 full hkups (30 amps). 2021 rates: $40.88 to $44.36. May 15 to Sep 30. (418)782-2924, 16 Biard St (C.P. 424), Perce, QC G0C 2L0

↖ CHALETS & CAMPING NATURE OCEAN **Ratings: 7/8/8** (Campground) 124 Avail: 64 full hkups, 15 W, 15 E (20/30 amps). 2021 rates: $29 to $40. May 23 to Oct 13. (418)782-2400, 400 Rte 132 Ouest, Perce, QC G0C 2L0

PLAISANCE — E3 *Outaouais*

PARC NATIONAL DE PLAISANCE (Public National Park) From jct Hwy 148 & Hwy 321: Go 7.7 km/4-3/4 mi W on Hwy 148, then 1.1 km/1/2 mi S on Chemin des Presquiles (R). 120 Avail. 2021 rates: $19.65 to $58.15. (819)427-5334

PLESSISVILLE — E6 *Centre du Quebec*

↓ CAMPING MON PLAISIR **Ratings: 8.5/9.5/8.5** (Campground) 98 Avail: 51 full hkups, 47 W, 47 E (15/30 amps). 2021 rates: $43.49 to $47.84. May 10 to Sep 08. (819)362-7591, 149 Sainte-Sophie Rd, Plessisville, QC G6L 2Y2

POINTE-A-LA-CROIX — C9 *Gaspesie*

↑ CAMPING LA MAISON VERTE DU PARC GASPESIEN **Ratings: 5.5/8★/7** (Campground) 103 Avail: 62 full hkups, 41 W, 41 E (20/30 amps). 2021 rates: $28.70 to $36.53. May 04 to Nov 18. (418)788-2342, 79 Rue Des Meandres, Pointe-A-La-Croix, QC G0C 1L0

POINTE-AUX-OUTARDES — B8 *Cote-Nord*

→ CAMPING PARC DE LA RIVE (Campground) (Phone Update) 83 Avail: 50 full hkups, 33 W, 33 E (15/30 amps). 2021 rates: $33.65 to $35.65. Jun 01 to Sep 07. (418)567-4021, 197 Chemin de la Baie, Les Buissons, QC G0H 1H0

POINTE-CALUMET — B2 *Laurentides*

← CAMPING L'ESCALE **Ratings: 8.5/9.5★/9.5** (Campground) 67 Avail: 27 full hkups, 40 W, 40 E (15/30 amps). 2021 rates: $47 to $62. Apr 20 to Oct 20. (450)472-6789, 880 - Rue Andre Soucy St., Pointe-Calumet, QC J0N 1G2

POINTE-LEBEL — B8 *Cote-Nord*

← CAMPING DE LA MER (Campground) (Phone Update) 65 Avail: 46 full hkups, 19 W, 19 E (15/30 amps). 2021 rates: $30.44 to $47.84. May 17 to Sep 22. (418)589-6576, 72 Rue Chounard, Baie-Comeau, QC G0H 1N0

PONT-ROUGE — D6 *Quebec*

→ UN AIR D'ETE **Ratings: 9/10★/9** (Campground) 95 Avail: 60 full hkups, 33 W, 33 E (15/30 amps). 2021 rates: $52.19 to $53.05. May 15 to Sep 22. (877)873-4791, 459 Rte Grand Capsa (Rt 358), Pont-Rouge, QC G3H 1L3

PORT-CARTIER — A9 *Cote-Nord*

← CAMPING LE PARADIS (Public) From Jct of Rte 138 & Boul Portage des Mosses (E end of town): Go .2 km/1/4 mi S on Boul Portage Des Mosses (R). 42 Avail: 25 full hkups, 2 W, 2 E (30 amps). 2021 rates: $25 to $37. Jun 07 to Sep 21. (418)766-7137

→ RESERVE FAUNIQUE DE PORT-CARTIER-SEPT-ILES/CAMPING LAC WALKER (Public National Park) From Hwy 138 E follow sign for Reserve. Avail: 9 W. 2021 rates: $27.55 to $30.80. May 31 to Sep 01. (418)766-4743

PORT-DANIEL — C10 *Gaspesie*

→ RESERVE FAUNIQUE DE PORT DANIEL/CAMPING PORT-DANIEL (Public National Park) In town, at church: Go 1 km/3/4 mi E on Hwy 132. Avail: 13 full hkups (30 amps). 2021 rates: $29.75 to $47.55. May 31 to Sep 28. (418)396-2789

PORTNEUF — D6 *Quebec*

← CAMPING PANORAMIQUE - PARKBRIDGE **Ratings: 9/9★/9** (Campground) Avail: 51 full hkups (30/50 amps). 2021 rates: $46.25 to $55.50. Apr 01 to Oct 15. (418)286-3655, 464 Francois-Gignac Rd, Portneuf, QC G0A 2Y0

RIVIERE FAUNIQUE DE PORTNEUF/CAMPING LAC BELLEVUE (Public National Park) From jct Hwy 153 & Hwy 367: Go 69.5 km/43 mi N on Hwy 367, then 33.5 km/21 mi NW on CRue Principale/Chemin St Laurent winding road (E). 45 Avail. 2021 rates: $29.75 to $33.05. Jun 17 to Sep 04. (418)323-2021

PRINCEVILLE — E6 *Centre du Quebec*

← CAMPING PLAGE DES SABLES **Ratings: 7.5/8.5★/8** (Campground) 75 Avail: 65 full hkups, 10 W, 10 E (15/30 amps). 2021 rates: $49.58 to $57.40. May 10 to Sep 08. (819)364-5769, 1450 Route 116 Ouest, Princeville, QC G6L 4K7

QUEBEC CITY — D6 *Quebec*

QUEBEC CITY See also Beaumont, Chateau-Richer, Fossambault-sur-le-Lac, Levis, Neuville, Pont-Rouge, St-Apollinaire, St-Augustin-de-Desmaures, St-François-dOrléans, St-Lambert-de-Lauzon, St-Michel-de-Bellechasse, St-Vallier, Ste-Anne-de-Beaupre, Scott, Stoneham & Valcartier.

↑ CAMPING DE LA JOIE **Ratings: 9/9.5★/8** (Campground) 88 Avail: 69 full hkups, 19 W, 19 E (30/50 amps). 2021 rates: $43 to $49. May 10 to Oct 14. (877)849-2264, 640 Georges Muir, Quebec City, QC G2N 2H3

↑ CAMPING QUEBEC EN VILLE **Ratings: 9/9★/8.5** (Campground) 38 Avail: 26 full hkups, 6 W, 6 E (30/50 amps). 2021 rates: $43 to $55. May 01 to Oct 31. (418)871-1574, 2050 Rte De L'Aeroport, Quebec, QC G2E 3L9

Say you saw it in our Guide!

↑ CENTER'S OUTDOOR BEAUPORT (Public) From Jct of Hwy 40 & Exit 321 (Boul Raymond)), E 0.1 mi on Yves Prevost St to Boul Raymond (Labelle St), N 2 mi to Boul Louis XIV, E 0.5 mi, follow signs (L). Avail: 55 full hkups (30 amps). 2021 rates: $38 to $47. Jun 06 to Sep 01. (418)641-6112

PARC NATIONAL RUSTIQUE DE LA JACQUES-CARTIER/CAMPING SECTEUR DE LA PALLIC (Public National Park) On Hwy 175 N. 158 Avail. 2021 rates: $23.20 to $30.70. May 01 to Sep 01. (418)848-3169

RESERVE FAUNIQUE DES LAURENTIDES/CAMPING LA LOUTRE (Public National Park) From town: Go 53.6 km/33 mi N on QC-175 (R). Avail: 36 full hkups (30 amps). 2021 rates: $29.75 to $47.55. May 23 to Aug 30. (418)846-2201

RACINE — E5 *Cantons de l'Est*

→ CAMPING PLAGE MCKENZIE **Ratings: 7.5/9★/8** (Campground) 55 Avail: 35 full hkups, 20 W, 20 E (30 amps). 2021 rates: $46.75 to $57. May 10 to Sep 22. (819)846-2011, 842 Rte 222, Racine, QC J0E 1Y0

RAWDON — A2 *Lanaudiere*

↓ CAMPING PARC ENSOLEILLE 2002 **Ratings: 8/6/6.5** (Campground) 27 Avail: 17 full hkups, 10 W, 10 E (30 amps). 2021 rates: $35 to $40. May 15 to Sep 30. (450)834-3332, 3137 1E Ave, Rawdon, QC J0K 1S0

RIGAUD — B1 *Monteregie*

↓ CAMPING CHOISY **Ratings: 9/10★/9** (Campground) 93 Avail: 70 full hkups, 17 W, 17 E (30/50 amps). 2021 rates: $61 to $65. May 01 to Oct 15. (450)458-4900, 209 Rte 201, Rigaud, QC J0P 1P0

← CAMPING TRANS-CANADIEN (Campground) (Rebuilding) Avail: 13 full hkups (30/50 amps). 2021 rates: $40 to $45. May 01 to Oct 30. (514)990-6647, 960 Chemin de la Baie, Rigaud, QC J0P 1P0

RIMOUSKI — C8 *Bas-Saint-Laurent*

← **CAMPING RIMOUSKI**

good sam park **Ratings: 8/9.5★/8.5** (Campground) Avail: 112 full hkups (30/50 amps). 2021 rates: $38.93 to $56.25. May 01 to Oct 14. (418)721-0322, 1105 Boul St-Germain, Rimouski, QC G5L 8Y9

→ RESERVE FAUNIQUE DE RIMOUSKI/CAMPING LAC RIMOUSKI (Public National Park) From jct Hwy 20 & Hwy 232: Go E on Hwy 232. 17 Avail. 2021 rates: $27.50 to $45.75. May 23 to Sep 01. (418)735-5672

RIVIERE-DU-LOUP — C7 *Bas-Saint-Laurent*

↑ CAMPING DU QUAI **Ratings: 9.5/9★/9** (Campground) 115 Avail: 80 full hkups, 16 W, 16 S (30/50 amps). 2021 rates: $32 to $48. May 05 to Oct 13. (418)860-3111, 70 Rue de L'Ancrage (70), Riviere-du-Loup, QC G5R 6B1

→ CAMPING MUNICIPAL DE LA POINTE (Public) From Jct of Hwy 20 & exit 507 (Boul. Cartier), NE 0.5 mi on Boul. Cartier (L). Avail: 116 full hkups (15/30 amps). 2021 rates: $26 to $42. May 09 to Sep 22. (418)862-4281

RIVIERE-ETERNITE — C6 *Saguenay-Lac-Saint-Jean*

PARC NATIONAL FJORD-DU-SAGUENAY/BAIE-ETERNITE (Public National Park) From town of La Baie at Hwy 170: Go 43 km/27 mi E on Hwy 170, then 1 km/1/2 mi NE on Rue Notre Dame to Riviere Eternite (L). Avail: 19 full hkups. 2021 rates: $29.75 to $35. May 16 to Oct 13. (877)272-1556

RIVIERE-OUELLE — D7 *Bas-Saint-Laurent*

↑ CAMPING RIVIERE-OUELLE (Public) From Jct of Hwy 20 & Exit 444, E 1.4 mi on Rte 132 to Chemin De La Pointe, N 2.3 mi (R). 225 Avail: (15/30 amps). 2021 rates: $33 to $48. May 04 to Oct 15. (418)856-1484

ROBERVAL — C5 *Saguenay-Lac-Saint-Jean*

← CAMPING MONT PLAISANT (Public) From town, N 2 mi on Rte 169 to De l'Aeroport Rd, W 0.6 mi (R). Avail: 165 full hkups (30 amps). 2021 rates: $34 to $48. May 09 to Oct 13. (418)275-0910

ROXTON FALLS — E5 *Monteregie*

↓ CAMPING DE L'ILE **Ratings: 8/9.5★/8.5** (Campground) 107 Avail: 30 full hkups, 77 W, 77 E (30/50 amps). 2021 rates: $48 to $58. May 03 to Oct 14. (450)548-2495, 238 chemin Pepin, Roxton Falls, QC J0H 1E0

SAGUENAY-LA BAIE — C6 *Saguenay-Lac-Saint-Jean*

CAMPING AU JARDIN DE MON PERE (Campground) (Phone Update) 125 Avail: 99 full hkups, 26 W, 26 E (30/50 amps). 2021 rates: $34.50 to $64.50. May 15 to Sep 15. (418)544-6486, 3736 Chemin St Louis, La Baie, QC G7B 4M8

SAINT-AIME-DES-LACS — D7 *Quebec*

PARC NATIONAL HAUTES-GORGES-DE-LA-RIVIERE-MALBAIE (Public National Park) From town: Go 24 km NE on Rang St Jerome/Route du Range B & C (L). 87 Avail. 2021 rates: $23 to $38.15. May 15 to Oct 30. (418)439-1227

SAINT-ALEXANDRE — D7 *Bas-Saint-Laurent*

CAMPING LE RAYON DE SOLEIL **Ratings: 8.5/8.5★/8** (Campground) 60 Avail: 12 full hkups, 23 W, 25 E (15/50 amps). 2021 rates: $39 to $46. May 16 to Oct 01. (418)495-2677, 571 Rang St Edouard Ouest, St Alexandre de Kamouraska, QC G0L 2G0

SAINT-ALEXIS-DES-MONTS — E5 *Mauricie*

RESERVE FAUNIQUE MASTIGOUCHE/LAC SAINT-BERNARD (Public National Park) From town: Go 20 km/12-1/2 mi NE on Rue Sainte Anne/Rang des Pins-Rouges, then 8.9 km/5-1/2 mi W on Chemin de Carufel (L). 74 Avail. 2021 rates: $32.50 to $33.65. May 09 to Oct 20. (819)265-6055

SAINT-ANDRE-AVELLIN — E3 *Outaouais*

CAMPING AU PETIT LAC SIMON **Ratings: 7/7.5★/8** (Campground) 71 Avail: 10 full hkups, 61 W, 61 E (20/30 amps). 2021 rates: $25 to $60. May 15 to Sep 25. (819)983-6584, 1203 Rte 321 Nord, Saint-Andre-Avellin, QC J0V 1W0

CAMPING ST ANDRE AVELLIN **Ratings: 8.5/UI/8.5** (Campground) 126 Avail: 123 full hkups, 3 W, 3 E (30 amps). 2021 rates: $47 to $56. May 17 to Oct 14. (819)983-3777, 20 Duquette St, Saint-Andre-Avellin, QC J0V 1W0

SAINT-ANTOINE-ABBE — C2 *Monteregie*

CAMPING LAC DES PINS **Ratings: 9.5/9.5★/8.5** (Campground) 280 Avail: 110 full hkups, 170 W, 170 E (20/30 amps). 2021 rates: $37.80 to $46. May 15 to Oct 01. (450)827-2353, 3625 Rte 201, Franklin, QC J0S 1N0

SAINT-ANTONIN — C7 *Bas-Saint-Laurent*

CAMPING CHEZ JEAN
Ratings: 9/10★/9.5 (Campground) 108 Avail: 68 full hkups, 40 W, 40 E (20/30 amps). 2021 rates: $31 to $47. May 17 to Sep 29. (418)862-3081, 434-A Principale, Saint-Antonin, QC G0L 2J0

CAMPING LIDO **Ratings: 8.5/9.5★/8.5** (Campground) 40 Avail: 36 full hkups, 4 W, 4 E (30/50 amps). 2021 rates: $38.27 to $41.75. May 10 to Sep 22. (418)862-6933, 928 Chemin Riviere Verte, Saint-Antonin, QC G0L 2J0

SAINT-APOLLINAIRE — D6 *Chaudiere-Appalaches*

DOMAINE DE LA CHUTE - PARKBRIDGE **Ratings: 9/UI/9** (Campground) 221 Avail: 163 full hkups, 58 W, 58 E (30/50 amps). 2021 rates: $46.25 to $55.50. May 15 to Oct 07. (418)831-1311, 74 Chemin de La Chute, Saint-Apollinaire, QC G0S 2E0

SAINT-AUGUSTIN-DE-DESMAURES — D6 *Quebec*

CAMPING JUNEAU CHALETS **Ratings: 7.5/8.5★/7** (Campground) 127 Avail: 54 full hkups, 50 W, 50 E (30/50 amps). 2021 rates: $43 to $62. May 01 to Oct 31. (866)871-9090, 155 Chemin du Lac, Saint-Augustin-De-Desmaures, QC G3A 1W7

CAMPING LE 209 **Ratings: 5.5/8.5★/8.5** (Campground) 31 Avail: 17 full hkups, 14 W, 14 E (20/30 amps). 2021 rates: $36 to $42. May 11 to Oct 29. (418)878-4254, 209 Rte 138, Saint-Augustin-De-Desmaures, QC G3A 1W7

SAINT-BARTHELEMY — E5 *Lanaudiere*

CAMPING DU VIEUX MOULIN
Ratings: 8/10★/9 (Campground) 140 Avail: 107 full hkups, 33 W, 33 E (30 amps). 2021 rates: $41.75 to $45.23. May 15 to Oct 10. (450)885-3591, 2780 Rue Buteau, St Barthelemy, QC J0K 1X0

We appreciate your business!

SAINT-BERNARD-DE-LACOLLE — C2 *Monteregie*

CAMPING COOLBREEZE **Ratings: 7/9.5★/9** (Campground) Avail: 14 full hkups (15/30 amps). 2021 rates: $40 to $48. Apr 21 to Oct 21. (450)246-3785, 144 Montee Glass, Saint-Bernard-De-Lacolle, QC J0J 1V0

CAMPING DU LAC CRISTAL **Ratings: 9/7.5/8** (Campground) 64 Avail: 48 full hkups, 16 W, 16 E (30 amps). 2021 rates: $40 to $60. May 15 to Oct 15. (450)246-3773, 38 Chemin Cristal, Saint-Bernard-De-Lacolle, QC J0J 1V0

SAINT-BONIFACE — E5 *Mauricie*

CAMPING ST BONIFACE **Ratings: 8/9.5★/10** (Campground) Avail: 37 full hkups (15/30 amps). 2021 rates: $37 to $42. May 10 to Oct 14. (819)535-7047, 1850 Boul Trudel Est, Saint-Boniface-de-Shawinigan, QC G0X 2L0

SAINT-CELESTIN — E5 *Centre du Quebec*

CAMPING VAL-LERO **Ratings: 8/10★/8.5** (Campground) 88 Avail: 80 full hkups, 8 W, 8 E (20/30 amps). 2021 rates: $46.97 to $51.97. May 10 to Sep 15. (819)229-3545, 1000 Rang Val-Lero, Saint-Celestin, QC J0C 1G0

SAINT-CHARLES-BORROMEE — A2 *Lanaudiere*

CAMPING DE LA RIVE **Ratings: 8/9★/8.5** (Campground) Avail: 43 full hkups (30/50 amps). 2021 rates: $42 to $47. May 01 to Oct 30. (450)755-6555, 45 Sansregret, Saint-Charles-Borromee, QC J6E 7Y8

SAINT-CHARLES-SUR-RICHELIEU — A3 *Monteregie*

DOMAINE MADALIE **Ratings: 7/9★/8** (Campground) Avail: 70 full hkups (15/30 amps). 2021 rates: $37 to $40. May 17 to Oct 17. (450)584-2444, 512-3e Rang N, Saint-Charles-Sur-Richelieu, QC J0H 2G0

SAINT-CHRYSOSTOME — B2 *Monteregie*

CAMPING RUSSELTOWN **Ratings: 8.5/9★/8** (Campground) 35 Avail: 27 full hkups, 8 W, 8 E (15/30 amps). 2021 rates: $45 to $60. May 13 to Oct 09. (450)826-4841, 258 Rang Notre Dame, Saint-Chrysostome, QC J0S 1R0

SAINT-COME — E4 *Lanaudiere*

CAMPING SUMMUM DE ST COME **Ratings: 7/10★/8** (Campground) 20 Avail: 10 full hkups, 10 W, 10 E (15/30 amps). 2021 rates: $39 to $50. May 17 to Oct 06. (800)559-1968, 2340 Rg Versaille (Hwy 347 N), Saint-Come, QC J0K 2B0

PARC NATIONAL DU MONT-TREMBLANT/CAMPING SECTEUR DE L'ASSOMPTION (Public National Park) From jct Hwy 117 & Hwy 327: Go 1.1 km to 1st roundabout exit/QC-117 S, then 7.7 m to 2nd roundabout exit/QC 117 S, then 750 m W on Rue Saint Faustin, then 2.3 km E on Rue Principale, then 800 m W on Chemin du Lac Superieur, then 12.4 km E on Chemin du Lac Superieur/Chemin du Moulin David (R). 76 Avail. 2021 rates: $23.20 to $33.05. May 09 to Oct 13. (877)688-2281

SAINT-DAMASE — B3 *Monteregie*

BASE PLEIN AIR SAINT-DAMASE **Ratings: 7/UI/8** (Campground) Avail: 84 full hkups (15/30 amps). 2021 rates: $29 to $40. May 17 to Sep 15. (418)776-2828, 302 Rte 297 Sud, Saint-Damase-De-Matapedia, QC G0J 2J0

SAINT-DAVID-DE-FALARDEAU — C6 *Saguenay-Lac-Saint-Jean*

MUNICIPAL L'OASIS (Campground) (Phone Update) 22 Avail: 5 full hkups, 11 W, 11 E (15/30 amps). 2021 rates: $35 to $40. May 22 to Sep 13. (418)673-3066, 694 Chemin du Lac Emmuraille, Saint-David-De-Falardeau, QC G0V 1C0

SAINT-DONAT — E4 *Lanaudiere*

PARC NATIONAL DU MONT-TREMBLANT/CAMPING SECTEUR DE LA PIMBINA (Public National Park) From jct Hwy 329 & Hwy 125: Go 8 km/5 mi N on Hwy 125 (L). Avail: 1 full hkups (30 amps). 2021 rates: $24.75 to $40.30. May 11 to Oct 08. (877)688-2281

SAINTE-AGATHE-DES-MONTS — A1 *Laurentides*

CAMPING DU DOMAINE LAUSANNE **Ratings: 6.5/9★/9** (Campground) 344 Avail: 267 full hkups, 77 W, 77 E (20/30 amps). 2021 rates: $35.16 to $65.23. May 10 to Oct 20. (819)326-3550, 150 Rte 117, Sainte-Agathe-Des-Monts, QC J8C 2Z8

SAINTE-ANGELE-DE-MONNOIR — B3 *Monteregie*

CAMPING DOMAINE DU REVE **Ratings: 9/10★/10** (Campground) 260 Avail: 75 full hkups, 80 W, 80 E (30/50 amps). 2021 rates: $52 to $59. May 01 to Oct 15. (450)469-2524, 85 Rang de la Cote-Double, Sainte-Angele-De-Monnoir, QC J0L 1P0

SAINTE-ANNE-DE-BEAUPRE — D6 *Quebec*

CAMPING LAC AUX FLAMBEAUX **Ratings: 6/8.5★/7** (Campground) 10 Avail: 5 full hkups, 5 W, 5 E (20/30 amps). 2021 rates: $43.50. May 01 to Oct 15. (418)456-8618, 9491 Boul Ste-Anne, Sainte-Anne-De-Beaupre, QC G0A 3C0

SAINTE-ANNE-DES-MONTS — B9 *Gaspesie*

CAMPING DU RIVAGE **Ratings: 5/8/6.5** (Campground) 24 Avail: 24 W, 24 E (15/30 amps). 2021 rates: $40 to $45. May 15 to Oct 15. (418)763-8387, 500 1Ere Ave Ouest, Sainte-Anne-Des-Monts, QC G4V 1H4

PARC NATIONAL DE LA GASPESIE/LAC CASCAPEDIA (Public National Park) From jct Hwy 132 & Hwy 299: Go 32 km/20 mi S on Hwy 299 to Gite Mont-Albert. 71 Avail. 2021 rates: $31. Jun 23 to Sep 29. (418)763-7494

PARC NATIONAL DE LA GASPESIE/MONT-ALBERT (Public National Park) From Hwy 132 E in Sainte-Anne-des-Monts: Go S on Hwy 299 to Gite du Mont-Albert. Avail: 23 E (20 amps). 2021 rates: $31 to $33.50. Jun 22 to Sep 29. (418)763-7494

SAINTE-CATHERINE-DE-HATLEY — F5 *Cantons de l'Est*

CAMPING HATLEY **Ratings: 7/8/7.5** (Campground) Avail: 48 full hkups (30/50 amps). 2021 rates: $36 to $50. May 10 to Oct 14. (819)843-5337, 250 Chemin Magog, Sainte-Catherine-de-Hatley, QC J0B 1W0

SAINTE-CECILE-DE-MASHAM — E3 *Outaouais*

GATINEAU PARK/PHILIPPE LAKE (Public Prov Park) From jct Hwy 105 & Hwy 366: Go 8 km/5 mi W on Hwy 366. 128 Avail. 2021 rates: $15.60 to $35.60. (819)456-3016

SAINTE-CECILE-DE-MILTON — B3 *Monteregie*

CAMPING OASIS **Ratings: 9.5/9.5★/8** (Campground) 91 Avail: 80 full hkups, 11 W, 11 E (30 amps). 2021 rates: $46 to $49. Apr 26 to Oct 14. (450)378-2181, 974-1st Rang Ouest, Sainte-Cecile-De-Milton, QC J0E 2C0

SAINTE-CROIX — E6 *Chaudiere-Appalaches*

CENTRE DE VILLEGIATURE BELLE-VUE **Ratings: 8.5/10★/9.5** (Campground) Avail: 21 full hkups (15/30 amps). 2021 rates: $32 to $54. May 01 to Oct 15. (418)926-3482, 6940 Pointe Platon, Sainte-Croix, QC G0S 2H0

SAINT-EDOUARD-DE-MASKINONGE — E5 *Mauricie*

CAMPING DE ST EDOUARD **Ratings: 8/9★/9** (Campground) Avail: 119 full hkups (30/50 amps). 2021 rates: $46.96 to $51.31. May 10 to Sep 29. (819)268-2422, 3371 Rang Des Chutes, Saint-Edouard-De-Maskinonge, QC J0K 2H0

SAINTE-EMELIE-DE-L'ENERGIE — E4 *Lanaudiere*

CAMPING SAINTE-EMILIE **Ratings: 7/8★/8** (Campground) Avail: 21 full hkups (15/30 amps). 2021 rates: $40 to $47.85. May 15 to Sep 15. (450)886-5879, 1551 Rte Saint-Joseph, Sainte-Emelie-de-L'Energie, QC J0K 2K0

SAINTE-FLAVIE — C8 *Bas-Saint-Laurent*

RESTO CAMPING CAPITAINE HOMARD **Ratings: 7/7.5/7.5** (Campground) Avail: 42 full hkups (15/30 amps). 2021 rates: $35 to $40. May 07 to Sep 20. (418)775-8046, 180 Rte de La Mer (Rte 132), Sainte-Flavie, QC G0J 2L0

SAINTE-GENEVIEVE-DE-BATISCAN — E5 *Mauricie*

CAMPING PARC DE LA PENINSULE **Ratings: 8.5/8.5★/9** (Campground) 197 Avail: 163 full hkups, 34 W, 34 E (20/30 amps). 2021 rates: $50 to $55. May 10 to Sep 22. (418)362-2043, 250 Grande Pointe Rd, Sainte-Genevieve-De-Batiscan, QC G0X 2R0

QC

SAINTE-JULIENNE — A2 *Lanaudiere*

CAMPING KELLY **Ratings: 7.5/7/8** (Campground) Avail: 30 full hkups (30 amps). 2021 rates: $45 to $50. May 15 to Sep 30. (450)831-2422, 2795 rue du Camping, Sainte-Julienne, QC J0K 2T0

SAINT-ELIE-DE-CAXTON — E5 *Mauricie*

FLORIBELL **Ratings: 6.5/8.5★/9** (Campground) 25 Avail: 15 full hkups, 10 W, 10 E (15/30 amps). 2021 rates: $37.50 to $53.50. May 10 to Oct 07. (819)221-5731, 391 Lac Bell, Saint-Elie-de-Caxton, QC G0X 2N0

SAINTE-LUCE — C8 *La Mitis*

CAMPING CHALETS LA LUCIOLE **Ratings: 5.5/9★/9** (Campground) Avail: 57 full hkups (20/30 amps). 2021 rates: $35 to $55. Jun 17 to Sep 07. (418)739-3258, 118 Route 132 West, Sainte-Luce, QC G0K 1P0

SAINTE-MADELEINE — B3 *Monteregie*

CAMPING SAINTE MADELEINE **Ratings: 8.5/10★/9** (Campground) Avail: 112 full hkups (30 amps). 2021 rates: $42 to $45. Apr 26 to Oct 07. (450)795-3888, 10 St Simon St, Sainte-Madeleine, QC J0H 1S0

SAINTE-MARCELLINE-DE-KILDARE — A2 *Lanaudiere*

CAMPING SOL AIR **Ratings: 7/9★/9** (Campground) Avail: 20 full hkups (30 amps). 2021 rates: $34.80 to $47.84. May 17 to Sep 29. (450)883-3400, 760 9e Rang, Sainte-Marcelline-De-Kildare, QC J0K 2Y0

SAINTE-MELANIE — A2 *Lanaudiere*

CAMPING A LA PLAGE BERNARD **Ratings: 7.5/7.5/7** (Campground) Avail: 33 full hkups (30/50 amps). 2021 rates: $29.99 to $35.99. May 03 to Sep 15. (450)756-2560, 100 Boul Bernard, Sainte-Melanie, QC J0K 3A0

CAMPING CAMPUS **Ratings: 7.5/10★/8** (Campground) Avail: 15 full hkups (15/30 amps). 2021 rates: $47.83 to $55. May 01 to Oct 31. (450)883-2337, 6571 Rte de Sainte-Beatrix, Sainte-Melanie, QC J0K 3A0

SAINTE-MONIQUE-DE-HONFLEUR — C6 *Saguenay-Lac-Saint-Jean*

CENTRE TOURISTIQUE SAINTE-MONIQUE (Public Prov Park) From S City Limit on Hwy 169: Go .05 km/1/4 mi S on Hwy 169, then 1 km/3/4 mi W on Rang 6 Ouest. 80 Avail: 34 full hkups, 12 W, 12 E. (418)347-3124

SAINTE-ROSE-DU-NORD — C6 *Saguenay-Lac-Saint-Jean*

CAMPING LA DESCENTE DES FEMMES (Campground) (Phone Update) Avail: 26 full hkups (15 amps). 2021 rates: $27 to $35. Jun 01 to Oct 15. (418)675-2581, 154 De La Montagne, Sainte-Rose-Du-Nord, QC G0V 1T0

SAINTE-SABINE — E7 *Chaudiere-Appalaches*

CAMPING CARAVELLE - PARKBRIDGE **Ratings: 8.5/9★/9** (Campground) Avail: 49 full hkups (30/50 amps). 2021 rates: $46.25 to $59.75. Apr 26 to Oct 27. (450)293-7637, 180 Rang de la Gare, Sainte-Sabine, QC J0J 2B0

SAINTE-SERAPHINE — E5 *Centre du Quebec*

CAMPING LAC DES CYPRES **Ratings: 7.5/9★/7.5** (Campground) Avail: 40 full hkups (30 amps). 2021 rates: $47.95 to $52.95. May 01 to Oct 13. (819)336-3443, 175 des Cypres, Sainte-Seraphine, QC J0A 1E0

SAINTE-SOPHIE — A2 *La Riviere-du-Nord*

CAMPING AU PIN D'ERABLE **Ratings: 7.5/9/8** (Campground) 44 Avail: 4 full hkups, 40 W, 40 E (15/30 amps). 2021 rates: $50 to $65. May 10 to Sep 10. (514)436-8319, 161 Chemin Du Lac Bertrand, Sainte-Sophie, QC J5J 2M1

SAINTE-SOPHIE-DE-LEVRARD — E5 *Centre du Quebec*

CAMPING PLAGE PARIS **Ratings: 7/9★/8.5** (Campground) 97 Avail: 68 full hkups, 29 W, 29 E (15/30 amps). 2021 rates: $49.95 to $54.95. May 16 to Sep 14. (819)288-5948, 315 Rang St-Antoine, Sainte-Sophie-de-Levrard, QC G0X 3C0

SAINTE-THECLE — D5 *Mauricie*

DOMAINE LAC ET FORET **Ratings: 7.5/9.5★/9.5** (Campground) 89 Avail: 77 full hkups, 12 W, 12 E (15/30 amps). 2021 rates: $49 to $69. May 17 to Sep 17. (418)289-3871, 131, 12e Av. du Lac-Croche Sud, Sainte-Thecle, QC G0X 3G0

SAINT-ETIENNE-DE-BOLTON — F5 *Cantons de l'Est*

DOMAINE DES CANTONS **Ratings: 9/10★/8.5** (RV Park) Avail: 92 full hkups (30/50 amps). 2021 rates: $49.95 to $51.95. (450)297-2444, 315 Rte 112 , Saint-Etienne-De-Bolton, QC J0E 2E0

DOMAINE DU LAC LIBBY **Ratings: 8/10★/9** (Campground) 90 Avail: 30 full hkups, 60 W, 60 E (15/30 amps). 2021 rates: $41 to $55. May 10 to Sep 09. (450)297-2221, 426 Rang 1 , Saint-Etienne-De-Bolton, QC J0E 2E0

SAINT-ETIENNE-DES-GRES — E5 *Mauricie*

CAMPING DU LAC BLAIS **Ratings: 7/8.5★/7.5** (Campground) Avail: 36 full hkups (15/30 amps). 2021 rates: $30 to $35. May 15 to Sep 15. (819)535-2783, 2191 7E Rang, Saint-Etienne-des-Gres, QC G0X 2P0

SAINTE-VERONIQUE — E3 *Laurentides*

MUNICIPAL DE STE VERONIQUE (Public) From town: Go 1 mi N on Hwy 117 (R). Avail: 32 full hkups (30/50 amps). 2021 rates: $41.24. May 11 to Oct 08. (819)275-2155

SAINT-FABIEN — C7 *Bas-Saint-Laurent*

BIC/ST FABIEN (Public) From town: Go 700 m/ 1/2 mi SW on 1re Rue, then 1.7 km/1 mi SW on 1 Rang O, then 2.7 km/1-1/2 mi E on QC-132 (R). 76 Avail: 18 W, 18 E (20/30 amps). 2021 rates: $20.38 to $36.79. May 01 to Oct 01. (418)869-3333

SAINT-FAUSTIN-LAC-CARRE — A1 *Laurentides*

DOMAINE DESJARDINS **Ratings: 7/7.5/7.5** (Campground) 33 Avail: 8 full hkups, 25 W, 25 E (20/30 amps). 2021 rates: $41 to $50. May 15 to Sep 02. (819)688-2179, 1045 Rue De La Pisciculture, Saint-Faustin-Lac-Carre, QC J0T 1J3

SAINT-FELICIEN — C5 *Saguenay-Lac-Saint-Jean*

CAMPING MUNICIPAL ST-FELICIEN (Public) From Jct of Rtes 167 & 169: Go 6.4 km/4 mi N on Rte 167 (R). 169 Avail: 59 full hkups, 110 W, 110 E (15/30 amps). 2021 rates: $25 to $46.74. May 16 to Oct 07. (418)679-1719

SAINT-FELIX-DE-VALOIS — A2 *Lanaudiere*

CAMPING AUX BOULEAUX **Ratings: 7/9.5★/9** (Campground) 82 Avail: 64 full hkups, 18 W, 18 E (15/30 amps). 2021 rates: $40.01 to $48.70. May 10 to Sep 15. (450)889-5809, 2294 Rg St-Leon, Saint-Felix-De-Valois, QC J0K 2M0

CAMPING AVENTURE SENTINELLE **Ratings: 6.5/8.5/8.5** (Campground) Avail: 48 full hkups (20/30 amps). 2021 rates: $52 to $66. May 15 to Sep 15. (450)889-2244, 201 Des Sources, Saint-Felix-De-Valois, QC J0K 2M0

CAMPING GLOBE TROTTER **Ratings: 6/10★/8** (Campground) Avail: 4 full hkups (30/50 amps). 2021 rates: $43 to $46. May 15 to Sep 15. (450)889-5832, 1200 Chemin de Ligne Brandon, Saint-Felix-De-Valois, QC J0K 2M0

SAINT-FELIX-D'OTIS — C6 *Charlevoix*

CAMPING MUNICIPAL DE ST-FELIX-D'OTIS (Public) From town: Go 9.7 km/6 mi W on Rte 170, then 1.6 km/1 mi NE on Sentier St-Hilaire (E). 218 Avail: 156 full hkups, 52 W, 52 E (20/30 amps). 2021 rates: $25 to $43. May 19 to Sep 20. (418)697-1617

SAINT-FERREOL-LES-NEIGES — D6 *Quebec*

CAMPING MONT STE-ANNE **Ratings: 7.5/7.5/8.5** (Campground) 88 Avail: 50 full hkups, 38 W, 38 E (20/30 amps). 2021 rates: $49 to $61. May 17 to Oct 14. (800)463-1568, 2000 Boul Beau-Pre, Beaupre, QC G0A 1E0

SAINT-FRANCOIS-D'ORLEANS — D6 *L'Ile-d' Orl'eans*

CAMPING ILE D'ORLEANS **Ratings: 9/10★/9.5** (Campground) 131 Avail: 26 full hkups, 105 W, 105 E (30 amps). 2021 rates: $45 to $75. May 17 to Oct 14. (418)829-2953, 357 Chemin Royal, Saint-Francois-D'Orleans, QC G0A 3S0

SAINT-GEDEON — C6 *Saguenay-Lac-Saint-Jean*

CAMPING 2 RIVIERES (Campground) (Phone Update) 90 Avail: 83 full hkups, 7 W, 7 E (30/50 amps). 2021 rates: $33 to $48. May 15 to Sep 15. (418)582-3278, 824, RR 204, Saint-Gedeon, QC G0M 1T0

SAINT-GEORGES-DE-MALBAIE — C10 *Gaspesie*

AUBERGE FORT - PREVEL (Public Prov Park) From Jct Rue Annett & Hwy 132 E: Go 3.5 km SE on Hwy 132/Boulevard de Douglas (L). 28 Avail: 28 W, 28 E. 2021 rates: $21 to $39. Jun 20 to Sep 21. (418)368-2281

CAMPING CAP-ROUGE **Ratings: 7/8.5★/8** (Campground) Avail: 49 full hkups (20/30 amps). 2021 rates: $32 to $41. May 15 to Sep 30. (418)645-3804, 2009, route 132 est, Saint-Georges-de-Malbaie, QC G0C 2X0

CAMPING TETE D'INDIEN **Ratings: 7/8/7.5** (Campground) Avail: 19 full hkups (30/50 amps). 2021 rates: $34 to $46. May 01 to Oct 10. (418)645-2333, 1669 Rte 132 E, Saint-Georges-de-Malbaie, QC G0C 2X0

SAINT-GODEFROI — C10 *Gaspesie*

CAMPING MUNICIPAL ST-GODEFROI (Public) In center town on Rte 132 (R). 17 Avail: 10 full hkups, 7 W, 7 E (15/30 amps). 2021 rates: $25 to $45. Jun 20 to Sep 10. (418)752-6316

SAINT-HENRI-DE-TAILLON — C6 *Saguenay-Lac-Saint-Jean*

CAMPING BELLEY (Campground) (Phone Update) 178 Avail: 111 full hkups, 67 W, 67 E (30/50 amps). 2021 rates: $48 to $62. May 25 to Oct 07. (418)347-3612, 100 Chemin Belley, Saint-Henri-de-Taillon, QC G0W 2X0

PARC NATIONAL DE LA POINTE-TAILLON (Public National Park) From town: Go 1.1 km/3/4 mi N on Hwy 169, then 5.7 km/3-1/2 mi W on 3e Rang O (L). 74 Avail: Pit toilets. 2021 rates: $24. (418)347-5371

SAINT-HONORE — C6 *Saguenay-Lac-Saint-Jean*

CAMPING LAC JOLY (Campground) (Phone Update) Avail: 215 full hkups (15 amps). 2021 rates: $25 to $46. May 25 to Sep 15. (418)673-4777, 901 Chemin du Cap, Saint-Honore-de-Chicoutimi, QC G0V 1L0

SAINT-HYACINTHE — B3 *Monteregie*

CAMPING DE L'ETE **Ratings: 8.5/10★/8.5** (Campground) 55 Avail: 37 full hkups, 18 W, 18 E (30/50 amps). 2021 rates: $34.20 to $100. May 01 to Oct 30. (450)799-1110, 5960-5e Rang, Saint-Hyacinthe, QC J2R 2A4

SAINT-JEAN-BAPTISTE — B3 *Monteregie*

CAMPING AU PIED DU MONT (Campground) (Phone Update) Avail: 15 full hkups (30 amps). 2021 rates: $34 to $44. Apr 20 to Oct 20. (450)467-6318, 3225 Rang du Cordon, Saint-Jean-Baptiste, QC J0L 2B0

CAMPING AUCLAIR **Ratings: 8.5/9★/9** (Campground) Avail: 151 full hkups (30 amps). 2021 rates: $45 to $50. May 01 to Sep 30. (450)467-1898, 4450 Rg. des Etangs, Saint-Jean-Baptiste, QC J0L 2B0

CAMPING LAC DU REPOS - PARKBRIDGE **Ratings: 8.5/8.5★/9.5** (Campground) Avail: 58 full hkups (30 amps). 2021 rates: $46.25 to $59.75. May 10 to Oct 14. (450)467-3671, 5715 Rang de La Riviere Nord, Saint-Jean-Baptiste, QC J0L 2B0

LE DOMAINE DE ROUVILLE **Ratings: 8.5/9.5★/10** (Campground) 192 Avail: 56 full hkups, 136 W, 136 E (30 amps). 2021 rates: $35.75 to $61.75. May 17 to Oct 14. (450)467-6867, 1925 Chemin Rouville, Saint-Jean-Baptiste, QC J0L 2B0

SAINT-JEAN-PORT-JOLI — D7 *Chaudiere-Appalaches*

CAMPING AU BONNET ROUGE **Ratings: 6/9★/8.5** (Campground) 36 Avail: 30 full hkups, 6 W, 6 E (30 amps). 2021 rates: $32.18 to $41.75. May 18 to Oct 14. (418)598-1919, 76 Ave de Gaspe Est, Saint-Jean-Port-Joli, QC G0R 3G0

CAMPING DE LA DEMI-LIEUE **Ratings: 8.5/10★/9.5** (Campground) 174 Avail: 129 full hkups, 45 W, 45 E (15/30 amps). 2021 rates: $44.59 to $49.99. May 10 to Sep 29. (418)598-6108, 589 ave de Gaspe Est, Saint-Jean-Port-Joli, QC G0R 3G0

SAINT-JEAN-SUR-RICHELIEU — B3 *Monteregie*

CAMPING LES CEDRES **Ratings: 8.5/10★/8.5** (Campground) 91 Avail: 76 full hkups, 8 W, 8 E (30/50 amps). 2021 rates: $47 to $60. May 01 to Nov 01. (450)346-9276, 658 Route 219, Saint-Jean-sur-Richelieu, QC J2Y 1C4

SAINT-JEROME — A2 *Laurentides*

CAMPING LAC LAFONTAINE - PARKBRIDGE **Ratings: 7.5/9.5/9** (Campground) 143 Avail: 36 full hkups, 107 W, 107 E (30/50 amps). 2021 rates: $38 to $59.75. (450)431-7373, 1100 Boulevard Du Grand-Heron, Saint-Jerome, QC J5L 1G2

SAINT-JOSEPH-DE-BEAUCE — E6 *Chaudiere-Appalaches*

CAMPING MUNICIPAL ST JOSEPH (Public) From Jct of Rtes 173 & 276, W 3 mi on Rte 276 (L). Avail: 28 full hkups (20/30 amps). 2021 rates: $26.09 to $38.27. May 10 to Sep 10. (418)397-5953

SAINT-LAMBERT-DE-LAUZON — E6 *Chaudiere-Appalaches*

CAMPING LE RUISSEAU BLEU **Ratings: 8/8.5★/8.5** (Campground) 34 Avail: 19 full hkups, 6 W, 6 E (30 amps). 2021 rates: $44 to $46. May 15 to Sep 15. (418)889-9100, 1635 des Erables St, Saint-Lambert-De-Lauzon, QC G0S 2W0

SAINT-LIBOIRE — A3 *Monteregie*

CAMPING PLAGE LA LIBERTE **Ratings: 8/10★/9** (Campground) 108 Avail: 92 full hkups, 16 W, 16 E (15/30 amps). 2021 rates: $48 to $52. May 01 to Sep 15. (450)793-2716, 129 Rang Charlotte, Saint-Liboire, QC J0H 1R0

SAINT-LOUIS-DE-BLANDFORD — E5 *Centre du Quebec*

DOMAINE DU LAC LOUISE **Ratings: 8.5/8.5★/9** (Campground) 88 Avail: 74 full hkups, 14 W, 14 E (30 amps). 2021 rates: $39 to $59. May 03 to Oct 14. (819)364-7002, 950 Rte 263 N, Saint-Louis-De-Blandford, QC G0Z 1B0

SAINT-MATHIEU-DE-BELOEIL — B3 *Monteregie*

CAMPING ALOUETTE - PARKBRIDGE **Ratings: 10/10★/10** (Campground) 203 Avail: 170 full hkups, 33 W, 33 E (30/50 amps). 2021 rates: $43 to $68.75. Apr 08 to Oct 31. (450)464-1661, 3449, de L'Industrie, Saint-Mathieu-De-Beloeil, QC J3G 4S5

SAINT-MATHIEU-DE-RIOUX — C7 *Bas-Saint-Laurent*

KOA BAS-ST-LAURENT CAMPGROUND **Ratings: 10/10★/10** (Campground) 153 Avail: 149 full hkups, 4 W, 4 E (30/50 amps). 2021 rates: $49 to $92. May 03 to Oct 06. (800)562-2482, 109 Chemin du Lac Sud, Saint-Mathieu-de-Rioux, QC G0L 3T0

SAINT-MICHEL-DE-BELLECHASSE — D6 *Chaudiere-Appalaches*

CAMPING PARC ST MICHEL **Ratings: 5/UI/8.5** (Campground) Avail: 25 full hkups (30/50 amps). 2021 rates: $32 to $45. May 15 to Sep 15. (418)884-2621, 7 Chemin des Campings, Saint-Michel-De-Bellechasse, QC G0R 3S0

SAINT-OMER — C9 *Gaspesie*

CAMPING AUX FLOTS BLEUS **Ratings: 5.5/8★/8.5** (Campground) Avail: 16 full hkups (15/30 amps). 2021 rates: $38 to $50. May 01 to Sep 30. (418)364-3659, 279 Rte 132 Ouest, Saint-Omer, QC G0C 2Z0

SAINT-OURS — A3 *Monteregie*

CAMPING BELLERIVE (MARINA) **Ratings: 9.5/10★/10** (Campground) Avail: 70 full hkups (30/50 amps). 2021 rates: $55 to $74. May 03 to Oct 14. (450)785-2272, 1992 Chemin des Patriotes, Saint-Ours, QC J0G 1P0

SAINT-PAULIN — E5 *Mauricie*

CAMPING BELLE MONTAGNE **Ratings: 7.5/9★/8.5** (Campground) 33 Avail: 24 full hkups, 9 W, 9 E (30 amps). 2021 rates: $34.79 to $43.49. May 17 to Oct 14. (819)268-2881, 2470 Belle Montagne, Saint-Paulin, QC J0K 3G0

SAINT-PHILIPPE — B2 *Monteregie*

CAMPING 15/30 **Ratings: 9.5/10★/9.5** (Campground) Avail: 44 full hkups (30/50 amps). 2021 rates: $59 to $69. Apr 25 to Oct 25. (450)659-8868, 110 Rang St Andre, Saint-Philippe, QC J0L 2K0

CAMPING AMERIQUE MONTREAL **Ratings: 7.5/8/7.5** (Campground) 20 Avail: 11 full hkups, 9 W, 9 E (30/50 amps). 2021 rates: $36.53 to $41.75. Apr 01 to Oct 31. (450)659-8282, 40 rang St Andre, Saint-Philippe, QC J0L 2K0

CAMPING LA CLE DES CHAMPS RV RESORT

good sam park

Ratings: 10/10★/10 (Campground) From Jct of Hwy 30 & Exit 104 (Rte 104), E 1.7 mi on Rte 104 to Rang St-Raphael, S 2 mi to Montee St-Claude, W 0.5 mi (R). **FAC:** paved rds. (201 spaces). Avail: 34 all weather, patios, 6 pull-thrus, (30x75), back-ins (30x45), 34 full hkups (30/50 amps), seasonal sites, WiFi @ sites, dump, laundry, groc, LP gas, fire rings, firewood, controlled access. **REC:** heated pool, hot tub, shuffleboard, playground. Pet restrict (B). Partial handicap access. No tents. Big rig sites, eco-friendly. 2021 rates: $63 to $78. Apr 05 to Oct 20.
(450)659-3389 Lat: 45.361975, Lon: -73.446600
415 Montee St Claude, Saint-Philippe, QC J0L 2K0
www.campinglacledeschamps.com
See ad this page

KOA MONTREAL SOUTH **Ratings: 8.5/10★/9** (Campground) 193 Avail: 147 full hkups, 46 W, 46 E (30/50 amps). 2021 rates: $40 to $105. May 01 to Oct 15. (450)659-8626, 130 Boul Monette, Saint-Philippe, QC J0L 2K0

SAINT-PIE — B3 *Monteregie*

CAMPING AQUA-PARC ST-PIE **Ratings: 9/10★/8** (Campground) Avail: 93 full hkups (30 amps). 2021 rates: $55. May 01 to Oct 31. (450)772-2614, 289 Chemin St-Dominique, Saint-Pie, QC J0H 1W0

CAMPING AU VIEUX FOYER ENR. **Ratings: 8/9★/8.5** (Campground) Avail: 70 full hkups (20/30 amps). 2021 rates: $35 to $45. May 01 to Sep 30. (450)772-5177, 105 Chemin St Dominique, Saint-Pie, QC J0H 1W0

SAINT-POLYCARPE — B1 *Monteregie*

CAMPING ST POLYCARPE **Ratings: 8.5/9★/9** (Campground) 69 Avail: 45 full hkups, 24 W, 24 E (20/30 amps). 2021 rates: $39.14 to $43.49. May 10 to Sep 15. (450)265-3815, 1400 St-Philippe Road, Saint-Polycarpe, QC J0P 1X0

SAINT-ROCH-DE-L'ACHIGAN — A2 *Lanaudiere*

CAMPING HORIZON **Ratings: 7/9★/8** (Campground) 20 Avail: 10 full hkups, 10 W, 10 E (30/50 amps). 2021 rates: $46 to $54. May 07 to Sep 15. (450)588-5607, 170 St Philippe Rd, Saint-Roch-De-L'Achigan, QC J0K 3H0

SAINT-ROCH-DE-RICHELIEU — A3 *Monteregie*

CAMPING DOMAINE DES ERABLES - PARKBRIDGE **Ratings: 9.5/10★/9.5** (Campground) 154 Avail: 123 full hkups, 31 W, 31 E (30/50 amps). 2021 rates: $46.75 to $59.75. Apr 26 to Oct 27. (450)785-2805, 500 rue St-Pierre, Saint-Roch-De-Richelieu, QC J0L 2M0

SAINT-ROCH-DES-AULNAIES — D7 *Chaudiere-Appalaches*

CAMPING DES AULNAIES **Ratings: 8.5/10★/9.5** (Campground) 191 Avail: 117 full hkups, 74 W, 74 E (30 amps). 2021 rates: $39 to $53. May 10 to Sep 22. (418)354-2225, 1399 Rte de La Seigneurie, Saint-Roch-Des-Aulnaies, QC G0R 4E0

SAINT-ROSAIRE — E5 *Centre du Quebec*

CAMPING DOMAINE DU LAC CRISTAL **Ratings: 9.5/10★/9** (Campground) Avail: 224 full hkups (30/50 amps). 2021 rates: $67.50 to $77.50. May 04 to Oct 15. (819)752-4275, 251 Rte 162, Chemin Grande-Ligne, Saint-Rosaire, QC G0Z 1K0

SAINT-SIMEON — C7 *Quebec*

CAMPING FAMILLE MORIN **Ratings: 7/7.5★/8** (Campground) Avail: 24 full hkups (30 amps). 2021 rates: $35. May 01 to Nov 01. (418)514-9268, 1640 Rte 138, Saint-Simeon, QC G0T 1X0

CAMPING LEVESQUE **Ratings: 6/8.5★/8.5** (Campground) 26 Avail: 10 full hkups, 16 W, 16 E (15/30 amps). 2021 rates: $30 to $35. May 17 to Oct 07. (418)638-5220, 40 Rte Port-Aux-Quilles (138), Saint-Simeon, QC G0T 1X0

CAMPING MUNICIPAL DE ST-SIMEON (Public) From Jct of Rtes 170 & 138, W 0.25 mi on Rte 138 to Ferry Rd (Festival St), S 0.5 mi (L). 112 Avail: 95 full hkups, 9 W, 9 E (30/50 amps). 2021 rates: $19.50 to $30. May 11 to Oct 08. (418)638-5253

SAINT-TITE — D5 *Mauricie*

CAMPING LA GERVAISIE **Ratings: 6.5/10★/8.5** (Campground) Avail: 96 full hkups (20/30 amps). 2021 rates: $52.25. May 15 to Sep 16. (418)365-7171, 1 Lac Trottier, Saint-Tite, QC G0X 3H0

SAINT-VALLIER — D6 *Chaudiere-Appalaches*

CAMPING LE DOMAINE CHAMPETRE **Ratings: 9/10★/9.5** (Campground) 110 Avail: 55 full hkups, 45 W, 45 E (30/50 amps). 2021 rates: $41 to $55. May 15 to Sep 08. (418)884-2270, 888 Montee de La Station, Saint-Vallier, QC G0R 4J0

SCOTT — E6 *Chaudiere-Appalaches*

CAMPING PARC DE LA CHAUDIERE **Ratings: 8.5/9.5★/8** (Campground) 57 Avail: 40 full hkups, 17 W, 17 E (30 amps). 2021 rates: $46.10 to $48.70. May 10 to Sep 22. (866)882-5759, 100 rue du Camping St, Scott, QC G0S 3G0

SHAWINIGAN — E5 *Mauricie*

CAMPING OTAMAC **Ratings: 9/9.5★/8.5** (Campground) 175 Avail: 130 full hkups, 45 W, 45 E (30/50 amps). 2021 rates: $45.23 to $62.62. May 15 to Sep 15. (819)538-9697, 5431 Av Tour Du Lac, Lac-a-la-Tortue, QC G0X 1L0

CAMPING ROUILLARD **Ratings: 7.5/9★/8.5** (Campground) 149 Avail: 114 full hkups, 35 W, 35 E (15/30 amps). 2021 rates: $43 to $55. Apr 26 to Oct 27. (819)538-2159, 5095 Ave Tour-du-Lac, Lac-a-la-Tortue, QC G0X 1L0

LA MAURICIE/MISTAGANCE (Public National Park) From jct Hwy 55 (exit 217) & Hwy 351 S: Go 24 km/15 mi N on Hwy 351. Avail: 26 E (15/30 amps). 2021 rates: $25.50 to $29.40. May 17 to Oct 07. (877)737-3783

LA MAURICIE/WAPIZAGONKE (Public National Park) From jct Hwy 55 (exit 217) & Hwy 351: Go 48 km/30 mi N on Hwy 351. 159 Avail. 2021 rates: $25.50. May 17 to Sep 30. (877)737-3783

PARC DE L'ILE MELVILLE (Public) From jct Hwy 55 & Exit 211 (Rte 153): Go 4.4 km/2-3/4 mi N on Rte 153, then .8 km/1/2 mi S on Rte 157 (L). 146 Avail: 107 full hkups, 19 W, 19 E (30/50 amps). 2021 rates: $27.50 to $45.50. May 15 to Oct 01. (819)536-0222

RESERVE FAUNIQUE DU SAINT-MAURICE/CAMPING LAC NORMAND (Public National Park) From jct Hwy 159 & Hwy 155: Go 65 km/40-1/4 mi N on Hwy 155 (R). Avail: 10 W. 2021 rates: $29.75 to $33.65. May 09 to Sep 01. (819)646-5687

QC

SHEFFORD — F5 *Cantons de l'Est*

CAMPING DE L'ESTRIE **Ratings: 8.5/9.5★/7** (Campground) 31 Avail: 10 full hkups, 21 W, 21 E (15/30 amps). 2021 rates: $42 to $55. Apr 30 to Oct 01. (450)539-3728, 630 Chemin de Frost Village, Shefford, QC J2M 1C1

SHERBROOKE — F5 *Cantons de l'Est*

CAMPING BEAU-LIEU **Ratings: 8.5/8.5★/8** (Campground) Avail: 53 full hkups (15/30 amps). 2021 rates: $43 to $48. May 01 to Oct 08. (819)864-4531, 5153 Chemin Ste Catherine , Sherbrooke, QC J1N 3B8

CAMPING ILE-MARIE **Ratings: 8/9★/7.5** (Campground) Avail: 119 full hkups (20/30 amps). 2021 rates: $40.88 to $45.23. May 15 to Sep 15. (819)820-0330, 225 Rue St Francis, Sherbrooke, QC J1M 0B3

CAMPING LAC MAGOG **Ratings: 8.5/9/8** (Campground) 82 Avail: 59 full hkups, 23 W, 23 E (15/30 amps). 2021 rates: $37.95 to $59.45. May 10 to Sep 29. (819)864-4401, 7255 Chemin Blanchette, Sherbrooke, QC J1N 0G7

Park owners and staff are rightly proud of their business. Let them know how much you enjoyed your stay.

STANSTEAD — F5 *Estrie*

CAMPING LAC FRONTIERE (BORDER LAKE) (Campground) (Phone Update) 76 Avail: 61 full hkups, 15 W, 15 E (15/30 amps). 2021 rates: $36 to $42. May 11 to Sep 30. (819)876-5505, 150, Route 143 North, Stanstead, QC J0B 3E1

STONEHAM — D6 *Quebec*

CAMPING STONEHAM **Ratings: 8.5/8.5★/7.5** (Campground) 293 Avail: 104 full hkups, 58 W, 84 E (30/50 amps). 2021 rates: $51 to $82. May 10 to Sep 08. (418)848-2233, 71 Chemin Saint-Edmond, Stoneham-et-Tewkesbury, QC G3C 1G3

TADOUSSAC — C7 *Manicouagan*

CAMPING TADOUSSAC (Campground) (Phone Update) 187 Avail: 52 full hkups, 135 W, 135 E (20/50 amps). 2021 rates: $33 to $58. May 29 to Sep 28. (855)708-4501, 428 Du Bateau Passeur (RtE 138), Tadoussac, QC G0T 2A0

TEMISCOUATA-SUR-LE-LAC — D7 *Bas-Saint-Laurent*

CAMPING CABANO **Ratings: 8.5/10★/8** (RV Park) Avail: 98 full hkups (15/30 amps). 2021 rates: $38 to $43. Apr 01 to Oct 31. (418)854-9133, 1155 Ch du Golf Quartier Cabano , Temiscouata-sur-le-Lac, QC G0L 1E0

TERREBONNE — A2 *Lanaudiere*

CAMPING AU PLATEAU 5 ETOILES **Ratings: 9/10★/8** (Campground) 31 Avail: 28 full hkups, 3 W, 3 E (15/30 amps). 2021 rates: $44 to $55. Apr 15 to Oct 15. (450)471-6266, 1770 Cote Terrebonne, Terrebonne, QC J6Y 1E2

TROIS-PISTOLES — C7 *Bas-Saint-Laurent*

CAMPING MUNICIPAL TROIS PISTOLES (Public) From Jct of Rtes 132 7 293 W 1 mi on Rte 132 to Rue Chanoine-Cote, N 0.6 mi (E). 160 Avail: 104 full hkups, 56 W, 56 E (15/30 amps). 2021 rates: $30 to $40. May 26 to Sep 06. (418)851-4515

CAMPING PLAGE TROIS-PISTOLES **Ratings: 8/9★/8** (Campground) 119 Avail: 90 full hkups, 29 W, 29 E (30/50 amps). 2021 rates: $38 to $42. Jun 01 to Sep 30. (418)851-2403, 130 Chemin Rioux, Trois-Pistoles, QC G0L 4K0

TROIS-RIVIERES — E5 *Centre du Quebec*

CAMPING LA ROCHELLE **Ratings: 8/8.5★/9.5** (Campground) 75 Avail: 70 full hkups, 5 W, 5 E (15/30 amps). 2021 rates: $44 to $49. May 01 to Nov 01. (819)372-9636, 471 Rue des Marguerites, Trois-Rivieres, QC G8W 2B6

CAMPING LAC ST MICHEL **Ratings: 8/9.5★/9.5** (Campground) 76 Avail: 51 full hkups, 25 W, 25 E (20/30 amps). 2021 rates: $44.59 to $48.99. May 10 to Sep 29. (819)374-8474, 11650 Du Clairon, Trois-Rivieres, QC G9A 5E1

DOMAINE AU GRAND 'R' **Ratings: 8/10★/9** (Campground) Avail: 150 full hkups (15/30 amps). 2021 rates: $68. May 11 to Sep 10. (819)378-3723, 761 Rue des Prairies, Trois-Rivieres, QC G8W 2E5

UPTON — A3 *Monteregie*

CAMPING WIGWAM **Ratings: 9/9★/9.5** (Campground) Avail: 75 full hkups (30 amps). 2021 rates: $46. May 03 to Oct 14. (450)549-4513, 425 Rue Principale St, Upton, QC J0H 2E0

VAL-ALAIN — E6 *Chaudiere-Appalaches*

CAMPING LAC GEORGES **Ratings: 8/9.5★/8.5** (Campground) 200 Avail: 131 full hkups, 69 W, 69 E (20/30 amps). 2021 rates: $61.73 to $66.75. May 09 to Oct 08. (418)744-3510, 150, Seigneuriale St, Val-Alain, QC G0S 3H0

VALCARTIER — D6 *Quebec*

CAMPING VALCARTIER (Campground) (Phone Update) 425 Avail: 124 full hkups, 301 W, 301 E (30/50 amps). 2021 rates: $38 to $70. Jun 11 to Sep 06. (418)844-2200, 1860 Boul Valcartier, Valcartier, QC G0A 4S0

VAL-DAVID — A1 *Laurentides*

CAMPING LAURENTIEN **Ratings: 8/7.5/8.5** (Campground) 44 Avail: 10 full hkups, 12 W, 12 E (20/30 amps). 2021 rates: $51 to $56. May 15 to Sep 09. (819)322-2281, 1949 Guertin St, Val-David, QC J0T 2N0

Had a great stay? Let us know by emailing us Parks@goodsam.com

VENISE-EN-QUEBEC — C3 *Monteregie*

CAMPING PLAGE CHAMPLAIN **Ratings: 9/9.5★/8.5** (Campground) 81 Avail: 26 full hkups, 18 W, 18 E (20/30 amps). 2021 rates: $44 to $47. May 15 to Sep 15. (450)244-5317, 29 Avenue Venise W, Venise-En-Quebec, QC J0J 2K0

CAMPING PLAGE KIRKLAND **Ratings: 9/9★/9** (Campground) 50 Avail: 23 full hkups, 15 W, 15 E (15/30 amps). 2021 rates: $38 to $62. May 01 to Sep 30. (450)244-5337, 39 Ave Venise Est, Venise-En-Quebec, QC J0J 2K0

CAMPING PLAGE VENISE **Ratings: 8.5/6.5/6.5** (Campground) 17 Avail: 16 full hkups, 1 W, 1 E (30/50 amps). 2021 rates: $35 to $40. May 15 to Oct 01. (514)979-5325, 94 Ave Venise Est, Venise-En-Quebec, QC J0J 2K0

DOMAINE FLORENT **Ratings: 8.5/8.5★/7.5** (Campground) Avail: 15 full hkups (15/30 amps). 2021 rates: $41 to $44.50. May 15 to Sep 15. (450)244-5607, 272 23 Avenue Est, Venise-en-Quebec, QC J0J 2K0

WEEDON — E6 *Cantons de l'Est*

CAMPING BEAU-SOLEIL **Ratings: 8/7/8** (Campground) 60 Avail: 40 full hkups, 20 W, 20 E (15/30 amps). 2021 rates: $37 to $50. May 11 to Sep 14. (819)877-5000, 1225 Route 112, Weedon, QC J0B 3J0

WEST BROME — B3 *Cantons de l'Est*

CAMPING VALLEE BLEUE **Ratings: 9/10★/8.5** (Campground) 45 Avail: 18 full hkups, 17 W, 17 E (30 amps). 2021 rates: $35 to $63. May 15 to Oct 15. (450)263-4804, 50 Haman, West Brome, QC J0E 2P0

YAMASKA — A3 *Centre du Quebec*

PARC NATIONAL DE LA YAMASKA (Public National Park) From I-10 (exit 68) & Hwy 139: Go 1.5 km/1 mi N on Hwy 139 (L). 147 Avail: 147 W, 147 E (15/30 amps). 2021 rates: $35. May 11 to Oct 08. (450)776-7182

County names help you follow the local weather report.

DID YOU KNOW ?

Purple sand beaches can be found in Prince Albert National Park, Hunter Bay and Candle Lake.

YOU ARE HERE

Saskatchewan

Getty Images/iStockphoto

SK

Saskatchewan is a virtual showcase for Canada's sprawling prairies and forests. Home to 100,000-plus lakes and rivers, endless prairies and untouched parkland, Saskatchewan is a doorway to untamed wilderness.

Meet the Mounties

In Regina, visitors can see where Mounties are made and glimpse the past. Swing by the RCMP Heritage Centre to see Mounties in training and hear the story of how the national police force came to be. The Royal Saskatchewan Museum goes even further back in time by unveiling the province's rich First Nations history and its dinosaur-filled past. You can also experience indigenous culture firsthand in Saskatoon's Wanuskewin Heritage Park. Tour Castle Butte in the badlands of the Big Muddy Valley in the south.

Perfect Park

Prince Albert National Park isn't a household word, but it should be. The park has been named by National Geographic as one of the country's "50 Places of a Lifetime." Scenic drives offer glimpses of wild bison; ziplines let you soar across boreal forest; and tranquil backcountry lakes provide the ultimate escape from city life. Grasslands National Park is worth a visit just for a prairie safari, which brings you close to bison, antelope and eagles.

Ride the White Water

Head to the Churchill River for high-speed rafting action on churning whitewater. It's also an excellent spot for catching walleye and northern pike. If you're set on trophy fish, make your way to the remote Milton Lake Lodge. Located in northern Saskatchewan, this renowned angling destination is where you go to battle gigantic trout and northern pike. Afterward, relax in salty Little Manitou Lake, known as the Dead Sea of Canada.

Saskatchewan Regina-Style Pizza

After a bite of this pie, you'll never see deep-dish pizza the same way again. This prairie dish features a thick and crispy pan crust, Greek-spiked tomato sauce, ample toppings and golden-brown cheese. In some restaurants, this dish is as thick as three inches. This pizza is served in several eateries in Regina. Many locals recommend Houston Pizza's "All Dressed" pie.

VISITOR CENTER

TIME ZONE
Central Standard

ROAD & HIGHWAY INFORMATION
888-335-7623
roadinfo.telenium.ca

FISHING & HUNTING INFORMATION
877-237-2273
tourismsaskatchewan.com/things-to-do/fishing

BOATING INFORMATION
800-267-6687
tc.gc.ca/boatingsafety

NATIONAL PARKS
pc.gc.ca/en/pn-np

PROVINCIAL PARKS
tourismsaskatchewan.com/places-to-go/provincial-parks

TOURISM INFORMATION
Tourism Saskatchewan
877-237-2273
tourismsaskatchewan.com

TOP TOURISM ATTRACTIONS
1) Royal Canadian Mounted Police Heritage Center
2) Prince Albert National Park
3) Fort Walsh National Historic Site

MAJOR CITIES
Saskatoon, Regina (capital), Prince Albert, Moose Jaw, Yorkton

good sam park

Featured Good Sam Parks

SASKATCHEWAN

When you stay with Good Sam, you can expect the highest degree of cleanliness and friendliness, and better yet, you get **10% off** overnight campground fees.

If you're not already a Good Sam member you can purchase your membership at one of these locations:

INDIAN HEAD
Indian Head Campground

SASKATOON
Campland RV Resort

Getty Images/iStockphoto

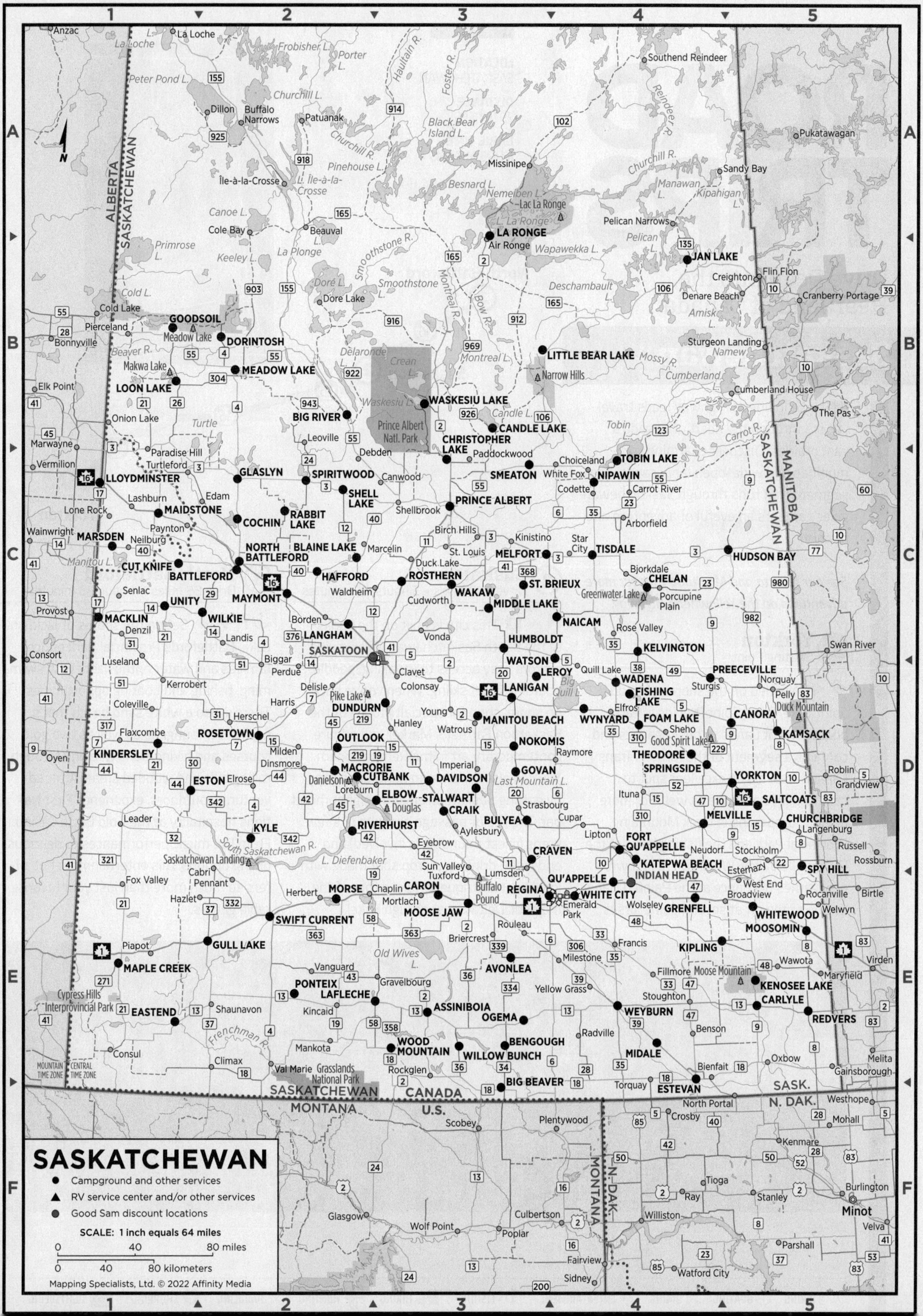
SASKATCHEWAN
Campground and other services
RV service center and/or other services
Good Sam discount locations
SCALE: 1 inch equals 64 miles
0 40 80 miles
0 40 80 kilometers
Mapping Specialists, Ltd. © 2022 Affinity Media
1 2 3 4 5
A B C D E F
N
ALBERTA
SASKATCHEWAN
MANITOBA
MONTANA
N. DAK.
SASK.
CANADA
U.S.
MOUNTAIN TIME ZONE
CENTRAL TIME ZONE
Anzac
La Loche
L. La Loche
Frobisher L.
Porter L.
Haultain R.
Foster R.
Southend Reindeer
Reindeer R.
Peter Pond L.
Churchill L.
Dillon
Buffalo Narrows
Patuanak
Black Bear Island L.
Churchill R.
Pukatawagan
Île-à-la-Crosse
L. Île-à-la-Crosse
Pinehouse L.
Missinipe
Sandy Bay
Besnard L.
Nemeiben L.
Lac La Ronge
L. La Ronge
Manawan L.
Kipahigan L.
Canoe L.
Cole Bay
Beauval
Pelican Narrows
Pelican L.
LA RONGE
Air Ronge
Wapawekka L.
Primrose L.
Keeley L.
La Plonge
Smoothstone R.
JAN LAKE
Creighton
Flin Flon
Cold L.
Doré L.
Dore Lake
Smoothstone L.
Montreal R.
Bow R.
Deschambault
Denare Beach
Amisk L.
Cranberry Portage
Cold Lake
Pierceland
Bonnyville
GOODSOIL
Meadow Lake
DORINTOSH
Beaver R.
Delaronde L.
Crean L.
Montreal L.
LITTLE BEAR LAKE
Mossy R.
Sturgeon Landing
Namew L.
Makwa Lake
MEADOW LAKE
LOON LAKE
Narrow Hills
Cumberland L.
Elk Point
Waskesiu L.
WASKESIU LAKE
Cumberland House
BIG RIVER
Onion Lake
Turtle L.
Prince Albert Natl. Park
Candle L.
CANDLE LAKE
Tobin L.
The Pas
Marwayne
Paradise Hill
Leoville
CHRISTOPHER LAKE
Paddockwood
Carrot R.
Vermilion
Turtleford
Debden
SMEATON
Choiceland
TOBIN LAKE
LLOYDMINSTER
GLASLYN
SPIRITWOOD
Canwood
White Fox
NIPAWIN
Lashburn
Edam
SHELL LAKE
Codette
Carrot River
Lone Rock
MAIDSTONE
RABBIT LAKE
Shellbrook
PRINCE ALBERT
COCHIN
Arborfield
Wainwright
Paynton
Birch Hills
MARSDEN
Neilburg
NORTH BATTLEFORD
BLAINE LAKE
Marcelin
Kinistino
Star City
TISDALE
HUDSON BAY
St. Louis
MELFORT
Manitou L.
CUT KNIFE
BATTLEFORD
Duck Lake
Bjorkdale
HAFFORD
ROSTHERN
CHELAN
ST. BRIEUX
Senlac
MAYMONT
Waldheim
WAKAW
Greenwater Lake
Porcupine Plain
Provost
UNITY
Cudworth
MIDDLE LAKE
MACKLIN
WILKIE
Borden
NAICAM
Denzil
Landis
LANGHAM
Vonda
Rose Valley
HUMBOLDT
SASKATOON
KELVINGTON
Swan River
Consort
Luseland
Biggar
Perdue
Clavet
WATSON
LEROY
Quill Lake
PREECEVILLE
Big Quill L.
Kerrobert
Delisle
Colonsay
LANIGAN
WADENA
Sturgis
Norquay
Pike Lake
FISHING LAKE
Pelly
Coleville
Harris
DUNDURN
Elfros
Duck Mountain
Herschel
Young
MANITOU BEACH
WYNYARD
FOAM LAKE
CANORA
Flaxcombe
ROSETOWN
Hanley
Watrous
Sheho
KAMSACK
KINDERSLEY
OUTLOOK
NOKOMIS
Good Spirit Lake
Oyen
Milden
Raymore
THEODORE
Dinsmore
Imperial
SPRINGSIDE
Roblin
MACRORIE
GOVAN
ESTON
Elrose
Danielson
CUTBANK
DAVIDSON
Last Mountain L.
YORKTON
Grandview
Loreburn
Ituna
ELBOW
STALWART
SALTCOATS
Douglas
CRAIK
Strasbourg
MELVILLE
Leader
CHURCHBRIDGE
KYLE
RIVERHURST
BULYEA
Cupar
Langenburg
Aylesbury
Lipton
FORT QU'APPELLE
Russell
Eyebrow
Neudorf
Stockholm
South Saskatchewan R.
CRAVEN
Rossburn
Saskatchewan Landing
L. Diefenbaker
KATEPWA BEACH
SPY HILL
Sun Valley
Lumsden
Esterhazy
Cabri
INDIAN HEAD
Fox Valley
Pennant
Tuxford
Buffalo Pound
QU'APPELLE
West End
Herbert
MORSE
Chaplin
CARON
REGINA
WHITE CITY
Broadview
Rocanville
Birtle
Hazlet
Mortlach
Emerald Park
Wolseley
GRENFELL
Welwyn
SWIFT CURRENT
MOOSE JAW
WHITEWOOD
Rouleau
MOOSOMIN
Briercrest
Francis
Piapot
GULL LAKE
KIPLING
Old Wives L.
Milestone
Wawota
Virden
MAPLE CREEK
Vanguard
AVONLEA
Fillmore
Moose Mountain
Maryfield
PONTEIX
Gravelbourg
Yellow Grass
KENOSEE LAKE
Cypress Hills Interprovincial Park
LAFLECHE
Stoughton
CARLYLE
EASTEND
Shaunavon
Kincaid
ASSINIBOIA
WEYBURN
REDVERS
OGEMA
Benson
Frenchman R.
Radville
Consul
Mankota
WOOD MOUNTAIN
WILLOW BUNCH
BENGOUGH
MIDALE
Melita
Climax
Oxbow
Val Marie
Grasslands National Park
Rockglen
Bienfait
Gainsborough
BIG BEAVER
Torquay
ESTEVAN
SASKATCHEWAN
North Portal
Westhope
Scobey
Plentywood
Crosby
Mohall
Kenmare
Tioga
Burlington
Glasgow
Ray
Stanley
Minot
Culbertson
Williston
Wolf Point
Poplar
Velva
Parshall
Fairview
Watford City
Sidney

ROAD TRIPS

Drive Deep Into the Heartland of Canada

Saskatchewan

LOCATION
SASKATCHEWAN

DISTANCE
292 MILES

DRIVE TIME
4 HRS 45 MINS

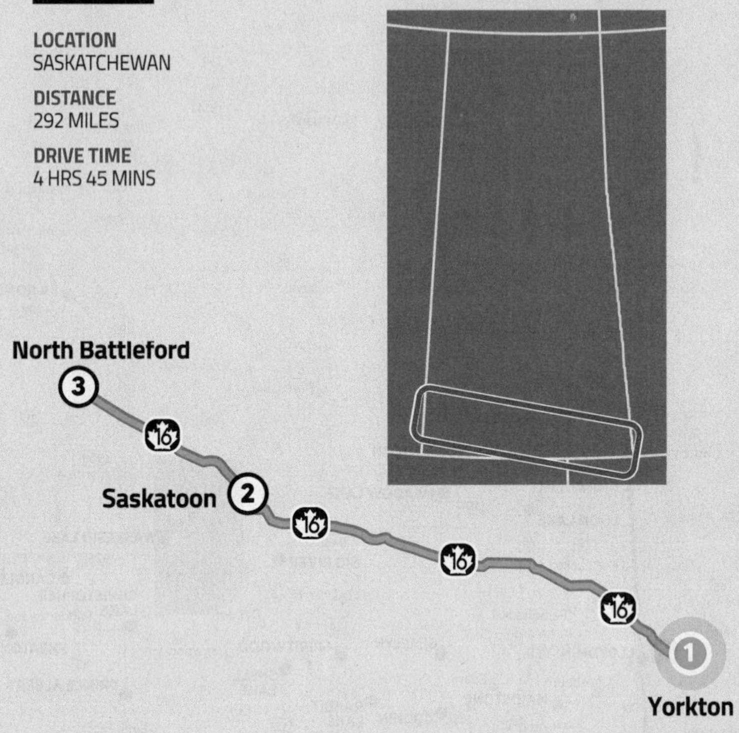

The Yellowhead Highway leads travelers through the heart of Canada's vast prairies. Discover charming communities and wide-open landscapes. The segment that runs through Saskatchewan gives campers an eyeful of adventure and history.

See our Alberta and Manitoba trips for more adventures on the Yellowhead Highway.

1 Yorkton
Starting Point

Nestled on the shores of Good Spirit Lake, Good Spirit Provincial Park boasts one of Canada's best beaches and contains a segment of the famous Trans Canada Trail. It's an excellent spot to catch walleye and pike as well. For more angling, drop a line in Duck Mountain Provincial Park and the fishing lakes of the Qu'Appelle Valley. While you're in town, play games of chance at the Painted Hand Casino or tee off at several golf courses.

2 Saskatoon
Drive 207 Miles ▪ 3 hours, 22 minutes

This city is built on the banks of the South Saskatchewan River, giving visitors easy access to kayaking, paddle-boarding or jet skiing. When you're back on shore, shop for specialty foods at the Saskatoon Farmer's Market and admire contemporary art in the Remai Modern. You can also become an honorary citizen by getting Saskatoon'ed at a neighborhood bar. The rite of passage consists of a few steps (chest pounding is involved) and ends with drinking a drop shot made with local beer and liqueur. Take a tour of the majestic Delta Bessborough Hotel.

3 North Battleford
Drive 85 miles ▪ 1 hour, 23 minutes

Set on the shores of Jackfish Lake, Battlefords Provincial Park entices families and water enthusiasts with swimming, fishing and boating opportunities. There's also a white sand beach that's perfect for lounging, as well as two golf courses and hiking trails weaving through rolling hills and wooded areas. After adventuring outdoors, experience First Nations hospitality at the Gold Eagle Casino. From live music performances to delicious dining options, this entertainment hub offers so much more than just your favorite table games.

Getty Images/iStockphoto

BIKING BOATING DINING ENTERTAINMENT FISHING HIKING HUNTING PADDLING SHOPPING SIGHTSEEING

Saskatchewan SPOTLIGHTS

Expect the Unexpected in Canada's Heartland

See where Mounties get made and walk the riverbanks of the "Paris of the Prairies." Saskatchewan is full of surprises for travelers eager to discover historic and natural treasures.

A MUTATION CAUSES THE TREES IN CROOKED BUSH TO BEND.

Aspens populate the Crooked Bush site in the Redberry Lake Biosphere Reserve.

Getty Images/iStockphoto

8 Hidden Gems in Saskatchewan

Driving through endless wheat fields may not sound like a grand adventure, but it can be if you know where to go. Hidden between flat stretches of grassland are surprises big and small — from dinosaur fossils and underground networks used during the Prohibition to ancient indigenous sites and Canada's own Dead Sea. Before you hit the road, make sure you add these eight hidden gems to your Saskatchewan itinerary.

See the Mysterious Crooked Bush

Northwest of Hafford in the Redberry Lake Biosphere Reserve is an eerie scene that looks straight out of a Tim Burton movie. Dubbed one of the 54 Wonders of Canada, the Crooked Bush is a collection of aspen trees with tangled trunks and twisted branches. Aspen trees usually grow straight, but local researchers believe these unusual woods were caused by a rare genetic mutation. The misshapen trees make a dramatic backdrop, especially during sunset, so follow the boardwalk with your camera in hand and capture this oddity.

Go back to Prohibition in Moose Jaw

Moose Jaw was a major railway hub in the early 20th century with routes south to Chicago via Minneapolis. The town also had a network of tunnels to help run local boiler rooms. Both of these factors made Moose Jaw a prime destination for bootleggers during Prohibition. Gangsters used the tunnels as gambling dens, brothels and liquor storage. According to local legend, even Al Capone made the trip north on occasion. See the historic tunnels for yourself by joining a guided theatrical tour with the Tunnels of Moose Jaw.

Discover Petroglyphs at the Ancient Echoes Interpretive Center

Not far from Herschel is the Ancient Echoes Interpretive Center, home to Indigenous artifacts and painting displays like "The Disappearance of Plains Buffalo" by Jo Cooper. After viewing the exhibits, take a guided tour to view three petroglyphs with ceremonial markings. You can also tour the nearby Coal Mine Ravine to see a buffalo rubbing stone, buffalo jump and a cluster of stone circles.

Step Inside a Traditional Ukrainian Church

Nicknamed the "perogy belt," the eastern part of the province has a long history of Ukrainian settlement. In Yorkton, admire the onion-shaped dome of St. Mary's Church and then go inside to see the painted ceiling depicting the heavenly coronation of the Virgin Mary. Afterward, stop by the Western Development Museum to hear the stories of early pioneers. Highlights include recreated rooms of settlers' homes, agricultural artifacts and two compelling carvings by Ukrainian settler Victor Humeniuk.

Hike the Valley of 1,000 Devils

The Killdeer Badlands within Grasslands National Park is home to the Valley of 1,000 Devils, a slice of dusty terrain teeming with dinosaur fossils and flat buttes. Start your

SK

LOCAL FAVORITE

Peanut Butter Chicken

Saskatchewan boasts an eclectic menu of food choices. Mix things up on your next visit with this delicious chicken dish. *Recipe by Sheena Pemberton.*

INGREDIENTS

- ☐ ¾ cup creamy peanut butter
- ☐ ¾ cup water
- ☐ ⅓ cup soy sauce
- ☐ 1 tsp garlic powder
- ☐ 4 Tbsp lemon juice
- ☐ ¼ cup packed brown sugar
- ☐ ½ tsp cayenne pepper
- ☐ 1 tsp ground ginger
- ☐ 2 lbs chicken breasts or thighs sliced into 1-inch strips
- ☐ Garlic salt and pepper to taste
- ☐ Skewers

DIRECTIONS

Combine first 8 items in the ingredients list in a small saucepan. Heat and mix until smooth and well combined. Remove a half cup for basting chicken and set the rest aside. Thread slices of chicken onto skewers and baste with a little of the peanut butter sauce. Oil the barbecue grill and place slices of chicken over open flame.

Cook 3-5 minutes, baste and flip skewers. Baste again, cook an additional 3-5 minutes or until cooked through. Remove from grill and serve with extra sauce for dipping.

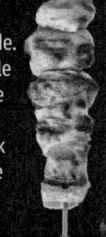

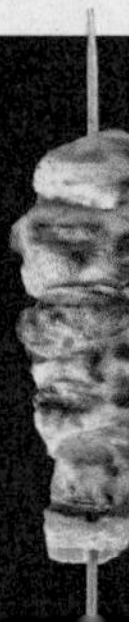

SPOTLIGHTS

journey from McGowan's Visitor Center at Rock Creek Campground and hike until the prairie landscape gives way to red hoodoos and wind-sculpted spires. Along the way, keep an eye out for mule deer, golden eagles and short-horned lizards. This stretch of badlands is known to be extremely hot, so it's best to hike early in the morning.

Learn about Indigenous History at Wanuskewin

First Nations history runs deep in the hills and valley of Opimihaw Creek. Dating back over 6,000 years, this area known as Wanuskewin has been used by Plains tribes as a trading hub, ceremonial site and settlement. Today, a large interpretative center lets you discover the past with a museum and restaurant serving traditional dishes such as muskeg tea and bison stew. You can also take part in archaeological digs and stay overnight in a traditional tipi. Cultural events like powwows are also held regularly.

Float in Canada's Dead Sea

Just a 90-minute drive from Saskatoon is Little Manitou Lake, Canada's own Dead Sea. The lake is fed by underground springs and is three times saltier than the ocean, allowing you to float weightlessly on the water. It's also famous for its healing properties – the water's high concentration of magnesium, potassium, sulfate, calcium, silica and sulfur can improve skin hydration, reduce inflammation and relieve joint pain. Go for a rejuvenating dip between June and August.

Visit the Cochin Lighthouse

A lighthouse in a landlocked prairie province? Yes, it's possible in Saskatchewan. Built in 1988, the Cochin Lighthouse rests on Pirot Hill and overlooks Jackfish Lake and Murray Lake. Climb 153 steps to the top of the hill for sweeping views of the white wooden structure and surrounding landscape.

Bright fall colors transform the foliage along the South Saskatchewan River in Saskatoon.

Regina

It's a good bet that many U.S. citizens associate the word "Mountie" with Dudley Do-Right, the TV cartoon character who fought arch-villain Snidely Whiplash on the Canadian frontier. However, the animated depiction couldn't be further from the truth. For more than a century, enforcers have brought criminals to justice to keep Canada safe.

Where Mounties Are Made

To learn more about the men and women who wear the iconic hats and bright-red blouses, tourists can visit the city of Regina, where the Royal Canadian Mounted Police Training Academy has been turning out mounties since the late 1800s. Regular tours take visitors to this facility, where cadets learn state-of-the-art crime-fighting techniques. Although many of today's Mounties wear navy blue uniforms, you can still catch them in their bright reds during parades and formal occasions. Close to the training facility, travelers can tour the RCMP Heritage Centre, where Mountie history is exhibited.

Saskatoon

With more sunny days per year than almost any other Canadian city, Canada's "Paris of the Prairies" boasts a vibrant downtown scene. Near the heart of the city, the palace-like Delta Bessborough Hotel, built in 1935, looms over the skyline.

Roaming the Riverbank

Nature lovers will find that outdoor experiences are close at hand in Saskatoon. Check out the Meewasin Valley, a green space that borders the South Saskatchewan River. Just over a half-hour south of the city, the twin watering holes of Blackstrap Lake and Brightwater Reservoir provide anglers the chance to land large walleye.

FOR MORE INFORMATION

Tourism Saskatchewan, 877-237-2273, www.sasktourism.com
Tourism Regina, 800-661-5099, www.tourismregina.com
Tourism Saskatoon, 800-567-2444, www.tourismsaskatoon.com

Saskatchewan

ASSINIBOIA — E3 *Assiniboia*

ASSINIBOIA REGIONAL PARK & GOLF COURSE (Public) From jct Hwy 13 & Hwy 2: Go .9 km/1/2 mi S on Hwy 2. Avail: 15 E. 2021 rates: $16.50 to $26.75. May 21 to Sep 30. (306)642-5442

AVONLEA — E3 *Moose Jaw*

DUNNET REGIONAL PARK (Public) From Jct SR-339 & SR-334: Go 3.2 km/2 mi S on SR-334, then 3.2 km/2 mi E on park access rd. 71 Avail: 2 full hkups, 48 W, 54 E (20/30 amps). 2021 rates: $20 to $40. (306)868-7664

BATTLEFORD — C2 *Battleford*

EILING KRAMER CAMPGROUND (Public) From Battleford: Go 1 mi S on SK-4 N. 74 Avail: 17 full hkups, 57 E (15/30 amps). 2021 rates: $30 to $40. May 01 to Sep 30. (306)937-6212

BENGOUGH — E3 *Weyburn*

BENGOUGH (Public) From jct Hwy 34 (3rd St) & 7th Ave: Go 1 block W on 7th Ave. 29 Avail: 29 W, 29 E (15/30 amps). 2021 rates: $22 to $30. May 01 to Oct 15. (306)268-2909

BIG BEAVER — F3 *Assiniboia*

BIG BEAVER CAMPGROUND (Public) From Jct of Hwy 18 & Hwy 34: Go 3/4 mi N on Hwy 34, then 1.9 km W on unnamed road, then 71 m N on Railway Ave, then 270 W on 2 Ave (R). Avail: 8 E (15/30 amps). 2021 rates: $15 to $20. Jun 01 to Sep 30. (306)267-4520

BIG RIVER — B2 *North Battleford*

BIG RIVER (Public) At west town limits. 65 Avail: 32 full hkups, 9 E (30/50 amps). 2021 rates: $24 to $35. May 13 to Sep 15. (306)469-2232

BLAINE LAKE — C2 *North Battleford*

MARTINS LAKE REGIONAL PARK (Public) From town: Go 24 km/15 mi NW on Hwy 12, then follow signs. Avail: 59 E (30 amps). 2021 rates: $20 to $25. May 18 to Sep 03. (306)466-4438

BULYEA — D3 *Last Mountain-Wascana*

ROWAN'S RAVINE (Public Prov Park) From Jct of Hwys 20 & 220: Go W 13 mi W on Hwy 220 (E). Avail: 301 E (30 amps). 2021 rates: $30. May 15 to Sep 01. (306)725-5200

CANDLE LAKE — B3 *Prince Albert*

CANDLE LAKE/SANDY BAY CAMPGROUND (Public Prov Park) From Jct of Hwy 120 & W Side Rd (MP-20): Go 9.7 km/6 mi W on W Side Rd (R). Avail: 225 E (15/30 amps). 2021 rates: $20 to $30. (306)929-8400

CANORA — D5 *Yorkton*

CANORA BEACH RESORT (Campground) (Phone Update) 89 Avail: 65 full hkups, 4 W, 20 E (15/30 amps), Pit toilets. 2021 rates: $42. May 15 to Sep 30. (306)563-6363, Albert Ave, Canora, SK S0A 0L0

CANORA CAMPGROUND (Public) On Roslyn Ave at north town limits. Avail: 13 E. 2021 rates: $16 to $20. May 15 to Oct 15. (306)563-5773

CARLYLE — E5 *Moose Mountain*

MOOSE MOUNTAIN/LYNWOOD (Public Prov Park) From town: Go 25.7 km/16 mi N on Hwy 9 to park rd, then .8 km/1/2 mi W on Hwy 209 (E). Avail: 11 full hkups (15/30 amps). 2021 rates: $10 to $20. (306)577-2600

CARON — E3 *Moose Jaw*

BESANT CAMPGROUND & RECREATION AREA **Ratings: 4/4.5/8** (Campground) Avail: 24 E (15/30 amps). 2021 rates: $35 to $40. May 07 to Sep 10. (306)756-2700, Parka Access Rd, Caron, SK S0H 0R0

CHELAN — C4 *Hudson Bay*

GREENWATER LAKE (Public Prov Park) From town: Go 16 km/10 mi S on Hwy 38 (R). Avail: 144 E (15/30 amps). 2021 rates: $17 to $27. May 15 to Sep 30. (306)278-3515

Directional arrows indicate the campground's position in relation to the nearest town.

CHRISTOPHER LAKE — C3 *Prince Albert*

GREAT BLUE HERON (ANDERSON POINT CAMPGROUND) (Public Prov Park) From jct Hwy 2N & Hwy 953: Go 8 km/5 mi W on Hwy 953. 32 Avail: Pit toilets. 2021 rates: $20 to $30. (306)982-6250

GREAT BLUE HERON (MURRAY POINT/NORTH CG) (Public Prov Park) From jct Hwy 2 & Hwy 263: Go 10 km/6-1/4 mi W on Hwy 263, then 5 km/3 mi N on Hwy 953. Avail: 169 E (30 amps). 2021 rates: $20 to $30. (306)982-2002

CHURCHBRIDGE — D5 *Yorkton*

CHURCHBRIDGE CAMPGROUND (Public) From Jct of Hwys 8, 16 & 80: Go .4 km/1/4 mi S on Hwy 80 (L). Avail: 29 E (15 amps). 2021 rates: $17 to $20. May 15 to Oct 09. (306)896-2240

COCHIN — C2 *Lloydminster*

THE BATTLEFORDS (Public Prov Park) From jct Hwy 26 & Hwy 4: Go 17.3 km/ 10-3/4 mi N on Hwy 4. Avail: 291 E (15/50 amps). 2021 rates: $20 to $30. (306)386-2212

CRAIK — D3 *Moose Jaw*

CRAIK & DISTRICT REGIONAL PARK (Public) From town (Craik Town exit): Go NW on Hwy 11, then 1-1/2 mi N on gravel park access rd (follow white sail signs) (E). 62 Avail: 6 full hkups, 56 W, 56 E (30 amps). 2021 rates: $14 to $22. May 15 to Sep 15. (306)734-5102

CRAVEN — D3 *Regina*

CRAVEN WORLD CAMPGROUND **Ratings: 5/8★/8.5** (Campground) 50 Avail: 45 full hkups, 5 W, 5 E (15/30 amps). 2021 rates: $35. May 01 to Sep 30. (306)731-3336, Hwy 20, Craven, SK S0G 0N0

CUT KNIFE — C1 *Battleford*

ATTON'S LAKE

(Public) From town: Go 10.5 km/6-1/2 mi E on Hwy 40, then 14 km/8-1/2 mi on Atton's Lake Rd (E). **FAC:** paved/dirt rds. Avail: 98 grass, back-ins (18x36), 97 W, 97 E (15/30 amps), tent sites, shower$, dump, laundry, groc, LP gas, firewood, restaurant, controlled access. **REC:** Atton's Lake: swim, fishing, golf, playground. Pets OK. Partial handicap access. 2021 rates: $29 to $35. May 15 to Sep 30. no cc.
(306)398-2814 Lat: 52.832528, Lon: -108.858250
Cut Knife, SK S0M 0N0
saskregionalparks.ca

TOMAHAWK CAMPGROUND (Public) In town on Hwy 40. 19 Avail: 10 W, 10 E (20/30 amps). 2021 rates: $15 to $30. Jun 01 to Sep 30. (306)398-2363

CUTBANK — D2 *Saskatoon*

DANIELSON (Public Prov Park) From Jct of Hwys 44 & 219: Go 4.8 km/3 mi S on park access rd (R). Avail: 48 E (15/30 amps). 2021 rates: $20 to $30. (306)857-5510

DAVIDSON — D3 *Saskatoon*

DAVIDSON CAMPGROUND (CITY PARK) (Public) From jct Hwy 11 & S Davidson exit: Go 2 km/1.3 mi N on Railway Ave, then 4 blocks E on Hamilton St. 38 Avail. 2021 rates: $18 to $25. May 15 to Sep 15. (306)567-2908

DORINTOSH — B2 *Meadow Lake*

MEADOW LAKE/FLOTTEN LAKE NORTH (Public Prov Park) From town: Go 4-1/2 mi N on Hwy 4 to 904 (L). 25 Avail: Pit toilets. 2021 rates: $18. May 15 to Sep 01. (306)236-7680

MEADOW LAKE/FLOTTEN LAKE SOUTH (Public Prov Park) From town: Go 4-1/2 mi N on Hwy 4 (L). 17 Avail: Pit toilets. 2021 rates: $18. May 15 to Sep 01. (306)236-7680

MEADOW LAKE/GREIG LAKE (Public Prov Park) From town: Go 4-1/2 mi N on Hwy 4 to Hwy 224 (L). 149 Avail: 9 full hkups, 130 E (15/30 amps). 2021 rates: $20 to $40. May 19 to Sep 05. (306)236-7680

MEADOW LAKE/KIMBALL LAKE (Public Prov Park) From town, N 4.5 mi on Hwy 4 to Hwy 224 (L). Avail: 167 E (15/30 amps). 2021 rates: $20 to $30. May 19 to Sep 05. (306)236-7680

MEADOW LAKE/MATHESON (Public Prov Park) From town: Go 4-1/2 mi N on Hwy 4 to Hwy 224 (L). 46 Avail: Pit toilets. 2021 rates: $20. May 19 to Sep 05. (306)236-7680

MEADOW LAKE/MISTOHAY (Public Prov Park) From town: Go 4-1/2 mi N on Hwy 4 to Hwy 224 (L). 20 Avail: Pit toilets. 2021 rates: $18. May 19 to Sep 05. (306)236-7680

MEADOW LAKE/MURRAY DOELL (Public Prov Park) From town: Go 4-1/2 mi N on Hwy 4 to Hwy 224 (L). Avail: 97 E (15/30 amps). 2021 rates: $18 to $30. May 19 to Sep 05. (306)236-7680

MEADOW LAKE/SANDY BEACH (Public Prov Park) From town: Go 4-1/2 mi N on Hwy 4 to Hwy 224 (L). Avail: 60 E (15/30 amps). 2021 rates: $20 to $30. May 15 to Sep 01. (306)236-7680

MEADOW LAKE/WATERHEN LAKE SOUTH (Public Prov Park) From town: Go 4-1/2 mi N on Hwy 4, N 10 mi on Hwy 904 (R). Avail: 22 E (15/30 amps). 2021 rates: $30. May 19 to Sep 05. (306)236-7680

DUNDURN — D3 *Saskatoon*

BLACKSTRAP (Public Prov Park) From town: Go 6.2 km/3-3/4 mi E on Hwy 211 (L). 143 Avail: 10 full hkups, 65 E (15 amps). 2021 rates: $20 to $30. (306)492-5675

EASTEND — E1 *Maple Creek*

EASTEND TOWN PARK (Public) From jct Hwy 13 (Red Coat Dr) & Tamarack Ave N: Go 2 blocks N on Tamarack Ave N. 31 Avail: 17 full hkups, 14 W, 14 E (30 amps). 2021 rates: $20 to $35. (306)295-3322

ELBOW — D3 *Moose Jaw*

DOUGLAS (Public Prov Park) From S end of town: Go 11 km/7 mi S on SR-19 (R). Avail: 140 E (15/30 amps). 2021 rates: $20 to $30. (306)854-6266

ESTEVAN — E4 *Weyburn*

WOODLAWN REGIONAL PARK (Public) From town, S 2 mi on Hwy 47 (L). Avail: 180 full hkups (15/30 amps). 2021 rates: $40. May 25 to Sep 07. (306)634-2324

ESTON — D1 *Swift Current*

ESTON RIVERSIDE REGIONAL PARK (Public) From south town limits on Hwy 30: Go 21 km/13 mi S on Hwy 30. 85 Avail: 25 full hkups, 40 E (15/30 amps). 2021 rates: $15 to $30. May 01 to Sep 30. (306)962-3845

FISHING LAKE — D4 *Quill Lakes*

LESLIE BEACH REGIONAL PARK (Public) From Jct SR-16 & CR-310: Go 16 km/10 mi N on CR-310 (R). Avail: 9 full hkups (30/50 amps). 2021 rates: $30 to $45. May 01 to Oct 31. (306)272-3968

FOAM LAKE — D4 *Wynyard*

FOAM LAKE CAMPGROUND (CITY PARK) (Public) In town at jct Hwy 16 & Hwy 310. Avail: 17 E (15/30 amps). 2021 rates: $18 to $35. (306)272-3538

FORT QU'APPELLE — D4 *Regina*

ECHO VALLEY (Public Prov Park) From town: Go 8.4 km/5-1/4 mi W on Hwy 210 (E). 308 Avail: 3 full hkups, 290 E (15/30 amps). 2021 rates: $20 to $40. (306)332-3215

Saskatchewan Privately Owned Campground Information Updated by our Good Sam Representatives

Dennis & Jackie Taylor

After rediscovering RVing following our retirement from our family publishing operation, we jumped at the opportunity to be part of Good Sam. We live in Alberta on a small ranch and enjoy traveling and spending time with our family.

SK

FORT QU'APPELLE (CONT)

↑ FORT CAMPGROUND (Public) From Jct of Hwy 10 & Boundary Rd: Go 1.6 km/1 mi N on Boundary Rd, then .18 km/200 yds W on Fort Trail (E). Avail: 24 E (15/30 amps). 2021 rates: $24 to $30. May 19 to Sep 07. (306)332-4614

GLASLYN — C2 *Lloydminster*

LITTLE LOON REGIONAL PARK (Public) From jct Hwy 4 & Hwy 3: Go 4-3/4 km/3 mi E on Hwy 3, then 1-1/2 km/1 mi S on gravel road. 61 Avail: 34 W, 34 E (15/30 amps). 2021 rates: $20 to $28. May 01 to Sep 30. (306)342-2176

GOODSOIL — B1 *Meadow*

← NORTHERN CROSS RESORT/LAC DES ISLES (Campground) (Phone Update) Avail: 13 E (15/30 amps). 2021 rates: $26 to $47. May 15 to Sep 07. (306)986-2618, Hwy 954, Goodsoil, SK S0M 1A0

GOVAN — D3 *Saskatoon*

LAST MOUNTAIN REGIONAL PARK (Public) From north town limits: Go 5 km/3 mi N on Hwy 20, then 14 km/8-3/4 mi W on grid road. Avail: 77 E (30/50 amps). 2021 rates: $30 to $35. May 05 to Sep 23. (306)484-4483

GRENFELL — E4 *Moose Mountain*

CROOKED LAKE (Public Prov Park) From jct Trans Canada Hwy 1 & Hwy 47: Go 31 km/19-1/4 mi N on Hwy 47. then E on Hwy 247. Avail: 94 E (30 amps). 2021 rates: $20 to $30. May 15 to Sep 01. (306)696-6253

← GRENFELL RECREATIONAL PARK (Public) From Jct of Trans-Canada Hwy & Desmond St: Go 1.2 km/3/4 mi N on Desmond St, then .8 km/1/2 mi W on Front St (L). 38 Avail: 9 full hkups, 29 E (20/50 amps). 2021 rates: $17 to $25. May 15 to Sep 30. (306)697-3055

GULL LAKE — E2 *Swift Current*

ANTELOPE LAKE (Public) From jct Hwy 1 & Hwy 37: Go 19 km/12 mi N on Hwy 37, then 3-1/4 km/2 mi E (follow signs). 52 Avail: 52 W, 52 E (30 amps). 2021 rates: $30. May 15 to Sep 15. (306)672-3933

→ GULL LAKE CAMPGROUND (Public) From Jct of Hwy 37 & 6th St (in town), E 0.3 mi on 6th St (L). Avail: 26 E (15/30 amps). 2021 rates: $30. May 15 to Oct 15. (306)672-3447

HAFFORD — C2 *Dundurn-Rosthern*

→ REDBERRY LAKE REGIONAL PARK (Public) From Hafford: Go 5 mi E on Hwy 40, then 3 mi S on park access rd (E). Avail: 43 E (15/50 amps). 2021 rates: $15 to $40. May 01 to Sep 30. (306)549-2149

HUDSON BAY — C5 *Hudson Bay*

↓ HUDSON BAY REGIONAL PARK (Public) From town: Go 2.4 km/1-1/2 mi S adjacent to Hwy 9 (R). Avail: 36 E (15/30 amps). 2021 rates: $20 to $30. May 15 to Sep 15. (306)865-4144

HUMBOLDT — C3 *Prince Albert*

HUMBOLDT CAMPGROUND (Public) From jct Hwys 20 & 5: Go 4 blks E on Hwy 5. Avail: 22 E (30/50 amps). 2021 rates: $23 to $35. May 01 to Oct 31. (306)682-4990

INDIAN HEAD — E4 *Wascana*

A SPOTLIGHT Introducing Hidden Gems' colorful attractions appearing at the front of this province section.

→ INDIAN HEAD CAMPGROUND

Ratings: 9/10★/9.5 (Campground) From Jct of Hwy 1 & East Entrance to Indian Head, N (across railway tracks) 0.3km/0.2 mi (L).

WE'RE #1 ON THE #1

First class RV park with all amenities imaginable! Heated pool, store, extra-large sites for Big Rigs! Full services. Amazing washrooms! Large play structure. Stay a night or stay a while. Easy access off of the TransCanada.

FAC: gravel rds. (146 spaces). Avail: 31 gravel, patios, 31 pull-thrus, (30x80), 31 full hkups (30/50 amps), seasonal sites, WiFi @ sites, dump, laundry, groc, LP bottles, fire rings, firewood, controlled access. **REC:** heated pool, boating nearby, playground. Pet restrict (B/Q) $. No tents. Big rig sites, eco-friendly. 2021 rates: $48 to $58. May 01 to Sep 30. **(855)695-3635 Lat: 50.530579, Lon: -103.656735 1100 McKay St., Indian Head, SK S0G 2K0 www.indianheadcampground.ca**

See ad page 1158

JAN LAKE — B4 *Pelican Narrows*

↑ JAN LAKE LODGE (Campground) (Phone Update) 13 Avail: 13 W, 13 E (15 amps). 2021 rates: $35. May 20 to Oct 01. (306)632-4416, Hwy 106-Hanson Lake Rd, Pelican Narrows, SK S7H 3A6

KAMSACK — D5 *Yorkton*

→ DUCK MOUNTAIN (Public Prov Park) From town: Go 21 km/13 mi E on Hwy 57, then 3 mi E on unnamed rd to park entry (E). 392 Avail: 15 full hkups, 351 E (30/50 amps). 2021 rates: $20 to $40. (306)542-5500

KATEPWA BEACH — D4 *Regina*

↓ SOUTH KATEPWA RV PARK **Ratings: 4.5/5.5/7.5** (RV Park) 18 Avail: 18 W, 18 E (30 amps). 2021 rates: $32 to $42. May 01 to Sep 30. (306)695-3330, Hwy 56 (RM156-Indian Head), Katepwa Beach, SK S0G 2K0

KELVINGTON — C4 *Melfort*

KELVINGTON LIONS PARK (Public) At south end of town on Hwy 38. Avail: 12 E (15 amps). (306)327-4482

KENOSEE LAKE — E5 *Estevan*

↑ MOOSE MOUNTAIN/FISH CREEK CAMPGROUND (Public Prov Park) From town, N 17 mi on Hwy 9 (L). 333 Avail: 11 full hkups, 11 W, 210 E (15/30 amps). 2021 rates: $20 to $40. May 01 to Oct 31. (306)577-2600

KINDERSLEY — D1 *Kindersley*

↘ GOLFVIEW MOBILE ACRES (RV Area in MH Park) (Phone Update) Avail: 43 full hkups (20/50 amps). 2021 rates: $35. (306)463-3839, 19 Golf View Tr. Crt, Kindersley, SK S0L 1S1

KINDERSLEY REGIONAL PARK (Public) From jct Hwy 7 & Ditson Dr: Go 1.5 km/1-1/4 mi S on Ditson Dr. 45 Avail: 20 full hkups, 25 W, 25 E (15/30 amps). 2021 rates: $30 to $35. May 01 to Sep 30. (306)463-2788

KIPLING — E4 *Melville*

↓ KIPLING CAMPGROUND (Public) From Jct Hwy 65 & Hwy 48: Go W 1/2 mi (.09 km) on Hwy 48, then S 1/2 mi (.08 km) on 6th Ave./Louisa Ave, then W 55 yards (50 meters) on Clare St. (E). 29 Avail: 18 full hkups, 11 W, 11 E (15/30 amps). 2021 rates: $25 to $30. May 15 to Oct 15. (306)736-8440

KYLE — D2 *Swift Current*

SASKATCHEWAN LANDING PROVINCIAL PARK (Public Prov Park) From town: Go 11 km/7 mi S on Hwy 4, then 4-3/4 km/3 mi E on park road. Avail: 255 E (30 amps). 2021 rates: $20 to $30. (306)375-5527

LA RONGE — B3 *La Ronge*

↑ LAC LA RONGE (Public Prov Park) From town: Go 24 km/15 mi N on Hwy 2 (L). Avail: 121 E (30/50 amps). 2021 rates: $18 to $30. (306)425-4234

LAFLECHE — E3 *Assiniboia*

THOMSON LAKE REGIONAL PARK (Public) From jct Hwy 13 & Hwy 58: Go 8 km/5 mi N on Hwy 58. 125 Avail: 69 full hkups, 40 E (20/50 amps). 2021 rates: $26 to $45. May 01 to Sep 30. (306)472-3752

LANGHAM — C2 *Saskatoon*

← RIVER VALLEY RV PARK **Ratings: 5.5/9★/9.5** (RV Park) Avail: 10 full hkups (30/50 amps). 2021 rates: $40. Apr 15 to Oct 31. (306)283-4672, 201 Service Rd West, Langham, SK S0K 2L0

LANIGAN — D3 *Saskatoon*

LANIGAN LIONS CAMPGROUND (Public) From jct Hwy 16 & Hoover St: Go 4 blocks N on Hoover St, then 3 blocks E on Downing Dr. 22 Avail: 16 W, 16 E (30 amps). 2021 rates: $12 to $20. May 01 to Oct 15. (306)365-2809

LEROY — D3 *Wynyard*

LEROY LEISURELAND REGIONAL PARK (Public) From Hwy 6: Go 12 mi W. 20 Avail: 20 W, 20 E (20/30 amps). 2021 rates: $30. May 15 to Sep 30. (306)286-3437

LITTLE BEAR LAKE — B3 *La Ronge*

↑ MOOSE HORN LODGE AND CAMPGROUND (Campground) (Phone Update) Avail: 26 E (15/30 amps). 2021 rates: $33. May 20 to Sep 05. (306)426-2700, Hwy 106, Smeaton, SK S0J 2J0

Be prepared! Bridge, Tunnel & Ferry Regulations and Rules of the Road can be found in the front of the Guide.

LLOYDMINSTER — C1 *Battleford*

→ WEAVER PARK CAMPGROUND (Public) From Jct of Hwy 17 & Hwy 16, E 1 mi on Hwy 16 to 45th Ave, S 0.1 mi (R). Avail: 57 full hkups (30/50 amps). 2021 rates: $44 to $52. May 01 to Sep 30. (306)825-3726

LOON LAKE — B1 *Meadow Lake*

← MAKWA LAKE/MEWASIN (Public Prov Park) From town: Go 3 mi SW on Grid 699. 36 Avail: Pit toilets. 2021 rates: $20. (306)837-2410

← MAKWA/JUMBO BEACH CAMPGROUND (Public Prov Park) From town: Go 3 mi SW on Grid 699 (L). 16 Avail: Pit toilets. 2021 rates: $20. May 19 to Sep 05. (306)837-2410

MACKLIN — C1 *Kindersley*

MACKLIN LAKE REGIONAL PARK (Public Prov Park) From jct Hwy 14 & Hwy 31: Go 3-1/4 km/2 mi S on Hwy 31 (through town), then 450 meters/500 yards SW. 193 Avail: 75 full hkups, 118 E (30 amps). 2021 rates: $26 to $30. May 01 to Oct 31. (306)753-3252

MACRORIE — D2 *Kindersley*

COLDWELL PARK REC SITE (Public Prov Park) From town: Go 8 mi SE on Hwy 44 (E). 19 Avail: Pit toilets. 2021 rates: $20. May 18 to Sep 03. (306)857-5510

MAIDSTONE — C1 *Battleford*

DELFRARI VICTORIA PARK (MAIDSTONE CITY PARK) (Public) From jct Hwy 21 & Hwy 16: Go 2.6 km/1-1/2 mi E on Hwy 16, then 1.7 km/1 mi S on Railroad Ave, then 200 m/4 blocks N on 4th St E (R). 27 Avail: 9 full hkups, 15 E (30 amps). 2021 rates: $25 to $30. May 01 to Sep 30. (306)893-2373

↑ SILVER LAKE REGIONAL PARK (Public) From Jct of Hwys 16 & 21: Go 9 mi N on Hwy 21, then 1 mi E on Silver Lake Cnty Rd, then 1/2 mi N on Regional Park access rd (E). 117 Avail: 117 W, 117 E (15/30 amps). 2021 rates: $27 to $30. Apr 15 to Oct 15. (306)893-2831

MANITOU BEACH — D3 *Quill Lakes*

↓ MANITOU & DISTRICT REGIONAL PARK (Public) From Watrous: Go 3-1/2 mi N on Hwy 365 (R). Avail: 154 E (15/30 amps). 2021 rates: $24 to $35. May 01 to Nov 27. (306)946-2588

MAPLE CREEK — E1 *Cypress Hills*

↓ CYPRESS HILLS (Public Prov Park) From town: Go 29 km/18 mi S on Hwy 21 (R). 560 Avail: 10 full hkups, 57 W, 411 E (15/30 amps). 2021 rates: $20 to $40. (306)662-5411

↑ EAGLE VALLEY PARK CAMPGROUND **Ratings: 7/9★/8** (Campground) 40 Avail: 11 full hkups, 22 W, 22 E (30 amps). 2021 rates: $45. May 01 to Sep 30. (306)662-2788, SW Q-8 of 12 of 26 W 3rd., Maple Creek, SK S0N 1N0

MARSDEN — C1 *Kindersley*

SUFFERN LAKE REGIONAL PARK (Public) From town: Go 6 km/3-3/4 mi SE on Hwy 40. 56 Avail: 24 W, 36 E (15/30 amps). 2021 rates: $15 to $20. May 01 to Sep 30. (306)210-8667

MAYMONT — C2 *North Battleford*

GLENBURN REGIONAL PARK (Public) From town: Go 8 km/5 mi S on Hwy 376. 61 Avail: 24 full hkups, 13 E (30/50 amps). 2021 rates: $15 to $32. May 01 to Sep 15. (306)389-4700

MEADOW LAKE — B2 *Lloydminster*

MEADOW LAKE LIONS PARK (Public) In town on Hwy 4. Avail: 30 E (15/30 amps). 2021 rates: $25. May 25 to Sep 07. (306)236-4447

MELFORT — C3 *Melfort*

MELFORT SOUTH CAMPGROUND (Public) From jct Hwys 3/6/41: Go 270 meters/300 yds W on Hwy 41. Avail: 16 E (15 amps). 2021 rates: $23 to $28. (306)752-7906

MELVILLE — D4 *Yorkton*

↗ MELVILLE REGIONAL PARK (Public) From Jct of Hwys 47 & 10 (Queen St), S 0.2 mi on Queen St to Halfax St, E 0.2 mi to Prince Edward St, S 0.1 mi (L). 105 Avail: 85 W, 85 E (20/30 amps). 2021 rates: $20 to $33. May 01 to Sep 30. (306)728-4111

Canada -- know the rules, regulations and tips before crossing the border. This is listed at the beginning of the country.

MIDALE — E4 *Weyburn*

MAINPRIZE REG PARK (Public) From Jct Hwy 39 & Hwy 606: Go .4 km/1/4 mi S on Hwy 606 to Stop Sign, then 8 km/5 mi W on Hwy 606 to Stop Sign, then 1.6 km/1 mi S on Hwy 606, then 6 km/3-3/4 mi W on Unnamed Access Rd (E). Avail: 33 E (30/50 amps). 2021 rates: $22 to $36. May 01 to Sep 30. (306)458-2865

MIDDLE LAKE — C3 *Quill Lakes*

LUCIEN LAKE REGIONAL PARK (Public) From Jct of Hwy 20 & Lucien Lake Rd: Go 1.6 km/1 mi W on Lucien Lake Rd (E). 94 Avail: 16 W, 86 E (15/30 amps). 2021 rates: $15 to $30. May 15 to Sep 15. (306)367-4300

MOOSE JAW — E3 *Moose Jaw*

BUFFALO POUND/ELMVIEW (Public Prov Park) From town: Go 17.7 km/11 mi N on Hwy 2, then 10.9 km/6-3/4 mi on Hwy 202 (L). Avail: 36 E (30 amps). 2021 rates: $20 to $40. (306)694-3229

BUFFALO POUND/MAPLE VALE (Public Prov Park) From town: Go 17.7 km/11 mi N on Hwy 2, then 10.9 km/6-3/4 mi on Hwy 202 (E). Avail: 46 E (30 amps). 2021 rates: $20 to $40. (306)694-3229

BUFFALO POUND/SHADY LANE (Public Prov Park) From town: Go 15.5 km/9-1/2 mi N on Hwy 2, then 16 km/10 mi E on Hwy 202 (E). Avail: 22 E (30 amps). 2021 rates: $20 to $40. (306)694-3229

PRAIRIE OASIS TOURIST COMPLEX **Ratings: 6/7.5/8** (RV Park) 54 Avail: 34 full hkups, 20 W, 20 E (15/50 amps). 2021 rates: $38 to $47. (800)854-8855, 955 Thatcher Dr E, Moose Jaw, SK S6H 4N9

MOOSOMIN — E5 *Moose Mountain*

MOOSOMIN & DISTRICT REGIONAL PARK (Public) From jct Hwy 1 & Hwy 8: Go 4-3/4 km/3 mi S on Hwy 8, then 3 mi W on Secondary Hwy 709, then 3-1/4 km/2 mi S. 120 Avail: 120 W, 120 E (15/30 amps). 2021 rates: $27.50 to $33. May 15 to Sep 30. (306)435-3531

MORSE — E2 *Moose Jaw*

MORSE CAMPGROUND (Public) From Hwy 1: Go N on Railway Ave. Avail: 12 E (30 amps). 2021 rates: $30. May 15 to Oct 31. (306)629-3300

NAICAM — C4 *Quill Lakes*

LAKE CHARRON REGIONAL PARK (Public) From town: Go 1.6 km/1 mi S on Hwy 6, then 12.8 km/8 mi E on access rd (R). Avail: 67 E (15/30 amps). 2021 rates: $10 to $25. May 15 to Sep 15. (306)874-8292

NIPAWIN — C4 *Prince Albert*

NIPAWIN & DISTRICT REGIONAL PARK (Public) From town: Go 1-1/2 mi S on Hwy 55 (L). 120 Avail: 28 full hkups, 92 W, 92 E (20/30 amps). 2021 rates: $33 to $40. May 15 to Oct 07. (306)862-3237

NOKOMIS — D3 *Saskatoon*

NOKOMIS CAMPGROUND (CITY PARK) (Public) From jct of Hwy 15 & Hwy 20: Go 1-1/2 km/1 mi N on Hwy 20 (through town to 7th Ave). 20 Avail: Pit toilets. 2021 rates: $6 to $15. May 31 to Oct 01. (306)528-2010

NORTH BATTLEFORD — C2 *North Battleford*

DAVID LAIRD CAMPGROUND (Public) From Jct of Hwy 40 & Hwy 16E: Go 1.6 km/1 mi E on Hwy 16, then 1.2 km/3/4 mi N on Unmarked Rd (L). 61 Avail: 17 full hkups, 21 W, 21 E (15/30 amps). 2021 rates: $21 to $37. May 01 to Sep 30. (306)445-3552

OGEMA — E3 *Weyburn*

OGEMA REGIONAL PARK (Public Prov Park) In town on Hwy 13. Avail: 50 E (15/30 amps). 2021 rates: $15 to $25. May 15 to Sep 13. (306)459-2537

OUTLOOK — D2 *Saskatoon*

OUTLOOK & DISTRICT REGIONAL PARK (Public Prov Park) From town: Go 45 km/28 mi S on Hwy 45. Avail: 84 E (15/30 amps). 2021 rates: $30. May 25 to Sep 07. (306)867-8846

PONTEIX — E2 *Assiniboia*

NOTUKEU REGIONAL PARK (Public Prov Park) From jct Hwy 13 & town access road (Centre St): Go 2.3 km/1-1/2 mi N on Centre St, then 1 block W on Railway Ave. Avail: 30 full hkups (15/30 amps). 2021 rates: $30 to $35. May 25 to Sep 30. (306)625-3222

The best things happen outdoors. Start your adventure today at GanderOutdoors.com

PREECEVILLE — D4 *Yorkton*

PREECEVILLE WILDLIFE CAMPGROUND (Public) Second street and eighth avenue NW in Preeceville. Avail: 7 E (30 amps). 2021 rates: $25. (306)547-2276

PRINCE ALBERT — C3 *North Central*

PRINCE ALBERT EXHIBITION RV CAMPGROUND (Public) From Jct of Hwy 2 & 15th St W: Go 3/4 mi E on 15th St W (becomes 15th St E), then 1/4 mi N on 6th Ave E, then 1/4 mi N on Exhibition Dr (E). Avail: 75 full hkups (30/50 amps). 2021 rates: $20 to $30. May 01 to Sep 30. (306)764-1611

PRINCE ALBERT EXHIBITION TRAILER & RV PARK (Campground) (Phone Update) Avail: 65 full hkups (15/30 amps). 2021 rates: $30. May 01 to Sep 30. (306)764-1711, Box 1538 - Exhibition Drive & 6th Ave East, Prince Albert, SK S6V 5T1

QU'APPELLE — E4 *Regina*

CREEKSIDE GARDENS (Campground) (Phone Update) 10 Avail: 10 W, 10 E (15/30 amps). 2021 rates: $35. May 01 to Sep 30. (306)699-7466, 95-9th Ave, Qu'Appelle, SK S0G 4A0

RABBIT LAKE — C2 *Battleford*

MEETING LAKE REGIONAL PARK (Public) From Jct Hwy 378 & Rabbit Lake Rd: Go 6 mi N on Hwy 378, then 1-1/2 mi N on Meeting Lake Rd (R). 30 Avail: 30 W, 30 E (30 amps). 2021 rates: $30. May 18 to Sep 04. (306)824-4812

REDVERS — E5 *Estevan*

REDVERS TOURISM & LOG CABIN CAMPGROUND (Public) From jct Hwy 8 & Hwy 13: Go .9 km/1/2 mi W on Hwy 13, then 100 metres/110 yds S on Methuen St. 56 Avail: 28 full hkups, 20 W, 28 E (30/50 amps). 2021 rates: $15 to $30. May 17 to Sep 01. (306)452-3276

REGINA — E3 *Wascana*

BUFFALO LOOKOUT RV PARK & CAMPING **Ratings: 5/5.5/6.5** (RV Park) 54 Avail: 46 full hkups, 8 W, 8 E (30/50 amps). 2021 rates: $39 to $50. Apr 01 to Nov 01. (306)525-1448, South East 201718 W 2, Regina, SK S4N 7L2

INDIAN HEAD CAMPGROUND

Ratings: 9/10★/9.5 (Campground) From jct SK 6 & Hwy 1: Go 65.5 km/40 mi E on Hwy 1, then 0.3 km/1000 feet N on SK 619 (L). **FAC:** gravel rds. (146 spaces). Avail: 31 gravel, patios, 31 pull-thrus, (30x80), 31 full hkups (30/50 amps), seasonal sites, WiFi @ sites, dump, laundry, groc, LP bottles, fire rings, firewood, controlled access. **REC:** heated pool, boating nearby, playground. Pet restrict (B/Q) $. No tents. Big rig sites, eco-friendly. 2021 rates: $48 to $58. May 01 to Sep 30.
(855)695-3635 Lat: 50.530579, Lon: -103.656735
1100 McKay St, Indian Head, SK S0G 2K0
www.indianheadcampground.ca
See primary listing at Indian Head and ad page 1158

KINGS ACRES CAMPGROUND **Ratings: 6/5.5/5.5** (RV Park) 60 Avail: 30 full hkups, 30 W, 30 E (20/50 amps). 2021 rates: $37 to $55. (306)522-1619, Hwy 1 E & East Gate Dr, Regina, SK S4L 7C6

RIVERHURST — D2 *Moose Jaw*

PALLISER REGIONAL PARK (Public) From Jct of Hwys 19 & 42: Go 18 mi W on Hwy 42, then 1-1/2 mi S on park access rd (R). 271 Avail: 68 full hkups, 160 E (30 amps). 2021 rates: $40 to $45. May 25 to Sep 07. (306)353-4604

ROSETOWN — D2 *Kindersley*

PRAIRIE VIEW PARK (RV Park) (Phone Update) Avail: 34 full hkups (30 amps). 2021 rates: $35. May 01 to Sep 30. (306)882-4257, Marshall Ave., Rosetown, SK S0L 2V0

ROSTHERN — C3 *Dundurn-Rosthern*

VALLEY REGIONAL PARK (Public) From town: Go 2 km N on Hwy 11 (R). 79 Avail: 41 full hkups, 32 E (30 amps). 2021 rates: $32. May 01 to Sep 30. (306)232-5000

SALTCOATS — D5 *Yorkton*

SALTCOATS & DISTRICT REGIONAL PARK (Public Prov Park) From town: Go 1/2 mi E on Hwy 16 (Yellowhead Hwy), then 1/4 mi N on access rd (E). Avail: 11 E (30 amps). 2021 rates: $15 to $20. May 15 to Sep 08. (306)744-2254

Read RV topics at blog.GoodSam.com

SASKATOON — C3 *Dundurn-Rosthern*

CAMPLAND RV RESORT

Ratings: 9/10★/9.5 (RV Park) From the city of Saskatoon, NW 9 km (5.5 mi) on Hwy 16 to Lutheran Rd, E 0.7 km (0.4 mi) on Lutheran Rd (R). **FAC:** gravel rds. Avail: 132 all weather, 132 pull-thrus, (30x70), 132 full hkups (30/50 amps), WiFi @ sites, tent sites, shower$, laundry, groc, LP bottles, fire rings, firewood. **REC:** heated pool $, playground, hunting nearby. Pet restrict (Q). Partial handicap access. Big rig sites, eco-friendly. 2021 rates: $44 to $48. Apr 14 to Oct 26.
(306)477-7444 Lat: 52.259534, Lon: -106.781449
Hwy 16 & Lutheran Rd, Saskatoon, SK S7K 3N2
www.camplandrvresort.com
See ad this page

GORDON HOWE CAMPGROUND (Public) From Jct of Idylwyld Dr & 22nd St, W 1.6km/1 mi on 22nd St to Ave P South, S 2.4km/1.5 mi (E). 135 Avail: 135 W, 135 E (30/50 amps). 2021 rates: $38.50 to $46. Apr 16 to Oct 14. (306)975-3328

PIKE LAKE (Public Prov Park) From town: Go 14-1/2 mi S on Hwy 60 (E). Avail: 210 E (15/30 amps). 2021 rates: $30. (306)933-6966

SHELL LAKE — C2 *Dundurn-Rosthern*

MEMORIAL LAKE REGIONAL PARK (Public) From Jct of Hwys 3 & 12, N 0.25 mi on Hwy 12/park access rd (R). Entrance fee required. Avail: 144 E (15/30 amps). 2021 rates: $30. May 01 to Sep 30. (306)427-2281

SMEATON — C3 *Melfort*

NARROW HILLS (Public Prov Park) From jct Hwy 55 & Hwy 106: Go 69 km/43 mi N on Hwy 106. Avail: 40 E (15/30 amps). 2021 rates: $18 to $30. (306)426-2622

SPIRITWOOD — C2 *Meadow Lake*

CHITEK LAKE (Public Prov Park) From town, NW 35 mi on Hwy 24 (E). Avail: 26 E (15/30 amps). 2021 rates: $20 to $30. Jun 24 to Sep 15. (306)984-2353

SPRINGSIDE — D4 *Yorkton*

GOOD SPIRIT LAKE (Public Prov Park) From town: Go 25.7 km/16 mi NE on Hwy 47, then 6.4 km/4 mi E on park access road (E). Avail: 126 E (30 amps). 2021 rates: $17 to $26. May 01 to Sep 30. (306)792-4750

SPY HILL — D5 *Yorkton*

CARLTON TRAIL (Public) From town: Go 6.4 km/4 mi N on Hwy 8 (L). 75 Avail: 75 W, 75 E (30 amps). 2021 rates: $29. May 01 to Sep 30. (306)534-4724

ST BRIEUX — C3 *Prince Albert*

ST BRIEUX REGIONAL PARK & GOLF COURSE (Public) At jct of Hwy 368 & Barbier Dr: Go 1 km/6/10 mi W of St. Brieux. Avail: 59 E (15/30 amps). 2021 rates: $28 to $32. May 18 to Sep 16. (306)275-4433

STALWART — D3 *Saskatoon*

RESORT VILLAGE AT ETTERS BEACH CAMPGROUND (Public Prov Park) From jct Hwy 2 & Hwy 11: Go N to Stalwart, then 7.2 km/4-1/2 mi E on Grid Rd. 12 Avail: 12 W, 12 E (30 amps). 2021 rates: $20 to $30. May 15 to Sep 27. (306)963-2532

So you're the one with ""pooch'' duty? Please make a clean sweep of it! Your fellow RVers will appreciate it!

SK

SWIFT CURRENT — E2 *Moose Jaw*

← KILTON HILL CAMPGROUND **Ratings: 3.5/8★/7** (RV Park) Avail: 19 full hkups (30/50 amps). 2021 rates: $38. (306)741-1538, Box 325 - Hwy 1 & Range Road 3144, Swift Current, SK S9H 3V8

LAC PELLETIER REGIONAL PARK (Public Prov Park) From east jct Hwy 1 & Hwy 4: Go 48 km/29 mi S on Hwy 4, then 14 km/10 mi W on grid road. 180 Avail. 2021 rates: $35 to $45. May 19 to Sep 17. (306)627-3595

↗ PONDAROSA MH & RV PARK **Ratings: 5/7/7** (Campground) 77 Avail: 70 full hkups, 7 W, 7 E (30/50 amps). 2021 rates: $40. (306)773-5000, Hwy 1 -Trans Canada Hwy-East side, Swift Current, SK S9H 3X6

↖ TRAIL CAMPGROUND **Ratings: 5/7.5/6** (Campground) 72 Avail: 31 full hkups, 20 W, 41 E (15/30 amps). 2021 rates: $32 to $40. Apr 01 to Oct 31. (306)773-8088, 53-701 11th Ave NW, Swift Current, SK S9H 4M5

THEODORE — D4 *Yorkton*

WHITESAND REGIONAL PARK (Public) From jct Hwy 16 & Grid Rd 651: Go 6.4 km/4 mi N on Grid Rd 651, then 2.4 km/1-1/2 mi E. Follow signs. 20 Avail: 3 full hkups, 15 E (30/50 amps). 2021 rates: $26.25 to $31.50. May 15 to Sep 15. (306)647-2191

TISDALE — C4 *Melfort*

KIPABISKAU REGIONAL PARK (Public) From town: Go 29 km/18 mi S on Hwy 35, then 11-1/4 km/7 mi W on gravel road. Avail: 17 E (15/30 amps). 2021 rates: $22.50 to $33. May 16 to Sep 07. (306)873-4335

TOBIN LAKE — C4 *Melfort*

↑ HILL TOP CAMPGROUND & RV PARK (Campground) (Phone Update) Avail: 10 full hkups (30/50 amps). 2021 rates: $49. May 15 to Oct 01. (306)862-4444, Hwy 255, Nipawin, SK S0E 1E0

UNITY — C1 *Kindersley*

UNITY AND DISTRICT REGIONAL PARK (Public) From west town limits on Hwy 14: Go 2 km/1-1/4 mi W on Hwy 14. 14 Avail: Pit toilets. 2021 rates: $15. Apr 01 to Sep 30. (306)228-2621

WADENA — D4 *Wynyard*

WADENA CAMPGROUND (Public) From jct Pamela Wallin Dr & Jim Headington Way: Go 1/2 block E on Pamela Wallin Drive. Follow signs. Avail: 60 E (30 amps). 2021 rates: $10 to $25. May 01 to Oct 31. (888)338-2145

WAKAW — C3 *Prince Albert*

WAKAW LAKE REGIONAL PARK (Public) From town: Go 3-1/4 km/2 mi N on Hwy 2, then 9-1/2 km/6 mi E on Secondary Rd. Avail: 45 E (20/50 amps). 2021 rates: $30 to $43. May 01 to Sep 30. (306)233-5744

Show Your Good Sam Membership Card!

WASKESIU LAKE — B3 *North Battleford*

PRINCE ALBERT/BEAVER GLEN (Public National Park) From jct Hwy 2 & Hwy 264: Go 12 km/7-1/2 mi NW on Hwy 264, then 1/2 km/1/3 mi W on Ajawaan St. Avail: 200 E (15/30 amps). 2021 rates: $23.50 to $29.40. (877)737-3783

PRINCE ALBERT/NAMEKUS LAKE (Public National Park) From jct Hwy 264 & Hwy 263: Go 15-1/4 km/9-1/2 mi S on Hwy 263. 15 Avail: Pit toilets. 2021 rates: $12.70 to $15.70. May 19 to Sep 30. (877)737-3783

PRINCE ALBERT/NARROWS (Public National Park) From Waskesiu Lake townsite: Go 25 km/15-1/2 mi NW on park road. 85 Avail. 2021 rates: $21.50. (877)737-3783

PRINCE ALBERT/RED DEER (Public National Park) From jct Hwy 2 & Hwy 264: Go 12 km/7-1/2 mi NW on Hwy 264, then 1/2 km/1/3 mi W on Ajawaan St. Avail: 161 full hkups (30/50 amps). 2021 rates: $29.40 to $35.30. (877)737-3783

PRINCE ALBERT/SANDY LAKE (Public National Park) From jct Hwy 240 & Hwy 263: Go 5 km/3 mi N on Hwy 263. 31 Avail: Pit toilets. 2021 rates: $12.70 to $15.70. (877)737-3783

WATSON — C4 *Wynyard*

MCNAB REGIONAL PARK (Public) From jct Hwy 5 & Hwy 6: Go .5 km/1/4 mi N on Hwy 6. Avail: 16 full hkups (15/50 amps). 2021 rates: $18 to $35. Apr 15 to Oct 15. (306)287-4240

WEYBURN — E4 *Weyburn*

↓ CITY OF WEYBURN RIVER PARK CAMPGROUND (Public) From jct Hwy 35 & Hwy 39: Go 300 m/300 yds E on Hwy 39, then 100 m/110 yds S on 3rd St S, then 200 m/220 yds E on 2nd Ave SE. 28 Avail: 28 W, 28 E (15/30 amps). 2021 rates: $18 to $30. May 25 to Sep 15. (306)848-3290

NICKLE LAKE REGIONAL PARK (Public Prov Park) From jct 16th St & Hwy 39: Go 6.6 km/4 mi S on Hwy 39, then 1.7 km/1 mi S on grid road, then .8 km/1/2 mi W on access road. 279 Avail: 31 full hkups, 240 W, 240 E (15/30 amps). 2021 rates: $23.75 to $30. May 15 to Sep 15. (306)842-7522

WHITE CITY — E4 *Regina*

→ COMFORT PLUS CAMPGROUND **Ratings: 7.5/6.5/7.5** (Campground) 50 Avail: 44 full hkups, 6 W, 6 E (15/30 amps). 2021 rates: $33 to $48. May 01 to Sep 30. (306)781-2810, North Service Road, Hwy 48 & Hwy 1 E., White City, SK S0G 5B0

How can you tell whether you're traveling in the right direction? The arrow in each listing denotes the compass direction of the facility in relation to the listed town. For example, an arrow pointing straight up indicates that the facility is located due north from town. An arrow pointing down and to the right indicates that the facility is southeast of town.

WHITEWOOD — E5 *Melville*

↑ WHITEWOOD CAMPGROUND (Public) From jct Hwy 1 & Hwy 9: Go 0.5 km/1/4 mi S on Hwy 9, then 0.8 km/1/2 mi NW on Service Rd, then 0.1 km/558 feet S on Lalonde St (R). 20 Avail: 6 full hkups, 12 W, 12 E (30 amps). 2021 rates: $24 to $32. May 01 to Sep 30. (306)735-2210

WILKIE — C2 *Kindersley*

WILKIE REGIONAL PARK (Public) From jct Hwy 14 & Hwy 29: Go 3/4 km/1/2 mi N on Hwy 29. Avail: 17 E (15/30 amps). 2021 rates: $15 to $25. May 15 to Sep 30. (306)843-2692

WILLOW BUNCH — E3 *Assiniboia*

JEAN LOUIS LEGARE REGIONAL PARK (Public) From Hwy 36 at south town limits: Go .5 km/1/4 mi W on grid road, then 1.8 km/1 mi SW on grid road. 59 Avail: 52 W, 52 E. 2021 rates: $40. May 16 to Sep 16. (306)640-7268

WOOD MOUNTAIN — E3 *Assiniboia*

WOOD MOUNTAIN REGIONAL PARK (Public) From town: Go 13 km/8 mi S on Hwy 18. Avail: 34 E (15/30 amps). 2021 rates: $23 to $30. May 19 to Sep 07. (306)266-4249

WYNYARD — D4 *Wynyard*

WYNYARD & DISTRICT REGIONAL PARK (Public) From jct Hwy 16 & Grid Rd 640: Go 2.4 km/1.5 mi S on Grid Rd 640. Avail: 27 E (15/30 amps). 2021 rates: $15 to $20. May 19 to Sep 30. (306)554-3661

YORKTON — D5 *Yorkton*

↖ CITY OF YORKTON CAMPGROUND (Public) From NW section of town: Go N on Gladstone Ave, W at York Rd/16A, past lake (L). 56 Avail: 56 W, 56 E (15/30 amps). 2021 rates: $20 to $27. Apr 15 to Sep 30. (306)786-1757

↓ YORK LAKE REGIONAL PARK (Public) From Jct of Hwys 16 & 9: Go 1/2 mi W on Queen St, then 2-1/2 mi S on Gladstone Ave (E). 31 Avail: 31 W, 31 E (15/30 amps). 2021 rates: $25. May 17 to Oct 10. (306)782-7080

RV Tech Tips - Awning Rod Storage: Tired of having to hunt for the awning rod buried under other items in the outside storage compartment? This RV tech tip can help. Cut two short pieces (about 6 inches long) of PVC pipe, drill two holes in each (enlarge the holes on one side for the screwdriver shaft) and attach them to the ceiling of the compartment. Measure the rod and place the pieces of pipe so that the rod tip (bent 90 degrees) will just hang out the end. That way, there is no room for the rod to slide back and forth. Now when you need your awning rod, you know right where it is; you don't have to hunt for it.

YOU ARE HERE
DID YOU KNOW?
The Sourtoe Cocktail is a time-honored tradition in Dawson City. It has a special ingredient: a mummified human toe.

Getty Images/iStockphoto

Yukon

The Yukon has never lost the frontier appeal first sparked in the days of the Klondike Gold Rush. From abundant wildlife to the dazzling lights in the skies, Yukon enchants visitors to the Land of the Midnight Sun.

Wild in the Yukon

In the Yukon, you don't have to go far to see larger-than-life wildlife. At the 700-acre Yukon Wildlife Preserve, in an accessible spot just north of Whitehorse, visitors can see musk, ox and bison trudge across rugged landscapes. Watch as mountain goats climb seemingly impossible slopes. Nearby, Miles Canyon offers majestic views of the Yukon River, which cuts dramatically through a forest-ed valley. Take a drive along the famed Dempster Highway to northern Yukon's Tombstone Territorial Park to explore a vast, untamed wilderness. Explore flora and fauna of the Arctic tundra and permafrost landforms.

Dawson City Dancers

Dawson has never lost the Gold Rush spirit. Back in the Klondike Days, dancing girls, rowdy bars and grizzled prospectors cavorted in saloons and along wooden sidewalks. Today, a visit to the historic town, further north along the Alaska/Klondike Highway, is a must. With many preserved buildings and costumed interpreters, the past truly comes to life in this rollicking town.

Wander to Whitehorse

White horse lies right on the Alaska Highway, and it stands out as one of the most popular stops on the route. Yukon's largest town preserves its gold rush past, and visitors will be awestruck at the mountains that tower in the horizon. Learn about the First Nations peoples, the Klondike Gold Rush and more at the MacBride Museum. The S.S. Klondike National Historic Site preserves a famous river vessel.

Yukon Bannock

In the 1800s, the First Nations people of the Yukon adopted the tasty bread brought to the region by Scottish employees of the Hudson Bay Company. Because bannock is so easy to prepare and transport, it became popular among the native hunters and trappers in the region. Visit Dänojà Zho Cultural Centre in Dawson City for a demonstration of cooking the flat cakes of barley and oatmeal dough.

YT

VISITOR CENTER

TIME ZONE
Pacific Standard

ROAD & HIGHWAY INFORMATION
867-667-5811
511yukon.ca

FISHING & HUNTING LICENSES
867-667-5721
yukon.ca/en/department-environment

BOATING INFORMATION
800-267-6687
tc.gc.ca/boatingsafety

NATIONAL PARKS
pc.gc.ca/en/pn-np

TERRITORIAL PARKS
yukon.ca/en/yukon-territorial-parks-and-other-conservation-areas

TOURISM INFORMATION
Tourism Yukon
800-661-0494
travelyukon.ca

TOP TOURISM ATTRACTIONS
1) Kluane National Park and Reserve
2) S.S. Klondike National Historic Site
3) Tombstone Territorial Park

MAJOR CITIES
Whitehorse (capital), Dawson City, Watson Lake, Haines Junction, Carmacks

Featured Good Sam Parks

YUKON

When you stay with Good Sam, you can expect the highest degree of cleanliness and friendliness, and better yet, you get **10% off** overnight campground fees.

If you're not already a Good Sam member you can purchase your membership at one of these locations:

CARMACKS
Carmacks Hotel & RV Park

WHITEHORSE
Caribou RV Park

Getty Images/iStockphoto

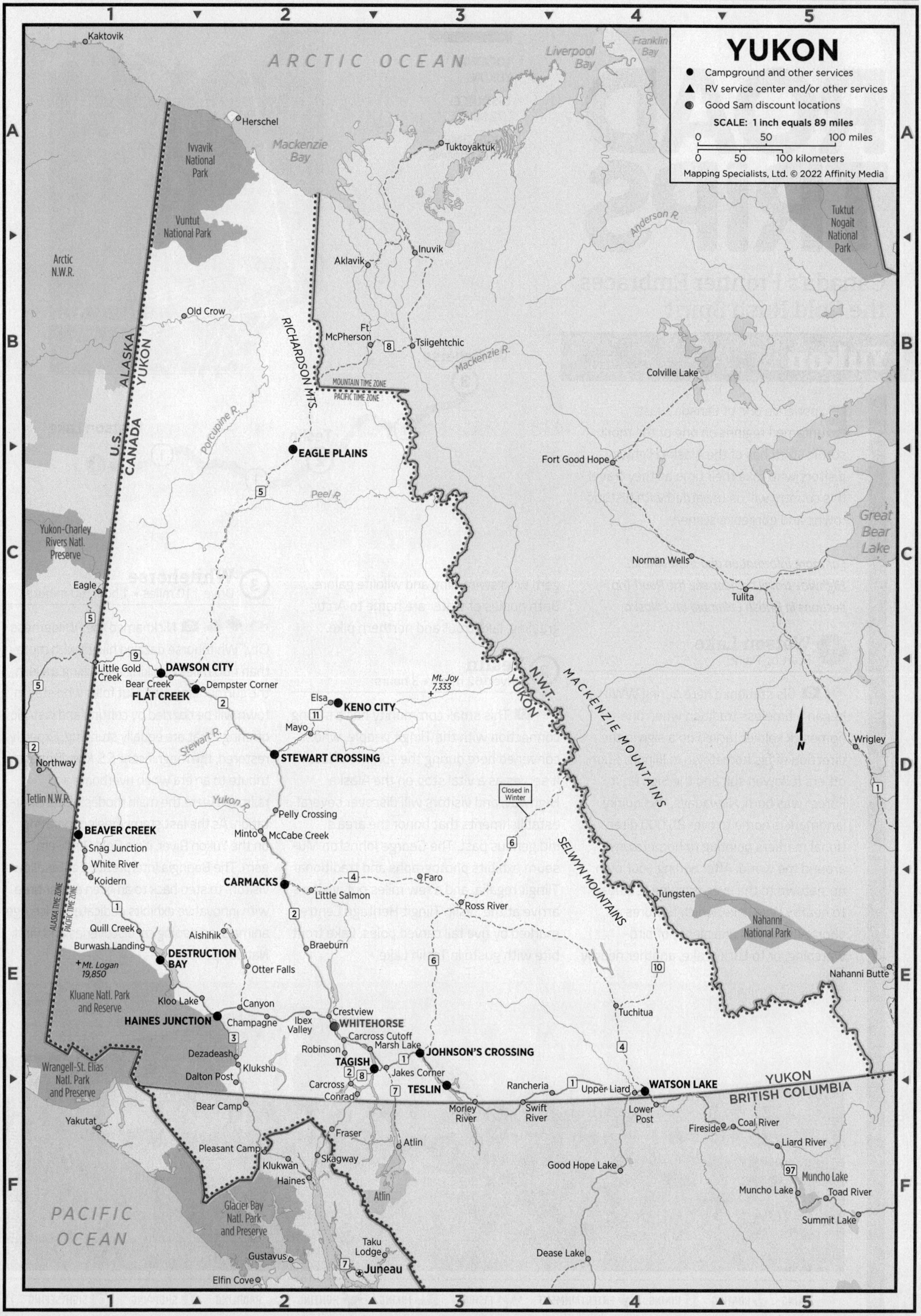
YUKON
Campground and other services
RV service center and/or other services
Good Sam discount locations
SCALE: 1 inch equals 89 miles
0 50 100 miles
0 50 100 kilometers
Mapping Specialists, Ltd. © 2022 Affinity Media
ARCTIC OCEAN
PACIFIC OCEAN
Kaktovik
Herschel
Mackenzie Bay
Liverpool Bay
Franklin Bay
Tuktoyaktuk
Ivvavik National Park
Vuntut National Park
Arctic N.W.R.
Tuktut Nogait National Park
Anderson R.
Inuvik
Aklavik
Old Crow
Ft. McPherson
Tsiigehtchic
Mackenzie R.
Colville Lake
RICHARDSON MTS.
MOUNTAIN TIME ZONE
PACIFIC TIME ZONE
ALASKA
YUKON
U.S.
CANADA
Porcupine R.
EAGLE PLAINS
Fort Good Hope
Peel R.
Great Bear Lake
Yukon-Charley Rivers Natl. Preserve
Norman Wells
Tulita
Eagle
Little Gold Creek
DAWSON CITY
Bear Creek
FLAT CREEK
Dempster Corner
Mt. Joy 7,333
Elsa
KENO CITY
Mayo
Stewart R.
N.W.T.
YUKON
MACKENZIE MOUNTAINS
Wrigley
Northway
STEWART CROSSING
Tetlin N.W.R.
Yukon R.
Closed in Winter
Pelly Crossing
Minto
McCabe Creek
BEAVER CREEK
Snag Junction
White River
Koidern
SELWYN MOUNTAINS
CARMACKS
Faro
Little Salmon
Tungsten
Ross River
Nahanni National Park
ALASKA TIME ZONE
PACIFIC TIME ZONE
Quill Creek
Aishihik
Burwash Landing
DESTRUCTION BAY
Braeburn
Mt. Logan 19,850
Otter Falls
Nahanni Butte
Kluane Natl. Park and Reserve
Kloo Lake
Canyon
Tuchitua
HAINES JUNCTION
Champagne
Ibex Valley
Crestview
WHITEHORSE
Carcross Cutoff
Marsh Lake
Robinson
JOHNSON'S CROSSING
Dezadeash
TAGISH
Klukshu
Wrangell-St. Elias Natl. Park and Preserve
Dalton Post
Jakes Corner
Carcross
TESLIN
Rancheria
Upper Liard
WATSON LAKE
YUKON
BRITISH COLUMBIA
Conrad
Bear Camp
Morley River
Swift River
Lower Post
Yakutat
Fireside
Coal River
Fraser
Atlin
Liard River
Pleasant Camp
Skagway
Good Hope Lake
Klukwan
Haines
Muncho Lake
Atlin
Muncho Lake
Toad River
Glacier Bay Natl. Park and Preserve
Summit Lake
Taku Lodge
Gustavus
Dease Lake
Juneau
Elfin Cove

YT

ROAD TRIPS

Canada's Frontier Embraces the Gold Rush Spirit

Yukon

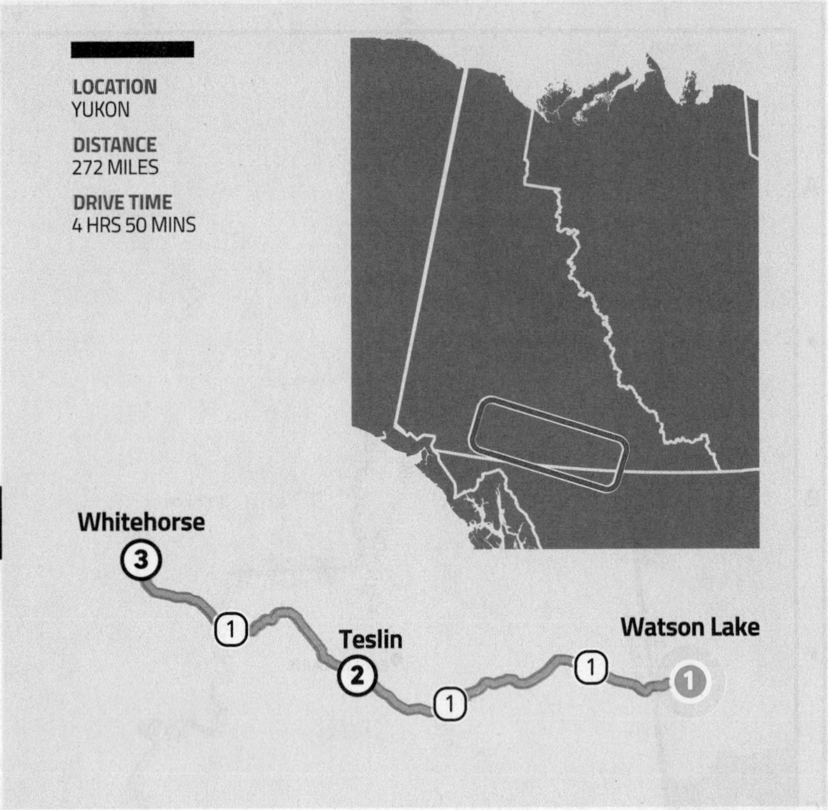

Experience one of Canada's last untamed regions on one of the most scenic stretches of the Alaska Highway. Visitors who take their time as they travel this country will be rewarded with historic towns and gorgeous scenery.

For more information about the Alaska Highway travel corridor, see the Road Trip sections in British Columbia and Alaska.

1 Watson Lake
Starting Point

GIs stationed here during WWII began a timeless tradition when one homesick soldier tacked up a sign in the direction of his hometown in Illinois. Soon, others followed suit and the Sign Post Forest was born. Nowadays, this quirky landmark is home to over 85,000 directional markers pointing to hometowns around the world. After adding your own hometown to the ever-growing list, head to nearby Wye Lake, which features a short nature trail and plenty of birdwatching, or to Lucky Lake, another nearby gem with swimming and wildlife galore. Both bodies of water are home to Arctic grayling, lake trout and northern pike.

2 Teslin
Drive 162 miles • 3 hours

This small community has a strong connection with the Tlingit people, who convened here during the summer. Now it serves as a vital stop on the Alaska Highway, and visitors will discover several establishments that honor the area's indigenous past. The George Johnston Museum exhibits photographs and traditional Tlingit regalia, and a few miles out, visitors arrive at the Teslin Tlingit Heritage Centre, marked by five tall carved poles. Lake trout bite with gusto in Teslin Lake.

3 Whitehorse
Drive 110 miles • 1 hour, 50 minutes

Nicknamed the "Wilderness City," Whitehorse dazzled hikers with more than 400 miles of hiking and biking trails in the surrounding area. But folks who stay in town will be dazzled by cultural and historic offerings that are equally stunning. Expertly restored, the magnificent *S.S. Klondike* pays tribute to an era when riverboats and railroads were the main modes of transportation. As the last sternwheeler operating on the Yukon River, it's a Gold Rush-era gem. The Beringia Interpretive Center allows visitors to step back to an even earlier time with innovative exhibits dedicated to Ice Age animals, archeological discoveries and First Nations people.

Getty Images/iStockphoto

BIKING BOATING DINING ENTERTAINMENT FISHING HIKING HUNTING PADDLING SHOPPING SIGHTSEEING

Yukon SPOTLIGHTS

Discover Larger Than Life Adventures

Prospectors flocked to Yukon in the 1800s in hopes of finding gold, and the region has never lost its wild vibe. Places like Whitehorse preserve history and serve as launch pads to wilderness adventure.

YUKON GOLD RUSH PROSPECTORS MINED $29 MILLION.

Everything from license plates to street signs hang in the Sign Post Forest in Watson Lake.

Getty Images/iStockphoto

So Many Signs

Don't get lost in the Sign Post Forest, a collection of 72,000 signs from around the world mounted on posts. The forest has its origins in directional signs set up by U.S. Army engineers to orient military drivers. One day, U.S. Army Private Carl K. Lindley felt homesick and posted a sign to his hometown of Danville, Illinois. Lindley set off a trend, and to this day, visitors regularly add their own contributions.

Look to the Skies

Northern night skies in the Yukon are home to the aurora borealis, the dancing lights caused by solar winds. Check out the Northern Lights Space and Science center, which educates visitors about this phenomenon.

Dawson City

In the 1800s, legions of eager prospectors flooded the Yukon region to strike it rich in the area's ample goldfields. That vibrant history is preserved in Dawson City's dirt streets and ramshackle boardwalks, where the spirit of carefree revelry prevails. Visitors are reminded that for a brief time in the 1800s, Dawson City was second only to San Francisco for the title of the West Coast's largest city. Walking tours, conducted by Parks Canada, provide entry to 26 restored buildings and National Historic Sites, including a gold dredge, the Jack London cabin, poet Robert Service's house and saloons.

Songs and Saloons

Summertime brings the midnight sun, along with the chance to party around the clock. Most saloons, lounge bars and pubs in town feature fine live music. As the final frontier before civilization gives way to wilderness, Dawson City entertains travelers and eccentrics at local restaurants, bars and cafés.

Watson Lake

Just north of the British Columbia border, the small community of Watson Lake has made a big name for itself. The city of around 1,500 residents, located on Mile 635 on the Alaska Highway, has compelling attractions.

Whitehorse

Named for roaring rapids in the Yukon River that resembled a white horse's mane, Whitehorse, like Dawson City, grew to prominence during the Klondike Gold Rush. The Klondike and Alaska Highways bring travelers to the town, which serves as the capital of Yukon. The surrounding wilderness serves up great adventures, from paddling on the Yukon River to biking along the trails.

FOR MORE INFORMATION

Department of Tourism Yukon, 800-661-0494, www.travelyukon.ca

Dawson City, 867-993-5566, DawsonCity.ca

Watson Lake, 867-536-8000, www.WatsonLake.ca

Whitehorse, travelyukon.com/en/discover/regions/whitehorse

LOCAL FAVORITE

Orange Yukon Jack Salmon

Finding this recipe for grilled salmon is like discovering culinary gold. Taste a bonanza of flavors. *Recipe by Wayne Jacobson.*

INGREDIENTS

- ☐ 1 skinned 4-20 lb salmon (or steelhead) fillet, dark back meat removed
- ☐ 1-2 jiggers of Canadian whiskey
- ☐ 2 Tbsp chopped fresh dill
- ☐ 1 Tbsp lemon pepper seasoning
- ☐ 1 can frozen concentrated orange juice
- ☐ ½ cup olive oil
- ☐ Salt and pepper to taste

DIRECTIONS

Make an aluminum foil boat with at least half-inch sides. Pour olive oil in the foil boat and spread around. Place the skinned salmon fillet in the foil, skin side down. Pour the whiskey over the fillet, sprinkle with dill, lemon pepper and season with salt and pepper to taste. Place dollops of frozen orange juice every inch over top of fillet and place the foil boat uncovered on a preheated grill. Close the grill cover and check frequently for doneness by looking for the whiskey to turn dark along the edges of the fillet.

YT

Yukon

BEAVER CREEK — D1 *Kluane Region*

↘ DISCOVERY YUKON LODGINGS & RV PARK **Ratings: 6.5/9.5★/9.5** (RV Park) Avail: 50 full hkups (20/30 amps). 2021 rates: $39.95 to $45.50. May 01 to Sep 30. (844)867-9030, KM 1818 Alaska Hwy, Beaver Creek, YT Y0B 1A0

LAKE CREEK (Public Prov Park) From Beaver Creek: Go 81 km/50 mi E on Alaska Hwy to km 1854/milepost 1152. 27 Avail: Pit toilets. 2021 rates: $12. (867)667-5652

CARMACKS — D2 *Klondike Region*

→ **CARMACKS HOTEL & RV PARK**

Ratings: 7.5/8.5/9 (RV Park) Avail: 15 full hkups (30/50 amps). 2021 rates: $40 to $57. May 15 to Sep 15. (867)863-5221, 35607 Klondike Hwy N, Carmacks, YT Y0B 1C0

← THE COAL MINE CAMPGROUND & CANTEEN **Ratings: 5.5/8.5/8** (Campground) Avail: 18 E (30 amps). 2021 rates: $28.95 to $32.95. May 15 to Sep 10. (867)863-6363, KM 359 Klondike Hwy N, Carmacks, YT Y0B 1C0

DAWSON CITY — C2 *Klondike Region*

↓ BONANZA GOLD MOTEL & RV PARK **Ratings: 7/9.5★/8.5** (RV Park) 102 Avail: 63 full hkups, 39 W, 39 E (30/50 amps). 2021 rates: $25.50 to $55.50. May 01 to Sep 30. (888)993-6789, KM 712 Klondike Hwy N, Dawson City, YT Y0B 1G0

↓ KLONDIKE RIVER (Public Prov Park) From town: Go S on Klondike Hwy 2 to km marker 697 (R). 35 Avail: Pit toilets. 2021 rates: $12. (867)667-5468

YUKON RIVER (Public Prov Park) In town on the Top of the World Hwy at km marker .3 (milepost 0). 102 Avail: Pit toilets. 2021 rates: $12. (867)667-5652

DESTRUCTION BAY — E1 *Kluane Region*

CONGDON CREEK (Public Prov Park) From town: Go 19 km/12 mi S on Alaska Hwy 1 to km marker 1724.3 (milepost 1071.5). 39 Avail: Pit toilets. 2021 rates: $12. (867)667-5200

↑ DESTRUCTION BAY RV LODGE **Ratings: 7.5/9★/8** (RV Park) 43 Avail: 43 W, 43 E (15/30 amps). 2021 rates: $29.95 to $39.95. May 15 to Sep 15. (867)841-4332, M 1083 Alaska Hwy, Destruction Bay, YT Y0B 1H0

From fishing along the Cape to boating on the Great Lakes, we've put the Spotlight on North America's most popular travel destinations. Turn to the Spotlight articles in our State and Province sections to learn more.

Yukon Privately Owned Campground Information Updated by our Good Sam Representatives

Tony & Nanette Martin

In 2014, Tony and I decided to sell everything we owned, buy a motorhome and travel for a year with our two dogs. That year turned into five, traveling from Mexico to Alaska. Along the way we met a couple of Good Sam rep teams, and we thought, "what a perfect job." And so it all began.

EAGLE PLAINS — C2 *North Yukon Region*

ROCK RIVER

(Public Prov Park) From Eagle Plains: Go 78 km/49 mi N on Dempster Hwy 5. **FAC:** Avail: 17 dirt, tent sites, pit toilets, fire rings, firewood. Pets OK. 2021 rates: $12. Jun 04 to Sep 15. no cc.
(867)667-5652 Lat: 66.912217, Lon: -136.356386
Eagle Plains, YT Y1A 3V5
www.env.gov.yk.ca

FLAT CREEK — D2 *Klondike Region*

TOMBSTONE MOUNTAIN (Public Prov Park) From town: Go 72 km/45 mi N on Dempster Hwy 5 to km marker 73 (milepost 45.4). 48 Avail: Pit toilets. 2021 rates: $12. (867)667-5652

HAINES JUNCTION — E2 *Kluane Region*

DEZADEASH LAKE (Public Prov Park) From jct Alaska Hwy 1 & Haines Rd 3: Go 50 km/3 mi S on Haines Rd 3. 20 Avail: Pit toilets. 2021 rates: $12. (867)667-5200

→ HAINES JUNCTION FAS GAS & RV PARK **Ratings: 5/9★/7.5** (RV Park) Avail: 22 full hkups (30 amps). 2021 rates: $36.75. (867)634-2505, 270 Alaska Hwy, Haines Junction, YT Y0B 1L0

KLUANE/KATHLEEN LAKE (Public National Park) From town: Go 27 km/17 mi S on the Haines Hwy 3 to km marker 229.4 (milepost 142). 38 Avail: Pit toilets. 2021 rates: $15.70. May 17 to Sep 22. (877)737-3783

MILLION DOLLAR FALLS (Public Prov Park) From town: Go S on the Haines Rd to km marker 167 (milepost 103.7). 34 Avail: Pit toilets. 2021 rates: $12. (867)667-5652

↓ OTTER FALLS CUTOFF RV PARK **Ratings: 6/8.5★/7** (RV Park) 46 Avail: 46 W, 46 E (15/30 amps). 2021 rates: $21.95 to $36.95. (867)634-2812, Km 1546 Alaska Hwy, Haines Junction, YT Y0B 1L0

PINE LAKE (Public Prov Park) In town on Alaska Hwy 1 at km marker 1628 (milepost 1013). 42 Avail: Pit toilets. 2021 rates: $12. (867)667-5652

JOHNSONS CROSSING — E3 *Johnsons Crossing*

QUIET LAKE (Public Prov Park) From jct Alaska Hwy 1 & Hwy 6 (Canol Rd): Go 77 km/48 mi N on Hwy 6 (Canol Rd). 22 Avail: Pit toilets. 2021 rates: $12. (867)667-5652

KENO CITY — D2 *Silver Trail Region*

KENO CITY CAMPGROUND (Public) From jct Hwy 2 (Klondike Hwy) & Hwy 11: Go 106.8 km/66-1/2 mi NE on Hwy 11, then 120 metres/130 yrds SE on Yukon Ave. 12 Avail: Pit toilets. 2021 rates: $10. (867)995-3103

STEWART CROSSING — D2 *Silver Trail Region*

MOOSE CREEK (Public Prov Park) From jct Hwy 11 (The Silver Trail) & Klondike Hwy 2: Go 24 km/15 mi NW on Klondike Hwy 2 to km marker 562 (milepost 349.2). 36 Avail: Pit toilets. 2021 rates: $12. (862)667-5652

TAGISH — E3 *Southern Lakes Region*

TAGISH (Public Prov Park) In town on Hwy 8 at km marker 21 (milepost 13). 15 Avail: Pit toilets. 2021 rates: $12. May 27 to Sep 04. (867)667-5652

TESLIN — E2 *Yukon*

TESLIN LAKE (Public Prov Park) From town: Go 15.5 km/9-1/2 mi W on Alaska Hwy to km 1309/milepost 813. 27 Avail: Pit toilets. 2021 rates: $12. (867)667-5652

↓ YUKON MOTEL & LAKESHORE RV PARK **Ratings: 7.5/9.5★/10** (RV Park) 58 Avail: 58 W, 58 E (15/30 amps). 2021 rates: $25 to $45. May 01 to Sep 30. (867)390-2575, Mile 804 Alaska Hwy (KM 1244), Teslin, YT Y0A 1B0

WATSON LAKE — E4 *Yukon*

↘ BABY NUGGET RV PARK **Ratings: 7/10★/9** (RV Park) 83 Avail: 83 W, 83 E (30/50 amps). 2021 rates: $40 to $68. May 15 to Sep 30. (867)536-2307, Milepost 627/KM 1003 Alaska Hwy, Watson Lake, YT Y0A 1C0

↗ DOWNTOWN RV PARK **Ratings: 7/9.5★/7** (RV Park) Avail: 78 full hkups (30/50 amps). 2021 rates: $40 to $58. Apr 15 to Oct 15. (867)536-2646, 105 8th St N, Watson Lake, YT Y0A 1C0

RV Park ratings you can rely on!

FRANCES LAKE (Public Prov Park) From jct Alaska Hwy 1 & Robert Campbell Hwy 4: Go N on Robert Campbell Hwy 4 to km 177/milepost 110. 24 Avail: Pit toilets. 2021 rates: $12. (867)667-5200

WATSON LAKE (Public Prov Park) Just outside of town on Alaska Hwy 1 at km marker 1025 (milepost 636.5), then 1.6 km/1 mi on access road. 40 Avail: Pit toilets. 2021 rates: $12. (867)667-5652

WHITEHORSE — E2 *Whitehorse Region*

→ **CARIBOU RV PARK**

Ratings: 7/10★/9 (Campground) 40 Avail: 28 W, 28 E (15/30 amps). 2021 rates: $39 to $45. May 01 to Sep 30. (867)668-2961, Mile 904/ KM 1403 Alaska Hwy, Whitehorse, YT Y1A 7A1

FOX LAKE (Public Prov Park) From town: Go N on Klondike Hwy 2 to km marker 248 (milepost 141.7). 43 Avail: Pit toilets. 2021 rates: $12. (867)667-5200

↓ HI COUNTRY RV PARK **Ratings: 7/10★/9.5** (RV Park) 125 Avail: 55 full hkups, 52 W, 52 E (20/30 amps). 2021 rates: $27 to $45. May 15 to Sep 15. (867)667-7445, 91374 Alaska Hwy, Whitehorse, YT Y1A 6E4

KUSAWA LAKE (Public Prov Park) From town: Go 67 km/42 mi W on Alaska Hwy 1 to km marker 1543.1 (milepost 959), then 22-1/2 km/14 mi S on Kusawa Lake Rd. 53 Avail: Pit toilets. 2021 rates: $12. (867)667-5652

MARSH LAKE (Public Prov Park) From town: Go 45 km/28 mi E on Alaska Hwy 1 to km marker 1429.6 (milepost 888.4). 59 Avail: Pit toilets. 2021 rates: $12. (867)667-5648

WOLF CREEK (Public Prov Park) From town: Go E on Alaska Hwy 1 to km marker 1458.6 (milepost 906). 46 Avail: Pit toilets. 2021 rates: $12. (867)667-5648

Exclusive! According to our research, restroom cleanliness is of the utmost importance to RVers. Of course, you knew that already. The cleanest campgrounds have a star in their restroom rating!

Find-it-Fast Index

All locations included in this Guide are listed alphabetically by state and province. A black dot (•) in front of a location indicates it is a Good Sam Park and offers a 10% discount to Good Sam members on an overnight stay. The facility name is followed by the listing city, and then the page number that the listing can be found.

USA

ALABAMA

ALASKA

ARIZONA

ARKANSAS

CALIFORNIA

INDEX

COLORADO

INDEX

CONNECTICUT

DELAWARE

FLORIDA

GEORGIA

IDAHO

ILLINOIS

INDIANA

IOWA

INDEX

KANSAS

KENTUCKY

LOUISIANA

INDEX

MAINE

MARYLAND

MASSACHUSETTS

MICHIGAN

INDEX

MINNESOTA

MISSISSIPPI

INDEX

MISSOURI

MONTANA

NEBRASKA

NEVADA

NEW HAMPSHIRE

NEW JERSEY

NEW MEXICO

INDEX

NEW YORK

NORTH CAROLINA

INDEX

NORTH DAKOTA

OHIO

OKLAHOMA

OREGON

PENNSYLVANIA

RHODE ISLAND

SOUTH CAROLINA

SOUTH DAKOTA

TENNESSEE

TEXAS

INDEX

UTAH

INDEX

VERMONT

VIRGINIA

WASHINGTON

INDEX

WEST VIRGINIA

WISCONSIN

INDEX

WYOMING

CANADA

ALBERTA

BRITISH COLUMBIA

MANITOBA

NEW BRUNSWICK

INDEX

NEWFOUNDLAND AND LABRADOR

NORTHWEST TERRITORIES

NOVA SCOTIA

ONTARIO

INDEX

PRINCE EDWARD ISLAND

QUEBEC

SASKATCHEWAN

INDEX

YUKON

2022 RESORT DIRECTORY

coast to coast

a good sam company

50TH ANNIVERSARY

est. 1972

Hopaway Holiday
coast to coast
a good sam company
DELUXE & PREMIER MEMBERS ONLY
START PLANNING YOUR Next Adventure
AROUND YOUR Favorite Time of Year!
Now is the time to book a "REAL" Vacation!
There are so many great places you can go on a vacation, and we are here to help. You might want to kick off your spring or summer laying out on a sunny beach. Maybe you prefer to see a fresh blanket of powder ready to ski down. No matter what season you love, we have lots of different options for you to choose from!
Choose Your Adventure:
• Discount Condo Vacations
• Houseboat Rentals
• Glamping Vacations
• Treehouses, Teepees, Yurts, and other Outdoor Resort Weekly Rentals
IT'S TIME TO PLAY!
Let us help you Book a Trip!
CALL 800-380-8939
Log into CoastResorts.com, under Benefits, click on Hopaway Holiday
Due to changing state regulations and requirements regarding Covid-19, please discuss your individual details with a representative.

CONTENTS

CHAIRMAN OF CAMPING WORLD HOLDINGS
Marcus Lemonis

CHIEF OPERATING OFFICER
Tamara Ward

PRESIDENT OF GOOD SAM MEDIA AND EVENTS
Vilma Fraguada

BUSINESS MANAGERS
Christine Distl & Christina Din

MARKETING COORDINATOR
MaryEllen Foster

COAST TO COAST PRESIDENT
Bruce Hoster
CCRPresident@coastresorts.com

MARKETING DIRECTOR
Kristin Moser

EDITORIAL DIRECTOR
Dee Whited

ART DIRECTOR
Nicole Wilson

COAST MEMBER SERVICES
64 Inverness Drive East
Englewood, Colorado 80112
800-368-5721
info@coastresorts.com

COAST TO COAST WEBSITE
CoastResorts.com

COAST FACEBOOK PAGE
Facebook.com/CoastResorts

Volume 41, Number 1. *Coast to Coast* (ISSN 1093-3581) is published quarterly for $14 per year as part of annual membership fees, by Coast to Coast Resorts, 64 Inverness Drive E., Englewood, Colorado 80112. Return undeliverable Canadian addresses to P.O. Box 875, Station A, Windsor, Ontario N92 6P2. U.S. POSTMASTER: Send address changes to Coast to Coast Resorts, P.O. Box 7028, Englewood, CO 80155-7028.

PRINTED IN THE USA.

CTC60894 - 1221

coast to coast
a good sam company

FEATURES

DIRECTORY

WELCOME TO OUR
GOLDEN ANNIVERSARY ISSUE!

This year is monumental in the history of Coast to Coast as it is our 50th anniversary. Anytime a business reaches 50 years, it is an occasion to celebrate. It also means that the business provides a product or service that people like. There are a lot of people to thank for helping Coast reach the 50-year milestone. But most of all we owe our deepest gratitude to our members, because it is you who have made this journey possible. Believe it or not, over 2.55 million people have been members of Coast to Coast over the last 50 years. That is perhaps the most amazing statistic of our 50-year history. We have dug into the Coast archives to provide you with a look back on our first 50 years, beginning on page 6. We hope you enjoy this feature story on the history of Coast to Coast as much as we enjoyed researching and writing it.

In terms of commemorating our 50th anniversary, how about our new home inside the 2022 Good Sam Campground and Coupon Guide! We feel honored to have our 2022 Coast Directory published inside the leading campground directory in North America. The guide includes over $1,500 in special coupon offers and information on over 12,000 campgrounds, RV parks, and services. A $29.95 retail value, it represents a great new Coast membership benefit and the best travel resource for any RVer planning their next travel adventure.

I am happy to report that our network of resorts and Good Neighbor Parks continued to grow in 2022. We added 72 new Good Neighbor Parks (GNPs) this year, many of them highly rated and some in states where we previously had no GNPs. We now have over 450 participating resorts and GNPs in the Coast network, which represents a 41% growth in just the last three years. Coast expects to continue this trend in 2022.

I want to take a moment to recognize a key individual in the membership camping industry, and a friend of Coast to Coast, that we lost this past year. Mike Pournoury, President of Ocean Canyon Properties, passed away in May 2021 at the age of 65. I attended Mike's celebration of life in Texarkana, Texas in July and learned a lot more about Mike's life outside our industry. I now realize just what an incredible life Mike lived. He immigrated to the U.S. from Iran in the 1970s and attended The Citadel, part of a U.S. program to train members of the Iran military for the Shah of Iran. However the Shah left in exile the same year Mike graduated The Citadel, Iran formed an Islamic Republic, and Mike could not return to Iran. Instead he stayed in the U.S. and built a career in membership camping, first in sales and later in sales management. He eventually formed his own resort group with partner Peter Graffman, Ocean Canyon Properties, which today includes eight resorts. Mike truly lived the American Dream. He was a supporter of Coast to Coast, someone that we counted on for his advice and the many ideas he would always contribute at our annual Coast Summit resort owner's meeting. His was a friendship that we were very fortunate to have, and one that we will miss greatly.

In closing, the year 2022 also marks my 15th anniversary at the helm of Coast to Coast. I am grateful to our parent company for the help and support they have provided to Coast over these 15 years. And I am grateful to all our members for continuing to support our business. One of the things I have always enjoyed about Coast is that we get to help members every day with their travel plans and with solving problems they may encounter along the way. There are always going to be problems, and I believe the mark of a good business is how, and how quickly, we resolve these issues. I hope that you find Coast very responsive to whatever membership needs you may have. As always, I welcome your feedback on this or any other subject at CCRPresident@CoastResorts.com.

Thank you for being a part of our journey during our first 50 years, and best wishes to all of you for safe and memorable travels in 2022.

MARCUS LEMONIS
Chairman and CEO
Camping World & Good Sam
MarcusVIP@goodsamfamily.com

BRUCE HOSTER
President
Coast to Coast Resorts
CCRPresident@coastresorts.com

coast to coast

a good sam company

50TH

ANNIVERSARY

est. 1972

CELEBRATING 50 YEARS

Coast to Coast is Golden

This year, 2022, Coast to Coast is marking 50 great years leading the membership campground industry. And while we celebrate the achievements of the last 50 years, we like to think that Coast to Coast is just getting better.

When you think back to what camping used to be like, most of us remember unpacking the station wagon and trying to set up a canvas Army surplus tent on a rocky campsite with no utilities. You struggled to find a campground near where you wanted to go and often had to settle for something with few amenities. After an uncomfortable night's sleep, it was time to haul out the stove and make breakfast. Fortunately, throughout the decades, campgrounds have improved and many of us traded in the old tent for a sleek recreational vehicle.

As campgrounds have evolved, so have recreational vehicles. The origins of the motorhome dates back to 1910, when the Pierce Arrow Motor Company introduced the Touring Landau model at the Madison Square Garden auto show. Pierce Arrow's entry was designed with the camper in mind—providing cargo compartments for camping equipment and even an on-board toilet. In the 1920s, individual builders and manufacturers began to convert panel trucks and buses to be used for camping. Designers patterned these "housecars" after airplanes, boats, and buses. RV production was halted during World War II and would not resume for the domestic market until the 1950s. When production did begin again, designers began grafting trailer bodies onto truck or bus chassis.

Travel News was the first Coast member publication, pictured here is the second issue published in the summer of 1982. At the same time Coast began publication of Resort News, this one is the third issue also from the summer of 1982.

Your choices of RVs are much greater now with Class A's, B's, C's, fifth wheels, and travel trailers, with numerous shapes, sizes and amenities available. And likewise your choices of campgrounds have expanded to include RV parks and campground resorts with many activities and amenities that make them a destination rather than a one-night stop. Fortunately for you, Coast to Coast has vetted the best and makes them available to our members in our resort and Good Neighbor Park network.

But how did it all start for Coast to Coast? In 1972, Denny Brown, co-founder of the American Land Development Association, came up with the then-revolutionary idea of a reciprocal-use camping

1972	1973	1981	1982	1983	1984	1985	1988
Founders Denny and A.C. Brown form Camp Coast to Coast with an initial network of 13 membership campground resorts.	First Coast to Coast Directory is published.	First Coast member newsletter is published.	Coast to Coast Resorts rental program is launched. First computer is purchased by Coast to manage the membership and resort databases. Coast grows from 4 employees to 24 employees as membership camping begins to boom.	Coast Travel Services is created as a new membership benefit.	Coast creates four regional offices to help manage the accelerating growth in membership camping.	Camp Coast to Coast is sold by Denny and A.C. Brown to the American Bakeries Company.	American Bakeries is acquired by the predecessor to The Affinity Group, the two companies included in the purchase are Coast to Coast and TL Enterprises. Camp Coast to Coast changes its name to Coast to Coast Resorts.

The 1910 Pierce Arrow Touring Landau, widely acknowledged as the first production motorhome.

network. With the help of his brother, A.C., Brown took the notion of membership camping one step further by putting a vast network of campground resorts within each member's reach - from Florida to Washington and from Maine to California – literally camping "from coast to coast."

Camp Coast to Coast started modestly enough in 1972 with 13 resorts, each anxious to provide their members with places to stay as they traveled across the continent. With the Coast to Coast reciprocal-use system, members at these resorts could stay at other affiliated parks for a mere one dollar a night. In 1973 the first annual Coast to Coast Directory was published.

Resort News, the club newsletter, was first published in 1981. This was later renamed Travel News, then Resort and Travel News, and eventually became the Coast to Coast Magazine we know today.

By 1982, A.C. Brown came up with the complementary idea of Coast to Coast Resorts, where members could lodge in resort rental units—everything from cabins to condos to country inns—if they chose not to travel with their RV. Coast only had four employees, but the membership camping industry really started to boom beginning at this time. As a result, that same year Coast hired 20 new employees and purchased their first computer to manage the growing member and the facility database. In 1984 four regional offices were added to help manage the rapid growth of the club.

The next 12 years saw not only rapid growth for Coast to Coast, but changes in the ownership and headquarters location of Coast as well. The company was purchased from the Browns in 1985 by the American Bakeries Company. Then in 1988 American Bakeries sold Coast to the company that owned Good Sam, which became the predecessor to our current parent company. That same year the company, which had been know as Camp Coast to Coast, changed its name to Coast to Coast Resorts. In 1990 Coast to Coast moved from a high-rise office building in Washington, D.C., to south-eastern Denver's sprawling 980-acre Inverness Business Park. Then in 1992 the Affinity Group was formed by Coast's parent company to manage TL Enterprises, Good Sam, and Coast to Coast. Finally in 1997 the Affinity Group also acquired Camping World to create a company with a single-minded focus on the needs of RV owners and outdoor enthusiasts.

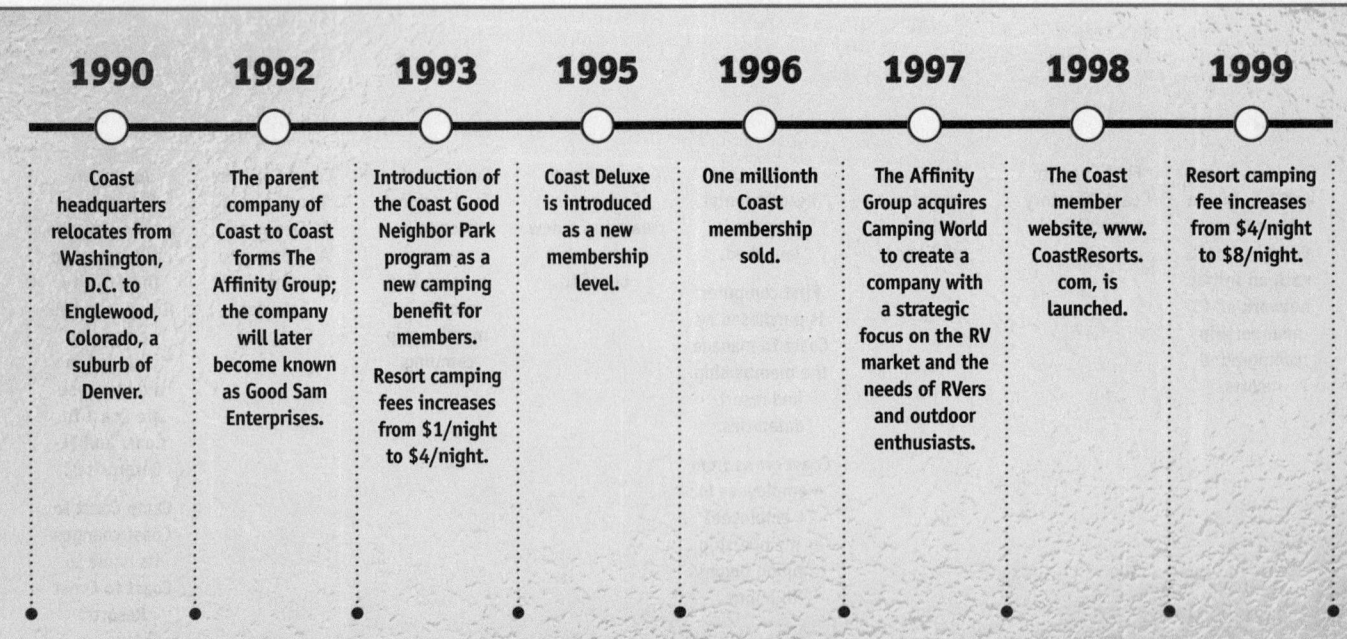

1990
Coast headquarters relocates from Washington, D.C. to Englewood, Colorado, a suburb of Denver.

1992
The parent company of Coast to Coast forms The Affinity Group; the company will later become known as Good Sam Enterprises.

1993
Introduction of the Coast Good Neighbor Park program as a new camping benefit for members.

Resort camping fees increases from $1/night to $4/night.

1995
Coast Deluxe is introduced as a new membership level.

1996
One millionth Coast membership sold.

1997
The Affinity Group acquires Camping World to create a company with a strategic focus on the RV market and the needs of RVers and outdoor enthusiasts.

1998
The Coast member website, www.CoastResorts.com, is launched.

1999
Resort camping fee increases from $4/night to $8/night.

While all this was happening, Coast continued to make enhancements to the membership with the creation of the Good Neighbor Parks program in 1993. Good Neighbor Parks are open-to-the-public RV campgrounds that welcome Coast to Coast members with a special discounted rate. In the same year the cost per night for staying at a network resort was increased from one dollar to four dollars. In the late 1990s it was increased to eight dollars per night, and today the cost is still arguably the greatest bargain in camping at ten dollars per night. In 1995 the first new product since the founding of the club, Coast Deluxe, was introduced.

GOOD NEIGHBOR PARK
COAST TO COAST

The Coast Good Neighbor Park program was first introduced as a member benefit in 1993.

Coast Deluxe
A HIGHER VACATION STANDARD PROGRAM

Coast Deluxe was launched in 1995 as the first new product since Coast was founded in 1972. The original Coast product was rebranded as Coast Classic, possibly in light of the "New Coke/Coke Classic" rebranding of the previous decade.

At the beginning of the new millennial, a new leadership group took the reigns at Coast to Coast and set about reinventing the club. They added exciting new benefits such as discounted week-long condo getaways, Coast Travel Services for airline, hotel, cruise, and rental car bookings, and a reservation system, Tripsetter, which enabled members to make resort reservations 24/7 and receive a printed confirmation. The reservation system was truly revolutionary as it was the first of its kind in the membership camping industry. Up until that time, members had to pre-purchase camping cards from Coast to Coast and then call or visit participating network resorts to make reservations. The cards came in several colors which determined the value of the card. Members paid for their resort reservations with the camping cards, and resorts had to send the cards back to Coast to receive reimbursement for member camping nights. The new reservation system accomplished all this with a few clicks and ensured that resorts were paid on a weekly basis for reservations checked out the previous week. These changes were implemented in January 2004 and were heralded by a new Coast to Coast logo affectionately known as the "wings" logo (see separate article on page CTC 16 showing the history of the Coast to Coast logo).

In 2004 a new leadership team at Coast reinvented the club, adding condo getaways as a member benefit and a revolutionary 24/7 reservation system branded as Tripsetter.

2000

After a few years spent preparing the company's computer systems for the switchover to the new millennial, Y2K (January 1,2000) comes and goes without affecting the Coast systems.

2004

A new leadership team completes a major overhaul of Coast to Coast Deluxe benefits, which now include discount week-long condo getaways, airline bookings, cruises, hotel reservations, rental car reservations, and Trip Plus powered by Entertainment with savings on restaurants, shopping, and recreation.

The Tripsetter reservation system is launched, the first of its kind in the membership camping industry, replacing Coast Camping Cards.

A new Coast to Coast "wings" logo is introduced.

Two millionth Coast membership sold.

2006

Marcus Lemonis becomes CEO of Camping World.

2007

Amenity icons are added to the annual directory to make it easier to see resort amenities at a glance.

2011

Camping World merges with Good Sam Enterprises, the parent company of Coast to Coast, with Marcus Lemonis appointed as Chairman and CEO.

2012

Coast Premier membership is introduced as the first new membership product in 17 years.

Resort and Good Neighbor Park listings are divided into separate sections in the annual directory to make a clearer distinction between the two types of participating parks.

Coast Resort News and Coast Travel News were combined to create Coast Resort & Travel News. Fess Parker, famous for his roles as Davey Crockett and Daniel Boone, was the spokesman for Coast to Coast in the late 1980s.

Since that time Coast to Coast has continued to evolve. In 2012 our third product, Coast Premier, was launched and in 2021 we introduced an updated brand identity. This clean new look for Coast to Coast projects a brand image that is modern, fun, and energetic. The new logo is part evolution in that the four horizontal lines on either side of our brand name call to mind the "wings" from our previous logo and give the new logo movement and energy. In addition, we acknowledge the strong bond to our parent company by adding the phrase "a Good Sam company" as a foundational element of the new logo.

Today your Coast to Coast membership is accepted at over 450 resorts and Good Neighbor Parks across the United States, Canada, and Mexico. Coast to Coast is the only membership campground network that annually inspects and rates the resorts and Good Neighbor Parks that participate in our program. To accomplish this, we utilize the campground inspectors from the Good Sam Campground and Coupon Guide who inspect thousands of campgrounds across the United States and Canada each year. The Good Sam rating system is the "gold standard" in the campground industry, and the Good Sam inspection teams are the recognized experts at inspecting and rating campgrounds.

Coast to Coast is part of Good Sam Enterprises, which includes not only the Good Sam Club but Good Sam Roadside Assistance, Good Sam Travel Assist, Good Sam Extended Service Plan, the Good Sam Campground and Coupon Guide, RV Magazine, and other related products and services. Coast still resides in the building we moved into 31 years ago in southeast Denver, which now also houses the largest member service center for Good Sam Enterprises. Good Sam Enterprises is part of Camping World Holdings, led by our dynamic Chairman and CEO Marcus Lemonis. Camping World Holdings went public with an initial public offering in October 2016 and is listed on the New York Stock Exchange under the symbol "CWH".

Coast moved its headquarters in 1990 from Washington, D.C., to Englewood in suburban Denver; the company is still headquartered in the same building today.

2013

The face of "Sammy", the longtime mascot of Good Sam, is added to the center of the Coast to Coast winged logo to convey that Coast is part of the Good Sam family of companies.

For the first time ratings of all network resorts are added to the annual directory; these rating are provided by the Good Sam Directory & Travel Guide, the "gold standard" in the campground industry.

2014

Good Neighbor Park pricing goes from $15/night to a special Coast member discount that is determined by each GNP.

2015

The CoastResorts.com member website undergoes a major upgrade, recognizing that more and more members are accessing their benefits online; the upgrades include a much cleaner look and feel, simplified site navigation, and enabling the website to adjust automatically to display correctly whether accessed from a computer, tablet, or smart phone.

2016

Camping World Holdings, parent company of Coast to Coast, holds an initial public offering on the New York Stock Exchange under the symbol CWH.

2017

Camping World Holdings acquires the assets of Gander Mountain, rebranding it as Gander Outdoors and later expanding RV sales to all locations under the new name Gander RV & Outdoors.

Due to growing interest in cabin rentals at resorts, the rental listings in the annual directory are expanded and moved into their own section.

Being part of such a large and successful parent company is a huge benefit to Coast and to our members, as it enables Coast to have state-of-the-art member service and technology systems to provide world-class service to our Coast members. Another advantage this brings to members is our ability to make continuous upgrades to our member website, www.CoastResorts.com. Recent updates include enabling the website to automatically resize to appear correctly on PCs, tablets, and smartphones, and updating our resort profile pages to include photos that provide a virtual tour of participating resorts and Good Neighbor Parks.

What does the next 50 years hold for Coast to Coast? Our parent company purchased a campground reservation company this past year, and we will soon be upgrading our Tripsetter reservation system to their updated and more user-friendly platform. We plan to explore bringing the Good Neighbor Park network onto this new reservation system as well to allow members to book online reservations at all our participating resorts and Good Neighbor Parks. Coast is continuously looking for new travel and savings benefits because we know our members love to travel and to save money doing it.

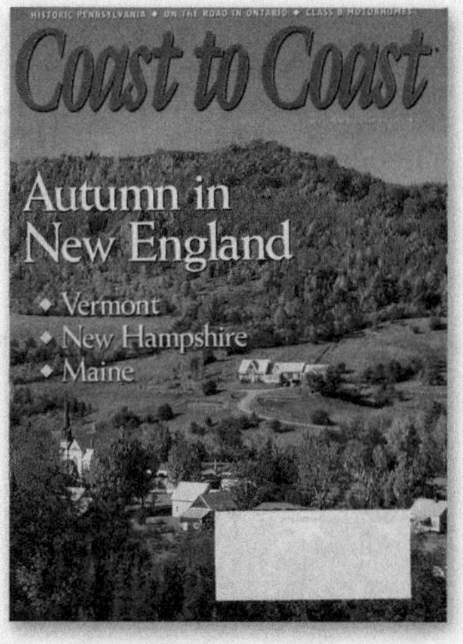

The magazine eventually changed to the title we know today, Coast to Coast Magazine.

To keep up with all the new developments at Coast to Coast, be sure you are receiving our quarterly Coast to Coast digital magazine and that you are signed up for our bi-monthly enewsletter, Coast to Coast Insider. This will ensure that you are among the first to know what's new at Coast.

When Coast started enrolling members way back in 1972, the first member number issued was 1, which was given to founder Denny Brown. Just recently we enrolled member number 2,551,100. That means that Coast over the last half century has helped over 2.5 million RVers expand their travel horizons, realize their vacation dreams, and create countless memories to last a lifetime. And that is without a doubt our greatest legacy. Thank you to all our current and former members for being a part of the first 50 years of Coast to Coast, and thanks as well to all the new members who will be joining us on our journey toward the next 50 years.

2018

Deluxe and Premier members receive the new benefit of Unique Getaways which include houseboat rentals, "glamping" accommodations such as safari tents, tree houses and teepees, and bed & breakfast reservations.

"How to" videos are created and added to the Coast member website to explain the benefits of the three membership types and to demonstrate how to use all key benefits.

2019

The resort and Good Neighbor Park profiles on the CoastResorts.com member website are upgraded to include a large rotating photo gallery at the top of each profile to serve as a virtual tour of each resort and Good Neighbor Park.

2020

2.5 millionth Coast membership sold.

Covid-19 global pandemic hits, with half of the Coast network resorts on emergency closure at one point mid-year due to local and state ordinances to limit the spread of the virus.

2021

Updated Coast to Coast brand identity and logo introduced.

2022

50th Anniversary Coast to Coast Directory published, and for the first time, the directory is distributed as a special section in the Good Sam Campground & Coupon Guide, the leading North American campground directory; all active Coast members receive a free copy as the newest membership benefit.

EXCERPTS FROM THE 20TH ANNIVERSARY COAST DIRECTORY IN 1992:

On what it was like to work in the original Washington, D.C. headquarters:

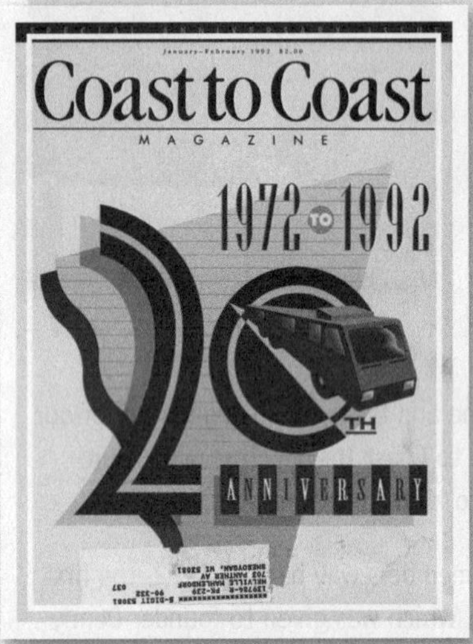

The cover of the 20th Anniversary Coast to Coast Magazine from January-February 1992.

"For the first 10 years a small seventh-floor suite in an otherwise undistinguished Washington, D.C., high-rise sufficed as Coast to Coast headquarters. And why shouldn't it? After all, Coast to Coast founders Denny and A.C. Brown were starting from scratch with 13 resorts and only a handful of members so the close confines seemed pretty big – for the time being.

But once Coast to Coast started to catch on in 1982, the company became as peripatetic as its traveling members. In the next two years, as business and the number of employees burgeoned, Coast to Coast shuffled between the seventh and eighth floors of 1000 16th Street. One year later, an entire floor of the building was acquired, leaving Coast to Coast with all of the second, half of the seventh and part of the eighth floor – a total of about 15,000 square feet, not including the 9,000-square-foot warehouse some 15 miles distant.

Coast was headquartered in Washington, D.C. for the first 18 years in the Solar Building at 1000 16th Street. This building was razed in 2003 and replaced by a newer office building.

But there was more to that building than met the eye. 'Because we were so close to the White House, we'd hear demonstrations going on all the time,' remembers Marketing Director Steve Vincent. Trying to conduct business surrounded by the pomp, history, and protest signs of a nation's capital was challenging, to say the least. Not only was the old Coast to Coast building a fixture on the capital parade route, it also stood just a block away from the Soviet Embassy, mere steps from where Mikhail Gorbachev made his famed unscheduled limousine exit to grip and grin with an astonished American public in the spring of 1990. What's more, members were occasionally put on hold while police-escort sirens screamed along busy 16th and K streets outside the Washington, D.C. high-rise that housed Coast to Coast."

On the company's early history with computer systems:

"Probably the most visible sign of Coast to Coast's high-tech commitment is its state-of-the-art computer system. Nicknamed "Thor", the current system is successor to "Zeus", the fledgling computer installed by Coast to Coast back in 1982. Consisting of a single video-display terminal and one dot-matrix printer, Zeus – unlike its mythic Greek namesake – was quickly rendered obsolete by the company's growth.

Today's VAX system runs 125 terminals and links nine Coast to Coast departments and four regional offices, performing tailor-made duties for each. The Member Services department uses the 12-gigabyte data base to log and capture member information and communications. Resort Services maintains resort statistics, and Marketing monitors the success of such programs as Roll on America! Everything from warehouse inventory to financial records to this very magazine story is but a few keystrokes away."

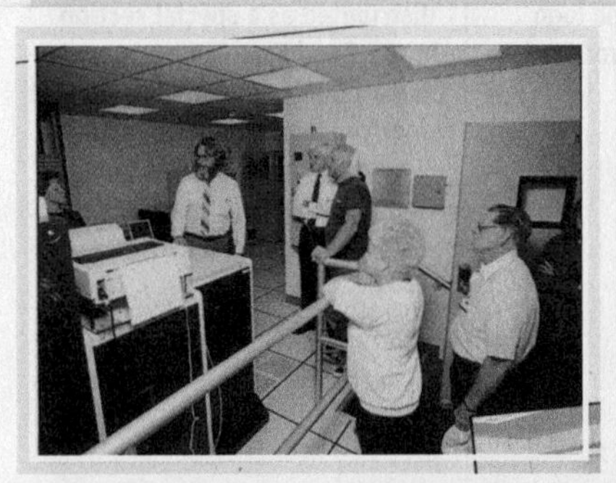

The Coast IT group admiring the new VAX system in 1992.

(editor note: The VAX system was replaced in the late 1990s by a system called AGIS (Affinity Group Information System). After many years and much re-programming and "tweaking", it was decided to re-write the AGIS system using newer technologies, adding more functionality and ultimately creating a new more robust user-friendly system for Marketing, the Call Center, and Order Processing. This system is still in use today but is scheduled to be replaced by a new system in the near future.)

EXCERPTS FROM THE 25TH ANNIVERSARY COAST DIRECTORY IN 1997:

On the priority given to Coast Member Service:

"From day one, Coast to Coast has made member service a top priority. Over the course of our 25-year history, our member services staff has grown from three part-time representatives in the mid '70s to 27 full-time representatives who regularly respond to more than 1,000 member calls a day, six days a week.

An event significant to our commitment to member service was our move from the cramped, antiquated quarters in downtown Washington, D.C., to our own spacious and modern office building in a quiet business park in a southeastern suburb of Denver, Colorado. The up-to-date facility enabled us to expand and enhance member services and related departments, including shipping and correspondence, by installing computer and telecommunication systems that put the power of leading-edge technology at everyone's fingertips.

Furthermore, Denver's central location made us more accessible for members to stop by our main office for a visit."

The 25th Anniversary issue of Coast to Coast Magazine from June 1997, featuring the 25th anniversary logo.

The somewhat cramped call center as it was in 1997. The Denver call center today is a state-of-the-art center with seats for 230 agents.

On the Brown brothers and the early days of Coast to Coast:

"The first-half of Coast to Coast's 25-year history, the company was run as a small entrepreneurial business under the direction of brothers Denny and A.C. Brown. The Browns pioneered the workings of the reciprocal-use network and laid the foundation for what was to follow. They recently shared some of their most memorable experiences from those formative years.

A.C. Brown remembers the time when he left their Washington, D.C., office for a two-day trip to sign up one park and ended up being gone six weeks and signing 13. 'I had to buy new clothes, and when I finally returned home, I had to hire a taxi to drive me around the airport parking lot until I found my car.'

Denny Brown recalls that some of his best moments were signing up companies that added multiple parks to the network. 'Our goal was to have a park in every state. Each addition was cause to kick up our heels.'

For A.C., his best and worst experiences were one and the same. It occurred at one of the early Coast to Coast conferences. Developers were bombarding A.C. with questions about how the reciprocal use exchange should work. 'We were supposed to be the experts, but actually we'd been feeling our way around the operation,' he says. The tense situation had a positive outcome when A.C. answered the questions with rules he made up on the spot. The rules made sense and were published quickly before they were forgotten. The network still uses many of those rules today.

Another incident that made a lasting impression on A.C happened during one of his regular visits to an affiliate. As he was walking through the park, a woman came up to him and gave him a big hug. She told A.C. that she was very thankful for him, because Coast to Coast had saved her family. She explained that now she and her husband and their two children could get out of the city and spend more quality time together."

Using one of the company's early computer terminals.

EXCERPTS FROM THE 30TH ANNIVERSARY COAST DIRECTORY IN 2002:

On visiting the home office in Colorado:

"The hub of Coast to Coast Resorts is the home office in Englewood, Colorado, a suburb of Denver. Whenever you're out this way exploring colorful Colorado, we invite you to stop by for a visit. You're always welcome and there's free parking for RVs of all sizes, as well as cars. We'll be happy to meet you and give you a behind-the-scenes tour. There is RV parking in the back of the building on the West side of the parking lot, and car parking is just outside the main entrance."

The cover of the 30th Anniversary Coast to Coast Directory from 2002.

On making resort reservations before the advent of the Tripsetter reservation system:

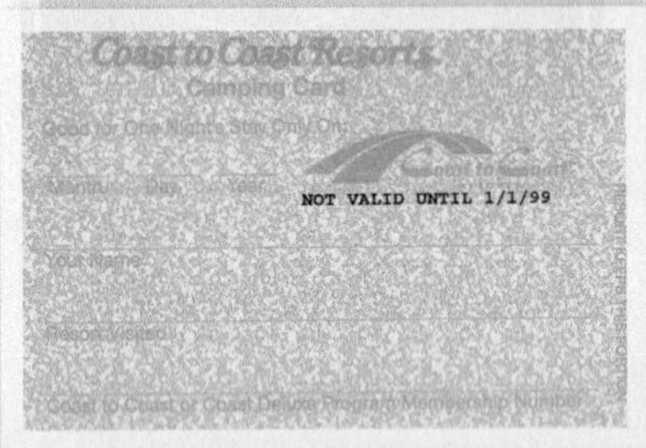

Before the Tripsetter system, Coast members used green, red, and blue camping cards for resort, cabin, and Good Neighbor Park reservations respectively.

"Coast to Coast accepts reservation requests from 7-60 days prior to the date of arrival, unless otherwise noted in the resort's directory entry. A standard $5 service fee is charged for each reservation except for Deluxe members. If you want to make reservations within seven days of arrival, you must call the resort directly. Obtain Green Cards in advance from Coast to Coast or from your home resort."

50 YEARS OF COAST LEADERSHIP

A look back at the leaders who helped found, grow, and manage Coast to Coast over the last 50 years.

1972 Founders Denny & A.C. Brown

1982 Dee Jacobs

1993 Roger Ryman

1985 Patrick Butler

1998 Gene Everett

2003 Grant Miller

2006 Marcos Strafacce

2007 Bruce Hoster

Wilderness Village at Crimson Lake was the 4th resort to join the Coast network.

The 12th resort to join the Coast network, Ghost Mountain Ranch.

RESORTS

Still at the Heart of Coast to Coast

When Denny & A.C. Brown founded Coast to Coast in 1972, their idea was to create a reciprocal use network of campground resorts that members of Coast could use when traveling away from their home resort. The original network contained only 13 resorts but grew from there as membership camping and Coast to Coast expanded rapidly in the 1980s and 1990s.

Any article on the 50-year history of Coast would be incomplete without giving our participating resorts their proper recognition. Camping at network resorts was then, and is today, the primary benefit of Coast to Coast membership. The resort network really is the heart and soul of Coast to Coast.

When the Brown brothers began acquiring those original 13 resorts, each resort was given a resort ID number, beginning with the number 1. The smaller the resort ID, the older the resort's start date in the Coast network. We are proud today to still have two of those original 13 resorts in our network, (4) Wilderness Village at Crimson Lake in Rocky Mountain House, Alberta, Canada and (12) Ghost Mountain Ranch in Pollock Pines, California. We owe our deepest gratitude to these two resorts for still being part of our resort network after 50 years.

Quinebaug Cove Resort was the 31st resort to join the Coast network.

We also wanted to take this opportunity to recognize the 10 resorts with the longest tenure in the resort network. The 10 resorts listed below joined the Coast network between 1972 and 1974, which is when the tenth resort listed below was affiliated. We know this because, while we could not find the affiliation documents for the first nine, we did find a letter from Coast founder Denny Brown dated August 16, 1974, welcoming Pathfinder Village – St. Croix in Minnesota to the resort network.

WE SALUTE THE TEN LONGEST-TENURED RESORTS STILL IN THE RESORT NETWORK, LISTED BY THEIR RESORT ID:

4 WILDERNESS VILLAGE AT CRIMSON LAKE
Rocky Mountain House, Alberta, Canada

12 GHOST MOUNTAIN RANCH
Pollock Pines, California

16 FISHERMAN'S RETREAT
Redlands, California

17 OAK GLEN RETREAT
Yucaipa, California

23 SUNDANCE MEADOWS
Aguanga, California

27 STATELINE CAMPRESORT & CABINS
East Killingly, Connecticut

31 QUINEBAUG COVE RESORT
Brimfield, Massachusetts

41 CUTTY'S DES MOINES CAMPING CLUB
Grimes, Iowa

43 ABITA SPRINGS RV RESORT
Abita Springs, Louisiana

54 PATHFINDER VILLAGE – ST. CROIX
Hinckley, Minnesota

ORIGINAL LOGO

1972 – 1997

This is the original logo for Coast to Coast which was in use for 25 years. The top part of the logo is comprised of mountains, sky, and either a sunrise or a sunset, no doubt signifying all the wonderful places in the great outdoors that you can visit with your Coast to Coast membership. The outline of the United States at the bottom of the logo along with the golden arch clearly conveys that you can travel "coast to coast" with Coast to Coast. The principle colors used are green, blue, and gold.

COAST TO COAST RESORTS LOGO

1998 – 2003

This logo retains the blue and green colors of the original logo but in a more streamline form that places more emphasis on the Coast to Coast name. The arch from the original logo now is a design element curving over the company name, but now it appears as a two-lane roadway. Like the original logo, this logo conveys that Coast to Coast can help you realize your travel dreams from coast to coast.

COAST "WINGS" LOGO

2004 – 2011

Coast to Coast was relaunched in 2004 with a 24/7 online reservation system as well as new benefits like condo vacation getaways. Along with this relaunch came a new logo that has become known as the Coast "wings" logo. The round center of the logo can be envisioned as one of the tires on your RV, complete with tire tread on the outside and a round hubcap in the middle. The "wings" on either side of the logo also convey travel, perhaps reflecting that Coast could now book air travel and condo vacation getaways for members in addition to RV travel. Added to the logo for the first time was the line "Est. 1972", reflecting the credibility of a company that had been in business for more than 30 years. This line also adds to the overall "retro" feel of this logo.

COAST "WINGS" LOGO WITH "SAM"

2012 – 2020

This logo retained most of the elements of the previous logo, while introducing the face of "Sam" to the center of the logo. Sam has been the mascot for Good Sam for many years, and the inclusion of Sam's face was meant to convey that Coast to Coast is a part of a much larger company (Good Sam/Camping World) that also has deep roots among RVers and outdoor travel enthusiasts. This logo also was redesigned with a more vibrant red color, a nod to Good Sam who has always used red as their primary logo color. Of course Sam has his halo, acknowledging the "Good Samaritan" foundation of Good Sam.

NEW COAST LOGO

2021

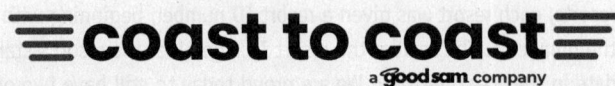

With a more contemporary design and typeface, this clean new look for Coast to Coast projects a brand image that is modern, fun, and energetic. The new logo is part evolution in that the four horizontal red lines on either side of our brand name call to mind the "wings" from our previous two logos and give the new logo movement and energy. In addition, we acknowledge the strong bond to our parent company by adding the phrase "a Good Sam company" as a foundational element of the new logo.

How many of these Coast to Coast logos can you remember? Email us at CCRPresident@CoastResorts.com with any thoughts or comments you have.

DREAM. PLAN. GO.

The 2022 Coast Directory is designed to give you everything you need to navigate the Coast to Coast network like a pro! Turn your travel dreams into reality by using the tools available to you in this directory including resort photos, maps, directions, descriptions, GPS coordinates, and ratings based on Good Sam's trusted 10/10★/10 rating system.

Coast to Coast continually updates our online directory throughout the year. Visit the Coast member website at CoastResorts.com for the most up-to-date information on participating parks and resorts.

If you'd like to keep current on the latest happenings at Coast to Coast and network resorts, or share your travel experiences with other members, visit the Coast Facebook page at Facebook.com/CoastResorts.

Happy Travels!

COAST TO COAST NETWORK

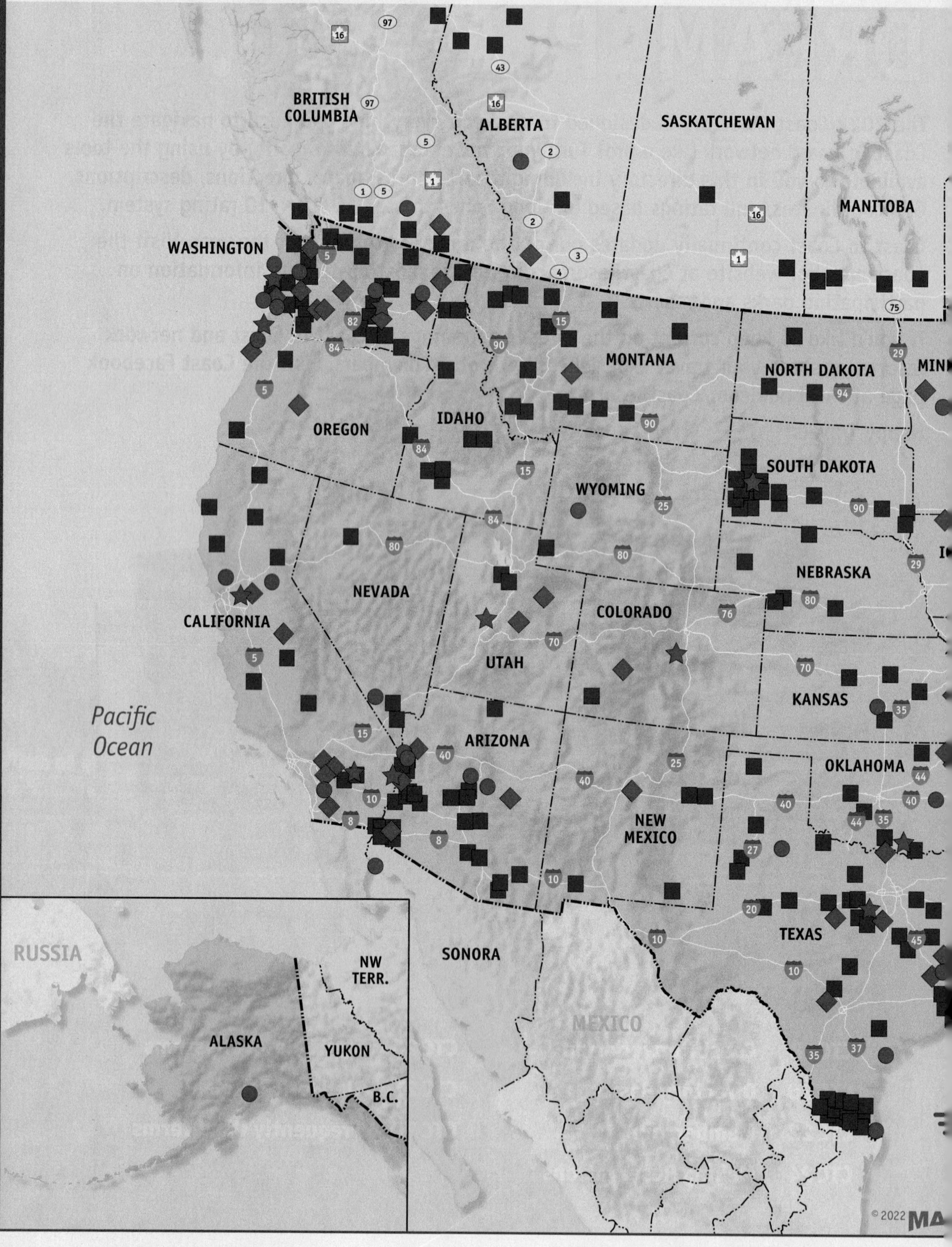

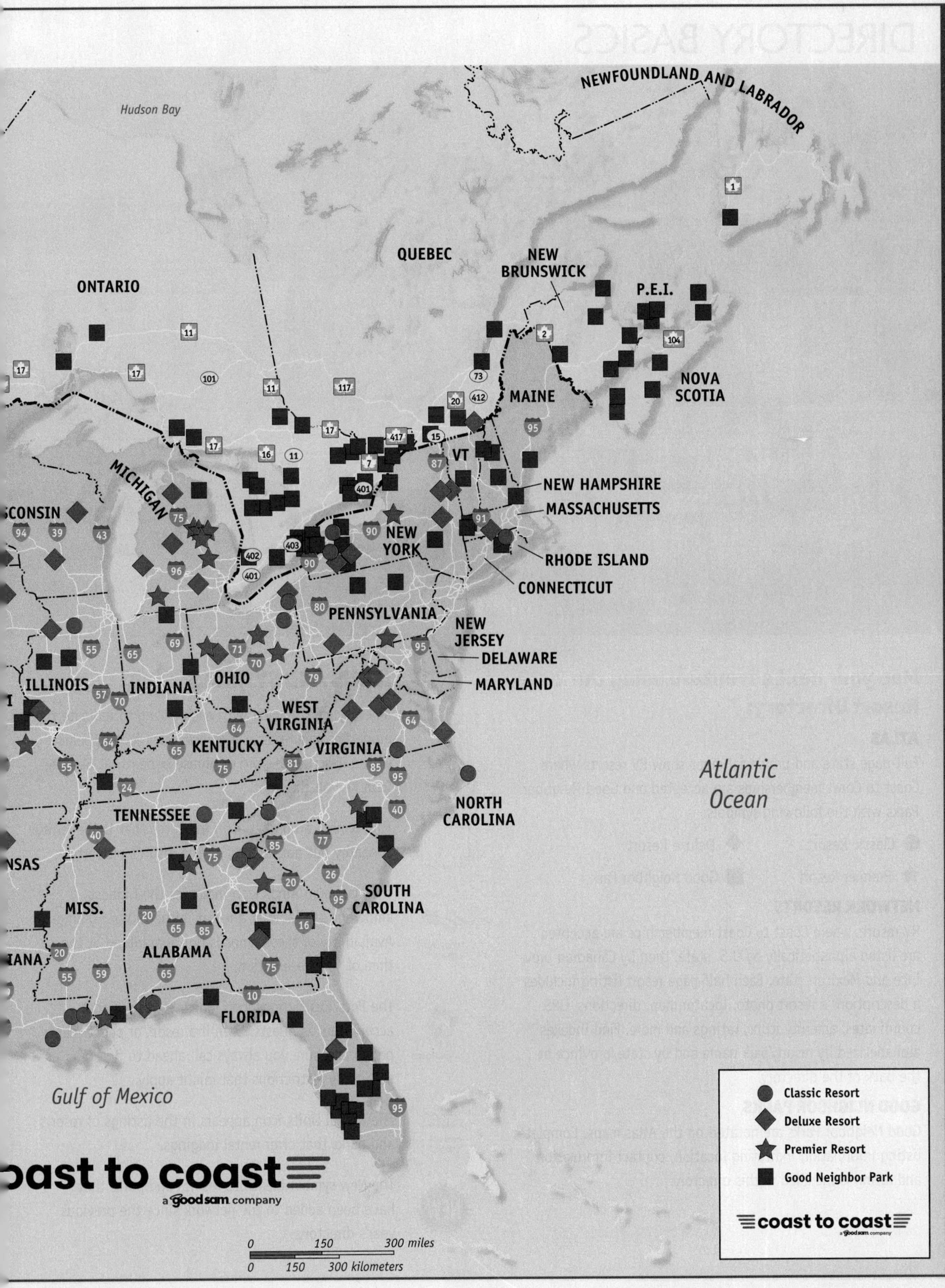

Hudson Bay
NEWFOUNDLAND AND LABRADOR
QUEBEC
ONTARIO
NEW BRUNSWICK
P.E.I.
NOVA SCOTIA
MAINE
VT
NEW HAMPSHIRE
MASSACHUSETTS
RHODE ISLAND
CONNECTICUT
NEW YORK
MICHIGAN
SCONSIN
PENNSYLVANIA
NEW JERSEY
DELAWARE
MARYLAND
ILLINOIS
INDIANA
OHIO
WEST VIRGINIA
VIRGINIA
KENTUCKY
TENNESSEE
NORTH CAROLINA
SOUTH CAROLINA
NSAS
MISS.
GEORGIA
ALABAMA
IANA
FLORIDA
Atlantic Ocean
Gulf of Mexico
Classic Resort
Deluxe Resort
Premier Resort
Good Neighbor Park
coast to coast
a good sam company
oast to coast
a good sam company
0 150 300 miles
0 150 300 kilometers

DIRECTORY BASICS

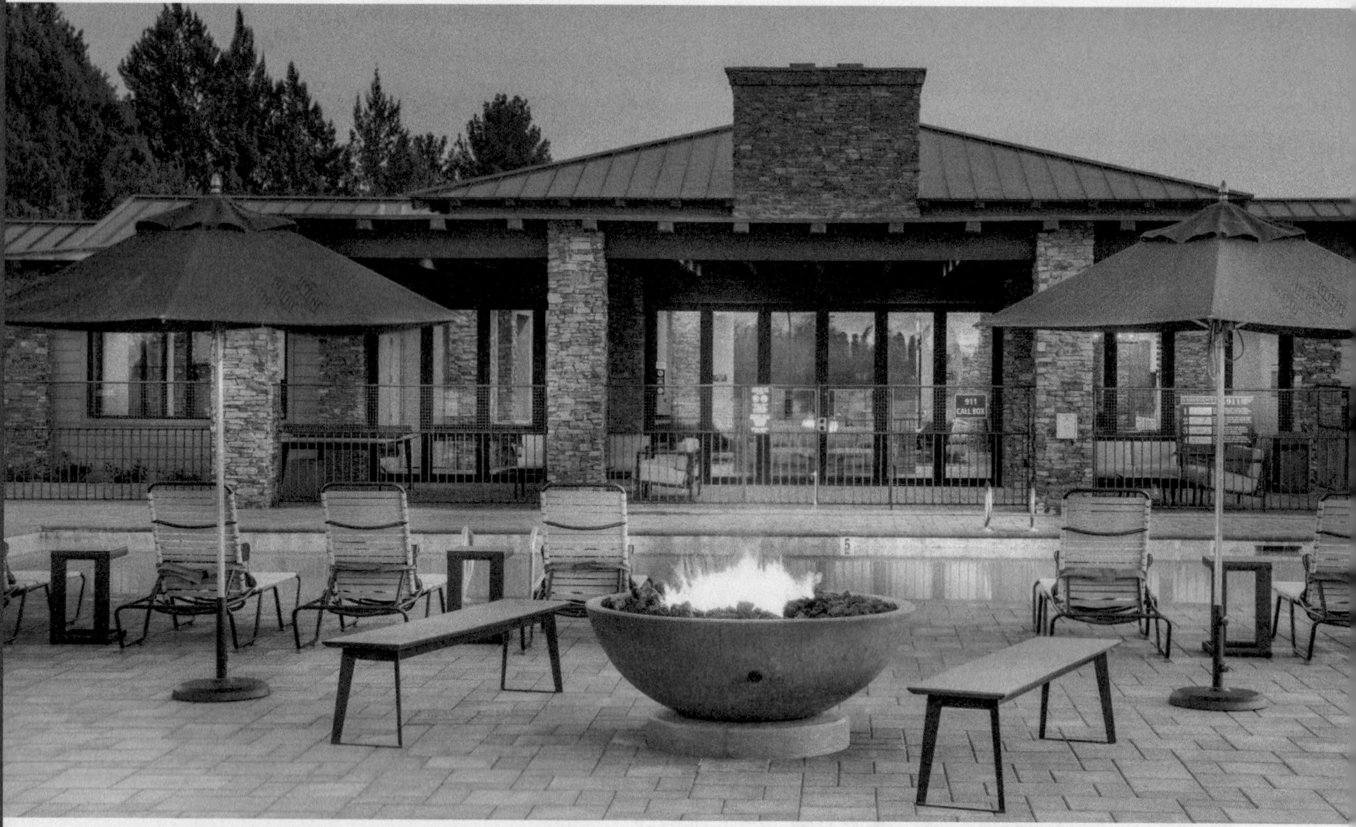

Map your next adventure using the 2022 Resort Directory:

ATLAS

Full-page state and provincial maps show RV resorts where Coast to Coast memberships are accepted and Good Neighbor Parks with the following symbols:

● Classic Resort ◆ Deluxe Resort

★ Premier Resort ■ Good Neighbor Park

NETWORK RESORTS

RV resorts where Coast to Coast memberships are accepted are listed alphabetically by U.S. state, then by Canadian province and Mexican state. Each half-page resort listing includes a description, a resort photo, locator map, directions, GPS coordinates, amenity icons, ratings and more. Find indexes alphabetized by resort/park name and by state/province at the back of the directory.

GOOD NEIGHBOR PARKS

Good Neighbor Parks are notated on the Atlas maps. Complete listing information indicating location, contact information and rating is included in this directory.

ICONS AND SYMBOLS

hot showers

Amenity icons appear with each listing to indicate the property's amenities at a glance. Each icon appears with a descriptive word or phrase beneath it. See the Icon Key on the right.

This symbol around an icon indicates that the amenity is nearby but not directly on the resort's property.

30 amps max

The Maximum Amps icon indicates the highest amperage available at a resort, either 30 or 50 amps. Availability of these amps is not guaranteed at the time of your reservation.

pets/ restrictions

The Pets/Restrictions icon indicates resorts that accept pets as guests. Even if a resort or park accepts pets, make sure you always call ahead to find out about any restrictions that might apply.

rental units

The Rental Units icon appears in the listings of resorts and parks that offer rental lodgings.

NEW

The New symbol identifies resorts and parks that have been added to the network since the previous year's directory.

ICON KEY

The following icons appear in the resort and park listings and indicate the amenities available at each property.

RATINGS

Coast to Coast utilizes the same Good Sam rating system featured in the *Good Sam Campground and Coupon Guide.* Based on a scale from one to 10, with 10 being the highest, Good Sam's three-part ratings give an overview of the amenities, cleanliness and environment that each facility has to offer.

THE FIRST rating judges facilities and amenities, such as interior roads, registration area, RV sites and hook-ups, security, recreational equipment, swimming, laundry facilities and building maintenance.

THE SECOND rating gauges cleanliness and completeness of bathrooms. Inspectors rate the tidiness of toilets, walls, showers, sinks, counters, mirrors and floor. Full points in each area earns a ★ following the second number.

THE THIRD rating deals with visual appearance and environmental quality, measuring the aesthetics of the entrance, landscaping and grounds and how harmoniously the facilities blend with the natural surroundings.

Good Sam ratings have a maximum score of 10/10★/10 and are determined by highly trained inspectors who annually visit and rate thousands of North American RV parks and campgrounds.

COAST TO COAST NETWORK

Get to know the resorts and parks that offer benefits to Coast to Coast members

NETWORK RESORTS

Classic, Deluxe and Premier Resorts are membership resorts where Coast to Coast memberships are accepted across North America with a full complement of amenities such as swimming pools, clubhouses, sport courts and lakes for fishing, boating and swimming. Exact amenities vary by resort. These resorts open their gates to Coast to Coast members for 1,000* Trip Points per RV night.

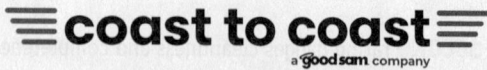

coast to coast
a good sam company

GOOD NEIGHBOR PARKS

Good Neighbor Parks (GNPs) enhance the Coast to Coast network by offering members additional high-quality places to stay. GNPs have their own set of operational guidelines because they are open-to-the-public parks rather than membership resorts. GNPs welcome Coast to Coast members for a special discounted rate* for Coast to Coast members, typically 20%-25% off normal pricing. All Good Neighbor Park reservations must be booked and paid directly with the Good Neighbor Park.

coast to coast
good neighbor park

*Subject to change. Additional fees, surcharges, or taxes may apply. Reservations are subject to availability at time of booking. GNP rate may not be available during peak seasons, holidays, and special events. Trip Points cannot be used to pay for GNP reservations.

GOOD SAM PARKS

good sam

All first-year Coast to Coast members are eligible for complimentary Good Sam membership. When you show your Good Sam membership card at any of the more than 2,000 Good Sam Parks across North America, you'll receive a 10 percent savings on nightly stays. Good Sam Parks are listed at GoodSam.com/camping.

MEMBER GET A PARK PROGRAM

If you've ever visited a resort or campground that you loved and wished that it was a part of the Coast to Coast network, here's your chance to nominate that park as a potential new resort or Good Neighbor Park. It's an opportunity for Coast members to help Coast to Coast grow our network, so there are more quality places to stay.

If a park or resort joins the Coast network as a result of a member recommendation, that member will receive from Coast to Coast a $50 merchandise certificate to use at Camping World or Gander RV retail locations. To recommend a new park or resort, Coast members must have recently stayed at the facility and must provide the following:

- Name, address, phone number, and contact at facility
- Indicate whether facility is a membership resort (potential resort) or an open-to-the-public park (potential Good Neighbor Park)
- Member's name and Coast member number
- Date that member visited the park or resort
- Submit Member Get a Park referrals to:
  - Email: CCRPresident@CoastResorts.com
  - Mail: Coast to Coast
Member Get a Park
PO Box 7028
Englewood, CO 80155-7028

All Coast members with active memberships are eligible to submit Member Get a Park referrals. In the case that Coast signs a new facility that is recommended by more than one member, only the first member recommending the new facility will be awarded the $50 merchandise certificate to use at Camping World or Gander RV retail locations.

MEMBER BILL OF RIGHTS

As a Coast to Coast member, you're among a group of savvy travelers who not only appreciate high-quality accommodations but also understand how to measure real value as you experience the outdoor lifestyle. We know this is true because you've already made the decision to become an active participant in resort membership, with all the benefits that membership provides.

Membership at your home resort and in Coast to Coast means you're entitled to great travel and vacation experiences all across North America. This is possible because your Coast to Coast membership provides access to participating network resorts and Good Neighbor Parks, as well as a host of other travel and savings benefits.

We want you to make the most of your Coast to Coast membership, taking full advantage of every benefit available to you. Coast to Coast expects a high standard from all of the participating network resorts. This translates to a number of things that you, as a valued member, can expect in return. The following Member Bill of Rights is a review of these points.

As a Coast to Coast member, you have the right to expect:

- Resort reservations can be booked and confirmed through Coast's Tripsetter reservation system. In the unlikely event you encounter a problem, please call the Coast to Coast Member Services Center immediately for resolution.
- Complaints will be taken seriously by Coast to Coast, with acknowledgement, resolution and follow-up with you handled on a timely basis.
- Your nightly network resort campsite fees will be paid using your available Trip Points.
- All Good Neighbor Park reservations must be booked and paid directly with the Good Neighbor Park.
- Sales tax and additional fees, not covered by your Trip Points and payable in cash, may be collected at check-in by the resort or park (see Fees and Surcharges on page CTC 28).
- Network resorts and Good Neighbor Parks are rated by the *Good Sam Campground and Coupon Guide* and monitored by Coast to Coast staff to ensure they meet our high standards for cleanliness, safety, amenities and customer service.
- Clear, concise and complete descriptions of Classic, Deluxe and Premier Resorts will be available in both the annual Resort Directory and on our website, CoastResorts.com. Please note: The most current information can be accessed on the website, since it is continually updated as changes occur.
- The two ways to make Tripsetter bookings for resorts are by Internet and through the Member Services Center (see page CTC 24).
- You'll be welcomed at the participating network resorts with the same warm hospitality you enjoy at your home resort.

PHONE NUMBER TO KNOW

MEMBER BENEFITS

Coast to Coast
Member Services Center: 800-368-5721

Tripsetter Reservations: 800-368-5721

COASTRESORTS.COM

- Reservations
- Trip Points
- Membership Renewals
- "How To" Videos
- Online Directory
- Member Benefits
- Digital Coast Magazines
- Plus Much More

Find us at Facebook.com/CoastResorts

2022 HOLIDAY SCHEDULE

Holidays are always popular travel times, with an increased use of resorts by their own home park members. Resorts will most likely have inventory restrictions during local events and major holidays, including the days before and after.

Here's a list of the major U.S. and Canadian holidays in 2022 to help with your travel planning:

UNITED STATES	CANADA
New Year's Day, January 1	New Year's Day, January 1
Easter, April 17	Easter Sunday, April 17
Memorial Day, May 30	Easter Monday, April 18
Independence Day, July 4	Victoria Day, May 23
Labor Day, September 5	Canada Day, July 1
Halloween, October 31	Civic Holiday, August 1
Thanksgiving, November 24	Labour Day, September 5
Christmas, December 25	Thanksgiving, October 10
	Halloween, October 31
	Christmas, December 25

TRIPSETTER

The Tripsetter Internet-based reservation system allows you to transact all your resort reservation business in real time, 24 hours a day, seven days a week, simply by using your computer, smartphone or other Internet-enabled device. All Good Neighbor Park reservations must be booked and paid directly with the Good Neighbor Park.

HOW TO USE TRIPSETTER

- Go to CoastResorts.com.
- Click on "Register".
- Register using your Coast membership number, last name, zip code, country and email address.
- Choose from a number of activities:
  - Check resort availability & book a resort reservation.
  - View your camping history.
  - View and change reservations.
  - Buy Trip Points & check your Trip Point balance.
  - Learn about Tripsetter Reservation System and Trip Points.

TRIP POINTS

Trip Points are electronic stored value instruments that are redeemable for overnight resort stays at participating resorts in the Coast to Coast network. Each participating resort has agreed to accept Trip Points instead of cash as payment for stays.

Members can either purchase Trip Points or earn Trip Points (for example, through promotional offers). Trips Points can be purchased online through Tripsetter or by calling Coast Member Services. Members can use the Good Sam Rewards Visa® or Coast to Coast Rewards Visa® credit card to earn Trip Points.

The basic Trip Point value is $1.00 = 100 Trip Points*. You can receive promotional points** when you buy certain higher-value Trip Point packages. Here's a sample of the currently available Trip Point packages:

PRICE	PURCHASED POINTS	PROMOTIONAL POINTS**	TOTAL POINTS
$5	500	0	500
$10	1,000	0	1,000
$25	2,500	0	2,500
$50	5,000	0	5,000
$100	10,000	0	10,000
$150	15,000	0	15,000
$200	20,000	0	20,000
$300	30,000	2,000	32,000
$500	50,000	5,000	55,000

*Prices are subject to change.
**Additional points received at no additional charge.

It's easy to review your Trip Points balance online anytime you wish, 24 hours a day, seven days a week, by logging into your member account on our website, CoastResorts.com. You may also check your Trip Points balance through Coast to Coast Member Services, weekdays between 8:00 a.m. and 9:00 p.m. and Saturdays between 10:00 a.m. and 6:30 p.m. Eastern Time.

CONDITIONS OF USE

Maintaining an active Coast membership is a condition that must be satisfied in order to be eligible to purchase, earn, gift, or otherwise redeem Trip Points. Trip Points that you purchase do not have an expiration date and may be used by you as long as you have a currently active Coast membership. In the event your membership becomes inactive or delinquent or you terminate your membership, your Trip Points will no longer be available for redemption; however, if you subsequently reactivate or renew your membership, your Trip Points balance will become available for use. Trip Points you receive free of charge as the result of a promotional offer and other points that you may receive that were not purchased will have an expiration date. Complete terms and condition of the Trip Points are provided in the membership terms and conditions.

GIFTING TRIP POINTS

Trip Points are easily gifted to anyone with a currently active Coast membership, but they are not refundable and may not be redeemed for cash (unless otherwise required by law). You can gift Trip Points only if you are an active Coast member and your Trip Points must be gifted to someone with a currently active Coast membership. When you gift your Trip Points to another Coast to Coast member, there is a $10 administrative fee. To gift Trip Points, call Coast Member Services at 800-368-5721.

MEMBER SERVICES

When you don't have internet access, you'll be glad to know that Coast to Coast Member Services is available weekdays between 8:00 a.m. and 9:00 p.m. and Saturdays between 10:00 a.m. and 6:30 p.m. Eastern Time for you to make resort reservations. Call 800-368-5721.

Resort reservations made within 72 hours of your arrival date must be made directly with the resort. Check the resort listing before calling: resorts that include the notation "drive-ups not accepted" will not accept reservations within 72 hours (three days). Good Sam Park or Good Neighbor Park reservations cannot be made thru Tripsetter and must be made directly with the Good Sam Park or Good Neighbor Park.

RESERVATION CANCELLATION POLICY

Be sure to cancel your reservation if you're unable to stay at a booked resort. If you don't change or cancel your reservation by 6:00 p.m. (resort time) the day prior to your arrival date, your account will be charged the amount of Trip Points equal to the resort's minimum-stay requirement. We enforce this rule because the resort may have turned away another guest to hold the space for you. Please be considerate—and save your Trip Points too.

HOSPITALITY CODE OF ETHICS

The mutual exchange of hospitality is fundamental to the Coast to Coast network. As a member, you're both a guest and a host. You're a host when other members visit your home resort; you're a guest when you're the one traveling away from your home resort. Either way, the Golden Rule of treating others as you wish to be treated definitely applies. All members are encouraged to follow the Coast to Coast Hospitality Code of Ethics:

WHEN YOU'RE A GUEST...

- Introduce yourself, listen to others and join in the fun.
- Follow the rules of the resort you're visiting, even if they differ from those of your home resort.
- Respect your host resort and treat all property as though it were your own.
- Unless it's an emergency, refrain from making unusual or excessive requests.
- Don't be afraid to explore! Ask questions about the surrounding area.
- Always leave your RV site or rental accommodations better than you found them.

WHEN YOU'RE A HOST...

- Be friendly and polite. Every happy guest who visits adds value and a new dimension to your home resort.
- It's fun to share your knowledge of the area and the resort. You're the local expert!
- You're likely to make some new friends when you invite guests to participate in activities.

LET US HEAR FROM YOU

If you visit a park or resort you think would be a good addition to the Coast to Coast network, please let us know. Likewise, if you have a concern or question about a resort stay, be sure to tell us. Contact us via postal mail or email:

- Coast to Coast Resorts
  P.O. Box 7028
  Englewood, Colorado 80155-7028
- CCRPresident@CoastResorts.com

DIRECTORY NOTES

The 2022 Resort Directory is structured to present the information members need in the most user-friendly, understandable way. As always, we'd love to hear from you at 800-368-5721, CCRPresident@CoastResorts.com, or Coast to Coast Resorts, P.O. Box 7028, Englewood, Colorado 80155-7028.

Directory information, including pricing and availability, is provided by resort management, is assumed to be correct and is subject to change. Coast to Coast shall not be liable for misrepresentation or any problems arising from accommodations at any network resort or Good Neighbor Park or any other matters that affect or inconvenience the user's vacation. Directory listings are continuously updated on CoastResorts.com.

Coast to Coast Resorts, P.O. Box 7028, Englewood, Colorado 80155-7028, is under agreement with the resorts within the Coast to Coast program to offer accommodations at member rates. Coast to Coast does not own or operate any participating network resorts or Good Neighbor Parks. Coast to Coast is not the provider of accommodations and is not responsible for the physical condition or any aspect of network resorts or Good Neighbor Parks at the time a membership is purchased or afterward.

Coast to Coast is not responsible for personal or property damage resulting from the acts, omissions or negligence of participating resorts, Good Neighbor Parks or their employees or agents. Coast to Coast's maximum liability to members in all respects is limited to the amount of annual membership fees for any calendar year.

Any dispute you may have with Coast to Coast will be finally decided by arbitration in accordance with the Rules of the American Arbitration Association's (AAA) U.S. Commercial Dispute Resolution Procedures and Supplementary Procedures for Consumer-Related Disputes by one arbitrator appointed in accordance with such rules. These rules and procedures are available by calling the AAA at 800-778-7879 or by visiting its website, adr.org. All deposits and fees required by the AAA to commence the arbitration shall be advanced by Coast to Coast. If at any time and/or for any reason you are dissatisfied with Coast to Coast's programs, you may immediately cancel your Coast to Coast membership.

MULTI-RESORT SYSTEMS

When an individual, company or corporation owns and operates two or more network resorts, we refer to that as a multi-resort system. Visits by Coast to Coast members to properties within these resort groups listed below have special restrictions. The restriction is that members cannot book back-to-back reservations at network resorts within a multi-resort system. After each stay in a multi-resort system, a member must be out of that multi-resort system for 7 days before starting another reservation/stay at a resort within that same multi-resort system.

ADVANCE RESORTS OF AMERICA		araresorts.com
Paradise Cove Resort and Marina	Rockaway Beach	Oregon
Willow Bay Resort and Marina	Nine Mile Falls	Washington
COLORADO RIVER ADVENTURES		coloradoriveradventures.com
Cherry Valley Lakes Resort	Beaumont	California
El Golfo RV Resort	El Golfo	Sonora, Mexico
Emerald Cove	Earp	California
Ghost Mountain Ranch	Pollock Pines	California
KQ Ranch Resort	Julian	California
Lake Havasu RV Park	Lake Havasu City	Arizona
Sunrise Adventures—Ridgeview	Bullhead City	Arizona
Yuma Lakes	Yuma	Arizona
ESCAPE RV RESORTS		escapervresorts.com
Lakeside RV Park	Duchesne	Utah
Pleasant Creek RV Park	Mount Pleasant	Utah
HALO RESORTS		haloresorts.com
Fisherman's Retreat	Redlands	California
Oak Glen Retreat	Yucaipa	California
K/M RESORTS OF AMERICA		kmresorts.com
Columbia Shores RV Park	Chinook	Washington
Diamond Point Resort	Sequim	Washington
Maple Grove Resort	Randle	Washington
Ocean Breeze Resort	Ocean City	Washington
Old American Kampground	Newport	Washington
Ponderosa Falls Resort	Cheney	Washington
Travel Inn Resort	Elma	Washington
MIDWEST OUTDOOR RESORTS		midwestoutdoorresorts.com
Ham Lake Resort	Ham Lake	Minnesota
Hidden Bluffs Resort	Spring Grove	Minnesota
Rushmore Shadows	Rapid City	South Dakota
St. Croix River Resort	Hinckley	Minnesota
OCEAN CANYON PROPERTIES		oceancanyon.com
Abita Springs RV Resort	Abita Springs	Louisiana
Branson Ridge RV Resort	Branson	Missouri
Hideaway Ponds RV Resort	Gibson	Louisiana
Millwood Landing Golf & RV Resort	Ashdown	Arkansas
Mountain Lakes RV Resort	Langston	Alabama
Styx River RV Resort	Robertsdale	Alabama
Texoma Shores RV Resort	Madill	Oklahoma
Tres Rios RV Resort	Glen Rose	Texas
OUTDOOR ADVENTURES		outdooradventuresinc.com
Benjamin's Beaver Creek Resort	Gaylord	Michigan
Grand Haven Resort	Grand Haven	Michigan
Kalamazoo Resort	Kalamazoo	Michigan
Lake of the North Resort	West Branch	Michigan
Lake Shore Resort	Davison	Michigan
Mt. Pleasant Resort	Mt. Pleasant	Michigan
Rifle River Resort	Sterling	Michigan
Saginaw Bay Resort	Standish	Michigan
Wilderness Resort	Omer	Michigan
SARATOGA/SCHROON RIVER ESCAPE RESORTS		schroonriverescape.com / saratogaescape.com
Saratoga Escape Lodges & RV Park	Greenfield Center	New York
Schroon River Escape Lodges & RV Resort	Diamond Point	New York
SOUND PACIFIC RESOURCES		soundpacificrv.com
Cascade Meadows RV Resort	La Pine	Oregon
Neskowin Creek RV Resort	Neskowin	Oregon
SUNRISE RESORTS		sunriseresorts.com
Clint's Well	Happy Jack	Arizona
Copalis Beach Resort	Copalis Beach	Washington
Dow Creek Resort	Hoodsport	Washington
Eagle's Nest RV Resort	Ilwaco	Washington
Edgewater RV Resort	Soldotna	Alaska
Lake Easton Resort	Easton	Washington
Pacific Holiday RV Resort	Long Beach	Washington
Page Springs	Cornville	Arizona
Pier 4 RV Resort	Moses Lake	Washington
White Mountain	Overgaard	Arizona
TRAVEL RESORTS OF AMERICA		travelresorts.com
Bass Lake Resort	Parish	New York
Gettysburg Battlefield Resort	Gettysburg	Pennsylvania
North Shore Landing	Greensboro	Georgia
Rocky Fork Ranch	Kimbolton	Ohio
Sycamore Lodge	Jackson Springs	North Carolina
Wally World Riverside Resort	Loudonville	Ohio
VENTURE OUT RESORTS		ventureoutresorts.com
Arrowhead Lakes Resort	Wapakoneta	Ohio
Indian Lake Resort	Huntsville	Ohio
VISTA RESORTS		vistaresorts.net
Canyon Creek Resort	Winters	California
Delta Shores Resort & Marina	Isleton	California

COAST TO COAST POLICIES

Reciprocity is at the heart of the Coast to Coast network. It's one of our foundational concepts that turns a membership in your home resort into privileges at scores of others. All network resorts are expected to treat traveling members the way they'd like their members to be treated when they travel. Therefore, restrictions adopted by your home resort, in addition to those identified in this directory, may be applied to you when you visit other resorts in the network.

SYSTEM USE

To use Coast to Coast's Tripsetter reservation system to book stays at network resorts, you must be an active member with both your home resort and Coast to Coast.

ANNUAL DUES

Annual Coast to Coast membership dues are paid directly to Coast to Coast prior to your enrollment anniversary. These are separate from the annual maintenance fees billed by your home resort.

RESORT ACCESS

- Access to network resorts and Good Neighbor Parks is on a space-available basis relative to the number of sites each resort designates for Coast to Coast membership use.
- Not all sites in every resort are devoted to the Coast to Coast network. Resorts can't guarantee availability.
- Coast to Coast cannot guarantee the availability of full hook-ups for reservations at resorts.

HIGH-DEMAND AREAS

At certain times, space may be difficult to secure in high-demand regions such as coastal areas in the summer and Sunbelt areas in the winter. It is highly recommended that you make reservations as early as possible when you'd like to visit these areas during peak season.

SITE OCCUPANCY

- Each RV site is limited to four persons, unless otherwise specified. This may include the member, family members and guest(s). Guests must travel with you in the same RV.
- Each rental unit is limited to the number of persons specified in the resort's directory listing, on the website or by the resort.

HOME RESORT TRANSFER

Home resort membership or ownership transfers must be discussed directly with the member's home resort prior to contacting Coast to Coast.

DAY-USE CAMPING

If you plan to visit a resort for day use only, call in advance. Resorts may not have space available. Day-use fees are charged at the resort's discretion.

DRIVE-UPS

Arriving at a network resort or Good Neighbor Park with no reservation is discouraged. It is at the discretion of each facility whether they will honor the Coast to Coast rate for any member who drives up without a valid reservation, including day-use RVers. Resorts may not have sites available. Those that do not accept drive-ups have the notation "drive-ups not accepted" in their directory listing.

LAST-MINUTE RESERVATIONS

Reservations within 72 hours of the arrival date must be made directly with the resort. This is considered a drive-up reservation, see the drive-ups paragraph above for restrictions.

LAST-MINUTE RESERVATION CHANGES

The resort's published reservation change policy will be honored by Coast to Coast.

EARLY DEPARTURES

Let the resort know if you're departing early; don't just drive off without checking out. The resort's published early-departure policy will be honored by Coast to Coast.

MULTI-RESORT SYSTEMS

When an individual, company or corporation owns and operates two or more network resorts, we refer to this as a multi-resort system. Visits by Coast to Coast members to properties within these resort groups have special restrictions. The restriction is that members cannot book back-to-back reservations at network resorts within a multi-resort system. After each stay at a resort in a multi-resort system, a member must be out of that multi-resort system for 7 days before starting another reservation/stay at a resort within that same multi-resort system. See page CTC 26 for more details.

NO-SHOWS

If you don't show up at a resort where you have a reservation and you didn't cancel by 6:00 p.m. (resort time) the day prior to your arrival date, you will be charged the amount of Trip Points equal to the resort's minimum-stay requirement. If you do not have sufficient Trip Points to pay the No-Show charge, Coast may suspend your membership privileges until you pay the No-Show charge. Contact the resort directly when a No-Show is disputed.

LATE CANCELLATIONS

If you cancel your reservation later than 6:00 p.m. (resort time) the day before your scheduled arrival date, you will be charged the amount of Trip Points equal to the resort's minimum-stay requirement.

SPECIAL NOTES

AVAILABILITY

Coast to Coast cannot guarantee that any particular resort or GNP will always be in the Coast to Coast network. Check CoastResorts.com for the most current list of participating resorts or GNPs.

CURRENCY

All dollar amounts quoted in the Resort Directory are in U.S. currency.

EMERGENCY CLOSURES

There are times when a network resort has to close temporarily because of a natural disaster. Reasons can include tornados, flooding, fires, hurricanes, bridge or roads that have washed out, etc. When this happens, Coast to Coast will make every attempt to contact any member(s) with upcoming reservations at the impacted resort to alert them to the closure. We will also attempt to redirect members affected by emergency closures to another network resort. To facilitate this, please make sure you have a phone number on file with us that we can use to contact you while you are on the road. If you are ever in doubt as to the status of a network resort, call Coast Member Services at 800-368-5721.

FEES AND SURCHARGES

- In addition to the nightly resort camping fee, other fee(s), surcharges or taxes may apply. Check the resort listings in this directory or on our website, CoastResorts.com, for more information, or check with the resort directly.
- 50-amp service is not available at all resorts in the Coast to Coast network. However, when and where available, 50-amp service may or may not be included in the nightly rate, and a surcharge, payable in cash, may be charged by the resort.
- Resorts in the Coast to Coast network reserve the right to charge visiting Coast to Coast members for the use of optional amenities such as golf courses, boating, waterslides, horseback riding, etc.
- Resorts are permitted to offer optional services to Coast to Coast members (i.e., cable TV, Wi-Fi) for an optional surcharge. Such amenities and surcharges cannot be paid with Trip Points and are payable in cash.

HANDICAP ACCESS

Members requiring handicap access should contact resorts directly to confirm handicap access availability.

LISTING ACCURACY

The information published for each network resort and Good Neighbor Park was provided by each property and is presumed to be accurate. If you need additional information about any specific resort or park, please contact them directly.

MAIL

Unless otherwise noted in each resort's directory listing, visitor mail is not accepted.

PET POLICIES

Many resorts in the Coast to Coast network welcome your pets as guests, but they do so with restrictions that vary from resort to resort. Some resorts in the network allow pets only in designated areas, and some limit number of pets, type of pets, pet size, weight and breed. The acceptance of pets with restrictions is noted in each network resort's directory listing with a Pets/Restrictions icon. When traveling with pets, it is essential that members do the following:

- Contact the resort directly prior to making a reservation to verify that resort's particular pet restrictions
- Attend to your pet at all times
- Keep your pet on a leash
- Clean up after your pet
- Keep your pet from disturbing others or destroying property
- Bring only non-dangerous breeds of dogs
- Leave exotic animals at home
- Provide a proof-of-vaccination record, if asked to do so

Reservations may not be honored for members who do not meet the resort's particular pet restrictions.

RV LENGTH

Not all network resorts can accommodate big rigs. Please specify your vehicle's length when making a reservation. The Maximum RV Length specification in the resort listings is designed to ensure that your vehicle can be accommodated at that particular resort. Reservations may not be honored for vehicles that exceed the listed maximum length.

RESORT OWNERSHIP

Coast to Coast does not own or operate any of the resorts in our network. The RV resorts where Coast to Coast memberships are accepted are independently owned and operated resort campgrounds. Some resorts may elect to permit nonmember public stays based upon availability.

RESTRICTIONS

Network resorts may block holidays, days surrounding holidays and special events. Note the 2022 Holiday Schedule on page CTC 23.

TAXES

Many resorts are subject to local sales tax, lodging tax or both. These taxes will be added to the charges published in the directory. Taxes cannot be paid with Trip Points and are payable in cash. Please contact the resorts directly for details.

WEBSITES

For the most current information on network resorts and Good Neighbor Parks, go to CoastResorts.com and click "Find A Resort". For current information about Good Sam Parks, go to GoodSam.com/camping.

COAST TO COAST GLOSSARY

CAMPING WORLD
The nation's largest network of RV sales, service and accessory centers that offer Coast to Coast members savings when they show their valid Good Sam membership card.

COAST TO COAST MEMBER
A member of Coast to Coast who is in good standing with their home resort and current with their Coast to Coast membership dues.

NETWORK RESORTS
Membership resorts with extensive amenities and services that participate in the Coast to Coast network and welcome Coast to Coast members in exchange for Trip Points.

DAY-USE CAMPING
Use of a resort's facilities and amenities during the day with no overnight stay.

DRIVE-UP
Arriving at a network resort with no reservation within 72 hours of the time you want to be accommodated.

DRY SITE
RV site with no water, sewer or electrical hook-ups.

FULL SITE
RV site that includes water, sewer and electrical hook-ups.

GOOD NEIGHBOR PARKS
High-quality, open-to-the-public parks that welcome Coast to Coast members at discounted rates. All Good Neighbor Park reservations must be booked and paid directly with the Good Neighbor Park.

GANDER RV
Leading outdoor and camping retailer providing outdoor enthusiasts with the RVs, camping and outdoor gear they need to fulfill their passion for the outdoors.

GOOD SAM MEMBERSHIP
The world's largest organization of RV owners. Membership in Good Sam provides savings at Camping World and Gander RV stores, discounts at over 2,000 Good Sam Parks, and much more!

GOOD SAM PARKS
A network of more than 2,000 open-to-the-public RV parks and resorts that offer Coast to Coast members 10 percent off nightly stays when they show their valid Good Sam membership card.

HOME RESORT
Membership resort through which a member joins Coast to Coast and gains access to the Coast to Coast network.

HOST RESORT
Resort within the Coast to Coast network other than the member's home resort.

MEMBER SERVICES CENTER
Coast to Coast representatives that answer member phone calls and respond to member email questions.

MULTI-RESORT SYSTEM
Two or more resorts owned and operated by a single individual, company or corporation and subject to special rules.

NO-SHOW
Making a reservation and not honoring it.

OPEN YEAR-ROUND
Open for business throughout the year, although the park may not have sites available every day for Coast to Coast members and services may be limited during certain seasons.

PARTIAL SITE
RV site that includes water and electrical hook-ups (no sewer hook-up).

PEAK SEASON
High-demand time period at resorts, with special reservation restrictions.

PULL-THROUGH
RV site where it is not necessary to back in or out.

RECIPROCAL USE
Right to access membership resorts in the Coast to Coast network by mutual agreement.

TRIP POINTS
Electronic stored value instruments that are used to book reservations at network resorts in the Tripsetter Reservation system. 100 Trip Points = $1 (rate is subject to change).

TRIPSETTER
Real-time reservation system accessed through CoastResorts.com or Coast to Coast Member Services.

RENTALS

If you don't own an RV, or plan to travel without your RV, Coast to Coast still has you covered with rentals at 85 outdoor resorts in 25 states and 3 Canadian Provinces that stretch from coast to coast. Review the listings on the following pages to choose your desired location and type of accommodation. Next call the Resort or Good Neighbor Park at the number indicated in the listing to make your reservation. Then get ready to enjoy a great outdoor resort experience!

RESORT LODGINGS

Coast to Coast gives you the flexibility of traveling without an RV and staying at resorts and Good Neighbor Parks that have a variety of rental units including cabins, condos, motel rooms and park-model trailers. Resorts and Good Neighbor Parks that offer rental accommodations are listed on the pages that follow.

RULES AND POLICIES

There are as many types of rental accommodations as there are different types of people to stay in them. When you plan your itinerary, make sure to call each resort directly for a detailed description of accommodations available for rent.

We've made every effort to provide the most complete and accurate information available about each resort in the rental program. However, we encourage you to call the resort directly for updated rental accommodation rates and requirements and to make reservations.

WHEN MAKING RESERVATIONS BE AWARE OF THE FOLLOWING:

- Some resorts may require a refundable cash security deposit and sales tax (not payable with Trip Points) upon check-in.
- Some resorts provide basic cooking utensils, tableware and linens. It's a good idea to confirm with the resort directly about what's provided so you can pack accordingly.
- If there is a specific item you must have in a rental accommodation, confirm directly with the resort whether it will be supplied.
- Some resorts may have premium rates at certain times of year or requirements for minimum stays (e.g., holidays, two-night stay during weekends, etc.). Contact the resort directly to confirm rates for a specific time period.
- Always verify the most current rental information with the resort.
- Rental inventory and rates are subject to change. Reservations subject to availability at time of booking.
- Coast to Coast cannot guarantee that any particular resort or GNP will always be in the Coast to Coast network. Check CoastResorts.com for the most current list of participating resorts or GNPs.

GUIDE TO RENTAL LISTINGS

Resorts and Good Neighbor Parks that offer rental accommodations are listed alphabetically by state in the Rental Accommodations directory that begins on page CTC 34. The guide on page CTC 33 explains the column headers.

UNIT TYPE	The Rental Unit for which the resort accepts Coast members.	
POLICIES	MINIMUM STAY/NIGHTS	The minimum number of nights for which a reservation will be accepted.
	CANCEL NOTICE/DAYS	The number of days in advance that a reservation cancellation must be received by the resort to avoid a cancellation charge.
	ADVANCE BOOKING/DAYS	The number of days in advance that members can make rental reservations through the resort.
DEPOSITS	DEPOSIT(S) REQUIRED	Resorts listing "Y" require some type of deposit(s) that must be paid at the time the reservation is made or at the time of check-in. These are not covered by Trip Points and are payable by cash, check or credit card. The types of deposits may include but are not limited to reservation, security, cleaning, pet, key, remote control, linen, pots, pans and dishes. The resort will provide details when a reservation is made.
OCCUPANCY	ADULTS INCLUDED	The number of adults the unit can accommodate.
	KIDS INCLUDED	The number of children the unit can accommodate.
	SLEEPS (MAXIMUM)	The maximum number of people the unit will sleep. If there is no distinction between the number of adults and children, the Adults Included and Kids Included columns are blank and a total number is indicated in Sleeps (Maximum).
RESTRICTIONS	PETS WELCOME	"Y" means pets are accepted in the unit, "N" means pets are not accepted. If both types of units are available, "Y/N" is indicated.
	SMOKING PERMITTED	"Y" means smoking is permitted in the unit, "N" means smoking is not permitted in the unit. If both types of units are available, "Y/N" is indicated.
PROVIDED	LINENS PROVIDED	"Y" means linens are provided in the unit, "N" means linens are not provided in the unit. If not provided, they may be available for rent.
	POTS, PANS, DISHES	"Y" means pots, pans and dishes are provided in the unit, "N" means pots, pans and dishes are not provided in the unit. If not provided, they may be available for rent.
PAYMENT	TRIP POINTS/CASH	Indicates whether Coast Trip Points "TP" or Cash "C" are accepted for payment.

ALABAMA

	MINIMUM STAY/DAYS	CANCEL NOTICE/DAYS	ADVANCE BOOKING/DAYS	DEPOSIT(S) REQUIRED	ADULTS INCLUDED	KIDS INCLUDED	SLEEPS (MAXIMUM)	PETS WELCOME	SMOKING PERMITTED	LINENS PROVIDED	POTS, PANS, DISHES	TRIP POINTS/CASH
MOUNTAIN LAKES RESORT, OCP • LANGSTON, AL 35755 • 256-582-5556 • PREMIER • CHECK-IN 4:00PM • CHECK-OUT 11:00AM												
Cabin	2	7	14	Y			4	Y/N	N	Y	Y	C
Cabinette	2	7	14	Y			4	Y/N	N	Y	N	C
Lake House	2	7	14	Y			6	Y/N	N	Y	Y	C
Bunk House	2	7	14	Y			25	N	N	Y	Y	C
STYX RIVER RESORT, OCP • ROBERTSDALE, AL 36567 • 251-202-4509 • CLASSIC • CHECK-IN 4:00PM • CHECK-OUT 11:00AM												
Cabin, 1 Bdrm	2	7	14	Y			4	Y/N	N	Y	Y	C
Cabin, 2 Bdrm	2	7	14	Y			6	Y/N	N	Y	Y	C
Cabin, 3 Bdrm	2	7	14	Y			8	Y/N	N	Y	Y	C
TALLADEGA CREEKSIDE RESORT • TALLADEGA, AL 35160 • 256-362-9053 • GNP • CHECK-IN 3:00PM • CHECK-OUT NOON												
Cabin, Efficiency, Non-Hndcp	1	30	365	Y			4	Y	N	Y	Y	C
Cabin, Sleeping Only, 1 Rm	1	30	365	Y	4		6	Y	N	Y	Y	C
Bunkhouse	1	30	365	Y	4		10	Y	N	Y	Y	C
Cabinette, Hndcp	1	30	365	Y	2		2	N	N	Y	Y	C

	MINIMUM STAY/DAYS	CANCEL NOTICE/DAYS	ADVANCE BOOKING/DAYS	DEPOSIT(S) REQUIRED	ADULTS INCLUDED	KIDS INCLUDED	SLEEPS (MAXIMUM)	PETS WELCOME	SMOKING PERMITTED	LINENS PROVIDED	POTS, PANS, DISHES	TRIP POINTS/CASH
ALASKA												
EDGEWATER RV RESORT, SUNRISE RESORTS • SOLDOTNA, AK 99669 • 907-262-7733 • CLASSIC • CHECK-IN 3:00PM • CHECK-OUT 11:00AM												
Lodge Room, Non-Hndcp	2	7	60	Y			4	N	N	Y	N	C
Lodge Room, Hndcp	2	7	60	Y			4	N	N	Y	N	C
Lodge Room, 1 Bdrm/Kitchen	2	7	60	Y			4	N	N	Y	Y	C
ARIZONA												
ARIZONA OASIS RV RESORT • EHRENBERG, AZ 85334 • 928-923-8230 • GNP • CHECK-IN 2:00PM • CHECK-OUT 11:00AM												
Cabin, 1 Bdrm, Rustic	1	7	365	Y			4	N	N	N	N	C
Cabin, 1 Bdrm, Rustic	1	7	365	Y			6	N	N	N	N	C
Cabin, 1 Bdrm, Rustic	1	7	365	Y			10	N	N	N	N	C
ARKANSAS												
MILLWOOD LANDING GOLF & RV RESORT, OCP • ASHDOWN, AR 71822 • 870-898-5320 • PREMIER • CHECK-IN 4:00PM • CHECK-OUT 11:00AM												
Cabin	2	7	14	Y			6	Y/N	N	Y	Y	C
CALIFORNIA												
BASS LAKE AT YOSEMITE RV PARK • BASS LAKE, CA 93604 • 559-642-3145 • DELUXE • CHECK-IN 3:00PM • CHECK-OUT 11:00AM												
Park Model, 1 Bdrm	2	2	60	Y			4	Y	N	N	Y	C
Park Model, 1 Bdrm	2	2	60	Y			5	Y	N	N	Y	C
CATALINA SPA AND RV RESORT • DESERT HOT SPRINGS, CA 92241 • 877-463-0355 • PREMIER • CHECK-IN 3:00PM • CHECK-OUT 11:00AM												
Cabin, 1 Bdrm, Non-Hndcp	2	30	60	Y	2	2	4	N	N	N	Y	C
DUTCH FLAT RV RESORT • GOLD RUN, CA 95717 • 530-389-8924 • GNP • CHECK-IN NOON • CHECK-OUT 3:00PM												
Motel, Mini-Room	1	2	1	Y	2	1	3	N	N	Y	N	C
EMERALD COVE, CRA • EARP, CA 92242 • 760-663-4968 • PREMIER • CHECK-IN 3:00PM • CHECK-OUT 11:00AM												
Park Model, 37 Ft	2	7	30	N			6	Y/N	N	N	Y	C
Cottage	2	7	30	N			4	Y/N	N	N	Y	C
LIGHTHOUSE MARINA, RESTAURANT & RESORT • ISLETON, CA 95641 • 916-777-5511 • DELUXE • CHECK-IN 3:00PM • CHECK-OUT 11:00AM												
Cabin 6	2	3	90	Y	Y	Y	6	N	N	Y	Y	C
Cabin 7	2	3	90	Y	Y	Y	6	Y	N	Y	Y	C
Cabin 8	2	3	90	Y	Y	Y	4	Y	N	Y	Y	C
Cabin 9	2	3	90	Y	Y	Y	4	N	N	Y	Y	C
Village 20	2	3	90	Y	Y	Y	4	Y	N	Y	Y	C

	MINIMUM STAY/DAYS	CANCEL NOTICE/DAYS	ADVANCE BOOKING/DAYS	DEPOSIT(S) REQUIRED	ADULTS INCLUDED	KIDS INCLUDED	SLEEPS (MAXIMUM)	PETS WELCOME	SMOKING PERMITTED	LINENS PROVIDED	POTS, PANS, DISHES	TRIP POINTS/CASH
Village 21	2	3	90	Y	Y	Y	4	Y	N	Y	Y	C
Village L1	2	3	90	Y	Y	Y	6	N	N	Y	Y	C
Village L2	2	3	90	Y	Y	Y	6	Y	N	Y	Y	C
Village L3	2	3	90	Y	Y	Y	6	N	N	Y	Y	C
Village L4	2	3	90	Y	Y	Y	6	N	N	Y	Y	C
Village L5	2	3	90	Y	Y	Y	6	N	N	Y	Y	C
FISHERMAN'S RETREAT, HALO RESORTS • REDLANDS, CA 92373 • 909-795-0171 • DELUXE • CHECK-IN 1:00PM • CHECK-OUT 11:00AM												
Trailer, 1 Bdrm	2	3	30	Y			4	Y	N	N	Y	C
Fifth Wheel, 1 Bdrm	2	3	30	Y			5	Y	N	N	Y	C
Park Model, 1 Bdrm	2	3	30	Y			4	Y	N	N	Y	C
COLORADO												
BLUE MESA RECREATIONAL RANCH • GUNNISON, CO 81230 • 970-642-4150 • DELUXE • CHECK-IN 2:00PM • CHECK-OUT 11:00AM												
Log Cabin, Sleeping Only, 1 Rm	2	1	60	N	2		2	N	N	N	Y	C
Log Cabin, Sleeping Only, 2 Rm	2	1	60	N			4	N	N	N	Y	C
Park Model, Dlx 2 Bdrm, Hndcp	2	1	60	N			4	N	N	N	Y	C
GEORGIA												
UNICOI SPRINGS CAMP RESORT • HELEN, GA 30545 • 706-878-2104 • CLASSIC • CHECK-IN 2:00PM • CHECK-OUT NOON												
RV, 29 Ft Dlx, 1 Bdrm, Non-Hndcp	1	1	60	Y	5		5	N	N	N	Y	TP
IOWA												
CUTTY'S DES MOINES CAMPING CLUB • GRIMES, IA 50111 • 515-986-3929 • CLASSIC • CHECK-IN 3:00PM • CHECK-OUT 1:00PM												
Park Model, 2 Bdrm, Non-Hndcp	2	2	7	Y			4	N	N	Y	Y	TP
Park Model, 3 Bdrm, Non-Hndcp	2	2	7	Y			8	N	N	Y	Y	TP
Chalet, 1 Bdrm/Loft, Non-Hndcp	2	2	7	Y			9	N	N	Y	Y	TP
Chalet, Efficiency/Loft, Non-Hndcp	2	2	7	Y			7	N	N	Y	Y	TP
Cabin, Loft, Non-Hndcp	2	2	7	Y			6	N	N	Y	Y	TP
CUTTY'S OKOBOJI RESORT CLUB • SPIRIT LAKE, IA 51360 • 712-336-2226 • DELUXE • CHECK-IN 4:00PM • CHECK-OUT NOON												
Lodge Room, Hndcp	1	2	30	N			10	N	N	Y	Y	TP
Lodge Room, Non-Hndcp	1	2	30	N			10	Y/N	N	Y	Y	TP
Lodge Room, Sm, Non-Hndcp	1	2	30	N			4	Y/N	N	Y	Y	TP

	MINIMUM STAY/DAYS	CANCEL NOTICE/DAYS	ADVANCE BOOKING/DAYS	DEPOSIT(S) REQUIRED	ADULTS INCLUDED	KIDS INCLUDED	SLEEPS (MAXIMUM)	PETS WELCOME	SMOKING PERMITTED	LINENS PROVIDED	POTS, PANS, DISHES	TRIP POINTS/CASH
LOUISIANA												
ABITA SPRINGS RV RESORT, OCP • ABITA SPRINGS, LA 70420 • 985-590-3926 • CLASSIC • CHECK-IN 4:00PM • CHECK-OUT 11:00AM												
Cabin	2	7	14	Y			4	Y/N	N	Y	Y	C
HIDEAWAY PONDS RV RESORT, OCP • GIBSON, LA 70356 • 985-255-4578 • CLASSIC • CHECK-IN 4:00PM • CHECK-OUT 11:00AM												
Cabin	2	7	14	Y			6	Y/N	N	Y	Y	C
Park Model	2	7	14	Y			4	Y/N	N	Y	Y	C
PASSPORT TO LEISURE • ROBERT, LA 70455 • 985-542-1507 • CLASSIC • CHECK-IN 3:00PM • CHECK-OUT 11:00AM												
Cabin, 2 Bdrm	2	3	60	Y			6	N	N	N	Y	C
MICHIGAN												
LAKE SHORE RESORT, OUTDOOR ADVENTURES • DAVISON, MI 48423 • 989-671-1125 • PREMIER • CHECK-IN 3:00PM • CHECK-OUT 11:00AM												
Cabinette, 1 Rm	1	14	30	Y			4	Y/N	N	Y	Y	C
Park Model, 3 Bdrm	1	14	30	Y			6	Y/N	N	Y	Y	C
A Frame Cabin, 1 Bdrm, Loft	1	14	30	Y			6	Y/N	N	Y	Y	C
Large Cabin, 2 Bdrm	1	14	30	Y			6	Y/N	N	Y	Y	C
Lodge, 1 Bdrm, Loft	1	14	30	Y			2	Y/N	N	Y	Y	C

	MINIMUM STAY/DAYS	CANCEL NOTICE/DAYS	ADVANCE BOOKING/DAYS	DEPOSIT(S) REQUIRED	ADULTS INCLUDED	KIDS INCLUDED	SLEEPS (MAXIMUM)	PETS WELCOME	SMOKING PERMITTED	LINENS PROVIDED	POTS, PANS, DISHES	TRIP POINTS/CASH
GRAND HAVEN RESORT, OUTDOOR ADVENTURES • GRAND HAVEN, MI 49417 • 989-671-1125 • DELUXE • CHECK-IN 3:00PM • CHECK-OUT 11:00AM												
Cabin, Rustic	1	14	30	Y			4	Y/N	N	Y	N	C
Lodge	1	14	30	Y			6	Y/N	N	Y	Y	C
Cottage	1	14	30	Y			6	Y/N	N	Y	Y	C
Park Model	1	14	30	Y			6	Y/N	N	Y	Y	C
House, 3 Bdrm	1	14	30	Y			10	N	N	Y	Y	C
KALAMAZOO RESORT, OUTDOOR ADVENTURES • KALAMAZOO, MI 49009 • 989-671-1125 • PREMIER • CHECK-IN 1:00PM • CHECK-OUT 11:00AM												
Cabinette, 1 Rm	1	14	30	Y			6	Y/N	N	Y	N	C
Park Model, 3 Bdrm	1	14	30	Y			6	Y	N	Y	Y	C
A Frame Cabin, 2 Bdrm	1	14	30	Y			6	Y	N	Y	Y	C
MT PLEASANT RESORT, OUTDOOR ADVENTURES • MT PLEASANT, MI 48749 • 989-671-1125 • DELUXE • CHECK-IN 3:00PM • CHECK-OUT 11:00AM												
A Frame Cabin, 1 Bdrm, Loft	1	14	30	Y			6	Y/N	N	Y	Y	C
WILDERNESS RESORT, OUTDOOR ADVENTURES • OMER, MI 48749 • 989-671-1125 • PREMIER • CHECK-IN 3:00PM • CHECK-OUT 11:00AM												
Cabinette, 1 Rm	1	14	30	Y			4	Y/N	N	Y	Y	C
Park Model, 3 Bdrm	1	14	30	Y			6	Y/N	N	Y	Y	C

	MINIMUM STAY/DAYS	CANCEL NOTICE/DAYS	ADVANCE BOOKING/DAYS	DEPOSIT(S) REQUIRED	ADULTS INCLUDED	KIDS INCLUDED	SLEEPS (MAXIMUM)	PETS WELCOME	SMOKING PERMITTED	LINENS PROVIDED	POTS, PANS, DISHES	TRIP POINTS/CASH
SAGINAW BAY RESORT, OUTDOOR ADVENTURES • STANDISH, MI 48658 • 989-671-1125 • PREMIER • CHECK-IN 3:00PM • CHECK-OUT 11:00AM												
Cabinette, 1 Rm	1	14	30	Y			4	Y/N	N	Y	Y	C
Park Model, 3 Bdrm	1	14	30	Y			6	Y/N	N	Y	Y	C
Lodge, 1 Bdrm, Loft	1	14	30	Y			4	N	N	Y	Y	C
A Frame Cabin, 1 Bdrm, Loft	1	14	30	Y			6	Y/N	N	Y	Y	C
RIFLE RIVER RESORT, OUTDOOR ADVENTURES • STERLING, MI 48659 • 989-671-1125 • PREMIER • CHECK-IN 3:00PM • CHECK-OUT 11:00AM												
Park Model, 3 Bdrm	1	14	30	Y			6	Y/N	N	Y	Y	C
The House, 2 Bdrm	1	14	30	Y			8	N	N	Y	Y	C
LAKE OF THE NORTH RESORT, OUTDOOR ADVENTURES • WEST BRANCH, MI 48661 • 989-671-1125 • PREMIER • CHECK-IN 3:00PM • CHECK-OUT 11:00AM												
Park Model, 3 Bdrm	1	14	30	Y			6	N	N	Y	Y	C
Travel Trailer, 1 Bdrm	1	14	30	Y			6	Y/N	N	Y	Y	C
MINNESOTA												
GOLDEN EAGLE RV VILLAGE • PERHAM, MN 56573 • 218-346-4386 • CLASSIC • CHECK-IN 4:00PM • CHECK-OUT 10:00AM												
A Frame, 1 Bdrm, Loft, Non-Hndcp	3	0	360	Y			6	N	N	N	Y	C
A Frame, Loft, Non-Hndcp	3	0	360	Y			6	N	N	N	Y	C
Duplex, 2 Bdrm, Non-Hndcp	7	0	360	Y			6	N	N	N	Y	C
MISSISSIPPI												
TLC WOLF RIVER RESORT • PASS-CHRISTIAN, MS 39571 • 228-452-9100 • PREMIER • CHECK-IN 2:00PM • CHECK-OUT 10:00AM												
Park Model, Hndcp	2	2	7	Y			4	N	N	Y	N	C
Park Model, Non-Hndcp	2	2	7	Y			4	Y	N	Y	N	C
MISSOURI												
BRANSON RIDGE RV RESORT, OCP • BRANSON, MO 65616 • 417-213-5801 • CLASSIC • CHECK-IN 4:00PM • CHECK-OUT 11:00AM												
Motel, 1 Bdrm	2	7	14	Y			4	Y/N	N	Y	N	C
Motel, 2 Bdrm, Kitchenette	2	7	14	Y			6	Y/N	N	Y	Y	C
Lodge	2	7	14	Y			4	Y/N	N	Y	N	C
Cabin	2	7	14	Y			6	Y/N	N	Y	Y	C
TREASURE LAKE RV RESORT • BRANSON, MO 65616 • 417-334-1040 • DELUXE • CHECK-IN 2:00PM • CHECK-OUT 11:00AM												
Cabin, Efficiency, Non-Hndcp	7	2	30	Y	4		4	N	N	Y	Y	C
Motel Room, Non-Hndcp	7	2	30	Y	4		4	Y/N	N	Y	Y	C
Park Model Std, 1 Bdrm, Non-Hndcp	7	2	30	Y			6	N	N	Y	Y	C

	MINIMUM STAY/DAYS	CANCEL NOTICE/DAYS	ADVANCE BOOKING/DAYS	DEPOSIT(S) REQUIRED	ADULTS INCLUDED	KIDS INCLUDED	SLEEPS (MAXIMUM)	PETS WELCOME	SMOKING PERMITTED	LINENS PROVIDED	POTS, PANS, DISHES	TRIP POINTS/CASH
Park Model Std, 1 Bdrm, Hndcp	7	2	30	Y			6	N	N	Y	Y	C
Park Model Std, 2 Bdrm, Non-Hndcp	7	2	30	Y			6	N	N	Y	Y	C
Park Model Std, 2 Bdrm, Hndcp	7	2	30	Y			6	N	N	Y	Y	C
Yurt	7	2	30	Y	2		2	N	N	Y	Y	C
TIEVOLI HILLS RESORT • CLARKSVILLE, MO 63336 • 573-242-3577 • DELUXE • CHECK-IN 4:00PM • CHECK-OUT 11:00AM												
Bunkhouse, Non-Hndcp	2	30	10	Y			8	N	N	Y	Y	C
Log Cabin, 2 Story, Non-Hndcp	2	30	10	Y			8	N	N	Y	Y	C
Cabin, Mini-Log, Non-Hndcp	2	30	10	Y			4	N	N	Y	Y	C
Cabin, Mini-Show, Non-Hndcp	2	30	10	Y			6	N	N	Y	Y	C
Condo, 1 Bdrm, Non-Hndcp	2	30	10	Y			4	N	N	Y	Y	C
Condo, 3 Bdrm, Non-Hndcp	2	30	10	Y			6	N	N	Y	Y	C
Penthouse, 2 Bdrm, Non-Hndcp	2	30	10	Y			6	N	N	Y	Y	C
Suite A, Non-Hndcp	2	30	10	Y			2	N	N	Y	Y	C
Suite B, Non-Hndcp	2	30	10	Y			4	N	N	Y	Y	C
LOST VALLEY LAKE RESORT • OWENSVILLE, MO 65066 • 800-865-2100 • PREMIER • CHECK-IN 3:00PM • CHECK-OUT 11:00AM												
Condo, 1 Bdrm	2	2	90	N			6	Y/N	Y/N	Y	Y	C
RV, 31 Ft	2	2	90	N			8	Y/N	Y/N	N	N	C
RV, 28 Ft	2	2	90	N			6	N	N	N	N	C
NEVADA												
PREFERRED RV RESORT • PAHRUMP, NV 89048 • 775-727-4414 • CLASSIC • CHECK-IN 2:00PM • CHECK-OUT 11:00AM												
Park Model, 1 Bdrm	1	0	60	Y			4	Y/N	N	Y	Y	C
NEW YORK												
SWAN BAY RESORT • ALEXANDRIA BAY, NY 13607 • 315-482-7926 • GNP • CHECK-IN 4:00PM • CHECK-OUT 11:00AM												
Cottage	1	14	365	Y			4	Y	N	Y	Y	C
Chalet	1	14	365	Y			10	Y	N	Y	Y	C
SCHROON RIVER ESCAPE LODGES & RV RESORT • DIAMOND POINT, NY 12824 • 518-504-4063 • DELUXE • CHECK-IN 3:00PM • CHECK-OUT 11:00AM												
Cabin, 1 Bdrm/Loft	2	14	30	Y			6	N	N	N	Y	C
Cabin, Loft	2	14	30	Y			4	N	N	N	Y	C
SARATOGA ESCAPE LODGES & RV PARK • GREENFIELD CENTER, NY 12833 • 518-893-0537 • DELUXE • CHECK-IN 3:00PM • CHECK-OUT 11:00AM												
Cabin, Studio	2	14	60	Y			4	N	N	N	Y	C

	MINIMUM STAY/DAYS	CANCEL NOTICE/DAYS	ADVANCE BOOKING/DAYS	DEPOSIT(S) REQUIRED	ADULTS INCLUDED	KIDS INCLUDED	SLEEPS (MAXIMUM)	PETS WELCOME	SMOKING PERMITTED	LINENS PROVIDED	POTS, PANS, DISHES	TRIP POINTS/CASH
Cabin, 1 Bdrm/Loft	2	14	60	Y			6	N	N	N	Y	C
Cabin, 1 Bdrm	2	14	60	Y			6	N	N	N	Y	C
NIAGARA'S LAZY LAKES RESORT • LOCKPORT, NY 14094 • 800-874-2957 • CLASSIC • CHECK-IN 3-5PM • CHECK-OUT 11:00AM												
Cabin, Studio	2	7	30	Y			2	N	N	N	Y	C
Cabin, Studio	2	7	30	Y			4	N	N	N	Y	C
Cabin, 1 Bdrm	2	7	30	Y			4	N	N	N	Y	C
Cabin, 2 Bdrm	2	7	30	Y			6	N	N	N	Y	C
BASS LAKE RESORT, TRA • PARISH, NY 13131 • 315-872-1293 • PREMIER • CHECK-IN 3:00PM • CHECK-OUT 11:00AM												
Park Model, 28 Ft	2	1	30	Y	2	2	4	N	N	N	Y	TP
RV, 29 Ft	2	1	30	Y	2	2	4	N	N	N	Y	TP
CHAMPS RV RESORT • WHITEHALL, NY 12887 • 518-499-5055 • DELUXE • CHECK-IN 11:00AM • CHECK-OUT 1:00PM												
Cabin, Sleeping Only, Open Floor Plan	3	7	60	Y			4	N	N	N	N	C
Cabin, Sleeping Only, 1 Rm	3	7	60	Y			4	N	N	N	N	C
NORTH CAROLINA												
SYCAMORE LODGE, TRA • JACKSON SPRINGS, NC 27281 • 910-420-3843 • PREMIER • CHECK-IN 3:00PM • CHECK-OUT 11:00AM												
Cabin, 1 Bdrm, Non-Hndcp	2	2	60	Y			4	N	N	Y	Y	TP

	MINIMUM STAY/DAYS	CANCEL NOTICE/DAYS	ADVANCE BOOKING/DAYS	DEPOSIT(S) REQUIRED	ADULTS INCLUDED	KIDS INCLUDED	SLEEPS (MAXIMUM)	PETS WELCOME	SMOKING PERMITTED	LINENS PROVIDED	POTS, PANS, DISHES	TRIP POINTS/CASH
CARROLLWOODS CAMPGROUND • TABOR CITY, NC 28463 • 910-653-5538 • GNP • CHECK-IN 1:00PM • CHECK-OUT 11:00AM												
Duplex Cabin, 1 Rm Std, Non-Hndcp	2	7	90	Y	2		2	N	N	Y	N	C
OHIO												
INDIAN LAKE RESORT, VOR • HUNTSVILLE, OH 43324 • 989-671-1125 • DELUXE • CHECK-IN 3:00PM • CHECK-OUT 11:00AM												
Cottage	1	14	30	Y			4	N	N	Y	Y	C
Park Model	1	14	30	Y			6	N	N	Y	Y	C
MILLBROOK OUTDOOR RESORT • JEFFERSON, OH 44047 • 440-484-4000 • DELUXE • CHECK-IN 3:00PM • CHECK-OUT 11:00AM												
Park Model, 2 Bdrm	2	2	60	N			6	Y	N	N	Y	C
Cabin, Dlx	2	2	60	N			5	Y	N	N	Y	C
ROCKY FORK RANCH, TRA • KIMBOLTON, OH 43749 • 740-498-4134 • PREMIER • CHECK-IN 3:00PM • CHECK-OUT 11:00AM												
Park Model Std, 1 Bdrm, Non-Hndcp	2	3	90	Y	4		4	N	N	N	Y	TP
Park Model Std, 2 Bdrm, Non-Hndcp	2	3	90	Y	6		6	N	N	N	Y	TP
SANDY SPRINGS CAMPGROUND • STOUT, OH 45684 • 701-640-7858 • GNP • CHECK-IN 3:00PM • CHECK-OUT NOON												
Cabin, 1 Rm, 1/2 Bath, Riverfront	2	2	90	Y			3	Y	N	N	Y	C
Cabin, 1 Rm, 1/2 Bath	2	2	90	Y			4	Y	N	N	Y	C
Cabin, 2 Rm, 1 Bath	2	2	90	Y			5	N	N	N	Y	C
Travel Trailer	2	2	90	Y			5	Y	N	N	Y	C
5th Wheel	2	2	90	Y			7	N	N	N	Y	C
ARROWHEAD LAKES, VOR • WAPAKONETA, OH 45895 • 989-671-1125 • PREMIER • CHECK-IN 3:00PM • CHECK-OUT 11:00AM												
Park Model, Loft	1	14	30	Y			6	Y/N	N	Y	Y	C
Park Model	1	14	30	Y			4	Y/N	N	Y	Y	C
A Frame, 1 Bdrm, Loft, Non-Hndcp	1	14	30	Y			8	Y	N	Y	Y	C
Log Cabin, Loft	1	14	30	Y			6	Y/N	N	Y	Y	C
OKLAHOMA												
PELICAN LANDING • AFTON, OK 74331 • 918-782-3295 • DELUXE • CHECK-IN 2:00PM • CHECK-OUT NOON												
Cabin, Duplex, 1 Bdrm, Non-Hndcp	1	2	90	Y			6	Y	N	N	Y	C
Park Model, 2 Bdrm, Non-Hndcp	1	2	90	Y			6	Y	N	N	Y	C
TERRA STARR PARK • CHECOTAH, OK 74426 • 918-689-7094 • CLASSIC • CHECK-IN 3:00PM • CHECK-OUT 11:00AM												
Cabin, Efficiency, Hndcp	1	3	60	Y			4	N	N	N	Y	C
Park Model, Std, 1 Bdrm, Non-Hndcp	1	3	60	Y			6	Y	N	N	Y	C

	MINIMUM STAY/DAYS	CANCEL NOTICE/DAYS	ADVANCE BOOKING/DAYS	DEPOSIT(S) REQUIRED	ADULTS INCLUDED	KIDS INCLUDED	SLEEPS (MAXIMUM)	PETS WELCOME	SMOKING PERMITTED	LINENS PROVIDED	POTS, PANS, DISHES	TRIP POINTS/CASH
Park Model, Std, 2 Bdrm, Non-Hndcp	1	3	60	Y			6	Y	Y/N	N	Y	C
EAGLES LANDING RESORT & RECREATION • GROVE, OK 74344 • 918-786-6196 • CLASSIC • CHECK-IN 3:00PM • CHECK-OUT 11:00AM												
Cabin, 1 Bdrm, Non-Hndcp	2	2	30	Y			4	Y/N	N	Y	Y	C
Cabin, 1 Bdrm, Hndcp Accessible	2	2	30	Y			4	Y/N	N	Y	Y	C
Cabin, 2 Bdrm, Non-Hndcp	2	2	30	Y			6	Y/N	N	Y	Y	C
Suite Cabin, 2 Bdrm, 2 Bath	2	2	30	Y			8	N	N	Y	Y	C
PINE ISLAND RV RESORT • JAY, OK 74346 • 918-786-9071 • DELUXE • CHECK-IN 3:00PM • CHECK-OUT 11:00AM												
Cabin, 1 Rm	1	2	90	Y			4	N	N	Y/N	Y	TP
TEXOMA SHORES RESORT, OCP • MADILL, OK 73446 • 580-795-3828 • PREMIER • CHECK-IN 4:00PM • CHECK-OUT 11:00AM												
Motel, Kitchen	2	7	14	Y			4	Y/ N	N	Y	Y	C
Cabin	2	7	14	Y			6	Y/ N	N	Y	Y	C
OREGON												
CASCADE MEADOWS RV RESORT • LA PINE, OR 97739 • 541-536-2244 • DELUXE • CHECK-IN 3:00PM • CHECK-OUT 10:00AM												
Log Cabin, 1 Bdrm, Non-Hndcp	2	3	30	Y			4	N	N	N	Y	C
Meadows House/Cabin, 3 Bdrm, Non-Hndcp	2	3	30	Y			9	Y	N	N	Y	C
NESKOWIN CREEK RV RESORT • NESKOWIN, OR 97149 • 503-392-3355 • CLASSIC • CHECK-IN 3:00PM • CHECK-OUT 11:00AM												
Park Model, 1 Bdrm, 19th Hole, Max 2 Dogs	2	5	30	Y			4	Y	N	N	Y	C
Park Model, 1 Bdrm, Salmon Run	2	5	30	Y			6	N	N	N	Y	C
Park Model, 1 Bdrm, Eagle's Nest	2	5	30	Y			6	N	N	N	Y	C
Park Model, 2 Bdrm, Elk View, Max 2 Dogs	2	5	30	Y			8	Y	N	N	Y	C
PARADISE COVE RESORT, ADVANCE RESORTS OF AMERICA • ROCKAWAY BEACH, OR 97136 • 503-368-6581 • PREMIER • CHECK-IN 4:00PM • CHECK-OUT NOON												
Park Model, 1 Bdrm	2	3	90	Y			4	N	N	Y	Y	C
SUNNY VALLEY RV PARK AND CAMPGROUND • SUNNY VALLEY, OR 97497 • 541-479-0209 • GNP • CHECK-IN 2:00PM • CHECK-OUT 11:00AM												
Cabin, Sleeping Only	1	2	1	Y			4	Y	N	N	N	C
Covered Wagon	1	7	1	Y			4	N	N	N	N	C
PENNSYLVANIA												
AUSTIN CAMPGROUND • AUSTIN, PA 16720 • 814-647-8777 • GNP • CHECK-IN 2:00PM • CHECK-OUT 11:00AM												
RV, Bunkhouse, 2 Bdrm	1	1	3	Y	2		2	Y	N	Y	Y	C
Log Cabin	1	1	3	Y	2		2	N	N	Y	Y	C
Cabin, Dlx, 2 Bdrm	1	1	3	Y	2		2	N	N	Y	Y	C

	MINIMUM STAY/DAYS	CANCEL NOTICE/DAYS	ADVANCE BOOKING/DAYS	DEPOSIT(S) REQUIRED	ADULTS INCLUDED	KIDS INCLUDED	SLEEPS (MAXIMUM)	PETS WELCOME	SMOKING PERMITTED	LINENS PROVIDED	POTS, PANS, DISHES	TRIP POINTS/CASH
Cabin, Dlx, 1 Bdrm	1	1	3	Y	2		2	Y	N	Y	Y	C
ROARING RUN RESORT • CHAMPION, PA 15622 • 724-593-7837 • DELUXE • CHECK-IN 3:00PM • CHECK-OUT 11:00AM												
Cabin, Cozy	2	1	30	Y			4	N	N	N	Y	C
Cabin, Cozy	2	1	30	Y			6	Y/N	N	N	Y	C
SOUTH DAKOTA												
RUSHMORE SHADOWS RESORT • RAPID CITY, SD 57702 • 800-231-0425 • PREMIER • CHECK-IN 2:00PM • CHECK-OUT 4:00PM												
Park Home	2	14	90	Y			8	Y/N	N	Y	Y	C
Park Model	2	14	90	Y			6	Y/N	N	Y	Y	C
Park Cabin	2	14	90	Y			4	Y/N	N	Y	Y	C
Camping Cabin	2	14	90	Y			5	N	N	Y	Y	C
TENNESSEE												
BIG BUCK CAMPING RESORT • HORNSBY, TN 38044 • 731-658-2246 • DELUXE • CHECK-IN 3:00PM • CHECK-OUT NOON												
Camping Cabin	1	4	90	Y	2		2	N	N	Y	N	C
Cabin, 1 Bdrm	1	4	90	Y			2	N	N	Y	Y	C
Cabin, 1 Bdrm/Loft	1	4	90	Y			6	N	N	Y	Y	C
TEXAS												
THE HIDEOUT RESORT & GOLF CLUB • BROWNWOOD, TX 76801 • 325-784-4653 • DELUXE • CHECK-IN 3:00PM • CHECK-OUT 11:00AM												
Cabin	2	7	90	N	4	2	6	N	N	Y	N	C
TRES RIOS RV RESORT, OCP • GLEN ROSE, TX 76043 • 254-221-0018 • PREMIER • CHECK-IN 4:00PM • CHECK-OUT 11:00AM												
Bunkroom	2	7	14	Y			4	Y/N	N	Y	N	C
Cabin	2	7	14	Y			2	Y/N	N	Y	Y	C
Cabin	2	7	14	Y			4	Y/N	N	Y	Y/N	C
Cabin	2	7	14	Y			6	Y/N	N	Y	Y	C
Cabin	2	7	14	Y			10	Y/N	N	Y	Y	C
Cabin	2	7	14	Y			11	Y/N	N	Y	Y	C
Cabin	2	7	14	Y			13	Y/N	N	Y	Y	C
MARINA VILLAGE RESORT • TRINITY, TX 75862 • 936-594-0149 • DELUXE • CHECK-IN 3:00PM • CHECK-OUT NOON												
Cabin, 2 Bdrm, Sleeping Only	2	2	30	Y			6	N	N	Y	N	C
Cabin, Open Floor Plan, Sleeping Only	2	2	30	Y			4	N	N	Y	N	C

	MINIMUM STAY/DAYS	CANCEL NOTICE/DAYS	ADVANCE BOOKING/DAYS	DEPOSIT(S) REQUIRED	ADULTS INCLUDED	KIDS INCLUDED	SLEEPS (MAXIMUM)	PETS WELCOME	SMOKING PERMITTED	LINENS PROVIDED	POTS, PANS, DISHES	TRIP POINTS/CASH
WATERS EDGE • WILLIS, TX 77318 • 936-856-2949 • DELUXE • CHECK-IN 3:00PM • CHECK-OUT 11:00AM												
Cabin, 1 Bdrm/Loft, Non-Hndcp	2	30	60	Y			6	N	N	Y	Y	C
VIRGINIA												
NORTH FORK RESORT • FRONT ROYAL, VA 22630 • 540-636-9449 • DELUXE • CHECK-IN 4:00PM • CHECK-OUT 11:00AM												
Park Model	1	1	7	Y	4		6	N	N	N	Y	C
Duplex Rental, 1 Rm	1	1	7	Y	4		4	Y/N	N	N	Y	C
River Park Model	1	1	7	Y	2		4	N	N	N	Y	C
SHENANDOAH CROSSING RESORT & COUNTRY CLUB • GORDONSVILLE, VA 22942 • CHOICEHOTELS.COM • DELUXE • CHECK-IN 4:00PM • CHECK-OUT 10:00AM												
Cabin, 2 Bdrm	2	3	45	Y			6	N	N	Y	Y	C
WILDERNESS PRESIDENTIAL RESORT • SPOTSYLVANIA, VA 22553 • 540-972-7471 • DELUXE • CHECK-IN 2:00PM • CHECK-OUT 10:00AM												
Park Model Dlx, 2 Bdrm, Non-Hndcp	2	1	30	N	2	4	6	Y	N	N	Y	TP
Park Model Std, 2 Bdrm, Non-Hndcp	2	1	30	N	2	4	6	Y	N	N	Y	TP
INDIAN COVE RESORT • VIRGINIA BEACH, VA 23456 • 757-426-2601 • DELUXE • CHECK-IN 2:00PM • CHECK-OUT 10:00AM												
Park Model, 2 Bdrm, Non-Hndcp	2	1	30	Y			4	N	N	N	Y	C

WASHINGTON

	MINIMUM STAY/DAYS	CANCEL NOTICE/DAYS	ADVANCE BOOKING/DAYS	DEPOSIT(S) REQUIRED	ADULTS INCLUDED	KIDS INCLUDED	SLEEPS (MAXIMUM)	PETS WELCOME	SMOKING PERMITTED	LINENS PROVIDED	POTS, PANS, DISHES	TRIP POINTS/CASH
PONDEROSA FALLS RESORT, K/M RESORTS • CHENEY, WA 99004 • 509-747-9415 • DELUXE • CHECK-IN 3:00PM • CHECK-OUT 11:00AM												
Park Model, 1 Bdrm/Loft, Non-Hndcp	2	2	30	N			4	Y/N	N	N	Y	C
Bungalow, Rustic	2	2	30	N			4	N	N	N	N	C
Cabin, 1 Bdrm/Loft	2	2	30	N			6	N	N	N	N	C
COLUMBIA SHORES RV PARK, K/M RESORTS • CHINOOK, WA 98614 • 253-896-4677 • CLASSIC • CHECK-IN 1:00PM • CHECK-OUT 11:00AM												
Travel Trailer	2	2	60	N			6	N	N	N	Y	C
COPALIS BEACH RESORT, SUNRISE RESORTS • COPALIS BEACH, WA 98535 • 360-289-4278 • CLASSIC • CHECK-IN 3:00PM • CHECK-OUT 11:00AM												
Park Model Dlx, 1 Bdrm, Non-Hndcp	2	7	90	Y			4	N	N	N	Y	C
LAKE EASTON RESORT, SUNRISE RESORTS • EASTON, WA 98925 • 509-656-2255 • DELUXE • CHECK-IN 3:00PM • CHECK-OUT 11:00AM												
A-Frame, Loft	2	7	90	Y			4	N	N	N	Y	C
DOW CREEK RESORT, SUNRISE RESORTS • HOODSPORT, WA 98548 • 360-877-5022 • CLASSIC • CHECK-IN 3:00PM • CHECK-OUT 11:00AM												
Cabin, 1 Bdrm, Non-Hndcp	2	7	60	Y	2	3	5	N	N	N	Y	C
EAGLE'S NEST RV RESORT, SUNRISE RESORTS • ILWACO, WA 98624 • 360-642-8351 • CLASSIC • CHECK-IN 3:00PM • CHECK-OUT 11:00AM												
Cabin, 2 Bdrm, Hndcp	2	7	60	Y			6	N	N	Y	Y	C

	MINIMUM STAY/DAYS	CANCEL NOTICE/DAYS	ADVANCE BOOKING/DAYS	DEPOSIT(S) REQUIRED	ADULTS INCLUDED	KIDS INCLUDED	SLEEPS (MAXIMUM)	PETS WELCOME	SMOKING PERMITTED	LINENS PROVIDED	POTS, PANS, DISHES	TRIP POINTS/CASH
Park Model Dlx, 1 Bdrm, Non-Hndcp	2	7	60	Y			4	N	N	N	Y	C
Park Model, 1 Bdrm/Loft, Non-Hndcp	2	7	60	Y	2	2	4	N	N	N	Y	C
Park Model, Std 1 Bdrm, Non-Hndcp	2	7	60	Y			4	N	N	N	Y	C
PACIFIC HOLIDAY RV RESORT, SUNRISE RESORTS • LONG BEACH, WA 98631 • 360-642-2770 • DELUXE • CHECK-IN 3:00PM • CHECK-OUT 11:00AM												
Cabin, 1 Bdrm, Hndcp	2	7	60	Y	2	3	5	N	N	N	Y	C
Park Model, Efficiency	2	7	60	Y	2	3	5	N	N	N	Y	C
PIER 4 RV RESORT, SUNRISE RESORTS • MOSES LAKE, WA 98837 • 509-765-6319 • PREMIER • CHECK-IN 3:00PM • CHECK-OUT 11:00AM												
Trailer, Lakeview	2	7	60	Y			6	N	N	N	Y	C
Cabin, 1 Bdrm, Non-Hndcp	2	7	60	Y	2	3	5	N	N	N	Y	C
OLD AMERICAN KAMPGROUND, K/M RESORTS • NEWPORT, WA 99156 • 509-447-3663 • DELUXE • CHECK-IN 1:00PM • CHECK-OUT 11:00AM												
Cabin, 1 Bdrm	2	2	60	N			6	N	N	N	Y	C
Cabin, Open Floor Plan	2	2	60	N			2	N	N	N	Y	C
WILLOW BAY RESORT, ADVANCE RESORTS • NINE MILE FALLS, WA 99026 • 800-445-9519 • CLASSIC • CHECK-IN 4:00PM • CHECK-OUT 11:00AM												
Park Model, 1 Bdrm	2	3	90	Y			4	N	N	Y	Y	C
OCEAN BREEZE RV RESORT, K/M RESORTS • OCEAN SHORES, WA 98569 • 360-289-0628 • PREMIER • CHECK-IN 1:00PM • CHECK-OUT 11:00AM												
Trailer, 2 Bdrm	2	2	60	N			6	N	N	N	Y	C
MAPLE GROVE RESORT, K/M RESORTS • RANDLE, WA 98377 • 253-896-4677 • DELUXE • CHECK-IN 1:00PM • CHECK-OUT 11:00AM												
Cabin, 1 Bdrm	2	2	60	N			6	Y/N	N	N	Y	C
Fifth Wheel	2	2	60	N			4	N	N	N	Y	C
Yurt	2	2	60	N			7	N	N	N	Y	C
DIAMOND POINT RESORT, K/M RESORTS • SEQUIM, WA 98382 • 253-896-4677 • DELUXE • CHECK-IN 1:00PM • CHECK-OUT 11:00AM												
Park Model	2	2	60	N			6	Y/N	N	N	Y	C
ALBERTA												
DINOSAUR TRAIL RV RESORT • DRUMHELLER, AB T0J 0Y0 • 403-823-9333 • GNP • CHECK-IN 3:00PM • CHECK-OUT 11:00AM												
Dino Dens	2	15	2	Y			4	N	N	Y	Y	C
Dino Dens	2	15	2	Y			6	N	N	Y	Y	C
WILDERNESS VILLAGE AT CRIMSON LAKE • ROCKY MOUNTAIN HOUSE, AB T4T 1A9 • 403-845-2145 • CLASSIC • CHECK-IN 4:00PM • CHECK-OUT 11:00AM												
Cabin, 1 Bdrm, Hndcp	2	30	60	Y			4	Y	N	Y	Y	C
Cabin, 2 Bdrm, Hndcp	2	30	60	Y			6	Y	N	Y	Y	C
Cabin, Efficiency, Non-Hndcp	2	30	60	Y			2	Y	N	Y	Y	C

	MINIMUM STAY/DAYS	CANCEL NOTICE/DAYS	ADVANCE BOOKING/DAYS	DEPOSIT(S) REQUIRED	ADULTS INCLUDED	KIDS INCLUDED	SLEEPS (MAXIMUM)	PETS WELCOME	SMOKING PERMITTED	LINENS PROVIDED	POTS, PANS, DISHES	TRIP POINTS/CASH
BRITISH COLUMBIA												
WOODBURY RESORT AND MARINA • AINSWORTH, BC VOG 1AO • 877-353-7717 • DELUXE • CHECK-IN 2:00PM • CHECK-OUT 11:00AM												
Motel Rm, Non-Hndcp	1	2	60	N	2		4	Y	N	Y	Y	TP
Motel Rm, 2 Bdrm, Hndcp	1	2	60	N	4		6	Y	N	Y	Y	TP
ONTARIO												
YOGI BEAR'S JELLYSTONE PARK NIAGARA FALLS, CANADA • NIAGARA FALLS, ON L2G 0J2 • 800-263-2570 • GNP• CHECK-IN 3:00PM • CHECK-OUT 11:00AM												
Cabin	2	14	1	Y	2	2	6	N	N	Y	Y	C
Cabin	2	14	1	Y	2	2	8	N	N	Y	Y	C
Park Model	2	14	1	Y	2	2	6	N	N	Y	Y	C
Cottage	2	14	1	Y	2	2	8	N	N	Y	Y	C

ATLAS

The following 32 pages contain maps illustrating more than 450 locations across the U.S., Canada, and Mexico where you can enjoy great savings using your Coast to Coast membership. Classic Resorts, Deluxe Resorts, Premier Resorts, and Good Neighbor Parks are all identified by their own unique symbol. Use the maps to plan your next great adventure!

Classic Resort
Deluxe Resort
Premier Resort
Good Neighbor Park
Numbers are used to locate the parks listed on this page.
coast to coast
a Good Sam company
MISSISSIPPI
Pass-Christian
1 TLC Wolf River Resort
Biloxi
2 Cajun RV Park
ALABAMA
Woodville
3 Parnell Creek RV Park
Langston
4 Mountain Lakes RV Resort
Talladega
5 Talladega Creekside Resort
Robertsdale
6 Wilderness RV Park
7 Styx River RV Resort
TENNESSEE
NC
GEORGIA
FLORIDA
LOUISIANA
ARKANSAS
MISSISSIPPI
ALABAMA
Gulf of Mexico
Jackson
Birmingham
Hoover
Montgomery
Mobile
Huntsville
Tuscaloosa
Meridian
Hattiesburg
Dothan
Biloxi
Pass-Christian
Woodville
Langston
Talladega
Robertsdale
0 25 50 miles
0 25 50 kilometers
© 2022 MAPS.com

Numbers are used to locate Coast Premier, Coast Deluxe and Coast Classic Resorts and Good Neighbor Parks.

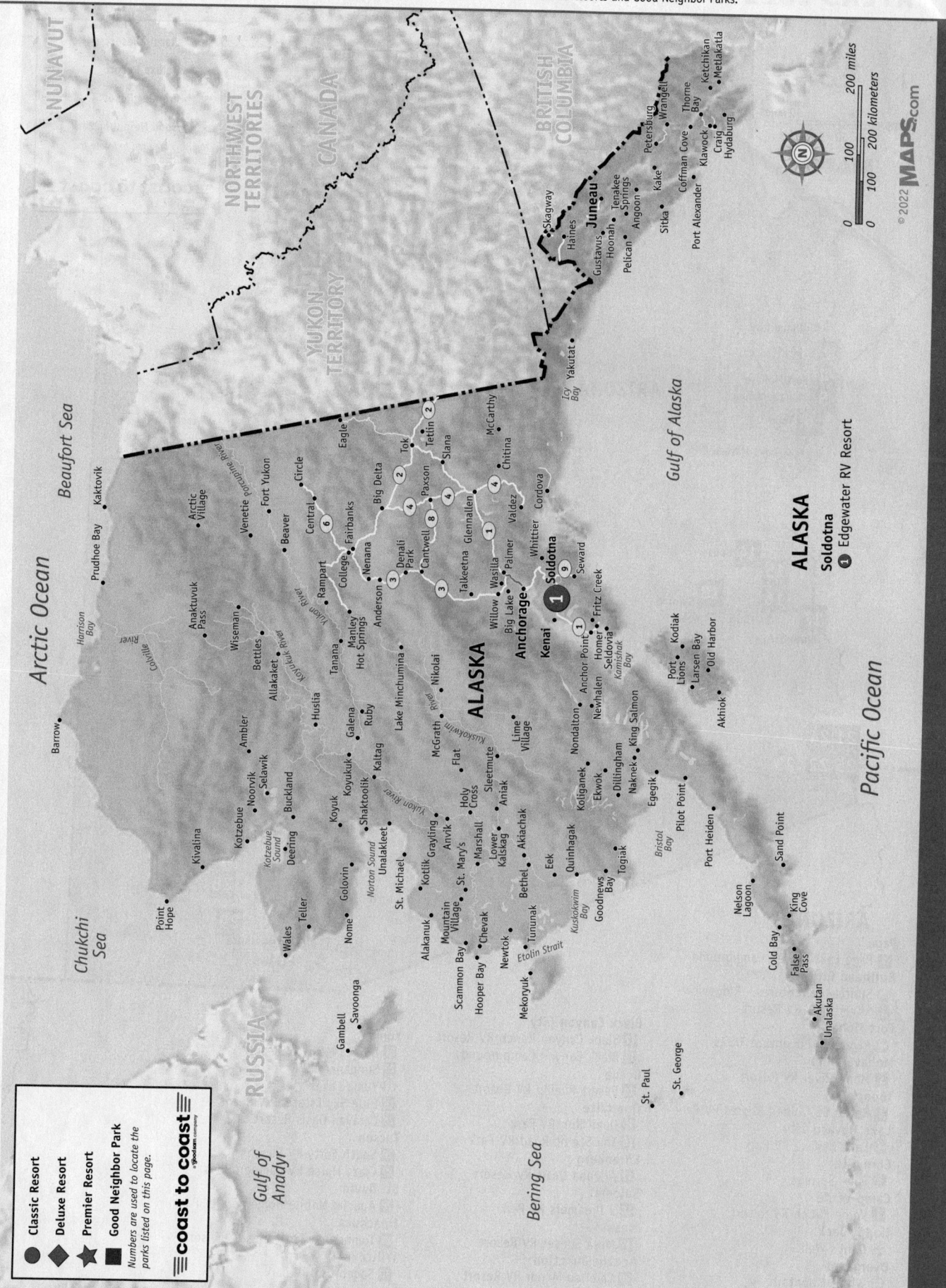

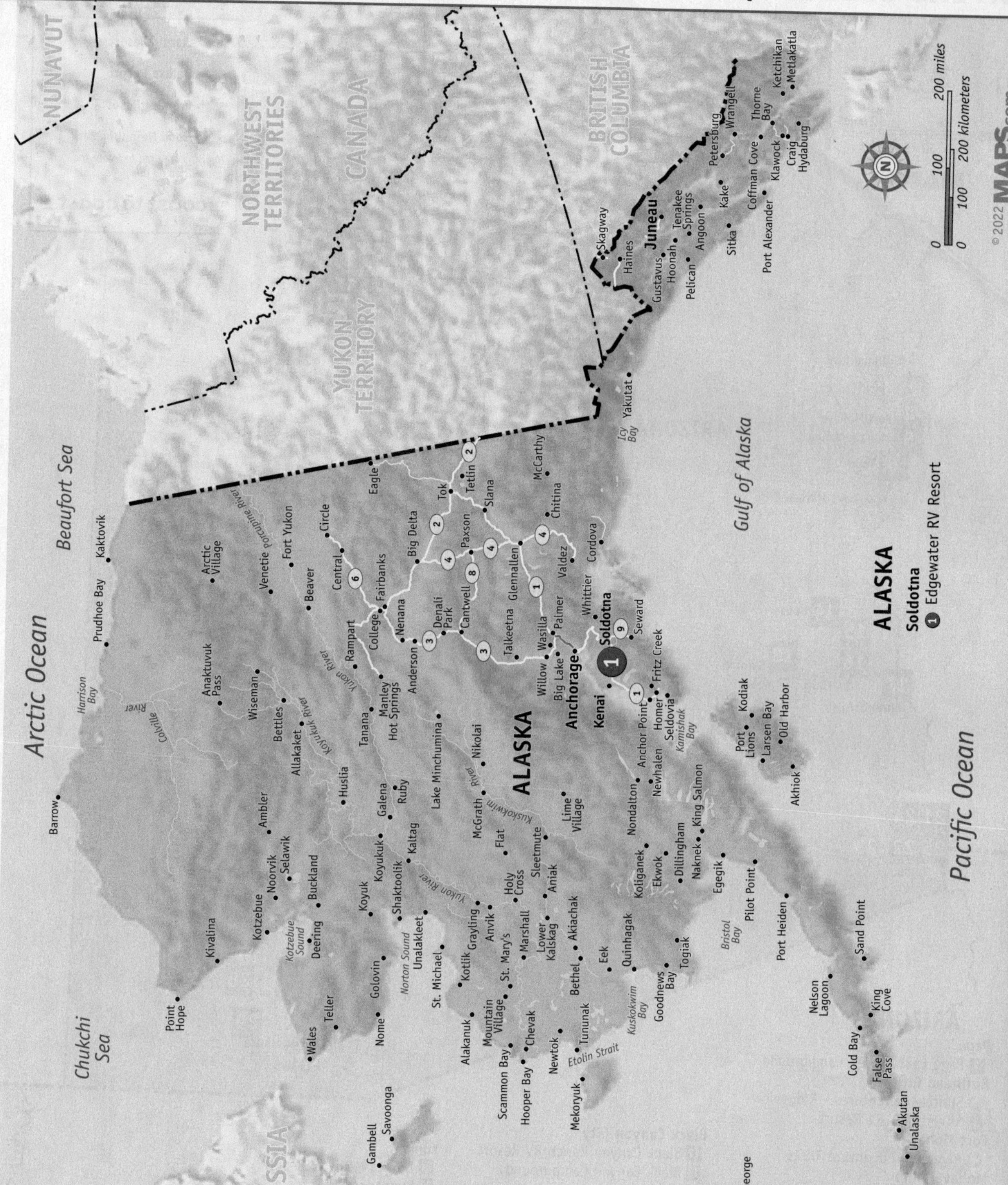

ARIZONA

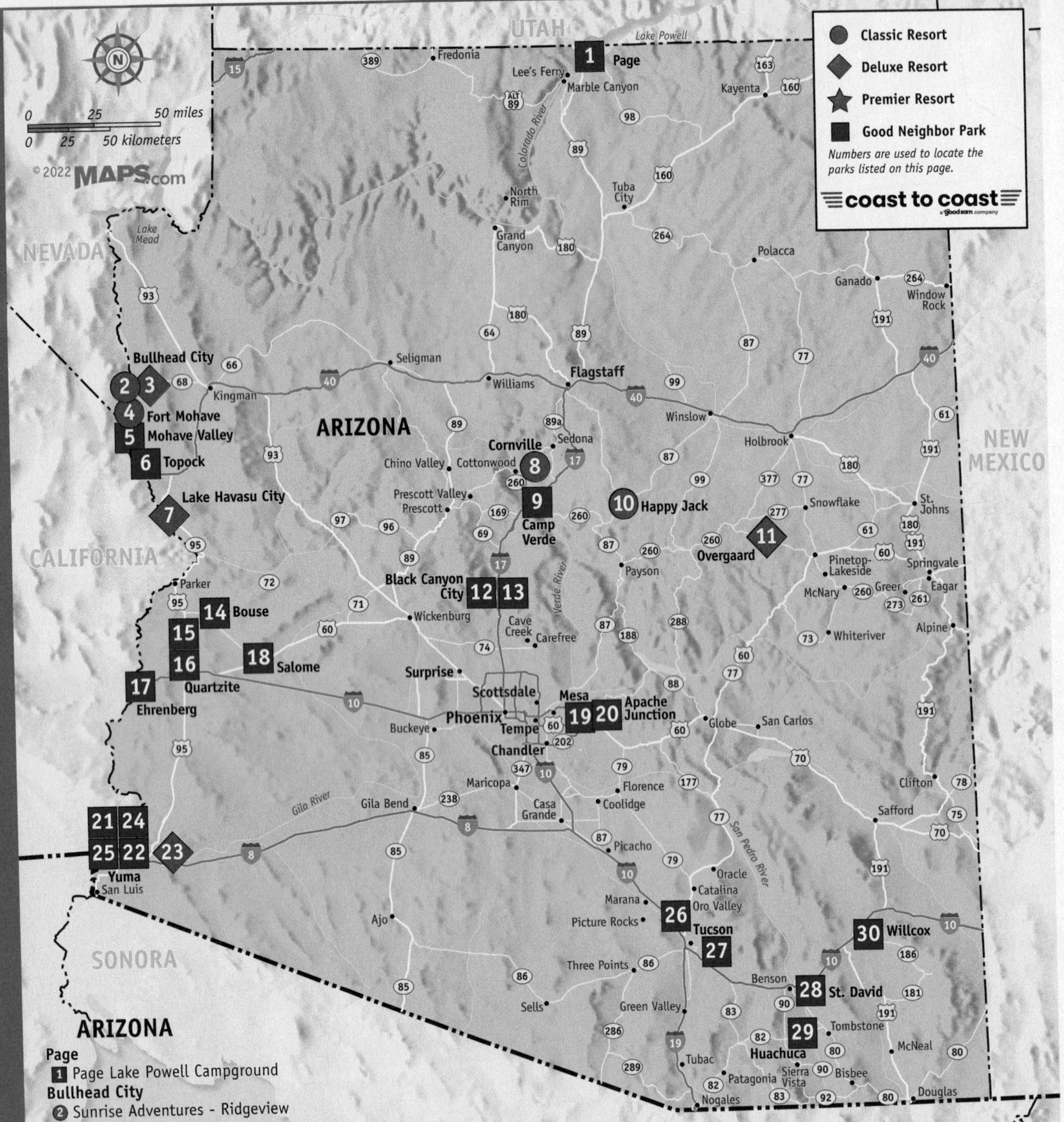

ARIZONA

Page
- 1 Page Lake Powell Campground

Bullhead City
- 2 Sunrise Adventures - Ridgeview
- 3 Silver View RV Resort

Fort Mohave
- 4 Riverside Adventure Trails

Mohave Valley
- 5 Moon River RV Resort

Topock
- 6 Route 66 Golden Shores RV Park

Lake Havasu City
- 7 Lake Havasu RV Park

Cornville
- 8 Page Springs

Camp Verde
- 9 Verde Ranch RV Resort

Happy Jack
- 10 Clint's Well

Overgaard
- 11 White Mountain

Black Canyon City
- 12 Black Canyon Ranch RV Resort
- 13 Black Canyon Campground

Bosue
- 14 Desert Pueblo RV Resort

Quartzite
- 15 Quail Run RV Park
- 16 The Scenic Road RV Park

Ehrenberg
- 17 Arizona Oasis RV Resort

Salome
- 18 3 Dreamers RV Park

Mesa
- 19 Mesa Sunset RV Resort

Apache Junction
- 20 Carefree Manor RV Resort

Yuma
- 21 Bonita Mesa RV Resort
- 22 Sundance RV Resort
- 23 Yuma Lakes
- 24 Blue Sky Estates/RV Resort
- 25 Caravan Oasis Resort

Tucson
- 26 South Forty RV Ranch
- 27 Crazy Horse RV Campgrounds

St. David
- 28 Apache Mobile Home and RV Park

Huachuca
- 29 Tombstone Territories RV Resort

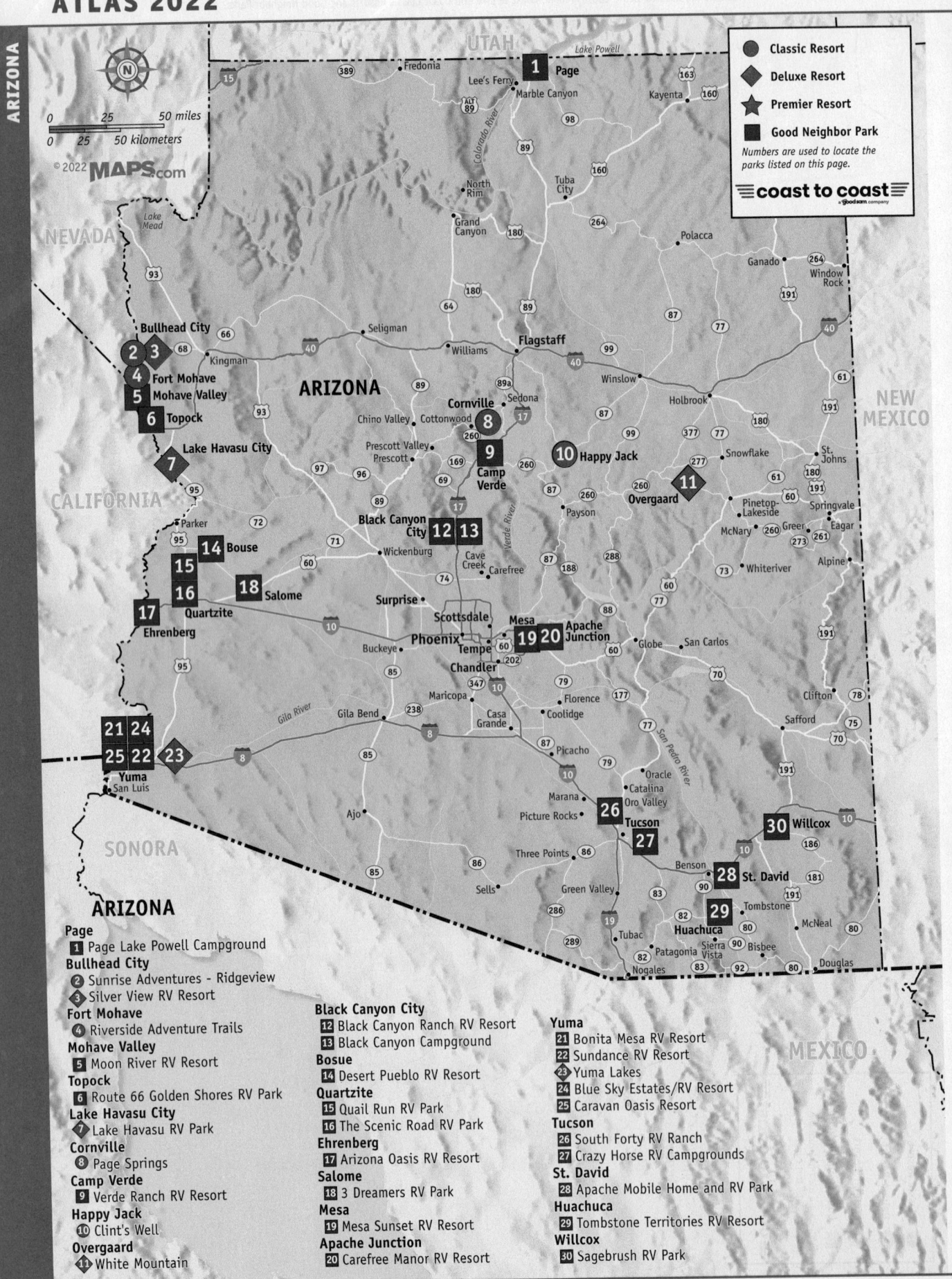

Willcox
- 30 Sagebrush RV Park

Numbers are used to locate Coast Premier, Coast Deluxe and Coast Classic Resorts and Good Neighbor Parks.

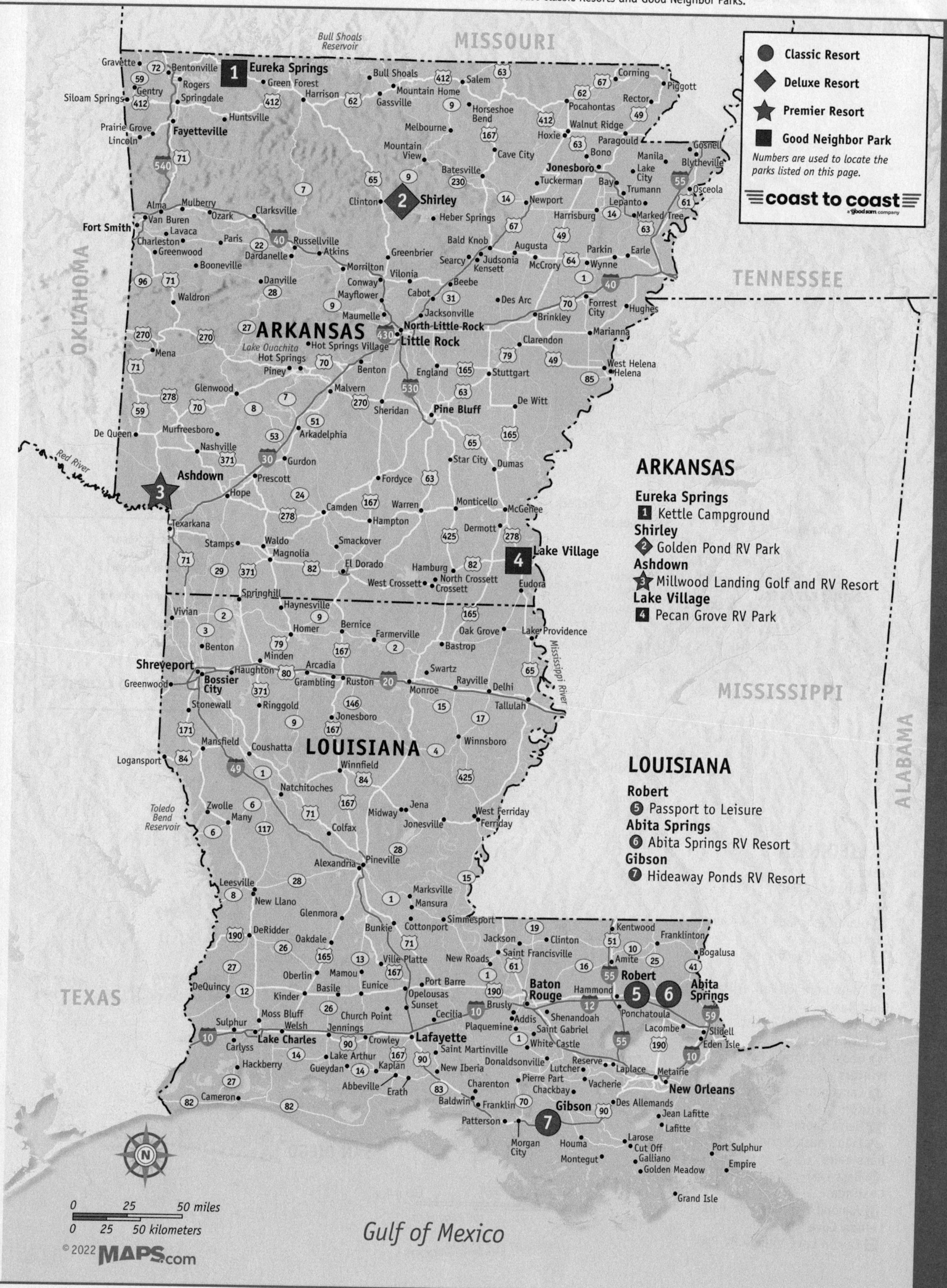

ARKANSAS

Eureka Springs

1 Kettle Campground

Shirley

2 Golden Pond RV Park

Ashdown

3 Millwood Landing Golf and RV Resort

Lake Village

4 Pecan Grove RV Park

LOUISIANA

Robert

5 Passport to Leisure

Abita Springs

6 Abita Springs RV Resort

Gibson

7 Hideaway Ponds RV Resort

OREGON
IDAHO
NEVADA
UTAH
ARIZ.
BAJA CALIFORNIA
SONORA
MEXICO
Gulf Of California
Pacific Ocean
CALIFORNIA
Lake Isabella
13 Lake Isabella RV Resort
Earp
14 Emerald Cove
Desert Hot Springs
15 Caliente Springs
16 Catalina Spa and RV Resort
17 Sky Valley Resort
Redlands
18 Fisherman's Retreat
Yucaipa
19 Oak Glen Retreat
Beaumont
20 Cherry Valley Lakes Resort
Aguanga
21 Sundance Meadows
Julian
22 KQ Ranch Resort
Winterhaven
23 Pilot Knob RV Resort
Classic Resort
Deluxe Resort
Premier Resort
Good Neighbor Park
Numbers are used to locate the parks listed on this page.
coast to coast
CALIFORNIA
Yreka
1 Waiiaka RV Park
Myers Flat
2 Giant Redwoods RV & Camp
Corning
3 Heritage RV Corning
Nice
4 The Aurora RV Park & Marina
Gold Run
5 Dutch Flat RV Resort
Pollock Pines
6 Ghost Mountain Ranch
Winters
7 Canyon Creek Resort
Isleton
8 Delta Shores Resort & Marina
9 Lighthouse Marina, Restaurant & Resort
Bass Lake
10 Bass Lake at Yosemite RV Park
Coalinga
11 Almond Tree Oasis RV Park
Lemon Cove
12 Lemon Cove Village RV Park
San Francisco
Oakland
San Jose
Sacramento
Stockton
Fresno
Bakersfield
LOS ANGELES
Long Beach
Anaheim
SAN DIEGO
0 50 100 miles
0 50 100 kilometers
© 2022 MAPS.com

Numbers are used to locate Coast Premier, Coast Deluxe and Coast Classic Resorts and Good Neighbor Parks.

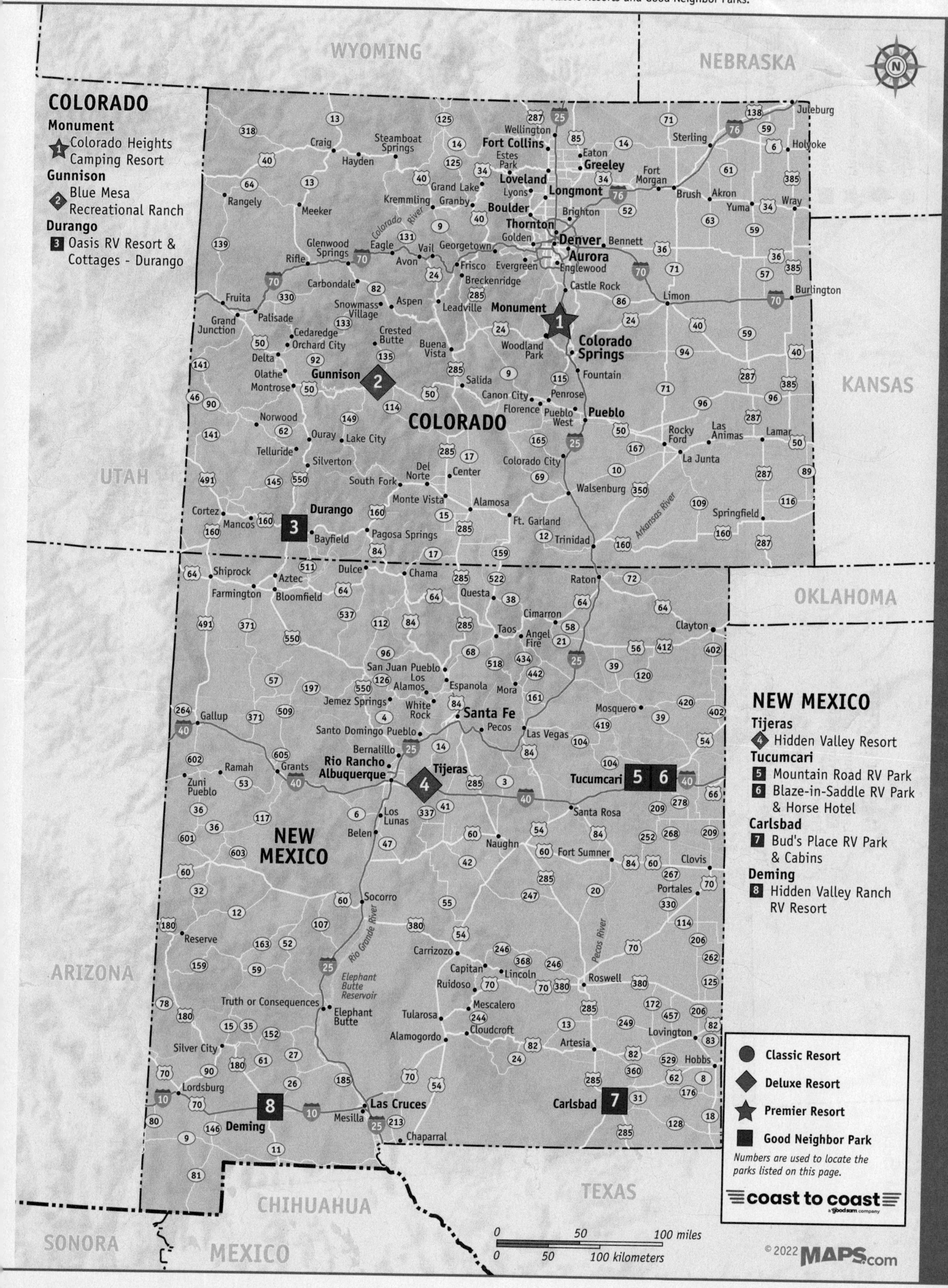

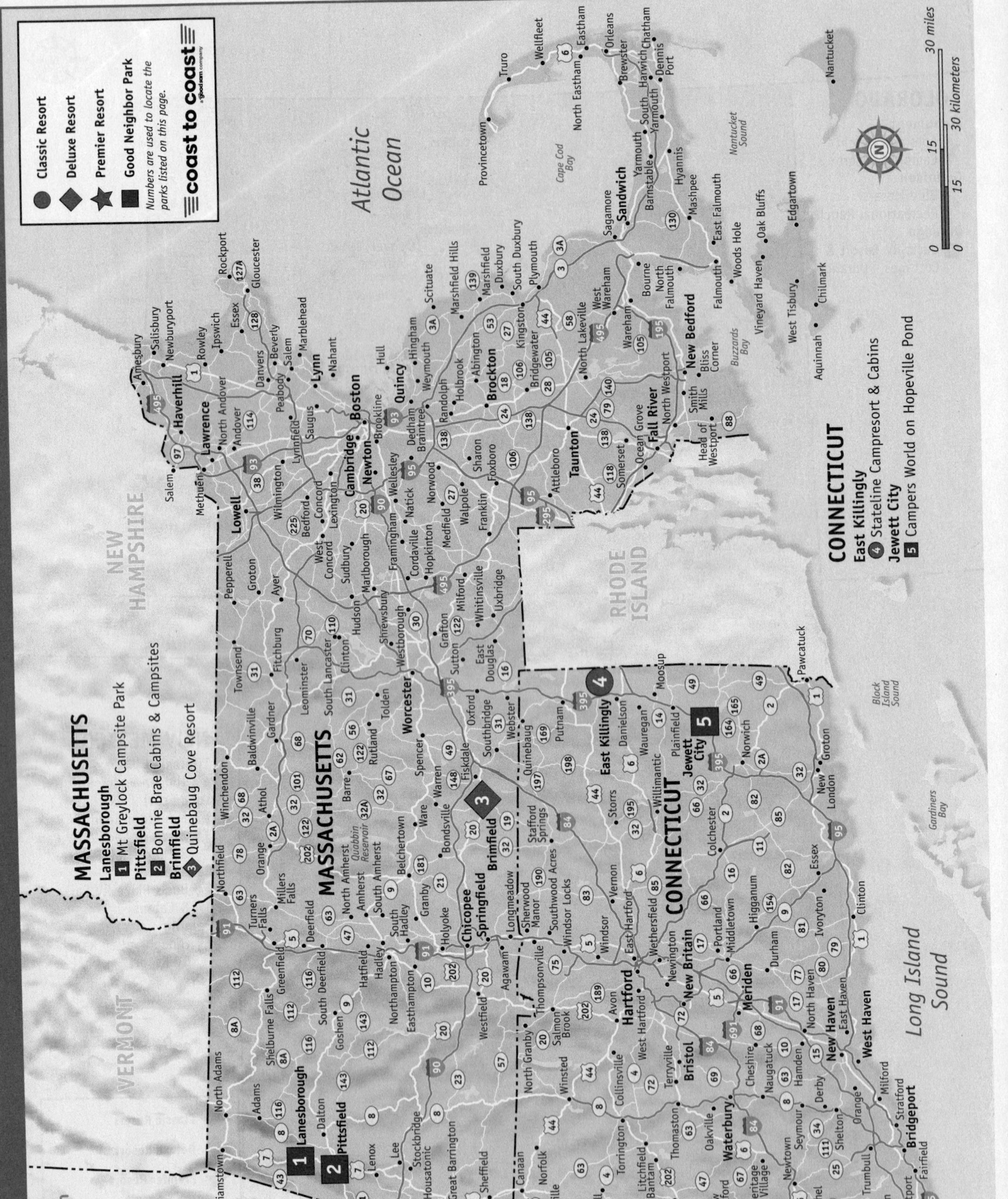
Classic Resort
Deluxe Resort
Premier Resort
Good Neighbor Park
Numbers are used to locate the parks listed on this page.
coast to coast
MASSACHUSETTS
Lanesborough
1 Mt Greylock Campsite Park
Pittsfield
2 Bonnie Brae Cabins & Campsites
Brimfield
3 Quinebaug Cove Resort
CONNECTICUT
East Killingly
4 Stateline Campresort & Cabins
Jewett City
5 Campers World on Hopeville Pond
Atlantic Ocean
Long Island Sound
NEW HAMPSHIRE
VERMONT
NEW YORK
RHODE ISLAND
0 15 30 miles
0 15 30 kilometers
© 2022 MAPS.com

Numbers are used to locate Coast Premier, Coast Deluxe and Coast Classic Resorts and Good Neighbor Parks.

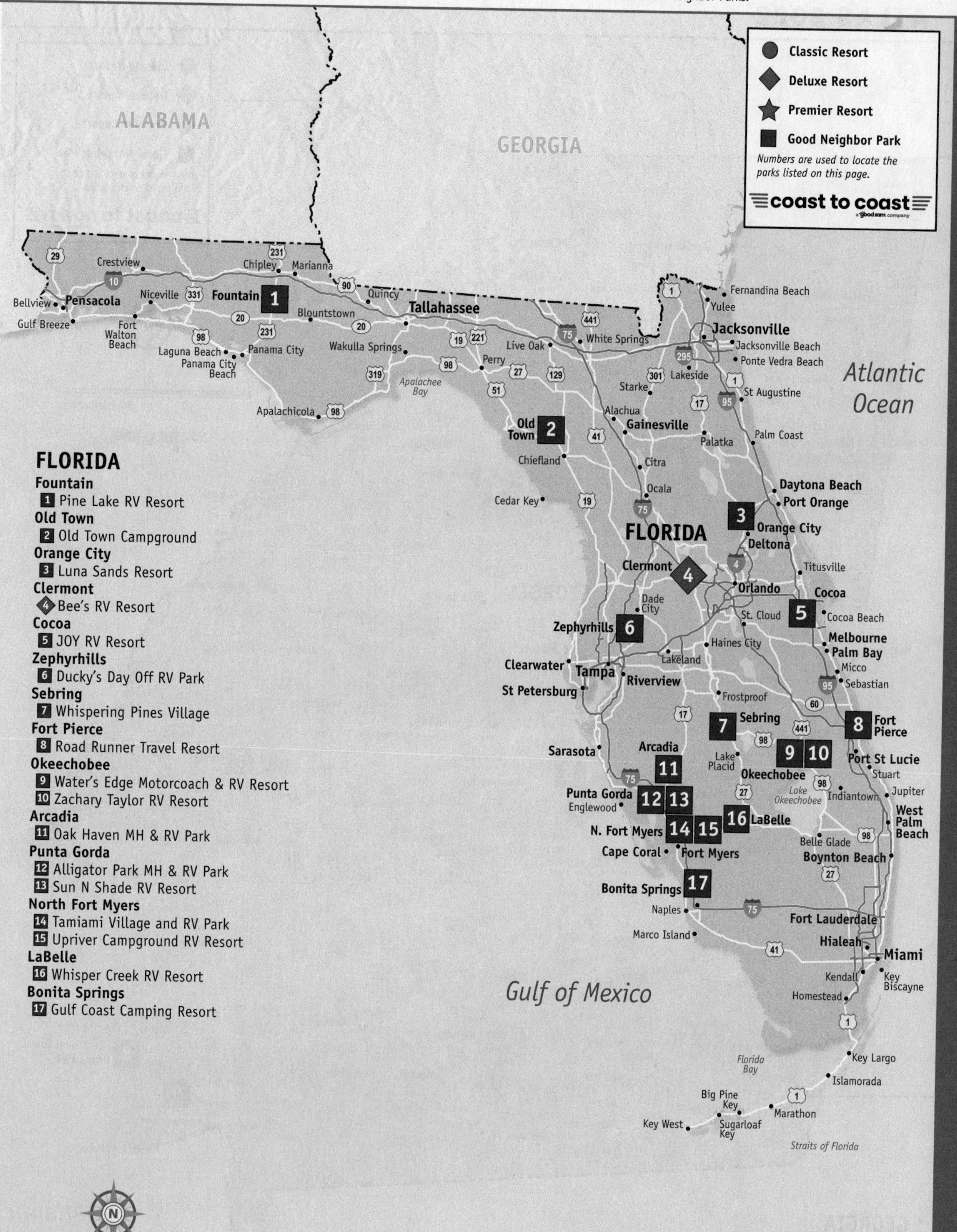

FLORIDA

Fountain
1 Pine Lake RV Resort

Old Town
2 Old Town Campground

Orange City
3 Luna Sands Resort

Clermont
4 Bee's RV Resort

Cocoa
5 JOY RV Resort

Zephyrhills
6 Ducky's Day Off RV Park

Sebring
7 Whispering Pines Village

Fort Pierce
8 Road Runner Travel Resort

Okeechobee
9 Water's Edge Motorcoach & RV Resort
10 Zachary Taylor RV Resort

Arcadia
11 Oak Haven MH & RV Park

Punta Gorda
12 Alligator Park MH & RV Park
13 Sun N Shade RV Resort

North Fort Myers
14 Tamiami Village and RV Park
15 Upriver Campground RV Resort

LaBelle
16 Whisper Creek RV Resort

Bonita Springs
17 Gulf Coast Camping Resort

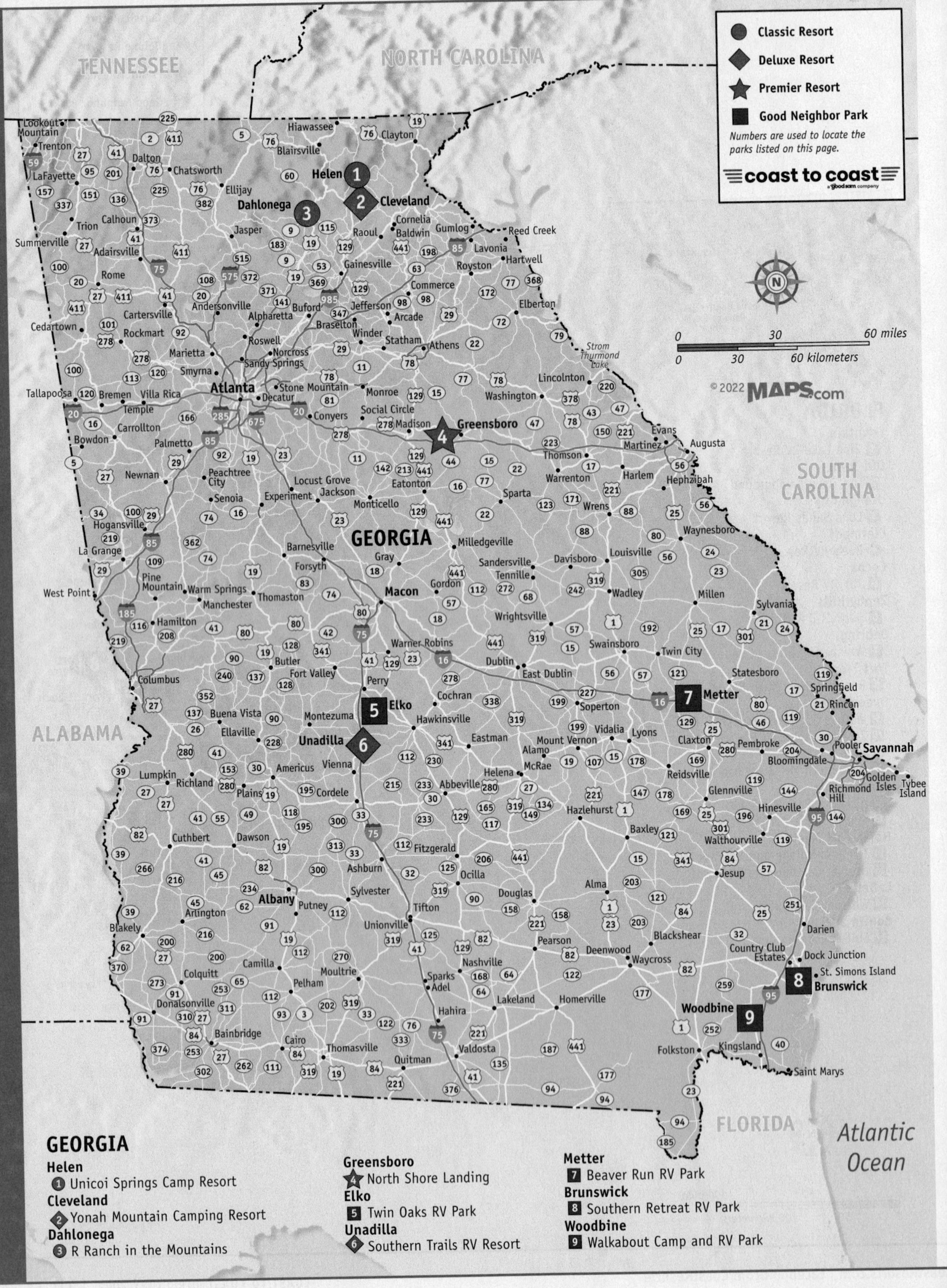

GEORGIA

Helen

1 Unicoi Springs Camp Resort

Cleveland

2 Yonah Mountain Camping Resort

Dahlonega

3 R Ranch in the Mountains

Greensboro

4 North Shore Landing

Elko

5 Twin Oaks RV Park

Unadilla

6 Southern Trails RV Resort

Metter

7 Beaver Run RV Park

Brunswick

8 Southern Retreat RV Park

Woodbine

9 Walkabout Camp and RV Park

Numbers are used to locate Coast Premier, Coast Deluxe and Coast Classic Resorts and Good Neighbor Parks.

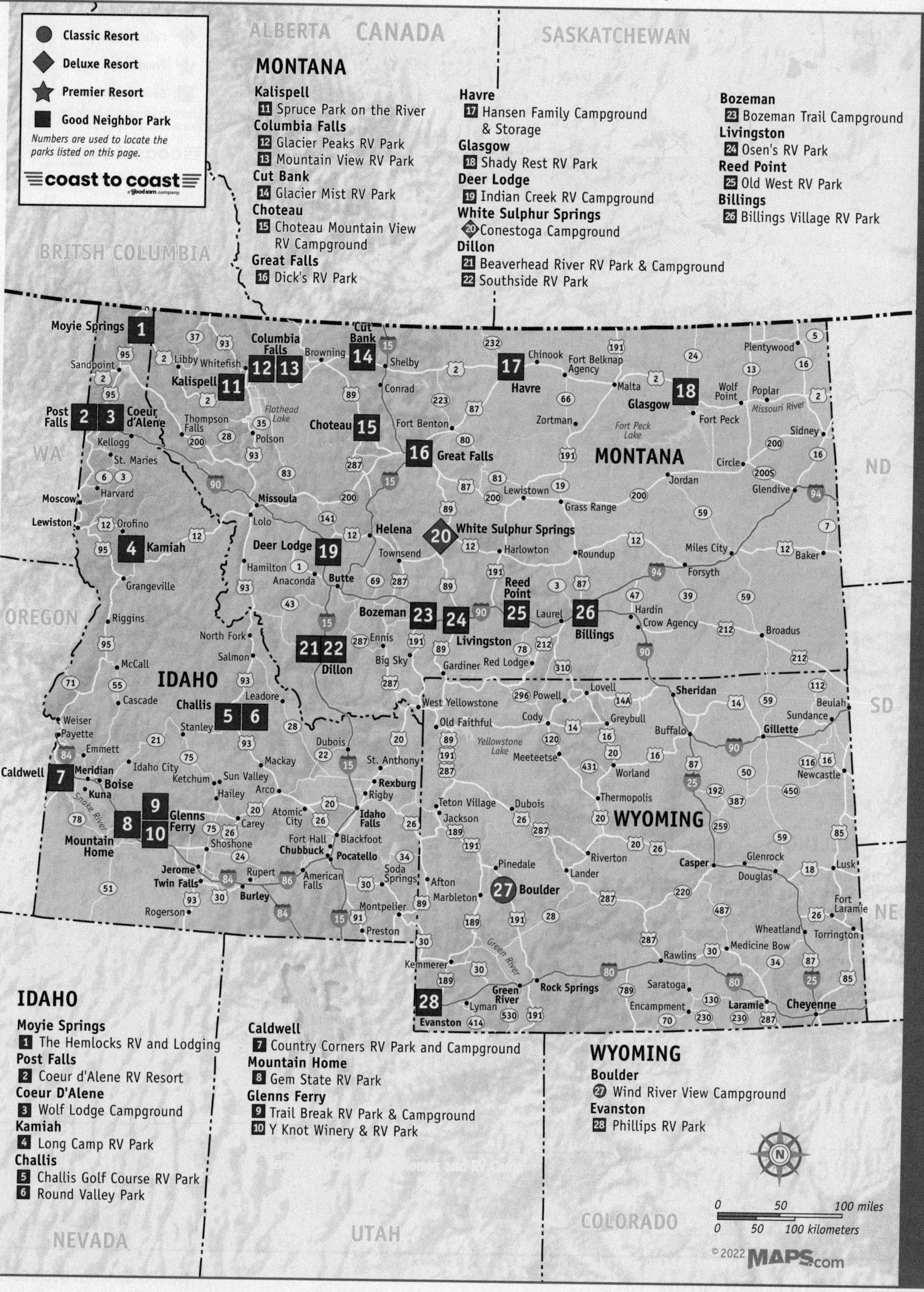

MONTANA

Kalispell
11 Spruce Park on the River

Columbia Falls
12 Glacier Peaks RV Park
13 Mountain View RV Park

Cut Bank
14 Glacier Mist RV Park

Choteau
15 Choteau Mountain View RV Campground

Great Falls
16 Dick's RV Park

Havre
17 Hansen Family Campground & Storage

Glasgow
18 Shady Rest RV Park

Deer Lodge
19 Indian Creek RV Campground

White Sulphur Springs
20 Conestoga Campground

Dillon
21 Beaverhead River RV Park & Campground
22 Southside RV Park

Bozeman
23 Bozeman Trail Campground

Livingston
24 Osen's RV Park

Reed Point
25 Old West RV Park

Billings
26 Billings Village RV Park

IDAHO

Moyie Springs
1 The Hemlocks RV and Lodging

Post Falls
2 Coeur d'Alene RV Resort

Coeur D'Alene
3 Wolf Lodge Campground

Kamiah
4 Long Camp RV Park

Challis
5 Challis Golf Course RV Park
6 Round Valley Park

Caldwell
7 Country Corners RV Park and Campground

Mountain Home
8 Gem State RV Park

Glenns Ferry
9 Trail Break RV Park & Campground
10 Y Knot Winery & RV Park

WYOMING

Boulder
27 Wind River View Campground

Evanston
28 Phillips RV Park

Classic Resort
Deluxe Resort
Premier Resort
Good Neighbor Park
Numbers are used to locate the parks listed on this page.
coast to coast
WISCONSIN
Lake Michigan
MICHIGAN
IOWA
ILLINOIS
INDIANA
MISSOURI
KENTUCKY
ARKANSAS
TENNESSEE
Kentucky Lake
Chicago
Rockford
Waukegan
Naperville
Aurora
Joliet
Gary
South Bend
Elkhart
Howe
Fort Wayne
Peoria
East Peoria
Bloomington
Champaign
Springfield
Decatur
Lafayette
Muncie
Indianapolis
Richmond
Terre Haute
Bloomington
North Vernon
Evansville
Hillsdale
Sublette
Bushnell
ILLINOIS
Hillsdale
1 Sunset Lakes RV Resort
Sublette
2 Woodhaven Lakes
Bushnell
3 Timber Lakes Campground
East Peoria
4 Mill Point Park
INDIANA
Howe
5 Grand View Bend
Richmond
6 Deer Ridge Camping Resort
North Vernon
7 Muscatatuck Park
0 25 50 miles
0 25 50 kilometers
© 2022 MAPS.com

Numbers are used to locate Coast Premier, Coast Deluxe and Coast Classic Resorts and Good Neighbor Parks.

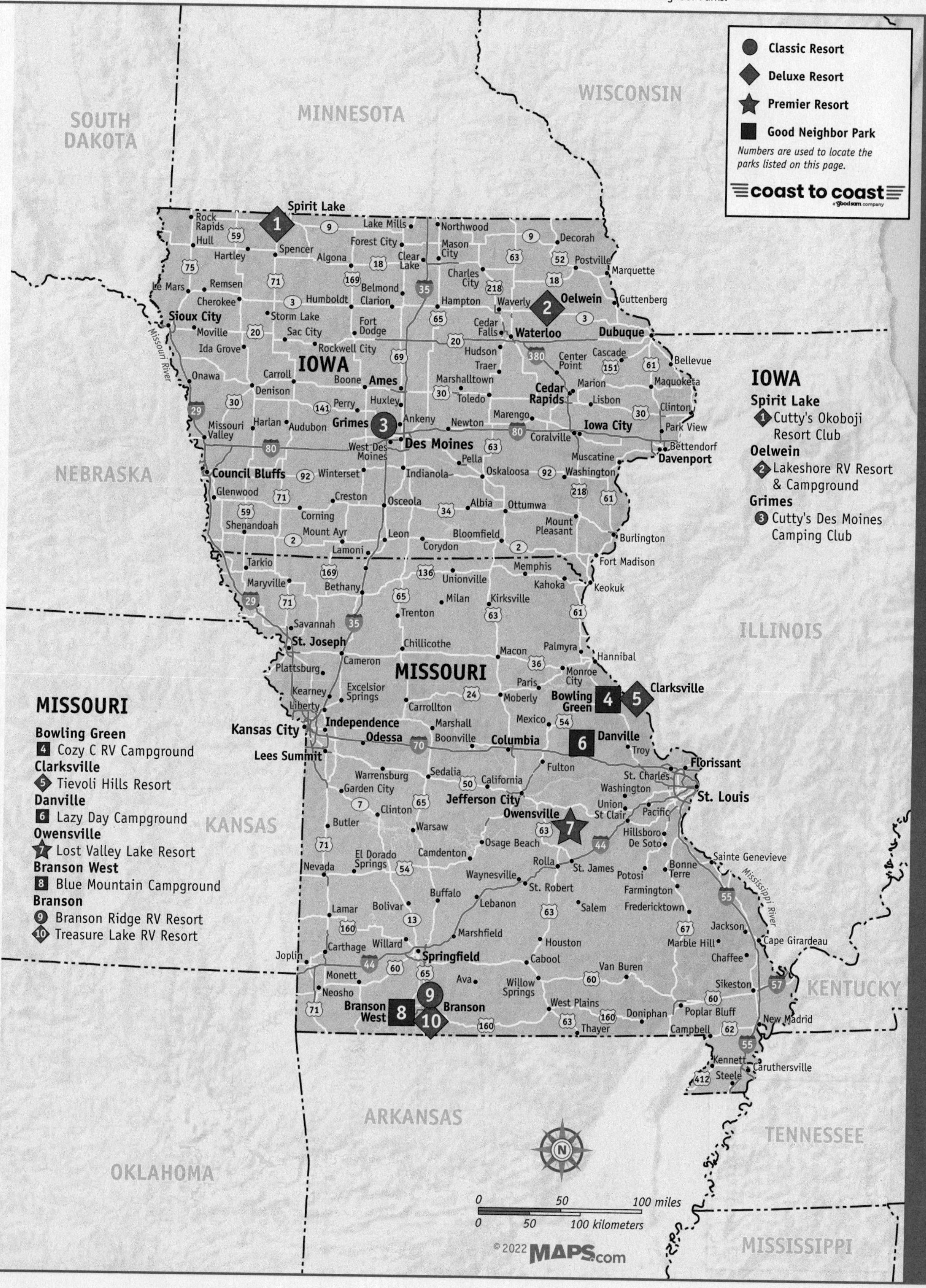
Classic Resort
Deluxe Resort
Premier Resort
Good Neighbor Park
Numbers are used to locate the parks listed on this page.
coast to coast
a Good Sam company
IOWA
Spirit Lake
1 Cutty's Okoboji Resort Club
Oelwein
2 Lakeshore RV Resort & Campground
Grimes
3 Cutty's Des Moines Camping Club
MISSOURI
Bowling Green
4 Cozy C RV Campground
Clarksville
5 Tievoli Hills Resort
Danville
6 Lazy Day Campground
Owensville
7 Lost Valley Lake Resort
Branson West
8 Blue Mountain Campground
Branson
9 Branson Ridge RV Resort
10 Treasure Lake RV Resort
SOUTH DAKOTA
MINNESOTA
WISCONSIN
NEBRASKA
ILLINOIS
KANSAS
KENTUCKY
ARKANSAS
TENNESSEE
OKLAHOMA
MISSISSIPPI
IOWA
MISSOURI
Missouri River
Mississippi River
Spirit Lake
Sioux City
Council Bluffs
Des Moines
Ames
Waterloo
Dubuque
Cedar Rapids
Iowa City
Davenport
St. Joseph
Kansas City
Independence
Lees Summit
Columbia
Jefferson City
Owensville
St. Louis
Florissant
Springfield
Branson
Branson West
Joplin
0 50 100 miles
0 50 100 kilometers
© 2022 MAPS.com

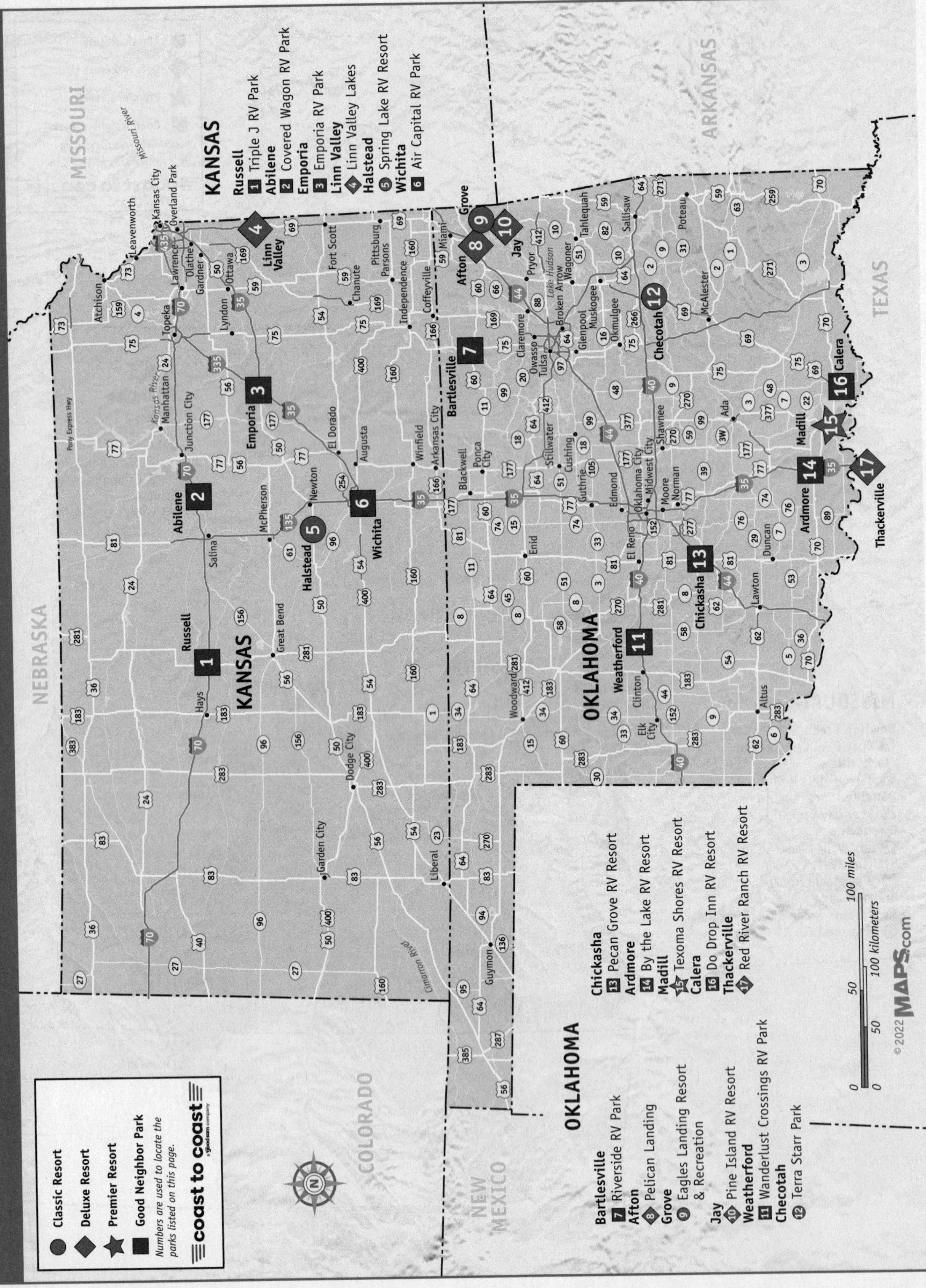
KANSAS/OKLAHOMA
Classic Resort
Deluxe Resort
Premier Resort
Good Neighbor Park
Numbers are used to locate the parks listed on this page.
coast to coast
KANSAS
Russell
1 Triple J RV Park
Abilene
2 Covered Wagon RV Park
Emporia
3 Emporia RV Park
Linn Valley
4 Linn Valley Lakes
Halstead
5 Spring Lake RV Resort
Wichita
6 Air Capital RV Park
OKLAHOMA
Bartlesville
7 Riverside RV Park
Afton
8 Pelican Landing
Grove
9 Eagles Landing Resort & Recreation
Jay
10 Pine Island RV Resort
Weatherford
11 Wanderlust Crossings RV Park
Checotah
12 Terra Starr Park
Chickasha
13 Pecan Grove RV Resort
Ardmore
14 By the Lake RV Resort
Madill
15 Texoma Shores RV Resort
Calera
16 Do Drop Inn RV Resort
Thackerville
17 Red River Ranch RV Resort
NEBRASKA
MISSOURI
ARKANSAS
TEXAS
COLORADO
NEW MEXICO
KANSAS
OKLAHOMA
0 50 100 miles
0 50 100 kilometers
© 2022 MAPS.com

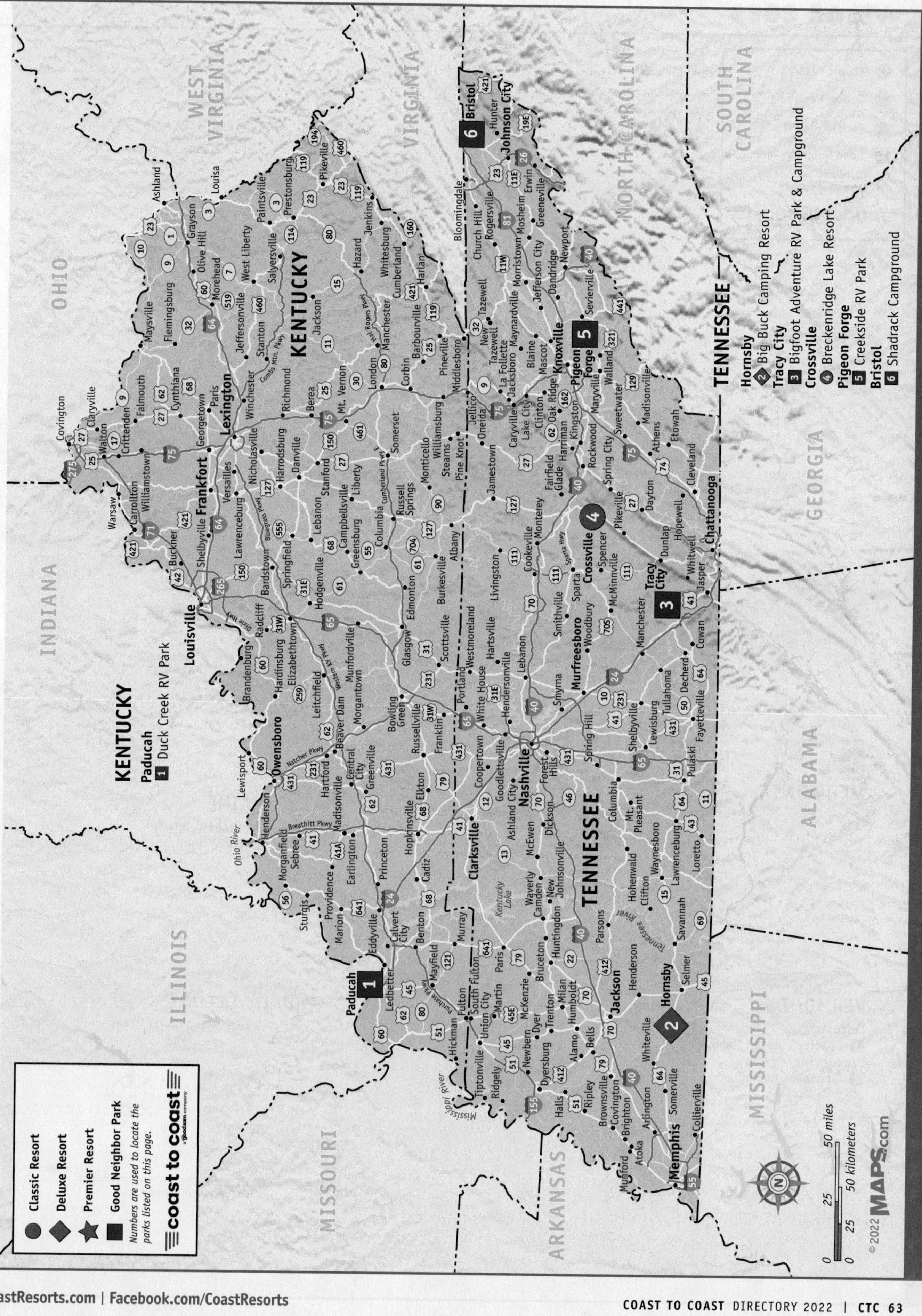
KENTUCKY
Paducah
1 Duck Creek RV Park
TENNESSEE
Hornsby
2 Big Buck Camping Resort
Tracy City
3 Bigfoot Adventure RV Park & Campground
Crossville
4 Breckenridge Lake Resort
Pigeon Forge
5 Creekside RV Park
Bristol
6 Shadrack Campground
Classic Resort
Deluxe Resort
Premier Resort
Good Neighbor Park
Numbers are used to locate the parks listed on this page.
coast to coast
OHIO
INDIANA
ILLINOIS
MISSOURI
ARKANSAS
MISSISSIPPI
ALABAMA
GEORGIA
SOUTH CAROLINA
NORTH CAROLINA
VIRGINIA
WEST VIRGINIA
Louisville
Lexington
Frankfort
Nashville
Knoxville
Memphis
Chattanooga
0 25 50 miles
0 25 50 kilometers
© 2022 MAPS.com

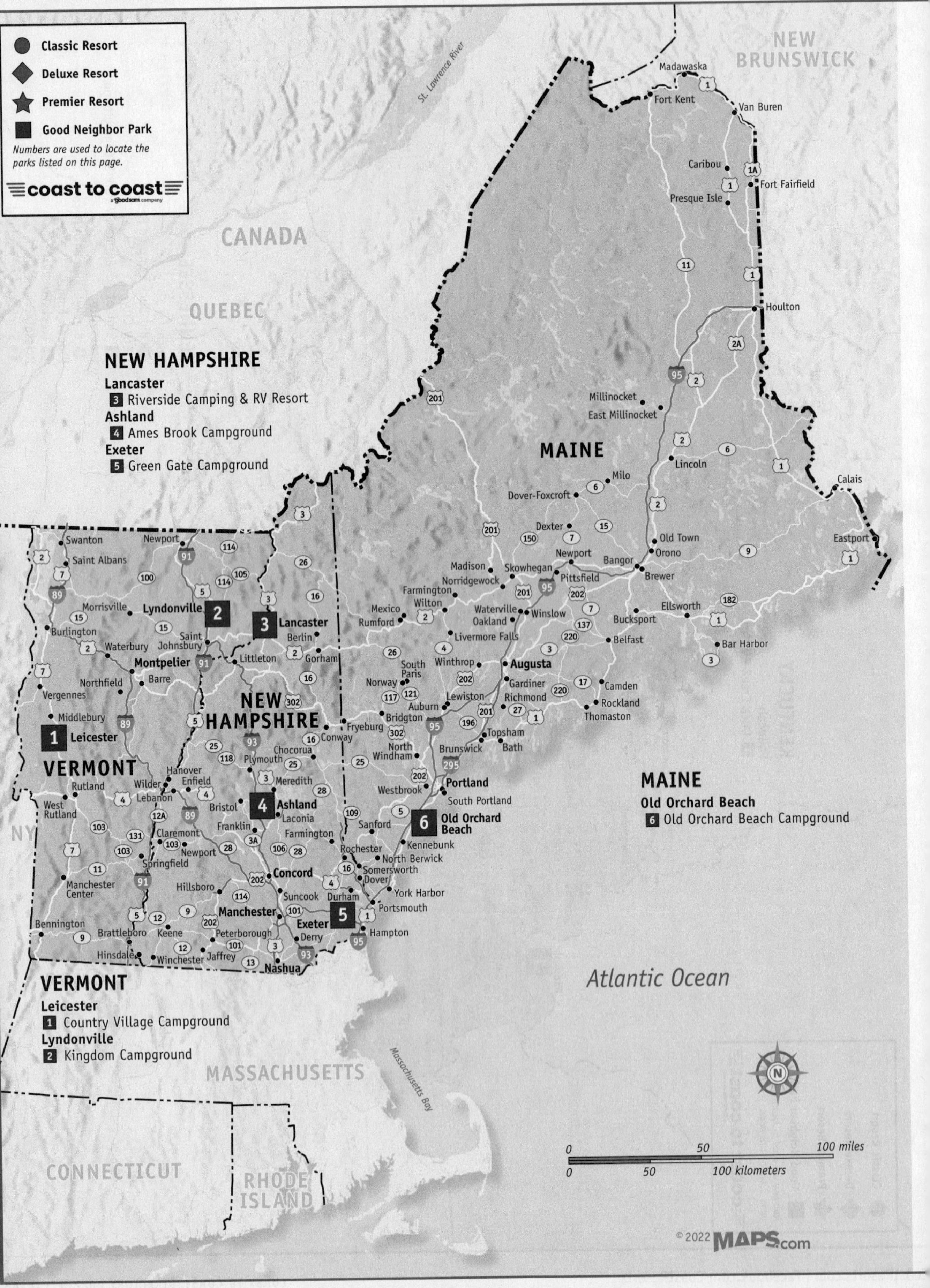

NEW HAMPSHIRE

Lancaster
3 Riverside Camping & RV Resort
Ashland
4 Ames Brook Campground
Exeter
5 Green Gate Campground

MAINE

Old Orchard Beach
6 Old Orchard Beach Campground

VERMONT

Leicester
1 Country Village Campground
Lyndonville
2 Kingdom Campground

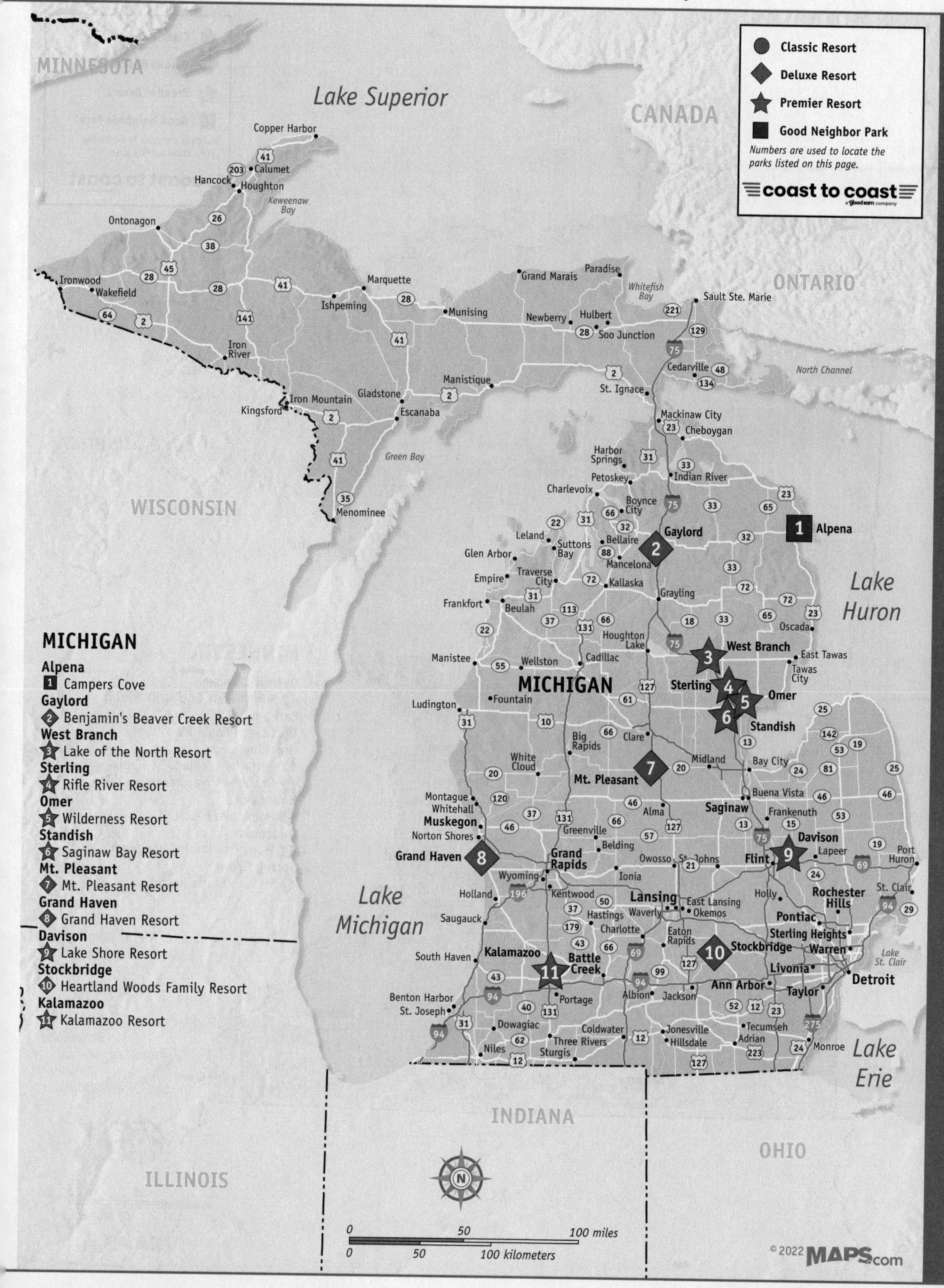
Classic Resort
Deluxe Resort
Premier Resort
Good Neighbor Park
Numbers are used to locate the parks listed on this page.
coast to coast
MICHIGAN
Alpena
1 Campers Cove
Gaylord
2 Benjamin's Beaver Creek Resort
West Branch
3 Lake of the North Resort
Sterling
4 Rifle River Resort
Omer
5 Wilderness Resort
Standish
6 Saginaw Bay Resort
Mt. Pleasant
7 Mt. Pleasant Resort
Grand Haven
8 Grand Haven Resort
Davison
9 Lake Shore Resort
Stockbridge
10 Heartland Woods Family Resort
Kalamazoo
11 Kalamazoo Resort
Lake Superior
Lake Michigan
Lake Huron
Lake Erie
CANADA
ONTARIO
MINNESOTA
WISCONSIN
ILLINOIS
INDIANA
OHIO
0 50 100 miles
0 50 100 kilometers
© 2022 MAPS.com

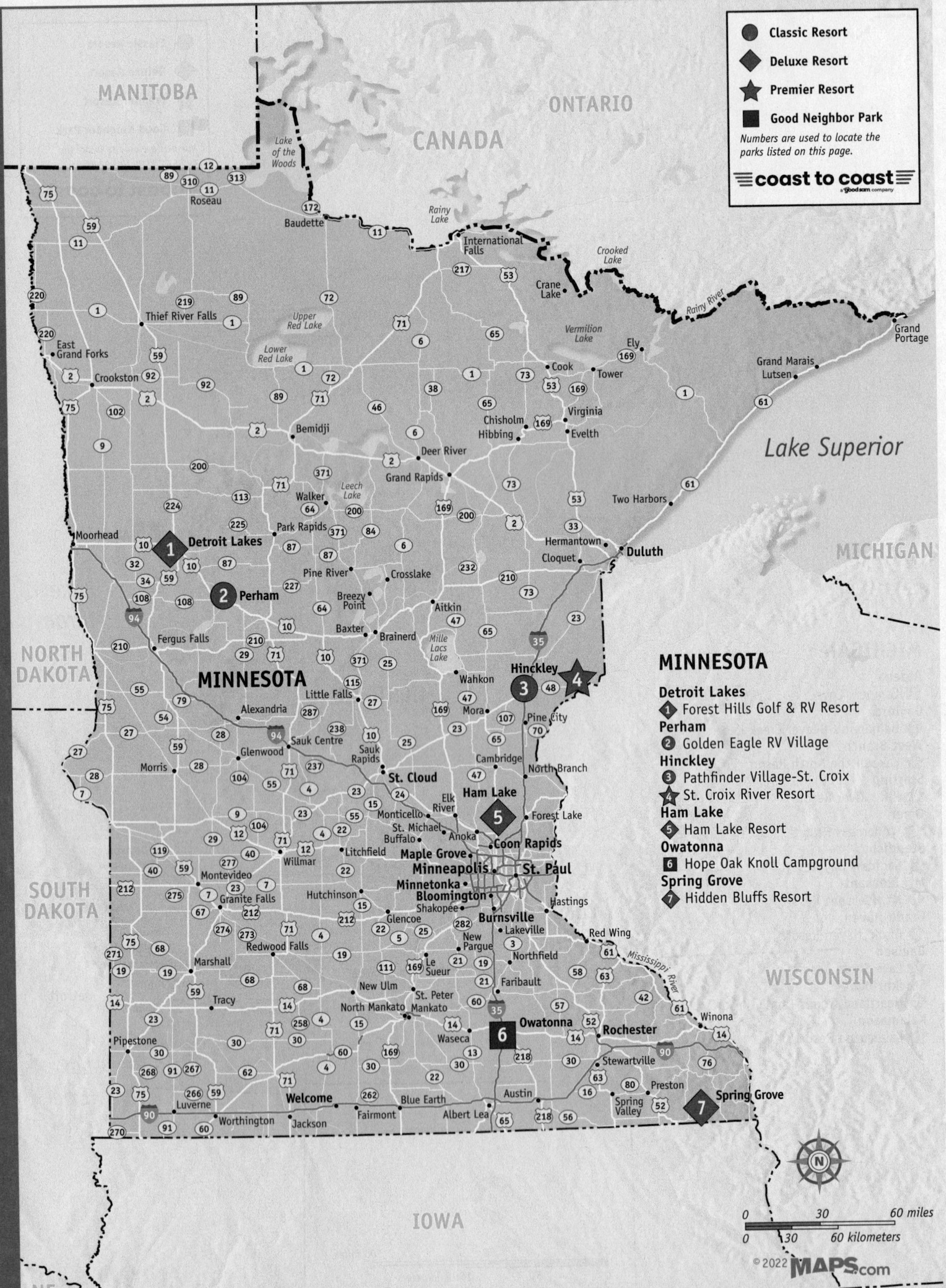
Classic Resort
Deluxe Resort
Premier Resort
Good Neighbor Park
Numbers are used to locate the parks listed on this page.
coast to coast
MINNESOTA
Detroit Lakes
1 Forest Hills Golf & RV Resort
Perham
2 Golden Eagle RV Village
Hinckley
3 Pathfinder Village-St. Croix
4 St. Croix River Resort
Ham Lake
5 Ham Lake Resort
Owatonna
6 Hope Oak Knoll Campground
Spring Grove
7 Hidden Bluffs Resort
MANITOBA
ONTARIO
CANADA
NORTH DAKOTA
SOUTH DAKOTA
IOWA
WISCONSIN
MICHIGAN
NE
MINNESOTA
Lake Superior
Lake of the Woods
Rainy Lake
Crooked Lake
Rainy River
Upper Red Lake
Lower Red Lake
Vermilion Lake
Leech Lake
Mille Lacs Lake
Mississippi River
Roseau
Baudette
International Falls
Crane Lake
Grand Portage
Grand Marais
Lutsen
Ely
Tower
Cook
Virginia
Eveleth
Chisholm
Hibbing
Thief River Falls
East Grand Forks
Crookston
Bemidji
Deer River
Grand Rapids
Two Harbors
Walker
Park Rapids
Moorhead
Detroit Lakes
Perham
Hermantown
Cloquet
Duluth
Pine River
Crosslake
Breezy Point
Aitkin
Baxter
Brainerd
Fergus Falls
Hinckley
Wahkon
Little Falls
Alexandria
Mora
Pine City
Sauk Centre
Glenwood
Morris
Sauk Rapids
St. Cloud
Cambridge
North Branch
Ham Lake
Elk River
Forest Lake
Monticello
St. Michael
Anoka
Coon Rapids
Buffalo
Maple Grove
Litchfield
Willmar
Minneapolis
St. Paul
Montevideo
Minnetonka
Bloomington
Hutchinson
Granite Falls
Shakopee
Hastings
Glencoe
Burnsville
Lakeville
Red Wing
Redwood Falls
New Prague
Northfield
Marshall
Le Sueur
Faribault
Tracy
New Ulm
St. Peter
North Mankato
Mankato
Winona
Owatonna
Rochester
Waseca
Pipestone
Stewartville
Preston
Austin
Spring Valley
Spring Grove
Luverne
Welcome
Blue Earth
Fairmont
Albert Lea
Worthington
Jackson
0
30
60 miles
60 kilometers
© 2022 MAPS.com

Numbers are used to locate Coast Premier, Coast Deluxe and Coast Classic Resorts and Good Neighbor Parks.

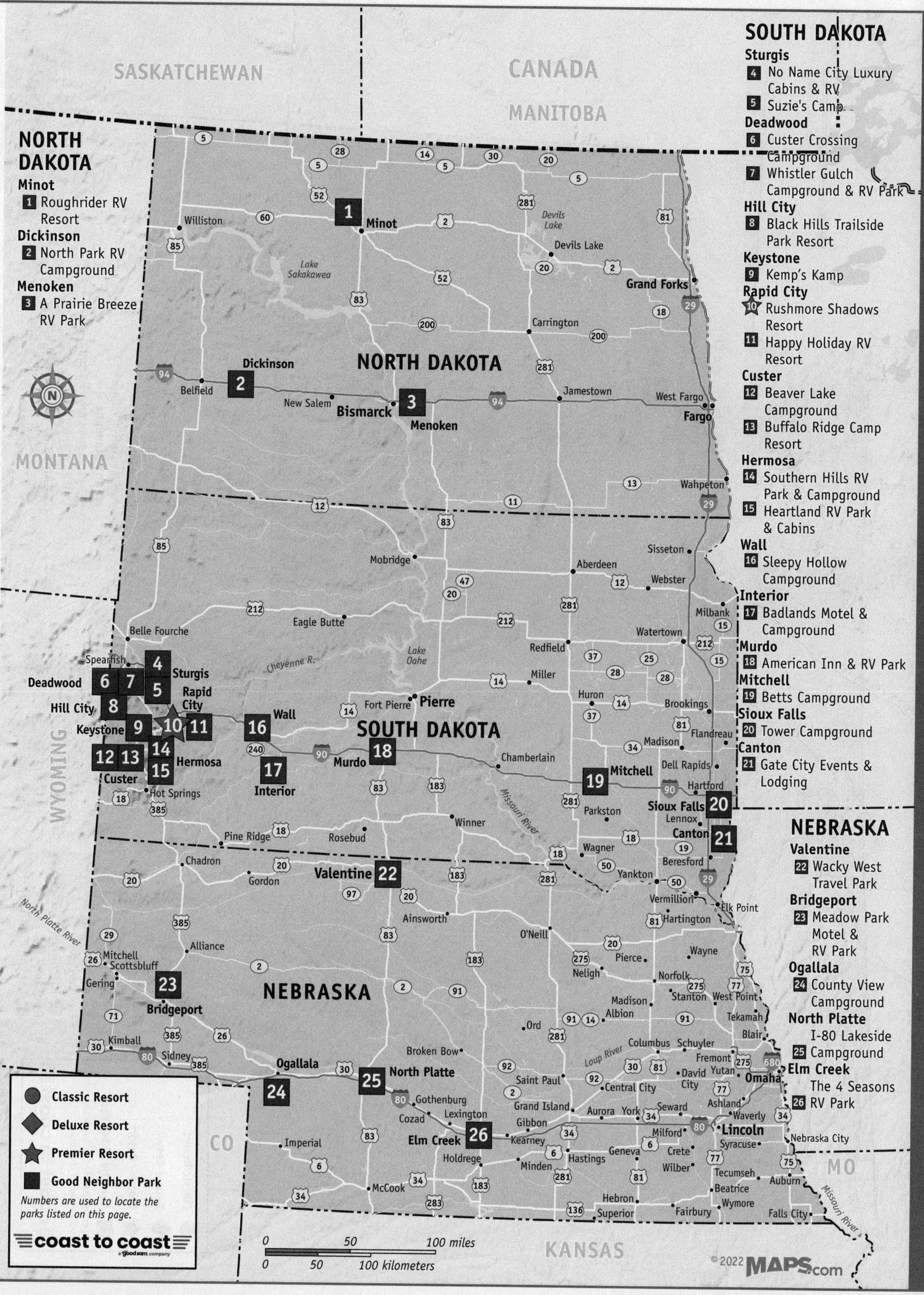
SOUTH DAKOTA
Sturgis
4 No Name City Luxury Cabins & RV
5 Suzie's Camp
Deadwood
6 Custer Crossing Campground
7 Whistler Gulch Campground & RV Park
Hill City
8 Black Hills Trailside Park Resort
Keystone
9 Kemp's Kamp
Rapid City
10 Rushmore Shadows Resort
11 Happy Holiday RV Resort
Custer
12 Beaver Lake Campground
13 Buffalo Ridge Camp Resort
Hermosa
14 Southern Hills RV Park & Campground
15 Heartland RV Park & Cabins
Wall
16 Sleepy Hollow Campground
Interior
17 Badlands Motel & Campground
Murdo
18 American Inn & RV Park
Mitchell
19 Betts Campground
Sioux Falls
20 Tower Campground
Canton
21 Gate City Events & Lodging
NORTH DAKOTA
Minot
1 Roughrider RV Resort
Dickinson
2 North Park RV Campground
Menoken
3 A Prairie Breeze RV Park
NEBRASKA
Valentine
22 Wacky West Travel Park
Bridgeport
23 Meadow Park Motel & RV Park
Ogallala
24 County View Campground
North Platte
25 I-80 Lakeside Campground
Elm Creek
26 The 4 Seasons RV Park
SASKATCHEWAN
CANADA
MANITOBA
MONTANA
WYOMING
CO
KANSAS
MO
Classic Resort
Deluxe Resort
Premier Resort
Good Neighbor Park
Numbers are used to locate the parks listed on this page.
coast to coast
0 50 100 miles
0 50 100 kilometers
© 2022 MAPS.com

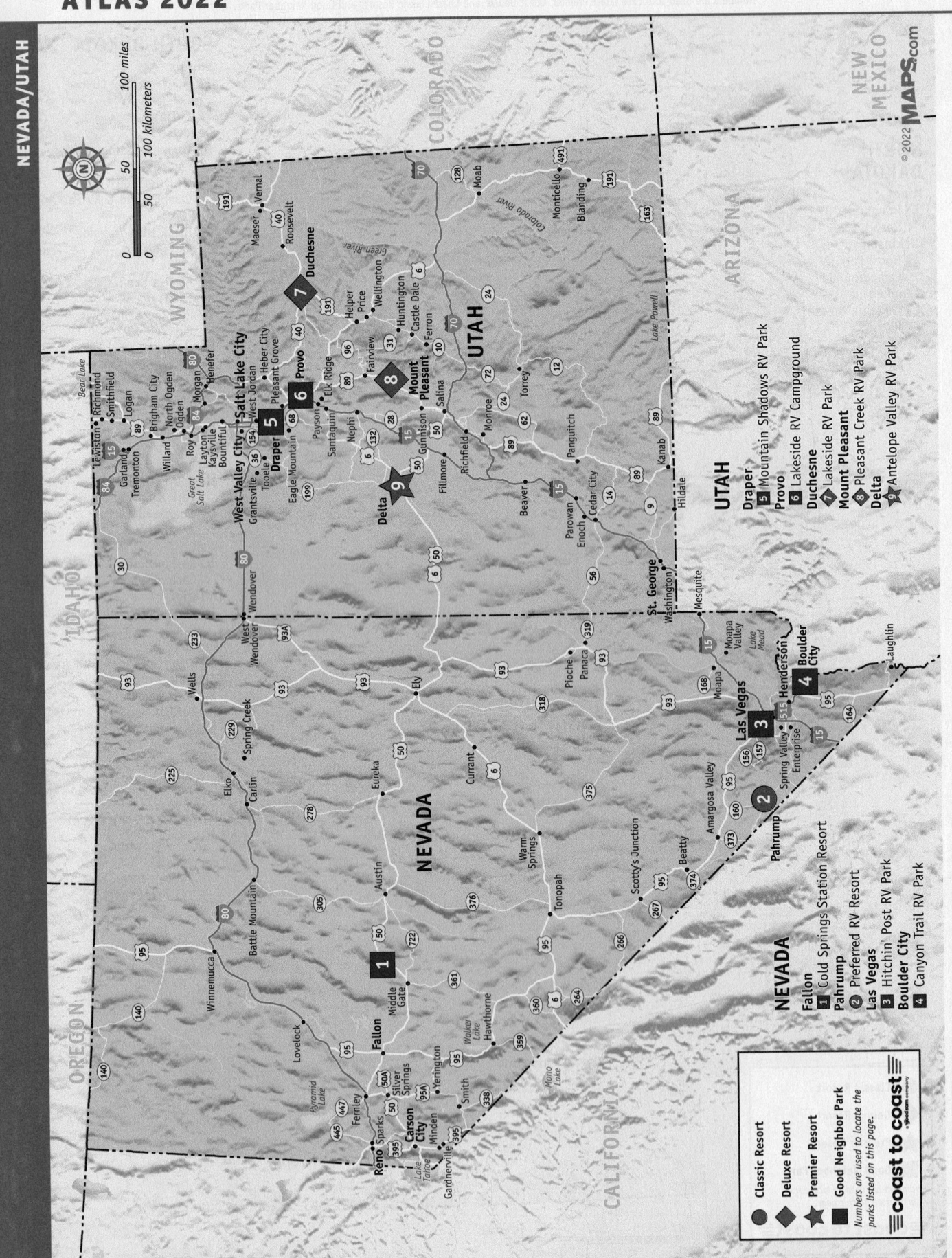

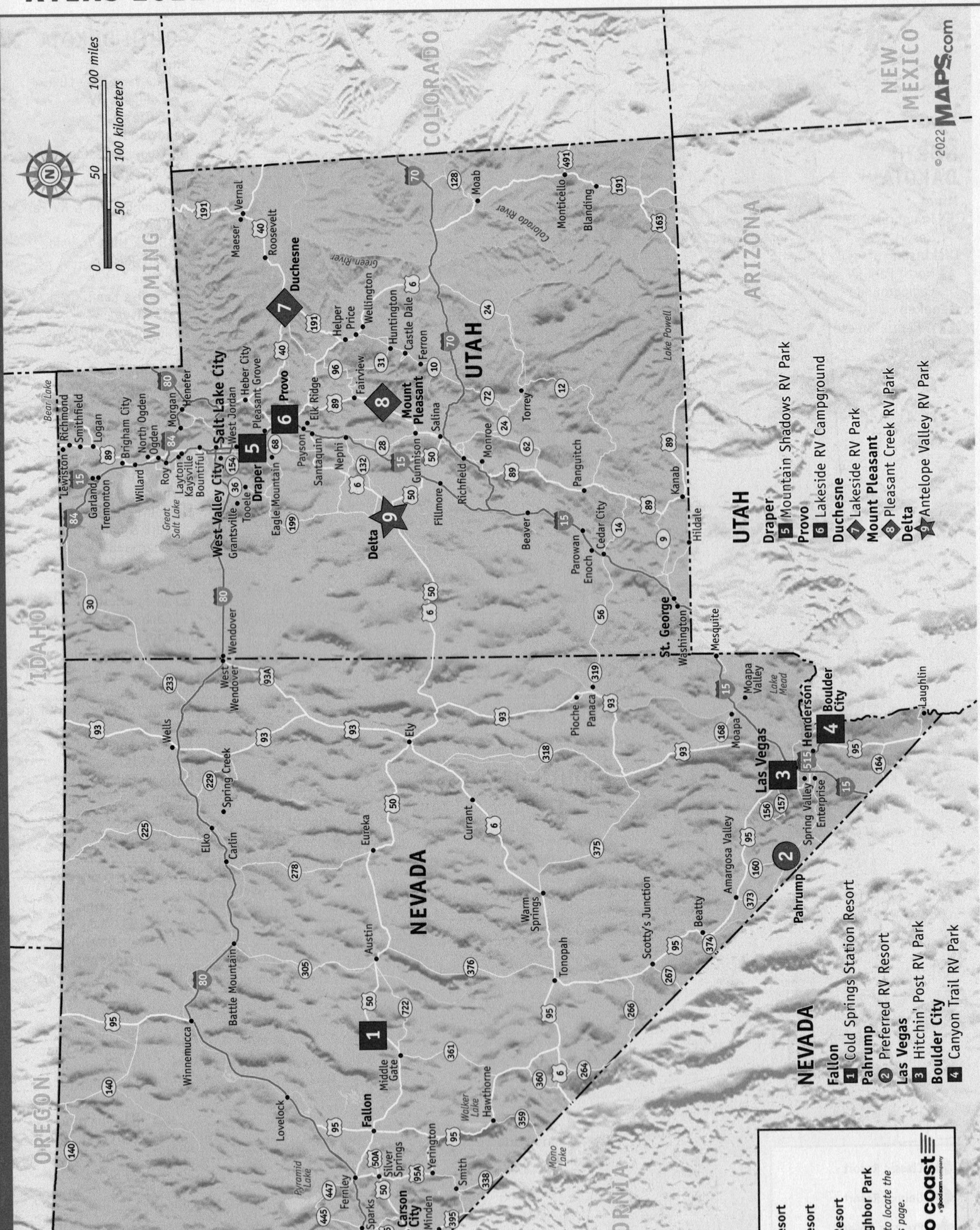
NEVADA
UTAH
IDAHO
OREGON
WYOMING
COLORADO
ARIZONA
NEW MEXICO
CALIFORNIA
0 50 100 miles
0 50 100 kilometers
NEVADA
Fallon
1 Cold Springs Station Resort
Pahrump
2 Preferred RV Resort
Las Vegas
3 Hitchin' Post RV Park
Boulder City
4 Canyon Trail RV Park
UTAH
Draper
5 Mountain Shadows RV Park
Provo
6 Lakeside RV Campground
Duchesne
7 Lakeside RV Park
Mount Pleasant
8 Pleasant Creek RV Park
Delta
9 Antelope Valley RV Park
Classic Resort
Deluxe Resort
Premier Resort
Good Neighbor Park
Numbers are used to locate the parks listed on this page.
coast to coast
© 2022 MAPS.com

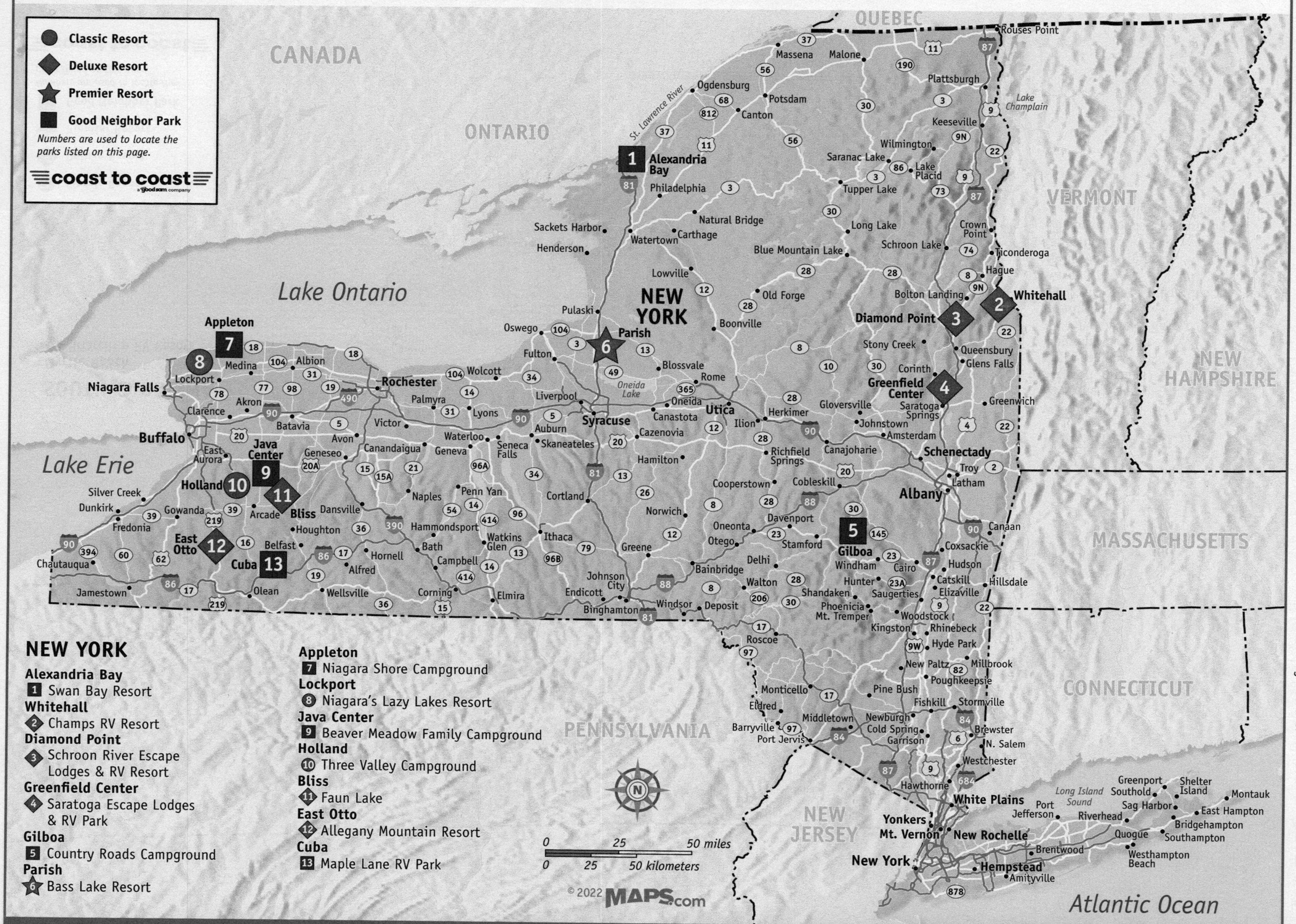

NEW YORK

Alexandria Bay
1 Swan Bay Resort
Whitehall
2 Champs RV Resort
Diamond Point
3 Schroon River Escape Lodges & RV Resort
Greenfield Center
4 Saratoga Escape Lodges & RV Park
Gilboa
5 Country Roads Campground
Parish
6 Bass Lake Resort
Appleton
7 Niagara Shore Campground
Lockport
8 Niagara's Lazy Lakes Resort
Java Center
9 Beaver Meadow Family Campground
Holland
10 Three Valley Campground
Bliss
11 Faun Lake
East Otto
12 Allegany Mountain Resort
Cuba
13 Maple Lane RV Park

NEW YORK

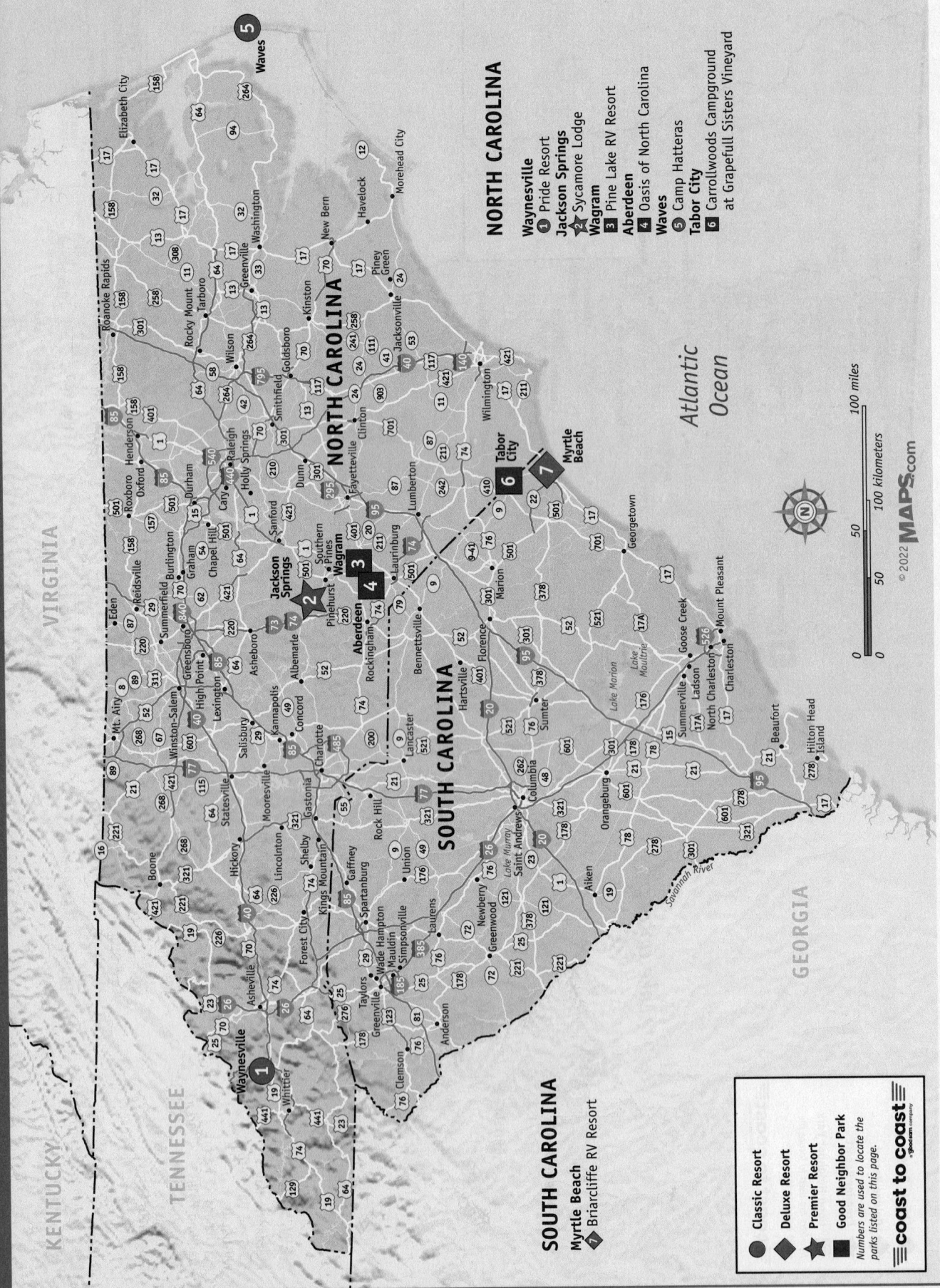

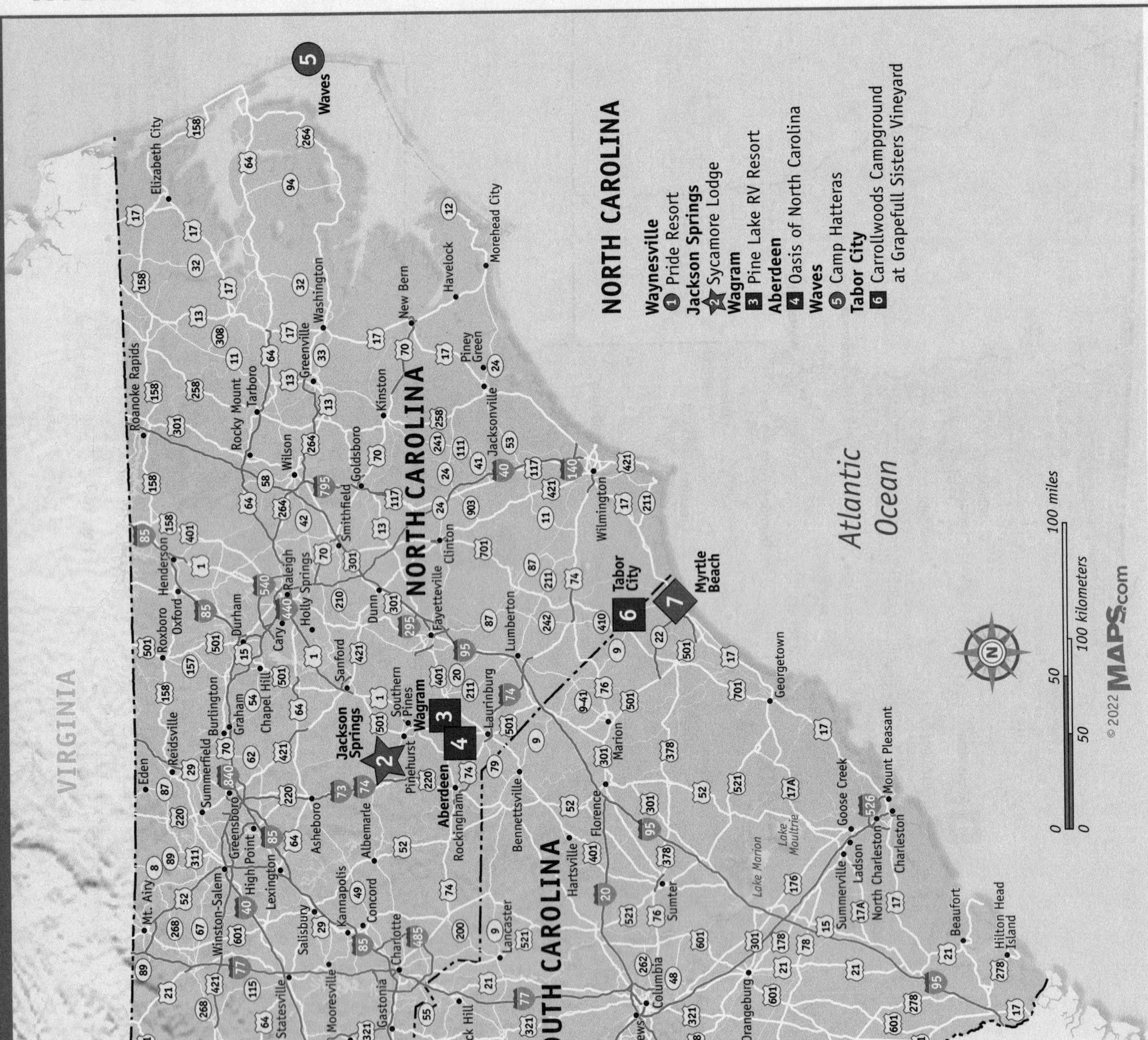
VIRGINIA
KENTUCKY
TENNESSEE
GEORGIA
NORTH CAROLINA
SOUTH CAROLINA
Atlantic Ocean
NORTH CAROLINA
Waynesville
1 Pride Resort
Jackson Springs
2 Sycamore Lodge
Wagram
3 Pine Lake RV Resort
Aberdeen
4 Oasis of North Carolina
Waves
5 Camp Hatteras
Tabor City
6 Carrollwoods Campground at Grapefull Sisters Vineyard
SOUTH CAROLINA
Myrtle Beach
7 Briarcliffe RV Resort
Classic Resort
Deluxe Resort
Premier Resort
Good Neighbor Park
Numbers are used to locate the parks listed on this page.
coast to coast
0 50 100 miles
0 50 100 kilometers
© 2022 MAPS.com

Numbers are used to locate Coast Premier, Coast Deluxe and Coast Classic Resorts and Good Neighbor Parks.

OHIO

Jefferson
1 MillBrook Outdoor Resort

Andover
2 Holiday Camplands

Diamond
3 Leisure Lake

Wapakoneta
4 Arrowhead Lakes

Huntsville
5 Indian Lake Resort

Loudonville
6 Wally World Riverside Resort

Kimbolton
7 Rocky Fork Ranch

Stout
8 Sandy Springs Campground

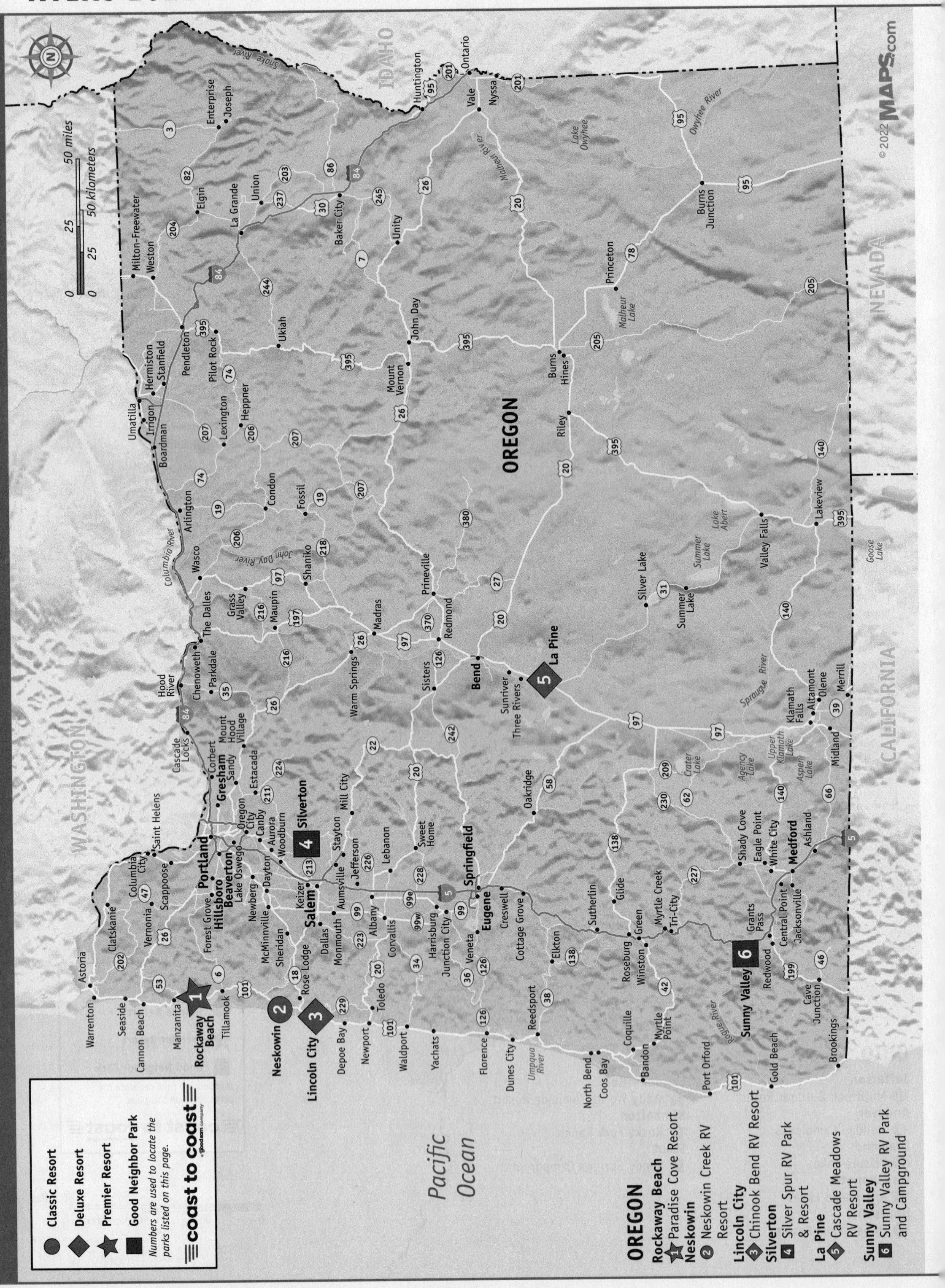
Classic Resort
Deluxe Resort
Premier Resort
Good Neighbor Park
Numbers are used to locate the parks listed on this page.
coast to coast
OREGON
Rockaway Beach
1 Paradise Cove Resort
Neskowin
2 Neskowin Creek RV Resort
Lincoln City
3 Chinook Bend RV Resort
Silverton
4 Silver Spur RV Park & Resort
La Pine
5 Cascade Meadows RV Resort
Sunny Valley
6 Sunny Valley RV Park and Campground
0 25 50 miles
0 25 50 kilometers
© 2022 MAPS.com
WASHINGTON
IDAHO
NEVADA
CALIFORNIA
OREGON
Pacific Ocean
Columbia River
Snake River
John Day River
Malheur River
Owyhee River
Lake Owyhee
Malheur Lake
Summer Lake
Lake Abert
Goose Lake
Crater Lake
Agency Lake
Upper Klamath Lake
Aspen Lake
Sprague River
Rogue River
Umpqua River
Astoria
Warrenton
Seaside
Cannon Beach
Manzanita
Rockaway Beach
Tillamook
Neskowin
Lincoln City
Depoe Bay
Newport
Toledo
Waldport
Yachats
Florence
Dunes City
Reedsport
North Bend
Coos Bay
Bandon
Coquille
Myrtle Point
Port Orford
Gold Beach
Brookings
Clatskanie
Vernonia
Columbia City
Saint Helens
Scappoose
Forest Grove
Hillsboro
Beaverton
Portland
Lake Oswego
Gresham
Corbett
Sandy
Estacada
Oregon City
Canby
Aurora
Woodburn
Silverton
Stayton
Mill City
Newberg
Dayton
McMinnville
Sheridan
Rose Lodge
Dallas
Monmouth
Salem
Keizer
Aumsville
Jefferson
Albany
Corvallis
Lebanon
Sweet Home
Harrisburg
Junction City
Veneta
Eugene
Springfield
Creswell
Cottage Grove
Oakridge
Elkton
Sutherlin
Glide
Roseburg
Winston
Green
Myrtle Creek
Tri-City
Grants Pass
Sunny Valley
Redwood
Cave Junction
Central Point
Jacksonville
Shady Cove
Eagle Point
White City
Medford
Ashland
Midland
Klamath Falls
Altamont
Olene
Merrill
Cascade Locks
Hood River
Chenoweth
Parkdale
Mount Hood Village
The Dalles
Wasco
Arlington
Boardman
Irrigon
Umatilla
Hermiston
Stanfield
Pendleton
Pilot Rock
Lexington
Heppner
Condon
Fossil
Shaniko
Grass Valley
Maupin
Warm Springs
Madras
Redmond
Prineville
Sisters
Bend
Sunriver
Three Rivers
La Pine
Silver Lake
Summer Lake
Valley Falls
Lakeview
Ukiah
Mount Vernon
John Day
Unity
Baker City
La Grande
Union
Elgin
Enterprise
Joseph
Milton-Freewater
Weston
Huntington
Ontario
Vale
Nyssa
Burns
Hines
Riley
Princeton
Burns Junction

Numbers are used to locate Coast Premier, Coast Deluxe and Coast Classic Resorts and Good Neighbor Parks.

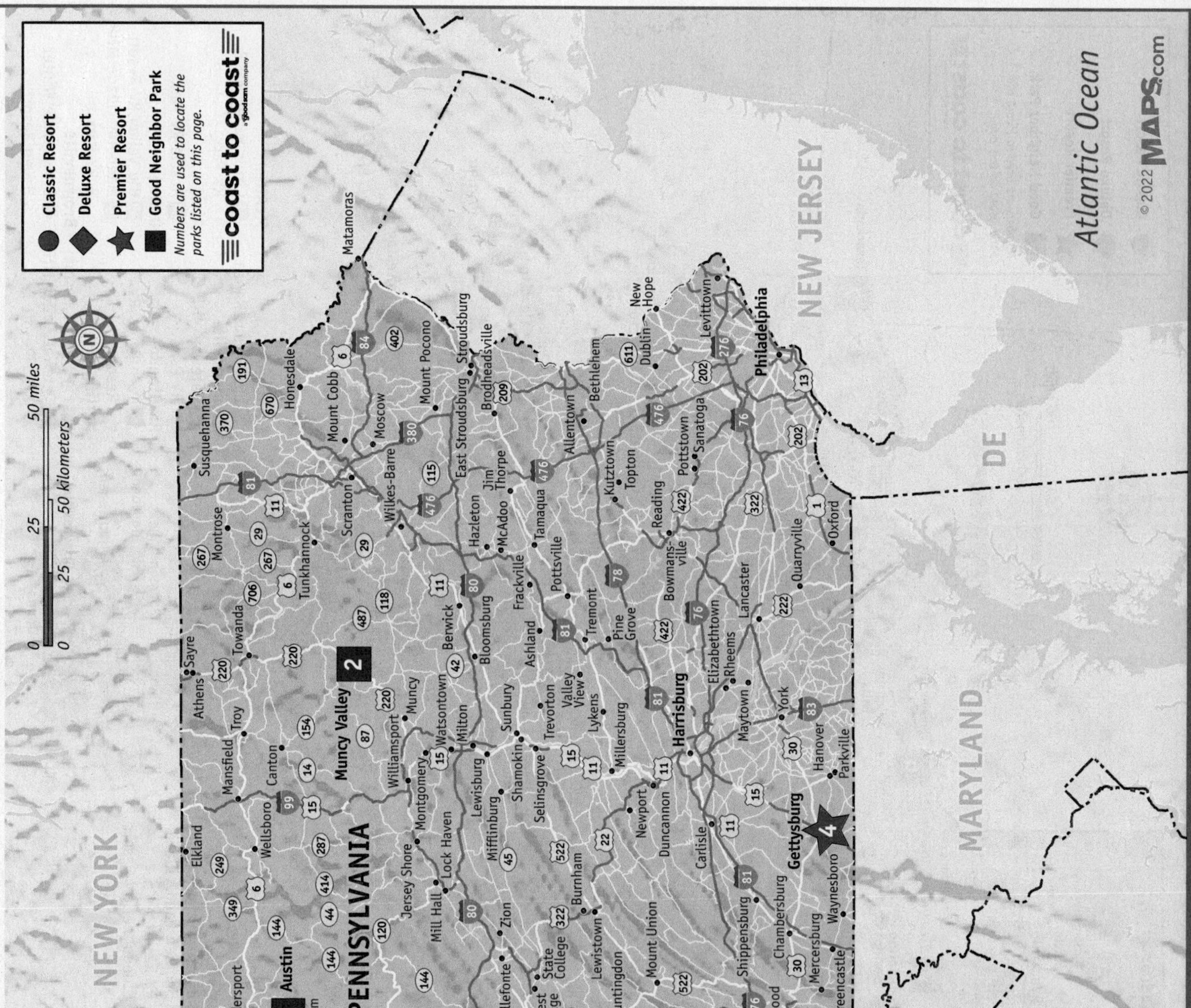

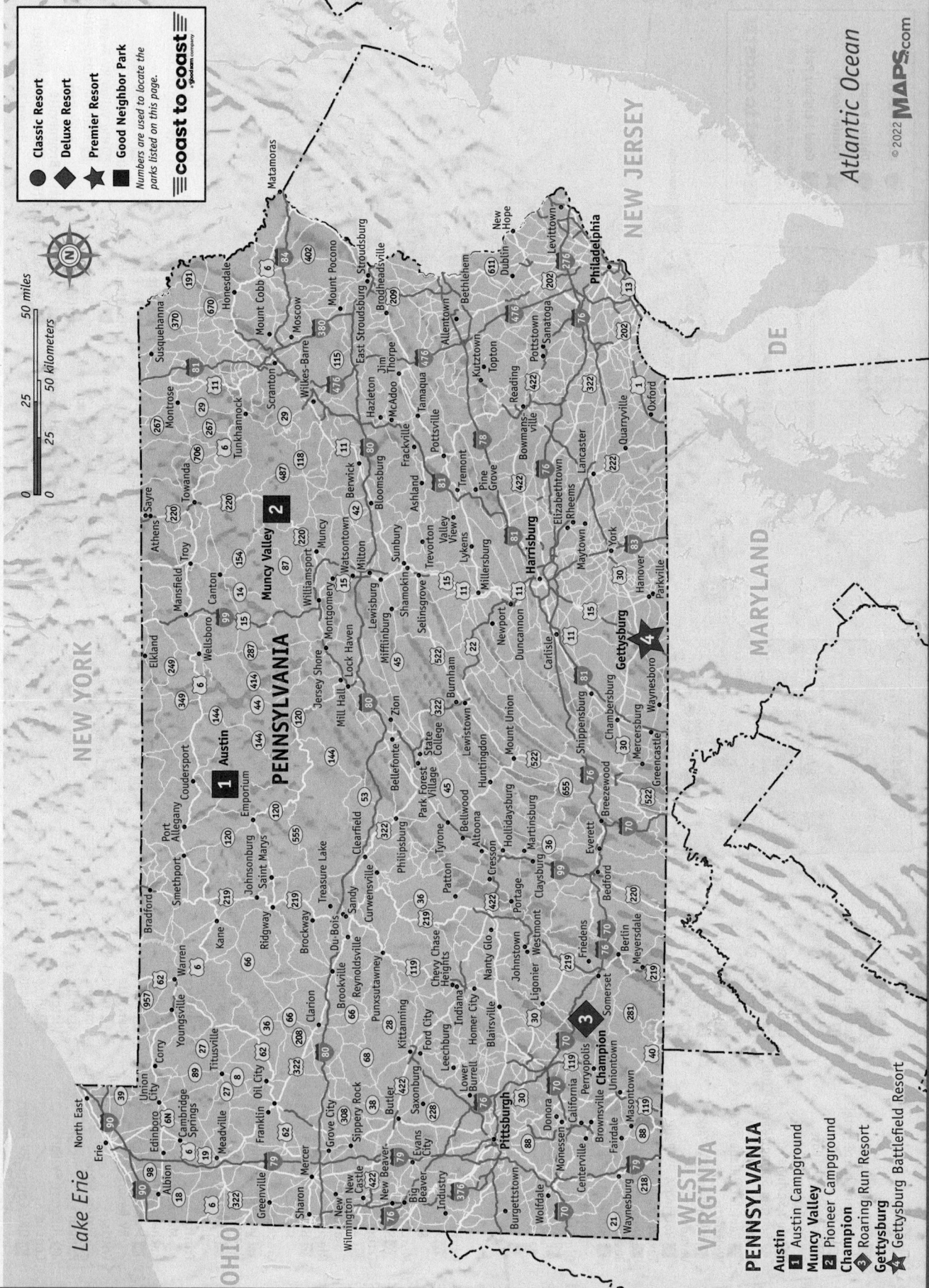

PENNSYLVANIA

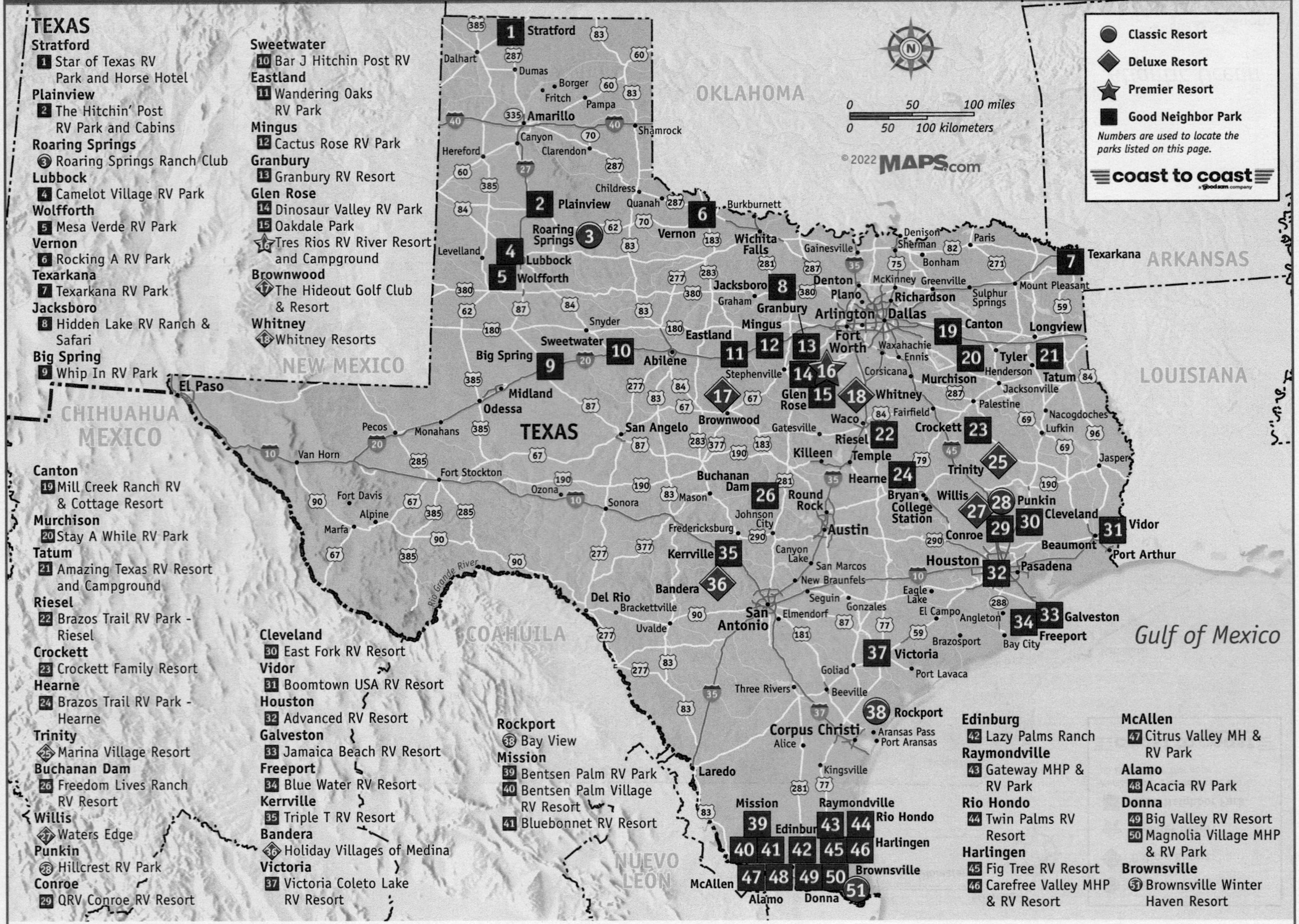

TEXAS

Stratford
1 Star of Texas RV Park and Horse Hotel
Plainview
2 The Hitchin' Post RV Park and Cabins
Roaring Springs
3 Roaring Springs Ranch Club
Lubbock
4 Camelot Village RV Park
Wolfforth
5 Mesa Verde RV Park
Vernon
6 Rocking A RV Park
Texarkana
7 Texarkana RV Park
Jacksboro
8 Hidden Lake RV Ranch & Safari
Big Spring
9 Whip In RV Park
Sweetwater
10 Bar J Hitchin Post RV
Eastland
11 Wandering Oaks RV Park
Mingus
12 Cactus Rose RV Park
Granbury
13 Granbury RV Resort
Glen Rose
14 Dinosaur Valley RV Park
15 Oakdale Park
16 Tres Rios RV River Resort and Campground
Brownwood
17 The Hideout Golf Club & Resort
Whitney
18 Whitney Resorts
Canton
19 Mill Creek Ranch RV & Cottage Resort
Murchison
20 Stay A While RV Park
Tatum
21 Amazing Texas RV Resort and Campground
Riesel
22 Brazos Trail RV Park - Riesel
Crockett
23 Crockett Family Resort
Hearne
24 Brazos Trail RV Park - Hearne
Trinity
25 Marina Village Resort
Buchanan Dam
26 Freedom Lives Ranch RV Resort
Willis
27 Waters Edge
Punkin
28 Hillcrest RV Park
Conroe
29 QRV Conroe RV Resort
Cleveland
30 East Fork RV Resort
Vidor
31 Boomtown USA RV Resort
Houston
32 Advanced RV Resort
Galveston
33 Jamaica Beach RV Resort
Freeport
34 Blue Water RV Resort
Kerrville
35 Triple T RV Resort
Bandera
36 Holiday Villages of Medina
Victoria
37 Victoria Coleto Lake RV Resort
Rockport
38 Bay View
Mission
39 Bentsen Palm RV Park
40 Bentsen Palm Village RV Resort
41 Bluebonnet RV Resort
Edinburg
42 Lazy Palms Ranch
Raymondville
43 Gateway MHP & RV Park
Rio Hondo
44 Twin Palms RV Resort
Harlingen
45 Fig Tree RV Resort
46 Carefree Valley MHP & RV Resort
McAllen
47 Citrus Valley MH & RV Park
Alamo
48 Acacia RV Park
Donna
49 Big Valley RV Resort
50 Magnolia Village MHP & RV Park
Brownsville
51 Brownsville Winter Haven Resort

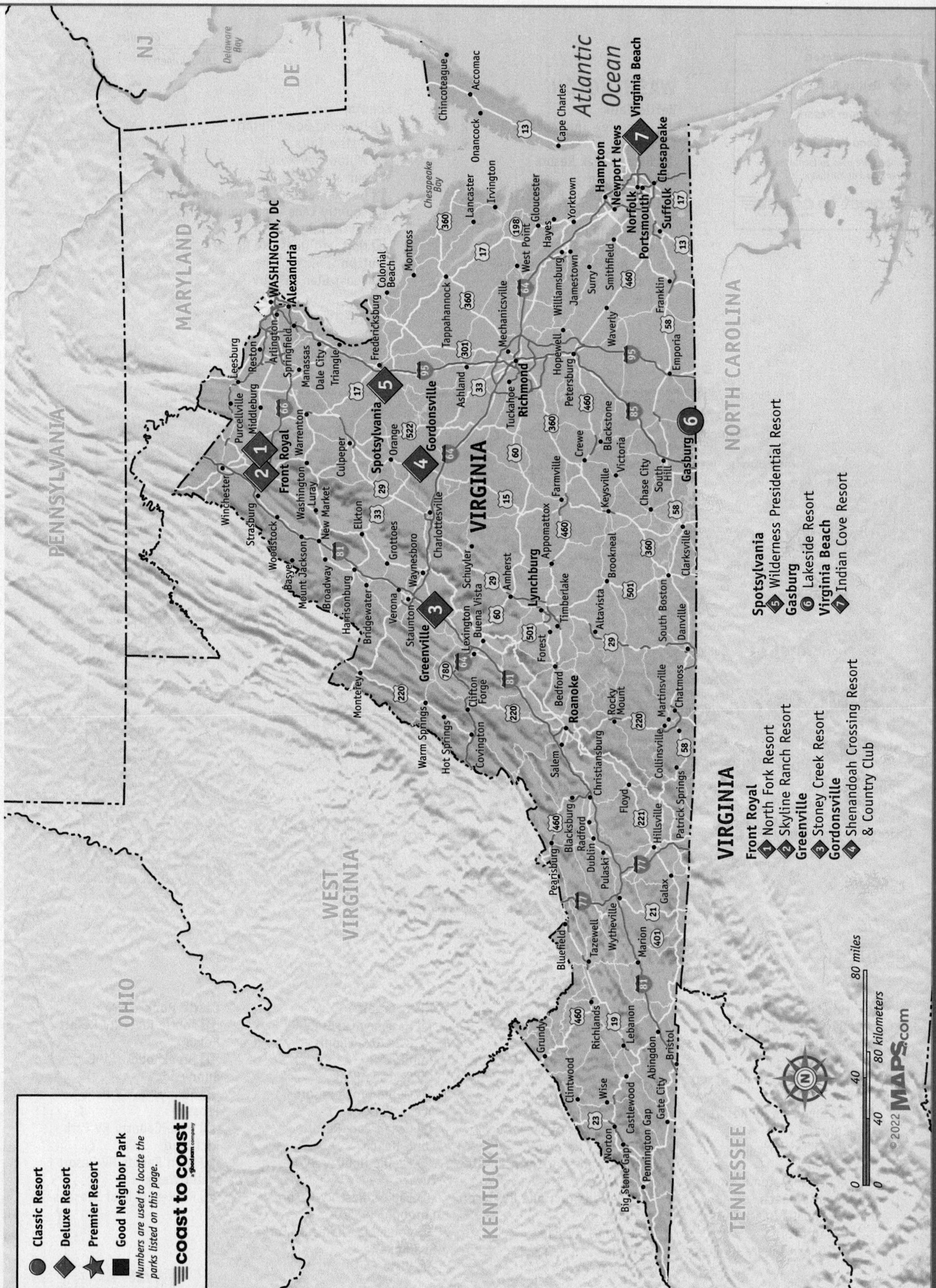

Classic Resort
Deluxe Resort
Premier Resort
Good Neighbor Park
Numbers are used to locate the parks listed on this page.
coast to coast
VIRGINIA
Front Royal
1 North Fork Resort
2 Skyline Ranch Resort
Greenville
3 Stoney Creek Resort
Gordonsville
4 Shenandoah Crossing Resort & Country Club
Spotsylvania
5 Wilderness Presidential Resort
Gasburg
6 Lakeside Resort
Virginia Beach
7 Indian Cove Resort
PENNSYLVANIA
MARYLAND
NJ
DE
Delaware Bay
WEST VIRGINIA
OHIO
KENTUCKY
TENNESSEE
NORTH CAROLINA
Atlantic Ocean
Chesapeake Bay
VIRGINIA
WASHINGTON, DC
Alexandria
Richmond
Roanoke
Lynchburg
Norfolk
Portsmouth
Chesapeake
Suffolk
Hampton
Newport News
Virginia Beach
Front Royal
Spotsylvania
Gordonsville
Greenville
Gasburg
80 miles
80 kilometers
© 2022 MAPS.com

- ● Classic Resort
- ◆ Deluxe Resort
- ★ Premier Resort
- ■ Good Neighbor Park

Numbers are used to locate the parks listed on this page.

coast to coast — a Good Sam company

0 30 60 miles
0 30 60 kilometers

WASHINGTON

Kettle Falls
1 Grandview Inn Motel & RV Park
Rockport
2 Glacier Peak Resort
Mount Vernon
3 Mount Vernon RV Park
Twisp
4 Riverbend RV Park
Newport
5 Old American Kampground
Port Angeles
6 Elwha Dam RV Park
Sequim
7 Diamond Point Resort
Nine Mile Falls
8 Willow Bay Resort
Wilbur
9 Goose Creek RV Park & Campground
10 Country Lane Campground & RV Park
Airway Heights
11 Northern Quest RV Resort
Poulsbo
12 Cedar Glen RV Park

Hoodsport
13 Dow Creek Resort
14 Glen Ayr Resort
Cheney
15 Ponderosa Falls Resort
Soap Lake
16 Smokiam RV Resort
Ephrata
17 Rimrock Meadows
Easton
18 Lake Easton Resort
Copalis Beach
19 Copalis Beach Resort
Ocean City
20 Ocean Breeze RV Resort

Hoquiam
21 Hoquiam River RV Park
Elma
22 Travel Inn Resort
Moses Lake
23 Pier 4 RV Resort
Othello
24 MarDon Resort on Potholes Reservoir
25 O'Sullivan Sportsman Resort
Warden
26 Sage Hills Golf and RV Resort
Grayland
27 Kenanna RV Park
Centralia
28 Midway RV Park

Silver Creek
29 Harmony Lakeside RV Park & Deluxe Cabins
Randle
30 Cascade Peaks
31 Maple Grove Resort
Ocean Park
32 Ocean Park Resort
Long Beach
33 Pacific Holiday RV Resort
Ilwaco
34 Eagle's Nest RV Resort
Chinook
35 Columbia Shores RV Park
Skamokawa
36 Vista Park

Castle Rock
37 Toutle River RV Resort
Kelso
38 Brookhollow RV Park
Sunnyside
39 Sunnyside RV Park
Prosser
40 Wine Country RV Park
Richland
41 Horn Rapids RV Resort
Walla Walla
42 RV Resort Four Seasons

WISCONSIN

Gresham

1 Captain's Cove Resort and Country Club

Wisconsin Dells

2 Christmas Mountain Village Campground

BRITISH COLUMBIA

Chemainus
1 Country Maples RV Resort
Rosedale
2 Camperland RV Resort & Cabins
Hope
3 Sunshine Valley RV Resort & Deluxe Cabins
Kelowna
4 Holiday Park Resort
Grand Forks
5 Riviera RV Park
Ainsworth
6 Woodbury Resort and Marina
Creston
7 Pair-A-Dice RV Park & Campground
Dawson Creek
8 Northern Lights RV Park

ALBERTA

County of Grande Prairie #1
9 Camp Tamarack RV Park
Valleyview
10 Sherk's RV Park
Peace River
11 Rendez-Vous RV Park & Storage
Rocky Mountain House
12 Wilderness Village at Crimson Lake
Drumheller
13 Dinosaur Trail RV Resort
Lethbridge
14 Bridgeview RV Resort

SASKATCHEWAN

Saskatoon
15 Campland RV Resort
Indian Head
16 Indian Head Campground

MANITOBA

Oak Lake
17 Aspen Grove Campground
Douglas
18 Bry-Mar RV Park and Campground
Portage La Prairie
19 Miller's Camping Resort
Lac Du Bonnet
20 Champagne's RV Park

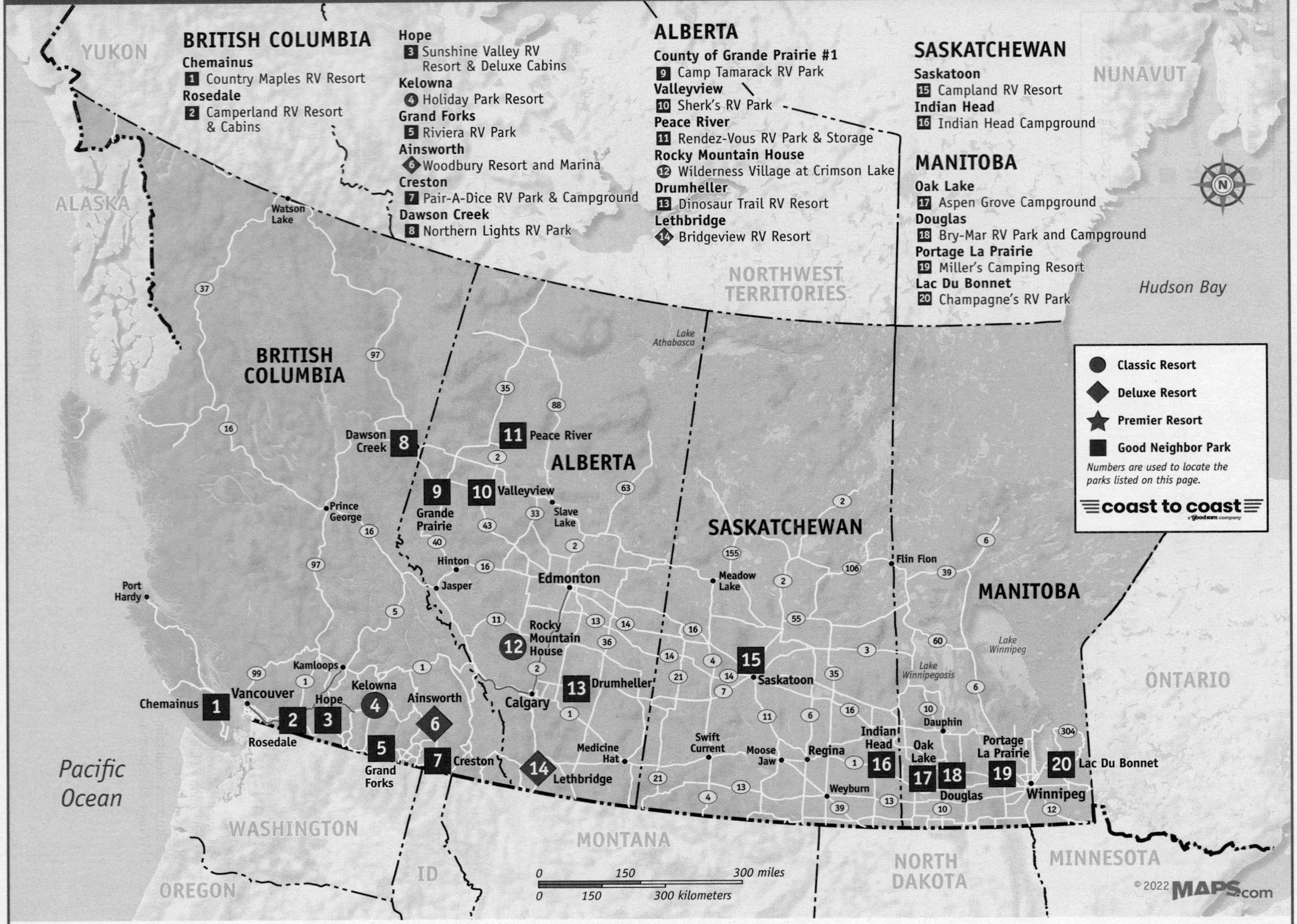

ONTARIO

Ignace
1 Davy Lake Campground
Nipigon
2 Stillwater Park Campground
Geraldton
3 Wild Goose Lake Campground
Sault Ste Marie
4 Glenview Cottages & Campground
Spragge
5 Serpent River Campground
Sturgeon Falls
6 Sturgeon Falls KOA
Mattawa
7 Sid Turcotte Park
Bracebridge
8 Santa's Whispering Pines Campground
Miller Lake
9 Summer House Park
Owen Sound
10 Sunny Valley Park Family Camping & Recreation
Kincardine
11 Aintree Trailer Park
Hanover
12 Saugeen Springs RV Park
Mono
13 Primrose Park
Alliston
14 Nicolston Dam Campground & Travellers Park
Wyoming
15 Country View Motel & RV Camping Resort
Eden
16 Red Oak Travel Park
Dunnville
17 Knight's Beach Resort
Niagara Falls
18 Campark Resorts Family Camping & RV Resort
19 Scott's Family RV Park
20 Yogi Bear's Jellystone Park Niagara Falls, Canada
21 Riverside Park Motel & Campground
Ridgeway
22 Windmill Point Park & Campground
Picton
23 Smugglers Cove RV Resort
Carrying Place
24 North Shore RV Park
Peterborough
25 Anchor Bay Camp
Lakefield
26 Lakefield Campground
Marmora
27 Heritage Trails Campground
Johnstown
28 Grenville Park Camping & RV Park
Morrisburg
29 Upper Canada Campground
Bainsville
30 Maplewood Acres RV Park
Ottawa
31 Camp Hither Hills
Cobden
32 Bona Vista Campground
Golden Lake
33 Golden Lake Campground
Combermere
34 Pine Cliff Resort

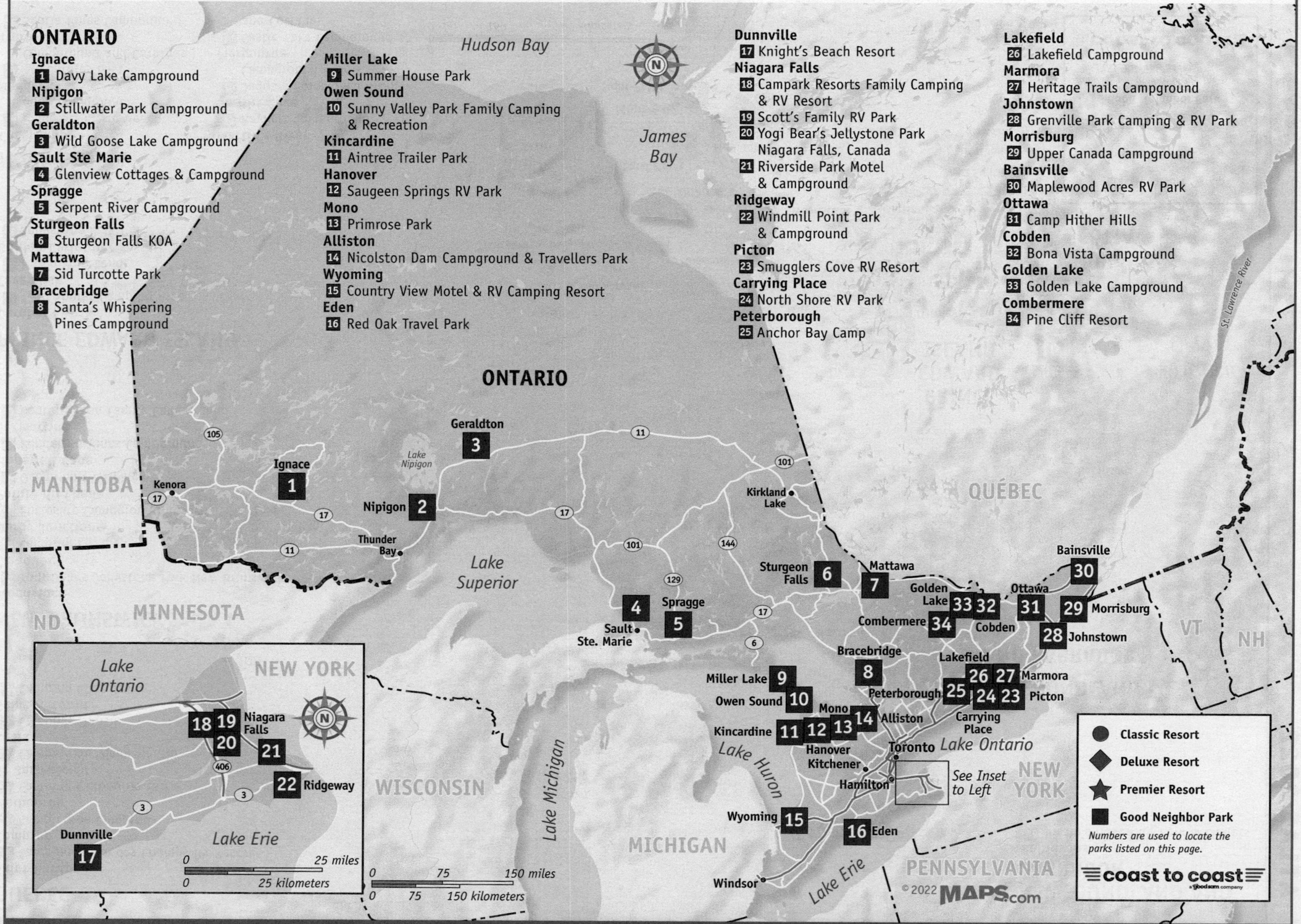

QUEBÉC

Saint-Philippe
1 Camping la Cle des Champs RV Resort
Compton
2 Camping de Compton
Melbourne
3 Camping Melbourne Estrie
St Barthelemy
4 Camping du Vieux Moulin
Levis
5 Camping Transit
Saint-Antonin
6 Camping Chez Jean

NEW BRUNSWICK

Woodstock
7 Yogi Bear's Jellystone Park New Brunswick
Caraquet
8 Camping Colibri
Derby Junction
9 Enclosure Campground Resort
Pointe du Chene
10 Ocean Surf RV Park
Hopewell Cape
11 Ponderosa Pines Campground
St. Martins
12 Century Farm Family Campground

PRINCE EDWARD ISLAND

Darnley
13 Twin Shores Camping Area
Cavendish
14 Marco Polo Land
Borden-Carleton
15 Jellystone Park PEI

NOVA SCOTIA

Cheticamp
16 Plage St. Pierre Beach and Campground
Baddeck
17 Adventures East Campground and Cottages
Truro
18 Scotia Pines Campground
Martin's River
19 RayPort Campground
Smiths Cove
20 Jaggars Point Oceanfront Campground Resort
Melbourne
21 Castle Lake Campground and Cottages

NEWFOUNDLAND AND LABRADOR

Robinsons
22 Pirate's Haven RV Park & Chalets

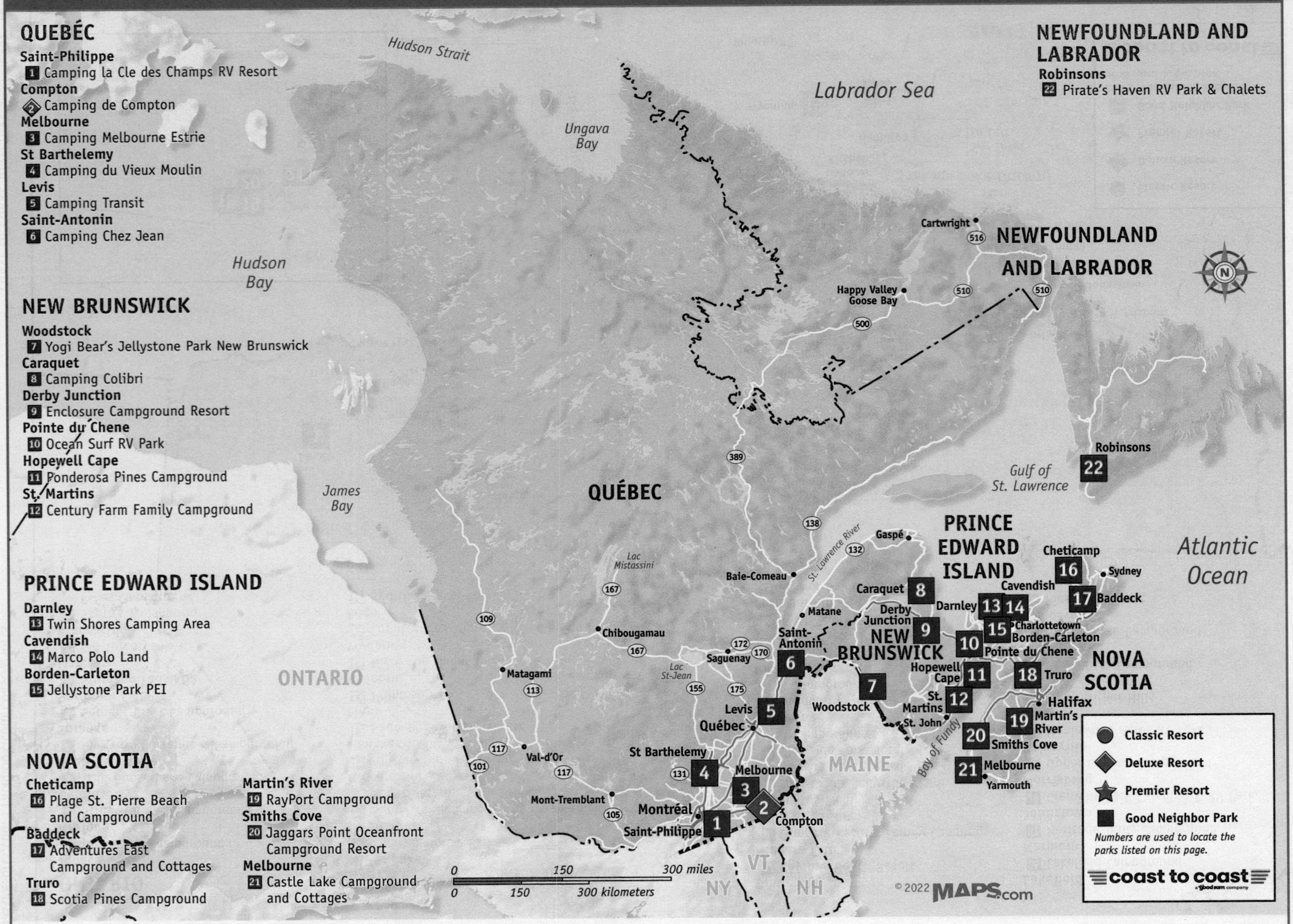

Numbers are used to locate Coast Premier, Coast Deluxe and Coast Classic Resorts and Good Neighbor Parks.

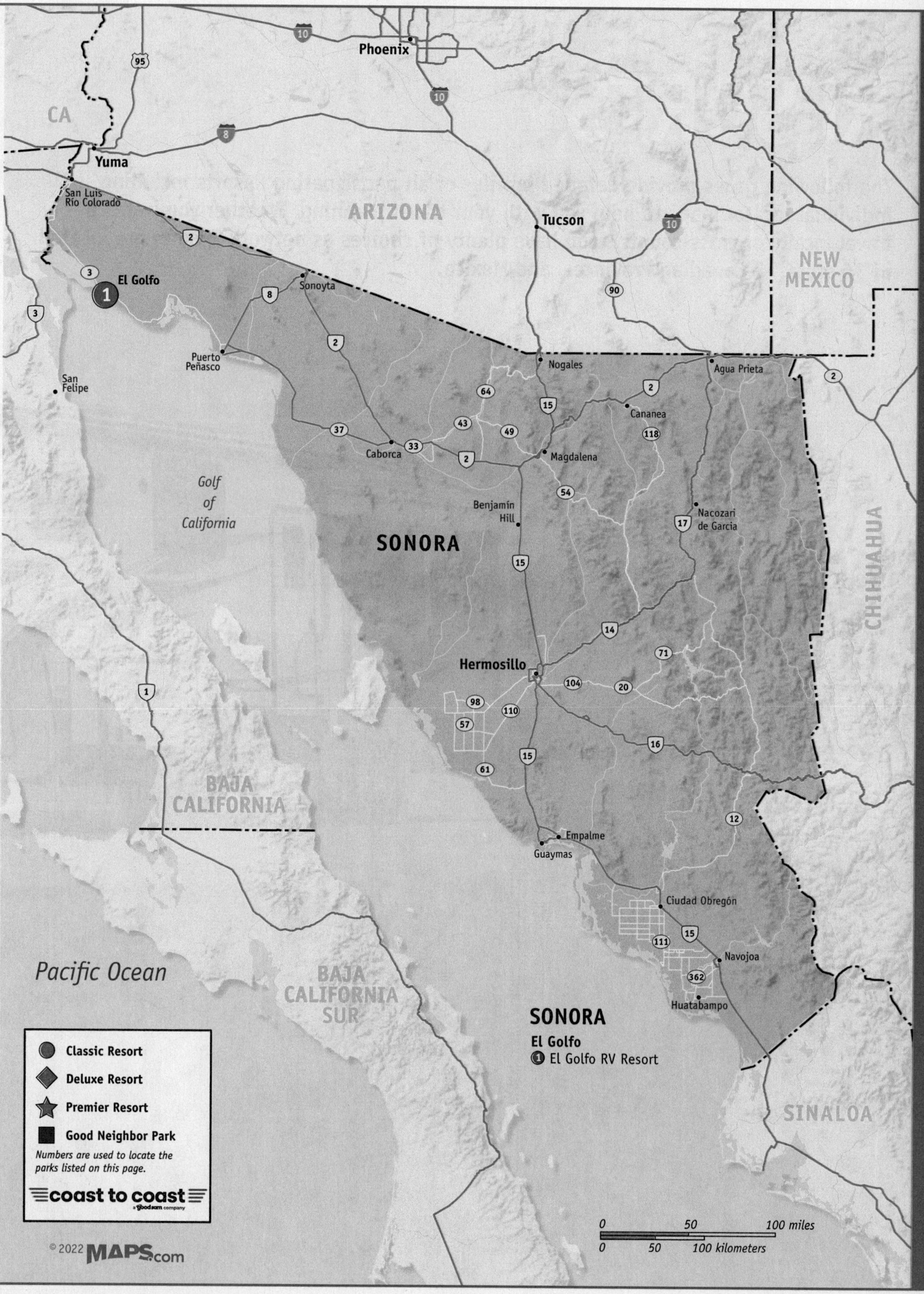

SONORA

El Golfo

1 El Golfo RV Resort

RESORTS

The following pages provide detailed profiles of all participating Resorts including individual locator maps to help you with your travel planning. Whether you want to travel locally or cross-country, you have plenty of choices as network Resorts are located in 36 states, 3 Canadian Provinces, and Mexico.

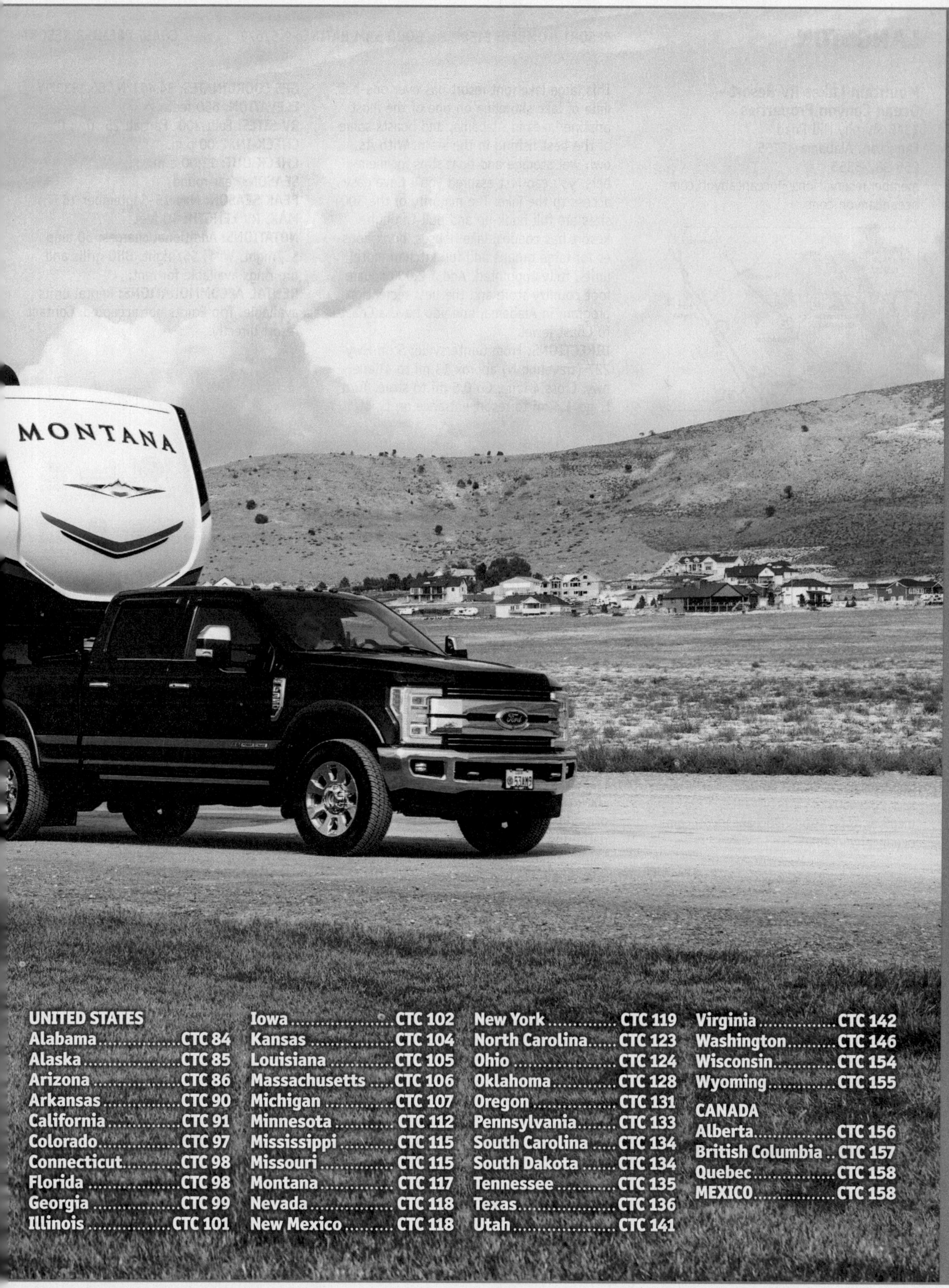
MONTANA

ALABAMA

LANGSTON

RESORT NUMBER: 2158 **GOOD SAM RATING:** 9.5/6/9 **COAST PREMIER RESORT**

Mountain Lakes RV Resort—
Ocean Canyon Properties
1345 Murphy Hill Road
Langston, Alabama 35755
256-582-5556
member.reservations@oceancanyon.com
oceancanyon.com

See page CTC 50 for state map.

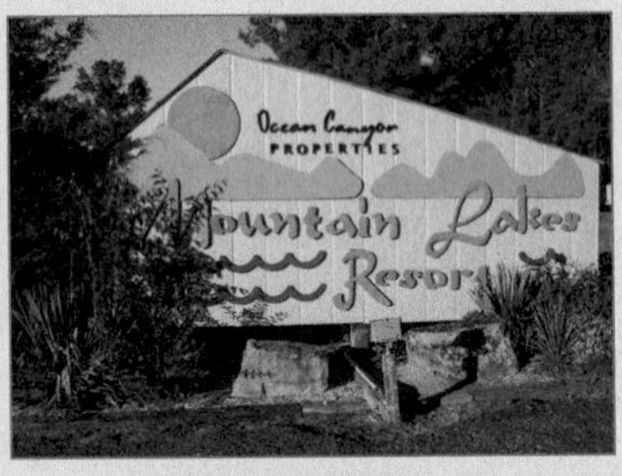

This large lakefront resort has over one-half mile of lake shoreline on one of the most pristine lakes in Alabama, and boasts some of the best fishing in the state. With its own wet storage and boat slips for members, you can rest assured you'll have easy access to the lake. The majority of the 300+ sites are full hook-up and pull-through. Resort has condos, lake houses, bunk houses for large groups and full kitchen motel units, fully appointed. Add a 2,000 square foot country store and the best recreation program in Alabama, and you have a Coast to Coast jewel.

DIRECTIONS: From Guntersville: S on Hwy 227 (traveling N) approx 13 mi to 4-lane hwy. Cross 4-lane. Go 0.5 mi to store. Turn L, go 1.4 mi to resort entrance on L.

GPS COORDINATES: 34.463°N/-86.1833°W
ELEVATION: 650 feet
RV SITES: Full: 200 Partial: 25 Dry: 0
CHECK-IN: 2:00 p.m.
CHECK-OUT: 11:00 a.m.
SEASON: Year-round
PEAK SEASON: May 15–September 15
MAX. RV LENGTH: 40 feet
NOTATIONS: Additional charges: 50 amp $5/night, Wi-Fi $5/night. BBQ grills and fire rings available for rent.
RENTAL ACCOMMODATIONS: Rental units available. Trip Points not accepted. Contact resort directly.

50 amps · pull-through · dump station · laundry · pets/restrictions · internet access · Wi-Fi access · playground · picnic tables · restaurant/snack bar · rental units · fishing · shuffleboard · horseshoes · group activities · boating · recreation hall · church services · outdoor pool · mini golf · basketball · tennis · volleyball · game room · tourist attraction · fitness · shopping · propane · spa · indoor pool · hot showers · fire rings · rv supplies · tenting · handicap access · ice · grills

ALABAMA

ROBERTSDALE

RESORT NUMBER: 222 **GOOD SAM RATING:** 9/8.5★/8 **COAST CLASSIC RESORT**

Styx River RV Resort—
Ocean Canyon Properties
25301 Waterworld Road
Robertsdale, Alabama 36567
251-202-4509
member.reservations@oceancanyon.com
oceancanyon.com

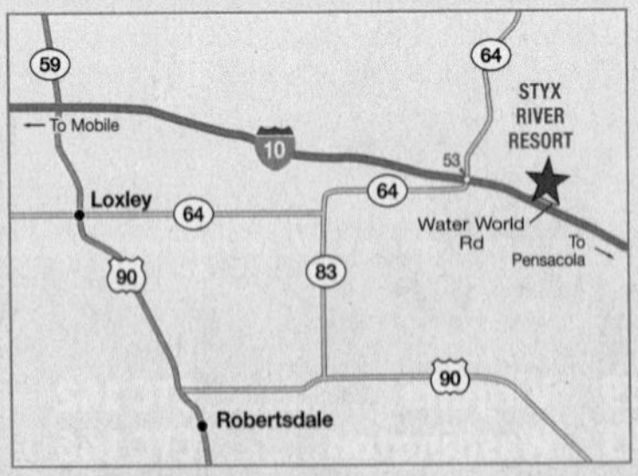

See page CTC 50 for state map.

Styx River takes you to the backwoods of Alabama with a resort experience. The resort sits on the Styx River, famous for recreation, floating, fishing and swimming. The outdoor pavilion hosts live bands, karaoke and the large screen TVs are a regular gathering spot for all of the Bama, LSU and Saints games. Resort has indoor and outdoor pools, a large clubhouse and scheduled activities including casino bus tours. Don't forget we're located 30 minutes from Gulf Shores and both Pensacola and Mobile. A great vacation spot!

DIRECTIONS: From I-10, take Wilcox Rd/Ex 53 to N side of I-10. R on service road at BP Station. E on service road (Water World Rd) 1.2 miles to entrance.

GPS COORDINATES: 30.6232°N/-87.5933°W
ELEVATION: 120 feet
RV SITES: Full: 136 Partial: 18 Dry: 0
CHECK-IN: 2:00 p.m.
CHECK-OUT: 11:00 a.m.
SEASON: Year-round
MAX. RV LENGTH: 40 feet
NOTATIONS: Additional charges: 50 amp $5/night, Wi-Fi $5/night.
RENTAL ACCOMMODATIONS: Rental units available. Trip Points not accepted. Contact resort directly.

50 amps · pull-through · dump station · laundry · pets/restrictions · internet access · Wi-Fi access · playground · picnic tables · restaurant/snack bar · rental units · fishing · shuffleboard · horseshoes · group activities · recreation hall · outdoor pool · mini golf · basketball · beach · volleyball · game room · tourist attraction · shopping · indoor pool · handicap access · ice

ROBERTSDALE

RESORT NUMBER: 750 **GOOD SAM RATING:** 8/9★/8.5 **COAST DELUXE RESORT**

ALABAMA

Wilderness RV Park—
Sugar Beach Resort
24280 Patterson Road
Robertsdale, Alabama 36567
251-960-1195; fax: 251-960-1196
wildernessrv@gulftel.com
wildernessrvpark.com

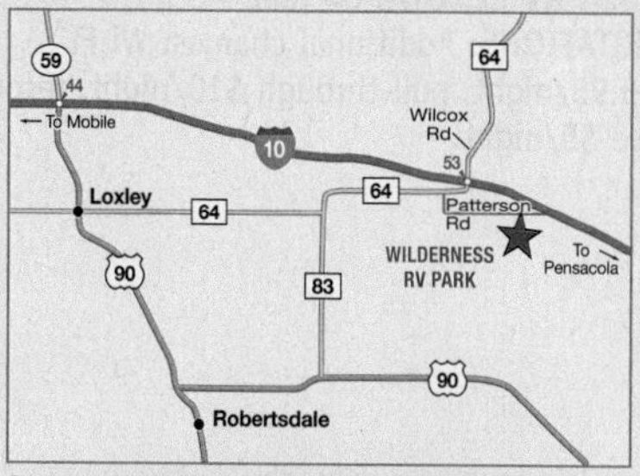

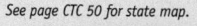

See page CTC 50 for state map.

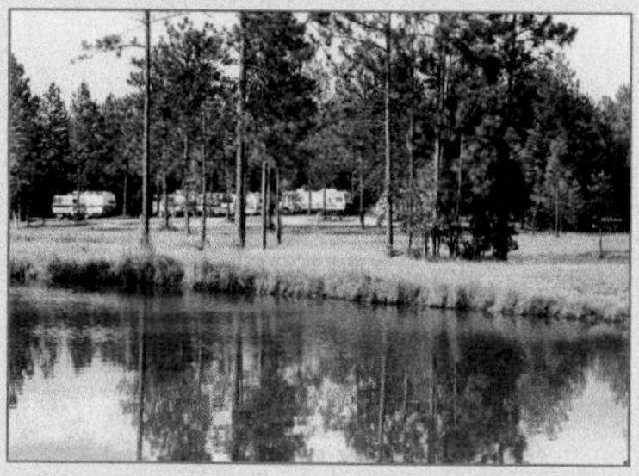

Located on I-10 22 miles west of Pensacola, Florida and 27 miles east of Mobile, Alabama. Miracle Strip beaches and other historic sights all within a short drive. Area attractions: Six golf courses, the Naval Aviation Museum, excellent deep sea and fresh water fishing, hunting, canoeing and other water sports.

DIRECTIONS: From I-10 (between Mobile and Pensacola): Ex 53/Wilcox Rd. S 0.2 mi, past Cheveron Station. L and follow Patterson Rd. 1.3 miles to resort.

GPS COORDINATES: 30.6187°N/-87.6113°W
RV SITES: Full: 71 Partial: 0 Dry: 6
CHECK-IN: 9:00 a.m.–6:00 p.m.
CHECK-OUT: Noon
SEASON: Year-round
PEAK SEASON: January 1–April 30
MAX. RV LENGTH: Unlimited
NOTATIONS: Additional charges: 50 amp $2.78/night including tax. Wi-Fi access in campground. No golf carts. No USPS mail accepted for campers.

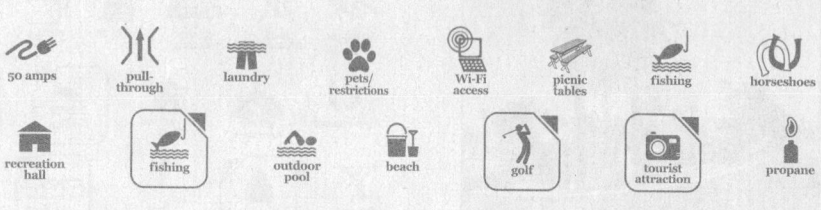

50 amps · pull-through · laundry · pets/restrictions · Wi-Fi access · picnic tables · fishing · horseshoes · recreation hall · fishing · outdoor pool · beach · golf · tourist attraction · propane

SOLDOTNA

RESORT NUMBER: 1301 **GOOD SAM RATING:** 6.5/8/7 **COAST CLASSIC RESORT**

ALASKA

Edgewater RV Resort—
Sunrise Resorts
48798 Funny River Road
Soldotna, Alaska 99669
907-262-7733
edgewaterlodge@sunriseresorts.com
sunriseresorts.com

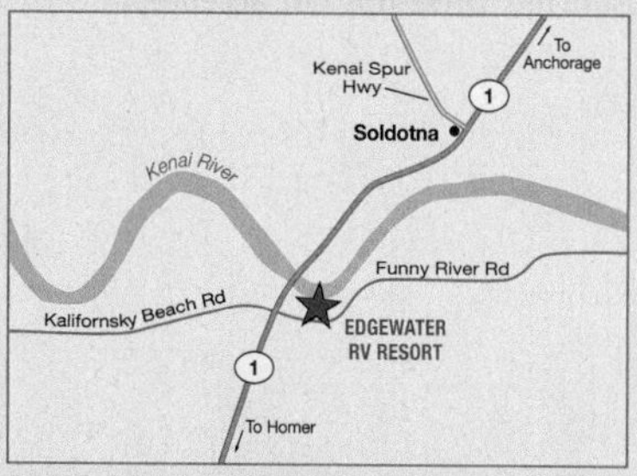

See page CTC 51 for state map.

Edgewater RV Park is located in Soldotna on the banks of the Kenai River known for its world-class salmon fishing. Soldotna is just a short drive to many points of interest on the Kenai Peninsula. Its central location offers fishermen and campers many modern conveniences while enjoying the beauty of Alaska.

DIRECTIONS: From Anchorage Seward Hwy: Ex on Sterling Hwy. S to Soldotna. Cross Kenai River Bridge. L at stoplight. Resort is 400 ft on L.

GPS COORDINATES: 60.4746°N/-151.0811°W
RV SITES: Full: 50 Partial: 18 Dry: 10
CHECK-IN: Noon–8:00 p.m.
CHECK-OUT: 11:00 a.m.
SEASON: May 15–September 1
MAX. RV LENGTH: 40 feet
NOTATIONS: Rate includes 1 RV, 1 vehicle and 4 people. Additional charges: Extra person over 4 $5/night, late check-out and early check-in $5-strictly enforced, resort fee $3/night, showers $1.50, Wi-Fi $1.95/day, extra vehicle $5/night, also add'l fees for cargo trailers, boats, etc. Sewer access is limited, must arrive with empty tanks or $15 dump fee.
RENTAL ACCOMMODATIONS: Rental units available. Trip Points not accepted. Contact resort directly.

30 amps · laundry · pets/restrictions · internet access · Wi-Fi access · rental units · fishing · shuffleboard · recreation hall · fishing · tourist attraction · hot showers

ARIZONA

BULLHEAD CITY

RESORT NUMBER: 2254 **GOOD SAM RATING:** 10/9.5★/10 **COAST DELUXE RESORT**

Silver View RV Resort
1501 Gold Rush Road
Bullhead City, Arizona 86442
928-763-5500; fax: 928-758-8631
office@silverviewrvresort.com
silverviewrvresort.com

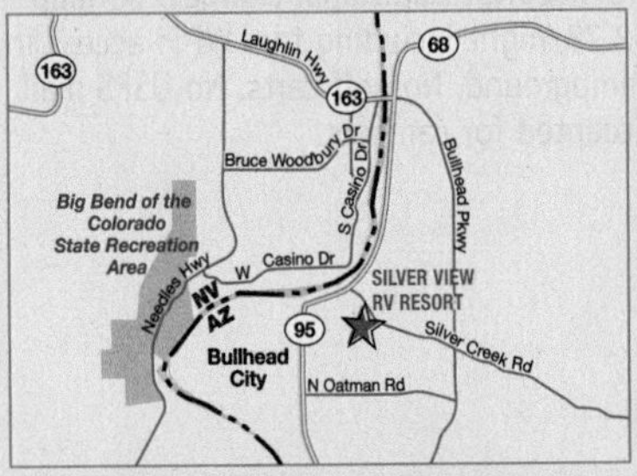

See page CTC 52 for state map.

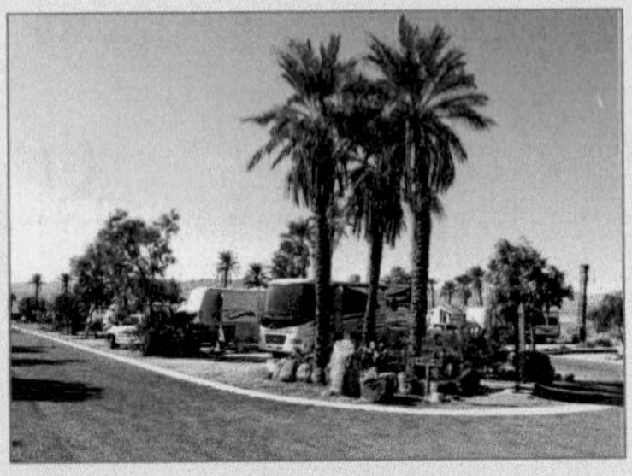

Resort sits on a ridge with a view of Laughlin, the Colorado River, and colorful casino lights. At sunset you can watch the mountains turn shades of pink, red and yellow. Resort is well maintained with beautiful landscaping, mature trees, and 260 sites with 30 and 50 amp. Two dog runs provide plenty of room for your dog. Deli has Boars Head meats and cheeses, come in or call for room service to your RV. Our friendly staff, large lots, paved roads, and plenty of small wildlife will make your stay one to remember.

DIRECTIONS: From Kingman: I-40 to Hwy 93 N to AZ 68 W to Bullhead City. At Laughlin Bridge S on Hwy 95 for 4.5 mi. L on Silver Creek Rd 0.7 mi, turn R on Goldrush Rd. GPS address: 1501 Goldrush Rd, Bullhead City, AZ.

GPS COORDINATES: 35.1134°N/-114.572°W
ELEVATION: 600 feet
RV SITES: Full: 266 Partial: 0 Dry: 100
CHECK-IN: 1:00 p.m.–5:00 p.m.
CHECK-OUT: Noon
SEASON: Year-round
PEAK SEASON: September 15–December 23
MAX. RV LENGTH: 64 feet
NOTATIONS: Additional charges: Wi-Fi $5.95/night, pull-through $10/night, resort fee $5/night.

50 amps · pull-through · dump station · cable tv · visitor mail · laundry · pets/restrictions · Wi-Fi access · restaurant/snack bar · hot tub · hiking trails · horseshoes · group activities · recreation hall · fishing · boating · outdoor pool · golf · game room · tourist attraction · fitness · shopping · hot showers · gambling casino · grocery · rv supplies · gift shop · handicap access · ice

ARIZONA

BULLHEAD CITY

RESORT NUMBER: 603 **GOOD SAM RATING:** 8/8/8 **COAST CLASSIC RESORT**

Sunrise Adventures—Ridgeview
775 Bullhead Parkway
Bullhead City, Arizona 86429
928-754-3809; res.: 760-663-4968
robinj@cramember.com
coloradoriveradventures.com

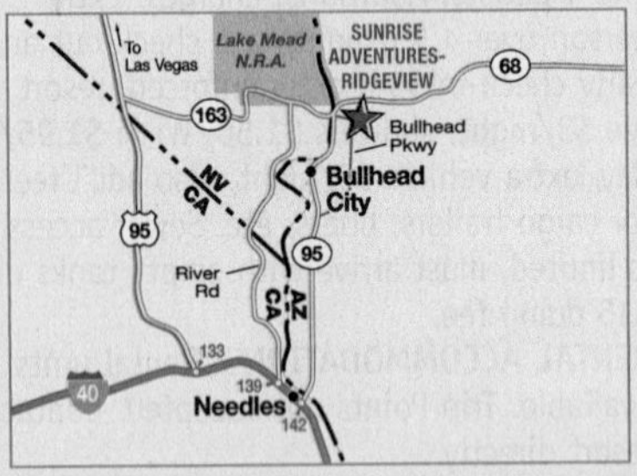

See page CTC 52 for state map.

Less than a mile from the Colorado River in the Mojave Valley, a mecca for boating, fishing and water skiing. Directly across the border from Laughlin, NV with 10 casinos. Just 2 hours from Las Vegas and 1 hour from the London Bridge in Lake Havasu City.

DIRECTIONS: From Las Vegas: Hwy 95 S to Hwy 163. E to Laughlin and cross Laughlin Bridge into AZ. E on Bullhead Pkwy for 0.5 mi to resort. From Needles: W Broadway-River Rd Ex. L at K St (flashing light). Cross Colorado River Bridge. N on Hwy 95. R on Bullhead Pkwy. Resort approx 9 mi on R.

GPS COORDINATES: 35.1719°N/-114.5554°W
RV SITES: Full: 302 Partial: 0 Dry: 0
CHECK-IN: Noon–6:00 p.m.
CHECK-OUT: 11:00 a.m.
SEASON: Year-round
MAX. RV LENGTH: 45 feet
NOTATIONS: Additional charges: $3 per day resort fee. Drive-ups not accepted.

50 amps · pets/restrictions · internet access · hot tub · shuffleboard · hiking trails · horseshoes · recreation hall · fishing · boating · outdoor pool · tourist attraction · gambling casino

CORNVILLE

RESORT NUMBER: 277 **GOOD SAM RATING:** 5/7/5.5 **COAST CLASSIC RESORT**

ARIZONA

Page Springs—Sunrise Resorts
1951 North Page Springs Road
Cornville, Arizona 86325
928-634-4309
pagesprings@sunriseresorts.com
sunriseresorts.com

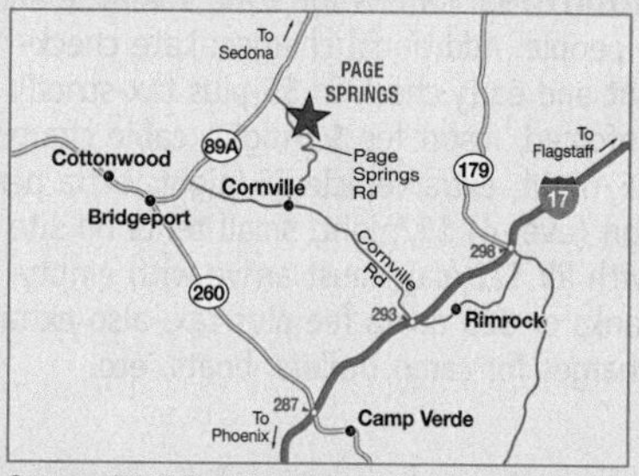

See page CTC 52 for state map.

Located on Oak Creek with old cottonwood trees and artesian streams. Restaurant for fine dining, four wineries and tasting rooms closeby.

DIRECTIONS: From Phoenix: I-17 N 90 mi to Cottonwood Ex 287. 14 mi on Hwy 260 to Cottonwood. R on Rte 89 A. 8 mi to CR 50 (Page Springs Fish Hatchery). R to resort 2 mi on L. Entrance is at Up The Creek Restaurant. From Flagstaff: I-17 S to Cottonwood Ex 287, follow directions above. Cornville Road and Rte 89 A from Flagstaff not recommended.

GPS COORDINATES: 34.7673°N/-111.8921°W
ELEVATION: 3,300 feet
RV SITES: Full: 25 Partial: 40 Dry: 0
CHECK-IN: Noon–6:00 p.m.
CHECK-OUT: 11:00 a.m.
SEASON: Year-round
MAX. RV LENGTH: 30 feet
NOTATIONS: Rate includes 1 RV, 1 vehicle, 4 people, water and electric. No 50 amp service. Additional charges: Late check-out and early check-in $5 plus tax-strictly enforced, resort fee $3/night, cable charge, extra vehicle $5/night, extra person (over 4) $5/night, no extra tent allowed on site. No boat or cargo trailer storage. No ATV's or ORV's allowed. Sewer access is limited, arrive with empty tanks or $25 dump fee.

30 amps | dump station | pets/restrictions | internet access | hiking trails | horseshoes | recreation hall | fishing | tourist attraction | shopping

FORT MOHAVE

RESORT NUMBER: 476 **GOOD SAM RATING:** 7.5/6.5/5.5 **COAST CLASSIC RESORT**

ARIZONA

Riverside Adventure Trails
4750 South Highway 95
Fort Mohave, Arizona 86426
928-763-8800; fax: 928-763-5514
rsatrvpark.com

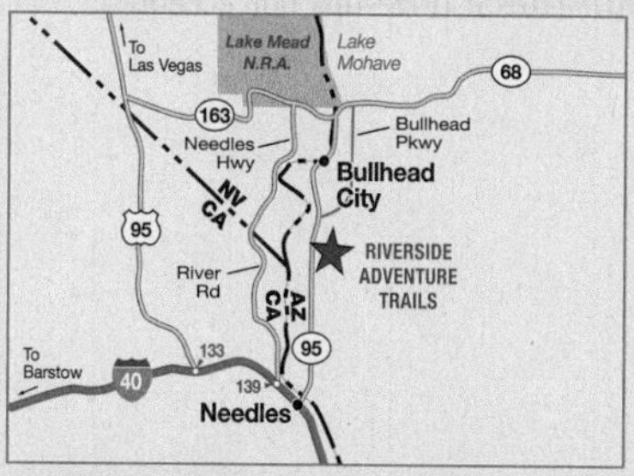

See page CTC 52 for state map.

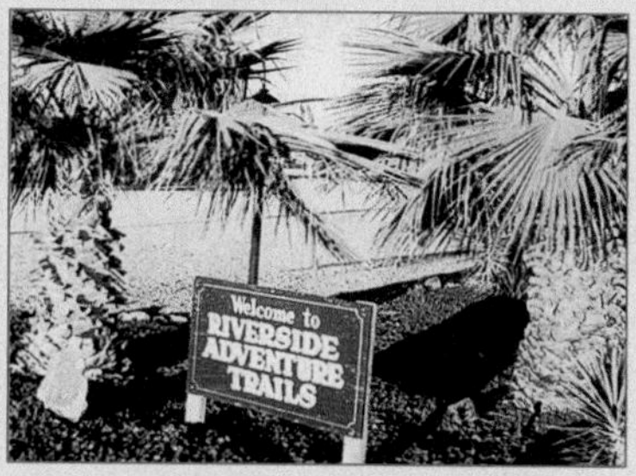

Located near the Colorado River, Lake Mojave and Davis Dam, where year-round boating, water skiing, swimming and fishing are available. Laughlin and Las Vegas, Nevada are easily accessible. Other nearby attractions include Hoover Dam, Oatman and the London Bridge at Lake Havasu City.

DIRECTIONS: From Las Vegas: Hwy 95 S to Hwy 163. Drive E on Hwy 163 to Laughlin, NV. Cross bridge to AZ. Cross Hwy 95 to Bullhead Pkwy and go to the end. L at signal (Hwy 95 again). 2 mi-100 ft past mi marker 238 to resort. From Barstow, CA: I-40 to Needles. Ex at W Broadway. Follow to signs that say Bullhead City. Cross bridge to AZ. N on Hwy 95 to 0.7 mi past mi marker 237 (on Hwy 95) or 100 ft S of mi marker 238.

GPS COORDINATES: 35.0189°N/-114.5965°W
RV SITES: Full: 350 Partial: 0 Dry: 0
CHECK-IN: 10:00 a.m.
CHECK-OUT: 10:00 a.m.
SEASON: Year-round
MAX. RV LENGTH: 60 feet
NOTATIONS: Credit cards and debit cards not accepted. Additional charges: Electric $1/night. Wi-Fi access in campground. Please contact resort directly for reservation.

50 amps | pets/restrictions | Wi-Fi access | hot tub | shuffleboard | hiking trails | horseshoes | recreation hall | fishing | boating | outdoor pool | tourist attraction | gambling casino

ARIZONA

HAPPY JACK

RESORT NUMBER: 154 **GOOD SAM RATING:** 5/7/6 **COAST CLASSIC RESORT**

Clint's Well—Sunrise Resorts
Junction of Highway 87 & FH3
Happy Jack, Arizona 86024
928-477-2299
clintswell@sunriseresorts.com
sunriseresorts.com

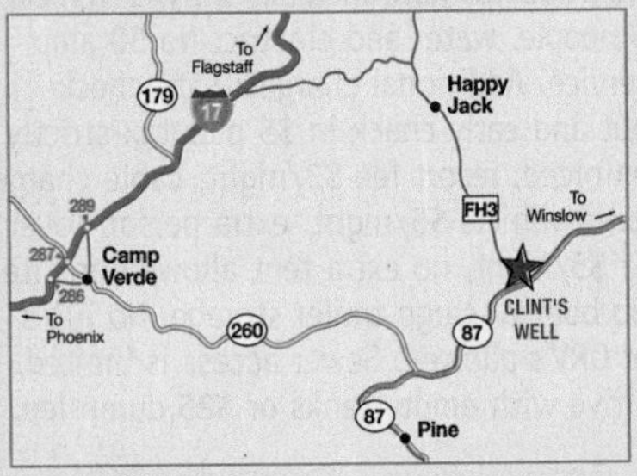

See page CTC 52 for state map.

Resort features mountain air and ponderosa pines of the Coconino National Forest. Deer, elk, and smaller wildlife visit the grounds, and lakes are ready for anglers and water sports. Perfect for a mountain getaway.

DIRECTIONS: From Phoenix: N on I-17 to Camp Verde (Ex 286 or 287). Hwy 260 E approx 40 mi to Jct with Hwy 87. L for approx 10 mi to Jct with FH 3. L approx 0.5 mi to first R. Part of Hwy 260 is winding and steep. From Winslow: Hwy 87 S approx 52 mi to FH 3. R 0.5 mi. 1st R to park. From Flagstaff: I-17 Lake Mary Rd Ex/FH 3. S approx 62 mi to last L before intersection with Hwy 87.

GPS COORDINATES: 34.5543°N/-111.3117°W
ELEVATION: 7,000 feet
RV SITES: Full: 40 Partial: 0 Dry: 0
CHECK-IN: Noon–6:00 p.m.
CHECK-OUT: 11:00 a.m.
SEASON: May 15–September 29
MAX. RV LENGTH: 34 feet
NOTATIONS: Rate is for 1 RV, 1 vehicle and 4 people. Additional charges: Late check-out and early check-in $5 plus tax-strictly enforced, resort fee $3/night, cable charge $5/night, extra vehicle $5/night, extra person (over 4) $5/night, small tents on site with RV $20/day, must arrive with empty tanks or $25 dump fee plus tax, also extra charges for cargo trailers, boats, etc.

30 amps · pets/restrictions · internet access · Wi-Fi access · hiking trails · horseshoes · recreation hall · fishing · boating · golf

ARIZONA

LAKE HAVASU CITY

RESORT NUMBER: 597 **GOOD SAM RATING:** 6.5/7.5/7 **COAST DELUXE RESORT**

Lake Havasu RV Park—
Colorado River Adventures
3829 London Bridge Road
Lake Havasu City, Arizona 86403
866-663-2727; fax: 760-663-4945
robinj@cramember.com
coloradoriveradventures.com

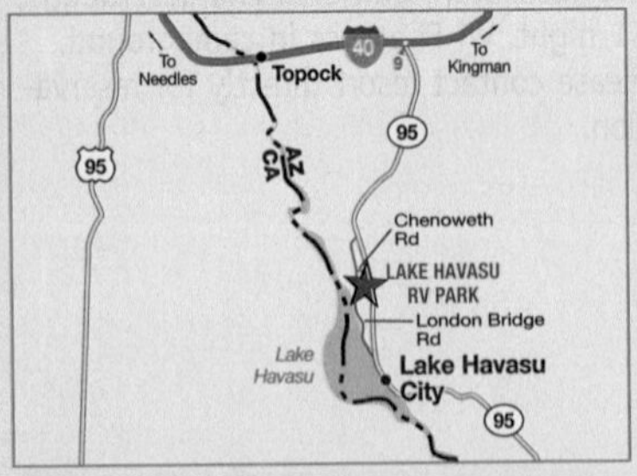

See page CTC 52 for state map.

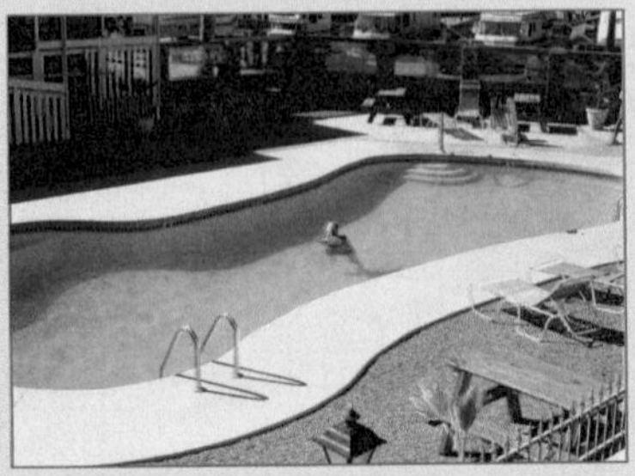

Near Old English Village and London Bridge, imported by Robert McCullough. This desert community has a beautiful lake for a playground as well as many fine desert activities. The city has three golf courses and many fine dining and shopping opportunities. The annual London Bridge Days are held each fall.

DIRECTIONS: From I-40: S on AZ Hwy 95 to Chenoweth Dr. R (W) on Chenoweth to London Bridge Rd. L (S) on London Bridge Rd, 0.2 mi to resort.

GPS COORDINATES: 34.5442°N/-114.3666°W
RV SITES: Full: 88 Partial: 0 Dry: 0
CHECK-IN: 9:00 a.m.–6:00 p.m.
CHECK-OUT: 11:00 a.m.
SEASON: September 15–May 15
PEAK SEASON: December 1–April 1
MAX. RV LENGTH: 40 feet
NOTATIONS: Drive-ups not accepted.

30 amps · pets/restrictions · picnic tables · hot tub · shuffleboard · horseshoes · recreation hall · outdoor pool · golf · tourist attraction · shopping

OVERGAARD

RESORT NUMBER: 278 **GOOD SAM RATING:** 5/6/6.5 **COAST DELUXE RESORT**

ARIZONA

White Mountain—Sunrise Resorts
2162 Camperland Road
Overgaard, Arizona 85933
928-535-5978
whitemountain@sunriseresorts.com
sunriseresorts.com

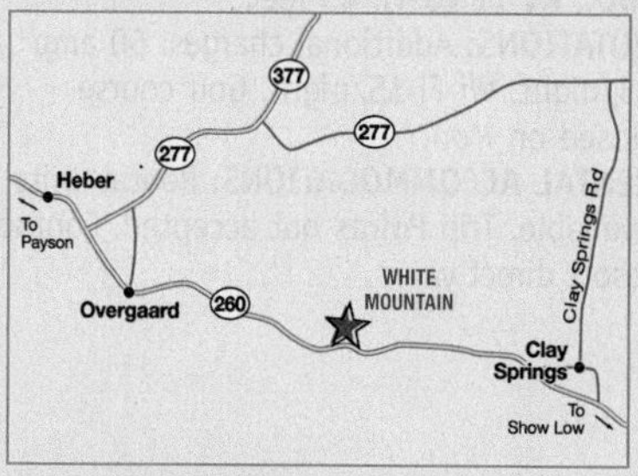

See page CTC 52 for state map.

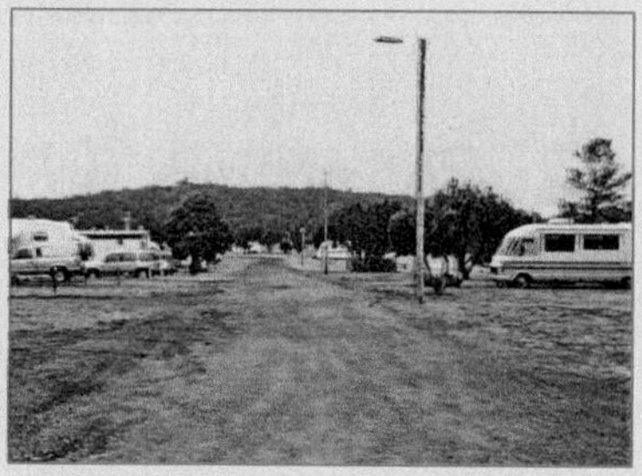

A peaceful retreat in the cool mountain air of a scenic recreation area. Scores of mountain lakes offer fishing challenges. Wildlife and miles of hiking trails with scattered Indian artifacts give nature lovers hours of enjoyment. Secrecy and seclusion a short drive from civilization.

DIRECTIONS: From Phoenix/Mesa: N on Hwy 87 to Payson to Rte 260 E. Through Heber. 7 mi past Overgaard on Rte 260 to resort on L near mi marker 317. Approx 23 mi from Show Low on Rte 260.

GPS COORDINATES: 34.3682°N/-110.4063°W
ELEVATION: 6,800 feet
RV SITES: Full: 30 Partial: 30 Dry: 25
CHECK-IN: Noon–6:00 p.m.
CHECK-OUT: 11:00 a.m.
SEASON: May 15–September 15
MAX. RV LENGTH: 40 feet
NOTATIONS: Rate includes RV, 1 vehicle, 2 adults, 2 children under 18, water and electric. No cable. Additional charges: Late check-out and early check-in $5 plus tax-strictly enforced, resort fee $3/night, cable charge, extra vehicle $5/night, extra person $5/night, small tent on site with RV $20/night, also extra charges for cargo trailers, boats, etc. Sewer access is limited, must arrive with empty tanks or $25 dump fee. Drive-ups not accepted.

YUMA

RESORT NUMBER: 525 **GOOD SAM RATING:** 7.5/8.5★/8 **COAST DELUXE RESORT**

ARIZONA

Yuma Lakes—
Colorado River Adventures
6275 South Avenue 8 1/2 East
Yuma, Arizona 85365
760-663-4968; fax: 760-663-4945
robinj@cramember.com
coloradoriveradventures.com

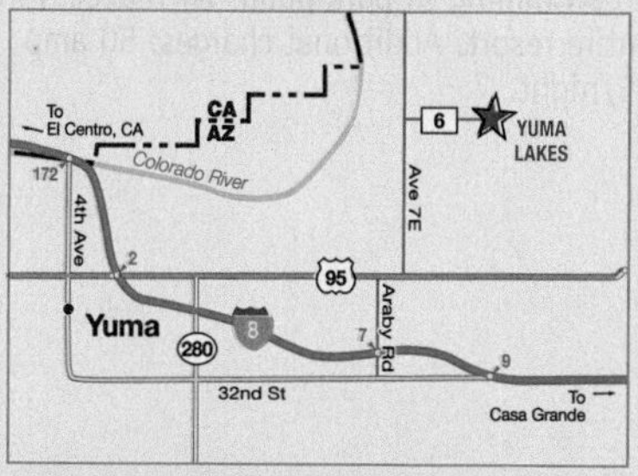

See page CTC 52 for state map.

In the southwest corner of Arizona, located just 6 miles from Yuma. On a refreshing lake offering canoeing, row boating and fishing as a contrast to the desert beauty of the area. Yuma offers shopping and dining. San Luis and Rio Colorado in Mexico are a short drive away for additional touring opportunities.

DIRECTIONS: From Yuma Hwy 95 N: 6 mi to 7E (near Circle K store). L for 3 mi. R on County 6 St. 1.5 mi to resort. From I-8: Araby Rd Ex. N to Hwy 95. R to Circle K. L and follow same as previous.

GPS COORDINATES: 32.7407°N/-114.4838°W
RV SITES: Full: 180 Partial: 0 Dry: 0
CHECK-IN: 9:00 a.m.–6:00 p.m.
CHECK-OUT: 11:00 a.m.
SEASON: September 15–May 15
PEAK SEASON: December 1–April 1
MAX. RV LENGTH: 40 feet
NOTATIONS: Drive-ups not accepted.

ASHDOWN

RESORT NUMBER: 574 **GOOD SAM RATING:** 9/8.5★/9 **COAST PREMIER RESORT**

Millwood Landing Golf & RV Resort—Ocean Canyon Properties
596 Highway 317
Ashdown, Arkansas 71822
870-898-5320
member.reservations@oceancanyon.com
oceancanyon.com

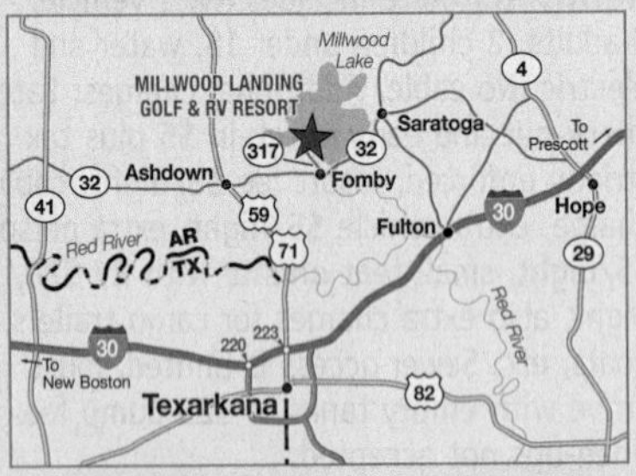

See page CTC 53 for state map.

Located in the southeast corner of Arkansas, Millwood Landing sits on one of Arkansas' premier bass lakes. The resort features southern Arkansas' longest 18-hole golf course, a par 72 challenging course woven through the tall and wispy pines. The resort has a great pool complex and 14 lakefront cabins.

DIRECTIONS: From Texarkana: Hwy 71 N 16 mi to Hwy 32. E on Hwy 32 at Ashdown. 7 mi to Hwy 317. N on 317 for 2.5 mi to resort on R.

GPS COORDINATES: 33.7131°N/-94.0139°W
ELEVATION: 266 feet
RV SITES: Full: 32 Partial: 0 Dry: 0
CHECK-IN: 2:00 p.m.
CHECK-OUT: 11:00 a.m.
SEASON: March 1–December 31
PEAK SEASON: May 15–September 15
MAX. RV LENGTH: 45 feet
NOTATIONS: Additional charges: 50 amp $5/night, Wi-Fi $5/night. Golf course closed on Mon.
RENTAL ACCOMMODATIONS: Rental units available. Trip Points not accepted. Contact resort directly.

50 amps, pull-through, dump station, visitor mail, laundry, pets/restrictions, internet access, Wi-Fi access, playground, picnic tables, rental units, horseshoes, recreation hall, boating, outdoor pool, basketball, volleyball, golf, tourist attraction, shopping, hot showers, handicap access

SHIRLEY

RESORT NUMBER: 1198 **GOOD SAM RATING:** 8.5/8.5★/9 **COAST DELUXE RESORT**

Golden Pond RV Park
241 Highway 330 South
Shirley, Arkansas 72153
501-723-8212; fax: 501-723-8414
goldenpondrvpark@gmail.com
goldenpondrvpark.com

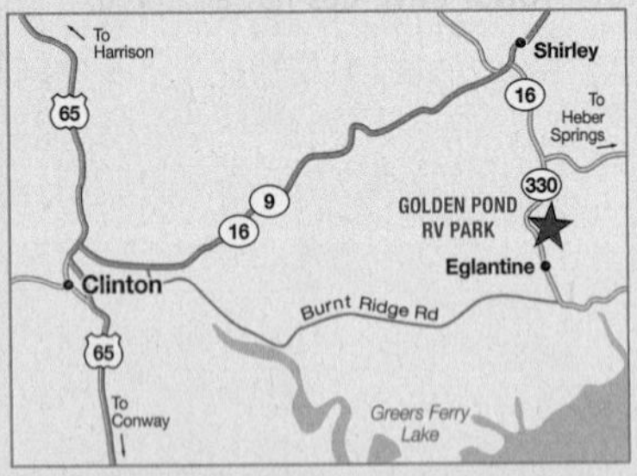

See page CTC 53 for state map.

In addition to enjoying Golden Pond's amenities take time to visit the town of Shirley and surrounding area including two golf courses and Greers Ferry Lake which is a local water playground.

DIRECTIONS: From Clinton: Jct of Hwy 65 and Hwy 16. E 2 mi on Hwy 16. R onto Burnt Ridge Rd. Approx 8 mi to Jct with Hwy 330 S (1st stop sign). L 2.5 mi to park at Jct of Hwy 16 and Hwy 330 S.

GPS COORDINATES: 35.6235°N/-92.3093°W
RV SITES: Full: 50 Partial: 3 Dry: 0
CHECK-IN: 9:00 a.m.–5:00 p.m.
CHECK-OUT: 3:00 p.m.
SEASON: Year-round
MAX. RV LENGTH: 65 feet
NOTATIONS: Rate includes full hook-up. No swimming in park pond. Wi-fi access in entire resort. Additional charges: 50 amp $5/night.

50 amps, pull-through, visitor mail, laundry, pets/restrictions, internet access, Wi-Fi access, hot tub, fishing, hiking trails, group activities, recreation hall, fishing, boating, outdoor pool, golf, spa, gift shop, handicap access

AGUANGA

RESORT NUMBER: 23 **GOOD SAM RATING:** 5.5/7/7 **COAST CLASSIC RESORT**

Sundance Meadows
43425 Sage Road
Aguanga, California 92536
951-767-0716; fax: 951-767-1718
sundancemeadows@earthlink.net
sundancemeadows.us

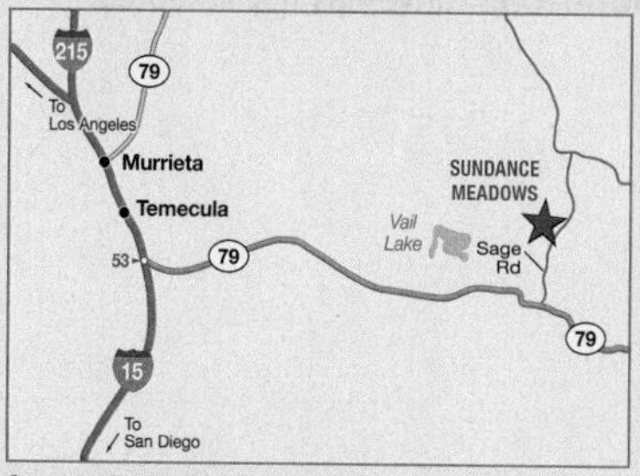

See page CTC 54 for state map.

Sundance Meadows, 70 miles east of Disneyland, is just 1 hour from world-famous Mt. Palomar Observatory. Nestled in a quiet, smog-free valley, the resort is 75 miles from Los Angeles and only 60 miles from San Diego. Favorite activities at the 400-acre ranch-resort are hiking and relaxation.

DIRECTIONS: From Riverside: I-15 S, winds through Corona to Ex for Temecula Pkwy/St Hwy 79. S to Indio. Hwy 79 S 15.5 mi. L on Rte 3 (look for Corner Cafe). Resort 1.7 mi on L on Rte 3/Sage Rd. Entrance is a 3 mi dirt road with a slight grade.

GPS COORDINATES: 33.494°N/-116.933°W
RV SITES: Full: 0 Partial: 60 Dry: 0
CHECK-IN: 9:00 a.m.–4:00 p.m.
CHECK-OUT: Noon
SEASON: Year-round
MAX. RV LENGTH: Unlimited
NOTATIONS: No arrivals/check-in on Mon or Tue. Arrival times Wed-Sat 9 a.m.-4 p.m. and Sun 9 a.m.-3 p.m. No after-hours check-in. Long entry drive. No Wi-Fi.

30 amps · pull-through · dump station · laundry · pets/restrictions · playground · picnic tables · fishing · hiking trails · horseshoes · outdoor pool · tennis · tourist attraction · ball field

BASS LAKE

RESORT NUMBER: 89 **GOOD SAM RATING:** 9.5/8★/9 **COAST DELUXE RESORT**

Bass Lake at Yosemite RV Park
39744 Road 274
Bass Lake, California 93604
559-642-3145; fax: 559-642-3792
info@basslakeatyosemite.com
basslakeatyosemite.com

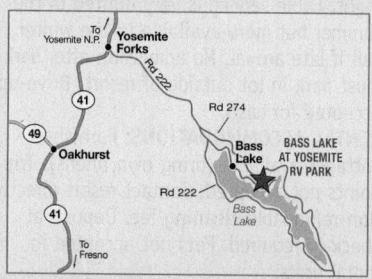

See page CTC 54 for state map.

Near the South Gate of Yosemite Park and next to Bass Lake, one of CA's most scenic lakes, offering fishing, boating, water skiing, sailing, and swimming. Fishermen find good fishing at Bass Lake as well as in the rivers and streams around the resort. Next to the resort is Pines Village, with stores and a marina.

DIRECTIONS: From Fresno: Hwy 41 N through Oakhurst. 3 mi past Oakhurst. R onto Rd 222. Follow winding Rd 222 for 2 mi to fork. L fork/Rd 274. 2.5 mi to resort on R.

GPS COORDINATES: 37.3236°N/-119.5547°W
ELEVATION: 3,500 feet
RV SITES: Full: 147 Partial: 6 Dry: 0
CHECK-IN: 11:00 a.m.–5:00 p.m.
CHECK-OUT: 11:00 a.m.
SEASON: Year-round
PEAK SEASON: May 1–September 30
MAX. RV LENGTH: 40 feet
NOTATIONS: Please contact resort directly to make reservations. Additional charges: Mandatory electric fee 0-49 amps $4.20/night, 50 amps $13.80/night. Wi-Fi access in campground, internet access in clubhouse.
RENTAL ACCOMMODATIONS: Rental units available. Trip Points not accepted. Contact resort directly.

50 amps · pull-through · cable tv · laundry · pets/restrictions · internet access · Wi-Fi access · playground · picnic tables · restaurant/snack bar · rental units · fishing · shuffleboard · hiking trails · horseshoes · recreation hall · fishing · boating · outdoor pool · game room · fitness · shopping · propane · hot showers · gift shop · ice

CALIFORNIA

BEAUMONT

RESORT NUMBER: 1874 **GOOD SAM RATING:** 7.5/8/7 **COAST DELUXE RESORT**

Cherry Valley Lakes Resort—Colorado River Adventures
36805 Brookside Avenue
Beaumont, California 92223
760-663-4968; fax: 760-663-4945
robinj@cramember.com
coloradoriveradventures.com

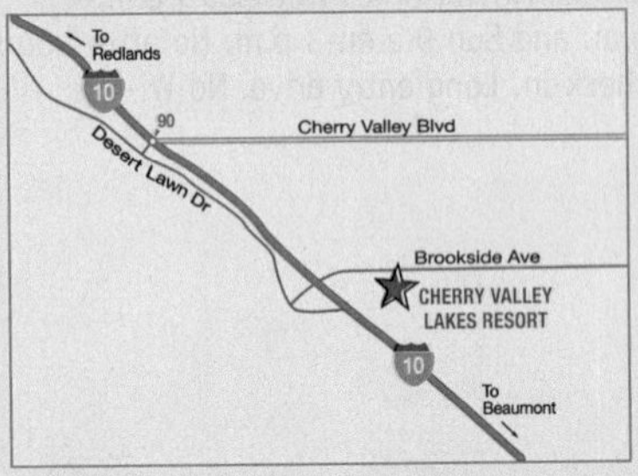

See page CTC 54 for state map.

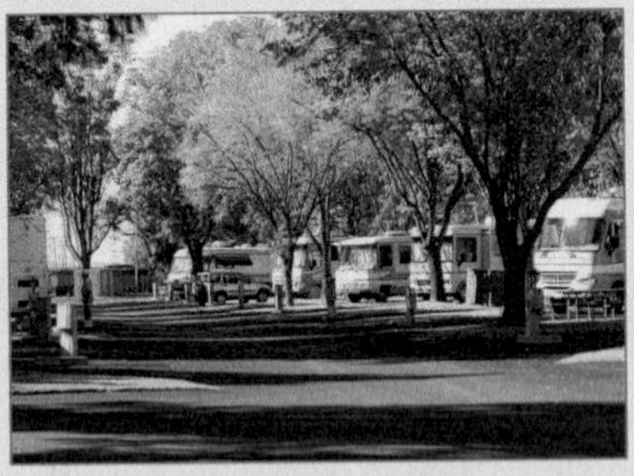

Located near Palm Springs with fishing ponds, swimming pool, covered Jacuzzi, a beautiful clubhouse and lots of trees and grass. Next door to Oak Valley PGA Golf Course and about 15 minutes from Cabazon Factory Outlet Mall (lots of shopping). It's also only 10 minutes from Casino Morongo (lots of fun).

DIRECTIONS: From Jct I-10 & Hwy 79 (Cherry Valley Blvd Ex): S over the Fwy, 1 mi E on Desert Lawn Dr, 0.5 mi N on Brookside Ave. Enter on R.

GPS COORDINATES: 33.9604°N/-117.0186°W
RV SITES: Full: 100 Partial: 0 Dry: 0
CHECK-IN: 9:00 a.m.
CHECK-OUT: 11:00 a.m.
SEASON: Year-round
PEAK SEASON: January 1–December 31
MAX. RV LENGTH: 40 feet
NOTATIONS: Drive-ups not accepted.

CALIFORNIA

DESERT HOT SPRINGS

RESORT NUMBER: 325 **GOOD SAM RATING:** 9.5/9.5★/9 **COAST PREMIER RESORT**

Catalina Spa and RV Resort
18800 Corkill Road
Desert Hot Springs, California 92241
760-329-4431; res.: 877-463-0355
frontdesk1@catalinasparvresort.com
catalinasparvresort.com

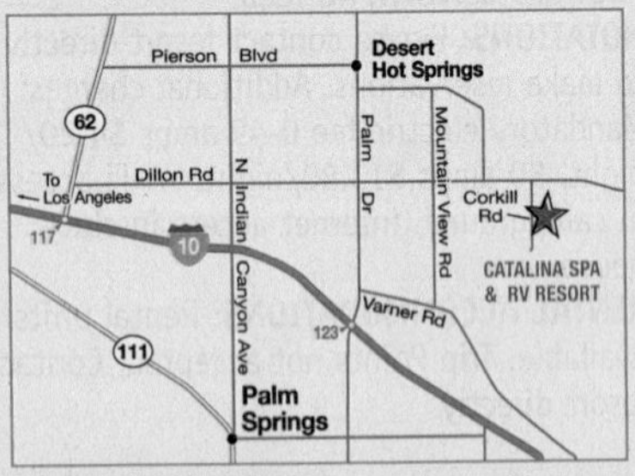

See page CTC 54 for state map.

Within an easy drive from anywhere in Southern California, we feature a combination of five odorless mineral hot springs pools and spas. We offer a wide array of winter seasonal activities and a resort open year-round featuring many recreational amenities for all ages. A short drive to the Greater Palm Springs area and Joshua Tree National Park.

DIRECTIONS: Between Palm Springs and Desert Hot Springs. From Phoenix I-10 W or from Los Angeles I-10 E: Ex 123 to Palm Dr N. R at Dillon Rd. R at Corkill Rd, resort on L. Resort 5.1 mi from Jct Dillon/Palm Dr.

GPS COORDINATES: 33.9134°N/-116.4405°W
RV SITES: Full: 482 Partial: 0 Dry: 0
CHECK-IN: Noon
CHECK-OUT: Noon
SEASON: Year-round
PEAK SEASON: October 1–March 31
MAX. RV LENGTH: 43 feet
NOTATIONS: Reservations not accepted through email. Additional charges: Lower level (30 amp/32 ft & under) $23.45/night, upper level (50 amp/over 32 ft) $28.45/night. Cable service is very limited in the summer but more available in the winter. Call if late arrival. No admission after dark must park in lot outside of resort. Drive-ups accepted for cash.
RENTAL ACCOMMODATIONS: Furnished cottages available (bring own linens). Trip Points not accepted. Contact resort directly. Non-refundable cleaning fee. Deposit at check-in required. Pets not accepted in rental units.

EARP

RESORT NUMBER: 181 **GOOD SAM RATING:** 7.5/7.5/8.5 **COAST PREMIER RESORT**

CALIFORNIA

Emerald Cove—
Colorado River Adventures
2715 Parker Dam Road
Earp, California 92242
760-663-4968; fax: 760-663-4945
robinj@cramember.com
coloradoriveradventures.com

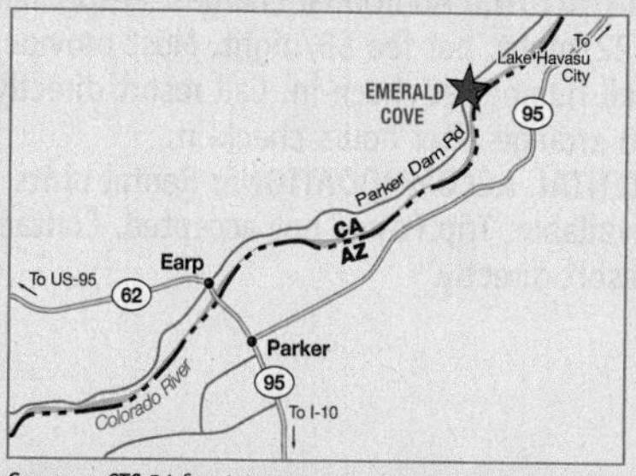

See page CTC 54 for state map.

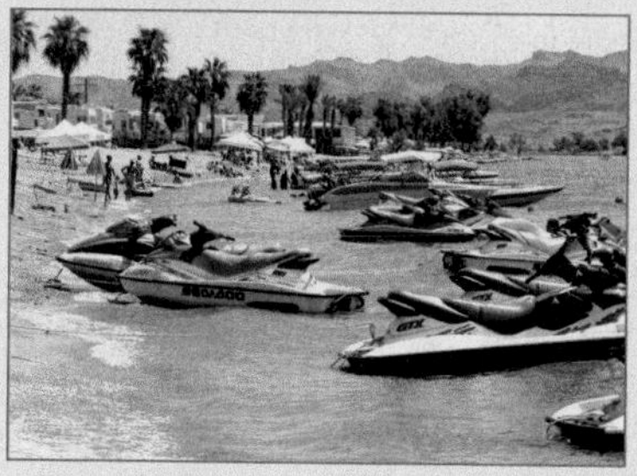

Located on the scenic Colorado River between California and Arizona. The town of Parker was Wyatt Earp's country. The area is replete with Old West names and history. The resort, a short distance from the London Bridge and Laughlin, Nevada, is in a desert setting, yet has lots of water activities.

DIRECTIONS: Between I-40 and I-10 on the Colorado River. 6.3 mi N of Earp, CA on Parker Dam Rd.

GPS COORDINATES: 34.2066°N/-114.2234°W
RV SITES: Full: 410 Partial: 0 Dry: 0
CHECK-IN: 9:00 a.m.–6:00 p.m.
CHECK-OUT: 11:00 a.m.
SEASON: Year-round
PEAK SEASON: December 1–April 1
MAX. RV LENGTH: 40 feet
NOTATIONS: Drive-ups not accepted.
RENTAL ACCOMMODATIONS: Rental units available. Trip Points not accepted. Contact resort directly.

30 amps · pull-through · pets/restrictions · Wi-Fi access · rental units · hot tub · fishing · hiking trails · boating
recreation hall · fishing · boating · outdoor pool · mini golf · beach · tourist attraction · gambling casino

ISLETON

RESORT NUMBER: 1914 **GOOD SAM RATING:** 8/9.5★/8 **COAST PREMIER RESORT**

CALIFORNIA

Delta Shores Resort & Marina
601 Brannan Island Road
Isleton, California 95641
916-777-5577; fax: 916-777-5779
delta_reservations@vistaresorts.net
vistaresorts.net

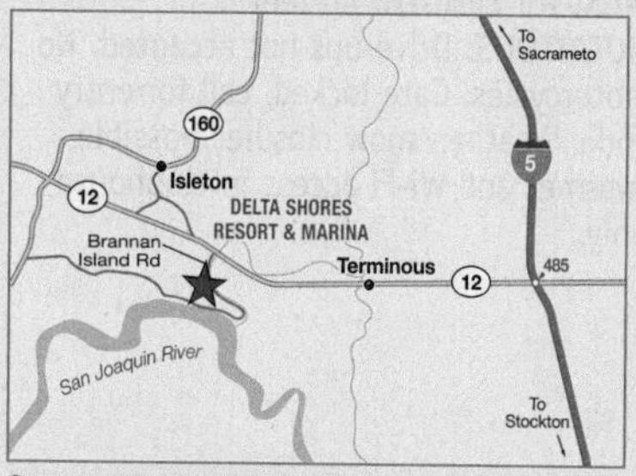

See page CTC 54 for state map.

Delta Shores is located on the Mokelumne River in the heart of the Sacramento Delta Region. This area is a favorite for boating, fishing and water-skiing enthusiasts alike.

DIRECTIONS: From I-5: Hwy 12 W approx 10 mi. Immediately after crossing 2nd bridge on Hwy 12, turn R onto Brannan Island Rd. Resort 1.25 mi on R. From San Francisco Bay area: Through city of Antioch on Hwy 4. Hwy 160 N (toll bridge). R on Hwy 12 approx 5 mi. L onto Brannan Island Rd. Resort 1.25 mi on R.

GPS COORDINATES: 38.1134°N/-121.5879°W
RV SITES: Full: 140 Partial: 35 Dry: 0
CHECK-IN: 10:00 a.m.–10:00 p.m.
CHECK-OUT: 3:00 p.m.
SEASON: Year-round
PEAK SEASON: April 1–September 3
MAX. RV LENGTH: 45 feet
NOTATIONS: Rate is for 30-amp site. Additional charge: Wi-Fi access in campground (fee).

30 amps · laundry · pets/restrictions · Wi-Fi access · playground · hot tub · fishing · horseshoes · group activities
boating · recreation hall · fishing · boating · outdoor pool · mini golf · basketball · hot showers · ice

CALIFORNIA

ISLETON

RESORT NUMBER: 241 **GOOD SAM RATING:** 8/8/8.5 **COAST DELUXE RESORT**

Lighthouse Marina, Restaurant & Resort
151 Brannan Island Road
Isleton, California 95641
916-777-5511; fax: 916-777-6120
info@lighthouseresortandmarina.com
lighthouseresortandmarina.com

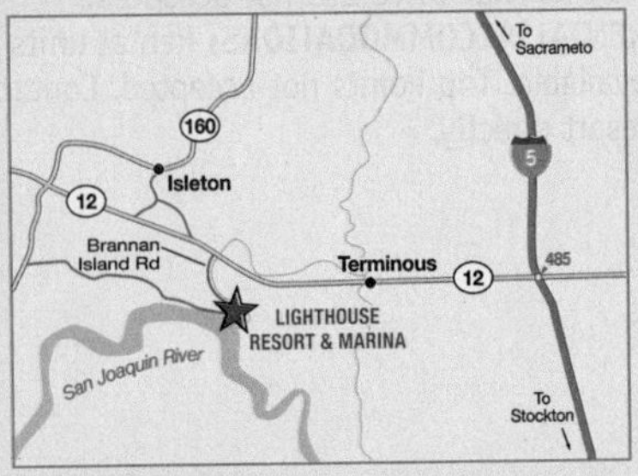

See page CTC 54 for state map.

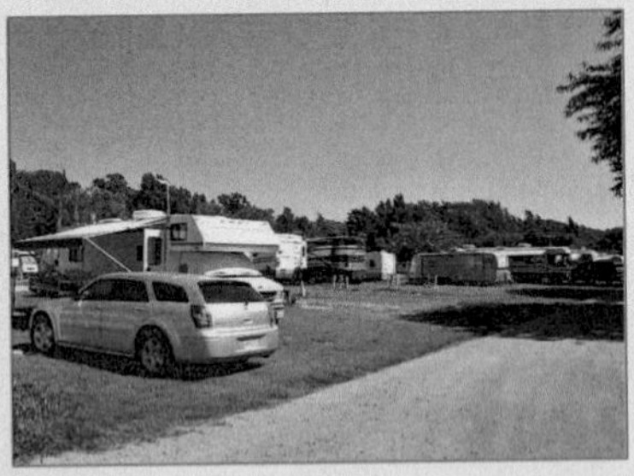

A beautifully landscaped resort located amidst the natural beauty of the Sacramento Delta region, with a marina and waterside bar/restaurant located on the north fork of the Mokolumne River. An hour drive from Napa Valley, Sacramento and the Central Valley with 1,100 miles of waterways to navigate.

DIRECTIONS: From I-5 N of Stockton: Hwy 12 W. Just past 2nd drawbridge R on Brannan Island Rd. 3 mi to resort. From coast: Hwy 12 E to Brannan Island Rd. L on Brannan Island Rd. 3 mi to resort.

GPS COORDINATES: 38.1031°N/-121.5708°W
RV SITES: Full: 120 Partial: 56 Dry: 0
CHECK-IN: 9:00 a.m.–5:00 p.m.
CHECK-OUT: Noon
SEASON: Year-round
PEAK SEASON: April 1–September 30
MAX. RV LENGTH: 45 feet
NOTATIONS: Additional charges: Resort fee $22/night, pet fee $5/night. Must provide cell number at check-in. Call resort directly to arrange after hours check-in.
RENTAL ACCOMMODATIONS: Rental units available. Trip Points not accepted. Contact resort directly.

CALIFORNIA

JULIAN

RESORT NUMBER: 471 **GOOD SAM RATING:** 7.5/7.5/7.5 **COAST DELUXE RESORT**

KQ Ranch Resort— Colorado River Adventures
449 KQ Ranch Road
Julian, California 92036
760-663-4968; fax: 760-663-4945
robinj@cramember.com
coloradoriveradventures.com

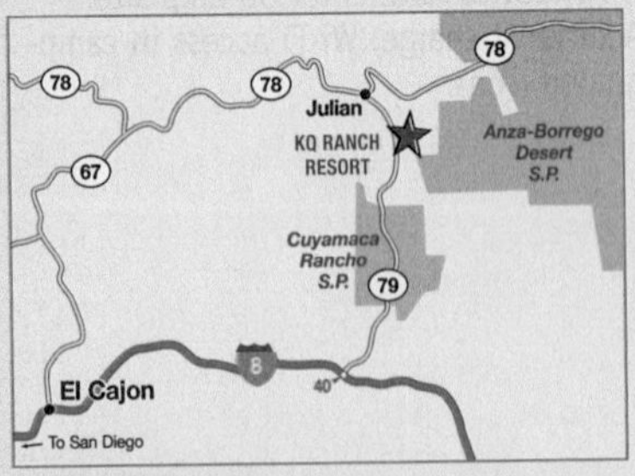

See page CTC 54 for state map.

In the San Diego mountains, the area is rich in natural beauty and interesting activities. Much local folklore centers on the gold rush over 100 years ago. Learn how Eagle Mine and other mines were run. Wild Flower Fair is in May, Apple Days Festival in September and October. Lake Cuyamaca is just down the road.

DIRECTIONS: E of San Diego from I-8: Hwy 79 N (L) toward Julian. Resort is on R approx 24 mi N of I-8. From Los Angeles: I-15 S to Temecula. Hwy 79 S to Julian. Resort approx 5 mi S of Julian on Hwy 79 on L. Roads are narrow and winding.

GPS COORDINATES: 33.0339°N/-116.5592°W
ELEVATION: 4,800 feet
RV SITES: Full: 125 Partial: 115 Dry: 0
CHECK-IN: 9:00 a.m.–4:00 p.m.
CHECK-OUT: 11:00 a.m.
SEASON: Year-round
PEAK SEASON: April 1–November 1
MAX. RV LENGTH: 40 feet
NOTATIONS: Drive-ups not accepted. No motorcycles. Gate locked, call for entry code. Weather/snow closures possible. Internet and Wi-Fi access in clubhouse only.

POLLOCK PINES

RESORT NUMBER: 12 **GOOD SAM RATING:** 8/9★/8.5 **COAST CLASSIC RESORT**

CALIFORNIA

Ghost Mountain Ranch—Colorado River Adventures
5560 Badger Hill Road
Pollock Pines, California 95726
760-663-4968; fax: 530-647-2981
robinj@cramember.com
coloradoriveradventures.com

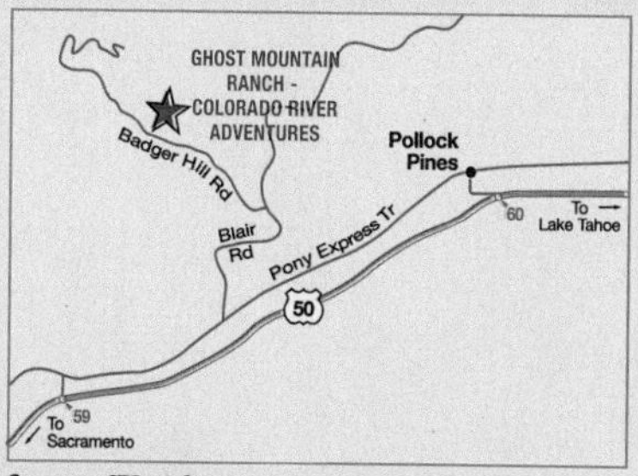

See page CTC 54 for state map.

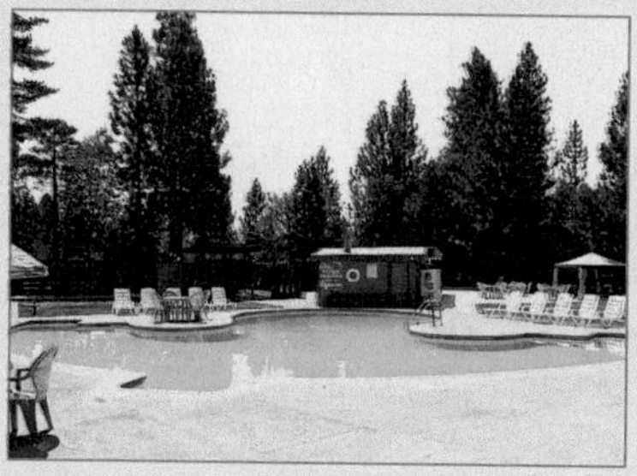

Ghost Mountain Ranch is a family orientated camping resort in the foothills of the Sierra Nevadas near the historic gold mining town of Placerville. It is situated right on the snow line, a half-hour from the rugged grandeur and beauty of Echo Summit and a half-hour from Lake Tahoe. An authentic ghost town and the remains of what was once one of the richest gold mines in the area are on the 325-acre pine preserve.

DIRECTIONS: From Sacramento: Hwy 50 E to first Pollock Pines Ex. Turn L under the freeway. Turn R on Pony Express Trl. Turn L on Blair Rd and L on Badger Hill Rd. Follow signs.

GPS COORDINATES: 39°N/-121°W
ELEVATION: 3,700 feet
RV SITES: Full: 4 Partial: 110 Dry: 30
CHECK-IN: 9:00 a.m.–5:00 p.m.
CHECK-OUT: 11:00 a.m.
SEASON: Year-round
MAX. RV LENGTH: 35 feet
NOTATIONS: Additional charges: Dump station $15 per use. Site includes water, electric and dump station. Drive-ups not accepted.

REDLANDS

RESORT NUMBER: 16 **GOOD SAM RATING:** 8.5/5.5/7 **COAST DELUXE RESORT**

CALIFORNIA

Fisherman's Retreat—Halo Resorts
32300 San Timoteo Canyon Road
Redlands, California 92373
909-795-0171; fax: 909-795-0169
hriinc@aol.com
haloresortsinc.com

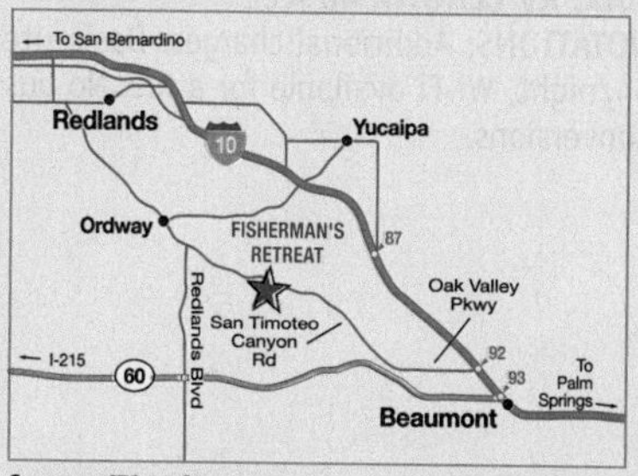

See page CTC 54 for state map.

One of the oldest vacation resorts in the Riverside County area. The 300-acre spot in the beautiful, secluded San Timoteo Canyon offers activity and quiet coves and corners. Man-made lakes are fully stocked with catfish and trout. Weekly bingo, activities and community dances provide exciting entertainment.

DIRECTIONS: From Hwy 60 E: Redlands-Moreno Blvd Ex. N to San Timoteo Canyon Rd. R 3 mi to resort. From I-10 E: Oak Valley Pkwy turnoff. R on San Timoteo Canyon Rd to resort on L.

GPS COORDINATES: 33.9752°N/-117.0991°W
RV SITES: Full: 189 Partial: 0 Dry: 20
CHECK-IN: 1:00 p.m.–7:00 p.m.
CHECK-OUT: 11:00 a.m.
SEASON: Year-round
PEAK SEASON: February 1–November 30
MAX. RV LENGTH: 35 feet
NOTATIONS: Additional charges: Basic site $4/night, Wi-Fi available for a fee. No bus conversions. Over 35 ft call resort for availability.
RENTAL ACCOMMODATIONS: Rental units available. Trip Points not accepted. Contact resort directly.

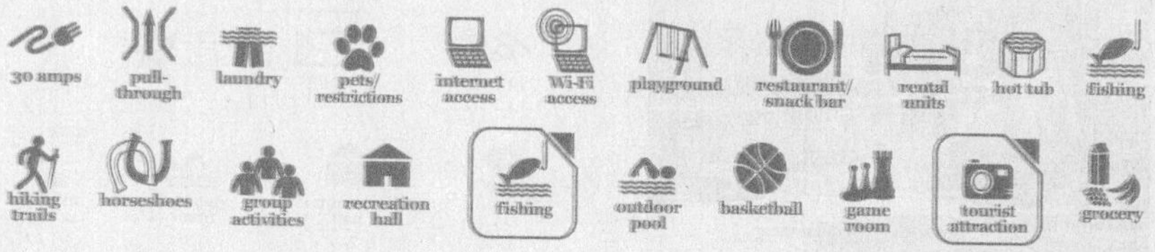

CALIFORNIA

WINTERS

RESORT NUMBER: 1800 **GOOD SAM RATING:** 7/6.5/7.5 **COAST CLASSIC RESORT**

Canyon Creek Resort
22074 State Highway 128
Winters, California 95694
530-795-4133; fax: 530-795-4141
reservations@vistaresorts.net
vistaresorts.net

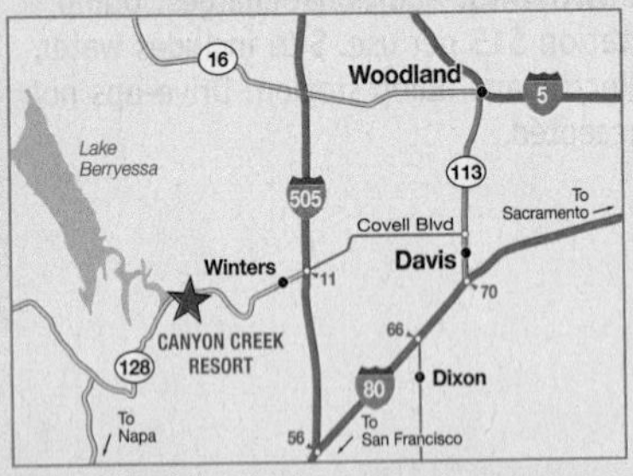

See page CTC 54 for state map.

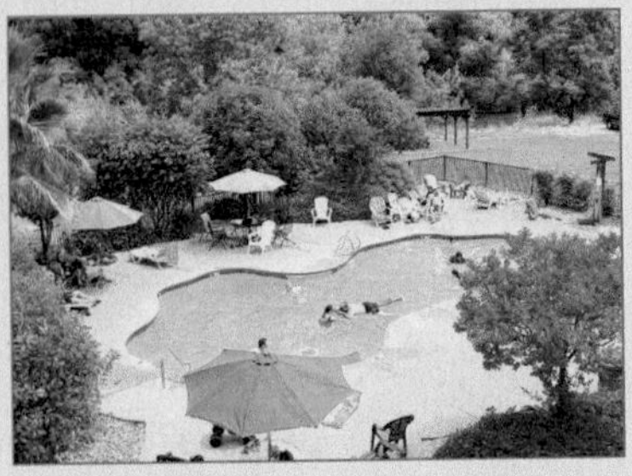

Canyon Creek is located on scenic Putah Creek close to Lake Berryessa, one of California's largest water sport and recreation areas. Lake Berryessa offers fishing, sailing, water-skiing and other sports all within minutes of the resort. The resort itself is known for its excellent trout fishing.

DIRECTIONS: From Sacramento, CA: I-80 W towards San Francisco. Ex Hwy 113/ Woodland. N to Covell Blvd/Hwy 128/ Winters Ex 11. Continue W on Hwy 128 approx 10 mi to the resort on L.

GPS COORDINATES: 38.5149°N/-122.0942°W
RV SITES: Full: 40 Partial: 74 Dry: 0
CHECK-IN: 10:00 a.m.–10:00 p.m.
CHECK-OUT: 3:00 p.m.
SEASON: Year-round
MAX. RV LENGTH: 40 feet
NOTATIONS: Wi-Fi access in campground (fee).

50 amps, pull-through, pets/restrictions, Wi-Fi access, playground, picnic tables, restaurant/snack bar, hot tub, fishing, hiking trails, horseshoes, recreation hall, fishing, boating, outdoor pool, basketball, game room, hot showers

CALIFORNIA

YUCAIPA

RESORT NUMBER: 17 **GOOD SAM RATING:** 6/7.5/6.5 **COAST DELUXE RESORT**

Oak Glen Retreat—Halo Resorts
38955 Oak Glen Road
Yucaipa, California 92399
909-790-1801; fax: 909-797-4103
hriinc@aol.com
haloresortsinc.com

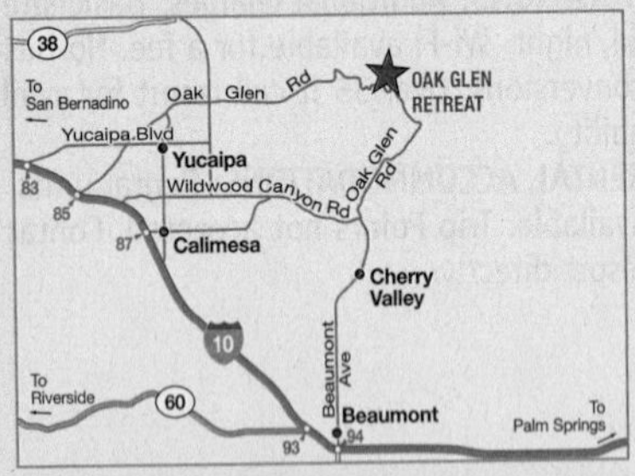

See page CTC 54 for state map.

In the heart of California's apple country, the resort features a full complement of activities and amenities, including a restaurant serving a supreme menu. Most sites have their own apple trees, in keeping with the theme of the park's location. Nearby: Antique shops, children's zoos and animal farms.

DIRECTIONS: From I-10 E from San Bernardino: Yucaipa Blvd to Oak Glen Rd. L 6 mi to resort. From Hwy 60 E: Beaumont Ave Ex. N 10 mi to resort.

GPS COORDINATES: 34.0525°N/-116.9544°W
ELEVATION: 4,800 feet
RV SITES: Full: 182 Partial: 32 Dry: 0
CHECK-IN: 1:00 p.m.–6:00 p.m.
CHECK-OUT: 11:00 a.m.
SEASON: Year-round
PEAK SEASON: March 1–November 30
MAX. RV LENGTH: 40 feet
NOTATIONS: Additional charges: Basic site $4/night, Wi-Fi available for a fee. No bus conversions.

30 amps, visitor mail, pets/restrictions, internet access, Wi-Fi access, playground, restaurant/snack bar, hot tub, recreation hall, outdoor pool, mini golf, game room, tourist attraction, shopping, grocery

GUNNISON

RESORT NUMBER: 375 **GOOD SAM RATING:** 9/10★/10 **COAST DELUXE RESORT**

Blue Mesa Recreational Ranch
27601 West Highway 50
Gunnison, Colorado 81230
970-642-4150; fax: 970-642-4592
info.bluemesaranch@gmail.com
bluemesarvcamping.com

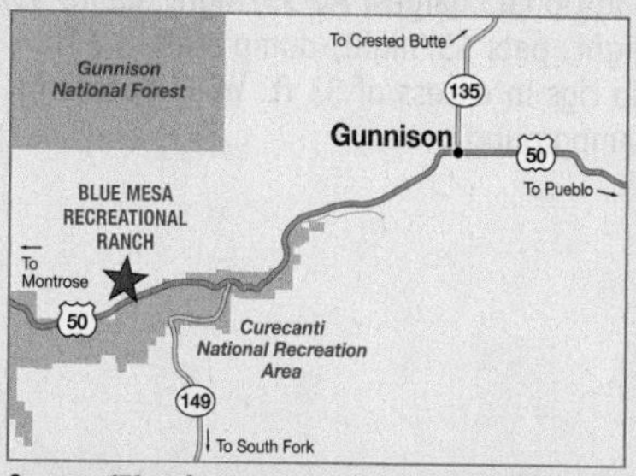

See page CTC 55 for state map.

In the heart of the Curecanti National Recreation Area on the Blue Mesa, Colorado's largest lake. A full complement of amenities supplement the activities available in the area. Nearby: Crested Butte, golf courses and river rapids. A total western environment on an unspoiled lake on the western slope of the Rockies.

DIRECTIONS: From Hwy 50: 12 mi W of Gunnison. 48 mi E of Montrose.

GPS COORDINATES: 38.5443°N/-106.9269°W
ELEVATION: 7,700 feet
RV SITES: Full: 267 Partial: 50 Dry: 0
CHECK-IN: 11:00 a.m.–5:00 p.m.
CHECK-OUT: 11:00 a.m.
SEASON: May 1–October 1
PEAK SEASON: June 15–September 15
MAX. RV LENGTH: 45 feet
NOTATIONS: Additional charges: Resort fee $5/night. Water and sewer available as weather permits.
RENTAL ACCOMMODATIONS: Rental units available. Trip Points not accepted. Contact resort directly.

COLORADO

MONUMENT

RESORT NUMBER: 143 **GOOD SAM RATING:** 8/7.5★/8.5 **COAST PREMIER RESORT**

Colorado Heights Camping Resort
19575 Monument Hill Road
Monument, Colorado 80132
719-481-2336; fax: 719-481-4091
richard@coloradoheights.com
coloradoheights.com

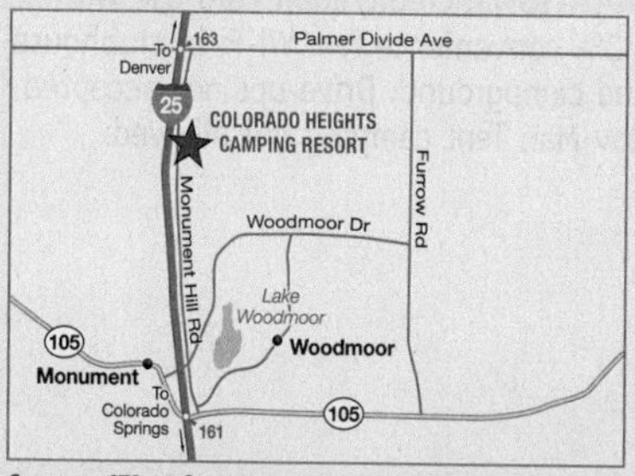

See page CTC 55 for state map.

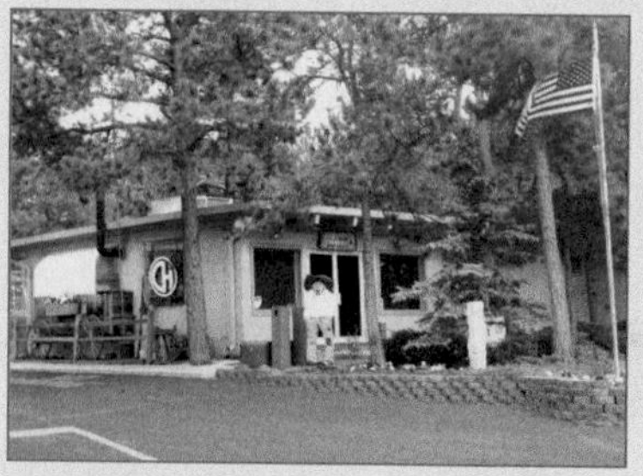

Situated with a panoramic view of the Front Range of the Rocky Mountains and Pike's Peak. Resort features 28 acres of pine-treed land, minutes from Colorado Springs, the U.S. Air Force Academy, and Cheyenne Mountain Zoo. Denver, churches, restaurants and shops just minutes away.

DIRECTIONS: From Denver: I-25 S, Exit 161, R at the light onto CO-105, take first L Woodmoor Dr, go 0.25 mi, turn L on Monument Hill Rd. Resort is 1 mi on R. From Colorado Springs: I-25 N, Ex 161, L at the light onto CO-105, take first R Woodmoor Dr, go 0.25 mi, turn L on Monument Hill Rd. Resort is 1 mi on R. Frontage Rd closed for improvements.

GPS COORDINATES: 39.1162°N/-104.8651°W
ELEVATION: 7,360 feet
RV SITES: Full: 166 Partial: 38 Dry: 0
CHECK-IN: 1:00 p.m.–8:00 p.m.
CHECK-OUT: 11:00 a.m.
SEASON: Year-round
PEAK SEASON: June 1–September 30
MAX. RV LENGTH: 45 feet
NOTATIONS: No tent camping. Weather closures possible. Limited accommodations Oct 1- Apr 1. No mail accepted Oct-Mar. Additional charges: Extra vehicle $5/day, Wi-Fi access in campground. Drive-ups not accepted.

COLORADO

CONNECTICUT

EAST KILLINGLY

RESORT NUMBER: 27 **GOOD SAM RATING:** 8.5/9.5★/9.5 **COAST CLASSIC RESORT**

Stateline Campresort & Cabins
1639 Hartford Pike
East Killingly, Connecticut 06243
860-774-3016; fax: 860-774-6470
camplands2@yahoo.com
statelinecampresort.com

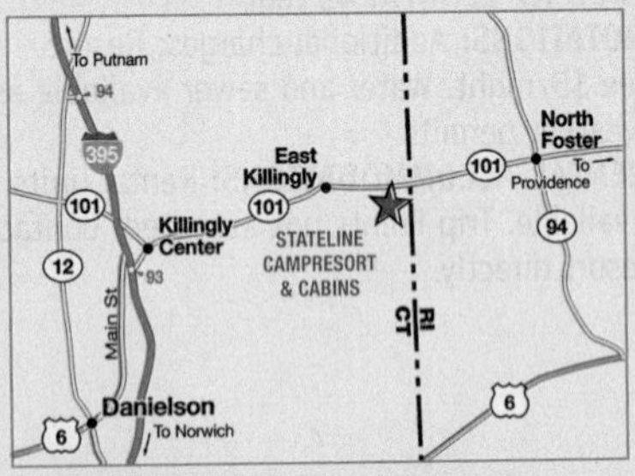

See page CTC 56 for state map.

1.5 hrs southwest of Boston at the Connecticut-Rhode Island northeast border. Minutes from churches, fine restaurants, antique shops, movie theater, shopping mall, county fair, stockcar racing. Nearby attractions include Mystic Seaport and Aquarium, Old Sturbridge Village, casinos, and a demanding golf course.

DIRECTIONS: From I-95 N-bound: Ex 76 onto I-395 N. From I-395: Ex 41, R at bottom of ramp onto Rte 101 E. 5 mi to resort on R.

GPS COORDINATES: 41.8487°N/-71.7952°W
RV SITES: Full: 0 Partial: 200 Dry: 0
CHECK-IN: 3:00 p.m.–6:00 p.m.
CHECK-OUT: 11:00 a.m.
SEASON: May 1–November 1
MAX. RV LENGTH: 33 feet
NOTATIONS: Drive-ups not accepted. Additional charges: AC $3/night, cable $5/night, pets $5/night, dump station $10. No rigs in excess of 33 ft. Wi-Fi access in campground.

FLORIDA

CLERMONT

RESORT NUMBER: 546 **GOOD SAM RATING:** 8.5/9.5★/7.5 **COAST DELUXE RESORT**

Bee's RV Resort
20260 U.S. Highway 27
Clermont, Florida 34715
352-429-2116; fax: 352-429-5791
beesrvresort@gmail.com
beesrvresort.com

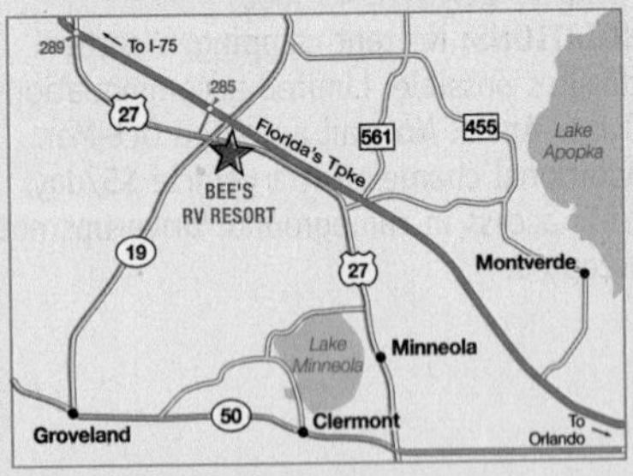

See page CTC 57 for state map.

The management and staff of the Bee's RV Resort want to make your visit as safe as possible. Please do not enter the office without a mask or if you are feeling ill. If this applies to you, please give us a call at 352-429-2116 upon arrival, and remote check-in can be arranged. Resort is in the heart of Florida, not only in geographical location but also in the middle of Florida's best. Nearby: Disney World, Epcot, Disney's Hollywood Studios, Universal Studios, Sea World, lakes, fishing, boating, swimming, and observing wildlife. In short, the perfect place for a family vacation any time of year.

DIRECTIONS: From FL Tpke N-bound: Ex 285. L on Hwy 27. 0.8 mi to resort. From FL Tpke S-bound: Ex 289. R on Hwy 27. 4.6 mi to resort. It will bee on the L.

GPS COORDINATES: 28.641°N/-81.7962°W
RV SITES: Full: 230 Partial: 15 Dry: 5
CHECK-IN: Noon–5:00 p.m.
CHECK-OUT: 11:00 a.m.
SEASON: Year-round
PEAK SEASON: December 1–April 30
MAX. RV LENGTH: 45 feet
NOTATIONS: Credit/debit card use will incur a 3% convenience fee. Wi-Fi in clubhouse and campground. Drive-ups not accepted Nov-Mar. Tent camping not allowed.

CLEVELAND

RESORT NUMBER: 668 **GOOD SAM RATING:** 9/10★/9 **COAST DELUXE RESORT**

Yonah Mountain Camping Resort
3678 Helen Highway
Cleveland, Georgia 30528
706-865-6546; fax: 706-865-9443
frontoffice@yonahcampground.com
yonahcampground.com

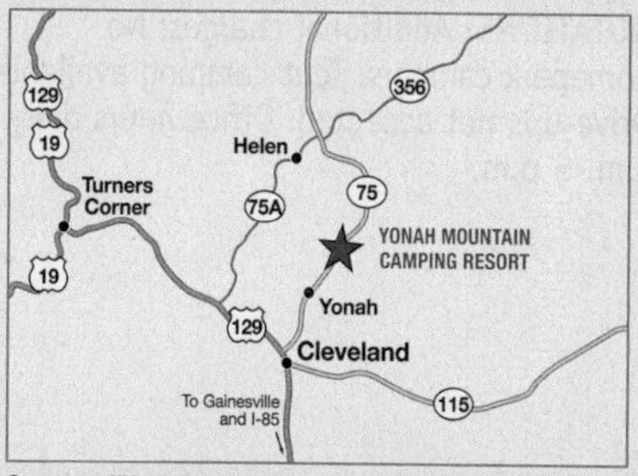

See page CTC 58 for state map.

Located in the North Georgia Mountains near the Chattahoochee River, known for trout fishing, rafting and tubing. Riding stables and hiking trails abound, extremely clean bathhouse, and weekend activities for children. Day trip to Lakes Burton, Lanier, and Rabun for skiing, boating, and fishing. **DIRECTIONS:** From I-985 N to Gainesville (Ex 24): N on Hwy 129 to Cleveland. From Cleveland: Hwy 75 N approx 4 mi to resort on R.

GPS COORDINATES: 34.64748°N/-83.73546°W
RV SITES: Full: 80 Partial: 27 Dry: 0
CHECK-IN: 1:00 p.m.
CHECK-OUT: Noon
SEASON: Year-round
PEAK SEASON: May 1–October 31
MAX. RV LENGTH: 33 feet
NOTATIONS: Full hook-up, 30 amp service only. Adaptors not accepted. Wi-Fi access in clubhouse only. Drive-ups not accepted.

GEORGIA

DAHLONEGA

RESORT NUMBER: 426 **GOOD SAM RATING:** 7.5/9★/9 **COAST CLASSIC RESORT**

R Ranch in the Mountains
65 R Ranch Road
Dahlonega, Georgia 30533
706-864-6444; fax: 706-864-9149
frontoffice@rranch.com
rranch.com

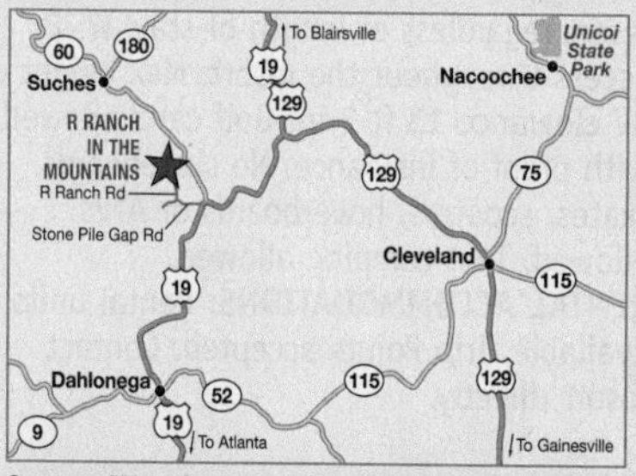

See page CTC 58 for state map.

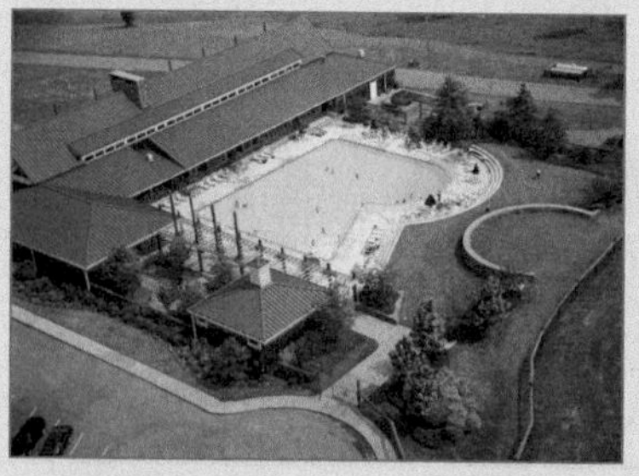

In the North Georgia Mountains amid the stunning wilds of the Chattahoochee National Forest lies a wealth of natural beauty, shining lakes, trout-laden streams, pastures, hardwood and pine woodlands. Only 200 of the resort's 834 acres are developed. The remaining property is kept natural to please nature lovers. **DIRECTIONS:** From Atlanta: GA 400 N to Hwy 60 N to Hwy 60/19 bypass. 5.5 miles L on Ridley Rd. L at dead end on Yahoola Rd. Next R onto Stone Pile Gap Rd. Follow to resort.

GPS COORDINATES: 34.6274°N/-83.9553°W
RV SITES: Full: 160 Partial: 12 Dry: 0
CHECK-IN: 4:00 p.m.
CHECK-OUT: Noon
SEASON: Year-round
MAX. RV LENGTH: 65 feet
NOTATIONS: Additional charges: Usage fee $5/night. Front desk (8 a.m.-5 p.m.), security manned 21 hrs. Majority of RV sites are full hook-up sites. Call for additional information. Wi-Fi access in clubhouse and campground bath houses. 1.5 hour trail rides $25.

GEORGIA

GEORGIA

GREENSBORO

RESORT NUMBER: 692 **GOOD SAM RATING:** 8.5/7.5/8.5 **COAST PREMIER RESORT**

North Shore Landing
2541 Carey Station Road
Greensboro, Georgia 30642
706-453-4505
nsl_reservations@travelresorts.com
travelresorts.com

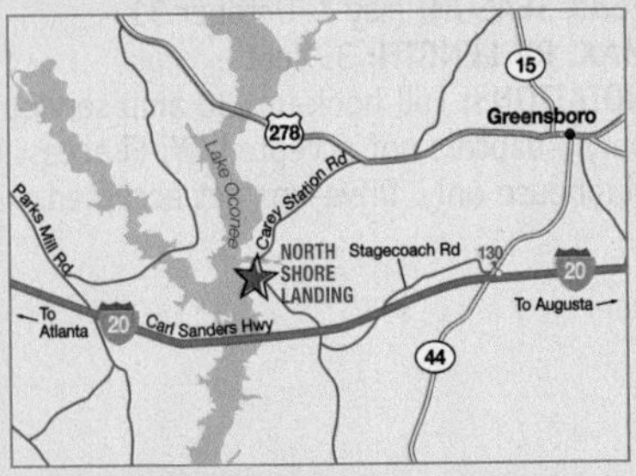

See page CTC 58 for state map.

North Shore Landing is located directly on beautiful Lake Oconee, Georgia's longest lake. The resort features 55 acres developed with a railroad theme including 13 railroad cars. The railroad cars are used for resort amenities and rental accommodations.
DIRECTIONS: I-20 east of Atlanta, Ex 130. S on GA 44 for 4 mi. R at light on Carey Station Rd. Resort on L 4.8 mi.

GPS COORDINATES: 33.54473°N/-83.26992°W
ELEVATION: 640 feet
RV SITES: Full: 100 Partial: 0 Dry: 0
CHECK-IN: 1:00 p.m.
CHECK-OUT: 11:00 a.m.
SEASON: Year-round
PEAK SEASON: May 27–September 5
MAX. RV LENGTH: 45 feet
NOTATIONS: Additional charges: No homepark campers. Tent camping available. Drive-ups not accepted. Office hours daily 9 a.m.-5 p.m.

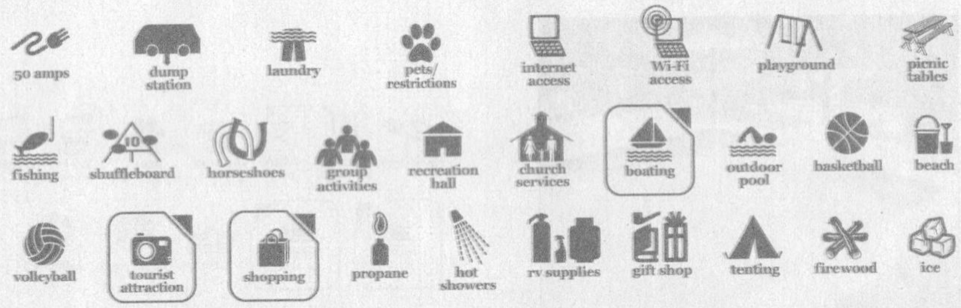

GEORGIA

SAUTEE NACOOCHEE

RESORT NUMBER: 286 **GOOD SAM RATING:** 9.5/8/9 **COAST CLASSIC RESORT**

Unicoi Springs Camp Resort
2444 Highway 356
Sautee Nacoochee, Georgia 30571
706-878-2104; fax: 706-878-1804
info@unicoisprings.com
unicoisprings.com

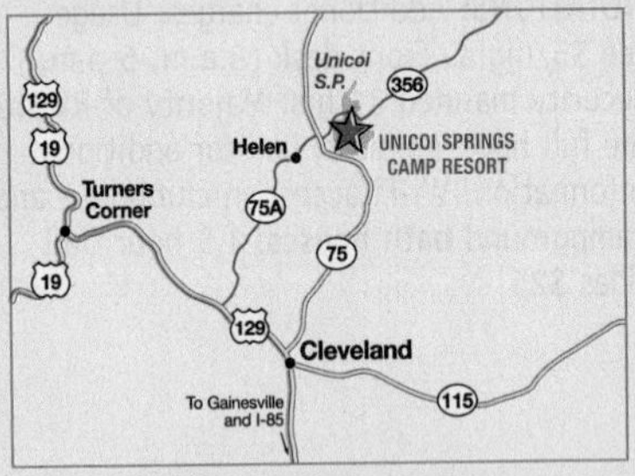

See page CTC 58 for state map.

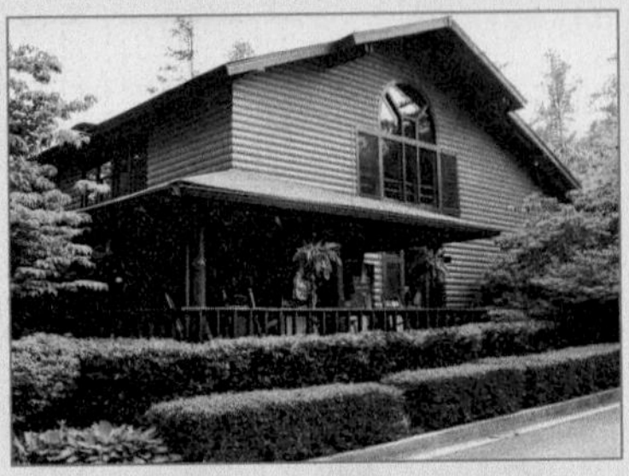

In the Northeast Georgia Mountains, near Helen's Alpine Village! Area recreation includes skiing, fishing, and boating on nearby lakes, tubing on Chattahoochee River, riding stables, miles of beautiful mountain biking and hiking trails, great restaurants, Brasstown Bald, Anna Ruby Falls, Unicoi State Park.
DIRECTIONS: From Atlanta: I-85/I-985 N to Gainesville. Hwy 129 N to Cleveland. N on Hwy 75 through Helen. N on Hwy 356. Continue 3 mi to resort. Avoid directions that include Bean Creek Rd.

GPS COORDINATES: 34.7212°N/-83.7116°W
RV SITES: Full: 284 Partial: 16 Dry: 0
CHECK-IN: 2:00 p.m.
CHECK-OUT: Noon
SEASON: Year-round
MAX. RV LENGTH: 35 feet
NOTATIONS: Additional charges: Mandatory $3/night amenities fee, storage fee $10 for any towing apparatus brought into the resort regardless of length of stay. Wi-Fi access throughout the resort. Max height of RV clearance 13 ft 3 in. Golf carts allowed with proof of insurance. No skateboards, skates, scooters, hoverboards or ATVs allowed. Tent camping allowed.
RENTAL ACCOMMODATIONS: Rental units available. Trip Points accepted. Contact resort directly.

UNADILLA

RESORT NUMBER: 711 **GOOD SAM RATING:** 7/9★/6 **COAST DELUXE RESORT**

Southern Trails RV Resort
2690 Arena Road
Unadilla, Georgia 31091
478-627-3254; fax: 478-627-9442
southerntrailsresort@gmail.com
southerntrailsresort.com

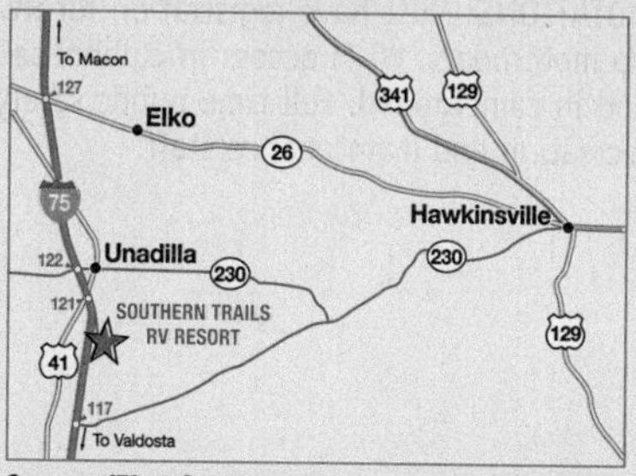

See page CTC 58 for state map.

Nestled in a pecan grove in the heart of the Old South, the resort provides a tranquil setting amidst plenty of activities. Favored attractions include the Andersonville Civil War Prison, Roosevelt's Little White House, Callaway Gardens, Lake Blackshear, and Plains, GA - the home of Jimmy Carter.

DIRECTIONS: Just off I-75 120 mi S of Atlanta and 120 mi N of the GA-FL state line. N or S on I-75, Ex 121. Turn L. First R (across from Subway Rest.). Cross RR tracks. R 0.2 mi to resort.

GPS COORDINATES: 32.2404°N/-83.7393°W
RV SITES: Full: 133 Partial: 58 Dry: 100
CHECK-IN: 8:00 a.m.–8:00 p.m.
CHECK-OUT: 11:00 a.m.
SEASON: Year-round
PEAK SEASON: May 1–September 30
MAX. RV LENGTH: Unlimited
NOTATIONS: Additional charges: 50 amp $4/night Mon-Thu & $5/night Fri-Sun plus tax. Wi-Fi access throughout park. If arrive after hours, call 478-627-3254. No cable avail.

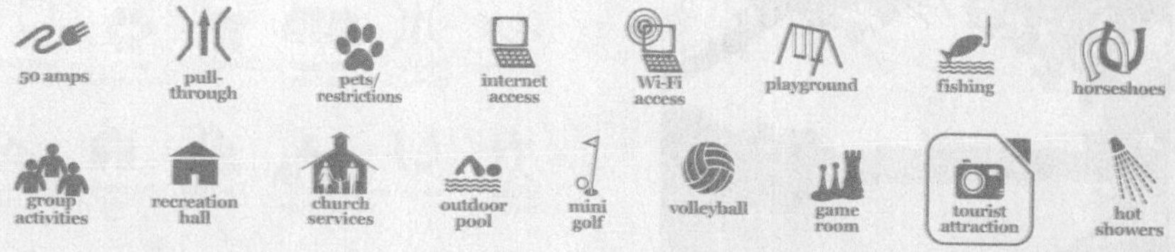

HILLSDALE

RESORT NUMBER: 187 **GOOD SAM RATING:** 9/10★/9 **COAST DELUXE RESORT**

Sunset Lakes RV Resort
3333 290th Street North
Hillsdale, Illinois 61257
855-430-7243; res.: 309-539-4149
sunsetlakes@suncommunities.com
sunsetlakesresort.com

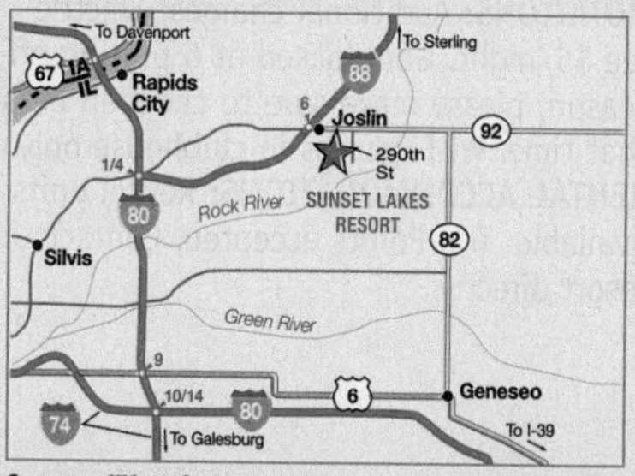

See page CTC 60 for state map.

Sunset Lakes Resort has spacious level sites with abundant recreational opportunities among its wooded areas and five fishing lakes. The 200-acre resort borders the Rock River with a 0.75 mile frontage. Nearby: John Deere Headquarters, riverboat gambling, Putnam Museum/Imax, Arsenal Island, and Niabi Zoo.

DIRECTIONS: From I-88: Exit 6/Joslin. E on Hwy 92. 1 mi to 290th St. R and 0.5 mi to the resort. From I-80 W: I-88 E and follow above. From I-80 E, Geneseo Ex. R (N) on Hwy 82 for 9 mi. At 1.6 mi follow truck route signs to avoid 10 foot underpass. L (W) on Hwy 92. 3 mi to 290th St. L (S) 0.5 mi to the resort.

GPS COORDINATES: 41.5488°N/-90.2159°W
RV SITES: Full: 50 Partial: 100 Dry: 0
CHECK-IN: 9:00 a.m.–6:00 p.m.
CHECK-OUT: 3:00 p.m.
SEASON: June 1–October 8
PEAK SEASON: June 1–September 7
MAX. RV LENGTH: 40 feet
NOTATIONS: Site includes 30 amp, water and electric only. ID required at check-in. Additional charges: Resort fee $12/night. Limited space for big rigs. No satellite reception available. No powerboats on lake.

ILLINOIS

SUBLETTE

RESORT NUMBER: 595 **GOOD SAM RATING:** 9/8.5★/9.5 **COAST CLASSIC RESORT**

Woodhaven Lakes
509 Lamoille Road
Sublette, Illinois 61367
815-849-5915; fax: 815-849-5116
maingate@woodhavenassociation.com
woodhavenassociation.com

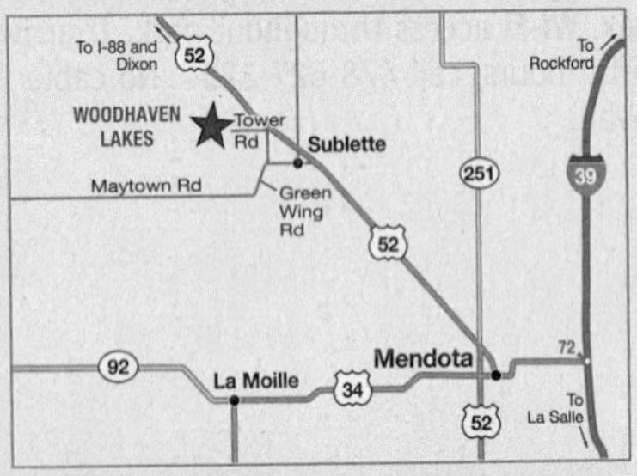

See page CTC 60 for state map.

Natural surroundings, seven lakes, hiking trails and wildlife within 1,756 acres of woodlands and prairie in North Central Illinois. Lakes stocked with bass, catfish and panfish. Recreational staff plans year-round activities and special events for campers of all ages.

DIRECTIONS: From Rte 52 to Green Wing Rd: W on Tower Rd (1st turn off Green Wing Rd). Park is 1 mi on Tower Rd. (GPS address: 499 LaMoille Rd, Amboy IL, 61310).

GPS COORDINATES: 41.6585°N/-89.2825°W
RV SITES: Full: 12 Partial: 18 Dry: 5
CHECK-IN: 24 hours
CHECK-OUT: Noon
SEASON: April 1–December 31
MAX. RV LENGTH: 40 feet
NOTATIONS: Must have registration for RV. No motorboats. Wi-Fi access in clubhouse and in campground. Full time public safety, recreation and maintenance staff.

IOWA

GRIMES

RESORT NUMBER: 41 **GOOD SAM RATING:** 7/8.5★/8 **COAST CLASSIC RESORT**

Cutty's Des Moines Camping Club
2500 Southeast 37th Street
Grimes, Iowa 50111
515-986-3929; fax: 515-986-9581
info@cuttys.com
cuttys.com

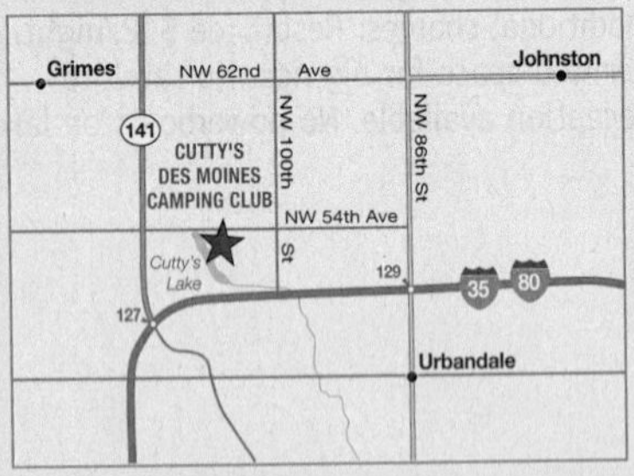

See page CTC 61 for state map.

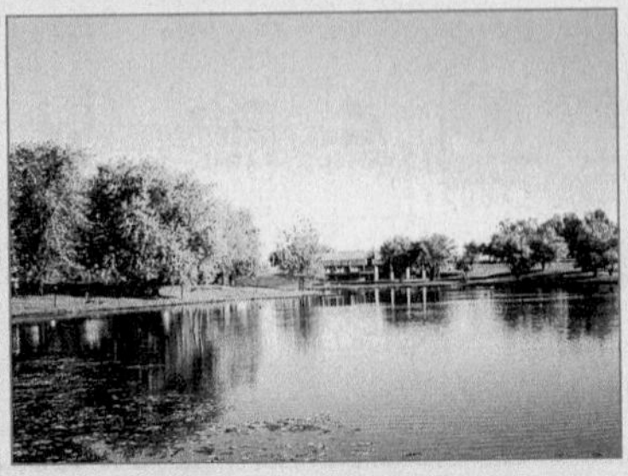

On the shores of Cutty's Lake, which is well-stocked with bass, channel cat, perch, and bluegill. Rolling countryside allows both serene and active RV sites. Nearby: Living History Farms, Saylorville Lake, indoor and outdoor tennis courts, Jester Park Golf Course (18-hole), amusement park, and Des Moines attractions.

DIRECTIONS: From any IA interstate to NW corner of greater Des Moines: I-35/80 Ex 127/Perry. Hwy 141 N for 0.5 mi. R at Quik Trip. 0.2 mi on SE 37th St to resort. Or 86th St Ex, N then L at first intersection and follow NW 54th Ave which becomes SE 37th St to resort.

GPS COORDINATES: 41.6584°N/-93.7642°W
RV SITES: Full: 205 Partial: 127 Dry: 0
CHECK-IN: 8:00 a.m.–5:00 p.m.
CHECK-OUT: 3:00 p.m.
SEASON: Year-round
MAX. RV LENGTH: 40 feet
NOTATIONS: Additional charges: Electric fee $5/night. Gate locked at 6 p.m. in off-season, please make sure to check-in before that time. Wi-Fi access in clubhouse only.
RENTAL ACCOMMODATIONS: Rental units available. Trip Points accepted. Contact resort directly.

OELWEIN

RESORT NUMBER: 780 **GOOD SAM RATING:** 8.5/9★/9.5 **COAST DELUXE RESORT**

IOWA

Lakeshore RV Resort & Campground
1418 Q Avenue
Oelwein, Iowa 50662
319-800-9968
mail@lakeshoreiowa.com
lakeshoreiowa.com

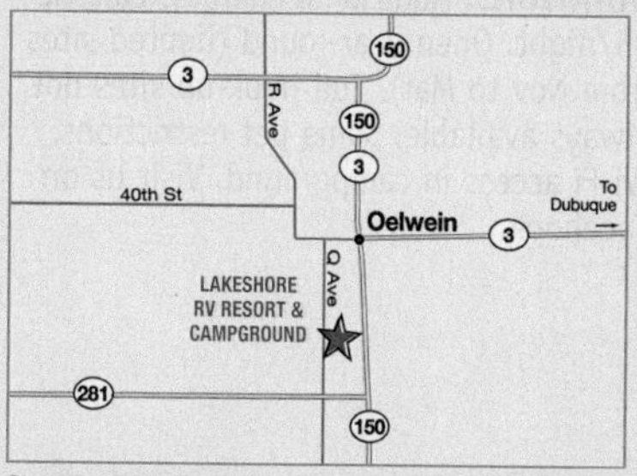

See page CTC 61 for state map.

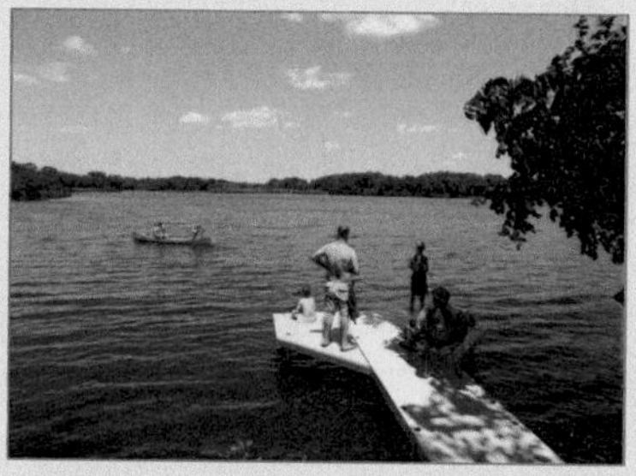

Lakeshore RV Resort & Campground is located on Lake Oelwein in northeast Iowa. We are a child/family friendly campground, privately owned, where our passion is to serve our camping guests with a high level of commitment and excellence. Our family has been camping here for more than 25 years and absolutely love it! We are confident you and your family will too. You will find it restful, relaxing, and peaceful-the way camping should be!

DIRECTIONS: From Hwy 150: W on Hwy 281, 0.7 mi. to Q Ave, R 0.3 mi, resort on R. From the N: Hwy 3 to T Ave/W 13 to Hwy 281. E approx 2.5 mi to Q Ave. N on Q Ave 0.3 mi to resort on R. Take entrance by resort sign and follow the lane down to the office for registration.

GPS COORDINATES: 42.6474°N/-91.9235°W
RV SITES: Full: 100 Partial: 0 Dry: 0
CHECK-IN: 3:00 p.m.
CHECK-OUT: Noon
SEASON: May 1–October 14
MAX. RV LENGTH: Unlimited
NOTATIONS: Additional charges: Energy surcharge $5/night, energy surcharge two or more AC units $10/night.

SPIRIT LAKE

RESORT NUMBER: 179 **GOOD SAM RATING:** 8/9★/10 **COAST DELUXE RESORT**

IOWA

Cutty's Okoboji Resort Club
1528 Iowa Highway 86
Spirit Lake, Iowa 51360
712-336-2226; fax: 712-336-6980
info@cuttysofokoboji.org
cuttysofokoboji.org

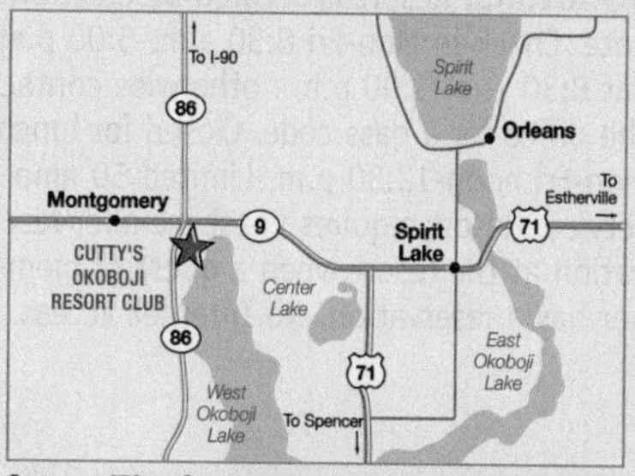

See page CTC 61 for state map.

In the Iowa Great Lakes area near West Lake Okoboji, named one of the three most beautiful blue water lakes in the world by the National Geographic Society. Big Spirit Lake connects to Okoboji. Nearby: Amusement and water parks, golf courses, trails, art centers, performing theatres, Spirit Lake Massacre Monument and museums.

DIRECTIONS: Located near the NW end of W Okoboji Lake. 0.5 mi S of Hwy 9 on Hwy 86.

GPS COORDINATES: 43.4254°N/-95.1826°W
RV SITES: Full: 243 Partial: 22 Dry: 0
CHECK-IN: 4:00 p.m.–10:00 p.m.
CHECK-OUT: 3:00 p.m.
SEASON: Year-round
PEAK SEASON: May 1–September 30
MAX. RV LENGTH: 44 feet
NOTATIONS: Minimum stay 2 nights. Sites may not be available for occupancy before 4 p.m. Phone ahead for arrival after 10 p.m. Reservations recommended for weekend stays. No water Oct 15-Apr 15. Additional charges: Cable $2/night, 50 amp $1/night. Internet and Wi-Fi access in clubhouse only.
RENTAL ACCOMMODATIONS: Rental units available. Trip Points accepted. Contact resort directly.

KANSAS

HALSTEAD

RESORT NUMBER: 90 **GOOD SAM RATING:** 8.5/9★/9 **COAST CLASSIC RESORT**

Spring Lake RV Resort
1308 South Spring Lake Road
Halstead, Kansas 67056
316-835-3443; fax: 316-835-2900
reservations@springlakervresort.com
springlakervresort.com

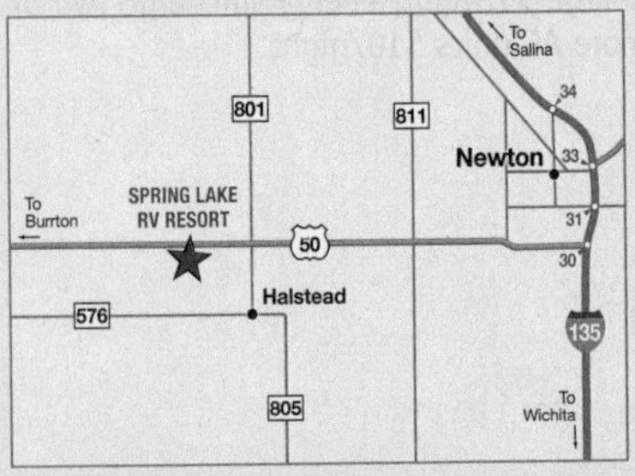

See page CTC 62 for state map.

Spring Lake RV Resort is a country park set in the beautiful Kansas Plains. It is a peaceful park with nature trails, wildlife, stocked ponds, entertainment and recreation. Plan a workout in the exercise room or just putt around on the mini golf course. Hutchinson Salt Museum, one of four in the world, the Kansas State Fair, Cosmosphere and Amish Community provide weekend seasonal activities.

DIRECTIONS: Do not use GPS for directions. From Wichita: I-135 N 20 mi to Hwy 50/ Newton Ex 30. W 12 mi to park sign. L 500 ft to resort. From Salina: I-135 S to Ex 48. S on 22nd Ave/N Halstead Rd for 14 mi to Hwy 50. R for 2 mi. L at sign. From Hutchinson: Hwy 50 E approx 20 mi. R at sign.

GPS COORDINATES: 38.0272°N/-97.9105°W
ELEVATION: 1,400 feet
RV SITES: Full: 123 Partial: 56 Dry: 0
CHECK-IN: 2:00 p.m.
CHECK-OUT: Noon
SEASON: Year-round
MAX. RV LENGTH: 48 feet
NOTATIONS: Additional charges: Electric $5/night. Open year-round (limited sites from Nov to Mar). Full hook-up sites not always available. Some pet restrictions. Wi-Fi access in campground. Visit us on Facebook.

KANSAS

LINN VALLEY

RESORT NUMBER: 415 **GOOD SAM RATING:** 8.5/7/8 **COAST DELUXE RESORT**

Linn Valley Lakes
9 Linn Valley Avenue
Linn Valley, Kansas 66040
913-757-4591; fax: 913-757-2991
office@linnvalleylakes.com
linnvalleylakes.com

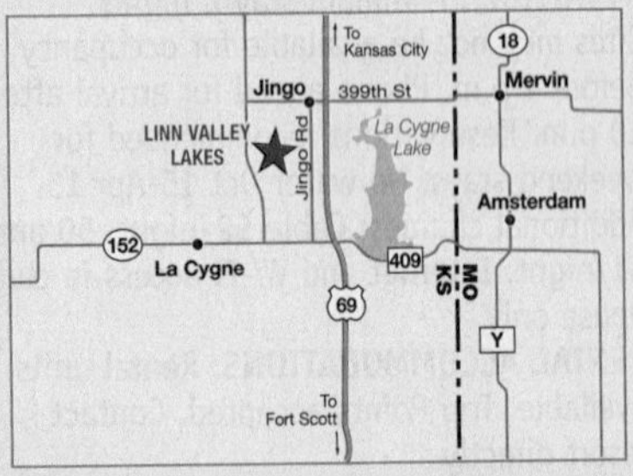

See page CTC 62 for state map.

Resort is 65 miles south of Kansas City on 2,000 acres of scenic rolling countryside near the Missouri border. Observe wild turkey, Canadian geese, ducks, deer, and bobcat at Marais des Cygnes Waterfowl Refuge. Spring and fall are favorite seasons because of the bird migrations.

DIRECTIONS: From Kansas City, KS, on I-435: Hwy 69 S to the 399th St Ex. W 0.5 mi to Jingo Rd. S at stop sign. At Linn County Line, Jingo Rd becomes Ullery Rd. S to the resort. Note: Google Maps will not get you to the front entrance.

GPS COORDINATES: 38.384°N/-94.716°W
RV SITES: Full: 47 Partial: 0 Dry: 0
CHECK-IN: 8:30 a.m.–5:00 p.m.
CHECK-OUT: 1:00 p.m.
SEASON: Year-round
PEAK SEASON: May 1–August 31
MAX. RV LENGTH: Unlimited
NOTATIONS: Resort is secured by electronic gate. Check-in Mon-Fri 8:30 a.m.-5:00 p.m., Sat 8:30 a.m.-1:00 p.m., otherwise contact the office for a pass code. Closed for lunch Mon-Fri noon-12:30 p.m. Limited 50 amp service. Resort requires Coast member reservation at the resort when a guest of member has a reservation. No Internet access.

ABITA SPRINGS

RESORT NUMBER: 43 **GOOD SAM RATING:** 9/10★/9.5 **COAST CLASSIC RESORT**

Abita Springs RV Resort—Ocean Canyon Properties
24150 Highway 435
Abita Springs, Louisiana 70420
985-590-3926
member.reservations@oceancanyon.com
oceancanyon.com

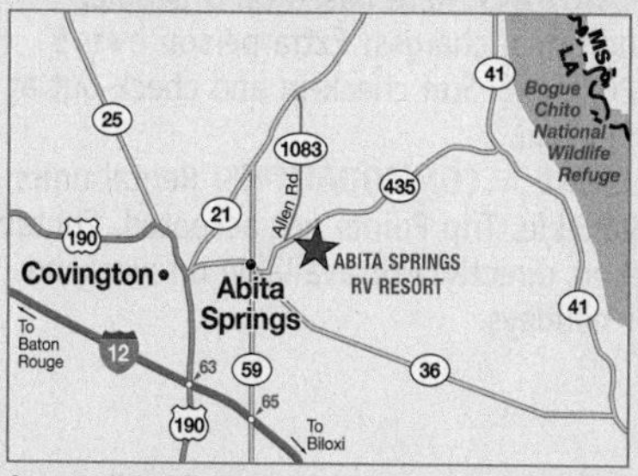

See page CTC 53 for state map.

This resort is located 40 miles from the French Quarter of New Orleans just across Lake Ponchatrain. It sits on its own well-stocked crappie and bass lake. Resort has a large clubhouse with scheduled activities and beautiful pool complex. The town of Abita Springs is an antebellum wonder and home of the famous Abita Springs Brewery with daily tours.
DIRECTIONS: From New Orleans: N on Hwy 190 to I-12 E. Ex 65. N on Hwy 59 through Abita Springs. E on Hwy 435. Resort approx. 2.5 mi on R.

GPS COORDINATES: 30.4943°N/-90.0029°W
ELEVATION: 62 feet
RV SITES: Full: 80 Partial: 20 Dry: 0
CHECK-IN: 2:00 p.m.
CHECK-OUT: 11:00 a.m.
SEASON: Year-round
MAX. RV LENGTH: 45 feet
NOTATIONS: Additional charges: Wi-Fi $5/night, 50 amps $5/night.
RENTAL ACCOMMODATIONS: Rental units available. Trip Points not accepted. Contact resort directly.

GIBSON

RESORT NUMBER: 1685 **GOOD SAM RATING:** 9/9.5★/8.5 **COAST CLASSIC RESORT**

Hideaway Ponds RV Resort—Ocean Canyon Properties
6367 Bayou Black Drive
Gibson, Louisiana 70356
985-255-4578; res.: 855-842-1469
member.reservations@oceancanyon.com
oceancanyon.com

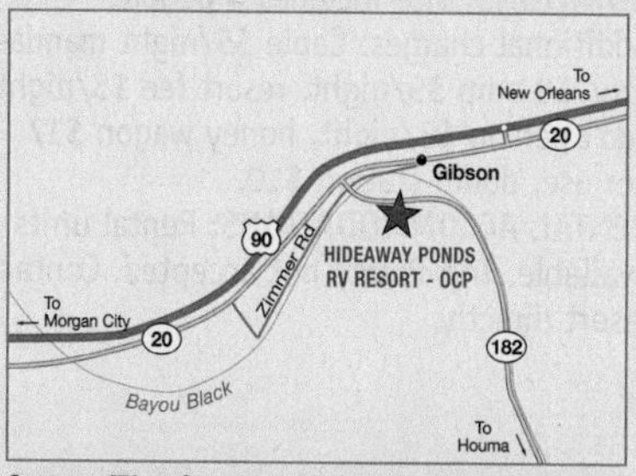

See page CTC 53 for state map.

Only 70 miles from New Orleans in the heart of Cajun Country, you'll find beautiful Hideaway Ponds Recreational Resort. If you want to experience life as a Cajun under the magnificent oak trees, come down to our family-oriented resort where you can swim, fish or just plain relax!
DIRECTIONS: From Hwy 90: Gibson Ex. L on Hwy 20. 1 mi. L on Hwy 182. Approx 0.5 mi to resort.

GPS COORDINATES: 29.6825°N/-90.9911°W
ELEVATION: 26 feet
RV SITES: Full: 99 Partial: 0 Dry: 0
CHECK-IN: 2:00 p.m.
CHECK-OUT: 11:00 a.m.
SEASON: Year-round
MAX. RV LENGTH: 35 feet
NOTATIONS: Additional charges: Cable $5/night, Wi-Fi $5/night, 50 amp $5/night, pull-through $5/night.
RENTAL ACCOMMODATIONS: Rental units available. Trip points not accepted. Contact resort directly.

LOUISIANA

ROBERT

RESORT NUMBER: 561 GOOD SAM RATING: 9/9★/8 COAST CLASSIC RESORT

Passport to Leisure
46049 Highway 445 North
Robert, Louisiana 70455
985-542-1507
yogibear@jellystonela.com
jellystonela.com

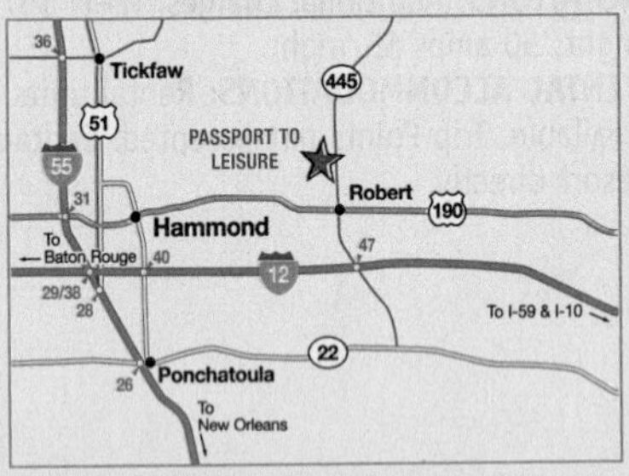

See page CTC 53 for state map.

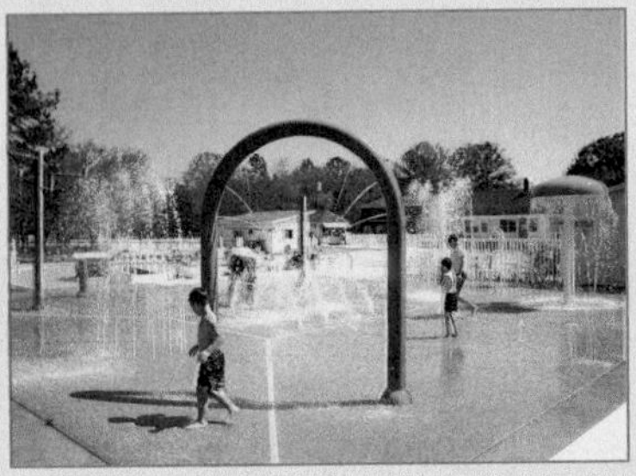

At the gateway to New Orleans and Cajun country, we offer a sampling of Louisiana lifestyle with diverse activities every weekend. An hour from New Orleans, Baton Rouge, and Gulf Coast beaches. Nearby: Sightseeing, historical sites, alligator farms, swamp tours and more. Ask us for tourist information.

DIRECTIONS: From I-12 Ex 47 (Robert): N 3 mi on Hwy 445 to resort. Register at Yogi Bear Ranger Station.

GPS COORDINATES: 30.5216°N/-90.3457°W
ELEVATION: 30 feet
RV SITES: Full: 60 Partial: 60 Dry: 0
CHECK-IN: 2:00 p.m.
CHECK-OUT: 2:00 p.m.
SEASON: Year-round
MAX. RV LENGTH: 40 feet
NOTATIONS: Rate based on 5 people. Additional charges: Extra person over 5 $20/night. Sun check-in and check-out at 3:30 p.m.
RENTAL ACCOMMODATIONS: Rental units available. Trip Points not accepted. Contact resort directly. Not available on weekends or holidays.

MASSACHUSETTS

BRIMFIELD

RESORT NUMBER: 31 GOOD SAM RATING: 8/9/9 COAST DELUXE RESORT

Quinebaug Cove Resort
49 East Brimfield Holland Road
Brimfield, Massachusetts 01010
413-245-9525; fax: 413-245-9259
quinebaugcoversort.com
quinebaugcove.com

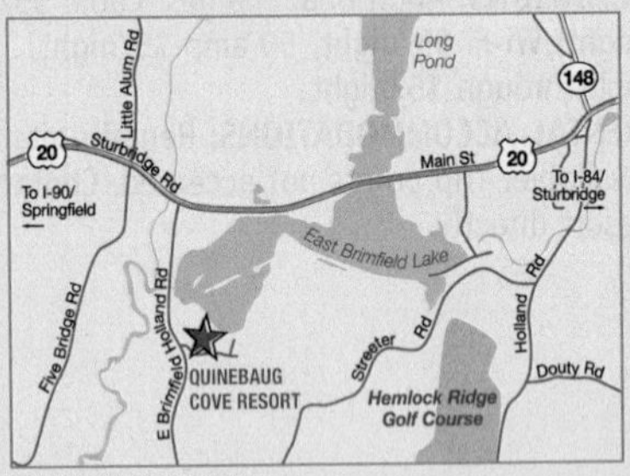

See page CTC 56 for state map.

In Central Massachusetts near historic Old Sturbridge Village, Quinebaug Cove Resort is a family friendly resort on a 420-acre reservoir with free boat ramp, 5-mile canoe/kayak trail, swimming pool, recreational center with meeting room, and much more.

DIRECTIONS: From the intersection of I-84 and US 20: US 20 W 4 mi. 1st L after the lake appears on both sides of highway (100 ft after Tru-Valu gas station). Resort on L.

GPS COORDINATES: 42.1036°N/-72.1475°W
RV SITES: Full: 14 Partial: 14 Dry: 0
CHECK-IN: 3:00 p.m.
CHECK-OUT: 11:00 a.m.
SEASON: April 14–October 5
PEAK SEASON: May 22–September 6
MAX. RV LENGTH: 45 feet
NOTATIONS: Site includes 4 people. Additional charges: Cable $5/night mandatory, 50 amp $5/night, resort fee $5/night, add'l person $5/night, honey wagon $17 per use, dump station $10.
RENTAL ACCOMMODATIONS: Rental units available. Trip Points not accepted. Contact resort directly.

DAVISON

RESORT NUMBER: 340 **GOOD SAM RATING:** 8.5/8.5★/8.5 **COAST PREMIER RESORT**

Lake Shore Resort—Outdoor Adventures
4392 North Irish Road
Davison, Michigan 48423
888-249-1995; fax: 810-653-7111
info@outdooradventuresinc.com
outdooradventuresinc.com

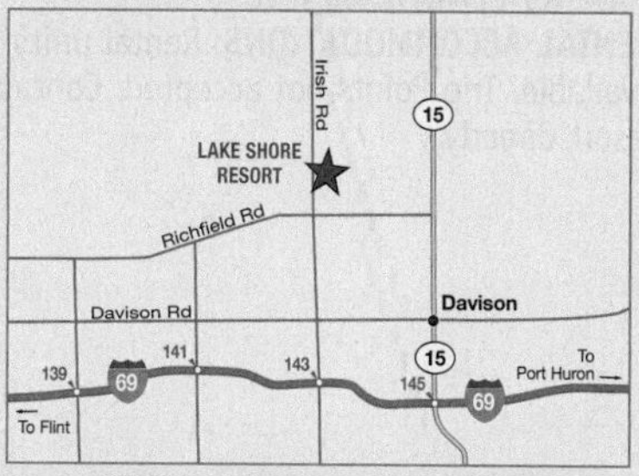

See page CTC 65 for state map.

Outdoor Adventures Lake Shore Resort offers a beautiful setting for fun and relaxation for the entire family. With a spring-fed lake, beach area, indoor pool, lazy river, and many planned activities, there is something for everyone.
DIRECTIONS: Approx 10 mi E of Flint. From I-69: Ex 143/Irish Rd N. 3.5 mi to resort on the R.

GPS COORDINATES: 43.0733°N/-83.5575°W
RV SITES: Full: 547 Partial: 41 Dry: 0
CHECK-IN: 3:00 p.m.
CHECK-OUT: Noon
SEASON: Year-round
PEAK SEASON: May 20–September 20
MAX. RV LENGTH: 40 feet
NOTATIONS: Tent camping available (fee). Drive-ups accepted.
RENTAL ACCOMMODATIONS: Rental units available. Trip Points not accepted. Contact resort directly.

30 amps, dump station, laundry, pets/restrictions, internet access, Wi-Fi access, playground, picnic tables, restaurant/snack bar, rental units, hot tub, fishing, shuffleboard, group activities, recreation hall, outdoor pool, mini golf, basketball, beach, golf, game room, fitness, propane, spa, canoes, indoor pool, hot showers, paddle boats, fire rings, tenting, firewood, ice

GAYLORD

RESORT NUMBER: 508 **GOOD SAM RATING:** 9/9★/9 **COAST DELUXE RESORT**

Benjamin's Beaver Creek Resort—Outdoor Adventures
5004 West Otsego Lake Drive
Gaylord, Michigan 49735
989-705-1055; res.: 888-249-1995
info@outdooradventuresinc.com
outdooradventuresinc.com

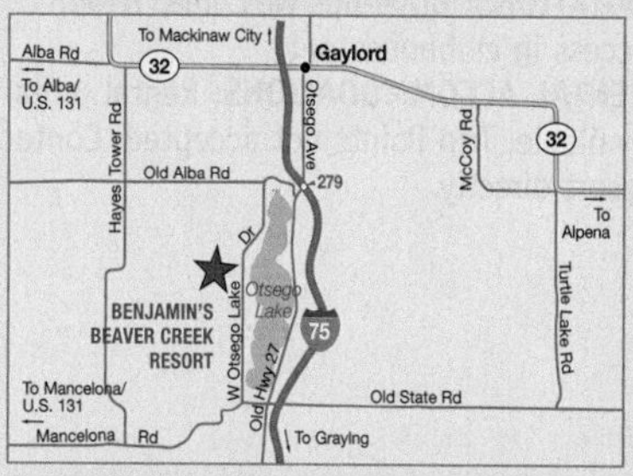

See page CTC 65 for state map.

In northern Lower Michigan near the Mackinac Bridge leading to the Michigan Upper Peninsula. Along 5-mile long Otsego Lake, popular for fishing and water sports. Area is famous for festivals during both winter and summer. Nearby: 22 championship golf courses, fishing, 5 major ski resorts, museums, forests for riding or cross-country skiing.
DIRECTIONS: From I-7 S of Mackinac Bridge: Exit 279/Old Hwy 27. S, then R on W. Otsego Lake Rd. 3 mi to resort.

GPS COORDINATES: 44.9595°N/-84.7082°W
RV SITES: Full: 0 Partial: 30 Dry: 0
CHECK-IN: 3:00 p.m.
CHECK-OUT: Noon
SEASON: Year-round
MAX. RV LENGTH: 40 feet
NOTATIONS: No tents or homemade campers. Electric only after Labor Day.

30 amps, pets/restrictions, internet access, horseshoes, recreation hall, fishing, mini golf, tennis, golf, indoor pool, winter sports

MICHIGAN

GRAND HAVEN

RESORT NUMBER: 2241 **GOOD SAM RATING:** 7.5/7.5/8.5 **COAST DELUXE RESORT**

Grand Haven Resort—Outdoor Adventures
10990 U.S. Highway 31
Grand Haven, Michigan 49417
888-249-1995; fax: 616-844-7491
info@outdooradventuresinc.com
outdooradventuresinc.com

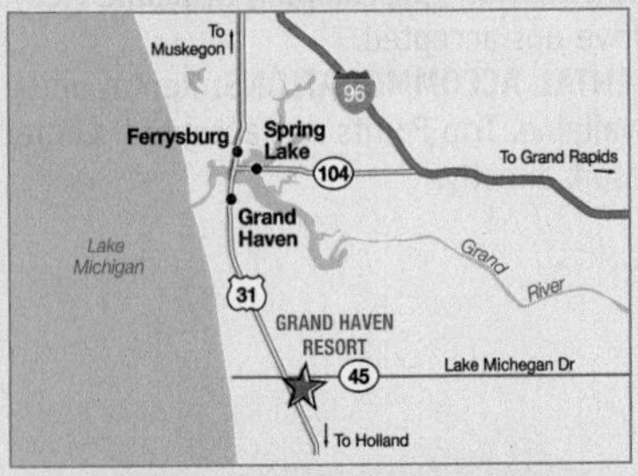

See page CTC 65 for state map.

A camper's paradise near the shores of Lake Michigan. Large wooded sites, adorable cabins and cozy cottages create a comfortable home away from home. Amenities include a large heated pool, indoor arcade and miniature golf. Historic town of Grand Haven has eight public beaches, a trolley ride, shopping, art galleries and wonderful restaurants. Don't forget to enjoy a leisurely stroll on the sandy beach!

DIRECTIONS: From the N: Located on L side of Hwy 31, 7 miles S of downtown Grand Haven. From the S: Located on the R side of Hwy 31, 13 miles N of Holland. From the E: Located off M45 (Lake Michigan Drive) and 158th St, 11 mi from Allendale.

GPS COORDINATES: 42.96835°N/-86.17801°W
RV SITES: Full: 80 Partial: 50 Dry: 0
CHECK-IN: 3:00 p.m.
CHECK-OUT: Noon
SEASON: May 2–October 10
PEAK SEASON: May 20–September 20
MAX. RV LENGTH: 40 feet
RENTAL ACCOMMODATIONS: Rental units available. Trip Points not accepted. Contact resort directly.

MICHIGAN

KALAMAZOO

RESORT NUMBER: 1607 **GOOD SAM RATING:** 7/8.5★/8.5 **COAST PREMIER RESORT**

Kalamazoo Resort—Outdoor Adventures
8368 West C Avenue
Kalamazoo, Michigan 49009
888-249-1995; fax: 269-888-2576
info@outdooradventuresinc.com
outdooradventuresinc.com

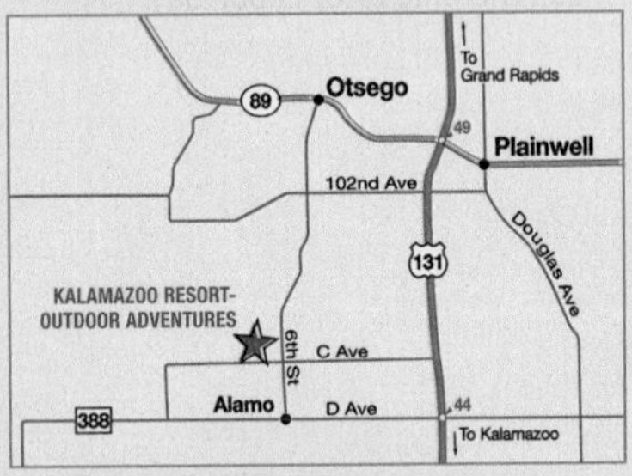

See page CTC 65 for state map.

Halfway between Chicago and Detroit. Ten miles from Kalamazoo stores, shops, restaurants, and malls, yet far enough away to be really in the country. One mile from Kal-Haven Trail, a 30-mile nature walk from Kalamazoo to South Haven for summer walking and winter cross-country skiing. Five miles from two ski resorts.

DIRECTIONS: From Kalamazoo: N on Hwy 131. Ex 44/D Ave. Turn L. 3 mi following signs. R (N) on 6th St. L on C Ave. Resort 0.5 mi on R.

GPS COORDINATES: 42.3897°N/-85.7182°W
RV SITES: Full: 75 Partial: 100 Dry: 0
CHECK-IN: 3:00 p.m.
CHECK-OUT: Noon
SEASON: Year-round
PEAK SEASON: May 20–September 25
MAX. RV LENGTH: 45 feet
NOTATIONS: Drive-ups welcome. Wi-Fi access in clubhouse only.
RENTAL ACCOMMODATIONS: Rental units available. Trip Points not accepted. Contact resort directly.

MT PLEASANT

RESORT NUMBER: 2237 **GOOD SAM RATING:** 9.5/9★/9 **COAST DELUXE RESORT**

Mt Pleasant Resort—Outdoor Adventures
340 North Loomis Road
Mt Pleasant, Michigan 48858
888-249-1995
info@outdooradventuresinc.com
outdooradventuresinc.com

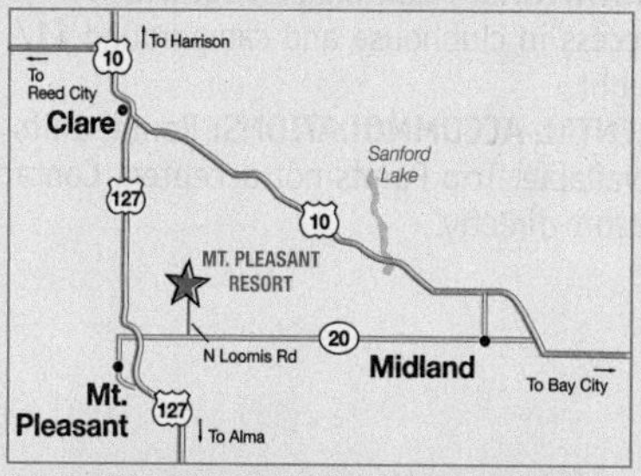

See page CTC 65 for state map.

Formerly known as Shardi's Hideaway. Located in Mount Pleasant, home of Central Michigan University and Soaring Eagle Casino and Entertainment Complex.
DIRECTIONS: From points E, S or N: I-75 to Hwy 10 W at Ex 162B towards Midland. Merge onto Hwy 10BR/M20 W (exit on the L) towards downtown Midland. Follow M-20 W 22 mi. Turn R onto Shepherd Rd. N 2 mi turn R onto E Baseline Rd. E 1 mi turn L onto N Loomis Rd. Resort 0.5 mi on the R.

GPS COORDINATES: 43.64603°N/-84.66797°W
RV SITES: Full: 160 Partial: 0 Dry: 0
CHECK-IN: 3:00 p.m.
CHECK-OUT: Noon
SEASON: Year-round
PEAK SEASON: May 20–September 30
MAX. RV LENGTH: 40 feet
RENTAL ACCOMMODATIONS: Rental units available. Trip Points not accepted. Contact resort directly.

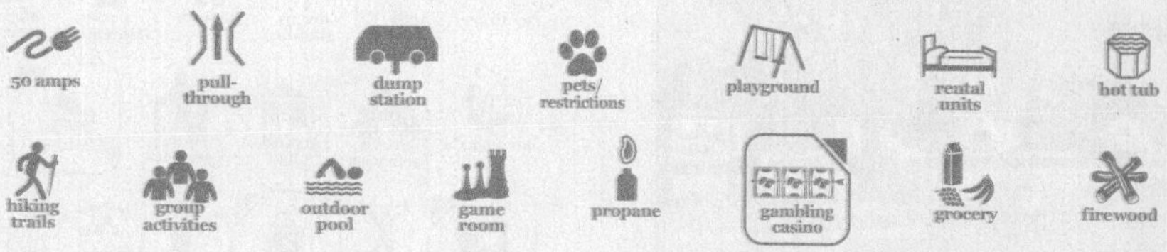

OMER

RESORT NUMBER: 1597 **GOOD SAM RATING:** 8/9★/8 **COAST PREMIER RESORT**

Wilderness Resort—Outdoor Adventures
1050 Husak Road
Omer, Michigan 48749
888-249-1995; fax: 989-653-3081
info@outdooradventuresinc.com
outdooradventuresinc.com

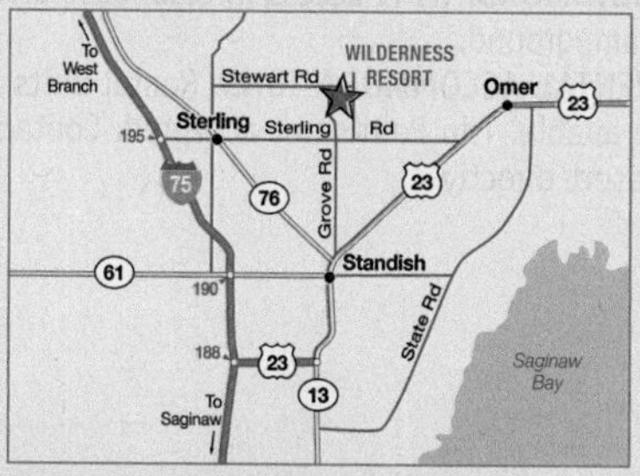

See page CTC 65 for state map.

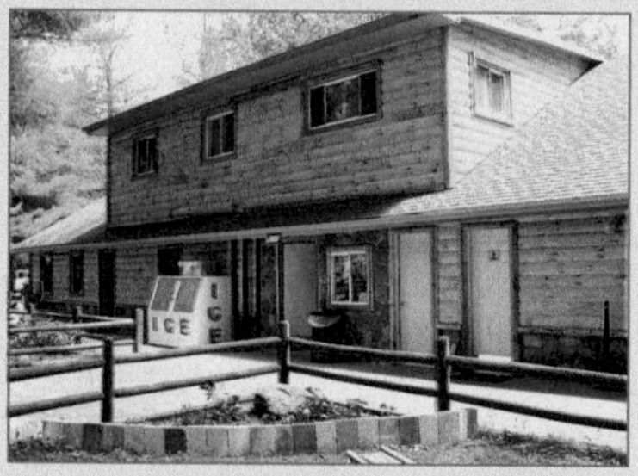

Outdoor Adventures Wilderness Resort offers a quiet, peaceful atmosphere with plenty of wildlife to enjoy. Abundant fishing and hunting areas make this a popular destination for sportsman and nature lovers as well. Nearby attractions include shopping, golfing, fun parks, and a flea market.
DIRECTIONS: From I-75: Ex 188. N on Hwy 23 approx 2.5 mi. L on Grove Rd. Approx 4.5 mi, R on Stewart Rd. Resort 0.5 mi on R.

GPS COORDINATES: 44.05436°N/-83.94762°W
RV SITES: Full: 29 Partial: 181 Dry: 0
CHECK-IN: 3:00 p.m.
CHECK-OUT: Noon
SEASON: May 2–October 10
PEAK SEASON: May 20–September 20
MAX. RV LENGTH: 40 feet
RENTAL ACCOMMODATIONS: Rental units available. Trip Points not accepted. Contact resort directly.

MICHIGAN

STANDISH

RESORT NUMBER: 1006 **GOOD SAM RATING:** 7.5/9★/7.5 **COAST PREMIER RESORT**

Saginaw Bay Resort—Outdoor Adventures
4738 Foco Road
Standish, Michigan 48658
888-249-1995; fax: 989-846-0942
info@outdooradventuresinc.com
outdooradventuresinc.com

See page CTC 65 for state map.

A pleasant family atmosphere, about 130 miles north of Detroit. The resort features shaded sites. Within minutes of golf courses, amusement parks, marinas and beaches. Area also offers some of the best fishing and hunting in Northern Michigan. Nearby are factory outlet shopping, auto racing and casinos.

DIRECTIONS: From I-75: Ex 188. 2.3 mi on Hwy 23. R onto Sagatoo Rd, 2 mi, R on Foco Rd. Resort is 0.5 mi on R.

GPS COORDINATES: 43.948°N/-83.9268°W
RV SITES: Full: 304 Partial: 92 Dry: 0
CHECK-IN: 3:00 p.m.
CHECK-OUT: Noon
SEASON: Year-round
PEAK SEASON: May 20–September 20
MAX. RV LENGTH: 40 feet
NOTATIONS: Additional charges: Wi-Fi access in clubhouse and campground $1/night.
RENTAL ACCOMMODATIONS: Rental units available. Trip Points not accepted. Contact resort directly.

MICHIGAN

STERLING

RESORT NUMBER: 1596 **GOOD SAM RATING:** 7.5/9★/9 **COAST PREMIER RESORT**

Rifle River Resort—Outdoor Adventures
334 North Melita Road
Sterling, Michigan 48659
888-249-1995; fax: 989-654-2325
info@outdooradventuresinc.com
outdooradventuresinc.com

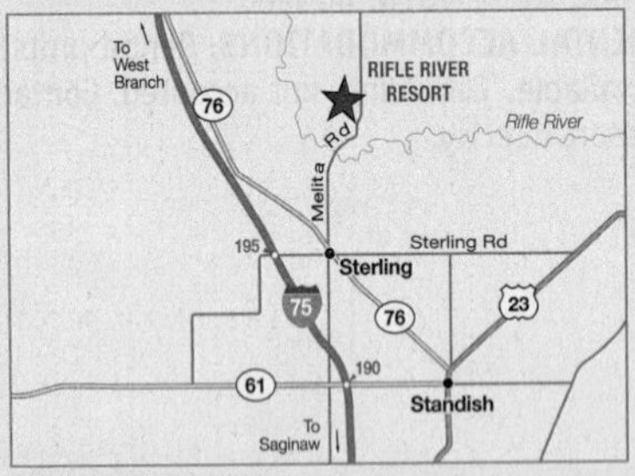

See page CTC 65 for state map.

Outdoor Adventures Rifle River Resort is located in the Saginaw lowlands of Eastern Michigan and offers a beautiful, quiet and secluded vacation spot. During your stay enjoy fishing, canoeing, tubing, and rafting on the Rifle River.

DIRECTIONS: From I-75: Ex 195. E to red flashing light. L to stop sign. Straight onto Melita Rd. Approx 3 mi. Resort on L across the bridge.

GPS COORDINATES: 44.0732°N/-84.0192°W
RV SITES: Full: 6 Partial: 159 Dry: 0
CHECK-IN: 3:00 p.m.
CHECK-OUT: Noon
SEASON: May 2–October 10
PEAK SEASON: May 20–September 20
MAX. RV LENGTH: 40 feet
NOTATIONS: Wi-Fi access in clubhouse and campground.
RENTAL ACCOMMODATIONS: Rental units available. Trip Points not accepted. Contact resort directly.

STOCKBRIDGE

RESORT NUMBER: 332 **GOOD SAM RATING:** 7.5/8.5/8 **COAST DELUXE RESORT**

Heartland Woods Family Resort
5120 Freiermuth Road
Stockbridge, Michigan 49285
517-565-3500; fax: 517-886-5998
heartlandresort@gmail.com
heartlandwoodsrv.com

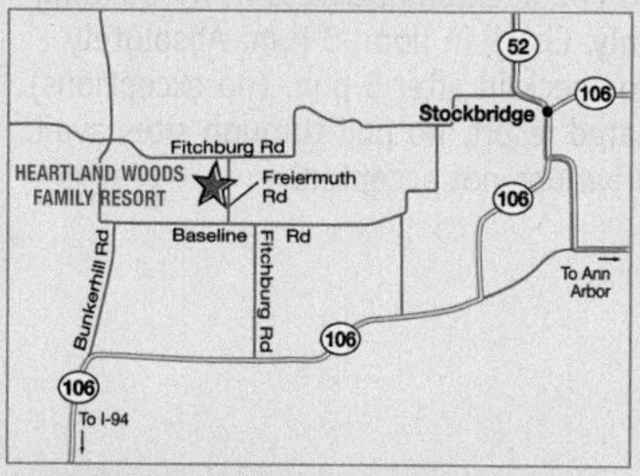

See page CTC 65 for state map.

A wonderful outdoor experience with its tall timber, scenic splendor and a large lawn amphitheatre and covered sound stage for outdoor concerts and special occasions. A few miles to fishing and boating lakes for a total outdoor experience. Michigan International Speedway is just south of Jackson for NASCAR enthusiasts.
DIRECTIONS: From Jackson: I-94, Ex 139. N 12.4 mi on M106/Cooper St. L on Fitchburg Rd for 2.5 mi. L on Baseland Rd for 0.2 mi. R on Freiermuth Rd. 0.7 mile to resort on L.

GPS COORDINATES: 42.4357°N/-84.278°W
RV SITES: Full: 12 Partial: 211 Dry: 0
CHECK-IN: 10:00 a.m.–9:00 p.m.
CHECK-OUT: Noon
SEASON: May 15–October 15
PEAK SEASON: June 15–September 3
MAX. RV LENGTH: 50 feet
NOTATIONS: Wi-Fi available.

50 amps · pets/restrictions · Wi-Fi access · playground · picnic tables · fishing · shuffleboard · biking trails · horseshoes · recreation hall · fishing · boating
outdoor pool · mini golf · basketball · beach · volleyball · golf · game room · tourist attraction · shopping · propane · fire rings · gift shop

WEST BRANCH

RESORT NUMBER: 1774 **GOOD SAM RATING:** 7.5/9★/8 **COAST PREMIER RESORT**

Lake of the North Resort—Outdoor Adventures
3070 Elm Drive
West Branch, Michigan 48661
888-249-1995; fax: 989-345-5362
info@outdooradventuresinc.com
outdooradventuresinc.com

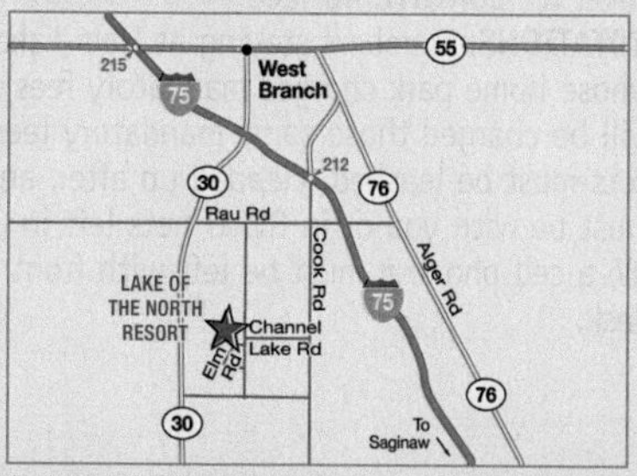

See page CTC 65 for state map.

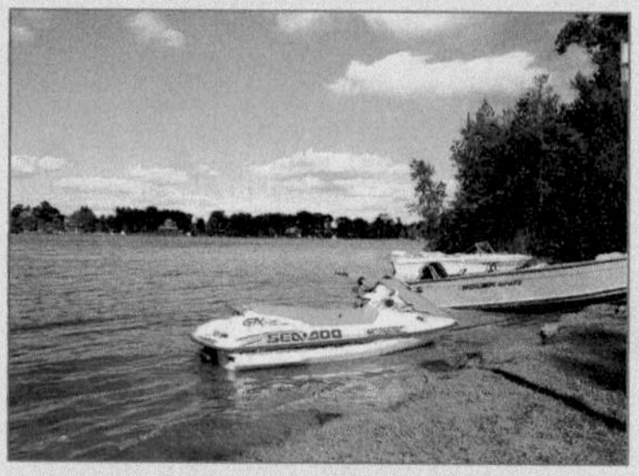

Lake of the North is located on beautiful Lake George near historic West Branch. Nearby attractions include outlet shopping, golf, a wildlife refuge, fishing and hunting.
DIRECTIONS: From I-75 Ex 212. S on Cook Rd approx 3 mi. R on Channel Lake Rd. 1 mi to Elm Dr and follow to resort.

GPS COORDINATES: 44.2037°N/-84.2498°W
RV SITES: Full: 42 Partial: 57 Dry: 0
CHECK-IN: 3:00 p.m.
CHECK-OUT: Noon
SEASON: May 2–October 10
PEAK SEASON: May 20–September 20
MAX. RV LENGTH: 40 feet
RENTAL ACCOMMODATIONS: Rental units available. Trip Points not accepted. Contact resort directly.

30 amps · dump station · laundry · pets/restrictions · playground · picnic tables · rental units · fishing · shuffleboard · horseshoes
group activities · boating · recreation hall · fishing · outdoor pool · mini golf · basketball · beach · volleyball
golf · game room · tourist attraction · shopping · propane · hot showers · fire rings · tenting · firewood · ice

MINNESOTA

DETROIT LAKES

RESORT NUMBER: 2138 **GOOD SAM RATING:** 9/9.5★/9 **COAST DELUXE RESORT**

Forest Hills Golf & RV Resort
22931 185th Street
Detroit Lakes, Minnesota 56501
800-482-3441; fax: 218-439-3971
office@foresthillsgolfrv.com
foresthillsgolfrv.com

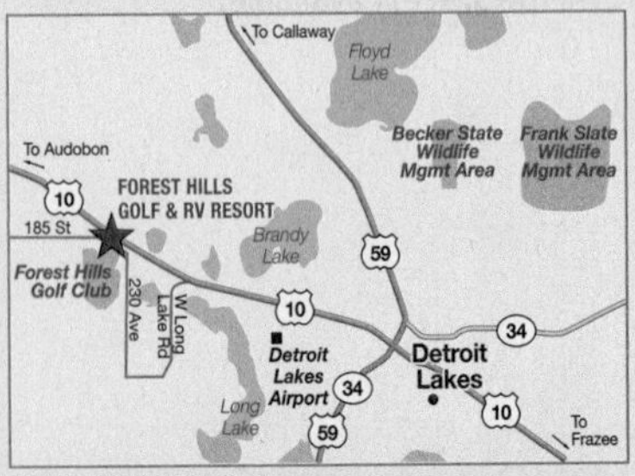

See page CTC 66 for state map.

In the heart of Lake Country with over 400 of Minnesota's 10,000 lakes within a 25-mile radius. Oak forests and natural wetlands are refuge to wildlife and make this one of the most beautiful resorts in northern Minnesota. An 18-hole golf course, amenities and location make this one of the finest family vacation spots.

DIRECTIONS: 3.5 mi W of Detroit Lakes, MN on S side of Hwy 10. Check-in time no later than 5 p.m.

GPS COORDINATES: 46.8403°N/-95.9259°W
RV SITES: Full: 167 Partial: 0 Dry: 0
CHECK-IN: Noon–5:00 p.m.
CHECK-OUT: 11:00 a.m.
SEASON: May 1–September 30
MAX. RV LENGTH: 44 feet
NOTATIONS: Rate includes full hook-up. Wi-Fi and Internet access in RV building only. Check in noon-5 p.m. Absolutely no check-in after 5 p.m. (no exceptions). Gated resort. No pull-through sites avail. Drive-ups not accepted.

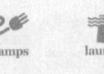

50 amps · laundry · pets/restrictions · internet access · Wi-Fi access · playground · restaurant/snack bar · hot tub · recreation hall · outdoor pool · mini golf · golf · fitness · shopping · hot showers · gambling casino

MINNESOTA

HAM LAKE

RESORT NUMBER: 2459 **GOOD SAM RATING:** 7.5/9★/8.5 **COAST DELUXE RESORT**

Ham Lake Resort—Midwest Outdoor Resorts
2400 Constance Boulevard Northeast
Ham Lake, Minnesota 55304
800-231-0425; fax: 605-343-3420
help@midwestoutdoorresorts.com
midwestoutdoorresorts.com

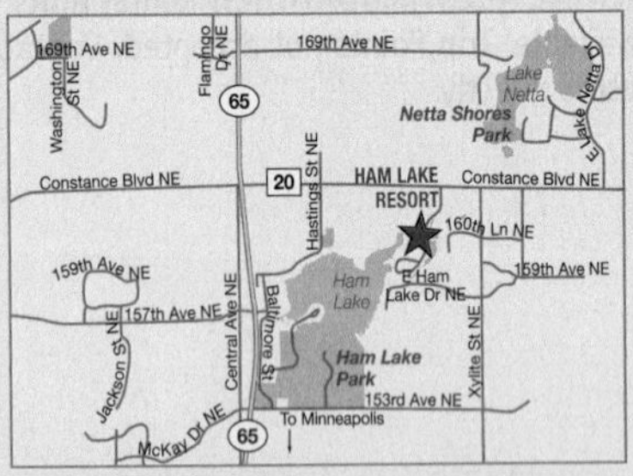

See page CTC 66 for state map.

Ham Lake Resort is a quiet getaway just minutes from the hustle and bustle of city life. Ham Lake Resort is located a mere 30 minutes from the Twin Cities. Come out and enjoy your morning coffee siting on the dock with a beautiful view of Ham Lake. The resort features a petting farm where you can feed the goats, sheep and alpacas. Don't miss the peacock, horse, mule and llama.

DIRECTIONS: From the Twin Cities: I-35 N to Blaine to MN-65/Central Ave Ex. R onto MN-65/Central Ave. R on Constance Blvd. Resort on R.

GPS COORDINATES: 45.26055°N/-93.21197°W
RV SITES: Full: 0 Partial: 0 Dry: 0
CHECK-IN: 11:00 a.m.
CHECK-OUT: 4:00 p.m.
SEASON: May 22–October 22
PEAK SEASON: May 22–September 7
MAX. RV LENGTH: 40 feet
NOTATIONS: Members staying at Ham Lake whose home park charges mandatory fees will be charged those same mandatory fees. Pets must be leashed, cleaned up after, and must be with you or in RV. If pets left in RV, a cell phone # must be left with front desk.

30 amps · dump station · visitor mail · laundry · pets/restrictions · internet access · playground · picnic tables · fishing · group activities · boating · fishing · boating · beach · canoes · hot showers · rv supplies · gift shop · tenting · firewood · ice

HINCKLEY

RESORT NUMBER: 54 **GOOD SAM RATING:** 8/9★/9.5 **COAST CLASSIC RESORT**

Pathfinder Village—St. Croix
49200 State Highway 48 #1
Hinckley, Minnesota 55037
320-384-7985; fax: 320-384-7728
pathfindervillage@yahoo.com
pathfindervillage.net

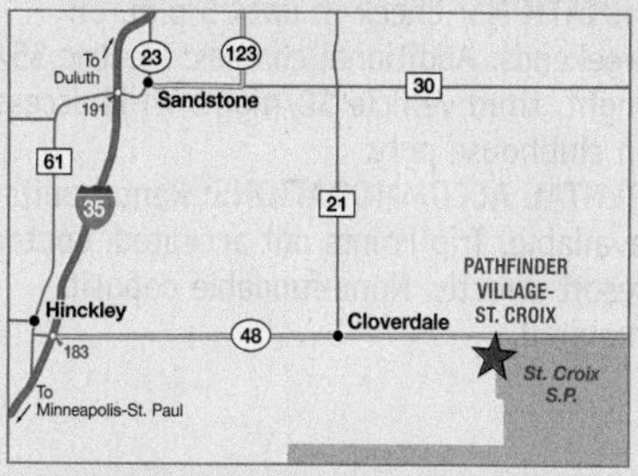

See page CTC 66 for state map.

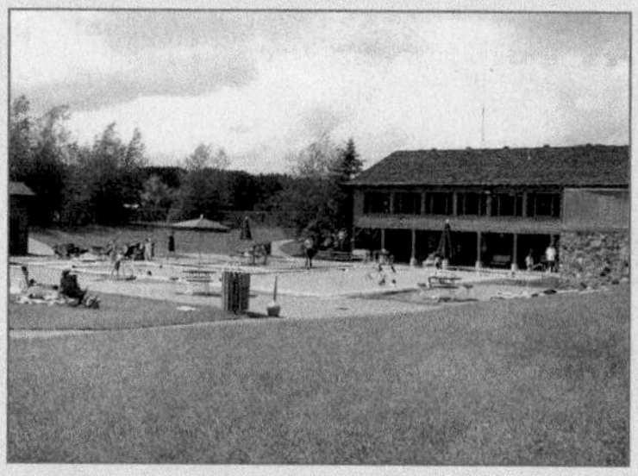

20-mile area around resort has 25 major and smaller fishing lakes. River canoeing and fishing available on five rivers, including St. Croix River. There are historical sites from the logging and mining era throughout the 500,000 acres of state and federal parks and forests. Nearby are 100 miles of registered trout streams.

DIRECTIONS: From Twin Cities: I-35 N, 77 mi to Hinckley. R (E) on paved SR 48. 14 mi to park on R.

GPS COORDINATES: 46.011°N/-92.6351°W
RV SITES: Full: 0 Partial: 30 Dry: 0
CHECK-IN: Noon
CHECK-OUT: 11:00 a.m.
SEASON: May 1–September 30
MAX. RV LENGTH: 35 feet
NOTATIONS: Resort office is closed after 5 p.m.

30 amps · pull-through · laundry · pets/restrictions · playground · fishing · hiking trails · fishing · outdoor pool · mini golf · tennis · golf · tourist attraction · canoes

HINCKLEY

RESORT NUMBER: 2243 **GOOD SAM RATING:** 8/10★/8.5 **COAST PREMIER RESORT**

St Croix River Resort—Midwest Outdoor Resorts
40756 Grace Lake Road
Hinckley, Minnesota 55037
320-655-0016; res.: 800-231-0425
stay@midwestoutdoorresorts.com
midwestoutdoorresorts.com

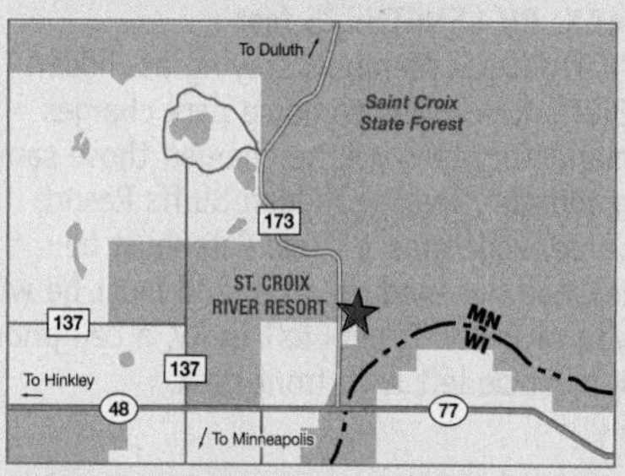

See page CTC 66 for state map.

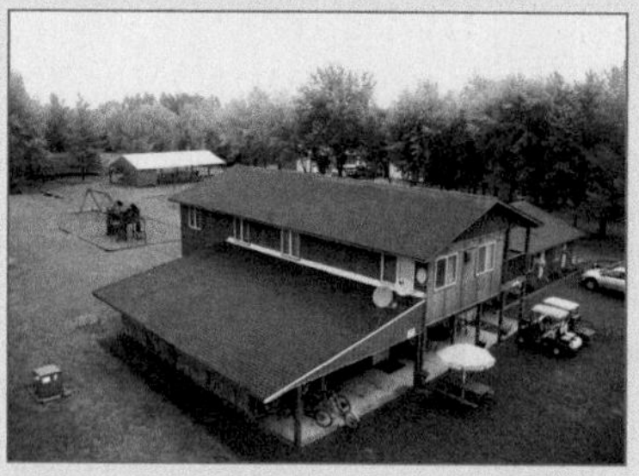

St. Croix River Resort is located near the St. Croix River and adjacent to the St. Croix State Forest. The spacious cul-du-sac campsites provide privacy not found elsewhere. You can choose quiet relaxation or get involved in as many planned activities as you wish.

DIRECTIONS: From the Twin Cities: I-35 N to Hinckley Ex. R on State Hwy 48 for 23 mi. Just before the St. Croix River turn L on Grace Lake Rd. Resort 1 mi on R.

GPS COORDINATES: 46.056°N/-92.467°W
RV SITES: Full: 15 Partial: 85 Dry: 0
CHECK-IN: 4:00 p.m.–close
CHECK-OUT: 11:00 a.m.
SEASON: May 22–October 18
PEAK SEASON: May 24–September 2
MAX. RV LENGTH: 44 feet
NOTATIONS: Members staying at St. Croix River Resort whose home park charges mandatory fees will be charged those same mandatory fees. Pets must be leashed, cleaned up after, and must be with you or in RV. If pets left in RV, a cell phone # must be left with front desk.

50 amps · pull-through · dump station · visitor mail · laundry · pets/restrictions · internet access · playground · picnic tables · hiking trails · horseshoes · group activities · fishing · volleyball · golf · tourist attraction · canoes · indoor pool · hot showers · gambling casino · fire rings · grocery · rv supplies · gift shop · tenting · firewood · ice

MINNESOTA

PERHAM

RESORT NUMBER: 279 **GOOD SAM RATING:** 7.5/8★/9 **COAST CLASSIC RESORT**

Golden Eagle RV Village
42492 480th Avenue
Perham, Minnesota 56573
218-346-4386
goldene2@arvig.net
goldeneaglervvillage.com

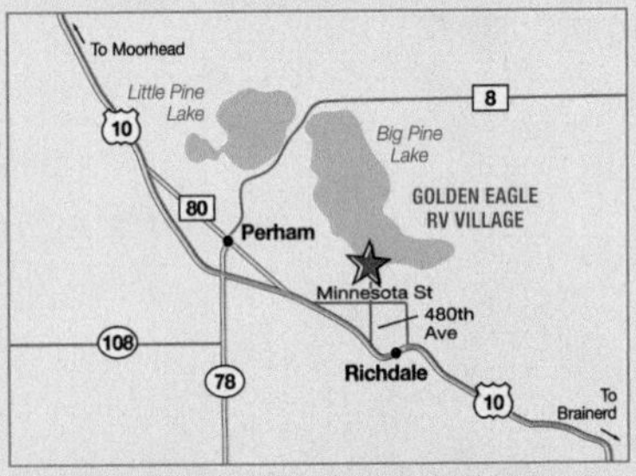

See page CTC 66 for state map.

The resort is located in west central Minnesota on the south end of 4,800-acre Big Pine Lake which is famous for its walleye fishing. Situated in the heart of the lake country, the resort offers large wooded sites on Big Pine Lake. Golden Eagle RV Village is a paradise for summer fun.

DIRECTIONS: From Moorhead: 72 mi E on Hwy 10, 3 mi E of Perham to Minnesota St. E on Minnesota St 2 mi. N on 480th Ave, 1 mi to resort.

GPS COORDINATES: 46.5796°N/-95.4915°W
RV SITES: Full: 150 Partial: 0 Dry: 8
CHECK-IN: 1:00 p.m.–5:00 p.m.
CHECK-OUT: 11:00 a.m.
SEASON: May 15–September 14
MAX. RV LENGTH: 40 feet
NOTATIONS: Check-in until 5 p.m. on weekends. Additional charges: Electric $5/night, third vehicle $2/night. Wi-Fi access in clubhouse only.
RENTAL ACCOMMODATIONS: Rental units available. Trip Points not accepted. Contact resort directly. Nonrefundable deposit required.

30 amps · laundry · pets/restrictions · Wi-Fi access · playground · rental units · fishing · boating · recreation hall · fishing · boating
outdoor pool · basketball · beach · golf · tourist attraction · shopping · hot showers · ball field · fire rings · firewood · ice

MINNESOTA

SPRING GROVE

RESORT NUMBER: 1932 **GOOD SAM RATING:** 8/8.5★/9 **COAST DELUXE RESORT**

Hidden Bluffs Resort—
Midwest Outdoor Resorts
22885 County Road 19
Spring Grove, Minnesota 55974
507-498-5880; res.: 800-231-0425
stay@midwestoutdoorresorts.com
midwestoutdoorresorts.com

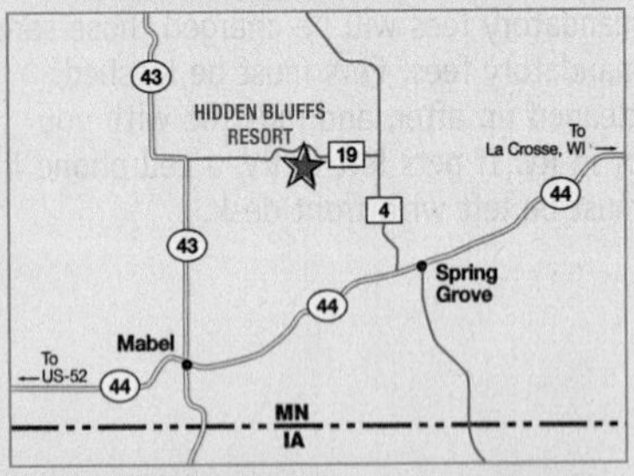

See page CTC 66 for state map.

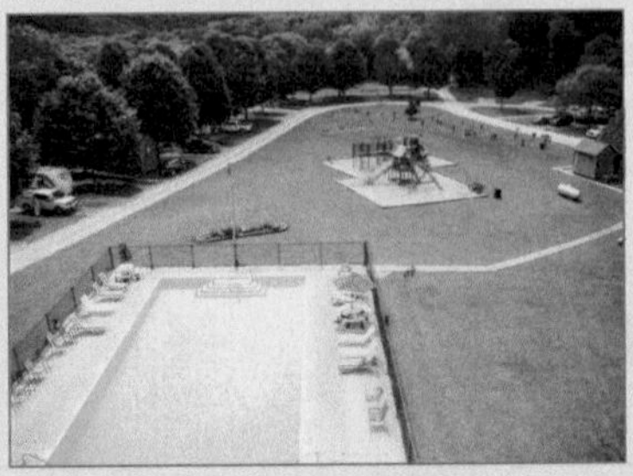

In the heart of Minnesota's Bluff Country surrounded by Amish communities and endless trout fishing. Nestled in a valley approximately 2.5 hours southeast of the Twin Cities. Hidden amongst a beautiful old growth of hardwood forest and bluffs, this resort offers the best of what are known as natural amenities.

DIRECTIONS: From Spring Grove: Take Hwy 44 out of Spring Grove and turn N onto County Rd 4, continue for 5 mi then turn W onto County Rd 19. Go 3 mi on gravel. Hidden Bluffs will be on the L.

GPS COORDINATES: 43.603°N/-91.7075°W
RV SITES: Full: 60 Partial: 16 Dry: 0
CHECK-IN: 4:00 p.m.
CHECK-OUT: 11:00 a.m.
SEASON: May 1–October 17
PEAK SEASON: May 24–September 4
MAX. RV LENGTH: 75 feet
NOTATIONS: Members staying at Hidden Bluffs Resort whose home park charges mandatory fees will be charged those same mandatory fees at Hidden Bluffs Resort. Large, wide grassy sites. Pets must be leashed, cleaned up after, and must be with you or in RV. If pets left in RV, a cell phone # must be left with front desk.

50 amps · pull-through · dump station · visitor mail · laundry · pets/restrictions · internet access · Wi-Fi access · playground · picnic tables · hot tub · fishing · biking trails · horseshoes
group activities · fishing · outdoor pool · mini golf · basketball · volleyball · shopping · hot showers · fire rings · gift shop · tenting · firewood · handicap access · ice

PASS-CHRISTIAN

RESORT NUMBER: 509 **GOOD SAM RATING:** 9/8/8 **COAST PREMIER RESORT**

MISSISSIPPI

TLC Wolf River Resort
23098 Freddie Frank Road
Pass-Christian, Mississippi 39571
228-452-9100; fax: 228-452-9190
tlcwolfriverresort@gmail.com
tlcwolfriverresort.com

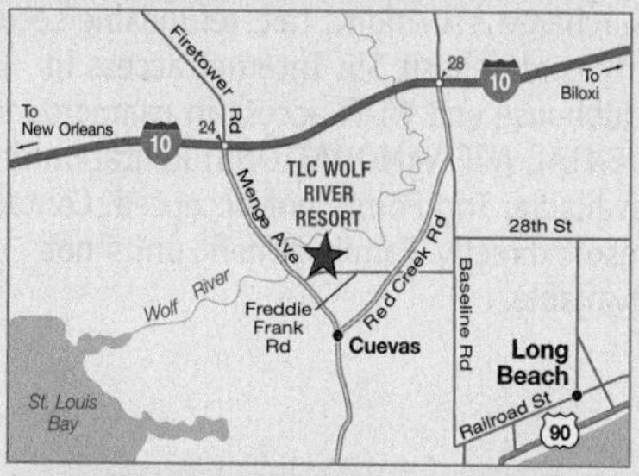

See page CTC 50 for state map.

Waterfront campsites along a private bayou with a private beach on the Wolf River. Five minutes from Mississippi's 26-mile sugar white sand gulf beach! Resort casinos line the coast, located only 10 minutes from Wolf River Resort. Charter fishing opportunities available along with excursions to barrier islands. Less than an hour from the New Orleans French Quarter.

DIRECTIONS: From I-10 E: Ex 24/Menge Ave S towards beach. 2.5 mi across Wolf River Bridge. First L on Freddie Frank Rd. Resort is 0.5 mi on L.

GPS COORDINATES: 30.384°N/-89.2655°W
RV SITES: Full: 140 Partial: 0 Dry: 50
CHECK-IN: 9:00 a.m.–5:00 p.m.
CHECK-OUT: Noon
SEASON: Year-round
PEAK SEASON: November 1–March 31
MAX. RV LENGTH: 45 feet
NOTATIONS: No check-in after 5 p.m. Central Time. Additional charges: 50 amp $5/night, Wi-Fi access in campground $1/night.
RENTAL ACCOMMODATIONS: Rental units available. Trip points not accepted. Contact resort directly.

BRANSON

RESORT NUMBER: 834 **GOOD SAM RATING:** 9.5/9★/8.5 **COAST CLASSIC RESORT**

MISSOURI

Branson Ridge RV Resort—Ocean Canyon Properties
5040 State Highway 265
Branson, Missouri 65616
417-213-5801; fax: 417-338-2949
member.reservations@oceancanyon.com
oceancanyon.com

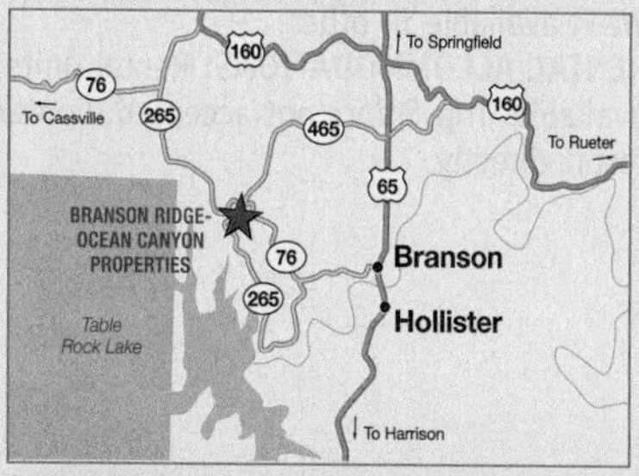

See page CTC 61 for state map.

We invite you to the Heart of the Ozarks for a Branson, Missouri camping experience like no other! Located a mile from Silver Dollar City, local to Table Rock Lake and minutes from Branson's shows. Our resort offers plenty of space and lush views from its sites, and picnic and recreation areas are also available. There is always something to do at Branson Ridge!

DIRECTIONS: From Springfield: Hwy 65 S to Hwy 465. Turn R onto Hwy 465, go 7 mi to Hwy 76. Turn L (W) at the stoplight onto Hwy 76. Go approx 0.5 mi to light at Hwy 265 turn L (S). Resort is approx 0.5 mi on the L. From Arkansas state line: Go N on Hwy 65. Turn L onto Hwy 465 and follow balance of directions above. From Hwy 13 Branson West: Go E on Hwy 76 approx 4 mi. Turn R onto Hwy 265 S.

GPS COORDINATES: 36.6659°N/-93.3287°W
ELEVATION: 1,070 feet
RV SITES: Full: 137 Partial: 42 Dry: 22
CHECK-IN: 2:00 p.m.
CHECK-OUT: 11:00 a.m.
SEASON: April 1–November 30
MAX. RV LENGTH: 45 feet
NOTATIONS: Additional charges: 50 amp $5/night, Wi-Fi $5/night, 7.475% tax.
RENTAL ACCOMMODATIONS: Rental units available. Trip Points not accepted. Contact resort directly.

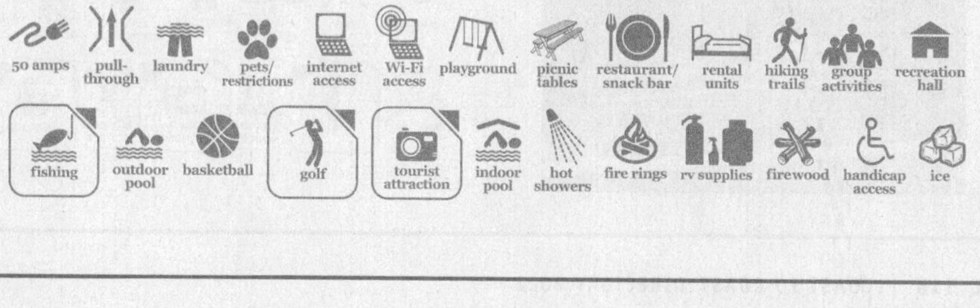

BRANSON

RESORT NUMBER: 144 **GOOD SAM RATING:** 9/9★/9 **COAST DELUXE RESORT**

Treasure Lake RV Resort
1 Treasure Lake Drive
Branson, Missouri 65616
417-334-1040; fax: 417-334-5522
reservations@tlresort.com
tlresort.com

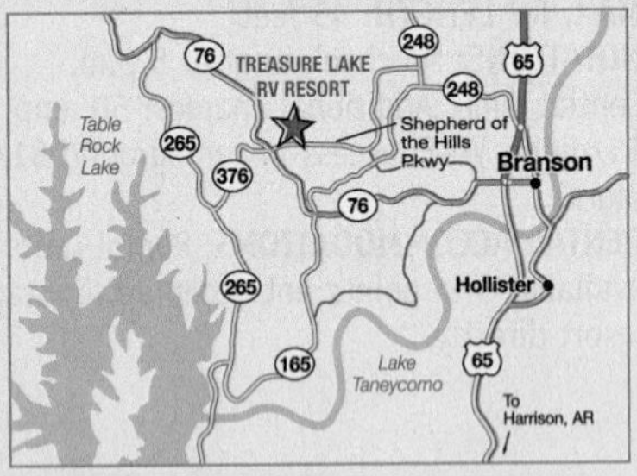

See page CTC 61 for state map.

This resort is deep in the heart of Ozark Mountain country and minutes away from a large variety of recreational facilities including the Tri-Lakes for fishing and boating. Less than three miles away are Shepherd of the Hills, Silver Dollar City, White Water, and many theaters.

DIRECTIONS: From Hwy 65: Ex Hwy 248 W. 2 mi (just past Hobby Lobby). R at the Y. L at SOH Expwy. Resort is on R next to IMAX. From Hwy 13: E at Hwy 76. Follow to SOH Expy (just past Butterfly Palace). L, then L again at bottom of hill.

GPS COORDINATES: 36.6549°N/-93.2879°W
RV SITES: Full: 587 Partial: 21 Dry: 0
CHECK-IN: 8:00 a.m.–9:00 p.m.
CHECK-OUT: 2:00 p.m.
SEASON: Year-round
MAX. RV LENGTH: 45 feet
NOTATIONS: Only one Coast Family & Friends benefit reservationallowed on property at a time. Additional charges: Surcharge $10/night, tax, refundable security card deposit $5. Internet access in clubhouse and Wi-Fi access in campground.
RENTAL ACCOMMODATIONS: Rental units available. Trip Points not accepted. Contact resort directly. Family benefit units not available.

CLARKSVILLE

RESORT NUMBER: 573 **GOOD SAM RATING:** 8/6/8.5 **COAST DELUXE RESORT**

Tievoli Hills Resort—
Family Resorts and Travel
25795 Highway N
Clarksville, Missouri 63336
573-242-3577; fax: 573-242-3288
ctucker@crowndiversified.com

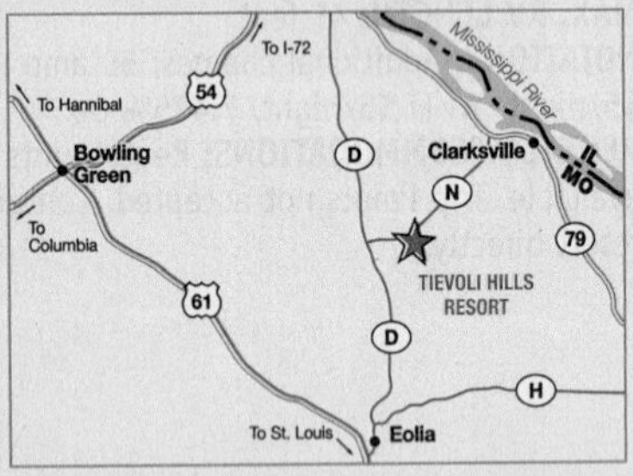

See page CTC 61 for state map.

Hidden in the Mississippi River countryside, one of the best amenity packages in the Midwest offering a country club theme over 160 acres, surrounded by thousands of acres of undeveloped, natural land. Day trip to Hannibal, Mark Twain Lake, or St. Louis.

DIRECTIONS: From I-70 W of St Louis: Hwy 79 N to Clarksville. 2 mi past Clarksville. Hwy N 4 mi W to resort on L.

GPS COORDINATES: 39.3306°N/-90.9867°W
RV SITES: Full: 32 Partial: 35 Dry: 0
CHECK-IN: 24 hours
CHECK-OUT: 11:00 a.m.
SEASON: Year-round
PEAK SEASON: May 26–September 5
MAX. RV LENGTH: 45 feet
NOTATIONS: Additional charges: Mandatory utility fee $18/night. Tent pads available. Wi-Fi available in office.
RENTAL ACCOMMODATIONS: Rental units available. Trip Points not accepted. Contact resort directly.

OWENSVILLE

RESORT NUMBER: 177 **GOOD SAM RATING:** 8/9/8.5 **COAST PREMIER RESORT**

Lost Valley Lake Resort
2334 Highway ZZ
Owensville, Missouri 65066
800-489-2100; res.: 800-865-2100
reservations@lostvalleylake.com
lostvalleylake.com

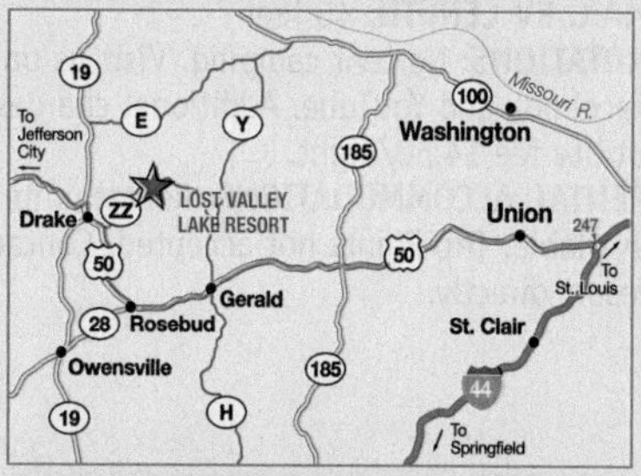

See page CTC 61 for state map.

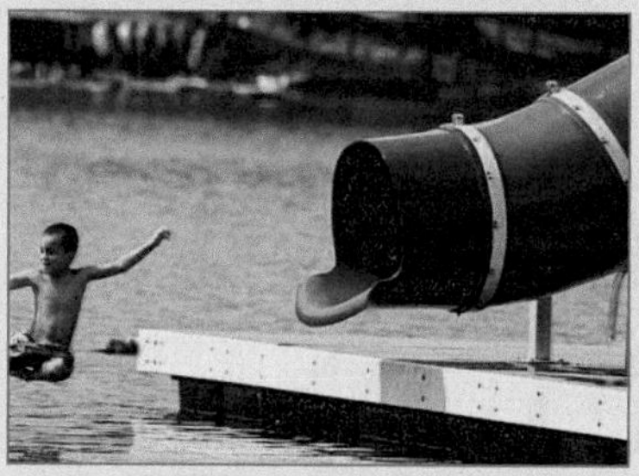

Located 75 miles west of St. Louis, this resort has 537 acres of gentle hills, rich foliage, four stocked lakes and a 44,000 square foot activity center with family activities scheduled year-round. Many must-see attractions located within a few miles. Nearby: Six Flags St. Louis, Meramec Caverns, and the German village of Hermann-famous for its wineries, Maifest and Octoberfest.

DIRECTIONS: From I-270 at St Louis: I-44 W 30 mi to Hwy 50. Hwy 50 W approx 28 mi. R on Hwy Y. L on Hwy ZZ. Resort 6 mi on L.

GPS COORDINATES: 38.4759°N/-91.3978°W
RV SITES: Full: 197 Partial: 82 Dry: 0
CHECK-IN: 3:00 p.m.–midnight
CHECK-OUT: 11:00 a.m.
SEASON: Year-round
MAX. RV LENGTH: 80 feet
NOTATIONS: Wi-Fi in public buildings and at a few sites.
RENTAL ACCOMMODATIONS: Rental units available. Trip Points not accepted. Contact resort directly.

WHITE SULPHUR SPRINGS

RESORT NUMBER: 1806 **GOOD SAM RATING:** 6.5/8.5/8 **COAST DELUXE RESORT**

Conestoga Campground
815 8th Avenue Southwest
White Sulphur Springs, Montana 59645
406-547-3890
info@conestoga-campground.com
conestoga-campground.com

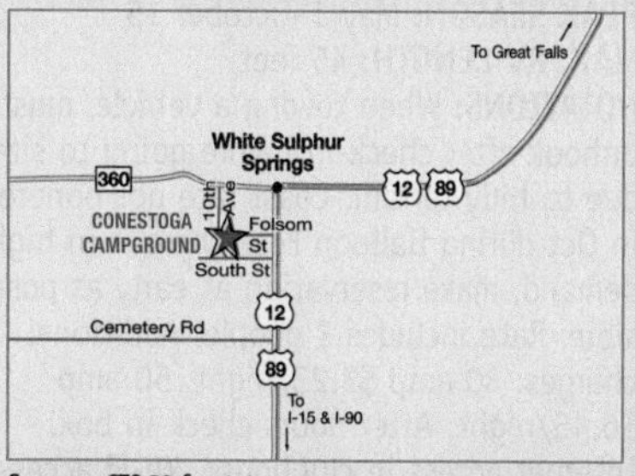

See page CTC 59 for state map.

Conestoga Campground is located four blocks from National Scenic Byway US Hwy 89, the shortest route between Glacier and Yellowstone National Parks. Our park is nestled in the heart of wonderful recreation and scenic opportunities in the Big Belt and Little Belt Mountains.

DIRECTIONS: From N-bound on Hwy 89: W (L) on Folsom St. 4 blocks to park. From center of White Sulphur Springs: S on Hwy 89/12 (SW 3rd Ave). W (R) on Folsom St. 4 blocks to park. Turns are well marked, follow signs.

GPS COORDINATES: 46.5425°N/-110.912°W
ELEVATION: 5,200 feet
RV SITES: Full: 27 Partial: 14 Dry: 29
CHECK-IN: 1:00 p.m.–dusk
CHECK-OUT: 11:00 a.m.
SEASON: April 1–November 30
PEAK SEASON: June 15–September 15
MAX. RV LENGTH: 42 feet
NOTATIONS: Additional charges: Daily member fee $5/night plus tax, extra person $3/night. Early check-in/late check-out $5/hr (2 hr max). All sites are pull-through. Rates include 1 RV, 1 vehicle/trailer, 2 people. Motorcycle friendly. Pet friendly but rules must be followed. Limited space avail for Big Rigs, please call resort for availability. Call office to arrange for after-hours check-in.

NEVADA

PAHRUMP

RESORT NUMBER: 349 GOOD SAM RATING: 9/10★/9.5 COAST CLASSIC RESORT

Preferred RV Resort
1801 Crawford Way
Pahrump, Nevada 89048
775-727-4414; fax: 775-727-4603
reservations@preferredrv.com
preferredrv.com

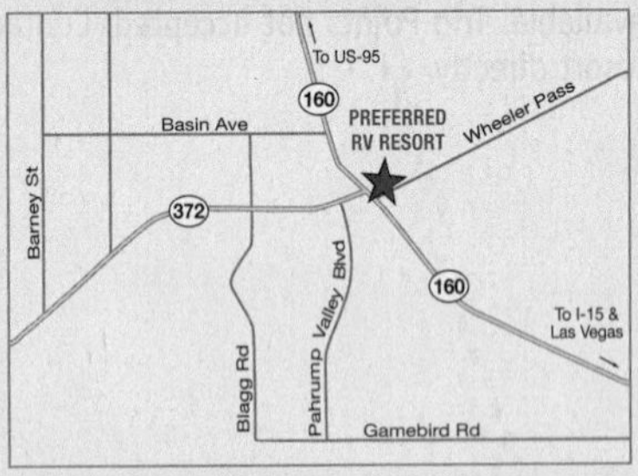

See page CTC 68 for state map.

The resort is located in the heart of downtown, in short walking distance of gambling, dining, shopping & bowling. Clean restrooms & showers, 100 pull-thru sites, 50 amp service at every site.

DIRECTIONS: From I-15 in Las Vegas: Ex 33/Blue Diamond Pahrump Hwy 160. NW 55 mi. R at Hwy 372 (Gold Town Casino). R 1,000 ft to resort.

GPS COORDINATES: 36.2113°N/-115.9821°W
ELEVATION: 2,695 feet
RV SITES: Full: 270 Partial: 0 Dry: 0
CHECK-IN: 10:00 a.m.–9:00 p.m.
CHECK-OUT: 11:00 a.m.
SEASON: April 1–December 31
MAX. RV LENGTH: 45 feet
NOTATIONS: No tent camping. Visit us on Facebook and YouTube. Additional charges: Utility fee $4.50/night.
RENTAL ACCOMMODATIONS: Rental units available. Trip Points not accepted. Contact resort directly.

50 amps · pull-through · dump station · visitor mail · laundry · pets/restrictions · internet access · Wi-Fi access · playground · picnic tables · rental units · hot tub · shuffleboard · horseshoes · group activities · outdoor pool · golf · fitness · shopping · propane · indoor pool · hot showers · gambling casino · ice

NEW MEXICO

TIJERAS

RESORT NUMBER: 164 GOOD SAM RATING: 6.5/7/6 COAST DELUXE RESORT

Hidden Valley Resort
844B State Highway 333
Tijeras, New Mexico 87059
505-281-3363; fax: 505-281-2026
info@hiddenvalley-rvpark.com
hiddenvalley-rvpark.com

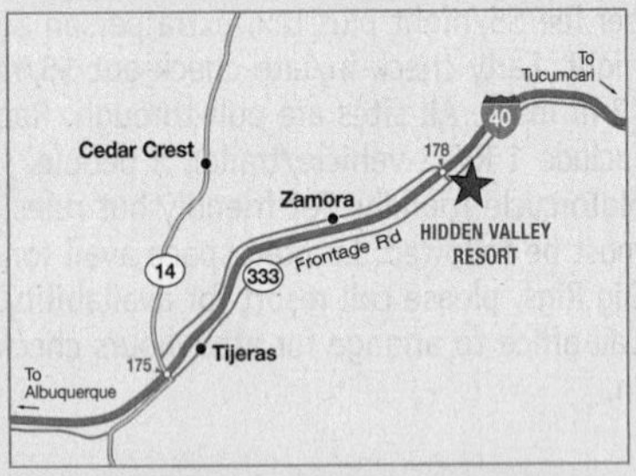

See page CTC 55 for state map.

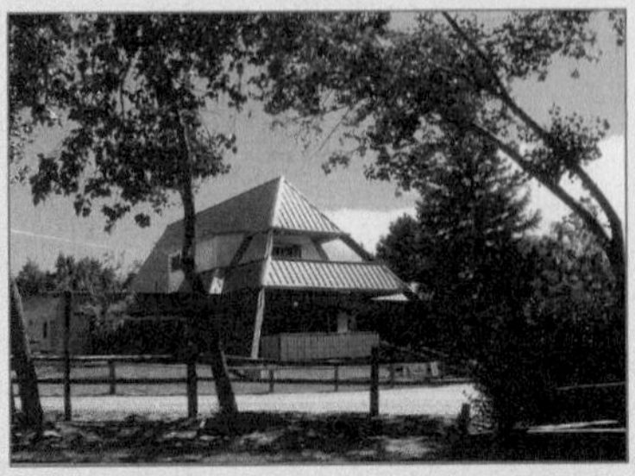

Resort is 10 miles east of Albuquerque, a short distance from the Sandia Crest Ski and Recreation Area. Nearby: national forest, ghost towns, Indian pueblos, Rio Grande Zoo, Coronado Ruins and Monument. Albuquerque's western edge reveals a history page of petroglyphs, volcano cliffs, and the Folsom Man Site.

DIRECTIONS: From I-40: Ex 178. At stop sign turn towards S Frontage Rd/Hwy 333 (old US 66) at Zuzax Gas Mart. Park on E side of Gas Mart. Entrance is uphill on R.

GPS COORDINATES: 35.105°N/-106.3394°W
ELEVATION: 6,607 feet
RV SITES: Full: 104 Partial: 2 Dry: 0
CHECK-IN: 1:00 p.m.–4:00 p.m.
CHECK-OUT: 11:00 a.m.
SEASON: Year-round
PEAK SEASON: May 1–October 15
MAX. RV LENGTH: 45 feet
NOTATIONS: When towing a vehicle, must unhook after check-in before going to site due to hilly terrain. Coast rate not honored in Oct during Balloon Fest. June is in high demand, make reservation as early as possible. Rate includes 2 people. Additional charges: 30 amp $3.23/night, 50 amp $6.45/night. After hours check-in box. Internet access in clubhouse, Wi-Fi access in lower level sites only.

50 amps · pull-through · dump station · visitor mail · laundry · pets/restrictions · internet access · Wi-Fi access · playground · picnic tables · hiking trails · recreation hall · outdoor pool · basketball · tourist attraction · hot showers · gift shop · tenting

BLISS

RESORT NUMBER: 71 **GOOD SAM RATING:** 7/9★/8 **COAST DELUXE RESORT**

Faun Lake
5124 Pleasant Valley Road
Bliss, New York 14024
585-322-7300; fax: 585-322-7330
faunlake.office@gmail.com
faunlake.com

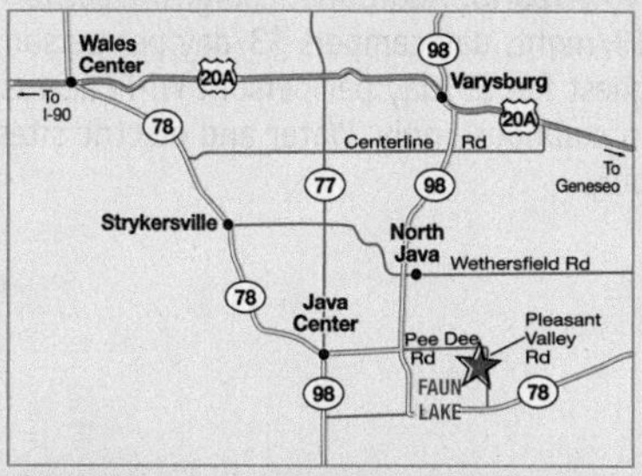

See page CTC 69 for state map.

In a scenic setting 38 mi southeast of Buffalo and 50 mi southwest of Rochester in beautiful Western New York. The wilderness surrounding the lake contains many nature trails, and the resort has many facilities for sports. Activities center, swimming, boating, and fishing in the lovely Faun Lake.

DIRECTIONS: From Buffalo: I-90 6 mi W to Ex 54. S (R) on SR 400. 11 mi to the town of E Aurora. Ex 28 E onto SR 20A. 2 mi, bear R on SR 78. S 14 mi to Jct of SR 78 and SR 98 E of Java Center. Straight on Pee Dee Rd. 3 mi to Pleasant Valley Rd. S (R) on Pleasant Valley Rd. 0.2 mi to entrance of park on the R. Do not pull in drive. Park on roadside to register at office.

GPS COORDINATES: 42.6462°N/-78.2837°W
RV SITES: Full: 0 Partial: 22 Dry: 0
CHECK-IN: 9:00 a.m.–4:00 p.m.
CHECK-OUT: Noon
SEASON: May 1–September 30
PEAK SEASON: July 1–September 30
MAX. RV LENGTH: 35 feet
NOTATIONS: Office hours 9 a.m.-4 p.m. until Labor Day. Must check-in at office. If after hours, come into office next business day to check-in. Clubhouse, pool and hot tub are 0.5 mi from our Coast to Coast area.

DIAMOND POINT

RESORT NUMBER: 2071 **GOOD SAM RATING:** 7/7/8 **COAST DELUXE RESORT**

Schroon River Escape Lodges & RV Resort
969 East Schroon River Road
Diamond Point, New York 12824
518-504-4063
schroonriverescape@gmail.com
schroonriverescape.com

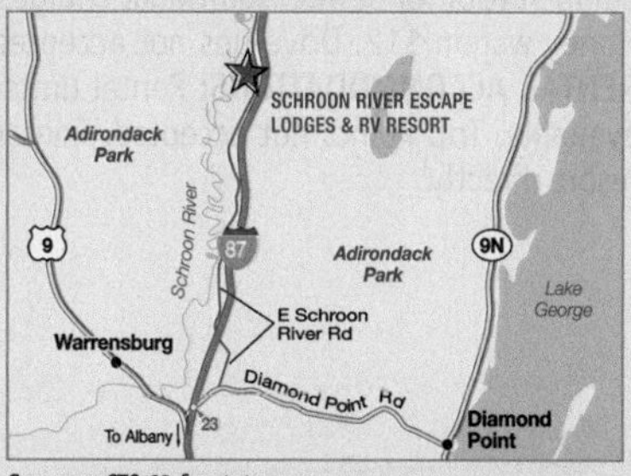

See page CTC 69 for state map.

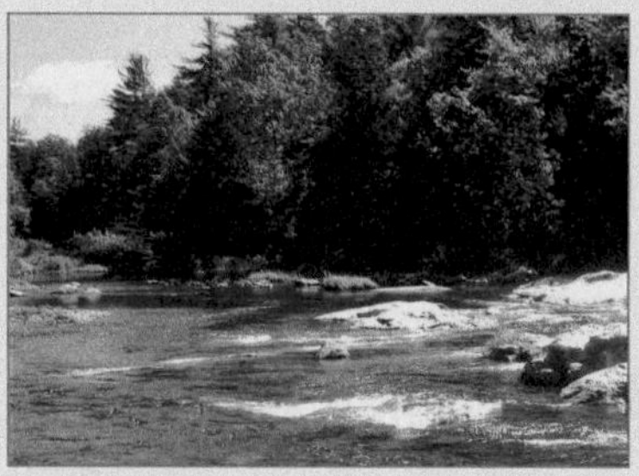

Nestled in the foothills of the Adirondack Mountains with almost a mile of river frontage. River-front sites afford you and your family the opportunity to get away from it all. Grab your fishing pole or one of our canoes and enjoy the peaceful flowing waters of the beautiful Schroon River.

DIRECTIONS: From I-87 N: Ex 23. R for 0.25 mi. L onto E Schroon River Rd. 4.6 mi to park on L. From Diamond Point: 4.5 mi N of intersection Diamond Point Rd (Cty Rte 35) and E Schroon River Rd.

GPS COORDINATES: 43.5506°N/-73.7383°W
ELEVATION: 727 feet
RV SITES: Full: 100 Partial: 50 Dry: 0
CHECK-IN: 3:00 p.m.–8:00 p.m.
CHECK-OUT: 11:00 a.m.
SEASON: May 20–October 10
MAX. RV LENGTH: 45 feet
NOTATIONS: Additional charges: Honey wagon $12, cable $5/day. No 50 amp service. No outside firewood permitted.
RENTAL ACCOMMODATIONS: Rental units available. Trip Points not accepted. Contact resort directly. Pet fee $25.

NEW YORK

EAST OTTO

RESORT NUMBER: 75 **GOOD SAM RATING:** 7.5/9★/8 **COAST DELUXE RESORT**

Allegany Mountain Resort
6994 Plato Road
East Otto, New York 14729
716-699-2352; fax: 716-699-2882
amrreservations@yahoo.com
alleganymountainresort.com

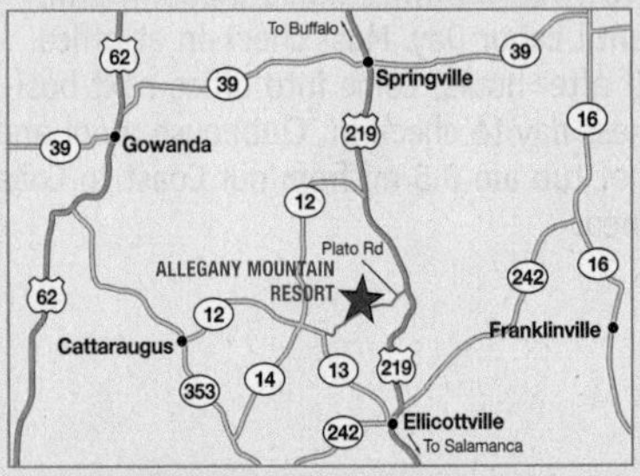

See page CTC 69 for state map.

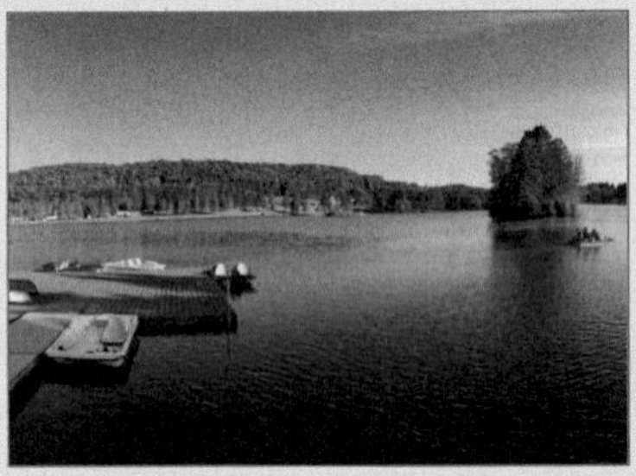

Allegany Mountain Resort surrounds a spring-fed, 66-acre lake with 2.5 miles of shoreline. Loads of free amenities for all ages are a perfect way to spend a hot summer day! You can soak up the sun at our two outdoor pools or go fishing in one of our rent-free boats where the bass and panfish are plentiful. Our resort is a short 10-minute drive to the quaint village of Ellicottville.

DIRECTIONS: Do not follow GPS. From Buffalo: Hwy 219 S off I-90 for 40 mi. R on Plato Rd, 3 mi to entrance. From Canada: Queen Elizabeth Way S to Peace Bridge to USA. I-90 S to I-90 interchange. I-90 W to Ex 55 at Hwy 219 Expy. Hwy 219 to the end of Expy. R to light and turn L. Stay on Hwy 219 S 12 mi S of Springville. R on Plato Rd. Follow signs to resort.

GPS COORDINATES: 42.4246°N/-78.6926°W
RV SITES: Full: 0 Partial: 230 Dry: 0
CHECK-IN: 11:00 a.m.–5:00 p.m.
CHECK-OUT: 2:00 p.m.
SEASON: May 1–October 14
PEAK SEASON: July 1–August 31
MAX. RV LENGTH: 37 feet
NOTATIONS: Additional charges: Electric $3/night, day campers $3/day per person, guest fee $3/day per person. Wi-Fi access in clubhouse only. Water and electric sites only.

NEW YORK

GREENFIELD CENTER

RESORT NUMBER: 1600 **GOOD SAM RATING:** 7.5/6.5/9.5 **COAST DELUXE RESORT**

Saratoga Escape Lodges & RV Park
265 Brigham Road
Greenfield Center, New York 12833
518-893-0537; fax: 518-893-5110
saratogaescapecamp@gmail.com
saratogaescape.com

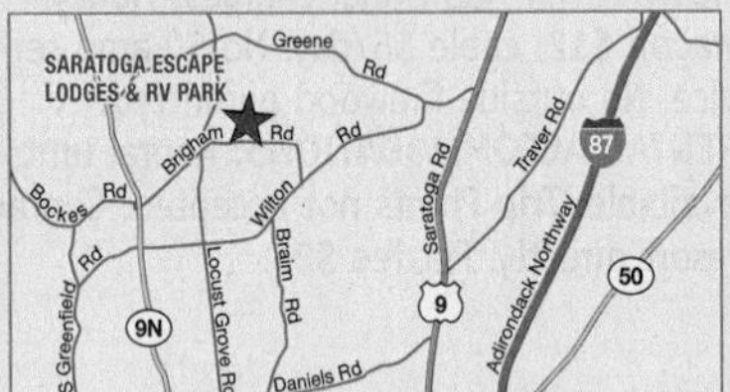

See page CTC 69 for state map.

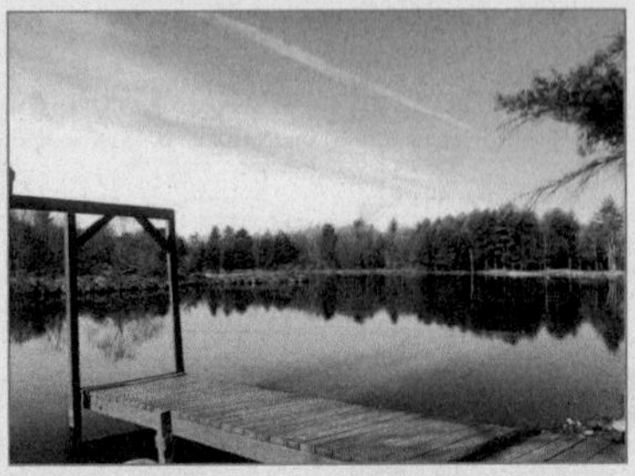

Our beautiful resort has a vast array of amenities for every age including a beautiful private spring-fed lake with beach area. We are just minutes from the famous Saratoga Race Track, SPAC, and downtown shopping on Broadway. Beautiful Lake George, Queen of the American Lakes, is an easy 20 minute drive. We are convenient to white water rafting, the beautiful Adirondack Mountains, and numerous historic sites.

DIRECTIONS: From NYS Trwy Ex 24: N onto N-Way (87N) to Ex 16. L to light. L onto Rte 9 to Gailor Rd. R to Brigham Rd. R to resort.

GPS COORDINATES: 43.1372°N/-73.8765°W
RV SITES: Full: 10 Partial: 110 Dry: 10
CHECK-IN: Noon
CHECK-OUT: Noon
SEASON: May 20–October 10
MAX. RV LENGTH: 40 feet
NOTATIONS: Rate includes water, 4 persons, dump station or sewer. Additional charges: Honey wagon $12. Drive-ups not accepted.
RENTAL ACCOMMODATIONS: Rental units available. Trip Points not accepted. Contact resort directly.

HOLLAND

RESORT NUMBER: 659 **GOOD SAM RATING:** 6/4.5/6.5 **COAST CLASSIC RESORT**

NEW YORK

Three Valley Campground
9766 Olean Road
Holland, New York 14080
716-537-2372; fax: 716-537-2095
info@threevalley.com
threevalley.com

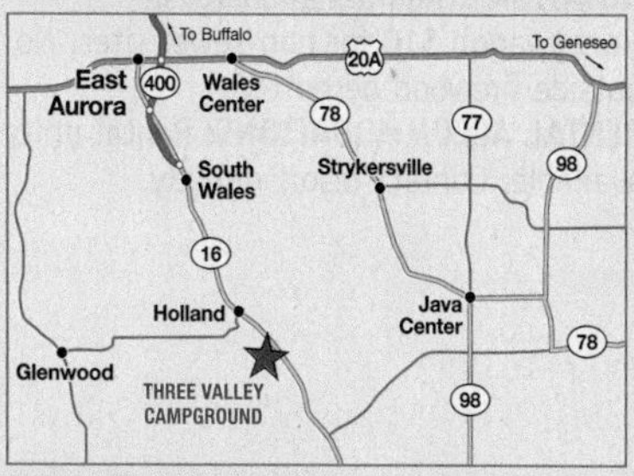

See page CTC 69 for state map.

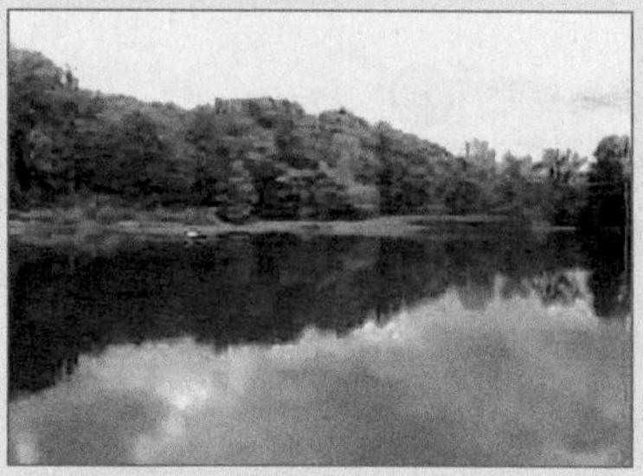

Three Valley is a 450-acre resort with sunny meadows, rolling hills and wooded areas. Fun for the whole family on two large lakes for water sports and 20 miles of nature and wildlife trails. Easy driving distance to Niagara Falls, Letchworth State Park, Lake Erie, downhill ski resorts and Holland International Speedway.

DIRECTIONS: From SE of Buffalo off I-90 Aurora Expwy (Hwy 400): 15 mi S to Hwy 16 through Holland. 2.5 mi to resort on Hwy 16.

GPS COORDINATES: 42.6137°N/-78.5088°W
RV SITES: Full: 0 Partial: 120 Dry: 0
CHECK-IN: 3:00 p.m.
CHECK-OUT: Noon
SEASON: June 1–September 1
MAX. RV LENGTH: 30 feet
NOTATIONS: 50 amp service not available.

30 amps · dump station · laundry · pets/restrictions · playground · picnic tables · fishing · hiking trails · horseshoes · group activities · recreation hall · fishing · outdoor pool · basketball · volleyball · game room · tourist attraction · propane · hot showers · ball field · fire rings · grocery · gift shop · firewood · ice

LOCKPORT

RESORT NUMBER: 646 **GOOD SAM RATING:** 8.5/9.5/10 **COAST CLASSIC RESORT**

NEW YORK

Niagara's Lazy Lakes Resort
4312 Church Road
Lockport, New York 14094
800-874-2957; fax: 716-433-2625
ccc@lazylakes.com
lazylakes.com

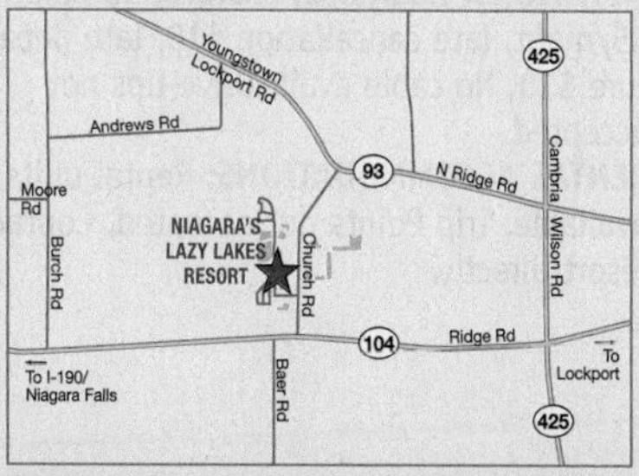

See page CTC 69 for state map.

Niagara's Lazy Lakes Resort is in the heart of Niagara and is known as Western New York's Best Kept Secret. Only 15 minutes from the Canadian border, plan on visiting many of the local and Canadian attractions such as Niagara Falls, Lake Ontario (salmon fishing), Old Fort Niagara, and Toronto.

DIRECTIONS: From 1-90 Wbnd: Ex 50 to I-290 to US Hwy 62, Ex 3 (Niagara Falls Blvd/US Hwy 62). Continue N to Rt 425, take Rt 425 to Rt 104. Turn W on Rt 104 for 1.5 mi to Church Rd. N on Church Rd, resort entrance is 1000 ft ahead on L.

GPS COORDINATES: 43.2067°N/-78.8526°W
ELEVATION: 300 feet
RV SITES: Full: 0 Partial: 265 Dry: 0
CHECK-IN: Noon–6:00 p.m.
CHECK-OUT: 11:00 a.m.
SEASON: May 1–October 31
MAX. RV LENGTH: 45 feet
NOTATIONS: Additional charges: 50 amp $4/night, arrival dump station fee $25, honeywagon $10. No sewer sites.
RENTAL ACCOMMODATIONS: Rental units available. Trip Points not accepted. Contact resort directly.

50 amps · pull-through · dump station · laundry · pets/restrictions · Wi-Fi access · playground · picnic tables · rental units · fishing · shuffleboard · horseshoes · group activities · boating · recreation hall · church services · fishing · boating · outdoor pool · basketball · beach · golf · game room · tourist attraction · shopping · propane · canoes · hot showers · gambling casino · fire rings · grocery · rv supplies · gift shop · firewood · handicap access · ice

NEW YORK

PARISH

RESORT NUMBER: 689 GOOD SAM RATING: 8.5/8/9.5 COAST PREMIER RESORT

Bass Lake Resort—Travel Resorts of America
132 Crim Road
Parish, New York 13131
315-728-9437
blrreservations@travelresorts.com
travelresorts.com

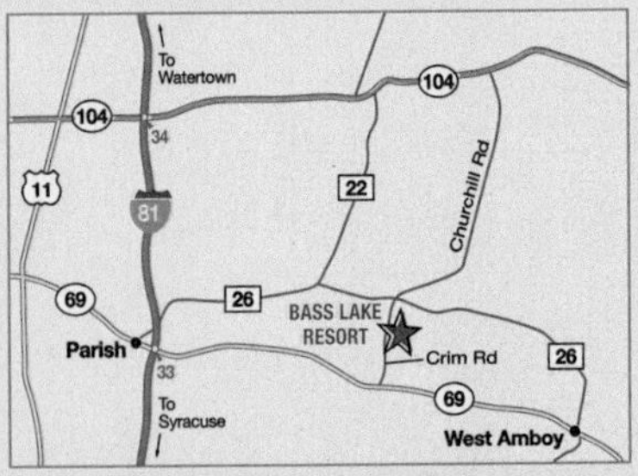

See page CTC 69 for state map.

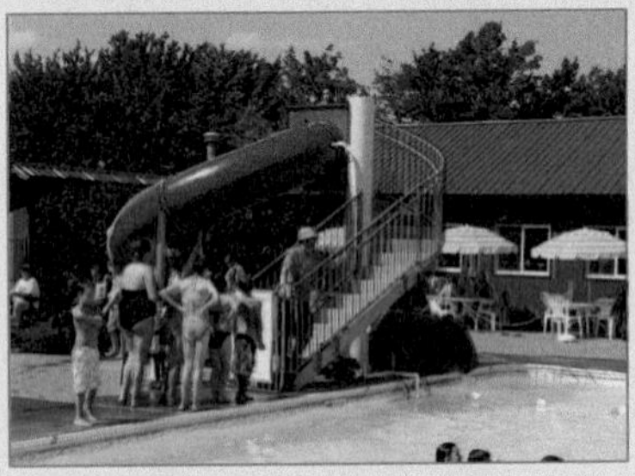

When glaciers moved out of the New York area, 244 acres of woodland and meadows, overlooking a sparkling, spring-fed pond were left behind. Little Salmon River makes its way from Lake Ontario. Evergreens, maple, and birch surround the campsites, with recreational amenities to make your vacation memorable.

DIRECTIONS: From I-81: Ex 33/Parish. Rte 69 3.5 mi E to Crim Rd. 0.5 mi N to resort.

GPS COORDINATES: 43.4033°N/-76.0451°W
ELEVATION: 100 feet
RV SITES: Full: 151 Partial: 155 Dry: 0
CHECK-IN: 1:00 p.m.
CHECK-OUT: 11:00 a.m.
SEASON: May 15–October 10
MAX. RV LENGTH: 40 feet
NOTATIONS: Additional charges: Honeywagon $10 for non-sewer sites. No outside firewood permitted.
RENTAL ACCOMMODATIONS: Rental units available. Contact resort directly.

50 amps, dump station, laundry, pets/restrictions, internet access, Wi-Fi access, playground, picnic tables, restaurant/snack bar, rental units, fishing, horseshoes, group activities, recreation hall, church services, fishing, outdoor pool, mini golf, basketball, volleyball, golf, game room, tourist attraction, canoes, hot showers, ball field, paddle boats, fire rings, grocery, rv supplies, gift shop, tenting, firewood, handicap access, ice

NEW YORK

WHITEHALL

RESORT NUMBER: 2252 GOOD SAM RATING: 3.5/5/4 COAST DELUXE RESORT

Champs RV Resort
1 Main Street
Whitehall, New York 12887
518-499-5055
me.campmoonlight@gmail.com

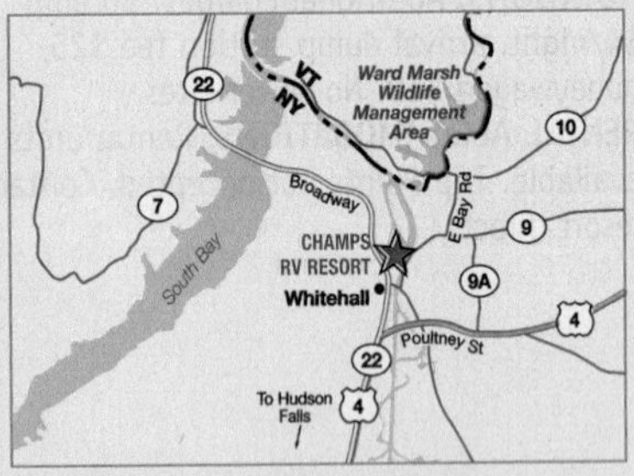

See page CTC 69 for state map.

Champs has it all. Nestled in the historic town of Whitehall, NY (birthplace of the US Navy) and 10 minutes from the VT border. Champs has a beautiful setting right on the Champlain Waterway and gorgeous mountain views. It's a nature lover's paradise and loaded with wildlife, as it borders a protected nature preserve. Champs is the perfect place to relax and make some priceless memories.

DIRECTIONS: From I-87: Ex 20, L on Hwy 9, R on Rte 149 to Rte 4. L on Rte 4. Rte 4 merges into Rte 22. Follow to Whitehall. R on Clinton St. L on Main St. Resort at the end of Main St.

GPS COORDINATES: 43.5608°N/-73.4012°W
ELEVATION: 144 feet
RV SITES: Full: 26 Partial: 0 Dry: 26
CHECK-IN: 1:00 p.m.–10:00 p.m.
CHECK-OUT: 11:00 a.m.
SEASON: June 1–October 12
MAX. RV LENGTH: 36 feet
NOTATIONS: Additional charges: 50 amp $5/night, late cancellation $10, late departure $10. No cable avail. Drive-ups not accepted.
RENTAL ACCOMMODATIONS: Rental units available. Trip Points not accepted. Contact resort directly.

50 amps, dump station, cable tv, visitor mail, laundry, pets/restrictions, internet access, Wi-Fi access, playground, picnic tables, restaurant/snack bar, rental units, fishing, hiking trails, horseshoes, group activities, boating, recreation hall, age restrictions, fishing, boating, golf, game room, tourist attraction, shopping, propane, canoes, hot showers, fire rings, rv supplies, gift shop, tenting, handicap access, ice

JACKSON SPRINGS

RESORT NUMBER: 379 **GOOD SAM RATING:** 8.5/10★/9 **COAST PREMIER RESORT**

Sycamore Lodge—
Travel Resorts of America
1059 Sycamore Lane
Jackson Springs, North Carolina 27281
855-332-9541
reservations@travelresorts.com
travelresorts.com

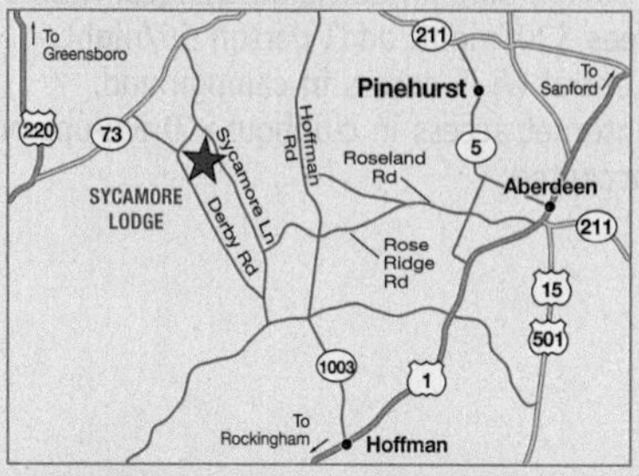

See page CTC 70 for state map.

Seventy miles south of Raleigh, Sycamore Lodge's large clubhouse sits among pines and overlooks the resort's terraced grounds and two-acre lake. The Golf Hall of Fame and other golf-oriented activities, including some of the best courses in the country, are nearby.

DIRECTIONS: From Hwy 15-501/Hwy 211 and Hwy 1 in Aberdeen: S 0.2 mi on Hwy 1 to Roseland Rd. W (R) 4.5 mi to Rose Ridge Rd. SW (L fork) 5.2 mi to Sycamore Ln. NW (R) 2.8 mi to resort.

GPS COORDINATES: 35.276°N/-79.6073°W
RV SITES: Full: 137 Partial: 39 Dry: 0
CHECK-IN: 1:00 p.m.
CHECK-OUT: 11:00 a.m.
SEASON: Year-round
PEAK SEASON: May 15–September 15
MAX. RV LENGTH: Unlimited
NOTATIONS: Additional charges: Honey wagon $7.
RENTAL ACCOMMODATIONS: Rental units available. Trip Points accepted. Contact resort directly.

50 amps · pull-through · visitor mail · laundry · pets/restrictions · internet access · Wi-Fi access · playground · rental units · hot tub · fishing · shuffleboard · horseshoes · recreation hall · church services · outdoor pool · mini golf · volleyball · golf · game room · tourist attraction · propane · canoes · paddle boats · grocery · gift shop

WAVES

RESORT NUMBER: 521 **GOOD SAM RATING:** 10/9.5★/9.5 **COAST CLASSIC RESORT**

Camp Hatteras
24798 North Carolina Highway 12
Waves, North Carolina 27968
252-987-2777
camping@camphatteras.com
camphatteras.com

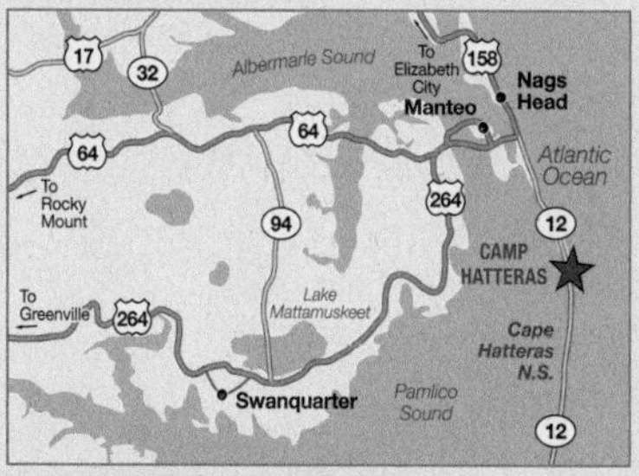

See page CTC 70 for state map.

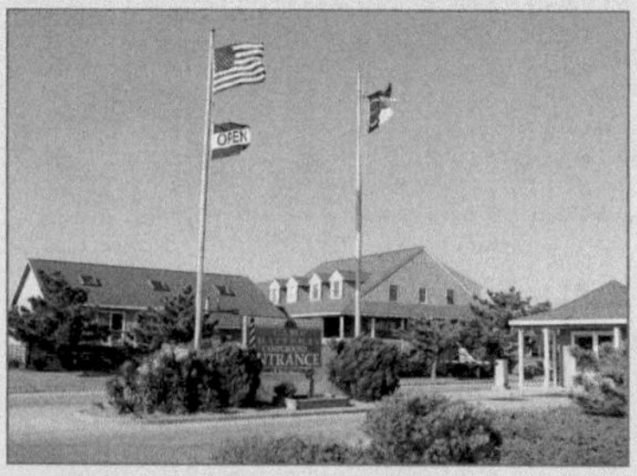

On the beautiful Outer Banks, just a few miles south of Nags Head Beach area. Less than an hour away are the Wright Brothers National Memorial, Fort Raleigh Historical Site, Cape Hatteras National Seashore, and Oregon Inlet Fishing Center. There is over 2,000 feet of unspoiled waterfront from sound to ocean.

DIRECTIONS: From Hwy 64 E or Hwy 158 E to Nags Head: S on Rte 12. 24 mi past Oregon Inlet on the S edge of Rodanthe.

GPS COORDINATES: 35.5782°N/-75.4666°W
RV SITES: Full: 400 Partial: 0 Dry: 0
CHECK-IN: 1:00 p.m.
CHECK-OUT: 11:00 a.m.
SEASON: Year-round
MAX. RV LENGTH: 45 feet
NOTATIONS: Late check-in available. Additional charges: Cable TV $3/night. Internet access in clubhouse, Wi-Fi access not guaranteed in campground. Coast sites are on the Soundside interior of the park. 1 p.m. check-in strictly enforced. Resort is using pre-pay and a remote check-in service. For cable TV call Camp Hatteras directly. Please allow 24 hrs for your reservation to be uploaded before calling the resort.

50 amps · cable tv · laundry · pets/restrictions · internet access · Wi-Fi access · playground · picnic tables · hot tub · fishing · shuffleboard · horseshoes · group activities · recreation hall · church services · fishing · boating · outdoor pool · mini golf · basketball · beach · tennis · golf · game room · tourist attraction · propane · indoor pool · hot showers · grocery · rv supplies · gift shop · tenting · handicap access · ice

NORTH CAROLINA

WAYNESVILLE

RESORT NUMBER: 588 **GOOD SAM RATING:** 9/9.5★/9.5 **COAST CLASSIC RESORT**

Pride Resort
4394 Jonathan Creek Road
Waynesville, North Carolina 28785
800-926-8191; fax: 828-926-3081
info@pridervresort.com
pridervresort.com

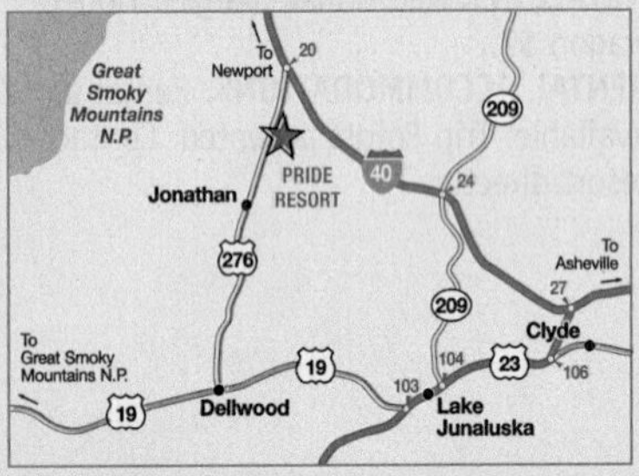

See page CTC 70 for state map.

Just outside the Great Smoky Mountains National Park near the most popular attractions in Western North Carolina. Nearby: Ghost town, Maggie Valley, Asheville, Cherokee Indian Reservation, Harrah's Casino, 1700s Cherokee Village, Cherokee Museum, and seasonal activities at the reservation.

DIRECTIONS: From I-40: Ex 20 to Hwy 276. 1.5 mi to resort on L.

GPS COORDINATES: 35.5834°N/-83.0124°W
RV SITES: Full: 140 Partial: 0 Dry: 0
CHECK-IN: Noon
CHECK-OUT: 11:30 a.m.
SEASON: Year-round
MAX. RV LENGTH: 45 feet
NOTATIONS: Site includes 6 guests total (no age limit). Additional charges: Resort fees $30/night, add'l person $6/night. Central Wi-Fi access in campground, Internet access in clubhouse. Drive-ups not accepted.

50 amps · pull-through · visitor mail · laundry · pets/restrictions · internet access · Wi-Fi access · hot tub · fishing · shuffleboard · horseshoes · recreation hall · outdoor pool · mini golf · tourist attraction · ball field · gambling casino

OHIO

ANDOVER

RESORT NUMBER: 80 **GOOD SAM RATING:** 8/8★/9 **COAST CLASSIC RESORT**

Holiday Camplands
4273 Pymatuning Lake Road
Andover, Ohio 44003
440-293-7116; fax: 440-293-6545
randyg130@gmail.com
holidaycamplands.com

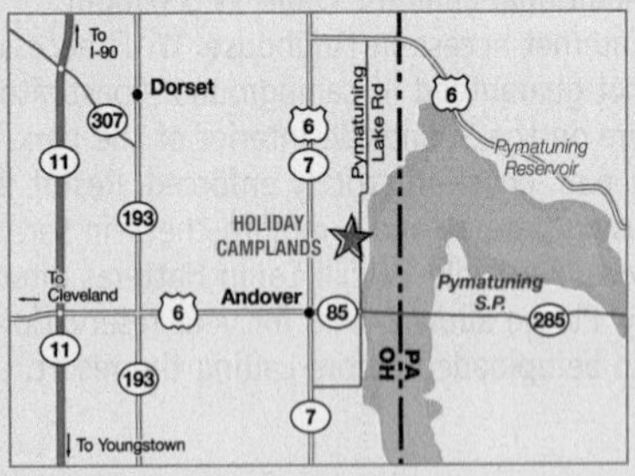

See page CTC 71 for state map.

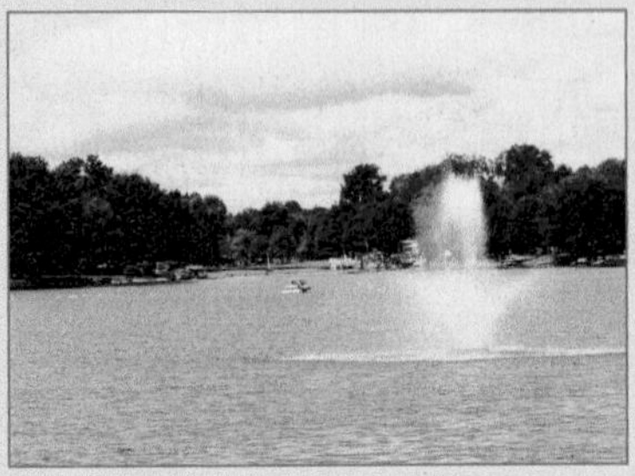

Resort is 25 miles from Lake Erie. Nearby Pymatuning Lake covers 16,000 acres and is 16 miles long with 70 miles of shoreline. Many free boating ramps for fishing and recreational boats. State beach on the lake. Deer, rabbit, squirrel, duck, and geese hunting in season. Conneaut Lake for water skiing.

DIRECTIONS: From Cleveland: Hwy 6 E to Andover. E on Rte 85 to Pymatuning Lake Rd. L 2 mi to resort.

GPS COORDINATES: 41.6358°N/-80.5422°W
RV SITES: Full: 0 Partial: 30 Dry: 0
CHECK-IN: 9:00 a.m.–10:00 p.m.
CHECK-OUT: 9:00 a.m.–10:00 p.m.
SEASON: April 24–October 16
MAX. RV LENGTH: 45 feet
NOTATIONS: Wi-Fi access available.

30 amps · dump station · laundry · pets/restrictions · Wi-Fi access · playground · picnic tables · fishing · shuffleboard · horseshoes · group activities · recreation hall · fishing · boating · outdoor pool · mini golf · basketball · beach · tennis · volleyball · golf · hot showers · ball field · fire rings · tenting · firewood · ice

DIAMOND

RESORT NUMBER: 83 **GOOD SAM RATING:** 5.5/10★/8.5 **COAST CLASSIC RESORT**

OHIO

Leisure Lake
5393 State Route 225
Diamond, Ohio 44412
330-953-9314; fax: 330-358-7419
info@leisurelakepark.com
leisurelakepark.com

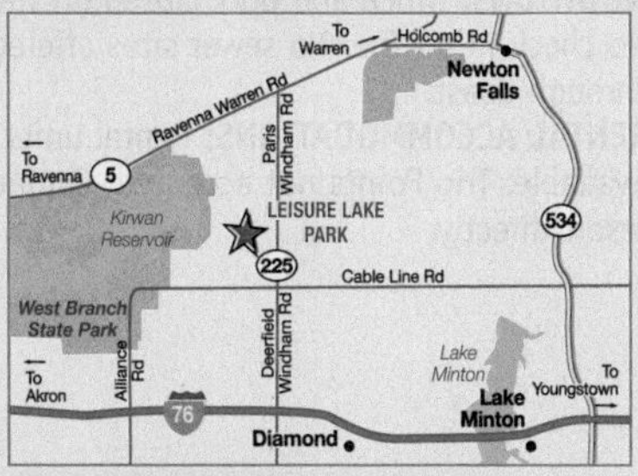

See page CTC 71 for state map.

We are located between Youngstown and Akron, two miles from West Branch Reservoir, a 2,650-acre lake in West Branch State Park. Marina and two boat ramps on the south shore, water skiing (unlimited horsepower), fishing for smallmouth bass, walleye, catfish, bluegill and crappie. 1,100 feet of swimming beach, picnic areas nearby, and Lake Milton also nearby.

DIRECTIONS: Midway between Youngstown and Akron off I-76. From I-76: Take Hwy 225 N, 2 mi to resort.

GPS COORDINATES: 41.0993°N/-81.0982°W
RV SITES: Full: 32 Partial: 279 Dry: 0
CHECK-IN: 10:00 a.m.–6:00 p.m.
CHECK-OUT: Noon
SEASON: April 1–September 30
MAX. RV LENGTH: 45 feet
NOTATIONS: Additional charges: Electric $5/night. We are a member-owned, volunteer park. A volunteer will contact you by text from 330-953-9314 with park info and ask for your ETA to better assist you the day of your arrival. Please use cell phone number for reservations. Office only open Sat & Sun. Pool hours 10 a.m.-9 p.m. Full hook-up sites avail (water, sewer, 30 and 50 amp). Drive-ups not accepted.

50 amps | laundry | pets/restrictions | playground | fishing | recreation hall | fishing | boating | mini golf | basketball | beach | indoor pool

HUNTSVILLE

RESORT NUMBER: 2428 **GOOD SAM RATING:** 9/8.5★/8 **COAST DELUXE RESORT**

OHIO

Indian Lake Resort—Venture Out Resorts
3939 County Road 37
Huntsville, Ohio 43324
888-249-1995
info@ventureoutresorts.com
ventureoutresorts.com

See page CTC 71 for state map.

Indian Lake Resort is a family-friendly outdoor resort located in West Central Ohio close to scenic Indian Lake. Modern amenities, indoor swimming pool, kid's playground, large mature trees, and peaceful creek provide the perfect setting for a memorable camping experience.

DIRECTIONS: From Columbus: 63 mi W on US-33. From Dayton: 50 mi N on I-75 to Ex 102. 20 mi on OH-274 E. 1 mi E on US-33. W on CR 37. 0.5 mi to resort on L.

GPS COORDINATES: 40.42634°N/-83.80933°W
RV SITES: Full: 115 Partial: 0 Dry: 0
CHECK-IN: 2:00 p.m.–5:00 p.m.
CHECK-OUT: Noon
SEASON: May 2–October 10
PEAK SEASON: May 2–October 10
MAX. RV LENGTH: Unlimited
RENTAL ACCOMMODATIONS: Rental units available. Trip Points not accepted. Contact resort directly.

50 amps | pull-through | pets/restrictions | playground | rental units | fishing | recreation hall | fishing | boating | golf | game room | indoor pool | hot showers

OHIO

JEFFERSON

RESORT NUMBER: 606 **GOOD SAM RATING:** 6.5/7.5/8 **COAST DELUXE RESORT**

Millbrook Outdoor Resort
4051 State Route 46 South
Jefferson, Ohio 44047
440-484-4000; fax: 440-294-3992
memberservices@gomillbrook.com
millbrookresortohio.com

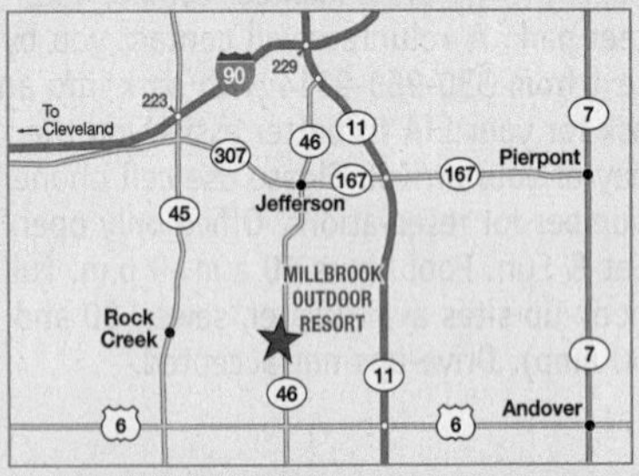

See page CTC 71 for state map.

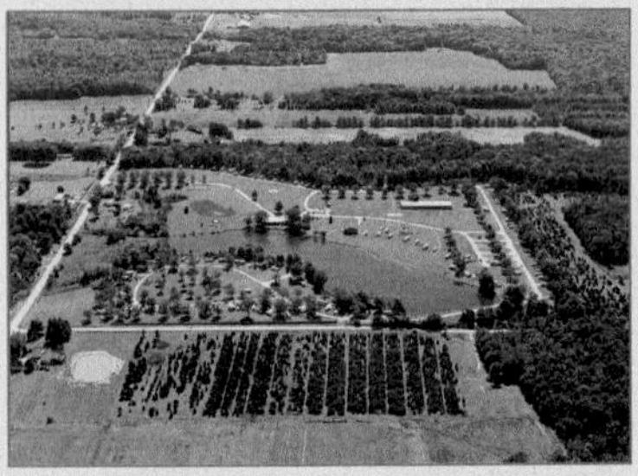

Located between Ohio's three largest recreational lakes; Erie, Pymatuning & Mosquito. Nearby: Historic train rides, wineries, covered bridge tours, animal, amusement and water fun parks, casino, canoe river, golf courses, historic lighthouse, beaches, marine & wildlife museums, historical landmarks.

DIRECTIONS: From Cleveland/Erie: I-90 to Hwy 11 S, to Ex SR 46 S. 18 mi to resort on R. From Youngstown/Pittsburgh: Hwy 11 N, to Ex Hwy 6 W, to SR 46 N. 2.5 mi to resort on L. From Akron/Canton: I-76 E, to I-80 E, to Hwy 11 N, to Ex Hwy 6 W, to SR 46 N. 2.5 mi to resort on L.

GPS COORDINATES: 41.6397°N/-80.7807°W
RV SITES: Full: 0 Partial: 150 Dry: 0
CHECK-IN: 3:00 p.m.–7:00 p.m.
CHECK-OUT: 11:00 a.m.
SEASON: May 1–October 14
PEAK SEASON: June 1–August 1
MAX. RV LENGTH: 39 feet
NOTATIONS: Office and pool closed on Tue. No check-in on Tue. No sewer sites offered through Coast.
RENTAL ACCOMMODATIONS: Rental units available. Trip Points not accepted. Contact resort directly.

30 amps, pull-through, dump station, laundry, pets/restrictions, internet access, playground, picnic tables, rental units, fishing, hiking trails, horseshoes, group activities, boating, recreation hall, mini golf, basketball, beach, volleyball, golf, game room, tourist attraction, fitness, propane, canoes, indoor pool, hot showers, ball field, paddle boats, gambling casino, fire rings, tenting, firewood, ice

OHIO

KIMBOLTON

RESORT NUMBER: 1566 **GOOD SAM RATING:** 7.5/8/8.5 **COAST PREMIER RESORT**

Rocky Fork Ranch—
Travel Resorts of America
74978 Broadhead Road
Kimbolton, Ohio 43749
855-332-9541
rfr_reservations@travelresorts.com
travelresorts.com

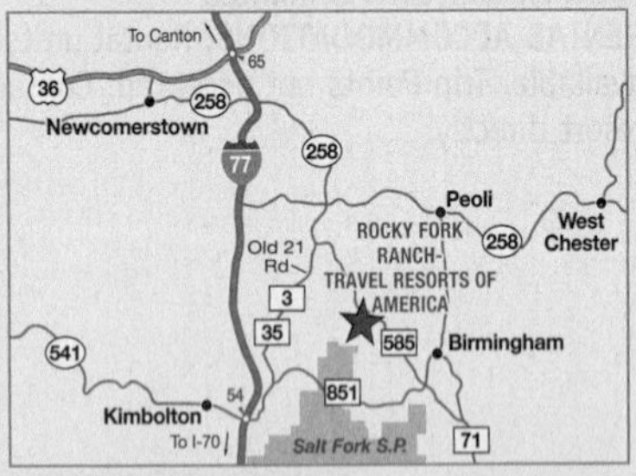

See page CTC 71 for state map.

Nestled in the wooded hillside of Southeastern Ohio. Next door at Salt Forks State Park is fabulous fishing and one of Ohio's premier 18-hole golf courses.

DIRECTIONS: Do not follow GPS. From the N: I-77 S to Ex 65 Newcomerstown/SR 36. SR 36 W. At the flashing caution light (SR 258) turn L. Follow SR 258 approx 8 mi. At the top of hill SR 258 will turn to L. Stay straight onto Salt Fork Rd for approx 1 mi. L on Broadhead Rd for approx 3.5 mi to the resort area. From the South: Take I-77 N to Kimbolton Ex 54. At stop sign, turn R. Go 0.5 mi to next stop sign at Old Hwy 21/Co Rd 35. Turn L onto Old Hwy 21 for approx 10 mi to the intersection of Broadhead Rd. Turn R 3.5 mi to Rocky Fork Rd.

GPS COORDINATES: 40.1891°N/-81.4858°W
RV SITES: Full: 49 Partial: 249 Dry: 0
CHECK-IN: 1:00 p.m.
CHECK-OUT: 11:00 a.m.
SEASON: Year-round
PEAK SEASON: May 15–September 15
MAX. RV LENGTH: 40 feet
NOTATIONS: Please give exact length of camper and if your camper has slide-outs. Site includes water and electric. We only accept Coast Trip Points. Nov 1-May 15 water not available to sites.
RENTAL ACCOMMODATIONS: Rental units available. Trip Points accepted. Contact resort directly.

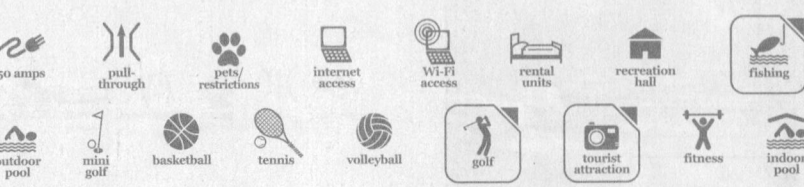

50 amps, pull-through, pets/restrictions, internet access, Wi-Fi access, rental units, recreation hall, fishing, outdoor pool, mini golf, basketball, tennis, volleyball, golf, tourist attraction, fitness, indoor pool

LOUDONVILLE

RESORT NUMBER: 416 **GOOD SAM RATING:** 8/8★/8 **COAST PREMIER RESORT**

Wally World Riverside Resort—Travel Resorts of Ohio
16121 County Road 23
Loudonville, Ohio 44842
855-559-2559
wwstore1@travelresorts.com
travelresorts.com

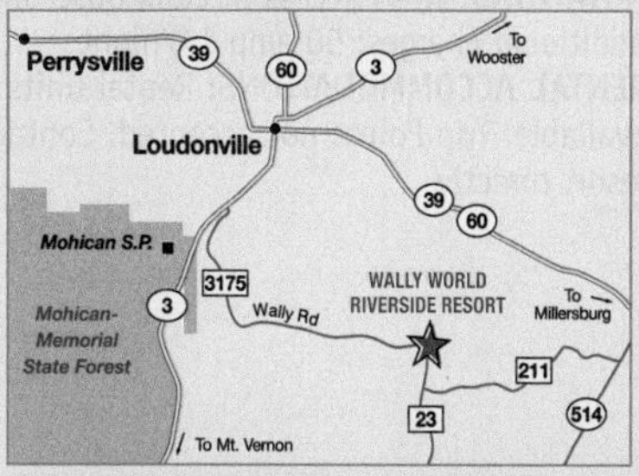

See page CTC 71 for state map.

Wally World Riverside Resort is set in a peaceful valley along the Mohican River in the heart of Amish country halfway between Columbus and Cleveland. The Mohican and Malabar Farm State Parks are nearby. Wally Road has been designated as an Ohio State Scenic Byway and the Mohican River an Ohio State Scenic River.
DIRECTIONS: From Cleveland: S on I-71 to Rte 30. E on Rte 30 to Rte 60. S on Rte 60 to Loudonville. S on SR 3 for 1 mi to Wally Rd. L on Wally Rd. 4.5 mi to resort. From Columbus: N on I-71 to Rte 97. E on Rte 97 to SR 3. N on SR 3 for 1 mi to Wally Rd. R on Wally Rd. 4.5 mi to resort. GPS: Use best route, not shortest route.

GPS COORDINATES: 40.5898°N/-82.19°W
RV SITES: Full: 5 Partial: 205 Dry: 10
CHECK-IN: 1:00 p.m.
CHECK-OUT: 11:00 a.m.
SEASON: April 1–November 14
PEAK SEASON: May 15–September 15
MAX. RV LENGTH: 40 feet
NOTATIONS: Additional charges: Honey wagon $15 on Mon & Thu, honey wagon emergency service $25. Water not turned on until Apr 30.

WAPAKONETA

RESORT NUMBER: 575 **GOOD SAM RATING:** 8/9★/9 **COAST PREMIER RESORT**

Arrowhead Lakes Resort—Venture Out Resorts
14296 Cemetery Road
Wapakoneta, Ohio 45895
419-738-5000; res.: 888-249-1995
info@ventureoutresorts.com
ventureoutresorts.com

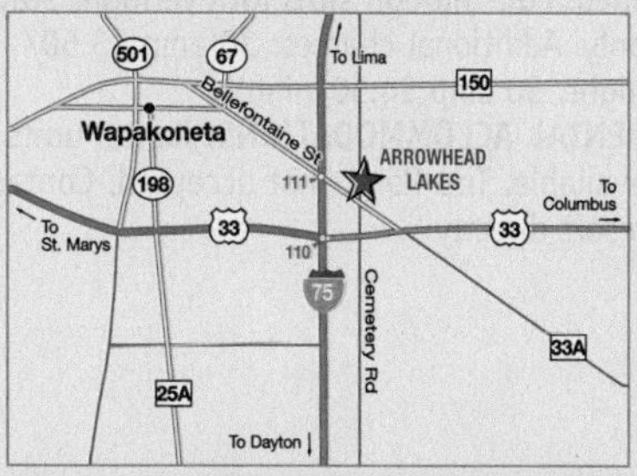

See page CTC 71 for state map.

In West Central Ohio, south of Lima and north of Dayton. Near the Neil Armstrong Air and Space Museum, Ohio Caverns, Indian and St. Mary's Lakes, and other attractions. Shopping is available in nearby Lima and Wapakoneta. Dayton, home of the Wright Brothers, is 50 miles away.
DIRECTIONS: From Dayton: 50 mi N on I-75. From Toledo: 90 mi S on I-75 to Ex 111. E approx 1,000 ft. L on Cemetery Rd (at Dodge City Restaurant). 500 ft to resort on R.

GPS COORDINATES: 40.5597°N/-84.1643°W
RV SITES: Full: 137 Partial: 66 Dry: 0
CHECK-IN: 2:00 p.m.–5:00 p.m.
CHECK-OUT: Noon
SEASON: Year-round
PEAK SEASON: May 1–November 1
MAX. RV LENGTH: 50 feet
NOTATIONS: Minimum stay 2 nights on weekends. Phone ahead for late arrival after 6 p.m.
RENTAL ACCOMMODATIONS: Rental units available. Trip Points not accepted. Contact resort directly.

OKLAHOMA

AFTON

RESORT NUMBER: 324 **GOOD SAM RATING:** 7.5/5.5/6.5 **COAST DELUXE RESORT**

Pelican Landing
32100 Highway 85
Afton, Oklahoma 74331
918-782-3295; fax: 918-782-3699
pelicanlandingrv@gmail.com
pelicanlanding.us

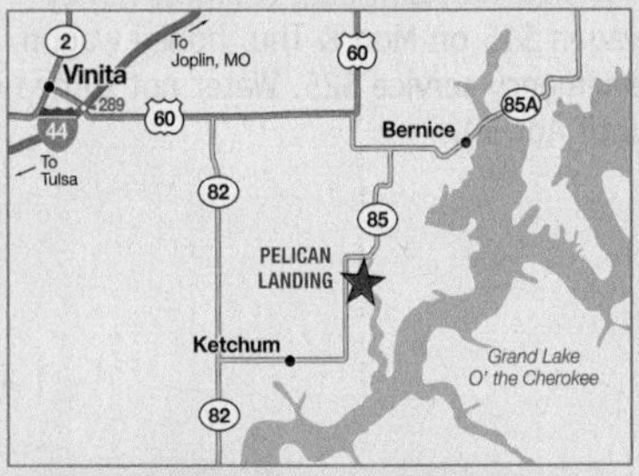

See page CTC 62 for state map.

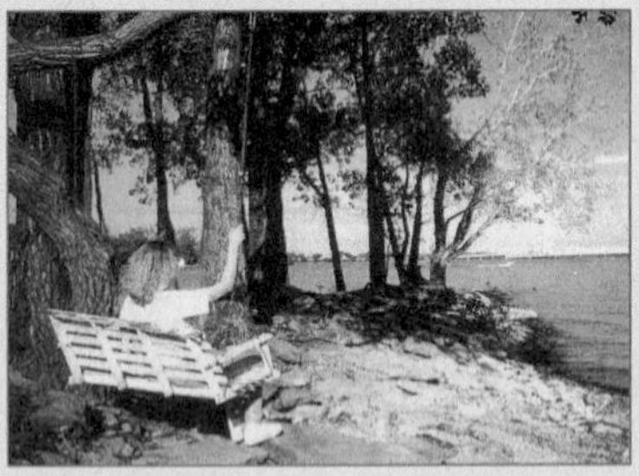

Located on Grand Lake O' The Cherokees, 66 miles long with over 1,300 miles of shoreline. Grand Lake is a sportsman's paradise for fishing, sailing, boating, water skiing, etc. The typical Southwest terrain abounds with deer and other wildlife. Nearby: Pensacola Dam, Har-Ber Village, golf courses, and casinos.

DIRECTIONS: From I-44: Vinita Ex. E on Hwy 60 for 5 mi to Hwy 82. S on Hwy 82 for 6 mi to Hwy 85. E on Hwy 85 through Ketchum. Resort is 4 mi NE of Ketchum.

GPS COORDINATES: 36.5525°N/-94.9878°W
RV SITES: Full: 35 Partial: 30 Dry: 0
CHECK-IN: 9:30 a.m.–4:00 p.m.
CHECK-OUT: Noon
SEASON: March 15–October 29
PEAK SEASON: May 1–October 29
MAX. RV LENGTH: 50 feet
NOTATIONS: Wi-Fi access in clubhouse only. Additional charges: 50 amp $4/night.
RENTAL ACCOMMODATIONS: Rental units available. Trip Points not accepted. Contact resort directly.

50 amps · pets/restrictions · internet access · Wi-Fi access · playground · rental units · fishing · hiking trails · horseshoes · boating · recreation hall

fishing · boating · outdoor pool · mini golf · basketball · golf · game room · tourist attraction · gambling casino

OKLAHOMA

CHECOTAH

RESORT NUMBER: 254 **GOOD SAM RATING:** 7.5/7/6 **COAST CLASSIC RESORT**

Terra Starr Park
420589 East 1147 Road
Checotah, Oklahoma 74426
918-689-7094; fax: 918-689-7244
terrastarrpark@gmail.com

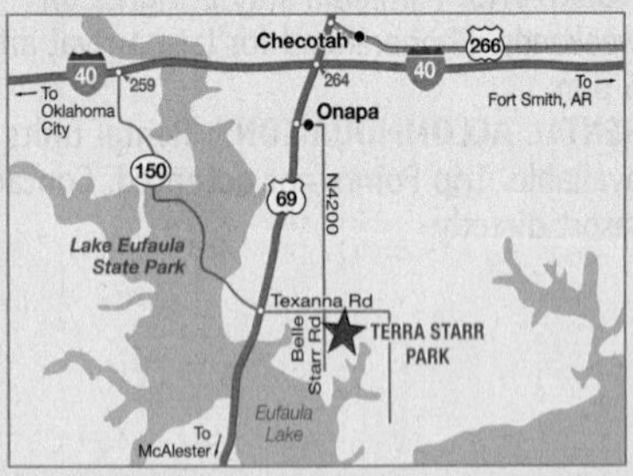

See page CTC 62 for state map.

At the gateway to Lake Eufaula, the largest lake in the southwest, with a total of 102,500 acres of water and 600 miles of shoreline. Terra Starr Park adjoins the lake, which has miles of sand beaches and a large marina. Lake Eufaula is renowned for its abundant black bass, crappie, and catfish.

DIRECTIONS: From I-40: Ex 264/Hwy 69 S. 7 mi S. E on Texanna Rd for 2 mi to Belle Starr Rd. R on Belle Starr (watch for signs) for 0.7 mi. L on Terra Park Dr. 0.4 mi to resort.

GPS COORDINATES: 35.3517°N/-95.5331°W
RV SITES: Full: 146 Partial: 154 Dry: 0
CHECK-IN: 9:00 a.m.–4:30 p.m.
CHECK-OUT: 1:00 p.m.
SEASON: Year-round
MAX. RV LENGTH: 40 feet
NOTATIONS: Limited number of 50 amp sites. Pull-through sites for overnight stays only. Additional charges: 30 amp $3.50/night, 50 amp $4.50/night.
RENTAL ACCOMMODATIONS: Rental units available. Trip Points not accepted. Contact resort directly.

50 amps · dump station · laundry · pets/restrictions · internet access · Wi-Fi access · playground · picnic tables · rental units

fishing · boating · recreation hall · fishing · boating · outdoor pool · basketball · tennis · golf · ball field

GROVE

RESORT NUMBER: 147 **GOOD SAM RATING:** 8/9.5★/8.5 **COAST CLASSIC RESORT**

OKLAHOMA

Eagles Landing Resort
25301 U.S. Highway 59 North
Grove, Oklahoma 74344
918-786-6196; fax: 918-801-7502
cchappell@eaglesresorts.net
eaglesresortok.com

See page CTC 62 for state map.

Eagle's Landing is located on one of Oklahoma's best fishing lakes, beautiful Grand Lake O' the Cherokees. All types of water sports and activities are available on this magnificent lake. The resort has a full range of amenities and a venue available for rent to complement the activities of the lake.

DIRECTIONS: Located on easy access paved roads 8 mi S of Afton. I-44, Ex 302 onto Hwy 59 S. Resort on R, 0.5 mi past Cherokee Casino. Approx 8 mi from I-44.

GPS COORDINATES: 36.653°N/-94.8221°W
ELEVATION: 786 feet
RV SITES: Full: 35 Partial: 98 Dry: 0
CHECK-IN: 3:00 p.m.
CHECK-OUT: 11:00 a.m.
SEASON: Year-round
MAX. RV LENGTH: 45 feet
NOTATIONS: Additional charges: Resort fee $10/night, early check-in $20, late check-out $20.
RENTAL ACCOMMODATIONS: Rental units available. Trip Points not accepted. Contact resort directly.

50 amps, pull-through, dump station, visitor mail, laundry, pets/restrictions, internet access, Wi-Fi access, playground, rental units, fishing, boating, fishing, boating, outdoor pool, mini golf, golf, game room, propane, canoes, paddle boats, gift shop

JAY

RESORT NUMBER: 256 **GOOD SAM RATING:** 8.5/8/7 **COAST DELUXE RESORT**

OKLAHOMA

Pine Island RV Resort
32501 South 571 Road
Jay, Oklahoma 74346
918-786-9071; fax: 918-786-7914
pineislandok@gmail.com
pineislandrvresort.com

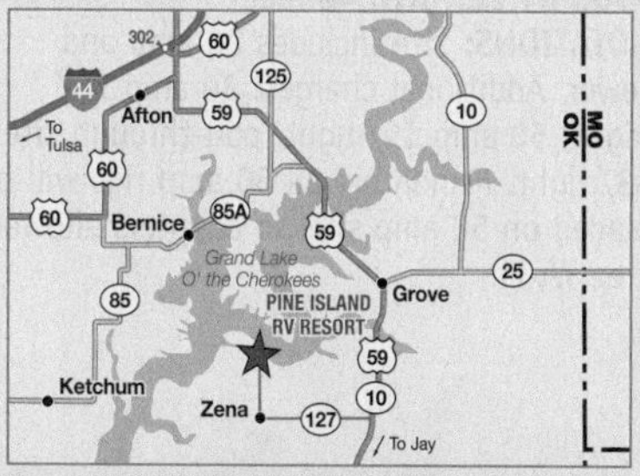

See page CTC 62 for state map.

Pine Island is located between Jay and Grove, on beautiful Grand Lake O' the Cherokees. Grand Lake is 66 miles long with 1,300 miles of shoreline. It's the home of the world's largest multiple arch dam. Shaded campsites are scattered among beautiful pine, oak, hickory, and walnut trees.

DIRECTIONS: From Tulsa: I-44 to Afton Ex. Hwy 59 S through Grove to SH 127. Go to Zena. R and follow signs to resort. From Jay: Hwy 59 N 5 mi to Hwy 127. Go to Zena. Follow signs to resort.

GPS COORDINATES: 36.5447°N/-94.8617°W
RV SITES: Full: 200 Partial: 66 Dry: 0
CHECK-IN: 9:00 a.m.–4:00 p.m.
CHECK-OUT: Noon
SEASON: Year-round
PEAK SEASON: May 1–September 30
MAX. RV LENGTH: 46 feet
NOTATIONS: Free Wi-Fi in campground. Additional charges: Surcharge $10/night to be paid to Pine Island RV Resort, includes Premier members. After hours check in at guard shack. After hours phone 918-964-1620.
RENTAL ACCOMMODATIONS: Rental units available. Trip Points accepted. Contact resort directly.

50 amps, pull-through, visitor mail, pets/restrictions, internet access, Wi-Fi access, rental units, fishing, boating, recreation hall, fishing, outdoor pool, mini golf, indoor pool, gift shop

OKLAHOMA

MADILL

RESORT NUMBER: 2163 **GOOD SAM RATING:** 6.5/5/6.5 **COAST PREMIER RESORT**

Texoma Shores RV Resort—Ocean Canyon Properties
16022 Cumberland Cove Road
Madill, Oklahoma 73446
580-795-3828; fax: 580-677-9726
member.reservations@oceancanyon.com
oceancanyon.com

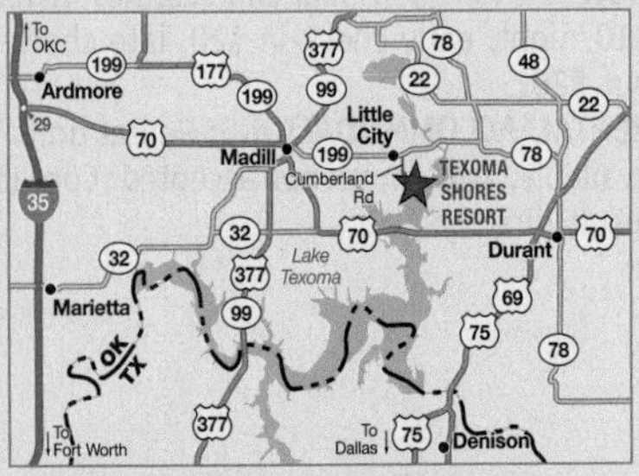

See page CTC 62 for state map.

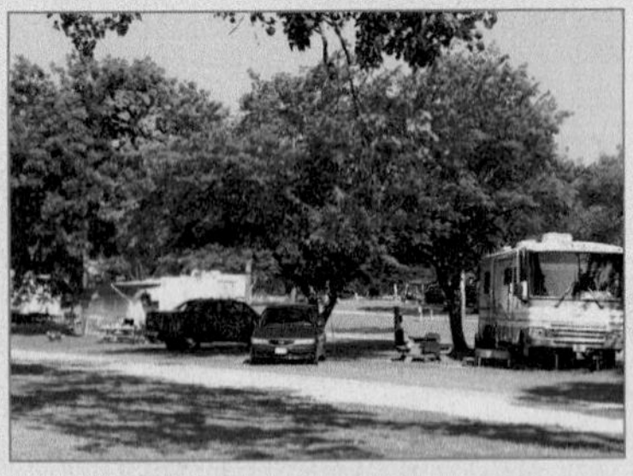

With over a mile of shoreline on one of the largest lakes in the South, and great views from everywhere on the resort, you will love your visit to OCP's Texoma Shores Resort. Whether you love to fish, spend your time on the lake, or relax by the beach, we have a spot for you. Our resort has over 38 full hook-up RV sites, a 7-unit motel, 4 two-bedroom cabins, swimming beach, boat launch, RV and boat storage, and a fishing pier. We are located between Madill and Durant, OK which both offer shopping, restaurants, and plenty of things to do.

DIRECTIONS: From Durant, OK: Take Hwy 69/75 to Lake Texoma Ex. N on Hwy 70 for 23 mi to Madill. In Madill Hwy 199 E to Cumberland Rd approx 13 mi from Madill. Follow signs to resort.

GPS COORDINATES: 34.0562°N/-96.5842°W
ELEVATION: 712 feet
RV SITES: Full: 30 Partial: 0 Dry: 0
CHECK-IN: 2:00 p.m.
CHECK-OUT: 11:00 a.m.
SEASON: April 1–November 1
PEAK SEASON: May 15–September 15
MAX. RV LENGTH: 40 feet
NOTATIONS: Additional charges: 50 amp $5/night.
RENTAL ACCOMMODATIONS: Rental units available. Trip Points not accepted. Contact resort directly.

50 amps · pull-through · visitor mail · laundry · pets/restrictions · playground · rental units · fishing · hiking trails · horseshoes · boating · recreation hall · basketball · beach · volleyball · tourist attraction · shopping · hot showers · gambling casino · tenting

OKLAHOMA

THACKERVILLE

RESORT NUMBER: 775 **GOOD SAM RATING:** 7/7/7 **COAST DELUXE RESORT**

Red River Ranch RV Resort
19691 U.S. Highway 77
Thackerville, Oklahoma 73459
580-276-4411; fax: 580-276-4424
redriverranch@brightok.net
redriverranchrvresort.org

See page CTC 62 for state map.

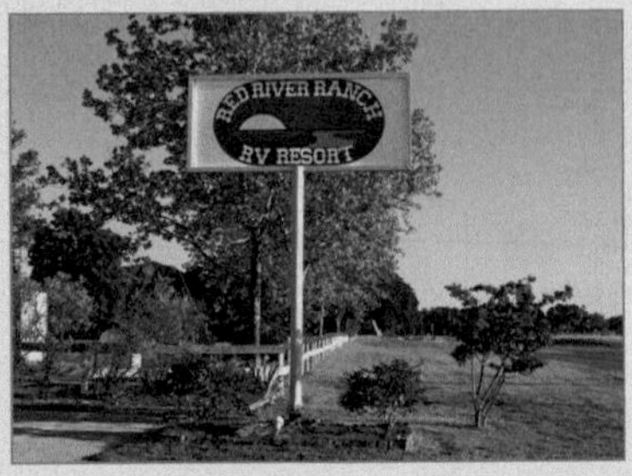

In Thackerville, South Central Oklahoma's lake country. Nearby: Red River, Turner Falls, Lake Arbuckle, Lake Texoma, Arbuckle Mountains and Wilderness, and Lake Murray. Winstar Casino only three miles away. Gene Autry Museum is nearby. Frank Buck Zoo in Gainesville, Texas. Antique stores along Hwy. 82, off Hwy 35 in Texas.

DIRECTIONS: Just off I-35 5 mi N of the Red River, 75 mi N of Dallas/Ft. Worth and 125 mi S of Oklahoma City. From the S: Ex 3 and go W 0.5 mi, then N on Hwy 77. From the N: Ex 5 and go W 0.5 mi, then S on Hwy 77. Resort is on E side of Hwy 77.

GPS COORDINATES: 33.7851°N/-97.1432°W
RV SITES: Full: 130 Partial: 85 Dry: 34
CHECK-IN: 9:00 a.m.–5:00 p.m.
CHECK-OUT: Noon
SEASON: Year-round
PEAK SEASONS: March 1–April 30
October 1–November 30
MAX. RV LENGTH: 48 feet
NOTATIONS: Site includes 20 amp and sewer. Additional charges: 30 amp $5/night, 50 amp $9/night, pull-through sites $3/night. Mandatory all 50 amp rigs will be placed on 50 amp site-no adapters allowed. Free Wi-Fi.

50 amps · pull-through · dump station · visitor mail · laundry · pets/restrictions · Wi-Fi access · hot tub · recreation hall · outdoor pool

LA PINE

RESORT NUMBER: 207 **GOOD SAM RATING:** 7.5/9.5★/7.5 **COAST DELUXE RESORT**

Cascade Meadows RV Resort
53750 Highway 97
La Pine, Oregon 97739
541-536-2244; fax: 541-536-2747
cascademeadows@soundpacificrv.com
soundpacificrv.com/cascade-meadows

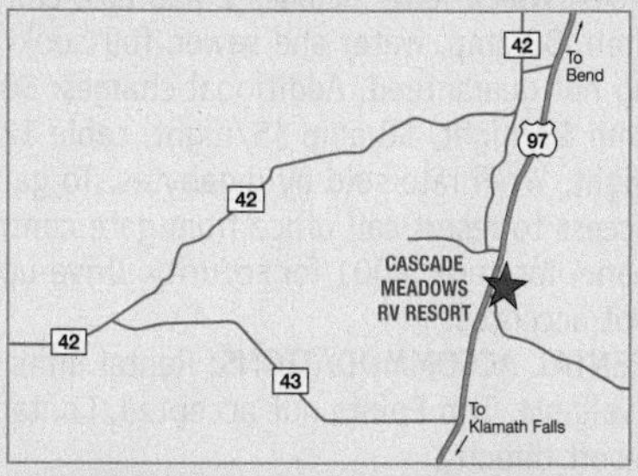

See page CTC 72 for state map.

Cascade Meadows is in the premiere recreation area of central Oregon with 156 crystal fishing lakes and miles of wilderness trails in the Deschutes National Forest. Paulina Lake is just a few miles from the resort as well as Mt Bachelor Ski Resort and Newberry National Volcanic Monument.
DIRECTIONS: From Bend: Hwy 97 S 22 mi to Paulina/East Lake Ex. Turn E (L) 0.1 mi to resort on R.
GPS COORDINATES: 43.7505°N/-121.4587°W
ELEVATION: 4,200 feet

RV SITES: Full: 102 Partial: 15 Dry: 60
CHECK-IN: 1:00 p.m.
CHECK-OUT: 11:00 a.m.
SEASON: Year-round
PEAK SEASON: May 1–September 30
MAX. RV LENGTH: 70 feet
NOTATIONS: Additional charges: 30 amp $3/night, 50 amp $5/night, lodging tax. Arrival instructions: Upon arrival at park, please pull to the right side of the driveway, stopping at the stop sign, or park in the parking lot of building on your right, if possible, so that the security gate is not blocked and is still accessible to checked-in guests.
RENTAL ACCOMMODATIONS: Rental units available. Trip Points not accepted. Contact resort directly.

50 amps · pull-through · pets/restrictions · internet access · Wi-Fi access · playground · rental units · hot tub
shuffleboard · hiking trails · horseshoes · recreation hall · fishing · outdoor pool · volleyball · tourist attraction · winter sports

LINCOLN CITY

RESORT NUMBER: 297 **GOOD SAM RATING:** 6/8/6.5 **COAST DELUXE RESORT**

Chinook Bend RV Resort
2920 Siletz Highway
Lincoln City, Oregon 97367
541-996-2032; res.: 800-203-6364
chinookrv@chinookbend.com
chinookbend.com

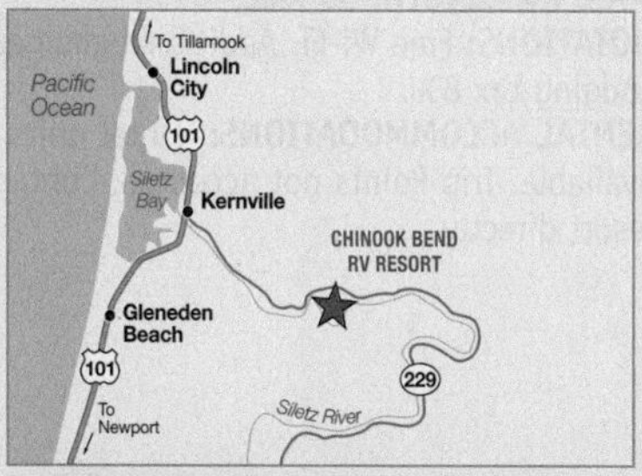

See page CTC 72 for state map.

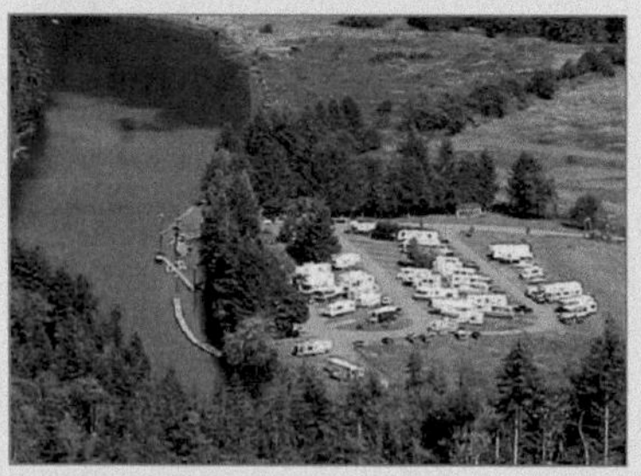

On the Oregon Coast, an 85-acre camping ranch and boat marina on the Siletz River with river access. Resort offers full hookups or remote tent camping, walking trails, wildlife viewing, acres of fishing and hiking, and a family environment. Secure, safe camping where the forest meets the ocean.
DIRECTIONS: On the Oregon coast, just S of Lincoln City. From Hwy 101 take Hwy 229 E, Kernville Siletz River turn-off. 3 mi to the resort (at the Big Red Barn). Check-in at the top of the hill.

GPS COORDINATES: 44.8°N/-123.9181°W
RV SITES: Full: 67 Partial: 20 Dry: 0
CHECK-IN: 2:00 p.m.–9:00 p.m.
CHECK-OUT: Noon
SEASON: Year-round
PEAK SEASON: June 1–September 30
MAX. RV LENGTH: 50 feet
NOTATIONS: Rate includes 5 people. Additional charges: Extra people $3/night, electric $8/night paid at check-in, Wi-Fi available, upgrade to riverside site if space available at check-in $8/night, upgrade to pull-through $10/night. Limited 50 amp sites available. Threaded sewer fittings required by county ordinance. Remote tent sites available. Life jackets required for all children while on docks, boats or near the river.

50 amps · pull-through · dump station · cable tv · visitor mail · laundry · pets/restrictions · internet access · Wi-Fi access · playground · fishing · hiking trails · horseshoes
boating · recreation hall · volleyball · fitness · shopping · propane · hot showers · fire rings · gift shop · tenting · firewood · ice

OREGON

NESKOWIN

RESORT NUMBER: 728 **GOOD SAM RATING:** 8.5/8.5★/8 **COAST CLASSIC RESORT**

Neskowin Creek RV Resort
50500 Highway 101 South
Neskowin, Oregon 97149
503-392-3355; fax: 503-392-4255
neskowincreek@soundpacificrv.com
soundpacificrv.com/neskowin-creek

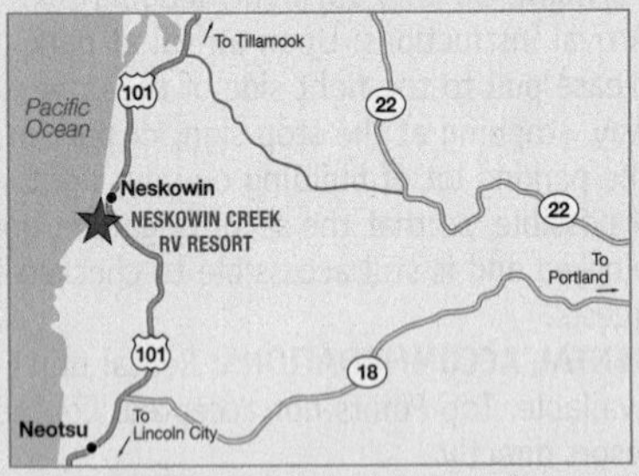

See page CTC 72 for state map.

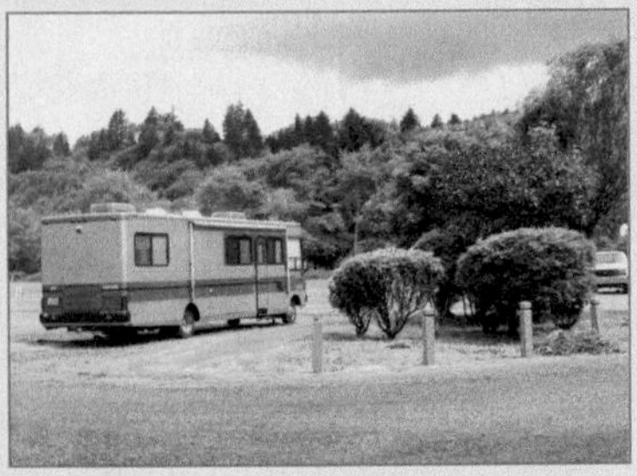

On the Central Oregon Coast, one-half mile south of Neskowin. Sandy beaches a short walk from the resort. Neskowin Creek runs through the property with catch and release fishing. Nearby: Golfing, fishing, surfing, diving, unique gift shops, restaurants, best hiking trails along the Oregon Coast.

DIRECTIONS: From Hwy 101 N: Approx 10 mi N of Lincoln City. Resort 7 mi N of Hwy 18. Just N of mi post 99. L into the resort.

GPS COORDINATES: 45.0932°N/-123.975°W
ELEVATION: 20 feet
RV SITES: Full: 99 Partial: 15 Dry: 29
CHECK-IN: 3:00 p.m.–8:00 p.m.
CHECK-OUT: Noon
SEASON: Year-round
MAX. RV LENGTH: 65 feet
NOTATIONS: Rate includes 2 adults/2 children, 50 amp, water and sewer, full hookup not guaranteed. Additional charges: 30 amp $3/night, 50 amp $5/night, cable $2/night, Wi-Fi rate sold by gigabytes. To gain access to resort call office from gate control panel for code, #001 for security. Drive-ups not accepted.
RENTAL ACCOMMODATIONS: Rental units available. Trip Points not accepted. Contact resort directly.

50 amps, laundry, pets/restrictions, internet access, Wi-Fi access, playground, rental units, hot tub, fishing, shuffleboard, hiking trails, horseshoes
recreation hall, fishing, basketball, beach, tennis, golf, game room, shopping, indoor pool, ball field, gambling casino

OREGON

ROCKAWAY BEACH

RESORT NUMBER: 2176 **GOOD SAM RATING:** 5/7.5/6.5 **COAST PREMIER RESORT**

Paradise Cove Resort—Advance Resorts of America
32455 Highway 101 North
Rockaway Beach, Oregon 97136
503-368-6581; res.: 800-445-9519
resort1214@gmail.com
araresorts.com

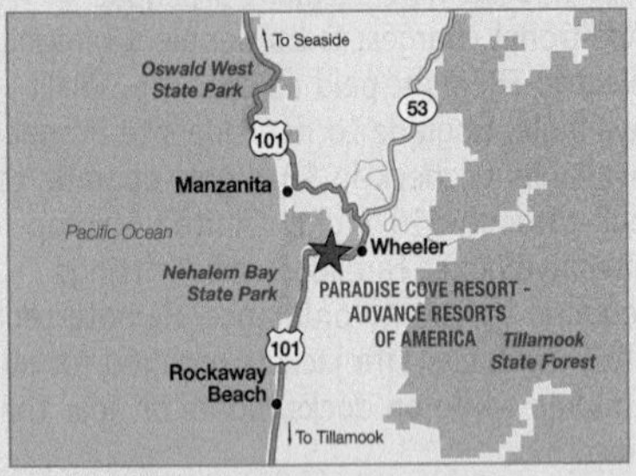

See page CTC 72 for state map.

Paradise Cove Resort and Marina is a quiet 68-acre waterfront RV park with fishing dock and a large crab cooker. The property is located on the Nehalem Bay near Rockaway Beach on the Oregon Coast between Seaside and Tillamook. The area's most popular activities include Chinook (King) salmon fishing, crabbing, clamming, hunting, golf, hiking, and enjoying the great local shops and restaurants.

DIRECTIONS: Paradise Cove Resort is 1 mi S of Wheeler on Nehalem Bay on Hwy 101.

GPS COORDINATES: 45.6884°N/-123.9227°W
ELEVATION: 65 feet
RV SITES: Full: 90 Partial: 0 Dry: 5
CHECK-IN: 4:00 p.m.
CHECK-OUT: Noon
SEASON: Year-round
PEAK SEASON: May 30–August 31
MAX. RV LENGTH: 50 feet
NOTATIONS: Free Wi-Fi. Additional charges: Lodging tax 8%.
RENTAL ACCOMMODATIONS: Rental units available. Trip Points not accepted. Contact resort directly.

30 amps, dump station, visitor mail, laundry, pets/restrictions, internet access, Wi-Fi access, picnic tables, rental units, hot tub, fishing, hiking trails
boating, recreation hall, age restrictions, fishing, boating, outdoor pool, beach, golf, tourist attraction
shopping, propane, hot showers, gambling casino, fire rings, tenting, firewood, ice

CHAMPION

RESORT NUMBER: 344 **GOOD SAM RATING:** 7.5/8/8.5 **COAST DELUXE RESORT**

Roaring Run Resort
194 Tannery Road
Champion, Pennsylvania 15622
724-593-7837; fax: 724-593-7838
roaringrunresort@hotmail.com
roaringrunresort.com

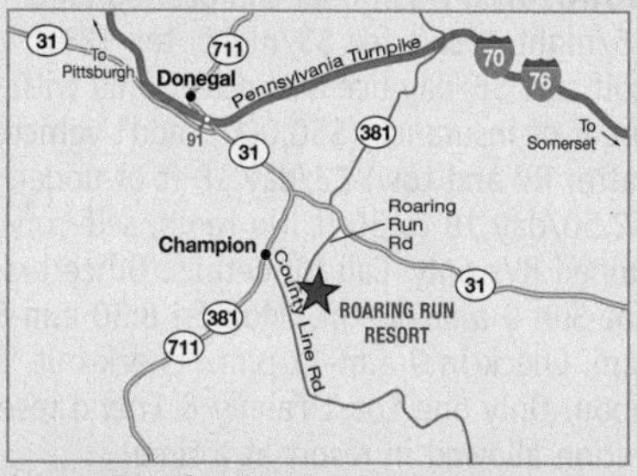

See page CTC 73 for state map.

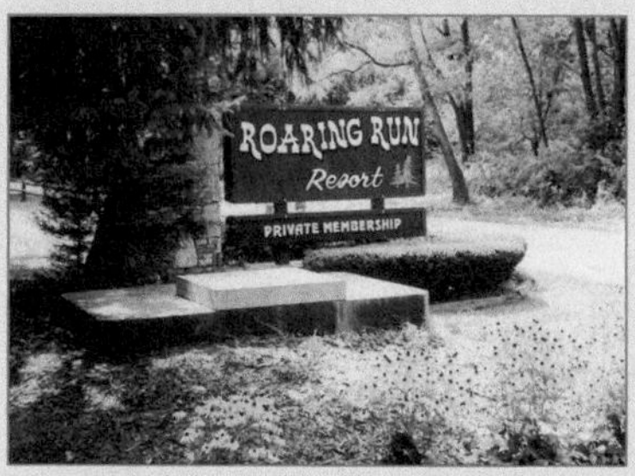

In the heart of Laurel Highlands, the playground of three western Pennsylvania counties. Nearby state parks: Laurel Mountain, Kooser, Laurel Ridge and Ohiopyle. Other resorts and places of interest include the Hidden Valley and Seven Springs Mountain Resorts, Falling Waters, and alpine ski resorts.

DIRECTIONS: From PA Tpke: Donegal Ex 91. Take Rte 31 E (L) 2 mi to Rte 711. S (R) 1 mi to Champion. L onto County Line Rd (Pennzoil Service Station). Cross bridge. 1st L onto Roaring Run Rd. 1 mi to main entrance. From S: Rte 711 N to Champion and follow directions above.

GPS COORDINATES: 40.0678°N/-79.3445°W
RV SITES: Full: 0 Partial: 140 Dry: 0
CHECK-IN: 9:00 a.m.–9:00 p.m.
CHECK-OUT: Noon
SEASON: May 15–October 15
PEAK SEASON: May 15–October 12
MAX. RV LENGTH: 38 feet
NOTATIONS: No minibikes, go-carts, or snowmobiles. 2 pets max per RV site.
RENTAL ACCOMMODATIONS: Rental units available. Trip Points not accepted. Contact resort directly.

PENNSYLVANIA

GETTYSBURG

RESORT NUMBER: 599 **GOOD SAM RATING:** 8.5/10★/9.5 **COAST PREMIER RESORT**

Gettysburg Battlefield Resort— Travel Resorts of America
1960 Emmitsburg Road
Gettysburg, Pennsylvania 17325
855-332-9541
trgreservations@travelresorts.com
travelresorts.com

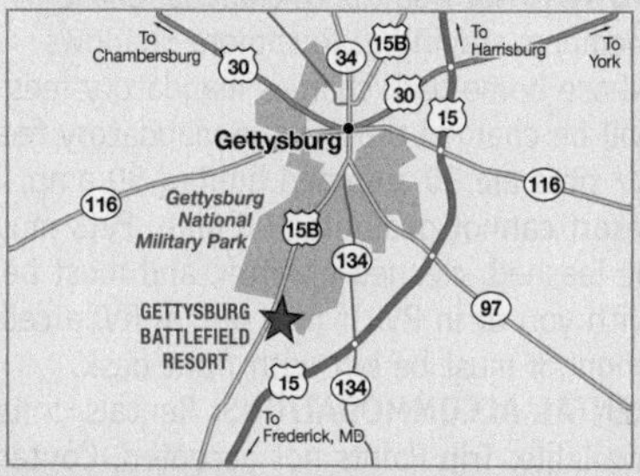

See page CTC 73 for state map.

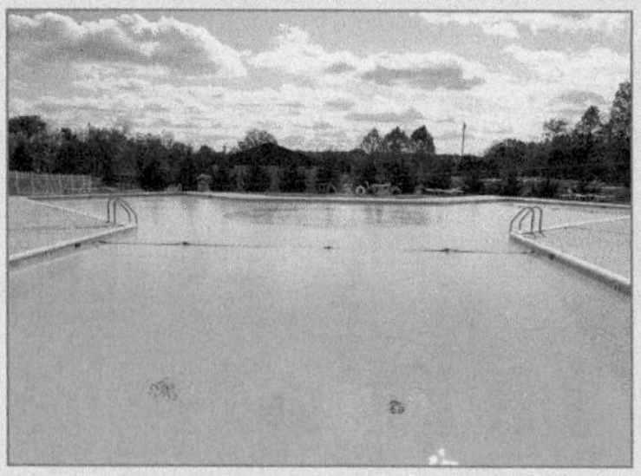

Located at the southern edge of the most famous battlefield in Civil War history, Gettysburg Battlefield Resort is convenient to Gettysburg, Hershey, Lancaster, and other Pennsylvania attractions, and is only two hours from the sights of Washington, D.C.

DIRECTIONS: From Hwy 15 in PA: Steinwehr Ave Ex US-Bus 15 N. 3 mi on US-Bus 15. Resort entrance on R.

GPS COORDINATES: 39.78°N/-77.2567°W
RV SITES: Full: 0 Partial: 180 Dry: 0
CHECK-IN: 1:00 p.m.
CHECK-OUT: 11:00 a.m.
SEASON: Year-round
PEAK SEASON: May 1–August 31
MAX. RV LENGTH: 45 feet
NOTATIONS: Additional charges: Honeywagon $18 Mon, Wed, Fri and $30 Sun, Tue, Thu, Sat. Limited sewer sites available.

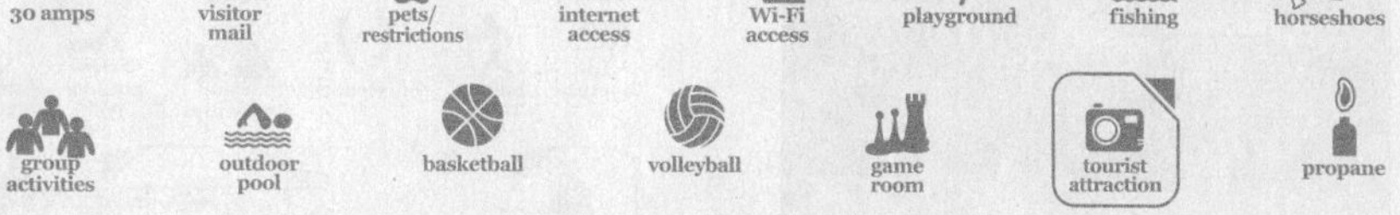

PENNSYLVANIA

SOUTH CAROLINA

MYRTLE BEACH

RESORT NUMBER: 327 **GOOD SAM RATING:** 10/9.5★/9.5 **COAST DELUXE RESORT**

Briarcliffe RV Resort
10495 North Kings Highway
Myrtle Beach, South Carolina 29572
843-272-2730; fax: 843-272-5188
briarcliffe@briarcliffervresort.com
briarcliffervresort.com

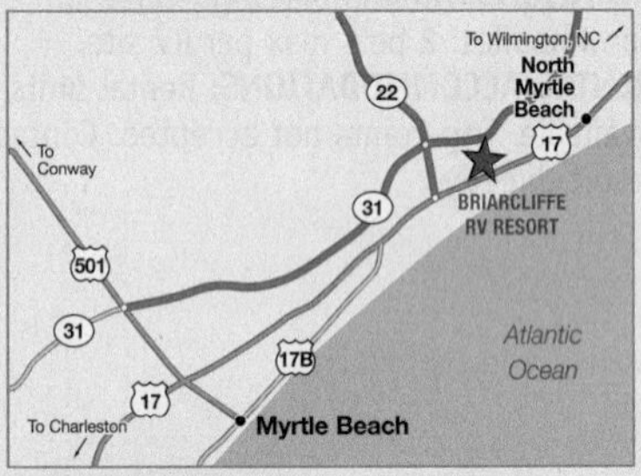

See page CTC 70 for state map.

On the Intracoastal Waterway in Myrtle Beach, known for its beaches, entertainment, shopping, recreation and over 100 golf courses. Walking distance to Barefoot Landing Shops, Alabama Theater and House of Blues.

DIRECTIONS: Hwy 17 between Myrtle Beach Mall and Barefoot Landing. From Hwy 501 S: Hwy 22 to Hwy 17/N Myrtle Beach. Ex to N Myrtle Beach. Resort is on L 1 mi N of Myrtle Beach Mall. Driving S on Hwy 17: Resort 2 blocks past Barefoot Landing on R.

GPS COORDINATES: 33.7955°N/-78.751°W
RV SITES: Full: 161 Partial: 0 Dry: 0
CHECK-IN: 9:00 a.m.–11:00 p.m.
CHECK-OUT: Noon
SEASON: Year-round
PEAK SEASON: June 1–September 30
MAX. RV LENGTH: 45 feet
NOTATIONS: Additional charges: 50 amp $5/night, resort fee $3/night, tax 12%, golf cart $5/day licensed driver only with proof of insurance ($50,000), add'l vehicles (after RV and tow) $2/day 18 ft or under, $2.50/day 18 to 30 ft. No tents, self-contained RVs only. Call for details. Office hrs Sat-Sun 9 a.m.-5 p.m., Mon-Fri 8:30 a.m-5 p.m. Check-in 9 a.m-11 p.m., check-out noon. Only one Coast Family & Friend reservation allowed in resort at a time.

SOUTH DAKOTA

RAPID CITY

RESORT NUMBER: 104 **GOOD SAM RATING:** 10/10★/10 **COAST PREMIER RESORT**

Rushmore Shadows Resort—Midwest Outdoor Resorts
23680 Busted Five Court
Rapid City, South Dakota 57702
605-399-7899; res.: 800-231-0425
stay@midwestoutdoorresorts.com
midwestoutdoorresorts.com

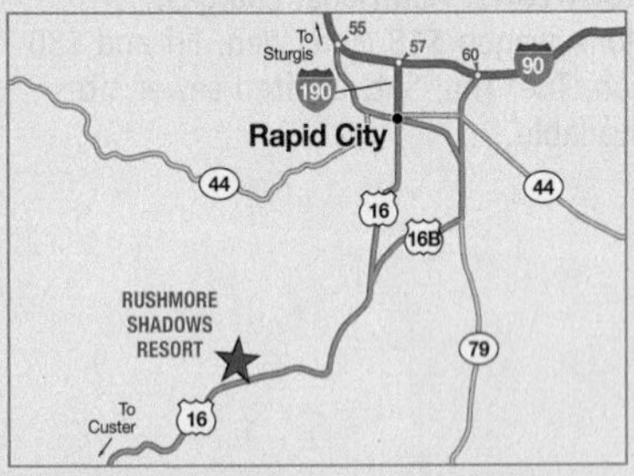

See page CTC 67 for state map.

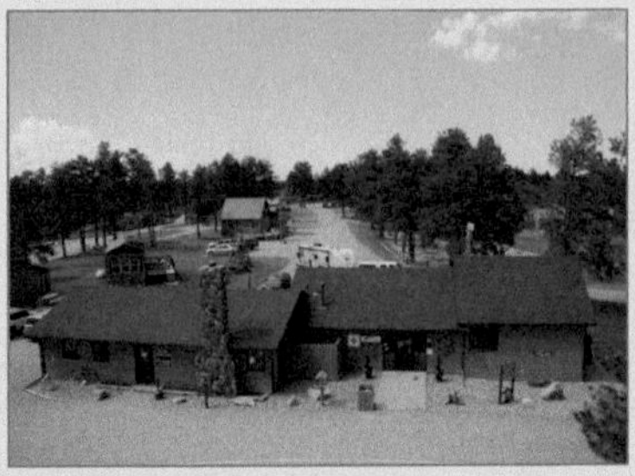

Centrally located in the heart of the Black Hills, between Mount Rushmore and Rapid City. Easy access to all area attractions including Mount Rushmore, Custer State Park, Crazy Horse Memorial and historic Deadwood. Rushmore Shadows is your quiet retreat in the Ponderosa Pines.

DIRECTIONS: From I-90: Take Ex 61 S (Hwy 16 Truck, Hwy 79 and Mt. Rushmore). Stay on Hwy 16 Truck for approx 9 mi, then turn L on Hwy 16. Travel SW approx 6 mi. Resort is on N side of Hwy 16 behind Old MacDonald's Farm.

GPS COORDINATES: 43.9731°N/-103.3272°W

ELEVATION: 4,130 feet
RV SITES: Full: 193 Partial: 0 Dry: 0
CHECK-IN: 4:00 p.m.–close
CHECK-OUT: 11:00 a.m.
SEASON: May 22–October 17
PEAK SEASON: May 24–September 2
MAX. RV LENGTH: 50 feet
NOTATIONS: Additional charges: Coast members staying at Rushmore Shadows whose home park charges mandatory fees will be charged those same mandatory fees. RV sites are 30 amp and limited 50 amp, resort cannot guarantee 50 amp. Pets must be leashed, cleaned up after, and must be with you or in RV. If pets left in RV, a cell phone # must be left with front desk.
RENTAL ACCOMMODATIONS: Rentals units available. Trip Points not accepted. Contact resort directly. No smoking in rental units.

CROSSVILLE

RESORT NUMBER: 275 **GOOD SAM RATING:** 6.5/7.5/7.5 **COAST CLASSIC RESORT**

Breckenridge Lake Resort
395 Oak Park Circle
Crossville, Tennessee 38572
931-788-1873; fax: 931-788-3839
breckenridgerv24@gmail.com
brlrvcamping.com

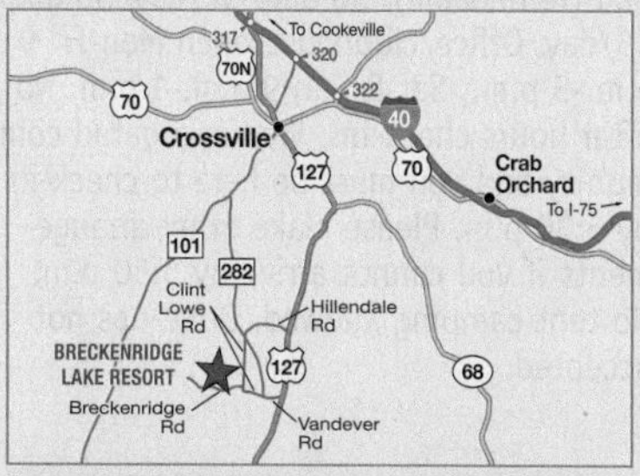

See page CTC 63 for state map.

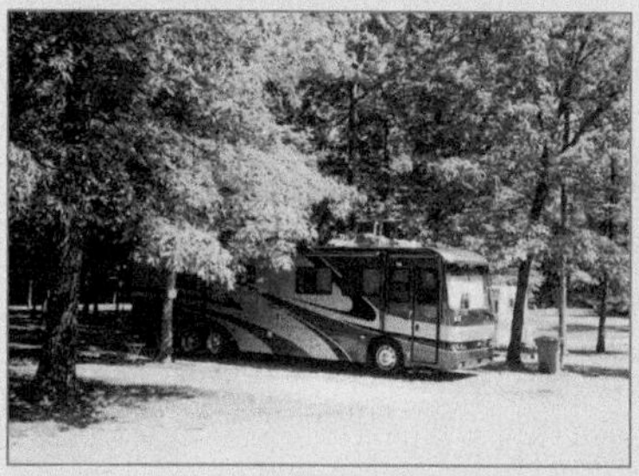

On the Cumberland Plateau between Knoxville, Nashville, & Chattanooga. Great area for fishing and hunting (licenses req.). Small campground with full hook-up, 30 & 50 amp sites. Lots of attractions nearby.
DIRECTIONS: From I-40: Ex 322 S to TN 392 bypass. 2.4 mi to Hwy 127. L on Hwy 127, 2.4 mi. R at fork on Hwy 127. Go 5 mi to Hillendale Rd. R for 2 mi. L on Dunbar, immediate R on Clint Lowe Rd. 2 mi to Breckenridge Rd. R 0.7 mi to park. Call if lost. GPS: park located just past 632 Breckenridge Rd.

GPS COORDINATES: 35.8095°N/-85.0623°W
ELEVATION: 1,980 feet
RV SITES: Full: 25 Partial: 18 Dry: 0
CHECK-IN: 10:00 a.m.–5:00 p.m.
CHECK-OUT: 11:00 a.m.
SEASON: Year-round
MAX. RV LENGTH: 45 feet
NOTATIONS: Rate includes 2 adults, 2 children under 14. Additional charges: 30 amp $2/night, 50 amp $4/night (limited sites), each add'l person $3/night. No pool, no pull-thrus. No unattended rigs overnight without mgmt knowledge. Late arrivals must notify park in advance or forfeit reservation. No arrivals after dark. Lake use requires pass-$5/day per person, fishing requires TN fishing license.

50 amps · dump station · visitor mail · laundry · pets/restrictions · internet access · Wi-Fi access · horseshoes · fishing · golf · tourist attraction · shopping · hot showers · tenting · grills

TENNESSEE

HORNSBY

RESORT NUMBER: 625 **GOOD SAM RATING:** 8/7.5/8.5 **COAST DELUXE RESORT**

Big Buck Camping Resort
205 Sparks Road
Hornsby, Tennessee 38044
731-658-2246
bigbuckresort@gmail.com
bigbuckresort.com

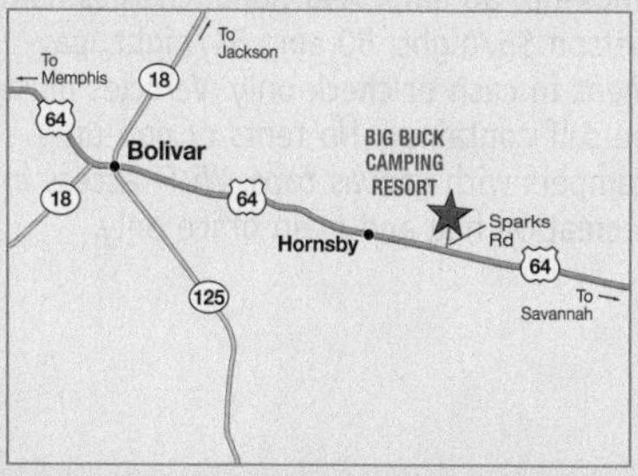

See page CTC 63 for state map.

Nestled on 212 acres in West Tennessee, Big Buck Resort is a little over an hour's drive to Graceland (home of Elvis Presley), the Bass Pro Shop on the Mississippi River, famous Beale Street and the festive Mud Island. We are 30 minutes from Shiloh Battleground, Standing Tall Sheriff Pusser Museum, and Pickwick Dam.
DIRECTIONS: From Jackson: Hwy 45 S to Hwy 64. R towards Memphis, follow for 10 mi (just past the Hardeman County Rd sign). R on Sparks Rd, the resort is 0.3 mi on the L. From Memphis: Hwy 64 E 10 mi E of Bolivar, L on Sparks Rd.

GPS COORDINATES: 35.2207°N/-88.7945°W
RV SITES: Full: 100 Partial: 20 Dry: 0
CHECK-IN: After Noon
CHECK-OUT: Noon
SEASON: Year-round
PEAK SEASON: May 26–September 7
MAX. RV LENGTH: 60 feet
NOTATIONS: Additional charges: 50 amp with sewer $5/night. Wi-Fi access in clubhouse, also some hot spots in campground.
RENTAL ACCOMMODATIONS: Rental units available. Trip Points not accepted. Contact resort directly.

50 amps · dump station · visitor mail · laundry · pets/restrictions · Wi-Fi access · playground · rental units · fishing · hiking trails · horseshoes · group activities · recreation hall · outdoor pool · basketball · volleyball · tourist attraction · hot showers · paddle boats · tenting · firewood · handicap access · ice · grills

TENNESSEE

TEXAS

BANDERA

RESORT NUMBER: 1912 **GOOD SAM RATING:** 8.5/8.5★/8.5 **COAST DELUXE RESORT**

Holiday Villages of Medina
234 Private Road 1501
Bandera, Texas 78003
830-796-8141; res.: 830-796-8142
hvmpoa@gmail.com
hvmpoa.com

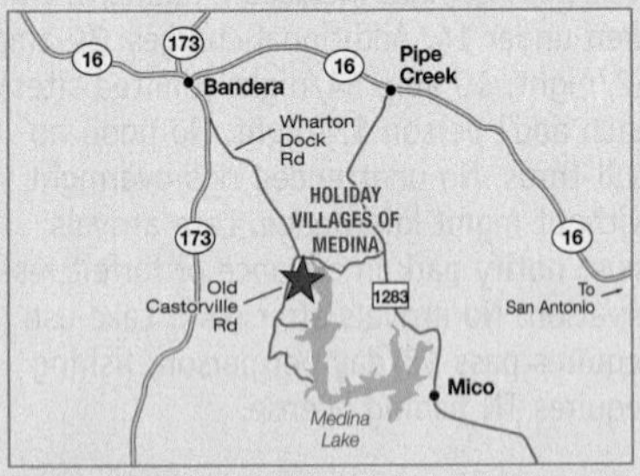

See page CTC 74 for state map.

Located on the shores of Medina Lake Hill County northwest of San Antonio, Texas. Lots of good fishing and hunting in the area. Convenient to nearby tourist attractions Sea World, Fiesta Texas and the River Walk.

DIRECTIONS: GPS latitude 29.617, longitude -98.99. From Loop 410: Hwy 16/Bandera, L at light onto Hwy 173 S for 1.2 mi. Turn L onto Whartons Dock Rd, in approx 7 mi the road will fork, stay R onto Old Castroville Rd for approx 2 mi. Holiday Village gate house will be on L.

GPS COORDINATES: 29.617°N/-98.99°W
RV SITES: Full: 30 Partial: 0 Dry: 0
CHECK-IN: Noon–5:30 p.m.
CHECK-OUT: Noon
SEASON: Year-round
MAX. RV LENGTH: 45 feet
NOTATIONS: Additional charges: Gate key $20 (refundable), 30 amp $2/day, 50 amp $5/day. Office/clubhouse open Mon-Fri 9 a.m.-5 p.m., Sat & Sun 9 a.m.-1 p.m. No after hours check-ins. We are a gated community and you must be here to check-in by 5:30 p.m. Please make other arrangements if you cannot arrive by 5:30 p.m. No tent camping allowed. Drive-ups not accepted.

50 amps · pull-through · visitor mail · laundry · pets/restrictions · internet access · Wi-Fi access · hot tub · fishing · horseshoes · recreation hall · fishing · outdoor pool · mini golf · basketball · volleyball · tourist attraction · hot showers

TEXAS

BROWNSVILLE

RESORT NUMBER: 540 **GOOD SAM RATING:** 10/9★/8.5 **COAST CLASSIC RESORT**

Brownsville Winter Haven Resort
3501 Old Port Isabel Road
Brownsville, Texas 78526
956-831-7755; fax: 956-831-7757
office@winterhavenresort.com
winterhavenresort.com

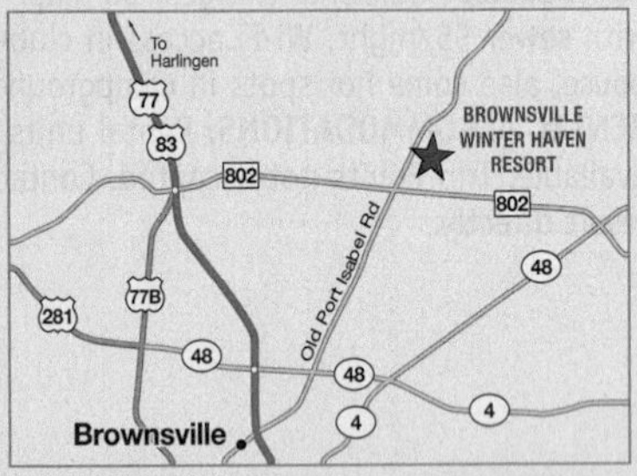

See page CTC 74 for state map.

In historic Brownsville, the southernmost city in Texas. The sub-tropical climate, proximity to Mexico, the beach at South Padre Island, fishing, boating, bird watching (three wildlife refuges in the area), and a top ten zoo make this the ideal destination. Enjoy mild winters in a relaxed two-nation atmosphere.

DIRECTIONS: From Hwy 77/83 N of Brownsville: Ex. E on FM 802 for 1.9 mi to Old Port Isabel Rd. L on Old Port Isabel Rd. 0.6 mi to resort on R.

GPS COORDINATES: 25.96°N/-97.46°W
RV SITES: Full: 29 Partial: 0 Dry: 0
CHECK-IN: Noon–6:00 p.m.
CHECK-OUT: 10:00 a.m.
SEASON: Year-round
MAX. RV LENGTH: 45 feet
NOTATIONS: Rate includes 4 people, full hook-up, 30 amp. Additional charges: Extra person $5/night, 50 amp $4/night, payment in cash or check only. Vehicles must be self-contained. No tents or pop-up campers with canvas tops. Wi-Fi access in recreation hall and main office only.

50 amps · dump station · cable tv · visitor mail · laundry · pets/restrictions · internet access · Wi-Fi access · hot tub · fishing · shuffleboard · group activities · recreation hall · church services · age restrictions · fishing · boating · outdoor pool · beach · tennis · golf · game room · tourist attraction · hot showers · handicap access · ice

BROWNWOOD

RESORT NUMBER: 2142 **GOOD SAM RATING:** 9.5/9.5★/9 **COAST DELUXE RESORT**

TEXAS

The Hideout Golf Club & Resort
185 Hideout Lane
Brownwood, Texas 76801
325-784-4653; fax: 325-784-8037
frontdesk@thehideouttexas.com
thehideouttexas.com

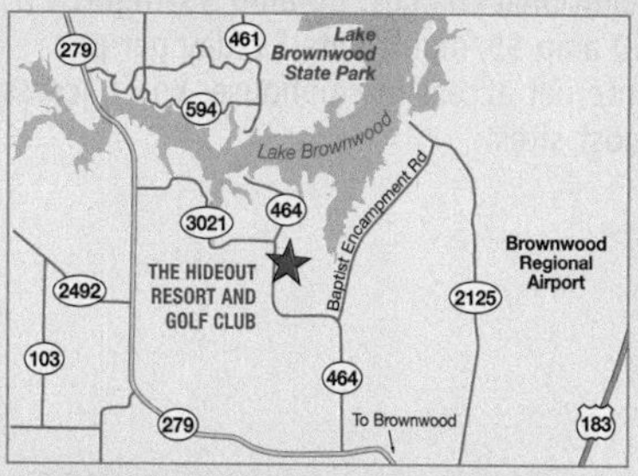

See page CTC 74 for state map.

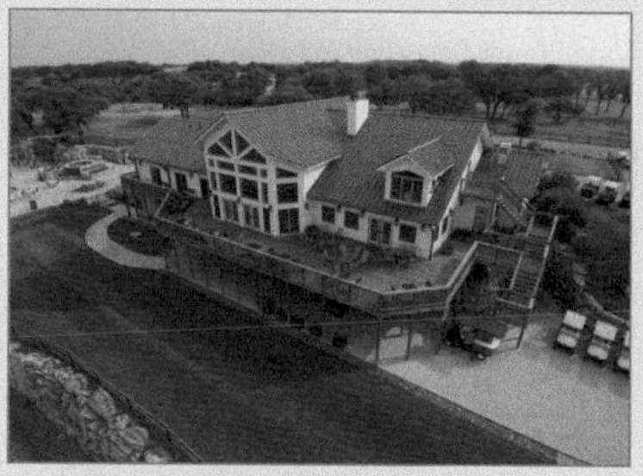

Situated in the heart of Central Texas on Lake Brownwood, offering a one-of-a-kind experience for golfers, RVers and their families. The 18-hole championship golf course is a top golf destination. Beautiful new 11,000 sq ft clubhouse has restaurant serving all three meals and a golf pro shop. Resort also has fully furnished cabins and a resort style pool and spa.

DIRECTIONS: From Abilene: TX 36 E to Cross Plains. R on S Main St/TX 279. Approx 3 mi from bridge, turn L on FM 3021. R on FM 2632. Resort on L. From Austin: I-35N to Ex 261, TX 29 W. Turn N on Hwy 183. In Goldthwaite L/N on Hwy 183/84 N. L on Early Blvd/Hwys 183/377/67/84. Follow Hwys 84/67, then R on Belle Plain St/TX 279. R on FM 2632. Resort on R. From Ft Worth: I-20-W, Ex 386, S on Hwy 281. R on Hwy 377 S. R on Belle Plain St/TX 279. R on FM 2632. Resort on R.

GPS COORDINATES: 31.6534°N/-98.9868°W
RV SITES: Full: 25 Partial: 0 Dry: 0
CHECK-IN: 9:00 a.m.
CHECK-OUT: 2:00 p.m.
SEASON: Year-round
PEAK SEASON: May 1–September 30
MAX. RV LENGTH: 48 feet
NOTATIONS: Drive-ups not accepted.
RENTAL ACCOMMODATIONS: Rental units available. Trip Points not accepted. Contact resort directly.

30 amps · pull-through · pets/restrictions · internet access · Wi-Fi access · playground · picnic tables · restaurant/snack bar · rental units · hot tub · fishing · recreation hall · fishing · boating · outdoor pool · volleyball · golf · paddle boats · grills

GLEN ROSE

RESORT NUMBER: 894 **GOOD SAM RATING:** 8.5/7/9 **COAST PREMIER RESORT**

TEXAS

Tres Rios RV Resort—
Ocean Canyon Properties
2322 County Road 312
Glen Rose, Texas 76043
214-306-6868; res.: 254-221-0018
member.reservations@oceancanyon.com
oceancanyon.com

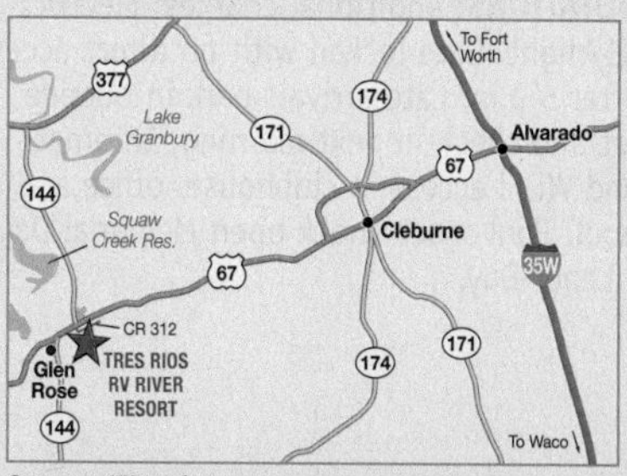

See page CTC 74 for state map.

Tres Rios is nestled at the confluence of three rivers, two miles from Glen Rose, Texas, which is known for its dinosaur museum and fossil grounds. The resort is known for its special events and local area events such as the annual music festival, blue bonnet festival and regularly scheduled arts, crafts, and antique shows. The resort has 50 years of history as a YMCA summer camp.

DIRECTIONS: From Cleburne: Hwy 67 S towards Glen Rose. L at intersection of Hwy 144. Quick L onto CR 312 (NW). Less than 1 mi on CR 312 across the Squaw Creek Bridge. R after bridge to resort.

GPS COORDINATES: 32.2518°N/-97.7214°W
RV SITES: Full: 160 Partial: 0 Dry: 0
CHECK-IN: 2:00 p.m.
CHECK-OUT: 11:00 a.m.
SEASON: Year-round
PEAK SEASON: January 1–December 31
MAX. RV LENGTH: 60 feet
NOTATIONS: Additional charges: 50 amp $5/night, Wi-Fi $5/night. No tent camping. BBQ grills for rent.
RENTAL ACCOMMODATIONS: Rental units available. Trip Points not accepted. Contact resort directly.

50 amps · pull-through · visitor mail · laundry · pets/restrictions · internet access · Wi-Fi access · playground · picnic tables · restaurant/snack bar · rental units · fishing · hiking trails · group activities · recreation hall · church services · fishing · boating · outdoor pool · basketball · volleyball · golf · game room · tourist attraction · shopping · hot showers · fire rings · rv supplies · firewood · handicap access · ice

TEXAS

PUNKIN

RESORT NUMBER: 1558 **GOOD SAM RATING:** 5/5/4.5 **COAST CLASSIC RESORT**

Hillcrest RV Park
5260 Highway 150 West
Punkin, Texas 77358
936-767-4101
5260hillcrestrvpark@gmail.com

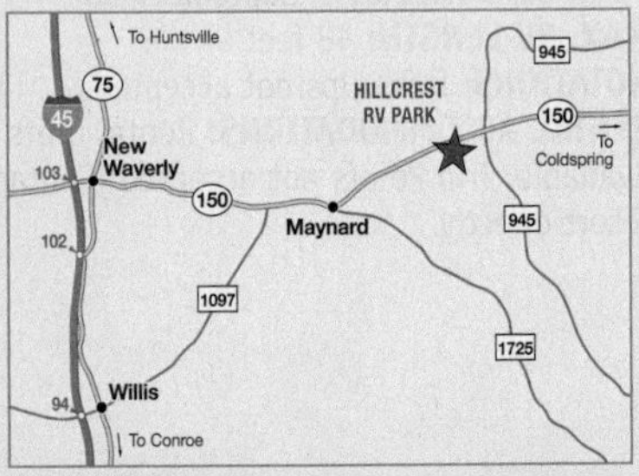

See page CTC 74 for state map.

Located in the heart of Sam Houston National Forest, the resort abounds in country charm. Between New Waverly and historic Coldspring and minutes from I-45 and US 59. Near Lake Conroe, Lake Livingston and one hour north of Houston. The clubhouse has a full kitchen and a fireplace for your comfort and enjoyment.

DIRECTIONS: From I-45: Ex 103 S-bound or Ex 102 N-bound onto Hwy 150. E 13.7 mi. Resort on R. Resort is 11 miles W of Coldspring.

GPS COORDINATES: 30.325°N/-95.2804°W
RV SITES: Full: 31 Partial: 0 Dry: 10
CHECK-IN: 11:00 a.m.
CHECK-OUT: 3:00 p.m.
SEASON: Year-round
MAX. RV LENGTH: Unlimited
NOTATIONS: Sites includes water and sewer. Additional charges: 30 amp $3/night, 50 amp $5/night, pets $1/day per pet. Internet access in clubhouse. Wi-Fi access most sites.

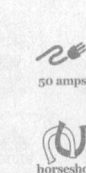

50 amps · pull-through · visitor mail · laundry · pets/restrictions · internet access · Wi-Fi access · picnic tables · hot tub · hiking trails · horseshoes · recreation hall · fishing · outdoor pool · golf · tourist attraction · shopping · fire rings · firewood

TEXAS

ROARING SPRINGS

RESORT NUMBER: 112 **GOOD SAM RATING:** 6.5/6.5/6.5 **COAST CLASSIC RESORT**

Roaring Springs Ranch Club
1001 FM 3203
Roaring Springs, Texas 79256
806-348-7292; fax: 806-348-7971
roaring@caprock-spur.com; info@rsrc.org
rsrc.org

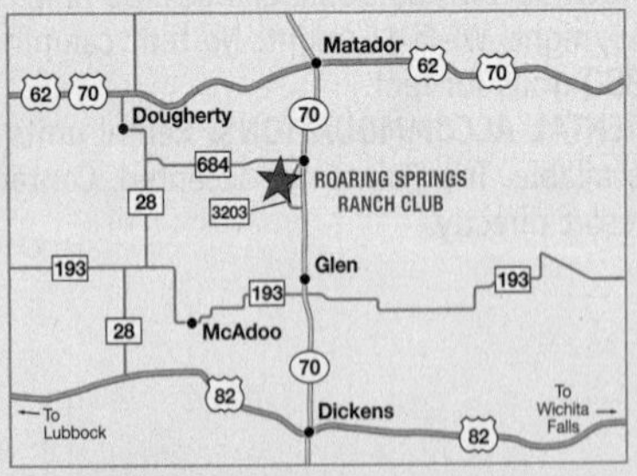

See page CTC 74 for state map.

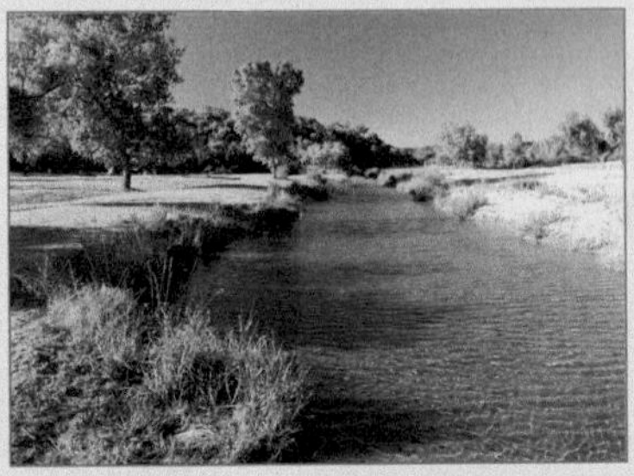

In northwest Texas on the South Pease River, with 746 acres of improved campsites and wilderness camping with ever-changing scenery, springs, bluffs, hidden valleys and nature trails. For centuries the ranch was the Comanche Indians' favorite campsite and was the heart of the famous 500,000-acre Matador Ranch.

DIRECTIONS: From Lubbock: Hwy 82 E 60 mi to Dickens. Hwy 70 N 18 mi. Pass golf course and cross bridge. L on FM 3203. Follow signs 0.5 mi to resort. If using GPS directions go to FM 3203.

GPS COORDINATES: 33.8604°N/-100.858°W
ELEVATION: 2,500 feet
RV SITES: Full: 0 Partial: 185 Dry: 0
CHECK-IN: 9:00 a.m.–4:00 p.m.
CHECK-OUT: Noon
SEASON: March 2–November 21
MAX. RV LENGTH: 48 feet
NOTATIONS: Additional charges: Electric $5/night. Gate locked with no direct access after 5 p.m. Late arrivals park in outside lot and check-in next morning. Internet and Wi-Fi access in clubhouse, office and at pool. Pool snack shack open Memorial Day - Labor Day.

50 amps · pull-through · visitor mail · pets/restrictions · internet access · Wi-Fi access · playground · picnic tables · fishing · hiking trails · horseshoes · recreation hall · outdoor pool · basketball · beach · volleyball · golf

ROCKPORT

RESORT NUMBER: 466 **GOOD SAM RATING:** 7.5/8.5★/7 **COAST CLASSIC RESORT**

TEXAS

Bay View
5451 Highway 35 North
Rockport, Texas 78382
361-400-6000; fax: 361-729-0576
resort@bayviewrockport.com
bayviewrockport.com

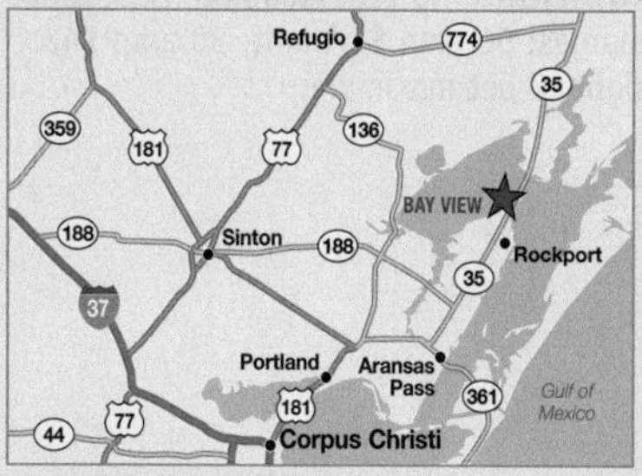

See page CTC 74 for state map.

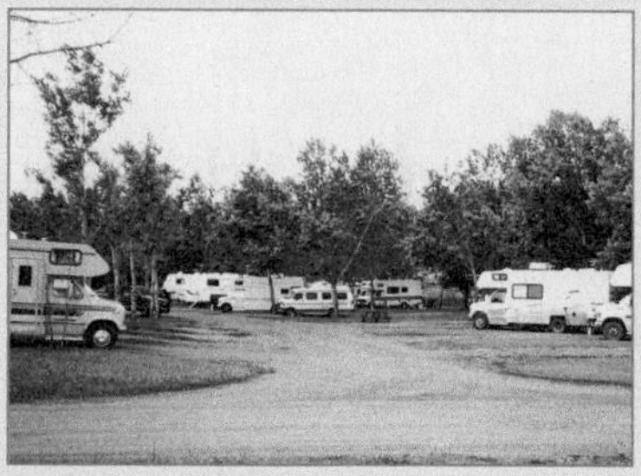

North of Corpus Christi, come relax under the oak trees. The weather is beautiful year round. Nearby are Fulton Mansion, Texas Maritime Museum, Rockport Center for the Arts, Aransas Wildlife Refuge, deep sea fishing, boat tours for birding, whooping cranes and dolphins, the USS Lexington, Texas State Aquarium, Bay Education Center, public beaches, boating, fun shops and many fine restaurants.

DIRECTIONS: From Rockport/Fulton area: 1 mi N of Aransas County Airport on Hwy 35 N. Resort is on L. GPS not recommended.

GPS COORDINATES: 28.1049°N/-97.0308°W
RV SITES: Full: 340 Partial: 100 Dry: 0
CHECK-IN: 1:00 p.m.–4:00 p.m.
CHECK-OUT: Noon
SEASON: Year-round
MAX. RV LENGTH: 45 feet
NOTATIONS: Additional charges: Utility fee $10/night, some sites have cable $3/night. If arriving after 4 p.m. please call resort. Credit cards not accepted. On-site amenities are limited at this time due to the virus, please call the resort for further information.

50 amps · cable tv · visitor mail · laundry · pets/restrictions · internet access · Wi-Fi access · playground · hot tub · shuffleboard · horseshoes · group activities · recreation hall · fishing · boating · outdoor pool · basketball · beach · tennis · game room · tourist attraction · hot showers · tenting · handicap access

TRINITY

RESORT NUMBER: 114 **GOOD SAM RATING:** 7.5/7/8.5 **COAST DELUXE RESORT**

TEXAS

Marina Village Resort
262 Westwood Drive East
Trinity, Texas 75862
936-594-0149
marinavillagers@fsresidential.com
marina-village.com

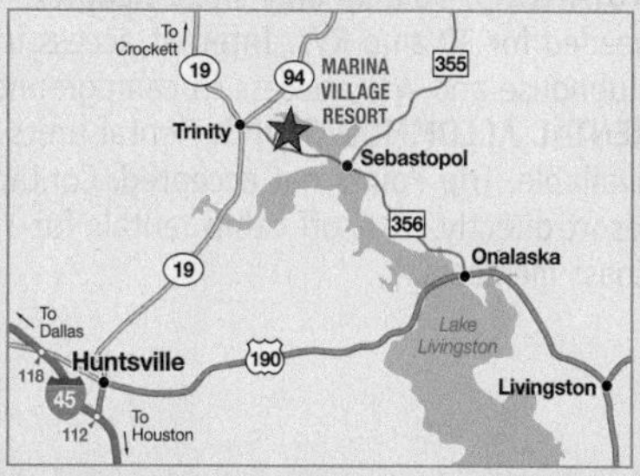

See page CTC 74 for state map.

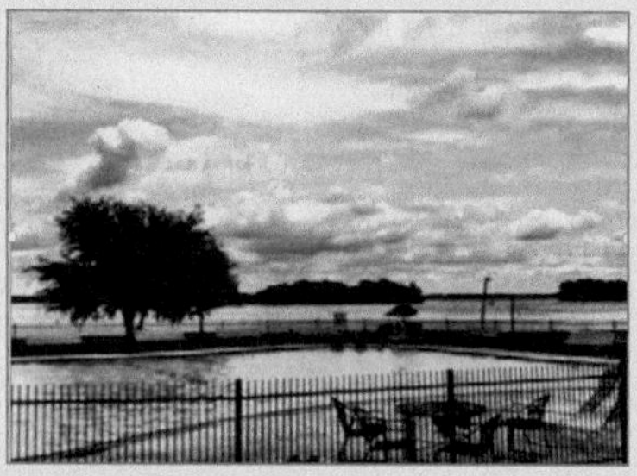

On 90,000-acre Lake Livingston, great for all watersports including fishing. Resort has a heavy tree cover of pine and oak, with many waterfront sites. Nearby: Sam Houston's home in Huntsville and Sam Houston National Forest. A beautiful resort for campers creating memories for a lifetime and dedicated to family fun for everyone.

DIRECTIONS: From Houston: I-45 N 86 mi to Ex 113 Trinity/Crockett. 20 mi on Hwy 19 to Trinity. S (R) on Hwy 94 for 3 blocks. S (R) on Hwy 356. 3 mi and L at Westwood Shores/Marina Village entrance. Office is located inside the campground over the bridge. Follow Westwood Drive E to the end of the road. Office is located in building adjacent to the restrooms.

GPS COORDINATES: 30.9398°N/-95.3106°W
RV SITES: Full: 189 Partial: 81 Dry: 0
CHECK-IN: 8:00 a.m.–5:00 p.m.
CHECK-OUT: Noon
SEASON: Year-round
MAX. RV LENGTH: 40 feet
NOTATIONS: Additional charges: Resort fee $5/night. No motorcycles or off-road vehicles. Internet and Wi-Fi access at community center.
RENTAL ACCOMMODATIONS: Rental units available. Trip Points not accepted. Contact resort directly.

50 amps · pull-through · pets/restrictions · internet access · Wi-Fi access · playground · restaurant/snack bar · rental units · fishing · shuffleboard · boating · recreation hall · fishing · outdoor pool · mini golf · basketball · tennis · golf · tourist attraction

TEXAS

WHITNEY

RESORT NUMBER: 210 **GOOD SAM RATING:** 7/8★/6.5 **COAST DELUXE RESORT**

Whitney Resorts
255 Suncountry Drive
Whitney, Texas 76692
254-694-4023; fax: 254-694-4027
info@whitneyresorts.com
whitneyresorts.com

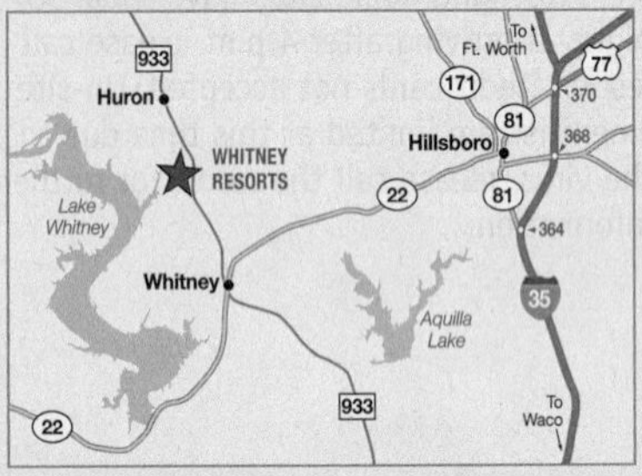

See page CTC 74 for state map.

Resort sits on 24,000-acre Lake Whitney. Nearby: Lake access at Juniper Cove, Texas Ranger Hall of Fame in Waco, Hillsboro Outlet Mall. One hour to Dallas/Fort Worth Metroplex, Dallas Cowboys, Texas Rangers, Dallas Mavericks, Dallas Stars and Texas Motor Speedway.

DIRECTIONS: From Dallas: I-35 E to Hillsboro. Hwy 22 W 12 mi to Whitney. R on FM 933. N 3.3 mi to resort and lighted entrance on L (going N).

GPS COORDINATES: 31.9935°N/-97.3418°W
ELEVATION: 900 feet
RV SITES: Full: 85 Partial: 0 Dry: 0
CHECK-IN: 8:00 a.m.–6:00 p.m.
CHECK-OUT: Noon
SEASON: Year-round
MAX. RV LENGTH: 45 feet
NOTATIONS: No tent camping. Additional charges: 50 amp $7/night, 30 amp $4/night, 2 pet maximum.

50 amps · pull-through · visitor mail · laundry · pets/restrictions · Wi-Fi access · hiking trails · horseshoes · group activities
recreation hall · church services · fishing · boating · outdoor pool · tourist attraction · shopping

TEXAS

WILLIS

RESORT NUMBER: 113 **GOOD SAM RATING:** 7/7/8 **COAST DELUXE RESORT**

Waters Edge
12922 Longstreet Road
Willis, Texas 77318
936-856-2949
watersedge.tthc@yahoo.com

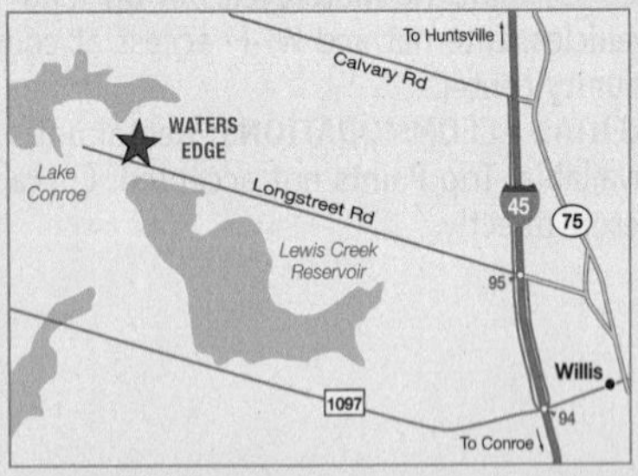

See page CTC 74 for state map.

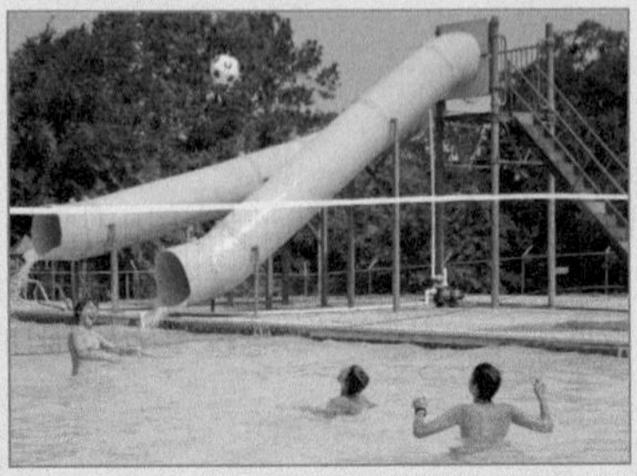

Nestled in a quiet cove, enjoy this beautiful resort just minutes away from the Sam Houston National Forest. Trails are available for hiking and biking, bird watching and nature enthusiasts. Only 35 miles N of Houston on beautiful Lake Conroe, a 30,000 acre lake for boating and fishing. Whether you are looking for a quiet, country family setting or a first-class fine dining experience, we are close to it all. Seasonal: The Texas Renaissance Festival, Catfish Festival, Crawfish Festival, outdoor concerts at the Cynthia Woods-Mitchell Pavilion.

DIRECTIONS: From S on I-45: Ex 95, L at stop sign onto Longstreet Rd, 3.2 mi to park on R. From N on I-45: Ex 95, R 3.2 mi, park is on the R.

GPS COORDINATES: 30.4494°N/-95.5514°W
RV SITES: Full: 130 Partial: 0 Dry: 0
CHECK-IN: 9:00 a.m.–9:00 p.m.
CHECK-OUT: Noon
SEASON: Year-round
PEAK SEASON: January 1–April 30
MAX. RV LENGTH: 42 feet
NOTATIONS: 50 amp only sites. Adapter needed for 30 amp RVs. Internet access in clubhouse and Wi-Fi access in campground.
RENTAL ACCOMMODATIONS: Rental units available. Trip Points not accepted. Contact resort directly. 10% off cabin rentals for Coast members.

50 amps · pull-through · laundry · pets/restrictions · internet access · Wi-Fi access · playground · rental units · fishing · horseshoes · boating
recreation hall · fishing · boating · outdoor pool · mini golf · basketball · tennis · volleyball · tourist attraction · hot showers · ball field

DELTA

RESORT NUMBER: 1542 **GOOD SAM RATING:** 7.5/9.5★/8 **COAST PREMIER RESORT**

UTAH

Antelope Valley RV Park
776 West Highway 6/50
Delta, Utah 84624
435-864-1813; fax: 435-864-2644
anteloperv@yahoo.com
antelopevalleyrvpark.com

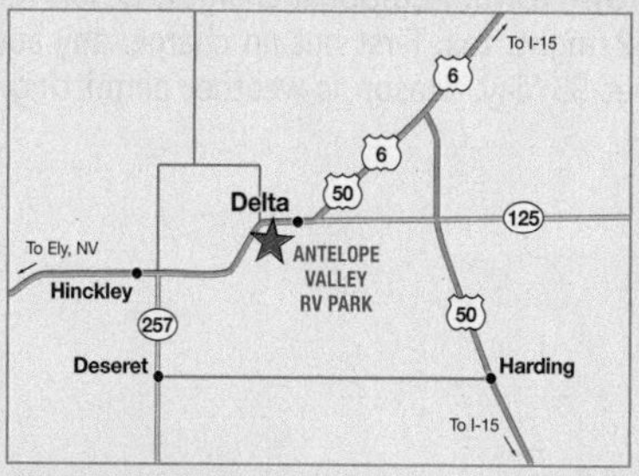

See page CTC 68 for state map.

A high country desert oasis with 30 Russian Olive trees. Bass fishing, swimming, boating and a lake beach are available at nearby Gunnison Bend Reservoir. Rock hounds find garnets, topaz, Apache tears, red beryl, and trilobites. Day trips are possible to Great Basin National Park, historical Gunnison Massacre Site, or craft shops.

DIRECTIONS: From Salt Lake City: I-15 S to Nephi. Hwy 132 W to Hwy 6. 15 mi to Delta. Resort is 0.2 mi W of Delta on Hwy 50. From the W: Hwy 50 E, 87 mi beyond the UT/NV border to resort 0.2 mi W of Delta.

GPS COORDINATES: 39.3525°N/-112.5913°W
ELEVATION: 4,600 feet
RV SITES: Full: 95 Partial: 0 Dry: 0
CHECK-IN: 9:00 a.m.–9:00 p.m.
CHECK-OUT: 1:00 p.m.
SEASON: Year-round
MAX. RV LENGTH: Unlimited
NOTATIONS: Self-registration is to be used between 9 p.m. and 9 a.m.

50 amps · pull-through · dump station · laundry · pets/restrictions · Wi-Fi access · horseshoes · fishing · boating · golf · tourist attraction · shopping · hot showers · tenting · handicap access

DUCHESNE

RESORT NUMBER: 536 **GOOD SAM RATING:** 6.5/7.5★/8 **COAST DELUXE RESORT**

UTAH

Lakeside RV Park
8850 South 26500 West
Duchesne, Utah 84021
435-823-2244; res.: 801-405-9427
lakeside@escapervresorts.com
escapervresorts.com

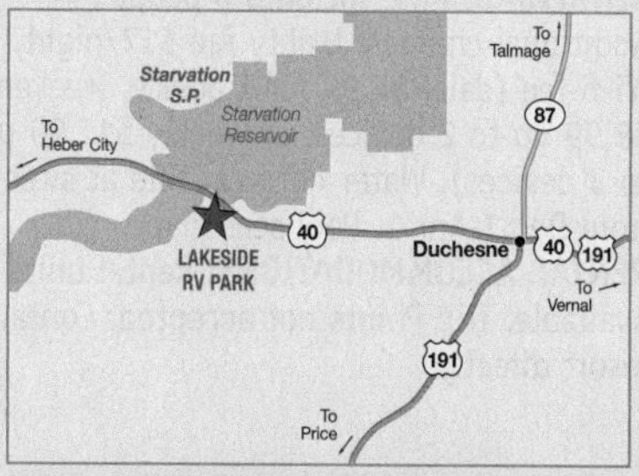

See page CTC 68 for state map.

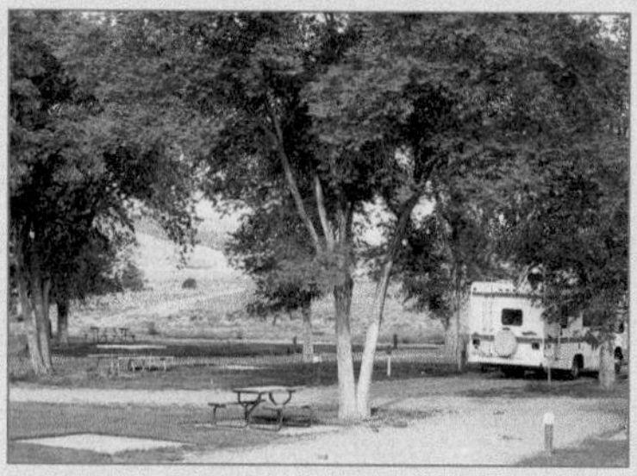

In Utah's mountain country next to Starvation Lake. The lake features 3,300 acres of water surface suitable for recreation, from peaceful canoe cruising to exhilarating water skiing. All season fishing, rock-hounding, and other activities are very popular in the area.

DIRECTIONS: From Salt Lake City: I-80 E onto Hwy 40/189 to Heber City. Hwy 40 past Heber City about 70 mi to the Starvation Reservoir Bridge. Cross bridge, resort on R. From the E: Approx 4 mi W of Duchesne. Resort on L (S). Do not cross bridge.

GPS COORDINATES: 40.1726°N/-110.4919°W
ELEVATION: 5,800 feet
RV SITES: Full: 18 Partial: 7 Dry: 0
CHECK-IN: 2:00 p.m.
CHECK-OUT: 11:00 a.m.
SEASON: March 15–October 15
MAX. RV LENGTH: 45 feet
NOTATIONS: Limited water in Oct. Additional charges: Resort fee $2/night, first pet no charge, any add'l pet $5/night, tax.

50 amps · pull-through · laundry · pets/restrictions · Wi-Fi access · picnic tables · hiking trails · fishing · boating · volleyball · game room · hot showers · tenting

UTAH

MT PLEASANT

RESORT NUMBER: 115 **GOOD SAM RATING:** 9/10★/8.5 **COAST DELUXE RESORT**

Pleasant Creek RV Park
2903 South 1700 East
Mt Pleasant, Utah 84647
801-903-9752; res.: 801-405-9427
tama@escapervresorts.com
escapervresorts.com

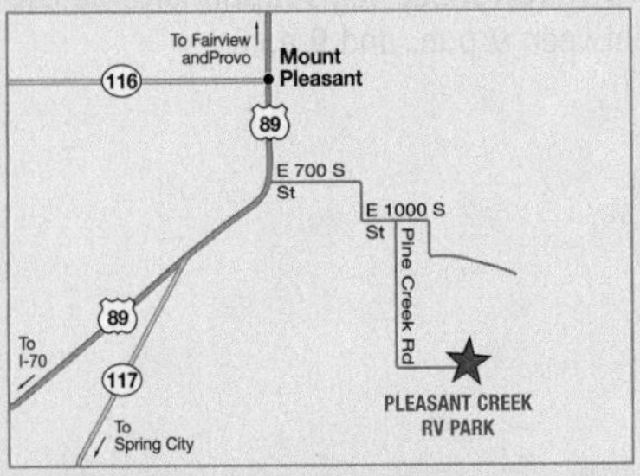

See page CTC 68 for state map.

Pleasant Creek is nestled against the Manti-La Sal National Forest in central Utah. The park is built on a mountainside with a commanding view of vast and rugged mountains and the picturesque valley below. Seasonal sports facilities are available.
DIRECTIONS: From I-15 S of Salt Lake City: Manti/Price Ex Hwys 6/89. Hwy 89 to Mt Pleasant. E on 700 S St/Hawks Blvd (look for N Sanpete High School sign) in Mt Pleasant. 4 mi to resort on L, staying on paved road.

GPS COORDINATES: 39.5053°N/-111.4225°W
ELEVATION: 6,800 feet
RV SITES: Full: 72 Partial: 12 Dry: 0
CHECK-IN: 2:00 p.m.
CHECK-OUT: 11:00 a.m.
SEASON: May 1–October 1
MAX. RV LENGTH: 40 feet
NOTATIONS: Additional charges: Resort fee $2/night, tax. First pet no charge, any add'l pet $5/day. Season is weather permitting.

50 amps · pull-through · laundry · pets/restrictions · Wi-Fi access · picnic tables · horseshoes · outdoor pool · basketball · volleyball · game room · hot showers · tenting

VIRGINIA

FRONT ROYAL

RESORT NUMBER: 120 **GOOD SAM RATING:** 9/8.5★/8.5 **COAST DELUXE RESORT**

North Fork Resort
301 North Fork Road
Front Royal, Virginia 22630
540-636-2995; res.: 540-636-9949
reservations@nfra.com
nfra.com

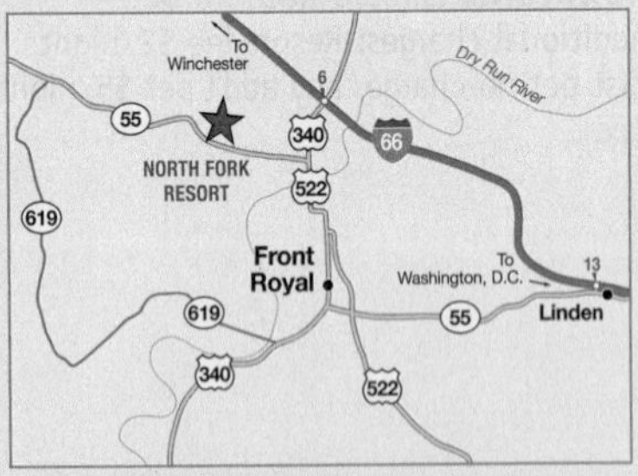

See page CTC 75 for state map.

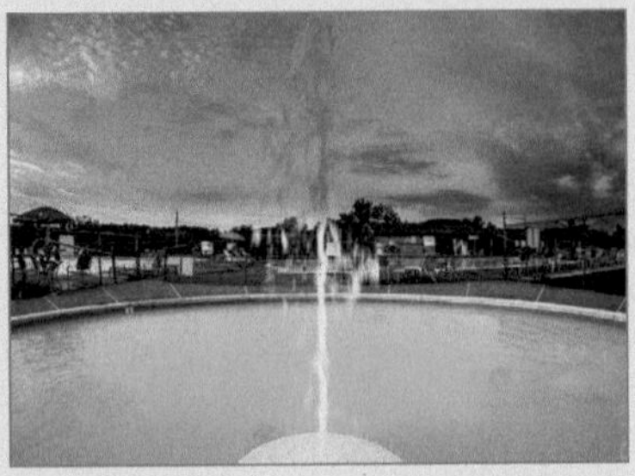

Resort is 69 miles west of Washington, D.C., on a mile-long shoreline of the Shenandoah River near the northern end of Skyline Drive. Minutes from Skyline Caverns and Skyline Drive. Activities include fishing the Shenandoah and hunting in George Washington National Forest. Nearby: Confederate museum, Civil War battlefields, the National Park, national monuments.
DIRECTIONS: From I-66 (near I-81): SR 340/522 S to SR 55 W (2nd traffic light). R onto SR 55. W 2 mi. Resort on R.

GPS COORDINATES: 38.9566°N/-78.2318°W
RV SITES: Full: 390 Partial: 60 Dry: 0
CHECK-IN: 2:00 p.m.
CHECK-OUT: 11:00 a.m.
SEASON: Year-round
PEAK SEASON: May 31–September 30
MAX. RV LENGTH: 40 feet
NOTATIONS: Rate includes 6 people. Additional charges: Utility fee $17/night, Wi-fi fee (daily $4.99 for 1 device, weekend $8.99 up to 2 devices, or weekly $17.99 up to 3 devices). Water not available at sites from Dec 1-Apr 1. Pool seasonal.
RENTAL ACCOMMODATIONS: Rental units available. Trip Points not accepted. Contact resort directly.

50 amps · pull-through · visitor mail · laundry · pets/restrictions · Wi-Fi access · playground · picnic tables · rental units · fishing · hiking trails · horseshoes · recreation hall · fishing · outdoor pool · mini golf · tennis · golf · game room · tourist attraction · shopping · propane · hot showers · rv supplies · firewood · ice

FRONT ROYAL

RESORT NUMBER: 386 **GOOD SAM RATING:** 8.5/8★/9 **COAST DELUXE RESORT**

VIRGINIA

Skyline Ranch Resort
751 Mountain Road
Front Royal, Virginia 22630
540-635-4169; fax: 540-635-7646
rezskylineranchresort@gmail.com
skylineranchresort.com

See page CTC 75 for state map.

A 90-minute drive from Washington, DC beltway. In the Shenandoah Valley, bordered by the Blue Ridge Mountains to the east and south and Massanutten Mountain Range to the west. View the inspiring scenery from the famous Skyline Drive, fish the Shenandoah River and visit the George Washington National Park.

DIRECTIONS: From I-81: Ex 300 to Rte 66E. Ex 6 to Rte 340S for 4.6 mi, then R on Rivermont Rd/Rte 619 for 4.6 mi to resort on L. Use these directions, not GPS directions, which will take you on difficult back roads. From I-66W E of Front Royal: Ex 13, turn L, then turn R on Rte 55W. Drive 5.2 mi and turn L on Rte 340S. Go 1 mi and turn R on Rivermont Rd/Rte 619. Resort is 5 mi ahead on L.

GPS COORDINATES: 38.906°N/-78.298°W
RV SITES: Full: 120 Partial: 0 Dry: 0
CHECK-IN: Noon–10:00 p.m.
CHECK-OUT: Noon
SEASON: Year-round
MAX. RV LENGTH: 34 feet
NOTATIONS: Additional charges: 50 amp $20/night cash only. Deposit required at check-in. One air conditioning unit per 30 amp. Drive-ups not accepted.

30 amps · pull-through · dump station · laundry · pets/restrictions · internet access · playground · picnic tables · restaurant/snack bar · hot tub · fishing · shuffleboard · hiking trails · horseshoes · group activities · recreation hall · fishing · outdoor pool · mini golf · volleyball · game room · tourist attraction · fitness · propane · hot showers · ball field · paddle boats · fire rings · grocery · gift shop · tenting · firewood · handicap access · ice · grills

GASBURG

RESORT NUMBER: 1516 **GOOD SAM RATING:** 8/7.5/6 **COAST CLASSIC RESORT**

VIRGINIA

Lakeside Resort
300 Lake Resort Drive
Gasburg, Virginia 23857
434-577-2194; fax: 434-577-2936
lakeside@lakegastonresort.com

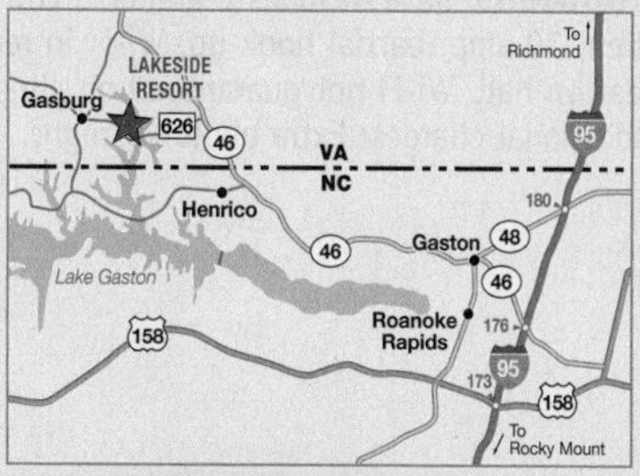

See page CTC 75 for state map.

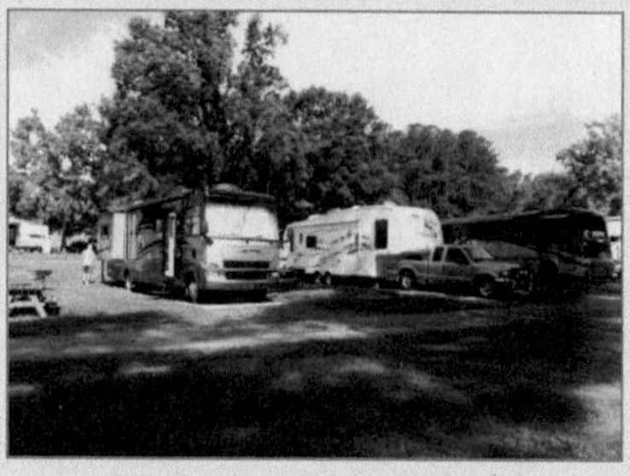

Located on the shores of beautiful Lake Gaston, Lakeside Resort offers members and guests some of the finest freshwater activities on the East Coast. Swimming, boating, water skiing and fishing are some of the most popular activities for outdoor enthusiasts.

DIRECTIONS: From I-95: Ex 176 to Hwy 46. W 17 mi to Rte 626. W 2 mi to resort on R.

GPS COORDINATES: 36.5583°N/-77.8643°W
RV SITES: Full: 130 Partial: 0 Dry: 0
CHECK-IN: 4:00 p.m.
CHECK-OUT: 11:00 a.m.
SEASON: April 1–October 15
MAX. RV LENGTH: 35 feet
NOTATIONS: Additional charges: 50 amp $3/night, Family Fun Center $10/day.

50 amps · laundry · pets/restrictions · internet access · playground · picnic tables · restaurant/snack bar · horseshoes · group activities · fishing · boating · outdoor pool · basketball · beach · tennis · volleyball · golf · game room · hot showers · fire rings · grocery · tenting · grills

VIRGINIA

GORDONSVILLE

RESORT NUMBER: 657 **GOOD SAM RATING:** 8.5/9★/9.5 **COAST DELUXE RESORT**

Shenandoah Crossing Resort & Country Club
174 Horseshoe Circle
Gordonsville, Virginia 22942
540-832-9506; res.: 540-832-9400
chelsea.bell@bluegreenvacations.com; perry.aaron@bluegreenvacations.com
bluegreenvacations.com/resorts/virginia/shenandoah-crossing

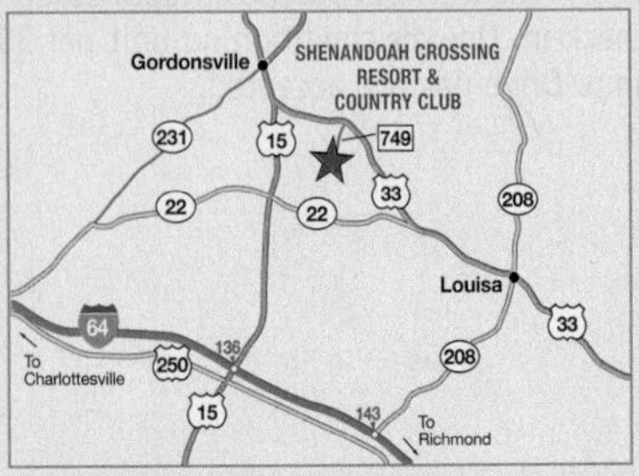

See page CTC 75 for state map.

Shenandoah Crossing Resort & Country Club features over 1,000 acres of rolling hillside and lush pastures with a 60-acre lake. The resort is a paradise for those who love the outdoors.

DIRECTIONS: From Washington DC: Hwy 29 S to Culpeper. Hwy 15 S to Gordonsville. Rte 33 E 4.5 mi to Rte 749. S 1.7 mi to resort. From Richmond: I-64 W to Hwy 15 N (Ex 136/Zion Crossroads). Rte 33 E approx 4.5 mi. S on Rte 749 1.7 mi. to resort.

GPS COORDINATES: 38.084°N/-78.1349°W

RV SITES: Full: 84 Partial: 0 Dry: 0

CHECK-IN: 2:00 p.m.

CHECK-OUT: Noon

SEASON: Year-round

MAX. RV LENGTH: 36 feet std site, 50 feet elite & deluxe sites

NOTATIONS: A $100 pre-authorization is required by a major credit card at check-in. Elite and Deluxe RV sites available at special rate. For Standard gravel RV sites, max RV length 36 ft. For Elite & Deluxe RV sites, max RV length 50 ft. No folding camping trailers (pop-ups), truck campers, or class B (van conversion). No tents in RV section. Credit card payment only for amenities and taxes. Golf cart restrictions apply, call resort if bringing personal golf cart. Drive-ups not accepted.

RENTAL ACCOMMODATIONS: Rental units available. Trip Points not accepted. Visit choicehotels.com to book rentals.

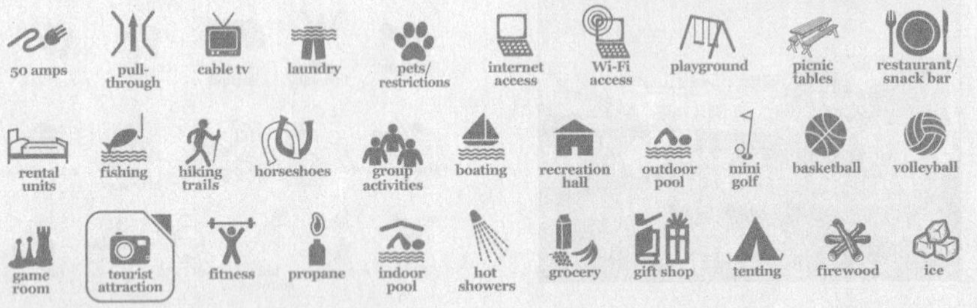

VIRGINIA

GREENVILLE

RESORT NUMBER: 422 **GOOD SAM RATING:** 7.5/7/6 **COAST DELUXE RESORT**

Stoney Creek Resort
277 Lake Drive
Greenville, Virginia 24440
540-337-1510; res.: 540-430-5547
stoneycreek325@gmail.com
stoneycreekresort.net

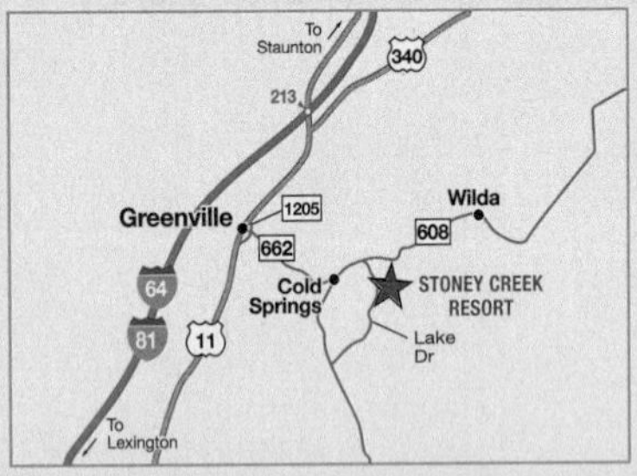

See page CTC 75 for state map.

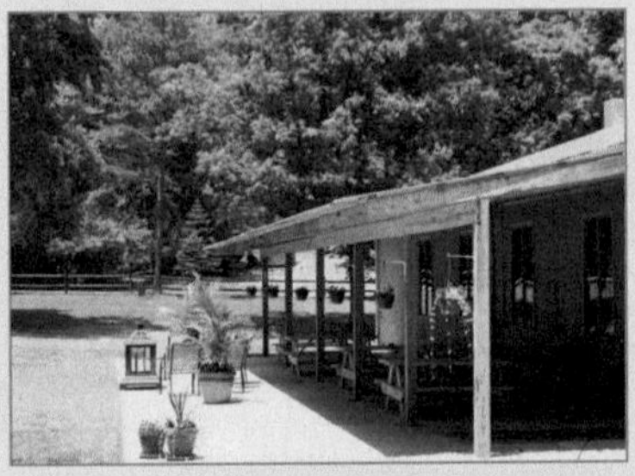

In the heart of the Shenandoah Valley and Blue Ridge Mountains. Nearby: Presidents Jefferson and Wilson homes, Walton Homestead, Crabtree Falls, Natural Bridge (Wonder of the World), American Frontier Museum, New Market Battlefield (Civil War), caverns and Lexington, VA.

DIRECTIONS: Do not use GPS. From I-81: Ex 217, E on White Hill Rd approx 3 mi. Turn onto Hwy 340 S approx 1 block. Next light turn L onto Indian Ridge Rd. This turns into Offliter Rd at a Y in the road. Bear L and follow to T intersection, turn R onto Cold Springs Rd, resort on L in approx 5 mi.

GPS COORDINATES: 37.9904°N/-79.1239°W

RV SITES: Full: 156 Partial: 36 Dry: 15

CHECK-IN: 1:00 p.m.

CHECK-OUT: Noon

SEASON: April 1–October 29

PEAK SEASON: April 1–October 29

MAX. RV LENGTH: 45 feet

NOTATIONS: Rate includes 2 adults/3 children, 30 amp, partial hook-up. Wi-Fi in recreation hall. Wi-Fi not guaranteed on sites. Additional charges: Extra adult $8/night.

SPOTSYLVANIA

RESORT NUMBER: 121 **GOOD SAM RATING:** 8/9.5★/8.5 **COAST DELUXE RESORT**

Wilderness Presidential Resort
9220 Plank Road
Spotsylvania, Virginia 22553
540-972-7433; fax: 540-972-3506
info@wpresort.com
wpresort.com

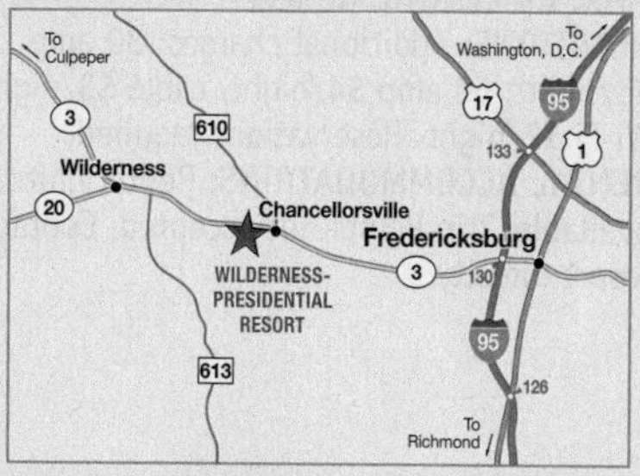

See page CTC 75 for state map.

Resort is 65 miles south of Washington, D.C. and borders the Wilderness and Chancellorsville Civil War Battlefields. Kings Dominion theme park is 40 miles south. Nearby: National monuments, George Washington's mother's and sister's homes and favorite tavern, James Monroe's law offices, The Chimneys, Spotsylvania and Fredericksburg Battlefields.
DIRECTIONS: From I-95: Culpeper Ex 130B/ Rte 3 W. 9 mi to resort on L. Resort is 0.3 mi past Chancellorsville Battlefield Visitors Center. From the W: Rte 3 E 23 mi from Culpeper.

GPS COORDINATES: 38.3103°N/-77.6551°W
RV SITES: Full: 166 Partial: 166 Dry: 0
CHECK-IN: 2:00 p.m.
CHECK-OUT: 10:00 a.m.
SEASON: Year-round
PEAK SEASON: May 1–September 30
MAX. RV LENGTH: 36 feet
NOTATIONS: Water turned off Nov through Mar. Internet and Wi-Fi access in clubhouse only. 50 amp not available.
RENTAL ACCOMMODATIONS: Rental units available. Trip Points accepted. Contact resort directly.

VIRGINIA BEACH

RESORT NUMBER: 119 **GOOD SAM RATING:** 9.5/8.5/9.5 **COAST DELUXE RESORT**

Indian Cove Resort
1053 Sandbridge Road
Virginia Beach, Virginia 23456
757-426-2601; fax: 757-721-6029
jlivingston@indian-cove.com
indian-cove.com

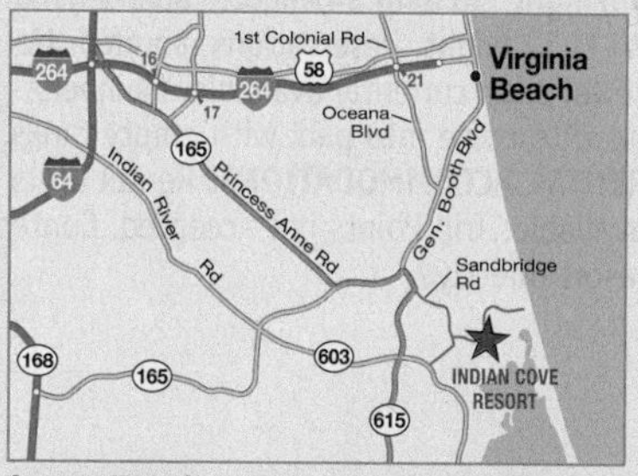

See page CTC 75 for state map.

Two minutes from the Atlantic Ocean at Sandbridge Beach, 20 minutes from Virginia Beach. Wooded and open campsites border a freshwater channel leading to the wildlife refuge at Back Bay, with largemouth bass, speckled perch, and channel cat. Nearby: Festival Park, Colonial Williamsburg, Busch Gardens, Outer Banks of North Carolina.
DIRECTIONS: From I-64: I-264 E to Ex 17A, Independence Blvd S, bear R. L on Princess Anne Rd. L to 2nd light where road becomes Sandbridge Rd. Approx 3 mi to resort. Sandbridge Rd is a narrow, twisting rural road.

GPS COORDINATES: 36.7271°N/-75.9726°W
RV SITES: Full: 300 Partial: 0 Dry: 0
CHECK-IN: 2:00 p.m.
CHECK-OUT: 10:00 a.m.
SEASON: Year-round
MAX. RV LENGTH: 40 feet
NOTATIONS: Additional charges: Park fee $20/night in Jan and Feb collected in cash or credit card; $15/night remainder of year. No gas powered golf carts. No pull-through sites. Drive-ups not accepted.
RENTAL ACCOMMODATIONS: Rental units available. Trip Points not accepted. Contact resort directly.

VIRGINIA

WASHINGTON

CHENEY

RESORT NUMBER: 1892 **GOOD SAM RATING:** 8/8/9 **COAST DELUXE RESORT**

Ponderosa Falls Resort—
K/M Resorts of America
7520 South Thomas Mallen Road
Cheney, Washington 99004
509-747-9415; fax: 509-459-0148
ponderosafalls@kmresorts.com
kmresorts.com

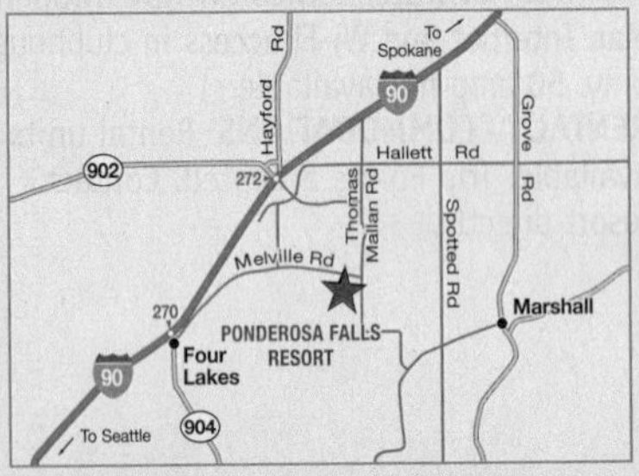

See page CTC 76 for state map.

Nestled among beautiful pines in the foothills of Eastern Washington, this year-round resort offers the very best in amenities and local attractions. It is famous for its style of camping where the fun never ends.
DIRECTIONS: 10 minutes W of Spokane. From I-90: Ex 272, S to roundabout by Petro truck stop. Ex roundabout at Aero Rd, you will be going through housing development. At stop sign turn R on Thomas Mallen Rd. Where the road turns to gravel, see our carved rock sign and turn R.

GPS COORDINATES: 47.5838°N/-117.5412°W
ELEVATION: 2,400 feet
RV SITES: Full: 168 Partial: 0 Dry: 0
CHECK-IN: 1:00 p.m.
CHECK-OUT: 11:00 a.m.
SEASON: Year-round
PEAK SEASON: April 1–September 30
MAX. RV LENGTH: 40 feet
NOTATIONS: Additional charges: 30 amp $3/night, 50 amp $4/night, cable $3/night, Wi-Fi $2/night. Reservations required.
RENTAL ACCOMMODATIONS: Rental units available. Trip Points not accepted. Contact resort directly.

50 amps, pull-through, cable tv, visitor mail, laundry, pets/restrictions, internet access, Wi-Fi access, playground, rental units, hot tub, horseshoes, group activities, mini golf, basketball, tennis, volleyball, game room, fitness, indoor pool, paddle boats

WASHINGTON

CHINOOK

RESORT NUMBER: 1655 **GOOD SAM RATING:** 4/7/6 **COAST CLASSIC RESORT**

Columbia Shores RV Park—
K/M Resorts of America
706 Highway 101
Chinook, Washington 98614
360-777-8581; res.: 253-896-4677
columbiashores@kmresorts.com
kmresorts.com

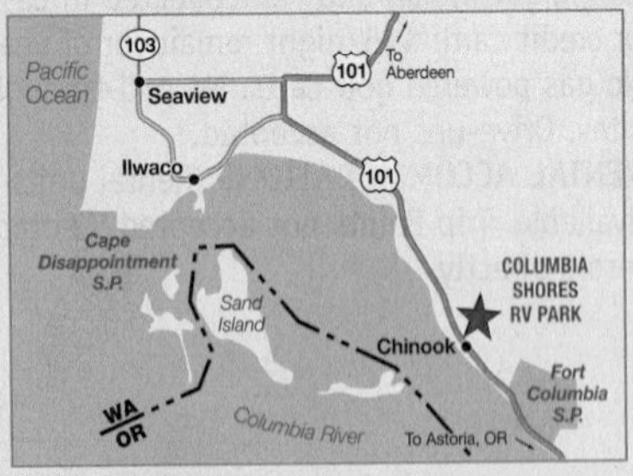

See page CTC 76 for state map.

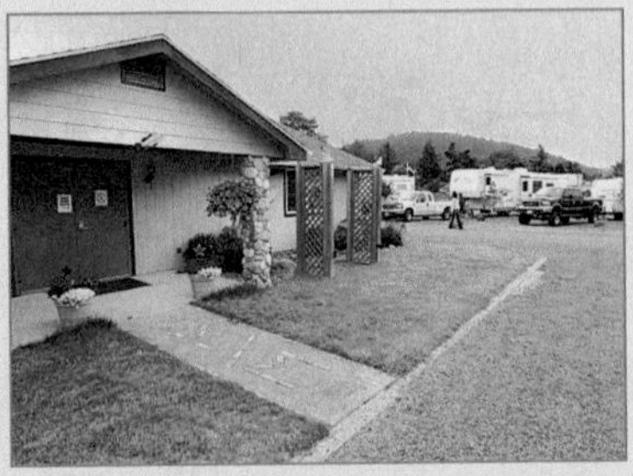

Long Beach peninsula is nine miles away and is a fisherman's paradise. Salmon, sturgeon, albacore, bottom fish, crab and clamming within 15 minutes. Area has one of the largest kite festivals in the world and some of the finest sand beaches anywhere. Nearby Ilwaco offers charter services and great restaurants.
DIRECTIONS: The resort is on the N side of Hwy 101 in downtown Chinook. From Olympia, WA: I-5 Ex 104 W. Hwy 101 to Hwy 8 to Elma. Hwy 12 to Aberdeen. Rejoin Hwy 101 S approx 85 mi to Chinook. From Portland, OR: Hwy 30 or Hwy 26 W to Astoria. N across the Astoria Bridge on Hwy 101. Approx 5 mi to Chinook, WA.

GPS COORDINATES: 46.269°N/-123.941°W
RV SITES: Full: 0 Partial: 53 Dry: 5
CHECK-IN: 1:00 p.m.
CHECK-OUT: 11:00 a.m.
SEASON: Year-round
MAX. RV LENGTH: 40 feet
NOTATIONS: Additional charges: 30 amp $3/night, 50 amp $4/night, cable $3/night, Wi-Fi $2/night. Reservations required. No sewer sites currently available. Members need to come into park with empty tanks.
RENTAL ACCOMMODATIONS: Rental units available. Trip Points not accepted. Contact resort directly.

30 amps, pets/restrictions, internet access, Wi-Fi access, rental units, recreation hall, fishing, beach, tourist attraction, grocery

COPALIS BEACH

RESORT NUMBER: 128 **GOOD SAM RATING:** 7/6/6.5 **COAST CLASSIC RESORT**

Copalis Beach Resort—Sunrise Resorts
14 Heath Road
Copalis Beach, Washington 98535
360-289-4278
copalisbeachresort@sunriseresorts.com
sunriseresorts.com

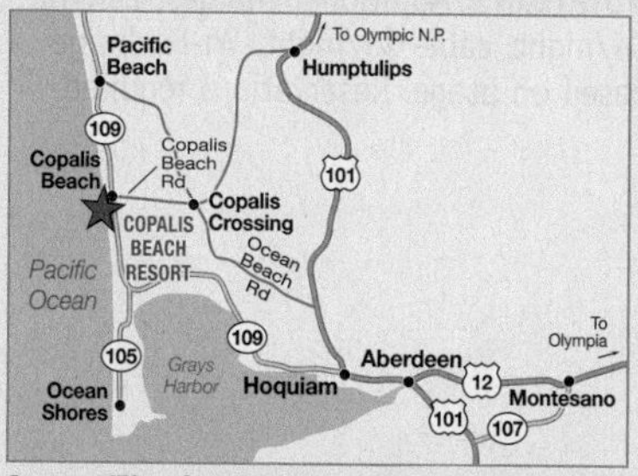

See page CTC 76 for state map.

On Copalis Beach, the premier razor clam beach in the Northwest. Minutes from deep-sea fishing, 18-hole golf course, horseback riding, restaurants, entertainment, salmon fishing, surf-fishing, beachcombing, hunting, and many other recreational activities.

DIRECTIONS: From I-5: W from Olympia on the Aberdeen Fwy. Hwy 109 through Aberdeen and Hoquiam. Copalis Beach 21 mi past Hoquiam. L on Heath Rd to the resort on the beach.

GPS COORDINATES: 47.1112°N/-124.176°W
ELEVATION: 8 feet
RV SITES: Full: 92 Partial: 0 Dry: 0
CHECK-IN: Noon–6:00 p.m.
CHECK-OUT: 11:00 a.m.

SEASON: Year-round
MAX. RV LENGTH: 38 feet
NOTATIONS: Rate includes 1 RV, 1 vehicle and 4 people. Additional charges: 50 amp $3/night plus tax, late check-out and early check-in $5 plus tax-strictly enforced, resort fee $3/night plus tax, cable charge $2/night plus tax, add'l vehicle $5/night, extra person (over 4) $5/night, small tent onsite with RV $20/night. Also add'l charges for cargo trailers, boats, etc. Sewer access is limited, must arrive with empty tanks or $25 dump fee plus tax. Gate hours vary throughtout season, but open 7 days/week.
RENTAL ACCOMMODATIONS: Rental units available. Trip Points not accepted. Contact resort directly.

30 amps · pets/restrictions · internet access · Wi-Fi access · picnic tables · rental units · fishing · recreation hall
fishing · beach · volleyball · golf · tourist attraction · ball field

WASHINGTON

EASTON

RESORT NUMBER: 558 **GOOD SAM RATING:** 7/6/5.5 **COAST DELUXE RESORT**

Lake Easton Resort—Sunrise Resorts
581 Lake Easton Road
Easton, Washington 98925
509-656-2255
lakeeaston@sunriseresorts.com
sunriseresorts.com

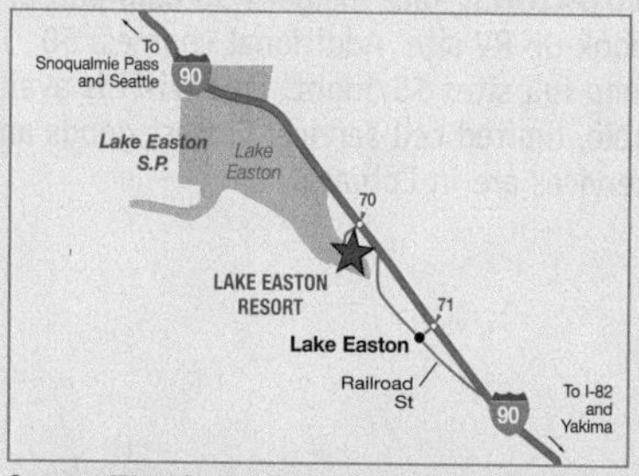

See page CTC 76 for state map.

On the eastern ridge of the Cascade Range, 70 miles from Seattle. Winter activities, while in summer four lakes offer fishing and water skiing. Yakima River offers some of the best fly fishing in Washington. Short drive to mining towns of Cle Elum and Roslyn, Yakima Valley wine country and the alpine town of Leavenworth.

DIRECTIONS: From Seattle: E on I-90 to Ex 70. Resort is adjacent to the Fwy, surrounded by Lake Easton State Park.

GPS COORDINATES: 47.2469°N/-121.187°W
ELEVATION: 2,100 feet

RV SITES: Full: 58 Partial: 150 Dry: 0
CHECK-IN: Noon
CHECK-OUT: Noon
SEASON: Year-round
PEAK SEASON: June 1–September 15
MAX. RV LENGTH: 35 feet
NOTATIONS: Rate includes 1 RV, 1 vehicle and 4 people. Limited space for RVs with slide-outs. Sewer access is limited-must arrive with empty tanks or $25 dump fee plus tax. Additional charges: Late check-out and early check-in $5 plus tax-strictly enforced, resort fee $3/night, extra person (over 4) $5/night, small tent on site with RV $20/night, and add'l charges for cargo trailers, boats, etc.
RENTAL ACCOMMODATIONS: Rental units available. Trip Points not accepted. Contact resort directly.

30 amps · pull-through · laundry · pets/restrictions · internet access · Wi-Fi access · playground · rental units · hot tub · hiking trails
horseshoes · recreation hall · fishing · outdoor pool · game room · tourist attraction · propane · gambling casino · winter sports

WASHINGTON

WASHINGTON

ELMA

RESORT NUMBER: 660 **GOOD SAM RATING:** 9/9★/9.5 **COAST DELUXE RESORT**

Travel Inn Resort—
K/M Resorts of America
801 East Main
Elma, Washington 98541
360-482-3877; fax: 360-482-1374
travelinn@kmresorts.com
kmresorts.com

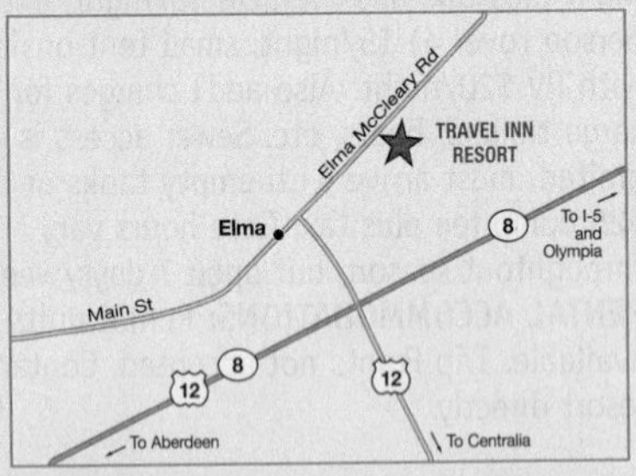

See page CTC 76 for state map.

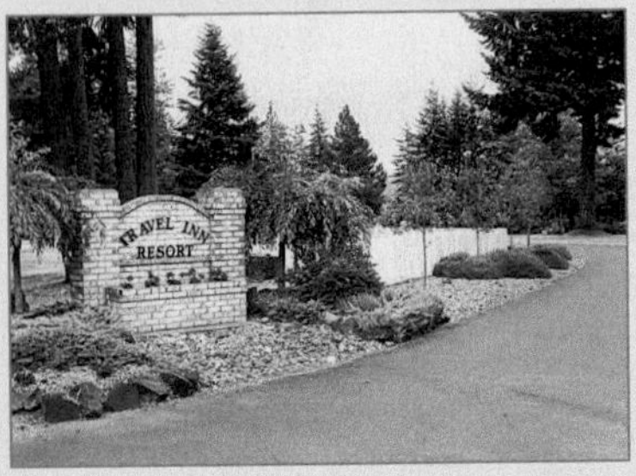

At the gateway to ocean and mountain recreation, 30 minutes from coastal beaches. Salmon, tuna, and bottom fishing, clamming and beach combing await you. Rivers and streams have steelhead and trout. Surrounding forests abound in game birds, deer and elk. Just minutes from public golfing and bowling.

DIRECTIONS: From I-5: Olympia Ex 104. Hwy 101 N to Hwy 8. W on Hwy 8, 20 mi to 1st Elma Ex/Hwy 12 E. R for 1 block. R 2 blocks. Resort on R.

GPS COORDINATES: 47.0095°N/-123.3864°W
RV SITES: Full: 130 Partial: 0 Dry: 0
CHECK-IN: 1:00 p.m.
CHECK-OUT: Noon
SEASON: Year-round
PEAK SEASON: May 1–September 30
MAX. RV LENGTH: 40 feet
NOTATIONS: Additional charges: Electric $4/night, cable $3/night. Wi-Fi charge based on usage. Reservations required.

WASHINGTON

EPHRATA

RESORT NUMBER: 404 **GOOD SAM RATING:** 7.5/7.5/6.5 **COAST CLASSIC RESORT**

Rimrock Meadows
4177 Tumbleweed Way
Ephrata, Washington 98823
509-632-9800
rimrockmeadows@gmail.com
rimrockmeadows.com

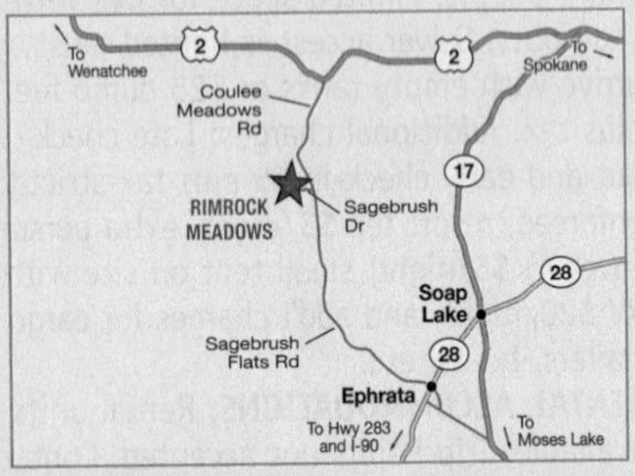

See page CTC 76 for state map.

Resort lies on the eastern slope of the Cascade Mountains and on the edge of the Moses Coulee, one of the West's most interesting geological phenomenon. The campground and Olympic-sized swimming pool provide a variety of family activities.

DIRECTIONS: From Seattle: I-90 E, Ex 151/ Hwy 283 to Ephrata. In Ephrata, L at 1st Ave NW. Approx 17 mi NW to Sagebrush Flats Rd and Coulee Meadows Rd (same rd). L on Sagebrush Dr (gravel), 1.5 mi to resort. From Hwy 2: S on Moses Coulee Rd, 20 mi from Waterville and Coulee City. Main entrance is framed by 4 basalt columns on each side of road. From I-90 Spokane: Hwy 17 Ex in Moses Lake and follow signs to Ephrata. R on Basin St and L on 1st Ave NW and follow directions above.

GPS COORDINATES: 47.4816°N/-119.7295°W
ELEVATION: 1,700 feet
RV SITES: Full: 24 Partial: 15 Dry: 0
CHECK-IN: 10:00 a.m.–2:00 p.m.
CHECK-OUT: 2:00 p.m.
SEASON: April 20–October 26
MAX. RV LENGTH: 40 feet
NOTATIONS: Rate includes 30 amp partial hook-up RV site. Additional charges: 50 amp full sites $5/night. Free Wi-Fi is available, limited cell service. Closest goods and services are in Ephrata.

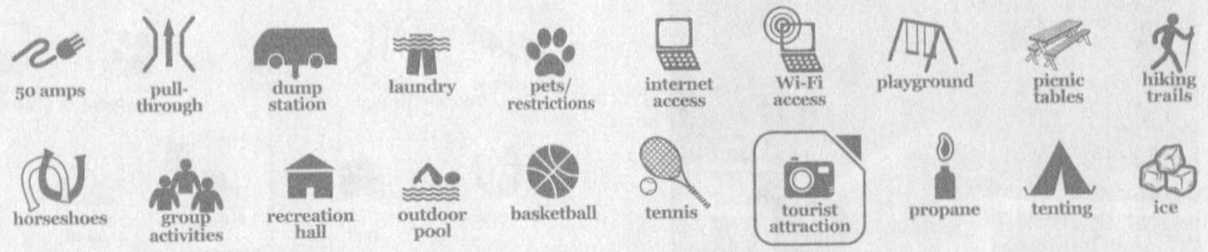

HOODSPORT

RESORT NUMBER: 129 **GOOD SAM RATING:** 7/8.5★/9 **COAST CLASSIC RESORT**

Dow Creek Resort—Sunrise Resorts
2670 North Lake Cushman Road
Hoodsport, Washington 98548
360-877-5022
dowcreek@sunriseresorts.com
sunriseresorts.com

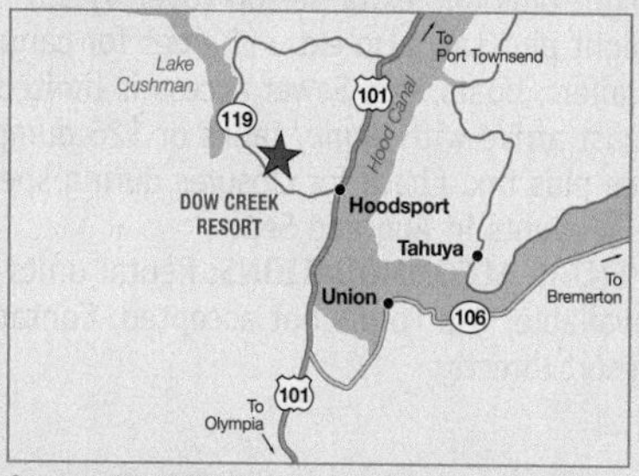

See page CTC 76 for state map.

97 miles from Seattle at the Olympic Mountains near Hood Canal and Lake Cushman with outdoor activities including hunting, fishing, golf and water skiing. Close to Olympic National Park and Olympic National Forest with the famous Staircase area.
DIRECTIONS: I-5 S of Seattle: Ex 104 to Hwy 101 past Shelton to Hoodsport. Cushman Rd/Hwy 119 (L off Hwy 101) 2.7 mi. R into resort after Lake Cushman grocery.
GPS COORDINATES: 47.4105°N/-123.1884°W
ELEVATION: 500 feet
RV SITES: Full: 20 Partial: 45 Dry: 29

CHECK-IN: Noon–6:00 p.m.
CHECK-OUT: 11:00 a.m.
SEASON: Year-round
MAX. RV LENGTH: 36 feet
NOTATIONS: Rate is for 1 RV, 1 vehicle, 4 people. Limited 50 amp. No sewer Jun 15-Sep 15. Additional charges: 50 amp $3/night plus tax, late check-out and early check-in $5/hour plus tax-strictly enforced, resort fee $3/night, cable fee $2/night plus tax, extra vehicle $5/night, extra person (over 4) $5/night, small tent onsite with RV $20/night, extra charges for cargo trailers, boats, etc. Sewer access is limited, arrive with empty tanks or $25 dump fee plus tax.
RENTAL ACCOMMODATIONS: Rental units available. Trip Points not accepted. Contact resort directly.

30 amps · pull-through · laundry · pets/restrictions · internet access · picnic tables · rental units · fishing · hiking trails · horseshoes · fishing · basketball · volleyball · golf · tourist attraction

ILWACO

RESORT NUMBER: 764 **GOOD SAM RATING:** 8.5/10★/8.5 **COAST CLASSIC RESORT**

Eagle's Nest RV Resort—Sunrise Resorts
700 West North Head Road
Ilwaco, Washington 98624
360-642-8351
eaglesnest@sunriseresorts.com
sunriseresorts.com

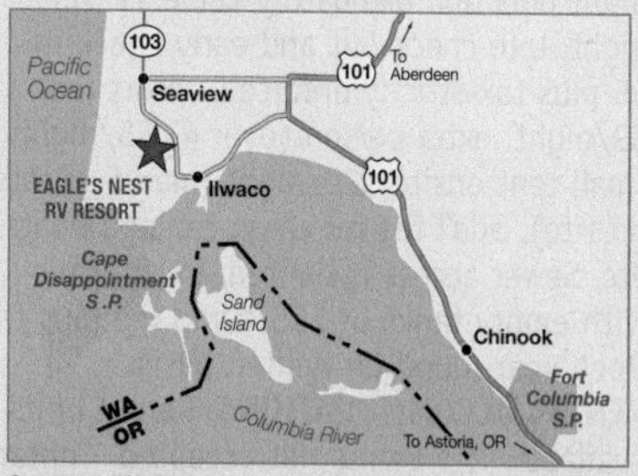

See page CTC 76 for state map.

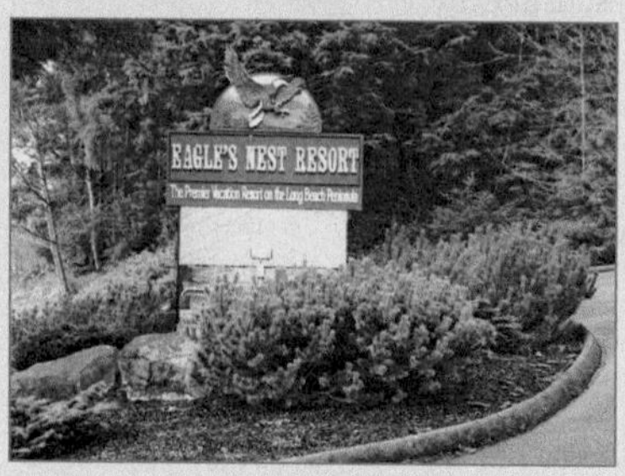

On Long Beach Peninsula's south end, 150 ft above sea level overlooking the Ilwaco Boat Harbor, Pacific Ocean beaches and more. The area harbors elk, deer and duck with seasons and limits controlled by Washington state.
DIRECTIONS: From Portland: I-5 N to Oregon Hwy 30. W to Astoria. Cross Columbia River Bridge. N to Ilwaco. From Seattle: I-5 S to Chealis. W on Hwy 6 to Raymond. S on Hwy 101 to Ilwaco. From Ilwaco: Follow signs to Cape Disappointment State Park. Resort 0.2 mi from Ilwaco on R.
GPS COORDINATES: 46.3103°N/-124.0487°W
ELEVATION: 150 feet

RV SITES: Full: 135 Partial: 0 Dry: 0
CHECK-IN: Noon
CHECK-OUT: 11:00 a.m.
SEASON: Year-round
MAX. RV LENGTH: 36 feet
NOTATIONS: Rate includes 1 RV, 1 vehicle, 4 people. Additional charges: 50 amp $3/night plus tax, late check-out and early check-in $5 plus tax-strictly enforced, extra vehicle $5/night, resort fee $3/night, cable $2/night, extra person (over 4) $5/night, small tent onsite with RV $20/night, add'l fee for cargo trailers, boats, etc. Sewer access limited-must arrive with empty tanks or $25 dump fee plus tax.
RENTAL ACCOMMODATIONS: Rental units available. Trip Points not accepted. Contact resort directly.

50 amps · pull-through · laundry · pets/restrictions · internet access · Wi-Fi access · playground · rental units · hot tub · shuffleboard · horseshoes · recreation hall · fishing · boating · mini golf · beach · volleyball · golf · game room · tourist attraction · indoor pool · gift shop

WASHINGTON

LONG BEACH

RESORT NUMBER: 264 **GOOD SAM RATING:** 9/8.5★/9 **COAST DELUXE RESORT**

Pacific Holiday RV Resort—Sunrise Resorts
12109 Pacific Way
Long Beach, Washington 98631
360-642-2770
pacificholiday@sunriseresorts.com
sunriseresorts.com

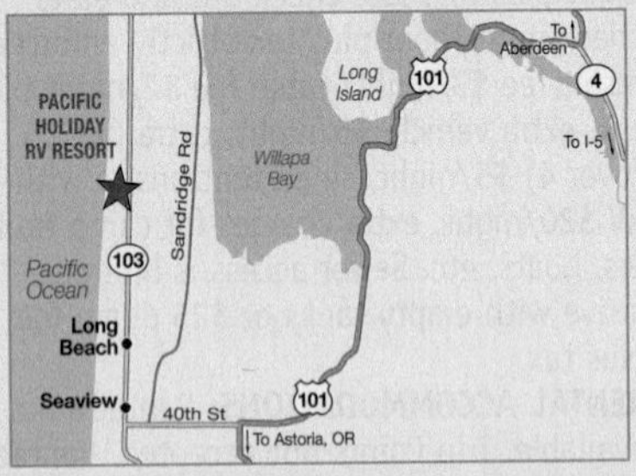

See page CTC 76 for state map.

On beautiful Long Beach Peninsula, one of the finest razor clam and surf fishing beaches. Nearby: Deep-sea fishing at Ilwaco, charter boats, Dungeness crab at Wilapa Bay, fishing, golf, dining.
DIRECTIONS: I-5 S from Olympia: Ex Hwy 6 at Chehalis. W to Raymond. Hwy 101 S to Seaview. R on Hwy 103 to Long Beach. Resort just past mile marker 4 on W side of hwy. Parts of Hwy 101 near resort are 25 mph with curves.
GPS COORDINATES: 46.3899°N/-124.0541°W
RV SITES: Full: 80 Partial: 12 Dry: 20
CHECK-IN: 1:00 p.m.–6:00 p.m.
CHECK-OUT: 11:00 a.m.
SEASON: Year-round
PEAK SEASON: May 15–September 30
MAX. RV LENGTH: 36 feet

NOTATIONS: Rate includes 1 RV, 1 vehicle and 4 people. Additional charges: Late check-out and early check-in $5 plus tax-strictly enforced, resort fee $3/night plus tax, small tent onsite with RV $20/night plus tax (max 6 guests on site), cable charge $3/night plus tax, extra vehicle $5/night plus tax, extra person (over 4) $5/night plus tax, also extra charges for cargo trailers, boats, etc. Sewer access is limited, must arrive with empty tanks or $25 dump fee plus tax. Check for closures during special events in Aug and Sep.
RENTAL ACCOMMODATIONS: Rental units available. Trip Points not accepted. Contact resort directly.

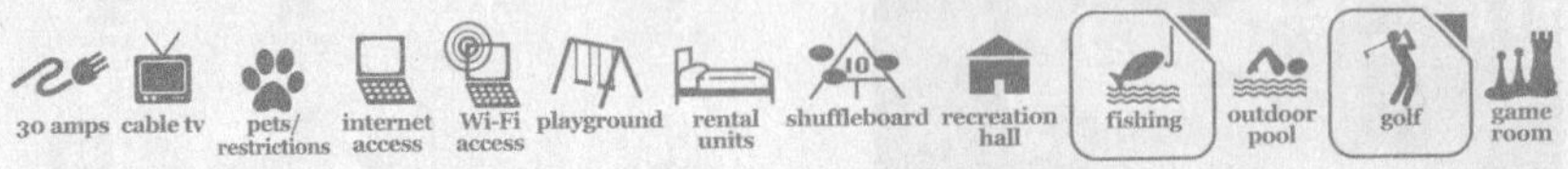

WASHINGTON

MOSES LAKE

RESORT NUMBER: 130 **GOOD SAM RATING:** 9/7.5/7 **COAST PREMIER RESORT**

Pier 4 RV Resort—Sunrise Resorts
3400 Sage Road
Moses Lake, Washington 98837
509-765-6319
pier4@sunriseresorts.com
sunriseresorts.com

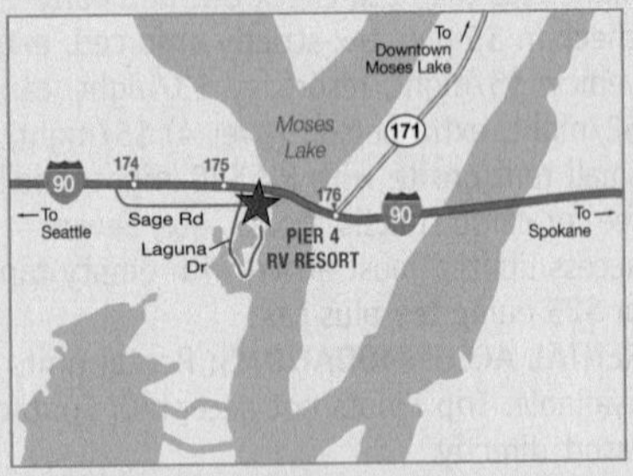

See page CTC 76 for state map.

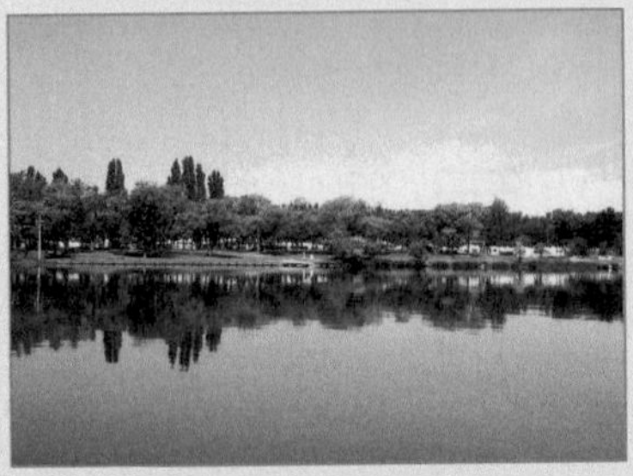

Sunrise-Pier 4 adjoins a city park and Moses Lake. The resort's shoreline, the city park's fine beach and 200-mile shoreline of the lake provide excellent access for lounging, exploring, water skiing, boating, sailing, and fishing. Nearby sand dunes provide a track for four-wheeling or bike riding.
DIRECTIONS: From Seattle I-90 E: Ex 174. Straight thru stop sign. R on Laguna Dr. Next L to resort. From Spokane on I-90 W: Ex 174. L at stop sign. Over fwy. L to resort.
GPS COORDINATES: 47.102°N/-119.3277°W
RV SITES: Full: 167 Partial: 29 Dry: 0

CHECK-IN: 1:00 p.m.
CHECK-OUT: 11:00 a.m.
SEASON: Year-round
PEAK SEASON: May 15–September 15
MAX. RV LENGTH: 38 feet
NOTATIONS: Rate is for 1 RV, 1 vehicle and 4 people. Additional charges: 50 amp $3/night plus tax, mandatory cable TV $2/night, late check-out and early check-in $5 plus tax-strictly enforced, resort fee $3/night, extra person (over 4) $5/night, small tent onsite $20/night (max 6 guests on site), add'l fee for cargo trailers, boats, etc. Sewer access is limited, must arrive with empty tanks or $25 dump fee plus tax. Open year-round on limited basis.
RENTAL ACCOMMODATIONS: Rental units available. Trip Points not accepted. Contact resort directly.

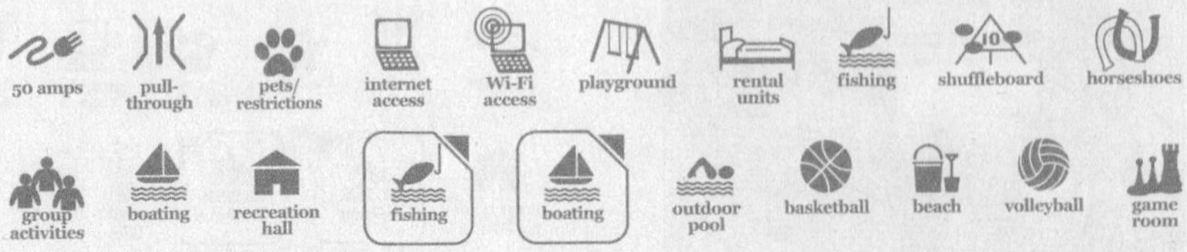

NEWPORT

RESORT NUMBER: 1024 **GOOD SAM RATING:** 7/10★/7 **COAST DELUXE RESORT**

Old American Kampground—
K/M Resorts of America
701 North Newport Avenue
Newport, Washington 99156
509-447-3663; fax: 509-447-0679
oldamerican@kmresorts.com
kmresorts.com

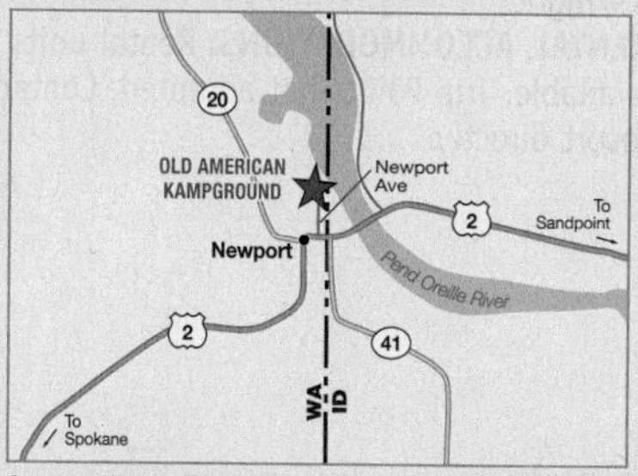

See page CTC 76 for state map.

On the Washington/Idaho border offering activities for everyone. Fish, boat, water ski and swim in Pend Oreille River. Hike or backpack in mountainous surroundings. Walking distance to Newport for shopping, restaurants and grocery stores. Nearby in winter: cross country skiing, ice skating, snow skiing, snowmobiling.
DIRECTIONS: From Spokane WA: I-90, Ex Hwy 2. N 6 mi on Division St. Hwy 2 to Newport for approx 35 mi. Hwy 2 through town toward Sandpoint. L on Newport Ave (McDonalds) to resort driveway. From Sandpoint, ID: Hwy 2 W to Newport, WA. R on Newport Ave (McDonalds) to resort. From Coeur d' Alene, ID: W on I-90 5 mi to Hwy 41, R on Hwy 41 to Newport, WA. L at light. R at McDonalds to resort.

GPS COORDINATES: 48.1863°N/-117.0407°W
ELEVATION: 3,200 feet
RV SITES: Full: 60 Partial: 0 Dry: 0
CHECK-IN: 1:00 p.m.
CHECK-OUT: 11:00 a.m.
SEASON: Year-round
PEAK SEASON: May 1–September 30
MAX. RV LENGTH: 40 feet
NOTATIONS: Reservations required. Additional charges: 30 amp $3/night, 50 amp $4/night, cable $3/night, Wi-Fi $2/night.
RENTAL ACCOMMODATIONS: Rental units available. Trip Points not accepted. Contact resort directly.

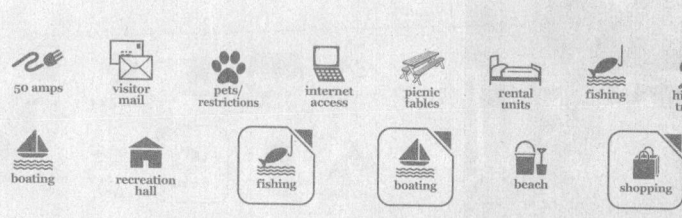

50 amps · visitor mail · pets/restrictions · internet access · picnic tables · rental units · fishing · hiking trails · horseshoes · boating · recreation hall · fishing · boating · beach · shopping · winter sports

NINE MILE FALLS

RESORT NUMBER: 2175 **GOOD SAM RATING:** 4/3/5.5 **COAST CLASSIC RESORT**

Willow Bay Resort—
Advance Resorts of America
6607 Highway 291
Nine Mile Falls, Washington 99026
509-276-2350; res.: 800-445-9519
resort1214@gmail.com
araresorts.com

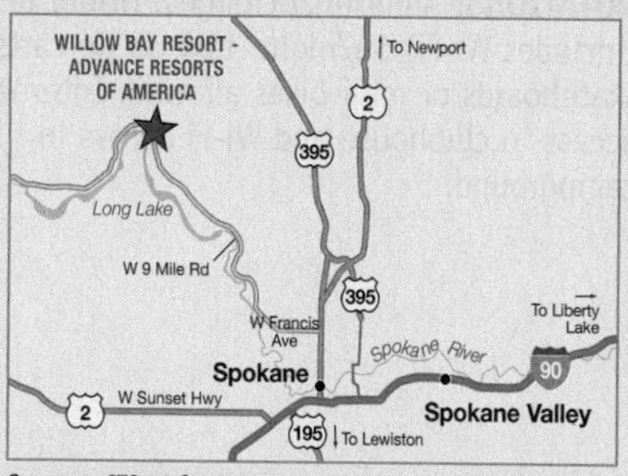

See page CTC 76 for state map.

Willow Bay Resort is located on Long Lake. The resort features onsite boat launch, multiple docks, boat storage, clubhouse with HD satellite, hiking trails, boathouse, and laundry facilities. At Willow Bay Resort and Marina swimming, waterskiing, and trophy bass fishing are right in your front yard.
DIRECTIONS: I-90 at Spokane take Division Ex 281. Follow 3 mi N to Hwy 291 (W Francis Ave). Turn L and continue approx 20 mi to resort.

GPS COORDINATES: 47.8804°N/-117.6571°W
RV SITES: Full: 0 Partial: 100 Dry: 0
CHECK-IN: 4:00 p.m.
CHECK-OUT: Noon
SEASON: April 1–November 1
MAX. RV LENGTH: 45 feet
RENTAL ACCOMMODATIONS: Rental units available. Trip Points not accepted. Contact resort directly.

30 amps · pull-through · visitor mail · laundry · pets/restrictions · picnic tables · rental units · fishing · hiking trails · horseshoes · boating · recreation hall · fishing · boating · beach · volleyball · golf · game room · tourist attraction · shopping · canoes · hot showers · paddle boats · gambling casino · tenting · winter sports · ice

WASHINGTON

OCEAN CITY

RESORT NUMBER: 463 **GOOD SAM RATING:** 8.5/8.5★/10 **COAST PREMIER RESORT**

Ocean Breeze RV Resort—K/M Resorts of America
2428 State Route 109
Ocean City, Washington 98569
360-289-0628; fax: 360-289-0394
oceanbreeze@kmresorts.com
kmresorts.com

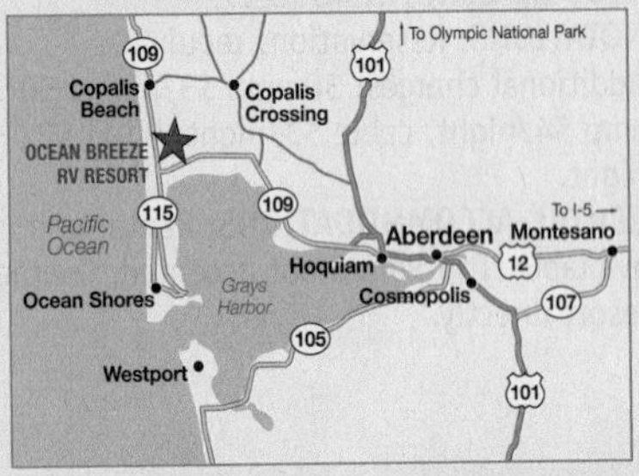

See page CTC 76 for state map.

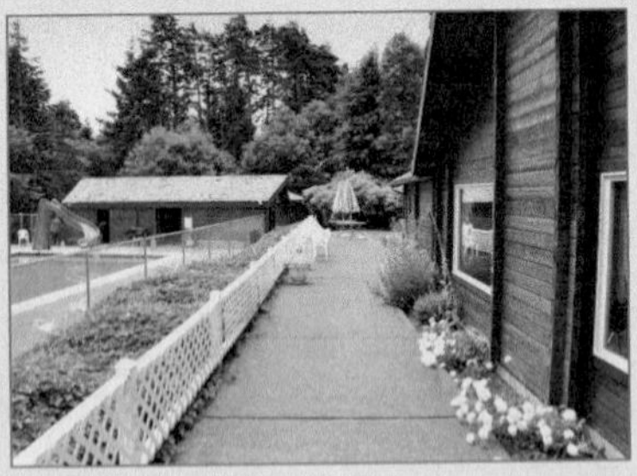

One of the state's most popular natural recreational areas is the razor clam capital of the world. Closest ocean beach to Everett, Tacoma, and the Seattle area. Surf fishing, horseback riding, oyster picking, and exploring. All this can be enjoyed from the beautiful 165 acres of trees at Ocean Breeze RV Resort.

DIRECTIONS: From I-5: W through Olympia. W onto the Aberdeen Fwy. Follow signs through Aberdeen on Hwy 109. 16 mi W of Hoquiam. Pass Hwy 115 turn off, staying on Hwy 109 for 0.7 mi to resort on R.

GPS COORDINATES: 47.0551°N/-124.1631°W
RV SITES: Full: 0 Partial: 220 Dry: 0
CHECK-IN: 1:00 p.m.
CHECK-OUT: 11:00 a.m.
SEASON: Year-round
MAX. RV LENGTH: 40 feet
NOTATIONS: Additional charges: 30 amp $3/night.
RENTAL ACCOMMODATIONS: Rental units available. Trip Points not accepted. Contact resort directly.

30 amps · dump station · laundry · pets/restrictions · internet access · Wi-Fi access · playground · rental units · hot tub · hiking trails · horseshoes · group activities · recreation hall · fishing · outdoor pool · mini golf · basketball · beach · game room · hot showers · ball field · firewood · handicap access

WASHINGTON

OTHELLO

RESORT NUMBER: 774 **GOOD SAM RATING:** 8.5/9★/9.5 **COAST DELUXE RESORT**

O'Sullivan Sportsman Resort
6897 Highway 262 Southeast
Othello, Washington 99344
509-346-2447; fax: 509-346-2497
osullivan@sosmail.us
osullivansportsmanresort.com

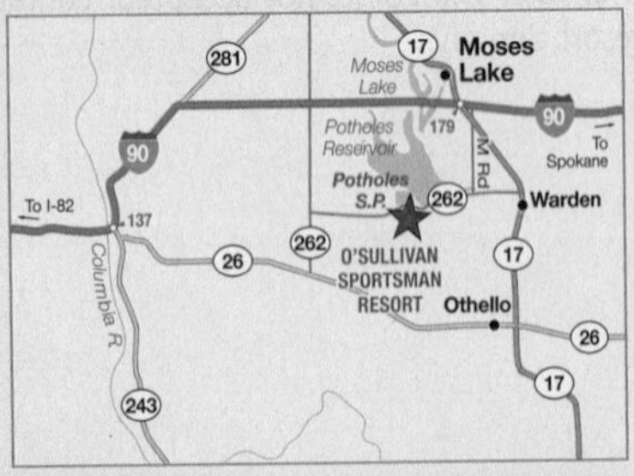

See page CTC 76 for state map.

Located on 23,000-acre Potholes Reservoir, perfect for fun in the sun. Most popular recreational area in Eastern Washington. Summer water sports, also ice fishing, snowmobiling and cross country skiing in winter. Public boat launch located one-quarter mile away at state park. Lakes provide excellent fishing. 18-hole golf course next to resort.

DIRECTIONS: From Seattle: I-90 E. Hwy 26 Ex just E of Vantage. Approx 26 mi. L on A St SE/SR 262. Approx 12 mi, resort on R just past Potholes State Park. From Spokane: I-90 W. Hwy 17 Ex at Moses Lake. Turn L. Approx 2 mi. R on M St SE. Approx 11 mi to stop sign. R on O'Sullivan Dam Rd SE/SR 262. Resort on L in 7 mi.

GPS COORDINATES: 46.9702°N/-119.3455°W
RV SITES: Full: 227 Partial: 0 Dry: 0
CHECK-IN: 8:00 a.m.–5:00 p.m.
CHECK-OUT: 11:00 a.m.
SEASON: Year-round
PEAK SEASON: May 1–September 1
MAX. RV LENGTH: 50 feet
NOTATIONS: Additional charges: Utility fee (includes Wi-Fi) $6/night, tax. No go-carts, skateboards or mini-bikes allowed. Internet access in clubhouse and Wi-Fi access in campground.

50 amps · visitor mail · pets/restrictions · internet access · Wi-Fi access · playground · picnic tables · restaurant/snack bar · hot tub · hiking trails · recreation hall · fishing · boating · outdoor pool · basketball · golf · tourist attraction · winter sports · winter sports

RANDLE

RESORT NUMBER: 1817 **GOOD SAM RATING:** 8/4/7 **COAST DELUXE RESORT**

Cascade Peaks
11519 U.S. Highway 12
Randle, Washington 98377
360-494-7931; fax: 360-494-2070
cascadepeaks@lewiscounty.com
cascadepeakscamping.com

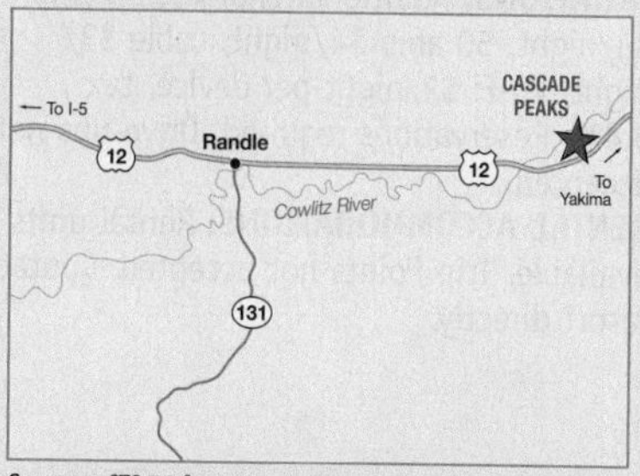

See page CTC 76 for state map.

The fun begins between Mt. Rainier, Mt. St. Helens, and Mt. Adams. 120 acres of wilderness beauty, 650 campsites and one-half mile of Cowlitz River frontage. Share your campsite with nature's beauty, deer and elk. Mountain climbing, fishing, hang gliding, guided boat trips, and white water rafting nearby.

DIRECTIONS: From Seattle (N) or Portland (S): I-5 Ex 68. E on Hwy 12 approx 58 mi. Resort on L. From Yakima: W on Hwy 12 approx 70 mi. Resort on R.

GPS COORDINATES: 46.5341°N/-121.7779°W
RV SITES: Full: 120 Partial: 300 Dry: 80
CHECK-IN: 9:00 a.m.–9:00 p.m.
CHECK-OUT: 7:00 a.m.–7:00 p.m.
SEASON: Year-round
PEAK SEASON: May 28–September 3
MAX. RV LENGTH: 45 feet

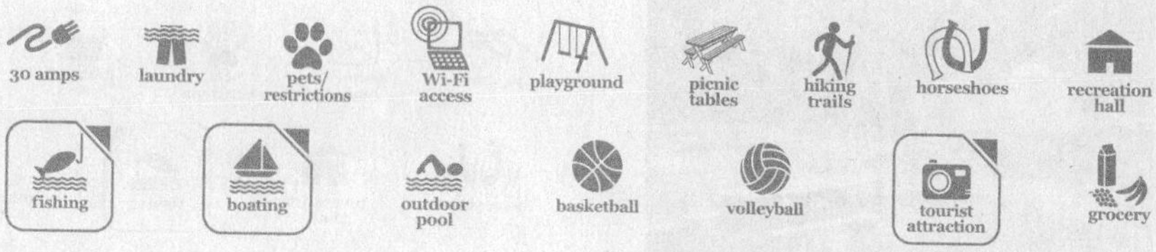

RANDLE

RESORT NUMBER: 724 **GOOD SAM RATING:** 8/8.5★/9.5 **COAST DELUXE RESORT**

Maple Grove Resort—
K/M Resorts of America
175 State Route 131
Randle, Washington 98377
360-497-2742; res.: 253-896-4677
maplegrove@kmresorts.com
kmresorts.com

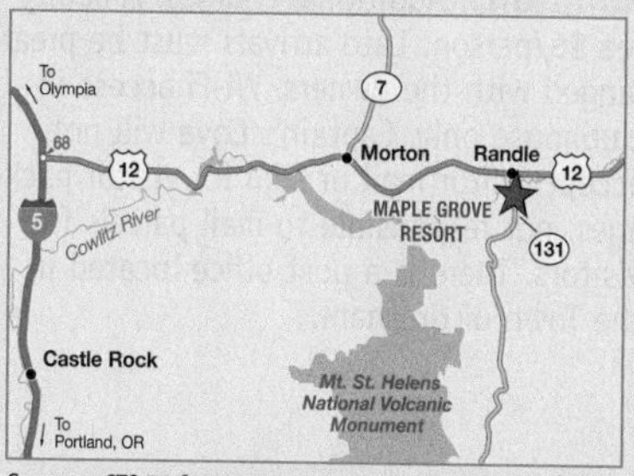

See page CTC 76 for state map.

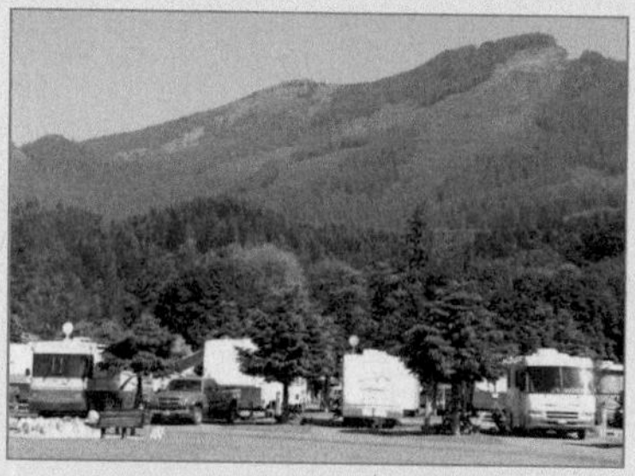

Adventure is never far with the triangle of Mounts Rainier, St. Helens and Adams around the resort. There are a total of 60 lakes within 40 miles offering salmon, steelhead and trout fishing. Activities include horseback riding, mountain climbing, hang gliding, guided boat trips, whitewater rafting, and scenic flights. Resort has 1,400 feet of frontage on Cowlitz River.

DIRECTIONS: From Seattle (N) or Portland (S) I-5: Ex 68. E on Hwy 12 approx 50 mi to Randle. S on Hwy 131. 0.1 mi to resort.

GPS COORDINATES: 46.5301°N/-121.9567°W
RV SITES: Full: 53 Partial: 146 Dry: 0
CHECK-IN: 1:00 p.m.
CHECK-OUT: 11:00 a.m.
SEASON: Year-round
PEAK SEASON: May 1–September 30
MAX. RV LENGTH: 40 feet
NOTATIONS: Additional charges: 30 amp $3/night, 50 amp $4/night, cable $3/night, Wi-Fi $2/night. Reservations required. Poolhouse closed Jan and Feb.
RENTAL ACCOMMODATIONS: Rental units available. Trip Points not accepted. Contact resort directly.

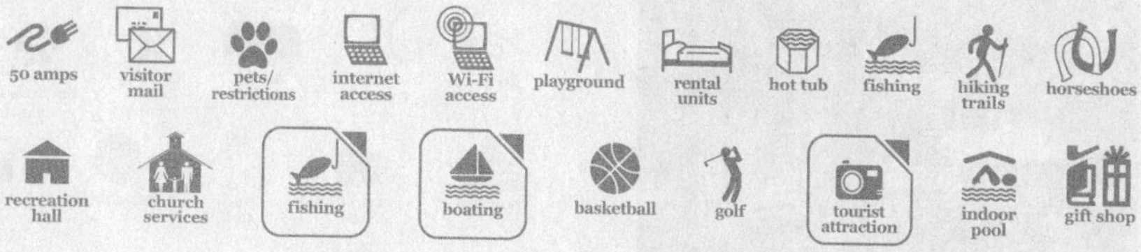

WASHINGTON

SEQUIM

RESORT NUMBER: 825 **GOOD SAM RATING:** 6/8★/8 **COAST DELUXE RESORT**

Diamond Point Resort—K/M Resorts of America
294 Industrial Parkway
Sequim, Washington 98382
360-681-0590; res.: 253-896-4677
diamondpoint@kmresorts.com
kmresorts.com

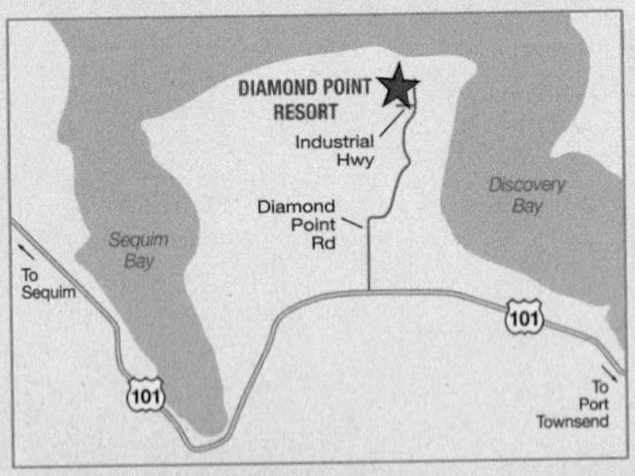

See page CTC 76 for state map.

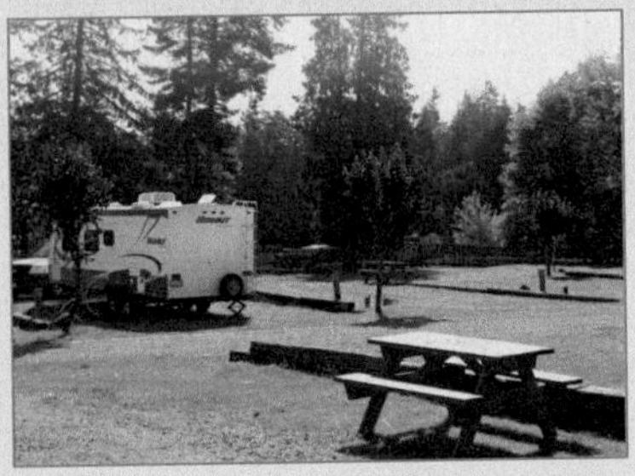

Diamond Point is in the Banana Belt of the Pacific Northwest. The resort is nestled between the Olympic Mountains and the Puget Sound, with beautiful views of the Canadian San Juan Islands. Area attractions include beach access, golf, fishing, mountain hiking and gambling at a nearby casino.

DIRECTIONS: From Sequim: Hwy 101. E approx 9 mi E of Sequim. Diamond Point Rd NW approx 3.5 mi. L on Industrial Pkwy to resort.

GPS COORDINATES: 48.0884°N/-122.9319°W
RV SITES: Full: 70 Partial: 11 Dry: 0
CHECK-IN: 1:00 p.m.
CHECK-OUT: 11:00 a.m.
SEASON: Year-round
PEAK SEASON: May 1–September 30
MAX. RV LENGTH: 35 feet
NOTATIONS: Additional charges: 30 amp $3/night, 50 amp $4/night, cable $3/night, Wi-Fi $2/night per device, tax 8.4%. Reservations required. Drive-ups not accepted.
RENTAL ACCOMMODATIONS: Rental units available. Trip Points not accepted. Contact resort directly.

WISCONSIN

GRESHAM

RESORT NUMBER: 768 **GOOD SAM RATING:** 6.5/7/7.5 **COAST DELUXE RESORT**

Captain's Cove Resort and Country Club
N9099 Big Lake Road
Gresham, Wisconsin 54128
715-787-3535; fax: 715-787-3517
captainscove@rocketmail.com
captaincove.com

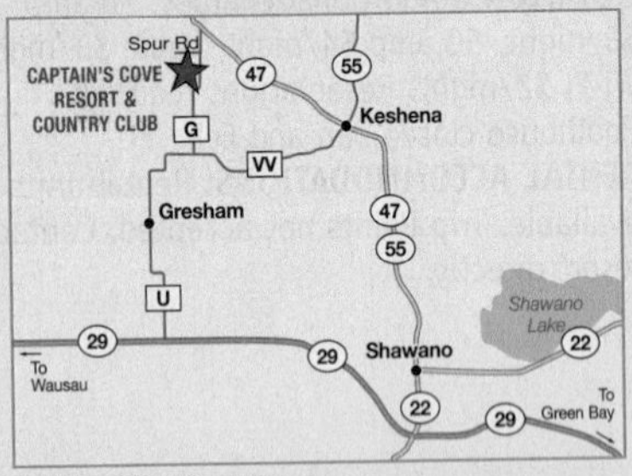

See page CTC 77 for state map.

Fill both your days and your nights with activities. Enjoy this cool, wooded lakeside resort, complete with two sandy beaches and a clubhouse overlooking the water. Or relax on the lake itself, which is closed to motorized boats. Come nightfall, try your luck at the popular casino located within eight miles.

DIRECTIONS: From E at Shawano: Hwy 47/55 N 7.5 mi past Menominee Casino. L on County G for 0.5 mi. R on Spur Rd. 0.7 mi to resort. From the W: Hwy 29 E. L on County U. Past Gresham 2 mi to Big Lake Rd. Go to intersection of Big Lake and Spur Rd.

GPS COORDINATES: 44.9215°N/-88.7669°W
RV SITES: Full: 50 Partial: 83 Dry: 0
CHECK-IN: 10:00 a.m.–6:00 p.m.
CHECK-OUT: Noon
SEASON: May 15–October 22
PEAK SEASON: May 15–September 15
MAX. RV LENGTH: 45 feet
NOTATIONS: Additional charges: Amenity fee $5/person. Late arrivals must be prearranged with the owners. Wi-Fi access in clubhouse only. Captain's Cove will not accept visitor mail or sign for visitor packages, not responsible to mail parcels for visitors. There is a post office located in the Town of Gresham.

WISCONSIN DELLS

RESORT NUMBER: 428 **GOOD SAM RATING:** 10/9.5★/10 **COAST DELUXE RESORT**

WISCONSIN

Christmas Mountain Village Campground
S944 Christmas Mountain Road
Wisconsin Dells, Wisconsin 53965
608-254-3940; fax: 608-254-3907
lori.seippel@bluegreencorp.com
christmasmountainvillage.com

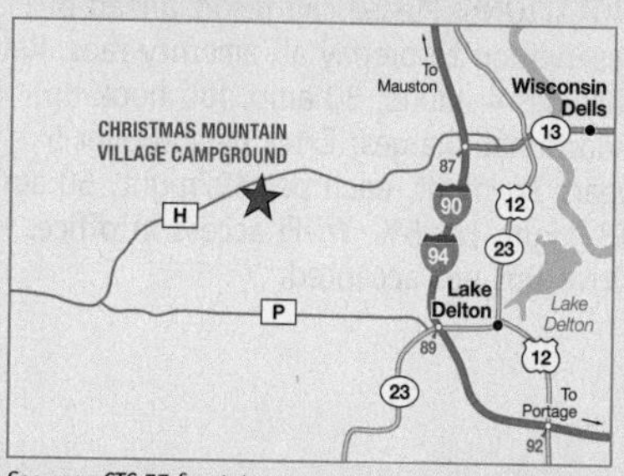

See page CTC 77 for state map.

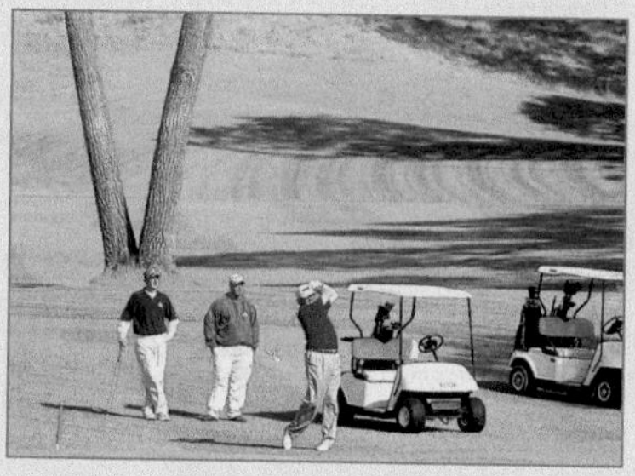

Located in the year-round Wisconsin Dells resort area. From quiet forests and scenic beauties to winter, summer, and water sports, to nightlife and fine dining, the Dells has it. The resort features a 27-hole golf course, alpine skiing and other outdoor activities, as well as organized activities.

DIRECTIONS: From I-90/94: Ex 87/Hwy 13. W on County Hwy H approx 3.5 mi. L on Lyndon Rd for 0.7 mi to entry gate. Press intercom button for registration and please pick up a welcome packet from the mail.

GPS COORDINATES: 43.6115°N/-89.848°W
RV SITES: Full: 91 Partial: 0 Dry: 0
CHECK-IN: Noon–9:00 p.m.
CHECK-OUT: 11:00 a.m.
SEASON: Year-round
PEAK SEASON: June 1–September 30
MAX. RV LENGTH: 40 feet
NOTATIONS: Credit card required at check-in.

BOULDER

RESORT NUMBER: 896 **GOOD SAM RATING:** 4.5/6/6.5 **COAST CLASSIC RESORT**

WYOMING

Wind River View Campground
8889 Highway 191
Boulder, Wyoming 82923
307-537-5453; fax: 307-537-5453
windriverview@outlook.com
windriverview.wixsite.com/mysite

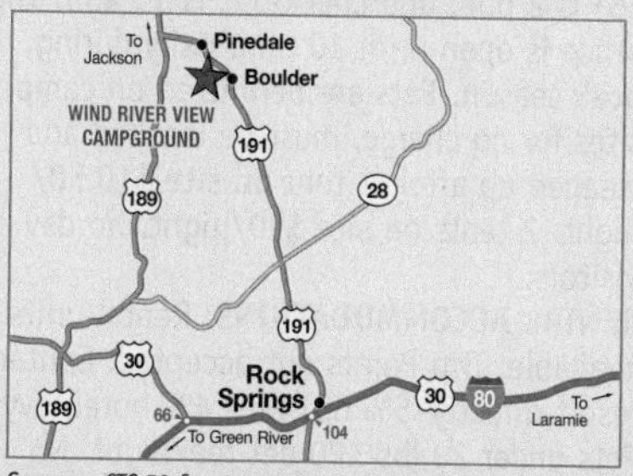

See page CTC 59 for state map.

Wind River View Campground is nestled at the base of the beautiful Wind River Mountain range of Wyoming. The park is about 100 miles south of Jackson Hole, Grand Teton, and Yellowstone Park areas. Numerous lakes and rivers are within a short drive from the park and offer exceptional fishing.

DIRECTIONS: From Rock Springs: 90 mi N on Hwy 191. Park on L 1 mi after crossing bridge at Boulder. From Jackson Hole: 90 mi S on Hwy 191. Park on R.

GPS COORDINATES: 42.7589°N/-109.7334°W
ELEVATION: 7,100 feet
RV SITES: Full: 50 Partial: 28 Dry: 0
CHECK-IN: 9:00 a.m.–8:00 p.m.
CHECK-OUT: 11:00 a.m.
SEASON: May 1–October 1
MAX. RV LENGTH: 50 feet

ALBERTA

LETHBRIDGE

RESORT NUMBER: 1872 **GOOD SAM RATING:** 8.5/10★/8.5 **COAST DELUXE RESORT**

Bridgeview RV Resort—Holiday Trails Resorts
1501 2nd Avenue West
Lethbridge, Alberta T1J 4S5
403-381-2357; fax: 403-328-1551
bridgeview@htr.ca
holidaytrailsresorts.ca

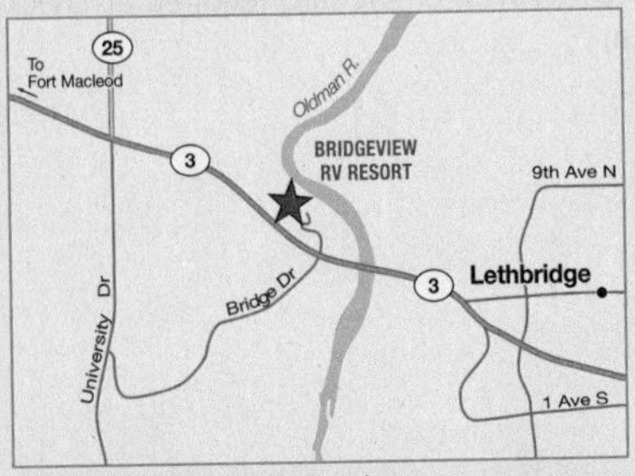

See page CTC 78 for Western Canada map.

In a picturesque river valley on the westerly outskirts of Lethbridge, Alberta. Plenty of opportunities for sightseeing, boating and fishing in the Oldman River. Nearby: Nikka Yuko Japanese Gardens, Indian Battle Park, Fort Whoop Up, Head-Smashed-In-Buffalo Jump, and other attractions.

DIRECTIONS: From the W: Ex S off Hwy 3 onto Bridge Drive. Follow to turn-around and reverse direction at golf course. N over Hwy 3. Follow signs to park. From the E: Ex R (N) off Hwy 3 after crossing Oldman River Bridge. Follow signs.

GPS COORDINATES: 49.7111°N/-112.8712°W
RV SITES: Full: 167 Partial: 55 Dry: 0
CHECK-IN: Noon–9:00 p.m.
CHECK-OUT: 11:00 a.m.
SEASON: Year-round
PEAK SEASON: May 15–September 15
MAX. RV LENGTH: Unlimited
NOTATIONS: Please call resort ahead of reservation to prepay all amenity fees. Rate includes 4 adults, 30 amp, full hook-up. Additional charges: Extra person over 5 years $4/night, each pet $3/night, 50 amp $3/night, tax 5%. Wi-Fi access in office. Drive-ups not accepted.

ALBERTA

ROCKY MOUNTAIN HOUSE

RESORT NUMBER: 4 **GOOD SAM RATING:** 8/10★/9 **COAST CLASSIC RESORT**

Wilderness Village at Crimson Lake
402034 Range Road 8-1
Rocky Mountain House, Alberta T4T 1A9
403-845-2145; fax: 403-845-2146
information@wildernessvillage.ca
wildernessvillage.ca

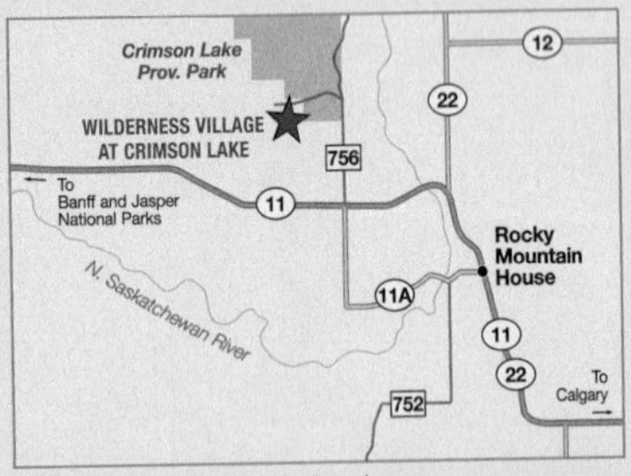

See page CTC 78 for Western Canada map.

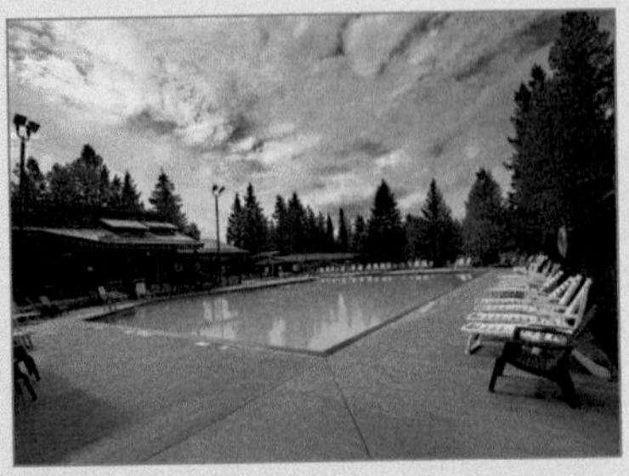

Set in a secluded wilderness northwest of Calgary and east of the Canadian Rockies. This resort offers an on site playground, bmx track, ball field and free petting zoo. Affordable horseback trail rides are offered from mid-May to mid-Sep. Resort has two pools and three hot tubs, and immaculate showers and washrooms. Enjoy trout fishing in the many lakes and streams and golf at nearby golf courses.

DIRECTIONS: Hwy 11 for 6 mi W of Rocky Mountain House, over the N Saskatchewan River to Hwy 756. 3 mi N on Hwy 756 to access shared with Crimson Lake Prov. Park. Resort 0.2 mi on L.

GPS COORDINATES: 52.4423°N/-115.0329°W
ELEVATION: 3,200 feet
RV SITES: Full: 0 Partial: 385 Dry: 0
CHECK-IN: 2:00 p.m.
CHECK-OUT: 11:00 a.m.
SEASON: January 2–December 31
MAX. RV LENGTH: 40 feet
NOTATIONS: Drive-ups not accepted due to gated community. Water and 30 amps only, mobile sewer service for nominal fee. Check-in during peak season (Jun 15-Sep 15) is 2 p.m. and check-out is 11 a.m. The office is open until 10 p.m. daily during peak season. Pets are permitted on campsites for no charge, must be leashed and cleaned up after. 1 tent on site $10.50/night, 2 tents on site $90/night. No day visitors.
RENTAL ACCOMMODATIONS: Rental units available. Trip Points not accepted. Contact resort directly. 5% GST plus 4% hotel levy. Pets under 20 lbs $20 pet fee/night. No pets over 20 lbs.

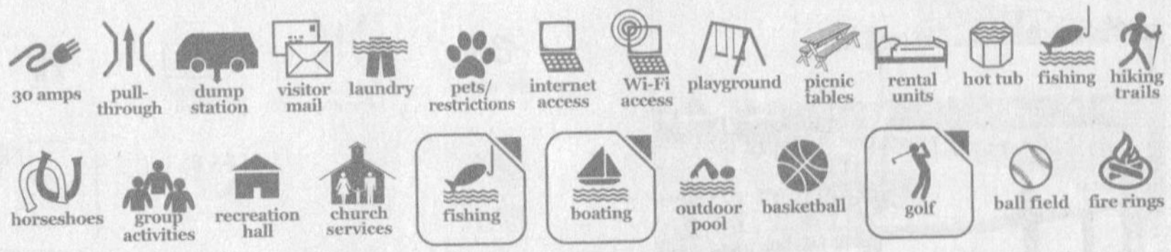

AINSWORTH

RESORT NUMBER: 491 **GOOD SAM RATING:** 7.5/6/7 **COAST DELUXE RESORT**

Woodbury Resort and Marina
4112 Highway 31
Ainsworth, British Columbia V0G 1A0
250-353-7717; res.: 877-353-7717
woodburyresort@netidea.com
woodburyresort.com

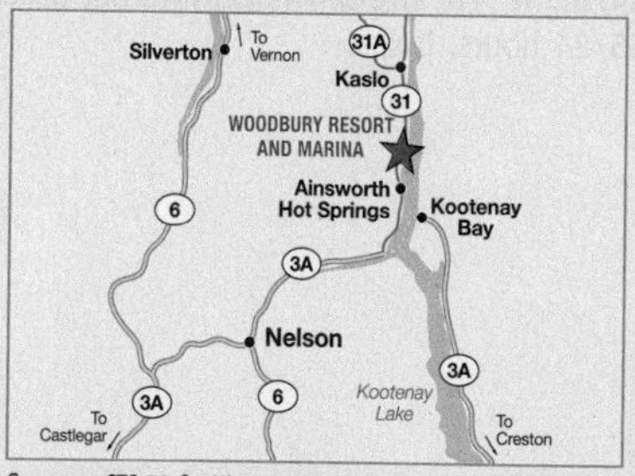

See page CTC 78 for Western Canada map.

Largest resort in the Kootenay Lakes area, 2.5 miles north of Ainsworth Hot Springs. Full service marina and rental boats. Famous JB's restaurant and pub on site. Lake hosts the over-10-pound Gerrard Rainbow Trout. Nearby are 60 miles of back roads to mountain lakes and old mines. Woodbury Canyon and Kokanee Glacier are a few miles from the resort.

DIRECTIONS: From Nelson: Rte 3A/31 NE to Balfour. Rte 31 N approx 9 mi to resort on R.

GPS COORDINATES: 49.7753°N/-116.9067°W
RV SITES: Full: 36 Partial: 30 Dry: 0
CHECK-IN: 2:00 p.m.
CHECK-OUT: 11:00 a.m.
SEASON: Year-round
PEAK SEASON: May 26–September 26
MAX. RV LENGTH: 40 feet
NOTATIONS: Check with park concerning Canadian holidays. Wi-Fi access in campground.
RENTAL ACCOMMODATIONS: Rental units available. Trip Points accepted. Contact resort directly.

30 amps · pull-through · pets/restrictions · internet access · Wi-Fi access · playground · restaurant/snack bar · rental units
fishing · boating · recreation hall · fishing · outdoor pool · beach · tourist attraction · winter sports

KELOWNA

RESORT NUMBER: 337 **GOOD SAM RATING:** 10/9.5★/9.5 **COAST CLASSIC RESORT**

Holiday Park Resort
1-415 Commonwealth Road
Kelowna, British Columbia V4V 1P4
250-766-4255; res.: 800-752-9678
holiday@sweetlife.com
sweetlife.com

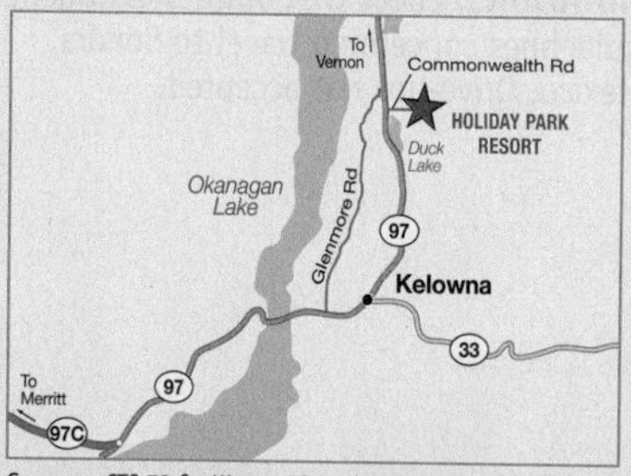

See page CTC 78 for Western Canada map.

Centrally located in the beautiful Okanagan Valley, Holiday Park is a four season RV & Condo Resort surrounded by championship golf courses, award-winning wineries, world-class ski hills, numerous recreation areas and facilities. This 67-acre playground offers landscaped RV sites, fully furnished condos, 4 pools, 3 hot tubs, 3 rec centers, plus a wide range of onsite activites with seasonal discounts and specials. Come discover the sweetlife!

DIRECTIONS: From Kelowna: On Hwy 97, 5 km N of Kelowna International Airport. From Winfield: On Hwy 97, 2 km S of Winfield turn onto Commonwealth Rd.

GPS COORDINATES: 50.0077°N/-119.3931°W
RV SITES: Full: 20 Partial: 0 Dry: 0
CHECK-IN: 1:00 p.m.–5:00 p.m.
CHECK-OUT: 11:00 a.m.
SEASON: Year-round
MAX. RV LENGTH: 40 feet
NOTATIONS: RVs with flush toilets and holding tanks only. No tents, pop-ups or porta-potties. Free Wi-Fi at hotspots. Wi-Fi access at RV site (fee).
RENTAL ACCOMMODATIONS: Rental units available. Trip Points not accepted. Contact resort directly.

50 amps · laundry · pets/restrictions · internet access · Wi-Fi access · playground · restaurant/snack bar · rental units
hot tub · fishing · shuffleboard · hiking trails · horseshoes · recreation hall · outdoor pool · golf · indoor pool · grocery · winter sports

QUEBEC

COMPTON

RESORT NUMBER: 189 **GOOD SAM RATING:** 9/10★/8.5 **COAST DELUXE RESORT**

Camping de Compton
24 Chemin de la Station
Compton, Quebec J0B 1L0
819-835-5277; fax: 819-835-5304
info@campingcompton.com
campingcompton.com

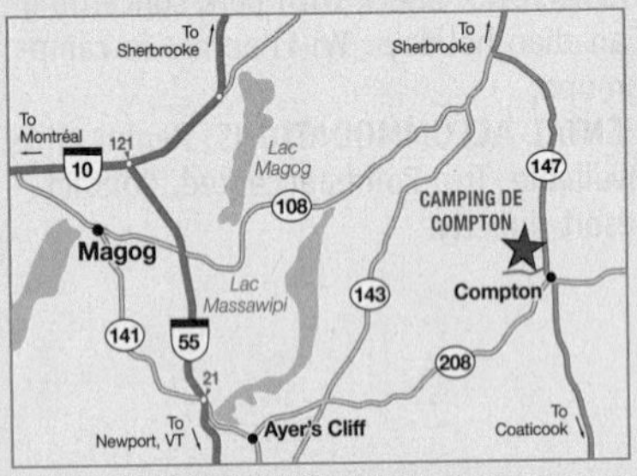

See page CTC 80 for Eastern Canada map.

Between Sherbrooke and the Vermont border. Located on rolling hills and offers remarkable scenic views for the great pleasure of golfers and cyclists. Nearby: Coaticook Gorge, Massawippi Lake, Saint-Benoit-du-Lac Abby, Mount Megantic Observatory. You will always remember Le Camping de Compton sunset on Mont-Orford.

DIRECTIONS: From Montreal: Hwy 10 towards Sherbrooke. Ex 121 towards Coaticook (Rte 55 S). Ex 21 towards Ayer's Cliff. In center of village, follow Rd 208 E to Compton. L on Rd 147 N. L on Chemin de la Station to resort 1,000 ft on L.

GPS COORDINATES: 45.243°N/-71.832°W
RV SITES: Full: 242 Partial: 45 Dry: 0
CHECK-IN: 2:00 p.m.
CHECK-OUT: Noon
SEASON: April 15–October 20
MAX. RV LENGTH: 50 feet
NOTATIONS: Additional charges: Electric fee $4/night, VIP site $5/night, internet access $5/24 hours, taxes.

50 amps · pull-through · dump station · laundry · pets/restrictions · internet access · Wi-Fi access · playground · picnic tables · fishing · shuffleboard · hiking trails · horseshoes · group activities · recreation hall · outdoor pool · basketball · volleyball · golf · tourist attraction · shopping · hot showers · fire rings · firewood · ice

SONORA

EL GOLFO DE SANTA CLARA

RESORT NUMBER: 1598 **GOOD SAM RATING:** N/A **COAST CLASSIC RESORT**

El Golfo RV Resort—
Colorado River Adventures
Los Cinco Amigos Del Golf, Clara S.A. de C.V.
El Golfo de Santa Clara, Sonora 83401
760-663-4941; res.: 760-663-4968
robinj@cramember.com
coloradoriveradventures.com

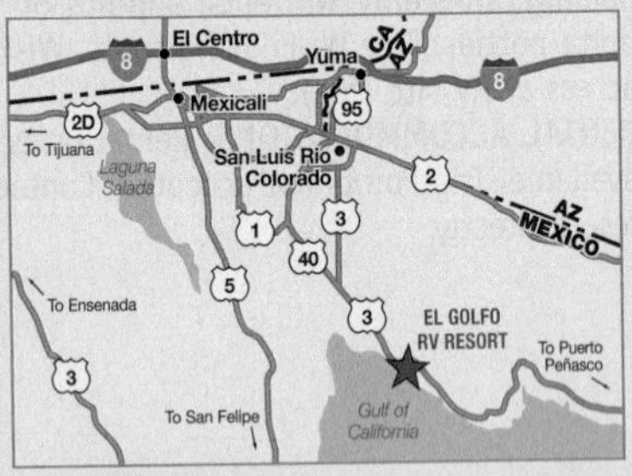

See page CTC 81 for Mexico map.

Located on the Sea of Cortez 70 miles south of Yuma, AZ, with miles of pristine white sand beach, tidepools and breath-taking area views. A fishing village with charter fishing available, great shrimp and just a few restaurants in town. Say hello to Teresa when you visit the famous El Capitan restaurant located right next door. For off-road enthusiasts El Golfo boasts sand dunes comparable to Glamis.

DIRECTIONS: From Yuma go 22 mi S following signs to San Luis Rio Colorado. Travel thru Riita to El Golfo. 70 mi from San Luis Rio Colorado to El Golfo de Santa Clara.

GPS COORDINATES: 31.67663°N/-114.48814°W
RV SITES: Full: 165 Partial: 0 Dry: 0
CHECK-IN: 8:00 a.m.
CHECK-OUT: 3:00 p.m.
SEASON: Year-round
MAX. RV LENGTH: 40 feet
NOTATIONS: Check U.S. State Department guidelines concerning travel to Sonora, Mexico. Drive-ups not accepted.

30 amps · laundry · pets/restrictions · hot tub · shuffleboard · recreation hall · fishing · outdoor pool · basketball · beach · volleyball · golf · game room

GOOD NEIGHBOR PARKS

Good Neighbor Parks provide additional quality locations across North America where you can stay at a discount when using your Coast to Coast membership. Good Neighbor Parks are located in 38 states and 10 Canadian Provinces.

ALABAMA

TALLADEGA

Talladega Creekside Resort
760 Lake Whitland Drive
Talladega, Alabama 35160
256-362-9053
info@talladegacreekside.com
talladegacreekside.com
RESORT NUMBER: 2064
GOOD SAM RATING: 3/UI/7
DIRECTIONS: From E or W I-20: Ex 173/ Eastaboga. S to CR 5. 4 mi to Lake Whitland Rd on L. From Hwy 21 in Talladega: N on Eastaboga Rd 5 mi and R on Lake Whitland Rd.
GPS COORDINATES: 33.5261°N/-86.0398°W
NOTATIONS: Check-in: 3:00 p.m.-7:00 p.m. Check-out: Noon. Special discount rate for Coast members. Coast rate not available NASCAR race weeks. Call if arriving later than 7 p.m. Rental units available. Trip Points not accepted. Contact resort directly. Max. RV length: 45 feet. Open: Year-round.
STATE MAP: See page CTC 50.

50 amps, pull-through, pets/restrictions, rental units, fishing, horseshoes, canoes, hot showers, tenting

WOODVILLE

Parnell Creek RV Park
115 Parnell Circle
Woodville, Alabama 35776
256-776-2348; res.: 256-508-7308
parnellcreekrvpark@yahoo.com
parnellcreekrvpark.com
RESORT NUMBER: 2070
GOOD SAM RATING: 9/8.5★/9
DIRECTIONS: Located near Huntsville and Scottsboro. Easy on/off hwy. From Huntsville: Hwy 72 E to mi marker 124. 2nd R past the log cabin store. Over ridge onto Parnell Cir. From Scottsboro: Hwy 72 W to mi marker 125. L onto Parnell Cir.
GPS COORDINATES: 34.6135°N/-86.235°W
NOTATIONS: Check-in: 1:00 p.m. Check-out: 11:00 a.m. Special discount rate for Coast members. Rate includes 2 adults, 2 children, 30 amp, full hook-ups. Additional charges: Extra person $2/night, 50 amp $5/night. Rental units available. Trip Points not accepted. Contact resort directly. Max. RV length: 50 feet. Open: Year-round.
STATE MAP: See page CTC 50.

50 amps, dump station, visitor mail, laundry, pets/restrictions, Wi-Fi access, playground, picnic tables, rental units, horseshoes, recreation hall, outdoor pool, mini golf, basketball, tourist attraction, fitness, propane, hot showers, fire rings, rv supplies, gift shop, firewood, ice, grills

ARIZONA

APACHE JUNCTION

Carefree Manor RV Resort
1615 North Delaware Drive Space 57
Apache Junction, Arizona 85120
480-982-4008
info@carefreerv.net
carefreerv.net
RESORT NUMBER: 1450
GOOD SAM RATING: 8.5/10★/9
DIRECTIONS: From Hwy 60: N on Ironwood Dr 3 mi to Teepee St. W on Teepee to Delaware. Resort on R.
GPS COORDINATES: 33.4297°N/-111.5698°W
NOTATIONS: Check-in: 9:00 a.m.– 4:00 p.m. Check-out: 11:00 a.m. 2021 Coast rate $39/ night. Rate includes 2 people, 30/50 amp, full hook-ups. Additional charges: Utilities $5/night. Applicable sales tax 11.1%. Lots are 30 ft x 50 ft. Max. RV length: 42 feet. Open: April 1–December 31.
STATE MAP: See page CTC 52.

50 amps, dump station, visitor mail, laundry, pets/restrictions, internet access, Wi-Fi access, hot tub, shuffleboard, outdoor pool

BLACK CANYON CITY

Black Canyon Campground
19600 East St Joseph Road
Black Canyon City, Arizona 85324
844-562-5314
bccampground@yahoo.com
blackcanyoncampground.com
RESORT NUMBER: 2482
GOOD SAM RATING: 8.5/8.5★/7.5
DIRECTIONS: From Jct of I-17 & Ex 242: N 0.5 mi on East Frntg Rd, campground on R.
GPS COORDINATES: 34.05976°N/-112.14213°W
NOTATIONS: Check-in: 3:00 p.m. Check-out: 10:00 a.m. Special 20% discount rate for Coast members. Discount available Jul 4-Sep 1. Rate includes 2 adults per site, full hook-ups, Wi-Fi, cable TV. Additional charges: Security deposit $60, tax 6.035%. Max. RV length: 60 feet. Open: July 4–September 1.
STATE MAP: See page CTC 52.

50 amps, pull-through, cable tv, laundry, pets/restrictions, Wi-Fi access, playground, hot tub, hiking trails, outdoor pool, tourist attraction, shopping, propane, hot showers, grocery, rv supplies, tenting, ice

BLACK CANYON CITY

Black Canyon Ranch RV Resort
33900 South Old Black Canyon Highway
Black Canyon City, Arizona 85324
623-374-9800; fax: 623-374-9801
manager@blackcanyonranchrv.com
blackcanyonranchrv.com
RESORT NUMBER: 2275
GOOD SAM RATING: 10/10★/10
DIRECTIONS: 25 mi N of Phoenix. Only 1 mi from either Ex 242 or Ex 244 off I-17. From Nbnd I-17 Ex 242: Turn L over Fwy, turn R, follow 1 mi, resort on L. From Sbnd I-17 Ex 244: Go straight 1 mi, resort on R.
GPS COORDINATES: 34.07178°N/-112.15338°W
ELEVATION: 2,200 feet
NOTATIONS: Check-in: Noon. Check-out: 11:00 a.m. 2022 Coast member rate $54/night good for up to 3 nights, avail Apr 1-Oct 31 only. Units must be self-contained. Drive-ups accepted. Max. RV length: 45 feet. Open: Year-round.
STATE MAP: See page CTC 52.

50 amps, pull-through, cable tv, visitor mail, laundry, pets/restrictions, internet access, Wi-Fi access, picnic tables, restaurant/snack bar, hot tub, hiking trails, horseshoes, group activities, recreation hall, outdoor pool, game room, propane, hot showers, handicap access, ice

BOUSE

Desert Pueblo RV Resort
28726 Highway 72
Bouse, Arizona 85325
928-851-2206
dprvresort@gmail.com
desertpueblorv.com
RESORT NUMBER: 2486
GOOD SAM RATING: 8.5/10★/10
DIRECTIONS: From Jct of Hwy 95 and Hwy 72: E 15 mi on Hwy 72, resort on R.
GPS COORDINATES: 33.91752°N/-113.99444°W
NOTATIONS: Check-in: 11:00 a.m. Check-out: 11:00 a.m. 2021 Coast rate $22.50. Rate includes 2 adults per site, 30 amp, full hook-ups, free Wi-Fi. Additional charges: Add'l adult $3/night, 50 amp $3.50/night, tax 7.7%. Wi-Fi in the clubhouse. Max. RV length: 50 feet. Open: October 1–April 15.
STATE MAP: See page CTC 52.

50 amps, pull-through, laundry, pets/restrictions, Wi-Fi access, hiking trails, group activities, recreation hall, fishing, boating, golf, tourist attraction, propane, hot showers, ice

CAMP VERDE

Verde Ranch RV Resort
1105 North Dreamcatcher Drive
Camp Verde, Arizona 86322
928-567-7126; res.: 928-567-7226
vrrvinfo@crrmgmt.com
campspot.com/book/verderanchrvresort
RESORT NUMBER: 2407
GOOD SAM RATING: 10/10★/10
DIRECTIONS: From Jct I-17 & Hwy 260 (Ex 287): Go 0.5 mi N on Hwy 260. Ex at 1st roundabout. Go 300 ft E on N Dreamcatcher Dr. Park on L.
GPS COORDINATES: 34.58443°N/-111.88563°W
NOTATIONS: Check-in: 2:00 p.m. Check-out: 11:00 a.m. 2022 Coast member rate 25% off nightly rate for RV site up to 3 nights on back-in and deluxe back-in sites. Rate includes 2 adults per site, full hook-ups, Wi-Fi, cable. Additional charges: $3 booking fee, tax 12.975%. Use code COAST when booking online. Discount not avail Jan-Apr and holiday weekends. Max. RV length: 54 feet. Open: Year-round.

STATE MAP: See page CTC 52.

50 amps · laundry · pets/restrictions · Wi-Fi access · playground · picnic tables · hot tub · fishing · hiking trails · horseshoes · group activities · recreation hall · outdoor pool · fitness · gambling casino · fire rings · gift shop

EHRENBERG

Arizona Oasis RV Resort
50238 Ehrenberg-Parker Highway
Ehrenberg, Arizona 85334
928-923-8230; fax: 928-923-7113
reservations@arizonaoasis.com
arizonaoasis.com
RESORT NUMBER: 1843
GOOD SAM RATING: 8.5/9/9
DIRECTIONS: From I-10: Ex 1. N 0.5 mi to Ehrenberg Rd. L, resort 3 blocks on R.
GPS COORDINATES: 33.606°N/-114.5238°W
NOTATIONS: Check-in: Noon. Check-out: 11:00 a.m. Special discount rate for Coast members. Rate includes 6 people. Additional charges: Extra vehicle $5/night, tax 7.7%. No drive-ups Dec, Jan & Feb. Rentals units available. Trip Points not accepted. Contact resort directly. Max. RV length: 65 feet. Open: Year-round.
STATE MAP: See page CTC 52.

50 amps · cable tv · laundry · pets/restrictions · internet access · Wi-Fi access · playground · rental units · hot tub · fishing · horseshoes · boating · recreation hall · fishing · boating · outdoor pool · beach · golf · tourist attraction · gambling casino

HUACHUCA

Tombstone Territories RV Resort
2111 East Highway 82
Huachuca, Arizona 85616
520-457-2584; res.: 877-316-6714
info@tombstoneterritories.com
tombstoneterritories.com
RESORT NUMBER: 2279
GOOD SAM RATING: 10/9.5★/10
DIRECTIONS: Located on the N side of Hwy 82 between mi posts 59 & 60. From I-10: Ex 302, S on Hwy 90 for 19 mi. L (E) on Hwy 82 for 8 mi. From Sierra Vista: N on Hwy 90. Turn R (E) on Hwy 82 for 8 mi. From Tombstone: N on Hwy 80. Turn L (W) on Hwy 82 for 10 mi. From Benson: S on Hwy 80. Turn R (W) on Hwy 82 for 10 mi.
GPS COORDINATES: 31.72107°N/-110.22435°W
ELEVATION: 4,000 feet
NOTATIONS: Check-in: 1:00 p.m. Check-out: 11:00 a.m. Coast member discount 25% for up to 3 days. Rate includes 2 people. Electricity metered at all sites. Additional charges: Extra person and dogs $2/night, electricity metered at all sites. Drive-ups accepted. Max. RV length: Unlimited. Open: May 15–October 14.
STATE MAP: See page CTC 52.

50 amps · pets/restrictions · Wi-Fi access · hot tub · shuffleboard · hiking trails · recreation hall · fitness · indoor pool

MESA

Mesa Sunset RV Resort
9252 East Broadway Road
Mesa, Arizona 85208
480-984-6731
msrvr@outlook.com
mesasunsetrvresort.com
RESORT NUMBER: 2450
GOOD SAM RATING: 9.5/8.5/9.5
DIRECTIONS: From Jct of US Hwy 60 & Ellsworth Rd (Ex 191): N 1.5 mi on Ellsworth Rd to Broadway Rd. E 500 ft. Resort on L.
GPS COORDINATES: 33.40834°N/-111.63074°W
NOTATIONS: Check-in: 1:00 p.m. Check-out: 11:00 a.m. Special discount rate for Coast members. Max. RV length: 40 feet. Open: April 1–September 30.
STATE MAP: See page CTC 52.

50 amps · laundry · pets/restrictions · hot tub · horseshoes · group activities · recreation hall · age restrictions · fishing · boating · outdoor pool · golf · tourist attraction · shopping

MOHAVE VALLEY

Moon River RV Resort
1325 Boundary Cone Road
(Bullhead City AZ/Laughlin NV area)
Mohave Valley, Arizona 86440
928-788-6666; fax: 928-768-9681
info@moonriverresort.com
moonriverresort.com
RESORT NUMBER: 2236
GOOD SAM RATING: 9/9★/9
DIRECTIONS: From Jct of Hwy 95 & Boundary Cone Rd: W to resort in 200 yds. From SR 68 & Hwy 95 (Laughlin Bridge): S 15.2 mi on Hwy 95 to Boundary Cone Rd. GPS users please call.
GPS COORDINATES: 34.9685°N/-114.6035°W
NOTATIONS: Check-in: 1:00 p.m. Check-out: Noon. Special discount rate for Coast members. Free Wi-Fi. Additional charges (cash only): Extra adult $5/night, additional child $3/night, pets $5/night, electrical $6/night, tax 5.78%. Max. RV length: 45 feet. Open: May 1–October 31.
STATE MAP: See page CTC 52.

50 amps · pull-through · laundry · pets/restrictions · Wi-Fi access · horseshoes · group activities · recreation hall · fishing · boating · outdoor pool · golf · tourist attraction · hot showers · gambling casino · grocery · rv supplies · ice

PAGE

NEW **Page Lake Powell Campground**
849 South Coppermine Road
Page, Arizona 86040
928-645-3374
cgmanager@baits.com
pagelakepowellcampground.com
RESORT NUMBER: 2553
GOOD SAM RATING: 8.5/9★/9
DIRECTIONS: From Jct of Hwy 89 & AZ 98 E, go E 2.6 mi on AZ 98 E to Coppermine Rd/N 20, then N 0.7 mi on Coppermine Rd. Park on R.
GPS COORDINATES: 36.90156°N/-111.45299°W
ELEVATION: 4,300 feet
NOTATIONS: Check-in: Noon. Check-out: 11:00 a.m. 2022 Coast rate 20% discount avail Nov-Jan. Rate includes 2 adults per site, full hook-ups. Additional charges: Tax 9.9%. Max. RV length: 40 feet. Open: Year-round.
STATE MAP: See page CTC 52.

50 amps · pull-through · dump station · laundry · pets/restrictions · Wi-Fi access · picnic tables · hiking trails · horseshoes · fitness · grocery · ice

QUARTZSITE

Quail Run RV Park
918 North Central Boulevard
Quartzsite, Arizona 85346
928-927-8810
info@quailrv.com
quailrv.com
RESORT NUMBER: 2496
GOOD SAM RATING: 9/10★/9
DIRECTIONS: From Jct of I-10 & Quartzsite Blvd (Ex 17), N 0.2 mi on Quartzsite Blvd to Bus Loop 10, E 1.4 mi on Bus Loop 10 to Central Blvd, N 0.9 mi, park on L.
GPS COORDINATES: 33.67998°N/-114.21742°W
NOTATIONS: Check-in: 1:00 p.m. Check-out: 11:00 a.m. Special 20% discount rate for Coast members. No discount avail Jan 1-31. Rate includes 2 adults per site, full hook-ups, Wi-Fi. Additional charges: Tax 13.2%. Max. RV length: 80 feet. Open: Year-round.
STATE MAP: See page CTC 52.

50 amps · pull-through · laundry · pets/restrictions · Wi-Fi access · group activities · recreation hall · tourist attraction · hot showers

QUARTZSITE

The Scenic Road RV Park
480 North Central Boulevard
Quartzsite, Arizona 85346
928-927-6443
info@thescenicroad.com
thescenicroad.com
RESORT NUMBER: 2497
GOOD SAM RATING: 7.5/8.5★/8
DIRECTIONS: From Jct of Bus. I-10 & AZ 95/N. Central Blvd, N 0.3 mi on AZ 95/N. Central Blvd, park on L.
GPS COORDINATES: 33.67459°N/-114.21806°W
NOTATIONS: Check-in: 1:00 p.m. Check-out: 11:00 a.m. Special 20% discount rate for Coast members. No avail Jan 2-31. Rate includes 2 adults per site, full hook-ups, Wi-Fi. Additional charges: Tax 13.2%. Max. RV length: 65 feet. Open: February 1–April 30; October 1–January 1.
STATE MAP: See page CTC 52.

50 amps · pull-through · laundry · pets/restrictions · Wi-Fi access · group activities · recreation hall · tourist attraction · hot showers

SALOME

3 Dreamers RV Park
54000 Highway 60
Salome, Arizona 85348
928-859-4145; fax: 928-859-3044
info@dreamersrvpark.com
dreamersrvpark.com
RESORT NUMBER: 2181
GOOD SAM RATING: 7/8★/8
DIRECTIONS: From Jct of I-10 & Hwy 60E (Ex 31): Go NE 11.1 mi on Hwy 60, at MP 42.5, park on R. Wbnd: From Jct of I-10 & Ex 45 (Vicksburg Rd): Go N 7 mi on Vicksburg Rd to Hwy 60, SW 3 mi, park on L. Do not use address for GPS.
GPS COORDINATES: 33.70647°N/-113.82067°W
NOTATIONS: Check-in: Noon. Check-out: 11:00 a.m. Special discount rate for Coast members. Rate includes 2 adults per site, full hook-ups. Additional charges: Add'l person $4/night, dump station fee $5/night, tax 7.7%. Discount available Feb 1 - Dec 31 only. Max. RV length: 120 feet. Open: February 1–December 31.
STATE MAP: See page CTC 52.

50 amps, pull-through, dump station, cable tv, visitor mail, laundry, pets/restrictions, Wi-Fi access, hiking trails, horseshoes, group activities, recreation hall, tourist attraction, hot showers

ST DAVID

Apache Mobile Home and RV Park
79 North Apache Trail
St David, Arizona 85630
520-720-4634; fax: 520-720-9408
apachemobilepark@gmail.com
apachemobilepark.com
RESORT NUMBER: 2402
GOOD SAM RATING: 7.5/8.5★/8
DIRECTIONS: From Jct 1-10 (Ex 303) & Hwy 80: Go 6.5 mi SE on Hwy 80. Park on L.
GPS COORDINATES: 31.90576°N/-110.22724°W
NOTATIONS: Check-in: 1:00 p.m. Check-out: 11:00 a.m. 2021 Coast rate 20% off nightly rate. Current rates are $25 plus tax for 30 amp single lot or $35 plus tax for 50 amp double lot. Rate includes 2 adults, full hook-ups, free Wi-Fi in clubhouse and office, and trash service. Additional charges: 6.05% tax. Max. RV length: 45 feet. Open: Year-round.
STATE MAP: See page CTC 52.

50 amps, visitor mail, laundry, pets/restrictions, Wi-Fi access, hiking trails, recreation hall, age restrictions, tourist attraction, propane

TOPOCK

Route 66 Golden Shores RV Park
13021 Waterreed Way
Topock, Arizona 86436
928-788-1001
mgr@goldenshores.info
route66goldenshores.com
RESORT NUMBER: 2501
GOOD SAM RATING: 7/8.5★/7.5
DIRECTIONS: From Jct of I-40 & Oatman/Topock Hwy (Ex 1), Go 5 mi N on Oatman/Topock Hwy, then 0.75 mi W on Powell Lake Rd, park on L.
GPS COORDINATES: 34.77838°N/-114.49193°W
NOTATIONS: Check-in: 1:00 p.m. Check-out: 11:00 a.m. Special 20% discount rate for Coast members. Rate includes 2 adults, max 6 children per site, full hook-ups. Additional charges: Tax 5.725%. Max. RV length: 45 feet. Open: April 1–November 1.
STATE MAP: See page CTC 52.

50 amps, pull-through, dump station, laundry, pets/restrictions, Wi-Fi access, recreation hall, fishing, boating, tourist attraction

TUCSON

Crazy Horse RV Campgrounds
6660 South Craycroft Road
Tucson, Arizona 85756
800-279-6279; fax: 520-664-0761
crazyhorservpark@gmail.com
crazyhorservcampgrounds.com
RESORT NUMBER: 2398
GOOD SAM RATING: 9.5/9★/9
DIRECTIONS: From Jct of I-10 & Craycroft Rd (Ex 268): Take Frontage Rd to Craycroft Rd, N 0.25 mi on Craycroft Rd, park on L.
GPS COORDINATES: 32.13072°N/-110.87533°W
NOTATIONS: Check-in: 1:00 p.m. Check-out: 11:00 a.m. Special discount rate for Coast members. Rate includes 2 adults, 1 RV, 1 vehicle, full hook-ups, 30 or 50 amp. Additional charges: Extra adult $4/night, add'l vehicle $4/night, tax 6.1%. Basic cable TV unavailable, currently being upgraded. Coast rate available May-Sep only. Max. RV length: 40 feet. Open: May 1–September 30.
STATE MAP: See page CTC 52.

50 amps, visitor mail, laundry, pets/restrictions, Wi-Fi access, hiking trails, recreation hall, fishing, outdoor pool, golf, tourist attraction, propane, spa, hot showers

TUCSON

South Forty RV Ranch
3600 West Orange Grove Road
Tucson, Arizona 85741
520-297-2503
southfortyrvresort@gmail.com
southfortyrvranch.com
RESORT NUMBER: 2412
GOOD SAM RATING: 9.5/10★/9.5
DIRECTIONS: From Jct of I-10 & Orange Grove Rd (Ex 250): Go 1/2 mi E on Orange Grove Rd, resort on L.
GPS COORDINATES: 32.32396°N/-111.04147°W
NOTATIONS: Check-in: 2:00 p.m. Check-out: 11:00 a.m. 2021 $48/night rate for Coast members May 1-Sep 30. Rate includes 2 adults per site, water, sewer, 30 or 50 amp electric. Max 2 pets per site. After business hours call camp host at 520-912-1388. RVs must be 15 years or newer. No pop-ups or tents. Max. RV length: 45 feet. Open: Year-round.
STATE MAP: See page CTC 52.

50 amps, pull-through, visitor mail, laundry, pets/restrictions, Wi-Fi access, picnic tables, hot tub, hiking trails, horseshoes, group activities, recreation hall, outdoor pool, golf, tourist attraction, fitness, shopping, ice, grills

WILLCOX

Sagebrush RV Park
200 West Lewis Street
Willcox, Arizona 85643
520-384-2872
sagebrushrvpark@gmail.com
sagebrushrvpark.com
RESORT NUMBER: 1201
GOOD SAM RATING: NA
DIRECTIONS: From I-10 W: Ex 344/Bus I-10 through town to last business on R leaving town. From I-10 E: Ex 336/Bus I-10. 3 mi to 1st business on L entering town.
GPS COORDINATES: 32.2441°N/-109.8392°W
NOTATIONS: Check-in: 24 hours. Check-out: 1:00 p.m. Special discount rate for Coast members. Rate includes 1-4 people, full hook-ups, free Wi-Fi. Large and level sites. Additional charges: 50 amp $3/night plus city & county tax. Max. RV length: Unlimited. Open: Year-round.
STATE MAP: See page CTC 52.

50 amps, pull-through, visitor mail, laundry, pets/restrictions, internet access, Wi-Fi access, recreation hall, hot showers

YUMA

Blue Sky Estates/RV Resort
10247 South Frontage Road
Yuma, Arizona 85365
928-342-1444; res.: 877-367-5220
managerbluesky@yahoo.com
blueskyyuma.com
RESORT NUMBER: 2276
GOOD SAM RATING: 9.5/10★/9.5
DIRECTIONS: Wbnd on I-8: Ex 12, make a L, turn R on S Frontage Rd. Approx 0.75 mi on L with Western landscape in front. Ebnd on I-8: Ex 12, make a R, turn R on S Frontage Rd. Approx 0.75 mi on L. From Hwy 95 Sbnd from Quartzite: L on S Ave 11 E, approx 1 mi, R on S Frontage Rd, approx 0.75 mi on L.
GPS COORDINATES: 32.67013°N/-114.45633°W
NOTATIONS: Check-in: 1:00 p.m. Check-out: 11:00 a.m. Special discount rate for Coast members. Additional charges: Each person over 2 $4/night, 2nd pet $1/night. Drive-ups accepted. Max. RV length: 40 feet. Open: Year-round.
STATE MAP: See page CTC 52.

50 amps, pull-through, cable tv, visitor mail, laundry, pets/restrictions, internet access, hot tub, shuffleboard, recreation hall, outdoor pool, fitness, hot showers, handicap access

YUMA

Bonita Mesa RV Resort
9400 North Frontage Road
Yuma, Arizona 85365
928-342-2999
info@bonitamesa.com
bonitamesa.com
RESORT NUMBER: 2451
GOOD SAM RATING: 10/10★/10
DIRECTIONS: From Jct of I-8 & Ex 12 (Fortuna Rd): N on Fortuna Rd to Frontage Rd, W 1.5 mi. Resort on R.
GPS COORDINATES: 32.67159°N/-114.47103°W
NOTATIONS: Check-in: 9:00 a.m. Check-out: Noon. 2021 Coast rate $37.81/night avail from Apr 16 - Oct 10. Additional charges: Tax. Max. RV length: 45 feet. Open: May 1–September 30.

STATE MAP: See page CTC 52.

50 amps, laundry, pets/restrictions, Wi-Fi access, hot tub, shuffleboard, horseshoes, group activities, recreation hall, fishing, boating, outdoor pool, golf, tourist attraction, fitness, shopping

YUMA

Caravan Oasis Resort
10500 North Frontage Road
Yuma, Arizona 85365
928-342-1480
contact@carvanoasisresort.com
caravanoasisresort.com
RESORT NUMBER: 2318
GOOD SAM RATING: 9.5/9★/9
DIRECTIONS: From Jct I-8 at Ex 12 (Fortuna Rd): N on Fortuna Rd to Frontage Rd. W 0.2 mi. Resort on R.
GPS COORDINATES: 32.67127°N/-114.44962°W
NOTATIONS: Check-in: 11:00 a.m. Check-out: 11:00 a.m. Special discount rate for Coast members. Additional charges: Extra adult $5/night, tax 7%. No tents. Max. RV length: 40 feet. Open: Year-round.
STATE MAP: See page CTC 52.

50 amps, pull-through, laundry, pets/restrictions, hot tub, shuffleboard, horseshoes, group activities, recreation hall, age restrictions, outdoor pool, tennis, game room, tourist attraction, fitness, shopping

YUMA

Sundance RV Resort—Cal-Am Properties
13502 North Frontage Road
Yuma, Arizona 85367
888-940-8989; fax: 928-305-3510
stormh@cal-am.com
cal-am.com/resorts
RESORT NUMBER: 2248
GOOD SAM RATING: 9.5/10★/9
DIRECTIONS: E of Yuma on I-8, Ex 14, turn E on I-8 Frontage Rd on N side of I-8, 0.5 mi to resort on L.
GPS COORDINATES: 32.6691°N/-114.403°W
ELEVATION: 141 feet
NOTATIONS: Check-in: Noon. Check-out: 11:00 a.m. Special discount rate for Coast members. Drive-ups not accepted. Max. RV length: 38 feet. Open: Year-round.
STATE MAP: See page CTC 52.

50 amps, laundry, pets/restrictions, Wi-Fi access, hot tub, shuffleboard, horseshoes, group activities, recreation hall, church services, outdoor pool, fitness

ARKANSAS

EUREKA SPRINGS

NEW **Kettle Campground**
4119 East Van Buren
Eureka Springs, Arkansas 72632
479-253-9100
kettlecampground@gmail.com
kettlecampground.net
RESORT NUMBER: 2529
GOOD SAM RATING: 8/9.5★/8.5
DIRECTIONS: From Jct US-62 & SR-23S: Go 3 mi E on US-62. Park on L.
GPS COORDINATES: 36.39627°N/-93.70579°W
NOTATIONS: Check-in: 1:00 p.m. Check-out: Noon. 2021 Coast rate 20% discount. Rate includes 2 adults per site, full hook-ups. Additional charges: Add'l adult over 4 people $5 per adult, $5 per child, $5 additional vehicle, 50 amp site $40-$44/night, tax 9.75%. Max. RV length: 47 feet. Open: Year-round.
STATE MAP: See page CTC 53.

50 amps, pull-through, dump station, laundry, pets/restrictions, Wi-Fi access, playground, picnic tables, horseshoes, fishing, boating, outdoor pool, fire rings, firewood, ice

LAKE VILLAGE

NEW **Pecan Grove RV Park**
3768 Highway 82 & 65 South
Lake Village, Arkansas 71653
870-265-3005
info@pecangrove.net
turnoninn.com
RESORT NUMBER: 2524
GOOD SAM RATING: 8/9★/9
DIRECTIONS: Sbnd: From Jct of US 65 & US 82 (in Lake Village), S 2.7 mi on US 65 & US 82 (R); or Nbnd: From Jct US 65 & US 82, 1.7 mi on US 65 & US 82. Park on L.
GPS COORDINATES: 26.31095°N/-98.23727°W
NOTATIONS: Check-in: 3:00 p.m. Check-out: 11:00 a.m. 2021 Coast rate 20% discount on daily rate from Jun 1-Mar 1. Rate includes 2 adults per site, full hook-ups. Additional charges: Tax 12%. Max. RV length: 90 feet. Open: Year-round.
STATE MAP: See page CTC 53.

50 amps, pull-through, dump station, laundry, pets/restrictions, Wi-Fi access, playground, restaurant/snack bar, horseshoes, boating, fishing, boating, firewood

CALIFORNIA

COALINGA

Almond Tree Oasis RV Park
41191 South Glenn Avenue
Coalinga, California 93210
559-935-0711
manager@almondtreeoasispark.com
almondtreeoasispark.com
RESORT NUMBER: 2499
GOOD SAM RATING: 9.5/9.5★/8
DIRECTIONS: From Jct I-5 & Jayne Ave (Ex 325): Go 0.25 mi W on Jayne Ave, then 0.1 mi S on Glenn Ave, park on R.
GPS COORDINATES: 36.13492°N/-120.1647°W
NOTATIONS: Check-in: Noon. Check-out: 11:00 a.m. Special 25% discount rate for Coast members up to 7 nights. Rate includes 2 adults per site, full hook-ups, Wi-Fi. Additional charges: Online booking fee $2.50, tax 7.975%. Check-in iPad kiosk. Max. RV length: 45 feet. Open: Year-round.
STATE MAP: See page CTC 54.

50 amps, pull-through, visitor mail, laundry, pets/restrictions, Wi-Fi access, outdoor pool, tourist attraction, propane, hot showers

CORNING

Heritage RV Corning
975 Highway 99 West
Corning, California 96021
530-824-6130
info@heritagervcorning.com
heritagervcorning.com
RESORT NUMBER: 2289
GOOD SAM RATING: 10/10★/9
DIRECTIONS: From Jct of I-5 and Corning Rd Ex 631 (CR-A9.): Ex E side of Hwy to CR-99 W, S 300 ft. Go through Heritage Square entrance, park on L. Do not use GPS as it does not give correct information.
GPS COORDINATES: 39.92682°N/-122.2024°W
NOTATIONS: Check-in: 1:00 p.m. Check-out: 11:00 a.m. 2021 Coast discount 15%: Back-in $39.86, pull-through $45.80. Additional charges: Extra adult $5/night, additional vehicle $5/night, dump station $10, tax 10%. Open year round, Coast discount available Jul 1-Sep 30, Nov 15-Jan 31. Park open 24/7 with night registration. Office open Mon-Sat 8:30 a.m.-5:30 p.m. Max. RV length: 45 feet. Open: Year-round.
STATE MAP: See page CTC 54.

50 amps, pull-through, laundry, outdoor pool, shopping, propane, gambling casino

DESERT HOT SPRINGS

Caliente Springs
70-200 Dillon Road
Desert Hot Springs, California 92241
760-329-8400; fax: 760-251-2672
guestcenter@calientesprings.com
calientesprings.com
RESORT NUMBER: 2131
GOOD SAM RATING: 8.5/8.5★/9
DIRECTIONS: From Los Angeles: I-10 E Ex Palm Dr. Turn L. R at Dillon Rd. Resort 4 mi ahead. From AZ: I-10 W Ex Washington St. R for 5 mi. R on Thousand Palms Canyon Rd. L on Dillon Rd. Resort 9 mi ahead.
GPS COORDINATES: 33.9258°N/-116.4368°W
ELEVATION: 1,100 feet
NOTATIONS: Check-in: 1:00 p.m. Check-out: Noon. 2021 Coast member rate 20% discount (off season only). Rate includes 4 adults (55+), full hook-ups. Additional charges: Extra adult $5/night. Open year round, Coast discount valid Mar 1-Dec 31. Max. RV length: 45 feet. Open: March 3–December 31.
STATE MAP: See page CTC 54.

50 amps, pull-through, cable tv, laundry, pets/restrictions, internet access, Wi-Fi access, hot tub, shuffleboard, hiking trails, horseshoes, group activities, recreation hall, church services, age restrictions, outdoor pool, tennis, golf, game room, tourist attraction, fitness, shopping, hot showers, gambling casino, handicap access

DESERT HOT SPRINGS

Sky Valley Resort
74711 Dillon Road
Desert Hot Springs, California 92241
760-329-2900; fax: 760-671-7025
guestcenter@skyvalleyresorts.com
skyvalleyresort.com
RESORT NUMBER: 2102
GOOD SAM RATING: 9/8.5★/9
DIRECTIONS: From Los Angeles: I-10 E Ex Palm Dr. Turn L. R at Dillon Rd. Resort 10 mi ahead. From AZ: I-10 W Ex Washington St. R and go 5 mi. R on Thousand Palms Canyon Rd. L on Dillon Rd. Resort 4 mi ahead.
GPS COORDINATES: 33.9035°N/-116.3623°W
ELEVATION: 1,000 feet
NOTATIONS: Check-in: 1:00 p.m. Check-out: Noon. 2021 Coast member rate 20% discount (off season only). Rate includes 4 people, full hook-ups and cable. Additional charges: Extra person $5/night. Open year round, Coast discount valid Mar 1-Dec 31. Max. RV length: 40 feet. Open: March 1–December 31.
STATE MAP: See page CTC 54.

50 amps, pull-through, dump station, cable tv, laundry, pets/restrictions, internet access, Wi-Fi access, hot tub, shuffleboard, hiking trails, horseshoes, group activities, recreation hall, church services, outdoor pool, basketball, tennis, game room, tourist attraction, fitness, shopping, spa, hot showers, gambling casino, grocery, handicap access

GOLD RUN

Dutch Flat RV Resort
55 Canyon Creek Road
Gold Run, California 95717
530-389-8924; fax: 530-389-8924
info@dutchflatrvresort.com
dutchflatrvresort.com
RESORT NUMBER: 2242
GOOD SAM RATING: NA
DIRECTIONS: From I-80 Ex 145/Dutch Flat. Go to S side of interstate. Proceed through gas station parking lot to park entrance. 60 mi E of Sacramento, 70 mi W of Reno.
GPS COORDINATES: 39.2484°N/-120.4743°W
ELEVATION: 3,000 feet
NOTATIONS: Check-in: Noon–8:00 p.m. Check-out: Noon. Special discount rate of $30/night for Coast members avail year round. Rate includes 2 people, water, dump station or sewer. Additional charges: Extra person $2/night, electrical fee $3/night, dump station $27. Credit cards accepted. Drive-ups not accepted. Rental units available. Trip Points not accepted. Contact resort directly. Max. RV length: 65 feet. Open: Year-round.
STATE MAP: See page CTC 54.

30 amps, pull-through, dump station, visitor mail, pets/restrictions, Wi-Fi access, picnic tables, rental units, hiking trails, recreation hall, fishing, boating, outdoor pool, beach, golf, tourist attraction, shopping, propane, hot showers, grocery, rv supplies, tenting, winter sports, ice

LAKE ISABELLA

Lake Isabella RV Resort
11936 Highway 178
Lake Isabella, California 93240
760-379-2046; fax: 760-379-1873
lakeisabellaresort.com
RESORT NUMBER: 2278
GOOD SAM RATING: 7.5/7.5/8
DIRECTIONS: From Jct of Hwy 178 and Hwy 155: Go 6 mi E on Hwy 178 (Mt. Mesa). Resort on R.
GPS COORDINATES: 35.64353°N/-118.41383°W
ELEVATION: 2,600 feet
NOTATIONS: Check-in: Noon. Check-out: 11:00 a.m. Drive-ups not accepted. Max. RV length: 45 feet. Open: Year-round.
STATE MAP: See page CTC 54.

50 amps, laundry, pets/restrictions, Wi-Fi access, picnic tables, horseshoes, recreation hall, fishing, boating, outdoor pool, tenting, grills

LEMON COVE

Lemon Cove Village RV Park
32075 Sierra Drive
Lemon Cove, California 93244
559-370-4152
info@lemoncovevillagervpark.com
lemoncovevillagervpark.com
RESORT NUMBER: 2285
GOOD SAM RATING: 9/9.5★/9.5
DIRECTIONS: From Hwy 99 and CA Hwy 198: Go 21 mi E on CA Hwy 198, park on L.
GPS COORDINATES: 36.36946°N/-119.03272°W
NOTATIONS: Check-in: 3:00 p.m. Check-out: 11:00 a.m. Coast rate 20% discount off current rate. Coast members must make reservation 48 hrs or more in advance to receive discount. Drive-ups not eligible for discount. Additional charges: Extra person $3/night RV site or $5/night tent site. Max. RV length: 45 feet. Open: Year-round.
STATE MAP: See page CTC 54.

50 amps, pull-through, dump station, laundry, pets/restrictions, Wi-Fi access, recreation hall, outdoor pool, hot showers, fire rings, tenting, firewood, ice

MYERS FLAT

Giant Redwoods RV & Camp
400 Myers Avenue #83
Myers Flat, California 95554
707-943-9999
info@giantredwoodsrv.com
giantredwoodsrv.com
RESORT NUMBER: 2292
GOOD SAM RATING: 9/9.5★/9.5
DIRECTIONS: Nbnd from Jct of Hwy 101/Myers Flat (Ex 656): Ex to Ave of Giants, N 0.2 mi to Myers Ave, SW 0.4 mi to park. Sbnd from Jct of Hwy 101/Myers Flat: Ex to Ave of Giants, NW 100 ft to Myers Ave, SW 0.4 mi to park. (Caution: Do not use Boy Scout Rd).
GPS COORDINATES: 40.26247°N/-123.87744°W
NOTATIONS: Check-in: 1:00 p.m. Check-out: 11:00 a.m. Special 10% discount rate for Coast members year-round. Rate includes water, electric, back-in, 2 people, 1 dog, 1 vehicle/RV. All RV sites are 20/30/50 amp. Additional charges: Extra person $5/night, extra dog $2/night, extra vehicle $5, 2% tourism tax. No more than 6 people per site. Gate closes at 10 p.m. Rental units available. Trip Points not accepted. Contact resort directly. 10% discount for Coast members, max 4 people, no pets in rental units. Max. RV length: 45 feet. Open: Year-round.
STATE MAP: See page CTC 54.

50 amps, pull-through, dump station, cable tv, visitor mail, laundry, pets/restrictions, Wi-Fi access, playground, rental units, fishing, hiking trails, horseshoes, volleyball, firewood, handicap access, ice

NICE

The Aurora RV Park & Marina
2985 Lakeshore Boulevard
Nice, California 95464
707-274-5531
bob@enjoyourpark.com
enjoyourpark.com
RESORT NUMBER: 2288
GOOD SAM RATING: 8/9.5★/8
DIRECTIONS: From Jct Hwy 101 & Hwy 20: Hwy 20 E 35 mi to Nice, R on Hammond Ave for 0.3 mi, L on Lakeshore Blvd, park on R in 0.5 mi.
GPS COORDINATES: 39.12088°N/-122.85671°W
NOTATIONS: Check-in: 11:00 a.m. Check-out: 11:00 a.m. Special discount rate for Coast members. For reservations call resort directly. Additional charges: Dump station $10, additional person over 4 $2.50/night, tax 9%. City water & sewer. Max. RV length: 60 feet. Open: Year-round.
STATE MAP: See page CTC 54.

50 amps, laundry, fishing, group activities, fishing, tourist attraction, shopping, canoes, hot showers, gambling casino, grills

WINTERHAVEN

Pilot Knob RV Resort
3707 U.S. Highway 80
Winterhaven, California 92283
928-750-3775; res.: 800-378-3709
info.pilotknobresort@gmail.com
pilotknobrvcamping.com
RESORT NUMBER: 1643
GOOD SAM RATING: 7.5/8.5/8
DIRECTIONS: From I-8 Ex at Sidewinder Rd (approx 8 mi W of Yuma), S to Frontage Rd. Turn R. Resort on L in 0.25 mi.
GPS COORDINATES: 32.7469°N/-114.7639°W
NOTATIONS: Check-in: 9:00 a.m.–5:00 p.m. Check-out: 11:00 a.m. 2021 Coast rates starting at $22.50/night, 14 night max stay with discount. Additional charges: Resort fee $5/night. Resort on AZ time. We permit formaldehyde-free products only, no formaldehyde in black tanks. Max. RV length: 42 feet. Open: November 1–April 1.
STATE MAP: See page CTC 54.

50 amps, pull-through, visitor mail, pets/restrictions, fishing, shuffleboard, hiking trails, horseshoes, group activities, recreation hall, outdoor pool, tourist attraction, shopping, spa

YREKA

Waiiaka RV Park
240 Sharps Road
Yreka, California 96097
530-842-4500
waiiakarvpark@gmail.com
waiiakarvpark.com
RESORT NUMBER: 2296
GOOD SAM RATING: 9/10★/8.5
DIRECTIONS: From Jct of I-5 and SR-3: Ex 773 (Fort Jones/Etna Ex at S end of town), Ex to E side of Hwy to Fairlane Rd. N 0.3 mi to Sharps Rd, E 0.2 mi, park on L.
GPS COORDINATES: 41.70952°N/-122.6381°W
ELEVATION: 2,600 feet
NOTATIONS: Check-in: 2:00 p.m. Check-out: Noon. 2021 Coast rate: 30 amp $36 plus tax, 50 amp $37.80 plus tax. Site includes 2 persons. Additional charges: Extra adult $2/night, extra child $2/night, tax 12%. Showers metered 25 cents. Max. RV length: 45 feet. Open: November 1–March 31.
STATE MAP: See page CTC 54.

30 amps · pull-through · cable tv · laundry · pets/restrictions · Wi-Fi access · playground · propane · hot showers · tenting · ice

COLORADO

DURANGO

Oasis RV Resort & Cottages—Durango
30090 Highway 160 East
Durango, Colorado 81303
970-247-0783
oasisrvresortdurango@gmail.com
myrvoasis.com/durango
RESORT NUMBER: 2475
GOOD SAM RATING: 10/9★/9.5
DIRECTIONS: From W Jct of US-550 & US-160 (in town): E 7 mi on US-160, resort on R. From E Jct of US-160 & US-550: E 2.5 mi on US-160, resort on R.
GPS COORDINATES: 37.22839°N/-107.80282°W
NOTATIONS: Check-in: 1:00 p.m. Check-out: 11:00 a.m. Special discount rate for Coast members. Rate includes 2 adults per site, electric, water, sewer. Additional charges: Add'l person $6.50/night, tax 6.8%. Discount available Apr and Oct only. Max. RV length: 45 feet. Open: April 1–April 30; October 1–October 31.
STATE MAP: See page CTC 55.

50 amps · pull-through · cable tv · laundry · pets/restrictions · Wi-Fi access · playground · hiking trails · fishing · boating · outdoor pool · mini golf · tourist attraction · shopping · propane · grocery · rv supplies · firewood

CONNECTICUT

JEWETT CITY

Campers World on Hopeville Pond
28 Nowakowski Road
Jewett City, Connecticut 06351
860-376-2340
tim@educationworks.com
campersworldcampground.com
RESORT NUMBER: 2488
GOOD SAM RATING: 7.5/6/7
DIRECTIONS: From Jct I-395 Hwy 201: Go 0.5 mi E on Hopeville Rd, then 1 mi S on Bishop Crossing Rd, then 1 mi SE on Nowakowski Rd.
GPS COORDINATES: 41.60856°N/-71.93858°W
NOTATIONS: Check-in: 1:00 p.m. Check-out: 11:00 a.m. 2021 Coast rate $40. Rate includes 2 adults per site, full hook-ups. Additional charges: Tax 6.8%. Max. RV length: 40 feet. Open: April 15–October 15.
STATE MAP: See page CTC 56.

50 amps · pull-through · laundry · pets/restrictions · Wi-Fi access · fishing · fishing · boating · basketball · beach · tourist attraction · hot showers · tenting

FLORIDA

ARCADIA

NEW **Oak Haven MH & RV Park**
10307 Southwest Lettuce Lake Avenue
Arcadia, Florida 34269
863-494-4578
oakhavenpark@yahoo.com
oakhavenrvpark.com
RESORT NUMBER: 2516
GOOD SAM RATING: 8/9★/8.5
DIRECTIONS: From Jct I-75 (Ex 170) & Hwy 769 (Kings Hwy): Go 6 mi N on Hwy 769 (Kings Hwy), then 2 mi E on Hwy 761, then 0.25 mi S on Lettuce Lake Ave, park is on L.
GPS COORDINATES: 27.07457°N/-81.98487°W
NOTATIONS: Check-in: 1:00 p.m. Check-out: Noon. Special 20% discount off nightly rate for Coast members. Rate includes 2 adults per site, electric, water, sewer. Discount available Jun 1-Nov 1 only. Max. RV length: 45 feet. Open: Year-round.
STATE MAP: See page CTC 57.

50 amps · laundry · pets/restrictions · Wi-Fi access · shuffleboard · horseshoes · group activities · recreation hall · fishing · boating · outdoor pool · beach · golf · tourist attraction · shopping · hot showers

BONITA SPRINGS

Gulf Coast Camping Resort
24020 Production Circle
Bonita Springs, Florida 34135
239-992-3808; fax: 239-992-1375
info@gulfcoastcampingresort.com
gulfcoastcampingresort.com
RESORT NUMBER: 2312
GOOD SAM RATING: 7.5/8.5★/7.5
DIRECTIONS: From I-75 Ex 123: W on Corkscrew Rd to US 41. S on US 41 for 3 mi. L on Production Cir. Look for big blue/white Gulf Coast sign.
GPS COORDINATES: 26.38475°N/-91.8053°W
NOTATIONS: Check-in: Noon. Check-out: Noon. Special discount rate for Coast members. Additional charges: Extra adult $3/night, extra child $3/night, dump station $10, tax 11%. All sites are level, back-in, grass. Max. RV length: 40 feet. Open: October 2–April 30.
STATE MAP: See page CTC 57.

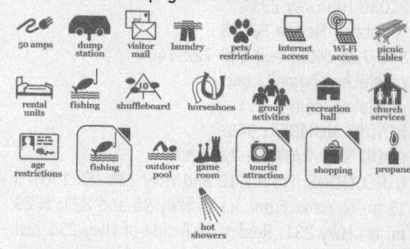

50 amps · dump station · visitor mail · laundry · pets/restrictions · internet access · Wi-Fi access · picnic tables · rental units · fishing · shuffleboard · horseshoes · group activities · recreation hall · church services · age restrictions · fishing · outdoor pool · game room · tourist attraction · shopping · propane · hot showers

COCOA

NEW **JOY RV Resort**
245 Flamingo Drive
Cocoa, Florida 32926
321-631-0305
info@joyrvpark.com
joyrvpark.com
RESORT NUMBER: 2586
GOOD SAM RATING: 9/9.5★/8.5
DIRECTIONS: From Jct I-95 & SR-520 (Ex 201): Go 0.25 mi W on SR-520, then 0.5 mi S on Tucker Ln, then 150 ft W on Flamingo Connector, then 0.5 mi S on Flamingo Dr. Park on E.
GPS COORDINATES: 44.36233°N/-103.4672°W
NOTATIONS: Check-in: 1:00 p.m. Check-out: 11:00 a.m. 2021 Coast rate $41-$51/night. Rate includes 2 adults per site, full hook-ups. Additional charges: Tax 7%. Max. RV length: 45 feet. Open: Year-round.
STATE MAP: See page CTC 57.

50 amps · pull-through · laundry · pets/restrictions · Wi-Fi access · picnic tables · hiking trails · fishing · boating · outdoor pool · beach

FORT PIERCE

Road Runner Travel Resort
5500 St Lucie Boulevard
Fort Pierce, Florida 34946
800-833-7108; fax: 772-464-0987
stay@roadrunnertravelresort.com
roadrunnertravelresort.com
RESORT NUMBER: 2188
GOOD SAM RATING: 9.5/10★/9
DIRECTIONS: From Jct of FL Tpke & SR 713 (Ex 152), N 5 mi on SR 713 to CR 608, E 1.2 mi, park on L. From Jct of I-95 & Indrio Rd (Ex 138), E 3.2 mi on Indrio Rd to SR 713, S 2.5 mi to CR 608 (St Lucie Blvd), E 1.2 mi, park on L.
GPS COORDINATES: 27.4854°N/-80.38°W
NOTATIONS: Check-in: 1:00 p.m. Check-out: 1:00 p.m. Special discount rate for Coast members. Rate includes one or two adult occupancy. Additional charges: Add'l person $3/night, tax 12%. Drive-ups not accepted. Max. RV length: 45 feet. Open: April 1–December 31.
STATE MAP: See page CTC 57.

50 amps · pull-through · dump station · laundry · pets/restrictions · internet access · Wi-Fi access · picnic tables · restaurant/snack bar · shuffleboard · horseshoes · group activities · recreation hall · church services · outdoor pool · tennis · golf · game room · propane · hot showers · grocery · rv supplies · ice

FOUNTAIN

Pine Lake RV Resort
21036 Highway 231
Fountain, Florida 32438
850-722-1401; fax: 850-722-1404
pinelakerv@gmail.com
pinelakerv.com
RESORT NUMBER: 943
GOOD SAM RATING: 7/8.5★/6
DIRECTIONS: From I-10 and Hwy 231 (Ex 130): S 15 mi to park. From Jct of Hwy 98 and 231: N 29 mi on Hwy 231. Resort on E side of Hwy 231 just N of an overpass.
GPS COORDINATES: 30.5302°N/-85.3957°W
NOTATIONS: Check-in: 1:00 p.m. Check-out: Noon. Special discount rate $27.50/night for Coast members avail year-round. Rate includes 2 adults, 2 children (under 12 yrs), partial hook-ups only (30 amp and water). Additional charges: Extra adult $4/night, extra child $2/night, add'l vehicle $2. No pop-ups or school buses. Max. RV length: 60 feet. Open: Year-round.
STATE MAP: See page CTC 57.

50 amps, pull-through, dump station, visitor mail, laundry, pets/restrictions, internet access, Wi-Fi access, picnic tables, fishing, hiking trails, horseshoes, group activities, recreation hall, fishing, tourist attraction, fitness, propane, hot showers, fire rings, rv supplies, gift shop, tenting, handicap access

LABELLE

NEW **Whisper Creek RV Resort**
1887 North State Road 29
LaBelle, Florida 33935
863-675-2323
whispercreek@whispercreek.com
inspirecom.com/communities/whisper-creek
RESORT NUMBER: 2531
GOOD SAM RATING: 9/10★/9.5
DIRECTIONS: From Jct of SR-80 & SR-29, N 1.8 mi on SR-29. Park on L.
GPS COORDINATES: 26.78713°N/-81.43482°W
NOTATIONS: Check-in: 2:00 p.m. Check-out: 11:00 a.m. 2021 Coast rate 20% discount from May 1-Sep 30. Rate includes 2 adults per site. Additional charges: Add'l adult $10. Max. RV length: 40 feet. Open: Year-round.
STATE MAP: See page CTC 57.

50 amps, pull-through, laundry, pets/restrictions, Wi-Fi access, playground, shuffleboard, horseshoes, recreation hall, fishing, outdoor pool, beach, golf, shopping, ice

NORTH FORT MYERS

Tamiami Village and RV Park
16555-A North Cleveland Avenue
North Fort Myers, Florida 33903
239-997-2697; fax: 239-997-3037
reservationist@tamiamicommunity.com
tamiamicommunity.com
RESORT NUMBER: 1876
GOOD SAM RATING: 9/9★/8
DIRECTIONS: From I-75 S: Take Ex 158 (old Ex 27), W to stoplight at US 41, turn L (S) and go 12 mi to park entrance opposite The Shell Factory entrance. Turn R into park, office on R. From I-75 N: Take Ex 143 (old Ex 26), W approx 7 mi to US 41 (Cleveland Ave). Turn R on US 41, go N 0.7 mi to park on L. Entrance is opposite The Shell Factory entrance. Turn L into park, office on R.
GPS COORDINATES: 26.6671°N/-81.8894°W
NOTATIONS: Check-in: 2:00 p.m. Check-out: 11:00 a.m. Special 10% discount rate for Coast members varies by site selection and is good for up to 2 weeks. Rate includes 2 people, full hook-ups. Additional charges: Extra adult $3/night, extra child $3/night, dump service $25, tax 6.5%. Dry site includes 1 dump free. No tenting. Quiet hours 10 p.m.-8 a.m. Max. RV length: 48 feet. Open: Year-round.
STATE MAP: See page CTC 57.

50 amps, dump station, visitor mail, laundry, pets/restrictions, internet access, Wi-Fi access, shuffleboard, horseshoes, group activities, recreation hall, fishing, boating, outdoor pool, beach, golf, tourist attraction, shopping

NORTH FORT MYERS

Upriver Campground RV Resort
17021 Upriver Drive
North Fort Myers, Florida 33917
239-543-3330; fax: 239-543-6663
info@upriver.com
upriver.com
RESORT NUMBER: 2234
GOOD SAM RATING: 9/9.5★/9.5
DIRECTIONS: From Jct I-75 and SR 78 (Ex 143/Bayshore Rd): E 1.6 mi on SR 78, resort on R.
GPS COORDINATES: 26.7116°N/-81.7852°W
NOTATIONS: Check-in: Noon. Check-out: 11:00 a.m. Special discount rate for Coast members: May 1-Oct 1 $44/night, Oct 1-Dec 1 $56/night. Rate includes 2 people and 2 pets. Additional charges: Extra person $5/night, extra pet $2/night. Max. RV length: 60 feet. Open: April 1–December 31.
STATE MAP: See page CTC 57.

50 amps, pull-through, laundry, pets/restrictions, internet access, Wi-Fi access, picnic tables, fishing, shuffleboard, hiking trails, horseshoes, group activities, boating, recreation hall, church services, outdoor pool, beach, tennis, golf, tourist attraction, fitness, shopping, propane, hot showers, gambling casino, rv supplies, ice

OKEECHOBEE

Water's Edge Motorcoach & RV Resort
12766 U.S. Highway 441 Southeast
Okeechobee, Florida 34974
863-357-5757; fax: 863-357-5756
info@okeervpark.com
okeechobeervpark.com
RESORT NUMBER: 2191
GOOD SAM RATING: 9/NA/10
DIRECTIONS: From Jct of SR 70 & SR 710 (E of town): E 5.9 mi on SR 710 to SE 86th Blvd. S 0.9 mi to Hwy 441. E 3.7 mi. Park on R. From Jct of SR 76 & SR 710 in Indiantown: W 11.5 mi on SR 76 to Hwy 441. N 5.3 mi. Park on L.
GPS COORDINATES: 27.1458°N/-80.6947°W
NOTATIONS: Check-in: 1:00 p.m.-3:00 p.m. Check-out: Noon. Special discount rate for Coast members Apr 1-Nov 15. 30 and 50 amp sites. Max. RV length: 45 feet. Open: Year-round.
STATE MAP: See page CTC 57.

50 amps, laundry, pets/restrictions, internet access, Wi-Fi access, shuffleboard, hiking trails, horseshoes, boating, recreation hall, fishing, boating, outdoor pool, tourist attraction, hot showers, gambling casino, handicap access

OKEECHOBEE

NEW **Zachary Taylor RV Resort**
2995 U.S. Highway 441 Southeast
Okeechobee, Florida 34974
863-763-3377
reserve@flrvresort.com
flrvresort.com
RESORT NUMBER: 2534
GOOD SAM RATING: 8.5/8.5★/8.5
DIRECTIONS: From Jct of SR-70 & US-Hwy 441, S 5.3 mi on US-Hwy 441 to SE 30th Terrace (across bridge), N 0.1 mi. Park on L.
GPS COORDINATES: 27.21231°N/-80.7983°W
NOTATIONS: Check-in: 1:00 p.m. Check-out: 11:00 a.m. 2021 Coast 20% discount avail May 1-Oct 15, min 2 nights, max 7 nights. Rate includes 2 adults per site, full hook-ups. Additional charges: Add'l adult $5/night. Max. RV length: Unlimited. Open: Year-round.
STATE MAP: See page CTC 57.

50 amps, pull-through, laundry, pets/restrictions, Wi-Fi access, shuffleboard, hiking trails, group activities, recreation hall, fishing, boating, shopping, indoor pool

OLD TOWN

Old Town Campground
2241 Southeast 349 Highway
Old Town, Florida 32680
352-542-9500
oldtowncampground@gmail.com
oldtowncampground.com
RESORT NUMBER: 2066
GOOD SAM RATING: NA
DIRECTIONS: 10 mi N. of Chiefland. 10 mi S. of Cross City. S on CR 349. Park 2 mi on L.
GPS COORDINATES: 29.5695°N/-82.9857°W
NOTATIONS: Check-in: Noon–6:00 p.m. Check-out: Noon. A 55+ campground. Special discount rate for Coast members of $24/night plus any upgrades. Discount can only be used a maximum of 5 nights. Rate includes 2 adults, partial hook-ups. Additional charges: 50 amp $3/night, sewer $4/night, add'l vehicle $2/night, tax 10%. Drive-ups not accepted. Max. RV length: 75 feet. Open: September 21–May 15.
STATE MAP: See page CTC 57.

50 amps, dump station, cable tv, visitor mail, laundry, pets/restrictions, internet access, Wi-Fi access, picnic tables, horseshoes, age restrictions, tourist attraction, hot showers, fire rings, firewood

ORANGE CITY

Luna Sands Resort
1440 East Minnesota Avenue
Orange City, Florida 32763
386-775-3996
lsr_reservations@travelresorts.com
lunasandsresort.com
RESORT NUMBER: 2255
GOOD SAM RATING: 8/8.5★/7.5
DIRECTIONS: From I-4 Ex 114: W on SR 472 1.5 mi. L on Minnesota Ave. Resort 0.5 mi on L. From Hwy 17-92: Ex SR 472 E for 1.5 mi. R on Minnesota Ave. Resort 0.5 mi on L.
GPS COORDINATES: 28.96829°N/-81.28802°W
ELEVATION: 49 feet
NOTATIONS: Check-in: 3:00 p.m. Check-out: Noon. 2021 Coast rate $37.50/night. Additional charges: Wi-Fi $10, add'l person $5/night, dump station $10, add'l vehicle $5, tax 6.5%. Limited 50 amp service. Drive-ups not accepted. Max. RV length: 35 feet. Open: Year-round.
STATE MAP: See page CTC 57.

50 amps · dump station · pets/restrictions · internet access · Wi-Fi access · playground · picnic tables · horseshoes · group activities · recreation hall · church services · fishing · boating · outdoor pool · basketball · golf · game room · tourist attraction · propane · hot showers · grocery · rv supplies · gift shop · firewood · ice

PUNTA GORDA

Alligator Park MH and RV Park
6400 Taylor Road Lot 112
Punta Gorda, Florida 33950
941-639-7000; fax: 941-575-8913
alligator-reception@comcast.net
alligatorpark.com
RESORT NUMBER: 1672
GOOD SAM RATING: 9.5/8.5/8.5
DIRECTIONS: From I-75 N or S: Ex 161. W on Jones Loop Rd. S on Taylor Rd (traffic light). S approx 2 mi. Park on L.
GPS COORDINATES: 26.8794°N/-82.0059°W
ELEVATION: 20 feet
NOTATIONS: Check-in: Noon. Check-out: 10:00 a.m. 2021 Coast rate $25/night. A senior resort park (55+), length of stay for children is restricted. Rate includes 2 adults, full hook-ups. 30 & 50 amp. Additional charges: Extra person $5/night. Credit cards accepted. Wi-Fi and cable access in campground for a fee with provider. Open year round, Coast discount available Apr 1-Dec 31, Apr & Dec 7 nights max. Max. RV length: 45 feet. Open: April 1–December 31.
STATE MAP: See page CTC 57.

50 amps · visitor mail · laundry · pets/restrictions · internet access · Wi-Fi access · shuffleboard · group activities · boating · recreation hall · church services · age restrictions · fishing · outdoor pool · beach · golf · game room · tourist attraction · hot showers · handicap access

PUNTA GORDA

NEW **Sun N Shade RV Resort**
14880 Tamiami Trail
Punta Gorda, Florida 33955
941-639-5388
sun_n_shade@hotmail.com
sunnshade.com
RESORT NUMBER: 2520
GOOD SAM RATING: 8/8/8.5
DIRECTIONS: From Jct of I-75 & CR-762/Tuckers Grade Rd (Ex 158), W 1 mi on CR-762 to US-41, S 3.4 mi. Park on L. Watch for tall American flag.
GPS COORDINATES: 26.8139°N/-81.95707°W
NOTATIONS: Check-in: 1:00 p.m. Check-out: 11:00 a.m. 2021 Coast discount 20% available May 1-Oct 31. Rate includes 2 adults per site, full hook-ups. Additional charges: Extra adult $3.50/night, Wi-Fi, tax 7%. Max. RV length: 45 feet. Open: Year-round.
STATE MAP: See page CTC 57.

50 amps · dump station · laundry · pets/restrictions · Wi-Fi access · horseshoes · fishing · boating · outdoor pool

SEBRING

NEW **Whispering Pines Village**
2323 Brunns Road
Sebring, Florida 33872
863-385-8806
info@whisperingpinesflorida.com
whisperingpinesflorida.com
RESORT NUMBER: 2532
GOOD SAM RATING: 8/8.5★/7
DIRECTIONS: From Jct of US 27 & Alt CR-634/Flare Rd: Go W 0.3 mi on Flare Rd, then S 0.3 mi on Brunns Rd. Park on R.
GPS COORDINATES: 27.48143°N/-81.48617°W
NOTATIONS: Check-in: 7:30 a.m. Check-out: 5:00 p.m. 2021 Coast rate 20% discount from May 1-Sep 30. Rate includes 2 adults per site, full hook-ups. Additional charges: Tax. Max. RV length: 42 feet. Open: Year-round.
STATE MAP: See page CTC 57.

50 amps · pull-through · laundry · pets/restrictions · Wi-Fi access · shuffleboard · horseshoes · group activities · fishing · outdoor pool · golf · game room · shopping

ZEPHYRHILLS

Ducky's Day Off RV Park
34408 State Road 54 West
Zephyrhills, Florida 33543
813-782-8223; res.: 866-234-2056
duckysdayoff@gmail.com
duckysdayoff.com
RESORT NUMBER: 1196
GOOD SAM RATING: 8/9★/7
DIRECTIONS: From I-75: Ex 279 (Wesley Chapel/Zephyrhills). E 6.8 mi to park on R, across from Home Depot.
GPS COORDINATES: 28.2185°N/-82.2472°W
NOTATIONS: Check-in: Noon–5:00 p.m. Check-out: Noon. Special discount rate for Coast members. Rate includes 2 people, 30-50 amp, full hook-ups. Additional charges: Extra person $2/night, 9% tax. Adult park, under 50 years limited to 30 days. No tent camping. If you have a reservation and the office is closed, an envelope containing a map, instructions and your name on the front will be placed on the front door. Drive-ups not accepted. Max. RV length: 50 feet. Open: Year-round.
STATE MAP: See page CTC 57.

50 amps · pull-through · visitor mail · pets/restrictions · internet access · Wi-Fi access · shuffleboard · horseshoes · group activities · recreation hall · age restrictions · outdoor pool · game room · shopping

GEORGIA

BRUNSWICK

Southern Retreat RV Park
7445 Blythe Island Highway
Brunswick, Georgia 31523
912-261-1025; fax: 912-265-5861
southernretreatrv@hotmail.com
southernretreatrvpark.com
RESORT NUMBER: 1324
GOOD SAM RATING: 9.5/9.5★/9
DIRECTIONS: From I-95: Ex 29. S-bound turn R, N-bound turn L. 0.5 mi to 2nd traffic light. R 0.2 mi to park on L.
GPS COORDINATES: 31.1444°N/-81.5793°W
NOTATIONS: Check-in: 1:00 p.m. Check-out: 11:00 a.m. Special discount rate of $38.08/night for Coast members subject to availability. Rate includes 4 people, 50 amp. Additional charges: Dump station $15, tax 12%. Rate not available holiday weekends or special events. Internet access in clubhouse and Wi-Fi access in campground. Max. RV length: 85 feet. Open: Year-round.
STATE MAP: See page CTC 58.

50 amps · pull-through · visitor mail · laundry · pets/restrictions · internet access · Wi-Fi access · playground · restaurant/snack bar · outdoor pool · propane

ELKO

NEW **Twin Oaks RV Park**
305 Georgia Highway 26 East
Elko, Georgia 31025
478-987-9361
info@twinoaksrvpark.com
twinoaksrvpark.com
RESORT NUMBER: 2544
GOOD SAM RATING: 9/9★/9.5
DIRECTIONS: From Jct of I-75 (Ex 127) & GA 26: Go 500 ft E on GA 26. Park on L.
GPS COORDINATES: 32.33598°N/-83.76465°W
NOTATIONS: Check-in: 1:00 p.m. Check-out: Noon. 2021 Coast rate $42/night. Rate includes 2 adults per site, full hook-ups. Additional charges: Add'l adult $5/night, add'l child $5/night, add'l vehicle $5/night, tax 6%. Max. RV length: 75 feet. Open: Year-round.
STATE MAP: See page CTC 58.

50 amps · pull-through · laundry · pets/restrictions · Wi-Fi access · playground · picnic tables · hiking trails · horseshoes · recreation hall · fishing · outdoor pool · tourist attraction · fire rings · rv supplies · firewood · ice

GEORGIA

METTER

NEW **Beaver Run RV Park**
22321 Excelsior Church Road
Metter, Georgia 30439
912-362-4737
camp@beaverrunrvpark.com
beaverrunrvpark.com
RESORT NUMBER: 2551
GOOD SAM RATING: 8.5/9.5★/9.5
DIRECTIONS: From Jct of I-16 (Ex 111) & Excelsior Church Rd, Go 0.25 mi S on Excelsior Church Rd. Park on R.
GPS COORDINATES: 32.33401°N/-81.95462°W
NOTATIONS: Check-in: 1:00 p.m. Check-out: Noon. 2021 Coast rate $38/night. Rate includes 2 adults per site, full hook-ups. Additional charges: Add'l adult $5/night; tax 8%. Max. RV length: 100 feet. Open: Year-round.
STATE MAP: See page CTC 58.

50 amps · pull-through · dump station · laundry · pets/restrictions · Wi-Fi access · picnic tables · hiking trails · basketball · propane · canoes · fire rings · rv supplies · firewood · ice

WOODBINE

Walkabout Camp and RV Park
742 Old Still Road
Woodbine, Georgia 31569
912-729-4110; fax: 912-729-4110
info@walkaboutcamp.com
walkaboutcamp.com
RESORT NUMBER: 813
GOOD SAM RATING: 8.5/8.5★/8.5
DIRECTIONS: From I-95: Ex 7 (Harrietts Bluff Rd). W 0.3 mi. L on Old Still Rd. S 0.3 mi to resort.
GPS COORDINATES: 30.8406°N/-81.6769°W
NOTATIONS: Check-in: 1:00 p.m.–8:00 p.m. Check-out: 11:00 a.m. Special discount rate for Coast members. Additional charges: 50 amp $3/night, extra adult $2/night, tax 10%. Call park for arrivals after 8 p.m. After 8 p.m. use late check-in box at office. Extra long rigs over 45 ft should call ahead to reserve longer sites. Max. RV length: 45 feet. Open: Year-round.
STATE MAP: See page CTC 58.

50 amps · pull-through · dump station · visitor mail · laundry · pets/restrictions · internet access · Wi-Fi access · playground · picnic tables · fishing · recreation hall · fishing · outdoor pool · beach · game room · tourist attraction · shopping · propane · hot showers · tenting

IDAHO

CALDWELL

NEW **Country Corners RV Park and Campground**
17671 Oasis Road
Caldwell, Idaho 83607
208-453-8791
manager@countrycornersrvpark.com
countrycornersrvpark.com
RESORT NUMBER: 2574
GOOD SAM RATING: 8/9.5★/9.5
DIRECTIONS: From Jct I-84 & Oasis Rd (Ex 17): Go 0.25 mi E Oasis on Rd. Park on R.
NOTATIONS: Check-in: 1:00 p.m. Check-out: Noon. 2021 Coast rate $44. Rate includes 2 adults per site, full hook-ups. Additional charges: Tax 8%. Max. RV length: 45 feet. Open: Year-round.
STATE MAP: See page CTC 59.

50 amps · pull-through · laundry · pets/restrictions · Wi-Fi access · picnic tables · hiking trails · horseshoes · recreation hall · fishing · boating · golf · fire rings · grocery · tenting · ice

CHALLIS

NEW **Challis Golf Course RV Park**
210 Golf Club Lane
Challis, Idaho 83226
208-879-5500
relax@golfcourserv.com
golfcourserv.com
RESORT NUMBER: 2552
GOOD SAM RATING: 6/9.5★/7.5
DIRECTIONS: From Jct US 93 & Hwy 75: Go 2.25 mi N on US 93, then 1.25 mi W on Main (becomes Garden Creek Rd), then 0.125 mi S on Emily Ln. Park on R.
GPS COORDINATES: 44.50391°N/-114.24709°W
ELEVATION: 5,355 feet
NOTATIONS: Check-in: 11:00 a.m. Check-out: 11:00 a.m. 2021 Coast rate $31-$36/night avail all year except 8/3-8/16. Rate includes 2 adults per site, full hook-ups. Additional charges: Tax 6%. Max. RV length: 45 feet. Open: April 15–October 15.
STATE MAP: See page CTC 59.

50 amps · pull-through · laundry · pets/restrictions · Wi-Fi access · picnic tables · hiking trails · horseshoes · fishing · golf · ice

CHALLIS

NEW **Round Valley Park**
211 Ramshorn Drive
Challis, Idaho 83226
208-879-2393
roundvalleypark@outlook.com
roundvalleyrv.com
RESORT NUMBER: 2572
GOOD SAM RATING: 7/9★/9
DIRECTIONS: From Jct US 93 & Hwy 75: Go 2 mi N on US 93, then 0.1 mi E on Ramshorn Ln. Park at end.
GPS COORDINATES: 44.50109°N/-114.22208°W
ELEVATION: 5,100 feet
NOTATIONS: Check-in: 1:00 p.m. Check-out: Noon. 2021 Coast rate $35.10/night, not avail Jul and Aug. Rate includes 2 adults per site, full hook-ups. Additional charges: Tax 8%. Max. RV length: 48 feet. Open: April 15–November 30.
STATE MAP: See page CTC 59.

50 amps · pull-through · laundry · pets/restrictions · Wi-Fi access · playground · picnic tables · hiking trails · fishing

COEUR D'ALENE

NEW **Wolf Lodge Campground**
12329 East Frontage Road
Coeur D'Alene, Idaho 83814
208-664-2812
info@wolflodgecampground.com
wolflodgecampground.com
RESORT NUMBER: 2578
GOOD SAM RATING: 8/8.5★/9
DIRECTIONS: From Jct I-90 & Hwy 97 (Ex 22): Go 0.1 mi N on Hwy 97, then 1.5 mi E on Frontage Rd. Park on L.
GPS COORDINATES: 47.63113°N/-116.6162°W
NOTATIONS: Check-in: 1:00 p.m. Check-out: 11:00 a.m. 2021 Coast rate $45-$54/night. Rate includes 2 adults per site, full hook-ups. Additional charges: Tax 8%. Max. RV length: 45 feet. Open: May 1–September 30.
STATE MAP: See page CTC 59.

50 amps · pull-through · dump station · laundry · pets/restrictions · Wi-Fi access · playground · picnic tables · hiking trails · horseshoes · boating · fishing · basketball · tourist attraction · shopping · grocery · rv supplies · firewood · ice

GLENNS FERRY

Trail Break RV Park & Campground
432 North Bannock Street
Glenns Ferry, Idaho 83623
208-366-7745
camp@trailbreakrvpark.com
trailbreakrvpark.com
RESORT NUMBER: 2331
GOOD SAM RATING: NA
DIRECTIONS: From Wbnd I-84: Ex 121, L at top of the ramp. R on frontage rd, 1 mi to flashing light at corner of Old Hwy 30 and Bannock. From Ebnd I-84: Ex #120, R at bottom of ramp. Resort down the street on L.
GPS COORDINATES: 42.95657°N/-115.30774°W
NOTATIONS: Check-in: 2:00 p.m. Check-out: Noon. Special discount rate for Coast members. Additional charges: Add'l adult $5, add'l child $2, tax. Max. RV length: 65 feet. Open: Year-round.
STATE MAP: See page CTC 59.

50 amps · pull-through · cable tv · laundry · pets/restrictions · Wi-Fi access · picnic tables · hiking trails · horseshoes · tourist attraction · tenting · firewood · ice · grills

GLENNS FERRY

NEW **Y Knot Winery & RV Park**
11204 North Bar 21 Drive
Glenns Ferry, Idaho 83623
208-366-2313
yknotwinery@gmail.com
yknotwinery.com/rv-park
RESORT NUMBER: 2542
GOOD SAM RATING: 6/NA/7.5
DIRECTIONS: From Jct of I-84 & I-84 Bus/East 1st Ave (Ex 121): Go 0.75 mi W on East 1st Ave to Commercial St, then 0.5 mi S on Commercial St to Madison Ave, then 0.75 mi W on Madison Ave. Park on R.
GPS COORDINATES: 42.94545°N/-115.31205°W

NOTATIONS: Check-in: 1:00 p.m. Check-out: 11:00 a.m. 2021 Coast rate $27-$32/night avail Sun-Thu Mar-Oct and all week in winter. Rate includes 2 adults per site, full hook-ups. Additional charges: Tax 8%. Max. RV length: 40 feet. Open: Year-round.
STATE MAP: See page CTC 59.

50 amps, pull-through, pets/restrictions, restaurant/snack bar, hiking trails, horseshoes, fishing, boating, golf, ice

KAMIAH

NEW Long Camp RV Park
4192 Highway 12
Kamiah, Idaho 83536
208-935-7922
connie@longcamprvpark.com
longcamprvpark.com
RESORT NUMBER: 2571
GOOD SAM RATING: 7/8.5★/9
DIRECTIONS: From Jct SR 13 & US 12 (W of Kooskia): Go 6 mi NW on US 12 (MP 68). Park on L.
GPS COORDINATES: 46.2171°N/-116.00657°W
NOTATIONS: Check-in: Noon. Check-out: 11:00 a.m. 2021 Coast rate $31.50-$36/night. Rate includes 2 adults per site, full hook-ups. Additional charges: Tax 8%. Max. RV length: 45 feet. Open: Year-round.
STATE MAP: See page CTC 59.

50 amps, pull-through, laundry, pets/restrictions, Wi-Fi access, picnic tables, restaurant/snack bar, hiking trails, gambling casino, fire rings, ice

MOUNTAIN HOME

NEW Gem State RV Park
220 East 10th North
Mountain Home, Idaho 83647
208-587-5111
gemstaterv.campground@gmail.com
gemstatervpark.com
RESORT NUMBER: 2577
GOOD SAM RATING: 7/9★/7
DIRECTIONS: From Jct I-84 & Hwy 51 (Ex 95): Go 1.75 mi S on Hwy 51 to 2nd St, then 0.75 mi N on 2nd St to E 10th St N, then 0.25 mi E on E 10th St N. Park on L.
GPS COORDINATES: 43.14156°N/-115.699°W
ELEVATION: 3,150 feet
NOTATIONS: Check-in: 2:00 p.m. Check-out: 11:00 a.m. 2021 Coast rate $33.75/night. Rate includes 2 adults per site, full hook-ups. Additional charges: Tax 8%. Max. RV length: 100 feet. Open: Year-round.
STATE MAP: See page CTC 59.

50 amps, pull-through, cable tv, laundry, pets/restrictions, Wi-Fi access, playground, picnic tables, hiking trails, horseshoes, recreation hall, fishing, rv supplies, ice

MOYIE SPRINGS

NEW The Hemlocks RV and Lodging
73400 U.S.-2
Moyie Springs, Idaho 83845
208-267-4363
johnneywalker@icloud.com
hemlockslodging.com
RESORT NUMBER: 2573
GOOD SAM RATING: 7/8.5★/8
DIRECTIONS: From Jct US Hwy 95 & US Hwy 2: Go 9.2 mi E on US Hwy 2. Park on R.
GPS COORDINATES: 48.70937°N/-116.12767°W
ELEVATION: 2,600 feet
NOTATIONS: Check-in: Noon. Check-out: 11:00 a.m. 2021 Coast rate $53.10-62.10/night avail Apr 1-Oct 31. Rate includes 2 adults per site, full hook-ups. Additional charges: Tax 8%. Max. RV length: 48 feet. Open: April 1–October 31.
STATE MAP: See page CTC 59.

50 amps, pull-through, dump station, laundry, pets/restrictions, Wi-Fi access, picnic tables, hiking trails, fishing, boating, propane, gambling casino, fire rings, firewood, ice

POST FALLS

NEW Coeur d'Alene RV Resort
2652 East Mullan Avenue
Post Falls, Idaho 83854
208-773-3527
cdarvparkmanager@gmail.com
RESORT NUMBER: 2570
GOOD SAM RATING: 9.5/9★/9.5
DIRECTIONS: From Jct I-90 & Hwy 41 (Ex 7): Go 0.25 mi N on Hwy 41 to E Mullan Ave, then 1 mi W on E Mullan Ave. Park on L.
GPS COORDINATES: 47.71564°N/-116.91235°W
NOTATIONS: Check-in: 1:00 p.m. Check-out: 11:00 a.m. 2021 Coast rate $45-$48.60/night. Rate includes 2 adults per site, full hook-ups. Additional charges: Tax 8%. Max. RV length: 45 feet. Open: Year-round.
STATE MAP: See page CTC 59.

50 amps, pull-through, dump station, cable tv, laundry, pets/restrictions, Wi-Fi access, playground, picnic tables, hiking trails, recreation hall, fishing, boating, basketball, propane, rv supplies, ice

ILLINOIS

BUSHNELL

Timber Lakes Campground
23200 North 2000 Road
Bushnell, Illinois 61422
309-772-3609
entlc@comcast.net
camptimberview.com
RESORT NUMBER: 2098
GOOD SAM RATING: NA
DIRECTIONS: From N on Rt 41: 0.5 mi past Jct of Rt 9 and turn L. 1 mi to stop. L approx 0.5 mi to front gate. From S: Rt 41 to N edge of Bushnell. 1 mi to 2000th Rd. R approx 1.75 mi to front gate.
GPS COORDINATES: 40.57°N/-90.4623°W
NOTATIONS: Check-in: 10:00 a.m. Check-out: 11:00 a.m. Rate includes 2 people, 30 amp, water. Additional charges: Extra adult $5/night, AC $2.50/night, 50 amp $2.50/night. Max. RV length: 40 feet. Open: April 15–October 14.
STATE MAP: See page CTC 60.

50 amps, dump station, laundry, pets/restrictions, playground, picnic tables, restaurant/snack bar, fishing, hiking trails, horseshoes, recreation hall, basketball, beach, volleyball, game room, fitness, propane, hot showers, paddle boats, fire rings, firewood, ice

EAST PEORIA

Mill Point Park
310 Ash Lane
East Peoria, Illinois 61611
309-231-6497; res.: 309-231-9495
camp@millpointrvpark.com
millpointrvpark.com
RESORT NUMBER: 2164
GOOD SAM RATING: 6.5/9.5★/8.5
DIRECTIONS: From Jct of I-74 (Ex 95) & Hwy 116: 5 mi E on Hwy 116, 3.5 mi N on Hwy 26, 0.75 mi W on Millpoint Rd.
GPS COORDINATES: 40.7565°N/-89.5578°W
NOTATIONS: Check-in: 24 hours. Check-out: Noon. Additional charges: Extra adult $3/night, extra child $3/night, 50 amp $5/night. Max. RV length: 85 feet. Open: Year-round.
STATE MAP: See page CTC 60.

50 amps, pull-through, visitor mail, pets/restrictions, internet access, Wi-Fi access, picnic tables, hiking trails, boating, tourist attraction, hot showers, gambling casino, fire rings, tenting, firewood

INDIANA

HOWE

Grand View Bend
4630 North 100 East
Howe, Indiana 46746
574-575-5927
grandviewbend@gmail.com
grandviewbend.com
RESORT NUMBER: 37
GOOD SAM RATING: 5.5/9★/8.5
DIRECTIONS: From IN Toll Rd: Ex 121/LaGrange. S (R) approx 2 mi on Hwy 9. E (L) on Hwy 120. 1 mi through the town of Howe. R on Hwy 100 E. 0.5 mi to the park on the R. Watch for signs.
GPS COORDINATES: 41.7088°N/-85.408°W
NOTATIONS: Check-in: 1:00 p.m. Check-out: Noon. Special discount rate for Coast members. Rate includes electric, water, 2 adults per site. Honey wagon available for fee. Max. RV length: 43 feet. Open: April 15–October 15.
STATE MAP: See page CTC 60.

50 amps, dump station, pets/restrictions, Wi-Fi access, playground, fishing, shuffleboard, hiking trails, horseshoes, group activities, boating, fishing, outdoor pool, mini golf, basketball, tennis, tourist attraction, shopping

INDIANA

NORTH VERNON

Muscatatuck Park
325 North State Highway 3 & 7
North Vernon, Indiana 47265
812-346-2953
greg.jcpr@frontier.com
muscatatuckpark.com
RESORT NUMBER: 980
GOOD SAM RATING: NA
DIRECTIONS: From S of N Vernon: St Hwy 3 and 7. Park is on R leaving N Vernon. From I-65 at Seymour: Approx 13 mi E to N Vernon on Hwy 50 to Jct of Hwy 3 and 7 at second stoplight. R (S) onto Hwy 3 and 7, park on R. Avoid 2 sharp turns from front entrance by using Gum St entrance (marked by signs on Hwy 50).
GPS COORDINATES: 38.9883°N/-85.6231°W
NOTATIONS: Check-in: 2:00 p.m. Check-out: 1:00 p.m. Special 25% discount rate for Coast members. Rate includes 6 people, 30 amp, water, electric. Sewer sites offered if available. Additional charges: Firewood $10/20 pcs, tax 7%. No showers Oct-Apr. Max. RV length: 65 feet. Open: Year-round.
STATE MAP: See page CTC 60.

30 amps, dump station, visitor mail, pets/restrictions, internet access, playground, picnic tables, fishing, hiking trails, horseshoes, fishing, basketball, volleyball, tourist attraction, canoes, hot showers, ball field, fire rings, tenting, firewood, handicap access

RICHMOND

Deer Ridge Camping Resort
3696 Smyrna Road
Richmond, Indiana 47374
765-939-0888
info@deerridgecampingresort.com
deerridgecampingresort.com
RESORT NUMBER: 2287
GOOD SAM RATING: 8.5/9★/8.5
DIRECTIONS: From Jct of I-70 & SR 227 (Ex 153): S 0.1 mi on SR 227 to Smyrna Rd, E 0.5 mi, resort on L.
GPS COORDINATES: 39.86586°N/-84.85122°W
NOTATIONS: Check-in: 2:00 p.m. Check-out: Noon. 20% discount rate for Coast members, holidays excluded. Rate includes 2 adults, children or grandchildren under 18, water, 30 amp and sewer. Additional charges: 50 amp $5/night, pull thru $5/night, extra adult over 18 $5/night, 12% tax. Max. RV length: 60 feet. Open: May 1–October 31.
STATE MAP: See page CTC 60.

50 amps, laundry, pets/restrictions, Wi-Fi access, playground, picnic tables, fishing, horseshoes, recreation hall, outdoor pool, mini golf, hot showers, grocery, rv supplies, firewood, ice

KANSAS

ABILENE

Covered Wagon RV Park
803 South Buckeye
Abilene, Kansas 67410
800-864-4053
reservations@coveredwagonrvks.com
coveredwagonrvks.com
RESORT NUMBER: 2481
GOOD SAM RATING: 8.5/10★/7.5
DIRECTIONS: From Jct I-70 (Ex 275) & Buckeye St: Go S 2.25 mi on Buckeye St, resort on R.
GPS COORDINATES: 38.90743°N/-97.21412°W
NOTATIONS: Check-in: Noon. Check-out: 11:00 a.m. Special discount rate for Coast members. Discount available Oct to Mar only. Rate includes 2 adults per site, full hook-ups, Wi-Fi, cable TV. Additional charges: Tax 8.75%. Max. RV length: 70 feet. Open: October 1–March 31.
STATE MAP: See page CTC 62.

50 amps, pull-through, dump station, cable tv, laundry, pets/restrictions, Wi-Fi access, playground, horseshoes, outdoor pool, tourist attraction, shopping, propane

EMPORIA

Emporia RV Park
4601 West U.S. Highway 50
Emporia, Kansas 66801
620-343-3422; res.: 800-343-3422
charlotte@emporiarvpark.net
emporiarvpark.com
RESORT NUMBER: 1538
GOOD SAM RATING: 7/9★/5.5
DIRECTIONS: From N-bound I-35: Ex 127A, 0.5 mi W on Hwy 50 to park on L. From S-bound I-35: Ex 127, W for 0.5 mi on Hwy 50 to park on L.
GPS COORDINATES: 38.41177°N/-96.24119°W
ELEVATION: 1,150 feet
NOTATIONS: Check-in: 1:00 p.m.–2:00 p.m. Check-out: Noon. Special discount rate for Coast members. Rate includes 2 adults, 30 amp, water. Additional charges: Extra person $5/night, AC $2/night, heat $2/night, 50 amp $2/night, cable $2/night, sewer $2/night. Max. RV length: 70 feet. Open: Year-round.
STATE MAP: See page CTC 62.

50 amps, pull-through, cable tv, laundry, pets/restrictions, internet access, Wi-Fi access, playground, fishing, rv supplies, tenting

RUSSELL

Triple J RV Park
187 East Edwards
Russell, Kansas 67665
785-483-4826; fax: 785-483-2172
triplejrv@ruraltel.net
triplejrvpark.com
RESORT NUMBER: 1504
GOOD SAM RATING: 7.5/10★/8.5
DIRECTIONS: From Jct I-70 (Ex 184) & US-281: Go 500 ft N on US-281 (at Cenex Gas), then 500 ft W on E Edwards Ave.
GPS COORDINATES: 38.8923°N/-98.8483°W
NOTATIONS: Check-in: Noon. Check-out: 11:00 a.m. Special discount rate for Coast members. Rate includes 2 adults per site, full hook-ups, Wi-Fi, cable TV. Additional charges: Add'l person $2/night. Max. RV length: 85 feet. Open: Year-round.
STATE MAP: See page CTC 62.

50 amps, pull-through, cable tv, laundry, pets/restrictions, Wi-Fi access, playground, picnic tables, hiking trails, recreation hall, fishing, golf, tourist attraction, shopping, hot showers, tenting

WICHITA

Air Capital RV Park
609 East 47th Street South
Wichita, Kansas 67216
316-201-1250; fax: 316-201-1257
aircapitalrvpark@yahoo.com
aircapital-rvpark.com
RESORT NUMBER: 2480
GOOD SAM RATING: 9/10★/9.5
DIRECTIONS: From Jct I-135 & 47th St (Ex 1A): Go 0.25 mi W on 47th St, then 300 ft S on Emporia St.
GPS COORDINATES: 37.60778°N/-97.33006°W
NOTATIONS: Check-in: 1:00 p.m. Check-out: 11:00 a.m. Special 10% discount rate for Coast members. Rate includes 2 adults per site, full hook-ups, Wi-Fi, cable TV. After hours check-in call 316-573-7958. Max. RV length: Unlimited. Open: Year-round.
STATE MAP: See page CTC 62.

50 amps, pull-through, cable tv, laundry, pets/restrictions, Wi-Fi access, tourist attraction, shopping, gambling casino, handicap access

KENTUCKY

PADUCAH

Duck Creek RV Park
2540 John L Puryear Drive
Paducah, Kentucky 42003
270-415-0404; fax: 270-415-0501
info@duckcreekrvpark.com
duckcreekrv.com
RESORT NUMBER: 2185
GOOD SAM RATING: 9.5/10★/7.5
DIRECTIONS: From Jct I-24 and SR 1954/Bus Loop 24 (Ex 11), N 0.5 mile on SR 1954. Park on R.
GPS COORDINATES: 37.0214°N/-88.5867°W
NOTATIONS: Check-in: Noon. Check-out: 11:00 a.m. 2022 Coast rate 30 amp $32/night plus tax, 50 amp $33/night plus tax avail year round. Additional charges: Add'l adult $2/night, tax. Max. RV length: 60 feet. Open: Year-round.
STATE MAP: See page CTC 63.

50 amps, pull-through, dump station, cable tv, laundry, pets/restrictions, internet access, Wi-Fi access, picnic tables, recreation hall, fishing, boating, outdoor pool, golf, tourist attraction, propane, hot showers, gambling casino, grocery, rv supplies, firewood, handicap access, ice

MAINE

OLD ORCHARD BEACH

Old Orchard Beach Campground
27 Ocean Park Road
Old Orchard Beach, Maine 04064
207-934-4477
reservations@gocamping.com
gocamping.com

RESORT NUMBER: 2429
GOOD SAM RATING: 10/9.5★/10
DIRECTIONS: From Jct I-95 (Ex 36) & I-195: Go 2 mi E on I-195, then Rte 5 joins I-195. Resort immediately on R.
GPS COORDINATES: 43.5094°N/-70.4291°W
NOTATIONS: Check-in: 1:00 p.m. Check-out: 11:00 a.m. 25% discount for Coast members. Additional charges: Extra adult $10/night, extra child $6/night, dump station $25, tax 9%. Drive-ups not accepted. Discount available from May 1-Jun 23, 2022 and Sep 6-Nov 1, 2022. Discount not available on holiday weekends. Max. RV length: 50 feet. Open: May 1–November 1; September 6–October 7.
STATE MAP: See page CTC 64.

50 amps, pull-through, dump station, laundry, pets/restrictions, Wi-Fi access, playground, picnic tables, horseshoes, group activities, fishing, boating, outdoor pool, basketball, golf, game room, tourist attraction, fire rings, grocery, rv supplies, tenting, firewood, ice

MASSACHUSETTS

LANESBOROUGH

Mt Greylock Campsite Park
15 Scott Road
Lanesborough, Massachusetts 01237
413-447-9419
info@mtgreylockcampsitepark.com
mtgreylockcampsitepark.com
RESORT NUMBER: 2473
GOOD SAM RATING: 8.5/10★/10
DIRECTIONS: From Jct of US 7 & N Main St, N 0.8 mi on N Main St to Scott Rd, N 0.2 mi, park on L. Use caution due to steep grade interior roads.
GPS COORDINATES: 42.55112°N/73.22956°W
NOTATIONS: Check-in: 2:00 p.m. Check-out: Noon. Special 25% discount rate for Coast members from Sun-Thu only. Rate includes 2 adults, up to 3 children per site, full hook-ups. Max 8 people per site. Additional charges: Add'l adult $12/night, add'l child (5 yrs and over) $6/night, Wi-Fi $5/night, tax 6.25%. Discount only available Sun-Thu from Sep 8-Oct 8. Max. RV length: 45 feet. Open: September 9–October 8.
STATE MAP: See page CTC 56.

50 amps, pull-through, pets/restrictions, Wi-Fi access, playground, picnic tables, fishing, horseshoes, group activities, recreation hall, boating, outdoor pool, basketball, volleyball, golf, tourist attraction, fire rings, firewood, ice

PITTSFIELD

Bonnie Brae Cabins & Campsites
108 Broadway
Pittsfield, Massachusetts 01201
413-442-3754
info@bonniebraecampground.com
bonniebraecampground.com
RESORT NUMBER: 2487
GOOD SAM RATING: 8/8.5★/9
DIRECTIONS: From Jct of Rte 20 & US-7 (in town): N 3.5 mi on US-7 to Broadway, E 0.5 mi, campground on R.
GPS COORDINATES: 42.4891°N/-73.23767°W
NOTATIONS: Check-in: 2:00 p.m. Check-out: 11:00 a.m. Special 25% discount rate for Coast members from Sun-Thu only. Rate includes 2 adults per site, full hook-ups. Additional charges: Cancellation processing fee $25. Max. RV length: 45 feet. Open: May 1–October 14.
STATE MAP: See page CTC 56.

30 amps, dump station, laundry, pets/restrictions, Wi-Fi access, picnic tables, fishing, boating, outdoor pool, golf, tourist attraction, canoes, hot showers, fire rings, tenting, firewood

MICHIGAN

ALPENA

Campers Cove
5005 Long Rapids Road
Alpena, Michigan 49707
989-356-3708; fax: 989-354-6023
info@camperscove.org
camperscovecampground.com
RESORT NUMBER: 1236
GOOD SAM RATING: 8.5/8.5★/7.5
DIRECTIONS: From Hwy 23 at N end of Alpena: W on Long Rapids Rd. 6 mi to park.
GPS COORDINATES: 45.1155°N/-83.5565°W
NOTATIONS: Check-in: 1:00 p.m.–10:00 p.m. Check-out: Noon. 25% discount for Coast members Sun-Thu only. Rate includes 2 people, 20/30 amp, water. Cannot guarantee availability of full hook-ups or 50 amp site. Max. RV length: 45 feet. Open: May 1–October 15.
STATE MAP: See page CTC 65.

50 amps, pull-through, visitor mail, laundry, pets/restrictions, internet access, Wi-Fi access, playground, fishing, horseshoes, boating, recreation hall, mini golf, beach, volleyball, propane, canoes, indoor pool, paddle boats, grocery

MINNESOTA

OWATONNA

NEW **Hope Oak Knoll Campground**
9545 County Road-3
Owatonna, Minnesota 55060
507-451-2998
hopeoakknoll@gmail.com
RESORT NUMBER: 2580
GOOD SAM RATING: 8/9★/9
DIRECTIONS: From Jct of I-35 & CR-4 (Ex 32), E 0.7 mi on CR-4 to CR-3, S 0.2 mi. Park on L.
GPS COORDINATES: 43.9543°N/-93.24379°W
NOTATIONS: Check-in: 1:00 p.m. Check-out: 11:00 a.m. 2021 Coast rate 15% discount avail Apr 15-May 1 and Sep 15-Oct 15. Rate includes 2 adults per site, full hook-ups. Additional charges: Tax 7.3%. Max. RV length: 45 feet. Open: April 15–October 15.
STATE MAP: See page CTC 66.

50 amps, pull-through, dump station, laundry, pets/restrictions, Wi-Fi access, playground, picnic tables, horseshoes, recreation hall, fishing, boating, game room, spa, grocery, rv supplies, firewood, ice

MISSISSIPPI

BILOXI

NEW **Cajun RV Park**
1860 Beach Boulevard
Biloxi, Mississippi 39531
877-225-8699
cajunrvpark@gmail.com
cajunpark.com
RESORT NUMBER: 2530
GOOD SAM RATING: 9.5/10★/9
DIRECTIONS: From Jct of I-10 (eEx 46B) & I-110: Go 5.5 mi S on I-110 then, 3.25 mi W on Hwy 90. Park on R.
GPS COORDINATES: 30.3938°N/-88.9491°W
NOTATIONS: Check-in: 1:00 p.m. Check-out: Noon. 2021 Coast rate 20% discount. Rate includes 2 adults per site, full hook-ups. Additional charges: Tax 7%. Max. RV length: Unlimited. Open: Year-round.
STATE MAP: See page CTC 50.

50 amps, pull-through, laundry, pets/restrictions, Wi-Fi access, playground, fishing, outdoor pool, beach, golf, shopping, gambling casino, ice

MISSOURI

BOWLING GREEN

Cozy C RV Campground
16733 Highway 54
Bowling Green, Missouri 63334
573-324-3055; fax: 573-324-3055
cozycampground@gmail.com
cozyccampground.com
RESORT NUMBER: 1480
GOOD SAM RATING: 9/10★/9
DIRECTIONS: From intersection of Hwy 61 and Hwy 54: E (toward Louisiana, MO) 2.5 mi on Hwy 54. Park on S side of Hwy 54.
GPS COORDINATES: 39.3732°N/-91.16425°W
NOTATIONS: Check-in: 3:00 p.m.–6:00 p.m. Check-out: Noon. Special 15% discount rate for Coast members not avail holiday weekends. Rate includes 2 adults, 30/50 amp, full hook-ups. Additional charges: Extra person $2/night. Stays over one week allowed with metered electric charge. Sewer donut required on sewer hook-ups. Must be checked in by 6 p.m. No water Nov-Mar 15. Hot showers available during Nov-Mar. Credit cards not accepted, cash or check only. Max. RV length: 45 feet. Open: Year-round.
STATE MAP: See page CTC 61.

50 amps, pull-through, cable tv, visitor mail, laundry, pets/restrictions, internet access, Wi-Fi access, fishing, mini golf, golf, tourist attraction, propane, rv supplies

BRANSON WEST

Blue Mountain Campground
8766 State Highway 76
Branson West, Missouri 65737
417-338-2114; fax: 417-338-8704
amainegem@yahoo.com
RESORT NUMBER: 1129
GOOD SAM RATING: 5.5/9★/9.5
DIRECTIONS: From Hwy 65: Hwy 465/Ozark Mountain Highroad to Hwy 76. W on Hwy 76 approx 1.5 -2 mi. Park on L. Call for more information on directions and best route.
GPS COORDINATES: 36.6803°N/-93.3406°W
NOTATIONS: Check-in: Noon. Check-out: Noon. Special discount rate for Coast members. Rate includes 2 people, 30 amp, full hook-ups. Additional charges: Extra person (over age 10) $2/night, 50 amp $4/night, cable $1.50/night, Wi-Fi $1/night. Wi-Fi access in campground. Max. RV length: 32 feet. Open: Year-round.
STATE MAP: See page CTC 61.

50 amps · pull-through · cable tv · visitor mail · pets/restrictions · Wi-Fi access · playground · outdoor pool · game room · tourist attraction · rv supplies · gift shop

DANVILLE

Lazy Day Campground
214 Highway J
Danville, Missouri 63361
573-564-2949; fax: 573-564-6039
lazydaycamping@gmail.com
lazydaycampground.com
RESORT NUMBER: 1628
GOOD SAM RATING: 10/10★/10
DIRECTIONS: From I-70: Ex 170, S on Hwy J 1.5 mi to park on L.
GPS COORDINATES: 38.89592°N/-91.55593°W
NOTATIONS: Check-in: Noon. Check-out: 11:00 a.m. 2022 Coast rate starting at $40/night avail all season. Rate includes 2 people, 50 amp, full hook-ups, pull-through sites. Additional charges: Extra person (12 and older) $2.50/person/night. Park offers large 1/2 acre fenced dog park, large pool, fishing pond & lake, free Wi-Fi. Max. RV length: 45 feet. Open: April 1–November 30.
STATE MAP: See page CTC 61.

50 amps · pull-through · visitor mail · laundry · pets/restrictions · Wi-Fi access · fishing · shuffleboard · horseshoes · recreation hall · outdoor pool · golf · tourist attraction · shopping · propane · fire rings · grocery · firewood · ice

MONTANA

BILLINGS

NEW **Billings Village RV Park**
325 South Billings Boulevard
Billings, Montana 59101
406-248-8685
grgw@bvrvmt.com
bvrvmt.com
RESORT NUMBER: 2560
GOOD SAM RATING: 8.5/9.5★/9
DIRECTIONS: From Jct I-90 & S Billings Blvd (Ex 447): Go 0.5 mi N on S Billings Blvd. Park on R.
GPS COORDINATES: 45.76357°N/-108.53542°W
NOTATIONS: Check-in: Noon. Check-out: 11:00 a.m. 2021 Coast rate $56/night. Rate includes 2 adults per site, full hook-ups. Additional charges: Tax 8%. Max. RV length: 45 feet. Open: Year-round.
STATE MAP: See page CTC 59.

50 amps · pull-through · cable tv · laundry · pets/restrictions · Wi-Fi access · playground · hiking trails · fishing · gambling casino

BOZEMAN

NEW **Bozeman Trail Campground**
31842 Frontage Road
Bozeman, Montana 59715
406-587-4797
bozemantrailcampground@gmail.com
bozemantrailcampground.com
RESORT NUMBER: 2563
GOOD SAM RATING: 8/8.5★/8
DIRECTIONS: From Jct of I-90 & E Main/Bus 90 (Ex 309): Go 0.5 mi E on frntg rd. Park on R.
GPS COORDINATES: 45.67352°N/-111.00343°W
ELEVATION: 4,600 feet
NOTATIONS: Check-in: Noon. Check-out: 11:00 a.m. 2021 Coast rate $40-$58.50/night avail Apr 1-Oct 31. Rate includes 2 adults per site, full hook-ups. Additional charges: Tax 8%. Max. RV length: 45 feet. Open: April 1–October 31.
STATE MAP: See page CTC 59.

50 amps · pull-through · dump station · laundry · pets/restrictions · Wi-Fi access · picnic tables · hiking trails · fishing · mini golf · propane

CHOTEAU

NEW **Choteau Mountain View RV Campground**
85 Montana-221
Choteau, Montana 59422
406-466-2615
campchoteaumt@gmail.com
campchoteaumt.com
RESORT NUMBER: 2584
GOOD SAM RATING: 7/9★/7.5
DIRECTIONS: From Jct Hwy 89 & Hwy 221: Go 1 mi E on Hwy 221. Park on L.
GPS COORDINATES: 47.81617°N/-112.16644°W
ELEVATION: 3,800 feet
NOTATIONS: Check-in: 1:00 p.m. Check-out: 11:00 a.m. 2021 Coast rate $36 -$48/night avail May 15-Oct 1. Rate includes 2 adults per site, full hook-ups. Additional charges: Tax 8%. Max. RV length: 45 feet. Open: May 15–October 1.
STATE MAP: See page CTC 59.

50 amps · pull-through · dump station · laundry · pets/restrictions · Wi-Fi access · playground · picnic tables · hiking trails · recreation hall · fishing · boating · mini golf · fire rings · rv supplies · firewood · ice

COLUMBIA FALLS

NEW **Glacier Peaks RV Park**
3185 Montana Highway 40 West
Columbia Falls, Montana 59912
406-892-2133
glacierpeaksrvpark@gmail.com
glacierpeaksrvpark.com
RESORT NUMBER: 2557
GOOD SAM RATING: 7/8.5★/8.5
DIRECTIONS: From Jct US 2 & Hwy 40: Go 0.25 mi W on Hwy 40 (R).
GPS COORDINATES: 48.37107°N/-114.24574°W
ELEVATION: 3,000 feet
NOTATIONS: Check-in: Noon. Check-out: 11:00 a.m. 2022 Coast rate $58.50/night avail Mar-Oct. Rate includes 2 adults per site, full hook-ups. Additional charges: Tax 8%. Max. RV length: 45 feet. Open: March 1–October 1.
STATE MAP: See page CTC 59.

50 amps · pull-through · laundry · pets/restrictions · Wi-Fi access · picnic tables · hiking trails · fishing · boating · winter sports · ice

COLUMBIA FALLS

NEW **Mountain View RV Park**
3621 Highway 40 West
Columbia Falls, Montana 59912
406-212-7811
rvparkmontana@gmail.com
rvparkmontana.com
RESORT NUMBER: 2561
GOOD SAM RATING: 8.5/8.5★/8
DIRECTIONS: From Jct of US 93 & Hwy 40: Go 3.25 mi E on Hwy 40. Park on L.
GPS COORDINATES: 48.37127°N/-114.26937°W
ELEVATION: 3,063 feet
NOTATIONS: Check-in: Noon. Check-out: 11:00 a.m. 2021 Coast rate $54-$58.50/night. Rate includes 2 adults per site, full hook-ups. Additional charges: Tax 8%. Max. RV length: 45 feet. Open: Year-round.
STATE MAP: See page CTC 59.

50 amps · pull-through · laundry · pets/restrictions · Wi-Fi access · picnic tables · hiking trails · fishing · boating · basketball · golf · gambling casino · rv supplies

CUT BANK

NEW **Glacier Mist RV Park**
1 McMisty Loop
Cut Bank, Montana 59427
406-548-2266
glaciermistrvpark@gmail.com
glaciermistrv.com
RESORT NUMBER: 2565
GOOD SAM RATING: 6/8.5★/6.5
DIRECTIONS: From Jct Hwy 2 & Hwy 213: Go 0.5 mi N on Hwy 213. Park on L.
GPS COORDINATES: 48.64269°N/-112.33066°W
ELEVATION: 3,800 feet
NOTATIONS: Check-in: 1:00 p.m. Check-out: 11:00 a.m. 2021 Coast rate $35 available Apr 1-Dec 1. Rate includes 2 adults per site, full hook-ups. Additional charges: tax 8% (included in rate). Max. RV length: 50 feet. Open: April 1–December 1.
STATE MAP: See page CTC 59.

50 amps · laundry · pets/restrictions · Wi-Fi access · hiking trails · fishing · gambling casino

DEER LODGE

Indian Creek RV Campground
745 Maverick Lane
Deer Lodge, Montana 59722
406-846-3848; res.: 800-294-0726
indiancreekdeerlodge@gmail.com
indiancreekcampground.net
RESORT NUMBER: 1348
GOOD SAM RATING: 7.5/10★/8
DIRECTIONS: From I-90: Ex 184/Business I-90. W 0.2 mi to access rd. S (L) 0.2 mi to park. Easy access on/off I-90.
GPS COORDINATES: 46.4086°N/-112.7252°W
ELEVATION: 4,600 feet
NOTATIONS: Check-in: Noon–7:00 p.m. Check-out: 11:00 a.m. 2021 Coast rate $29.75 for 30 amp site, $33.75 for 50 amp site. Rate includes 2 people, full hook-ups, free Wi-Fi. Additional charges: Cable $4/night, tax 8%. Extra wide/long pull-through sites. Max. RV length: 125 feet. Open: April 15–October 15.
STATE MAP: See page CTC 59.

50 amps · pull-through · cable tv · visitor mail · laundry · pets/restrictions · internet access · Wi-Fi access · golf · tourist attraction · hot showers · tenting

DILLON

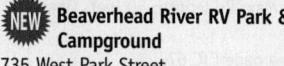

NEW **Beaverhead River RV Park & Campground**
735 West Park Street
Dillon, Montana 59725
855-683-2749
beaverheadrvpark@outlook.com
beaverheadriverrvpark.com
RESORT NUMBER: 2559
GOOD SAM RATING: 8/9★/8.5
DIRECTIONS: From Jct I-15 & Atlantic St/Bus 15 (Ex 62): Go 1.25 mi N on Atlantic St/Bus 15, then 1 mi W on Reeder St. Park on R.
GPS COORDINATES: 45.21954°N/-112.65019°W
ELEVATION: 5,050 feet
NOTATIONS: Check-in: 11:00 a.m. Check-out: 11:00 a.m. 2022 Coast rate $46.54 - $49.81/night avail Oct 1-Apr 30. Rate includes 2 adults per site, full hook-ups. Additional charges: Add'l pet $2/day, tax 8%. Max. RV length: 42 feet. Open: Year-round.
STATE MAP: See page CTC 59.

30 amps · pull-through · dump station · laundry · pets/restrictions · Wi-Fi access · picnic tables · hiking trails · fishing · gambling casino · fire rings · rv supplies · ice · grills

DILLON

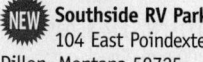

NEW **Southside RV Park**
104 East Poindexter
Dillon, Montana 59725
406-683-2244
info@southsidervpark.com
southsidervpark.com
RESORT NUMBER: 2546
GOOD SAM RATING: 8/9★/9
DIRECTIONS: From Jct I-15 & Bus Loop 15/S Atlantic St (Ex 62) : Go 0.75 mi N on Bus Loop 15, then 0.25 mi W on E Poindexter St. Park on E.
GPS COORDINATES: 45.21014°N/-112.64606°W
NOTATIONS: Check-in: Noon. Check-out: 11:00 a.m. 2021 Coast rate $45/night. Rate includes 2 adults per site, full hook-ups. Additional charges: Tax 8%. Max. RV length: 45 feet. Open: March 1–December 1.
STATE MAP: See page CTC 59.

50 amps · pull-through · laundry · pets/restrictions · Wi-Fi access · picnic tables · hiking trails · fishing · boating · golf · ice

GLASGOW

NEW **Shady Rest RV Park**
8 Lasar Drive, #15
Glasgow, Montana 59230
406-228-2769
cody-pederson@hotmail.com
shadyrestrvparkmt.com
RESORT NUMBER: 2558
GOOD SAM RATING: 6/8.5★/9
DIRECTIONS: From Jct US 2 & Hwy 24 (Glasgow): Go 1.25 mi W on US 2, then 0.1 mi N on Lasar Dr. Park at end.
GPS COORDINATES: 48.19673°N/-106.62061°W
NOTATIONS: Check-in: 1:00 p.m. Check-out: Noon. 2022 Coast rate $40/night. Rate includes 2 adults per site, full hook-ups. Additional charges: Tax 8% included in rate. Max. RV length: 50 feet. Open: Year-round.
STATE MAP: See page CTC 59.

50 amps · pull-through · laundry · pets/restrictions · Wi-Fi access · picnic tables · hiking trails · fishing · boating · gambling casino · rv supplies · ice

GREAT FALLS

NEW **Dick's RV Park**
1403 11th Street Southwest
Great Falls, Montana 59404
406-452-0333
reservations@dicksrvpark.com
dicksrvpark.com
RESORT NUMBER: 2585
GOOD SAM RATING: 7.5/9★/8.5
DIRECTIONS: From Jct I-15 & 10th Ave S (Ex 278): Go 0.1 mi E on 10th Ave S to Ex 0, then 0.25 mi N on 14th St SW, then 0.25 mi E on 13th Ave SW (dead end). Park on R. From Jct of US-87 (15th St) & 10th Ave S: Go 2 .5 mi W on 10th Ave S to Ex 0, then follow directions above from Ex 0. Park on R.
GPS COORDINATES: 47.49077°N/-111.33057°W
ELEVATION: 3,300 feet
NOTATIONS: Check-in: 11:00 a.m. Check-out: 11:00 a.m. 2021 Coast rate $40.50/night. Rate includes 2 adults per site, full hook-ups. Additional charges: Tax 8%. Max. RV length: 50 feet. Open: Year-round.
STATE MAP: See page CTC 59.

50 amps · pull-through · dump station · laundry · pets/restrictions · Wi-Fi access · picnic tables · hiking trails · fishing · boating · mini golf · propane

HAVRE

NEW **Hansen Family Campground & Storage**
39180 U.S. Highway 2 East
Havre, Montana 59501
406-945-6629
hfcs.llc@hotmail.com
hansenfamilycampground.com
RESORT NUMBER: 2567
GOOD SAM RATING: 7/NA/8.5
DIRECTIONS: From Jct US 87 N & US Hwy 2 E: Go 13 mi E on Hwy 2 E. Park on R.
GPS COORDINATES: 48.56356°N/-109.47986°W
NOTATIONS: Check-in: 1:00 p.m. Check-out: 11:00 a.m. 2021 Coast rate $36/night. Rate includes 2 adults per site, full hook-ups. Additional charges: Tax 8%. Max. RV length: 50 feet. Open: Year-round.
STATE MAP: See page CTC 59.

50 amps · pull-through · pets/restrictions · Wi-Fi access · picnic tables · hiking trails · fishing · gambling casino · ice

KALISPELL

NEW **Spruce Park on the River**
1985 Montana Highway 35
Kalispell, Montana 59901
406-752-6321
spruceparkrv@gmail.com
spruceparkrv.com
RESORT NUMBER: 2564
GOOD SAM RATING: 9/8.5★/8
DIRECTIONS: From Jct US 2 & MT Hwy 35: Go 1.75 mi E on MT Hwy 35. Park on L.
GPS COORDINATES: 48.22343°N/-114.24483°W
ELEVATION: 2,920 feet
NOTATIONS: Check-in: 11:00 a.m. Check-out: 11:00 a.m. 2021 Coast rate $40.50-$67.50/night avail Apr 1-Nov 15. Rate includes 2 adults per site, full hook-ups. Additional charges: Tax 8%. Max. RV length: 45 feet. Open: April 1–November 15.
STATE MAP: See page CTC 59.

50 amps · pull-through · dump station · cable tv · laundry · pets/restrictions · Wi-Fi access · playground · picnic tables · hiking trails · fishing · golf · fire rings · firewood · ice

LIVINGSTON

NEW **Osen's RV Park**
20 Merrill Lane
Livingston, Montana 59047
406-222-0591
info@osensrvpark.com
osensrvpark.com
RESORT NUMBER: 2562
GOOD SAM RATING: 8/10★/9
DIRECTIONS: From Jct I-90 & US 89 (Ex 333): Go 0.5 mi S on US 89, then 0.1 mi W on Merrill Ln. Park on R.
GPS COORDINATES: 45.63677°N/-110.58023°W
ELEVATION: 4,500 feet
NOTATIONS: Check-in: Noon. Check-out: 11:00 a.m. 2021 Coast rate $41.40-$53.10/night avail Apr 15-Oct 10. Rate includes 2 adults per site, full hook-ups. Additional charges: Tax 8%. Max. RV length: 45 feet. Open: April 15–October 10.
STATE MAP: See page CTC 59.

50 amps · pull-through · dump station · cable tv · laundry · pets/restrictions · Wi-Fi access · picnic tables · hiking trails · horseshoes · fishing · boating · basketball · ice

MONTANA

REED POINT

NEW **Old West RV Park**
5 South Division Street
Reed Point, Montana 59069
406-326-2394
oldwestrvpark@gmail.com
oldwestrv.com
RESORT NUMBER: 2566
GOOD SAM RATING: 6.5/8.5★/8
DIRECTIONS: From Jct I-90 & Division St (Ex 392): Go 0.1 mi N on Division St. Park on R.
GPS COORDINATES: 45.7065°N/-109.54175°W
ELEVATION: 3,800 feet
NOTATIONS: Check-in: 1:00 p.m. Check-out: 11:00 a.m. 2021 Coast rate $38.70-$48.60/night avail May-Oct. Rate includes 2 adults per site, full hook-ups. Additional charges: Tax 8%. Max. RV length: 45 feet. Open: May 1–October 31.
STATE MAP: See page CTC 59.

50 amps, pull-through, dump station, cable tv, laundry, pets/restrictions, Wi-Fi access, picnic tables, hiking trails, fishing

NEBRASKA

BRIDGEPORT

Meadow Park Motel & RV Park
9868 Highway 385
Bridgeport, Nebraska 69336
308-279-1176
meadowpark385@yahoo.com
meadowparkmotelrv.com
RESORT NUMBER: 2404
GOOD SAM RATING: 7/8/7
DIRECTIONS: From Jct NE 26 & US 385: Go 2.5 mi N. Then NW on US 385. Park on L.
GPS COORDINATES: 41.70825°N/-103.11975°W
NOTATIONS: Check-in: Noon. Check-out: 11:00 a.m. Special discount rate for Coast members. Rate includes 2 adults, full hook-ups, free Wi-Fi. Additional charges: Tax. Kids under 2 free. Max 6 people/site. Max. RV length: 40 feet. Open: Year-round.
STATE MAP: See page CTC 67.

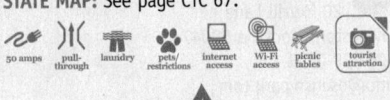

50 amps, pull-through, laundry, pets/restrictions, internet access, Wi-Fi access, picnic tables, tourist attraction, tenting

ELM CREEK

The 4 Seasons RV Park
2005 Highway 183
Elm Creek, Nebraska 68836
308-962-4168; fax: 308-856-4164
michellestretch@yahoo.com
the4seasonsrvpark.godaddysites.com
RESORT NUMBER: 1788
GOOD SAM RATING: 4/4.5/5.5
DIRECTIONS: From I-80: Ex 257/Elm Creek. N 0.2 mi on Hwy 183. Park on R.
GPS COORDINATES: 40.6987°N/-99.3793°W
NOTATIONS: Check-in: 3:00 p.m. Check-out: 11:00 a.m. 2022 special Coast rate of $32/night avail year round. Rate includes 4 people, 30 or 50 amp, full hook-ups and taxes. All pull-through sites. Wi-Fi access in campground. Max. RV length: 75 feet. Open: Year-round.
STATE MAP: See page CTC 67.

50 amps, pull-through, dump station, laundry, pets/restrictions, internet access, Wi-Fi access, playground, picnic tables, fishing, tourist attraction, hot showers

NORTH PLATTE

I-80 Lakeside Campground
3800 Hadley Drive
North Platte, Nebraska 69101
877-648-2267
i80lakesidecampground@yahoo.com
i80lakesidecampground.com
RESORT NUMBER: 2465
GOOD SAM RATING: 6/8★/6
DIRECTIONS: From Jct I-80 & Newberry Rd (56G) (Ex 179): Go 1000 ft N on Newberry Rd, then 1000 ft E on Haldley Dr. East of La Quinta Hotel.
GPS COORDINATES: 41.1075°N/-100.71956°W
ELEVATION: 2,800 feet
NOTATIONS: Check-in: 2:00 p.m. Check-out: 1:00 p.m. Special 20% discount rate for Coast members. Rate includes 2 adults per site, full water, sewer, and electric. No availability major holiday weekends. Additional charges: Add'l adult $3/night, add'l child $2/night, cancellation fee, tax 14%. No Wi-fi or cable TV. Open via dropbox only Oct 1-Apr 15. Showerhouse, laundry & boat rentals closed Oct 1-Apr 15. Discount rate available Apr 15-Sep 15 only. Max. RV length: 100 feet. Open: April 15–September 15; October 1–March 31.
STATE MAP: See page CTC 67.

50 amps, pull-through, dump station, laundry, pets/restrictions, playground, fishing, horseshoes, volleyball, golf, shopping, canoes, paddle boats, grocery, tenting, firewood, ice

OGALLALA

Country View Campground
120 Road East 80
Ogallala, Nebraska 69153
308-284-2415
camp@cvcampground.com
cvcampground.com
RESORT NUMBER: 2349
GOOD SAM RATING: 9/10★/9.5
DIRECTIONS: From Jct of I-80 & NE 61 (Ex 126): Go 0.5 mi S on NE 61, then 0.25 mi E on CR East 80, campground on R.
GPS COORDINATES: 41.10519°N/-101.71488°W
NOTATIONS: Check-in: 1:00 p.m. Check-out: 11:00 a.m. Special discount rate for Coast members. Rate includes 4 people per site. Additional charges: Tax 10.5%. No credit cards accepted. Max. RV length: 45 feet. Open: October 1–April 30.
STATE MAP: See page CTC 67.

50 amps, pull-through, cable tv, laundry, pets/restrictions, Wi-Fi access, playground, picnic tables, fishing, boating, golf, tourist attraction, shopping, fire rings, rv supplies, tenting, ice

VALENTINE

Wacky West Travel Park
702 East C Street
Valentine, Nebraska 69201
402-376-1771
wackywst@hotmail.com
RESORT NUMBER: 1871
GOOD SAM RATING: 6/4/3.5
DIRECTIONS: E from Jct of Hwy 83/20 in town: 3 blocks E. N on Government St, 50 ft to C St, E on C St 2 blocks. Park on N side across from the Bomgarrs store.
GPS COORDINATES: 42.86817°N/-100.54142°W
NOTATIONS: Check-in: 24 hours. Check-out: 11:00 a.m. Special discount rate for Coast members. Rate includes 2 people, 20/30 amp, water and sewer, all sites 50 ft long. Additional charges: Extra person $3/night, 50 amp $3/night, AC or heat $3/night per unit, dump station $5.50/non-guest, tax. Tent sites available. Cash or check only, no credit cards. Limited services in the winter: 12 freezeless sites but no showers or laundry. Max. RV length: 50 feet. Open: Year-round.
STATE MAP: See page CTC 67.

50 amps, pull-through, dump station, cable tv, visitor mail, laundry, pets/restrictions, internet access, Wi-Fi access, playground, picnic tables, horseshoes, propane, fire rings, rv supplies, gift shop, tenting, firewood

NEVADA

BOULDER CITY

NEW **Canyon Trail RV Park**
1200 Industrial Road
Boulder City, Nevada 89005
702-293-1200
info@canyontrailrvpark.com
canyontrailrvpark.com
RESORT NUMBER: 2568
GOOD SAM RATING: 9.5/10★/9.5
DIRECTIONS: From Jct of US 93 & US 95: Go 1.25 mi S on US 93, then 1.25 mi N on Veteran's Memorial (Industrial Rd), bridge clearance 14 ft 6 in. (L). From Jct of Boulder Dam & US 93: Go 7.5 mi W on US 93, then 600 yds W on Industrial Rd. Park on R.
GPS COORDINATES: 35.9775°N/-114.8503°W
NOTATIONS: Check-in: 1:00 p.m. Check-out: 11:00 a.m. 2021 Coast rate 20% discount avail Jul 1- Aug 31. Rate includes 2 adults per site, full hook-ups. Additional charges: Tax 8.375%. Max. RV length: 45 feet. Open: Year-round.
STATE MAP: See page CTC 68.

50 amps, pull-through, dump station, cable tv, laundry, pets/restrictions, Wi-Fi access, hiking trails, fishing, boating, rv supplies

FALLON

Cold Springs Station Resort
52300 Austin Highway
Fallon, Nevada 89406
775-423-1233
coldsprings@cssresort.com
cssresort.com
RESORT NUMBER: 2485
GOOD SAM RATING: 7/8.5★/7
DIRECTIONS: From Jct US-95 & US-50: Go 61 mi E on US-50, resort on R.
GPS COORDINATES: 39.4154°N/-117.84117°W
NOTATIONS: Check-in: 1:00 p.m. Check-out: Noon. Special 20% discount rate for Coast members from Sun-Thu only. Rate includes 2 adults per site, full hook-ups. Max 6 people per site. Additional charges: Tax 7%, service fee. Max. RV length: 60 feet. Open: Year-round.
STATE MAP: See page CTC 68.

50 amps · pull-through · laundry · pets/restrictions · Wi-Fi access · restaurant/snack bar · tourist attraction · gift shop

LAS VEGAS

NEW **Hitchin' Post RV Park**
3640 Las Vegas Boulevard North
Las Vegas, Nevada 89115
888-433-8402
office@hprvp.com
hprvp.com
RESORT NUMBER: 2554
GOOD SAM RATING: 9.5/9.5★/9.5
DIRECTIONS: Sbnd: From Jct of I-15 & Ex 50 (Lamb): Go 2 mi S on Lamb, then 500 ft S on Las Vegas Blvd (L). N-bnd: From Jct of I-15 & Craig Rd (Ex 48): Go 1.25 mi E on Craig Rd, then 1 mi SE on Lamb Blvd, then 500 ft on Las Vegas Blvd. Park on L.
GPS COORDINATES: 36.22266°N/-115.08447°W
NOTATIONS: Check-in: 1:00 p.m. Check-out: 11:00 a.m. 2021 Coast rate 20% discount available Jun-Aug. Rate includes 2 adults per site, full hook-ups. Additional charges: Tax 8.25%. Max. RV length: 45 feet. Open: Year-round.
STATE MAP: See page CTC 68.

50 amps · pull-through · dump station · laundry · pets/restrictions · Wi-Fi access · picnic tables · restaurant/snack bar · hiking trails · gambling casino · rv supplies · ice

NEW HAMPSHIRE

ASHLAND

Ames Brook Campground
104 Winona Road
Ashland, New Hampshire 03217
603-968-7998
info@amesbrook.com
amesbrook.com
RESORT NUMBER: 2390
GOOD SAM RATING: 10/10★/9.5
DIRECTIONS: From Jct of I-93 & Ex 24 (Rtes 3 & 25): Go 0.75 mi S on Rte 3 & 25 to Rte 132, then 0.25 mi S to Winona Rd, then 0.5 mi S, campground on R. Avoid S end of Winona Rd, low bridge.
GPS COORDINATES: 43.68811°N/-71.6229°W
NOTATIONS: Check-in: 2:00 p.m. Check-out: Noon. Special discount for Coast members. Rate includes 2 adults, 2 children (3 years or less free), max 2 pets, water, electric, sewer, cable TV. Wi-Fi complimentary-cannot guarantee high speed internet at all times. Coast rate only available Sun-Thu, no availability holidays, Bike Week Jun 7-17, week of July 4. Max. RV length: 45 feet. Open: May 15–October 17.
STATE MAP: See page CTC 64.

50 amps · pull-through · dump station · laundry · pets/restrictions · internet access · Wi-Fi access · playground · fishing · hiking trails · horseshoes · group activities · recreation hall · fishing · boating · outdoor pool · basketball · beach · volleyball · golf · game room · tourist attraction · fitness · shopping · propane · hot showers · firewood

EXETER

Green Gate Campground
185 Court Street
Exeter, New Hampshire 03833
603-772-2100
info@thegreengatecampground.com
thegreengatecampground.com
RESORT NUMBER: 2495
GOOD SAM RATING: 9/8★/9
DIRECTIONS: From Jct of I-95 & Rte 107 (Ex 1), Go 2.6 mi NW on Rte 107 to Rte 150, then 4.1 mi NW to Rte 108, then 0.2 mi N, campground on L.
GPS COORDINATES: 42.95924°N/-70.95898°W
NOTATIONS: Check-in: 1:00 p.m. Check-out: Noon. Special discount rate of $44 for Coast members from Sun-Thu only. No avail Jul-Aug. Rate includes 2 adults, 3 children, 1 camping unit per site, 30 amp, full hook-ups. Additional charges: 50 amp $5/night, add'l adult $12/night, add'l child (16 yrs and under) $8/night. Max. RV length: 44 feet. Open: May 1–June 30; September 7–October 1.
STATE MAP: See page CTC 64.

50 amps · pull-through · laundry · pets/restrictions · Wi-Fi access · playground · picnic tables · outdoor pool · golf · game room · tourist attraction · shopping · fire rings · tenting

LANCASTER

Riverside Camping & RV Resort
94 Bridge Street
Lancaster, New Hampshire 03584
603-631-7433
manager@riversidecampingnh.com
riversidecampingnh.com
RESORT NUMBER: 2388
GOOD SAM RATING: 9/10★/9.5
DIRECTIONS: From Jct US 2 & US 3 (in town at traffic cir): Go 0.75 mi W on US 2, resort on L.
GPS COORDINATES: 44.4957°N/-71.58964°W
NOTATIONS: Check-in: 2:00 p.m. Check-out: 11:00 a.m. 2022 Coast 10% discount, not valid on holidays or weekends. Rate includes 2 adults, 2 children, water, sewer, electric hook-ups. Additional charges: Extra person $5/night. Cash or check only. Due to NH firewood quarantine, all firewood must be purchased at resort-no outside wood. Max. RV length: Unlimited. Open: May 15–October 15.
STATE MAP: See page CTC 64.

50 amps · pull-through · laundry · pets/restrictions · Wi-Fi access · playground · picnic tables · fishing · shuffleboard · hiking trails · horseshoes · group activities · boating · fishing · boating · outdoor pool · beach · volleyball · tourist attraction · propane · fire rings · tenting · firewood

NEW MEXICO

CARLSBAD

Bud's Place RV Park & Cabins
900 Standpipe Road
Carlsbad, New Mexico 88220
575-200-1865
budsplacervpark@gmail.com
RESORT NUMBER: 2504
GOOD SAM RATING: 7/10★/8
DIRECTIONS: From Jct of Canal St & NM-524/W Lea St: Go W 1.5 mi on NM 524/ W Lea St to Standpipe Rd, then S 0.2 mi, park on L. From Jct of US 285 & NM 524 (N of Carlsbad): Go SW 7 mi on NM 524 to Standpipe Rd (S 6th St), then S 0.2 mi, park on L.
GPS COORDINATES: 32.4117°N/-104.25501°W
ELEVATION: 3 feet
NOTATIONS: Check-in: 2:00 p.m. Check-out: Noon. Special 10% discount rate for Coast members. Rate includes 2 adults per site, electric, water, sewer, Wi-Fi. Additional charges: Tax 5.275%. Max. RV length: 70 feet. Open: Year-round.
STATE MAP: See page CTC 55.

50 amps · pull-through · laundry · pets/restrictions · Wi-Fi access · fishing · tourist attraction · shopping

DEMING

Hidden Valley Ranch RV Resort
12100 Hidden Valley Road Northwest
Deming, New Mexico 88030
575-546-3071; fax: 575-544-2134
hiddenvalleyrvranch@gmail.com
hiddenvalleyranchrv.com
RESORT NUMBER: 1149
GOOD SAM RATING: NA
DIRECTIONS: From Deming: 3 mi N on Hwy 180. R (E) on Keeler Rd 2.8 mi, crossing cattle guard at end of pavement. Veer R at Hidden Valley sign. 5.5 mi to the ranch on gravel country road.
GPS COORDINATES: 32.4284°N/-107.761°W
ELEVATION: 4,841 feet
NOTATIONS: Check-in: 2:00 p.m. Check-out: Noon. Office hours 9 a.m.-4 p.m. 2021 Coast rate $16/night includes 2 people, 30/50 amp, full hook-ups. Additional charges: Extra person $2.23/night. Maximum stay 2 weeks. No tents. No washer, dryer or electric heater use in RV. Wi-Fi access in campground. Cash or check only. Max. RV length: Unlimited. Open: Year-round.
STATE MAP: See page CTC 55.

50 amps · visitor mail · laundry · pets/restrictions · internet access · Wi-Fi access · picnic tables · restaurant/snack bar · hiking trails · horseshoes · group activities · recreation hall · propane · ice · grills

TUCUMCARI

NEW **Blaze-in-Saddle RV Park & Horse Hotel**
2500 East Route 66 Boulevard
Tucumcari, New Mexico 88401
575-815-4085
blazeinsaddlervpark@hughes.net
blaze-in-saddle.com
RESORT NUMBER: 2556
GOOD SAM RATING: 6/9★/8.5
DIRECTIONS: From Jct I-40W (Ex 335)/Historic Rt 66 & E Tucumcari Blvd: Go 1.25 mi W on Historic Rt 66/E Tucumcari Blvd. Park on R.
GPS COORDINATES: 35.17177°N/-103.69361°W
ELEVATION: 4,030 feet
NOTATIONS: Check-in: 1:00 p.m. Check-out: 11:00 a.m. 2022 Coast rate 15% discount. Rate includes 2 adults per site, full hook-ups. Additional charges: Add'l adult $2/night, add'l child $2/night, add'l vehicle $5/night, tax 8.35%. Max. RV length: 70 feet. Open: Year-round.
STATE MAP: See page CTC 55.

50 amps · pull-through · dump station · laundry · pets/restrictions · Wi-Fi access · hiking trails · fishing · boating · rv supplies · ice

TUCUMCARI

Mountain Road RV Park
1701 Mountain Road
Tucumcari, New Mexico 88401
575-461-9628
mountainroadrvpark@yahoo.com
RESORT NUMBER: 2506
GOOD SAM RATING: 7/9★/9
DIRECTIONS: From Jct of I-40 & US-54/Mountain Rd (Ex 333): Go 0.5 mi N on US-54, park on L.
GPS COORDINATES: 35.16258°N/-103.70305°W
NOTATIONS: Check-in: 11:00 a.m. Check-out: 10:30 a.m. Special 10% discount rate for Coast members. Rate includes 2 adults per site, 30 amp, water, sewer, cable TV, W-Fi. Additional charges: 50 amp $3/night, tax 13.75%. Max. RV length: Unlimited. Open: Year-round.
STATE MAP: See page CTC 55.

50 amps · pull-through · cable tv · visitor mail · laundry · pets/restrictions · Wi-Fi access · tourist attraction · shopping · hot showers · tenting

NEW YORK

ALEXANDRIA BAY

Swan Bay Resort
43615 State Route 12
Alexandria Bay, New York 13607
315-482-7926
manager@swanbayresort.com
swanbayresort.com
RESORT NUMBER: 2316
GOOD SAM RATING: 10/10★/10
DIRECTIONS: From I-81 N: Ex 50 N (Alexandria Bay/Rte 12 N). Resort is on L after Price Chopper entrance. From Canada: Rte 401 to Ex 661. Follow signs to USA and Thousand Islands Bridge. Cross the bridge into the USA and follow I-81 S to Ex 50 N. Resort is on L after Price Chopper entrance.
GPS COORDINATES: 44.3009°N/-75.96533°W
NOTATIONS: Check-in: 2:00 p.m. Check-out: 11:00 a.m. Coast member rate 25% discount during off season only: rate avail May 1-Jun 17 & Sep 7-Oct 31 only. Site includes 6 persons (over 6 yrs), park view site. Additional charges: 30 amp $5/night, 50 amp $10/night, dump station $20 (non-guest). Credit card kept on file for additional charges. Free Wi-Fi all sites. 48 hr advanced notice required. Rental units available. Trip Points not accepted. Contact resort directly. Rental check-in 4 p.m., check-out 11 a.m. Pets allowed in rental units. Max. RV length: Unlimited. Open: May 1–October 31.
STATE MAP: See page CTC 69.

50 amps · pull-through · visitor mail · laundry · pets/restrictions · internet access · Wi-Fi access · picnic tables · rental units · hiking trails · boating · fishing · outdoor pool · golf · tourist attraction · shopping · gambling casino · fire rings · grocery · rv supplies

APPLETON

Niagara Shores Campground
6419 Lake Road
Appleton, New York 14008
716-778-8568
niagarashorescampground@gmail.com
niagarashorescampground.com
RESORT NUMBER: 2437
GOOD SAM RATING: NA
DIRECTIONS: From Appleton: W on W Somerset Rd 341 ft to Hess Rd. R onto Hess Rd 1.3 mi, then L on NY-18W 1.6 mi, then R onto Kingfisher Ct (restricted usage rd), 315 ft turn R. Resort on L.
GPS COORDINATES: 43.34685°N/-78.67789°W
NOTATIONS: Check-in: 1:00 p.m. Check-out: 11:00 a.m. Special discount rate for Coast members. Additional charges: Add'l adult $15/night, add'l pet $7/night, tax 8%. Discount not available long holiday weekends. Drive-ups not accepted. Max. RV length: 40 feet. Open: May 1–May 30; September 1–September 26.
STATE MAP: See page CTC 69.

50 amps · cable tv · pets/restrictions · Wi-Fi access · playground · restaurant/snack bar · shuffleboard · horseshoes · church services · fishing · boating · outdoor pool · mini golf · basketball · volleyball · game room · tourist attraction · shopping · ball field · gambling casino · grocery

CUBA

Maple Lane RV Park
5233 Maple Lane
Cuba, New York 14727
585-968-1677
dadnapa@hotmail.com
maple-lane-r-v-park.my-free.website
RESORT NUMBER: 2408
GOOD SAM RATING: NA
DIRECTIONS: From Jct of I-86 (SR-17) & SR-305 (Ex 28), N 600 ft on SR-305 to Maple Lane, park on L.
GPS COORDINATES: 42.2279°N/-78.27831°W
NOTATIONS: Check-in: Noon. Check-out: 11:00 a.m. Coast rate is 20% off nightly rate. Current rate is $40 plus tax. Rate includes water, electric, septic, free Wi-Fi. Additional charges: Tax. Kids under 2 free. Max 8 people per site. Max. RV length: 100 feet. Open: April 1–October 10.
STATE MAP: See page CTC 69.

50 amps · pull-through · dump station · laundry · pets/restrictions · Wi-Fi access · fishing · boating · tourist attraction · shopping · hot showers · tenting · grills

GILBOA

Country Roads Campground
144 Peaceful Road
Gilboa, New York 12076
518-827-6397
camp@countryroadscampground.com
countryroadscampground.com
RESORT NUMBER: 2454
GOOD SAM RATING: 8/7.5/8
DIRECTIONS: From Jct of SR-23 & SR-30 (Grand Gorge): N 3 mi on SR-30 to SR-990V (Gilboa), N on Wycoff Rd (changes to Kingsley Rd), N 1.7 mi to Peaceful Rd, W 0.3 mi.
GPS COORDINATES: 42.43206°N/-74.42739°W
ELEVATION: 2,175 feet
NOTATIONS: Check-in: 2:00 p.m. Check-out: 1:00 p.m. Special 10% discount rate for Coast members avail non holiday weekends. Rate includes 2 adults, up to 4 children under 18, 30 amp electric, water and sewer. Additional charges: Add'l person $5/night, 50 amp $7/night, tax 8%. Max 6 people/site & 1 camping unit. No check-ins after 10 p.m. Max. RV length: 45 feet. Open: May 15–October 10.
STATE MAP: See page CTC 69.

50 amps · dump station · laundry · pets/restrictions · Wi-Fi access · playground · picnic tables · hot tub · hiking trails · horseshoes · group activities · recreation hall · fishing · boating · outdoor pool · volleyball · golf · tourist attraction · hot showers · ball field · fire rings · rv supplies · ice

JAVA CENTER

Beaver Meadow Family Campground
1455 Beaver Meadow Road
Java Center, New York 14082
585-457-3101; fax: 585-457-3101
beavermeadowcampground@yahoo.com
beavermeadowcampground.com
RESORT NUMBER: 2025
GOOD SAM RATING: 8.5/9★/9.5
DIRECTIONS: From Buffalo/I-90 (NYS Trwy): W to Rt 400 S/Ex 54. S to Rt 20A/Rt 78 (E Aurora) Ex. L on Rt 20A/Rt 78. R on Rt 77 (S). L on Beaver Meadow Rd. From Rochester I-90 (NYS Trwy): W to Rt 77/Ex 48A. R on Rt 77 (S). L on Beaver Meadow Rd. From S tier or PA: Rt 16 AAA N. R on Rt 39. L on Rt 98 (N) (stay straight). R on Beaver Meadow Rd.

GPS COORDINATES: 42.6611°N/-78.3855°W
ELEVATION: 1,400 feet
NOTATIONS: Check-in: 1:00 p.m. Check-out: Noon. 2022 Coast rate $37.50/night not avail during holiday periods. Rate includes 2 adults/3 dependent children, standard 20/30/50 amp site with water. No sewer sites. Additional charges: Extra adult (up to 4 max) $10/night, add'l child $3/night, honeywagon, Wi-Fi at site, dump station free. Max. RV length: 45 feet. Open: May 6–October 10.
STATE MAP: See page CTC 69.

50 amps, dump station, laundry, pets/restrictions, internet access, Wi-Fi access, playground, picnic tables, fishing, hiking trails, horseshoes, group activities, recreation hall, outdoor pool, basketball, volleyball, tourist attraction, propane, ball field, fire rings, grocery, tenting, firewood, ice

NORTH CAROLINA

ABERDEEN

Oasis of North Carolina
15340 Palmer Road
Aberdeen, North Carolina 28363
910-266-8372
oasisofnorthcarolina.us
RESORT NUMBER: 2351
GOOD SAM RATING: 7/9★/9.5
DIRECTIONS: From Jct of US-15/501 & NC 211: Go SE 14.5 mi on US-15/501 to Palmer Rd, W 2 mi, park on L. From Jct of US-74 & US-15/501: Go N 12 mi on US-15/501 to Palmer, W 2 mi, park on L. Do not use GPS.
GPS COORDINATES: 34.9044°N/-79.4676°W
NOTATIONS: Check-in: 1:00 p.m. Check-out: 11:00 a.m. Special discount rate for Coast members. Rate includes 4 people per site. Additional charges: 50 amp $2/night, extra vehicle over two $5/night each. Coast rate available Nov 10-Feb 28. Max. RV length: 80 feet. Open: Year-round.
STATE MAP: See page CTC 70.

50 amps, laundry, pets/restrictions, picnic tables, hiking trails, golf, tourist attraction, hot showers, fire rings, rv supplies, tenting, firewood

TABOR CITY

Carrollwoods Campground at Grapefull Sisters Vineyard
95 Dots Drive
Tabor City, North Carolina 28463
910-653-5538; fax: 910-653-2538
info@grapefullsistersvineyard.com
myrtlebeachcampingwest.com
RESORT NUMBER: 2130
GOOD SAM RATING: 8/8.5★/9.5
DIRECTIONS: From Myrtle Beach: 501-W to Hwy 31-N to Hwy 9-N. R after Black Bear Golf on Camp Swamp Rd. R on Dothan Rd. L on Ramsey Ford Rd. Enter on R. From I-95: Ex 193 to Hwy 9-S. 49 mi, L at Black Bear Golf and follow above directions.
GPS COORDINATES: 34.05°N/-78.73°W
ELEVATION: 39 feet
NOTATIONS: Check-in: 1:00 p.m. Check-out: 11:00 a.m. Rate includes 2 adults/2 children under 10, electric and water. Additional charges: Extra adult $4/night, extra child $2/night, cable $2/night, 50 amp $5/night, tax. Resort requires advance notice of check-in after 8 p.m. Rental units available. Trip Points not accepted. Contact resort directly. Max. RV length: 75 feet. Open: Year-round.
STATE MAP: See page CTC 70.

50 amps, pull-through, cable tv, visitor mail, laundry, pets/restrictions, internet access, Wi-Fi access, playground, picnic tables, rental units, fishing, hiking trails, horseshoes, group activities, recreation hall, fishing, boating, outdoor pool, volleyball, golf, tourist attraction, shopping, propane, hot showers, gambling casino, fire rings, gift shop, tenting, firewood, handicap access, ice, grills

WAGRAM

Pine Lake RV Resort
32482 Hillcreek Road
Wagram, North Carolina 28396
910-281-3319
spooky.88@icloud.com
pinelakervresorts.com
RESORT NUMBER: 955
GOOD SAM RATING: 8/8★/7.5
DIRECTIONS: From Aberdeen: 10 miles S on 15-501, 2 mi E on Hillcreek Rd. From Laurinburg: 15 miles N on 15-501, 2 mi E on Hillcreek Rd.
GPS COORDINATES: 34.9098°N/-79.467°W
NOTATIONS: Check-in: 11:00 a.m. Check-out: 5:00 p.m. Special discount rate for Coast members. Rate includes 2 adults, 2 children under 18 years per site. Additional charges: Extra adult $10/night, extra child $5/night. Max. RV length: 45 feet. Open: Year-round.
STATE MAP: See page CTC 70.

50 amps, pull-through, dump station, laundry, pets/restrictions, Wi-Fi access, playground, picnic tables, fishing, hiking trails, horseshoes, boating, fishing, boating, outdoor pool, golf, tourist attraction, propane, hot showers, fire rings, firewood, ice, grills

NORTH DAKOTA

DICKINSON

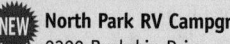

NEW **North Park RV Campground**
2320 Buckskin Drive
Dickinson, North Dakota 58601
701-227-8498
campnorthpark@yahoo.com
campnorthpark.com
RESORT NUMBER: 2579
GOOD SAM RATING: 8/9.5★/8.5
DIRECTIONS: From Jct I-94 (Ex 61) & 3rd Ave/Hwy 22: Go 0.5 mi N on 3rd Ave/Hwy 22, then 0.5 mi E on 21st St, then 500 ft N on 5th Ave. Park on R.
GPS COORDINATES: 46.90662°N/-102.77717°W
ELEVATION: 2,536 feet
NOTATIONS: Check-in: Noon. Check-out: 11:00 a.m. 2021 Coast rate $38/night. Rate includes 2 adults per site, full hook-ups. Additional charges: Tax. Max. RV length: 50 feet. Open: Year-round.
STATE MAP: See page CTC 67.

50 amps, pull-through, dump station, laundry, pets/restrictions, Wi-Fi access, picnic tables, hiking trails, fishing

MENOKEN

NEW **A Prairie Breeze RV Park**
2810 158th Street Northeast
Menoken, North Dakota 58558
701-224-8215
RESORT NUMBER: 2582
GOOD SAM RATING: 5/9★/8
DIRECTIONS: From Jct of I-94 & Ex 170 (Menoken Ex): Go 1000 ft S on Rd to Menoken. Park on R.
GPS COORDINATES: 46.83446°N/-100.54261°W
NOTATIONS: Check-in: 1:00 p.m. Check-out: 1:00 p.m. 2021 Coast rate $25-$30/night. Rate includes 2 adults per site, full hook-ups. Additional charges: Tax. Max. RV length: 45 feet. Open: April 1–November 1.
STATE MAP: See page CTC 67.

50 amps, pull-through, dump station, laundry, pets/restrictions, Wi-Fi access, picnic tables, horseshoes, fishing, boating

MINOT

Roughrider RV Resort
500 54th Street Northwest
Minot, North Dakota 58703
701-852-8442; fax: 701-837-1262
manager@roughriderrvresort.com
roughriderrvresort.com
RESORT NUMBER: 2281
GOOD SAM RATING: 8/9.5★/9
DIRECTIONS: From Jct of Hwy 83 & Hwy 2/Hwy 52: Go 4 mi W on Hwy 2/Hwy 52, then 0.5 mi N on paved CR 17 (54th St). Resort on R.
GPS COORDINATES: 48.24172°N/-101.37104°W
NOTATIONS: Check-in: 2:00 p.m. Check-out: Noon. Coast rate $33.75, max 7 days, only one discount per stay. Full hook-ups daily rate includes electric, water, sewer, trash, and Wi-Fi. Additional charges: Dump station $20 if not hooked up to full hook-ups. Drive-ups accepted. Max. RV length: 45 feet. Open: September 7–May 21.
STATE MAP: See page CTC 67.

50 amps, pull-through, dump station, visitor mail, laundry, pets/restrictions, Wi-Fi access, playground, picnic tables, fishing, horseshoes, basketball, volleyball, propane, hot showers, fire rings, tenting, firewood, ice

OHIO

STOUT

Sandy Springs Campground
27719 U.S. Highway 52
Stout, Ohio 45684
701-640-7858
sandyspringscampground@gmail.com
sandyspringscampground.com
RESORT NUMBER: 2143
GOOD SAM RATING: 4.5/9★/8.5
DIRECTIONS: From Cincinnati: Approx 90 mi. E on Hwy 52. From Portsmouth, OH: Approx 20 mi W on Hwy 52.
GPS COORDINATES: 38.6068°N/-83.2859°W
ELEVATION: 520 feet
NOTATIONS: Check-in: 24 hours. Check-out: Noon. Special 10% discount for Coast members. Rate includes 2 adults, 3 children, full hook-ups. Additional charges: Honeywagon $10, add'l adult $5, add'l child $2. Rental units available. Trip Points not accepted. Contact resort directly. No smoking in rental units. Optional linen fee $5. Rental check-in 3 p.m., rental check-out noon. Max. RV length: Unlimited. Open: Year-round.
STATE MAP: See page CTC 71.

50 amps, pull-through, dump station, visitor mail, laundry, pets/restrictions, playground, picnic tables, rental units, fishing, group activities, boating, basketball, tourist attraction, propane, hot showers, fire rings, tenting, firewood

OKLAHOMA

ARDMORE

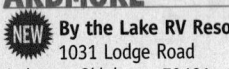

NEW **By the Lake RV Resort**
1031 Lodge Road
Ardmore, Oklahoma 73401
580-798-4721
bythelakervpark@gmail.com
bythelakerv.com
RESORT NUMBER: 2535
GOOD SAM RATING: 10/10★/10
DIRECTIONS: From Jct of I-35 (Ex 24) Lodge Rd: Go 0.5 mi E on Lodge Rd. Park on L.
GPS COORDINATES: 34.07169°N/-97.13291°W
NOTATIONS: Check-in: 1:00 p.m. Check-out: Noon. 2021 Coast rate $36-$40/night on daily rate year round. Rate includes 2 adults per site, full hook-ups. Additional charges: Add'l adult $2/night, tax 8.375%. Max. RV length: 75 feet. Open: Year-round.
STATE MAP: See page CTC 62.

50 amps, pull-through, laundry, pets/restrictions, Wi-Fi access, playground, fishing, fishing, boating, outdoor pool, game room, shopping, gambling casino, fire rings

BARTLESVILLE

NEW **Riverside RV Park**
1211 Southeast Adams Boulevard.
Bartlesville, Oklahoma 74003
918-336-6431; fax: 918-336-3892
riverside@takemetoriverside.com
resortrv.com
RESORT NUMBER: 1322
GOOD SAM RATING: 9/9.5★/8.5
DIRECTIONS: From Jct of US-75 & W US-60 (Pawhuska exit): Go W 1.5 mi on US-60, then S 1 blk on Quapaw Ave. Park on L.
GPS COORDINATES: 36.7498°N/-95.9689°W
NOTATIONS: Check-in: Noon. Check-out: Noon. 2022 Coast rate 20% discount. Rate includes 2 adults per site, full hook-ups. Additional charges: Add'l adult $2/night, add'l child $2/night, tax 8.9%. Max. RV length: 50 feet. Open: Year-round.
STATE MAP: See page CTC 62.

50 amps, pull-through, dump station, cable tv, laundry, pets/restrictions, picnic tables, hiking trails, horseshoes, fishing, gambling casino, ice

CALERA

NEW **Do Drop Inn RV Resort**
560 Platter Dike Road
Calera, Oklahoma 74730
580-965-3600
dodropinnrv@gmail.com
dodropinn.com
RESORT NUMBER: 2541
GOOD SAM RATING: 10/10★/10
DIRECTIONS: From Jct US-75 & W Main St: Go 2.5 mi S on US-75, then 4.5 mi W on Platter Rd, then 0.5 mi S on Platter Dike Rd. Park on R.
GPS COORDINATES: 33.90364°N/-96.54089°W
NOTATIONS: Check-in: 1:00 p.m. Check-out: Noon. 2021 Coast rate $33.60-$39.20/night. Rate includes 2 adults per site, full hook-ups. Additional charges: Add'l adult $5/night, taxes. Max. RV length: 72 feet. Open: Year-round.
STATE MAP: See page CTC 62.

50 amps, pull-through, laundry, pets/restrictions, Wi-Fi access, restaurant/snack bar, recreation hall, fishing, boating, outdoor pool, volleyball, fitness, gambling casino, fire rings, ice

CHICKASHA

NEW **Pecan Grove RV Resort**
600 West Almar Drive
Chickasha, Oklahoma 73018
405-320-5690
info@pecangrovervresort.com
pecangrovervresort.com
RESORT NUMBER: 2540
GOOD SAM RATING: 8.5/10★/8.5
DIRECTIONS: From Jct of I-44 (H.E. Bailey Turnpike) & US-81/US-277: Go S 0.25 mi on US-81/US-277, then W 0.25 mi on W Almar Dr. Park on R.
GPS COORDINATES: 35.0205°N/-97.93952°W
NOTATIONS: Check-in: Noon. Check-out: 11:00 a.m. 2021 Coast rate $28-$32/night. Rate includes 2 adults per site. Additional charges: Taxes. Max. RV length: 85 feet. Open: Year-round.
STATE MAP: See page CTC 62.

50 amps, pull-through, laundry, pets/restrictions, Wi-Fi access, horseshoes, game room, gambling casino, rv supplies, ice

WEATHERFORD

NEW **Wanderlust Crossings RV Park**
1038 Airport Road
Weatherford, Oklahoma 73096
580-772-2800
info@wanderlustcrossings.com
wanderlustcrossings.com
RESORT NUMBER: 2528
GOOD SAM RATING: 9/9.5★/10
DIRECTIONS: From Jct I-40 (Ex 84) & Airport Rd: Go 0.25 mi S on Airport Rd. Park on L before bridge.
GPS COORDINATES: 35.52939°N/-98.65717°W
NOTATIONS: Check-in: 1:00 p.m. Check-out: 11:00 a.m. 2021 Coast rate $33.60-$37.80/night. Rate includes 2 adults per site, full hook-ups. Additional charges: Add'l adult $3/night, tax 5%. Max. RV length: 50 feet. Open: Year-round.
STATE MAP: See page CTC 62.

50 amps, pull-through, laundry, pets/restrictions, Wi-Fi access, playground, picnic tables, recreation hall, golf, game room, spa, grocery, firewood, ice

OREGON

SILVERTON

NEW **Silver Spur RV Park & Resort**
12622 Silverton Road Northeast
Silverton, Oregon 97381
503-873-2020
info@silverspurrvpark.com
silverspurrvpark.com
RESORT NUMBER: 2543
GOOD SAM RATING: 9.5/10★/10
DIRECTIONS: Nbnd: From Jct of I-5 & Chemawa Rd (Ex 260) or Sbnd (Ex 260B): Go E 5.6 mi on Chemawa/Hazel Green Rd to Howell Prairie Rd, then S 1.3 mi to Silverton Rd, then E 3.6 mi. Park on R. Note: Follow Oregon Gardens signs.
GPS COORDINATES: 45.00263°N/-122.80305°W
NOTATIONS: Check-in: 1:00 p.m. Check-out: 11:00 a.m. 2021 Coast rate 10% discount avail Oct 1-Feb 28. Rate includes 2 adults per site, full hook-ups, Wi-Fi, cable. Additional charges: Add'l adult $2/night, tax 1.5%. Max. RV length: 42 feet. Open: Year-round.
STATE MAP: See page CTC 72.

50 amps, pull-through, laundry, pets/restrictions, Wi-Fi access, playground, hiking trails, recreation hall, boating, outdoor pool, shopping, rv supplies, firewood, ice

SUNNY VALLEY

Sunny Valley RV Park and Campground
140 Old Stage Road
Sunny Valley, Oregon 97497
541-479-0209
info@sunnyvalleycampground.com
sunnyvalleycampground.com
RESORT NUMBER: 2317
GOOD SAM RATING: 8.5/10★/9.5
DIRECTIONS: From Sunny Valley I-5: Ex 71. Follow signs 0.5 mi.
GPS COORDINATES: 42.639°N/-123.3753°W
ELEVATION: 1,260 feet
NOTATIONS: Check-in: 2:00 p.m. Check-out: 11:00 a.m. Special Coast discount 10% off peak season, 25% off shoulder months. Rate includes 4 adults per site, electric, water, limited sewer. 50 & 30 amp sites available. Limited 50 amp sites (6 total). Additional charges: Extra adults $5/night, cancellation fee, tax 1.8%. Free Wi-Fi throughout park. Rental units available. Trip Points not accepted. Contact resort directly. Max.

RV length: 45 feet. Open: March 1–October 31.
STATE MAP: See page CTC 72.

50 amps · pull-through · laundry · pets/restrictions · Wi-Fi access · playground · picnic tables · rental units · horseshoes · fishing · boating · outdoor pool · golf · game room · tourist attraction · shopping · hot showers · fire rings · grocery · tenting · firewood · ice

PENNSYLVANIA

AUSTIN

Austin Campground
364 Nelson Run Road
Austin, Pennsylvania 16720
814-647-8777; fax: 814-647-8855
camping@austincampground.com
austincampground.com
RESORT NUMBER: 2077
GOOD SAM RATING: 5.5/9★/9
DIRECTIONS: From SE: I-80 Lock Haven Ex 178. Hwy 220 to Rt 120. W to Sinnemahoning. R on Rt 872. N 21 mi. At camp sign R on Nelson Run Rd for 1 mi. From N: Rt 6 to Rt 872 S 19.8 mi. L at camp sign.
GPS COORDINATES: 41.5688°N/-78.0214°W
ELEVATION: 1,200 feet
NOTATIONS: Check-in: 2:00 p.m. Check-out: 11:00 a.m. 2021 Coast rate $35/night, includes 2 adults/2 children under 13, 30 amp, partial hook-ups. Additional charges: Extra person $5/night, 50 amp $3/night, AC $3/night, honey-wagon $10, dump station $5/one night stay. Day users $5/person. Rental units available. Trip Points not accepted. Contact resort directly. Rental unit additional charges: $10/night extra person. Max. RV length: Unlimited. Open: April 15–December 14.
STATE MAP: See page CTC 73.

50 amps · dump station · pets/restrictions · internet access · picnic tables · rental units · fishing · horseshoes · volleyball · tourist attraction · propane · hot showers · ball field · fire rings · grocery · rv supplies · gift shop · tenting · winter sports · winter sports · firewood · ice

MUNCY VALLEY

Pioneer Campground
307 Pioneer Trail
Muncy Valley, Pennsylvania 17758
570-946-9971
pioneercg@epix.net
pioneercampground.com
RESORT NUMBER: 2491
GOOD SAM RATING: 9.5/9★/10
DIRECTIONS: From Jct US 220 & Hwy 42 (in Laporte): Go S 2 mi on US 220, campground is on R.
GPS COORDINATES: 41.39969°N/-76.50537°W
NOTATIONS: Check-in: 3:00 p.m. Check-out: Noon. Special 20% discount rate for Coast members for Tue-Thu only with max 2 night stay. Rate includes 2 adults per site, water, electric, no sewer. Additional charges: Add'l person $10/night, cancellation fee, honey wagon service fee. Max. RV length: 42 feet. Open: April 15–December 15.
STATE MAP: See page CTC 73.

50 amps · dump station · laundry · pets/restrictions · Wi-Fi access · playground · picnic tables · hiking trails · horseshoes · group activities · fishing · outdoor pool · game room · shopping · propane · hot showers · ball field · fire rings

SOUTH DAKOTA

CANTON

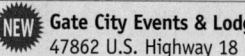

NEW **Gate City Events & Lodging**
47862 U.S. Highway 18
Canton, South Dakota 57013
602-214-4604
gceventsllc@gmail.com
gceventsllc.com
RESORT NUMBER: 2581
GOOD SAM RATING: 5/NA/9.5
DIRECTIONS: From Jct I-29 & US-18/5th St: Go 8.75 mi E on US-18/5th St. Park on R.
GPS COORDINATES: 43.30426°N/-96.61837°W
NOTATIONS: Check-in: 1:00 p.m. Check-out: 11:00 a.m. 2021 Coast rate $35/night. Rate includes 2 adults per site, full hook-ups. Additional charges: Tax 9%. Max. RV length: 50 feet. Open: Year-round.
STATE MAP: See page CTC 67.

50 amps · pull-through · dump station · laundry · pets/restrictions · Wi-Fi access · playground · picnic tables · hiking trails · horseshoes · recreation hall · fishing · boating

CUSTER

NEW **Beaver Lake Campground**
12005 U.S. Highway 16
Custer, South Dakota 57730
605-673-2464
beaverres@goldenwest.net
beaverlakecampground.net
RESORT NUMBER: 2537
GOOD SAM RATING: 9/10★/10
DIRECTIONS: From Jct US 385 & US 16 (in town): Go 3.5 mi W on US 16. Park on L.
GPS COORDINATES: 43.73967°N/-103.65685°W
NOTATIONS: Check-in: 1:00 p.m. Check-out: Noon. 2021 Coast rate $51-$55/night avail Aug 20-Sep 3 and Sep 8-Nov 10. Rate includes 2 adults per site, full hook-ups. Additional charges: Add'l adult $6/night, add'l child $6/night, tax 6%. Coast discount not avail July 1-Aug 19. Max. RV length: 80 feet. Open: April 1–November 1.
STATE MAP: See page CTC 67.

pull-through · laundry · pets/restrictions · Wi-Fi access · playground · hiking trails · horseshoes · recreation hall · fishing · outdoor pool · tourist attraction · shopping

CUSTER

Buffalo Ridge Camp Resort
245 Centennial Drive
Custer, South Dakota 57730
605-673-2305
buffaloridge@custerhospitality.com
custerhospitality.com/buffalo-ridge-camp-resort
RESORT NUMBER: 2477
GOOD SAM RATING: 9/10★/10
DIRECTIONS: From Jct US-16/385 & 16-A: Go 0.75 mi W on US-16 to U.S. 385, go S 2 blocks on US-385, resort on R.
GPS COORDINATES: 43.75746°N/-103.61069°W
NOTATIONS: Check-in: 3:00 p.m. Check-out: 11:00 a.m. Special discount rate of $60 for Coast members. Rate includes 2 adults per site, full hook-ups, free Wi-Fi. Additional charges: Tax 6%. No discount available Jul 4 long holiday weekend. Max. RV length: 65 feet. Open: May 21–October 1.
STATE MAP: See page CTC 67.

50 amps · pull-through · laundry · pets/restrictions · Wi-Fi access · playground · hot tub · outdoor pool · tourist attraction · hot showers

DEADWOOD

NEW **Custer Crossing Campground**
22036 U.S. Highway 385
Deadwood, South Dakota 57732
605-584-1009
laurie@custercrossingcampground.com
custercrossingcampground.com
RESORT NUMBER: 2538
GOOD SAM RATING: 5.5/9★/9
DIRECTIONS: From Jct Custer Crossing Rd & US Hwy 385: Go 0.25 mi S on US Hwy 385. Park on L; From Jct US Hwy 44 & US Hwy 385: Go 8 mi N on US Hwy 385. Park on R.
GPS COORDINATES: 44.20562°N/-103.64984°W
ELEVATION: 5,434 feet
NOTATIONS: Check-in: 1:00 p.m. Check-out: Noon. 2021 Coast rate $35-$55/night. Not avail July 4th weekend, Sturgis Rally week in Aug and Labor Day weekend. Rate includes 2 adults per site. Additional charges: Add'l adult $5/night, add'l child $5/night, tax 6%. Max. RV length: 60 feet. Open: Year-round.
STATE MAP: See page CTC 67.

50 amps · pull-through · pets/restrictions · Wi-Fi access · picnic tables · fishing · boating · tourist attraction · fire rings · grocery · ice

DEADWOOD

Whistler Gulch Campground & RV Park
235 Cliff Street
Deadwood, South Dakota 57732
800-704-7139
whistlergulch@gmail.com
whistlergulch.com
RESORT NUMBER: 2492
GOOD SAM RATING: 9.5/9.5★/9
DIRECTIONS: From Jct US-85 & US-14A: Go 3 mi S on US-85, campground on L. From Jct US-385 & US-85: Go 0.5 mi E on US-85, campground on R.
GPS COORDINATES: 44.36383°N/-103.73485°W
NOTATIONS: Check-in: 1:00 p.m. Check-out: 11:00 a.m. 2021 Coast rate 20% discount. Rate includes 2 adults per site, full hook-ups, free Wi-Fi. Additional charges: Tax 9.5%. No discount avail Jun 1- Aug 31. Coast discount avail May and Sep. Max. RV length: 60 feet. Open: May 1–September 30.
STATE MAP: See page CTC 67.

50 amps · pull-through · laundry · pets/restrictions · Wi-Fi access · picnic tables · hiking trails · fishing · outdoor pool · tourist attraction · grocery · rv supplies · firewood

HERMOSA

Heartland RV Park & Cabins
24743 Highway 79
Hermosa, South Dakota 57744
605-255-5460; fax: 605-225-5460
reservations@heartlandrvpark.com
heartlandrvpark.com
RESORT NUMBER: 2140
GOOD SAM RATING: 10/10★/10
DIRECTIONS: From I-90 take Ex 61 S for 5.5 mi to SD-79 S, 15.5 mi S on SD-79 to resort. Located on new 4-lane divided hwy at mi marker 59 just past intersections of Hwy 79 & Hwy 36.
GPS COORDINATES: 43.8205°N/-103.202°W
ELEVATION: 3,338 feet
NOTATIONS: Check-in: 1:00 p.m. Check-out: 11:00 a.m. Coast member 25% discount avail Apr 15-May 26 & Sep 1-Oct 31. Rate includes 2 guests per site. Children 6 & younger free. Additional charges: Each extra guest $5/night, extra child $5/night, tax 6%. Max. RV length: 120 feet. Open: April 15–October 31.
STATE MAP: See page CTC 67.

50 amps, pull-through, cable tv, visitor mail, laundry, pets/restrictions, Wi-Fi access, playground, picnic tables, restaurant/snack bar, hot tub, recreation hall, tourist attraction, fitness, propane, hot showers, gambling casino, fire rings, rv supplies, gift shop, tenting, firewood, handicap access, ice, grills

HERMOSA

Southern Hills RV Park & Campground
24549 Highway 79
Hermosa, South Dakota 57744
605-939-7609
kstyles907@msn.com
RESORT NUMBER: 2343
GOOD SAM RATING: 8/9.5★/8.5
DIRECTIONS: From I-90 & Elk Vale Rd (US-16 Truck bypass): S 5.4 mi to Hwy 79, then 14 mi S on Hwy 79 to mi marker 61. Resort on R.
GPS COORDINATES: 43.84587°N/-103.2022°W
NOTATIONS: Check-in: 1:00 p.m. Check-out: 11:00 a.m. Special discount rate for Coast members. Additional charges: Extra adult $5/night, extra child $5/night, tax 9%. Max. RV length: 45 feet. Open: May 1–May 31; September 1–September 30.
STATE MAP: See page CTC 67.

50 amps, pull-through, dump station, laundry, pets/restrictions, picnic tables, tourist attraction, hot showers, tenting, ice

HILL CITY

NEW **Black Hills Trailside Park Resort**
24024 Highway 16/385
Hill City, South Dakota 57745
605-574-9079
reserve@trailsideparkresort.com
trailsideparkresort.com
RESORT NUMBER: 2569
GOOD SAM RATING: 6.5/9.5★/7.5
DIRECTIONS: At South city limit of Hill City on US-16/385 (East side).
GPS COORDINATES: 43.92564°N/-103.57831°W
ELEVATION: 5,000 feet
NOTATIONS: Check-in: 1:00 p.m. Check-out: 11:00 a.m. 2021 Coast rate 15% discount available May -Sep. Rate includes 2 adults per site, full hook-ups. Additional charges: Tax 10%. Max. RV length: 40 feet. Open: May 1–October 30.
STATE MAP: See page CTC 67.

50 amps, pull-through, dump station, cable tv, pets/restrictions, Wi-Fi access, picnic tables, hiking trails, fishing, boating, basketball, gambling casino, fire rings, firewood

INTERIOR

Badlands Motel & Campground
900 South Dakota Highway 377
Interior, South Dakota 57750
605-433-5335; fax: 605-433-5598
badlandsmotelcampground@gmail.com
badlandsbudgethostmotel.com
RESORT NUMBER: 1761
GOOD SAM RATING: 7/9★/8.5
DIRECTIONS: From I-90 Ex 131, S on Hwy 240 Badlands Loop for 8.5 miles. Just past Badlands Visitor Center turn L on Hwy 377 toward Interior, 2 mi, park on R.
GPS COORDINATES: 43.72909°N/-101.97857°W
NOTATIONS: Check-in: 1:00 p.m. Check-out: 11:30 a.m. 2022 Coast rate $35-$45 avail all season. RV site is limited to 2 adults and 3 children. Drive-ups not accepted. Max. RV length: 75 feet. Open: April 9–October 9.
STATE MAP: See page CTC 67.

50 amps, pull-through, dump station, laundry, pets/restrictions, playground, fishing, outdoor pool, basketball

KEYSTONE

Kemp's Kamp
1022 Old Hill City Road
Keystone, South Dakota 57751
888-466-6282
kempskamp.com
RESORT NUMBER: 2438
GOOD SAM RATING: 6.5/9★/7.5
DIRECTIONS: From Jct US-16 Alt & CR-323/Old Hill City Rd (N edge of town): Go 1.5 mi W on CR-323/Old Hill City Rd, resort on R.
GPS COORDINATES: 43.91846°N/-103.51098°W
NOTATIONS: Check-in: 1:00 p.m. Check-out: 11:00 a.m. Special discount rate for Coast members. Limited Wi-Fi access. Discount not available major holiday or special event weekends. Max. RV length: 40 feet. Open: May 10–June 10; September 5–September 30.
STATE MAP: See page CTC 67.

50 amps, pull-through, laundry, pets/restrictions, Wi-Fi access, fishing, hiking trails, fishing, outdoor pool, tourist attraction, shopping, canoes

MITCHELL

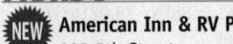

Betts Campground
25473 403rd Avenue
Mitchell, South Dakota 57301
605-996-8983
bettscampground@outlook.com
bettscampground.com
RESORT NUMBER: 2474
GOOD SAM RATING: 9/9.5★/9.5
DIRECTIONS: From Jct of I-90 & Ex 325 (Betts Rd): S 0.2 mi on Betts Rd, campground on R.
GPS COORDINATES: 43.69179°N/-98.14728°W
NOTATIONS: Check-in: 3:00 p.m. Check-out: 1:00 p.m. Special discount rate of $26.25 for Coast members only available Mon-Thu from Apr 15 -Oct 31. Rate includes 2 adults per site, full hook-ups, 30 or 50 amp. Additional charges: Tax 4.5% + 1.5% tourism. Max. RV length: 75 feet. Open: April 15–October 31.
STATE MAP: See page CTC 67.

50 amps, pull-through, laundry, pets/restrictions, Wi-Fi access, horseshoes, recreation hall, outdoor pool, mini golf, basketball, volleyball, game room, tourist attraction, fire rings, tenting, firewood, ice

MURDO

NEW **American Inn & RV Park**
305 5th Street
Murdo, South Dakota 57559
605-530-0120
RESORT NUMBER: 2484
GOOD SAM RATING: 5/8.5★/9
DIRECTIONS: From Jct I-90 (Ex 192) & Hwy 83: Go 2 blks N on US-83, then 2 blks W on 5th St, park on L.
GPS COORDINATES: 43.88562°N/-100.70991°W
NOTATIONS: Check-in: Noon. Check-out: 11:00 a.m. 2021 Coast rate $38. Rate includes 2 adults per site, full hook-ups. Additional charges: Tax 9%. Max. RV length: 65 feet. Open: May 1–November 1.
STATE MAP: See page CTC 67.

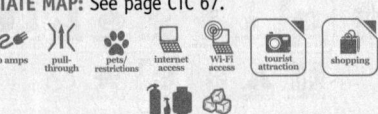

50 amps, pull-through, pets/restrictions, internet access, Wi-Fi access, tourist attraction, shopping, rv supplies, ice

RAPID CITY

NEW **Happy Holiday RV Resort**
8990 South Highway 16
Rapid City, South Dakota 57702
605-342-7365
camp@happyholidayrvresort.com
happyholidayrvresort.com
RESORT NUMBER: 2575
GOOD SAM RATING: 9/9★/7.5
DIRECTIONS: From Jct I-90 & Ex 61 (Elkvale Rd): Go 8.8 mi S on Elkvale Rd (turns into Catron Blvd/US-16 Truck BYP) to US 16, then 2.2 mi S on US-16. Park on L.
GPS COORDINATES: 43.9903°N/-103.2687°W
ELEVATION: 3,200 feet
NOTATIONS: Check-in: 1:00 p.m. Check-out: Noon. 2021 Coast rate 15% discount. Rate includes 2 adults per site, full hook-ups. Additional charges: Tax 6%. Max. RV length: 40 feet. Open: Year-round.

STATE MAP: See page CTC 67.

50 amps, pull-through, dump station, laundry, pets/restrictions, Wi-Fi access, playground, picnic tables, hiking trails, horseshoes, recreation hall, fishing, outdoor pool, golf, fire rings, grocery, gift shop, ice

SIOUX FALLS

NEW **Tower Campground**
4609 West 12th Street
Sioux Falls, South Dakota 57106
605-332-1173
towercampground@gmail.com
towercampground.com
RESORT NUMBER: 2545
GOOD SAM RATING: 8/9.5★/8.5
DIRECTIONS: Nbnd: From Jct I-29 (Ex 78) & 26th St: Go 0.5 mi W on 26th St, then 1 mi N on Marion Rd, then 0.3 mi E on W 12th St/SD-42 (R). Sbnd: From Jct I-29 (Ex 80) & W Madison St: Go 0.5 mi W on Madison St, then 1 mi S on S Ebenezer, then 0.3 mi E on W 12th St/SD-42. Park on R.
GPS COORDINATES: 43.54361°N/-96.78177°W
NOTATIONS: Check-in: 1:00 p.m. Check-out: 11:00 a.m. 2021 Coast 15% discount. Rate includes 2 adults per site, full hook-ups and Wi-Fi. Max. RV length: 55 feet. Open: Year-round.
STATE MAP: See page CTC 67.

50 amps, pull-through, dump station, laundry, pets/restrictions, Wi-Fi access, playground, picnic tables, hiking trails, golf, shopping, propane, firewood, ice

STURGIS

No Name City Luxury Cabins & RV
20899 Pleasant Valley Drive
I-90 Ex 34
Sturgis, South Dakota 57785
605-347-8891
camping@nonamecity.com
nonamecity.com
RESORT NUMBER: 2245
GOOD SAM RATING: 9/9★/8
DIRECTIONS: Do not use GPS, use Google Maps or phone. I-90 Ex 34, S on Service Rd (Pleasant Valley Dr), 0.75 mi to park on R.
GPS COORDINATES: 44.3634°N/-103.4658°W
NOTATIONS: Check-in: 1:00 p.m. Check-out: 11:00 a.m. Rate includes 2 people, full hook-ups, 30 amp. Additional charges: 50 amp $3/night, extra adult $5/night, extra child $3/night, early check-in/check-out $15, tax 6%. Max. RV length: 90 feet. Open: May 1–October 14.
STATE MAP: See page CTC 67.

50 amps, pull-through, dump station, visitor mail, laundry, pets/restrictions, internet access, Wi-Fi access, playground, picnic tables, hot tub, hiking trails, recreation hall, outdoor pool, tourist attraction, propane, hot showers, tenting, handicap access, ice

STURGIS

NEW **Suzie's Camp**
20983 Pleasant Valley Drive
Sturgis, South Dakota 57785
605-347-8677
randyhanson56chevy@yahoo.com
suziescamp.com
RESORT NUMBER: 2539
GOOD SAM RATING: 6/9.5★/6.5
DIRECTIONS: From Jct US-14A & I-90: Go 4 mi SE on I-90 (Ex 34), then 1 mi E on Pleasant Valley Dr/Service Rd. Park on R.
GPS COORDINATES: 44.36233°N/-103.4672°W
ELEVATION: 3,600 feet
NOTATIONS: Check-in: 1:00 p.m. Check-out: Noon. 2021 Coast rate $38-$48/night not avail during Aug. Rate includes 2 adults per site, full hook-ups. Additional charges: Add'l adult $5/night, add'l child 5-11 years $5/night, add'l child 12-16 years $10/night, tax 6.5%. Max. RV length: 80 feet. Open: Year-round.
STATE MAP: See page CTC 67.

50 amps, pull-through, dump station, laundry, pets/restrictions, Wi-Fi access, picnic tables, hiking trails, tourist attraction

WALL

NEW **Sleepy Hollow Campground**
118 4th Avenue West
Wall, South Dakota 57790
605-279-2100
sleepyhollowsd@gmail.com
sleepyhollowcampgroundsd.com
RESORT NUMBER: 2547
GOOD SAM RATING: 7.5/10★/8.5
DIRECTIONS: From Jct I-90 (Ex 110): Go 0.5 mi N on Glenn, then 0.25 mi W on 4th Ave. Park on R.
GPS COORDINATES: 43.99471°N/-102.24374°W
NOTATIONS: Check-in: 1:00 p.m. Check-out: 11:00 a.m. 2021 Coast rate 15% discount avail Apr, May, Sep and Oct. Rate includes 2 adults per site, full hook-ups. Additional charges: Tax 9%. Max. RV length: 45 feet. Open: April 15–October 31.
STATE MAP: See page CTC 67.

50 amps, pull-through, dump station, laundry, pets/restrictions, Wi-Fi access, playground, picnic tables, hiking trails, fishing, boating, fire rings, grocery, firewood, ice

TENNESSEE

BRISTOL

Shadrack Campground
2537 Volunteer Parkway
Bristol, Tennessee 37620
423-217-1181
camp@shadrack.com
shadrackcampground.com
RESORT NUMBER: 2401
GOOD SAM RATING: 7.5/9.5★/6.5
DIRECTIONS: From Jct I-81 & SR-394 (Ex 69): Go 5.5 mi S on SR 394, then 2 mi E on US-19 (US-11E). Park on R.
GPS COORDINATES: 36.52906°N/-82.24979°W
NOTATIONS: Check-in: 1:00 p.m. Check-out: Noon. Special discount rate for Coast members. Rate includes full hook-ups, Wi-Fi. Additional charges: Tax 9.3%. Rate not available for the Apr NASCAR, Jun NHRA, or Aug NASCAR race weeks. Max. RV length: 45 feet. Open: Year-round.
STATE MAP: See page CTC 63.

50 amps, dump station, laundry, pets/restrictions, Wi-Fi access, recreation hall, fishing, boating, golf, tourist attraction, shopping, hot showers, rv supplies, tenting, firewood

PIGEON FORGE

Creekside RV Park
2475 Henderson Springs Road
Pigeon Forge, Tennessee 37863
865-428-4801
creeksidervpark@yahoo.com
creeksidervpark.com
RESORT NUMBER: 2315
GOOD SAM RATING: 9.5/9.5★/9.5
DIRECTIONS: From Jct US-441 & US 321: SW 0.7 mi on US 321 to Henderson Springs Rd. R 0.2 mi. 2nd resort on R. From Parkway: W on Wears Valley Road at traffic light #3. Pass Kroger and Pigeon Forge School on R. At 2nd traffic light, turn R on Henderson Springs Rd. Approx 0.3 mi 2nd resort on R.
GPS COORDINATES: 35.80174°N/-83.58911°W
NOTATIONS: Check-in: 1:00 p.m. Check-out: 11:00 a.m. 2021 Coast rate $40.80-$42.40/night. Rate includes 4 people. Additional charges: 50 amp $2/night, add'l adult $2/night, tax 12.75%. No tents. Rate not available Jun, Jul, Sep and Oct. Max. RV length: 40 feet. Open: April 1–December 31.
STATE MAP: See page CTC 63.

50 amps, pull-through, cable tv, laundry, pets/restrictions, Wi-Fi access, picnic tables, fishing, outdoor pool, tourist attraction, shopping, fire rings, grocery, rv supplies, firewood

TRACY CITY

NEW **Bigfoot Adventure RV Park & Campground**
514 Brawley Road
Tracy City, Tennessee 37387
931-488-8652
info@bigfootadventuretn.com
bigfootadventuretn.com
RESORT NUMBER: 2576
GOOD SAM RATING: 7/9.5★/9.5
DIRECTIONS: From Jct I-24 & US 41 (Ex 134): Go 3.25 mi N on US 41, then 2.75 mi NW on Summerfield Rd, then 1.5 mi E on Clouse Hill Rd, then 1 mi N on Brawley Rd. Park on E.
GPS COORDINATES: 35.30324°N/-85.77099°W
NOTATIONS: Check-in: 1:00 p.m. Check-out: Noon. 2021 Coast rate 20% discount available Nov 1-Apr 30. Rate includes 2 adults per site, full hook-ups. Additional charges: Tax 7%. Max. RV length: 80 feet. Open: Year-round.
STATE MAP: See page CTC 63.

50 amps, pull-through, dump station, pets/restrictions, Wi-Fi access, playground, picnic tables, hiking trails, horseshoes, tourist attraction, shopping, fire rings, gift shop, ice

TEXAS

ALAMO

Acacia RV Park
89 East Business Highway 83
Alamo, Texas 78516
956-884-0202
info@rvacacia.com
rvacacia.com
RESORT NUMBER: 2396
GOOD SAM RATING: 7.5/8.5★/8
DIRECTIONS: From I-2: Ex Val Verde, go S on Val Verde. Turn R onto Bus 83 and go approx 1 mi to park on L.
GPS COORDINATES: 26.17824°N/-98.09372°W
NOTATIONS: Check-in: 3:00 p.m. Check-out: 11:00 a.m. 2022 Coast rate $28. Rate includes 2 people per RV site, full hook-ups. Additional charges: Add'l adults $2/night, add'l children $2/night. No extra charge for 50 amp. Max. RV length: 46 feet. Open: Year-round.
STATE MAP: See page CTC 74.

50 amps · laundry · pets/restrictions · Wi-Fi access · group activities · recreation hall · tourist attraction · shopping · hot showers

BIG SPRINGS

NEW **Whip In RV Park**
7000 South Service Road I-20
Big Springs, Texas 79720
432-393-5242
whipinrvpark@yahoo.com
whipinrvpark.com
RESORT NUMBER: 2519
GOOD SAM RATING: 7/8.5/7.5
DIRECTIONS: From Jct I-20: Go 200 ft S on Moss Lake Rd Ex 184. Park on L.
GPS COORDINATES: 32.27412°N/-101.36983°W
NOTATIONS: Check-in: 11:00 a.m. Check-out: 11:00 a.m. 2021 Coast rate $28/night. Rate includes 2 adults per site, full hook-ups, Wi-Fi, cable TV. Additional charges: Tax 8.25%. Max. RV length: 45 feet. Open: Year-round.
STATE MAP: See page CTC 74.

50 amps · pull-through · laundry · pets/restrictions · Wi-Fi access · picnic tables · golf · tourist attraction · shopping

BUCHANAN DAM

Freedom Lives Ranch RV Resort
9606 West Rural Route 1431
Buchanan Dam, Texas 78609
512-793-2171
mwilke@ctesc.net
freedomlivesranchrvresort.com
RESORT NUMBER: 2509
GOOD SAM RATING: 8.5/9★/8.5
DIRECTIONS: From Jct Hwy 29 & Ranch Rd 1431: Go 1 mi N on Ranch Rd 1431, resort on R.
GPS COORDINATES: 30.74983°N/-98.466°W
NOTATIONS: Check-in: 1:00 p.m. Check-out: Noon. Special discount rate of $36 for Coast members. Rate includes 2 adults per site, electric, water, sewer, Wi-Fi. Max. RV length: 48 feet. Open: Year-round.
STATE MAP: See page CTC 74.

50 amps · pull-through · visitor mail · laundry · pets/restrictions · Wi-Fi access · hot tub · recreation hall · fishing · boating · tourist attraction

CANTON

Mill Creek Ranch RV & Cottage Resort
1880 North Trade Days Boulevard
Canton, Texas 75103
903-567-7275; res.: 877-927-3439
lesli@millcreekranchresort.com
millcreekranchresort.com
RESORT NUMBER: 2080
GOOD SAM RATING: 9.5/10★/10
DIRECTIONS: From Dallas (60 mi): I-20 E. Ex 527 to TX 19. R (S) at Trade Days Blvd/TX 19. Resort on L. From Shreveport (120 mi): I-20 W. Ex 527 to TX 19. L (S) at Trade Days Blvd/TX 19. Resort on L.
GPS COORDINATES: 32.5732°N/-95.8502°W
ELEVATION: 505 feet
NOTATIONS: Check-in: 1:00 p.m. Check-out: Noon. Coast discount of 15% includes 2 adults, full hook-ups, 20/30/50 amp, concrete pad, water, sewer, children free. Coast discount not avail holidays & First Monday Trade Days. Additional charges for extra guests 12 yrs & older. Optional resort fee $5 for amenities & activities. Monthly spots avail. Drive-ups accepted. Max. RV length: 60 feet. Open: Year-round.
STATE MAP: See page CTC 74.

50 amps · laundry · pets/restrictions · Wi-Fi access · playground · picnic tables · hot tub · fishing · hiking trails · horseshoes · outdoor pool · golf · game room · tourist attraction · paddle boats · fire rings · grocery · rv supplies · firewood · ice

CLEVELAND

East Fork RV Resort
1626 Highway 59 S
Cleveland, Texas 77327
281-593-2053
info@eastforkrvresort.com
eastforkrvresort.com
RESORT NUMBER: 2512
GOOD SAM RATING: 10/9.5★/9
DIRECTIONS: From Jct Hwy 105 & US 69: Go 0.5 mi S on US 69, then 1 mi S on US 59 N, resort on R.
GPS COORDINATES: 30.3257°N/-95.10248°W
NOTATIONS: Check-in: 1:00 p.m. Check-out: 11:00 a.m. Coast members receive special discounted rate. Rate includes 2 adults, 2 children per site, electric, water, sewer, free Wi-Fi. Max. RV length: 45 feet. Open: Year-round.
STATE MAP: See page CTC 74.

50 amps · pull-through · laundry · pets/restrictions · Wi-Fi access · fishing · hiking trails · boating · fishing · boating · outdoor pool · golf · shopping · hot showers

CONROE

QRV Conroe RV Resort
3043 Waukegan Road
Conroe, Texas 77306
844-728-7278
conroe@qualityrvresorts.com
qualityrvresorts.com
RESORT NUMBER: 2476
GOOD SAM RATING: 9/9★/9.5
DIRECTIONS: From Jct of E Loop 336 & SR-105: E 3.7 mi on SR-105 to Waukegan Rd, S 0.6 mi to resort on L.
GPS COORDINATES: 30.32497°N/-95.34041°W
NOTATIONS: Check-in: Noon. Check-out: 11:00 a.m. Coast 2021 rate 20% discount on daily rates only. Rate includes up to 4 persons, 6 max per site, full hook-ups, Wi-Fi. Additional charges: Add'l person $5/night. Max. RV length: 75 feet. Open: Year-round.
STATE MAP: See page CTC 74.

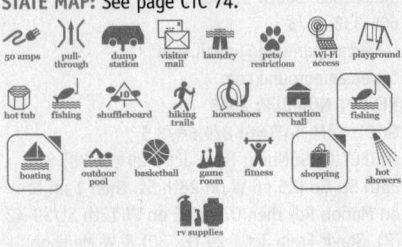

50 amps · pull-through · dump station · visitor mail · laundry · pets/restrictions · Wi-Fi access · playground · hot tub · fishing · shuffleboard · hiking trails · horseshoes · recreation hall · fishing · boating · outdoor pool · basketball · game room · fitness · shopping · hot showers · rv supplies

CROCKETT

Crockett Family Resort
75 Dogwood Lane West
Crockett, Texas 75835
936-544-8466
marina@crockettresort.com
crockettresort.com
RESORT NUMBER: 2458
GOOD SAM RATING: 8/8/8
DIRECTIONS: From Jct of Loop 304 & FM 229 (NW of town): W 6.8 mi on FM 229 to CR 2140, N 2 mi.
GPS COORDINATES: 31.41133°N/-95.57894°W
NOTATIONS: Check-in: 2:00 p.m. Check-out: 2:00 p.m. Special discount rate of $28.80 for Coast members. Rate includes 2 people. Additional charges: Add'l adult $3/night, add'l child over 6 yrs $3/night, add'l vehicle $3/night, 50 amp $3/night, cable $3/night. Max. RV length: 41 feet. Open: Year-round.
STATE MAP: See page CTC 74.

50 amps · pull-through · cable tv · visitor mail · laundry · pets/restrictions · internet access · Wi-Fi access · playground · fishing · group activities · boating · outdoor pool · paddle boats · tenting · firewood · ice

DONNA

NEW **Big Valley RV Resort**
109 West Business Highway 83
Donna, Texas 78537
956-464-4159
bigvalley@vineyardsmg.com
bigvalleymhrvpark.com
RESORT NUMBER: 2526
GOOD SAM RATING: 9.5/9★/8.5
DIRECTIONS: From Jct of FM 493 & Bus 83: Go 0.75 mi W on Bus 83. Park on L.
GPS COORDINATES: 26.17253°N/-98.06458°W
NOTATIONS: Check-in: 11:00 a.m. Check-out: Noon. 2021 Coast rate $27/night. Rate includes 2 adults per site, full hook-ups. Additional charges: Tax 8.25%. Max. RV length: 45 feet. Open: Year-round.

STATE MAP: See page CTC 74.

50 amps · cable tv · laundry · pets/restrictions · Wi-Fi access · shuffleboard · group activities · fishing · shopping · indoor pool · ice

DONNA

NEW **Magnolia Village MHP & RV Park**
3707 East Highway Business 83
Donna, Texas 78537
956-464-2421
magnolia@vineyardsmg.com
RESORT NUMBER: 2525
GOOD SAM RATING: 7.5/7.5/7
DIRECTIONS: From Jct of US Bus 83 & Victoria Rd go E 0.5 mi. Park on R.
GPS COORDINATES: 26.16535°N/-98.02419°W
NOTATIONS: Check-in: 11:00 a.m. Check-out: 11:00 a.m. 2021 Coast rate $40.50/night. Rate includes 2 adults per site, full hook-ups. Additional charges: Tax 8.25%. Max. RV length: 40 feet. Open: Year-round.
STATE MAP: See page CTC 74.

50 amps · laundry · pets/restrictions · Wi-Fi access · shuffleboard · group activities · fishing · outdoor pool · fitness · shopping

EASTLAND

Wandering Oaks RV Park
10502 Interstate Highway 20, exit 343
Eastland, Texas 76448
254-433-9090
wanderingoaksrvpark@gmail.com
wanderingoaksrvpark.com
RESORT NUMBER: 2502
GOOD SAM RATING: 6.5/9.5★/8
DIRECTIONS: From Jct Hwy 112 (E Main St) & I-20: Go 0.5 mi SW on IH 20 W Service Rd, park on R. Entrance is located at the end of a dead end road.
GPS COORDINATES: 32.3946°N/-98.79566°W
NOTATIONS: Check-in: Noon. Check-out: 11:00 a.m. 2021 Coast rate $40. Rate includes 2 adults, 2 children per site, 1 main camping unit, full hook-ups, free Wi-Fi. All payments accepted. Max. RV length: 60 feet. Open: Year-round.
STATE MAP: See page CTC 74.

50 amps · pull-through · laundry · pets/restrictions · Wi-Fi access · playground · fishing · hiking trails · golf · tourist attraction · shopping · hot showers

EDINBURG

Lazy Palms Ranch
35100 Lazy Palms Drive
Edinburg, Texas 78541
956-383-1020; fax: 956-383-2007
manager@lazypalmsranch.com
lazypalmsranch.com
RESORT NUMBER: 1587
GOOD SAM RATING: 8/9★/7
DIRECTIONS: From Linn, TX: 1.7 mi S on Hwy 281. R on Floral Rd, exactly 2 mi N on paved road. Then 0.5 mi to resort. From Edinburg: 18 mi N on Hwy 281.
GPS COORDINATES: 26.541°N/-98.1575°W
NOTATIONS: Check-in: 10:00 a.m.–7:00 p.m. Check-out: 11:00 a.m. Special discount rate for Coast members. Additional charges: 50 amp $2/night, add'l person $1/night. Over 50 resort (no children). Drive-ups not accepted. Max. RV length: 45 feet. Open: Year-round.
STATE MAP: See page CTC 74.

50 amps · pull-through · visitor mail · laundry · pets/restrictions · internet access · Wi-Fi access · hot tub · fishing · shuffleboard · horseshoes · recreation hall · age restrictions · fishing · outdoor pool · game room · tourist attraction · shopping · propane

FREEPORT

Blue Water RV Resort
11511 Blue Water Highway
Freeport, Texas 77541
979-239-4301
info@bluewaterrvpark.com
bluewaterrvpark.com
RESORT NUMBER: 2391
GOOD SAM RATING: 10/9.5★/10
DIRECTIONS: From Galveston via San Luis Pass Rd and County Rd 257: 1 mi, R on Seawall Blvd. Continue straight staying on Seawall Blvd. 0.8 mi Seawall Blvd turns slightly R becoming San Luis Pass Rd/Termini-San Luis Pass Rd. 18.5 mi San Luis Pass Rd turns slightly R becoming County Rd 257. Resort on L.
GPS COORDINATES: 29.00504°N/-95.22077°W
NOTATIONS: Check-in: 1:00 p.m. Check-out: 11:00 a.m. 2021 Coast rate $55 to $100. Tax 8.25%. Rental units available. Trip Points not accepted. Contact resort directly. Rental check-in 3:00 p.m. Max. RV length: 65 feet. Open: Year-round.
STATE MAP: See page CTC 74.

50 amps · cable tv · visitor mail · pets/restrictions · Wi-Fi access · restaurant/snack bar · rental units · fishing · boating · recreation hall · outdoor pool · beach · tourist attraction · shopping · propane

GALVESTON

Jamaica Beach RV Resort
17200 Farm to Market Road 3005
Galveston, Texas 77554
409-632-0200
rongustafson@hotmail.com
jbrv.net
RESORT NUMBER: 2470
GOOD SAM RATING: 10/10★/10
DIRECTIONS: From Jct of I-45 & 61 St: Ex 1A, S 1.7 mi to Seawall Blvd (FM-3005), W 11 mi, resort on R.
GPS COORDINATES: 29.17832°N/-94.9825°W
NOTATIONS: Check-in: 1:00 p.m. Check-out: Noon. Special discount rate for Coast members. Rate includes 2 adults, 1 vehicle per site, full hook-ups. Additional charges: Add'l adult $9/night, add'l child (age 4-15) $5/night, extra vehicle $10, tax. Kids 3 and under free. Quiet time 10 p.m.-8 a.m. Coast rate available Sep 1-Nov 10 and Apr 1-May 20. Max. RV length: 65 feet. Open: April 1–May 20; September 1–November 10.
STATE MAP: See page CTC 74.

50 amps · pull-through · laundry · pets/restrictions · Wi-Fi access · playground · restaurant/snack bar · hot tub · shuffleboard · horseshoes · recreation hall · fishing · boating · outdoor pool · mini golf · basketball · beach · golf · tourist attraction · fitness · propane · ice

GLEN ROSE

Dinosaur Valley RV Park
1099 Park Road 59
Glen Rose, Texas 76043
888-996-3466
admin@dinosaurvalleyrvpark.com
dinosaurvalleyrvpark.com
RESORT NUMBER: 2463
GOOD SAM RATING: 10/9.5★/8.5
DIRECTIONS: From Jct US Hwy 67 & FM 205: Go 3 mi W on FM 205, then 1 blk N on Park Rd 59, park is on R.
GPS COORDINATES: 32.24109°N/97.80795°W
NOTATIONS: Check-in: 3:00 p.m. Check-out: 11:00 a.m. 2022 Coast 10% discount. Rate includes 2 adults per site, 1 vehicle, electric, water, sewer, picnic table, fire ring. Additional charges: Add'l vehicle $10, tax 6.25%. Max. RV length: 80 feet. Open: Year-round.
STATE MAP: See page CTC 74.

50 amps · pets/restrictions · Wi-Fi access · playground · hot tub · outdoor pool · golf · grocery · rv supplies

GLEN ROSE

Oakdale Park
1019 Northeast Barnard Street
Glen Rose, Texas 76043
254-897-2321
oakdaleparkinfo@glenrosetexas.org
oakdalepark.com
RESORT NUMBER: 2399
GOOD SAM RATING: 9.5/9.5★/8
DIRECTIONS: From Jct TX 144 & US 67: Go 1 mi SW on US 67, then 0.5 mi S on NE Barnard St. Park is on R.
GPS COORDINATES: 32.23958°N/-97.74521°W
NOTATIONS: Check-in: 1:00 p.m. Check-out: 11:00 a.m. Special discount rate for Coast members. Rate includes 2 adults, 1 vehicle per site, full hook-ups, free Wi-Fi. Additional charges: Extra vehicle $5/night. Quiet time from 10 p.m. to 7 a.m. Credit card charged 1st night site charge prior to arrival. $20 cancellation fee if within 48 hrs. Max. RV length: 45 feet. Open: October 8–March 7.
STATE MAP: See page CTC 74.

50 amps · pull-through · dump station · laundry · pets/restrictions · Wi-Fi access · playground · horseshoes · recreation hall · fishing · outdoor pool · mini golf · basketball · volleyball · golf · tourist attraction · shopping · propane · hot showers · rv supplies · tenting · ice

GRANBURY

Granbury RV Resort
1800 Mambrino Highway
Granbury, Texas 76048
817-776-1902
granburyrvresort@gmail.com
granburyrvresort.com
RESORT NUMBER: 2464
GOOD SAM RATING: NA
DIRECTIONS: From jct Hwy 144 (Glen Rose Hwy) & Mambrino Hwy: Go 2 mi W on Mambrino Hwy, resort is on L.
GPS COORDINATES: 32.37646°N/-97.74215°W
NOTATIONS: Check-in: 9:00 a.m. Check-out: 11:00 a.m. Special discount rate for Coast members. Rate includes 2 adults per site, water, sewer, electric. Max. RV length: 45 feet. Open: Year-round.
STATE MAP: See page CTC 74.

50 amps, laundry, pets/restrictions, Wi-Fi access, playground, hot tub, fishing, boating, outdoor pool, tourist attraction

HARLINGEN

NEW **Carefree Valley MHP & RV Resort**
4506 North Bus 77
Harlingen, Texas 78552
956-335-9396
carefree@vineyardsmg.com
RESORT NUMBER: 2522
GOOD SAM RATING: 7.5/7/6
DIRECTIONS: From Jct of I-69 S & Primera Ex: Go 0.4 mi N (right) on US-77 Business N. Park is on R.
GPS COORDINATES: 26.23621°N/-97.72578°W
NOTATIONS: Check-in: 11:00 a.m. Check-out: Noon. 2021 Coast rate $27/night. Rate includes 2 adults per site, full hook-ups. Additional charges: Tax 8.25%. Max. RV length: 45 feet. Open: Year-round.
STATE MAP: See page CTC 74.

50 amps, laundry, pets/restrictions, Wi-Fi access, group activities, recreation hall, fishing, boating, outdoor pool, fitness, shopping

HARLINGEN

Fig Tree RV Resort
15257 North Expressway 83
Harlingen, Texas 78552
956-423-6699; fax: 956-622-3580
info@figtreervresort.com
figtreervresort.com
RESORT NUMBER: 2462
GOOD SAM RATING: 9.5/9★/8.5
DIRECTIONS: From Jct of W US-83 Expy & Altas Palmas Ex, W 0.3 mi on N Frntg Rd to resort on R. GPS: Plug in Fig Tree Blvd (no street number needed).
GPS COORDINATES: 26.18678°N/-97.77838°W
NOTATIONS: Check-in: 10:00 a.m. Check-out: 1:00 p.m. 2021 Coast rate $32. Rate includes 2 adults per site, water, electric, Wi-Fi. Age restrictions lifted during off season May-Sep. Max. RV length: 42 feet. Open: Year-round.
STATE MAP: See page CTC 74.

50 amps, visitor mail, laundry, pets/restrictions, Wi-Fi access, hot tub, shuffleboard, group activities, recreation hall, age restrictions, outdoor pool, golf, game room, tourist attraction, fitness, shopping, propane, hot showers, firewood

HEARNE

Brazos Trail RV Park—Hearne
901 North Market Street
Hearne, Texas 77859
979-977-7275
info@brazostrailrvpark.com
brazostrailrvpark.com
RESORT NUMBER: 2510
GOOD SAM RATING: NA
DIRECTIONS: From Jct Franklin St & North Market St: Go 0.5 mi N on North Market St, park on L.
GPS COORDINATES: 30.89008°N/-96.59994°W
NOTATIONS: Check-in: Noon. Check-out: Noon. 2021 Coast rate $28. Rate includes 2 adults per site, electric, water, sewer, free Wi-Fi. Additional charges: Add'l person $5/night, tax 8.25%. Anyone in the office under 21 yrs old must be accompanied by a parent or guardian. Max. RV length: 50 feet. Open: Year-round.
STATE MAP: See page CTC 74.

50 amps, pull-through, visitor mail, laundry, pets/restrictions, Wi-Fi access, tourist attraction, propane, ice

HOUSTON

Advanced RV Resort
2850 South Sam Houston Parkway East
Houston, Texas 77047
713-433-6950
beichenlaub.advancedrv@gmail.com
advancedrvpark.com
RESORT NUMBER: 2469
GOOD SAM RATING: 10/10★/10
DIRECTIONS: From Jct I-610 & Hwy 288: Go 5.5 mi S on US 288, then 0.5 mi SE on Beltway 8 Frontage Rd, resort on R.
GPS COORDINATES: 29.5937°N/-95.38083°W
NOTATIONS: Check-in: 1:30 p.m. Check-out: Noon. Special 20% discount on current daily rates for Coast members. Rate includes up to 6 guests per site, all amenities. Additional charges: Extra person $2/night, tax 8.25%. 3 pets max per site. Wi-Fi in resort and hardwire internet at select sites. Max. RV length: Unlimited. Open: Year-round.
STATE MAP: See page CTC 74.

50 amps, pull-through, dump station, laundry, pets/restrictions, internet access, Wi-Fi access, hot tub, fishing, recreation hall, outdoor pool, golf, tourist attraction, fitness, shopping, propane, rv supplies, gift shop, handicap access

JACKSBORO

NEW **Hidden Lake RV Ranch & Safari**
3100 Lowrance Road
Jacksboro, Texas 76458
940-567-6900
info@hiddenlakervranch.com
hiddenlakervranch.com
RESORT NUMBER: 2533
GOOD SAM RATING: 7.5/8★/6.5
DIRECTIONS: From Jct Hwy 148 & US 281: Go 5.25 mi NW on US 281, then 0.5 mi E on Lowrance Rd. Park on L.
GPS COORDINATES: 33.25252°N/-98.23735°W
NOTATIONS: Check-in: Noon. Check-out: Noon. 2021 Coast rate $40/night. Rate includes 2 adults per site, full hook-ups. Additional charges: Tax. Max. RV length: 45 feet. Open: Year-round.
STATE MAP: See page CTC 74.

50 amps, pull-through, laundry, pets/restrictions, Wi-Fi access, picnic tables, fishing, hiking trails, horseshoes, fishing, outdoor pool, shopping, fire rings

KERRVILLE

Triple T RV Resort
3900 Bandera Highway
Kerrville, Texas 78028
830-634-3000
info@tripletrvresort.com
tripletrvresort.com
RESORT NUMBER: 2167
GOOD SAM RATING: 9/10★/9
DIRECTIONS: From I-10: Ex 508. S on Hwy 16 for 0.4 mi. L on Veterans Hwy (Loop 534) for 4.2 mi. L (S) on Hwy 173 (Bandera Hwy) 5.1 mi. Resort on R. If using GPS, enter 5000 Bandera Hwy instead of 3900.
GPS COORDINATES: 29.9536°N/-99.1039°W
ELEVATION: 1,700 feet
NOTATIONS: Check-in: 2:00 p.m. Check-out: 11:00 a.m. 2022 special discount rate of $50/night for Coast members available during the week. Rate includes 2 adults, 2 children under age 12. Additional charges: Extra adult $5/night, extra child $5/night. Wi-Fi access in campground. Max. RV length: 75 feet. Open: Year-round.
STATE MAP: See page CTC 74.

50 amps, pull-through, dump station, laundry, pets/restrictions, internet access, Wi-Fi access, picnic tables, hot tub, horseshoes, recreation hall, outdoor pool, tourist attraction, fitness, hot showers

LUBBOCK

NEW **Camelot Village RV Park**
6001 34th Street
Lubbock, Texas 79407
806-792-6477
camelot@evergreenmh.com
camelotvillagelubbock.com
RESORT NUMBER: 2517
GOOD SAM RATING: 8.5/9★/10
DIRECTIONS: From Jct Loop 289W & 34th St Ex: Go 500 ft W on 34th St, park on L.
GPS COORDINATES: 33.56308°N/-101.94703°W
NOTATIONS: Check-in: Noon. Check-out: 1:00 p.m. 2021 Coast rate $35/night. Rate includes 2 adults per site, electric, water, sewer. Additional charges: Tax 8.25%. Max. RV length: 45 feet. Open: Year-round.
STATE MAP: See page CTC 74.

50 amps, pull-through, laundry, pets/restrictions, Wi-Fi access, picnic tables, outdoor pool, basketball, volleyball, tourist attraction, shopping, hot showers, grills

MCALLEN

NEW Citrus Valley MH & RV Park
2901 Highway 107 West
McAllen, Texas 78504
956-383-8189
citrusvalley@vineyardsmg.com
citrusvalleymhrvpark.com
RESORT NUMBER: 2523
GOOD SAM RATING: 8/8.5★/7
DIRECTIONS: From Jct of US 281 & Monte Cristo Rd, W 6.1 mi on Monte Cristo Rd to Ware Rd (FM 1925), S 2 mi to US 107, E 0.4 mi. Park on R.
GPS COORDINATES: 26.31095°N/-98.23727°W
NOTATIONS: Check-in: 11:00 a.m. Check-out: Noon. 2021 Coast rate $36/night. Rate includes 2 adults per site, full hook-ups. Additional charges: Tax 8.25%. Max. RV length: 45 feet. Open: Year-round.
STATE MAP: See page CTC 74.

50 amps, laundry, pets/restrictions, Wi-Fi access, playground, shuffleboard, hiking trails, recreation hall, outdoor pool, fitness, shopping

MINGUS

Cactus Rose RV Park
115 West I-20
Mingus, Texas 76463
254-693-5976
reservations@cactusroserv.com
cactusroserv.com
RESORT NUMBER: 2397
GOOD SAM RATING: 8/9.5★/8
DIRECTIONS: From Jct of I-20 & Ex 370: Go 500 ft W on S Frontage Rd. Park on L.
GPS COORDINATES: 32.51334°N/-98.36957°W
NOTATIONS: Check-in: Noon. Check-out: 11:00 a.m. Special Coast discount rate of $30/night for Coast members. Rate includes 2 adults per site, full hook-ups, 2 vehicles. Free Wi-Fi hotspot and TV in clubhouse. Wi-Fi at all sites. Max. RV length: 60 feet. Open: Year-round.
STATE MAP: See page CTC 74.

50 amps, pull-through, dump station, laundry, pets/restrictions, Wi-Fi access, picnic tables, recreation hall, fishing, boating, outdoor pool, tourist attraction, hot showers, tenting

MISSION

Bentsen Palm RV Park
3501 North Bentsen Palm Drive
Mission, Texas 78574
956-585-0541
manager@bentsenpalmrvpark.com
bentsenpalmrvpark.com
RESORT NUMBER: 2507
GOOD SAM RATING: 9/8.5★/8.5
DIRECTIONS: From Jct US 83 & Bentsen Palm Dr: Go 1.5 mi N on Bentsen Palm Dr, park on L.
GPS COORDINATES: 26.25393°N/-98.36753°W
NOTATIONS: Check-in: Noon. Check-out: 11:00 a.m. Special 20% discount rate for Coast members. Rate includes 2 adults per site, full hook-ups. Max. RV length: 42 feet. Open: Year-round.
STATE MAP: See page CTC 74.

50 amps, laundry, pets/restrictions, Wi-Fi access, hot tub, fishing, shuffleboard, group activities, recreation hall, tourist attraction, shopping, hot showers

MISSION

Bentsen Palm Village RV Resort
2500 South Bentsen Palm Drive
Mission, Texas 78572
956-585-5568
jon@mlrhodes.com
bentsenpalm.com
RESORT NUMBER: 2461
GOOD SAM RATING: 10/10★/10
DIRECTIONS: From Jct of US-83 Expy & Conway, go S 4 mi on Conway to Military, go W 3 mi on Military to Bentsen Palm Dr, go S 0.25 mi on Bentsen Palm Dr to resort on L.
GPS COORDINATES: 26.18841°N/-98.37857°W
NOTATIONS: Check-in: 3:00 p.m. Check-out: 10:00 a.m. Special discount rate of 15% off nightly rate for Coast members. Rate includes 2 adults per site, electric, water, sewer and free cable TV. Additional charges: Tax 8.25%. Max 2 pets of any kind. Special discount rate for Coast members available Apr 1-Oct 1. Max. RV length: 50 feet. Open: April 1–October 1.
STATE MAP: See page CTC 74.

50 amps, laundry, pets/restrictions, Wi-Fi access, hot tub, hiking trails, horseshoes, group activities, recreation hall, boating, outdoor pool, golf, tourist attraction, fitness, shopping

MISSION

Bluebonnet RV Resort
3366 North Bentsen Palm Drive
Mission, Texas 78574
956-585-7630
bluebonnet@rvresorts.com
rvresorts.com/blue-bonnet.html
RESORT NUMBER: 2460
GOOD SAM RATING: 9/9★/8
DIRECTIONS: From Ebnd: Jct of US 83 Expy/I-2 & Bentsen Palm Dr, go 1.2 mi N to resort on R. From Wbnd: Jct of US 83 Expy & Lahoma Ex, Go 1 block W on N Frontage Rd, then 1.2 mi N on Bentsen Palm Dr to resort on R.
GPS COORDINATES: 26.25057°N/-98.36747°W
NOTATIONS: Check-in: 3:00 p.m. Check-out: 11:00 a.m. 2021 Coast 10% discount for first 3 nights. Rate includes 2 adults per site, 1 RV, 1 vehicle, electric, water, and sewer. Additional charges: Add'l person $3, electric at .13kw. Max. RV length: 50 feet. Open: Year-round.
STATE MAP: See page CTC 74.

50 amps, pets/restrictions, Wi-Fi access, shuffleboard, horseshoes, group activities, recreation hall, golf, game room, tourist attraction, fitness, shopping, indoor pool

MURCHISON

Stay A While RV Park
10101 State Highway 31 East
Murchison, Texas 75778
903-469-4477
stayawhilerv@yahoo.com
stayawhilervpark.com
RESORT NUMBER: 2514
GOOD SAM RATING: 7.5/9★/9.5
DIRECTIONS: From Jct Hwy 773 & State Hwy 31 E: Go 4 mi E on State Hwy 31 E, park on L.
GPS COORDINATES: 32.29105°N/-95.68926°W
NOTATIONS: Check-in: Noon. Check-out: 10:00 a.m. Special 20% discount rate for Coast members. Rate includes 2 adults per site, electric, water, limited sewer, Wi-Fi. Max. RV length: 40 feet. Open: Year-round.
STATE MAP: See page CTC 74.

50 amps, pull-through, dump station, laundry, pets/restrictions, Wi-Fi access, playground, fishing, hiking trails, propane, gift shop, tenting, firewood

PLAINVIEW

The Hitchin' Post RV Park and Cabins
4018 North I-27
Plainview, Texas 79072
806-789-3066; fax: 806-409-8040
thehitchinpostrvpark@gmail.com
thehitchinpostrvpark.com
RESORT NUMBER: 2380
GOOD SAM RATING: NA
DIRECTIONS: From Jct I-27 & Ex 51: Go 1 mi N on I-27 Frontage Rd. Park on R.
GPS COORDINATES: 34.22507°N/-101.71784°W
NOTATIONS: Check-in: 1:00 p.m. Check-out: 11:00 a.m. 2022 Coast member rate $30. Rate includes electric, water, and sewer. 30 & 50 amp sites. 1 night deposit due when reservation made. Max. RV length: 45 feet. Open: Year-round.
STATE MAP: See page CTC 74.

50 amps, pull-through, laundry, Wi-Fi access, playground, picnic tables, horseshoes, tourist attraction, propane, hot showers, fire rings, grocery, rv supplies, gift shop, tenting, firewood

RAYMONDVILLE

NEW Gateway MHP & RV Park
400 Farm to Market Road 3168
Raymondville, Texas 78580
956-689-6658
gateway@vineyardsmg.com
gatewayrvtexas.com
RESORT NUMBER: 2521
GOOD SAM RATING: 8.5/8.5★/8
DIRECTIONS: From Jct US 77 & FM 3168: Go 0.25 mi S on Frontage Rd, then 0.5 mi W on FM. Park on L.
GPS COORDINATES: 26.46442°N/-97.77254°W
NOTATIONS: Check-in: 11:00 a.m. Check-out: Noon. 2021 Coast rate $36/night. Rate includes 2 adults per site, full hook-ups. Additional charges: Tax 8.25%. Max. RV length: 45 feet. Open: Year-round.
STATE MAP: See page CTC 74.

50 amps, pull-through, dump station, laundry, pets/restrictions, Wi-Fi access, fishing, boating, golf, shopping

RIESEL

Brazos Trail RV Park—Riesel
219 Rice Road
Riesel, Texas 76682
254-277-7275
info@brazostrailrvpark.com
brazostrailrvpark.com
RESORT NUMBER: 2511
GOOD SAM RATING: 7.5/10★/8
DIRECTIONS: From Jct FM 1860 & Hwy 6: Go 1 mi S on Hwy 6, then 1 blk W on Rice Road, park on L.
GPS COORDINATES: 31.46081°N/-96.92574°W
NOTATIONS: Check-in: Noon. Check-out: Noon. 2021 Coast rate $36/night. Rate includes 2 adults per site, electric, water, sewer, free W-Fi. Additional charges: Add'l person $5/night, tax 8.25%. Anyone in the office under 12 yrs old must be accompanied by a parent or guardian. Max. RV length: 50 feet. Open: Year-round.
STATE MAP: See page CTC 74.

50 amps · pull-through · cable tv · visitor mail · laundry · pets/restrictions · Wi-Fi access · fishing · horseshoes · tourist attraction · hot showers · ice

RIO HONDO

NEW **Twin Palms RV Resort**
107 East Colorado
Rio Hondo, Texas 78583
956-748-0800
twinpalmsrvresort@yahoo.com
twinpalmsrvresort.net
RESORT NUMBER: 2527
GOOD SAM RATING: 9/8★/7.5
DIRECTIONS: From Jct of FM-508 & FM-106, E 1 mi on FM-106. Park on L.
GPS COORDINATES: 26.23506°N/-97.57737°W
NOTATIONS: Check-in: 11:00 a.m. Check-out: 11:00 a.m. 2021 Coast rate $45/night includes 2 adults per site, full hook-ups, water, trash & sewer. Additional charges: Tax 8.25%. Max. RV length: 45 feet. Open: Year-round.
STATE MAP: See page CTC 74.

50 amps · pull-through · laundry · pets/restrictions · Wi-Fi access · hot tub · shuffleboard · group activities · fishing · outdoor pool · beach · shopping

STRATFORD

Star of Texas RV Park and Horse Hotel
5680 Texas Highway 15
Stratford, Texas 79084
806-366-7827
staroftexasrvsandhorses@gmail.com
staroftexasrv.com
RESORT NUMBER: 2383
GOOD SAM RATING: NA
DIRECTIONS: Park is 5.25 blocks south of US 287 and US 54 intersection.
GPS COORDINATES: 36.32779°N/-102.06939°W
ELEVATION: 3,800 feet
NOTATIONS: Check-in: Noon. Check-out: Noon. Special discount rate for Coast members. Max. RV length: Unlimited. Open: Year-round.
STATE MAP: See page CTC 74.

50 amps · pull-through · pets/restrictions · Wi-Fi access

SWEETWATER

NEW **Bar J Hitchin Post RV**
50 North Hopkins Road
Sweetwater, Texas 79556
325-236-3889
barjrv@gmail.com
barjhitchinpostrv.com
RESORT NUMBER: 2518
GOOD SAM RATING: 8.5/10★/8.5
DIRECTIONS: From Jct I-20 & Ex 242: Go 1 blk N on CR142, resort on L.
GPS COORDINATES: 32.45279°N/-100.4429°W
ELEVATION: 7,860 feet
NOTATIONS: 2021 Coast rate $35.20. Rate includes 2 adults per site, full hook-ups. Additional charges: Tax 8.25%. Max. RV length: 45 feet. Open: Year-round.
STATE MAP: See page CTC 74.

50 amps · pull-through · laundry · pets/restrictions · Wi-Fi access · fishing · boating · shopping

TATUM

Amazing Texas RV Resort and Campground
17506 Farm to Market Road 782 North
Tatum, Texas 75691
903-836-4444; res.: 936-204-0397
amazingtexasrvresort@gmail.com
amazingtexasrvresort.com
RESORT NUMBER: 2347
GOOD SAM RATING: 8/8/7.5
DIRECTIONS: From Shreveport: I-20 W to Ex 614 for TX-43. L on TX-43 S. Follow TX-43 S for 40.4 mi, turn R on TX-149 W/Hill St. Continue 5.5 mi, L onto FM 782 W, then 1.5 mi to resort on L.
GPS COORDINATES: 32.3397°N/-94.60086°W
NOTATIONS: Check-in: Noon. Check-out: Noon. Special discount rate for Coast members. Rate includes 2 adults, 2 children, 2 pets per site. Additional charges: Extra adult $5/night, extra child $5/night. Max. RV length: 40 feet. Open: Year-round.
STATE MAP: See page CTC 74.

50 amps · laundry · pets/restrictions · Wi-Fi access · playground · fishing · boating · outdoor pool

TEXARKANA

Texarkana RV Park
5000 U.S. Highway 59 S
Texarkana, Texas 75501
903-306-1364
txkarvpark20200@gmail.com
texarkanarvparkandeventcenter.com
RESORT NUMBER: 2515
GOOD SAM RATING: 8.5/10★/8.5
DIRECTIONS: From Jct I-30 & US 369: Go 4 mi S on US 369, then 1 mi SW on US 59, park on R.
GPS COORDINATES: 33.38554°N/-94.11184°W
NOTATIONS: Check-in: Noon. Check-out: Noon. Coast members receive 20% discount. Rate includes full hook-ups, electric, water, sewer, Wi-Fi, cable, and use of amenities. Gated community. Max. RV length: 45 feet. Open: Year-round.
STATE MAP: See page CTC 74.

50 amps · pull-through · cable tv · laundry · pets/restrictions · Wi-Fi access · playground · fishing · recreation hall · outdoor pool · game room · tourist attraction · shopping · hot showers

VERNON

Rocking A RV Park
3725 Harrison Street
Vernon, Texas 76384
940-552-2821
main@rockingarvpark.com
rockingarvpark.com
RESORT NUMBER: 2513
GOOD SAM RATING: 9/9.5★/8.5
DIRECTIONS: From Jct of US 70 & US 287 (W of town): Go 0.25 mi NW on N Service Rd, then 1 block E on Harrison St past Walmart, park is on R.
GPS COORDINATES: 34.16567°N/-99.31147°W
NOTATIONS: Check-in: 2:00 p.m. Check-out: Noon. Special discount rate for Coast members. Rate includes 2 adults per site, electric, water, sewer, free Wi-Fi. Additional charges: Add'l adult $5/night. Max. RV length: 45 feet. Open: Year-round.
STATE MAP: See page CTC 74.

50 amps · pull-through · cable tv · laundry · pets/restrictions · Wi-Fi access · playground · picnic tables · horseshoes · fishing · boating · outdoor pool · golf · tourist attraction · shopping · propane · hot showers · grocery · rv supplies · tenting

VICTORIA

Victoria Coleto Lake RV Resort
500 Coleto Park Road
Victoria, Texas 77905
361-582-0222; fax: 361-582-0024
coletolake@gmail.com
coletolakervpark.com
RESORT NUMBER: 2468
GOOD SAM RATING: 9.5/9.5★/10
DIRECTIONS: From Jct US Hwy 59 & Coleto Park Rd, go W 0.5 mi, resort on L.
GPS COORDINATES: 28.71468°N/-97.17813°W
NOTATIONS: Check-in: Noon. Check-out: 11:00 a.m. Special discount rate of $34.40 for Coast members. Rate includes 2 adults/2 children, 1 RV, 2 vehicles per site, water, sewer, electric, cable, Wi-Fi, picnic table, grill. Additional charges: Add'l adult $5/night, add'l child $5/night, cancellation fee, tax 6.25%. 2 pets max. Wi-Fi throughout campground. Wi-Fi code given at registration. Quiet hours 10 p.m.-7 a.m. Max. RV length: 100 feet. Open: Year-round.

STATE MAP: See page CTC 74.

50 amps, pull-through, cable tv, laundry, pets/restrictions, Wi-Fi access, playground, restaurant/snack bar, fishing, horseshoes, group activities, recreation hall, boating, outdoor pool, volleyball, golf, hot showers

VIDOR

Boomtown USA RV Resort
23030 Interstate Highway 10
Vidor, Texas 77662
409-769-6105
boomtownreservations@gmail.com
boomtownusarvresort.com
RESORT NUMBER: 2467
GOOD SAM RATING: 9.5/10★/8
DIRECTIONS: From Jct I-10 & FM 105 (Ex 859): Go 0.5 mi W on Freeway Blvd, resort on R.
GPS COORDINATES: 30.11291°N/-94.04553°W
NOTATIONS: Check-in: Noon. Check-out: 11:00 a.m. Special discount rate for Coast members. Rate includes 2 adults per site, electric, water, limited sewer. Additional charges: Add'l adult $5/night, dump station fee $5, tax 8.25%. Max. RV length: 70 feet. Open: Year-round.
STATE MAP: See page CTC 74.

50 amps, pull-through, dump station, laundry, pets/restrictions, Wi-Fi access, hot tub, fishing, outdoor pool, beach, game room, fitness, paddle boats, tenting

WOLFFORTH

Mesa Verde RV Park
503 East Highway 62/82
Wolfforth, Texas 79382
806-773-3135
mesaverde@nts-online.net
rvlubbock.com
RESORT NUMBER: 2395
GOOD SAM RATING: 9.5/9.5★/9
DIRECTIONS: From Jct W Loop 289 & US 62/82 (Lubbock): Go 5 mi SW on US 62/82 (Ex FM 179), then 1.25 mi N on E Service Rd. Park on R.
GPS COORDINATES: 33.51436°N/-101.99803°W
ELEVATION: 3,312 feet
NOTATIONS: Check-in: 1:00 p.m. Check-out: Noon. Special Coast rate $35.20/night. Rate includes 2 adults, 2 children per site, or 3 adults no kids, full hook-ups, free cable, and free Wi-Fi. Additional charges: Tax 8.25%. Max. RV length: 45 feet. Open: Year-round.
STATE MAP: See page CTC 74.

50 amps, laundry, pets/restrictions, Wi-Fi access, outdoor pool, tourist attraction, fitness, shopping, hot showers, rv supplies

UTAH

DRAPER

Mountain Shadows RV Park
13275 South Minuteman Drive
Draper, Utah 84020
801-571-4024; fax: 801-571-4056
apage@mountain-shadows.com
mountain-shadows.com
RESORT NUMBER: 2374
GOOD SAM RATING: 9.5/10★/8.5
DIRECTIONS: From Jct of I-15 & 12300 South St (Draper Ex 291): E 150 ft on 12300 South St to Minuteman Dr, S 1.2 mi, park on L.
GPS COORDINATES: 40.51053°N/-111.8896°W
ELEVATION: 4,100 feet
NOTATIONS: Check-in: 1:00 p.m. Check-out: 11:00 a.m. Special discount rate for Coast members. Rate includes 2 adults per site, full hook-ups. Additional charges: 50 amp $5/night, tax 11%. Max. RV length: 45 feet. Open: Year-round.
STATE MAP: See page CTC 68.

50 amps, pull-through, dump station, laundry, pets/restrictions, internet access, Wi-Fi access, playground, hot tub, recreation hall, outdoor pool, basketball, volleyball, golf, game room, tourist attraction, shopping, propane, hot showers, grocery

PROVO

Lakeside RV Campground
4000 West Center Street
Provo, Utah 84601
801-373-5267; fax: 801-373-8624
lakesiderv@aol.com
lakesidervcampground.com
RESORT NUMBER: 2354
GOOD SAM RATING: 9.5/10★/9
DIRECTIONS: From Jct of I-15 & Center St (Ex 265): W 2.2 mi on Center St, park on R.
GPS COORDINATES: 40.2356°N/-111.7281°W
ELEVATION: 4,650 feet
NOTATIONS: Check-in: 1:00 p.m. Check-out: 11:00 a.m. Special Coast discount rate includes 2 people per site. Additional charges: Extra adult $3/night, extra child 6 years and over $3/night, pets $3/night, 50 amp $5/night, tax 13%. No drive-ups accepted. All reservations must be made by phone. Max. RV length: 40 feet. Open: October 1–March 31.
STATE MAP: See page CTC 68.

50 amps, pull-through, dump station, cable tv, laundry, pets/restrictions, Wi-Fi access, playground, picnic tables, fishing, horseshoes, fishing, boating, volleyball, golf, game room, tourist attraction, shopping, propane, hot showers, grocery, rv supplies

VERMONT

LEICESTER

Country Village Campground
40 U.S. Route 7
Leicester, Vermont 05733
802-247-3333
countryvillagevt@aol.com
countryvillagecampground.com
RESORT NUMBER: 2453
GOOD SAM RATING: 7.5/8.5★/8.5
DIRECTIONS: From Jct of Rte 73 & US 7 (in town): N 3 mi on US 7, park on L.
GPS COORDINATES: 43.84482°N/-73.10656°W
NOTATIONS: Check-in: Noon. Check-out: 11:00 a.m. Coast member rate 20% discount, available Sep 2-Sep 30 only. Rate includes water and 30 amp electric. Additional charges: Add'l adult or child $3/night, tax 6%. Max. RV length: 40 feet. Open: May 1–September 30.
STATE MAP: See page CTC 64.

30 amps, dump station, pets/restrictions, Wi-Fi access, playground, picnic tables, shuffleboard, horseshoes, group activities, fishing, boating, outdoor pool, basketball, shopping, tenting

LYNDONVILLE

Kingdom Campground
972 Lynburke Road
Lyndonville, Vermont 05850
802-626-1151
kingdomcampground@gmail.com
kingdomcampground.com
RESORT NUMBER: 2489
GOOD SAM RATING: 8/10★/9
DIRECTIONS: From Jct I-91 & US-5 N: Go 3 mi N on US-5/Lynburke Rd, campground on R.
GPS COORDINATES: 44.5565°N/-71.9967°W
NOTATIONS: Check-in: 1:00 p.m. Check-out: 11:00 a.m. Special discount rate of $40/night for Coast members from Mon-Wed only. Rate includes 2 adults per site, 1 RV, full hook-ups. Additional charges: Add'l person $5/night, tax 6%. Wi-Fi in general store. Max. RV length: 70 feet. Open: May 7–October 13.
STATE MAP: See page CTC 64.

50 amps, pull-through, laundry, pets/restrictions, playground, outdoor pool, tourist attraction, hot showers, grocery

WASHINGTON

AIRWAY HEIGHTS

Northern Quest RV Resort
303 South Kalispel Way
Airway Heights, Washington 99001
509-481-4300; res.: 833-702-2082
info@nqrvresort.com
nqrvresort.com
RESORT NUMBER: 2409
GOOD SAM RATING: 10/10★/10
DIRECTIONS: From Jct of I-90 and US-2 at Ex 277: Go 4.5 mi W on US-2, then 1 mi N on S Hayford Rd, 0.25 mi W on Sprague Ave. Ex roundabout on Kalispel. Resort on L.
GPS COORDINATES: 47.65841°N/-117.56262°W
NOTATIONS: Check-in: 1:00 p.m. Check-out: Noon. Special discount rate for Coast members. Rate includes 2 adults, full hook-ups. Additional charges: Extra adult $5/night, lodging fee $2, tax 9.1%. Max 5 adults, 2 pets. Deposit of first night required for reservation. Max. RV length: 80 feet. Open: Year-round.
STATE MAP: See page CTC 76.

50 amps, pull-through, laundry, pets/restrictions, Wi-Fi access, outdoor pool, golf, tourist attraction, fitness, shopping, spa, hot showers, gambling casino, handicap access

CASTLE ROCK

Toutle River RV Resort
150 Happy Trails
Castle Rock, Washington 98611
360-274-8373
info@greatrvresort.com
greatrvresort.com
RESORT NUMBER: 2447
GOOD SAM RATING: 10/10★/9
DIRECTIONS: From Jct of I-5 (Ex 52) & Barnes Rd: Go W on Barnes Rd to first L, Happy Trails Rd. Resort on L.
GPS COORDINATES: 46.32526°N/-122.91478°W
NOTATIONS: Check-in: 1:00 p.m. Check-out: Noon. 20% discount off regular rate for Coast members. Max. RV length: 100 feet. Open: November 1–April 30.
STATE MAP: See page CTC 76.

50 amps, pull-through, visitor mail, laundry, pets/restrictions, Wi-Fi access, playground, picnic tables, hot tub, hiking trails, horseshoes, group activities, recreation hall, fishing, outdoor pool, volleyball, golf, propane, hot showers, fire rings, grocery, rv supplies, tenting, firewood, ice

CENTRALIA

Midway RV Park
3200 Galvin Road
Centralia, Washington 98531
360-736-3200
info@midwayrvparkwa.com
midwayrvparkwa.com
RESORT NUMBER: 2455
GOOD SAM RATING: 9/10★/9.5
DIRECTIONS: From Jct of I-5 & Harrison Ave (Ex 82): Go W 0.8 mi on Harrison Av to Galvin Rd, S 0.3 mi on Galvin Rd, park on L.
GPS COORDINATES: 46.73467°N/-122.99532°W
NOTATIONS: Check-in: 1:00 p.m. Check-out: Noon. 20% discount rate for Coast members available Nov 1 to Mar 31. Rate includes full hook-ups, 2 adults, 1 RV. Additional charges: Add'l adult $5/night, tax 8.2%. Max. RV length: 60 feet. Open: Year-round.
STATE MAP: See page CTC 76.

50 amps, pull-through, visitor mail, laundry, pets/restrictions, Wi-Fi access, restaurant/snack bar, hiking trails, horseshoes, group activities, recreation hall, fishing, golf, game room, shopping, propane, hot showers, gambling casino, grocery, rv supplies

GRAYLAND

Kenanna RV Park
2959 State Route 105
Grayland, Washington 98547
360-267-3515
reservations@kenannarv.com
kenannarv.com
RESORT NUMBER: 2442
GOOD SAM RATING: 7.5/10★/9
DIRECTIONS: From Grayland: Go 3 mi S on SR-105 to Kenanna RV Park Rd. Resort on R.
GPS COORDINATES: 46.75393°N/-124.08686°W
NOTATIONS: Check-in: Noon. Check-out: 11:00 a.m. 20% discount for Coast members. Additional charges: Showers $0.25/3 min, restrooms, tax 10.1%. Drive-ups not accepted. Max. RV length: 50 feet. Open: October 1–March 31.
STATE MAP: See page CTC 76.

50 amps, pull-through, dump station, visitor mail, laundry, pets/restrictions, Wi-Fi access, playground, picnic tables, fishing, hiking trails, horseshoes, recreation hall, fishing, boating, tourist attraction, propane, hot showers, fire rings, rv supplies, firewood, ice

HOODSPORT

Glen Ayr Resort
25381 North U.S. Highway 101
Hoodsport, Washington 98548
360-877-9522
office@garesort.com
garesort.com
RESORT NUMBER: 2326
GOOD SAM RATING: 8.5/9.5★/9
DIRECTIONS: From Jct of US Hwy 101 and SR-119 N Lake Cushman Rd (in town): Go 1.2 mi N on US Hwy 101 between MP 330 and 331. Resort on L.
GPS COORDINATES: 47.42031°N/-123.13204°W
NOTATIONS: Check-in: 1:00 p.m. Check-out: Noon. Special Coast rate avail Oct 1-Apr 1 and varies from $35-$45 per type of site. Max 6 guests/site, no tent camping, campfires allowed. Max. RV length: 45 feet. Open: Year-round.
STATE MAP: See page CTC 76.

50 amps, pull-through, laundry, pets/restrictions, Wi-Fi access, picnic tables, hot tub, fishing, hiking trails, recreation hall, fishing, boating, beach, tourist attraction, hot showers, gambling casino, firewood, ice, grills

HOQUIAM

Hoquiam River RV Park
425 Queen Avenue
Hoquiam, Washington 98550
360-538-2870
contact@hoquiamriverrvpark.com
hoquiamriverrvpark.com
RESORT NUMBER: 2449
GOOD SAM RATING: 8/9.5★/9
DIRECTIONS: From downtown Hoquiam: Go N 1.2 mi on Hwy 101 to Queen Ave, then E 0.1 mi on Queen Ave. Resort on L.
GPS COORDINATES: 46.9939°N/-123.89246°W
NOTATIONS: Check-in: 1:00 p.m. Check-out: 11:00 a.m. Special discount rate for Coast members. Max. RV length: 45 feet. Open: November 1–March 1.
STATE MAP: See page CTC 76.

50 amps, pull-through, dump station, cable tv, laundry, pets/restrictions, Wi-Fi access, picnic tables, fishing, hiking trails, horseshoes, group activities, recreation hall, fishing, beach, golf, propane, canoes, hot showers, gambling casino, fire rings, rv supplies, tenting, firewood, ice

KELSO

Brookhollow RV Park
2506 Allen Street
Kelso, Washington 98626
360-577-6474
brookhollowrv@ipgmhc.com
brookhollowrvpark.com
RESORT NUMBER: 2444
GOOD SAM RATING: 9/10★/10
DIRECTIONS: From Jct of I-5 & Allen St (Ex 39): Go 1 mi E on Allen St (just past mobile home park). Resort on R.
GPS COORDINATES: 46.14472°N/-122.87946°W
NOTATIONS: Check-in: Noon. Check-out: 11:00 a.m. Special 10% discount rate for Coast members. Rate includes 1 RV, 1 or 2 vehicles, 2 people, full hook-ups, cable TV. Additional charges: Add'l person $1/night, dog $1/night, extra vehicle $1/night, tax 8.1%. Min 1 day reservation fee for cancellations within 2 days of check-in. Max. RV length: 45 feet. Open: Year-round.
STATE MAP: See page CTC 76.

50 amps, pull-through, laundry, pets/restrictions, Wi-Fi access, picnic tables, fishing, tourist attraction, fitness, shopping, hot showers

KETTLE FALLS

Grandview Inn Motel & RV Park
978 Highway 395 North
Kettle Falls, Washington 99141
509-738-6733
gvmotel@gmail.com
grandviewinnmotelandrvpark.com
RESORT NUMBER: 2375
GOOD SAM RATING: 7.5/9.5★/8.5
DIRECTIONS: From Jct of WA-25 & SR-20/US-395: Go 0.8 mi N on US-395, park on R.
GPS COORDINATES: 48.60642°N/-118.07698°W
NOTATIONS: Check-in: 2:00 p.m. Check-out: 11:00 a.m. Special discount rate for Coast members. Rate includes 2 adults per site, full hook-ups. Max. RV length: 66 feet. Open: Year-round.
STATE MAP: See page CTC 76.

30 amps, dump station, cable tv, laundry, pets/restrictions, Wi-Fi access, hiking trails, fishing, boating, golf, tourist attraction, shopping, hot showers, gambling casino, fire rings, tenting, winter sports, grills

MOUNT VERNON

Mount Vernon RV Park
1229 Memorial Highway
Mount Vernon, Washington 98273
800-385-9895
mountvernonrvpark@hotmail.com
RESORT NUMBER: 2369
GOOD SAM RATING: 8.5/9★/9.5
DIRECTIONS: From Jct of I-5 & Kincaid St (Ex 226): Go 0.8 mi W on Kincaid St to SR-536 (Third St), then 1 mi N on SR-536 (becomes Memorial Hwy) over bridge, park on R.
GPS COORDINATES: 48.4234°N/-122.35087°W

NOTATIONS: Check-in: 1:00 p.m. Check-out: 11:00 a.m. Special discount rate for Coast members. Rate includes 2 adults per site. Additional charges: Tax 10.7%. Max. RV length: 82 feet. Open: Year-round.
STATE MAP: See page CTC 76.

50 amps | pull-through | laundry | Wi-Fi access | picnic tables | hiking trails | recreation hall | fishing
boating | golf | tourist attraction | hot showers

OCEAN PARK

Ocean Park Resort
25904 R Street
Ocean Park, Washington 98640
360-665-4585; res.: 800-835-4634
info@opresort.com
opresort.com
RESORT NUMBER: 2448
GOOD SAM RATING: 7.5/9★/6.5
DIRECTIONS: From Jct of US-101 & WA-103/Pacific Way (in Seaview): Go 11 mi N on WA-103/Pacific Way to 259th Pl, then 3 blocks.
GPS COORDINATES: 46.48992°N/-124.0473°W
NOTATIONS: Check-in: 1:00 p.m. Check-out: 11:00 a.m. Special discount rate for Coast members. Additional charges: Add'l person $3/night, tax, showers. Drive-ups not accepted. Max. RV length: 60 feet. Open: January 1–September 23.
STATE MAP: See page CTC 76.

30 amps | cable tv | laundry | pets/restrictions | Wi-Fi access | playground | picnic tables | group activities
recreation hall | fishing | boating | basketball | tourist attraction | shopping
propane | hot showers | firewood

OTHELLO

MarDon Resort on Potholes Reservoir
8198 Highway 262 Southeast
Othello, Washington 99344
509-346-2651
info@mardonresort.com
mardonresort.com
RESORT NUMBER: 2384
GOOD SAM RATING: 9/9★/9
DIRECTIONS: From Jct I-90 (Ex 179) & Hwy 17: Go 1.5 mi S on Hwy 17 to Rd M, then 7 mi W to Hwy 262/Old O'Sullivan Dam Rd, then 6 mi W on Hwy 262, resort on R.
GPS COORDINATES: 46.96601°N/-119.32121°W
NOTATIONS: Check-in: 3:00 p.m. Check-out: 1:00 p.m. Special discount rate for Coast members includes full hook-ups, 50 amp. Summer rates 20% off Mon-Wed only. Spring/Fall rates 20% off anytime except event or holiday weekends. Only 1 discount at a time. Extra charges for pets and extra cars/people. Max. RV length: 45 feet. Open: Year-round.
STATE MAP: See page CTC 76.

50 amps | pull-through | visitor mail | pets/restrictions | Wi-Fi access | playground | picnic tables | restaurant/snack bar
fishing | horseshoes | boating | fishing | boating | basketball | volleyball
golf | tourist attraction | shopping | fire rings | grocery | tenting | firewood

PORT ANGELES

Elwha Dam RV Park
47 Lower Dam Road
Port Angeles, Washington 98363
360-452-7054
paradise@elwhadamrvpark.com
elwhadamrvpark.com
RESORT NUMBER: 2356
GOOD SAM RATING: 9/10★/9.5
DIRECTIONS: From Jct of US 101 & Lincoln St (in town): Go 5.5 mi W on US 101 to SR-112, then 0.75 mi W on SR-112 to Lower Dam Rd, then 0.8 mi S on Dam Rd, park on L.
GPS COORDINATES: 48.09775°N/-123.55268°W
NOTATIONS: Check-in: 1:00 p.m. Check-out: 11:00 a.m. Special discount rate for Coast members varies per site. Rate includes full hook-ups, 2 adults, 2 children under 10, 2 pets, 1 tow or towed vehicle per site. Additional charges: Extra adult $2/night, extra pet $2/night, extra vehicle $2/night. Max. RV length: 82 feet. Open: Year-round.
STATE MAP: See page CTC 76.

50 amps | pull-through | laundry | pets/restrictions | Wi-Fi access | playground | picnic tables | hiking trails
horseshoes | recreation hall | fishing | boating | basketball | volleyball
tourist attraction | hot showers | fire rings | grocery | rv supplies | gift shop | tenting | ice

POULSBO

Cedar Glen RV Park
16300 Northeast State Highway 305
Poulsbo, Washington 98370
360-779-4305; fax: 360-779-1838
admin@cedarglenmhp.com
cedarglenmhp.com
RESORT NUMBER: 2353
GOOD SAM RATING: 9/9.5★/9.5
DIRECTIONS: From Jct Hwy 3 & Hwy 305 (Poulsbo): Go 5 mi SE on Hwy 305, park office on L.
GPS COORDINATES: 47.70603°N/-122.5944°W
NOTATIONS: Check-in: 2:00 p.m. Check-out: 11:00 a.m. 2021 Coast rate $44/night avail Nov 1-Apr 30 only. Rate includes 2 adults, 2 children, 2 non-aggressive dogs per site. All RVs must be 2011 or newer. No pop-up trailers, vans or campers. Max. RV length: 50 feet. Open: Year-round.
STATE MAP: See page CTC 76.

50 amps | laundry | pets/restrictions | Wi-Fi access | recreation hall | boating | golf
tourist attraction | hot showers | gambling casino

PROSSER

Wine Country RV Park
330 Merlot Drive
Prosser, Washington 99350
509-786-5192
winecountry@winecountryrvpark.com
winecountryrvpark.com
RESORT NUMBER: 2443
GOOD SAM RATING: 10/10★/10
DIRECTIONS: From Jct of I-82 & Wine Country Rd (Ex 80): Go 0.8 mi SE on Wine Country Rd to Merlot Dr, then 0.25 mi E. Resort on R.
GPS COORDINATES: 46.21976°N/-119.78389°W
NOTATIONS: Check-in: 1:00 p.m. Check-out: Noon. 20% discount for Coast members. Rate includes 2 adults, full hook-ups, picnic table. Additional charges: Add'l adult $3/night, add'l car $3/night, showers, tax 10.2% plus TPA $1/night. Max 8 people per site. Drive-ups not accepted. Max. RV length: 55 feet. Open: November 1–February 1.
STATE MAP: See page CTC 76.

50 amps | pull-through | cable tv | laundry | pets/restrictions | Wi-Fi access | playground | picnic tables
hot tub | hiking trails | horseshoes | group activities | recreation hall | fishing | outdoor pool | basketball
propane | hot showers | fire rings | grocery | rv supplies | tenting | firewood | ice

RICHLAND

Horn Rapids RV Resort
2640 Kingsgate Way
Richland, Washington 99354
866-557-9637; fax: 509-375-9953
info@hornrapidsrvresort.com
hornrapidsrvresort.com
RESORT NUMBER: 2446
GOOD SAM RATING: 10/10★/10
DIRECTIONS: From Jct of I-182 & Hwy 240W (Ex 4): Go 4 mi NE on Hwy 240W, then 2 mi NW on Hwy 240W to Kingsgate Way, then 0.8 mi NE on Kingsgate Way, resort on R.
GPS COORDINATES: 46.3274°N/-119.31495°W
NOTATIONS: Check-in: Noon. Check-out: 11:00 a.m. Special discount rate for Coast members. Rate includes 2 adults, 2 children, full hook-ups, cable. Additional charges: Tax. No tenting. Max. RV length: 70 feet. Open: Year-round.
STATE MAP: See page CTC 76.

50 amps | pull-through | cable tv | pets/restrictions | Wi-Fi access | playground | hot tub | shuffleboard
horseshoes | group activities | recreation hall | fishing | boating | outdoor pool | volleyball
golf | tourist attraction | propane | hot showers | gambling casino | grocery | rv supplies

ROCKPORT

Glacier Peak Resort
58468 Clark Cabin Road
Rockport, Washington 98283
360-873-2250
glacierpeakresort@icloud.com
glacierpeakresort.com
RESORT NUMBER: 2365
GOOD SAM RATING: 8.5/10★/9
DIRECTIONS: From Jct of Hwy 20 and WA 530 at Rockport: Go 7 mi E on Hwy 20, resort on L.
GPS COORDINATES: 48.51211°N/-121.46998°W
NOTATIONS: Check-in: 1:00 p.m. Check-out: 11:00 a.m. Special discount Coast rate includes 2 adults per site. Max. RV length: 50 feet. Open: Year-round.
STATE MAP: See page CTC 76.

50 amps | pull-through | dump station | laundry | pets/restrictions | Wi-Fi access | playground | picnic tables
restaurant/snack bar | fishing | hiking trails | boating | fishing | boating | game room
tourist attraction | hot showers | tenting | ice

SILVER CREEK

Harmony Lakeside RV Park & Deluxe Cabins
563 State Route 122
Silver Creek, Washington 98585
877-780-7275
harmonyrvpark@aol.com
harmonylakesidervpark.com
RESORT NUMBER: 2456
GOOD SAM RATING: 8.5/10★/10
DIRECTIONS: From Jct of I-5 & US-12 (Ex 68): Go 13.75 mi E on US-12 to SR-122 (MP 86-87), then 5.5 mi NE on SR-122, park on R.
GPS COORDINATES: 46.55791°N/-122.50372°W
NOTATIONS: Check-in: 2:00 p.m. Check-out: 2:00 p.m. 10% discount for Coast members. Rate includes full hook-ups, TV, Wi-Fi. Additional charges: Add'l person $5/night, add'l vehicle $11/night, tax 9.8%. Max 6 people per site. No tent sites. 1 night deposit required for reservation. $29 cancellation fee less your deposit if cancel 14 days or more prior to check-in. Full deposit fee if cancel within 13 days or less of arrival. No shows charged entire reservation fee. Quiet hours 11 p.m.-8 a.m. Max. RV length: 60 feet. Open: Year-round.
STATE MAP: See page CTC 76.

50 amps, pull-through, cable tv, laundry, pets/restrictions, Wi-Fi access, playground, fishing, hiking trails, horseshoes, boating, fishing, boating, basketball, volleyball, tourist attraction, canoes, paddle boats, fire rings

SKAMOKAWA

Vista Park
13 Vista Park Road
Skamokawa, Washington 98647
360-795-8605
info@wahport2.org
wahport2.org
RESORT NUMBER: 2483
GOOD SAM RATING: 7.5/8.5★/8.5
DIRECTIONS: From Jct WA 4 & Vista Park Rd: Go 0.75 mi W on Vista Park Rd, park is on R.
GPS COORDINATES: 46.27135°N/-123.4591°W
NOTATIONS: Check-in: 2:00 p.m. Check-out: Noon. 2021 Coast rate $30 available Oct 31-Apr 1 only. Rate includes 6 persons max per site, 1 vehicle, 1 RV, full hook-ups. Additional charges: Extra vehicle $5/night, cancellation fee $10, tax 9.8%. Max. RV length: 50 feet. Open: Year-round.
STATE MAP: See page CTC 76.

50 amps, pets/restrictions, Wi-Fi access, playground, fishing, hiking trails, horseshoes, fishing, boating, basketball, beach, tennis, hot showers, ball field, gift shop, firewood, ice

SOAP LAKE

Smokiam RV Resort
22818 Highway 17 North
Soap Lake, Washington 98851
509-246-0413
camp@smokiamrvresort.com
smokiamrvresort.com
RESORT NUMBER: 2494
GOOD SAM RATING: 8.5/10★/8.5
DIRECTIONS: From Jct of WA Hwy 17 & WA Hwy 28 (in Soap Lake): Go 2 mi N on Hwy 17, resort on L.
GPS COORDINATES: 47.42464°N/-119.49758°W
NOTATIONS: Check-in: 1:00 p.m. Check-out: 11:00 a.m. Special 20% discount rate for Coast members. Rate includes 6 people per site, full hook-ups, cable TV. Additional charges: Add'l person $10/night after 6 people, children under 2 free, add'l vehicle $20/night, tax 10%. Max. RV length: 60 feet. Open: November 1–May 1.
STATE MAP: See page CTC 76.

50 amps, pull-through, laundry, pets/restrictions, Wi-Fi access, playground, picnic tables, hot tub, hiking trails, horseshoes, recreation hall, fishing, boating, outdoor pool, mini golf, beach, fire rings, grocery, gift shop

SUNNYSIDE

Sunnyside RV Park
609 Scoon Road
Sunnyside, Washington 98944
509-837-8486
sunnysidervpark.com
RESORT NUMBER: 2441
GOOD SAM RATING: 9.5/9★/8.5
DIRECTIONS: From I-82 (Ex 63) & WA-241: Go 0.3 mi S on WA-241 to Yakima Valley Highway, then 2.5 mi W to N 1st St, then N on N 1st St/Scoon Rd. Resort on L.
GPS COORDINATES: 46.3325°N/-120.0217°W
NOTATIONS: Check-in: 1:00 p.m. Check-out: 11:00 a.m. 20% discount for Coast members. Additional charges: Tax 7.9%. Drive-ups not accepted. Max. RV length: 55 feet. Open: Year-round.
STATE MAP: See page CTC 76.

50 amps, laundry, pets/restrictions, Wi-Fi access, playground, picnic tables, horseshoes, group activities, recreation hall, outdoor pool, rv supplies

TWISP

Riverbend RV Park
19961 Highway 20
Twisp, Washington 98856
509-997-3500
reservations@riverbendrv.com
riverbendrv.com
RESORT NUMBER: 2372
GOOD SAM RATING: 9/10★/9.5
DIRECTIONS: From town: Go 2 mi N on SR 20 (between MM 199 & 200), park on R. From Winthrop: Go 6 mi S on SR 20, park on L.
GPS COORDINATES: 48.39143°N/-120.1357°W
NOTATIONS: Check-in: 2:00 p.m. Check-out: 11:00 a.m. 2022 Coast rate $44-$50/night avail all season. Rate includes 2 adults. Additional charges: Extra child ages 7-14 $5/night, extra adult $7/night, dog $2, tax 10.5%. Max. RV length: 45 feet. Open: April 15–October 15.
STATE MAP: See page CTC 76.

50 amps, pull-through, dump station, pets/restrictions, Wi-Fi access, playground, picnic tables, horseshoes, fishing, boating, basketball, tourist attraction, propane, fire rings, rv supplies, gift shop, tenting, winter sports, firewood

WALLA WALLA

RV Resort Four Seasons
1440 The Dalles Military Road
Walla Walla, Washington 99362
509-529-6072
rvresortfourseasonsww@gmail.com
rvresortfourseasons.com
RESORT NUMBER: 2439
GOOD SAM RATING: 8.5/9.5★/10
DIRECTIONS: From Jct of US 12 & Prescott/Pendleton Ex: Go 2 mi S on NE Myra Rd to The Dalles Military Rd, then 0.5 mi E (L) on The Dalles Military Rd. Resort on L. Do not use GPS.
GPS COORDINATES: 46.04847°N/-118.35761°W
NOTATIONS: Check-in: 1:00 p.m. Check-out: 11:00 a.m. Special discount rate for Coast members avail Nov 1-March 1. Additional charges: Tax 8.9%. Drive-ups not accepted. Max. RV length: 65 feet. Open: Year-round.
STATE MAP: See page CTC 76.

50 amps, cable tv, laundry, pets/restrictions, Wi-Fi access, hiking trails, horseshoes, group activities, fishing, rv supplies, ice

WARDEN

Sage Hills Golf Club & RV Resort
10400 Sage Hill Road Southeast
Warden, Washington 98857
509-349-2088
reservations@sagehillsgolf.com
sagehillsgolf.com
RESORT NUMBER: 2498
GOOD SAM RATING: 9/8.5★/9
DIRECTIONS: From Jct of I-90 & Hwy 17 (Ex 179): Go 14.1 mi S mi on Hwy 17, resort on R.
GPS COORDINATES: 46.93321°N/-119.13385°W
NOTATIONS: Check-in: 2:00 p.m. Check-out: 2:00 p.m. Special 20% discount rate for Coast members. Rate includes 2 adults per site, 1 vehicle, full hook-ups, free Wi-Fi. Additional charges: Add'l adult $10/night, pet $10/night, add'l vehicle $10/night, tax 9.8%. Max. RV length: 60 feet. Open: November 1–May 1.
STATE MAP: See page CTC 76.

50 amps, pull-through, laundry, pets/restrictions, Wi-Fi access, restaurant/snack bar, horseshoes, recreation hall, outdoor pool, golf, tourist attraction, propane, hot showers

WILBUR

Country Lane Campground & RV Park
14 Portland Street Northwest
Wilbur, Washington 99185
509-647-0100
clrv.wilburwa@gmail.com
countrylanecampground.com
RESORT NUMBER: 2387
GOOD SAM RATING: 8/8.5★/7.5

DIRECTIONS: From Jct of Hwy 2 & Hwy 174/21 (W of Wilbur): Go 0.8 mi E on Hwy 2 to Portland St, then N on Portland St, park on L.
GPS COORDINATES: 47.76084°N/-118.71348°W
NOTATIONS: Check-in: 1:00 p.m. Check-out: 11:00 a.m. Coast rate $26-$34 plus 8% tax. Rate includes 2 adults, kids under 2 free, full hook-ups. Night check-in is available on front of office during closed hours. Max. RV length: 45 feet. Open: Year-round.
STATE MAP: See page CTC 76.

50 amps · pull-through · dump station · laundry · pets/restrictions · Wi-Fi access · picnic tables · restaurant/snack bar · recreation hall · fishing · boating · golf · tourist attraction · fire rings · tenting

WILBUR

Goose Creek RV Park & Campground
712 Southeast Railroad Avenue
Wilbur, Washington 99185
509-647-5888; fax: 509-647-5888
info@goosecreekrvpark.com
goosecreekrvpark.com
RESORT NUMBER: 2386
GOOD SAM RATING: 7.5/8★/8.5
DIRECTIONS: From Hwy 2: Turn S on Bell St (at Blue Footbridge). Use second driveway on L for entrance to park.
GPS COORDINATES: 47.75657°N/-118.70035°W
ELEVATION: 2,145 feet
NOTATIONS: Check-in: 2:00 p.m. Check-out: 11:00 a.m. 2022 Coast rate $32.40 for back-in only. Rate includes 2 people, city water and sewer hook-up, 30 amp, picnic table. Additional charges: 50 amp site $3, tax 8%. For arrivals after 6 p.m., call ahead for approval. No check-in after 9 p.m. Discount not available a week before or a week after major holidays. Max. RV length: 45 feet. Open: April 1–October 31.
STATE MAP: See page CTC 76.

50 amps · pull-through · visitor mail · laundry · pets/restrictions · Wi-Fi access · playground · picnic tables · fishing · boating · golf · tourist attraction · shopping · hot showers · gambling casino · rv supplies · tenting

WYOMING

EVANSTON

Phillips RV Park
225 Bear River Drive
Evanston, Wyoming 82930
307-789-3805
phillipsrvpark@nglconnection.net
phillipsrvpark.com
RESORT NUMBER: 2393
GOOD SAM RATING: 8/9.5★/8
DIRECTIONS: From Jct of I-80 & I-80 Bus Loop (E Evanston Ex 6): W 0.6 mi on I-80 Bus Loop/Bear River Dr, park on L. Note: Do not use GPS.
GPS COORDINATES: 41.27096°N/-110.94778°W
NOTATIONS: Check-in: Noon. Check-out: 11:00 a.m. Special discount rate for Coast members. Rate includes 2 people per site, full hook-ups, 30 amp. Additional charges: Extra adult $2/night, extra child $1/night, 50 amp $2/night, extra vehicle $3/night, tax 8%. Availability Apr, May, Jun, Sep, Oct. No availability Jul or Aug. Do not use GPS directions. Max. RV length: 40 feet. Open: April 15–June 30; September 1–October 15.
STATE MAP: See page CTC 59.

50 amps · pull-through · cable tv · laundry · pets/restrictions · Wi-Fi access · playground · picnic tables · hiking trails · horseshoes · fishing · basketball · golf · tourist attraction · rv supplies · tenting · ice

ALBERTA

COUNTY OF GRANDE PRAIRIE #1

Camp Tamarack RV Park
704063 Range Road 62
County of Grande Prairie #1, Alberta T8W 5B3
780-532-9998; fax: 780-532-9439
reservations@camptamarackrv.com
camptamarackrv.com
RESORT NUMBER: 2366
GOOD SAM RATING: 8/10★/9
DIRECTIONS: From Jct Hwy 43 & Hwy 40: S 5.5 mi (9 km) on Hwy 40, park on L.
GPS COORDINATES: 55.09466°N/-118.81274°W
NOTATIONS: Check-in: 1:00 p.m. Check-out: 11:00 a.m. Special discount rate for Coast members. Rate includes 1 RV, 1 vehicle, 2 adults, any children under 16. Additional charges: Extra adult $5/night, 50 amp $2/night, tax 5% + DMF 2%. No availability Jun, Jul, Aug. Mastercard or Visa required for reservation. Max. RV length: 40 feet. Open: April 15–May 30; September 1–October 15.
WESTERN CANADA MAP: See page CTC 78.

50 amps · pull-through · dump station · laundry · pets/restrictions · Wi-Fi access · playground · picnic tables · hiking trails · horseshoes · golf · shopping · propane · fire rings · grocery · rv supplies · firewood

DRUMHELLER

Dinosaur Trail RV Resort & Cabins—Holiday Trails Resorts
Highway 838 North Dinosaur Trail at 11 km pt
Drumheller, Alberta T0J 0Y0
403-823-9333; fax: 403-823-3626
dinosaur@htr.ca
htr.ca
RESORT NUMBER: 2043
GOOD SAM RATING: 8/8/8
DIRECTIONS: From Drumheller: Watch for Tyrell Museum signs. W 11 km from Drumheller on N Dinosaur Trl/Hwy 838. 5 km past Tyrell Museum.
GPS COORDINATES: 51.5034°N/-112.8292°W
NOTATIONS: Check-in: 1:00 p.m.–8:00 p.m. Check-out: 11:00 a.m. Special discount rate for Coast members. Rate includes 2 adults, 30 or 50 amp, full hook-ups. Additional charges: Extra person over 5 yrs $5/night, each pet $3/night, Wi-Fi $3/night, reservation fee $6, GST of 5%. Drive-ups not accepted. Rental units available. Trip Points not accepted. Contact resort directly. Max. RV length: 45 feet. Open: May 1–September 30.
WESTERN CANADA MAP: See page CTC 78.

50 amps · dump station · laundry · pets/restrictions · internet access · Wi-Fi access · playground · restaurant/snack bar · rental units · horseshoes · fishing · outdoor pool · game room · tourist attraction · propane · canoes

PEACE RIVER

Rendez-Vous RV Park & Storage
950 Woods Road
Peace River, Alberta T8S 1Y9
877-250-4284
support@rvpeaceriver.com
rvpeaceriver.com
RESORT NUMBER: 2416
GOOD SAM RATING: 9/9.5★/7.5
DIRECTIONS: From Jct of AB 2 N & AB 688: Go 1 km (0.5 mi) NE on AB 688. Then 230 m (750 feet) NW on Sunrise Rd. Then 800 m (0.5 mi) W on Sunrise Road S. Then 300 m (0.25 mi) N on Woods Road. Resort on R.
GPS COORDINATES: 56.20773°N/-117.1996°W
NOTATIONS: Check-in: 1:00 p.m. Check-out: Noon. Special 10% discount rate for Coast members. Additional charges: Tax 5%. Drive-ups not accepted. Max. RV length: 45 feet. Open: Year-round.
WESTERN CANADA MAP: See page CTC 78.

50 amps · pull-through · laundry · pets/restrictions · Wi-Fi access · playground · hiking trails · group activities · propane · rv supplies · winter sports · firewood · ice

VALLEYVIEW

Sherk's RV Park
22362 Township Road 702
Valleyview, Alberta T0H 3N0
780-524-4949; fax: 780-524-4346
skye.dietzen@gmail.com
sherksrvpark.com
RESORT NUMBER: 2392
GOOD SAM RATING: 8.5/10★/10
DIRECTIONS: From E Jct Hwy 43 & Hwy 49: S 0.5 mi on Hwy 43 to Twp Range Rd 702. W 0.6 mi on Range Rd 702. Resort on R.
GPS COORDINATES: 55.05417°N/-117.2983°W
ELEVATION: 2,284 feet
NOTATIONS: Check-in: 11:00 a.m. Check-out: 11:00 a.m. Special 20% discount rate for Coast members. Additional charges: Tax 5%. Site includes gravel parking pad, picnic table, full hook-ups. Max. RV length: 60 feet. Open: May 1–September 30.
WESTERN CANADA MAP: See page CTC 78.

30 amps · pull-through · laundry · pets/restrictions · Wi-Fi access · playground · picnic tables · hiking trails · horseshoes · fishing · golf · shopping · hot showers · ball field · tenting · firewood · handicap access

BRITISH COLUMBIA

CHEMAINUS

Country Maples RV Resort—
Holiday Trails Resorts
9010 Trans Canada Highway
Chemainus, British Columbia V0R 1K4
250-246-2078; fax: 250-246-2038
countrymaples@htr.ca
htr.ca
RESORT NUMBER: 2042
GOOD SAM RATING: 8/7.5/8.5
DIRECTIONS: From Hwy 1 N: Park is 18 km (11 mi) N of Duncan on L of Hwy. N and follow designated u-turn route at Henry Rd. From Hwy 1 S: 1.5 km (1 mi) past Fuller Lake Motel at Henry Rd. Ex lane allows slowing before park entrance.
GPS COORDINATES: 48.8961°N/-123.7148°W
NOTATIONS: Check-in: Noon. Check-out: 11:00 a.m. Call for special 25% discount rate for Coast members avail year round. Rate includes 4 adults, 30 amp, full hook-ups. Additional charges: Extra person over 5 yrs $4/night, each pet $3/night, Wi-Fi $3/night, reservation fee $6, dump station $10, tax 5%. Sun & Mon holidays 3 p.m. check-in. Drive-ups not accepted. Max. RV length: 45 feet. Open: Year-round.
WESTERN CANADA MAP: See page CTC 78.

50 amps · pull-through · dump station · laundry · pets/restrictions · internet access · Wi-Fi access · playground · horseshoes · recreation hall · outdoor pool · mini golf · fitness · gift shop · handicap access

CRESTON

Pair-A-Dice RV Park & Campground
1322 North West Boulevard Highway 3
Creston, British Columbia V0B 1G6
250-428-2347; res.: 866-223-3423
pairadice@shaw.ca
pairadicepark.com
RESORT NUMBER: 2452
GOOD SAM RATING: 7/9.5★/8
DIRECTIONS: From Jct Hwy 3A & Hwy 3 (W side of town): Go 0.8 km (0.5 mi) E on Hwy 3, park on L.
GPS COORDINATES: 49.11124°N/-116.52311°W
NOTATIONS: Check-in: Noon. Check-out: 11:00 a.m. Special discount rate for Coast members. Additional charges: Add'l adult or child $3/night, cable $3/night, 50 amp $8/night, tax 5%. Coast member discount avail Apr 1-Jun 15, Aug 15-Oct 31. Max. RV length: 65 feet. Open: April 1–June 15; August 15–October 31.
WESTERN CANADA MAP: See page CTC 78.

50 amps · pull-through · dump station · cable tv · laundry · pets/restrictions · Wi-Fi access · playground · picnic tables · hiking trails · horseshoes · fishing · boating · grocery · tenting

DAWSON CREEK

Northern Lights RV Park
9636 Friesen Sub
Dawson Creek, British Columbia V1G 4T9
250-782-9433
nlrv2010@gmail.com
nlrv.com
RESORT NUMBER: 2419
GOOD SAM RATING: 8.5/9.5★/7.5
DIRECTIONS: From Jct Hwy 97 N & Hwy 97 S: Go 2.6 km (1.5 mi) W on Hwy 97 S. Resort on L.
GPS COORDINATES: 55.76532°N/-120.2912°W
NOTATIONS: Check-in: 1:00 p.m. Check-out: 11:00 a.m. Special discount rate for Coast members. Additional charges: 50 amp $5/night, tax 5%. Max. RV length: 45 feet. Open: June 1–August 31.
WESTERN CANADA MAP: See page CTC 78.

50 amps · pull-through · laundry · pets/restrictions · Wi-Fi access · hiking trails · recreation hall · golf · gambling casino · rv supplies · firewood

GRAND FORKS

Riviera RV Park
6331 Highway 3 East
Grand Forks, British Columbia V0H 1H9
250-442-2158; res.: 855-442-2158
reservations@grandforksrivierarvpark.com
grandforksrivierarvpark.com
RESORT NUMBER: 2417
GOOD SAM RATING: 8/9.5★/8
DIRECTIONS: From Jct Hwy 3 & Kettle River Bridge: Go 2 km (1.5 mi) E on Hwy 3. Resort on R.
GPS COORDINATES: 49.02472°N/-118.4193°W
NOTATIONS: Check-in: 24 hr. Check-out: 24 hr. Toll-free reservations number (855) 442-2158. Special discount rate for Coast members. Additional charges: Extra person. Max. RV length: 100 feet. Open: Year-round.
WESTERN CANADA MAP: See page CTC 78.

30 amps · pull-through · visitor mail · laundry · pets/restrictions · Wi-Fi access · playground · picnic tables · fishing · hiking trails · horseshoes · group activities · fishing · boating · canoes · fire rings · firewood · ice

HOPE

Sunshine Valley RV Resort & Cabins—
Holiday Trails Resorts
14850 Alpine Boulevard
Hope, British Columbia V0X 1L5
604-869-0066; fax: 604-869-0040
sunshinevalley@htr.ca
htr.ca
RESORT NUMBER: 2166
GOOD SAM RATING: 9/10★/9
DIRECTIONS: From W on Hwy BC-3: L into Sunshine Valley and onto Alpine Blvd. Park entrance is 28.6 mi. From Manning Park: E on Hwy BC-3 Ex 177. Park entrance is 8.7 mi E of Hope.
GPS COORDINATES: 49.1645°N/-121.3944°W
ELEVATION: 138 feet
NOTATIONS: Check-in: Noon–9:00 p.m. Check-out: Noon. Special discount rate for Coast members. Rate includes 4 people, 50 amp, full hook-ups. Additional charges: Extra person over 5 yrs $4/night, Wi-Fi $3/night, each pet $3/night, firewood, dump station $10, tax 5%. Reservation deposit $6 plus tax at time of booking. Sunday check-in 3 p.m. to 9 p.m. Max. RV length: 70 feet. Open: January 15–December 31.
WESTERN CANADA MAP: See page CTC 78.

50 amps · pull-through · visitor mail · laundry · pets/restrictions · Wi-Fi access · playground · picnic tables · hot tub · shuffleboard · hiking trails · recreation hall · outdoor pool · game room · fitness · propane · indoor pool · hot showers · fire rings · grocery · rv supplies · winter sports · firewood · handicap access · ice

ROSEDALE

Camperland RV Resort & Cabins—
Holiday Trails Resorts
53730 Bridal Falls Road
Rosedale, British Columbia V0X 1X1
604-794-7361; fax: 604-794-3756
kristina@htr.ca
htr.ca
RESORT NUMBER: 2044
GOOD SAM RATING: 9.5/8/9
DIRECTIONS: From Hope/Hwy 1: W 21.7 mi, Ex 138. L across overpass to N side of Hwy. Frontage Rd to park, just past waterslide. From Vancouver/Hwy 1: E to Bridal Falls/Ex 135, approx 10 mi past Chilliwack. Frontage Rd to park.
GPS COORDINATES: 49.1882°N/-121.7427°W
NOTATIONS: Check-in: Noon–9:00 p.m. Check-out: Noon. Coast member rate 25% discount off nightly rate. Rate includes 2 adults, 30 amps, full hook-ups. Additional charges: Extra person over 5 yrs $4/night, each pet $3/night, dump station $10, reservation fee $6, Wi-Fi $3/night, tax 5%. Many 50 amp sites available. Max. RV length: 45 feet. Open: April 1–October 31.
WESTERN CANADA MAP: See page CTC 78.

50 amps · pull-through · laundry · pets/restrictions · internet access · Wi-Fi access · playground · restaurant/snack bar · hot tub · shuffleboard · horseshoes · outdoor pool · game room · tourist attraction

MANITOBA

DOUGLAS

Bry-Mar RV Park and Campground
Site 520 Road 102 (Highway 1)
Douglas, Manitoba R7A 5Y5
204-573-7067
info@brymarrvpark.com
brymarrvpark.com
RESORT NUMBER: 2413
GOOD SAM RATING: 7.5/8.5★/8.5
DIRECTIONS: Ebnd from Jct MB 110 (S) & TC 1: Go 4.9 km (3 mi) E on TC 1, park on L. Wbnd from MB 5 & TC 1: Go 31.9 km (20 mi) W on TC 1, park on R.
GPS COORDINATES: 49.88887°N/-99.80151°W
NOTATIONS: Check-in: Noon. Check-out: 11:00 a.m. Special discount rate for Coast members. Rate includes 2 adults per site, full hook-ups, free Wi-Fi. Additional charges: Extra adult $5/night, tax 5% GST, dump station $21, water fill $21. $8 reservation fee for specific site. Max of 6 people per site. Max. RV length: 60 feet. Open: April 15–September 26.

WESTERN CANADA MAP: See page CTC 78.

30 amps, pull-through, visitor mail, laundry, pets/restrictions, Wi-Fi access, playground, picnic tables, hiking trails, horseshoes, fishing, boating, golf, fitness, hot showers, gambling casino, fire rings, rv supplies, tenting, firewood, ice

LAC DU BONNET

Champagne's RV Park
102 Tinant Road
Lac Du Bonnet, Manitoba R0E 1A0
204-345-2414
champagnesrv@hotmail.com
RESORT NUMBER: 2411
GOOD SAM RATING: 8/9.5★/10
DIRECTIONS: From Jct Hwy 11 & Hwy 313: Go 0.4 km (0.25 mi) W on gravel road.
GPS COORDINATES: 50.28096°N/-96.03726°W
NOTATIONS: Check-in: Noon. Check-out: 11:00 a.m. Special discount rate for Coast members. Rate includes 2 adults per site, full hook-ups. Additional charges: Extra adult $5/night, extra child $5/night, tax 5%. No availability over long holiday weekends. Max. RV length: 60 feet. Open: May 1–October 1.
WESTERN CANADA MAP: See page CTC 78.

30 amps, pull-through, dump station, laundry, pets/restrictions, Wi-Fi access, playground, picnic tables, hiking trails, horseshoes, fishing, boating, basketball, volleyball, golf, fire rings, tenting

OAK LAKE

Aspen Grove Campground
Northwest 25-9-25W
Oak Lake, Manitoba R0M 1P0
204-855-2260
aspengrovecampground@gmail.com
aspengrovecampground.com
RESORT NUMBER: 2418
GOOD SAM RATING: 8/8★/8
DIRECTIONS: From Jct Hwy 254S & Trans Canada Hwy: Go 3.6 km (2 mi) W on Trans Canada Hwy.
GPS COORDINATES: 49.77177°N/-100.75238°W
NOTATIONS: Check-in: 1:00 p.m. Check-out: 11:00 a.m. 20% discount for Coast members. Additional charges: Wi-Fi $7, tax 5%. No long holiday weekends. Drive-ups not accepted. Max. RV length: 60 feet. Open: May 1–June 26; September 8–September 26.
WESTERN CANADA MAP: See page CTC 78.

50 amps, dump station, laundry, pets/restrictions, playground, picnic tables, hiking trails, horseshoes, group activities, fishing, boating, outdoor pool, mini golf, propane, canoes, fire rings, rv supplies, tenting, firewood, ice

PORTAGE LA PRAIRIE

Miller's Camping Resort
29081 Highway 1 East
Portage La Prairie, Manitoba R1N 3C3
204-857-4255
info@millerscampground.com
millerscampground.com
RESORT NUMBER: 2434
GOOD SAM RATING: 8.5/9.5★/10
DIRECTIONS: From town, E 6 mi on Hwy 1, follow signs. Resort on L.
GPS COORDINATES: 49.97557°N/-98.13661°W
NOTATIONS: Check-in: 1:00 p.m. Check-out: Noon. Special discount rate for Coast members. Additional charges: 50 amp $5/night, add'l adult $3/night. Max. RV length: 90 feet. Open: May 1–June 30; September 1–October 9.
WESTERN CANADA MAP: See page CTC 78.

50 amps, pull-through, dump station, laundry, pets/restrictions, Wi-Fi access, playground, picnic tables, restaurant/snack bar, horseshoes, group activities, recreation hall, fishing, boating, outdoor pool, game room, gambling casino, fire rings, grocery, tenting, firewood

NEW BRUNSWICK

CARAQUET

Camping Colibri
913 Boul des Acadiens Route 11
Caraquet, New Brunswick E1W 1H5
506-727-2222
info@lecolibri.ca
lecolibri.ca
RESORT NUMBER: 2325
GOOD SAM RATING: 10/10★/10
DIRECTIONS: From Caraquet: W end of town on Rte 11. Resort on L.
GPS COORDINATES: 47.7628°N/-65.04816°W
NOTATIONS: Check-in: 2:00 p.m. Check-out: 11:00 a.m. Special discount rate for Coast members. Additional charges: Tax 15%. Not available Jul, Aug, long holiday weekends. Max. RV length: 75 feet. Open: May 15–September 15.
EASTERN CANADA MAP: See page CTC 80.

50 amps, pull-through, laundry, pets/restrictions, Wi-Fi access, playground, restaurant/snack bar, horseshoes, group activities, recreation hall, outdoor pool, basketball, volleyball, fire rings, rv supplies, tenting, firewood, ice

DERBY JUNCTION

Enclosure Campground Resort
8 Enclosure Road
Derby Junction, New Brunswick E1V 5B2
506-622-8638; res.: 800-363-1733
enclosurecampground92@gmail.com
enclosurecampground.ca
RESORT NUMBER: 888
GOOD SAM RATING: 8/7/7.5
DIRECTIONS: From Rt 8: Ex 163 to NB 108. Just W of Miramichi City. Follow signs to park.
GPS COORDINATES: 46.4067°N/-65.5937°W
NOTATIONS: Check-in: 1:00 p.m.–9:00 p.m. Check-out: Noon. Special discount rate for Coast members. Rate includes 4 people, 30 amp and water. Additional charges: Extra person (over age 19) $5/night, 15% tax. Max. RV length: 45 feet. Open: May 15–October 13.
EASTERN CANADA MAP: See page CTC 80.

30 amps, pull-through, visitor mail, laundry, pets/restrictions, internet access, playground, restaurant/snack bar, hiking trails, fishing, outdoor pool, volleyball, tourist attraction

HOPEWELL CAPE

Ponderosa Pines Campground
4325 Route 114
Hopewell Cape, New Brunswick E4H 3P1
800-822-8800; fax: 506-734-2978
ponderosa.pines.campground@gmail.com
ponderosapines.ca
RESORT NUMBER: 2379
GOOD SAM RATING: 8.5/10★/9.5
DIRECTIONS: From Jct of Rte 114 & Hopewell Rock Entrance (in town): W 1 mi on Rte 114, campground on L.
GPS COORDINATES: 45.81907°N/-64.59628°W
NOTATIONS: Check-in: 2:00 p.m–8:00 p.m. Check-out: 11:00 a.m. Special discount rate for Coast members. Rate includes 2 adults, electric, water, sewer each RV site. Additional charges: Extra adult $10, tax 15%. No availability Jul, Aug, or long holiday weekends. Max. RV length: 90 feet. Open: May 12–June 30; September 1–October 22.
EASTERN CANADA MAP: See page CTC 80.

50 amps, pull-through, laundry, pets/restrictions, Wi-Fi access, playground, picnic tables, fishing, hiking trails, horseshoes, fishing, boating, outdoor pool, basketball, volleyball, tourist attraction, canoes, hot showers, paddle boats, gambling casino, fire rings, grocery, rv supplies, tenting, firewood

POINTE DU CHENE

Ocean Surf RV Park
73 Belliveau Beach Road
Pointe du Chene, New Brunswick E4P 3W2
506-532-5480; res.: 888-532-5480
reservations@oceansurf.ca
oceansurf.ca
RESORT NUMBER: 2346
GOOD SAM RATING: 10/10★/10
DIRECTIONS: From Jct of Hwy 15 & Ex 37 (Parlee Beach Rd-Rte 140), NE 1 mi on Rte 140 to Rte 133, E 0.3 mi to Belliveau Beach Rd, N 0.5 mi, resort on R.
GPS COORDINATES: 46.2296°N/-64.5014°W
NOTATIONS: Check-in: 1:00 p.m. Check-out: 11:00 a.m. Special discount rate for Coast members. Rate includes 2 adults, 1 camping unit. Additional charges: 50 amp $6/night, extra vehicle $6/night, tax 15%. No availability Jul, Aug, and all long holiday weekends. Max. RV length: 75 feet. Open: May 1–June 30; September 1–October 1.
EASTERN CANADA MAP: See page CTC 80.

50 amps, pull-through, dump station, laundry, pets/restrictions, Wi-Fi access, playground, picnic tables, group activities, boating, recreation hall, fishing, boating, outdoor pool, beach, volleyball, tourist attraction, canoes, fire rings

ST. MARTINS

Century Farm Family Campground
67 Ocean Wave Drive
St. Martins, New Brunswick E5R 2E8
506-833-2357; res.: 866-394-4400
reservecffc@nb.aibn.com
centuryfarmcampground.com
RESORT NUMBER: 1334
GOOD SAM RATING: 8.5/9.5★/8.5
DIRECTIONS: From Bangor, ME: US 9 or 1 to St Stephen, NB, Canada. Rt 1 to Ex 137A. E of St John to Rt 111. 20 mi past airport to Main St, St Martins. R on Ocean Wave Dr. From Sussex: Ex 198. Rt 111 W. Exit L onto Main St, St Martins.
GPS COORDINATES: 45.3527°N/-65.5436°W
NOTATIONS: Check-in: 1:00 p.m. Check-out: 11:00 a.m. Special discount rate for Coast members, cash only. Rate includes 2 adults and children under 16, 30 amp only. Additional charges: Extra person $5/night, tax 15%. No availability Jul, Aug, and all long holiday weekends. Max. RV length: 80 feet. Open: May 15–September 26.
EASTERN CANADA MAP: See page CTC 80.

30 amps, pull-through, dump station, laundry, pets/restrictions, Wi-Fi access, playground, picnic tables, horseshoes, recreation hall, fishing, basketball, beach, game room, tourist attraction, shopping, hot showers, fire rings, rv supplies, tenting, firewood

WOODSTOCK

Yogi Bear's Jellystone Park New Brunswick
174 Hemlock Street
Woodstock, New Brunswick E7M 4E5
506-328-6287; fax: 506-328-0015
jellystonepark96@gmail.com
jellystoneparknb.com
RESORT NUMBER: 2339
GOOD SAM RATING: 9.5/9.5★/9
DIRECTIONS: From Jct of TCH-2 & Ex 191 (Beardsley Rd), N 0.25 mi on Beardsley Rd to Hemlock St, W 0.25 mi, follow signs. Resort on R.
GPS COORDINATES: 46.13077°N/-67.60752°W
NOTATIONS: Check-in: 1:00 p.m. Check-out: Noon. 2021 Coast rate 20% discount available Jun 1-Jun 15 and Aug 15-Sep 3. Rate includes 2 adults, 2 children under 18 years. Additional charges: Extra adult $15/night, extra child $15/night, 50 amp $2/night, tax 15%. Max. RV length: 80 feet. Open: June 1–September 3.
EASTERN CANADA MAP: See page CTC 80.

50 amps, pull-through, dump station, laundry, pets/restrictions, Wi-Fi access, playground, group activities, recreation hall, boating, outdoor pool, mini golf, basketball, beach, volleyball, golf, game room, shopping, hot showers, fire rings, rv supplies, tenting, firewood, ice

NEWFOUNDLAND AND LABRADOR

ROBINSONS

Pirate's Haven RV Park & Chalets
229 Main Road
Robinsons, Newfoundland and Labrador A0N 1V0
709-649-0601
paulandruth@nf.sympatico.ca
pirateshavenadventures.com
RESORT NUMBER: 2378
GOOD SAM RATING: 9/10★/9
DIRECTIONS: From Port-Aux-Basques on Hwy 1: Go 100 km to Rte 404, turn L, go 11 km, park on R. From Deer Lake on Hwy 1: Go 168 km to Rte 404, turn R, go 6 km to intersection, turn L, park on L.
GPS COORDINATES: 48.24719°N/-58.78768°W
NOTATIONS: Check-in: 1:00 p.m. Check-out: 11:00 a.m. Special discount rate for Coast members. Rate includes 2 adults, water, 50 amp, sewer. Additional charges: Extra adult $5/night, tax 15%. No availability Jul, Aug. Max. RV length: 60 feet. Open: May 1–June 30; September 1–October 15.
EASTERN CANADA MAP: See page CTC 80.

50 amps, pull-through, dump station, laundry, pets/restrictions, Wi-Fi access, playground, picnic tables, restaurant/snack bar, fishing, hiking trails, fishing, boating, outdoor pool, volleyball, game room, tourist attraction, firewood

NOVA SCOTIA

BADDECK

Adventures East Campground and Cottages
9585 Highway 105
Baddeck, Nova Scotia B0E 1B0
902-295-2417
info@adventureseast.ca
adventures-east.com
RESORT NUMBER: 729
GOOD SAM RATING: 9.5/10★/10
DIRECTIONS: Located on the Trans-Canada Hwy 105. 0.5 mi E of Ex 7 (but still on the Hwy) 5 mi W of Baddeck.
GPS COORDINATES: 46.089°N/-60.8586°W
NOTATIONS: Check-in: 3:00 p.m. Check-out: 11:00 a.m. 2022 Coast member rate $33.20-$53.48. Electric and water hook-ups only guaranteed. Sewer hook-ups are space available only. Wi-Fi access in campground. Max. RV length: 45 feet. Open: May 15–October 15.
EASTERN CANADA MAP: See page CTC 80.

30 amps, laundry, pets/restrictions, Wi-Fi access, playground, restaurant/snack bar, hiking trails, group activities, fishing, boating, outdoor pool, tourist attraction, fire rings, tenting, grills

CHETICAMP

Plage St Pierre Beach and Campground
635 ChetiCamp Island Road
Cheticamp, Nova Scotia B0E 1H0
902-224-2112; fax: 902-224-2357
plagestpierre@ns.sympatico.ca
plagestpierrebeachandcampground.com
RESORT NUMBER: 2340
GOOD SAM RATING: 7.5/9★/9.5
DIRECTIONS: From town: S 2.5 mi on Cabot Trail Rd to Cheticamp Island, W 2 mi. Resort on L.
GPS COORDINATES: 46.60778°N/-61.04781°W
NOTATIONS: Check-in: 1:00 p.m. Check-out: 11:00 a.m. Special discount rate for Coast members. Additional charges: Extra person $10/night, extra child $10/night, tax 15%. No availability Jul and Aug. Max. RV length: 60 feet. Open: May 14–June 30; September 1–October 13.
EASTERN CANADA MAP: See page CTC 80.

30 amps, pull-through, laundry, pets/restrictions, Wi-Fi access, playground, picnic tables, hiking trails, horseshoes, fishing, boating, mini golf, beach, tennis, golf, game room, tourist attraction, fire rings, rv supplies, tenting, firewood, ice

MARTIN'S RIVER

RayPort Campground
165 Shingle Mill Road
Martin's River, Nova Scotia B0J 2E0
902-627-2678; fax: 902-627-1144
rayport@hotmail.com
rayport.ca
RESORT NUMBER: 2341
GOOD SAM RATING: 8.5/8.5★/9.5
DIRECTIONS: From Jct of Hwy 103 & Ex 10 (Rte 3), S. 0.5 mi on access rd to Rte 3, E 2 mi, follow signs to resort on L.
GPS COORDINATES: 44.48876°N/-64.34227°W
NOTATIONS: Check-in: 1:00 p.m. Check-out: Noon. Special discount rate for Coast members. Rate includes 2 adults, 2 children per site. Additional charges: Extra adult $5/night, tax 15%. Max. RV length: 50 feet. Open: May 10–October 14.
EASTERN CANADA MAP: See page CTC 80.

50 amps, pull-through, dump station, laundry, pets/restrictions, Wi-Fi access, playground, picnic tables, fishing, group activities, fishing, boating, outdoor pool, game room, tourist attraction, hot showers, fire rings, firewood, ice

MELBOURNE

Castle Lake Campground and Cottages
83 Comeaus Hill Road
Melbourne, Nova Scotia B0W 1B0
902-749-1739
castlelakecampground@gmail.com
castlelakecampground.com
RESORT NUMBER: 2342
GOOD SAM RATING: 8.5/10★/10
DIRECTIONS: From Jct of Hwy 103 and Rte 3 (in Yarmouth): Go 2.4 km/1.5 mi S on Rte 3, then 5.5 km/3 mi E on Rte 334, then 4.5 km/2.5 mi E on Melbourne Rd, then 2.2 km/1.25 mi S on Comeaus Hill Rd. Resort on L.
GPS COORDINATES: 43.82492°N/-66.07284°W
NOTATIONS: Check-in: 1:00 p.m. Check-out: 11:00 a.m. Special discount rate for Coast members avail May, Jun, Sep, & Oct. Additional charges: 50 amp $10/night, tax 15%. No availability Jul or Aug. Max. RV length: 80 feet. Open: May 21–October 11.
EASTERN CANADA MAP: See page CTC 80.

50 amps, pull-through, dump station, pets/restrictions, Wi-Fi access, picnic tables, restaurant/snack bar, fishing, hiking trails, boating, mini golf, tourist attraction, canoes, paddle boats, fire rings, firewood, ice

SMITHS COVE

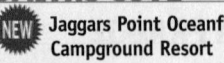

NEW **Jaggars Point Oceanfront Campground Resort**
57 Cross Road
Smiths Cove, Nova Scotia B0S 1S0
902-245-4814

jpcampground@gmail.com
campinnovascotia.com
RESORT NUMBER: 2583
GOOD SAM RATING: 8/8.5★/8.5
DIRECTIONS: From Jct Hwy 101 & Hwy 1 (Ex 24): Go 1.4 km (1 mi) W on Hwy 1, then 0.4 km (0.25 mi) W on N Old Post Rd, then 0.3 km (0.25 mi) N on Smiths Cove Crossing Rd. Park on R.
GPS COORDINATES: 44.6119°N/-65.71703°W
NOTATIONS: Check-in: 2:00 p.m. Check-out: Noon. 2021 Coast rate 20% discount available May 8-Jun 15 and Sep 15-Oct 15. Rate includes 2 adults per site, full hook-ups. Additional charges: Add'l adult $5/night, tax 15%. Max. RV length: 60 feet. Open: May 8–October 15.
EASTERN CANADA MAP: See page CTC 80.

30 amps, pull-through, dump station, laundry, pets/restrictions, Wi-Fi access, playground, picnic tables, horseshoes, group activities, fishing, boating, outdoor pool, mini golf, basketball, volleyball, fire rings, rv supplies, firewood, ice

TRURO

Scotia Pines Campground
1911 Highway 2
Truro, Nova Scotia B0N 1C0
877-893-3666
info@scotiapine.ca
scotiapine.ca
RESORT NUMBER: 2329
GOOD SAM RATING: 9/10★/10
DIRECTIONS: From Jct of Hwy 102 & Ex 12 (Rte 289), E 0.6 mi on Rte 289 to Rte 2, N 2.4 mi. Resort on R.
GPS COORDINATES: 45.28642°N/-63.2894°W
NOTATIONS: Check-in: 1:00 p.m. Check-out: 1:00 p.m. Special discount rate for Coast members avail May 15-Jun 30 & Sep 1-Oct 15. Site rates are for one RV, trailer, or tent per site. Additional charges: Tax 15%. No availability Jul, Aug, or long holiday weekends. Max. RV length: 80 feet. Open: May 15–October 15.
EASTERN CANADA MAP: See page CTC 80.

50 amps, pull-through, dump station, laundry, pets/restrictions, Wi-Fi access, playground, picnic tables, hiking trails, horseshoes, outdoor pool, tourist attraction, fire rings, grocery, rv supplies, tenting, firewood, handicap access, ice

ONTARIO

ALLISTON

Nicolston Dam Campground and Travellers Park
5140 5th Line Essa
Alliston, Ontario L9R 1V2
705-435-7946
nicolstondam@gmail.com
nicolstondam.com
RESORT NUMBER: 2337
GOOD SAM RATING: 8.5/9.5★/8.5
DIRECTIONS: From Jct Hwy 400 & 89: Go 11 km/7 mi W on Hwy 89. Use Essa as town if using GPS.
GPS COORDINATES: 44.16745°N/-79.80716°W
NOTATIONS: Check-in: 1:00 p.m. Check-out: 11:00 a.m. Special Coast member 20% discount. Rate includes 2 adults, 1 RV, 1 kitchen tent, 1 vehicle. Additional charges: Extra adult $10, extra child over 9 years $3, extra vehicle $20, tax 13%. Max. RV length: 45 feet. Open: May 1–October 28.
CENTRAL CANADA MAP: See page CTC 79.

30 amps, pull-through, dump station, laundry, pets/restrictions, Wi-Fi access, playground, picnic tables, fishing, horseshoes, fishing, outdoor pool, mini golf, volleyball, golf, tourist attraction, shopping, canoes, paddle boats, fire rings, gift shop, tenting, firewood, ice

BAINSVILLE

Maplewood Acres RV Park
21848 Concession Road 3
Bainsville, Ontario K0C 1E0
613-347-2130
info@maplewoodacres.com
maplewoodacres.com
RESORT NUMBER: 2362
GOOD SAM RATING: 9/10★/9.5
DIRECTIONS: From Hwy 401 E Ex 825/4th Line Rd (last Ex in ON): 4th Line Rd N for 3 km (1.8 mi). R on Concession Rd 3, park on R.
GPS COORDINATES: 45.22564°N/-74.40518°W
NOTATIONS: Check-in: 1:00 p.m. Check-out: 11:00 a.m. Special discount rate for Coast members. Rate includes 2 adults, 3 children, 1 vehicle, 1 RV, 1 tent per site. Additional charges: Extra adult $8/night, extra child $6/night, tax 13%. No availability Jul, Aug, or long holiday weekends. Max. RV length: 80 feet. Open: May 5–October 9.
CENTRAL CANADA MAP: See page CTC 79.

50 amps, pull-through, dump station, laundry, pets/restrictions, Wi-Fi access, playground, picnic tables, horseshoes, group activities, fishing, boating, outdoor pool, basketball, beach, golf, game room, tourist attraction, shopping, gambling casino, fire rings, firewood, ice

BRACEBRIDGE

Santa's Whispering Pines Campground
1623 Golden Beach Road
Bracebridge, Ontario P1L 1W8
705-645-5682; fax: 705-645-9791
camping@santasvillage.ca
santasvillage.ca
RESORT NUMBER: 2335
GOOD SAM RATING: 8.5/10★/8.5
DIRECTIONS: From Jct Hwy 11 N and Hwy 118 W: Go 1.5 km/1 mi on Hwy 118 N, then 4 km/2.5 mi W on Santa's Village Road. Resort on R.
GPS COORDINATES: 45.02451°N/-79.36179°W
NOTATIONS: Check-in: 2:00 p.m. Check-out: 11:00 a.m. Special discount rate for Coast members. Rate includes 4 people, 1 sleeping structure, 1 dining structure. Additional charges: Extra adult $5/night, extra child $5/night, tax 13%. Max. RV length: 45 feet. Open: May 19–October 9.
CENTRAL CANADA MAP: See page CTC 79.

30 amps, pull-through, pets/restrictions, Wi-Fi access, playground, fishing, hiking trails, group activities, boating, recreation hall, outdoor pool, mini golf, beach, volleyball, tourist attraction, canoes, firewood, ice

CARRYING PLACE

North Shore RV Park
1675 County Road 64
Carrying Place, Ontario K0K 1L0
613-475-2036
nshore@northshorepark.com
northshorepark.com
RESORT NUMBER: 2336
GOOD SAM RATING: NA
DIRECTIONS: From E on Hwy 401: Ex 522 at Hwy 40 (Wooler Rd). Go S until Hwy 40 ends at Hwy 33. Turn R, cross Murray Canal, enter Carrying Place. Turn R at CR 64 at traffic lights. Follow CR 64 for approx 4 km/2.5 mi. Resort on L. From W on Hwy 401: Ex 509 at Hwy 30 S into Brighton. At 2nd light continue on CR 64, cross Murray Canal. Keep L. Resort on R 0.5 km/0.3 mi past golf club.
GPS COORDINATES: 44.03331°N/-77.62472°W
NOTATIONS: Check-in: 2:00 p.m. Check-out: Noon. Special discount rate for Coast members. Rate includes 4 people. Additional charges: Extra adult $6/night, extra child over 4 years $6/night, 50 amp $5/night, Wi-Fi $3/night, tax 13%. Max. RV length: 80 feet. Open: May 1–May 17; September 3–October 15.
CENTRAL CANADA MAP: See page CTC 79.

50 amps, pull-through, laundry, pets/restrictions, Wi-Fi access, playground, picnic tables, fishing, horseshoes, group activities, boating, recreation hall, fishing, boating, outdoor pool, beach, golf, tourist attraction, shopping, canoes, fire rings, firewood, ice

COBDEN

Bona Vista Campground
18070A Highway 17
Cobden, Ontario K0J 1K0
613-646-2716
bonavistacamp@bell.net
bonavistacampground.ca
RESORT NUMBER: 2431
GOOD SAM RATING: NA
DIRECTIONS: From Jct CR 8 & Hwy 17: Go 3 km (2 mi) N on Hwy 17, park on R.
GPS COORDINATES: 45.64113°N/-76.88945°W
NOTATIONS: Check-in: 2:00 p.m. Check-out: Noon. Special discount rate for Coast members. Tax 13%. Drive-ups not accepted. Max. RV length: 48 feet. Open: April 15–June 30; September 14–October 30.
CENTRAL CANADA MAP: See page CTC 79.

50 amps, laundry, pets/restrictions, Wi-Fi access, playground, fishing, horseshoes, group activities, boating, recreation hall, outdoor pool, game room, grocery, firewood, ice

COMBERMERE

Pine Cliff Resort
21 Allingham Lane
Combermere, Ontario K0J 1L0
888-756-3014
info@pinecliff.com
pinecliff.com
RESORT NUMBER: 2324
GOOD SAM RATING: 8.5/8.5★/8.5
DIRECTIONS: From Jct of CR 517 & CR 62: N 2.6 km (1.6 mi) on CR 62 to Pine Cliff Rd. W 0.4 km (0.25 mi). Resort on L.
GPS COORDINATES: 45.3831°N/-77.62529°W
NOTATIONS: Check-in: Noon. Check-out: 11:00 a.m. Special discount rate for Coast members. Additional charges: Add'l adult, add'l child, 50 amp, tax 13%. Unavailable weekends and holidays. No tents. Max. RV length: Unlimited. Open: May 8–October 19.
CENTRAL CANADA MAP: See page CTC 79.

50 amps · laundry · Wi-Fi access · playground · hot tub · shuffleboard · hiking trails · horseshoes · boating · recreation hall · outdoor pool · basketball · beach · fitness · propane · spa · indoor pool · rv supplies · firewood · ice

DUNNVILLE

Knight's Beach Resort
2190 Lakeshore Road
Dunnville, Ontario N1A 2W8
905-774-4566
info@knightsbeach.com
knightsbeach.com
RESORT NUMBER: 2425
GOOD SAM RATING: 8/10★/9.5
DIRECTIONS: From Jct of Rainham & Reg Rd 50: S 1.9 km (1.2 mi) on Reg Rd 50 to Lakeshore Rd, W 1 km (0.6 mi). Resort on L.
GPS COORDINATES: 42.84447°N/-79.75511°W
NOTATIONS: Check-in: 1:00 p.m. Check-out: 11:00 a.m. Special discount rate for Coast members. Additional charges: Extra person $20, tax 13%. Discount not available long holiday weekends. Drive-ups not accepted. Max. RV length: 45 feet. Open: May 1–June 15; September 15–October 10.
CENTRAL CANADA MAP: See page CTC 79.

30 amps · dump station · laundry · pets/restrictions · Wi-Fi access · playground · picnic tables · restaurant/snack bar · fishing · hiking trails · horseshoes · group activities · boating · recreation hall · game room · fire rings · grocery · tenting · firewood · ice

EDEN

Red Oak Travel Park
54428 Talbot Line (Highway 3)
Eden, Ontario N0J 1H0
519-866-3504
camp@redoaktravelpark.com
redoaktravelpark.com
RESORT NUMBER: 2426
GOOD SAM RATING: 8.5/8.5★/8.5
DIRECTIONS: From Jct of Hwy 3 & Culloden Rd: W 0.4 km (0.25 mi) on Hwy 3. Resort on L.
GPS COORDINATES: 42.79233°N/-80.8338°W
NOTATIONS: Check-in: 1:00 p.m. Check-out: 11:00 a.m. Special Coast member rate 20% discount. Additional charges: Tax 13%. Drive-ups not accepted. Max. RV length: 55 feet. Open: May 1–June 15; September 3–October 30.
CENTRAL CANADA MAP: See page CTC 79.

30 amps · laundry · pets/restrictions · Wi-Fi access · playground · picnic tables · horseshoes · group activities · recreation hall · fishing · boating · outdoor pool · mini golf · game room · tourist attraction · fire rings · grocery · rv supplies · tenting · firewood · ice

GERALDTON

Wild Goose Lake Campground
8 Kueng's Road
Geraldton, Ontario P0T 1M0
866-465-4404
wildgooselake@yahoo.ca
wildgooselakecampground.com
RESORT NUMBER: 2363
GOOD SAM RATING: 7/8★/8.5
DIRECTIONS: From Jct of Hwy 11 & CR 584: W 19.3 km (12 mi) on Hwy 11 to Kueng's Rd, N 1.2 km (0.75 mi), campground on L. Once on Kueng's Rd stay right past resort with similar name.
GPS COORDINATES: 49.71114°N/-87.18449°W
NOTATIONS: Check-in: Noon. Check-out: Noon. Coast member rate 10% discount. Rate includes 2 adults, water, electric & sewer. Additional charges: Tax 13%. Max. RV length: 110 feet. Open: May 15–September 30.
CENTRAL CANADA MAP: See page CTC 79.

30 amps · pull-through · dump station · laundry · pets/restrictions · Wi-Fi access · playground · picnic tables · fishing · hiking trails · boating · fishing · beach · golf · shopping · canoes · hot showers · fire rings · tenting · firewood

GOLDEN LAKE

Golden Lake Campground
13685 Highway 60
Golden Lake, Ontario K0J 1X0
613-757-0018
inquiry@goldenlakepark.ca
goldenlakepark.ca
RESORT NUMBER: 2430
GOOD SAM RATING: 8/8★/8
DIRECTIONS: From Jct Hwy 30 and Hwy 60: 12.4 km (7 mi) W on Hwy 60. Resort on L.
GPS COORDINATES: 45.60154°N/-77.38323°W
NOTATIONS: Check-in: 1:00 p.m. Check-out: 11:00 a.m. Special discount rate for Coast members. Rates are for 2 adults, dependant children (under 18) and 1 vehicle. Extra guests and extra vehicles permitted for a fee. Tax 13%. Coast rate not available long holiday weekends. Drive-ups not accepted. Max. RV length: 45 feet. Open: May 20–June 14; September 10–October 10.
CENTRAL CANADA MAP: See page CTC 79.

30 amps · pull-through · laundry · pets/restrictions · internet access · Wi-Fi access · playground · fishing · horseshoes · group activities · recreation hall · game room · paddle boats · rv supplies · firewood

HANOVER

Saugeen Springs RV Park
173844 Mulock Road, Rural Route #3
Hanover, Ontario N4N 3B9
519-369-5136; res.: 888-241-2686
saugeenspringspark@gmail.com
saugeenspringspark.com
RESORT NUMBER: 2333
GOOD SAM RATING: 8.5/8.5★/10
DIRECTIONS: From Hanover: S on 11th Ave toward 10th St/Grey County Rd 4. L at 1st cross street on 10th St/Grey County Rd 4. L on Mulock Rd. Resort on L.
GPS COORDINATES: 44.2118°N/-80.9179°W
NOTATIONS: Check-in: 2:00 p.m. Check-out: Noon. Special discount rate for Coast members. Rate includes 2 adults, 4 children (to age 17 years), 1 RV, 1 dining tent, 1 vehicle. Additional charges: Add'l adult, Wi-Fi, tax 13%. Max. RV length: 45 feet. Open: April 1–November 10.
CENTRAL CANADA MAP: See page CTC 79.

30 amps · pull-through · dump station · laundry · pets/restrictions · Wi-Fi access · playground · fishing · shuffleboard · hiking trails · horseshoes · recreation hall · church services · beach · volleyball · tourist attraction · fire rings · firewood · ice

IGNACE

Davy Lake Campground
400 Davy Lake Road
Ignace, Ontario P0T 1T0
877-374-3113; fax: 807-934-0036
smorin@davylakecampground.com
davylakecampground.com
RESORT NUMBER: 2368
GOOD SAM RATING: 8.5/10★/9.5
DIRECTIONS: From Jct of Hwy 17 & Hwy 599: W 0.5 km (0.3 mi) on Hwy 17 to Davy Lake Rd, SW 0.8 km (0.5 mi), campground on L.
GPS COORDINATES: 49.41009°N/-91.65237°W
NOTATIONS: Check-in: 4:00 p.m. Check-out: 11:00 a.m. Special discount rate for Coast members. Rate includes 2 adults, electric, city water, sewer. Additional charges: Extra adult $5/night, tax 13%. Max. RV length: 100 feet. Open: May 15–September 30.
CENTRAL CANADA MAP: See page CTC 79.

50 amps · dump station · laundry · pets/restrictions · Wi-Fi access · playground · restaurant/snack bar · fishing · hiking trails · horseshoes · fishing · boating · beach · golf · canoes · fire rings · grocery · firewood

JOHNSTOWN

Grenville Park Camping and RV Park
2323 County Road 2
Johnstown, Ontario K0E 1T1
613-925-5055
contact-us@gocampgrenvillepark.com
gocampgrenvillepark.com
RESORT NUMBER: 2432
GOOD SAM RATING: 7.5/9★/8.5
DIRECTIONS: From Jct of Hwys 401 & 16/416, Ebnd on Hwy 401 (Ex 721B); or Wbnd on Hwy 401 (Ex 721); or Sbnd on Hwy 416 (Ex 1): S 3 km (1.9 mi) on Hwy 16/416 to Hwy 2, E 1 km (0.6 mi). Park on R.
GPS COORDINATES: 44.74954°N/-75.45465°W
NOTATIONS: Check-in: 1:00 p.m-6:00 p.m. Check-out: Noon. Special discounted rate for Coast members. Wi-Fi at rec hall only. Site includes 4 adults maximum, total 6 people. Tax rate 13%. Fri and Sat check-in from 1 p.m.-8 p.m. Max. RV length: 45 feet. Open: May 1–June 15; September 8–October 15.
CENTRAL CANADA MAP: See page CTC 79.

30 amps · pull-through · laundry · pets/restrictions · Wi-Fi access · playground · fishing · horseshoes · group activities · boating · recreation hall · mini golf · game room · fitness · paddle boats · grocery · rv supplies · firewood · ice

KINCARDINE

Aintree Trailer Park
2435 Huron Concession 12 Road
Kincardine, Ontario N2Z 2X3
877-396-8533
aintreepark@hotmail.com
aintreepark.com
RESORT NUMBER: 2421
GOOD SAM RATING: 8/8.5★/9
DIRECTIONS: From Jct Hwy 21 & Hwy 9: SW 3.2 km (2 mi) on Hwy 21 to Conc #12, NW 1.9 km (1.2 mi). Resort on L.
GPS COORDINATES: 44.14894°N/-81.66752°W
NOTATIONS: Check-in: 1:30 p.m. Check-out: 1:00 p.m. Coast member rate 20% discount available Apr 15-Jun 29 & Sep 6-Oct 10. Extra adult $12/night. Max. RV length: 40 feet. Open: April 15–October 10.
CENTRAL CANADA MAP: See page CTC 79.

30 amps · pull-through · laundry · pets/restrictions · Wi-Fi access · playground · shuffleboard · horseshoes · group activities · recreation hall · fishing · boating · basketball · golf · game room · tourist attraction · shopping · propane · firewood

LAKEFIELD

Lakefield Campground
59 Hague Boulevard
Lakefield, Ontario K0L 2H0
705-652-8610; res.: 800-316-8841
cindyloumac@outlook.com
lakefieldcampgrounds.ca
RESORT NUMBER: 1387
GOOD SAM RATING: 6.5/7/7.5
DIRECTIONS: From Peterborough: Ex Hwy 115/35 at Pkwy. Follow Trent University signs through Peterborough past University and Buckhorne signs into Lakefield. L on Clementi St (1st light). Follow signs to park.
GPS COORDINATES: 44.4295°N/-78.2737°W
NOTATIONS: Check-in: 11:00 a.m.–7:00 p.m. Check-out: 3:00 p.m. Special 20% discount rate for Coast members not avail long holiday weekends. Additional charges: Family children $2/day, non-family children $4/day, tax. Optional Ontario phone 800-316-8841. Max. RV length: 40 feet. Open: May 1–October 6.
CENTRAL CANADA MAP: See page CTC 79.

30 amps · pets/restrictions · internet access · playground · fishing · shuffleboard · horseshoes · boating · beach · tennis · shopping · ball field

MARMORA

Heritage Trails Campground
178 KOA Campground Road, Rural Route 2
Marmora, Ontario K0K 2M0
800-792-0223; res.: 613-472-2233
reservations@heritagetrailscampground.com
heritagetrailscampground.com
RESORT NUMBER: 2436
GOOD SAM RATING: 9/9★/8.5
DIRECTIONS: From Jct of Hwy 62 & Hwy 7 (in Madoc): W 8 km (4.8 mi) on Hwy 7 to KOA Campground Rd. S 1 km (0.5 mi). Resort on R.
GPS COORDINATES: 44.48864°N/-77.62587°W
NOTATIONS: Check-in: 2:00 p.m. Check-out: 11:00 a.m. Special 10% discount rate for Coast members, must present member card at check-in. Additional charges: Tax 13%, Wi-Fi. Drive-ups accepted. Max. RV length: 60 feet. Open: April 29–October 16.
CENTRAL CANADA MAP: See page CTC 79.

30 amps · pull-through · pets/restrictions · Wi-Fi access · playground · restaurant/snack bar · fishing · hiking trails · horseshoes · group activities · recreation hall · outdoor pool · mini golf · game room · tourist attraction · shopping · propane · grocery · rv supplies · firewood · ice

MATTAWA

Sid Turcotte Park
750 Mattawan Street
Mattawa, Ontario P0H 1V0
705-744-5375; fax: 705-744-1081
stp@sidturcottepark.com
sidturcottepark.com
RESORT NUMBER: 2323
GOOD SAM RATING: 8/9★/9.5
DIRECTIONS: From Jct of Hwy 17 & Turcotte Park Rd: N 0.3 km (0.2 mi) on Turcotte Park Rd to Mattawan St. E 46 meters (50 yds). Resort on L.
GPS COORDINATES: 46.3118°N/-78.7156°W
NOTATIONS: Check-in: 11:00 a.m. Check-out: 11:00 a.m. Special discount rate for Coast members. Site includes electric, water, sewer, 2 adults and children under 18. Additional charges: Add'l adult, add'l vehicle, tax 13%. Max. RV length: 60 feet. Open: May 11–October 6.
CENTRAL CANADA MAP: See page CTC 79.

30 amps · pull-through · dump station · laundry · pets/restrictions · Wi-Fi access · playground · picnic tables · fishing · horseshoes · boating · recreation hall · beach · volleyball · golf · tourist attraction · shopping · canoes · fire rings · tenting · firewood · ice

MILLER LAKE

Summer House Park
197 Miller Lake Shore Road
Miller Lake, Ontario N0H 1Z0
519-795-7712; res.: 800-265-5557
info@summerhousepark.ca
summerhousepark.ca
RESORT NUMBER: 2358
GOOD SAM RATING: 8.5/10★/10
DIRECTIONS: From Hwy 6: Follow Hwy 6 N to Miller Lake Rd. Turn R (E) on Miller Lake Rd, go 3.2 km (2 mi) to end, park on L.
GPS COORDINATES: 45.09863°N/-81.40217°W
NOTATIONS: Check-in: 2:00 p.m. Check-out: 1:00 p.m. Special discount rate for Coast members. Rate includes 2 adults, 1 vehicle, 1 camping unit, water, electric and sewer hook-ups. Additional charges: Extra adult $5/night, extra vehicle $5/night, tax 13%. No availability Jul 1 to Labor Day. Max. RV length: 60 feet. Open: May 1–June 30; September 5–October 16.
CENTRAL CANADA MAP: See page CTC 79.

50 amps · pull-through · dump station · laundry · pets/restrictions · Wi-Fi access · playground · picnic tables · restaurant/snack bar · fishing · shuffleboard · hiking trails · horseshoes · group activities · boating · recreation hall · fishing · boating · basketball · beach · tennis · volleyball · golf · tourist attraction · hot showers · fire rings · grocery · rv supplies · tenting · firewood · ice

MONO

Primrose Park
635687 Highway 10
Mono, Ontario L9V 0Z8
519-925-2848
primrosepark@outlook.com
primrosepark.ca
RESORT NUMBER: 2410
GOOD SAM RATING: 8/9/8.5
DIRECTIONS: From Jct of Hwys 89 & 10, S 0.4 km (0.25 mi) on Hwy 10. Park on L.
GPS COORDINATES: 44.08821°N/-80.13763°W
NOTATIONS: Check-in: 1:00 p.m. Check-out: Noon. Special discount rate for Coast members. Rate includes 2 adults per site, kids under 12, full hook-ups. Additional charges: Extra adult $5/night, tax 13%. Quiet time 11 p.m.-7 a.m. No firewood permitted from outside park. Max. RV length: 45 feet. Open: May 1–October 14.
CENTRAL CANADA MAP: See page CTC 79.

30 amps · dump station · laundry · pets/restrictions · Wi-Fi access · playground · picnic tables · hiking trails · horseshoes · group activities · fishing · outdoor pool · basketball · volleyball · tourist attraction · hot showers · tenting · firewood

MORRISBURG

Upper Canada Campground
13390 Upper Canada Road
Morrisburg, Ontario K0C 1X0
613-543-2201
info@uppercanadacampground.com
uppercanadacampground.com
RESORT NUMBER: 2321
GOOD SAM RATING: 8/9★/9
DIRECTIONS: From Ottawa: Hwy 31 or Hwy 416 S to Hwy 401. E to Ex 758. N 0.25 mi. From Toronto: Hwy 401 E to Ex 758. N 0.25 mi. From Montreal: Hwy 401 W to Ex 758. N 0.25 mi.
GPS COORDINATES: 44.95336°N/-75.11371°W
NOTATIONS: Check-in: 2:00 p.m. Check-out: 11:00 a.m. Special discount rate for Coast members. Additional charges: 50 amp, add'l adult, showers, tax 13%. Age of RV must be 20 yrs or newer. Guests must be 25 yrs or older. Local firewood only. Weekends require minimum stay. Max. RV length: 45 feet. Open: May 1–September 19.
CENTRAL CANADA MAP: See page CTC 79.

50 amps, pull-through, dump station, laundry, pets/restrictions, Wi-Fi access, playground, picnic tables, restaurant/snack bar, horseshoes, group activities, recreation hall, fishing, boating, outdoor pool, basketball, volleyball, golf, tourist attraction, shopping, fire rings, grocery, tenting, firewood, ice

NIAGARA FALLS

Campark Resorts Family Camping & RV Resort
9387 Lundy's Lane
Niagara Falls, Ontario L2E 6S4
877-226-7275
info@campark.com
campark.com
RESORT NUMBER: 2427
GOOD SAM RATING: 8.5/9★/9
DIRECTIONS: Sbnd Jct of QEW & Ex 30B: W 0.16 km (0.1 mi) to Montrose Rd, S 0.8 km (0.5 mi) to Lundy's Ln, W 2.6 km (1.6 mi). Resort on R. From Nbnd: Jct of QEW & McLeod Rd (Ex 27): W 0.5 km (0.3 mi) on McLeod Rd to Montrose Rd, N 2 km (1.3 mi) to Lundy's Ln, W 2.6 km (1.6 mi). Resort on R.
GPS COORDINATES: 43.08631°N/-79.15514°W
NOTATIONS: Check-in: 1:00 p.m. Check-out: 11:00 a.m. Special Coast member rate 20% discount. Additional charges: Extra adult $6/night, extra child $4/night, tax 13%. Discount not available long holiday weekends. Drive-ups not accepted. Max. RV length: 45 feet. Open: May 1–June 15; September 1–October 30.
CENTRAL CANADA MAP: See page CTC 79.

50 amps, pull-through, dump station, laundry, pets/restrictions, Wi-Fi access, playground, picnic tables, restaurant/snack bar, hot tub, hiking trails, horseshoes, group activities, recreation hall, fishing, outdoor pool, mini golf, golf, game room, propane, canoes, gambling casino, fire rings, grocery, rv supplies, tenting, firewood, ice

NIAGARA FALLS

Riverside Park Motel & Campground
13541 Niagara Parkway
Niagara Falls, Ontario L2E 6S6
905-382-2204
camp@riversidepark.net
riversidepark.net
RESORT NUMBER: 2424
GOOD SAM RATING: 8.5/9★/10
DIRECTIONS: Nbnd from Peace Bridge: N 11.7 km (7.25 mi) on QEW to Netherby Rd (RR 25) Ex 12, E 1.3 km (0.8 mi) to Niagara Pkwy, N 0.4 km (0.25 mi). Resort on L.
GPS COORDINATES: 42.98485°N/-79.02689°W
NOTATIONS: Check-in: 1:00 p.m. Check-out: 11:00 a.m. Special 10% discount for Coast members. Additional charges: Extra adult $7/night, extra child $3/night, Wi-Fi $2/night, 50 amp $5/night, dump station $10, tax 13%. Discount not available long holiday weekends. Drive-ups not accepted. Max. RV length: 45 feet. Open: May 1–May 31; October 1–October 10.
CENTRAL CANADA MAP: See page CTC 79.

50 amps, pull-through, dump station, laundry, pets/restrictions, Wi-Fi access, playground, fishing, hiking trails, horseshoes, group activities, boating, fishing, boating, outdoor pool, mini golf, game room, tourist attraction, canoes, gambling casino, rv supplies, tenting, firewood, ice

NIAGARA FALLS

Scott's Family RV Park
8845 Lundy's Lane
Niagara Falls, Ontario L2H 1H5
905-356-6988; res.: 800-649-9497
scottscamping@outlook.com
campingatscotts.com
RESORT NUMBER: 2322
GOOD SAM RATING: 8/9.5★/8
DIRECTIONS: From S Jct QEW and Ex 30B: W 0.1 mi to Montrose Rd. S 0.5 mi to Lundy's Ln. W 1.2 mi. Resort on R. From N Jct QEW and McLeod Rd (Ex 27): W 0.3 mi on McLeod Rd to Montrose Rd. N 1.3 mi to Lundy's Ln. W 1.2 mi. Resort on R.
GPS COORDINATES: 43.08843°N/-79.14705°W
NOTATIONS: Check-in: 1:00 p.m. Check-out: 11:00 a.m. Special discount rate for Coast members. Site includes water, sewer and electric. Additional charges: Add'l adult, add'l child, tax 13%. Unavailable weekends and holidays. Max. RV length: 60 feet. Open: May 1–October 30.
CENTRAL CANADA MAP: See page CTC 79.

50 amps, pull-through, laundry, Wi-Fi access, playground, picnic tables, outdoor pool, basketball, tourist attraction, shopping, propane, fire rings, grocery, tenting, firewood, ice

NIAGARA FALLS

Yogi Bear's Jellystone Park Niagara Falls, Canada
8676 Oakwood Drive
Niagara Falls, Ontario L2G 0J2
800-263-2570; fax: 905-374-4493
yogibear@jellystoneniagara.ca
jellystoneniagara.ca
RESORT NUMBER: 2319
GOOD SAM RATING: 9/10★/9.5
DIRECTIONS: From Jct QEW & McLeod Rd (Ex 27): E 200 yds on McLeod Rd to Oakwood Dr. S 1.5 mi. Resort is the last driveway on the L side of the road, past the car dealerships & landscaping businesses.
GPS COORDINATES: 43.051°N/-79.12155°W
NOTATIONS: Check-in: 3:00 p.m. Check-out: 11:00 a.m. Special discount rate for Coast members. Site includes 2 adults, 1 RV, 1 car. Additional charges: Extra adult, children (3-17), Wi-Fi, tax 13%. No tents. Minimum stay required, deposit required. Rental units available. Trip Points not accepted. Contact resort directly. Max. RV length: 80 feet. Open: April 29–June 14; September 3–October 13.
CENTRAL CANADA MAP: See page CTC 79.

50 amps, pull-through, dump station, laundry, pets/restrictions, Wi-Fi access, playground, picnic tables, restaurant/snack bar, rental units, shuffleboard, horseshoes, group activities, recreation hall, outdoor pool, mini golf, basketball, volleyball, game room, tourist attraction, hot showers, fire rings, grocery, rv supplies, firewood, ice

NIPIGON

Stillwater Park Campground
358 Highway 11-17
Nipigon, Ontario P0T 2J0
807-887-3701
info@stillwaterpark.ca
stillwaterpark.ca
RESORT NUMBER: 2361
GOOD SAM RATING: 7/8.5★/8.5
DIRECTIONS: From town: W 2.6 km (1.6 mi) on TCH 11-17, campground on R. From E: 106 km (66 mi) E of Thunder Bay, campground on L.
GPS COORDINATES: 49.01191°N/-88.31826°W
NOTATIONS: Check-in: 1:00 p.m.–8:00 p.m. Check-out: Noon. Special discount rate for Coast members. Rate includes 2 adults, 3 children up to 12 years. Additional charges: Extra adult $5/night, extra child $5/night, 50 amp $9/night, tax 13%. Max. RV length: 80 feet. Open: May 1–October 1.
CENTRAL CANADA MAP: See page CTC 79.

50 amps, pull-through, dump station, laundry, pets/restrictions, Wi-Fi access, playground, picnic tables, fishing, hiking trails, fishing, boating, tourist attraction, shopping, fire rings, grocery, gift shop, tenting, firewood, ice

OTTAWA

Camp Hither Hills
5227 Bank Street
Ottawa, Ontario K1X 1H2
613-822-0509; fax: 613-822-0196
info@ottawarvparks.ca
ottawarvparks.ca
RESORT NUMBER: 2320
GOOD SAM RATING: 9/10★/9

DIRECTIONS: From E Jct Hwy 417 & 416S (Ex 131): S 11 mi on 416S to Bankfield Rd (Ex 57). E 2.8 mi to Manotick Main St. SE 0.2 m to Bridge St. NE 6.8 mi to Bank St. NW 0.8 mi. Resort on R.
GPS COORDINATES: 45.2908°N/-75.5753°W
NOTATIONS: Check-in: 1:00 p.m. Check-out: 11:00 a.m. Special discount rate for Coast members. Additional charges: Showers, 50 amp, add'l adult, add'l child, tax 13%. Site includes full hook-ups. Staff bilingual. Minimum stay required on weekends. Not available long holiday weekends. Max. RV length: 45 feet. Open: April 15–October 30.
CENTRAL CANADA MAP: See page CTC 79.

50 amps · pull-through · dump station · cable tv · visitor mail · laundry · pets/restrictions · Wi-Fi access · playground · horseshoes · recreation hall · outdoor pool · basketball · tourist attraction · shopping · fire rings · tenting · firewood

OWEN SOUND

Sunny Valley Park Family Camping & Recreation
62703 Sunny Valley Road
Owen Sound, Ontario N4K 5N6
519-794-3297
info@sunnyvalleypark.com
sunnyvalleypark.com
RESORT NUMBER: 2420
GOOD SAM RATING: NA
DIRECTIONS: From Jct Hwy 10 & Hwy 6: Go 10 km (6 mi) S on Hwy 6, then 0.7 km (0.5 mi) W on Sunny Valley Rd.
GPS COORDINATES: 44.48982°N/-80.92151°W
NOTATIONS: Check-in: 1:00 p.m. Check-out: 11:00 a.m. Special discount rate for Coast members. Additional charges: Extra adult $10/night, Wi-Fi $7/night, tax 13%. Drive-ups not accepted. Max. RV length: 40 feet. Open: May 1–June 15; September 8–October 10.
CENTRAL CANADA MAP: See page CTC 79.

50 amps · pull-through · dump station · laundry · pets/restrictions · Wi-Fi access · playground · picnic tables · fishing · hiking trails · horseshoes · group activities · recreation hall · outdoor pool · ball field · fire rings · grocery · rv supplies · tenting · firewood · ice

PETERBOROUGH

Anchor Bay Camp
197 Anchor Bay Road
Peterborough, Ontario K9J 6X2
705-657-8439
info@anchorbaycamp.net
anchorbaycamp.net
RESORT NUMBER: 2433
GOOD SAM RATING: 8/9.5★/8.5
DIRECTIONS: From Jct of Hwy 36 & 23 & Lakehurst Rd (in Buckhorn): SW 14.5 km (9 mi) on Lakehurst Rd, follow signs to resort on R.
GPS COORDINATES: 44.49961°N/-78.43151°W
NOTATIONS: Check-in: 1:00 p.m. Check-out: 11:00 a.m. Special discount rate for Coast members. Additional charges: Add'l adult $20/night, tax 13%. Discount not available long holiday weekends. Drive-ups not accepted. Max. RV length: 45 feet. Open: May 15–June 15; September 10–October 14.
CENTRAL CANADA MAP: See page CTC 79.

30 amps · Wi-Fi access · playground · fishing · hiking trails · horseshoes · group activities · boating · recreation hall · outdoor pool · game room · canoes · gambling casino

PICTON

Smugglers Cove RV Resort
3187 County Road 13, Rural Route 3
Picton, Ontario K0K 2T0
613-476-4125
smugglerscoverv@outlook.com
smugglerscove.ca
RESORT NUMBER: 2435
GOOD SAM RATING: 8/8.5★/9
DIRECTIONS: From Jct of CR-17 & CR-10: SE 4.5 km (2.8 mi) on CR-10 to CR-13, S 5.4 km (3.4 mi). Resort on L.
GPS COORDINATES: 43.93485°N/-77.01492°W
NOTATIONS: Check-in: 1:00 p.m. Check-out: 11:00 a.m. Special Coast member rate 20% discount. Additional charges: Add'l adult $10/night, tax 13%. Discount not available long holiday weekends. Drive-ups not accepted. Max. RV length: 40 feet. Open: May 1–June 15; September 9–October 10.
CENTRAL CANADA MAP: See page CTC 79.

30 amps · dump station · laundry · Wi-Fi access · playground · fishing · horseshoes · group activities · boating · recreation hall · outdoor pool · beach · volleyball · game room · tourist attraction · shopping · propane · grocery · ice

RIDGEWAY

Windmill Point Park and Campground
2409 Dominion Road
Ridgeway, Ontario L0S 1N0
888-977-8888
info@windmillpointpark.com
windmillpointpark.com
RESORT NUMBER: 2422
GOOD SAM RATING: 7.5/8.5/8.5
DIRECTIONS: From Jct QEW & Thompson Rd (1 mi north of Peace Bridge): Go 0.5 mi S on Thompson Rd, 2.5 mi W on Hwy 3, then 1.25 mi S on Stonemill Rd (Reg Rd 120), then 0.25 mi W on Dominion Rd, then 0.25 mi S on paved road.
GPS COORDINATES: 42.88306°N/-79.00467°W
NOTATIONS: Check-in: 1:00 p.m. Check-out: 11:00 a.m. Special discount rate for Coast members. Additional charges: Extra adult $27, extra child $15, tax 13%. Discount not available long holiday weekends. Drive-ups not accepted. Max. RV length: 45 feet. Open: May 1–June 15; September 3–October 14.
CENTRAL CANADA MAP: See page CTC 79.

50 amps · dump station · laundry · pets/restrictions · Wi-Fi access · playground · picnic tables · restaurant/snack bar · fishing · hiking trails · horseshoes · group activities · boating · fishing · boating · canoes · paddle boats · gambling casino · fire rings · grocery · rv supplies · tenting · firewood · ice

SAULT STE MARIE

Glenview Cottages & Campground
2611 Great Northern Road
Sault Ste Marie, Ontario P6A 5K7
705-759-3436; fax: 705-759-9060
info@glenviewcottages.com
glenviewcottages.com
RESORT NUMBER: 2360
GOOD SAM RATING: 9/9★/8
DIRECTIONS: From Jct of International Bridge & Queen St W: W 259 meters (850 ft) on Queen St W to Carmens Way, N 2.3 km (1.4 mi) to Second Line, E 2.1 km (1.3 mi) to Great Northern Rd/Hwy 17 N, N 8.1 km (5 mi), campground on L.
GPS COORDINATES: 46.6015°N/-84.2947°W
NOTATIONS: Check-in: 3:00 p.m. Check-out: 11:00 a.m. Special discount rate for Coast members. Rate includes 2 adults per site. Additional charges: Extra adult $5/night, tax 13%. Max. RV length: 50 feet. Open: May 15–October 15.
CENTRAL CANADA MAP: See page CTC 79.

30 amps · pull-through · dump station · laundry · pets/restrictions · Wi-Fi access · playground · picnic tables · hot tub · hiking trails · horseshoes · fishing · outdoor pool · basketball · volleyball · tourist attraction · hot showers · fire rings · firewood · ice

SPRAGGE

Serpent River Campground
4696 Highway 17 West
Spragge, Ontario P0R 1K0
705-849-2210; fax: 705-849-2211
mail@serpentrivercampground.com
serpentrivercampground.com
RESORT NUMBER: 2359
GOOD SAM RATING: 8.5/9.5★/10
DIRECTIONS: From Jct of Hwys 17 & 108: W 2.3 km (1.4 mi) on Hwy 17, campground on L.
GPS COORDINATES: 46.21069°N/-82.60069°W
NOTATIONS: Check-in: 1:00 p.m. Check-out: 11:00 a.m. Special 20% discount rate for Coast members not avail Jul, Aug, or long holiday weekends. Rate includes 2 adults per site. Additional charges: Extra adult $10/night, extra child $5/night, tax 13%. Max. RV length: 90 feet. Open: May 1–October 8.
CENTRAL CANADA MAP: See page CTC 79.

30 amps · pull-through · laundry · pets/restrictions · Wi-Fi access · playground · picnic tables · fishing · hiking trails · boating · fishing · boating · outdoor pool · golf · game room · tourist attraction · shopping · canoes · fire rings · rv supplies · gift shop · tenting · firewood · ice

STURGEON FALLS

Sturgeon Falls KOA
818 Lalande Road
Sturgeon Falls, Ontario P2B 2V4
705-753-5759; res.: 800-562-7798
sturgeonfalls@koa.com
koa.com/campgrounds/sturgeon-falls
RESORT NUMBER: 2357
GOOD SAM RATING: 8/10★/9.5
DIRECTIONS: From town: Hwy 17 (S) to Leblanc Rd 2 km (1.8 m), to Lalande Rd 1 km (0.6 m), resort on L.
GPS COORDINATES: 46.3495°N/-79.96832°W
NOTATIONS: Check-in: 1:00 p.m. Check-out: 11:00 a.m. Special discount rate for Coast members. Rate includes up to 2 adults and 2 children, full hook-ups, waterfront deluxe patio site. Additional charges: Extra adult $5/night, extra child $3/night, extra vehicle $5/night, tax 13%. No discount available Jun 15-Sep 5. Max. RV length: 110 feet. Open: May 14–October 10.
CENTRAL CANADA MAP: See page CTC 79.

WYOMING

Country View Motel & RV Camping Resort
4569 London Line
Wyoming, Ontario N0N 1T0
519-845-3394
evcoulbeck@gmail.com
countryviewmotelandrvresort.com
RESORT NUMBER: 2334
GOOD SAM RATING: 8.5/10★/9.5
DIRECTIONS: From Jct of Hwy 402 & Hwy 21 (Ex 25): S 1.2 km (0.75 mi) on Hwy 21 to CR 22 (London Line). E 91 meters (300 ft). Resort on R.
GPS COORDINATES: 42.97945°N/-82.11344°W
NOTATIONS: Check-in: 2:00 p.m. Check-out: 11:00 a.m. Special discount rate for Coast members. Additional charges: Wi-Fi, firewood, tax 13%. Not available Jul, Aug, and long holiday weekends. Max. RV length: 75 feet. Open: April 21–June 30; September 1–October 23.
CENTRAL CANADA MAP: See page CTC 79.

PRINCE EDWARD ISLAND

BORDEN-CARLETON

Jellystone Park PEI
23714 Trans Canada Highway
Borden-Carleton, Prince Edward Island C0B 1X0
902-855-3492; res.: 844-734-9644
jellystonepei@gmail.com
jellystonepei.com
RESORT NUMBER: 2330
GOOD SAM RATING: 9.5/9.5★/10
DIRECTIONS: From town, NE 1.25 mi on Hwy 1. Resort on L.
GPS COORDINATES: 46.2543°N/-63.6732°W
NOTATIONS: Check-in: 11:00 a.m. Check-out: 3:00 p.m. Special discount rate for Coast members. Additional charges: Add'l adult, add'l child, tax 15%. No availability Jul, Aug, or long holiday weekends. Max. RV length: 85 feet. Open: June 1–June 30; September 1–September 29.
EASTERN CANADA MAP: See page CTC 80.

CAVENDISH

Marco Polo Land
7406 Route 13
Cavendish, Prince Edward Island C0A 1N0
902-963-2352; fax: 902-963-2384
questions@marcopololand.com
marcopololand.com
RESORT NUMBER: 2345
GOOD SAM RATING: 8.5/10★/10
DIRECTIONS: From Jct of Rtes 6 & 13: S 0.5 mi on Rte 13, resort on L.
GPS COORDINATES: 46.4834°N/-63.37547°W
NOTATIONS: Check-in: Noon. Check-out: 11:30 a.m. Special discount rate for Coast members. Rate includes 4 persons, 1 camping unit, 1 vehicle. Additional charges: 50 amp $5/night, tax 15%. No availability Jul, Aug, or long holiday weekends. Max. RV length: 80 feet. Open: May 28–June 23; September 1–October 14.
EASTERN CANADA MAP: See page CTC 80.

DARNLEY

Twin Shores Camping Area
702 Lower Darnley Road
Darnley, Prince Edward Island C0B 1M0
902-836-4142; res.: 877-734-2267
info@twinshores.com
twinshores.com
RESORT NUMBER: 2370
GOOD SAM RATING: 9/10★/10
DIRECTIONS: In Kensington: From Jct of Hwy 2 & Rte 20, N 10 mi on Rte 20 to Lower Darnley Rd, W 2.5 mi to property.
GPS COORDINATES: 46.56299°N/-63.66493°W
NOTATIONS: Check-in: 1:00 p.m. Check-out: 11:00 a.m. Special 25% discount rate for Coast members avail Jun 1-23, Sep 11-30. Rate includes 2 adults, up to 4 children, 1 vehicle + HST. Additional charges: Extra adult $10/night, extra child $7/night, extra vehicle $10/night, tax 15%. No discount available Jun 25-Sep 10. Max. RV length: 50 feet. Open: June 1–October 1.
EASTERN CANADA MAP: See page CTC 80.

QUEBEC

LEVIS

Camping Transit
600 Chemin St. Roch
Levis, Quebec G6Y 0W3
418-838-0948
info@campingtransit.com
campingtransit.com
RESORT NUMBER: 2350
GOOD SAM RATING: 9.5/10★/10
DIRECTIONS: From Jct of Hwy 20 & Ex 330 (Rte Lallemand/Chemin St-Roch): E 2.5 mi on Chemin St-Roch, follow signs, resort on L. From Jct of Hwy 20 & Exit 337 (Rte 279): S 0.5 mi on Rte 279 to Chemin St-Roch Rd, W 2 mi, resort on R.
GPS COORDINATES: 46.81218°N/-71.05149°W
NOTATIONS: Check-in: 1:00 p.m. Check-out: Noon. Special 30% discount rate for Coast members. Rate includes 2 adults, 2 children per site. Additional charges: Extra adult $6/night, extra child $3/night, Wi-Fi $2.60/night, tax 15%. Discount available Apr 26-Jun 13 & Sep 13-Oct 22. No discount long holiday weekends. Bilingual resort. Max. RV length: 75 feet. Open: April 15–June 30; September 1–October 30.
EASTERN CANADA MAP: See page CTC 80.

MELBOURNE

NEW **Camping Melbourne Estrie**
1185 Chemin du camping
Melbourne, Quebec J0B 2B0
819-826-6222
campingmelbourne@hotmail.com
campingmelbourne.com
RESORT NUMBER: 2548
GOOD SAM RATING: 8/10★/9
DIRECTIONS: From Jct of Hwy 55 & Ex 85 (Rte 243), N 1.5 mi on Rte 243 to Belmont St, W 0.6 mi. Park on R.
GPS COORDINATES: 45.6533°N/-72.16031°W
NOTATIONS: Check-in: 1:00 p.m. Check-out: 1:00 p.m. 2021 Coast 10% discount avail May, Jun, Aug and Sep. Full hook-up sites avail May, Jun, Sep and Oct. Rate includes 2 adults per site. Additional charges: Tax 15%. Max. RV length: 40 feet. Open: May 10–September 15.
EASTERN CANADA MAP: See page CTC 80.

SAINT-ANTONIN

NEW **Camping Chez Jean**
434-A Principale
Saint-Antonin, Quebec G0L 2J0
418-862-3081
info@campingchezjean.com
campingchezjean.com
RESORT NUMBER: 2555
GOOD SAM RATING: 9/10★/9.5
DIRECTIONS: From Jct of Rte 185 & St Antonin Ex, Go 2.3 mi W on Rue Principale, follow signs. Park on R.
GPS COORDINATES: 47.75024°N/-69.49055°W
NOTATIONS: Check-in: 1:00 p.m. Check-out: 1:00 p.m. 2022 Coast rate 20% discount available May 15-Jun 10 and Sep 10-27. Rate includes 2 adults per site, full hook-ups. Additional charges: Add'l adult $5/night, add'l child 5-11 years $5/night, add'l child 12-16 years $5/night, tax 15%. Max. RV length: 43 feet. Open: May 21–September 27.
EASTERN CANADA MAP: See page CTC 80.

50 amps · pull-through · dump station · laundry · pets/restrictions · Wi-Fi access · playground · picnic tables · hiking trails · horseshoes · fishing · boating · outdoor pool · golf · propane · fire rings · firewood · ice

SAINT-PHILIPPE

NEW **Camping la Cle des Champs RV Resort**
415 Montee St Claude
Saint-Philippe, Quebec J0L 2K0
450-659-3389
info@campinglacledeschamps.com
campinglacledeschamps.com
RESORT NUMBER: 2549
GOOD SAM RATING: 10/10★/10
DIRECTIONS: From Jct of Hwy 30 & Ex 104 (Rte 104), E 1.7 mi on Rte 104 to Rang St-Raphael, S 2 mi to Montee St-Claude, W 0.5 mi. Park on R.
GPS COORDINATES: 45.36198°N/-73.4466°W
NOTATIONS: Check-in: 2:00 p.m. Check-out: 1:00 p.m. Special discount rate for Coast members. Rate includes 2 adults per site, full hook-ups. Additional charges: Add'l adult $7.50/night, add'l child $4.50/night, tax 14.75%. Max. RV length: 38 feet. Open: April 21–October 20.
EASTERN CANADA MAP: See page CTC 80.

50 amps · pull-through · dump station · laundry · pets/restrictions · Wi-Fi access · playground · picnic tables · hiking trails · horseshoes · group activities · recreation hall · outdoor pool · game room · fitness · grocery · firewood · ice

ST BARTHELEMY

NEW **Camping du Vieux Moulin**
2780 Rue Buteau
St Barthelemy, Quebec J0K 1X0
450-885-3591
reservation@campingduvieuxmoulin.ca
campingduvieuxmoulin.com
RESORT NUMBER: 2550
GOOD SAM RATING: 8/10★/9
DIRECTIONS: From Jct of Hwy 40 & Ex 155, N 5 mi on Ex rd (Mtee St-Laurent-Mtee Des Laurentides) to St-Joachim Rd, E 1 mi. Follow signs to park.
GPS COORDINATES: 46.22409°N/-73.13798°W
NOTATIONS: Check-in: 1:00 p.m. Check-out: 1:00 p.m. 2021 Coast 10% discount. Rate includes 2 adults and 2 child per site, full hook-ups. Additional charges: Add'l adult $7.50/night, add'l child $7.50/night, tax 15%. Max. RV length: 42 feet. Open: May 15–October 10.
EASTERN CANADA MAP: See page CTC 80.

30 amps · dump station · laundry · pets/restrictions · Wi-Fi access · picnic tables · restaurant/snack bar · horseshoes · recreation hall · boating · basketball · tennis · fire rings · firewood · ice

SASKATCHEWAN

INDIAN HEAD

Indian Head Campground
1100 McKay Street
Indian Head, Saskatchewan S0G 2K0
855-695-3635
indianheadcampground@sasktel.net
indianheadcampground.ca
RESORT NUMBER: 2415
GOOD SAM RATING: 9/10★/9.5
DIRECTIONS: From Jct Hwy 1 and E entrance to Indian Head: N (across railway tracks) 0.2 mi. Resort on L.
GPS COORDINATES: 50.53058°N/-103.65674°W
NOTATIONS: Check-in: 1:00 p.m. Check-out: Noon. Special discount rate for Coast members. Rate includes 2 adults. Additional charges: Extra adult $5/night, extra child $3/night, pet $2 per pet, tax 5%. Rate not available major holidays. Drive-ups not accepted. Max. RV length: 80 feet. Open: May 1–June 10; September 8–September 26.
WESTERN CANADA MAP: See page CTC 78.

50 amps · pull-through · dump station · laundry · pets/restrictions · Wi-Fi access · playground · restaurant/snack bar · fishing · outdoor pool · tourist attraction · shopping · propane · hot showers · fire rings · tenting · firewood

SASKATOON

Campland RV Resort
Highway 16 & Lutheran Road
Saskatoon, Saskatchewan S7K 3N2
306-477-7444
camplandrvresort@sasktel.net
camplandrvresort.com
RESORT NUMBER: 2414
GOOD SAM RATING: 9/10★/9.5
DIRECTIONS: From city of Saskatoon: NW 9 km (5.5 mi) on Hwy 16 to Lutheran Rd, E 0.7 km (0.4 mi) on Lutheran Rd. Resort on R.
GPS COORDINATES: 52.25953°N/-106.78145°W
NOTATIONS: Check-in: 1:00 p.m. Check-out: 11:00 a.m. 20% discount for Coast members. Rate includes pull-through, full hook-ups. Payment in full at check-in. No refunds. Additional charges: Tax 5%. Max. RV length: Unlimited. Open: April 15–October 15.
WESTERN CANADA MAP: See page CTC 78.

50 amps · pull-through · laundry · pets/restrictions · internet access · Wi-Fi access · playground · picnic tables · hiking trails · outdoor pool · propane · fire rings · grocery · rv supplies · tenting · firewood · ice

INDEX

INDEX

T

U

V

W

Y

Z

INDEX

STATE AND PROVINCE INDEX

INDEX

STATE AND PROVINCE INDEX

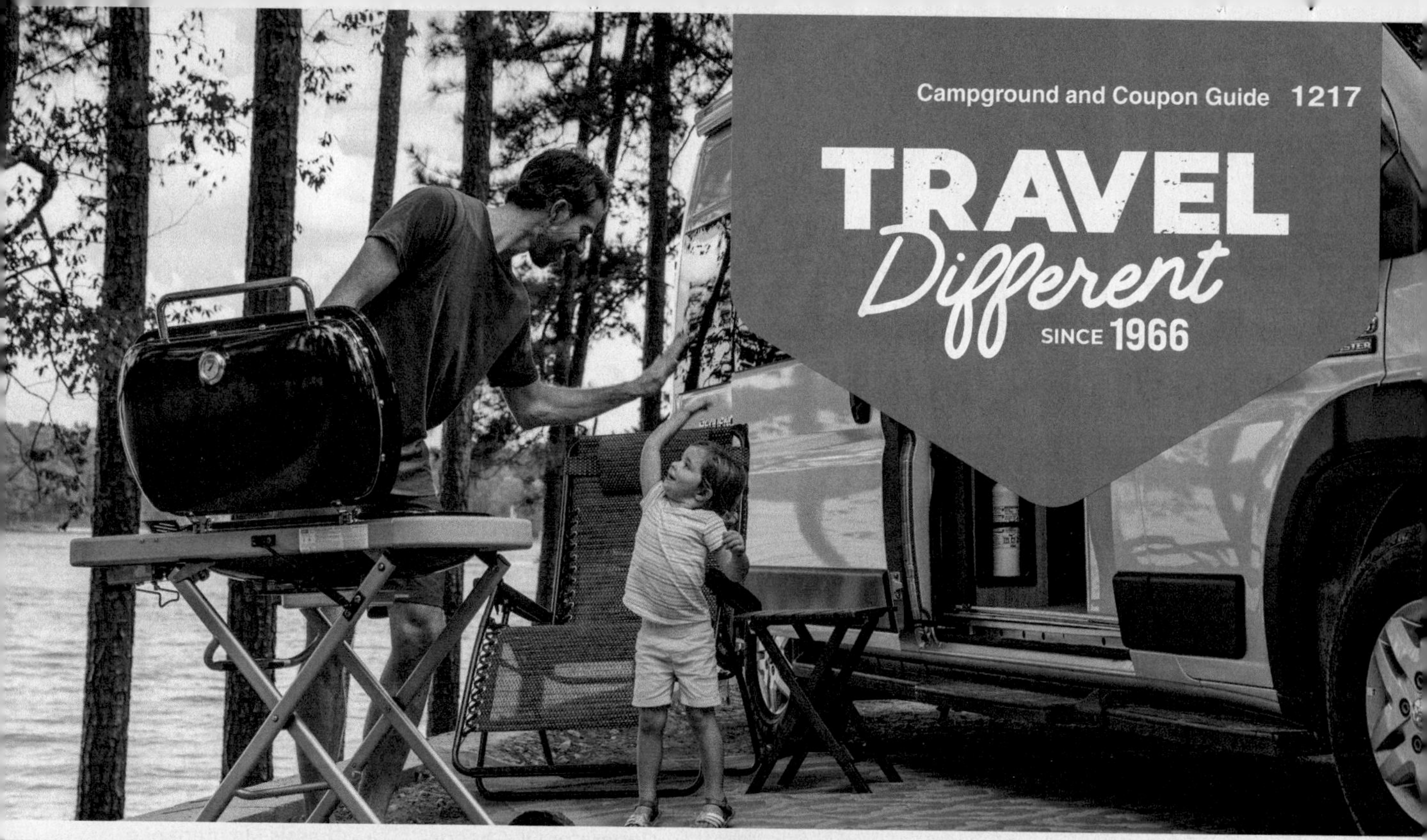
TRAVEL
Different
SINCE 1966

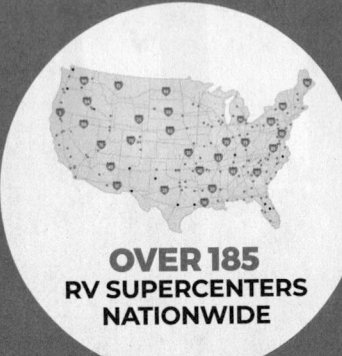

good sam member exclusive offers!

JANUARY MEMBERS EXCLUSIVE

ONLINE ONLY

Buy One Year of RV Magazine, Get One Year FREE

Visit **RV.com/GS2for1** to redeem this exclusive offer

Offer valid 1/1/22-1/31/22 only.

JANUARY MEMBERS EXCLUSIVE

$30 OFF

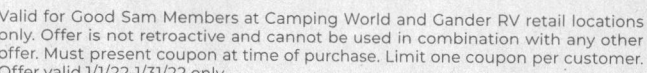

Installed Satellite Antennas

Valid for Good Sam Members at Camping World and Gander RV retail locations only. Offer is not retroactive and cannot be used in combination with any other offer. Must present coupon at time of purchase. Limit one coupon per customer. Offer valid 1/1/22-1/31/22 only.

Coupon Code: 2757

FEBRUARY MEMBERS EXCLUSIVE

FREE

Night of Camping

(Up to $25)

To redeem this offer, stay at any Good Sam Park of your choice and pay the camping fee. **Mail your original campground receipt along with this coupon, your name, address and Good Sam Membership Number to: Good Sam Park Network, PO Box 6547, Englewood, CO 80155-6547.** Information must be received by 4/16/22. ***Your rebate check for your free night of camping (up to $25) will arrive at the address you provide within 4-6 weeks.*** Offer valid for one-time use only. Offer valid for one night only. Limit one coupon per membership number. Qualifying campground stay must occur between 2/1/22-2/28/22.

FEBRUARY MEMBERS EXCLUSIVE

$10 OFF

Heaters

Valid for Good Sam Members at Camping World and Gander RV retail locations only. Offer is not retroactive and cannot be used in combination with any other offer. Must present coupon at time of purchase. Limit one coupon per customer. Offer valid 2/1/22-2/28/22 only.

CC2705

FEBRUARY MEMBERS EXCLUSIVE

TUESDAY-THURSDAY ONLY

$5 OFF

Any Purchase

Valid for Good Sam Members at Camping World and Gander RV retail locations only. Offer redeemable on merchandise only excluding generators, electronics and RV covers. Offer is not retroactive and cannot be used in combination with any other offer. Must present coupon at time of purchase. Limit one coupon per customer. Any unused portion of this dollar amount cannot be exchanged for cash or used on a later transaction. Offer valid Tuesdays thru Thursdays 2/1/22-2/28/22 only.

CC2706

FEBRUARY MEMBERS EXCLUSIVE

TUESDAY-THURSDAY ONLINE ONLY

$10 OFF

Purchase of $75 or More

Must use promo code TRAVELGUIDE10 at online checkout

Valid for Good Sam Members at CampingWorld.com only. Offer redeemable on merchandise only excluding generators, electronics and RV covers. Offer is not retroactive and cannot be used in combination with any other offer. Limit one coupon per customer. Offer valid Tuesdays thru Thursdays 2/1/22-2/28/22 only.

FEBRUARY MEMBERS EXCLUSIVE

$20 OFF

Ultra-Shield RV Covers

Valid for Good Sam Members at Camping World and Gander RV retail locations only. Offer is not retroactive and cannot be used in combination with any other offer. Must present coupon at time of purchase. Limit one coupon per customer. Offer valid 2/1/22-2/28/22 only.

CC2708

FEBRUARY MEMBERS EXCLUSIVE

$30 OFF

Awnings

Valid for Good Sam Members at Camping World and Gander RV retail locations only. Offer is not retroactive and cannot be used in combination with any other offer. Must present coupon at time of purchase. Limit one coupon per customer. Offer valid 2/1/22-2/28/22 only.

CC2709

For More Exclusive Offers Visit: **CampingWorld.com**

Yosemite National Park

Half Dome - Sunset from Glacier Point

Known for its vast terrain and breathtaking waterfalls, Yosemite is home to many different views of cliffs, lakes, mountains, glaciers and overall diverse wildlife. Over 800 miles of trails can be hiked throughout the park to various landmarks including the popular Half Dome rock formation.

good sam member exclusive offers!

FEBRUARY MEMBERS EXCLUSIVE

10% OFF
Stabilizer Jacks

Valid for Good Sam Members at Camping World and Gander RV retail locations only. Offer is not retroactive and cannot be used in combination with any other offer. Must present coupon at time of purchase. Limit one coupon per customer. Offer valid 2/1/22-2/28/22 only.

CC2710

FEBRUARY MEMBERS EXCLUSIVE

15% OFF
RV Cleaning Supplies

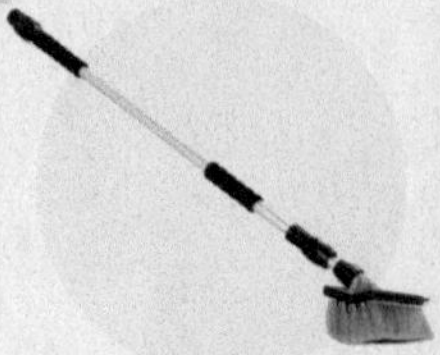

Valid for Good Sam Members at Camping World and Gander RV retail locations only. Offer is not retroactive and cannot be used in combination with any other offer. Must present coupon at time of purchase. Limit one coupon per customer. Offer valid 2/1/22-2/28/22 only.

CC2711

MARCH MEMBERS EXCLUSIVE

$10 OFF
Any Two Chairs

Valid for Good Sam Members at Camping World and Gander RV retail locations only. Offer is not retroactive and cannot be used in combination with any other offer. Must present coupon at time of purchase. Limit one coupon per customer. Offer valid 3/1/22-3/31/22 only.

CC2712

MARCH MEMBERS EXCLUSIVE

20% OFF
Small Appliances

Valid for Good Sam Members at Camping World and Gander RV retail locations only. Offer is not retroactive and cannot be used in combination with any other offer. Must present coupon at time of purchase. Limit one coupon per customer. Offer valid 3/1/22-3/31/22 only.

CC2713

MARCH MEMBERS EXCLUSIVE

$10 OFF
Outdoor Fire Pits

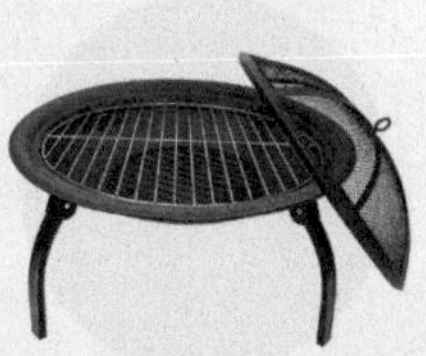

Valid for Good Sam Members at Camping World and Gander RV retail locations only. Offer is not retroactive and cannot be used in combination with any other offer. Must present coupon at time of purchase. Limit one coupon per customer. Offer valid 3/1/22-3/31/22 only.

CC2714

MARCH MEMBERS EXCLUSIVE

$10 OFF
Outdoor Mats

Valid for Good Sam Members at Camping World and Gander RV retail locations only. Offer is not retroactive and cannot be used in combination with any other offer. Must present coupon at time of purchase. Limit one coupon per customer. Offer valid 3/1/22-3/31/22 only.

CC2715

MARCH MEMBERS EXCLUSIVE

$20 OFF
Adult Bikes

Valid for Good Sam Members at Camping World and Gander RV retail locations only. Offer is not retroactive and cannot be used in combination with any other offer. Must present coupon at time of purchase. Limit one coupon per customer. Offer valid 3/1/22-3/31/22 only.

CC2716

MARCH MEMBERS EXCLUSIVE

$10 OFF
Tents

Valid for Good Sam Members at Camping World and Gander RV retail locations only. Offer is not retroactive and cannot be used in combination with any other offer. Must present coupon at time of purchase. Limit one coupon per customer. Offer valid 3/1/22-3/31/22 only.

CC2717

For More Exclusive Offers Visit: **CampingWorld.com**

Yellowstone National Park

Old Faithful Geyser

America's first national park, Yellowstone's geothermal features – specifically the Old Faithful geyser – brings millions of visitors annually to its nearly 3,500 square miles of terrain. Comprised of lakes, canyons and mountains, Yellowstone is home to over half of the world's geysers and is home to the largest supervolcano in North America – the Yellowstone Caldera.

good sam member exclusive offers!

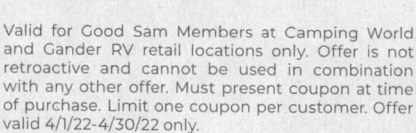

MARCH MEMBERS EXCLUSIVE

TUESDAY-THURSDAY ONLY

$20 OFF

Purchase of $50 or More

Valid for Good Sam Members at Camping World and Gander RV retail locations only. Offer redeemable on merchandise only excluding generators, electronics and RV covers. Offer is not retroactive and cannot be used in combination with any other offer. Must present coupon at time of purchase. Limit one coupon per customer. Offer valid Tuesdays thru Thursdays 3/1/22-3/31/22 only.

CC2718

MARCH MEMBERS EXCLUSIVE

$500

RV Trade-In Bonus

Trade-in bonus applied as discount on purchase of new units only. Must present this advertisement at time of purchase. Prior sales excluded. Not applicable on wholesale units. Cannot be combined with any other promotion or used as a down payment. Valid only at participating Camping World RV Sales and Gander RV Sales locations. See dealer for full details. Void where prohibited. Offer valid 3/1/22-3/31/22.

APRIL MEMBERS EXCLUSIVE

$20 OFF

Furniture

Valid for Good Sam Members at Camping World and Gander RV retail locations only. Offer is not retroactive and cannot be used in combination with any other offer. Must present coupon at time of purchase. Limit one coupon per customer. Offer valid 4/1/22-4/30/22 only.

CC2719

APRIL MEMBERS EXCLUSIVE

$15 OFF

Watersports Purchase of $99+

Valid for Good Sam Members at Camping World and Gander RV retail locations only. Offer is not retroactive and cannot be used in combination with any other offer. Must present coupon at time of purchase. Limit one coupon per customer. Offer valid 4/1/22-4/30/22 only.

CC2720

APRIL MEMBERS EXCLUSIVE

TUESDAY-THURSDAY ONLY

$20 OFF

Purchase of $100 or More

Valid for Good Sam Members at Camping World and Gander RV retail locations only. Offer redeemable on merchandise only excluding generators, electronics and RV covers. Offer is not retroactive and cannot be used in combination with any other offer. Must present coupon at time of purchase. Limit one coupon per customer. Offer valid Tuesdays thru Thursdays 4/1/22-4/30/22 only.

CC2721

APRIL MEMBERS EXCLUSIVE

$30 OFF

Large Appliances

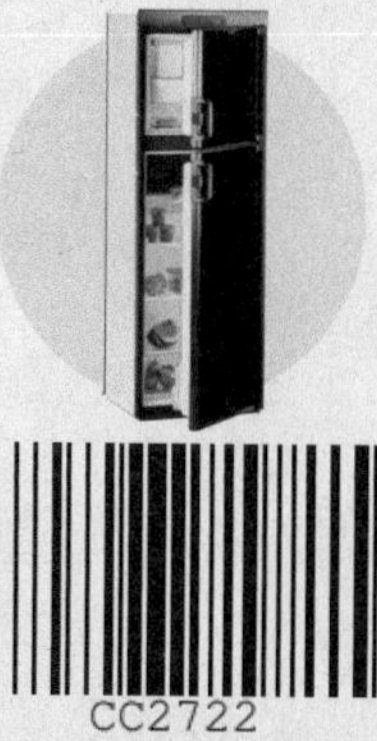

Valid for Good Sam Members at Camping World and Gander RV retail locations only. Offer is not retroactive and cannot be used in combination with any other offer. Must present coupon at time of purchase. Limit one coupon per customer. Offer valid 4/1/22-4/30/22 only.

CC2722

APRIL MEMBERS EXCLUSIVE

ONLINE ONLY

$15 OFF

Purchase of $99 or More

Must use promo code TRAVELGUIDE15 at online checkout

Valid for Good Sam Members at CampingWorld.com only. Offer redeemable on merchandise only excluding generators, electronics and RV covers. Offer is not retroactive and cannot be used in combination with any other offer. Limit one coupon per customer. Offer valid 4/1/22-4/30/22 only.

APRIL MEMBERS EXCLUSIVE

$30 OFF

Ultra-Shield RV Covers

Valid for Good Sam Members at Camping World and Gander RV retail locations only. Offer is not retroactive and cannot be used in combination with any other offer. Must present coupon at time of purchase. Limit one coupon per customer. Offer valid 4/1/22-4/30/22 only.

CC2724

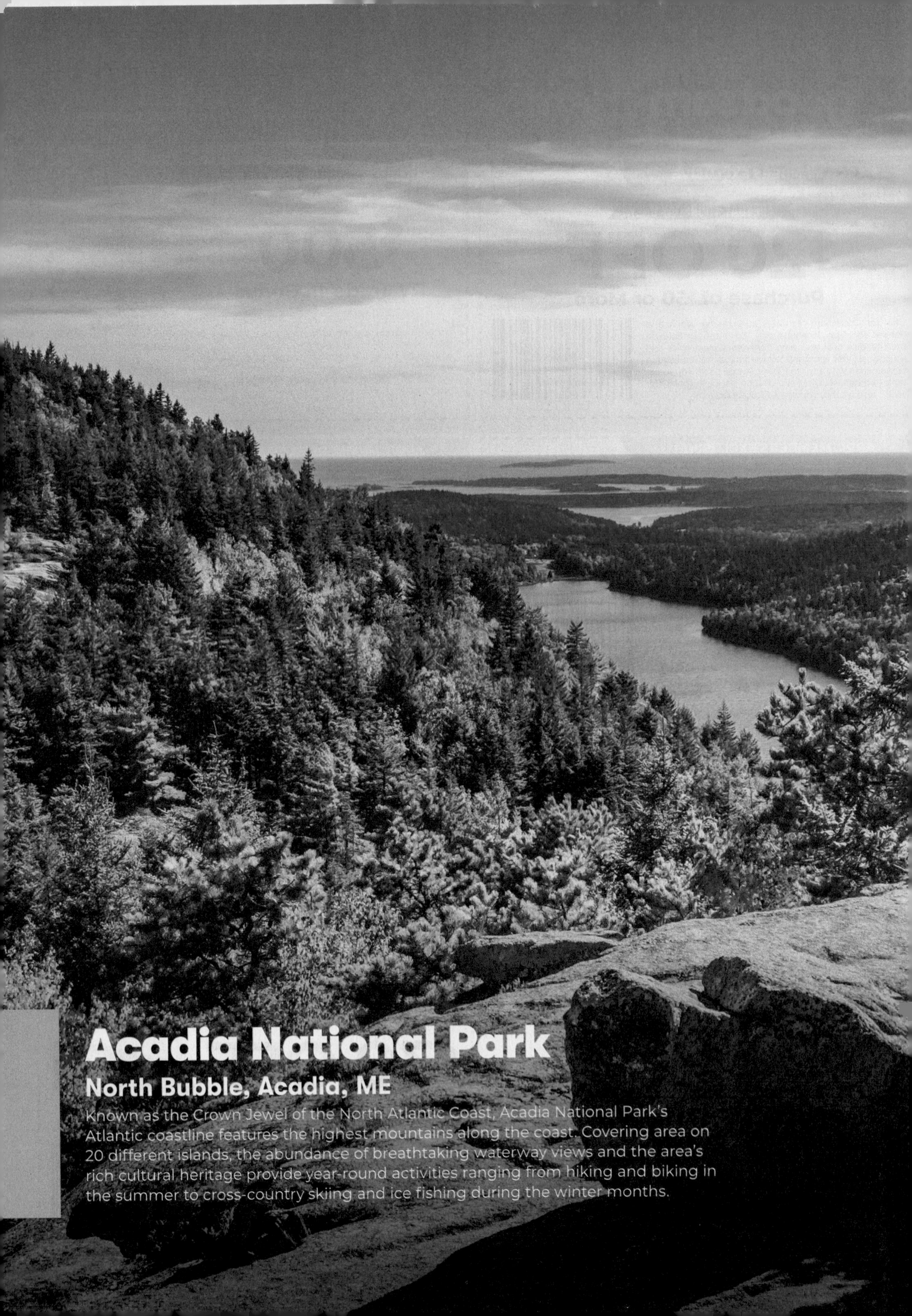

Acadia National Park

North Bubble, Acadia, ME

Known as the Crown Jewel of the North Atlantic Coast, Acadia National Park's Atlantic coastline features the highest mountains along the coast. Covering area on 20 different islands, the abundance of breathtaking waterway views and the area's rich cultural heritage provide year-round activities ranging from hiking and biking in the summer to cross-country skiing and ice fishing during the winter months.

good sam member exclusive offers!

APRIL MEMBERS EXCLUSIVE

$40 OFF
Air Conditioners

Valid for Good Sam Members at Camping World and Gander RV retail locations only. Offer is not retroactive and cannot be used in combination with any other offer. Must present coupon at time of purchase. Limit one coupon per customer. Offer valid 4/1/22-4/30/22 only.

CC2725

APRIL MEMBERS EXCLUSIVE

IN STORES AND ONLINE

10% OFF
Any Purchase

Must use promo code **APRIL10** at online checkout

Valid for Good Sam Members at Camping World and Gander RV retail and online locations. Offer redeemable on merchandise only excluding generators, electronics, RV covers and firearms. Offer is not retroactive and cannot be used in combination with any other offer. Must present coupon at time of purchase. Limit one coupon per customer. Good for one time, one use only. Offer valid Tuesdays thru Thursdays 4/1/22-4/30/22 only.

CC2726

APRIL MEMBERS EXCLUSIVE

$50 OFF
Service

Valid for Good Sam Members at Camping World RV Sales and Gander RV Sales service locations only. Offer is not retroactive and cannot be used in combination with any other offer. Must present coupon prior to service. Limit one coupon per customer. Additional shop supplies and taxes may apply. Service must be scheduled between 4/1/22-4/30/22.

Coupon Code: 2759

MAY MEMBERS EXCLUSIVE

TUESDAY-THURSDAY ONLY

$10 OFF
Purchase of $25 or More

Valid for Good Sam Members at Camping World and Gander RV retail locations only. Offer redeemable on merchandise only excluding generators, electronics and RV covers. Offer is not retroactive and cannot be used in combination with any other offer. Must present coupon at time of purchase. Limit one coupon per customer. Offer valid Tuesdays thru Thursdays 5/1/22-5/31/22 only.

CC2727

MAY MEMBERS EXCLUSIVE

$20 OFF
Mattresses

Valid for Good Sam Members at Camping World and Gander RV retail locations only. Offer is not retroactive and cannot be used in combination with any other offer. Must present coupon at time of purchase. Limit one coupon per customer. Offer valid 5/1/22-5/31/22 only.

CC2728

MAY MEMBERS EXCLUSIVE

$25 OFF
Awnings

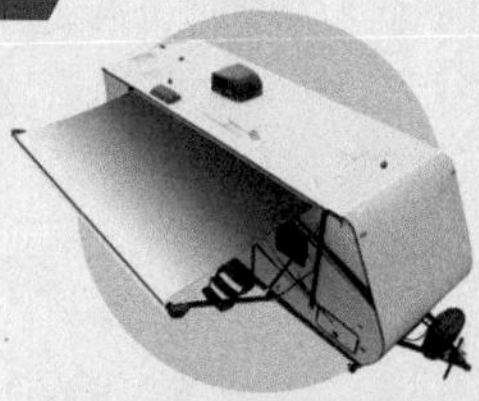

Valid for Good Sam Members at Camping World and Gander RV retail locations only. Offer is not retroactive and cannot be used in combination with any other offer. Must present coupon at time of purchase. Limit one coupon per customer. Offer valid 5/1/22-5/31/22 only.

CC2729

MAY MEMBERS EXCLUSIVE

$30 OFF
Backup Cameras

Valid for Good Sam Members at Camping World and Gander RV retail locations only. Offer is not retroactive and cannot be used in combination with any other offer. Must present coupon at time of purchase. Limit one coupon per customer. Offer valid 5/1/22-5/31/22 only.

CC2730

MAY MEMBERS EXCLUSIVE

10% OFF
RV Bedding

Valid for Good Sam Members at Camping World and Gander RV retail locations only. Offer is not retroactive and cannot be used in combination with any other offer. Must present coupon at time of purchase. Limit one coupon per customer. Offer valid 5/1/22-5/31/22 only.

CC2731

For More Exclusive Offers Visit: **CampingWorld.com**

Big Bend National Park

Big Bend National Park, TX

Big Bend's desert landscape sits along the United States' border with Mexico, with approximately 118 miles of the Rio Grande running through it. The park is home to nearly 10,000 years of archeological history and features the Chisos Mountains – the only mountain range in the country to be fully contained within the boundary of a national park.

good sam member exclusive offers!

JUNE MEMBERS EXCLUSIVE

$10 OFF
Surge Protectors

Valid for Good Sam Members at Camping World and Gander RV retail locations only. Offer is not retroactive and cannot be used in combination with any other offer. Must present coupon at time of purchase. Limit one coupon per customer. Offer valid 6/1/22-6/30/22 only.

CC2732

JUNE MEMBERS EXCLUSIVE

TUESDAY-THURSDAY ONLY

$20 OFF
Purchase of $50 or More

Valid for Good Sam Members at Camping World and Gander RV retail locations only. Offer redeemable on merchandise only excluding generators, electronics and RV covers. Offer is not retroactive and cannot be used in combination with any other offer. Must present coupon at time of purchase. Limit one coupon per customer. Any unused portion of this dollar amount cannot be exchanged for cash or used on a later transaction. Offer valid Tuesdays thru Thursdays 6/1/22-6/30/22 only.

CC2733

JUNE MEMBERS EXCLUSIVE

TUESDAY-THURSDAY ONLY

$30 OFF
Purchase of $200 or More

Valid for Good Sam Members at Camping World and Gander RV retail locations only. Offer redeemable on merchandise only excluding generators, electronics and RV covers. Offer is not retroactive and cannot be used in combination with any other offer. Must present coupon at time of purchase. Limit one coupon per customer. Any unused portion of this dollar amount cannot be exchanged for cash or used on a later transaction. Offer valid Tuesdays thru Thursdays 6/1/22-6/30/22 only.

CC2734

JUNE MEMBERS EXCLUSIVE

$5 OFF
RV Vent Covers

Valid for Good Sam Members at Camping World and Gander RV retail locations only. Offer is not retroactive and cannot be used in combination with any other offer. Must present coupon at time of purchase. Limit one coupon per customer. Offer valid 6/1/22-6/30/22 only.

CC2735

JUNE MEMBERS EXCLUSIVE

15% OFF
Kitchen Accessories

Valid for Good Sam Members at Camping World and Gander RV retail locations only. Offer is not retroactive and cannot be used in combination with any other offer. Must present coupon at time of purchase. Limit one coupon per customer. Offer valid 6/1/22-6/30/22 only.

CC2736

JULY MEMBERS EXCLUSIVE

10% OFF
Watersports Purchase

Valid for Good Sam Members at Camping World and Gander RV retail locations only. Offer is not retroactive and cannot be used in combination with any other offer. Must present coupon at time of purchase. Limit one coupon per customer. Offer valid 7/1/22-7/31/22 only.

CC2737

JULY MEMBERS EXCLUSIVE

TUESDAY-THURSDAY ONLY

$5 OFF
Any Purchase

Valid for Good Sam Members at Camping World and Gander RV retail locations only. Offer redeemable on merchandise only excluding generators, electronics and RV covers. Offer is not retroactive and cannot be used in combination with any other offer. Must present coupon at time of purchase. Limit one coupon per customer. Any unused portion of this dollar amount cannot be exchanged for cash or used on a later transaction. Offer valid Tuesdays thru Thursdays 7/1/22-7/31/22 only.

CC2738

JULY MEMBERS EXCLUSIVE

$10 OFF
Coolers

Valid for Good Sam Members at Camping World and Gander RV retail locations only. Offer is not retroactive and cannot be used in combination with any other offer. Must present coupon at time of purchase. Limit one coupon per customer. Offer valid 7/1/22-7/31/22 only.

CC2739

For More Exclusive Offers Visit: **CampingWorld.com**

Rocky Mountain National Park

Rocky Mountain National Park, CO

One of the most visited national parks in the country, Rocky Mountain National Park may be known for its amazing mountain ranges, but it also features gorgeous alpine lakes and a vast variety of wildlife throughout its various climates. In addition to it's numerous hiking trails, the park also features challenging rock climbing spots and fishing in many of the lakes and streams.

good sam member exclusive offers!

JULY MEMBERS EXCLUSIVE

$50 OFF
Coleman Powersports

Valid for Good Sam Members at Camping World and Gander RV retail locations only. Offer is not retroactive and cannot be used in combination with any other offer. Must present coupon at time of purchase. Limit one coupon per customer. Offer valid 7/1/22-7/31/22 only.

CC2740

JULY MEMBERS EXCLUSIVE

$50 OFF
Installed Braking System

Valid for Good Sam Members at Camping World and Gander RV retail locations only. Offer is not retroactive and cannot be used in combination with any other offer. Must present coupon at time of purchase. Limit one coupon per customer. Offer valid 7/1/22-7/31/22 only.

Coupon Code: 2760

AUGUST MEMBERS EXCLUSIVE

ONLINE ONLY

$20 OFF
Purchase of $150 or More

Must use promo code **TRAVELGUIDE20** at online checkout

Valid for Good Sam Members at CampingWorld.com only. Offer redeemable on merchandise only excluding generators, electronics and RV covers. Offer is not retroactive and cannot be used in combination with any other offer. Limit one coupon per customer. Offer valid 8/1/22-8/31/22 only.

AUGUST MEMBERS EXCLUSIVE

$25 OFF
Portable Satellites

Valid for Good Sam Members at Camping World and Gander RV retail locations only. Offer is not retroactive and cannot be used in combination with any other offer. Must present coupon at time of purchase. Limit one coupon per customer. Offer valid 8/1/22-8/31/22 only.

CC2742

AUGUST MEMBERS EXCLUSIVE

TUESDAY-THURSDAY ONLY

$5 OFF
Any Purchase

Valid for Good Sam Members at Camping World and Gander RV retail locations only. Offer redeemable on merchandise only excluding generators, electronics and RV covers. Offer is not retroactive and cannot be used in combination with any other offer. Must present coupon at time of purchase. Limit one coupon per customer. Any unused portion of this dollar amount cannot be exchanged for cash or used on a later transaction. Offer valid Tuesdays thru Thursdays 8/1/22-8/31/22 only.

CC2743

SEPTEMBER MEMBERS EXCLUSIVE

$20 OFF
Outdoor Recliners

Valid for Good Sam Members at Camping World and Gander RV retail locations only. Offer is not retroactive and cannot be used in combination with any other offer. Must present coupon at time of purchase. Limit one coupon per customer. Offer valid 9/1/22-9/30/22 only.

CC2744

SEPTEMBER MEMBERS EXCLUSIVE

TUESDAY-THURSDAY ONLY

$20 OFF
Purchase of $150 or More

Valid for Good Sam Members at Camping World and Gander RV retail locations only. Offer redeemable on merchandise only excluding generators, electronics and RV covers. Offer is not retroactive and cannot be used in combination with any other offer. Must present coupon at time of purchase. Limit one coupon per customer. Any unused portion of this dollar amount cannot be exchanged for cash or used on a later transaction. Offer valid Tuesdays thru Thursdays 9/1/22-9/30/22 only.

CC2745

SEPTEMBER MEMBERS EXCLUSIVE

TUESDAY-THURSDAY ONLY

$20 OFF
Purchase of $50 or More

Valid for Good Sam Members at Camping World and Gander RV retail locations only. Offer redeemable on merchandise only excluding generators, electronics and RV covers. Offer is not retroactive and cannot be used in combination with any other offer. Must present coupon at time of purchase. Limit one coupon per customer. Any unused portion of this dollar amount cannot be exchanged for cash or used on a later transaction. Offer valid Tuesdays thru Thursdays 9/1/22-9/30/22 only.

CC2746

For More Exclusive Offers Visit: **CampingWorld.com**

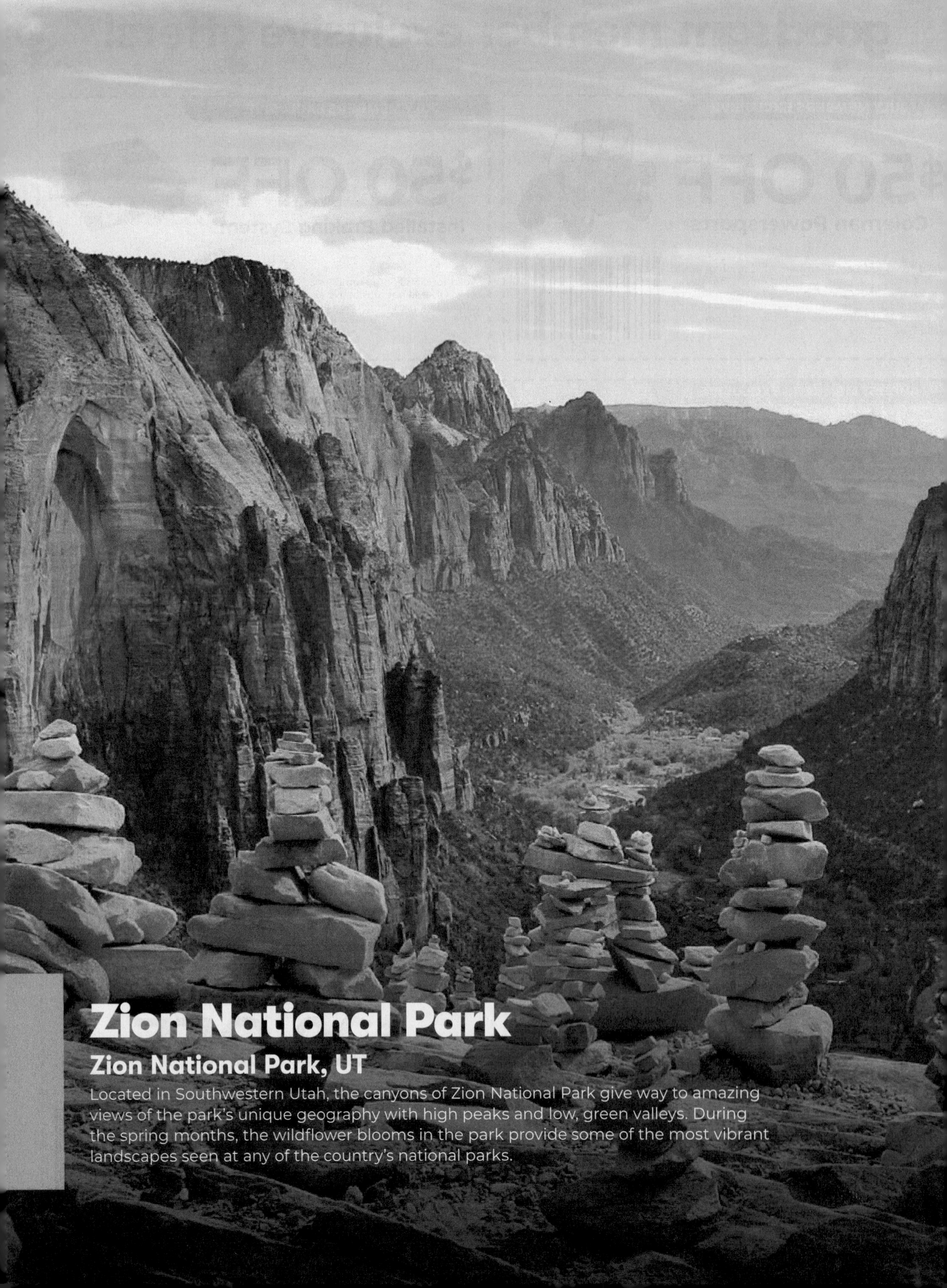

Zion National Park

Zion National Park, UT

Located in Southwestern Utah, the canyons of Zion National Park give way to amazing views of the park's unique geography with high peaks and low, green valleys. During the spring months, the wildflower blooms in the park provide some of the most vibrant landscapes seen at any of the country's national parks.

good sam
Insurance Agency

For your free quote
Call **833-408-0433**
mention savings code **TD-Z5**
GoodSamRVInsurance.com/code/Z5

Don't settle for less, get full RV coverage!

Many auto insurance companies cover your rig like it's a big car. Unfortunately, these gaps in coverage could cost you thousands in the event of a claim!

The Good Sam Insurance Agency offers top-of-the-line specialized RV coverage that fits your needs and your budget with options and features like:

- **Great Rates** | Customers that switch save an average of $321 each year!
- **Storage Option** | Save as much as 53% when you're not using your RV
- **Automatic Coverage** of personal belongings and attachments
- **Full-Timer Coverage** tailored for people who use their RVs at least 6 months out of the year
- **And much more!**

We represent the nation's top RV specialty carriers!

FOREMOST INSURANCE GROUP
PROGRESSIVE
National General – Auto, Home & Health Insurance
Safeco Insurance – A Liberty Mutual Company

Availability, eligibility, coverages, features and benefits may vary by state and carrier. The content herein is for descriptive purposes only. The exact protection provided is subject to the terms, conditions, and expectations of the policy contract issued. The Good Sam Vehicle Insurance Plan (VIP) is provided by a member company of the National General Insurance Group. Savings data is based on new policyholder surveys taken between 2018 and 2019.

good sam member exclusive offers!

SEPTEMBER MEMBERS EXCLUSIVE

$250 OFF

New Travel Trailer Purchase

Discount can be applied to new units only. Discount taken off Special Online Price. Must present this coupon at time of purchase. Prior sales excluded. Not applicable on wholesale units. Cannot be combined with any other promotion or used as a down payment. Valid only at Camping World RV Sales, Gander RV Sales or Freedom Roads RV Sales location. Offer valid 9/1/22-9/30/22.

SEPTEMBER MEMBERS EXCLUSIVE

FREE

Night of Camping

(Up to $25)

To redeem this offer, stay at any Good Sam Park of your choice and pay the camping fee. **Mail your original campground receipt along with this coupon, your name, address and Good Sam Membership Number to: Good Sam Park Network, PO Box 6547, Englewood, CO 80155-6547.** Information must be received by 11/16/22. ***Your rebate check for your free night of camping (up to $25) will arrive at the address you provide within 4-6 weeks.*** Offer valid for one-time use only. Offer valid for one night only. Limit one coupon per membership number. Qualifying campground stay must occur between 9/1/22-9/30/22.

OCTOBER MEMBERS EXCLUSIVE

TUESDAY-THURSDAY ONLY

$10 OFF

Any Purchase

/alid for Good Sam Members at Camping World and Gander RV etail locations only. Offer redeemable on merchandise only excluding generators, electronics and RV covers. Offer is not retroactive and cannot be used in combination with any other offer. Must present coupon at ime of purchase. Limit one coupon per customer. Any unused portion of this dollar amount cannot be exchanged for cash or used on a later ransaction. Offer valid Tuesdays thru Thursdays 10/1/22-10/31/22 only.

CC2747

OCTOBER MEMBERS EXCLUSIVE

$15 OFF

WiFi/Cellular Systems

Valid for Good Sam Members at Camping World and Gander RV retail locations only. Offer is not retroactive and cannot be used in combination with any other offer. Must present coupon at time of purchase. Limit one coupon per customer. Offer valid 10/1/22-10/31/22 only.

CC2748

OCTOBER MEMBERS EXCLUSIVE

$15 OFF

Sofas

/alid for Good Sam Members at Camping World and Gander RV retail locations only. Offer is not etroactive and cannot be used in combination with any other offer. Must present coupon at time of purchase. Limit one coupon per customer. Offer valid 10/1/22-10/31/22 only.

CC2749

OCTOBER MEMBERS EXCLUSIVE

TUESDAY-THURSDAY ONLY

$50 OFF

Purchase of $300 or More

Valid for Good Sam Members at Camping World and Gander RV retail locations only. Offer redeemable on merchandise only excluding generators, electronics and RV covers. Offer is not retroactive and cannot be used in combination with any other offer. Must present coupon at time of purchase. Limit one coupon per customer. Any unused portion of this dollar amount cannot be exchanged for cash or used on a later transaction. Offer valid Tuesdays thru Thursdays 10/1/22-10/31/22 only.

CC2750

OCTOBER MEMBERS EXCLUSIVE

$100 OFF

New Travel Trailer Purchase

Discount can be applied to new units only. Discount taken off Special Online Price. Must present this coupon at time of purchase. Prior sales excluded. Not applicable on wholesale units. Cannot be combined with any other promotion or used as a down payment. Valid only at Camping World RV Sales, Gander RV Sales or Freedom Roads RV Sales location. Offer valid 10/1/22-10/31/22.

NOVEMBER MEMBERS EXCLUSIVE

ONLINE ONLY

$15 OFF

GPS Systems

Must use promo code GPS15 at online checkout

Valid for Good Sam Members at CampingWorld.com only. Offer is not retroactive and cannot be used in combination with any other offer. Limit one coupon per customer. Offer valid 11/1/22-11/30/22 only.

For More Exclusive Offers Visit: **CampingWorld.com**

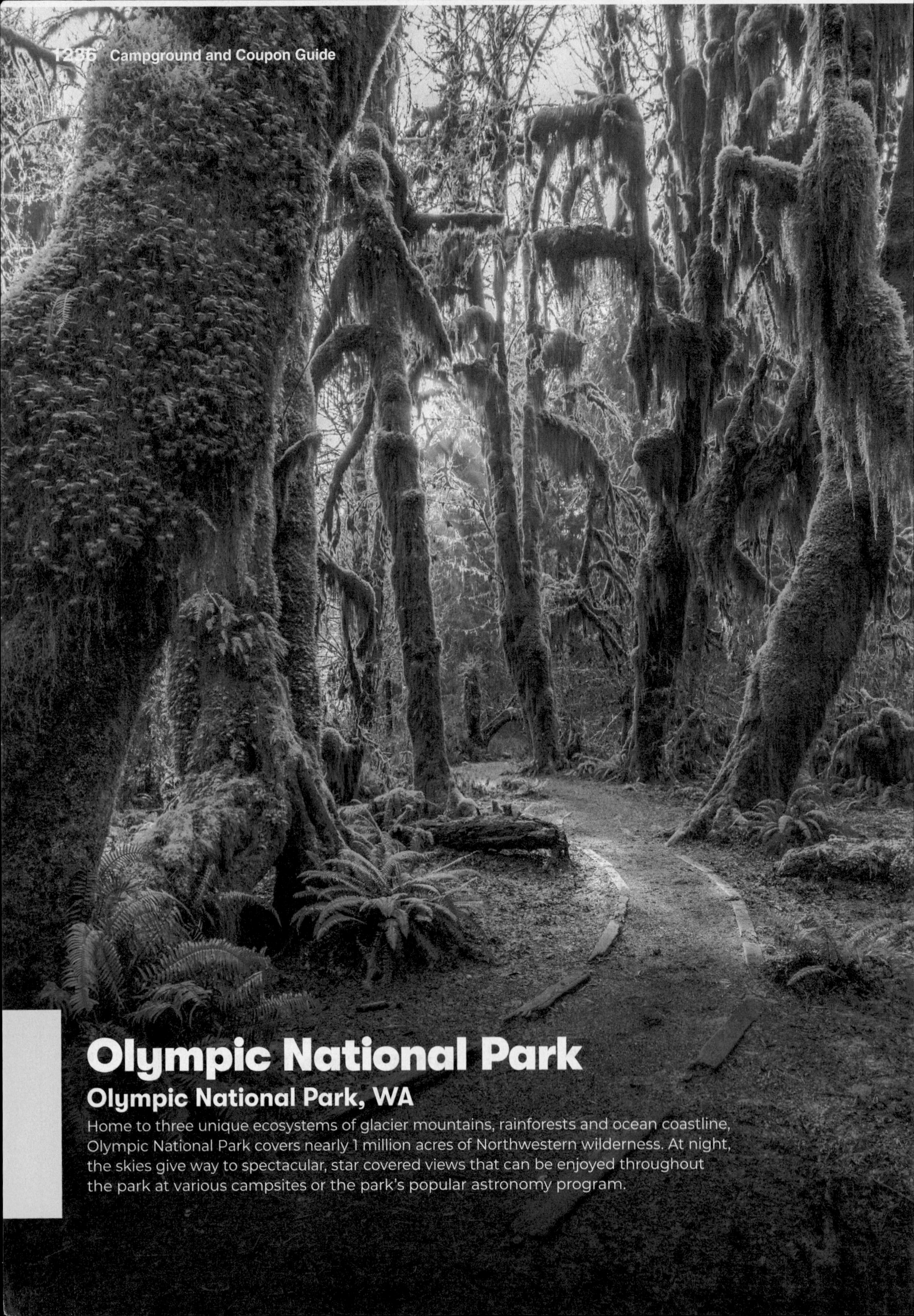

Olympic National Park

Olympic National Park, WA

Home to three unique ecosystems of glacier mountains, rainforests and ocean coastline, Olympic National Park covers nearly 1 million acres of Northwestern wilderness. At night, the skies give way to spectacular, star covered views that can be enjoyed throughout the park at various campsites or the park's popular astronomy program.

good sam member exclusive offers!

NOVEMBER MEMBERS EXCLUSIVE

FREE

Night of Camping

(Up to $25)

To redeem this offer, stay at any Good Sam Park of your choice and pay the camping fee. **Mail your original campground receipt along with this coupon, your name, address and Good Sam Membership Number to: Good Sam Park Network, PO Box 6547, Englewood, CO 80155-6547.** Information must be received by 1/15/23. ***Your rebate check for your free night of camping (up to $25) will arrive at the address you provide within 4-6 weeks.*** Offer valid for one-time use only. Offer valid for one night only. Limit one coupon per membership number. Qualifying campground stay must occur between 11/1/22-11/30/22.

NOVEMBER MEMBERS EXCLUSIVE

$25 OFF

Boat Covers

Valid for Good Sam Members at Camping World and Gander RV retail locations only. Offer is not retroactive and cannot be used in combination with any other offer. Must present coupon at time of purchase. Limit one coupon per customer. Offer valid 11/1/22-11/30/22 only.

CC2752

NOVEMBER MEMBERS EXCLUSIVE

TUESDAY-THURSDAY ONLY

$40 OFF

Purchase of $150 or More

Valid for Good Sam Members at Camping World and Gander RV retail locations only. Offer redeemable on merchandise only excluding generators, electronics and RV covers. Offer is not retroactive and cannot be used in combination with any other offer. Must present coupon at time of purchase. Limit one coupon per customer. Any unused portion of this dollar amount cannot be exchanged for cash or used on a later transaction. Offer valid Tuesdays thru Thursdays 11/1/22-11/30/22 only.

CC2753

NOVEMBER MEMBERS EXCLUSIVE

$500 OFF

New Fifth Wheel Purchase

Discount can be applied to new units only. Discount taken off Special Online Price. Must present this coupon at time of purchase. Prior sales excluded. Not applicable on wholesale units. Cannot be combined with any other promotion or used as a down payment. Valid only at Camping World RV Sales, Gander RV Sales or Freedom Roads RV Sales location. Offer valid 11/1/22-11/30/22.

DECEMBER MEMBERS EXCLUSIVE

TUESDAY-THURSDAY ONLY

$10 OFF

Any Purchase

Valid for Good Sam Members at Camping World and Gander RV retail locations only. Offer redeemable on merchandise only excluding generators, electronics and RV covers. Offer is not retroactive and cannot be used in combination with any other offer. Must present coupon at time of purchase. Limit one coupon per customer. Any unused portion of this dollar amount cannot be exchanged for cash or used on a later transaction. Offer valid Tuesdays thru Thursdays 12/1/22-12/31/22 only.

CC2754

DECEMBER MEMBERS EXCLUSIVE

TUESDAY-THURSDAY ONLY

$20 OFF

Any Purchase

Valid for Good Sam Members at Camping World and Gander RV retail locations only. Offer redeemable on merchandise only excluding generators, electronics and RV covers. Offer is not retroactive and cannot be used in combination with any other offer. Must present coupon at time of purchase. Limit one coupon per customer. Any unused portion of this dollar amount cannot be exchanged for cash or used on a later transaction. Offer valid Tuesdays thru Thursdays 12/1/22-12/31/22 only.

CC2755

DECEMBER MEMBERS EXCLUSIVE

TUESDAY-THURSDAY ONLY

$20 OFF

Purchase of $125 or More

Valid for Good Sam Members at Camping World and Gander RV retail locations only. Offer redeemable on merchandise only excluding generators, electronics and RV covers. Offer is not retroactive and cannot be used in combination with any other offer. Must present coupon at time of purchase. Limit one coupon per customer. Any unused portion of this dollar amount cannot be exchanged for cash or used on a later transaction. Offer valid Tuesdays thru Thursdays 12/1/22-12/31/22 only.

CC2756

DECEMBER MEMBERS EXCLUSIVE

$500

RV Trade-In Bonus

Trade-in bonus applied as discount on purchase of new units only. Must present this advertisement at time of purchase. Prior sales excluded. Not applicable on wholesale units. Cannot be combined with any other promotion or used as a down payment. Valid only at participating Camping World RV Sales and Gander RV Sales locations. See dealer for full details. Void where prohibited. Offer valid 12/1/22-12/31/22.

For More Exclusive Offers Visit: **CampingWorld.com**

Grand Teton National Park

Grand Teton National Park, WY

The southern neighbor to Yellowstone National Park, Grand Teton features a unique mix of wildlife, glacier-made waterways, and incredible mountain ranges. During the fall months, the mix of color in the park brings about vibrant scenes and active wildlife migration patterns. In addition to the over 200 miles of hiking trails that lead to backcountry camping areas, Grand Teton is also world-renowned for trout fishing.

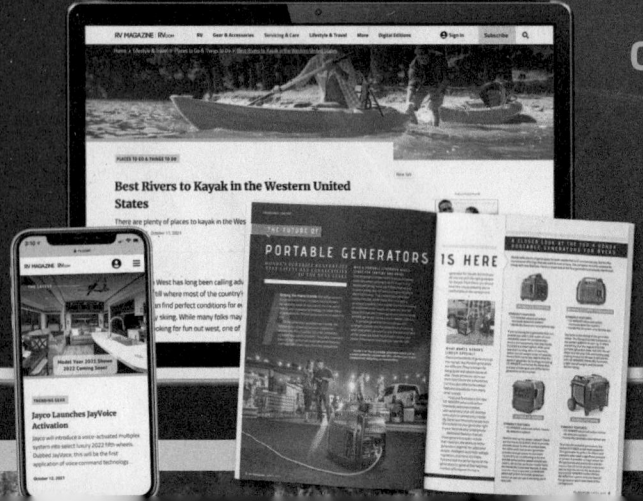